A DICTIONARY OF THE ENGLISH LANGUAGE

A DICTIONARY OF THE ENGLISH LANGUAGE

SAMUEL JOHNSON

ARNO PRESS

New York 1979

This edition published 1979 by Arno Press Inc.

Library of Congress Cataloging in Publication Data

Johnson, Samuel, 1709-1784.
Dictionary of the English language.

Reprint of the 1755 ed. printed by W. Strahan, London.
SUMMARY: A dictionary with more than 40,000 entries which was a primary reference source for scholars and writers of the 18th and 19th century.
1. English language—Dictionaries. [1. English language—Dictionaries] I. Title.
PE1620.J6 1979 423 79-14941
ISBN 0-405-12414-7

Manufactured in the United States of America

Preface to this edition

It is a daunting task to write a Preface to a facsimile edition of a dictionary which itself contains a Preface describing the noble purpose of one of the greatest of all English writers.

A Dictionary of the English Language by Samuel Johnson was published in two large folio volumes by a group of London booksellers on 15 April 1755. It was made up of some 2,300 pages, printed at intervals from 1750 onwards, and contained about 40,000 entries. In the dictionary the words, as the title-page states, are 'deduced from their originals' and 'illustrated in their different significations by examples from the best writers.' Between the Preface and the dictionary itself are two sections of small value then as now, a history of the English language and an English grammar, also written by Johnson.

The dictionary was printed by William Strahan,[1] who as King's Printer and the owner of the largest printing house in London, was one of the leading figures in the book trade of the eighteenth century. The dictionary, with tall pages of type set in two elegant columns, is an excellent example of his work.[2] Strahan, whose portrait by Sir Joshua Reynolds is deposited in London's National Portrait Gallery, printed many of Johnson's works, including his *Lives of the Poets, Rasselas,* and *Journey to the Western Islands of Scotland,* as well as some of the more famous works of David Hume, Adam Smith, Edward Gibbon, and others. The two men became friends during the printing of the dictionary and the friendship lasted, with a single short break, until Johnson's death in 1784.[3]

The contract for the preparation and publication of the dictionary, dated 18 June 1746, according to Sir John Hawkins's life of Johnson, was between Johnson and five London bookselling firms, those of Robert Dodsley, Charles Hitch, Andrew Millar, J. & P. Knapton, and T. and T. Longman. Johnson received a sum of £1,575 for his work, which it was hoped he would complete in three years, but which took nine. As Boswell commented 'When the expence of amanuenses and paper, and other articles are deducted, his clear profit was very inconsiderable. I once said to him, "I am sorry, Sir, you did not get more for your Dictionary." His answer was, "I am sorry, too. But it was very well. The booksellers are generous, liberal-minded men."'[4] In 1747 Johnson issued a work entitled *The Plan of a Dictionary of the English Language; Addressed to the Right Honourable Philip Dormer, Earl of Chesterfield; One of His Majesty's Principal Secretaries of State.* In this he set down his main aims, resolutely refusing to place much merit upon the art of lexicography:

"The work in which I engaged is generally considered as drudgery for the blind, as the proper toil of artless industry, a task that requires neither the light of learning, nor the activity of genius, but may be successfully performed without any higher quality than that of bearing burthens with dull patience, and beating the track of the alphabet with sluggish resolution." (p.1)

It was to be a work of preservation and of ascertainment, and restrictions were to be firmly placed on the type of vocabulary included:

"The chief intent of it is to preserve the purity and ascertain the meaning of our English idiom; and this seems to require nothing more than that our language be considered so far as it is our own; that the words and phrases used in the general intercourse of life, or found in the works of those whom we commonly stile polite writers, be selected, without including the terms of particular professions, since, with the arts to which they relate, they are generally derived from other nations..." (p.4).

[1] J. A. Cochrane *Dr. Johnson's Printer: The Life of William Strahan* (1964), esp. pp. 21-29.

[2] 'It cannot be claimed that the Dictionary is an example of superlatively good printing, but it is a worthy piece of bookwork, handsome if not resplendent.' *Ibid.* 29.

[3] *Ibid.* 22.

[4] G. B. Hill and L. F. Powell *Boswell's Life of Johnson* (Oxford, 1934) I.304.

"When I survey the Plan which I have laid before you," said Johnson, "I cannot, my Lord, but confess, that I am frighted at its extent, and, like the soldiers of Cæsar, look on Britain as a new world, which it is almost madness to invade." (p.33). He took a house in Gough Square, off Fleet Street, in London, fitted up the upper room for six amanuenses or copyists, and made a start. By December 1750 the first 70 sheets of the dictionary were printed, and in 1755 the first edition was issued in some 2,000 copies.[5]

It should be kept in mind that during the period 1749-55 Johnson was not continuously employed on the dictionary to the exclusion of all else. In 1749 he published 'The Vanity of Human Wishes,' described by Boswell as 'as high an effort of ethick poetry as any language can show.' In 1750 he started the *Rambler*, and wrote most of the pieces in it himself. It appeared twice a week until 1752 (when his wife Tetty died and his way of life changed). From March 1753 for a year he contributed regularly to Hawkesworth's *Adventurer*, and in 1754 he published his life of Edward Cave, the printer, in the *Gentleman's Magazine.*

In the two centuries and more since Johnson's dictionary appeared this great work has settled into legend as being one of the greatest works of the language. It is fitting now that it should be reproduced in facsimile so that the actual book can become more widely known in its first form, rather than in its later abridgements and adaptations.

It was not the first English dictionary, far less the first dictionary of a European language. It contributed little to the theory of the compilation of dictionaries, and it derived much of its factual content from earlier ones. More than most contemporary or later dictionaries, it displays a cluster of personal beliefs and precepts that stand far from the kind of objectivity that lexicographers count among their primary aims. Dr. Johnson is insular, prescriptive, and unscientific. Its relative antiquity as a dictionary is underlined by the entry under X: 'X is a letter, which, though found in Saxon words, begins no word in the English language.' Even if he had wished to do so he could not have delved into the vocabulary of English before the sixteenth century because it mostly lay in unedited and uncollected works in monastery libraries and great private houses. He therefore decided to restrict his illustrative quotations to those from the period from Sidney to the Restoration, that is from the 1580s to 1660:

> 'My purpose was to admit no testimony of living authours, that I might not be misled by partiality, and that none of my cotemporaries might have reason to complain; nor have I departed from this resolution, but when some performance of uncommon excellence excited my veneration... So far have I been from any care to grace my pages with modern decorations, that I have studiously endeavoured to collect examples and authorities from the writers before the restoration, whose works I regard as the wells of English undefiled, as the pure sources of genuine diction.'

And yet the dictionary that emerged from the restless pen of the great essayist remains as a potent monument whereas the influential lexicons of his predecessors, Cawdrey, Cockeram, Phillips, Bailey, and the rest, gently gather dust in the stacks of the great libraries, unstudied except by a band of historically minded scholars. The reason is not hard to find. In the whole tradition of English language and literature the *only* dictionary compiled by a writer of the first rank is that of Dr. Johnson. The muses spared him a while from his main literary work before letting him return to his poems, his essays, and his tracts. If Dryden in the seventeenth century, Macaulay in the nineteenth, and T. S. Eliot in the twentieth had found it possible to withdraw from their main pursuits for a similar interval, and diverted their own 'intolerable wrestle with words' to the realm of lexicography, the result would very likely have been as beguiling, and as influential.

The history of English lexicography up to and including 1755 has been studied in great detail by several scholars, notably (in chronological order) James A. H. Murray (the founding editor of the *O.E.D.*) in the Romanes Lectures of 1900, *The Evolution of English Lexicography* (Oxford, 1900); DeWitt T. Starnes and Gertrude E. Noyes *The English Dictionary from Cawdrey to Johnson, 1604-1755* (Chapel Hill, 1946); James H. Sledd and Gwin J. Kolb *Dr. Johnson's Dictionary: Essays in the Biography of a Book* (Chicago, 1955); and W. K. Wimsatt Jr. 'Johnson's Dictionary' in *New Light on Dr. Johnson: Essays on the Occasion of his 250th Birthday* edited by Frederick W. Hilles (New Haven, 1959). Criticism is not spared:

[5]The figure is not certain: see J. A. Cochrane, *op. cit.*, p.29.

"It must all along have been fairly obvious that Johnson was not the first to write a history of the English language, or a grammar, or a preface to a dictionary, and that his efforts under the first two of these heads were even somewhat perfunctory. His etymological notions were unlearned by modern standards, and in places even comic. His attempts to discourage some words by applying a kind of linguistic weedkiller, or notation of censure, were not very successful; even in his Preface he reports his loss of faith in that campaign. Johnson was not the first to write definitions of English words nor the first to subdivide and number his definitions. In short, . . . Johnson wrote his Dictionary in an age when 'many men, at work on different undertakings, were thinking in similar ways.'" (Wimsatt, *op. cit.*, p.66).

One key to Johnson's success lay in the diligence with which he read the works of the writers to whom he looked for his vocabulary:

"I therefore extracted from philosophers principles of science; from historians remarkable facts; from chymists complete processes; from divines striking exhortations; and from poets beautiful descriptions . . .

If the language of theology were extracted from Hooker and the translation of the Bible; the terms of natural knowledge from Bacon; the phrases of policy, war, and navigation from Raleigh; the dialect of poetry and fiction from Spenser and Sidney; and the diction of common life from Shakespeare, few ideas would be lost to mankind, for want of English words, in which they might be expressed . . .

The chief glory of every people arises from its authours . . . I shall not think my employment useless or ignoble . . . if my labours afford light to the repositories of science, and add celebrity to Bacon, to Hooker, to Milton, and to Boyle." (Preface to the Dictionary).

I should be remiss if I let the opportunity pass to draw attention to the 'numerous whimsical and licentious manifestations of [Johnson's] personality' that he allowed himself. Johnson entered a vexatious definition of 'oats' because he 'meant to vex [the Scots]'[6]. The definitions of *dedicator, excise, favourite, Grubstreet, lexicographer, patron, pension,* and *Tory* are splendidly prejudicial. The words *leeward* and *windward*, though of opposite meaning, are defined identically. His definition of *network*, as Boswell pointed out, is 'often quoted with sportive malignity, as obscuring a thing in itself very plain.' Johnson hated Gallicisms, and therefore hated Bolingbroke who used them in profusion. As a result Bolingbroke's name appears, censoriously presented, in the entry for *Gallicism*. The definition of *irony* reads: 'a mode of speech in which the meaning is contrary to the words: as, *Bolingbroke was a holy man.*'

He frequently quoted from his own works, as, for example, under *dissipate*, and, at least once, even attributed a couplet from Pope's *Essay on Man* to himself:

Some safer world in depth of woods embrac'd,
Some happier *island* in the wat'ry waste.

The name of his birthplace is explained under *lich* 'a dead carcase': *Lichfield*, the field of the dead, a city in Staffordshire, so named from martyred christians.

Johnson's dictionary is an outstanding example of literary lexicography. In the second half of the eighteenth century and well into the nineteenth, in its various editions and adaptations, it remained a primary work of reference for scholars and writers of the day until it came to be superseded by the great dictionaries of Charles Richardson and Noah Webster, and in due course by the *Oxford English Dictionary* itself. In its sturdy Englishness – American vocabulary, for example, is almost all deliberately excluded – in its steady belief in the superiority of the vocabulary of the best writers, in its rejection of foreign expressions, dialectal words, and the more detailed terminology of the sciences and of technology, in its notes on usage and its rejection of illiterate or modish vocabulary, Johnson's dictionary set standards of lexicography to which future generations of lexicographers may yet return when current doctrines of descriptive lexicography pass into desuetude like the doctrines they supplanted.

September 1978

Robert W. Burchfield, CBE
Chief Editor
The Oxford English Dictionaries

[6]It is of interest to compare James A. H. Murray's definition of *kohlrabi* in the *O.E.D.:* A cabbage with a turnip-shaped stem, varieties of which are cultivated as food for cattle in England, and as a vegetable in India and Germany.

A

DICTIONARY

OF THE

ENGLISH LANGUAGE:

IN WHICH

The WORDS are deduced from their ORIGINALS,

AND

ILLUSTRATED in their DIFFERENT SIGNIFICATIONS

BY

EXAMPLES from the beſt WRITERS.

TO WHICH ARE PREFIXED,

A HISTORY of the LANGUAGE,

AND

AN ENGLISH GRAMMAR.

BY SAMUEL JOHNSON, A. M.

IN TWO VOLUMES.

VOL. I.

Cum tabulis animum cenſoris ſumet honeſti:
Audebit quæcunque parum ſplendoris habebunt,
Et ſine pondere erunt, et honore indigna ferentur.
Verba movere loco; quamvis invita recedant,
Et verſentur adhuc intra penetralia Veſtæ:
Obſcurata diu populo bonus eruet, atque
Proferet in lucem ſpecioſa vocabula rerum,
Quæ priſcis memorata Catonibus atque Cethegis,
Nunc ſitus informis premit et deſerta vetuſtas. HOR.

LONDON,
Printed by W. STRAHAN,
For J. and P. KNAPTON; T. and T. LONGMAN; C. HITCH and L. HAWES;
A. MILLAR; and R. and J. DODSLEY.
MDCCLV.

Manufactured in the United States of America

P R E F A C E.

IT is the fate of thoſe who toil at the lower employments of life, to be rather driven by the fear of evil, than attracted by the proſpect of good; to be expoſed to cenſure, without hope of praiſe; to be diſgraced by miſcarriage, or puniſhed for neglect, where ſucceſs would have been without applauſe, and diligence without reward.

Among theſe unhappy mortals is the writer of dictionaries; whom mankind have conſidered, not as the pupil, but the ſlave of ſcience, the pioneer of literature, doomed only to remove rubbiſh and clear obſtructions from the paths of Learning and Genius, who preſs forward to conqueſt and glory, without beſtowing a ſmile on the humble drudge that facilitates their progreſs. Every other authour may aſpire to praiſe; the lexicographer can only hope to eſcape reproach, and even this negative recompence has been yet granted to very few.

I have, notwithſtanding this diſcouragement, attempted a dictionary of the *Engliſh* language, which, while it was employed in the cultivation of every ſpecies of literature, has itſelf been hitherto neglected, ſuffered to ſpread, under the direction of chance, into wild exuberance, reſigned to the tyranny of time and faſhion, and expoſed to the corruptions of ignorance, and caprices of innovation.

When I took the firſt ſurvey of my undertaking, I found our ſpeech copious without order, and energetick without rules: wherever I turned my view, there was perplexity to be diſentangled, and confuſion to be regulated; choice was to be made out of boundleſs variety, without any eſtabliſhed principle of ſelection; adulterations were to be detected, without a ſettled teſt of purity, and modes of expreſſion to be rejected or received, without the ſuffrages of any writers of claſſical reputation or acknowledged authority.

Having therefore no aſſiſtance but from general grammar, I applied myſelf to the peruſal of our writers; and noting whatever might be of uſe to aſcertain or illuſtrate any word or phraſe, accumulated in time the materials of a dictionary, which, by degrees, I reduced to method, eſtabliſhing to myſelf, in the progreſs of the work, ſuch rules as experience and analogy ſuggeſted to me; experience, which practice and obſervation were continually increaſing; and analogy, which, though in ſome words obſcure, was evident in others.

In adjuſting the ORTHOGRAPHY, which has been to this time unſettled and fortuitous, I found it neceſſary to diſtinguiſh thoſe irregularities that are inherent in our tongue, and perhaps coeval with it, from others which the ignorance or negligence of later writers has produced. Every language has its anomalies, which, though inconvenient, and in themſelves once unneceſſary, muſt be tolerated among the imperfections of human things, and which require only to be regiſtred, that they may not be increaſed, and aſcertained, that they may not be confounded: but every language has likewiſe its improprieties and abſurdities, which it is the duty of the lexicographer to correct or proſcribe.

As language was at its beginning merely oral, all words of neceſſary or common uſe were ſpoken before they were written; and while they were unfixed by any viſible ſigns, muſt have been ſpoken with great diverſity, as we now obſerve thoſe who cannot read to catch ſounds imperfectly, and utter them negligently. When this wild and barbarous jargon was firſt reduced to an alphabet, every penman endeavoured to expreſs, as he could, the ſounds which he was accuſtomed to pronounce or to receive, and vitiated in writing ſuch words as were already vitiated in ſpeech. The powers of the letters, when they were applied to a new language, muſt have been vague and unſettled, and therefore different hands would exhibit the ſame ſound by different combinations.

From this uncertain pronunciation ariſe in a great part the various dialects of the ſame country, which will always be obſerved to grow fewer, and leſs different, as books are multiplied; and from this arbitrary repreſentation of ſounds by letters, proceeds that diverſity of ſpelling obſervable in the *Saxon* remains, and I ſuppoſe in the firſt books of every nation, which perplexes or deſtroys analogy, and produces anomalous formations, which, being once incorporated, can never be afterward diſmiſſed or reformed.

Of this kind are the derivatives *length* from *long*, *ſtrength* from *ſtrong*, *darling* from *dear*, *breadth* from *broad*, from *dry*, *drought*, and from *high*, *height*, which *Milton*, in zeal for analogy, writes *highth*; *Quid te exempta juvat ſpinis de pluribus una*; to change all would be too much, and to change one is nothing.

This

This uncertainty is moſt frequent in the vowels, which are ſo capriciouſly pronounced, and ſo differently modified, by accident or affectation, not only in every province, but in every mouth, that to them, as is well known to etymologiſts, little regard is to be ſhewn in the deduction of one language from another.

Such defects are not errours in orthography, but ſpots of barbarity impreſſed ſo deep in the *Engliſh* language, that criticiſm can never waſh them away; theſe, therefore, muſt be permitted to remain untouched: but many words have been altered by accident, or depraved by ignorance, as the pronunciation of the vulgar has been weakly followed; and ſome ſtill continue to be variouſly written, as authours differ in their care or ſkill: of theſe it was proper to enquire the true orthography, which I have always conſidered as depending on their derivation, and have therefore referred them to their original languages: thus I write *enchant, enchantment, enchanter*, after the *French*, and *incantation* after the *Latin*; thus *entire* is choſen rather than *intire*, becauſe it paſſed to us not from the *Latin integer*, but from the *French entier*.

Of many words it is difficult to ſay whether they were immediately received from the *Latin* or the *French*, ſince at the time when we had dominions in *France*, we had *Latin* ſervice in our churches. It is, however, my opinion, that the *French* generally ſupplied us; for we have few *Latin* words, among the terms of domeſtick uſe, which are not *French*; but many *French*, which are very remote from *Latin*.

Even in words of which the derivation is apparent, I have been often obliged to ſacrifice uniformity to cuſtom; thus I write, in compliance with a numberleſs majority, *convey* and *inveigh*, *deceit* and *receipt*, *fancy* and *phantom*; ſometimes the derivative varies from the primitive, as *explain* and *explanation*, *repeat* and *repetition*.

Some combinations of letters having the ſame power are uſed indifferently without any diſcoverable reaſon of choice, as in *choak, choke*; *ſoap, ſope*; *fewel, fuel*, and many others; which I have ſometimes inſerted twice, that thoſe who ſearch for them under either form, may not ſearch in vain.

In examining the orthography of any doubtful word, the mode of ſpelling by which it is inſerted in the ſeries of the dictionary, is to be conſidered as that to which I give, perhaps not often raſhly, the preference. I have left, in the examples, to every authour his own practice unmoleſted, that the reader may balance ſuffrages, and judge betwixt us: but this queſtion is not always to be determined by reputed or by real learning; ſome men, intent upon greater things, have thought little on ſounds and derivations; ſome, knowing in the ancient tongues, have neglected thoſe in which our words are commonly to be ſought. Thus *Hammond* writes *fecibleneſs* for *feaſibleneſs*, becauſe I ſuppoſe he imagined it derived immediately from the *Latin*; and ſome words, ſuch as *dependant, dependent*; *dependance, dependence*, vary their final ſyllable, as one or other language is preſent to the writer.

In this part of the work, where caprice has long wantoned without controul, and vanity ſought praiſe by petty reformation, I have endeavoured to proceed with a ſcholar's reverence for antiquity, and a grammarian's regard to the genius of our tongue. I have attempted few alterations, and among thoſe few, perhaps the greater part is from the modern to the ancient practice; and I hope I may be allowed to recommend to thoſe, whoſe thoughts have been, perhaps, employed too anxiouſly on verbal ſingularities, not to diſturb, upon narrow views, or for minute propriety, the orthography of their fathers. It has been aſſerted, that for the law to be *known*, is of more importance than to be *right*. Change, ſays *Hooker*, is not made without inconvenience, even from worſe to better. There is in conſtancy and ſtability a general and laſting advantage, which will always overbalance the ſlow improvements of gradual correction. Much leſs ought our written language to comply with the corruptions of oral utterance, or copy that which every variation of time or place makes different from itſelf, and imitate thoſe changes, which will again be changed, while imitation is employed in obſerving them.

This recommendation of ſteadineſs and uniformity does not proceed from an opinion, that particular combinations of letters have much influence on human happineſs; or that truth may not be ſucceſſfully taught by modes of ſpelling fanciful and erroneous: I am not yet ſo loſt in lexicography, as to forget that *words are the daughters of earth, and that things are the ſons of heaven*. Language is only the inſtrument of ſcience, and words are but the ſigns of ideas: I wiſh, however, that the inſtrument might be leſs apt to decay, and that ſigns might be permanent, like the things which they denote.

In ſettling the orthography, I have not wholly neglected the pronunciation, which I have directed, by printing an accent upon the acute or elevated ſyllable. It will ſometimes be found, that the accent is placed by the authour quoted, on a different ſyllable from that marked in the alphabetical ſeries; it is then to be underſtood, that cuſtom has varied, or that the authour has, in my opinion, pronounced wrong. Short directions are ſometimes given where the ſound of letters is irregular; and if they are ſometimes omitted, defect in ſuch minute obſervations will be more eaſily excuſed, than ſuperfluity.

In the inveſtigation both of the orthography and ſignification of words, their ETYMOLOGY was neceſſarily to be conſidered, and they were therefore to be divided into primitives and derivatives. A primitive word, is that which can be traced no further to any *Engliſh* root; thus *circumſpect, circum-*

vent,

vent, *circumſtance*, *delude*, *concave*, and *complicate*, though compounds in the *Latin*, are to us primitives. Derivatives, are all thoſe that can be referred to any word in *Engliſh* of greater ſimplicity.

The derivatives I have referred to their primitives, with an accuracy ſometimes needleſs; for who does not ſee that *remoteneſs* comes from *remote*, *lovely* from *love*, *concavity* from *concave*, and *demonſtrative* from *demonſtrate*? But this grammatical exuberance the ſcheme of my work did not allow me to repreſs. It is of great importance, in examining the general fabrick of a language, to trace one word from another, by noting the uſual modes of derivation and inflection; and uniformity muſt be preſerved in ſyſtematical works, though ſometimes at the expence of particular propriety.

Among other derivatives I have been careful to inſert and elucidate the anomalous plurals of nouns and preterites of verbs, which in the *Teutonick* dialects are very frequent, and, though familiar to thoſe who have always uſed them, interrupt and embarraſs the learners of our language.

The two languages from which our primitives have been derived are the *Roman* and *Teutonick*: under the *Roman* I comprehend the *French* and provincial tongues; and under the *Teutonick* range the *Saxon*, *German*, and all their kindred dialects. Moſt of our polyſyllables are *Roman*, and our words of one ſyllable are very often *Teutonick*.

In aſſigning the *Roman* original, it has perhaps ſometimes happened that I have mentioned only the *Latin*, when the word was borrowed from the *French*; and conſidering myſelf as employed only in the illuſtration of my own language, I have not been very careful to obſerve whether the *Latin* word be pure or barbarous, or the *French* elegant or obſolete.

For the *Teutonick* etymologies I am commonly indebted to *Junius* and *Skinner*, the only names which I have forborn to quote when I copied their books; not that I might appropriate their labours or uſurp their honours, but that I might ſpare a perpetual repetition by one general acknowledgment. Of theſe, whom I ought not to mention but with the reverence due to inſtructors and benefactors, *Junius* appears to have excelled in extent of learning, and *Skinner* in rectitude of underſtanding. *Junius* was accurately ſkilled in all the northern languages, *Skinner* probably examined the ancient and remoter dialects only by occaſional inſpection into dictionaries; but the learning of *Junius* is often of no other uſe than to ſhow him a track by which he may deviate from his purpoſe, to which *Skinner* always preſſes forward by the ſhorteſt way. *Skinner* is often ignorant, but never ridiculous: *Junius* is always full of knowledge; but his variety diſtracts his judgment, and his learning is very frequently diſgraced by his abſurdities.

The votaries of the northern muſes will not perhaps eaſily reſtrain their indignation, when they find the name of *Junius* thus degraded by a diſadvantageous compariſon; but whatever reverence is due to his diligence, or his attainments, it can be no criminal degree of cenſoriouſneſs to charge that etymologiſt with want of judgment, who can ſeriouſly derive *dream* from *drama*, becauſe *life is a drama, and a drama is a dream*; and who declares with a tone of defiance, that no man can fail to derive *moan* from *μόνος*, *monos*, who conſiders that grief naturally loves to be *alone* *.

Our knowledge of the northern literature is ſo ſcanty, that of words undoubtedly *Teutonick* the original is not always to be found in any ancient language; and I have therefore inſerted *Dutch* or *German* ſubſtitutes, which I conſider not as radical but parallel, not as the parents, but ſiſters of the *Engliſh*.

The words which are repreſented as thus related by deſcent or cognation, do not always agree in ſenſe; for it is incident to words, as to their authours, to degenerate from their anceſtors, and to change their manners when they change their country. It is ſufficient, in etymological enquiries, if the ſenſes of kindred words be found ſuch as may eaſily paſs into each other, or ſuch as may both be referred to one general idea.

The etymology, ſo far as it is yet known, was eaſily found in the volumes where it is particularly and profeſſedly delivered; and, by proper attention to the rules of derivation, the orthography was ſoon adjuſted. But to COLLECT the WORDS of our language was a taſk of greater difficulty: the deficiency of dictionaries was immediately apparent; and when they were exhauſted, what was yet wanting muſt be ſought by fortuitous and unguided excurſions into books, and gleaned as induſtry

* That I may not appear to have ſpoken too irreverently of *Junius*, I have here ſubjoined a few Specimens of his etymological extravagance.

BANISH, *religare, ex banno vel territorio exigere*, in *exilium agere*. G. *bannir*. It. *bandire*, *bandeggiare*. H. *bandir*. B. bannen. Ævi medii ſcriptores bannire dicebant. V. Spelm. in Bannum & in Banleuga. Quoniam verò regionum urbiumq; limites arduis plerumq; montibus, altis fluminibus, longis deniq; flexuoſiſq; anguſtiſſimarum viarum amfractibus includebantur, fieri poteſt id genus limites *ban* dici ab eo quod Βαννάται & Βάνναῖροι Tarentinis olim, ſicuti tradit Heſychius, vocabantur αἱ λοξοὶ καὶ μὴ ἰθυτενεῖς ὁδοι, " obliquæ ac minimè in rectum tendentes viæ." Ac fortaſſe quoque huc facit quod Βανὸς, eodem Heſychio teſte, dicebant ὄρη ϛρογγύλη, montes arduos.

EMPTY, emtie, *vacuus*, *inanis*. A. S. Æmtiȝ. Neſcio an ſint ab ἐμέω vel εμεῖάω. Vomo, evomo, vomitu evacuo. Videtur interim etymologiam hanc non obſcurè firmare codex Ruſh. Mat. xii. 22. ubi antiquè ſcriptum invenimus ȝemoeteð hit emetiȝ. " Invenit eam vacantem."

HILL, *mons*, *collis*. A. S. hȳll. Quod videri poteſt abſciſſum ex κολώνη vel κολωνὸς. Collis, tumulus, locus in plano editior. Hom. Il. b. v. 811, ἔϛι δέ τις προπάροιθε πόλεος αἰπεῖα, κολώνη. Ubi authori brevium ſcholiorum κολώνη exp. τόπος εις ὕψος ἀνήκων, γεώλοφος ἐξοχή.

NAP, *to take a nap. Dormire*, *condormiſcere*. Cym. heppian. A. S. hnæppan. Quod poſtremum videri poteſt deſumptum ex κνέφας, obſcuritas, tenebræ: nihil enim æque ſolet conciliare ſomnum, quàm caliginoſa profundæ notis obſcuritas.

STAMMERER, Balbus, blæſus. Goth. STAMMS. A. S. ſtamen, ſtamun. D. ſtam. B. ſtameler. Su. ſtamma. Iſl. ſtamr. Sunt à ϛωμυλεῖν vel ϛωμύλλειν, nimiâ loquacitate alios offendere; quod impeditè loquentes libentiſſimè garrire ſoleant; vel quod aliis nimii ſemper videantur, etiam parciſſimè loquentes.

ſhould find, or chance ſhould offer it, in the boundleſs chaos of a living ſpeech. My ſearch, however, has been either ſkilful or lucky; for I have much augmented the vocabulary.

As my deſign was a dictionary common or appellative, I have omitted all words which have relation to proper names; ſuch as *Arian*, *Socinian*, *Calviniſt*, *Benedictine*, *Mahometan*; but have retained thoſe of a more general nature, as *Heathen*, *Pagan*.

Of the terms of art I have received ſuch as could be found either in books of ſcience or technical dictionaries; and have often inſerted, from philoſophical writers, words which are ſupported perhaps only by a ſingle authority, and which being not admitted into general uſe, ſtand yet as candidates or probationers, and muſt depend for their adoption on the ſuffrage of futurity.

The words which our authours have introduced by their knowledge of foreign languages, or ignorance of their own, by vanity or wantonneſs, by compliance with faſhion, or luſt of innovation, I have regiſtred as they occurred, though commonly only to cenſure them, and warn others againſt the folly of naturalizing uſeleſs foreigners to the injury of the natives.

I have not rejected any by deſign, merely becauſe they were unneceſſary or exuberant; but have received thoſe which by different writers have been differently formed, as *viſcid*, and *viſcidity*, *viſcous*, and *viſcoſity*.

Compounded or double words I have ſeldom noted, except when they obtain a ſignification different from that which the components have in their ſimple ſtate. Thus *highwayman*, *woodman*, and *horſecourſer*, require an explication; but of *thieflike* or *coachdriver* no notice was needed, becauſe the primitives contain the meaning of the compounds.

Words arbitrarily formed by a conſtant and ſettled analogy, like diminutive adjectives in *iſh*, as *greeniſh*, *bluiſh*, adverbs in *ly*, as *dully*, *openly*, ſubſtantives in *neſs*, as *vileneſs*, *faultineſs*, were leſs diligently ſought, and many ſometimes have been omitted, when I had no authority that invited me to inſert them; not that they are not genuine and regular offſprings of *Engliſh* roots, but becauſe their relation to the primitive being always the ſame, their ſignification cannot be miſtaken.

The verbal nouns in *ing*, ſuch as the *keeping* of the *caſtle*, the *leading* of the *army*, are always neglected, or placed only to illuſtrate the ſenſe of the verb, except when they ſignify things as well as actions, and have therefore a plural number, as *dwelling*, *living*; or have an abſolute and abſtract ſignification, as *colouring*, *painting*, *learning*.

The participles are likewiſe omitted, unleſs, by ſignifying rather qualities than action, they take the nature of adjectives; as a *thinking* man, a man of prudence; a *pacing* horſe, a horſe that can pace: theſe I have ventured to call *participial adjectives*. But neither are theſe always inſerted, becauſe they are commonly to be underſtood, without any danger of miſtake, by conſulting the verb.

Obſolete words are admitted, when they are found in authours not obſolete, or when they have any force or beauty that may deſerve revival.

As compoſition is one of the chief characteriſticks of a language, I have endeavoured to make ſome reparation for the univerſal negligence of my predeceſſors, by inſerting great numbers of compounded words, as may be found under *after*, *fore*, *new*, *night*, and many more. Theſe, numerous as they are, might be multiplied, but that uſe and curioſity are here ſatisfied, and the frame of our language and modes of our combination are amply diſcovered.

Of ſome forms of compoſition, ſuch as that by which *re* is prefixed to note *repetition*, and *un* to ſignify *contrariety* or *privation*, all the examples cannot be accumulated, becauſe the uſe of theſe particles, if not wholly arbitrary, is ſo little limited, that they are hourly united to new words as occaſion requires, or is imagined to require them.

There is another kind of compoſition more frequent in our language than perhaps in any other, from which ariſes to foreigners the greateſt difficulty. We modify the ſignification of many verbs by a particle ſubjoined; as to *come off*, to eſcape by a fetch; to *fall on*, to attack; to *fall off*, to apoſtatize; to *break off*, to ſtop abruptly; to *bear out*, to juſtify; to *fall in*, to comply; to *give over*, to ceaſe; to *ſet off*, to embelliſh; to *ſet in*, to begin a continual tenour; to *ſet out*, to begin a courſe or journey; to *take off*, to copy; with innumerable expreſſions of the ſame kind, of which ſome appear wildly irregular, being ſo far diſtant from the ſenſe of the ſimple words, that no ſagacity will be able to trace the ſteps by which they arrived at the preſent uſe. Theſe I have noted with great care; and though I cannot flatter myſelf that the collection is complete, I have perhaps ſo far aſſiſted the ſtudents of our language, that this kind of phraſeology will be no longer inſuperable; and the combinations of verbs and particles, by chance omitted, will be eaſily explained by compariſon with thoſe that may be found.

Many words yet ſtand ſupported only by the name of *Bailey*, *Ainſworth*, *Philips*, or the contracted *Dict.* for *Dictionaries* ſubjoined: of theſe I am not always certain that they are ſeen in any book but the works of lexicographers. Of ſuch I have omitted many, becauſe I had never read them; and many I have inſerted, becauſe they may perhaps exiſt, though they have eſcaped my notice: they are, however,

however, to be yet considered as resting only upon the credit of former dictionaries. Others, which I considered as useful, or know to be proper, though I could not at present support them by authorities, I have suffered to stand upon my own attestation, claiming the same privilege with my predecessors of being sometimes credited without proof.

The words, thus selected and disposed, are grammatically considered: they are referred to the different parts of speech; traced, when they are irregularly inflected, through their various terminations; and illustrated by observations, not indeed of great or striking importance, separately considered, but necessary to the elucidation of our language, and hitherto neglected or forgotten by *English* grammarians.

That part of my work on which I expect malignity most frequently to fasten, is the *Explanation*; in which I cannot hope to satisfy those, who are perhaps not inclined to be pleased, since I have not always been able to satisfy myself. To interpret a language by itself is very difficult; many words cannot be explained by synonimes, because the idea signified by them has not more than one appellation; nor by paraphrase, because simple ideas cannot be described. When the nature of things is unknown, or the notion unsettled and indefinite, and various in various minds, the words by which such notions are conveyed, or such things denoted, will be ambiguous and perplexed. And such is the fate of hapless lexicography, that not only darkness, but light, impedes and distresses it; things may be not only too little, but too much known, to be happily illustrated. To explain, requires the use of terms less abstruse than that which is to be explained, and such terms cannot always be found; for as nothing can be proved but by supposing something intuitively known, and evident without proof, so nothing can be defined but by the use of words too plain to admit a definition.

Other words there are, of which the sense is too subtle and evanescent to be fixed in a paraphrase; such are all those which are by the grammarians termed *expletives*, and, in dead languages, are suffered to pass for empty sounds, of no other use than to fill a verse, or to modulate a period, but which are easily perceived in living tongues to have power and emphasis, though it be sometimes such as no other form of expression can convey.

My labour has likewise been much increased by a class of verbs too frequent in the *English* language, of which the signification is so loose and general, the use so vague and indeterminate, and the senses detorted so widely from the first idea, that it is hard to trace them through the maze of variation, to catch them on the brink of utter inanity, to circumscribe them by any limitations, or interpret them by any words of distinct and settled meaning: such are *bear*, *break*, *come*, *cast*, *full*, *get*, *give*, *do*, *put*, *set*, *go*, *run*, *make*, *take*, *turn*, *throw*. If of these the whole power is not accurately delivered, it must be remembered, that while our language is yet living, and variable by the caprice of every one that speaks it, these words are hourly shifting their relations, and can no more be ascertained in a dictionary, than a grove, in the agitation of a storm, can be accurately delineated from its picture in the water.

The particles are among all nations applied with so great latitude, that they are not easily reducible under any regular scheme of explication: this difficulty is not less, nor perhaps greater, in *English*, than in other languages. I have laboured them with diligence, I hope with success; such at least as can be expected in a task, which no man, however learned or sagacious, has yet been able to perform.

Some words there are which I cannot explain, because I do not understand them; these might have been omitted very often with little inconvenience, but I would not so far indulge my vanity as to decline this confession: for when *Tully* owns himself ignorant whether *lessus*, in the twelve tables, means a *funeral song*, or *mourning garment*; and *Aristotle* doubts whether οὔρευς, in the Iliad, signifies a *mule*, or *muleteer*, I may freely, without shame, leave some obscurities to happier industry, or future information.

The rigour of interpretative lexicography requires that *the explanation, and the word explained, should be always reciprocal*; this I have always endeavoured, but could not always attain. Words are seldom exactly synonimous; a new term was not introduced, but because the former was thought inadequate: names, therefore, have often many ideas, but few ideas have many names. It was then necessary to use the proximate word, for the deficiency of single terms can very seldom be supplied by circumlocution; nor is the inconvenience great of such mutilated interpretations, because the sense may easily be collected entire from the examples.

In every word of extensive use, it was requisite to mark the progress of its meaning, and show by what gradations of intermediate sense it has passed from its primitive to its remote and accidental signification; so that every foregoing explanation should tend to that which follows, and the series be regularly concatenated from the first notion to the last.

This is specious, but not always practicable; kindred senses may be so interwoven, that the perplexity cannot be disentangled, nor any reason be assigned why one should be ranged before the other. When the radical idea branches out into parallel ramifications, how can a consecutive series be formed of senses in their nature collateral? The shades of meaning sometimes pass imperceptibly into each other; so that though on one side they apparently differ, yet it is impossible to mark the point of contact. Ideas of the same race, though not exactly alike, are sometimes so little different, that no words can express the dissimilitude, though the mind easily perceives it, when they are exhibited

bited together; and ſometimes there is ſuch a confuſion of acceptations, that diſcernment is wearied, and diſtinction puzzled, and perſeverance herſelf hurries to an end, by crouding together what ſhe cannot ſeparate.

Theſe complaints of difficulty will, by thoſe that have never conſidered words beyond their popular uſe, be thought only the jargon of a man willing to magnify his labours, and procure veneration to his ſtudies by involution and obſcurity. But every art is obſcure to thoſe that have not learned it: this uncertainty of terms, and commixture of ideas, is well known to thoſe who have joined philoſophy with grammar; and if I have not expreſſed them very clearly, it muſt be remembered that I am ſpeaking of that which words are inſufficient to explain.

The original ſenſe of words is often driven out of uſe by their metaphorical acceptations, yet muſt be inſerted for the ſake of a regular origination. Thus I know not whether *ardour* is uſed for *material heat*, or whether *flagrant*, in *Engliſh*, ever ſignifies the ſame with *burning*; yet ſuch are the primitive ideas of theſe words, which are therefore ſet firſt, though without examples, that the figurative ſenſes may be commodiouſly deduced.

Such is the exuberance of ſignification which many words have obtained, that it was ſcarcely poſſible to collect all their ſenſes; ſometimes the meaning of derivatives muſt be ſought in the mother term, and ſometimes deficient explanations of the primitive may be ſupplied in the train of derivation. In any caſe of doubt or difficulty, it will be always proper to examine all the words of the ſame race; for ſome words are ſlightly paſſed over to avoid repetition, ſome admitted eaſier and clearer explanation than others, and all will be better underſtood, as they are conſidered in greate. variety of ſtructures and relations.

All the interpretations of words are not written with the ſame ſkill, or the ſame happineſs: things equally eaſy in themſelves, are not all equally eaſy to any ſingle mind. Every writer of a long work commits errours, where there appears neither ambiguity to miſlead, nor obſcurity to confound him; and in a ſearch like this, many felicities of expreſſion will be caſually overlooked, many convenient parallels will be forgotten, and many particulars will admit improvement from a mind utterly unequal to the whole performance.

But many ſeeming faults are to be imputed rather to the nature of the undertaking, than the negligence of the performer. Thus ſome explanations are unavoidably reciprocal or circular, as *hind, the female of the ſtag*; *ſtag, the male of the hind*: ſometimes eaſier words are changed into harder, as *burial* into *ſepulture* or *interment*, *drier* into *deſiccative*, *dryneſs* into *ſiccity* or *aridity*, *fit* into *paroxyſm*; for the eaſieſt word, whatever it be, can never be tranſlated into one more eaſy. But eaſineſs and difficulty are merely relative, and if the preſent prevalence of our language ſhould invite foreigners to this dictionary, many will be aſſiſted by thoſe words which now ſeem only to increaſe or produce obſcurity. For this reaſon I have endeavoured frequently to join a *Teutonick* and *Roman* interpretation, as to CHEER to *gladden*, or *exhilarate*, that every learner of *Engliſh* may be aſſiſted by his own tongue.

The ſolution of all difficulties, and the ſupply of all defects, muſt be ſought in the examples, ſubjoined to the various ſenſes of each word, and ranged according to the time of their authours.

When firſt I collected theſe authorities, I was deſirous that every quotation ſhould be uſeful to ſome other end than the illuſtration of a word; I therefore extracted from philoſophers principles of ſcience; from hiſtorians remarkable facts; from chymiſts complete proceſſes; from divines ſtriking exhortations; and from poets beautiful deſcriptions. Such is deſign, while it is yet at a diſtance from execution. When the time called upon me to range this accumulation of elegance and wiſdom into an alphabetical ſeries, I ſoon diſcovered that the bulk of my volumes would fright away the ſtudent, and was forced to depart from my ſcheme of including all that was pleaſing or uſeful in *Engliſh* literature, and reduce my tranſcripts very often to cluſters of words, in which ſcarcely any meaning is retained; thus to the wearineſs of copying, I was condemned to add the vexation of expunging. Some paſſages I have yet ſpared, which may relieve the labour of verbal ſearches, and interſperſe with verdure and flowers the duſty deſarts of barren philology.

The examples, thus mutilated, are no longer to be conſidered as conveying the ſentiments or doctrine of their authours; the word for the ſake of which they are inſerted, with all its appendant clauſes, has been carefully preſerved; but it may ſometimes happen, by haſty detruncation, that the general tendency of the ſentence may be changed: the divine may deſert his tenets, or the philoſopher his ſyſtem.

Some of the examples have been taken from writers who were never mentioned as maſters of elegance or models of ſtile; but words muſt be ſought where they are uſed; and in what pages, eminent for purity, can terms of manufacture or agriculture be found? Many quotations ſerve no other purpoſe, than that of proving the bare exiſtence of words, and are therefore ſelected with leſs ſcrupulouſneſs than thoſe which are to teach their ſtructures and relations.

My purpoſe was to admit no teſtimony of living authours, that I might not be miſled by partiality, and that none of my cotemporaries might have reaſon to complain; nor have I departed from this reſolution, but when ſome performance of uncommon excellence excited my veneration, when my memory ſupplied me, from late books, with an example that was wanting, or when my heart, in the tenderneſs of friendſhip, ſolicited admiſſion for a favourite name.

So

PREFACE.

So far have I been from any care to grace my pages with modern decorations, that I have ſtudiouſly endeavoured to collect examples and authorities from the writers before the reſtoration, whoſe works I regard as *the wells of Engliſh undefiled*, as the pure ſources of genuine diction. Our language, for almoſt a century, has, by the concurrence of many cauſes, been gradually departing from its original *Teutonick* character, and deviating towards a *Gallick* ſtructure and phraſeology, from which it ought to be our endeavour to recal it, by making our ancient volumes the ground-work of ſtile, admitting among the additions of later times, only ſuch as may ſupply real deficiencies, ſuch as are readily adopted by the genius of our tongue, and incorporate eaſily with our native idioms.

But as every language has a time of rudeneſs antecedent to perfection, as well as of falſe refinement and declenſion, I have been cautious leſt my zeal for antiquity might drive me into times too remote, and croud my book with words now no longer underſtood. I have fixed *Sidney*'s work for the boundary, beyond which I make few excurſions. From the authours which roſe in the time of *Elizabeth*, a ſpeech might be formed adequate to all the purpoſes of uſe and elegance. If the language of theology were extracted from *Hooker* and the tranſlation of the Bible; the terms of natural knowledge from *Bacon*; the phraſes of policy, war, and navigation from *Raleigh*; the dialect of poetry and fiction from *Spenſer* and *Sidney*; and the diction of common life from *Shakeſpeare*, few ideas would be loſt to mankind, for want of *Engliſh* words, in which they might be expreſſed.

It is not ſufficient that a word is found, unleſs it be ſo combined as that its meaning is apparently determined by the tract and tenour of the ſentence; ſuch paſſages I have therefore choſen, and when it happened that any authour gave a definition of a term, or ſuch an explanation as is equivalent to a definition, I have placed his authority as a ſupplement to my own, without regard to the chronological order, that is otherwiſe obſerved.

Some words, indeed, ſtand unſupported by any authority, but they are commonly derivative nouns or adverbs, formed from their primitives by regular and conſtant analogy, or names of things ſeldom occurring in books, or words of which I have reaſon to doubt the exiſtence.

There is more danger of cenſure from the multiplicity than paucity of examples; authorities will ſometimes ſeem to have been accumulated without neceſſity or uſe, and perhaps ſome will be found, which might, without loſs, have been omitted. But a work of this kind is not haſtily to be charged with ſuperfluities: thoſe quotations which to careleſs or unſkilful peruſers appear only to repeat the ſame ſenſe, will often exhibit, to a more accurate examiner, diverſities of ſignification, or, at leaſt, afford different ſhades of the ſame meaning: one will ſhew the word applied to perſons, another to things; one will expreſs an ill, another a good, and a third a neutral ſenſe; one will prove the expreſſion genuine from an ancient authour; another will ſhew it elegant from a modern: a doubtful authority is corroborated by another of more credit; an ambiguous ſentence is aſcertained by a paſſage clear and determinate; the word, how often ſoever repeated, appears with new aſſociates and in different combinations, and every quotation contributes ſomething to the ſtability or enlargement of the language.

When words are uſed equivocally, I receive them in either ſenſe; when they are metaphorical, I adopt them in their primitive acceptation.

I have ſometimes, though rarely, yielded to the temptation of exhibiting a genealogy of ſentiments, by ſhewing how one authour copied the thoughts and diction of another: ſuch quotations are indeed little more than repetitions, which might juſtly be cenſured, did they not gratify the mind, by affording a kind of intellectual hiſtory.

The various ſyntactical ſtructures occurring in the examples have been carefully noted; the licence or negligence with which many words have been hitherto uſed, has made our ſtile capricious and indeterminate; when the different combinations of the ſame word are exhibited together, the preference is readily given to propriety, and I have often endeavoured to direct the choice.

Thus have I laboured to ſettle the orthography, diſplay the analogy, regulate the ſtructures, and aſcertain the ſignification of *Engliſh* words, to perform all the parts of a faithful lexicographer: but I have not always executed my own ſcheme, or ſatisfied my own expectations. The work, whatever proofs of diligence and attention it may exhibit, is yet capable of many improvements: the orthography which I recommend is ſtill controvertible, the etymology which I adopt is uncertain, and perhaps frequently erroneous; the explanations are ſometimes too much contracted, and ſometimes too much diffuſed, the ſignifications are diſtinguiſhed rather with ſubtilty than ſkill, and the attention is harraſſed with unneceſſary minuteneſs.

The examples are too often injudiciouſly truncated, and perhaps ſometimes, I hope very rarely, alleged in a miſtaken ſenſe; for in making this collection I truſted more to memory, than, in a ſtate of diſquiet and embarraſſment, memory can contain, and purpoſed to ſupply at the review what was left incomplete in the firſt tranſcription.

Many terms appropriated to particular occupations, though neceſſary and ſignificant, are undoubtedly omitted; and of the words moſt ſtudiouſly conſidered and exemplified, many ſenſes have eſcaped obſervation.

Yet theſe failures, however frequent, may admit extenuation and apology. To have attempted much is always laudable, even when the enterprize is above the ſtrength that undertakes it: To reſt below his own aim is incident to every one whose fancy is active, and whose views are comprehensive; nor is any man satisfied with himself because he has done much, but because he can conceive little. When first I engaged in this work, I resolved to leave neither words nor things unexamined, and pleased myself with a prospect of the hours which I should revel away in feasts of literature, the obscure recesses of northern learning, which I should enter and ransack, the treasures with which I expected every search into those neglected mines to reward my labour, and the triumph with which I should display my acquisitions to mankind. When I had thus enquired into the original of words, I resolved to show likewise my attention to things; to pierce deep into every science, to enquire the nature of every substance of which I inserted the name, to limit every idea by a definition strictly logical, and exhibit every production of art or nature in an accurate description, that my book might be in place of all other dictionaries whether appellative or technical. But these were the dreams of a poet doomed at last to wake a lexicographer. I soon found that it is too late to look for instruments, when the work calls for execution, and that whatever abilities I had brought to my task, with those I must finally perform it. To deliberate whenever I doubted, to enquire whenever I was ignorant, would have protracted the undertaking without end, and, perhaps, without much improvement; for I did not find by my first experiments, that what I had not of my own was easily to be obtained: I saw that one enquiry only gave occasion to another, that book referred to book, that to search was not always to find, and to find was not always to be informed; and that thus to persue perfection, was, like the first inhabitants of Arcadia, to chace the sun, which, when they had reached the hill where he seemed to rest, was still beheld at the same distance from them.

I then contracted my design, determining to confide in myself, and no longer to solicit auxiliaries, which produced more incumbrance than assistance: by this I obtained at least one advantage, that I set limits to my work, which would in time be finished, though not completed.

Despondency has never so far prevailed as to depress me to negligence; some faults will at last appear to be the effects of anxious diligence and persevering activity. The nice and subtle ramifications of meaning were not easily avoided by a mind intent upon accuracy, and convinced of the necessity of disentangling combinations, and separating similitudes. Many of the distinctions which to common readers appear useless and idle, will be found real and important by men versed in the school philosophy, without which no dictionary ever shall be accurately compiled, or skilfully examined.

Some senses however there are, which, though not the same, are yet so nearly allied, that they are often confounded. Most men think indistinctly, and therefore cannot speak with exactness; and consequently some examples might be indifferently put to either signification: this uncertainty is not to be imputed to me, who do not form, but register the language; who do not teach men how they should think, but relate how they have hitherto expressed their thoughts.

The imperfect sense of some examples I lamented, but could not remedy, and hope they will be compensated by innumerable passages selected with propriety, and preserved with exactness; some shining with sparks of imagination, and some replete with treasures of wisdom.

The orthography and etymology, though imperfect, are not imperfect for want of care, but because care will not always be successful, and recollection or information come too late for use.

That many terms of art and manufacture are omitted, must be frankly acknowledged; but for this defect I may boldly allege that it was unavoidable: I could not visit caverns to learn the miner's language, nor take a voyage to perfect my skill in the dialect of navigation, nor visit the warehouses of merchants, and shops of artificers, to gain the names of wares, tools and operations, of which no mention is found in books; what favourable accident, or easy enquiry brought within my reach, has not been neglected; but it had been a hopeless labour to glean up words, by courting living information, and contesting with the sullenness of one, and the roughness of another.

To furnish the academicians *della Crusca* with words of this kind, a series of comedies called *la Fiera*, or *the Fair*, was professedly written by *Buonaroti*; but I had no such assistant, and therefore was content to want what they must have wanted likewise, had they not luckily been so supplied.

Nor are all words which are not found in the vocabulary, to be lamented as omissions. Of the laborious and mercantile part of the people, the diction is in a great measure casual and mutable; many of their terms are formed for some temporary or local convenience, and though current at certain times and places, are in others utterly unknown. This fugitive cant, which is always in a state of increase or decay, cannot be regarded as any part of the durable materials of a language, and therefore must be suffered to perish with other things unworthy of preservation.

Care will sometimes betray to the appearance of negligence. He that is catching opportunities which seldom occur, will suffer those to pass by unreguarded, which he expects hourly to return; he that is searching for rare and remote things, will neglect those that are obvious and familiar: thus many of the most common and cursory words have been inserted with little illustration, because in gathering the authorities, I forbore to copy those which I thought likely to occur whenever they were wanted. It is remarkable that, in reviewing my collection, I found the word SEA unexemplified.

Thus

Thus it happens, that in things difficult there is danger from ignorance, and in things easy from confidence; the mind, afraid of greatness, and disdainful of littleness, hastily withdraws herself from painful searches, and passes with scornful rapidity over tasks not adequate to her powers, sometimes too secure for caution, and again too anxious for vigorous effort; sometimes idle in a plain path, and sometimes distracted in labyrinths, and dissipated by different intentions.

A large work is difficult because it is large, even though all its parts might singly be performed with facility; where there are many things to be done, each must be allowed its share of time and labour, in the proportion only which it bears to the whole; nor can it be expected, that the stones which form the dome of a temple, should be squared and polished like the diamond of a ring.

Of the event of this work, for which, having laboured it with so much application, I cannot but have some degree of parental fondness, it is natural to form conjectures. Those who have been persuaded to think well of my design, require that it should fix our language, and put a stop to those alterations which time and chance have hitherto been suffered to make in it without opposition. With this consequence I will confess that I flattered myself for a while; but now begin to fear that I have indulged expectation which neither reason nor experience can justify. When we see men grow old and die at a certain time one after another, from century to century, we laugh at the elixir that promises to prolong life to a thousand years; and with equal justice may the lexicographer be derided, who being able to produce no example of a nation that has preserved their words and phrases from mutability, shall imagine that his dictionary can embalm his language, and secure it from corruption and decay, that it is in his power to change sublunary nature, or clear the world at once from folly, vanity, and affectation.

With this hope, however, academies have been instituted, to guard the avenues of their languages, to retain fugitives, and repulse intruders; but their vigilance and activity have hitherto been vain; sounds are too volatile and subtile for legal restraints; to enchain syllables, and to lash the wind, are equally the undertakings of pride, unwilling to measure its desires by its strength. The *French* language has visibly changed under the inspection of the academy; the stile of *Amelot*'s translation of father *Paul* is observed by *Le Courayer* to be *un peu passé*; and no *Italian* will maintain, that the diction of any modern writer is not perceptibly different from that of *Boccace*, *Machiavel*, or *Caro*.

Total and sudden transformations of a language seldom happen; conquests and migrations are now very rare: but there are other causes of change, which, though slow in their operation, and invisible in their progress, are perhaps as much superiour to human resistance, as the revolutions of the sky, or intumescence of the tide. Commerce, however necessary, however lucrative, as it depraves the manners, corrupts the language; they that have frequent intercourse with strangers, to whom they endeavour to accommodate themselves, must in time learn a mingled dialect, like the jargon which serves the traffickers on the *Mediterranean* and *Indian* coasts. This will not always be confined to the exchange, the warehouse, or the port, but will be communicated by degrees to other ranks of the people, and be at last incorporated with the current speech.

There are likewise internal causes equally forcible. The language most likely to continue long without alteration, would be that of a nation raised a little, and but a little, above barbarity, secluded from strangers, and totally employed in procuring the conveniencies of life; either without books, or, like some of the *Mahometan* countries, with very few: men thus busied and unlearned, having only such words as common use requires, would perhaps long continue to express the same notions by the same signs. But no such constancy can be expected in a people polished by arts, and classed by subordination, where one part of the community is sustained and accommodated by the labour of the other. Those who have much leisure to think, will always be enlarging the stock of ideas, and every increase of knowledge, whether real or fancied, will produce new words, or combinations of words. When the mind is unchained from necessity, it will range after convenience; when it is left at large in the fields of speculation, it will shift opinions; as any custom is disused, the words that expressed it must perish with it; as any opinion grows popular, it will innovate speech in the same proportion as it alters practice.

As by the cultivation of various sciences, a language is amplified, it will be more furnished with words deflected from their original sense; the geometrician will talk of a courtier's zenith, or the excentrick virtue of a wild hero, and the physician of sanguine expectations and phlegmatick delays. Copiousness of speech will give opportunities to capricious choice, by which some words will be preferred, and others degraded; vicissitudes of fashion will enforce the use of new, or extend the signification of known terms. The tropes of poetry will make hourly encroachments, and the metaphorical will become the current sense: pronunciation will be varied by levity or ignorance, and the pen must at length comply with the tongue; illiterate writers will at one time or other, by publick infatuation, rise into renown, who, not knowing the original import of words, will use them with colloquial licentiousness, confound distinction, and forget propriety. As politeness increases, some expressions will be considered as too gross and vulgar for the delicate, others as too formal and ceremonious for the gay and airy; new phrases are therefore adopted, which must, for the same reasons, be in time dismissed. *Swift*, in his petty treatise on the *English* language, allows that new words must sometimes be introduced, but proposes that none should be suffered to become obsolete. But what makes a word obsolete, more than general agreement to forbear it? and how shall it be continued, when it conveys an offensive idea, or recalled again into the mouths of mankind, when it has once by disuse become unfamiliar, and by unfamiliarity unpleasing.

There is another cause of alteration more prevalent than any other, which yet in the present state of the world cannot be obviated. A mixture of two languages will produce a third distinct from both; and they will always be mixed, where the chief part of education, and the most conspicuous accomplishment, is skill in ancient or in foreign tongues. He that has long cultivated another language, will find its words and combinations croud upon his memory; and haste or negligence, refinement or affectation, will obtrude borrowed terms and exotick expressions.

The great pest of speech is frequency of translation. No book was ever turned from one language into another, without imparting something of its native idiom; this is the most mischievous and comprehensive innovation; single words may enter by thousands, and the fabrick of the tongue continue the same, but new phraseology changes much at once; it alters not the single stones of the building, but the order of the columns. If an academy should be established for the cultivation of our stile, which I, who can never wish to see dependance multiplied, hope the spirit of *English* liberty will hinder or destroy, let them, instead of compiling grammars and dictionaries, endeavour, with all their influence, to stop the licence of translatours, whose idleness and ignorance, if it be suffered to proceed, will reduce us to babble a dialect of *France*.

If the changes we fear be thus irresistible, what remains but to acquiesce with silence, as in the other insurmountable distresses of humanity? it remains that we retard what we cannot repel, that we palliate what we cannot cure. Life may be lengthened by care, though death cannot be ultimately defeated: tongues, like governments, have a natural tendency to degeneration; we have long preserved our constitution, let us make some struggles for our language.

In hope of giving longevity to that which its own nature forbids to be immortal, I have devoted this book, the labour of years, to the honour of my country, that we may no longer yield the palm of philology without a contest to the nations of the continent. The chief glory of every people arises from its authours: whether I shall add any thing by my own writings to the reputation of *English* literature, must be left to time: much of my life has been lost under the pressures of disease; much has been trifled away; and much has always been spent in provision for the day that was passing over me; but I shall not think my employment useless or ignoble, if by my assistance foreign nations, and distant ages, gain access to the propagators of knowledge, and understand the teachers of truth; if my labours afford light to the repositories of science, and add celebrity to *Bacon*, to *Hooker*, to *Milton*, and to *Boyle*.

When I am animated by this wish, I look with pleasure on my book, however defective, and deliver it to the world with the spirit of a man that has endeavoured well. That it will immediately become popular I have not promised to myself: a few wild blunders, and risible absurdities, from which no work of such multiplicity was ever free, may for a time furnish folly with laughter, and harden ignorance in contempt; but useful diligence will at last prevail, and there never can be wanting some who distinguish desert; who will consider that no dictionary of a living tongue ever can be perfect, since while it is hastening to publication, some words are budding, and some falling away; that a whole life cannot be spent upon syntax and etymology, and that even a whole life would not be sufficient; that he, whose design includes whatever language can express, must often speak of what he does not understand; that a writer will sometimes be hurried by eagerness to the end, and sometimes faint with weariness under a task, which *Scaliger* compares to the labours of the anvil and the mine; that what is obvious is not always known, and what is known is not always present; that sudden fits of inadvertency will surprize vigilance, slight avocations will seduce attention, and casual eclipses will darken learning; and that the writer shall often in vain trace his memory at the moment of need, for that which yesterday he knew with intuitive readiness, and which will come uncalled into his thoughts to-morrow.

In this work, when it shall be found that much is omitted, let it not be forgotten that much likewise is performed; and though no book was ever spared out of tenderness to the authour, and the world is little solicitous to know whence proceeded the faults of that which it condemns; yet it may gratify curiosity to inform it, that the *English Dictionary* was written with little assistance of the learned, and without any patronage of the great; not in the soft obscurities of retirement, or under the shelter of academick bowers, but amidst inconvenience and distraction, in sickness and in sorrow: and it may repress the triumph of malignant criticism to observe, that if our language is not here fully displayed, I have only failed in an attempt which no human powers have hitherto completed. If the lexicons of ancient tongues, now immutably fixed, and comprised in a few volumes, are yet, after the toil of successive ages, inadequate and delusive; if the aggregated knowledge, and co-operating diligence of the *Italian* academicians, did not secure them from the censure of *Beni*; if the embodied criticks of *France*, when fifty years had been spent upon their work, were obliged to change its oeconomy, and give their second edition another form, I may surely be contented without the praise of perfection, which, if I could obtain, in this gloom of solitude, what would it avail me? I have protracted my work till most of those whom I wished to please, have sunk into the grave, and success and miscarriage are empty sounds: I therefore dismiss it with frigid tranquillity, having little to fear or hope from censure or from praise.

THE

HISTORY

OF THE

ENGLISH LANGUAGE.

THOUGH the *Britains* or *Welsh* were the first possessors of this island, whose names are recorded, and are therefore in civil history always considered as the predecessors of the present inhabitants; yet the deduction of the *English* language, from the earliest times of which we have any knowledge to its present state, requires no mention of them: for we have so few words, which can, with any probability, be refered to *British* roots, that we justly regard the *Saxons* and *Welsh*, as nations totally distinct. It has been conjectured, that when the *Saxons* seized this country, they suffered the *Britains* to live among them in a state of vassalage, employed in the culture of the ground, and other laborious and ignoble services. But it is scarcely possible, that a nation, however depressed, should have been mixed in considerable numbers with the *Saxons* without some communication of their tongue, and therefore it may, with great reason, be imagined, that those, who were not sheltered in the mountains, perished by the sword.

The whole fabrick and scheme of the *English* language is *Gothick* or *Teutonick*: it is a dialect of that tongue, which prevails over all the northern countries of *Europe*, except those where the *Sclavonian* is spoken. Of these languages Dr. *Hickes* has thus exhibited the genealogy.

GOTHICK,

- ANGLO-SAXON,
  - Dutch,
  - Frisick,
  - English.
- FRANCICK,
  - German.
- CIMBRICK,
  - Islandick,
  - Norwegian,
  - Swedish.
  - Danish.

Of the *Gothick*, the only monument remaining is a copy of the gospels somewhat mutilated, which, from the silver with which the characters are adorned, is called the *silver book*. It is now preserved at *Upsal*, and has been twice published. Whether the diction of this venerable manuscript be purely *Gothick*, has been doubted; it seems however to exhibit the most ancient dialect now to be found of the *Teutonick* race, and the *Saxon*, which is the original of the present *English*, was either derived from it, or both descended from some common parent.

What was the form of the *Saxon* language, when, about the year 450, they first entred *Britain*, cannot now be known. They seem to have been a people without learning, and very probably without an alphabet; their speech therefore, having been always cursory and extemporaneous, must have been artless and unconnected, without any modes of transition or involution of clauses; which abruptness and inconnection may be observed even in their later writings. This barbarity may be supposed to have continued during their wars with the *Britains*, which for a time left them no leisure for softer studies; nor is there any reason for supposing it abated, till the year 570, when *Augustine* came from *Rome* to convert them to Christianity. The Christian religion always implies or produces a certain degree of civility and learning; they then became by degrees acquainted with the *Roman* language, and so gained, from time to time, some knowledge and elegance, till in three centuries they had formed a language capable of expressing all the sentiments of a civilised people, as appears by king *Alfred*'s paraphrase or imitation of *Boethius*, and his short preface, which I have selected as the first specimen of ancient *English*.

CAP. I.

ON ðære tide þe Gotan of Sciððiu mægþe ƿiþ Romana rice geƿin upahofon. ⁊ miþ heora cyningum. Rædgota and Eallerica ƿæron hatne. Romane burig abræcon. and eall Italia rice ꝥ is betƿux þam muntum ⁊ Sicilia ðam ealonde in anƿald gerehton. ⁊ þa æfter þam foresprecenan cyningum Ðeodric feng to þam ilcan rice se Ðeodric ƿæs Amulinga. he ƿæs Cristen þeah he on þam Arrianiscan gedƿolan ðurhƿunode. Ðe gehet Romanum his freondscipe. sƿa ꝥ hi mostan heora ealdrihta ƿyrðe beon. Ac he þa gehat sƿiðe yfele gelæste. ⁊ sƿiðe ƿraþe geendode mid manegum mane. ꝥ ƿæs to eacan oþrum unarimedum yflum. ꝥ he Iohannes þone papan het ofslean. Ða ƿæs sum consul. ꝥ ƿe heretoha hataþ. Boetius ƿæs haten. se ƿæs in boccræftum ⁊ on poruld þeaƿum se rihtƿisesta. Se ða ongeat þa manigfealdan yfel þe se cyning Ðeodric ƿiþ þam Cristenandome ⁊ ƿiþ þam Romaniscum ƿitum dyde. he þa gemunde ðara eþnessa ⁊ þara ealdrihta ðe hi under ðam Caserum hæfdon heora ealdhlafordum. Ða ongan he smeagan ⁊ leornigan on him selfum hu he ꝥ rice ðam unrihtƿisan cyninge aferran mihte. ⁊ on ryht geleaffulra and on rihtƿisra anƿald gebringan. Sende þa digellice ærendgeƿritu to þam Casere to Constantinopolim. þær is Creca heah burg ⁊ heora cynestol. forþam se Casere ƿæs heora ealdhlaford cynnes. bædon hine þæt he him to heora Cristendome ⁊ to heora ealdrihtum gefultumede. Ða ꝥ ongeat se ƿælhreoƿa cyning Ðeodric. ða het he hine gebringan on carcerne ⁊ þær inne belucan. Ða hit ða gelomp ꝥ se arƿyrða ƿær on sƿa micelre nearanesse becom. þa ƿæs he sƿa micle sƿiðor on his Mode gedrefed. sƿa his Mod ær sƿiðor to þam poruld sælþum ungeƿod ƿæs. ⁊ he ða nanre frofre be innan þam carcerne ne gemunde. ac he gefeoll niƿol of dune on þa flor. ⁊ hine astrehte sƿiþe unrot. and ormod hine selfne ongan ƿepan ⁊ þus singende cƿæþ.

CAP. II.

ÐA hoð þe ic ƿrecca geo lustbærlice song. ic sceal nu heofiende singan. ⁊ mid sƿi ungeradum ƿordum gesettan. þeah ic geo hƿilum gecoplice funde. ac ic nu ƿepende ⁊ gisciende of geradra ƿorda misso. me ablendan þas ungetreoƿan ƿoruld sælþa. ⁊ me þa forletan sƿa blindne on þis dimme hol. Ða bereafodon ælcere lustbærnesse þa ða ic him æfre betst truƿode, ða ƿendon hi me heora bæc to and me mid ealle fromgeƿitan. To ƿhon sceoldan la mine friend seggan þæt ic gesælig mon ƿære. hu mæg se beon gesælig se ðe on ðam gesælþum ðurhƿuman ne mot:·

CAP. III.

ÐA ic þa ðis leoþ. cƿæð Boetius. geomriende asungen hæfde. ða com ðær gan in to me heofencund ƿisdom. ⁊ þ min murnende Mod mid his ƿordum gegrette. ⁊ þus cƿæþ. Þu ne eart þu se mon þe on minre scole ƿære afed ⁊ gelæred. Ac hƿonon ƿurde þu mid þissum ƿoruld sorgum þus sƿiþe geƿenced. buton ic ƿat þ þu hæfst ðara ƿæpna to hraþe forgiten ðe ic þe ær sealde. Ða clipode se Ƿisdom ⁊ cƿæþ. Geƿitaþ nu aƿirgede ƿoruld sorga of mines þegenes Mode. forþam ge sind þa mæstan sceaþan. Lætaþ hine eft hƿeorfan to minum larum. Ða eode se Ƿisdom near. cƿæþ Boetius. minum hreoƿsiendan geþohte. ⁊ hit sƿa moƿolil hƿæt hƿega uparærde. adrigde þa minenes Modes eagan. and hit fran bliþum ƿordum. hƿæþer hit oncneoƿe his fostermodor. mid ðam þe ða þ Mod ƿiþ beƿende. ða gecneoƿ hit sƿiþe sƿeotele his agne modor. þ ƿæs se Ƿisdom þe hit lange ær tyde ⁊ lærde. ac hit ongeat his lare sƿiþe totorenne ⁊ sƿiþe tobrocenne mid dysigra hondum. ⁊ hine þa fran hu þ geƿurde. Ða andsƿyrde se Ƿisdom him ⁊ sæde. þ his gingran hæfdon hine sƿa totorenne. þær þær hi teohhodon þ hi hine eallne habban sceoldon. ac hi gegaderiað monifeald dysig on þære fortruƿunga. ⁊ on þam gilpe butan heora hƿelc eft to hyre bote gecirre:·

This may perhaps be considered as a specimen of the *Saxon* in its highest state of purity, for here are scarcely any words borrowed from the *Roman* dialects.

Of the following version of the gospels the age is not certainly known, but it was probably written between the time of *Alfred* and that of the *Norman* conquest, and therefore may properly be inserted here.

Translations seldom afford just specimens of a language, and least of all those in which a scrupulous and verbal interpretation is endeavoured, because they retain the phraseology and structure of the original tongue; yet they have often this convenience, that the same book, being translated in different ages, affords opportunity of marking the gradations of change, and bringing one age into comparison with another. For this purpose I have placed the *Saxon* version and that of *Wickliffe*, written about the year 1380, in opposite columns; because the convenience of easy collation seems greater than that of regular chronology.

LUCÆ Cap. I.

FORÐAM þe ƿitodlice manega þohton þara þinga race ge-endebyrdan þe on us gefyllede synt.

2 Sƿa us betæhtun þa ðe hit of fruman gesaƿon. and þære spræce þenas ƿæron.

3 Me geþuhte [of-fyligde fram fruma] geornlice eallum. [mid] endebyrdnesse ƿritan ðe. þu ðe selusta Theophilus.

4 Ðæt þu oncnaƿe þara ƿorda soðfæstnesse. of þam ðe þu gelæred eart:·

5 On Herodes dagum Iudea cyninges. ƿæs sum sacerd on naman Zacharias. of Abian tune. ⁊ his ƿif ƿæs of Aarones dohtrum. and hyre nama ƿæs Elizabeth:·

6 Soðlice hig ƿæron butu rihtƿise beforan Gode. gangende on eallum his bebodum ⁊ rihtƿisnessum butan ƿrohte:·

7 And hig næfdon nan bearn. forþam ðe Elizabeth ƿæs unberende. ⁊ hy on hyra dagum butu forð-eodun:·

8 Soðlice ƿæs geƿorden þa Zacharias hys sacerdhades breac on his geƿrixles endebyrdnesse beforan Gode.

9 Æfter geƿunan þæs sacerdhades hlotes. he eode þ he his offrunge sette. ða he on Godes tempel eode.

10 Eall ƿerod þæs folces ƿæs ute gebiddende on þære offrunge timan:·

11 Ða ætyƿde him Drihtnes engel standende on þæs ƿeofodes sƿiðran healfe.

12 Ða ƿearð Zacharias gedrefed þ geseonde. ⁊ him ege onhreas:·

13 Ða cƿæð se engel him to. Ne ondræd þu ðe Zacharias. forþam þin ben is gehyred. ⁊ þin ƿif Elizabeth þe sunu cenð. and þu nemst hys naman Iohannes.

14 ⁊ he byð þe to gefean ⁊ to blisse. ⁊ manega on hys acennednesse gefagniað:·

15 Soðlice he byð mære beforan Drihtne. and he ne drincð ƿin ne beor. ⁊ he bið gefylled on haligum Gaste. þonne gyt of his modor innoðe.

16 And manega Israhela bearna he gecyrð to Drihtne hyra Gode.

17 And he gæð toforan him on gaste ⁊ Elias mihte. þ he fædera heortan to hyra bearnum gecyrre. ⁊ ungeleaffulle to rihtƿisra gleaƿscype. Drihtne fulfremed folc gegearƿian:·

LUK, Chap. I.

IN the dayes of Eroude kyng of Judee ther was a prest Zacarye by name: of the sort of Abia, and his wyf was of the doughtris of Aaron: and hir name was Elizabeth.

2 An bothe weren juste bifore God: goynge in alle the maundementis and justifyingis of the Lord withouten playnt.

3 And thei hadden no child, for Elizabeth was bareyn and bothe weren of greet age in her dayes.

4 And it bifel that whanne Zacarye schould do the office of presthod in the ordir of his course to fore God.

5 Aftir the custom of the presthod, he wente forth by lot and entride into the temple to encensen.

6 And at the multitude of the puple was without forth and preyede in the our of encensying.

7 And an aungel of the Lord apperide to him: and stood on the right half of the auter of encense.

8 And Zacarye seynge was afrayed: and drede fel upon him.

9 And the aungel sayde to him, Zacarye drede thou not: for thy preier is herd, and Elizabeth thi wif schal bere to thee a sone: and his name schal be clepid Jon.

10 And joye and gladyng schal be to thee: and manye schulen have joye in his natyvyte.

11 For he schal be great bifore the Lord: and he schal not drinke wyn ne sydyr, and he schal be fulfild with the holy gost yit of his modir wombe.

12 And he schal converte manye of the children of Israel to her Lord God.

13 And he schal go bifore in the spiryte and vertu of Helye: and he schal turne the hertis of the fadris to the sonis, and men out of beleeve: to the prudence of just men, to make redy a perfyt puple to the Lord.

18 Ða cwæð Zacharias to þam engele. Hwanun wat ic þis. ic eom nu eald. and min wif on hyre dagum forðeode:·

19 Ða andswarode him se engel. Ic eom Gabriel. ic þe stande beforan Gode. and ic eom asend wið þe sprecan. ⁊ þe þis bodian.

20 And nu þu bist suwigende. ⁊ þu sprecan ne miht oð þone dæg þe þas þing gewurðað. forþam þu minum wordum ne gelyfdest. þa beoð on hyra timan gefyllede:·

21 And þ folc wæs Zachariam ge-anbidigende. and wundrodon þ he on þam temple læt wæs:·

22 Ða he ut-eode ne mihte he him to-sprecan. ⁊ hig oncneowon þ he on þam temple sume gesihðe geseah. ⁊ he wæs bicniende hym. ⁊ dumb þurhwunede:·

23 Ða wæs geworden þa his þenunga dagas gefyllede wæron. he ferde to his huse:·

24 Soðlice æfter dagum Elizabeth his wif geeacnode. and heo bediglude hig fif monþas. ⁊ cwæð.

25 Soðlice me Drihten gedyde þus. on þam dagum þe he geseah minne hosp betwux mannum afyrran:·

26 Soðlice on þam syxtan monðe wæs asend Gabriel se engel fram Drihtne on Galilea ceastre. þære nama wæs Nazareth.

27 To beweddudre fæmnan anum were. þæs nama wæs Iosep. of Dauides huse. ⁊ þære fæmnan nama wæs Maria:·

28 Ða cwæð se engel ingangende. Hal wes þu mid gyfe gefylled. Drihten mid þe. ðu eart gebletsud on wifum:·

29 Þa wearð heo on his spræce gedrefed. and þohte hwæt seo greting wære:·

30 Ða cwæð se engel. Ne ondræd þu ðe Maria. soðlice þu gyfe mid Gode gemettest.

31 Soðlice nu. þu on innoðe ge-eacnast. and sunu censt. and his naman Hælend genemnest.

32 Se bið mære. ⁊ þæs hehstan sunu genemned. and him syld Drihten God his fæder Dauides setl.

33 And he ricsað on ecnesse on Iacobes huse. ⁊ his rices ende ne bið:·

34 Ða cwæð Maria to þam engle. hu gewyrð þis. forþam ic were ne oncnawe:

35 Ða andswarode hyre se engel. Se halga Gast on þe becymð. ⁊ þæs heahstan miht þe ofer-sceadað. and forþam þ halige þe of þe acenned bið. bið Godes sunu genemned.

36 And nu. Elizabeth þin mage sunu on hyre ylde geacnode. and þes monað is hyre syxta. seo is unberende genemned.

37 Forþam nis ælc word mid Gode unmihtelic:·

38 Ða cwæð Maria. Her is Drihtnes þinen. gewurðe me æfter þinum worde:· And se engel hyre fram-gewat:·

39 Soðlice on þam dagum aras Maria ⁊ ferde on muntland mid ofste. on Iudeisce ceastre.

40 ⁊ eode into Zacharias huse. ⁊ grette Elizabeth:·

41 Ða wæs geworden þa Elizabeth gehyrde Marian gretinge. ða gefagnude þ cild on hyre innoðe. and þa wearð Elizabeth haligum Gaste gefylled.

42 ⁊ heo clypode mycelre stefne. and cwæð. Þu eart betwux wifum gebletsud. and gebletsud is þines innoðes wæstm.

43 ⁊ hwanun is me þis. þ mines Drihtnes modor to me cume:·

44 Sona swa þinre gretinge stefn on minum earum geworden wæs. þa fahnude [in glædnisse] min cild on minum innoþe.

45 And eadig þu eart þu þe gelyfdest. þ fulfremede synt þa þing þe þe fram Drihtne gesæde synd:·

46 Ða cwæð Maria. Min sawel mærsað Drihten.

14 And Zacarye ſeyde to the aungel: wherof ſchal Y wyte this? for Y am old: and my wyf hath gon fer in hir dayes.

15 And the aungel anſwerde and ſeyde to him, for Y am Gabriel that ſtonde nygh bifore God, and Y am ſent to thee to ſpeke and to evangeliſe to thee theſe thingis, and lo thou ſchalt be doumbe.

16 And thou ſchalt not mowe ſpeke, til into the day in which theſe thingis ſchulen be don. for thou haſt not beleved to my wordis, whiche ſchulen be fulfild in her tyme.

17 And the puple was abidynge Zacarye: and thei wondriden that he taryede in the temple.

18 And he gede out and myghte not ſpeke to hem: and thei knewen that he hadde ſeyn a viſioun in the temple, and he bekenide to hem: and he dwellide ſtille doumbe.

19 And it was don whanne the dayes of his office weren fulfillid: he wente into his hous.

20 And aftir theſe dayes Elizabeth his wif conſeyvede and hidde hir fyve monethis and ſeyde.

21 For ſo the Lord dide to me in the dayes in whiche he biheld to take awey my reprof among men.

22 But in the ſixte monethe the aungel Gabriel was ſent from God: into a cytee of Galilee whos name was Nazareth.

23 To a maydun weddid to a man: whos name was Joſeph of the hoūs of Dauith, and the name of the maydun was Marye.

24 And the aungel entride to hir, and ſayde, heil ful of grace the Lord be with thee: bleſſid be thou among wymmen.

25 And whanne ſche hadde herd: ſche was troublid in his word, and thoughte what manner ſalutacioun this was.

26 And the aungel ſeid to hir, ne drede not thou Marye: for thou haſt founden grace anentis God.

27 Lo thou ſchalt conſeyve in wombe, and ſchalt bere a ſone: and thou ſchalt clepe his name Jheſus.

28 This ſhall be gret: and he ſchal be clepid the ſone of higheſte, and the Lord God ſchal geve to him the ſeete of Dauith his fadir.

29 And he ſchal regne in the hous of Jacob withouten ende, and of his rewme ſchal be noon ende.

30 And Marye ſeyde to the aungel, on what maner ſchal this thing be don? for Y knowe not man.

31 And the aungel anſwerde and ſeyde to hir, the holy Goſt ſchal come fro above into thee: and the vertu of the higheſte ſchal ouer ſchadowe thee: and therfore that holy thing that ſchal be borun of thee: ſchal be clepide the ſone of God.

32 And to Elizabeth thi coſyn, and ſche alſo hath conſeyved a ſone in hir eelde, and this monethe is the ſixte to hir that is clepid bareyn.

33 For every word ſchal not be impoſſyble anentis God.

34 And Marye ſeide to the hond maydun of the Lord: be it doon to me aftir thi word; and the aungel departide fro hir.

35 And Marye roos up in tho dayes and wente with haſte into the mountaynes into a citee of Judee.

36 And ſche entride into the hous of Zacarye and grette Elizabeth.

37 And it was don as Elizabeth herde the ſalutacioun of Marye the young childe in hir wombe gladide, and Elizabeth was fulfild with the holy Goſt.

38 And cryede with a gret voice and ſeyde, bleſſid be thou among wymmen and bleſſid be the fruyt of thy wombe.

39 And wherof is this thing to me, that the modir of my Lord come to me?

40 For lo as the vois of thi ſalutacioun was maad in myn eeris: the yong child gladide in joye in my wombe.

41 And bleſſid be thou that haſt beleeved: for thilke thingis that ben ſeid of the Lord to thee ſchulen be parfytly don.

42 And Marye ſeyde, my ſoul magnifieth the Lord.

47 ⁊ min gast geblissude on Gode minum Hælende.
48 Forþam þe he geseah his þinene ead-modnesse. soðlice heonun-forð me eadige secgað ealle cneoressa.
49 Forþam þe me mycele þing dyde se ðe mihtig is. ⁊ his nama is halig.
50 ⁊ his mild-heortnes of cneoresse on cneoresse hine ondrædendum:
51 He worhte mægne on his earme. he to-dælde þa ofer-modan on mode hyra heortan.
52 He awearp þa rican of setle. and þa eað-modan upahof.
53 Hingrigende he mid godum gefylde. ⁊ ofer-mode idele forlet.
54 He afeng Israhel his cniht. ⁊ gemunde his mild-heortnesse.
55 Swa he spræc to urum fæderum. Abrahame and his sæde on á weoruld.
56 Soðlice Maria wunude mid hyre swylce þry monðas. ⁊ gewende þa to hyre huse:·
57 Ða wæs gefylled Elizabethe cenning-tid. and heo sunu cende.
58 ⁊ hyre nehchebuas ⁊ hyre cuðan ꝥ gehyrdon. ꝥ Drihten his mild-heortnesse mid hyre mærsude ⁊ hig mid hyre blissodon:·
59 Ða on þam ehteoðan dæge hig comon ꝥ cild ymbsniðan. and nemdon hine his fæder naman Zachariam:·
60 Ða andswarode his modor. Ne se soðes. ac he bið Iohannes genemned:·
61 Ða cwædon hi to hyre. Nis nan on þinre mægðe þyssum naman genemned:·
62 Ða bicnodon hi to his fæder. hwæt he wolde hyne genemnedne beon:·
63 Ða wrat he gebedenum wex-brede. Iohannes is his nama. ða wundrodon hig ealle:·
64 Ða wearð sona his muð ⁊ his tunge ge-openod. ⁊ he spræc. Drihten bletsigende:·
65 Ða wearð ege geworden ofer ealle hyra nehchebuas. and ofer ealle Iudea munt-land wæron þas word gewidmærsode.
66 ⁊ ealle þa ðe hit gehyrdon. on hyra heortan settun ⁊ cwædon. Wenst ðu hwæt byð þes cnapa. witodlice Drihtnes hand wæs mid him:·
67 And Zacharias his fæder wæs mid halegum Gaste gefylled. ⁊ he witegode and cwæð.
68 Gebletsud sy Drihten Israhela God. forþam þe he geneosude. ⁊ his folces alysednesse dyde.
69 And he us hæle horn arærde on Dauides huse his cnihtes.
70 Swa he spræc þurh his halegra witegena muð. þa ðe of worldes frym ðe spræcon.
71 ⁊ he alysde us of urum feondum. and of ealra þara handa þe us hatedon.
72 Mild-heortnesse to wyrcenne mid urum fæderum. ⁊ gemunan his halegan cyðnesse.
73 Hyne wy to syllenne þone að þe he urum fæder Abrahame swor.
74 Ðæt we butan ege. of ure feonda handa alysede. him þeowian
75 On halignesse beforan him eallum urum dagum:·
76 And þu cnapa bist þæs hehstan witega genemned. þu gæst beforan Drihtnes ansyne. his wegas gearwian.
77 To syllene his folce hæle gewit on hyra synna forgyfnesse.
78 Ðurh innoðas ures Godes mild-heortnesse. on þam he us geneosude of eastdæle up-springende.
79 Onlyhtan þam þe on þystrum ⁊ on deaðes sceade sittað. ure fet to gereccenne on sibbe weg:·
80 Soðlice se cnapa weox. ⁊ wæs on gaste gestrangod. ⁊ wæs on westenum oð þone dæg hys ætywednessum on Israhel:·

43 And my ſpiryt hath gladid in God myn helthe.
44 For he hath behulden the mekeneſſe of his handmayden: for lo for this alle generatiouns ſchulen ſeye that I am bleſſid.
45 For he that is mighti hath don to me grete thingis, and his name is holy.
46 And his merſy is fro kyndrede into kyndredis to men that dreden him.
47 He made myght in his arm, he ſcateride proude men with the thoughte of his herte.
48 He ſette doun myghty men fro ſeete and enhaunſide meke men.
49 He hath fulfillid hungry men with goodis, and he has left riche men voide.
50 He havynge mynde of his mercy took up Iſrael his child,
51 As he hath ſpokun to oure fadris, to Abraham, and to his ſeed into worldis.
52 And Marye dwellide with hir as it were thre monethis and turned agen into his hous.
53 But the tyme of beringe child was fulfillid to Elizabeth, and ſche bar a ſon.
54 And the neyghbouris and coſyns of hir herden that the Lord hadde magnyfied his mercy with hir, and thei thankiden him.
55 And it was doon in the eightithe day thei camen to circumſide the child, and thei clepiden him Zacarye by the name of his fadir.
56 And his modir anſweride and ſeide, nay; but he ſchal be clepid Jon.
57 And thei ſeiden to hir, for no man is in thi kynrede that is clepid this name.
58 And thei bikenyden to his fadir, what he wolde that he were clepid.
59 And he axinge a poyntel wroot ſeiynge, Jon is his name, and alle men wondriden.
60 And annoon his mouth was openyd and his tunge, and he ſpak and bleſſide God.
61 And drede was maad on all hir neighbouris, and all the wordis weren pupliſchid on alle the mounteynes of Judee.
62 And alle men that herden puttiden in her herte, and ſeiden what manner child ſcal this be, for the hond of the Lord was with him.
63 And Zacarye his fadir was fulfillid with the holy Goſt, and profeciede and ſeide.
64 Bleſſid be the Lord God of Iſrael, for he has viſitid and maad redempcioun of his puple.
65 And he has rered to us an horn of helthe in the hous of Dauith his child.
66 As he ſpak by the mouth of hiſe holy prophetis that weren fro the world.
67 Helth fro oure enemyes, and fro the hond of alle men that hatiden us.
68 To do merſy with oure fadris, and to have mynde of his holy teſtament.
69 The grete ooth that he ſwoor to Abraham our fadir,
70 To geve himſelf to us, that we without drede delyvered fro the hond of oure enemyes ſerve to him,
71 In holyneſſe and rightwiſneſſe before him, in alle our dayes.
72 And thou child ſchalt be clepid the profete of the higheſte, for thou ſchalt go before the face of the Lord to make redy hiſe weyes.
73 To geve ſcience of heelth to his puple into remiſſioun of her ſynnes.
74 By the inwardeneſs of the merſy of oure God, in the which he ſpringyng up fro on high hath viſited us.
75 To geve light to them that ſitten in derkneſſis, and in ſchadowe of deeth, to dreſſe oure feet into the weye of pees;
76 And the child wexide, and was confortid in ſpiryt, and was in deſert placis till to the day of his ſchewing to Yſrael.

Of the *Saxon* poetry some specimen is necessary, though our ignorance of the laws of their metre and the quantities of their syllables, which it would be very difficult, perhaps impossible, to recover, excludes us from that pleasure which the old bards undoubtedly gave to their contemporaries.

The first poetry of the *Saxons* was without rhyme, and consequently must have depended upon the quantity of their syllables; but they began in time to imitate their neighbours, and close their verses with correspondent sounds.

The two passages, which I have selected, contain apparently the rudiments of our present lyrick measures, and the writers may be justly considered as the genuine ancestors of the *English* poets.

He mai him sore adreden,
Ðæt he ðanne ore bidde ne muȝen,
Uor ꝥ bilimpeð ilome.
He is ƿis ꝥ bit and bote
And bet biuoren dome.
Deað com on ðis midelard
Ðurð ðær defles onde,
And senne and sorȝe and isƿinc,
On se and on londe.

Ic am elder ðanne ic ƿes,
A ƿintre ⁊ ec à lore.
Ic ealdi more ðanne ic dede,
Mi ƿit oȝhte to bi more.
Se ꝥ hine selue uorȝet,
Uor ƿiue oþer uor childe.
He sal comen on euele stede,
Bute ȝod him bi milde.
Ne hopie ƿif to hire ƿere,
Ne ƿere to his ƿiue.
Bi for him selue eurich man,
Ðær ƿile he bieð alíue.
Eurich man mid ꝥ he haueð,
Mai beȝȝen heueriche.
Se ðe lesse ⁊ se ðe more,
Here aider iliche.
Heuene and erðe he ouersieð,
His eȝhen bið fulbriht.
Sunne ⁊ mone ⁊ alle sterren,
Bieð ðiestre on his lihte.
He ƿot hƿet ðencheð and hƿet doþ,
Alle quike ƿihte.
Nis no louerd sƿich is x̄ist,
Ne no king sƿich is drihte.
Heuene ⁊ erðe ⁊ all ðat is,
Biloken is on his honde.
He deð al ꝥ his ƿille is,
On sea and ec on londe.
He is ord albuten orde,
And ende albuten ende.
He one is eure on eche stede,
Wende ƿer ðu ƿende.
He is buuen us and bineðen,
Biuoren and ec bihind.
Se man ꝥ ȝodes ƿille deð,
Hie mai hine aihƿar uinde.
Eche rune he iherð,
And ƿot eche dede.
He ðurh siȝð eches iðanc,
Wai hƿat sel us to rede.
Se man neure nele don ȝod,
Ne neure ȝod lif leden.
Er deð ⁊ dom come to his dure,
He mai him sore adreden.
Hunger ⁊ ðurst hete ⁊ chele,
Ecðe and all unhelðe.
Ðurh deð com on ðis midelard,
And oðer uniselðe.
Ne mai non herte hit iþenche,
Ne no tunge telle.
Hu muchele ƿinum and hu uele,
Bieð inne helle.
Louie God mid ure hierte.
And mid all ure mihte.
And ure emcristene sƿo us self,
Sƿo us lereð drihte.

Sume ðer habbeð lesse merȝðe,
And sume ðer habbeð more.
Ech efter ðan ꝥ he dede,
Efter ꝥ he sƿanc sore.
Ne sel ðer bi bred ne ƿin,
Ne oþer kennes este.
God one sel bi eches lif,
And blisce and eche reste.
Ne sal ðar bi scete ne scrud,
Ne ƿorlder ƿele none.
Ac si merȝþe ꝥ men us bihat,
All sall ben ȝod one.
Ne mai no merȝþe bi sƿo muchel,
Sƿo is ȝodes isihðe.
Hi is soþ sune and briht,
And dai bute nihte.
Ðer is ƿele bute ƿane,
And reste buten isƿinche.
Se ꝥ mai and nele ðeder come,
Sore hit sel uorðenche.
Ðer is blisce buten treȝe,
And lif buten deaðe.
Ðet eure sullen ƿunie ðer,
Bliðe hi bieþ and eaðe.
Ðer is ȝeuȝeþe buten elde,
And elde buten unhelþe.
Nis ðer sorȝe ne sor non,
Ne non uniselðe.
Ðer me sel drihten isen,
Sƿo ase he is mid iƿisse.
He one mai and sel al bien,
Engles and mannes blisce.
To ðare blisce us bring ȝod,
Ðet rixeð buten ende.
Ðanne he ure saula unbint,
Of lichamlice bend.
Crist ȝeue us lede sƿich lif,
And habbe sƿichne ende.
Ðet ƿe moten ðider cumen,
Ðanne ƿe hennes ƿende.

About the year 1150, the *Saxon* began to take a form in which the beginning of the present *English* may be plainly discovered; this change seems not to have been the effect of the *Norman* conquest, for very few *French* words are found to have been introduced in the first hundred years after it; the language must therefore have been altered by causes like those which, notwithstanding the care of writers and societies instituted to obviate them, are even now daily making innovations in every living language. I have exhibited a specimen of the language of this age from the year 1135 to 1140 of the *Saxon* chronicle, of which the latter part was apparently written near the time to which it relates.

Ðis gære for þe king Stephne ofer sæ to Normandi. ⁊ þer ƿes underfangen. forði ꝥ hi ƿenden ꝥ he sculde ben alsuic alse þe eom ƿes. ⁊ for he hadde get his tresor. ac he to-deld it ⁊ scatered sotlice. Micel hadde Henri king gadered gold ⁊ sÿluer. and na god ne dide me for his saule þar of. Ða þe king Stephne to Engla-land com þa macod he his gadering æt Oxene-ford. ⁊ þar he nam þe biscop Roger of Seres-beri. ⁊ Alexander biscop of Lincoln. ⁊ te Canceler Roger hise neues. ⁊ dide ælle in prisun. til hi jafen up here castles. Ða þe suikes undergæton ꝥ he milde man ƿas ⁊ softe ⁊ god. ⁊ na justise ne dide. þa diden hi alle ƿunder. Hi hadden him manred maked and aðes suoren. ac hi nan treuðe ne heolden. alle he ƿæron for-sƿoren. ⁊ here treoðes for-loren. for æuric rice man his castles makede and agænes him heolden. and fÿlden þe land full of castles. Hi suencten suiðe þe ƿrecce men of þe land mid castel-ƿeorces. þa þe castles ƿaren maked. þa fÿlden hi mid deoules and ẏuele men. Ða namen hi þa men þe hi ƿenden ꝥ ani god hefden. baðe be nihtes and be dæies. carl-men ⁊ ƿimmen. and diden heom in prisun efter gold and sÿluer. ⁊ pined heom un-tellendlice pining. for ne ƿæren næure nan martÿrs sƿa pined alse hi ƿæron. Me henged up bi þe fet and smoked heom mid ful smoke. me henged bi þe þumbes.

oðer bi þe hefed. ⁊ hengen bryniges on her fet. Me dide cnotted strenges abuton here hæued. ⁊ uuryðen to ꝥ it gæde to þe hærnes. Hi diden heom in quarterne þar nadres ⁊ snakes ⁊ pades pæron inne. ⁊ drapen heom spa. Sume hi diden in crucet hus. ꝥ is in an ceste ꝥ pas scort ⁊ nareu. ⁊ un-dep. ⁊ dide scærpe stanes þer inne. ⁊ þrengde þe man þær inne. ꝥ hi bræcon alle þe limes. In mani of þe castles pæron lof ⁊ grī. ꝥ pæron sachenteges ꝥ tpa oðer þre men hadden onoh to bæron onne. ꝥ pas spa maced ꝥ is fæstned to an beom. ⁊ diden an scærp iren abuton þa mannes þrote ⁊ his hals. ꝥ he ne mihte nopiderpardes ne sitten. ne lien. ne slepen. oc bæron al ꝥ iren. Mani þusen hi drapen mid hungær. I ne canne. ⁊ ne mai tellen alle þe punders. ne alle þe pines ꝥ hi diden precce men on his land. ⁊ ꝥ lastede þa xix. pintre pile Stephne pas king. ⁊ æure it pas uuerse and uuerse. Hi læidengæildes on þe tunes æureū pile. ⁊ clepeden it tenserie. þa þe precce men ne hadden nan more to giuen. þa ræueden hi and brendon alle þe tunes. ꝥ pel þu mihtes faren all adæis fare sculdest þu neure finden man in tune sittende. ne land tiled. Ða pas corn dære. ⁊ flec. ⁊ cæse. ⁊ butere. for nan ne pæs o þe land. Wrecce men sturuen of hungær. sume jeden on æimes þe paren sum pile rice men. sum flugen ut of lande. Wes næure gæt mare preccehed on land. ne næure heðen men perse ne diden þan hi diden. for ouer siðon ne for-baren hi nouðer circe. ne cyrce-iærd. oc nam al þe god ꝥ þar inne pas. ⁊ brenden syðen þe cyrce ⁊ altegædere. Ne hi ne for-baren biscopes land. ne abbotes. ne preostes. ac ræueden munecces. ⁊ clerekes. ⁊ æuric man oðer þe ouer myhte. Gif tpa men oðer þre coman ridend to an tun. al þe tunscipe flugæn for heom. penden ꝥ hi pæron ræueres. Ðe biscopes ⁊ lered men heom cursede æure. oc pas heom naht þar of. for hi pæron all for-cursæd ⁊ for-suoren ⁊ forloren. War sæ me tilede. þe erðe ne bar nan corn. for þe land pas all for-don mid suilce dædes. ⁊ hi sæden openlice ꝥ Crist slep. ⁊ his halechen. Suilc ⁊ mare þanne pe cunnen sæin. pe þolenden xix. pintre for ure sinnes.

On al þis yuele time heold Martin abbot his abbotrice xx. pinter. ⁊ half gær. ⁊ viii. dæis. mid micel suinc. ⁊ fand þe munekes. ⁊ te gestes al ꝥ heom behoued. ⁊ heold mycel carited in the hus. and þoð peðere prohte on þe circe ⁊ sette þar to landes ⁊ rentes. ⁊ goded it suyðe and læt it refen. and brohte heom into þe nepæ mynstre on s. Petres mæsse-dæi mid micel purtscipe. ꝥ pas anno ab incarnatione Dom. MCXL. a combustione loci XXIII. And he for to Rome ⁊ þær pæs pæl under-fangen fram þe Pape Eugenie. ⁊ begæt thare priuileges. an of alle þe landes of þabbot-rice. ⁊ an oðer of þe landes þe lien to þe circe-pican. ⁊ gif he leng moste liuen. alse he mint to don of þe horder-pycan. And he begæt in landes ꝥ rice men herden mid strengþe. of Willelm Malduit þe heold Rogingham þæ castel he pan Cotingham ⁊ Estun. ⁊ of Hugo of Waltuile he pan Hyrtlingb. ⁊ Stanepig. ⁊ LX. sol. of Aldepingle ælc gær. And he makede manie munekes. ⁊ plantede piniærd. ⁊ makede manie peorkes. ⁊ pende þe tun betere þan it ær pæs. and pæs god munec ⁊ god man. ⁊ forði hi luueden God and gode men. Nu pe pillen sægen sum del· pat belamp on Stephne kinges time. On his time þe Judeus of Nor-pic bohton an Cristen cild beforen Estren. and pineden him alle þe ilce pining ꝥ ure Drihten pas pined. and on lang-fridæi him on rode hengen for ure Drihtnes luue. ⁊ syðen byrieden him. Wenden ꝥ it sculde ben for-holen. oc ure Drihtin atypede ꝥ he pas hali martyr. ⁊ to munekes him namen. ⁊ bebyried him heglice. in ðe mynstre. ⁊ he maket þur ure Drihtin punderlice and mani-fældlice miracles. ⁊ hatte he s. Willelm:·

On þis gær com Dauid king of Scotland mid ormete færd to þis land polde pinnan þis land. ⁊ him com togænes Willelm eorl of Albamar þe þe king adde beteht Euor-pic. ⁊ to oðer æuez men mid fæu men ⁊ fuhten pid heom. ⁊ flemden þe king æt te standard. ⁊ slogen suiðe micel of his genge:·

On þis gær polde þe king Stephne tæcen Rodbert eorl of Gloucestre. þe kinges sune Henries. ac he ne mihte for he part it par. Ða efter hi þe lengten þesterede þe sunne ⁊ te dæi abuton nontid dæies. þa men eten ꝥ me lihtede candles to æten bi. ⁊ ꝥ pas XIII. kł. April. pæron men suiðe ofpundred. Ðer efter ford-ferde Willelm Ærce-biscop of Cant-par-byrig. ⁊ te king makede Teobald Ærce-biscop. þe pas abbot in þe Bec. Ðer efter pæx suiðe micel uuerre betuyx þe king ⁊ Randolf eorl of Cæstre noht forði ꝥ he ne iaf him al ꝥ he cuðe axen him. alse he dide alle oðre. oc æfre þe mare iaf heom þe pærse hi pæron him. Ðe eorl heold Lincol agænes þe king. ⁊ benam him al ꝥ he ahte to hauen. ⁊ te king for þider ⁊ besætte him ⁊ his broðer Willelm de R . . . are in þe castel. ⁊ te eorl stæl ut ⁊ ferde efter Rodbert eorl of Gloucestre. ⁊ broht him þider mid micel ferd. and fuhten spiðe on Candel-masse-dæi agenes heore lauerd. ⁊ namen him. for his men him suyken ⁊ flugæn. and læd him to Bris-tope and diden þar in prisun. ⁊ . . . teres. Ða pas all Engle-land styred mar þan ær pæs. and all yuel pæs in lande. Ðer efter com þe kinges dohter Henries þe hefde ben Emperic on Alamanie. ⁊ nu pæs cuntesse in Angou. ⁊ com to Lundene. ⁊ te Lundenissce folc hire polde tæcen ⁊ scæ fleh. ⁊ forles þar micel:· Ðer efter þe biscop of Win-cestre Henri. þe kinges broðer Stephnes. spac pid Rodbert eorl ⁊ pid þemperice and spor heom aðas ꝥ he neure ma mid te king his broðer polde halden. ⁊ cursede alle þe men þe mid him heolden. and sæde heom ꝥ he polde iiuen heom up Win-cestre. ⁊ dide heom cumen þider. Ða hi þær inne pæren þa com þe kinges cuen . . . hire strengðe ⁊ besæt heom. ꝥ þer pæs inne micel hungær. Ða hi ne leng ne muhten þolen. þa stali hi ut ⁊ flugen. ⁊ hi purðen par piðuten ⁊ folecheden heom. and namen Rodbert eorl of Glou-cestre and ledden him to Roue-cestre. and diden him þare in prisun. and te emperice fleh into an mynstre. Ða feorden ða pise men betpyx. þe kinges freond ⁊ te eorles freond. and sahtlede sua ꝥ me sculde leten ut þe king of prisun for þe eorl. ⁊ te eorl for þe king. ⁊ sua diden. Siðen ðer efter sathleden þe king ⁊ Randolf eorl at Stan-ford ⁊ aðes sporen and treuðes fæston ꝥ her nouðer sculde besuiken oðer. ⁊ it ne for-stod naht. for þe king him siðen nam in Hamtun. þurhe picci ræd. ⁊ dide him in prisun. ⁊ ef sones he let him ut þurhe pærse red to ꝥ forepard ꝥ he suor on halidom. ⁊ gysles fand. ꝥ he alle his castles sculde iiuen up. Sume he iaf up and sume ne iaf he noht. and dide þanne pærse ðanne he hær sculde. Ða pas Engle-land suiðe to-deled. sume helden mid te king. ⁊ sume mid þemperice. for þa þe king pas in prisun. þa penden þe eorles ⁊ te rice men ꝥ he neure mare sculde cumme ut. ⁊ sæhtleden pyd þemperice. ⁊ brohten hire into Oxen-ford. and iauen hire þe burch:· Ða ðe king pas ute. þa herde ꝥ sægen. and toc his feord ⁊ besæt hire in þe tur. ⁊ me læt hire dun on niht of þe tur mid rapes. ⁊ stal ut ⁊ scæ fleh ⁊ iæde on fote to Waling-ford. Ðær efter scæ ferde ofer sæ. ⁊ hi of Normandi penden alle fra þe king to þe eorl of Angæu. sume here þankes ⁊ sume here un þankes. for he besæt heom til hi aiauen up here castles. ⁊ hi nan helpe ne hæfden of þe king. Ða ferde Eustace þe kinges sune to France. ⁊ nam þe kinges suster of France to pife. pende to bigæton Normandi þær þurh. oc he spedde litel. ⁊ be gode rihte. for he pas an yuel man. for pare se he . . . . dide mare yuel þanne god. he reuede þe landes ⁊ læide mic . . . . s on. he brohte his pif to Engle-land. ⁊ dide hire in þe caste . . . . . . teb. god pimman scæ pæs. oc scæ hedde litel blisse mid him. ⁊ xpist ne polde ꝥ he sculde lange rixan. ⁊ pærd ded and his moder beien. ⁊ te eorl of Angæu pærd ded. ⁊ his sune Henri toc to þe rice. And te cuen of France to-dælde fra þe king. ⁊ scæ com to þe iunge eorl Henri. ⁊ he toc hire to piue. ⁊ al Peitou mid hire. Ða ferde he mid micel færd into Engle-land. ⁊ pan castles. ⁊ te king ferde agenes him mi-

cel

cel mare ferð. ⁊ þoðwæþere suten hi noht. oc fer-
den þe Ærce-biscop ⁊ te wise men betwux heom. ⁊
makede ꝥ sahte ꝥ te king sculde ben lauerd ⁊ king
wile he liuede. ⁊ æfter his dæi ware Henri king. ⁊ he
helde him for fader ⁊ he him for sune. and sib ⁊
sæhte sculde ben betwyx heom ⁊ on al Engle-land.
Ðis and te oðre forwuarder þet hi makeden suoren
to halden þe king ⁊ te eorl. and te biscop. ⁊ te
eorles. ⁊ ricemen alle. Ða was þe eorl underfangen
æt Win-cestre and æt Lundene mid micel wurtscipe.
and alle diden him man-red. and suoren þe pais to
halden. and hit ward sone suiðe god pais sua ꝥ neure
was here. Ða was ðe king strengere þanne he æuert
her was. ⁊ te eorl ferde ouer sæ. ⁊ al folc him
luuede. for he dide god justise ⁊ makede pais:.

Nearly about this time, the following pieces of poetry seem to have been written, of which I have inserted only short fragments; the first is a rude attempt at the present measure of eight syllables, and the second is a natural introduction to *Robert of Gloucester*, being composed in the same measure, which, however rude and barbarous it may seem, taught the way to the *Alexandrines* of the *French* poetry.

FUR in see bi west spaynge.
Is a lond ihote cokaygne.
Ðer nis lond under heuenriche.
Of wel of godnis hit iliche.
Ðoy paradis be miri and briyt.
Cokaygn is of fairir siyt.
What is þer in paradis.
Bot grasse and flure and greneris.
Ðoy þer be ioi and gret dute.
Ðer nis met bote frute.
Ðer nis halle bure no bench.
Bot watir man is þursto quench.
Beþ þer no men but two.
Þely and enok also.
Clinglich may hi go.
Whar þer woniþ men no mo.
In cokaygne is met and drink.
Wiþute care how and swink.
Ðe met is trie þe drink so clere.
To none russin and sopper.
I sigge for soþ boute were.
Ðer nis lond on erþe is pere.
Under heuen nis lond i wisse.
Of so mochil ioi and blisse.
Ðer is mani swete siyte.
Al is dai nis þer no niyte.
Ðer nis baret noþer strif.
Nis þer no deþ ac euer lif.
Ðer nis lac of met no cloþ.
Ðer nis no man no woman wroþ.
Ðer nis serpent wolf no fox.
Þors no capil. kowe no ox.
Ðer nis schepe no swine no gote.
No non horwyla god it wote.
Noþer harate noþer stode.
Ðe land is ful of oþer gode.
Nis þer flei fle no lowse.
In cloþ in toune bed no house.
Ðer nis dunnir slete no hawle.
No non vile worme no snawile.
No non storm rein no winde.
Ðer nis man no woman blinde.
Ok al is game ioi ant gle.
Wel is him þat þer mai be.
Ðer beþ rivers gret and fine.
Of oile melk honi and wine.
Watir seruiþ þer to noþing.
Bot to siyt and to waussing.

SANCTA MARGARETTA.

OLDE ant yonge i preit ou oure folies for to lete.
Ðenchet on god þat yef ou wit oure sunnes to bete.
Þere mai tellen ou. wid wordes feire ant swete.
Ðe vie of one meidan. was hoten Maregrete.
Þire fader was a patriac. as ic ou tellen may.
In auntioge wif eches i ðe false lay.
Deve godes ant doumbe. he served nitt ant day.
So deden mony oþere. þat singet weilawey.
Theodosius was is nome. on crist ne levede he noutt.
Þe levede on þe false godes. ðat weren wid honden wroutt.
Ðo þat child sculde christine ben. ic com him well in þoutt.
E bed wen it were ibore. to deþe it were ibroutt.
Ðe moder was an heþene wif þat hire to wyman bere.
Ðo þat child ibore was. nolde ho hit furfare.
Þo sende it into asye. wid messagers ful yare.
To a norice þat hire wiste. ant sette hire to lore.
Ðe norice þat hire wiste. children aheuede seuene.
Ðe eitteþe was maregrete. cristes may of heuene.
Tales ho ani tolde. ful feire ant ful euene.
Wou ho þoleden martirdom. sein Laurence ant seinte Steuene.

In these fragments, the adulteration of the *Saxon* tongue, by a mixture of the *Norman*, becomes apparent; yet it is not so much changed by the admixture of new words, which might be imputed to commerce with the continent, as by changes of its own forms and terminations; for which no reason can be given.

Hitherto the language used in this island, however different in successive time, may be called *Saxon*; nor can it be expected, from the nature of things gradually changing, that any time can be assigned, when the *Saxon* may be said to cease, and the *English* to commence. *Robert of Gloucester* however, who is placed by the criticks in the thirteenth century, seems to have used a kind of intermediate diction, neither *Saxon* nor *English*; in his work therefore we see the transition exhibited, and, as he is the first of our writers in rhyme, of whom any large work remains, a more extensive quotation is extracted. He writes apparently in the same measure with the foregoing authour of St. *Margarite*, which polished into greater exactness, appeared to our ancestors so suitable to the genius of the *English* language, that it was continued in use almost to the middle of the seventeenth century.

OF þe batayles of Denemarch, þat hii dude in þys londe
þat worst were of alle oþere, we mote abbe an honde.
Worst hii were. vor oþere adde somwanne ydo,
As Romeyns & Saxons, & wel wuste þat lond þerto.
Ac hii ne kepte yt holde noȝt, bote robby, and sfende,
And destrue, & berne, & sle, & ne couþe abbe non ende.
And bote lute yt nas worþ, þey hii were ouercome ylome.
Vor myd ssypes and gret poer as prest essone hii come.
Kyng Adelwolf of þys lond kyng was tuenty ȝer.
þe Deneys come by hym ryuor þan hii dude er.
Vor in þe al our vorst ȝer of ys kynedom
Myd þre & þrytty ssypuol men her prince hyder come,
And at Souþhamtone aryued, an hauene by Souþe.
Anoþer gret ost þulke tyme aryuede at Portesmouþe.
þe kyng nuste weþer kepe, at delde ys ost atuo.
þe Denes adde þe maystre. þo al was ydo,
And by Estangle & Lyndeseye hii wende vorþ atte laste,
And so hamward al by Kent, & slowe & barnde vaste.
Aȝen wynter hii wende hem. anoþer ȝer eft hii come.
And destrude Kent al out, and Londone nome.
þus al an ten ȝer þat lond hii broȝte þer doune,
So þat in þe teþe ȝer of þe kynge's croune,
Al bysouþe hii come alond, and þet folc of Somersete
þoru þe byssop Alcston and þet folc of Dorsete
Hii come & smyte an batayle, & þere, þoru Gode's grace,
þe Deneys were al byneþe, & þe lond folc adde þe place,
And more prowesse dude þo, þan þe kyng myȝte byuore,
þeruore gode lond men ne beþ noȝt al verlore.
þe kyng was þe boldore þo, & aȝen hem þe more drou,
And ys foure godes sones woxe vaste y nou,
Edelbold and Adelbryȝt, Edelred and Alfred.
þys was a stalwarde tem, & of gret wysdom & red,
And kynges were al foure, & defendede wel þys lond,
An Deneys dude ssame ynou, þat me volwel vond.
In syxteþe ȝere of þe kynge's kynedom
Is eldeste sone Adelbold gret ost to hym nome,
And ys fader also god, and oþere heye men al so,
And wende aȝen þys Deneys, þat muche wo adde y do.

Vor

Vor mýd tuo hondred ſſýpes & an alf at Temſe mouþ hii come,
And Londone, and Kanterburý, and oþer tounes nome,
And ſo vorþ in to Soþereýe, & ſlowe & barnde vaſte,
þere þe kyng and ýs ſone hem mette atte laſte.
þere was batayle ſtrong ýnou ýſmýte in an þrowe.
þe godes kýnȝtes leýe adoun as gras, wan medeþ mowe.
Heueden, (þat were of ýſmýte,) & oþer lýmes alſo,
Flete in blode al fram þe grounde, ar þe batayle were ýdo.
Wanne þat blod ſtod al abrod, vas þer gret wo ý nou.
Nýs ýt reuþe vorto hure, þat me ſo volc ſlou ?
Ac our ſuete Louerd atte laſte ſſewede ýs ſuete grace,
And ſende þe Criſtýne Englýſſe men þe maýſtrýe in þe place,
And þe heþene men of Denemarch býneþe were echon.
Nou nas þer ȝut in Denemarch Criſtendom non;
þe kýng her after to holý chýrche ýs herte þe more drou,
And teþeȝede wel & al ýs lond, as hii aȝte, wel ý nou.
Seýn Swýthýn at Wýncheſtre býſſop þo was,
And Alcſton at Sýrebourne, þat amendede muche þýs cas.
þe kýng was wel þe betere man þoru her beýre red,
Tuentý wýnter he was kýng, ar he were ded.
At Wýncheſtre he was ýbured, as he ȝut lýþ þere.
Hýs tueýe ſones he ȝef ýs lond, as he býȝet ham ere.
Adelbold, the eldore, þe kýnedom of Eſtſex,
And ſuþþe Adelbrýȝt, Kent and Weſtſex.
Eýȝte hondred ȝer ýt was and ſeuene and fýftý al ſo,
After þat God anerþe com, þat þýs dede was ýdo.
Boþe hii wuſte bý her týme wel her kýnedom,
At þe vyfte ȝer Adelbold out of þýs lyue nome.
At Sſýrebourne he was ýbured, & ýs broþer Adelbrýȝt
His kýnedom adde after hým, as lawe was and rýȝt.
Bý ýs daye þe verde com of þe heþene men wel prout,
And Hamteſſyre and deſtrude Wýncheſtre al out.
And þat lond folc of Hamteſſyre her red þo nome
And of Barcſſýre, and foȝte and þe ſſrewen ouercome.
Adelbrýȝt was kýng of Kent ȝeres folle tene,
And of Weſtſex bote výue, þo he deýde ých wene.

ADELRED was after hým kýng ý mad in þe place,
Eýȝte hondred & ſeuene & ſýxtý as in þe ȝer of grace.
þe vorſte ȝer of ýs kýnedom þe Deneýs þýcke com,
And robbede and deſtrude, and cýtes vaſte nome.
Maýſtres hii adde of her oſt, as ýt were dukes, tueýe,
Hýnguar and Hubba, þat ſſrewen were beýe.
In Eſt Angle hii býleuede, to reſt hem as ýt were,
Mýd her oſt al þe wynter, of þe vorſt ȝere.
þe oþer ȝer hii dude hem vorþ, & ouer Homber come,
And ſlowe to grounde & barnde, & Euerwýk nome.
þer was batayle ſtrong ý nou, vor ýſlawe was þere
Oſryc kýng of Homberlond, & monýe þat with hým were.
þo Homberlond was þus ýſſend, hii wende & tounes nome.
So þat atte laſte to Eſtangle aȝen hým come.
þer hii barnde & robbede, & þat folc to grounde ſlowe,
And, as wolues among ſſep, reulých hem to drowe.
Seýnt Edmond was þo her kýng, & þo he ſeý þat deluol cas
þat me morþrede ſo þat folc, & non amendement nas,
He ches leuere to deýe hýmſulf, þat ſuch ſorwe to ýſeý.
He dude hým vorþ among ýs fon, nolde he noþýg fle.
Hii nome hým & ſcourged hým, & ſuþþe naked hým bounde
To a tre, & to hým ſſote, & made hým moný a wounde,
þat þe arewe were on hým þo þýcce, þat no ſtede nas býleuede.
Atte laſte hii martred hým, & ſmýte of ýs heued.
þe ſýxte ȝer of þe crounement of Aldered þe kýng
A nýwe oſt com into þys lond, gret þoru alle þýng,
And anon to Redýnge robbede and ſlowe.
þe king and Alfred ýs broþer nome men ýnowe,
Mette hem, and a batayle ſmýte vp Aſſeſdoune.
þer was mony moder chýld, þat ſone laý þer doune.
þe batayle ýlaſte vorte nýȝt, and þer were aſlawe
Výf dukes of Denemarch, ar hii wolde wyþ drawe,
And mony þouſend of oþer men, & þo gonne hii to fle;
Ac hii adde alle ýbe aſſend, ȝýf þe nýȝt nadde y be.
Tueye batayles her after in þe ſulf ȝere
Hii ſmyte, and at boþe þe heþene maýſtres were.
þe kýng Aldered ſone þo þen weý of deþ nome,
As ýt vel, þe výftý ȝer of ýs kýnedom.
At Wýmbourne he was ýbured, as God ȝef þat cas,
þe gode Alfred, ýs broþer, after hým kýng was.

ALFRED, þýs noble man, as in þe ȝer of grace he nom
Eýȝte hondred & ſýxtý & tuelue þe kýnedom.
Arſt he adde at Rome ýbe, &, vor ýs grete wýſdom,
þe pope Leon hým bleſſede, þo he þuder com,
And þe kynge's croune of hýs lond, þat in þýs lond ȝut ýs:
And he led hým to be kýng, ar he kýng were ýwýs.
An he was kýng of Engelond, of alle þat þer come,
þat vorſt þus ýlad was of þe pope of Rome,
An ſuþþe oþer after hým of þe erchebýſſopes echon.
So þat hýuor hým pore kýng nas þer non.
In þe Souþ ſýde of Temeſe nýne batayles he nome
Aȝen þe Deneýs þe vorſt ȝer of ýs kýnedom.
Nýe ȝer he was þus in þýs lond in batayle & in wo,
An ofte ſýþe aboue was, and býneþe oftor mo;
So longe, þat hým nere bý leuede bote þre ſſýren in ýs hond,
Hamteſſyre, and Wýlteſſyre, and Somerſete, of al ýs lond.
A daý as he werý was, and aſuoddrýnge hým nome
And ýs men were ýwend auýſſeþ, Seyn Cutbert to hym com.
" Ich am," he ſeyde, " Cutbert, to þe ýcham ýwend
" To brýnge þe gode týtýnges. Fram God ýcham ýſend.
" Vor þat folc of þýs lond to ſýnne her wýlle al ȝeue,
" And ȝut nolle herto her ſýnnes býleue
" þoru me & oþer halewen, þat in þýs lond were ýbore;
" þan vor ȝou býddeþ God, wanne we beþ hým býuore,
" Hour Louerd mýd ýs eýen of milce on þe lokeþ þeruore,
" And þý poer þe wole ȝýue aȝen, þat þou aſt neý verlore.
" And þat þou þer of ſoþ ýſe, þou ſſalt abbe tokýnýnge.
" Vor þým men, þat beþ ago to daý auýſſynge,
" In lepes & in couſles ſo muche vyſs hii ſſolde hým brynge,
" þat ech man wondrý ſſal of ſo gret cacchýnge.
" And þe mor vor þe harde vorſte, þat þe water ýfrore hýs,
" þat þe more aȝen þe kunde of vyſſýnge ýt ýs.
" Of ſerue ýt wel aȝen God, and ýlef me ys meſſager,
" And þou ſſall þý wýlle abýde, as ýcham ýtold her."
As þýs kýng herof awoc, and of þýs ſýȝte þoȝte,
Hys vyſſares come to hým, & ſo gret won of fyſs hým broȝte,
þat wonder ýt was, & namelýche vor þe weder was ſo colde.
þo lýuede þe god man wel, þat Seyn Cutbert adde ýtold.
In Deuenýſſyre þer after arýuede of Deneýs
þre and tuentý ſſýpuol men, all aȝen þe peýs,
þe kýnge's broþer of Denemarch duc of oſt was.
Oure kýnge's men of Engelond mette hem bý cas,
And ſmýte þer an bataýe, and her gret duc ſlowe,
And eyȝte hondred & fourtý men, & her caronýes to drowe.
þo kyng Alfred hurde þýs, ýs herte gladede þo,
þat lond folc to hým come ſo þýcke ſo ýt mýȝte go,
Of Somerſete, of Wýlteſſýre, of Hamteſſýre þerto,
Euere as he wende, and of ýs owe folc al ſo.
So þat he adde poer ýnou, and atte laſte hii come,
And a batayle at Edendone aȝen þe Deneýs nome,
And ſlowe to grounde, & wonne þe maýſtre of the velde.
þe kýng & ýs grete duke býgonne hem to ȝelde
To þe kýng Alfred to ýs wýlle, and oſtages toke,
Vorto wende out of ýs lond, ȝýf he ýt wolde loke;
And ȝut þerto, vor ýs loue, to auonge Criſtendom.
Kýng Gurmund, þe hexte kýng, vorſt þer to come.
Kýng Alfred ýs godfader was. & ýbaptýſed ek þer were
þrettý of her hexte dukes. and muche of þat folc þere
Kýng Alfred hem huld wýþ hým tuelf dawes as he hende,
And ſuþþe he ȝef hem large ȝýftes, and let hým wende.
Hii, þat nolde Criſtyn be, of lande ſlowe þo,
And byȝonde ſee in France dude wel muche wo.
ȝut þe ſſrewen come aȝen, and muche wo here wroȝte.
Ac þe kýng Alfred atte laſte to ſſame hem euere broȝte.

 Kýng

Kẏng Alfred was þe wẏſoſt kẏnȝ, þat long was bẏuore.
Vor þeẏ me ſegge þe lawes beþ in worre tẏme vorlore,
Nas ẏt noȝt ſo hiis daẏe. vor þeẏ he in worre were,
Lawes he made rẏȝtuollore, and ſtrengore þan er were.
Clerc he was god ynou, and ȝut, as me telleþ me,
He was more þan ten ȝer old, ar he couþe ẏs abece.
Ac ẏs gode moder ofte ſmale ȝẏftes hẏm tok,
Vor to byleue oþer ple, and lokẏ on ẏs boke.
So þat bẏ por clergẏe ẏs rẏȝt lawes he wonde,
þat neuerc er nere ẏ mad, to gouernẏ ẏs lond.
And vor þe worre was ſo muche of þe luþer Deneẏs,
þe men of þẏs ſulue lond were of þe worſe peẏs.
And robbede and ſlowe oþere, þeruor he bẏuonde,
þat þer were hondredes in eche contreẏe of ẏs lond,
And in ech toune of þe hondred a teþẏnge were alſo,
And þat ech man wyþoute gret lond in teþẏnge were ẏdo,
And þat ech man knewe oþer þat in teþẏnge were,
And wuſte ſomdel of her ſtat, ȝẏf me þu vp hem bere.
So ſtreẏt he was, þat þeẏ me ledde amẏdde weẏes heẏe
Seluer, þat non man ne dorſte ẏt nẏme, þey he ẏt ſeẏe.
Abbeẏs he rerde monẏ on, and monẏ ſtudes ẏwẏs.
AcWyncheſtrye he rerdeon, þat nẏwe munſtre ẏcluped ẏs.
Hẏs lẏf eẏȝte and tuentẏ ȝer in ẏs kẏnedom ẏlaſte.
After ẏs deþ he was ẏbured at Wẏncheſtre atte laſte.

Sir *John Mandeville* wrote, as he himſelf informs us, in the fourteenth century, and his work, which compriſing a relation of many different particulars, conſequently required the uſe of many words and phraſes, may be properly ſpecified in this place. Of the following quotations, I have choſen the firſt, becauſe it ſhows, in ſome meaſure, the ſtate of *European* ſcience as well as of the *Engliſh* tongue; and the ſecond, becauſe it is valuable for the force of thought and beauty of expreſſion.

IN that lond, ne in many othere bezonde that, no man may ſee the ſterre tranſmontane, that is clept the ſterre of the ſee, that is unmevable, and that is toward the Northe, that we clepen the lode ſterre. But men ſeen another ſterre, the contrarie to him, that is toward the Southe, that is clept Antartyk. And right as the ſchip men taken here avys here, and governe hem be the lode ſterre, right ſo don ſchip men bezonde the parties, be the ſterre of the Southe, the which ſterre apperethe not to us. And this ſterre, that is toward the Northe, that wee clepen the lode ſterre, ne apperethe not to hem. For whiche cauſe, men may wel perceyve, that the lond and the ſee ben of rownde ſchapp and forme. For the partie of the firmament ſchewethe in o contree, that ſchewethe not in another contree. And men may well preven be experience and ſotyle compaſſement of wytt, that zif a man fond paſſages be ſchippes, that wolde go to ſerchen the world, men myghte go be ſchippe alle aboute the world, and aboven and benethen. The whiche thing I prove thus, aftre that I have ſeyn. For I have been toward the parties of Braban, and beholden the Aſtrolabre, that the ſterre that is clept the transmontayne, is 53 degrees highe. And more forthere in Almayne and Bewme, it hathe 58 degrees. And more forthe toward the parties ſeptemtrioneles, it is 62 degrees of heghte, and certyn mynutes. For I my ſelf have meſured it by the Aſtrolabre. Now ſchulle ze knowe, that azen the Tranſmontayne, is the tother ſterre, that is clept Antartyke; as I have ſeyd before. And tho 2 ſterres ne meeven nevere. And be hem turnethe alle the firmament, righte as dothe a wheel, that turnethe be his axille tree: ſo that tho ſterres beren the firmament in 2 egalle parties; ſo that it hathe als mochel aboven, as it hathe benethen. Aftre this, I have gon toward the parties meridionales, that is toward the Southe: and I have founden, that in Lybye, men ſeen firſt the ſterre Antartyk. And ſo fer I have gon more in tho contrees, that I have founde that ſterre more highe; ſo that toward the highe Lybye, it is 18 degrees of heghte, and certeyn minutes (of the whiche, 60 minutes maken a degree) aftre goynge be ſee and be londe, toward this contree, of that I have ſpoke, and to other yles and londes bezonde that contree, I have founden the ſterre Antartyk of 33 degrees of heghte, and mo mynutes. And zif I hadde had companye and ſchippynge, for to go more bezonde, I trowe wel in certyn, that wee ſcholde have ſeen alle the roundneſſe of the firmament alle abou e. For as I have ſeyd zou be forn, the half of the firmament is betwene tho 2 ſterres: the whiche halfondelle I have ſeyn. And of the tother halfondelle, I have ſeyn toward the Northe, undre the Tranſmontane 62 degrees and 10 mynutes; and toward the partie meridionalle, I have ſeen undre the Antartyk 33 degrees and 16 mynutes: and thanne the halfondelle of the firmament in alle, ne holdethe not but 180 degrees. And of tho 180, I have ſeen 62 on that o part, and 33 on that other part, that ben 95 degrees, and nyghe the halfondelle of a degree; and ſo there ne faylethe but that I have ſeen alle the firmament, ſaf 84 degrees and the halfondelle of a degree; and that is not the fourthe part of the firmament. For the 4 partie of the roundneſſe of the firmament holt 90 degrees: ſo there faylethe but 5 degrees and an half, of the fourthe partie. And alſo I have ſeen the 3 parties of alle the roundneſſe of the firmament, and more zit 5 degrees and an half. Be the whiche I ſeye zou certeynly, that men may envirowne alle the erthe of alle the world, as wel undre as aboven, and turnen azen to his contree, that hadde companye and ſchippynge and conduyt: and alle weyes he ſcholde fynde men, londes, and yles, als wel as in this contree. For zee wyten welle, that thei that ben toward the Antartyk, thei ben ſtreghte, feet azen feet of hem, that dwellen undre the tranſmontane; als wel as wee and thei that dwellyn under us, ben feet azenſt feet. For alle the parties of ſee and of lond han here appoſitees, habitables or trepaſſables, and thei of this half and bezond half. And wytethe wel, that aftre that, that I may parceyve and comprehende, the londes of Preſtre John, emperour of Ynde ben undre us. For in goynge from Scotlond or from Englond toward Jeruſalem, men gon upward alweys. For oure lond is in the lowe partie of the erthe, toward the Weſt: and the lond of Preſtre John is the lowe partie of the erthe, toward the Eſt: and thei han there the day, whan wee have the nyghte, and alſo highe to the contrarie, thei han the nyghte, whan wee han the day. For the erthe and the ſee ben of round forme and ſchapp, as I have ſeyd beforn. And that that men gon upward to o coſt, men gon dounward to another coſt. Alſo zee have herd me ſeye, that Jeruſalem is in the myddes of the world; and that may men preven and ſchewen there, be a ſpere, that is pighte in to the erthe, upon the hour of mydday, whan it is equenoxium, that ſchewethe no ſchadwe on no ſyde. And that it ſcholde ben in the myddes of the world, David wytneſſethe it in the Pſautre, where he ſeythe, Deus operatus eſt ſalutē in medio terre. Thanne thei that parten fro the parties of the Weſt, for to go toward Jeruſalem, als many iorneyes as thei gon upward for to go thidre, in als many iorneyes may thei gon fro Jeruſalem, unto other confynyes of the ſuperficialtie of the erthe bezonde. And whan men gon bezonde tho iourneyes, towarde Ynde and to the foreyn yles, alle is envyronynge the roundneſſe of the erthe and of the ſee, undre oure contrees on this half. And therfore hathe it befallen many tymes of o thing, that I have herd cownted, whan I was zong; how a worthi man departed ſometyme from oure contrees, for to go ſerche the world. And ſo he paſſed Ynde, and the yles bezonde Ynde, where ben mo than 5000 yles: and ſo longe he wente be ſee and lond, and ſo enviround the world be many ſeyſons, that he fond an yle, where he herde ſpeke his owne langage, callynge on oxen in the plowghe, ſuche wordes as men ſpeken to beſtes in his owne contree: whereof he hadde gret mervayle: for he knewe not how it myghte be. But I ſeye, that he had gon ſo longe, be londe and be ſee, that he had envyround alle the erthe, that he was comen azen envirounynge, that is to ſeye, goynge aboute, unto his owne marches, zif he wolde have paſſed forthe, til he had founden his contree and his owne knouleche. But he turned azen from thens, from whens he was come fro; and ſo he loſte moche peyneſulle labour, as him ſelf ſeyde, a gret while aftre, that he was comen hom. For it befelle aftre, that he wente in to Norweye; and there tempeſt of the ſee toke him; and he arryved in an yle; and whan he was in that yle, he knew wel, that it was the yle, where he had herd ſpeke his owne langage before, and the callynge of the oxen at the plowghe: and that was poſſible thinge. But how it ſemethe to ſymple men unlerned, that men ne mowe not go undre the erthe, and alſo that men ſcholde falle toward the hevene, from undre! But that may not be, upon leſſe, than wee mowe falle toward hevene, fro the erthe, where wee ben. For fro what partie of the erthe, that men duelle, outher aboven or benethen, it ſemethe alweyes to hem that duellen, that thei gon more righte than ony other folk. And righte as it ſemethe to us, that thei ben undre us, righte ſo it ſemethe hem, that wee ben undre hem. For zif a man myghte falle fro the erthe unto the firmament; be grettere reſoun, the erthe and the ſee, that ben ſo grete and ſo hevy, ſcholde fallen to the firmament: but that may not be: and therfore ſeithe oure Lord God, Non timeas me, qui ſuſpendi terrā ex nichilo? And alle be it, that it be poſſible thing, that men may ſo envyronne alle the world, natheles of a 1000 perſones, on ne myghte not happen to returnen in to his contree. For, for the gretneſſe of the erthe and of the ſee, men may go be a 1000 and a 1000 other weyes, that no man cowde redye him perfitely toward the parties that he cam fro, but zif it were be aventure and happ, or be the grace of God. For the erthe is fulle large and fulle gret, and holt in roundneſſe and aboute envyroun, be aboven and be benethen 20425 myles, aftre the opynyoun of the olde wiſe aſtronomeres. And here ſeyenges I repreve noughte. But aftre my lytylle wyt, it ſemethe me, ſavynge here reverence, that it is more. And for to have bettere underſtondynge, I ſeye thus, be ther ymagyned a figure, that hathe a gret compas; and aboute the poynt of the gret compas, that is clept the centre, be made another litille compas: than aftre, be the gret compaſs deviſed be lines in manye parties; and that alle the lynes meeten at the centre; ſo that in as many parties, as the grete compas ſchal be departed, in als manye, ſchalle be departed the litille, that is aboute the centre, alle be it, that the ſpaces ben leſſe. Now thanne, be the gret compas repreſented for the firmament, and the litille compas repreſented for the erthe. Now thanne the firmament is devyſed, be aſtronomeres, in 12 ſignes; and every ſigne is devyſed in 30 degrees, that is 360 degrees, that the firmament hathe aboven. Alſo, be the erthe devyſed in als many parties, as the firmament; and lat every partye anſwere to a degree of the firmament: and wytethe it wel, that aftre the auctoures of aſtronomye, 700 furlonges of erthe anſweren to a degree of the firmament; and tho ben 87 miles and 4 furlonges. Now be that here multiplyed be 360 ſithes; and than thei ben 31500 myles, every of 8 furlonges, aftre myles of oure contree. So moche hathe the erthe in roundneſſe, and of heghte enviroun, aftre myn opynyoun and myn undirſtondynge. And zee ſchulle undirſtonde, that aftre the opynyoun of olde wiſe philoſophres and aſtronomeres, oure contree ne Irelond ne Wales ne Scotlond ne Norweye ne the other yles coſtynge to hem, ne ben not in the ſuperficyalte cownted aboven the erthe; as it ſchewethe be alle the bokes of aſtronomye. For the ſuperficialtee of the erthe is departed in 7 parties, for the 7 planetes: and tho parties ben clept clymates. And oure parties be not of the 7 clymates: for thei ben deſcendynge toward the Weſt. And alſo theſe yles of Ynde, which beth evene azenſt us, beth noght reckned in the climates: for thei ben azenſt us, that ben in the lowe contree. And the 7 clymates ſtrecchen hem envyrounynge the world.

II. And I John Maundevylle knyghte aboveſeyd, (alle thoughe I bē unworthi) that departed from oure contrees and paſſed the ſee, the zeer of grace 1322. that have paſſed manye londes and manye yles and contrees, and cerched manye fulle ſtraunge places, and have ben in many a fulle gode honourable companye, and at many a faire dede of armes, (alle be it that I dide none myſelf, for myn unable inſuffiſance) now I am comen hom (mawgree my ſelf) to reſte: for gowtes, artetykes, that me diſtreynen, tho diffynen the ende of my labour, azenſt my wille (God knowethe.) And thus takynge ſolace in my wrecched reſte, recordynge the tyme paſſed, I have fulfilled theiſe thinges and putte hem wryten in this boke, as it wolde come in to my mynde, the zeer of grace 1356 in the 34 zeer that I departede from oure contrees. Wherfore I preye to alle the rederes and hereres of this boke, zif it pleſe hem, that thei wolde preyen to God for me: and I ſchalle preye for hem. And alle tho that ſeyn for me a Pater noſter, with an Ave Maria, that God forzeve me my ſynnes, I make hem partneres and graunte hem part of alle the gode pilgrymages and of alle the gode dedes, that I have don, zif ony be to his pleſance: and noghte only of tho, but of alle that evere I ſchalle do unto my lyfes ende. And I beſeche Almyghty God, fro whom alle godeneſſe and grace comethe fro, that he vouchesaf, of his excellent mercy and habundant grace, to fulle fylle hire ſoules with inſpiracioun of the Holy Goſt, in makynge defence of alle hire goſtly enemyes here in erthe, to hire ſalvacioun, bothe of body and ſoule; to worſchipe and thankynge of him, that is three and on, with outen begynnynge and withouten endynge; that is, with outen qualitee, good, and with outen quantytee, gret; that in alle places is preſent, and alle thinges contenynynge; the whiche that no goodneſſe may amende, ne non evelle empeyre; that in perfeyte trynytee lyvethe and regnethe God, be alle worldes and be alle tymes. Amen, Amen, Amen.

The firſt of our authours, who can be properly ſaid to have written *Engliſh*, was Sir *John Gower*, who, in his *Confeſſion of a Lover*, calls *Chaucer* his diſciple, and may therefore be conſidered as the father of our poetry.

NOWE for to ſpeke of the commune,
It is to drede of that fortune,
Which hath befalle in ſondrye londes:
But ofte for defaute of bondes
All ſodeinly, er it be wiſt,
A tunne, whan his lie ariſt
Tobreketh, and renneth all aboute,
Whiche els ſhulde nought gone out.
And eke full ofte a littell ſkare
Vpon a banke, er men be ware,
Let in the ſtreme, whiche with gret peine,
If any man it ſhall reſtreine.
Where lawe failleth, errour groweth.
He is not wiſe, who that ne troweth.
For it hath proued oft er this.
And thus the common clamour is
In euery londe, where people dwelleth:
And eche in his complainte telleth,
How that the worlde is miſwent,
And thervpon his argument
Yeueth euery man in ſondrie wiſe:
But what man wolde him ſelfe auiſe
His conſcience, and nought miſuſe,
He maie well at the firſt excuſe
His god, whiche euer ſtant in one,
In him there is defaute none
So muſt it ſtande vpon vs ſelue,
Nought only vpon ten ne twelue,
But plenarly vpon vs all.
For man is cauſe of that ſhall fall.

The hiſtory of our language is now brought to the point at which the hiſtory of our poetry is generally ſuppoſed to commence, the time of the illuſtrious *Geoffry Chaucer*, who may perhaps, with great juſtice, be ſtiled the firſt of our verſifyers who wrote poetically. He does not however appear to have deſerved all the praiſe which he has received, or all the cenſure that he has ſuffered. *Dryden*, who miſtakes genius for learning, and, in confidence of his abilities, ventured to write of what he had not examined, aſcribes to *Chaucer* the firſt refinement of our numbers, the firſt production of eaſy and natural rhymes, and the improvement of our language, by words borrowed from the more poliſhed languages of the continent. *Skinner* contrarily blames him in harſh terms for having vitiated his native ſpeech by *whole cartloads of foreign words*. But he that reads the works of *Gower* will find ſmooth numbers and eaſy rhymes, of which *Chaucer* is ſuppoſed to have been the inventor, and the *French* words, whether good or bad,

of

of which *Chaucer* is charged as the importer. Some innovations he might probably make, like others, in the infancy of our poetry, which the paucity of books does allow us to discover with particular exactneſs; but the works of *Gower* and *Lydgate* ſufficiently evince, that his diction was in general like that of his contemporaries: and ſome improvements he undoubtedly made by the various diſpoſitions of his rhymes, and by the mixture of different numbers, in which he ſeems to have been happy and judicious. I have ſelected ſeveral ſpecimens both of his proſe and verſe; and among them, part of his tranſlation of *Boetius*, to which another verſion, made in the time of queen *Mary*, is oppoſed. It would be improper to quote very ſparingly an authour of ſo much reputation, or to make very large extracts from a book ſo generally known.

CHAUCER.

ALAS! I wepyng am conſtrained to begin verſe of ſorowfull matter, that whilom in floriſhyng ſtudie made delitable ditees. For lo! rendyng muſes of Poetes enditen to me thinges to be writen, and drerie teres. At laſte no drede ne might overcame tho muſes, that thei ne werren fellowes, and foloweden my waie, that is to ſaie, when I was exiled, thei that weren of my youth whilom welfull and grene, comforten now ſorowfull wierdes of me olde man: for elde is comen unwarely upon me, haſted by the harmes that I have, and ſorowe hath commaunded his age to be in me. Heres hore aren ſhad overtimeliche upon my hed: and the ſlacke ſkinne trembleth of mine empted bodie. Thilke deth of men is welefull, that he ne cometh not in yeres that be ſwete, but cometh to wretches often icleped: Alas, alas! with how deſe an ere deth cruell turneth awaie fro wretches, and naieth for to cloſe wepyng eyen. While fortune unfaithfull favoured me with light godes, that ſorowfull houre, that is to ſaie, the deth, had almoſte drente myne hedde: but now for fortune cloudie hath chaunged her decevable chere to mewarde, myne unpitous life draweth along ungreable dwellynges. O ye my frendes, what, or whereto avaunted ye me to ben welfull? For he that hath fallin, ſtode in no ſtedfaſt degre.

COLVILE.

I THAT in tyme of proſperite, and floryſhing ſtudye, made pleaſaunte and delectable dities, or verſes: alas now beyng heauy and ſad ouerthrowen in aduerſitie, am compelled to fele and taſt heuines and greif. Beholde the muſes Poeticall, that is to ſaye: the pleaſure that is in poetes verſes, do appoynt me, and compel me to writ theſe verſes in meter, and the ſorowfull verſes do wet my wretched face with very waterye teares, yſſuinge out of my eyes for ſorowe. Whiche muſes no feare without doute could ouercome, but that they wold folow me in my iourney of exile or baniſhment. Sometyme the ioye of happy and luſty delectable youth dyd comfort me, and nowe the courſe of ſorowfull olde age causeth me to reioyſe. For haſty old age vnloked for is come vpon me with al her incommodities and euyls, and ſorow hath commaunded and broughte me into the ſame old age, that is to ſay: that ſorowe cauſeth me to be olde, before my time come of olde age. The hoer heares do growe vntimely vpon my heade, and my reuiled ſkynne trembleth my fleſh, cleane conſumed and waſted with ſorowe. Mannes death is happy, that cometh not in youth, when a man is luſtye, and in pleaſure or welth: but in time of aduerſitie, when it is often deſyred. Alas Alas howe dull and deffe be the eares of cruel death vnto men in miſery that would fayne dye: and yet refuſythe to come and ſhutte vp theyr carefull wepyng eyes. Whiles that falſe fortune fauoryd me with her tranſitorye goodes, then the howre of death had almoſt ouercom me. That is to ſay deathe was redy to oppreſſe me when I was in proſperitie. Nowe for by cauſe that fortune beynge turned, from proſperitie into aduerſitie (as the clere day is darkyd with cloudes) and hath chaungyd her deceyuable countenaunce: my wretched life is yet prolonged and doth continue in dolour. O my frendes why haue you ſo often boſted me, ſayinge that I was happy when I had honor poſſeſſions riches, and authoritie whych be tranſitory thynges. He that hath fallen was in no ſtedefaſt degre.

IN the mene while, that I ſtill record theſe thynges with my ſelf, and marked my wepelie complainte with office of poinctell: I ſaugh ſtondyng aboven the hight of myn hed a woman of full grete reverence, by ſemblaunt. Her eyen brennyng, and clere, ſeyng over the common might of menne, with a lively colour, and with ſoche vigour and ſtrength that it ne might not be nempned, all were it ſo, that ſhe were full of ſo grete age, that menne woulden not trowen in no manere, that ſhe were of our elde.

The ſtature of her was of doutous Judgemente, for ſometyme ſhe conſtrained and inronke her ſelven, like to the common meſure of menne: And ſometyme it ſemed, that ſhe touched the heven with the hight of her hedde. And when ſhe hove her hedde higher, ſhe perced the ſelf heven, ſo that the ſight of menne lokyng was in ydell: her clothes wer maked of right delie thredes, and ſubtel craft of perdurable matter. The whiche clothes ſhe had woven with her owne handes, as I knewe well after by her ſelf declaryng, and ſhewyng to me the beautie: The whiche clothes a darkneſſe of a forleten and diſpiſed elde had duſked and darked, as it is wonte to darke by ſmoked Images.

In the nethereſt hemme and border of theſe clothes menne redde iwoven therein a Grekiſhe A. that ſignifieth the life active, and above that letter, in the hieſt bordure, a Grekiſhe C. that ſignifieth the life contemplatiſe. And betwene theſe two letters there were ſeen degrees nobly wrought, in maner of ladders, by whiche degrees menne might climben from the nethereſt letter to the uppereſt: natheleſſe handes of ſome men hadden kerve that clothe, by violence or by ſtrength, and

WHYLES that I conſiderydde pryuylye with my ſelfe the thynges before ſayd, and deſcrybed my wofull complaynte after the maner and offyce of a wrytter, me thought I ſawe a woman ſtand ouer my head of a reuerend countenaunce, hauyng quycke and glyſteryng clere eye, aboue the common ſorte of men in lyuely and delectable coloure, and ful of ſtrength, although ſhe ſemed ſo olde that by no meanes ſhe is thought to be one of this oure tyme, her ſtature is of douteful knowledge, for nowe ſhe ſhewethe herſelſe at the commen length or ſtatur of men, and other whiles ſhe ſemeth ſo high, as though ſhe touched heuen with the crown of her hed. And when ſhe wold ſtretch fourth her hed hygher, it alſo perced thorough heauen, ſo that mens ſyghte coulde not attaine to behold her. Her veſtures or cloths were perfyt of the finyſte thredes, and ſubtyll workemanſhyp, and of ſubſtaunce permament, whych veſturs ſhe had wouen with her own hands as I perceyued after by her owne ſaiynge. The kynde or beawtye of the whyche veſtures, a certayne darkenes or rather ignoraunce of oldenes ſorgotten hadde obſcuryd and darkened, as the ſmoke is wont to darken Images that ſtand nyghe the ſmoke. In the lower parte of the ſaid veſtures was read the greke letter P. wouen whych ſignifyeth practiſe or actyffe, and in the hygher part of the veſtures the greke letter. T. whych eſtandeth for theorica, that ſignifieth ſpeculacion or contemplation. And betwene both the ſayd letters were ſene certayne degrees, wrought after the maner of ladders, wherein was as it were a paſſage or waye in ſteppes or degrees from the lower part wher the letter. P. was which is vnderſtand from practys or actyf, unto

everiche

everiche manne of 'hem had borne awaie soche peces, as he might getten. And forsothe this foresaied woman bare smale bokes in her right hande, and in her left hand she bare a scepter. And when she sawe these Poeticall muses approchyng about my bed, and endityng wordes to my wepynges, she was a litle amoved, and glowed with cruell eyen. Who (qđ she) hath suffered approchen to this sike manne these commen strompettes, of which is the place that menne callen Theatre, the whiche onely ne asswagen not his sorowes with remedies, but thei would feden and norishe hym with swete venime? Forsothe, that ben tho that with thornes, and prickynges of talentes of affeccions, whiche that ben nothyng fructuous nor profitable, distroien the Corne, plentuous of fruictes of reson. For thei holden hertes of men in usage, but thei ne deliver no folke fro maladie. But if ye muses had withdrawen fro me with your flatteries any unconnyng and unprofitable manne, as ben wont to finde commenly among the peple, I would well suffre the lasse grevously. For why, in soche an unprofitable man myne ententes were nothyng endamaged. But ye withdrowen fro me this man, that hath ben nourished in my studies or scoles of Eleaticis, and of Academicis in Grece. But goeth now rather awaie ye Mermaidens, whiche that ben swete, till it be at the last, and suffreth this man to be cured and heled by my muses, that is to say, by my notefull sciences. And thus this companie of muses iblamed casten wrothly the chere dounward to the yerth, and shewing by rednesse ther shame, thei passeden sorowfully the thresholde. And I of whom the sight plounged in teres was darked, so that I ne might not know what that woman was, of so Imperial aucthoritie, I woxe all abashed and stonied, and cast my sight doune to the yerth, and began still for to abide what she would doen afterward. Then came she nere, and set her doune upon the utterest corner of my bed, and she beholdyng my chere, that was cast to the yerth, hevie and grevous of wepyng, complained with these wordes (that I shall saine) the perturbacion of my thought.

the hygher parte wher the letter T. was whych is vnderstand speculacion or contemplacion. Neuertheles the handes of some vyolente persones had cut the sayde vestures and had taken awaye certayne pecis thereof, such as euery one coulde catch. And she her selfe dyd bare in her ryght hand litel bokes, and in her lefte hande a scepter, which foresayd phylosophy (when she saw the muses poetycal present at my bed, spekyng sorrowful wordes to my wepynges) beyng angry sayd (with terrible or frownynge countenaunce) who suffred these crafty harlottes to com to thys sycke man? whych can help hym by no means of hys griefe by any kind of medicines, but rather increase the same with swete poyson. These be they that doo dystroye the fertile and plentious commodytyes of reason and the fruytes therof wyth their pryckynge thornes, or barren affectes, and accustome or subdue mens myndes with sickenes, and heuynes, and do not delyuer or heale them of the same. But yf your flatterye had conueyed or wythdrawen from me, any vnlernyd man as the comen sorte of people are wonte to be, I coulde haue ben better contentyd, for in that my worke should not be hurt or hynderyd. But you haue taken and conueyed from me thys man that hath ben broughte vp in the studyes of Aristotel and of Plato But yet get you hence maremaids (that seme swete untyll you haue brought a man to deathe) and suffer me to heale thys my man wyth my muses or scyences that be holsome and good. And after that philosophy had spoken these wordes the sayd companye of the musys poeticall beynge rebukyd and sad, caste down their countenaunce to the grounde, and by blussyng confessed their shamfastnes, and went out of the dores. But I (that had my syght dull and blynd wyth wepyng, so that I knew not what woman this was hauyng soo great aucthoritie) was amasyd or astonyed, and lokyng downeward, towarde the grounde, I began pryvylye to look what thyng she would saye ferther, then she had said. Then she approching and drawynge nere vnto me, sat downe vpon the vttermost part of my bed, and lokyng vpon my face sad with weping, and declynyd toward the earth for sorow, bewayled the trouble of my minde wyth these sayinges folowynge.

The conclusions of the Astrolabie.

This book (written to his son in the year of our Lord 1391, and in the 14 of King Richard II.) standeth so good at this day, especially for the horizon of Oxford, as in the opinion of the learned it cannot be amended, says an Edit. of Chaucer.

LYTEL Lowys my sonne, I perceve well by certaine evidences thyne abylyte to lerne scyences, touching nombres and proporcions, and also well consydre I thy besye prayer in especyal to lerne the tretyse of the astrolabye. Than for as moche as a philosopher saithe, he wrapeth hym in his frende, that condiscendeth to the ryghtfull prayers of his frende: therfore I have given the a sufficient astrolabye for oure orizont, compowned after the latitude of Oxenforde: upon the whiche by mediacion of this lytell tretise, I purpose to teche the a certaine nombre of conclusions, pertainynge to this same instrument. I say a certaine nombre of conclusions for thre causes, the first cause is this. Truste wel that al the conclusions that have be founden, or ells possiblye might be founde in so noble an instrument as in the astrolabye, ben unknowen perfitely to anye mortal man in this region, as I suppose. Another cause is this, that sothely in any cartes of the astrolabye that I have ysene, ther ben some conclusions, that wol not in al thinges perfourme ther behestes: and some of 'hem ben to harde to thy tender age of ten yere to conceve. This tretise divided in five partes, wil I shewe the wondir light rules and naked wordes in Englishe, for Latine ne canst thou nat yet but smale, my litel sonne. But nevertheless suffiseth to the these trewe conclusyons in Englishe, as well as suffiseth to these noble clerkes grekes these same conclusions in greke, and to the Arabines in Arabike, and to Jewes in Hebrewe, and to the Latin folke in Latyn: whiche Latyn folke had 'hem firste out of other divers langages, and write 'hem in ther owne tonge, that is to saine in Latine.

And God wote that in all these languages and in manye mo, have these conclusyons ben sufficientlye lerned and taught, and yet by divers rules, right as divers pathes leden divers folke the right waye to Rome.

Now wol I pray mekely every person discrete, that redeth or hereth this lityl tretise to have my rude ententing excused, and my superfluite of wordes, for two causes. The first cause is, for that curious endityng and harde sentences is ful hevy at ones, for soch a childe to lerne. And the seconde cause is this, that sothely me semeth better to writen unto a childe twise a gode sentence, than he foriete it ones. And, Lowis, if it be so that I shewe the in my lith Englishe, as trew conclusions touching this mater, and not only as trewe but as many and subtil conclusions as ben yshewed in latin, in any comon tretise of the astrolabye, conne me the more thanke, and praye God save the kinge, that is lorde of this langage, and all that him faith bereth, and obeieth everiche in his degree, the more and the lasse. But consydreth well, that I ne usurpe not to have founden this werke of my labour or of myne engin. I n'ame but a leude compilatour of the laboure of olde astrologiens, and have it translated in myn englishe onely for thy doctrine: and with this swerde shal I slene envy.

The first party.

The first partye of this tretise shall reherce the figures, and the membres of thyne astrolaby, bycause that thou shalte have the greter knowinge of thine owne instrument.

The seconde party.

The seconde partye shal teche the to werken the very practike of the foresaid conclusions, as ferforthe and also narowe as may be shewed in so smale an instrument portatife aboute. For wel wote every astrologien, that smallest fractions ne wol not be shewed in so smal an instrument, as in subtil tables calculed for a cause.

The

The Prologue of the Testament of LOVE.

MANY men there ben, that with eres openly ſprad ſo moche ſwalowen the deliciouſneſſe of jeſtes and of ryme, by queint knittinge coloures, that of the godeneſſe or of the badneſſe of the ſentence take they litel hede or els none.

Sothelye dulle witte and a thoughtfulle ſoule ſo ſore have mined and graffed in my ſpirites, that ſoche craft of enditinge woll nat ben of mine acquaintaunce. And for rude wordes and boiſtous percen the herte of the herer to the inreſt point, and planten there the ſentence of thinges, ſo that with litel helpe it is able to ſpring, this boke, that nothynge hath of the grete flode of wytte, ne of ſemelyche colours, is dolven with rude wordes and boiſtous, and ſo drawe togiðer to maken the catchers therof ben the more redy to hent ſentence.

Some men there ben, that painten with colours riche and ſome with wers, as with red inke, and ſome with coles and chalke: and yet is there gode matter to the leude peple of thylke chalkye purtreyture, as 'hem thinketh for the time, and afterward the ſyght of the better colours yeven to 'hem more joye for the firſt leudeneſſe. So ſothly this leude clowdy occupacyon is not to prayſe, but by the leude, for comenly leude leudeneſſe commendeth. Eke it ſhal yeve ſight that other precyous thynges ſhall be the more in reverence. In Latin and French hath many ſoveraine wittes had grete delyte to endite, and have many noble thinges fulfilde, but certes there ben ſome that ſpeken ther poiſye mater in Frenche, of whiche ſpeche the Frenche men have as gode a fantaſye as we have in heryng of Frenche mens Engliſhe. And many termes there ben in Englyſhe, whiche unneth we Engliſhe men connen declare the knowleginge: howe ſhould than a Frenche man borne? ſoche termes connejumpere in his matter, but as the jay chatereth Engliſhe. Right ſo truely the underſtandyn of Engliſhmen woll not ſtretche to the privie termes in Frenche, what ſo ever we boſten of ſtraunge langage. Let than clerkes enditen in Latin, for they have the propertie of ſcience, and the knowinge in that facultie: and lette Frenche men in ther Frenche alſo enditen ther queint termes, for it is kyndely to ther mouthes; and let us ſhewe our fantaſies in ſuch wordes as we lerneden of our dame's tonge. And although this boke be lytel thank worthy for the leudneſſe in travaile, yet ſoch writing exiten men to thilke thinges that ben neceſſarie: for every man therby may as by a perpetual myrrour ſene the vices or vertues of other, in whyche thynge lightly may be conceved to eſchue perils, and neceſſaries to catch, after as aventures have fallen to other peple or perſons.

Certes the ſoverainſt thinge of deſire and moſt creture reſonable, have or els ſhuld have full appetite to ther perfeccyon: unreſonable beſtes mowen not, ſithe reſon hath in 'hem no workinge: than reſonable that wol not, is compariſoned to unreſonable, and made lyke 'hem. Forſothe the moſt ſoveraine and finall perfeccion of man is in knowynge of a ſothe, withouten any entent decevable, and in love of one very God, that is inchaungeable, that is to knowe, and love his creator.

Nowe principally the mene to brynge in knowleging and lovynge his creatour, is the conſideracyon of thynges made by the creatour, wher through by thylke thinges that ben made, underſtandynge here to our wyttes, arne the unſene pryvities of God made to us ſyghtfull and knowinge, in our contemplacion and underſtondinge. Theſe thinges than forſothe moche bringen us to the ful knowleginge ſothe, and to the parfyte love of the maker of hevenly thynges. Lo! David ſaith: thou haſte delited me in makinge, as who ſaith, to have delite in the tune how God hat lent me in conſideracion of thy makinge. Wherof Ariſtotle in the boke de Animalibus, ſaith to naturell philoſophers: it is a grete likynge in love of knowinge ther cretoure: and alſo in knowinge of cauſes in kindelye thynges, conſidrid forſothe the formes of kindelye thinges and the ſhap, a gret kyndely love we ſhulde have to the werkman that 'hem made. The crafte of a werkman is ſhewed in the werk. Herefore trulie the philoſophers with a lyvely ſtudie manie noble thinges, righte precious, and worthy to memorye, writen, and by a gret ſwet and travaille to us leften of cauſes the properties in natures of thinges, to whiche therfore philoſophers it was more joy, more lykinge, more herty luſt in kindely vertues and matters of reſon the perfeccion by buſy ſtudy to knowe, than to have had all the treſour, al the richeſſe, al the vaine glory, that the paſſed emperours, princes, or kinges hadden. Therfore the names of 'hem in the boke of perpetuall memorie in vertue and pece arne writen; and in the contrarie, that is to ſaine, in Styxe the foule pitte of helle arne thilke preſſed that ſoch godenes hated. And bicauſe this boke ſhall be of love, and the prime cauſes of ſtering in that doinge with paſſions and diſeſes for wantinge of deſire, I wil that this boke be cleped the teſtament of love.

But nowe thou reder, who is thilke that will not in ſcorne laughe, to here a dwarſe or els halfe a man, ſay he wil rende out the ſwerde of Hercules handes, and alſo he ſhulde ſet Hercules Gades a mile yet ferther, and over that he had power of ſtrength to pull up the ſpere, that Aliſander the noble might never wagge, and that paſſinge al thinge to ben mayſter of Fraunce by might, there as the noble gracious Edwarde the thirde for al his grete proweſſe in victories ne might al yet conquere?

Certes I wote well, ther ſhall be made more ſcorne and jape of me, that I ſo unworthely clothed altogither in the cloudie cloude of unconning, wil putten me in prees to ſpeak of love, or els of the cauſes in that matter, ſithen al the gretteſt clerkes han had ynough to don, and as who ſaith gathered up clene toforne 'hem, and with ther ſharp ſithes of conning al mowen and made therof grete rekes and noble, ful of al plenties to fede me and many an other. Envye forſothe commendeth noughte his reſon, that he hath in hain, be it never ſo truſty. And although theſe noble repers, as gode workmen and worthy ther hier, han al draw and bounde up in the ſheves, and made many ſhockes, yet have I enſample to gaðer the ſmale crommes, and fullin ma walet of tho that fallen from the bourde among the ſmalle houndes, notwithſtanding the travaile of the almoigner, that hath draw up in the cloth al the remiſſailes, as trenchours, and the relefe to bere to the almeſſe. Yet alſo have I leve of the noble huſbande Boece, although I be a ſtraunger of conninge to come after his doctrine, and theſe grete workmen, and glene my handfuls of the ſhedynge after ther handes, and yf me faile ought of my ful, to encreſe my porcion with that I ſhal drawe by privyties out of ſhockes; a ſlye ſervaunte in his owne helpe is often moche commended; knowynge of trouthe in cauſes of thynges, was more hardier in the firſte ſechers, and ſo ſayth Ariſtotle, and lighter in us that han folowed after. For ther paſſing ſtudy han freſhed our wittes, and oure underſtandynge han excited in conſideracion of trouth by ſharpenes of ther reſons. Utterly theſe thinges be no dremes ne japes, to throwe to hogges, it is lyfelych mete for children of trouth, and as they me betiden whan I pilgramed out of my kith in wintere, whan the wether out of meſure was boiſtous, and the wyld wynd Boreas, as his kind aſketh, with dryinge coldes maked the wawes of the ocean ſe ſo to ariſe unkindely over the commune bankes that it was in point to ſpill all the erthe.

The Prologues of the Canterbury Tales of CHAUCER, from the MSS.

WHEN that Aprilis with his ſhouris ſote,
The drought of March had percid to the rote,
And bathid every veyn in ſuch licour,
Of which vertue engendrid is the flour.
When Zephyrus eke, with his ſwetè breth
Enſpirid hath, in every holt and heth
The tender croppis; and that the yong Sunn
Hath in the Ramm his halvè cours yrunn;
And ſmalè foulis makin melodye,
That ſlepin allè night with opin eye,
(So prickith them nature in ther corage)
Then longin folk to go on pilgrimage:
And palmers for to ſekin ſtrangè ſtrondes,
To ſervin hallowes couth in ſondry londes:
And ſpecially fro every ſhir'is end
Of England, to Canterbury they wend,

The holy blisfull martyr for to seke,
That them hath holpin, whan that they were seke:
Befell that in that seson on a day
In Southwerk at the Tabberd as I lay,
Redy to wendin on my pilgrimage
To Canterbury, with devote corage,
At night wer come into that hostery
Wele nine and twenty in a cumpany
Of sundrie folk, by aventure ysall
In felaship; and pilgrimes wer they all;
That toward Canterbury wouldin ride.
The chambers and the stablis werin wide,
And well we werin esid at the best:
And shortly whan the sunnè was to rest,
So had I spokin with them everych one,
That I was of ther felaship anone;
And madè forward erli for to rise,
To take our weye, ther as I did devise.
But nathless while that I have time and space,
Er' that I farther in this talè pace,
Methinkith it accordaunt to reson,
To tell you allè the condition
Of ech of them, so as it semid me,
And which they werin, and of what degree,
And eke in what array that they wer in:
And at a knight then woll I first begin.

The KNIGHT.

A knight ther was, and that a worthy man,
That fro the timè that he first began
To ridin out, he lovid Chevalrie,
Trouth and honour, fredome and curtesy.
Full worthy was he in his lord'is werre,
And thereto had he riddin nane more ferre
As well in Christendom, as in Hethness;
And evyr honoured for his worthiness.
At Alessandre' he was whan it was won;
Full oft timis he had the bord begon
Abovin allè naciouns in Pruce;
In Lettow had he riddin, and in Luce,
No Christen-man so oft of his degree
In Granada; in the sege had he be
Of Algezir, and ridd in Belmary;
At Leyis was he, and at Sataly,
Whan that they wer won; and in the grete see
At many'a noble army had he be:
At mortal battails had he ben fiftene,
And foughtin for our feith at Tramesene,
In listis thrys, and alwey slein his fo.
This ilke worthy knight had ben also
Sometimis with the lord of Palathy,
Ayens anothir hethin in Turky;
And evirmore he had a sov'rane prize;
And though that he was worthy, he was wise;
And of his port as meke as is a maid,
He nevir yet no villany ne said
In all his life unto no manner wight:
He was a very parfit gentil knight.
But for to tellin you of his array,
His hors wer good; but he was nothing gay,
Of fustian he werid a gipon,
Allè besmottrid with his haburgeon.
For he was late ycome from his viage,
And wentè for to do his pilgrimage.

The HOUSE of FAME.
The First Boke.

NOW herkin, as I have you saied,
What that I mette or I abraied,
Of December the tenith daie,
When it was night, to slepe I laie,
Right as I was wonte for to doen,
And fill aslepè wondir sone,
As he that was werie forgo
On pilgrimagè milis two
To the corps of sainct Leonarde,
To makin lithe that erst was harde.
But as me slept me mette I was
Within a temple' imade of glas,
In whiche there werin mo images
Of golde, standyng in sondrie stages,
Sette in mo riche tabirnacles,
And with perrè mo pinnacles,
And mo curious portraituris,
And queint manir of figuris
Of golde worke, then I sawe evir.
But certainly I n'ist nevir
Where that it was, but well wist I
It was of Venus redily
This temple, for in purtreiture
I sawe anone right her figure
Nakid yfletyng in a se,
And also on her hedde parde
Her rosy garland white and redde,
And her combe for to kembe her hedde,
Her dovis, and Dan Cupido
Her blindè sonne, and Vulcano,
That in his face ywas full broune.
But as I romid up and doune,
I founde that on the wall there was
Thus writtin on a table' of bras.
I woll now syng, if that I can,
The armis, and also the man,
That first came through his destine
Fugitife fro Troye the countre
Into Itaile, with full moche pine,
Unto the strondis of Lavine,
And tho began the storie' anone,
As I shall tellin you echone.
First sawe I the distruccion
Of Troie, thorough the Greke Sinon,
With his falsе untrue forsweryngеs,
And with his chere and his lesynges,
That made a horse, brought into Troye,
By whiche Trojans loste all ther joye.
And aftir this was graved, alas!
How Ilions castill assailed was,
And won, and kyng Priamus slain,
And Polites his sonne certain,
Dispitously of Dan Pyrrhus.
And next that sawe I howe Venus,
When that she sawe the castill brende,
Doune from hevin she gan discende,
And bade her sonne Æneas fle,
And how he fled, and how that he
Escapid was from all the pres,
And toke his fathre', old Anchises,
And bare hym on his backe awaie,
Crying alas and welawaie!
The whiche Anchises in his hande,
Bare tho the goddis of the lande
I mene thilke that unbrennid were.
Then sawe I next that all in fere
How Creusa, Dan Æneas wife,
Whom that he lovid all his life,
And her yong sonne clepid Julo,
And eke Ascanius also,
Fleddin eke, with full drerie chere,
That it was pite for to here,
And in a forest as thei went
How at a tournyng of a went
Creüsa was iloste, alas!
That rede not I, how that it was
How he her sought, and how her ghoste
Bad hym to flie the Grekis hoste,
And saied he must into Itaile,
As was his destinie, sauns faile,
That it was pitie for to here,
When that her spirite gan appere,
The wordis that she to hym saied,
And for to kepe her sonne hym praied.
There sawe I gravin eke how he
His fathir eke, and his meinè,
With his shippis began to saile
Toward the countrey of Itaile,
As streight as ere thei mightin go.
There sawe I eke the, cruill Juno,
That art Dan Jupiter his wife,
That hast ihatid all thy life

Merciless

Merciless all the Trojan blode,
Rennin and crie as thou were wode
On Æolus, the god of windes,
To blowin out of allè kindes
So loudè, that he should ydrenche
Lorde, and ladie, and grome, and wenche
Of all the Trojanis nacion,
Without any' of ther savacion.
There sawe I soche tempest arise,
That evèry herte might agrise
To se it paintid on the wall.
There sawe I eke gravin withall,
Venus, how ye, my ladie dere,
Ywepyng with full wofull chere
Yprayid Jupiter on hie,
To save and kepin that navie
Of that dere Trojan Æneas,
Sithins that he your sonne ywas.

Gode counsaile of CHAUCER.

FLIE fro the prese and dwell with sothfastnesse,
Suffise unto thy gode though it be small,
For horde hath hate, and climbyng tikilnesse,
Prece hath envie, and wele it brent oer all,
Savour no more then the behovin shall,
Rede well thy self, that othir folke canst rede,
And trouthe the shall delivir it 'is no drede.
Painè the not eche crokid to redresse,
In trust of her that tournith as a balle,
Grete rest standith in litil businesse,
Beware also to spurne again a nalle,
Strive not as doith a crocke with a walle,
Demith thy self that demist othir's dede,
And trouthe the shall deliver it 'is no drede.
That the is sent receve in buxomenesse;
The wrastlyng of this worlde askith a fall;
Here is no home, here is but wildirnesse,
Forthe pilgrim, forthe o best out of thy stall,
Loke up on high, and thanke thy God of all,
Weivith thy luste and let thy ghost the lede,
And trouthe the shall delivir, it 'is no drede.

Balade of the village without paintyng.

THIS wretchid world'is transmutacion
As wele and wo, nowe pore, and now honour,
Without ordir or due discrecion
Govirnid is by fortun'is errour,
But nathèlesse the lacke of her favour
Ne maie not doe me syng though that I die,
J'ay tout perdu, mon temps & mon labeur
For finally fortune I doe defie.
Yet is me left the sight of my resoun
To knowin frende fro foe in thy mirrour,
So moche hath yet thy tournyng up and doun,
I taughtin me to knowin in an hour,
But truily no force of thy reddour
To hym that ovir hymself hath maistrie,
My suffisaunce yshal be my succour,
For finally fortune I do defie.
O Socrates, thou stedfast champion,
She ne might nevir be thy turmentour,
Thou nevir dreddist her oppression,
Ne in her chere foundin thou no favour,
Thou knewe wele the disceipt of her colour,
And that her moste worship is for to lie,
I knowe her eke a false dissimulour,
Tor finally fortune I do defie.

The answere of Fortune.

No man is wretchid but hymself it wene,
He that yhath hymself hath suffisaunce,
Why saiest thou then I am to the so kene,
That hast thy self out of my govirnaunce?
Saie thus grant mercie of thin habundaunce,
That thou hast lent or this, thou shalt not strive,
What wost thou yet how I the woll avaunce?
And eke thou hast thy bestè frende alive.
I have the taught division betwene
Frende of effecte, and frende of countinaunce,
The nedith not the gallê of an hine,
That curith eyin derke for ther penaunce,
Now seest thou clere that wer in ignoraunce,
Yet holt thine anker, and thou maiest arive
There bountie bereth the key of my substaunce,
And eke thou haste thy bestè frende alive.
How many have I refused to sustene,
Sith I have the fostrid in thy plesaunce?
Wolt thou then make a statute on thy quene,
That I shall be aie at thine ordinaunce?
Thou born art in my reign of variaunce,
About the whele with othir must thou drive
My lore is bet, then wicke is thy grevaunce,
And eke thou hast thy bestè frende alive.

The answere to Fortune.

Thy lore I dampne, it is adversitie,
My frend maist thou not revin blind goddesse,
That I thy frendis knowe I thanke it the,
Take 'hem again, let 'hem go lie a presse,
The nigardis in kepyng ther richesse
Pronostike is thou wolt ther toure assaile,
Wicke appetite cometh aie before sickenesse,
In generall this rule ne maie not faile.

Fortune.

Thou pinchist at my mutabilitie,
For I the lent a droppe of my richesse,
And now me likith to withdrawin me,
Why shouldist thou my roialtie oppresse?
The se maie ebbe and flowin more and lesse,
The welkin hath might to shine, rain, and haile,
Right so must I kithin my brotilnesse,
In generall this rule ne maie not faile.

The Plaintiffe.

Lo, the' execucion of the majestie,
That all purveighith of his rightwisenesse,
That samè thyng fortune yclepin ye,
Ye blindè bestis full of leudènes!
The heven hath propirtie of sikirnes,
This worldè hath evir restlesse travaile,
The last daie is the ende of myne entresse,
In generall this rule ne maie not faile.

Th' envoye of Fortune.

Princes I praie you of your gentilnesse,
Let not this man and me thus crie and plain,
And I shall quitin you this businesse,
And if ye liste releve hym of his pain,
Praie ye his best frende of his noblenesse
That to some bettir state he maie attain.

Lydgate was a monk of *Bury*, who wrote about the same time with *Chaucer*. Out of his prologue to his third book of the *Fall of Princes* a few stanzas are selected, which, being compared with the style of his two contemporaries, will show that our language was then not written by caprice, but was in a settled state.

LIKE a pilgrime which that goeth on foote,
And hath none horse to releue his trauayle,
Whote, drye and wery, and may find no bote
Of wel cold whan thrust doth hym assayle,
Wine nor licour, that may to hym auayle,
Tight so fare I which in my businesse,
No succour fynde my rudenes to redresse.
I meane as thus, I haue no fresh licour
Out of the conduites of Calliope,
Nor through Clio in rhethorike no floure,
In my labour for to refresh me:
Nor of the susters in noumber thrise three,
Which with Cithera on Parnaso dwell,
They neuer me gaue drinke once of their wel.
Nor of theyr springes clere and christaline,
That sprange by touchyng of the Pegase,
Their fauour lacketh my making ten lumine
I fynde theyr bawme of so great scarcitie,
To tame their tunnes with some drop of plentie
For Poliphemus throw his great blindnes,
Hath in me derked of Argus the brightnes.

I

Our

Our life here short of wit the great dulnes
The heuy soule troubled with trauayle,
And of memorye the glasyng brotelnes,
Drede and vncunning haue made a strong batail
With werines my spirite to assayle,
And with their subtil creping in most queint
Hath made my spirit in makyng for to feint.
And ouermore, the ferefull frowardnes
Of my stepmother called obliuion,
Hath a bastyll of foryetfulnes,
To stoppe the passage, and shadow my reason
That I might haue no clere direccion,
In translating of new to quicke me,
Stories to write of olde antiquite.
Thus was I set and stode in double werre
At the metyng of feareful wayes tweyne,
The one was this, who euer list to lere,
Whereas good wyll gan me constrayne,
Bochas taccomplish for to doe my payne,
Came ignoraunce, with a menace of drede,
My penne to rest I durst not procede.

Fortescue was chief justice of the Common-Pleas, in the reign of king *Henry* VI. He retired in 1471. after the battle of Tewkesbury, and probably wrote most of his works in his privacy. The following passage is selected from his book of the *Difference between an absolute and limited Monarchy.*

HYT may peraventure be marvelid by some men, why one Realme is a Lordshyp only *Royall*, and the Prynce thereof rulyth yt by his Law, callid *Jus Regale*; and another Kyngdome is a Lordschip, *Royal and Politike*, and the Prince thereof rulyth by a Lawe, callyd *Jus Politicum & Regale*; sythen thes two Princes beth of egall Astate.

To this dowte it may be answeryd in this manner; The first Institution of thes twoo Realmys, upon the Incorporation of them, is the Cause of this diversyte.

When Nembroth by Might, for his own Glorye, made and incorporate the first Realme, and subduyd it to hymself by Tyrannye, he would not have it governyd by any other Rule or Lawe, but by his own Will; by which and for th' accomplishment thereof he made it. And therfor, though he had thus made a Realme, holy Scripture denyyd to cal hym a Kyng, *Quia Rex dicitur a Regendo*; Whych thyng he dyd not, but oppressyd the People by Myght, and therfor he was a Tyrant, and callid *Primus Tyrannorum.* But holy Writ callith hym *Robustus Venator coram Deo.* For as the Hunter takyth the wyld beste for to scle and eate hym; so Nembroth subduyd to him the People with Might, to have their service and their goods, using upon them the Lordschip that is callid *Dominium Regale tantum.* After hym Belus that was callid first a Kyng, and after hym his Sone Nynus, and after hym other Panyms; They, by Example of Nembroth, made them Realmys, would not have them rulyd by other Lawys than by their own Wills. Which Lawys ben right good under good Princes; and their Kyngdoms a then most resemblyd to the Kyngdome of God, which reynith upon Man, rulyng him by hys own Will. Wherfor many Crystyn Princes usen the same Lawe; and therfor it is, that the Lawys sayen, *Quod Principi placuit Legis habet vigorem.* And thus I suppose first beganne in Realmys, *Dominium tantum Regale.* But afterward, whan Mankynd was more mansuete, and better disposyd to Vertue, Grete Communalties, as was the Feliship, that came into this Lond with Brute, wyllyng to be unyed and made a Body Politike callid a Realme, havyng an Heed to governe it; as after the Saying of the Philosopher, every Communaltie unyed of many parts must needs have an Heed; than they chose the same Brute to be their Heed and Kyng. And they and he upon this Incorporation and Institution, and onyng of themself into a Realme, ordeynyd the same Realme so to be rulyd and justyfyd by such Lawys, as they al would assent unto; which Law therfor is callid *Politicum*; and bycause it is mynystrid by a Kyng, it is callid *Regale. Dominium Politicum dicitur quasi Regimen, plurium Scientia, sive Consilio ministratum* The Kyng of Scotts reynith upon his People by this Lawe, *videlicet, Regimine Politico & Regali.* And as Diodorus Syculus saith, in his Boke *de priscis Historiis*, The Realme of Egypte is rulid by the same Lawe, and therfor the Kyng therof chaungith not his Lawes, without the Assent of his People. And in like forme as he saith is ruled the Kyngdome of Saba, in Felici Arabia, and the Lond of *Libie*; And also the more parte of al the Realmys in *Afrike.* Which manner of Rule and Lordship, the sayd Diodorus in that Boke, praysith gretely. For it is not only good for the Prince, that may thereby the more sewerly do Justice, than by his owne Arbitriment; but it is also good for his People that receyve therby, such Justice as they desyer themself. Now as me seymth, it ys shewyd opinly ynough, why one Kyng rulyth and reynith on his People *Dominio tantum Regali*, and that other reynith *Dominio Politico & Regali*: For that one Kyngdome beganne, of and by, the Might of the Prince, and that other beganne, by the Desier and Institution of the People of the same Prince.

Of the works of Sir *Thomas More* it was necessary to give a larger specimen, both because our language was then in a great degree formed and settled, and because it appears from *Ben Johnson*, that his works were considered as models of pure and elegant style. The tale, which is placed first, because earliest written, will show what an attentive reader will, in perusing our old writers, often remark, that the familiar and colloquial part of our language, being disused among those classes who had no ambition of refinement, or affectation of novelty, has suffered very little change. There is another reason why the extracts from this authour are more copious: his works are carefully and correctly printed, and may therefore be better trusted than any other edition of the *English* books of that, or the preceding ages.

A merry iest how a sergeant would learne to playe the frere. Written by maister Thomas More in hys youth.

WYSE men alway,
Affyrme and say,
That best is for a man:
Diligently,
For to apply,
The busines that he can,
And in no wyse,
To enterpryse,
An other faculte,
For he that wyll,
And can no skyll,
Is neuer lyke to the.
He that hath lafte,
The hosiers crafte,
And falleth to making shone,
The smythe that shall,
To payntyng fall,
His thrift is well nigh done.
A blacke draper,
With whyte paper,
To goe to writyng scole,
An olde butler,
Becum a cutler,
I wene shall proue a fole.
And an olde trot,
That can I wot,
Nothyng but kysse the cup,
With her phisick,
Wil kepe one sicke,
Tyll she haue soused hym vp.
A man of lawe,
That neuer sawe,
The wayes to bye and sell,
Wenyng to ryse,
By marchaundise,
I wish to spede hym well.
A marchaunt eke,
That wyll goo seke,
By all the meanes he may,
To fall in sute,
Tyll he dispute,
His money cleane away,

Pletyng

Pletyng the lawe,
For euery ſtrawe,
Shall proue a thrifty man,
With bate and ſtrife,
But by my life,
I cannot tell you whan.
Whan an hatter
Wyll go ſmatter,
In philoſophy,
Or a pedlar,
Ware a medlar,
In theology,
All that enſue,
Suche craftes new,
They driue ſo farre a caſt,
That euermore,
They do therfore,
Beſhrewe themſelfe at laſt.
This thing was tryed
And verefyed,
Here by a ſergeaunt late,
That thriftly was,
Or he coulde pas,
Rapped about the pate,
Whyle that he would
See how he could,
A little play the frere:
Now yf you wyll,
Knowe how it fyll,
Take hede and ye ſhall here.
It happed ſo,
Not long ago,
A thrifty man there dyed,
An hundred pounde,
Of nobles rounde,
That had he layd a ſide:
His ſonne he wolde,
Should haue this golde,
For to beginne with all:
But to ſuffiſe
His chylde, well thriſe,
That money was to ſmal.
Yet or this day
I have hard ſay,
That many a man certeſſe,
Hath with good caſt,
Be ryche at laſt,
That hath begonne with leſſe.
But this yonge manne,
So well beganne,
His money to imploy,
That certainly,
His policy,
To ſee it was a joy,
For leſt ſum blaſt,
Myght ouer caſt,
His ſhip, or by miſchaunce,
Men with ſum wile,
Myght hym begyle,
And miniſh his ſubſtaunce,
For to put out,
All maner dout,
He made a good puruay,
For euery whyt,
By his owne wyt,
And toke an other way:
Firſt fayre and wele,
Therof much dele,
He dygged it in a pot,
But then him thought,
That way was nought,
And there he left it not.
So was he faine,
From thence agayne,
To put it in a cup,
And by and by,
Couetouſly,
He ſupped it fayre vp,
In his owne breſt,
He thought it beſt,
His money to encloſe,
Then wiſt he well,
What euer fell,
He coulde it neuer loſe.
He borrowed then,
Of other men,
Money and marchaundiſe:
Neuer payd it,
Up he laid it,
In like maner wyſe.
Yet on the gere,
That he would were,
He reight not what he ſpent,
So it were nyce,
As for the price,
Could him not miſcontent.
With luſty ſporte,
And with reſort,
Of ioly company,
In mirth and play,
Full many a day,
He liued merely.
And men had ſworne,
Some man is borne,
To haue a lucky howre,
And ſo was he,
For ſuch degre,
He gat and ſuche honour,
That without dout,
Whan he went out,
A ſergeaunt well and fayre,
Was redy ſtrayte,
On him to wayte,
As ſone as on the mayre.
But he doubtleſſe,
Of his mekeneſſe,
Hated ſuch pompe and pride,
And would not go,
Companied ſo,
But drewe himſelf a ſide,
To ſaint Katharine,
Streight as a line,
He gate him at a tyde,
For deuocion,
Or promocion,
There would he nedes abyde.
There ſpent he faſt,
Till all were paſt,
And to him came there meny,
To aſke theyr det,
But none could get,
The valour of a peny.
With viſage ſtout,
He bare it out,
Euen vnto the harde hedge,
A month or twaine,
Tyll he was faine,
To laye his gowne to pledge.
Than was he there,
In greater feare,
Than ere that he came thither,
And would as fayne,
Depart againe,
But that he wiſt not whither.
Than after this,
To a frende of his,
He went and there abode,
Where as he lay,
So ſick alway,
He myght not come abrode.
It happed than,
A marchant man,
That he ought money to,
Of an officere,
Than gan enquere,
What him was beſt to do.
And he anſwerde,
Be not aferde,
Take an accion therfore,
I you beheſte,
I ſhall hym reſte,
And than care for no more.

I feare

I feare quod he,
It wyll not be,
For he wyll not come out.
The ſergeaunt ſaid,
Be not afrayd.
It ſhall be brought about.
In many a game,
Lyke to the ſame,
Haue I bene well in vre,
And for your ſake,
Let me be bake,
But yf I do this cure.
Thus part they both,
And foorth then goth,
A pace this officere,
And for a day,
All his array,
He chaunged with a frere.
So was he dight,
That no man might,
Hym for a frere deny,
He dopped and dooked,
He ſpake and looked,
So religiouſly.
Yet in a glaſſe,
Or he would paſſe,
He toted and he peered,
His harte for pryde,
Lepte in his ſyde,
To ſee how well he freered.
Than forth a pace,
Unto the place,
He goeth withouten ſhame
To do this dede,
But now take hede,
For here begynneth the game.
He drew hym ny,
And ſoftely,
Streyght at the dore he knocked:
And a damſell,
That hard hym well,
There came and it vnlocked.
The frere ſayd,
Good ſpede fayre mayd,
Here lodgeth ſuch a man,
It is told me:
Well ſyr quod ſhe,
And yf he do what than.
Quod he mayſtreſſe,
No harme doutleſſe:
It longeth for our order,
To hurt no man,
But as we can,
Euery wight to forder.
With hym truly,
Fayne ſpeake would I.
Sir quod ſhe by my fay,
He is ſo ſike,
Ye be not lyke,
To ſpeake with hym to day.
Quod he fayre may,
Yet I you pray,
This much at my deſire,
Vouchesafe to do,
As go hym to,
And ſay an auſten frere
Would with hym ſpeke,
And matters breake,
For his auayle certayn.
Quod ſhe I wyll,
Stonde ye here ſtyll,
Tyll I come downe agayn.
Vp is ſhe go,
And told hym ſo,
As ſhe was bode to ſay,
He miſtruſtying,
No maner thyng,
Sayd mayden go thy way,
And fetch him hyder,
That we togyder,
May talk. A downe ſhe gothe,
Vp ſhe hym brought,
No harme ſhe thought,
But it made ſome fol
This officere,
This fayned frere,
Whan he was come al
He dopped than,
And grete this man,
Religiouſly and oft.
And he agayn,
Ryght glad and fayn.
Toke hym there by the hande,
The frere than ſayd,
Ye be diſmayd,
With trouble I underſtande.
In dede quod he,
It hath with me,
Bene better than it is.
Syr quod the frere,
Be of good chere,
Yet ſhall it after this.
But I would now,
Comen with you,
In counſayle yf you pleaſe,
Or ellys nat
Of matters that,
Shall ſet your heart at eaſe.
Downe went the mayd,
The marchaunt ſayd,
Now ſay on gentle frere,
Of thys tydyng,
That ye me bryng,
I long full ſore to here.
Whan there was none,
But they alone,
The frere with euyll grace,
Sayd, I reſt the,
Come on with me,
And out he toke his mace:
Thou ſhalt obay,
Come on thy way,
I have the in my clouche,
Thou goeſt not hence,
For all the penſe,
The mayre hath in his pouche.
This marchaunt there,
For wrath and fere,
He waxyng welnygh wood,
Sayd horſon thefe,
With a miſchefe,
Who hathtaught the thy good.
And with his fiſt,
Vpon the lyſt,
He gaue hym ſuch a blow,
That backward downe,
Almoſt in ſowne,
The frere is ouerthrow.
Yet was this man,
Well fearder than,
Leſt he the frere had ſlayne,
Tyll with good rappes,
And heuy clappes,
He dawde hym vp agayne.
The frere toke harte,
And vp he ſtarte,
And well he layde about,
And ſo there goth,
Betwene them both,
Many a luſty clout.
They rent and tere,
Eche others here,
And claue togyder faſt,
Tyll with luggyng,
And with tuggyng,
They fell downe bothe at laſt.
Than on the grounde,
Togyder rounde,
With many a ſadde ſtroke,
They roll and rumble,
They turne and tumble,
As pygges do in a poke.

So

So long aboue,
They heue and ſhoue,
Togider that at laſt,
The mayd and wyfe,
To breake the ſtrife,
Hyed them vpward faſt.
And whan they ſpye,
The captaynes lye,
Both waltring on the place,
The freres hood,
They pulled a good,
Adowne about his face.
Whyle he was blynde,
The wenche behynde,
Lent him leyd on the flore,
Many a ioule,
About the noule,
With a great batyldore.
The wyfe came yet,
And with her fete,
She holpe to kepe him downe,
And with her rocke,
Many a knocke,
She gaue hym on the crowne.
They layd his mace,
About his face,
That he was wood for payne:
The fryre frappe,
Gate many a ſwappe,
Tyll he was full nygh ſlayne.
Vp they hym lift,
And with yll thrift,
Hedlyng a long the ſtayre,
Downe they hym threwe,
And ſayde adewe,
Commende us to the mayre.
The frere aroſe,
But I ſuppoſe,
Amaſed was his hed,
He ſhoke his eares,
And from grete feares,
He thought hym well yfled.
Quod he now loſt,
Is all this coſt,
We be neuer the nere.
Ill mote he be,
That cauſed me,
To make my ſelf a frere.
Now maſters all,
Here now I ſhall,
Ende there as I began,
In any wyſe,
I would auyſe,
And counſayle euery man,
His owne craft vſe,
All newe refuſe,
And lyghtly let them gone:
Play not the frere,
Now make good chere,
And welcome euerych one.

A ruful lamentacion (writen by maſter Thomas More in his youth) of the deth of quene Eliſabeth mother to king Henry the eight, wife to king Henry the ſeuenth, and eldeſt doughter to king Edward the fourth, which quene Eliſabeth dyed in childbed in February in the yere of our Lord 1503, and in the 18 yere of the raigne of king Henry the ſeuenth.

O Ye that put your truſt and confidence,
In worldly ioy and frayle proſperite,
That ſo lyue here as ye ſhould neuer hence,
Remember death and loke here vppon me.
Enſaumple I thynke there may no better be.
Your ſelfe wotte well that in this realme was I,
Your quene but late, and lo now here I lye.
Was I not borne of olde worthy linage?
Was not my mother queene my father kyng?
Was I not a kinges fere in marriage?
Had I not plenty of euery pleaſaunt thyng?
Mercifull god this is a ſtraunge reckenyng:
Rycheſſe, honour, welth, and aunceſtry?
Hath me forſaken and lo now here I ly.
If worſhip myght haue kept me, I had not gone.
If wyt myght haue me ſaued, I neded not fere.
If money myght haue holpe, I lacked none.
But O good God what vayleth all this gere.
When deth is come thy mighty meſſangere,
Obey we muſt there is no remedy,
Me hath he ſommoned, and lo now here I ly.
Yet was I late promiſed otherwyſe,
This yere to liue in welth and delice.
Lo where to commeth thy blandiſhyng promyſe,
O falſe aſtrolagy and deuynatrice,
Of goddes ſecretes makyng thy ſelfe ſo wyſe.
How true is for this yere thy prophecy.
The yere yet laſteth, and lo nowe here I ly.
O bryttill welth, as full of bitterneſſe,
Thy ſingle pleaſure doubled is with payne.
Account my ſorow firſt and my diſtreſſe,
In ſondry wyſe, and recken there agayne,
The ioy that I haue had, and I dare ſayne,
For all my honour, endured yet haue I,
More wo then welth, and lo now here I ly.
Where are our caſtels, now where are our towers,
Goodly Rychmonde ſone art thou gone from me,
At Weſtminſter that coſtly worke of yours,
Myne owne dere lorde now ſhall I neuer ſee.
Almighty god voucheſafe to graunt that ye,
For you and your children well may edefy.
My palyce bylded is, and lo now here I ly.
Adew myne owne dere ſpouſe my worthy lorde,
The faithfull loue, that dyd vs both combyne,
In mariage and peaſable concorde,
Into your handes here I cleane reſyne,
To be beſtowed vppon your children and myne.
Erſt wer you father, and now muſt ye ſupply,
The mothers part alſo, for lo now here I ly.
Farewell my doughter lady Margerete.
God wotte full oft it greued hath my mynde,
That ye ſhould go where we ſhould ſeldome mete.
Now am I gone, and haue left you behynde.
O mortall folke that we be very blynde.
That we leaſt feare, full oft it is moſt nye,
From you depart I fyrſt, and lo now here I lye.
Farewell Madame my lordes worthy mother,
Comfort your ſonne, and be ye of good chere.
Take all a worth, for it will be no nother.
Farewell my doughter Katherine late the fere,
To prince Arthur myne owne chyld ſo dere,
It booteth not for me to wepe or cry,
Pray for my ſoule, for lo now here I ly.
Adew lord Henry my louyng ſonne adew.
Our lorde encreaſe your honour and eſtate,
Adew my doughter Mary bright of hew,
God make you vertuous wyſe and fortunate.
Adew ſwete hart my litle doughter Kate,
Thou ſhalt ſwete babe ſuche is thy deſteny,
Thy mother neuer know, for lo now here I ly.
Lady Cicyly Anne and Katheryne,
Farewell my welbeloved ſiſters three,
O lady Briget other ſiſter myne,
Lo here the ende of worldly vanitee.
Now well are ye that earthly foly flee,
And heuenly thynges loue and magnify,
Farewell and pray for me, for lo now here I ly.
A dew my lordes, a dew my ladies all,
A dew my faithful ſeruauntes euerych one,
A dew my commons whom I neuer ſhall,
See in this world wherfore to the alone,
Immortall god verely three and one,
I me commende. Thy infinite mercy,
Shew to thy ſeruant, for lo now here I ly.

Certain meters in Engliſh written by maſter Thomas More in hys youth for the boke of fortune, and cauſed them to be printed in the begynnyng of that boke.

The wordes of Fortune to the people.

MINE high eſtate power and auctoritie,
If ye ne know, enſerche and ye ſhall ſpye,
That richeſſe, worſhip, welth, and dignitie,
Joy, reſt, and peace, and all thyng fynally,
That any pleaſure or profit may come by,
To mannes comfort, ayde, and ſuſtinaunce,
Is all at my deuyſe and ordinaunce.

Without

Without my fauour there is nothyng wonne.
Many a matter haue I brought at last,
To good conclusion, that fondly was begonne.
And many a purpose, bounden sure and fast
With wise prouision, I haue ouercast.
Without good happe there may no wit suffise.
Better is to be fortunate than wyse.
And therefore hath there some men bene or this,
My deadly foes and written many a boke,
To my disprayse. And other cause there nys,
But for me list not frendly on them loke.
Thus lyke the fox they fare that once forsoke,
The pleasaunt grapes, and gan for to defy them,
Because he lept and yet could not come by them.
But let them write theyr labour is in vayne.
For well ye wote, myrth, honour, and richesse,
Much better is than penury and payne.
The nedy wretch that lingereth in distresse,
Without myne helpe is euer comfortlesse,
A wery burden odious and loth,
To all the world, and eke to him selfe both.
But he that by my fauour may ascende,
To mighty power and excellent degree,
A common wele to gouerne and defende,
O in how blist condicion standeth he:
Him self in honour and felicite,
And ouer that, may forther and increase,
A region hole in ioyfull rest and peace.
Now in this poynt there is no more to say,
Eche man hath of him self the gouernaunce.
Let euery wight than folowe his owne way,
And he that out of pouertee and mischaunce,
List for to liue, and wyll him selfe enhaunce,
In wealth and richesse, come forth and wayte on me.
And he that wyll be a beggar, let hym be.

THOMAS MORE to them that trust in Fortune.

THOU that are prowde of honour shape or kynne,
That hepest vp this wretched worldes treasure,
Thy fingers shrined with gold, thy tawny skynne,
With fresh apparyle garnished out of measure,
And wenest to haue fortune at thy pleasure,
Cast vp thyne eye, and loke how slipper chaunce,
Illudeth her men with chaunge and varyaunce.
Sometyme she loketh as louely fayre and bright,
As goodly Uenus mother of Cupyde.
She becketh and she smileth on euery wight.
But this chere fayned, may not long abide.
There cometh a cloude, and farewell all our pryde.
Like any serpent she beginneth to swell,
And looketh as fierce as any fury of hell.
Yet for all that we brotle men are fayne,
(So wretched is our nature and so blynde)
As soone as Fortune list to laugh agayne,
With fayre countenaunce and disceitfull mynde,
To crouche and knele and gape after the wynde,
Not one or twayne but thousandes in a rout,
Lyke swarmyng bees come flickeryng her aboute.
Then as a bayte she bryngeth forth her ware,
Siluer, gold, riche perle, and precious stone:
On whiche the mased people gase and stare,
And gape therefore, as dogges doe for the bone.
Fortune at them laugheth, and in her trone
Amyd her treasure and waueryng rychesse,
Prowdly she houeth as lady and empresse.
Fast by her syde doth wery labour stand,
Pale fere also, and sorow all bewept,
Disdayn and hatred on that other hand,
Eke restles watche fro slepe with trauayle kept,
His eyes drowsy and lokyng as he slept.
Before her standeth daunger and enuy,
Flattery, dysceyt, mischiefe and tiranny.
About her commeth all the world to begge.
He asketh lande, and he to pas would bryng,
This toye and that, and all not worth an egge:
He would in loue prosper aboue all thyng:
He kneleth downe and would be made a kyng:
He forceth not so he may money haue,
Though all the worlde accompt hym for a knaue.
Lo thus ye see diuers heddes, diuers wittes.
Fortune alone as diuers as they all,
Vnstable here and there among them flittes:
And at auenture downe her giftes fall,
Catch who so may she throweth great and small
Not to all men, as commeth sonne or dewe,
But for the most part, all among a fewe.
And yet her brotell giftes long may not last.
He that she gaue them, loketh prowde and hye.
She whirlth about and pluckth away as fast,
And geueth them to an other by and by.
And thus from man to man continually,
She vseth to geue and take, and slily tosse,
One man to wynnyng of an others losse.
And when she robbeth one, down goth his pryde.
He wepeth and wayleth and curseth her full sore.
But he that receueth it, on that other syde,
Is glad, and blesth her often tymes therefore.
But in a whyle when she loueth hym no more,
She glydeth from hym, and her giftes to.
And he her curseth, as other fooles do,
Alas the folysh people can not cease,
Ne voyd her trayne, tyll they the harme do fele.
About her alway, besely they preace.
But lord how he doth thynk hym self full wele.
That may set once his hande vppon her whele.
He holdeth fast: but vpward as he flieth,
She whippeth her whele about, and there he lyeth.
Thus fell Julius from his mighty power.
Thus fell Darius the worthy kyng of Perse.
Thus fell Alexander the great conquerour.
Thus many mo then I may well reherse.
Thus double fortune, when she lyst reuerse
Her slipper fauour fro them that in her trust,
She fleeth her wey and leyeth them in the dust.
She sodeinly enhaunceth them aloft.
And sodeynly mischeueth all the flocke.
The head that late lay easily and full soft,
In stede of pylows lyeth after on the blocke.
And yet alas the most cruell proude mocke:
The deynty mowth that ladyes kissed haue,
She bryngeth in the case to kysse a knaue.
In chaungyng of her course, the chaunge shewth this,
Vp startth a knaue, and downe there falth a knight,
The beggar ryche, and the ryche man pore is.
Hatred is turned to loue, loue to despyght.
This is her sport, thus proueth she her myght.
Great boste she maketh yf one be by her power,
Welthy and wretched both within an howre.
Pouertee that of her giftes wyl nothing take,
Wyth mery chere, looketh vppon the prece,
And seeth how fortunes houshold goeth to wrake.
Fast by her standeth the wyse Socrates.
Arristippus, Pythagoras, and many a lese,
Of olde philosophers. And eke agaynst the sonne
Bekyth h.m poore Diogenes in his tonne.
With her is Byas, whose countrey lackt defence,
And whylom of their foes stode so in dout,
That eche man hastely gan to cary thence,
And asked hym why he nought caryed out.
I bere quod he all myne with me about:
Wisedom he ment, not fortunes brotle fees.
For nought he counted his that he might leese.
Heraclitus eke, lyst felowship to kepe
With glad pouertee, Democritus also:
Of which the fyrst can neuer cease but wepe,
To see how thick the blynded people go,
With labour great to purchase care and wo.
That other laugheth to see the foolysh apes,
Howe earnestly they walk about theyr capes.
Of this poore sect, it is comen vsage,
Onely to take that nature may sustayne,
Banishing cleane all other surplusage,
They be content, and of nothyng complayne.
No nygarde eke is of his good so fayne.
But they more pleasure haue a thousande folde,
The secrete draughtes of nature to beholde.
Set fortunes servauntes by them and ye wull,
That one is free, that other euer thrall,
That one content, that other neuer full.
That one in suretye, that other lyke to fall.
Who lyst to aduise them bothe, parceyue he shall,
As great difference between them as we see,
Betwixte wretchednes and felicite.

Nowe

Nowe haue I shewed you bothe: these whiche ye lyst,
Stately fortune, or humble pouertee:
That is to say, nowe lyeth it in your fyst,
To take here bondage, or free libertee.
But in thys poynte and ye do after me,
Draw you to fortune, and labour her to pleasé,
If that ye thynke your selfe to well at ease.
And fyrst vppon the louely shall she smile,
And frendly on the cast her wandering eyes,
Embrace the in her armes, and for a whyle,
Put the and kepe the in a fooles paradise:
And foorth with all what so thou lyst deuise,
She wyll the graunt it liberally parhappes:
But for all that beware of after clappes.
Recken you neuer of her fauoure sure:
Ye may in clowds as easily trace an hare,
Or in drye lande cause fishes to endure,
And make the burnyng fyre his heate to spare,
And all thys worlde in compace to forfare,
As her to make by craft or engine stable,
That of her nature is euer variable.
Serue her day and nyght as reuerently,
Vppon thy knees as any seruaunt may,
And in conclusion, that thou shalt winne thereby
Shall not be worth thy seruyce I dare say.
And looke yet what she geueth the to day,
With labour wonne she shall happly to morow
Pluck it agayne out of thyne hande with sorow.
Wherefore yf thou in suretye lyst to stande,
Take pouerties parte and let prowde fortune go,
Receyue nothyng that commeth from her hande.
Loue maner and vertue: they be onely tho.
Whiche double fortune may not take the fro.
Then mayst thou boldly defye her turnyng chaunce:
She can the neyther hynder nor auaunce.
But and thou wylt nedes medle with her treasure,
Trust not therein, and spende it liberally.
Beare the not proude, nor take not out of measure.
Bylde not thyne house on heyth vp in the skye.
None falleth farre, but he that climbeth hye,
Remember nature sent the hyther bare,
The gyftes of fortune count them borowed ware.

THOMAS MORE to them that seke Fortune.

WHO so delyteth to prouen and assay,
Of waueryng fortune the vncertayne lot,
If that the aunswere please you not alway,
Blame ye not me: for I commaunde you not,
Fortune to trust, and eke full well ye wot,
I haue of her no brydle in my fist,
She renneth loose, and turneth where she lyst.
The rollyng dyse in whome your lucke doth stande,
With whose vnhappy chaunce ye be so wroth,
Ye knowe your selfe came neuer in myne hande.
Lo in this ponde be fyshe and frogges both.
Cast in your nette: but be you liefe or lothe,
Hold you content as fortune lyst assyne:
For it is your owne fishyng and not myne.
And though in one chaunce fortune you offend,
Grudge not there at, but beare a mery face.
In many an other she shall it amende.
There is no manne so farre out of her grace,
But he sometyme hath comfort and solace:
Ne none agayne so farre foorth in her fauour,
That is full satisfyed with her behauiour.
Fortune is stately, solemne, prowde, and hye:
And rychesse geueth, to haue seruyce therefore.
The nedy begger catcheth an halfpeny:
Some manne a thousande pounde, some lesse some more.
But for all that she kepeth euer in store,
From euery manne some parcell of his wyll,
That he may pray therfore and serue her styll.
Some manne hath good, but chyldren hath he none.
Some man hath both, but he can get none health.
Some hath al thre, but vp to honours trone,
Can he not crepe, by no maner of stelth.
To some she sendeth, children, ryches, welthe,
Honour, woorshyp, and reuerence all hys lyfe:
But yet she pyncheth hym with a shrewde wyfe.
Then for asmuch as it is fortunes guyse,
To graunt no manne all thyng that he wyll axe,
But as her selfe lyst order and deuyse,
Doth euery manne his parte diuide and tax,
I counsayle you eche one trusse vp your packes,
And take no thyng at all, or be content,
With suche rewarde as fortune hath you sent.
All thynges in this boke that ye shall rede,
Doe as ye lyst, there shall no manne you bynde,
Them to beleue, as surely as your crede.
But notwithstandyng certes in my mynde,
I durst well swere, as true ye shall them fynde,
In euery poynt eche answere by and by,
As are the iudgementes of astronomye.

The Descripcion of RICHARD the thirde.

RICHARDE the third sonne, of whom we nowe entreate, was in witte and courage egall with either of them, in bodye and prowesse farre vnder them bothe, little of stature, ill fetured of limmes, croke backed, his left shoulder much higher than his right, hard fauoured of visage, and such as is in states called warlye, in other menne otherwise, he was malicious, wrathfull, enuious, and from afore his birth, euer frowarde. It is for trouth reported, that the duches his mother had so much a doe in her trauaile, that shee coulde not bee deliuered of hym vncutte: and that hee came into the worlde with the feete forwarde, as menne bee borne outwarde, and (as the fame runneth) also not vntothed, whither menne of hatred reporte aboue the trouthe, or elles that nature chaunged her course in hys beginninge, whiche in the course of his lyfe many thinges vnnaturallye committed. None euill captaine was hee in the warre, as to whiche his disposicion was more metely then for peace. Sundrye victories hadde hee, and sommetime ouerthrowes, but neuer in defaulte as for his owne parsone, either of hardinesse or polytike order, free was hee called of dyspence, and sommewhat aboue hys power liberall, with large giftes hee get him vnstedfaste frendeshippe, for whiche hee was fain to pil and spoyle in other places, and get him stedfast hatred. Hee was close and secrete, a deepe dissimuler, lowlye of counteynaunce, arrogant of heart, outwardly coumpinable where he inwardely hated, not letting to kisse whome hee thoughte to kyll: dispitious and cruell, not for euill will alway, but after for ambicion, and either for the suretie or encrease of his estate. Frende and foo was muche what indifferent, where his aduauntage grew, he spared no mans deathe, whose life withstoode his purpose. He slewe with his owne handes king Henry the sixt, being prisoner in the Tower, as menne constantly saye, and that without commaundement or knoweledge of the king, whiche woulde vndoubtedly yf he had entended that thinge, haue appointed that boocherly office, to some other then his owne borne brother.

Somme wise menne also weene, that his drift couertly conuayde, lacked not in helping furth his brother of Clarence to his death: whiche hee resisted openly, howbeit somwhat (as menne deme) more faintly then he that wer hartely minded to his welth. And they that thus deme, think that he long time in king Edwardes life, forethought to be king in that case the king his brother (whose life hee looked that euil dyete shoulde shorten) shoulde happen to decease (as in dede he did) while his children wer yonge. And thei deme, that for thys intente he was gladde of his brothers death the duke of Clarence, whose life must nedes haue hindered hym so entendynge, whither the same duke of Clarence hadde kepte him true to his nephew the yonge king, or enterprised to be kyng himselfe. But of al this pointe, is there no certaintie, and whoso diuineth vppon coniectures, maye as wel shote to farre as to short. How beit this haue I by credible informacion learned, that the selfe nighte in whiche kynge Edwarde died, one Mystlebrooke longe ere mornynge, came in greate haste to the house of one Pottyer dwellyng in Reddecrosse strete without Crepulgate: and when he was with hastye rappyng quickly letten in, hee shewed vnto Pottyer that kynge Edwarde was departed. By my trouthe manne quod Pottier then wyll my mayster the duke of Gloucester bee kynge. What cause hee hadde soo to thynke harde it is to saye, whyther hee being toward him, anye thynge knewe that hee suche thynge purposed, or otherwyse

wyse had anye inkelynge thereof: for hee was not likelye to speake it of noughte.

But nowe to returne to the course of this hystorye, were it that the duke of Gloucester hadde of old foreminded this conclusion, or was nowe at erste thereunto moued, and putte in hope by the occasion of the tender age of the younge princes, his nephues (as opportunitye and lykelyhoode of spede, putteth a manne in courage of that hee neuer entended) certayn is it that hee contriued theyr destruccion, with the vsurpacion of the regal dignitye vppon hymselfe. And for as muche as hee well wiste and holpe to mayntayn, a long continued grudge and hearte brennynge betwene the quenes kinred and the kinges blood eyther partye enuying others authoritye, he nowe thought that their deuision shoulde bee (as it was in dede) a fortherlye begynnynge to the pursuite of his intente, and a sure ground for the foundacion of al his building yf he might firste vnder the pretext of reuengynge of olde displeasure, abuse the anger and ygnoraunce of the tone partie, to the destruccion of the tother: and then wynne to his purpose as manye as he coulde: and those that coulde not be wonne, myght be loste ere they looked therefore. For of one thynge was hee certayne, that if his entente were perceiued, he shold soone haue made peace beetwene the bothe parties, with his owne bloude.

Kynge Edwarde in his life, albeit that this discencion beetwene hys frendes sommewhat yrked hym: yet in his good health he sommewhat the lesse regarded it, because hee thought whatsoeuer busines shoulde falle betwene them, hymselfe should alwaye bee hable to rule bothe the parties.

But in his last sicknesse, when hee receiued his naturall strengthe soo sore enfebled, that hee dyspayred all recouerye, then hee consyderynge the youthe of his chyldren, albeit hee nothynge lesse mistrusted then that that happened, yet well forseynge that manye harmes myghte growe by theyr debate, whyle the youth of hys children shoulde lacke discrecion of themself and good counsayle, of their frendes, of whiche either party shold counsayle for their owne commodity and rather by pleasaunte aduyse too wynne themselfe fauour, then by profitable aduertisemente to do the children good, he called some of them before him that were at variaunce, and in especyall the lorde marques Dorsette the quenes sonne by her fyrste housebande, and Richarde the lorde Hastynges, a noble man, than lorde chaumberlayne agayne whome the quene specially grudged, for the great fauoure the kyng bare hym, and also for that shee thoughte hym secretelye familyer with the kynge in wanton coumpanye. Her kynred also bare hym sore, as well for that the kynge hadde made hym captayne of Calyce (whiche office the lorde Ryuers, brother to the quene claimed of the kinges former promyse as for diuerse other great giftes whiche hee receyued, that they loked for. When these lordes with diuerse other of bothe the parties were comme in presence, the kynge liftinge vppe himselfe and vndersette with pillowes, as it is reported on this wyse sayd vnto them, My lordes, my dere kinsmenne and alies, in what plighte I lye you see, and I feele. By whiche the lesse whyle I looke to lyue with you, the more depelye am I moued to care in what case I leaue you, for such as I leaue you, suche bee my children lyke to fynde you. Whiche if they shoulde (that Godde forbydde) fynde you at varyaunce, myght happe to fall themselfe at warre ere their discrecion woulde serue to sette you at peace. Ye se their youthe, of whiche I recken the onely suretie to reste in youre concord, For it suffiseth not that al you loue them, yf eche of you hate other, If they wer menne, your faithfulnesse happelye woulde suffise. But childehood must be maintained by mens authoritye, and slipper youth vnderpropped with elder counsayle, which neither they can haue, but ye geue it, nor ye geue it, yf ye gree not. For wher eche laboureth to breake that the other maketh, and for hatred of ech of others parson, impugneth eche others counsayle, there must it nedes bee long ere anye good conclusion goe forwarde. And also while either partye laboureth to be chiefe, flattery shall haue more place then plaine and faithfull aduyse, of whyche muste needes ensue the euyll bringing vppe of the prynce, whose mynd in tender youth infect, shal redily fal to mischief and riot, and drawe down with this noble realme to ruine, but if grace turn him to wisdom: which if God send, then thei that by euill menes before pleased him best, shal after fall farthest out of fauour, so that euer at length euil driftes dreue to nought, and good plain wayes prosper. Great variaunce hath ther long bene betwene you, not alway for great causes. Sometime a thing right wel intended, our misconstruccion turneth vnto worse or a smal displeasure done vs, eyther our owne affeccion or euil tongues agreueth. But this wote I well ye neuer had so great cause of hatred, as ye haue of loue. That we be al men, that we be christen men, this shall I leaue for prechers to tel you (and yet I wote nere whither any preachers wordes ought more to moue you, then his that is by and by gooying to the place that thei all preache of.) But this shal I desire you to remember, that the one parte of you is of my bloode, the other of myne alies, and eche of yow with other, eyther of kinred or affinitie, whiche spirytuall kynred of affynyty, if the sacramentes of Christes churche, beare that weyghte with vs that woulde Godde thei did, shoulde no lesse moue vs to charitye, then the respecte of fleshlye consanguinitye. Oure Lorde forbydde, that you loue together the worse, for the selfe cause that you ought to loue the better. And yet that happeneth. And no where fynde wee so deadlye debate, as amonge them, whyche by nature and lawe moste oughte to agree together. Suche a pestilente serpente is ambicion and desyre of vaine glorye and soueraintye, whiche amonge states where he once entreth crepeth foorth so farre, tyll with deuision and variaunce hee turneth all to mischiefe. Firste longing to be nexte the best, afterwarde egall with the beste, and at laste chiefe and aboue the beste. Of which immoderate appetite of woorship, and thereby of debate and dissencion what losse, what sorowe, what trouble hathe within these fewe yeares growen in this realme, I praye Godde as well forgeate as wee well remember.

Whiche thinges yf I coulde as well haue foresene as I haue with my more payne then pleasure proued, by Goddes blessed Ladie (that was euer his othe) I woulde neuer haue won the courtesye of mennes knees, with the losse of soo many heades. But sithen thynges passed cannot be gaine called, muche oughte wee the more beware, by what occasion we haue taken soo greate hurte afore, that we eftesoones fall not in that occasion agayne. Nowe be those griefes passed, and all is (Godde be thanked) quiete, and likelie righte wel to prosper in wealthfull peace vnder youre coseyns my children, if Godde sende them life and you loue. Of whyche twoo thinges, the lesse losse wer they by whome thoughe Godde dydde hys pleasure, yet shoulde the realme alway finde kinges and paraduenture as good kinges. But yf you among youre selfe in a childes reygne fall at debate, many a good man shall perish and happely he to, and ye to, ere thys land finde peace again. Wherfore in these last wordes that euer I looke to speak with you: I exhort you and require you al, for the loue that you haue euer borne to me, for the loue that I haue euer born to you, for the loue that our Lord beareth to vs all, from this time forwarde, all grieues forgotten, eche of you loue other. Whiche I verelye truste you will, if ye any thing earthly regard, either Godde or your king, affinitie or kinred, this realme, your owne countrey, or your owne surety. And therewithal the king no longer enduring to sitte vp, laide him down on his right side, his face towarde them: and none was there present that coulde refrain from weping. But the lordes recomforting him with as good wordes as they could, and answering for the time as thei thought to stand with his pleasure, there in his presence (as by their wordes appered ech forgaue other, and ioyned their hands together, when (as it after appeared by their dedes) their hearts wer far a sonder. As sone as the king was departed, the noble prince his sonne drew toward London, which at the time of his decease, kept his houshold at Ludlow in Wales. Which countrey being far of from the law and recourse to iustice, was begon to be farre oute of good wyll and waxen wild, robbers and riuers walking at libertie vncorrected. And for this encheason the

the prince was in the life of his father sente thither, to the end that the authoritie of his presence, ſhould refraine euill diſpoſed parſons fro the boldnes of their formar outerages, to the gouernaunce and ordering of this yong princé at his ſending thyther, was there appointed Sir Antony Woduile lord Riuers and brother vnto the quene, a right honourable man, as valiaunte of hande as politike in counſayle. Adioyned wer there vnto him other of the ſame partie, and in effect euery one as he was nereſt of kin vnto the quene, ſo was planted next about the prince. That drifte by the quene not vnwiſely deuiſed, whereby her bloode mighte of youth be rooted in the princes fauor, the duke of Glouceſter turned vnto their deſtruccion, and vpon that grounde ſet the foundacion of all his vnhappy building. For whom ſoeuer he perceiued, either at variance with them, or bearing himſelf their fauor, hee brake vnto them, ſome by mouth, ſom by writing and ſecret meſſengers, that it neyther was reaſon nor in any wiſe to be ſuffered, that the yong king their maſter and kinſmanne, ſhoold bee in the handes and cuſtodye of his mothers kinred, ſequeſtred in maner from theyr compani and attendance, of which eueri one ought him as faithful ſeruice as they, and manye of them far more honorable part of kin then his mothers ſide: whoſe blood (quod he) ſauing the kinges pleaſure, was ful vnmetely to be matched with his: whiche nowe to be as who ſay remoued from the kyng, and the leſſe noble to be left aboute him, is (quod he) neither honorable to hys mageſtie, nor vnto vs, and alſo to his grace no ſurety to haue the mightieſt of his frendes from him, and vnto vs no little ieopardy, to ſuffer our welproued euil willers, to grow in ouergret authoritie with the prince in youth, namely which is lighte of beliefe and ſone perſwaded. Ye remember I trow king Edward himſelf, albeit he was a manne of age and of diſcrecion, yet was he in manye thynges ruled by the bende, more then ſtode either with his honour, or our profite, or with the commoditie of any manne els, except onely the immoderate aduauncement of them ſelfe. Whiche whither they ſorer thirſted after their owne weale, or our woe, it wer hard I wene to geſſe. And if ſome folkes frendſhip had not holden better place with the king, then any reſpect of kinred, thei might peraduenture eaſily haue be trapped and brought to confuſion ſomme of vs ere this. Why not as eaſily as they haue done ſome other alreadye, as neere of his royal bloode as we. But our Lord hath wrought his wil, and thanke be to his grace that peril is paſte. Howe be it as great is growing, yf wee ſuffer this yonge kyng in oure enemyes hande, whiche without his wyttyng, might abuſe the name of his commaundement, to ani of our vndoing, which thyng God and good prouiſion forbyd. Of which good prouiſion none of us hath any thing the leſſe nede, for the late made attonemente, in whiche the kinges pleaſure hadde more place then the parties willes. Nor none of vs I beleue is ſo vnwyſe, ouerſone to truſte a newe frende made of an olde foe, or to think that an houerly kindnes, ſodainely contract in one houre continued, yet ſcant a fortnight, ſhold be deper ſetled in their ſtomackes: then a long accuſtomed malice many yeres rooted.

With theſe wordes and writynges and ſuche other, the duke of Glouceſter ſone ſet a fyre, them that were of themſelf ethe to kindle, and in eſpeciall twayne, Edwarde duke of Buckingham, and Richarde lorde Haſtinges and chaumberlayn, both men of honour and of great power. The tone by longe ſucceſſion from his anceſtrie, the tother by his office and the kinges fauor. Theſe two not bearing eche to other ſo muche loue, as hatred bothe vnto the quenes parte: in this poynte accorded together wyth the duke of Glouceſter, that they wolde vtterlye amoue fro the kynges companye, all his mothers frendes, vnder the name of their enemyes. Vpon this concluded, the duke of Glouceſter vnderſtandyng, that the lordes whiche at that tyme were aboute the kyng, entended to bryng him vppe to his coronacion, accoumpanied with ſuche power of theyr frendes, that it ſhoulde bee harde for hym to brynge his purpoſe to paſſe, without the gathering and great aſſemble of people and in maner of open warre, whereof the ende he wiſte was doubtuous, and in which the kyng being on their ſide, his part ſhould haue the face and name of a rebellion: he ſecretly therefore by diuers meanes, cauſed the quene to be perſwaded and brought in the mynd, that it neither wer nede, and alſo ſhold be ieopardous, the king to come vp ſtrong. For where as nowe euery lorde loued other, and none other thing ſtudyed vppon, but aboute the coronacion and honoure of the king: if the lordes of her kinred ſhold aſſemble in the kinges name muche people, thei ſhould geue the lordes atwixte whome and them hadde bene ſommetyme debate, to feare and ſuſpecte, leſte they ſhoulde gather thys people, not for the kynges ſauegarde whome no manne enpugned, but for theyr deſtruccion, hauying more regarde to their olde variaunce, then their newe attonement. For whiche cauſe thei ſhoulde aſſemble on the other partie muche people agayne for their defence, whoſe power ſhe wyſte wel farre ſtretched. And thus ſhould all the realme fall on a rore. And of al the hurte that therof ſhould enſue, which was likely not to be litle, and the moſt harme there like to fal wher ſhe leſt would, all the worlde woulde put her and her kinred in the wyght, and ſay that thei had vnwyſelye and vntrewlye alſo, broken the amitie and peace that the kyng her huſband ſo prudentelye made, betwene hys kinne and hers in his death bed, and whiche the other party faithfully obſerued.

The quene being in this wiſe perſwaded, ſuche woorde ſente vnto her ſonne, and vnto her brother being aboute the kynge, and ouer that the duke of Glouceſter hymſelfe and other lordes the chiefe of hys bende, wrote vnto the kynge ſoo reuerentelye, and to the queenes frendes, there ſoo louyngelye, that they nothynge earthelye myſtruſtynge, broughte the kynge vppe in greate haſte, not in good ſpede, with a ſober coumpanye. Nowe was the king in his waye to London gone, from Northampton, when theſe dukes of Glouceſter and Buckyngham came thither. Where remained behynd, the lorde Ryuers the kynges vncle, entendyng on the morowe to folow the kynge, and bee with hym at Stonye Stratford miles thence, earely or hee departed. So was there made that nyghte muche frendely chere betwene theſe dukes and the lorde Riuers a greate while. But incontinente after that they were oppenlye with greate courteſye departed, and the lorde Riuers lodged, the dukes ſecretelye with a fewe of their moſte priuye frendes, ſette them downe in counſayle, wherin they ſpent a great parte of the nyght. And at their riſinge in the dawnyng of the day, thei ſent about priuily to their ſeruantes in their innes and lodgynges about, geuinge them commaundemente to make them ſelfe ſhortely readye, for their lordes wer to horſebackward. Vpon whiche meſſages, manye of their folke were attendaunt, when manye of the lorde Riuers ſeruantes were vnreadye. Nowe hadde theſe dukes taken alſo into their cuſtodye the kayes of the inne, that none ſhoulde paſſe foorth without theyr licence.

And ouer this in the hyghe waye towarde Stonye Stratforde where the kynge laye, they hadde beeſtowed certayne of theyr folke, that ſhoulde ſende backe agayne, and compell to retourne, anye manne that were gotten oute of Northampton toward Stonye Stratforde, tyll they ſhould geue other lycence. For as muche as the dukes themſelfe entended for the ſhewe of theire dylygence, to bee the fyrſte that ſhoulde that daye attende vppon the kynges highneſſe oute of that towne: thus bare they folke in hande. But when the lorde Ryuers vnderſtode the gates cloſed, and the wayes on euerye ſide beſette, neyther hys ſeruauntes nor hymſelf ſuffered to go oute, parceiuyng well ſo greate a thyng without his knowledge not begun for noughte, comparyng this maner preſent with this laſt nightes chere, in ſo few houres ſo gret a chaunge marueylouſlye miſliked. How be it ſithe hee coulde not geat awaye, and keepe himſelfe cloſe, hee woulde not, leſte he ſhoulde ſeeme to hyde himſelfe for ſome ſecret feare of hys owne faulte, whereof he ſaw no ſuch cauſe in hym ſelf: he determined vppon the ſuretie of his own conſcience, to goe boldelye to them, and inquire what thys matter myghte meane. Whome as ſoone as they ſawe, they beganne to quarrell with hym, and ſaye, that hee intended to ſette diſtaunce

beetweene

beetweene the kynge and them, and to brynge them to confusion, but it shoulde not lye in hys power. And when hee beganne (as hee was a very well spoken manne) in goodly wise to excuse himself, they taryed not the ende of his aunswere, but shortely tooke him and putte him in warde, and that done, foorthwyth wente to horsebacke, and tooke the waye to Stonye Stratforde. Where they founde the kinge with his companie readye to leape on horsebacke, and departe forwarde, to leaue that lodging for them, because it was to streighte for bothe coumpanies. And as sone as they came in his presence, they lighte adowne with all their companie aboute them. To whome the duke of Buckingham saide, goe afore gentlemenne and yeomen, kepe youre rowmes. And thus in goodly arraye, thei came to the kinge, and on theire knees in very humble wise, salued his grace; whiche receyued them in very ioyous and amiable maner, nothinge earthlye knowing nor mistrustinge as yet. But euen by and by in his presence, they piked a quarell to the lorde Richard Graye, the kynges other brother by his mother, sayinge that hee with the lorde marques his brother and the lorde Riuers his vncle, hadde coumpassed to rule the kinge and the realme, and to sette variaunce among the states, and to subdewe and destroye the noble blood of the realm. Toward the accoumplishinge whereof, they sayde that the lorde Marques hadde entered into the Tower of London, and thence taken out the kinges treasor, and sent menne to the sea. All whiche thinge these dukes wiste well were done for good purposes and necessari by the whole counsaile at London, sauing that sommewhat thei must sai. Vnto whiche woordes, the king aunswered, what my brother Marques hath done I cannot saie. But in good faith I dare well aunswere for myne vncle Riuers and my brother here, that thei be innocent of any such matters. Ye my liege quod the duke of Buckingham thei haue kepte theire dealing in these matters farre fro the knowledge of your good grace. And foorthwith thei arrested the lord Richarde and Sir Thomas Waughan knighte, in the kinges presence, and broughte the king and all backe vnto Northampton, where they tooke againe further counsaile. And there they sent awaie from the kinge whom it pleased them, and sette newe seruantes aboute him, suche as lyked better them than him. At whiche dealinge hee wepte and was nothing contente, but it booted not. And at dyner the duke of Gloucester sente a dishe from his owne table to the lord Riuers, prayinge him to bee of good chere, all should be well inough. And he thanked the duke, and prayed the messenger to beare it to his nephewe the lorde Richard with the same message for his comfort, who he thought had more nede of coumfort, as one to whom such aduersitie was straunge. But himself had been al his dayes in vre therewith, and therfore coulde beare it the better. But for al this coumfortable courtesye of the duke of Gloucester he sent the lord Riuers and the lorde Richarde with Sir Thomas Vaughan into the Northe countrey into diuers places to prison, and afterward al to Pomfrait, where they were in conclusion beheaded.

A letter written with a cole by Sir THOMAS MORE to hys doughter maistres MARGARET ROPER, within a whyle after he was prisoner in the Towre.

MYNE own good doughter, our lorde be thanked I am in good helthe of bodye, and in good quiet of minde: and of worldly thynges I no more desyer then I haue. I beseche hym make you all mery in the hope of heauen. And such thynges as I somewhat longed to talke with you all, concerning the worlde to come, our Lorde put theim into your myndes, as I truste he dothe and better to by hys holy spirite: who blesse you and preserue you all. Written wyth a cole by your tender louing father, who in hys pore prayers forgetteth none of you all nor your babes, nor your nurses, nor your good husbandes, nor your good husbandes shrewde wyues, nor your fathers shrewde wyfe neither, nor our other frendes. And thus fare ye hartely well for lacke of paper.

THOMAS MORE, knight.

Two short ballettes which Sir THOMAS MORE made for hys pastime while he was prisoner in the Tower of London.

LEWYS the lost louer.

EY flatering fortune, loke thou neuer so fayre,
Or neuer so plesantly begin to smile,
As though thou wouldst my ruine all repayre,
During my life thou shalt me not begile.
Trust shall I God, to entre in a while.
Hys hauen or heauen sure and vniforme.
Euer after thy calme, loke I for a storme.

DAUY the dycer.

LONG was I lady Lucke your seruing man,
And now haue lost agayne all that I gat,
Wherfore whan I thinke on you nowe and than,
And in my mynde remember this and that,
Ye may not blame me though I beshrew your cat,
But in fayth I blesse you agayne a thousand times,
For lending me now some laysure to make rymes.

At the same time with Sir *Thomas More* lived *Skelton*, the poet laureate of *Henry* VIII. from whose works it seems proper to insert a few stanzas, though he cannot be said to have attained great elegance of language.

The prologue to the Bouge of Courte.

IN Autumpne whan the sonne in vyrgyne
By radyante hete enryped hath our corne
Whan Luna full of mutabylyte
As Emperes the dyademe hath worne
Of our pole artyke, smylynge halfe in scorne
At our foly, and our vnstedfastnesse
The time whan Mars to warre hym dyd dres,
I callynge to mynde the greate auctoryte
Of poetes olde, whiche full craftely
Vnder as couerte termes as coulde be
Can touche a trouth, and cloke subtylly
With freshe vtteraunce full sentencyously
Dyuerse in style some spared not vyce to wryte
Some of mortalitie nobly dyd endyte
Whereby I rede, theyr renome and theyr fame
Maye neuer dye, but euermore endure
I was sore moued to a forse the same
But ignoraunce full soone dyde me dyscure
And shewed that in this arte I was not sure
For to illumine she sayd I was to dulle
Aduysynge me my penne awaye to pulle
And not to wryte, for he so wyll atteyne
Excedyng ferther than his connynge is
His heed maye be harde, but feble is brayne
Yet haue I knowen suche er this
But of reproche surely he maye not mys
That clymmeth hyer than he may fotinge haue
What and he slyde downe, who shall him saue?
Thus vp and downe my mynde was drawen and cast
That I ne wyste what to do was beste
So sore enwered that I was at the laste
Enforsed to slepe, and for to take some reste
And to lye downe as soone as I my dreste
At Harwyche porte slumbrynge as I laye
In myne hostes house called powers keye

Of the wits that flourished in the reign of *Henry* VIII. none has been more frequently celebrated than the earl of *Surry*; and this history would therefore have been imperfect without some specimens of his works, which yet it is not easy to distinguish from those of Sir *Thomas Wyat* and others, with which they are confounded in the edition that has fallen into my hands. The three first are, I believe, *Surry*'s; the rest, being of the same age, are selected, some as examples of different measures, and one as the oldest composition which I have found in blank verse.

Description of Spring, wherein eche thing renewes, save only the lover.

THE soote season that bud, and bloome fourth bringes,
With grene hath cladde the hyll, and eke the vale,
The Nightingall with fethers new she singes;
The turtle to her mate hath told her tale:

Somer

Somer is come, for every ſpray now ſpringes.
The hart hath hunge hys olde head on the pale,
The bucke in brake his winter coate he flynges;
The fiſhes flete with newe repayred ſcale:
The adder all her ſlough away ſhe flynges,
The ſwift ſwallow purſueth the flyes ſmalle,
The buſy bee her honey how ſhe mynges;
Winter is worne that was the floures bale.
And thus I ſee among theſe pleaſant thynges
Eche care decayes, and yet my ſorrow ſprynges.

Deſcripcion of the reſtleſs eſtate of a lover.

WHen youth had led me half the race,
That Cupides ſcourge had made me runne;
I looked back to meet the place,
From whence my weary courſe begunne:
And then I ſaw howe my deſyre
Miſguiding me had led the waye,
Myne eyne to greedy of theyre hyre,
Had made me loſe a better prey.
For when in ſighes I ſpent the day,
And could not cloake my grief with game;
The boyling ſmoke dyd ſtill bewray,
The preſent heat of ſecret flame:
And when ſalt teares do bayne my breaſt,
Where love his pleaſent traynes hath ſown,
Her beauty hath the fruytes oppreſt,
Ere that the buddes were ſpronge and blowne.
And when myne eyen dyd ſtill purſue,
The flying chaſe of theyre requeſt;
Theyre greedy looks dyd oft renew,
The hydden wounde within my breſte.
When every loke theſe cheekes might ſtayne,
From dedly pale to glowing red;
By outward ſignes appeared playne,
To her for helpe my hart was fled.
But all to late Love learneth me,
To paynt all kynd of Colours new;
To blynd theyre eyes that elſe ſhould ſee
My ſpeckled chekes with Cupids hew.
And now the covert breſt I clame,
That worſhipt Cupide ſecretely;
And nouriſhed hys ſacred flame,
From whence no blairing ſparks do flye.

Deſcripcion of the fickle Affections, Pangs, and Sleightes of Love.

SUCH wayward wayes hath Love, that moſt part in diſcord
Our willes do ſtand, whereby our hartes but ſeldom do accord:
Decyte is hys delighte, and to begyle and mocke
The ſimple hartes which he doth ſtrike with froward divers ſtroke.
He cauſeth th' one to rage with golden burning darte,
And doth alay with Leaden cold, again the others harte.
Whoſe gleames of burning fyre and eaſy ſparkes of flame,
In balance of unequal weyght he pondereth by ame
From eaſye ford where I myghte wade and paſs full well,
He me withdrawes and doth me drive, into a depe dark hell:
And me witholdes where I am calde and offred place,
And willes me that my mortal foe I do beſeke of Grace;
He lettes me to purſue a conqueſt welnere wonne
To follow where my paynes were loſt, ere that my ſute begunne.
So by this means I know how ſoon a hart may turne
From warre to peace, from truce to ſtryſe, and ſo agayne returne.
I know how to content my ſelf in others luſt,
Of little ſtuffe unto my ſelf to weave a webbe of truſt:
And how to hyde my harmes with ſole dyſſembling chere,
Whan in my face the painted thoughtes would outwardly appeare.
I know how that the bloud forſakes the face for dred,
And how by ſhame it ſtaynes agayne the Chekes with flamyng red:
I know under the Grene, the Serpent how he lurkes:
The hammer of the reſtleſs forge I wote eke how it workes.
I know and con by roate the tale that I woulde tell
But ofte the woordes come fourth awrye of him that loveth well.
I know in heate and colde the Lover how he ſhakes,
In ſynging how he doth complayne, in ſleeping how he wakes
To languiſh without ache, ſickeleſſe for to conſume,
A thouſand thynges for to devyſe, reſolvynge of his fume;
And though he lyſte to ſee his Ladyes Grace full ſore
Such pleaſures as delyght hys Eye, do not his helthe reſtore.
I know to ſeke the tracte of my deſyred foe,
And fere to fynde that I do ſeek, but chiefly this I know,
That Lovers muſt transfourme into the thynge beloved,
And live (alas! who would believe?) with ſprite from Lyfe removed.
I knowe in harty ſighes and laughters of the ſpleene,
At once to chaunge my ſtate, my will, and eke my colour clene.
I know how to deceyve my ſelf wythe others helpe,
And how the Lyon chaſtiſed is, by beatynge of the whelpe.
In ſtandynge nere the fyre, I know how that I freaſe;
Farre of I burne, in bothe I waſte, and ſo my Lyfe I leeſe.
I know how Love doth rage upon a yeylding mynde,
How ſmalle a nete may take and maſe a harte of gentle kynde:
Or elſe with ſeldom ſwete to ſeaſon hepes of gall,
Revived with a glympſe of Grace old ſorrowes to let fall.
The hydden traynes I know, and ſecret ſnares of Love,
How ſoone a loke will prynte a thoughte that never may remove.
The ſlypper ſtate I know, the ſodein turnes from welthe
The doubtfull hope, the certaine wooe, and ſure deſpaired helthe.

A praiſe of his ladie.

GEVE place you ladies and be gone,
Boaſt not your ſelves at all,
For here at hande approcheth one,
Whoſe face will ſtayne you all.
The vertue of her lively lookes
Excels the precious ſtone,
I wiſhe to have none other bookes
To reade or look upon.
In eche of her two chriſtall eyes,
Smyleth a naked boy;
It would you all in heart ſuffiſe
To ſee that lampe of joye.
I think nature hath loſt the moulde,
Where ſhe her ſhape did take;
Or elſe I doubte if nature coulde
So fayre a creature make.
She may be well comparde
Unto the Phenix kinde,
Whoſe like was never ſeene nor heard,
That any man can fynde.
In lyfe ſhe is Diana chaſt
In trouth Penelopey,
In woord and eke in dede ſtedfaſt;
What will you more we ſay:
If all the world were ſought ſo farre,
Who could finde ſuche a wight,
Her beauty twinkleth lyke a ſtarre
Within the froſty night.

The Lover refuſed of his love, embraceth vertue.

MY youthfull yeres are paſt,
My joyfull dayes are gone,
My lyfe it may not laſt,
My grave and I am one.
My Myrth and joyes are fled,
And I a Man in wo,
Deſirous to be ded,
My miſciefe to forgo.

I burne

I burne and am a colde,
I freeſe amyddes the fyer,
I ſee ſhe doth witholde
That is my honeſt deſyre.
I ſee my helpe at hande,
I ſee my lyfe alſo,
I ſee where ſhe doth ſtande
That is my deadly fo.
I ſee how ſhe doth ſee,
And yet ſhe wil be blynde,
I ſee in helpyng me,
She ſekes and will not fynde.
I ſee how ſhe doth wrye,
When I begynne to mone,
I ſee when I come nye,
How fayne ſhe would be gone;
I ſee what wil ye more,
She will me gladly kill,
And you ſhall ſee therfore
That ſhe ſhall have her will.
I cannot live with ſtones,
It is too hard a foode,
I wil be dead at ones
To do my Lady good.

The Death of ZOROAS, an Egiptian aſtronomer, in the firſt fight that Alexander had with the Perſians.

NOW clattring armes, now raging broyls of warre,
Gan paſſe the noys of dredfull trumpetts clang,
Shrowded with ſhafts, the heaven with cloude of dartes,
Covered the ayre. Againſt full fatted bulles.
As forceth kyndled yre the lyons keene,
Whoſe greedy gutts the gnawing hunger prickes;
So Macedons againſt the Perſians fare,
Now corpſes hyde the purpurde ſoyle with blood;
Large ſlaughter on eche ſide, but Perſes more,
Moyſt fieldes bebled, theyr heartes and numbers bate,
Fainted while they gave backe, and fall to flighte.
The litening Macedon by ſwordes, by gleaves,
By bandes and troupes of footemen, with his garde,
Speedes to Dary, but hym his mereſt kyn,
Oxate preſerves with horſemen on a plumpe
Before his carr, that none his charge ſhould give.
Here grunts, here groans, eche where ſtrong youth is ſpent:
Shaking her bloudy hands, Bellone among
The Perſes ſoweth all kind of cruel death:
With throte yent he roares, he lyeth along
His entrailes with a launce through gryded quyte,
Hym ſmytes the club, hym woundes farre ſtryking bowe,
And him the ſling, and him the ſhining ſword;
He dyeth, he is all dead, he pantes, he reſtes.
Right over ſtoode in ſnowwhite armour brave,
The Memphite Zoroas, a cunnyng clarke,
To whom the heaven lay open as his booke;
And in celeſtiall bodies he could tell
The moving meeting light, aſpect, eclips,
And influence, and conſtellations all;
What earthly chaunces would betyde, what yere,
Of plenty ſtorde, what ſigne forewarned death,
How winter gendreth ſnow, what temperature
In the prime tyde doth ſeaſon well the ſoyle,
Why ſummer burnes, why autumne hath ripe grapes,
Whither the circle quadrate may become,
Whether our tunes heavens harmony can yelde
Of four begyns among themſelves how great
Proportion is; what ſway the erryng lightes
Doth ſend in courſe gayne that fyrſt movyng heaven;
What, grees one from another diſtant be,
What ſtarr doth lett the hurtfull fyre to rage,
Or him more mylde what oppoſition makes,
What fyre doth qualifye Mavorſes fyre,
What houſe eche one doth ſeeke, what plannett raignes
Within this heaven ſphere, nor that ſmall thynges
I ſpeake, whole heaven he cloſeth in his breſt.
This ſage then in the ſtarres hath ſpyed the fates
Threatned him death without delay, and, ſith,
He ſaw he could not fatall order chaunge,
Foreward he preſt in battayle, that he might
Mete with the rulers of the Macedons,
Of his right hand deſirous to be ſlain,
The bouldeſt borne, and worthieſt in the feilde;
And as a wight, now wery of his lyfe,
And ſeking death, in fyrſt front of his rage,
Comes deſperately to Alexanders face,
At him with dartes one after other throwes,
With reckleſſe wordes and clamour him provokes,
And ſayth, Nectanaks baſtard ſhamefull ſtayne
Of mothers bed, why loſeſt thou thy ſtrokes,
Cowardes among, Turn thee to me, in caſe
Manhood there be ſo much left in thy heart,
Come fight with me, that on my helmet weare
Apollo's laurell both for learninges laude,
And eke for martiall praiſe, that in my ſhielde
The ſeven fold Sophie of Minerve contein,
A match more mete, Syr King, then any here.
The noble prince amoved takes ruth upon
The wilfull wight, and with ſoft words ayen,
O monſtrous man (quoth he) what ſo thou art,
I pray thee live, ne do not with thy death
This lodge of Lore, the Muſes manſion marre;
That treaſure houſe this hand ſhall never ſpoyle,
My ſword ſhall never bruiſe that ſkilfull brayne,
Long gather'd heapes of ſcience ſone to ſpill;
O how fayre fruites may you to mortall men
From Wiſdoms garden give; how many may
By you the wiſer and the better prove:
What error, what mad moode, what frenzy thee
Perſwades to be downe, ſent to depe Averne,
Where no artes flouriſh, nor no knowledge vailes
For all theſe ſawes. When thus the ſovereign ſaid,
Alighted Zoroas with ſword unſheathed,
The careleſs king there ſmoate above the greve,
At th' opening of his quiſhes wounded him,
So that the blood down trailed on the ground:
The Macedon perceiving hurt, gan gnaſhe,
But yet his mynde he bent in any wiſe
Hym to forbeare, ſett ſpurrs unto his ſtede,
And turnde away, leſt anger of his ſmarte
Should cauſe revenger hand deale balefull blowes;
But of the Macedonian chieftaines knights,
One Meleager could not bear this ſight,
But ran upon the ſaid Egyptian rude,
And cutt him in both knees: he fell to ground,
Wherewith a whole rout came of ſouldiours ſterne,
And all in pieces hewed the ſely ſeg,
But happely the ſoule fled to the ſtarres,
Where, under him, he hath full ſight of all,
Whereat he gazed here with reaching looke.
The Perſians waild ſuch ſapience to forgoe,
The very fone the Macedonians wiſht
He would have lived, king Alexander ſelfe
Demde him a man unmete to dye at all;
Who wonne like praiſe for conqueſt of his Yre,
As for ſtoute men in field that day ſubdued,
Who princes taught how to diſcerne a man,
That in his head ſo rare a jewel beares,
But over all thoſe ſame Camenes, thoſe ſame,
Divine Camenes, whoſe honour he procurde,
As tender parent doth his daughters weale,
Lamented, and for thankes, all that they can,
Do cheriſh hym deceaſt, and ſett him free,
From dark oblivion of devouring death.

Barclay wrote about 1550; his chief work is the *Ship of Fooles*, of which the following extract will ſhew his ſtyle.

Of Mockers and Scorners, and falſe Accuſers.

O Heartleſs fooles, haſte here to our doctrine,
Leaue off the wayes of your enormitie,
Enforce you to my preceptes to encline,
For here ſhall I ſhewe you good and veritie:
Encline, and ye finde ſhall great proſperitie,
Enſuing the doctrine of our fathers olde,
And godly lawes in valour worth great golde.
Who that will followe the graces manyfolde
Which are in vertue, ſhall finde auauncement:
Wherfore ye fooles that in your ſinne are bolde,
Enſue ye wiſdome, and leaue your lewde intent,
Wiſdome is the way of men moſt excellent:
Therfore haue done, and ſhortly ſpede your pace,
To quaynt your ſelf and company with grace.

Learne

Learne what is vertue, therin is great solace,
Learne what is truth, sadnes and prudence,
Let grutche be gone, and grauitie purchase,
Forsake your folly and inconuenience,
Cease to be fooles, and ay to sue offence,
Followe ye vertue, chiefe roote of godlynes,
For it and wisedome is ground of clenlynes.
Wisedome and vertue two thinges are doubtles,
Whiche man endueth with honour speciall,
But suche heartes as slepe in foolishnes
Knoweth nothing, and will nought know at all:
But in this little barge in principall
All foolish mockers I purpose to repreue,
Clawe he his backe that feeleth itche or greue.
Mockers and scorners that are harde of beleue,
With a rough combe here will I clawe and grate,
To proue if they will from their vice remeue,
And leaue their folly, which causeth great debate:
Suche caytiues spare neyther poore man nor estate,
And where their selfe are moste worthy derision,
Other men to scorne is all their most condition.
Yet are mo fooles of this abusion,
Whiche of wise men despiseth the doctrine,
With mowes, mockes, scorne, and collusion,
Rewarding rebukes for their good discipline:
Shewe to suche wisdome, yet shall they not encline
Unto the same, but set nothing therby,
But mocke thy doctrine, still or openly.
So in the worlde it appeareth commonly,
That who that will a foole rebuke or blame,
A mocke or mowe shall he haue by and by:
Thus in derision haue fooles their speciall game.
Correct a wise man that woulde eschue ill name,
And fayne would learne, and his lewde life amende,
And to thy wordes he gladly shall intende.
If by misfortune a rightwise man offende,
He gladly suffereth a iuste correction,
And him that him teacheth taketh for his frende,
Him selfe putting mekely unto subiection,
Folowing his preceptes and good direction:
But yf that one a foole rebuke or blame,
He shall his teacher hate, slaunder and diffame.
Howbeit his wordes oft turne to his own shame,
And his owne dartes retourne to him agayne,
And so is he sore wounded with the same,
And in wo endeth, great misery and payne.
It also proued full often is certayne,
That they that on mockers alway their mindes cast,
Shall of all other be mocked at the last.
He that goeth right, stedfast, sure, and fast,
May him well mocke that goeth halting and lame,
And he that is white may well his scornes cast,
Agaynst a man of Inde: but no man ought to blame
Anothers vice, while he vseth the same.
But who that of sinne is cleane in deede and thought,
May him well scorne whose liuing is starke nought.
The scornes of Naball full dere should haue been bought,
If Abigayl his wife discrete and sage,
Had not by kindnes right crafty meanes sought,
The wrath of Dauid to temper and asswage.
Hath not two beares in their fury and rage
Two and fortie children rent and torne,
For they the prophete Helyseus did scorne.
So might they curse the time that they were borne,
For their mocking of this prophete diuine:
So many other of this sort often mourne
For their lewde mockes, and fall into ruine.
Thus is it foly for wise men to encline,
To this lewde flocke of fooles, for see thou shall
Them moste scorning that are most bad of all.

The Lenuoy of Barclay to the fooles.

Ye mocking fooles that in scorne set your ioy,
Proudly despising Gods punition:
Take ye example by Cham the sonne of Noy,
Which laughed his father vnto derision,
Which him after cursed for his transgression,
And made him seruaunt to all his lyne and stocke.
So shall ye caytifs at the conclusion,
Since ye are nought, and other scorne and mocke.

About the year 1553 wrote Dr. *Wilson*, a man celebrated for the politeness of his style, and the extent of his knowledge: what was the state of our language in his time, the following may be of use to show.

PRonunciation is an apte orderinge bothe of the voyce, countenaunce, and all the whole bodye, accordynge to the worthines of suche woordes and mater as by speache are declared. The vse hereof is suche for anye one that liketh to haue prayse for tellynge his tale in open assemblie, that hauing a good tongue, and a comelye countenaunce, he shalbe thought to passe all other that haue the like vtteraunce: thoughe they haue much better learning. The tongue geueth a certayne grace to euerye matter, and beautifieth the cause in like maner, as a swete soundynge lute muche setteth forthe a meane deuised ballade. Or as the sounde of a good instrumente styrreth the hearers, and moueth muche delite, so a cleare soundyng voice comforteth muche our deintie eares, with muche swete melodie, and causeth vs to allowe the matter rather for the reporters sake, then the reporter for the matters sake. Demosthenes therfore, that famouse oratour, beyng asked what was the chiefest point in al oratorie, gaue the chiefe and onely praise to Pronunciation; being demaunded, what was the seconde, and the thirde, he stil made answere. Pronunciation, and would make none other aunswere, till they lefte askyng, declaryng hereby that arte without vtteraunce can dooe nothyng, vtteraunce without arte can dooe right muche. And no doubte that man is in outwarde apparaunce halfe a good clarke, that hath a cleane tongue, and a comely gesture of his body. Æschines lykwyse beyng bannished his countrie through Demosthenes, when he had redde to the Rhodians his own oration, and Demosthenes aunswere thereunto, by force whereof he was bannished, and all they marueiled muche at the excellencie of the same: then (q d Æschines) you would have marueiled muche more if you had heard hymselfe speak it. Thus beyng cast in miserie and bannished for euer, he could not but geue such great reporte of his deadly and mortal ennemy.

Thus have I deduced the *English* language from the age of *Alfred* to that of *Elizabeth*; in some parts imperfectly for want of materials; but I hope, at least, in such a manner that its progress may be easily traced, and the gradations observed, by which it advanced from its first rudeness to its present elegance.

A GRAMMAR OF THE ENGLISH TONGUE.

GRAMMAR, which is *the art of uſing words properly*, compriſes four parts; Orthography, Etymology, Syntax, and Proſody.

In this diviſion and order of the parts of grammar I follow the common grammarians, without enquiring whether a fitter diſtribution might not be found. Experience has long ſhown this method to be ſo diſtinct as to obviate confuſion, and ſo comprehenſive as to prevent any inconvenient omiſſions. I likewiſe uſe the terms already received, and already underſtood, though perhaps others more proper might ſometimes be invented. Sylburgius, and other innovators, whoſe new terms have ſunk their learning into neglect, have left ſufficient warning againſt the trifling ambition of teaching arts in a new language.

ORTHOGRAPHY is *the art of combining letters into ſyllables, and ſyllables into words.* It therefore teaches previouſly the form and ſound of letters.

The letters of the Engliſh language are,

Roman.	Italick.	Old Engliſh.	Name.
A a	*A a*	𝔄 𝔞	*a*
B b	*B b*	𝔅 𝔟	*be*
C c	*C c*	ℭ 𝔠	*ſee*
D d	*D d*	𝔇 𝔡	*dee*
E e	*E e*	𝔈 𝔢	*e*
F f	*F f*	𝔉 𝔣	*eff*
G g	*G g*	𝔊 𝔤	*jee*
H h	*H h*	ℌ 𝔥	*aitch*
I i	*I i*	𝔦	*i* (or *ja*
J j	*J j*	𝔍 𝔧	*j* conſonant,
K k	*K k*	𝔎 𝔨	*ka*
L l	*L l*	𝔏 𝔩	*el*
M m	*M m*	𝔐 𝔪	*em*
N n	*N n*	𝔑 𝔫	*en*
O o	*O o*	𝔒 𝔬	*o*
P p	*P p*	𝔓 𝔭	*pee*
Q q	*Q q*	𝔔 𝔮	*cue*
R r	*R r*	ℜ 𝔯	*ar*
S ſ s	*S ſ s*	𝔖 ſ 𝔰	*eſs*
T t	*T t*	𝔗 𝔱	*tee*
U u	*U u*	𝔲	*u* (or *va*
V v	*V v*	𝔙 𝔳	*v* conſonant,
W w	*W w*	𝔚 𝔴	double *u*
X x	*X x*	𝔛 𝔵	*ex*
Y y	*Y y*	𝔜 𝔶	*wy*
Z z	*Z z*	ℨ 𝔷	*zed*, more commonly *izzard* or *uzzard*, that is, *ſ hard.*

To theſe may be added certain combinations of letters univerſally uſed in printing; as ct, ſt, ſl, fl, ſb, ſk, ff, ſſ, ſi, ſſi, fi, ffi, ffl, and &, or *and per ſe, and.* *ct, ſt, ſl, fl, ſb, ſk, ff, ſſ, ſi, ſſi, fi, ffi, ffl, &.* ct, ſt, ſl, fl, ff, ſſ, ſi, ſſi, fi, ffi, &.

Our letters are commonly reckoned twenty-four, becauſe anciently *i* and *j*, as well as *u* and *v*, were expreſſed by the ſame character; but as thoſe letters, which had always different powers, have now different forms, our alphabet may be properly ſaid to conſiſt of twenty-ſix letters.

None of the ſmall conſonants have a double form, except *ſ*, *s*; of which *ſ* is uſed in the beginning and middle, and *s* at the end.

Vowels are five, a, e, i, o, u.

Such is the number generally received; but for *i* it is the practice to write *y* in the end of words, as *thy*, *holy*; before *i*, as from *die*, *dying*; from *beautify*, *beautifying*; in the words *ſays*, *days*, *eyes*; and in words derived from the Greek, and written originally with υ, as *ſyſtem*, σύςημα, *ſympathy*, συμπάθεια.

For *u* we often write *w* after a vowel, to make a diphthong; as *raw*, *grew*, *view*, *vow*, *flowing*, *lowneſs*.

The ſounds of all the letters are various.

In treating on the letters, I ſhall not, like ſome other grammarians, enquire into the original of their form as an antiquarian; nor into their formation and prolation by the organs of ſpeech, as a mechanick, anatomiſt, or phyſiologiſt; nor into the properties and gradation of ſounds, or the elegance or harſhneſs of particular combinations, as a writer of univerſal and tranſcendental grammar. I conſider the Engliſh alphabet only as it is Engliſh; and even in this narrow view I follow the example of former grammarians, perhaps with more reverence than judgment, becauſe by writing in Engliſh I ſuppoſe my reader already acquainted with the Engliſh language; and becauſe of ſounds in general it may be obſerved, that words are unable to deſcribe them. An account therefore of the primitive and ſimple letters is uſeleſs almoſt alike to thoſe who know their ſound, and thoſe who know it not.

Of VOWELS.

A.

A has three ſounds, the ſlender, open, and broad.

A ſlender is found in moſt words, as *face*, *mane*; and in words ending in *ation*, as *creation*, *ſalvation*, *generation*.

The *a* ſlender is the proper Engliſh *a*, called very juſtly by Erpenius, in his Arabick Grammar, *a Anglicum cum e miſtum*, as having a middle ſound between the open *a* and the *e*. The French have a ſimilar ſound in the word *pais*, and in their *e* maſculine.

A open is the *a* of the Italian, or nearly reſembles it; as *father*, *rather*, *congratulate*, *fancy*, *glaſs*.

A broad reſembles the *a* of the German; as *all*, *wall*, *call*.

Many words pronounced with *a* broad were anciently written with *au*, as *fault*, *mault*; and we ſtill ſay *fault*, *vault*. This was probably the Saxon ſound, for it is yet retained in the northern dialects, and in the ruſtick pronunciation; as *maun* for *man*, *haund* for *hand*.

The ſhort *a* approaches to the *a* open, as *graſs*.

The long *a*, if prolonged by *e* at the end of the word, is always ſlender, as *graze*, *fame*.

A forms a diphthong only with *i* or *y*, and *u* or *w*. *Ai* or *ay*, as in *plain*, *wain*, *gay*, *clay*, has only the ſound of the long and ſlender *a*, and differs not in the pronunciation from *plane*, *wane*.

Au or *aw* has the ſound of the German *a*, as *raw*, *naughty*.

Ae is ſometimes found in Latin words not compleatly naturaliſed or aſſimilated, but is no Engliſh diphthong; and is more properly expreſſed by ſingle *e*, as *Ceſar*, *Eneas*.

E.

E is the letter which occurs moſt frequently in the Engliſh language.

E is long, as in *ſcēne*; or ſhort, as in *cĕllar*, *ſĕparate*, *cĕlebrate*, *mĕn*, *thĕn*.

It is always ſhort before a double conſonant, or two conſonants, *relĕnt*, *mĕdlar*, *rĕptile*, *ſĕrpĕnt*, *cĕllar*, *cĕſſation*, *blĕſſing*, *fĕll*, *fĕlling*, *dĕbt*.

E is always mute at the end of a word, except in monoſyllables that have no other vowel, as *the*; or proper names, as *Penelope*, *Phebe*, *Derbe*; being uſed to modify the foregoing conſonant, as *ſince*, *once*, *hedge*, *oblige*; or to lengthen the preceding vowel, as *băn*, *bāne*; *căn*, *cāne*; *pĭn*, *pīne*; *tŭn*, *tūne*; *rŏb*, *rōbe*; *pŏp*, *pōpe*; *fĭr*, *fīre*; *cŭr*, *cūre*; *tŭb*, *tūbe*.

Almoſt all words which now terminate in conſonants ended anciently in *e*, as *year*, *yeare*; *wildneſs*, *wildneſſe*; which *e* probably had the force of the French *e* feminine, and conſtituted a ſyllable with its aſſociate conſonant; for, in old editions, words are ſometimes divided thus, *clea-re*, *fel-le*, *knowled-ge*. This *e* was perhaps for a time vocal or ſilent in poetry as convenience required; but it has been long wholly mute. Camden calls it the ſilent *e*.

It does not always lengthen the foregoing vowel, as *glŏve*, *lĭve*, *gĭve*.

It has ſometimes in the end of words a ſound obſcure, and ſcarcely perceptible, as *open*, *ſhapen*, *ſhotten*, *thiſtle*, *participle*, *metre*, *lucre*.

E forms a diphthong with *a*, as *near*; with *i*, as *deign*, *receive*; and with *u* or *w*, as *new*, *flew*.

Ea ſounds like *e* long, as *mean*; or like *ee*, as *dear*, *clear*, *near*.

Ei is ſounded like *e* long, as *ſeize*, *perceiving*.

Eu ſounds as *u* long and ſoft.

E, *a*, *u* are combined in *beauty* and its derivatives, but have only the ſound of *u*.

E may be ſaid to form a diphthong by reduplication, as *agree*, *ſleeping*.

Eo is found in *yeomen*, where it is ſounded as *e* ſhort; and in *people*, where it is pronounced like *ee*.

I.

I has a ſound, long, as *fīne*; and ſhort, as *fĭn*.

That is eminently obſervable in *i*, which may be likewiſe remarked in other letters, that the ſhort ſound is not the long ſound contracted, but a ſound wholly different.

The long ſound in monoſyllables is always marked by the *e* final, as *thĭn*, *thīne*.

I is often ſounded before *r* as a ſhort *u*; as *flirt*, *firſt*, *ſhirt*.

It forms a diphthong only with *e*, as *field*, *ſhield*, which is ſounded as the double *ee*; except *friend*, which is ſounded as *frĕnd*.

I is joined with *eu* in *lieu*, and *ew* in *view*; which triphthongs are ſounded as the open *u*.

O.

O is long, as *bōne*, *ōbedient*, *corrōding*; or ſhort, as *blŏck*, *knŏck*, *ŏblique*, *lŏll*.

Women is pronounced *wimen*.

The ſhort *o* has ſometimes the ſound of a cloſe *u*, as *ſon*, *come*.

O coaleſces into a diphthong with *a*, as *moan*, *groan*, *approach*; *oa* has the ſound of *o* long.

O is united to *e* in ſome words derived from Greek, as *œconomy*; but *œ* being not an Engliſh diphthong, they are better written as they are ſounded, with only *e*, *economy*.

With *i*, as *oil*, *ſoil*, *moil*, *noiſome*.

This coalition of letters ſeems to unite the ſounds of the two letters as far as two ſounds can be united without being deſtroyed, and therefore approaches more nearly than any combination in our tongue to the notion of a diphthong.

With *o*, as *boot*, *hoot*, *cooler*; *oo* has the ſound of the Italian *u*.

With *u* or *w*, as *our*, *power*, *flower*; but in ſome words has only the ſound of *o* long, as in *ſoul*, *bowl*, *ſow*, *grow*. Theſe different ſounds are uſed to diſtinguiſh different ſignifications; as *bow*, an inſtrument for ſhooting; *bow*, a depreſſion of the head: *ſow*, the ſhe of a boar; *ſow*, to ſcatter ſeed: *bowl*, an orbicular body; *bowl*, a wooden veſſel.

Ou is ſometimes pronounced like *o* ſoft, as *court*; ſometimes like *o* ſhort, as *cough*; ſometimes like *u* cloſe, as *could*; or *u* open, as *rough*, *tough*; which uſe only can teach.

Ou is frequently uſed in the laſt ſyllable of words which in Latin end in *or*, and are made Engliſh, as *honour*, *labour*, *favour*, from *honor*, *labor*, *favor*.

Some late innovators have ejected the *u*, without conſidering that the laſt ſyllable gives the ſound neither of *or* nor *ur*, but a ſound between them, if not compounded of both; beſides that they are probably derived to us from the French nouns in *eur*, as *honeur*, *faveur*.

U.

U is long in *ūſe*, *confūſion*; or ſhort, as *ŭs*, *concŭſſion*.

It coaleſces with *a*, *e*, *i*, *o*; but has rather in theſe combinations the force of the *w* conſonant, as *quaff*, *queſt*, *quit*, *quite*, *languiſh*; ſometimes in *ui* the *i* loſes its ſound, as in *juice*. It is ſometimes mute before *a*, *e*, *i*, *y*, as *guard*, *gueſt*, *guiſe*, *buy*.

U is followed by *e* in *virtue*, but the *e* has no ſound.

Ue is ſometimes mute at the end of a word, in imitation of the French, as *prorogue*, *ſynagogue*, *plague*, *vague*, *harangue*.

Y.

Y is a vowel, which, as Quintilian obſerves of one of the Roman letters, we might want without inconvenience, but that we have it. It ſupplies the place of *i* at the end of words, as *thy*; before an *i*, as *dying*; and is commonly retained in derivative words where it was part of a diphthong in the primitive; as *deſtroy*, *deſtroyer*; *betray*, *betrayed*, *betrayer*; *pray*, *prayer*; *ſay*, *ſayer*; *day*, *days*.

Y being the Saxon vowel ẏ, which was commonly uſed where *i* is now put, occurs very frequently in all old books.

GENERAL RULES.

A vowel in the beginning or middle ſyllable, before two conſonants, is commonly ſhort, as *ŏpportunity*.

In monoſyllables a ſingle vowel before a ſingle conſonant is ſhort, as *ſtag*, *frog*.

Of CONSONANTS.

B.

B has one unvaried ſound, ſuch as it obtains in other languages.

It is mute in *debt*, *debtor*, *ſubtle*, *doubt*, *lamb*, *limb*, *dumb*, *thumb*, *climb*, *comb*, *womb*.

It is uſed before *l* and *r*, as *black*, *brown*.

C.

C has before *e* and *i* the ſound of *ſ*; as *ſincerely*, *centrick*, *century*, *circular*, *ciſtern*, *city*, *ſiccity*: before *a*, *o*, and *u*, it ſounds like *k*, as *calm*, *concavity*, *copper*, *incorporate*, *curioſity*, *concupiſcence*.

C might be omitted in the language without loſs, ſince one of its ſounds might be ſupplied by *ſ*, and the other by *k*, but that it preſerves to the eye the etymology of words, as *face* from *facies*, *captive* from *captivus*.

Ch has a ſound which is analyſed into *tſh*, as *church*, *chin*, *crutch*. It is the ſame ſound which the Italians give to the *c* ſimple before *i* and *e*, as *citta*, *cerro*.

Ch is ſounded like *k* in words derived from the Greek, as *chymiſt*, *ſcheme*, *choler*. *Arch* is commonly ſounded *ark* before a vowel, as *archangel*; and with the Engliſh ſound of *ch* before a conſonant, as *archbiſhop*.

Ch, in ſome French words not yet aſſimilated, ſounds like *ſh*, as *machine*, *chaiſe*.

C, according to Engliſh orthography, never ends a word; therefore we write *ſtick*, *block*, which were originally *ſticke*, *blocke*, in ſuch words. *C* is now mute.

It is uſed before *l* and *r*, as *clock*, *croſs*.

D

Is uniform in its ſound, as *death*, *diligent*.

It is uſed before *r*, as *draw*, *droſs*; and *w*, as *dwell*.

F.

F, though having a name beginning with a vowel, it is numbered by the grammarians among the ſemivowels, yet has this quality of a mute, that it is commodiouſly ſounded before a liquid, as *flaſk*, *fly*, *freckle* It has an unvariable ſound, except that *of* is ſometimes ſpoken nearly as *ov*.

G.

G has two ſounds, one hard, as in *gay*, *go*, *gun*; the other ſoft, as in *gem*, *giant*.

At

At the end of a word it is always hard, *ring*, *ſnug*, *ſong*, *frog*.

Before *e* and *i* the ſound is uncertain.

G before *e* is ſoft, as *gem*, *generation*, except in *gear*, *gold*, *geeſe*, *get*, *gewgaw*, and derivatives from words ending in *g*, as *ſinging*, *ſtronger*, and generally before *er* at the end of words, as *finger*.

G is mute before *n*, as *gnaſh*, *ſign*, *foreign*.

G before *i* is hard, as *give*, except in *giant*, *gigantick*, *gibbet*, *gibe*, *giblets*, *giles*, *gill*, *gilliflower*, *gin*, *ginger*, *gingle*, *gipſy*.

Gh in the beginning of a word has the ſound of the hard *g*, as *ghoſtly*; in the middle, and ſometimes at the end, it is quite ſilent, as *though*, *right*, *ſought*, ſpoken *tho'*, *rite*, *ſoute*.

It has often at the end the ſound of *f*, as *laugh*; whence *laughter* retains the ſame ſound in the middle; *cough*, *trough*, *ſough*, *tough*, *enough*, *ſlough*.

It is not to be doubted, but that in the original pronunciation *gh* had the force of a conſonant, deeply guttural, which is ſtill continued among the Scotch.

G is uſed before *h*, *l*, and *r*.

H.

H is a note of aſpiration, and ſhows that the following vowel muſt be pronounced with a ſtrong emiſſion of the breath, as *hat*, *horſe*.

It ſeldom, perhaps never, begins any but the firſt ſyllable, in which it is always ſounded with a full breath, except in *heir*, *herb*, *hoſtler*, *honour*, *humble*, *honeſt*, *humour*, and their derivatives.

J.

J conſonant ſounds uniformly like the ſoft *g*, and is therefore a letter uſeleſs, except in etymology, as *ejaculation*, *jeſter*, *jocund*, *juice*.

K.

K has the ſound of hard *c*, and is uſed before *e* and *i*, where, according to Engliſh analogy, *c* would be ſoft, as *kept*, *king*, *ſkirt*, *ſkeptick*, for ſo it ſhould be written, not *ſceptick*.

It is uſed before *n*, as *knell*, *knot*, but totally loſes its ſound.

K is never doubled; but *c* is uſed before it to ſhorten the vowel by a double conſonant, as *cŏckle*, *pĭckle*.

L.

L has in Engliſh the ſame liquid ſound as in other languages.

The cuſtom is to double the *l* at the end of monoſyllables, as *kill*, *will*, *full*. Theſe words were originally written *kille*, *wille*, *fulle*; and when the *e* firſt grew ſilent, and was afterwards omitted, the *ll* was retained, to give force, according to the analogy of our language, to the foregoing vowel.

L is ſometimes mute, as in *calf*, *half*, *halves*, *calves*, *could*, *would*, *ſhould*, *pſalm*, *talk*, *ſalmon*, *falcon*.

The Saxon, who delighted in guttural ſounds, ſometimes aſpirated the *l* at the beginning of words, as hlaꝼ, *a loaf*, or *bread*; hlaꝼoꞃd, *a lord*; but this pronunciation is now diſuſed.

Le at the end of words is pronounced like a weak *el*, in which the *e* is almoſt mute, as *table*, *ſhuttle*.

M.

M has always the ſame ſound, as *murmur*, *monumental*.

N.

N has always the ſame ſound, as *noble*, *manners*.

N is ſometimes mute after *m*, as *damn*, *condemn*, *hymn*.

P.

P has always the ſame ſound, which the Welſh and Germans confound with *B*.

P is ſometimes mute, as in *pſalm*, and between *m* and *t*, as *tempt*.

Ph is uſed for *f* in words derived from the Greek, as *philoſopher*, *philanthropy*, *Philip*.

Q.

Q, as in other languages, is always followed by *u*, and has a ſound which our Saxon anceſtors well expreſſed by *cp*, *cw*, as *quadrant*, *queen*, *equeſtrian*, *quilt*, *enquiry*, *quire*, *quotidian*. *Qu* is never followed by *u*

Qu is ſometimes ſounded, in words derived from the French, like *k*, as *conquer*, *liquor*, *riſque*, *chequer*.

R.

R has the ſame rough ſnarling ſound as in other tongues.

The Saxons uſed often to put *h* before it, as before *l* at the beginning of words.

Rh is uſed in words derived from the Greek, as *myrrh*, *myrrhine*, *catarrhous*, *rheum*, *rheumatick*, *rhyme*.

Re, at the end of ſome words derived from the Latin or French, is pronounced like a weak *er*, as *theatre*, *ſepulchre*.

S.

S has a hiſſing ſound, as *ſibilation*, *ſiſter*.

A ſingle *s* ſeldom ends any word, except the third perſon of verbs, as *loves*, *groves*; and the plurals of nouns, as *trees*, *buſhes*, *diſtreſſes*, the pronouns *this*, *his*, *ours*, *yours*, *us*; the adverb *thus*; and words derived from Latin, as *rebus*, *ſurplus*; the cloſe being always either in *ſe*, as *houſe*, *horſe*, or in *ſs*, as *graſs*, *dreſs*, *bliſs*, *leſs*, anciently *graſſe*, *dreſſe*.

S ſingle, at the end of words, has a groſſer ſound, like that of *z*, as *trees*, *eyes*, except *this*, *thus*, *us*, *rebus*, *ſurplus*.

It ſounds like *z* before *ion*, if a vowel goes before, as *intruſion*; and like *ſ*, if it follows a conſonant, as *converſion*.

It ſounds like *z* before *e* mute, as *refuſe*, and before *y* final, as *roſy*; and in thoſe words, *boſom*, *deſire*, *wiſdom*, *priſon*, *priſoner*, *préſent*, *preſènt*, *damſel*, *caſement*.

It is the peculiar quality of *ſ*, that it may be ſounded before all conſonants, except *x* and *z*, in which *ſ* is compriſed, *x* being only *ks*, and *z* a hard or groſs *ſ*. This *ſ* is therefore termed by grammarians *ſuæ poteſtatis litera*; the reaſon of which the learned Dr. Clarke erroneouſly ſuppoſed to be, that in ſome words it might be doubled at pleaſure. Thus we find in ſeveral languages:

Σβέννυμι, *ſcatter*, *ſdegno*, *ſdrucciolo*, *ſfavellare*, σφίγξ, *ſgombrare*, *ſgranare*, *ſhake*, *ſlumber*, *ſmell*, *ſnipe*, *ſpace*, *ſplendour*, *ſpring*, *ſqueeze*, *ſhrew*, *ſtep*, *ſtrength*, *ſtramen*, *ſventura*, *ſwell*.

S is mute in *iſle*, *iſland*, *demeſne*, *viſcount*.

T.

T has its cuſtomary ſound, as *take*, *temptation*.

Ti before a vowel has the ſound of *ſi*, as *ſalvation*, except an *ſ* goes before, as *queſtion*, excepting likewiſe derivatives from *y*, as *mighty*, *mightier*.

Th has two ſounds; the one ſoft, as *thus*, *whether*; the other hard, as *thing*, *think*. The ſound is ſoft in theſe words, *then*, *thence*, and *there*, with their derivatives and compounds, *that*, *theſe*, *thou*, *thee*, *thy*, *thine*, *their*, *they*, *this*, *theſe*, *them*, *though*, *thus*, and in all words between two vowels, as *father*, *whether*; and beween *r* and a vowel, as *burthen*.

In other words it is hard, as *thick*, *thunder*, *faith*, *faithful*. Where it is ſoftened at the end of a word, an *e* ſilent muſt be added, as *breath*, *breathe*; *cloth*, *clothe*.

V.

V has a ſound of near affinity to that of *f*, *vain*, *vanity*.

From *f* in the Iſlandick alphabet, *v* is only diſtinguiſhed by a diacritical point.

W.

Of *w*, which in diphthongs is often an undoubted vowel, ſome grammarians have doubted whether it ever be a conſonant; and not rather as it is called a double *u* or *ou*, as *water* may be reſolved into *ouater*; but letters of the ſame ſound are always reckoned conſonants in other alphabets: and it may be obſerved, that *w* follows a vowel without any hiatus or difficulty of utterance, as *froſty winter*.

Wh has a ſound accounted peculiar to the Engliſh, which the Saxons better expreſſed by *hp*, *hw*, as *what*, *whence*, *whiting*; in *whore* only, and ſometimes in *wholeſome*, *wh* is ſounded like a ſimple *h*.

X.

X begins no Engliſh word; it has the ſound of *ks*, as *axle*, *extraneous*.

Y.

Y, when it follows a conſonant, is a vowel; when it precedes either vowel or diphthong, is a conſonant,

ye,

ye, *young*. It is thought by ſome to be in all caſes a vowel. But it may be obſerved of *y* as of *w*, that it follows a vowel without any hiatus, as *roſy youth*.

Z.

Z begins no word originally Engliſh; it has the ſound as its name *izzard* or *ſ hard* expreſſes, of an *ſ* uttered with cloſer compreſſion of the palate by the tongue, as *freeze*, *froze*.

In orthography I have ſuppoſed *orthoepy*, or *juſt utterance of words*, to be included; orthography being only the art of expreſſing certain ſounds by proper characters. I have therefore obſerved in what words any of the letters are mute.

Moſt of the writers of Engliſh grammar have given long tables of words pronounced otherwiſe than they are written, and ſeem not ſufficiently to have conſidered, that of Engliſh, as of all living tongues, there is a double pronunciation, one curſory and colloquial, the other regular and ſolemn. The curſory pronunciation is always vague and uncertain, being made different in different mouths by negligence, unſkilfulneſs, or affectation. The ſolemn pronunciation, though by no means immutable and permanent, is yet always leſs remote from the orthography, and leſs liable to capricious innovation. They have however generally formed their tables according to the curſory ſpeech of thoſe with whom they happened to converſe; and concluding that the whole nation combines to vitiate language in one manner, have often eſtabliſhed the jargon of the loweſt of the people as the model of ſpeech.

For pronunciation the beſt general rule is, to conſider thoſe as the moſt elegant ſpeakers who deviate leaſt from the written words.

There have been many ſchemes offered for the emendation and ſettlement of our orthography, which, like that of other nations, being formed by chance, or according to the fancy of the earlieſt writers in rude ages, was at firſt very various and uncertain, and is yet ſufficiently irregular. Of theſe reformers ſome have endeavoured to accommodate orthography better to the pronunciation, without conſidering that this is to meaſure by a ſhadow, to take that for a model or ſtandard which is changing while they apply it. Others, leſs abſurdly indeed, but with equal unlikelihood of ſucceſs, have endeavoured to proportion the number of letters to that of ſounds, that every ſound may have its own character, and every character a ſingle ſound. Such would be the orthography of a new language to be formed by a ſynod of grammarians upon principles of ſcience. But who can hope to prevail on nations to change their practice, and make all their old books uſeleſs? or what advantage would a new orthography procure equivalent to the confuſion and perplexity of ſuch an alteration?

Some of theſe ſchemes I ſhall however exhibit, which may be uſed according to the diverſities of genius, as a guide to reformers, or terrour to innovators.

One of the firſt who propoſed a ſcheme of regular orthography, was Sir Thomas Smith, ſecretary of ſtate to Queen Elizabeth, a man of real learning, and much practiſed in grammatical diſquiſitions. Had he written the following lines according to his ſcheme, they would have appeared thus.

At length Eraſmus, that great injur'd name,
The glory of the prieſthood, and the ſhame,
Stemm'd the wild torrent of a barb'rous age,
And drove thoſe holy Vandals off the ſtage.

At lengð Eraſmus, ðat grët ïnʒurd nâm,
Δe glorï of ðe prëſthüd, and ðe zâm,
Stemmd ðe *w*ild torrent of a barb'rous âʒ.
And dröv ðös höli Vandals öff ðe ſtâʒ.

After him another mode of writing was offered by Dr. Gill, the celebrated maſter of St. Paul's ſchool in London; which I cannot repreſent exactly for want of types, but will approach as nearly as I can by means of characters now in uſe as to make it underſtood, exhibiting two ſtanzas of Spenſer in the reformed orthography.

Spenſer, book iii. canto 5.

Unthankful wretch, ſaid he, is this the meed,
With which her ſovereign mercy thou doſt quite?
Thy life ſhe ſaved by her gracious deed;
But thou doſt ween with villanous deſpight,
To blot her honour, and her heav'nly light.
Die, rather die, than ſo diſloyally,
Deem of her high deſert, or ſeem ſo light.
Fair death it is to ſhun more ſhame; then die.
Die, rather die, than ever love diſloyally.
But if to love diſloyalty it be,
Shall I then hate her, that from deathes door
Me brought? ah! far be ſuch reproach from me.
What can I leſs do, than her love therefore.
Sith I her due reward cannot reſtore?
Die, rather die, and dying do her ſerve,
Dying her ſerve, and living her adore.
Thy life ſhe gave, thy life ſhe doth deſerve;
Die, rather die, than ever from her ſervice ſwerve.

Vnђ*a*nkful wrɛɔ, ſ*a*id hj, iz ðis ðe mjd,
Wiђ ƀiɔ hɛr ſoƀɛr*a*in mɛrſi ðou duſt qujt?
Ðj ljf ɼj ſ*a*ƀɛd bj hɛr graſius djd;
But ðou duſt wen wiђ ƀilɛnus diſpjt,
Tu blot hɛr honor, *a*nd hɛr heƀnlj li*b*t.
Dj, r*a*ðɛr dj, ðɛn ſo diſloi*a*lj.
Djm of hɛr hi*b* dɛzɛrt, or ſjm ſo li*b*t.
F*a*ir deђ it iz tu ɼun m*ω*r ɼãm; ðɛn dj.
Dj, raðer dj, ðɛn ɛƀɛr luƀ diſloi*a*lj.
But if tu luƀ diſloi*a*ltj it bj,
Sal I ðɛn hãt hɛr ðat from dɛðez d*ω*r
Mj brou*b*t? *a*h! f*a*r bj ſuɔ rɛproɔ from mj.
W*a*t k*a*n I lɛs du ðɛn hɜr luƀ ðɛrf*ω*r,
Si*b* I her du rɛw*a*rd kanot reſt*ω*r?
Dj, r*a*ðer dj, and djiʒ du hɛr ſɛrƀ,
Djiʒ hɛr ſɛrƀ, and liƀiʒ hɛr ad*ω*r.
Ðj ljf ɼj gãƀ, ðj ljf ɼj du*b* dɛzɛrƀ.
Dj, r*a*ðɛr di, ðɛn ɛƀɛr from hɛr ſɛrƀis ſwɛrƀ.

Dr. Gill was followed by Charles Butler, a man who did not want an underſtanding which might have qualified him for better employment. He ſeems to have been more ſanguine than his predeceſſors, for he printed his book according to his own ſcheme; which the following ſpecimen will make eaſily underſtood.

But whenſoever you have occaſion to trouble their patience, or to come among them being troubled, it is better to ſtand upon your guard, than to truſt to their gentleneſs. For the ſafeguard of your face, which they have moſt mind unto, provide a purſehood, made of coarſe boultering, to be drawn and knit about your collar, which for more ſafety is to be lined againſt the eminent parts with woollen cloth. Firſt cut a piece about an inch and a half broad, and half a yard long, to reach round by the temples and forehead, from one ear to the other; which being ſowed in his place, join unto it two ſhort peces of the ſame breadth under the eyes, for the balls of the cheeks, and then ſet an other piece about the breadth of a ſhilling againſt the top of the noſe. At other times, when they are not angered, a little piece half a quarter broad, to cover the eyes and parts about them, may ſerve though it be in the heat of the day.

Bet ƿenſoëver you hav' occaſion to trubble ðeir patienc', or to coom among ðem b*ee*ing trubled, it is better to ſtand upon your gard, ðan to truſt to ðeir gentlenes. For ðe ſaf'gard of your fac', ƿiɔ ðey hav' moſt mind' unto, provid' a purſehood, mad' of *coo*rſe boultering, to b*ee* drawn and knit about your collar, ƿiɔ for mor' ſaf'ty is to b*ee* lined againſt ð' eminent parts wiτ w*oo*llen cloτ. Firſt cut a peec' about an inɔ and a half broad, and half a yard long, to reaɔ round by ðe temples and for'head, from one ear to ðe oðer; ƿiɔ b*ee*ing ſowed in his plac', join unto it two ɼort p*ee*ces of the ſam breadτ under ðe eys, for the bals of ðe *cheeks*, and then ſet an oðer peec' about ðe breadτ of a ɼilling againſt the top of ðe noſe. At oðer tim's, ƿen ðey ar' not angered, a little piec' half a quarter broad, to cover ðe eys and parts about them, may ſerve ðowʒ it be in the heat of ðe day. *Butler on the Nature and Properties of Bees*, 1634.

In the time of Charles I. there was a very prevalent inclination to change the orthography; as appears, among other books, in ſuch editions of the works of Milton as were publiſhed by himſelf. Of theſe reformers every man had his own ſcheme; but they agreed in one general deſign of accommodating the letters to the pronunciation, by ejecting ſuch as they thought ſuperfluous. Some of them would have written theſe lines thus:

——All the erth
Shall then be paradis, far happier place
Than this of Eden, and far happier dais.

Biſhop Wilkins afterwards, in his great work of the philoſophical language, propoſed, without expecting to be followed, a regular orthography; by which the Lord's prayer is to be written thus:

Yɤr Fádher hɤitſh art in héven, hɑlloed bi dhyi nám, dhyi cingdy̆m cy̆m, dhy ɤill bi dy̆n in erth as it is in héven, &c.

We have ſince had no general reformers; but ſome ingenious men have endeavoured to deſerve well of their country, by writing *honor* and *labor* for *honour* and *labour*, *red* for *read* in the preter-tenſe, *sais* for *ſays*, *repete* for *repeat*, *explane* for *explain*, or *declame* for *declaim*. Of theſe it may be ſaid, that as they have done no good, they have done little harm; both becauſe they have innovated little, and becauſe few have followed them.

ETYMOLOGY.

ETYMOLOGY teaches the deduction of one word from another, and the various modifications by which the ſenſe of the ſame word is diverſified; as *horſe*, *horſes*; I *love*, I *loved*.

Of the ARTICLE.

The Engliſh have two articles, *an* or *a*, and *the*.

AN, A.

A has an indefinite ſignification, and means *one*, with ſome reference to more; as, *This is a good book*, that is, *one among the books that are good*. *He was killed by a ſword*, that is, *ſome ſword*. *This is a better book for a man than a boy*, that is, *for one of thoſe that are men than one of thoſe that are boys*. *An army might enter without reſiſtance*, that is, *any army*.

In the ſenſes in which we uſe *a* or *an* in the ſingular, we ſpeak in the plural without an article; as, *theſe are good books*.

I have made *an* the original article, becauſe it is only the Saxon [illegible]n, *one*, applied to a new uſe, as the German *ein*, and the French

French *un*; the *n* being cut off before a consonant in the speed of utterance.

Grammarians of the last age direct, that *an* should be used before *h*; whence it appears that the English anciently aspirated less. *An* is still used before the silent *h*, as *an herb*, *an honest man*: but otherwise *a*; as,

A horse, *a* horse, my kingdom for *a* horse.
Shakespeare.

THE has a particular and definite signification.

The fruit
Of that forbidden tree, whose mortal taste
Brought death into *the* world. *Milton.*

That is, *that particular fruit*, and *this world in which we live*. So *He giveth fodder for* the *cattle, and green herbs for* the *use of man*; that is, for *those beings that are cattle*, and *his use that is man.*

The is used in both numbers.

I am as free as Nature first made man,
Ere *the* base laws of servitude began,
When wild in woods *the* noble savage ran. *Dryd.*

Many words are used without articles; as,

1. Proper names, as *John*, *Alexander*, *Longinus*, *Aristarchus*, *Jerusalem*, *Athens*, *Rome*, *London*. GOD is used as a proper name.

2. Abstract names, as *blackness*, *witchcraft*, *virtue*, *vice*, *beauty*, *ugliness*, *love*, *hatred*, *anger*, *goodnature*, *kindness*.

3. Words in which nothing but the mere being of any thing is implied: This is not *beer*, but *water*; This is not *brass*, but *steel*.

Of NOUNS SUBSTANTIVES.

The relations of English nouns to words going before or following are not expressed by *cases*, or changes of termination, but as in most of the other European languages by prepositions, unless we may be said to have a genitive case.

Singular.

Nom.	Magister,	*a* Master, *the* Master.
Gen.	Magistri,	*of a* Master, *of the* Master, *or* Masters, *the* Masters.
Dat.	Magistro,	*to a* Master, *to the* Master.
Acc.	Magistrum,	*a* Master, *the* Master.
Voc.	Magister,	Master, *O* Master.
Abl.	Magistro,	*from a* Master, *from the* Master.

Plural.

Nom.	Magistri,	Masters, *the* Masters.
Gen.	Magistrorum,	*of* Masters, *of the* Masters.
Dat.	Magistris,	*to* Masters, *to the* Masters.
Acc.	Magistros,	Masters, *the* Masters.
Voc.	Magistri,	Masters, *O* Masters.
Abl.	Magistris,	*from* Masters, *from the* Masters.

Our nouns are therefore only declined thus:

Master,	*Gen.* Masters.	*Plur.* Masters.
Scholar,	*Gen.* Scholars.	*Plur.* Scholars.

These genitives are always written with a mark of elision, *master's*, *scholar's*, according to an opinion long received, that the *'s* is a contraction of *his*, as *the soldier's valour*, for *the soldier* his *valour*: but this cannot be the true original, because *'s* is put to female nouns, *Woman's beauty*; the *Virgin's delicacy*; *Haughty Juno's unrelenting hate*: and collective nouns, as *Women's passions*; *the rabble's insolence*; *the multitude's folly*; in all these cases it is apparent that *his* cannot be understood. We say likewise, *the foundation's strength*, *the diamond's lustre*, *the winter's severity*; but in these cases *his* may be understood, *he* and *his* having formerly been applied to neuters in the place now supplied by *it* and *its*.

The learned, the sagacious Wallis, to whom every English grammarian owes a tribute of reverence, calls this modification of the noun an *adjective possessive*; I think with no more propriety than he might have applied the same to the genitive in *equitum decus*, *Trojæ oris*, or any other Latin genitive.

This termination of the noun seems to constitute a real genitive indicating possession. It is derived to us from those who declined ꞅmið, *a smith*; Gen. ꞅmiðeꞅ, *of a smith*; Plur. ꞅmiðeꞅ, or ꞅmiðaꞅ, *smiths*; and so in two other of their seven declensions.

It is a further confirmation of this opinion, that in the old poets both the genitive and plural were longer by a syllable than the original word; *knitis*, for *knight's*, in Chaucer; *leavis*, for *leaves*, in Spenser.

When a word ends in *s*, the genitive may be the same with the nominative, as *Venus temple*.

The plural is formed by adding *s*, as *table*, *tables*; *fly*, *flies*; *sister*, *sisters*; *wood*, *woods*; or *es* where *s* could not otherwise be sounded, as after *ch*, *s*, *sh*, *x*, *z*; after *c* sounded like *s*, and *g* like *j*; the mute *e* is vocal before *s*, as *lance*, *lances*; *outrage*, *outrages*.

The formation of the plural and genitive singular is the same.

A few words yet make the plural in *n*, as *men*, *women*, *oxen*, *swine*, and more anciently *eyen* and *shoon*. This formation is that which generally prevails in the Teutonick dialects.

Words that end in *f* commonly form their plural by *ves*, as *loaf*, *loaves*; *calf*, *calves*.

Except a few, *muff*, *muffs*; *chief*, *chiefs*. So *hoof*, *roof*, *proof*, *relief*, *mischief*, *puff*, *cuff*, *dwarf*, *handkerchief*, *grief*.

Irregular plurals are *teeth* from *tooth*, *lice* from *louse*, *mice* from *mouse*, *geese* from *goose*, *feet* from *foot*, *dice* from *die*, *pence* from *penny*, *brethren* from *brother*, *children* from *child*.

Plurals ending in *s* have no genitives; but we say, Womens *excellencies*, and *Weigh the* mens *wits against the* ladies *hairs*. Pope.

Dr. Wallis thinks *the Lords' house* may be said for *the house of Lords*; but such phrases are not now in use; and surely an English ear rebels against them.

Of ADJECTIVES.

Adjectives in the English language are wholly indeclinable; having neither case, gender, nor number, and being added to substantives in all relations without any change; as, *a good woman*, *good women*, *of a good woman*; *a good man*, *good men*, *of good men*.

The Comparison of Adjectives.

The comparative degree of adjectives is formed by adding *er*, the superlative by adding *est*, to the positive; as, *fair*, fairer, fair*est*; *lovely*, lovelier, loveliest; *sweet*, sweeter, sweet*est*; *low*, lower, low*est*; *high*, higher, high*est*.

Some words are irregularly compared; as *good*, *better*, *best*; *bad*, *worse*, *worst*; *little*, *less*, *least*; *near*, *nearer*, *next*; *much*, *more*, *most*; *many* (or *moe*), *more* (for *moer*), *most* (for *moest*); *late*, *latter*, *latest* or *last*.

Some comparatives form a superlative by adding *most*, as *nether*, *nethermost*; *outer*, *outmost*; *under*, *undermost*; *up*, *upper*, *uppermost*; *fore*, *former*, *foremost*.

Most is sometimes added to a substantive, as *topmost*, *southmost*.

Many adjectives do not admit of comparison by terminations, and are only compared by *more* and *most*, as *benevolent*, *more benevolent*, *most benevolent*.

All adjectives may be compared by *more* and *most*, even when they have comparatives and superlatives regularly formed; as *fair*; *fairer*, or *more fair*; *fairest*, or *most fair*.

In adjectives that admit a regular comparison, the comparative *more* is oftener used than the superlative *most*, as *more fair* is oftener written for *fairer*, than *most fair* for *fairest*.

The comparison of adjectives is very uncertain; and being much regulated by commodiousness of utterance, or agreeableness of sound, is not easily reduced to rules.

Monosyllables are commonly compared.

Polysyllables, or words of more than two syllables, are seldom compared otherwise than by *more* and *most*, as *deplorable*, *more deplorable*, *most deplorable*.

Dissyllables are seldom compared if they terminate in *some*, as *fulsome*, *toilsome*; in *ful*, as *careful*, *spleenful*, *dreadful*; in *ing*, as *trifling*, *charming*; in *ous*, as *porous*; in *less*, as *careless*, *harmless*; in *ed*, as *wretched*; in *id*, as *candid*; in *al*, as *mortal*; in *ent*, as *recent*, *fervent*; in *ain*, as *certain*; in *ive*, as *missive*; in *dy*, as *woody*; in *fy*, as *puffy*; in *ky*, as *rocky*, except *lucky*; in *my*, as *roomy*; in *ny*, as *skinny*; in *py*, as *ropy*, except *happy*; in *ry*, as *hoary*.

Some comparatives and superlatives are yet found in good writers formed without regard to the foregoing rules; but in a language subjected so little and so lately to grammar, such anomalies must frequently occur.

So *shady* is compared by *Milton*.

She in *shadiest* covert hid,
Tun'd her nocturnal note. *Parad. Lost.*

And *virtuous*.

What she wills to say or do,
Seems wisest, *virtuousest*, discreetest, best. *Parad. Lost.*

So

So *trifling*, by *Ray*, who is indeed of no great authority.

It is not so decorous, in respect of God, that he should immediately do all the meanest and *triflingest* things himself, without making use of any inferior or subordinate minister. *Ray on the Creaiton.*

Famous, by *Milton*.

I shall be named among the *famousest*
Of women, sung at solemn festivals. *Milton's Agonistes.*

Inventive, by *Ascham*.

Those have the *inventivest* heads for all purposes, and roundest tongues in all matters. *Ascham's Schoolmaster.*

Mortal, by *Bacon*.

The *mortalest* poisons practised by the West Indians, have some mixture of the blood, fat, or flesh of man. *Bacon.*

Natural, by *Wotton*.

I will now deliver a few of the properest and *naturallest* considerations that belong to this piece. *Wotton's Architecture.*

Wretched, by *Johnson*.

The *wretcheder* are the contemners of all helps; such as presuming on their own naturals, deride diligence, and mock at terms when they understand not things. *B. Johnson.*

Powerful, by *Milton*.

We have sustain'd one day in doubtful fight,
What heav'n's great King hath *pow'rfullest* to send
Against us from about his throne. *Paradise Lost.*

The termination in *ish* may be accounted in some sort a degree of comparison, by which the signification is diminished below the positive, as *black*, *blackish*, or tending to blackness; *salt*, *saltish*, or having a little taste of salt: they therefore admit no comparison. This termination is seldom added but to words expressing sensible qualities, nor often to words of above one syllable, and is scarcely used in the solemn or sublime style.

Of PRONOUNS.

Pronouns, in the English language, are, *I*, *thou*, *he*, with their plurals *we*, *ye*, *they*, *it*, *who*, *which*, *what*, *whether*, *whosoever*, *whatsoever*, *my*, *mine*, *our*, *ours*, *thy*, *thine*, *your*, *yours*, *his*, *her*, *hers*, *their*, *theirs*, *this*, *that*, *other*, *another*, the *same*.

The pronouns personal are irregularly inflected.

	Singular.	Plural.
Nom.	I	We
Accus. and other oblique cases.	Me	Us
Nom.	Thou	Ye
Oblique.	Thee	You

You is commonly used in modern writers for *ye*, particularly in the language of ceremony, where the second person plural is used for the second person singular, *You are my friend.*

	Singular.	Plural.	
Nom.	He	They	Applied to masculines.
Oblique.	Him	Them	
Nom.	She	They	Applied to feminines.
Oblique.	Her	Them	
Nom.	It	They	Applied to neuters or things.
Oblique.	Its	Them	

For *it* the practice of ancient writers was to use *he*, and for *its*, *his*.

The possessive pronouns, like other adjectives, are without cases or change of termination.

The possessive of the first person is *my*, *mine*, *our*, *ours*; of the second, *thy*, *thine*, *you*, *yours*; of the third, from *he*, *his*, from *she*, *her*, and *hers*, and in the plural *their*, *theirs*, for both sexes.

Our, *yours*, *hers*, *theirs*, are used when the substantive preceding is separated by a verb, as *These are* our *books*. *These books are* ours. Your *children excel* ours *in stature*, *but* ours *surpass* yours *in learning*.

Ours, *yours*, *hers*, *theirs*, notwithstanding their seeming plural termination, are applied equally to singular and plural substantives, as *This book is* ours. *These books are* ours.

Mine and *thine* were formerly used before a vowel, as *mine amiable lady*; which though now disused in prose, might be still properly continued in poetry, they are used as *ours* and *yours*, when they are referred to a substantive preceding.

Their and *theirs* are the possessives likewise of *it*, and are therefore applied to things.

Pronouns relative are, *who*, *which*, *what*, *whether*, *whosoever*, *whatsoever*.

	Sing. and Plur.		Sing. and Plur.
Nom.	Who	*Nom.*	Which
Gen.	Whose	*Gen.*	Of which, *or* whose
Other oblique cases.	Whom	*Other oblique cases.*	Which

Who is now used in relation to persons, and *which* in relation to things; but they were anciently confounded.

Whose is rather the poetical than regular genitive of *which*:

The fruit
Of that forbidden tree, *whose* mortal taste
Brought death into the world. *Milton.*

Whether is only used in the nominative and accusative cases; and has no plural, being applied only to *one* of a number, commonly to one of two, as, Whether *of these is left I know not.* Whether *shall I choose?* It is now almost obsolete.

What, whether relative or interrogative, is without variation.

Whosoever, *whatsoever*, being compounded of *who* or *what*, and *soever*, follow the rule of their primitives.

	Singular.	Plural.
In all cases,	This	These
	That	Those
	Other	Others
	Whether	

The plural *others* is not used but when it is referred to a substantive preceding, as *I have sent* other *horses*. *I have not sent the same horses*, *but* others.

Another, being only *an other*, has no plural.

Here, *there*, and *where*, joined with certain particles, have a relative and pronominal use. *Hereof*, *herein*, *hereby*, *hereafter*, *herewith*, *thereof*, *therein*, *thereby*, *thereupon*, *therewith*, *whereof*, *wherein*, *whereby*, *whereupon*, *wherewith*, which signify, *of this*, *in this*, &c. *of that*, *in that*, &c. *of which*, *in which*, &c.

Therefore and *wherefore*, which are properly, *there for* and *where for*, *for that*, *for which*, are now reckoned conjunctions, and continued in use. The rest seem to be passing by degrees into neglect, though proper, useful, and analogous. They are referred both to singular and plural antecedents.

There are two more words used only in conjunction with pronouns, *own* and *self*.

Own is added to possessives, both singular and plural, as *my* own *hand*, *our* own *house*. It is emphatical, and implies a silent contrariety or opposition; as, *I live in my own house*, that is, *not in a hired house*. *This I did with my own hand*, that is, *without help*, or *not by proxy*.

Self is added to possessives, as *myself*, *yourselves*; and sometimes to personal pronouns, as *himself*, *itself*, *themselves*. It then, like *own*, expresses emphasis and opposition, as *I did this myself*, that is, *not another*; or it forms a reciprocal pronoun, as *We hurt ourselves by vain rage*.

Himself, *itself*, *themselves*, is supposed by Wallis to be put by corruption, for *his self*, *it' self*, *their selves*; so that *self* is always a substantive. This seems justly observed, for we say, *He came himself*; *Himself shall do this*; where *himself* cannot be an accusative.

Of the VERB.

English verbs are active, as *I love*; or neuter, as *I languish*. The neuters are formed like the actives.

Most verbs signifying *action*, may likewise signify *condition* or *habit*, and become *neuters*, as *I love*, I am in love; *I strike*, I am now striking.

Verbs have only two tenses inflected in their terminations, the present, and simple preterite; the other tenses are compounded of the auxiliary verbs *have*, *shall*, *will*, *let*, *may*, *can*, and the infinitive of the active or neuter verb.

The passive voice is formed by joining the participle preterite to the substantive verb, as *I am loved*.

To Have. Indicative Mood.

Present Tense.

Sing. *I* have, *thou* hast, *he* hath *or* has;
Plur. *We* have, *ye* have, *they* have.

Has is a termination corrupted from *hath*, but now more frequently used both in verse and prose.

Simple Preterite.

Sing. *I* had, *thou* hadst, *he* had;
Plur. *We* had, *ye* had, *they* had.

Compound Preterite.

Sing. *I* have had, *thou* hast had, *he* has had;
Plur. *We* have have had, *ye* have had, *they* have had.

Preterpluperfect.

Preterpluperfect.
Sing. *I* had had, *thou* hadſt had, *he* had had;
Plur. *We* had had, *ye* had had, *they* had had.

Future.
Sing. *I* ſhall have, *thou* ſhalt have, *he* ſhall have;
Plur. *We* ſhall have, *ye* ſhall have, *they* ſhall have.

Second Future.
Sing. *I* will have, *thou* wilt have, *he* will have;
Plur. *We* will have, *ye* will have, *they* will have.

By reading theſe future tenſes may be obſerved the variations of *ſhall* and *will*.

Imperative Mood.
Sing. Have *or* have *thou*, let *him* have;
Plur. Let *us* have, have *or* have *ye*, let *them* have.

Conjunctive Mood.

Preſent.
Sing. *I* have, *thou* have, *he* have;
Plur. *We* have, *ye* have, *they* have.

Preterite ſimple as in the Indicative.

Preterite compound.
Sing. *I* have had, *they* have had, *he* have had;
Plur. *We* have had, *ye* have had, *they* have had.

Future.
Sing. *I* ſhall have, as in the Indicative.

Second Future.
Sing. *I* ſhall have had, *thou* ſhalt have had, *he* ſhall have had;
Plur. *We* ſhall have had, *ye* ſhall have had, *they* ſhall have had.

Potential.

The potential form of ſpeaking is expreſſed by *may*, *can*, in the preſent; and *might*, *could*, or *ſhould*, in the preterite, joined with the infinitive mood of the verb.

Preſent.
Sing. *I* may have, *thou* mayſt have, *he* may have;
Plur. *We* may have, *ye* may have, *they* may have.

Preterite.
Sing. *I* might have, *thou* mightſt have, *he* might have;
Plur. *We* might have, *ye* might have, *they* might have.

Preſent.
Sing. *I* can have, *thou* canſt have, *he* can have;
Plur. *We* can have, *ye* can have, *they* can have.

Preterite.
Sing. *I* could have, *thou* couldſt have, *he* could have;
Plur. *We* could have, *ye* could have, *they* could have.

In like manner *ſhould* is united to the verb.

There is likewiſe a double *Preterite.*
Sing. *I* ſhould have had, *thou* ſhouldſt have had, *he* ſhould have had;
Plur. *We* ſhould have had, *ye* ſhould have had, *they* ſhould have had.

In like manner we uſe, *I might* have had; *I could* have had, &c.

Infinitive Mood.
Preſent. To have. *Preterite.* To have had.
Participle preſent. Having. *Participle preter.* Had.

Verb Active. *To Love.*

Indicative. *Preſent.*
Sing. *I* love, *thou* loveſt, *he* loveth *or* loves;
Plur. *We* love, *ye* love, *they* love.

Preterite ſimple.
Sing. *I* loved, *thou* lovedſt, *he* loved;
Plur. *We* loved, *ye* loved, *they* loved.
Preterperfect compared. *I* have loved, &c.
Preterpluperfect. *I* had loved, &c.
Future. *I* ſhall love, &c. *I* will love, &c.

Imperative.
Sing. Love *or* love *thou*, let *him* love;
Plur. Let *us* love, love *or* love *ye*, let *them* love.

Conjunctive. *Preſent,*
Sing. *I* love, *thou* love, *he* love;
Plur. *We* love, *ye* love, *they* love.
Preterite ſimple, as in the Indicative.
Preterite compound. *I* have loved, &c.

1

Future. *I* ſhall love, &c.
Second Future. I ſhall have loved, &c.

Potential.
Preſent. *I* may *or* can love, &c.
Preterite. *I* might, could, *or* ſhould love, &c.
Double Pret. *I* might, could, *or* ſhould have loved, &c.

Infinitive.
Preſent. To love. *Preterite.* To have loved.
Participle preſent. Loving. *Participle paſt.* Loved.

The paſſive is formed by the addition of the participle preterite, to the different tenſes of the verb *to be*, which muſt therefore be here exhibited.

Indicative. *Preſent.*
Sing. *I* am, *thou* art, *he* is;
Plur. *We* are *or* be, *ye* are *or* be, *they* are *or* be.

The plural *be* is now little in uſe.

Preterite.
Sing. *I* was, *thou* waſt *or* wert, *he* was;
Plur. *We* were, *ye* were, *they* were.

Wert is properly of the conjunctive mood, and ought not to be uſed in the indicative.

Preterite compound. *I* have been, &c.
Preterpluperfect. *I* had been, &c.
Future. *I* ſhall or will be, &c.

Imperative.
Sing. Be *thou*; let *him* be;
Plur. Let *us* be; be *ye*; let *them* be.

Conjunctive. *Preſent.*
Sing. *I* be, *thou* beeſt, *he* be;
Plur. *We* be, *ye* be, *they* be.

Preterite.
Sing. *I* were, *thou* wert, *he* were;
Plur. *We* were, *ye* were, *they* were.
Preterite compound. *I* have been, &c.
Future. *I* ſhall have been, &c.

Potential.
I may *or* can; would, could, *or* ſhould be; could, would, *or* ſhould have been, &c.

Infinitive.
Preſent. To be. *Preterite.* To have been.
Participle preſ. Being. *Participle preter.* Having been.

Paſſive Voice. Indicative Mood.
I am loved, &c. *I* was loved, &c. *I* have been loved, &c.

Conjunctive Mood.
If *I* be loved, &c. If *I* were loved, &c. If *I* ſhall have been loved, &c.

Potential Mood.
I may *or* can be loved, &c. *I* might, could, *or* ſhould be loved, &c. *I* might, could, *or* ſhould have been loved, &c.

Infinitive.
Preſent. To be loved. *Preterite.* To have been loved.
Participle. Loved.

There is another form of Engliſh verbs, in which the infinitive mood is joined to the verb *do* in its various inflections, which are therefore to be learned in this place.

To Do.

Indicative. *Preſent.*
Sing. *I* do, *thou* doſt, *he* doth;
Plur. *We* do, *ye* do, *they* do.

Preterite.
Sing. *I* did, *thou* didſt, *he* did;
Plur. *We* did, *ye* did, *they* did.
Preterite, &c. *I* have done, &c. *I* had done, &c.
Future. *I* ſhall *or* will do, &c.

Imperative.
Sing. Do *thou*, let *him* do;
Plur. Let *us* do, do *ye*, let them do.

Conjunctive. *Preſent.*
Sing. *I* do, *thou* do, *he* do;
Plur. *We* do, *ye* do, *they* do.

The reſt are as in the indicative.

Infinitive. To do; to have done.
Participle preſ. Doing, *Participle preter.* Done.

I do is ſometimes uſed ſuperfluouſly, as, *I* do *love*, *I* did *love*; ſimply for *I love*, or *I loved*; but this is conſidered as a vitious mode of ſpeech.

It is ſometimes uſed emphatically; as,

I do *love thee, and when I love thee not,*
Chaos is come again. Shakeſpeare.

It is frequently joined with a negative; as, *I like her, but I* do *not love her*; *I wiſhed him ſucceſs, but* did *not help him.*

The Imperative prohibitory is ſeldom applied in the ſecond perſon, at leaſt in proſe, without the word *do*; as, *Stop him, but* do *not hurt him*; *Praiſe beauty, but* do *not dote on it.*

Its chief uſe is in interrogative forms of ſpeech, in which it is uſed through all the perſons; as, Do *I live?* Doſt *thou ſtrike me?* Do *they rebel?* Did *I complain?* Didſt *thou love her?* Did *ſhe die?* So likewiſe in negative interrogations; Do *I not yet grieve?* Did *ſhe not die?*

Do is thus uſed only in the ſimple tenſes.

There is another manner of conjugating neuter verbs, which, when it is uſed, may not improperly denominate them *neuter paſſives*, as they are inflected according to the paſſive form by the help of the verb ſuſtantive *to be.* They anſwer nearly to the reciprocal verbs in French; as,

I am riſen, ſurrexi, *Latin*; Je me ſuis levé, *French.*
I was walked out, exieram; Je m'etois promené.

In like manner we commonly expreſs the preſent tenſe; as, I am going, *eo.* I am grieving, *doleo.* She is dying, *illa moritur.* The tempeſt is raging, *furit procella.* I am purſuing an enemy, *hoſtem inſequor.* So the other tenſes, as, *We were walking*, ἐτυγχάνομεν περιπατοῦντες, *I have been walking, I had been walking, I ſhall* or *will be walking.*

There is another manner of uſing the active participle, which gives it a paſſive ſignification; as, The grammar is now printing, *grammatica jam nunc chartis imprimitur.* The braſs is forging, *æra excuduntur.* This is, in my opinion, a vitious expreſſion, probably corrupted from a phraſe more pure, but now ſomewhat obſolete: *The book is* a *printing, The braſs is* a *forging*; *a* being properly *at*, and *printing* and *forging* verbal nouns ſignifying action, according to the analogy of this language.

The indicative and conjunctive moods are by modern writers frequently confounded, or rather the conjunctive is wholly neglected, when ſome convenience of verſification does not invite its revival. It is uſed among the purer writers after *if, though, ere, before, whether, except, unleſs, whatſoever, whomſoever*, and words of wiſhing; as, *Doubtleſs thou art our father*, though *Abraham* be *ignorant of us, and Iſrael* acknowledge *us not.*

Of IRREGULAR VERBS.

The Engliſh verbs were divided by Ben Johnſon into four conjugations, without any reaſon ariſing from the nature of the language, which has properly but one conjugation, ſuch as has been exemplified; from which all deviations are to be conſidered as anomalies, which are indeed in our monoſyllable Saxon verbs and the verbs derived from them very frequent; but almoſt all the verbs which have been adopted from other languages, follow the regular form.

Our verbs are obſerved by Dr. Wallis to be irregular only in the formation of the preterite, and its participle. Indeed, in the ſcantineſs of our conjugations, there is ſcarcely any other place for irregularity.

The firſt irregularity, is a ſlight deviation from the regular form, by rapid utterance or poetical contraction: the laſt ſyllable *ed* is often joined with the former by ſuppreſſion of *e*; as, *lov'd* for *loved*; after *c, ch, ſh, f, k, x*, and after the conſonants *ſ, th*, when more ſtrongly pronounced, and ſometimes after *m, n, r*, if preceded by a ſhort vowel, *t* is uſed in pronunciation, but very ſeldom in writing, rather than *d*; as *plac't, ſnatch't, fiſh't, wak't, dwel't, ſmel't*; for *plac'd ſnatch'd, fiſh'd, wak'd, dwel'd, ſmel'd*; or *placed, ſnatched, fiſhed, waked, dwelled, ſmelled.*

Thoſe words which terminate in *l* or *ll*, or *p*, make their preterite in *t*, even in ſolemn language; as *crept, felt, dwelt*; ſometimes after *x*, *ed* is changed into *t*; as, *vext*: this is not conſtant.

A long vowel is often changed into a ſhort one; thus, *kept, ſlept, wept, crept, ſwept*; from the verbs, to *keep*, to *ſleep*, to *weep*, to *creep*, to *ſweep.*

Where *d* or *t* go before, the additional letter *d* or *t*, in this contracted form, coaleſce into one letter with the radical *d* or *t*: if *t* were the radical, they coaleſce into *t*; but if *d* were the radical, then into *d* or *t*, as the one or the other letter may be more eaſily pronounced: as, *read, led, ſpread, ſhed, ſhred, bid, hid, chid, fed, bled, bred, ſped, ſtrid, rid*; from the verbs, to *read*, to *lead*, to *ſpread*, to *ſhed*, to *ſhread*, to *bid*, to *hide*, to *chide*, to *feed*, to *bleed*, to *breed*, to *ſpeed*, to *ſtride*, to *ſlide*, to *ride.* And thus, *caſt, hurt, coſt, burſt, eat, beat, ſweat, ſit, quit, ſmit, writ, bit, hit, met, ſhot*; from the verbs, to *caſt*, to *hurt*, to *coſt*, to *burſt*, to *eat*, to *beat*, to *ſweat*, to *ſit*, to *quit*, to *ſmite*, to *write*, to *bite*, to *hit*, to *meet*, to *ſhoot.* And in like manner, *lent, ſent, rent, girt*; from the verbs, to *lend*, to *ſend*, to *rend*, to *gird.*

The participle preterite or paſſive is often formed in *en*, inſtead of *ed*; as *been, taken, given, ſlain, known*, from the verbs to *be*, to *take*, to *give*, to *ſlay*, to *know.*

Many words have two or more participles, as not only *written, bitten, eaten, beaten, hidden, chidden, ſhotten, choſen, broken*; but likewiſe *writ, bit, eat, beat, hid, chid, ſhot, choſe, broke*, are promiſcuouſly uſed in the participle, from the verbs to *write*, to *bite*, to *eat*, to *beat*, to *hide*, to *chide*, to *ſhoot*, to *chooſe*, to *break*, and many ſuch like.

In the ſame manner *ſown, ſhewn, hewn, mown, loaden, laden*, as well as *ſow'd, ſhew'd, hew'd, mow'd, loaded, laded*, from the verbs to *ſow*, to *ſhew*, to *hew*, to *mow*, to *load*, or *lade.*

Concerning theſe double participles it is difficult to give any rule; but he ſhall ſeldom err who remembers, that when a verb has a participle diſtinct from its preterite, as *write, wrote, written*, that diſtinct participle is more proper and elegant, as *The book is* written, is better than *The book is* wrote, though *wrote* may be uſed in poetry.

There are other anomalies in the preterite.

1. *Win, ſpin, begin, ſwim, ſtrike, ſtick, ſing, ſting, fling, ring, wring, ſpring, ſwing, drink, ſink, ſhrink, ſtink, come, run, find, bind, grind, wind*, both in the preterite imperfect and participle paſſive, give *won, ſpun, begun, ſwum, ſtruck, ſtuck, ſung, ſtung, flung, rung, wrung, ſprung, ſwung, drunk, ſunk, ſhrunk, hung, come, run, found, bound, ground, wound.* And moſt of them are alſo formed in the preterite by *a*, as *began, rang, ſang, ſprang, drank, came, ran*, and ſome others; but moſt of theſe are now obſolete. Some in the participle paſſive likewiſe take *en*, as *ſtricken, ſtrucken, drunken, bounden.*

2. *Fight, teach, reach, ſeek, beſeech, catch, buy, bring, think, work*, make *fought, taught, raught, ſought, beſought, caught, bought, brought, thought, wrought.*

But a great many of theſe retain likewiſe the regular form, as *teached, reached, beſeeched, catched, worked.*

3. *Take, ſhake, forſake, wake, awake, ſtand, break, ſpeak, bear, ſhear, ſwear, tear, weave, cleave, ſtrive, thrive, drive, ſhine, riſe, ariſe, ſmite, write, bide, abide, ride, chooſe, chuſe, tread, get, beget, forget, ſeethe*, make in both preterite and participle *took, forſook, woke, awoke, ſtood, broke, ſpoke, bore, ſhore, ſwore, tore, wore, wove, clove, ſtrove, throve, drove, ſhone, roſe, aroſe, ſmote, wrote, bode, abode, rode, choſe, trode, got, begot, forgot, ſod.* But we ſay likewiſe, *thrive, riſe, ſmit, writ, abid, rid.* In the preterite ſome are likewiſe formed by *a*, as *brake, ſpake, bare, ſhare, ſware, tare, ware, clave, gat, begat, forgat*, and perhaps ſome others, but more rarely. In the participle paſſive are many of them formed by *en*, as *taken, ſhaken, forſaken, broken, ſpoken, born, ſhorn, ſworn, torn, worn, woven, cloven, thriven, driven, riſen, ſmitten, ridden, choſen, trodden, gotten, begotten, forgotten, ſodden.* And many do likewiſe retain the analogy in both, as *waked, awaked, ſheared, weaved, leaved, abided, ſeethed.*

4. *Give, bid, ſit*, make in the preterite *gave, bade, ſate*; in the participle paſſive, *given, bidden, ſitten*; but in both *bid.*

5. *Draw, know, grow, throw, blow, crow* like a cock, *fly, ſlay, ſee, ly*, make their preterite *drew, knew, grew, threw, blew, crew, flew, ſlew, ſaw, lay*; their participles paſſive by *n*, *drawn, known, ſnown, grown, thrown, blown, flown, ſlain, ſeen, lien, lain.* Yet from *flee* is made *fled*; from *go*, *went*, from the old *wend*, and the participle *gone.*

Of DERIVATION.

That the Engliſh language may be more eaſily underſtood, it is neceſſary to enquire how its derivative words are deduced from their primitives, and how the primitives are borrowed from other languages. In this enquiry I ſhall ſometimes copy Dr. Wallis, and ſometimes endeavour to ſupply his defects, and rectify his errours.

Nouns are derived from verbs.

The thing implied in the verb as done or produced, is commonly either the preſent of the verb; as, to love, *love*; to fright, a *fright*; to fight, a *fight*; or the preterite of the verb, as, to ſtrike, I ſtrick *or* ſtrook, a *ſtroke*.

The action is the ſame with the participle preſent, as *loving*, *frighting*, *fighting*, *ſtriking*.

The agent, or perſon acting, is denoted by the ſyllable *er* added to the verb, as *lover*, *frighter*, *ſtriker*.

Subſtantives, adjectives, and ſometimes other parts of ſpeech, are changed into verbs: in which caſe the vowel is often lengthened, or the conſonant ſoftened; as, a houſe, *to houſe*; braſs, *to braze*; glaſs, *to glaze*; graſs, *to graze*; price, *to prize*; breath, *to breathe*; a fiſh, *to fiſh*; oyl, *to oyl*; further, *to further*; forward, *to forward*; hinder, *to hinder*.

Sometimes the termination *en* is added, eſpecially to adjectives; as, haſte, *to haſten*; length, *to lengthen*; ſtrength, *to ſtrengthen*; ſhort, *to ſhorten*; faſt, *to faſten*; white, *to whiten*; black, *to blacken*; hard, *to harden*; ſoft, *to ſoften*.

From ſubſtantives are formed adjectives of plenty, by adding the termination *y*; as, a louſe, *louſy*; wealth, *wealthy*; health, *healthy*; might, *mighty*; worth, *worthy*; wit, *witty*; luſt, *luſty*; water, *watery*; earth, *earthy*; wood, a wood, *woody*; air, *airy*; a heart, *hearty*; a hand, *handy*.

From ſubſtantives are formed adjectives of plenty, by adding the termination *ful*, denoting abundance; as, joy, *joyful*; fruit, *fruitful*; youth, *youthful*; care, *careful*; uſe, *uſeful*; delight, *delightful*; plenty, *plentiful*; help, *helpful*.

Sometimes, in almoſt the ſame ſenſe, but with ſome kind of diminution thereof, the termination *ſome* is added, denoting *ſomething*, or *in ſome degree*; as, delight, *delightſome*; game, *gameſome*; irk, *irkſome*; burden, *burdenſome*; trouble, *troubleſome*; light, *lightſome*; hand, *handſome*; alone, *loneſome*; toil, *toilſome*.

On the contrary, the termination *leſs* added to ſubſtantives, makes adjectives ſignifying want; as *worthleſs*, *witleſs*, *heartleſs*, *joyleſs*, *careleſs*, *helpleſs*. Thus comfort, *comfortleſs*; ſap, *ſapleſs*.

Privation or contrariety is very often denoted by the particle *un* prefixed to many adjectives, or *in* before words derived from the Latin; as, pleaſant, *unpleaſant*; wiſe, *unwiſe*; profitable, *unprofitable*; patient, *impatient*. Thus *unworthy*, *unhealthy*, *unfruitful*, *unuſeful*, and many more.

The original Engliſh privative is *un*; but as we often borrow from the Latin, or its deſcendants, words already ſignifying privation, as *inefficacious*, *impious*, *indiſcreet*, the inſeparable particles *un* and *in* have fallen into confuſion, from which it is not eaſy to diſentangle them.

Un is prefixed to all words originally Engliſh, as *untrue*, *untruth*, *untaught*, *unhandſome*.

Un is prefixed to all participles made privative adjectives, as *unfeeling*, *unaſſiſting*, *unaided*, *undelighted*, *unendeared*.

Un ought never to be prefixed to a participle preſent, to mark a forbearance of action, as *unſighing*; but a privation of habit, as *unpitying*.

Un is prefixed to moſt ſubſtantives which have an Engliſh termination, as *unfertileneſs*, *unperfectneſs*, which, if they have borrowed terminations, take *in* or *im*, as *infertility*, *imperfection*; *uncivil*, *incivility*; *unactive*, *inactivity*.

In borrowing adjectives, if we receive them already compounded, it is uſual to retain the particle prefixed, as *indecency*, *inelegant*, *improper*; but if we borrow the adjective, and add the privative particle, we commonly prefix *un*, as *unpolite*, *ungallant*.

The prepoſitive particles *dis* and *mis*, derived from the *des* and *mes* of the French, ſignify almoſt the ſame as *un*; yet *dis* rather imports contrariety than privation, ſince it anſwers to the Latin prepoſition *de*. *Mis* inſinuates ſome error, and for the moſt part may be rendered by the Latin words *male* or *perperam*. To like, *to diſlike*; honour, *diſhonour*; to honour, to grace, *to diſhonour*, *to diſgrace*; to deign, *to diſdeign*; chance, hap, *miſchance*, *miſhap*; to take, *to miſtake*; deed, *miſdeed*; to uſe, *to miſuſe*; to employ, *to miſemploy*; to apply, *to miſapply*.

Words derived from Latin written with *de* or *dis* retain the ſame ſignification, as *diſtinguiſh*, diſtinguo; *detract*, detraho; *defame*, defamo; *detain*, detineo.

The termination *ly* added to ſubſtantives, and ſometimes to adjectives, forms adjectives that import ſome kind of ſimilitude or agreement, being formed by contraction of *lick* or *like*.

A giant, *giantly*, *giantlike*; earth, *earthly*; heaven, *heavenly*; world, *worldly*; God, *godly*; good, *goodly*.

The ſame termination *ly* added to adjectives, forms adverbs of like ſignification; as, beautiful, *beautifully*; ſweet, *ſweetly*; that is, *in a beautiful manner*; *with ſome degree of ſweetneſs*.

The termination *iſh* added to adjectives, imports diminution; and added to ſubſtantives, imports ſimilitude or tendency to a character; as, green, *greeniſh*; white, *whitiſh*; ſoft, *ſoftiſh*; a thief, *thieviſh*; a wolf, *wolviſh*; a child, *childiſh*.

We have forms of diminutives in ſubſtantives, though not frequent; as, a hill, *a hillock*; a cock, *a cockrel*; a pike, *pickrel*; this is a French termination: a gooſe, *a goſling*; this is a German termination: a lamb, *a lambkin*; a chick, *a chicken*; a man, *a manikin*; a pipe, *a pipkin*; and thus *Halkin*, whence the patronimick *Hawkins*, *Wilkin*, *Thomkin*, and others.

Yet ſtill there is another form of diminution among the Engliſh, by leſſening the ſound itſelf, eſpecially of vowels; as there is a form of augmenting them by enlarging, or even lengthening it; and that ſometimes not ſo much by change of the letters, as of their pronunciation; as, *ſup*, *ſip*, *ſoop*, *ſop*, *ſippet*, where, beſides the extenuation of the vowel, there is added the French termination *et*; *top*, *tip*; *ſpit*, *ſpout*; *babe*, *baby*, *booby*, βȣ̃παις; *great* pronounced long, eſpecially if with a ſtronger ſound, *grea-t*; *little* pronounced long, *lee-tle*; *ting*, *tang*, *tong*, imports a ſucceſſion of ſmaller and then greater ſounds; and ſo in *jingle*, *jangle*, *tingle*, *tangle*, and many other made words.

Much however of this is arbitrary and fanciful, depending wholly on oral utterance, and therefore ſcarcely worthy the notice of Wallis.

Of concrete adjectives are made abſtract ſubſtantives, by adding the termination *neſs*, and a few in *hood* or *head*, noting character or qualities; as, white, *whiteneſs*; hard, *hardneſs*; great, *greatneſs*; ſkilful, *ſkilfulneſs*, *unſkilfulneſs*; *godhead*, *manhood*, *maidenhead*, *widowhood*, *knighthood*, *prieſthood*, *likelihood*, *falſehood*.

There are other abſtracts, partly derived from adjectives, and partly from verbs, which are formed by the addition of the termination *th*, a ſmall change being ſometimes made; as, long, *length*; ſtrong, *ſtrength*; broad, wide, *breadth*, *width*; deep, *depth*; true, *truth*; warm, *warmth*; dear, *dearth*; ſlow, *ſlowth*; merry, *mirth*; heal, *health*; well, weal, *wealth*; dry, *droughth*; young, *youth*; and ſo moon, *month*.

Like theſe are ſome words derived from verbs; dy, *death*; till, *tilth*; grow, *growth*; mow, later *mowth*, after *mow'th*; commonly ſpoken and written later *math*, after *math*; ſteal, *ſtealth*; bear, *birth*; rue, *ruth*; and probably *earth* from to *ear* or *plow*; fly, *flight*; weigh, *weight*; fray, *fright*; to draw, *draught*.

Theſe ſhould rather be written *flighth*, *frighth*, only that cuſtom prevails, leſt *h* ſhould be twice repeated.

The ſame form retain *faith*, *ſpight*, *wreathe*, *wrath*, *broth*, *froth*, *breath*, *ſooth*, *worth*, *light*, *wight*, and the like, whoſe primitives are either entirely obſolete, or ſeldom occur. Perhaps they are derived from *fey* or *foy*, *ſpry*, *wry*, *wreak*, *brew*, *mow*, *fry*, *bray*, *ſay*, *work*.

Some ending in *ſhip* imply an office, employment, or condition; as, *kingſhip*, *wardſhip*, *guardianſhip*, *partnerſhip*, *ſtewardſhip* *headſhip*, *lordſhip*.

Thus *worſhip*, that is, *worthſhip*; whence *worſhipful*, *to worſhip*.

Some few ending in *dom*, *rick*, *wick*, do eſpecially denote dominion, at leaſt ſtate or condition; as *kingdom*, *dukedom*, *earldom*, *princedom*, *popedom*, *chriſtendom*, *freedom*, *wiſdom*, *whoredom*, *biſhoprick*, *bailywick*.

Ment and *age* are plainly French terminations, and are of the ſame import with us as among them, ſcarcely ever occuring, except in words derived from the French, as *commandment*, *uſage*.

There

There are in English often long trains of words allied by their meaning and derivation; as, *to beat, a bat, batoon, a battle, a beetle, a battle-door, to batter, butter*, a kind of glutinous composition for food. All these are of similar signification, and perhaps derived from the Latin *batuo*. Thus *take, touch, tickle, tack, tackle*; all imply a local conjunction, from the Latin *tango, tetigi, tactum*.

From *two* are formed *twain, twice, twenty, twelve, twins, twine, twist, twirl, twig, twitch, twinge, between, betwixt, twilight, twibil*.

The following remarks, extracted from Wallis, are ingenious, but of more subtlety than solidity, and such as perhaps might in every language be enlarged without end.

Sn usually implies the *nose*, and what relates to it. From the Latin *nasus* are derived the French *nes* and the English *nose*; and *nesse*, a promontory, as projecting like a nose. But as if from the consonants *ns* taken from *nasus*, and transposed, that they may the better correspond, *sn* denotes *nasus*; and thence are derived many words that relate to the nose, as *snout, sneeze, snore, snort, snear, snicker, snot, snevil, snite, snuff, snuffle, snaffle, snarle, snudge*.

There is another *sn*, which may perhaps be derived from the Latin *sinuo*, as *snake, sneak, snail, snare*; so likewise *snap* and *snatch, snib, snub*.

Bl implies a *blast*; as, *blow, blast, to blast, to blight*, and, metaphorically, *to blast* one's reputation; *bleat, bleak*, a *bleak* place, to look *bleak* or weather-beaten, *bleak, blay, bleach, bluster, blurt, blister, blab, bladder, bleb, blister, blabber-lip't, blubber-cheek't, bloted, blote-herrings, blast, blaze, to blow*, that is, *blossom, bloom*; and perhaps *blood* and *blush*.

In the native words of our tongue is to be found a great agreement between the letters and the thing signified; and therefore the sounds of letters smaller, sharper, louder, closer, softer, stronger, clearer, more obscure, and more stridulous, do very often intimate the like effects in the things signified.

Thus words that begin with *str* intimate the force and effect of the thing signified, as if probably derived from ςρώννυμι, or *strenuus*; as, *strong, strength, strew, strike, streake, stroke, stripe, strive, strife, struggle, strout, strut, stretch, strait, strict, streight*, that is, narrow, *distrain, stress, distress, string, strap, stream, streamer, strand, strip, stray, struggle, strange, stride, straddle*.

St in like manner implies strength, but in a less degree, so much only as is sufficient to preserve what has been already communicated, rather than acquire any new degree; as if it were derived from the Latin *sto*: for example, *stand, stay*, that is, to remain, or to prop; *staff, stay*, that is, to oppose; *stop, to stuff, stifle, to stay*, that is, to stop; *a stay*, that is, an obstacle; *stick, stut, stutter, stammer, stagger, stickle, stick, stake*, a sharp pale, and any thing deposited at play; *stock, stem, sting, to sting, stink, stitch, stud, stanchion, stub, stubble, to stub* up, *stump*, whence *stumble, stalk, to stalk, step, to stamp* with the feet, whence *to stamp*, that is, to make an impression and a stamp; *stow, to stow, to bestow, steward* or *stoward, stead, steady, steadfast, stable, a stable, a stall, to stall, stool, stall, still, stall, stallage, stall, stage, still* adj. and *still* adv. *stale, stout, sturdy, steed, stoat, stallion, stiff, stark-dead, to starve* with hunger or cold; *stone, steel, stern, stanch, to stanch* blood, *to stare, steep, steeple, stair, standard*, a stated measure, *stately*. In all these, and perhaps some others, *st* denotes something firm and fixed.

Thr implies a more violent degree of motion, as *throw, thrust, throng, throb, through, threat, threaten, thrall, throws*.

Wr imply some sort of obliquity or distortion, as *wry, to wreathe, wrest, wrestle, wring, wrong, wrinch, wrench, wrangle, wrinkle, wrath, wreak, wrack, wretch, wrist, wrap*.

Sw imply a silent agitation, or a softer kind of lateral motion; as *sway, swag, to sway, swagger, swerve, sweat, sweep, swill, swim, swing, swift, sweet, switch, swinge*.

Nor is there much difference of *sm* in *smoothe, smug, smile, smirk, smite*, which signifies the same as to *strike*, but is a softer word; *small, smell, smack, smother, smart*, a *smart* blow properly signifies such a kind of stroke as with an originally silent motion implied in *sm*, proceeds to a quick violence, denoted by *ar* suddenly ended, as is shewn by *t*.

Cl denote a kind of adhesion or tenacity, as in *cleave, clay, cling, climb, clamber, clammy, clasp, to clasp, to clip, to clinch, cloak, clog, close, to close, a clod, a clot*, as a *clot* of blood, *clouted* cream, *a clutter, a cluster*.

Sp implies a kind of dissipation or expansion, especially a quick one, particularly if there be an *r*, as if it were from *spargo* or *separo*: for example, *spread, spring, sprig, sprout, sprinkle, split, splinter, spill, spit, sputter, spatter*.

Sl denotes a kind of silent fall, or a less observable motion; as in *slime, slide, slip, slipper, sly, sleight, slit, slow, slack, slight, sling, slap*.

And so likewise *ash*, in *crash, rash, gash, flash, clash, lash, slash, plash, trash*, indicates something acting more nimbly and sharply. But *ush*, in *crush, rush, gush, flush, blush, brush, hush, push*, implies something as acting more obtusely and dully. Yet in both there is indicated a swift and sudden motion, not instantaneous, but gradual, by the continued sound *sh*.

Thus in *fling, sling, ding, swing, cling, sing, wring, sting*, the tingling of the termination *ng*, and the sharpness of the vowel *i*, imply the continuation of a very slender motion or tremor, at length indeed vanishing, but not suddenly interrupted. But in *tink, wink, sink, clink, chink, think*, that end in a mute consonant, there is also indicated a sudden ending.

If there be an *l*, as in *jingle, tingle, tinkle, mingle, sprinkle, twinkle*, there is implied a frequency, or iteration of small acts. And the same frequency of acts, but less subtile by reason of the clearer vowel *a*, is indicated in *jangle, tangle, spangle, mangle, wrangle, brangle, dangle*; as also in *mumble, grumble, jumble, tumble, stumble, rumble, crumble, fumble*. But at the same time the close *u* implies something obscure or obtunded; and a congeries of consonants *mbl*, denotes a confused kind of rolling or tumbling, as in *ramble, scamble, scramble, wamble, amble*; but in these there is something acute.

In *nimble*, the acuteness of the vowel denotes celerity. In *sparkle, sp* denotes dissipation, *ar* an acute crackling, *k* a sudden interruption, *l* a frequent iteration; and in like manner in *sprinkle*, unless *in* may imply the subtility of the dissipated guttules. *Thick* and *thin* differ, in that the former ends with an obtuse consonant, and the later with an acute.

In like manner, in *squeek, squeak, squeal, squall, braul, wraul, yaul, spaul, screek, shreek, shril, sharp, shrivel, wrinkle, crack, crash, clash, gnash, plash, crush, hush, hisse, fisse, whist, soft, jarr, hurl, curl, whirl, buz, bussle, spindle, dwindle, twine, twist*, and in many more, we may observe the agreement of such sort of sounds with the things signified: and this so frequently happens, that scarce any language which I know can be compared with ours. So that one monosyllable word, of which kind are almost all ours, emphatically expresses what in other languages can scarce be explained but by compounds, or decompounds, or sometimes a tedious circumlocution.

We have many words borrowed from the Latin; but the greatest part of them were communicated by the intervention of the French; as *grace, face, elegant, elegance, resemble*.

Some verbs, which seem borrowed from the Latin, are formed from the present tense, and some from the supines.

From the present are formed *spend, expend*, expendo; *conduce*, conduco; *despise*, despicio; *approve*, approbo; *conceive*, concipio.

From the supines, *supplicate*, supplico; *demonstrate*, demonstro; *dispose*, dispono; *expatiate*, expatior; *suppress*, supprimo; *exempt*, eximo.

Nothing is more apparent, than that Wallis goes too far in quest of originals. Many of these which seem selected as immediate descendents from the Latin, are apparently French, as *conceive, approve, expose, exempt*.

Some words purely French, not derived from the Latin, we have transferred into our language; as, *garden, garter, buckler, to advance, to cry, to plead*, from the French *jardin, jartier, bouclier, avancer, cryer, plaider*; though indeed, even of these, part is of Latin original.

As to many words which we have in common with the Germans, it is doubtful whether the old Teutons borrowed them from the Latins, or the Latins from the Teutons, or both had them from some common original; as, *wine*, vinum; *wind*, ventus; *went*, veni; *way*, via; *wall*, vallum; *wallow*, volvo; *wool*, vellus; *will*, volo; *worm*, vermis; *worth*, virtus; *wasp*, vespa; *day*, dies; *draw*, traho; *tame*, domo, δαμάω; *yoke*, jugum, ζεῦγος; *over, upper*, super, ὑπερ; *am*, sum, ειμι; *break*, frango; *fly*, volo; *blow*, fio. I make no doubt but the Teutonick is more ancient than the Latin: and it is no less certain, that the Latin, which borrowed a great number of words, not only from the Greek, especially the Æolick, but from other neighbouring languages, as the Oscan and others, which have long become obsolete, received not a few from the Teutonick. It is certain, that the English, German, and other Teutonick languages, retained some derived fom the Greek, which the Latin has not; as *path, pfad, ax, achs, mit, ford, pfurd, daughter, tochter, mickle, mingle, moon, sear, grave, graff, to grave, to scrape, whole, heal*, from πάγος, ἀξίνη, μέλα, πορθμος, μεγάλος, μιγνύω, μήνη, ξηρός, γράφω, ὅλος, ειλέω. Since they received these immediately from the Greeks, without the intervention of the Latin language, why may not other words be derived immediately from the same fountain, though they be likewise found among the Latins.

Our ancestors were studious to form borrowed words, however long, into monosyllables; and not only cut off the formative terminations, but cropped the first syllable, especially in words beginning with a vowel; and rejected not only vowels in the middle, but likewise consonants of a weaker sound, retaining the stronger, which seem the bones of words, or changing them for others of the same organ, in order that the sound might become the softer; but especially transposing their order, that they might the more readily be pronounced without the intermediate vowels. For example, in expendo, *spend*; exemplum, *sample*; excipio, *scape*; extraneus, *strange*; extractum, *stretch'd*; excrucio, *to screw*; exscorio, *to scour*; excorio, *to scourge*; excortico, *to scratch*; and others beginning with *ex*: as also, emendo, *to mend*; episcopus, *bishop*; in Danish *Bisp*; epistola, *pistle*; hospitale, *spittle*; Hispania, *Spain*; historia, *story*.

Many of these etymologies are doubtful, and some evidently mistaken.

The following are somewhat harder, *Alexander, Sander*; *Elisabetha, Betty*; apis, *bee*; aper, *bar*; *p* passing into *b*, as in *bishop*; and by cutting

ENGLISH TONGUE.

cutting off *a* from the beginning, which is reſtored in the middle; but for the old *bar* or *bare*, we now ſay *boar*; as for *lang*, *long*; for *bain*, *bane*; for *ſtane*, *ſtone*; aprugna, *brawn*, *p* being changed into *b*, and *a* tranſpoſed, as in *aper*, and *g* changed into *w*, as in pignus, *pawn*; lege, *law*; ἀλωπήξ, *fox*, cutting off the beginning, and changing *p* into *f*, as in pellis, *a fell*; pullus, *a foal*; pater, *father*; pavor, *fear*; polio, *file*; pleo, impleo, *fill*, *full*; piſcis, *fiſh*; and tranſpoſing *o* into the middle, which was taken from the beginning; apex, *a piece*; peak, *pike*; zophorus, *freeſe*; muſtum, *ſtum*; defenſio, *fence*; diſpenſator, *ſpencer*; aſculto, eſcouter, Fr. *ſcout*; exſcalpo, *ſcrape*, reſtoring *l* inſtead of *r*, and hence *ſcrap*, *ſcrable*, *ſcrawl*; exculpo, *ſcoop*; exterritus, *start*; extonitus, attonitus, *stonn'd*; ſtomachus, *maw*; offendo, *fined*; obſtipo, *stop*; audere, *dare*; cavere, *ware*, whence *a-ware*, *be-ware*, *wary*, *warn*, *warning*; for the Latin *v* conſonant formerly ſounded like our *w*, and the modern ſound of the *v* conſonant was formerly that of the letter *f*, that is, the Æolick digamma, which had the ſound of φ, and the modern ſound of the letter *f* was that of the Greek φ or *ph*; ulcus, ulcere, *ulcer*, *ſore*, and hence *ſorry*, *ſorrow*, *ſorrowful*; ingenium, *engine*, *gin*; ſcalenus, *leaning*, unleſs you would rather derive it from χλίνω, whence inclino; infundibulum, *funnel*; gagates, *jett*; projectum, *to jett forth*, *a jetty*; cucullus, *a cowl*.

There are ſyncopes ſomewhat harder; from tempore, *time*; from nomine, *name*; domina, *dame*; as the French *homme*, *femme*, *nom*, from homine, fœmina, nomine. Thus pagina, *page*; ποτήριον, *pot*; κύπελλα, *cup*; cantharus, *can*; tentorium, *tent*; precor, *pray*; præda, *prey*; ſpecio, ſpeculor, *ſpy*; plico, *ply*: implico, *imply*; replico, *reply*; complico, *comply*; ſedes epiſcopalis, *ſee*.

A vowel is alſo cut off in the middle, that the number of the ſyllables may be leſſened; as, amita, *aunt*; ſpiritus, *ſpright*; debitum, *debt*; dubito, *doubt*; comes, comitis, *count*; clericus, *clerk*; quietus, *quit*, *quite*; acquieto, *to acquit*; ſeparo, *to ſpare*; ſtabilis, *stable*; ſtabulum, *stable*; pallacium, *palace*, *place*; rabula, *rail*, *rawl*, *wraul*, *brawl*, *rable*, *brable*; quæſitio, *quest*.

As alſo a conſonant, or at leaſt one of a ſofter ſound, or even a whole ſyllable; rotundus, *round*; fragilis, *frail*; ſecurus, *ſure*; regula, *rule*; tegula, *tile*; ſubtilis, *ſubtle*; nomen, *noun*; decanus, *dean*; computo, *count*; ſubitaneus, *ſuddain*, *ſoon*; ſuperare, *to ſoar*; periculum, *peril*; mirabile, *marvel*; as magnus, *main*; dignor, *deign*; tingo, *stain*; tinctum, *taint*; pingo, *paint*; prædari, *reach*.

The contractions may ſeem harder, where many of them meet, as κυριακὸς, *kyrk*, *church*; preſbyter, *priest*; ſacriſtanus, *ſexton*; frango, fregi, *break*, *breach*; fagus, φηγα, *beech*, *f* changed into *b*, and *g* into *ch*, which are letters near-a-kin; frigeſco, *freeze*; frigeſco, *freſh*, *ſc* into *ſh*, as above in *biſhop*, *fiſh*, ſo in *ſcapha*, *ſkiff*, *ſkip*, and refrigeſco, *refreſh*; but vireſco, *freſh*; phlebotomus, *fleam*; bovina, *beef*; vitulina, *veal*; ſcutifer, *ſquire*; pœnitentia, *penance*; ſanctuarium, *ſanctuary*, *ſentry*; quæſitio, *chaſe*; perquiſitio, *purchaſe*; anguilla, *eel*; inſula, *iſle*, *ile*, *iſland*, *iland*; inſuletta, *iſlet*, *ilet*; *eyght* and more contractedly *ey*, whence *Owſney*, *Ruley*, *Ely*; examinare, *to ſcan*, namely, by rejecting from the beginning and end *e* and *o*, according to the uſual manner, the remainder *xamin*, which the Saxons, who did not uſe *x*, writ *cſamen*, or *ſcamen* is contracted into *ſcan*; as from dominus, *don*; nomine, *noun*; abomino, *ban*; and indeed *apum examen* they turned into *ſciame*; for which we ſay *ſwarme*, by inſerting *r* to denote the murmuring; theſaurus, *store*; ſedile, *stool*; ὑετὸς, *wet*; ſudo, *ſweat*; gaudium, *gay*; jocus, *joy*; ſuccus, *juice*; catena, *chain*; caliga, calga; chauſe, chauſſe, Fr. *hoſe*; extinguo, *stanch*, *ſquench*, *quench*, *stint*; foras, *forth*; ſpecies, *ſpice*; recito, *read*; adjuvo, *aid*; αἰὼν, ævum, *ay*, *age*, *ever*; floccus, *lock*; excerpo, *ſcrape*, *ſcrabble*, *ſcrawl*; extravagus, *stray*, *straggle*; collectum, *clot*, *clutch*; colligo, *coil*; recolligo, *recoil*; ſevero, *ſwear*; ſtridulus, *ſhrill*; procurator, *proxy*; pulſo, *to puſh*; calamus, *a quill*; impetere, *to impeach*; augeo, auxi, *wax*; and vaneſco, vanui, *wane*; ſyllabare, *to ſpell*; puteus, *pit*; granum, *corn*; comprimo, *cramp*, *crump*, *crumple*, *crinkle*.

Some may ſeem harſher, yet may not be rejected, for it at leaſt appears, that ſome of them are derived from proper names, and there are others whoſe etymology is acknowledged by every body; as, Alexander, *Elick*, *Scander*, *Sander*, *Sandy*, *Sanny*; Elizabeth, *Elizabeth*, *Eliſabeth*, *Betty*, *Beſs*; Margareta, *Margaret*, *Marget*, *Meg*, *Peg*; Maria, *Mary*, *Mal*. *Pal*, *Malkin*, *Mawkin*, *Mawkes*; Matthæus, *Mattha*, *Matthew*; Martha, *Matt*. *Pat*; Gulielmus, *Wilhelmus*, *Girolamo*, *Guillaume*, *William*, *Will*, *Bill*, *Wilkin*, *Wicken*, *Wicks*, *Weeks*.

Thus cariophyllus, flos; gerofilo, Ital. giriflee, gilofer, Fr. *gilliflower*, which the vulgar call *julyflower*, as if derived from the month *July*; petroſelinum, *parſly*; portulaca, *purſlain*; cydonium, *quince*; cydoniatum, *quiddeny*; perſicum, *peach*; eruca, *eruke*, which they corrupt to *ear-wig*, as if it took its name from the ear; annulus geminus, *a gimmal* or *gimbal ring*; and thus the word *gimbal* and *jumbal* is transferred to other things thus interwoven; quelques choſes, *kickſhaws*. Since the origin of theſe, and many others, however forced, is evident, it ought to appear no wonder to any one if the ancients have thus disfigured many, eſpecially as they ſo much affected monoſyllables; and, to make them ſound the ſofter, took this liberty of maiming, taking away, changing, tranſpoſing, and ſoftening them.

But while we derive theſe from the Latin, I do not mean to ſay, that many of them did not immediately come to us from the Saxon, Daniſh, Dutch, and Teutonick languages, and other dialects, and ſome taken more lately from the French or Italians, or Spaniards.

The ſame word, according to its different ſignifications, often has a different origin; as, *to bear a burden*, from *fero*; but to *bear*, whence *birth*, *born*, *bairn*, comes from *pario*; and a *bear*, at leaſt if it be of Latin original, from *fera*. Thus *perch*, a fiſh, from *perca*; but *perch*, a meaſure, from *pertica*, and likewiſe *to perch*. *To ſpell* is from *ſyllaba*; but *ſpell*, an inchantment, by which it is believed that the boundaries are ſo fixed in lands, that none can paſs them againſt the maſter's will, from *expello*; and *ſpell*, a meſſenger, from *epistola*; whence *goſpel*, *good-ſpel*, or *god-ſpell*. Thus *freeſe*, or *freeze*, from *frigeſco*; but *freeze*, an architectonic word, from *zophorus*; but *freeſe*, for *cloth*, from *Friſia*, or perhaps from *frigeſco*, as being more fit than any other for keeping out the cold.

There are many words among us, even monoſyllables, compounded of two or more words,, at leaſt ſerving inſtead of compounds, and compriſing the ſignification of more words than one; as, from *ſcrip* and *roll* comes *ſcroll*; from *proud* and *dance*, *prance*; from *st* of the verb *stay*, or *stand* and *stout*, is made *stout*; from *stout* and *hardy*, *ſturdy*; from *ſp* of *ſpit* or *ſpew*, and *out*, comes *ſpout*; from the ſame *ſp*, with the termination *in*, is *ſpin*; and adding *out*, *ſpin out*; and from the ſame *ſp*, with *it*, is *ſpit*, which only differs from *ſpout* in that it is ſmaller, and with leſs noiſe and force; but *ſputter* is, becauſe of the obſcure *u*, ſomething between *ſpit* and *ſpout*; and by reaſon of adding *r*, it intimates a frequent iteration and noiſe, but obſcurely confuſed: whereas *ſpatter*, on account of the ſharper and clearer vowel *a*, intimates a more diſtinct noiſe, in which it chiefly differs from *ſputter*. From the ſame *ſp*, and the termination *ark*, comes *ſpark*, ſignifying a ſingle emiſſion of fire with a noiſe; namely, *ſp* the emiſſion, *ar* the more acute noiſe, and *k*, the mute conſonant, intimates its being ſuddenly terminated; but adding *l*, is made the frequentative *ſparkle*. The ſame *ſp*, by adding *r*, that is *ſpr*, implies a more lively impetus of diffuſing or expanding itſelf; to which adding the termination *ing*, it becomes *ſpring*; its vigour *ſpr* imports, its ſharpneſs the termination *ing*, and laſtly *in* acute and tremulous, ends in the mute conſonant *g*, denotes the ſudden ending of any motion, that it is meant in its primary ſignification, of a ſingle, not a complicated exilition. Hence we call *ſpring* whatever has an elaſtick force; as alſo a fountain of water, and thence the origin of any thing; and to *ſpring*, to germinate; and *ſpring*, one of the four ſeaſons. From the ſame *ſpr* and *out*, is formed *ſprout*, and with the termination *ig*, *ſprig*; of which the following, for the moſt part, is the difference: *ſprout*, of a groſſer ſound, imports a fatter or croſſer bud; *ſprig*, of a ſlenderer ſound, denotes a ſmaller ſhoot. In like manner, from *str* of the verb *strive*, and *out*, comes *strout* and *strut*. From the ſame *str*, and the termination *uggle*, is made *struggle*; and this *gl* imports, but without any great noiſe, by reaſon of the obſcure ſound of the vowel *u*. In like manner, from *throw* and *roll* is made *trull*; and almoſt in the ſame ſenſe is *trundle*, from *throw* or *thrust*, and *rundle*. Thus *graff* or *grough* is compounded of *grave* and *rough*; and *trudge* from *tread* or *trot*, and *drudge*.

In theſe obſervations it is eaſy to diſcover great ſagacity and great extravagance, an ability to do much defeated by the deſire of doing more than enough. It may be remarked,

1. That Wallis's derivations are often ſo made, that by the ſame licence any language may be deduced from any other.

2. That he makes no diſtinction between words immediately derived by us from the Latin, and thoſe which being copied from other languages, can therefore afford no example of the genius of the Engliſh language, or its laws of derivation.

3. That he derives from the Latin, often with great harſhneſs and violence, words apparently Teutonick; and therefore, according to his own declaration, probably older than the tongue to which he refers them.

4. That ſome of his derivations are apparently erroneous.

SYNTAX.

The eſtabliſhed practice of grammarians requires that I ſhould here treat of the Syntax; but our language has ſo little inflection, or variety of terminations, that its conſtruction neither requires nor admits many rules. Wallis therefore has totally omitted it; and Johnſon, whoſe deſire of following the writers upon the learned languages made him think a ſyntax indiſpenſably neceſſary, has publiſhed ſuch petty obſervations as were better omitted.

The verb, as in other languages, agrees with the nominative in number and perſon; as, *Thou flieſt from good*; *He runs to death.*

Our adjectives and pronouns are invariable.

Of two ſubſtantives the noun poſſeſſive is the genitive; as, *His father's glory*; *The ſun's heat.*

Verbs tranſitive require an oblique caſe; as, *He loves me*; *You fear him.*

All prepoſitions require an oblique caſe: *He gave this* to *me*; *He took this* from *me*; *He ſays this* of *me*; *He came* with *me.*

PROSODY.

It is common for thoſe that deliver the grammar of modern languages, to omit their Proſody. So that of the Italians is neglected by *Buomattei*; that of the French by *Deſmarais*; and that of the Engliſh by *Wallis*, *Cooper*, and even by *Johnſon* though a poet. But as the laws of metre are included in the idea of a grammar, I have thought it proper to inſert them.

Proſody compriſes *orthoepy*, or the rules of pronunciation; and *orthometry*, or the laws of verſification.

PRONUN-

Pronunciation is juſt, when every letter has its proper ſound, and when every ſyllable has its proper accent, or which in Engliſh verſification is the ſame, its proper quantity.

The ſounds of the letters have been already explained; and rules for the accent or quantity are not eaſily to be given, being ſubject to innumerable exceptions. Such however as I have read or formed, I ſhall here propoſe.

1. Of diſſyllables formed by affixing a termination, the former ſyllable is commonly accented, as *chíldiſh*, *kíngdom*, *áctest*, *ácted*, *tóilſome*, *lóver*, *ſcóffer*, *faírer*, *forémoſt*, *zéalous*, *fúlneſs*, *gódly*, *méekly*, *ártiſt*.

2. Diſſyllables formed by prefixing a ſyllable to the radical word, have commonly the accent on the latter; as, *to begét*, *to beſeém*, *to beſtów*.

3. Of diſſyllables, which are at once nouns and verbs, the verb has commonly the accent on the latter, and the noun on the former ſyllable; as, *to deſcánt*, *a déſcant*; *to cemént*, *a cément*; *to contráct*, *a cóntract*.

This rule has many exceptions. Though verbs ſeldom have their accent on the former, yet nouns often have it on the latter ſyllable; as, *delíght*, *perfúme*.

4. All diſſyllables ending in *y*, as *cranny*; in *our*, as *labour*, *favour*; in *ow*, as *willow*, *wállow*, except *allów*; in *le*, as *báttle*, *bíble*; in *iſh*, as *bániſh*; in *ck*, as *cámbrick*, *cáſſock*; in *ter*, as *to bátter*; in *age*, as *coúrage*; in *en*, as *fáſten*; in *et*, as *quíet*, accent the former ſyllable.

5. Diſſyllable nouns in *er*, as *cánker*, *bútter*, have the accent on the former ſyllable.

6 Diſſyllable verbs terminating in a conſonant and *e* final, as *comprı́ſe*, *eſcápe*; or having a diphthong in the laſt ſyllable, as *appéaſe*, *revéal*; or ending in two conſonants, as *att
énd*; have the accent on the latter ſyllable.

7. Diſſyllable nouns having a diphthong in the latter ſyllable, have commonly their accent on the latter ſyllable, as *applaúſe*; except words in *ain*, *cértain*, *moúntain*.

8. Triſſyllables formed by adding a termination, or prefixing a ſyllable, retain the accent of the radical word, as *lóvelineſs*, *ténderneſs*, *contémner*, *wágonner*, *phýſical*, *beſpátter*, *comménting*, *comménding*, *aſſúrance*.

9. Triſſyllables ending in *ous*, as *grácious*, *árduous*; in *al*, as *cápital*; in *ion*, as *méntion*, accent the firſt.

10. Triſſyllables ending in *ce*, *ent*, and *ate*, accent the firſt ſyllable, as *coúntenance*, *cóntinence*, *ármament*, *ímminent*, *élegant*, *própagate*, except they be derived from words having the accent on the laſt, as *connívence*, *acquáintance*; or the middle ſyllable hath a vowel before two conſonants, as *promúlgate*.

11. Triſſyllables ending in *y*, as *éntity*, *ſpécify*, *líberty*, *víctory*, *ſúbſidy*, commonly accent the firſt ſyllable.

12. Triſſyllables in *re* or *le* accent the firſt ſyllable, as *légible*, *théatre*, except *diſcíple*, and ſome words which have a poſition, as *exámple*, *epíſtle*.

13. Triſſyllables in *ude* commonly accent the firſt ſyllable, as *plénitude*.

14. Triſſyllables ending in *ator* or *atour*, as *creátour*, or having in the middle ſyllable a diphthong, as *endeávour*; or a vowel before two conſonants, as *doméſtick*, accent the middle ſyllable.

15. Triſſyllables that have their accent on the laſt ſyllable are commonly French, as *acquieſce*, *repartée*, *magazíne*, or words formed by prefixing one or two ſyllables to an acute ſyllable, as *immatúre*, *overchárge*.

16. Polyſyllables, or words of more than three ſyllables, follow the accent of the words from which they are derived, as *árrogating*, *cóntinency*, *incóntinently*, *comméndable*, *commúnicableneſs*.

17. Words in *ion* have the accent upon the antepenult, as *ſalvátion*, *perturbátion*, *concóction*; words in *atour* or *ator* on the penult, as *dedicátor*.

18. Words ending in *le* commonly have the accent on the firſt ſyllable, as *ámicable*, unleſs the ſecond ſyllable have a vowel before two conſonants, as *combúſtible*.

19. Words ending in *ous* have the accent on the antepenult, as *uxórious*, *volúptuous*.

20. Words ending in *ty* have their accent on the antepenult, as *puſillanímity*, *actívity*.

Theſe rules are not advanced as compleat or infallible, but propoſed as uſeful. Almoſt every rule of every language has its exceptions; and in Engliſh, as in other tongues, much muſt be learned by example and authority. Perhaps more and better rules may be given that have eſcaped my obſervation.

Versification is the arrangement of a certain number of ſyllables according to certain laws.

The feet of our verſes are either iambick, as *alóft*, *creáte*; or trochaick, as *hóly*, *lófty*.

Our iambick meaſure compriſes verſes

Of four ſyllables,

Moſt good, moſt fair,
Or things as rare,
To call you's loſt;
For all the coſt
Words can beſtow,
So poorly ſhow
Upon your praiſe,
That all the ways
Senſe hath, come ſhort. *Drayton.*

With raviſh'd ears
The monarch hears. *Dryden.*

Of ſix,

This while we are abroad,
Shall we not touch our lyre?
Shall we not ſing an ode?
Shall that holy fire,
In us that ſtrongly glow'd,
In this cold air expire?

Though in the utmoſt Peak
A while we do remain,
Amongſt the mountains bleak,
Expos'd to ſleet and rain,
No ſport our hours ſhall break,
To exerciſe our vein.

Who though bright Phœbus' beams
Refreſh the ſouthern ground,
And though the princely Thames
With beauteous nymphs abound,
And by old Camber's ſtreams
Be many wonders found;

Yet many rivers clear
Here glide in ſilver ſwathes,
And what of all moſt dear,
Buxton's delicious baths,
Strong ale and noble chear,
T' aſſwage breem winter's ſcathes.

In places far or near,
Or famous, or obſcure,
Where wholeſom is the air,
Or where the moſt impure,
All times, and every where,
The muſe is ſtill in ure. *Drayton.*

Of eight, which is the uſual meaſure for ſhort poems,

And may at laſt my weary age
Find out the peaceful hermitage,
The hairy gown, and moſſy cell,
Where I may ſit, and nightly ſpell
Of ev'ry ſtar the ſky doth ſhew,
And ev'ry herb that ſips the dew. *Milton.*

Of ten, which is the common meaſure of heroick and tragick poetry.

Full in the midſt of this created ſpace,
Betwixt heav'n, earth, and ſkies, there ſtands a place
Confining on all three; with triple bound;
Whence all things, though remote, are view'd around,
And thither bring their undulating ſound.
The palace of loud Fame, her ſeat of pow'r,
Plac'd on the ſummit of a lofty tow'r;
A thouſand winding entries long and wide
Receive of freſh reports a flowing tide.

A thousand crannies in the walls are made;
Nor gate nor bars exclude the busy trade.
'Tis built of brass, the better to diffuse
The spreading sounds, and multiply the news;
Where echo's in repeated echo's play:
A mart for ever full; and open night and day.
Nor silence is within, nor voice express,
But a deaf noise of sounds that never cease;
Confus'd, and chiding, like the hollow rore
Of tides, receding from th' insulted shore;
Or like the broken thunder, heard from far,
When Jove to distance drives the rolling war.
The courts are fill'd with a tumultuous din
Of crouds, or issuing forth, or entring in:
A thorough-fare of news; where some devise
Things never heard, some mingle truth with lies:
The troubled air with empty sounds they beat,
Intent to hear, and eager to repeat. *Dryden.*

In all these measures the accents are to be placed on even syllables; and every line considered by itself is more harmonious, as this rule is more strictly observed.

Our trochaick measures are

Of three syllables,

Here we may
Think and pray,
Before death
Stops our breath:
Other joys
Are but toys.

Of five,

In the days of old,
Stories plainly told,
Lovers felt annoy.

Of seven,

Fairest piece of welform'd earth,
Urge not thus your haughty birth.

In these measures the accent is to be placed on the odd syllables.

These are the measures which are now in use, and above the rest those of seven, eight, and ten syllables. Our ancient poets wrote verses sometimes of twelve syllables, as Drayton's Polyolbion.

Of all the Cambrian shires their heads that bear so high,
And farth'st survey their soils with an ambitious eye,
Mervinia for her hills, as for their matchless crowds,
The nearest that are said to kiss the wand'ring clouds,
Especial audience craves, offended with the throng,
That she of all the rest neglected was so long;
Alledging for herself, when through the Saxons pride,
The godlike race of Brute to Severn's setting side
Were cruelly inforc'd, her mountains did relieve
Those whom devouring war else every where did grieve.
And when all Wales beside (by fortune or by might)
Unto her ancient foe resign'd her ancient right,
A constant maiden still she only did remain,
The last her genuine laws which stoutly did retain.
And as each one is prais'd for her peculiar things;
So only she is rich, in mountains, meres, and springs,
And holds herself as great in her superfluous waste,
As others by their towns, and fruitful tillage grac'd.

And of fourteen, as Chapman's Homer.

And as the mind of such a man, that hath a long way gone,
And either knoweth not his way, or else would let alone
His purpos'd journey, is distract.

The verse of twelve lines, called an *Alexandrine*, is now only used to diversify heroick lines.

Waller was smooth, but Dryden taught to join
The varying verse, the full-resounding line,
The long majestick march, and energy divine.

The pause in the Alexandrine must be at the sixth syllable.

The verse of fourteen syllables is now broken into a soft lyrick measure of verses, consisting alternately of eight syllables and six.

She to receive thy radiant name,
Selects a whiter space.

When all shall praise, and ev'ry lay
Devote a wreath to thee,
That day, for come it will, that day
Shall I lament to see.

We have another measure very quick and lively, and therefore much used in songs, which may be called the *anapestick*, in which the accent rests upon every third syllable.

May I góvern my pássions with ábsolute swáy,
And grow wíser and bétter as life wears awáy.

In this measure a syllable is often retrenched from the first foot, as

Diógenes súrly and proúd.

I think not of I'ris, nor I'ris of mé.

These measures are varied by many combinations, and sometimes by double endings, either with or without rhyme, as in the heroick measure.

'Tis heav'n itself that points out an hereafter,
And intimates eternity to man.

So in that of eight syllables,

They neither added nor confounded,
They neither wanted nor abounded.

In that of seven,

For resistance I could fear none,
But with twenty ships had done,
What thou, brave and happy Vernon,
Hast atchiev'd with six alone.

In that of six,

'Twas when the seas were roaring,
With hollow blasts of wind,
A damsel lay deploring,
All on a rock reclin'd.

In the anapestick,

When terrible tempests assail us,
And mountainous billows affright,
Nor power nor wealth can avail us,
But skilful industry steers right.

To these measures, and their laws, may be reduced every species of English verse.

Our versification admits of few licences, except a *synalœpha*, or elision of *e* in *the* before a vowel, as *th'eternal*; and more rarely of *o* in *to*, as *t'accept*; and a *synæresis*, by which two short vowels coalesce into one syllable, as *question*, *special*; or a word is contracted by the expulsion of a short vowel before a liquid, as *av'rice*, *temp'rance*.

Thus have I collected rules and examples, by which the English language may be learned, if the reader be already acquainted with grammatical terms, or taught by a master to those that are more ignorant. To have written a grammar for such as are not yet initiated in the schools, would have been tedious, and perhaps at last ineffectual.

Directions to the BOOK-BINDER.

The First Volume contains, —— The Preface; History of the English Language; The Grammar; and, The Letters A to K inclusive.

The Second Volume contains, —— L to Z inclusive.

A

DICTIONARY

OF THE

ENGLISH LANGUAGE.

A, The first letter of the European alphabets, has, in the English language, three different sounds, which may be termed the broad, open, and slender.

The broad sound, resembling that of the German *a*, is found in many of our monosyllables, as *all, wall, malt, salt*; in which *a* is pronounced as *au* in *cause*, or *aw* in *law*. Many of these words were anciently written with *au*, as *sault, waulk*; which happens to be still retained in *fault*. This was probably the ancient sound of the Saxons, since it is almost uniformly preserved in the rustick pronunciation, and the northern dialects, as *maun* for *man*, *haund* for *hand*.

A open, not unlike the *a* of the Italians, is found in *father, rather*, and more obscurely in *fancy, fast*, &c.

A slender or close, is the peculiar *a* of the English language, resembling the sound of the French *e* masculine, or diphthong *ai* in *païs*, or perhaps a middle sound between them, or between the *a* and *e*; to this the Arabic *a* is said nearly to approach. Of this sound we have examples in the words *place, face, waste*, and all those that terminate in *ation*, as, *relation, nation, generation*.

A is short, as, *glass, grass*; or long, as, *glaze, graze*: it is marked long, generally, by an *e* final, *plane*, or by an *i* added, as, *plain*.

A, an article set before nouns of the singular number; *a* man, *a* tree; denoting the number *one*, as, *a* man is coming, that is, *no more than one*; or an indefinite indication, as, *a* man may come this way; that is, *any* man. This article has no plural signification. Before a word beginning with a vowel, it is written *an*, as, *an* ox, *an* egg, of which *a* is the contraction.

A is sometimes a noun; as, a great *A*, a little *a*.

A is placed before a participle, or participial noun; and is considered by Wallis as a contraction of *at*, when it is put before a word denoting some action not yet finished; as, I am *a* walking. It also seems to be anciently contracted from *at*, when placed before local surnames; as, Thomas *a* Becket. In other cases, it seems to signify *to*, like the French *à*.

A hunting Chloë went. *Prior.*

They go *a* begging to a bankrupt's door. *Dryd.*

May pure contents for ever pitch their tents
Upon these downs, these meads, these rocks, these mountains,
And peace still slumber by these purling fountains!
Which we may every year
Find when we come *a* fishing here. *Wotton.*

Now the men fell *a* rubbing of armour, which a great while had lain oiled; the magazines of munition are viewed; the officers of remains called to account. *Wotton.*

Another falls *a* ringing a Pescennius Niger, and judiciously distinguishes the sound of it to be modern. *Addison on medals.*

A has a peculiar signification, denoting the proportion of one thing to another. Thus we say, The landlord hath a hundred *a* year; The ship's crew gained a thousand pounds *a* man.

The river Inn, that had been hitherto shut up among mountains, passes generally through a wide open country, during all its course through Bavaria; which is a voyage of two days, after the rate of twenty leagues *a* day. *Addison on Italy.*

A is used in burlesque poetry to lengthen out a syllable, without adding to the sense.

For cloves and nutmegs to the line-*a*,
And even for oranges to China. *Dryden.*

A is sometimes, in familiar writings, put by a barbarous corruption for *he*.

A, in composition, seems to have sometimes the power of the French *a* in these phrases, *a droit, a gauche*, &c. and sometimes to be contracted from *at*; as, *aside, aslope, afoot, asleep, athirst, aware*.

If this, which he avouches, does appear,
There is no flying hence, nor tarrying here.
I gin to be *a weary* of the sun;
And wish the state of the world were now undone.
Shakespeare's Macbeth.

And now a breeze from shore began to blow,
The sailors ship their oars, and cease to row;
Then hoist their yards *a-trip*, and all their sails
Let fall, to court the wind, and catch the gales.
Dryden's Ceyx and Alcyone.

A is sometimes redundant; as, *arise, arouse, awake*; the same with rise, rouse, wake.

A, in abbreviations, stands for *artium*, or arts; as, A. B. bachelor of arts, *artium baccalaureus*; A. M. master of arts, *artium magister*; or, *anno*; as, A. D. *anno domini*.

AB, at the beginning of the names of places, generally shews that they have some relation to an abbey.

ABA'CKE. *adv.* Backwards. Obsolete.

But when they came where thou thy skill didst show,
They drew *abacke*, as half with shame confound,
Shepherds to see them in their art outgo. *Spens. Past.*

ABA'CTOR. n. s. [Lat. *abactor*, a driver away.] Those who drive away or steal cattle in herds, or great numbers at once, in distinction from those that steal only a sheep or two. *Blount.*

A'BACUS. n. s. [Lat.]

1. A counting-table, anciently used in calculations.
2. In architecture, it is the uppermost member of a column, which serves as a sort of crowning both to the capital and column. *Dict.*

ABA'FT. *adv.* [of abaꝼtan, Sax. behind.] From the fore-part of the ship, towards the stern. *Dict.*

ABAI'SANCE. *n. s.* [from the French *abaiser*, to depress, to bring down.] An act of reverence, a bow. *Obeisance* is considered by Skinner as a corruption of *abaisance*, but is now universally used.

To ABA'LIENATE. *v. a.* [from *abalieno*, Lat.] To make that another's which was our own before. *Calv. Lex. Jur.*

A term of the civil law, not much used in common speech.

ABALIENA'TION. *n. s.* [*abalienatio*, Lat.] A giving up one's right to another person; or a making over an estate, goods, or chattels by sale, or due course of law. *Dict.*

To ABA'ND. *v. a.* [A word contracted from abandon, but not now in use. See ABANDON.] To forsake.

Those foreigners which came from far
Grew great, and got large portions of land,
That in the realm, ere long, they stronger are
Than they which sought at first their helping hand,
And Vortiger enforced the kingdom to *aband*.
Spenser's Fairy Queen, b. ii. *cant.* 10.

To ABA'NDON. *v. a.* [*abandonner*. Fr. Derived, according to *Menage*, from the Italian *abandonare*, which signifies to forsake his colours; *bandum* [*vexillum*] *deserere*. *Pasquier* thinks it it a coalition of *a ban donner*, to give up to a proſcription; in which ſenſe we, at this day, mention the ban of the empire. *Ban*, in our own old dialect, ſignifies a curſe; and to *abandon*, if conſidered as compounded between French and Saxon, is exactly equivalent to *diris devovere.*]

1. To give up, reſign, or quit; often followed by the particle *to*.

  The paſſive gods behold the Greeks defile
  Their temples, and *abandon to* the ſpoil
  Their own abodes; we, feeble few, conſpire
  To ſave a ſinking town, involv'd in fire. *Dryd. Æneid.*

2. To deſert.

The princes uſing the paſſions of fearing evil, and deſiring to eſcape, only to ſerve the rule of virtue, not to *abandon* one's ſelf, leapt to a rib of the ſhip. *Sidney, b.* ii.

  Then being alone,
  Left and *abandon'd* of his velvet friends,
  'Tis right, quoth he; thus miſery doth part
  The flux of company. *Shakeſp. As you like it.*

  What fate a wretched fugitive attends,
  Scorn'd by my foes, *abandon'd* by my friends. *Dryd. Æn.* 2.

3. To forſake, generally with a tendency to an ill ſenſe.

  When he in preſence came, to Guyon firſt
  He boldly ſpake, Sir knight, if knight thou be,
  Abandon this forſtalled place at erſt,
  For fear of further harm, I counſel thee.
  Spenſer's Fairy Queen, b. ii. *cant.* 4. *ſtanz.* 39.

  But to the parting goddeſs thus ſhe pray'd;
  Propitious ſtill be preſent to my aid,
  Nor quite *abandon* your once favour'd maid. *Dryd. Fab.*

To ABANDON OVER. *v. a.* [a form of writing not uſual, perhaps not exact.] To give up to, to reſign.

  Look on me as a man *abandon'd o'er*
  To an eternal lethargy of love;
  To pull, and pinch, and wound me, cannot cure,
  And but diſturb the quiet of my death. *Dryd. Sp. Friar.*

ABANDONED. *particip. adj.*

1. Given up.

  If ſhe be ſo *abandon'd* to her ſorrow,
  As it is ſpoke, ſhe never will admit me.
  Shakeſp. Twelfth Night.

Who is he ſo *abandoned* to ſottiſh credulity, as to think, upon that principle, that a clod of earth in a ſack, may ever, by eternal ſhaking, receive the fabric of man's body? *Bentley's Sermons.*

  Muſt he, whoſe altars on the Phrygian ſhore,
  With frequent rites, and pure, avow'd thy pow'r,
  Be doom'd the worſt of human ills to prove,
  Unbleſs'd, *abandon'd* to the wrath of Jove?
  Pope's Odyſſey, b. i. *l.* 80.

2. Forſaken, deſerted.
3. Corrupted in the higheſt degree. In this ſenſe, it is a contraction of a longer form, abandoned [given up] to wickedneſs.

ABA'NDONING. [A verbal noun from *abandon.*] Deſertion, forſaking.

He hoped his paſt meritorious actions might outweigh his preſent, *abandoning* the thought of future action. *Clarend. b.* viii.

ABA'NDONMENT. *n. ſ.* [*abandonnement*, Fr.]

1. The act of abandoning.
2. The ſtate of being abandoned. *Dict.*

ABANNI'TION. *n. ſ.* [*abannitio*, Lat.] A baniſhment for one or two years, among the ancients, for manſlaughter. *Dict.*

A'BARCY. *n. ſ.* Inſatiableneſs. *Dict.*

To ABA'RE. *v. a.* [abaꞃian, Sax.] To make bare, uncover, or diſcloſe. *Dict.*

ABARTICULA'TION. *n. ſ.* [from *ab*, from, and *articulus*, a joint, Lat.] A good and apt conſtruction of the bones, by which they move ſtrongly and eaſily; or that ſpecies of articulation that has manifeſt motion.

To ABA'SE. *v. a.* [*abaiſſer*, Fr. from the Lat. *baſis*, or *baſſus*, a barbarous word, ſignifying low, baſe.] To caſt down, to depreſs, to bring low, almoſt always in a figurative and perſonal ſenſe.

Happy ſhepherd, with thanks to the gods, ſtill think to be thankful, that to thy advancement their wiſdoms have thee *abaſed*. *Sidney, b.* i.

  With unreſiſted might the monarch reigns;
  He levels mountains, and he raiſes plains;
  And, not regarding diff'rence of degree,
  Abas'd your daughter, and exalted me. *Dryd. Fables:*

Behold every one that is proud, and *abaſe* him. *Job*, xl. 11.

If the mind be curbed and humbled too much in children; if their ſpirits be *abaſed* and broken much by too ſtrict an hand over them; they loſe all their vigour and induſtry, and are in a worſe ſtate than the former. *Locke on Education*, § 46.

ABA'SED. *adj.* [with heralds] is a term uſed of the wings of eagles, when the top looks downwards towards the point of the ſhield; or when the wings are ſhut; the natural way of bearing them being ſpread with the top pointing to the chief of the angle. *Bailey. Chambers.*

ABA'SEMENT. *n. ſ.* The ſtate of being brought low; the act of bringing low; depreſſion.

There is an *abaſement* becauſe of glory; and there is that lifteth up his head from a low eſtate. *Eccleſiaſticus*, xx. 11.

To ABA'SH. *v. a.* [See BASHFUL.] To put into confuſion; to make aſhamed. It generally implies a ſudden impreſſion of ſhame.

  They heard, and were *abaſh'd*, and up they ſprung
  Upon the wing. *Milton's Paradiſe Loſt, b.* i. *l.* 331.

  This heard, th' imperious queen ſat mute with fear;
  Nor further durſt incenſe the gloomy thunderer.
  Silence was in the court at this rebuke:
  Nor could the gods, *abaſh'd*, ſuſtain their ſovereign's look.
  Dryden's Fables.

The paſſive admits the particle *at*, ſometimes *of*, before the cauſal noun.

In no wiſe ſpeak againſt the truth, but be *abaſhed of* the error of thy ignorance. *Eccleſiaſticus*, iv. 25.

I ſaid unto her, from whence is this kid? Is it not ſtolen? Render it to the owners, for it is not lawful to eat any thing that is ſtolen. But ſhe replied upon me, it was given for a gift, more than the wages: however, I did not believe her, but bad her render it to the owners: and I was *abaſhed at* her. *Tob.* ii. 13, 14.

  The little Cupids hov'ring round,
  (As pictures prove) with garlands crown'd,
  Abaſh'd at what they ſaw and heard,
  Flew off, nor ever more appear'd. *Swift's Miſcellanies.*

To ABA'TE. *v. a.* [from the French *abbatre*, to beat down.]

1. To leſſen, to diminiſh.

Who can tell whether the divine wiſdom, to *abate* the glory of thoſe kings, did not reſerve this work to be done by a queen, that it might appear to be his own immediate work? *Sir John Davies on Ireland.*

  If you did know to whom I gave the ring,
  And how unwillingly I left the ring,
  You would *abate* the ſtrength of your diſpleaſure.
  Shakeſp. Merchant of Venice.

Here we ſee the hopes of great benefit and light from expoſitors and commentators are in a great part *abated*; and thoſe who have moſt need of your help, can receive but little from them, and can have very little aſſurance of reaching the Apoſtle's ſenſe, by what they find in them.
Locke's Eſſay on St. Paul's Epiſtles.

2. To deject, or depreſs the mind.

  This iron world (the ſame he weeping ſays)
  Brings down the ſtouteſt hearts to loweſt ſtate:
  For miſery doth braveſt minds *abate*. *Spenſ. Hubberd's Tale.*

  ——— Have they power ſtill
  To baniſh your defenders, till at length
  Your ignorance deliver you,
  As moſt *abated* captives to ſome nation
  That won you without blows? *Shakeſp. Coriolanus.*

  Time that changes all, yet changes us in vain,
  The body, not the mind; nor can controul
  Th' immortal vigour, or abate the ſoul. *Dryden's Æneid.*

3. In commerce, to let down the price in ſelling, ſometimes to beat down the price in buying.

To ABA'TE. *v. n.* To grow leſs; as, his paſſion abates; the ſtorm abates. It is uſed ſometimes with the particle *of* before the thing leſſened.

Our phyſicians have obſerved, that, in proceſs of time, ſome diſeaſes have *abated* of their virulence, and have, in a manner, worn out their malignity, ſo as to be no longer mortal. *Dryden's Hind and Panth.*

To ABA'TE. [In common law.]

It is in law uſed both actively and neuterly; as, to *abate* a caſtle, to beat it down. To *abate* a writ, is, by ſome exception, to defeat or overthrow it. A ſtranger *abateth*, that is, entereth upon a houſe or land void by the death of him that laſt poſſeſſed it, before the heir take his poſſeſſion, and ſo keepeth him out. Wherefore, as he that putteth out him in poſſeſſion, is ſaid to diſſeiſe: ſo he that ſteppeth in between the former poſſeſſor and his heir, is ſaid to *abate*. In the neuter ſignification thus; The writ of the demandment ſhall *abate*, that is, ſhall be diſabled, fruſtrated, or overthrown. The appeal *abateth* by covin, that is, that the accuſation is defeated by deceit. *Cowel.*

To ABA'TE. [In horſemanſhip.] A horſe is ſaid to abate or take down his curvets, when working upon curvets, he puts his two hind-legs to the ground both at once, and obſerves the ſame exactneſs in all the times. *Dict.*

ABA'TEMENT. *n. ſ.* [*abatement*, Fr.]

1. The act of abating or leſſening.

The law of works then, in ſhort, is that law, which requires perfect obedience, without remiſſion or *abatement*; ſo that, by that law, a man cannot be juſt, or juſtified, without an exact performance of every tittle. *Locke.*

2. The ſtate of being abated.

Coffee has, in common with all nuts, an oil ſtrongly combined and entangled with earthy particles. The moſt noxious part of oil exhales in roaſting to the *abatement* of near one quarter of its weight. *Arbuthnot on Aliments.*

3. The ſum or quantity taken away by the act of abating.

Xenophon tells us, that the city contained about ten thou-

ſand

fand houfes, and allowing one man to every houfe, who could have any fhare in the government, (the reft, confifting of women, children and fervants) and making other obvious *abatements*, thefe tyrants, if they had been careful to adhere together, might have been a majority even of the people collective. *Swift on the Contefts in Athens and Rome.*

4. The caufe of abating; extenuation.

As our advantages towards practifing and promoting piety and virtue were greater than thofe of other men; fo will our excufe be lefs, if we neglect to make ufe of them. We cannot plead, in *abatement* of our guilt, that we were ignorant of our duty, under the prepoffeffion of ill habits, and the biafs of a wrong education. *Atterbury's Sermons.*

5. ABA'TEMENT. [In law.]

The act of the abator; as, the *abatement* of the heir into the land before he hath agreed with the lord. The affection or paffion of the thing abated; as, *abatement* of the writ. *Cowel.*

ABA'TEMENT [with heralds] is an accidental mark, which being added to a coat of arms, the dignity of it is abafed, by reafon of fome ftain or difhonourable quality of the bearer. *Dict.*

ABA'TER. *n. f.* The agent or caufe by which an abatement is procured.

Abaters of acrimony or fharpnefs: expreffed oils of ripe vegetables, and all preparations of fuch; as of almonds, piftachoes, and other nuts. *Arbuthnot on diet.*

ABA'TOR. *n. f.* [a law-term.] One who intrudes into houfes or land, that is void by the death of the former poffeffour, as yet not entered upon or taken up by his heir. *Dict.*

A'BATUDE. *n. f.* [old records.] Any thing diminifhed. *Bailey.*

A'BATURE. *n. f.* [a hunting term.] Thofe fprigs of grafs which are thrown down by a ftag in his paffing by. *Dict.*

ABB. *n. f.* The yarn on a weaver's warp; a term among clothiers. *Chambers.*

ABBA. n. f. [Heb. אב] A Syriac word, which fignifies father.

A'BBACY. *n. f.* [*abbatia*, Lat.] The rights or privileges of an abbot. See ABBEY.

According to Felinus, an *abbacy* is the dignity itfelf, fince an abbot is a term or word of dignity, and not of office; and, therefore, even a fecular perfon, who has the care of fouls, is fometimes, in the canon law, alfo ftiled an abbot. *Ayliffe's Parergon Juris Canonici.*

A'BBESS. *n. f.* [*abbatiffa*, Lat. from whence the Saxon abubiррe, then probably *abbatefs*, and by contraction *abbeffe* in Fr. and *abbefs*, Eng.] The fuperiour or governefs of a nunnery or monaftery of women.

They fled
Into this abbey, whither we purfued them;
And here the *abbefs* fhuts the gate on us,
And will not fuffer us to fetch him out.
Shakefp. Comedy of Errours.

I have a fifter, *abbefs* in Terceras,
Who loft her lover on her bridal-day. *Dryd. D. Sebaft.*

Conftantia's heart was fo elevated with the difcourfe of Father Francis, that the very next day fhe entered upon her vow. As foon as the folemnities of her reception were over, we retired, as it is ufual, with the *abbefs* into her own apartment. *Addifon's Spect.* N° 164.

A'BBEY, or ABBY. *n. f.* [*abbatia*, Lat. from whence probably firft ABBACY; which fee.] A monaftery of religious perfons, whether men or women; diftinguifhed from religious houfes of other denominations by larger privileges. See ABBOT.

With eafy roads he came to Leicefter;
Lodg'd in the *abbey*, where the reverend abbot,
With all his convent, honourably receiv'd him.
Shakefp. Henry VIII.

A'BBEY-LUBBER. *n. f.* [See LUBBER.] A flothful loiterer in a religious houfe, under pretence of retirement and aufterity.

This is no Father Dominic, no huge overgrown *abbey-lubber*; this is but a diminutive fucking friar. *Dryd. Sp. Fr.*

A'BBOT. *n. f.* [in the lower Latin *abbas*, from אב father, which fenfe was implied; fo that the abbots were called *patres*, and abbeffes *matres monafterii*. Thus Fortunatus to the abbot Paternus: *Nominis officium jure, Paterne, geris.*] The chief of a convent, or fellowfhip of canons. Of thefe, fome in England were mitred, fome not: thofe that were mitred, were exempted from the jurifdiction of the diocefan, having in themfelves epifcopal authority within their precincts, and being alfo lords of parliament. The other fort were fubject to the diocefan in all fpiritual government. *Cowel.* See ABBEY.

A'BBY. See ABBEY.

A'BBOTSHIP. *n. f.* The ftate or privilege of an abbot. *Dict.*

To ABBRE'VIATE. *v. a.* [*abbreviare*, Lat.]

1. To fhorten by contraction of parts without lofs of the main fubftance.

It is one thing to *abbreviate* by contracting, another by cutting off. *Bacon, Effay* 26.

The only invention of late years, which hath any way contributed towards politenefs in difcourfe, is that of *abbreviating* or reducing words of many fyllables into one, by lopping off the reft. *Swift's Introduction to Genteel Converfation.*

2. To fhorten, to cut fhort.

Againft this opinion we may very well fet the length of their days before the flood; which were *abbreviated* after, and in half this fpace contracted into hundreds and threefcores. *Brown's Vulgar Errours, b.* vi. *c.* 6.

ABBREVIA'TION. *n. f.*

1. The act of abbreviating.
2. The means ufed to abbreviate, as characters fignifying whole words.

Such is the propriety and energy of expreffion in them all, that they never can be changed, but to difadvantage, except in the circumftance of ufing *abbreviations.* *Swift's Introduction to Genteel Converfation.*

ABBREVIA'TOR. *n. f.* [*abbreviateur*, Fr.] One who abbreviates, or abridges.

ABBRE'VIATURE. *n. f.* [*abbreviatura*, Lat.]

1. A mark ufed for the fake of fhortening.
2. A compendium or abridgement.

He is a good man, who grieves rather for him that injures him, than for his own fuffering; who prays for him, that wrongs him, forgiving all his faults; who fooner fhews mercy than anger; who offers violence to his appetite, in all things endeavouring to fubdue the flefh to the fpirit. This is an excellent *abbreviature* of the whole duty of a chriftian. *Taylor's Guide to Devotion.*

ABBREUVOI'R. [in French, a watering-place. This word is derived by *Menage*, not much acquainted with the Teutonic dialects, from *adbibare* for *adbibere*; but more probably it comes from the fame root with brew. See BREW.] It fignifies, among mafons, the joint or juncture of two ftones, or the interftice between two ftones to be filled up with mortar. *Dict.*

A, B, C.

1. Is taken for the alphabet; as, he has not learned his *a, b, c.*
2. Sometimes for the little book by which the elements of reading are taught.

To A'BDICATE. *v. a.* [*abdico*, Lat.] To give up right; to refign; to lay down an office.

Old Saturn, here, with upcaft eyes,
Beheld his *abdicated* fkies. *Addifon.*

ABDICA'TION. *n. f.* [*abdicatio*, Lat.] The act of abdicating; refignation; quitting an office by one's own proper act before the ufual or ftated expiration.

Neither doth it appear how a prince's *abdication* can make any other fort of vacancy in the throne, than would be caufed by his death; fince he cannot *abdicate* for his children, otherwife than by his own confent in form to a bill from the two houfes. *Swift on the Sentiments of a Church of England-man.*

A'BDICATIVE. *adj.* That which caufes or implies an *abdication.* *Dict.*

A'BDITIVE. *adj.* [from *abdo*, to hide.] That which has the power or quality of hiding. *Dict.*

ABDO'MEN. *n. f.* [Lat. from *abdo*, to hide.] A cavity commonly called the lower venter or belly: It contains the ftomach, guts, liver, fpleen, bladder, and is within lined with a membrane called the peritonæum. The lower part is called the hypogaftrium; the foremoft part is divided into the epigaftrium, the right and left hypochondria, and the navel; 'tis bounded above by the cartilago enfiformis and the diaphragm, fideways by the fhort or lower ribs, and behind by the vertebræ of the loins, the bones of the coxendix, that of the pubes and os facrum. It is covered with feveral mufcles, from whofe alternate relaxations and contractions in refpiration, digeftion is forwarded, and the due motion of all the parts therein contained promoted, both for fecretion and expulfion. *Quincy.*

The *abdomen* confifts moreover of parts containing and contained. *Wifeman's Surgery.*

ABDO'MINAL. } *adj.* Relating to the abdomen.
ABDO'MINOUS. }

To ABDU'CE. *v. a.* [*abduco*, Lat.] To draw to a different part; to withdraw one part from another. A word chiefly ufed in phyfick or fcience.

And if we *abduce* the eye unto either corner, the object will not duplicate; for, in that pofition, the axis of the cones remain in the fame plain, as is demonftrated in the optics delivered by Galen. *Brown's Vulgar Errours, b.* iii. *c.* 20.

ABDU'CENT. *adj.* Mufcles abducent, are thofe which ferve to open or pull back divers parts of the body; their oppofites being called adducent. *Dict.*

ABDU'CTION. *n. f.* [Latin.]

1. The act of drawing apart, or withdrawing one part from another.
2. A particular form of argument.

ABDU'CTOR. n. f. [Latin.] The name given by anatomifts to the mufcles, which ferve to draw back the feveral members.

In purfuance of this theory, he fuppofed the conftrictors of the eyelids muft be ftrengthened in the fupercilious; the *abductors* in drunkards, and contemplative men, who have the fame fteady and grave motion of the eye. *Arbuthnot and Pope's Martinus Scriblerus.*

ABECEDA'RIAN. *n. ſ.* [from the names of *a*, *b*, *c*, the three firſt letters of the alphabet.] He that teaches or learns the alphabet, or firſt rudiments of literature.

This word is uſed by *Wood* in his *Athenæ Oxonienſes*, where mentioning Farnaby the critic, he relates, that, in ſome part of his life, he was reduced to follow the trade of an *abecedarian* by his misfortunes.

A'BECEDARY. *adj.* [See ABECEDARIAN.]

1. Belonging to the alphabet.
2. Inſcribed with the alphabet.

This is pretended from the ſympathy of two needles touched with the loadſtone, and placed in the center of two *abecedary* circles, or rings of letters, deſcribed round about them, one friend keeping one, and another the other, and agreeing upon an hour wherein they will communicate.
Brown's Vulgar Errours, *b.* ii. *c.* 2.

ABE'D *adv.* [from *a*, for *at*. See (A) and BED.] In bed.

It was a ſhame for them to mar their complexions, yea and conditions too, with long lying *abed*: and that, when ſhe was of their age, ſhe trowed, ſhe would have made a handkerchief by that time o' day. *Sidney*, *b.* ii.

She has not been *abed*, but in her chapel
All night devoutly watch'd, and brib'd the ſaints
With prayers for her deliverance. *Dryd. Span. Friar.*

ABE'RRANCE. *n. ſ.* [from *aberro*, Lat. to wander from the right way.] A deviation from the right way; an errour; a miſtake; a falſe opinion.

Could a man be compoſed to ſuch an advantage of conſtitution, that it ſhould not at all adulterate the images of his mind; yet this ſecond nature would alter the craſis of his underſtanding, and render it as obnoxious to *aberrances*, as now.
Glanville's Scepſis Scientifica, *c.* 16.

ABE'RRANCY. The ſame with ABERRANCE.

They do not only ſwarm with errors, but vices depending thereon. Thus they commonly affect no man any farther than he deſerts his reaſon, or complies with their *aberrancies*.
Brown's Vulgar Errours, *b.* i. *c.* 3.

ABE'RRANT. *adj.* [from *aberrans*, Lat.] Deviating, wandering from the right or known way. *Dict.*

ABERRA'TION. *n. ſ.* [from *aberratio*, Lat.] The act of deviating from the common track.

And if it be a miſtake, it is only ſo; there is no hereſy in ſuch an harmleſs *aberration*; at the worſt, with the ingenuous, the probability of it will render it a lapſe of eaſy pardon.
Glanville's Scepſis Scientifica, *c.* 11.

ABE'RRING. *part.* [from the verb *aberr*, of *aberro*, Lat.] Wandering, going aſtray.

Though there were a fatality in this year, yet divers were, and others might be, out in their account, *aberring* ſeveral ways from the true and juſt compute, and calling that one year, which perhaps might be another.
Brown's Vulgar Errours, *b.* iv. *c.* 12.

Of the verb *aberr* I have found no example.

To ABERU'NCATE. *v. a.* [*averunco*, Lat.] To pull up by the roots; to extirpate utterly. *Dict.*

To ABE'T. *v. a.* [from betan, Sax. ſignifying to enkindle or animate.] To puſh forward another, to ſupport him in his deſigns by connivance, encouragement, or help. It is generally taken, at leaſt by modern writers, in an ill ſenſe; as may be ſeen in ABETTER.

To *abet* ſignifieth, in our common law, as much as to encourage or ſet on. *Cowel.*

Then ſhall I ſoon, quoth he, return again,
Abet that virgin's cauſe diſconſolate,
And ſhortly back return unto this place,
To walk this way in pilgrim's poor eſtate. *Fairy Q. b.* i.

A widow who by ſolemn vows,
Contracted to me, for my ſpouſe,
Combin'd with him to break her word,
And has *abetted* all.——— *Hudibras*, *p.* iii. *cant.* 3.

Men lay ſo great weight upon their being of right opinions, and their eagerneſs of *abetting* them, that they account that the unum neceſſarium. *Decay of Piety.*

In the reign of king Charles the firſt, though that prince was married to a daughter of France, and was perſonally beloved and eſteemed in the French court; it is well known that they *abetted* both parties in the civil war, and always furniſhed ſupplies to the weaker ſide, leſt there ſhould be an end put to theſe fatal diviſions. *Addiſon's Freeholder*, N° 28.

ABE'TMENT. *n. ſ.* The act of abetting. *Dict.*

ABE'TTER, or ABE'TTOR. *n. ſ.* He that abets; the ſupporter or encourager of another.

You ſhall be ſtill plain Torriſmond with me,
Th' *abettor*, partner, (if you like the name)
The huſband of a tyrant, but no king;
Till you deſerve that title by your juſtice.
Dryden's Spaniſh Friar.

Whilſt this ſin of calumny has two ſuch potent *abetters*, we are not to wonder at its growth: as long as men are malicious and deſigning, they will be traducing. *Govern. of the Tongue.*

Theſe and the like conſiderations, though they may have no influence on the headſtrong unruly multitude, ought to ſink into the minds of thoſe who are their *abettors*, and who, if they eſcape the puniſhment here due to them, muſt very well know, that theſe ſeveral miſchiefs will be one day laid to their charge. *Addiſon's Freeholder*, N° 50.

ABEY'ANCE. *n. ſ.* [from the French *aboyer*, *allatrare*, to bark at.] This word, in *Littleton*, cap. Diſcontinuance, is thus uſed. The right of fee-ſimple lieth in *abeyance*, when it is all only in the remembrance, intendment, and conſideration of the law. The frank tenement of the glebe of the parſonage, is in no man during the time that the parſonage is void, but is in *abeyance*. *Cowel.*

ABGREGA'TION *n. ſ.* [*abgregatio*, Lat.] A ſeparation from the flock. *Dict.*

To ABHO'R. *v. a.* [*abhorreo*, Lat.] To hate with acrimony; to deteſt to extremity; to loath.

Whilſt I was big in clamour, came there a man,
Who having ſeen me in my worſer ſtate,
Shunn'd my *abhorr'd* ſociety. *Shakeſpear's K. Lear.*

To whom thus Michael: juſtly thou *abhorr'ſt*
That ſon, who on the quiet ſtate of men
Such trouble brought, affecting to ſubdue
Rational liberty. *Milt. Parad. Loſt*, *b.* xii. *l.* 79.

The ſelf-ſame thing they will *abhor*
One way, and long another for. *Hudibras*, *p.* i. *cant.* 1.

A church of England man *abhors* the humour of the age, in delighting to fling ſcandals upon the clergy in general; which, beſides the diſgrace to the reformation, and to religion itſelf, caſt an ignominy upon the kingdom that it doth not deſerve.
Swift on the Sentiments of a Church of England-man.

ABHO'RRENCE *n. ſ.* [from *abhor*.]

1. The act of abhorring, deteſtation.

It draws upon him the juſt and univerſal hatred and *abhorrence* of all men here; and, finally, ſubjects him to the wrath of God, and eternal damnation hereafter. *South's Serm.*

2. The diſpoſition to abhor; hatred.

He knew well that even a juſt and neceſſary offence does, by giving men acquaintance with war, take off ſomewhat from the *abhorrence* of it, and inſenſibly diſpoſe them to farther hoſtilities. *Decay of Piety.*

ABHO'RRENCY. *n. ſ.* The ſame with ABHORRENCE.

The firſt tendency to any injuſtice that appears, muſt be ſuppreſſed with a ſhow of wonder and *abhorrency* in the parents and governours. *Locke on Education*, § 110.

ABHO'RRENT. *adj.* [from *abhor*.]

1. Struck with abhorrence.

——— For if the worlds
In worlds incloſ'd would on his ſenſes burſt,
He would *abhorrent* turn. *Thomſon's Summer*, *l.* 310.

2. Contrary to, foreign, inconſiſtent with. It is uſed with the particles *from* or *to*, but more properly with *from*.

This I conceive to be an hypotheſis, well worthy a rational belief; and yet is it ſo *abhorrent from* the vulgar, that they would as ſoon believe Anaxagoras, that ſnow is black, as him that ſhould affirm it is not white; and if any ſhould in effect aſſert, that the fire is not formally hot, it would be thought that the heat of his brain had fitted him for Anticyra, and that his head were ſo to madneſs. *Glanville's Scepſis Scient. c.* 12.

Why then theſe foreign thoughts of ſtate employments,
Abhorrent to your function and your breeding?
Poor droning truants of unpractis'd cells,
Bred in the fellowſhip of beardleſs boys,
What wonder is it if you know not men?
Dryden's Don Sebaſtian.

ABHO'RRER. *n. ſ.* [from *abhor*.] The perſon that abhors; a hater, deteſter.

The repreſentatives of the lower clergy were railed at, for diſputing the power of the biſhops, by the known *abhorrers* of epiſcopacy, and abuſed for doing nothing in the convocations, by theſe very men who wanted to bind up their hands.
Swift's Examiner, N° 21.

ABHO'RRING. The object of abhorrence. This ſeems not to be the proper uſe of the participial noun.

And they ſhall go forth, and look upon the carcaſes of the men that have tranſgreſſed againſt me: for their worm ſhall not die, neither ſhall their fire be quenched, and they ſhall be an *abhorring* unto all fleſh. *Iſaiah*, lxvi. 44.

To ABI'DE. *v. n.* I abode or abid. [from bidian, or aubidian, Sax.]

1. To dwell in a place, not remove.

Thy ſervant became ſurety for the lad unto my father, ſaying, if I bring him not unto thee, then I ſhall bear the blame to my father for ever. Now therefore I pray thee, let thy ſervant *abide* inſtead of the lad, a bondman to my lord; and let the lad go up with his brethren. *Gen.* xliv. 32, 33.

2. To dwell.

The Marquis Dorſet, as I hear, is fled
To Richmond, in the parts where he *abides*.
Shakeſp. Richard III.

3. To remain, not ceaſe or fail.

They that truſt in the Lord ſhall be as mount Zion, which cannot be removed, but *abideth* for ever. *Pſalm* cxxv. 1.

4. To continue in the same state.

The fear of the Lord tendeth to life; and he that hath it shall *abide* satisfied. *Prov.* xix. 23.

Those who apply themselves to learning, are forced to acknowledge one God, incorruptible and unbegotten; who is the only true being, and *abides* for ever above the highest heavens, from whence he beholds all the things that are done in heaven and earth. *Stillingfl. Defence of Disc. on Rom. Idolat.*

There can be no study without time; and the mind must *abide* and dwell upon things, or be always a stranger to the inside of them. *South.*

5. It is used with the particle *with* before a person, and *at* or *in* before a place.

It is better that I give her to thee, than that I should give her to another man: *abide with* me. *Gen.* xxix. 19.

For thy servant vowed a vow, while I *abode at* Geshur in Syria, saying, if the Lord shall bring me again indeed to Jerusalem, then I will serve the Lord. 2 *Sam.* xv. 8.

6. It is used with *by* before a thing; as, to *abide by* his testimony; to *abide by* his own skill; that is, *to rely upon them*; to *abide by* an opinion, to *maintain it*; to *abide by* a man, is also, *to defend or support him*. But these forms are something low.

Of the participle *abid*, I have found only the example in Woodward.

To ABIDE. *v. a.*

1. To bear or support, without being conquered or destroyed.

But the Lord he is the true God, he is the living God, and an everlasting King: at his wrath the earth shall tremble, and the nations shall not be able to *abide* his indignation. *Jer.* x. 10.

It must be allowed a fair presumption in favour of the truth of my doctrines, that they have *abid* a very rigorous test now for above thirty years, stand yet firm; and the longer and more strictly they are look'd into, the more they are confirmed to this very day. *Woodward, Letter* i.

2. To bear or suffer.

That chief (rejoin'd the God) his race derives
From Ithaca, and wond'rous woes survives;
Laertes' son: girt with circumfluous tides
He still calamitous constraint *abides*. *Pope's Odyss. b.* iv. *l.* 750.

3. To bear without aversion; in which sense it is commonly used with a negative.

Thou can'st not *abide* Tiridates; this is but love of thyself. *Sidney, b.* ii.

Thy vile race,
Though thou didst learn, had that in't, which good natures
Could not *abide* to be with; therefore wast thou
Deservedly confin'd into this rock. *Shakesp. Tempest.*

4. To wait for, expect, attend, wait upon, await; used of things prepared for persons, as well as of persons expecting things.

Home is he brought, and laid in sumptuous bed,
Where many skilful leeches him *abide*,
To salve his hurts. *Fairy Queen, b.* i. *cant.* 5. *stanz.* 17.

While lions war, and battle for their dens,
Poor harmless lambs *abide* their enmity. *Shakesp. Hen.* VI.

Bonds and afflictions *abide* me. *Acts* xx. 23.

5. To bear or support the consequences of a thing.

Ah me! they little know.
How dearly I *abide* that boast so vain. *Milton's Par. Lost.*

ABI'DER. *n. s.* [from *abide*] The person that abides or dwells in a place; perhaps that lives or endures. A word little in use.

ABI'DING. *n. s.* [from *abide.*] Continuance; duration.

We are strangers before thee and sojourners, as were all our fathers: our days on the earth are as a shadow, and there is none *abiding*. 1 *Chron.* xxix. 15.

The air in that region is so violently removed, and carried about with such swiftness, as nothing in that place can consist or have *abiding*. *Raleigh's History of the World.*

A'BJECT. *adj.* [*abjectus*, Lat. thrown away as of no value.]

1. Mean, or worthless, spoken of persons.

That rebellion
Came like itself in base and *abject* routs,
Led on by bloody youth goaded with rage,
And countenanc'd by boys and beggary. *Shakesp. Hen.* IV.

Honest men, who tell their sovereigns what they expect from them, and what obedience they shall be always ready to pay them, are not upon an equal foot with such base and *abject* flatterers; and are therefore always in danger of being the last in the royal favour. *Addison's Whig Examiner.*

2. Contemptible, or of no value; used of things.

I was at first, as other beasts that graze
The troden herb, of *abject* thoughts and low.
Milt. Paradise Lost, b. ix. *l.* 571.

3. Without hope or regard; used of condition.

The rarer thy example stands,
By how much from the top of wond'rous glory,
Strongest of mortal men,
To lowest pitch of *abject* fortune thou art fall'n.
Milton's Sampson Agonistes.

We see man and woman in the highest innocence and perfection, and in the most *abject* state of guilt and infirmity. *Addison, Spectator,* Nº. 273.

4. Destitute, mean and despicable; used of actions.

To what base ends, and by what *abject* ways,
Are mortals urg'd thro' sacred lust of praise?
Pope's Essay on Criticism.

The rapine is so *abject* and profane,
They not from trifles, nor from gods refrain.
Dryden's Juvenal, Sat. 8.

A'BJECT. *n. s.* A man without hope; a man whose miseries are irretrievable.

But in mine adversity they rejoiced, and gathered themselves together: yea, the *abjects* gathered themselves together against me, and I knew it not; they did tear me, and ceased not. *Psalm* xxxv. 15.

To ABJE'CT. *v. a.* [*abjicio*, Lat.] To throw away. A word rarely used.

ABJ'ECTEDNESS. *n. s.* [from *abject.*] The state of an abject.

He would love at no less rate than death; and, from the supereminent height of glory, stooped and abased himself to the sufferance of the extremest of indignities, and sunk himself to the bottom of *abjectedness*, to exalt our condition to the contrary extreme. *Boyle's Works.*

ABJE'CTION. *n. s.* [from *abject.*] Meanness of mind; want of spirit; servility; baseness.

That this should be termed baseness, *abjection* of mind, or servility, is it credible? *Hooker, b.* v. § 47.

Now the just medium of this case lies betwixt the pride and the *abjection*, the two extremes. *L'Estrange.*

A'BJECTLY *adv.* [from *abject.*] In an abject manner, meanly, basely, servilely, contemptibly.

A'BJECTNESS. *n. s.* [from *abject.*] The same with abjection; servility, meanness.

Servility and *abjectness* of humour is implicitely involved in the charge of lying; the condescending to that, being a mark of a disingenuous spirit. *Government of the Tongue,* § 8.

By humility I mean not the *abjectness* of a base mind: but a prudent care not to over-value ourselves upon any account. *Grew's Cosmologia Sacra, b.* ii. *c.* 7.

ABI'LITY. *n. s.* [*habilité*, Fr.]

1. The power to do any thing, whether depending upon skill, or riches, or strength, or any other quality.

Of singing thou hast got the reputation,
Good Thyrsis, mine I yield to thy *ability*;
My heart doth seek another estimation. *Sidney, b.* i.

If aught in my *ability* may serve
To heighten what thou suffer'st, and appease
Thy mind with what amends is in my pow'r.
Milton's Sampson Agonistes, l. 744.

They gave after their *ability* unto the treasure of the work. *Ezra* ii. 69.

If any man minister, let him do it as of the *ability* which God giveth: that God in all things may be glorified through Jesus Christ. 1 *Pet.* iv. 11.

2. Capacity.

Children in whom there was no blemish, but well-favoured, and skilful in all wisdom, and cunning in knowledge, and understanding science, and such as had *ability* in them to stand in the king's palace. *Dan.* i. 4.

3. When it has the plural number, *abilities*, it frequently signifies the faculties or powers of the mind, and sometimes the force of understanding given by nature, as distinguished from acquired qualifications.

Wherever we find our *abilities* too weak for the performance, he assures us of the assistance of his holy spirit. *Rogers's Sermons.*

Whether it may be thought necessary, that in certain tracts of country, like what we call parishes, there should be one man, at least, of *abilities* to read and write? *Swift's Arguments against abolishing Christianity.*

ABINTE'STATE. *adj.* [of *ab*, from, and *intestatus*, Lat.] A term of law, implying him that inherits from a man, who, though he had the power to make a will, yet did not make it.

To A'BJUGATE. *v. a.* [*abjugo*, Lat.] To unyoke, to uncouple. *Dict.*

To ABJU'RE. *v. a.* [*abjuro*, Lat.]

1. To cast off upon oath, to swear not to do something.

Either to die the death, or to *abjure*
For ever the society of man. *Shakesp. Midsum. Night's Dream.*

No man, therefore, that hath not *abjured* his reason, and sworn allegiance to a preconceived fantastical hypothesis, can undertake the defence of such a supposition. *Hale's Origin of Mankind.*

2. To retract, or recant, or abnegate, a position upon oath.

ABJURA'TION. *n. s.* [from *abjure.*] The act of abjuring. The oath taken for that end.

Until Henry VIII. his time, if a man, having committed felony, could go into a church or church-yard, before he were apprehended, he might not be taken from thence to the usual trial of law, but confessing his fault to the justices, or to the coroner, gave his oath to forsake the realm for ever, which was called *abjuration*.

There are some *abjurations* still in force among us here in England; as, by the statute of the 25th of king Charles II. all persons that are admitted into any office, civil or military, must

must take the test; which is an *abjuration* of some doctrines of the church of Rome.

There is likewise another oath of *abjuration*, which laymen and clergymen are both obliged to take; and that is, to abjure the Pretender. *Ayliffe's Parergon Juris Canonici.*

To ABLA'CTATE. *v. a.* [*ablacto*, Lat.] To wean from the breast.

ABLACTA'TION. *n. s.* One of the methods of grafting; and, according to the signification of the word, as it were a weaning of a cyon by degrees from its mother stock, not cutting it off wholly from the stock, till it is firmly united to that on which it is grafted.

ABLAQUEA'TION. *n. s.* [*ablaqueatio*, Lat.] The act or practice of opening the ground about the roots of trees, to let the air and water operate upon them.

Trench the ground, and make it ready for the spring; prepare also soil, and use it where you have occasion: Dig borders. Uncover as yet roots of trees, where *ablaqueation* is requisite. *Evelyn's Kalendar.*

The tenure in chief ought to be kept alive and nourished; the which, as it is the very root that doth maintain this silver stem, that by many rich and fruitful branches spreadeth itself into the chancery, exchequer, and court of wards: so if it be suffered to starve, by want of *ablaqueation*, and other good husbandry, not only this yearly fruit will much decrease from time to time, but also the whole body and boughs of that precious tree itself, will fall into danger of decay and dying. *Bacon.*

ABLA'TION. *n. s.* [*ablatio*, Lat.] The act of taking away.

A'BLATIVE. *n. a.* [*ablativus*, Lat.]

1. That which takes away.
2. The sixth case of the Latin nouns; the case which, among other significations, includes the person from whom something is taken away. A term of grammar.

A'BLE. *adj.* [*habile*, Fr. *habilis*, Lat. skilful, ready.]

1. Having strong faculties, or great strength or knowledge, riches, or any other power of mind, body, or fortune.

He was not afraid of an able man, as Lewis the Eleventh was. But, contrariwise, he was served by the *ablest* men that were to be found; without which his affairs could not have prospered as they did. *Bacon's Henry* VII.

Such other gambol faculties he hath, that shew a weak mind and an *able* body, for the which the prince admits him: for the prince himself is such another: the weight of an hair will turn the scales. *Shakesp. Henry* IV. *p.* ii.

2. Having power sufficient; enabled.

All mankind acknowledge themselves *able* and sufficient to do many things, which actually they never do. *South's Serm.*

Every man shall give as he is *able*, according to the blessing of the Lord thy God, which he hath given thee. *Deut.* xvi. 17.

3. Before a verb, with the participle *to*, it signifies generally having the power; before a noun with *for*, it means *qualified*.

Wrath is cruel, and anger is outrageous; but who is *able to* stand before envy? *Prov.* xxvii. 4.

There have been some inventions also, which have been *able for* the utterance of articulate sounds, as the speaking of certain words. *Wilkins's Mathematical Magick.*

To A'BLE. *v. a.* To make able; to enable, which is the word commonly used. See ENABLE.

Plate sin with gold,
And the strong lance of justice hurtless breaks:
Arm it with rags, a pigmy's straw doth pierce it.
None does offend, none, I say none; I'll *able* 'em;
Take that of me, my friend, who have the pow'r
To seal th' accuser's lips. *Shakespeare's King Lear.*

ABLE-BODIED. *adj.* Strong of body.

It lies in the power of every fine woman, to secure at least half a dozen *able-bodied* men to his majesty's service. *Addison, Freeholder*, Nº 4.

To A'BLEGATE. *v. a.* [*ablego*, Lat.] To send abroad upon some employment; also to send a person out of the way that one is weary of. *Dict.*

ABLEGA'TION. *n. s.* [from *ablegate*.] A sending abroad, or out of the way. *Dict.*

A'BLENESS. *n. s.* [from *able*.] Ability of body or mind; vigour, force; faculties.

That nation doth so excel, both for comeliness and *ableness*, that from neighbour countries they ordinarily come, some to strive, some to learn, some to behold. *Sidney, b.* ii.

A'BLEPSY. *n. s.* [Αβλεψία, Gr.] Want of sight, natural blindness; also unadvisedness. *Dict.*

ABLIGURI'TION. *n. s.* [*abligurritio*, Lat.] A prodigal spending on meat and drink. *Dict.*

To A'BLIGATE. *v. a.* [*abligo*, Lat.] To bind or tye up from. *D.*

To A'BLOCATE. *v. a.* [*abloco*, Lat.] To let out to hire. Perhaps properly by him who has hired it from another. *Calvin's Lexicon Juridicum.*

ABLOCA'TION. *n. s.* [from *ablocate*.] A letting out to hire.

To ABLU'DE. *v. n.* [*abludo*, Lat.] To be unlike. *Dict.*

A'BLUENT. *adj.* [*abluens*, Lat. from *abluo*, to wash away.]

1. That which washes clean.
2. That which has the power of cleansing. *Dict.*

ABLU'TION. *n. s.* [*ablutio*, Lat.]

1. The act of cleansing, or washing clean.

There is a natural analogy between the *ablution* of the body and the purification of the soul; between eating the holy bread and drinking the sacred chalice, and a participation of the body and blood of Christ. *Taylor's Worthy Communicant.*

Wash'd by the briny wave, the pious train
Are cleans'd, and cast th' *ablutions* in the main. *Pope's Iliad.*

2. The rinsing of chymical preparations in water, to dissolve and wash away any acrimonious particles.
3. The cup given, without consecration, to the laity in the popish churches.

To A'BNEGATE. *v. a.* [from *abnego*, Lat.] To deny.

ABNEGA'TION. *n. s.* [*abnegatio*, Lat. denial, from *abnego*, to deny.] Denial, renunciation.

The *abnegation* or renouncing of all his own holds and interests, and trusts of all that man is most apt to depend upon, that he may the more expeditely follow Christ. *Hammond's Practical Catechism.*

ABNODA'TION. *n. s.* [*abnodatio*, Lat.] The act of cutting away knots from trees; a term of gardening. *Dict.*

ABNO'RMOUS. *adj.* [*abnormis*, Lat. out of rule.] Irregular, misshapen. *Dict.*

ABO'ARD. *adv.* [a sea term, but adopted into common language; derived immediately from the French *à bord*, as *aller à bord*, *envoyer à bord*. *Bord* is itself a word of very doubtful original, and perhaps, in its different acceptions, deducible from different roots. Borð, in the ancient Saxon, signified a *house*; in which sense, *to go aboard*, is to take up residence in a ship.] In a ship.

Which, when far off, Cymocles heard and saw,
He loudly call'd to such as were *aboard*,
The little bark unto the shore to draw,
And him to ferry over that deep ford. *Fairy Queen.*

I made this answer, that he might land them, if it pleased him, or otherwise keep them *aboard*. *Sir W. Raleigh's Essays.*

When morning rose, I sent my mates to bring
Supplies of water from a neighb'ring spring;
Whilst I the motions of the winds explor'd;
Then summon'd in my crew, and went *aboard*.
Addison's Ovid's Metamorphoses, b. iii.

ABO'DE. *n. s.* [from *abide*.]

1. Habitation, dwelling place of residence.

But I know thy *abode*, and thy going out, and thy coming in and thy rage against me. *2 Kings*, xix. 27.

Others may use the ocean as their road,
Only the English make it their *abode*;
Whose ready sails with every wind can fly,
And make a cov'nant with th' unconstant sky. *Waller.*

2. Stay, continuance in a place.

Sweet friends, your patience for my long *abode*;
Not I, but my affairs, have made you wait.
Shakespeare's Merchant of Venice.

Making a short *abode* in Sicily the second time, landing in Italy, and making the war, may be reasonably judged the business but of ten months. *Dryden's Dedicat. to Æneid.*

The woodcocks early visit, and *abode*
Of long continuance in our temp'rate clime,
Foretel a liberal harvest. *Phillips.*

3. To make abode; to dwell, to reside, to inhabit.

Deep in a cave the Sibyl makes *abode*;
Thence full of fate returns, and of the god. *Dryd. Æn.* 6.

To ABO'DE. *v. a.* [See BODE.] To foretoken or foreshow; to be a prognostic, to be ominous. It is taken, with its derivatives, in the sense either of good or ill.

Every man,
After the hideous storm that follow'd, was
A thing inspir'd; and, not consulting, broke
Into a general prophecy, that this tempest,
Dashing the garment of this peace, *aboded*
The sudden breach of it. *Shakespeare's Henry* VIII.

ABO'DEMENT. *n. s.* [from *to abode*.] A secret anticipation of something future; an impression upon the mind of some event to come; prognostication; omen.

I like not this.
For many men that stumble at the threshold,
Are well foretold that danger lurks within.—
—Tush! man, *abodements* must not now affright us.
Shakespeare's Henry VI. *p.* iii.

My lord bishop, being somewhat troubled, took the freedom to ask him, Whether he had never any secret *abodement* in his mind? No, replied the duke: but I think some adventure may kill me as well as another man. *Wotton.*

To ABO'LISH. *v. a.* [from *aboleo*, Lat. to blot out.]

1. To annul.

For us to *abolish* what he hath established, were presumption most intolerable. *Hooker, b.* iii. § 10.

On the parliament's part it was proposed, that all the bishops, deans, and chapters, might be immediately taken away, and *abolished*. *Clarendon, b.* viii.

2. To put an end to; to destroy.

The long continued wars, between the English and the Scots, had then raised invincible jealousies and hate, which long continued peace hath since *abolished*. *Sir John Hayward.*

That

That shall Pericles well requite, I wot,
And, with thy blood, *abolish* so reproachful blot.
Fairy Queen, b. ii. *cant.* 4. *stanza* 45.

More destroy'd than they,
We should be quite *abolish'd*, and expire.
Milton's Paradise Lost, b. ii. *l.* 92.

Or wilt thou thyself
Abolish thy creation, and unmake
For him, what for thy glory thou hast made? *Id. b.* iii. *l.* 163.

Fermented spirits contract, harden, and consolidate many fibres together, *abolishing* many canals; especially where the fibres are the tenderest, as in the brain. *Arbuth. on Aliments.*

Nor could Vulcanian flame
The stench *abolish*, or the savour tame. *Dryd. Virg. Geo.* iii.

ABO'LISHABLE. *adj.* [from *abolish.*] That which may be abolished.

ABO'LISHER. *n. s.* [from *abolish.*] He that abolishes.

ABO'LISHMENT. *n. s.* [from *abolish.*] The act of abolishing.

The plain and direct way against us herein, had been only to prove, that all such ceremonies, as they require to be abolished, are retained by us with the hurt of the church, or with less benefit than the *abolishment* of them would bring. *Hooker, b.* iv.

He should therefore think the *abolishment* of that order among us, would prove a mighty scandal and corruption to our faith, and manifestly dangerous to our monarchy.
Swift on the Sentiments of a Church of England-man.

ABOLI'TION. *n. s.* [from *abolish.*] The act of abolishing. This is now more frequently used than *abolishment.*

From the total *abolition* of the popular power, may be dated the ruin of Rome: for had the reducing hereof to its ancient condition, proposed by Agrippa, been accepted instead of Mæcenas's model, that state might have continued unto this day.
Grew's Cosmologia Sacra, b. iii. *c.* 4.

An apoplexy is a sudden *abolition* of all the senses, external and internal, and of all voluntary motion, by the stoppage of the flux and reflux of the animal spirits through the nerves destined for those motions. *Arbuthnot on Diet.*

ABO'MINABLENESS. *n. s.* [from *abominable.*] The quality of being abominable; hatefulness, odiousness.

Till we have proved, in its proper place, the eternal and essential difference between virtue and vice, we must forbear to urge atheists with the corruption and *abominableness* of their principles. *Bentley's Sermons.*

ABO'MINABLE. *adj.* [*abominabilis*, Lat.]

1. Hateful, detestable.

Return'd
Successful beyond hope, to lead thee forth
Triumphant out of this infernal pit
Abominable, accurs'd, the house of woe. *Par. Lost, b.* x.

It is not to be questioned, but the queen and ministry might easily redress this *abominable* grievance, by enlarging the number of justices of the peace, by endeavouring to choose men of virtuous principles. *Swift's Project for the Advancement of Religion.*

2. Unclean.

The soul that shall touch any unclean thing, as the uncleanness of man, or any unclean beast, or any *abominable* unclean thing, and eat of the flesh of the sacrifice of peace-offerings, which pertain unto the Lord, even that soul shall be cut off from his people. *Leviticus*, vii. 21.

3. In low and ludicrous language, it is a word of loose and indeterminate censure.

They say you are a melancholy fellow.—I am so; I do love it better than laughing.—Those that are in extremity of either, are *abominable* fellows, and betray themselves to every modern censure, worse than drunkards. *Shakespeare's As you like it.*

ABO'MINABLY. *adv.* [from *abominable.*] A word of low or familiar language, signifying excessively, extremely, exceedingly; in the ill sense.

Since I have been your wife, I have observed great abuses and disorders in your family; your servants are mutinous and quarrelsome, and cheat you most *abominably.*
Arbuthnot's History of John Bull.

To ABO'MINATE. *v. a.* [*abominor*, Lat.] To abhor, detest, hate utterly.

We are not guilty of your injuries,
No way consent to them; but abhor,
Abominate, and loath this cruelty. *Southern's Oroonoko.*

He professed both to *abominate* and despise all mystery, refinement, and intrigue, either in a prince or minister. He could not tell what I meant by secrets of state, where an enemy, or some rival nation, were not in the case. *Swift's Gulliv. Travels.*

ABOMINA'TION. *n. s.*

1. Hatred, detestation; as, *to have in abomination.*

To assist king Charles by English or Dutch forces, would render him odious to his new subjects, who have nothing in so great *abomination*, as those whom they hold for hereticks.
Swift's Miscellanies.

2. The object of hatred.

That ye shall say, thy servant's trade hath been about cattle, from our youth even until now, both we and also our fathers: that ye may dwell in the land of Goshen; for every shepherd is an *abomination* to the Egyptians. *Genesis*, xlvi. 34.

3. Pollution, defilement.

And there shall in no wise enter into it any thing that defileth, neither whatsoever worketh *abomination*, or maketh a lie. *Rev.* xxi. 27.

Each heart in Rome does love and pity you;
Only th' adulterous Antony, most large
In his *abominations*, turns you off,
And gives his potent regiment to a trull,
That noses it against us. *Shakesp. Antony and Cleopatra.*

4. The cause of pollution.

And the high places that were before Jerusalem, which were on the right hand of the mount of corruption, which Solomon the king of Israel had builded for Ashteroth the *abomination* of the Zidonians, and for Chemosh the *abomination* of the Moabites, and for Milcom the *abomination* of the children of Ammon, did the king defile. *2 Kings*, xxiii. 13.

ABORI'GINES. *n. s.* [Lat.] The earliest inhabitants of a country; those of whom no original is to be traced; as the Welsh in Britain.

To ABO'RT. *v. n.* [*aborto*, Lat.] To bring forth before the time; to miscarry. *Dict.*

ABO'RTION. *n. s.* [*abortio*, Lat.]

1. The act of bringing forth untimely.

2. The produce of an untimely birth.

His wife miscarried; but as the *abortion* proved only a female fœtus, he comforted himself, that, had it arrived to perfection, it would not have answered his account.
Arbuthnot and Pope's Martinus Scriblerus.

Behold my arm thus blasted, dry and wither'd,
Shrunk like a foul *abortion*, and decay'd,
Like some untimely product of the seasons,
Robb'd of its properties of strength and office.
Rowe's Jane Shore.

ABO'RTIVE. *n. s.* That which is born before the due time. See ABORTIVE, *adj.*

No common wind, no customed event,
But they will pluck away its nat'ral causes,
And call them meteors, prodigies, and signs,
Abortives, and presages, tongues of heav'n
Plainly denouncing vengeance upon John. *Shakes. K. John.*

Take the fine skin of an *abortive*, and, with starch thin laid on, prepare your ground or tablet. *Peacham on Drawing.*

This is certain, that many are, by this means, preserved, and do signal service to their country, who, without such a provision, might have perished as *abortives*, or have come to an untimely end, and perhaps have brought, upon their guilty parents, the like destruction. *Addison, Guardian*, Nº 106.

ABO'RTIVE. *adj.* [*abortivus*, Lat.]

1. That which is brought forth before the due time of birth.

If ever he have child, *abortive* be it,
Prodigious, and untimely brought to light. *Shakesp. Rich.* III.

All th' unaccomplish'd works of nature's hand,
Abortive, monstrous, or unkindly mix'd,
Dissolv'd on earth, fleet hither. *Paradise Lost, b.* iii. *l.* 456.

2. Figuratively, that which fails for want of time.

This is the true cause, why so many politic conceptions, so elaborately formed and wrought, and grown at length ripe for delivery, do yet, in the issue, miscarry and prove *abortive.*
South's Sermons.

False hopes
He cherishes, nor will his fruit expect
Th' autumnal season, but, in summer's pride
When other orchards smile, *abortive* fail. *Phillips.*

How often hast thou waited at my cup,
Fed from my trencher, kneel'd down at the board,
When I have feasted with queen Margaret?
Remember it, and let it make thee crest-faln;
Ay, and allay this thy *abortive* pride. *Shakesp. Hen.* VI. *p.* ii.

3. That which brings forth nothing.

These pass'd, if any pass, the void profound
Of unessential night receives him next,
Wide-gaping! and with utter loss of being
Threatens him, plung'd in that *abortive* gulf.
Milton's Paradise Lost, b. ii. *l.* 451.

ABO'RTIVELY *adv.* [from *abortive.*] Born without the due time; immaturely, untimely.

ABO'RTIVENESS. *n. s.* [from *abortive.*] The state of abortion.

ABO'RTMENT. *n. s.* [from *abort.*] The thing brought forth out of time; an untimely birth.

I shall not then doubt the happy issue of my undertakings in this design, whereby concealed treasures, which now seem utterly lost to mankind, shall be confined to so universal a piety, and brought into use by the industry of converted penitents, whose wretched carcases the impartial laws have, or shall, dedicate, as untimely feasts, to the worms of the earth, in whose womb those deserted mineral riches must ever lie buried as lost *abortments*, unless those be made the active midwives to deliver them. *Bacon's Physical Remains.*

ABO'VE. *prep.* [from *a*, and buran, Saxon; *boven*, Dutch.]

1. Higher in place.

So when with crackling flames a cauldron fries,
The bubbling waters from the bottom rise;

Above the brims they force their firy way;
Black vapours climb aloft, and cloud the day.
Dryden, Æneid vii. *l.* 643.

2. More in quantity or number.

Every one that passeth among them, that are numbered from twenty years old and *above*, shall give an offering unto the Lord. *Exodus*, xxx. 14.

3. Higher in rank, power or excellence.

The Lord is high *above* all nations, and his glory *above* the heavens. *Psalm* cxiii. 4.

The public power of all societies is *above* every soul contained in the same societies. *Hooker*, *b.* i.

There is no riches *above* a sound body, and no joy *above* the joy of the heart. *Ecclesiasticus*, xxx. 16.

To her
Thou didst resign thy manhood, and the place
Wherein God set thee *above* her, made of thee,
And for thee: whose perfection far excell'd
Her's, in all real dignity. *Milton's Paradise Lost*, *b.* x. *l.* 147.

Latona sees her shine *above* the rest,
And feeds with secret joy her silent breast. *Dryden's Æneid.*

4. Superiour to, unattainable by.

It is an old and true distinction, that things may be *above* our reason, without being contrary to it. Of this kind are the power, the nature, and the universal presence of God, with innumerable other points. *Swift.*

5. Beyond; more than.

We were pressed out of measure, *above* strength; insomuch that we despaired even of life. 2 *Cor.* i. 8.

In this, of having thoughts unconfused, and being able nicely to distinguish one thing from another, where there is but the least difference, consists, in a great measure, the exactness of judgment and clearness of reason, which is to be observed in one man above another. *Locke.*

The inhabitants of Tirol have many particular privileges *above* those of the other hereditary countries of the emperor. *Addison on Italy.*

6. Too proud for; too high for. A phrase chiefly used in familiar expression.

Kings and princes, in the earlier ages of the world, laboured in arts and occupations, and were *above* nothing that tended to promote the conveniences of life. *Pope's Odyssey, Notes.*

ABO'VE. *adv.*

1. Over-head.

To men standing below, men standing aloft seem much lessened; to those *above*, men standing below, seem not so much lessened. *Bacon.*

When he established the clouds *above*; when he strengthened the fountains of the deep; when he gave to the sea his decree, that the waters should not pass his commandment: when he appointed the foundations of the earth: then I was by him, as one brought up with him: and I was daily his delight, rejoicing always before him. *Proverbs*, viii. 28.

2. In the regions of heaven.

Your praise the birds shall chant in every grove,
And winds shall waft it to the pow'rs *above*. *Pope's Pastorals.*

3. Before. [See ABOVE-CITED.]

I said *above*, that these two machines of the balance, and the dira, were only ornamental, and that the success of the duel had been the same without them. *Dryd. Dedicat. Æneid.*

FROM ABOVE.

1. From an higher place.

The Trojans *from above* their foes beheld;
And with arm'd legions all the rampires fill'd. *Dryd. Æneid.*

2. From heaven.

Every good gift, and every perfect gift is *from above*, and cometh down from the father of lights, with whom is no variableness, neither shadow of turning. *James*, i. 17.

ABOVE ALL. In the first place; chiefly.

I had also studied Virgil's design, his disposition of it, his manners, his judicious management of the figures, the sober retrenchments of his sense, which always leaves somewhat to gratify our imagination, on which it may enlarge at pleasure; but *above all*, the elegance of his expression, and the harmony of his numbers. *Dryden's Dedication to the Æneid.*

ABOVE-BOARD. In open sight; without artifice or trick. A figurative expression, borrowed from gamesters, who, when they put their hands under the table, are changing their cards. It is used only in familiar language.

It is the part also of an honest man to deal *above-board*, and without tricks. *L'Estrange.*

Though there have not been wanting such heretofore, as have practised these unworthy arts (for as much as there have been villains in all places, and all ages) yet now-a-days they are owned *above-board*. *South's Sermons.*

ABOVE-CITED. Cited before. A figurative expression, taken from the ancient manner of writing books on scrolls; as whatever is cited or mentioned before in the same page, must be above.

Nor would I mention this particular, did it not appear from the authority *above-cited*, that this was a fact confessed by heathens themselves. *Addison on the Christian Religion.*

ABOVE-GROUND. An expression used to signify, that a man is alive; not in the grave.

ABOVE-MENTIONED. See ABOVE-CITED.

I do not remember, that Homer any-where falls into the faults *above-mentioned*, which were indeed the false refinements of latter ages. *Addison, Spectator*, Nº 279.

To ABO'UND. *v. n.* [*abundo*, Lat. *abonder*, French.]

1. To have in great plenty; used sometimes with the particle *in*, and sometimes the particle *with*.

The king-becoming graces,
I have no relish of them, but *abound*
In the division of each several crime,
Acting it many ways. *Shakespeare's Macbeth.*

Corn, wine, and oil, are wanting to this ground,
In which our countries fruitfully *abound*. *Dryd. Indian Emp.*

A faithful man shall *abound with* blessings: but he that maketh haste to be rich, shall not be innocent. *Prov.* xxviii. 20.

Now that languages are made, and *abound with* words, standing for such combinations, an usual way of getting these complex ideas, is by the explication of those terms that stand for them. *Locke.*

2. To be in great plenty.

And because iniquity shall *abound*, the love of many shall wax cold. *Matthew*, xxiv. 12.

Words are like leaves, and where they most *abound*,
Much fruit of sense beneath is rarely found.
Pope's Essay on Criticism.

ABO'UT. *prep.* [abutan, or abuton, Sax. which seems to signify encircling on the outside.]

1. Round, surrounding, encircling.

Let not mercy and truth forsake thee. Bind them *about* thy neck; write them upon the table of thy heart. *Proverbs*, iii. 3.

At this she loudly shrieks,
'Tis he, 'tis he, she cries, and tears her cheeks,
Her hair, her vest; and, stooping to the sands,
About his neck she cast her trembling hands. *Dryd. Fables.*

2. Near to.

Speak unto the congregetion, saying, get you up from *about* the tabernacle of Korah, Dathan, and Abiram. *Exodus.*

Thou dost nothing, Sergius,
Thou canst endeavour nothing, nay, not think,
But I both see and hear it; and am with thee,
By and before, *about* and in thee too. *Benj. Johnson's Catiline.*

3. Concerning, with regard to, relating to.

When Constantine had finished an house for the service of God at Jerusalem, the dedication he judged a matter not unworthy, *about* the solemn performance whereof, the greatest part of the bishops in christendom should meet together. *Hooker*, *b.* v. § 12.

The painter is not to take so much pains *about* the drapery as *about* the face, where the principal resemblance lies. *Dryd. Pref. to Dufresnoy.*

They are most frequently used as words equivalent, and do both of them indifferently signify either a speculative knowledge of things, or a practical skill *about* them, according to the exigency of the matter or thing spoken of. *Tillot. Sermon* i.

Theft is always a sin, although the particular species of it, and the denomination of particular acts, doth suppose positive laws *about* dominion and property.
Stillingfleet's Defence of Discourses on Romish Idolatry.

They should always be heard, and fairly and kindly answered, when they ask after any thing they would know, and desire to be informed *about*. Curiosity should be as carefully cherished in children, as other appetites suppressed.
Locke on Education, § 108.

It hath been practised as a method of making men's court, when they are asked *about* the rate of lands, the abilities of tenants, the state of trade and manufacture, to answer, that, in their neighbourhood, all things are in a flourishing condition. *Swift's short View of Ireland.*

4. Engaged in, employed upon.

Our blessed Lord was pleased to command the representation of his death and sacrifice on the cross, should be made by breaking of bread and effusion of wine; to signify to us the nature and sacredness of the liturgy we are *about*.
Taylor's Worthy Communicant.

Labour, for labour's sake, is against nature. The understanding, as well as all the other faculties, chooses always the shortest way to its end, would presently obtain the knowledge it is *about*, and then set upon some new enquiry. But this, whether laziness or haste, often misleads it. *Locke.*

They ought, however, to be provided with secretaries, and assisted by our foreign ministers, to tell their story for them in plain English, and to let us know, in our mother-tongue, what it is our brave countrymen are *about*. *Addison, Spect.* Nº 309.

5. Appendant to the person; as, cloaths, &c.

If you have this *about* you,
As I will give you when we go, you may
Boldly assault the necromancer's hall. *Milton's Comus.*

It is not strange to me, that persons of the fairer sex should like, in all things *about* them, that handsomeness for which they find themselves most liked. *Boyle on Colours.*

6. Relating

6. Relating to the person, as a servant.

Liking very well the young gentleman, such I took him to be, admitted this Deiphantes *about* me, who well shewed there is no service like his that serves because he loves. *Sidney, b.* ii.

Good master, corporal, captain, for my old dame's sake, stand my friend: she hath no body to do any thing *about* her when I am gone, and she is old and cannot help herself.
Shakespeare's Henry IV. *p.* ii.

ABO'UT. *adv.*

1. Circularly.

The weyward sisters, hand in hand,
Posters of the sea and land,
Thus do go *about, about*,
Thrice to thine, and thrice to mine,
And thrice again to make up nine. *Shakesp. Macbeth.*

2. In circuit.

My honest lads, I'll tell you what I am *about*.—Two yards and more.—No quips now Pistol: indeed I am in the waste two yards *about*; but I am about no waste, I am about thrift.
Shakespeare's Merry Wives of Windsor.

A tun *about* was ev'ry pillar there,
A polish'd mirrour shone not half so clear. *Dryd. Fables.*

3. Nearly.

When the boats were come within *about* sixty yards of the pillar, they found themselves all bound, and could go no farther; yet so as they might move to go about, but might not approach nearer. *Bacon's New Atalantis.*

4. Here and there; every way.

Up rose the gentle virgin from her place,
And looked all *about*, if she might spy
Her lovely knight to move his manly pace.
Fairy Queen, b. i. *cant.* 2. *stanz.* 33.

A wolf that was past labour, had the wit in his old age, yet to make the best of a bad game; he borrows a habit, and so *about* he goes, begging charity, from door to door, under the disguise of a pilgrim. *L'Estrange.*

5. With *to* before a verb; as, *about to fly*; upon the point, within a small distance of.

These dying lovers, and their floating sons,
Suspend the fight, and silence all our guns:
Beauty and youth, *about* to perish, finds
Such noble pity in brave English minds. *Waller.*

6. The longest way, in opposition to the short straight way.

Gold hath these natures; greatness of weight; closeness of parts; fixation; pliantness, or softness; immunity from rust; colour, or tincture of yellow: Therefore the sure way (though most *about*) to make gold, is to know the causes of the several natures before rehearsed. *Bacon's Natural Hist.* N° 328.

Spies of the Volscians
Held me in chase, that I was forc'd to wheel
Three or four miles *about*; else had I, Sir,
Half an hour since brought my report. *Shakesp. Coriolanus.*

7. To bring about; to bring to the point or state desired; as, *he has brought about his purposes.*

Whether this will be brought *about*, by breaking his head, I very much question. *Spectator.*

8. To come about; to come to some certain state or point.

Wherefore it came to pass, when the time was come *about*, after Hannah had conceived, that she bare a son. 1 *Sam.* i. 20.

One evening it befel, that looking out,
The wind they long had wish'd was come *about*;
Well pleas'd they went to rest; and if the gale
'Till morn continu'd, both resolv'd to sail. *Dryd. Fables.*

9. To go about a thing; to prepare to do it.

Did not Moses give you the law, and yet none of you keepeth the law? Why go ye *about* to kill me? *John* vii. 19.

In common language, they say, to *come about* a man, to *circumvent* him.

Some of these phrases seem to derive their original from the French *à bout*; *venir à bout d'une chose*; *venir bout de quelqu'un.*

A. Bp. for Archbishop; which see.

ABRACADA'BRA. A superstitious charm against agues.

To ABRA'DE. *v. a.* [*abrado*, Lat.] To rub off; to wear away from the other parts; to waste by degrees.

By this means there may be a continued supply of what is successively *abraded* from them by decursion of waters.
Hale's Origin of Mankind.

ABRAHAM'S BALM. The name of an herb.

ABRA'SION. [See ABRADE.]

1. The act of abrading; a rubbing off.

2. [In medicine.] The wearing away of the natural mucus, which covers the membranes, particularly those of the stomach and guts, by corrosive or sharp medicines, or humours. *Quincy.*

3. The matter worn off by the attrition of bodies.

ABRE'AST. *adv.* [See BREAST.] Side by side; in such a position that the breasts may bear against the same line.

My cousin Suffolk,
My soul shall thine keep company to heaven:
Tarry, sweet soul, for mine, then fly *abreast*. *Shak. Henry* V.
For honour travels in a streight so narrow,
Where one but goes *abreast*. *Shakesp. Troilus and Cressida.*

The riders rode *abreast*, and one his shield,
His lance of cornel-wood another held;
The third his bow, and glorious to behold!
The costly quiver, all of burnish'd gold. *Dryden's Fables.*

ABRI'COT. See APRICOT.

To ABRI'DGE. *v. a.* [*abreger*, Fr. *abbrevio*, Lat.]

1. To make shorter in words, keeping still the same substance.

All these sayings, being declared by Jason of Cyrene in five books, we will essay to *abridge* in one volume. 2 *Macc.* ii. 23.

2. To contract, to diminish, to cut short.

The determination of the will, upon enquiry, is following the direction of that guide; and he, that has a power to act or not to act, according as such determination directs, is free. Such determination *abridges* not that power wherein liberty consists. *Locke.*

3. To deprive of; in which sense it is followed by the particle *from* or *of*, preceding the thing taken away.

I have disabled mine estate,
By shewing something a more swelling port,
Than my faint means would grant continuance;
Nor do I now make moan to be *abridg'd*
From such a noble rate. *Shakespeare's Merchant of Venice.*

They were formerly, by the common law, discharged from pontage and murage; but this privilege has been *abridged* them since by several statutes. *Ayliffe's Parergon Juris Canonici.*

ABRI'DGED OF. *part.* Deprived of, debarred from, cut short.

An ABRIDGER.

1 He that abridges; a shortener.

2. A writer of compendiums or abridgments.

ABRI'DGMENT. *n. s.* [*abregement*, Fr.]

1. The contraction of a larger work into a small compass.

Surely this commandment containeth the law and the prophets; and, in this one word, is the *abridgment* of all volumes of scripture. *Hooker, b.* ii. § 5.

Myself have play'd
The int'rim, by remembring you 'tis past;
Then brook *abridgment*, and your eyes advance
After your thought, straight back again to France?
Shakespeare's Henry V.

Idolatry is certainly the first-born of folly, the great and leading paradox; nay, the very *abridgment* and sum total of all absurdities. *South's Sermons.*

2. A diminution in general.

All trying, by a love of littleness,
To make *abridgments*, and to draw to less,
Even that nothing which at first we were. *Donne.*

3. Restraint, or abridgment of liberty.

The constant desire of happiness, and the constraint it puts upon us, no body, I think, accounts an *abridgment* of liberty, or at least an *abridgment* of liberty, to be complained of. *Locke.*

ABRO'ACH. *adv.* [See *To* BROACH.]

1. In a posture to run out; to yield the liquor contained; properly spoken of vessels.

The Templer spruce, while ev'ry spout's *abroach*,
Stays 'till 'tis fair, yet seems to call a coach. *Swift's Misc.*
The jarrs of gen'rous wine (Acestes' gift,
When his Trinacrian shores the navy left)
He set *abroach*, and for the feast prepar'd,
In equal portions with the ven'son shar'd.
Dryden's Virgil's Æneid, vol. ii.

2. In a figurative sense: in a state to be diffused or advanced; in a state of such beginning as promises a progress.

That man, that sits within a monarch's heart,
And ripens in the sunshine of his favour,
Would he abuse the count'nance of the king,
Alack! what mischiefs might be set *abroach*,
In shadow of such greatness? *Shakespeare's Henry* IV. *p.* ii.

ABRO'AD. *adv.* [compounded of *a* and *broad*. See BROAD.]

1. Without confinement; widely; at large.

Intermit no watch
Against a wakeful foe, while I *abroad*,
Thro' all the coasts of dark destruction, seek
Deliverance. *Milton's Paradise Lost, b.* ii. *l.* 463.
Again, the lonely fox roams far *abroad*,
On secret rapine bent, and midnight fraud;
Now haunts the cliff, now traverses the lawn,
And flies the hated neighbourhood of man. *Prior.*

2. Out of the house.

Welcome, sir;
This cell's my court; here have I few attendants,
And subjects none *abroad*. *Shakespeare's Tempest.*

Lady——walked a whole hour *abroad*, without dying after it; at least in the time I staid; though she seemed to be fainting, and had convulsive motions several times in her head. *Pope's Letters.*

3. In another country.

They thought it better to be somewhat hardly yoked at home, than for ever *abroad*, and discredited. *Hooker. Pref.*

Whosoever offers at verbal translation, shall have the misfortune of that young traveller, who lost his own language *abroad*, and brought home no other instead of it. *Sir J. Denham.*

What learn our youth *abroad*, but to refine
The homely vices of their native land? *Dryd. Span. Friar.*

He who sojourns in a foreign country, refers what he sees and hears *abroad*, to the state of things at home. *Atterb. Serm.*

4. In all directions, this way and that.

Full in the midst of this infernal road,
An elm displays her dusky arms *abroad*. *Dryd. Virgil. Æn.* vi.

5. Without, not within.

Bodies politic, being subject, as much as natural, to dissolution, by divers means, there are undoubtedly more states overthrown through diseases bred within themselves, than through violence from *abroad*. *Hooker, Dedication.*

To A'BROGATE *v. a.* [*abrogo*, Lat.] To take away from a law its force, to repeal, to annul.

Such laws, as have been made upon special occasions, which occasions ceasing, laws of that kind do *abrogate* themselves. *Hooker, b.* iv. § 14.

The negative precepts of men may cease by many instruments, by contrary customs, by public disrelish, by long omission: but the negative precepts of God never can cease, but when they are expresly *abrogated* by the same authority. *Taylor's Rule of Living Holy.*

Abroga'tion. *n. s.* [*abrogatio*, Lat.] The act of abrogating; the repeal of a law.

The commissioners from the confederate Roman catholics, demanded the *abrogation* and repeal of all those laws, which were in force against the exercise of the Roman religion. *Clarendon, b.* viii.

To Abro'ok. *v. a.* [from *To brook*, with *a* superabundant, a word not in use.] To brook, to bear, to endure.

Sweet Nell, ill can thy noble mind *abrook*
The abject people gazing on thy face
With envious looks, still laughing at thy shame.
Shakespeare's Henry VI. *p.* ii.

ABRU'PT. *adj.* [*abruptus*, Lat.] Broken off.

1. Broken, craggy.

Resistless, roaring, dreadful down it comes
From the rude mountain, and the mossy wild,
Tumbling through rocks *abrupt*. *Thomson's Winter.*

2. Divided, without any thing intervening.

Or spread his airy flight,
Upborn with indefatigable wings,
Over the vast *abrupt*, ere he arrive
The happy isle. *Milton's Paradise Lost, b.* ii. *l.* 409.

3. Sudden, without the customary or proper preparatives.

My lady craves
To know the cause of your *abrupt* departure.
Shakespeare's Henry VI.

The *abrupt* and unkind breaking off the two first parliaments, was wholly imputed to the duke of Buckingham. *Clar.*

Abrupt, with eagle-speed she cut the sky;
Instant invisible to mortal eye.
Then first he recogniz'd th' ethereal guest. *Pope's Odyss. b.* i.

4. Unconnected.

The *abrupt* stile, which hath many breaches, and doth not seem to end but fall. *Ben. Johnson's Discov.*

Abru'pted. *adj.* [*abruptus*, Lat. a word little in use.] Broken off suddenly.

The effects of whose activity are not precipitously *abrupted*, but gradually proceed to their cessations. *Brown's Vulgar Errours, b.* vi. 10.

Abru'ption. *n. s.* [*abruptio*, Lat.] Breaking off, violent and sudden separation.

Those which are inclosed in stone, marble, or such other solid matter, being difficultly separable from it, because of its adhesion to all sides of them, have commonly some of that matter still adhering to them, or at least marks of its *abruption* from them, on all their sides. *Woodward's Nat. Hist.*

Abru'ptly. *adv.* [See Abrupt.] Hastily, without the due forms of preparation.

The sweetness of virtue's disposition, jealous even over itself, suffered her not to enter *abruptly* into questions of Musidorus. *Sidney, b.* ii.

Now missing from their joy so lately found,
So lately found and so *abruptly* gone. *Par. Regain. b.* ii.

They both of them punctually observed the time thus agreed upon, and that in whatever company or business they were engaged, they left it *abruptly*, as soon as the clock warned them to retire. *Addison, Spectator,* Nº 241.

Abru'ptness. *n. s.* [from *abrupt.*]

1. An abrupt manner, haste, suddenness, untimely vehemence.
2. The state of an abrupt thing; unconnectedness, roughness, cragginess.

The crystallized bodies found in the perpendicular intervals, are easily known from those that are lodged in the strata. The former have always their root, as the jewellers call it, which is only the *abruptness*, at the end of the body whereby it adhered to the stone, or sides of the intervals; which *abruptness* is caused by its being broke off from the said stone. *Woodward's Natural History, p.* 4.

Ab'scess. *n. s.* [*abscessus*, Lat.] A morbid cavity in the body; a tumour filled with matter; a term of chirurgery.

If the patient is not relieved, nor dies in eight days, the inflammation ends in a suppuration and an *abscess* in the lungs, and sometimes in some other part of the body. *Arbuth. of Diet.*

Lindanus conjectured it might be some hidden *abscess* in the mesentery, which, breaking some few days after, was discovered to be an apostem of the mesentery. *Harvey on Consumptions.*

To Absci'nd. *v. a.* To cut off, either in a natural or figurative sense.

ABSCI'SSA. [Lat.] Part of the diameter of a conic section, intercepted between the vertex and a semi-ordinate.

Absci'ssion. *n. s.* [*abscissio*, Lat.]

1. The act of cutting off.

Fabricius ab Aquapendente renders the *abscission* of them difficult enough, and not without danger. *Wiseman's Surgery.*

2. The state of being cut off.

By cessation of oracles, with Montacutius, we may understand this intercision, not *abscission*, or consummate desolation. *Brown's Vulgar Errours, b.* vi. *c.* 12.

To ABSCO'ND. *v. n.* [*abscondo*, Lat.] To hide one's self; to retire from the public view: generally used of persons in debt, or criminals eluding the law.

Absco'nder. *n. s.* [from *abscond.*] The person that absconds.

A'bsence. *n. s.* [See Absent.]

1. The state of being absent, opposed to presence.

Sir, 'tis fit
You have strong party to defend yourself
By calmness, or by *absence*: all's in danger. *Shakesp. Coriol.*

His friends beheld, and pity'd him in vain,
For what advice can ease a lover's pain?
Absence, the best expedient they could find,
Might save the fortune, if not cure the mind. *Dryd. Fab.*

2. Want of appearance, in the legal sense.

Absence is of a fourfold kind or species. The first is a necessary *absence*, as in banished persons; this is entirely necessary. A second, necessary and voluntary; as, upon the account of the commonwealth, or in the service of the church. The third kind the civilians call a probable *absence*; as, that of students on the score of study. And the fourth, an *absence* entirely voluntary; as, on the account of trade, merchandise, and the like. Some add a fifth kind of *absence*, which is committed *cum dolo & culpâ*, by a man's non-appearance on a citation; as, in a contumacious person, who, in hatred to his contumacy, is, by the law, in some respects, reputed as a person present. *Ayliffe's Parergon Juris Canonici.*

You have given no dissertation upon the *absence* of lovers, nor laid down any methods how they should support themselves under those separations. *Addison, Spectator,* Nº 241.

3. Inattention, heedlessness, neglect of the present object.

I continued my walk, reflecting on the little *absences* and distractions of mankind. *Addison, Spectator,* Nº 77.

4. It is used with the particle *from.*

His *absence from* his mother oft he'll mourn,
And, with his eyes, look wishes to return. *Dryd. Juv.*

A'BSENT. *adj.* [*absens*, Lat.]

1. Not present; used with the particle *from.*

In spring the fields, in autumn hills I love;
At morn the plains, at noon the shady grove;
But Delia always: *absent from* her sight,
Nor plains at morn, nor groves at noon delight. *Pope's Past.*

Where there is advantage to be given,
Both more and less have given him the revolt;
And none serve with him but constrained things,
Whose hearts are *absent* too. *Shakespeare's Macbeth.*

Whether they were *absent* or present, they were vexed alike. *Wisd.* xi. 11.

2. Absent in mind; inattentive; regardless of the present object.

I distinguish a man that is *absent*, because he thinks of something else, from him that is *absent*, because he thinks of nothing. *Addison, Spectator,* Nº 77.

To Abse'nt. *v. a.* To withdraw, to forbear to come into presence.

If thou didst ever hold me in thy heart,
Absent thee from felicity a while,
And in this harsh world draw thy breath in pain,
To tell my tale. *Shakespeare's Hamlet.*

But if thou think'st trial unsought may find
Us both securer, than thus warn'd thou seem'st,
Go—for thy stay, not free, *absents* thee more.
Milton's Paradise Lost, b. ix. *l.* 372.

Tho' I am forc'd, thus to *absent* myself
From all I love, I shall contrive some means,
Some friendly intervals, to visit thee.
Southern's Spartan Dame.

The Arengo, however, is still called together in cases of extraordinary importance; and if, after due summons any member *absents* himself, he is to be fined to the value of about a penny English. *Addison's Rem. on Italy.*

Absenta'neous. *adj.* Relating to absence; absent. *Dict.*

Absente'e. *n. s.* He that is absent from his station, or employment, or country. A word used commonly with regard to Irishmen living out of their country.

Then

Then was the first statute made against *absentees*, commanding all such as had land in Ireland, to return and reside thereupon. *Sir John Davies on Ireland.*

A great part of estates in Ireland are owned by absentees, and such as draw over the profits raised out of Ireland, refunding nothing. *Child's Discourse on Trade.*

ABSI'NTHIATED. *part.* [from *absinthium*, Lat. wormwood.] Imbittered, impregnated with wormwood. *Dict.*

ABSIS. See *APSIS.*

To ABSI'ST. *v. n.* [*absisto*, Lat.] to stand off, to leave off. *Dict.*

To ABSO'LVE. *v. a.* [*absolvo.* Lat.]

1. To clear, to acquit of a crime in a judicial sense.

Your great goodness, out of holy pity,
Absolv'd him with an axe. *Shakespeare's Henry* VIII.

Our victors, blest in peace, forget their wars,
Enjoy past dangers, and *absolve* the stars. *Tickell.*

As he hopes, and gives out, by the influence of his wealth, to be here *absolved*; in condemning this man, you have an opportunity of belying that general scandal, of redeeming the credit lost by former judgments. *Swift's Miscellanies.*

2. To set free from an engagement or promise.

Compell'd by threats to take that bloody oath,
And the act ill, I am *absolv'd* by both. *Waller's Maid's Trag.*

This command, which must necessarily comprehend the persons of our natural fathers, must mean a duty we owe them, distinct from our obedience to the magistrate, and from which the most absolute power of princes cannot absolve us. *Locke.*

3. To pronounce a sin remitted, in the ecclesiastical sense.

But all is calm in this eternal sleep;
Here grief forgets to groan, and love to weep;
Ev'n superstition loses ev'ry fear;
For God, not man, *absolves* our frailties here.
Pope's Eloisa to Abelard.

4. To finish, to complete.

If that which is so supposed infinitely distant from what is now current, is distant from us by a finite interval, and not infinitely, then that one circulation which preceded it must necessarily be like ours, and consequently *absolved* in the space of twenty-four hours. *Hale's Origin of Mankind.*

What cause
Mov'd the creator, in his holy rest
Through all eternity, so late to build
In chaos; and the work begun, how soon
Absolv'd. *Milton's Paradise Lost, b.* vii. *l.* 94.

A'BSOLUTE. *adj.* [*absolutus*, Lat.]

1. Complete; applied as well to persons as things.

Because the things that proceed from him are perfect, without any manner of defect or maim; it cannot be, but that the words of his mouth are *absolute*, and lack nothing which they should have, for performance of that thing whereunto they tend. *Hooker, b.* ii. § 6.

2. Unconditional; as, an *absolute* promise.

Although it runs in forms *absolute*, yet it is indeed conditional, as depending upon the qualification of the person to whom it is pronounced. *South's Sermons.*

3. Not relative; as, *absolute* space.

I see still the distinctions of sovereign and inferior, of *absolute* and relative worship, will bear any man out in the worship of any creature with respect to God, as well at least as it doth in the worship of images. *Stillingfl. Def. of Disc. on Rom. Idol.*

An *absolute* mode is that which belongs to its subject, without respect to any other beings whatsoever: but a relative mode is derived from the regard that one being has to others. *Watts's Logic.*

In this sense we speak of the ablative case *absolute* in grammar.

4. Not limited; as, *absolute* power.

My crown is *absolute*, and holds of none;
I cannot in a base subjection live,
Nor suffer you to take, though I would give. *Dryd. Ind. Emp.*

5. Positive, certain, without any hesitation. In this sense it rarely occurs.

—— Long is it since I saw him,
But time hath nothing blurr'd those lines of favour,
Which then he wore; the snatches in his voice,
And burst of speaking were as his: I'm *absolute*,
'Twas very Cloten. *Shakespeare's Cymbeline.*

What is his strength by land?—
—Great and increasing: but by sea
He is an *absolute* master. *Shakespeare's Antony and Cleopatra.*

A'BSOLUTELY. *adv.* [from *absolute.*]

1. Completely, without restriction.

All the contradictions which grow in those minds, that neither *absolutely* climb the rock of virtue, nor freely sink into the sea of vanity. *Sidney.*

What merit they can build upon having joined with a protestant army, under a king they acknowledged, to defend their own liberties and properties, is, to me, *absolutely* inconceivable; and, I believe, will equally be so for ever. *Swift's Presb. Plea.*

2. Without relation.

Absolutely we cannot discommend, we cannot *absolutely* approve either willingness to live, or forwardness to die. *Hooker, b.* v.

These then being the perpetual causes of zeal; the greatest good, or the greatest evil; either *absolutely* so in themselves, or relatively so to us; it is therefore good to be zealously affected for the one against the other. *Spratt's Sermons.*

No sensible quality, as light, and colour, and heat, and sound, can be subsistent in the bodies themselves, *absolutely* considered, without a relation to our eyes and ears, and other organs of sense. These qualities are only the effects of our sensation, which arise from the different motions, upon our nerves, from objects without, according to their various modifications and positions. *Bentley's Sermons.*

3. Without limits or dependance.

The prince long time had courted fortune's love,
But once possess'd, did *absolutely* reign:
Thus, with their Amazons, the heroes strove,
And conquer'd first those beauties they would gain.
Dryden's Annus Mirabilis.

4. Without condition.

And of that nature, for the most part, are things *absolutely* unto all mens salvation necessary, either to be held or denied, either to be done or avoided. *Hooker's Preface.*

5. Peremptorily, positively.

Being as I am, why didst not thou
Command me *absolutely* not to go,
Going into such danger, as thou saidst? *Parad. Lost, b.* ix.

A'BSOLUTENESS. *n. s.* [from *absolute.*]

1. Completeness.

2. Freedom from dependance, or limits.

The *absoluteness* and illimitedness of his commission was generally much spoken of. *Clarendon, b.* viii.

There is nothing that can raise a man to that generous *absoluteness* of condition, as neither to cringe, to fawn, or to depend meanly; but that which gives him that happiness within himself, for which men depend upon others. *South's Serm.*

3. Despoticism.

He kept a strait hand on his nobility, and chose rather to advance clergymen and lawyers, which were more obsequious to him, but had less interest in the people; which made for his *absoluteness*, but not for his safety. *Bacon's Henry* VII.

ABSOLU'TION. *n. s.* [*absolutio*, Lat.]

1. Acquittal.

Absolution, in the civil law, imports a full acquittal of a person by some final sentence of law; also, a temporary discharge of his farther attendance upon a mesne process, through a failure or defect in pleading; as it does likewise in the canon law, where, and among divines, it likewise signifies a relaxation of him from the obligation of some sentence pronounced either in a court of law, or else *in foro pœnitentiali.* Thus there is, in this kind of law, one kind of *absolution*, termed judicial, and another, stiled a declaratory or extrajudicial *absolution.* *Ayliffe's Parergon Juris Canonici.*

2. The remission of sins, or penance, declared by ecclesiastical authority.

The *absolution* pronounced by a priest, whether papist or protestant, is not a certain infallible ground to give the person, so absolved, confidence towards God. *South's Sermons.*

A'BSOLUTORY. *adj.* [*absolutorius*, Lat.] That which absolves.

Though an *absolutory* sentence should be pronounced in favour of the persons, upon the account of nearness of blood; yet, if adultery shall afterwards be truly proved, he may be again proceeded against as an adulterer. *Ayliffe's Parergon.*

A'BSONANT. *adj.* [See ABSONOUS.] Contrary to reason, wide from the purpose.

A'BSONOUS. *adj.* [*absonus*, Lat. ill-sounding.] Absurd, contrary to reason.

To suppose an uniter of a middle constitution, that should partake of some of the qualities of both, is unwarranted by any of our faculties; yea, most *absonous* to our reason.
Glanville's Scepsis Scientifica, c 4.

To ABSO'RB. *v. a.* [*absorbeo*, Lat. preter. *absorbed*; part. pret. *absorbed*, or *absorpt.*]

1. To swallow up.

Some tokens shew
Of fearless friendship, and their sinking mates
Sustain; vain love, tho' laudable, *absorpt*
By a fierce eddy, they together found
The vast profundity. *Phillips.*

Moses imputed the deluge to the disruption of the abyss; and St. Peter, to the particular constitution of that earth, which made it obnoxious to be *absorpt* in water. *Burn. Theory.*

2. To suck up. See ABSORBENT.

Supposing the forementioned consumption should prove so durable, as to *absorb* and extenuate the said sanguine parts to an extreme degree, it is evident, that the fundamental parts must necessarily come into danger. *Harvey on Consumptions.*

ABSO'RBENT. *n. s.* [*absorbens*, Lat.]

A medicine that, by the softness or porosity of its parts, either causes the asperities of pungent humours, or dries away superfluous moisture in the body. *Quincy.*

There is a third class of substances, commonly balled *absorbents*; as, the various kinds of shells, coral, chalk, crabs eyes, &c. which likewise raise an effervescence, and are therefore called

called alkalies, though not so properly, for they are not salts.
Arbuthnot on Aliments.

ABSO'RPT. *part.* [from *absorb.*] Swallowed up; used as well, in a figurative sense, of persons, as in the primitive, of things.

What can you expect from a man, who has not talked these five days; who is withdrawing his thoughts, as far as he can, from all the present world, its customs and its manners, to be fully possessed and *absorpt* in the past. *Pope's Letters.*

ABSO'RPTION. *n. s.* [from *absorb.*] The act of swallowing up.

It was below the dignity of those sacred penmen, or the spirit of God that directed them, to shew us the causes of this disruption, or of this *absorption*; this is left to the enquiries of men. *Burnet's Theory of the Earth.*

To ABSTA'IN. *v. n.* [*abstineo*, Lat.] To forbear, to deny one's self any gratification; with the particle *from*.

If thou judge it hard and difficult,
Conversing, looking, loving, to *abstain*
From love's due rites, nuptial embraces sweet;
And, with desires, to languish without hope.
Milton's Paradise Lost, b. x. *l.* 993.

To be perpetually longing, and impatiently desirous of any thing, so that a man cannot *abstain from* it, is to lose a man's liberty, and to become a servant of meat and drink, or smoke.
Taylor's Rule of Living Holy.

Even then the doubtful billows scarce *abstain*
From the toss'd vessel on the troubled main. *Dryden's Virgil.*

ABSTE'MIOUS. *adj.* [*abstemius*, Lat.] Temperate, sober, abstinent, refraining from excess or pleasures. It is used of persons; as, an *abstemious* hermit: and of things; as, an *abstemious* diet. It is spoken likewise of things that cause temperance.

The instances of longevity are chiefly amongst the *abstemious*. Abstinence in extremity will prove a mortal disease; but the experiments of it are very rare. *Arbuthnot on Aliments.*

Clytorean streams the love of wine expel,
(Such is the virtue of th' *abstemious* well)
Whether the colder nymph that rules the flood,
Extinguishes, and balks the drunken god:
Or that Melampus (so have some assur'd)
When the mad Prætides with charms he cur'd,
And pow'rful herbs, both charms and simples cast
Into the sober spring, where still their virtues last. *Dryd. Fab.*

ABSTE'MIOUSLY. *adv.* [from *abstemious.*] Temperately, soberly, without indulgence.

ABSTE'MIOUSNESS. *n. s.* [See ABSTEMIOUS.] The quality of being abstemious.

ABSTE'NTION. *n. s.* [from *abstineo*, Lat.] The act of holding off, or restraining; restraint. *Dict.*

To ABSTE'RGE. *v. a.* [*abstergo*, Lat.] To cleanse by wiping; to wipe.

ABSTE'RGENT. *adj.* Cleansing; having a cleansing quality.

To ABSTE'RSE. [See ABSTERGE.] To cleanse, to purify: a word very little in use, and less analogical than *absterge*.

Nor will we affirm, that iron receiveth, in the stomach of the ostrich, no alteration; but we suspect this effect rather from corrosion than digestion; not any tendence to chilification by the natural heat, but rather some attrition from an acid and vitriolous humidity in the stomach, which may *absterse* and shave the scorious parts thereof. *Brown's Vulgar Errours, b.* iii.

ABSTE'RSION *n. s.* [*abstersio*, Lat.] The act of cleansing. See ABSTERGE.

The seventh cause is *abstersion*; which is plainly a scouring off, or incision of the more viscous humours, and making the humours more fluid, and cutting between them and the part; as is found in nitrous water, which scoureth linen cloth speedily from the foulness. *Bacon's Natural History*, N° 42.

ABSTE'RSIVE. *adj.* [from *absterge.*] That has the quality of absterging or cleansing.

It is good, after purging, to use apozemes and broths, not so much opening as those used before purging; but *abstersive* and mundifying clysters also are good to conclude with, to draw away the reliques of the humours. *Bacon's Nat. History.*

A table stood of that *abstersive* tree,
Where Æthiop's swarthy bird did build to nest. *Sir J. Denh.*
There, many a flow'r *abstersive* grew,
Thy fav'rite flow'rs of yellow hue. *Swift's Miscellanies.*

A'BSTINENCE. *n. s.* [*abstinentia*, Lat.]

1. Forbearance of any thing; with the particle *from*.

Because the *abstinence from* a present pleasure, that offers itself, is a pain, nay, oftentimes a very great one: it is no wonder that that operates after the same manner pain does, and lessens, in our thoughts, what is future; and so forces us, as it were blindfold into its embraces. *Locke.*

2. Fasting, or forbearance of necessary food. It is generally distinguished from temperance, as the greater degree from the less; sometimes as single performances from habits; as, a day of *abstinence*, and a life of temperance.

Say, can you fast? your stomachs are too young:
And *abstinence* ingenders maladies. *Shakesp. Love's Lab. Lost.*
Religious men, who hither must be sent
As awful guides of heavenly government;
To teach you penance, fasts, and *abstinence*,
To punish bodies for the souls offence. *Dryden's Ind. Emp.*

And the faces of them, which have used *abstinence*, shall shine above the stars; whereas our faces shall be blacker than darkness. 2 *Esdras*, vii. 55.

A'BSTINENCY. *n. s.* The same with ABSTINENCE.

Were our rewards for the *abstinencies*, or riots, of this present life, under the prejudices of short or finite, the promises and threats of Christ would lose much of their virtue and energy. *Hammond's Fundam.*

A'BSTINENT. *adj.* [*abstinens*, Lat.] That uses abstinence, in opposition to covetous, rapacious, or luxurious. It is used chiefly of persons.

ABSTO'RTED. *adj.* [*abstortus*, Lat.] Forced away, wrung from another by violence. *Dict.*

To ABSTRA'CT. *v. a.* [*abstraho*, Lat.]

1. *To* take one thing from another.

Could we *abstract* from these pernicious effects, and suppose this were innocent, it would be too light to be matter of praise.
Decay of Piety.

2. To separate ideas.

Those, who cannot distinguish, compare and *abstract*, would hardly be able to understand and make use of language, or judge or reason to any tolerable degree. *Locke.*

3. To reduce to a epitome.

If we would fix in the memory the discourses we hear, or what we design to speak, let us *abstract* them into brief compends, and review them often. *Watts's Improv. of the Mind.*

A'BSTRACT. *adj.* [*abstractus*, Lat. See the verb *To* ABSTRACT.]

1. Separated from something else, generally used with relation to mental perceptions; as, *abstract* mathematics, *abstract* terms, in opposition to concrete.

Mathematics, in its latitude, is usually divided into pure and mixed. And though the pure do handle only *abstract* quantity in general, as geometry, arithmetic; yet that which is mixed, doth consider the quantity of some particular determinate subject. So astronomy handles the quantity of heavenly motions, music of sounds; and mechanics, of weights and powers. *Wilkins's Mathematical Magick.*

Abstract terms signify the mode or quality of a being, without any regard to the subject in which it is; as, whiteness, roundness, length, breadth, wisdom, mortality, life, death.
Watts's Logick.

2. With the particle *from*.

Another fruit from the considering things in themselves, *abstract from* our opinions and other mens notions and discourses on them, will be, that each man will pursue his thoughts in that method, which will be most agreeable to the nature of the thing, and to his apprehension of what it suggests to him. *Locke.*

A'BSTRACT. *n. s.* [from the verb.]

1. A smaller quantity, containing the virtue or power of a greater.

You shall there find a man, who is the *abstract*
Of all faults all men follow. *Shakesp. Antony and Cleopatra.*
If you are false, these epithets are small;
You're then the things, and *abstract* of them all. *Dryd. Aur.*

2. An epitome made by taking out the principal parts.

When Mnemon came to the end of a chapter, he recollected the sentiments he had remarked; so that he could give a tolerable analysis and *abstract* of every treatise he had read, just after he had finished it. *Watts's Improvement of the Mind.*

3. The state of being abstracted.

The hearts of great princes, if they be considered, as it were in *abstract*, without the necessity of states, and circumstances of time, can take no full and proportional pleasure in the exercise of any narrow bounty. *Wotton.*

ABSTRA'CTED. *part. adj.* [from *abstract.*]

1. Separated.

That space the evil one *abstracted* stood
From his own evil, and for the time remain'd
Stupidly good. *Milton.*

2. Refined, abstruse.

Abstracted spiritual love, they like
Their souls exhal'd. *Donne.*

3. Absent of mind, inattentive to present objects; as, an *abstracted* scholar.

ABSTRA'CTEDLY. *adv.* With abstraction, simply, separately from all contingent circumstances.

Or whether more *abstractedly* we look,
Or on the writers, or the written book:
Whence, but from heav'n, could men unskill'd in arts,
In several ages born, in several parts,
Weave such agreeing truths? or how, or why
Should all conspire to cheat us with a lie?
Unask'd their pains, ungrateful their advice,
Starving their gain, and martyrdom their price.
Dryden's Religio Laici.

ABSTRA'CTION. *n. s.* [*abstractio*, Lat.]

1. The act of abstracting.

The word *abstraction* signifies a withdrawing some part of

An idea from other parts of it; by which means, such abstracted ideas are formed, as neither represent any thing corporeal or spiritual; that is, any thing peculiar or proper to mind or body. *Watts's Logick.*

2. The state of being abstracted.
3. Absence of mind, inattention.
4. Disregard of worldly objects.

ABSTRA'CTIVE. *adj.* [from *abstract.*] Having the power or quality of abstracting.

ABSTRA'CTLY. *adv.* [from *abstract.*] In an abstract manner, absolutely, without reference to any thing else.

Matter *abstractly* and absolutely considered, cannot have born an infinite duration now past and expired. *Bentley's Sermons.*

ABSTRI'CTED. *part. adj.* [*abstrictus*, Lat.] Unbound. *Dict.*

To ABSTRI'NGE *v. a* [*abstringo*, Lat.] To unbind. *Dict.*

To ABSTRU'DE. *v. a.* [*abstrudo*, Lat.] To thrust off, or pull away. *Dict.*

ABSTRU'SE. *adj.* [*abstrusus*, Lat. thrust out of sight.]

1. Hidden.

Th' eternal eye, whose sight discerns
Abstrusest thoughts, from forth his holy mount,
And from within the golden lamps that burn
Nightly before him, saw, without their light,
Rebellion rising. *Milton's Paradise Lost, b.* v. *l.* 712.

2. Difficult, remote from conception or apprehension. It is opposed to *obvious* and *easy*.

So spake our sire, and, by his count'nance, seem'd
Ent'ring on studious thoughts *abstruse*. *Parad. Lost, b.* viii.

The motions and figures within the mouth are *abstruse*, and not easy to be distinguished, especially those of the tongue, which is moved, through the help of many muscles, so easily, and habitually, and variously, that we are scarce able to give a judgment of motions and figures thereby framed. *Holder's Elements of Speech.*

No man could give a rule of the greatest beauties, and the knowledge of them was so *abstruse*, that there was no manner of speaking which could express them. *Dryden's Dufresnoy.*

ABSTRU'SELY. *adv.* In an abstruse manner; obscurely, not plainly, or obviously.

ABSTRU'SENESS. *n. s.* [from *abstruse.*] The quality of being abstruse; difficulty, obscurity.

It is not oftentimes so much what the scripture says, as what some men persuade others it says, that makes it seem obscure; and that as to some other passages that are so indeed, since it is the *abstruseness* of what is taught in them, that makes them almost inevitably so; it is little less saucy, upon such a score, to find fault with the style of the scripture, than to do so with the author for making us but men. *Boyle on the Scripture.*

ABSTRU'SITY. *n. s.* [from *abstruse.*]

1. Abstruseness.
2. That which is abstruse. A word seldom used.

Authors are also suspicious, nor greedily to be swallowed, who pretend to write of secrets, to deliver antipathies, sympathies, and the occult *abstrusities* of things. *Brown's Vulg. Err.*

To ABSU'ME. *v. a.* [*absumo*, Lat.] To bring to an end by a gradual waste; to eat up.

That which had been burning an infinite time could never be burnt, no not so much as any part of it; for if it had burned part after part, the whole must needs be *absumed* in a portion of time. *Hale's Origin of Mankind.*

ABSU'RD. *adj.* [*absurdus*, Lat.]

1. Unreasonable, without judgment, as used of men.

Seeming wise men may make shift to get opinion; but let no man choose them for employment; for certainly you had better take for business a man somewhat *absurd*, than over formal. *Bacon's Essay* 27.

2. Inconsistent, contrary to reason, used of sentiments or practices.

The thing itself appeared desirable to him, and accordingly he could not but like and desire it; but then, it was after a very irrational *absurd* way, and contrary to all the methods and principles of a rational agent; which never wills a thing really and properly, but it applies to the means, by which it is to be acquired. *South's Sermons.*

A man who cannot write with wit on a proper subject, is dull and stupid; but one who shews it in an improper place, is as impertinent and *absurd*. *Addison, Spectator,* Nº 291.

But grant that those can conquer, these can cheat;
'Tis phrase *absurd* to call a villain great:
Who wickedly is wise, or madly brave,
Is but the more a fool, the more a knave. *Pope's Essay on Man.*

ABSU'RDITY. *n. s.* [from *absurd.*]

1. The quality of being absurd; want of judgment applied to men; want of propriety applied to things.

How clear soever this idea of the infinity of number be, there is nothing more evident than the *absurdity* of the actual idea of an infinite number. *Locke.*

2. That which is *absurd*; as, his travels were full of *absurdities*. In which sense it has a plural.

That satisfaction we receive from the opinion of some pre-eminence in ourselves, when we see the *absurdities* of another, or when we reflect on any past *absurdities* of our own. *Addison, Spectator,* Nº 249.

ABSU'RDLY. *adv.* [from *absurd.*] After an absurd manner; improperly, unreasonably.

But man we find the only creature,
Who, led by folly, combats nature;
Who, when she loudly cries, forbear,
With obstinacy fixes there;
And where his genius least inclines,
Absurdly bends his whole designs. *Swift's Miscellanies.*

We may proceed yet further with the atheist, and convince him, that not only his principle is absurd, but his consequences also as *absurdly* deduced from it. *Bentley's Sermons.*

ABSU'RDNESS. *n. s.* [from *absurd.*] The quality of being absurd; injudiciousness, impropriety. See ABSURDITY; which is more frequently used.

ABU'NDANCE. *n. s.* [*abondance*, Fr.]

1. Plenty; a sense chiefly poetical.

At the whisper of thy word,
Crown'd *abundance* spreads my board. *Crashaw.*

The doubled charge his subjects love supplies,
Who, in that bounty, to themselves are kind;
So glad Egyptians see their Nilus rise,
And, in his plenty, their *abundance* find. *Dryd. Ann. Mir.*

2. Great numbers.

The river Inn, during its course through the Tyrol, is generally shut up between a double range of mountains, that are most of them covered with woods of fir-trees. *Abundance* of peasants are employed in hewing down the largest of these trees, that, after they are barked and cut into shape, are tumbled down. *Addison on Italy.*

3. A great quantity.

Their chief enterprize was the recovery of the Holy land; in which worthy, but extremely difficult, action, it is lamentable to remember what *abundance* of noble blood hath been shed with very small benefit unto the Christian state. *Sir Walter Raleigh's Essays.*

4. Exuberance, more than enough.

For well I wot, most mighty sovereign,
That all this famous antique history,
Of some, th' *abundance* of an idle brain
Will judged be, and painted forgery. *Spens. Fairy Q. b.* ii.

ABU'NDANT. *adj.* [*abundans*, Lat.]

1. Plentiful.

Good the more
Communicated, more *abundant* grows;
The author not impair'd, but honour'd more. *Par. Lost, b.* v.

2. Exuberant.

If the vessels are in a state of too great rigidity, so as not to yield, a strong projectile motion occasions their rupture, and hæmorrhages; especially in the lungs, where the blood is *abundant*. *Arbuthnot on Aliments.*

3. Full stored. It is followed sometimes by *in*, commonly by *with*.

The world began but some ages before these were found out, and was *abundant with* all things at first; and men not very numerous; and therefore were not put so much to the use of their wits, to find out ways for living commodiously. *Burnet's Theory of the Earth.*

4. It is applied generally to things, sometimes to persons.

The Lord, the Lord God, merciful and gracious, long-suffering and *abundant in* goodness and truth. *Exod.* xxxiv. 6.

ABU'NDANTLY. *adv.* [from *abundant.*]

1. In plenty.

Let the waters bring forth *abundantly* the moving creature that hath life. *Genesis,* i. 20.

God on thee
Abundantly his gifts hath also pour'd;
Inward and outward both, his image fair. *Par. Lost, b.* viii.

2. Amply, liberally, more than sufficiently.

What the example of our equals wants of authority, is *abundantly* supplied in the imaginations of friendship, and the repeated influences of a constant conversation. *Rogers's Serm.*

Heroic poetry has ever been esteemed the greatest work of human nature. In that rank has Aristotle placed it; and Longinus is so full of the like expressions, that he *abundantly* confirms the other's testimony. *Dryden's State of Innocence, Pref.*

To ABU'SE. *v. a.* [*abutor*, Lat.]

In *abuse* the verb, *s* has the sound of *z*; in the noun, the common sound.

1. To make an ill use of.

They that use this world, as not *abusing* it; for the fashion of this world passeth away. 1 *Cor.* vii. 31.

He has fixed and determined the time for our repentance, beyond which he will no longer await the perverseness of men, no longer suffer his compassion to be *abused*. *Rogers's Sermons.*

2. To deceive, to impose upon.

The world hath been much *abused* by the opinion of making gold: the work itself I judge to be possible; but the means hitherto propounded are, in the practice, full of error. *Bacon's Natural History,* Nº 126.

He perhaps,
Out of my weakness and my melancholy,
As he is very potent with such spirits,
Abuses me to damn me. *Shakespeare's Hamlet.*

It imports the misrepresentation of the qualities of things and actions, to the common apprehensions of men, *abusing* their minds with false notions; and so, by this artifice, making evil pass for good, and good for evil, in all the great concerns of life. *South's Sermons.*

Nor be with all these tempting words *abus'd*;
These tempting words were all to Sappho us'd.
Pope's Sappho to Phaon.

3. To treat with rudeness, to reproach.

I am no strumpet, but of life as honest
As you that thus *abuse* me. *Shakespeare's Othello.*

But he mocked them, and laughed at them, and *abused* them shamefully, and spake proudly. 1 *Mac.* vii. 34.

Some praise at morning what they blame at night,
But always think the last opinion right.
A muse by these is like a mistress us'd,
This hour she's idoliz'd, the next *abus'd*. *Pope's Ess. on Crit.*

The next criticism upon the stars seems to be introduced for no other reason, but to mention Mr. Bickerstaff, whom the author every-where endeavours to imitate and *abuse*. *Addison.*

ABU'SE. *n. s.* [from the verb *abuse*.]

1. The ill use of any thing.

The casting away things profitable for the sustenance of man's life, is an unthankful *abuse* of the fruits of God's good providence towards mankind. *Hooker, b.* v. § 9.

Little knows
Any, but God alone, to value right
The good before him, but perverts best things
To worst *abuse*, or to their meanest use. *Parad. Lost, b.* iv.

2. A corrupt practice, bad custom.

The nature of things is such, that, if *abuses* be not remedied, they will certainly encrease. *Swift, Advancem. of Relig.*

3. Seducement.

Was it not enough for him to have deceived me, and through the deceit abused me, and, after the *abuse*, forsaken me, but that he must now, of all the company, and before all the company, lay want of beauty to my charge. *Sidney, b.* ii.

4. Unjust censure, rude reproach, contumely.

I dark in light, expos'd
To daily fraud, contempt, *abuse*, and wrong. *Sampſ. Agon.*

ABU'SER. *n. s.* [from the verb *abuse*.]

1. He that make an ill use.
2. He that deceives.

Next thou, th' *abuser* of thy prince's ear. *Denh. Sophy.*

3. He that reproaches with rudeness.
4. A ravisher, a violater.

ABU'SIVE. *adj.* [from *abuse*.]

1. Practising abuse.

The tongue mov'd gently first, and speech was low,
Till wrangling science taught it noise and show,
And wicked wit arose, thy most *abusive* foe. *Pope's Miscell.*

Dame Nature, as the learned show,
Provides each animal its foe;
Hounds hunt the hare, the wily fox
Devours your geese, the wolf your flocks.
Thus envy pleads a natural claim,
To persecute the muse's fame,
On poets in all times *abusive*,
From Homer down to Pope inclusive. *Swift's Miscellanies.*

2. Containing abuse; as, an *abusive* lampoon.

Next, Comedy appear'd with great applause,
Till her licentious and *abusive* tongue
Waken'd the magistrates coercive pow'r. *Roscommon.*

3. Deceitful; a sense little used, yet not improper.

It is verified by a number of examples, that whatsoever is gained by an *abusive* treaty, ought to be restored *in integrum*.
Bacon's Considerations on War with Spain.

ABU'SIVELY. *adv.* [from *abuse*.]

1. Improperly, by a wrong use.

The oil, *abusively* called spirit, of roses swims at the top of the water, in the form of a white butter; which I remember not to have observed in any other oil drawn in any limbeck.
Boyle's Sceptical Chymistry.

2. Reproachfully.

ABU'SIVENESS. *n. s.* [from *abuse*.] The quality of being abusive; foulness of language.

Pick out of mirth, like stones out of thy ground,
Profaneness, filthiness, *abusiveness*.
These are the scum, with which coarse wits abound:
The fine may spare these well, yet not go less. *Herbert.*

To ABU'T. *v. n.* obsolete. [*aboutir*, to touch at the end, Fr.] To end at, to border upon; to meet, or approach to, with the particle *upon*.

Two mighty monarchies,
Whose high upreared and *abutting* fronts
Perilous the narrow ocean parts asunder. *Shakesp. Henry* V.

In entring the same, we will first pitch at the Looes, two several corporations, distinguished by the addition of east and west, *abutting* upon a navigable creek, and joined by a fair bridge of many arches. *Carew's Survey of Cornwall.*

ABUTTAL. *n. s.* [from *abut.*] The butting or boundaries of any land. A writing declaring on what lands, highways, or other places, it does abut. *Dict.*

ABU'TMENT. *n. s.* [from *abut.*] That which abuts, or borders upon another.

ABY'SM. *n. s.* [*abysme*, old Fr. now written contractedly *abîme.*] A gulf; the same with *abyss*.

My good stars, that were my former guides,
Have empty left their orbs, and shot their fires
Into the *abysm* of hell. *Shakespeare's Antony and Cleopatra.*

ABY'SS. *n. s.* [*abyssus*, Lat. Ἄβυσσος, bottomless, Gr.]

1. A depth without bottom.

Who shall tempt with wand'ring feet
The dark, unbottom'd, infinite *abyss*,
And, through the palpable obscure, find out
This uncouth way. *Milton's Paradise Lost, b.* ii. *l.* 405.

2. A great depth, a gulph.

The yawning earth disclos'd th' *abyss* of hell:
The weeping statues did the wars foretell,
And holy sweat from brazen idols fell. *Dryd. Virg. Georg.* i.

3. In a figurative sense, that in which any thing is lost.

For sepulchres themselves must crumbling fall
In time's *abyss*, the common grave of all. *Dryd. Juv. Sat.* x.

If, discovering how far we have clear and distinct ideas, we confine our thoughts within the contemplation of those things that are within the reach of our understandings, and launch not out into that *abyss* of darkness, out of a presumption, that nothing is beyond our comprehension. *Locke.*

4. The body of waters supposed at the center of the earth.

We are here to consider what is generally understood by the great *abyss*, in the common explication of the deluge; and 'tis commonly interpreted either to be the sea, or subterraneous waters hid in the bowels of the earth. *Burnet's Theor. Earth.*

5. In the language of divines, hell.

From what insatiable *abyss*,
Where flames devour, and serpents hiss,
Promote me to thy seat of bliss. *Roscommon.*

AC, AK, or AKE.

Being initials in the names of places, as *Acton*, signify an oak, from the Saxon ac, an oak. *Gibson's Camden.*

ACA'CIA. n. s. [Lat.]

1. A drug brought from Egypt, which, being supposed the inspissated juice of a tree, is imitated by the juice of sloes, boiled to the same consistence. *Dictionaire de Comm. Savary. Trevoux.*

2. A tree commonly so called here, though different from that which produces the true *acacia*; and therefore termed *pseudacacia*, or *Virginian acacia*.

It hath a papilionaceous flower, from whose flower-cup rises the pointal, wrapped in a fimbriated membrane, which afterwards becomes a pod, opening into two parts, in which are contained several kidney-shaped seeds. *Miller.*

ACADE'MIAL. *adj.* [from *academy.*] Relating to an academy, belonging to an academy.

ACADE'MIAN. *n. s.* [from *academy.*] A scholar of an academy or university; a member of an university. *Wood*, in his *Athenæ Oxonienses*, mentions a great feast made for the *academians*.

ACADE'MICK. *n. s.* [from *academy.*] A student of an university.

A young *academic* shall dwell upon a journal that treats of trade in a dictatorial style, and shall be lavish in the praise of the author; while, at the same time, persons well skilled in those different subjects, hear the tattle with contempt.
Watts's Improvement of the Mind, p. i. *c.* 5.

ACADE'MICK. *adj.* [*academicus*, Lat.] Relating to an university.

While through poetic scenes the genius roves,
Or wanders wild in *academic* groves. *Dunciad, b.* iv. *l.* 481.

ACADE'MICAL. *adj.* [*academicus*, Lat.] Belonging to an university.

He drew him first into the fatal circle, from a kind of resolved privateness at his house at Lampsie in South Wales; where, after the *academical* life, he had taken such a taste of the rural, as I have heard him say, that he could well have bent his mind to a retired course. *Wotton.*

ACADEMI'CIAN. *n. s.* [*academicien*, Fr.] The member of an academy. It is generally used in speaking of the professors in the academies of France.

ACA'DEMIST. *n. s.* [from *academy.*] The member of an academy.

It is observed by the Parisian *academists*, that some amphibious quadrupeds, particularly the sea-calf, or seal, hath his epiglottis extraordinarily large. *Ray on the Creation.*

A'CADEMY. *n. s.* [anciently, and properly, with the accent on first syllable, now frequently on the second. *Academia*, Lat. from *Academus* of Athens, whose house was turned into a school, from whom the *Groves of Academe* in Milton.]

1. An assembly or society of men, uniting for the promotion of some art.

Our court shall be a little *academy*,
Still and contemplative in living arts. *Shak. Love's Lab. Lost.*

2. The place were sciences are taught.

Amongst the *academies*, which were composed by the rare genius of those great men, these four are reckoned as the principal; namely, the Athenian school, that of Sicyon, that of Rhodes, and that of Corinth. *Dryden's Dufresnoy.*

3. An university.
4. A place of education, in contradistinction to the universities or public schools.

ACA'NTHUS.

ACA'NTHUS. *n.ſ.* [Lat.] The name of the herb bears-foot; remarkable for being the model of the foliage on the Corinthian chapiter.

On either ſide
Acanthus, and each od'rous buſhy ſhrub,
Fenc'd up the verdant wall. *Milt. Parad. Loſt, b.* iv. *l.* 696.

ACATALE'CTIC. *n.ſ.* [ἀκαταλήκτικος, Gr.] A verſe which has the complete number of ſyllables, without defect or ſuperfluity.

To ACCE'DE. *v.n.* [*accedo*, Lat.] To be added to, to come to; generally uſed in political accounts: as, another power has *acceded* to the treaty; that is, has become a party.

To ACCE'LERATE. *v.a.* [*accelero*, Lat.]

1. To make quick, to haſten, to quicken motion; to give a continual impulſe to motion, ſo as perpetually to encreaſe.

Take new beer, and put in ſome quantity of ſtale beer into it; and ſee whether it will not *accelerate* the clarification, by opening the body of the beer, whereby the groſſer parts may fall down into lees. *Bacon's Natural Hiſtory*, Nº 307.

If the rays endeavour to recede from the denſeſt part of the vibration, they may be alternately *accelerated* and retarded by the vibrations overtaking them. *Newton's Optics.*

Spices quicken the pulſe, and *accelerate* the motion of the blood, and diſſipate the fluids; from whence leanneſs, pains in the ſtomach, loathings, and fevers. *Arbuthnot on Aliments.*

Lo! from the dread immenſity of ſpace
Returning, with *accelerated* courſe,
The ruſhing comet to the ſun deſcends. *Thomſ. Sum. l.* 1690.

2. It is generally applied to matter, and uſed chiefly in philoſophical language; but is ſometimes uſed on other occaſions.

In which council the king himſelf, whoſe continual vigilancy did ſuck in ſometimes cauſeleſs ſuſpicions, which few elſe knew, inclined to the *accelerating* a battle. *Bacon's Henry* VII.

Perhaps it may point out to a ſtudent now and then, what may employ the moſt uſeful labours of his thoughts, and *accelerate* his diligence in the moſt momentous enquiries. *Watts's Impr.*

ACCELERA'TION. *n.ſ.* [*acceleratio*, Lat.]

1. The act of quickening motion.

The law of the *acceleration* of falling bodies, diſcovered firſt by Galileo, is, that the velocities acquired by falling, being as the time in which the body falls, the ſpaces through which it paſſes will be as the ſquares of the velocities, and the velocity and time taken together, as in a quadruplicate ratio of the ſpaces.

2. The ſtate of the body accelerated, or quickened in its motion.

The degrees of *acceleration* of motion, the gravitation of the air, the exiſtence or non-exiſtence of empty ſpaces, either coacervate or interſperſed, and many the like, have taken up the thoughts and times of men in diſputes concerning them. *Hale's Origin of Mankind.*

To ACCE'ND. *v.a.* [*accendo*, Lat.] To kindle, to ſet on fire; a word very rarely uſed.

Our devotion, if ſufficiently *accended*, would, as theirs, burn up innumerable books of this ſort. *Decay of Piety.*

ACCE'NSION. *n.ſ.* [*accenſio*, Lat.] The act of kindling, or the ſtate of being kindled.

The fulminating damp will take fire at a candle, or other flame, and, upon its *accenſion*, gives a crack or report, like the diſcharge of a gun, and makes likewiſe an exploſion ſo forcible as ſometimes to kill the miners, break their limbs, ſhake the earth, and force coals, ſtones, and other bodies, even though they be of very great weight and bulk, from the bottom of the pit or mine. *Woodward's Natural Hiſtory, p.* iv.

A'CCENT. *n.ſ.* [*accentus*, Lat.]

1. The manner of ſpeaking or pronouncing, with regard either to force or elegance.

I know, ſir, I am no flatterer; he that beguiled you in a plain *accent* was a plain knave; which, for my part, I will not be. *Shakeſpeare's King Lear.*

Your *accent* is ſomething finer than you could purchaſe in ſo removed a dwelling. *Shakeſpeare's As you like it.*

2. In grammar, the marks made upon ſyllables to regulate their pronunciation.

Accent, as in the Greek names and uſage, ſeems to have regarded the tune of the voice; the acute *accent* raiſing the voice in ſome certain ſyllables to a higher, *i.e.* more acute pitch or tone, and the grave depreſſing it lower, and both having ſome emphaſis, *i.e.* more vigorous pronunciation. *Holder's Elem.*

3. Poetically, language or words.

How many ages hence
Shall this our lofty ſcene be acted o'er,
In ſtates unborn, and *accents* yet unknown. *Shak. Jul. Cæſar.*

Winds, on your wings to heav'n her *accents* bear;
Such words as heav'n alone is fit to hear. *Dryd. Virg. Paſt.* 3.

4. A modification of the voice, expreſſive of the paſſions or ſentiments.

The tender *accent* of a woman's cry
Will paſs unheard, will unregarded die;
When the rough ſeaman's louder ſhouts prevail,
When fair occaſion ſhews the ſpringing gale. *Prior.*

To ACCE'NT, *v.a.* [from *accentus*, Lat.]

1. To pronounce, to ſpeak words with particular regard to the grammatical marks or rules.

Having got ſomebody to mark the laſt ſyllable but one, where it is long, in words above two ſyllables (which is enough to regulate her pronunciation, and *accenting* the words) let her read daily in the goſpels, and avoid underſtanding them in Latin, if ſhe can. *Locke on Education*, § 177.

2. In poetry, to pronounce or utter in general.

O my unhappy lines! you that before
Have ſerv'd my youth to vent ſome wanton cries,
And, now congeal'd with grief, can ſcarce implore
Strength to *accent*, Here my Albertus lies! *Wotton.*

3. To write or note the accents.

To ACCE'NTUATE. *v.a.* [*accentuer*, Fr.] To place the proper accents over the vowels.

ACCENTUA'TION. *n.ſ.* [from *accentuate.*]

1. The act of placing the accent in pronunciation.

2. Marking the accent in writing.

To ACCE'PT, *v.a.* [*accipio*, Lat. *accepter*, Fr.]

1. To take with pleaſure; to receive kindly; to admit with approbation. It is diſtinguiſhed from *receive*, as *ſpecific* from *general*; noting a particular manner of receiving.

Neither do ye kindle fire on my altar for nought. I have no pleaſure in you, ſaith the Lord of hoſts, neither will I *accept* an offering at your hand. *Malachi*, i. 10.

Then Peter opened his mouth, and ſaid, Of a truth I perceive that God is no reſpecter of perſons: but, in every nation, he that feareth him, and worketh righteouſneſs, is *accepted* with him. *Acts*, x. 34, 35.

You have been graciouſly pleaſed to *accept* this tender of my duty. *Dryden's Dedication to his Fables.*

Charm by *accepting*, by ſubmitting ſway,
Yet have your humour moſt when you obey. *Pope.*

2. It is uſed in a kind of juridical ſenſe; as, to *accept* terms, *accept* a treaty.

His promiſe Palamon *accepts*, but pray'd
To keep it better than the firſt he made. *Dryden's Fables.*

3. In the language of the bible, to *accept* perſons, is to act with perſonal and partial regard.

He will ſurely reprove you, if ye do ſecretly *accept* perſons. *Job*, xiii. 10.

4. It is ſometimes uſed with the particle *of.*

I will appeaſe him with the preſent that goeth before me, and afterward I will ſee his face; peradventure he will *accept of* me. *Geneſis*, xxxii. 20.

ACCEPTABI'LITY. *n.ſ.* The quality of being acceptable. See ACCEPTABLE.

He hath given us his natural blood to be ſhed, for the remiſſion of our ſins, and for the obtaining the grace and *acceptability* of repentance. *Taylor's Worthy Communicant.*

ACCE'PTABLE. *adj.* [*acceptable*, Fr. from the Latin.] It is pronounced by ſome with the accent on the firſt ſyllable, as by Milton; by others, with the accent on the ſecond.

1. That which is likely to be accepted; grateful; pleaſing. It is uſed with the particle *to* before the perſon *accepting.*

This woman, whom thou mad'ſt to be my help,
And gav'ſt me as thy perfect gift, ſo good,
So fit, ſo *acceptable*, ſo divine,
That from her hand I could expect no ill. *Parad. Loſt, b.*ii.

I do not ſee any other method left for men of that function to take, in order to reform the world, than by uſing all honeſt arts to make themſelves *acceptable to* the laity. *Swift's Proj. &c.*

After he had made a peace ſo *acceptable to* the church, and ſo honourable to himſelf, he ſpent the remainder of his life at Ripaille, and died with an extraordinary reputation of ſanctity. *Addiſon on Italy.*

ACCE'PTABLENESS. *n.ſ.* [from *acceptable.*] The quality of being acceptable.

It will thereby take away the *acceptableneſs* of that conjunction. *Grew's Coſmologia Sacra, b.* ii. *c.* 2.

ACCE'PTABLY. *adv.* [from *acceptable.*] In an acceptable manner; ſo as to pleaſe; with the particle *to.* For the accent, ſee ACCEPTABLE.

Do not omit thy prayers, for want of a good oratory; for he that prayeth upon God's account, cares not what he ſuffers, ſo he be the friend of Chriſt; nor where nor when he prays, ſo he may do it frequently, fervently, and *acceptably.* *Taylor's Guide to Devotion.*

If you can teach them to love and reſpect other people, they will, as your age requires it, find ways to expreſs it *acceptably to* every one. *Locke on Education*, § 145.

ACCE'PTANCE. *n.ſ.* [*acceptance*, Fr.]

1. Reception with approbation.

By that *acceptance* of his ſovereignty, they alſo accepted of his laws; why then ſhould any other laws be now uſed amongſt them? *Spenſer's State of Ireland.*

If he tells us his noble deeds, we muſt alſo tell him our noble *acceptance* of them. *Shakeſpeare's Coriolanus.*

Some men cannot be fools with ſo good *acceptance* as others. *South's Sermons.*

Thus I imbolden'd ſpake, and freedom us'd
Permiſſive, and *acceptance* found. *Par. Loſt, b.* viii. *l.* 435.

2. The meaning of a word as it is received or underſtood; acceptation.

That pleaſure is man's chiefeſt good, becauſe indeed it is the perception of good that is properly pleaſure, is an aſſertion most certainly true, though, under the common *acceptance* of it, not only false but odious: for, according to this, pleasure and sensuality pass for terms equivalent; and therefore he, who takes it in this sense, alters the subject of the discourse. *South.*

ACCE'PTANCE. [in law.] The receiving of a rent, whereby the giver binds himself, for ever, to allow a former fact done by another, whether it be in itself good or not. *Cowel.*

ACCEPTA'TION. *n. s.* [from *accept.*]

1. Reception, whether good or bad. This large sense seems now wholly out of use.

Yet, poor soul! knows he no other, but that I do suspect, neglect, yea, and detest him: for, every day, he finds one way or other to set forth himself unto me; but all are rewarded with like coldness of *acceptation.* *Sidney, b.* ii.

What is new finds better *acceptation,* than what is good or great. *Denham's Sophy.*

2. Good reception, acceptance.

Cain, envious of the *acceptation* of his brother's prayer and sacrifice, slew him; making himself the first manslayer, and his brother the first martyr. *Raleigh's History of the World, b.* i.

3. The state of being acceptable, regard.

Some things, although not so required of necessity, that, to leave them undone, excludeth from salvation, are, notwithstanding, of so great dignity and *acceptation* with God, that most ample reward in heaven is laid up for them. *Hooker, b.* ii.

They have those enjoyments only as the consequences of the state of esteem and *acceptation* they are in with their parents and governours. *Locke on Education,* § 53.

5. Acceptance in the juridical sense. This sense occurs rarely.

As, in order to the passing away a thing by gift, there is required a surrender of all right on his part that gives; so there is required also an *acceptation* on his part to whom it is given. *South's Sermons.*

5. The meaning of a word, as it is commonly received.

Thereupon the earl of Lauderdale made a discourse upon the several questions, and what *acceptation* these words and expressions had. *Clarendon, b.* viii.

All matter is either fluid or solid, in a large *acceptation* of the words, that they may comprehend even all the middle degrees between extreme fixedness and coherency, and the most rapid intestine motion of the particles of bodies. *Bentl. Serm.*

An ACCE'PTER. *n. s.* [from *accept.*] The person that accepts.

ACCEPTILA'TION, *n. s.* [*acceptilatio,* Lat.] A term of the civil law, importing the remission of a debt by an acquittance from the creditor, testifying the receipt of money which has never been paid.

ACCE'PTION. *n. s.* [*acception,* Fr. from *acceptio,* Lat.] The received sense of a word; the meaning.

That this hath been esteemed the due and proper *acception* of this word, I shall testify by one evidence, which gave me the first hint of this notion. *Hammond on Fundamentals.*

ACCE'SS. *n. s.* [In some of its senses, it seems derived from *accessus,* in others, from *accessio,* Lat. *acces,* Fr.]

1. The way by which any thing may be approached.

There remained very advantageous *accesses* for temptations to enter and invade men, the fortifications being very slender, little knowledge of immortality, or any thing beyond this life, and no assurance that repentance would be admitted for sin. *Hammond on Fundamentals.*

And here th' *access* a gloomy grove defends;
And here th' unnavigable lake extends,
O'er whose unhappy waters, void of light,
No bird presumes to steer his airy flight. *Dryd. Æneid* vi.

2. The means, or liberty, of approaching either to things or men.

When we are wrong'd, and would unfold our griefs,
We are deny'd *access* unto his person,
Ev'n by those men that most have done us wrong. *Shakespeare's Henry* IV. *p.* ii.

They go commission'd to require a peace,
And carry presents to procure *access.* *Dryden, Æneid* vii.

He grants what they besought;
Instructed, that to God is no *access*
Without Mediator, whose high office now
Moses in figure bears. *Milton's Paradise Lost, b.* xii.

3. Encrease, enlargement, addition.

The gold was accumulated, and store treasure, for the most part; but the silver is still growing. Besides, infinite is the *access* of territory and empire by the same enterprize. *Bacon's Holy War.*

Although to opinion, there be many gods, may seem an *access* in religion, and such as cannot at all consist with atheism, yet doth it deductively, and upon inference, include the same; for unity is the inseparable and essential attribute of Deity. *Brown's Vulgar Errours, b.* i. *c.* 10.

Nor think superfluous their aid;
I, from the influence of thy looks, receive
Access in every virtue; in thy sight
More wise, more watchful, stronger. *Paradise Lost.*

The reputation
Of virtuous actions past, if not kept up
With an *access,* and fresh supply, of new ones,
Is lost and soon forgotten. *Denham's Sophy.*

4. It is sometimes used, after the French, to signify the returns of fits of a distemper; but this sense seems yet scarcely received into our language.

For as relapses make diseases
More desperate than their first *accesses.* *Hudibras.*

A'CCESSARINESS. *n. s.* [from *accessary.*] The state of being accessary.

Perhaps this will draw us into a negative *accessariness* to the mischiefs. *Decay of Piety.*

A'CCESSARY. *adj.* [A corruption, as it seems, of the word *accessory,* which see; but now more commonly used than the proper word.]

That which, without being the chief agent in a crime, contributes to it. But it had formerly a good and general sense.

As for those things that are *accessary* hereunto, those things that so belong to the way of salvation. *Hooker.*

He had taken upon him the government of Hull, without any apprehension or imagination, that it would ever make him *accessary* to rebellion. *Clarendon, b.* viii.

ACCE'SSIBLE. *adj.* [*accessibilis,* Lat. *accessible,* Fr.] That which may be approached; that which we may reach or arrive at.

It is applied both to persons and things, with the particle *to.*

In conversation, the tempers of men are open and *accessible,* their attention is awake, and their minds disposed to receive the strongest impressions; and what is spoken is generally more affecting, and more apposite to particular occasions. *Rogers.*

As an island, we are *accessible* on every side, and exposed to perpetual invasions; against which it is impossible to fortify ourselves sufficiently, without a power at sea. *Addison's Freeholder.*

Those things, which were indeed inexplicable, have been rackt and tortured to discover themselves, while the plainer and more *accessible* truths, as if despicable while easy, are clouded and obscured. *Decay of Piety.*

Some lie more open to our senses and daily observation; others are more occult and hidden, and though *accessible,* in some measure, *to* our senses, yet not without great search and scrutiny, or some happy accident. *Hale's Origin of Mankind.*

ACCE'SSION. *n. s.* [*accessio,* Lat. *accession,* Fr.]

1. Encrease by something added, enlargement, augmentation.

There would not have been found the difference here set down betwixt the force of the air, when expanded, and what that force should have been according to the theory, but that the included inch of air received some little *accession* during the trial. *Boyle's Spring of the Air.*

The wisest among the nobles began to apprehend the growing power of the people; and therefore, knowing what an *accession* thereof would accrue to them, by such an addition of property, used all means to prevent it. *Swift on the Contests in Athens and Rome.*

Charity, indeed, and works of munificence, are the proper discharge of such over-proportioned *accessions,* and the only virtuous enjoyment of them. *Rogers's Sermons.*

2. The act of coming to, or joining one's self to; as, *accession* to a confederacy.

Beside, what wise objections he prepares
Against my late *accession* to the wars?
Does not the fool perceive his argument
Is with more force against Achilles bent? *Dryden's Fables.*

3. The act of arriving at; as, the king's *accession* to the throne.

A'CCESSORILY. *adv.* [from *accessory.*] In the manner of an accessory.

A'CCESSORY. *adj.* Joined to another thing, so as to encrease it; additional.

In this kind there is not the least action, but it doth somewhat make to the *accessory* augmentation of our bliss. *Hooker.*

A'CCESSORY. *n. s.* [*accessorius,* Lat. *accessoire,* Fr. This word, which had anciently a general signification, is now almost confined to forms of law.]

1. Applied to persons.

A man that is guilty of a felonious offence, not principally, but by participation; as, by commandment, advice, or concealment. And a man may be *accessory* to the offence of another, after two sorts, by the common law, or by statute: and, by the common law, two ways also; that is, before or after the fact. Before the fact; as, when one commandeth or adviseth another to commit a felony, and is not present at the execution thereof; for his presence makes him also a principal: wherefore there cannot be an *accessory* before the fact in manslaughter; because manslaughter is sudden and not prepensed. *Accessory* after the fact, is, when one receiveth him, whom he knoweth to have committed felony. *Accessory,* by statute, is he that abets, counsels, or hides any man committing, or having committed an offence made felony by statute. *Cowel.*

By the common law, the *accessories* cannot be proceeded against till the principal has received his trial. *Spenser's State of Irel.*

But pause, my soul! and study, ere thou fall
On accidental joys, th' essential.
Still before *accessories* to abide
A trial, must the principal be try'd. *Donne.*

Now were all transform'd
Alike, to serpents all, as *accessories*
To his bold riot. *Milton's Paradise Lost, b.* x. *l.* 520.

2. Applied

2. Applied to things.

An *acceſſory* is ſaid to be that which does accede unto ſome principal fact or thing in law; and, as ſuch, generally ſpeaking, follows the reaſon and nature of its principal. *Ayliffe's Parergon Juris Canonici.*

A'CCIDENCE. *n. ſ.* [a corruption of *accidents*, from *accidentia*, Lat.] The little book containing the firſt rudiments of grammar, and explaining the properties of the eight parts of ſpeech.

I do confeſs I do want eloquence,
And never yet did learn mine *accidence*. *Taylor the Water-poet.*

A'CCIDENT. *n. ſ.* [*accidens*, Lat.]

1. The property or quality of any being, which may be ſeparated from it, at leaſt in thought.

If ſhe were but the body's *accident*,
And her ſole being did in it ſubſiſt,
As white in ſnow, ſhe might herſelf abſent,
And in the body's ſubſtance not be miſs'd. *Sir John Davies.*

An accidental mode, or an *accident*, is ſuch a mode as is not neceſſary to the being of a thing; for the ſubject may be without it, and yet remain of the ſame nature that it was before; or it is that mode which may be ſeparated or aboliſhed from its ſubject. *Watts's Logick.*

2. In grammar, the property of a word.

The learning of a language is nothing elſe but the informing of ourſelves, what compoſures of letters are, by conſent and inſtitution, to ſignify ſuch certain notions of things, with their modalities and *accidents*. *Holder's Elements of Speech.*

3. That which happens unforeſeen; caſualty, chance.

General laws are like general rules in phyſick, according whereunto, as no wiſe man will deſire himſelf to be cured, if there be joined with his diſeaſe ſome ſpecial *accident*, in regard whereof, that whereby others in the ſame infirmity, but without the like *accident*, recover health, would be, to him, either hurtful, or, at the leaſt, unprofitable. *Hooker, b.* v. § 9.

The flood, and other *accidents* of time, made it one common field and paſture with the land of Eden. *Raleigh's Hiſt. World.*

Thus we rejoic'd, but ſoon our joy is turn'd
Into perplexity, and new amaze;
For whither is he gone? What *accident*
Hath rapt him from us? *Paradiſe Regained, b.* i.

And trivial *accidents* ſhall be forborn,
That others may have time to take their turn. *Dryd. Fables.*

The reformation owed nothing to the good intentions of king Henry. He was only an inſtrument of it (as the logicians ſpeak) by *accident*. *Swift's Miſcellanies.*

ACCIDE'NTAL. *n. ſ.* [*accidental*, Fr. See ACCIDENT.] A property noneſſential.

Conceive, as much as you can, of the eſſentials of any ſubject, before you conſider its *accidentals*. *Watts's Logick.*

ACCIDE'NTAL. *adj.* [from *accident*.]

1. Having the quality of an accident, noneſſential; uſed with the particle *to*, before that in which the accident inheres.

A diſtinction is to be made between what pleaſes naturally in itſelf, and what pleaſes upon the account of machines, actors, dances, and circumſtances, which are merely *accidental to* the tragedy. *Rymer's Tragedies of the laſt Age.*

This is *accidental to* a ſtate of religion, and therefore ought to be reckoned among the ordinary difficulties of it. *Tillotſon.*

2. Caſual, fortuitous, happening by chance.

Thy ſin's not *accidental*, but a trade. *Shakeſp. Meaſ. for Meaſ.*

So ſhall you hear
Of *accidental* judgments, caſual ſlaughters;
Of deaths put on by cunning, and forc'd cauſe. *Shakeſ. Ham.*

Look upon things of the moſt *accidental* and mutable nature; *accidental* in their production, and mutable in their continuance; yet God's preſcience of them is as certain in him, as the memory of them is, or can be, in us. *South's Sermons.*

3. In the following paſſage it ſeems to ſignify *adventitious*.

Ay, ſuch a miniſter as wind to fire,
That adds an *accidental* fierceneſs to
Its natural fury. *Denham's Sophy.*

ACCIDE'NTALLY. *adv.* [from *accidental*.]

1. After an accidental manner; noneſſentially.

Other needful points of publick matters, no leſs concerning the good of the commonwealth, though but *accidentally* depending upon the former. *Spenſer's State of Ireland.*

I conclude choler *accidentally* better, and acrimonious, but not in itſelf. *Harvey on Conſumptions.*

2. Caſually, fortuitouſly.

Although virtuous men do ſometimes *accidentally* make their way to preferment, yet the world is ſo corrupted, that no man can reaſonably hope to be rewarded in it, merely upon account of his virtue. *Swift's Miſcellanies.*

ACCIDE'NTALNESS. *n. ſ.* [from *accidental*.] The quality of being accidental. *Dict.*

ACCI'PIENT. *n. ſ.* [*accipiens*, Lat.] A receiver, perhaps ſometimes uſed for *recipient*. *Dict.*

To ACCI'TE. *v. a.* [*accito*, Lat.] To call, to ſummons; a word not in uſe now.

Our coronation done, we will *accite*
No prince, no peer, ſhall have juſt cauſe to ſay,
Heav'n ſhorten Harry's happy life one day. *Shakeſ. Henry* IV.

ACCLA'IM. *n. ſ.* [*acclamo*, Lat. from which probably firſt the verb *acclaim*, now loſt, and then the noun.] A ſhout of praiſe, acclamation.

Back from purſuit thy pow'rs, with loud *acclaim*,
Thee only extoll'd. *Milton's Par. Loſt, b.* iii. *l.* 397.

The herald ends; the vaulted firmament
With loud *acclaims*, and vaſt applauſe, is rent. *Dryd. Fables.*

ACCLAMA'TION. *n. ſ.* [*acclamatio*, Lat.] Shouts of applauſe; ſuch as thoſe with which a victorious army ſalutes the general.

It hath been the cuſtom of chriſtian men, in token of the greater reverence, to ſtand, to utter certain words of *acclamation*, and, at the name of Jeſus, to bow. *Hooker, b. v.* § 29.

Gladly then he mix'd
Among thoſe friendly pow'rs, who him receiv'd
With joy, and *acclamations* loud, that one,
That, of ſo many myriads fall'n, yet one
Return'd, not loſt. *Milt. Parad. Loſt. b.* vi. *l.* 23.

Such an enchantment is there in words, and ſo fine a thing does it ſeem to ſome, to be ruined plauſibly, and to be uſhered to their deſtruction with panegyric and *acclamation*. *South.*

ACCLI'VITY. *n. ſ.* [from *acclivus*, Lat.] The ſteepneſs or ſlope of a line inclining to the horizon, reckoned upwards; as, the aſcent of an hill is the *acclivity*, the deſcent is the declivity. *Quincy.*

The men, leaving their wives and younger children below, do, not without ſome difficulty, clamber up the *acclivities*, dragging their kine with them, where they feed them, and milk them, and make butter and cheeſe, and do all the dairy-work. *Ray on the Creation.*

ACCLI'VOUS. *adj.* [*acclivus*, Lat.] Riſing with a ſlope.

To ACCLO'Y. *v. a.* [See CLOY.]

1. To fill up, in an ill ſenſe; to croud, to ſtuff full: a word almoſt obſolete.

At the well-head the pureſt ſtreams ariſe:
But mucky filth his branching arms annoys,
And with uncomely weeds the gentle wave *accloys*. *Fairy Q.*

2. To fill to ſatiety; in which ſenſe *cloy* is ſtill in uſe.

They that eſcape beſt in the temperate zone, would be *accloyed* with long nights, very tedious, no leſs than forty days. *Ray on the Creation.*

To ACCO'IL. *v. n.* [See COIL.] To croud, to keep a *coil* about, to buſtle, to be in a hurry; a word now out of uſe.

About the cauldron many cooks *accoil'd*,
With hooks and ladles, as need did require;
The while the viands in the veſſel boil'd,
They did about their buſineſs ſweat, and ſorely toil'd. *Fairy Q.*

A'CCOLENT. *n. ſ.* [*accolens*, Lat.] He that inhabits near a place; a borderer. *Dict.*

ACCO'MMODABLE. *adj.* [*accommodabilis*, Lat.] That which may be fitted; with the particle *to*.

As there is infinite variety in the circumſtances of perſons, things, actions, times and places; ſo we muſt be furniſhed with ſuch general rules as are *accommodable to* all this variety, by a wiſe judgment and diſcretion. *Watts's Logick.*

To ACCO'MMODATE. *v. a.* [*accommodo*, Lat.]

1. To ſupply with conveniencies of any kind.

Theſe three,
Three thouſand confident, in act as many;
For three performers are the file, when all
The reſt do nothing; with this word ſtand, ſtand,
Accommodated by the place, (more charming
With their own nobleneſs, which could have turn'd
A diſtaff to a lance) gilded pale looks. *Shakeſp. Cymbeline.*

2. With the particle *to*, to adapt, to fit, to make conſiſtent with.

He had altered many things, not that they were not natural before, but that he might *accommodate* himſelf *to* the age in which he lived. *Dryden on Dramatic Poetry.*

'Twas his misfortune to light upon an hypotheſis, that could not be *accommodated to* the nature of things, and human affairs; his principles could not be made to agree with that conſtitution and order which God hath ſettled in the world. *Locke.*

ACCO'MMODATE. *adj.* [*accommodatus*, Lat.] Suitable, fit; uſed ſometimes with the particle *for*, but more frequently with *to*.

They are ſo acted and directed by nature, as to caſt their eggs in ſuch places as are moſt *accommodate for* the excluſion of their young, and where there is food ready for them ſo ſoon as they be hatched. *Ray on the Creation.*

In theſe caſes, we examine the why, the what, and the how, of things, and propoſe means *accommodate to* the end. *L'Eſtrange.*

God did not primarily intend to appoint this way of worſhip, and to impoſe it upon them as that which was moſt proper and agreeable to him, but that he condeſcended to it as moſt *accommodate to* their preſent ſtate and inclination. *Tillotſ. Serm.* v.

ACCO'MMODATELY. *adv.* [from *accommodate*.] Suitably, fitly.

ACCOMMODA'TION. *n. ſ.* [from *accommodate*.]

1. Proviſion of conveniencies.

2. In the plural, conveniencies, things requiſite to eaſe or refreſhment.

The king's commiſſioners were to have ſuch *accommodations*, as the other thought fit to leave to them; who had been very civil to the king's commiſſioners. *Clarendon, b.* viii.

3. Adaptation, fitneſs; with the particle *to*.

The organization of the body, with *accommodation to* its functions,

tions, is fitted with the most curious mechanism. *Hale.*

4. Composition of a difference, reconciliation, adjustment.

Acco'mpanable. *adj.* [from *accompany.*] Sociable; a word now not used.

A show, as it were, of an *accompanable* solitariness, and of a civil wildness. *Sidney.*

Acco'mpanier. *n. s.* [from *accompany.*] The person that makes part of the company; companion. *Dict.*

To ACCO'MPANY. *v. a.* [*accompagner*, Fr.]

1. To be with another as a companion.

Go visit her, in her chaste bower of rest,
Accompany'd with angel-like delights. *Spenser.*

The great business of the senses being to make us take notice of what hurts or advantages the body, it is wisely ordered by nature, that pain should *accompany* the reception of several ideas. *Locke.*

2. To join with.

With regard to sheep, as folly is usually *accompanied* with perverseness, so it is here. There is something so monstrous to deal in a commodity, which we are not allowed to export; there is, I say, something so sottish, that it wants a name, in our language, to express it by. *Swift.*

Acco'mplice. *n. s.* [*complice*, Fr. from *complex*, a word in the barbarous Latin, much in use, *Complices fertæ prudentius.*]

1. An associate, a partaker; usually in an ill sense.

There were several scandalous reports industriously spread by Wood, and his *accomplices*, to discourage all opposition against his infamous project. *Swift.*

2. A partner, or co-operator; in a sense indifferent.

If a tongue would be talking without a mouth, what could it have done, when it had all its organs of speech, and *accomplices* of sound, about it. *Addison.*

3. It is used with the particle *to* before a thing, and *with* before a person.

Childless Arturius, vastly rich before,
Thus by his losses multiplies his store,
Suspected for *accomplice to* the fire,
That burnt his palace but to build it higher. *Dryd. Juv.*
Who, should they steal, for want of his relief,
He judg'd himself *accomplice with* the thief. *Dryden.*

To ACCO'MPLISH. *v. a.* [*accomplir*, Fr. from *compleo*, Lat.]

1. To complete, to execute fully; as, to *accomplish* a design.

He that is far off shall die of the pestilence, and he that is near shall fall by the sword, and he that remaineth, and is besieged, shall die by the famine. Thus will I *accomplish* my fury upon them. *Ezekiel.*

2. To complete a period of time.

He would *accomplish* seventy years in the desolations of Jerusalem. *Daniel.*

3. To fulfil; as, a prophecy.

The vision,
Which I made known to Lucius ere the stroke
Of this yet scarce cold battle, at this instant
Is full *accomplish'd.* *Shakespeare's Cymbeline.*

We see every day those events exactly *accomplished*, which our Saviour foretold at so great a distance. *Addison on the Christian Religion.*

4. To gain, to obtain.

Tell him from me (as he will win my love)
He bear himself with honourable action;
Such as he hath observ'd in noble ladies,
Unto their lords, by them *accomplished.* *Shakespeare.*
I'll make my heaven in a lady's lap,
And deck my body in gay ornaments.
Oh miserable thought, and more unlikely,
Than to *accomplish* twenty golden crowns. *Shak. Henry V.*

5. To adorn, or furnish, either mind or body.

From the tents
The armourers *accomplishing* the knights,
With busy hammers closing rivets up,
Give dreadful note of preparation. *Shakespeare's Henry V.*

Acco'mplished. *participial adj.*

1. Complete in some qualification.

For who expects, that, under a tutor, a young gentleman should be an *accomplished* publick orator or logician. *Locke.*

2. Elegant, finished in respect of embellishments; used commonly with respect to acquired qualifications, without including moral excellence.

The next I took to wife,
O that I never had! fond wish too late,
Was in the vale of Sorec, Dalila,
That specious monster, my *accomplish'd* snare. *Samson Agon.*

Acco'mplisher. *n. s.* [from *accomplish.*] The person that accomplishes. *Dict.*

Acco'mplishment. *n. s.* [*accomplissement*, Fr.]

1. Completion, full performance, perfection.

Thereby he might evade the *accomplishment* of those afflictions, he now but gradually endureth. *Brown's Vulg. Errours.*

This would be the *accomplishment* of their common felicity, in case, by their evil, either through destiny or advice, they suffered not the occasion to be lost. *Haywood.*

He thought it impossible to find, in any one body, all those perfections which he sought for the *accomplishment* of a Helena; because nature, in any individual person, makes nothing that is perfect in all its parts. *Dryden.*

2. Completion; as, of a prophecy.

The miraculous success of the apostles preaching, and the *accomplishment* of many of their predictions, which, to those early christians, were matters of faith only, are, to us, matters of sight and experience. *Atterbury.*

3. Embellishment, elegance, ornament of mind or body.

Young heirs, and elder brothers, from their own reflecting upon the estates they are born to, and therefore thinking all other *accomplishments* unnecessary, are of no manner of use but to keep up their families. *Addison.*

4. The act of obtaining any thing.

The means suggested by policy and worldly wisdom, for the attainment of those earthly enjoyments, are unfit for that purpose, not only upon the account of their insufficiency for, but also of their frequent opposition and contrariety to, the *accomplishment* of such ends. *South.*

Acco'mpt. *n. s.* [Fr. *compter* and *compte*, anciently *accompter. Skinner.*] An account, a reckoning. See Account.

The soul may have time to call itself to a just *accompt* of all things past, by means whereof repentance is perfected. *Hooker.*

Each Christmas they *accompts* did clear;
And wound their bottom round the year. *Prior.*

Acco'mptant. *n. s.* [*accomptant*, Fr.] A reckoner, computer. See Accountant.

As the accompt runs on, generally the *accomptant* goes backward. *South's Sermons.*

Acco'mpting-day. The day on which the reckoning is to be settled.

To whom thou much dost owe, thou much must pay;
Think on the debt against th' *accompting-day.* *Denham.*

To ACCO'RD. *v. a.* [derived, by some, from *corda* the string of a musical instrument, by others, from *corda* hearts; in the first, implying *harmony*, in the other, *unity.*]

To make agree to adjust one thing to another; with the particle *to.*

The first sports the shepherds showed, were full of such leaps and gambols, as being *accorded to* the pipe which they bore in their mouths, even as they danced, made a right picture of their chief god Pan, and his companions the satyrs. *Sidney.*

Her hands *accorded* the lute's music *to* the voice; her panting heart danced to the music. *Sidney.*

The lights and shades, whose well *accorded* strife,
Gives all the strength and colour of our life. *Pope.*

To Acco'rd. *v. n.* To agree, to suit one with another; with the particle *with.*

Things are often spoke, and seldom meant;
But that my heart *accordeth with* my tongue,
Seeing the deed is meritorious,
And to preserve my sovereign from his foe. *Shak. Hen. VI.*

Several of the main parts of Moses's history, as concerning the flood, and the first fathers of the several nations of the world, do very well *accord with* the most ancient accounts of profane history. *Tillotson.*

Acco'rd. *n. s.* [*accord*, Fr.]

1. A compact; an agreement.

If both are satisfy'd with this *accord*,
Swear by the laws of knighthood on my sword. *Dryden.*

2. Concurrence, union of mind.

At last such grace I found, and means I wrought,
That I that lady to my spouse had won,
Accord of friends, consent of parents sought,
Affiance made, my happiness begun. *Spenser's Fairy Queen.*

They gathered themselves together, to fight with Joshua and Israel, with one *accord.* *Joshua.*

3. Harmony, symmetry, just correspondence of one thing with another.

Beauty is nothing else but a just *accord* and mutual harmony of the members, animated by a healthful constitution. *Dryden's Dufresnoy.*

4. Musical note.

Try if there were in one steeple two bells of unison, whether the striking of the one would move the other, more than if it were another *accord.* *Bacon's Natural History.*

We must not blame Apollo, but his lute,
If false *accords* from her false strings be sent. *Davies.*

5. Voluntary motion.

Ne Guyon yet spake word,
Till that they came unto an iron door,
Which to them open'd of its own *accord.* *Fairy Queen.*

Will you blame any man for doing that of his own *accord*, which all men should be compelled to do, that are not willing of themselves. *Hooker.*

All animal substances, exposed to the air, turn alkaline of their own *accord*; and some vegetables, by heat, will not turn acid, but alkaline. *Arbuthnot.*

6. Action

6. Action in speaking, correspondent to the words.

Titus, I am come to talk with thee.—
—No, not a word: how can I grace my talk,
Wanting a hand to give it that *accord?* *Shakespeare.*

ACCO'RDANCE *n. s.* [from *accord.*]

1. Agreement with a person; with the particle *with*.

And prays he may in long *accordance* bide,
With that great worth which hath such wonders wrought. *Fairfax.*

2. Conformity to something.

The only way of defining of sin, is, by the contrariety to the will of God; as of good, by the *accordance with* that will. *Hammond's Fundamentals.*

ACCO'RDANT. *adj.* [*accordant*, Fr.] Willing; in a good humour.

The prince discovered to Claudio, that he loved your niece my daughter, and meant to acknowledge it this night in a dance; and, if he found her *accordant*, he meant to take the present time by the top, and instantly break with you of it. *Shakespeare's Much ado about Nothing.*

ACCO'RDING. *prep.* [from *accord.*]

1. In a manner suitable to, agreeably to, in proportion.

Our churches are places provided, that the people might there assemble themselves in due and decent manner, *according* to their several degrees and orders. *Hooker.*

Our zeal, then, should be *according* to knowledge. And what kind of knowledge? Without all question, first, *according* to the true, saving, evangelical knowledge. It should be *according* to the gospel, the whole gospel: not only *according* to its truths, but precepts: not only *according* to its free grace, but necessary duties: not only *according* to its mysteries, but also its commandments. *Sprat's Sermons.*

How much more noble is the fame that is built on candour and ingenuity, *according* to those beautiful lines of Sir John Denham, in his Poem on Fletcher's works. *Addison.*

A man may, with prudence and a good conscience, approve of the professed principles of one party more than the other, *according* as he thinks they best promote the good of church and state. *Swift.*

2. With regard to.

God made all things in number, weight, and measure, and gave them to be considered by us *according* to these properties which are inherent in created beings. *Holder on Time.*

ACCO'RDINGLY. *adv.* [from *accord.*] Agreeably, suitably, conformably.

Sirrah, thou'rt said to have a stubborn soul,
That apprehends no further than this world;
And squar'st thy life *accordingly*. *Shakespeare.*

As the actions of men are of sundry distinct kinds, so the laws thereof must *accordingly* be distinguished. *Hooker.*

Whoever is so assured of the authority and sense of scripture, as to believe the doctrine of it, and to live *accordingly*, shall be saved. *Tillotson.*

Mealy substances, fermented, turn sour. *Accordingly*, given to a weak child, they still retain their nature; for bread will give them the cholic. *Arbuthnot on Aliments.*

To ACCOST. *v. a.* [*accoster*, Fr.] To speak to first; to address; to salute.

You mistake, knight: *accost* her, front her, board her, woo her, assail her. *Shakespeare's Twelfth Night.*

At length, collecting all his serpent wiles,
With soothing words renew'd, him thus *accosts*. *Milton.*

I first *accosted* him: I su'd, I sought,
And, with a loving force, to Pheneus brought. *Dryden.*

ACCO'STABLE. *adj.* [from *accost.*] Easy of access; familiar.

They were both indubitable, strong, and high-minded men, yet of sweet and *accostable* nature, almost equally delighting in the press and affluence of dependents and suitors. *Wotton.*

ACCO'UNT. *n. s.* [from the old French *accompt*, from *computus*, Lat. originally written *accompt*, which see; but, by gradually softening the pronunciation, in time the orthography changed to *account.*]

1. A computation of debts or expences; a register of facts relating to money.

At many times I brought in my *accounts*,
Laid them before you; you would throw them off,
And say you found them in mine honesty. *Shakespeare.*

When my young master has once got the skill of keeping *accounts* (which is a business of reason more than arithmetic) perhaps is will not be amiss, that his father from thenceforth require him to do it in all his concernments. *Locke.*

2. The state or result of a computation; as, the *account* stands thus between us.

Behold this have I found, saith the Preacher, counting one by one, to find out the *account*. *Ecclesiasticus.*

3. Such a state of persons or things, as may make them more or less worthy of being considered in the reckoning. Value, or estimation.

For the care that they took for their wives and their children, their brethren and kinsfolks, was in least *account* with them: but the greatest and principal fear was for the holy temple. 2 *Maccab.* xv. 18.

That good affection, which things of smaller *account* have once set on work, is by so much the more easily raised higher. *Hooker, b.* v. §. 35.

I should make more *account* of their judgment, who are men of sense, and yet have never touched a pencil, than of the opinion given by the greatest part of painters. *Dryden's Dufresn.*

We would establish our souls in such a solid and substantial virtue, as will turn to *account* in that great day, when it must stand the test of infinite wisdom and justice. *Addison.*

4. Distinction, dignity, rank.

There is such a peculiarity in Homer's manner of apostrophizing Eumæus, and speaking of him in the second person: it is generally applied, by that poet, only to men of *account* and distinction. *Pope's Odyssey.*

5. A reckoning verified by finding the value of a thing equal to what was accounted.

Considering the usual motives of human actions, which are pleasure, profit, and ambition, I cannot yet comprehend how those persons find their *account* in any of the three. *Swift's Address to Parliament.*

6. A reckoning referred to, or sum charged upon any particular person; and thence, figuratively, regard, consideration, sake.

If he hath wronged thee, or oweth thee ought, put that on my *account*. *Philemon*, i. 8.

This must be always remembered, that nothing can come into the *account* of recreation, that is not done with delight. *Locke.*

In matters where his judgment led him to oppose men on a public *account*, he would do it vigorously and heartily. *Atterbury.*

The assertion is our Saviour's, though uttered by him in the person of Abraham, the father of the faithful; who, on the *account* of that character, is very fitly introduced. *Idem.*

These tribunes, a year or two after their institution, kindled great dissensions between the nobles and the commons, on the *account* of Coriolanus, a nobleman, whom the latter had impeached. *Swift.*

Nothing can recommend itself to our love, on any other *account*, but either as it promotes our present, or is a means to assure to us a future happiness. *Rogers.*

Sempronius gives no thanks on this *account*. *Addison.*

7. A narrative, relation; in this use it may seem to be derived from *conte*, Fr. a tale, a narration.

8. The review or examination of an affair taken by authority; as, the magistrate took an *account* of the tumult.

Therefore is the kingdom of heaven likened unto a certain king, which would take *account* of his servants; and when he had begun to reckon, one was brought unto him, which owed him ten thousand talents. *Matt.* xix. 23, 24.

9. The relation and reasons of a transaction given to a person in authority.

Fie, my lord, fie! a soldier, and afraid! What need we fear who knows it, when none can call our power to *account?* *Shakespeare's Macbeth.*

The true ground of morality can only be the will and law of a God, who sees men in the dark, has in his hands rewards and punishments, and power enough to call to *account* the proudest offender.

10. Explanation; assignment of causes.

It is easy to give *account*, how it came to pass, that though all men desire happiness, yet their wills carry them so contrarily. *Locke.*

It being in our author's *account*, a right acquired by begetting, to rule over those he had begotten, it was not a power possible to be inherited, because the right, being consequent to, and built on, an act perfectly personal, made that power so too, and impossible to be inherited. *Locke.*

11. An opinion concerning things previously established.

These were designed to join with the forces at sea, there being prepared a number of flat-bottomed boats to transport the land-forces, under the wing of the great navy: for they made no *account*, but that the navy should be absolutely master of the seas. *Bacon's Considerations on War with Spain.*

A prodigal young fellow, that had sold his clothes, upon the sight of a swallow, made *account* that summer was at hand, and away went his shirt too. *L'Estrange.*

12. The reasons of any thing collected.

Being convinced, upon all *accounts*, that they had the same reason to believe the history of our Saviour, as that of any other person to which they themselves were not actually eyewitnesses, they were bound, by all the rules of historical faith, and of right reason, to give credit to this history. *Addison on the Christian Religion.*

13. In law.

Account is, in the common law, taken for a writ or action brought against a man, that, by means of office or business undertaken, is to render an *account* unto another; as, a baliff toward his master, a guardian to his ward. *Cowell.*

To ACCO'UNT. *v. n.* [See ACCOUNT.]

1. To esteem, to think, to hold in opinion.

That also was *accounted* a land of giants. *Deut.*

2. To

2. To reckon, to compute.

The calendar months are likewise arbitrarily and unequally settled by the same power; by which months we, to this day, *account*, and they measure, and make up, that which we call the Julian year. *Holder on Time.*

3. To give an account, to assign the causes; in which sense it is followed by the particle *for*.

If any one should ask, why our general continued so easy to the last? I know no other way to *account for* it, but by that unmeasurable love of wealth, which his best friends allow to be his predominant passion. *Swift.*

4. To make up the reckoning; to answer for practices.

Then thou shalt see him plung'd when least he fears,
At once *accounting for* his deep arrears. *Dryden.*

They have no uneasy presages of a future reckoning, wherein the pleasures they now taste, must be *accounted for*; and may, perhaps, be outweighed by the pains, which shall then lay hold of them. *Atterbury.*

5. To appear as the medium by which any thing may be explained.

Such as have a faulty circulation through the lungs, ought to eat very little at a time; because the increase of the quantity of fresh chyle, must make that circulation still more uneasy; which, indeed, is the case of consumptive and some asthmatic persons, and *accounts for* the symptoms they are troubled with after eating. *Arbuthnot on Aliments.*

6. To assign to, with the particle *to*.

For some years, really accrued the yearly sum of two hundred thousand pounds to the king's coffers: and it was, in truth, the only project that was *accounted to* his own service. *Clarendon.*

7. To hold in esteem.

Silver was nothing *accounted* of in the days of Solomon. *Chron.*

ACCO'UNTABLE. *adj.* [from *account.*] Of whom an account may be required; who must answer for: followed by the particle *to* before the person, and *for* before the thing.

Accountable to none,
But to my conscience and my God alone. *Oldham.*

Thinking themselves excused from standing upon their own legs, or being *accountable for* their own conduct, they very seldom trouble themselves with enquiries. *Locke.*

The good magistrate will make no distinction; for the judgment is God's; and he will look upon himself as *accountable* at his bar *for* the equity of it. *Atterbury.*

ACCOU'NTANT. *adj.* [from *account.*] Accountable to; responsible for.

His offence is so, as it appears
Accountant to the law upon that pain. *Shakespeare.*
I love her too,
Not out of absolute lust (though, peradventure,
I stand *accountant* for as great a sin)
But partly led to diet my revenge. *Shakespeare.*

ACCOU'NTANT. *n. s.* [See ACCOMPTANT.] A computer; a man skilled or employed in accounts.

The different compute of divers states; the short and irreconcileable years of some; the exceeding errour in the natural frame of others; and the false deductions of ordinary *accountants* in most. *Brown's Vulgar Errours.*

ACCO'UNT-BOOK. *n. s.* A book containing accounts.

I would endeavour to comfort myself upon the loss of friends, as I do upon the loss of money; by turning to my *account-book*, and seeing whether I have enough left for my support. *Swift.*

ACCO'UNTING. *n. s.* [from *account*] The act of reckoning, or making up of accounts.

This method faithfully observed, must keep a man from breaking, or running behind hand in his spiritual estate; which, without frequent *accountings*, he will hardly be able to prevent. *South's Sermons.*

To ACCO'UPLE. *v. a.* [*accoupler*, Fr.] To join; to link together.

He sent a solemn embassage to treat a peace and league with the king; *accoupling* it with an article in the nature of a request. *Bacon.*

To ACCO'URAGE. *v. a.* [obsolete. See COURAGE.] To animate.

That forward pair she ever would assuage,
When they would strive due reason to exceed;
But that same forward twain would *accourage*,
And of her plenty add unto her need. *Fairy Queen.*

To ACCO'URT. *v. a.* [See *To* COURT.] To entertain with courtship, or courtesy; a word now not in use.

Who all this while were at their wanton rest,
Accourting each her friend with lavish feast. *Fairy Queen.*

To ACCOUTRE. *v. a.* [*accoûtrer*, Fr.] To dress, to equip.

Is it for this they study? to grow pale,
And miss the pleasures of a glorious meal?
For this, in rags *accoutred* are they seen,
And made the may-game of the public spleen? *Dryden.*

ACCO'UTREMENT. *n. s.* [*accoûtrement*, Fr.] Dress, equipage, furniture relating to the person; trappings, ornaments.

I profess requital to a hair's breadth; not only in the simple office of love, but in all the *accoutrement*, complement, and ceremony of it. *Shakespeare's Merry Wives of Windsor.*

I have seen the pope officiate at St. Peter's, where, for two hours together, he was busied in putting on or off his different *accoutrements*, according to the different parts he was to act in them. *Addison.*

How gay with all th' *accoutrements* of war,
The Britons come, with gold well-fraught they come. *Phil.*

Christianity is lost among them, in the trappings and *accoutrements* of it; with which, instead of adorning religion, they have strangely disguised it, and quite stifled it in the croud of external rites and ceremonies. *Tillotson.*

ACCRE'TION. *n. s.* [*accretio*, Lat.] The act of growing to another, so as to encrease it.

Plants do nourish; inanimate bodies do not: they have an *accretion*, but no alimentation. *Bacon.*

The changes seem to be effected by the exhaling of the moisture, which may leave the tinging corpuscles more dense, and something augmented by the *accretion* of the oily and earthy parts of that moisture. *Newton's Optics.*

Infants support abstinence worst, from the quantity of aliment consumed in *accretion.* *Arbuthnot on Aliments.*

ACCRE'TIVE. *adj.* [from *accretion.*] Growing; that which by growth is added.

If the motion be very slow, we perceive it not: we have no sense of the *accretive* motion of plants and animals: and the sly shadow steals away upon the dial; and the quickest eye can discover no more but that it is gone. *Glanv. Scepsis Scient.*

To ACCRO'ACH. *v. a.* [*accrocher*, Fr.] To draw to one as with a hook; to gripe, to draw away by degrees what is another's.

ACCRO'ACHMENT. *n. s.* [from *accroach.*] The act of accroaching. *Dict.*

To ACCRUE. *v. n.* [from the participle *accrû*, formed from *accroître*, Fr.]

1. To accede to, to be added to; as, a natural production or effect, without any particular respect to good or ill.

The Son of God, by his incarnation, hath changed the manner of that personal subsistence; no alteration thereby *accruing* to the nature of God. *Hooker.*

2. To be added, as an advantage or improvement, in a sense inclining to good rather than ill; in which meaning it is more frequently used by later authors.

From which compact there arising an obligation upon every one, so to convey his meaning, there *accrues* also a right to every one, by the same signs, to judge of the sense or meaning of the person so obliged to express himself. *South's Sermons.*

Let the evidence of such a particular miracle be never so bright and clear, yet it is still but particular; and must therefore want that kind of force, that degree of influence, which *accrues* to a standing general proof, from its having been tried or approved, and consented to, by men of all ranks and capacities, of all tempers and interests, of all ages and nations. *Atterbury.*

3. To append to, or arise from; as, an ill consequence. This sense seems to be less proper.

His scholar Aristotle, as in many other particulars, so likewise in this, did justly oppose him, and became one of the authors; choosing a certain benefit, before the hazard that might *accrue* from the disrespects of ignorant persons. *Wilk. Math. Mag.*

4. In a commercial sense, to be produced, or arise; as, profits.

The yearly benefit, that, out of those his works, *accrueth* to her majesty, amounteth to one thousand pounds. *Carew's Surv.*

The great profits which have *accrued* to the duke of Florence from his free port, have set several of the states of Italy on the same subject. *Addison.*

5. Sometimes to follow, as loss; but less properly.

The benefit or loss of such a trade *accruing* to the government, until it comes to take root in the nation. *Temple's Misc.*

ACCUBA'TION. *n. s.* [from *accubo*, to lye down to, Lat.] The antient posture of leaning at meals.

It will appear, that *accubation*, or lying down at meals, was a gesture used by very many nations. *Brown.*

To ACCU'MB. *v. a.* [*accumbo*, Lat.] To lie at the table, according to the ancient manner. *Dict.*

To ACCU'MULATE. *v. a.* [from *accumulo*, Lat.] To heap one thing upon another; to pile up, to heap together. It is used either literally, as, to *accumulate* money, or, figuratively, as, to *accumulate* merit or wickedness.

If thou dost slander her, and torture me,
Never pray more; abandon all remorse;
On horrors head horrors *accumulate*;
For nothing can'st thou to damnation add. *Shakespeare.*
Crusht by imaginary treason's weight,
Which too much merit did *accumulate*. *Sir John Denham.*

ACCUMULA'TION. *n. s.* [from *accumulate.*]

1. The act of accumulating.

Some, perhaps, might otherwise wonder at such an *accumulation* of benefits, like a kind of embroidering, or listing of one favour upon another. *Wotton.*

One of my place in Syria, his lieutenant,
For quick *accumulation* of renown,
Which he achiev'd by th' minute, lost his favour.
Shakespeare's Antony and Cleopatra.

2. The

2. The ſtate of being accumulated.

By the regular returns of it in ſome people, and their freedom from it after the morbid matter is exhauſted, it looks as there were regular *accumulations* and gatherings of it, as of other humours in the body, growing perhaps on ſome people as corns. *Arbuthnot on Diet.*

ACCU'MULATIVE. *adj.* [from *accumulate.*]

1. That which accumulates.

2. That which is accumulated.

If the injury meet not with meekneſs, it then acquires another *accumulative* guilt, and ſtands anſwerable not only for its own poſitive ill, but for all the accidental, which it cauſes in the ſufferer. *Government of the Tongue.*

ACCUMULA'TOR *n. ſ.* [from *accumulate.*] He that accumulates; a gatherer or heaper together.

Injuries may fall upon the paſſive man, yet there would be no broils and quarrels, the great *accumulators* and multipliers of injuries; which demonſtrates how unjuſtly meekneſs is charged with ſo much as accidental production of them. *Decay of Piety.*

A'CCURACY. *n. ſ.* [*accuratio*, Lat.] Exactneſs, nicety.

The man who hath the ſtupid ignorance, or hardened effrontery! to inſult the revealed will of God; or the petulant conceit to turn it into ridicule; or the arrogance to make his own perfections the meaſure of the Divinity; or, at beſt, that can collate a text, or quote an authority, with an inſipid *accuracy*; or demonſtrate a plain propoſition, in all the formality of A's and B's; theſe now are the only men worth mentioning. *Delany.*

We conſider the uniformity of the whole deſign, *accuracy* of the calculations, and ſkill in reſtoring and comparing paſſages of ancient authors. *Arbuthnot on Coins.*

A'CCURATE. *adj.* [*accuratus*, Lat.]

1. Exact, as oppoſed to negligence or ignorance, applied to perſons.

2. Exact, without defect or failure, applied to things.

No man living has made more *accurate* trials than Reaumure, that brighteſt ornament of France. *Colſon.*

A'CCURATELY. *adv.* [from *accurate.*] In an acurate manner; exactly, without errour, nicely.

The ſin of incidence is either *accurately*, or very nearly, in a given ratio to the ſine of refraction. *Newt. Opt.*

That all theſe diſtances, motions, and quantities of matter, ſhould be ſo *accurately* and harmoniouſly adjuſted in this great variety of our ſyſtem, is above the fortuitous hits of blind material cauſes, and muſt certainly flow from that eternal fountain of wiſdom. *Bentley.*

A'CCURATENESS. *n. ſ.* [from *accurate.*] Exactneſs, nicety.

But ſometime after, ſuſpecting that in making this obſervation I had not determined the diameter of the ſphere with ſufficient *accurateneſs*, I repeated the experiment. *Newton's Opt.*

To ACCU'RSE. *v. a.* [See CURSE.] To doom to miſery; to invoke miſery upon any one.

As if it were an unlucky comet, or as if God had ſo *accurſed* it, that it ſhould never ſhine to give light in things concerning our duty any way towards him. *Hooker.*

ACCU'RSED. *part adj.*

1. That which is curſed or doomed to miſery.

'Tis the moſt certain ſign the world's *accurſt*,
That the beſt things corrupted are and worſt. *Denham.*

2. That which deſerves the curſe; execrable; hateful; deteſtable; and, by conſequence, wicked; malignant.

Some holy angel
Fly to the court of England, and unfold
His meſſage ere he come; that a ſwift bleſſing
May ſoon return to this our ſuffering country,
Under a hand *accurs'd!* *Shakeſpeare's Macbeth.*

The chief part of the miſery of wicked men, and thoſe *accurſed* ſpirits, the devils, is this, that they are of a diſpoſition contrary to God. *Tillotſon.*

They, like the ſeed from which they ſprung, *accurſt*,
Againſt the gods immortal hatred nurſt. *Dryden's Ovid.*

ACCU'SABLE. *adj.* [from the verb *accuſe.*] That which may be cenſured; blamable; culpable.

There would be a manifeſt defect, and her improviſion juſtly *accuſable*; if animals, ſo ſubject unto diſeaſes from bilious cauſes, ſhould want a proper conveyance for choler. *Brown's Vulgar Errours.*

ACCUSA'TION. *n. ſ.* [from *accuſe.*]

1. The act of accuſing.

Thus they in mutual *accuſation* ſpent
The fruitleſs hours, but neither ſelf-condemning,
And of their vain conteſt appear'd no end. *Milton.*

2. The charge brought againſt any one by the accuſer.

You read
Theſe *accuſations*, and theſe grievous crimes
Committed by your perſon, and your followers.
Shakeſpeare's Richard II.

All *accuſation*, in the very nature of the thing, ſtill ſuppoſing, and being founded upon ſome law: for where there is no law, there can be no trangreſſion; and where there can be no tranſgreſſion, I am ſure there ought to be no *accuſation*. *South.*

3. In the ſenſe of the courts—

A declaration of ſome crime preferred before a competent judge, by the intervention of an inſcription lawfully made, in order to inflict ſome judgment on the guilty perſon. *Ayl. Parer.*

ACCU'SATIVE. *adj.* [*accuſativus*, Lat.] A term of grammar, ſignifying the relation of the noun, on which the action implied in the verb terminates.

ACCU'SATORY. *adj.* [from *accuſe.*] That which produceth or containeth an accuſation.

In a charge of adultery, the accuſer ought to ſet forth, in the *accuſatory* libel, ſome certain and definite time. *Ayl. Parer.*

To ACCU'SE. *v. a.* [*accuſo*, Lat.]

1. To charge with a crime. It requires the particle *of* before the ſubject of accuſation.

He ſtripp'd the bears-foot of its leafy growth;
And, calling weſtern winds, *accus'd* the ſpring *of* ſloth.
Dryden's Virgil.

The profeſſors are *accuſed of* all the ill practices which may ſeem to be the ill conſequences of their principles. *Addiſon.*

2. It ſometimes admits the particle *for*.

Never ſend up a leg of a fowl at ſupper, while there is a cat or dog in the houſe, that can be *accuſed for* running away with it: but, if there happen to be neither, you muſt lay it upon the rats, or a ſtrange greyhound. *Swift.*

3. To blame or cenſure, in oppoſition to applauſe or juſtification.

Their conſcience bearing witneſs, and their thoughts the mean while *accuſing* or elſe excuſing one another. *Rom.* ii. 15.

Your valour would your ſloth too much *accuſe*,
And therefore, like themſelves, they princes chooſe.
Dryden's Tyrannick Love.

ACCU'SER. *n. ſ.* [from *accuſe.*] He that brings a charge againſt another.

There are ſome perſons forbidden to be *accuſers*, on the ſcore of their ſex, as women; others, of their age, as pupils and infants; others, upon the account of ſome crimes committed by them; and others, on the ſcore of ſome filthy lucre to propoſe to gain thereby; others, on the ſcore of their conditions, as libertines againſt their patrons; and others, through a ſuſpicion of calumny, as having once already given falſe evidence; and, laſtly, others on account of their poverty, as not being worth more than fifty aurei. *Ayliffe's Parergon.*

—That good man, who drank the pois'nous draught,
With mind ſerene, and could not wiſh to ſee
His vile *accuſer* drink as deep as he. *Dryd. Juv.*

If the perſon accuſed maketh his innocence plainly to appear upon his trial, the *accuſer* is immediately put to an ignominious death; and, out of his goods and lands, the innocent perſon is quadruply recompenſed. *Gulliver's Travels.*

To ACCU'STOM. *v. a.* [*accoûtumer*, Fr.] To habituate, to enure, with the particle *to*. It is uſed chiefly of perſons.

How ſhall we breathe in other air
Leſs pure, *accuſtom'd to* immortal fruits? *Milton.*

It has been ſome advantage to *accuſtom* one's ſelf *to* books of the ſame edition. *Watts's Improvement of the Mind.*

ACCU'STOMABLE. *adj.* [from *accuſtom.*] Of long cuſtom or habit; habitual; cuſtomary.

Animals even of the ſame original, extraction, and ſpecies, may be diverſified by *accuſtomable* reſidence in one climate, from what they are in another. *Hale's Origin of Mankind.*

ACCU'STOMABLY. *adv.* According to cuſtom.

Touching the king's fines *accuſtomably* paid for the purchaſing of writs original, I find no certain beginning of them, and do therefore think that they alſo grew up with the chancery. *Bacon's Alienation.*

ACCU'STOMANCE. *n. ſ.* [*accoutûmance*, Fr.] Cuſtom, habit, uſe.

Through *accuſtomance* and negligence, and perhaps ſome other cauſes, we neither feel it in our own bodies, nor take notice of it in others. *Boyle.*

ACCU'STOMARILY. *adv.* In a cuſtomary manner; according to common or cuſtomary practice.

ACCU'STOMARY. *adj.* [from *accuſtom.*] Uſual, practiſed; according to cuſtom.

ACCU'STOMED. [from *accuſtom.*] According to cuſtom; frequent; uſual.

Look how ſhe rubs her hands.—It is an *accuſtomed* action with her, to ſeem thus waſhing her hands: I have known her continue in this a quarter of an hour. *Shakeſp. Macbeth.*

A'CE. *n. ſ.* [*As* not only ſignified a piece of money, but any integer, from whence is derived the word *ace*, or unit. Thus *As* ſignified the whole inheritance. *Arbuthnot on Coins.*]

1. An unit; a ſingle point on cards or dice.

When lots are ſhuffled together in a lap, urn or pitcher; or if a man blindfold caſts a die, what reaſon in the world can he have to preſume, that he ſhall draw a white ſtone rather than a black, or throw an *ace* rather than a ſiſe. *South.*

2. A ſmall quantity.

He will not bate an *ace* of abſolute certainty; but however doubtful or improbable the thing is, coming from him it muſt go for an indiſputable truth. *Government of the Tongue.*

I'll not wag an *ace* farther: the whole world shall not bribe me to it. *Dryden's Spanish Friar.*

ACE'PHALOUS. *adj.* [ἀκέφαλος, Gr.] Without a head. *Dict.*

ACE'RB. *adj.* [*acerbus*, Lat.] Acid, with an addition of roughness, as most fruits are before they are ripe. *Quincy.*

ACE'RBITY. *n. s.* [*acerbitas*, Lat.]

1. A rough sour taste.

2. Applied to men, sharpness of temper; severity.

True it is, that the talents for criticism, namely, smartness, quick censure, vivacity of remark, indeed all but *acerbity*, seem rather the gifts of youth than of old age. *Pope.*

To ACERVATE. *v. a.* [*acervo*, Lat.] To heap up. *Dict.*

ACERVA'TION. *n. s.* [from *acervate.*] The act of heaping together.

ACE'RVOSE. *adj.* Full of heaps. *Dict.*

ACE'SCENT. *adj.* [*acescens*, Lat.] That which has a tendency to sourness or acidity.

The same persons, perhaps, had enjoyed their health as well with a mixture of animal diet, qualified with a sufficient quantity of *acescents*; as, bread, vinegar, and fermented liquors. *Arbuthnot on Aliments.*

ACETO'SE. *adj.* That which has in it acids or vinegar. *Dict.*

ACETO'SITY. *n. s.* [from *acetose.*] The state of being acetose, or of containing vinegar. *Dict.*

ACE'TOUS. *adj.* [from *acetum*, vinegar, Lat.] Having the quality of vinegar, sour.

Raisins, which consist chiefly of the juice of grapes, inspissated in the skins or husks by the avolation of the superfluous moisture through their pores, being distilled in a retort, did not afford any vinous, but rather an *acetous* spirit. *Boyle.*

ACHE. *n. s.* [ace, Sax. ἄχος, Gr. now generally written *ake*, and in the plural *akes*, of one syllable; the primitive manner being preserved chiefly in poetry, for the sake of the measure.]

A continued pain. See AKE.

I'll rack thee with old cramps;
Fill all thy bones with *aches*, make thee roar,
That beasts shall tremble at thy din. *Shakespeare.*
A coming show'r your shooting corns presage,
Old *aches* throb, your hollow tooth will rage. *Swift.*

To ACHE. *v. n.* [See ACHE.] To be in pain.

Upon this account, our senses are dulled and spent by any extraordinary intention, and our very eyes will *ache*, if long fixed upon any difficultly discerned object. *Glanville.*

To ACHI'EVE. *v. a.* [*achever*, Fr. to complete.]

1. To perform, to finish a design prosperously.

Our toils, my friends, are crown'd with sure success:
The greater part perform'd, *achieve* the less. *Dryden.*

2. To gain, to obtain.

Experience is by industry *achiev'd*,
And perfected by the swift course of time.
Shakespeare's Two Gentlemen of Verona.
Tranio, I burn, I pine, I perish, Tranio,
If I *achieve* not this young modest girl.
Shakespeare's Taming the Shrew.
Thou hast *achiev'd* our liberty, confin'd
Within hell-gates till now. *Milton's Paradise Lost.*
Show all the spoils by valiant kings *achiev'd*,
And groaning nations by their arms reliev'd. *Prior.*

An ACHI'EVER. *n. s.* He that performs; he that obtains what he endeavours after.

A victory is twice itself, when the *achiever* brings home full numbers. *Shakespeare's Much ado about Nothing.*

An ACHI'EVEMENT. *n. s.* [*achevement*, Fr.]

1. The performance of an action.

From every coast that heaven walks about,
Have thither come the noble martial crew,
That famous hard *achievements* still pursue. *Fairy Queen.*

2. The escutcheon, or ensigns armorial, granted to any man for the performance of great actions.

Then shall the war, and stern debate, and strife
Immortal, be the bus'ness of my life;
And in thy fane, the dusty spoils among,
High on the burnish'd roof, my banner shall be hung;
Rank'd with my champions bucklers, and below
With arms revers'd, th' *achievements* of the foe. *Dryden.*

Achievement, in the first sense, is derived from *achive*, as it signifies *to perform*; in the second, from *achieve*, as it imports *to gain*.

A'CHOR. n. s. [*achor*, Lat. ἄχωρ, Gr. *furfur.*]

A species of the herpes; it appears with a crusty scab, which causes an itching on the surface of the head, occasioned by a salt sharp serum oozing through the skin. *Quincy.*

A'CID. *adj. acidus*, Lat. *acide*, Fr.] Sour, sharp.

Wild trees last longer than garden trees; and in the same kind, those whose fruit is *acid*, more than those whose fruit is sweet. *Bacon's Natural History*, Nº 585.

Acid, or sour, proceeds from a salt of the same nature, without mixture of oil; in austere tastes the oily parts have not disentangled themselves from the salts and earthy parts; such is the taste of unripe fruits. *Arbuthnot on Aliments.*

Liquids and substances are called *acids*, which being composed of pointed particles, affect the taste in a sharp and piercing manner. The common way of trying, whether any particular liquor hath in it any particles of this kind, is by mixing it with syrup of violets, which it will turn of a red colour; but if it contains alkaline or lixivial particles, it changes that syrup green. *Quincy.*

ACI'DITY. *n. s.* [from *acid.*] The quality of being acid; an acid taste; sharpness; sourness.

Fishes, by the help of a dissolvent liquor, corrode and reduce their meats, skin, bones, and all, into a chylus or cremor; and yet this liquor manifests nothing of *acidity* to the taste. *Ray on the Creation.*

When the taste of the mouth is bitter, it is a sign of a redundance of a bilious alkali, and demands a quite different diet from the case of *acidity* or sourness. *Arbuthnot on Aliments.*

A'CIDNESS. *n. s.* [from *acid.*] The quality of being acid; acidity. See ACIDITY.

ACI'DULÆ. n. s. [that is, *aquæ acidulæ.*]

Medicinal springs impregnated with sharp particles, as all the nitrous, chalybeate, and alum-springs are. *Quincy.*

The *acidulæ*, or medical springs, emit a greater quantity of their minerals than usual; and even the ordinary springs, which were before clear, fresh and limpid, become thick and turbid, and are impregnated with sulphur and other minerals, as long as the earthquake lasts. *Woodward's Natural History, p.* 4.

To ACIDULATE. *v. a.* [*aciduler*, Fr.] To impregnate or tinge with acids in a slight degree.

The muriatic scurvy is evidently a diet of fresh unsalted things, watery liquors *acidulated*, farinaceous emollient substances, sour milk, butter, and acid fruits. *Arbuthnot.*

To ACKNO'WLEDGE. *v. a.* [a word formed, as it seems, between the Latin and English, from *agnosco*, and *knowledge*, which is deduced from the Saxon, cnapan, *to know.*]

1. To own the knowledge of; to own any thing or person in a particular character.

My people do already know my mind,
And will *acknowledge* you and Jessica,
In place of lord Bassanio and myself. *Shakespeare.*
None that *acknowledge* God, or providence,
Their souls eternity did ever doubt. *Sir John Davies.*

2. To confess; as a fault.

For I *acknowledge* my transgressions; and my sin is ever before me. *Psalm* li. 3.

3. To own; as, a benefit; sometimes with the particle *to* before the person conferring the benefit.

His spirit
Taught them; but they his gifts *acknowledg'd* not. *Par. Lost.*

In the first place, therefore, I thankfully *acknowledge* to the Almighty power the assistance he has given me in the beginning, and the prosecution of my present studies. *Dryden.*

ACKNO'WLEDGING. *adj.* [from *acknowledge.*] Grateful; ready to acknowledge benefits received.

He has shewn his hero *acknowledging* and ungrateful, compassionate and hard hearted; but, at the bottom, fickle and self-interested. *Dryden's Virgil.*

ACKNO'WLEDGMENT. *n. s.* [from *acknowledge.*]

1. Concession of any character in another, as existence, superiority.

The due contemplation of the human nature doth, by a necessary connexion and chain of causes, carry us up to the unavoidable *acknowledgment* of the Deity; because it carries every thinking man to an original of every successive individual. *Hale's Origin of Mankind.*

2. Concession of the truth of any position.

Immediately upon the *acknowledgment* of the christian faith, the eunuch was baptized by Philip. *Hooker.*

3. Confession of a fault.

4. Confession of a benefit received; gratitude.

5. Act of attestation to any concession; such as homage.

There may be many wide countries in Ireland, in which the laws of England were never established, nor any *acknowledgment* of subjection made. *Spenser's State of Ireland.*

The second is an *acknowledgment* to his majesty for the leave of fishing upon his coasts; and though this may be grounded upon any treaty, yet, if it appear to be an ancient right on our side and custom on theirs, not determined or extinguished by any treaty between us, it may with justice be insisted on. *Temple's Miscellanies.*

A'CME. n. s. [ἀκμή, Gr.]

The height of any thing; more especially used to denote the height of a distemper, which is divided into four periods. 1. The *arche*, the beginning or first attack. 2. *Anabasis*, the growth. 3. *Acme*, the height. And, 4. *Paracme*, which is the declension of the distemper. *Quincy.*

ACO'LOTHIST. *n. s.* [ἀκολουθέω, Gr.] One of the lowest order in the Romish church, whose office is to prepare the elements for the offices, to light the church, &c.

In the Romish communion it is duty, according to the papal law, when the bishop sings mass, to order all the inferior clergy to appear in their proper habits; and to see that all the offices of the church be rightly performed; to ordain the *acolothist*, to keep the sacred vessels, &c. *Ayliffe's Parergon.*

A'COLYTE. *n. s.* The same with ACOLOTHIST.

A'CONITE. *n. s.* [*aconitum*, Lat.] Properly the herb wolfs-bane, but commonly used in poetical language for poison in general.

Our land is from the rage of tygers freed,
Nor nourishes the lion's angry seed;
Nor pois'nous *aconite* is here produc'd,
Or grows unknown, or is, when known, refus'd. *Dryden.*

Despair, that *aconite* does prove,
And certain death to others, love,
That poison never yet withstood,
Does nourish mine, and turns to blood. *Glanville.*

A'CORN. *n. s.* [Æcepn, Sax. from ac, an oak, and copn, corn or grain; that is, the grain of the oak.]

The seed or fruit born by the oak.

What roots old-age contracteth into errours, and how such as are but *acorns* in our younger brows, grow oaks in our older heads, and become inflexible. *Brown's Vulgar Errours.*

Content with food which nature freely bred,
On wildings and on strawberries they fed;
Cornels and bramble-berries gave the rest,
And falling *acorns* furnish'd out a feast. *Dryden's Ovid.*

He that is nourished by the *acorns* he picked up under an oak, or the apples he gathered from the trees in the wood, has certainly appropriated them to himself. *Locke.*

ACO'USTICKS. *n. s.* ['Ακουστικα of ἀκούω, Gr. to hear.]

1. The doctrine or theory of sounds.

2. Medicines to help the hearing. *Quincy.*

To ACQUAINT. *v. a.* [*accointer*, Fr.]

1. To make familiar with; applied either to persons or things.

We that *acquaint* ourselves with ev'ry zone,
And pass the tropicks, and behold each pole;
When we come home, or to ourselves unknown,
And unacquainted still with our own soul. *Davies.*

There with thee, new welcome saint,
Like fortunes may her soul *acquaint*;
With thee there clad in radiant sheen. *Milton.*

Before a man can speak on any subject, it is necessary to be *acquainted* with it. *Locke on Education.*

Acquaint yourselves with things ancient and modern, natural, civil, and religious, domestic and national; things of your own and foreign countries; and, above all, be well *acquainted* with God and yourselves; learn animal nature, and the workings of your own spirits. *Watts's Logick.*

2. To inform.

But for some other reasons, my grave Sir,
Which is not fit you know, I not *acquaint*
My father of this business. *Shakespeare's Twelfth Night.*

I have lately received a letter from a friend in the country, wherein he *acquaints* me, that two or three men of the town are got among them, and have brought down particular words and phrases, which were never before in those parts. *Tatler.*

ACQUA'INTANCE. *n. s.* [*accointre*, Fr.]

1. The state of being acquainted with; familiarity, knowledge. It is applied as well to persons as things, with the particle *with*.

Nor was his *acquaintance* less *with* the famous poets or his age, than *with* the noblemen and ladies. *Dryden.*

Our admiration of a famous man lessens upon our nearer *acquaintance with* him; and we seldom hear of a celebrated person, without a catalogue of some notorious weaknesses and infirmities. *Addison, Spectator*, N° 256.

Would we be admitted into an *acquaintance with* God: let us study to resemble him. We must be partakers of a divine nature, in order to partake of this high privilege and alliance. *Atterbury's Sermons.*

2. Familiar knowledge, simply without a preposition.

Brave soldier, pardon me,
That any accent breaking from my tongue,
Should 'scape the true *acquaintance* of mine ear. *Shakesp.*

This keeps the understanding long in converse with an object, and long converse brings *acquaintance*. *South.*

In what manner he lived with those who were of his neighbourhood and *acquaintance*, how obliging his carriage was to them, what kind offices he did, and was always ready to do them, I forbear particularly to say. *Atterbury.*

3. A slight or initial knowledge, short of friendship, as applied to persons.

I hope I am pretty near seeing you, and therefore I would cultivate an *acquaintance*; because if you do not know me when we meet, you need only keep one of my letters, and compare it with my face; for my face and letters are counterparts of my heart. *Swift to Pope.*

A long noviciate of *acquaintance* should precede the vows of friendship. *Bolingbroke.*

4. The person with whom we are acquainted; him of whom we have some knowledge, without the intimacy of friendship.

In this sense, the plural is, in some authours, *acquaintance*, in others *acquaintances*.

But she, all vow'd unto the red-cross knight,
His wand'ring peril closely did lament,
Ne in this new *acquaintance* could delight,
But her dead heart with anguish did torment. *F. Queen.*

That young men travel under some tutor, I allow well, so that he be such a one that may be able to tell them, what *acquaintances* they are to seek, what exercises or discipline the place yieldeth. *Bacon.*

This, my lord, has justly acquired you as many friends, as there are persons who have the honour to be known to you; meer *acquaintance* you have none, you have drawn them all into a nearer line; and they who have conversed with you, are for ever after inviolably yours. *Dryden.*

We see he is ashamed of his nearest *acquaintances*. *Boyle against Bentley.*

ACQUA'INTED. [from *acquaint.*] Familiar, well known; not new.

Now call we our high court of parliament;
That war or peace, or both at once, may be
As things *acquainted* and familiar to us. *Sha'esp. Henry* IV.

ACQU'EST. *n. s.* [*acquest*, Fr. from *acquerir*, written by some *acquist*, with a view to the word *acquire*, or *acquisita.*] Attachment, acquisition; the thing gained.

New *acquests* are more burden than strength. *Bacon.*

Mud, reposed near the ostia of those rivers, makes continual additions to the land, thereby excluding the sea, and preserving these shells as trophies and signs of its new *acquests* and encroachments. *Woodward.*

To ACQUIE'SCE. *v. n.* [*acquiescer*, Fr. *acquiescere*, Lat.] To rest in, or remain satisfied with, without opposition or discontent.

Neither a bare approbation of, nor a mere wishing, nor unactive complacency in; nor, lastly, a natural inclination to things virtuous and good, can pass before God for a man's willing of such things; and, consequently, if men, upon this account, will needs take up and *acquiesce* in an airy ungrounded persuasion, that they will those things which really they not will, they fall thereby into a gross and fatal delusion. *South.*

He hath employed his transcendent wisdom and power, that by these he might make way for his benignity, as the end wherein they ultimately *acquiesce*. *Grew.*

ACQUIE'SCENCE. *n. s.* [from *acquiesce.*]

1. A silent appearance of content, distinguished on one side from avowed consent, on the other from opposition.

Neither from any of the nobility, nor of the clergy, who were thought most averse from it, there appeared any sign of contradiction to that; but an entire *acquiescence* in all the bishops thought fit to do. *Clarendon.*

2. Satisfaction, rest, content.

Many indeed have given over their pursuits after fame, either from disappointment, or from experience of the little pleasure which attends it, or the better informations or natural coldness of old-age; but seldom from a full satisfaction and *acquiescence* in their present enjoyments of it. *Addison.*

3. Submission.

The greatest part of the world take up their persuasions concerning good and evil, by an implicit faith, and a full *acquiescence* in the word of those, who shall represent things to them under these characters. *South.*

ACQUI'RABLE. *adj.* [from *acquire.*] That which may be acquired or obtained; attainable.

Those rational instincts, the connate principles engraven in the human soul, though they are truths *acquirable* and deducible by rational consequence and argumentation, yet they seem to be inscribed in the very crasis and texture of the soul, antecedent to any acquisition by industry or the exercise of the discursive faculty in man. *Hale.*

If the powers of cogitation and volition, and sensation, are neither inherent in matter as such, nor *acquirable* to matter by any motion or modification of it; it necessarily follows, that they proceed from some cogitative substance, some incorporeal inhabitant within us, which we call spirit and soul. *Bentley.*

To ACQU'IRE. *v. a.* [*acquerir*, Fr. *acquiro*, Lat.] To gain by one's own labour or power; to obtain what is not received from nature, or transmitted by inheritance.

I've done enough. A lower place not well,
May make too great an act: for learn this, Silius,
Better to leave undone, than by our deed
Acquire too high a fame, while he, we serve, 's away.
Shakespeare's Anthony and Cleopatra.

ACQU'IRED. *particip. adj.* [from *acquire.* Gained by one's self, in opposition to those things which are bestowed by nature.

We are seldom at ease, and free enough from the solicitation of our natural or adopted desires; but a constant succession of uneasinesses, out of that stock, which natural wants, or *acquired* habits, have heaped up, take the will in their turns. *Locke.*

An ACQUI'RER. *n. s.* [from *acquire.*] The person that acquires; a gainer.

An ACQUI'REMENT. *n. s.* [from *acquire.*] That which is acquired; gain; attainment. The word may be properly used in opposition to the gifts of nature.

These his *acquirements*, by industry, were exceedingly both enriched and enlarged by many excellent endowments of nature. *Hayward on Edward* VI.

By a content and acquiescence in every species of truth, we embrace

embrace the ſhadow thereof: or ſo much as may palliate its juſt and ſubſtantial *acquirements*. *Brown's Vulgar Errours.*

It is very difficult to lay down rules for the *acquirement* of ſuch a taſte as that I am here ſpeaking of. The faculty muſt, in ſome degree, be born with us. *Addiſon.*

ACQUISI'TION. *n. ſ.* [*acquiſitio*, Lat.]

1. The act of acquiring or gaining.

Each man has but a limited right to the good things of the world; and the natural allowed way, by which he is to compaſs the poſſeſſion of theſe things, is by his own induſtrious *acquiſition* of them. *South.*

2. The thing gained; acquirement.

Great Sir, all *acquiſition*
Of glory as of empire, here I lay before
Your royal feet. *Denham's Sophy.*

A ſtate can never arrive to its period in a more deplorable criſis, than when ſome prince lies hovering like a vulture to diſmember its dying carcaſe; by which means it becomes only an *acquiſition* to ſome mighty monarchy, without hopes of a reſurrection. *Swift.*

ACQU'ISITIVE. *adj.* [*acquiſitivus*, Lat.] That which is acquired or gained.

He died not in his *acquiſitive* but in his native ſoil; nature herſelf, as it were, claiming a final intereſt in his body, when fortune had done with him. *Wotton.*

ACQU'IST. *n. ſ.* [See ACQUEST.] Acquirement; attainment; gain.

His ſervant he with new *acquiſt*
Of true experience from this great event,
With peace and conſolation hath diſmiſt. *Milton.*

To ACQU'IT. *v. a.* [*acquiter*, Fr. See QUIT.]

1. To ſet free.

Ne do I wiſh (for wiſhing were but vain)
To be *acquit* from my continual ſmart;
But joy her thrall for ever to remain,
And yield for pledge my poor captived heart. *Spenſer.*

2. To clear from a charge of guilt; to abſolve; oppoſed to *condemn*, either ſimply with an accuſative, as, *the jury acquitted him*, or with the particles *from* or *of*, which is more common, before the crime.

If I ſin, then thou markeſt me, and thou wilt not *acquit* me *from* mine iniquity. *Job*, x. 14.

By the ſuffrage of the moſt and beſt he is already *acquitted*, and, by the ſentence of ſome, condemned.
Dryden's Conqueſt of Granada, Dedic.

He that judges, without informing himſelf to the utmoſt that he is capable, cannot *acquit* himſelf *of* judging amiſs. *Locke.*

Neither do I reflect upon the memory of his majeſty, whom I entirely *acquit of* any imputation upon this matter. *Swift.*

3. To clear from any obligation.

Steady to my principles, and not diſpirited with my afflictions, I have, by the bleſſing of God on my endeavours, overcome all difficulties; and, in ſome meaſure, *acquitted* myſelf *of* the debt which I owed the publick, when I undertook this work. *Dryden.*

4. In a ſimilar ſenſe, it is ſaid, *The man hath acquitted himſelf well*; that is, he diſcharged his duty.

ACQU'ITMENT. *n. ſ.* [from *acquit.*] The ſtate of being acquitted; or act of acquitting.

The word imports properly an *acquitment* or diſcharge of a man upon ſome precedent accuſation, and a full trial and cognizance of his cauſe had thereupon. *South.*

ACQU'ITTAL. *n. ſ.* in law, is a deliverance and ſetting free from the ſuſpicion or guiltineſs of an offence. *Cowell.*

The conſtant deſign of both theſe orators, was to drive ſome one particular point, either the condemnation or *acquittal* of an accuſed perſon, a perſuaſive to war, and the like. *Swift.*

To ACQU'ITTANCE. *v. n.* To procure an acquittance; to acquit; a word not in preſent uſe.

But if black ſcandal and foul-fac'd reproach,
Attend the ſequel of your impoſition,
Your meer enforcement ſhall *acquittance* me
From all the impure blots and ſtains thereof *Shak. Rich.* III.

ACQU'ITTANCE. *n. ſ.* [from *acquit.*]

1. The act of diſcharging from a debt.

But ſoon ſhall find
Forbearance, no *acquittance*, ere day end
Juſtice ſhall not return, as beauty, ſcorn'd. *Paradiſe Loſt.*

2. A writing teſtifying the receipt of a debt.

You can produce *acquittances*
For ſuch a ſum, from ſpecial officers
Of Charles his father. *Shakeſp. Love's Labour Loſt.*

They quickly pay their debt, and then
Take no *acquittances*, but pay again. *Donne.*

They had got a worſe trick than that; the ſame man bought and ſold to himſelf, paid the money, and gave the *acquittance*. *Arbuthnot.*

A'CRE. *n. ſ.* [Æcre, Sax.] A quantity of land containing in length forty perches, and four in breadth, or four thouſand eight hundred and forty ſquare yards. *Dict.*

Search ev'ry *acre* in the high-grown field,
And bring him to our eye. *Shakeſpeare's K. Lear.*

A'CRID. *adj.* [*acer*, Lat.] Of a hot biting taſte; bitter, ſo as to leave a painful heat upon the organs of taſte.

Bitter and *acrid* differ only by the ſharp particles of the firſt, being involved in a greater quantity or oil than thoſe of the laſt. *Arbuthnot on Aliments.*

ACRIMO'NIOUS. *adj.* Abounding with acrimony; ſharp; corroſive.

If gall cannot be rendered *acrimonious*, and bitter of itſelf, then whatever acrimony or amaritude redounds in it, muſt be from the admixture of melancholy. *Harvey on Conſumptions.*

A'CRIMONY. *n. ſ.* [*acrimonia*, Lat.]

1. Sharpneſs, corroſiveneſs.

There be plants that have a milk in them when they are cut; as, figs, old lettuce, ſow-thiſtles, ſpurge, &c. The cauſe may be an inception of putrefaction: for thoſe milks have all an *acrimony*, though one would think they ſhould be lenitive. *Bacon.*

The chymiſts define ſalt, from ſome of its properties, to be a body fuſible in the fire, congeable again by cold into brittle glebes or cryſtals, ſoluble in water, ſo as to diſappear, not malleable, and having ſomething in it which affects the organs of taſte with a ſenſation of *acrimony* or ſharpneſs.
Arbuthnot on Aliments.

2. Sharpneſs of temper, ſeverity, bitterneſs of thought or language.

This made John the Baptiſt ſet himſelf, with ſo much *acrimony* and indignation, to baffle this ſenſeleſs arrogant conceit of theirs, which made them huff at the doctrine of repentance, as a thing below them, and not at all belonging to them. *South.*

A'CRITUDE. *n. ſ.* [from *acrid.*] An acrid taſte; a biting heat on the palate.

Green vitriol, mixed with ſome rays of a pale blue, from the ſame place; with its aſtringent and ſweetiſh taſtes, is joined ſome *acritude*. *Grew's Muſæum.*

ACROAMA'TICAL. *adj.* [ἀκροάομαι, Gr. I bear.] Of or pertaining to deep learning; the oppoſite of exoterical.

ACROA'TICKS. *n. ſ.* [Ἀκροατικὰ, Gr.] Ariſtotle's lectures on the more nice and principal parts of philoſophy, to whom none but friends and ſcholars were admitted by him.

ACRO'NYCAL. *adj.* [from ἄκρος, *ſummus*, and νὺξ, *nox*; importing the beginning of night.] A term of aſtronomy, applied to the ſtàrs, of which the riſing or ſetting is called *acronical*, when they either appear above or ſink below the horizon at the time of ſunſet. It is oppoſed to *coſmical*.

ACRO'NYCALLY. *adv.* [from *acronical.*] At the acronycal time.

He is tempeſtuous in the ſummer, when he riſes heliacally, and rainy in the winter, when he riſes *acronycally*.
Dryden's Æneid.

A'CROSPIRE. *n. ſ.* [from ἄκρος and σπεῖρα, Gr.] A ſhoot or ſprout from the end of ſeeds before they are put in the ground.

Many corns will ſmilt, or have their pulp turned into a ſubſtance like thick cream; and moſt of thoſe which come without extraordinary pains, will ſend forth their ſubſtance in an *acroſpire*. *Mortimer.*

A'CROSPIRED. *part. adj.* Having ſprouts, or having ſhot out.

For want of turning, when the malt is ſpread on the floor, it comes and ſprouts at both ends, which is called *acroſpired*, and is fit only for ſwine. *Mortimer.*

ACRO'SS. *adv.* [from *a* for *at*, or the French *à*, as it is uſed in *à travers*, and *croſs*.] Athwart, laid over ſomething ſo as to croſs it.

The harp hath the concave not along the ſtrings, but *acroſs* the ſtrings; and no harp hath the ſound ſo melting and prolonged as the Iriſh harp. *Bacon.*

This view'd, but not enjoy'd, with arms *acroſs*,
He ſtood, reflecting on his country's loſs. *Dryden.*

There is a ſet of artiſans, who, by the help of ſeveral poles, which they lay *acroſs* each others ſhoulders, build themſelves up into a kind of pyramid; ſo that you ſee a pile of men in the air of four or five rows riſing one above another. *Addiſon.*

An ACRO'STICK. *n. ſ.* [from ἄκρος and ςίχος, Gr.] A poem in which the firſt letter of every line being taken, makes up the name of the perſon or thing on which the poem is written.

ACRO'STICK. *adj.*

1. That which relates to an acroſtick.

2. That which contains acroſticks.

Leave writing plays, and chooſe for thy command
Some peaceful province in *acroſtick* land:
There thou may'ſt wings diſplay, and altars raiſe,
And torture one poor word ten thouſand ways. *Dryden.*

A'CROTERS, or *ACROTERIA*. *n. ſ.* [In architecture; from ὄκρον, Gr. the extremity of any body.] Little pedeſtals without baſes, placed at the middle and the two extremes of pediments, ſometimes ſerving to ſupport ſtatues.

To ACT. *v. a.* [*ago*, *actum*, Lat.]

1. To be in action, not to reſt.

He hangs between in doubt to *act* or reſt. *Pope.*

2. To perform the proper functions.

Albeit the will is not capable of being compelled to any of its actings, yet it is capable of being made to *act* with more or leſs difficulty, according to the different impreſſions it receives from motives or objects. *South.*

'Tis

3. To practise the arts or duties of life; to conduct one's self.
'Tis plain, that she who, for a kingdom now,
Would sacrifice her love, and break her vow,
Not out of love, but interest, *acts* alone,
And would, ev'n in my arms, lie thinking of a throne.
Dryden's Conquest of Granada.

The desire of happiness, and the constraint it puts upon us to *act* for it, no body accounts an abridgment of liberty. *Locke.*

The splendor of his office, is the token of that sacred character which he inwardly bears: and one of these ought constantly to put him in mind of the other, and excite him to *act* up to it, through the whole course of his administration. *Atterbury's Sermons.*

It is our part and duty to co-operate with this grace, vigorously to exert those powers, and *act* up to those advantages to which it restores us. He has given eyes to the blind, and feet to the lame. *Rogers's Sermons.*

4. To bear a borrowed character, as, a stage-player.
Honour and shame from no condition rise;
Act well your part, there all the honour lies.
Pope's Essay on Man.

5. To counterfeit; to feign by action.
His former trembling once again renew'd,
With *acted* fear the villain thus pursu'd. *Dryd. Æneid.*

6. To produce effects in some passive subject.
Hence 'tis we wait the wond'rous cause to find
How body *acts* upon impassive mind. *Garth's Dispensary.*

The stomach, the intestines, the muscles of the lower belly, all *act* upon the aliment; besides, the chyle is not sucked, but squeezed into the mouths of the lacteals, by the action of the fibres of the guts. *Arbuthnot on Aliments.*

7. To actuate; to put in motion; to regulate the movements.
Most people in the world are *acted* by levity and humour, by strange and irrational changes. *South.*

Perhaps they are as proud as Lucifer, as covetous as Demas, as false as Judas, and, in the whole course of their conversation, *act*, and are *acted*, not by devotion, but design. *South.*

We suppose two distinct incommunicable consciousnesses *acting* the same body, the one constantly by day, the other by night; and, on the other side, the same consciousness *acting* by intervals two distinct bodies. *Locke.*

ACT. *n. s.* [*actum*, Lat.]

1. Something done; a deed; an exploit, whether good or ill.
I've done enough. A lower place, not well,
May make too great an *act*: for learn this, Silius,
Better to leave undone, than by our deed
Acquire too high a fame, when he, we serve, 's away.
Shakespeare's Antony and Cleopatra.

The conscious wretch must all his *acts* reveal;
Loth to confess, unable to conceal;
From the first moment of his vital breath,
To his last hour of unrepenting death. *Dryd. Æneid.*

2. Agency; the power of producing an effect.
I will try the forces
Of these thy compounds on such creatures as
We count not worth the hanging; but none human;
To try the vigour of them, and apply
Allayments to their *act*; and by them gather
Their several virtues and effects. *Shakespeare's Cymbeline.*

3. Action; the performance of exploits; production of effects.
'Tis so much in your nature to do good, that your life is but one continued *act* of placing benefits on many, as the sun is always carrying his light to some part or other of the world. *Dryden's Fables.*

Who forth from nothing call'd this comely frame,
His will and *act*, his word and work the same. *Prior.*

4. The doing of some particular thing; a step taken; a measure executed.
This *act* persuades me,
That this remotion of the duke and her,
Is practice only. *Shakespeare's King Lear.*

5. A state of action.
The seeds of herbs and plants at the first are not in *act*, but in possibility that which they afterwards grow to be. *Hooker.*

God alone excepted, who actually and everlastingly is whatsoever he may be, and which cannot hereafter be that which now he is not; all other things besides are somewhat in possibility, which as yet they are not in *act*. *Hooker.*

Sure they're conscious
Of some intended mischief, and are fled
To put it into *act*. *Denham's Sophy.*

Her legs were buskin'd, and the left before;
In *act* to shoot, a silver bow she bore. *Dryd. Fables.*

6. A part of a play, during which the action proceeds without interruption.
Many never doubt but the whole condition required by Christ, the repentance he came to preach, will, in that last scene of their last *act*, immediately before the exit, be as opportunely and acceptably performed, as at any other point of their lives. *Hammond's Fundamentals.*

Five *acts* are the just measure of a play. *Roscommon.*

7. A decree of a court of justice, or edict of a legislature.
They make edicts for usury to support usurers, repeal daily any wholesome *act* established against the rich, and provide more piercing statutes daily to chain up and restrain the poor. *Shakespeare's Coriolanus.*

You that are king, though he do wear the crown,
Have caus'd him, by new *act* of parliament,
To blot out me. *Shakespeare's Henry VI.*

8. Record of judicial proceedings.
Judicial *acts* are all those matters, which relate to judicial proceedings; and being reduced into writing by a publick notary, are recorded by the authority of the judge. *Ayliffe's Parergon.*

A'CTION, *n. s.* [*action*, Fr. *actio*, Lat.]

1. The quality or state of acting, opposite to *rest*.
O noble English, that could entertain
With half their forces the full power of France;
And let another half stand laughing by,
All out of work, and cold for *action*. *Shakesp. Henry V.*

2. An act or thing done; a deed.
This *action*, I now go on,
Is for my better grace. *Shakespeare's Winter's Tale.*

God never accepts a good inclination instead of a good *action*, where that *action* may be done; nay, so much the contrary, that, if a good inclination be not seconded by a good *action*, the want of that *action* is made so much the more criminal and inexcusable. *South's Sermons.*

3. Agency, operation.
It is better therefore, that the earth should move about its own center, and make those useful vicissitudes of night and day, than expose always the same side to the *action* of the sun. *Bentley's Sermons.*

He has settled laws, and laid down rules, conformable to which natural bodies are governed in their *actions* upon one another. *Cheyne's Philosophical Principles.*

4. The series of events represented in a fable.
This *action* should have three qualifications. First, it should be but one *action*; secondly, it should be an entire *action*; and, thirdly, it should be a great *action*. *Addison.*

5. Gesticulation; the accordance of the motions of the body with the words spoken; a part of oratory.
—He that speaks doth gripe the hearer's wrist,
While he that hears makes fearful *action*
With wrinkled brows. *Shakesp. King John.*

Our oratours are observed to make use of less gesture or *action* than those of other countries. *Addison.*

6. [In law.] It is used with the preposition *against* before the person, and *for* before the thing.
Actions are personal, real, and mixt: *action* personal belongs to a man *against* another, by reason of any contract, offence, or cause, of like force with a contract or offence made or done by him or some other, for whose fact he is to answer. *Action* real is given to any man *against* another, that possesses the thing required or sued for in his own name, and no other man's. *Action* mixt is that which lies as well *against* or *for* the thing which we seek, as *against* the person that hath it; called *mixt*, because it hath a mixt respect both to the thing and to the person.

Action is divided into civil, penal, and mixt. *Action* civil is that which tends only to the recovery of that which is due to us; as, a sum of money formerly lent. *Action* penal is that which aims at some penalty or punishment in the party sued, be it corporal or pecuniary: as, in common law, the next friends of a man feloniously slain shall pursue the law *against* the murderer. *Action* mixt is that which seeks both the thing whereof we are deprived, and a penalty also for the unjust detaining of the same.

Action upon the case, is an *action* given for redress of wrongs done without force *against* any man, by law not specially provided for.

Action upon the statute, is an *action* brought *against* a man upon breach of a statute. *Cowell.*

There was never man could have a juster *action against* filthy fortune than I, since all other things being granted me, her blindness is the only lett. *Sidney.*

For our reward then,
First, all our debts are paid; dangers of law,
Actions, decrees, judgments, *against* us quitted.
Ben. Johnson's Catiline.

7. In the plural, in France, the same as *stocks* in England.

A'CTIONABLE. *adj.* [from *action*.] That which admits an action in law to be brought against it; punishable.
After he had been thus, as a man would think, quite extinguished, his process was formed; whereby he was found guilty of nought else, that I could learn, which was *actionable*, but of ambition. *Howel's Vocal Forest.*

A'CTIONARY, or A'CTIONIST. *n. s.* [from *action*.] One that has a share in *actions* or stocks.

A'CTION-TAKING. *adj.* Accustomed to resent by means of law; litigious.
A knave, a rascal, an eater of broken meats, a filthy worsted-stocking knave; a lily-liver'd *action-taking* knave.
Shakespeare's King Lear.

ACTITA'TION. *n. s.* [from *actito*, Lat.] Action quick and frequent. *Dict.*

To A'CTIVATE. *v. a.* [from *active.*] To make active. This word is perhaps used only by the author alleged.

As snow and ice, especially being holpen, and their cold *activated* by nitre or salt, will turn water into ice, and that in a few hours: so it may be, it will turn wood or stiff clay into stone, in longer time. *Bacon's Nat. Hist.*

A'CTIVE. *adj.* [*activus*, Lat.]

1. That which has the power or quality of acting.

These particles have not only a *vis inertiæ*, accompanied with such passive laws of motion, as naturally result from that force, but also they are moved by certain *active* principles, such as is that of gravity, and that which causes fermentation, and the cohesion of bodies. *Newton's Opticks.*

2. That which acts, opposed to *passive*, or that which suffers.

—When an even flame two hearts did touch,
His office was indulgently to fit
Actives to passives, correspondency
Only his subject was. *Donne.*

If you think that by multiplying the additaments in the same proportion, that you multiply the ore, the work will follow, you may be deceived: for quantity in the passive will add more resistance than the quantity in the *active* will add force. *Bacon's Physical Remains.*

3. Busy, engaged in action; opposed to *idle* or *sedentary*, or any state of which the duties are performed only by the mental powers.

'Tis virtuous action that must praise bring forth,
Without which, slow advice is little worth;
Yet they who give good counsel, praise deserve,
Though in the *active* part they cannot serve. *Denham.*

4. Practical; not merely theoretical.

The world hath had in these men fresh experience, how dangerous such *active* errors are. *Hooker, Preface.*

5. Nimble; agile; quick.

Some bend the stubborn bow for victory;
And some with darts their *active* sinews try. *Dryd. Æn.*

6. In grammar.

A verb *active* is that which signifies action, as does, *I teach.* *Clarke's Latin Grammar.*

A'CTIVELY. *adv.* [from *active.*] In an active manner; busily; nimbly. In an active signification; as *the word is used actively.*

A'CTIVENESS. *n. s.* [from *active.*] The quality of being active; quickness; nimbleness. This is a word more rarely used than *activity.*

What strange agility and *activeness* do our common tumblers and dancers on the rope attain to, by continual exercise? *Wilkins's Mathematical Magick.*

ACTI'VITY. *n. s.* [from *active.*] The quality of being active, applied either to things or persons.

Salt put to ice, as in the producing of the artificial ice, increaseth the *activity* of cold. *Bacon's Nat. Hist.*

Our adversary will not be idle, though we are; he watches every turn of our soul, and incident of our life; and, if we remit our *activity*, will take advantage of our indolence. *Rogers.*

A'CTOR. *n. s.* [*actor*, Lat.]

1. He that acts, or performs any thing.

The virtues of either age may correct the defects of both: and good for succession, that young men may be learners, while men in age are *actors.* *Bacon.*

He, who writes an *Encomium Neronis*, if he does it heartily, is himself but a transcript of Nero in his mind, and would, no doubt, gladly enough see such pranks, as he was famous for, acted again, though he dares not be the *actor* of them himself. *South's Sermons.*

2. He that personates a character; a stage-player.

Would you have
Such an Herculean *actor* in the scene,
And not this hydra? They must sweat no less
To fit their properties, than t'express their parts.
Ben Johnson's Catiline.

When a good *actor* doth his part present,
In every act he our attention draws,
That at the last he may find just applause. *Denham.*

These false beauties of the stage are no more lasting than a rain-bow; when the *actor* ceases to shine upon them, when he gilds them no longer with his reflection, they vanish in a twinkling. *Dryd. Spanish Friar.*

A'CTRESS. *n. s.* [*actrice*, Fr.]

She that performs any thing.

Virgil has, indeed, admitted Fame as an *actress* in the *Æneid*; but the part she acts is very short, and none of the most admired circumstances of that divine work. *Addis. Spect.*

2. A woman that plays on the stage.

We sprights have just such natures
We had, for all the world, when human creatures;
And therefore I that was an *actress* here,
Play all my tricks in hell, a goblin there. *Dryd. Tyr. Love.*

A'CTUAL. *adj.* [*actuel*, Fr.]

1. That which comprises action.

In this slumbry agitation, besides her walking and other *actual* performances, what, at any time, have you heard her say? *Shakespeare's Macbeth.*

2. Really in act; not merely potential.

Sin, there in pow'r before
Once *actual*; now in body, and to dwell
Habitual habitant. *Milt. Paradise Lost.*

3. In act; not purely in speculation.

For he that but conceives a crime in thought,
Contracts the danger of an *actual* fault:
Then what must he expect, that still proceeds
To finish sin, and work up thoughts to deeds?
Dryden's Juvenal.

ACTUA'LITY. *n. s.* [from *actual.*] The state of being actual.

The *actuality* of these spiritual qualities is thus imprisoned, though their potentiality be not quite destroyed; and thus a crass, extended, impenetrable, passive, divisible, unintelligent substance is generated, which we call matter. *Cheyne.*

A'CTUALLY. *adv.* [from *actual.*] In act; in effect; really.

All mankind acknowledge themselves able and sufficient to do many things, which *actually* they never do. *South.*

Read one of the chronicles written by an author of this frame of mind, and you will think you were reading a history of the kings of Israel or Judah, where the historians were *actually* inspired, and where, by a particular scheme of providence, the kings were distinguished by judgments or blessings, according as they promoted idolatry, or the worship of the true God. *Addison.*

Though our temporal prospects should be full of danger, or though the days of sorrow should *actually* overtake us, yet still we must repose ourselves on God. *Rogers.*

A'CTUALNESS. *n. s.* [from *actual.*] The quality of being actual.

A'CTUARY. *n. s.* [*actuarius*, Lat.] The register who compiles the minutes of the proceedings of a court; a term of the civil law.

Suppose the judge should say, that he would have the keeping of the acts of court remain with him, and the notary will have the custody of them with himself: certainly, in this case, the *actuary* or writer of them ought to be preferred. *Ayliffe's Parergon.*

A'CTUATE. *adj.* [from the verb *To actuate.*] Put into action; animated; brought into effect.

The active informations of the intellect, filling the passive reception of the will, like form closing with matter, grew *actuate* into a third and distinct perfection of practice. *South.*

To A'CTUATE. *v. a.* [from *ago*, *actum*, Lat.] To put into action; to invigorate or encrease the powers of motion.

The light made by this animal depends upon a living spirit, and seems, by some vital irradiation, to be *actuated* into this lustre. *Brown's Vulgar Errours.*

Such is every man, who has not *actuated* the grace given him, to the subduing of every reigning sin. *Decay of Piety.*

Men of the greatest abilities are most fired with ambition; and, on the contrary, mean and narrow minds are the least *actuated* by it. *Addison.*

Our passions are the springs which *actuate* the powers of our nature. *Rogers.*

ACTUO'SE. *adj.* [from *act.*] That which hath strong powers of action; a word little used.

To A'CUATE. *v. a.* [*acuo*, Lat.] To sharpen, to invigorate with any powers of sharpness.

AC'ULEATE. *adj.* [*aculeatus*, Lat.] That which has a point or sting; prickly; that which terminates in a sharp point.

ACU'MEN. *n. s.* [Lat.] A sharp point; figuratively, quickness of intellects.

The word was much affected by the learned Aristarchus in common conversation, to signify genius or natural *acumen.* *Pope's Dunciad.*

ACU'MINATED. *particip. adj.* Ending in a point; sharp-pointed.

This is not *acuminated* and pointed, as in the rest, but seemeth, as it were, cut off. *Brown's Vulgar Errours.*

I appropriate this word, *Noli me tangere*, to a small round *acuminated* tubercle, which hath not much pain, unless it be touched or rubbed, or otherways exasperated by topicks. *Wiseman's Surgery.*

ACU'TE. *adj.* [*acutus*, Lat.]

1. Sharp, ending in a point; opposed to *obtuse* or *blunt.*

Having the ideas of an obtuse and an *acute* angled triangle, both drawn from equal bases and between parallels, I can, by intuitive knowledge, perceive the one not to be the other, but cannot that way know whether they be equal. *Locke.*

2. In a figurative sense applied to men; ingenious; penetrating; opposed to *dull* or *stupid.*

The *acute* and ingenious author, among many very fine thoughts, and uncommon reflections, has started the notion of seeing all things in God. *Locke.*

3. Spoken of the senses, vigorous; powerful in operation.

Were our senses altered, and made much quicker and *acuter*, the appearance and outward scheme of things would have quite another face to us. *Locke.*

4. Acute disease. Any disease, which is attended with an increased velocity of blood, and terminates in a few days. *Quincy.*

5. Acute accent; that which raises or sharpens the voice.

ACU'TELY.

ACU'TELY. *adv.* [from *acute.*] After an acute manner; sharply; it is used as well in the figurative as primitive sense.

He that will look into many parts of Asia and America, will find men reason there, perhaps, as *acutely* as himself, who yet never heard of a syllogism. *Locke.*

ACU'TENESS. *n. s.* [from *acute*, which see.]

1. Sharpness.
2. Force of intellects.

They would not be so apt to think, that there could be nothing added to the *acuteness* and penetration of their understandings. *Locke.*

3. Quickness and vigour of senses.

If eyes so framed could not view at once the hand and the hour plate, their owner could not be benefited by that *acuteness*; which, whilst it discovered the secret contrivance of the machine, made him lose its use. *Locke.*

4. Violence and speedy crisis of a malady.

We apply present remedies according to indications, respecting rather the *acuteness* of the disease, and precipitancy of the occasion, than the rising and setting of stars. *Brown's Vulgar Errours.*

5. Sharpness of sound.

This *acuteness* of sound will shew, that whilst, to the eye, the bell seems to be at rest, yet the minute parts of it continue in a very brisk motion, without which they could not strike the air. *Boyle.*

ADA'CTED. *participial adj.* [*adactus*, Lat.] Driven by force; a word little used. *Dict.*

A'DAGE. *n. s.* [*adagium*, Lat.] A maxim handed down from antiquity; a proverb.

Shallow unimproved intellects, that are confident pretenders to certainty; as if, contrary to the *adage*, science had no friend but ignorance. *Glanville's Scepsis Scientifica.*

Fine fruits of learning! old ambitious fool,
Dar'st thou apply that *adage* of the school;
As if 'tis nothing worth that lies conceal'd;
And science is not science till reveal'd? *Dryd.*

ADAGIO. *n. s.* [Italian.] A term used by musicians, to mark a slow time.

A'DAMANT. *n. s.* [*adamas*, Lat. from α and δαμάω, Gr. that is *insuperable, infrangible.*]

1. A stone, imagined by writers, of impenetrable hardness.

So great a fear my name amongst them spread,
That they suppos'd I could rend bars of steel,
And spurn in pieces posts of *adamant.* *Shakesp.*

Satan, with vast and haughty strides advanc'd,
Came tow'ring, arm'd in *adamant*, and gold. *Milton.*

Eternal Deities,
Who rule the world with absolute decrees,
And write whatever time shall bring to pass,
With pens of *adamant*, on plates of brass. *Dryd.*

2. The diamond.

Hardness, wherein some stones exceed all other bodies, and among them the *adamant* all other stones, being exalted to that degree thereof, that art in vain endeavours to counterfeit it, the factitious stones of chymists, in imitation, being easily detected by an ordinary lapidist. *Ray on the Creation.*

3. Adamant is taken for the loadstone.

Let him change his lodging from one end and part of the town to another, which is a great *adamant* of acquaintance. *Bacon's Essays.*

You draw me, you hard-hearted *adamant!*
But yet you draw not iron; for my heart
Is true as steel. *Shakespeare.*

ADAMANTE'AN. *adj.* [from *adamant.*] Hard as adamant.

He ran on embattl'd armies clad in iron,
And weaponless himself,
Made arms ridiculous, useless the forgery
Of brazen shield and spear, the hammer'd cuirass,
Chalybean temper'd steel, and frock of mail
Adamantean proof. *Milton's Samson Agonistes.*

This word occurs perhaps only in this passage.

ADAMA'NTINE. *adj.* [*adamantinus*, Lat.]

1. Made of adamant.

Wide is the fronting gate, and rais'd on high
With *adamantine* columns, threats the sky. *Dryd.*

2. Having the qualities of adamant; as, hardness, indissolubility.

Could Eve's weak hand, extended to the tree,
In sunder rend that *adamantine* chain,
Whose golden links, effects and causes be,
And which to God's own chair doth fix'd remain? *Davies.*

An eternal sterility must have possessed the world, where all things had been fixed and fastened everlastingly with the *adamantine* chains of specific gravity; if the Almighty had not spoken and said, Let the earth bring forth grass, the herb yielding seed, and the fruit-tree yielding fruit after its kind; and it was so. *Bentley's Sermons.*

In *adamantine* chains shall death be bound,
And hell's grim tyrant feel th' eternal wound. *Pope.*

Tho' *adamantine* bonds the chief restrain,
The dire restraint his wisdom will defeat,
And soon restore him to his regal seat. *Pope.*

A'DAM'S-APPLE. *n. s.* [in anatomy.] A prominent part of the throat.

To ADA'PT. *v. a.* [*adapto*, Lat.] To fit one thing to another; to suit; in proportion.

'Tis true, but let it not be known,
My eyes are somewhat dimmish grown;
For nature, always in the right,
To your decays *adapts* my sight. *Swift.*

It is not enough that nothings offends the ear, but a good poet will *adapt* the very sounds, as well as words, to the things he treats of. *Pope's Letters.*

ADAPTA'TION. *n. s.* [from *adapt.*] The act of fitting one thing to another; the fitness of one thing to another.

Some species there be of middle natures, that is, of bird and beast, as batts; yet are their parts so set together, that we cannot define the beginning or end of either, there being a commixtion of both, rather than *adaptation* or cement of the one unto the other. *Brown's Vulgar Errours.*

Their adhesion may be in part ascribed, either to some elastical motion in the pressed glass, or to the exquisite *adaptation* of the almost numberless, though very small, asperities of the one, and the numerous little cavities of the other; whereby the surfaces do lock in with one another, or are, as it were, clasped together. *Boyle.*

ADA'PTION. *n. s.* [from *adapt.*] The act of fitting.

It were alone a sufficient work to shew all the necessities, the wise contrivances, and prudent *adaptions*, of these admirable machines, for the benefit of the whole. *Cheyne.*

To ADCO'RPORATE. *v. a.* [from *ad* and *corpus.*] To unite one body with another; more usually wrote *accorporate*; which see.

To ADD. *v. a.* [*addo*, Lat.]

1. To join something to that which was before.

Mark if his birth makes any difference,
If to his words it *adds* one grain of sense. *Dryd.*

They, whose muses have the highest flown,
Add not to his immortal memory,
But do an act of friendship to their own. *Dryd.*

2. To perform the mental operation of adding one number or conception to another.

Whatsoever positive ideas a man has in his mind, of any quantity, he can repeat it, and *add* it to the former, as easily as he can *add* together the ideas of two days, or two years. *Locke.*

A'DDABLE. *adj.* [from *add.*] That which may be added. *Addible* is more proper.

The first number in every addition is called the *addable* number, the other, the number or numbers added, and the number invented by the addition, the aggregate or sum. *Cocker's Arithmetick.*

To ADDE'CIMATE. *v. a.* [*addecimo*, Lat.] To take or ascertain tithes. *Dict.*

To ADDE'EM. *v. a.* [from *deem.*] To esteem; to account. This word is now out of use.

She scorns to be *addeem'd* so worthless-base,
As to be mov'd to such an infamy. *Daniel's Civil Wars.*

A'DDER. *n. s.* [Æττeꝛ, Æττoꝛ, Naꝺꝺꝛe, as it seems from eιττeꝛ, Sax. poison.] A serpent, a viper, a poisonous reptile; perhaps of any species. In common language, *adders* and *snakes* are not the same.

Or is the *adder* better than the eel,
Because his painted skin contents the eye. *Shakesp.*

An *adder* did it; for, with doubler tongue
Than thine, thou serpent, never *adder* stung.
Shakespeare's Midsum. Night's Dream.

The *adder* teaches us where to strike, by her curious and fearful defending of her head. *Taylor of Living holy.*

A'DDER'S-GRASS. *n. s.* The name of a plant, imagined by *Skinner* to be so named, because serpents lurk about it.

A'DDER'S-TONGUE. *n. s.* [*ophioglossum*, Lat.] The name of an herb.

It hath no visible flower; but the seeds are produced on a spike, which resembles a serpent's tongue; which seed is contained in many longitudinal cells, which open, and cast forth the seeds when ripe. It grows wild in moist meadows, and is used in medicine. *Miller.*

The most common simples with us in England, are comfrey, bugle, agrimony, sanicle, paul's-betony, fluellin, periwinkle, *adder's-tongue.* *Wiseman's Surgery.*

A'DDER'S-WORT. *n. s.* An herb so named, on account of its virtue, real or supposed, of curing the bite of serpents.

A'DDIBLE. *adj.* [from *add.*] Possible to be added. See ADDABLE.

The clearest idea it can get of infinity, is the confused, incomprehensible remainder of endless, *addible* numbers, which affords no prospect of stop, or boundary. *Locke.*

ADDIBI'LITY. *n. s.* [from *addible.*] The possibility of being added.

This endless addition, or *addibility* (if any one like the word better) of numbers, so apparent to the mind, is that which gives us the clearest and most distinct idea of infinity. *Locke.*

A'DDICE. *n. s.* [for which we corruptly speak and write *adz*, from adeꝛe, Sax. an axe.]

The *addice* hath its blade made thin and somewhat arching.

As

As the axe hath its edge parallel to its handle, so the *addice* hath its edge athwart the handle, and is ground to a basil on its inside to its outer edge. *Moxon's Mechanical Exercises.*

To ADDICT. *v. a.* [*addico*, Lat.]

1. To devote, to dedicate, in a good sense; which is rarely used.

Ye know the house of Stephanus, that they have *addicted* themselves to the ministry of the saints. 1 *Cor.* xvi. 15.

2. It is commonly taken in a bad sense; as, *he addicted himself to vice.*

A'DDICTEDNESS. *n. s.* [from *addicted.*] The quality or state of being addicted.

Those, that know how little I have remitted of my former *addictedness* to make chymical experiments, will believe, that the design was to give occasion to the more knowing artists to lay aside their reservedness. *Boyle.*

ADDI'CTION. *n. s.* [*addictio*, Lat.]

1. The act of devoting, or giving up.

2. The state of being devoted.

It is a wonder how his grace should glean it,
Since his *addiction* was to courses vain;
His companies unletter'd, rude and shallow;
His hours fill'd up with riots, banquets, sports. *Shakesp.*

An A'DDITAMENT. *n. s.* [*additamentum*, Lat.] The addition, or thing added.

Iron will not incorporate with brass, nor other metals, of itself, by simple fire: so as the enquiry must be upon the calcination, and the *additament*, and the charge of them. *Bacon.*

In such a palace there is first the case or fabrick, or moles of the structure itself; and, besides that, there are certain *additaments* that contribute to its ornament and use; as, various furniture, rare fountains and aqueducts, curious motions of divers things appendicated to it. *Hale's Origin of Mankind.*

ADDI'TION. *n. s.* [from *add.*]

1. The act of adding one thing to another; opposed to *diminution.*

The infinite distance between the Creator and the noblest of all creatures, can never be measured, nor exhausted by endless *addition* of finite degrees. *Bentley's Sermons.*

2. Additament, or the thing added.

It will not be modestly done, if any of our own wisdom intrude or interpose, or be willing to make *additions* to what Christ and his Apostles have designed. *Hammond's Fundam.*

Some such resemblances, methinks, I find
Of our last even'ing's talk, in this thy dream,
But with *addition* strange! *Milton.*

The abolishing of villanage, together with the custom permitted, among the nobles, of selling their lands, was a mighty *addition* to the power of the commons.
Swift on the Dissensions in Athens and Rome.

3. In arithmetick.

Addition is the reduction of two or more numbers of like kind, together into one sum or total. *Cocker's Arith.*

4. In law. A title given to a man over and above his christian name and surname, shewing his estate, degree, occupation, trade, age, place of dwelling. *Cowell.*

Only retain
The name, and all th' *addition* to a king;
The sway, revenue, execution of th' last,
Beloved sons, be yours; which to confirm,
This coronet part between you. *Shakespeare.*
From this time,
For what he did before Corioli, call him,
With all th' applause and clamour of the host,
Caius Marcius Coriolanus. Bear th' *addition* nobly ever.
Shakespeare's Coriolanus.

There arose new disputes upon the persons named by the king, or rather against the *additions* and appellations of title, which were made to their names. *Clarendon.*

ADDI'TIONAL. *adj.* [from *addition.*] That which is added.

Our kalendar being once reformed and set right, it may be kept so, without any considerable variation, for many ages, by omitting one leap-year; *i. e.* the *additional* day, at the end of every 134 years. *Holder on Time.*

The greatest wits, that ever were produced in one age, lived together in so good an understanding, and celebrated one another with so much generosity, that each of them receives an *additional* lustre from his cotemporaries. *Addison.*

They include in them that very kind of evidence, which is supposed to be so powerful; and do, withal, afford us several other *additional* proofs, of great force and clearness. *Atter.*

ADDI'TORY. *adj.* [from *add.*] That which has the power or quality of adding.

The *additory* fiction gives to a great man a larger share of reputation than belongs to him, to enable him to serve some good end or purpose. *Arbuthnot.*

A'DDLE. *adj.* [from adel, a disease, Sax. according to *Skinner* and *Junius*; perhaps from ydel, idle, barren, unfruitful.] Originally applied to eggs, and signifying such as produce nothing, but grow rotten under the hen; thence transferred to brains that produce nothing.

There's one with truncheon, like a ladle,
That carries eggs too fresh or *addle*;
And still at random, as he goes,
Among the rabble rout bestows. *Hudibras.*

After much solitariness, fasting, or long sickness, their brains were *addle*, and their bellies as empty of meat as their heads of wit. *Burton on Melancholy.*

Thus far the poet; but his brains grow *addle*:
And all the rest is purely from this noddle. *Dryd.*

To A'DDLE. *v. a.* [from *addle*, *adj.*] To make addle; to corrupt; to make barren.

This is also evidenced in eggs, whereof the sound one sinks, and such as are *addled* swim; as do also those that are termed *hypenemiæ*, or wind-eggs. *Brown's Vulgar Errours.*

A'DDLE-PATED *adj.* Having addled brains. See ADDLE.

Poor slaves in metre, dull and *addle-pated*,
Who rhyme below even David's psalms translated.
Dryden's Absalom and Achitophel.

To ADDRE'SS. *v. a* [*addresser*, Fr. from *dereçar*, Span. from *dirigo*, *directum*, Lat.]

1. To prepare one's self to enter upon any action; as, *he addressed himself to the work.*

It lifted up its head, and did *address*
Itself to motion, like as it would speak. *Shakesp.*
With him the Palmer eke, in habit sad,
Himself *addrest* to that adventure hard;
So to the river's side they both together far'd. *Fairy Q.*
Then Turnus, from his chariot leaping light,
Address'd himself on foot to single fight. *Dryd.*

2. To get ready; to put in a state for immediate use.

By this means they fell directly on head on the English battle; whereupon the earl of Warwick *addressed* his men to take the flank. *Sir J. Hayward.*

Duke Frederick hearing, how that every day
Men of great worth resorted to this forest,
Address'd a mighty power, which were on foot,
In his own conduct purposely to take
His brother here. *Shakespeare, As you like it.*
To-night in Harfleur we will be your guest,
To-morrow for the march we are *addrest.* *Shak.*

3. To apply to another by words, with various forms of construction.

4. Sometimes without a preposition.

Are not your orders to *address* the senate? *Addison.*

5. Sometimes with *to.*

Addressing to Pollio, his great patron, and himself no vulgar poet, he no longer could restrain the freedom of his spirit; but began to assert his native character, which is sublimity.
Dryden's Dedication of Virgil's Past.

Among the croud, but far above the rest,
Young Turnus *to* the beauteous maid *addrest.* *Dryd.*

6. Sometimes with the reciprocal pronoun; as, *he addressed himself to the general.*

7. Sometimes with the accusative of the matter of the address, which may be the nominative to the passive.

The young hero had *addressed* his *prayers* to him for his assistance. *Dryd. Æneid.*

The prince himself, with awful dread possess'd,
His *vows* to great Apollo thus *addrest.* *Dryd.*
His suit was common; but, above the rest,
To both the *brother-princes* thus *addrest.* *Dryd.*

8. To address, is to apply to the king in form.

The representatives of the nation in parliament, and the privy-council, *address'd* the king to have it recalled. *Swift.*

ADDRE'SS. *n. s.* [*addresse*, Fr.]

1. Verbal application to any one, by way of persuasion, petition.

Henry, in knots involving Emma's name,
Had half confess'd and half conceal'd his flame
Upon this tree; and as the tender mark
Grew with the year, and widen'd with the bark,
Venus had heard the virgin's soft *address*,
That, as the wound, the passion might encrease. *Prior.*

Most of the persons, to whom these *addresses* are made, are not wise and skilful judges, but are influenced by their own sinful appetites and passions. *Watts's Improvement of the Mind.*

2. Courtship.

They both behold thee with their sisters eyes,
And often have reveal'd their passion to me:
But, tell me, whose *address* thou favour'st most;
I long to know, and yet I dread to hear it. *Addison.*

About three years since, a gentleman, whom, I am sure, you yourself would have approved, made his *addresses* to me.
Addison. Spectator.

3. Manner of addressing another; as, we say, *a man of an happy or a pleasing address*; *a man of an aukward address.*

4. Skill, dexterity.

I could produce innumerable instances from my own memory and observation, of events imputed to the profound skill and *address* of a minister, which, in reality, were either mere effects of negligence, weakness, humour, passion, or pride, or, at best, but the natural course of things left to themselves.
Swift's Thoughts on the present Posture of Affairs.

5. Manner of directing a letter; a sense chiefly mercantile.

ADDRE'SSER. *n. s.* [from *address.*] The person that addresses or petitions.

ADDU'CENT. *adj.* [*adducens*, Lat.]
A word applied to those muscles that bring forward, close, or draw together the parts of the body to which they are annexed. *Quincy.*

To ADDU'LCE. *v. a.* [*addoucir*, Fr. *dulcis*, Lat.] To sweeten; a word not now in use.
Thus did the French embassadors, with great shew of their king's affection, and many sugared words, seek to *addulce* all matters between the two kings. *Bacon's Henry* VII.

A'DELING. *n. s.* [from æbel, Sax. illustrious.] A word of honour among the Angles, properly appertaining to the king's children: king Edward the Confessor, being without issue, and intending to make Edgar his heir, called him *adeling*. *Cowell.*

ADENO'GRAPHY. *n. s.* [from ἀδηνον and γράφω, Gr.] A treatise of the glands.

ADE'MPTION. *n. s.* [*adimo*, *ademptum*, Lat.] Taking away; privation. *Dict.*

ADE'PT. *n. s.* [from *adeptus*, Lat. that is *adeptus artem.*]
He that is completely skilled in all the secrets of his art. It is, in its original signification, appropriated to the chymists, but is now extended to other artists.
The preservation of chastity is easy to true *adepts*. *Pope.*

ADE'PT. *adj.* Skilful; throughly versed.
If there be really such *adept* philosophers as we are told of, I am apt to think, that, among their arcana, they are masters of extremely potent menstruums. *Boyle.*

A'DEQUATE. *adj.* [*adequatus*, Lat.] Equal to; proportionate; correspondent to, so as to bear an exact resemblance or proportion. It is used generally in a figurative sense, and often with the particle *to*.
Contingent death seems to be the whole *adequate* object of popular courage; but a necessary and unavoidable coffin strikes paleness into the stoutest heart. *Harvey on Consumptions.*
The arguments were proper, *adequate*, and sufficient to compass their respective ends. *South's Sermons.*
All our simple ideas are *adequate*; because, being nothing but the effects of certain powers in things, fitted and ordained by God to produce such sensations in us, they cannot but be correspondent and *adequate to* those powers. *Locke.*
Those are *adequate* ideas, which perfectly represent their archetypes or objects. Inadequate are but a partial, or incomplete, representation of those archetypes to which they are referred. *Watts's Logick.*

A'DEQUATELY. *adv.* [from *adequate.*]
1. In an adequate manner; with justness of representation; with exactness of proportion.
Gratitude consists *adequately* in these two things: first, that it is a debt; and, secondly, that it is such a debt as is left to every man's ingenuity, whether he will pay or no. *South.*
2. It is used with the particle *to*.
Piety is the necessary christian virtue, proportioned *adequately to* the omniscience and spirituality of that infinite Deity. *Hammond's Fundamentals.*

A'DEQUATENESS. *n. s.* [from *adequate.*] The state of being adequate; justness of representation; exactness of proportion.

ADESPO'TICK. *adj.* Not absolute; not despotick. *Dict.*

To ADHE'RE. *v. n.* [*adhæreo*, Lat.]
1. To stick to; as, wax to the finger.
2. To stick, in a figurative sense; to be consistent; to hold together.
Why every thing *adheres* together, that no dram of a scruple, no scruple of a scruple, no obstacle, no incredulous or unsafe circumstance—— *Shakesp. Twelfth Night.*
3. To remain firmly fixed to a party, person, or opinion.
Good gentlemen, he hath much talk'd of you;
And sure I am, two men there are not living,
To whom he more *adheres*. *Shakesp. Ham.*
Every man of sense will agree with me, that singularity is laudable, when, in contradiction to a multitude, it *adheres* to the dictates of conscience, morality, and honour. *Boyle.*

ADHE'RENCE. *n. s.* [from *adhere.*] See ADHESION.
1. The quality of adhering, or sticking; tenacity.
2. In a figurative sense, fixedness of mind; attachment; steadiness.
Their firm *adherence* to their religion is no less remarkable than their dispersion; considering it as persecuted or contemned over the whole earth. *Addison, Spectator*, Nº 495.
A constant *adherence* to one sort of diet may have bad effects on any constitution. *Arbuthnot on Aliments.*
Plain good sense, and a firm *adherence* to the point, have proved more effectual than those arts, which are contemptuously called the spirit of negociating. *Swift.*

ADHE'RENCY. *n. s.* [The same with *adherence.*]
1. Steady attachment.
2. That which adheres.
Vices have a native *adherency* of vexation. *Decay of Piety.*

ADHE'RENT. *adj.* [from *adhere.*]
1. Sticking to.
Close to the cliff with both his hands he clung,
And stuck *adherent*, and suspended hung. *Pope's Odyssey.*
2. United with.
Modes are said to be inherent or *adherent*; that is, proper or improper. *Adherent* or improper modes arise from the joining of some accidental substance to the chief subject, which yet may be separated from it; so when a bowl is wet, or a boy is cloathed, these are *adherent* modes; for the water and the clothes are distinct substances which adhere to the bowl, or to the boy. *Watts's Logick.*

ADHE'RENT. *n. s.* [from *adhere.*] The person that adheres; one that supports the cause, or follows the fortune of another; a follower; a partisan;
Princes must give protection to their subjects and *adherents*, when worthy occasion shall require it. *Sir W. Raleigh.*
A new war must be undertaken upon the advice of those, who, with their partisans and *adherents*, were to be the sole gainers by it. *Swift's Miscellanies.*

ADHE'RER. *n. s.* [from *adhere.*] He that adheres.
He ought to be indulgent to tender consciences; but, at the same time, a firm *adherer* to the established church. *Swift.*

ADHE'SION. *n. s.* [*adhæsio*, Lat.]
1. The act or state of sticking to something. *Adhesion* is generally used in the natural, and *adherence* in the metaphorical sense; as, *the adhesion of iron to the magnet*; and *adherence of a client to his patron*.
Why therefore may not the minute parts of other bodies, if they be conveniently shaped for *adhesion*, stick to one another, as well as stick to this spirit? *Boyle.*
The rest consisting wholly in the sensible configuration as smooth and rough; or else more, or less, firm *adhesion* of the parts, as hard and soft, tough and brittle, are obvious. *Locke.*
— Prove that all things, on occasion,
Love union, and desire *adhesion*. *Prior.*
2. It is sometimes taken, like *adherence*, figuratively, for firmness in an opinion, or steadiness in practice.
The same want of sincerity, the same *adhesion* to vice, and aversion from goodness, will be equally a reason for their rejecting any proof whatsoever. *Atterbury's Sermons.*

ADHE'SIVE. *adj.* [from *adhesion.*] Sticking; tenacious; with *to*.
If slow, yet sure, *adhesive to* the tract,
Hot steaming up. *Thomson's Autumn, l.* 440.

To ADHI'BIT. *v. a.* [*adhibeo*, Lat.] To apply; to make use of.

ADHIBI'TION. *n. s.* [from *adhibit.*] Application; use. *Dict.*

ADJA'CENCY. *n. s.* [from *adjaceo*, Lat.]
1. The state of lying close to another thing.
2. That which is adjacent. See ADJACENT.
Because the Cape hath sea on both sides near it, and other lands, remote as it were, equidistant from it; therefore, at that point, the needle is not distracted by the vicinity of *adjacencies*. *Brown's Vulgar Errours, b.* ii. *c.* 2.

ADJA'CENT. *adj.* [*adjacens*, Lat.] Lying close; bordering upon something.
It may corrupt within itself, although no part of it issue into the body *adjacent*. *Bacon's Nat. History*, Nº 71.
Uniform pellucid mediums, such as water, have no sensible reflection but in their external superficies, where they are *adjacent* to other mediums of a different density. *Newton's Opt.*

ADJA'CENT. *n. s.* That which lies next another.
The sense of the author goes visibly in its own train, and the words receiving a determined sense from their companions and *adjacents*, will not consent to give countenance and colour to what must be supported at any rate. *Locke's Ess. upon S. Paul.*

ADIA'PHOROUS. *adj.* [ἀδιάφορος, Gr.] Neutral; particularly used of some spirits and salts, which are neither of an acid nor alkaline nature. *Quincy.*
Our *adiaphorous* spirit may be obtained, by distilling the liquor that is afforded by woods and divers other bodies. *Boyle.*

ADIA'PHORY. *n. s.* [ἀδιαφορία, Gr.] Neutrality; indifference.

To ADJE'CT. *v. a.* [*adjicio*, *adjectum*, Lat.] To add to; to put to another thing.

ADJE'CTION. *n. s.* [*adjectio*, Lat.]
1. The act of adjecting, or adding.
2. The thing adjected, or added.
That unto every pound of sulphur, an *adjection* of one ounce of quicksilver; or unto every pound of petre, one ounce of sal-armoniac, will much intend the force, and consequently the report, I find no verity. *Brown's Vulgar Errours, b.* ii.

ADJECTI'TIOUS. *adj.* [from *adjection.*] Added; thrown in upon the rest.

A'DJECTIVE. *n. s.* [*adjectivum*, Lat.]
A word added to a noun, to signify the addition or separation of some quality, cirumstance, or manner of being; as, *good*, *bad*, are *adjectives*, because, in speech, they are applied to nouns, to modify their signification, or intimate the manner of existence in the things signified thereby. *Clarke's Latin Gram.*
All the versification of Claudian is included within the compass of four or five lines; perpetually closing his sense at the end of a verse, and that verse commonly which they call golden, or two substantives and two *adjectives*, with a verb betwixt them, to keep the peace. *Dryden.*

A'DJECTIVELY. *adv.* [from *adjective.*] After the manner of an adjective; a term of grammar.

ADIEU'. *adv.* [from *à Dieu*, used elliptically for *à Dieu je vous commende*, used at the departure of friends.] The form of parting, originally importing a commendation to the Divine care, but now used, in a popular sense, sometimes to things inanimate; farewell.

Ne gave him leave to bid that aged sire
Adieu, but nimbly ran her wonted course. *Fairy Queen.*

Use a more spacious ceremony to the noble lords; you restrained yourself within the list of too cold an *adieu*; be more expressive to them. *Shakespeare's All's well that ends well.*

While now I take my last *adieu*,
Heave thou no sigh, nor shed a tear;
Lest yet my half-clos'd eye may view
On earth an object worth its care. *Prior.*

To ADJO'IN. *v. a* [*adjoindre*, Fr. *adjungo*, Lat.] To join to; to unite to; to put to.

Corrections or improvements should be as remarks *adjoined*, by way of note or commentary, in their proper places, and superadded to a regular treatise. *Watts's Improvem. of the Mind.*

To ADJO'IN. *v. n.* To be contiguous to; to lye next so as to have nothing between.

Th' *adjoining* fane, th' assembled Greeks express'd,
And hunting of the Caledonian beast. *Dryden's Fables.*

In learning any thing, as little should be proposed to the mind at once as is possible; and, that being understood and fully mastered, proceed to the next *adjoining*, yet unknown, simple, unperplexed proposition, belonging to the matter in hand, and tending to the clearing what is principally designed. *Locke.*

To ADJO'URN. *v. a.* [*adjourner*, Fr.]

1. To put off to another day, naming the time; a term used in juridical proceedings; as, of parliaments, or courts of justice.

The queen being absent, 'tis a needful fitness,
That we *adjourn* this court to further day. *Shakesp. Hen.* VIII.

By the king's authority alone, and by his writs they are assembled, and by him alone are they prorogued and dissolved; but each house may *adjourn* itself. *Bac. Advice to Sir G. Villiers.*

2. To put off; to defer; to let stay to another time.

Then, Jupiter, thou king of gods,
Why hast thou thus *adjourn'd*
The graces for his merits due,
Being all to dolours turn'd. *Shakesp. Cymbeline.*

Crown high the goblets with a chearful draught;
Enjoy the present hour, *adjourn* the future thought.
Dryden, Æneid vii. *l.* 181.

The formation of animals being foreign to my purpose, I shall *adjourn* the consideration of it to another occasion.
Woodward's Nat History, p. iii.

ADJO'URNMENT. *n. s.* [*adjournement*, Fr.] An assignment of a day, or a putting off till another day. *Adjournement in eyre*, an appointment of a day, when the justices in eyre mean to sit again. *Cowell.*

We will and we will not, and then we will not again, and we will. At this rate we run our lives out in *adjournments* from time to time, out of a fantastical levity that holds us off and on, betwixt hawk and buzzard. *L'Estrange.*

A'DIPOUS. *adj.* [*adiposus*, Lat.] Fat. *Dict.*

A'DIT. *n. s.* [*aditus*, Lat.] A passage for the conveyance of water under ground; a passage under ground in general: a term among the minemen.

For conveying away the water, they stand in aid of sundry devices; as, *adits*, pumps, and wheels, driven by a stream, and interchangeably filling and emptying two buckets. *Carew's Surv.*

The delfs would be so flown with waters (it being impossible to make any *adits* or soughs to drain them) that no gins or machines could suffice to lay and keep them dry. *Ray on the Creat.*

ADI'TION. *n. s.* [from *adeo*, *aditum*, Lat.] The act of going to another. *Dict.*

To ADJU'DGE. *v. a.* [*adjudico*, Lat.]

1. To give the thing controverted to one of the parties by a judicial sentence; with the particle *to* before the person.

The way of disputing in the schools leads from it, by insisting on one topical argument; by the success of which, victory is *adjudged to* the opponent, or defendant. *Locke.*

The great competitors for Rome,
Cæsar and Pompey on Pharsalian plains,
Where stern Bellona, with one final stroke,
Adjudg'd the empire of this globe *to* one. *Phillips.*

2. To sentence, or condemn to a punishment; with *to* before the thing.

But though thou art *adjudged to* the death;
Yet I will favour thee in what I can. *Shakesp. Com. of Err.*

3. Simply, to judge; to decree; to determine.

He *adjudged* him unworthy of his friendship and favour; purposing sharply to revenge the wrong he had received.
Knolles's History of the Turks.

ADJUDICA'TION. *n. s.* [*adjudicatio*, Lat.] The act of judging, or of granting something to a litigant, by a judicial sentence.

To ADJU'DICATE. *v. a.* [*adjudico*, Lat.] To adjudge; to give something controverted to one of the litigants, by a sentence or decision.

To A'DJUGATE. *v. a.* [*adjugo*, Lat.] To yoke to; to join to another by a yoke. *Dict.*

A'DJUMENT. *n. s.* [*adjumentum*, Lat.] Help; support. *Dict.*

A'DJUNCT. *n. s.* [*adjunctum*, Lat.]

1. Something adherent or united to another, though not essentially part of it.

Learning is but an *adjunct* to ourself,
And where we are, our learning likewise is.
Shakesp. Love's Labour Lost.

But I make haste to consider you as abstracted from a court, which (if you will give me leave to use a term of logick) is only an *adjunct*, not a propriety, of happiness. *Dryd. Aureng. Ded.*

The talent of discretion, as I have described it in its several *adjuncts* and circumstances, is no where so serviceable as to the clergy. *Swift's Miscellanies.*

2. A person joined to another. This sense rarely occurs.

He made him the associate of his heir apparent, together with the lord Cottington (as an *adjunct* of singular experience and trust) in foreign travels, and in a business of love. *Wotton.*

A'DJUNCT. *adj.* United with; immediately consequent.

So well, that what you bid me undertake,
Though that my death were *adjunct* to my act,
I'd do't. *Shakesp. King John.*

ADJU'NCTION. *n. s.* [*adjunctio*, Lat.]

1. The act of adjoining, or coupling together.
2. The thing joined.

ADJU'NCTIVE. *n. s.* [*adjunctivus*, Lat.]

1. He that joins.
2. That which is joined.

ADJURA'TION. *n. s.* [*adjuratio*, Lat.]

1. The act of adjuring, or proposing an oath to another.
2. The form of oath proposed to another.

When these learned men saw sickness and phrenzy cured, the dead raised, the oracles put to silence, the dæmons and evil spirits forced to confess themselves no gods, by persons, who only made use of prayer and *adjurations* in the name of their crucified Saviour; how could they doubt of their Saviour's power on the like occasions? *Addison on the Christian Religion.*

To ADJU'RE. *v. a.* [*adjuro* Lat.] To impose an oath upon another, prescribing the form in which he shall swear.

Thou know'st, the magistrates
And princes of my country came in person,
Solicited, commanded, threaten'd, urg'd,
Adjur'd by all the bonds of civil duty,
And of religion, press'd how just it was,
How honourable. *Milton's Sampson's Agonistes, l.* 853.

Ye lamps of heav'n! he said, and lifted high
His hands now free, thou venerable sky!
Inviolable pow'rs! ador'd with dread,
Ye fatal fillets! that once bound this head,
Ye sacred altars! from whose flames I fled,
Be all of you *adjured*. *Dryden, Æneid* ii.

To ADJU'ST. *v. a.* [*adjuster*, Fr.]

1. To regulate; to put in order; to settle in the right form.

Your lordship removes all our difficulties, and supplies all our wants, faster than the most visionary projector can *adjust* his schemes. *Swift to the Lord High Treasurer.*

2. To reduce to the true state or standard; to make accurate.

The names of mixed modes, for the most part, want standards in nature, whereby men may rectify and *adjust* their signification; therefore they are very various and doubtful. *Locke.*

3. To make conformable. It requires the particle *to* before the thing to which the conformity is made.

As to the accomplishment of this remarkable prophecy, whoever reads the account given by Josephus, without knowing his character, and compares it with what our Saviour foretold, would think the historian had been a Christian, and that he had nothing else in view, but to *adjust* the event *to* the prediction.
Addison on the Christian Religion.

ADJU'STMENT. *n. s.* [*adjustement*, Fr.]

1. Regulation; the act of putting in method; settlement.

The farther and clearer *adjustment* of this affair, I am constrained to adjourn to the larger treatise. *Woodward's Nat. Hist.*

2. The state of being put in method, or regulated.

It is a vulgar idea we have of a watch or clock, when we conceive of it as an instrument made to shew the hour; but it is a learned idea which the watch-maker has of it, who knows all the several parts of it, together with the various connexions and *adjustments* of each part. *Watts's Logick.*

A'DJUTANT. *n. s.* A petty officer, whose duty is to assist the major, by distributing the pay, and overseeing the punishment, of the common men.

To ADJU'TE. *v. a.* [*adjuvo*, *adjutum*, Lat.] To help; to concur: a word not now in use.

For if there be
Six bachelors as bold as he,
Adjuting to his company;
And each one hath his livery. *Ben. Johnson's Under-woods.*

ADJU'TOR. *n. s.* [*adjutor*, Lat.] A helper. *Dict.*

ADJU'TORY. *adj.* [*adjutorius*, Lat.] That which helps. *Dict.*

An ADJU'TRIX. *n. s.* [Lat.] She who helps. *Dict.*

A'DJUVANT. *adj.* [*adjuvans*, Lat.] Helpful; useful. *Dict.*

 To

To A'DJUVATE. *v. a* [*adjuvo*, Lat.] To help; to further; to put forward. *Dict.*

ADMEA'SUREMENT. *n. ſ.* [See MEASURE.] The adjuſtment of proportions; the act or practice of meaſuring according to rule.

Admeaſurement is a writ, which lieth for the bringing of thoſe to a mediocrity, that uſurp more than their part. It lieth in two caſes: one is termed *admeaſurement* of dower, where the widow of the deceaſed holdeth from the heir, or his guardian, more in the name of her dower, than belongeth to her. The other is *admeaſurement* of paſture which lieth between thoſe that have common of paſture appendant to their freehold, or common by vicinage, in caſe any one of them, or more, do ſurcharge the common with more cattle than they ought. *Cowell.*

In ſome counties they are not much more acquainted with *admeaſurement* by acre; and thereby the writs of thoſe counties contain twice or thrice ſo many acres more than the land hath. *Bacon's Hiſt. Off. Alienat.*

ADMENSURA'TION. *n. ſ.* [*ad* and *menſura*, Lat.] The act, or practice, of meaſuring out to each his part.

ADMI'NICLE. *n. ſ.* [*adminiculum*, Lat.] Help; ſupport; furtherance. *Dict.*

ADMINI'CULAR. *adj.* [from *adminiculum*, Lat.] That which gives help. *Dict.*

To ADMINISTER. *v. a.* [*adminiſtro*, Lat.]

1. To give; to afford; to ſupply.

Let Zephyrs bland
Adminiſter their tepid genial airs;
Naught fear he from the weſt, whoſe gentle warmth
Diſcloſes well the earth's all-teeming womb. *Philips.*

2. To act as the miniſter or agent in any employment or office; generally, but not always, with ſome hint of ſubordination, to adminiſter the government.

For forms of government let fools conteſt,
Whate'er is beſt *adminiſter'd*, is beſt. *Pope's Eſſay on Man.*

3. To adminiſter juſtice.

4. To adminiſter the ſacraments.

Have not they the old popiſh cuſtom of *adminiſtering* the bleſſed ſacrament of the holy euchariſt with wafer-cakes? *Hooker, b.* iv. § 10.

5. To adminiſter an oath.

Swear by the duty that you owe to heav'n,
To keep the oath that we *adminiſter*. *Shakeſp. Richard* II.

6. To adminiſter phyſick.

I was carried on men's ſhoulders, *adminiſtering* phyſick and phlebotomy. *Wafers's Voyage.*

7. To adminiſter to; to contribute; to bring ſupplies.

I muſt not omit, that there is a fountain riſing in the upper part of my garden, which forms a little wandering rill, and *adminiſters* to the pleaſure, as well as the plenty, of the place. *Spectator*, N° 477.

8. To perform the office of an adminiſtrator, in law. See ADMINISTRATOR.

Neal's order was never performed, becauſe the executors durſt not *adminiſter*. *Arbuthnot and Pope's Martin. Scribler.*

To ADMI'NISTRATE. *v. a.* [*adminiſtro*, Lat.] To exhibit; to give as phyſick.

They have the ſame effects in medicine, when inwardly *adminiſtrated* to animal bodies. *Woodward's Nat. Hiſt.*

ADMINISTRA'TION. *n. ſ.* [*adminiſtratio*, Lat.]

1. The act of adminiſtering or conducting any employment; as, the conducting the publick affairs; diſpenſing the laws.

I then did uſe the perſon of your father;
The image of his pow'r lay then in me:
And in th' *adminiſtration* of his law,
While I was buſy for the commonwealth,
Your highneſs pleaſed to forget my place. *Shakeſp. Hen.* IV.

In the ſhort time of his *adminiſtration*, he ſhone ſo powerfully upon me, that, like the heat of a Ruſſian ſummer, he ripened the fruits of poetry in a cold climate. *Dryden's Dedication of Virgil's Paſtorals.*

2. The active or executive part of government.

It may paſs for a maxim in ſtate, that the *adminiſtration* cannot be placed in too few hands, nor the legiſlator in too many. *Swift's Sentiments of a Church of England-man.*

3. Thoſe to whom the care of publick affairs is committed.

4. Diſtribution; exhibition; diſpenſation.

There is, in ſacraments, to be obſerved their force, and their form of *adminiſtration*. *Hooker, b.* v.

By the univerſal *adminiſtration* of grace, begun by our bleſſed Saviour, enlarged by his apoſtles, carried on by their immediate ſucceſſors, and to be compleated by the reſt to the world's end; all types that darkened this faith are enlightened. *Sprat's Sermons.*

ADMI'NISTRATIVE. *adj.* [from *adminiſtrate*.] That which adminiſters; that by which any one adminiſters.

ADMINISTRA'TOR. *n. ſ.* [*adminiſtrator*, Lat.]

1. Is properly taken for him that has the goods of a man dying inteſtate, committed to his charge by the ordinary, and is accountable for the ſame, whenever it ſhall pleaſe the ordinary to call upon him thereunto. *Cowell.*

He was wonderfully diligent to enquire and obſerve what became of the king of Arragon, in holding the kingdom of Caſtile, and whether he did hold it in his own right, or as *adminiſtrator* to his daughter. *Bacon's Henry* VII.

2. He that officiates in divine rites.

I feel my conſcience bound to remember the death of Chriſt, with ſome ſociety of Chriſtians or other, ſince it is a moſt plain command; whether the perſon, who diſtributes theſe elements, be only an occaſional or a ſettled *adminiſtrator*. *Watts's Improvement of the Mind, p.* i. *c.* 18.

3. He that conducts the government.

The reſidence of the prince, or chief *adminiſtrator*, of the civil power. *Swift's Short View of Ireland.*

ADMI'NISTRATRIX. *n. ſ.* [Lat.] She who adminiſters in conſequence of a will.

ADMINISTRA'TORSHIP. *n. ſ.* [from *adminiſtrator*.] The office of adminiſtrator.

A'DMIRABLE. *adj.* [*admirabilis*, Lat.] To be admired; worthy of admiration; of power to excite wonder; always taken in a good ſenſe, and applied either to perſons or things.

The more power he hath to hurt, the more *admirable* is his praiſe, that he will not hurt. *Sidney, b.* ii.

God was with them in all their afflictions, and, at length, by working their *admirable* deliverance, did teſtify that they ſerved him not in vain. *Hooker, b.* iv. § 2.

What *admirable* things occur in the remains of ſeveral other philoſophers? Short, I confeſs, of the rules of Chriſtianity, but generally above the lives of Chriſtians. *South's Sermons.*

You can at moſt
To an indiff'rent lover's praiſe pretend:
But you would ſpoil an *admirable* friend. *Dry. Aurengz.*

A'DMIRABLENESS. *n. ſ.* [from *admirable*.] The quality of being admirable; the power of raiſing wonder.

ADMIRABI'LITY. *n. ſ.* [*admirabilis*, Lat.] The quality or ſtate of being admirable. *Dict.*

A'DMIRABLY. *adv.* [from *admirable*.] So as to raiſe wonder; in an admirable manner.

The theatre is, I think, the moſt ſpacious of any I ever ſaw, and, at the ſame time, ſo *admirably* well contrived, that, from the very depth of the ſtage, the loweſt ſound may be heard diſtinctly to the fartheſt part of the audience, as in a whiſpering place; and yet, if you raiſe your voice as high as you pleaſe, there is nothing like an echo to cauſe in it the leaſt confuſion. *Addiſon on Italy.*

A'DMIRAL. *n. ſ.* [*amiral*, Fr. of uncertain etymology.]

1. An officer or magiſtrate that has the government of the king's navy, and the hearing and determining all cauſes, as well civil as criminal, belonging to the ſea. *Cowell.*

2. The chief commander of a fleet.

He alſo, in battle at ſea, overthrew Rodericus Rotundus, *admiral* of Spain; in which fight the *admiral*, with his ſon, were both ſlain, and ſeven of his gallies taken. *Knolles's Hiſt. Turks.*

Make the ſea ſhine with gallantry, and all
The Engliſh youth flock to their *admiral*. *Waller.*

3. The ſhip which carries the admiral or commander of the fleet.

The *admiral* galley, wherein the emperor himſelf was, by great miſchance ſtruck upon a ſand. *Knolles's Hiſt. of the Turks.*

A'DMIRALSHIP. *n. ſ.* [from *admiral*.] The office or power of an admiral.

ADMIRA'LTY. *n. ſ.* [*amirauté*, Fr.] The power, or officers, appointed for the adminiſtration of naval affairs.

ADMIRA'TION. *n. ſ.* [*admiratio*, Lat.]

1. Wonder; the act of admiring or wondering.

Indu'd with human voice, and human ſenſe,
Reaſoning to *admiration*. *Milton's Paradiſe Loſt, b.* ix.

They are imitations of the paſſions, which always move, and therefore, conſequently, pleaſe; for, without motion, there can be no delight; which cannot be conſidered but as an active paſſion. When we view thoſe elevated ideas of nature, the reſult of that view is *admiration*, which is always the cauſe of pleaſure. *Dryd. Dufreſnoy, Pref.*

There is a pleaſure in *admiration*, and this is that which properly cauſeth *admiration*, when we diſcover a great deal in an object, which we underſtand to be excellent; and yet we ſee, we know not how much more beyond that, which our underſtandings cannot fully reach and comprehend. *Tillotſon's Serm.*

2. It is taken ſometimes in a bad ſenſe, though generally in a good.

Your boldneſs I with *admiration* ſee;
What hope had you to gain a queen like me?
Becauſe a hero forc'd me once away,
Am I thought fit to be a ſecond prey? *Dryden.*

To ADMI'RE. *v. a.* [*admiro*, Lat. *admirer*, Fr.]

1. To regard with wonder; generally in a good ſenſe.

'Tis here that knowledge wonders, and there is an admiration that is not the daughter of ignorance. This indeed ſtupidly gazeth at the unwonted effect; but the philoſophic paſſion truly *admires* and adores the ſupreme efficient. *Glanville.*

2. It is ſometimes uſed, in more familiar ſpeech, for *to regard with love.*

3. It is uſed, but rarely, in an ill ſenſe.

You have diſplac'd the mirth, broke the good meeting
With moſt *admir'd* diſorder. *Shakeſp. Macbeth.*

To ADMI'RE. *v. n.* To wonder; sometimes with the particle *at.*

The eye is already so perfect, that I believe the reason of a man would easily have rested here, and *admir'd at* his own contrivance. *Ray on the Creation.*

An ADMI'RER. *n. s.* [from *admire.*]

1. The person that wonders, or regards with admiration.

Neither Virgil nor Horace would have gained so great reputation, had they not been the friends and *admirers* of each other. *Addison, Spectator.*

Who most to shun or hate mankind pretend,
Seek an *admirer*, or would fix a friend. *Pope's Essay on Man.*

2. In common speech, a lover.

ADMI'RINGLY. *adv.* [from *admire.*] With admiration; in the manner of an admirer.

The king very lately spoke of him *admiringly* and mournfully. *Shakespeare's All's well that ends well.*

We may yet further *admiringly* observe, that though men usually give freeliest where they have not given before, and make it an excuse of their desistance from giving, that they have given it otherwise. *Boyle.*

ADMI'SSIBLE. *adj.* [*admitto, admissum,* Lat.] That which may be admitted.

Suppose that this supposition were *admissible*, yet this would not any way be inconsistent with the eternity of the divine nature and essence. *Hale's Origin of Mankind.*

ADMI'SSION. *n. s.* [*admissio,* Lat.]

1. The act or practice of admitting.

There was also enacted that charitable law, for the *admission* of poor suitors without fee; whereby poor men became rather able to vex, than unable to sue. *Bacon's Henry VII.*

By means of our solitary situation, and our rare *admission* of strangers, we know most part of the habitable world, and are ourselves unknown. *Bacon's New Atalantis.*

2. The state of being admitted.

My father saw you ill designs pursue;
And my *admission* show'd his fear of you. *Dryd. Aurengzebe.*

God did then exercise man's hopes with the expectations of a better paradise, or a more intimate *admission* to himself. *South's Sermons.*

3. Admittance; the power of entering, or being admitted.

All springs have some degree of heat, none ever freezing, no not in the longest and severest frosts; especially those, where there is such a site and disposition of the strata as gives free and easy *admission* to this heat. *Woodward's Natural History.*

Our king descends from Jove:
And hither are we come, by his command,
To crave *admission* in your happy land. *Dryd. Æneid* vii.

4. In the ecclesiastical law.

It is, when the patron presents a clerk to a church that is vacant, and the bishop, upon examination, admits and allows of such clerk to be fitly qualified, by saying, *Admitto te habilem, &c. Ayliffe's Parergon.*

5. The allowance of an argument; the grant of a position not fully proved.

To ADMIT. *v. a.* [*admitto,* Lat.]

1. To suffer to enter; to grant entrance.

Does not one table Bavius still *admit?*

2. To suffer to enter upon an office; in which sense, the phrase of *admission into a college,* &c. is used.

The treasurer found it no hard matter so far to terrify him, that, for the king's service, as was pretended, he *admitted*, for a six-clerk, a person recommended by him. *Clarendon.*

3. To allow an argument or position.

Suppose no weapon can thy valour's pride
Subdue, that by no force thou may'st be won,
Admit no steel can hurt or wound thy side,
And be it heav'n hath thee such favour done. *Fairfax, b.* ii.

This argument is like to have the less effect on me, seeing I cannot easily *admit* the inference. *Locke.*

4. To allow, or grant in general; sometimes with the particle *of.*

If you once *admit* of a latitude, that thoughts may be exalted, and images raised above the life, that leads you insensibly from your own principles to mine. *Dryden on Heroic Poetry.*

ADMI'TTABLE. *adj.* [from *admit.*] The person or thing which may be admitted.

The clerk, who is presented, ought to prove to the bishop, that he is a deacon, and that he has orders; otherwise, the bishop is not bound to admit him: for, as the law then stood, a deacon was *admittable. Ayliffe's Parergon Juris Canonici.*

ADMI'TTANCE. *n. s.* [from *admit.*]

1. The act of admitting; allowance or permission to enter.

It cannot enter any man's conceit to think it lawful, that every man which listeth should take upon him charge in the church; and therefore a solemn *admittance* is of such necessity, that, without it, there can be no church-polity. *Hooker b.* iii.

As to the *admittance* of the weighty elastic parts of the air into the blood through the coats of the vessels, it seems contrary to experiments upon dead bodies. *Arbuthnot on Aliments.*

2. The power or right of entering.

What
If I do line one of their hands?——'tis gold
Which buys *admittance. Shakespeare's Cymbeline.*

Surely a daily expectation at the gate, is the readiest way to gain *admittance* into the house. *South's Sermons.*

There's news from Bertran; he desires
Admittance to the king, and cries aloud,
This day shall end our fears. *Dryden's Spanish Friar.*

There are some ideas which have *admittance* only through one sense, which is peculiarly adapted to receive them. *Locke.*

3. Custom, or prerogative, of being admitted to great persons; a sense now out of use.

Now, Sir John, here is the heart of my purpose: you are a gentleman of excellent breeding, of great *admittance*, authentick in your place and person, generally allowed for your many warlike, courtlike, and learned preparations. *Shakespeare's Merry Wives of Windsor.*

4. Concession of a position.

Nor could the Pythagorean give easy *admittance* thereto; for, holding that separate souls successively supplied other bodies, they could hardly allow the raising of souls from other worlds. *Brown's Vulgar Errours, b.* i.

To ADMI'X. *v. a.* [*admisceo,* Lat.] To mingle with something else.

ADMI'XTION. *n. s.* [from *admix.*] The union of one body with another, by mingling them.

All metals may be calcined by strong waters, or by *admixtion* of salt, sulphur, and mercury. *Bacon's Physical Remains.*

The elements are no where pure in these lower regions; and if there is any free from the *admixtion* of another, sure it is above the concave of the moon. *Glanville's Scepsis Scientifica.*

There is no way to make a strong and vigorous powder of saltpetre, without the *admixtion* of sulphur. *Brown's Vulg. Err.*

ADMI'XTURE. *n. s.* [from *admix.*] The body mingled with another; perhaps sometimes the act of mingling.

A mass which to the eye appears to be nothing but mere simple earth, shall, to the smell or taste, discover a plentiful *admixture* of sulphur, alum, or some other mineral. *Woodward's Natural History, p.* iv.

Whatever acrimony, or amaritude, at any time redounds in it, must be derived from the *admixture* of another sharp bitter substance. *Harvey on Consumptions.*

To ADMO'NISH. *v. a.* [*admoneo,* Lat.]

To warn of a fault; to reprove gently; to counsel against wrong practices; to put in mind of a fault or a duty; with the particle *of*, or *against*, which is more rare, or the infinitive mood of a verb.

One of his cardinals, who better knew the intrigues of affairs, *admonished* him *against* that unskilful piece of ingenuity. *Decay of Piety.*

He of their wicked ways
Shall them *admonish*, and before them set
The paths of righteousness. *Milt. Par. Lost, b.* xi.

But when he was *admonished* by his subject *to descend*, he come down, gently circling in the air, and singing, to the ground. *Dryden's Dedication of Virgil's Past.*

ADMO'NISHER. *n. s.* [from *admonish.*] The person that admonishes, or puts another in mind of his faults or duty.

Horace was a mild *admonisher*; a court-satyrist fit for the gentle times of Augustus. *Dryden's Juvenal, Dedicat.*

ADMO'NISHMENT. *n. s.* [from *admonish.*] Admonition; the notice by which one is put in mind of faults or duties: a word not often used.

But yet be wary in thy studious care.—
—Thy grave *admonishments* prevail with me. *Shakespeare's Henry V. p.* i.

To th' infinitely Good we owe
Immortal thanks, and his *admonishment*
Receive, with solemn purpose to observe
Immutably his sovereign will, the end
Of what we are. *Milton's Paradise Lost, b.* vii. *l.* 77.

ADMONI'TION. *n. s.* [*admonitio,* Lat.] The hint of a fault or duty; counsel; gentle reproof.

They must give our teachers leave, for the saving of those souls, to intermingle sometimes, with other more necessary things, *admonition* concerning these not unnecessary. *Hooker.*

From this *admonition* they took only occasion to redouble their fault, and to sleep again; so that, upon a second and third *admonition*, they had nothing to plead for their unseasonable drowsiness. *South's Sermons.*

ADMONI'TIONER. *n. s.* [from *admonition.*] A liberal dispenser of admonition; a general adviser. A ludicrous term.

Albeit the *admonitioners* did seem at first to like no prescript form of prayer at all, but thought it the best that their minister should always be left at liberty to pray, as his own discretion did serve, their defender, and his associates, have since proposed to the world a form as themselves did like. *Hooker, b.* v. § 27.

ADMO'NITORY. *adj.* [*admonitorius,* Lat.] That which admonishes.

The sentence of reason is either mandatory, shewing what must be done; or else permissive, declaring only what may be done; or, thirdly, *admonitory*, opening what is the most convenient for us to do. *Hooker's Ecclesiastical Polity, b.* i.

ADMURMURA'TION. *n. s.* [*admurmuro,* Lat.] The act of murmuring, or whispering to another. *Dict.*

To

To ADMO'VE. *v. a.* [*admoveo*, Lat.] To bring one thing to another.

If, unto the powder of loadstone or iron, we *admove* the north-pole of the loadstone, the powders, or small divisions, will erect and conform themselves thereto. *Brown's Vulgar Errours, b.* ii.

ADO'. *n. s.* [from the verb *to do*, with *a* before it, as the French *affaire*, from *à* and *faire*.]

1. Trouble, difficulty.

He took Clitophon prisoner, whom, with much *ado*, he keepeth alive; the Helots being villainously cruel. *Sidney, b.* i.

They moved, and in the end persuaded, with much *ado*, the people to bind themselves by solemn oath. *Hooker, Pref.*

He kept the borders and marches of the pale with much *ado*; he held many parliaments, wherein sundry laws were made. *Sir John Davies on Ireland.*

With much *ado*, he partly kept awake;
Not suff'ring all his eyes repose to take:
And ask'd the stranger, who did reeds invent,
And whence began so rare an instrument. *Dryden.*

2. Bustle; tumult; business; sometimes with the particle *about*.

Let's follow, to see the end of this *ado*. *Shakesp. Taming of the Shrew.*

All this *ado about* Adam's fatherhood, and the greatness of its power, helps nothing to establish the power of those that govern. *Locke.*

3. It has a light and ludicrous sense, implying more tumult and shew of business, than the affair is worth; in this sense it is generally used.

I made no more *ado*, but took all their seven points in my target, thus. *Shakesp. Henry* IV.

We'll keep no great *ado*—a friend or two—
For, hark, Tybalt being slain so late,
It may be thought we held him carelesly,
Being our kinsman, if we revel much. *Shakesp. Rom. and Jul.*

Come, come, says Puss, without any more *ado*, 'tis time for me to go to breakfast; for cats don't live upon dialogues. *L'Estrange, Fab.* ii.

ADOLE'SCENCE. *n. s.* [*adolescentia*, Lat.]

The age succeeding childhood, and succeeded by puberty; more largely, that part of life in which the body has not yet reached its full perfection. See ADOLESCENCY.

The sons must have a tedious time of childhood and *adolescence*, before they can either themselves assist their parents, or encourage them with new hopes of posterity. *Bentley's Serm.*

ADOLE'SCENCY. *n. s.* The same with *adolescence*.

He was so far from a boy, that he was a man born, and at his full stature, if we believe Josephus, who places him in the last *adolescency*, and makes him twenty-five years old. *Brown's Vulgar Errours, b.* v. *c.* 8.

To ADO'PT. *v. a.* [*adopto*, Lat.]

1. To take a son by choice; to make him a son, who was not so by birth.

Were none of all my father's sisters left;
Nay, were I of my mother's kin bereft;
None by an uncle's or a grandame's side,
Yet I cou'd some *adopted* heir provide. *Dryd. Pers. Sat* vi.

2. To place any person or thing in a nearer relation, than they have by nature, to something else.

Whether, *adopted* to some neighb'ring star,
Thou roll'st above us, in thy wand'ring race,
Or, in procession fix'd and regular,
Mov'd with the heav'ns majestic pace;
Or call'd to more celestial bliss,
Thou tread'st, with seraphims, the vast abyss. *Dryd.*

We are seldom at ease from the solicitation of our natural or *adopted* desires; but a constant succession of uneasinesses, out of that stock, which natural wants, or acquired habits, have heaped up, take the will in their turns. *Locke.*

ADO'PTEDLY. *adv.* [from *adopted.*] After the manner of something adopted.

Adoptedly, as school-maids change their names,
By vain, though apt, affection. *Shakesp. Measure for Meas.*

ADO'PTER. *n. s.* [from *adopt.*]

He that gives some one by choice the rights of a son.

ADO'PTION. *n. s.* [*adoptio*, Lat.]

1. The act of adopting, or taking to one's self what is not native.

See the hell of having a false woman! My bed shall be abused, my coffers ransacked, my reputation gnawn at; and I shall not only receive this villainous wrong, but stand under the *adoption* of abominable terms, and by him that does me the wrong. *Shakesp. Merry Wives of Windsor.*

2. The state of being adopted.

In which time she purpos'd,
By watching, weeping, tendance, kissing, to
O'ercome you with her shew: yes, and in time
(When she had fitted you with her craft) to work
Her son into th' *adoption* of the crown. *Shakesp. Cymbeline.*

In every act of our christian worship, we are taught to call upon him under the endearing character of our Father, to remind us of our *adoption*, that we are made heirs of God, and joint heirs of Christ. *Rogers's Sermons.*

ADO'PTIVE. *adj.* [*adoptivus*, Lat.]

1. He that is adopted by another, and made his son.

It is impossible an elective monarch should be so free and absolute as an hereditary; no more than it is possible for a father to have so full power and interest in an *adoptive* son, as in a natural. *Bacon's Considerations on a War with Spain.*

2. He that adopts another, and makes him his son.

An adopted son cannot cite his *adoptive* father into court, without his leave. *Ayliffe's Parergon Juris Canonici.*

ADO'RABLE. *adj.* [*adorable*, Fr.] That which ought to be adored; that which is worthy of divine honours.

On these two, *viz.* the love of God, and our neighbour, hang both the law and the prophets, says the *adorable* Author of christianity; and the Apostle says, the end of the law is charity. *Cheyne's Philosophical Principles.*

ADO'RABLENESS. *n. s.* [from *adorable.*] The quality of being adorable; worthiness of divine honours.

ADO'RABLY. *adv.* [from *adorable.*] In a manner worthy of adoration.

ADORA'TION. *n. s.* [*adoratio*, Lat.]

1. The external homage paid to the Divinity, distinct from mental reverence.

Solemn and serviceable worship we name, for distinction sake, whatsoever belongeth to the church, or publick society, of God, by way of external *adoration*. *Hooker, b.* v. § 4.

It is possible to suppose, that those who believe a supreme excellent Being, may yet give him no external *adoration* at all. *Stillingfleet's Defence of Discourses on Rom. Idolatry.*

2. Homage paid to persons in high place or esteem.

O ceremony, shew me but thy worth:
What is thy toll, O *adoration!*
Art thou nought else but place, degree, and form,
Creating awe and fear in other men?
Wherein thou art less happy, being fear'd,
Than they in fearing.
What drink'st thou oft, instead of homage sweet,
But poison'd flattery? *Shakespeare's Henry* V.

To ADO'RE. *v. a.* [*adoro*, Lat.]

1. To worship with external homage; to pay divine honours.

The mountain nymphs and Themis they *adore*,
And from her oracles relief implore. *Dryden.*

2. It is used, popularly, to denote a high degree of reverence or regard; to reverence; to honour; to love.

The people appear *adoring* their prince, and their prince *adoring* God. *Tatler,* N° 57.

ADO'REMENT. *n. s.* [from *adore.*] Adoration; worship: a word scarcely used.

The priests of elder times deluded their apprehensions with sooth-saying, and such oblique idolatries, and won their credulities to the literal and downright *adorement* of cats, lizzards, and beetles. *Brown's Vulgar Errours, b.* i. *c.* 3.

ADO'RER. *n. s.* [from *adore.*]

He that adores; a worshiper: a term generally used in a low sense; as, by lovers, or admirers.

Being so far provoked as I was in France, I would abate her nothing; though I profess myself her *adorer*, not her friend. *Shakespeare's Cymbeline.*

Whilst as th' approaching pageant does appear,
And echoing crouds speak mighty Venus near;
I, her *adorer*, too devoutly stand
Fast on the utmost margin of the land. *Prior.*

2. A worshipper, in a serious sense.

He was so severe an *adorer* of truth, as not to dissemble; or to suffer any man to think that he would do any thing, which he resolved not to do. *Clarendon.*

To ADO'RN. *v. a.* [*adorno*, Lat.]

1. To dress; to deck the person with ornaments.

He hath clothed me with the garments of salvation, he hath covered me with the robe of righteousness, as a bridegroom decketh himself with ornaments, and as a bride *adorneth* herself with her jewels. *Isaiah*, lxi. 10.

Yet 'tis not to *adorn* and gild each part,
That shews more cost than art;
Jewels at nose and lips, but ill appear. *Cowley.*

2. To set out any place or thing with decorations.

A gallery *adorned* with the pictures or statues of the invention of things useful to human life. *Cowley.*

3. To embellish with oratory or elegance of language.

This will supply men's tongues with many new things, to be named, *adorned*, and described, in their discourse. *Sprat's History of the Royal Society.*

Thousands there are in darker fame that dwell,
Whose names some nobler poem shall *adorn*;
For, though unknown to me, they sure fought well. *Dryd.*

ADO'RNMENT. *n. s.* [from *adorn.*] Ornament; embellishment; elegance

Which attribute was not given to the earth, while it was confused; nor to the heavens, before they had motion and *adornment*. *Raleigh's History of the World.*

She held the very garment of Posthumus in more respect than my noble and natural person, together with the *adornment* of my qualities. *Shakespeare's Cymbeline.*

ADO'WN. *adv.* [from *a* and *down.*] Down; on the ground.

Thrice did ſhe ſink *adown* in deadly ſound,
And thrice he her reviv'd with buſy pain. *Fairy Queen, b.* i.

Ado'wn. *prep.* Down; towards the ground; from a higher ſituation towards a lower.

In this remembrance Emily ere day
Aroſe, and dreſs'd herſelf in rich array;
Freſh as the month, and as the morning fair,
Adown her ſhoulders fell her length of hair. *Dryd. Fables.*

Adre'ad. *adv.* [from *a* and *dread*; as, *aſide, athirſt, aſleep.*] In a ſtate of fear; frighted; terrified: now obſolete.

And thinking to make all men *adread* to ſuch a one an enemy, who would not ſpare, nor fear to kill ſo great a prince. *Sidney, b.* ii.

Adri'ft. *adv.* [from *a* and *drift*, from *drive.*] Floating at random; as, any impulſe may drive.

Then, ſhall this mount
Of paradiſe, by might of waves, be mov'd
Out of his place, puſh'd by the horned flood;
With all his verdure ſpoil'd, and trees *adrift*
Down the great river, to the opening gulf,
And there take root. *Milton's Paradiſe Loſt, b.* xi. *l.* 832.

It ſeem'd a corps *adrift* to diſtant ſight;
But at a diſtance who could judge aright. *Dryd. Fables.*

The cuſtom of frequent reflection will keep their minds from running *adrift*, and call their thoughts home from uſeleſs unattentive roving. *Locke on Education,* § 176.

ADRO'IT. adj. [French.] Dextrous; active; ſkilful.

An *adroit* ſtout fellow would ſometimes deſtroy a whole family, with juſtice apparently againſt him the whole time. *Jervas's Introduct. to Don Quixote.*

Adro'itness. *n. ſ.* [from *adroit.*] Dexterity; readineſs; activity. Neither this word, nor *adroit*, ſeem yet completely naturalized.

Adry'. *adv.* [from *a* and *dry.*] Athirſt; thirſty; in want of drink.

He never told any of them, that he was his humble ſervant, but his well-wiſher; and would rather be thought a malecontent, than drink the king's health when he was not *adry. Spect.*

Adsciti'tious. *adj.* [*adſcititius*, Lat.] That which is taken in to complete ſomething elſe, though originally extrinſick; ſupplemental; additional.

Adstri'ction. *n. ſ.* [*adſtrictio*, Lat.] The act of binding together; and applied, generally, to medicaments and applications, which have the power of making the part contract.

To ADVA'NCE. *v. a.* [*avancer*, Fr.]

1. To bring forward, in the local ſenſe.

Now morn, her roſy ſteps in th' eaſtern clime
Advancing, ſow'd the earth with orient pearl. *Parad. Loſt.*

2. To raiſe to preferment; to aggrandize.

The declaration of the greatneſs of Mordecai, whereunto the king *advanced* him. *Eſther,* x. 2.

3. To improve.

What laws can be adviſed more proper and effectual to *advance* the nature of man to its higheſt perfection, than theſe precepts of chriſtianity? *Tillotſon.*

4. To heighten; to grace; to give luſtre to.

As the calling dignifies the man, ſo the man much more *advances* his calling. As a garment, though it warms the body, has a return with an advantage, being much more warmed by it. *South's Sermons.*

5. To forward; to accelerate.

Theſe three laſt were ſlower than the ordinary Indian wheat of itſelf; and this culture did rather retard than *advance. Bacon.*

6. To propoſe; to offer to the publick.

I dare not *advance* my opinion againſt the judgment of ſo great an author; but I think it fair to leave the deciſion to the publick. *Dryden's Fables, Pref.*

Some ne'er *advance* a judgment of their own,
But catch the ſpreading notion of the town. *Pop. Eſſ. on Crit.*

To Adva'nce. *v. n.*

1. To come forward.

At this the youth, whoſe vent'rous ſoul
No fears of magick art controul,
Advanc'd in open ſight. *Parnel.*

2. To make improvement.

They who would *advance* in knowledge, and not deceive and ſwell themſelves with a little articulated air, ſhould not take words for real entities in nature, till they can frame clear and diſtinct ideas of thoſe entities. *Locke.*

Adva'nce. *n. ſ.* [from *to advance.*]

1. The act of coming forward.

All the foot were put into Abington, with a reſolution to quit, or defend, the town, according to the manner of the enemy's *advance* towards it. *Clarendon, b.* viii.

So, like the ſun's *advance*, your titles ſhow;
Which, as he riſes, does the warmer grow. *Waller.*

2. A tendency to come forward to meet a lover; an act of invitation.

In vain are all the practis'd wiles,
In vain thoſe eyes would love impart;
Not all th' *advances*, all the ſmiles,
Can move one unrelenting heart. *Walſh.*

His genius was below
The ſkill of ev'ry common beau;
Who, tho' he cannot ſpell, is wiſe
Enough to read a lady's eyes;
And will each accidental glance
Interpret for a kind *advance*. *Swift's Miſcell.*

He has deſcribed the unworthy paſſion of the goddeſs Calypſo, and the indecent *advances* ſhe made to detain him from his own country. *Pope's Odyſſey, b.* vii. *notes.*

3. Progreſſion; riſe from one point to another.

Our Saviour raiſed the ruler's daughter, the widow's ſon, and Lazarus; the firſt of theſe, when ſhe had juſt expired; the ſecond, as he was carried to the grave on his bier; and the third, after he had been ſome time buried. And having, by theſe gradual *advances*, manifeſted his divine power, he at laſt exerted the higheſt and moſt glorious degree of it; and raiſed himſelf alſo by his own all-quickening virtue, and according to his own expreſs prediction. *Atterbury's Sermons.*

Men of ſtudy and thought, that reaſon right, and are lovers of truth, do make no great *advances* in their diſcoveries of it. *Locke of Human Underſtanding,* § 3.

4. Improvement; progreſs towards perfection.

The principle and object of the greateſt importance in the world to the good of mankind, and for the *advance* and perfecting of human nature. *Hale's Origin of Mankind.*

Adva'ncement. *n. ſ.* [*avancement*, Fr.]

1. The act of coming forward.

This refinement having begun about the time of the revolution, I had ſome ſhare in the honour of promoting it; and I obſerve, that it makes daily *advancements*, and, I hope, in time, will raiſe our language to the utmoſt perfection. *Swift.*

2. The ſtate of being advanced; preferment.

During whoſe reign, the Percies of the North
Finding his uſurpation moſt unjuſt,
Endeavour'd my *advancement* to the throne.
Shakeſpeare's Henry VI. *p.* i.

3. The act of advancing another.

In his own grace he doth exalt himſelf
More than in your *advancement*. *Shakeſpeare's K. Lear.*

4. Improvement.

Nor can we conceive it may be unwelcome unto thoſe honoured worthies, who endeavour the *advancement* of learning. *Brown's Pref. to Vulgar Errours.*

Adva'ncer. *n. ſ.* [from *advance.*] He that advances any thing; a promoter; forwarder.

Soon after the death of a great officer, who was judged no *advancer* of the king's matters, the king ſaid to his ſolicitor Bacon, who was his kinſman, How, tell me truly, what ſay you of your couſin that is gone? *Bacon's Apothegms.*

Let us add only this concerning this latter ſort, that they are greater *advancers* of defamatory deſigns, than the very firſt contrivers. *Government of the Tongue,* § 5.

ADVA'NTAGE. *n. ſ.* [*avantage*, Fr.]

1. Superiority; often with *of* or *over* before a perſon.

In the practical prudence of managing ſuch gifts, the laity may have ſome *advantage over* the clergy; whoſe experience is, and ought to be, leſs of this world than the others. *Sprat.*

All other ſorts and ſects of men would evidently have the *advantage of* us, and a much ſurer title to happineſs than we. *Atterbury's Preface to his Sermons.*

2. Superiority gained by ſtratagem, or unlawful means.

The common law hath left them this benefit, whereof they make *advantage*, and wreſt it to their bad purpoſes. *Spenſer's State of Ireland.*

But ſpecially he took *advantage* of the night for ſuch privy attempts, inſomuch that the bruit of his manlineſs was ſpread every-where. 2 *Macc.* viii. 7.

It is a noble and a ſure defiance of a great malice, backed with a great intereſt; which yet can have no *advantage* of a man, but from his own expectations of ſomething that is without him. *South's Sermons.*

As ſoon as he was got to Sicily, they ſent for him back; deſigning to take *advantage*, and proſecute him in the abſence of his friends. *Swift on the Diſſent. in Athens and Rome.*

3. Opportunity; convenience.

I beſeech you,
If you think fit, or that it may be done,
Give me *advantage* of ſome brief diſcourſe
With Deſdemona alone. *Shakeſpeare's Othello.*

4. Favourable circumſtances.

Like jewels to *advantage* ſet,
Her beauty by the ſhade does get. *Waller.*

A face, which is over-fluſhed, appears to *advantage* in the deepeſt ſcarlet, and the darkeſt complexion is not a little alleviated by a black hood. *Addiſon. Spectator,* N° 265.

True wit is nature to *advantage* dreſs'd,
What oft was thought, but ne'er ſo well expreſs'd.
Pope's Eſſay on Criticiſm.

5. Gain; profit.

For thou ſaidſt, what *advantage* will it be unto thee, and what profit ſhall I have, if I be cleanſed from my ſin? *Job,* xxxv. 3.

Certain

Certain it is, that *advantage* now sits in the room of conscience, and steers all. *South's Sermons.*

6. Overplus; something more than the mere lawful gain.

O my gentle Hubert,
We owe thee much; within this wall of flesh
There is a soul counts thee her creditor,
And with *advantage* means to pay thy love.
Shakespeare's King John.

You said, you neither lend nor borrow
Upon *advantage*. *Shakesp. Merchant of Venice.*

7. Preponderation on one side of the comparison.

Much more should the consideration of this pattern arm us with patience against ordinary calamities; especially if we consider his example with this *advantage*, that though his sufferings were wholly undeserved, and not for himself but for us, yet he bore them patiently. *Tillotson.*

To ADVA'NTAGE. *v. a.* [from the noun.]

1. To benefit.

Convey what I set down to my lady: it shall *advantage* more than ever the bearing of letter did. *Shakespeare's Twelfth-Night.*

The great business of the senses being to make us take notice of what hurts or *advantages* the body, it is wisely ordered by nature, that pain should accompany the reception of several ideas. *Locke.*

We should have pursued some other way, more effectual, for distressing the common enemy, and *advantaging* ourselves. *Swift.*

The trial hath endamag'd thee no way,
Rather more honour left, and more esteem;
Me naught *advantag'd*, missing what I aim'd. *Par. Regained.*

2. To promote; to bring forward; to gain ground.

To ennoble it with the spirit that inspires the Royal Society, were to *advantage* it in one of the best capacities in which it is improveable. *Glanville's Scepsis Scientifica, Pref.*

ADVA'NTAGED. *adj.* [from *to advantage.*]

Possessed of advantages.

In the most *advantaged* tempers, this disposition is but comparative; whereas the most of men labour under disadvantages, which nothing can rid them off. *Glanv. Scepsis Scientifica.*

ADVA'NTAGE-GROUND. *n. s.* Ground that gives superiority, and opportunities of annoyance or resistance.

This excellent man, who stood not upon the *advantage-ground* before, from the time of his promotion to the archbishoprick, or rather from that of his being commissioner of the treasury, exceedingly provoked, or underwent the envy, and reproach, and malice of men of all qualities and conditions; who agreed in nothing else. *Clarendon.*

ADVANTA'GEOUS. *adj.* [*avantageux*, Fr.]

1. Of advantage; profitable; useful; opportune; convenient.

The time of sickness, or affliction, is, like the cool of the day to Adam, a season of peculiar propriety for the voice of God to be heard; and may be improved into a very *advantageous* opportunity of begetting or increasing spiritual life in the soul. *Hammond's Fundamentals.*

Here perhaps
Some *advantageous* act may be atchiev'd
By sudden onset, either with hell-fire
To waste his whole creation; or possess
All as our own. *Milton's Paradise Lost, b.* ii. *l.* 363.

2. It is used with relation to persons, and followed by *to*.

Since every painter paints himself in his own works, 'tis *advantageous to* him to know himself, to the end that he may cultivate those talents which make his genius. *Dryd. Dufresnoy.*

ADVANTA'GEOUSLY. *adv.* [from *advantageous.*]

Conveniently; opportunely; profitably.

It was *advantageously* situated, there being an easy passage from it to Ægypt, Æthiopia, Persia, and India, by sea. *Arbuth.*

ADVANTA'GEOUSNESS. *n. s.* [from *advantageous.*]

Quality of being advantageous; profitableness; usefulness; convenience.

The last property, which qualifies God for the fittest object of our love, is, the *advantageousness* of his to us, both in the present and the future life. *Boyle's Seraphic Love.*

To ADVE'NE. *v. n.* [*advenio*, Lat.]

To accede to something; to become part of something else, without being essential; to be superadded.

A sixth cause considered in judicature, is stiled an accidental cause; and the accidental of any act, is said to be whatever *advenes* to the act itself already substantiated. *Ayliffe's Parergon.*

ADVE'NIENT. *adj.* [*adveniens*, Lat.]

Advening; coming from outward causes; superadded.

If to suppose the soul a distinct substance from the body, and extrinsecally *advenient*, be a great error in philosophy, almost all the world hath hitherto been mistaken. *Glanville's Vanity of Dogmatism.*

Being thus divided from truth in themselves, they are yet farther removed by *advenient* deception; for they are daily mocked into error by subtler devisers. *Brown's Vulg. Errours.*

A'DVENT. *n. s.* [from *adventus*; that is, *adventus Redemptoris.*]

The name of one of the holy seasons, signifying the *coming*; that is, the *coming* of our Saviour; which is made the subject of our devotion during the four weeks before Christmas.

ADVE'NTINE. *adj.* [from *advenio, adventum.*]

Adventitious; that which is extrinsically added; that which comes from outward causes: a word scarcely in use.

As for the peregrine heat, it is thus far true, that, if the proportion of the *adventine* heat be greatly predominant to the natural heat and spirits of the body, it tendeth to dissolution or notable alteration. *Bacon's Natural History,* N° 836.

ADVENTI'TIOUS. *adj.* [*adventitius*, Lat.]

That which advenes; accidental; supervenient; extrinsically added, not essentially inherent.

Diseases of continuance get an *adventitious* strength from custom, besides their material cause from the humours. *Bacon.*

Though we may call the obvious colours natural, and the others *adventitious*; yet such changes of colours, from whatsoever cause they proceed, may be properly enough taken in, to illustrate the present subject. *Boyle on Colours.*

If his blood boil, and th' *adventitious* fire
Rais'd by high meats, and higher wines, require
To temper and allay the burning heat;
Waters are brought, which by decoction get
New coolness. *Dryd. Juvenal, Sat.* v.

Of this we have an instance in the gem-kind; where, of all the many sorts reckoned up by lapidaries, there are not above three or four that are original; their diversities, as to lustre, colour, and hardness, arising from the different admixture of other *adventitious* mineral matter. *Woodward's Natural Hist.*

ADVE'NTIVE. *n. s.* [from *advenio*, Lat.] The thing or person that comes from without: a word not now in use.

That the natives be not so many, but that there may be elbow-room enough for them, and for the *adventives* also. *Bacon's Advice to Sir George Villiers.*

ADVE'NTUAL. *adj.* [from *advent.*]

Relating to the season of advent.

I do also daily use one other collect; as, namely, the collects *advental*, quadragesimal, paschal, or pentecostal, for their proper seasons. *Bishop Saunderson upon Submission to Usurpers.*

ADVE'NTURE. *n. s.* [French.]

1. An accident; a chance; a hazard; an event of which we have no direction.

The general summoned three castles that were near: one desperate of succour, and not desirous to dispute the defence, presently yielded; but two stood upon their *adventure*. *Sir John Hayward.*

2. In this sense is used the phrase, *at all adventures*; [*à l'adventure*, Fr.] By chance; without any rational scheme.

Blows flew *at all adventures*, wounds and deaths given and taken unexpected; many scarce knowing their enemies from their friends. *Sir John Hayward.*

Where the mind does not perceive this probable connection, there men's opinions are the effects of chance and hazard, of a mind floating *at all adventures*, without choice and without direction. *Locke.*

3. The occasion of casual events; an enterprise in which something must be left to hazard.

For I must love, and am resolv'd, to try
My fate, or, failing in th' *adventure*, die. *Dryden's Fables.*

This noun, with all its derivatives, are frequently written without *ad*; as, *venture, venturous.*

To ADVE'NTURE. *v. n.* [*adventurer*, Fr.]

1. To try the chance; to dare.

Be not angry,
Most mighty princess, that I have *adventur'd*
To try your taking of a false report. *Shakesp. Cymbeline.*

The tender and delicate woman among you, which would not *adventure* to set the sole of her foot upon the ground, for delicateness and tenderness. *Deuter.* xxviii. 26.

2. In an active sense, to put into the power of chance.

For my father fought for you, and *adventured* his life for, and delivered you out of the hand of Midian. *Judges*, ix. 17.

3. It is often used with the reciprocal pronoun; as, *he adventured himself.*

ADVE'NTURER. *n. s.* [*adventurier*, Fr.]

He that seeks occasions of hazard; he that puts himself in the hands of chance.

He is a great *adventurer*, said he,
That hath his sword through hard assay forgone,
And now hath vow'd, till he avenged be
Of that despight, never to wear none. *Fairy Queen, b.* ii.

The kings of England did not make the conquest of Ireland their own work; it was begun by particular *adventurers*, and other voluntaries, who came to seek their fortunes in Ireland. *Sir John Davies on Ireland.*

In this action, highly commendable, he intended to hazard his own action, that so the more easily he might win *adventurers*, who else were like to be less forward. *Sir W. Raleigh's Ess.*

Had it not been for the British, which the late wars drew over, and of *adventurers* or soldiers seated here, the country had, by the last war, and plague, been left, in a manner, destitute. *Temple's Miscellanies.*

Their wealthy trade from pirate's rapine free,
Our merchants shall no more *advent'rers* be. *Dryden.*

Adve'nturous. *adj.* [*adventureux*, Fr.]

1. He that is inclined to adventures; and, conſequently, bold, daring, courageous.

  At land and ſea, in many a doubtful fight,
  Was never known a more *advent'rous* knight;
  Who oftner drew his ſword, and always for the right.
  Dryd. Hind and Panther.

2. Applied to things; that which is full of hazard; which requires courage; dangerous.

  But I've already troubled you too long,
  Nor dare attempt a more *advent'rous* ſong.
  My humble verſe demands a ſofter theme;
  A painted meadow, or a purling ſtream. *Addiſon.*

Adve'nturously. *adv.* [from *adventurous.*]

After an adventurous manner; boldly; daringly.

They are both hanged; and ſo would this be, if he durſt ſteal any thing *adventurouſly.* *Shakeſpeare's Henry* V.

Adve'nturesome. *adj.* [from *adventure.*]

The ſame with *adventurous*: a low word, ſcarcely uſed in writing.

Adve'nturesomeness. *n. ſ.* [from *adventureſome*]

The quality of being adventureſome. *Dict.*

A'DVERB. *n. ſ.* [*adverbium*, Lat.]

A word joined to a verb or adjective, and ſolely applied to the uſe of qualifying and reſtraining the latitude of their ſignification, by the intimation of ſome circumſtance thereof; as, of quality, manner, degree. *Clarke's Latin Grammar.*

Thus we ſay, he runs *ſwiftly*; the bird flies *aloft*; he lives *virtuouſly*.

Adve'rbial. *adj.* [*adverbialis*, Lat.]

That which has the quality or ſtructure of an adverb.

Adve'rbially. *adv.* [*adverbialiter*, Lat.]

Like an adverb; in the manner of an adverb.

I ſhould think *alta* was joined *adverbially* with *tremit*, did Virgil make uſe of ſo equivocal a ſyntax. *Addiſ. Rem. on Italy.*

Adve'rsable. *adj.* [from *adverſe.*]

Contrary to; oppoſite to. *Dict.*

ADVERSA'RIA. n. ſ. [Lat. A book, as it ſhould ſeem, in which *Debtor* and *Creditor* were ſet in oppoſition.] A common-place; a book to note in.

Theſe parchments are ſuppoſed to have been St. Paul's *adverſaria.* *Bull's Sermons.*

A'dversary. *n. ſ.* [*adverſaire*, Fr. *adverſarius*, Lat.]

An opponent; antagoniſt; enemy: generally applied to thoſe that have verbal or judicial quarrels; as, controvertiſts or litigants: ſometimes to an opponent in ſingle combat. It may ſometimes imply an open profeſſion of enmity; as we ſay, a ſecret enemy is worſe than an open *adverſary*.

  Yet am I noble, as the *adverſary*
  I come to cope. *Shakeſpeare's King Lear.*

Thoſe rites and ceremonies of the church, therefore, which were the ſelf-ſame now that they were, when holy and virtuous men maintained them againſt profane and deriding *adverſaries*, her own children have in deriſion. *Hooker, b.* i. § 1.

  Mean while th' *adverſary* of God and man,
  Satan, with thoughts inflam'd, of higheſt deſign,
  Puts on ſwift wings. *Milton's Paradiſe Loſt, b.* ii. *l.* 620.

An *adverſary*, on the contrary, makes a ſtricter ſearch into us, and diſcovers every flaw and imperfection in our tempers. A friend exaggerates a man's virtues; an enemy inflames his crimes. *Addiſon. Spectator,* N° 399.

Adve'rsative. *adj.* [*adverſativus*, Lat.]

A term of grammar, applied to a word which makes ſome oppoſition or variety; as in this ſentence: *This diamond is orient*, but *it is rough*. *But* is an *adverſative* conjunction.

A'DVERSE. *adj.* [*adverſus*, Lat.]

In proſe it has now the accent on the firſt ſyllable; in verſe it is accented on the firſt by *Shakeſpeare*; on either, indifferently, by *Milton*; on the laſt, by *Dryden*; on the firſt, by *Roſcommon*.

1. Acting with contrary directions; as, two bodies in colliſion.

  Was I for this nigh wreckt upon the ſea,
  And twice, by *adverſe* winds, from England's bank
  Drove back again unto my native clime. *Shakeſp. Henry* VI.

  As when two polar winds blowing *adverſe*,
  Upon the Cronian ſea together drive
  Mountains of ice. *Milton's Paradiſe Loſt, b.* x. *l.* 289.

  With *adverſe* blaſt up-turns them from the South,
  Notus and Afer. *Ibid. l.* 701.

  A cloud of ſmoke envelopes either hoſt,
  And all at once the combatants are loſt;
  Darkling they join *adverſe*, and ſhock unſeen;
  Courſers with courſers juſtling, men with men. *Dryd.*

2. Figuratively, contrary to the wiſh or deſire; thence, calamitous; afflictive; pernicious. It is oppoſed to *proſperous*.

  What if he hath decreed, that I ſhall firſt
  Be try'd in humble ſtate, and things *adverſe*;
  By tribulations, injuries, inſults,
  Contempts, and ſcorns, and ſnares, and violence. *Par. Reg.*

  Some the prevailing malice of the great,
  Unhappy men, or *adverſe* fate,
  Sunk deep into the gulfs of an afflicted ſtate. *Roſcommon.*

3. Perſonally opponent; the perſon that counteracts another, or conteſts any thing.

Well ſhe ſaw her father was grown her *adverſe* party; and yet her fortune ſuch, as ſhe muſt favour her rivals. *Sidney.*

Adve'rsity. *n. ſ.* [*adverſité*, Fr.]

Affliction; calamity; that is, oppoſition to our wiſhes.

1. The cauſe of our ſorrow; affliction; misfortune. In this ſenſe it may have a plural.

  Let me embrace theſe ſour *adverſities*,
  For wiſe men ſay, it is the wiſeſt courſe. *Shakeſp. Hen.* VI.

2. The ſtate of uuhappineſs; miſery.

  Sweet are the uſes of *adverſity*,
  Which like the toad, ugly and venomous,
  Wears yet a precious jewel in his head. *Shak. As you like it.*

Concerning deliverance itſelf from all *adverſity*, we uſe not to ſay men are in *adverſity*, whenſoever they feel any ſmall hinderance of their welfare in this world, but when ſome notable affliction or croſs, ſome great calamity or trouble, befalleth them. *Hooker, b.* v. § 48.

A remembrance of the good uſe he had made of proſperity, contributed to ſupport his mind under the heavy weight of *adverſity*, which then lay upon him. *Atterbury's Sermons.*

Adve'rsly. *adv.* [from *adverſe.*]

In an adverſe manner; oppoſitely; unfortunately.

What I think, I utter, and ſpend my malice in my breath. Meeting two ſuch wealſmen as you are, (I cannot call you Lycurguſſes) if the drink you give me touch my palate *adverſly*, I make a crooked face at it. *Shakeſp. Coriolanus.*

To ADVE'RT. *v. n.* [*adverto*, Lat.]

To attend to; to regard; to obſerve; with the particle *to* before the object of regard.

The mind of man being not capable at once to *advert to* more than one thing, a particular view and examination of ſuch an innumerable number of vaſt bodies, will afford matter of admiration. *Ray on the Creation.*

  Now *to* the univerſal whole *advert*;
  The earth regard as of that whole a part;
  In which wide frame more noble worlds abound;
  Witneſs, ye glorious orbs, which hang around. *Blackmore.*

We ſometimes ſay, *To* advert *the mind* to *an object.*

Adve'rtence. *n. ſ.* [from *advert.*]

Attention to; regard to; conſideration.

Chriſtianity may make Archimedes his challenge; give it but where it may ſet its foot; allow but a ſober *advertence* to its propoſals, and it will move the whole world. *Decay of Piety.*

Adve'rtency. *n. ſ.* [from *advert.*]

The ſame with *advertence.* Attention; regard; heedfulneſs.

Too much *advertency* is not your talent; or elſe you had fled from that text, as from a rock. *Swift.*

To ADVERTI'SE. *v. a.* [*advertir*, Fr.]

It is now ſpoken with the accent upon the laſt ſyllable; but appears to have been anciently accented on the ſecond.

1. To inform another; to give intelligence; with an accuſative of the perſon informed.

  The biſhop did require a reſpite,
  Wherein he might the *king* his lord *advertiſe*,
  Whether our daughter were legitimate.
  Shakeſpeare's Henry VIII.

  As I by friends am well *advertiſed*,
  Sir Edmund Courtney, and the haughty prelate,
  Biſhop of Exeter, his elder brother,
  With many more confederates are in arms.
  Shakeſpeare's Richard III.

2. To inform; to give notice; with *of* before the ſubject of information.

The death of Selymus nothing ſuſpected, Ferhates, underſtanding that Solyman expected more aſſured advertiſement, ſent unto the other Baſſas; unto whom he declared the death of the emperor: *of* which they, by another meſſenger, *advertiſed* Solyman; firming thoſe letters with all their hands and ſeals. *Knolles's Hiſtory of the Turks.*

They were to *advertiſe* the chief hero *of* the diſtreſſes of his ſubjects, occaſioned by his abſence, to crave his ſuccour, and ſolicite him to haſten his return. *Dryd. Pref. Dufreſn.*

3. To give notice of any thing, by means of an advertiſement in the publick prints; as, *He* advertiſed *his loſs.*

Adverti'sement, or Adve'rtisement. *n. ſ.* [*advertiſſement*, Fr.]

1. Inſtruction; admonition.

  —'Tis all men's office to ſpeak patience
  To thoſe, that wring under the load of ſorrow;
  But no man's virtue nor ſufficiency,
  To be ſo moral, when he ſhall endure
  The like himſelf: therefore give me no counſel;
  My griefs are louder than *advertiſement.*
  Shakeſpeare's Much ado about Nothing.

2. Intelligence; information.

  Then, as a cunning prince that uſeth ſpies,
  If they return no news, doth nothing know;
  But if they make *advertiſement* of lies,
  The prince's counſel all awry do go. *Sir John Davies.*

He had received *advertisement*, that the party, which was sent for his relief from London, had received some brush in Somersetshire, which would much retard their march. *Clarendon.*

The drum and trumpet, by their several sounds, serve for many kinds of *advertisements*, in military affairs: the bells serve to proclaim a scare-fire; and, in some places, water-breaches; the departure of a man, woman, or child; time of divine service; the hour of the day; day of the month. *Holder.*

3. Notice of any thing published in a paper of intelligence.

ADVERTI'SER. *n. s.* [*advertiseur*, Fr.]

1. He that gives intelligence or information.

2. The paper in which advertisements are published.

ADVE'RTISING, or ADVERTI'SING. *part. adj.* [from *advertise.*] Active in giving intelligence; monitory: a word not now in use.

As I was then
Advertising, and holy to your business,
Not changing heart with habit, I am still
Attornied at your service. *Shakesp. Measure for Measure.*

To ADVE'SPERATE. *v. n.* [*advespero*, Lat.] To draw towards evening. *Dict.*

ADVI'CE. *n. s.* [*avis*, *advis*, Fr. from *adviso*, low Latin.]

1. Counsel; instruction: except that instruction implies superiority, and advice may be given by equals or inferiors.

Break we our match up, and, by my *advice*,
Let us impart what we have seen to-night
Unto young Hamlet. *Shakesp. Hamlet.*

O troubled, weak and coward, as thou art!
Without thy poor *advice*, the lab'ring heart
To worse extremes with swifter steps would run;
Not sav'd by virtue, yet by vice undone. *Prior.*

2. Reflection; prudent consideration; as, he always acts with good *advice*.

What he hath won, that he hath fortified:
So hot a speed, with such *advice* dispos'd,
Such temperate order, in so fierce a course,
Doth want example. *Shakesp. King John.*

3. Consultation; deliberation; with the particle *with*.

Great princes, for the most part, taking *advice with* workmen, with no less cost, set their things together. *Bacon's Ess.*

4. Intelligence; as, the merchants received *advice* of their loss. This sense is somewhat low, and chiefly commercial.

ADVI'CE-BOAT. *n. s.* A vessel employed to bring intelligence.

ADVI'SABLE. *adj.* [from *advise.*] Prudent; fit to be advised.

Some judge it *advisable* for a man to account with his heart every day; and this, no doubt, is the best and surest course; for still the oftner, the better. *South's Sermons.*

It is not *advisable* to reward, where men have the tenderness not to punish. *L'Estrange's Fables.*

ADVI'SABLENESS. *n. s.* [from *advisable.*] The quality of being advisable, or fit; fitness; propriety.

To ADVI'SE. *v. a.* [*adviser*, Fr.]

1. To counsel; with the particle *to* before the thing advised.

If you do stir abroad, go arm'd.——
—— Arm'd, brother!——
—— Brother, I *advise* you *to* the best. *Shak. K. Lear.*

I would *advise* all gentlemen *to* learn merchants accounts, and not to think it a skill that belongs not to them. *Locke.*

When I consider the scruples and cautions I here lay in your way, methinks it looks as if I *advised* you *to* something which I would have offered at, but in effect not done. *Idem.*

2. To give information; to inform; to make acquainted with any thing; often with the particle *of* before the thing told.

You were *advis'd*, his flesh was capable
Of wounds and scars; and that his forward spirit
Would lift him, where most trade of danger rang'd.
Shakespeare's Henry IV. *p.* ii.

Such discourse bring on,
As may *advise* him *of* his happy state;
Happiness in his pow'r, left free to will. *Paradise Lost.*

A posting messenger dispatch'd from hence,
Of this fair troop *advis'd* their aged prince. *Dryden's Æneid.*

To ADVI'SE. *v. n.*

1. To consult; with the particle *with* before the person consulted; as, *he advised with his companions.*

2. To consider; to deliberate.

Advise if this be worth
Attempting, or to sit in darkness here,
Hatching vain empires. *Milton's Paradise Lost, b.* ii.

ADVI'SED. *participial adj.* [from *advise.*]

1. Acting with deliberation and design; prudent; wise.

Let his travel appear rather in his discourse, than in his apparel or gesture; and, in his discourse, let him be rather *advised* in his answers, than forward to tell stories. *Bacon's Ess.*

Th' Almighty Father, where he sits
Shrin'd in his sanctuary of heav'n secure,
Consulting on the sum of things foreseen,
This tumult, and permitted all, *advis'd. Paradise Lost, b.* vi.

2. Performed with deliberation; done on purpose; acted with design.

By that which we work naturally, as, when we breathe, sleep, and move, we set forth the glory of God, as natural agents do; albeit we have no express purpose to make that our end, nor any *advised* determination therein to follow a law. *Hooker, b.* i. *p.* 49.

In my school-days, when I had lost one shaft,
I shot his fellow of the self-same flight,
The self-same way, with more *advised* watch,
To find the other forth; by vent'ring both,
I oft found both. *Shakesp. Merchant of Venice.*

ADVI'SEDLY. *adv.* [from *advised.*] Deliberately; purposely; by design; prudently.

Surprize may be made by moving things, when the party is in haste, and cannot stay to consider *advisedly* of that which is moved. *Bacon, Essay* xxiii.

Thou stilest second thoughts (which are by all allowed the best) a relapse; and talkest of a quagmire, where no man ever stuck fast; and accusest constancy of mischief in what is natural, and *advisedly* undertaken. *Sir John Suckling.*

ADVI'SEDNESS. *n. s.* [from *advised.*] Deliberation; cool and prudent procedure.

While things are in agitation, private men may modestly tender their thoughts to the consideration of those that are in authority; to whose care it belongeth, in prescribing concerning indifferent things, to proceed with all just *advisedness* and moderation. *Saunderson's Judgment in one View.*

ADVI'SEMENT. *n. s.* [*advisement*, Fr.]

1. Counsel; information.

Mote I wote,
What strange adventure do ye now pursue?
Perhaps my succour, or *advisement* meet,
Mote stead you much your purpose to subdue. *Fairy Queen.*

I will, according to your *advisement*, declare the evils, which seem most hurtful. *Spenser's State of Ireland.*

2. It is taken likewise, in old writers, for prudence and circumspection. It is now, in both senses, antiquated.

ADVI'SER. *n. s.* [from *advise.*] The person that advises, or gives counsel; a counsellor.

Here, free from court-compliances, he walks,
And with himself, his best *adviser*, talks. *Waller.*

They never fail of their most artful and indefatigable address, to silence this impertinent *adviser*, whose severity awes their excesses. *Rogers's Sermons.*

ADULA'TION. *n. s.* [*adulation*, Fr. *adulatio*, Lat.] Flattery; high compliment.

O be sick, great Greatness!
And bid thy ceremony give thee cure.
Think'st thou the firy fever will go out,
With titles blown from *adulation?* *Shakesp. Henry* V.

They who flattered him most before, mentioned him now with the greatest bitterness, and called him now the corrupter of the king, and betrayer of the people; without imputing the least crime to him, committed since the time of that exalted *adulation*, or that was not then as much known to them, as it could be now. *Clarendon.*

ADULA'TOR. *n. s.* [*adulator*, Lat.] A flatterer. *Dict.*

A'DULATORY. *adj.* [*adulatorius*, Lat.] Flattering; full of compliments.

ADU'LT. *adj.* [*adultus*, Lat.] Grown up; past the age of infancy and weakness.

They would appear less able to approve themselves, not only to the confessor, but even to the catechist, in their *adult* age, than they were in their minority; as having scarce ever thought of the principles of their religion, since they conned them to avoid correction. *Decay of Piety.*

The earth, by these applauded schools, 'tis said,
This single crop of men and women bred;
Who grown *adult*, (so chance, it seems, enjoin'd)
Did, male and female, propagate their kind. *Blackmore.*

ADU'LT. *n. s.* A person above the age of infancy, or grown to some degree of strength; sometimes full grown: a word used chiefly by medicinal writers.

The depression of the cranium, without a fracture, can but seldom occur; and then it happens to children, whose bones are more pliable and soft than those of *adults*. *Sharp's Surgery.*

ADU'LTNESS. *n. s.* [from *adult.*] The state of being adult. See ADOLESCENCE. *Dict.*

To ADU'LTER. *v. a.* [*adulterer*, Fr. *adultero*, Lat.] To commit adultery with another: a word not classical.

His chaste wife
He *adulters* still: his thoughts lye with a whore. *Ben. Johns.*

ADU'LTERANT. *n. s.* [*adulterans*, Lat.] The person or thing which adulterates.

To ADU'LTERATE. *v. a.* [*adulterer*, Fr. *adultero*, Lat.]

1. To commit adultery.

But fortune, oh!
Adulterates hourly with thine uncle John;
And with her golden hand hath pluckt on France.
Shakesp. King John.

2. To corrupt by some foreign admixture; to contaminate.

Common pot-ashes, bought of them that sell it in shops, who are not so foolishly knavish, as to *adulterate* them with saltpetre, which is much dearer than pot-ashes. *Boyle.*

Could a man be composed to such an advantage of constitution,

tion, that it should not at all *adulterate* the images of his mind; yet this second nature would alter the crasis of his understanding. *Glanville's Scepsis Scientifica, c.* xvi.

The present war has so *adulterated* our tongue with strange words, that it would be impossible for one of our great grandfathers to know what his posterity have been doing. *Spectator.*

ADU'LTERATE. *adj.* [from *To adulterate.*]

1. Tainted with the guilt of adultery.

I am possess'd with an *adulterate* blot;
My blood is mingled with the grime of lust;
Being strumpeted by thy contagion. *Shakesp. Comedy of Err.*
—That incestuous, that *adulterate* beast. *Idem, Hamlet.*

2. Corrupted with some foreign mixture.

It does indeed differ no more, than the maker of *adulterate* wares does from the vender of them. *Governm. of the Tongue.*

They will have all their gold and silver, and may keep their *adulterate* copper at home; for we are determined not to purchase it with our manufactures. *Swift's Miscellanies.*

ADU'LTERATENESS. *n. s.* [from *adulterate.*] The quality or state of being adulterate, or counterfeit.

ADULTERA'TION. *n. s.* [from *adulterate.*]

1. The act of adulterating or corrupting by foreign mixture; contamination.

To make the compound pass for the rich metal simple, is an *adulteration*, or counterfeiting: but if it be done avowedly, and without disguising, it may be a great saving of the richer metal. *Bacon's Natural History*, N° 798.

2. The state of being adulterated, or contaminated.

Such translations are like the *adulteration* of the noblest wines, where something of the colour, spirit, and flavour, will remain; and, while they please some injudicious palates, do only raise the indignation of every good taste. *Felton on the Class.*

ADU'LTERER. *n. s.* [*adulter*, Lat.] The person guilty of adultery.

With what impatience must the muse behold,
The wife by her procuring husband sold;
For tho' the law makes null th' *adulterer*'s deed
Of lands to her, the cuckold may succeed. *Dryd. Juvenal.*

ADU'LTERESS. *n. s.* [from *adulterer.*] A woman that commits adultery.

The Spartan lady replied, when she was asked, What was the punishment for *adulteresses*? There are no such things here. *Government of the Tongue*, § 3.

A robe of tissue, stiff with golden wire;
An upper vest, once Helen's rich attire;
From Argos by the fam'd *adult'ress* brought;
With golden flow'rs and winding foliage wrought. *Dry. Vir.*

ADU'LTERINE. *n. s.* [*adulterine*, Fr. *adulterinus*, Lat.] A child born of an adulteress: a term of canon law.

ADU'LTEROUS. *adj.* [*adulter*, Lat.] Guilty of adultery.

Th' *adulterous* Antony, most large
In his abominations, turns you off,
And gives his potent regiment to a trull,
That noses it against us. *Shakesp. Antony and Cleopatra.*

An *adulterous* person is tied to restitution of the injury, so far as it is reparable; and to make provision for the children, that they may not injure the legitimate. *Taylor.*

Think on whose faith th' *adult'rous* youth rely'd;
Who promis'd, who procur'd the Spartan bride? *Dryd. Æn.*

ADU'LTERY. *n. s.* [*adulterium*, Lat.] The act of violating the bed of a married person.

All thy domestic griefs at home be left,
The wife's *adult'ry*, with the servant's theft;
And (the most racking thought, which can intrude)
Forget false friends, and their ingratitude. *Dryd. Juven.*

ADU'MBRANT. *adj.* [from *adumbrate.*] That which gives a slight resemblance.

To ADU'MBRATE. *v. a.* [*adumbro*, Lat.]

To shadow out; to give a slight likeness; to exhibit a faint resemblance, like that which shadows afford of the bodies which they represent.

Heaven is designed for our reward, as well as rescue; and therefore is *adumbrated* by all those positive excellencies, which can endear or recommend. *Decay of Piety.*

ADUMBRA'TION. *n. s.* [from *adumbrate.*]

1. The act of adumbrating, or giving a slight and imperfect representation. See ADUMBRATE.

To make some *adumbration* of that we mean, the interiour is rather an impulsion or contusion of the air, than an elision or section of the same. *Bacon's Nat. Hist.* N° 187.

2. The slight and imperfect representation of a thing; a faint sketch.

The observers view but the backside of the hangings; the right one is on the other side the grave: and our knowledge is but like those broken ends; at best a most confused *adumbration*. *Glanville's Scepsis Scientifica.*

Those of the first sort have some *adumbration* of the rational nature, as vegetables have of the sensible. *Hales's Origin.*

ADUNA'TION. *n. s.* [from *ad* and *unus*, Lat.] The state of being united; union: a word of little use.

When, by glaciation, wood, straw, dust, and water, are supposed to be united into one lump, the cold does not cause any real union or *adunation*, but only hardening the aqueous parts of the liquor into ice; the other bodies, being accidentally present in that liquor, are frozen up in it, but not really united. *Boyle.*

ADU'NCITY. *n. s.* [*aduncitas*, Lat.] Crookedness; flexure inwards; hookedness.

There can be no question, but the *aduncity* of the pounces, and beaks of the hawks, is the cause of the great and habitual immorality of those animals. *Arbuthnot and Pope's Mart. Scrib.*

ADU'NQUE. *adj.* [*aduncus*, Lat.] Crooked; bending inwards; hooked.

The birds that are speakers, are parrots, pies, jays, daws, and ravens; of which parrots have an *adunque* bill, but the rest not. *Bacon's Nat. Hist.* N° 238.

A'DVOCACY. *n. s.* [from *advocate.*] The act of pleading; vindication; defence; apology: a word in little use.

If any there are who are of opinion, that there are no antipodes, or that the stars do fall, they shall not want herein the applause or *advocacy* of Satan. *Brown's Vulgar Errours, b.* i.

A'DVOCATE. *n. s.* [*advocatus*, Lat.]

1. He that pleads the cause of another in a court of judicature.

An *advocate*, in the general import of the word, is that person who has the pleading and management of a judicial cause. In a strict way of speaking, only that person is stiled *advocate*, who is the patron of the cause, and is often, in Latin, termed *togatus*, and, in English, a person of the long robe. *Ayl. Par.*

Learn what thou ow'st thy country and thy friend;
What's requisite to spare, and what to spend:
Learn this; and, after, envy not the store
Of the greas'd *advocate* that grinds the poor. *Dryd. Perseus.*

2. He that pleads any cause, in whatever manner, as a controvertist or vindicator.

If she dares trust me with her little babe,
I'll shew't the king, and undertake to be
Her *advocate* to th' loudest. *Shakesp. Hamlet.*

Of the several forms of government that have been, or are, in the world, that cause seems commonly the better, that has the better *advocate*, or is advantaged by fresher experience. *Temple's Miscellanies.*

3. It is used with the particle *for* before the person or thing, in whose favour the plea is offered.

Foes to all living worth except your own,
And *advocates for* folly dead and gone. *Pope's Epistles.*

4. In the scriptural and sacred sense, it stands for one of the offices of our Redeemer.

Me his *advocate*,
And propitiation; all his works on me,
Good, or not good, ingraft. *Milton's Paradise Lost.*

ADVOCA'TION. *n. s.* [from *advocate.*] The office of pleading; plea; apology.

Alas! thrice gentle Cassio,
My *advocation* is not now in tune;
My lord is not my lord; nor should I know him,
Were he in favour, as in humour, alter'd. *Shakesp. Othello.*

ADVOLA'TION. *n. s.* [*advolo*, *advolatum*, Lat.] The act of flying to something. *Dict.*

ADVOLU'TION. *n. s.* [*advolutio*, Lat.] The act of rolling to something.

ADVO'UTRY. *n. s.* [*avoutrie*, Fr.] Adultery.

He was the most perfidious man upon the earth, and he had made a marriage compounded between an *advoutry* and a rape. *Bacon's Henry* VII.

ADVOWE'. *n. s.* He that has the right of advowson. See ADVOWSON.

ADVO'WSON, or ADVO'WZEN. *n. s.* [In common law.]

A right to present to a benefice, and signifies as much as *Jus Patronatûs.* In the canon law, it is so termed, because they that originally obtained the right of presenting to any church, were great benefactors thereto; and are therefore termed sometimes *Patroni*, sometimes *Advocati.* *Cowell.*

To ADU'RE. *v. n.* [*aduro*, Lat.] To burn up.

Such a degree of heat, which doth neither melt nor scorch, doth mellow, and not *adure.* *Bacon's Nat. Hist.* N° 319.

ADU'ST. *adj.* [*adustus*, Lat.]

1. Burnt up; hot as with fire, scorched.

By this means, the virtual heat of the water will enter; and such a heat as will not make the body *adust*, or *fragile.* *Bacon.*

Which with torrid heat,
And vapours as the Libyan air *adust*,
Began to parch that temperate clime. *Milton's Par. Lost.*

2. It is generally now applied, in a medicinal or philosophical sense, to the complexion and humours of the body.

Such humours are *adust*, as, by long heat, become of a hot and fiery nature, as choler, and the like. *Quincy.*

To ease the soul of one oppressive weight,
This quits an empire, that embroils a state.
The same *adust* complexion has impell'd
Charles to the convent, Philip to the field. *Pope.*

ADU'STED. *adj.* [See ADUST.]

1. Burnt; scorch'd; dried with fire.

Sulphurous and nitrous foam
They found, they mingled, and with subtle art,
Concocted, and *adusted*, they reduc'd
To blackest grain, and into store convey'd. *Paradise Lost.*

2. Hot,

2. Hot, as the complexion.

In regard they are but the fruits of *aduſted* choler, and the evaporations of a vindicative ſpirit, Helia needs not much care for them; beſides, ſhe muſt give loſers leave to ſpeak. *Howell.*

Adu'stible. *adj.* [from *aduſt.*] That which may be aduſted, or burnt up. *Dict.*

Adu'stion. *n. ſ.* [from *aduſt.*] The act of burning up, or drying, as by fire.

This is ordinarily a conſequent of a burning colliquative fever; the ſofter parts being melted away, the heat continuing its *aduſtion*, upon the drier and fleſhy parts, changes into a marcid fever. *Harvey on Conſumptions.*

Adz. *n. ſ.* See Addice.

AE, or Æ. A diphthong of very frequent uſe in the Latin language, which ſeems not properly to have any place in the Engliſh; ſince the *æ* of the Saxons has been long out of uſe, being changed to *e* ſimple, to which, in words frequently occurring, the *æ* of the Romans is, in the ſame manner, altered, as in *equator*, *equinoctial*, and even in *Eneas*.

Æ'glogue. *n. ſ.* [written inſtead of *eclogue*, from a miſtaken etymology.] A paſtoral; a dialogue in verſe between goatherds.

Which moved him rather in *æglogues* otherwiſe to write, doubting, perhaps, his ability, which he little needed, or minding to furniſh our tongue with this kind wherein it faulteth. *Spenſer's Paſtorals.*

Æ'gilops. *n. ſ.* [αἰγίλωψ, Gr. ſignifying goat-eyed, the goat being ſubject to this ailment.]

A tumour or ſwelling in the great corner of the eye, by the root of the noſe, either with or without an inflammation: alſo a plant ſo called, for its ſuppoſed virtues againſt ſuch a diſtemper. *Quincy.*

Ægilops is a tubercle in the inner canthus of the eye. *Wiſeman's Surgery.*

Ægypti'acum. *n. ſ.* An ointment conſiſting only of honey, verdigreaſe and vinegar. *Quincy.*

Æl, or Eal, or Al.

In compound names, as πᾶν in the Greek compounds, ſignifies *all*, or *altogether*. So *Ælwin* is a *compleat conqueror*: *Albert*, *all illuſtrious*: *Aldred*, *altogether reverend*: *Alfred*, *altogether peaceful*. To theſe *Pammachius*, *Pancratius*, *Pamphilius*, &c. do in ſome meaſure anſwer. *Gibſon's Camden.*

Ælf, (which, according to various dialects, is pronounced *ulf*, *welph*, *hulph*, *hilp*, *helfe*, and, at this day, *helpe*) implies aſſiſtance. So *Ælfwin* is *victorious*, and *Ælfwold*, an *auxiliary governour*; *Ælfgiſa*, a *lender of aſſiſtance*: with which *Boetius*, *Symmachus*, *Epicurus*, &c. bear a plain analogy. *Gibſon's Camden.*

Æni'gma. See Enigma.

Ae'rial. *adj.* [*aërius*, Lat.]

1. Belonging to the air, as conſiſting of it.

The thunder, when to roll
With terrour through the dark *aerial* hall. *Paradiſe Loſt.*
From all that can with fins or feathers fly,
Thro' the *aerial* or the wat'ry ſky. *Prior.*

I gathered the thickneſs of the air, or *aerial* interval, of the glaſſes at that ring. *Newton's Opticks.*

Vegetables abound more with *aerial* particles, than animal ſubſtances. *Arbuthnot on Aliments.*

2. Produced by the air.

The gifts of heav'n my foll'wing ſong purſues,
Aerial honey, and ambroſial dews. *Dryd. Virg. Georg.*

3. Inhabiting the air.

Where thoſe immortal ſhapes
Of bright *aerial* ſpirits live inſpher'd,
In regions mild, of calm and ſerene air. *Paradiſe Regained.*

Aerial animals may be ſubdivided into birds and flies. *Locke.*

4. Placed in the air.

Here ſubterranean works and cities ſee,
There towns *aerial* on the waving tree. *Pope's Eſſay on Man.*

5. High; elevated in ſituation, and therefore in the air.

A ſpacious city ſtood, with firmeſt walls,
Sure mounded, and with numerous turrets crown'd,
Aerial ſpires, and citadels, the ſeat
Of kings and heroes reſolute in war. *Philips.*

A'erie. *n. ſ.* [*airie*, Fr.]

The proper word in hawks and other birds of prey for that which we generally call a neſt in other birds. *Cowell.*

Aero'logy. *n. ſ.* [ἀὴρ and λόγος, Gr.] The doctrine of the air.

A'eromancy. *n. ſ.* [ἀὴρ and μάντις, Gr.] The art of divining by the air. *Dict.*

Aero'metry. *n. ſ.* [ἀὴρ and μετρέω.] The art of meaſuring the air. *Dict.*

Aero'scopy. *n. ſ.* [ἀὴρ and σκέπτω, Gr.] The obſervation of the air. *Dict.*

Æ'thiops-mineral. *n. ſ.*

A medicine ſo called, from its dark colour, prepared of quickſilver and ſulphur, ground together in a marble mortar to a black powder. Such as have uſed it moſt, think its virtues not very great. *Quincy.*

Æti'tes. *n. ſ.* [ἀετὸς, an eagle.] Eagle-ſtone. It is about the bigneſs of a cheſnut, and hollow, with ſomewhat in it that rattles upon ſhaking. *Quincy.*

Afa'r. *adv.* [from *a* for *at*, and *far*.] See Far.

1. At a great diſtance.

So ſhaken as we are, ſo wan with care,
Find we a time for frighted peace to pant,
And breathe ſhort-winded accents of new broils,
To be commenc'd in ſtrouds *afar* remote? *Shakeſpeare's Henry IV.*

We hear better when we hold our breath than contrary; inſomuch as in liſtening to attain a ſound *afar* off, men hold their breath. *Bacon's Natural Hiſtory, N° 284.*

2. To a great diſtance.

Hector haſtened to relieve his boy;
Diſmiſs'd his burniſh'd helm that ſhone *afar*,
The pride of warriours, and the pomp of war. *Dryd.*

3. From afar; from a diſtant place.

The rough Vulturnus, furious in its courſe,
With rapid ſtreams divides the fruitful grounds,
And *from afar* in hollow murmur ſounds. *Addiſon on Italy.*

4. Afar off; remotely diſtant.

Much ſuſpecting his ſecret ends, he entertained a treaty of peace with France, but ſecretly and *afar off*, and to be governed as occaſions ſhould vary. *Sir John Hayward.*

Afe'ard. *participial adj.* [from *to fear*, for *to fright*, with *a* redundant.]

1. Frighted; terrified; afraid.

He loudly bray'd, that like was never heard,
And from his wide devouring oven ſent
A flake of fire, that flaſhing in his beard,
Him all amaz'd, and almoſt made *afeard*. *Fairy Queen.*

But tell me, Hal, art thou not horridly *afeard*? Thou being heir apparent, could the world pick thee out three ſuch enemies again, as Douglas, Percy, and Glendower. *Shakeſp. Henry IV.*

Till he cheriſh'd too much beard,
And make Love, or me *afeard*. *Ben. Johnſon's Underwoods.*

2. It has the particle *of* before the object of fear.

Fear is deſcribed by Spenſer to ride in armour, at the claſhing whereof he looks *afeard of* himſelf. *Peacham.*

It is now obſolete; the laſt authour whom I have found uſing it, is *Sedley*.

A'*fer*. *n. ſ.* [Lat.] The ſouthweſt wind.

With adverſe blaſt upturns them from the ſouth,
Notus, and Afer, black with thund'rous clouds,
From Sierra Liona. *Milton's Paradiſe Loſt, b.* x.

Affabi'lity. *n. ſ.* [*affabilité*, Fr. *affabilitas*, Lat.] See Affable.

The quality of being affable; eaſineſs of manners; courteouſneſs; civility; condeſcenſion. It is commonly uſed of ſuperiours.

Hearing of her beauty and her wit,
Her *affability* and baſhful modeſty,
Her wond'rous qualities, and mild behaviour. *Shakeſpeare's Taming of the Shrew.*

He was of a moſt flowing courteſy and *affability* to all men, and ſo deſirous to oblige them, that he did not enough conſider the value of the obligation, or the merit of the perſon. *Clarend.*

All inſtances of charity, ſweetneſs of converſation, *affability*, admonition, all ſignifications of tenderneſs, care and watchfulneſs, muſt be expreſſed towards children. *Taylor.*

It is impoſſible for a publick miniſter to be ſo open and eaſy to all his old friends, as he was in his private condition; but this may be helped out by an *affability* of addreſs. *L'Eſtrange.*

A'ffable. *adj.* [*affable*, Fr. *affabilis*, Lat.]

1. Eaſy of manners; accoſtable; courteous; complaiſant. It is uſed of ſuperiours.

He was *affable*, and both well and fair ſpoken, and would uſe ſtrange ſweetneſs and blandiſhment of words, where he deſired to affect or perſuade any thing that he took to heart. *Bacon.*

Her father is Baptiſta Minola,
An *affable* and courteous gentleman. *Shakeſp. Tam. Shrew.*
Gentle to me, and *affable* hath been
Thy condeſcenſion, and ſhall be honour'd ever
With grateful memory. *Milton's Paradiſe Loſt, b.* viii.

2. It is applied to the external appearance; benign; mild; favourable.

Auguſtus appeared, looking round him with a ſerene and *affable* countenance upon all the writers of his age. *Tatler.*

A'ffableness. *n. ſ.* [from *affable.*] Courteſy; affability.

A'ffably. *adv.* [from *affable.*] In an affable manner; courteouſly; civilly.

A'ffabrous. *adj.* [*affabre*, Fr.] Skilfully made; complete; finiſhed in a workman-like manner. *Dict.*

Affabula'tion. *n. ſ.* [*affabulatio*, Lat.] The moral of a fable. *Dict.*

Affa'ir. *n. ſ.* [*affaire*, Fr.] Buſineſs; ſomething to be managed or tranſacted. It is uſed for both private and publick matters.

I was not born for courts or great *affairs*;
I pay my debts, believe, and ſay my prayers. *Pope.*

A good acquaintance with method will greatly aſſiſt every one in ranging, diſpoſing, and managing all human *affairs*. *Watts's Logick.*

What

What St. John's skill in state *affairs*,
What Ormond's valour, Oxford's cares,
To aid their sinking country lent,
Was all destroy'd by one event. *Swift.*

To AFFE'AR. *v. n.* [from *affier*, Fr.] To confirm; to give a sanction to; to establish: an old term of law.

Bleed, bleed, poor country!
Great tyranny, lay thou thy basis sure;
For goodness dares not check thee!
His title is *affear'd*. *Shakesp. Macbeth.*

AFFE'CT. *n. s.* [from the verb *affect*.]

1. Affection; passion; sensation.

It seemeth that as the feet have a sympathy with the head; so the wrists have a sympathy with the heart; we see the *affects* and passions of the heart and spirits are notably disclosed by the pulse. *Bacon's Natural History*, N° 97.

2. Quality; circumstance.

I find it difficult to make out one single ulcer, as authors describe it, without other symptoms or *affects* joined to it. *Wisem.*

This is only the antiquated word for *affection*.

To AFFE'CT. *v. a.* [*affecter*, Fr. *afficio*, *affectum*, Lat.]

1. To act upon; to produce effects in any other thing.

The sun
Had first his precept so to move, so shine,
As might *affect* the earth with cold, and heat,
Scarce tolerable. *Milton's Paradise Lost, b.* x.

The generality of men are wholly governed by names, in matters of good and evil; so far as these qualities relate to, and *affect*, the actions of men. *South's Sermons.*

Yet even those two particles do reciprocally *affect* each other with the same force and vigour, as they would do at the same distance in any other situation imaginable. *Bentley's Sermons.*

2. To move the passions.

As a thinking man cannot but be very much *affected* with the idea of his appearing in the presence of that Being, whom none can see and live; he must be much more *affected*, when he considers, that this Being whom he appears before, will examine the actions of his life, and reward or punish him accordingly. *Addison. Spectator*, N° 513.

3. To aim at; to endeavour after: spoken of persons.

Atrides broke
His silence next, but ponder'd ere he spoke:
Wise are thy words, and glad I would obey,
But this proud man *affects* imperial sway. *Dryden's Iliad.*

4. To tend to; to endeavour after: spoken of things.

The drops of every fluid *affect* a round figure, by the mutual attraction of their parts; as, the globe of the earth and sea *affects* a round figure, by the mutual attraction of its parts by gravity. *Newton's Opticks.*

5. To be fond of; to be pleased with; to love; to regard with fondness.

That little which some of the heathen did chance to hear, concerning such matter as the sacred Scripture plentifully containeth, they did in wonderful sort *affect*. *Hooker, b.* i.

There is your crown;
And he that wears the crown immortally,
Long guard it yours! If I *affect* it more,
Than as your honour, and as your renown,
Let me no more from this obedience rise. *Shak. Henry* IV.

Think not that wars we love, and strife *affect*;
Or that we hate sweet peace. *Fairfax, b.* ii.

None but a woman could a man direct
To tell us women what we most *affect*. *Dryd. Wife of Bath.*

6. To make a shew of something; to study the appearance of any thing; with some degree of hypocrisy.

Another nymph, amongst the many fair,
Before the rest *affected* still to stand,
And watch'd my eye preventing my command. *Prior.*

These often carry the humour so far, till their *affected* coldness and indifference quite kills all the fondness of a lover. *Addison. Spectator*, N° 171.

The conscious husband, whom like symptoms seize,
Charges on her the guilt of their disease;
Affecting fury, acts a madman's part,
He'll rip the fatal secret from her heart. *Granville.*

7. To imitate in an unnatural and constrained manner.

Spenser, in *affecting* the ancients, writ no language; yet I would have him read for his matter, but as Virgil read Ennius. *Ben. Johnson's Discoveries.*

8. To convict of some crime; to attaint with guilt: a phrase merely juridical.

By the civil law, if a dowry with a wife be promised and not paid, the husband is not obliged to allow her alimony. But if her parents shall become insolvent by some misfortune, she shall have alimony, unless you can *affect* them with fraud, in promising what they knew they were not able to perform. *Ayliffe's Parergon.*

AFFECTA'TION. *n. s.* [*affectatio*, Lat.] The act of making an artificial appearance.

In things of their own nature indifferent, if either councils or particular men have at any time, with sound judgment, misliked conformity between the church of God and infidels, the cause thereof hath been somewhat else than only *affectation* of dissimilitude. *Hooker, b.* iv. § 7.

It has been, from age to age, an *affectation* to love the pleasure of solitude, among those who cannot possibly be supposed qualified for passing life in that manner. *Spectator*, N° 264.

AFFE'CTED. *participial adj.* [from *affect*.]

1. Moved; touched with affection; internally disposed or inclined.

No marvel then if he were ill *affected*;
'Tis they have put him on the old man's death,
To have th' expence and waste of his revenues.
Shakesp. King Lear.

He was assured, that the model they seemed *affected* to in their directory, was not like to any of their foreign reformed churches now in the world. *Clarendon.*

2. Studied with over-much care, or with hypocritical appearance.

These antick, lisping, *affected* phantasies, these new tuners of accents. *Shakesp. Romeo and Juliet.*

3. In a personal sense, full of affectation; as, *an affected lady*.

AFFE'CTEDLY. *adv.* [from *affected*.] In an affected manner; hypocritically; with more appearance than reality.

Perhaps they are *affectedly* ignorant; they are so willing it should be true, that they have not attempted to examine it.
Government of the Tongue, § 5.

Some indeed have been so *affectedly* vain, as to counterfeit immortality, and have stolen their death, in hopes to be esteemed immortal. *Brown's Vulgar Errours, b.* vii. *c.* 10.

By talking so familiarly of one hundred and ten thousand pounds, by a tax upon a few commodities, it is plain, you are either naturally or *affectedly* ignorant of our condition. *Swift.*

AFFE'CTEDNESS. *n. s.* [from *affected*.] The quality of being affected, or of making false appearances.

AFFE'CTION. *n. s.* [*affection*, Fr. *affectio*, Lat.]

1. The state of being affected by any cause, or agent. This general sense is little in use.

Some men there are love not a gaping pig;
Some that are mad if they behold a cat;
And others, when the bag-pipe sings i' th' nose,
Cannot contain their urine, for *affection*.
Shakesp. Merchant of Venice.

2. Passion of any kind.

Then gan the Palmer thus: most wretched man,
That to *affections* does the bridle lend;
In their beginning they are weak and wan,
But soon through sufferance grow to fearful end. *Fairy Q.*

Impute it to my late solitary life, which is prone to *affections*. *Sidney, b.* i.

Affections, as joy, grief, fear, and anger, with such like, being, as it were, the sundry fashions and forms of appetite, can neither rise at the conceit of a thing indifferent, nor yet choose but rise at the sight of some things. *Hooker. b.* i.

To speak truth of Cæsar,
I have not known when his *affections* sway'd
More than his reason. *Shakesp. Julius Cæsar.*

Zeal ought to be composed of the highest degrees of pious *affections*; of which some are milder and gentler, some sharper and more vehement. *Sprat's Sermons.*

I can present nothing beyond this to your *affections*, to excite your love and desire. *Tillotson.*

3. Love; kindness; good-will to some person; often with *to*, or *towards*, before the person.

I have acquainted you
With the dear love I bear to fair Anne Page,
Who mutually hath answer'd my *affection*.
Shakesp. Merry Wives of Windsor.

My king is tangl'd in *affection to*
A creature of the queen's lady Anne Bullen. *Sh. Henry* VIII.

What warmth is there in your *affection towards* any of these princely suitors? *Shakesp. Merchant of Venice.*

Make his interest depend upon mutual *affection* and good correspondence with others. *Collier on General Kindness.*

Nor at first sight, like most, admires the fair;
For you he lives, and you alone shall share
His last *affection*, as his early care. *Pope.*

4. Good-will to any object; zeal; passionate regard.

I have reason to distrust mine own judgment, as that which may be overborn by my zeal and *affection to* this cause.
Bacon's Holy War.

Set your *affection* upon my words; desire them, and ye shall be instructed. *Wisdom*, vi. 11.

His integrity to the king was without blemish, and his *affection to* the church so notorious, that he never deserted it. *Cla.*

All the precepts of christianity command us to moderate our passions, to temper our *affections towards* all things below.
Temple.

Let not the mind of a student be under the influence of warm *affection to* things of sense, when he comes to the search of truth. *Watts's Improvement of the Mind.*

5. State of the mind, in general.

There grows,
In my most ill compos'd *affection*, such

A ſtanchleſs avarice, that, were I king,
I ſhould cut off the nobles for their lands. *Shak. Macbeth.*

The man that hath no muſick in himſelf,
Nor is not mov'd with concord of ſweet ſounds,
Is fit for treaſons, ſtratagems, and ſpoils;
The motions of his ſpirit are dull as night,
And his *affections* dark as Erebus:
Let no ſuch man be truſted. *Shakeſp. Merchant of Venice.*

6. Quality; property.

The certainty and accurateneſs which is attributed to what they deliver, muſt be reſtrained to what they teach, concerning thoſe purely mathematical diſciplines, arithmetick and geometry, where the *affections* of quantity are abſtractedly conſidered. *Boyle.*

The mouth being neceſſary to conduct the voice to the ſhape of its cavity, neceſſarily gives the voice ſome particular *affection* of ſound in its paſſage before it come to the lips. *Holder's Elements of Speech.*

God may have joined immaterial ſouls to other kinds of bodies, and in other laws of union; and, from thoſe different laws of union, there will ariſe quite different *affections*, and natures, and ſpecies of the compound beings. *Bentley's Sermons.*

7. State of the body, as acted upon by any cauſe.

It ſeemed to me a venereal gonorrhæa, and others thought it aroſe from ſome ſcorbutical *affection*. *Wiſeman's Surgery.*

8. Lively repreſentation in painting.

Affection is the lively repreſentment of any paſſion whatſoever, as if the figures ſtood not upon a cloth or board, but as if they were acting upon a ſtage. *Wotton's Architecture.*

AFFE'CTIONATE. *adj.* [*affectionné*, Fr. from *affection.*]

1. Full of affection; ſtrongly moved; warm; zealous.

In their love of God, and deſire to pleaſe him, men can never be too *affectionate*; and it is as true, that, in their hatred of ſin, men may be ſometimes too paſſionate. *Sprat's Sermons.*

2. Strongly inclined to; diſpoſed to; with the particle *to.*

As for the parliament, it preſently took fire, being *affectionate*, of old, *to* the war of France. *Bacon's Henry* VII.

3. Fond; tender.

He found me ſitting, beholding this picture, I know not with how *affectionate* countenance, but, I am ſure, with a moſt *affectionate* mind. *Sidney.*

Away they fly
Affectionate, and undeſiring bear
The moſt delicious morſel to their young. *Thomſon's Spring.*

4. Benevolent; tender.

When we reflect on all this *affectionate* care of providence for our happineſs, with what wonder muſt we obſerve the little effect it has on men. *Rogers's Sermons.*

AFFE'CTIONATELY. *adv.* [from *affectionate.*] In an affectionate manner; fondly; tenderly; benevolently.

AFFE'CTIONATENESS. *n. ſ.* [from *affectionate.*] The quality or ſtate of being affectionate; fondneſs; tenderneſs; good-will; benevolence.

AFFE'CTIONED. *adj.* [from *affection.*]

1. Affected; conceited. This ſenſe is now obſolete.

An *affectioned* aſs that cons ſtate without book, and utters it by great ſwaths. *Shakeſp. Twelfth Night.*

2. Inclined; mentally diſpoſed.

Be kindly *affectioned* one to another. *Rom.* xii. 10.

AFFE'CTIOUSLY. *adv.* [from *affect.*] In an affecting manner. *Dict.*

AFFE'CTIVE. *adj.* [from *affect.*] That which affects; that which ſtrongly touches. It is generally uſed for painful.

Pain is ſo uneaſy a ſentiment, that very little of it is enough to corrupt every enjoyment: and the effect God intends this variety of ungrateful and *affective* ſentiments ſhould have on us, is to reclaim our affections from this valley of tears. *Rogers.*

AFFECTUO'SITY. *n. ſ.* [from *affectuous.*] Paſſionateneſs. *Dict.*

AFFE'CTUOUS. *adj.* [from *affect.*] Full of paſſion; as, an *affectuous* ſpeech: a word little uſed.

To AFFE'RE. *v. a.* [*affier*, Fr.] A law term, ſignifying to confirm. See AFEARD.

AFFE'RORS. *n. ſ.* [from *affere.*]

Such as are appointed in court-leets, &c. upon oath, to mulct ſuch as have committed faults arbitrarily puniſhable, and have no expreſs penalty ſet down by ſtatute. *Cowell.*

AFFI'ANCE. *n. ſ.* [*affiance*, from *affier*, Fr.]

1. A marriage-contract.

At laſt ſuch grace I found, and means I wrought,
That I that lady to my ſpouſe had won,
Accord of friends, conſent of parents ſought,
Affiance made, my happineſs begun. *Fairy Queen, b.* ii.

2. Truſt in general; confidence; ſecure reliance.

The duke is virtuous, mild, and too well given
To dream on evil, or to work my downfal.—
—Ah! what's more dangerous than this fond *affiance?*
Seems he a dove? his feathers are but borrowed. *Shakeſp. Henry* VI.

3. Truſt in the divine promiſes and protection. To this ſenſe it is now almoſt confined.

It receives him into a covenant of grace, where there is pardon reached out to all truly penitent ſinners, and aſſiſtance promiſed, and engaged, and beſtowed upon very eaſy conditions, *viz.* humility, prayer, and *affiance* in him. *Hammond's Fund.*

There can be no ſurer way to ſucceſs, than by diſclaiming all confidence in ourſelves, and referring the events of things to God with an implicit *affiance.* *Atterbury's Sermons.*

To AFFI'ANCE. *v. a.* [from the noun *affiance.*]

1. To betroth; to bind any one by promiſe to marriage.

To me, ſad maid, or rather widow ſad,
He was *affianced* long time before,
And ſacred pledges he both gave and had;
Falſe, errant knight, infamous, and foreſwore. *Fairy Queen.*

Her ſhould Angelo have married; was *affianced* to her by oath, and the nuptial appointed; between which time of the contract, and limit of the ſolemnity, his brother was wrecked, having, in that veſſel, the dowry of his ſiſter. *Sh. Meaſ. for M.*

2. To give confidence.

Stranger! whoe'er thou art, ſecurely reſt,
Affianc'd in my faith, a friendly gueſt. *Pope's Odyſſey.*

AFFI'ANCER. *n. ſ.* [from *affiance.*] He that makes a contract of marriage between two parties. *Dict.*

AFFIDA'TION. } *n. ſ.* [from *affido*, Lat. See AFFIED.] Mutual
AFFIDA'TURE. } contract; mutual oath of fidelity. *Dict.*

AFFIDA'VIT. *n. ſ.* [*affidavit* ſignifies, in the language of the common law, *he made oath.*] A declaration upon oath.

You ſaid, if I return'd next 'ſize in Lent,
I ſhould be in remitter of your grace;
In th' interim my letters ſhould take place
Of *affidavits.* *Donne.*

Count Rechteren ſhould have made *affidavit*, that his ſervants had been affronted, and then Monſieur Meſnager would have done him juſtice. *Spectator*, Nº 481.

AFFI'ED. *participial adj.* [from the verb *affy*, derived from *affido*, Lat. Bracton uſing the phraſe *affidare mulieres.*] Joined by contract; affianced.

Be we *affied*, and ſuch aſſurance ta'en,
As ſhall with either part's agreement ſtand. *Shakeſp. Taming of a Shrew.*

AFFILIA'TION. *n. ſ.* [from *ad* and *filius*, Lat.] Adoption; the act of taking a ſon. *Chambers.*

A'FFINAGE. *n. ſ.* [*affinage*, Fr.] The act of refining metals by the cupel. *Dict.*

AFFI'NED. *adj.* [from *affinis*, Lat.] Joined by affinity to another; related to another.

If partially *affin'd*, or leagu'd in office,
Thou doſt deliver more or leſs than truth,
Thou art no ſoldier. *Shakeſp. Othello.*

AFFI'NITY. *n. ſ.* [*affinité*, Fr. from *affinis*, Lat.]

1. Relation by marriage; relation contracted by the huſband to the kindred of the wife, and by the wife to thoſe of the huſband. It is oppoſed to *conſanguinity*, or relation by birth.

In this ſenſe it has ſometimes the particle *with*, and ſometimes *to*, before the perſon to whom the relation is contracted.

And Solomon made *affinity with* Pharaoh king of Egypt, and took Pharaoh's daughter. 1 *Kings*, iii. 1.

They had left none alive, who had ſet his hand to their ſervitude, by the blindneſs of rage killing many guiltleſs perſons, either for *affinity to* the tyrant, or enmity to the tyrant-killers. *Sidney, b.* ii.

A breach firſt with Spain, and not long after with France itſelf, notwithſtanding ſo ſtrait an *affinity*, ſo lately treated with the one, and actually accompliſhed with the other; as if indeed (according to that pleaſant maxim of ſtate) kingdoms were never married. *Wotton.*

2. Relation to; connexion with; reſemblance to: ſpoken of things.

The Britiſh tongue, or Welſh, as we now call it, was in uſe only in this iſland, having great *affinity with* the old Gallick. *Camden.*

All things that have *affinity with* the heavens, move upon the center of another, which they benefit. *Bacon, Eſſay* xxiv.

The art of painting hath wonderful *affinity* with that of poetry. *Dryd. Dufreſnoy. Pref.*

Man is more diſtinguiſhed by devotion than by reaſon, as ſeveral brute creatures diſcover ſomething like reaſon, though they betray not any thing that bears the leaſt *affinity to* devotion. *Addiſon. Spect.* Nº 201.

To AFFI'RM. *v. n.* [*affirmo*, Lat.] To declare; to tell confidently: oppoſed to the word *deny.*

Yet their own authors faithfully *affirm*,
That the land Salike lies in Germany,
Between the floods of Sala and of Elve. *Shakeſp. Henry* V.

To AFFI'RM. *v. a.* To ratify or approve a former law, or judgment: oppoſed to *reverſe* or *repeal.*

The houſe of peers hath a power of judicature in ſome caſes, properly to examine and then to *affirm*; or, if there be cauſe, to reverſe the judgments which have been given in the court of king's bench. *Bacon's Advice to Sir G. Villiers.*

In this ſenſe we ſay, *to affirm the truth.*

AFFI'RMABLE. *adj.* [from *affirm.*] That which may be affirmed.

Thoſe attributes and conceptions that were applicable and *affirmable* of him when preſent, are now *affirmable* and applicable to him though paſt. *Hale's Origin of Mankind.*

AFFI'RMANCE. *n. s.* [from *affirm.*] Confirmation: opposed to *repeal.*

This statute did but restore an ancient statute, which was itself also made but in *affirmance* of the common law. *Bacon.*

AFFI'RMANT. *n. s.* [from *affirm.*] The person that affirms; a declarer. *Dict.*

AFFIRMA'TION. *n. s.* [*affirmatio*, Lat.]

1. The act of affirming or declaring: opposed to negation or denial.

This gentleman vouching, upon warrant of bloody *affirmation*, his to be more virtuous, and less attemptable, than any of our ladies. *Shakesp. Cymbeline.*

2. The position affirmed.

That he shall receive no benefit from Christ, is the *affirmation*, whereon his despair is founded; and one way of removing this dismal apprehension, is, to convince him, that Christ's death, if he perform the condition required, shall certainly belong to him. *Hammond's Fundamentals.*

3. Confirmation: opposed to *repeal.*

The learned in the laws of our land observe, that our statutes sometimes are only the *affirmation*, or ratification, of that which, by common law, was held before. *Hooker.*

AFFI'RMATIVE. *adj.* [from *affirm.*]

1. That which affirms, opposed to *negative*; in which we use the *affirmative*, that is, *the affirmative position.*

For the *affirmative*, we are now to answer such proofs of theirs as have been before alleged. *Hooker.*

Whether there are such beings or not, 'tis sufficient for my purpose, that many have believed the *affirmative*.
Dryden's Preface to Tyrannick Love.

2. That which can or may be affirmed: a sense used chiefly in science.

As in algebra, where *affirmative* quantities vanish or cease, there negative ones begin: so in mechanicks, where attraction ceases, there a repulsive virtue ought to succeed. *Newt. Opt.*

3. Applied to persons; he who has the habit of affirming with vehemence; positive; dogmatical.

Be not confident and *affirmative* in an uncertain matter, but report things modestly and temperately, according to the degree of that persuasion, which is, or ought to be, begotten by the efficacy of the authority, or the reason, inducing thee. *Taylor.*

AFFI'RMATIVELY. *adv.* [from *affirmative.*] In an affirmative manner; on the positive side; not negatively.

The reason of man hath no such restraint: concluding not only *affirmatively*, but negatively; not only affirming, there is no magnitude beyond the last heavens, but also denying, there is any vacuity within them. *Brown's Vulgar Errours.*

AFFI'RMER. *n. s.* [from *affirm.*] The person that affirms.

If by the word virtue, the *affirmer* intends our whole duty to God and man, and the denier, by the word virtue, means only courage, or, at most, our duty toward our neighbour, without including, in the idea of it, the duty which we owe to God.
Watts's Logick.

To AFFI'X. *v. a.* [*affigo*, *affixum*, Lat.] To unite to the end, or *à posteriori*; to subjoin.

He that has settled in his mind determined ideas, with names *affixed* to them, will be able to discern their differences one from another. *Locke.*

If men constantly *affixed* applause and disgrace where they ought, this principle would have a very good influence on the publick conduct of men; though on secret villanies it lays no restraint. *Rogers's Sermons.*

AFFI'X. *n. s.* [*affixum*, Lat.] A term of grammar; something united to the end of a word.

In the Hebrew language, the noun has its *affixa*, to denote the pronouns possessive or relative. *Clarke's Latin Grammar.*

AFFI'XION. *n. s.* [from *affix.*]

1. The act of affixing.

2. The state of being affixed. *Dict.*

AFFLA'TION. *n. s.* [*afflo*, *afflatum*, Lat.] The act of breathing upon any thing. *Dict.*

AFFLA'TUS. *n. s.* [Lat.] Communication of the power of prophecy. *Dict.*

To AFFLI'CT. *v. a.* [*afflicto*, *afflictum*, Lat.]

1. To put to pain; to grieve; to torment.

In the seventh month, on the tenth day of the month, ye shall *afflict* your souls, and do no work at all, whether it be one of your own country, or a stranger that sojourneth among you. *Leviticus*, xvi. 29.

Give not over thy mind to heaviness, and *afflict* not thyself in thine own counsel. *Ecclus*, xxx. 21.

For a father *afflicted* with untimely mourning, when he hath made an image of his child soon taken away, now honoured him as a God, which was then a dead man, and delivered to those that were under him, ceremonies and sacrifices. *Wisdom.*

It teacheth us, how God thought fit to plague and *afflict* them, it doth not appoint in what form and manner we ought to punish the sin of idolatry in others. *Hooker*, *b.* v. § 17.

O coward conscience! how dost thou *afflict* me?
The lights burn blue—Is it not dead midnight?
Cold fearful drops stand on my trembling flesh.
Shakesp. Richard III.

A melancholy tear *afflicts* my eye,
And my heart labours with a sudden sigh. *Prior.*

2. The passive *to be afflicted*, has often *at* before the causal noun.

The mother was so *afflicted at* the loss of a fine boy, who was her only son, that she died for grief of it. *Addison. Spect.*

AFFLI'CTEDNESS. *n. s.* [from *afflicted.*] The state of affliction, or of being afflicted; sorrowfulness; grief.

AFFLI'CTER. *n. s.* [from *afflict.*] The person that afflicts.

AFFLI'CTION. *n. s.* [*afflictio*, Lat.]

1. The cause of pain or sorrow; calamity.

To the flesh, as the Apostle himself granteth, all *affliction* is naturally grievous: therefore nature, which causeth fear, teacheth to pray against all adversity. *Hooker*, *b.* v. § 48.

We'll bring you to Windsor, to one Mr. Brook, that you have cozened of money; I think, to repay that money will be a biting *affliction*. *Shakesp. Merry Wives of Windsor.*

2. The state of sorrowfulness; misery: opposed to *prosperity.*

Besides you know,
Prosperity's the very bond of love,
Whose fresh complexion, and whose heart together
Affliction alters. *Shakesp. Winter's Tale.*

Where shall we find the man that bears *affliction*,
Great and majestic in his griefs, like Cato? *Addis. Cato.*

Some virtues are only seen in *affliction*, and some in prosperity. *Addison. Spectator*, N° 257.

AFFLI'CTIVE. *adj.* [from *afflict.*] That which causes affliction; painful; tormenting.

They found martyrdom a duty dressed up indeed with all that was terrible and *afflictive* to human nature, yet not at all the less a duty. *South.*

Nor find
Where to retire themselves, or where appease
Th' *afflictive* keen desire of food, expos'd
To winds, and storms, and jaws of savage death. *Philips.*

Restless Proserpine—
— On the spacious land and liquid main,
Spreads slow disease, and darts *afflictive* pain. *Prior.*

A'FFLUENCE. *n. s.* [*affluence*, Fr. *affluentia*, Lat.]

1. The act of flowing to any place; concourse. It is almost always used figuratively.

I shall not relate the *affluence* of young nobles from hence into Spain, after the voice of our prince being there had been noised. *Wotton.*

2. Exuberance of riches; stream of wealth; plenty.

Those degrees of fortune, which give fulness and *affluence* to one station, may be want and penury in another. *Rogers.*

Let joy or ease, let *affluence* or content,
And the gay conscience of a life well spent,
Calm ev'ry thought, inspirit ev'ry grace. *Pope.*

A'FFLUENCY. *n. s.* The same with *affluence.*

A'FFLUENT. *adj.* [*affluent*, Fr. *affluens*, Lat.]

1. Flowing to any part.

These parts are no more than foundation-piles of the ensuing body; which are afterwards to be increased and raised to a greater bulk by the *affluent* blood, that is transmitted out of the mother's body. *Harvey on Consumptions.*

2. Abundant; exuberant; wealthy.

I see thee, Lord and end of my desire,
Loaded and blest with all the *affluent* store,
Which human vows at smoaking shrines implore. *Prior.*

A'FFLUENTNESS. *n. s.* [from *affluent.*] The quality of being affluent. *Dict.*

A'FFLUX. *n. s.* [*affluxus*, Lat.]

1. The act of flowing to some place; affluence.

2. That which flows to another place.

The cause hereof cannot be a supply by procreations; *ergo*, it must be by new *affluxes* to London out of the country. *Graunt.*

The infant grows bigger out of the womb, by agglutinating one *afflux* of blood to another. *Harvey on Consumptions.*

AFFLU'XION. *n. s.* [*affluxio*, Lat.]

1. The act of flowing to a particular place.

2. That which flows from one place to another.

An inflammation either simple, consisting of an hot and sanguineous *affluxion*, or else denominable from other humours, according unto the predominancy of melancholy, phlegm or choler. *Brown's Vulgar Errours.*

To AFFO'RD. *v. a.* [*affourrer*, *affourrager*, Fr.]

1. To yield or produce; as, *the soil affords grain*; *the trees afford fruits.* This seems to be the primitive signification.

2. To grant, or confer any thing; generally in a good sense, and sometimes in a bad, not properly.

So soon as Maurmon there arrived, the door
To him did open, and *afforded* way. *Fairy Queen.*

This is the consolation of all good men, unto whom his ubiquity *affordeth* continual comfort and security; and this is the affliction of hell, to whom it *affordeth* despair and remediless calamity. *Brown's Vulgar Errours*, *b.* i. *c.* 2.

3. To be able to sell. It is used always with reference to some certain price; as, *I can afford this for less than the other.*

They fill their magazines in times of the greatest plenty, that so they may *afford* cheaper, and increase the public revenue at a small expence of its members. *Addison on Italy.*

4. To be able to bear expences; as, *traders can afford more finery in peace than war.*

The same errours run through all families, where there is wealth enough to *afford* that their sons may be good for nothing. *Swift on Modern Education.*

To AFFO'REST. *v. a.* [*afforestare*, Lat.] To turn ground into forest.

It appeareth, by *Charta de Foresta*, that he *afforested* many woods and wastes, to the grievance of the subject, which by that law were disafforested. *Sir John Davies on Ireland.*

AFFORESTA'TION. *n. s.* [from *afforest.*]

The charter *de Foresta* was to reform the encroachments made in the time of *Richard* I. and *Henry* II. who had made new *afforestations*, and much extended the rigour of the forest laws. *Hales's Common Law of England.*

To AFFRA'NCHISE. *v. a.* [*affrancher*, Fr.] To make free.

To AFFRA'Y. *v. a.* [*effrayer*, or *effriger*, Fr. which *Menage* derives from *frayer*; perhaps it comes from *frigus.*]

To fright; to terrify; to strike with fear. This word is not now in use.

The same to wight he never won't disclose,
But when as monsters huge he would dismay,
Or daunt unequal armies of his foes,
Or when the flying heavens he would *affray*. *Fairy Queen.*

AFFRA'Y, or AFFRA'YMENT. *n. s.* [from the verb.]

A tumultuous assault of one or more persons upon others; a law term. A battle: in this sense it is written *fray.*

AFFRI'CTION. *n. s.* [*affrictio*, Lat.] The act of rubbing one thing upon another.

I have divers times observed, in wearing silver-hilted swords, that, if they rubbed upon my cloaths, if they were of a light-coloured cloth, the *affriction* would quickly blacken them; and, congruously hereunto, I have found pens blacked almost all over, when I had a while carried them about me in a silver case. *Boyle.*

To AFFRI'GHT. *v. a.* [See FRIGHT.]

1. To affect with fear; to terrify: it generally implies a sudden impression of fear.

Thy name *affrights* me, in whose sound is death.
Shakespeare's Henry VI.

God-like his courage seem'd, whom nor delight
Could soften, nor the face of death *affright*. *Waller.*

He, when his country (threaten'd with alarm)
Requires his courage and his conqu'ring Arm,
Shall, more than once, the Punic bands *affright*. *Dryd. Æn.*

2. It is used in the passive, sometimes with *at* before the thing feared.

Thou shalt not be *affrighted at* them: for the Lord thy God is among you. *Deut.* vii. 21.

3. Sometimes with the particle *with* before the thing feared.

As one *affright*
With hellish fiends, or furies mad uproar,
He then uprose. *Fairy Queen, b.* ii. *cant.* 5.

AFFRI'GHT. *n. s.* [from the verb.]

1. Terrour; fear. This word is chiefly poetical.

As the moon, cloathed with cloudy night,
Does shew to him, that walks in fear and sad *affright*. *F. Q.*

Wide was his parish, not contracted close
In streets, but here and there a straggling house;
Yet still he was at hand, without request,
To serve the sick; to succour the distress'd:
Tempting, on foot, alone, without *affright*,
The dangers of a dark tempestuous night. *Dryd. Fab.*

2. The cause of fear; a terrible object.

I see the gods
Upbraid our suff'rings, and would humble them,
By sending these *affrights*, while we are here,
That we might laugh at their ridiculous fear. *B. Johns. Catil.*

The war at hand appears with more *affright*,
And rises ev'ry moment to the sight. *Dryden's Æneid.*

AFFRI'GHTFUL. *adj.* [from *affright.*] Full of affright or terrour; terrible.

We shall find there is an absence of all that is destructive or *affrightful* to human nature. *Decay of Piety.*

AFFRI'GHTMENT. *n. s.* [from *affright.*]

1. The impression of fear; terrour.

Hearing she was at rest, he attended till she should awake of herself; which she did with the *affrightment* of a dream. *Wotton.*

Passionate words or blows from the tutor, fill the child's mind with terrour and *affrightment*; which immediately takes it wholly up, and leaves no room for other impression. *Locke.*

2. The state of fearfulness.

Whether those that, under any anguish of mind, return to *affrightments* or doubtings, have not been hypocrites. *Hammond.*

To AFFRO'NT. *v. a.* [*affronter*, Fr. that is, *ad frontem stare*; *ad frontem & contumeliam allidere*, to insult a man to his face.]

1. To meet face to face; to encounter. This seems the genuine and original sense of the word, which was formerly indifferent to good or ill.

We have closely sent for Hamlet hither,
That he, as 'twere by accident, may here
Affront Ophelia. *Shakespeare's Hamlet.*

The seditious, the next day, *affronted* the king's forces at the entrance of a highway; whom when they found both ready and resolute to fight, they desired enterparlance, and in the meantime they began to fortify. *Sir John Hayward.*

2. To meet, in an hostile manner, front to front.

His holy rites and solemn feasts profan'd,
And with their darkness durst *affront* his light. *Parad. Lost.*

3. To offer an open insult; to offend avowedly. With respect to this sense, it is observed by Cervantes, that, if a man strikes another on the back, and then runs away, the person so struck is injured, but not *affronted*; an *affront* always implying a justification of the act.

But harm precedes not sin only our foe,
Tempting *affronts* us with his foul esteem
Of our integrity. *Milton's Paradise Lost, b.* ix.

I would learn the cause, why Torrismond,
Within my palace walls, within my hearing,
Almost within my sight, *affronts* a prince,
Who shortly shall command him. *Dryden's Spanish Friar.*

This brings to mind Faustina's fondness for the gladiator, and is interpreted as satire. But how can one imagine, that the Fathers would have dared to *affront* the wife of Aurelius. *Addison.*

AFFRO'NT. *n. s.* [from the verb *affront.*]

1. Insult offered to the face; contemptuous or rude treatment.

He would often maintain Plantianus, in doing *affronts* to his son. *Bacon's Essays.*

You've done enough; for you design'd my chains:
The grace is vanish'd, but th' *affront* remains. *Dryd. Aureng.*

He that is found reasonable in one thing, is concluded to be so in all; and to think or say otherwise, is thought so unjust an *affront*, and so senseless a censure, that no body ventures to do it. *Locke.*

There is nothing which we receive with so much reluctance as advice: we look upon the man who gives it us, as offering an *affront* to our understanding, and treating us like children or ideots. *Addison, Spectator*, N° 512.

2. Outrage; act of contempt, in a more general sense.

Oft have they violated
The temple, oft the law with foul *affronts*,
Abominations rather. *Milton's Paradise Regained.*

3. Open opposition; encounter: a sense not frequent, though regularly deducible from the derivation.

Far beyond
The sons of Anak, famous now and blaz'd,
Fearless of danger, like a petty god
I walk'd about admir'd of all, and dreaded
On hostile ground, none daring my *affront*. *Samson Agonist.*

4. Disgrace; shame. This sense is rather peculiar to the Scottish dialect.

Antonius attacked the pirates of Crete, and, by his too great presumption, was defeated; upon the sense of which *affront* he died with grief. *Arbuthnot on Coins.*

AFFRO'NTER. *n. s.* [from *affront.*] The person that affronts.

AFFRO'NTING. *participial adj.* [from *affront.*] That which has the quality of affronting.

Among words which signify the same principal ideas, some are clean and decent, others unclean; some are kind, others are *affronting* and reproachful, because of the secondary idea which custom has affixed to them. *Watts's Logick.*

To AFFU'SE. *v. a.* [*affundo*, *affusum*, Lat.] To pour one thing upon another.

I fruitlessly poured on them acid liquors, to try if they contained any volatile salt or spirit, which would probably have discovered itself, by making an ebullition with the *affused* liquor. *Boyle.*

AFFU'SION. *n. s.* [*affusio*, Lat.] The act of pouring one thing upon another.

Upon the *affusion* of a tincture of galls, it immediately became as black as ink. *Grew's Musæum.*

To AFFY'. *v. a.* [*affier*, Fr. *affidare mulierem*, Bracton.] To betroth in order to marriage.

Wedded be thou to the hags of hell,
For daring to *affy* a mighty lord
Unto the daughter of a worthless king. *Shakesp. Henry* VI.

To AFFY'. *v. n.* To put confidence in; to put trust in.

Marcus Andronicus, so I do *affy*
In thy uprightness and integrity,
That I will here dismiss my loving friends. *Shak. Tit. Andr.*

AFI'ELD. *adv.* [from *a* and *field.* See FIELD.] To the field.

We drove *afield*, and both together heard
What time the grey fly winds her sultry horn,
Batt'ring our flocks with the fresh dews of night. *Milton.*

Afield I went, amid the morning dew,
To milk my kine, for so should housewives do. *Gay.*

AFLA'T. *adv.* [from *a* and *flat.* See FLAT.] Level with the ground.

When you would have many new roots of fruit-trees, take a low tree, and bow it, and lay all his branches *aflat* upon the ground, and cast earth upon them; and every twig will take root. *Bacon's Natural History.*

AFLO'AT. *adv.* [from *a* and *float.* See FLOAT.] Floating; born up in the water: in a figurative sense, within view; in motion.

There

There is a tide in the affairs of men,
Which taken at the flood, leads on to fortune;
Omitted, all the voyage of their life
Is bound in ſhallows and in miſeries.
On ſuch a full ſea are we now *afloat*;
And we muſt take the current when it ſerves,
Or loſe our ventures. *Shakeſpeare's Julius Cæſar.*

Take any paſſion of the ſoul of man, while it is predominant and *afloat*, and, juſt in the critical height of it, nick it with ſome lucky or unlucky word, and you may as certainly over-rule it to your own purpoſe, as a ſpark of fire, falling upon gun-powder, will infallibly blow it up. *South.*

There are generally ſeveral hundred loads *afloat*, for they begin to cut above twenty-five leagues up the river above Hall; and there are other rivers that flow into the Inn, which bring in their contributions. *Addiſon's Italy.*

AFO'OT. *adv.* [from *a* and *foot.*]

1. On foot; not on horſeback.

He thought it beſt to return, for that day, to a village not far off; and diſpatching his horſe in ſome ſort, the next day early, to come *afoot* thither. *Shakeſpeare's Hamlet.*

2. In action; as, *a deſign is afoot.*

I pr'ythee, when thou ſeeſt that act *afoot*,
Ev'n with the very comment of thy ſoul
Obſerve mine uncle. *Idem, ibid.*

3. In motion.

Of Albany's and Cornwall's pow'rs you heard not—
'Tis ſaid they are *afoot*. *Shakeſpeare's K. Lear.*

AFO'RE. *prep.* [from *a* and *fore.* See BEFORE.]

1. Before; nearer in place to any thing; as, *he ſtood* afore *him.*

2. Sooner in time.

If your diligence be not ſpeedy, I ſhall be there *afore* you. *Shakeſpeare's King Lear.*

AFO'RE. *adv.*

1. In time foregone or paſt.

Whoſoever ſhould make light of any thing *afore* ſpoken or written, out of his own houſe a tree ſhould be taken, and he thereon be hanged. *Eſdras*, vi. 22.

If he never drank wine *afore*, it will go near to remove his fit. *Shakeſpeare's Tempeſt.*

2. Firſt in the way.

Æmilia, run you to the citadel,
And tell my lord and lady what hath hap'd;
Will you go on *afore*? *Shakeſpeare's Othello.*

3. In front; in the fore-part.

Approaching nigh, he reared high *afore*
His body monſtrous, horrible and vaſt. *Fairy Queen.*

AFO'REGOING. *participial adj.* [from *afore* and *going.*] Going before.

AFOREHAND. *adv.* [from *afore* and *hand.*].

1. By a previous proviſion.

Many of the particular ſubjects of diſcourſe are occaſional, and ſuch as cannot *aforehand* be reduced to any certain account. *Government of the Tongue.*

2. Provided; prepared; previouſly fitted.

For it will be ſaid, that in the former times, whereof we have ſpoken, Spain was not ſo mighty, as now it is; and England, on the other ſide, was more *aforehand* in all matters of power. *Bacon's Conſiderations on War with Spain.*

AFO'REMENTIONED. *adj.* [from *afore* and *mentioned.*] Mentioned before.

Among the nine other parts, five are not in a condition to give alms or relief to thoſe *aforementioned*; being very near reduced themſelves to the ſame miſerable condition. *Addiſon.*

AFO'RENAMED. *adj.* [from *afore* and *named.*] Named before.

Imitate ſomething of circular form, in which, as in all other *aforenamed* proportions, you ſhall help yourſelf by the diameter. *Peacham on drawing.*

AFO'RESAID. *adj.* [from *afore* and *ſaid.*] Said before.

It need not go for repetition, if we reſume again that which we ſaid in the *aforeſaid* experiment concerning annihilation. *Bacon's Natural Hiſtory*, N° 771.

AFO'RETIME. *adv.* [from *afore* and *time.*] In time paſt.

O thou that art waxen old in wickedneſs, now thy ſins which thou haſt committed *aforetime*, are come to light. *Suſanna.*

AFRA'ID. *participial adj.* [from the verb *affray*: it ſhould therefore properly be written with *ff.*]

1. Struck with fear; terrified; fearful.

So perſecute them with thy tempeſt, and make them *afraid* with thy ſtorm. *Pſalm* lxxxiii. 15.

2. It has often the particle *of* before the object of fear.

There, loathing life, and yet *of* death *afraid*,
In anguiſh of her ſpirit, thus ſhe pray'd. *Dryden's Fables.*

If, while this wearied fleſh draws fleeting breath,
Not ſatisfy'd with life, *afraid of* death,
It hap'ly be thy will, that I ſhould know
Glimpſe of delight, or pauſe from anxious woe;
From now, from inſtant now, great Sire, diſpel
The clouds that preſs my ſoul. *Prior.*

AFRE'SH. *adv.* [from *a* and *freſh.* See FRESH.] Anew; again, after intermiſſion.

The Germans now uſing no ſuch light horſemen, but ſerving upon great horſes, and charged with heavy armour, received great hurt by theſe light ſkirmiſhes; the Turks, with their light horſes, eaſily ſhunning their charge, and again, at their pleaſure, charging them *afreſh*, when they ſaw the heavy horſes almoſt weary. *Knolles's Hiſtory of the Turks.*

When once we have attained theſe ideas, they may be excited *afreſh* by the uſe of words. *Watts's Logick.*

AFRO'NT. *adv.* [from *a* and *front.*] In front; in direct oppoſition to the face.

Theſe four came all *afront*, and mainly thruſt at me. *Shakeſpeare's Henry* IV. *p.* i.

A'FTER. *prep.* [æꝼꞇeꞃ, Sax.]

1. Following in place. *After* is commonly applied to words of motion; as, he came *after*, and ſtood *behind* him. It is oppoſed to *before.*

What ſays lord Warwick, ſhall we *after* them?—
— *After* them! nay, *before* them, if we can. *Shak. Henry* VI.

2. In purſuit of.

After whom is the king of Iſrael come out? *After* whom doſt thou purſue? *After* a dead dog, *after* a flea. 1 *Sam.* xxiv. 14.

3. Behind.

Sometimes I placed a third priſm *after* a ſecond, and ſometimes alſo a fourth *after* the third, by all which the image might be often refracted ſideways. *Newton's Opticks.*

4. Poſteriour in time.

Good *after* ill, and *after* pain delight;
Alternate, like the ſcenes of day and night. *Dryden's Fab.*

We ſhall examine the ways of conveyance of the ſovereignty of Adam to princes that were to reign *after* him. *Locke.*

5. According to.

He that thinketh Spain our over-match, is no good mintman, but takes greatneſs of kingdoms according to bulk and currency, and not *after* their intrinſic value. *Bacon.*

6. In imitation of.

There are, among the old Roman ſtatues, ſeveral of Venus, in different poſtures and habits; as there are many particular figures of her made *after* the ſame deſign. *Addiſon's Italy.*

This alluſion is *after* the oriental manner: thus in the pſalms, how frequently are perſons compared to cedars. *Pope's Od. notes.*

A'FTER. *adv.*

1. In ſucceeding time. It is uſed of time mentioned as ſucceeding ſome other. So we cannot ſay, I ſhall be happy *after*, but *hereafter*; but we ſay, I was firſt made miſerable by the loſs, but was *after* happier.

Far be it from me, to juſtify the cruelties which were at firſt uſed towards them, which had their reward ſoon *after*. *Bacon.*

The chief were thoſe who, from the pit of hell
Roaming to ſeek their prey on earth, durſt fix
Their ſeats long *after* next the ſeat of God. *Paradiſe Loſt.*

2. Following another.

Let go thy hold, when a great wheel runs down a hill, leſt it break thy neck with following it; but the great one that goes upward, let him draw thee *after*. *Shakeſpeare's King Lear.*

AFTER is compounded with many words, but almoſt always in its genuine and primitive ſignification; ſome, which occurred, will follow, by which others may be explained.

A'FTER ACCEPTATION. [from *after* and *acceptation.*] A ſenſe afterwards, not at firſt admitted.

'Tis true, ſome doctors in a ſcantier ſpace,
I mean, in each apart, contract the place:
Some, who to greater length extend the line,
The church's *after acceptation* join. *Dryd. Hind and Panther.*

A'FTERAGES. *n. ſ.* [from *after* and *ages.*] Succeſſive times; poſterity. This word has no ſingular.

Not the whole land, which the Chuſites ſhould, or might in future time, conquer; ſeeing, in *afterages*, they became lords of many nations. *Raleigh's Hiſtory of the World.*

Nor to philoſophers is praiſe deny'd,
Whoſe wiſe inſtructions *afterages* guide. *Sir J. Denham.*

What an opinion will *afterages* entertain of their religion, who bid fair for a gibbet, by endeavouring to bring in a ſuperſtition, which their forefathers periſhed in flames to keep out. *Addiſon's Freeholder*, N° 1.

A'FTER ALL. When all has been taken into the view; when there remains nothing more to be added; at laſt; in fine; in concluſion.

They have given no good proof in aſſerting this extravagant principle; for which, *after all*, they have no ground or colour, but a paſſage or two of ſcripture, miſerably perverted, in oppoſition to many expreſs texts. *Atterbury's Sermons.*

But, *after all*, if they have any merit, it is to be attributed to ſome good old authors, whoſe works I had leiſure to ſtudy. *Pope on Paſtoral Poetry.*

A'FTERBIRTH. *n. ſ.* [from *after* and *birth.*] The membrane in which the birth was involved, which is brought away after; the ſecundine.

The exorbitances or degenerations of that, whether from a hurt in labour, or from part of the *after-birth* left behind, produce ſuch virulent diſtempers of the blood, as make it caſt out a tumour. *Wiſeman's Surgery.*

A'FTERCLAP. *n. ſ.* [from *after* and *clap.*] Unexpected events happening after an affair is ſuppoſed to be at an end.

For the next morrow's meed they closely went,
For fear of *afterclaps* to prevent. *Spens. Hub. Tale.*

It is commonly taken in an ill sense.

A'FTERCOST. *n. s.* [from *after* and *cost.*] The latter charges; the expence incurred after the original plan is executed.

You must take care to carry off the land-floods and streams, before you attempt draining; lest your *aftercost* and labour prove unsuccessful. *Mortimer's Husbandry.*

A'FTERCROP. *n. s.* [from *after* and *crop.*] The second crop or harvest of the same year.

Aftercrops I think neither good for the land, nor yet the hay good for cattle. *Mortimer's Husbandry.*

A'FTER-DINNER. *n. s.* [from *after* and *dinner.*] The hour passing just after dinner, which is generally allowed to indulgence and amusement.

Thou hast nor youth nor age,
But, as it were, an *afterdinner*'s sleep,
Dreaming on both. *Shakesp. Measure for Measure.*

A'FTER-ENDEAVOUR. *n. s.* [from *after* and *endeavour.*] Endeavours made after the first effort or endeavour.

There is no reason why the sound of a pipe should leave traces in their brains, which, not first, but by their *after-endeavours*, should produce the like sounds. *Locke.*

A'FTER-ENQUIRY. *n. s.* [from *after* and *enquiry.*] Enquiry made after the fact committed, or after life.

You must either be directed by some that take upon them to know, or to take upon yourself that, which, I am sure, you do not know, or lump the *after-enquiry* on your peril; and how you shall speed in your journey's end, I think, you'll never return to tell me. *Shakespeare's Cymbeline.*

To A'FTEREYE. *v. a.* [from *after* and *eye.*] To keep one in view; to follow in view.

Thou shouldst have made him
As little as a crow, or less, ere left
To *aftereye* him. *Shakespeare's Cymbeline.*

A'FTERGAME. *n. s.* [from *after* and *game.*] The scheme which may be laid, or the expedients which are practised after the original design has miscarried; methods taken after the first turn of affairs.

This earl, like certain vegetables, did bud and open slowly; nature sometimes delighting to play an *aftergame*, as well as fortune, which had both their turns and tides in course. *Wotton.*

The fables of the ax-handle and the wedge, serve to precaution us not to put ourselves needlessly upon an *aftergame*, but to weigh beforehand what we say and do. *L'Estrange's Fab.*

Our first design, my friend, has prov'd abortive;
Still there remains an *aftergame* to play. *Addison's Cato.*

A'FTERHOURS. *n. s.* [from *after* and *hours.*] The hours that succeed.

So smile the heav'ns upon this holy act,
That *afterhours* with sorrow chide us not.
Shakespeare's Romeo and Juliet.

A'FTER-LIVER. *n. s.* [from *after* and *live.*] He that lives in succeeding times.

By thee my promise sent
Unto myself, let *after-livers* know. *Sidney, b.* ii.

A'FTERLOVE. *n. s.* [from *after* and *love.*] The second or later love.

Intended, or committed, was this fault?
If but the first, how heinous ere it be,
To win thy *after-love*, I pardon thee. *Shakesp. Richard* II.

A'FTERMATH. *n. s.* [from *after*, and *math*, from *mow.*] The latter math; the second crop of grass mown in autumn. See AFTERCROP.

A'FTERNOON. *n. s.* [from *after* and *noon.*] The time from the meridian to the evening.

A beauty-waining and distressed widow,
Ev'n in the *afternoon* of her best days,
Made prize and purchase of his wanton eye.
Shakespeare's Richard III.

However, keep the lively taste you hold
Of God; love him now, but fear him more;
And, in your *afternoons*, think what you told
And promis'd him at morning-prayer before. *Donne.*

Such, all the morning, to the pleadings run;
But when the bus'ness of the day is done,
On dice, and drink, and drabs, they spend the *afternoon.*
Dryden's Persius, Sat. i.

A'FTERPAINS. *n. s.* [from *after* and *pain.*]

The pains after birth, by which women are delivered of the secundine.

A'FTERPART. *n. s.* [from *after* and *part.*] The latter part.

The flexibleness of the former part of a man's age, not yet grown up to be headstrong, makes it more governable and safe; and, in the *afterpart*, reason and foresight begin a little to take place, and mind a man of his safety and improvement. *Locke.*

A'FTERPROOF. *n. s.* [from *after* and *proof.*] Evidence posteriour to the thing in question.

All know, that he likewise at first was much under the expectation of his *afterproof*; such a solar influence there is in the solar aspect. *Wotton.*

A'FTERTASTE. *n. s.* [from *after* and *taste.*] A taste remaining upon the tongue after the draught, which was not perceived in the act of drinking.

A'FTERTHOUGHT. *n. s.* [from *after* and *thought.*] Reflections after the act; expedients formed too late. It is not properly to be used for *secondthought.*

Expence, and *afterthought*, and idle care,
And doubts of motely hue, and dark despair;
Suspicions, and fantastical surmise,
And jealousy suffus'd with jaundice in her eyes,
Discolouring all she view'd, in tawny dress'd,
Downlook'd, and with a cuckow on her fist. *Dryd. Fables.*

A'FTER-TIMES. *n. s.* [from *after* and *time.*] Succeeding times. See AFTERAGES.

You promis'd once, a progeny divine
Of Romans, rising from the Trojan line,
In *aftertimes* should hold the world in awe,
And to the land and ocean give the law. *Dryd. Virg. Æn.*

A'FTERTOSSING. *n. s.* [from *after* and *toss.*] The motion of the sea after a storm.

Confusions and tumults are only the impotent remains of an unnatural rebellion, and are no more than the *aftertossings* of a sea, when the storm is laid. *Addison's Freeholder*, N° 25.

A'FTERWARD. *adv.* [from *after*, and peaꞃb, Sax.] In succeeding time; sometimes written *afterwards*, but less properly.

Uses not thought upon before, may *afterward* spring up, and be reasonable causes of retaining that, which former considerations did formerly procure to be instituted. *Hooker.*

An anxious distrust of the divine goodness, makes a man more and more unworthy of it; and miserable beforehand, for fear of being so *afterward.* *L'Estrange.*

A'FTERWIT. *n. s.* [from *after* and *wit.*] The contrivance of expedients after the occasion of using them is past. See AFTERTHOUGHT.

There is no recalling of what's gone and past; so that *afterwit* comes too late, when the mischief is done. *L'Estrange.*

A'FTER-WRATH. *n. s.* [from *after* and *wrath.*] Anger when the provocation seems past.

I hear him mock
The luck of Cæsar, which the gods give men
T' excuse their *after-wrath.* *Shakesp. Antony and Cleopatra.*

A'GA. *n. s.* The title of a Turkish military officer.

AGA'IN. *adv.* [agen, Sax.]

1. A second time; once more; marking the repetition of the same thing.

The poor remnant of human seed, which remained in their mountains, peopled their country *again* slowly, by little and little. *Bacon's New Atalantis.*

Go now, deluded man, and seek *again*
New toils, new dangers, on the dusty plain. *Dryd. Æn.*

Some are already retired into foreign countries; and the rest, who possess lands, are determined never to hazard them *again*, for the sake of establishing their superstition. *Swift.*

2. On the other hand; marking some opposition or contrariety.

His wit encreased upon the occasion; and so much the more, if the occasion were sharpened with danger. *Again*, whether it were the shortness of his foresight, or the strength of his will, certain it is, that the perpetual trouble of his fortunes could not have been without defects in his nature. *Bacon.*

Those things that we know not what to do withal, if we had them, and those things, *again*, which another cannot part with, but to his own loss and shame, are the very conditions of this fable. *L'Estrange's Fables.*

3. On another part; marking a transition to some new consideration.

Behold yon mountain's hoary height,
Made higher with new mounts of snow;
Again, behold the winter's weight
Oppress the lab'ring woods below. *Dryden.*

4. In return, noting re-action, or reciprocal action; as, his fortune worked upon his nature, and his nature *again* upon his fortune.

5. Back; in restitution.

When your head did but ake,
I knit my handkerchief about your brows;
The best I had, a princess wrought it me,
And I did never ask it you *again.* *Shakesp. King John.*

6. In return for any thing; in recompence.

That he hath given will he pay *again.* *Prov.* xix. 27.

7. In order of rank or succession; marking distribution.

Question was asked of Demosthenes, What was the chief part of an orator? He answered, Action. What next? Action. What next, *again?* Action. *Bacon's Essays.*

The cause of the holding green, is the close and compact substance of their leaves, and the pedicles of them: and the cause of that *again* is either the tough and viscous juice of the plant, or the strength and heat thereof. *Bacon's Nat. History.*

8. Besides; in any other time or place.

They have the Walloons, who are tall soldiers; yet that is but a spot of ground. But, on the other side, there is not in the world *again* such a spring and seminary of brave military people, as in England, Scotland, and Ireland. *Bacon.*

9. Twice as much; marking the same quantity once repeated.

There are whom heav'n has blest with store of wit,
Yet want as much *again* to manage it;
For wit and judgment ever are at strife,
Tho' meant each other's aid, like man and wife. *Pope.*

I should not be sorry to see a chorus on a theatre, more than as large and as deep *again* as ours, built and adorned at a king's charges. *Dryden's Dufresnoy.*

10. Again and again; with frequent repetition; often.

This is not to be obtained by one or two hasty readings; it must be repeated *again and again*, with a close attention to the tenour of the discourse. *Locke's Essay on St. P. Epistles.*

11. In opposition; by way of resistance.

Who art thou that answerest *again?* *Rom.* ix. 20.

12. Back; as, returning from some message.

Bring us word *again* which way we shall go. *Deut.* i. 22.

AGA'INST. *prep.* [ænᵹeon, onᵹeonδ, Sax.]

1. In opposition to any person.

And he will be a wild man; his hand will be *against* every man, and every man's hand *against* him. *Gen.* xvi. 12.

2. Contrary; opposite, in general.

That authority of men should prevail with men either *against* or above reason, is no part of our belief. *Hooker.*

He is melancholy without cause, and merry *against* the hair. *Shakesp. Troilus and Cressida.*

We might work any effect without and *against* matter; and this not holpen by the co-operation of angels or spirits, but only by the unity and harmony of nature. *Bacon's Natural Hist.*

The preventing goodness of God does even wrest him from himself, and save him, as it were, *against* his will. *South.*

The god, uneasy till he slept again,
Resolv'd, at once, to rid himself of pain;
And, tho' *against* his custom, call'd aloud,
Exciting Morpheus from the sleepy crowd. *Dryden.*

Men often say a thing is *against* their conscience, when really it is not. *Swift's Miscellanies.*

3. In contradiction to any opinion.

After all that can be said *against* a thing, this will still be true, that many things possibly are, which we know not of; and that many more things may be than are: and if so, after all our arguments *against* a thing, it will be uncertain whether it be or not. *Tillotson.*

The church-clergy have written the best collection of tracts *against* popery, that ever appeared in England. *Swift.*

4. With contrary motion or tendency; used of material action.

Boils and plagues
Plaister you o'er, that you may be abhorr'd
Farther than seen, and one infect another
Against the wind a mile. *Shakesp. Coriolanus.*

The kite being a bird of prey, and therefore hot, delighteth in the fresh air; and many times flieth *against* the wind, as trouts and salmons swim *against* the stream. *Bacon.*

5. Contrary to rule or law.

If aught *against* my life
Thy country sought of thee, it sought unjustly,
Against the law of nature, law of nations. *M. Sam. Agon.*

Against the public sanctions of the peace,
Against all omens of their ill success;
With fates averse, the rout in arms resort,
To force their monarch, and insult the court. *Dryden's Æn.*

6. Opposite to, in place.

Against the Tiber's mouth, but far away. *Dryden.*

7. To the hurt of another.

And when thou think'st of her eternity,
Think not that death *against* her nature is;
Think it a birth: and when thou go'st to die,
Sing like a swan, as if thou went'st to bliss. *Sir J. Davies.*

8. In provision for; in expectation of.

This mode of speaking probably had its original from the idea of making provision *against*, or in opposition to a time of misfortune, but by degrees acquired a neutral sense.

Thence she them brought into a stately hall,
Wherein were many tables fair dispred,
And ready dight with drapets festival,
Against the viands should be ministred. *Fairy Queen.*

The like charge was given them *against* the time they should come to settle themselves in the land promised unto their fathers. *Hooker, b.* v. § 11.

Some say, that ever *'gainst* that season comes,
Wherein our Saviour's birth is celebrated,
The bird of dawning singeth all night long:
And then they say no spirit walks abroad;
The nights are wholesome, then no planets strike,
No fairy tales, no witch hath power to charm;
So hallowed and so gracious is the time. *Shakesp. Hamlet.*

To that purpose, he made haste to Bristol, that all things might be ready *against* the prince came thither. *Clarendon.*

Against the promis'd time provides with care,
And hastens in the woof, the robes he was to wear. *Dryd.*

All which I grant to be reasonably and truly said, and only desire they may be remembered *against* another day. *Stillingfl.*

A'GALAXY. *n. s.* [from α and γάλα, Gr.] Want of milk. *Dict.*

AGA'PE. *adv.* [from *a* and *gape.*] Staring with eagerness; as, a bird gapes for meat.

In himself was all his state;
More solemn than the tedious pomp that waits
On princes, when their rich retinue long
Of horses led, and grooms besmear'd with gold,
Dazzles the crowd, and sets them all *agape.* *Paradise Lost.*

Dazzle the crowd, and set them all *agape.* *Philips.*

The whole crowd stood *agape*, and ready to take the doctor at his word. *Spectator,* Nº 572.

A'GARICK. *n. s.* [*agaricum*, Lat.] A drug of use in physick, and the dying trade. It is divided into male and female; the male is used only in dying, the female in medicine: the male grows on oaks, the female on larches.

There are two excrescences which grow upon trees; both of them in the nature of mushrooms: the one the Romans call *boletus*, which groweth upon the roots of oaks, and was one of the dainties of their table; the other is medicinal, that is called *agarick*, which groweth upon the tops of oaks; though it be affirmed by some, that it groweth also at the roots. *Bacon.*

AGA'ST. *adj.* [This word, which is usually, by later authours, written *aghast*, is, not improbably, the true word derived from *agaze*, which has been written *aghast*, from a mistaken etymology. See AGHAST.]

Struck with terrour; amazed; frighted to astonishment.

Thus roving on
In confus'd march forlorn, th' advent'rous bands,
With shudd'ring horrour pale, and eyes *agast*,
View'd first their lamentable lot, and found
No rest. *Milton's Paradise Lost, b.* ii. *l.* 616.

A'GATE. *n. s.* [*agate*, Fr. *achates*, Lat.] A precious stone of the lowest class, often clouded with beautiful variegations.

In shape no bigger than an *agate* stone,
On the forefinger of an alderman. *Shak. Romeo and Juliet.*

Agates are only varieties of the flint kind; they have a grey horny ground, clouded, lineated, or spotted with different colours, chiefly dusky, black, brown, red, and sometimes blue. *Woodward's Method of Fossils.*

A'GATY. *adj.* [from *agate.*] Partaking of the nature of agate.

An *agaty* flint was above two inches in diameter; the whole covered over with a friable cretaceous crust. *Woodward.*

To AGA'ZE. *v. a.* [from *a* and *gaze*, to set *a gazing*; as, *amaze*, *amuse*, and others.] To strike with amazement; to stupify with sudden terrour. The verb is now out of use.

So as they travell'd, so they gan espy
An armed knight toward them gallop fast,
That seemed from some feared foe to fly,
Or other grisly thing that him *agast.* *Fairy Queen.*

AGA'ZED. *participial adj.* [from *agaze*; which see.] Struck with amazement; terrified to stupidity.

Hundreds he sent to hell, and none durst stand him;
Here, there, and every where, enrag'd he slew:
The French exclaim'd; "The devil was in arms!"
All the whole army stood *agazed* on him. *Shak. Henry* VI.

AGE. *n. s.* [*age*, Fr. anciently *eage*, or *aage*; it is deduced by *Menage*, from *ætatium*, of *ætas*; by *Junius*, from *aa*, which, in the Teutonic dialects, signified long duration.]

1. Any period of time attributed to something as the whole, or part, of its duration: in this sense, we say, the *age* of man, the several *ages* of the world, the golden or iron *age.*

One man in his time plays many parts,
His life being seven *ages.* *Shakespeare.*

And Jacob lived in the land of Egypt seventeen years; so the whole *age* of Jacob was an hundred forty and seven years. *Genesis,* xlvii. 28.

2. A succession or generation of men.

Hence, lastly, springs care of posterities,
For things their kind would everlasting make.
Hence is it, that old men do plant young trees,
The fruit whereof another *age* shall take. *Sir J. Davies.*

Next, to the Son,
Destin'd Restorer of mankind, by whom
New heav'n, and earth, shall to the *ages* rise,
Or down from heav'n descend. *Milton's Paradise Lost.*

No declining *age*
E'er felt the raptures of poetic rage. *Roscommon.*

3. The time in which any particular man, or race of men, lived, or shall live; as, the *age* of heroes.

4. The space of a hundred years; a secular period; a century.

5. The latter part of life; old-age; oldness.

You see how full of change his *age* is: the observation we have made of it hath not been little; he always loved our sister most, and with what poor judgment he hath now cast her off. *Shakespeare's King Lear.*

Boys must not have th' ambitious care of men,
Nor men the weak anxieties of *age.* *Roscommon.*

And on this forehead, where your verse has said,
The loves delighted, and the graces play'd;
Insulting *age* will trace his cruel way,
And leave sad marks of his destructive sway. *Prior.*

6. Maturity; ripeneſs; full ſtrength of life.

A ſolemn admiſſion of proſelytes, all that either, being of *age*, deſire that admiſſion for themſelves, or that, in infancy, are by others preſented to that charity of the church. *Hammond.*

We thought our ſires, not with their own content,
Had, ere we came to *age*, our portion ſpent. *Dryd.*

7. In law.

In a man, the *age* of fourteen years is the *age* of diſcretion; and twenty-one years is the full *age*: In a woman, at ſeven years of *age*, the lord her father may diſtrain his tenants for aid to marry her; at the *age* of nine years, ſhe is dowable; at twelve years, ſhe is able finally to ratify and confirm her former conſent given to matrimony; at fourteen, ſhe is enabled to receive her land into her own hands, and ſhall be out of ward at the death of her anceſtor; at ſixteen, ſhe ſhall be out of ward, though, at the death of her anceſtor, ſhe was within the *age* of fourteen years; at twenty-one, ſhe is able to alienate her lands and tenements. At the *age* of fourteen, a ſtripling is enabled to chooſe his own guardian; at the *age* of fourteen, a man may conſent to marriage. *Cowell.*

A'GED. *adj.* [from *age*. It makes two ſyllables in poetry.]

1. Old; ſtricken in years; applied generally to animate beings.

If the compariſon do ſtand between man and man, which ſhall hearken unto other, ſith the *aged*, for the moſt part, are beſt experienced, leaſt ſubject to raſh and unadviſed paſſions. *Hooker, b.* v. § 7.

Novelty is only in requeſt; and it is as dangerous to be *aged* in any kind of courſe, as it is virtuous to be conſtant in any undertaking. *Shakeſp. Meaſure for Meaſure.*

Kindneſs itſelf too weak a charm will prove,
To raiſe the feeble fires of *aged* love. *Prior.*

2. Old; applied to inanimate things. This uſe is rare, and commonly with ſome tendency to the *proſopopœia*.

The people did not more worſhip the images of gold and ivory, than they did the groves; and the ſame Quintilian ſaith of the *aged* oaks. *Stillingfleet's Defence of Diſc. on Rom. Idol.*

A'GEDLY. *adv.* [from *aged.*] After the manner of an aged perſon.

AGE'N. *adv.* [aȝen, Sax.] Again; in return. See AGAIN.

This word is only written in this manner, though it be in reality the true orthography, for the ſake of rhime.

Thus Venus: Thus her ſon reply'd *agen*;
None of your ſiſters have we heard or ſeen. *Dryden's Æn.*

A'GENCY. *n. ſ.* [from *agent.*]

1. The quality of acting; the ſtate of being in action; action.

A few advances there are in the following papers, tending to aſſert the ſuperintendence and *agency* of providence in the natural world. *Woodward's Preface to Nat. Hiſtory.*

2. The office of an agent or factor for another; buſineſs performed by an agent.

Some of the purchaſers themſelves may be content to live cheap in a worſe country, rather than be at the charge of exchange and *agencies*. *Swift.*

A'GENT. *adj.* [*agens*, Lat.] That which acts; oppoſed to *patient*, or that which is acted upon.

This ſucceſs is oft truly aſcribed unto the force of imagination upon the body *agent*; and then, by a ſecondary means, it may upon a diverſe body; as, for example, if a man carry a ring, or ſome part of a beaſt, believing ſtrongly that it will help him to obtain his love, it may make him more induſtrious, and again more confident and perſiſting than otherwiſe he would be. *Bacon's Natural Hiſtory*, N° 902.

A'GENT. *n. ſ.*

1. An actor; he that acts; he that profeſſes the faculty of action.

Where there is no doubt, deliberation is not excluded as impertinent unto the thing, but as needleſs in regard of the *agent*, which ſeeth already what to reſolve upon. *Hooker.*

To whom nor *agent*, from the inſtrument,
Nor pow'r of working, from the work is known. *Davies.*

Heav'n made us *agents* free to good or ill,
And forc'd it not, tho' he foreſaw the will.
Freedom was firſt beſtow'd on human race,
And preſcience only held the ſecond place. *Dryden.*

A miracle is a work exceeding the power of any created *agent*, conſequently being an effect of the divine omnipotence. *South's Sermons.*

2. A ſubſtitute; a deputy; a factor; a perſon employed to tranſact the buſineſs of another.

— All hearts in love, uſe your own tongues;
Let every eye negotiate for itſelf,
And truſt no *agent*. *Shakeſpeare.*

They had not the wit to ſend to them, in any orderly faſhion, *agents* or choſen men, to tempt them, and to treat with them. *Bacon's Henry* VII.

Remember, Sir, your fury of a wife,
Who, not content to be reveng'd on you,
The *agents* of your paſſion will purſue. *Dryden's Aureng.*

3. That which has the power of operating, or producing effects upon another thing.

They produced wonderful effects, by the proper application of *agents* to patients. *Temple.*

AGGENERA'TION. *n. ſ.* [from *ad* and *generatio*, Lat.] The ſtate of growing or uniting to another body.

To make a perfect nutrition, there is required a tranſmutation of nutriment; now where this converſion or *aggeneration* is made, there is alſo required, in the aliment, a ſimilarity of matter. *Brown's Vulgar Errours.*

To A'GGERATE. *v. a.* [from *agger*, Lat.] To heap up. *Dict.*

AGGERO'SE. *adj.* [from *agger*, Lat.] Full of heaps. *Dict.*

To AGGLO'MERATE. *v. a.* [*agglomero*, Lat.]

1. To gather up in a ball, as thread.

2. To gather together.

To AGGLO'MERATE. *v. n.*

Beſides, the hard *agglomerating* ſalts,
The ſpoil of ages, would impervious choke
Their ſecret channels. *Thomſon's Autumn.*

AGGLU'TINANTS. *n. ſ.* [from *agglutinate.*] Thoſe medicines or applications which have the power of uniting parts together.

To AGGLU'TINATE. *v. n.* [from *ad* and *gluten*, glue, Lat.] To unite one part to another; to join together, ſo as not to fall aſunder. It is a word almoſt appropriated to medicine.

It has got room enough to grow into its full dimenſions, which is performed by the daily ingeſtion of food that is digeſted into blood; which being diffuſed through the body, is *agglutinated* to thoſe parts that were immediately *agglutinated* to the foundation-parts of the womb. *Harvey on Conſumptions.*

AGGLUTINA'TION. *n. ſ.* [from *agglutinate.*] Union; coheſion; the act of agglutinating; the ſtate of being agglutinated.

The occaſion of its not healing by *agglutination*, as the other did, was from the alteration the ichor had begun to make in the bottom of the wound. *Wiſeman's Surgery.*

AGGLU'TINATIVE. *adj.* [from *agglutinate.*] That which has the power of procuring agglutination.

Rowl up the member with the *agglutinative* rowler. *Wiſem.*

To AGGRANDI'ZE. *v. a.* [*aggrandiſer*, Fr.] To make great; to enlarge; to exalt; to improve in power, honour, or rank. It is applied to perſons generally, ſometimes to things.

If the king ſhould uſe it no better than the pope did, only to *aggrandize* covetous churchmen, it cannot be called a jewel in his crown. *Ayliffe's Parergon.*

Theſe furniſh us with glorious ſprings and mediums, to raiſe and *aggrandize* our conceptions, to warm our ſouls, to awaken the better paſſions, and to elevate them even to a divine pitch, and that for devotional purpoſes. *Watts's Improv. of the Mind.*

A'GGRANDIZEMENT. *n. ſ.* [*aggrandiſſement*, Fr.] The ſtate of being aggrandized; the act of aggrandizing.

A'GGRANDIZER. *n. ſ.* [from *aggrandize.*] The perſon that aggrandizes or makes great another.

To AGGRA'TE. *v. a.* [*aggratare*, Ital.] To pleaſe; to treat with civilities: a word not now in uſe.

And in the midſt thereof, upon the floor,
A lovely bevy of fair ladies ſate,
Courted of many a jolly paramour;
The which them did in modeſt wiſe amate,
And each one ſought his lady to *aggrate*. *Fairy Queen.*

To A'GGRAVATE. *v. a.* [*aggravo*, Lat.]

1. To make heavy; uſed only in a metaphorical ſenſe; as, to *aggravate* an accuſation, or a puniſhment.

A grove hard by, ſprung up with this their change,
His will who reigns above! to *aggravate*
Their penance, laden with fruit, like that
Which grew in paradiſe, the bait of Eve
Us'd by the tempter. *Milton's Paradiſe Loſt, b.* x.

Ambitious Turnus in the preſs appears,
And *aggravating* crimes augment their fears. *Dryd. Æneid.*

2. To make any thing worſe, by the addition of ſome particular circumſtance, not eſſential.

This offence, in itſelf ſo heinous, was yet in him *aggravated* by the motive thereof, which was not malice or diſcontent, but an aſpiring mind to the papacy. *Bacon's Henry* VII.

AGGRAVA'TION. *n. ſ.* [from *aggravate.*]

1. The act of aggravating, or making heavy.

2. The extrinſecal circumſtances or accidents, which encreaſe the guilt of a crime, or the miſery of a calamity.

If it be weigh'd
By itſelf, with *aggravations* not ſurcharg'd,
Or elſe with juſt allowance counterpois'd,
I may, if poſſible, thy pardon find
The eaſier towards me, or thy hatred leſs. *M. Sampſ. Ag.*

He, to the ſins which he commits, hath the *aggravation* ſuperadded of committing them againſt knowledge, againſt conſcience, againſt ſight of the contrary law. *Hammond's Fundam.*

A'GGREGATE. *adj.* [*aggregatus*, Lat.] Framed by the collection of any particular parts into one maſs, body, or ſyſtem.

They had, for a long time together, produced many other inept combinations, or *aggregate* forms of particular things, and nonſenſical ſyſtems of the whole. *Ray on the Creation.*

A'GGREGATE. *n. ſ.* [from the verb.] The complex or collective reſult of the conjunction or acervation of many particulars.

The reaſon of the far greateſt part of mankind, is but an *aggregate* of miſtaken phantaſms, and, in things not ſenſible, a conſtant deluſion. *Glanville's Scepſis Scientifica.*

A

A great number of ſuch living and thinking particles could n t poſſibly, by their mutual contact, and preſſing, and ſtriking, compoſe one greater individual animal, with one mind and underſtanding, and a vital conſenſion of the whole body; any more than a ſwarm of bees, or a crowd of men and women, can be conceived to make up one particular living creature, compounded and conſtituted of the *aggregate* of them all. *Bentl.*

To AGGREGATE. *v. a.* [*aggrego*, Lat.] To collect together; to heap many particulars into one maſs.

The *aggregated* ſoil
Death, with his mace petrifick, cold, and dry,
As with a trident, ſmote. *Milton's Paradiſe Loſt, b.* x.

AGGREGA'TION. *n. ſ.* [from *aggregate.*]

1. The collection, or act of collecting many particulars into one whole.

The water reſident in the abyſs is, in all parts of it, ſtored with a conſiderable quantity of heat, and more eſpecially in thoſe where theſe extraordinary *aggregations* of this fire happen. *Woodward's Nat. Hiſtory.*

2. The whole compoſed by the coacervation of many particulars; an aggregate.

3. Collection, or ſtate of being collected.

Their individual imperfections being great, they are moreover enlarged by their *aggregation*; and being erroneous in their ſingle numbers, once huddled together, they will be errour itſelf. *Brown's Vulgar Errours, b.* i.

To AGGRE'SS. *v. n.* [*aggredior*, *aggreſſum*, Lat.] To commit the firſt act of violence; to begin the quarrel.

The rage diſpers'd, the glorious pair advance
With mingl'd anger, and collected might,
To turn the war, and tell *aggreſſing* France,
How Britain's ſons, and Britain's friends can fight. *Prior.*

AGGRE'SSION. *n. ſ.* [*aggreſſio*, Lat.] The firſt act of injury; commencement of a quarrel by ſome act of iniquity.

There is no reſiſting of a common enemy, without an union for a mutual defence; and there may be alſo, on the other hand, a conſpiracy of common enmity and *aggreſſion*. *L'Eſtr.*

AGGRE'SSOR. *n. ſ.* [from *aggreſs.*] The perſon that firſt commences hoſtility; the aſſaulter or invader, oppoſed to the *defendant*.

Fly in nature's face?
But how, if nature fly in my face firſt?
Then nature's the *aggreſſor*: Let her look to't.
Dryden's Spaniſh Friar.

It is a very unlucky circumſtance, to be obliged to retaliate the injuries of ſuch authours, whoſe works are ſo ſoon forgotten, that we are in danger already of appearing the firſt *aggreſſors*. *Pope and Swift's Preface to Miſcellanies.*

AGGRI'EVANCE. *n. ſ.* [See GRIEVANCE.] Injury; hardſhip inflicted; wrong endured.

To AGGRI'EVE. *v. a.* [from *gravis*, Lat. See *To grieve.*]

1. To give ſorrow; to cauſe grief; to vex. It is not improbable, that *to grieve* was originally neuter, and *aggrieve* the active.

But while therein I took my chief delight,
I ſaw, alas! the gaping earth devour
The ſpring, the place, and all clean out of ſight:
Which yet *aggrieves* my heart even to this hour. *Spenſer.*

2. To impoſe ſome hardſhips upon; to harraſs; to hurt in one's right. This is a kind of juridical ſenſe; and whenever it is uſed now, it bears ſome alluſion to forms of law.

Sewall, archbiſhop of York, much *aggrieved* with ſome practices of the pope's collectors, took all patiently. *Cambden.*

The landed man finds himſelf *aggrieved*, by the falling of his rents, and the ſtreightening of his fortune; whilſt the monied man keeps up his gain, and the merchant thrives and grows rich by trade. *Locke.*

Of injur'd fame, and mighty wrongs receiv'd,
Cloë complains, and wond'rouſly's *aggriev'd*. *Granville.*

To AGGRO'UP. *v. a.* [*aggropare*, Ital.] To bring together into one figure; to croud together: a term of painting.

Bodies of divers natures, which are *aggrouped* (or combined) together, are agreeable and pleaſant to the ſight; as alſo thoſe things which appear to be performed with eaſe. *Dryd. Dufr.*

AGHA'ST. *adj.* [either the participle of *agaze*, (ſee AGAZE.) and then to be written *agazed*, or *agaſt*, or from *a* and ȝaȝꞇ, a ghoſt, which the preſent orthography favours; perhaps they were originally different words.]

Struck with horrour, as at the ſight of a ſpectre; ſtupified with terrour. It is generally applied to the external appearance.

Who ſighing ſore, as if her heart in twaine
Had riven been, and all her heart-ſtrings braſt,
With dreary drooping eyne look'd up like one *aghaſt*. *Spenſ.*

The aged earth *aghaſt*,
With terrour of that blaſt,
Shall from the ſurface to the centre ſhake. *Mil. Chr. Nat.*

Aghaſt he wak'd, and, ſtarting from his bed,
Cold ſweat in clammy drops his limbs o'erſpread. *Dryd. Æn.*

I laugh to think how your unſhaken Cato
Will look *aghaſt*, while unforeſeen deſtruction
Pours in upon him thus from every ſide. *Addiſon. Cato*

A'GILE. *adj.* [*agile*, Fr. *agilis*, Lat.] Nimble; ready; having the quality of being ſpeedily put in motion; active.

With that he gave his able horſe the head,
And bending forward ſtruck his *agile* heels
Againſt the panting ſides of his poor jade,
Up to the rowel-head. *Shakeſp. Henry* IV.

The immediate and *agile* ſubſervience of the ſpirits to the empire of the mind or ſoul. *Hale's Origin of Mankind.*

To guide its actions with informing care,
In peace to judge, to conquer in the war,
Render it *agile*, witty, valiant, ſage,
As fits the various courſe of human age. *Prior.*

A'GILENESS. *n. ſ.* [from *agile.*] The quality of being agile; nimbleneſs; readineſs for motion; quickneſs; activity; agility.

AGI'LITY. *n. ſ.* [*agilitas*, Lat. from *agilis*, *agile.*] Nimbleneſs; readineſs to move; quickneſs; activity.

A limb over-ſtrained by lifting a weight above its power, may never recover its former *agility* and vigour. *Watts.*

AGI'LLOCHUM. *n. ſ.* Aloes-wood.

A tree in the Eaſt-Indies, brought to us in ſmall bits, of a very fragrant ſcent. It is hot, drying, and accounted a ſtrengthener of the nerves in general. The beſt is of a blackiſh purple colour, and ſo light as to ſwim upon water. *Quincy.*

A'GIO. *n. ſ.* [an Italian word, ſignifying eaſe or conveniency.]

A mercantile term, uſed chiefly in Holland and Venice, for the difference between the value of bank notes, and the current money. *Chambers.*

To AGI'ST. *v. a.* [from *giſte*, Fr. a bed or reſting-place, or from *giſter*, i. e. *ſtabulari.*]

To take in and feed the cattle of ſtrangers in the king's foreſt, and to gather the money. The officers that do this, are called *agiſtors*, in Engliſh *gueſt* or *giſt-takers*. Their function is termed *agiſtment*; as, *agiſtment* upon the ſea banks. This word *agiſt* is alſo uſed, for the taking in of other men's cattle into any man's ground, at a certain rate *per* week. *Blount.*

AGI'STMENT. *n. ſ.* [See AGIST.]

It is taken by the canon lawyers in another ſenſe than is mentioned under *agiſt*. They ſeem to intend by it, a *modus* or compoſition, or mean rate, at which ſome right or due may be reckoned: perhaps it is corrupted from *addouciſſement*, or *adjuſtment*.

AGI'STOR. *n. ſ.* [from *agiſt.*] An officer of the king's foreſt. See AGIST.

A'GITABLE. *n. ſ.* [from *agitate*; *agitabilis*, Lat.] That which may be agitated, or put in motion; perhaps that which may be diſputed. See AGITATE, and AGITATION.

To A'GITATE. *v. a.* [*agito*, Lat.]

1. To put in motion; to ſhake; to move nimbly; as, the ſurface of the waters is *agitated* by the wind; the veſſel was broken by *agitating* the liquour.

2. To be the cauſe of motion; to actuate; to move.

Where dwells this ſov'reign arbitrary ſoul,
Which does the human animal controul,
Informs each part, and *agitates* the whole? *Blackmore.*

3. To affect with perturbation; as, the mind of man is *agitated* by various paſſions.

4. To ſtir; to bandy from one to another; to diſcuſs; to controvert; as, to *agitate* a queſtion.

Though this controverſy be revived, and hotly *agitated* among the moderns; yet I doubt whether it be not, in a great part, a nominal diſpute. *Boyle on Colours.*

AGITA'TION. *n. ſ.* [from *agitate*, *agitatio*, Lat.]

1. The act of moving, or ſhaking any thing.

Putrefaction aſketh reſt; for the ſubtle motion which putrefaction requireth, is diſturbed by any *agitation*. *Bacon.*

2. The ſtate of being moved or agitated; as, the waters, after a ſtorm, are ſometime in a violent *agitation*.

3. Diſcuſſion; controverſial examination.

A kind of a ſchool queſtion is ſtarted in this fable, upon reaſon and inſtinct: and whether this deliberative proceeding of the crow, was not rather a logical *agitation* of the matter. *L'Eſtrange's Fables.*

4. Violent motion of the mind; perturbation; diſturbance of the thoughts.

A great perturbation in nature! to receive at once the benefit of ſleep, and do the effects of watching. In this ſlumbry *agitation*, beſides her walking, and other actual performances, what, at any time, have you heard her ſay? *Shakeſp. Macbeth.*

His mother could no longer bear the *agitations* of ſo many paſſions as thronged upon her. *Tatler, N° 55.*

5. Deliberation; contrivance; the ſtate of being conſulted upon.

The project now in *agitation* for repealing of the teſt act, and yet leaving the name of an eſtabliſhment to the preſent national church, is inconſiſtent *Swift's Miſcell.*

AGITA'TOR. *n. ſ.* [from *agitate.*] He that agitates any thing; he who manages affairs: in which ſenſe ſeems to be uſed the *agitators* of the army.

A'GLET. *n. ſ.* [A word which ſome derive from αἴγλη, ſplendour, but which is apparently to be deduced from *aiguletté*, Fr. a tag to a point, and that from *aigu*, ſharp.]

A tag of a point curved into some representation of an animal, generally of a man.

He thereupon gave for the garter a chain worth 200 l. and his gown addressed with *aglets*, esteemed worth 25 l. *Hayward.*

Why, give him gold enough, and marry him to a puppet, or an *aglet* baby, or an old trot, and ne'er a tooth in her head. *Shakesp. Taming of the Shrew.*

2. The pendants at the ends of the chieves of flowers, as in tulips.

A'GMINAL. *adj.* [from *agmen*, Lat.] Belonging to a troop. *Dict.*

A'GNAIL. *n. s.* [from anȝe, grieved, and naȝle, a nail.]
A disease of the nails; a whitlow; an inflammation round the nails.

AGNA'TION. *n. s.* [from *agnatus*, Lat.] Descent from the same father, in a direct male line, distinct from *cognation*, or consanguinity, which includes descendants from females.

AGNI'TION. *n. s.* [from *agnitio*, Lat.] Acknowledgment.

To AGNI'ZE. *v. a.* [from *agnosco*, Lat.] To acknowledge; to own; to avow. This word is now obsolete.

I do *agnize*
A natural and prompt alacrity
I find in hardness; and do undertake
This present war against the Ottomites. *Shakesp. Othello.*

AGNOMINA'TION. *n. s.* [*agnominatio*, Lat.] Allusion of one word to another, by resemblance of sound.

The British continueth yet in Wales, and some villages of Cornwall, intermingled with provincial Latin, being very significative, copious, and pleasantly running upon *agnominations*, although harsh in aspirations. *Camden.*

AGNUS CASTUS. n. s. [Lat.] The name of the tree commonly called the *Chaste Tree*, from an imaginary virtue of preserving chastity.

Of laurel some, of woodbine many more,
And wreathes of *agnus castus* others bore. *Dryden.*

AGO'. *adv.* [aȝan, Sax. past or gone; whence writers formerly used, and in some provinces the people still use, *agone* for *ago.*]
Past; as, *long ago*; that is, long time has past since. Reckoning time towards the present, we use *since*; as, it is a year *since* it happened: reckoning from the present, we use *ago*; as, it happened a year *ago*. This is not, perhaps, always observed.

Be of good comfort: for the great supply,
That was expected by the Dauphin here,
Are wreck'd three nights *ago* on Godwin sands. *Sh. K. John.*

This both by others and myself I know,
For I have serv'd their sovereign long *ago*;
Oft have been caught within the winding train. *Dryd. Fab.*

I shall set down an account of a discourse I chanced to have with one of them some time *ago*. *Addison. Freeholder.*

AGO'G. *adv.* [a word of uncertain etymology; the French have the term *à gogo*, in low language; as, *ils vivent à gogo*, they live to their wish: from this phrase our word may be, perhaps, derived.]

1. In a state of desire; in a state of imagination; heated with the notion of some enjoyment; longing.

As for the sense and reason of it, that has little or nothing to do here; only let it sound full and round, and chime right to the humour, which is at present *agog*, (just as a big, long, rattling name is said to command even adoration from a Spaniard) and, no doubt, with this powerful, senseless engine, the rabble-driver, shall be able to carry all before him. *South's Sermons.*

2. It is used with the verbs *to be*, or *to set*; as, he *is agog*, or you may *set* him *agog*.

The gawdy gossip, when she's set *agog*,
In jewels drest, and at each ear a bob,
Goes flaunting out, and, in her trim of pride,
Thinks all she says or does, is justify'd. *Dryd. Juv. Sat.* 6.

This maggot has no sooner set him *agog*, but he gets him a ship, freights her, builds castles in the air, and conceits both the Indies in his coffers. *L'Estrange.*

3. It has the particles *on*, or *for*, before the object of desire.

On which the saints are all *agog*,
And all this for a bear and dog. *Hudibras, cant.* ii.

They generally straggle into these parts about this time of the year; and set the heads of our servant-maids so *agog for* husbands, that we do not expect to have any business done as it should be, whilst they are in the country. *Addison. Spectator.*

AGO'NE. *adv.* [aȝan, Sax.] Ago; past. See AGO.

Is he such a princely one,
As you speak him long *agone*? *Ben. Johnson's Fairy Prince.*

A'GONISM. *n. s.* [ἀγωνισμὸς, Gr.] Contention for a prize. *Dict.*

AGO'ING. *participial adj.* [from *a* and *going*.] In action.

Their first movement, and impressed motions, demanded the impulse of an almighty hand to set them first *agoing*. *Tatler.*

A'GONIST. *n. s.* [ἀγωνιστής, Gr.] A contender for prizes. *Dict.*

AGONI'STES. *n. s.* [ἀγωνιστής, Gr.] A prize-fighter; one that contends at any public solemnity for a prize. *Milton* has so stiled his tragedy, because *Sampson* was called out to divert the Philistines with feats of strength.

AGONI'STICAL. *adj.* [from *agonistes*.] Relating to prize-fighting. *Dict.*

To A'GONIZE. *v. n.* [from *agonizo*, low Latin, ἀγωνίζω, Gr. *agoniser*, Fr.] To feel agonies; to be in excessive pain.

Dost thou behold my poor distracted heart,
Thus rent with *agonizing* love and rage,
And ask me what it means? Art thou not false? *Rowe's J. Sh.*

Or touch, if, tremblingly alive all o'er,
To smart and *agonize* at ev'ry pore? *Pope's Essay on Man.*

AGONOTHE'TICK. *adj.* [ἀγων and τίθημι, Gr.] Proposing publick contentions for prizes; giving prizes; presiding at publick games. *Dict.*

A'GONY. *n. s.* [ἀγών, Gr. *agon*, low Lat. *agonie*, Fr.]

1. The pangs of death; properly the last contest between life and death.

Never was there more pity in saving any than in ending me, because therein my *agony* shall end. *Sidney, b.* ii.

Thou who for me did feel such pain,
Whose precious blood the cross did stain,
Let not those *agonies* be vain. *Roscommon.*

2. Any violent or excessive pain of body or mind.

Betwixt them both, they have me done to dy,
Through wounds and strokes, and stubborn handeling,
That death were better than such *agony*,
As grief and fury unto me did bring. *Fairy Queen, b.* ii.

Thee I have miss'd, and thought it long, depriv'd
Thy presence, *agony* of love! till now
Not felt, nor shall be twice. *Milton's Paradise Lost, b.* ix.

3. It is particularly used in devotions for our Redeemer's conflict in the garden.

To propose our desires, which cannot take such effect as we specify, shall, notwithstanding, otherwise procure us his heavenly grace, even as this very prayer of Christ obtained angels to be sent him as comforters in his *agony*. *Hooker, b.* v.

AGO'OD. *adv.* [*a* and *good.*] In earnest; not fictitiously.

At that time I made her weep *agood*,
For I did play a lamentable part. *Shak. Two Gent. of Ver.*

AGO'UTY. *n. s.* An animal of the Antilles, of the bigness of a rabbet, with bright red hair, and a little tail without hair. He has but two teeth in each jaw, holds his meat in his fore-paws like a squirrel, and has a very remarkable cry. When he is angry, his hair stands on end, and he strikes the earth with his hindfeet, and, when chased, he flies to a hollow tree, whence he is expelled by smoke. *Trevoux.*

To AGRA'CE. *v. a.* [from *a* and *grace.*] To grant favours to; to confer benefits upon: a word not now in use.

She granted, and that knight so much *agrac'd*,
That she him taught celestial discipline. *Fairy Queen.*

AGRA'MMATIST. *n. s.* [α, *priv.* and γράμμα, Gr.] An illiterate man. *Dict.*

AGRA'RIAN. *adj.* [*agrarius*, Lat.] Relating to fields or grounds; a word seldom used but in the Roman history, where there is mention of the *agrarian* law.

To AGRE'ASE. *v. a.* [from *a* and *grease.*] To daub; to grease; to pollute with filth.

The waves thereof so slow and sluggish were,
Engross'd with mud, which did them foul *agrease. Fairy Q.*

To AGRE'E. *v. n.* [*agreer*, Fr. from *gré*, liking or good-will; *gratia* and *gratus*, Lat.]

1. To be in concord; to live without contention; not to differ.

The more you *agree* together, the less hurt can your enemies do you. *Pope's View of Epic Poetry.*

2. To grant; to yield to; to admit; with the particles *to* or *upon.*

And persuaded them to *agree to* all reasonable conditions. *2 Maccabees*, xi. 14.

We do not prove the origin of the earth from a chaos; seeing that is *agreed on* by all that give it any origin. *Burnet's Theo.*

3. To settle terms by stipulation; to accord.

Agree with thine adversary quickly, whilst thou art in the way with him; lest at any time the adversary deliver thee to the judge, and the judge deliver thee to the officer, and thou be cast into prison. *Matt.* v. 25.

4. To settle a price between buyer and seller.

Friend, I do thee no wrong: didst not thou *agree* with me for a penny. *Matt.* xx. 13.

5. To be of the same mind or opinion.

He exceedingly provoked, or underwent the envy, and reproach, and malice of men of all qualities and conditions, who *agreed* in nothing else. *Clarendon.*

Milton is a noble genius, and the world *agrees* to confess it. *Watts's Improvement of the Mind.*

6. To settle some point among many.

Strifes and troubles would be endless, except they gave their common consent all to be ordered by some whom they should *agree upon*. *Hooker, b.* i.

If judicious men, skilled in chymical affairs, shall *agree* to write clearly, and keep men from being stunned by dark or empty words, it is hoped, they will be reduced either to write nothing, or books that may teach us something. *Boyle.*

7. To be consistent; not to contradict.

For many bare false witness against him, but their witness *agreed* not together. *Mark*, xiv. 56.

They that stood by said again to Peter, surely thou art one of them: for thou art a Galilean, and thy speech *agreeth* thereto. *Mark*, xiv. 70.

Which testimony I the less scruple to allege, because it *agrees* very well with what has been affirmed to me by a physician at Moscow. *Boyle's History of Colours.*

8. To suit with; to be accommodated to.

Thou feedest thine own people with angels food, and didst send them from heaven bread *agreeing* to every taste. *Wisdom.*

His principles could not be made to *agree* with that constitution and order, which God had settled in the world; and, therefore, must needs clash with common sense and experience. *Locke.*

9. To cause no disturbance in the body.

I have often thought, that our prescribing asses milk in such small quantities, is injudicious; for, undoubtedly, with such as it *agrees* with, it would perform much greater and quicker effects, in greater quantities. *Arbuthnot on Coins.*

To Agree. *v. a.*

1. To put an end to a variance.

He saw from far, or seemed for to see,
Some troublous uproar, or contentious fray,
Whereto he drew in haste it to *agree.* *Fairy Queen, b.* ii.

2. To make friends; to reconcile.

The mighty rivals, whose destructive rage
Did the whole world in civil arms engage,
Are now *agreed.* *Roscommon.*

Agre'eable. *adj.* [*agreable*, Fr.]

1. Suitable to; consistent with. It has the particle *to*, or *with.*

What you do, is not at all *agreeable* either *with* so good a christian, or so reasonable and so great a person. *Temple.*

That which is *agreeable to* the nature of one thing, is many times contrary to the nature of another. *L'Estrange.*

As the practice of all piety and virtue is *agreeable to* our reason, so is it likewise the interest both of private persons and of publick societies. *Tillotson.*

Agreeable hereunto, perhaps it might not be amiss, to make children, as soon as they are capable of it, often to tell a story. *Locke on Education.*

2. Pleasing; that is suitable to the inclination, faculties, or temper. It is used in this sense both of persons and things.

And while the face of outward things we find
Pleasing and fair, *agreeable* and sweet,
These things transport. *Sir J. Davies.*

I recollect in my mind the discourses which have passed between us, and call to mind a thousand *agreeable* remarks, which he has made on these occasions. *Addison. Spectator*, N° 241.

3. It has also the particle *to.*

The delight which men have in popularity, fame, submission, and subjection of other men's minds, seemeth to be a thing, in itself, without contemplation of consequence, *agreeable* and grateful *to* the nature of man. *Bacon's Natural Hist.*

Agre'eableness. *n. s.* [from *agreeable.*]

1. Consistency with; suitableness to; with the particle *to.*

Pleasant tastes depend not on the things themselves, but their *agreeableness to* this or that particular palate, wherein there is great variety. *Locke.*

2. The quality of pleasing. It is used in an inferiour sense, to mark the production of satisfaction, calm and lasting, but below rapture or admiration.

There will be occasion for largeness of mind and *agreeableness* of temper. *Collier of Friendship.*

It is very much an image of that author's writing, who has an *agreeableness* that charms us, without correctness; like a mistress, whose faults we see, but love her with them all. *Pope.*

3. Resemblance; likeness; sometimes with the particle *between.*

This relation is likewise seen in the *agreeableness between* man and the other parts of the universe; and that in sundry respects. *Grew's Cosmologia Sacra.*

Agre'eably. *adv.* [from *agreeable.*]

1. Consistently with; in a manner suitable to.

They may look into the affairs of Judea and Jerusalem, *agreeably to* that which is in the law of the Lord. 1 *Esd.* xviii. 12.

2. Pleasingly.

I did never imagine, that so many excellent rules could be produced so advantageously and *agreeably.* *Swift.*

Agre'ed. *participial adj.* [from *agree.*] Settled by consent.

When they had got known and *agreed* names, to signify those internal operations of their own minds, they were sufficiently furnished to make known by words all their ideas. *Locke.*

Agre'eingness. *n. s.* [from *agree.*] Consistence; suitableness.

Agre'ement. *n. s.* [*agrement*, Fr. in law Latin *agreeamentum*, which Coke would willingly derive from *aggregatio mentium.*]

1. Concord.

What *agreement* is there between the hyena and the dog? and what peace between the rich and the poor? *Ecclus*, xiii. 18.

2. Resemblance of one thing to another.

Expansion and duration have this farther *agreement*, that though they are both considered by us as having parts, yet their parts are not separable one from another. *Locke.*

3. Compact; bargain; conclusion of controversy; stipulation.

And your covenant with death shall be disannulled, and your *agreement* with hell shall not stand; when the overflowing scourge shall pass through, then ye shall be trodden down by it. *Isaiah*, xxviii. 18.

Make an *agreement* with me by a present, and come out to me, and then eat ye every man of his own vine, and every one of his fig-tree, and drink ye every one the waters of his cistern. 2 *Kings*, xviii. 31.

Frog had given his word, that he would meet the abovementioned company at the Salutation, to talk of this *agreement.* *Arbuthnot's History of John Bull.*

Agre'stick, or Agre'stical. *adj.* [from *agrestis*, Lat.] Having relation to the country; rude; rustick. *Dict.*

Agricola'tion. *n. s.* [from *agricola*, Lat.] Culture of the ground. *Dict.*

A'griculture. *n. s.* [*agricultura*, Lat.] The art of cultivating the ground; tillage; husbandry.

He strictly adviseth not to begin to sow before the setting of the stars; which notwithstanding, without injury to *agriculture*, cannot be observed in England. *Brown's Vulgar Errours.*

That there was tillage bestowed upon the ground, Moses does indeed intimate in general; as also, what sort of tillage that was, is not expressed: I hope to shew, that their *agriculture* was nothing near so laborious and troublesome, nor did it take up so much time as ours doth. *Woodward's Nat. History.*

The disposition of Ulysses inclined him to war, rather than the more lucrative, but more secure, method of life, by *agriculture* and husbandry. *Pope's Odyssey; notes.*

A'grimony. *n. s.* [*agrimonia*, Lat.] The name of a plant.

The leaves are rough, hairy, pennated, and grow alternately on the branches; the flower-cup consists of one leaf, which is divided into five segments; the flowers have five or six leaves, and are formed into a long spike, which expand in form of a rose; the fruit is oblong, dry, and prickly, like the burdock; in each of which are contained two kernels.

The species are; 1. The common or medicinal *agrimony.* 2. The sweet-smelling *agrimony.* 3. Lesser *agrimony*, with a white flower.

The first is common in the hedges, in many parts, and is the sort commonly used in medicine. It will grow in almost any soil or situation; and is increased by parting the roots in autumn, or by sowing the seeds soon after they are ripe. *Mill.*

Agro'und. *adv.* [from *a* and *ground.*]

1. Stranded; hindered by the ground from passing farther.

With our great ships we durst not approach the coast, we having been all of us *aground.* *Sir W. Raleigh's Essays.*

Say what you seek, and whether were you bound?
Were you, by stress of weather, cast *aground?* *Dryden's Æn.*

2. It is likewise figuratively used, for being hindered in the progress of affairs; as, the negotiators were *aground* at that objection.

A'GUE. *n. s.* [*aigu*, Fr. *acute.*] An intermitting fever, with cold fits succeeded by hot. The cold fit is, in popular language, more particularly called the *ague*, and the hot the fever.

Our castle's strength
Will laugh a siege to scorn. Here let them lie,
Till famine and the *ague* eat them up. *Shakesp. Macbeth.*

Though
He feels the heats of youth, and colds of age,
Yet neither tempers nor corrects the other;
As if there were an *ague* in his nature,
That still inclines to one extreme. *Denham's Sophy.*

A'gued. *adj.* [from *ague.*] Struck with an ague; shivering; chill; cold: a word in little use.

All hurt behind, backs red, and faces pale,
With flight and *agued* fear! mind and charge home.
Shakespeare's Coriolanus.

A'gue fit. *n. s.* [from *ague* and *fit.*] The paroxysm of the ague.

This *ague fit* of fear is overblown;
An easy task it is to win our own. *Shakesp. Richard* II.

A'gue proof. *adj.* [from *ague* and *proof.*] Proof against agues; able to resist the causes which produce agues, without being affected.

When the rain came to wet me once, and the wind to make me chatter; when the thunder would not peace at my bidding; there I found 'em, there I smelt 'em out. Go to, they are not men o' their words; they told me I was every thing: 'tis a lie; I am not *ague proof.* *Shakespeare's King Lear.*

A'gue-tree. *n. s.* [from *ague* and *tree.*] A name sometimes given to sassafras. *Dict.*

To Agu'ise. *v. a.* [from *a* and *guise.* See Guise.] To dress; to adorn; to deck: a word now not in use.

At other whiles she would devise,
As her fantastick wit did most delight;
Sometimes her head she fondly would *aguise*
With gaudy garlands, or fresh flowers dight
About her neck, or rings of rushes plight. *Fairy Queen.*

A'guish. *adj.* [from *ague.*] Having the qualities of an ague.

So calm, and so serene, but now,
What means this change on Myra's brow?
Her *aguish* love now glows and burns,
Then chills and shakes, and the cold fit returns. *Granville.*

A'guishness. *n. s.* [from *aguish.*] The quality of resembling an ague.

AH. *interjection.*

1. A word noting sometimes dislike and censure.

Ah! sinful nation, a people laden with iniquity, a seed of evil-doers, children that are corrupters, they have forsaken the Lord. *Isaiah*, i. 4.

2. Sometimes contempt and exultation.

Let them not say in their hearts, *Ah!* so we would have it: let them not say, we have swallowed him up. *Psalm* xxxv. 25.

3. Sometimes, and most frequently, compassion and complaint.

In youth alone, unhappy mortals live;
But, *ah!* the mighty bliss is fugitive:
Discolour'd sickness, anxious labour come,
And age and death's inexorable doom. *Dryd. Virg. Georg.* iii.

Ah me! the blooming pride of May,
And that of beauty, are but one:
At morn both flourish bright and gay,
Both fade at evening, pale, and gone. *Prior.*

4. When it is followed by *that*, it expresses vehement desire.

In goodness, as in greatness, they excell;
Ah that! we loved ourselves but half so well. *Dryd. Juven.*

AHA', AHA'! *interjection.* A word intimating triumph and contempt.

They opened their mouth wide against me, and said, *Aha, aha!* our eye hath seen it. *Psalm* xxxv. 21.

AHE'AD. *adv.* [from *a* and *head.*]

1. Farther onward than another: a sea term.

And now the mighty Centaur seems to lead,
And now the speedy dolphin gets *ahead.* *Dryden's Æn.*

2. Headlong; precipitant: used of men.

It is mightily the fault of parents, guardians, tutors, and governours, that so many men miscarry. They suffer them at first to run *ahead*, and, when perverse inclinations are advanced into habits, there is no dealing with them. *L'Estrange's Fab.*

AHE'IGHT. *adv.* [from *a* and *height.*] Aloft; on high.

But have I fall'n or no?—
—From the dread summit of this chalky bourne!
Look up *aheight*, the shrill-gorg'd lark so far
Cannot be seen or heard. *Shakespeare's King Lear.*

AHOUA'I. n. s. The name of a plant.

It hath funnel-shaped flowers of one leaf, divided into several parts at the top; the pointal, which rises from the cup, is fixed, like a nail, to the inner part of the flower, and becomes a pear-shaped fleshy fruit, inclosing a three-cornered nut.

There are two species of this plant abounding on the continent of South America: the first grows to the height of our common cherry-tree; its leaves are three or four inches long, and almost two inches broad; the wood of it stinks most abominably, and the kernel of the nut is a most deadly poison; to expel which, the Indians know no antidote, nor will they use the wood for fuel. The second sort, with an oleander leaf, and a yellow flower, does not grow higher than ten or twelve feet; its fruit is of a beautiful red colour when ripe, and equally poisonous with the former. Both plants abound in every part with a milky juice. *Millar.*

To AID. *v. a.* [*aider*, Fr. from *adjutare*, Lat.] To help; to support; to succour.

Into the lake he leapt, his lord to *aid*,
(So love the dread of danger doth despise)
And of him catching hold, him strongly staid
From drowning. *Fairy Queen, b.* ii. *c.* 6.

Neither shall they give any thing unto them that make war upon them, or *aid* them with victuals, weapons, money, or ships. *Maccabees*, viii. 26.

By the loud trumpet, which our courage *aids*,
We learn that sound as well as sense persuades. *Roscommon.*

AID. *n. s.* [from *To aid.*]

1. Help; support.

The memory of useful things may receive considerable *aid*, if they are thrown into verse. *Watts's Improvement of the Mind.*

Your patrimonial stores in peace possess;
Undoubted all your filial claim confess:
Your private right should impious power invade,
The peers of Ithaca would arm in *aid.* *Pope's Odyssey, b.* i.

2. The person that gives help or support; a helper.

Thou hast said, it is not good that man should be alone; let us make unto him an *aid*, like unto himself. *Tobit*, viii. 6.

3. In law.

A subsidy. *Aid* is also particularly used in matter of pleading, for a petition made in court, for the calling in of help from another, that hath an interest in the cause in question; and is likewise both to give strength to the party that prays in *aid* of him, and also to avoid a prejudice accruing toward his own right, except it be prevented: as, when a tenant for term of life, courtesy, &c. being impleaded touching his estate, he may pray in *aid* of him in the reversion; that is, entreat the court, that he may be called in by writ, to allege what he thinks good for the maintenance both of his right and his own. *Cowell.*

A'IDANCE. *n. s.* [from *aid.*] Help; support: a word little used.

Oft have I seen a timely parted ghost,
Of ashy semblance, meagre, pale, and bloodless,
Being all descended to the lab'ring heart,
Who, in the conflict that it holds with death,
Attracts the same for *aidance* 'gainst the enemy. *Sh. Hen.* VI.

A'IDANT. *adj.* [*aidant*, Fr.] Helping; helpful.

All you unpublish'd virtues of the earth,
Spring with my tears; be *aidant* and remediate
In the good man's distress. *Shakesp. King Lear.*

A'IDER. *n. s.* [from *aid.*] He that brings aid or help; a helper; an ally.

All along as he went, were punished the adherents and *aiders* of the late rebels. *Bacon's Henry* VII.

A'IDLESS. *adj.* [from *aid* and *less*, an inseparable particle.] Helpless; unsupported; undefended.

Alone he enter'd
The mortal gate o' the city, which he painted
With shunless destiny: *aidless* came off,
And, with a sudden re-enforcement, struck
Corioli, like a planet. *Shakesp. Coriolanus.*

Had met
Already, ere my best speed could prevent,
The *aidless* innocent lady, his wish'd prey. *Milt. Comus.*

A'IGULET. *n. s.* [*aigulet*, Fr.] A point with tags; points of gold at the end of fringes.

Which all above besprinkled was throughout
With golden *aigulets* that glister'd bright,
Like twinkling stars, and all the skirt about
Was hemm'd with golden fringes. *Fairy Queen, b.* ii.

To AIL. *v. a.* [eglan, Sax. to be troublesome.]

1. To pain; to trouble; to give pain.

And the angel of God called to Hagar out of heaven, and said unto her, what *aileth* thee, Hagar? fear not: for God hath heard the voice of the lad where he is. *Gen.* xxi. 17.

2. It is used, in a sense less determinate, for *to affect* in any manner; as, *something* ails *me that I cannot sit still*; *what* ails *the man that he laughs without reason?*

Love smil'd, and thus said, Want join'd to desire is unhappy;
But if he nought do desire, what can Heraclitus *ail?* *Sidney.*

What *ails* me, that I cannot lose thy thought!
Command the empress hither to be brought,
I, in her death, shall some diversion find,
And rid my thoughts at once of woman-kind.
Dryden's Tyrannick Love.

3. To feel pain; to be incommoded.

4. It is remarkable, that this word is never used but with some indefinite term, or the word *nothing*; as, *What ails* him? *What* does he *ail?* He *ails something*; he *ails nothing*. *Something ails* him; *nothing ails* him. Thus we never say, a fever *ails* him, or he *ails* a fever, or use definite terms with this verb.

AIL. *n. s.* [from the verb.] A disease.

Or heal, O Narses, thy obscener *ail.* *Pope.*

A'ILMENT. *n. s.* [from *ail.*] Pain; disease.

Little *ailments* oft attend the fair,
Not decent for a husband's eye or ear. *Granville.*

I am never ill, but I think of your *ailments*, and repine that they mutually hinder our being together. *Swift's Letters.*

A'ILING. *participial adj.* [from *To ail.*] Sickly; full of complaints.

To AIM. *v. a.* [It is derived by *Skinner* from *esmer*, to point at; a word which I have not found.]

1. To endeavour to strike with a missive weapon; to direct towards; with the particle *at.*

Aim'st thou *at* princes, all amaz'd they said,
The last of games? *Pope's Odyssey.*

2. To point the view, or direct the steps towards any thing; to tend towards; to endeavour to reach or obtain; with *to* formerly, now only with *at.*

Lo, here the world is bliss; so here the end
To which all men do *aim*, rich to be made,
Such grace now to be happy is before thee laid. *Fairy Q.*

Another kind there is, which although we desire for itself, as health, and virtue, and knowledge, nevertheless they are not the last mark *whereat* we *aim*, but have their further end whereunto they are referred. *Hooker, b.* i.

Swoln with applause, and *aiming* still *at* more,
He now provokes the sea gods from the shore. *Dryden's Æn.*

Religion tends to the ease and pleasure, the peace and tranquillity of our minds, which all the wisdom of the world did always *aim at*, as the utmost felicity of this life. *Tillotson.*

3. To direct the missile weapon; more particularly taken for the act of pointing the weapon by the eye, before its dismission from the hand.

And proud Ideus, Priam's charioteer,
Who shakes his empty reins, and *aims* his airy spear. *Dryd.*

4. To guess.

AIM. *n. s.* [from the verb.]

1. The direction of a missile weapon.

Ascanius, young and eager of his game,
Soon bent his bow, uncertain of his *aim*;
But the dire fiend the fatal arrow guides,
Which pierc'd his bowels through his parting sides.
Dryden, Æn. vii. *l.* 691.

2. The point to which the thing thrown is directed.

That

That arrows fled not ſwifter toward their *aim*,
Than did our ſoldiers, aiming at their ſafety,
Fly from the field. *Shakeſp. Henry* IV. *p.* ii.

3. In a figurative ſenſe, a purpoſe; a ſcheme; an intention; a deſign.

He truſted to have equall'd the moſt High,
If he oppos'd: and, with ambitious *aim*
Againſt the throne, and monarchy of God,
Rais'd impious war. *Milton's Parad. Loſt, b.* i. *l.* 41.

But ſee, how oft ambitious *aims* are croſt,
And chiefs contend till all the prize is loſt. *Pope.*

4. The object of a deſign; the thing after which any one endeavours.

The ſafeſt way is to ſuppoſe, that the epiſtle has but one *aim*, till, by a frequent peruſal of it, you are forced to ſee there are diſtinct independent parts. *Locke's Eſſay on St. Paul's Epiſtles.*

5. Conjecture; gueſs.

It is impoſſible, by *aim*, to tell it; and, for experience and knowledge thereof, I do not think that there was ever any of the particulars thereof. *Spenſer on Ireland.*

There is a hiſtory in all mens lives,
Figuring the nature of the times deceas'd;
The which obſerv'd, a man may propheſy,
With a near *aim*, of the main chance of things,
As yet not come to life, which, in their ſeeds
And weak beginnings, lie intreaſur'd. *Shakeſp. Henry* IV.

AIR. *n. ſ.* [*air*, Fr. *aër*, Lat.]

1. The element encompaſſing the terraqueous globe.

If I were to tell what I mean by the word *air*, I may ſay, it is that fine matter which we breathe in and breathe out continually; or it is that thin fluid body, in which the birds fly, a little above the earth; or it is that inviſible matter, which fills all places near the earth, or which immediately encompaſſes the globe of earth and water. *Watts's Logick.*

2. The ſtate of the air; or the air conſidered with regard to health.

There be many good and healthful *airs*, that do appear by habitation and other proofs, that differ not in ſmell from other *airs*. *Bacon's Natural Hiſtory*, N° 904.

3. Air in motion; a ſmall gentle wind.

Freſh gales, and gentle *airs*,
Whiſper'd it to the woods, and from their wings
Flung roſe, flung odours from the ſpicy ſhrub
Diſporting! *Milton's Paradiſe Loſt, b.* viii. *l.* 515.

But ſafe repoſe, without an *air* of breath,
Dwells here, and a dumb quiet next to death. *Dryden.*

Let vernal *airs* through trembling oſiers play,
And Albion's cliffs reſound the rural lay. *Pope's Paſtorals.*

4. Blaſt.

All the ſtor'd vengeancies of heaven fall
On her ingrateful top! ſtrike her young bones,
You taking *airs*, with lameneſs. *Shakeſp. King Lear.*

5. Any thing light or uncertain; that is as light as air.

O momentary grace of mortal men,
Which we more hunt for than the grace of God!
Who builds his hope in *air* of your fair looks,
Lives like a drunken ſailor on a maſt,
Ready, with ev'ry nod, to tumble down
Into the fatal bowels of the deep. *Shakeſp. Rich.* III.

6. The open weather; air unconfined.

The garden was inclos'd within the ſquare,
Where young Emilia took the morning *air*. *Dryd. Fables.*

7. Vent; utterance; emiſſion into the air.

I would have aſk'd you, if I durſt for ſhame,
If ſtill you lov'd? you gave it *air* before me.
But ah! why were we not both of a ſex?
For then we might have lov'd without a crime. *Dryd. D.Seb.*

8. Publication; expoſure to the publick view and knowledge.

I am ſorry to find it has taken *air*, that I have ſome hand in theſe papers. *Pope's Letters.*

9. Intelligence; information.

It grew alſo from the *airs*, which the princes and ſtates abroad received from their ambaſſadors and agents here; which were attending the court in great number. *Bacon's Henry* VII.

10. Poetry; a ſong.

And the repeated *air*
Of ſad Electra's poet, had the pow'r
To ſave th' *Athenian* walls from ruin bare. *Parad. Regain.*

11. Muſick, whether light or ſerious.

This muſick crept by me upon the waters,
Allaying both their fury and my paſſion,
With its ſweet *air*. *Shakeſpeare's Tempeſt.*

Call in ſome muſick; I have heard, ſoft *airs*
Can charm our ſenſes, and expel our cares. *Denh. Sophy.*

The ſame *airs*, which ſome entertain with moſt delightful tranſports, to others are importune. *Glanville's Sceyſis Scient.*

Since we have ſuch a treaſury of words, ſo proper for the *airs* of muſick, I wonder that perſons ſhould give ſo little attention. *Addiſon. Spectator*, N° 406.

Born on the ſwelling notes, our ſouls aſpire,
While ſolemn *airs* improve the ſacred fire;
And angels lean from heav'n to hear! *Pope's St. Cæcilia.*

— When the ſoul is ſunk with cares,
Exalts [illegible] enliv'ning *airs*. *Pope's Cæcilia.*

12. The mien, or manner, of the perſon.

Her graceful innocence, her ev'ry *air*,
Of geſture, or leaſt action, over-aw'd
His malice. *Milton's Paradiſe Loſt, b.* ix. *l.* 459.

For the *air* of youth
Hopeful and chearful, in thy blood ſhall reign
A melancholy damp of cold and dry,
To weigh thy ſpirits down; and laſt conſume
The balm of life. *Milt. Par. Loſt, b.* xi. *l.* 452.

But, having the life before us, beſides the experience of all they knew, it is no wonder to hit ſome *airs* and features, which they have miſſed. *Dryden on Dramatick Poetry.*

There is ſomething wonderfully divine in the *airs* of this picture. *Addiſon on Italy.*

Yet ſhould the Graces all thy figures place,
And breathe an *air* divine on ev'ry face. *Pope.*

13. An affected or laboured manner or geſture; as, a lofty *air*, a gay *air*.

Whom Ancus follows, with a fawning *air*;
But vain within, and proudly popular. *Dryd. Æn.* vi.

There are of theſe ſort of beauties, which laſt but for a moment; as, the different *airs* of an aſſembly, upon the ſight of an unexpected and uncommon object, ſome particularity of a violent paſſion, ſome graceful action, a ſmile, a glance of an eye, a diſdainful look, a look of gravity, and a thouſand other ſuch like things. *Dryden's Dufreſnoy.*

Their whole lives were employed in intrigues of ſtate, and they naturally give themſelves *airs* of kings and princes, of which the miniſters of other nations are only the repreſentatives. *Addiſon's Remarks on Italy.*

To curl their waving hairs,
Aſſiſt their bluſhes, and inſpire their *airs*. *Pope.*

He aſſumes and affects an entire ſet of very different *airs*; he conceives himſelf a being of a ſuperiour nature. *Swift.*

14. Appearance.

As it was communicated with the *air* of a ſecret, it ſoon found its way into the world. *Pope's Ded. to Rape of the Lock.*

15. [In horſemanſhip.] *Airs* denote the artificial or practiſed motions of a managed horſe. *Chambers.*

To AIR. *v. a.* [from the noun *air*.]

1. To expoſe to the air.

Fleas breed principally of ſtraw or mats, where there hath been a little moiſture, or the chamber and bed-ſtraw kept cloſe, and not *aired*. *Bacon's Natural Hiſtory*, N° 696.

We have had, in our time, experience twice or thrice, when both the judges that ſat upon the jail, and numbers of thoſe that attended the buſineſs, or were preſent, ſickened upon it, and died. Therefore, it were good wiſdom, that, in ſuch caſes, the jail were *aired*, before they were brought forth. *Bacon's Natural Hiſtory*, N° 914.

As the ants were *airing* their proviſions one winter, up comes a hungry graſhopper to them, and begs a charity. *L'Eſtrange's Fables.*

Or wicker-baſkets weave, or *air* the corn,
Or grinded grain, betwixt two marbles turn. *Dryd. Virgil.*

2. To take the air, or enjoy the open air, with the reciprocal pronoun.

Nay, ſtay a little———
Were you but riding forth to *air yourſelf*,
Such parting were too petty. *Shakeſp. Cymbeline.*

I aſcended the higheſt hills of Bagdat, in order to paſs the reſt of the day in meditation and prayer. As I was here *airing myſelf* on the tops of the mountains, I fell into a profound contemplation on the vanity of human life. *Addiſon. Spect.*

3. To open to the air; as, clothes.

The others make it a matter of ſmall commendation in itſelf, if they, who wear it, do nothing elſe but *air* the robes, which their place requireth. *Hooker, b.* v. § 29.

4. To air liquors; to warm them by the fire: a term uſed in converſation.

5. To make neſts. In this ſenſe, it is derived from *aery*, a neſt. It is now out of uſe.

You may add their buſy, dangerous, diſcourteous, yea, and ſometimes deſpiteful ſtealing, one from another, of the eggs and young ones; who, if they were allowed to *air* naturally and quietly, there would be ſtore ſufficient, to kill not only the partridges, but even all the good houſewives chickens in a country. *Carew's Survey of Cornwall.*

A'IRBLADDER. *n. ſ.* [from *air* and *bladder*.]

1. Any cuticle or veſicle filled with air.

The pulmonary artery and vein paſs along the ſurfaces of theſe *airbladders*, in an infinite number of ramifications. *Arbuthnot on Aliments.*

2. The bladder in fiſhes, by the contraction and dilatation of which, they vary the properties of their weight to that of their bulk, and riſe or fall.

Though the *airbladder* in fiſhes ſeems neceſſary for ſwimming, yet ſome are ſo formed as to ſwim without it. *Cudworth.*

A'IRBUILT. *adj.* [from *air* and *build*.] Built in the air, without any ſolid foundation.

Hence the fool's paradiſe, the ſtateſman's ſcheme,
The *airbuilt* caſtle, and the golden dream,

The maid's romantick wish, the chymist's flame,
And poet's vision of eternal fame. *Pope's Dunciad, b.* iii.

AIR-DRAWN. *adj.* [from *air* and *drawn.*] Drawn or painted in air.

This is the very painting of your fear,
This is the *air-drawn* dagger, which, you said,
Led you to Duncan. *Shakesp. Macbeth.*

A'IRER. *n. s.* [from *To air.*] He that exposes to the air.

A'IRHOLE. *n. s.* [from *air* and *hole.*] A hole to admit the air.

A'IRINESS. *n. s.* [from *airy.*]

1. Openness; exposure to the air.

2. Lightness; gaiety; levity.

The French have indeed taken worthy pains to make classick learning speak their language; if they have not succeeded, it must be imputed to a certain talkativeness and *airiness* represented in their tongue, which will never agree with the sedateness of the Romans, or the solemnity of the Greeks. *Felton.*

A'IRING. *n. s.* [from *air.*] A short journey or ramble to enjoy the free air.

This little fleet serves only to fetch them wine and corn, and to give their ladies an *airing* in the summer-season. *Add. on It.*

A'IRLESS. *adj.* [from *air.*] Without communication with the free air.

Nor stony tower, nor walls of beaten brass,
Nor *airless* dungeon, nor strong links of iron,
Can be retentive to the strength of spirit. *Shakesp. J. Cæsar.*

A'IRLING. *n. s.* [from *air*, for *gayety.*] A young, light, thoughtless, gay person.

Some more there be, slight *airlings*, will be won
With dogs, and horses, and perhaps a whore. *B. John. Catil.*

A'IRPUMP. *n. s.* [from *air* and *pump.*]

A machine by whose means the air is exhausted out of proper vessels. The principle on which it is built, is the elasticity of the air; as that on which the waterpump is founded, is on the gravity of the air. The invention of this curious instrument is ascribed to Otto de Guerick, consul of Magdebourg, who exhibited his first publick experiments before the emperour and the states of Germany, in 1654. But his machine laboured under several defects, in the force necessary to work it, which was very great, and the progress very slow; besides, it was to be kept under water, and allowed of no change of subjects for experiments. However, Mr. Boyle, with the assistance of Dr. Hooke, removed several of these inconveniencies; though, still, the working of this pump was laborious, by reason of the pressure of the atmosphere at every exsuction, after a vacuum was nearly obtained. This labour has been since removed by Mr. Hawksbee; who, by adding a second barrel and piston, to rise as the other fell, and fall as it rose, made the pressure of the atmosphere on the descending one, of as much service as it was of disservice in the ascending one. Vream made a further improvement in Hawksbee's air-pump, by reducing the alternate motion of the hand and winch to a circular one. *Chambers.*

For the air that, in exhausted receivers of *airpumps*, is exhaled from minerals, and flesh, and fruits, and liquours, is as true and genuine as to elasticity and density, or rarefaction, as that we respire in; and yet this factitious air is so far from being fit to be breathed in, that it kills animals in a moment, even sooner than the very absence of all air, or a vacuum itself. *Bentley's Sermons.*

A'IRSHAFT. *n. s.* [from *air* and *shaft.*] A passage for the air into mines and subterraneous places.

By the sinking of an *airshaft*, the air hath liberty to circulate, and carry out the steams both of the miners breath and the damps, which would otherwise stagnate there. *Ray.*

A'IRY. *adj.* [from *air*; *aëreus*, Lat.]

1. Composed of air.

The first is the transmission, or emission, of the thinner and more *airy* parts of bodies; as, in odours and infections: and this is, of all the rest, the most corporeal. *Bacon.*

2. Relating to the air; belonging to the air.

There are fishes that have wings, that are no strangers to the *airy* region. *Boyle.*

3. High in air.

Whole rivers here forsake the fields below,
And, wond'ring at their height, through *airy* channels flow. *Addison.*

4. Light as air; thin; unsubstantial; without solidity.

I hold ambition of so *airy* and light a quality, that it is but a shadow's shadow. *Shakesp. Hamlet.*

Still may the dog the wand'ring troops constrain
Of *airy* ghosts, and vex the guilty train;
And, with her grisly lord, his lovely queen remain. *Dr. Æn.*

5. Without reality; without any steady foundation in truth or nature; vain; trifling.

Nor think with wind
Of *airy* threats to awe whom yet with deeds
Thou can'st not. *Milton's Paradise Lost, b.* vi.

Nor (to avoid such meanness) soaring high,
With empty sound, and *airy* notions, fly. *Roscommon.*

I have found a complaint concerning the scarcity of money, which occasioned many *airy* propositions for the remedy of it. *Temple's Miscellanies.*

6. Fluttering; loose; as if to catch the air; full of levity.

But the epick poem is too stately to receive those little ornaments. The painters draw their nymphs in thin and *airy* habits; but the weight of gold and of embroideries is reserved for queens and goddesses. *Dryd. Æneid, Dedicat.*

By this name of ladies, he means all young persons, slender, finely shaped, *airy*, and delicate: such as are nymphs and Naïads. *Dryden's Dufresnoy.*

7. Gay; sprightly; full of mirth; vivacious; lively; spirited; light of heart.

He that is merry and *airy* at shore, when he sees a sad and a loud tempest on the sea, or dances briskly when God thunders from heaven, regards not when God speaks to all the world. *Taylor's Rule of living holy.*

AISLE. *n. s.* [Thus the word is written by Addison, but perhaps improperly; since it seems deducible only from either *aile*, a wing, or *allée*, a path; and is therefore to be written *aile.*] The walks in a church, or wings of a quire.

The abbey is by no means so magnificent as one would expect from its endowments. The church is one huge nef, with a double *aisle* to it; and, at each end, is a large quire. *Addison.*

AIT, or EYGHT. *n. s.* [supposed, by *Skinner*, to be corrupted from *islet.*] A small island in a river.

A'JUTAGE. n. s. [*ajutage*, Fr.] An additional pipe to waterworks. *Dict.*

To AKE. *v. n.* [from ἄχος, Gr. and therefore more grammatically written *ache*. See ACHE.]

1. To feel a lasting pain, generally of the internal pains; distinguished from smart, which is commonly used of uneasiness in the external parts; but this is no accurate account.

To sue, and be deny'd, such common grace,
My wounds *ake* at you! *Shakesp. Timon.*

Let our finger *ake*, and it endues
Our other healthful members with a sense
Of pain. *Shakesp. Othello.*

Were the pleasure of drinking accompanied, the very moment, with that sick stomach and *aking* head, which, in some men, are sure to follow, I think, no body would ever let wine touch his lips. *Locke.*

His limbs must *ake*, with daily toils opprest,
Ere long-wish'd night brings necessary rest. *Prior.*

2. It is frequently applied, in an improper sense, to the heart; as, *the heart akes*; to imply grief or fear. *Shakespeare* has used it, still more licentiously, of the soul.

Here shame dissuades him, there his fear prevails,
And each, by turns, his *aking* heart assails. *Addis. Ov. Met.*

My soul *akes*
To know when two authorities are up,
Neither supreme, how soon confusion
May enter. *Shakesp. Coriolanus.*

AKI'N. *adj.* [from *a* and *kin.*]

1. Related to; allied to by blood; used of persons.

I do not envy thee, dear Pamela; only I could wish, that, being thy sister in nature, I were not so far off *akin* in fortune. *Sidney, b.* ii.

2. Allied to by nature; partaking of the same properties; used of things.

The cankered passion of envy is nothing *akin* to the silly envy of the ass. *L'Estrange, Fab.* xxxviii.

Some limbs again in bulk or stature
Unlike, and not *akin* by nature,
In concert act, like modern friends,
Because one serves the other's ends. *Prior.*

He separates it from questions with which it may have been complicated, and distinguishes it from questions which may be *akin* to it. *Watts's Improvement of the Mind, p.* i. *c.* 13.

AL, ATTLE, ADLE, do all seem to be corruptions of the Saxon Æpel, *noble*, *famous*; as also, *Alling* and *Adling*, are corruptions of Æpelinȝ, *noble*, *splendid*, *famous*. *Gibson's Camden.*

Al, *Ald*, being initials, are derived from the Saxon Ealb, *ancient*; and so, oftentimes, the initial *all*, being melted by the Normans, from the Saxon ealb. *Idem, ibid.*

A'LABASTER. *n. s.* [ἀλάβαστρον.]

A kind of soft marble, easier to cut, and less durable, than the other kinds; some is white, which is most common; some of the colour of horn, and transparent; some yellow, like honey, marked with veins. The ancients used it to make boxes for perfumes. *Savary.*

Yet I'll not shed her blood,
Nor scar that whiter skin of hers than snow,
And smooth as monumental *alabaster*. *Shakesp. Othello.*

A'LABASTER. *adj.* Made of alabaster.

I cannot forbear reckoning part of an *alabaster* column, found in the ruins of Livia's portico. It is of the colour of fire, and may be seen over the high altar of St. Maria in Campitello; for they have cut it into two pieces, and fixed it, in the shape of a cross, in a hole of the wall; so that the light passing through it, makes it look to those in the church, like a huge transparent cross of amber. *Addison on Italy.*

ALA'CK. *interject.* [This word seems only the corruption of *alas.*] Alas; an expression of sorrow.

Alack! when once our grace we have forgot,
Nothing goes right; we would, and we would not.
Shakeſp. Meaſure for Meaſure.

At thunder now no more I ſtart,
Than at the rumbling of a cart:
Nay, what's incredible, *alack!*
I hardly hear a woman's clack. *Swift.*

ALA'CKADAY. *interjection.* [This, like the former, is for *alas the day.*] A word noting ſorrow and melancholy.

ALA'CRIOUSLY. *adv.* [from *alacrious*, ſuppoſed to be formed from *alacris*; but of *alacrious* I have found no example.] Cheerfully; without dejection.

Epaminondas *alacriouſly* expired, in confidence that he left behind him a perpetual memory of the victories he had atchieved for his country. *Government of the Tongue*, § 4.

ALA'CRITY. *n. ſ.* [*alacritas*, Lat.] Cheerfulneſs, expreſſed by ſome outward token; ſprightlineſs; gayety; livelineſs; cheerful willingneſs.

Wherefore, in the end, theſe orders were, on all ſides, aſſented unto with no leſs *alacrity* of mind, than cities, unable to hold out any longer, are wont to ſhew when they take conditions, ſuch as it liketh him to offer them, which hath them in the narrow ſtraits of advantage. *Hooker's Preface.*

Give me a bowl of wine;
I have not that *alacrity* of ſpirit,
Nor cheer of mind, that I was wont to have. *Sh. Rich.* III.

But glad, that now his ſea ſhould find a ſhore,
With freſh *alacrity*, and force renew'd,
Springs upward. *Milton's Paradiſe Loſt, b.*ii. *l.* 1011.

Never did men more joyfully obey,
Or ſooner underſtood the ſign to fly:
With ſuch *alacrity* they bore away,
As if, to praiſe them all, the ſtates ſtood by. *Dryd. Ann. Mir.*

ALAMI'RE. n. ſ. The loweſt note but one in Guido Aretine's ſcale of muſick.

ALAMO'DE. *adv.* [*à la mode*, Fr.] According to the faſhion: a low word. It is uſed likewiſe by ſhopkeepers for a kind of thin ſilken manufacture.

ALA'ND. *adv.* [from *a* for *at*, and *land.*] At land; landed; on the dry ground.

He only, with the prince his couſin, were caſt *aland*, far off from the place whither their deſires would have guided them.
Sidney, b. ii.

Three more, fierce Eurus, in his angry mood,
Daſh'd on the ſhallows of the moving ſand,
And, in mid ocean, left them moor'd *aland. Dryd. Virg. Æn.*

ALA'RM. *n. ſ.* [from the French, *à l'arme*, to arms; as, *crier à l'arme*, to call to arms.]

1. A cry by which men are ſummoned to their arms; as, at the approach of an enemy.

When the congregation is to be gathered together, you ſhall blow, but you ſhall not ſound an *alarm.* *Numbers*, x. 7.

Behold, God himſelf is with us for our captain, and his prieſts with ſounding trumpets, to cry *alarms* againſt you.
2 *Chron.* xiii. 12.

The trumpets loud clangour
Excites us to arms,
With ſhrill notes of anger,
And mortal *alarms.* *Dryden's Cæcilia.*

Taught by this ſtroke, renounce the wars *alarms*,
And learn to tremble at the name of arms. *Pope's Iliad.*

2. A cry, or notice, of any danger approaching; as, an *alarm* of fire.

3. Any tumult or diſturbance.

Is it then true, as diſtant rumours run,
That crowds of rivals, for thy mothers charms,
Thy palace fill with inſults and *alarms.* *Pope's Odyſſ. b.* iii.

To ALA'RM. *v. a.* [from *alarm*, the noun.]

1. To call to arms; to diſturb; as, with the approach of an enemy.

The waſp the hive *alarms*
With louder hums, and with unequal arms. *Addiſon.*

2. To ſurpriſe with the apprehenſion of any danger.

When rage miſguides me, or when fear *alarms*,
When pain diſtreſſes, or when pleaſure charms. *Tickell on Add.*

3. To diſturb in general.

His ſon, Cupavo, bruſh'd the briny flood;
Upon his ſtern a brawny Centaur ſtood,
Who heav'd a rock, and threat'ning ſtill to throw,
With lifted hands *alarm'd* the ſeas below. *Dryd. Æneid*

ALARMBELL. *n. ſ.* [from *alarm* and *bell.*] The bell that is rung at the approach of an enemy.

The *alarmbell* rings from our Alhambra walls,
And, from the ſtreets, ſound drums and ataballes.
Dryden's Conqueſt of Granada.

ALA'RMING. *particip. adj.* [from *alarm.*] Terrifying; awakening; ſurpriſing; as, an *alarming* meſſage; an *alarming* pain.

ALARMPOST. *n. ſ.* [from *alarm* and *poſt.*] The poſt or place appointed to each body of men, to appear at, when an alarm ſhall happen.

ALA'RUM. *n. ſ.* [corrupted, as it ſeems, from *alarm.* See ALARM.]

Now are our brows bound with victorious wreaths,
Our bruiſed arms hung up for monuments,
Our ſtern *alarums* chang'd to merry meetings.
Shakeſpeare's Richard III.

Hence too, that ſhe might better hear,
She ſets a drum at either ear;
And loud or gentle, harſh or ſweet,
Are but th' *alarums* which they beat. *Prior.*

To ALA'RUM. *v. a.* [corrupted from *To alarm.* See ALARM.]

Withered murder
(*Alarum'd* by his ſentinel the wolf,
Whoſe howl's his watch) thus with his ſtealthy pace,
With Tarquin's raviſhing ſtrides, tow'rds his deſign
Moves like a ghoſt. *Shakeſp. Macbeth.*

ALA'S. *interject.* [*helas*, Fr. *eylaes*, Dutch.]

1. A word expreſſing lamentation, when we uſe it of ourſelves.

But yet, *alas!* O but yet *alas!* our haps be but hard haps.
Sidney, b. i.

Alas! how little from the grave we claim?
Thou but preſerv'ſt a form, and I a name. *Pope's Epiſt.*

2. A word of pity, when uſed of other perſons.

Alas! poor Protheus, thou haſt entertain'd
A fox to be the ſhepherd of thy lambs.
Shakeſp. Two Gentlemen of Verona.

3. A word of ſorrow and concern, when uſed of things.

Thus ſaith the Lord God, Smite with thine hand, and ſtamp with thy foot, and ſay, *Alas!* for all the evil abominations of the houſe of Iſrael. *Ezekiel*, vi. 11.

Alas! both for the deed, and for the cauſe!
Milton's Paradiſe Loſt, b. xi. *l.* 461.

Alas! for pity of this bloody field;
Piteous indeed muſt be, when I, a ſpirit,
Can have ſo ſoft a ſenſe of human woes. *Dryd. K. Arthur.*

ALAS THE DAY. *interject.* Ah, unhappy day!

Alas the day! I never gave him cauſe. *Shakeſp. Othello.*

Alas a day! you have ruined my poor miſtreſs: you have made a gap in her reputation; and can you blame her, if ſhe make it up with her huſband? *Congreve's Old Bachelor.*

ALAS THE WHILE. *interject.* Ah, unhappy time!

All as the ſheep, ſuch was the ſhepherd's look;
For pale and wan he was, (*alas the while!*)
May ſeem he loved, or elſe ſome care he took. *Spenſ. Paſtor.*

ALA'TE. *adv.* [from *a* and *late.*] Lately; no long time ago.

ALB. *n. ſ.* [*album*, Lat.] A ſurplice; a white linen veſtment worn by prieſts.

ALBE'IT. *adv.* [a coalition of the words *all be it ſo. Skinner.*] Although; notwithſtanding; though it ſhould be.

This very thing is cauſe ſufficient, why duties belonging to each kind of virtue, *albeit* the law of reaſon teach them, ſhould, notwithſtanding, be preſcribed even by human law. *Hooker.*

Of one, whoſe eyes,
Albeit unuſed to the melting mood,
Drop tears, as faſt as the Arabian trees
Their medicinal gum. *Shakeſp. Othello.*

He, who has a probable belief, that he ſhall meet with thieves in ſuch a road, thinks himſelf to have reaſon enough to decline it, *albeit* he is ſure to ſuſtain ſome leſs, though yet conſiderable, inconvenience by his ſo doing. *South's Sermons.*

ALBUGI'NEOUS. *adj.* [*albugo*, Lat. the white of an egg.]

Eggs, I obſerve, will freeze in the *albugineous* part thereof.
Brown's Vulgar Errours, b. ii.

I opened it by inciſion, giving vent firſt to an *albugineous*, then to white concocted matter: upon which the tumour ſunk.
Wiſeman's Surgery.

ALBU'GO. n. ſ. [Lat.] A diſeaſe in the eye, by which the cornea contracts a whiteneſs. The ſame with *leucoma.*

A'LBURN COLOUR. *n. ſ.* See AUBURN.

A'LCAHEST. *n. ſ.* An Arabick word, to expreſs an univerſal diſſolvent, which was pretended to by Paracelſus and Helmont.
Quincy.

ALCA'ID. *n. ſ.* [from *al*, Arab. and קדקד, the head.]

1. In Barbary, the governour of a caſtle.

Th' *alcaid*
Shuns me, and, with a grim civility,
Bows, and declines my walks. *Dryd. Don Sebaſtian.*

2. In Spain, the judge of a city, firſt inſtituted by the Saracens.
Du Cange.

ALCA'NNA. n. ſ. An Egyptian plant uſed in dying; the leaves making a yellow, infuſed in water, and a red in acid liquours.

The root of *alcanna*, though green, will give a red ſtain.
Brown's Vulgar Errours.

ALCHY'MICAL. *adj.* [from *alchymy.*] Relating to alchymy; produced by alchymy.

The roſe noble, then current for ſix ſhillings and eight pence, the alchymiſts do *affirm* as an unwritten verity, was made by projection or multiplication *alchymical* of Raymond Lully in the tower of London. *Camden's Remains.*

ALCHY'MICALLY. *adv.* [from *alchymical.*] In the manner of an alchymiſt; by means of alchymy.

Raymond Lully would prove it *alchymically.* *Camden.*

A'LCHYMIST. *n. ſ.* [from *alchymy.*] One who purſues or profeſſes the ſcience of alchymy.

To

To solemnize this day, the glorious sun
Stays in his course, and plays the *alchymist*,
Turning, with splendour of his precious eye,
The meagre cloddy earth to glitt'ring gold. *Shak. K. John.*

Every *alchymist* knows, that gold will endure a vehement fire for a long time, without any change; and that after it has been divided by corrosive liquours, into invisible parts, yet may presently be precipitated, so as to appear in its own form. *Grew.*

A'LCHYMY. *n. s.* [of *al*, Arab. and χημεία.]

1. The more sublime and occult part of chymistry, which proposes, for its object, the transmutation of metals, and other important operations.

There is nothing more dangerous than this licentious and deluding art, which changeth the meaning of words, as *alchymy* doth, or would do, the substance of metals, maketh of any thing what it listeth, and bringeth, in the end, all truth to nothing. *Hooker, b.* v. § 58.

O he sits high in all the people's hearts;
And that which would appear offence in us,
His countenance, like richest *alchymy*,
Will change to virtue, and to worthiness. *Shakesp. J. Cæsar.*

Princes do but play us; compared to this,
All honours mimick, all wealth *alchymy*. *Donne.*

2. A kind of mixed metal used for spoons, and kitchen utensils.

The golden colour may be some mixture of orpiment, such as they use to brass in the yellow *alchymy*. *Bacon.*

White *alchymy* is made of pan-brass one pound, and arsenicum three ounces; or *alchymy* is made of copper and auripigmentum. *Bacon's Physical Remains.*

They bid cry,
With trumpets regal sound, the great result:
Tow'rds the four winds, four speedy cherubim
Put to their mouths the sounding *alchymy*,
By herald's voice explain'd. *Milton's Paradise Lost, b.* ii.

A'LCOHOL. *n. s.* An Arabick term used by chymists for a high rectified dephlegmated spirit of wine, or for any thing reduced into an impalpable powder. *Quincy.*

If the same salt shall be reduced into *alcohol*, as the chymists speak, or an impalpable powder, the particles and intercepted spaces will be extremely lessened. *Boyle.*

Sal volatile oleosum will coagulate the serum on account of the *alcahol*, or rectified spirit which it contains. *Arbuthnot.*

ALCOHOLIZA'TION. *n. s.* [from *alcoholize.*] The act of alcoholizing or rectifying spirits; or of reducing bodies to an impalpable powder.

To A'LCOHOLIZE. *v. a.* [from *alcohol.*]

1. To make an alcohol; that is, to rectify spirits till they are wholly dephlegmated.

2. To comminute powder till it is wholly without roughness.

A'LCORAN. *n. s.* [*al* and *koran*, Arab.] The book of the Mahometan precepts, and credenda.

If this would satisfy the conscience, we might not only take the present covenant, but subscribe to the council of Trent; yea, and to the Turkish *alcoran*; and swear to maintain and defend either of them. *Sanderson against the Covenant.*

ALCO'VE. *n. s.* [*alcoba*, Span.]

A recess, or part of a chamber, separated by an estrade, or partition of a column, and other correspondent ornaments; in which is placed a bed of state, and sometimes seats to entertain company. *Trevoux.*

The weary'd champion lulls in soft *alcoves*,
The noblest boast of thy romantick groves.
Oft, if the muse presage, shall he be seen
By Rosamonda fleeting o'er the green,
In dreams be hail'd by heroes' mighty shades,
And hear old Chaucer warble through the glades. *Tickell.*

Deep in a rich *alcove* the prince was laid,
And slept beneath the pompous colonnade. *Pope's Odyssey.*

A'LDER. *n. s.* [*alnus*, Lat.] A tree having leaves resembling those of the hazel; the male flowers, or katkins, are produced at remote distances from the fruit, on the same tree; the fruit is squamose, and of a conical figure.

The species are; 1. The common or round-leaved *alder*. 2. The long-leaved *alder*. 3. The scarlet *alder*.

These trees delight in a very moist soil, where few others will thrive, and are a great improvement to such lands. They may be also planted on the sides of brooks, and cut for poles every third or fourth year. The wood is used by turners, and will endure long under ground, or in water. These trees are propagated either by planting layers, or truncheons, about three feet in length, in February or March. *Millar.*

Without the grot, a various silver scene
Appear'd around, and groves of living green;
Poplars and *alders* ever quivering play'd,
And nodding cypress form'd a fragrant shade. *Pope's Odyss.*

ALDERLI'EVEST. *adj. superl.* [from *ald*, *alder*, old, elder, and *lieve*, dear, beloved.] Most beloved; which has held the longest possession of the heart.

The mutual conference that my mind hath had,
By day, by night, waking, and in my dreams,
In courtly company, or at my beads,
With you, mine *alderlievest* sovereign;
Makes me the bolder to salute my king
With ruder terms. *Shakesp. Henry* VI. *p.* ii.

A'LDERMAN. *n. s.* [from *ald*, old, and *man.*]

1. The same as senator. *Cowell.* A governour or magistrate, originally, as the name imports, chosen on account of the experience which his age had given him.

Tell him, myself, the mayor, and *aldermen*,
Are come to have some conf'rence with his grace. *Sh. R.* III.

Though my own *aldermen* conferr'd my bays,
To me committing their eternal praise;
Their full-fed heroes, their pacifick may'rs,
Their annual trophies, and their monthly wars. *Pope's Dun.*

2. In the following passage it is, I think, improperly used.

But if the trumpet's clangour you abhor,
And dare not be an *alderman* of war,
Take to a shop, behind a counter lie. *Dryd. Juv. Sat.*

A'LDERMANLY. *adv.* [from *alderman.*] Like an alderman; belonging to an alderman.

These, and many more, suffered death, in envy to their virtues and superiour genius, which emboldened them, in exigencies (wanting an *aldermanly* discretion) to attempt service out of the common forms. *Swift's Miscellanies.*

A'LDERN. *adj.* [from *alder.*] Made of alder.

Then *aldern* boats first plow'd the ocean;
The sailors number'd then, and nam'd each star. *May's Virg.*

ALE. *n. s.* [eale, Sax.]

1. A liquour made by infusing malt [See MALT.] in hot water, and then fermenting the liquour.

I'll scratch your heads; you must be seeing christenings. Do you look for *ale* and cakes here, you rude rascals? *Shakesp. Henry* VIII.

The fertility of the soil in grain, and its being not proper for vines, put the Egyptians upon drinking *ale*, of which they were the inventors. *Arbuthnot on Coins.*

2. A merry meeting used in country places.

And all the neighbourhood, from old records
Of antick proverbs drawn from Whitson lords,
And their authorities at wakes and *ales*,
With country precedents, and old wives tales,
We bring you now. *Ben. Johnson.*

A'LEBERRY. *n. s.* [from *ale* and *berry.*] A beverage made by boiling ale with spice and sugar, and sops of bread: a word only used in conversation.

ALE BREWER. *n. s.* [from *ale* and *brewer.*] One that professes to brew ale.

The summer-made malt brews ill, and is disliked by most of our *ale brewers*. *Mortimer's Husbandry.*

A'LECONNER. *n. s.* [from *ale* and *con.*] An officer in the city of London, whose business is to inspect the measures of publick houses. Four of them are chosen or rechosen annually by the common-hall of the city; and whatever might be their use formerly, their places are now regarded only as sine-cures for decayed citizens.

A'LECOST. *n. s.* [perhaps from *ale*, and *costus*, Lat.] The name of an herb. *Dict.*

ALE'CTRYOMANCY, or ALE'CTOROMANCY. *n. s.* [ἀλεκτρυὼν and μάντις.] Divination by a cock. *Dict.*

A'LEGAR. *n. s.* [from *ale* and *eager*, sour.] Sour ale; a kind of acid made by ale, as vinegar by wine, which has lost its spirit.

A'LEGER. *adj.* [*allegre*, Fr. *alacris*, Lat.] Gay; chearful; sprightly: a word not now used.

Certainly, this berrycoffee, the root and leaf betle, and leaf tobacco, of which the Turks are great takers, do all condense the spirits, and make them strong and *aleger*. *Bacon's Nat. Hist.*

A'LEHOOF. *n. s.* [from *ale* and hoop, head.] Groundivy, so called by our Saxon ancestors, as being their chief ingredient in ale. See GROUNDIVY.

Alehoof or groundivy, is, in my opinion, of the most excellent and most general use and virtue, of any plants we have among us. *Temple.*

A'LEHOUSE. *n. s.* [from *ale* and *house.*] A house where ale is publickly sold; a tipling-house. It is distinguished from a tavern, where they sell wine.

Thou most beauteous inn,
Why should hard-favour'd grief be lodg'd in thee,
When triumph is become an *alehouse* guest? *Sh. Rich.* II.

One would think it should be no easy matter to bring any man of sense in love with an *alehouse*; indeed of so much sense, as seeing and smelling amounts to; there being such strong encounters of both, as would quickly send him packing, did not the love of good fellowship reconcile to these nusances. *South.*

Thee shall each *alehouse*, thee each gilhouse mourn,
And answ'ring ginshops sowrer sighs return. *Pope's Dun.*

A'LEHOUSE KEEPER. *n. s.* [from *alehouse* and *keeper.*] He that keeps ale publickly to sell.

You resemble perfectly the two *alehouse keepers* in Holland, who were at the same time burgomasters of the town, and taxed one another's bills alternately. *Bolingbroke to Swift.*

A'LEKNIGHT. *n. s.* [from *ale* and *knight.*] A pot-companion; a tippler: a word now out of use.

The old *aleknights* of England were well depainted out of him, in the ale-house colours of that time, in this manner. *Camden.*

ALE'MBICK. *n. ſ.* A veſſel uſed in diſtilling, conſiſting of a veſſel placed over a fire, in which is contained the ſubſtance to be diſtilled, and a concave cloſely fitted on, into which the fumes ariſe by the heat; this cover has a beak or ſpout, into which the vapours riſe, and by which they paſs into a ſerpentine pipe, which is kept cool by making many convolutions in a tub of water; here the vapours are condenſed, and what entered the pipe in fumes, comes out in drops.

Though water may be rarefied into inviſible vapours, yet it is not changed into air, but only ſcattered into minute parts; which meeting together in the *alembick*, or in the receiver, do preſently return into ſuch water as they conſtituted before. *Boyle.*

ALE'NGTH. *adv.* [from *a* for *at*, and *length.*] At full length; along; ſtretched along the ground.

ALE'RT. *adj.* [*alerte*, Fr. perhaps from *alacris*, but probably from *à l'art*, according to art or rule.]

1. In the military ſenſe, on guard; watchful; vigilant; ready at a call.
2. In the common ſenſe, briſk; pert; petulant; ſmart; implying ſome degree of cenſure and contempt.

I ſaw an *alert* young fellow, that cocked his hat upon a friend of his, and accoſted him after the following manner: Well, Jack, the old prig is dead at laſt. *Addiſon. Spect.* N° 403.

ALE'RTNESS. *n. ſ.* [from *alert.*] The quality of being alert; ſprightlineſs; pertneſs.

That *alertneſs* and unconcern for matters of common life, which a campaign or two would infallibly have given him. *Addiſon. Spectator.*

ALE TASTER. *n. ſ.* [from *ale* and *taſter.*] An officer appointed in every courtleet, and ſworn to look to the aſſize and the goodneſs of bread and ale, or beer, within the precincts of that lordſhip. *Cowell.*

A'LEVAT. *n. ſ.* [from *ale* and *vat.*] The tub in which the ale is fermented.

A'LEWASHED. *adj.* [from *ale* and *waſh.*] Steeped or ſoaked in ale.

What a beard of the general's cut, and a horrid ſuit of the camp, will do among foaming battles and *alewaſhed* wits, is wonderful to be thought on. *Shakeſp. Henry* V.

ALEWIFE. *n. ſ.* [from *ale* and *wife.*] A woman that keeps an alehouſe.

Perhaps he will ſwagger and hector, and threaten to beat and butcher an *alewife*, or take the goods by force, and throw them the bad halfpence. *Swift's Draper's Letters.*

A'LEXANDERS. *n. ſ.* [*Smyrnium*, Lat.] The name of a plant.

The flowers are produced in umbels, conſiſting of ſeveral leaves, which are placed orbicularly, and expand in form of a roſe; theſe reſt upon the empalement, which afterward becomes an almoſt globular fruit, compoſed of two pretty thick ſeeds, ſometimes ſhaded like a creſcent, gibbous, and ſtreaked on one ſide, and plain on the other.

The ſpecies are; 1. Common *Alexanders.* 2. Foreign *Alexanders*, with a round leaf, &c.

The firſt of theſe ſorts, which is that ordered by the college for medicinal uſe, grows wild in divers parts of England, and may be propagated by ſowing their ſeeds upon an open ſpot of ground in Auguſt. *Millar.*

A'LEXANDER'S FOOT. *n. ſ.* The name of an herb.

ALEXA'NDRINE. *n. ſ.* A kind of verſe borrowed from the French, firſt uſed in a poem called *Alexander.* They conſiſt, among the French, of twelve and thirteen ſyllables, in alternate couplets; and, among us, of twelve.

Our numbers ſhould, for the moſt part, be lyrical. For variety, or rather where the majeſty of thought requires it, they may be ſtretched to the Engliſh heroick of five feet, and to the French *Alexandrine* of ſix. *Dryd.*

Then, at the laſt, an only couplet fraught
With ſome unmeaning thing they call a thought,
A needleſs *Alexandrine* ends the ſong,
That, like a wounded ſnake, drags it ſlow length along.
Pope's Eſſay on Criticiſm.

ALEXIPHA'RMICK. *adj.* [from ἀλεξέω and φάρμακον.] That which drives away poiſon; antidotal; that which oppoſes infection.

That ſome antidotal quality it may have, we have no reaſon to deny; for ſince elke's hoofs and horns are magnified for epilepſies, ſince not only the bone in the heart, but the horn of a deer, is *alexipharmick.* *Brown's Vulgar Errours.*

ALEXITE'RICAL, or ALEXITE'RICK. *adj.* [from ἀλεξέω.] That which drives away poiſon; that which reſiſts in fevers.

A'LGATES. *adv.* [from *all* and *gate. Skinner. Gate* is the ſame as *via*; and ſtill uſed for *way* in the Scottiſh dialect.] On any terms; every way: now obſolete.

Nor had the boaſter ever riſen more,
But that Rinaldo's horſe ev'n then down fell,
And with the fall his leg oppreſs'd ſo ſore,
That, for a ſpace, there muſt he *algates* dwell. *Fairfax.*

A'LGEBRA. *n. ſ.* [an Arabick word of uncertain etymology; derived, by ſome, from *Geber* the philoſopher; by ſome, from *geſr*, parchment; by others, from *algebiſta*, a bone-ſetter; by *Menage*, from *algiatarat*, the reſtitution of things broken.]

This is a peculiar kind of arithmetick, which takes the quantity ſought, whether it be a number or a line, or any other quantity, as if it were granted, and, by means of one or more quantities given, proceeds by conſequence, till the quantity at firſt only ſuppoſed to be known, or at leaſt ſome power thereof, is found to be equal to ſome quantity or quantities which are known, and conſequently itſelf is known. The origin of this art is very obſcure. It was in uſe, however, among the Arabs, long before it came into this part of the world; and they are ſuppoſed to have borrowed it from the Perſians, and the Perſians from the Indians. The firſt Greek author of *algebra* was Diophantus, who, about the year 800, wrote thirteen books. In 1494, Lucas Pacciolus, or Lucas de Burgos, a cordelier, printed a treatiſe of *algebra*, in Italian, at Venice. He ſays, that *algebra* came originally from the Arabs, and never mentions Diophantus; which makes it probable, that that author was not yet known in Europe; whoſe method was very different from that of the Arabs, obſerved by Pacciolus and his firſt European followers. His *algebra* goes no farther than ſimple and quadratick equations; and only ſome of the others advanced to the ſolution of culick equations. After ſeveral improvements by Vieta, Oughtred, Harriot, Deſcartes, Sir Iſaac Newton brought this art to the height at which it ſtill continues. *Trevoux. Chambers.*

It would ſurely require no very profound ſkill in *algebra*, to reduce the difference of ninepence in thirty ſhillings. *Swift.*

ALGEBRA'ICK. } *adj.* [from *algebra.*]
ALGEBRA'ICAL. }

1. Relating to algebra; as, an *algebraical* treatiſe.
2. Containing operations of algebra; as, an *algebraical* computation.

ALGEBRA'IST. *n. ſ.* [from *algebra.*] A perſon that underſtands or practiſes the ſcience of algebra.

When any dead body is found in England, no *algebraiſt* or uncipherer can uſe more ſubtle ſuppoſitions, to find the demonſtration or cipher, than every unconcerned perſon doth to find the murderers. *Graunt's Bills of Mortality.*

Confining themſelves to deſcribe almoſt nothing elſe but the ſynthetick and analytick methods of geometricians and *algebraiſts*, they have too much narrowed the rules of method, as though every thing were to be treated in mathematical forms. *Watts's Logick.*

A'LGID. *adj.* [*algidus*, Lat.] Cold; chill. *Dict.*

ALGI'DITY, } *n. ſ.* [from *algid.*] Chilneſs; cold. *Dict.*
A'LGIDNESS. }

ALGI'FIC. *adj.* [from *algor*, Lat.] That which produces cold. *D.*

A'LGOR. *n. ſ.* [Lat.] Extreme cold; chilneſs. *Dict.*

A'LGORISM, } *n. ſ.* Arabick words, which are uſed to imply
A'LGORITHM. } the ſix operations of arithmetick, or the ſcience of numbers. *Dict.*

ALGO'SE. *adj.* [from *algor*, Lat.] Extremely cold; chill. *Dict.*

A'LIAS. *adv.* A Latin word, ſignifying otherwiſe; often uſed in the trials of criminals, whoſe danger has obliged them to change their names; as, Simpſon *alias* Smith, *alias* Baker; that is, *otherwiſe* Smith, *otherwiſe* Baker.

A'LIBLE. *adj.* [*alibilis*, Lat.] Nutritive; nouriſhing; that which may be nouriſhed. *Dict.*

A'LIEN. *adj.* [*alienus*, Lat.]

1. Foreign, or not of the ſame family or land.

The mother plant admires the leaves unknown
Of *alien* trees, and apples not her own. *Dryd. Virg. Georg.*
But who can tell, what pangs, what ſharp remorſe,
Torment the Boian prince? from native ſoil
Exil'd by fate, torn from the tender embrace
Of weeping conſort, and depriv'd the ſight
Of his young guiltleſs progeny, he ſeeks
Inglorious ſhelter in an *alien* land. *Philips.*

2. Eſtranged from; not allied to; adverſe to; with the particle *from*, and ſometimes *to*, but improperly.

To declare my mind to the diſciples of the fire, by a ſimilitude not *alien from* their profeſſion. *Boyle.*

The ſentiment that ariſes, is a conviction of the deplorable ſtate of nature, to which ſin reduced us; a weak, ignorant creature, *alien from* God and goodneſs, and a prey to the great deſtroyer. *Rogers's Sermons.*

They encouraged perſons and principles, *alien from* our religion and government, in order to ſtrengthen their faction. *Swift's Miſcellanies.*

A'LIEN. *n. ſ.* [*alienus*, Lat.]

1. A foreigner; not a deniſon; a man of another country or family; not allied; a ſtranger.

In whomſoever theſe things are, the church doth acknowledge them for her children; them only ſhe holdeth for *aliens* and ſtrangers, in whom theſe things are not found. *Hooker.*

If it be prov'd againſt an *alien*,
He ſeeks the life of any citizen,
The party, 'gainſt the which he doth contrive,
Shall ſeize on half his goods. *Shakeſp. Merch. of Venice.*

The mere Iriſh were not only accounted *aliens*, but enemies, and altogether out of the protection of the law; ſo as it was no capital offence to kill them. *Sir John Davies on Ireland.*

Thy place in council thou haſt rudely loſt,
Which by thy younger brother is ſupply'd,
And art almoſt an *alien to* the hearts
Of all the court and princes of my blood. *Shak. Henry IV.*

Their famous lawgiver condemned the persons, who sat idle in divisions dangerous to the government, as *aliens to* the community, and therefore to be cut off from it. *Addison. Freeholder.*

2. In law.

An *alien* is one born in a strange country, and never enfranchised. A man born out of the land, so it be within the limits beyond the seas, or of English parents out of the king's obedience, so the parents, at the time of the birth, be of the king's obedience, is not *alien*. If one born out of the king's allegiance, come and dwell in England, his children (if he beget any here) are not *aliens*, but denizens. *Cowell.*

To A'LIEN. *v. a.* [*aliener*, Fr. *alieno*, Lat.]

1. To make any thing the property of another.

If the son *alien* those lands, and then repurchase them again in fee, now the rules of descents are to be observed, as if he were the original purchaser. *Hale's History of Common Law.*

2. To estrange; to turn the mind or affection; to make averse to; with *from*.

The king was wonderfully disquieted, when he found, that the prince was totally *aliened from* all thoughts of, or inclination to, the marriage. *Clarendon.*

A'LIENABLE. *adj.* [from *To alienate.*] That of which the property may be transferred.

Land is *alienable*, and treasure is transitory, and both must, at one time or other, pass from him, either by his own voluntary act, or by the violence and injustice of others, or at least by fate. *Dennis's Letters.*

To A'LIENATE. *v. a.* [*aliener*, Fr. *alieno*, Lat.]

1. To transfer the property of any thing to another.

The countries were once christian, and members of the church and where the golden candlesticks did stand, though now they be utterly *alienated*, and no christians left. *Bacon.*

2. To withdraw the heart or affections; with the particle *from*, where the first possessor is mentioned.

The manner of mens writing must not *alienate* our hearts *from* the truth. *Hooker's Preface.*

Be it never so true which we teach the world to believe, yet if once their affections begin to be *alienated*, a small thing persuadeth them to change their opinions. *Hooker, Dedicat.*

His eyes survey'd the dark idolatries
Of *alienated* Judah. *Milton's Paradise Lost, b.* i. *l.* 457.

Any thing that is apt to disturb the world, and to *alienate* the affections of men *from* one another, such as cross and distasteful humours, is, either expresly, or by clear consequence and deduction, forbidden in the New Testament. *Tillotson.*

Her mind was quite *alienated from* the honest Castilian, whom she was taught to look upon as a formal old fellow. *Add. Spectat.*

A'LIENATE. *adj.* [*alienatus*, Lat.] Withdrawn from; stranger to; with the particle *from*.

They are most damnably wicked; impatient for the death of the queen; ready to gratify their ambition and revenge, by all desperate methods; wholly *alienate from* truth, law, religion, mercy, conscience, or honour. *Swift's Miscellanies.*

ALIENA'TION. *n. s.* [*alienatio*, Lat.]

1. The act of transferring property.

The beginning of this ordinance was for the maintenance of their lands in their posterity, and for excluding all innovation or *alienation* thereof unto strangers. *Spenser's State of Ireland.*

God put it into the heart of one of our princes, towards the close of her reign, to give a check to that sacrilege. Her successour passed a law, which prevented absolutely all future *alienations* of the church revenues. *Atterbury.*

Great changes and *alienations* of property, have created new and great dependencies. *Swift on Athens and Rome.*

2. The state of being alienated; as, the estate was wasted during its *alienation*.

3. Change of affection.

It is left but in dark memory, what the case of this person was, and what was the ground of his defection, and the *alienation* of his heart from the king. *Bacon's Henry* VII.

4. Applied to the mind, it means disorder of the faculties.

Some things are done by man, though not through outward force and impulsion, though not against, yet without their wills; as in *alienation* of mind, or any like inevitable utter absence of wit and judgment. *Hooker, b.* i. *p.* 23.

ALI'FEROUS. *adj.* [from *ala* and *fero*, Lat.] Having wings. *D.*

ALI'GEROUS. *adj.* [*aliger*, Lat.] Having wings; winged. *Dict.*

To ALI'GGE. *v. a.* [from *a*, and *lig*, to lye down.] To lay; to allay; to throw down; to subdue: an old word even in the time of Spenser, now wholly forgotten.

Thomalin, why sitten we so,
As weren overwent with woe:
Upon so fair a morrow,
The joyous time now nigheth fast,
That shall *aligge* this bitter blast,
And slake the winter sorrow. *Spenser's Pastorals.*

To ALI'GHT. *v. n.* [alihtan, Sax. *af-lichten*, Dutch.]

1. To come down, and stop. The word implies the idea of *descending*; as, of a bird from the wing; a traveller from his horse or carriage, and generally of resting or stopping.

There ancient night arriving, did *alight*
From her high weary waine. *Fairy Queen, b.* i. *c.* v.

There is *alighted* at your gate
A young Venetian. *Shakesp. Merchant of Venice.*

Slackness breeds worms; but the sure traveller,
Though he *alights* sometimes, still goeth on. *Herbert.*

When marching with his foot he walks till night;
When with his horse he never will *alight*. *Denham.*

When Dedalus, to fly the Cretan shore,
His heavy limbs on jointed pinions bore;
The first that sail'd in air, 'tis sung by Fame,
To the Cumean coast at length he came,
And here *alighting* built this costly frame. *Dryden's Æneid.*

When he was admonished by his subject to descend, he came down gently and circling in the air, and singing to the ground. Like a lark, melodious in her mounting, and continuing her song till she *alights*; still preparing for a higher flight at her next sally. *Dryden.*

When finish'd was the fight,
The victors from their lusty steeds *alight*;
Like them dismounted all the warlike train. *Dryd. Fables.*

Should a spirit of superiour rank, a stranger to human nature, *alight* upon the earth, what would his notions of us be? *Addison. Spectator.*

2. It is used also of any thing thrown or falling; to fall upon.

But storms of stones from the proud temple's height,
Pour down, and on our batter'd helms *alight*. *Dryd. Æneid.*

ALI'KE. *adv.* [from *a* and *like.*] With resemblance; without difference; in the same manner; in the same form.

The darkness hideth not from thee; but the night shineth as the day: the darkness and the light are both *alike* to thee. *Psalm* cxxxix. 12.

With thee conversing, I forget all time;
All seasons, and their change, all please *alike*. *Parad. Lost.*

Riches cannot rescue from the grave,
Which claims *alike* the monarch and the slave. *Dryd. Juv.*

Let us unite at least in an equal zeal for those capital doctrines, which we all equally embrace, and are *alike* concerned to maintain. *Atterbury's Preface to his Sermons.*

Two handmaids wait the throne: *alike* in place,
But diff'ring far in figure and in face. *Pope's Rape of the Lock.*

A'LIMENT. *n. s.* [*alimentum*, Lat.] Nourishment; that which nourishes; nutriment; food.

New parts are added to our substance; and as we die, we are born daily; nor can we give an account, how the *aliment* is so prepared for nutrition, or by what mechanism it is distributed. *Glanville's Scepsis Scientifica, Pref.*

All bodies which, by the animal faculties, can be changed into the fluids and solids of our bodies, are called *aliments*. But, to take it in the largest sense, by *aliment*, I understand every thing which a human creature takes in common diet; as, meat, drink; and seasoning, as, salt, spice, vinegar, &c. *Arbuthnot.*

ALIME'NTAL. *adj.* [from *aliment.*] That which has the quality of aliment; that which nourishes; that which feeds.

The sun, that light imparts to all, receives
From all his *alimental* recompense,
In humid exhalations. *Milton's Paradise Lost, b.* v.

Except they be watered from higher regions, these weeds must lose their *alimental* sap, and wither themselves. *Brown's Preface to Vulgar Errours.*

Th' industrious, when the sun in Leo rides,
And darts his sultriest beams, portending drought,
Forget not, at the foot of ev'ry plant,
To sink a circling trench, and daily pour
A just supply of *alimental* streams,
Exhausted sap recruiting. *Philips.*

ALIME'NTARINESS. *n. s.* [from *alimentary.*] The quality of being alimentary, or of affording nourishment. *Dict.*

ALIME'NTARY. *adj.* [from *aliment.*]

1. That which belongs or relates to aliment.

The solution of the aliment by mastication is necessary; without it, the aliment could not be disposed for the changes, which it receives as it passeth through the *alimentary* duct. *Arbuthnot on Aliments.*

2. That which has the quality of aliment, or the power of nourishing.

I do not think that water supplies animals, or even plants, with nourishment, but serves for a vehicle to the *alimentary* particles, to convey and distribute them to the several parts of the body. *Ray on the Creation.*

Of *alimentary* roots, some are pulpy and very nutritious; as, turneps and carrots. These have a fattening quality, which they manifest in feeding of cattle. *Arbuthnot on Aliments.*

ALIMENTA'TION. *n. s.* [from *aliment.*] The power of affording aliment; the quality of nourishing.

Plants do nourish; inanimate bodies do not: they have an accretion, but no *alimentation*. *Bacon's Natural History*, Nº 54.

ALIMO'NIOUS. *adj.* [from *alimony.*] That which nourishes: a word very little in use.

The plethora renders us lean, by suppressing our spirits, whereby they are incapacitated of digesting the *alimonious* humours into flesh. *Harvey on Consumptions.*

A'LIMONY. *n. s.* [*alimonia*, Lat.]

Alimony signifies that legal proportion of the husband's estate, which, by the sentence of the ecclesiastical court, is allowed to the

the wife for her maintenance, upon the account of any ſeparation from him, provided it be not cauſed by her elopement or adultery. *Ayliffe's Parergon.*

Before they ſettled hands and hearts,
Till *alimony* or death them parts. *Hudibras, p.* iii. *c.* iii.

A'LIQUANT. *adj.* [*aliquantus*, Lat.] Parts of a number, which, however repeated, will never make up the number exactly; as, 3 is an aliquant of 10, thrice 3 being 9, four times 3 making 12.

A'LIQUOT. *adj.* [*aliquot*, Lat.] Aliquot parts of any number or quantity, ſuch as will exactly meaſure it without any remainder: as, 3 is an alquot part of 12, becauſe, being taken four times, it will juſt meaſure it.

A'LISH. *adj.* [from *ale.*] Reſembling ale; having qualities of ale.

They let it ſtand five days before they put it into the caſk, ſtirring it and beating down the yeaſt into it; this gives it the ſweet *aliſh* taſte. *Mortimer's Husbandry.*

A'LITURE. *n. ſ.* [*alitura*, Lat.] Nouriſhment. *Dict.*

ALI'VE. *adj.* [from *a* and *live.*]

1. In the ſtate of life; not dead.

Nor well *alive*, nor wholly dead they were,
But ſome faint ſigns of feeble life appear. *Dryd. Fables.*
Not youthful kings in battle ſeiz'd *alive*,
Not ſcornful virgins who their charms ſurvive. *Pope.*

2. In a figurative ſenſe, unextinguiſhed; undeſtroyed; active; in full force.

Thoſe good and learned men had reaſon to wiſh, that their proceedings might be favoured, and the good affection of ſuch as inclined toward them, kept *alive*. *Hooker, b.* v.

3. Chearful; ſprightly; full of alacrity.

She was not ſo much *alive* the whole day, if ſhe ſlept more than ſix hours. *Clariſſa.*

4. In a popular ſenſe, it is uſed only to add an emphaſis, like the French *du monde*; as, the *beſt* man *alive*; that is, the *beſt*, with an emphaſis.

And to thoſe brethren ſaid, riſe, riſe by-live,
And unto battle do yourſelves addreſs;
For yonder comes the proweſt knight *alive*,
Prince Arthur, flower of grace and nobileſs. *Fairy Queen.*

The earl of Northumberland, who was the proudeſt man *alive*, could not look upon the deſtruction of monarchy with any pleaſure. *Clarendon, b.* viii.

John was quick and underſtood his buſineſs very well; but no man *alive* was more careleſs in looking into his accounts. *Arbuthnot's Hiſtory of John Bull.*

A'LKAHEST. *n. ſ.* A word uſed firſt by Paracelſus, and adopted by his followers, to ſignify an univerſal diſſolvent, or liquour, which has the power of reſolving all things into their firſt principles.

ALKALE'SCENT. *adj.* [from *alkali.*] That which has a tendency to the properties of an alkali.

All animal diet is *alkaleſcent* or anti-acid. *Arbuthnot on Alim.*

A'LKALI. *n. ſ.* [The word *alkali* comes from an herb, called by the Egyptians *kali*; by us glaſswort.] This herb they burnt to aſhes, boiled them in water, and, after having evaporated the water, there remained at the bottom a white ſalt; this they called *ſal kali*, or *alkali*. It is corroſive, producing putrefaction in animal ſubſtances, to which it is applied. *Arbuthnot on Aliments.*

Any ſubſtance, which, when mingled with acid, produces efferveſcence and fermentation. See ALKALIZATE.

A'LKALINE. *adj.* [from *alkali.*] That which has the qualities of alkali.

Any watery liquour will keep an animal from ſtarving very long, by diluting the fluids, and conſequently keeping them from this *alkaline* ſtate, which is confirmed by experience; for people have lived twenty-four days upon nothing but water. *Arbuthnot upon Aliments.*

To ALKA'LIZATE. *v. a.* [from *alkali.*] To make bodies alkaline, by changing their nature, or by mixing alkalies with them.

ALKA'LIZATE. *adj.* [from *alkali.*] That which has the qualities of alkali; that which is impregnated with alkali.

The odour of the fixed nitre is very languid; but that, which it diſcovers, being diſſolved in hot water, is different, being of kin to that of other *alkalizate* ſalts. *Boyle.*

The colour of violets ſeems to be of that order, becauſe their ſyrup, by acid liquours, turns red, and, by urinous and *alkalizate*, turns green. *Newton's Opticks.*

ALKALIZA'TION. *n. ſ.* [from *alkali.*] The act of alkalizating, or impregnating bodies with alkali.

A'LKANET. *n. ſ.* [*Anchuſa*, Lat.] The name of a plant.

This plant is a ſpecies of bugloſs, with a red root, brought from the ſouthern parts of France, and uſed in medicine. It will grow in almoſt any ſoil, and muſt be ſown in March. *Mil.*

A'LKEKE'NGI. *n. ſ.* A medicinal fruit or berry, produced by a plant of the ſame denomination; popularly alſo called *winter-cherry*; of conſiderable uſe as an aſtringent, diſſolvent, and diuretick. The plant bears a near reſemblance to Solanum, or Nightſhade; whence it is frequently called in Latin by that name, with the addition or epithet of *veſicarium*. *Chambers.*

ALKE'RMES. *n. ſ.* In medicine, a term borrowed from the Arabs, denoting a celebrated remedy, of the form and conſiſtence of a confection; whereof the *kermes* berries are the baſis. The other ingredients are pippin-cyder, roſe-water, ſugar, ambergreaſe, muſk, cinnamon, aloes-wood, pearls, and leaf-gold; but the ſweets are uſually omitted. The *confectio alkermes* is chiefly made at Montpelier, which ſupplies moſt part of Europe therewith. The grain, which gives it the denomination, is nowhere found ſo plentifully as there. *Chambers.*

ALL. *adv.* [See ALL, *adj.*]

1. Quite; completely.

How is my love *all* ready forth to come. *Spenſer's Epithal.*
Know, Rome, that *all* alone Marcus did fight
Within Corioli gates. *Shakeſp. Coriolanus.*
And ſwore ſo loud,
That, *all* amaz'd, the prieſt let fall the book. *Sh.Tam.Shrew.*

They could call a comet a faxed ſtar, which is *all* one with *ſtella crinita*, or *cometa*. *Camden's Remains.*

For a large conſcience is *all* one,
And ſignifies the ſame with none. *Hudibras, p.* iii. *c.* i.
Balm, from a ſilver box diſtill'd around,
Shall *all* bedew the roots, and ſcent the ſacred ground. *Dryd.*

I do not remember he any where mentions expreſly the title of the firſt-born, but *all* along keeps himſelf under the ſhelter of the indefinite term, heir. *Locke.*

Juſtice, indeed, may be furniſhed out of this element, as far as her ſword goes; and courage may be *all* over a continued blaze, if the artiſt pleaſes. *Addiſon. Guardian*, N° 103.

If e'er the miſer durſt his farthings ſpare,
He thinly ſpreads them through the publick ſquare,
Where, *all* beſide the rail, rang'd beggars lie,
And from each other catch the doleful cry. *Gay's Trivia.*

2. Altogether; wholly; without any other conſideration.

I am of the temper of moſt kings, who love to be in debt, are *all* for preſent money, no matter how they pay it afterward. *Dryd. Fab. Preface.*

3. Only; without admiſſion of any thing elſe.

When I ſhall wed,
That lord, whoſe hand muſt take my plight, ſhall carry
Half my love with him, half my care and duty.
Sure I ſhall never marry, like my ſiſter,
To love my father *all*. *Shakeſp. King Lear.*

4. Although. This ſenſe is truly Teutonick, but now obſolete.

Do you not think th' accompliſhment of it
Sufficient work for one man's ſimple head,
All were it as the reſt but ſimply writ. *Spenſer, Son.* xxxii.

5. It is ſometimes a word of emphaſis; nearly the ſame with *juſt*.

A ſhepherd's ſwain, ſay, did thee bring,
All as his ſtraying flock he fed;
And, when his honour hath thee read,
Crave pardon for thy hardy head. *Spenſer's Paſtorals.*

ALL. *adj.* [Æll, Æal, ealle, alle. Sax. oll, Welſh; al, Dutch; alle, Germ. ὅλος, Gr.]

1. The whole number; every one.

Brutus is an honourable man;
So are they *all*, *all* honourable men. *Shakeſp. Jul. Cæſar.*
To graze the herb *all* leaving,
Devour'd each other. *Milton's Paradiſe Loſt, b.* x.

The great encouragement of *all*, is the aſſurance of a future reward. *Tillotſon, Sermon* vi.

2. The whole quantity; every part.

Six days thou ſhalt labour, and do *all* thy work. *Deut.* v. 13.

Political power, I take to be a right of making laws with penalties, and of employing the force of the community in the execution of ſuch laws, and in the defence of the commonwealth; and *all* this only for the publick good. *Locke.*

3. The whole duration of time.

On whoſe paſtures cheerful ſpring,
All the year doth ſit and ſing;
And, rejoicing, ſmiles to ſee,
Their green backs wear his livery. *Craſhaw.*

4. The whole extent of place.

Gratiano ſpeaks an infinite deal of nothing, more than any man in *all* Venice. *Shak. Merch. of Venice.*

ALL. *n. ſ.*

1. The whole; oppoſed to part, or nothing.

And will ſhe yet debaſe her eyes on me;
On me, whoſe *all* not equals Edward's moiety?
On me that halt, and am miſhapen thus? *Shak. Rich.* III.
Nought's had, *all*'s ſpent,
Where our deſire is got without content. *Shak. Macbeth.*
The youth ſhall ſtudy, and no more engage
Their flatt'ring wiſhes for uncertain age;
No more with fruitleſs care, and cheated ſtrife,
Chace fleeting pleaſure through the maze of life;
Finding the wretched *all* they here can have,
But preſent food, and but a future grave. *Prior.*

Our *all* is at ſtake, and irretrieveably loſt, if we fail of ſucceſs. *Addiſon on the State of the War.*

2. Every thing.

Then ſhall we be news-cramm'd.—*All* the better; we ſhall be the more remarkable. *Shakeſp. As you like it.*

Up

Up with my tent, here will I lie to night;
But where to morrow?—Well, *all's* one for that. *Sh. R.* III.
All the fitter, Lentulus: our coming
Is not for salutation; we have bus'ness. *Ben. Johns. Catiline.*

That is, *every thing is the better, the same, the fitter.*

Sceptre and pow'r, thy giving, I assume;
And glad her shall resign, when in the end
Thou shalt be *all* in *all*, and I in thee,
For ever; and in me all whom thou lov'st. *Parad. Lost.*

They all fell to work at the roots of the tree, and left it so little foothold, that the first blast of wind laid it flat upon the ground, nest, eagles, and *all*. *L'Estrange.*

They that do not keep up this indifferency for *all* but truth, put coloured spectacles before their eyes, and look through false glasses. *Locke.*

A torch, snuff and *all*, goes out in a moment, when dipped in the vapour. *Addison's Remarks on Italy.*

All is much used in composition; but, in most instances, it is merely arbitrary; as, *all-commanding*. Sometimes the words compounded with it, are fixed and classical; as, *Almighty*.

When it is connected with a participle, it seems to be a noun; as, *all-surrounding*: in other cases, an adverb; as, *all-accomplished*, or completely accomplished.

Of these compounds, a small part of those which may be found is inserted.

ALL-BEARING. *adj.* [from *all* and *bear*.] That which bears every thing; omniparous.

Thus while he spoke, the sovereign plant he drew,
Where on th' *all-bearing* earth unmark'd it grew. *Pope's Od.*

ALL-CHEERING. *adj.* [from *all* and *cheer*.] That which gives gayety and cheerfulness to all.

Soon as the *all-cheering* sun
Should, in the farthest east, begin to draw
The shady curtains from Aurora's bed. *Sh. Romeo and Jul.*

ALL-COMMANDING. *adj.* [from *all* and *command*.] Having the sovereignty over all.

He now sets before them the high and shining idol of glory, the *all-commanding* image of bright gold. *Raleigh's History.*

ALL-COMPOSING. *adj.* [from *all* and *compose*.] That which quiets all men, or every thing.

Wrapt in embow'ring shades, Ulysses lies,
His woes forgot! but Pallas now addrest,
To break the bands of *all-composing* rest. *Pope's Odyssey, b.* vi.

ALL-CONQUERING. *adj.* [from *all* and *conquer*.] That which subdues every thing.

Second of Satan sprung, *all-conquering* death!
What think'st thou of our empire now? *Paradise Lost, b.* x.

ALL-CONSUMING. *adj.* [from *all* and *consume*.] That which consumes every thing.

By age unbroke—but *all-consuming* care
Destroys perhaps the strength, that time would spare. *Pope.*

ALL-DEVOURING. *adj.* [from *all* and *devour*.] That which eats up every thing.

Secure from flames, from envy's fiercer rage,
Destructive war, and *all-devouring* age. *Pope's Essay on Crit.*

ALL FOURS. *n. s.* [from *all* and *four*.] A low game at cards, played by two; so named from the four particulars by which it is reckoned, and which, joined in the hand of either of the parties, are said to make *all fours*.

ALL HAIL. *n. s.* [from *all*, and *hail*, for *health*.] All health. This is therefore not a compound, though, perhaps usually reckoned among them.

All hail, ye fields, where constant peace attends!
All hail, ye sacred, solitary groves!
All hail, ye books, my true, my real friends,
Whose conversation pleases and improves. *Walsh.*

ALL-HALLOWN. *n. s.* [from *all* and *hallow*, to make holy.] The time about Allsaintsday.

Farewell, thou latter spring! farewell,
All-hallown summer. *Shakesp. Henry* IV. *p.* i.

ALLHALLOWTIDE. *n. s.* [See ALL-HALLOWN.] The term near Allsaints, or the first of November.

Cut off the bough about *Allhallowtide*, in the bare place, and set it in the ground, and it will grow to be a fair tree in one year. *Bacon's Natural History*, N° 427.

ALL-HEAL. *n. s.* [*Panax*, Lat.] A species of *ironwort*; which see.

ALL-JUDGING. *adj.* [from *all* and *judge*.] That which has the sovereign right of judgment.

I look with horrour back,
That I detest my wretched self, and curse
My past polluted life. *All-judging* heav'n,
Who knows my crimes, has seen my sorrow for them.
Rowe's Jane Shore.

ALL-KNOWING. *adj.* [from *all* and *know*.] Omniscient; all-wise.

Shall we repine at a little misplaced charity, we, who could no way foresee the effect; when an *all-knowing*, all-wise Being, showers down every day his benefits on the unthankful and undeserving? *Atterbury's Sermons.*

ALL-MAKING. *adj.* [from *all* and *make*.] That created all; omnifick. [See ALL-SEEING.]

ALL-POWERFUL. *adj.* [from *all* and *powerful*.] Almighty; omnipotent; possessed of infinite power.

2

O *all-powerful* Being, the least motion of whose will can create or destroy a world; pity us, the mournful friends of thy distressed servant. *Swift.*

ALL SAINTS DAY. *n. s.* The day on which there is a general celebration of the saints. The first of November.

ALL-SEER. *n. s.* [from *all* and *see*.] He that sees or beholds every thing; he whose view comprehends all things.

That high *All-seer*, which I dallied with,
Hath turn'd my feigned prayer on my head,
And giv'n in earnest, what I begg'd in jest. *Shak. Rich.* III.

ALL-SEEING. *adj.* [from *all* and *see*.] That beholds every thing.

The same First Mover certain bounds has plac'd,
How long those perishable forms shall last;
Nor can they last beyond the time assign'd
By that *all-seeing* and *all making* mind. *Dryd. Fables.*

ALL SOULS DAY. *n. s.* The day on which supplications are made for all souls by the church of Rome; the second of November.

This is *all souls day*, fellows, is it not?—
It is, my lord.—
Why then, *all souls day* is my body's doomsday. *Shak. R.* III.

ALL-SUFFICIENT. *adj.* [from *all* and *sufficient*.] Sufficient to every thing.

The testimonies of God are perfect, the testimonies of God are *all-sufficient* unto that end for which they were given *Hooker.*

He can more than employ all our powers in their utmost elevation; for he is every way perfect and *all-sufficient*. *Norris.*

ALL-WISE. *adj.* [from *all* and *wise*.] Possest of infinite wisdom.

There is an infinite, eternal, *all-wise* Mind governing the affairs of the world. *South.*

Supreme, *all-wise*, eternal, potentate!
Sole authour, sole disposer of our fate! *Prior.*

ALLANTO'IS, or *ALLANTO'IDES*. *n. s.* [from ἀλλᾶς, a gut, and εἶδος, shape.] The urinary tunick placed between the amnion and chorion, which, by the navel and urachus, or passage by which the urine is conveyed from the infant in the womb, receives the urine that comes out of the bladder. *Quincy.*

To ALLA'Y. *v. a.* [from *alloyer*, Fr. to mix one metal with another in order to coinage; it is therefore derived by some from *à la loi*, *according to law*; the quantity of metals being mixed according to law; by others, from *allier*, to unite; perhaps from *allocare*, to put together.]

1. To mix one metal with another, to make it fitter for coinage. In this sense, most authours preserve the original French orthography, and write *alloy*. See ALLOY.

2. To join any thing to another, so as to abate its predominant qualities.

Being brought into the open air,
I would *allay* the burning quality
Of that fell poison. *Shakesp. King John.*

No friendly offices shall alter or *allay* that rancour, that frets in some hellish breasts, which, upon all occasions, will foam out at its foul mouth in slander and invective. *South.*

3. To quiet; to pacify; to repress. The word, in this sense, I think not to be derived from the French *alloyer*, but to be the English word *lay*, with *a* before it, according to the old form.

If, by your art, you have
Put the wild waters in this roar, *allay* them. *Shak. Tempest.*

ALLA'Y. *n. s.* [*alloy*, Fr.]

1. The metal of a baser kind mixed in coins, to harden them, that they may wear less. Gold is allayed with silver and copper, two carats to a pound Troy; silver with copper only, of which eighteen pennyweight is mixed with a pound. *Cowel* thinks the allay is added, to countervail the charge of coining; which might have been done only by making the coin less.

For fools are stubborn in their way,
As coins are harden'd by th' *allay*. *Hudibras, p.* iii. *c.* 2.

2. Any thing which, being added, abates the predominant qualities of that with which it is mingled; in the same manner, as the admixture of baser metals allay the qualities of the first mass.

Dark colours easily suffer a sensible *allay*, by little scattering light. *Newton's Opticks.*

3. Allay being taken from baser metals, commonly implies something worse than that with which it is mixed.

The joy has no *allay* of jealousy, hope and fear. *Roscommon.*

ALLA'YER. *n. s.* [from *allay*.] The person or thing which has the power or quality of allaying.

Phlegm and pure blood are reputed *allayers* of acrimony; and, upon that account, Avicen countermands letting blood in cholerick bodies; because he esteems the blood a *frænum bilis*, or a bridle of gall, obtunding its acrimony and fierceness.
Harvey on Consumptions.

ALLA'YMENT. *n. s.* [from *allay*.] That which has the power of allaying or abating the force of another.

If I could temporize with my affection,
Or brew it to a weak and colder palate,
The like *allayment* would I give my grief. *Sh. Troilus and Cr.*

ALLEGA'TION. *n. s.* [from *allege*.]

1. Affirmation; declaration.

2. The thing alleged or affirmed.

Hath he not twit our sovereign lady here
With ignominious words, though darkly coucht?

As

As if ſhe had ſuborned ſome to ſwear
Falſe *allegations*, to o'erthrow his ſtate. *Shakeſp. Henry* VI.

3. An excuſe; a plea.

I omitted no means in my power, to be informed of my errours; and I expect not to be excuſed in any negligence on account of youth, want of leiſure, or any other idle *allegations*. *Pope's Preface to his Works.*

To ALLE'GE. *v. a.* [*allego*, Lat.]

1. To affirm; to declare; to maintain.
2. To plead as an excuſe, or produce as an argument.

Surely the preſent form of church-government is ſuch, as no law of God, or reaſon of man, hath hitherto been *alleged*, of force ſufficient to prove they do ill, who, to the utmoſt of their power, withſtand the alteration thereof. *Hooker's Preface.*

If we forſake the ways of grace or goodneſs, we cannot *allege* any colour of ignorance, or want of inſtruction; we cannot ſay we have not learned them, or we could not. *Sprat.*

He hath a clear and full view, and there is no more to be *alleged* for his better information. *Locke.*

Alle'geable. *adj.* [from *allege.*] That which may be alleged.

Upon this interpretation all may be ſolved, that is *allegeable* againſt it. *Brown's Vulgar Errours, b.* vi. *c.* 7.

Alle'gement. *n. ſ.* [from *allege.*] The ſame with *allegation*. *D.*

Alle'ger. *n. ſ.* [from *allege.*] He that alleges.

Which narrative, if we may believe it as confidently as the famous *alleger* of it, Pamphilio, appears to do, would ſeem to argue, that there is, ſometimes, no other principle requiſite, than what may reſult from the lucky mixture of the parts of ſeveral bodies. *Boyle.*

Alle'giance. *n. ſ.* [*allegeance*, Fr.] The duty of ſubjects to the government.

I did pluck *allegiance* from mens hearts,
Loud ſhouts and ſalutations from their mouths,
Even in the preſence of the crowned king. *Shak. Henry* IV.

We charge you on *allegiance* to ourſelves,
To hold your ſlaught'ring hands, and keep the peace.
Shakeſpeare's Henry VI. *p.* i.

The houſe of commons, to whom every day petitions are directed by the ſeveral counties of England, profeſſing all *allegiance* to them, govern abſolutely; the lords concurring, or rather ſubmitting to whatſoever is propoſed. *Clarendon.*

Alle'giant. *adj.* [from *allege.*] Loyal; conformable to the duty of *allegiance*: a word not now uſed.

For your great graces
Heap'd upon me, poor undeſerver, I
Can nothing render but *allegiant* thanks,
My pray'rs to heav'n for you. *Shakeſp. Henry* VIII.

Allego'rick. *adj.* [from *allegory.*] After the manner of an allegory; not real; not literal.

A kingdom they portend thee; but what kingdom,
Real or *allegorick*, I diſcern not. *Milton's Par. Loſt, b.* iv.

Allego'rical. *adj.* [from *allegory.*] In the form of an allegory; not real; not literal; myſtical.

When our Saviour ſaid, in an *allegorical* and myſtical ſenſe, Except ye eat the fleſh of the Son of man, and drink his blood, ye have no life in you; the hearers underſtood him literally and groſly. *Bentley's Sermons.*

The epithet of Apollo for ſhooting, is capable of two applications; one literal, in reſpect of the darts and bow, the enſigns of that god; the other *allegorical*, in regard to the rays of the ſun. *Pope's Preface to Iliad.*

Allego'rically. *adv.* [from *allegory.*] After an allegorical manner.

Virgil often makes Iris the meſſenger of Juno, *allegorically* taken for the air. *Peacham on Drawing.*

The place is to be underſtood *allegorically*; and what is thus ſpoken by a Phæacian with wiſdom, is, by the Poet, applied to the goddeſs of it. *Pope's Odyſſey, b.* viii. *notes.*

Allego'ricalness. *n. ſ.* [from *allegorical.*] The quality of being allegorical. *Dict.*

To A'llegorize. *v. a.* [from *allegory.*] To turn into allegory; to form an allegory; to take in a ſenſe not literal.

He hath very wittily *allegorized* this tree, allowing his ſuppoſition of the tree itſelf to be true. *Raleigh's Hiſtory.*

As ſome would *allegorize* theſe ſigns, which we noted before; ſo others would confine them to the deſtruction of Jeruſalem. *Burnet's Theory of the Earth.*

An alchymiſt ſhall reduce divinity to the maxims of his laboratory, explain morality by ſal, ſulphur, and mercury; and *allegorize* the ſcripture itſelf, and the ſacred myſteries thereof into the philoſopher's ſtone. *Locke.*

A'LLEGORY. *n. ſ.* [ἀλληγορία.] A figurative diſcourſe, in which ſomething other is intended, than is contained in the words literally taken; as, *wealth is the daughter of diligence, and the parent of authority.*

Neither muſt we draw out our *allegory* too long, leſt either we make ourſelves obſcure, or fall into affectation, which is childiſh. *Ben. Johnſon's Diſcovery.*

This word nympha meant nothing elſe but, by *allegory*, the vegetative humour or moiſture that quickeneth and giveth life to trees and flowers, whereby they grow. *Peacham.*

ALLE'GRO. n. ſ. A word, denoting one of the ſix diſtinctions of time. It expreſſes a ſprightly motion, the quickeſt of all, except Preſto. It originally means *gay*, as in *Milton.*

ALLELU'JAH. n. ſ. [This word is falſely written for *Hallelujah*, הללו and יה.] A word of ſpiritual exultation, uſed in hymns; it ſignifies, *Praiſe God.*

He will ſet his tongue to thoſe pious divine ſtrains, which may be a proper præludium to thoſe *allelujahs* he hopes eternally to ſing. *Government of the Tongue.*

ALLEMA'NDE. n. ſ. [Ital.] A grave kind of muſick. *Dict.*

To ALLE'VIATE. *v. a.* [*allevo*, Lat.]

1. To make light; to eaſe; to ſoften.

Moſt of the diſtempers are the effects of abuſed plenty and luxury, and muſt not be charged upon our Maker; who, notwithſtanding, hath provided excellent medicines, to *alleviate* thoſe evils which we bring upon ourſelves. *Bentley's Sermons.*

2. To extenuate, or ſoften; as, he *alleviates* his fault by an excuſe.

Allevia'tion. *n. ſ.* [from *alleviate.*]

1. The act of making light; of allaying, or extenuating.

All apologies for, and *alleviations* of faults, though they are the heights of humanity, yet they are not the favours, but the duties of friendſhip. *South's Sermons.*

2. That by which any pain is eaſed, or fault extenuated.

This loſs of one fifth of their debts and income will ſit heavy on them, who ſhall feel it, without the *alleviation* of any profit. *Locke.*

A'lley. *n. ſ.* [*allée*, Fr.]

1. A walk in a garden.

And all within were walks and *alleys* wide,
With footing worn, and leading inward far. *Fairy Queen.*

It is common from experience, that where *alleys* are cloſe gravelled, the earth putteth forth the firſt year knotgraſs, and after ſpiregraſs. *Bacon's Natural Hiſtory*, Nº 565.

Yonder *alleys* green,
Our walk at noon, with branches overgrown. *Parad. Loſt.*

Come, my fair love, our morning's taſk we loſe;
Some labour ev'n the eaſieſt life would chooſe:
Ours is not great: the dangling bows to crop,
Whoſe too luxuriant growth our *alleys* ſtop. *Dryden.*

The thriving plants, ignoble broomſticks made,
Now ſweep thoſe *alleys* they were born to ſhade. *Pope.*

2. A paſſage in towns narrower than a ſtreet.

A back friend, a ſhoulder clapper, one that commands
The paſſages of *alleys*, creeks, and narrow lands.
Shakeſp. Comedy of Errours.

Alli'ance. *n. ſ.* [*alliance*, Fr.]

1. The ſtate of connection with another by confederacy; a league. In this ſenſe, our hiſtories of Queen Anne mention *the grand alliance.*
2. Relation by marriage.

A bloody Hymen ſhall th' *alliance* join
Betwixt the Trojan and th' Auſonian line. *Dryden's Æneid.*

3. Relation by any form of kindred.

For my father's ſake,
In honour of a true Plantagenet,
And, for *alliance'* ſake, declare the cauſe
My father loſt his head. *Shakeſp. Henry* VI. *p.* i.

4. The act of forming or contracting relation to another; the act of making a confederacy.

Dorſet, your ſon, that with a fearful ſoul
Leads diſcontented ſteps in foreign ſoil,
This fair *alliance* quickly ſhall call home
To high promotions. *Shakeſp. Richard* III.

Adraſtus ſoon, with gods averſe, ſhall join
In dire *alliance* with the Theban line;
Thence ſtrife ſhall riſe, and mortal war ſucceed. *Pope.*

5. The perſons allied to each other.

I would not boaſt the greatneſs of my father,
But point out new *alliances* to Cato. *Addiſon's Cato.*

Alli'ciency. *n. ſ.* [*allicio*, Lat. to entice or draw.] The power of attracting any thing; magnetiſm; attraction.

The feigned central *alliciency* is but a word, and the manner of it ſtill occult. *Glanville's Sceps̃is Scientifica.*

To A'LLIGATE. *v. a.* [*alligo*, Lat.] To tie one thing to another; to unite.

Alliga'tion. *n. ſ.* [from *alligate.*]

1. The act of tying together; the ſtate of being ſo tied.
2. The arithmetical rule that teaches to adjuſt the price of compounds, formed of ſeveral ingredients of different value.

Alliga'tor. *n. ſ.* The crocodile. This name is chiefly uſed for the crocodile of America, between which, and that of Africa, naturaliſts have laid down this difference, that one moves the upper, and the other the lower jaw; but this is now known to be chimerical, the lower jaw being equally moved by both. See Crocodile.

In his needy ſhop a tortoiſe hung,
An *alligator* ſtuff'd, and other ſkins
Of ill-ſhap'd fiſhes. *Shakeſp. Romeo and Juliet.*

Aloft in rows large poppy-heads were ſtrung,
And here a ſcaly *alligator* hung. *Garth's Diſpenſary.*

A'lligature. *n. ſ.* [from *alligate.*] The link, or ligature, by which two things are joined together. *Dict.*

ALLI'SION. *n. s.* [*allido, allisum*, Lat.] The act of striking one thing against another.

There have not been any islands of note, or considerable extent, torn and cast off from the continent by earthquakes, or severed from it by the boisterous *allision* of the sea. *Woodward.*

ALLOCA'TION. *n. s.* [*alloco*, Lat.]

1. The act of putting one thing to another.
2. The admission of an article in reckoning, and addition of it to the account.
3. An allowance made upon an account; a term used in the exchequer. *Chambers.*

ALLOCU'TION. *n. s.* [*allocutio*, Lat.] The act of speaking to another.

ALLO'DIAL. *adj.* [from *allodium.*] Held without any acknowledgment of superiority; not feudal; independent.

ALLO'DIUM. n. s. [A word of very uncertain derivation, but most probably of German original.]

A possession held in absolute independence, without any acknowledgment of a lord paramount. It is opposed to *fee*, or *feudum*, which intimates some kind of dependance. There are no allodial lands in England, all being held either mediately or immediately of the king.

ALLO'NGE. *n. s.* [*allonge*, Fr.] A pass or thrust with a rapier, so called from the lengthening of the space taken up by the fencer.

To ALLO'O. *v. a.* [This word is generally spoke *halloo*, and is used to dogs, when they are incited to the chase or battle; it is commonly imagined to come from the French *allons*; perhaps from *all lo*, look all; shewing the object.] To set on; to incite a dog, by crying *alloo*.

Alloo thy furious mastiff; bid him vex
The noxious herd, and print upon their ears
A sad memorial of their past offence. *Philips.*

A'LLOQUY. *n. s.* [*alloquium*, Lat.] The act of speaking to another; converse; conversation. *Dict.*

To ALLO'T. *v. a.* [from *lot.*]

1. To distribute by lot.
2. To grant.

Five days we do *allot* thee for provision,
To shield thee from disasters of the world;
And, on the sixth, to turn thy hated back
Upon our kingdom. *Shakesp. King Lear.*

I shall deserve my fate, if I refuse
That happy hour, which heaven *allots* to peace. *Dryden.*

3. To distribute; to parcel out; to give each his share.

Since fame was the only end of all their new enterprizes and studies, a man cannot be too scrupulous in *allotting* them their due portion of it. *Tatler*, N° 81.

ALLO'TMENT. *n. s.* [from *allot.*] That which is alloted to any one; the part; the share; the portion granted.

There can be no thought of security or quiet in this world, but in a resignation to the *allotments* of God and nature. *L'Estr.*

Though it is our duty to submit with patience to more scanty *allotments*, yet thus much we may reasonably and lawfully ask of God. *Rogers's Sermons.*

ALLO'TTERY. *n. s.* [from *allot.*] That which is granted to any particular person in a distribution. See ALLO'TMENT.

Allow me such exercises as may become a gentleman, or give me the poor *allottery* my father left me by testament.
Shakespeare, As you like it.

To ALLO'W. *v. a.* [*allouer*, Fr. from *allaudare.*]

1. To admit; as, to *allow* a position; not to contradict; not to oppose.

The principles, which all mankind *allow* for true, are innate; those, that men of right reason admit, are the principles *allowed* by all mankind. *Locke.*

The pow'r of musick all our hearts *allow*;
And what Timotheus was, is Dryden now. *Pope's Ess. Crit.*

As to what is alleged, that some of the Presbyterians declared openly against the king's murder, I *allow* it to be true. *Swift.*

2. To grant; to yield; to own any one's title to.

We will not, in civility, *allow* too much sincerity to the professions of most men; but think their actions to be interpreters of their thoughts. *Locke.*

I will help you to enough of them, and shall be ready to *allow* the pope as little power here as you please. *Swift.*

3. To grant licence to; to permit.

Let's follow the old earl, and get the beldam
To lead him where he would; his roguish madness
Allows itself to any thing. *Shakespeare's King Lear.*

But as we were *allowed* of God to be put in trust with the gospel, even so we speak, not as pleasing men, but God, which trieth our hearts. *1 Thess.* ii. 4.

They referred all laws, that were to be passed in Ireland, to be considered, corrected and *allowed* first by the state of England. *Sir John Davies on Ireland.*

4. To give a sanction to; to authorize.

There is no slander in an *allow'd* fool. *Shakesp. Tw. Night.*

5. To give to; to pay to.

Ungrateful then! if we no tears *allow*
To him that gave us peace and empire too. *Waller.*

6. To appoint for; to set out to a certain use; as, he *allowed* his son the third part of his income.

7. To make abatement, or provision; or to settle any thing, with some concessions or cautions, regarding something else.

If we consider the different occasions of ancient and modern medals, we shall find they both agree in recording the great actions and successes in war; *allowing* still for the different ways of making it, and the circumstances that attended it. *Addison.*

ALLO'WABLE. *adj.* [from *allow.*]

1. That which may be admitted without contradiction.

It is not *allowable*, what is observable in many pieces of Raphael, where Magdalen is represented, before our Saviour, washing his feet, on her knees; which will not consist with the text. *Brown's Vulgar Errours.*

2. That which is permitted or licensed; lawful; not forbidden.

In actions of this sort, the very light of nature alone may discover that which is so far forth in the sight of God *allowable*. *Hooker, b.* ii. § 8.

I was, by the freedom *allowable* among friends, tempted to vent my thoughts with negligence. *Boyle on the Scriptures.*

Reputation becomes a signal and a very peculiar blessing to magistrates; and their pursuit of it is not only *allowable*, but laudable. *Atterbury's Sermons.*

ALLO'WABLENESS. *n. s.* [from *allowable.*] The quality of being allowable; lawfulness; exemption from prohibition.

I cannot think myself engaged to discourse of lots, as to their nature, use, and *allowableness*, in matters of recreation; which is indeed impugned by some, though better defended by others.
South's Sermons.

ALLO'WANCE. *n. s.* [from *allow.*]

1. Admission without contradiction.

Without the notion and *allowance* of spirits, our philosophy will be lame and defective in one main part of it. *Locke.*

2. Sanction; licence; authority.

That which wisdom did first begin, and hath been with good men long continued, challengeth *allowance* of them that succeed, although it plead for itself nothing. *Hooker, b.* v. § 7.

You sent a large commission
To Gregory de Cassado, to conclude,
Without the king's will, or the state's *allowance*,
A league between his highness and Ferrara. *Shak. Henry* VIII.

3. Permission; freedom from restraint.

They should therefore be accustomed betimes to consult and make use of their reason, before they give *allowance* to their inclinations. *Locke.*

4. A settled rate; or appointment for any use.

The victual in plantations ought to be expended almost as in a besieged town; that is, with certain *allowance*. *Bacon.*

And his *allowance* was a continual *allowance* given him of the king; a daily rate for every day all his life. *2 Kings*, xxv. 30.

5. Abatement from the strict rigour of a law, or demand.

The whole poem, though written in that which they call heroick verse, is of the Pindarick nature, as well in the thought as the expression; and, as such, requires the same grains of *allowance* for it. *Dryden.*

Parents never give *allowances* for an innocent passion. *Swift.*

6. Established character; reputation.

His bark is stoutly timber'd, and his pilot
Of very expert and approved *allowance*;
Therefore my hopes, not surfeited to death,
Stand in bold awe. *Shakesp. Othello.*

ALLO'Y. *n. s.* [See ALLAY.]

1. Baser metal mixed in coinage.

That precise weight and fineness, by law appropriated to the pieces of each denomination, is called the standard. Fine silver is silver without the mixture of any baser metal. *Alloy* is baser metal mixed with it. *Locke.*

For let another piece be coined of the same weight, wherein half the silver is taken out, and copper, or other *alloy*, put into the place, every one knows it will be worth but half as much; for the value of the *alloy* is so inconsiderable as not to be reckoned. *Locke.*

2. Abatement; diminution.

The pleasures of sense are probably relished by beasts in a more exquisite degree, than they are by men; for they taste them sincere and pure always, without mixture or *alloy*.
Atterbury's Sermons.

ALLUBE'SCENCY. *n. s.* [*allubescentia*, Lat.] Willingness; content. *Dict.*

To ALLU'DE. *v. n* [*alludo*, Lat.] To have some reference to a thing, without the direct mention of it; to hint at; to insinuate. It is used of persons; as, *he* alludes *to an old story*; or of things, as, *the lampoon* alludes *to his mother's faults*.

These speeches of Jerom and Chrysostom do seem plainly to *allude* unto such ministerial garments as were then in use.
Hooker, b. v. § 29.

True it is, that many things of this nature be *alluded* unto, yea, many things declared. *Hooker, b.* iv. § 2.

Then just proportions were taken, and every thing placed by weight and measure: and this I doubt not was that artificial structure here *alluded* to. *Burnet's Theory of the Earth.*

ALLU'MINOR. *n. s.* [*allumer*, Fr. to light.] One who colours or paints upon paper or parchment; because he gives graces, light an ornament, to the letters or figures coloured. *Cowell.*

To ALLU'RE. *v. a.* [*leurrer*, Fr. *looren*, Dutch, belæ͞pen, Sax.] To entice to any thing whether good or bad; to draw towards any thing by enticement.

Unto laws that men make for the benefit of men, it hath ſeemed always needful to add rewards, which may more *allure* unto good, than any hardneſs deterreth from it, and puniſhments, which may more deter from evil, than any ſweetneſs thereto *allureth*. *Hooker, b.* i. *p.* 28.

Above them all
The golded ſun, in ſplendour likeſt heav'n,
Allur'd his eye. *Milton's Paradiſe Loſt, b.* iii. *l.* 572.

Each flatt'ring hope, and each *alluring* joy. *Lyttleton.*

ALLU'RE. *n. ſ.* [from the verb *allure.*] Something ſet up to entice birds, or other things, to it. We now write *lure.*

The rather to train them to his *allure*, he told them both often, and with a vehement voice, how they were over-topped and trodden down by gentlemen. *Sir John Hayward.*

ALLU'REMENT. *n. ſ.* [from *allure.*]

That which allures, or has the force of alluring: enticement; temptation of pleaſure.

Againſt *allurement*, cuſtom, and a world
Offended; fearleſs of reproach, and ſcorn,
Or violence. *Milton's Paradiſe Loſt, b.* xi.

——Adam, by his wife's *allurement*, fell. *Par. Reg. b.* ii.

To ſhun th' *allurement* is not hard
To minds reſolv'd, forewarn'd, and well prepar'd;
But wond'rous difficult, when once beſet,
To ſtruggle through the ſtraits, and break th' involving net. *Dryden.*

ALLU'RER. *n. ſ.* [from *allure.*] The perſon that allures; enticer; enveigler.

ALLU'RINGLY. *adv.* [from *allure.*] In an alluring manner; enticingly.

ALLU'RINGNESS. *n. ſ.* [from *alluring.*] The quality of alluring or enticing; incitation; temptation by propoſing pleaſure.

ALLU'SION. *n. ſ.* [*alluſio*, Lat.] That which is ſpoken with reference to ſomething ſuppoſed to be already known, and therefore not expreſſed; a hint; an implication. It has the particle *to.*

Here are manifeſt *alluſions* and footſteps of the diſſolution of the earth, as it was in the deluge, and will be in its laſt ruin. *Burnet's Theory.*

This laſt *alluſion* gall'd the Panther more,
Becauſe indeed it rubb'd upon the ſore. *Dryden.*

Expreſſions now out of uſe, *alluſions to* cuſtoms loſt to us, and various particularities, muſt needs continue ſeveral paſſages in the dark. *Locke's Eſſay on St. Paul's Epiſtles.*

ALLU'SIVE. *adj.* [*alludo, alluſum*, Lat.] Hinting at ſomething not fully expreſſed.

Where the expreſſion in one place is plain, and the ſenſe affixed to it agreeable to the proper force of the words, and no negative objection requires us to depart from it; and the expreſſion, in the other, is figurative or *alluſive*, and the doctrine, deduced from it, liable to great objections; it is reaſonable, in this latter place, to reſtrain the extent of the figure and alluſion, to a conſiſtency with the former. *Rogers's Sermons.*

ALLU'SIVELY. *adv.* [from *alluſive.*] In an alluſive manner; by implication; by inſinuation.

The Jewiſh nation, that rejected and crucified him, within the compaſs of one generation, were, according to his prediction, deſtroyed by the Romans, and preyed upon by thoſe eagles, (*Matt.* xxiv. 28.) by which, *alluſively*, are noted the Roman armies, whoſe enſign was the eagle. *Hammond's Pr. Cat.*

ALLU'SIVENESS. *n. ſ.* [from *alluſive.*] The quality of being alluſive.

ALLU'VION. *n. ſ.* [*alluvio*, Lat.]

1. The carrying of any thing to ſomething elſe by the motion of the water.

2. The thing carried by water to ſomething elſe.

The civil law gives the owner of land a right to that increaſe which ariſes from *alluvion*, which is defined an inſenſible increment, brought by the water.

ALLU'VIOUS. *adj.* [from *alluvion.*] That which is carried by water to another place, and lodged upon ſomething elſe.

To ALLY'. *v. a.* [*allier*, Fr.]

1. To unite by kindred, friendſhip, or confederacy.

All theſe ſepts are *allied* to the inhabitants of the North, ſo as there is no hope that they will ever ſerve faithfully againſt them. *Spenſer on Ireland.*

Wants, frailties, paſſions, cloſer ſtill *ally*
The common int'reſt, or endear the tye. *Pope's Eſſ. on Man.*

To the ſun *ally'd*,
From him they draw the animating fire. *Thomſon's Summer.*

2. To make a relation between two things, by ſimilitude, or reſemblance, or any other means.

Two lines I cannot excuſe: they are indeed remotely *allied* to Virgil's ſenſe; but they are too like the tenderneſs of Ovid. *Dryden.*

ALLY'. *n. ſ.* [*allie*, Fr.] One united by ſome means of connexion; as, marriage; friendſhip; confederacy.

We could hinder the acceſſion of Holland to France, either as ſubjects, with great immunities for the encouragement of trade, or as an inferiour and dependent *ally* under their protection. *Temple.*

ALMACA'NTAR. n. ſ. [An Arabick word, written variouſly by various authours; by D'Herbelot, *almocantar*; by others, *almucantar.*] A circle drawn parallel to the horizon. It is generally uſed in the plural, and means a ſeries of parallel circles drawn through the ſeveral degrees of the meridian.

ALMACA'NTAR'S STAFF. *n. ſ.* An inſtrument commonly made of pear-tree or box, with an arch of fifteen degrees, uſed to take obſervations of the ſun, about the time of its riſing and ſetting, in order to find the amplitude, and conſequently the variation of the compaſs. *Chambers.*

A'LMANACK. *n. ſ.* [Derived, by ſome, from the Arabick, *al*, and *manah*, Heb. to *count*, or *compute*; but others, from *al*, Arabick, and μὴν, a *month*, or μαναχὸς, the *courſe of the months*; by others, from a Teutonick original, *al* and *maan*, the *moon*, an account of every moon, or month: all of them are probable.]

A calendar; a book in which the revolutions of the ſeaſons, with the return of feaſts and faſts, is noted for the enſuing year.

It will be ſaid, this is an *almanack* for the old year; all hath been well; Spain hath not aſſailed this kingdom. *Bacon.*

This aſtrologer made his *almanack* give a tolerable account of the weather, by a direct inverſion of the common prognoſticators. *Government of the Tongue.*

Beware the woman too, and ſhun her ſight,
Who in theſe ſtudies does herſelf delight;
By whom a greaſy *almanack* is born,
With often handling like chaft amber worn. *Dryd. Juvenal.*

I'll have a faſting *almanack* printed on purpoſe for her uſe. *Dryden's Spaniſh Friar.*

A'LMANDINE. n. ſ. [Fr. *almandina*, Ital.] A ruby coarſer and lighter than the oriental, and nearer the colour of the granate. *Dict.*

ALMI'GHTINESS. *n. ſ.* [from *almighty.*] Unlimited power; omnipotence; one of the attributes of God.

It ſerveth to the world for a witneſs of his *almightineſs*, whom we outwardly honour with the chiefeſt of outward things. *Hooker, b.* v. § 15.

In creating and making exiſtent the world univerſal, by the abſolute act of his own word, his power and *almightineſs*. *Sir Walter Raleigh.*

In the wilderneſs, the bittern and the ſtork, the unicorn and the elk, live upon his proviſions, and revere his power, and feel the force of his *almightineſs*. *Taylor's Rule of holy living.*

ALMI'GHTY. *adj.* [from *all* and *mighty.*] Of unlimited power; omnipotent.

The Lord appeared unto Abram, and ſaid unto him, I am the *almighty* God; walk before me, and be thou perfect. *Geneſis*, xvii. 1.

He wills you in the name of God *almighty*,
That you diveſt yourſelf, and lay apart
The borrow'd glories, that, by gift of heav'n,
By law of nature and of nations 'long
To him and to his heirs. *Shakeſpeare's Henry* V.

A'LMOND. *n. ſ.* [*amand*, Fr. derived by *Menage* from *amandala*, a word in low Latin; by others, from *Allemand*, a German; ſuppoſing that almonds come to France from Germany.]

The nut of the almond tree, either ſweet or bitter.

Pound an *almond*, and the clear white colour will be altered into a dirty one, and the ſweet taſte into an oily one. *Locke.*

A'LMOND TREE. *n. ſ.* [*amygdalus*, Lat.]

It has leaves and flowers very like thoſe of the peach tree, but the fruit is longer and more compreſſed; the outer green coat is thinner and drier when ripe, and the ſhell is not ſo rugged.

The ſpecies are, 1. The common large *almond*. 2. The ſweet *almond*, with tender ſhells. 3. The bitter *almond*. 4. The white flowering *almond*.

The three firſt ſorts are chiefly cultivated in England, for the beauty of their flowers; and the firſt ſort yields large quantities of fruit yearly, little inferiour to what we receive from abroad, if not kept too long. They are propagated in July, by inoculating a bud into a plum ſtock, for wet ground, or an *almond* or peach ſtock for dry. The fourth is a greater curioſity; it will not ſucceed on a plum, but muſt be budded on a peach or *almond*. *Millar.*

Like to an *almond tree*, you're mounted high
On top of green Selinis, all alone,
With bloſſoms brave bedecked daintily,
Whoſe tender locks do tremble every one,
At every little breath that under heav'n is blown. *Fairy Q.*

Mark well the flow'ring *almonds* in the wood,
If od'rous blooms the bearing branches load,
The glebe will anſwer to the ſylvan reign;
Great heats will follow, and large crops of grain. *Dryden.*

A'LMONDS OF THE THROAT, or TONSILS, called improperly *Almonds of the ears*; are two round glands placed on the ſides of the baſis of the tongue, under the common membrane of the fauces; each of them has a large oval ſinus, which opens into the fauces, and in it are a great number of leſſer ones, which diſcharge themſelves through the great ſinus of a mucous and the ſlippery matter into the fauces, larynx, and œſophagus, for the moiſtening and lubricating thoſe parts. When the œſophagus muſcle acts, it compreſſes the *almonds*, and they frequently are the occaſion of a ſore throat. *Quincy.*

The tonſils, or *Almonds of the Ears*, are alſo frequently ſwelled in the king's evil; which tumour may be very well reckoned a ſpecies of it. *Wiſeman's Surgery.*

A'LMOND-FURNACE, or A'LMAN-FURNACE, called alſo the *Sweep*, is a peculiar kind of furnace uſed in refining, to ſeparate metals from cinders and other foreign ſubſtances. *Chambers.*

A'LMONER, or ALMNER. *n. ſ.* [*eleemoſynarius*, Lat.] The officer of a prince, or other perſon, employed in the diſtribution of charity.

I enquired among the Jacobins for an *almoner*; and the general fame has pointed out your reverence as the worthieſt man. *Dryden's Spaniſh Friar.*

A'LMONRY. *n. ſ.* [from *almoner.*] The place where the almoner reſides, or where the alms are diſtributed.

ALMO'ST. *adv.* [from *all* and *moſt*; that is, *moſt part of all. Skinner.*] Nearly; well nigh; in the next degree to the whole, or to univerſality.

Who is there *almoſt*, whoſe mind, at ſome time or other, love or anger, fear or grief, has not ſo faſtened to ſome clog, that it could not turn itſelf to any other object. *Locke.*

There can be no ſuch thing or notion, as an *almoſt* infinite; there can be nothing next or ſecond to an omnipotent God. *Bentley's Sermons.*

Atlas becomes unequal to his freight,
And *almoſt* faints beneath the glowing weight. *Addiſ. Ovid.*

ALMS. *n. ſ.* [in Saxon, elmeȝ, from *eleemoſyna*, Lat.] What is given gratuitouſly in relief of the poor. It has no ſingular.

My arm'd knees,
Which bow'd but in my ſtirrup, bend like his
That hath received an *alms*. *Shakeſp. Coriolanus.*

The poor beggar hath a juſt demand of an *alms* from the rich man; who is guilty of fraud, injuſtice and oppreſſion, if he does not afford relief according to his abilities. *Swift.*

ALMS-BASKET. *n. ſ.* [from *alms* and *basket.*] The basket in which proviſions are put to be given away.

There ſweepings do as well,
As the beſt order'd meal;
For who the reliſh of theſe gueſts will fit,
Needs ſet them but the *alms-basket* of wit. *Ben. Johnſon.*

We'll ſtand up for our properties, was the beggar's ſong that lived upon the *alms-basket*. *L'Eſtrange's Fables.*

ALMSDEED. *n. ſ.* [from *alms* and *deed.*] An act of charity; a charitable gift.

This woman was full of good works, and *almſdeeds* which ſhe did. *Acts*, ix. 36.

Hard favour'd Richard, where art thou?
Thou art not here: murder is thy *almsdeed*;
Petitioner for blood thou ne'er put'ſt back.
Shakeſpeare's Henry VI.

ALMS-GIVER. *n. ſ.* [from *alms* and *giver.*] He that gives alms; he that ſupports others by his charity.

He built and endowed many religious foundations, beſides his memorable hoſpital of the Savoy. And yet was he a great *alms-giver* in ſecret, which ſhewed that his works in publick were dedicated rather to God's glory than his own. *Bacon.*

ALMSHOUSE. *n. ſ.* [from *alms* and *houſe.*] A houſe devoted to the reception and ſupport of the poor; an hoſpital for the poor.

The way of providing for the clergy by tithes, the device of *almshouſes* for the poor, and the ſorting out of the people into their ſeveral pariſhes, are manifeſt unto men of underſtanding. *Hooker's Preface.*

And to relief of lazars, and weak age
Of indigent faint ſouls, paſt corporal toil,
A hundred *almshouſes* right well ſupplied. *Shakeſp. Henry* V.

Many penitents, after the robbing of temples, and other violences of rapine, build an hoſpital, or ſome *alms-houſe*, out of the ruins of the church, and the ſpoils of widows and orphans. *L'Eſtrange's Fables.*

Behold yon *almshouſe*, neat, but void of ſtate,
Where age and want ſit ſmiling at the gate. *Pope.*

ALMSMAN. *n. ſ.* [from *alms* and *man.*] A man who lives upon alms; who is ſupported by charity.

I'll give my jewels for a ſet of beads;
My gorgeous palace, for a hermitage;
My gay apparel for an *almsman*'s gown. *Shakeſp. Rich.* II.

A'LMUG-TREE. *n. ſ.* A tree mentioned in ſcripture.

Of its wood were made muſical inſtruments, and it was uſed alſo in rails, or in a ſtaircaſe. The Rabbins generally render it *coral*, others *ebony*, *brazil*, or *pine*. In the Septuagint it is tranſlated *wrought wood*, and in the Vulgate, *Ligna Thyina*. But coral could never anſwer the purpoſes of the almugim; the pine-tree is too common in Judea to be imported from Ophir; and the Thyinum, or citron-tree, much eſteemed by the ancients for its fragrance and beauty, came from Mauritania. By the wood *almugim*, or *algumim*, or, ſimply, *gummim*, taking *al* for a kind of article, may be underſtood oily and gummy ſorts of wood, and particularly the trees which produce gum ammoniac, or gum arabick; and is, perhaps, the ſame with the Shittim wood mentioned by Moſes. *Calmet.*

And the navy alſo of Hiram that brought gold from Ophir, brought in from Ophir great plenty of *almug-trees* and precious trees. 1 *Kings*, x. 11.

A'LNAGAR, A'LNAGER, or A'LNEGER. *n. ſ.* [from *alnage.*] A meaſurer by the ell; a ſworn officer, whoſe buſineſs formerly was to inſpect the aſſize of woollen cloth, and to fix the ſeals appointed upon it for that purpoſe; but there are now three officers belonging to the regulation of cloth-manufactures, the *ſearcher*, *meaſurer*, and *alneger*. *Dict.*

A'LNAGE. *n. ſ.* [from *aulnage*, or *aunage*, Fr.] Ell-meaſure, or rather the meaſuring by the ell or yard. *Dict.*

A'LNIGHT. *n. ſ.* [from *all* and *night.*]

There is a ſervice which they call *alnight*, which is a great cake of wax, with the wick in the midſt; whereby it cometh to paſs, that the wick fetcheth the nouriſhment farther off. *Bacon's Natural Hiſtory*, N° 372.

A'LOES. *n. ſ.* [אחלם, as it is ſuppoſed.] A term applied to three different things.

1. A precious wood uſed, in the Eaſt, for perfumes, of which the beſt ſort is of higher price than gold, and was the moſt valuable preſent given by the king of Siam, in 1686, to the king of France. It is called *Tambac*, and is the heart, or innermoſt part, of the *aloetree*; the next part to which is called *Calembac*, which is ſometimes imported into Europe, and, though of inferiour value to the *Tambac*, is much eſteemed: the part next the bark is termed, by the Portugueſe, *Pao d'aquila*, or eagle-wood; but ſome account the eagle-wood not the outer part of the *Tambac*, but another ſpecies. Our knowledge of this wood is yet very imperfect. *Savary.*

2. *Aloes* is a tree which grows in hot countries, and even in the mountains of Spain.

The leaves are thick, ſucculent, and generally beſet with ſpines on the edges; the flower conſiſts of one leaf, is tubulous, and cut into ſix ſegments at the top, like the hyacinth; the fruit is oblong and cylindrical, divided into three cells, containing flat, and, for the moſt part, ſemicircular ſeeds.

The ſpecies are 39; 1. The common large American *aloe*. 2. The narrow-leaved *aloe*, from Vera Cruz. 3. The American *aloe*, which produces young plants out of the flower ſtems, &c.

Many of theſe plants, in Engliſh gardens, are natives of the Eaſt and Weſt Indies; but the moſt curious are brought from the Cape of Good Hope.

The firſt of theſe *aloes* is very hardy, and has endured the air, in mild winters, in a very dry ſoil, and under a ſouth wall; but they may be kept in a common greenhouſe, giving them very little moiſture in winter. The other ſorts are preſerved in an airy glaſs-caſe, with a ſtove. The *aloes* are all increaſed by off-ſets.

Moſt of the African ſpecies, after the ſecond, third, or fourth year's growth, produce flowers with us annually; but the American *aloes* flower but once during the life of the plant, producing the flower-ſtems from the centre of the plant, of a conſiderable ſize, and ſometimes fifteen feet in height.

A common error, relating to the firſt ſpecies, is, that it never flowers till it be an hundred years old; but experience has proved, that ſome have flowered in fifty years. Another errour is, that, when the flower opens, it makes a report like a gun. *Millar.*

3. *Aloes* is a medicinal juice extracted not from the odoriferous, but the common *aloes tree*, by cutting the leaves, and expoſing the juice that drops from them to the ſun. It is diſtinguiſhed into Socotorine and Caballine, or horſe *aloes*; the firſt is ſo called from *Socotora*; the ſecond, becauſe, being coarſer, it ought to be confined to the uſe of farriers. It is a warm and ſtrong cathartick, and uſed in moſt purgative compoſitions.

ALOE'TICAL. *adj.* [from *aloes.*] Conſiſting chiefly of aloes.

It may be excited by *aloetical*, ſcammoniate, or acrimonious medicines. *Wiſeman's Surgery.*

ALO'ETICK. *n. ſ.* [from *aloes.*] Any medicine is ſo called, which chiefly conſiſts of aloes. *Quincy.*

ALO'FT. *adv.* [*loffter*, to lift up, *Dan. Loft* air, *Icelandiſh*; ſo that *aloft* is, into the air.] On high; above; in the air: a word uſed chiefly in poetry.

For I have read in ſtories oft,
That love has wings, and ſoars *aloft*. *Suckling.*

Upright he ſtood, and bore *aloft* his ſhield,
Conſpicuous from afar, and overlook'd the field. *Dryd. Fab.*

AL'OFT. *prep.* Above.

The great luminary
Aloft the vulgar conſtellations thick,
That from his lordly eye keep diſtance due,
Diſpenſes light from far. *Milton's Paradiſe Loſt*, *b.* iii.

A'LOGY. *n. ſ.* [αλογος.] Unreaſonableneſs; abſurdity. *Dict.*

ALO'NE. *adj.* [*alleen*, Dutch; from *al* and *een*, or *one*, that is, *ſingle.*]

1. Without another.

The quarrel toucheth none but us *alone*;
Betwixt ourſelves let us decide it then. *Shakeſp. Henry* VI.

If by a mortal hand my father's throne
Could be defended, 'twas by mine *alone*. *Dryden, Æneid* ii.

God, by whoſe *alone* power and conſervation, we all live, and move, and have our being. *Bentley.*

2. Without company; ſolitary.

Eagles we ſee fly *alone*, and they are but ſheep which always herd together. *Sidney, b.* i.

Alone, for other creature in this place
Living, or lifeleſs, to be found was none. *Paradiſe Loſt.*
I never durſt in darkneſs be *alone.* *Dryden's Ind. Emp.*

ALO'NE. *adv.*

1. This word is ſeldom uſed but with the word *let*, if even then it be an adverb, and implies ſometimes an ironical prohibition, to help a man who is able to manage the affair himſelf.

Let us *alone* to guard Corioli,
If they ſet down before's; 'fore they remove,
Bring up your army. *Shakeſpeare's Coriolanus.*

Let you *alone*, cunning artificer;
See how his gorget peers above his gown,
To tell the people in what danger he was. *Ben. Johnſ. Catil.*

2. To let alone; to forbear; to leave unfiniſhed.

His client ſtole it, but he had better have *let* it *alone*; for he loſt his cauſe by his jeſt. *Addiſon. Spectator*, N° 408.

ALO'NG. *adv.* [*au longue*, Fr.]

1. At length.

Some rowl a mighty ſtone; ſome laid *along*,
And, bound with burning wires, on ſpokes of wheels are hung. *Dryden, Æneid* vi.

2. Through any ſpace meaſured lengthwiſe.

A firebrand carried *along*, leaveth a train of light behind it. *Bacon's Natural Hiſtory*, N° 274.

Where Ufens glides *along* the lowly lands,
Or the black water of Pomptina ſtands. *Dryd. Æneid* vii.

3. Throughout; in the whole; with *all* prefixed.

They were *all along* a croſs, untoward ſort of people. *South.*

Solomon, *all along* in his Proverbs, gives the title of fool to a wicked man. *Tillotſon.*

4. Joined with the particle *with*; in company; joined with.

I your commiſſion will forthwith diſpatch,
And he to England ſhall *along with* you. *Shakeſp. Hamlet.*

Hence then! and Evil go *with* thee *along*,
Thy offspring, to the place of evil, Hell;
Thou and thy wicked crew! *Milton's Par. Loſt, b.* vi.

Religious zeal is ſubject to an exceſs, and to a defect, when ſomething is mingled with it, which it ſhould not have; or when it wants ſomething that ought to go *along with* it. *Sprat.*

5. Sometimes *with* is underſtood.

Command thy ſlaves: my free-born ſoul diſdains
A tyrant's curb; and reſtive breaks the reins.
Take this *along*; and no diſpute ſhall riſe
(Though mine the woman) for my raviſh'd prize. *Dryden.*

6. Forward; onward. In this ſenſe it is derived from *allons*, French.

Come then, my friend, my genius, come *along*,
Thou maſter of the poet and the ſong. *Pope.*

ALO'NGST. *adv.* [a corruption, as it ſeems, from *along.*] Along; through the length.

The Turks did keep ſtrait watch and ward in all their ports thereabout *alongſt* the ſea-coaſt. *Knolles's Hiſt. of the Turks.*

ALO'OF. *adv.* [*all off*, that is, *quite off.*]

1. At a diſtance; with the particle *from.* It generally implies a ſmall diſtance, ſuch as is within view or obſervation.

Then bad the knight this lady yede *aloof*,
And to an hill herſelf withdrew aſide,
From whence ſhe might behold the battle's proof,
And elſe be ſafe from danger far deſcried. *Fairy Queen, b.* i.

As next in worth,
Came ſingly where he ſtood, on the bare ſtrand,
While the promiſcuous croud ſtood yet *aloof.* *Parad. Loſt.*

The noiſe approaches, though our palace ſtood
Aloof from ſtreets, encompaſs'd with a wood. *Dryden.*

2. Applied to perſons, it often inſinuates caution and circumſpection.

Turn on the bloody hounds with heads of ſteel,
And make the cowards ſtand *aloof* at bay. *Shak. Henry* VI.

Going northwards, *aloof*, as long as they had any doubt of being purſued, at laſt when they were out of reach, they turned and croſſed the ocean to Spain. *Bacon.*

The king would not, by any means, enter the city, until he had *aloof* ſeen the croſs ſet up upon the greater tower of Granada, whereby it became Chriſtian ground. *Bacon's Hen.* VII.

Two pots ſtood by a river, one of braſs, the other of clay. The water carried them away; the earthen veſſel kept *aloof from* t'other. *L'Eſtrange's Fables.*

The ſtrong may fight *aloof*; Ancæus try'd
His force too near, and by preſuming dy'd. *Dryd. Fables.*

3. In a figurative ſenſe, it is uſed to import art or cunning in converſation, by which a man holds the principal queſtion at a diſtance.

Nor do we find him forward to be ſounded;
But with a crafty madneſs keeps *aloof*,
When we would bring him on to ſome confeſſion
Of his true ſtate. *Shakeſp. Hamlet.*

4. It is uſed metaphorically of perſons that will not be ſeen in a deſign.

It is neceſſary the queen join; for, if ſhe ſtand *aloof*, there will be ſtill ſuſpicions: it being a received opinion in the world, that ſhe hath a great intereſt in the king's favour and power. *Suckling.*

5. It is applied to things not properly belonging to each other.

Love's not love,
When it is mingled with regards that ſtand
Aloof from th' entire point. *Shakeſp. King Lear.*

ALO'UD. *adv.* [from *a* and *loud.*] Loudly; with a ſtrong voice; with a great noiſe.

Strangled he lies! yet ſeems to cry *aloud*,
To warn the mighty, and inſtruct the proud;
That of the great, neglecting to be juſt,
Heav'n in a moment makes an heap of duſt. *Waller.*

Then heav'n's high monarch thund'red thrice *aloud*,
And thrice he ſhook aloft a golden cloud. *Dryd. Æneid* vii.

ALO'W. *adv.* [from *a* and *low.*] In a low place; not aloft.

And now *alow*, and now aloft they fly,
As born through air, and ſeem to touch the ſky. *Dryden.*

A'LPHA. *n. ſ.* The firſt letter in the Greek alphabet, anſwering to our A; therefore uſed to ſignify the firſt.

I am *alpha* and omega, the beginning and the ending, ſaith the Lord, which is, and which was, and which is to come, the Almighty. *Revelat.*

A'LPHABET. *n. ſ.* [from ἄλφα, *alpha*, and βῆτα, *beta*, the two firſt letters of the Greeks.] The order of the letters, or elements of ſpeech.

Thou ſhalt not ſigh,
Nor wink, nor nod, nor kneel, nor make a ſign,
But I of theſe will reſt an *alphabet*,
And by ſtill practice learn to know thy meaning. *Shakeſpeare's Titus Andronicus.*

The letters of the *alphabet*, formed by the ſeveral motions of the mouth, and the great variety of ſyllables compoſed of letters, and formed with almoſt equal velocity, and the endleſs number of words capable of being framed out of the *alphabet*, either of more ſyllables, or of one. *Holder.*

Taught by their nurſes, little children get
This ſaying, ſooner than their *alphabet.* *Dryd jun. Juv.*

To A'LPHABET. *v. a.* [from *alphabet*, noun.] To range in the order of the alphabet.

ALPHABE'TICAL. } *adj.* [from *alphabet*; *alphabetique*, Fr.] In the
ALPHABE'TICK. } order of the alphabet; according to the ſeries of letters.

I have now by me, digeſted in an *alphabetical* order, all the counties, corporations, and boroughs in Great Britain, with their reſpective tempers. *Swift.*

ALPHABE'TICALLY. *adv.* [from *alphabetical.*] In an alphabetical manner; according to the order of the letters.

I had once in my thoughts to contrive a grammar, more than I can now compriſe in ſhort hints; and a dictionary, *alphabetically* containing the words of the language, which the deaf perſon is to learn. *Holder's Elements of Speech.*

ALRE'ADY. *adv.* [from *all* and *ready.*] At this preſent time, or at ſome time paſt; oppoſed to futurity; as, *Will he come ſoon? He is come* already. *Will it be done? It is done* already.

Touching our uniformity, that which hath been *already* anſwered, may ſerve for anſwer to that exception. *Hooker.*

You warn'd me ſtill of loving two;
Can I love him, *already* loving you? *Dryd. Indian Emp.*

See, the guards, from yon far eaſtern hill
Already move, no longer ſtay afford;
High in the air, they wave the flaming ſword,
Your ſignal to depart. *Dryden's State of Innocence.*

I confine myſelf to methods for the advancement of piety, which are in the power of a prince limited like ours, by a ſtrict execution of the laws *already* in force. *Swift.*

Methinks, *already* I your tears ſurvey,
Already hear the horrid things they ſay,
Already ſee you a degraded toaſt,
And all your honour in a whiſper loſt! *Pope.*

ALS. *adv.* [*als*, Dutch.] Alſo; likewiſe: a word now out of uſe.

The golden ſun his gliſtering head gan ſhew,
And ſad remembrance now the prince amoves
With freſh deſire his voyage to purſue;
Als Una earn'd her travel to renew. *Fairy Queen, b.* i.

A'LSO. *adv.* [from *all* and *ſo.*]

1. In the ſame manner; likewiſe.

In theſe two, no doubt, are contained the cauſes of the great deluge, as according to Moſes, ſo *alſo* according to neceſſity; for our world affords no other treaſures of water. *Burnet's Theo.*

2. *Alſo* is ſometimes nearly the ſame with *and*, and only conjoins the members of the ſentence.

God do ſo to me, and more *alſo.* 1 *Samuel*, xiv. 44.

A'LTAR. *n. ſ.* [*altare*, Lat. It is obſerved by *Junius*, that the word *altar* is received, with chriſtianity, in all the European languages; and that *altare* is uſed by one of the Fathers, as appropriated to the Chriſtian worſhip, in oppoſition to the *ara* of gentiliſm.]

1. The place where offerings to heaven are laid.

The goddeſs of the nuptial bed,
Tir'd with her vain devotions for the dead,
Reſolv'd the tainted hand ſhould be repell'd,
Which incenſe offer'd, and her *altar* held. *Dryd. Fab.*

2. The table in Chriſtian churches where the communion is adminiſtered.

Her

Her grace roſe, and, with modeſt paces,
Came to the *altar*, where ſhe kneel'd, and, ſaintlike,
Caſt her fair eyes to heav'n, and pray'd devoutly.
Shakeſpeare's Henry VIII.

A'LTARAGE. *n. ſ.* [*altaragium*, Lat.] An emolument ariſing to the prieſt from oblations, through the means of the altar. *Ayliffe's Parergon.*

A'LTAR-CLOTH. *n. ſ.* [from *altar* and *cloth.*] The cloth thrown over the altar in churches.

I ſhould ſet down the wealth, books, hangings, and *altar-cloths*, which our kings gave this abbey. *Peacham on Drawing.*

To A'LTER. *v. a.* [*alterer*, Fr. from *alter*, Lat.]

1. To change; to make otherwiſe than it is. *To alter*, ſeems more properly to imply a change made only in ſome part of a thing; as, to *alter* a writing, may be, to blot or interpolate it; to *change* it, may be, to ſubſtitute another in its place.

Do you note
How much her grace is *alter'd* on the ſudden?
How long her face is drawn? how pale ſhe looks,
And of an earthly cold? *Shak. Hen.* VIII.

Acts appropriated to the worſhip of God by his own appointment, muſt continue ſo, till himſelf hath otherwiſe declared: for who dares *alter* what God hath appointed?
Stillingfleet's Defence of Diſc. on Romiſh Idolatry.

2. To take off from a perſuaſion or ſect.

For the way of writing plays in verſe, I find it troubleſome and ſlow; but I am no way *altered* from my opinion of it, at leaſt with any reaſons which have oppoſed it. *Dryden.*

To ALTER. *v. n.* To become otherwiſe than it was; as, *the weather* alters *from bright to cloudy.*

A'LTERABLE. *adj.* [from *alter*; *alterable*, Fr.] That which may be altered or changed by ſomething elſe; diſtinct from changeable, or that which changes, or may change itſelf.

That *alterable* reſpects are realities in nature, will never be admitted by a conſiderate diſcerner. *Glanville.*

Our condition in this world is mutable and uncertain, *alterable* by a thouſand accidents, which we can neither foreſee nor prevent. *Rogers.*

I wiſh they had been more clear in their directions to him upon that mighty point, Whether the ſettlement of the ſucceſſion in the Houſe of Hanover be *alterable* or no? *Swift.*

A'LTERABLENESS. *n. ſ.* [from *alterable.*] The quality of being alterable, or admitting change from external cauſes.

A'LTERABLY. *adv.* [from *alterable.*] In ſuch a manner as may be altered.

A'LTERANT. *adj.* [*alterant*, Fr.] That which has the power of producing changes in any thing.

And whether the body be *alterant* or altered, evermore a perception precedeth operation; for elſe all bodies would be alike one to another. *Bacon's Natural Hiſtory.*

ALTERA'TION. *n. ſ.* [from *alter*; *alteration*, Fr.]

1. The act of altering or changing.

Alteration, though it be from worſe to better, hath in it inconveniencies, and thoſe weighty. *Hooker.*

2. The change made.

Why may we not preſume, that God doth even call for ſuch change or *alteration*, as the very condition of things themſelves doth make neceſſary. *Hooker, b.* ii. § 10.

So he, with difficulty and labour hard,
Mov'd on:
But he once paſt, ſoon after, when man fell,
Strange *alteration!* Sin, and death, amain
Following his track (ſuch was the will of heav'n!)
Pav'd after him a broad and beaten way. *Parad. Loſt, b.* ii.

No other *alteration* will ſatisfy; nor this neither, very long, without an utter abolition of all order. *South.*

Appius Claudius admitted to the ſenate the ſons of thoſe who had been ſlaves; by which, and ſucceeding *alterations*, that council degenerated into a moſt corrupt body. *Swift.*

A'LTERATIVE. *adj.* [from *alter.*]

Medicines called *alterative*, are ſuch as have no immediate ſenſible operation, but gradually gain upon the conſtitution, by changing the humours from a ſtate of diſtemperature to health. They are oppoſed to *evacuants.* *Quincy.*

When there is an eruption of humour in any part, it is not cured merely by outward applications, but by ſuch *alterative* medicines as purify the blood. *Government of the Tongue.*

ALTERCA'TION. *n. ſ.* [*altercation*, Fr. from *altercor*, Lat.] Debate; controverſy; wrangle.

By this hot purſuit of lower controverſies amongſt men profeſſing religion, and agreeing in the principal foundations thereof, they conceive hope, that, about the higher principles themſelves, time will cauſe *altercation* to grow. *Hooker.*

Their whole life was, in a manner, little elſe than a perpetual wrangling and *altercation*; and that, many times, rather for victory and oſtentation of wit, than a ſober and ſerious ſearch of truth. *Hakewell on Providence.*

ALTE'RN. *adj.* [*alternus*, Lat.] Acting by turns, in ſucceſſion each to the other.

And God made two great lights, great for their uſe
To man; the greater to have rule by day,
The leſs by night, *altern.* *Milton's Par. Loſt, b.* vii.

ALTE'RNACY. *n. ſ.* [from *alternate.*] Action performed by turns.

ALTE'RNATE. *adj.* [*alternus*, Lat.] Being by turns; one after another; reciprocal.

Friendſhip conſiſts properly in mutual offices, and a generous ſtrife in *alternate* acts of kindneſs. *South.*

Hear how Timotheus' various lays ſurpriſe,
And bid *alternate* paſſions fall and riſe!
While, at each change, the ſon of Lybian Jove
Now burns with glory, and then melts with love. *Pope.*

ALTE'RNATE ANGLES. [In geometry.] Are the internal angles made by a line cutting two parallels, and lying on the oppoſite ſides of the cutting line; the one below the firſt parallel, and the other above the ſecond.

ALTERNATE RATIO, or PROPORTION, is where the antecedent of one is to its conſequent, as the antecedent of another to its conſequent; the very ſame ratio, in this caſe, holding alternately in reſpect of the antecedents to each other, and the conſequents to each other. *Chambers.*

ALTE'RNATE. *n. ſ.* [from *alternate, adj.*] That which happens alternately; viciſſitude.

And rais'd in pleaſure, or repos'd in eaſe,
Grateful *alternates* of ſubſtantial peace,
They bleſs the long nocturnal influence ſhed
On the crown'd goblet, and the genial bed. *Prior.*

To ALTE'RNATE. *v. a.* [*alterno*, Lat.]

1. To perform alternately.

Thoſe who, in their courſe,
Melodious hymns about the ſov'reign throne
Alternate all night long. *Milton's Paradiſe Loſt, b.* v.

2. To change one thing for another reciprocally.

The moſt high God, in all things appertaining unto this life, for ſundry wiſe ends, *alternates* the diſpoſition of good and evil. *Grew's Coſmologia Sacra, b.* iii.

ALTE'RNATELY. *adv.* [from *alternate.*] In reciprocal ſucceſſion, ſo that each ſhall be ſucceeded by that which it ſucceeds, as, light follows darkneſs, and darkneſs follows light.

The princeſs Meleſinda, bath'd in tears,
And toſs'd *alternately* with hopes and fears,
Would learn from you the fortunes of her lord. *Dryden.*

Unhappy man! whom ſorrow thus and rage
To different ills *alternately* engage. *Prior.*

The rays of light are, by ſome cauſe or other, *alternately* diſpoſed to be reflected or refracted for many viciſſitudes. *Newton.*

ALTE'RNATENESS. *n. ſ.* [from *alternate.*] The quality of being alternate, or of happening in reciprocal ſucceſſion. *Dict.*

ALTERNA'TION. *n. ſ.* [from *alternate.*] The reciprocal ſucceſſion of things.

The one would be oppreſſed with conſtant heat, the other with inſufferable cold; and ſo the defect of *alternation* would utterly impugn the generation of all things. *Brown's Vul. Err.*

ALTE'RNATIVE. *n. ſ.* [*alternatif*, Fr.] The choice given of two things; ſo that if one be rejected, the other muſt be taken.

A ſtrange *alternative*——
Muſt ladies have a doctor, or a dance? *Young.*

ALTE'RNATIVELY. *adv.* [from *alternative.*] In alternate manner; by turns; reciprocally.

An appeal *alternatively* made may be tolerated by the civil law as valid. *Ayliffe's Parergon.*

ALTE'RNATIVENESS. *n. ſ.* [from *alternative.*] The quality or ſtate of being alternative; reciprocation. *Dict.*

ALTE'RNITY. *n. ſ.* [from *altern.*] Reciprocal ſucceſſion; viciſſitude; turn; change of one thing for another; reciprocally.

They imagine, that an animal of the vaſteſt dimenſions, and longeſt duration, ſhould live in a continual motion, without the *alternity* and viciſſitude of reſt, whereby all other animals continue. *Brown's Vulgar Errours, b.* viii. *c.* 1.

ALTHO'UGH. *conj.* [from *all* and *though.* See THOUGH.] Notwithſtanding; however it may be granted; however it may be that.

We all know, that many things are believed, *although* they be intricate, obſcure, and dark; *although* they exceed the reach and capacity of our wits; yea, *although* in this world they be no way poſſible to be underſtood. *Hooker, b.* v. § 22.

Me the gold of France did not ſeduce,
Although I did admit it as a motive
The ſooner to effect what I intended. *Shakeſp. Hen.* V.

The ſtreſs muſt be laid upon a majority; without which the laws would be of little weight, *although* they be good additional ſecurities. *Swift.*

A'LTIGRADE. *adj.* [from *altus* and *gradior*, Lat.] Riſing on high. *Dict.*

ALTI'LOQUENCE. *n. ſ.* [*altus* and *loquor*, Lat.] High ſpeech; pompous language.

ALTI'METRY. *n. ſ.* [*altimetria*, Lat. from *altus* and μέτρον.] The art of taking or meaſuring altitudes or heights, whether acceſſible, or inacceſſible, generally performed by a quadrant.

ALTI'SONANT. } *adj.* [*altiſonus*, Lat.] High ſounding; pom-
ALTI'SONOUS. } pous or lofty in ſound. *Dict.*

A'LTITUDE. *n. ſ.* [*altitudo*, Lat.]

1. Height of place; ſpace meaſured upward.

Ten maſts attach'd make not the *altitude*,
Which thou haſt perpendicularly fall'n. *Shak. King Lear.*

Some define the perpendicular *altitude* of the higheſt mountains to be four miles; others but fifteen furlongs *Brown.*

She ſhines above, we know, but in what place,
How near the throne, and heav'n's imperial face,
By our weak opticks is but vainly gueſs'd;
Diſtance and *altitude* conceal the reſt. *Dryden.*

2. The elevation of any of the heavenly bodies above the horizon.

Even unto the latitude of fifty-two, the efficacy thereof is not much conſiderable, whether we conſider its aſcent, meridian, *altitude*, or abode above the horizon. *Brown's Vulgar Errours.*

Has not a poet more virtues and vices within his circle, cannot he obſerve them and their influences in their ſeveral ſituations, in their oppoſitions and conjunctions, in their *altitudes* and depreſſions? *Rymer's Tragedies of laſt Age.*

3. Situation with regard to lower things.

Thoſe members which are pairs, ſtand by one another in equal *altitude*, and anſwer on each ſide one to another. *Ray.*

4. Height of excellence; ſuperiority.

Your *altitude* offends the eyes
Of thoſe who want the power to riſe.
The world, a willing ſtander-by,
Inclines to aid a ſpecious lye. *Swift.*

5. Height of degree; higheſt point.

He did it to pleaſe his mother, and to be partly proud; which he is, even to the *altitude* of his virtue. *Shakeſp. Coriolanus.*

ALTI'VOLANT. *adj.* [*altivolans*, Lat. from *altus* and *volo.*] High flying. *Dict.*

A'LTOGETHER. *adv.* [from *all* and *together.*]

1. Completely; without reſtriction; without exception.

It is in vain to ſpeak of planting laws, and plotting policy, till they be *altogether* ſubdued. *Spenſer's State of Ireland.*

We find not in the world any people that hath lived *altogether* without religion. *Hooker, b.* v. § 18.

If death and danger are things that really cannot be endured, no man could ever be obliged to ſuffer for his conſcience, or to die for his religion; it being *altogether* as abſurd to imagine a man obliged to ſuffer, as to do impoſſibilities. *South.*

I do not *altogether* diſapprove of the manner of interweaving texts of ſcripture through the ſtyle of your ſermon. *Swift.*

2. Conjunctly; in company. This is rather *all together.*

Couſin of Somerſet, join you with me,
And *altogether* with the duke of Suffolk,
We'll quickly hoiſt duke Humphry from his ſeat.
Shakeſpeare's Henry VI. *p.* ii.

A'LUDEL. n. ſ. [from *a* and *lutum*; that is, *without lute.*]

Aludels are ſubliming pots uſed in chemiſtry, without bottoms, and fitted into one another, as many as there is occaſion for, without luting. At the bottom of the furnace is a pot that holds the matter to be ſublimed; and, at the top is a head, to retain the flowers that riſe up. *Quincy.*

A'LUM. *n. ſ.* [*alumen*, Lat.]

A kind of mineral ſalt, of an acid taſte, leaving in the mouth a ſenſe of ſweetneſs, accompanied with a conſiderable degree of aſtringency. The ancient naturaliſts allow of two ſorts of *alum*, natural and factitious. The natural is found in the iſland of Milo, being a kind of whitiſh ſtone, very light, friable, and porous, and ſtreaked with filaments reſembling ſilver. The factitious *alum* is prepared in different manners, according to the different materials of which it is made. Hence ariſe red, Roman, and citron *alums*; alſo plumoſe, ſaccharine, and burnt *alums*. England, Italy, and Flanders, are the countries where *alum* is principally produced; and the Engliſh *roche-alum* is made from a bluiſh mineral ſtone, frequent in the hills of Yorkſhire and Lancaſhire. *Alum* is uſed in medicine as an abſorbent; but, being apt to excite vomiting, it is ſeldom preſcribed inwardly. It is uſed outwardly in aſtringent lotions, and is an ingredient in ſeveral dentifrices and coſmeticks. It is a principal ingredient in dying and colouring; neither of which can be well performed without it. It ſerves to bind the colour upon the ſtuffs, and has the ſame uſes there, that gum water and glutinous oils have in painting. It alſo diſpoſes ſtuffs to take the colour, and adds a degree of briſkneſs and delicacy to it. This effect of *alum* ſeems to proceed from its ſtyptick or aſtringent quality, by which it binds the finer parts of colours together, and prevents their exhaling. Hence alſo it preſerves paper, that has been dipped in its water, from ſinking when wrote upon.

Saccharine alum bears a near reſemblance to ſugar, and is a compoſition of common *alum*, with roſe-water and whites of eggs boiled together, to the conſiſtence of a paſte, and thus moulded at pleaſure. As it cools, it grows hard as a ſtone, and is uſed as a coſmetick.

Burnt alum is *alum* calcined over the fire, and thus rendered whiter, more light, and more eaſily pulverized.

Plumoſe or *plume alum* is a ſort of ſaline mineral ſtone, of various colours, moſt commonly white, bordering on green, reſembling Venetian talc, except that, inſtead of ſcales, it riſes in threads or fibres, reſembling thoſe of a feather; whence its name from *pluma*, a feather. Some will have this to be the lapis amianthus of the ancients. *Chambers.*

By long beating the white of an egg with a lump of *alum*, you may bring it, for the moſt part, into white curds. *Boyle.*

ALUM STONE. *n. ſ.* A ſtone or calx uſed in ſurgery; perhaps alum calcined, which then becomes corroſive.

She gargled with oxycrate, and was in a few days cured, by touching it with the vitriol and *alum ſtones. Wiſeman's Surgery.*

ALU'MINOUS. *adj.* [from *alum.*] Relating to alum, or conſiſting of alum.

Nor do we reaſonably conclude, becauſe, by a cold and *aluminous* moiſture, it is able a while to reſiſt the fire, that, from a peculiarity of nature, it ſubſiſteth and liveth in it. *Brown.*

The tumour may have other mixture with it, to make it of a vitriolick or *aluminous* nature. *Wiſeman's Surgery.*

A'LWAYS. *adv.* [It is ſometimes written *alway*, compounded of *all* and *way*; eallepæᵹa, Sax. *tuttavia*, Ital.]

1. Perpetually; throughout all time; oppoſed to *ſometime*, or to *never.*

That, which ſometime is expedient, doth not *always* ſo continue. *Hooker, b.* iv. § 14.

Man never is, but *always* to be bleſt. *Pope.*

2. Conſtantly; without variation; oppoſed to *ſometimes*, or to *now and then.*

He is *always* great, when ſome great occaſion is preſented to him. *Dryden.*

A. M. Stands for *artium magiſter*, or maſter of arts; the ſecond degree of our univerſities, which, in ſome foreign countries, is called doctor of philoſophy.

AM. The firſt perſon of the verb *to be.* [See TO BE.]

And God ſaid unto Moſes, I *am* that I *am*: and he ſaid, thus ſhalt thou ſay unto the children of Iſrael, *I am* hath ſent me unto you. *Exodus*, iii. 14.

Come then, my ſoul: I call thee by that name,
Thou buſy thing, from whence I know I *am*:
For knowing what I *am*, I know thou art;
Since that muſt needs exiſt, which can impart. *Prior.*

AMABI'LITY. *n. ſ.* [from *amabilis*, Lat.] Lovelineſs; the power of pleaſing.

No rules can make *amability*, our minds and apprehenſions make that; and ſo is our felicity. *Taylor.*

AMADE'TTO. n. ſ. A ſort of pear [See PEAR.] ſo called, ſays *Skinner*, from the name of him who cultivated it.

A'MADOT. n. ſ. A ſort of pear. [See PEAR.]

AMA'IN. *adv.* [from *maine*, or *maigne*, old Fr. derived from *magnus*, Lat.] With vehemence; with vigour; fiercely; violently. It is uſed of any action performed with precipitation, whether of fear or courage, or of any violent effort.

Great lords, from Ireland am I come *amain*,
To ſignify that rebels there are up,
And put the Engliſhmen unto the ſword. *Shak. Henry* VI.

What! when we fled *amain*, purſued, and ſtruck
With heav'n's afflicting thunder, and beſought
The deep to ſhelter us? *Milton's Paradiſe Loſt, b.* ii.

The hills, to their ſupply,
Vapour and exhalation duſk and moiſt,
Sent up *amain.* *Par. Loſt.*

From hence the boar was rous'd, and ſprung *amain*,
Like light'ning ſudden, on the warriour train,
Beats down the trees before him, ſhakes the ground;
The foreſt echoes to the crackling ſound,
Shout the fierce youth, and clamours ring around. *Dry.*

AMA'LGAM. } *n. ſ.* [ἅμα and γαμεῖν.] The mixture of metals
AMA'LGAMA. } procured by amalgamation. See AMALGAMATION.

The induration of the *amalgam* appears to proceed from the new texture reſulting from the coalition of the mingled ingredients, that make up the *amalgam.* *Boyle.*

To AMA'LGAMATE. *v. a.* [from *amalgam.*]

To unite metals with quickſilver, which may be practiſed upon all metals, except iron and copper. The uſe of this operation is, to make the metal ſoft and ductile. Gold is, by this method, drawn over other materials by the gilders.

AMALGAMA'TION. *n. ſ.* [from *amalgamate.*] The act or practice of amalgamating metals.

Amalgamation is the mixing of mercury with any of the metals. The manner is thus in gold, the reſt are anſwerable: Take ſix parts of mercury, mix them hot in a crucible, and pour them to one part of gold made red hot in another crucible; ſtir theſe well that they may incorporate; then caſt the maſs into cold water, and waſh it. *Bacon's Phyſical Remains.*

AMANDA'TION. *n. ſ.* [from *amando*, Lat.] The act of ſending on a meſſage, or employment.

AMANUE'NSIS. n. ſ. [Lat.] A perſon who writes what another dictates.

A'MARANTH. *n. ſ.* [*amaranthus*, Lat. from α and μαραίνω.] The name of a plant.

The flowers have no petals; the cup of the flower is dry and multifid; the ſeeds are included in membranaceous veſſels, which, when come to maturity, burſt open tranſverſely or horizontally, like purſlane, each of which contains one or more roundiſh ſeeds.

Among the many ſpecies, the moſt beautiful are, 1. The tree *amaranth.* 2. The long pendulous *amaranth*, with reddiſh coloured ſeeds, commonly called *Love lies a bleeding.* All theſe plants muſt be ſown on a good hotbed in February, or the beginning

ginning of March. They produce large beautiful flowers, and perfect their ſeed in September. *Millar.*

2. In poetry, it is ſometimes an imaginary flower, ſuppoſed, according to its name, never to fade.

Immortal *amaranth!* a flower which once
In paradiſe, faſt by the tree of life,
Began to bloom; but ſoon, for man's offence,
To heav'n remov'd, where firſt it grew, there grows,
And flow'rs aloft, ſhading the fount of life;
And where the river of bliſs, thro' midſt of heav'n,
Rowls o'er Elyſian flow'rs her amber ſtream:
With theſe, that never fade, the ſpirits elect
Bind their reſplendent locks, inwreath'd with beams.
Milton's Paradiſe Loſt, b. iii. *l.* 353.

AMARA'NTHINE. *adj.* [*amaranthinus*, Lat.] Relating to amaranths; conſiſting of amaranths.

By the ſtreams that ever flow,
By the fragrant winds that blow
O'er the Elyſian flow'rs,
By thoſe happy ſouls who dwell
In yellow meads of Aſphodel,
Or *amaranthine* bow'rs. *Pope's St. Cæcilia.*

AMA'RITUDE. *n. ſ.* [*amaritudo*, Lat.] Bitterneſs.

What *amaritude* or acrimony is deprehended in choler, it acquires from a commixture of melancholy, or external malign bodies. *Harvey on Conſumptions.*

AMA'RULENCE. *n. ſ.* [*amaritudo*, Lat.] Bitterneſs. *Dict.*

AMA'SMENT. *n. ſ.* [from *amaſs.*] A heap; an accumulation; a collection.

What is now in the ſubject, is but an *amaſment* of imaginary conceptions, prejudices, ungrounded opinions, and infinite impoſtures. *Glanville's Scepſis Scientifica.*

To AMA'SS. *v. a.* [*amaſſer*, Fr.]

1. To collect together into one heap or maſs.

The rich man is not blamed, as having made uſe of any unlawful means to *amaſs* riches, as having thriven by fraud and injuſtice. *Atterbury's Sermons.*

When we would think of infinite ſpace, or duration, we, at firſt ſtep, uſually make ſome very large idea, as perhaps of millions of ages, or miles, which poſſibly we double and multiply ſeveral times. All that we thus *amaſs* together in our thoughts, is poſitive, and the aſſemblage of a great number of poſitive ideas of ſpace or duration. *Locke.*

2. In a figurative ſenſe, to add one thing to another, generally with ſome ſhare of reproach, either of eagerneſs or indiſcrimination.

Such as *amaſs* all relations, muſt err in ſome, and be unbelieved in many. *Brown's Vulgar Errours, b.* i.

Do not content yourſelves with mere words, leſt your improvements only *amaſs* a heap of unintelligible phraſes. *Watts's Improvement of the Mind.*

The life of Homer has been written, by *amaſſing* of all the traditions and hints the writers could meet with, in order to tell a ſtory of him to the world. *Pope's Eſſay on Homer.*

To AMA'TE. *v. n.* [from *a* and *mate.* See MATE.]

1. To accompany; to entertain as a companion. It is now obſolete.

A lovely bevy of fair ladies ſate,
Courted of many a jolly paramour,
The which did them immodeſt way *amate*,
And each one ſought his lady to aggrate. *Fairy Queen, b.*ii.

2. To terrify; to ſtrike with horrour. In this ſenſe, it is derived from the old French, *matter*, to cruſh or ſubdue.

AMATO'RCULIST. *n. ſ.* [*amatorculus*, Lat.] A little inſignificant lover; a pretender to affection. *Dict.*

A'MATORY. *adj.* [*amatorius*, Lat.] Relating to love; cauſing love.

It is the ſame thing whether one raviſh Lucretia by force, as Tarquin, or by *amatory* potions, not only allure her, but neceſſitate her to ſatisfy his luſt, and incline her effectually, and draw her inevitably to follow him ſpontaneouſly. *Bramham againſt Hobbes.*

AMAURO'SIS. n. ſ. [ἀμαυρόω.] A dimneſs of ſight, not from any viſible defect in the eye, but from ſome diſtemperature of the inner parts, occaſioning the repreſentations of flies and duſt floating before the eyes: which appearances are the parts of the retina hid and compreſſed by the blood-veſſels being too much diſtended; ſo that, in many of its parts, all ſenſe is loſt; and therefore no images can be painted upon them, whereby the eyes, continually rolling round, many parts of objects falling ſucceſſively upon them, are obſcure. The cure of this depends upon a removal of the ſtagnations in the extremities of thoſe arteries which run over the bottom of the eye. *Quincy.*

To AMA'ZE. *v. a.* [from *a* and *maze*, perplexity.]

1. To confuſe with terrour.

Yea, I will make many people *amazed* at thee, and their kings ſhall be horribly afraid for thee, when I ſhall brandiſh my ſword before them, and they ſhall tremble at every moment; every man for his own life in the day of the fall. *Ezek.* xxxii. 10.

2. To put into confuſion with wonder.

Go, heav'nly pair, and with your dazling virtues,
Your courage, truth, your innocence and love,
Amaze and charm mankind. *Smith's Phædr. and Hippol.*

3. To put into perplexity.

That cannot chooſe but *amaze* him. If he be not *amazed*, he will be mocked; if he be *amazed*, he will every way be mocked. *Shakeſpeare's Merry Wives of Windſor.*

AMA'ZE. *n. ſ.* [from the verb *amaze.*] Aſtoniſhment; confuſion, either of fear or wonder.

Fairfax, whoſe name in arms thro' Europe rings,
And fills all mouths with envy or with praiſe,
And all her jealous monarchs with *amaze*,
And rumours loud. *Milton's Paradiſe Regained.*

Meantime the Trojan cuts his wat'ry way,
Fix'd on his voyage thro' the curling ſea,
Then caſting back his eyes with dire *amaze*,
Sees, on the Punick ſhore, the mounting blaze. *Dryden.*

AMA'ZEDLY. *adv.* [from *amazed.*] Confuſedly; with amazement; with confuſion.

I ſpeak *amazedly*, and it becomes
My marvel, and my meſſage. *Shakeſp. Winter's Tale.*

Why
Stands Macbeth thus *amazedly!*
Come, ſiſters, cheer we up his ſprights. *Macbeth.*

AMA'ZEDNESS. *n. ſ.* [from *amazed.*] The ſtate of being amazed; aſtoniſhment; wonder; confuſion.

I was by at the opening of the farthel, heard the old ſhepherd deliver the manner how he found it; whereupon, after a little *amazedneſs*, we were all commanded out of the chamber. *Shakeſp. Winter's Tale.*

AMA'ZEMENT. *n. ſ.* [from *amaze.*]

1. Such a confuſed apprehenſion as does not leave reaſon its full force; extreme fear; horrour.

He anſwer'd nought at all; but adding new
Fear to his firſt *amazement*, ſtaring wide,
With ſtony eyes, and heartleſs hollow hue,
Aſtoniſh'd ſtood, as one that had eſpy'd
Infernal furies, with their chains unty'd. *Fairy Queen.*

But look! *amazement* on thy mother ſits;
O ſtep between her and her fighting ſoul:
Conceit in weakeſt bodies ſtrongeſt works. *Shak. Hamlet.*

2. Extreme dejection.

He ended, and his words impreſſion left
Of much *amazement* to th' infernal crew,
Diſtracted and ſurpris'd with deep diſmay
At theſe ſad tidings. *Milton's Paradiſe Regained, b.* i.

3. Height of admiration.

Had you, ſome ages paſt, this race of glory
Run, with *amazement* we ſhould read your ſtory;
But living virtue, all atchievements paſt,
Meets envy ſtill to grapple with at laſt. *Waller.*

4. Aſtoniſhment; wonder at an unexpected event.

They knew that it was he which ſat for alms at the Beautiful gate of the temple, and they were filled with wonder and *amazement* at that which had happened unto him. *Acts*, iii. 10.

AMA'ZING. *participial adj.* [from *amaze.*] Wonderful; aſtoniſhing.

It is indeed an *amazing* thing to ſee the preſent deſolation of Italy, when one conſiders what incredible multitudes of people it abounded with during the reigns of the Roman emperours. *Addiſon's Remarks on Italy.*

AMA'ZINGLY. *adv.* [from *amazing.*] To a degree that may excite aſtoniſhment; wonderfully.

If we ariſe to the world of ſpirits, our knowledge of them muſt be *amazingly* imperfect, when there is not the leaſt grain of ſand but has too many difficulties belonging to it, for the wiſeſt philoſopher to anſwer. *Watts's Logick.*

A'MAZON. n. ſ. [α and μαζός.] The Amazons were a race of women famous for valour, who inhabited Caucaſus; they are ſo called from their cutting off their breaſts, to uſe their weapons better. A warlike woman; a virago.

Stay, ſtay thy hands, thou art an *amazon*,
And fighteſt with the ſword. *Shakeſp. Henry* VI.

AMBA'GES. n. ſ. [Lat.] A circuit of words; a circumlocutory form of ſpeech; a multiplicity of words; an indirect manner of expreſſion.

They gave thoſe complex ideas names, that they might the more eaſily record and diſcourſe of things they were daily converſant in, without long *ambages* and circumlocutions; and that the things, they were continually to give and receive information about, might be the eaſier and quicker underſtood. *Locke.*

AMBA'GIOUS. *adj.* [from *ambages.*] Circumlocutory; perplexed; tedious. *Dict.*

AMBASSA'DE. *n. ſ.* [*ambaſſade*, Fr.] Embaſſy; character or buſineſs of an ambaſſador; a word not now in uſe.

When you diſgraced me in my *ambaſſade*,
Then I degraded you from being king. *Shak. Henry* VI.

AMBA'SSADOUR. *n. ſ.* [*ambaſſadeur*, Fr. *embaxador*, Span. It is written differently, as it is ſuppoſed to come from the French or Spaniſh language; and the original derivation being uncertain, it is not eaſy to ſettle its orthography. Some derive it from the Hebrew בשר, *to tell*, and מבשר, a *meſſenger*; others from *ambactus*, which, in the old Gauliſh, ſignified a *ſervant*; whence *ambaſcia*, in low Latin, is found to ſignify *ſervice*, and *ambaſciator*, a *ſervant*; others deduce it from *ambacht*, in old

* Teutonick,

Teutonick, signifying a *government*, and *Junius* mentions a possibility of its descent from ἀναβάινω; and others from *am* for *ad*, and *bassus*, low, as supposing the act of sending an ambassadour, to be in some sort an act of submission. All these derivations lead to write *ambassadour*, not *embassadour*.]

A person sent in a publick manner from one sovereign power to another, and supposed to represent the power from which he is sent. The person of an ambassadour is inviolable.

Ambassador is, in popular language, the general name of a messenger from a sovereign power, and sometimes, ludicrously, from common persons. In the juridical and formal language, it signifies particularly a minister of the highest rank residing in another country, and is distinguished from an *envoy*, who is of less dignity.

Give first admittance to th' *ambassadours*. *Shak. Hamlet.*

Rais'd by these hopes, I sent no news before,
Nor ask'd you leave, nor did your faith implore;
But come, without a pledge, my own *ambassadour*. *Dryden.*

Oft have their black *ambassadours* appear'd
Loaden with gifts, and fill'd the courts of Zama. *Add. Cato.*

AMBA'SSADRESS. *n. s.* [*ambassadrice*, Fr.]

1. The lady of an ambassadour.
2. In ludicrous language, a woman sent on a message.

Well, my *ambassadress*——
Come you to menace war, and loud defiance?
Or does the peaceful olive grace your brow? *Rowe's Penit.*

A'MBASSAGE. *n. s.* [from *ambassadour.*] An embassy; the business of an ambassadour.

Maximilian entertained them with dilatory answers; so as the formal part of their *ambassage* might well warrant their further stay. *Bacon's Henry* VII.

A'MBER. *n. s.* [from *ambar*, Arab. whence the lower writers formed *ambarum.*]

A yellow transparent substance of a gummous or bituminous consistence, but a resinous taste, and a smell like oil of turpentine; chiefly found in the Baltick sea, along the coasts of Prussia. Some naturalists refer it to the vegetable, others to the mineral, and some even to the animal kingdom. Pliny describes it as a resinous juice, oozing from aged pines and firs, and discharged thence into the sea; where, undergoing some alteration, it is thrown, in this form, upon the shores of Prussia, which lie very low. He adds, that it was hence the ancients gave it the denomination of *succinum*, from *succus*, juice. This opinion of the ancient naturalist is confirmed by the observation of many of the moderns, particularly Father Camelli. *Philos. Transact.* N° 290. Some have imagined it a concretion of the tears of birds; others, the urine of a beast; others, the scum of the lake Cephisis, near the Atlantick; others, a congelation formed in the Baltick, and in some fountains, where it is found swimming like pitch. Others suppose it a bitumen trickling into the sea from subterraneous sources; but this opinion is also discarded, as good *amber* having been found in digging at a considerable distance from the sea, as that gathered on the coast. Boerhaave ranks it with camphire, which is a concrete oil of aromatick plants, elaborated by heat into a crystalline form. *Amber* assumes all figures in the ground; that of a pear, an almond, a pea; and, among others, there have been found letters very well formed, and even Hebrew and Arabick characters. Within some pieces of *amber* have been found leaves, and insects included; which seems to indicate, either that the *amber* was originally in a fluid state, or, that having been exposed to the sun, it was softened, and rendered susceptible of the leaves and insects. *Amber*, when rubbed, draws or attracts bodies to it; and, by friction, is brought to yield light pretty copiously in the dark. Some distinguish *amber* into yellow, white, brown, and black: but the two latter are supposed to be of a different nature and denomination; the one called *jet*, the other *ambergris*. The white is most valued for medicinal uses, and the yellow for being wrought into beads and toys, because of its transparency. *Trev. Chamb.*

Liquid amber, is a kind of native balsam or resin, like turpentine; clear, reddish, or yellowish; of a pleasant smell, almost like ambergris. It flows from an incision made in the bark of a fine large tree in New Spain, called by the natives *ososol*; but it hardens, as it grows older, into a solid form, and is brought to us in barrels. It is reputed an excellent balsam. *Chambers.*

If light penetrateth any clear body, that is coloured, as painted glass, *amber*, water, and the like, it gives the light the colour of its medium. *Peacham on Drawing.*

No interwoven reeds a garland made,
To hide his brows within the vulgar shade;
But poplar wreathes around his temples spread,
And tears of *amber* trickled down his head. *Addis. Italy.*

The spoils of elephants the roofs inlay,
And studded *amber* darts a golden ray. *Pope's Odyssey.*

A'MBER. *adj.* Consisting of amber.

With scarfs, and fans, and double charge of brav'ry,
With *amber* bracelets, beads, and all this knav'ry.
Shakespeare's Taming of the Shrew.

AMBER DRINK. *n. s.* Drink of the colour of amber, or resembling amber in colour and transparency.

All your clear *amber drink* is flat. *Bacon's Nat. History.*

A'MBERGRIS. *n. s.* [from *amber* and *gris*, or *grey*; that is, *grey amber.*]

A fragrant drug, that melts almost like wax, commonly of a greyish or ash colour, used both as a perfume and a cordial. It is found on the sea coasts of several warm countries, and on the western coasts of Ireland. Some imagine it to be the excrement of a bird, which, being melted by the heat of the sun, and washed off the shore by the waves, is swallowed by whales, who return it back in the condition we find it. Others conclude it to be the excrement of a cetaceous fish, because sometimes found in the intestines of such animals. But we have no instance of any excrement capable of melting like wax; and if it were the excrement of a whale, it should rather be found where these animal abound, as about Greenland. Others take it for a kind of wax or gum, which distils from trees, and drops into the sea, where it congeals. Many of the orientals imagine it springs out of the sea, as naphtha does out of some fountains. Others suppose it a sea mushroom, torn up from the bottom by the violence of tempests. Others assert it to be a vegetable production, issuing out of the root of a tree, whose roots always shoot toward the sea, and discharge themselves into it. Others maintain, that *ambergris* is made from the honey-combs, which fall into the sea from the rocks, where the bees had formed their nests; several persons having seen pieces that were half *ambergris*, and half plain honey-comb; and others have found large pieces of *ambergris*, in which, when broke, honey-comb, and honey too, were found in the middle. Some affirm it to be a true animal concrete, formed in balls in the body of the male spermaceti whale, and lodged in a large oval bag over the testicles. But, besides that it is not one spermaceti whale in a hundred, that is found to have *ambergris*, Neumann, chemist to the king of Prussia, absolutely denies it to be an animal substance, as not yielding in the analysis, any one animal principle. It may indeed be found in whales, but it must have been swallowed by them. He concludes it to be a bitumen issuing out of the earth into the sea; at first of a viscous consistence, but hardening, by its mixture with some liquid naphtha, into the form in which we find it. *Trevoux. Chambers.*

Bermudas wall'd with rocks, who does not know
That happy island, where huge lemons grow,
Where shining pearl, coral, and many a pound,
On the rich shore, of *ambergris* is found. *Waller.*

AMBER SEED, or *musk seed*, resembles millet, is of a bitterish taste, and brought dry from Martinico and Egypt. The Egyptians use it internally as a cordial. It gives a grateful scent to the breath after eating. *Chambers.*

AMBER TREE. *n. s.* [*frutex Africanus ambram spirans.*] A shrub, whose beauty is in its small evergreen leaves, which grow as close as heath, and, being bruised between the fingers, emit a very fragrant odour. *Millar.*

AMBIDE'XTER. n. s. [Lat.]

1. A man who has equally the use of both his hands.

Rodiginus, undertaking to give a reason of *ambidexters*, and left-handed men, delivereth a third opinion. *Brown's Vul. Err.*

2. A man who is equally ready to act on either side, in party disputes. This sense is ludicrous.

AMBIDEXTE'RITY. *n. s.* [from *ambidexter.*]

1. The quality of being able equally to use both hands.
2. Double dealing.

AMBIDE'XTROUS. *adj.* [from *ambidexter*, Lat.]

1. Double dealing; practising on both sides.

Æsop condemns the double practices of trimmers, and all false, shuffling, and *ambidextrous* dealings. *L'Estrange's Fab.*

2. Having, with equal facility, the use of either hand.

Others, not considering *ambidextrous* and left-handed men, do totally submit unto the efficacy of the liver. *Vulgar Err.*

AMBIDE'XTROUSNESS. *n. s.* [from *ambidextrous.*] The quality of being ambidextrous. *Dict.*

A'MBIENT. *adj.* [*ambiens*, Lat.] Surrounding; encompassing; investing.

This which yields or fills
All space, the *ambient* air wide-interfus'd. *Paradise Lost.*

The thickness of a plate requisite to produce any colour, depends only on the density of the plate, and not on that of the *ambient* medium. *Newton's Opticks.*

Around him dance the rosy hours,
And damasking the ground with flow'rs,
With *ambient* sweets perfume the morn. *Fenton to L. Gower.*

Illustrious virtues, who by turns have rose,
With happy laws her empire to sustain,
And with full pow'r assert her *ambient* main. *Prior.*

The *ambient* æther is too liquid and empty, to impel horizontally with that prodigious celerity. *Bentley's Sermons.*

A'MBIGU. n. s. [French.] An entertainment, consisting not of regular courses, but of a medley of dishes set on together.

When straiten'd in your time, and servants few,
You'd richly then compose an *ambigu*;
Where first and second course, and your desert,
All in our single table have their part. *King's Art of Cookery.*

AMBIGU'ITY. *n. s.* [from *ambiguous.*] Doubtfulness of meaning; uncertainty of signification; double meaning.

With *ambiguities* they often entangle themſelves, not marking what doth agree to the word of God in itſelf, and what in regard of outward accidents. *Hooker, b.* v.

We can clear theſe *ambiguities*,
And know their ſpring, their head, their true deſcent.
Shakeſpeare's Romeo and Juliet.

The words are of ſingle ſignification, without any *ambiguity*; and therefore I ſhall not trouble you, by ſtraining for an interpretation, where there is no difficulty; or diſtinction, where there is no difference. *South.*

AMBI'GUOUS. *adj.* [*ambiguus*, Lat.]

1. Doubtful; having two meanings; of uncertain ſignification.

But what have been thy anſwers, what but dark,
Ambiguous, and with doubtful ſenſe deluding. *Par. Regain.*

Some expreſſions in the covenant were *ambiguous*, and were left ſo; becauſe the perſons who framed them, were not all of one mind. *Clarendon, b.* viii.

2. Applied to perſons uſing doubtful expreſſions. It is applied to expreſſions, or thoſe that uſe them, not to a dubious, or ſuſpended ſtate of mind.

Th' *ambiguous* god, who rul'd her lab'ring breaſt,
In theſe myſterious words his mind expreſt;
Some truths reveal'd, in terms involv'd the reſt. *Dryd.*

Silence at length the gay Antinous broke,
Conſtrain'd a ſmile, and thus *ambiguous* ſpoke. *Pope's Odyſſ.*

AMBI'GUOUSLY. *adv.* [from *ambiguous.*] In an ambiguous manner; doubtfully; uncertainly; with double meaning.

AMBI'GUOUSNESS. *n. ſ.* [from *ambiguous.*] The quality of being ambiguous; uncertainty of meaning; duplicity of ſignification.

AMBI'LOGY. *n. ſ.* [from *ambo*, Lat. and λόγος.] Talk of ambiguous or doubtful ſignification. *Dict.*

AMBI'LOQUOUS. *adj.* [from *ambo* and *loquor*, Lat.] Uſing ambiguous and doubtful expreſſions. *Dict.*

AMBI'LOQUY. *n. ſ.* [*ambiloquium*, Lat.] The uſe of doubtful and indeterminate expreſſions; diſcourſe of doubtful meaning. *D.*

A'MBIT. *n. ſ.* [*ambitus*, Lat.] The compaſs or circuit of any thing; the line that encompaſſes any thing.

The tuſk of a wild boar winds about almoſt into a perfect ring or hoop; only it is a little writhen. In meaſuring by the *ambit*, it is long or round about a foot and two inches; its baſis an inch over. *Grew's Muſæum.*

AMBI'TION. *n. ſ.* [*ambitio*, Lat.] The deſire of ſomething higher than is poſſeſſed at preſent.

1. The deſire of preferment or honour.

Who would think, without having ſuch a mind as Antiphilus, that ſo great goodneſs could not have bound gratefulneſs? and ſo high advancement not have ſatisfied his *ambition?* *Sidn.*

2. The deſire of any thing great or excellent.

The quick'ning power would be, and ſo would reſt;
The ſenſe would not be only, but be well:
But wit's *ambition* longeth to the beſt,
For it deſires in endleſs bliſs to dwell. *Sir J. Davies.*

Urge them, while their ſouls
Are capable of this *ambition*;
Leſt zeal, now melted by the windy breath
Of ſoft petitions, pity and remorſe,
Cool and congeal again to what it was. *Shakeſp. K. John.*

3. It is uſed with *to* before a verb, and *of* before a noun.

I had a very early *ambition to* recommend my ſelf to your Lordſhip's patronage. *Addiſon.*

There was an *ambition of* wit, and an affectation of gayety. *Pope's Preface to his Letters.*

AMBI'TIOUS. *adj.* [*ambitioſus*, Lat.]

1. Seized or touched with ambition; deſirous of advancement; eager of honours; aſpiring. It has the particle *of* before the object of ambition.

The neighb'ring monarchs, by thy beauty led,
Contend in crouds, *ambitious of* thy bed:
The world is at thy choice, except but one,
Except but him thou canſt not chooſe alone. *Dryd. Fables.*

You have been pleaſed not to ſuffer an old man to go diſcontented out of the world, for want of that protection, *of* which he had been ſo long *ambitious.* *Dryden.*

Trajan, a prince *ambitious of* glory, deſcended to the mouths of the Tigris and Euphrates, and went upon the ocean, where, ſeeing a veſſel trading to the Indies, he had thoughts of outdoing Alexander. *Arbuthnot on Coins.*

2. Eager to grow bigger; aſpiring.

I have ſeen
Th' *ambitious* ocean ſwell, and rage, and foam,
To be exalted with the threatening clouds. *Shakeſp. J. Cæſ.*

AMBI'TIOUSLY. *adv.* [from *ambitious.*] In an ambitious manner; with eagerneſs of advancement or preference.

With ſuch glad hearts did our deſpairing men
Salute th' appearance of the prince's fleet;
And each *ambitiouſly* would claim the ken,
That with firſt eyes did diſtant ſafety meet. *Dryd. Ann. Mir.*

Here Flecknoe, as a place to fame well known,
Ambitiouſly deſign'd his Sh—'s throne. *Dryden.*

AMBI'TIOUSNESS. *n. ſ.* [from *ambitious.*] The quality of being ambitious.

AMBI'TUDE. *n. ſ.* [*ambio*, Lat.] Compaſs; circuit; circumference.

To A'MBLE. *v. n.* [*ambler*, Fr. *ambulo*, Lat.]

1. To move upon an amble. [See AMBLE.]

It is good, on ſome occaſions, to enjoy as much of the preſent, as will not endanger our futurity; and to provide ourſelves of the virtuoſo's ſaddle, which will be ſure to *amble*, when the world is upon the hardeſt trot. *Dryden's Virgil, Dedication.*

2. To move eaſily, without hard ſhocks, or ſhaking.

Who *ambles* time withal?—A rich man that hath not the gout; for he lives merrily, becauſe he feels no pain; knowing no burden of heavy tedious penury: him time *ambles* withal. *Shakeſpeare's As you like it.*

3. In a ludicrous ſenſe, to move with ſubmiſſion, and by direction; as, a horſe that *ambles*, uſes a gait not natural.

A laughing, toying, wheedling, whimpering ſhe,
Shall make him *amble* on a goſſip's meſſage,
And take the diſtaff with a hand as patient,
As ere did Hercules. *Rowe's Jane Shore.*

4. To walk daintily and affectedly.

I am rudely ſtampt, and want love's majeſty,
To ſtrut before a wanton *ambling* nymph. *Shakeſp. Ric. III.*

A'MBLE. *n. ſ.* [from *to amble.*] A pace or movement in which the horſe removes both his leg on one ſide; as, on the far ſide, he removes his fore and hinder leg of the ſame ſide at one time, whilſt the legs on the near ſide ſtand ſtill; and when the far legs are upon the ground, the near ſide removes the fore leg and hinder leg, and the legs on the far ſide ſtand ſtill. An *amble* is the firſt pace of young colts, but when they have ſtrength to trot, they quit it. There is no *amble* in the manage; riding-maſters allow only of walk, trot, and gallop. A horſe may be put from a trot to a gallop without ſtopping; but cannot be put from an *amble* to a gallop without a ſtop, which interrupts the juſtneſs of the manage. *Farrier's Dict.*

A'MBLER. *n. ſ.* [from *to amble.*] A horſe that has been taught to amble; a pacer.

A'MBLINGLY. *adv.* [from *ambling.*] With an ambling movement.

AMBRO'SIA. n. ſ. [ἀμβροσία.]

1. The imaginary food of the gods, from which every thing eminently pleaſing to the ſmell or taſte, is called *ambroſia.*

2. The name of a plant.

It has male floſculous flowers, produced on ſeparate parts of the ſame plant from the fruit, having no viſible petals; the fruit which ſucceeds the female flowers, is ſhaped like a club, and is prickly, containing one oblong ſeed in each.

The ſpecies are, 1. The marine or ſea *ambroſia.* 2. Taller unſavoury ſea *ambroſia.* 3. The talleſt Canada *ambroſia*, with rough plane tree leaves. The firſt ſort ſhould be ſown early in the ſpring, under a warm wall. The ſecond and third are common American weeds, which ſhould be ſown upon a gentle hotbed in the ſpring. None of them have much beauty to recommend them. *Millar.*

AMBRO'SIAL. *adj.* [from *ambroſia.*] Partaking of the nature or qualities of ambroſia; fragrant; delicious; delectable.

Thus while God ſpake, *ambroſial* fragrance fill'd
All heaven, and in the bleſſed ſpirits elect
Senſe of new joy ineffable diffus'd. *Milton's Parad. Loſt.*

The gifts of heaven my following ſong purſues,
Aerial honey, and *ambroſial* dews. *Dryden's Virg. Georg.*

To fartheſt ſhores th' *ambroſial* ſpirit flies,
Sweet to the world, and grateful to the ſkies. *Pope.*

A'MBRY. *n. ſ.* [a word corrupted from *almonry.*]

1. The place where the almoner lives, or where alms are diſtributed.

2. The place where plate, and utenſils for houſekeeping, are kept; alſo a cupboard for keeping cold victuals: a word ſtill uſed in the northern counties, and in Scotland.

AMBS ACE. *n. ſ.* [from *ambo*, Lat. and *ace.*] A double ace; ſo called when two dice turn up the ace.

I had rather be in this choice, than throw *ambs ace* for my life. *Shakeſp. All's well that ends well.*

This will be yet clearer, by conſidering his own inſtance of caſting *ambs ace*, though it partake more of contingency than of freedom. Suppoſing the poſture of the party's hand who did throw the dice, ſuppoſing the figure of the table, and of the dice themſelves, ſuppoſing the meaſure of force applied, and ſuppoſing all other things which did concur to the production of that caſt, to be the very ſame they were, there is no doubt but in this caſe the caſt is neceſſary. *Bramh. againſt Hobbes.*

AMBULA'TION. *n. ſ.* [*ambulatio*, Lat.] The act of walking.

From the occult and inviſible motion of the muſcles in ſtation, proceed more offenſive laſſitudes, than from *ambulation.* *Brown's Vulgar Errours, b.* iii. *c.* 1.

A'MBULATORY. *adj.* [*ambulo*, Lat.]

1. That which has the power or faculty of walking.

The gradient, or *ambulatory*, are ſuch as require ſome baſis, or bottom, to uphold them in their motions: ſuch were thoſe ſtrange inventions, commonly attributed to Dædalus, or ſelf-moving ſtatues, which, unleſs violently detained, would of themſelves run away. *Wilkins's Mathemat. Magick.*

2. That which happens during a passage or walk.

He was sent to conduce hither the princess Henrietta Maria, of whom his majesty had an *ambulatory* view in his travels. *Wotton.*

3. Moveable; as, an *ambulatory* court; a court which removes from place to place for the exercise of its jurisdiction.

A'MBURY. *n. s.* A bloody wart on any part of a horse's body.

AMBUSCA'DE. *n. s.* [*embuscade*, Fr. See AMBUSH.] A private station in which men lie to surprise others; ambush.

Then waving high her torch, the signal made,
Which rous'd the Grecians from their *ambuscade*. *Dryden.*

When I behold a fashionable table set out, I fancy that gouts, fevers, and lethargies, with innumerable distempers, lie in *ambuscade* among the dishes. *Addison. Spect.* N° 195.

AMBUSCA'DO. *n. s.* [*emboscada*, Span.] A private post, in order to surprise an enemy.

Sometimes she driveth o'er a soldier's neck,
And then he dreams of cutting foreign throats,
Of breaches, *ambuscadoes*, Spanish blades,
Of healths five fathom deep. *Shakesp. Romeo and Juliet.*

A'MBUSH. *n. s.* [*embusche*, Fr. from *bois* a wood; whence *embuscher*, to hide in woods, ambushes being commonly laid under the concealment of thick forests.]

1. The post where soldiers or assassins are placed, in order to fall unexpectedly upon an enemy.

Charge, charge, their ground the faint Taxallans yield,
Bold in close *ambush*, base in open field.
Dryden's Indian Emperour.

2. The act of surprising another, by lying in wait, or lodging in a secret post.

Nor shall we need,
With dangerous expedition, to invade
Heav'n, whose high walls fear no assault or siege,
Or *ambush* from the deep. *Milton's Par. Lost, b.* ii.

3. The state of being posted privately, in order to surprise; the state of lying in wait.

The residue retired deceitfully towards the place of their *ambush*, whence issued more. Then the earl gathered his small company about him, and maintained the fight. But the enemy, whether perceiving some succours advancing, or whether intending to draw the English further into their *ambush*, turned away at an easy pace. *Hayward.*

4. Perhaps the persons placed in private stations.

For you, my noble lord of Lancaster,
Once did I lay an *ambush* for your life. *Shakesp. Richard* II.

A'MBUSHED. *adj.* [from *ambush.*] Placed in ambush; lying in wait.

Thick as the shades, there issue swarming bands
Of *ambush'd* men, whom, by their arms and dress,
To be Taxallan enemies I guess. *Dryd. Ind. Emp.*

AMBU'SHMENT. *n. s.* [from *ambush*; which see.] Ambush; surprize: a word now not used.

Like as a wily fox, that having spied
Where on a sunny bank the lambs do play,
Full closely creeping by the hinder side,
Lies in *ambushment* of his hoped prey. *Spenser's Muiopotmos.*

AMBU'ST. *adj.* [*ambustus*, Lat.] Burnt; scalded. *Dict.*

AMBU'STION. *n. s.* [*ambustio*, Lat.] A burn; a scald.

A'MEL. *n. s.* [*email*, Fr.] The matter with which the variegated works are overlaid, which we call *enamelled.*

The materials of glass melted with calcined tin, compose an undiaphanous body. This white *amel* is the basis of all those fine concretes that goldsmiths and artificers employ in the curious art of enamelling. *Boyle on Colours.*

AME'N. adv. [A word of which the original has given rise to many conjectures. *Scaliger* writes, that it is Arabick; and the Rabbies make it the compound of the initials of three words, signifying *the Lord is a faithful king*; but the word seems merely Hebrew, אמן, which, with a long train of derivatives, signifies firmness, certainty, fidelity.]

A term used in devotions, by which, at the end of a prayer, we mean, *so be it*, at the end of a creed, *so it is.*

One cried, God bless us! and, *Amen!* the other,
As they had seen me with these hangman's hands.
Listening their fear, I could not say *Amen*,
When they did say God bless us. *Shakesp. Macbeth.*

Blessed be the Lord God of Israel, from everlasting and to everlasting, *Amen* and *amen*. *Psalm* xli. 13.

AME'NABLE. *adj.* [*amesnable*, Fr. *amener quelqu'un*, in the French courts, signifies, to oblige one to appear to answer a charge exhibited against him.] Responsible; subject so as to be liable to enquiries or accounts.

Again, because the inferiour sort were loose and poor, and not *amenable* to the law, he provided, by another act, that five of the best and eldest persons of every sept, should bring in all the idle persons of their surname, to be justified by the law.
Sir John Davies on Ireland.

A'MENANCE. *n. s.* [It seems to come from *amener*, Fr.] Conduct; behaviour; mien: a word disused.

For he is fit to use in all assays,
Whether for arms and warlike *amenance*,
Or else for wise and civil governance. *Spens. Hubb. Tale.*

Well kend him so far space,
Th' enchanter, by his arms and *amenance*,
When under him he saw his Lybian steed to prance.
Fairy Queen, b. ii. *c.* vi.

To AME'ND. *v. a.* [*amender*, Fr. *emendo*, Lat.]

1. To correct; to change any thing that is wrong to something better.

2. To reform the life, or leave wickedness.

In these two cases we usually write *mend.* See MEND.

Amend your ways and your doings, and I will cause you to dwell in this place. *Jerem.* vii. 3.

3. To restore passages in writers which the copiers are supposed to have depraved; to recover the true reading.

To AME'ND. *v. n.* To grow better. To *amend* differs from to *improve*; to *improve* supposes or not denies that the thing is well already, but to *amend* implies something wrong.

As my fortune either *amends* or impairs, I may declare it unto you. *Sidney.*

At his touch
Such sanctity hath heaven given his hand,
They presently *amend*. *Shakesp. Macbeth.*

AME'NDE. n. s. [French.] This word, in French, signifies a fine, by which recompense is supposed to be made for the fault committed. We use, in a cognate signification, the word *amends.*

AME'NDMENT. *n. s.* [*amendement*, Fr.]

1. A change from bad for the better.

Before it was presented on the stage, some things in it have passed your approbation and *amendment*. *Dryd. Aureng. Pref.*

Man is always mending and altering his works; but nature observes the same tenour, because her works are so perfect, that there is no place for *amendments*; nothing that can be reprehended. *Ray on the Creation.*

There are many natural defects in the understanding, capable of *amendment*, which are overlooked and wholly neglected. *Locke.*

2. Reformation of life.

Our Lord and Saviour was of opinion, that they which would not be drawn to *amendment* of life, by the testimony which Moses and the prophets have given, concerning the miseries that follow sinners after death, were not likely to be persuaded by other means, although God from the dead should have raised them up preachers. *Hooker, b.* v. § 22.

Behold! famine and plague, tribulation and anguish, are sent as scourges for *amendment*. 2 *Esdras*, xvi. 19.

Though a serious purpose of *amendment*, and true acts of contrition, before the habit, may be accepted by God; yet there is no sure judgment whether this purpose be serious, or these acts true acts of contrition. *Hammond's Practical Catechism.*

3. Recovery of health.

Your honour's players hearing your *amendment*,
Are come to play a pleasant comedy. *Shakesp. Tam. Shrew.*

AME'NDMENT. [*emendatio*, Lat.] It signifies, in law, the correction of an errour committed in a process, and espied before or after judgment; and sometimes after the party's seeking advantage by the errour. *Blount.*

AME'NDER. *n. s.* [from *amend.*] The person that amends any thing.

AME'NDS. *n. s.* [*amende*, Fr. from which it seems to be accidentally corrupted.] Recompense; compensation; attonement.

If I have too austerely punished you,
Your compensation makes *amends*. *Shakesp. Tempest.*

Of the *amends* recovered, little or nothing returns to those that had suffered the wrong, but commonly all runs into the prince's coffers. *Sir W. Raleigh's Essays.*

Where I a pris'ner chain'd, scarce freely draw
The air imprison'd also, close and damp,
Unwholsome draught; but here I feel *amends*,
The breath of heav'n fresh blowing, pure and sweet,
With day-spring born; here leave me to respire.
Milton's Sampson Agonistes.

Some little hopes I have yet remaining, that I make the world some part of *amends* for many ill plays, by an heroick poem. *Dryden's Aureng. Preface.*

If our souls be immortal, this makes abundant *amends* and compensation for the frailties of life, and sufferings of this state. *Tillotson.*

It is a strong argument for retribution hereafter, that virtuous persons are very often unfortunate, and vicious persons prosperous; which is repugnant to the nature of a Being, who appears infinitely wise and good in all his works; unless we may suppose that such a promiscuous distribution, which was necessary for carrying on the designs of providence in this life, will be rectified and made *amends* for in another. *Spect.* N° 483.

AME'NITY. *n. s.* [*amenité*, Fr. *amoenitas*, Lat.] Pleasantness; agreeableness of situation.

If the situation of Babylon was such at first, as it was in the days of Herodotus, it was rather a seat of *amenity* and pleasure, than conducing unto this intention. *Brown's Vulgar Errours.*

To AME'RCE. *v. a.* [*amercier*, Fr. Ὀφθαλμῶν μὲν ἄμερσε, seems to give the original.]

1. To punish with a pecuniary penalty; to exact a fine; to inflict

flict a forfeiture. It is a word originally juridical, but adopted by other writers.

But I'll *amerce* you with ſo ſtrong a fine,
That you ſhall all repent the loſs of mine.
Shakeſp. Romeo and Juliet.

All the ſuitors were conſiderably *amerced*; yet this proved but an ineffectual remedy for thoſe miſchiefs. *Hale's Law of Engl.*

2. Sometimes with the particle *in* before the fine.

They ſhall *amerce* him *in* an hundred ſhekels of ſilver, and give them unto the father of the damſel, becauſe he hath brought up an evil name upon a virgin of Iſrael. *Deut.* xxii. 19.

3. Sometimes it is uſed, in imitation of the Greek conſtruction, with the particle *of*.

Millions of ſpirits, for his fault *amerc'd*
Of heav'n, and from eternal ſplendours flung
For his revolt. *Milton's Paradiſe Loſt, b.* i.

AME'RCER. *n. ſ.* [from *amerce*.] He that ſets a fine upon any miſdemeanour; he that decrees or inflicts any pecuniary puniſhment or forfeiture.

AME'RCEMENT. } *n. ſ.* [from *amerce*.] The pecuniary puniſhment of an offender, who ſtands at the mercy of the king, or other lord in his court. *Cowell.*
AME'RCIAMENT. }

All *amercements* and fines that ſhall be impoſed upon them, ſhall come unto themſelves. *Spenſer's State of Ireland.*

AMES ACE. *n. ſ.* [a corruption of the word *ambs ace*, which appears, from very old authorities, to have been early ſoftened by omitting the *b*.] Two aces on two dice.

But then my ſtudy was to cog the dice,
And dext'rouſly to throw the lucky ſice:
To ſhun *ames ace*, that ſwept my ſtakes away;
And watch the box, for fear they ſhould convey
Falſe bones, and put upon me in the play. *Dryd. Perſius.*

A'MESS. *n. ſ.* [corrupted from *amice*.] A prieſt's veſtment. *Dict.*

AMETHO'DICAL. *adj.* [from *a* and *method*.] Out of method; without method; irregular.

A'METHYST. *n. ſ.* [ἀμέθυςος, contrary to wine, or contrary to drunkenneſs; ſo called, either becauſe it is not quite of the colour of wine, or becauſe it was imagined to prevent inebriation.]

A precious ſtone of a violet colour, bordering on purple. The oriental *amethyſt* is the hardeſt, ſcarceſt, and moſt valuable; it is generally of a dove colour, though ſome are purple, and others white like the diamond. The German is of a violet colour, and the Spaniſh are of three ſorts; the beſt are the blackeſt or deepeſt violet; others are almoſt quite white, and ſome few tinctured with yellow. They are found in a hill named St. Sigminont, in Catalonia, by following the vein of reddiſh or black earth, or a vein in a rock ſo coloured, and are all hexangular, and pointed like cryſtal. Sometimes a great number is found ſticking together, like the Briſtol diamonds; but the beſt are found looſe in the chinks of the rock. Beautiful ones are alſo found in the Pyreneans, and in the mountains of Auvergne. The *amethyſt* is not extremely hard, but eaſy to be engraved upon, and is next in value to the emerald. *Savary. Chambers.*

I obſerved ſome ſtones that nearly approached the granate complection; and ſeveral very nearly reſembling the *amethyſt*. *Woodward on Foſſils.*

A'METHYST [in heraldry] ſignifies the ſame colour in a nobleman's coat, that *purpure* does in a gentleman's.

AMETHY'STINE. *adj.* [from *amethyſt*.] Reſembling an amethyſt in colour.

A'MIABLE. *adj.* [*aimable*, Fr.]

1. Lovely; pleaſing.

That which is good in the actions of men, doth not only delight as profitable, but as *amiable* alſo. *Hooker.*

She told her, while ſhe kept it,
'Twould make her *amiable*, ſubdue my father
Intirely to her love; but if ſhe loſt it,
Or made a gift of it, my father's eye
Should hold her loathed. *Shakeſp. Othello.*

2. Pretending love; ſhewing love.

Spend all, only give me ſo much time in exchange, as to lay *amiable* ſiege to the honeſty of this Ford's wife; uſe your art of wooing. *Shakeſpeare's Merry Wives of Windſor.*

A'MIABLENESS. *n. ſ.* [from *amiable*.] The quality of being amiable; lovelineſs; power of raiſing love.

As ſoon as the natural gaiety and *amiableneſs* of the young man wears off, they have nothing left to commend them, but lie by among the lumber and refuſe of the ſpecies. *Addiſ. Guard.*

A'MIABLY. *adv.* [from *amiable*.] In an amiable manner; in ſuch a manner as to excite love.

A'MICABLE. *adj.* [*amicabilis*, Lat.] Friendly; kind. It is commonly uſed of more than one; as, they live in an *amicable* manner; but we ſeldom ſay, an *amicable* action, or an *amicable* man, though it be ſo uſed in this paſſage.

O grace ſerene! oh virtue heav'nly fair,
Divine oblivion of low-thoughted care!
Freſh blooming hope, gay daughter of the ſky!
And faith, our early immortality!
Enter each mild, each *amicable* gueſt;
Receive and wrap me in eternal reſt. *Pope's Elo. to Abelard.*

A'MICABLENESS. *n. ſ.* [from *amicable*.] The quality of being amicable; friendlineſs; goodwill.

A'MICABLY. *adv.* [from *amicable*.] In an amicable manner; in a friendly way; with goodwill and concord.

They ſee
Through the dun miſt, in blooming beauty freſh,
Two lovely youths, that *amicably* walkt
O'er verdant meads, and pleas'd, perhaps, revolv'd
Anna's late conqueſts. *Philips.*

I found my ſubjects *amicably* join,
To leſſen their defects, by citing mine. *Prior.*

In Holland itſelf, where it is pretended that the variety of ſects live ſo *amicably* together, it is notorious how a turbulent party, joining with the Arminians, did attempt to deſtroy the republick. *Swift on the Sentiments of a Church of England man.*

A'MICE. *n. ſ.* [*amictus*, Lat. *amict*, Fr. *Primum ex ſex indumentis epiſcopo & presbyteriis communibus ſunt*, amictus, *alba*, *cingulum*, *ſtola*, *manipulus*, *& planeta*. Du Cange. *Amictus quo collum ſtringitur*, *& pectus tegitur*, *caſtitatem interioris hominis deſignat*; *tegit enim cor*, *ne vanitates cogitet*, *ſtringit autem collum*, *ne inde ad linguam tranſeat mendacium.* Bruno.] The firſt or undermoſt part of a prieſt's habit, over which he wears the alb.

Thus paſs'd the night ſo foul, till morning fair
Came forth with pilgrim ſteps in *amice* grey. *Paradiſe Reg.*

On ſome a prieſt, ſuccinct in *amice* white,
Attends. *Pope's Dunciad, b.* iv. *l.* 441.

AMI'D. } *prep.* [from *a* and *mid*, or *midſt*.]
AMI'DST. }

1. In the midſt; equally diſtant from either extremity.

Of the fruit
Of each tree in the garden we may eat;
But of the fruit of this fair tree, *amidſt*
The garden, God hath ſaid, ye ſhall not eat. *Paradiſe Loſt.*

The two ports, the bagnio, and Donatelli's ſtatue of the great duke, *amidſt* the four ſlaves, chained to his pedeſtal, are very noble ſights. *Addiſon on Italy.*

2. Mingled with; ſurrounded by; in the abmit of another thing.

Amid my flock with woe my voice I tear,
And, but bewitch'd, who to his flock would moan? *Sidney.*

So hills *amid* the air encounter'd hills,
Hurl'd to and fro, with jaculation dire. *Milt. Parad. Loſt.*

What have I done, to name that wealthy ſwain,
The boar *amidſt* my cryſtal ſtreams I bring;
And ſouthern winds to blaſt my flow'ry ſpring. *Dryd. Virg.*

Amata's breaſt the fury thus invades,
And fires with rage *amid* the ſylvan ſhades. *Dryd. Æneid.*

3. Amongſt; conjoined with.

What tho' no real voice nor ſound
Amid their radiant orbs be found?
In reaſon's ear they all rejoice,
And utter forth a glorious voice,
For ever ſinging, as they ſhine,
"The hand that made us is divine." *Addiſ. Spect.* Nº 465.

AMI'SS. *adv.* [from *a*, which, in this form of compoſition, often ſignifies *according to*, and *miſs*, the Engliſh particle, which ſhews any thing, like the Greek παρά, to be wrong; as, to *miſcount*, to count erroneouſly; to *miſdo*, to commit a crime: *amiſs* therefore ſignifies *not right*, or *out of order*.]

1. Faulty; criminal.

For that which thou haſt ſworn to do *amiſs*,
Is yet *amiſs* when it is truly done. *Shakeſp. King John.*

2. Faultily; criminally.

We hope therefore to reform ourſelves, if at any time we have done *amiſs*, is not to ſever ourſelves from the church we were of before. *Hooker, b.* iii. § 1.

O ye powers that ſearch
The heart of man, and weigh his inmoſt thoughts,
If I have done *amiſs*, impute it not. *Addiſon's Cato.*

3. In an ill ſenſe.

She ſigh'd withal, they conſtru'd all *amiſs*,
And thought ſhe wiſh'd to kill who long'd to kiſs. *Fairfax.*

4. Wrong; improper; unfit.

Examples have not generally the force of laws, which all men ought to keep, but of counſels only and perſuaſions, not *amiſs* to be followed by them, whoſe caſe is the like. *Hooker.*

Methinks, though a man had all ſcience, and all principles, yet it might not be *amiſs* to have ſome conſcience. *Tillotſ. Pref.*

5. Wrong; not according to the perfection of the thing, whatever it be.

Your kindred is not much *amiſs*, 'tis true;
Yet I am ſomewhat better born than you. *Dryden.*

I built a wall, and when the maſons plaid the knaves, nothing delighted me ſo much as to ſtand by, while my ſervants threw down what was *amiſs*. *Swift.*

6. Reproachful; irreverent.

Every people, nation, and language, which ſpeak any thing *amiſs* againſt the God of Shadrach, Meſhach, and Abednego, ſhall be cut in pieces, and their houſes ſhall be made a dunghil; becauſe there is no other God that can deliver after this ſort. *Daniel*, iii. 29.

7. Impaired in health; as, I was ſomewhat *amiſs* yeſterday, but am well to day.

8. *Amiſs* is marked as an adverb, though it cannot always be adverbially rendered; becauſe it always follows the ſubſtantive to which

which it relates, contrary to the nature of adjectives in English; and though we say the action was *amiss*, we never say an *amiss* action.

9. *Amiss* is used by *Shakespeare* as a noun substantive.

To my sick soul, as sin's true nature is,
Each toy seems prologue to some great *amiss*. *Hamlet.*

AMI'SSION. *n. s.* [*amissio*, Lat.] Loss.

To AMI'T. *v. a.* [*amitto*, Lat.] To lose: a word little in use.

Ice is water congealed by the frigidity of the air, whereby it acquireth no new form, but rather a consistence or determination of its diffluency, and *amitteth* not its essence, but condition of fluidity. *Brown's Vulgar Errours, b.* ii.

A'MITY. *n. s.* [*amitie*, Fr. *amicitia*, Lat.] Friendship, whether publick between nations, opposed to *war*, or among the people, opposed to *discord*, or between private persons.

The prophet David did think, that the very meeting of men together, and their accompanying one another to the house of God, should make the bond of their love insoluble, and tie them in a league of inviolable *amity*. *Hooker, b.* v. § 38.

The monarchy of Great Britain was in league and *amity* with all the world. *Sir John Davies on Ireland.*

You have a noble and a true conceit
Of godlike *amity*; which appears most strongly
In bearing thus the absence of your lord. *Shak. Merch. of Ven.*

And ye, oh Tyrians, with immortal hate
Pursue this race, this service dedicate
To my deplored ashes; let there be
'Twixt us and them no league nor *amity*. *Sir John Denham.*

AMMONI'AC. *n. s.* The name of a drug.

GUM AMMONIAC is brought from the East Indies, and is supposed to ooze from an umbelliferous plant. Dioscorides says, it is the juice of a kind of ferula growing in Barbary, and the plant is called *agasyllis*. Pliny calls the tree *metopion*, which, he says, grows near the temple of Jupiter Ammon, whence the gum takes its name. It ought to be in dry drops, white within, yellowish without, easily fusible, resinous, somewhat bitter, and of a very sharp taste and smell, somewhat like garlick. This gum is said to have served the ancients for incense, in their sacrifices. It enters several medicinal compositions, as an attenuant and detergent; and, outwardly applied, it is resolutive and suppurative. *Savary. Trevoux.*

SAL AMMONIAC is a volatile salt of two kinds, ancient and modern. The ancient sort, described by Pliny and Dioscorides, was a native salt, generated in those large inns or caravanseras, where the crouds of pilgrims, coming from the temple of Jupiter Ammon, used to lodge; who, in those parts, travelling upon camels, and those creatures when in Cyrene, a province of Egypt, where that celebrated temple stood, urining in the stables, or, say some, in the parched sands, out of this urine, which is remarkably strong, arose a kind of salt, denominated sometimes from the temple, *Ammoniac*, and sometimes from the country, *Cyreniac*. Since the cessation of these pilgrimages, no more of this salt is produced there; and, from this deficiency, some suspect there never was any such thing: but this suspicion is removed, by the large quantities of a salt, nearly of the same nature, thrown out by mount Ætna. The characters of the ancient *sal ammoniac* are, that it cools water, turns aqua fortis into aqua regia, and consequently dissolves gold.

The modern *sal ammoniac* is entirely factitious, and made in Egypt; where several long-necked glass bottles, being filled with soot, a little sea salt, and the urine of cattle, and having their mouths luted with a piece of wet cotton, are placed over an oven or furnace, contrived for the purpose, in a thick bed of ashes, nothing but the necks appearing, and kept there two days and a night, with a continual strong fire. The steam swells up the cotton, and forms a paste at the vent-hole, hindering the salts from evaporating; which, being confined, stick to the top of the bottle, and are, upon breaking it, taken out in those large cakes, which they send to England. Only soot exhaled from dung, is the proper ingredient in this preparation; and the dung of camels affords the strongest and best.

Our chymists imitate the Egyptian *sal ammoniac*, by adding one part of common salt to five of urine; with which some mix that quantity of soot, and putting the whole in a vessel, they raise from it, by sublimation, a white, friable, farinaceous substance, which they call *sal ammoniac*. There are various preparations of this salt used in pharmacy; as, *sublimate of sal ammoniac*, and *flowers of sal ammoniac*, used as sudorificks, diureticks, and good aperients; *volatile sal ammoniac*, used against malignant fevers, as a sudorifick, and in pocket bottles; *spirit of sal ammoniac*, of various kinds. *Chambers.*

AMMONI'ACAL. *adj.* [from *ammoniac*.] Having the properties of ammoniac salt.

Human blood calcin'd, yields no fixed salt; nor is it a sal ammoniack; for that remains immutable after repeated distillations; and distillation destroys the *ammoniacal* quality of animal salts, and turns them alkaline: so that it is a salt neither quite fixed, nor quite volatile, nor quite acid, nor quite alkaline, nor quite *ammoniacal*; but soft and benign, approaching nearest to the nature of sal ammoniac. *Arbuthnot.*

AMMUNI'TION. *n. s.* [supposed by some to come from *amonitio*, which, in the barbarous ages, seems to have signified supply of provision; but it, surely, may be more reasonably derived from *munitio*, fortification; *choses à munitions*, things for the fortresses.] Military stores.

They must make themselves defensible against strangers; and must have the assistance of some able military man, and convenient arms and *ammunition* for their defence. *Bacon.*

The colonel staid to put in the *ammunition* he brought with him; which was only twelve barrels of powder, and twelve hundred weight of match. *Clarendon, b.* viii.

All the rich mines of learning ransackt are,
To furnish *ammunition* for this war. *Denham.*

But now his stores of *ammunition* spent,
His naked valour is his only guard:
Rare thunders are from his dumb cannon sent,
And solitary guns are scarcely heard. *Dryden's Annus Mir.*

AMMUNI'TION BREAD. *n. s.* Bread for the supply of the armies or garrisons.

A'MNESTY. *n. s.* [ἀμνηστία.] An act of oblivion; an act by which crimes against the government, to a certain time, are so obliterated, that they can never be brought into charge.

I never read of a law enacted to take away the force of all laws, by which a man may safely commit upon the last of June, what he would infallibly be hanged for, if he committed it on the first of July; by which the greatest criminals may escape, provided they continue long enough in power, to antiquate their crimes, and, by stifling them a while, deceive the legislature into an *amnesty*. *Swift.*

AMNI'COLIST. *n. s.* [*amnicola*, Lat.] Inhabiting near a river. *D.*

AMNI'GENOUS. *n. s.* [*amnigenus*, Lat.] Born of a river. *Dict.*

A'MNION. } *n. s.* [Lat. perhaps from ἀμνός.]
A'MNIOS. }

The innermost membrane with which the fœtus in the womb is most immediately covered, and with which the rest of the secundines, the chorion, and alantois, are ejected after birth. It is whiter and thinner than the chorion. It also contains a nutritious humour, separated by glands for that purpose, with which the fœtus is preserved. It is outwardly cloathed with the urinary membrane, and the chorion, which sometimes stick so close to one another, that they can scarce be separated. It has also its vessels from the same origin as the chorion. *Quincy.*

AMO'MUM. *n. s.* [Lat.] A sort of fruit.

The commentators on Pliny and Dioscorides differ about the ancient *amomum*; but the generality of them suppose it to be a fruit different from ours. Scaliger is confident, that the *amomum* was no fruit; but the wood, which bore some resemblance to a bunch of grapes, and was used in embalming of bodies; whence the name *mummy* was given to bodies embalmed with it. The modern *amomum* appears to be the *sison*, or *sium*, of the ancients, or *bastard stone-parsley*. It resembles the muscat grape, grows in clusters, and is about the thickness of a pea, round, membranous, and divided into three cells, that contain several brown angular grains, of a very strong aromatick taste and smell. This fruit is brought from the East Indies, and makes part of the composition of treacle. It is of a hot spicy taste and smell. There is likewise another paler seed, named *amomum*; but neither are in much repute in physick.

Trevoux. Chambers.

AMO'NG. } *prep.* [amanᵹ, ᵹemanᵹ, Saxon.]
AMO'NGST. }

1. Mingled with; placed with other persons or things; on every side.

Amongst strawberries sow here and there some borage-seed; and you shall find the strawberries under those leaves far more large than their fellows. *Bacon's Natural Hist.* N° 441.

The voice of God they heard,
Now walking in the garden, by soft winds
Brought to their ears, while day declin'd: they heard,
And from his presence hid themselves, *among*
The thickest trees, both man and wife. *Paradise Lost.*

2. Conjoined with others, so as to make part of the number.

I have then, as you see, observed the failings of many great wits *amongst* the moderns, who have attempted to write an epic poem. *Dryden's Juvenal, Dedicat.*

There were, *among* the old Roman statues, several of Venus in different postures and habits; as there are many particular figures of her made after the same design. *Addison on Italy.*

A'MORIST. *n. s.* [from *amour*.] An inamorato; a galant; a man professing love.

Female beauties are as fickle in their faces as their minds; though casualties should spare them, age brings in a necessity of decay; leaving doters upon red and white, perplexed by incertainty both of the continuance of their mistress's kindness, and her beauty, both which are necessary to the *amorist's* joys and quiet. *Boyle.*

AMORO'SO. *n. s.* [Ital.] A man enamoured. *Dict.*

A'MOROUS. *adj.* [*amoroso*, Ital.]

1. In love; enamoured; with the particle *of* before the thing loved; in *Shakespeare*, *on*.

Sure, my brother is *amorous on* Hero; and hath withdrawn her father to break with him about it.

Shakespeare's Much ado about nothing.

Apes, as soon as they have brought forth their young, keep their eyes

eyes faſtened on them, and are never weary of admiring their beauty: ſo *amorous* is nature *of* whatſoever ſhe produces. *Dryden's Dufreſnoy.*

2. Naturally inclined to love; diſpoſed to fondneſs; fond.

The *am'rous* maſter own'd her potent eyes,
Sigh'd when he look'd, and trembl'd as he drew;
Each flowing line confirm'd his firſt ſurprize,
And as the piece advanc'd, the paſſion grew. *Prior.*

3. Relating, or belonging to love.

I that am not ſhap'd for ſportive tricks,
Nor made to court an *am'rous* looking-glaſs,
I, that am rudely ſtampt. *Shakeſp. Rich.* III.

And into all things from her air inſpir'd
The ſpirit of love, and *amorous* delight. *Parad. Loſt, b.* viii.

In the *amorous* net
Firſt caught they lik'd; and each his liking choſe. *Milton's Paradiſe Loſt, b.* xi. *l.* 586.

O! how I long my careleſs limbs to lay
Under the plantane's ſhade, and all the day
With *am'rous* airs my fancy entertain,
Invoke the muſes, and improve my vein! *Waller.*

A'MOROUSLY. *adv.* [from *amorous.*] Fondly; lovingly.

When thou wilt ſwim in that live-bath,
Each fiſh, which every channel hath,
Will *amorouſly* to thee ſwim,
Gladder to catch thee, than thou him. *Donne.*

A'MOROUSNESS. *n. ſ.* [from *amorous.*] The quality of being amorous; fondneſs; lovingneſs; love.

All Gynecia's actions were interpreted by Baſilius, as proceeding from jealouſy of his *amorouſneſs.* *Sidney, b.* ii.

I can readily believe that Lindamor has wit, and *amorouſneſs* enough, to make him find it more eaſy to defend fair ladies, than to defend himſelf againſt them. *Boyle on Colours.*

AMO'RT. *adv.* [*à la mort,* Fr.] In the ſtate of the dead; dejected; depreſſed; ſpiritleſs.

How fares my Kate? what, ſweeting, all *amort?* *Shakeſpeare's Taming of the Shrew.*

AMORTIZA'TION. } AMO'RTIZEMENT. } *n. ſ.* [*amortiſſement, amortiſſable,* Fr.] The right or act of transferring lands to mortmain; that is, to ſome community, that never is to ceaſe.

Every one of the religious orders was confirmed by one pope or other; and they made an eſpecial proviſion for them, after the laws of *amortization* were deviſed and put in uſe by princes. *Ayliffe's Parergon Juris Canonici.*

To AMO'RTIZE. *v. a.* [*amortir,* Fr.] To alien lands or tenements to any corporation, guild or fraternity, and their ſucceſſors; which cannot be done without licence of the king, and the lord of the manour. *Blount.*

This did concern the kingdom to have farms ſufficient to maintain an able body out of penury, and to *amortize* part of the lands unto the yeomanry, or middle part of the people. *Bacon's Henry* VII.

To AMO'VE. *v. a.* [*amoveo,* Lat.]

1. To remove from a poſt or ſtation: a juridical ſenſe.

2. To remove; to move; to alter: a ſenſe now out of uſe.

Therewith, *amoved* from his ſober mood,
And lives he yet, ſaid he, that wrought this act?
And do the heavens afford him vital food? *Fairy Queen.*

To AMO'UNT. *v. n.* [*monter,* Fr.]

1. To riſe to in the accumulative quantity; to compoſe in the whole; with the particle *to.* It is uſed of ſeveral ſums in quantities added together.

Let us compute a little more particularly how much this will *amount to,* or how many oceans of water would be neceſſary to compoſe this great ocean rowling in the air, without bounds or banks. *Burnet's Theory of the Earth.*

2. It is uſed, figuratively, of the conſequence riſing from any thing taken altogether.

The errours of young men are the ruin of buſineſs; but the errours of aged men *amount* but *to* this, that more might have been done, or ſooner. *Bacon's Eſſays Civil and Moral.*

Judgments that are made on the wrong ſide of the danger, *amount to* no more than an affectation of ſkill, without either credit or effect. *L'Eſtrange.*

AMO'UNT. *n. ſ.* [from *To amount.*] The ſum total; the reſult of ſeveral ſums or quantities accumulated.

And now, ye lying vanities of life,
Where are you now, and what is your *amount?*
Vexation, diſappointment, and remorſe. *Thomſon's Winter.*

AMO'UR. *n. ſ.* [*amour,* Fr. *amor,* Lat.] An affair of gallantry; an intrigue: generally uſed of vicious love. The *ou* ſounds like *oo* in *poor.*

No man is of ſo general and diffuſive a luſt, as to proſecute his *amours* all the world over; and let it burn never ſo outrageouſly, yet the impure flame will either die of itſelf, or conſume the body that harbours it. *South's Sermons.*

The reſtleſs youth ſearch'd all the world around;
But how can Jove in his *amours* be found? *Addiſon's Ovid's Metam.*

A'MPER. *n. ſ.* [ampre, Sax.] A tumour, with inflammation; bile: a word ſaid, by *Skinner,* to be much in uſe in Eſſex; but, perhaps, not found in books.

AMPHI'BIOUS. *adj.* [ἀμφι and βίος.] That which partakes of two natures, ſo as to live in two elements; as, in air and water.

A creature of *amphibious* nature,
On land a beaſt, a fiſh in water. *Hudibras, cant.* iii.

Thoſe are called *amphibious,* which live freely in the air, upon the earth, and yet are obſerved to live long upon water, as if they were natural inhabitants of that element; though it be worth the examination to know, whether any of thoſe creatures that live at that eaſe, and by choice, a good while, or at any time upon the earth, can live, a long time together, perfectly under water. *Locke.*

Fiſhes contain much oil, and *amphibious* animals participate ſomewhat of the nature of fiſhes, and are oily. *Arbuthnot.*

AMPHI'BIOUSNESS. *n. ſ.* [from *amphibious.*] The quality of being able to live in different elements.

AMPHIBOLO'GICAL. *adj.* [from *amphibology.*] Doubtful.

AMPHIBOLO'GICALLY. *adv.* [from *amphibological.*] Doubtfully; with a doubtful meaning.

AMPHIBO'LOGY. *n. ſ.* [ἀμφιβολογία.] Diſcourſe of uncertain meaning. It is diſtinguiſhed from *equivocation,* which means the double ſignification of a ſingle word; as, *noli regem occidere, timere bonum eſt,* is *amphibology*; *captare lepores,* meaning by *lepores,* either hares or jeſts, is *equivocation.*

Now the fallacies, whereby men deceive others, and are deceived themſelves, the ancients have divided into verbal and real; of the verbal, and ſuch as conclude from miſtakes of the word, there are but two worthy our notation; the fallacy of equivocation and *amphibology.* *Brown's Vulgar Errours.*

In defining obvious appearances, we are to uſe what is moſt plain and eaſy; that the mind be not miſled by *amphibologies,* or ill conceived notions, into fallacious deductions. *Glanville's Scepſis Scientifica.*

AMPHI'BOLOUS. *adj.* [ἀμφι and βάλλω.] Toſſed from one to another; ſtriking each way.

Never was there ſuch an *amphibolous* quarrel, both parties declaring themſelves for the king, and making uſe of his name in all their remonſtrances, to juſtify their actions. *Howell.*

AMPHI'LOGY. *n. ſ.* [ἀμφι and λόγος.] Equivocation; ambiguity. *D.*

AMPHISBÆ'NA. *n. ſ.* [Lat. ἀμφισβαίνη.] A ſerpent ſuppoſed to have two heads.

That the *amphisbæna,* that is, a ſmaller kind of ſerpent, which moveth forward and backward, hath two heads, or one at either extreme, was affirmed by Nicander, and others. *Brown's Vulgar Errours, b.* iii.

Scorpion, and aſp, and *amphisbæna* dire,
Ceraſtes horn'd, hydrus, and ellops drear,
And dipſas. *Milton's Paradiſe Loſt, b.* x.

AMPHI'SCII. *n. ſ.* [Lat. ἀμφίσκιοι, of ἀμφι and σκία, a ſhadow.] Thoſe people dwelling in climates, wherein the ſhadows, at different times of the year, fall both ways; to the north pole, when the ſun is in the ſouthern ſigns, and to the ſouth pole, when he is in the northern ſigns. Theſe are the people who inhabit the torrid zone.

AMPHITHE'ATRE. *n. ſ.* [of ἀμφιθέατρον, of ἀμφι and θεάομαι.] A building in a circular or oval form, having its area encompaſſed with rows of ſeats one above another; where ſpectators might behold ſpectacles, as ſtage-plays, or gladiators. The theatres of the ancients were built in the form of a ſemicircle, only exceeding a juſt ſemicircle by one fourth part of the diameter; and the amphitheatre is two theatres joined together; ſo that the longeſt diameter of the amphitheatre, was to the ſhorteſt, as one and a half to one.

Within, an *amphitheatre* appear'd
Rais'd in degrees; to ſixty paces rear'd,
That when a man was plac'd in one degree,
Height was allow'd for him above to ſee. *Dryd. Fables.*

Conceive a man placed in the burning iron chair at Lyons, amid the inſults and mockeries of a crouded *amphitheatre,* and ſtill keeping his ſeat; or ſtretched upon a grate of iron, over coals of fire, and breathing out his ſoul, among the exquiſite ſufferings of ſuch a tedious execution, rather than renounce his religion, or blaſpheme his Saviour. *Addiſ. on the Chr. Rel.*

A'MPLE. *adj.* [*amplus,* Lat.]

1. Large; wide; extended.

Heav'n deſcends
In univerſal bounty, ſhedding herbs,
And fruits, and flowers, on nature's *ample* lap. *Thomſon.*

2. Great in bulk.

Did your letters pierce the queen to any demonſtration of grief?——

She took 'em, and read 'em in my preſence,
And now and then an *ample* tear trill'd down
Her delicate cheeks. *Shakeſp. King Lear.*

3. Unlimited; without reſtriction.

Have what you aſk, your preſents I receive;
Land where, and when you pleaſe, with *ample* leave. *Dryd.*

4. Liberal; large; without parſimony.

If we ſpeak of ſtrict juſtice, God could no way have been bound to require man's labours in ſo large and *ample* manner as human felicity doth import; in as much as the dignity of this exceedeth ſo far the other's value. *Hooker.*

5. Large; splendid; without reservation.

To dispose the prince the more willingly to undertake his relief, the earl made *ample* promises, that, within so many days after the siege should be raised, he would advance his highness's levies with two thousand men. *Clarendon, b.* viii.

6. Diffusive; not contracted; as, an *ample* narrative; that is, not an epitome.

A'MPLENESS. *n. s.* [from *ample.*] The quality of being ample; largeness; splendour.

Impossible it is for a person of my condition to produce any thing in proportion either to the *ampleness* of the body you represent, or of the places you bear. *South.*

To A'MPLIATE. *v. a.* [*amplio,* Lat.] To enlarge; to make greater; to extend.

He shall solemnly look upon it, not only to destroy ours, but to establish his own; not to traduce or extenuate, but to explain and dilucidate, to add and *ampliate,* according to the custom of the ancients. *Brown's Preface to Vulgar Errours.*

AMPLIA'TION. *n. s.* [from *ampliate.*]

1. Enlargement; exaggeration; extension.

Odious matters admit not of an *ampliation,* but ought to be restrained and interpreted in the mildest sense. *Ayliffe's Parer.*

2. Diffuseness; enlargement.

The obscurity of the subject, and the prejudice and prepossession of most readers, may plead excuse for any *ampliations* or repetitions that may be found, whilst I labour to express myself plain and full. *Holder's Elements of Speech, Preface.*

To AMPLI'FICATE. *v. a.* [*amplifico,* Lat.] To enlarge; to spread out; to amplify. *Dict.*

AMPLIFICA'TION. *n. s.* [*amplification,* Fr. *amplificatio,* Lat.]

1. Enlargement; extension.

2. It is usually taken in a rhetorical sense, and implies exaggerated representation, or diffuse narrative; an image heightened beyond reality; a narrative enlarged with many circumstances.

I shall summarily, without any *amplification* at all, shew in what manner defects have been supplied. *Sir J. Davies.*

Things unknown seem greater than they are, and are usually received with *amplifications* above their nature. *Brown's Vulgar Errours, b.* vi.

Is the poet justifiable for relating such incredible *amplifications?* It may be answered, if he had put these extravagances into the mouth of Ulysses, he had been unpardonable; but they suit well with the character of Alcinous. *Pope's Od. notes.*

A'MPLIFIER. *n. s.* [from *To amplify.*] One that enlarges any thing; one that exaggerates; one that represents any thing with a large display of the best circumstances; it being usually taken in a good sense.

Dorillaus could need no *amplifier's* mouth for the highest point of praise. *Sidney, b.* ii.

To A'MPLIFY. *v. a.* [*amplifier,* Fr.]

1. To enlarge; to encrease any material substance, or object of sense.

So when a great moneyed man hath divided his chests, and coins, and bags, he seemeth to himself richer than he was: and therefore a way to *amplify* any thing, is to break it, and to make anatomy of it in several parts, and to examine it according to the several circumstances. *Bacon's Essays.*

All concaves that proceed from more narrow to more broad, do *amplify* the sound at the coming out. *Bacon's Nat. History.*

2. To enlarge, or extend any thing incorporeal.

For as the reputation of the Roman prelates grew up in these blind ages, so grew up in them withal, a desire of *amplifying* their power, that they might be as great in temporal forces, as mens opinions have formed them in spiritual matters. *Raleigh.*

3. To exaggerate any thing; to enlarge it by the manner of representation.

Since I have plainly laid open the negligence and errours of every age that is past, I would not willingly seem to flatter the present, by *amplifying* the diligence and true judgment of those servitours that have laboured in this vineyard. *Davies on Irel.*

Thy general is my lover; I have been
The book of his good acts; whence men have read
His fame unparallel'd, haply *amplified.* *Shakesp. Coriolanus.*

4. To enlarge; to improve by new additions.

I feel age advancing, and my health is insufficient to increase and *amplify* these remarks, to confirm and improve these rules, and to illuminate the several pages. *Watts.*

To A'MPLIFY. *v. n.* Frequently with the particle *on.*

1. To speak largely in many words; to lay one's self out in diffusion.

When you affect to *amplify on* the former branches of a discourse, you will often lay a necessity upon yourself of contracting the latter, and prevent yourself in the most important part of your design. *Watts's Logick.*

2. To form large or pompous representations.

I have sometimes been forced to *amplify on* others; but here where the subject is so fruitful, that the harvest overcomes the reaper, I am shortened by my chain. *Dryd. Fab. Ded.*

Homer *amplifies,* not invents; and as there was really a people called Cyclopeans, so they might be men of great stature, or giants. *Pope's Odyssey, notes.*

A'MPLITUDE. *n. s.* [*amplitude,* Fr. *amplitudo,* Lat.]

1. Extent.

Whatever I look upon, within the *amplitude* of heaven and earth, is evidence of human ignorance. *Glanville's Scepsis.*

2. Largeness; greatness.

Men should learn how severe a thing the true inquisition of nature is, and accustom themselves, by the light of particulars, to enlarge their minds to the *amplitude* of the world, and not reduce the world to the narrowness of their minds. *Bacon.*

3. Capacity.

With more than human gifts from heaven adorn'd,
Perfections absolute, graces divine,
And *amplitude* of mind to greatest deeds. *Parad. Regained.*

4. Splendour; grandeur; dignity.

In the great frame of kingdoms and commonwealths, it is in the power of princes, or estates, to add *amplitude* and greatness to their kingdoms. *Bacon's Essays.*

5. Copiousness; abundance.

You should say every thing which has a proper and direct tendency to this end; always proportioning the *amplitude* of your matter, and the fulness of your discourse, to your great design; the length of your time, to the convenience of your hearers. *Watts's Logick.*

6. *Amplitude of the range of a projectile,* denotes the horizontal line subtending the path in which it moved.

7. *Amplitude,* in astronomy, an arch of the horizon, intercepted between the true east and west point thereof, and the centre of the sun or star at its rising or setting. It is eastern or ortive, when the star rises, and western or occiduous, when the star sets. The eastern or western *amplitude,* are also called northern or southern, as they fall in the northern or southern quarters of the horizon.

8. *Magnetical amplitude,* is an arch of the horizon contained between the sun at his rising, and the east or west point of the compass; or, it is the difference of the rising or setting of the sun, from the east or west parts of the compass. *Chambers.*

A'MPLY. *adv.* [*amplè,* Lat.]

1. Largely; liberally.

For whose well-being,
So *amply,* and with hands so liberal,
Thou hast provided all things. *Milton's Par. Lost, b.* viii.

The evidence they had before was enough, *amply* enough, to convince them; but they were resolved not to be convinced: and to those, who are resolved not to be convinced, all motives, all arguments are equal. *Atterbury's Sermons.*

2. At large; without reserve.

At return
Of him so lately promis'd to thy aid,
The woman's seed; obscurely then foretold,
Now *amplier* known, thy Saviour, and thy Lord. *Par. Lost.*

3. At large; copiously; with a diffusive detail.

Some parts of a poem require to be *amply* written, and with all the force and elegance of words; others must be cast into shadows; that is, passed over in silence, or but faintly touched. *Dryden's Dufresnoy, Pref.*

To A'MPUTATE. *v. a.* [*amputo,* Lat.] To cut off a limb: a word used only in chirurgery.

Amongst the cruizers in private frigates from Dunkirk, it was complained, that their surgeons were too active in *amputating* those fractured members. *Wiseman's Surgery.*

AMPUTA'TION. *n. s.* [*amputatio,* Lat.]

The operation of cutting off a limb, or other part of the body, with an instrument of steel. The usual method of performing it, in the instance of a leg, is as follows. The proper part for the operation being four or five inches below the knee, the skin and flesh are first to be drawn very tight upwards, and secured from returning by a ligature two or three fingers broad: above this ligature another loose one is passed, for the gripe; which being twisted by means of a stick, may be straitened to any degree at pleasure. Then the patient being conveniently situated, and the operator placed to the inside of the limb, which is to be held by one assistant above, and another below the part designed for the operation, and the gripe sufficiently twisted, to prevent too large an hæmorrhage, the flesh is, with a stroke or two, to be separated from the bone with the dismembering knife. Then the periostium being also divided from the bone with the back of the knife, saw the bone asunder, with as few strokes as possible. When two parallel bones are concerned, the flesh that grows between them must likewise be separated before the use of the saw. This being done, the gripe may be slackened, to give an opportunity of searching for the large blood vessels, and securing the hæmorrhage at their mouths. After making proper applications to the stump, loosen the first ligature, and pull both the skin and the flesh, as far as conveniently may be, over the stump, to cover it; and secure them with the cross stitch made at the depth of half or three quarters of an inch in the skin. Then apply pledgets, astringents, plaisters, and other necessaries. *Chambers.*

The Amazons, by the *amputation* of their right breast, had the freer use of their bow. *Brown's Vulgar Errours, b.* iv.

A'MULET. *n. s.* [*amulette,* Fr. *amuletum,* Lat.] An appended remedy,

remedy, or preservative: a thing hung about the neck, or any other part of the body, for preventing or curing of some particular diseases.

That spirits are corporeal, seems at first view a conceit derogative unto himself; yet herein he establisheth the doctrine of lustrations, *amulets*, and charms. *Brown's Vulgar Errours.*

They do not certainly know the falsity of what they report; and their ignorance must serve you as an *amulet* against the guilt both of deceit and malice. *Government of the Tongue.*

AMURCO'SITY. *n. s.* [*amurca*, Lat.] The quality of lees or mother of any thing.

To AMU'SE. *v. a.* [*amuser*, Fr.]

1. To entertain with tranquillity; to fill with thoughts that engage the mind, without distracting it. To *divert* implies something more lively, and to *please*, something more important. It is therefore frequently taken in a sense bordering on contempt.

They think they see visions, and are arrived to some extraordinary revelations; when, indeed, they do but dream dreams, and *amuse* themselves with the fantastick ideas of a busy imagination. *Decay of Piety.*

I cannot think it natural for a man, who is much in love, to *amuse* himself with trifles. *Walsh.*

2. To draw on from time to time; to keep in expectation; as, he *amused* his followers with idle promises.

AMU'SEMENT. *n. s.* [*amusement*, Fr.] That which amuses; entertainment.

Every interest or pleasure of life, even the most trifling *amusement*, is suffered to postpone the one thing necessary. *Rogers.*

During his confinement, his *amusement* was to give poison to dogs and cats, and see them expire by slower or quicker torments. *Pope's Eth. Epist. notes.*

I was left to stand the battle, while others, who had better talents than a draper, thought it no unpleasant *amusement* to look on with safety, whilst another was giving them diversion, at the hazard of his liberty. *Swift.*

AMU'SER. *n. s.* [*amuseur*, Fr.] He that amuses, as with false promises. The French word is always taken in an ill sense.

AMU'SIVE. *adj.* [from *amuse*.] That which has the power of amusing.

But amaz'd,
Beholds th' *amusive* arch before him fly,
Then vanish quite away. *Thomson's Spring.*

AMY'GDALATE. *adj.* [*amygdala*, Lat.] Made of almonds.

AMY'GDALINE. *adj.* [*amygdala*, Lat.] Relating to almonds; resembling almonds.

AN. *article.* [ane, Saxon. een, Dutch, *eine*, German.] The article indefinite, used before a vowel, or *h* mute. See A.

1. One, but with less emphasis; as, there stands *a* house.

Since he cannot be always employed in study, reading, and conversation, there will be many *an* hour, besides what his exercises will take up. *Locke.*

2. Any, or some; as, *an* elephant might swim in this water.

He was no way at *an* uncertainty, nor ever in the least at *a* loss concerning any branch of it. *Locke on St. Paul's Epistles.*

A wit's a feather, and a chief *a* rod,
An honest man's the noblest work of God. *Pope.*

3. Sometimes it signifies, like *a*, some particular state; but this is now disused.

It is certain, that odours do, in a small degree, nourish; especially the odour of wine; and we see men *an* hungred do love to smell hot bread. *Bacon's Natural History.*

4. *An* is sometimes, in old authours, a contraction of *and if*.

He can't flatter, he!
An honest mind and plain, he must speak truth;
An they will take it so; if not, he's plain. *Shakesp. K. Lear.*

5. Sometimes a contraction of *and* before *if*.

Well I know
The clerk will ne'er wear hair on's face that had it.
——— He will *an' if* he live to be a man.
Shakesp. Merchant of Venice.

6. Sometimes it is a contraction of *as if*.

My next pretty correspondent, like Shakespeare's lion in Pyramus and Thisbe, roars *an'* it were any nightingale.
Addison. Guardian, N° 121.

A'NA. adv. [ἀνά.] A word used in the prescriptions of physick, importing the like quantity; as, wine and honey, ā or *ana* ℥ii; that is, of wine and honey each two ounces.

In the same weight prudence and innocence take,
Ana of each does the just mixture make. *Cowley.*
He'll bring an apothecary, with a chargeable long bill of *anas*.
Dryden's Spanish Friar.

A'NA. n. s. Books so called from the last syllables of their titles; as, *Scaligerana*, *Thuaniana*; they are loose thoughts, or casual hints, dropped by eminent men, and collected by their friends.

ANACA'MPTICK. *adj.* [ἀνακάμπτω.] Reflecting, or reflected: an *anacamptick* sound, an echo; an *anacamptick* hill, a hill that produces an echo.

ANACA'MPTICKS. *n. s.* The doctrine of reflected light, or catoptricks. It has no singular.

ANACATHA'RTICK. *n. s.* [See CATHARTICK.] Any medicine that works upwards. *Quincy.*

ANACEPHALÆO'SIS. n. s. [ἀνακεφαλαίωσις.] Recapitulation, or summary of the principal heads of a discourse. *Dict.*

ANA'CHORETE. } *n. s.* [sometimes viciously writen *anchorite*;
ANA'CHORITE. } ἀναχωρήτης.] A monk, who, with the leave of his superiour, leaves the convent for a more austere and solitary life.

Yet lies not love dead here, but here doth sit,
Vow'd to this trench, like an *anachorite*. *Donne.*

ANA'CHRONISM. *n. s.* [from ἀνά and χρόνος.] An errour in computing time, by which events are misplaced with regard to each other. It seems properly to signify an errour by which an event is placed too early; but is generally used for any errour in chronology.

This leads me to the defence of the famous *anachronism*, in making Æneas and Dido cotemporaries: for it is certain, that the hero lived almost two hundred years before the building of Carthage. *Dryden's Virgil, Dedicat.*

ANACLA'TICKS. *n. s.* [ἀνά and κλάω.] The doctrine of refracted light; dioptricks. It has no singular.

ANADIPLO'SIS. n. s. [ἀναδίπλωσις.] Reduplication; a figure in rhetorick, in which the last word of a foregoing member of a period becomes the first of the following; as, *he retained his virtues amidst all his* misfortunes, misfortunes *which only his virtue* brought upon him.

ANAGOGE'TICAL. *adj.* [ἀναγωγή.] That which contributes or relates to spiritual elevation, or religious raptures; mysterious; elevated above humanity. *Dict.*

ANAGO'GICAL. *adj.* [*anagogique*, Fr.] Mysterious; elevated; religiously exalted. *Dict.*

ANAGO'GICALLY. *adv.* [from *anagogical*.] Mysteriously; with religious elevation.

A'NAGRAM. *n. s.* [ἀνά and γράμμα.] A conceit arising from the letters of a name transposed; as this, of *W,i,l,l,i,a,m, N,o,y,* attorney-general to Charles I. a very laborious man, *I moyl in law.*

Though all her parts be not in th' usual place,
She hath yet the *anagrams* of a good face:
If we might put the letters but one way,
In that lean dearth of words, what could we say? *Donne.*
Thy genius calls thee not to purchase fame
In keen iambicks, but mild *anagram*. *Dryden.*

ANAGRA'MMATISM. *n. s.* [from *anagram*.] The act or practice of making anagrams.

The only quintessence that hitherto the alchymy of wit could draw out of names, is *anagrammatism*, or metagrammatism, which is a dissolution of a name truly written into his letters, as his elements, and a new connexion of it by artificial transposition, without addition, substraction, or change of any letter into different words, making some perfect sense appliable to the person named. *Camden.*

ANAGRA'MMATIST. *n. s.* [from *anagram*.] A maker of anagrams.

To ANAGRA'MMATIZE. *v. n.* [*anagrammatiser*, Fr.] To make anagrams.

ANALE'PTICK. *adj.* [ἀναληπτικός.] Comforting; corroborating: a term of physick.

Analeptick medicines cherish the nerves, and renew the spirits and strength. *Quincy.*

ANALO'GICAL. *adj.* [from *analogy*.]

1. Used by way of analogy. It seems properly distinguished from *analogous*, as words from things; *analogous* signifies having relation, and *analogical* having the quality of representing relation.

It is looked on only as the image of the true God, and that not as a proper likeness, but by *analogical* representation.
Stillingfleet's Def. of Disc. on Rom. Idolatry.

When a word, which originally signifies any particular idea or object, is attributed to several other objects, not by way of resemblance, but on the account of some evident reference to the original idea, this is peculiarly called an *analogical* word; so a sound or healthy pulse, a sound digestion, sound sleep, are so called, with reference to a sound and healthy constitution; but if you speak of sound doctrine, or sound speech, this is by way of resemblance to health, and the words are metaphorical.
Watts's Logick.

2. Analogous; having resemblance or relation.

There is placed the minerals between the inanimate and vegetable province, participating something *analogical* to either.
Hales's Origin of Mankind.

ANALO'GICALLY. *adv.* [from *analogical*.] In an analogical manner; in an analogous manner.

I am convinced, from the simplicity and uniformity of the Divine Nature, and of all his works, that there is some one universal principle, running through the whole system of creatures *analogically*, and congruous to their relative natures.
Cheyne's Philosoph. Principles.

ANALO'GICALNESS. *n. s.* [from *analogical*.] The quality of being analogical; fitness to be applied for the illustration of some analogy.

ANA'LOGISM. *n. s.* [ἀναλογισμός.] An argument from the cause to the effect.

To ANA'LOGIZE. *v. a.* [from *analogy*.] To explain by way of analogy;

analogy; to form ſome reſemblance between different things; to conſider ſomething with regard to its analogy with ſomewhat elſe.

We have ſyſtems of material bodies, diverſly figured and ſituated, if ſeparately conſidered; they repreſent the object of the deſire, which is *analogized* by attraction or gravitation. *Cheyne's Philoſ. Principles.*

ANA'LOGOUS. *adj.* [ἀνὰ and λόγος.]

1. Having analogy; bearing ſome reſemblance or proportion; having ſomething parallel.

Exerciſe makes things eaſy, that would be otherwiſe very hard; as, in labour, watchings, heats, and colds; and then there is ſomething *analogous* in the exerciſe of the mind, to that of the body. It is folly and infirmity that makes us delicate and froward. *L'Eſtrange.*

Many important conſequences may be drawn from the obſervation of the moſt common things, and *analogous* reaſonings from the cauſes of them. *Arbuthnot on Aliments.*

2. It has the word *to* before the thing to which the reſemblance is noted.

This incorporeal ſubſtance may have ſome ſort of exiſtence, *analogous to* corporeal extenſion: though we have no adequate conception hereof. *Locke.*

ANA'LOGY. *n. ſ.* [ἀναλογία.]

1. Reſemblance between things with regard to ſome circumſtances or effects; as, *learning* is ſaid to *enlighten* the mind; that is, it is to the mind what light is to the eye, by enabling it to diſcover that which was hidden before.

From God it hath proceeded, that the church hath evermore held a preſcript form of common prayer, although not in all things every where the ſame, yet, for the moſt part, retaining the ſame *analogy*. *Hooker, b.* v. § 25.

What I here obſerve of extraordinary revelation and prophecy, will, by *analogy* and due proportion, extend even to thoſe communications of God's will, that are requiſite to ſalvation. *South.*

2. When the thing to which the analogy is ſuppoſed, happens to be mentioned, *analogy* has after it the particles *to* or *with*; when both the things are mentioned after *analogy*, the particle *between* or *betwixt* is uſed.

If the body politick have any *analogy to* the natural, an act of oblivion were neceſſary in a hot diſtemper'd ſtate. *Dryd. Pref. to Abſalom and Achitop.*

By *analogy with* all other liquours and concretions, the form of the chaos, whether liquid or concrete, could not be the ſame with that of the preſent earth. *Burnet's Theory of the Earth.*

If we make him expreſs the cuſtoms of our country, rather than of Rome, it is either when there was ſome *analogy betwixt* the cuſtoms, or to make him more eaſy to vulgar underſtanding. *Dryden's Juvenal, Dedication.*

3. By grammarians, it is uſed to ſignify the agreement of ſeveral words in one common mode; as, from *love* is formed *loved*, from *hate*, *hated*, from *grieve*, *grieved*.

ANA'LYSIS. *n. ſ.* [ἀνάλυσις.]

1. A ſeparation of a compound body into the ſeveral parts of which it conſiſts.

There is an account of dew falling, in ſome places, in the form of butter, or greaſe, which grows extremely fetid; ſo that the *analyſis* of the dew of any place, may, perhaps, be the beſt method of finding ſuch contents of the ſoil as are within the reach of the ſun. *Arbuthnot.*

2. A conſideration of any thing in parts, ſo as that one particular is firſt conſidered, then another.

Analyſis conſiſts in making experiments and obſervations, and in drawing general concluſions from them by induction, and admitting of no objections againſt the concluſions, but ſuch as are taken from experiments, or other certain truths. *Newton's Opticks.*

3. A ſolution of any thing, whether corporeal or mental, to its firſt elements; as, of a ſentence to the ſingle words; of a compound word, to the particles and words which form it; of a tune, to ſingle notes; of an argument, to ſimple propoſitions.

We cannot know any thing of nature, but by an *analyſis* of its true initial cauſes; till we know the firſt ſprings of natural motions, we are ſtill but ignorants. *Glanville's Scepſis Scientif.*

ANALY'TICAL. *adj.* [from *analyſis*.]

1. That which reſolves any thing into firſt principles; that which ſeparates any compound. See ANALYSIS.

Either may be probably maintained againſt the inaccurateneſs of the *analytical* experiments vulgarly relied on. *Boyle.*

2. That which proceeds by analyſis, or by taking the parts of a compound into diſtinct and particular conſideration.

Deſcartes hath here infinitely outdone all the philoſophers that went before him, in giving a particular and *analytical* account of the univerſal fabrick: yet he intends his principles but for hypotheſes. *Glanville's Scepſis Scientifica.*

ANALY'TICALLY. *adv.* [from *analytical*.] In ſuch a manner as ſeparates compounds into ſimples. See ANALYSIS.

ANALY'TICK. *adj.* [ἀναλυτικὸς.] The manner of reſolving compounds into the ſimple conſtituent or component parts, applied chiefly to mental operations.

He was in logick a great critick,
Profoundly ſkill'd in *analytick*. *Hudibras.*

Analytick method takes the whole compound as it finds it, whether it be a ſpecies or an individual, and leads us into the knowledge of it, by reſolving into its firſt principles, or parts, its generick nature, and its ſpecial properties; and therefore it is called the method of reſolution. *Watts's Logick.*

To A'NALYZE. *v. a.* [ἀναλύω.] To reſolve a compound into its firſt principles. See ANALYSIS.

Chymiſtry enabling us to depurate bodies, and, in ſome meaſure, to *analyze* them, and take aſunder their heterogeneous parts, in many chymical experiments, we may, better than in others, know what manner of bodies we employ; art having made them more ſimple or uncompounded, than nature alone is wont to preſent them us. *Boyle.*

To *analyze* the immorality of any action into its laſt principles; if it be inquired, why ſuch an action is to be avoided, the immediate anſwer is, becauſe it is ſin. *Norris's Miſcell.*

When the ſentence is diſtinguiſhed into ſubject and predicate, propoſition, argument, act, object, cauſe, effect, adjunct, oppoſite, &c. then it is *analyzed* analogically and metaphyſically. This laſt is what is chiefly meant in the theological ſchools, when they ſpeak of *analyzing* a text of ſcripture. *Watts's Logick.*

A'NALYZER. *n. ſ.* [from *To analyze.*] That which has the power of analyzing.

Particular reaſons incline me to doubt, whether the fire be the true and univerſal *analyzer* of mixt bodies. *Boyle.*

ANAMORPHO'SIS. n. ſ. [ἀνὰ and μορφόω.] Deformation; a perſpective projection of any thing, ſo that to the eye, at one point of view, it ſhall appear deformed, in another, an exact and regular repreſentation. Sometimes it is made to appear confuſed to the naked eye, and regular, when viewed in a mirrour of a certain form.

ANA'NAS. n. ſ. The pine apple.

It has a flower conſiſting of one leaf, divided into three parts, and funnel-ſhaped; the embryos produced in the tubercles, afterwards become fruit; the ſeeds in the tubercles are ſmall, and almoſt kidney-ſhaped.

The ſpecies are, 1. Oval-ſhaped pine apple, with a whitiſh fleſh. 2. Pyramidal pine apple, with a yellow fleſh. 3. Pine apple, with ſmooth leaves. 4. Pine apple, with ſhining green leaves, and ſcarce any ſpines on their edges. 5. The olive-coloured pine.

The firſt ſort is moſt common in Europe, but the fruit of the ſecond is larger, better flavoured, and its juice not ſo aſtringent. The fifth ſort is the moſt rare in Europe, but eſteemed above all the reſt. Theſe plants are propagated by ſuckers; and from the crowns which grow on the top of the fruit. *Mill.*

Witneſs thou beſt *anana*, thou the pride
Of vegetable life, beyond whate'er
The poets imag'd in the golden age. *Thomſ. Summer.*

ANA'NAS, wild. The ſame with *penguin*. See *PENGUIN.*

ANA'PHORA. n. ſ. [ἀναφορά.] A figure, when ſeveral clauſes of a ſentence are begun with the ſame word, or ſound; as,—*Where is the wiſe? Where is the ſcribe? Where is the diſputer of this world?*

ANAPLERO'TICK. *adj.* [ἀναπληρόω.] That which fills up any vacuity; uſed of applications which promote fleſh.

A'NARCH. *n. ſ.* [See ANARCHY.] An authour of confuſion.

Him thus the *anarch* old,
With fault'ring ſpeech, and viſage incompos'd,
Anſwer'd. *Milton's Paradiſe Loſt, b.* ii.

ANA'RCHICAL. *adj.* [from *anarchy.*] Confuſed; without rule or government.

In this *anarchical* and rebellious ſtate of human nature, the faculties belonging to the material world preſume to determine the nature of ſubjects belonging to the ſupreme Spirit. *Cheyne's Philoſophical Principles.*

A'NARCHY. *n. ſ.* [ἀναρχία.] Want of government; a ſtate in which every man is unaccountable; a ſtate without magiſtracy.

Where eldeſt night
And chaos, anceſtors of nature, hold
Eternal *anarchy*, amidſt the noiſe
Of endleſs wars, and by confuſion ſtand. *Paradiſe Loſt.*

Arbitrary power is but the firſt natural ſtep from *anarchy*, or the ſavage life; the adjuſting power and freedom being an effect and conſequence of maturer thinking. *Swift.*

ANASA'RCA. n. ſ. [from ἀνὰ and σὰρξ.] A ſort of dropſy, where the whole ſubſtance is ſtuffed with pituitous humours. *Quincy.*

When the lympha ſtagnates, or is extravaſated under the ſkin, it is called an *anaſarca*. *Arbuthnot on Diet.*

ANASA'RCOUS. *adj.* [from *anaſarca.*] Relating to an anaſarca; partaking of the nature of an anaſarca.

A gentlewoman laboured of an aſcites, with an *anaſarcous* ſwelling on her belly, thighs, and legs. *Wiſeman.*

ANASTOMA'TICK. *adj.* [from ἀνὰ and στόμα.] That which has the quality of opening the veſſels, or of removing obſtructions.

ANASTOMO'SIS. n. ſ. [from ἀνὰ and στόμα.] The inoſculation of veſſels, or the opening of one veſſel into another; as, of the arteries into the veins.

ANA'STROPHE. *n. s.* [ἀναστροφὴ, a prepoſterous placing, from ἀναστρέφω.] A figure whereby words which ſhould have been precedent, are poſtponed.

ANA'THEMA. *n. s.* [ἀνάθεμα.]

1. A curſe pronounced by eccleſiaſtical authority; excommunication.

Her bare *anathemas* fall but like ſo many *bruta fulmina* upon the ſchiſmatical; who think themſelves ſhrewdly hurt, forſooth, by being cut off from the body, which they chooſe not to be of. *South's Sermons.*

2. The object of the curſe, or perſon curſed. This ſeems the original meaning, though now little uſed.

ANATHEMA'TICAL. *adj.* [from *anathema.*] That which has the properties of an anathema; that which relates to an anathema.

ANATHEMA'TICALLY. *adv.* [from *anathematical.*] In an anathematical manner.

To ANATHE'MATIZE. *v. a.* [from *anathema.*] To pronounce accurſed by eccleſiaſtical authority; to excommunicate.

They were therefore to be *anathematized* after this manner, and, with deteſtation, branded and baniſhed out of the church. *Hammond's Fundamentals.*

ANATI'FEROUS. *adj.* [from *anas* and *fero*, Lat.] Producing ducks.

If there be *anatiferous* trees, whoſe corruption breaks forth into barnacles; yet, if they corrupt, they degenerate into maggots, which produce not them again. *Brown's Vulgar Errours.*

ANA'TOCISM. *n. s.* [*anatociſmus*, Lat. ἀνατοκισμός.] The accumulation of intereſt upon intereſt; the addition of the intereſt due for money lent, to the original ſum. A ſpecies of uſury generally forbidden.

ANATO'MICAL. *adj.* [from *anatomy.*]

1. Relating or belonging to anatomy.

When we are taught by logick to view a thing completely in all its parts, by the help of diviſion, it has the uſe of an *anatomical* knife, which diſſects an animal body, and ſeparates the veins, arteries, nerves, muſcles, membranes, &c. and ſhews us the ſeveral parts which go to the compoſition of a complete animal. *Watts's Logick.*

2. Proceeding upon principles taught in anatomy; conſidered as the object of anatomy.

There is a natural, involuntary diſtortion of the muſcles, which is the *anatomical* cauſe of laughter; but there is another cauſe of laughter, which decency requires. *Swift.*

3. Anatomized; diſſected; ſeparated.

The continuation of ſolidity is apt to be confounded with, and, if we will look into the minute *anatomical* parts of matter, is little different from, hardneſs. *Locke.*

ANATO'MICALLY. *adv.* [from *anatomical.*] In an anatomical manner; in the ſenſe of an anatomiſt; according to the doctrine of anatomy.

While ſome affirmed it had no gall, intending only thereby no evidence of anger or fury, others have conſtrued *anatomically*, and denied that part at all. *Brown's Vulgar Errours, b.* iii.

ANA'TOMIST. *n. s.* [ἀνατόμος.] He that ſtudies the ſtructure of animal bodies, by means of diſſection; he that divides the bodies of animals, to diſcover the various parts.

Anatomiſts adjudged, that if nature had been ſuffered to run her own courſe, without this fatal interruption, he might have doubled his age. *Howel's Vocal Foreſt.*

Hence when *anatomiſts* diſcourſe,
How like brutes organs are to ours;
They grant, if higher powers think fit,
A bear might ſoon be made a wit;
And that, for any thing in nature,
Pigs might ſqueak love odes, dogs bark ſatire. *Prior.*

To ANA'TOMIZE. *v. a.* [ἀνατέμνω.]

1. To diſſect an animal; to divide the body into its component or conſtituent parts.

Our induſtry muſt even *anatomize* every particle of that body, which we are to uphold. *Hooker, Dedicat.*

2. To lay any thing open diſtinctly, and by minute parts.

I ſpeak but brotherly of him, but ſhould I *anatomize* him to thee as he is, I muſt bluſh and weep, and then muſt look pale and wonder. *Shakeſpeare's As you like it.*

Then dark diſtinctions reaſon's light diſguis'd,
And into atoms truth *anatomiz'd.* *Denham.*

ANA'TOMY. *n. s.* [ἀνατομία.]

1. The art of diſſecting the body.

It is therefore in the *anatomy* of the mind, as in that of the body; more good will accrue to mankind, by attending to the large, open, and perceptible parts, than by ſtudying too much ſuch finer nerves and veſſels, as will for ever eſcape our obſervation. *Pope's Eſſay on Man, Pref.*

2. The doctrine of the ſtructure of the body, learned by diſſection.

Let the muſcles be well inſerted and bound together, according to the knowledge of them which is given us by *anatomy.* *Dryden's Dufreſnoy.*

3. The act of dividing any thing, whether corporeal or intellectual.

When a moneyed man hath divided his cheſts, he ſeemeth to himſelf richer than he was; therefore, a way to amplify any thing, is to break it, and to make *anatomy* of it in ſeveral parts. *Bacon's Eſſays.*

4. The body ſtripped of its integuments; a ſkeleton.

O that my tongue were in the thunder's mouth,
Then with a paſſion I would ſhake the world,
And rouze from ſleep that fell *anatomy*,
Which cannot hear a feeble lady's voice. *Shakeſp. K. John.*

5. By way of irony or ridicule, a thin meagre perſon.

They brought one Pinch, a hungry lean-fac'd villain,
A meer *anatomy*, a mountebank,
A thread-bare juggler, and a fortune-teller,
A needy hollow-ey'd, ſharp-looking wretch,
A living dead man. *Shakeſpeare's Comedy of Errours.*

A'NATRON. *n. s.* The ſcum which ſwims upon the molten glaſs in the furnace, which, when taken off, melts in the air, and then coagulates into common ſalt. It is likewiſe that ſalt which gathers upon the walls of vaults.

A'NBURY. *n. s.* See AMBURY.

A'NCESTOR. *n. s.* [*anceſtor*, Lat. *anceſtre*, Fr.] One from whom a perſon deſcends, either by the father or the mother. It is diſtinguiſhed from *predeceſſor*; which is not, like *anceſtor*, a natural, but civil denomination. An hereditary monarch ſucceeds to his *anceſtors*; an elective, to his *predeceſſors.*

And ſhe lies buried with her *anceſtors*,
O, in a tomb where never ſcandal ſlept,
Save this of hers. *Shakeſp. Much ado about Nothing.*

Cham was the paternal *anceſtor* of Ninus, the father of Chus, the grandfather of Nimrod; whoſe ſon was Belus, the father of Ninus. *Raleigh's Hiſtory of the World.*

Obſcure! why pr'ythee what am I? I know
My father, grandſire, and great grandſire too:
If farther I derive my pedigree,
I can but gueſs beyond the fourth degree.
The reſt of my forgotten *anceſtors*,
Were ſons of earth like him, or ſons of whores.
Dryden's Perſius, ſat. vi.

A'NCESTREL. *adj.* [from *anceſtor.*] Claimed from anceſtors; relating to anceſtors: a term of law.

Limitation in actions *anceſtrel*, was anciently ſo here in England. *Hale's Law of England.*

A'NCESTRY. *n. s.* [from *anceſtor.*]

1. Lineage; a ſeries of anceſtors, or progenitors; the perſons who compoſe the lineage.

Phedon I hight, quoth he; and do advance
Mine *anceſtry* from famous Coradin,
Who firſt to raiſe our houſe to honour did begin. *Fairy Q.*

A tenacious adherence to the rights and liberties tranſmitted from a wiſe and virtuous *anceſtry*, publick ſpirit, and a love of one's country, are the ſupport and ornaments of government. *Addiſon's Freeholder, N° 5.*

Say from what ſcepter'd *anceſtry* ye claim,
Recorded eminent in deathleſs fame? *Pope's Odyſſey.*

2. The honour of deſcent; birth.

Title and *anceſtry* render a good man more illuſtrious, but an ill one, more contemptible. *Addiſon. Guardian, N° 123.*

A'NCHENTRY. *n. s.* [from *ancient*, and therefore properly to be written *ancientry.*] Antiquity of a family; ancient dignity; appearance or proof of antiquity.

Wooing, wedding, and repenting, is a Scotch jig, a meaſure and a cinque pace; the firſt ſuit is hot and haſty, like a Scotch jig, and full as fantaſtical; the wedding mannerly modeſt, as a meaſure full of ſtate and *anchentry*; and then comes repentance, and with his bad legs falls into the cinque pace faſter and faſter, till he ſinks into his grave.
Shakeſp. Much ado about Nothing.

A'NCHOR. *n. s.* [*anchora*, Lat.]

1. A heavy iron, compoſed of a long ſhank, having a ring at one end to which the cable is faſtened, and at the other, branching out into two arms or flooks, tending upwards, with barbs or edges on each ſide. Its uſe is to hold the ſhip, by being fixed to the ground.

He ſaid, and wept; then ſpread his ſails before
The winds, and reach'd at length the Cuman ſhore:
Their *anchors* dropt, his crew the veſſels moor. *Dryd. Æn.*

2. It is uſed, by a metaphor, for any thing which confers ſtability or ſecurity.

Which hope we have as an *anchor* of the ſoul, both ſure and ſtedfaſt, and which entereth not into that within the veil.
Hebrews, vi. 19.

3. The forms of ſpeech in which it is moſt commonly uſed, are, to *caſt anchor*, to *lye* or *ride at anchor.*

The Turkiſh general, deceived of his expectations, and perceiving that the Rhodians would not be drawn forth to battle at ſea, withdrew his fleet, when *caſting anchor*, and landing his men, he burnt the corn. *Knolles's Hiſtory of the Turks.*

Ent'ring with the tide,
He *dropp'd his anchors*, and his oars he ply'd:
Furl'd every ſail, and drawing down the maſt,
His veſſel moor'd, and made with haulſers faſt. *Dryd. Homer.*

Far from your capital my ſhip reſides
At Reithrus, and ſecure at *anchor rides.* *Pope's Odyſſey.*

To A'NCHOR. *v. n.* [from *anchor.*]

1. To caſt anchor; to lie at anchor.

The fiſhermen that walk upon the beach
Appear like mice; and yon tall *anchoring* bark
Diminiſh'd to her cock; her cock, a buoy
Almoſt too ſmall for ſight. *Shakeſp. King Lear.*

Near Calais the Spaniards *anchored*, expecting their land-forces, which came not. *Bacon.*

Or the ſtrait courſe to rocky Chios plow,
And *anchor* under Mimos' ſhaggy brow. *Pope's Odyſſey.*

2. To ſtop at; to reſt on.

My intention, hearing not my tongue,
Anchors on Iſabel. *Shakeſp.*

My tongue ſhould to my ears not name my boys,
'Till that my nails were *anchor'd* in thine eyes. *Shak. R.* III.

A'NCHOR. *n. ſ. Shakeſpeare* ſeems to have uſed this word for *anchoret*, or an abſtemious recluſe perſon.

To deſperation turn my truſt and hope!
An *anchor*'s cheer in priſon be my ſcope! *Shakeſp. Hamlet.*

A'NCHOR-HOLD. *n. ſ.* [from *anchor* and *hold.*] The hold or faſtneſs of the anchor; and, figuratively, ſecurity.

The old Engliſh could expreſs moſt aptly all the conceits of the mind in their own tongue, without borrowing from any; as for example: the holy ſervice of God, which the Latins called *religion*, becauſe it knitted the minds of men together, and moſt people of Europe have borrowed the ſame from them, they called moſt ſignificantly *ean-faſtneſs*, as the one and only aſſurance and faſt *anchor-hold* of our ſouls health. *Cambden.*

A'NCHOR-SMITH. *n. ſ.* [from *anchor* and *ſmith.*] The maker or forger of anchors.

Smithing comprehends all trades, which uſe either forge or file, from the *anchor-ſmith* to the watchmaker; they all working by the ſame rules, though not with equal exactneſs, and all uſing the ſame tools, though of ſeveral ſizes. *Moxon's Mechanical Exerciſes.*

A'NCHORAGE. *n. ſ.* [from *anchor.*]

1. The hold of the anchor.

Let me reſolve whether there be indeed ſuch efficacy in nurture and firſt production; for if that ſuppoſal ſhould fail us, all our *anchorage* were looſe, and we ſhould but wander in a wild ſea. *Wotton.*

2. The ſet of anchors belonging to a ſhip.

Lo as the bark that hath diſcharg'd her freight,
Returns with precious lading to the bay
From whence at firſt ſhe weigh'd her *anchorage*;
Cometh Andronicus. *Shakeſp. Titus Andronicus.*

3. The duty paid for the liberty of anchoring in a port.

A'NCHORED. *participial adj.* [from *To anchor.*] Held by the anchor.

Like a well twiſted cable, holding faſt
The *anchor'd* veſſel in the loudeſt blaſt. *Waller.*

A'NCHORET. } *n. ſ.* [contracted from *anachoret*, ἀναχωρητὴς.] A
A'NCHORITE. } recluſe; a hermit; one that retires to the more ſevere duties of religion.

His poetry indeed he took along with him; but he made that an *anchorite* as well as himſelf. *Sprat.*

You deſcribe ſo well your hermitical ſtate of life, that none of the ancient *anchorites* could go beyond you, for a cave in a rock, with a fine ſpring, or any of the accommodations that befit a ſolitary life. *Pope's Letters.*

ANCHO'VY. *n. ſ.* [from *anchova*, Span. or *anchioe*, Ital. of the ſame ſignification.] A little ſea-fiſh, much uſed by way of ſauce, or ſeaſoning. Scaliger deſcribes the *anchovy* as of the herring kind, about the length of a finger, having a pointed ſnout, a wide mouth, no teeth, but gums as rough as a ſaw. Others make it a ſort of ſardine, or pilchard; but others, with better reaſon, hold it a peculiar ſpecies, very different from either. It is caught in the months of May, June, and July, on the coaſts of Catalonia, Provence, &c. when it conſtantly repairs up the Straits of Gibraltar into the Mediterranean. The fiſhing is chiefly in the night time; when a light being put on the ſtern of their little fiſhing veſſels, the *anchovies* flock round, and are caught in nets. When the fiſhery is over, they cut off the heads, take out the galls and guts, then lay them in barrels, and ſalt them. *Savary.*

We invent new ſauces and pickles, which reſemble the animal ferment in taſte and virtue, as the ſalſo-acid gravies of meat; the ſalt pickles of fiſh, *anchovies*, oyſters. *Floyer on the Humours.*

A'NCIENT. *adj.* [*ancien*, Fr. *antiquus*, Lat.]

1. Old; that happened long ſince; of old time; not modern. *Ancient* and *old* are diſtinguiſhed; *old* relates to the duration of the thing itſelf, as, an *old* coat, a coat much worn; and *ancient*, to time in general, as, an *ancient* dreſs, a habit uſed in former times. But this is not always obſerved; for we mention *old cuſtoms*; but though old be ſometimes oppoſed to *modern*, *ancient* is ſeldom oppoſed to *new*.

Ancient tenure is that whereby all the manours belonging to the crown, in St. Edward's or William the Conquerour's days, did hold. The number and names of which manours, as all others belonging to common perſons, he cauſed to be written in a book, after a ſurvey made of them, now remaining in the exchequer, and called doomſday book; and ſuch as by that book appeared to have belonged to the crown at that time, are called *ancient* demeſnes. *Cowell.*

2. Old; that has been of long duration.

With the *ancient* is wiſdom, and in length of days underſtanding. *Job*, xii. 12.

Thales affirms, that God comprehended all things, and that God was of all things the moſt *ancient*, becauſe he never had any beginning. *Raleigh's Hiſtory of the World.*

Induſtry
Gave the tall *ancient* foreſt too his axe. *Thomſon's Summer.*

3. Paſt; former.

I ſee thy fury: if I longer ſtay,
We ſhall begin our *ancient* bickerings. *Shakeſp. Henry* VI.

A'NCIENT. *n. ſ.* [from *ancient*, *adj.*] Thoſe that lived in old time were called *ancients*, oppoſed to the moderns.

And though the *ancients* thus their rules invade,
As kings diſpenſe with laws themſelves have made;
Moderns, beware! or if you muſt offend
Againſt the precept, ne'er tranſgreſs its end. *Pop. Eſſ. on Crit.*

A'NCIENT. *n. ſ.* The flag or ſtreamer of a ſhip, and, formerly, of a regiment.

A'NCIENT. *n. ſ.* The bearer of a flag, as was *Ancient Piſtol*; whence in preſent uſe, enſign.

A'NCIENTLY. *adv.* [from *ancient.*] In old times.

Not far from this is the great city of Trebiſond, which, with the territory about it, *anciently* pertained unto this crown; now unjuſtly poſſeſſed, and as unjuſtly abuſed, by thoſe who have neither title to hold it, nor virtue to rule it. *Sidney, b.* ii.

The colewort is not an enemy, though that were *anciently* received, to the vine only; but it is an enemy to any other plant, becauſe it draweth ſtrongly the fatteſt juice of the earth. *Bacon's Natural Hiſtory*, N° 480.

A'NCIENTNESS. *n. ſ.* [from *ancient.*] Antiquity; exiſtence from old times.

The Feſcenine and Saturnian were the ſame; they were called Saturnian from their *ancientneſs*, when Saturn reigned in Italy. *Dryden's Dedication to Juvenal.*

A'NCIENTRY. *n. ſ.* [from *ancient.*] The honour of ancient lineage; the dignity of birth.

Of all nations under heaven, the Spaniard is the moſt mingled, and moſt uncertain. Wherefore, moſt fooliſhly do the Iriſh think to ennoble themſelves, by wreſting their *ancientry* from the Spaniard, who is unable to derive himſelf from any in certain. *Spenſer on Ireland.*

There is nothing in the between, but getting wenches with child, wronging the *ancientry*, ſtealing, fighting. *Shakeſp. Winter's Tale.*

ANCLE. See ANKLE.

A'NCONY. *n. ſ.* [in the iron mills.] A bloom wrought into the figure of a flat iron bar, about three foot long, with two ſquare rough knobs, one at each end. *Chambers.*

AND. *conjunction.*

1. The particle by which ſentences or terms are joined, which it is not eaſy to explain by any ſynonimous word.

Sure his honeſty
Got him ſmall gains, but ſhameleſs flattery
And filthy beverage, *and* unſeemly thift,
And borrow baſe, *and* ſome good lady's gift. *Spenſ. Hubb.*

What ſhall I do to be for ever known,
And make the age to come my own? *Cowley.*

The Danes unconquer'd offspring march behind;
And Morini, the laſt of human kind. *Dryd.*

It ſhall ever be my ſtudy to make diſcoveries of this nature in human life, *and* to ſettle the proper diſtinctions between the virtues *and* perfections of mankind, *and* thoſe falſe colours *and* reſemblances of them that ſhine alike in the eyes of the vulgar. *Addiſon. Tatler.*

2. *And* ſometimes ſignifies *though*, and ſeems a contraction of *and if.*

It is the nature of extreme ſelf-lovers, as they will ſet an houſe on fire, *and* it were but to roaſt their eggs. *Bacon.*

3. In *and if*, the *and* is redundant, and is omitted by all later writers.

I pray thee, Launce, *an' if* thou ſeeſt my boy,
Bid him make haſte. *Shakeſp. Two Gentlemen of Verona.*

A'NDIRON. *n. ſ.* [ſuppoſed by *Skinner* to be corrupted from *hand-iron*; an iron that may be moved by the hand, or may ſupply the place of a hand.] Irons at the end of a fire-grate, in which the ſpit turns; or irons in which wood is laid to burn.

If you ſtrike an entire body, as an *andiron* of braſs, at the top, it maketh a more treble ſound, and at the bottom a baſer. *Bacon's Natural Hiſtory*, N° 178.

ANDRO'GYNAL. *adj.* [from ἀνὴρ and γυνὴ.] Having two ſexes; hermaphroditical.

ANDRO'GYNALLY. *adv.* [from *androgynal.*] In the form of hermaphrodites; with two ſexes.

The examples hereof have undergone no real or new tranſexion, but were *androgynally* born, and under ſome kind of hermaphrodites. *Brown's Vulgar Errours, b.* iii.

ANDRO'-

Andro'gynous. *adj.* The ſame with *androgynal.*

ANDRO'GYNUS. *n. ſ.* [Lat. See Androgynal.] An hermaphrodite; one that is of both ſexes.

Andro'tomy. *n. ſ.* [from ἀνὴρ and τέμνω.] The practice of cutting human bodies. *Dict.*

A'necdote. *n. ſ.* [ἀνέκδοτον.] Something yet unpubliſhed; ſecret hiſtory.

Some modern *anecdotes* aver,
He nodded in his elbow-chair. *Prior.*

Anemo'graphy. *n. ſ.* [ἄνεμος and γράφω.] The deſcription of the winds.

Anemo'meter. *n. ſ.* [ἄνεμος and μέτρον.] An inſtrument contrived to meaſure the ſtrength or velocity of the wind.

ANE'MONE. *n. ſ.* [ἀνεμώνη.] The wind flower.

Upon the top of its ſingle ſtalk, ſurrounded by a leaf, is produced one naked flower, of many petals, with many ſtamina in the center; the ſeeds are collected into an oblong head, and ſurrounded with a copious down. The principal colours in *anemonies*, are white, red, blue, and purple ſometimes curiouſly intermixed. *Millar.*

Wind flowers are diſtinguiſhed into thoſe with broad and hard leaves, and thoſe with narrow and ſoft ones; of both which ſorts there are great variety of colours, ſome being double, and others ſingle flowered. The broad leaved *anemony* roots ſhould be planted about the end of September, and the ſmall eminences which put forth the leaves ſet uppermoſt. Theſe with ſmall leaves muſt be ſet after the ſame manner, but not put into the ground till the end of October. *Mortimer's Art of Husbandry.*

From the ſoft wing of vernal breezes ſhed,
Anemonies, auriculas, enrich'd
With ſhining meal o'er all their velvet leaves. *Thomſon.*

A'nemoscope. *n. ſ.* [ἄνεμος and σκόπος.] A machine invented to foretel the changes of the wind. It has been obſerved, that hygroſcopes made of cat's gut proved very good *anemoſcopes*, ſeldom failing, by the turning the index about, to foretel the ſhifting of the wind. *Chambers.*

Ane'nt. *prep.* A word uſed in the Scotch dialect.

1. Concerning; about; as, *he ſaid nothing* anent *this particular.*
2. Over againſt; oppoſite to; as, *he lives* anent *the market-houſe.*

Anes. } *n. ſ.* The ſpires or beards of corn. *Dict.*
Awns. }

A'neurism. *n. ſ.* [ἀνευρύνω.] A diſeaſe of the arteries, in which, either by a preternatural weakneſs of any part of them, they become exceſſively dilated, or by a wound through their coats, the blood is extravaſated amongſt the adjacent cavities. *Sharp's Surgery.*

In the orifice, there was a throbbing of the arterial blood, as in an *aneuriſm.* *Wiſeman's Surgery.*

Ane'w. *adv.* [from *a* and *new.*]

1. Over again; another time; repeatedly. This is the moſt common uſe.

Nor, if at miſchief taken, on the ground
Be ſlain, but pris'ners to the pillar bound,
At either barrier plac'd; nor, captives made,
Be freed, or, arm'd *anew*, the fight invade. *Dryden's Fables.*

That as in birth, in beauty you excel,
The muſe might dictate, and the poet tell:
Your art no other art can ſpeak; and you
To ſhow how well you play, muſt play *anew.* *Prior.*

The miſeries of the civil war did, for many years, deter the inhabitants of our iſland from the thoughts of engaging *anew* in ſuch deſperate undertakings. *Addiſon's Freeholder,* Nº 28.

2. Newly; in a new manner.

He who begins late, is obliged to form *anew* the whole diſpoſition of his ſoul, to acquire new habits of life, to practiſe duties to which he is utterly a ſtranger. *Rogers's Sermons.*

Anfra'ctuose. } *adj.* [from *anfractus*, Lat.] Winding; mazy;
Anfra'ctuous. } full of turnings and winding paſſages.

Behind the drum are ſeveral vaults and *anfractuoſe* cavities in the ear-bone, ſo to intend the leaſt ſound imaginable, that the ſenſe might be affected with it; as we ſee in ſubterraneous caves and vaults, how the ſound is redoubled. *Ray.*

Anfra'ctuousness. *n. ſ.* [from *anfractuous.*] Fulneſs of windings and turnings.

Anfra'cture. *n. ſ.* [from *anfractus*, Lat.] A turning; a mazy winding and turning. *Dict.*

A'NGEL. *n. ſ.* [Ἄγγελος; *angelus*, Lat.]

1. Originally a meſſenger. A ſpirit employed by God in the adminiſtration of human affairs.

Some holy *angel*
Fly to the court of England, and unfold
His meſſage ere he come. *Shakeſpeare's Macbeth.*

Had we ſuch a knowledge of the conſtitution of man, as it is poſſible *angels* have, and it is certain his Maker has; we ſhould have a quite other idea of his eſſence. *Locke.*

See Hierarchy.

2. *Angel* is ſometimes uſed in a bad ſenſe; as, *angels of darkneſs.*

And they had a king over them, which was the *angel* of the bottomleſs pit. *Revelat.* ix. 11.

3. *Angel*, in ſcripture, ſometimes means *man of God, prophet.*
4. *Angel* is uſed, in the ſtile of love, for a beautiful perſon.

A N G

Heav'n bleſs thee!
Thou haſt the ſweeteſt face I ever look'd on.
Sir, as I have a ſoul, ſhe is an *angel.* *Shakeſp. Henry* VIII.

5. A piece of money anciently coined and impreſſed with an angel, in memory of an obſervation of Pope Gregory, that the pagan *Angli*, or Engliſh, were ſo beautiful, that, if they were chriſtians, they would be *Angeli*, or *angels.* The coin was rated at ten ſhillings.

Take an empty baſon, put an *angel* of gold, or what you will, into it; then go ſo far from the baſon, till you cannot ſee the *angel*, becauſe it is not in a right line; then fill the baſon with water, and you will ſee it out of its place, becauſe of the reflection. *Bacon's Natural Hiſtory,* Nº 762.

Couſin, away for England; haſte before,
And, ere our coming, ſee thou ſhake the bags
Of hoarding abbots; their impriſon'd *angels*
Set thou at liberty. *Shakeſpeare's King John.*

A'ngel. *adj.* Reſembling angels; angelical.

I have mark'd
A thouſand bluſhing apparitions
To ſtart into her face; a thouſand innocent ſhames
In *angel* whiteneſs bear away thoſe bluſhes. *Shakeſpeare's Much ado about Nothing.*

Or virgins viſited by *angel* powers,
With golden crowns and wreathes of heav'nly flow'rs. *Pope's Rape of the Lock.*

A'ngel-like. *adj.* [from *angel* and *like.*] Reſembling an angel.

In heav'n itſelf thou ſure wer't dreſt
With that *angel-like* diſguiſe. *Waller.*

A'ngel shot. *n. ſ.* [from *angel* and *ſhot.*] Chain ſhot, being a cannon bullet cut in two, and the halves being joined together by a chain. *Dict.*

ANGE'LICA. *n. ſ.* [Lat. *ab angelica virtute.*] The name of a plant.

It has winged leaves divided into large ſegments; its ſtalks are hollow and jointed; the flowers grow in an umbel upon the tops of the ſtalks, and conſiſt of five leaves, ſucceeded by two large channelled ſeeds.

The ſpecies are, 1. Common or manured *angelica.* 2. Greater wild *angelica.* 3. Shining Canada *angelica.* 4. Mountain perennial *angelica*, with columbine leaves.

The common *angelica* delights to grow in a very moiſt ſoil, and its ſeeds ſhould be ſown ſoon after it is ripe. This plant is uſed in medicine, as are its ſeeds; and the confectioners make a ſweetmeat with its tender ſtalks, cut in May. The ſecond ſort grows wild; and the two laſt ſorts may be propagated like the firſt. *Millar.*

ANGE'LICA. (Berry-bearing) [*Aralia*, Lat.]

The flower conſiſts of many leaves, expanding in form of a roſe, which are naked, growing on the top of the ovary: theſe flowers are ſucceeded by globular fruits, which are ſoft and ſucculent, and full of oblong ſeeds.

The ſpecies are, 1. Canada berry-bearing *angelica.* 2. Berry-bearing *angelica*, with a naked ſtalk and creeping root. 3. *Angelica* tree.

The two firſt are propagated either by ſowing their ſeeds, or by parting of their roots. The third ſort grows with us to the height of ſeven or eight feet, and is only propagated by ſeeds, which are frequently brought from America. *Millar.*

Ange'lical. *adj.* [*angelicus*, Lat.]

1. Reſembling angels.

It diſcovereth unto us the glorious works of God, and carrieth up, with an *angelical* ſwiftneſs, our eyes, that our mind, being informed of his viſible marvels, may continually travel upward. *Raleigh's Hiſtory of the World.*

2. Partaking of the nature of angels.

Others more mild
Retreated in a ſilent valley, ſing
With notes *angelical* to many a harp,
Their own heroick deeds, and hapleſs fall
By doom of battle. *Milton's Paradiſe Loſt, b.* ii.

3. Belonging to angels.

It may be encouragement to conſider the pleaſure of ſpeculations, which do raviſh and ſublime the thoughts with more clear *angelical* contentments. *Wilkins's Dædalus.*

Ange'licalness. *n. ſ.* [from *angelical.*] The quality of being angelical; reſemblance of angels; excellence more than human.

Ange'lick. *adj.* [*angelicus*, Lat.] Partaking of the nature of angels; angelical; above human.

Here, happy creature, fair *angelick* Eve,
Partake thou alſo. *Milton's Paradiſe Loſt, b.* v.

My fancy form'd thee of *angelick* kind,
Some emanation of th' all beauteous mind. *Pop. Elo. to Abel.*

A'ngelot. *n. ſ.* A muſical inſtrument, ſomewhat reſembling a lute. *Dict.*

A'NGER. *n. ſ.* [a word of no certain etymology, but, with moſt probability, derived by *Skinner* from anᵹe, Sax. *vexed*; which, however, ſeems to come originally from the Latin *ango.*]

1. *Anger* is uneaſineſs or diſcompoſure of the mind, upon the receipt of any injury, with a preſent purpoſe of revenge. *Locke.*

Anger

Anger is like
A full hot horſe, who being allow'd his way,
Self-mettle tires him. *Shakeſp. Henry* VIII.

Was the Lord diſpleaſed againſt the rivers? was thine *anger* againſt the rivers? was thy wrath againſt the ſea, that thou didſt ride upon thine horſes and thy chariots of ſalvation? *Habb.* iii. 8.

Anger is, according to ſome, a tranſient hatred, or at leaſt very like it. *South.*

2. Pain, or ſmart, of a ſore or ſwelling. In this ſenſe it ſeems plainly deducible from *angor.*

I made the experiment, ſetting the moxa where the firſt violence of my pain began, and where the greateſt *anger* and ſoreneſs ſtill continued, notwithſtanding the ſwelling of my foot. *Temple's Miſcellanies.*

To A'NGER. *v. a.* [from the noun.] To make angry; to provoke; to enrage.

Who would *anger* the meaneſt artiſan, which carrieth a good mind? *Hooker, b.* iv. § 12.

Sometimes he *angers* me,
With telling me of the moldwarp and the ant.
Shakeſp. Henry IV. *p.* i.

There were ſome late taxes and impoſitions introduced, which rather *angered* than grieved the people. *Clarendon.*

It *anger'd* Turenne, once upon a day,
To ſee a footman kick'd that took his pay. *Pope's Dial.* ii.

A'NGERLY. *adv.* [from *anger.*] In an angry manner; like one offended.

Why, how now, Hecat, you look *angerly. Shak. Macbeth.*

Such jeſter's diſhoneſt indiſcretion, is rather charitably to be pitied, than their exception either *angerly* to be grieved at, or ſeriouſly to be confuted. *Carew's Survey of Cornwal.*

ANGIO'GRAPHY. *n. ſ.* [from ἀγγεῖον and γράφω.] A deſcription of veſſels in the human body; nerves, veins, arteries, and lymphaticks.

ANGIO'LOGY. *n. ſ.* [from ἀγγεῖον and λόγος.] A treatiſe or diſcourſe of the veſſels of a human body.

ANGIOMONOSPE'RMOUS. *adj.* [from ἀγγεῖον, μόνος, and σπέρμα.] Such plants as have but one ſingle ſeed in the ſeed-pod.

ANGIO'TOMY. *n. ſ.* [from ἀγγεῖον and τέμνω, to cut.] A cutting open of the veſſels, as in the opening of a vein or artery.

A'NGLE. *n. ſ.* [*angle,* Fr. *angulus,* Lat.] The ſpace intercepted between two lines interſecting each other.

Angle of the centre of a circle, is an *angle* whoſe vertex, or angular point is at the centre of a circle, and whoſe legs are two ſemidiameters of that circle. *Stone's Dict.*

A'NGLE. *n. ſ.* [*angel,* Germ. and Dutch.] An inſtrument to take fiſh, conſiſting of a rod, a line, and a hook.

She alſo had an *angle* in her hand; but the taker was ſo taken, that ſhe had forgotten taking. *Sidney.*

Give me mine *angle,* we'll to the river there,
My muſick playing far off, I will betray
Tawny finn'd fiſh; my bended hook ſhall pierce
Their ſlimy jaws. *Shakeſp. Antony and Cleopatra.*

The patient fiſher takes his ſilent ſtand,
Intent, his *angle* trembling in his hand;
With looks unmov'd, he hopes the ſcaly breed,
And eyes the dancing cork, and bending reed. *Pop. Windſ.*

To A'NGLE. *v. n.* [from the noun.]

1. To fiſh with a rod and hook.

The ladies *angling* in the cryſtal lake,
Feaſt on the waters with the prey they take. *Waller.*

2. To try to gain by ſome inſinuating artifices, as fiſhes are caught by a bait.

By this face,
This ſeeming brow of juſtice, did he win
The hearts of all that he did *angle* for. *Shak. Henry* IV.

The pleaſant'ſt angling is to ſee the fiſh
Cut with her golden oars the ſilver ſtream,
And greedily devour the treacherous bait;
So *angle* we for Beatrice. *Shak. Much ado about Nothing.*

A'NGLE-ROD. *n. ſ.* [*angel roede,* Dutch.] The ſtick to which the line and hook are hung.

It differeth much in greatneſs; the ſmalleſt being fit for thatching of houſes; the ſecond bigneſs is uſed for *angle-rods,* and, in China, for beating of offenders upon the thighs. *Bacon's Natural Hiſtory,* N° 656.

He makes a May-fly to a miracle, and furniſhes the whole country with *angle-rods.* *Addiſon. Spectator,* N° 108.

A'NGLER. *n. ſ.* [from *angle.*] He that fiſhes with an angle.

He, like a patient *angler,* ere he ſtrook,
Would let them play a while upon the hook. *Dryden.*

Neither do birds alone, but many ſorts of fiſhes, feed upon inſects; as is well known to *anglers,* who bait their hooks with them. *Ray on the Creation.*

A'NGLICISM. *n. ſ.* [from *Anglus,* Lat.] A form of ſpeech peculiar to the Engliſh language; an Engliſh idiom.

A'NGOBER. *n. ſ.* A kind of pear. See PEAR.

A'NGRILY. *adv.* [from *angry.*] In an angry manner; furiouſly; peeviſhly.

I will ſit as quiet as a lamb;
I will not ſtir, nor wince, nor ſpeak a word,
Nor look upon the iron *angrily.* *Shakeſp. King John.*

A'NGRY. *adj.* [from *anger.*]

1. Touched with anger; provoked.

Oh let not the Lord be *angry,* and I will ſpeak: peradventure there ſhall be thirty found there. *Gen.* xviii. 30.

2. It ſeems properly to require, when the object of anger is mentioned, the particle *at* before a thing, and *with* before a perſon; but this is not always obſerved.

Your Coriolanus is not much miſſed, but with his friends; the commonwealth doth ſtand, and ſo would do, were he *angry at* it. *Shakeſpeare's Coriolanus.*

Now therefore be not grieved, nor *angry with* yourſelves, that ye ſold me hither: for God did ſend me before you to preſerve life. *Gen.* xlv. 5.

I think it a vaſt pleaſure, that whenever two people of merit regard one another, ſo many ſcoundrels envy and are *angry at* them. *Swift.*

3. Having the appearance of anger; having the effect of anger.

The north wind driveth away rain: ſo doth an *angry* countenance a backbiting tongue. *Prov.* xxv. 23.

4. In chirurgery, painful; inflamed; ſmarting.

This ſerum, being accompanied by the thinner parts of the blood, grows red and *angry;* and, wanting its due regreſs into the maſs, firſt gathers into a hard ſwelling, and, in a few days, ripens into matter, and ſo diſchargeth. *Wiſeman's Surgery.*

A'NGUISH. *n. ſ.* [*angoiſſe,* Fr. *angor,* Lat.] Exceſſive pain either of mind or body; applied to the mind, it means the pain of *ſorrow,* and is ſeldom uſed to ſignify other paſſions.

Not all ſo cheerful ſeemed ſhe of ſight,
As was her ſiſter; whether dread did dwell,
Or *anguiſh* in her heart, is hard to tell. *Fairy Queen, b.* i.

Virtue's but *anguiſh,* when 'tis ſeveral,
By occaſion wak'd, and circumſtantial;
True virtue's ſoul, always in all deeds all. *Donne.*

They had perſecutors, whoſe invention was as great as their cruelty. Wit and malice conſpired to find out ſuch deaths, and thoſe of ſuch incredible *anguiſh,* that only the manner of dying was the puniſhment, death itſelf the deliverance. *South.*

Perpetual *anguiſh* fills his anxious breaſt,
Not ſtopt by buſineſs, nor compos'd by reſt;
No muſick cheers him, nor no feaſt can pleaſe. *Dryd. Juv.*

A'NGUISHED. *adj.* [from *anguiſh.*] Seized with anguiſh; tortured; exceſſively pained.

Feel no touch
Of conſcience, but of fame, and be
Anguiſh'd, not that 'twas ſin, but that 'twas ſhe. *Donne.*

A'NGULAR. *adj.* [from *angle.*] Having angles or corners; cornered.

As for the figure of cryſtal, it is for the moſt part hexagonal, or ſix cornered, being built upon a confuſed matter, from whence, as it were from a root, *angular* figures ariſe, even as in the amethyſt and baſaltes. *Brown's Vulgar Errours, b.* ii.

The diſtance of the edges of the knives from one another, a the diſtance of four inches from the *angular* point, where the edges of the knives meet, was the eight part of an inch. *Newton's Opticks.*

ANGULA'RITY. *n. ſ.* [from *angular.*] The quality of being angular, or having corners.

A'NGULARLY. *adv.* [from *angular.*] With angles or corners.

Another part of the ſame ſolution afforded us an ice *angularly* figured. *Boyle.*

A'NGULARNESS. *n. ſ.* [from *angular.*] The quality of being angular.

A'NGULATED. *adj.* [from *angle.*] Formed with angles or corners.

Topazes, amethyſts, or emeralds, which grow in the fiſſures, are ordinarily cryſtallized, or ſhot into *angulated* figures; whereas, in the ſtrata, they are found in rude lumps, like yellow, purple, and green pebbles. *Woodward's Nat. Hiſtory.*

ANGULO'SITY. *n. ſ.* [from *angulous.*] Angularity; cornered form. *Dict.*

A'NGULOUS. *adj.* [from *angle.*] Hooked; angular.

Nor can it be a difference, that the parts of ſolid bodies are held together by hooks, and *angulous* involutions; ſince the coherence of the parts of theſe will be of as difficult a conception. *Glanville's Scepſis Scientifica.*

ANGU'ST. *adj.* [*anguſtus,* Lat.] Narrow; ſtrait. *Dict.*

ANGUSTA'TION. *n. ſ.* [from *anguſtus.*] The act of making narrow; ſtraitening; the ſtate of being narrowed.

The cauſe may be referred either to the grumouſneſs of the blood, or to obſtruction of the vein ſomewhere in its paſſage, by ſome *anguſtation* upon it by part of the tumour. *Wiſeman.*

ANHELA'TION. *n. ſ.* [*anhelo,* Lat.] The act of panting; the ſtate of being out of breath.

ANHELO'SE. *adj.* [*anhelus,* Lat.] Out of breath; panting; labouring of being out of breath. *Dict.*

A'NIENTED. *adj.* [*anneantir,* Fr.] Fruſtrated; brought to nothing.

ANI'GHTS. *adv.* [from *a* for *at,* and *night.*] In the night time.

Sir Toby, you muſt come in earlier *anights;* your niece, my lady, takes great exceptions at your ill hours. *Shakeſp. Twelfth Night.*

A'NIL. *n. ſ.* The ſhrub from whoſe leaves and ſtalks indigo is prepared.

ANI'LENESS. } *n. ſ.* [*anilitas*, Lat.] The ſtate of being an old
ANI'LITY. } woman; the old age of women.

A'NIMABLE. *adj.* [from *animate.*] That which may be put into life, or receive animation. *Dict.*

ANIMADVE'RSION. *n. ſ.* [*animadverſio*, Lat.]

1. Reproof; ſevere cenſure; blame.

He diſmiſſed their commiſſioners with ſevere and ſharp *animadverſions.* *Clarendon, b.* viii.

2. Puniſhment. When the object of *animadverſion* is mentioned, it has the particle *on* or *upon* before it.

When a bill is debating in parliament, it is uſual to have the controverſy handled by pamphlets on both ſides; without the leaſt *animadverſion upon* the authours. *Swift.*

3. In law.

An eccleſiaſtical cenſure, and an eccleſiaſtical *animadverſion*, are different things; for a cenſure has a relation to a ſpiritual puniſhment, but an *animadverſion* has only a reſpect to a temporal one; as, degradation, and the delivering the perſon over to the ſecular court. *Ayliffe's Parergon Juris Canonici.*

ANIMADVE'RSIVE. *adj.* [from *animadvert.*] That has the power of judging.

The repreſentation of objects to the ſoul, the only *animadverſive* principle, are conveyed by motions made on the immediate organs of ſenſe. *Glanville's Scepſis Scientifica, c.* 12.

ANIMADVE'RSIVENESS. *n. ſ.* [from *animadverſive.*] The power of animadverting, or making judgment. *Dict.*

To ANIMADVERT. *v. n.* [*animadverto*, Lat.]

1. To paſs cenſures upon.

I ſhould not *animadvert on* him, who was otherwiſe a painful obſerver of the decorum of the ſtage, if he had not uſed extreme ſeverity in his judgment of the incomparable Shakeſpeare for that fault. *Dryden on Dramatick Poeſy.*

2. To inflict puniſhments. In both ſenſes with the particle *upon.*

If the Authour of the univerſe *animadverts upon* men here below, how much more will it become him to do it upon their entrance into a higher ſtate of being. *Grew's Coſmolog. Sacra.*

ANIMADVE'RTER. *n. ſ.* [from *animadvert.*] He that paſſes cenſures, or inflicts puniſhments.

God is a ſtrict obſerver of, and a ſevere *animadverter upon*, ſuch as preſume to partake of thoſe myſteries, without ſuch a preparation. *South.*

A'NIMAL. *n. ſ.* [*animal*, Lat.]

1. A living creature corporeal, diſtinct, on the one ſide, from pure ſpirit, on the other, from mere matter.

Animals are ſuch beings, which, beſides the power of growing, and producing their like, as plants and vegetables have, are endowed alſo with ſenſation and ſpontaneous motion. Mr. *Ray* gives two ſchemes of tables of them.

Animals are either
- Sanguineous, that is, ſuch as have blood, which breathe either by
  - Lungs, having either
    - Two ventricles in their heart, and thoſe either
      - Viviparous,
        - Aquatick, as the whale kind,
        - Terreſtrial, as quadrupeds;
      - Oviparous, as birds.
    - But one ventricle in the heart, as frogs, tortoiſes, and ſerpents.
  - Gills, as all ſanguineous fiſhes, except the whale kind.
- Exſanguineous, or without blood, which may be divided into
  - Greater, and thoſe either,
    - Naked,
      - Terreſtrial, as naked ſnails.
      - Aquatick, as the poulp, cuttle-fiſh, &c.
    - Covered with a tegument, either
      - Cruſtaceous, as lobſters and crab-fiſh.
      - Teſtaceous, either
        - Univalve, as limpets;
        - Bivalve, as oyſters, muſcles, cockles;
        - Turbinate, as periwinkles, ſnails, &c.
  - Leſſer, as inſects of all ſorts.

Viviparous hairy *animals*, or quadrupeds, are either
- Hoofed, which are either
  - Whole-footed or hoofed, as the horſe and aſs;
  - Cloven-footed, having the hoof divided into
    - Two principal parts, called biſulca, either
      - Such as chew not the cud, as ſwine;
      - Ruminant, or ſuch as chew the cud; divided into
        - Such as have perpetual and hollow horns.
          - Beef-kind,
          - Sheep-kind,
          - Goat-kind.
        - Such as have ſolid, branched and deciduous horns, as the deer-kind.
    - Four parts, or quadriſulca, as the rhinoceros and hippopotamus.
- Clawed or digitate, having the foot divided into
  - Two parts or toes, having two nails, as the camel kind;
  - Many toes or claws; either
    - Undivided, as the elephant;
    - Divided, which have either
      - Broad nails, and an human ſhape, as apes;
      - Narrower, and more pointed nails, which, in reſpect of their teeth, are divided into ſuch as have
        - Many fore-teeth, or cutters in each jaw;
          - The greater, which have
            - A ſhorter ſnout and rounder head, as the cat-kind;
            - A longer ſnout and head, as the dog-kind.
          - The leſſer, the vermin or weazel kind
        - Only two large and remarkable fore-teeth, all which are phytivorous, and are called the hare kind. *Ray.*

Vegetables are proper enough to repair *animals*, as being near of the ſame ſpecifick gravity with the animal juices, and as conſiſting of the ſame parts with animal ſubſtances, ſpirit, water, ſalt, oil, earth; all which are contained in the ſap they derive from the earth. *Arbuthnot on Aliments.*

Some of the animated ſubſtances have various organical or inſtrumental parts, fitted for a variety of motions from place to place, and a ſpring of life within themſelves, as beaſts, birds, fiſhes, and inſects; theſe are called *animals.* Other animated ſubſtances are called vegetables, which have within themſelves the principles of another ſort of life and growth, and of various productions of leaves and fruit, ſuch as we ſee in plants, herbs, and trees. *Watts's Logick.*

2. By way of contempt, we ſay of a ſtupid man, that he is a *ſtupid animal.*

A'NIMAL. *adj.* [*animalis*, Lat.]

1. That which belongs or relates to animals.

There are other things in the world of ſpirits, wherein our ideas are very dark and confuſed; ſuch as their union with *animal* nature, the way of their acting on material beings, and their converſe with each other. *Watts's Logick.*

2. *Animal* functions, diſtinguiſhed from *natural* and *vital*, are the lower powers of the mind, as, the will, memory, and imagination.

3. *Animal* life is oppoſed, on one ſide, to *intellectual*, and, on the other, to *vegetable.*

4. *Animal* is uſed in oppoſition to *ſpiritual* or *rational*; as, the *animal* nature.

ANIMA'LCULE. *n. ſ.* [*animalculum*, Lat.] A ſmall animal; particularly thoſe which are in their firſt and ſmalleſt ſtate.

We are to know, that they all come of the ſeed of *animalcules* of their own kind, that were before laid there. *Ray.*

ANIMA'LITY. *n. ſ.* [from *animal.*] The ſtate of animal exiſtence.

The word animal there only ſignifies human *animality.* In the minor propoſition, the word animal, for the ſame reaſon, ſignifies the *animality* of a gooſe: thereby it becomes an ambiguous term, and unfit to build the concluſion upon. *Watts.*

To A'NIMATE. *v. a.* [*animo*, Lat.]

1. To quicken; to make alive; to give life to: as, the ſoul *animates* the body; man muſt have been *animated* by a higher power.

2. To give powers to; to heighten the powers or effect of any thing.

But none, ah! none can *animate* the lyre,
And the mute ſtrings with vocal ſouls inſpire;
Whether the learn'd Minerva be her theme,
Or chaſte Diana bathing in the ſtream;
None can record their heav'nly praiſe ſo well
As Helen, in whoſe eyes ten thouſand Cupids dwell. *Dryd.*

3. To encourage; to incite.

The more to *animate* the people, he ſtood on high, from whence he might be beſt heard, and cried unto them with a loud voice. *Knolles's Hiſtory of the Turks.*

A'NIMATE. *adj.* [from *To animate.*] Alive; poſſeſſing animal life.

All bodies have ſpirits and pneumatical parts within them; but the main differences between *animate* and inanimate, are two: the firſt is, that the ſpirit of things *animate* are all contained within themſelves, and are branched in veins and ſecret canals, as blood is; and, in living creatures, the ſpirits have not only branches, but certain cells or ſeats, where the principal ſpirits do reſide, and whereunto the reſt do reſort: but the ſpirits in things inanimate are ſhut in, and cut off by the tangible parts, and are not pervious one to another, as air is in ſnow. *Bacon's Natural Hiſtory,* N° 601.

Nobler birth
Of creatures *animate* with gradual life,
Of growth, ſenſe, reaſon, all ſumm'd up in man.
Milton's Par. Loſt, b. ix. *l.* 112.

There are ſeveral topicks there uſed againſt the atheiſm and idolatry of the heathens; ſuch as the viſible marks of divine wiſdom and goodneſs in the works of the creation, the vital union of ſouls with matter, and the admirable ſtructure of *animate* bodies, and the like. *Bentley's Sermons.*

A'NIMATED. *participial adj.* [from *animate.*] Lively; vigorous.

Warriours ſhe fires with *animated* ſounds;
Pours balm into the bleeding lover's wounds. *Pope.*

A'NIMATENESS. *n. ſ.* [from *animate.*] The ſtate of being animated. *Dict.*

ANIMA'TION. *n. ſ.* [from *animate.*]

1. The act of animating or enlivening.

Plants or vegetables are the principal part of the third day's work. They are the first *producat*, which is the word of *animation*. *Bacon's Natural History, cent.* v.

2. The state of being enlivened.

A'NIMATIVE. *adj.* [from *animate.*] That which has the power of giving life, or animating.

ANIMA'TOR. *n. s.* [from *animate.*] That which gives life; that which implants a principle of life.

Those bodies being of a congenerous nature, do readily receive the impressions of their motor, and, if not fettered by their gravity, conform themselves to situations, wherein they best unite to their *animator*. *Brown's Vul. Err. b.* ii. *c.* 2.

ANIMO'SE. *adj.* [*animositas*, Lat.] Full of spirit; hot; vehement. *Dict.*

ANIMO'SENESS. *n. s.* [from *animose.*] Spirit; heat; vehemence of temper. *Dict.*

ANIMO'SITY. *n. s.* [*animositas*, Lat.] Vehemence of hatred; passionate malignity. It implies rather the disposition to break out into outrages, than the outrage itself.

They were sure to bring passion, *animosity*, and malice enough of their own, what evidence soever they had from others. *Clarendon, b.* viii.

If there is not some method found out for allaying these heats and *animosities* among the fair sex, one does not know to what outrages they may proceed. *Addison's Freeholder*, N° 23.

No religious sect ever carried their aversions for each other to greater heights than our state parties have done; who, the more to inflame their passions, have mixed religious and civil *animosities* together; borrowing one of their appellations from the church. *Swift on the Sentiments of a Church of England man.*

A'NISE. *n. s.* [*anisum*, Lat.] A species of apium or parsley, with large sweet scented seeds. This plant is not worth propagating in England for use, because the seeds can be had much better and cheaper from Italy. *Millar.*

The seed of this plant has a sweetish taste, intermixed with something pungent and bitter, is reputed an aromatick, and prescribed not barely as a carminative against wind, but also as a pectoral, stomachick, and digestive. *Chambers.*

Ye pay the tithe of mint, and *anise*, and cummin, and have omitted the weightier matters of the law, judgment, mercy, and faith: these ought ye to have done, and not to leave the other undone. *Matt.* xxv. 25.

A'NKER. *n. s.* [*ancker*, Dut.] A liquid measure chiefly used at Amsterdam. It is the fourth part of the awm, and contains two stekans: each stekan consists of sixteen mengles; the mengle being equal to two of our wine quarts. *Chambers.*

A'NKLE. *n. s.* [ancleop, Sax. *anckel*, Dutch.] The joint which joins the foot to the leg.

One of his *ankles* was much swelled and ulcerated on the inside, in several places. *Wiseman.*

My simple system shall suppose,
That Alma enters at the toes;
That then she mounts by just degrees
Up to the *ankles*, legs and knees. *Prior.*

A'NKLE-BONE. *n. s.* [from *ankle* and *bone.*] The bone of the ankle.

The shin-bone, from the knee to the instep, is made by shadowing one half of the leg with a single shadow, the *ankle-bone* will shew itself by a shadow given underneath, as the knee. *Peacham on Drawing.*

A'NNALIST. *n. s.* [from *annals.*] A writer of annals.

I wonder my author should be offended, especially since their own *annalist* has given the same title to that of *Syrmium*. *Atterb.*

A'NNALS. *n. s. without singular number.* [*annales*, Lat.] Histories digested in the exact order of time; narratives in which every event is recorded under its proper year.

Could you with patience hear, or I relate,
O nymph! the tedious *annals* of our fate!
Through such a train of woes if I should run,
The day wou'd sooner than the tale be done! *Dryd. Virg.*

We are assured, by many glorious examples in the *annals* of our religion, that every one, in the like circumstances of distress, will not act and argue thus; but thus will every one be tempted to act. *Rogers's Sermons.*

A'NNATS. *n. s. without singular.* [*annates*, Lat.]

1. First fruits; because the rate of first fruits paid of spiritual livings, is after one year's profit. *Cowell.*
2. Masses said in the Romish church for the space of a year, or for any other time, either for the soul of a person deceased, or for the benefit of a person living. *Ayliffe's Parergon.*

To ANNE'AL. *v. a.* [ælan, to heat, Saxon.]

1. To heat glass, that the colours laid on it may pierce through.

But when thou dost *anneal* in glass thy story,
——— ——— then the light and glory
More rev'rend grows, and more doth win,
Which else shews wat'rish, bleak, and thin. *Herbert.*

When you purpose to *anneal*, take a plate of iron made fit for the oven; or, for want thereof, take a blue stone, which being made fit for the aforesaid oven, lay it upon the cross bars of iron. *Peacham on Drawing.*

Which her own inward symmetry reveal'd,
And like a picture shone, in glass *anneal'd*. *Dryden's Fables.*

2. To heat glass after it is blown, that it may not break.
3. To heat any thing in such a manner as to give it the true temper.

To ANNE'X. *v. a.* [*annecto*, *annexum*, Lat. *annexer*, Fr.]

1. To unite to at the end; as, he *annexed* a codicil to his will.
2. To unite; as, a smaller thing to a greater; as, he *annexed* a province to his kingdom.
3. To unite *à posteriori*; annexion always presupposing something: thus we may say, punishment is *annexed* to guilt; but not guilt to punishment.

Concerning fate or destiny, of which the opinions of those learned men, that have written thereof, may be safely received, had they not thereunto *annexed* and fastened an inevitable necessity, and made it more general and universally powerful than it is. *Raleigh's History of the World.*

Nations will decline so low
From virtue, which is reason, that no wrong,
But justice, and some fatal curse *annex'd*,
Deprives them of their outward liberty. *Milton's Par. Lost.*

I mean not the authority, which is *annexed* to your office; I speak of that only which is inborn and inherent to your person. *Dryden's Juvenal, Dedication.*

He cannot but love virtue wherever it is, and *annex* happiness always to the exercise of it. *Atterbury's Sermons.*

The temporal reward is *annexed* to the bare performance of the action, but the eternal to the obedience. *Rogers's Sermons.*

ANNE'X. *n. s.* [from *To annex.*] The thing annexed; additament. *Blount.*

Failing in his first attempt to be but like the highest in heaven, he hath obtained of men to be the same on earth, and hath accordingly assumed the *annexes* of divinity. *Brown's Vulgar Errours, b.* i. *c.* 10.

ANNEXA'TION. *n. s.* [from *annex.*]

1. Conjunction; addition.

If we can return to that charity and peaceable mindedness, which Christ so vehemently recommends to us, we have his own promise, that the whole body will be full of light. *Matt.* vi. that all other christian virtues will, by way of concomitance or *annexation*, attend them. *Hammond's Fundamentals.*

2. Union; coalition; conjunction.

How these *annexations* of benefices first came into the church, whether by the prince's authority, or the pope's licence, is a very great dispute. *Ayliffe's Parergon Juris Canonici.*

ANNE'XION. *n. s.* [from *annex.*] The act of annexing; addition.

It is necessary to engage the fears of men, by the *annexion* of such penalties as will overbalance temporal pleasure. *Rogers.*

ANNE'XMENT. *n. s.* [from *annex.*]

1. The act of annexing.
2. The thing annexed.

When it falls,
Each small *annexment*, petty consequence,
Attends the boist'rous ruin. *Shakespeare's Hamlet.*

ANNI'HILABLE. *adj.* [from *annihilate.*] That which may be reduced to nothing; that which may be put out of existence.

To ANNI'HILATE. *v. a.* [*ad* and *nihilum*, Lat.]

1. To reduce to nothing; to put out of existence.

It is impossible for any body to be utterly *annihilated*; but that as it was the work of the omnipotency of God, to make somewhat of nothing; so it requireth the like omnipotency to turn somewhat into nothing. *Bacon's Nat. Hist.* N° 100.

Thou taught'st me, by making me
Love her, who doth neglect both me and thee,
T' invent and practise this one way, t' *annihilate* all three. *Donne.*

He despaired of God's mercy; he, by a decollation of all hope, *annihilated* his mercy. *Brown's Vulgar Errours, b.* i. *c.* 2.

Whose friendship can stand against assaults, strong enough to *annihilate* the friendship of puny minds; such an one has reached true constancy. *South.*

Some imagined, water sufficient to a deluge was created, and, when the business was done, disbanded, and *annihilated*. *Woodward's Natural History.*

2. To destroy, so as to make the thing otherwise than it was.

The flood that hath altered, deformed, or rather *annihilated*, this place, so as no man can find any mark or memory thereof. *Raleigh's History of the World.*

3. To annul; to destroy the agency of any thing.

There is no reason, that any one commonwealth should *annihilate* that whereupon the whole world has agreed. *Hooker.*

ANNIHILA'TION. *n. s.* [from *annihilate.*] The act of reducing to nothing. The state of being reduced to nothing.

God hath his influence into the very essence of things, without which their utter *annihilation* could not choose but follow. *Hooker, b.* v. § 56.

That knowledge, which as spirits we obtain,
Is to be valu'd in the midst of pain:
Annihilation were to lose heav'n more:
We are not quite exil'd, where thought can soar. *Dryden.*

ANNIVE'RSARY. *n. s.* [*anniversarius*, Lat.]

1. A day celebrated as it returns in the course of the year.

For encouragement to follow the example of martyrs, the primitive

primitive christians met at the places of their martyrdom, to praise God for them, and to observe the *anniversary* of their sufferings. *Stillingfleet's Defence of Disc. on Romish Idolatry.*

2. The act of celebration, or performance, in honour of the anniversary day.

Donne had never seen Mrs. Drury, whom he has made immortal in his admirable *anniversaries.* *Dryden.*

3. *Anniversary* is an office in the Romish church, celebrated not only once a year, but which ought to be said daily through the year, for the soul of the deceased. *Ayliffe's Parergon.*

ANNIVE'RSARY. *adj.* [*anniversarius*, Lat.] Returning with the revolution of the year; annual; yearly.

The heaven whirled about with admirable celerity, most constantly finishing its *anniversary* vicissitudes. *Ray.*

They deny giving any worship to a creature, as inconsistent with christianity; but confess the honour and esteem for the martyrs, which they expressed by keeping their *anniversary* days, and recommending their example. *Stillingfl. Defence.*

A'NNO DOMINI. [Lat.] In the year of our Lord; as, *anno domini*, or *A. D.* 1751; that is, in the seventeen hundred and fifty first year from the birth of our Saviour.

ANNO'ISANCE. *n. s.* [from *annoy*, but not now in use.]

It hath a double signification, being as well for any hurt done either to a publick place, as highway, bridge, or common river, or to a private, by laying any thing that may breed infection, by encroaching, or such like means; as also, for the writ that is brought upon this transgression. See NUSANCE, the word now used. *Blount.*

A'NNOLIS. *n. s.* An American animal, like a lizard.

ANNOTA'TION. *n. s.* [*annotatio*, Lat.] Explications or remarks written upon books; notes.

It might appear very improper to publish *annotations*, without the text itself whereunto they relate. *Boyle.*

ANNOTA'TOR. *n. s.* [Lat.] A writer of notes, or annotations; a scholiast; a commentator.

I have not that respect for the *annotators*, which they generally meet with in the world. *Felton on the Classicks.*

To ANNO'UNCE. *v. a.* [*annoncer*, Fr. *annuncio*, Lat.]

1. To publish; to proclaim.

Of the Messiah I have heard foretold
By all the prophets; of thy birth at length
Announc'd by Gabriel with the first I knew. *Paradise Reg.*

2. To pronounce; to declare by a judicial sentence.

Those, mighty Jove, mean time, thy glorious care,
Who model nations, publish laws, *announce*
Or life or death. *Prior.*

To ANNO'Y. *v. a.* [*annoyer*, Fr.] To incommode; to vex; to teaze; to molest.

Woe to poor man; each outward thing *annoys* him;
He heaps in inward grief, that most destroys him. *Sidney.*

Her joyous presence and sweet company,
In full content he there did long enjoy;
Ne wicked envy, nor vile jealousy,
His dear delights were able to *annoy.* *Fairy Queen, b.* i.

As one who long in populous city pent,
Where houses thick, and sewers, *annoy* the air,
Forth issuing on a summer's morn to breathe
Among the pleasant villages, and farms
Adjoin'd, from each thing met conceives delight.
Milton's Paradise Lost, b. ix. *l.* 445.

Insects seldom use their offensive weapons, unless provoked: let them but alone, and *annoy* them not. *Ray on the Creation.*

ANNO'Y. *n. s.* [from the verb.] Injury; molestation; trouble.

Sleep, Richmond, sleep in peace, and wake in joy;
Good angels guard thee from the boar's *annoy.* *Shakesp. R.* III.

All pain and joy is in their way;
The things we fear bring less *annoy*
Than fear, and hope brings greater joy;
But in themselves they cannot stay. *Donne.*

What then remains, but, after past *annoy*,
To take the good vicissitude of joy. *Dryden's Fables.*

ANNO'YANCE. *n. s.* [from *annoy.*]

1. That which annoys; that which hurts.

A grain, a dust, a gnat, a wand'ring hair,
Any *annoyance* in that precious sense. *Shakesp. King John.*

Crows, ravens, rooks, and magpies, are great *annoyances* to corn. *Mortimer's Husbandry.*

2. The state of being annoyed; or act of annoying.

The spit venom of their poisoned hearts breaketh out to the *annoyance* of others. *Hooker, b.* v. § 2.

The greatest *annoyance* and disturbance of mankind, has been from one of those two things, force or fraud. *South.*

For the further *annoyance* and terrour of any besieged place, they would throw into it dead bodies. *Wilkins's Math. Mag.*

ANNO'YER. *n. s.* [from *To annoy.*] The person that annoys.

A'NNUAL. *adj.* [*annuel*, Fr. from *annus*, Lat.]

1. That which comes yearly.

Annual for me, the grape, the rose, renew,
The juice nectareous, and the balmy dew. *Pope's Ess. on M.*

2. That which is reckoned by the year.

The king's majesty
Does purpose honour to you; to which
A thousand pounds a year, *annual* support,
Out of his grace he adds. *Shakesp. Henry* VIII.

3. That which lasts only a year.

The dying in the winter of the roots of plants that are *annual*, seemeth to be caused by the over-expence of the sap; which being prevented, they will superannuate, if they stand warm. *Bacon's Natural History*, N° 448.

Every tree may, in some sense, be said to be an *annual* plant, both leaf, flower, and fruit, proceeding from the coat that was superinduced over the wood the last year. *Ray on the Creation.*

A'NNUALLY. *adv.* [from *annual.*] Yearly; every year.

By two drachms, they thought it sufficient to signify a heart; because the heart at one year weigheth two drachms, that is, a quarter of an ounce; and unto fifty years *annually* encreaseth the weight of one drachm. *Brown's Vulgar Errours, b.* v. *c.* 20.

The whole strength of a nation is the utmost that a prince can raise *annually* from his subjects. *Swift.*

ANNU'ITANT. *n. s.* [from *annuity.*] He that possesses or receives an annuity.

ANNU'ITY. *n. s.* [*annuité*, Fr.]

1. A yearly rent to be paid for term of life or years. The differences between a rent and an *annuity* are, that every rent is going out of land; but an *annuity* charges only the granter, or his heirs, that have assets by descent. The second difference is, that, for the recovery of an *annuity*, no action lies, but only the writ of *annuity* against the granter, his heirs, or successors; but of a rent, the same actions lie as do of land. The third difference is, that an *annuity* is never taken for assets, because it is no freehold in law; nor shall be put in execution upon a statute merchant, statute staple, or elegit, as a rent may. *Cowel.*

2. A yearly allowance.

He was generally known to be the son of one earl, and brother to another, who supplied his expence, beyond what his *annuity* from his father would bear. *Clarendon.*

To ANNU'L. *v. a.* [from *nullus.*]

1. To make void; to nullify; to abrogate; to abolish.

That which gives force to the law, is the authority that enacts it; and whoever destroys this authority, does, in effect, *annul* the law. *Rogers's Sermons.*

2. To reduce to nothing; to obliterate.

Light the pure work of God to me 's extinct,
And all her various objects of delight
Annull'd, which might in part my grief have eas'd.
Milton's Sampson Agonistes, l. 72.

A'NNULAR. *adj.* [from *annulus*, Lat.] In the form of a ring.

That they might not, in bending the arm or leg, rise up, he has tied them to the bones by *annular* ligaments. *Cheyne.*

A'NNULARY. *adj.* [from *annulus*, Lat.] In the form of rings.

Because continual respiration is necessary, the wind-pipe is made with *annulary* cartilages, that the sides of it may not flag and fall together. *Ray on the Creation.*

A'NNULET. *n. s.* [from *annulus*, Lat.]

1. A little ring.

2. [In heraldry.] A difference or mark of distinction, which the fifth brother of any family ought to bear in his coat of arms.

3. *Annulets* are also a part of the coat-armour of several families; they were anciently reputed a mark of nobility and jurisdiction, it being the custom of prelates to receive their investiture *per baculum & annulum.*

4. [In architecture.] The small square members, in the Dorick capital, under the quarter round, are called *annulets.*

5. *Annulet* is also used for a narrow flat moulding common to other parts of the column; so called, because it encompasses the column round. *Chambers.*

To ANNU'MERATE. *v. a.* [*annumero*, Lat.] To add to a former number; to unite to something beforementioned.

ANNUMERA'TION. *n. s.* [*annumeratio*, Lat.] Addition to a former number.

To ANNU'NCIATE. *v. a.* [*annuncio*, Lat.] To bring tidings; to relate something that has fallen out: a word not in popular use.

ANNUNCIA'TION DAY. *n. s.* [from *annunciate.*] The day celebrated by the church, in memory of the angel's salutation of the blessed virgin; solemnized with us on the twenty-fifth of March.

Upon the day of the *annunciation*, or Lady-day, meditate on the incarnation of our blessed Saviour: and so upon all the festivals of the year. *Taylor's Guide to Devotion.*

A'NODYNE. *adj.* [from ἀ and ὀδύνη.] That which has the power of mitigating pain.

Yet durst she not too deeply probe the wound,
As hoping still the nobler parts were found:
But strove with *anodynes* t' assuage the smart,
And mildly thus her med'cine did impart. *Dryd. Hind and P.*

Anodynes, or abaters of pain of the alimentary kind, are such things as relax the tension of the affected nervous fibres, as decoctions of emollient substances; those things which destroy the particular acrimony which occasions the pain, or what deadens the sensation of the brain, by procuring sleep. *Arbuthnot.*

To ANO'INT. *v. a.* [*oindre, enoindre*; part. *oint, enoint*, Fr.]

1. To rub over with unctuous matter, as oil, or unguents.

Anointed let me be with deadly venom,
And die, ere men can ſay, God ſave the queen. *Shak. R.* III.

Thou ſhalt have olive trees throughout all thy coaſts, but thou ſhalt not *anoint* thyſelf with the oil: for thine olive ſhall caſt his fruit. *Deut.* xxviii. 40.

2. To ſmear; to be rubbed upon.

Warm waters then in brazen caldrons born,
Are pour'd to waſh his body, joint by joint,
And fragrant oils the ſtiffen'd limbs *anoint*. *Dryd. Æn.* vi.

3. To conſecrate by unction.

I would not ſee thy cruel nails
Pluck out his poor old eyes; nor thy fierce ſiſter
In his *anointed* fleſh ſtick boariſh fangs. *Shakeſp. King Lear.*

ANO'INTER. *n. ſ.* [from *anoint.*] The perſon that anoints.

ANO'MALISM. *n. ſ.* [from *anomaly.*] Anomaly; irregularity; deviation from the common rule. *Dict.*

ANOMALI'STICAL. *adj.* [from *anomaly.*] Irregular; applied in aſtronomy to the year, taken for the time in which the earth paſſeth through its orbit, diſtinct from the tropical year.

ANO'MALOUS. *adj.* [α *priv.* and ὁμαλός.] Irregular; out of rule; deviating from the general method or analogy of things: It is applied, in grammar, to words deviating from the common rules of inflection; and, in aſtronomy, to the ſeemingly irregular motions of the planets.

There will ariſe *anomalous* diſturbances not only in civil and artificial, but alſo in military officers. *Brown's Vulgar Errours.*

He being acquainted with ſome characters of every ſpeech, you may at pleaſure make him underſtand *anomalous* pronunciation. *Holder's Elements of Speech.*

Metals are gold, ſilver, copper, tin, lead, and iron: to which we may join that *anomalous* body, quickſilver or mercury. *Locke's Elements of Natural Philoſophy.*

ANO'MALOUSLY. *adv.* [from *anomalous.*] Irregularly; in a manner contrary to rule.

Eve was not ſolemnly begotten, but ſuddenly framed, and *anomalouſly* proceeded from Adam. *Brown's Vulgar Errours.*

ANO'MALY. *n. ſ.* [*anomalie*, Fr. *anomalia*, Lat. ἀνωμαλία.] Irregularity; deviation from the common rule.

If we ſhould chance to find a mother debauching her daughter, as ſuch monſters have been ſeen, we muſt charge this upon a peculiar *anomaly* and baſeneſs of nature. *South.*

I do not purſue the many pſeudographies in uſe, but intend to ſhew how moſt of theſe *anomalies* in writing might be avoided, and better ſupplied. *Holder's Elements of Speech.*

A'NOMY. *n. ſ.* [α *priv.* and νόμος.] Breach of law.

If ſin be good, and juſt, and lawful, it is no more evil, it is no ſin, no *anomy*. *Bramham againſt Hobbes.*

ANO'N. *adv.* [*Junius* imagines it to be an elliptical form of ſpeaking for *in one*, that is, *in one minute*; *Skinner* from *a* and *nean*, or *near*; *Minſhew* from *on on.*]

1. Quickly; ſoon; in a ſhort time.

A little ſnow, tumbled about,
Anon becomes a mountain. *Shakeſpeare's King John.*

Will they come abroad *anon?*
Shall we ſee young Oberon? *Ben Johnſon's Fairy Prince.*

However, witneſs, heav'n!
Heav'n, witneſs thou *anon!* while we diſcharge
Freely our part. *Milton's Par. Loſt, b.* vi. *l.* 564.

He was not without deſign at that preſent, as ſhall be made out *anon*; meaning by that device to withdraw himſelf. *Clarend.*

Still as I did the leaves inſpire,
With ſuch a purple light they ſhone,
As if they had been made of fire,
And ſpreading ſo, would flame *anon.* *Waller.*

2. Sometimes; now and then; at other times. In this ſenſe is uſed *ever and anon.*

Full forty days he paſs'd, whether on hill
Sometimes, *anon* in ſhady vale, each night,
Or harbour'd in one cave, is not revealed. *Par. Regained.*

ANO'NYMOUS. *adj.* [α *priv.* and ὄνομα.] Wanting a name.

Theſe animalcules ſerve alſo for food to another *anonymous* inſect of the waters. *Ray on the Creation.*

They would forthwith publiſh ſlanders unpuniſhed, the authors being *anonymous*, the immediate publiſhers thereof ſculking. *Notes on the Dunciad.*

ANO'NYMOUSLY. *adv.* [from *anonymous.*] Without a name.

I would know, whether the edition is to come out *anonymouſly*, among complaints of ſpurious editions? *Swift.*

ANORE'XY. *n. ſ.* [ἀνορεξία.] Inappetency, or loathing of food. *Quincy.*

ANO'THER. *adj.* [from *an* and *other.*]

1. Not the ſame.

He that will not lay a foundation for perpetual diſorder, muſt of neceſſity find *another* riſe of government than that. *Locke.*

2. One more; a new addition to the former number.

——— A fourth? ———
Start eye!
What! will the line ſtretch out to th' crack of doom?
Another yet?—a ſeventh! I'll ſee no more. *Shak. Macbeth.*

3. Any other; any one elſe.

If one man ſin againſt *another*, the judge ſhall judge him. *1 Samuel*, ii. 25.

Why not of her? preferr'd above the reſt,
By him with knightly deeds, and open love profeſs'd;
So had *another* been, where he his vows addreſs'd.
Dryden's Fables.

4. Not one's ſelf.

A man ſhall have diffuſed his life, his ſelf, and his whole concernments ſo far, that he can weep his ſorrows with *another's* eyes; when he has another heart beſides his own, both to ſhare, and to ſupport his grief. *South.*

5. Widely different; much altered.

When the ſoul is beaten from its ſtation, and the mounds of virtue are broken down, it becomes quite *another* thing from what it was before. *South.*

ANO'THERGAINES. *adj.* [See ANOTHERGUESS.] Of another kind. This word I have found only in *Sidney.*

If my father had not plaid the haſty fool, I might have had *anothergaines* huſband than Dametas. *Sidney.*

ANO'THERGUESS. *adj.* [This word, which though rarely uſed in writing, is ſomewhat frequent in colloquial language, I conceive to be corrupted from *another guiſe*; that is, of a different *guiſe*, or manner, or form.] Of a different kind.

Oh Hocus! where art thou? It uſed to go in *anothergueſs* manner in thy time. *Arbuthnot's Hiſtory of John Bull.*

A'NSATED. *adj.* [*anſatus*, Lat.] Having handles; or ſomething in the form of handles.

To A'NSWER. *v. n.* [The etymology is uncertain; the Saxons had anbꝥpaꝛian, but in another ſenſe; the Dutch have *antwoorden.*]

1. To ſpeak in return to a queſtion.

Are we ſuccour'd? are the Moors remov'd?
Anſwer theſe queſtions firſt, and then a thouſand more,
Anſwer them altogether. *Dryden's Spaniſh Friar.*

2. To ſpeak in oppoſition.

No man was able to *anſwer* him a word. *Matt.* xxii. 46.

If it be ſaid, we may diſcover the elementary ingredients of things, I *anſwer*, that it is not neceſſary that ſuch a diſcovery ſhould be practicable. *Boyle.*

3. To be accountable for.

Some men have ſinned in the principles of humanity, and muſt *anſwer* for not being men. *Brown's Vulgar Errours.*

If there be any abſurdity in this, our author muſt *anſwer* for it. *Locke.*

4. To vindicate; to give a juſtificatory account of.

The night, ſo impudently fixed for my laſt, made little impreſſion on myſelf; but I cannot *anſwer* for my family. *Swift.*

5. To give an account.

How they have been ſince received, and ſo well improved, let thoſe *anſwer* either to God or man, who have been the authors and promoters of ſuch wiſe council. *Temple.*

He wants a father to protect his youth,
And rear him up to virtue. You muſt bear
The future blame, and *anſwer* to the world,
When you refuſe the eaſy honeſt means
Of taking care of him. *Southern's Innocent Adultery.*

6. To correſpond to; to ſuit with.

In water face *anſwereth* to face: ſo the heart of man to man. *Prov.* xxvii. 19.

7. To be equivalent to; to ſtand for ſomething elſe.

A feaſt is made for laughter, and wine maketh merry: but money *anſwereth* all things. *Eccl.* x. 19.

8. To ſatisfy any claim or petition.

Revenge the jeering and diſdain'd contempt
Of this proud king, who ſtudies day and night
To *anſwer* all the debt he owes unto you,
Ev'n with the bloody payments of your deaths. *Sh. Hen.* IV.

Men no ſooner find their appetites *unanſwered*, than they complain the times are injurious. *Raleigh's Hiſt. of the World.*

9. To act reciprocally upon.

Say, do'ſt thou yet the Roman harp command?
Do the ſtrings *anſwer* to thy noble hand? *Dryden's Perſius.*

10. To ſtand as oppoſite or correlative to ſomething elſe.

There can but two things create love, perfection and uſefulneſs; to which *anſwer*, on our part, 1. Admiration; and, 2. Deſire: and both theſe are centered in love. *Taylor.*

11. To bear proportion to.

He deſired, that proper officers might ſearch me; for probably I might carry ſeveral weapons, which muſt needs be dangerous things, if they *anſwered* the bulk of ſo prodigious a perſon. *Swift's Gulliver's Travels.*

12. To perform what is endeavoured or intended by the agent.

Our part is, to chooſe out the moſt deſerving objects, and the moſt likely to *anſwer* the ends of our charity; and when that is done, all is done that lies in our power: the reſt muſt be left to providence. *Atterbury's Sermons.*

13. To comply with.

He dies that touches of this fruit,
Till I and my affairs are *anſwered.* *Shakeſp. As you like it.*

14. To ſucceed; to produce the wiſhed event.

Jaſon followed her counſel, whereto, when the event had *anſwered*, he again demanded the fleece. *Raleigh's Hiſt. of the W.*

We ſee likewiſe, that much water draweth forth the juice of the body infuſed; but little water is imbibed by the body: and this

this is a principal cause, why, in operations upon bodies for their version or alteration, the trial in great quantities doth not *answer* the trial in small; and so deceiveth many.
Bacon's Natural History, N° 92.

15. To appear to any call, or authoritative summons; in which sense, though figuratively, the following passage may be, perhaps, taken.

Thou wert better in thy grave, than to *answer*, with thy uncovered body, this extremity of the skies. *Shakesp. K. Lear.*

16. To be over-against any thing.

Fire *answers* fire, and, by their paly beams,
Each battle sees the other's umber'd face. *Shakesp. Henry* V.

A'NSWER. *n. s.* [from *To answer.*]

1. That which is said, whether in speech or writing, in return to a question, or position.

It was a right *answer* of the physician to his patient, that had sore eyes: If you have more pleasure in wine than in your sight, wine is good. *Locke.*

How can we think of appearing at that tribunal, without being able to give a ready *answer* to the questions which he shall then put to us, about the poor and the afflicted, the hungry and the naked, the sick and imprisoned? *Atterbury's Sermons.*

2. In law, a confutation of a charge exhibited against a person.

A personal *answer* ought to have three qualities; it ought to be pertinent to the matter in hand; it ought to be absolute and unconditional; it ought to be clear and certain. *Ayliffe's Par.*

A'NSWER-JOBBER. *n. s.* [from *answer* and *jobber.*] He that makes a trade of writing answers.

What disgusts me from having any thing to do with *answer-jobbers*, is, that they have no conscience. *Swift.*

A'NSWERABLE. *adj.* [from *answer.*]

1. That to which a reply may be made; that which may be answered; as, the argument, though subtle, is yet *answerable.*

2. Obliged to give an account, or stand the trial of an accusation.

Every chief of every kindred or family should be *answerable*, and bound to bring forth every one of that kindred, at all times to be justified, when he should be required, or charged with any treason, felony, &c. *Spenser's State of Ireland.*

Will any man argue, that if a physician should manifestly prescribe poison to all his patients, he cannot be justly punished, but is *answerable* only to God? *Swift.*

He cannot think ambition more justly laid to their charge, than to other men; because that would be to make church government *answerable* for the errours of human nature. *Swift.*

3. Correspondent.

It was but such a likeness as an imperfect glass doth give, *answerable* enough in some features and colours, but erring in others. *Sidney.*

The daughters of Atlas were ladies, who, accompanying such as came to be registered among the worthies, brought forth children *answerable* in quality to those that begot them.
Raleigh's History of the World.

4. Proportionate.

Only add
Deeds to thy knowledge *answerable*; add faith,
Add virtue, patience, temperance; add love
By name to come call'd charity, the soul
Of all the rest. *Milton's Paradise Lost, b.* xii.

5. Suitable; suited.

The following, by certain estates of men, *answerable* to that which a great person himself professeth, as of soldiers to him that hath been employed in the wars, hath been a thing well taken even in monarchies. *Bacon's Essays.*

If *answerable* style I can obtain
Of my celestial patroness, who deigns
Her mighty visitation unimplor'd. *Milt. Parad. Lost, b.* ix.

6. Equal.

There be no kings whose means are *answerable* unto other mens desires. *Raleigh's History of the World.*

7. Relative; correlative.

That, to every petition for things needful, there should be some *answerable* sentence of thanks provided particularly to follow, is not requisite. *Hooker, b.* v. § 43.

A'NSWERABLY. *adv.* [from *answerable.*] In due proportion; with proper correspondence; suitably.

The broader seas are, if they be intire, and free from islands, they are *answerably* deeper. *Brerewood on Languages.*

It bears light, and more active sorts, into the atmosphere, to a greater or lesser height, *answerably* to the greater or lesser intenseness of the heat. *Woodward's Nat. History.*

A'NSWERABLENESS. *n. s.* [from *answerable.*] The quality of being answerable. *Dict.*

A'NSWERER. *n. s.* [from *answer.*]

1. He that answers; he that speaks in return to what another has spoken.

2. He that manages the controversy against one that has written first.

It is very unfair in any writer to employ ignorance and malice together; because it gives his *answerer* double work. *Swift.*

ANT. *n. s.* [æmett, Sax. which *Junius* imagines, not without probability, to have been first contracted to æmt, and then softened to *ant.*] An emmet; a pismire. A small insect that lives in great numbers together in hillocks.

We'll set thee to school to an *ant*, to teach thee there's no lab'ring in the winter. *Shakesp. King Lear.*

Methinks, all cities now but ant-hills are,
Where when the several labourers I see
For children, house, provision, taking pain,
They're all but *ants*, carrying eggs, straw, and grain. *Donne.*

Learn each small people's genius, policies;
The *ant*'s republick, and the realm of bees;
How those in common all their stores bestow,
And anarchy without confusion know. *Pope's Ess. on Man.*

ANT-BEAR. *n. s.* [from *ant* and *bear.*] An animal that feeds on ants.

Divers quadrupeds feed upon insects; and some live wholly upon them; as two sorts of tamanduas upon ants, which therefore are called in English *ant-bears.* *Ray on Creation.*

A'NT-HILL, or HILLOCK. *n. s.* [from *ant* and *hill.*] The small protuberances of earth in which ants make their nests.

Put blue flowers into an *ant-hill*, they will be stained with red; because the ants drop upon them their stinging liquour, which hath the effect of oil of vitriol. *Ray on Creation.*

Those who have seen *ant-hillocks*, have easily perceived those small heaps of corn about their nests. *Addison. Guardian.*

AN'T. A contraction for *and it*, or rather *and if it*; as, *an't please you*; that is, *and if it please you.*

ANTA'GONIST. *n. s.* [ἀντὶ and ἀγωνίζω.]

1. One who contends with another; an opponent. It implies generally a personal and particular opposition.

Our *antagonists* in these controversies may have met with some not unlike to Ithacius. *Hooker's Dedication.*

What was set before him,
To heave, pull, draw, and break, he still perform'd,
None daring to appear *antagonist.* *Milton's Sampson Agon.*

Is it not fit, that the history of a person should appear, till the prejudice both of his *antagonists* and adherents be softened and subdued. *Addison. Freeholder*, N° 35.

2. Contrary.

The short club consists of those who are under five feet; ours is to be composed of such as are above six. These we look upon as the two extremes and *antagonists* of the species; considering all these as neuters, who fill up the middle space.
Addison. Guardian, N° 108.

3. In anatomy, the *antagonist* is that muscle which counteracts some others.

A relaxation of a muscle must produce a spasm in its *antagonist*, because the equilibrium is destroyed. *Arbuthnot on Diet.*

To ANTA'GONIZE. *v. n.* [ἀντὶ and ἀγωνίζω.] To contend against another. *Dict.*

ANTA'LGICK. *adj.* [from ἀντὶ, against, and ἄλγος, pain.] That which softens pain; anodyne.

ANTANACLA'SIS. n. s. [Lat. from ἀντανάκλασις, from ἀντανακλάω, to drive back.]

1. A figure in rhetorick, when the same word is repeated in a different, if not in a contrary signification; as, *In thy youth learn some* craft, *that in old age thou mayst get thy living without* craft. *Craft*, in the first place, signifies science or occupation; in the second, deceit or subtilty.

2. It is also a returning to the matter at the end of a long parenthesis; as, Shall that heart (*which does not only feel them, but hath all motion of his life placed in them*) shall that heart, *I say*, &c.
Smith's Rhetorick.

ANTAPHRODI'TICK. *adj.* [from ἀντὶ, against, and ἀφροδίτη, Venus.] That which is efficacious against the venereal disease.

ANTAPOPLE'CTICK. *adj.* [ἀντὶ, against, and ἀποπληξις, an apoplexy.] Good against an apoplexy.

ANTA'RCTICK. *adj.* [ἀντὶ, against, and ἄρκτος, the bear or northern constellation.] The southern pole, so called, as opposite to the northern.

Downward as far as *antarctick.* *Milton's Par. Lost, b.* ix.

They that had sail'd from near th' *antarctick* pole,
Their treasure safe, and all their vessels whole,
In sight of their dear country ruin'd be,
Without the guilt of either rock or sea. *Waller.*

ANTARTHRI'TICK. *adj.* [ἀντὶ, against, and ἀρθρῖτις, the gout.] Good against the gout.

ANTASTHMA'TICK. *adj.* [from ἀντὶ and ἆσθμα.] Good against the asthma.

A'NTE. A Latin particle signifying *before*, which is frequently used in compositions; as, *antediluvian*, before the flood; *antechamber*, a chamber leading into another apartment.

A'NTEACT. *n. s.* [from *ante* and *act.*] A former act.

ANTEAMBULA'TION. *n. s.* [from *ante* and *ambulatio*, Lat.] A walking before. *Dict.*

To ANTECE'DE. *v. n.* [from *ante*, before, and *cedo*, to go.] To precede; to go before.

It seems more consonant to reason, that the fabrick of the world did not long *antecede* its motion. *Hale's Orig. of Mank.*

ANTECE'DENCE. *n. s.* [from *antecede.*] The act or state of going before; precedence.

It is impossible that mixed bodies can be eternal, because there is necessarily a pre-existence of the simple bodies, and an an *antecedence* of their constitution preceding the existence of mixed bodies. *Hale's Origin of Mankind.*

ANTECE'DENT. *adj.* [*antecedens*, Lat.]

1. Going before; preceding. *Antecedent* is used, I think, only with regard to time; *precedent*, with regard both to time and place.

To assert, that God looked upon Adam's fall as a sin, and punished it, when, without any *antecedent* sin of his, it was impossible for him not to fall, seems a thing that highly reproaches essential equity and goodness. *South.*

2. It has *to* before the thing which is supposed to follow.

No one is so hardy as to say, God is in his debt; that he owed him a nobler being: for existence must be *antecedent to* merit. *Collier of Envy.*

Did the blood first exist, *antecedent to* the formation of the heart? But that is to set the effect before the cause. *Bentley.*

ANTECE'DENT. *n. s.* [*antecedens*, Lat.]

1. That which goes before.

A duty of so mighty an influence, that it is indeed the necessary *antecedent*, if not also the direct cause of a sinner's return to God. *South.*

2. In grammar, the noun to which the relative is subjoined; as, the *man* who comes hither.

3. In logick, the first proposition of an enthymeme or argument, consisting only of two propositions.

Conditional or hypothetical propositions are those whose parts are united by the conditional particle *if*; as, *if* the sun be fixed, the earth must move: *if* there be no fire, there will be no smoke. The first part of these propositions, or that wherein the condition is contained, is called the *antecedent*, the other is called the *consequent*. *Watts's Logick.*

ANTECE'DENTLY. *adv.* [from *antecedent*.] In the state of antecedence, or going before; previously.

We consider him *antecedently* to his creation, while he yet lay in the barren womb of nothing, and only in the number of possibilities. *South.*

ANTECE'SSOR. *n. s.* [Latin.] One who goes before, or leads another. *Dict.*

ANTECHA'MBER. *n. s.* [from *ante* before, and *chamber*; it is generally written, improperly, *antichamber*.] The chamber that leads to the chief apartment.

The empress has the *antichambers* past,
And this way moves with a disorder'd haste. *Dryd. Aurengz.*

His *antichamber*, and room of audience, are little square chambers wainscoted. *Addison on Italy.*

ANTECU'RSOR. *n. s.* [Latin.] One who runs before. *Dict.*

To A'NTEDATE. *v. a.* [from *ante* and *do*, *datum*, Lat.]

1. To date earlier than the real time, so as to confer a fictitious antiquity.

Now thou hast lov'd me one whole day,
To-morrow when thou leav'st, what wilt thou say?
Wilt thou then *antedate* some new-made vow,
Or say, that now
We are not just those persons, which we were? *Donne.*

By reading, a man does, as it were, *antedate* his life, and makes himself contemporary with the ages past. *Collier's Essays.*

2. To take something before the proper time.

Our joys below it can improve,
And *antedate* the bliss above. *Pope's St. Cæcilia.*

ANTEDILU'VIAN. *adj.* [from *ante* before, and *diluvium* a deluge.]

1. Existing before the deluge.

During the time of the deluge, all the stone and marble of the *antediluvian* earth were totally dissolved. *Woodw. Nat. History.*

2. Relating to things existing before the deluge.

The text intends only the line of Seth, conduceable unto the genealogy of our Saviour, and the *antediluvian* chronology. *Brown's Vulgar Errours, b.* vii. *c.* 4.

ANTEDILU'VIAN. *n. s.* One that lived before the flood.

We are so far from repining at God, that he hath not extended the period of our lives to the longevity of the *antediluvians*, that we give him thanks for contracting the days of our trial. *Bentley's Sermons.*

A'NTELOPE. *n. s.* [The etymology is uncertain.] A goat with curled or wreathed horns.

The *antelope*, and wolf both fierce and fell. *Fairy Queen.*

ANTEMERI'DIAN. *adj.* [from *ante*, before, and *meridian*, noon.] Before noon.

ANTEME'TICK. *adj.* [ἀντὶ, against, and ἠμέω, to vomit.] That which has the power of calming the stomach; of preventing or stopping vomiting.

ANTEMU'NDANE. *adj.* [*ante*, before, and *mundus*, the world.] That which was before the creation of the world.

ANTENU'MBER. *n. s.* [from *ante* and *number*.] The number that precedes another.

Whatsoever virtue is in numbers, for conducing to consent of notes, is rather to be ascribed to the *antenumber*, than to the entire number, as that the sound returneth after six, or after twelve; so that the seventh or thirteenth is not the matter, but the sixth or the twelfth. *Bacon's Natural History*, N° 106.

A'NTEPAST. *n. s.* [from *ante*, before, and *pastum*, to feed.] A foretaste; something taken before the proper time.

Were we to expect our bliss only in the satiating our appetites, it might be reasonable, by frequent *antepasts*, to excite our gust for that profuse perpetual meal. *Decay of Piety.*

A'NTEPENULT. *n. s.* [*antepenultima*, Lat.] The last syllable but two, as the syllable *te* in *antepenult*: a term of grammar.

ANTEPILE'PTICK. *adj.* [ἀντὶ and ἐπίληψις.] A medicine against convulsions.

That bezoar is antidotal, lapis judaicus diuretical, coral *antepileptical*, we will not deny. *Brown's Vulgar Errours, b.* ii.

To A'NTEPONE. *v. a.* [*antepono*, Lat.] To set one thing before another; to prefer one thing to another. *Dict.*

ANTEPREDI'CAMENT. *n. s.* [*antepredicamentum*, Lat.] Something to be known in the study of logick, previously to the doctrine of the predicament.

ANTERIO'RITY. *n. s.* [from *anteriour*.] Priority; the state of being before either in time or situation.

ANTE'RIOUR. *adj.* [*anterior*, Lat.] Going before, either with regard to time or place.

If that be the *anteriour* or upper part wherein the senses are placed, and that the posteriour and lower part, which is opposite thereunto, there is no inferiour or former part in this animal; for the senses being placed at both extremes, make both ends *anteriour*, which is impossible. *Brown's Vulgar Errours.*

ANTES. *n. s.* [Latin.] Pillars of large dimensions that support the front of a building.

ANTESTO'MACH. *n. s.* [from *ante*, before, and *stomach*.] A cavity which leads into the stomach.

In birds there is no mastication or comminution of the meat in the mouth; but it is immediately swallowed into a kind of *antestomach*, which I have observed in piscivorous birds. *Ray.*

ANTHELMI'NTHICK. *adj.* [ἀντὶ, against, and ἕλμινθος, a worm.] That which kills worms.

Anthelminthicks, or contrary to worms, are things which are known by experience to kill them, as oils, or honey taken upon an empty stomach. *Arbuthnot on Diet.*

A'NTHEM. *n. s.* [ἄνθυμνος, a hymn sung in alternate parts, and should therefore be written *anthymn*.] A holy song; a song performed as part of divine service.

God Moses first, then David did inspire,
To compose *anthems* for his heavenly quire. *Denham.*

There is no passion that is not finely expressed in those parts of the inspired writings, which are proper for divine songs and *anthems*. *Addison. Spectator*, N° 405.

ANTHO'LOGY. *n. s.* [ἀνθολογία, from ἄνθος, a flower, and λέγω, to gather.]

1. A collection of flowers.
2. A collection of devotions in the Greek church.
3. A collection of poems.

A'NTHONY'S FIRE. *n. s.* A kind of erysipelas.

ANTHRAX. *n. s.* [ἄνθραξ, a burning coal.] A scab or blotch that is made by a corrosive humour, which burns the skin, and occasions sharp pricking pains. *Quincy.*

ANTHROPO'LOGY. *n. s.* [from ἄνθρωπος, man, and λέγω, to discourse.] The doctrine of anatomy; the doctrine of the form and structure of the body of man.

ANTHROPO'PATHY. *n. s.* [ἄνθρωπος, man, and πάθος, passion.] The sensibility of man; the passions of man.

ANTHROPO'PHAGI. *n s. It has no singular.* [ἄνθρωπος, man, and φάγω, to eat.]

Man-eaters; cannibals; those that live upon human flesh.

The cannibals that each other eat,
The *anthropophagi*, and men whose heads
Do grow beneath their shoulders. *Shakesp. Othello.*

ANTHROPOPHAGI'NIAN. *n. s.* A ludicrous word, formed by *Shakespeare* from *anthropophagi*, for the sake of a formidable sound.

Go, knock, and call; he'll speak like an *anthropophaginian* unto thee: knock, I say. *Shakesp. Merry Wives of Windsor.*

ANTHROPO'PHAGY. *n. s.* [ἄνθρωπος, a man, and φάγω, to eat.] The quality of eating human flesh, or man-eating.

Upon slender foundations was raised the *anthropophagy* of Diomedes his horses. *Brown's Vulgar Errours, b.* i. *c.* 6.

ANTHROPO'SOPHY. *n. s.* [ἄνθρωπος, man, and σοφία, wisdom.] The knowledge of the nature of man.

ANTHYPNO'TICK. *adj.* [from ἀντὶ, against, and ὕπνος, sleep.] That which has the power of preventing sleep; that which is efficacious against a lethargy.

ANTHYPOCHONDRI'ACK. *adj.* [from ἀντὶ, against, and ὑποχονδριακὸς.] Good against hypochondriack maladies.

ANTHYPO'PHORA. *n. s.* [ἀνθυποφορα.] A figure in rhetorick, which signifies a contrary illation, or inference, and is when an objection is refuted or disproved by the opposition of a contrary sentence. *Smith's Rhetorick.*

ANTHYSTE'RICK. *adj.* [from ἀντὶ, against, and ὑστερος.] Good against hystericks.

ANTI. [ἀντὶ.] A particle much used in composition w[illegible] words derived from the Greek, and signifies *contrary to*; as, *antimonarchical*, opposite to monarchy.

ANTIA'CID. *adj.* [from ἀντὶ, and *acidus*, sour.] Contrary to sourness; alkalis.

Oils are *antiacids*, so far as they blunt acrimony; but as they are hard of digestion, they produce acrimony of another sort. *Arbuthnot on Aliments.*

ANTICHACHE'CTICK. *adj.* [from ἀντὶ, againſt, and καχεξία, a bad habit.] Things adapted to the cure of a bad conſtitution.

ANTICHA'MBER. *n. ſ.* This word is corruptly written for *antechamber*; which ſee.

ANTICHRI'STIAN. *adj.* [from ἀντὶ, againſt, and χριστιανὸς.] Oppoſite to chriſtianity.

That deſpiſed, abject, oppreſſed ſort of men, the miniſters, whom the world would make *antichriſtian*, and ſo deprive them of heaven. *South.*

ANTICHRI'STIANISM. *n. ſ.* [from *antichriſtian*.] Oppoſition or contrariety to chriſtianity.

Have we not ſeen many, whoſe opinions have faſtened upon one another the brand of *antichriſtianiſm?* *Decay of Piety.*

ANTICHRISTIA'NITY. *n. ſ.* [from *antichriſtian*.] Contrariety to chriſtianity.

ANTI'CHRONISM. *n. ſ.* [ἀντὶ, againſt, and χρόνος, time.] Deviation from the right order or account of time.

To ANTI'CIPATE. *v. a.* [*anticipo*, Lat.]

1. To take ſomething ſooner than another, ſo as to prevent him that comes after.

God hath taken care to *anticipate* and prevent every man, to draw him early into his church; to give piety the prepoſſeſſion, and ſo to engage him in holineſs. *Hammond's Fundamentals.*

2. To take up before the time, at which any thing might be regularly had.

I find I have *anticipated* already, and taken up from Boccace, before I come to him; but I am of the temper of kings, who are for preſent money, no matter how they pay it. *Dryd. Fab.*

3. To foretaſte, or take an impreſſion of ſomething, which is not yet, as if it really was.

The life of the deſperate equals the anxiety of death, who but act the life of the damned, and *anticipate* the deſolations of hell. *Brown's Vulgar Errours, b.* i. *c.* 2.

Why ſhould we
Anticipate our ſorrows? 'tis like thoſe
That die for fear of death. *Denham's Sophy.*

4. To prevent any thing by crouding in before it; to preclude.

Time, thou *anticipat'ſt* my dread exploits:
The flighty purpoſe never is o'ertook,
Unleſs the deed go with it. *Shakeſpeare's Macbeth.*

I am ſo far from pretending to inſtruct the profeſſion, or *anticipating* their directions to ſuch as are under their government. *Arbuthnot on Aliments.*

If our Apoſtle had maintained ſuch an *anticipating* principle engraven upon our ſouls before all exerciſe of reaſon; what did he talk of ſeeking the Lord, ſeeing that the knowledge of him was innate and perpetual. *Bentley's Sermons.*

ANTICIPA'TION. *n. ſ.* [from *anticipate*.]

1. The act of taking up ſomething before its time.

The golden number gives the new moon four days too late, by reaſon of the aforeſaid *anticipation*, and our neglect of it. *Holder on Time.*

2. Foretaſte.

It is not enough to be miſerable when the time comes, unleſs we make ourſelves ſo beforehand, and by *anticipation*. *L'Eſtrange.*

If we really live under the hope of future happineſs, we ſhall taſte it by way of *anticipation* and forethought, an image of it will meet our minds often, and ſtay there, as all pleaſing expectations do. *Atterbury's Sermons.*

3. Opinion implanted before the reaſons of that opinion can be known.

The eaſt and weſt, the north and ſouth, have the ſame *anticipation* concerning one ſupreme diſpoſer of things. *Stillingfleet.*

What nation is there, that, without any teaching, have not a kind of *anticipation*, or preconceived notion of a Deity? *Derham's Phyſico-Theology.*

A'NTICK. *adj.* [probably from *antiquus*, ancient, as things out of uſe appear old.] Odd; ridiculouſly wild; buffoon in geſticulation.

What! dares the ſlave
Come hither cover'd with an *antick* face,
And fleer and ſcorn at our ſolemnity? *Shakeſp. Rom. & Jul.*

Of all our *antick* ſights, and pageantry,
Which Engliſh idiots run in crouds to ſee. *Dryden.*

The prize was to be conferred upon the whiſtler, that could go through his tune without laughing, though provoked by the *antick* poſtures of a merry Andrew, who was to play tricks. *Addiſon. Spectator,* N° 179.

A'NTICK. *n. ſ.*

1. He that plays anticks; he that uſes odd geſticulation: a buffoon.

Within the hollow crown,
That rounds the mortal temples of a king,
Keeps death his court; and there the *antick* ſits,
Scoffing his ſtate. *Shakeſp. Richard* II.

If you ſhould ſmile, he grows impatient.—
Fear not, my lord, we can contain ourſelves,
Were he the verieſt *antick* in the world. *Shakeſp. Tam. Shr.*

2. Odd appearance.

A work of rich entail, and curious mold,
Woven with *anticks*, and wild imagery. *Fairy Queen, b.* ii.

For ev'n at firſt reflection ſhe eſpies
Such toys, ſuch *anticks*, and ſuch vanities,
As ſhe retires and ſhrinks for ſhame and fear. *Sir J. Davies.*

To A'NTICK. *v. a.* [from *antick*.] To make anticks.

Mine own tongue
Splits what it ſpeaks; the wild diſguiſe hath almoſt
Antickt us all. *Shakeſp. Antony and Cleopatra.*

A'NTICKLY. *adv.* [from *antick*.] In an antick manner; with odd poſtures, or wild geſticulations.

Scrambling, outfacing, faſhion-mongring boys,
That lye, and cog, and flout, deprave, and ſlander,
Go *anticklly*, and ſhew an outward hideouſneſs,
And ſpeak of half a dozen dangerous words.
Shakeſp. Much ado about Nothing.

ANTICLI'MAX. *n. ſ.* [from ἀντὶ and κλίμαξ.] A ſentence in which the laſt part is lower than the firſt.

A certain figure which was unknown to the ancients, is called by ſome an *anticlimax*. *Addiſon's Whig Examiner.*

This diſtich is frequently mentioned as an example.

Next comes Dalhouſſey the great god of war,
Lieutenant col'nel to the earl of Mar.

ANTICONVU'LSIVE. *adj.* [from ἀντὶ, againſt, and *convulſive*.] Good againſt convulſions.

Whatſoever produces an inflammatory diſpoſition in the blood, produces the aſthma, as *anticonvu'ſive* medicines. *Floyer.*

A'NTICOR. *n. ſ.* [from ἀντὶ, againſt, and *cor*, the heart.]

A preternatural ſwelling of a round figure, occaſioned by a ſanguine and bilious humour, and appearing in a horſe's breaſt, oppoſite to his heart. An *anticor* may kill a horſe, unleſs it be brought to a ſuppuration by good remedies. *Farrier's Dict.*

ANTICO'URTIER. *n. ſ.* [from ἀντὶ, againſt, and *courtier*.] One that oppoſes the court.

ANTI'DOTAL. *adj.* [from *antidote*.] That which has the quality of an antidote, or the power of counteracting poiſon.

That bezoar is *antidotal*, we ſhall not deny. *Brown's V. Err.*

A'NTIDOTE. *n. ſ.* [ἀντίδοτος, *antidotus*, Lat. a thing given in oppoſition to ſomething elſe.]

A medicine given to expel the miſchiefs of another, as of poiſon. *Quincy.*

Truſt not the phyſician,
His *antidotes* are poiſon, and he ſlays
More than you rob. *Shakeſp. Timon.*

What fool would believe that *antidote* delivered by Pierus againſt the ſting of a ſcorpion; to ſit upon an aſs, with one's face towards his tail. *Brown's Vulgar Errours, b.* i. *c.* 7.

Poiſon will work againſt the ſtars: beware;
For ev'ry meal an *antidote* prepare. *Dryden jun. Juv. Sat.*

ANTIDYSENTE'RICK. *adj.* [from ἀντὶ, againſt, and *dyſenteria*, a bloody flux.] Good againſt the bloody flux.

ANTIFE'BRILE. *adj.* [from ἀντὶ, againſt, and *febris*, a fever.] Good againſt fevers.

Antifebrile medicines check the ebullition. *Floyer.*

ANTILO'GARITHM. *n. ſ.* [from ἀντὶ, againſt, and *logarithm*.]

The complement of the logarithm of a ſine, tangent, or ſecant; or the difference of that logarithm from the logarithm of ninety degrees. *Chambers.*

ANTI'LOGY. *n. ſ.* [ἀντιλογία.] A contradiction between any words and paſſages in an authour. *Dict.*

ANTI'LOQUIST. *n. ſ.* [from ἀντὶ, againſt, and *loquor*, to ſpeak.] A contradictor. *Dict.*

ANTIMONA'RCHICAL. *adj.* [from ἀντὶ, againſt, and μοναρχία, government by a ſingle perſon.] Againſt government by a ſingle perſon.

When he ſpied the ſtatue of king Charles in the middle of the croud, and moſt of the kings ranged over their heads, he concluded that an *antimonarchical* aſſembly could never chooſe ſuch a place. *Addiſon. Freeholder,* N° 47.

ANTIMONA'RCHICALNESS. *n. ſ.* [from *antimonarchical*.] The quality of being an enemy to regal power.

ANTIMO'NIAL. *adj.* [from *antimony*.] Made of antimony; having the qualities of antimony; relating to antimony.

They were got out of the reach of *antimonial* fumes. *Grew.*

Though *antimonial* cups prepar'd with art,
Their force to wine through ages ſhould impart;
This diſſipation, this profuſe expence,
Nor ſhrinks their ſize, nor waſtes their ſtores immenſe.
Blackmore on the Creation.

A'NTIMONY. *n. ſ.* [The ſtibium of the ancients, by the Greeks called στίμμι. The reaſon of its modern denomination is referred to Baſil Valentine, a German monk; who, as the tradition relates, having thrown ſome of it to the hogs, obſerved, that, after it had purged them heartily, they immediately fattened; and therefore, he imagined, his fellow monks would be the better for a like doſe. The experiment, however, ſucceeded ſo ill, that they all died of it; and the medicine was thenceforward called *antimoine*; *antimonk*.]

Antimony is a mineral ſubſtance, of a metalline nature, having all the ſeeming characters of a real metal, except malleability; and may be called a ſemimetal, being a foſſile glebe of ſome undetermined metal, combined with a ſulphurous and ſtony ſubſtance. Mines of all metals afford it; but chiefly thoſe

thoſe of ſilver and lead; that in gold mines is reckoned beſt. It has alſo its own mines in Hungary, Germany, and France. It is found in clods or ſtones of ſeveral ſizes, bearing a near reſemblance to black lead, only being lighter and harder. Its texture is full of little ſhining veins or threads, like needles; brittle as gaſs. Sometimes veins of a red or golden colour are intermixed, which is called *male antimony*; that without them being denominated *female antimony*. It fuſes in the fire, though with ſome difficulty; and diſſolves more eaſily in water. When dug out of the earth, it is put into large crucibles, fuſed by a violent fire, and then poured into cones, which make the crude *antimony* of the ſhops. Of theſe cones the top is the pureſt part, and the baſe the fouleſt. It deſtroys and diſſipates all metals fuſed with it, except gold; and is therefore uſeful in refining. It is a common ingredient in ſpeculums, or burning concaves; ſerving to give them a finer poliſh. It makes a part in bell metal; and renders the ſound more clear. It is mingled with tin, to make it more hard, white, and ſound; and with lead, in the caſting of printers letters, to render them more ſmooth and firm. It is a general help in the melting of metals, and eſpecially in caſting of cannon balls. In pharmacy it is uſed under various forms, and with various intentions, chiefly as an emetick. It had no place in medicine before the fourteenth century; and was generally neglected, till Paracelſus brought it into eſteem, in the beginning of the ſixteenth century; but much miſchief was done by it, till the proper methods of preparing it were, after a long courſe of experiments, diſcovered. *Chambers.*

ANTINEPHRI'TICK. *adj.* [from ἀντὶ and νεφριτικὸς.] Medicines good againſt diſeaſes of the reins and kidneys.

A'NTINOMY. *n. ſ.* [from ἀντὶ and νόμος.] A contradiction between two laws, or two articles of the ſame law.

ANTIPARALY'TICK. *adj.* [from ἀντὶ and παράλυσις.] Efficacious againſt the palſy.

ANTIPATHE'TICAL. *adj.* [from *antipathy.*] Having a natural contrariety to any thing.

The ſoil is fat and luxurious, and *antipathetical* to all venemous creatures. *Howel's Vocal Foreſt.*

ANTIPATHE'TICALNESS. *n. ſ.* [from *antipathetical.*] The quality or ſtate of having a natural contrariety to any thing. *Dict.*

ANTI'PATHY. *n. ſ.* [from ἀντὶ, againſt, and πάθος, feeling; *antipathie*, Fr.]

1. A natural contrariety to any thing, ſo as to ſhun it involuntarily; averſion; diſlike. It is oppoſed to *ſympathy*.

No contraries hold more *antipathy*,
Than I and ſuch a knave. *Shakeſpeare's King Lear.*

To this perhaps might be juſtly attributed moſt of the ſympathies and *antipathies* obſervable in men. *Locke.*

2. It has ſometimes the particle *againſt* before the object of antipathy.

I had a mortal *antipathy againſt* ſtanding armies in times of peace; becauſe I took armies to be hired by the maſter of the family, to keep his children in ſlavery. *Swift.*

3. Sometimes *to.*

Ask you, what provocation I have had?
The ſtrong *antipathy* of good *to* bad.
When truth, or virtue, an affront endures,
Th' affront is mine, my friend, and ſhould be yours. *Pope.*

4. Formerly *with*; but improperly.

Tangible bodies have an *antipathy with* air; and any liquid body, that is more denſe, they will draw, condenſe, and, in effect, incorporate. *Bacon's Natural Hiſtory*, Nº 80.

ANTIPERI'STASIS. *n. ſ.* [from ἀντιπερίστασις, formed of ἀντὶ and περιίσταμαι, to ſtand round.] The oppoſition of a contrary quality, by which the quality it oppoſes, becomes heightened or intended; or the action, by which a body attacked by another, collects itſelf, and becomes ſtronger by ſuch oppoſition: or an intention of the activity of one quality cauſed by the oppoſition of another. Thus quicklime is ſet on fire by the affuſion of cold water; ſo water becomes warmer in winter than in ſummer; and thunder and lightening are excited in the middle region of the air, which is continually cold, and all by *antiperiſtaſis*. This is an exploded principle in the Peripatetick philoſophy.

Th' *antiperiſtaſis* of age
More inflam'd his am'rous rage. *Cowley.*

The riotous prodigal deteſts covetouſneſs; yet let him find the ſprings grow dry, which feed his luxury, covetouſneſs ſhall be called in; and ſo, by a ſtrange *antiperiſtaſis*, prodigality ſhall beget rapine. *Decay of Piety.*

ANTIPESTILE'NTIAL. *adj.* [from ἀντὶ, againſt, and *peſtilential.*] Efficacious againſt the infection of the plague.

Perfumes correct the air before it is attracted by the lungs; or, rather, *antipeſtilential* unguents, to anoint the noſtrils with. *Harvey on the Plague.*

ANTI'PHRASIS. *n. ſ.* [from ἀντὶ, againſt, and φράσις, a form of ſpeech.] The uſe of words in a ſenſe oppoſite to their proper meaning.

You now find no cauſe to repent, that you never dipt your hands in the bloody high courts of juſtice, ſo called only by *antiphraſis*. *South's Dedication to his Sermons.*

ANTI'PODAL. *adj.* [from *antipodes.*] Relating to the countries inhabited by the antipodes.

The Americans are *antipodals* unto the Indians. *Brown's Vulgar Errours, b.* vi. *c.* 7.

ANTI'PODES. *n. ſ. It has no ſingular.* [from ἀντὶ, againſt, and πόδες, feet.] Thoſe people who, living on the other ſide of the globe, have their feet directly oppoſite to ours.

We ſhould hold day with the *antipodes*,
If you would walk in abſence of the ſun. *Shakeſpeare's Merchant of Venice.*

So ſhines the ſun, tho' hence remov'd, as clear
When his beams warm th' *antipodes*, as here. *Waller.*

A'NTIPOPE. *n. ſ.* [from ἀντὶ, againſt, and *pope.*] He that uſurps the popedom, in oppoſition to the right pope.

This houſe is famous in hiſtory, for the retreat of an *antipope*, who called himſelf Felix V. *Addiſon on Italy.*

ANTIPTO'SIS. *n. ſ.* [ἀντίπτωσις.] A figure in grammar, by which one caſe is put for another.

A'NTIQUARY. *n. ſ.* [*antiquarius*, Lat.] A man ſtudious of antiquity; a collector of ancient things.

All thoſe arts, rarities, and inventions, are but the relicts of an intellect defaced with ſin. We admire it now, only as *antiquaries* do a piece of old coin, for the ſtamp it once bore. *South's Sermons.*

With ſharpen'd ſight pale *antiquaries* pore,
Th' inſcription value, but the ruſt adore. *Pope.*

The rude Latin of the monks is ſtill very intelligible; had their records been delivered in the vulgar tongue, they could not now be underſtood, unleſs by *antiquaries*. *Swift.*

A'NTIQUARY. *adj.* [This word is improper.] Old; antique.

Here's Neſtor,
Inſtructed by the *antiquary* times;
He muſt, he is, he cannot but be wiſe. *Shakeſpeare's Troilus and Creſſida.*

To A'NTIQUATE. *v. a.* [*antiquo*, Lat.] To put out of uſe; to make obſolete.

The growth of chriſtianity in this kingdom might reaſonably introduce new laws, and *antiquate* or abrogate ſome old ones, that ſeemed leſs conſiſtent with the chriſtian doctrines. *Hale's Common Law of England.*

Milton's Paradiſe Loſt is admirable. But cannot I admire the height of his invention, and the ſtrength of his expreſſion, without defending his *antiquated* words, and the perpetual harſhneſs of their ſound? *Dryden.*

Almighty Latium, with her cities crown'd,
Shall like an *antiquated* fable ſound. *Addiſon on Italy.*

A'NTIQUATEDNESS. *n. ſ.* [from *antiquated.*] The ſtate of being antiquated, worn out of uſe, or obſolete.

ANTI'QUE. *adj.* [*antique*, Fr. *antiquus*, Lat. It was formerly pronounced according to the Engliſh analogy, with the accent on the firſt ſyllable; but now after the French, with the accent on the laſt, at leaſt in proſe; the poets uſe it variouſly.]

1. Ancient; old; not modern.

Now, good Ceſario, but that piece of ſong,
That old and *antique* ſong we heard laſt night. *Shakeſp. Twelfth Night.*

Such truth in love as th' *antique* world did know,
In ſuch a ſtile as courts might boaſt of now. *Waller.*

2. Of genuine antiquity.

The ſeals which we have remaining of Julius Cæſar, which we know to be *antique*, have the ſtar of Venus over them. *Dryden's Virgil's Æneis, Pref.*

My copper lamps at any rate,
For being true *antique* I bought;
Yet wiſely melted down my plate,
On modern models to be wrought;
And trifles I alike purſue,
Becauſe they're old, becauſe they're new. *Prior.*

3. Of old faſhion.

Forth came that ancient lord and aged queen,
Array'd in *antique* robes down to the ground.
And ſad habiliments right well beſeen. *Fairy Queen, b.* i.

Muſt he no more divert the tedious day?
Nor ſparkling thoughts in *antique* words convey? *Smith to the Memory of Philips.*

4. Odd; wild; antick.

Name not theſe living death-heads unto me;
For theſe not ancient but *antique* be. *Donne.*

And ſooner may a gulling weather-ſpy
By drawing forth heav'n's ſcheme, tell certainly
What faſhion'd hats or ruffs, or ſuits next year,
Our giddy-headed *antique* youth will wear. *Donne.*

ANTI'QUE. *n. ſ.* [from *antique*, adj.] An antiquity; a remain of ancient times; an ancient rarity.

I leave to Edward, now early of Oxford, my ſeal of Julius Cæſar; as alſo another ſeal, ſuppoſed to be a young Hercules; both very choice *antiques*, and ſet in gold. *Swift's Laſt Will.*

ANTI'QUENESS. *n. ſ.* [from *antique.*] The quality of being antique; an appearance of antiquity.

We may diſcover ſomething venerable in the *antiqueneſs* of the work; but we would ſee the deſign enlarged, the figures reformed, and the colour laid on. *Addiſon on the Georgicks.*

Anti'quity. *n. ſ.* [*antiquitas*, Lat.]

1. Old times; time paſt long ago.

I mention Ariſtotle, Polybius, and Cicero, the greateſt philoſopher, the moſt impartial hiſtorian, and the moſt conſummate ſtateſman of all *antiquity*. *Addiſon. Freeholder*, N° 51.

2. The people of old times; the ancients.

That ſuch pillars were raiſed by Seth, all *antiquity* has avowed. *Raleigh's Hiſtory of the World.*

3. The works or remains of old times.

As for the obſervation of Machiavel, traducing Gregory the Great, that he did what in him lay, to extinguiſh all heathen *antiquities*: I do not find that thoſe zeals laſt long; as it appeared in the ſucceſſion of Sabinian, who did revive the former *antiquities*. *Bacon's Eſſays.*

4. Old age: a ludicrous ſenſe.

Is not your voice broken? your wind ſhort? your chin double? your wit ſingle? and every part about you blaſted with *antiquity*? and will you yet call yourſelf young? *Shakeſpeare's Henry* IV.

5. Ancientneſs; as, this ring is valuable for its *antiquity*.

ANTI'SCII. *n. ſ.* *It has no ſingular.* [from ἀντὶ and σκιὰ.] In geography, the people who inhabit on different ſides of the equator, who, conſequently, at noon have their ſhadows projected oppoſite ways. Thus the people of the north are *Antiſcii* to thoſe of the ſouth; the one projecting their ſhadows at noon toward the north pole, and the other toward the ſouth pole. *Chambers.*

Antiscorbu'tical. *adj.* [from ἀντὶ, againſt, and *ſcorbutum*, the ſcurvy.] Good againſt the ſcurvy.

The warm *antiſcorbutical* plants, in quantities, will occaſion ſtinking breath, and corrupt the blood. *Arbuth. on Aliments.*

Antiscorbu'tick. *adj.* [from ἀντὶ, againſt, and *ſcorbutum*, the ſcurvy.] Good againſt the ſcurvy.

The warm *antiſcorbuticks*, animal diet, and animal ſalts, are proper. *Arbuthnot on Diet.*

ANTI'SPASIS. *n. ſ.* [from ἀντὶ, againſt, and σπάω, to draw.] The revulſion of any humour into another part.

Antispasmo'dick. *adj.* [from ἀντὶ, againſt, and σπασμὸς, the cramp.] That which has the power of relieving the cramp.

Antispa'stick. *adj.* [from ἀντὶ and σπαστικὸς.] Medicines which cauſe a revulſion of the humours.

Antisplene'tick. *adj.* [from ἀντὶ and *ſplenetick*.] Efficacious in diſeaſes of the ſpleen.

Antiſpleneticks open the obſtructions of the ſpleen. *Floyer.*

ANTI'STROPHE. *n. ſ.* [ἀντιστροφὴ, from ἀντὶ, the contrary way, and στροφὴ, turning.] In an ode ſuppoſed to be ſung in parts, the ſecond ſtanza of every three, or ſometimes every ſecond ſtanza; ſo called becauſe the dance turns about.

Antistruma'tick. *adj.* [from ἀντὶ and *ſtruma*, a ſcrophulous ſwelling.] Good againſt the king's evil.

I preſcribed him a diſtilled milk, with *antiſtrumaticks*, and purged him. *Wiſeman's Surgery.*

ANTI'THESIS. *n. ſ.* in the plural *antitheſes*. [ἀντίθεσις, placing in oppoſition.] Oppoſition of words or ſentiments; contraſt; as in theſe lines:

Though gentle, yet not dull,
Strong without rage, without o'erflowing, full. *Denham.*

I ſee a chief, who leads my choſen ſons,
All arm'd with points, *antitheſes*, and puns. *Pope's Dunciad.*

A'ntitype. *n. ſ.* [ἀντίτυπος.] That which is reſembled or ſhadowed out by the type; that of which the type is the repreſentation. It is a term of theology. See Type.

When once upon the wing, he ſoars to an higher pitch, from the type to the *antitype*, to the days of the Meſſiah, the aſcenſion of our Saviour, and, at length, to his kingdom and dominion over all the earth. *Burnet's Theory of the Earth.*

He brought forth bread and wine, and was the prieſt of the moſt high God; and imitating the *antitype*, or the ſubſtance, Chriſt himſelf. *Taylor's Worthy Communicant.*

Antity'pical. *adj.* [from *antitype*.] That which relates to an antitype; that which explains the type.

Antivene'real. *adj.* [from ἀντὶ and *venereal*.] Good againſt the venereal diſeaſe.

If a lues be joined with it, you will ſcarce cure your patient without exhibiting *antivenereal* remedies. *Wiſeman's Surgery.*

A'ntler. *n. ſ.* [*andouillier*, Fr.] Properly the firſt branches of a ſtag's horns; but, popularly and generally, any of his branches.

Grown old, they grow leſs branched, and firſt loſe their brow *antlers*, or loweſt furcations next to the head. *Brown's Vulgar Errours, b.* iii. *c.* 9.

A well grown ſtag, whoſe *antlers* riſe
High o'er his front, his beams invade the ſkies. *Dryden.*

Bright Diana
Brought hunted wild goats heads, and branching *antlers*
Of ſtags, the fruit and honour of her toil. *Prior.*

ANTŒ'CI. *n. ſ.* *It has no ſingular.* [Lat. from ἀντὶ and οἰκέω, to inhabit.] In geography, thoſe inhabitants of the earth, who live under the ſame meridian, and at the ſame diſtance from the equator; the one toward the north, and the other to the ſouth. Hence they have the ſame longitude, and their latitude is alſo the ſame, but of a different denomination. They are in the ſame ſemicircle of the meridian, but oppoſite parallels. They have preciſely the ſame hours of the day and night, but oppoſite ſeaſons; and the night of the one is always equal to the day of the other. *Chambers.*

ANTONOMA'SIA. *n. ſ.* [from ἀντὶ and ὄνομα, a name.] A form of ſpeech, in which, for a proper name, is put the name of ſome dignity, office, profeſſion, ſcience, or trade; or when a proper name is put in the room of an appellative. Thus a king is called his majeſty; a nobleman, his lordſhip. We ſay the philoſopher inſtead of Ariſtotle, and the orator for Cicero: thus a man is called by the name of his country, a German, an Italian; and a grave man is called a Cato, and a wiſe man a Solomon. *Smith's Rhetorick.*

A'ntre. [*antre*, Fr. *antrum*, Lat.] A cavern; a cave; a den.

With all my travels hiſtory:
Wherein of *antres* vaſt, and deſarts idle,
It was my hent to ſpeak. *Shakeſp. Othello.*

A'nvil. *n. ſ.* [ænfille, Sax.]

1. The iron block on which the ſmith lays his metal to be forged.

I ſaw a ſmith ſtand with his hammer, thus,
The whilſt his iron did on the *anvil* cool. *Shak. King John.*

On their eternal *anvils* here he found
The brethren beating, and the blows go round. *Dryden.*

2. Any thing on which blows are laid.

Here I clip
The *anvil* of my ſword, and do conteſt
Hotly and nobly. *Shakeſpeare's Coriolanus.*

3. Figuratively; to be upon the *anvil*, is to be in a ſtate of formation or preparation.

Several members of our houſe knowing, ſome time ago, what was upon the *anvil*, went to the clergy, and deſired their judgment. *Swift.*

Anxi'ety. *n. ſ.* [*anxietas*, Lat.]

1. Trouble of mind about ſome future event; ſuſpenſe with uneaſineſs; perplexity; ſolicitude.

To be happy, is not only to be freed from the pains and diſeaſes of the body, but from *anxiety* and vexation of ſpirit; not only to enjoy the pleaſures of ſenſe, but peace of conſcience, and tranquillity of mind. *Tillotſon.*

2. In the medical language, depreſſion; lowneſs of ſpirits.

In *anxieties* which attend fevers, when the cold fit is over, a warmer regimen may be allowed; and becauſe *anxieties* often happen by ſpaſms from wind, ſpices are uſeful. *Arbuthnot.*

A'NXIOUS. *adj.* [*anxius*, Lat.]

1. Diſturbed about ſome uncertain event; ſolicitous.

His penſive cheek upon his hand reclin'd,
And *anxious* thoughts revolving in his mind. *Dryden.*

With beating hearts the dire event they wait,
Anxious, and trembling for the birth of fate. *Pope.*

2. Careful; full of inquietude; unquiet.

In youth alone, unhappy mortals live;
But ah! the mighty bliſs is fugitive;
Diſcolour'd ſickneſs, *anxious* labour come,
And age, and death's inexorable doom. *Dryden's Virgil.*

3. Careful, as of a thing of great importance.

There being no writings we need to be ſolicitous about the meaning of, but thoſe that contain truths we are to believe, or laws we are to obey, we may be leſs *anxious about* the ſenſe of other authours. *Locke.*

4. It has generally *for* or *about* before the object, but ſometimes *of*.

Who *anxious of* neglect, ſuſpecting change,
Conſults her pride, and meditates revenge. *Granville.*

A'nxiously. *adv.* [from *anxious*.] In an anxious manner; ſolicitouſly; unquietly; carefully.

But where the loſs is temporal, every probability of it needs not put us ſo *anxiouſly* to prevent it, ſince it might be repaired again. *South.*

Thou what befits the new lord mayor,
And what the Gallick arms will do,
Art *anxiouſly* inquiſitive to know. *Dryden.*

A'nxiousness. *n. ſ.* [from *anxious*.] The quality of being anxious; ſuſceptibility of anxiety.

A'ny. *adj.* [ænig, ænig, Sax.]

1. Every; whoever he be; whatever it be. It is, in all its ſenſes, applied indifferently to perſons or things.

I know you are now, Sir, a gentleman born—Ay and have been ſo *any* time theſe four hours. *Shakeſpeare's Winter's Tale.*

You contented yourſelf with being capable, as much as *any* whoſoever, of defending your country with your ſword. *Dryd.*

How fit is this retreat for uninterrupted ſtudy? *Any* one that ſees it will own, I could not have choſen a more likely place to converſe with the dead in. *Pope's Letters.*

2. Whoſoever; whatſoever; as diſtinguiſhed from ſome other.

What warmth is there in your affection towards *any* of theſe princely ſuitors that are already come. *Shakeſp. Merch. of Ven.*

An inverted motion being begun *any* where below, continues itſelf all the whole length. *Locke.*

3. It is uſed in oppoſition to *none*.

I wound and I heal: neither is there *any* that can deliver out of my hand. *Deut.* xxxii. 39.

A'orist. *n. ſ.* [ἀόριστος.] Indefinite; a term in the Greek grammar.

AORTA. *n. ſ.* [ἀορτὴ.] The great artery which riſes immediately out of the left ventricle of the heart. *Quincy.*

APA'CE. *adv.* [from *a* and *pace*; that is, with a great pace.]

1. Quick; ſpeedily: uſed of things in motion.

Or when the flying libbard ſhe did chace,
She could them nimbly move, and after fly *apace.* *F. Queen.*

Ay, quoth my uncle Glo'ſter,
Small herbs have grace, great weeds do grow *apace.*
And ſince methinks, I would not grow ſo faſt,
Becauſe ſweet flow'rs are ſlow, and weeds make haſte.
Shakeſp. Richard III.

He promis'd in his eaſt a glorious race;
Now ſunk from his meridian, ſets *apace.* *Dryden's Aurengz.*

Is not he imprudent, who, ſeeing the tide making haſte towards him *apace*, will ſleep till the ſea overwhelm him. *Tillotſon.*

2. With haſte; applied to ſome action.

The baron now his diamonds pours *apace*;
Th' embroider'd king who ſhows but half his face,
And his refulgent queen. *Pope's Rape of the Lock.*

3. Haſtily; with ſpeed: ſpoken of any kind of progreſſion from one ſtate to another.

This ſecond courſe of men,
With ſome regard to what is juſt and right,
Shall lead their lives, and multiply *apace.* *Milton's Par. Loſt,*

The life and power of religion decays *apace* here and at home, while we are ſpreading the honour of our arms far and wide through foreign nations. *Atterbury's Sermons.*

If ſenſible pleaſure, or real grandeur, be our end, we ſhall proceed *apace* to real miſery. *Watts's Improv. of the Mind.*

APAGO'GICAL. *adj.* [from ἀπαγωγὴ; compounded of ἀπὸ, from, and ἄγω, to bring or draw.] An *apagogical* demonſtration is ſuch as does not prove the thing directly; but ſhews the impoſſibility, or abſurdity, which ariſes from denying it; and is alſo called *reductio ad impoſſibile*, or *ad abſurdum.* *Chambers.*

APA'RT. *adv.* [*apart*, Fr.]

1. Separately from the reſt in place.

Since I enter into that queſtion, it behoveth me to give reaſon for my opinion, with circumſpection; becauſe I walk aſide, and in a way *apart* from the multitude. *Raleigh's Hiſtory.*

The party diſcerned, that the earl of Eſſex would never ſerve their turn, they reſolved to have another army *apart*, that ſhould be at their devotion. *Clarendon, b.* viii.

2. In a ſtate of diſtinction; as, to ſet *apart* for any uſe.

He is ſo very figurative, that he requires a grammar *apart*, to conſtrue him. *Dryden.*

The tyrant ſhall demand yon ſacred load,
And gold and veſſels ſet *apart* for God. *Prior.*

3. Diſtinctly.

Moſes firſt nameth heaven and earth, putting waters but in the third place, as comprehending waters in the word earth; but afterwards he nameth them *apart.* *Raleigh's Hiſtory.*

4. At a diſtance; retired from the other company.

So pleaſe you, madam,
To put *apart* theſe your attendants, I
Shall bring Emilia forth. *Shakeſp. Winter's Tale.*

APA'RTMENT. *n. ſ.* [*apartement*, Fr.] A part of the houſe allotted to the uſe of any particular perſon; a room; a ſet of rooms.

A private gallery 'twixt th' *apartments* led,
Not to the foe yet known. *Sir J. Denham.*

Pale as death, deſpoil'd of his array,
Into the queen's *apartment* takes his way. *Dryden's Fables.*

The moſt conſiderable ruin is that on the eaſtern promontory, where are ſtill ſome *apartments* left, very high and arched at top. *Addiſon's Remarks on Italy.*

A'PATHY. *n. ſ.* [α, not, and πάθος, feeling.] The quality of not feeling; exemption from paſſion; freedom from mental perturbation.

Of good and evil much they argued then,
Paſſion, and *apathy*, and glory, and ſhame.
Milton's Paradiſe Loſt.

To remain inſenſible of ſuch provocations, is not conſtancy, but *apathy.* *South.*

In lazy *apathy* let ſtoicks boaſt
Their virtue fix'd; 'tis fixed as in froſt,
Contracted all, retiring to the breaſt;
But ſtrength of mind is exerciſe, not reſt. *Pope.*

APE. *n. ſ.* [*ape*, Icelandiſh.]

1. A kind of monkey remarkable for imitating what he ſees.

I will be more newfangled than an *ape*, more giddy in my deſires than a monkey. *Shakeſp. As you like it.*

Writers report, that the heart of an *ape* worn near the heart, comforteth the heart, and increaſeth audacity. It is true, that the *ape* is a merry and bold beaſt. *Bacon's Natural Hiſtory.*

With glittering gold and ſparkling gems they ſhine,
But *apes* and monkeys are the gods within. *Granville.*

2. An imitator; uſed generally in the bad ſenſe.

Julio Romano, who, had he himſelf eternity, and could put breath into his work, would beguile nature of her cuſtom: ſo perfectly he is her *ape.* *Shakeſp. Winter's Tale.*

To APE. *v. a.* [from *ape.*] To imitate, as an ape imitates human actions.

Aping the foreigners in every dreſs,
Which, bought at greater coſt, becomes him leſs. *Dryden.*

Curſe on the ſtripling! how he *apes* his ſire!
Ambitiouſly ſententious! *Addiſon's Cato.*

APE'AK, or APE'EK. *adv.* [probably from *à pique.*] In a poſture to pierce the ground.

A'PEPSY. *n. ſ.* [ἀπεψία.] A loſs of natural concoction. *Quincy.*

A'PER. *n. ſ.* [from *ape.*] A ridiculous imitator or mimick.

APE'RIENT. *adj.* [*aperio*, Lat. to open.] That which has the quality of opening; chiefly uſed in medicine for gently purgative.

There be bracelets fit to comfort the ſpirits; and they be of three intentions; refrigerant, corroborant, and *aperient.* *Bacon.*

Of the ſtems of plants, ſome contain a fine *aperient* ſalt, and are diuretick and ſaponaceous. *Arbuthnot on Aliments.*

APE'RITIVE. *adj.* [from *aperio*, Lat. to open.] That which has the quality of opening the excrementious paſſages of the body.

They may make broth, with the addition of *aperitive* herbs.
Harvey on Conſumptions.

APE'RT. *adj.* [*apertus*, Lat.] Open.

APE'RTION. *n. ſ.* [from *apertus*, Lat.]

1. An opening; a paſſage through any thing; a gap.

The next now in order are the *apertions*; under which term I do comprehend doors, windows, ſtaircaſes, chimneys, or other conduits: in ſhort, all inlets or outlets. *Wotton's Archit.*

2. The act of opening; or ſtate of being opened.

The plenitude of veſſels, otherways called the plethora, when it happens, cauſeth an extravaſation of blood, either by ruption or *apertion* of them. *Wiſeman's Surgery.*

APE'RTLY. *adv.* [*apertè*, Lat.] Openly; without covert.

APE'RTNESS. *n. ſ.* [from *apert.*] Openneſs.

In general, the freedom, or *apertneſs* and vigour of pronouncing, and the cloſeneſs and muffling, and, as I may ſay, lazineſs of ſpeaking, render the ſound conſiderably different.
Holder's Elements of Speech.

A'PERTURE. *n. ſ.* [from *apertus*, open.]

1. The act of opening.

Hence ariſeth the facility of joining a conſonant to a vowel, becauſe from an appulſe to an *aperture* is eaſier, than from one appulſe to another. *Holder's Elements of Speech.*

2. An open place.

If memory be made by the eaſy motion of the ſpirits through the opened paſſages, images, without doubt, paſs through the ſame *apertures.* *Glanville's Scepſis Scientifica, Preface.*

3. The hole next the object glaſs of a teleſcope or microſcope.

The concave metal bore an *aperture* of an inch; but the *aperture* was limited by an opaque circle, perforated in the middle. *Newton's Opticks.*

4. Enlargement; explanation: a ſenſe ſeldom found.

It is too much untwiſted by the doctors, and, like philoſophy, made intricate by explications, and difficult by the *aperture* and diſſolution of diſtinctions. *Taylor's Worthy Communic.*

APE'TALOUS. *adj.* [of α, *priv.* and πέταλον, a leaf.] Without petala or flower leaves.

APE'TALOUSNESS. *n. ſ.* [from *apetalous.*] Being without leaves.

APEX. *n. ſ.* *apices*, plur. [Lat.] The tip or point of any thing.

The *apex*, or leſſer end of it, is broken off. *Woodward.*

APHÆ'RESIS. *n. ſ.* [ἀφαίρεσις.] A figure in grammar that takes away a letter or ſyllable from the beginning of a word.

APHE'LION. *n. ſ.* *aphelia*, plur. [from ἀπὸ, and ἥλιος, the ſun.] That part of the orbit of a planet, in which it is at the point remoteſt from the ſun.

The reaſon why the comets move not in the zodiack, is, that, in their *aphelia*, they may be at the greateſt diſtances from one another; and conſequently diſturb one another's motions the leaſt that may be. *Cheyne's Philoſoph. Principles.*

APHE'TA. *n. ſ.* [with aſtrologers.] The name of the plant, which is imagined to be the giver or diſpoſer of life in a nativity. *Dict.*

APHE'TICAL. *adj.* [from *apheta.*] Relating to the apheta.

APHILA'NTHROPY. *n. ſ.* [ἀ, without, and φιλανθρωπία, love of mankind.] Want of love to mankind.

A'PHONY. *n. ſ.* [ἀ, without, and φωνὴ, ſpeech.] A loſs of ſpeech.
Quincy.

A'PHORISM. *n. ſ.* [ἀφορισμὸς.] A maxim; a precept contracted in a ſhort ſentence; an unconnected poſition.

He will eaſily diſcern how little of truth there is in the multitude; and though ſometimes they are flattered with that *aphoriſm*, will hardly believe the voice of the people to be the voice of God. *Brown's Vulgar Errours, b.* i. *c.* 3.

I ſhall at preſent conſider the *aphoriſm*, that a man of religion and virtue is a more uſeful, and conſequently a more valuable member of a community. *Rogers's Sermons.*

APHORI'STICAL. *adj.* [from *aphoriſm.*] In the form of an aphoriſm; in ſeparate and unconnected ſentences.

APHORI'STICALLY. *adv.* [from *aphoriſtical.*] In the form of an aphoriſm.

Theſe being carried down, do ſeldom miſs a cure of the former, as Hippocrates doth likeways *aphoriſtically* tell us.
Harvey on Conſumptions.

Aphrodisi'acal. } *adj.* [from ἀφροδίτη, Venus.] Relating to
Aphrodisi'ack. } the venereal disease.

A'piary. *n. s.* [from *apis*, Lat. a bee.] The place where bees are kept.

Those who are skilled in bees, when they see a foreign swarm approaching to plunder their hives, have a trick to divert them into some neighbouring *apiary*, there to make what havock they please. *Swift.*

API'CES of a flower. [Lat. from *apex* the top.] Little knobs that grow on the tops of the stamina, in the middle of a flower. They are commonly of a dark purplish colour. By the microscope they have been discovered to be a sort of *capsulæ seminales*, or seed vessels, containing in them small globular, and often oval particles, of various colours, and exquisitely formed. *Quincy.*

Api'ece. *adv.* [from *a* for *each*, and *piece*, or share.] To the part or share of each.

Men, in whose mouths at first sounded nothing but mortification, were come to think they might lawfully have six or seven wives *apiece*. *Hooker, Preface.*

I have to night dispatched sixteen businesses, a month's length *apiece*, by an abstract of success. *Shak. All's well that ends well.*

One copy of this paper may serve a dozen of you, which will be less than a farthing *apiece*. *Swift.*

A'pish. *adj.* [from *ape.*]

1. Having the qualities of an ape; imitative.

Report of fashions in proud Italy,
Whose manners still our tardy, *apish* nation
Limps after, in base aukward imitation. *Shak. Richard* II.

2. Foppish; affected.

Because I cannot flatter, and look fair,
Duck with French nods and *apish* courtesy,
I must be held a rancorous enemy. *Shakesp. Richard* III.

3. Silly; trifling; insignificant.

All this is but *apish* sophistry; and, to give it a name divine and excellent, is abusive and unjust. *Glanville's Scepsis Scient.*

4. Wanton; playful.

Gloomy sits the queen;
Till happy chance reverts the cruel scene;
And *apish* folly, with her wild resort
Of wit and jest, disturbs the solemn court. *Prior.*

A'pishly. *adv.* [from *apish.*] In an apish manner; foppishly; conceitedly.

A'pishness. *n. s.* [from *apish.*] Mimickry; foppery; insignificance; playfulness.

Api'tpat. *adv.* [a word formed from the motion.] With quick palpitation.

O there he comes—Ay, my Hector of Troy, welcome my bully, my back; agad my heart has gone *apitpat* for you. *Congreve's Old Batchelor.*

APLU'STRE. *n. s.* [Latin.] The ancient ensign carried in sea vessels.

The one holds a sword in her hand, to represent the Iliad, as the other has an *aplustre*, to represent the Odyssey, or voyage of Ulysses. *Addison.*

APO'CALYPSE. *n. s.* [from ἀποκαλύπτω.] Revelation; discovery: a word used only of the sacred writings.

O for that warning voice, which he who saw
Th' *apocalypse* heard cry in heav'n aloud. *Milton's Par. Lost.*

With this throne, of the glory of the Father, compare the throne of the Son of God, as seen in the *apocalypse*. *Burnet's Theory of the Earth.*

Apocaly'ptical. *adj.* [from *apocalypse.*] Concerning revelation; containing revelation.

If we could understand that scene, at the opening of this *apocalyptical* theatre, we should find it a representation of the majesty of our Saviour. *Burnet's Theory of the Earth.*

Apocaly'ptically. *adv.* [from *apocalyptical.*] In such a manner as to reveal something secret.

APO'COPE. *n. s.* [ἀποκοπή.] A figure in grammar, when the last letter or syllable of a word is taken away; as, *ingeni* for *ingenii*.

Apocru'stick. *adj.* [ἀποκρουστικά, from ἀποκρούω, to drive.] Remedies endued with a repelling and astringent power, by which they prevent the too great afflux of humours to a part diseased. *Chambers.*

APO'CRYPHA. *n. s.* [from ἀποκρύπτω, to put out of sight.] Books whose authours are not known. It is used for the books appended to the sacred writings, which, being of doubtful authours, are less regarded.

We hold not the *apocrypha* for sacred, as we do the holy scripture, but for human compositions. *Hooker, b.* v.

Apo'cryphal. *adj.* [from *apocrypha.*]

1. Not canonical; of uncertain authority.

Jerom, who saith, that all writings not canonical are *apocryphal*, uses not the title *apocryphal*, as the rest of the fathers ordinarily have done, whose custom is so to name, for the most part, only such as might not publickly be read or divulged. *Hooker, b.* v. § 20.

2. Contained in the apocrypha.

To speak of her in the words of the *apocryphal* writers, wisdom is glorious, and never fadeth away. *Addison. Spectator.*

3. It is sometimes used for an account of uncertain credit.

Apo'cryphally. *adv.* [from *apocryphal.*] Uncertainly; not indisputably.

Apo'cryphalness. *n. s.* [from *apocryphal.*] Uncertainty; doubtfulness of credit.

Apodi'ctical. *adj.* [from ἀπόδειξις, evident truth; demonstration.] Demonstrative; evident beyond contradiction.

Holding an *apodictical* knowledge, and an assured knowledge of it; verily, to persuade their apprehensions otherwise, were to make Euclid believe, that there were more than one centre in a circle. *Brown's Vulgar Errours, b.* i. *c.* 10.

We can say all at the number three; therefore the world is perfect. Tobit went, and his dog followed him; therefore there is a world in the moon, were an argument as *apodictical*. *Glanville's Scepsis, c.* 19.

APODI'XIS. *n. s.* [ἀπόδειξις.] Demonstration. *Dict.*

APOGÆ'ON. } *n. s.* [from ἀπὸ, from, and γῆ, the earth.] A
A'pogee. } point in the heavens, in which the sun, or a
APOGE'UM. } planet, is at the greatest distance possible from the earth in its whole revolution. The ancient astronomers regarding the earth as the centre of the system, chiefly regarded the apogæon and perigæon, which the moderns, making the sun the centre, change for the aphelion and perihelion. *Chamb.*

Thy sin is in his *apogæon* placed,
And when it moveth next, must needs descend. *Fairfax.*

It is not yet agreed in what time, precisely, the *apogeum* absolveth one degree. *Brown's Vulgar Errours, b.* vi. *c.* i.

Apologe'tical. } *adj.* [from ἀπολογέω, to defend.] That which
Apologe'tick. } is said in defence of any thing or person.

I design to publish an essay, the greater part of which is *apologetical*, for one sort of chymists. *Boyle.*

Apologe'tically. *adv.* [from *apologetical.*] In the way of defence or excuse.

Apo'logist. *n. s.* [from *To apologize.*] He that makes an apology; a pleader in favour of another.

To **Apo'logize.** *v. n.* [from *apology.*]

1. To plead in favour of any person or thing.

It will be much more seasonable to reform than *apologize* or rhetoricate; and therefore it imports those, who dwell secure, to look about them. *Decay of Piety.*

2. It has the particle *for* before the subject of apology.

I ought to *apologize for* my indiscretion in the whole undertaking. *Wake's Preparation for Death.*

The translator needs not *apologize for* his choice of this piece, which was made in his childhood. *Pope's Preface to Statius.*

A'pologue. *n. s.* [ἀπόλογος.] Fable; story contrived to teach some moral truth.

An *apologue* of Æsop is beyond a syllogism, and proverbs more powerful than demonstration. *Brown's Vulgar Errours.*

Some men are remarked for pleasantness in raillery; others for *apologues* and apposite diverting stories. *Locke.*

APO'LOGY. *n. s.* [*apologia*, Lat. ἀπολογία.]

1. Defence; excuse. *Apology* generally signifies rather excuse than vindication, and tends rather to extenuate the fault, than prove innocence. This is, however, sometimes unregarded by writers.

In her face excuse
Came prologue; and *apology* too prompt;
Which with bland words at will she thus address'd.
Milton's Parad. Lost, b. ix. *l.* 854.

2. It has *for* before the object of excuse.

It is not my intention to make an *apology for* my poem: some will think it needs no excuse, and others will receive none. *Dryden's Pref. to Abs. and Achit.*

I shall neither trouble the reader, nor myself, with any *apology for* publishing of these sermons; for if they be, in any measure, truly serviceable to the end for which they are designed, I do not see what apology is necessary; and if they be not so, I am sure none can be sufficient. *Tillotson.*

Apomeco'metry. *n. s.* [ἀπὸ, from, μῆκος, distance, and μετρέω, to measure.] The art of measuring things at a distance.

APONEURO'SIS. *n. s.* [from ἀπὸ, from, and νεῦρον, a nerve.] An expansion of a nerve into a membrane.

When a cyst rises near the orifice of the artery, it is formed by the *aponeurosis* that runs over the vessel, which becomes excessively expanded. *Sharp's Surgery.*

APO'PHASIS. *n. s.* [Lat. ἀπόφασις, a denying.] A figure in rhetorick, by which the orator, speaking ironically, seems to wave what he would plainly insinuate; as, *Neither will I mention those things, which if I should, you notwithstanding could neither confute or speak against them.* *Smith's Rhetorick.*

Apophle'gmatick. *adj.* [ἀπὸ and φλέγμα.] That which has the quality of drawing away phlegm.

Apophle'gmatism. *n. s.* [ἀπὸ and φλέγμα.] A medicine of which the intention is to draw phlegm from the blood.

And so it is in *apophlegmatisms* and gargarisms, that draw the rheum down by the palate. *Bacon's Natural Hist.* N° 38.

Apophlegma'tizant. *n. s.* [ἀπὸ and φλέγμα.] Any remedy which causes an evacuation of serous or mucous humour by the nostrils, as particular kinds of sternutatories. *Quincy.*

A'pophthegm. *n. s.* [ἀπόφθεγμα.] A remarkable saying; a valuable maxim uttered on some sudden occasion.

We may magnify the *apophthegms*, or reputed replies of wisdom,

dom, whereof many are to be seen in Laertius and Lycosthenes. *Brown's Vulgar Errours, b.* i. *c.* 6.

I had a mind to collect and digest such observations and *apophthegms*, as tend to the proof of that great assertion, All is vanity. *Prior's Pref. to Solomon.*

APOPHYGE. *n. s.* [ἀποφυγὴ, flight, or escape.] Is, in architecture, that part of a column, where it begins to spring out of its base; and was originally no more than the ring or ferrel, which anciently bound the extremities of wooden pillars, to keep them from splitting, and were afterward imitated in stone work. We sometimes call it the spring of the column. *Chambers.*

APO'PHYSIS. *n. s.* [ἀπόφυσις.] The prominent parts of some bones; the same as process. It differs from an epiphysis, as that is a continuance of the bone itself; whereas the latter is somewhat adhering to a bone, and of which it is not properly a part. *Quincy.*

It was the *apophysis*, or head of the os tibiæ,which makes the knee. *Wiseman's Surgery.*

APOPLE'CTICAL. *adj.* [from *apoplexy.*] Relating to an apoplexy.

We meet with the same complaints of gravity in living bodies, when the faculty locomotive seems abolished; as may be observed in supporting persons inebriated, *apoplectical*, or in lipothymies and swoonings. *Brown's Vulgar Errours, b.* iv.

In an *apoplectical* case, he found extravasated blood, making way from the ventricles of the brain. *Derham's Physico-Theol.*

APOPLE'CTICK. *adj.* [from *apoplexy.*] Relating to an apoplexy.

A lady was seized with an *apoplectick* fit, which afterward terminated in some kind of lethargy. *Wiseman's Surgery.*

A'POPLEX. *n. s.* [See APOPLEXY.] Apoplexy. The last syllable is cut away; but this is only in poetry.

Present punishment pursues his maw,
When surfeited and swell'd, the peacock raw,
He bears into the bath; whence want of breath,
Repletions, *apoplex*, intestate death. *Dryden's Juvenal.*

A'POPLEXED. *adj.* [from *apoplex.*] Seized with an apoplexy.

Sense, sure, you have,
Else could you not have motion: but sure that sense
Is *apoplex'd*. *Shakesp. Hamlet.*

A'POPLEXY. *n. s.* [ἀποπληξις.] A sudden deprivation of all internal and external sensation, and of all motion, unless of the heart and thorax. The cause is generally a repletion, and indicates evacuation, joined with stimuli. *Quincy.*

Apoplexy is a sudden abolition of all the senses, external and internal, and of all voluntary motion, by the stoppage of the flux and reflux of the animal spirits through the nerves destined for those motions. *Arbuthnot on Diet.*

Peace is a very *apoplexy*, lethargy, mulled, deaf, sleepy, insensible. *Shakesp. Coriolanus.*

A fever may take away my reason, or memory, and an *apoplexy* leave neither sense nor understanding. *Locke.*

APO'RIA. *n. s.* [ἀπορία.] Is a figure in rhetorick, by which the speaker shews, that he doubts where to begin for the multitude of matter, or what to say in some strange and ambiguous thing; and doth, as it were, argue the case with himself. Thus Cicero says, *Whether he took them from his fellows more impudently, gave them to a harlot more lasciviously, removed them from the Roman people more wickedly, or altered them more presumptuously, I cannot well declare.* *Smith's Rhetorick.*

APORRHOE'A. *n. s.* [ἀποῤῥοια.] Effluvium; emanation; something emitted by another.

The reason of this he endeavours to make out by atomical *aporrhœas*, which passing from the cruentate weapon to the wound, and being incorporated with the particles of the salve, carry them to the affected part. *Glanville's Scepsis, c.* 24.

APOSIOPE'SIS. *n. s.* [ἀποσιώπησις, from ἀπὸ, after, and σιωπάω, to be silent.] A form of speech, by which the speaker, through some affection, as sorrow, bashfulness, fear, anger, or vehemency, breaks off his speech before it be all ended. A figure, when, speaking of a thing, we yet seem to conceal it, though indeed we aggravate it; or when the course of the sentence begun is so stayed, as thereby some part of the sentence not being uttered, may be understood; as, *I might say much more, but modesty commands silence.* *Smith's Rhetorick.*

APO'STASY. *n. s.* [ἀπόστασις.] Departure from what a man has professed: it is generally applied to religion; sometimes with the particle *from.*

The canon law defines *apostasy* to be a wilful departure from that state of faith, which any person has professed himself to hold in the christian church. *Ayliffe's Parergon.*

The affable archangel had forewarn'd
Adam, by due example, to beware
Apostasy, by what befel in heav'n
To those apostates. *Milton's Paradise Lost, b.* vi. *l.* 43.

Vice in us were not only wickedness, but *apostasy*, degenerate wickedness. *Sprat.*

Whoever do give different worships, must bring in more gods; which is an *apostasy from* one God. *Stillingfleet.*

APO'STATE. *n. s.* [*apostata*, Lat. ἀποστατης.] One that has forsaken his profession; generally applied to one that has left his religion.

The angels, for disobedience, thou hast reserved to a miserable immortality; but unto man, equally rebellious, equally *apostate* from thee and goodness, thou hast given a Saviour. *Rogers's Sermons.*

Apostates in point of faith, are, according to the civil law, subject unto all punishments ordained against hereticks. *Ayliffe's Parergon Juris Canonici.*

APOSTA'TICAL. *adj.* [from *apostate.*] After the manner of an apostate.

To APO'STATIZE. *v. n.* [from *apostate.*] To forsake one's profession; it is commonly used of one who departs from his religion.

None revolt from the faith; not because they must not look upon a woman to lust after her, but because they are restrained from the perpetration of their lusts. If wanton glances, and libidinous thoughts, had been permitted by the gospel, they would have *apostatized* nevertheless. *Bentley's Sermons.*

To APO'STEMATE. *v. n.* [from *aposteme.*] To become an aposteme; to swell and corrupt into matter.

There is care to be taken in abscesses of the breast and belly, in danger of breaking inwards; yet, by opening these too soon, they some times *apostemate* again, and become crude. *Wiseman.*

APOSTEMA'TION. *n. s.* [from *apostemate.*] The formation of an aposteme; the gathering of a hollow purulent tumour.

Nothing can be more admirable than the many ways nature hath provided for preventing, or curing of fevers; as, vomitings, *apostemations*, salivations, *&c.* *Grew's Cosmologia Sacra.*

A'POSTEME. } *n. s.* [ἀπόστημα.] A hollow swelling, filled with
A'POSTUME. } purulent matter; an abscess.

With equal propriety we may affirm, that ulcers of the lungs, or *apostemes* of the brain, do happen only in the left side. *Brown's Vulgar Errours, b.* iii. *c.* 3.

The opening of *apostemes*, before the suppuration be perfected, weakeneth the heat, and renders them crude. *Wiseman.*

APO'STLE. *n. s.* [*apostolus*, Lat. ἀπόστολος.] A person sent with mandates by another. It is particularly applied to them whom our Saviour deputed to preach the gospel.

But all his mind is bent to holiness;
His champions are the prophets and *apostles.* *Shak. Hen.* IV.

I am far from pretending infallibility; that would be to erect myself into an *apostle*: a presumption in any one that cannot confirm what he says by miracles. *Locke.*

We know but a small part of the notion of an *apostle*, by knowing barely that he is sent forth. *Watts's Logick.*

APO'STLESHIP. *n. s.* [from *apostle.*] The office or dignity of an apostle.

Where, because faith is in too low degree,
I thought it some *apostleship* in me
To speak things, which by faith alone I see. *Donne.*

God hath ordered it, that St. Paul hath writ epistles; which are all confined within the business of his *apostleship*; and so contain nothing but points of christian instruction. *Locke's Essay on St. Paul's Epistles.*

APOSTO'LICAL. *adj.* [from *apostolick.*] Delivered or taught by the apostles; belonging to the apostles.

They acknowledge not, that the church keeps any thing as *apostolical*, which is not found in the apostles writings, in what other records soever it be found. *Hooker, b.* iv. § 2.

Declare yourself for that church, which is founded upon scripture, reason, *apostolical* practice and antiquity. *Hooker.*

APOSTO'LICALLY. *adv.* [from *apostolical.*] In the manner of the apostles.

APOSTO'LICALNESS. *n. s.* [from *apostolical.*] The quality of relating to the apostles; apostolical authority.

APOSTO'LICK. *adj.* [from *apostle.*] Taught by the apostles; belonging to an apostle.

Their oppositions in maintenance of publick superstition against *apostolick* endeavours, were vain and frivolous. *Hooker.*

Or where did I at sure tradition strike,
Provided still it were *apostolick*? *Dryden's Hind and Panther.*

APO'STROPHE. *n. s.* [ἀποστροφὴ, from ἀπὸ, from, and στρέφω, to turn.]

1. In rhetorick, a diversion of speech to another person, than the speech appointed did intend or require; or it is a turning of the speech from one person to another, many times abruptly. A figure when we break off the course of our speech, and speak to some new person, present or absent, as to the people or witnesses, when it was before directed to the judges, or opponent. This diversion or speech is made many ways. 1. To God. 2. To angels. 3. To men in their several ranks, whether absent or present, dead or alive. 4. To the adversary. 5. To the heavenly bodies and meteors. 6. To the earth and things in it. 7. To the sea and things in it. 8. To beasts, birds, and fishes. 9. To inanimate things. *Smith's Rhetorick.*
2. In grammar, the contraction of a word by the use of a comma; as, *tho'*, for *though*; *rep'*, for *reputation.*

Many laudable attempts have been made, by abbreviating words with *apostrophes*; and by lopping polysyllables, leaving one or two words at most. *Swift.*

To APO'STROPHIZE. *v. a.* [from *apostrophe.*] To address by an apostrophe.

There is a peculiarity in Homer's manner of *apostrophizing* Eumæus,

Eumæus; and ſpeaking of him in the ſecond perſon, it is generally applied only to men of account. *Pope's Odyſſey; notes.*

A'POSTUME. *n. ſ.* See APOSTEME. [This word is properly *apoſtem.*] A hollow tumour filled with purulent matter.

How an *apoſtume* in the meſentery breaking, cauſes a conſumption in the parts, is apparent. *Harvey on Conſumptions.*

To A'POSTUME. *v. n.* [from *apoſtume.*] To apoſtemate. *Dict.*

A'POTHECARY. *n. ſ.* [*apotheca*, Lat. a repoſitory.] A man whoſe employment it is to keep medicines for ſale.

Give me an ounce of civet, good *apothecary*, to ſweeten my imagination. *Shakeſp. King Lear.*

They have no other doctor but the ſun and the freſh air, and that ſuch an one, as never ſends them to the *apothecary*. *South.*

Wand'ring in the dark,
Phyſicians, for the tree, have found the bark;
They, lab'ring for relief of human kind,
With ſharpen'd ſight ſome remedies may find;
Th' *apothecary*-train is wholly blind. *Dryd. Fab.*

APO'THEGM. *n. ſ.* [properly *apophthegm*; which ſee.] A remarkable ſaying.

By frequent converſing with him, and ſcattering ſhort *apothegms*, and little pleaſant ſtories, and making uſeful applications of them, his ſon was, in his infancy, taught to abhor vanity and vice as monſters. *Watſon's Life of Sanderſon.*

APOTHE'OSIS. *n. ſ.* [from ἀπὸ and θεός.] Deification; the rite of adding any one to the number of gods.

As if it could be graved and painted omnipotent, or the nails and the hammer could give it an *apotheoſis*. *South.*

Allots the prince of his celeſtial line,
An *apotheoſis*, and rites divine. *Garth.*

APO'TOME. *n. ſ.* [from ἀποτέμνω, to cut off.]

1. In mathematicks, the remainder or difference of two incommenſurable quantities.

2. In muſick, it is the part remaining of an entire tone, after a greater ſemitone has been taken from it. The proportion in numbers of the *apotome*, is that of 2048 to 2187. The Greeks thought that the greater tone could not be divided into two equal parts; for which reaſon they called the firſt part ἀποτομη, and the other λῆμμα. *Chambers.*

A'POZEM. *n. ſ.* [ἀπὸ, from, and ζέω, to boil.] A decoction; an infuſion made by boiling ingredients.

During this evacuation, he took opening broths and apozems. *Wiſeman's Surgery.*

To APPA'L. *v. a.* [*appalir*, Fr. It might more properly have been written *appale.*] To fright; to ſtrike with ſudden fear; to depreſs; to diſcourage.

Whilſt ſhe ſpake, her great words did *appal*
My feeble courage, and my heart oppreſs,
That yet I quake and tremble over all. *Fairy Queen, b. ii.*

Give with thy trumpet a loud note to Troy,
Thou dreadful Ajax; that th' *appalled* air
May pierce the head of thy great combatant. *Shakeſp.*

The houſe of peers was ſomewhat *appalled* at this alarum; but took time to conſider of it till next day. *Clarendon.*

Does neither rage inflame, nor fear *appal*,
Nor the black fear of death that ſaddens all. *Pope.*

The monſter curls
His flaming creſt, all other thirſt *appall'd*,
Or ſhiv'ring flies, or choak'd at diſtance ſtands. *Thomſon.*

APPA'LEMENT. *n. ſ.* [from *appal.*] Depreſſion; diſcouragement; impreſſion of fear.

As the furious ſlaughter of them was a great diſcouragement and *appalement* to the reſt. *Bacon's Henry VII.*

A'PPANAGE. *n. ſ.* [*appanagium*, low Latin; probably from *panis*, bread.] Lands ſet apart by princes for the maintenance of their younger children.

He became ſuitor for the earldom of Cheſter, a kind of *appanage* to Wales, and uſing to go to the king's ſon. *Bacon.*

Had he though it fit,
That wealth ſhould be the *appanage* of wit,
The God of light could ne'er have been ſo blind,
To deal it to the worſt of human kind. *Swift.*

APPARA'TUS. *n. ſ.* [Latin.] Things provided as means to any certain end, as the tools of a trade; the furniture of a houſe; ammunition for war; equipage; ſhow.

There is an *apparatus* of things previous, to be adjuſted before I come to the calculation itſelf. *Woodward's Nat. Hiſt.*

Ourſelves are eaſily provided for; it is nothing but the circumſtantials, the *apparatus* or equipage of human life, that coſts ſo much. *Pope's Letters to Gay.*

APPA'REL. *n. ſ. It has no plural.* [*appareil*, Fr.]

1. Dreſs; veſture.

I cannot cog and ſay, that thou art this and that, like many of thoſe liſping hawthorn buds, that come like women in mens *apparel*, and ſmell like Buckleſbury in ſimpling time.
Shakeſpeare's Merry Wives of Windſor.

2. External habiliments.

Our late burnt London, in *apparel* new,
Shook off her aſhes to have treated you. *Waller.*

At publick devotion, his reſigned carriage made religion appear in the natural *apparel* of ſimplicity. *Tatler*, N° 54.

To APPA'REL. *v. a.* [from *apparel*, the noun.]

1. To dreſs; to cloath.

With ſuch robes were the king's daughters that were virgins *apparelled.* *2 Sam.* xiii. 18.

2. To adorn with dreſs.

She did *apparel* her apparel, and with the preciousneſs of her body made it moſt ſumptuous. *Sidney.*

3. To cover or deck, as with dreſs.

You may have trees *apparelled* with flowers, by boring holes in them, and putting into them earth, and ſetting ſeeds of violets. *Bacon's Natural Hiſtory*, N° 504.

Shelves, and rocks, and precipices, and gulfs, being *apparelled* with a verdure of plants, would reſemble mountains and valleys. *Bentley's Sermons.*

APPARENT. *adj.* [*apparent*, Fr. *apparens*, Lat.]

1. Plain; indubitable.

The main principles of reaſon are in themſelves *apparent*. For to make nothing evident of itſelf unto man's underſtanding, were to take away all poſſibility of knowing any thing. *Hooker, b.* i.

2. Seeming; in appearance; not real.

The perception intellective often corrects the report of phantaſy, as in the *apparent* bigneſs of the ſun, the *apparent* crookedneſs of the ſtaff in air and water. *Hale's Origin of Mankind.*

3. Viſible; in oppoſition to *ſecret.*

What ſecret imaginations we entertained is known to God: this is *apparent*, that we have not behaved ourſelves, as if we preſerved a grateful remembrance of his mercies. *Atterbury.*

The outward and *apparent* ſanctity of actions ſhould flow from purity of heart. *Rogers.*

4. Open; diſcoverable; known.

As well the fear of harm, as harm *apparent*,
In my opinion ought to be prevented. *Shakeſp. Richard* III.

5. Certain; not preſumptive.

He is the next of blood,
And heir *apparent* to the Engliſh crown. *Shakeſp. Henry* VI.

APPA'RENT. *n. ſ.* Elliptically uſed for *heir apparent.*

Ariſe a knight;
And learn this leſſon, Draw thy ſword in right.—
—I'll draw it as *apparent* to the crown,
And in that quarrel uſe it. *Shakeſp. Henry* VI.

APPA'RENTLY. *adv.* [from *apparent.*] Evidently; openly.

Arreſt him, officer;
I would not ſpare my brother in this caſe,
If he ſhould ſcorn me ſo *apparently*. *Shakeſp. Comedy of Err.*

Vices *apparently* tend to the impairing of mens health. *Tillot.*

APPARI'TION. *n. ſ.* [from *appareo*, Lat. to appear.]

1. Appearance; viſibility.

When ſuddenly ſtood at my head a dream,
Whoſe inward *apparition* gently mov'd
My fancy. *Milton's Paradiſe Loſt, b.* viii.

2. The thing appearing; a form; a viſible object.

I have mark'd
A thouſand bluſhing *apparitions*
To ſtart into her face; a thouſand innocent ſhames
In angel whiteneſs bear away thoſe bluſhes.
Shakeſpeare's Much ado about Nothing.

A glorious *apparition!* had not doubt,
And carnal fear, that day dimm'd Adam's eyes. *Parad. Loſt.*

Any thing beſides may take from me the ſenſe of what appeared; which *apparition*, it ſeems, was you. *Tatler*, N° 55.

3. A ſpectre; a walking ſpirit.

Horatio ſays 'tis but our phantaſy,
Touching this dreaded ſight twice ſeen of us;
Therefore I have intreated him,
That if again this *apparition* come,
He may approve our eyes, and ſpeak to it. *Shakeſp. Hamlet.*

Tender minds ſhould not receive early impreſſions of goblins, ſpectres, and *apparitions*, wherewith maids fright them into compliance. *Locke.*

One of thoſe *apparitions* had his right hand filled with darts, which he brandiſhed in the face of all who came up that way. *Tatler*, N° 81.

4. Something only apparent, not real.

Still there's ſomething
That checks my joys————
—Nor can I yet diſtinguiſh
Which is an *apparition*, this or that. *Denham's Sophy.*

5. Aſtronomically, the viſibility of ſome luminary, oppoſed to *occultation.*

A month of *apparition* is the ſpace wherein the moon appeareth, deducting three days wherein it commonly diſappeareth; and this containeth but twenty-ſix days and twelve hours. *Brown's Vulgar Errours, b.* iv. *c.* 12.

APPA'RITORS. *n. ſ.* [from *appareo*, Lat. to be at hand.]

1. Such perſons as are at hand to execute the proper orders of the magiſtrate or judge of any court of judicature. *Ayliffe's Parerg.*

2. The loweſt officer of the eccleſiaſtical court.

They ſwallowed all the Roman hierarchy, from the pope to the *apparitor*. *Ayliffe's Parergon.*

To APPA'Y. *v. a.* [*appayer*, old Fr. to ſatisfy.] To ſatisfy; to content: whence *well appayed*, is *pleaſed*; *ill appayed*, is *uneaſy.* It is now obſolete.

How well *appaid* she was her bird to find? *Sidney.*
Ay, Willy, when the heart is ill assay'd,
How can bagpipe or joints be well *appaid.* *Spenser's Past.*
I am well *appaid* that you had rather believe, than take the pain of a long pilgrimage, you will never be so stiff in any opinion. *Camden.*
So only can high justice rest *appaid.* *Parad. Lost, b.* xii.

To APPE'ACH. *v. a.*

1. To accuse; to inform against any person.
He did, amongst many others, *appeach* Sir William Stanley, the lord chamberlain. *Bacon's Henry* VII.
Were he twenty times
My son, I would *appeach* him. *Shakesp. Richard* II.
Disclose
The state of your affection; for your passions
Have to the full *appeached.* *Shak. All's well that ends well.*

2. To censure; to reproach; to taint with accusation.
For when Cymochles saw the foul reproach,
Which them *appeached*; prick'd with guilty shame,
And inward grief, he fiercely gen approach,
Resolv'd to put away that lordly shame. *Fairy Queen, b.* ii.
Nor canst, nor durst thou, traitor, on the pain,
Appeach my honour, or thine own maintain. *Dryd. Fables.*

APPE'ACHMENT. *n. s.* [from *appeach.*] Charge exhibited against any man; accusation.
A busy headed man gave first light to this *appeachment*; but the earl did avouch it. *Sir J. Hayward.*
The duke's answers to his *appeachments*, in number thirteen, I find civilly couched. *Wotton.*

To APPE'AL. *v. n.* [*appello*, Lat.]

1. To transfer a cause from one to another; with the particles *to* and *from.*
From the ordinary therefore they *appeal to* themselves. *Hooker.*

2. To refer to another as judge.
Force, or a declared design of force, upon the person of another, where there is no common superior on earth to *appeal to* for relief, is the state of war; and it is the want of such an appeal gives a man the right of war, even against an aggressor, though he be in society and a fellow subject. *Locke.*
They knew no foe, but in the open field,
And *to* their cause and *to* the gods *appealed.* *Stepney.*

3. To call another as witness.
Whether this, that the soul always thinks, be a self-evident proposition, I *appeal to* mankind. *Locke.*

4. To charge with a crime; to accuse.
One but flatters us,
As well appeareth by the cause you come,
Namely, t' *appeal* each other of high treason. *Shak. Rich.* II.

APPE'AL. *n. s.* [from the verb *To appeal.*]

1. An *appeal* is a provocation from an inferior to a superior judge, whereby the jurisdiction of the inferior judge is for a while suspended, in respect of the cause; the cognizance being devolved to the superior judge. *Ayliffe's Parergon.*
This ring
Deliver them, and your *appeal to* us
There make before them. *Shakesp. Henry* VIII.
Our reason prompts us to a future state,
The last *appeal from* fortune and *from* fate,
Where God's all righteous ways will be declar'd. *Dryden.*
There are distributers of justice, from whom there lies an *appeal to* the prince. *Addison on Italy.*

2. In the common law.
An accusation; which is a lawful declaration of another man's crime before a competent judge, by one that sets his name to the declaration, and undertakes to prove it, upon the penalty that may ensue of the contrary; more commonly used for the private accusation of a murderer, by a party who had interest in the party murdered, and of any felon, by one of his accomplices in the fact. *Cowell.*
The duke's unjust,
Thus to retort your manifest *appeal*,
And put your trial in the villain's mouth,
Which here you come to accuse. *Shak. M.Wives of Windsor.*
Hast thou, according to thy oath and bond,
Brought hither Henry Hereford, thy bold son,
Here to make good the boist'rous late *appeal*
Against the duke of Norfolk? *Shakespeare.*

3. A summons to answer a charge.
Nor shall the sacred character of king
Be urg'd to shield me from thy bold *appeal*,
If I have injur'd thee, that makes us equal. *Dryd. Don Seb.*

4. A call upon any as witness.
The casting up of the eyes, and lifting up of the hands, is a kind of *appeal to* the Deity, the authour of wonders. *Bacon.*

APPE'ALANT. *n. s.* [from *appeal.*] He that appeals.
Lords *appealants*,
Your diff'rences shall all rest under gage,
Till we assign you to your days of trial. *Shakesp. Rich.* III.

APPE'ALER. *n. s.* [from *appeal.*] One who makes an appeal.

To APPE'AR. *v. n.* [*appareo*, Lat.]

1. To be in sight; to be visible; sometimes with the particle *in.*
As the leprosy *appeareth in* the skin of the flesh. *Lev.* xiii. 43.
And half her knee, and half her breast *appear*,
By art, like negligence, disclos'd and bare. *Prior.*

2. To become visible as a spirit.
For I have *appeared* unto thee for this purpose, to make thee a minister and a witness. *Acts* xxvi. 16.

3. To stand in the presence of another; generally used of standing before some superiour.
When shall I come and *appear* before God? *Psalm* xlii. 2.

4. To be the object of observation.
Let thy work *appear* unto thy servants, and thy glory unto their children. *Psalm* xc. 16.

5. To exhibit one's self before a court of justice.
Keep comfort to you, and this morning see
You do *appear* before them. *Shakesp. Henry* VIII.

6. To be made clear by evidence.
Egfrid did utterly waste and subdue it, as *appears* out of Beda's complaint against him; and Edgar brought it under his obedience, as *appears* by an ancient record. *Spenser's Ireland.*

7. To seem in opposition to reality.
His first and principal care being to *appear* unto his people, such as he would have them be, and to be such as he *appeared.* *Sidney, b.* ii.
My noble master will *appear*
Such as he is, full of regard and honour. *Shak. Julius Cæs.*

8. To be plain beyond dispute.
From experiments, useful indications may be taken, as will *appear* by what follows. *Arbuthnot on Aliments.*

APPE'ARANCE. *n. s.* [from *To appear.*]

1. The act of coming into sight; as, they were surprised by the sudden *appearance* of the enemy.
2. The thing seen; as, the remarkable *appearances* in the sky.
3. Phœnomena; that quality of any thing which is visible.
The advancing day of experimental knowledge discloseth such *appearances*, as will not lie even in any model extant. *Glanville's Scepsis Scientifica, Pref.*

4. Semblance; not reality.
He encreased in estimation, whether by destiny, or whether by his virtues, or at least by his *appearances* of virtues. *Hayw.*
Heroic virtue did his actions guide,
And he the substance not th' *appearance* chose. *Dryden.*
The hypocrite would not put on the *appearance* of virtue, if it was not the most proper means to gain love. *Addison. Spectat.*

5. Outside; show.
Under a fair and beautiful *appearance* there should ever be the real substance of good. *Rogers.*

6. Entry into a place or company.
Do the same justice to one another, which will be done us hereafter by those, who shall make their *appearance* in the world, when this generation is no more. *Addison's Freeholder*, N° 35.

7. Apparition; supernatural visibility.
I think a person terrified with the imagination of spectres, more reasonable than one who thinks the *appearance* of spirits fabulous. *Addison. Spectator*, N° 110.

8. Exhibition of the person to a court.
I will not tarry; no, nor ever more
Upon this business my *appearance* make
In any of their courts. *Shakesp. Henry* VIII.

9. Open circumstance of a case.
Or grant her passion be sincere,
How shall his innocence be clear?
Appearances were all so strong,
The world must think him in the wrong. *Swift.*

10. Presence; mien.
Health, wealth, victory, and honour, are introduced; wisdom enters the last, and so captivates with her *appearance*, that he gives himself up to her. *Addison. Guardian*, N° 111.

11. Probability; seeming; likelihood.
There is that which hath no *appearance*, that this priest being utterly unacquainted with the true person, according to whose pattern he should shape his counterfeit, should think it possible for him to instruct his player. *Bacon's Henry* VII.

APPE'ARER. *n. s.* [from *To appear.*] The person that appears.
That owls and ravens are ominous *appearers*, and presignify unlucky events, was an augurial conception. *Brown's Vul. Err.*

APPE'ASABLE. *adj.* [from *To appease.*] That may be pacified; reconcileable.

APPE'ASABLENESS. *n. s.* [from *To appease.*] The quality of being easily appeased; reconcileableness.

To APPE'ASE. *v. a.* [*appaiser*, Fr.]

1. To quiet; to put in a state of peace.
By his counsel he *appeaseth* the deep, and planteth islands therein. *Ecclus*, xliii. 23.
England had no leisure to think of reformation, till the civil wars were *appeased*, and peace settled. *Sir J. Davies on Irel.*

2. To pacify; to reconcile; to still wrath.
So Simon was *appeased* towards them, and fought no more against them. *1 Mac.* xiii. 47.
O God! if my deep prayers cannot *appease* thee,
Yet execute thy wrath on me alone. *Shakesp. Richard* III.
The rest shall hear me call, and oft be warn'd
Their sinful state, and to *appease* betimes
Th' incensed Deity. *Milton's Paradise Lost, b.* iii.

APPE'ASEMENT. *n. f.* [from *To appease.*] A ftate of peace.

Being neither in numbers nor in courage great, partly by authority, partly by entreaty, they were reduced to fome good *appeafements.* *Sir J. Hayward.*

APPE'ASER. *n. f.* [from *To appeafe.*] He that pacifies others; he that quiets difturbances.

APPE'LLANT. *n. f.* [*appello*, Lat. to call.]

1. A challenger; one that fummons another to anfwer either in the lifts or in a court of juftice.

In the devotion of a fubject's love,
And free from other mifbegotten hate,
Come I *appellant* to this princely prefence. *Shakefp. Rich.* II.
This is the day appointed for the combat,
And ready are th' *appellant* and defendant,
Th' armourer and his man, to enter the lifts. *Shak. Hen.* IV.
Thefe fhifts refuted, anfwer thy *appellant,*
Though by his blindnefs maim'd for high attempts,
Who now defies thee thrice to fingle fight.

2. One that appeals from a lower to a higher power. *Milton's Samfon Agonistes.*

An appeal transfers the cognizance of the caufe to the fuperior judge; fo that, pending the appeal, nothing can be attempted in prejudice of the *appellant.* *Ayliffe's Parergon.*

APPE'LLATE. *n. f.* [*appellatus*, Lat.] The perfon appealed againft.

An appellatory libel ought to contain the name of the party appellant; the name of him from whofe fentence it is appealed; the name of him to whom it is appealed; from what fentence it is appealed; the day of the fentence pronounced, and appeal interpofed; and the name of the party *appellate*, or perfon againft whom the appeal is lodged. *Ayliffe's Parergon.*

APPELLA'TION. *n. f.* [*appellatio*, Lat.] Name; word by which any thing is called.

Nor are always the fame plants delivered under the fame name and *appellations.* *Brown's Vulgar Errours.*

Good and evil commonly operate upon the mind of man, by refpective names or *appellations*, by which they are notified and conveyed to the mind. *South.*

APPE'LLATIVE. *n. f.* [*appellativum*, Lat.]

Words and names are either common or proper. Common names are fuch as ftand for univerfal ideas, or a whole rank of beings, whether general or fpecial. Thefe are called *appellatives.* So fifh, bird, man, city, river, are common names; and fo are trout, eel, lobfter; for they all agree to many individuals, and fome to many fpecies. *Watts's Logick.*

APPE'LLATIVELY. *adv.* [from *appellative.*] According to the manner of nouns appellative; as, *this man is a Hercules. Hercules* is ufed *appellatively* to fignify *a ftrong man.*

APPE'LLATORY. *adj.* [from *appeal.*] That which contains an appeal. See APPELLATE.

APPE'LLEE. *n. f.* [from *appeal.*] One who is appealed againft, and accufed. *Dict.*

To APPE'ND. *v. a.* [*appendo*, Lat. to hang to any thing.]

1. To hang any thing upon another; as, the infcription was *appended* to the column.

2. To add to fomething as an acceffory, not a principal part.

APPE'NDAGE. *n. f.* [French] Something added to another thing, without being neceffary to its effence, as a portico to the houfe.

Modefty is the *appendage* of fobriety, and is to chaftity, to temperance, and to humility, as the fringes are to a garment. *Taylor's Rule of living holy.*

None of the laws of motion now eftablifhed, will ferve to account for the production, motion, or number of bodies, nor their *appendages*, though they may help us a little to conceive their appearances. *Cheyne's Philofophical Principles.*

He was fo far from over-valuing any of the *appendages* of life, that the thoughts of life did not affect him. *Atterbury's Serm.*

APPE'NDANT. *adj.* [French.]

1. Hanging to fomething elfe.

2. Belonging to; annexed; concomitant.

He that defpifes the world, and all its *appendant* vanities, is the moft fecure. *Taylor's Rule of holy living.*

He that looks for the bleffings *appendant* to the facrament, muft expect them upon no terms, but of a worthy communion. *Taylor's Worthy Communicant.*

Riches multiplied beyond the proportion of our character, and the wants *appendant* to it, naturally difpofe men to forget God. *Rogers.*

3. In law.

Appendant is any thing belonging to another, as *acceſſorium principali*, with the civilians, or *adjunctum fubjecto*, with the logicians. An hofpital may be *appendant* to a manour; a common of fifhing *appendant* to a freehold. *Cowell.*

APPE'NDANT. *n. f.* That which belongs to another thing, as an accidental or adventitious part.

Pliny gives an account of the inventors of the forms and *appendants* of fhipping. *Hale's Origin of Mankind.*

A word, a look, a tread, will ftrike, as they are *appendants* to external fymmetry, or indications of the beauty of the mind. *Grew's Cofmologia Sacra, b.* ii. *c.* 6.

To APPE'NDICATE. *v. a.* [*appendo*, Lat.] To add to another thing.

In a palace there is the cafe or fabrick of the ftructure, and there are certain additaments; as, various furniture, and curious motions of divers things *appendicated* to it. *Hale's Origin of Mankind.*

APPENDICA'TION. *n. f.* [from *appendicate.*] Adjunct; appendage; annexion.

There are confiderable parts and integrals, and *appendications* unto the *mundus afpectabilis*, impoffible to be eternal. *Hale's Origin of Mankind.*

APPE'NDIX. *n. f. appendices*, plur. [Lat.]

1. Something appended, or added to another thing.

The cherubim were never intended as an object of worfhip, becaufe they were only the *appendices* to another thing. But a thing is then propofed as an object of worfhip, when it is fet up by itfelf, and not by way of addition or ornament to another thing. *Stillingfleet's Defence of Difcourfes on Romifh Idolatry.*

Normandy became an *appendix* to England, the nobler dominion, and received a greater conformity of their laws to the Englifh, than they gave to it. *Hale's Civil Law of England.*

2. An adjunct or concomitant.

All concurrent *appendices* of the action ought to be furveyed, in order to pronounce with truth concerning it. *Watts.*

To APPERTA'IN. *v. n.* [*appartenir*, Fr.]

1. To belong to as of right.

The honour of devifing this doctrine, that religion ought to be inforced by the fword, would be found *appertaining* to Mahomed the falfe prophet. *Raleigh's Effays.*

The Father, t' whom in heav'n fupreme
Kingdom, and power, and glory *appertains*,
Hath honour'd me, according to his will. *Paradife Loft, b.* vi.

2. To belong to by nature or appointment.

If the foul of man did ferve only to give him being in this life, then things *appertaining* to this life would content him, as we fee they do other creatures. *Hooker, b.* i.

And they roafted the paffover with fire, as *appertaineth*: as for the facrifices they fod them in brafs pots. 1 *Efdras*, i. 2.

Both of them feem not to generate any other effect, but fuch as *appertaineth* to their proper objects and fenfes. *Bacon.*

Is it expected, I fhould know no fecrets
That *appertain* to you? *Shakefp. Julius Cæfar.*

APPERTA'INMENT. *n. f.* [from *appertain.*] That which belongs to any rank or dignity.

He fhent our meffengers, and we lay by
Our *appertainments*, vifiting of him. *Shakefpeare's Troilus and Creffida.*

APPE'RTENANCE. *n. f.* [*appartenance*, Fr.] That which belongs or relates to another thing.

Can they which behold the controverfy of divinity condemn our enquiries in the doubtful *appertenancies* of arts, and receptaries of philofophy? *Brown's Vulgar Errours, Preface.*

APPE'RTINENT. *adj.* [from *To appertain.*] Belonging; relating.

You know how apt our love was to accord
To furnifh him with all *appertinents*
Belonging to his honour. *Shakefpeare's Henry* V.

A'PPETENCE. } *n. f.* [*appetentia*, Lat.] Carnal defire; fenfual
A'PPETENCY. } defire.

Bred only and completed to the tafte
Of luftful *appetence*; to fing, to dance,
To drefs, to troule the tongue, and roll the eye.
Milton's Paradife Loft, b. xi. *l.* 619.

APPETIBI'LITY. *n. f.* [from *appetible.*] The quality of being defirable.

That elicitation which the fchools intend, is a deducing of the power of the will into act, merely from the *appetibility* of the object, as a man draws a child after him with the fight of a green bough. *Bramham againft Hobbes.*

A'PPETIBLE. *adj.* [*appetibilis*, Lat.] Defirable; that which may be the object of appetite.

Power both to flight the moft *appetible* objects, and to controul the moft unruly paffions. *Bramham againft Hobbes.*

A'PPETITE. *n. f.* [*appetitus*, Lat.]

1. The natural defire of good; the inftinct by which we are led to feek pleafure.

The will properly and ftrictly taken, as it is of things which are referred unto the end that men defireth, differeth greatly from that inferiour natural defire, which we call *appetite.* The object of *appetite* is whatfoever fenfible good may be wifhed for; the object of will is that good which reafon does lead us to feek. *Hooker, b.* i. § 7.

2. The defire of fenfual pleafure.

Why, fhe fhould hang on him,
As if increafe of *appetite* had grown
By what it fed on. *Shakefp. Hamlet.*
Urge his hateful luxury,
And beftial *appetite* in change of luft. *Shakefp. Richard* III.
Each tree
Loaden with faireft fruit, that hung to th' eye
Tempting, ftirr'd in me fudden *appetite*
To pluck and eat. *Milton's Paradife Loft, b.* viii.

There is continual abundance, which creates fuch an *appetite* in your reader, that he is not cloyed with any thing, but fatisfied with all. *Dryden's Juvenal, Dedicat.*

3. Vio-

3. Violent longing; eagerneſs after any thing.

No man could enjoy his life, his wife, or goods, if a mightier man had an *appetite* to take the ſame from him. *Davies on Irel.*

Hopton had an extraordinary *appetite* to engage Waller in a battle. *Clarendon, b.* viii.

Power being the natural *appetite* of princes, a limited monarch cannot gratify it. *Swift.*

4. Keenneſs of ſtomach; hunger; deſire of food.

There be four principal cauſes of *appetite*; the refrigeration of the ſtomach, joined with ſome dryneſs; contraction; vellication, and abſterſion; beſides hunger, which is an emptineſs. *Bacon's Natural Hiſtory*, N° 831.

5. It has ſometimes *of* before the object of deſire.

The new officer's nature needed ſome reſtraint to his immoderate *appetite of* power. *Clarendon.*

6. Sometimes *to.*

We have generally ſuch an *appetite to* praiſe, that we greedily ſuck it in. *Government of the Tongue*, § 8.

APPETI'TION. *n. ſ.* [*appetitio*, Lat.] Deſire.

The actual *appetition* or faſtening our affections on him. *Hammond's Practical Catechiſm.*

A'PPETITIVE. *adj.* [from *appetite.*] That which deſires; that which has the quality of deſiring.

The will is not a bare *appetitive* power as that of the ſenſual appetite, but is a rational appetite. *Hale's Origin of Mankind.*

To APPLA'UD. *v. a.* [*applaudo*, Lat.]

1. To praiſe by clapping the hand.

2. To praiſe in general.

I would *applaud* thee to the very echo,
That ſhould *applaud* again. *Shakeſp. Macbeth.*
Nations unborn your mighty names ſhall ſound,
And worlds *applaud* that muſt not yet be found! *Pope.*

APPLA'UDER. *n. ſ.* [from *applaud.*] He that praiſes or commends.

I had the voice of my ſingle reaſon againſt it, drowned in the noiſe of a multitude of *applauders.* *Glanville's Scepſis.*

APPLA'USE. *n. ſ.* [*applauſus*, Lat.] Approbation loudly expreſſed; praiſe.

This general *applauſe*, and chearful ſhout,
Argues your wiſdom and your love to Richard. *Shak. R.* III.
Sylla wept,
And chid her barking waves into attention;
And fell Charybdis murmur'd ſoft *applauſe.* *Milton's Comus.*

Thoſe that are ſo fond of *applauſe*, how little do they taſte it when they have it? *South.*

See their wide ſtreaming wounds; they neither came
For pride of empire, nor deſire of fame;
Kings fight for kingdoms, madmen for *applauſe*,
But love for love alone, that crowns the lover's cauſe.
Dryden's Fables.

A'PPLE. *n. ſ.* [æppel, Saxon.]

1. The fruit of the apple tree.

Tall thriving trees confeſs'd the fruitful mold;
The red'ning *apple* ripens here to gold. *Pope's Odyſſey.*

2. The pupil of the eye.

He inſtructed him; he kept him as the *apple* of his eye. *Deut.* xxxii. 10.

APPLE *of Love.*

Apples of love are of three ſorts; the moſt common having long trailing branches, with rough leaves and yellow joints, ſucceeded by apples, as they are called, at the joints, not round, but bunched; of a pale orange ſhining pulp, and ſeeds within. *Mortimer's Art of Huſbandry.*

APPLE-GRAFT. *n. ſ.* [from *apple* and *graft.*] A twig of apple tree grafted upon the ſtock of another tree.

We have ſeen three and twenty ſorts of *apple-grafts* upon the ſame old plant, moſt of them adorned with fruit. *Boyle.*

APPLE-TART. [from *apple* and *tart.*] A tart made of apples.

What, up and down carv'd like an *apple-tart.*
Shakeſpeare's Taming of the Shrew.

APPLE TREE. *n. ſ.* [from *apple* and *tree.*]

The fruit of this tree is for the moſt part hollowed about the foot ſtalk; the cells incloſing the ſeed are ſeparated by cartilaginous partitions; the juice of the fruit is ſowriſh, the tree large and ſpreading; the flowers conſiſt of five leaves, expanding in form of a roſe. There is a great variety of theſe fruits. Thoſe for the deſſert are, the white juniting, Margaret apple, ſummer pearmain, ſummer queening, embroidered apple, golden reinette, ſummer white Colville, ſummer red Colville, ſilver pippin, aromatick pippin, the gray reinette, la haute-bonté, royal ruſſeting, Wheeler's ruſſet, Sharp's ruſſet, ſpice apple, golden pippin, nonpareil, and l'api. Thoſe for the kitchen uſe are, codling, ſummer marigold, ſummer red pearmain, Holland pippin, Kentiſh pippin, the hanging body, Loan's pearmain, French reinette, French pippin, royal ruſſet, monſtruous reinette, winter pearmain, pomme violette, Spencer's pippin, ſtone pippin, oakenpin. And thoſe generally uſed for cyder are, Devonſhire royal wilding, redſtreaked apple, the whitſour, Herefordſhire underleaf, John apple, &c. *Millar.*

Thus *apple trees*, whoſe trunks are ſtrong to bear
Their ſpreading boughs exert themſelves in air. *Dryden.*

APPLE WOMAN. *n. ſ.* [from *apple* and *woman.*] A woman that ſells apples.

Yonder are two *apple women* ſcolding, and juſt ready to uncoif one another. *Arbuthnot and Pope's Mart. Scribl.*

APPLI'ABLE. *adj.* [from *apply.*] That which may be applied. For this word the moderns uſe *applicable*; which ſee.

Limitations all ſuch principles have, in regard of the varieties of the matter whereunto they are *appliable.* *Hooker, b.* v.

All that I have ſaid of the heathen idolatry is *appliable* to the idolatry of another ſort of men in the world. *South.*

APPLI'ANCE. *n. ſ.* [from *apply.*] The act of applying; the thing applied to.

Diſeaſes deſp'rate grown,
By deſperate *appliance* are relieved. *Shakeſp. Hamlet.*

APPLICABI'LITY. *n. ſ.* [from *applicable.*] The quality of being fit to be applied to ſomething.

The action of cold is compoſed of two parts; the one preſſing, the other penetration, which require *applicability.* *Digby.*

A'PPLICABLE. *adj.* [from *apply.*] That which may be applied, as properly relating to ſomething.

What he ſays of the portrait of any particular perſon, is *applicable* to poetry. In the character, there is a better or a worſe likeneſs; the better is a panegyrick, and the worſe a libel. *Dryden's Dufreſnoy, Preface.*

It were happy for us, if this complaint were *applicable* only to the heathen world. *Rogers.*

A'PPLICABLENESS. *n. ſ.* [from *applicable.*] Fitneſs to be applied.

The knowledge of ſalts may poſſibly, by that little part which we have already delivered of its *applicableneſs*, be of uſe in natural philoſophy. *Boyle.*

A'PPLICABLY. *adv.* [from *applicable.*] In ſuch a manner as that it may be properly applied.

A'PPLICATE. *n. ſ.* [from *apply.*] A right line drawn acroſs a curve, ſo as to biſect the diameter thereof. *Chambers.*

APPLICA'TION. *n. ſ.* [from *apply.*]

1. The act of applying any thing to another; as, he mitigated his pain by the *application* of emollients.

2. The thing applied; as, he invented a new *application*, by which blood might be ſtaunched.

3. The act of applying to any perſon, as a ſolicitor, or petitioner.

It ſhould ſeem very extraordinary, that a patent ſhould be paſſed, upon the *application* of a poor, private, obſcure mechanick. *Swift.*

4. The employment of any means for a certain end.

If a right courſe be taken with children, there will not be much need of the *application* of the common rewards and puniſhments. *Locke.*

5. Intenſeneſs of thought; cloſe ſtudy.

I have diſcovered no other way to keep our thoughts cloſe to their buſineſs, but by frequent attention and *application*, getting the habit of attention and *application.* *Locke.*

6. Attention to ſome particular affair; with the particle *to.*

His continued *application to* ſuch publick affairs, as may conduce to the benefit of his kingdoms, diverts him from pleaſures. *Addiſon's Freeholder*, N° 46.

This crime certainly deſerves the utmoſt *application* and wiſdom of a people to prevent it. *Addiſon.*

7. The condition of being uſed as means to an end.

There is no ſtint which can be ſet to the value or merit of the ſacrificed body of Chriſt; it hath no meaſured certainty of limits, bounds of efficacy unto life it knoweth none, but is alſo itſelf infinite in poſſibility of *application.* *Hooker, b.* v.

This principle acts with the greateſt force in the worſt *application*; and the familiarity of wicked men more ſucceſsfully debauches, than that of good men reforms. *Rogers.*

A'PPLICATIVE. *adj.* [from *apply.*] That which applies.

The directive command for counſel is in the underſtanding, and the *applicative* command for putting in execution, is in the will. *Bramhal againſt Hobbes.*

A'PPLICATORY. *adj.* [from *apply.*] That which comprehends the act of application.

A'PPLICATORY. *n. ſ.* That which applies.

There are but two ways of applying the death of Chriſt: faith is the inward *applicatory*, and if there be any outward, it muſt be the ſacraments. *Taylor's Worthy Communicant.*

To APPLY'. *v. a.* [*applico*, Lat.]

1. To put one thing to another.

He ſaid, and to the ſword his throat *applied.* *Dryd. Æn.*

2. To lay medicaments upon a wound.

Apply ſome ſpeedy cure, prevent our fate,
And ſuccour nature ere it be too late. *Addiſon's Ovid's Met.*

God has addreſſed every paſſion of our nature, *applied* remedies to every weakneſs, warned us of every enemy. *Rogers.*

3. To make uſe of as relative or ſuitable to ſomething.

This brought the death of your father into remembrance, and I repeated the verſes which I formerly *applied* to him. *Dryden's Fables, Ded.*

4. To put to a certain uſe.

The profits thereof might be applied towards the ſupport of the year. *Clarendon.*

5. To uſe as means to an end.

Theſe glorious beings are inſtruments in the hands of God, who

who *applies* their services, and governs their actions, and disposes even their wills and affections. *Rogers.*

6. To fix the mind upon; to study; with *to.*

Apply thine heart *unto* instruction, and thine ears *to* the words of knowledge. *Prov.* xxiii. 12.

Every man is conscious to himself that he thinks; and that which his mind is *applied* about, whilst thinking, is the ideas that are there. *Locke.*

It is a sign of a capacious mind, when the mind can *apply* itself *to* several objects with a swift succession. *Watts.*

7. To have recourse to, as a solicitor or petitioner; with *to.*

I had no thoughts of *applying to* any but himself; he desired I would speak to others. *Swift.*

8. To endeavour to work upon.

God knows every faculty and passion, and in what manner they can most successfully be *applied to.* *Rogers.*

9. To ply; to busy; to keep at work: an antiquated sense.

She was skilful in *applying* his humours; never suffering fear to fall to despair, nor hope to hasten to assurance. *Sidney.*

Far away they spy'd
A varlet running towards hastily,
Whose flying feet so fast their way *apply'd,*
That round about a cloud of dust did fly. *Fairy Queen, b.* ii.

To APPO'INT. *v. a.* [*appointer*, Fr.]

1. To fix any thing, as to settle the exact time for some transaction.

The time *appointed* of the father. *Galat.* iv. 2.

2. To settle any thing by compact.

He said, *Appoint* me thy wages, and I will pay it. *Gen.* xxx. 20.

Now there was an *appointed* sign between the men of Israel and the liers in wait. *Judges*, xx. 38.

3. To establish any thing by decree.

It was before the Lord, which chose me before thy father, and before all his house, to *appoint* me ruler over the people of the Lord. 2 *Sam.* vi. 21.

Unto him thou gavest commandment, which he transgressed, and immediately thou *appointedst* death in him, and in his generations. 2 *Esdras*, iii. 7.

O Lord, that art the God of the just, thou hast not *appointed* repentance to the just. *Manasseh's Prayer.*

4. To furnish in all points; to equip; to supply with all things necessary: used anciently in speaking of soldiers.

The English being well *appointed*, did so entertain them, that their ships departed terribly torn. *Hayward.*

APPO'INTER. *n. s.* [from *appoint.*] He that settles or fixes any thing or place.

APPO'INTMENT. *n. s.* [*appointement*, Fr.]

1. Stipulation; the act of fixing something in which two or more are concerned.

They had made an *appointment* together, to come to mourn with him, and to comfort him. *Job*, ii. 11.

2. Decree; establishment.

The ways of death be only in his hands, who alone hath power over all flesh, and unto whose *appointment* we ought with patience meekly to submit ourselves. *Hooker, b.* v.

3. Direction; order.

That good fellow,
If I command him, follows my *appointment*;
I will have none so near else. *Shakesp. Henry* VIII.

4. Equipment; furniture.

They have put forth the haven: further on,
Where their *appointment* we may best discover,
And look on their endeavour. *Shakesp. Ant. and Cleopatra.*

Here art thou in *appointment* fresh and fair,
Anticipating time with starting courage. *Shak. Tr. and Cress.*

5. An allowance paid to any man, commonly used of allowances to publick officers.

To APPO'RTION. *v. a.* [from *portio*, Lat.] To set out in just proportions.

Try the parts of the body, which of them issue speedily, and which slowly; and, by *apportioning* the time, take and leave that quality which you desire. *Bacon's Natural History.*

And to these it were good, that some proper prayer were *apportioned*, and they taught it. *South.*

An office cannot be *apportioned* out like a common, and shared among distinct proprietors. *Collier of Envy.*

APPO'RTIONMENT. *n. s.* [from *apportion.*] A dividing of a rent into two parts or portions, according as the land whence it issues, is divided among two or more proprietors. *Chambers.*

To APPO'SE. *v. a.* [*appono*, Lat.] To put questions to. This word is not now in use, except that, in some schools, to put grammatical questions to a boy is called, to *pose* him; and we now use *pose* for *puzzle.*

Some procure themselves to be surprised at such times as it is like the party that they work upon, will come upon them: and to be found with a letter in their hand, or doing somewhat which they are not accustomed; to the end they may be *apposed* of those things which of themselves they are desirous to utter. *Bacon.*

A'PPOSITE. *adj.* [*appositus*, Lat.] Proper; fit; well adapted to time, place, or circumstances.

The duke's delivery of his mind was not so sharp, as solid and grave, and *apposite* to the times and occasions. *Wotton.*

Neither was Perkin, for his part, wanting to himself, either in gracious and princely behaviour, or in ready and *apposite* answers. *Bacon's Henry* VII.

Remarkable instances of this kind have been; but it will administer reflections very *apposite* to the design of this present solemnity. *Atterbury's Sermons.*

A'PPOSITELY. *adv.* [from *apposite.*] Properly; fitly; suitably.

When we come into a government, and see this place of honour allotted to a murderer, another filled with an atheist or a blasphemer, may we not *appositely* and properly ask, Whether there be any virtue, sobriety, or religion, amongst such a people? *South.*

We may *appositely* compare this disease, of a proper and improper consumption, to a decaying house. *Harvey on Cons.*

A'PPOSITENESS. *n. s.* [from *apposite.*] Fitness; propriety; suitableness.

Judgment is either concerning things to be known, or of things done, of their congruity, fitness, rightness, *appositeness.* *Hale's Origin of Mankind.*

APPOSI'TION. *n. s.* [*appositio*, Lat.]

1. The addition of new matter, so as that it may touch the first mass.

Urine inspected with a microscope, will discover a black sand; wherever this sand sticks, it grows still bigger, by the *apposition* of new matter. *Arbuthnot on Diet.*

2. In grammar, the putting of two nouns in the same case; as, *Liber Mariæ matris*, the book of his mother Mary.

To APPRA'ISE. *v. a.* [*apprecier*, Fr.] To set a price upon any thing, in order to sale.

APPRA'ISER. *n. s.* [from *appraise.*] A person appointed to set a price upon things to be sold.

To APPREHE'ND. *v. a.* [*apprehendo*, Lat. to take hold of.]

1. To lay hold on.

There is nothing but hath a double handle, or at least we have two hands to *apprehend* it. *Taylor's Rule of living holy.*

2. To seize in order for trial or punishment.

The governour kept the city with a garrison, desirous to *apprehend* me. 2 *Cor.* xi. 32.

It was the rabble, of which no body was named; and, which is more strange, not one *apprehended.* *Clarendon.*

3. To conceive by the mind.

The good which is gotten by doing, causeth not action; unless, *apprehending* it as good, we like and desire it. *Hooker.*

Yet this I *apprehend* not, why to those
Among whom God will deign to dwell on earth,
So many, and so various laws are giv'n. *Milton's Par. Lost.*

The First Being is invisible and incorruptible, and can only be *apprehended* by our minds. *Stillingfleet.*

4. To think on with terrour; to fear.

From my grandfather's death I had reason to *apprehend* the stone; and, from my father's life, the gout. *Temple.*

APPREHE'NDER. *n. s.* [from *apprehend.*] Conceiver; thinker.

Gross *apprehenders* may not think it any more strange, than that a bullet should be moved by the rarified fire. *Glanville.*

APPREHE'NSIBLE. *adj.* [from *apprehend.*] That which may be apprehended, or conceived.

The north and southern poles are incommunicable and fixed points, whereof the one is not *apprehensible* in the other. *Brown's Vulgar Errours, b.* vi. *c.* 7.

APPREHE'NSION. *n. s.* [*apprehensio*, Lat.]

1. The mere contemplation of things, without affirming or denying any thing concerning them. So we think of a horse, high, swift, animal, time, matter, mind, death, &c. *Watts.*

Simple *apprehension* denotes no more than the soul's naked intellection of an object, without either composition or deduction. *Glanville's Scepsis Scientifica, c.* iv.

2. Opinion; sentiments; conception.

To be false, and to be thought false, is all one in respect of men who act not according to truth, but *apprehension.* *South.*

The expressions of scripture are commonly suited in those matters to the vulgar *apprehensions* and conceptions of the place and people where they were delivered. *Locke on St. Paul's Ep.*

3. The faculty by which we conceive new ideas, or power of conceiving them.

I nam'd them as they pass'd, and understood
Their nature, with such knowledge God indu'd
My sudden *apprehension.* *Milton's Paradise Lost, b.* viii.

4. Fear.

It behoveth that the world should be held in awe, not by a vain surmise, but a true *apprehension* of somewhat which no man may think himself able to withstand. *Hooker, b.* v. § 2.

And he the future evil shall no less
In *apprehension*, than in substance, feel. *Milt. Paradise Lost.*

The *apprehension* of what was to come from an unknown, at least unacknowledged successour to the crown, clouded much of that prosperity. *Clarendon.*

After the death of his nephew Caligula, Claudius was in no small *apprehension* for his own life. *Addison on ancient Medals.*

5. Suspicion of something to happen, or be done.

I'll note you in my book of memory,
And scourge you for this *apprehension.* *Shakesp. Henry* VI.

That he might take away the *apprehension*, that he meant suddenly to depart, he sent out orders, which he was sure would come into the enemies hands, to two or three villages next the house, that they should, by the next day noon, send proportions of corn into Basinghouse. *Clarendon, b.* viii.

As they have no *apprehension* of these things, so they need no comfort against them. *Tillotson.*

6. Seizure.

See that he be convey'd unto the tower:
And go we brothers to the man that took him,
To question of his *apprehension*. *Shakesp. Henry* VI.

APPREHE'NSIVE. *adj.* [from *apprehend.*]

1. Quick to understand.

And gives encouragement to those who teach such *apprehensive* scholars. *Holder's Elements of Speech.*

If conscience be naturally *apprehensive* and sagacious, certainly we should trust and rely upon the reports of it. *South.*

2. Fearful.

The inhabitants of this country, when I passed through it, were extremely *apprehensive* of seeing Lombardy the seat of war. *Addison's Remarks on Italy.*

They are not at all *apprehensive* of evils at a distance, nor tormented with the fearful prospect of what may befal them hereafter. *Tillotson.*

APPREHE'NSIVELY. *adv.* [from *apprehensive.*] In an apprehensive manner.

APPREHE'NSIVENESS. *n. s.* [from *apprehensive.*] The quality of being apprehensive.

Whereas the vowels are much more difficult to be taught, you will find, by falling upon them last, great help by the *apprehensiveness* already gained in learning the consonants. *Holder's Elements of Speech.*

APPRE'NTICE. *n. s.* [*apprenti*, Fr.] One that is bound by covenant, to serve another man of trade, for a certain term of years, upon condition, that the artificer, or tradesman, shall, in the mean time, endeavour to instruct him in his art or mystery. *Cowell.*

Love enjoined such diligence, that no *apprentice*, no, no bond slave could ever be more ready than that young princess was. *Sidney, b.* ii.

He found him such an *apprentice*, as knew well enough how to set up for himself. *Wotton.*

This rule sets the painter at liberty; it teaches him, that he ought not to be subject himself servilely, and be bound like an *apprentice* to the rules of his art. *Dryden's Dufresnoy.*

To APPRE'NTICE. *v. a.* [from the noun.] To put out to a master as an apprentice.

Him portion'd maids, *apprentic'd* orphans blest,
The young who labour, and the old who rest. *Pope's Epist.*

APPRE'NTICEHOOD. *n. s.* [from *apprentice.*] The years of an apprentice's servitude.

Must I not serve a long *apprenticehood*
To foreign passages, and in the end,
Having my freedom, boast of nothing else
But that I was a journeyman to grief? *Shakesp. Richard* II.

APPRE'NTICESHIP. *n. s.* [from *apprentice.*] The years which an apprentice is to pass under a master.

In every art, the simplest that is, there is an *apprenticeship* necessary, before it can be expected one should work it in a fashionable piece. *Digby on the Soul, Dedication.*

Many rushed into the ministry, as being the only calling that they could profess, without serving any *apprenticeship*. *South.*

To APPRI'ZE. *v. a.* [*apprendre*; part. *appris*, Fr.] To inform; to give the knowledge of any thing.

He considers the tendency of such a virtue or vice; he is well *apprized*, that the representation of some of these things may convince the understanding, and some may terrify the conscience. *Watts's Improvement of the Mind.*

It is fit he be *apprized* of a few things, that may prevent his mistaking. *Cheyne's Philosophical Principles.*

But if *appriz'd* of the severe attack,
The country be shut up, lur'd by the scent
On church yard drear (inhuman to relate),
The disappointed prowlers fall. *Thomson's Winter.*

To APPRO'ACH. *v. n.* [*approcher*, Fr.]

1. To draw near locally.

'Tis time to look about: the powers of the kingdom *approach* apace. *Shakesp. King Lear.*

We suppose Ulysses *approaching* toward Polypheme. *Notes on Odyssey.*

2. To draw near, as time.

Hark! I hear the sound of coaches,
The hour of attack *approaches*. *Gay's Beggar's Opera.*

3. To make a progress towards, in the figurative sense, as mentally.

He shall *approach* unto me: for who is this that engaged his heart to *approach* unto me? *Jer.* xxx. 21.

He was an admirable poet, and thought even to have *approached* Homer. *Temple's Miscellanies.*

To have knowledge in all the objects of contemplation, is what the mind can hardly attain unto; the instances are few of those who have, in any measure, *approached* towards it. *Locke.*

To APPRO'ACH. *v. a.* To bring near to. This sense is rather French than English.

This they will nimbly perform, if objected to the extremes, but slowly and not at all, if *approached* unto their roots. *Brown's Vulgar Errours, b.* iii. *c.* 20.

By plunging paper thoroughly in weak spirit of wine, and *approaching* it to a candle, the spirituous parts will burn, without harming the paper. *Boyle.*

Approach'd, and looking underneath the sun,
He saw proud Arcite. *Dryden's Fables.*

APPRO'ACH. *n. s.* [from the verb.]

1. The act of drawing near.

If I could bid the seventh welcome with so good heart as I can bid the other five farewel, I should be glad of his *approach*. *Shakespeare's Merchant of Venice.*

'Tis with our souls
As with our eyes, that after a long darkness
Are dazzled at th' *approach* of sudden light. *Denh. Sophy.*

2. Access.

Honour hath in it the vantage ground to do good; the *approach* to kings and principal persons; and the raising of a man's own fortunes. *Bacon's Essays.*

3. Hostile advance.

For England his *approaches* makes as fierce
As waters to the sucking of a gulph. *Shakesp. Henry* V.

4. Means of advancing.

Against beleagur'd heav'n the giants move,
Hills pil'd on hills, on mountains mountains lie,
To make their mad *approaches* to the sky. *Dryden's Ovid.*

APPRO'ACHER. *n. s.* [from *approach.*] The person that approaches or draws near.

Thou gav'st thine ears, like tapsters, that bid welcome
To knaves and all *approachers*. *Shakesp. Timon.*

APPRO'ACHMENT. *n. s.* [from *approach.*] The act of coming near.

As for ice, it will not concrete, but in the *approachment* of the air, as we have made trial in glasses of water, which will not easily freeze. *Brown's Vulgar Errours, b.* ii. *c.* 1.

APPROBA'TION. *n. s.* [*approbatio*, Lat.]

1. The act of approving, or expressing himself pleased.

That not past me, but
By learned *approbation* of my judges. *Shakesp. Henry* VIII.

2. The liking of any thing.

There is no positive law of men, whether received by formal consent, as in councils, or by secret *approbation*, as in customs, but may be taken away. *Hooker, b.* iv. § 14.

The bare *approbation* of the worth and goodness of a thing, is not properly the willing of that thing; yet men do very commonly account it so. *South.*

3. Attestation; support.

How many now in health
Shall drop their blood in *approbation*
Of what your reverence shall incite us to. *Shak. Henry* V.

APPRO'OF. *n. s.* [from *approve*, as *proof* from *prove.*] Approbation; commendation: a word rightly derived, but old.

O most perilous mouths,
That bear in them one and the self-same tongue
Either of condemnation or *approof*! *Shak. Measure for M.*

To APPRO'PERATE. *v. a.* [*appropero*, Lat.] To hasten; to set forward. *Dict.*

To APPROPI'NQUATE. *v. n.* [*appropinquo*, Lat.] To draw nigh unto; to approach.

To APPROPI'NQUE. *v. n.* [*appropinquo*, Lat.] To approach; to draw near to.

The clotted blood within my hose,
That from my wounded body flows,
With mortal crisis doth portend
My days to *appropinque* an end. *Hudibras.*

APPRO'PRIABLE. *adj.* [from *appropriate.*] That which may be appropriated; that which may be restrained to something particular.

This conceit applied unto the original of man, and the beginning of the world, is more justly *appropriable* unto its end. *Brown's Vulgar Errours, b.* vi. *c.* 1.

To APPRO'PRIATE. *v. a.* [*approprier*, Fr. *approprio*, low Lat.]

1. To consign to some particular use or person.

Things sanctified were thereby in such sort *appropriated* unto God, as that they might never afterwards again be made common. *Hooker, b.* v. § 20.

As for this spot of ground, this person, this thing, I have selected and *appropriated*, I have inclosed it to myself and my own use; and I will endure no sharer, no rival or companion in it. *South.*

Some they *appropriated* to the gods,
And some to publick, some to private ends. *Roscommon.*

Marks of honour are *appropriated* to the magistrate, that he might be invited to reverence himself. *Atterbury.*

2. To claim or exercise an exclusive right.

To themselves *appropriating*
The spirit of God, promis'd alike, and giv'n
To all believers. *Milton's Paradise Lost, b.* xii.

Why ſhould people engroſs and *appropriate* the common benefits of fire, air, and water, to themſelves? *L'Eſtrange.*

Every body elſe has an equal title to it; and therefore he cannot *appropriate*, he cannot incloſe, without the conſent of all his fellow commoners, all mankind. *Locke.*

3. To make peculiar to ſomething; to annex.

He need but be furniſhed with verſes of ſacred ſcripture; and his ſyſtem, that has *appropriated* them to the orthodoxy of his church, makes them immediately irrefragable arguments. *Locke's Eſſay on St. Paul's Epiſtles.*

We, by degrees, get ideas and names, and learn their *appropriated* connection one with another. *Locke.*

4. In law, to alienate a benefice. See APPROPRIATION.

Before Richard II. it was lawful to *appropriate* the whole fruits of a benefice to any abbey, the houſe finding one to ſerve the cure; that king redreſſed that horrid evil. *Ayliffe's Parerg.*

APPRO'PRIATE. *adj.* [from the verb.] Peculiar; conſigned to ſome particular uſe or perſon.

He did inſtitute a band of fifty archers, by the name of yeomen of his guard; and that it might be thought to be rather a matter of dignity, than any matter of diffidence *appropriate* to his own caſe, he made an ordinance not temporary, but to hold in ſucceſſion for ever. *Bacon's Henry* VII.

The heathens themſelves had an apprehenſion of the neceſſity of ſome *appropriate* acts of divine worſhip. *Stillingfleet.*

APPROPRIA'TION. *n. ſ.* [from *appropriate.*]

1. The application of ſomething to a particular purpoſe.

The mind ſhould have diſtinct ideas of the things, and retain the particular name, with its peculiar *appropriation* to that idea. *Locke.*

2. The claim of any thing as peculiar.

He doth nothing but talk of his horſe, and make a great *appropriation* to his good parts, that he can ſhoe him himſelf. *Shakeſp. Merchant of Venice.*

3. The fixing a particular ſignification to a word.

The name of faculty may, by an *appropriation* that diſguiſes its true ſenſe, palliate the abſurdity. *Locke.*

4. In law, a ſevering of a benefice eccleſiaſtical to the proper and perpetual uſe of ſome religious houſe, or dean, and chapter, biſhoprick, or college; becauſe, as perſons ordinarily have no right of fee ſimple, theſe, by reaſon of their perpetuity, are accounted owners of the fee ſimple; and therefore are called proprietors. To an *appropriation*, after the licence obtained of the king in chancery, the conſent of the dioceſan, patron, and incumbent, are neceſſary, if the church be full: but if the church be void, the dioceſan and the patron, upon the king's licence, may conclude. *Cowel.*

APPROPRIA'TOR. *n. ſ.* [from *appropriate.*] He that is poſſeſſed of an appropriated benefice.

Theſe *appropriators*, by reaſon of their perpetuities, are accounted owners of the fee ſimple; and therefore are called proprietors. *Ayliffe's Parergon Juris Canonici.*

APPRO'VABLE. *adj.* [from *approve.*] That which merits approbation.

The ſolid reaſon, or confirmed experience, of any men, is very *approvable* in what profeſſion ſoever. *Brown's Vulgar Err.*

APPRO'VAL. *n. ſ.* [from *approve.*] Approbation: a word not much uſed.

There is a cenſor of juſtice and manners, without whoſe *approval* no capital ſentences are to be executed. *Temple.*

APPRO'VANCE. *n. ſ.* [from *approve.*] Approbation: a word not much uſed.

Should ſhe ſeem
Soft'ning the leaſt *approvance* to beſtow,
Their colours burniſh, and, by hope inſpir'd,
They briſk advance. *Thomſon's Spring.*

To APPROVE. *v. a.* [*approuver*, Fr. *approbo*, Lat.]

1. To like; to be pleaſed with.

There can be nothing poſſibly evil which God *approveth*, and that he *approveth* much more than he doth command. *Hooker.*

What power was that, whereby Medea ſaw,
And well *approv'd*, and prais'd the better courſe,
When her rebellious ſenſe did ſo withdraw
Her feeble pow'rs, that ſhe purſu'd the worſe? *Davies.*

2. To expreſs liking.

It is looked upon as inſolence for a man to ſet up his own opinion againſt that of ſome learned doctor, or otherwiſe *approved* writer. *Locke.*

3. To prove; to ſhow; to juſtify.

His meaning was not, that Archimedes could ſimply in nothing be deceived; but that he had in ſuch ſort *approved* his skill, that he ſeemed worthy of credit for ever after, in matters appertaining to the ſcience he was skilful in. *Hooker, b.* ii.

In religion,
What damned errour, but ſome ſober brow
Will bleſs it, and *approve* it with a text. *Shak. M. of Venice.*

I'm ſorry
That he *approves* the common liar, Fame,
Who ſpeaks him thus at Rome. *Shak. Antony and Cleop.*

Would'ſt thou *approve* thy conſtancy? *Approve*
Firſt thy obedience. *Milton's Paradiſe Loſt, b.* ix.

Refer all the actions of this ſhort life to that ſtate which will never end; and this will *approve* itſelf to be wiſdom at the laſt, whatever the world judge of it now. *Tillotſon.*

4. To experience.

Oh, 'tis the curſe in love, and ſtill *approv'd*,
When women cannot love, where they're belov'd.
Shakeſp. Two Gentlemen of Verona.

5. To make worthy of approbation.

The firſt care and concern muſt be to *approve* himſelf to God by righteouſneſs, holineſs, and purity. *Rogers.*

6. It has *of* before the object.

I ſhewed you a piece of black and white ſtuff, juſt ſent from the dyer; which you were pleaſed to *approve of*, and be my cuſtomer for. *Swift.*

APPRO'VEMENT. *n. ſ.* [from *approve.*] Approbation; liking.

It is certain that at the firſt you were all of my opinion, and that I did nothing without your *approvement*. *Hayward.*

APPRO'VER. *n. ſ.* [from *approve.*]

1. He that approves.

2. He that makes trial.

Their diſcipline,
Now mingled with their courages, will make known
To their *approvers*, they are people ſuch
As mend upon the world. *Shakeſp. Cymbeline.*

3. In our common law, one that confeſſing felony of himſelf, appealeth or accuſeth another, one or more, to be guilty of the ſame: and he is called ſo, becauſe he muſt prove what he hath alleged in his appeal. *Cowel.*

APPRO'XIMATE. *adj.* [from *ad*, to, and *proximus*, near, Lat.] Near to.

Theſe receive a quick converſion, containing *approximate* diſpoſitions unto animation. *Brown's Vulgar Errours, b.* iii. *c.* 21.

APPROXIMA'TION. *n. ſ.* [from *approximate.*]

1. Approach to any thing.

Unto the latitude of Capricorn, or the winter ſolſtice, it had been a ſpring; for, unto that poſition, it had been in a middle point, and that of aſcent or *approximation*. *Brown's Vulg. Err.*

The fiery region gains upon the inferiour elements; a neceſſary conſequent of the ſun's gradual *approximation* towards the earth. *Hale's Origin of Mankind.*

Quadrupeds are better placed according to the degrees of their *approximation* to the human ſhape. *Grew's Muſæum.*

2. In ſcience, a continual approach nearer ſtill, and nearer to the quantity ſought, without a poſſibility of ever arriving at it exactly.

APPU'LSE. *n. ſ.* [*appulſus*, Lat.] The act of ſtriking againſt any thing.

An hectick fever is the innate heat kindled into a deſtructive fire, violently abſorbing the radical moiſture, through the *appulſe* of ſaline ſteams. *Harvey on Conſumptions.*

In vowels, the paſſage of the mouth is open and free, without any *appulſe* of an organ of ſpeech to another: but, in all conſonants, there is an *appulſe* of the organs. *Holder.*

To A'PRICATE. *v. n.* [*apricor*, Lat.] To bask in the ſun. *Dict.*

APRI'CITY. *n. ſ.* [*apricitas*, Lat.] Warmth of the ſun; ſunſhine. *Dict.*

A'PRICOT, or A'PRICOCK. *n. ſ.* [from *apricus*, Lat. ſunny.] A kind of wall fruit.

The ordinary ſorts of this fruit cultivated in Engliſh gardens are, 1. The maſculine *apricock*. 2. The orange *apricock*. 3. The Algier *apricock*. 4. The Roman *apricock*. 5. The Turkey *apricock*. 6. The tranſparent *apricock*. 7. The Breda *apricock*. 8. The Bruxelles *apricock*. They are generally propagated by budding them on plum ſtocks, and will readily take upon almoſt any ſort of plum, provided the ſtock be free and thriving. *Millar.*

APRIL. *n. ſ.* [*Aprilis*, Lat. *Avril*, Fr.] The fourth month of the year, January counted firſt.

April is repreſented by a young man in green, with a garland of myrtle and hawthorn buds; in one hand primroſes and violets, in the other the ſign Taurus. *Peacham on Drawing.*

Men are *April* when they woo, December when they wed: Maids are May when they are maids, but the sky changes when they are wives. *Shakeſp. As you like it.*

A'PRON. *n. ſ.* [A word of uncertain etymology, but ſuppoſed by ſome to be contracted from *afore one.*] A cloth hung before, to keep the other dreſs clean.

Give us gold, good Timon: haſt thou more?———
————— Hold up, you ſluts,
Your *aprons* mountant. *Shakeſp. Timon.*

The nobility think ſcorn to go in leather *aprons*. *Shak. H.* VI.

How might we ſee Falſtaff, and not ourſelves be ſeen?——
Put on two leather jerkins and *aprons*, and wait upon him at his table as drawers. *Shakeſp. Henry* IV.

In both theſe figures the veſt is gathered up before them, like an *apron*, which you muſt ſuppoſe filled with fruits, as well as the cornucopiæ. *Addiſon on Medals.*

APRON. [in gunnery.] A piece of lead which covers the touchhole of a great gun.

APRON *of a gooſe.* The fat ſkin which covers the belly.

A'PRON-MAN. *n. ſ.* [from *apron* and *man.*] A man that wears an apron; a workman; an artificer.

You

You have made good work,
You and your *apron-men*, that ſtood ſo much
Upon the voice of occupation, and
The breath of garlick eaters. *Shakeſp. Coriolanus.*

APRONED. *adj.* [from *apron.*] Wearing an apron.

The cobler *apron'd*, and the parſon gown'd. *Pope's Eſſ. on M.*

A'PSIS. *n. ſ.* *apſides*, plural. [ἀψίς.]

Is applied, in aſtronomy, to two points in the orbits of planets, in which they are at the greateſt, and the leaſt diſtance from the ſun or earth. The higher *apſis* is more particularly denominated aphelion, or apogee; the lower, perihelion, or perigee. *Chambers.*

If bodies revolve in orbits that are pretty near circles, and the *apſides* of theſe orbits be fixed, then the centripetal forces of thoſe bodies will be reciprocally as the ſquares of the diſtances. *Cheyne's Philoſophical Principles.*

APT. *adj.* [*aptus*, Lat.]

1. Fit.

This ſo eminent induſtry in making proſelytes, more of that ſex than of the other, groweth; for that they are deemed *apter* to ſerve as inſtruments in the cauſe. *Apter* they are through the eagerneſs of their affection; *apter* through a natural inclination unto piety; *apter* through ſundry opportunities, *&c.* Finally, *apter* through a ſingular delight which they take in giving very large and particular intelligence how all near about them ſtand affected as concerning the ſame cauſe. *Hooker, Pr.*

2. Having a tendency to.

Things natural, as long as they keep thoſe forms which give them their being, cannot poſſibly be *apt* or inclinable to do otherwiſe than they do. *Hooker.*

3. Inclined to; led to.

You may make her you love, believe it; which, I warrant, ſhe is *apter* to do, than confeſs ſhe does. *Shak. As you like it.*

Men are *apt* to think well of themſelves, and of their nation, of their courage and ſtrength. *Temple.*

One, who has not theſe lights, is a ſtranger to what he reads, and *apt* to put a wrong interpretation upon it. *Addiſon. Spect.*

Even thoſe who are near the court, are *apt* to deduct wrong conſequences, by reaſoning upon the motives of actions. *Swift.*

What we have always ſeen to be done in one manner, we are *apt* to imagine there was but that one way. *Bentl. Sermons.*

4. Ready; quick; as, an apt wit.

I have a heart as little *apt* as yours,
But yet a brain that leads my uſe of anger
To better vantage. *Shakeſp. Coriolanus.*

5. Qualified for.

All that were ſtrong and *apt* for war, even them the king of Babylon brought captive to Babylon. *2 Kings*, xxiv. 16.

To APT. *v. a.* [*apto*, Lat.]

1. To ſuit; to adapt.

We need a man that knows the ſeveral graces
Of hiſtory, and how to *apt* their places;
Where brevity, where ſplendour, and where height,
Where ſweetneſs is required, and where weight. *B. Johnſon.*

2. To fit; to qualify.

The king is melancholy,
Apted for any ill impreſſions. *Denham's Sophy.*

To A'PTATE. *v. a.* [*aptatum*, Lat.] To make fit.

To *aptate* a planet, is to ſtrengthen the planet in poſition of houſe and dignities to the greateſt advantage, in order to bring about the deſired end. *Bailey.*

A'PTITUDE. *n. ſ.* [French.]

1. Fitneſs.

This evinces its perfect *aptitude* and fitneſs for the end to which it was aimed, the planting and nouriſhing all true virtue among men. *Decay of Piety.*

2. Tendency.

In an abortion, the mother, beſides the fruſtration of her hopes, acquires an *aptitude* to miſcarry for the future. *Decay of Piety.*

3. Diſpoſition.

He that is about children, ſhould ſtudy their nature and *aptitudes*, what turns they eaſily take, and what becomes them; what their native ſtock is, and what it is fit for. *Locke.*

A'PTLY. *adv.* [from *apt.*]

1. Properly; with juſt connection, or correſpondence; fitly.

That part
Was *aptly* fitted, and naturally perform'd. *Sh. As you like it.*

But what the maſs nutritious does divide?
What makes them *aptly* to the limbs adhere,
In youth encreaſe them, and in age repair? *Blackmore.*

2. Juſtly; pertinently.

Irenæus very *aptly* remarks, that thoſe nations, who were not poſſeſt of the goſpels, had the ſame accounts of our Saviour, which are in the Evangeliſts. *Addiſon on the Chriſtian Relig.*

3. Readily; acutely; as, he learned his buſineſs very *aptly*.

A'PTNESS. *n. ſ.* [from *apt.*]

1. Fitneſs; ſuitableneſs.

The nature of every law muſt be judged of by the *aptneſs* of things therein preſcribed, unto the ſame end. *Hooker.*

There are antecedent and independent *aptneſſes* in things; with reſpect to which, they are fit to be commanded or forbidden. *Norris's Miſcel.*

2. Diſpoſition to any thing.

The nobles receive ſo to heart the baniſhment of that worthy Coriolanus, that they are in a ripe *aptneſs* to take all power from the people. *Shakeſp. Coriolanus.*

3. Quickneſs of apprehenſion; readineſs to learn.

What ſhould be the *aptneſs* of birds, in compariſon of beaſts, to imitate ſpeech, may be enquired. *Bacon's Nat. Hiſtory.*

4. Tendency.

Some ſeeds of goodneſs give him a reliſh of ſuch reflections, as have an *aptneſs* to improve the mind. *Addiſon. Spectator.*

A'PTOTE. *n. ſ.* [of α and πτῶσις.] A noun which is not declined with caſes.

A'QUA. *n. ſ.* [Latin.] A word ſignifying *water*, very much uſed in chymical writings.

AQUA FORTIS. [Latin.] A corroſive liquor made by diſtilling purified nitre with calcined vitriol, or rectified oil of vitriol in a ſtrong heat: the liquor, which riſes in fumes red as blood, being collected, is the ſpirit of nitre or *aqua fortis*; which ſerves as a menſtruum for diſſolving of ſilver, and all other metals, except gold. But if ſea ſalt, or ſal ammoniack, be added to *aqua fortis*, it commences *aqua regia*, and will then diſſolve no metal but gold. *Aqua fortis* is commonly held to have been invented about the year 1300; though others will have it to have been known in the time of Moſes. It is ſerviceable to refiners, in ſeparating ſilver from gold and copper; to the workers in moſaick, for ſtaining and colouring their woods; to dyers, in their colours, particularly ſcarlet; and to other artiſts, for colouring bone and ivory. With *aqua fortis* bookbinders marble the covers of books, and diamond cutters ſeparate diamonds from metalline powders. It is alſo uſed in etching copper or braſs plates. *Chambers.*

The diſſolving of ſilver in *aqua fortis*, and gold in aqua regia, and not *vice verſâ*, would not be difficult to know. *Locke.*

AQUA MARINA, *of the Italian lapidaries*, is of a ſea or bluiſh green. This ſtone ſeems to me to be the beryllus of Pliny. *Woodward's Meth. of Foſſils.*

AQUA MIRABILIS. [Latin.] The wonderful water, is prepared of cloves, galangals, cubebs, mace, cardomums, nutmegs, ginger, and ſpirit of wine, digeſted twenty four hours, then diſtilled. It is a good and agreeable cordial.

AQUA REGIA, or *AQUA REGALIS.* [Latin.] An acid corroſive ſpirit or water, ſo called becauſe it ſerves as a menſtruum to diſſolve gold, commonly eſteemed the king of metals. Its baſis, or eſſential ingredient, is common ſea ſalt, the only ſalt in nature which will operate on gold. It is commonly prepared by mixing common ſea ſalt, or ſal ammoniack, or the ſpirit of them, with ſpirit of nitre, or common aqua fortis. *Chambers.*

He adds to his complex idea of gold, that of fixedneſs or ſolubility in *aqua regia*. *Locke.*

AQUA-VITÆ. [Latin.] It is commonly underſtood of what is otherwiſe called brandy, or ſpirit of wine, either ſimple or prepared with aromaticks. But ſome appropriate the term brandy to what is procured from wine, or the grape; *aqua-vitæ*, to that drawn after the ſame manner from malt. *Chambers.*

I will rather truſt a Fleming with my butter, parſon Hugh the Welchman with my cheeſe, an Iriſhman with my *aqua vitæ* bottle, or a thief to walk with my ambling gelding, than my wife with herſelf. *Shakeſp. Merry Wives of Windſor.*

AQUA'TICK. *adj.* [*aquaticus*, Lat. from *aqua*, water.]

1. That which inhabits the water.

The vaſt variety of worms found in animals, as well terreſtrial as *aquatick*, are taken into their bodies by meats and drinks. *Ray on Creation.*

Brutes may be conſidered as either aerial, terreſtrial, *aquatick*, or amphibious. *Aquatick* are thoſe whoſe conſtant abode is upon the water. *Locke.*

2. Applied to plants, that which grows in the water.

Flags, and ſuch like *aquaticks*, are beſt deſtroyed by draining. *Mortimer's Husbandry.*

A'QUATILE. *adj.* [*aquatilis*, Lat.] That which inhabits the water.

A'QUEDUCT. *n. ſ.* [*aquæductus*, Lat.] A conveyance made for carrying water from one place to another; made on uneven ground, to preſerve the level of the water, and convey it by a canal. Some aqueducts are under ground, and others above it, ſupported by arches.

Among the remains of old Rome, the grandeur of the commonwealth ſhews itſelf chiefly in temples, highways, *aqueducts*, walls and bridges of the city. *Addiſon's Remarks on Italy.*

Hither the rills of water are convey'd
In curious *aqueducts*, by nature laid
To carry all the humour. *Blackmore, Creation.*

A'QUEOUS. *adj.* [from *aqua*, water, Lat.] Watery.

The vehement fire requiſite to its fuſion, forced away all the *aqueous* and fugitive moiſture. *Ray on Creation.*

A'QUEOUSNESS. *n. ſ.* [*aquoſitas*, Lat.] Wateriſhneſs.

A'QUILINE. *adj.* [*aquilinus*, Lat. from *aquila*, an eagle.] Reſembling an eagle; when applied to the noſe, hooked.

His noſe was *aquiline*, his eyes were blue,
Ruddy his lips, and freſh and fair his hue. *Dryden's Fables.*

Gryps ſignifies ſome kind of eagle or vulture; from whence the epithet *grypus* for an hooked or *aquiline* noſe. *Br. Vul. Err.*

Aquo'se. *adj.* [from *aqua*, Lat.] Watery; having the qualities of water. *Dict.*

Aquo'sity. *n. ſ.* [from *aquoſe.*] Waterineſs. *Dict.*

A. R. *anno regni*; that is, the year of the reign: as, *A. R. G. R.* 20. *Anno regni Georgii regis vigeſimo*, in the twentieth year of the reign of king George.

A'rable. *adj.* [from *aro*, Lat. to plow.] Fit for the plough; fit for tillage; productive of corn.

His eyes he open'd, and beheld a field,
Part *arable*, and tilth; whereon were ſheaves
New reap'd. *Milton's Paradiſe Loſt, b.* xi.

'Tis good for *arable*, a glebe that asks
Tough teams of oxen, and laborious tasks. *Dryden's Virgil.*

Having but very little *arable* land, they are forced to fetch all their corn from foreign countries. *Addiſon's Rem. on Italy.*

ARACHNOIDES. *n. ſ.* [from ἀράχνη, a ſpider, and εἶδος, form.]

1. One of the tunicks of the eye, ſo called from its reſemblance to a cobweb.

As to the tunicks of the eye, many things might be taken notice of; the prodigious fineneſs of the *arachnoides*, the acute ſenſe of the retina, &c. *Derham's Phyſico-Theology.*

2. It is alſo a fine thin tranſparent membrane, which, lying between the dura and the pia mater, is ſuppoſed to inveſt the whole ſubſtance of the brain. *Chambers.*

ARA'IGNEE. *n. ſ.* [French.] A term in fortification, which ſometimes denotes a branch, return, or gallery of a mine. *Dict.*

Ara'neous. *adj.* [from *aranea*, Lat. a cobweb.] Reſembling a cobweb.

The curious *araneous* membrane of the eye conſtringeth and dilateth it, and ſo varieth its focus. *Derham's Ph. Theol.*

Ara'tion. *n. ſ.* [*aratio*, Lat.] The act or practice of plowing.

A'ratory. *adj.* [from *aro*, Lat. to plow.] That which contributes to tillage. *Dict.*

A'rbalist. *n. ſ.* [from *arcus*, a bow, and *baliſta*, an engine to throw ſtones.] A croſs-bow.

It is reported by William Brito, that the arcubaliſta, or *arbaliſt*, was firſt ſhewed to the French by our king Richard the firſt, who was ſhortly after ſlain by a quarrel thereof. *Camden.*

A'RBITER. *n. ſ.* [Lat.]

1. A judge appointed by the parties, to whoſe determination they voluntarily ſubmit.

He would put himſelf into the king's hands, and make him *arbiter* of the peace. *Bacon's Henry* VII.

2. One who has the power of deciſion or regulation; a judge.

Next him, high *arbiter*,
Chance governs all. *Milton's Par. Loſt, b.* ii. *l.* 909.

His majeſty, in this great conjuncture, ſeems to be generally allowed for the ſole *arbiter* of the affairs of chriſtendom. *Temple.*

A'rbitrable. *adj.* [from *arbitror*, Lat.] Arbitrary; depending upon the will.

The ordinary revenue of a parſonage is in land, called the glebe; in tythe, a ſet part of our goods rendered to God; in other offerings beſtowed upon God by the people, either in ſuch *arbitrable* proportion as their own devotion moveth them, or as the laws or cuſtoms of particular places do require them. *Spelman.*

Arbi'trament. *n. ſ.* [from *arbitror*, Lat.] Will; determination; choice.

Stand faſt! to ſtand or fall,
Free in thine own *arbitrament* it ſtands,
Perfect within, no outward aid require;
And all temptation to tranſgreſs repel. *Milton's Par. Loſt.*

A'rbitrarily. *adv.* [from *arbitrary.*] With no other rule than the will; deſpotically; abſolutely.

He governed *arbitrarily*, he was expelled; and came to the deſerved end of all tyrants. *Dryden's Virgil's Æneid, Pref.*

Arbitra'rious. *adj.* [from *arbitrarius*, Lat.] Arbitrary; depending on the will.

Theſe are ſtanding and irrepealable truths, ſuch as have no precarious exiſtence, or *arbitrarious* dependance upon any will or underſtanding whatſoever. *Norris's Miſcellanies.*

Arbitra'riously. *adv.* [from *arbitrarious.*] Arbitrarily; according to mere will and pleaſure.

Where words are impoſed *arbitrariouſly*, diſtorted from their common uſe, the mind muſt be led into miſpriſion. *Glanville.*

A'rbitrary. *adj.* [*arbitrarius*, Lat.]

1. Deſpotick; abſolute; bound by no law; following the will without reſtraint. It is applied both to perſons and things.

In vain the Tyrian queen reſigns her life
For the chaſte glory of a virtuous wife,
If lying bards may falſe amours rehearſe,
And blaſt her name with *arbitrary* verſe. *Walſh.*

Their regal tyrants ſhall with bluſhes hide
Their little luſts of *arbitrary* pride,
Nor bear to ſee their vaſſals ty'd. *Prior.*

2. Depending on no rule; capricious.

It may be perceived, with what inſecurity we aſcribe effects depending on the natural period of time, unto *arbitrary* calculations, and ſuch as vary at pleaſure. *Brown's Vulgar Err.*

To A'rbitrate. *v. a.* [*arbitror*, Lat.]

1. To decide; to determine.

This might have been prevented, and made whole,
With very eaſy arguments of love,
Which now the manage of two kingdoms muſt
With fearful bloody iſſue *arbitrate*. *Shakeſp. King John.*

2. To judge of.

Yet where an equal poiſe of hope and fear
Does *arbitrate* th' event, my nature is
That I incline to hope, rather than fear. *Milton's Comus.*

To A'rbitrate. *v. n.* To give judgment.

It did *arbitrate* upon the ſeveral reports of ſenſe, not like a drowſy judge, only hearing, but alſo directing their verdict. *South.*

A'rbitrariness. *n. ſ.* [from *arbitrary.*] Deſpoticalneſs; tyranny.

He that by harſhneſs of nature, and *arbitrarineſs* of commands, uſes his children like ſervants, is what they mean by a tyrant. *Temple's Miſcellanies.*

Arbitra'tion. *n. ſ.* [from *arbitror*, Lat.] The determination of a cauſe by a judge mutually agreed on by the parties contending.

Arbitra'tor. *n. ſ.* [from *arbitrate.*]

1. An extraordinary judge between party and party, choſen by their mutual conſent. *Cowel.*

Be a good ſoldier, or upright truſtee,
An *arbitrator* from corruption free. *Dryd. Juv.*

2. A governour; a preſident.

Though heav'n be ſhut,
And heav'n's high *arbitrator* ſit ſecure
In his own ſtrength, this place may be expos'd. *M. Par. Loſt.*

3. He that has the power of acting by his own choice without limit or controul.

Another Blenheim or Ramillies will make the confederates maſters of their own terms, and *arbitrators* of a peace. *Addiſon on the State of the War.*

4. The determiner; he that puts an end to any affair.

But now the *arbitrator* of deſpairs,
Juſt death, kind umpire of man's miſeries,
With ſweet enlargement doth diſmiſs me hence. *Sh. H.* VI.

The end crowns all;
And that old common *arbitrator*, time,
Will one day end it. *Shakeſp. Troilus and Creſſida.*

Arbi'trement. *n. ſ.* [from *arbitror*, Lat.]

1. Deciſion; determination.

I know the knight is incenſed againſt you, even to a mortal *arbitrement*; but nothing of the circumſtance more. *Shakeſp. Twelfth Night.*

Aid was granted, and the quarrel brought to the *arbitrement* of the ſword. *Hayward.*

2. Compromiſe.

Lukewarm perſons think they may accommodate points of religion by middle ways, and witty reconcilements; as if they would make an *arbitrement* between God and man. *Bacon's Eſſ.*

A'rborary. *adj.* [*arborarius*, Lat.] Of or belonging to a tree. *D.*

A'rboret. *n. ſ.* [*arbor*, Lat. a tree.] A ſmall tree or ſhrub.

No *arboret* with painted bloſſoms dreſt,
And ſmelling ſweet, but there it might be found,
To bud out fair, and her ſweet ſmells throw all around. *Fairy Queen, b.* ii. *cant.* 6.

Now hid, now ſeen,
Among thick woven *arborets*, and flow'rs,
Imbroider'd on each bank. *Milton's Paradiſe Loſt, b.* ix.

Arbo'reous. *adj.* [*arboreus*, Lat.]

1. Belonging to trees.

2. A term in botany, to diſtinguiſh ſuch funguſes or moſſes as grow upon trees, from thoſe that grow on the ground. *Quincy.*

They ſpeak properly, who make it an *arboreous* excreſcence, or rather a ſuperplant bred of a viſcous and ſuperfluous lopp, which the tree itſelf cannot aſſimilate. *Brown's Vulgar Err.*

A'rborist. *n. ſ.* [*arboriſte*, Fr. from *arbor*, a tree.] A naturaliſt who makes trees his ſtudy.

The nature of the mulberry, which the *arboriſts* obſerve to be long in the begetting his buds; but the cold ſeaſons being paſt, he ſhoots them all out in a night. *Howel's Vocal Foreſt.*

A'rborous. *adj.* [from *arbor*, Lat.] Belonging to a tree.

From under ſhady *arborous* roof
Soon as they forth were come to open ſight
Of day-ſpring, and the ſun. *Milton's Par. Loſt, b.* v.

A'rbour. *n. ſ.* [from *arbor*, Lat. a tree.] A bower; a place covered with green branches of trees.

Nay you ſhall ſee mine orchard, where, in an *arbour*, we will eat a laſt year's pippin of my own graffing. *Shak. Henry* IV.

Let us divide our labours: thou, where choice
Leads thee, or where moſt needs, whether to wind
The woodbine round this *arbour*, or direct
The claſping ivy where to climb. *Milton's Par. Loſt, b.* ix.

For noon-day's heat are cloſer *arbours* made,
And for freſh ev'ning air the op'ner glade. *Dryd. State of Inn.*

Arbour vine. A ſpecies of bind weed; which ſee.

A'rbuscle. *n. ſ.* [*arbuſcula*, Lat.] Any little ſhrub. *Dict.*

A'RBUTE. *n. ſ.* [*arbutus*, Lat.]

Arbute, or ſtrawberry tree, grows common in Ireland. It is difficult to be raiſed from the ſeeds, but may be propagated by layers. It grows to a goodly tree, endures our climate, unleſs the weather be very ſevere, and makes beautiful hedges. *Mortimer's Art of Husbandry.*

Rough *arbute* ſlips into a hazel bough
Are oft ingrafted; and good apples grow
Out of a plain tree ſtock. *May's Virgil's Georg.*

ARC. *n. ſ.* [*arcus*, Lat.]

1. A ſegment; a part of a circle; not more than a ſemicircle.

Their ſegments, or *arcs*, for the moſt part, exceeded not the third part of a circle. *Newton's Opticks.*

2. An arch.

Load ſome vain church with old theatrick ſtate,
Turn *arcs* of triumph to a garden gate;
Reverſe your ornaments, and hang them all
On ſome patch'd dog-hole ek'd with ends of wall. *Pope.*

ARCA'DE. *n. ſ.* [French.] A continued arch; a walk arched over.

Or call the winds through long *arcades* to roar,
Proud to catch hold at a Venetian door. *Pope's Epiſtles.*

ARCA'NUM. n. ſ. in the plural arcana. A Latin word, ſignifying a ſecret.

ARCH. *n. ſ.* [*arcus*, Lat.]

1. Part of a circle, not more than the half.

The mind perceives, that an *arch* of a circle is leſs than the whole circle, as clearly as it does the idea of a circle. *Locke.*

2. A building in form of a ſegment of a circle, uſed for bridges and other works.

Ne'er through an *arch* ſo hurried the blown tide,
As the recomforted through the gates. *Shakeſp. Coriolanus.*
Let Rome in Tiber melt, and the wide *arch*
Of the rais'd empire fall! here is my ſpace.
Shakeſpeare's Antony and Cleopatra.
The royal ſquadron marches,
Erect triumphal *arches*
For Albion and Albanius. *Dryden's Albion.*

3. The ſky, or vault of heaven.

Hath nature given them eyes
To ſee this vaulted *arch*, and the rich cope
Of ſea and land. *Shakeſp. Cymbeline.*

4. [from ἄρχος.] A chief: obſolete.

The noble duke, my maſter,
My worthy *arch* and patron comes to night. *Sh. King. Lear.*

To ARCH. *v. a.* [*arcuo*, Lat.]

1. To build arches.

The nations of the field and wood
Build on the wave, or *arch* beneath the ſand. *Pope.*

2. To cover with arches.

Gates of monarchs
Are *arch'd* ſo high, that giants may jet through. *Sh. Cymbel.*

The proud river which makes her bed at her feet, is *arched* over with ſuch a curious pile of ſtones, that conſidering the rapid courſe of the deep ſtream that roars under it, it may well take place among the wonders of the world. *Howel's Voc. For.*

ARCH. *adj.* [from ἄρχος, chief.]

1. Chief; of the firſt claſs.

The tyrannous and bloody act is done;
The moſt *arch* deed of piteous maſſacre,
That ever yet this land was guilty of. *Shakeſp. Richard* III.
There is ſprung up
An heretick, an *arch* one, Cranmer. *Shakeſp. Henry* VIII.

2. Waggiſh; mirthful; triflingly miſchievous. This ſignification it ſeems to have gained, by being frequently applied to the boy moſt remarkable for his pranks; as the *arch* rogue, *&c.*

Eugenio ſet out from the ſame univerſity, and about the ſame time with Coruſades; he had the reputation of an *arch* lad at ſchool. *Swift's Fates of Clergy.*

ARCH, in compoſition, ſignifies chief, or of the firſt claſs, [from ἄρχος, or ἀρχὴ.] as, *archangel*, *archbiſhop*. It is pronounced variouſly with regard to the *ch*, which before a conſonant ſound as in *cheeſe*, as *archdeacon*; before a vowel like *k*, as *archangel.*

ARCHA'NGEL. *n. ſ.* [*archangelus*, Lat.] One of the higheſt order of angels.

His form had yet not loſt
All her original brightneſs, nor appear'd
Leſs than *archangel* ruin'd, and th' exceſs
Of glory obſcur'd. *Milton's Paradiſe Loſt, b.* i.
'Tis ſure th' *archangel*'s trump I hear,
Nature's great paſſing-bell, the only call
Of gods that will be heard by all. *Norris's Miſcellanies.*

ARCHANGEL. *n. ſ.* [*lamium*, Lat.] The name of a plant, called alſo *Dead nettle.*

It hath a labiated flower of one leaf, whoſe upper lip is hollow like a ſpoon; but the under one divided into two ſegments, in the form of a heart, and both end in chaps brimmed and edged; out of the flower cup, which is fiſtulous and cut into ſegments, riſes the pointal, fixed, like a nail, to the hinder part of the flower, with four embryoes which become triangular ſeeds incloſed in a huſk formed of the flower cup. The ſpecies are fourteen, and ſeven of them grow wild on dry banks, or under hedges, two ſorts of which are uſed in medicine. *Millar.*

ARCHANGE'LICK. *adj.* [from *archangel.*] Belonging to archangels.

He ceas'd, and th' *archangelick* pow'r prepar'd
For ſwift deſcent; with him the cohort bright
Of watchful cherubim. *Milton's Paradiſe Loſt, b.* x.

ARCHBE'ACON. *n. ſ.* [from *arch* and *beacon.*] The chief place of proſpect, or of ſignal.

You ſhall win the top of the Corniſh *archbeacon* Hainborough, which may for proſpect compare with Rama in Paleſtina. *Carew's Survey of Cornwal.*

ARCHBI'SHOP. *n. ſ.* [from *arch* and *biſhop.*] A biſhop of the firſt claſs, who ſuperintends the conduct of other biſhops his ſuffragans.

Cranmer is return'd with welcome,
Inſtall'd lord *archbiſhop* of Canterbury. *Shakeſ. Henry* VIII.

The *archbiſhop* was the known architect of this new fabrick. *Clarendon.*

ARCHBI'SHOPRICK. *n. ſ.* [from *archbiſhop.*] The ſtate or juriſdiction of an archbiſhop.

'Tis the cardinal;
And merely to revenge him on the emperor,
For not beſtowing on him, at his aſking,
The *archbiſhoprick* of Toledo this is purpos'd. *Sh. H.* VIII.

This excellent man, from the time of his promotion to the *archbiſhoprick*, underwent the envy and malice of men who agreed in nothing elſe. *Clarendon.*

ARCHCHA'NTER. *n. ſ.* [from *arch* and *chanter.*] The chief chanter.

ARCHDE'ACON. *n. ſ.* [*archidiaconus*, Lat.] One that ſupplies the biſhop's place and office in ſuch matters as do belong to the epiſcopal function. The law ſtiles him the biſhop's vicar, or vicegerent. *Ayliffe's Parergon.*

Leſt negligence might foiſt in abuſes, an *archdeacon* was appointed to take account of their doings. *Carew's Surv. of Irel.*

ARCHDE'ACONRY. *n. ſ.* [*archidiaconatus*, Lat.] The office or juriſdiction of an archdeacon.

It oweth ſubjection to the metropolitan of Canterbury, and hath one only *archdeaconry.* *Carew's Survey of Cornwall.*

ARCHDE'ACONSHIP. *n. ſ.* [from *archdeacon.*] The office of an archdeacon.

ARCHDU'KE. *n. ſ.* [*archidux*, Lat.] A title given to ſome ſovereign princes, as of Auſtria and Tuſcany.

Philip *archduke* of Auſtria, during his voyage from the Netherlands towards Spain, was weather-driven into Weymouth. *Carew's Survey of Cornwal.*

ARCHDU'CHESS. *n. ſ.* [from *arch* and *ducheſs.*] A title given to the ſiſter or daughter of the archduke of Auſtria, or to the wife of an archduke of Tuſcany.

ARCH-PHILO'SOPHER. *n. ſ.* [from *arch* and *philoſopher.*] Chief philoſopher.

It is no improbable opinion therefore, which the *arch-philoſopher* was of, that the chiefeſt perſon in every houſhold was always as it were a king. *Hooker, b.* i.

ARCH-PRE'LATE. *n. ſ.* [from *arch* and *prelate.*] Chief prelate.

May we not wonder, that a man of St. Baſil's authority and quality, an *arch-prelate* in the houſe of God, ſhould have his name far and wide called in queſtion. *Hooker, b.* v. § 42.

ARCH-PRE'SBYTER. *n. ſ.* [from *arch* and *preſbyter.*] Chief preſbyter.

As ſimple deacons are in ſubjection to preſbyters, according to the canon law; ſo are alſo preſbyters and *arch-preſbyters* in ſubjection to theſe archdeacons. *Ayliffe's Parergon.*

ARCH-PRI'EST. *n. ſ.* [from *arch* and *prieſt.*] Chief prieſt.

The word decanus was extended to an eccleſiaſtical dignity, which included the *arch-prieſts.* *Ayliffe's Parergon.*

ARCHAIO'LOGY. *n. ſ.* [from ἀρχαῖος, ancient, and λόγος, a diſcourſe.] A diſcourſe on antiquity.

ARCHAIOLO'GICK. *adj.* [from *archaiology.*] Relating to a diſcourſe on antiquity.

A'RCHAISM. *n. ſ.* [ἀρχαισμὸς] An ancient phraſe, or mode of expreſſion.

I ſhall never uſe *archaiſms*, like Milton. *Watts.*

A'RCHED. *participial adj.* [from *To arch.*] Bent in the form of an arch.

I ſee how thine eye would emulate the diamond; thou haſt the right *arched* bent of the brow. *Shak. Merry Wives of Windſ.*

A'RCHER. *n. ſ.* [*archer*, Fr. from *arcus*, Lat. a bow.] He that ſhoots with a bow; he that carries a bow in battle.

Fight, gentlemen of England; fight, bold yeomen!
Draw, *archers*, draw your arrows to the head:
Spur your proud horſes hard. *Shakeſp. Richard* III.

This Cupid is no longer an *archer*, his glory ſhall be ours, for we are the only love-gods. *Shakeſp. Much ado about Noth.*

Thou frequent bring'ſt the ſmitten deer;
For ſeldom, *archers* ſay, thy arrows err. *Prior.*

A'RCHERY. *n. ſ.* [from *archer.*]

1. The uſe of the bow.

Among the Engliſh artillery, *archery* challengeth the preeminence, as peculiar to our nation. *Camden's Remains.*

2. The

2. The act of ſhooting with the bow.

Flower of this purple dye,
Hit with Cupid's *archery*,
Sink in apple of his eye! *Shakeſ. Midſ. Night's Dr.*

3. The art of an archer.

Bleſt ſeraphims ſhall leave their quire,
And turn love's ſoldiers upon thee,
To exerciſe their *archery*. *Craſhaw's Steps to Temple.*

A'RCHES-COURT. *n. ſ.* [from *arches* and *court.*] The chief and moſt ancient conſiſtory that belongs to the archbiſhop of Canterbury, for the debating of ſpiritual cauſes, ſo called from Bow-church in London, where it is kept, whoſe top is raiſed of ſtone-pillars, built arch-wiſe. The judge of this court is termed the dean of the arches, or official of the *arches-court*: dean of the arches, becauſe with this office is commonly joined a peculiar juriſdiction of thirteen pariſhes in London, termed a deanery, being exempted from the authority of the biſhop of London, and belonging to the archbiſhop of Canterbury; of which the pariſh of Bow is one. Some others ſay, that he was firſt called dean of the arches, becauſe the official to the archbiſhop, the dean of the arches, was his ſubſtitute in his court; and by that means the names became confounded. The juriſdiction of this judge is ordinary, and extends through the whole province of Canterbury: ſo that, upon any appeal, he forthwith, and without any further examination of the cauſe, ſends out his citation to the party appealed, and his inhibition to the judge from whom the appeal is made. *Cowell.*

A'RCHETYPE. *n. ſ.* [*archetypum*, Lat.] The original of which any reſemblance is made.

Our ſouls, though they might have perceived images themſelves by ſimple ſenſe; yet it ſeems inconceivable, how they ſhould apprehend their *archetypes*. *Glanville's Sceпſis Scientifica.*

As a man, a tree, are the outward objects of our perception, and the outward *archetypes* or patterns of our ideas; ſo our ſenſations of hunger, cold, are alſo inward *archetypes* or patterns of our ideas. But the notions or pictures of theſe things, as they are in the mind, are the ideas. *Watts's Logick.*

ARCHE'TYPAL. *adj.* [*archetypus*, Lat.] Original; being a pattern from which copies are made.

Through contemplation's opticks I have ſeen
Him who is fairer than the ſons of men:
The ſource of good, the light *archetypal*. *Norris's Miſcell.*

ARCHE'US. *n. ſ.* [probably from ἀρχὸς.] A word by which Paracelſus ſeems to have meant a power that preſides over the animal œconomy, diſtinct from the rational ſoul.

ARCHIDIA'CONAL. *adj.* [from *archidiaconus*, Lat. an archdeacon.] Belonging to an archdeacon; as, this offence is liable to be cenſured in an *archidiaconal* viſitation.

ARCHIEPI'SCOPAL. *adj.* [from *archiepiſcopus*, Lat. an archbiſhop.] Belonging to an archbiſhop; as, Canterbury is an *archiepiſcopal* ſee; the ſuffragans are ſubject to *archiepiſcopal* juriſdiction.

A'RCHITECT. *n. ſ.* [*architectus*, Lat.]

1. A profeſſor of the art of building.

The *architect's* glory conſiſts in the deſignment and idea of the work; his ambition ſhould be to make the form triumph over the matter. *Wotton.*

2. A contriver of a building; a builder.

The haſty multitude
Admiring enter'd, and the work ſome praiſe,
And ſome the *architect*: his hand was known
In heav'n, by many a tow'red ſtructure high,
Where ſcepter'd angels held their reſidence,
And ſat as princes. *Milton's Paradiſe Loſt, b.* i.

3. The contriver or former of any compound body.

This inconvenience the divine *architect* of the body obviated. *Ray on the Creation.*

4. The contriver of any thing.

An irreligious Moor,
Chief *architect* and plotter of theſe woes. *Shak. Tit. Andron.*

ARCHITE'CTIVE. *adj.* [from *architect.*] That performs the work of architecture.

How could the bodies of many of them, particularly the laſt mentioned, be furniſhed with *architective* materials? *Derham's Phyſico-Theology.*

ARCHITECTO'NICK. *adj.* [from ἀρχὸς, chief, and τέκτων, an artificer.] That which has the power or ſkill of an architect; that which can build or form any thing.

To ſay that ſome more fine part of either, or all the hypoſtatical principle, is the architect of this elaborate ſtructure, is to give occaſion to demand, what proportion of the tria prima afforded this *architectonick* ſpirit, and what agent made ſo ſkilful and happy a mixture. *Boyle's Scept. Chym.*

ARCHITE'CTURE. *n. ſ.* [*architectura*, Lat.]

1. The art or ſcience of building.

Architecture is divided into *civil architecture*, called by way of eminence *architecture*; *military architecture*, or fortification; and *naval architecture*, which, beſides building of ſhips and veſſels, includes alſo ports, moles, docks, &c. Some think the Tyrians were the firſt improvers of *architecture*; but others contend, that the rules of this art were delivered by God himſelf to Solomon, from whom the Tyrians had their inſtruction, which they afterwards communicated to the Egyptians; theſe to the Grecians, and theſe again to the Romans. Under Auguſtus, *architecture* arrived to its greateſt glory; but it afterwards dwindled by degrees, and at laſt fell with the weſtern empire, in the fifth century, when the Viſigoths deſtroyed all the moſt beautiful monuments of antiquity; and a new manner of building took its riſe, called the Gothick, coarſe, artleſs, and maſſive. Of the ſame kind was the Arabeſk, Mooriſk or Mooriſh *architecture*, brought from the South by the Moors and Saracens. The architects of the thirteenth, fourteenth, and fifteenth centuries, who had ſome knowledge of ſculpture, ſeemed to make perfection conſiſt altogether in the delicacy and multitude of ornaments, which they frequently beſtowed on their buildings without any conduct or taſte. In the two laſt centuries, the architects of Italy and France were wholly bent upon retrieving the primitive ſimplicity and beauty of ancient *architecture*, in which they did not fail of ſucceſs. This art is divided into five orders; the Tuſcan, Dorick, Ionick, Corinthian, and Compoſite; which took their riſe from the different proportions that the different kinds of buildings rendered neceſſary, according to the bulk, ſtrength, delicacy, richneſs, or ſimplicity required. *Chambers.*

Our fathers next in *architecture* ſkill'd,
Cities for uſe, and forts for ſafety build:
Then palaces and lofty domes aroſe,
Theſe for devotion, and for pleaſure thoſe. *Blackm. Creat.*

2. The effect or performance of the ſcience of building.

The formation of the firſt earth being a piece of divine *architecture*, aſcribed to a particular providence. *Burnet's Theory.*

A'RCHITRAVE. *n. ſ.* [from ἀρχὴ, chief, and *trabs*, Lat. a beam; becauſe it is ſuppoſed to repreſent the principal beam in timber buildings.] That part of a column, or order of a column, which lies immediately upon the capital, and is the loweſt member of the entablature. This member is different in the different orders; and, in building *architrave* doors and windows, the workman frequently follows his own fancy. The *architrave* is ſometimes called the reaſon piece, or maſter beam, in timber buildings, as porticos, cloiſters, &c. In chimnies it is called the mantle piece; and over jambs of doors, and lintels of windows, hyperthyron. *Builders Dict.*

The materials laid over this pillar were of wood; through the lightneſs whereof the *architrave* could not ſuffer, nor the column itſelf, being ſo ſubſtantial. *Wotton's Architecture.*

Weſtward a pompous frontiſpiece appear'd,
On Dorick pillars of white marble rear'd,
Crown'd with an *architrave* of antique mold,
And ſculpture riſing on the roughen'd gold. *Pope's T. of F.*

A'RCHIVES. *n. ſ. without a ſingular.* [*archiva*, Lat.] The places where records or ancient writings are kept. It is perhaps ſometimes uſed for the writings themſelves.

Though we think our words vaniſh with the breath that utters them, yet they become records in God's court, and are laid up in his *archives*, as witneſſes either for or againſt us. *Government of the Tongue*, § 1.

I ſhall now only look a little into the Moſaick *archives*, to obſerve what they furniſh us with upon this ſubject. *Woodward.*

A'RCHWISE. *adv.* [from *arch* and *wiſe.*] In the form of an arch.

The court of arches, ſo called *ab arcuata eccleſia*, or from Bow church in London, which is dedicated to the Virgin Mary, by reaſon of the ſteeple or clochier thereof, raiſed at the top with ſtone pillars in faſhion of a bow bent *archwiſe*. *Ayliffe's Par.*

ARCI'TENENT. *adj.* [*arcitenens*, Lat.] Bow-bearing. *Dict.*

ARCTA'TION. *n. ſ.* [from *arcto*, to ſtreighten.] Streightening; confinement to a narrower compaſs.

A'RCTICK. *n. ſ.* [from Ἄρκτος, the northern conſtellation.] Northern; lying under the Arctos, or bear. See ARTICK.

Ever during ſnows, perpetual ſhades
Of darkneſs, would congeal their livid blood,
Did not the *arctick* tract ſpontaneous yield
A cheering purple berry big with wine. *Philips.*

A'RCTICK *Circle.* See CIRCLE.

A'RCUATE. *adj.* [*arcuatus*, Lat.] Bent in the form of an arch.

The cauſe of the confuſion in ſounds, and the inconfuſion of ſpecies viſible, is, for that the ſight worketh in right lines; but ſounds that move in oblique and *arcuate* lines, muſt needs encounter and diſturb the one the other. *Bacon's Nat. Hiſt.*

In the gullet, where it perforateth the midriff, the carneous fibres are inflected and *arcuate*. *Ray on Creation.*

A'RCUATILE, *adj.* [from *arcuate.*] Bent; inflected. *Dict.*

ARCUA'TION. *n. ſ.* [from *arcuate.*]

1. The act of bending any thing; incurvation.

2. The ſtate of being bent; curvity, or crookedneſs.

3. [In gardening.] The method of raiſing by layers ſuch trees as cannot be raiſed from ſeed, or that bear no ſeed, as the elm, lime, alder, willow; and is ſo called from bending down to the ground the branches which ſpring from the offsets or ſtools after they are planted. *Chambers.*

A'RCUATURE. *n. ſ.* [*arcuatura*, low Latin.] The bending or curvature of an arch. *Dict.*

ARCUBA'LISTER. *n. ſ.* [from *arcus*, a bow, and *baliſta*, an engine.] A croſsbow man.

King John was eſpied by a very good *arcubaliſter*, who ſaid, that he would ſoon diſpatch the cruel tyrant. God forbid, vile varlet, quoth the earl, that we ſhould procure the death of the holy one of God. *Camden's Remains.*

ARD. [Saxon.] Signifies natural diſpoſition; as, *Goddard* is a divine temper; *Reinard*, a ſincere temper; *Giffard*, a bountiful and liberal diſpoſition; *Bernard*, filial affection, *&c.* *Gibſon's Camden.*

A'RDENCY. *n. ſ.* [from *ardent.*] Ardour; eagerneſs; warmth of affection.

Accepted they ſhall be, if qualified with humility, and *ardency*, and perſeverance, ſo far as concerns the end immediate to them. *Hammond's Pract. Catechiſm.*

The ineffable happineſs of our dear Redeemer muſt needs bring an increaſe to ours, commenſurate to the *ardency* of our love for him. *Boyle.*

A'RDENT. *adj.* [*ardens*, Lat. burning.]

1. Hot; burning; fiery.

Chymiſts obſerve, that vegetables, as lavender, rue, marjoram, *&c.* diſtilled before fermentation, yield oils without any burning ſpirits; but, after fermentation, yield *ardent* ſpirits without oils; which ſhews, that their oil is, by fermentation, converted into ſpirit. *Newton's Opticks.*

2. Fierce; vehement.

A knight of ſwarthy face,
High on a cole-black ſteed purſued the chace;
With flaſhing flames his *ardent* eyes were filled. *Dryd. Fab.*

3. Paſſionate; affectionate: uſed generally of deſire.

Another nymph with fatal pow'r may riſe,
To damp the ſinking beams of Cælia's eyes;
With haughty pride may hear her charms confeſt,
And ſcorn the *ardent* vows that I have bleſt. *Prior.*

A'RDENTLY. *adv.* [from *ardent.*] Eagerly; affectionately.

With true zeal may our hearts be moſt *ardently* inflamed to our religion. *Sprat's Sermons.*

A'RDOUR. *n. ſ.* [*ardor*, Lat. heat.]

1. Heat.

2. Heat of affection, as love, deſire, courage.

Joy, like a ray of the ſun, reflects with a greater *ardour* and quickneſs, when it rebounds upon a man from the breaſt of his friend. *South.*

The ſoldiers ſhout around with gen'rous rage;
He prais'd their *ardour*, inly pleas'd to ſee
His hoſt. *Dryden's Fables.*

Unmov'd the mind of Ithacus remain'd,
And the vain *ardours* of our love reſtrain'd. *Pope's Odyſſey.*

3. The perſon ardent or bright. This is only uſed by *Milton.*

Nor delay'd the winged ſaint,
After his charge receiv'd; but from among
Thouſand celeſtial *ardours*, where he ſtood
Veil'd with his gorgeous wings, up-ſpringing light,
Flew thro' the midſt of heav'n. *Paradiſe Loſt, b.* v.

ARDU'ITY. *n. ſ.* [from *arduous.*] Height; difficulty. *Dict.*

A'RDUOUS. *adj.* [*arduus*, Lat.]

1. Lofty; hard to climb.

High on Parnaſſus' top her ſons ſhe ſhow'd,
And pointed out thoſe *arduous* paths they trod. *Pope.*

2. Difficult.

It was a means to bring him up in the ſchool of arts and policy, and ſo to fit him for that great and *arduous* employment that God deſigned him to. *South.*

A'RDUOUSNESS. *n. ſ.* [from *arduous.*] Height; difficulty.

ARE. The third perſon plural of the preſent tenſe of the verb *to be*; as, young men *are* raſh, old *are* cautious.

ARE, or *Alamire.* The loweſt note but one in Guido's ſcale of muſick.

Gamut I am, the ground of all accord,
Are to plead Hortenſio's paſſion;
B mi Bianca take him for thy lord,
C faut, that loves with all affection. *Shakeſp. Tam. Shrew.*

A'REA. *n. ſ.* [Latin.]

1. The ſurface contained between any lines or boundaries.

The *area* of a triangle is found by knowing the height and the baſe. *Watts's Logick.*

2. Any open ſurface, as the floor of a room; the open part of a church; the vacant part or ſtage of an amphitheatre. An incloſed place, as liſts, or a bowling-green, or graſs-plot.

Let us conceive a floor or *area* of goodly length, with the breadth ſomewhat more than half the longitude. *Wotton.*

The Alban lake is of an oval figure, and, by reaſon of the high mountains that encompaſs it, looks like the *area* of ſome vaſt amphitheatre. *Addiſon on Italy.*

In *areas* vary'd with Moſaic art,
Some whirl the diſk, and ſome the jav'lin dart. *Pope's Odyſſ.*

To ARE'AD, or ARE'ED. *v. a.* [aꞃeban, Sax. to counſel.] To adviſe; to direct.

Knights and ladies gentle deeds,
Whoſe praiſes having ſlept in ſilence long,
Me, all too meane, the ſacred muſe *areeds*
To blazon broad. *Fairy Queen, b.* i.

But mark what I *aread* thee now: avant,
Fly thither whence thou fled'ſt! If from this hour
Within theſe hallow'd limits thou appear,
Back to th' infernal pit I drag thee chain'd. *Paradiſe Loſt.*

AREFA'CTION. *n. ſ.* [*arefacio*, Lat. to dry.] The ſtate of growing dry; the act of drying.

From them, and their motions, principally proceed *arefaction*, and moſt of the effects of nature. *Bacon's Nat. Hiſtory.*

To A'REFY. *v. a.* [*arefacio*, Lat. to dry.] To dry; to exhale moiſture.

Heat drieth bodies that do eaſily expire, as parchment, leaves, roots, clay, *&c.* and ſo doth time or age *arefy*, as in the ſame bodies, *&c.* *Bacon's Nat. Hiſt.* N° 294.

ARENA'CEOUS. *adj.* [*arena*, Lat. ſand.] Sandy; having the qualities of ſand.

A piece of the ſtone of the ſame mines, of a yellowiſh brown colour, an *arenaceous* friable ſubſtance, and with ſome white ſpar mixed with it. *Woodward on Foſſils.*

ARENA'TION. *n. ſ.* [from *arena*, Lat. ſand.] Is uſed by ſome phyſicians for a ſort of dry bath, when the patient ſits with his feet upon hot ſand. *Dict.*

ARENO'SE. *adj.* [from *arena*, Lat.] Sandy; full of ſand. *Dict.*

ARE'NULOUS. *adj.* [from *arenula*, Lat. ſand.] Full of ſmall ſand; gravelly. *Dict.*

AREO'TICK. *adj.* [ἀραιωτικὰ.] Such medicines as open the pores of the ſkin, ſo that the morbifick matter may be carried off by ſweat, or inſenſible perſpiration. *Dict.*

ARETO'LOGY. *n. ſ.* [from ἀρετὴ, virtue, and λέγω, to diſcourſe.] That part of moral philoſophy which treats of virtue, its nature, and the means of arriving at it. *Dict.*

A'RGAL. *n. ſ.* Hard lees ſticking to the ſides of wine veſſels, more commonly called tartar. *Dict.*

A'RGENT. *adj.* [from *argentum*, Lat. ſilver.]

1. The white colour uſed in the coats of gentlemen, knights, and baronets, ſuppoſed to be the repreſentation of that metal.

Rinaldo flings
As ſwift as fiery light'ning kindled new,
His *argent* eagle with her ſilver wings
In field of azure, fair Erminia knew. *Fairfax, b.* iii.

In an *argent* field, the god of war
Was drawn triumphant on his iron car. *Dryden's Fables.*

2. Silver; bright like ſilver.

Thoſe *argent* fields more likely habitants,
Tranſlated ſaints, or middle ſpirits hold,
Betwixt th' angelical and human kind. *Milton.*

Or aſk of yonder *argent* fields above,
Why Jove's ſatellites are leſs than Jove. *Pope's Eſſ. on Man.*

ARGENTA'TION. *n. ſ.* [from *argentum*, Lat. ſilver.] An overlaying with ſilver. *Dict.*

A'RGENTINE. *adj.* [*argentin*, Fr.] Sounding like ſilver. *Dict.*

A'RGIL. *n. ſ.* [*argilla*, Lat.] Potters clay; a fat ſoft kind of earth of which veſſels are made.

ARGILLA'CEOUS. *adj.* [from *argil.*] Clayey; partaking of the nature of argil; conſiſting of argil, or potter's clay.

ARGI'LLOUS. *adj.* [from *argil.*] Conſiſting of clay; clayiſh; containing clay.

Albuquerque derives this redneſs from the ſand and *argillous* earth at the bottom. *Brown's Vulgar Errours, b.* vi.

A'RGOSY. *n. ſ.* [derived by *Pope* from *Argo*, the name of Jaſon's ſhip.] A large veſſel for merchandiſe; a carrack.

Your mind is toſſing on the ocean;
There where your *argoſies* with portly ſail,
Like ſigniors and rich burghers on the flood,
Or as it were the pageants of the ſea
Do overpeer the petty traffickers. *Shakeſ. Merch. of Venice.*

To A'RGUE. *v. n.* [*arguo*, Lat.]

1. To reaſon; to offer reaſons.

I know your majeſty has always lov'd her
So dear in heart, not to deny her what
A woman of leſs place might aſk by law;
Scholars allow'd freely to *argue* for her. *Shakeſp. Hen.* VIII.

Publick *arguing* oft ſerves not only to exaſperate the minds, but to whet the wits of hereticks. *Decay of Piety.*

An idea of motion, not paſſing on, would perplex any one, who ſhould *argue* from ſuch an idea. *Locke.*

2. To perſuade by argument.

It is a ſort of poetical logick which I would make uſe of, to *argue* you into a protection of this play. *Congr. Ded to Old Bat.*

3. To diſpute; with the particles *with* or *againſt* before the opponent, and *againſt* before the thing oppoſed.

Why do chriſtians, of ſeveral perſuaſions, ſo fiercely *argue againſt* the ſalvability of each other. *Decay of Piety.*

He that by often *arguing againſt* his own ſenſe, impoſes falſehoods on others, is not far from believing himſelf. *Locke.*

I do not ſee how they can *argue with* any one, without ſetting down ſtrict boundaries. *Locke.*

To A'RGUE. *v. a.*

1. To prove any thing by argument.

If the world's age and death be *argued* well,
By the ſun's fall, which now toward's earth doth bend,
Then we might fear that virtue, ſince ſhe fell
So low as woman, ſhould be near her end. *Donne.*

2. To debate any queſtion; as, to *argue* a cauſe.

3. To prove, as an argument.

So many laws *argue* ſo many ſins
Among them: how can God with ſuch reſide? *Parad. Loſt.*

It

It *argues* diſtemper of the mind as well as of the body, when a man is continually toſſing from one ſide to the other. *South.*

This *argues* a virtue and diſpoſition in thoſe ſides of the rays, which anſwers to that virtue and diſpoſition of the cryſtal. *Newton's Opticks.*

4. To charge with, as a crime; with *of*.

I have pleaded guilty to all thoughts and expreſſions of mine, which can be truly *argued of* obſcenity, profaneneſs, or immorality, and retract them. *Dryden's Fables, Preface.*

The accidents are not the ſame, which would have *argued* him *of* a ſervile copying, and total barrenneſs of invention; yet the ſeas were the ſame. *Dryden's Fab. Pref.*

A'RGUER. *n. ſ.* [from *argue.*] A reaſoner; a diſputer; a controvertiſt.

Men are aſhamed to be proſelytes to a weak *arguer*, as thinking they muſt part with their reputation as well as their ſin. *Decay of Piety.*

A'RGUMENT. *n. ſ.* [*argumentum*, Lat.]

1. A reaſon alleged for or againſt any thing.

We ſometimes ſee, on our theatres, vice rewarded, at leaſt unpuniſhed; yet it ought not to be an *argument* againſt the art. *Dryden's Pref. to Tyrannick Love.*

When any thing is proved by as good *arguments* as that thing is capable of, ſuppoſing it were; we ought not in reaſon to make any doubt of the exiſtence of that thing. *Tillotſon's Preface.*

And thus we have our author's two great and only *arguments* to prove, that heirs are lords over their brethren. *Locke.*

2. The ſubject of any diſcourſe or writing.

That ſhe who ev'n but now was your beſt object,
Your praiſe's *argument*, balm of your age,
Deareſt and beſt. *Shakeſp. King Lear.*

To the height of this great *argument*
I may aſſert eternal providence,
And juſtify the ways of God to man. *Milton's Par. Loſt, b.* i.

Sad task! yet *argument*
Not leſs, but more heroick than the wrath
Of ſtern Achilles. *Milton's Par. Loſt, b.* ix.

A much longer diſcourſe my *argument* requires; your merciful diſpoſitions a much ſhorter. *Sprat's Sermons.*

3. The contents of any work ſummed up by way of abſtract.

The *argument* of the work, that is, its principal action, the œconomy and diſpoſition of it, are the things which diſtinguiſh copies from originals. *Dryden's Æn. Pref.*

4. A controverſy.

This day, in *argument* upon a caſe,
Some words there grew 'twixt Somerſet and me. *Sh: H.* VI.

If the idea be not agreed on betwixt the ſpeaker and hearer, the *argument* is not about things, but names. *Locke.*

It was much like an *argument* that fell out laſt night, where each of us fell in praiſe of our country miſtreſſes. *Sh. Cymbeline.*

5. It has ſometimes the particle *to* before the thing to be proved, but generally *for.*

The beſt moral *argument to* patience, in my opinion, is the advantage of patience itſelf. *Tillotſon.*

This, before that revelation had enlightened the world, was the very beſt *argument for* a future ſtate. *Atterbury's Sermons.*

6. [In aſtronomy.] An arch by which we ſeek another unknown arch, proportional to the firſt. *Chambers.*

ARGUME'NTAL. *adj.* [from *argument.*] Belonging to argument; reaſoning.

Afflicted ſenſe thou kindly doſt ſet free,
Oppreſs'd with *argumental* tyranny,
And routed reaſon finds a ſafe retreat in thee. *Pope.*

ARGUMENTA'TION. *n. ſ.* [from *argument.*] Reaſoning; the act of reaſoning.

Argumentation is that operation of the mind, whereby we infer one propoſition from two or more propoſitions premiſed. Or it is the drawing a concluſion, which before was unknown, or doubtful, from ſome propoſitions more known and evident; ſo when we have judged that matter cannot think, and that the mind of man doth think, we conclude, that therefore the mind of man is not matter. *Watts's Logick.*

I ſuppoſe it is no ill topick of *argumentation*, to ſhew the prevalence of contempt, by the contrary influences of reſpect. *South.*

His thoughts muſt be maſculine, full of *argumentation*, and that ſufficiently warm. *Dryden.*

It is certain, that the whole courſe of his *argumentation* comes to nothing. *Addiſon. Freeholder*, N° 31.

ARGUME'NTATIVE. *adj.* [from *argument.*] Conſiſting of argument; containing argument.

This omiſſion, conſidering the bounds within which the *argumentative* part of my diſcourſe was confined, I could not avoid. *Atterb. Pref. to his Sermons.*

ARGUTA'TION. *n. ſ.* [from *arguo*, Lat.] A proving by argument; a diſputing for and againſt. *Dict.*

A'RGUTE. *adj.* [*arguto*, Ital. *argutus*, Lat.]

1. Subtile; witty; ſharp.

2. Shrill.

A'RIA. n. ſ. [Ital. in muſick.] An air, ſong, or tune.

A'RID. *adj.* [*aridus*, Lat. dry.] Dry; parched up.

My complexion is become aduſt, and my body *arid*, by viſiting lands. *Arbuthnot and Pope's M. Scribl.*

His harden'd fingers deck the gaudy ſpring,
Without him ſummer were an *arid* waſte. *Thomſ. Autumn.*

ARI'DITY. *n. ſ.* [from *arid.*]

1. Dryneſs; ſiccity.

Salt taken in great quantities will reduce an animal body to the great extremity of *aridity*, or dryneſs. *Arbuth. on Aliments.*

2. In the theological ſenſe, a kind of inſenſibility in devotion, contrary to melting.

Strike my ſoul with lively apprehenſions of thy excellencies, to bear up my ſpirit under the greateſt *aridities* and dejections, with the delightful proſpect of thy glories. *Norris.*

A'RIES. n. ſ. [Lat.] The Ram; one of the twelve ſigns of the zodiack.

At laſt from *Aries* rolls the bounteous ſun,
And the bright Bull receives him. *Thomſon's Spring.*

To ARI'ETATE. *v. n.* [*arieto*, Lat.]

1. To butt like a ram.

2. To ſtrike in imitation of the blows which rams give with their heads.

ARIETA'TION. *n. ſ.* [from *arietate.*]

1. The act of butting like a ram.

2. The act of battering with an engine called a ram.

The ſtrength of the percuſſion, wherein ordnance do exceed all *arietations* and ancient inventions. *Bacon's Eſſays.*

3. The act of ſtriking, or conflicting in general.

Now thoſe heterogeneous atoms, by themſelves, hit ſo exactly into their proper reſidence, in the midſt of ſuch tumultuary motions, and *arietations* of other particles. *Glanv. Scepſis.*

ARIE'TTA. n. ſ. [Ital. in muſick.] A ſhort air, ſong, or tune.

ARI'GHT. *adv.* [from *a* and *right.*]

1. Rightly; without mental errour.

How him I lov'd, and love with all my might;
So thought I eke of him, and think I thought *aright. F. Q.*

Theſe were thy thoughts, and thou could'ſt judge *aright*,
Till intereſt made a jaundice in thy ſight. *Dryden's Fables.*

The motions of the tongue are ſo eaſy, and ſo ſubtile, that you can hardly conceive or diſtinguiſh them *aright*. *Holder.*

2. Rightly; without crime.

A generation that ſet not their heart *aright*. *Pſ.* lxxviii. 8.

3. Rightly; without failing of the end deſigned.

Guardian of groves, and goddeſs of the night,
Fair queen, he ſaid, direct my dart *aright*. *Dryden's Æneid.*

ARIOLA'TION, or HARIOLA'TION. *n. ſ.* [*hariolus*, Lat. a ſoothſayer.] Soothſaying; vaticination.

The prieſts of elder time have deluded their apprehenſions with *ariolation*, ſoothſaying, and ſuch oblique idolatries. *Brown's Vulgar Errours, b.* i. *c.* 3.

ARIO'SO. n. ſ. [Ital. in muſick.] The movement of a common air, ſong, or tune. *Dict.*

To ARI'SE. *v. n.* pret. *aroſe*, particip. *ariſen.* [from *a* and *riſe.*]

1. To mount upward as the ſun.

He roſe, and, looking up, beheld the ſkies
With purple bluſhing, and the day *ariſe*. *Dryden's Æneid.*

2. To get up as from ſleep, or from reſt.

So Eſdras *aroſe* up, and ſaid unto them, ye have tranſgreſſed the law. 1 *Eſd.* ix. 7.

How long wilt thou ſleep, O ſluggard; when wilt thou *ariſe* out of thy ſleep? *Prov.* vi. 9.

3. To come into view, as from obſcurity.

There ſhall *ariſe* falſe Chriſts and falſe prophets. *Matt.* xxiv.

4. To revive from death.

Thy dead men ſhall live, together with my body ſhall they *ariſe*: awake and ſing, ye that dwell in duſt. *Iſaiah* xxvi. 19.

5. To proceed, or have its original.

They which were ſcattered abroad upon the perſecution that *aroſe* about Stephen, travelled as far as Phœnice. *Acts* xi. 19.

I know not what miſchief may *ariſe* hereafter from the example of ſuch an innovation. *Dryden.*

6. To enter upon a new ſtation.

Another Mary then *aroſe*,
And did rig'rous laws impoſe. *Cowley.*

7. To commence hoſtility.

And when he *aroſe* againſt me, I caught him by his beard, and ſmote him. 1 *Sam.* xvii. 35.

For the various ſenſes of this word, ſee RISE.

ARISTO'CRACY. *n. ſ.* [ἄριστος, greateſt, and κρατέω, to govern.] That form of government which places the ſupreme power in the nobles, without a king, and excluſively of the people.

The *ariſtocracy* of Venice hath admitted ſo many abuſes through the degeneracy of the nobles, that the period of its duration ſeems to approach. *Swift.*

ARISTOCRA'TICAL, or ARISTOCRA'TICK. *adj.* [from *ariſtocracy.*] Relating to ariſtocracy; including a form of government by the nobles.

Ockham diſtinguiſhes, that the papacy, or eccleſiaſtical monarchy, may be changed in an extraordinary manner, for ſome time, into an *ariſtocratical* form of government. *Ayliffe's Par.*

ARISTOCRA'TICALNESS. *n. ſ.* [from *ariſtocratical.*] An ariſtocratical ſtate. *Dict.*

ARI'THMANCY. *n. ſ.* [from ἀριθμός, number, and μαντεία, divination.] A foretelling future events by numbers. *Dict.*

ARITHME'TICAL. *adj.* [from *arithmetick.*] According to the rules or method of arithmetick.

The principles of bodies may be infinitely ſmall, not only beyond all naked or aſſiſted ſenſe, but beyond all *arithmetical* operation or conception. *Grew's Coſm. Sacra.*

The ſquares of the diameters of theſe rings, made by any priſmatick colour, were in *arithmetical* progreſſion, as in the fifth obſervation. *Newton's Opticks.*

ARITHME'TICALLY. *adv.* [from *arithmetical.*] In an arithmetical manner; according to the principles of arithmetick.

Though the fifth part of a xeſtes being a ſimple fraction, and *arithmetically* regular, it is yet no proper part of that meaſure. *Arbuthnot on Coins.*

ARITHMETI'CIAN. *n. ſ.* [from *arithmetick.*] A maſter of the art of numbers.

A man had need be a good *arithmetician*, to underſtand this author's works. His deſcription runs on like a multiplication table. *Addiſon on ancient Medals.*

ARI'THMETICK. *n. ſ.* [ἀριθμὸς, number, and μετρέω, to meaſure.] The ſcience of numbers; the art of computation.

We have very little intelligence about the origin and invention of *arithmetick*; but probably it muſt have taken its riſe from the introduction of commerce, and conſequently be of Tyrian invention. From Aſia it paſſed into Egypt, where it was greatly cultivated. From thence it was tranſmitted to the Greeks, who conveyed it to the Romans with additional improvements. But, from ſome treatiſes of the ancients remaining on this ſubject, it appears that their *arithmetick* was much inferiour to that of the moderns. *Chambers.*

On fair ground I could beat forty of them;
But now 'tis odds beyond *arithmetick*. *Shakeſp. Coriolanus.*

The chriſtian religion, according to the Apoſtle's *arithmetick*, hath but theſe three parts of it; ſobriety, juſtice, religion. *Taylor.*

ARK. *n. ſ.* [*arca*, Lat. a cheſt.]

1. A veſſel to ſwim upon the water, uſually applied to that in which Noah was preſerved from the univerſal deluge.

Make thee an *ark* of gopher wood; rooms ſhalt thou make in the *ark*, and ſhalt pitch it within and without. *Gen.* vi. 14.

The one juſt man alive, by his command,
Shall build a wond'rous *ark*, as thou beheld'ſt,
To ſave himſelf and houſhold, from amidſt
A world devote to univerſal wreck. *Milton's Par. Loſt, b.* xi.

2. The repoſitory of the covenant of God with the Jews.

This coffer was of ſhittim wood, covered with plates or leaves of gold, being two cubits and an half in length, a cubit and a half wide, and a cubit and a half high. It had two rings of gold on each ſide, through which the ſtaves were put for carrying it. Upon the top of it was a kind of gold crown all around it, and two cherubim were faſtened to the cover. It contained the two tables of ſtone, written by the hand of God. *Calmet.*

ARM. *n. ſ.* [eaꝛm, eoꝛm, Sax.]

1. The limb which reaches from the hand to the ſhoulder.

If I have lift up my hand againſt the fatherleſs, when I ſaw my help in the gate, then let mine *arm* fall from my ſhoulder-blade, and mine *arm* be broken from the bone. *Job*, xxxi. 21.

Like helpleſs friends, who view from ſhore
The labouring ſhip, and hear the tempeſt roar,
So ſtood they with their *arms* acroſs. *Dryden.*

2. The bough of a tree.

The trees ſpred out their *arms* to ſhade her face,
But ſhe on elbow lean'd. *Sidney.*

Hide me, ye foreſts, in your cloſeſt bowers,
Where the tall oak his ſpreading *arms* entwines,
And with the beech a mutual ſhade combines. *Gay.*

3. An inlet of water from the ſea.

Full in the centre of the ſacred wood,
An *arm* ariſeth of the Stygian flood. *Dryden's Æneid.*

We have yet ſeen but an *arm* of this ſea of beauty. *Norris.*

4. Power; might. In this ſenſe is uſed the ſecular *arm*, &c.

Curſed be the man that truſteth in man, and maketh fleſh his *arm*, and whoſe heart departeth from the Lord. *Jer.* xvii. 5.

O God, thy *arm* was here!
And not to us, but to thy *arm* alone,
Aſcribe we all. *Shakeſp. Hen.* V.

ARM'S END. *n. ſ.* A phraſe taken from boxing, in which the weaker man may overcome the ſtronger, if he can keep him from cloſing.

Such a one as can keep him at *arm's end*, need never wiſh for a better companion. *Sidney's Arcad.*

For my ſake be comfortable, hold death awhile at the *arm's end*. *Shakeſp. As you like it.*

To ARM. *v. a.* [*armo*, Lat.]

1. To furniſh with armour of defence, or weapons of offence.

And when Abram heard that his brother was taken captive, he *armed* his trained ſervants, born in his own houſe, three hundred and eighteen, and purſued them unto Dan. *Gen.* xiv. 14.

True conſcious honour is to feel no ſin;
He's *arm'd* without, that's innocent within. *Pope.*

2. To plate with any thing that may add ſtrength.

Their wounded ſteeds
Yerk out their *armed* heels at their dead maſters. *Sh. H.* V.

3. To furniſh; to fit up; as, to *arm* a loadſtone, is to caſe it with iron.

You muſt *arm* your hook with the line in the inſide of it. *Walton's Angler.*

Having waſted the callus, I left off thoſe tents, and dreſſed it with others *armed* with digeſtives. *Wiſeman's Surgery.*

To ARM. *v. n.*

1. To take arms.

Think we king Harry ſtrong;
And, princes, look you ſtrongly *arm* to meet him. *Sh. H.V.*

2. To provide againſt.

His ſervant, throughly *arm'd* againſt ſuch coverture,
Reported unto all, that he was ſure
A noble gentleman of high regard. *Spenſer's Hubb. Tale.*

ARMA'DA. n. ſ. [Span. a fleet of war.] An armament for ſea; a fleet of war. It is often erroneouſly ſpelt *armado.*

In all the mid-earth ſeas was left no road
Wherein the pagan his bold head untwines,
Spred was the huge *armado* wide and broad,
From Venice, Genes, and towns which them confines.
Fairfax, b. i. *ſtanza* 79.

So by a roaring tempeſt on the flood,
A whole *armado* of collected ſail
Is ſcatter'd and disjoin'd from fellowſhip. *Shak. King John.*

At length reſolv'd t' aſſert the wat'ry ball,
He in himſelf did whole *armados* bring:
Him aged ſeamen might their maſter call,
And chooſe for general, were he not their king. *Dryden.*

ARMADI'LLO. n. ſ. [Spaniſh.] A four-footed animal of Braſil, as big as a cat, with a ſnout like a hog, a tail like a lizard, and feet like a hedge-hog. He is armed all over with hard ſcales like armour, whence he takes his name, and retires under them like the tortoiſe. He lives in holes, or in the water, being of the amphibious kind. His ſcales are of a bony or cartilaginous ſubſtance; but they are eaſily pierced. This animal hides himſelf a third part of the year under ground. He feeds upon roots, ſugar-canes, fruits, and poultry. When he is caught, he draws up his feet and head to his belly, and rolls himſelf up in a ball, which the ſtrongeſt hand cannot open; and he muſt be brought near the fire before he will ſhew his noſe. His fleſh is white, fat, tender, and more delicate than that of a ſucking pig. *Trevoux.*

A'RMAMENT. *n. ſ.* [*armamentum*, Lat.] A force equipped for war; generally uſed of a naval force.

ARMAME'NTARY. *n. ſ.* [*armamentarium*, Lat.] An armoury; a magazine or arſenal of warlike implements. *Dict.*

A'RMAN. *n. ſ.* A confection for reſtoring loſt appetite in horſes. *D.*

A'RMATURE. *n. ſ.* [*armatura*, Lat.] Armour; ſomething to defend the body from hurt.

Others ſhould be armed with hard ſhells; others with prickles; the reſt that have no ſuch *armature*, ſhould be endued with great ſwiftneſs and pernicity. *Ray on the Creation.*

A'RMED. *adj.* [in heraldry.] Is uſed in reſpect of beaſts and birds of prey, when their teeth, horns, feet, beak, talons, or tuſks, are of a different colour from the reſt; as, he bears a cock or a falcon *armed*, or. *Chambers.*

ARMED *Chair. n. ſ.* [from *armed* and *chair.*] An elbow chair, or a chair with reſts for the arms.

ARME'NIAN *Bole. n. ſ.* A fatty medicinal kind of earth, of a pale reddiſh colour, of conſiderable uſe as an abſorbent, aſtringent, and vulnerary; which takes its name from the country of Armenia, whence it is chiefly brought.

ARMENIAN *Stone. n. ſ.* A mineral ſtone or earth of a blue colour, ſpotted with green, black and yellow; anciently brought only from Armenia, but now found in Germany, and the Tyrol. It bears a near reſemblance to lapis lazuli, from which it ſeems only to differ in degree of maturity; it being ſofter, and ſpeckled with green inſtead of gold. Boerhaave ranks it among ſemimetals; and ſuppoſes it compoſed of a metal and earth. Woodward ſays, it owes its colour to an admixture of copper. Its chief uſe is in moſaick work, though it has ſome place alſo in phyſick. *Chambers.*

ARME'NTAL. } *adj.* [*armentalis*, or *armentinus*, Lat.] Belong-
A'RMENTINE. } ing to a drove or herd of cattle. *Dict.*

ARMENTO'SE. *adj.* [*armentoſus*, Lat.] Abounding with cattle. *D.*

A'RMGAUNT. *adj.* [from *arm* and *gaunt.*] Slender as the arm.

So he nodded,
And ſoberly did mount an *armgaunt* ſteed. *Sh. Ant. and Cl.*

ARM-HOLE. *n. ſ.* [from *arm* and *hole.*] The cavity under the ſhoulder.

Tickling is moſt in the ſoles of the feet, and under the *armholes*, and on the ſides. The cauſe is the thinneſs of the ſkin in thoſe parts, joined with the rareneſs of being touched there. *Bacon's Natural Hiſt.* N° 766.

ARMI'GEROUS. *adj.* [from *armiger*, Lat. an armour-bearer.] Bearing arms.

A'RMILLARY. *adj.* [from *armilla*, Lat. a bracelet.] Reſembling a bracelet.

When the circles of the mundane ſphere are ſuppoſed to be deſcribed on the convex ſurface of a ſphere, which is hollow within, and, after this, you imagine all parts of the ſphere's ſurface to be cut away, except thoſe parts on which ſuch circles are deſcribed; then that ſphere is called an *armillary* ſphere, becauſe it appears in the form of ſeveral circular rings, or bracelets, put together in a due position. *Harris's Description of the Globes.*

A'RMILLATED. *adj.* [*armillatus*, Lat.] Wearing bracelets. *Dict.*

A'RMINGS. *n. s.* [in a ship.] The same with wasteclothes, being red clothes, hung about the outside of the ship's upper works fore and aft, and before the cubbrige heads. Some are also hung round the tops, called *top armings.* *Chambers.*

ARMI'POTENCE. *n. s.* [from *arma*, arms, and *potentia*, power, Lat.] Power in war.

ARMI'POTENT. *adj.* [*armipotens*, Lat.] Powerful in arms; mighty in war.

This is your devoted friend, Sir, the manifold linguist, and the *armipotent* soldier. *Shakesp. All's well that ends well.*

For if our God the Lord *armipotent*,
Those armed angels in our aid down send,
That were at Dathan to his prophet sent,
Thou wilt come down with them, and well defend
Our host. *Fairfax, b. iii. stan. 70.*

Beneath the low'ring brow, and on a bent,
The temple stood of Mars *armipotent.* *Dryden's Fab.*

ARMI'SONOUS. *adj.* [*armisonus*, Lat.] Rustling with armour.

A'RMISTICE. *n. s.* [*armistitium*, Lat.] A short truce; a cessation of arms for a short time.

A'RMLET. *n. s.* [from *arm.*]

1. A little arm; as, an *armlet* of the sea.
2. A piece of armour for the arm.
3. A bracelet for the arm.

And, when she takes thy hand, and doth seem kind,
Doth search what rings and *armlets* she can find. *Donne.*

ARMONI'ACK. *n. s.* [erroneously so written for *ammoniac.*] A sort of volatile salt. See AMMONIAC.

A'RMORER. *n. s.* [*armorier*, Fr.]

1. He that makes armour, or weapons.

Now thrive the *armorers*, and honour's thought
Reigns solely in the breast of every man. *Shakesp. Henry V.*

The *armorers* make their steel more tough and pliant, by aspersion of water and juice of herbs. *Bacon's Phys. Remains.*

The whole division that to Mars pertains,
All trades of death that deal in steel for gains
Were there: The butcher, *armorer*, and smith,
Who forges sharpen'd fauchions, or the scythe. *Dryd. Fab.*

When *arm'rers* temper in the ford
The keen-edg'd pole-ax, or the shining sword,
The red-hot metal hisses in the lake. *Pope's Odyssey, b. ix.*

2. He that dresses another in armour.

The *armorers* accomplishing the knights,
With busy hammers closing rivets up,
Give dreadful note of preparation. *Shakesp. Henry V.*

The morning he was to join battle with Harold, his *armorer* put on his backpiece before, and his breastplate behind. *Cambd.*

ARMO'RIAL. *adj.* [*armorial*, Fr.] Belonging to the arms or escutcheon of a family, as ensigns *armorial.*

A'RMORIST. *n. s.* [from *armour.*] A person skilled in heraldry. *Dict.*

A'RMORY. *n. s.* [from *armour.*]

1. The place in which arms are reposited for use.

The sword
Of Michael, from the *armory* of God,
Was giv'n him temper'd so, that neither keen,
Nor solid, might resist that edge. *Milton's Par. Lost, b. vi.*

With plain heroick magnitude of mind,
And celestial vigour arm'd,
Their *armories* and magazines contemns. *Sampson Agonist.*

Let a man consider these virtues, with the contrary sins, and then, as out of a full *armory*, or magazine, let him furnish his conscience with texts of scripture. *South.*

2. Armour; arms of defence.

Nigh at hand
Celestial *armory*, shields, helms, and spears,
Hung high, with diamond flaming, and with gold. *Par. Lost.*

3. Ensigns armorial.

Well worthy be you of that *armory*,
Wherein you have great glory won this day. *Fairy Queen.*

A'RMOUR. *n. s.* [*armateur*, Fr. *armatura*, Lat.] Defensive arms.

Your friends are up, and buckle on their *armour.* *Shakesp. Richard III.*

That they might not go naked among their enemies, the only *armour* that Christ allows them, is prudence and innocence. *South.*

A'RMOUR BEARER. *n. s.* [from *armour* and *bear.*] He that carries the armour of another.

His *armour bearer* first, and next he kills
His charioteer. *Dryden's Æneis.*

A'RMPIT. *n. s.* [from *arm* and *pit.*] The hollow place under the shoulder.

The handles to these gouges are made so long, that the handle may reach under the *armpit* of the workman. *Moxon's Mechanical Exercises.*

Others hold their plate under the left *arm-pit*, the best situation for keeping it warm. *Swift's Direct. to the Footman.*

ARMS. *n. s. without the singular number.* [*arma*, Lat.]

1. Weapons of offence, or armour of defence.

Those *arms* which Mars before
Had giv'n the vanquish'd, now the victor bore. *Pope's Iliad.*

2. A state of hostility.

Sir Edward Courtney, and the haughty prelate,
With many more confed'rates, are in *arms.* *Shakes. R. III.*

3. War in general.

Arms and the man I sing. *Dryd. Virgil.*

Him Paris follow'd to the dire alarms,
Both breathing slaughter, both resolv'd in *arms. Pope's Iliad.*

4. Action; the act of taking arms.

Up rose the victor angels, and to *arms*
The matin trumpet sung. *Milton's Paradise Lost, b. vi.*

5. The ensigns armorial of a family.

A'RMY. *n. s.* [*armée*, Fr.]

1. A collection of armed men, obliged to obey one man. *Locke.*

Number itself importeth not much in *armies*, where the people are of weak courage. *Bacon.*

The meanest soldier, that has fought often in an *army*, has a truer knowledge of war, than he that has writ whole volumes, but never was in any battle. *South.*

The Tuscan leaders, and their *army* sing,
Which follow'd great Æneas to the war;
Their arms, their numbers, and their names declare. *Dryd.*

2. A great number.

The fool hath planted in his memory an *army* of good words. *Shakesp. Merchant of Venice.*

AROMA'TICAL. *adj.* [from *aromatick.*] Spicy; fragrant; high scented.

All things that are hot and *aromatical* do preserve liquors or powders. *Bacon's Natural Hist.* N° 346.

Volatile oils refresh the animal spirits, but likewise are endued with all the bad qualities of such substances, producing all the effects of an oily and *aromatical* acrimony. *Arbuthnot on Aliment.*

AROMA'TICK. *adj.* [from *aroma*, Lat. spice.]

1. Spicy.

Amidst whole heaps of spices lights a ball,
And now their odours arm'd against them fly:
Some preciously by shatter'd porcelain fall,
And some by *aromatick* splinters die. *Dryden's Ann. Mirab.*

2. Fragrant; strong scented.

Or quick effluvia darting through the brain,
Dye of a rose in *aromatick* pain. *Pope's Essay on Man.*

AROMA'TICKS. *n. s.* Spices.

They were furnished for exchange of their *aromaticks*, and other proper commodities. *Raleigh's Hist. of the World.*

AROMATIZA'TION. *n. s.* [from *aromatize.*] The mingling of a due proportion of aromatick spices or drugs with any medicine.

To ARO'MATIZE. *v. a.* [from *aroma*, Lat. spice.]

1. To scent with spices; to impregnate with spices.

Drink the first cup at supper hot, and half an hour before supper something hot and *aromatized.* *Bacon's Phys. Remains.*

2. To scent; to perfume.

Unto converted Jews no man imputeth this unsavoury odour, as though *aromatized* by their conversion. *Brown's Vulg. Err.*

ARO'SE. The preterite of the verb *arise.* See ARISE.

ARO'UND. *adv.* [from *a* and *round.*]

1. In a circle.

He shall extend his propagated sway,
Where Atlas turns the rowling heav'ns *around*,
And his broad shoulders with their lights are crown'd. *Dryd.*

2. On every side.

AROUND. *prep.* About.

From young Iülus head
A lambent flame arose, which gently spread
Around his brows, and on his temples fed. *Dryden's Æn.*

To ARO'USE. *v. a.* [from *a* and *rouse.*]

1. To wake from sleep.
2. To raise up; to excite.

But absent, what fantastick woes *arous'd*
Rage in each thought, by restless musing fed,
Chill the warm cheek, and blast the bloom of life. *Thomson.*

ARO'W. *adv.* [from *a* and *row.*] In a row; with the breasts all bearing against the same line.

Then some green gowns are by the lasses worn
In chastest plays, till home they walk *arow.* *Sidney.*

But with a pace more sober and more slow,
And twenty, rank in rank, they rode *arow.* *Dryden's Fab.*

ARO'YNT. *adv.* [a word of uncertain etymology, but very ancient use.] Be gone; away: a word of expulsion, or avoiding.

Saint Withold footed thrice the wold,
He met the night-mare, and her name told,
Bid her alight, and her troth plight,
And *aroynt* thee, witch, *aroynt* thee right. *Shak. King Lear.*

A'RQUEBUSE. *n. s.* [Fr. spelt falsely *harquebuss.*] A hand gun. It seems to have anciently meant much the same as our carabine, or fusee.

A *harquebuse*, or ordnance, will be farther heard from the mouth of the piece, than backwards or on the sides. *Bacon's Nat. Hist.* N° 204.

A'RQUEBUSIER. *n. s.* [from *arquebuse*.] A soldier armed with an arquebuse.

He compassed them in with fifteen thousand *arquebusiers*, whom he had brought with him well appointed. *Knolles's History of the Turks.*

ARRA'CK, or ARA'CK. *n. s.* A spirituous liquor imported from the East Indies, used by way of dram and in punch. The word *arack* is an Indian name for strong waters of all kinds; for they call our spirits and brandy English *arack*. But what we understand by the name *arack*, is really no other than a spirit procured by distillation from a vegetable juice called toddy, which flows by incision out of the cocoa-nut tree. There are divers kinds of it; single, double, and treble distilled. The double distilled is commonly sent abroad, and is preferred to all other *aracks* of India. *Chambers.*

I send this to be better known for choice of china, tea, *arrack*, and other Indian goods. *Spectator*, N° 288.

A'RRACH, O'RRACH, or O'RRAGE. *n. s.* One of the quickest plants both in coming up and running to feed. Its leaves are very good in pottage. It should be used as soon as it peeps out, because it decays quickly. It thrives very well in all sorts of ground. See ORRAGE. *Mortimer's Art of Husbandry.*

To ARRA'IGN. *v. a.* [*arranger*, Fr. to set in order.]

1. To set a thing in order, or in its place. One is said to *arraign* a writ in a county, that fits it for trial before the justices of the circuit. A prisoner is said to be *arraigned*, where he is indicted and brought forth to his trial. *Cowel.*

Summon a session, that we may *arraign*
Our most disloyal lady; for as she hath
Been publickly accused, so shall she have
A just and open trial. *Shakesp. Winter's Tale.*

2. To accuse; to charge with faults in general, as in controversy, in a satire.

Reverse of nature! shall such copies then
Arraign th' originals of Maro's pen? *Roscommon.*

He that thinks a man to the ground, will quickly endeavour to lay him there: for while he despises him, he *arraigns* and condemns him in his heart. *South.*

3. It has *for* before the fault.

My own enemies I shall never answer; and if your lordship has any, they will not *arraign* you *for* want of knowledge. *Dryden's Dedication to the Æneid.*

ARRA'IGNMENT. *n. s.* [from *arraign*.] The act of arraigning; an accusation; a charge.

In the sixth satire, which seems only an *arraignment* of the whole sex, there is a latent admonition to avoid ill women. *Dryden's Juv. Dedication.*

To ARRA'NGE. *v. a.* [*arranger*, Fr.] To put in the proper order for any purpose.

I chanc'd this day
To see two knights in travel on my way,
(A sorry sight!) *arrang'd* in battle new. *Fairy Queen, b.* i.

How effectually are its muscular fibres *arranged*, and with what judgment are its columns and furrows disposed! *Cheyne.*

ARRA'NGEMENT. *n. s.* [from *arrange*.] The act of putting in proper order; the state of being put in order.

There is a proper *arrangement* of the parts to be brought about in elastick bodies, which may be facilitated by use. *Cheyne's Philosophical Principles.*

A'RRANT. *adj.* [a word of uncertain etymology, but probably from *errant*, which being at first applied to its proper signification to vagabonds, as an *errant* or *arrant rogue*, that is, a *rambling rogue*, lost, in time, its original signification, and being by its use understood to imply something bad, was applied at large to any thing that was mentioned with hatred or contempt.] Bad in a high degree.

Country folks, who hallooed and hooted after me, as at the *arrantest* coward that ever shewed his shoulders to the enemy. *Sidney, b.* ii.

A vain fool grows forty times an *arranter* sot than before. *L'Estrange's Fables.*

And let him every deity adore,
If his new bride prove not an *arrant* whore. *Dryd. Juven.*

A'RRANTLY. *adv.* [from *arrant*.] Corruptly; shamefully.

Funeral tears are as *arrantly* hired out as mourning clokes. *L'Estrange.*

A'RRAS. *n. s.* [from *Arras*, a town in Artois, where hangings are woven.] Tapestry; hangings woven with images.

Thence to the hall, which was on every side
With rich array and costly *arras* dight. *Fairy Queen, b.* i.

He's going to his mother's closet;
Behind the *arras* I'll convey myself,
To hear the process. *Shakesp. Hamlet.*

As he shall pass the galleries, I'll place
A guard behind the *arras*. *Denham's Sophy.*

ARRA'UGHT. *v. a.* [a word used by *Spenser* in the preter tense, of which I have not found the present, but suppose he derived *arreach* from *arracher*, Fr.] Seized by violence.

His ambitious sons unto them twain
Arraught the rule, and from their father drew. *Fairy Q.*

ARRA'Y. *n. s.* [*arroy*, Fr. *arreo*, Sp. *arredo*, Ital. from *reye*, Teut. order. It was adopted into the middle Latin, *mille hominum arraitorum*, Knighton.]

1. Order, chiefly of war.

The earl espying them scattered near the army, sent one to command them to their *array*. *Sir J. Hayward.*

Wer't thou sought to deeds,
That might require th' *array* of war, thy skill
Of conduct would be such, that all the world
Could not sustain thy prowess. *Milton's Par. Lost, b.* iii.

A gen'ral sets his army in *array*
In vain, unless he fight and win the day. *Sir J. Denham.*

2. Dress.

A rich throne, as bright as sunny day,
On which there sat most brave embellished
With royal robes, and gorgeous *array*,
A maiden queen. *Fairy Queen, b.* i.

In this remembrance, Emily ere day
Arose, and dress'd herself in rich *array*;
Fresh as the month, and as the morning fair. *Dryd. Fables.*

3. In law. *Array*, of the Fr. *array*, i. e. *ordo*, the ranking or setting forth of a jury or inquest of men impannelled upon a cause. Thence is the verb *to array* a pannel, that is, to set forth one by another the men impannelled. *Cowel.*

To ARRA'Y. *v. a.* [*arroyer*, old Fr.]

1. To put in order.

2. To deck; to dress; to adorn the person; with the particle *with*.

Deck thyself now with majesty and excellency, and *array* thyself *with* glory and beauty. *Job*, xl. 10.

Now went forth the morn,
Such as in highest heav'n, *array'd* in gold
Empyreal. *Milton's Paradise Lost, b.* vi.

One vest *array'd* the corps, and one they spread
O'er his clos'd eyes, and wrapp'd around his head. *Dryden.*

3. In law. See ARRAY in law.

ARRA'YERS. *n. s.* [from *array*.] Officers who anciently had the care of seeing the soldiers duly appointed in their armour. *Cowel.*

ARRE'AR. *adv.* [*arriere*, Fr. behind.] Behind. This is the primitive signification of the word, which, though not now in use, seems to be retained by *Spenser*. See REAR.

To leave with speed Atlanta swift *arrear*,
Through forests wild and unfrequented land,
To chase the lion, boar, or rugged bear. *Fairy Queen, b.* ii.

ARRE'AR. *n. s.* That which remains behind unpaid, though due. See ARREARAGE.

His boon is giv'n; his knight has gain'd the day,
But lost the prize; th' *arrears* are yet to pay. *Dryd. Fables.*

If a tenant run away in *arrear* of some rent, the land remains; that cannot be carried away, or lost. *Locke.*

It will comfort our grand-children, when they see a few rags hung up in Westminster-hall, which cost an hundred millions, whereof they are paying the *arrears*, and boasting as beggars do, that their grandfathers were rich. *Swift.*

ARRE'ARAGE. *n. s.* *a word now little used.* [from *arriere*, Fr. behind.]

Arrearage is the remainder of an account, or a sum of money remaining in the hands of an accountant; or, more generally, any money unpaid at the due time, as *arrearage* of rent. *Cowel.*

Paget set forth the king of England's title to his debts and pension from the French king; with all *arrearages*. *Hayward.*

I think,
He'll grant the tribute, send th' *arrearages*,
Ere look upon our Romans. *Shakesp. Cymbeline.*

The old *arrearages* under which that crown had long groaned, being defrayed, he hath brought Lurana to uphold and maintain herself. *Howel's Vocal Forest.*

ARRE'ARANCE. *n. s.* The same with *arrear*. See ARREAR. *D.*

ARRENTA'TION. *n. s.* [from *arrendar*, Span. to farm.] Is, in the forest law, the licensing an owner of lands in the forest, to inclose them with a low hedge and small ditch, in consideration of a yearly rent. *Dict.*

ARREPTI'TIOUS. *adj.* [*arreptus*, Lat.]

1. Snatched away.

2. Crept in privily. *Dict.*

ARRE'ST. *n. s.* [from *arrester*, Fr. to stop.]

1. In law.

A stop or stay; as, a man apprehended for debt, is said to be arrested. To plead in *arrest* of judgment, is to shew cause why judgment should be stayed, though the verdict of the twelve be passed. To plead in *arrest* of taking the inquest upon the former issue, is to shew cause why an inquest should not be taken. An *arrest* is a certain restraint of a man's person, depriving him of his own will, and binding it to become obedient to the will of the law, and may be called the beginning of imprisonment. *Cowel.*

If I could speak so wisely under an *arrest*, I would send for my creditors; yet I had as lief have the foppery of freedom, as the morality of imprisonment. *Shakesp. Measure for Measure.*

2. Any caption.

To the rich man, who had promised himself ease for many years, it was a sad *arrest*, that his soul was surprised the first night. *Taylor's Holy Living.*

3. A stop.

The stop and *arrest* of the air sheweth, that the air hath little appetite of ascending. *Bacon's Nat. History*, N° 24.

To ARREST. *v. a.* [*arrester*, Fr. to stop.]

1. To seize by a mandate from a court or officer of justice. See ARREST.

Good tidings, my lord Hastings, for the which
I do *arrest* thee, traitor, of high treason. *Shak. Hen.* IV.

Well, well; there's one yonder *arrested*, and carried to prison, was worth five thousand of you all. *Shakes. Meas for M.*

2. To seize any thing by law.

He h th enjoyed nothing of Ford's but twenty pounds of money, which must be paid to master Brook; his horses are *arrested* for it. *Shakesp. Merry Wives of Windsor.*

3. To seize; to lay hands on.

But when as Morpheus had with leaden maze
Arrested all that goodly company. *Fairy Queen, b.* i.

Age itself, which, of all things in the world, will not be baffled or defied, shall begin to *arrest*, seize, and remind us of our mortality. *South.*

4. To with-hold; to hinder.

This defect of the English justice was the main impediment that did *arrest* and stop the course of the conquest. *Sir John Davies.*

As often as my dogs with better speed
Arrest her flight, is she to death decreed. *Dryd. Fables.*

Nor could her virtues, nor repeated vows
Of thousand lovers, the relentless hand
Of death *arrest*. *Philips.*

5. To stop motion.

To manifest the coagulative power, we have *arrested* the fluidity of new milk, and turned it into a curdled substance. *Boyle.*

ARRE'ST. *n. s.* [In horsemanship.] A mangey humour between the ham and pastern of the hinder legs of a horse. *Dict.*

A'RRETED. *adj.* [*arrectatus*, low Lat.] He that is convened before a judge, and charged with a crime. It is used sometimes for *imputed* or *laid unto*; as, no folly may be *arreted* to one under age. *Cowel.*

To ARRI'DE. *v. a.* [*arrideo*, Lat.]

1. To laugh at.

2. To smile; to look pleasantly upon one.

ARRI'ERE. *n. s.* [French.] The last body of an army, for which we now use *rear*.

The horsemen might issue forth without disturbance of the foot, and the avant-guard without shuffling with the battail or *arriere*. *Sir J. Hayward.*

ARRI'ERE BAN. *n. s.* [*Casseneuve* derives this word from *arriere* and *ban*; *ban* denotes the convening of the noblesse or vassals, who hold fees immediately of the crown; and *arriere*, those who only hold of the king mediately.] A general proclamation, by which the king of France summons to the war all that hold of him, both his own vassals or the noblesse, and the vassals of his vassals.

ARRI'ERE FEE, or FIEF. Is a fee dependant on a superior one. These fees commenced, when the dukes and counts, rendering their governments hereditary in their families, distributed to their officers parts of the royal domains, which they found in their respective provinces; and even permitted those officers to gratify the soldiers under them, in the same manner.

ARRI'ERE VASSAL. The vassal of a vassal. *Trevoux.*

ARRI'SION. *n. s.* [*arrisio*, Lat.] A smiling upon. *Dict.*

ARRI'VAL. *n. s.* [from *arrive.*]

The act of coming to any place; and, figuratively, the attainment of any purpose.

How are we changed, since we first saw the queen?
She, like the sun, does still the same appear,
Bright as she was at her *arrival* here. *Waller.*

The unravelling is the *arrival* of Ulysses upon his own island. *Broom's View of Epick Poetry.*

ARRI'VANCE. *n. s.* [from *arrive.*] Company coming.

Every minute is expectancy
Of more *arrivance*. *Shakesp. Othello.*

To ARRI'VE. *v. n.* [*arriver*, Fr. to come on shore.]

1. To come to any place by water.

At length *arriving* on the banks of Nile,
Wearied with length of ways, and worn with toil,
She laid her down. *Dryden.*

2. To reach any place by travelling.

When we were *arrived* upon the verge of his estate, we stopped at a little inn, to rest ourselves and our horses.

3. To reach any point.

The bounds of all body we have no difficulty to *arrive* at; but when the mind is there, it finds nothing to hinder its progress. *Locke.*

4. To gain any thing.

It is the highest wisdom by despising the world to *arrive* at heaven; they are blessed who converse with God. *Taylor.*

The virtuous may know in speculation, what they could never *arrive* at by practice, and avoid the snares of the crafty. *Addison. Spectator*, N° 245.

5. The thing at which we *arrive* is always supposed to be good.

6. To happen; with *to* before the person. This sense seems not proper.

Happy! *to* whom this glorious death *arrives*,
More to be valued than a thousand lives. *Waller.*

To ARRO'DE. *v. a.* [*arrodo*, Lat.] To gnaw or nibble. *Dict.*

A'RROGANCE. } *n. s.* [*arrogantia*, Lat.] The act or quality of
A'RROGANCY. } taking much upon one's self; that species of pride which consists in exorbitant claims.

Stanley, notwithstanding she's your wife,
And loves not me; be you, good lord, assur'd,
I hate not you for her proud *arrogance*. *Shakesp. Rich.* III.

Pride hath no other glass
To shew itself but pride; for supple knees
Feed *arrogance*, and are the proud man's fees. *Sh. Tr. and Cr.*

Pride and *arrogance*, and the evil way, and the froward mouth do I hate. *Prov* viii. 13.

Discoursing of matters dubious, and on any controvertible truths, we cannot, without *arrogancy*, entreat a credulity. *Brown's Vulgar Errours, b.* i.

Humility it expresses by the stooping and bending of the head; *arrogance*, when it is lifted, or, as we say, tossed up. *Dryd. Dufresn.*

A'RROGANT. *adj.* [*arrogans*, Lat.] Given to make exorbitant claims; haughty; proud.

Feagh's right unto that country which he claims, or the signiory therein, must be vain and *arrogant*. *Spenser on Ireland.*

An *arrogant* way of treating with other princes and states, is natural to popular governments. *Temple.*

A'RROGANTLY. *adv.* [from *arrogant.*] In an arrogant manner.

Our poet may
Himself admire the fortune of his play;
And *arrogantly*, as his fellows do,
Think he writes well, because he pleases you. *Dryden's Prol. to Indian Emperour.*

Another, warm'd
With high ambition, and conceit of prowess
Inherent, *arrogantly* thus presum'd;
What if this sword, full often drench'd in blood,
Should now cleave sheer the execrable head
Of Churchill. *Philips.*

A'RROGANTNESS. *n. s.* [from *arrogant.*] The same with *arrogance*; which see. *Dict.*

To A'RROGATE. *v. a* [*arrogo*, Lat.] To claim vainly; to exhibit unjust claims only prompted by pride.

I intend to describe this battle fully, not to derogate any thing from one nation, or to *arrogate* to the other. *Sir J. Hayw.*

The popes *arrogated* unto themselves, that the empire was held of them in homage. *Sir Walter Raleigh's Essays.*

Who, not content
With fair equality, fraternal state,
Will *arrogate* dominion undeserv'd,
Over his brethren. *Milton's Paradise Lost, b.* xii.

Rome never *arrogated* to herself any infallibility, but what she pretended to be founded upon Christ's promise. *Tillot. Pr.*

ARROGA'TION. *n. s.* [from *arrogate.*] A claiming in a proud unjust manner. *Dict.*

ARRO'SION. *n. s.* [from *arrosus*, Lat.] A gnawing. *Dict.*

A'RROW. *n. s.* [arepe, Sax.] The pointed weapon which is shot from a bow. Darts are thrown by the hand, but in poetry they are confounded.

I swear to thee by Cupid's strongest bow,
By his best *arrow* with the golden head. *Shakesp. Midsummer Night's Dream.*

Here were boys so desperately resolved, as to pull *arrows* out of their flesh, and deliver them to be shot again by the archers on their side. *Sir J. Hayward.*

A'RROWHEAD. *n. s.* [from *arrow* and *head.*] A water plant, so called from the resemblance of its leaves to the head of an arrow. *Dict.*

A'RROWY. *adj.* [from *arrow.*] Consisting of arrows.

He saw them in their forms of battle rang'd,
How quick they wheel'd, and flying, behind them shot
Sharp sleet of *arrowy* show'r against the face
Of their pursuers, and o'ercame by flight. *Par. Lost, b.* iii.

ARSE. *n. s.* [eappe, Sax.] The buttocks, or hind part of an animal.

To hang an ARSE. A vulgar phrase, signifying to be tardy, sluggish, or dilatory.

For Hudibras wore but one spur,
As wisely knowing, could he stir
To active trot one side of 's horse,
The other would not *hang an arse*. *Hudibras, cant.* i.

ARSE FOOT. *n. s.* A kind of water fowl, called also a *didapper*. *D.*

ARSE-SMART. [*Persicaria*, Lat.]

It is a plant with an apetalous flower, having several chives from the multifid calyx: the pointal becomes an oval pointed smooth seed, inclosed in the capsule, which was before the flower-cup; it hath jointed stalks, and the flowers are produced in spikes. Several species of this plant grow wild upon moist soils and dunghills. *Millar.*

A'RSENAL. *n. s.* [*arsenale*, Ital.] A repository of things requisite to war; a magazine.

I would have a room for the old Roman inſtruments of war, where you might ſee all the ancient military furniture, as it might have been in an *arſenal* of old Rome. *Add. on An. Med.*

ARSE'NICAL. *adj.* [from *arſenick.*] Containing arſenick; conſiſting of arſenick.

An hereditary conſumption, or one engendered by *arſenical* fumes under ground, is incapable of cure. *Harvey on Conſump.*

There are *arſenical*, or other like noxious minerals lodged underneath. *Woodward's Natural Hiſtory.*

A'RSENICK. *n. ſ.* [ἀρσενικὸν.] A ponderous mineral ſubſtance, volatile and uninflammable, which gives a whiteneſs to metals in fuſion, and proves a violent corroſive poiſon; of which there are three ſorts. *Native* or *yellow arſenick*, called alſo auripigmentum or orpiment, is chiefly found in copper mines, in a ſort of glebes or ſtones of different figures and ſizes. Its colour, though always yellow, yet admits of different ſhades and mixtures, as a golden yellow, a reddiſh yellow, or a green yellow. It contains a ſmall portion of gold, but not worth the expence of ſeparating it. *White* or *cryſtalline arſenick* is extracted from the native kind, by ſubliming it with a proportion of ſea ſalt, and is chiefly uſed among us. It is ſaid to be found native in ſome German mines. The ſmalleſt quantity of cryſtalline *arſenick*, being mixed with any metal, abſolutely deſtroys its malleability; and a ſingle grain will turn a pound of copper into a beautiful ſeeming ſilver, but without ductility. There is a method practiſed in Hungary, of procuring yellow and white *arſenick* from cobalt. *Red arſenick* is a preparation of the white, made by adding to it a mineral ſulphur. There are ſeveral chymical preparations of *arſenick*, intended to blunt its corroſive ſalts, and render it a ſafe medicine; but experience proves that it ſhould never be uſed inwardly, in any form. *Chambers.*

Arſenick is a very deadly poiſon; held to the fire, it emits fumes, but liquates very little. *Woodw. on Foſſ.*

ART. *n. ſ.* [*arte*, Fr. *ars*, Lat.]

1. The power of doing ſomething not taught by nature and inſtinct; as, to *walk* is natural, to *dance* is an *art*.

Art is properly an habitual knowledge of certain rules and maxims, by which a man is governed and directed in his actions. *South.*

Bleſt with each grace of nature and of *art*. *Pope.*

Ev'n copious Dryden wanted, or forgot,
The laſt and greateſt *art*, the *art* to blot. *Pope.*

2. A ſcience; as, the liberal *arts*.

Arts that reſpect the mind were ever reputed nobler than thoſe that ſerve the body. *Ben. Johnſon's Diſcovery.*

3. A trade.

This obſervation is afforded us by the *art* of making ſugar. *Boyle.*

4. Artfulneſs; ſkill; dexterity.

The *art* of our neceſſities is ſtrange,
That can make vile things precious. *Shak. King Lear.*

5. Cunning.

6. Speculation.

I have as much of this in *art* as you;
But yet my nature could not bear it ſo. *Shakeſp. J. Cæſar.*

ARTE'RIAL. *adj.* [from *artery.*] That which relates to the artery; that which is contained in the artery.

Had not the Maker wrought the ſpringy frame,
The blood, defrauded of its nitrous food,
Had cool'd and languiſh'd in th' *arterial* road. *Blackmore.*

As this mixture of blood and chyle paſſeth through the *arterial* tube, it is preſſed by two contrary forces; that of the heart driving it forward againſt the ſides of the tube, and the elaſtick force of the air, preſſing it on the oppoſite ſides of thoſe air-bladders; along the ſurface of which this *arterial* tube creeps. *Arbuthnot on Aliments.*

ARTERIO'TOMY. *n. ſ.* [from ἀρτηρία, and τέμνω, to cut.] The operation of letting blood from the artery: a practice much in uſe among the French.

A'RTERY. *n. ſ.* [*arteria*, Lat.] An *artery* is a conical canal, conveying the blood from the heart to all parts of the body. Each *artery* is compoſed of three coats; of which the firſt ſeems to be a thread of fine blood veſſels and nerves, for nouriſhing the coats of the *artery*; the ſecond is made up of circular, or rather ſpiral fibres, of which there are more or fewer ſtrata, according to the bigneſs of the *artery*. Theſe fibres have a ſtrong elaſticity, by which they contract themſelves with ſome force, when the power by which they have been ſtretched out ceaſes. The third and inmoſt coat is a fine tranſparent membrane, which keeps the blood within its canal, that otherwiſe, upon the dilatation of an *artery*, would eaſily ſeparate the ſpiral fibres from one another. As the *arteries* grow ſmaller, theſe coats grow thinner, and the coats of the veins ſeem only to be continuations of the capillary *arteries*. *Quincy.*

The *arteries* are elaſtick tubes, endued with a contractile force, by which they drive the blood ſtill forward; it being hindered from going backward by the valves of the heart. *Arb.*

A'RTFUL. *adj.* [from *art* and *full.*]

1. Performed with art.

The laſt of theſe was certainly the moſt eaſy, but, for the ſame reaſon, the leaſt *artful*. *Dryden's Don Sebaſtian.*

2. Artificial; not natural.

3. Cunning; ſkilful; dexterous.

O ſtill the ſame, Ulyſſes, ſhe rejoin'd,
In uſeful craft ſucceſsfully refin'd,
Artful in ſpeech, in action, and in mind. *Pope's Od.*

A'RTFULLY. *adv.* [from *artful.*] With art; ſkilfully; dexterouſly.

The reſt in rank: Honoria chief in place,
Was *artfully* contriv'd to ſet her face,
To front the thicket, and behold the chace. *Dryd. Fab.*

Vice is the natural growth of our corruption. How irreſiſtibly muſt it prevail, when the ſeeds of it are *artfully* ſown, and induſtriouſly cultivated? *Rogers's Sermons.*

A'RTFULNESS. *n. ſ.* [from *artful.*]

1. Skill.

Conſider with how much *artfulneſs* his bulk and ſituation is contrived, to have juſt matter to draw round him theſe maſſy bodies. *Cheyne's Philoſophical Principles.*

2. Cunning.

ARTHRI'TICK. }
ARTHRI'TICAL. } *adj.* [from *arthritis.*]

1. Gouty; relating to the gout.

Frequent changes produce all the *arthritick* diſeaſes. *Arbuth.*

2. Relating to joints.

Serpents, worms, and leaches, though ſome want bones, and all extended articulations, yet have they *arthritical* analogies; and, by the motion of fibrous and muſculous parts, are able to make progreſſion. *Brown's Vulgar Errours, b.* iii. *c.* i.

ARTHRI'TIS. n. ſ. [ἀρθρῖτις, from ἄρθρον, a joint.] Any diſtemper that affects the joints, but the gout moſt particularly. *Quin.*

A'RTICHOKE. *n. ſ.* [*artichault*, Fr.]

This plant is very like the thiſtle, but hath large ſcaly heads ſhaped like the cone of the pine tree; the bottom of each ſcale, as alſo at the bottom of the florets, is a thick fleſhy eatable ſubſtance. The ſpecies are, 1. The garden *artichoke*, with prickly and ſmooth leaves. 2. Garden *artichoke*, without prickles, and reddiſh heads. 3. The wild *artichoke* of Bœotia. There is at preſent but one ſort of *artichoke* cultivated in the gardens near London, which is commonly known by the name of the red *artichoke*. It is propagated from ſlips or ſuckers taken from the old roots in February or March. *Millar.*

No herbs have curled leaves, but cabbage and cabbage lettuce; none have double leaves, one belonging to the ſtalk, another to the fruit or ſeed, but the *artichoke*. *Bacon's Nat. Hiſt.*

Artichokes contain a rich, nutritious, ſtimulating juice. *Arbuthnot on Aliments.*

A'RTICHOKE *of Jeruſalem.* See SUN-FLOWER, of which it is a ſpecies.

A'RTICK. *adj.* [It ſhould be written *arctick*, from ἄρκτος.] Northern; under the Bear. See ARCTICK.

But they would have winters like thoſe beyond the *artick* circle; for the ſun would be 80 degrees from them. *Brown's Vulgar Errours, b.* i. *c.* 5.

In the following example it is, contrary to cuſtom, ſpelt after the French manner, and accented on the laſt ſyllable.

To you, who live in chill degree,
As map informs, of fifty three,
And do not much for cold atone,
By bringing thither fifty one,
Methinks all climes ſhould be alike,
From tropick e'en to pole *artique*. *Dryden.*

A'RTICLE. *n. ſ.* [*articulus*, Lat.]

1. A part of ſpeech, as *the*, *an*; *the* man, *an* ox.

2. A ſingle clauſe of an account; a particular part of any complex thing.

Laws touching matters of order are changeable by the power of the church; *articles* concerning doctrine not ſo. *Hooker.*

Have the ſummary of all our griefs,
When time ſhall ſerve to ſhew in *articles*. *Shak. Henry* IV.

Many believe the *article* of remiſſion of ſins, but believe it without the condition of repentance. We believe the *article* otherwiſe than God intended it. *Taylor's Holy Living.*

All the precepts, promiſes, and threatenings of the goſpel will riſe up in judgment againſt us; and the *articles* of our faith will be ſo many *articles* of accuſation; and the great weight of our charge will be this, that we did not obey the goſpel which we profeſſed to believe; that we made confeſſion of the chriſtian faith, but lived like heathens. *Tillotſon.*

You have ſmall reaſon to repine upon that *article* of life. *Swift.*

3. Terms; ſtipulations.

I embrace theſe conditions; let us have *articles* between us. *Shakeſpeare's Cymbeline.*

It would have gall'd his ſurly nature,
Which eaſily endures not *article*,
Tying him to aught. *Shakeſpeare's Coriolanus.*

4. Point of time; exact time.

If Cansfield had not, in that *article* of time, given them that briſk charge, by which other troops were ready, the king himſelf had been in danger. *Clarendon, b.* viii.

To A'RTICLE. *v. n.* [from the noun *article.*] To ſtipulate; to make terms.

Such in love's warfare is my caſe,
I may not *article* for grace,
Having put love at laſt to ſhow this face. *Donne.*

He had not infringed the leaſt tittle of what was *articled*, that they aimed at one mark, and their ends were concentrick. *Howel's Vocal Foreſt.*

If it be ſaid, God choſe the ſucceſſor, that is manifeſtly not ſo in the ſtory of Jephtha, where he *articled* with the people, and they made him judge over them. *Locke.*

To Article. *v. a.* To draw up in particular articles.

He, whoſe life ſeems fair, yet if all his errours and follies were *articled* againſt him, the man would ſeem vicious and miſerable. *Taylor's Rule of living holy.*

Arti'cular. *adj.* [*articularis*, Lat. belonging to the joints.] Is, in medicine, an epithet applied to a diſeaſe, which more immediately infeſts the joints. Thus the gout is called *morbus articularis.*

Arti'culate. *adj.* [from *articulus*, Lat.]

1. Diſtinct, as the parts of a limb by joints; not continued in one tone, as *articulate* ſounds; that is, ſounds varied and changed at proper pauſes, in oppoſition to the voice of animals, which admit no ſuch variety. An *articulate* pronunciation, a manner of ſpeaking clear and diſtinct, in which one ſound is not confounded with another.

In ſpeaking under water, when the voice is reduced to an extreme exility, yet the *articulate* ſounds, the words, are not confounded. *Bacon's Nat. Hiſt.* N° 195.

The firſt, at leaſt, of theſe I thought deny'd
To beaſts; whom God, on their creation-day,
Created mute to all *articulate* ſound. *Milton's Parad. Loſt.*

2. Branched out into articles. This is a meaning little in uſe.

His inſtructions were extreme curious and *articulate*; and, in them, more articles touching inquiſition, than negotiation: requiring from his ambaſſadors an anſwer in diſtinct articles to his queſtions. *Bacon's Henry* VII.

To Arti'culate. *v. a.* [from *article*]

1. To form words; to ſpeak as a man.

The dogmatiſt knows not by what art he directs his tongue, in *articulating* ſounds into voices. *Glanvile's Scepſis Scientifica.*

Pariſian academiſts, in their anatomy of apes, tell us, that the muſcles of the tongue, which do moſt ſerve to *articulate* a word, were wholly like to thoſe of man. *Ray on Creation.*

They would advance in knowledge, and not deceive themſelves with a little *articulated* air. *Locke.*

2. To draw up in articles.

Theſe things, indeed, you have *articulated*,
Proclaim'd at market-croſſes, read in churches,
To face the garment of rebellion
With ſome fine colour. *Shakeſp. Henry* IV.

3. To make terms. Theſe two latter ſignifications are unuſual.

Send us to Rome
The beſt, with whom we may *articulate*
For their own good and ours. *Shakeſp. Coriolanus.*

Arti'culately. *adv.* [from *articulate.*] In an articulate voice.

The ſecret purpoſe of our heart, no leſs *articulately* ſpoken to God, who needs not our words to diſcern our meaning. *Decay of Piety.*

Arti'culateness. *n. ſ.* [from *articulate.*] The quality of being articulate.

Articula'tion. *n. ſ.* [from *articulate.*]

1. The juncture, or joint of bones.

With relation to the motion of the bones in their *articulations*, there is a twofold liquor prepared for the inunction and lubrification of their heads, an oily one, and a mucilaginous, ſupplied by certain glandules ſeated in the *articulations.* *Ray.*

2. The act of forming words.

I conceive that an extreme ſmall, or an extreme great ſound, cannot be articulate, but that the *articulation* requireth a mediocrity of ſound. *Bacon's Nat. Hiſt.* N° 196.

By *articulation* I mean a peculiar motion and figure of ſome parts belonging to the mouth, between the throat and lips. *Holder's Elements of Speech.*

3. [In botany.] The joints or knots in ſome plants, as the cane.

A'rtifice. *n. ſ.* [*artificium*, Lat.]

1. Trick; fraud; ſtratagem.

It needs no legends, no ſervice in an unknown tongue; none of all theſe laborious *artifices* of ignorance; none of all theſe cloaks and coverings. *South.*

2. Art; trade.

Arti'ficer. *n. ſ.* [*artifex*, Lat.]

1. An artiſt; a manufacturer; one by whom any thing is made.

The lights, doors, and ſtairs, rather directed to the uſe of the gueſt, than to the eye of the *artificer.* *Sidney.*

The great *artificer* would be more than ordinarily exact in drawing his own picture. *South.*

So in the practices of *artificers*, and the manufactures of ſeveral kinds, the end being propoſed, we find out ways. *Locke.*

2. A forger; a contriver.

He ſoon aware,
Each perturbation ſmooth'd with outward calm,
Artificer of fraud! and was the firſt
That practis'd falſehood under ſaintly ſhew. *Paradiſe Loſt.*

Th' *artificer* of lies
Renews th' aſſault, and his laſt batt'ry tries. *Dryden's Fab.*

3. A dexterous or artful fellow.

Let you alone, cunning *artificer.* *Ben. Johnſon.*

Artificial. *adj.* [*artificiel*, Fr.]

1. Made by art; not natural.

Baſilius uſed the *artificial* day of torches to lighten the ſports their inventions could contrive. *Sidney, b.* i.

The curtains cloſely drawn the light to ſkreen,
As if he had contriv'd to lie unſeen:
Thus cover'd with an *artificial* night,
Sleep did his office. *Dryden's Fables.*

There is no natural motion perpetual; yet it doth not hinder but that it is poſſible to contrive ſuch an *artificial* revolution. *Wilkins's Dædalus.*

2. Fictitious; not genuine.

Why, I can ſmile, and murder while I ſmile,
And cry, content, to that which grieves my heart,
And wet my cheeks with *artificial* tears. *Shakeſp. Hen.* VI.

3. Artful; contrived with ſkill.

Theſe ſeem to be the more *artificial*, as thoſe of a ſingle perſon the more natural governments, orders, and inſtitutions. *Temple.*

Artificial *Arguments.* [in rhetorick.] Are proofs on conſiderations which ariſe from the genius, induſtry, or invention of the orator; ſuch are definitions, cauſes, effects, &c. which are thus called, to diſtinguiſh them from laws, authorities, citations, and the like, which are ſaid to be *inartificial* arguments.

Artificial *Lines*, on a ſector or ſcale, are lines ſo contrived as to repreſent the logarithmick ſines and tangents; which, by the help of the line of numbers, ſolve, with tolerable exactneſs, queſtions in trigonometry, navigation, &c. *Chambers.*

Artificial *Numbers*, are the ſame with logarithms.

Artifi'cially. *adv.* [from *artificial.*]

1. Artfully; with ſkill; with good contrivance.

How cunningly he made his faultineſs leſs, how *artificially* he ſet out the torments of his own conſcience. *Sidney.*

Should any one be caſt upon a deſolate iſland, and find there a palace *artificially* contrived, and curiouſly adorned. *Ray.*

2. By art; not naturally.

It is covered on all ſides with earth, crumbled into powder, as if it had been *artificially* ſifted. *Addiſon's Remarks on Italy.*

Artifi'cialness. *n. ſ.* [from *artificial.*] Artfulneſs. *Dict.*

Artifi'cious. *adj.* [from *artifice.*] The ſame with *artificial.*

Arti'llery. *n. ſ. It has no plural.* [*artillerie*, Fr.]

1. Weapons of war.

And Jonathan gave his *artillery* unto his lad, and ſaid unto him, Go, carry them unto the city.

2. Cannon; great ordnance.

Have I not heard great ordnance in the field?
And heav'n's *artillery* thunder in the ſkies? *Shak. T. Shrew.*

I'll to the Tower with all the haſte I can,
To view th' *artillery* and ammunition. *Shak. Henry* VI.

Upon one wing the *artillery* was drawn, being ſixteen pieces, every piece having pioneers to plain the ways. *Hayward.*

He that views a fort to take it,
Plants his *artillery* 'gainſt the weakeſt place. *Denh. Sophy.*

Artisa'n. *n. ſ.* [French.]

1. Artiſt; profeſſor of an art.

What are the moſt judicious *artiſans*, but the mimicks of nature? *Wotton's Architecture.*

Beſt and happieſt *artiſan*,
Beſt of painters, if you can,
With your many-colour'd art,
Draw the miſtreſs of my heart. *Guardian.*

2. Manufacturer; low tradeſman.

I who had none but generals to oppoſe me, muſt have an *artiſan* for my antagoniſt. *Addiſon. Whig Examiner.*

A'rtist. *n. ſ.* [*artiſte*, Fr.]

1. The profeſſor of an art, generally of an art manual.

How to build ſhips, and dreadful ordnance caſt,
Inſtruct the *artiſts*, and reward their haſte. *Waller.*

Rich with the ſpoils of many a conquer'd land,
All arts and *artiſts* Theſeus could command,
Who ſold for hire, or wrought for better fame:
The maſter painters and the carvers came. *Dryden's Fables.*

When I made this, an *artiſt* undertook to imitate it; but uſing another way, fell much ſhort. *Newton's Opticks.*

2. A ſkilful man; not a novice.

If any one thinks himſelf an *artiſt* at this, let him number up the parts of his child's body. *Locke.*

A'rtlesly. *adv.* [from *artleſs.*] In an artleſs manner; naturally; ſincerely.

Nature and truth, though never ſo low or vulgar, are yet pleaſing when openly and *artleſly* repreſented. *Pope's Letters.*

A'rtless. *adj.* [from *art* and *leſs.*]

1. Unſkilful; ſometimes with the particle *of.*

The high-ſhoo'd plowman, ſhould he quit the land,
Artleſs of ſtars, and of the moving ſand. *Dryden's Perſ.*

2. Without fraud; as, an *artleſs* maid.

3. Contrived without ſkill; as, an *artleſs* tale.

To A'rtuate. *v. a.* [*artuatus*, Lat.] To tear limb from limb. *D.*

ARUNDINA'CEOUS. *adj.* [*arundinaceus*, Lat.] Of or like reeds. *Dict.*

ARUNDI'NEOUS. *adj.* [*arundineus*, Lat.] Abounding with reeds.

As. *conjunct.* [*als*, Teut.]

1. In the same manner with something else.

When thou dost hear I am *as* I have been,
Approach me, and thou shalt be *as* thou wast.
Shakespeare' Henry IV.

In singing, *as* in piping, you excel;
And scarce your master could perform so well. *Dryden.*

I live *as* I did, I think *as* I did, I love you *as* I did; but all these are to no purpose: the world will not live, think, or love *as* I do. *Swift's Letters.*

2. In the manner that.

Mad *as* I was, I could not bear his fate
With silent grief, but loudly blam'd the state. *Dryden's Æn.*

The landlord, in his shirt *as* he was, taking a candle in one hand, and a drawn sword in the other, ventured out of the room. *Arbuthnot and Pope's Mart. Scriblerus.*

3. That; in a consequential sense.

The cunningest mariners were so conquered by the storm, *as* they thought it best with stricken sails to yield to be governed by it. *Sidney, b.* ii.

He had such a dexterous proclivity, *as* his teachers were fain to restrain his forwardness. *Wotton.*

The relations are so uncertain, *as* they require a great deal of examination. *Bacon's Nat. Hist.* N° 986.

God shall by grace prevent sin so soon, *as* to keep the soul in the virginity of its first innocence. *South.*

4. In the state of another.

Madam, were I *as* you, I'd take her counsel;
I'd speak my own distress. *A. Philips, Distrest Mother.*

5. Under a particular consideration; with a particular respect.

Besides that law which concerneth men *as* men, and that which belongs unto men *as* they are men, linked with others in some society; there is a third which touches all several bodies politick, so far forth as one of them hath publick concerns with another. *Hooker's Ecclesiastical Polity, b.* i.

I say 'tis copper. Dar'st thou be as good as thy word now?—
—— Why, Hal, thou knowest, *as* thou art but a man, I dare; but *as* thou art a prince, I fear thee, as I fear the roaring of the lion's whelp. *Shakesp. Henry IV.*

The objections that are raised against it *as* a tragedy, are as follow. *Gay's Pref. to What d'ye call it.*

6. Like; of the same kind with.

A simple idea is one uniform idea, *as* sweet, bitter. *Watts.*

7. In the same degree with.

Where you, unless you are *as* matter blind,
Conduct and beauteous disposition find. *Blackmore.*

Well hast thou spoke, the blue-eyed maid replies,
Thou good old man, benevolent *as* wise. *Pope's Odyssey.*

8. As if; in the same manner.

The squire began nigher to approach,
And wind his horn under the castle-wall,
That with the noise it shook *as* it would fall. *Fairy Queen.*

They all contended to creep into his humour, and to do that, *as* of themselves, which they conceived he desired they should do. *Sir J. Hayward.*

Contented in a nest of snow
He lies, *as* he his bliss did know,
And to the wood no more would go. } *Waller.*

So hot th' assault, so high the tumult rose,
As all the Dardan and Argolick race
Had been contracted in that narrow space. *Dryden's Æn.*

Can misery no place of safety know,
The noise pursues me wheresoe'er I go,
As fate sought only me. *Dryden's Aurengz.*

According to what.

Who then is Paul, and who is Apollos, but ministers by whom ye believed, even *as* the Lord gave to every man.
1 Cor. iii. 5.

Their figure being printed,
As just before, I think, I hinted,
Alma inform'd can try the case,
As she had been upon the place. *Prior.*

The republick is shut up in the great duke's dominions, who at present is very much incensed against it. The occasion is *as* follows. *Addison on Italy.*

). As it were; in some sort.

As for the daughters of king Edward IV. they thought king Richard had said enough for them; and took them to be but *as* of the king's party, because they were in his power, and at his disposal. *Bacon's Henry VII.*

. While; at the same time that.

At either end, it whistled *as* it flew,
And as the brands were green, so dropp'd the dew;
Infected *as* it fell with sweat of sanguine hue. *Dryd. Fab.*

These haughty words Alecto's rage provoke,
And frighted Turnus trembled *as* she spoke. *Dryden's Æn.*

So the pure limpid stream, when foul with stains
Of rushing torrents, and descending rains,
Works itself clear, and *as* it runs refines. *Addison's Cato.*

12. Because.

He that commanded the injury to be done, is first bound; then he that did it; and they also are obliged who did so assist, *as* without them the thing could not have been done. *Taylor.*

13. As being.

The kernels draw out of the earth juice fit to nourish the tree, *as* those that would be trees themselves. *Bacon's Nat Hist.*

14. Equally.

Before the place
A hundred doors a hundred entries grace;
As many voices issue, and the sound
Of Sibyl's word *as* many times rebound. *Dryden's Æn.*

15. How; in what manner.

Men are generally permitted to publish books, and contradict others, and even themselves, *as* they please, with as little danger of being confuted, as of being understood. *Boyle.*

16. With; answering to *like* or *same*.

Sister, well met; whither away so fast?—
—No further than the Tower; and, as I guess,
Upon the like devotion *as* yourselves,
To gratulate the gentle princes there. *Shakesp. Richard III.*

17. In a reciprocal sense, answering to *as*.

Every offence committed in the state of nature, may, in the state of nature, be also punished, and *as* far forth *as* it may in a commonwealth. *Locke.*

As sure *as* it is good, that human nature should exist; so certain it is, that the circular revolutions of the earth and planets, rather than other motions which might as possibly have been, do declare God. *Bentley's Sermons.*

18. Going before *as*, in a comparative sense; the first *as* being sometimes understood.

Sempronius is *as* brave a man *as* Cato. *Addison's Cato.*
Bright *as* the sun, and like the morning fair. *Granville.*

19. Answering to *such*.

Is it not every man's interest, that there should be *such* a governour of the world *as* designs our happiness, *as* would govern us for our advantage. *Tillotson.*

20. Having *so* to answer it; in a conditional sense.

As far *as* they carry light and conviction to any other man's understanding, *so* far, I hope, my labour may be of use to him. *Locke.*

21. *So* is sometimes understood.

As in my speculations I have endeavoured to extinguish passion and prejudice, I am still desirous of doing some good in this particular. *Spectator,* N° 126.

22. Answering to *so* conditionally.

So may th' auspicious queen of love,
To thee, O sacred ship, be kind;
As thou to whom the muse commends,
The best of poets and of friends,
Dost thy committed pledge restore. *Dryden.*

23. Before *how* it is sometimes redundant; but this is in low language.

As how, dear Syphax? *Addison's Cato.*

24. It seems to be redundant before *yet*; to this time.

Though that war continued nine years, and this hath *as* yet lasted but six, yet there hath been much more action in the present war. *Addison.*

25. In a sense of comparison, followed by *so*.

As when a dab-chick waddles through the copse
On feet and wings, and flies, and wades, and hops;
So lab'ring on, with shoulders, hands, and head,
Wide as a windmill all his figure spread. *Pope's Dunciad.*

26. As FOR; with respect to.

As for the rest of those who have written against me, they deserve not the least notice. *Dryden's Fables, Preface.*

27. As IF; in the same manner that it would be, if.

Answering their questions, *as if* it were a matter that needed it. *Locke.*

28. As TO; with respect to.

I pray thee, speak to me *as to* thy thinkings,
As thou dost ruminate; and give thy worst of thoughts
The worst of words. *Shakesp. Othello.*

They pretend, in general, to great refinements, *as to* what regards christianity. *Addison on Italy.*

I was mistaken *as to* the day, placing that accident about thirty-six hours sooner than it happened. *Swift.*

29. As WELL AS; equally with.

Each man's mind has some peculiarity, *as well as* his face, that distinguishes him from all others. *Locke.*

It is adorned with admirable pieces of sculpture, *as well* modern *as* ancient. *Addison on Italy.*

30. As THOUGH; as if.

These should be at first gently treated, *as though* we expected an imposthumation. *Sharp's Surgery.*

A'SA DULCIS. See BENZOIN.

A'SA FOETIDA. } *n. s.* A gum or resin brought from the East
A'SSA FOETIDA. } Indies, of a sharp taste, and a strong offensive smell; which is said to distil, during the heat of summer, from a little shrub, frequent in Media, Persia, Assyria, and Arabia. It is at first white, bordering on yellow, then on red, and, lastly, violet; and melts under the fingers like wax. It is of

of known efficacy in ſome uterine diſorders; but the rankneſs of its ſmell occaſions it to be ſeldom uſed but by farriers; yet, in the Eaſt Indies, it makes an ingredient in their ragouts. *Chambers.*

ASARABA'CCA. *n. ſ.* [*aſarum*, Lat.] The name of a plant.

The flower cup is divided into four parts, and the fruit into ſix cells, filled with oblong ſeeds. The leaves are roundiſh, thick, and almoſt of the colour of thoſe of the ivy tree. There are two ſorts, the common *aſarabacca*, and that of Canada. The firſt ſort is uſed in medicine. It delights in a moiſt ſhady place, and is increaſed by parting the roots in autumn. *Millar.*

ASBE'STINE. *adj.* [from *asbeſtos.*] Something incombuſtible, or that partakes of the nature and qualities of the *lapis asbeſtos*.

ASBE'STOS. *n. ſ.* [ἄσβεϛος.] A ſort of native foſſile ſtone, which may be ſplit into threads and filaments, from one inch to ten inches in length, very fine, brittle, yet ſomewhat tractable, ſilky, and of a greyiſh colour, not unlike talc of Venice. It is almoſt inſipid to the taſte, indiſſoluble in water, and endued with the wonderful property of remaining unconſumed in the fire, which only whitens it. But, notwithſtanding the common opinion, in two trials before the Royal Society, a piece of cloth made of this ſtone was found to loſe a dram of its weight each time. Paper as well as cloth has been made of this ſtone; and Pliny ſays he had ſeen napkins of it, which, being taken foul from the table, were thrown into the fire, and better ſcowered than if they had been waſhed in water. This ſtone is found in many places of Aſia and Europe; particularly in the iſland of Angleſey in Wales, and in Aberdeenſhire in Scotland. *Chambers.*

ASCA'RIDES *n. ſ.* [ἀσκαρίδες, from ἀσκαρίζω, to leap.] Little worms in the rectum, ſo called from their continual troubleſome motion, cauſing an intolerable itching. *Quincy.*

To ASCE'ND. *v. n.* [*aſcendo*, Lat.]

1. To mount upwards.

Then to the heav'n of heav'ns ſhall he *aſcend*
With victory, triumphing through the air
Over his foes and thine. *Milton's Par. Loſt, b.* xii.

2. To proceed from one degree of knowledge to another.

By theſe ſteps we ſhall *aſcend* to more juſt ideas of the glory of Jeſus Chriſt, who is intimately united to God, and is one with him. *Watts's Improvement of the Mind.*

3. To ſtand higher in genealogy.

The only inceſt was in the *aſcending*, not collateral or deſcending branch; as when parents and children married, this was accounted inceſt. *Broome's Notes on the Odyſſey.*

To ASCEND. *v. a.* To climb up any thing.

They *aſcend* the mountains, they deſcend the vallies. *Delane's Revelation examined.*

ASCE'NDABLE. *adj.* [from *aſcend.*] That may be aſcended. *Dict.*

ASCE'NDANT. *n. ſ.* [from *aſcend.*]

1. The part of the ecliptick at any particular time above the horizon, which is ſuppoſed by aſtrologers to have great influence.

2. Height; elevation.

He was initiated, in order to gain inſtruction in ſciences that were there in their higheſt *aſcendant.* *Temple.*

3. Superiority; influence.

By the *aſcendant* he had in his underſtanding, and the dexterity of his nature, he could perſuade him very much. *Claren.*

What ſtar I know not, but ſome ſtar I find,
Has giv'n thee an *aſcendant* o'er my mind. *Dryden's Perſ.*

When they have got an *aſcendant* over them, they ſhould uſe it with moderation, and not make themſelves ſcarecrows. *Locke.*

4. One of the degrees of kindred reckoned upwards.

The moſt nefarious kind of baſtards, are inceſtuous baſtards, which are begotten between *aſcendants* and deſcendants *in infinitum*; and between collaterals, as far as the divine prohibition. *Ayliffe's Parergon.*

ASCE'NDANT. *adj.*

1. Superiour; predominant; overpowering.

Chriſt outdoes Moſes, before he diſplaces him; and ſhews an *aſcendant* ſpirit above him. *South.*

2. In an aſtrological ſenſe, above the horizon.

Let him ſtudy the conſtellation of Pegaſus, which is about that time *aſcendant.* *Brown's Vulgar Errours, b.* iv.

ASCE'NDENCY. *n. ſ.* [from *aſcend.*] Influence; power.

Cuſtom has ſome *aſcendency* over underſtanding, and what at one time ſeemed decent, appears diſagreeable afterwards. *Watts.*

ASCE'NSION. *n. ſ.* [*aſcenſio*, Lat.]

1. The act of aſcending or riſing; frequently applied to the viſible elevation of our Saviour to heaven.

Then riſing from his grave,
Spoil'd principalities, and pow'rs, triumph'd
In open ſhew; and, with *aſcenſion* bright,
Captivity led captive through the air. *Paradiſe Loſt, b.* x.

2. The thing riſing, or mounting.

Men err in the theory of inebriation, conceiving the brain doth only ſuffer from vaporous *aſcenſions* from the ſtomach. *Brown's Vulgar Errours.*

ASCE'NSION, in aſtronomy, is either *right* or *oblique*. *Right aſcenſion* of the ſun, or a ſtar, is that degree of the equinoctial, counted from the beginning of Aries, which riſes with the ſun or ſtar in a right ſphere. *Oblique aſcenſion* is an arch of the equator intercepted between the firſt point of Aries, and that point of the equator which riſes together with a ſtar in an oblique ſphere.

ASCE'NSION DAY. The day on which the aſcenſion of our Saviour is commemorated, commonly called Holy Thurſday; the Thurſday but one before Whitſuntide.

ASCE'NSIONAL *Difference*, is the difference between the right and oblique aſcenſion, of the ſame point to the ſurface of the ſphere. *Chambers.*

ASCE'NSIVE. *adj.* [from *aſcend.*] In a ſtate of aſcent.

The cold augments when the days begin to encreaſe, though the ſun be then *aſcenſive*, and returning from the winter tropick. *Brown's Vulgar Errours, b.* iv.

ASCE'NT. *n. ſ.* [*aſcenſus*, Lat.]

1. Riſe; the act of riſing.

To him with ſwift *aſcent* he up return'd,
Into his bliſsful boſom reaſſum'd
In glory, as of old. *Milton's Par. Loſt, b.* x.

2. The way by which one aſcends.

The temple, and the ſeveral degrees of *aſcent*, whereby men did climb up to the ſame, as if it had been a *ſcala cœli*, be all poetical and fabulous. *Bacon's New Atlant.*

It was a rock
Conſpicuous far; winding with one *aſcent*
Acceſſible from earth, one ent'rance high. *Par. Loſt, b.* iv.

3. An eminence, or high place.

No land like Italy erects the ſight,
By ſuch a vaſt *aſcent*, or ſwells to ſuch a height. *Addiſon.*

A wide flat cannot be pleaſant in the Elyſian fields, unleſs it be diverſified with depreſſed valleys and ſwelling *aſcents*. *Bentl.*

To ASCERTA'IN. *v. a.* [*acertener*, Fr.]

1. To make certain; to fix; to eſtabliſh.

The divine law both *aſcertaineth* the truth, and ſupplieth unto us the want of other laws. *Hooker, b.* i.

Money differs from uncoined ſilver in this, that the quantity of ſilver in each piece is *aſcertained* by the ſtamp. *Locke.*

2. To make confident; to take away doubt; often with *of.*

If it be on right judgment of myſelf, it may give me the other certainty, that is, *aſcertain* me that I am in the number of God's children. *Hammond's Practical Catechiſm.*

This makes us act with a repoſe of mind and wonderful tranquillity, becauſe it *aſcertains* us *of* the goodneſs of our work. *Dryden's Dufreſnoy.*

ASCERTA'INER. *n. ſ.* [from *aſcertain.*] The perſon that proves or eſtabliſhes.

ASCERTA'INMENT. *n. ſ.* [from *aſcertain.*] A ſettled rule; an eſtabliſhed ſtandard.

For want of *aſcertainment*, how far a writer may expreſs his good wiſhes for his country, innocent intentions may be charged with crimes. *Swift to Lord Middleton.*

ASCE'TICK. *adj.* [ἀσκητικὸς.] Employed wholly in exerciſes of devotion and mortification.

None lived ſuch long lives as monks and hermits, ſequeſtered from plenty to a conſtant *aſcetick* courſe of the ſevereſt abſtinence and devotion. *South.*

ASCE'TICK. *n. ſ.* He that retires to devotion and mortification; a hermit.

I am far from commending thoſe *aſceticks*, that, out of a pretence of keeping themſelves unſpotted from the world, take up their quarters in deſarts. *Norris.*

He that preaches to man, ſhould underſtand what is in man; and that ſkill can ſcarce be attained by an *aſcetick* in his ſolitudes. *Atterbury's Sermons.*

A'SCII. *n. ſ. It has no ſingular.* [from α, without, and σκιὰ, a ſhadow.] Thoſe people who, at certain times of the year, have no ſhadow at noon; ſuch are the inhabitants of the torrid zone, becauſe they have the ſun twice a year vertical to them. *Dict.*

ASCI'TES. *n. ſ.* [from ἀσκὸς, a bladder.] A particular ſpecies of dropſy; a ſwelling of the lower belly and depending parts, from an extravaſation and collection of water broke out of its proper veſſels. This caſe, when certain and inveterate, is univerſally allowed to admit of no cure but by means of the manual operation of tapping. *Quincy.*

There are two kinds of dropſy, the anaſarca, called alſo leucophlegmacy, when the extravaſated matter ſwims in the cells of the membrana adipoſa; and the *aſcites*, when the water poſſeſſes the cavity of the abdomen. *Sharp's Surgery.*

ASCI'TICAL. } *adj.* [from *aſcites.*] Belonging to an aſcites; dropſical; hydropical.
ASCI'TICK. }

When it is part of another tumour, it is hydropical, either anaſarcous or *aſcitical.* *Wiſeman's Surgery.*

ASCITI'TIOUS. *adj.* [*aſcititius*, Lat.] Supplemental; additional; not inherent; not original.

Homer has been reckoned an *aſcititious* name, from ſome accident of his life. *Pope's Eſſay on Homer.*

ASCRI'BABLE. *adj.* [from *aſcribe.*] That which may be aſcribed.

The greater part have been forward to reject it, upon a miſtaken perſuaſion, that thoſe phœnomena are the effects of nature's abhorrency of a vacuum, which ſeem to be more fitly *aſcribable* to the weight and ſpring of the air. *Boyle.*

To ASCRI'BE. *v. a.* [*aſcribo*, Lat.]

1. To attribute to as a cauſe.

The cause of his banishment is unknown, because he was unwilling to provoke the emperor, by *ascribing* it to any other reason than what was pretended. *Dryden.*

To this we may justly *ascribe* those envies, jealousies, and encroachments, which render mankind uneasy to one another. *Rogers's Sermons.*

2. To attribute to as a possessor, or substance receiving accidents.

These perfections must be somewhere, and therefore may much better be *ascribed* to God, in whom we suppose all other perfections to meet, than to any thing else. *Tillotson.*

ASCRI'PTION. *n. s.* [*ascriptio*, Lat.] The act of ascribing. *Dict.*

ASCRIPTI'TIOUS. *adj.* [*ascriptitius*, Lat.] That which is ascribed. *Dict.*

ASH. *n. s.* [*fraxinus*, Lat. æsc, Saxon.]

This tree hath pennated leaves, which end in an odd lobe. The male flowers, which grow at a remote distance from the fruit, have no petals, but consist of many stamina. The ovary becomes a seed vessel, containing one seed at the bottom, shaped like a bird's tongue. The species are, 1. The common *ash tree.* 2. The striped *ash.* 3. The manna *ash*, &c. The first sort is a common timber tree in every part of England. The second is a variety of the first. The third sort is supposed to be the tree from whence the true Calabrian manna is taken. The timber is of excellent use to the wheelwright and cartwright. *Millar.*

Let me twine
Mine arms about that body, where against
My grained *ash* an hundred times hath broke,
And scar'd the moon with splinters. *Shakesp. Coriolanus.*

With which of old he charm'd the savage train,
And call'd the mountain *ashes* to the plain. *Dryd. Silenus.*

ASH COLOURED. *adj.* [from *ash* and *colour.*] Coloured between brown and grey, like the bark of an ashen branch.

Clay, *ash coloured*, was part of a stratum which lay above the strata of stone. *Woodward on Fossils.*

ASHA'MED. *adj.* [from *shame.*] Touched with shame; generally with *of* before the cause of shame.

Profess publickly the doctrine of Jesus Christ, not being *ashamed of* the word of God, or *of* any practices enjoined by it. *Taylor's Holy Living.*

One wou'd have thought she would have stirr'd; but strove
With modesty, and was *asham'd* to move. *Dryd. Fables.*

This I have shadowed, that you may not be *ashamed of* that hero, whose protection you undertake. *Dryd. Conq. of Gr. Ded.*

A'SHEN. *adj.* [from *ash.*] Made of ash wood.

At once he said, and threw
His *ashen* spear; which quiver'd as it flew. *Dryden.*

A'SHES. *n. s. wants the singular.* [asca, Sax. *asche*, Dutch.]

1. The remains of any thing burnt.

Some relicks would be left of it, as when *ashes* remain of burned bodies. *Digby on Bodies.*

This late dissension, grown betwixt the peers,
Burns under feigned *ashes* of forg'd love,
And will at last break out into a flame. *Shakesp. Henry* VI.

Ashes contain a very fertile salt, and are the best manure for cold lands, if kept dry, that the rain doth not wash away their salt. *Mortimer's Husbandry.*

. The remains of the body; often used in poetry for the carcase, from the ancient practice of burning the dead.

Poor key-cold figure of a holy king!
Pale *ashes* of the house of Lancaster!
Thou bloodless remnant of that royal blood! *Shak. R.* III.

To great Laërtes I bequeath
A task of grief, his ornaments of death;
Lest, when the fates his royal *ashes* claim,
The Grecian matrons taint my spotless name. *Pope.*

ASHWEDNESDAY. *n. s.* The first day of Lent, so called from the ancient custom of sprinkling ashes on the head.

A'SHLAR. *n. s.* [with masons.] Free stones as they come out of the quarry, of different lengths, breadths, and thicknesses.

A'SHLERING. *n. s.* [with builders.] Quartering to tack to in garrets, about two foot and a half or three foot high, perpendicular to the floor, and reaching to the underside of the rafters. *Builder's Dict.*

ASHO'RE. *adv.* [from *a* and *shore.*]

1. On shore; on the land.

The poor Englishman riding in the road, having all that he brought thither *ashore*, would have been undone. *Raleigh*

Moor'd in a Chian creek, *ashore* I went,
And all the following night in Chios spent. *Addison's Ovid.*

2. To the shore; to the land.

We may as bootless spend our vain command,
As send our precepts to the leviathan
To come *ashore.* *Shakesp. Henry* V.

May thy billows rowl *ashore*
The beryl, and the golden ore. *Milton's Comus.*

A'SHWEED. *n. s.* [from *ash* and *weed.*] An herb.

A'SHY. *adj.* [from *ash.*] Ash coloured; pale; inclining to a whitish grey.

Oft have I seen a timely parted ghost
Of *ashy* semblance, meagre, pale, and bloodless. *Sh. H.* VI.

ASI'DE. *adv.* [from *a* and *side.*]

1. To one side; out of the perpendicular direction.

The storm rush'd in, and Arcite stood aghast;
The flames were blown *aside*, yet shone they bright,
Fann'd by the wind, and gave a ruffled light. *Dryd. Fables.*

2. To another part; out of the true direction.

He had no brother; which though it be a comfortable thing for kings to have, yet it draweth the subjects eyes a little *aside.* *Bacon's Henry* VIII.

3. From the company; as, to speak *aside.*

He took him *aside* from the multitude. *Mark*, vii. 33.

A'SINARY. *adj.* [*asinarius*, Lat.] Belonging to an ass. *Dict.*

A'SININE. *adj.* [from *asinus*, Lat.] Belonging to an ass.

You shall have more ado to drive our dullest youth, our stocks and stubs, from such nurture, than we have now to hale our choicest and hopefullest wits to that *asinine* feast of sow thistles and brambles. *Milt. on Education.*

To ASK. *v. a.* [ascian, Saxon.]

1. To petition; to beg; sometimes with an *accusative* only; sometimes with *for.*

When thou dost *ask* me *blessing*, I'll kneel down,
And *ask* of thee *forgiveness.* *Shakesp. King Lear.*

We have nothing else to *ask*, but that
Which you deny already: yet will *ask*,
That, if we fail in our request, the blame
May hang upon your hardness. *Shakesp. Coriolanus.*

My son, hast thou sinned? do so no more, but *ask* pardon *for* thy former sins. *Ecclus*, xxi. 1.

If he *ask for bread*, will he give him a stone? *Matt.* vii. 9.

In long journies, *ask* your master *leave* to give ale to the horses. *Swift.*

2. To demand; to claim; as, to *ask* a price for goods.

Ask me never so much dowry and gift, and I will give according as ye shall say unto me: but give me the damsel to wife. *Gen.* xxxiv. 12.

He saw his friends, who, whelm'd beneath the waves,
Their funeral honours claim'd, and *ask'd* their quiet graves. *Dryden's Æneid.*

3. To enquire; to question; with *for* before the thing, and sometimes *of* before the person.

Stand ye in the ways, and see, and *ask for* the old paths, where is the good way, and walk therein, and ye shall find rest for your souls. *Jerem.* vi. 16.

For *ask* now of the days that are past, which were before thee, since the day that God created man upon the earth, and *ask* from the one side of heaven unto the other, whether there hath been any such thing as this great thing is, or hath been heard like it. *Deut.* iv. 32.

O inhabitant of Aroer, stand by the way and espy, *ask* him that flieth, and her that escapeth, and say, what is done? *Jeremiah*, xlviii. 19.

4. To enquire; with *after* before the thing.

He said, wherefore is it that thou dost *ask after* my name? And he blessed him there. *Genesis*, xxxii. 29.

5. To require, as physically necessary.

A lump of ore in the bottom of a mine will be stirred by two men's strength; which, if you bring it to the top of the earth, will *ask* six men to stir it. *Bacon's Natural History.*

The administration passes into different hands at the end of two months, which contributes to dispatch: but any exigence of state *asks* a much longer time to conduct any design to its maturity. *Addison's Rem. on Italy.*

ASK, ASH, AS, do all come from the Saxon æsc, an ash tree. *Gibson's Camden.*

ASKA'NCE. } *adv.* Sideways; obliquely.
ASKA'UNCE. }

Zelmane, keeping a countenance *askance*, as she understood him not, told him, it became her evil. *Sidney, b.* i.

His wannish eyes upon them bent *askance.*
And when he saw their labours well succeed,
He wept for rage, and threaten'd dire mischance. *Fairfax.*

Some say, he bid his angels turn *askance*
The poles of earth, twice ten degrees, and more,
From the sun's axle; they with labour push'd
Oblique the centrick globe. *Milton's Par. Lost, b.* x.

ASKA'UNT. *adv.* Obliquely; on one side.

At this Achilles roll'd his furious eyes,
Fix'd on the king *askaunt*; and thus replies,
O, impudent. *Dryden's Iliad.*

Since the space, that lies on either side
The solar orb, is without limits wide,
Grant that the sun had happen'd to prefer
A seat *askaunt*, but one diameter:
Lost to the light by that unhappy place,
This globe had lain a frozen lonesome mass. *Blackmore.*

A'SKER. *n. s.* [from *ask.*]

1. Petitioner.

Have you
Ere now denied the *asker?* and, now again
On him that did not ask, but mock, bestow
Your su'd for tongues. *Shakesp. Coriolanus.*

The greatness of the *asker*, and the smallness of the thing asked, had been sufficient to enforce his request. *South.*

2. En-

2. Enquirer.

Every *asker* being satisfied, we may conclude, that all their conceptions of being in a place are the same. *Digby of Bodies.*

ASKER. *n. s.* A water newt.

ASKE'W. *adv.* [from *a* and *skew.*] Aside; with contempt; contemptuously; disdainfully.

For when ye mildly look with lovely hue,
Then is my soul with life and love inspir'd:
But when ye lowre, or look on me *askew*,
Then do I die. *Spenser, Sonnet* vii.

Then take it, Sir, as it was writ,
Nor look *askew* at what it saith;
There's no petition in it.——— *Prior.*

To ASLA'KE. *v. a.* [from *a* and *slake*, or *slack.*] To remit; to mitigate; to slacken.

But this continual, cruel, civil war,
No skill can stint, nor reason can *aslake*. *Spenser, Son.* xliv.
Whilst seeking to *aslake* thy raging fire,
Thou in me kindlest much more great desire. *Spenser.*

ASLA'NT. *adv.* [from *a* and *slant.*] Obliquely; on one side; not perpendicularly.

There is a willow grows *aslant* a brook,
That shews his hoar leaves in the glassy stream. *Sh. Hamlet.*

He fell; the shaft
Drove through his neck *aslant*; he spurns the ground,
And the soul issues through the weazon's wound. *Dryden.*

Aslant the dew-bright earth, and colour'd air,
He looks in boundless majesty abroad. *Thomson's Summer.*

ASLE'EP. *adv.* [from *a* and *sleep.*]

1. Sleeping; at rest.

How many thousands of my poorest subjects
Are at this hour *asleep!* O gentle sleep,
Nature's soft nurse, how have I frighted thee! *Sh. H.* IV.

The diligence of trade, and noiseful gain,
And luxury more late *asleep* were laid:
All was the night's, and, in her silent reign,
No sound the rest of nature did invade. *Dryden's Ann. M.*

There is no difference between a person *asleep*, and in an apoplexy, but that the one can be awaked, and the other cannot. *Arbuthnot on Diet.*

2. To sleep.

If a man watch too long, it is odds but he will fall *asleep*. *Bacon's Essays.*

Thus done the tales, to bed they creep,
By whispering winds soon lull'd *asleep*. *Milton's l'Allegro.*

ASLO'PE. *adv.* [from *a* and *slope.*] With declivity; obliquely; not perpendicularly.

Set them not upright, but *aslope*, a reasonable depth under the ground. *Bacon's Nat. History,* N° 425.

The curse *aslope*
Glanc'd on the ground; with labour I must earn
My bread: what harm? Idleness had been worse:
My labour will sustain me. *Milt. Par. Lost, b.* x.

The knight did stoop,
And sate on further side *aslope*. *Hudibras.*

ASO'MATOUS. *adj.* [from α, priv. and σῶμα, a body.] Incorporeal, or without a body.

ASP. } *n. s.* [*aspis*, Lat.] A kind of serpent, whose poison
A'SPICK. } is so dangerous and quick in its operation, that it kills without a possibility of applying any remedy. It is said to be very small, and peculiar to Egypt and Lybia. Those that are bitten by it, die within three hours; and the manner of their dying being by sleep and lethargy, without any pain, Cleopatra chose it, as the easiest way of dispatching herself. *Calmet.*

High-minded Cleopatra, that with stroke
Of *asp*'s sting, herself did kill. *Fairy Queen, b.* i.

Scorpion, and *asp*, and amphisbæna dire,
And dipsas. *Milton's Par. Lost, b.* x.

ASP. *n. s.* A tree. See ASPEN.

ASPA'LATHUS. n. s. [Latin.]

1. A plant called the rose of Jerusalem, or our lady's rose.

2. The wood of a prickly tree, heavy, oleaginous, somewhat sharp and bitter to the taste, and anciently in much repute as an astringent, but now little used. There are four kinds of this wood; the first of the colour of box, hard, solid, heavy, and smelling like roses; which is therefore called rosewood. The second, red like yew, and of a very agreeable smell. The third, hard, twisted, knotty, of a rank smell, like that of a goat, and a disagreeable taste. The fourth has an ash coloured bark, and the wood is of a purple dye. *Aspalathus* affords an oil of admirable scent, reputed one of the best perfumes. *Chambers.*

I gave a sweet smell like cinnamon and *aspalathus*, and I yielded a pleasant odour like the best myrrh. *Ecclus*, xxiv. 15.

ASPA'RAGUS. *n. s.* [Lat.] The name of a plant. It has a rosaceous flower of six leaves, placed orbicularly, out of whose center rises the pointal, which turns to a soft globular berry, full of hard seeds. The leaves are finely cut. The species are twelve, of which all but the two first are exoticks. 1. Garden *asparagus*. 2. Wild *asparagus*, with narrow leaves. The first sort is cultivated for the table, and propagated by the seeds, which should be sown in the beginning of February. The next year they should be planted out; the third spring, after planting, they may be begun to be cut, and, by proper management, a plot of *asparagus* may be continued ten or twelve years in cutting. The second sort grows wild in some parts, but, producing slender shoots, it is rarely cultivated. *Millar.*

Asparagus affects the urine with a fetid smell, especially if cut when they are white; and therefore have been suspected by some physicians, as not friendly to the kidneys; when they are older, and begin to ramify, they lose this quality; but then they are not so agreeable. *Arbuthnot on Aliments.*

A'SPECT. *n. s.* [*aspectus*, Lat. It appears anciently to have been pronounced with the accent on the last syllable, which is now placed on the first.]

1. Look; air; appearance.

I have presented the tongue under a double *aspect*, such as may justify the definition, that it is the best and worst part. *Government of the Tongue.*

They are both, in my judgment, the image or picture of a great ruin, and have the true *aspect* of a world lying in its rubbish. *Burnet's Theory of the Earth.*

2. Countenance; look.

Fairer than fairest, in his faining eye,
Whose sole *aspect* he counts felicity. *Spens. Hymn on Love.*

Those eyes of thine from mine have drawn salt tears,
Sham'd their *aspects* with store of childish drops. *Sh. R.* III.

I am fearful: wherefore frowns he thus?
'Tis his *aspect* of terrour. All's not well. *Sh. Richard* III.

Yet had his *aspect* nothing of severe,
But such a face as promis'd him sincere. *Dryden's Fables.*

Then shall thy Craggs (and let me call him mine)
On the cast ore another Pollio shine;
With *aspect* open shall erect his head. *Pope.*

3. Glance; view; act of beholding.

When an envious or an amorous *aspect* doth infect the spirits of another, there is joined both affection and imagination. *Bacon's Natural Hist.* N° 908.

The setting sun
Slowly descended; and with right *aspect*
Against the eastern gate of paradise,
Levell'd his ev'ning rays. *Paradise Lost, b.* iv.

4. Direction towards any point; view; position.

I have built a strong wall, faced to the south *aspect* with brick. *Swift's Last Will.*

5. Disposition of any thing to something else; relation.

The light got from the opposite arguings of men of parts, shewing the different sides of things, and their various *aspects* and probabilities, would be quite lost, if every one were obliged to assent to, and say after the speaker. *Locke.*

6. Disposition of a planet to other planets.

There's some ill planet reigns,
I must be patient till the heavens look
With an *aspect* more favourable. *Shakesp. Winter's Tale.*

Not unlike that which astrologers call a conjunction of planets, of no very benign *aspect* the one to the other. *Wotton.*

To the blank moon
Her office they prescrib'd: to th' other five
Their planetary motions, and *aspects*,
In sextile, square, and trine, and opposite. *Paradise Lost.*

Why does not every single star shed a separate influence, and have *aspects* with other stars of their own constellation? *Bentley's Sermons.*

To ASPE'CT. *v. a.* [*aspicio*, Lat.] To behold.

Happy in their mistake, those people whom
The northern pole *aspects*; whom fear of death
(The greatest of all human fears) ne'er moves. *Temple.*

ASPE'CTABLE. *adj.* [*aspectabilis*, Lat.] Visible; being the object of sight.

He was the sole cause of this *aspectable* and perceivable universal. *Raleigh's Hist. of the World.*

To this use of informing us what is in this *aspectable* world, we shall find the eye well fitted. *Ray on Creation.*

ASPE'CTION. *n. s.* [from *aspect.*] Beholding; view.

A Moorish queen, upon *aspection* of the picture of Andromeda, conceived and brought forth a fair one. *Brown's V. Err.*

A'SPEN, or ASP. *n. s.* [*espe*, Dutch; *asp*, Dan. epſe, trembling, Sax. *Somner.*] See POPLAR, of which it is a species. The leaves of this tree always tremble.

The *aspen* or *asp* tree hath leaves much the same with the poplar, only much smaller, and not so white. *Mortim. Husb.*

The builder oak sole king of forests all,
The *aspen*, good for statues, the cypress funeral. *Spenser.*

ASPEN. *adj.* [from *asp* or *aspen.*]

1. Belonging to the asp tree.

Oh! had the monster seen those lily hands
Tremble like *aspen* leaves upon a lute. *Shak. Titus Andron.*

No gale disturbs the trees,
Nor *aspen* leaves confess the gentlest breeze. *Gay.*

2. Made of aspen wood.

A'SPER. adj. [Lat.] Rough; rugged. This word I have found only in the following passage.

All base notes, or very treble notes, give an *asper* sound; for that the base striketh more air than it can well strike equally. *Bacon.*

To

To A'SPERATE. *v. a.* [*aspero*, Lat.] To roughen; to make rough or uneven.

Those corpuscles of colour, insinuating themselves into all the pores of the body to be dyed, may *asperate* its superficies, according to the bigness and texture of the corpuscles. *Boyle.*

ASPERA'TION. *n. s.* [from *asperate.*] A making rough. *Dict.*

ASPERIFO'LIOUS. *adj.* [from *asper*, rough, and *folium*, a leaf, Lat.] One of the divisions of plants, so called from the roughness of their leaves.

ASPE'RITY. *n. s.* [*asperitas*, Lat.]

1. Unevenness; roughness of surface.

Sometimes the pores and *asperities* of dry bodies are so incommensurate to the particles of the liquor, that they glide over the surface. *Boyle.*

2. Roughness of sound; harshness of pronunciation.

3. Roughness, or ruggedness of temper; moroseness; sourness; crabbedness.

The charity of the one, like kindly exhalations, will descend in showers of blessings; but the rigour and *asperity* of the other, in a severe doom upon ourselves. *Govern. Tongue.*

Avoid all unseemliness and *asperity* of carriage; do nothing that may argue a peevish or froward spirit. *Rogers.*

ASPERNA'TION. *n. s.* [*aspernatio*, Lat.] Neglect; disregard. *D.*

A'SPEROUS. *adj.* [*asper*, Lat.] Rough; uneven.

Black and white are the most *asperous* and unequal of colours; so like, that it is hard to distinguish them: black is the most rough. *Boyle.*

To ASPE'RSE. *v. a.* [*aspergo*, Lat.] To bespatter with censure or calumny.

In the business of Ireland, besides the opportunity to *asperse* the king, they were safe enough. *Clarendon, b.* viii.

Curb that impetuous tongue, nor rashly vain,
And singly mad, *asperse* the sov'reign reign. *Pope's Iliad.*
Unjustly poets we *asperse*,
Truth shines the brighter clad in verse. *Swift.*

ASPE'RSION. *n. s.* [*aspersio*, Lat.]

1. A sprinkling.

If thou dost break her virgin knot, before
All sanctimonious ceremonies,
No sweet *aspersions* shall the heav'ns let fall,
To make this contract grow. *Shakesp. Tempest.*

It exhibits a mixture of new conceits and old; whereas the instauration gives the new unmixed, otherwise than with some little *aspersion* of the old, for taste's sake. *Bacon's Holy War.*

2. Calumny; censure.

The same *aspersions* of the king, and the same grounds of a rebellion. *Dryden's Epistle to the Whigs.*

ASPHA'LTICK. *adj.* [from *asphaltos.*] Gummy; bituminous.

And with *asphaltick* slime, broad as the gate,
Deep to the roots of hell, the gather'd beach
They fasten'd. *Milton's Paradise Lost, b.* ix.

ASPHA'LTOS. *n. s.* [ἄσφαλτος, bitumen.] A solid, brittle, black, bituminous, inflammable substance, resembling pitch, and chiefly found swimming on the surface of the *Lacus Asphaltites*, or Dead sea, where anciently stood the cities of Sodom and Gomorrah. It is cast up from time to time, in the nature of liquid pitch, from the earth at the bottom of this sea; and, being thrown upon the water, swims like other fat bodies, and condenses gradually by the heat of the sun, and the salt that is in it. It burns with great vehemence. The Arabs use it for pitching their ships; and much of it was employed in the embalming of the ancients.

ASPHA'LTUM. *n. s.* [Lat.] A bituminous stone found near the ancient Babylon, and lately in the province of Neufchâtel; which, mixed with other matters, makes an excellent cement, incorruptible by air, and impenetrable by water; supposed to be the mortar so much celebrated among the ancients, with which the walls of Babylon were laid. *Chambers.*

A'SPHODEL. *n. s.* [*lilio-asphodelus*, Lat.] Day-lily.

The characters are; It hath a root like kingspear; the flower consists of one leaf, which is deeply cut into six segments, and expands in form of a lily; the flower is succeeded by an oval fruit, which contains several roundish seeds. The species are, 1. The yellow *asphodel*. 2. The red *asphodel*. These two sorts are very common in most of the English gardens; the first is often called by the gardeners the yellow tuberose, from its having a very agreeable scent; but the other is called the day-lily, or the tuberose orange-lily, in most places. They are both hardy plants, and multiply exceedingly, if suffered to remain two or three years undisturbed; especially the red sort, which sends forth offsets. The best time to transplant their roots is in September or October. They will grow in any soil or situation; the yellow produces its flowers in May and June; the red a month later. *Millar.*

Asphodels were by the ancients planted near burying-places, in order to supply the manes of the dead with nourishment.

By those happy souls who dwell
In yellow meads of *asphodel*. *Pope's St. Cæcilia.*

A'SPICK. *n. s.* [See ASP.] The name of a serpent.

Why did I 'scape th' invenom'd *aspick's* rage,
And all the fiery monsters of the desart,
To see this day? *Addison's Cato.*

To A'SPIRATE. *v. a.* [*aspiro*, Lat.] To pronounce with aspiration, or full breath; as we aspirate *horse*, *house*, and *hog*.

To A'SPIRATE. *v. n.* [*aspiro*, Lat.] To be pronounced with full breath.

Where a vowel ends a word, the next begins either with a consonant, or what is its equivalent; for our *w* and *h aspirate*. *Dryd. Dedication to Æneid.*

A'SPIRATE. *adj.* [*aspiratus*, Lat.] Pronounced with full breath.

For their being pervious, you may call them, if you please, perspirate; but yet they are not *aspirate*, i. e. with such an aspiration as *h*. *Holder's Elements of Speech.*

ASPIRA'TION. *n. s.* [*aspiratio*, Lat.]

1. A breathing after; an ardent wish; used generally of a wish for spiritual blessings.

A soul inspired with the warmest *aspirations* after celestial beatitude, keeps its powers attentive. *Watts's Impr. of the Mind.*

2. The act of aspiring, or desiring something high and great.

'Tis he; I ken the manner of his gate;
He rises on his toe; that spirit of his
In *aspiration* lifts him from the earth. *Shak. Troil. and Cress.*

3. The pronunciation of a vowel with full breath.

H is only a guttural *aspiration*, i. e. a more forcible impulse of the breath from the lungs. *Holder's Elements of Speech.*

To ASPI'RE. *v. n.* [*aspiro*, Lat.]

1. To desire with eagerness; to pant after something higher; sometimes with the particle *to*.

Most excellent lady, no expectation in others, nor hope in himself, could *aspire to* a higher mark, than to be thought worthy to be praised by you. *Sidney, b.* ii.

Hence springs that universal strong desire,
Which all men have of immortality:
Not some few spirits *unto* this thought *aspire*,
But all men's minds in this united be. *Sir J. Davies.*
Horace did ne'er *aspire to* epic bays:
Nor lofty Maro stoop to lyrick lays. *Roscommon.*
Till then a helpless, hopeless, homely swain;
I sought not freedom, nor *aspir'd to* gain. *Dryden's Virgil.*
Aspiring to be gods, if angels fell,
Aspiring to be angels, men rebel. *Pope's Essay on Man.*

2. Sometimes with *after*.

Those are raised above sense, and *aspire after* immortality, who believe the perpetual duration of their souls. *Tillotson.*

There is none of us but who would be thought, throughout the whole course of his life, to *aspire after* immortality. *Atterbury's Sermons, Pref.*

3. To rise higher.

There is betwixt that smile we would *aspire to*,
That sweet aspect of princes and our ruin,
More pangs and fears than war or women have. *Sh. H.* VIII.
My own breath still foment the fire,
Which flames as high as fancy can *aspire*. *Waller.*

ASPORTA'TION. *n. s.* [*asportatio*, Lat.] A carrying away. *D.*

ASQU'INT. *adv.* [from *a* and *squint.*] Obliquely; not in the strait line of vision.

A single guide may direct the way better than five hundred, who have contrary views, or look *asquint*, or shut their eyes. *Swift's Project for the Advancement of Religion.*

ASS. *n. s.* [*asinus*, Lat.]

1. An animal of burden, remarkable for sluggishness, patience, hardiness, coarseness of food, and long life.

You have among you many a purchas'd slave,
Which, like your *asses*, and your dogs and mules,
You use in abject and in slavish part,
Because you bought them. *Shakesp. Merchant of Venice.*

2. A stupid, heavy, dull fellow; a dolt.

I do begin to perceive that I am made an *ass*. *Shakesp. Merry Wives of Windsor.*

That such a crafty mother
Should yield the world to this *ass!*—a woman that
Bears all down with her brain; and her son
Cannot take two from twenty for his heart,
And leave eighteen. *Shakesp. Cymbeline.*

To ASSA'IL. *v. a.* [*assailler*, Fr.]

1. To attack in a hostile manner; to assault; to fall upon; to invade.

So when he saw his flatt'ring arts to fail,
With greedy force he 'gan the fort t' *assail*. *Fairy Queen.*

2. To attack with argument; censure; or motives applied to the passions.

My gracious lord, here in the parliament
Let us *assail* the family of York. *Shakesp. Henry* VI.
She will not stay the siege of loving terms,
Nor bide th' encounter of *assailing* eyes. *Sh. Romeo and Jul.*
How have I fear'd your fate! but fear'd it most,
When love *assail'd* you on the Libyan coast. *Dryden's Æn.*
All books he reads, and all he reads *assails*,
From Dryden's Fables down to D—y's Tales. *Pope.*
In vain Thalestris with reproach *assails*;
For who can move when fair Belinda fails? *Pope.*

ASSA'ILABLE. *adj.* [from *assail.*] That which may be attacked.

Banquo, and his Fleance, lives.——
— But in them nature's copy's not eternal.—
— There's comfort yet, they are *assailable*. *Shak. Macbeth.*

ASSA'ILANT. *n. s.* [*assaillant*, Fr.] He that attacks; in opposition to *defendant*.

The same was so well encountered by the defendants, that the obstinacy of the *assailants* did but increase the loss. *Sir J. Hayward.*

I'll put myself in poor and mean attire,
And with a kind of umber smirch my face,
The like do you; so shall we pass along,
And never stir *assailants*. *Shakesp. As you like it.*

ASSA'ILANT. *adj.* Attacking; invading.

And as ev'ning dragon came,
Assailant on the perched roosts
Of tame villatick fowl. *Milton's Sampson Agonistes.*

ASSA'ILER. *n. s.* [from *assail.*] One who attacks another.

Palladius heated, so pursued our *assailers*, that one of them slew him. *Sidney, b.* ii.

ASSAPA'NICK. *n. s.* A little animal of Virginia, which is said to fly by stretching out its shoulders and its skin, and is called in English the flying squirrel. *Trevoux.*

ASSARABA'CCA. See ASARABACCA.

ASSA'RT. *n. s.* [*essart*, from *essarter*, Fr. to clear away wood in a forest.] An offence committed in the forest, by plucking up those woods by the roots, that are thickets or coverts of the forest, and by making them as plain as arable land. *Cowel.*

To ASSA'RT. *v. a.* [*essartir*, Fr.] To commit an assart. See ASSART.

ASSA'SSIN. } ASSA'SSINATE. } *n. s.* [*assassin*, Fr. a word brought originally from Asia, where, about the time of the holy war, there was a set of men called *assassins*, as is supposed for *Arsacidæ*, who killed any man, without regard to danger, at the command of their chief.] A murderer; one that kills by treachery, or sudden violence.

In the very moment as the knight withdrew from the duke, this *assassinate* gave him, with a back blow, a deep wound into his left side. *Wotton.*

The Syrian king, who, to surprize
One man, *assassin* like, had levy'd war,
War unproclaim'd. *Milton's Paradise Lost, b.* xi.

Here hir'd *assassins* for their gain invade,
And treach'rous pois'ners urge their fatal trade. *Dryd. Juv.*

When she hears of a murder, she enlarges more on the guilt of the suffering person, than of the *assassin*. *Addison. Spectator.*

Orestes brandish'd the revenging sword,
Slew the dire pair, and gave to fun'ral flame
The vile *assassin*, and adult'rous dame. *Pope's Odyssey.*

Useful, we grant, it serves what life requires,
But dreadful too, the dark *assassin* hires. *Pope, Epist.* iii.

ASSA'SINATE. *n. s.* [from *assassin.*] The crime of an assassin; murder.

Were not all *assassinates* and popular insurrections wrongfully chastised, if the meanness of the offenders indemnified them from punishment? *Pope's Dunciad.*

To ASSA'SSINATE. *v. a.* [from *assassin.*]

1. To murder by violence.

Help, neighbours, my house is broken open by force, and I am ravished, and like to be *assassinated*. *Dryd. Span. Friar.*

What could provoke thy madness
To *assassinate* so great, so brave a man! *A. Philips, D. Moth.*

2. To way-lay; to take by treachery. This meaning is perhaps peculiar to *Milton*.

Such usage as your honourable lords
Afford me, *assassinated* and betray'd,
Who durst not, with your whole united pow'rs,
In fight withstand one single and unarm'd. *Sampf. Agonist.*

ASSASSINA'TION. *n. s.* [from *assassinate.*] The act of assassinating; murder by violence.

If it were done, when 'tis done, then 'twere well
It were done quickly: if th' *assassination*
Could trammel up the consequence, and catch,
With its surcease, success. *Shakesp. Macbeth.*

The duke finish'd his course by a wicked *assassination*. *Claren.*

ASSASSINA'TOR. *n. s.* [from *assassinate.*] Murderer; mankiller; the person that kills by violence.

ASSA'TION. *n. s.* [*assatus*, roasted, Lat.] Roasting.

The egg expiring less in the elixation or boiling; whereas, in the *assation* or roasting, it will sometimes abate a drachm. *Brown's Vulgar Errours, b.* iii.

ASSA'ULT. *n. s.* [*assault*, French.]

1. Attack; hostile onset; opposed to *defence*.

Her spirit had been invincible against all *assaults* of affection. *Shakesp. Much ado about Nothing.*

Not to be shook thyself, but all *assaults*
Baffling, like thy hoar cliffs the loud sea wave. *Thomson.*

2. Storm; opposed to *sap* or *siege*.

Jason took at least a thousand men, and suddenly made an *assault upon* the city. 2 *Macc.* v. 5.

After some days siege, he resolved to try the fortune of an *assault*: he succeeded therein so far, that he had taken the principal tower and fort. *Bacon's Henry* VII.

3. Violence.

Themselves at discord fell,
And cruel combat join'd in middle space,
With horrible *assault*, and fury fell. *Fairy Queen, b.* ii.

4. Invasion; hostility; attack.

After some unhappy *assaults upon* the prerogative by the parliament, which produced its dissolution, there followed a composure. *Clarendon.*

Theories built upon narrow foundations, are very hard to be supported against the *assaults* of opposition. *Locke.*

5. In law. A violent kind of injury offered to a man's person. It may be committed by offering of a blow, or by a fearful speech. *Cowel.*

6. It has *upon* before the thing assaulted.

To ASSA'ULT. *v. a.* [from the noun.] To attack; to invade; to fall upon with violence.

The king granted the Jews to gather themselves together, and to stand for their life, to destroy all the power that would *assault* them. *Esth.* viii. 11.

Before the gates the cries of babes new-born,
Whom fate had from their tender mothers torn,
Assault his ears. *Dryd. Æneid* vi.

Curs'd steel, and more accursed gold,
Gave mischief birth, and made that mischief bold:
And double death did wretched man invade,
By steel *assaulted*, and by gold betray'd. *Dryden's Ovid.*

ASSA'ULTER. *n. s.* [from *assault.*] One who violently assaults another.

Neither liking their eloquence, nor fearing their might, we esteemed few swords in a just defence, able to resist many unjust *assaulters*. *Sidney, b.* ii.

ASSA'Y. *n. s.* [*essaye*, Fr. from which the ancient writers borrowed *assay*, according to the sound, and the latter, *essay*, according to the writing; but the senses now differing, they may be considered as two words.]

1. Examination.

This cannot be
By no *assay* of reason. 'Tis a pageant,
To keep us in false gaze. *Shakesp. Othello.*

2. In law. The examination of measures and weights used by the clerk of the market. *Cowel.*

3. The first enterance upon any thing; a taste.

For well he weened, that so glorious bait
Would tempt his guest to take thereof *assay*. *Fairy Queen.*

4. Attack; trouble.

She heard with patience all unto the end,
And strove to master sorrowful *assay*. *Fairy Queen, b.* i.

The men he prest from Tours and Blois but late,
To hard *assays* unfit, unsure at need,
Yet arm'd to point in well attempted plate. *Fairfax, b.* i.

Be sure to find,
What I foretel thee, many a hard *assay*
Of dangers, and adversities, and pains,
Ere thou of Israel's sceptre get fast hold. *Parad. Lost, b.* iv.

To ASSA'Y. *v. a.* [*essayer*, Fr.]

1. To make trial of; to make experiment of.

Gray and Bryan obtained leave of the general a little to *assay* them; and so with some horsemen charged them home. *Sir J. Hayward.*

What unweighed behaviour hath this drunkard picked out of my conversation, that he dares in this manner *assay* me? *Shakesp. Merry Wives of Windsor.*

2. To apply to, as the touchstone in *assaying* metals.

Whom thus afflicted, when sad Eve beheld,
Desolate where she sat, approaching nigh,
Soft words to his fierce passion she *assay'd*. *Par. Lost, b.* x.

3. To try; to endeavour.

David girded his sword upon his armour, and he *assayed* to go, for he had not proved it. 1 *Sam.* xvii. 39.

ASSA'YER. *n. s.* [from *assay.*] An officer of the mint, for the due trial of silver, appointed between the master of the mint and the merchants that bring silver thither for exchange. *Cowel.*

The smelters come up to the *assayers* within one in twenty. *Woodward on Fossils.*

ASSECTA'TION. *n. s.* [*assectatio*, Lat.] Attendance, or waiting upon. *Dict.*

ASSECU'TION. *n. s.* [from *assequor*, *assecutum*, to obtain.] Acquirement; the act of obtaining.

By the canon law, a person, after he has been in full possession of a second benefice, cannot return again to his first; because it is immediately void by his *assecution* of a second. *Ayliffe's Parergon Juris Canonici.*

ASSE'MBLAGE. *n. s.* [*assemblage*, Fr.] A collection; a number of individuals brought together. It differs from *assembly*, by being applied only, or chiefly, to things; *assembly* being used only, or generally, of persons.

All that we amass together in our thoughts is positive, and the *assemblage* of a great number of positive ideas of space or duration. *Locke.*

O Hartford, fitted or to shine in courts
With unaffected grace, or walk the plains,

With innocence and meditation join'd
In soft *assemblage*, listen to my song. *Thomson's Spring.*

To ASSE'MBLE. *v. a.* [*assembler*, Fr.] To bring together into one place. It is used both of persons and things.

And he shall set up an ensign for the nations, and shall *assemble* the outcasts of Israel, and gather together the dispersed of Judah. *Job*, xi. 12.

He wonders for what end you have *assembled*
Such troops of citizens to come to him. *Shak. Richard* III.

To ASSEMBLE. *v. n.* To meet together.

These men *assembled*, and found Daniel praying. *Dan.* vi. 11.

ASSE'MBLY. *n. s.* [*assemblée*, Fr.] A company met together.

Having heard, by fame,
Of this so noble, and so fair *assembly*,
This night to meet here, they could do no less,
Out of the great respect they bear to beauty. *Shak. H.* VIII.

ASSE'NT. *n. s.* [*assensus*, Lat.]

1. The act of agreeing to any thing.

All the arguments on both sides must be laid in balance, and, upon the whole, the understanding determine its *assent*. *Locke.*

2. Consent; agreement.

To urge any thing upon the church, requiring thereunto that religious *assent* of christian belief, wherewith the words of the holy prophets are received, and not to shew it in scripture; this did the Fathers evermore think unlawful, impious, and execrable. *Hooker, b.* ii. § 5.

The evidence of God's own testimony, added unto the natural *assent* of reason concerning the certainty of them, doth not a little comfort and confirm the same. *Hooker, b.* i. § 12.

Without the king's *assent* or knowledge,
You wrought to be a legate. *Shakesp. Henry* VIII.

Faith, on the other side, is the *assent* to any proposition, not thus made out by the deduction of reason, but upon the credit of the proposer. *Locke.*

To ASSE'NT. *v. n.* [*assentire*, Lat.] To concede; to yield to, or agree to.

And the Jews also *assented*, saying, that these things were so. *Acts*, xxiv. 9.

ASSENTA'TION. *n. s.* [*assentatio*, Lat.] Compliance with the opinion of another out of flattery or dissimulation. *Dict.*

ASSE'NTMENT. *n. s.* [from *assent*.] Consent.

We may shrink at their bare testimonies, whose arguments are but precarious, and subsist upon the charity of our *assentments*. *Brown's Vulgar Errours, b.* i.

To ASSE'RT. *v. a.* [*assero*, Lat.]

1. To maintain; to defend either by words or actions.

Your forefathers have *asserted* the party which they chose till death, and died for its defence. *Dryden's Virgil, Dedication.*

2. To affirm.

3. To claim; to vindicate a title to.

Nor can the grovelling mind,
In the dark dungeon of the limbs confin'd,
Assert the native skies, or own its heav'nly kind. *Dryden.*

ASSE'RTION. *n. s.* [from *assert*.] The act of asserting.

If any affirm the earth doth move, and will not believe with us it standeth still; because he hath probable reasons for it, and I no infallible sense or reason against it, I will not quarrel with his *assertion*. *Brown's Vulgar Errours, b.* i.

ASSE'RTIVE. *adj.* [from *assert*.] Positive; dogmatical; peremptory.

He was not so fond of the principles he undertook to illustrate, as to boast their certainty; proposing them not in a confident and *assertive* form, but as probabilities and hypotheses. *Glanv.*

ASSE'RTOR. *n. s.* [from *assert*.] Maintainer; vindicator; supporter; affirmer.

Among th' *assertors* of free reason's claim,
Our nation's not the least in worth or fame. *Dryden.*

Faithful *assertor* of thy country's cause,
Britain with tears shall bathe thy glorious wound. *Prior.*

It is an usual piece of art to undermine the authority of fundamental truths, by pretending to shew how weak the proofs are, which their *assertors* employ in defence of them. *Atterbury.*

To ASSE'RVE. *v. a.* [*asservio*, Lat.] To serve, help, or second. *Dict.*

To ASSE'SS. *v. a.* [from *assestare*, Ital. To make an equilibrium, or balance.] To charge with any certain sum.

Before the receipt of them in this office, they were *assessed* by the affidavit from the time of the inquisition found. *Bacon.*

ASSE'SSION. *n. s.* [*assessio*, Lat.] A sitting down by one; a giving assistance or advice. *Dict.*

ASSE'SSMENT. *n. s.* [from *to assess*.]

1. The sum levied on certain property.

2. The act of assessing.

What greater immunity and happiness can there be to a people, than to be liable to no laws, but what they make themselves? To be subject to no contribution, *assessment*, or any pecuniary levy whatsoever, but what they vote, and voluntarily yield unto themselves? *Howel's Pre-eminence of Parliam.*

ASSE'SSOR. *n. s.* [*assessor*, Lat.]

1. The person that sits by another; generally used of those who assist the judge.

Minos, the strict inquisitor, appears;
And lives and crimes, with his *assessors*, hears.
Round in his urn the blended balls he rowls,
Absolves the just, and dooms the guilty souls. *Dryden's Æn.*

2. He that sits by another as next in dignity.

To his Son,
Th' *assessor* of his throne, he thus began. *Par. Lost, b.* vi.

Twice stronger than his sire, who sat above,
Assessor to the throne of thund'ring Jove. *Dryden's Iliad.*

3. He that lays taxes; derived from *assess*.

A'SSETS. *n. s. without the singular.* [*assez*, Fr.] Goods sufficient to discharge that burden, which is cast upon the executor or heir, in satisfying the testators or ancestors debts or legacies. Whoever pleads *assets*, sayeth nothing; but that the person against whom he pleads, hath enough come to his hands, to discharge what is in demand. *Cowel.*

To ASSE'VER. } *v. a.* [*assevero*, Lat.] To affirm with great
To ASSE'VERATE. } solemnity, as upon oath.

ASSEVERA'TION. *n. s.* [from *asseverate*.] Solemn affirmation, as upon oath.

That which you are persuaded of, ye have it no otherwise than by your own only probable collection; and therefore such bold *asseverations*, as in him were admirable, should, in your mouths, but argue rashness. *Hooker, Preface.*

Another abuse of the tongue I might add; vehement *asseverations* upon slight and trivial occasions. *Ray on Creation.*

The repetition gives a greater emphasis to the words, and agrees better with the vehemence of the speaker in making his *asseveration*. *Broome's Notes on Odyssey.*

A'SSHEAD. *n. s.* [from *ass* and *head*.] One slow of apprehension; a blockhead.

Will you help an *asshead*, and a coxcomb, and a knave, a thin-faced knave, a gull. *Shakesp. Hamlet.*

ASSIDU'ITY. *n. s.* [*assiduité*, Fr. *assiduitas*, Lat.] Diligence; closeness of application.

Can he, who has undertaken this, want conviction of the necessity of his utmost vigour and *assiduity* to acquit himself of it? *Rogers.*

We observe the address and *assiduity* they will use to corrupt us. *Rogers.*

I have, with much pains and *assiduity*, qualified myself for a nomenclator. *Addison. Guardian*, N° 107.

ASSI'DUOUS. *adj.* [*assiduus*, Lat.] Constant in application.

And if by pray'r
Incessant I could hope to change the will
Of him who all things can, I would not cease
To weary him with my *assiduous* cries. *Parad. Lost, b.* xi.

The most *assiduous* talebearers, and bitterest revilers, are often half-witted people. *Government of the Tongue*, § 6.

In summer, you see the hen giving herself greater freedoms, and quitting her care for above two hours together; but in winter, when the rigour of the season would chill the principles of life, and destroy the young one, she grows more *assiduous* in her attendance, and stays away but half the time. *Addison. Spectator.*

Each still renews her little labour,
Nor justles her *assiduous* neighbour. *Prior.*

ASSI'DUOUSLY. *adv.* [from *assiduous*.] Diligently; continually.

The trade, that obliges artificers to be *assiduously* conversant with their materials, is that of glass-men. *Boyle.*

The habitable earth may have been perpetually the drier, seeing it is *assiduously* drained and exhausted by the seas. *Bentley.*

To ASSI'EGE. *v. a.* [*assieger*, Fr.] To besiege. *Dict.*

ASSIE'NTO. *n. s.* [In Spanish a contract or bargain.] A contract or convention between the king of Spain and other powers, for furnishing the Spanish dominions in America with negro slaves. This contract was transferred from the French to the English South-Sea company, by the treaty of 1713, for thirty years; who were likewise permitted to send a register ship, of 500 tuns, yearly to the Spanish settlements, with European goods. *Chambers.*

To ASSI'GN. *v. a.* [*assigner*, Fr. *assigno*, Lat.]

1. To mark out; to appoint.

He *assigned* Uriah unto a place where he knew that valiant men were. 2 *Sam.* xi. 16.

Both joining,
As join'd in injuries, one enmity
Against a foe by doom express *assign'd* us,
That cruel serpent. *Milt. Par. Lost, b.* x.

True quality is neglected, virtue is oppressed, and vice triumphant. The last day will *assign* to every one a station suitable to his character. *Addison. Spect.* N° 219.

2. To fix with regard to quantity or value.

There is no such intrinsick, natural, settled value in any thing, as to make any *assigned* quantity of it constantly worth any *assigned* quantity of another. *Locke.*

3. In law. In general, to appoint a deputy, or make over a right to another; in particular, to appoint or set forth, as to *assign* error, is to shew in what part of the process error is committed: to *assign* false judgment, is to declare how and where the judgment is unjust: to *assign* the cessor, is to shew how the plaintiff had cessed, or given over: to *assign* waste, is to shew wherein especially the waste is committed. *Cowel.*

ASSI'GNABLE. *adj.* [from *assign*.] That which may be marked out, or fixed.

Aristotle

Aristotle held that it streamed by connatural result and emanation from God; so that there was no instant *assignable* of God's eternal existence, in which the world did not also coexist. *South.*

ASSIGNA'TION. *n. s.* [*assignation*, French.]

1. An appointment to meet; used generally of love appointments.

The lovers expected the return of this stated hour with as much impatience as if it had been a real *assignation*. *Spectator.*

Or when a whore, in her vocation,
Keeps punctual to an *assignation*. *Swift.*

2. A making over a thing to another.

ASSIGNEE'. *n. s.* [*assigné*, Fr.] He that is appointed or deputed by another, to do any act, or perform any business, or enjoy any commodity. And an *assignee* may be either in deed or in law; *assignee* in deed, is he that is appointed by a person; *assignee* in law, is he whom the law maketh so, without any appointment of the person. *Cowel.*

ASSI'GNER. *n. s.* [from *assign.*] He that appoints.

The Gospel is at once the *assigner* of our tasks, and the magazine of our strength. *Decay of Piety.*

ASSI'GNMENT. *n. s.* [from *assign.*] Appointment of one thing with regard to another thing or person.

The only thing which maketh any place publick, is the publick *assignment* thereof unto such duties. *Hooker, b.* v. § 12.

This institution, which assigns it to a person, whom we have no rule to know, is just as good as an *assignment* to no body at all. *Locke.*

ASSI'MILABLE. *adj.* [from *assimilate.*] That which may be converted to the same nature with something else.

The spirits of many, long before that time, will find but naked habitations; and meeting no *assimilables* wherein to react their natures, must certainly participate such natural desolations. *Brown's Vulgar Errours, b.* vi.

To ASSI'MILATE. *v. a.* [*assimilo*, Lat.]

1. To convert to the same nature with another thing.

Birds *assimilate* less, and excern more, than beasts; for their excrements are ever liquid, and their flesh generally more dry. *Bacon's Nat. History.*

Birds be commonly better meat than beasts, because their flesh doth *assimilate* more finely, and secerneth more subtely. *Bacon's Nat. Hist.* N° 680.

Tasting concoct, digest, *assimilate*,
And corporeal to incorporeal turn. *Milt. Parad. Lost.*

Hence also animals and vegetables may *assimilate* their nourishment; moist nourishment easily changing its texture, till it becomes like the dense earth. *Newton.*

2. To bring to a likeness, or resemblance.

A ferine and necessitous kind of life would easily *assimilate* at least the next generation to barbarism and ferineness. *Hale's Origin of Mankind.*

They are not over patient of mixture; but such, whom they cannot *assimilate*, soon find it their interest to remove. *Swift.*

ASSI'MILATENESS. *n. s.* [from *assimilate.*] Likeness. *Dict.*

ASSIMILA'TION. *n. s.* [from *assimilate.*]

1. The act of converting any thing to the nature or substance of another.

It furthers the very act of *assimilation* of nourishment, by some outward emollients that make the parts more apt to assimilate. *Bacon's Natural History*, N° 59.

2. The state of being assimilated.

A nourishment in a large acceptation, but not in propriety, conserving the body, not repairing it by *assimilation*, but preserving it by ventilation. *Brown's Vulgar Errours, b.* iii.

3. The act of growing like some other being.

It is as well the instinct as duty of our nature, to aspire to an *assimilation* with God; even the most laudable and generous ambition. *Dec. of Piety.*

To ASSI'MULATE. *v. a.* [*assimulo*, Lat.] To feign; to counterfeit. *Dict.*

ASSIMULA'TION. *n. s.* [*assimulatio*, Lat.] A dissembling; a counterfeiting. *Dict.*

To ASSI'ST. *v. a.* [*assister*, Fr. *assisto*, Lat.] To help.

Receive her in the Lord, as becometh saints, and *assist* her in whatsoever business she hath need. *Rom.* xvi. 2.

It is necessary and *assisting* to all our other intellectual faculties. *Locke.*

Acquaintance with method will *assist* one in ranging human affairs. *Watts's Logick.*

She no sooner yielded to adultery, but she agreed to *assist* in the murder of her husband. *Broome on Odyssey.*

ASSI'STANCE. *n. s.* [*assistance*, French.] Help; furtherance.

The council of Trent commends recourse, not only to the prayers of the saints, but to their aid and *assistance*: What doth this aid and *assistance* signify? *Stillingfleet.*

You have abundant *assistances* for this knowledge, in excellent books. *Wake's Preparation for Death.*

Let us entreat this necessary *assistance*, that by his grace he would lead us. *Rogers.*

ASSI'STANT. *adj.* [from *assist.*] Helping; lending aid.

Some perchance did adhere to the duke, and were *assistant* to him openly, or at least under hand. *Hale's Com. Law of Engl.*

ASSI'STANT. *n. s.* [from *assist.*]

1. A person engaged in an affair not as principal, but as auxiliary or ministerial.

Some young towardly noblemen or gentlemen were usually sent as *assistants* or attendants, according to the quality of the persons. *Bacon's Advice to Sir George Villiers.*

2. Sometimes it is only a softer word for an attendant.

The pale *assistants* on each other star'd,
With gaping mouths for issuing words prepar'd. *Dryden.*

ASSI'ZE. *n. s.* [*assise*, a sitting, Fr.]

1. An assembly of knights and other substantial men, with the bailiff or justice, in a certain place, and at a certain time.

2. A jury.

3. An ordinance or statute.

4. The court, place, or time, where and when the writs and processes of *assize* are taken. *Cowel.*

The law was never executed by any justices of *assize*, but the people left to their own laws. *Sir J. Davies on Ireland.*

At each *assize* and term we try
A thousand rascals of as deep a dye. *Dryden's Juvenal.*

5. Any court of justice.

The judging God shall close the book of fate,
And there the last *assizes* keep,
For those who wake, and those who sleep. *Dryden.*

6. *Assize of bread, ale*, &c. Measure, or quantity. Thus it is said, *when wheat is of such a price, the bread shall be of such* assize.

7. Measure; rate: for which we now use *size*. See SIZE.

On high hill's top I saw a stately frame,
An hundred cubits high by just *assize*,
With hundred pillars. *Spen. Vision of Bellay.*

To ASSI'ZE. *v. a.* [from the noun.] To fix the rate of any thing by an *assize* or writ.

ASSI'ZER, or ASSISER. *n. s.* [from *assize.*] Is an officer that has the care and oversight of weights and measures. *Chambers.*

ASSO'CIABLE. *adj.* [*associabilis*, Lat.] That which may be joined to another.

To ASSO'CIATE. *v. a.* [*associer*, Fr. *associo*, Lat.]

1. To unite with another as a confederate.

A fearful army led by Caius Marcius,
Associated with Aufidius, rages
Upon our territories. *Shakesp. Coriolanus.*

2. To adopt as a friend upon equal terms.

Associate in your town a wand'ring train,
And strangers in your palace entertain. *Dryden's Æneid.*

3. To accompany; to keep company with another.

Friends should *associate* friends in grief and woe. *Shakesp. Titus Andronicus.*

4. It has generally the particle *with*; as, he *associated with* his master's enemies.

ASSO'CIATE. *adj.* [from the verb.] Confederate; joined in interest or purpose.

While I descend through darkness,
To my *associate* pow'rs, them to acquaint
With these successes. *Milt. Par. Lost, b.* x.

ASSO'CIATE. *n. s.* [from the verb.]

1. A person joined with another; a partner.

They persuade the king, now in old age, to make Plangus his *associate* in government with him. *Sidney, b.* ii.

2. A confederate.

Their defender, and his *associates*, have sithence proposed to the world a form such as themselves like. *Hooker, b.* v. § 27.

3. A companion; implying some kind of equality.

He was accompanied with a noble gentleman, no unsuitable *associate*. *Wotton.*

Sole Eve, *associate* sole, to me beyond
Compare, above all living creatures dear. *Milton's Paradise Lost, b.* ix.

But my *associates* now my stay deplore,
Impatient. *Pope's Odyssey.*

ASSOCIA'TION. *n. s.* [from *associate.*]

1. Union; conjunction; society.

The church being a society, hath the self-same original grounds, which other politick societies have; the natural inclination which all men have unto sociable life, and consent to some certain bond of *association*; which bond is the law that appointeth what kind of order they shall be associated in. *Hooker, b.* i.

2. Confederacy; union for particular purposes.

This could not be done but with mighty opposition: against which, to strengthen themselves, they secretly entered into a league of *association*. *Hooker, Preface.*

3. Partnership.

Self-denial is a kind of holy *association* with God; and, by making you his partner, interests you in all his happiness. *Boyle.*

4. Connection.

Association of ideas is of great importance, and may be of excellent use. *Watts's Improvement of the Mind.*

5. Apposition; union of matter.

The changes of corporeal things are to be placed only in the various separations, and new *associations* and motions of these permanent particles. *Newton's Opticks.*

A'SSONANCE. *n. s.* [*assonance*, Fr.] Reference of one sound to another resembling it. *Dict.*

A'SSONANT. *adj.* [*assonant*, French.] Sounding in a manner resembling another sound. *Dict.*

To ASSO'RT. *v. a.* [*assortir*, Fr.] To range in classes, as one thing suits with another.

To ASSO'T. *v. a.* [from *sot*; *assoter*, Fr.] To infatuate; to besot: a word out of use.

> But whence they sprung, or how they were begot,
> Uneath is to assure, uneath to weene
> That monstrous errour which doth some *assot*. *Fairy Queen.*

To ASSUA'GE. *v. a.* [The derivation of this word is uncertain; *Minshew* deduces it from *adsuadere*, or *assuaviare*; *Junius*, from ꞅꝩæꞅ, sweet; from whence *Skinner* imagines aꞅꝩæꞅan might have been formed.]

1. To mitigate; to soften; to allay.

> Refreshing winds the summer's heats *assuage*,
> And kindly warmth disarms the winter's rage. *Addison.*

2. To appease; to pacify.

> Yet is his hate, his rancour ne'er the less,
> Since nought *assuageth* malice when 'tis told. *Fairfax, b.* iv.

This was necessary for the securing the people from their fears; which were capable of being *assuaged* by no other means. *Clarendon, b.* viii.

> Shall I, t' *assuage*
> Their brutal rage,
> The regal stem destroy? *Dryden's Albion.*

3. To ease; as, the medecine *assuages* pain.

To ASSUA'GE. *v. n.* To abate.

God made a wind to pass over the earth, and the waters *assuaged*. *Gen.* viii. 1.

ASSUA'GEMENT. *n. s.* [from *assuage.*] What mitigates or softens.

> Tell me, when shall these weary woes have end,
> Or shall their ruthless torment never cease?
> But all my days in pining languor spend,
> Without hope of *assuagement* or release. *Spenser's Sonnets.*

ASSUA'GER. *n. s.* [from *assuage.*] One who pacifies or appeases.

ASSUA'SIVE. *adj.* [from *assuage.*] Softening; mitigating.

> If in the breast tumultuous joys arise.
> Musick her soft *assuasive* voice applies. *Pope's St. Cæcilia.*

To ASSU'BJUGATE. *v. a.* [*subjugo*, Lat.] To submit to.

> This valiant lord
> Must not so state his palm, nobly acquir'd;
> Nor by my will *assubjugate* his merit,
> By going to Achilles. *Shakesp. Troilus and Cressida.*

ASSUEFA'CTION. *n. s.* [*assuefacio*, Lat.] The state of being accustomed to any thing.

Right and left, as parts inservient unto the motive faculty, are differenced by degrees from use and *assuefaction*, or according whereto the one grows stronger. *Brown's Vulgar Errours.*

ASSU'ETUDE. *n. s.* [*assuetudo*, Lat.] Accustomance; custom.

We see that *assuetude* of things hurtful, doth make them lose the force to hurt. *Bacon's Nat. Hist.* N° 67.

To ASSU'ME. *v. a.* [*assumo*, Lat.]

1. To take.

> This when the various God had urg'd in vain,
> He strait *assum'd* his native form again. *Pope.*

2. To take upon one's self.

> With ravish'd ears,
> The monarch hears,
> *Assumes* the God,
> Affects to nod,
> And seems to shake the spheres. *Dryden's St. Cæcilia.*

3. To arrogate; to claim or seize unjustly.

This makes him over-forward in business, *assuming* in conversation, and peremptory in answers. *Collier of Confidence.*

4. To suppose something granted without proof.

In every hypothesis, something is allowed to be *assumed*. *Boyle.*

5. To apply to one's own use; to appropriate.

His majesty might well *assume* the complaint and expression of king David. *Clarendon, b.* viii.

ASSU'MER. *n. s.* [from *assume.*] An arrogant man; a man who claims more than his due.

Can man be wise in any course, in which he is not safe too? But can these high *assumers* and pretenders to reason, prove themselves so? *South.*

ASSU'MING. *participial adj.* [from *assume.*] Arrogant; haughty.

> His haughty looks, and his *assuming* air,
> The son of Isis could no longer bear. *Dryden.*

ASSU'MPSIT. n. s. [*assumo*, Lat.] A voluntary promise made by word, whereby a man taketh upon him to perform or pay any thing to another: It contains any verbal promise made upon consideration. *Cowel.*

ASSU'MPTION. *n. s.* [*assumptio*, Lat.]

1. The act of taking any thing to one's self.

The personal descent of God himself, and his *assumption* of our flesh to his divinity, more familiarly to insinuate his pleasure to us, was an enforcement beyond all methods of wisdom. *Hammond's Fundamentals.*

2. The supposition, or act of supposing of any thing without farther proof.

These by way of *assumption*, under the two general propositions, are intrinsically and naturally good or bad. *Norris.*

For the *assumption*, that Christ did such miraculous and supernatural works, to confirm what he said, we need only repeat the message sent by him to John the Baptist. *South.*

3. The thing supposed; a postulate.

> Hold, says the Stoick, your *assumption*'s wrong:
> I grant, true freedom you have well defin'd. *Dryd Persius.*

4. The taking up any person into heaven, which is supposed by the Romish church of the Blessed Virgin.

Upon the feast of the *assumption* of the Blessed Virgin, the pope and cardinals keep the vespers. *Stillingfl. on Rom. Idolat.*

Had Adam done this after a certain period of years, he would have been rewarded with an *assumption* to eternal felicity. *Wake's Preparation for Death.*

ASSU'MPTIVE. *adj.* [*assumptivus*, Lat.] That may be assumed.

ASSU'RANCE. *n. s.* [*assurance*, French.]

1. Certain expectation.

Though hope be, indeed, a lower and lesser thing than *assurance*, yet, as to all the purposes of a pious life, it may prove more useful. *South.*

What encouragement can be given to goodness, beyond the hopes of heaven, and the *assurance* of an endless felicity? *Tillot.*

2. Secure confidence; trust.

> What man is he, that boasts of fleshly might,
> And vain *assurance* of mortality,
> Which all so soon as it doth come to fight
> Against spiritual foes, yields by and by. *Fairy Queen, b.* i.

3. Freedom from doubt; certain knowledge.

I grant that proof from the authority of man's judgment, is not able to work that *assurance*, which doth grow by a stronger proof. *Hooker, b.* ii.

> 'Tis far off,
> And rather like a dream, than an *assurance*
> That my remembrance warrants. *Shakesp. Tempest.*

The obedient, and the man of practice, shall outgrow all their doubts and ignorances, till persuasion pass into knowledge, and knowledge advance into *assurance*. *South.*

Hath he found, in an evil course, that comfortable *assurance* of God's favour, and good hopes of his future condition, which a religious life would have given him? *Tillotson.*

4. Firmness; undoubting steadiness.

Men whose consideration will relieve our modesty, and give us courage and *assurance* in the duties of our profession. *Rogers.*

5. Confidence; want of modesty; exemption from awe or fear.

My behaviour ill governed, gave you the first comfort; my affection ill hid, hath given you this last *assurance*. *Sidney.*

Conversation, when they come into the world, will add to their knowledge and *assurance*. *Locke.*

6. Ground of confidence; security given.

The nature of desire itself is no easier to receive belief, than it is hard to ground belief; for as desire is glad to embrace the first shew of comfort, so is desire desirous of perfect *assurance*. *Sidney, b.* ii.

As the conquest was but slight and superficial, so the pope's donation to the Irish submissions were but weak and fickle *assurances*. *Sir J. Davies on Ireland.*

> None of woman born
> Shall harm Macbeth.———
> — Then live, Macduff, what need I fear of thee?
> But yet I'll make *assurance* double sure,
> And take a bond of fate; Thou shalt not live. *Shak. Macb.*
> I must confess your offer is the best;
> And, let your father make her the *assurance*,
> She is your own, else you must pardon me,
> If you should die before him, where's her dower.
> *Shakesp. Taming of the Shrew.*

7. Spirit; intrepidity.

> With all th' *assurance* innocence can bring,
> Fearless without, because secure within;
> Arm'd with my courage, unconcern'd I see
> This pomp, a shame to you, a pride to me. *Dryd. Aureng.*

8. Sanguinity; readiness to hope.

This is not the grace of hope, but a good natural *assurance* or confidence, which Aristotle observes young men to be full of, and old men not so inclined to. *Hammond's Pract. Cat.*

9. Testimony of credit.

> I am a gentleman of blood and breeding,
> And from some knowledge and *assurance* of you,
> Offer this office. *Shakesp. King Lear.*

We have as great *assurance* that there is a God, as we could expect to have, supposing that he were. *Tillotson, Preface.*

10. Conviction.

Such an *assurance* of things as will make men careful to avoid a lesser danger, ought to awaken men to avoid a greater. *Tillot.*

11. The same with *insurance*. See INSURANCE.

To ASSU'RE. *v. a.* [*asseurer*, Fr. from *assecurare*, low Latin.]

1. To give confidence by a firm promise.

So when he had *assured* them with many words, that he would restore them without hurt, according to the agreement, they let him go for the saving of their brethren. 2 *Mac.* xii. 25.

2. To secure to another.

And, for that dowry, I'll *assure* her of
Her widowhood, be it that she survives me,
In all my lands and leases whatsoever.
Shakesp. Taming of the Shrew.

So irresistible an authority cannot be reflected on, without the most awful reverence, even by those whose piety *assures* its favour to them. *Rogers.*

3 To make confident; to exempt from doubt or fear; to confer security.

And hereby we know, that we are of the truth, and shall *assure* our hearts before him. *1 John*, iii. 19.

I revive
At this last sight; *assur'd* that man shall live
With all the creatures, and their seed preserve. *Parad. Lost.*

4. To make secure.

But what on earth can long abide in state?
Or who can him *assure* of happy day? *Spens. Muiopotmos.*

5. To affiance; to betroth.

This diviner laid claim to me, called me Dromio, swore I was *assured* to her. *Shakesp. Comedy of Errours.*

Assu'red. *participial adj.* [from *assure.*]

1. Certain; indubitable.

It is an *assured* experience, that flint laid about the bottom of a tree makes it prosper. *Bacon's Nat. Hist.* N° 422.

2. Certain; not doubting.

Young princes, close your hands,
—— And your lips too; for, I am well assured,
That I did so, when I was first *assur'd.* *Shak. King John.*

As when by night the glass
Of Galilæo, less *assur'd*, observes
Imagin'd lands, and regions, in the moon. *Par. Lost*, b. v.

3. Immodest; viciously confident.

Assu'redly. *adv.* [from *assured.*] Certainly; indubitably.

They promis'd me eternal happiness,
And brought me garlands, Griffith, which I feel
I am not worthy yet to wear: I shall *assuredly.*
Shakesp. Henry VIII.

God is absolutely good, and so, *assuredly*, the cause of all that is good; but, of any thing that is evil, he is no cause at all. *Raleigh's Hist. of the World.*

Assuredly he will stop our liberty, till we restore him his worship. *South.*

Assu'redness. *n. s.* [from *assured.*] The state of being assured; certainty.

Assu'rer. *n. s.* [from *assure.*]

1. He that gives assurance.
2. He that gives security to make good any loss.

To ASSWAGE. See ASSUAGE.

A'sterisk. *n. s.* [ἀστερίσκος.] A mark in printing or writing, in form of a little star; as *.

He also published the translation of the Septuagint by itself, having first compared it with the Hebrew, and noted by *asterisks* what was defective, and by obelisks what was redundant. *Grew's Cosmol. Sacra*, b. iv.

A'sterism. *n. s.* [*asterismus*, Lat.]

1. A constellation.

Poetry had filled the skies with *asterisms*, and histories belonging to them; and then astrology devises the feigned virtues and influences of each. *Bentley's Sermons.*

2. An asterisk, or mark. This is a very improper use.

Dwell particularly on passages with an *asterism* *; for the observations which follow such a note, will give you a clear light. *Dryden's Dufresnoy.*

A'sthma. *n. s.* [ἆσθμα.] A frequent, difficult, and short respiration, joined with a hissing sound and a cough, especially in the night-time, and when the body is in a prone posture; because then the contents of the lower belly bear so against the diaphragm, as to lessen the capacity of the breast, whereby the lungs have less room to move. *Quincy.*

An *asthma* is the inflation of the membranes of the lungs, and of the membranes covering the muscles of the thorax, but does not continue long. *Floyer on the Humours.*

Asthma'tical. } *adj.* [from *asthma.*] Troubled with an
Asthma'tick. } asthma.

In *asthmatical* persons, we often see, that though the lungs be very much stuffed with tough phlegm, yet the patient may live some months, if not some years. *Boyle.*

After drinking, our horses are most *asthmatick*; and, for avoiding the watering of them, we wet their hay.
Floyer on the Humours.

Aste'rn. *adv.* [from *a* and *stern.*] In the hinder part of the ship; behind the ship.

The galley gives her side, and turns her prow,
While those *astern* descending down the steep,
Thro' gaping waves behold the boiling deep. *Dryden.*

To Aste'rt. *v. a.* [a word used by *Spenser*, as it seems, for *start*, or *startle.*] To terrify; to startle; to fright.

We deem of death, as doom of ill desert;
But knew we fools what it us brings until,
Die would we daily, once it to expert;
No danger there the shepherd can *astert.* *Spenser's Past.*

Asto'nied. *particip. adj.* A word used in the version of the bible for *astonished.*

Many were *astonied* at thee. *Isaiah*, lii. 14.

To ASTO'NISH. *v. a.* [*estonner*, Fr. from *attonitus*, Lat] To confound with some sudden passion, as with fear or wonder; to amaze; to surprise.

It is the part of men to fear and tremble,
When the most mighty gods, by tokens, send
Such dreadful heralds to *astonish* us. *Shak. Julius Cæsar.*

Astonish'd at the voice, he stood amaz'd,
And all around with inward horror gaz'd. *Addison's Ovid.*

A genius universal as his theme,
Astonishing as chaos. *Thomson's Summer.*

Asto'nishingness. *n. s.* [from *astonish.*] Of a nature to excite astonishment.

Asto'nishment. *n. s.* [*estonnement*, Fr.] Amazement; confusion of mind from fear or wonder.

We found, with no less wonder to us, than *astonishment* to themselves, that they were the two valiant and famous brothers. *Sidney*, b. ii.

She esteemed this as much above his wisdom, as *astonishment* is beyond bare admiration. *South.*

To Asto'und. *v. a.* [*estonner*, Fr.] To astonish; to confound with fear or wonder. This word is now somewhat obsolete.

These thoughts may startle well, but not *astound*
The virtuous mind, that ever walks attended
By a strong siding champion, conscience. *Paradise Regain.*

Astra'ddle. *adv.* [from *a* and *straddle.*] With one's legs across any thing. *Dict.*

A'stragal. *n. s.* [ἀστράγαλος, the ankle, or ankle-bone.] A little round member, in the form of a ring or bracelet, serving as an ornament at the tops and bottoms of columns. *Build. Dict.*

We see none of that ordinary confusion, which is the result of quarter rounds of the *astragal*, and I know not how many other intermingled particulars. *Spectator*, N° 415.

A'stral. *adj.* [from *astrum*, Lat.] Starry; relating to the stars.

Some *astral* forms I must invoke by pray'r,
Fram'd all of purest atoms of the air;
Not in their natures simply good or ill;
But most subservient to bad spirits will. *Dryd. Tyran. Love.*

Astra'y. *adv.* [from *a* and *stray.*] Out of the right way.

May seem the wain was very evil led,
When such an one had guiding of the way,
That knew not, whether right he went, or else *astray.* *F. Q.*

You run *astray*, for whilst we talk of Ireland, you rip up the original of Scotland. *Spenser on Ireland.*

Like one that had been led *astray*
Through the heav'n's wide pathless way. *Milt. Il Penseroso.*

To ASTRI'CT. *v. a.* [*astringo*, Lat.] To contract by applications, in opposition to *relax*: a word not so much used as *constringe.*

The solid parts were to be relaxed or *astricted*, as they let the humours pass either in too small or too great quantities.
Arbuthnot on Aliments.

Astri'ction. *n. s.* [*astrictio*, Lat.] The act or power of contracting the parts of the body by applications.

Astriction is in a substance that hath a virtual cold; and it worketh partly by the same means that cold doth. *Bacon.*

This virtue requireth an *astriction*, but such an *astriction* as is not grateful to the body; for a pleasing *astriction* doth rather bind in the nerves than expel them: and therefore such *astriction* is found in things of a harsh taste. *Bacon's Nat. History.*

Such lenitive substances are proper for dry atrabilarian constitutions, who are subject to *astriction* of the belly and the piles.
Arbuthnot on Diet.

Astri'ctive. *adj.* [from *astrict.*] Stiptick; of a binding quality. *Dict.*

Astri'ctory. *adj.* [*astrictorius*, Lat.] Astringent; apt to bind. *Dict.*

Astri'de. *adv.* [from *a* and *stride.*] With the legs open.

To lay their native arms aside,
Their modesty, and ride *astride.* *Hudibras.*

I saw a place, where the Rhone is so straitened between two rocks, that a man may stand *astride* upon both at once. *Boyle.*

Astri'ferous. *adj.* [*astrifer*, Lat.] Bearing, or having stars *D.*

Astri'gerous. *adj.* [*astriger*, Lat.] Adorned with stars. *Dict.*

To ASTRI'NGE. *v. a.* [*astringo*, Lat.] To press by contraction; to make the parts draw together.

Tears are caused by a contraction of the spirits of the brain; which contraction, by consequence, *astringeth* the moisture of the brain, and thereby sendeth tears into the eyes. *Bacon.*

Astri'ngency. *n. s.* [from *astringe.*] The power of contracting the parts of the body; opposed to the power of *relaxation.*

Astriction prohibiteth dissolution; as, in medicines, astringents inhibit putrefaction: and, by *astringency*, some small quantity of oil of vitriol will keep fresh water long from putrefying.
Bacon's Natural History, N° 342.

Acid, acrid, austere, and bitter substances, by their *astringency*, create horrour, that is, stimulate the fibres. *Arbuthnot.*

Astri'ngent. *adj.* [*astringens*, Lat.] Binding; contracting; opposed to *laxative.*

Aſtringent medicines are binding, which act by the aſperity of their particles, whereby they corrugate the membranes, and make them draw up cloſer. *Quincy.*

The juice is very *aſtringent*, and therefore of ſlow motion. *Bacon's Nat. Hiſt.* Nº 641.

What diminiſheth ſenſible perſpiration, encreaſeth the inſenſible; for that reaſon a ſtrengthening and *aſtringent* diet often conduceth to this purpoſe. *Arbuthnot on Aliments.*

A'STROGRAPHY. *n. ſ.* [from ἄϛρον and γραφω.] The ſcience of deſcribing the ſtars. *Dict.*

A'STROLABE. *n. ſ.* [ἀϛρολάβιον, of ἀϛὴρ, and λαβεῖν, to take.]

1. An inſtrument chiefly uſed for taking the altitude of the pole, the ſun or ſtars, at ſea.

2. A ſtereographick projection of the circles of the ſphere upon the plain of ſome great circle. *Chambers.*

ASTRO'LOGER. *n. ſ.* [*aſtrologus*, Lat. from ἄϛρον and λόγος.]

1. One that, ſuppoſing the influences of the ſtars to have a cauſal power, profeſſes to foretel or diſcover events depending on thoſe influences.

Not unlike that which *aſtrologers* call a conjunction of planets, of no very benign aſpect the one to the other. *Wotton.*

A happy genius is the gift of nature: it depends on the influence of the ſtars, ſay the *aſtrologers*; on the organs of the body, ſay the naturaliſts; it is the particular gift of heaven, ſay the divines, both chriſtians and heathens. *Dryd. Pr. Dufr.*

Aſtrologers, that future fates foreſhew. *Pope.*

I never heard a finer ſatire againſt lawyers, than that of *aſtrologers*, when they pretend, by rules of art, to tell when a ſuit will end, and whether to the advantage of the plaintiff or defendant. *Swift.*

2. It was antiently uſed for one that underſtood or explained the motions of the planets, without including prediction.

A worthy *aſtrologer* now living, who, by the help of perſpective glaſſes, hath found in the ſtars many things unknown to the ancients, affirms much to have been diſcovered in Venus. *Raleigh's Hiſt. of the World.*

ASTROLO'GIAN. *n. ſ.* [from *aſtrology*.] The ſame with *aſtrologer*.

The twelve houſes of heaven, in the form which *aſtrologians* uſe. *Camden.*

The ſtars, they ſay, cannot diſpoſe,
No more than can the *aſtrologian*. *Hudibras.*

ASTROLO'GICAL. } *adj.* [from *aſtrology*.] Relating to aſtrology;
ASTROLO'GICK. } profeſſing aſtrology.

Some ſeem a little *aſtrological*, as when they warn us from places of malign influence. *Wotton.*

No *aſtrologick* wizard honour gains,
Who has not oft been baniſh'd, or in chains. *Dryd. Juv.*

Aſtrological prayers ſeem to me to be built on as good reaſon as the predictions. *Stillingfl. Def. of Diſc. on R. Idol.*

The poetical fables are more ancient than the *aſtrological* influences, that were not known to the Greeks till after Alexander the Great. *Bentley's Sermons.*

ASTROLO'GICALLY. *adv.* [from *aſtrology*.] In an aſtrological manner.

To ASTRO'LOGIZE. *v. n.* [from *aſtrology*.] To practiſe aſtrology.

ASTRO'LOGY. *n. ſ.* [*aſtrologia*, Lat.] The practice of foretelling things by the knowledge of the ſtars; an art now generally exploded, as without reaſon.

I know it hath been the opinion of the learned, who think of the art of *aſtrology*, that the ſtars do not force the actions or wills of men. *Swift.*

ASTRO'NOMER. *n. ſ.* [from ἄϛρον, a ſtar, and νόμος, a rule or law.] He that ſtudies the celeſtial motions, and the rules by which they are governed.

The motions of factions under kings, ought to be like the motions, as the *aſtronomers* ſpeak of, in the inferiour orbs. *Bacon.*

The old and new *aſtronomers* in vain
Attempt the heav'nly motions to explain. *Blackmore.*

Since *aſtronomers* no longer doubt of the motion of the planets about the ſun, it is fit to proceed upon that hypotheſis. *Locke.*

ASTRONO'MICAL. } *adj.* [from *aſtronomy*.] Belonging to aſtro-
ASTRONO'MICK. } nomy.

Our forefathers marking certain mutations to happen in the ſun's progreſs through the zodiack, they regiſtrate and ſet them down in their *aſtronomical* canons. *Brown's Vulgar Errours.*

Can he not paſs an *aſtronomick* line,
Or does he dread th' imaginary ſign,
That he ſhould ne'er advance to either pole. *Blackmore.*

ASTRONO'MICALLY. *adv.* [from *aſtronomical*.] In an aſtronomical manner.

ASTRO'NOMY. *n. ſ.* [ἀϛρονομία, from ἄϛρον, a ſtar, and νόμος, a law, or rule.] A mixed mathematical ſcience teaching the knowledge of the celeſtial bodies, their magnitudes, motions, diſtances, periods, eclipſes, and order. The origin of *aſtronomy* is uncertain; but from Egypt it travelled into Greece, where Pythagoras was the firſt European who taught that the earth and planets turn round the ſun, which ſtands immoveable in the center; as he himſelf had been inſtructed by the Egyptian prieſts. From the time of Pythagoras, *aſtronomy* ſunk into neglect, till it was revived by the Ptolemys, kings of Egypt; and the Saracens, after their conqueſt of that country, having acquired ſome knowledge of it, brought it from Africa to Spain, and again reſtored this ſcience to Europe, where it has ſince received very conſiderable improvements. *Chambers.*

To this muſt be added the underſtanding of the globes, and the principles of geometry and *aſtronomy*. *Cowley.*

A'STROSCOPY. *n. ſ.* [ἀϛὴρ, a ſtar, and σκοπέω, to view.] Obſervation of the ſtars. *Dict.*

ASTRO-THEOLOGY. *n. ſ.* [from *aſtrum*, a ſtar, and *theologia*, divinity.] Divinity founded on the obſervation of the celeſtial bodies.

That the diurnal and annual revolutions are the motions of the terraqueous globe, not of the ſun, I ſhew in the preface of my *Aſtro-Theology*. *Derham's Phyſico-Theology.*

ASU'NDER. *adv.* [aſunꝺnan, Sax.] Apart; ſeparately; not together.

Two indirect lines, the further that they are drawn out, the further they go *aſunder*. *Spenſer on Ireland.*

Senſe thinks the planets ſpheres not much *aſunder*;
What tells us then their diſtance is ſo far. *Sir J. Davies.*

Greedy hope to find
His wiſh, and beſt advantage, us *aſunder*. *Paradiſe Loſt, b.* ix.

The fall'n archangel, envious of our ſtate,
Seeks hid advantage to betray us worſe;
Which, when *aſunder*, will not prove too hard,
For both together are each other's guard. *Dryd. State of Inn.*

Born far *aſunder* by the tides of men,
Like adamant and ſteel they meet agen. *Dryd. Fables.*

All this metallick matter, both that which continued *aſunder*, and in ſingle corpuſcles, and that which was amaſſed and concreted into nodules, ſubſided. *Woodward's Nat. Hiſt.*

ASY'LUM. *n. ſ.* [Lat. ἄσυλον, from α. not, and συλάω, to pillage.] A place out of which he that has fled to it, may not be taken; a ſanctuary; a refuge.

So ſacred was the church to ſome, that it had the right of an *aſylum*, or ſanctuary. *Ayliffe's Parergon.*

ASY'MMETRY. *n. ſ.* [from α, without, and συμμετρία, ſymmetry.]

1. Contrariety to ſymmetry; diſproportion.

The *aſymmetries* of the brain, as well as the deformities of the legs or face, may be rectified in time. *Grew's Coſm. Sacra.*

2. This term is ſometimes uſed in mathematicks, for what is more uſually called incommenſurability; when between two quantities there is no common meaſure.

A'SYMPTOTE. *n. ſ.* [from α, priv. σὺν, with, and πτόω, to fall; which never meet; incoincident.] *Aſymptotes* are right lines, which approach nearer and nearer to ſome curve; but which, though they and their curve were infinitely continued, would never meet; and may be conceived as tangents to their curves at an infinite diſtance. *Chambers.*

Aſymptote lines, though they may approach ſtill nearer together, till they are nearer than the leaſt aſſignable diſtance, yet, being ſtill produced infinitely, will never meet. *Grew's Coſm.*

ASYMPTO'TICAL. *adj.* [from *aſymptote*.] Curves are ſaid to be *aſymptotical*, when they continually approach, without a poſſibility of meeting.

ASY'NDETON. *n. ſ.* [ἀσύνδετον, of α, priv. and συνδέω, to bind together.] A figure in grammar, when a conjunction copulative is omitted in a ſentence; as in *veni, vidi, vici,* &c is left out.

AT. *prep.* [æt, Saxon.]

1. *At* before a place, notes the nearneſs of the place; as, a man is *at* the houſe before he is *in* it.

This cuſtom continued among many, to ſay their prayers *at* fountains. *Stillingfleet's Def. of Diſc. on Romiſh Idolatry.*

To all you ladies now *at* land
We men *at* ſea indite. *Buckhurſt.*

2. *At* before a word ſignifying time, notes the coexiſtenceof the time with the event; the word *time* is ſometimes included in the adjective.

We thought it *at* the very firſt a ſign of cold affection. *Hooker.*

How frequent to deſert him, and *at* laſt
To heap ingratitude on worthieſt deeds. *Milt. Samp. Agon.*

At the ſame time that the ſtorm beats upon the whole ſpecies, we are falling foul upon one another. *Addiſon. Spect.*

We made no efforts at all, where we could have moſt weakened the common enemy, and, *at* the ſame time, enriched ourſelves. *Swift.*

3. *At* before a cauſal word ſignifies nearly the ſame as *with*.

At his touch,
Such ſanctity hath heav'n giv'n his hand,
They preſently amend. *Shakeſp. Macbeth.*

O ſir, when he ſhall hear of your approach,
If that young Arthur be not gone already,
Ev'n *at* this news he dies. *Shakeſp. King John.*

Much *at* the ſight was Adam in his heart
Diſmay'd. *Milton's Paradiſe Loſt, b.* xi.

High o'er their heads a moulding rock is plac'd,
That promiſes a fall, and ſhakes *at* ev'ry blaſt. *Dryden.*

4. *At* before a ſuperlative adjective implies *in the ſtate*, as *at moſt*, in the ſtate of moſt perfection, &c.

Consider any man as to his personal powers, they are not great; for, *at* greatest, they must still be limited. *South.*

We bring into the world with us a poor needy uncertain life, short *at* the longest, and unquiet *at* the best. *Temple.*

5. *At* before a person, is seldom used otherwise than ludicrously; as, he longed to be *at* him, that is, to attack him.

6. *At* before a substantive sometimes signifies the particular condition or circumstances of the person; as, *at* peace, in a state of peace.

Under pardon,
You are much more *at* task for want of wisdom,
Than prais'd for harmful mildness. *Shakesp. King Lear.*

It bringeth the treasure of a realm into a few hands: for the usurer being *at* certainties, and others *at* uncertainties, at the the end of the game most of the money will be in the box. *Bac.*

Hence walk'd the fiend *at* large in spacious field. *P. Lost.*

The rest, for whom no lot is yet decreed,
May run in pastures, and *at* pleasure feed. *Dryden's Virgil.*

Deserted, *at* his utmost need,
By those his former bounty fed. *Dryden's St. Cæcilia.*

What hinder'd either in their native soil,
At ease to reap the harvest of their toil. *Dryden's Fables.*

Wise men are sometimes over-borne, when they are taken *at* a disadvantage. *Collier of Confidence.*

These have been the maxims they have been guided by: take these from them, and they are perfectly *at* a loss, their compass and pole-star then are gone, and their understanding is perfectly *at* a nonplus. *Locke.*

One man manages four horses at once, and leaps from the back of another *at* full speed. *Pope's Essay on Homer's Battles.*

They will not let me be *at* quiet in my bed, but pursue me to my very dreams. *Swift.*

7. *At* before a substantive sometimes marks employment or attention.

We find some arrived to that sottishness, as to own roundly what they would be *at*. *South.*

How d'ye find yourself, says the doctor to his patient? A little while after he is *at* it again, with a pray how d'ye find your body? *L'Estrange.*

But she who well enough knew what,
Before he spoke, he would be *at*,
Pretended not to apprehend. *Hudibras.*

The creature's *at* his dirty work again. *Pope.*

8. *At* sometimes the same with *furnished with*, after the French *a.*

Infuse his breast with magnanimity,
And make him naked foil a man *at* arms. *Shak. Henry VI.*

9. *At* sometimes notes the place where any thing is, or acts.

Your husband is *at* hand, I hear his trumpet. *Sh. M. of Ven.*

He that in tracing the vessels began *at* the heart, though he thought not at all of a circulation; yet made he the first true step towards the discovery. *Grew's Cosmologia Sacra.*

There various news I heard, of love and strife,
Of storms *at* sea, and travels on the shore. *Pope.*

10. *At* sometimes signifies in consequence of.

Impeachments *at* the prosecution of the house of commons, have received their determinations in the house of lords. *Hale.*

11. *At* marks sometimes the effect proceeding from an act.

Rest in this tomb, rais'd *at* thy husband's cost. *Dryden.*

Tom has been *at* the charge of a penny upon this occasion. *Addison. Spectator*, N° 482.

Those may be of use to confirm by authority, what they will not be *at* the trouble to deduce by reasoning. *Arbuth. on Alim.*

12. *At* sometimes is nearly the same as *in*, noting situation.

She hath been known to come *at* the head of these rascals, and beat her lover. *Swift.*

13. *At* sometimes marks the occasion, like *on.*

Others, with more helpful care,
Cry'd out aloud, Beware, brave youth, beware!
At this he turn'd, and, as the bull drew near,
Shunn'd, and receiv'd him on his pointed spear. *Dryden.*

14. *At* sometimes seems to signify in the power of, or obedient to.

But thou of all the kings, Jove's care below,
Art least *at* my command, and most my foe. *Dryd. Iliad.*

15. *At* sometimes notes the relation of a man to an action.

To make pleasure the vehicle of health, is a doctor *at* it in good earnest. *Collier of Friendship.*

16. *At* sometimes imports the manner of an action.

One warms you by degrees, the other sets you on fire all *at* once, and never intermits his heat. *Dryden's Fables, Pref.*

Not with less ruin than the Bajan mole,
At once comes tumbling down. *Dryden's Æneid.*

17. *At*, like the French *chez*, means sometimes application to, or dependence on.

The worst authors might endeavour to please us, and in that endeavour deserve something *at* our hands. *Pope.*

18. *At all.* In any manner; in any degree.

Nothing more true than what you once let fall,
Most women have no characters *at all.* *Pope.*

A'TABAL. *n. s.* A kind of tabour used by the Moors.

Children shall beat our *atabals* and drums,
And all the noisy trades of war no more
Shall wake the peaceful morn. *Dryden's Don Sebastian.*

ATARA'XIA. } *n. s.* [ἀταραξία.] Exemption from vexation;
A'TARAXY. } tranquillity.

The scepticks affected an indifferent equiponderous neutrality, as the only means to their *ataraxia*, and freedom from passionate disturbances. *Glanville's Scepsis Scientifica.*

ATE. The preterite of *eat.* See TO EAT.

And by his side, his steed the grassy forage *ate.* *Fairy Q.*

Even our first parents *ate* themselves out of paradise; and Job's children junketted and feasted together often. *South.*

ATHA'NOR. *n. s.* [a chymical term, borrowed from ἀθάνατος; or, as others think, תנור.] A digesting furnace, to keep heat for some time; so that it may be augmented or diminished at pleasure, by opening or shutting some apertures made on purpose with sliders over them, called registers. *Quincy.*

A'THEISM. *n. s.* [from *atheist.* It is only of two syllables in poetry.] The disbelief of a God.

God never wrought miracles to convince *atheism*, because his ordinary works convince it. *Bacon's Essays.*

It is the common interest of mankind, to punish all those who would seduce men to *atheism.* *Tillotson.*

A'THEIST. *n. s.* [ἄθεος, without God.] One that denies the existence of God.

To these, that sober race of men, whose lives
Religious, titled them the sons of God,
Shall yield up all their virtue, all their fame,
Ignobly! to the trains, and to the smiles
Of these fair *atheists.* *Milton's Paradise Lost, b.* xi.

Though he were really a speculative *atheist*, yet if he would but proceed rationally, he could not however be a practical *atheist*, nor live without God in this world. *South.*

Atheist, use thine eyes,
And having view'd the order of the skies,
Think, if thou canst, that matter blindly hurl'd,
Without a guide, should frame this wond'rous world. *Creech.*

No *atheist*, as such, can be a true friend, an affectionate relation, or a loyal subject. *Bentley's Sermons.*

ATHEIST. *adj.* Atheistical; denying God.

Nor stood unmindful Abdiel to annoy
The *atheist* crew. *Milton's Paradise Lost, b.* vi.

ATHEI'STICAL. *adj.* [from *atheist.*] Given to atheism; impious.

Men are *atheistical*, because they are first vicious; and question the truth of christianity, because they hate the practice. *South.*

ATHEI'STICALLY. *adv.* [from *atheistical.*] In an atheistical manner.

Is it not enormous, that a divine, hearing a great sinner talk *atheistically*, and scoff profanely at religion, should, instead of vindicating the truth, tacitely approve the scoffer. *South.*

I entreat such as are *atheistically* inclined, to consider these things. *Tillotson.*

ATHEI'STICALNESS. *n. s.* [from *atheistical.*] The quality of being atheistical.

Lord, purge out of all hearts profaneness and *atheisticalness.* *Hammond's Fundamentals.*

ATHEI'STICK. *adj.* [from *atheist.*] Given to atheism.

This argument demonstrated the existence of a Deity, and convinced all *atheistick* gainsayers. *Ray on the Creation.*

A'THEL, ATHELING, ADEL, and ÆTHEL. [from *adel*, noble, Germ.] So *Æthelred* is *noble for counsel*; *Æthelard, a noble genius*; *Æthelbert, eminently noble*; *Æthelward, a noble protector.* *Gibson's Camden.*

A'THEOUS. *adj.* [ἄθεος.] Atheistick; godless.

Thy Father, who is holy, wise, and pure,
Suffers the hypocrite, or *atheous* priest,
To tread his sacred courts. *Paradise Regained, b.* i.

ATHERO'MA. *n. s.* [ἀθέρωμα, from ἀθέρα, pap or pulse.] A species of wen, which neither causes pain, discolours the skin, nor yields easily to the touch.

If the matter forming them, resembles milk curds, the tumour is called *atheroma*; if it be like honey, meliceris; and if composed of fat, or a suety substance, steatoma. *Sharp.*

ATHERO'MATOUS. *adj.* [from *atheroma.*] Having the qualities of an atheroma, or curdy wen.

Feeling the matter fluctuating, I thought it *atheromatous.* *Wiseman's Surgery.*

ATHI'RST. *adv.* [from *a* and *thirst.*] Thirsty; in want of drink.

With scanty measure then supply their food;
And, when *athirst*, restrain 'em from the flood. *Dryden.*

ATHLE'TICK. *adj.* [from *athleta*, Lat. ἀθλητής, a wrestler.]

1. Belonging to wrestling.

2. Strong of body; vigorous; lusty; robust.

Seldom shall one see in rich families that *athletick* soundness and vigour of constitution, which is seen in cottages, where nature is cook, and necessity caterer. *South.*

Science distinguishes a man of honour from one of those *athletick* brutes, whom undeservedly we call heroes. *Dryden.*

ATHWA'RT. *prep.* [from *a* and *thwart.*]

1. Across; transverse to any thing.

Themistocles made Xerxes post out of Grecia, by giving out a purpose to break his bridge *athwart* the Hellespont. *Bacon's Essays.*

Execrable

Execrable shape!
That dar'st, though grim and terrible, advance
Thy miscreated front *athwart* my way. *Parad. Lost, b.* ii.

2. Through.
Now, *athwart* the terrors that thy vow
Has planted round thee, thou appear'st more fair. *Add. Cato.*

ATHW'ART. *adv.*

1. In a manner vexatious and perplexing; crossly.
All *athwart* there came
A post from Wales, loaden with heavy news. *Sh. Hen.* IV.

2. Wrong.
The baby beats the nurse, and quite *athwart*
Goes all decorum. *Shakesp. Measure for Measure.*

ATI'LT. *adv.* [from *a* and *tilt.*]

1. In the manner of a tilter; with the action of a man making a thrust at an antagonist.
In the city Tours,
Thou ran'st *atilt*, in honour of my love,
And stol'st away the ladies hearts from France. *Sh. Hen.* VI.
To run *atilt* at men, and wield
Their naked tools in open field. *Hudibras, p.* i. *c.* i.

2. In the posture of a barrel raised or tilted behind, to make it run out.
Such a man is always *atilt*; his favours come hardly from him. *Spectator.*

A'TLAS. *n. s.*

1. A collection of maps, so called probably from a picture of *Atlas* supporting the heavens, prefixed to some collection.
2. A large square folio; so called from these folios, which, containing maps, were made large and square.
3. Sometimes the supporters of a building.
4. A rich kind of silk or stuff made for women's cloaths.
I have the conveniency of buying Dutch *atlasses* with gold and silver, or without. *Spectator*, N° 288.

A'TMOSPHERE. *n. s.* [ἀτμὸς, vapour, and σφαῖρα, a sphere.]
The exteriour part of this our habitable world is the air, or *atmosphere*; a light, thin, fluid, or springy body, that encompasses the solid earth on all sides. *Locke.*
It is generally supposed to be about forty-five miles high.
Immense the whole excited *atmosphere*
Impetuous rushes o'er the sounding world. *Thomson's Aut.*

[A]TMOSPHE'RICAL. *adj.* [from *atmosphere.*] Consisting of the atmosphere; belonging to the atmosphere.
We did not mention the weight of the incumbent *atmospherical* cylinder, as a part of the weight resisted. *Boyle.*

[A]'TOM. *n. s.* [*atomus*, Lat. ἄτομος.]

[1]. Such a small particle as cannot be physically divided: and these are the first rudiments, or the component parts of all bodies. *Quin.*
Innumerable minute bodies are called *atoms*, because, by reason of their perfect solidity, they were really indivisible. *Ray.*
See plastick nature working to this end,
The single *atoms* each to other tend,
Attract, attracted to, the next in place,
Form'd and impell'd its neighbour to embrace. *Pope.*

[2]. Any thing extremely small.
It is as easy to count *atoms*, as to resolve the propositions of a lover. *Shakesp. As you like it.*

[A]TO'MICAL. *adj.* [from *atom.*]

[1]. Consisting of atoms.
Vitrified and pellucid bodies are clearer in their continuities, than in powders and *atomical* divisions. *Brown's Vulgar Err.*

[2]. Relating to atoms.
Vacuum is another principal doctrine of the *atomical* philosophy. *Bentley's Sermons.*

[A']TOMIST. *n. s.* [from *atom.*] One that holds the *atomical* philosophy, or doctrine of atoms.
The *atomists*, who define motion to be a passage from one place to another, what do they more than put one synonymous word for another? *Locke.*
Now can judicious *atomists* conceive,
Chance to the sun could his just impulse give? *Blackmore.*

[A']TOMY. *n. s.* An obsolete word for *atom.*
Drawn with a team of little *atomies*,
Athwart men's noses, as they be asleep. *Shak. Rom. and Jul.*

[T]o ATO'NE. *v. n.* [from *at one*, as the etymologists remark, *to be at one*, is the same as *to be in concord.* This derivation is much confirmed by the following passage.]

[1]. To agree; to accord.
He and Aufidus can no more *atone*,
Than violentest contrariety. *Shakesp. Coriolanus.*

[2]. To stand as an equivalent for something; and particularly used of expiatory sacrifices; with the particle *for* before the thing for which something else is given.
From a mean stock the pious Decii came;
Yet such their virtues, that their loss alone,
For Rome and all our legions did *atone.* *Dryden's Juvenal.*
The good intention of a man of weight and worth, or a real friend, seldom *atones for* the uneasiness produced by his grave representations. *Locke.*
Let thy sublime meridian course
For Mary's setting rays *atone*:
Our lustre, with redoubl'd force,
Must now proceed from thee alone. *Prior.*

His virgin sword Ægysthus' veins imbru'd;
The murd'rer fell, and blood *aton'd for* blood. *Pope's Odyss.*

To ATO'NE. *v. a.* To expiate; to answer for.
Soon should yon' boasters cease their haughty strife,
Or each *atone* his guilty love with life. *Pope's Odyssey.*

ATO'NEMENT. *n. s.* [from *atone.*]

1. Agreement; concord.
He seeks to make *atonement*
Between the duke of Glo'ster and your brothers. *Sh. R.* III.

2. Expiation; expiatory equivalent; with *for.*
And the Levites were purified, and they washed their cloaths: and Aaron offered them as an offering before the Lord; and Aaron made an *atonement for* them to cleanse them. *Num.* viii. 21.
Surely it is not a sufficient *atonement for* the writers, that they profess loyalty to the government, and sprinkle some arguments in favour of the dissenters, and, under the shelter of popular politicks and religion, undermine the foundations of all piety and virtue. *Swift on the Sentiments of a Church of England man.*

ATO'P. *adv.* [from *a* and *top.*] On the top; at the top.
Atop whereof, but far more rich, appear'd
The work as of a kingly palace-gate. *Par. Lost, b.* iii.
What is extracted by water from coffee is the oil, which often swims *atop* of the decoction. *Arbuthnot on Aliments.*

ATRABILA'RIAN. *adj.* [from *atra bilis*, black choler.] Melancholy; replete with black choler.
The *atrabilarian* constitution, or a black, viscous, pitchy consistence of the fluids, makes all secretions difficult and sparing. *Arbuthnot on Diet.*

ATRABILA'RIOUS. *adj.* [from *atra bilis*, black choler.] Melancholick.
The blood, deprived of its due proportion of serum, or finer and more volatile parts, is *atrabilarious*; whereby it is rendered gross, black, unctuous, and earthy. *Quincy.*
From this black adust state of the blood, they are *atrabilarious.* *Arbuthnot on Air.*

ATRABILA'RIOUSNESS. *n. s.* [from *atrabilarious.*] The state of being melancholy; repletion with melancholy.

ATRAME'NTAL. *adj.* [from *atramentum*, ink. Lat.] Inky; black.
If we enquire in what part of vitriol this *atramental* and denigrating condition lodgeth, it will seem especially to lie in the more fixed salt thereof. *Brown's Vulgar Errours, b.* vi.

ATRAME'NTOUS. *adj.* [from *atramentum*, ink, Lat.] Inky; black.
I am not satisfied, that those black and *atramentous* spots, which seem to represent them, are ocular. *Brown's Vulg. Err.*

ATRO'CIOUS. *adj.* [*atrox*, Lat.] Wicked in a high degree; enormous; horribly criminal.
An advocate is necessary, and therefore audience ought not to be denied him in defending causes, unless it be an *atrocious* offence. *Ayliffe's Parergon.*

ATRO'CIOUSLY. *adv.* [from *atrocious.*] In an atrocious manner; with great wickedness.

ATRO'CIOUSNESS. *n. s.* [from *atrocious.*] The quality of being enormously criminal.

ATRO'CITY. *n. s.* [*atrocitas*, Lat.] Horrible wickedness; excess of wickedness.
I never recall it to mind, without a deep astonishment of the very horrour and *atrocity* of the fact in a christian court. *Wotton.*
They desired justice might be done upon offenders, as the *atrocity* of their crimes deserved. *Clarendon.*

A'TROPHY. *n. s.* [ἀτροφία.] Want of nourishment; a disease in which what is taken at the mouth cannot contribute to the support of the body.
Pining *atrophy*,
Marasmus, and wide-wasting pestilence. *Par. Lost, b.* xi.
The mouths of the lacteals may be shut up by a viscid mucus, in which case the chyle passeth by stool, and the person falleth into an *atrophy.* *Arbuthnot on Aliments.*

To ATTA'CH. *v. a.* [*attacher*, Fr.]

1. To arrest; to take or apprehend by commandment or writ. *Cowel.*
Eftsoons the guard, which on his state did wait,
Attach'd that traitor false, and bound him strait. *Fairy Q.*
The Tower was chosen, that if Clifford should accuse great ones, they might, without suspicion or noise, be presently *attached.* *Bacon's Henry* VII.
Bohemia greets you,
Desires you to *attach* his son, who has
His dignity and duty both cast off. *Shakesp. Winter's Tale.*

2. Sometimes with the particle *of*, but not in present use.
You, lord archbishop, and you, lord Mowbray,
Of capital treason I *attach* you both. *Shakesp. Henry* IV.

3. To seize.
France hath flaw'd the league, and hath *attach'd*
Our merchants goods at Bourdeaux. *Shakesp. Henry* VIII.

4. To lay hold on.
I cannot blame thee,
Who am myself *attach'd* with weariness,
To th' dulling of my spirits. *Shakesp. Tempest.*

5. To win; to gain over; to enamour.
Songs, garlands, flow'rs,
And charming symphonies, *attach'd* the heart
Of Adam. *Milton's Paradise Lost, b.* xi.

6. To

6. To fix to one's intereſt.

The great and rich depend on thoſe whom their power or their wealth *attaches* to them. *Rogers.*

ATTA'CHMENT. *n. ſ.* [*attachement*, Fr.]

1. Adherence; attention; regard.

The Jews are remarkable for an *attachment* to their own country. *Addiſon. Freeholder*, N° 5.

The Romans burnt this laſt fleet, which is another mark of their ſmall *attachment* to the ſea. *Arbuthnot on Coins.*

2. An apprehenſion of a man to bring him to anſwer an action; and ſometimes it extends to his moveables.

3. *Foreign attachment*, is the attachment of a foreigner's goods found within a city, to ſatisfy creditors within a city.

To ATTA'CK. *v. a.* [*attaquer*, Fr.]

1. To aſſault an enemy; oppoſed to *defence.*

The front, the rear
Attack, while Yvo thunders in the center. *A.Philips's Briton.*

Thoſe that *attack*, generally get the victory, though with diſadvantage of ground. *Cane's Campaigns.*

2. To impugn in any manner, as with ſatire, confutation, calumny; as, the declaimer *attacked* the reputation of his adverſaries.

ATTA'CK. *n. ſ.* [from the verb.] An aſſault upon an enemy.

Hector oppoſes, and continues the *attack*; in which, after many actions, Sarpedon makes the firſt breach in the wall. *Pope's Iliad, argum. b.* xii.

If appriz'd of the ſevere *attack*,
The country be ſhut up. *Thomſon.*

I own 'twas wrong, when thouſands call'd me back,
To make that hopeleſs, ill-adviſ'd *attack*. *Young.*

ATTA'CKER. *n. ſ.* [from *attack*.] The perſon that attacks.

To ATTA'IN. *v. a.* [*atteindre*, Fr. *attineo*, Lat.]

1. To gain; to procure; to obtain.

Such knowledge is too wonderful for me; it is high; I cannot *attain* unto it. *Pſ.* cxxxix. 6.

Is he wiſe who hopes to *attain* the end without the means, nay by means that are quite contrary to it? *Tillotſon.*

2. To overtake; to come up with: a ſenſe now little in uſe.

The earl hoping to have overtaken the Scottiſh king, and to have given him battle; but not *attaining* him in time, ſet down before the caſtle of Aton. *Bacon's Henry* VII.

3. To come to; to enter upon.

Canaan he now *attains*; I ſee his tents
Pitch'd above Sichem. *Milton's Paradiſe Loſt, b.* xii.

4. To reach :to equal.

So the firſt precedent, if it be good, is ſeldom *attained* by imitation. *Bacon's Eſſays.*

To have knowledge in moſt objects of contemplation, is what the mind of one man can hardly *attain* unto. *Locke.*

To ATTA'IN. *v. n.*

1. To come to a certain ſtate.

Milk will ſoon ſeparate itſelf into a cream, and a more ſerous liquor, which, after twelve days, *attains* to the higheſt degree of acidity. *Arbuthnot on Aliments.*

2. To arrive at.

ATTA'IN. *n. ſ.* [from the verb.] The thing attained; attainment: a word notin uſe.

Crowns and diadems, the moſt ſplendid terrene *attains*, are akin to that which to-day is in the field, and to-morrow is cut down. *Glanville's Sceſis.*

ATTA'INABLE. *adj.* [from *attain.*] That which may be attained; procurable.

He wilfully neglects the obtaining unſpeakable good, which he is perſuaded is certain and *attainable*. *Tillotſon.*

None was propoſed that appeared certainly *attainable*, or of value enough. *Rogers.*

ATTA'INABLENESS. *n. ſ.* [from *attainable.*] The quality of being attainable.

Perſons become often enamoured of outward beauty, without any particular knowledge of its poſſeſſor, or its *attainableneſs* by them. *Cheyne's Philoſophical Principles.*

ATTA'INDER. *n. ſ.* [from *to attaint.*]

1. The act of attainting in law; conviction of a crime. See To ATTAINT.

The ends in calling a parliament were chiefly to have the *attainders* of all of his party reverſed; and, on the other ſide, to attaint by parliament his enemies. *Bacon's Henry* VII.

2. Taint.

So ſmooth he daub'd his vice with ſhew of virtue,
He liv'd from all *attainder* of ſuſpect. *Shakeſp. Richard* III.

ATTA'INMENT. *n. ſ.* [from *attain.*]

1. That which is attained; acquiſition.

We diſpute with men that count it a great *attainment* to be able to talk much, and little to the purpoſe. *Glanville's Sceſis.*

Our *attainments* are mean, compared with the perfection of the univerſe. *Grew's Coſmologia Sacra, b.* ii.

2. The act or power of attaining.

The Scripture muſt be ſufficient to imprint in us the character of all things neceſſary for the *attainment* of eternal life. *Hooker, b.* v.

Education in extent, more large, of time ſhorter, and of *attainment* more certain. *Milton on Education.*

Government is an art above the *attainment* of an ordinary genius. *South.*

If the ſame actions be the inſtruments, both of acquiring fame and procuring this happineſs, they would nevertheleſs fail in the *attainment* of this laſt end, if they proceeded from a deſire of the firſt. *Addiſon. Spectator*, N° 257.

The great care of God for our ſalvation muſt appear in the concern he expreſſed for our *attainment* of it. *Rogers.*

To ATTA'INT. *v. a.* [*attenter*, Fr.]

1. To *attaint* is particularly uſed for ſuch as are found guilty of ſome crime or offence, and eſpecially of felony or treaſon. A man is *attainted* two ways, by appearance, or by proceſs. Attainder by appearance is by confeſſion, battle, or verdict. Confeſſion is double; one at the bar before the judges, when the priſoner, upon his indictment read, being aſked guilty or not guilty, anſwers guilty, never putting himſelf upon the verdict of the jury. The other is before the coroner in ſanctuary, where he, upon his confeſſion, was in former times conſtrained to abjure the realm; which kind is called attainder by abjuration. Attainder by battle is, when the party appealed, and chooſing to try the truth by combat rather than by jury, is vanquiſhed. Attainder by verdict is, when the priſoner at the bar, anſwering to the indictment not guilty, hath an inqueſt of life and death paſſing upon him, and is by the verdict pronounced guilty. Attainder by proceſs is, where a party flies, and is not found till five times called publickly in the county, and at laſt outlawed upon his default. *Cowel.*

Were it not an endleſs trouble, that no traitor or felon ſhould be *attainted*, but a parliament muſt be called. *Spenſer on Ireland.*

I muſt offend before I be *attainted*. *Shakeſp. Hen.* VI.

2. To taint; to corrupt.

My tender youth was never yet *attaint*
With any paſſion of inflaming love. *Shakeſp. Henry* VI.

ATTA'INT. *n. ſ.* [from the verb.]

1. Any thing injurious, as illneſs, wearineſs. This ſenſe is now obſolete.

Nor doth he dedicate one jot of colour
Unto the weary and all-watched night;
But freſhly looks, and overbears *attaint*
With chearful ſemblance. *Shakeſp. Henry* V.

2. Stain; ſpot; taint.

No man hath a virtue that he has not a glimpſe of; nor any man an *attaint*, but he carries ſome ſtain of it. *Shakeſp. Troilus and Creſſida.*

3. In horſemanſhip. A blow or wound on the hinder feet of an horſe. *Farrier's Dict.*

ATTA'INTURE. *n. ſ.* [from *attaint.*] Reproach; imputation.

Hume's knavery will be the ducheſs's wreck,
And her *attainture* will be Humphry's fall. *Shakeſpeare's Henry* VI.

To ATTA'MINATE. *v. a.* [*attamino*, Lat.] To corrupt; to ſpoil.

To ATTE'MPER. *v. a.* [*attempero*, Lat.]

1. To mingle; to weaken by the mixture of ſomething elſe; to dilute.

Nobility *attempers* ſovereignty, and draws the eyes of the people ſomewhat aſide from the line royal. *Bacon's Eſſays.*

Attemper'd ſuns ariſe,
Sweet-beam'd, and ſhedding oft thro' lucid clouds
A pleaſing calm. *Thomſon's Summer.*

2. To regulate; to ſoften.

His early providence could likewiſe have *attempered* his nature therein. *Bacon's Henry* VII.

Thoſe ſmiling eyes, *attemp'ring* ev'ry ray,
Shone ſweetly lambent with celeſtial day. *Pope's El. to Abel.*

3. To mix in juſt proportions.

Alma, like a virgin queen moſt bright,
And to her gueſts doth bounteous banquet dight,
Attemper'd, goodly, well for health and for delight. *F. Queen.*

4. To fit to ſomething elſe.

Phemius! let arts of gods and heroes old,
Attemper'd to the lyre, your voice employ. *Pope's Odyſſey.*

To ATTE'MPERATE. *v. a.* [*attempero*, Lat.] To proportion to ſomething.

Hope muſt be proportioned and *attemperate* to the promiſe; if it exceed that temper and proportion, it becomes a tumour and tympany of hope. *Hammond's Pract. Catechiſm.*

To ATTE'MPT. *v. a.* [*attenter*, Fr.]

1. To attack; to invade; to venture upon.

He flatt'ring his diſpleaſure,
Tript me behind, got praiſes of the king,
For him *attempting* who was ſelf-ſubdu'd. *Shak. K. Lear.*

Who, in all things wiſe and juſt,
Hinder'd not Satan to *attempt* the mind
Of man; with ſtrength entire, and free-will, arm'd. *Milton's Paradiſe Loſt, b.* x.

I have been ſo hardy to *attempt* upon a name, which among ſome is yet very ſacred. *Glanville's Sceſis, Preface.*

2. To try; to endeavour.

I have nevertheleſs *attempted* to ſend unto you, for the renewing of brotherhood and friendſhip. 1 *Macc.* xii. 17.

Atte'mpt. *n. s.* [from the verb.]

1. An attack.

If we be always prepared to receive an enemy, we shall long live in peace and quietness, without any *attempts* upon us. *Bacon.*

2. An essay; an endeavour.

Alack! I am afraid, they have awak'd;
And 'tis not done, th' *attempt*, and not the deed,
Confounds us. *Shakesp. Macbeth.*

He would have cry'd; but hoping that he dreamt,
Amazement ty'd his tongue, and stopp'd th' *attempt*. *Dryd.*

I subjoin the following *attempt* towards a natural history of fossils. *Woodward on Fossils.*

Atte'mptable. *adj.* [from *attempt.*] Liable to attempts or attacks.

The gentleman vouching his to be more fair, virtuous, wise, and less *attemptable* than the rarest of our ladies. *Shak. Cymbel.*

Atte'mpter. *n. s.* [from *attempt.*]

1. The person that attempts; an invader.

The Son of God, with godlike force endu'd
Against th' *attempter* of thy Father's throne. *Par. Lost, b.* iv.

2. An endeavourer.

You are no factors for glory or treasure, but disinterested *attempters* for the universal good. *Glanville's Sceps. Scientifica.*

To ATTE'ND. *v. a.* [*attendre*, Fr. *attendo*, Lat.]

1. To regard; to fix the mind upon.

The crow doth sing as sweetly as the stork,
When neither is *attended*. *Shakesp. Merch. of Venice.*

2. To wait on; to accompany as an inferiour.

His companion, youthful Valentine,
Attends the emperour in his royal court. *Sh. T. Gent. of Ver.*

3. To accompany as an enemy.

He was at present strong enough to have stopped or *attended* Walter in his western expedition. *Clarendon, b.* viii.

4. To be present with, upon a summons.

If any minister refused to admit a lecturer recommended by him, he was required to *attend* upon the committee, and not discharged till the houses met again. *Clarendon.*

5. To accompany; to be appendant to.

England is so idly king'd,
Her sceptre so fantastically born,
That fear *attends* her not. *Shakesp. Henry* V.

My pray'rs and wishes always shall *attend*
The friends of Rome. *Addison's Cato.*

A vehement, burning, fixed, pungent pain in the stomach, *attended* with a fever. *Arbuthnot on Diet.*

6. To expect. This sense is French.

So dreadful a tempest, as all the people *attended* therein the very end of the world, and judgment-day. *Raleigh's Hist.*

7. To wait on, as on a charge.

The fifth had charge sick persons to *attend*,
And comfort those in point of death which lay. *Fairy Q.*

8. To be consequent to.

The duke made that unfortunate descent upon Rhée, which was afterwards *attended* with many unprosperous attempts. *Clar.*

9. To remain to; to await; to be in store for.

To him, who hath a prospect of the state that *attends* all men after this, the measures of good and evil are changed. *Locke.*

10. To wait for insidiously.

Thy interpreter, full of despight, bloody as the hunter, *attends* thee at the orchard end. *Shakesp. Twelfth Night.*

11. To be bent upon any object.

Their hunger thus appeas'd, their care *attends*
The doubtful fortune of their absent friends. *Dryd. Virgil.*

12. To stay for.

I died whilst in the womb he staid,
Attending nature's law. *Shakesp. Cymbeline.*

I hasten to our own; nor will relate
Great Mithridates, and rich Crœsus' fate;
Whom Solon wisely counsell'd to *attend*
The name of happy, till he knew his end. *Dryden's Juv.*

To Atte'nd. *v. n.*

1. To yield attention.

But, thy relation now! for I *attend*,
Pleas'd with thy words. *Milton's Par. Lost, b.* viii.

Since man cannot at the same time *attend* to two objects, if you employ your spirit upon a book or a bodily labour, you have no room left for sensual temptation. *Taylor's Holy Living.*

2. To stay; to delay.

This first true cause, and last good end,
She cannot here so well, and truly see;
For this perfection she must yet *attend*,
Till to her Maker she espoused be. *Sir J. Davies.*

Plant anemonies after the first rains, if you will have flowers very forward; but it is surer to *attend* till October, or the month after. *Evelyn's Kalendar.*

Atte'ndance. *n. s.* [*attendance*, Fr.]

1. The act of waiting on another; or of serving.

I dance *attendance* here,
I think the duke will not be spoke withal. *Shakesp. R.* III.

For he, of whom these things are spoken, pertaineth to another tribe, of which no man gave *attendance* at the altar. *Heb.* vii. 13.

The other, after many years *attendance* upon the duke, was now one of the bedchamber to the prince. *Clarendon.*

2. Service.

Why might not you, my lord, receive *attendance*
From those that she calls servants? *Shakesp. King Lear.*

3. The persons waiting; a train.

Attendance none shall need, nor train; where none
Are to behold the judgment, but the judg'd,
Those two. *Milton's Paradise Lost, b.* x. *l.* 80.

4. Attention; regard.

Give *attendance* to reading, to exhortation, to doctrine. *1 Tim.* iv. 13.

5. Expectation; a sense now out of use.

That which causeth bitterness in death, is the languishing *attendance* and expectation thereof ere it come. *Hooker, b.* i.

Atte'ndant. *adj.* [*attendant*, Fr.] Accompanying as subordinate.

Other suns, perhaps,
With their *attendant* moons, thou wilt descry,
Communicating male and female light. *Par. Lost, b.* viii.

Atte'ndant. *n. s.*

1. One that attends.

I will be returned forthwith; dismiss your *attendant* there; look it be done. *Shakesp. Othello.*

2. One that belongs to the train.

When some gracious monarch dies,
Soft whispers first and mournful murmurs rise
Among the sad *attendants*. *Dryden.*

3. One that waits the pleasure of another, as a suitor or agent.

I endeavour that my reader may not wait long for my meaning: to give an *attendant* quick dispatch is a civility. *Burnet's Theory, Preface.*

4. One that is present at any thing.

He was a constant *attendant* at all meetings relating to charity, without contributing. *Swift's Fates of Clergymen.*

5. In law. One that oweth a duty or service to another; or, after a sort, dependeth upon another. *Cowel.*

6. That which is united with another; a concomitant; a consequent.

Beware,
And govern well thy appetite, lest sin
Surprize thee, and her black *attendant*, death. *Par. L. b.* vii.

They secure themselves first from doing nothing, and then from doing ill; the one being so close an *attendant* on the other, that it is scarce possible to sever them. *Decay of Piety.*

He had an unlimited sense of fame, the *attendant* of noble spirits, which prompted him to engage in travels. *Pop. Ess. on H.*

It is hard to take into view all the *attendants* or consequents that will be concerned in the determination of a question. *Watts's Improvement of the Mind.*

Atte'nder. *n. s.* [from *attend.*] Companion; associate.

The gypsies were there,
Like lords to appear,
With such their *attenders*,
As you thought offenders. *Ben Johnson's Gypsies.*

Att'ent. *adj.* [*attentus*, Lat.] Intent; attentive; heedful; regardful.

Now mine eyes shall be open, and mine ears *attent* unto the prayer that is made in this place. *2 Chron.* vii. 15.

What can then be less in me than desire,
To see thee, and approach thee, whom I know,
Declar'd the Son of God, to hear *attent*
Thy wisdom, and behold thy godlike deeds. *Par. Regained.*

Read your chapter in your prayers; little interruptions will make your prayers less tedious, and yourself more *attent* upon them. *Taylor's Guide to Devotion.*

To want of judging abilities, we may add their want of leisure to apply their minds to such a serious and *attent* consideration. *South.*

Being denied communication by their ear, their eyes are more vigilant, *attent*, and heedful. *Holder's El. of Speech.*

A'ttentates. *n. s.* [*attentata*, Lat.] Proceedings in a court of judicature, pending suit, and after an inhibition is decreed and gone out; those things which are done after an extrajudicial appeal, may likewise be stiled *attentates*. *Ayliff. Par.*

Atte'ntion. *n. s.* [*attention*, Fr.] The act of attending or heeding; the act of bending the mind upon any thing.

They say the tongues of dying men
Inforce *attention* like deep harmony. *Shakesp. Richard* II.

He perceived nothing but silence, and signs of *attention* to what he would further say. *Bacon's Holy War.*

But him the gentle angel by the hand
Soon rais'd, and his *attention* thus recall'd. *Par. Lost, b.* xi.

By *attention* the ideas, that offer themselves, are taken notice of, and, as it were, registered in the memory. *Locke.*

Attention is a very necessary thing; truth doth not always strike the soul at first sight. *Watts's Improv. of the Mind.*

Atte'ntive. *adj.* [from *attent.*] Heedful; regardful; full of attention.

Being moved with these and the like your effectual discourses, whereunto we gave most *attentive* ear, till they entered even unto our souls. *Hooker, Preface.*

I'm never merry when I hear ſweet muſick.
— The reaſon is, your ſpirits are *attentive.* *Sh. M. of Venice.*

I ſaw moſt of them *attentive* to three Sirens, diſtinguiſhed by the names of Sloth, Ignorance, and Pleaſure. *Tatler*, N° 81.

A critick is a man who, on all occaſions, is more *attentive* to what is wanting than what is preſent. *Addiſon. Guardian.*

Muſick's force can tame the furious beaſt;
Can make the wolf, or foaming boar, reſtrain
His rage; the lion drop his creſted main,
Attentive to the ſong. *Prior.*

ATTE'NTIVELY. *adv.* [from *attentive.*] Heedfully; carefully.

If a man look ſharply and *attentively*, he ſhall ſee Fortune; for though ſhe be blind, ſhe is not inviſible. *Bacon.*

The cauſe of cold is a quick ſpirit in a cold body; as will appear to any that ſhall *attentively* conſider of nature. *Bacon.*

ATTE'NTIVENESS. *n. ſ.* [from *attentive.*] The ſtate of being attentive; heedfulneſs; attention.

At the relation of the queen's death, bravely confeſſed and lamented by the king, how *attentiveneſs* wounded his daughter. *Shakeſp. Winter's Tale.*

ATTE'NUANT. *adj.* [*attenuans*, Lat.] What has the power of making thin, or diluting.

To ATTE'NUATE. *v. a.* [*attenuo*, Lat.] To make thin, or ſlender.

The finer part belonging to the juice of grapes, being *attenuated* and ſubtilized, was changed into an ardent ſpirit. *Boyle.*

Vinegar curd, put upon an egg, not only diſſolves the ſhell, but alſo *attenuates* the white contained in it into a limpid water. *Wiſeman's Surgery.*

It is of the nature of acids to diſſolve or *attenuate*, and of alkalies to precipitate or incraſſate. *Newton's Opticks.*

The ingredients are digeſted and *attenuated* by heat; they are ſtirred and conſtantly agitated by winds. *Arbuth. on Air.*

ATTE'NUATE. *adj.* [from the verb.] Made thin, or ſlender.

Vivification ever conſiſteth in ſpirits *attenuate*, which the cold doth congeal and coagulate. *Bacon's Natural Hiſtory.*

ATTENUA'TION. *n. ſ.* [from *attenuate.*] The act of making any thing thin or ſlender; leſſening.

Chiming with a hammer upon the outſide of a bell, the ſound will be according to the inward concave of the bell; whereas the eliſion or *attenuation* of the air, can be only between the hammer and the outſide of the bell. *Bacon's Nat. Hiſtory.*

A'TTER. *n. ſ.* [aꞇeꞃ, Sax. venom.] Corrupt matter. A word much uſed in Lincolnſhire. *Skinner.*

To ATTE'ST. *v. a.* [*atteſtor*, Lat.]

1. To bear witneſs of; to witneſs.

Many particular facts are recorded in holy writ, *atteſted* by particular pagan authors. *Addiſon on the Chriſtian Religion.*

2. To call to witneſs; to invoke as conſcious.

The ſacred ſtreams, which heav'n's imperial ſtate
Atteſts in oaths, and fears to violate. *Dryden's Æneid.*

ATTE'ST. *n. ſ.* [from the verb.] Witneſs; teſtimony; atteſtation.

With the voice divine
Nigh thunderſtruck, th' exalted man, to whom
Such high *atteſt* was giv'n, a while ſurvey'd
With wonder. *Paradiſe Regained, b.* i.

ATTESTA'TION. *n. ſ.* [from *atteſt.*] Teſtimony; witneſs; evidence.

There remains a ſecond kind of peremptorineſs, of thoſe who can make no relation without an *atteſtation* of its certainty. *Government of the Tongue.*

The next coal-pit, mine, quarry, or chalk-pit, will give *atteſtation* to what I write, theſe are ſo obvious that I need not ſeek for a compurgator. *Woodward's Nat. Hiſtory.*

We may derive a probability from the *atteſtation* of wiſe and honeſt men by word or writing, or the concurring witneſs of multitudes who have ſeen and known what they relate. *Watts.*

ATTI'GUOUS. *adj.* [*attiguus*, Lat.] Hard by; adjoining. *Dict.*

To ATTI'NGE. *v. a.* [*attingo*, Lat.] To touch lightly or gently. *Dict.*

To ATTI'RE. *v. a.* [*attirer*, Fr.] To dreſs; to habit; to array.

Let it likewiſe your gentle breaſt inſpire
With ſweet infuſion, and put you in mind
Of that proud maid, whom now thoſe leaves *attire*,
Proud Daphne. *Spenſer, Sonnet* xxxvii.

My Nan ſhall be the queen of all the fairies;
Finely *attired* in a robe of white. *Shakeſp. M. W. of Windſ.*

With the linen mitre ſhall he be *attired.* *Lev.* xvi. 4.

Now the ſappy boughs
Attire themſelves with blooms. *Philips.*

ATTI'RE. *n. ſ.* [from the verb.]

1. Clothes; dreſs; habit.

It is no more diſgrace to Scripture to have left things free to be ordered by the church, than for nature to have left it to the wit of man to deviſe his own *attire.* *Hooker, b.* iii.

After that the Roman *attire* grew to be in account, and the gown to be in uſe among them. *Sir John Davies on Ireland.*

Thy ſumptuous buildings, and thy wife's *attire*,
Hath coſt a maſs of publick treaſury.
Shakeſpeare's Henry VI. *p.* ii.

And in this coarſe *attire*, which I now wear,
With God and with the Muſes I confer. *Donne.*

When laviſh nature, with her beſt *attire*,
Cloaths the gay ſpring, the ſeaſon of deſire. *Waller.*

I paſs their form, and ev'ry charming grace,
But their *attire*, like liveries of a kind,
All rich and rare, is freſh within my mind. *Dryd.*

2. In hunting. The horns of a buck or ſtag.

3. In botany. The flower of a plant is divided into three parts, the empalement, the foliation, and the *attire*, which is either florid or ſemiform. *Florid attire*, called thrums or ſuits, as in the flowers of marigold and tanſey, conſiſt ſometimes of two, but commonly of three parts. The outer part is the floret, the body of which is divided at the top, like the cowſlip flower, into five diſtinct parts. *Semiform attire* conſiſts of two parts, the chives and apices; one upon each *attire.* *Dict.*

ATTI'RER. *n. ſ.* [from *attire.*] One that attires another; a dreſſer. *Dict.*

A'TTITUDE. *n. ſ.* [*attitude*, Fr. from *atto*, Ital.] The poſture or action in which a ſtatue or painted figure is placed.

Bernini would have taken his opinion upon the beauty and *attitude* of a figure. *Prior's Dedication.*

They were famous originals that gave riſe to ſtatues, with the ſame air, poſture, and *attitudes.* *Addiſon.*

ATTO'LLENT. *adj.* [*attollens*, Lat.] That which raiſes or lifts up.

I ſhall farther take notice of the exquiſite libration of the *attollent* and depriment muſcles. *Derham's Phyſico-Theology.*

ATTO'RNEY. *n. ſ.* [*attornatus*, low Lat. from *tour*, Fr. *Celui qui vient à tour d'autrui; qui alterius vices ſubit.*]

1. Such a perſon as by conſent, commandment, or requeſt, takes heed, ſees, and takes upon him the charge of other men's buſineſs, in their abſence. *Attorney* is either general or ſpecial: *Attorney general* is he that by general authority is appointed to all our affairs or ſuits; as the *attorney general* of the king, which is nearly the ſame with *Procurator Cæſaris* in the Roman empire. *Attorneys general* are made either by the king's letters patent, or by our appointment before juſtices in eyre, in open court. *Attorney ſpecial* or *particular*, is he that is employed in one or more cauſes particularly ſpecified. There are alſo, in reſpect of the divers courts, *attorneys at large*, and *attorneys ſpecial*, belonging to this or that court only. *Cowel.*

Attorneys in common law, are nearly the ſame with proctors in the civil law, and ſolicitors in courts of equity. *Attorneys* ſue out writs or proceſs, or commence, carry on, and defend actions, or other proceedings, in the names of other perſons, in the courts of common law. None are admitted to act without having ſerved a clerkſhip for five years, taking the proper oath, being enrolled, and examined by the judges. The *attorney general* pleads within the bar. To him come warrants for making out patents, pardons, &c. and he is the principal manager of all law affairs of the crown. *Chambers.*

I am a ſubject,
And challenge law: *attorneys* are deny'd me,
And therefore perſonally I lay my claim
To mine inheritance. *Shakeſp. Richard* II.

The king's *attorney*, on the contrary,
Urg'd on examinations, proofs, confeſſions,
Of divers witneſſes. *Shakeſp. Henry* VIII.

Deſpairing quacks with curſes fled the place,
And vile *attorneys*, now an uſeleſs race. *Pope, Epiſt.* iii.

2. It was anciently uſed for thoſe who did any buſineſs for another; now only in law.

I will attend my huſband; it is my office;
And will have no *attorney* but myſelf;
And therefore let me have him home. *Shak. Com. of Err.*

Why ſhould calamity be full of words?——
— Windy *attorneys* to their client woes,
Airy ſucceeders of inteſtate joys. *Shakeſp. Richard* III.

To ATTO'RNEY. *v. a.* [from the noun; the verb is now not in uſe.]

1. To perform by proxy.

Their encounters, though not perſonal, have been royally *attornied* with interchange of gifts. *Shakeſp. Winter's Tale.*

2. To employ as a proxy.

As I was then
Advertiſing, and holy to your buſineſs,
Not changing heart with habit, I am ſtill
Attornied to your ſervice. *Shakeſp. Meaſure for Meaſure.*

ATTO'RNEYSHIP. *n. ſ.* [from *attorney.*] The office of an attorney.

But marriage is a matter of more worth,
Than to be dealt in by *attorneyſhip.* *Shakeſp. Henry* VI.

ATTO'URNMENT. *n. ſ.* [*attournement*, Fr.] An yielding of the tenant to a new lord, or acknowledgment of him to be his lord; for, otherwiſe, he that buyeth or obtaineth any lands or tenements of another, which are in the occupation of a third, cannot get poſſeſſion. *Cowel.*

To ATTRA'CT. *v. a.* [*attraho*, *attractum*, Lat.]

1. To draw to ſomething.

A man ſhould ſcarce perſuade the affections of the loadſtone, or that jet and amber *attracteth* ſtraws and light bodies. *Brown's Vulgar Errours.*

The

The single atoms each to other tend,
Attract, *attracted* to, the next in place,
Form'd and impell'd its neighbour to embrace. *Pope.*

2. To allure; to invite.

Adorn'd
She was indeed, and lovely, to *attract*
Thy love; not thy subjection. *Milton's Par. Lost, b.* x.

Shew the care of approving all actions so, as may most effectually *attract* all to this profession. *Hammond's Fundam.*

Deign to be lov'd, and ev'ry heart subdue!
What nymph could e'er *attract* such crowds as you! *Pope.*

ATTRA'CT. *n. s.* [from *to attract.*] Attraction; the power of drawing.

Feel darts and charms, *attracts* and flames,
And woe and contract in their names. *Hudibras.*

ATTRA'CTICAL. *adj.* [from *attract.*] Having the power to draw to it.

Some stones are endued with an electrical or *attractical* virtue. *Ray on the Creation.*

ATTRA'CTION. *n. s.* [from *attract.*]

1. The power of drawing any thing.

The drawing of amber and jet, and other electrick bodies, and the *attraction* in gold of the spirit of quicksilver at distance; and the attraction of heat at distance; and that of fire to naphtha; and that of some herbs to water, though at distance; and divers others, we shall handle. *Bacon's Nat. Hist.*

Loadstones and touched needles, laid long in quicksilver, have not admitted their *attraction*. *Brown's Vulgar Errours.*

Attraction may be performed by impulse, or some other means; I use that word, to signify any force by which bodies tend towards one another. *Newton's Opticks.*

2. The power of alluring or enticing.

Setting the *attraction* of my good parts aside, I have no other charms. *Shakesp. Merry Wives of Windsor.*

ATTRA'CTIVE. *adj.* [from *attract.*]

1. Having the power to draw any thing.

What if the sun
Be centre to the world; and other stars,
By his *attractive* virtue, and their own,
Incited, dance about him various rounds. *Paradise Lost.*

Some the round earth's cohesion to secure,
For that hard task employ magnetick power;
Remark, say they, the globe, with wonder own
Its nature, like the fam'd *attractive* stone. *Blackmore.*

Bodies act by the attractions of gravity, magnetism, and electricity; and these instances make it not improbable but there may be more *attractive* powers than these. *Newt. Opt.*

2. Inviting; alluring; enticing.

Happy is Hermia, wheresoe'er she lies;
For she hath blessed and *attractive* eyes.
Shakesp. Midsum. Night's Dream.

I pleas'd, and with *attractive* graces won,
The most averse, thee chiefly. *Paradise Lost, b.* ii.

ATTRA'CTIVE. *n. s.* [from *attract.*] That which draws or incites allurement; except that *attractive* is of a good or indifferent sense, and *allurement* generally bad.

The condition of a servant staves him off to a distance; but the gospel speaks nothing but *attractives* and invitation. *South.*

ATTRA'CTIVELY. *adv.* [from *attractive.*] With the power of attracting or drawing.

ATTRA'CTIVENESS. *n. s.* [from *attractive.*] The quality of being attractive.

ATTRA'CTOR. *n. s.* [from *attract.*] The agent that attracts; a drawer.

If the straws be in oil, amber draweth them not; oil makes the straws to adhere so, that they cannot rise unto the *attractor*. *Brown's Vulgar Errours, b.* ii.

A'TTRAHENT. *n. s.* [*attrahens*, Lat.] That which draws.

Our eyes will inform us of the motion of the steel to its *attrahent*. *Glanville's Scepsis.*

ATTRECTA'TION. *n. s.* [*attrectatio*, Lat.] Frequent handling. *D.*

ATTRI'BUTABLE. *adj.* [*attribuo*, Lat.] That which may be ascribed or attributed; ascribable; imputable.

Much of the origination of the Americans seems to be *attributable* to the migrations of the Seri. *Hale's Origin of Mankind.*

To ATTRI'BUTE. *v. a.* [*attribuo*, Lat.]

1. To ascribe; to give; to yield.

To their very bare judgment somewhat a reasonable man would *attribute*, notwithstanding the common imbecillities which are incident unto our nature. *Hooker, b.* ii.

We *attribute* nothing to God that hath any repugnancy or contradiction in it. Power and wisdom have no repugnancy in them. *Tillotson.*

2. To impute, as to a cause.

I have observed a Campania determine contrary to appearances, by the caution and conduct of a general, which were *attributed* to his infirmities. *Temple.*

The imperfection of telescopes is *attributed* to spherical glasses; and mathematicians have propounded to figure them by the conical sections. *Newton's Opticks.*

A'TTRIBUTE. *n. s.* [from *to attribute.*]

1. The thing attributed to another, as perfection to the Supreme Being.

Power, light, virtue, wisdom, and goodness, being all but *attributes* of one simple essence, and of one God, we in all admire, and in part discern. *Sir Walter Raleigh.*

Your vain poets after did mistake,
Who ev'ry *attribute* a god did make. *Dryden's Tyr. Love.*

All the perfections of God are called his *attributes*; for he cannot be without them. *Watts's Logick.*

2. Quality; adherent.

They must have these three *attributes*; they must be men of courage, fearing God, and hating covetousness. *Bacon.*

3. A thing belonging to another; an appendant.

His sceptre shews the force of temporal pow'r,
The *attribute* to awe and majesty;
But mercy is above this scepter'd sway,
It is an attribute to God himself. *Shak. Merchant of Venice.*

The sculptor, to distinguish him, gave him, what the medallists call his proper *attributes*, a spear and a shield. *Addison.*

4. Reputation; honour.

It takes
From our atchievements, though perform'd at height,
The pith and marrow of our *attribute*. *Shakesp. Hamlet.*

ATTRIBU'TION. *n. s.* [from *to attribute.*] Commendation.

If speaking truth,
In this fine age, were not thought flattery,
Such *attribution* should the Douglas have,
As not a soldier of this season's stamp
Should go so general current through the world.
Shakesp. Henry IV. *p.* i.

ATTRI'TE. *adj.* [*attritus*, Lat.] Ground; worn by rubbing.

Or by collision of two bodies, grind
The air *attrite* to fire. *Milton's Paradise Lost, b.* x.

ATTRI'TENESS. *n. s.* [from *attrite.*] The being much worn.

ATTRI'TION. *n. s.* [*attritio*, Lat.]

1. The act of wearing things, by rubbing one against another.

This vapour, ascending incessantly out of the abyss, and pervading the strata of gravel, and the rest, decays the bones and vegetables lodged in those strata; this fluid, by its continual *attrition*, fretting the said bodies. *Woodw. Nat. History.*

The change of the aliment is effected by *attrition* of the inward stomach, and dissolvent liquor assisted with heat.
Arbuthnot on Aliments.

2. [With divines.] Grief for sin, arising only from the fear of punishment; the lowest degree of repentance.

To ATTU'NE. *v. a.* [from *tune.*]

1. To make any thing musical.

Airs, vernal airs,
Breathing the smell of field and grove, *attune*
The trembling leaves. *Milton's Par. Lost, b.* iv.

2. To tune one thing to another; as, he *attunes* his voice to his harp.

ATTU'RNEY. *n. s.* See ATTORNEY.

ATWE'EN. *adv.* or *prep.* [See BETWEEN.] Betwixt; between; in the midst of two things.

Her loose long yellow locks, like golden wire,
Sprinkled with pearl, and perling flowers *atween*,
Do, like a golden mantle, her attire. *Spenser's Epithalam.*

ATWI'XT. *prep.* [See BETWIXT.] In the middle of two things.

But with outrageous strokes did him restrain,
And with his body barr'd the way *atwixt* them twain.
Fairy Queen, b. i.

To AVA'IL. *v. a.* [from *valoir*, Fr. *to avail* being nearly the same thing with *faire valoir.*]

1. To profit; to turn to profit; with *of* before the thing used.

Then shall they seek t' *avail* themselves *of* names,
Places, and titles; and with these to join
Secular pow'r. *Milton's Par. Lost, b.* xii.

Both of them *avail* themselves *of* those licences, which Apollo has equally bestowed on them. *Dryden's Dufresnoy.*

2. To promote; to prosper; to assist.

Meantime he voyag'd to explore the will
Of Jove on high Dodona's holy hill,
What means might best his safe return *avail*. *Pope's Odyss.*

To AVA'IL. *v. n.* To be of use; to be of advantage.

Nor can my strength *avail*, unless by thee
Endu'd with force, I gain the victory. *Dryden's Fables.*

When real merit is wanting, it *avails* nothing to have been encouraged by the great. *Pope's Preface to his Works.*

AVA'IL. *n. s.* [from *to avail.*] Profit; advantage; benefit.

For all that else did come, were sure to fail;
Yet would he further none but for *avail*.
Spenser's Hubbard's Tale.

I charge thee,
As heav'n shall work in me for thine *avail*,
To tell me truly. *Shakesp. All's well that ends well.*

Truth, light upon this way, is of no more *avail* to us than errour. *Locke.*

AVA'ILABLE. *adj.* [from *avail.*]

1. Profitable; advantageous.

All things subject to action, the will does so far incline unto, as reason judges them more *available* to our bliss. *Hooker, b.* i.

2. Powerful; in force.

Laws human are *available* by consent. *Hooker, b* i.

Mighty is the efficacy of such intercessions to avert judgments; how much more *available* then may they be to secure the continuance of blessings? *Atterbury's Serm.*

AVA'ILABLENESS. *n. s.* [from *available.*] Power of promoting the end for which it is used.

We differ from that supposition of the efficacy or *availableness*, or suitableness of these to the end *Hale's Origin of Man.*

AVA'ILABLY. *adv.* [from *available.*] Powerfully; profitably; advantageously.

AVA'ILMENT. *n. s.* [from *avail.*] Usefulness; advantage; profit.

To AVA'LE. *v. a.* [*avaler*, to let sink, Fr.] To let fall; to depress; to make abject; to sink: a word out of use.

He did abase and *avale* the sovereignty into more servitude towards that see, than had been among us. *Wotton.*

To AVA'LE. *v. n.* To sink.

But when his latter ebb 'gins to *avale*,
Huge heaps of mud he leaves. *Spenser.*

AVA'NT. See VAN.

AVA'NT-GUARD. *n. s.* [*avantgarde*, Fr.] The van; the first body of an army.

The horsemen might issue forth without disturbance of the foot, and the *avant-guard* without shuffling with the battail or arriere. *Sir J. Hayward.*

A'VARICE. *n. s.* [*avarice*, Fr. *avaritia*, Lat.] Covetousness; insatiable desire.

There grows
In my most ill compos'd affection, such
A stanchless *avarice*, that were I king,
I should cut off the nobles for their lands. *Shakesp. Macbeth.*
This *avarice* of praise in times to come,
Those long inscriptions crouded on the tomb. *Dryd. Juv.*
Nor love his peace of mind destroys,
Nor wicked *avarice* of wealth. *Dryden.*

Avarice is insatiable; and so he went still pushing on for more. *L'Estrange.*

AVARI'CIOUS. *adj.* [*avaricieux*, Fr.] Covetous; insatiably desirous.

I grant him bloody,
Luxurious, *avaricious*, false, deceitful. *Shakesp. Macbeth.*

This speech has been condemned, as *avaricious*; and Eustathius judges it to be spoken artfully. *Broome on the Odyssey.*

AVARI'CIOUSLY. *adv.* [from *avaricious.*] Covetously.

AVARI'CIOUSNESS. *n. s.* [from *avaricious.*] The quality of being avaricious.

AVA'ST. *adv.* [from *basta*, Ital. it is enough.] Enough; cease. A word used among seamen.

AVA'UNT. *interject.* [*avaunt*, Fr.] A word of abhorrence, by which any one is driven away.

O, he is bold, and blushes not at death;
Avaunt, thou hateful villain, get thee gone! *Sh. King John.*
After this process
To give her the *avaunt!* it is a pity
Would move a monster. *Shakesp. Henry VIII.*
Mistress! dismiss that rabble from your throne.
Avaunt!—is Aristarchus yet unknown? *Dunciad, b.* iv.

A'UBURNE. *adj.* [from *aubour*, bark, Fr.] Brown; of a tan colour.

Her hair is *auburne*, mine is perfect yellow. *Sh. T. G. of Ver.*
His *auburne* locks on either shoulder flow'd,
Which to the fun'ral of his friend he vow'd. *Dryd. Fables.*
Lo, how the arable with barley grain
Stands thick, o'ershadow'd, these, as modern use
Ordains, infus'd, an *auburne* drink compose,
Wholesome, of deathless fame. *Philips.*

A'UCTION. *n. s.* [*auctio*, Lat.]

1. A manner of sale in which one person bids after another, till so much is bid as the seller is content to take.

2. The things sold by auction.

Ask you why Phrine the whole *auction* buys;
Phrine foresees a general excise. *Pope.*

To A'UCTION. *v. a.* [from *auction.*] To sell by auction

A'UCTIONARY. *adj.* [from *auction.*] Belonging to an auction.

And much more honest, to be hir'd, and stand,
With *auctionary* hammer in thy hand,
Provoking to give more, and knocking thrice
For the old houshold stuff of picture's price. *Dryd. Juven.*

A'UCTIONIER. *n. s.* [from *auction.*] The person that manages an auction.

A'UCTIVE. *adj.* [from *auctus*, Lat.] Of an increasing quality. *D.*

AUCUPA'TION. *n. s.* [*aucupatio*, Lat.] Fowling; bird-catching.

AUDA'CIOUS. *adj.* [*audacieux*, Fr. *audax*, Lat.] Bold; impudent; daring; always in a bad sense.

Such is thy *audacious* wickedness,
Thy leud, pestif'rous, and dissentious pranks. *Shak. H.* VI.
Till Jove, no longer patient, took his time
T' avenge with thunder their *audacious* crime. *Dryden.*

Young students, by a constant habit of disputing, grow impudent and *audacious*, proud and disdainful. *Watts's Improvement of the Mind.*

AUDA'CIOUSLY. *adv.* [from *audacious.*] Boldly; impudently.

An angel shalt thou see,
Yet fear not thou, but speak *audaciously*. *Sh. Love's Lab. L.*

AUDA'CIOUSNESS. *n. s.* [from *audacious.*] Impudence.

AUDA'CITY. *n. s.* [from *audax*, Lat.] Spirit; boldness; confidence.

Lean, raw-bon'd rascals! who would e'er suppose,
They had such courage and *audacity*. *Shakesp. Henry* VI.

Great effects come of industry and perseverance; for *audacity* doth almost bind and mate the weaker sort of minds. *Bacon's Natural History*, N° 902.

For want of that freedom and *audacity*, necessary in commerce with men, his personal modesty overthrew all his publick actions. *Tatler*, N° 52.

A'UDIBLE. *adj.* [*audibilis*, Lat.]

1. That which may be perceived by hearing.

Visibles work upon a looking-glass, and *audibles* upon the places of echo, which resemble in some sort the cavern of the ear. *Bacon's Nat. History*, N° 263.

Eve, who unseen,
Yet all had heard, with *audible* lament
Discover'd soon the place of her retire. *Paradise Lost, b.* xi.

Every sense doth not operate upon fancy with the same force. The conceits of visibles are clearer and stronger than those of *audibles*. *Grew's Cosmologia Sacra, b.* ii.

2. Loud enough to be heard.

One leaning over a wall twenty-five fathom deep, and speaking softly, the water returned an *audible* echo. *Bacon.*

A'UDIBLENESS. *n. s.* [from *audible.*] Capableness of being heard.

A'UDIBLY. *adv.* [from *audible.*] In such a manner as to be heard.

And last, the sum of all, my Father's voice
Audibly heard from heav'n, pronounc'd me his. *Par. Reg.*

A'UDIENCE. *n. s.* [*audience*, Fr.]

1. The act of hearing or attending to any thing.

Now I breathe again
Aloft the flood, and can give *audience*
To any tongue, speak it of what it will. *Shak. King John.*
Thus far his bold discourse, without controul,
Had *audience*. *Milton's Par. Lost, b.* v.
His look
Drew *audience*, and attention still as night,
Or summer's noon-tide air. *Milton's Par. Lost, b.* ii.

2. The liberty of speaking granted; a hearing.

Were it reason to give men *audience*, pleading for the overthrow of that which their own deed hath ratified? *Hooker.*

According to the fair play of the world,
Let me have *audience*: I am sent to speak,
My holy lord of Milan, from the king. *Shakesp. K. John.*

3. An auditory; persons collected to hear.

Or, if the star of ev'ning, and the moon,
Haste to thy *audience*, night with her will bring
Silence. *Milton's Par. Lost, b.* vii.

The hall was filled with an *audience* of the greatest eminence for quality and politeness. *Addison. Guard.* N° 115.

It proclaims the triumphs of goodness in a proper *audience*, even before the whole race of mankind. *Atterbury's Sermons.*

4. The reception of any man who delivers a solemn message.

In this high temple, on a chair of state,
The seat of *audience*, old Latinus sate. *Dryden's Æneid.*

AUDIENCE *Court.* A court belonging to the archbishop of Canterbury, of equal authority with the arches court, though inferiour both in dignity and antiquity. The original of this court was, because the archbishop of Canterbury heard several causes extrajudicially at home in his own palace; in which, before he would finally determine any thing, he usually committed them to be discussed by men learned in the civil and canon laws, whom thereupon he called his auditors: and so in time it became the power of the man, who is called *causarum negotiorumque audientiæ Cantuariensis auditor, seu officinalis.* *Cowel.*

A'UDIT. *n. s.* [from *audit*, he hears, Lat.] A final account.

If they, which are accustomed to weigh all things, shall here sit down to receive our *audit*, the sum, which truth amounteth to, will appear to be but this. *Hooker, b.* v.

He took my father grossly, full of bread,
With all his crimes broad blown, and flush as May;
And how his *audit* stands, who knows save heav'n? *Hamlet.*
I can make my *audit* up, that all
From me do back receive the flow'r of all,
And leave me but the bran. *Shakesp. Coriolanus.*

To A'UDIT. *v. a.* [from *audit.*] To take an account finally.

Bishops ordinaries *auditing* all accounts, take twelve pence. *Ayliffe's Parergon.*

I love exact dealing, and let Hocus *audit*; he knows how the money was disbursed. *Arbuthnot's Hist. of J. Bull.*

AUDI'TION. *n. s.* [*auditio*, Lat.] Hearing.

A'UDITOR. *n. s.* [*auditor*, Lat.]

1. A hearer.

Dear cousin, you that were last day so high in the pulpit against lovers, are you now become so mean an *auditor?* *Sidney, b.* ii.

What a play tow'rd? I'll be an *auditor*;
An actor too, perhaps. *Shakesp. Midsummer Night's Dream.*

This

This first doctrine, though admitted by many of his *auditors*, is expresly against the Epicureans. *Bentley's Sermons.*

2. A person employed to take an account ultimately.

If you suspect my husbandry,
Call me before th' exactest *auditors*,
And set me on the proof. *Shakesp. Timon.*

3. In ecclesiastical law.

The archbishop's usage was to commit the discussing of causes to certain persons learned in the law, stiled his *auditors*. *Ayliffe's Parergon.*

4. In the state.

A king's officer, who, yearly examining the accounts of all under-officers accountable, makes up a general book. *Cowel.*

A'UDITORY. *adj.* [*auditorius*, Lat.] That which has the power of hearing.

Is not hearing performed by the vibrations of some medium, excited in the *auditory* nerves by the tremours of the air, and propagated through the capillaments of those nerves? *Newton.*

A'UDITORY. *n. s.* [*auditorium*, Lat.]

1. An audience; a collection of persons assembled to hear.

Met in the church, I look upon you as an *auditory* fit to be waited on, as you are, by both universities. *South.*

Demades never troubled his head to bring his *auditory* to their wits, by dry reason. *L'Estrange.*

Several of this *auditory* were, perhaps, entire strangers to the person whose death we now lament. *Atterbury's Sermons.*

2. A place where lectures are to be heard.

A'UDITRESS. *n. s.* [from *auditor.*] The woman that hears; a she hearer.

Yet went she not, as not with such discourse
Delighted, or not capable her ear
Of what was high: such pleasure she reserv'd,
Adam relating, she sole *auditress*. *Milt. Par. Lost, b.* viii.

To AVE'L. *v. a.* [*avello*, Lat.] To pull away.

The beaver in chase makes some divulsion of parts, yet are not these parts *avelled* to be termed testicles. *Brown's Vulg. Err.*

A'VE MARY. *n. s.* [from the first words of the salutation to the Blessed Virgin, *Ave Maria.*] A form of worship repeated by the Romanists in honour of the Virgin Mary.

All his mind is bent on holiness,
To number *Ave Maries* on his beads. *Shakesp. Henry* VI.

A'VENAGE. *n. s.* [of *avena*, oats, Lat.] A certain quantity of oats paid to a landlord, instead of some other duties, or as a rent by the tenant. *Dict.*

To AVE'NGE. *v. a.* [*venger*, Fr.]

1. To revenge.

I will *avenge* me of mine enemies. *Isaiah*, i. 24.

They stood against their enemies, and were *avenged* of their adversaries. *Wisd.* xi. 3.

I will *avenge* the blood of Jezreel upon the house of Jehu. *Hosea*, i. 4.

2. To punish.

Till Jove, no longer patient, took his time
T' *avenge* with thunder your audacious crime. *Dryden.*

AVE'NGEANCE. *n. s.* [from *avenge.*] Punishment.

This neglected fear
Signal *avengeance*, such as overtook
A miser. *Philips.*

AVE'NGEMENT. *n. s.* [from *avenge.*] Vengeance; revenge.

That he might work th' *avengement* for his shame
On those two caitives which had bred him blame.
Spenser's Hubberd's Tale.

All those great battles which thou boasts to win
Through strife and bloodshed, and *avengement*
Now praised, hereafter thou shalt repent. *Fairy Queen, b.* i.

AVE'NGER. *n. s.* [from *avenge.*]

1. Punisher.

That no man go beyond his brother, because that the Lord is the *avenger* of all such. 1 *Thess.* iv. 6.

Ere this he had return'd, with fury driv'n
By his *avengers*; since no place like this
Can fit his punishment, or their revenge. *Par. Lost, b.* x.

2. Revenger; taker of vengeance for.

The just *avenger* of his injured ancestors, the victorious Louis was darting his thunder. *Dryden's Dufresnoy.*

But just disease to luxury succeeds,
And ev'ry death its own *avenger* breeds. *Pope's Ess. on M.*

A'VENS. *n. s.* [*caryophyllata*, Lat.] The same with herb bennet. The characters are; It hath pennated or winged leaves; the cup of the flower consists of one leaf, cut into ten segments; the flower consists of five leaves, spreading open; the seeds are formed into a globular figure, each having a tail; the roots are perennial, and smell sweet. The species are, 1. Common *avens*. 2. Mountain *avens*, with large yellow flowers, &c. The first sort grows wild in England, Scotland and Ireland; but the second sort came from the Alps. The first is used in medicine, and in confectionary for seed-cakes. *Millar.*

AVE'NTURE. *n. s.* [*aventure*, Fr.] A mischance, causing a man's death, without felony; as when he is suddenly drowned, or burnt, by any sudden disease falling into the fire or water. See ADVENTURE. *Cowel.*

A'VENUE. *n. s.* [*avenue*, Fr. It is sometimes pronounced with the accent on the second syllable, as *Watts* observes; but it is generally placed on the first.]

1. A way by which any place may be entered.

Good guards were set up at all the *avenues* of the city, to keep all people from going out. *Clarendon, b.* viii.

Truth is a strong-hold, and diligence is laying siege to it: so that it must observe all the *avenues* and passes to it. *South.*

2. An alley, or walk of trees before a house.

To AVER. *v. a.* [*averer*, Fr. from *verum*, truth, Lat.] To declare positively, or peremptorily.

The reason of the thing is clear;
Would Jove the naked truth *aver*. *Prior.*

Then vainly the philosopher *avers*,
That reason guides our deed, and instinct theirs.
How can we justly diff'rent causes frame,
When the effects entirely are the same? *Prior.*

We may *aver*, though the power of God be infinite, the capacities of matter are within limits. *Bentley's Sermons.*

A'VERAGE. *n. s.* [*averagium*, Lat.]

1. In law, that duty or service which the tenant is to pay to the king, or other lord, by his beasts and carriages. *Chambers.*

2. In navigation, a certain contribution that merchants and others proportionably make towards the losses of such as have their goods cast overboard for the safety of the ship; or of the goods and lives of those in the ship, in a tempest; and this contribution seems to be so called, because it is so proportioned, after the rate of every man's *average* or goods carried. *Cowel.*

3. A small duty which merchants, who send goods in another man's ship, pay to the master thereof for his care of them, over and above the freight. *Chambers.*

4. A medium; a mean proportion.

AVE'RMENT. *n. s.* [from *aver.*]

1. Establishment of any thing by evidence.

To avoid the oath, for *averment* of the continuance of some estate, which is eigne, the party will sue a pardon. *Bacon on Alien.*

2. An offer of the defendant to justify an exception, and the act as well as the offer. *Blount.*

AVE'RNAT. *n. s.* A sort of grape. See VINE.

AVERRUNCA'TION. *n. s.* [from *averruncate.*] The act of rooting up any thing.

To AVERRU'NCATE. *v. a.* [*averrunco*, Lat.] To root up; to tear up by the roots.

Sure some mischief will come of it,
Unless by providential wit,
Or force, we *averruncate* it. *Hudibras.*

AVERSA'TION. *n. s.* [from *aversor*, Lat.]

1. Hatred; abhorrence; turning away with detestation.

Hatred is the passion of defiance, and there is a kind of *aversation* and hostility included in its essence. *South.*

2. It is most properly used with *from* before the object of hate.

There was a stiff *aversation* in my lord of Essex *from* applying himself to the earl of Leicester. *Wotton.*

3. Sometimes with *to*, less properly.

There is such a general *aversation* in human nature *to* contempt, that there is scarce any thing more exasperating. I will not deny, but the excess of the *aversation* may be levelled against pride. *Government of the Tongue*, § 7.

4. Sometimes, very improperly, with *towards.*

A natural and secret hatred and *aversation towards* society, in any man, hath somewhat of the savage beast. *Bacon.*

AVE'RSE. *adj.* [*aversus*, Lat.]

1. Malign; not favourable.

Their courage languish'd, as their hopes decay'd,
And Pallas, now *averse*, refus'd her aid. *Dryden's Æneid.*

2. Not pleased with; unwilling to; having such a hatred as to turn away.

Has thy uncertain bosom ever strove
With the first tumults of a real love?
Hast thou now dreaded, and now bless'd his sway,
By turns *averse*, and joyful to obey? *Prior.*

Averse alike to flatter, or offend,
Not free from faults, nor yet too vain to mend. *Pope.*

3. It has most properly *from* before the object of aversion.

Laws politick are never framed as they should be, unless presuming the will of man to be inwardly obstinate, rebellious, and *averse from* all obedience unto the sacred laws of his nature. *Hooker, b.* i.

They believed all who objected against their undertaking to be *averse from* peace. *Clarendon, b.* viii.

These cares alone her virgin breast employ,
Averse from Venus and the nuptial joy. *Pope.*

4. Very frequently, but improperly, *to.*

He had, from the beginning of the war, been very *averse to* any advice of the privy council. *Clarendon, b.* viii.

Diodorus tells us of one Charondos, who was *averse to* all innovation, especially when it was to proceed from particular persons. *Swift on the Dissensions in Athens and Rome.*

AVE'RSELY. *adv.* [from *averse.*]

1. Unwillingly.

2. Backwardly.

Not only they want those parts of secretion, but it is emitted *aversely*, or backward, by both sexes. *Brown's Vulgar Err.*

AVE'RSE-

Ave'rsenes. *n. s.* [from *averse.*] Unwillingness; backwardness.
The corruption of man is in nothing more manifest, than in his *averseness* to entertain any friendship or familiarity with God. *Atterbury's Sermons.*

Ave'rsion. *n. s.* [*aversion*, Fr. *aversio*, Lat.]
1. Hatred; dislike; detestation; such as turns away from the object.
What if with like *aversion* I reject
Riches and realms? *Milton's Par. Lost, b.* ii.
2. It is used most properly with *from* before the object of hate.
They had an inward *aversion from* it, and were resolved to prevent it by all possible means. *Clarendon, b.* viii.
With men these considerations are usually causes of despite, disdain, or *aversion from* others; but with God, so many reasons of our greater tenderness towards others. *Sprat's Sermons.*
The same adhesion to vice, and *aversion from* goodness, will be a reason for rejecting any proof whatsoever. *Atterbury.*
3. Sometimes, less properly, with *to.*
A freeholder is bred with an *aversion to* subjection. *Addison.*
I might borrow illustrations of freedom and *aversion to* receive new truths from modern astronomy. *Watts.*
4. Sometimes with *for.*
The Lucquese would rather throw themselves under the government of the Genoese, than submit to a state *for* which they have so great *aversion.* *Addison on Italy.*
This *aversion* of the people *for* the late proceedings of the commons, might be improved to good uses. *Swift.*
5. Sometimes, very improperly, with *towards.*
His *aversion towards* the house of York was so predominant, as it found place not only in his councils but in his bed. *Bacon.*
6. The cause of aversion.
They took great pleasure in compounding law-suits among their neighbours; for which they were the *aversion* of the gentlemen of the long robe. *Arbuthnot's History of J. Bull.*
Self-love and reason to one end aspire;
Pain their *aversion*, pleasure their desire. *Pope's Ess. on Man.*

To AVE'RT. *v. a.* [*averto*, Lat.]
1. To turn aside; to turn off.
I beseech you
T' *avert* your liking a more worthy way,
Than on a wretch. *Shakesp. King Lear.*
At this, for the last time, she lifts her hand,
Averts her eyes, and half unwilling drops the brand. *Dryden.*
2. To put by, as a calamity.
O Lord! *avert* whatsoever evil our swerving may threaten unto his church. *Hooker, b.* iv.
Diversity of conjectures made many, whose conceits *averted* from themselves the fortune of that war, to become careless and secure. *Knolles's History of the Turks.*
These affections earnestly fix our minds on God, and forcibly *avert* from us those things which are displeasing to him, and contrary to religion. *Sprat's Sermons.*
Thro' threaten'd lands they wild destruction throw,
Till ardent prayer *averts* the publick woe. *Prior.*

Auf. *n. s.* [of *alf*, Dutch.] A fool, or silly fellow. *Dict.*

A'uger. *n. s.* [*egger*, Dut.] A carpenter's tool to bore holes with.
The *auger* hath a handle and bit; its office is to make great round holes. When you use it, the stuff you work upon is commonly laid low under you, that you may the easier use your strength; for in twisting the bit about by the force of both your hands, on each end of the handle one, it cuts great chips out of the stuff. *Moxon's Mechanical Exercises.*

Aught. *pronoun.* [auht, apht, Saxon. It is sometimes, improperly, written *ought.*] Any thing.
If I can do it,
By *aught* that I can speak in his dispraise,
She shall not long continue love to him. *Sh. T. G. of Verona.*
They may, for *aught* I know, obtain such substances as may induce the chymists to entertain other thoughts. *Boyle.*
But go, my son, and see if *aught* be wanting
Among thy father's friends. *Addison's Cato.*

To AUGME'NT. *v. a.* [*augmenter*, Fr.] To encrease; to make bigger, or more.
Some cursed weeds her cunning hand did know,
That could *augment* his harm, encrease his pain. *Fairfax.*
Rivers, though they continue the denomination of their first stream, have streams added to them in their passage, which enlarge and *augment* them. *Hale's Common Law of England.*

To Augme'nt. *v. n.* To encrease; to grow bigger.
But as his heat with running did *augment*,
Much more his sight encreas'd his hot desire. *Sidney.*
The rocks are from their old foundations rent;
The winds redouble, and the rains *augment*;
The waves on heaps are dash'd. *Dryd. Virgil, Georg.*

A'ugment. *n. s.* [*augmentum*, Lat.]
1. Encrease.
You shall find this *augment* of the tree to be without the diminution of one drachm of the earth. *Walton's Angler.*
2. State of encrease.
Discutients are improper in the beginning of inflammations but proper, when mixed with repellents, in the *augment. Wisem.*

Augmenta'tion. *n. s.* [from *augment.*]
1. The act of encreasing or making bigger.
Those who would be zealous against regular troops after a peace, will promote an *augmentation* of those on foot. *Addison.*
2. The state of being made bigger.
What modification of matter can make one embryo capable of so prodigiously vast *augmentation*, while another is confined to the minuteness of an insect. *Bentley's Sermons.*
3. The thing added, by which another is made bigger.
By being glorified, it does not mean that he doth receive any *augmentation* of glory at our hands; but his name we glorify, when we testify our acknowledgment of his glory. *Hooker.*

Augmentation *Court.* A court erected by king Henry the eight, for the increase of the revenues of his crown, by the suppression of monasteries. *Dict.*

A'ugre. *n. s.* A carpenter's tool. See Auger.
Your temples burned in the cement, and
Your franchises, whereon you stood, confin'd
Into an *augre's* bore. *Shakesp. Coriolanus.*

Augre-hole. *n. s.* [from *augre* and *hole.*] A hole made by boring with an augre.
What should be spoken here,
Where our fate hid within an *augre-hole*,
May rush and seize us? *Shakesp. Macbeth.*

A'UGUR. *n. s.* [*augur*, Lat.] One who pretends to predict by omens, particularly by the flight of birds.
What say the *augurs?*———
—They would not have you stir forth to-day:
Plucking the entrails of an offering forth,
They could not find a heart within the beast. *Shak. J. Cæs.*
Calchas, the sacred seer, who had in view
Things present and the past, and things to come foreknew:
Supreme of *augurs.* *Dryden's Fables.*
As I and mine consult thy *augur*,
Grant the glad omen; let thy fav'rite rise
Propitious, ever soaring from the right. *Prior.*

To A'ugur. *v. n.* [from *augur.*] To guess; to conjecture by signs.
The people love me, and the sea is mine,
My pow'r's a crescent, and my *aug'ring* hope
Says it will come to the full. *Shakesp. Ant. and Cleopat.*
Fought for a crown and bright Lavinia's bed;
So will I meet thee hand to hand oppos'd;
My *aug'ring* mind assures the same success. *Dryd. K. Arthur.*

To A'ugurate. *v. n.* [*auguror.* Lat.] To judge by augury.

Augura'tion. *n s.* [from *augur.*] The practice of augury, or of foretelling by events and prodigies.
And Claudius Pulcher underwent the like success, when he continued the tripudiary *augurations. Brown's Vulgar Errours.*

A'ugurer. *n. s.* [from *augur.*] The same with *augur.*
These apparent prodigies,
The unaccustom'd terrour of this night,
And the persuasion of his *augurers*,
May hold him from the capitol to-day. *Shakesp. Julius Cæs.*

A'ugurial. *adj.* [from *augury.*] Relating to augury.
On this foundation were built the conclusions of southsayers, in their *augurial* and tripudiary divinations. *Brown's Vulg. Err.*

To A'ugurise. *v. n.* [from *augur.*] To practise divination by augury. *Dict.*

A'ugurous. *adj.* [from *augur.*] Predicting; prescient; foreboding.
So fear'd
The fair-man'd horses, that they flew back, and their chariots turn'd,
Presaging in their *augurous* hearts the labours that they mourn'd. *Chapman's Iliad.*

A'ugury. *n. s.* [*augurium*, Lat.]
1. The act of prognosticating by omens or prodigies.
The winds are chang'd, your friends from danger free,
Or I renounce my skill in *augury.* *Dryden's Æneid.*
She knew by *augury* divine,
Venus would fail in her design. *Swift.*
2. The rules observed by augurs.
The goddess has such an aversion to ye, that you are particularly excluded out of all *auguries.* *L'Estrange.*
3. An omen or prediction.
Thy face and thy behaviour,
Which, if my *augury* deceive me not,
Witness good breeding. *Shakesp. Two Gentlemen of Verona.*
What if this death, which is for him design'd,
Had been your doom (far be that *augury!*)
And you not, Aurengzebe, condemn'd to die. *Dryden.*
The pow'rs we both invoke,
To you, and yours, and mine, propitious be,
And firm our purpose with an *augury.* *Dryden's Æneid.*

Augu'st. *adj.* [*augustus*, Lat.] Great; grand; royal; magnificent; awful.
There is nothing so contemptible, but antiquity can render it *august* and excellent. *Glanville's Scepsis, c.* 22.
The Trojan chief appear'd in open sight,
August in visage, and serenely bright;
His mother goddess, with her hands divine,
Had form'd his curling locks, and made his temples shine. *Dry.*

A'ugust. *n. s.* [*augustus*, Lat.] The name of the eight month from January inclusive.

August was dedicated to the honour of Augustus Cæsar, because, in the same month, he was created consul, thrice triumpher in Rome, subdued Egypt to the Roman empire, and made an end of civil wars; being before called *Sextilis*, or the sixth from March. *Peacham.*

AUGU'STNESS. *n. s.* [from *august.*] Elevation of look; dignity; loftiness of mien or aspect.

A'VIARY. *n. s.* [from *avis*, Lat. a bird.] A place inclosed to keep birds in.

In *aviaries* of wire, to keep birds of all sorts, the Italians bestow vast expence; including great scope of ground, variety of bushes, trees of good height, running waters, and sometimes a stove annexed, to contemper the air in the winter. *Wotton's Architecture.*

Look now to your *aviary*; for now the birds grow sick of their feathers. *Evelyn's Kalendar.*

AVI'DITY. *n. s.* [*avidité*, Fr. *aviditas*, Lat.] Greediness; eagerness; appetite; insatiable desire.

A'VITOUS. *adj.* [*avitus*, Lat.] Left by a man's ancestors; ancient. *Dict.*

To AVI'ZE. *v. a.* [*aviser*, Fr.] A word out of use.

1. To counsel.

With that, the husbandman 'gan him *avize*,
That it for him was fittest exercise. *Spens. Hubb. Tale.*

2. With a reciprocal pronoun, to bethink himself; *s'aviser*, Fr.

But *him avizing*, he that dreadful deed
Forbore, and rather chose, with scornful shame,
Him to avenge. *Spenser's Hubberd's Tale.*

3. To consider.

No power he had to stir, nor will to rise,
That when the careful knight 'gan well *avize*,
He lightly left the foe. *Fairy Queen, b.* i.

A'UKWARD. See AWKWARD.

AULD. *adj.* [alb, Sax.] A word now obsolete; but still used in the Scotch dialect.

'Tis pride that pulls the country down;
Then take thine *auld* cloak about thee. *Shakesp. Othello.*

AULE'TICK. *adj.* [*auleticus*, Lat.] Belonging to pipes. *Dict.*

A'ULICK. *adj.* [*aulicus*, Lat.] Belonging to the court.

AULN. *n. s.* [*aulne*, Fr.] A French measure of length; an ell.

To AUMA'IL. *v. a.* [from *maille*, Fr. the mesh of a net; whence a coat of *amail*, a coat with network of iron.] To variegate; to figure.

In golden buskins of costly cordwaine,
All hard with golden bendes, which were entail'd
With curious anticks, and full fair *aumail'd*. *Fairy Queen.*

AU'MBRY. See AMBRY.

AUNT. *n. s.* [*tante*, Fr. *amita*, Lat.] A father or mother's sister; correlative to nephew or niece.

Who meets us here? my niece Plantagenet,
Led in the hand of her kind *aunt* of Glo'ster. *Shak. R.* III.

She went to plain work, and to purling brooks,
Old fashion'd halls, dull *aunts*, and croaking rooks. *Pope.*

AVOCA'DO. n. s. [Span. *Persica*, Lat.] The name of a plant.

This plant hath a rose-shaped flower, consisting of several leaves, which are ranged in a circle; from whose middle rises the pointal, which afterwards becomes a soft, fleshy, pear-shaped fruit, in which is an hard stone or seed, having two lobes, which is included in a membrane or pericardium.

The tree grows in great plenty in the Spanish West Indies, as also in the island of Jamaica; and hath been transplanted into the English settlements in America, upon account of its fruit, which is very necessary for the support of life. The fruit is of itself very insipid, for which reason they generally eat it with the juice of lemons and sugar, to give it a poignancy. This tree, in warm countries where it is planted, grows to the height of thirty feet, with a trunk as large as common apple-trees; the bark smooth and of an ash colour; the branches are beset with pretty large oblong smooth leaves, of a deep green colour throughout the year. The flowers and fruit are produced towards the extremity of the branches. *Millar.*

To A'VOCATE. *v. a.* [*avoco*, Lat.] To call off from business; to call away.

Their divesture of mortality dispenses them from those laborious and *avocating* duties to distressed christians, and their secular relations, which are here requisite. *Boyle.*

AVOCA'TION. *n. s.* [from *avocate.*]

1. The act of calling aside.

The bustle of business, the *avocations* of our senses, and the din of a clamorous world, are impediments. *Glanville's Scep.*

Stir up that remembrance, which his many *avocations* of business have caused him to lay aside. *Dryd. Aurengz. Pref.*

2. The business that calls; or the call that summons away.

It is a subject that we may make some progress in its contemplation within the time, that the ordinary time of life, and the permission of necessary *avocations*, a man may employ in such a contemplation. *Hale's Origin of Mankind.*

God does frequently inject into the soul blessed impulses to duty, and powerful *avocations* from sin. *South.*

By the secular cares and *avocations* which accompany marriage, the clergy have been furnished with skill in common life. *Atterbury.*

To AVO'ID. *v. a.* [*vuider*, Fr.]

1. To shun; to escape.

The wisdom of pleasing God, by doing what he commands, and *avoiding* what he forbids. *Tillotson.*

2. To endeavour to shun.

The fashion of the world is to *avoid* cost, and you encounter it. *Shakesp. Much ado about Nothing.*

3. To evacuate; to quit.

What have you to do here, fellow? pray you, *avoid* the house. *Shakesp. Coriolanus.*

If any rebel should be required of the prince confederate, the prince confedederate should command him to *avoid* the country. *Bacon's Henry* VII.

He desired to speak with some few of us: whereupon six of us only stayed, and the rest *avoided* the room. *Bacon's N. Atl.*

4. To oppose; to hinder effect.

The removing that which caused putrefaction, doth prevent and *avoid* putrefaction. *Bacon's Nat. Hist.* N° 340.

To AVOID. *v. n.*

1. To retire.

And Saul cast the javelin; for he said, I will smite David even to the wall with it: and David *avoided* out of his presence twice. 1 *Sam.* xviii. 11.

2. To become void or vacant.

Bishopricks are not included under benefices: so that if a person takes a bishoprick, it does not *avoid* by force of that law of pluralities, but by the ancient common law.

Ayliffe's Parergon Juris Canonici.

AVO'IDABLE. *adj.* [from *avoid.*] That which may be avoided, shunned, or escaped.

Want of exactness in such nice experiments is scarce *avoidable*. *Boyle.*

To take several things for granted, is hardly *avoidable* to any one, whose task it is to shew the falsehood or improbability of any truth. *Locke.*

AVO'IDANCE. *n. s.* [from *avoid.*]

1. The act of avoiding.

It is appointed to give us vigour in the pursuit of what is good, or in the *avoidance* of what is hurtful. *Watts's Logick.*

2. The course by which any thing is carried off.

For *avoidances*, and drainings of water, where there is too much, we shall speak of. *Bacon's Nat. History,* N° 600.

AVO'IDER. *n. s.* [from *avoid.*]

1. The person that avoids or shuns any thing.
2. The person that carries any thing away.
3. The vessel in which things are carried away.

AVO'IDLESS. *adj.* [from *avoid.*] Inevitable; that which cannot be avoided.

That *avoidless* ruin in which the whole empire would be involved. *Dennis's Letters.*

AVOIRDUPO'IS. *n. s.* [*avoir du poids*, Fr.] A kind of weight, of which a pound contains sixteen ounces, and is in proportion to a pound Troy, as seventeen to fourteen. All the larger and coarser commodities are weighed by *avoirdupois* weight. *Chambers.*

Probably the Romans left their ounce in Britain, which is now our *avoirdupois* ounce: for our Troy ounce we had elsewhere. *Arbuthnot on Coins.*

AVOLA'TION. *n. s.* [from *avolo*, to fly away, Lat.] The act of flying away; flight; escape.

These airy vegetables are made by the relicks of plantal emissives, whose *avolation* was prevented by the condensed enclosure. *Glanville's Scepsis, c.* vii.

Strangers, or the fungous parcels about candles, only signify a pluvious air hindering the *avolation* of the favillous particles. *Brown's Vulgar Errours.*

To AVO'UCH. *v. a.* [*avouer*, Fr. for this word we now generally say *vouch.*]

1. To affirm; to maintain; to declare peremptorily.

They boldly *avouched* that themselves only had the truth, which they would at all times defend. *Hooker, Pref.*

Wretched though I seem,
I can produce a champion that will prove
What is *avouched* here. *Shakesp. King Lear.*

2. To produce in favour of another.

Such antiquities could have been *avouched* for the Irish. *Spenser's Ireland.*

3. To vindicate; to justify.

You will think you made no offence, if the duke *avouch* the justice of your dealing. *Shakesp. Measure for Measure.*

AVO'UCH. *n. s.* [from the verb.] Declaration; evidence.

I might not this believe,
Without the sensible and try'd *avouch*
Of mine own eyes. *Shakesp. Hamlet.*

AVO'UCHABLE. *adj.* [from *avouch.*] That may be avouched.

AVO'UCHER. *n. s.* [from *avouch.*] He that avouches.

To AVO'W. *v. a.* [*avouer*, Fr.] To declare with confidence; to justify; not to dissemble.

His cruel stepdame seeing what was done,
Her wicked days with wretched knife did end;
In death *avowing* th' innocence of her son. *Fairy Queen.*

He that delivers them mentions his doing it upon his own

particular knowledge, or the relation of ſome credible perſon, *avowing* it upon his own experience. *Boyle.*

Left to myſelf, I muſt *avow*, I ſtrove,
From publick ſhame to ſkreen my ſecret love. *Dryden.*

Such aſſertions proceed from principles which cannot be *avowed* by thoſe who are for preſerving church and ſtate. *Swift.*

Then blaz'd his ſmother'd flame, *avow'd* and bold. *Thomſ.*

AVO'WABLE. *adj.* [from *avow.*] That which may be openly declared; that which may be declared without ſhame.

AVO'WAL. *n. ſ.* [from *avow.*] Juſtificatory declaration; open declaration.

AVO'WEDLY. *adv.* [from *avow.*] In an avowed manner.

Wilmot could not *avowedly* have excepted againſt the other. *Clarendon, b.* viii.

AVOWE'E. *n. ſ.* [*avoué*, Fr.] He to whom the right of advowſon of any church belongs. *Dict.*

AVO'WER. *n. ſ.* [from *avow.*] He that avows or juſtifies.

Virgil makes Æneas a bold *avower* of his own virtues. *Dryd.*

AVO'WRY. *n. ſ.* [from *avow.*] In law, is where one takes a diſtreſs for rent, or other thing, and the other ſues replevin. In which caſe the taker ſhall juſtify, in his plea, for what cauſe he took it; and, if he took it in his own right, is to ſhew it, and ſo avow the taking, which is called his *avowry*. *Chambers.*

AVO'WSAL. *n. ſ.* [from *avow.*] A confeſſion. *Dict.*

AVO'WTRY. *n. ſ.* [See ADVOWTRY.] Adultery.

A'URATE. *n. ſ.* A ſort of pear; which ſee.

AURE'LIA. *n. ſ.* [Lat.] A term uſed for the firſt apparent change of the eruca, or maggot of any ſpecies of inſects. *Chambers.*

The ſolitary maggot, found in the dry heads of teaſel, is ſometimes changed into the *aurelia* of a butterfly, ſometimes into a fly-caſe. *Ray on Creation.*

A'URICLE. *n. ſ.* [*auricula*, Lat.]

1. The external ear, or that part of the ear which is prominent from the head.
2. Two appendages of the heart; being two muſcular caps, covering the two ventricles thereof; thus called from the reſemblance they bear to the external ear. They move regularly like the heart, only in an inverted order; their ſyſtole correſponding to the diaſtole of the heart. *Chambers.*

Blood ſhould be ready to join with the chyle, before it reaches the right *auricle* of the heart. *Ray on Creation.*

AURI'CULA. *n. ſ.* See BEARS EAR.

AURI'CULAR. *n. ſ.* [from *auricula*, Lat. the ear.]

1. Within the ſenſe or reach of hearing.

You ſhall hear us confer, and by an *auricular* aſſurance have your ſatisfaction. *Shakeſp. King Lear.*

2. Secret; told in the ear; as *auricular* confeſſion.

AURI'CULARLY. *adv.* [from *auricular.*] In a ſecret manner.

Theſe will ſoon confeſs, and that not *auricularly*, but in a loud and audible voice. *Decay of Piety.*

AURI'FEROUS. *adj.* [*aurifer*, Lat.] That which produces gold.

Rocks rich in gems, and mountains big with mines,
Whence many a burſting ſtream *auriferous* plays. *Thomſon.*

AURIGA'TION. *n. ſ.* [*auriga*, Lat.] The act or practice of driving carriages. *Dict.*

AURI'PIGMENTUM. See ORPIMENT.

AURO'RA. *n. ſ.* [Lat.]

1. A ſpecies of crowfoot; which ſee.
2. The goddeſs that opens the gates of day; poetically, the morning.

Aurora ſheds,
On Indus' ſmiling banks the roſy ſhower. *Thomſon's Summ.*

AURO'RA Borealis. See STREAMERS.

AURUM fulminans. [Latin.] A preparation made by diſſolving gold in aqua regia, and precipitating it with ſalt of tartar; whence a very ſmall quantity of it becomes capable, by a moderate heat, of giving a report like that of a piſtol. *Quincy.*

Some *aurum fulminans* the fabrick ſhook. *Garth.*

AUSCULTA'TION. *n. ſ.* [from *auſculto*, Lat.] A hearkening or liſtening to. *Dict.*

A'USPICE. *n. ſ.* [*auſpicium*, Lat.]

1. The omens of any future undertaking drawn from birds.
2. Protection; favour ſhewn by proſperous men.

Great father Mars, and greater Jove,
By whoſe high *auſpice* Rome hath ſtood
So long. *Ben Johnſon's Catiline.*

3. Influence; good derived to others from the piety of their patron.

But ſo may he live long, that town to ſway,
Which by his *auſpice* they will nobler make,
As he will hatch their aſhes by his ſtay. *Dryd. Ann. Mir.*

AUSPI'CIAL. *adj.* [from *auſpice.*] Relating to prognoſticks.

AUSPI'CIOUS. *adj.* [from *auſpice.*]

1. With omens of ſucceſs.

You are now, with happy and *auſpicious* beginnings, forming a model of a chriſtian charity. *Sprat.*

2. Proſperous; fortunate; applied to perſons.

Auſpicious chief! thy race in times to come,
Shall ſpread the conqueſts of imperial Rome. *Dryd. Æneid.*

3. Favourable; kind; propitious; applied to perſons.

Fortune play upon thy proſp'rous helm,
As thy *auſpicious* miſtreſs! *Shakeſp. All's well that ends well.*

4. Lucky; happy; applied to things.

I'll deliver all,
And promiſe you calm ſeas, *auſpicious* gales,
And ſails expeditious. *Shakeſp. Tempeſt.*

A pure, an active, an *auſpicious* flame,
And bright as heav'n from whence the bleſſing came. *Roſcommon.*

Two battles your *auſpicious* cauſe has won;
Thy ſword can perfect what it has begun;
And, from your walls, diſlodge that haughty ſon. *Dryden.*

AUSPI'CIOUSLY. *adv.* [from *auſpicious.*] Happily; proſperouſly; with proſperous omens.

AUSPI'CIOUSNESS. *n. ſ.* [from *auſpicious.*] Proſperity; happineſs.

AUSTE'RE. *adj.* [*auſterus*, Lat.]

1. Severe; harſh; rigid.

When men repreſent the Divine nature, as an *auſtere* and rigorous maſter, always lifting up his hand to take vengeance; ſuch conceptions muſt unavoidably raiſe terrour. *Rogers.*

Auſtere Saturnius, ſay,
From whence this wrath? or who controuls thy ſway? *Pope.*

2. Sower of taſte; harſh.

Th' *auſtere* and pond'rous juices they ſublime,
Make them aſcend the porous ſoil, and climb
The orange-tree, the citron, and the lime. *Blackm.*

Auſtere wines, diluted with water, cool more than water alone, and at the ſame time do not relax. *Arbuth. on Aliments.*

AUSTE'RELY. *adv.* [from *auſtere.*] Severely; rigidly.

Ah! Luciana, did he tempt thee ſo?
Might'ſt thou perceive *auſterely* in his eye,
That he did plead in earneſt, yea or no?
Look'd he or red, or pale, or ſad, or merrily? *Shakeſp. Comedy of Errours.*

Hypocrites *auſterely* talk
Of purity, and place, and innocence. *Paradiſe Loſt, b.* iv.

AUSTE'RENESS. *n. ſ.* [from *auſtere.*]

1. Severity; ſtrictneſs; rigour.

My unſoil'd name, th' *auſtereneſs* of my life,
May vouch againſt you; and my place i' th' ſtate
Will ſo your accuſation overweigh. *Shak. Meaſure for M.*

2. Roughneſs in taſte.

AUSTE'RITY. *n. ſ.* [from *auſtere.*]

1. Severity; mortified life; ſtrictneſs.

Now, Marcus Cato, our new conſul's ſpy,
What is your ſower *auſterity* ſent t'explore? *B. Johnſ. Catil.*

What was that ſnaky-headed Gorgon ſhield
That wiſe Minerva wore, unconquer'd virgin,
Wherewith ſhe freez'd her foes to congeal'd ſtone,
But rigid looks of chaſte *auſterity*,
And noble grace, that daſh'd brute violence
With ſudden adoration and blank awe? *Milton.*

This prince kept the government, and yet lived in this convent with all the rigour and *auſterity* of a capuchin. *Add. Italy.*

2. Cruelty; harſh diſcipline.

Let not *auſterity* breed ſervile fear;
No wanton ſound offend her virgin ear. *Roſcommon.*

A'USTRAL. *adj.* [*auſtralis*, Lat.] Southern; as the *auſtral* ſigns.

To A'USTRALIZE. *v. n.* [from *auſter*, the ſouth wind, Lat.] To tend towards the ſouth.

Steel and good iron diſcover a verticity, or polary faculty; whereby they do ſeptentriate at one extreme, and *auſtralize* at another. *Brown's Vulgar Errours, b.* ii. *c.* 2.

A'USTRINE. *adj.* [from *auſtrinus*, Lat.] Southern; ſouthernly.

AUTHE'NTICAL. *adj.* [from *authentick.*] The ſame with *authentick.*

Of ſtatutes made before time of memory, we have no *authentical* records, but only tranſcripts. *Hale's Common Law of Engl.*

AUTHE'NTICALLY. *adv.* [from *authentical.*] After an authentick manner; with all the circumſtances requiſite to procure authority.

This point is dubious, and not yet *authentically* decided. *Brown's Vulgar Errours, b.* ii. *c.* 5.

Conſcience never commands or forbids any thing *authentically*, but there is ſome law of God which commands or forbids it firſt. *South.*

AUTHE'NTICALNESS. *n. ſ.* [from *authentical.*] The quality of being authentick; genuineneſs; authority.

Nothing can be more pleaſant than to ſee a circle of theſe virtuoſo's about a cabinet of medals, deſcanting upon the value, rarity, and *authenticalneſs* of the ſeveral pieces. *Addiſon on ancient Medals.*

AUTHENTI'CITY. *n. ſ.* [from *authentick.*] Authority; genuineneſs; the being authentick.

AUTHE'NTICK. *adj.* [*authenticus*, Lat.] That which has every thing requiſite to give it authority, as an *authentick* regiſter. It is uſed in oppoſition to any thing by which authority is deſtroyed, as *authentick*, not *counterfeit*. It is never uſed of perſons.

Thou art wont his great *authentick* will
Interpreter through higheſt heav'n to bring. *Par. Loſt, b.* iii.

She joy'd th' *authentick* news to hear,
Of what ſhe gueſs'd before, with jealous fear. *Cowley.*

But censure's to be understood
Th' *authentick* mark of the elect,
The publick stamp heav'n sets on all that's great and good. *Swift.*

AUTHE'NTICKLY. *adv.* [from *authentick.*] After an authentick manner.

AUTHE'NTICKNESS. *n. s.* [from *authentick.*] The same with *authenticity.*

A'UTHOR. *n. s.* [*auctor*, Lat.]

1. The first beginner or mover of any thing; he to whom any thing owes its original.

That law, the *author* and observer whereof is one only God, to be blessed for ever. *Hooker, b.* i.

The *author* of that which causeth another thing to be, is *author* of that thing also which thereby is caused. *Hooker, b.* iii.

I'll never
Be such a gosling to obey instinct; but stand
As if a man was *author* of himself,
And knew no other kin. *Shakesp. Coriolanus.*

Thou art my father, thou my *author*, thou
My being gav'st me; whom should I obey,
But thee? *Milton's Paradise Lost, b.* ii.

But Faunus came from Picus, Picus drew
His birth from Saturn, if records be true.
Thus king Latinus, in the third degree,
Had Saturn *author* of his family. *Dryden, Æneid* vii.

If the worship of false Gods had not blinded the heathen, instead of teaching to worship the sun, and dead heroes, they would have taught us to worship our true *Author* and benefactor, as their ancestors did under the government of Noah and his sons, before they corrupted themselves. *Newton's Opticks.*

2. The efficient; he that effects or produces any thing.

That which is the strength of their amity, shall prove the immediate *author* of their variance. *Shakesp. Antony and Cleopat.*

Now while the tortur'd savage turns around,
And flings about his foam, impatient of the wound;
The wound's great *author* close at hand provokes
His rage. *Dryden's Fables.*

From his loins
New *authors* of dissention spring; from him
Two branches, that in hosting long contend
For sov'reign sway. *Philips.*

3. The first writer of any thing; distinct from the *translator* or *compiler.*

To stand upon every point in particulars, belongeth to the first *author* of the story. 2 *Macc.* ii. 30.

An *author* has the choice of his own thoughts and words, which a translator has not. *Dryden.*

4. A writer in general.

Yet their own *authors* faithfully affirm,
That the land Salike lies in Germany. *Shakesp. Henry* V.

AUTHO'RITATIVE. *adj.* [from *authority.*]

1. Having due authority.

2. Having an air of authority.

I dare not give them the *authoritative* title of aphorisms, which yet may make a reasonable moral prognostick. *Wotton.*

The two worthies have done mischief, the mock *authoritative* manner of the one, and the insipid mirth of the other. *Swift's Examiner*, N° 15.

AUTHO'RITATIVELY. *adv.* [from *authoritative.*]

1. In an authoritative manner; with a shew of authority.

2. With due authority.

No law that is foreign binds here in England, till it be received, and *authoritatively* engrafted, into the law of England. *Hale's History of Law.*

AUTHO'RITATIVENESS. *n. s.* [from *authoritative.*] An acting by authority; authoritative appearance. *Dict.*

AUTHO'RITY. *n. s.* [*auctoritas*, Lat.]

1. Legal power.

Idle old man,
That still would manage those *authorities*,
That he hath given away! *Shakes. King Lear.*

I know, my lord,
If law, *authority*, and pow'r deny not,
It will go hard with poor Antonio. *Shakesp. Merch. of Ven.*

Power arising from strength, is always in those that are governed, who are many: but *authority* arising from opinion, is in those that govern, who are few. *Temple.*

Adam's sovereignty, that by virtue of being proprietor of the whole world, he had any *authority* over men, could not have been inherited by any of his children. *Locke.*

2. Influence; credit.

The woods are fitter to give rules than cities, where those that call themselves civil and rational, go out of their way, by the *authority* of example. *Locke.*

3. Power; rule.

But I suffer not a woman to teach, nor to usurp *authority* over the man, but to be in silence. 1 *Tim.* ii. 12.

4. Support; justification; countenance.

Do'st thou expect th' *authority* of their voices,
Whose silent wills condemn thee? *Ben. Johns. Catiline.*

5. Testimony.

Something I have heard of this, which I would be glad to find by so sweet an *authority* confirmed. *Sidney, b.* ii.

We urge *authorities* in things that need not, and introduce the testimony of ancient writers, to confirm things evidently believed. *Brown's Vulgar Errours, b.* i. *c.* 6.

Having been so hardy as to undertake a charge against the philosophy of the schools, I was liable to have been overborn by a torrent of *authorities.* *Glanville's Scepsis Scientifica, Pref.*

6. Weight of testimony; credibility.

They consider the main consent of all the churches in the whole world, witnessing the sacred *authority* of scriptures, ever sithence the first publication thereof, even till this present day and hour. *Hooker, b.* v. § 22.

AUTHORIZA'TION. *n. s.* [from *authorize.*] Establishment by authority.

The obligation of laws arises not from their matter, but from their admission and reception, and *authorization* in this kingdom. *Hale's History of Law.*

To A'UTHORIZE. *v. a.* [*autoriser*, Fr.]

1. To give authority to any person.

Making herself an impudent suitor, *authorizing* herself very much, with making us see, that all favour and power depended upon her. *Sidney, b.* ii.

Deaf to complaints they wait upon the ill,
Till some safe crisis *authorize* their skill. *Dryden.*

2. To make any thing legal.

Yourself first made that title which I claim,
First bid me love, and *authoriz'd* my flame. *Dryd. Aurengz.*

My prayers are heard,
And I have nothing farther to desire,
But Sancho's leave to *authorize* our marriage. *Dryd. Sp. Fr.*

To have countenanced in him irregularity and disobedience to that light which he had, would have been, to have *authorized* disorder, confusion, and wickedness in his creatures. *Locke.*

3. To establish any thing by authority.

Lawful it is to devise any ceremony, and to *authorize* any kind of regiment, no special commandment being thereby violated. *Hooker, b.* iii. § 4.

Those forms are best which have been longest received and *authorized* in a nation by custom and use. *Temple.*

4. To justify; to prove a thing to be right.

All virtue lies in a power of denying our own desires, where reason does not *authorize* them. *Locke.*

5. To give credit to any person or thing.

Although their intention be sincere, yet doth it notoriously strengthen vulgar errour, and *authorize* opinions injurious unto truth. *Brown's Vulgar Errours, b.* i. *c.* 9.

Be a person in vogue with the multitude, he shall *authorize* any nonsense, and make incoherent stuff, seasoned with twang and tautology, pass for rhetorick. *South.*

AUTO'CRASY. *n. s.* [αὐτοκρατεῖα, from αὐτὸς, self, and κρατὸς, power.] Independent power; supremacy. *Dict.*

AUTOGRA'PHICAL. *adj.* [from *autography.*] Of one's own writing. *Dict.*

AUTO'GRAPHY. *n. s.* [αὐτογραφὸν, from αὐτὸς, and γράφω, to write.] A particular person's own writing; or the original of a treatise, in opposition to a copy.

AUTO'LOGY. *n. s.* [αὐτολογία.] A speaking of, or to one's own self. *Dict.*

AUTOMA'TICAL. *adj.* [from *automaton.*] Belonging to an automaton; having the power of moving themselves.

AUTO'MATON. *n. s.* [αὐτόματον. *In the plural*, automata.] A machine that hath the power of motion within itself, and which stands in need of no foreign assistance. *Quincy.*

For it is greater to understand the art, whereby the Almighty governs the motions of the great *automaton*, than to have learned the intrigues of policy. *Glanville's Scepsis Scientifica, Pref.*

The particular circumstances for which the *automata* of this kind are most eminent, may be reduced to four. *Wilkins's Mathematical Magick.*

AUTO'MATOUS. *adj.* [from *automaton.*] Having in itself the power of motion.

Clocks, or *automatous* organs, whereby we distinguish of time, have no mention in ancient writers. *Vulgar Err. b.* v.

AUTO'NOMY. *n. s.* [αὐτονομία.] The living according to one's mind and prescription. *Dict.*

A'UTOPSY. *n. s.* [αὐτοψία.] Ocular demonstration; seeing a thing one's self. *Quincy.*

In those that have forked tails, *autopsy* convinceth us, that it hath this use. *Ray on the Creation.*

AUTO'PTICAL. *adj.* [from *autopsy.*] Perceived by one's own eyes.

AUTO'PTICALLY. *adv.* [from *autoptical.*] By means of one's own eyes.

Were this true, it would *autoptically* silence that dispute, out of which Eve was framed. *Brown's Vulgar Errours, b.* vii.

That the galaxy is a meteor, was the account of Aristotle; but the telescope hath *autoptically* confuted it: and he, who is not Pyrrhonian enough to the disbelief of his senses, may see that it is no exhalation. *Glanville's Scepsis, c.* 20.

AUTOTHE'IST. *n. s.* [from αὐτὸς and Θεὸς, God.] One who believes God's self-subsistence. *Dict.*

A'UTUMN. *n. s.* [*autumnus*, Lat.] The season of the year between summer and winter, beginning astronomically at the equi-

equinox, and ending at the ſolſtice; popularly, *autumn* compriſes Auguſt, September, and October.

For I will board her, though ſhe chide as loud
As thunder, when the clouds in *autumn* crack. *As you like it.*

I would not be over confident, till he hath paſſed a ſpring or *autumn*. *Wiſeman's Surgery.*

The ſtarving brood,
Void of ſufficient ſuſtenance, will yield
A ſlender *autumn*. *Philips.*
While *autumn* nodding o'er the yellow plain,
Comes jovial on; the Dorick reed once more
Well pleas'd I'll tune. *Thomſon's Autumn.*

AUTU'MNAL. *adj.* [from *autumn.*] Belonging to autumn; produced in autumn.

No ſpring, or ſummer's beauty, hath ſuch grace,
As I have ſeen in one *autumnal* face. *Donne.*
Thou ſhalt not long
Rule in the clouds; like an *autumnal* ſtar,
Or light'ning, thou ſhalt fall. *Milt. Par. Loſt, b.* iv. *l.* 620.

Bind now up your *autumnal* flowers, to prevent ſudden guſts, which will proſtrate all. *Evelyn's Kalendar.*

Not the fair fruit that on yon branches glows,
With that ripe red th' *autumnal* ſun beſtows. *Pope.*

AVU'LSION. *n. ſ.* [*avulſio*, Lat.] The act of pulling one thing from another.

Spare not the little offsprings, if they grow
Redundant; but the thronging cluſters thin
By kind *avulſion*. *Philips.*

The preſſure of any ambient fluid can be no intelligible cauſe of the coheſion of matter; though ſuch a preſſure may hinder the *avulſion* of two poliſhed ſuperficies one from another, in a line perpendicular to them. *Locke.*

AUXE'SIS. n. ſ. [Latin.] An encreaſing; an exornation, when, for amplification, a more grave and magnificent word is put inſtead of the proper word. *Smith's Rhetorick.*

AUXI'LIAR. } *n. ſ.* [from *auxilium*, Lat.] Helper; aſſiſtant;
AUXI'LIARY. } confederate.

In the ſtrength of that power, he might, without the *auxiliaries* of any further influence, have determined his will to a full choice of God. *South.*

There are, indeed, a ſort of underling *auxiliars* to the difficulty of a work, called commentators and criticks. *Pope.*

AUXI'LIAR. } *adj.* [from *auxilium*, Lat.] Aſſiſtant; helping;
AUXI'LIARY. } confederate.

The giant brood,
That fought at Thebes and Ilium on each ſide,
Mix'd with *auxiliar* gods. *Milton's Paradiſe Loſt, b.* i.

Their tractates are little *auxiliary* unto ours, nor afford us any light to detenebrate this truth. *Brown's Vulgar Errours.*

There is not the ſmalleſt capillary vein but it is preſent with, and *auxiliary* to it, according to its uſe. *Hale's Orig. of Mank.*

Nor from his patrimonial heav'n alone
Is Jove content to pour his vengeance down;
Aid from his brother of the ſeas he craves,
To help him with *auxiliary* waves. *Dryden.*

AUXILIARY *Verb.* A verb that helps to conjugate other verbs.

In almoſt all languages, ſome of the commoneſt nouns and verbs have many irregularities; ſuch are the common *auxiliary* verbs, *to be* and *to have*, *to do* and *to be done*, &c. *Watts.*

AUXILIA'TION. *n. ſ.* [from *auxiliatus*, Lat.] Help; aid; ſuccour. *Dict.*

To AWA'IT. *v. a.* [from *a* and *wait.* See WAIT.]

1. To expect; to wait for.

Even as the wretch condemn'd to loſe his life,
Awaits the falling of the murd'ring knife. *Fairfax, b.* iv.
Betwixt the rocky pillars Gabriel ſat,
Chief of th' angelick guards, *awaiting* night. *Par. Loſt, b.* iv.

2. To attend; to be in ſtore for.

To ſhew thee what reward
Awaits the good; the reſt, what puniſhment. *Par. L. b.* xi.

Unleſs his wrath be appeaſed, an eternity of torments *awaits* the objects of his diſpleaſure. *Rogers.*

AWA'IT. *n. ſ.* [from the verb.] Ambuſh. See WAIT.

And leaſt miſhap the moſt bliſs alter may?
For thouſand perils lie in cloſe *await*
About us daily, to work our decay. *Spenſer's Muiopotmos.*

To AWA'KE. *v. a.* [peccian, Sax. *To awake* has the preterite *awoke*, or, as we now more commonly ſpeak, *awaked.*]

1. To rouſe out of ſleep.

Take heed,
How you *awake* our ſleeping ſword of war. *Shakeſp. Hen.* V.

Our friend Lazarus ſleepeth; but I go that I may *awake* him out of ſleep. *John*, xi. 11.

2. To raiſe from any ſtate reſembling ſleep.

Hark, hark, the horrid ſound
Has rais'd up his head:
As *awak'd* from the dead,
And amaz'd he ſtairs round. *Dryden's St. Cæcilia.*

3. To put into new action.

The fair
Repairs her ſmiles, *awakens* ev'ry grace,
And calls forth all the wonders of her face. *Pope.*

To AWA'KE. *v. n.* To break from ſleep; to ceaſe to ſleep.

Alack, I am afraid, they have *awak'd*;
And 'tis not done. *Shakeſp. Macbeth.*

I *awaked* up laſt of all, as one that gathereth after the grape-gatherers. *Ecclus*, xxxiii. 16.

AWA'KE. *adj.* [from the verb.] Without ſleep; not ſleeping.

Imagination is like to work better upon ſleeping men, than men *awake.* *Bacon's Nat. Hiſtory*, Nº 955.

Cares ſhall not keep him on the throne *awake*,
Nor break the golden ſlumbers he would take. *Dryden.*

To AWA'KEN. *v. a.* and *v. n.* See AWAKE.

To AWA'RD. *v. a.* [derived by *Skinner*, ſomewhat improbably, from peaꞃð, Sax. towards.]

1. To adjudge; to give any thing by a judicial ſentence.

A pound of that ſame merchant's fleſh is thine;
The court *awards* it, and the law doth give it.
Shakeſp. Merchant of Venice.

A church which allows ſalvation to none without it, nor *awards* damnation to almoſt any within it. *South.*

It advances that grand buſineſs, and according to which their eternity hereafter will be *awarded.* *Decay of Piety.*

Satisfaction for every affront cannot be *awarded* by ſtated laws. *Collier on Duelling.*

2. To judge; to determine.

Th' unwiſe *award* to lodge it in the tow'rs,
An off'ring ſacred. *Pope's Odyſſey, b.* viii. *l.* 555.

AWA'RD. *n. ſ.* [from the verb.] Judgment; ſentence; determination.

Now hear th' *award*, and happy may it prove
To her, and him who beſt deſerves her love. *Dryden's Fab.*

Affection bribes the judgment, and we cannot expect an equitable *award*, where the judge is made a party. *Glanville's Sceps.*

To urge the foe,
Prompted by blind revenge and wild deſpair,
Were to refuſe th' *awards* of providence. *Addiſon's Cato.*

AWA'RE. *adv.* [from *a* and *ware*; an old word for *cautious*; it is however, perhaps an *adjective*; ȝepaꞃian, Sax.] Vigilant; in a ſtate of alarm; attentive.

Ere I was *aware*, I had left myſelf nothing but the name of a king. *Sidney.*

Ere ſorrow was *aware*, they made his thoughts bear away ſomething elſe beſides his own ſorrow. *Sidney's Arcadia.*

Temptations of proſperity inſinuate themſelves; ſo that we are but little *aware* of them, and leſs able to withſtand them.
Atterbury's Sermons.

To AWA'RE. *v. n.* To beware; to be cautious.

So warn'd he them, *aware* themſelves; and
Inſtant, without diſturb, they took alarm. *Par. Loſt, b.* vi.

AWA'Y. *adv.* [apeȝ, Saxon.]

1. Abſent.

They could make
Love to your dreſs, although your face were *away.*
Ben. Johnſon's Catiline.

It is impoſſible to know properties that are ſo annexed to it, that any of them being *away*, that eſſence is not there. *Locke.*

2. From any place or perſon.

I have a pain upon my forehead here———
—Why that's with watching; 'twill *away* again.
Shakeſp. Othello.

When the fowls came down upon the carcaſes, Abraham drove them *away* again. *Gen.* xv. 11.

Would you youth and beauty ſtay,
Love hath wings, and will *away.* *Waller.*
Summer ſuns roll unperceiv'd *away.* *Pope.*

3. Let us go.

Away, old man; give me thy hand; *away*;
King Lear hath loſt, he and his daughter ta'en;
Give me thy hand. Come on. *Shakeſp. King Lear.*

4. Begone.

Away, and gliſter like the god of war,
When he intendeth to become the field. *Shakeſp. King John.*
I'll to the woods among the happier brutes:
Come, let's *away*; hark, the ſtill horn reſounds.
Smith's Phædra and Hippolitus.
Away, you flatt'rer!
Nor charge his gen'rous meaning. *Rowe's Jane Shore.*

5. Out of one's own hands; into the power of ſomething elſe.

It concerns every man, who will not trifle *away* his ſoul, and fool himſelf into irrecoverable miſery, to enquire into theſe matters. *Tillotſon.*

6. It is often uſed with a verb; as, to *drink away* an eſtate; to *idle away* a manor; that is, to drink or idle till an eſtate or manor is gone.

He *play'd* his life *away.* *Pope.*

7. On the way; on the road: perhaps this is the original import of the following phraſe.

Sir Valentine, whither *away* ſo faſt? *Sh. T. G. of Verona.*

8. Perhaps the phraſe, *he cannot away with*, may mean *he cannot travel with*; *he cannot bear the company.*

She never could *away* with me.———Never, never: ſhe would always ſay, ſhe could not abide maſter Shallow.
Shakeſp. Henry IV.

9. *Away with.* Throw away; take away.

If you dare think of deserving our charms,
Away with your sheephooks, and take to your arms. *Dryd.*

AWE. *n. s.* [eze, oza, Saxon.] Reverential fear; reverence.

They all be brought up idly, without *awe* of parents, without precepts of masters, and without fear of offence. *Spenser's State of Ireland.*

It fixed upon him who is only to be feared, God: and yet with a filial fear, which at the same time both fears and loves. It was *awe* without amazement, and dread without distraction. *South.*

What is the proper *awe* and fear, which is due from man to God? *Rogers.*

To AWE. *v. a.* [from the noun.] To strike with reverence, or fear.

If you will work on any man, you must either know his nature and fashions, and so lead him; or his ends, and so persuade him; or his weaknesses and disadvantages, and so *awe* him; or those that have interest in him, and so govern him. *Bacon.*

Why then was this forbid? Why, but to *awe*?
Why, but to keep you low, and ignorant,
His worshippers? *Milton's Paradise Lost, b.* ix.

Heav'n that hath plac'd this island to give law,
To balance Europe, and her states to *awe*. *Waller.*

The rods and axes of princes, and their deputies, may *awe* many into obedience; but the fame of their goodness, justice, and other virtues, will work on more. *Atterbury's Sermons.*

A'WEBAND. *n. s.* [from *awe* and *band*] A check. *Dict.*

A'WFUL. *adj.* [from *awe* and *full.*]

1. That which strikes with awe, or fills with reverence.

So *awful*, that with honour thou may'st love
Thy mate; who sees, when thou art seen least wise.
Milt. Par. Lost, b. viii. *l.* 577.

I approach thee thus, and gaze
Insatiate; I thus single; nor have fear'd
Thy *awful* brow, more *awful* thus retir'd,
Fairest resemblance of thy Maker fair!
Milton's Paradise Lost, b. ix.

2. Worshipful; in authority; invested with dignity. This sense is obsolete.

Know then, that some of us are gentlemen,
Such as the fury of ungovern'd youth
Thrust from the company of *awful* men.
Shakesp. Two Gentlemen of Verona.

3. Struck with awe; timorous; scrupulous. This sense occurs but rarely.

It is not nature and strict reason, but a weak and *awful* reverence for antiquity, and the vogue of fallible men. *Watts's Improvement of the Mind.*

A'WFULLY. *adv* [from *awful.*] In a reverential manner.

It will concern a man, to treat this great principle *awfully* and warily, by still observing what it commands, but especially what it forbids. *South.*

A'WFULNESS. *n. s.* [from *awful.*]

1. The quality of striking with awe; solemnity.

These objects naturally raise seriousness; and night heightens the *awfulness* of the place, and pours out her supernumerary horrours upon every thing. *Addison. Spect.* N° 110.

2. The state of being struck with awe.

An help to prayer, producing in us reverence and *awfulness* to the divine majesty of God. *Taylor's Rule of living holy.*

To AWHA'PE. *v. a.* [This word I have met with only in *Spenser*, nor can I discover whence it is derived; but imagine, that the Teutonick language had anciently *wapen*, to strike, or some such word, from which *weapons*, or offensive arms, took their denomination.] To strike; to confound.

Ah! my dear gossip, answer'd then the ape,
Deeply do your sad words my wits *awhape*,
Both for because your grief doth great appear,
And eke because myself am touched near. *Hubberd's Tale.*

AWHI'LE. *adv.* [This word, generally reputed an *adverb*, is only *a while*, that is, a time, an interval.] Some time; some space of time.

Stay, stay, I say;
And if you love me, as you say you do,
Let me persuade you to forbear *awhile*. *Shakesp. Henry* VI.

Into this wild abyss the wary fiend
Stood on the brink of hell, and look'd *awhile*,
Pond'ring his voyage. *Milt. Paradise Lost, b.* ii. *l.* 918.

AWK. *adj.* [a barbarous contraction of the word *awkward.*] Odd; out of order.

We have heard as arrant jangling in the pulpits, as the steeples; and professors ringing as *awk* as the bells to give notice of the conflagration. *L'Estrange.*

A'WKWARD. *adj.* [[æpapd, Saxon; that is, backward, untoward.]

1. Inelegant; unpolite; untaught; ungenteel.

Proud Italy,
Whose manners still our tardy, apish nation
Limps after in base *awkward* imitation. *Shak. Rich.* II.

Their own language is worthy their care; and they are judged of by their handsome or *awkward* way of expressing themselves in it. *Locke.*

An *awkward* shame, or fear of ill usage, has a share in this conduct. *Swift.*

2. Unready; unhandy; not dexterous; clumsy.

Slow to resolve, but in performance quick:
So true, that he was *awkward* at a trick. *Dryd. Hind and P.*

3. Perverse; untoward.

A kind and constant friend
To all that regularly offend;
But was implacable, and *awkward*,
To all that interlop'd and hawker'd. *Hudibras.*

A'WKWARDLY. *adv.* [from *awkward.*] Clumsily; unreadily; inelegantly; ungainly.

Dametas nodding from the waste upwards, and swearing he never knew man go more *awkwardly* to work. *Sidney.*

If any pretty creature is void of genius, and would perform her part but *awkwardly*, I must nevertheless insist upon her working. *Addison. Spectator,* N° 606.

And when any thing is done *awkwardly*, the common saying will pass upon them, that it is suitable to their breeding. *Locke.*

She still renews the ancient scene;
Forgets the forty years between;
Awkwardly gay, and oddly merry;
Her scarf pale pink, her head-knot cherry. *Prior.*

If a man be taught to hold his pen *awkwardly*, yet writes sufficiently well, it is not worth while to teach him the accurate methods of handling that instrument. *Watts's Imp. of the Mind.*

A'WKWARDNESS. *n. s.* [from *awkward.*] Inelegance; want of gentility; oddness; unsuitableness.

One may observe *awkwardness* in the Italians, which easily discovers their airs not to be natural. *Addis. Rem. on Italy.*

All his airs of behaviour have a certain *awkwardness* in them; but these awkward airs are worn away by degrees in company. *Watts's Improvement of the Mind.*

AWL. *n. s.* [æle, ale, Sax.] A pointed instrument to bore holes with.

He which was minded to make himself a perpetual servant, should, for a visible token thereof, have also his ear bored through with an *awl*. *Hooker, b.* iv. § 1.

You may likewise prick many holes with an *awl*, about a joint that will lie in the earth. *Mortimer's Husbandry.*

A'WLESS. *adj.* [from *awe*, and the negative *less.*]

1. Without reverence.

Against whose fury, and th' unmatched force,
The *awless* lion could not wage the fight. *Shak. King John.*

He claims the bull with *awless* insolence,
And having seiz'd his horns, accosts the prince. *Dryden.*

2. Without the power of causing reverence.

Ah me! I see the ruin of my house;
The tyger now hath seiz'd the gentle hind:
Insulting tyranny begins to jut
Upon the innocent and *awless* throne. *Shakesp. Rich.* III.

AWME, or AUME. *n. s.* A Dutch measure of capacity for liquids, containing eight steckans, or twenty verges or verteels; answering to what in England is called a tierce, or one sixth of a ton of France, or one seventh of an English ton. *Arbuth Tab.*

AWN. *n. s.* [*arista*, Lat.] The beard growing out of the corn or grass. *Chambers.*

A'WNING. *n. s.* A cover spread over a boat or vessel, to keep off the weather.

Of these boards I made an *awning* over me. *Robinson Cruso.*

AWO'KE. The preterite from *awake*.

And she said, the Philistines be upon thee, Samson. And he *awoke* out of his sleep. *Judges,* xvi. 20.

A'WORK. *adv.* [from *a* and *work.*] On work; into a state of labour.

So after Pyrrhus' pause,
Aroused vengeance sets him new *awork*. *Shakesp. Hamlet.*

By prescribing the condition, it sets us *awork* to the performances of it, and that by living well. *Hammond's Pract. Cat.*

A'WORKING. *adj.* [from *awork.*] In the state of working.

Long they thus travelled, yet never met
Adventure which might them *aworking* set. *Hubberd's Tale.*

AWRY'. *adv.* [from *a* and *wry.*]

1. Not in a strait direction; obliquely.

But her sad eyes still fast'ned on the ground,
Are governed with goodly modesty;
That suffers not one look to glance *awry*,
Which may let in a little thought unsound. *Spens. Epithal.*

Like perspectives which rightly gaz'd upon,
Shew nothing but confusion; ey'd *awry*,
Distinguish form. *Shakesp. Richard* II.

When lo!
A violent cross wind, from either coast,
Blows them transverse; ten thousand leagues *awry*
Into the devious air. *Milton's Paradise Lost, b.* ii.

2. Asquint; with oblique vision.

You know the king
With jealous eyes has look'd *awry*
On his son's actions. *Denham's Sophy.*

3. Not

3 Not level; unevenly.

I hap to ſtep *awry*, where I ſee no path, and can diſcern but few ſteps afore me. *Brerewood on Languages.*

4. Not equally between two points.

Not tyrants fierce that unrepenting die,
Not Cynthia when her manteau's pinn'd *awry*,
Ere felt ſuch rage. *Pope's Rape of the Lock.*

5. Not in a right ſtate; perverſely.

All *awry*, and which wried it to the moſt wry courſe of all, wit abuſed, rather to feign reaſon why it ſhould be amiſs, than how it ſhould be amended. *Sidney, b.* ii.

Much of the ſoul they talk, but all *awry*,
And in themſelves ſeek virtue, and to themſelves
All glory arrogate, to God give none. *Paradiſe Regained.*

Axe. *n. ſ.* [eax, acſe, Sax. *aſcia*, Lat.] An inſtrument conſiſting of a metal head, with a ſharp edge, fixed in a helve or handle, to cut with.

No metal can,
No, not the hangman's *axe*, bear half the keenneſs
Of thy ſharp envy. *Shakeſp. Merchant of Venice.*

There ſtood a foreſt on the mountain's brow,
Which overlook'd the ſhaded plains below;
No ſounding *axe* preſum'd theſe trees to bite,
Coeval with the world; a venerable ſight. *Dryden's Fables.*

AXI'LLA. n. ſ. [*axilla*, Lat.] The cavity under the upper part of the arm, called the arm-pit. *Quincy.*

Axi'llar. } *adj.* [from *axilla*, Lat.] Belonging to the arm-
A'xillary. } pit.

In the ſame manner is the *axillary* artery diſtributed unto the hand; below the cubit, it divideth unto two parts. *Brown's Vulgar Errours.*

A'xiom. *n. ſ.* [*axioma*, Lat. ἀξίωμα, from ἀξιόω.]

1. A propoſition evident at firſt ſight, that cannot be made plainer by demonſtration.

Axioms, or principles more general, are ſuch as this, that the greater good is to be choſen before the leſſer. *Hooker, b.* i.

2. An eſtabliſhed principle to be granted without new proof.

The *axioms* of that law, whereby natural agents are guided, have their uſe in the moral. *Hooker, b.* i.

Their affirmations are unto us no *axioms*; we eſteem thereof as things unſaid, and account them but in liſt of nothing. *Brown's Vulgar Errours, b.* i.

A'xis. *n. ſ.* [*axis*, Lat.] The line real or imaginary that paſſes through any thing, on which it may revolve.

But ſince they ſay our earth, from morn to morn,
On its own *axis* is oblig'd to turn;
That ſwift rotation muſt diſperſe in air
All things which on the rapid orb appear. *Blackmore.*

It might annually have compaſſed the ſun, and yet never have once turned upon its *axis*. *Bentley's Sermons.*

On their own *axis* as the planets run,
And make at once their circle round the ſun;
So two conſiſtent motions act the ſoul,
And one regards itſelf, and one the whole.
Pope's Eſſay on Man, epiſt. iii. *l.* 313.

A'xle. } *n. ſ.* [*axis*, Lat.] The pin which paſſes through
A'xle-tree. } the midſt of the wheel, on which the circumvolutions of the wheel are performed.

Venerable Neſtor
Should with a bond of air, ſtrong as the *axle-tree*
On which heav'n rides, knit all the Grecians ears
To his experienc'd tongue. *Shakeſp. Troilus and Creſſida.*

The fly ſate upon the *axle-tree* of the chariot-wheel, and ſaid, what a duſt do I raiſe? *Bacon's Eſſays.*

And the gilded car of day
His glowing *axle* doth allay
In the ſteep Atlantick ſtream. *Milton's Comus.*

He ſaw a greater ſun appear,
Than his bright throne or burning *axle-tree* could bear.
Milton's Chriſt's Nativity.

Ay. *adv.* [perhaps from *aio*, Lat.]

1. Yes; an *adverb* of anſwering affirmatively.

Return you thither?———
—*Ay*, madam, with the ſwifteſt wing of ſpeed.
Shakeſp. All's well that ends well.

What ſay'ſt thou? Wilt thou be of our conſort?
Say *ay*; and be the captain of us all.
Shakeſp. Two Gentlemen of Verona.

2. It is a word by which the ſenſe is enforced; even; yes, certainly; and more than that.

Remember it, and let it make thee creſt-fall'n;
Ay, and allay this thy abortive pride. *Shakeſp. Henry* VI.

Aye. *adv.* [apa, Saxon.] Always; to eternity; for ever.

And now in darkſome dungeon, wretched thrall,
Remedyleſs for *aye* he doth him hold. *Fairy Queen, b.* i.

Either prepare to die,
Or on Diana's altar to proteſt,
For *aye*, auſterity and ſingle life.
Shakeſpeare's Midſummer Night's Dream.

The ſoul, though made in time, ſurvives for *aye*;
And, though it hath beginning, ſees no end.
Sir John Davies.

And hears the muſes, in a ring,
Aye round about Jove's altar ſing. *Milton's Il Penſeroſo.*

Th' aſtoniſh'd mariners *aye* ply the pump;
No ſtay, nor reſt, till the wide breach is clos'd. *Philips.*

A'ygreen. *n. ſ.* The ſame with *houſeleek*; which ſee. *Dict.*

A'yry. *n. ſ.* [See Airy.]

I ſhould diſcourſe on the brancher, the haggard, and then treat of their ſeveral *ayries*. *Walton's Angler.*

A'zimuth. *n. ſ.* [Arab.]

1. The *azimuth* of the ſun, or of a ſtar, is an arch between the meridian of the place and any given vertical line.

2. *Magnetical azimuth*, is an arch of the horizon contained between the ſun's *azimuth* circle and the magnetical meridian; or it is the apparent diſtance of the ſun from the north or ſouth point of the compaſs.

3. *Azimuth Compaſs*, is an inſtrument uſed at ſea for finding the ſun's magnetical *azimuth*.

4. *Azimuth Dial*, is a dial whoſe ſtyle or gnomon is at right angles to the plane of the horizon.

5. *Azimuths*, called alſo vertical circles, are great circles interſecting each other in the zenith and nadir, and cutting the horizon at right angles, in all the points thereof. *Chambers.*

Azu're. *adj.* [*azur*, Fr. *azurro*, Span. *lazur*, Arab. from *lazuli*, a blue ſtone.] Blue; faint blue.

The blue of the firſt order, though very faint and little, may be the colour of ſome ſubſtances; and the *azure* colour of the ſkies ſeems to be of this order. *Newton's Opticks.*

Thus replies
Minerva, graceful with her *azure* eyes. *Pope's Odyſſey, b.* i.

The ſea,
Far through his *azure* turbulent domain,
Your empire owns. *Thomſon's Spring.*

B.

B, The ſecond letter of the Engliſh alphabet, is pronounced as in moſt other European languages, by preſſing the whole length of the lips together, and forcing them open with a ſtrong breath. It has a near affinity with the other labial letters, and is confounded by the Germans with *P*, and by the Gaſcons with *V*; from which an epigrammatiſt remarks, that *bibere* and *vivere* are in Gaſcony the ſame. The Spaniards, in moſt words, uſe *B* or *V* indifferently.

BAA. *n. ſ.* [See the verb.] The cry of a ſheep.

To BAA. *v. n.* [*balo*, Lat.] To cry like a ſheep.

Or like a lamb, whoſe dam away is ſet,
He treble *baas* for help, but none can get. *Sidney.*

To BA'BBLE. *v. n.* [*babbelen*, Germ. *babiller*, Fr.]

1. To prattle like a child; to prate imperfectly.

My *babbling* praiſes I repeat no more,
But hear, rejoice, ſtand ſilent, and adore. *Prior.*

2. To talk idly, or irrationally.

John had conned over a catalogue of hard words; theſe he uſed to *babble* indifferently in all companies. *Arbuthn. J. Bull.*

Let the ſilent ſanctuary ſhow,
What from the *babbling* ſchools we may not know. *Prior.*

3. To talk thoughtleſsly; to tell ſecrets.

There is more danger in a reſerved and ſilent friend, than in a noiſy *babbling* enemy. *L'Eſtrange.*

4. To talk much.

The *babbling* echo mocks the hounds,
Replying ſhrilly to the well tun'd horns,
As if a double hunt were heard at once. *Shakeſp. Tit. Andr.*

And had I pow'r to give that knowledge birth,
In all the ſpeeches of the *babbling* earth. *Prior.*

The *babbling* echo had deſcry'd his face;
She, who in others words her ſilence breaks. *Addiſon's Ovid.*

BA'BBLE. *n. ſ.* [*babil*, Fr.] Idle talk; ſenſeleſs prattle.

This *babble* ſhall not henceforth trouble me;
Here is a coil with proteſtation! *Shakeſp. Two G. of Verona.*

Come, no more,
This is mere moral *babble*. *Milton.*

With volleys of eternal *babble*,
And clamour more unanſwerable. *Hudibras.*

The *babble*, impertinence, and folly, I have taken notice of in diſputes. *Glanville's Scepſis Scientifica.*

BA'BBLEMENT. *n. ſ.* [from *babble.*] Senſeleſs prate.

Deluded all this while with ragged notions and *babblements*, while they expected worthy and delightful knowledge. *Milton.*

BA'BBLER. *n. ſ.* [from *babble.*]

1. An idle talker; an irrational prattler.

We hold our time too precious to be ſpent
With ſuch a *babbler*. *Shakeſp. King John.*

Great *babblers*, or talkers, are not fit for truſt. *L'Eſtrange.*

The apoſtle of my text had no ſooner propoſed it to the greater maſters at Athens, but he himſelf was ridiculed as a *babbler*. *Rogers.*

2. A teller of ſecrets.

Utterers of ſecrets he from thence debarr'd;
Babblers of folly, and blazers of crime. *Fairy Queen, b.* ii.

BABE. *n. ſ.* [*baban*, Welch; *babbaerd*, Dutch.] An infant; a child of either ſex.

Thoſe that do teach your *babes*,
Do it with gentle means, and eaſy taſks;
He might have chid me ſo: for, in good faith,
I am a child to chiding. *Shakeſp. Othello.*

Nor ſhall Sebaſtian's formidable name
Be longer uſ'd, to lull the crying *babe*. *Dryden's Don Seb.*

The *babe* had all that infant care beguiles,
And early knew his mother in her ſmiles. *Dryden.*

BA'BERY. *n. ſ.* [from *babe.*] Finery to pleaſe a babe or child.

So have I ſeen trim books in velvet dight,
With golden leaves and painted *babery*
Of ſeely boys, pleaſe unacquainted ſight. *Sidney.*

BA'BISH. *adj.* [from *babe.*] Childiſh.

If he be baſhful, and will ſoon bluſh, they call him a *babiſh* and ill brought up thing. *Aſcham's Schoolmaſter.*

BABO'ON. *n. ſ.* [*babouin*, Fr. It is ſuppoſed by *Skinner* to be the augmentation of *babe*, and to import a *great babe.*] A monkey of the largeſt kind.

You had looked through the grate like a geminy of *baboons*. *Shakeſp. Merry Wives of Windſor.*

He caſt every human feature out of his countenance, and became a *baboon*. *Addiſon. Spect.* N° 174.

BA'BY. *n. ſ.* [See BABE.]

1. A child; an infant.

The *baby* beats the nurſe, and quite athwart
Goes all decorum. *Shakeſp. Meaſure for Meaſure.*

The child muſt have ſugar plumbs, rather than make the poor *baby* cry. *Locke.*

He muſt marry, and propagate: the father cannot ſtay for the portion, nor the mother for *babies* to play with. *Locke.*

2. A ſmall image in imitation of a child, which girls play with.

The archduke ſaw that Perkin would prove a runnagate; and that it was the part of children to fall out about *babies*. *Bacon's Henry* VII.

Since no image can repreſent the great Creator, never think to honour him by your fooliſh puppets, and *babies* of dirt and clay. *Stillingfleet's Def. of Diſc. on Rom. Idolatry.*

BA'CCATED. *adj.* [*baccatus*, Lat.] Beſet with pearls; having many berries. *Dict.*

BACCHANA'LIAN. *n. ſ.* [from *bacchanalia*, Lat.] A riotous perſon; a drunkard.

BA'CCHANALS. *n. ſ.* [*bacchanalia*, Lat.] The drunken feaſts and revels of Bacchus, the god of wine.

Ha, my brave emperor, ſhall we dance now the Egyptian *bacchanals*, and celebrate our drink? *Shakeſp. Ant. and Cleop.*

What wild fury was there in the heathen *bacchanals*, which we have not ſeen equalled. *Decay of Piety.*

Both extremes were baniſhed from their walls,
Carthuſian faſts, and fulſome *bacchanals*. *Pope.*

B'ACCHUS BOLE. *n. ſ.* A flower not tall, but very full and broad-leaved; of a ſad light purple, and a proper white; having the three outmoſt leaves edged with a crimſon colour, bluiſh bottom, and dark purple. *Mortimer.*

BACCI'FEROUS. *adj.* [from *bacca*, a berry, and *fero*, to bear, Lat.] Berry-bearing.

Bacciferous trees are of four kinds.

1. Such as bear a calculate or naked berry; the flower and calix both falling off together, and leaving the berry bare; as the ſaſſafras trees.
2. Such as have a naked monoſpermous fruit, that is, containing in it only one ſeed; as the arbutes.
3. Such as have but polyſpermous fruit, that is, containing two or more kernels or ſeeds within it; as the jaſminum, liguſtrum.
4. Such as have their fruit compoſed of many acini, or round ſoft balls ſet cloſe together like a bunch of grapes; as the uva marina. *Ray.*

BACCI'VOROUS. *adj.* [from *bacca*, a berry, and *voro*, to devour, Lat.] A devourer of berries. *Dict.*

BA'CHELOR. *n. ſ.* [This is a word of very uncertain etymology, it not being well known what was its original ſenſe. *Junius* derives it from βάκηλος, fooliſh; *Menage*, from *bas chevalier*, a knight of the loweſt rank; *Spelman*, from *baculus*, a ſtaff; *Cujas*, from *buccella*, an allowance of proviſion. The moſt probable derivation ſeems to be from *bacca laurus*, the berry of a laurel or bay; bachelors being young, are of good hopes, like laurels in the berry. In Latin, *baccalaureus.*]

1. A man unmarried.

Such ſeparation
Becomes a virtuous *bachelor* and a maid.
Shakeſp. Midſummer Night's Dream.

The haunting of thoſe diſſolute places, or reſort to courteſans, are no more puniſhed in married men than in *bachelors*. *Bacon's New Atlantis.*

A true painter naturally delights in the liberty which belongs to the *bachelor's* eſtate. *Dryden's Dufreſnoy.*

Let ſinful *bachelors* their woes deplore,
Full well they merit all they feel, and more. *Pope.*

2. A man who takes his firſt degrees at the univerſity in any profeſſion.

Being a boy, new *bachelor* of arts, I chanced to ſpeak againſt the pope. *Aſcham's Schoolmaſter.*

I appear before your honour, in behalf of Martinus Scriblerus, *bachelor* of phyſick. *Arbuthn. and Pope's Mart. Scriblerus.*

3. A knight of the loweſt order. This is a ſenſe now little uſed.

BA'CHELORS *Button.* [See CAMPION, of which it is a ſpecies.] All the ſorts of this plant are hardy; they grow above two foot, and produce their flower in June and July. *Millar.*

BA'CHELORSHIP. *n. ſ.* [from *bachelor.*] The condition of a bachelor.

Her mother, living yet, can teſtify,
She was the firſt fruit of my *bachelorſhip*. *Shakeſp. Hen.* VI.

BACK. *n. ſ.* [bac, bæc, Sax. *bach*, Germ.]

1. The hinder part of the body, from the neck to the thighs.

As the voice goeth round, as well towards the *back* as towards the front of him that ſpeaketh, ſo likewiſe doth the echo: for you have many *back* echoes to the place where you ſtand. *Bacon's Nat. Hiſt.* N° 247.

Part following enter, part remain without,
With envy hear their fellow's conqu'ring ſhout;
And mount on others *backs*, in hope to ſhare. *Dryden.*

2. The outer part of the hand when it is ſhut; oppoſed to the *palm.*

Methought love pitying me, when he ſaw this,
Gave me your hands, the *backs* and palms to kiſs. *Donne.*

3. The outward part of the body; that which requires cloaths; opposed to the *belly*.

Those who, by their ancestors, have been set free from a constant drudgery to their *backs* and their bellies, should bestow some time on their heads. *Locke.*

4. The rear; opposed to the *van*.

He might conclude, that Walter would be upon the king's *back*, as his majesty was upon his. *Clarendon, b.* viii.

5. The place behind.

Antheus, Sergestus grave, Cleanthus strong,
And at their *backs* a mighty Trojan throng. *Dryden.*

6. The part of any thing out of sight.

Trees set upon the *backs* of chimneys do ripen fruit sooner. *Bacon's Nat. Hist.* N° 856.

7. The thick part of any tool, opposed to the edge; as the *back* of a knife or sword; whence *backsword*, or sword with a *back*; as,

Bull dreaded not old Lewis either at *backsword*, single faulchion, or cudgel-play. *Arbuthnot's History of J. Bull.*

8. To turn the *back* on one, is to forsake him, or neglect him.

At the hour of death, all the friendships of the world shall bid him adieu, and the whole creation turn its *back* upon him. *South.*

9. To turn the *back*, is to go away; to be not within the reach of taking cognizance.

His *back* was no sooner turned, but they returned to their former rebellion. *Sir J. Davies on Ireland.*

ACK. *adv.* [from the noun.]

. To the place from which one came.

Back you shall not to the house, unless
You undertake that with me. *Shakesp. Twelfth Night.*

He sent many to seek the ship Argo, threatening that if they brought not *back* Medea, they should suffer in her stead. *Raleigh's History of the World.*

But where they are, and why they came not *back*,
Is now the labour of my thoughts. *Milton.*

Back to thy native island might'st thou sail,
And leave half-heard the melancholy tale. *Pope's Odyssey.*

Backward; from the present station.

I've been surprised in an unguarded hour,
But must not now go *back*; the love that lay
Half smother'd in my breast, has broke through all
Its weak restraints. *Addison's Cato.*

Behind; not coming forward.

I thought to promote thee unto great honour; but lo the Lord hath kept thee *back* from honour. *Numb.* xxiv. 11.

Constrains the glebe, keeps *back* the hurtful weed. *Blackmore's Creation, b.* ii.

Toward things past.

I had always a curiosity to look *back* unto the sorrows of things, and to view in my mind the beginning and progress of a rising world. *Burnet's Theory of the Earth.*

Again; in return.

The lady's mad; yet if 'twere so,
She could not sway her house, command her followers,
Take and give *back* affairs, and their despatch,
With such a smooth, discreet, and stable bearing. *Shakesp. Twelfth Night.*

Again; a second time.

This Cæsar found, and that ungrateful age,
With losing him, went *back* to blood and rage. *Waller.*

The epistles being written from ladies forsaken by their lovers, many thoughts came *back* upon us in divers letters. *Dryd.*

o BACK. *v. a.* [from the noun *back*.]

To mount on the back of a horse.

That roan shall be my throne.
Well I will *back* him strait. O Esperance!
Bid Butler lead him forth into the park. *Shak. Henry* IV.

To break a horse; to train him to bear upon his back.

Direct us how to *back* the winged horse;
Favour his flight, and moderate his course. *Roscommon.*

To place upon the back.

As I slept, methought
Great Jupiter, upon his eagle *back'd*,
Appear'd to me. *Shakesp. Cymbeline.*

To maintain; to strengthen.

Belike, he means,
Back'd by the pow'r of Warwick, that false peer,
T' aspire unto the crown. *Shakesp. Henry* VI.

You are strait enough in the shoulders, you care not who sees your back: call you that *backing* of your friends? a plague upon such *backing!* give me them that will face me. *Sh. H.* VI.

These were seconded by certain demilaunces, and both *backed* with men at arms. *Sir J. Hayward.*

Did they not swear, in express words,
To prop and *back* the house of lords?
And after turn'd out the whole houseful. *Hudibras.*

A great malice, *backed* with a great interest, can have no advantage of a man, but from his expectations of something without himself. *South.*

How shall we treat this bold aspiring man?
Success still follows him, and *backs* his crimes. *Addis. Cato.*

5. To justify; to support.

The patrons of the ternary number of principles, and those that would have five elements, endeavour to *back* their experiments with a specious reason. *Boyle.*

We have I know not how many adages to *back* the reason of this moral. *L'Estrange.*

6. To second.

Factious, and fav'ring this or t'other side,
Their wagers *back* their wishes. *Dryden's Fables.*

To BA'CKBITE. *v. a.* [from *back* and *bite*.] To censure or reproach the absent.

Most untruly and maliciously do these evil tongues *backbite* and slander the sacred ashes of that most just and honourable personage. *Spenser's Ireland.*

I will use him well; a friend i' th' court is better than a penny in purse. Use his men well, Davy, for they are arrant knaves, and will *backbite*. *Shakesp. Henry* IV.

BA'CKBITER. *n. s.* [from *backbite*.] A privy calumniator; a censurer of the absent.

No body is bound to look upon his *backbiter*, or his underminer, his betrayer, or his oppressor, as his friend. *South.*

BA'CKBONE. *n. s.* [from *back* and *bone*.] The bone of the back.

The *backbone* should be divided into many vertebres for commodious bending, and not be one entire rigid bone. *Ray.*

BA'CKCARRY. Having on the back.

Manwood, in his forest laws, noteth it for one of the four circumstances, or cases, wherein a forester may arrest an offender against vert or venison in the forest, *viz.* stable-stand, dog-draw, *backcarry*, and bloody hand. *Cowel.*

BA'CKDOOR. *n. s.* [from *back* and *door*.] The door behind the house; privy passage.

The procession durst not return by the way it came; but, after the devotion of the monks, passed out at a *backdoor* of the convent. *Addison on Italy.*

Popery, which is so far shut out as not to re-enter openly, is stealing in by the *backdoor* of atheism. *Atterbury.*

BA'CKED. *adj.* [from *back*.] Having a back.

Lofty-neck'd,
Sharp headed, barrel-belly'd, broadly *back'd*. *Dryd. Virgil.*

BA'CKFRIEND. *n. s.* [from *back* and *friend*.] A friend backwards; that is, an enemy in secret.

Set the restless importunities of talebearers and *backfriends* against fair words and professions. *L'Estrange.*

Far is our church from encroaching upon the civil power; as some who are *backfriends* to both, would maliciously insinuate. *South.*

BACKGA'MMON. *n. s.* [from *bach gammon*, Welch, a little battle.] A play or game at tables, with box and dice.

In what esteem are you with the vicar of the parish? can you play with him at *backgammon?* *Swift.*

BA'CKHOUSE. *n. s.* [from *back* and *house*.] The buildings behind the chief part of the house.

Their *backhouses*, of more necessary than cleanly service, as kitchens, stables, are climbed up unto by steps. *Carew's Survey of Cornwal.*

BA'CKPIECE. *n. s.* [from *back* and *piece*.] The piece of armour which covers the back.

The morning that he was to join battle, his armourer put on his *backpiece* before, and his breastplate behind. *Camden.*

BA'CKROOM. *n. s.* [from *back* and *room*.] A room behind; not in the front.

If you have a fair prospect backwards of gardens, it may be convenient to make *backrooms* the larger. *Mox. Mech. Exerc.*

BA'CKSIDE. *n. s.* [from *back* and *side*.]

1. The hinder part of any thing.

If the quicksilver were rubbed from the *backside* of the speculum, the glass would cause the same rings of colours, but more faint; the phænomena depends not upon the quicksilver, unless so far as it encreases the reflection of the *backside* of the glass. *Newton's Opticks.*

2. The hind part of an animal.

A poor ant carries a grain of corn, climbing up a wall with her head downwards and her *backside* upwards. *Addison.*

3. The yard or ground behind a house.

The wash of pastures, fields, commons, roads, streets, or *backsides*, are of great advantage to all sorts of land. *Mortimer.*

To BACKSLI'DE. *v. n.* [from *back* and *slide*.] To fall off; to apostatize: a word only used by divines.

Hast thou seen that which *backsliding* Israel hath done? She is gone up upon every high mountain, and under every green tree. *Jeremiah,* iii. 6.

BACKSLI'DER. *n. s.* [from *backslide*.] An apostate.

The *backslider* in heart shall be filled. *Prov.* xiv. 14.

BA'CKSTAFF. *n. s.* [from *back* and *staff*; because, in taking an observation, the observer's back is turned towards the sun.] An instrument useful in taking the sun's altitude at sea; invented by Captain Davies.

BA'CKSTAIRS. *n. s.* [from *back* and *stairs*.] The private stairs in the house.

I condemn the practice which hath lately crept into the court at the *backstairs*, that some pricked for sheriffs get out of the bill. *Bacon's Advice to Sir George Villiers.*

BA'CKSTAYS. *n. ſ.* [from *back* and *ſtay.*] Ropes or ſtays which keep the maſts of a ſhip from pitching forward or overboard.

BA'CKSWORD. *n. ſ.* [from *back* and *ſword.*] A ſword with one ſharp edge.

Bull dreaded not old Lewis at *backſword.* *Arbuth. J. Bull.*

BA'CKWARD. } *adv.* [from *back* and ƿeaꞃd, Sax. that is, to-
BA'CKWARDS. } wards the back.]

1. With the back forwards.

They went *backward,* and their faces were *backward.* *Gen.* ix.

2. Towards the back.

In leaping with weights, the arms are firſt caſt *backwards,* and then forwards, with ſo much the greater force; for the hands go *backward* before they take their riſe. *Bacon's Nat. H.*

3. On the back.

Then darting from her malignant eyes,
She caſt him *backward* as he ſtrove to riſe. *Dryden's Æneid.*

4. From the preſent ſtation to the place behind the back.

We might have met them dareful, beard to beard,
And beat them *backward* home. *Shakeſp. Macbeth.*
The monſtrous ſight
Struck them with horrour *backward;* but far worſe
Urg'd them behind. *Milton's Paradiſe Loſt, b.* vi.

5. Regreſſively.

Are not the rays of light, in paſſing by the edges and ſides of bodies, bent ſeveral times *backwards* and forwards with a motion like that of an eel? *Newton's Opticks.*

6. Towards ſomething paſt.

To prove the poſſibility of a thing, there is no argument to that which looks *backwards;* for what has been done or ſuffered, may certainly be done or ſuffered again. *South.*

7. Out of the progreſſive ſtate; reflex.

No, doubtleſs; for the mind can *backward* caſt
Upon herſelf, her underſtanding light. *Sir J. Davies.*

8. From a better to a worſe ſtate.

The work went *backward;* and the more he ſtrove
T' advance the ſuit, the farther from her love. *Dryden.*

9. Paſt; in time paſt.

They have ſpread one of the worſt languages in the world, if we look upon it ſome reigns *backwards.* *Locke.*

10. Perverſely; from the wrong end.

I never yet ſaw man,
But ſhe would ſpell him *backward;* if fair-fac'd,
She'd ſwear the gentleman ſhould be her ſiſter;
If black, why, nature, drawing of an antick,
Made a foul blot; if tall, a launce ill-headed.
Shakeſp. Much ado about Nothing.

BA'CKWARD. *adj.*

1. Unwilling; averſe.

Cities laid waſte, they ſtorm'd the dens and caves;
For wiſer brutes are *backward* to be ſlaves. *Pope.*

We are ſtrangely *backward* to lay hold of this ſafe, this only method of cure. *Atterbury.*

Our mutability makes the friends of our nation *backward* to engage with us in alliances. *Addiſon. Freeholder.*

2. Heſitating.

All things are ready, if our minds be ſo;
Periſh the man, whoſe mind is *backward* now. *Shak. H.* V.

3. Sluggiſh; dilatory.

The mind is *backward* to undergo the fatigue of weighing every argument. *Watts's Improvement of the Mind.*

4. Dull; not quick or apprehenſive.

It often falls out, that the *backward* learner makes amends another way. *South.*

BA'CKWARD. *n. ſ.* The things or ſtate behind or paſt.

What ſeeſt thou elſe
In the dark *backward* or abyſm of time? *Shakeſp. Tempeſt.*

BA'CKWARDLY. *adv.* [from *backward.*]

1. Unwillingly; averſely; with the back forward.

Like Numid lions by the hunters chas'd,
Though they do fly, yet *backwardly* do go
With proud aſpect, diſdaining greater haſte. *Sidney.*

2. Perverſely.

I was the firſt man
That e'er receiv'd gift from him;
And does he think ſo *backwardly* of me,
That I'll requite it laſt? *Shakeſp. Timon.*

BA'CKWARDNESS. *n. ſ.* [from *backward.*] Dulneſs; unwillingneſs; ſluggiſhneſs.

The thing by which we are apt to excuſe our *backwardneſs* to good works, is the ill ſucceſs that hath been obſerved to attend well deſigned charities. *Atterbury.*

BA'CON. *n. ſ.* [probably from *baken,* that is, dried fleſh.]

1. The fleſh of a hog ſalted and dried.

High o'er the hearth a chine of *bacon* hung,
Good old Philemon ſeiz'd it with a prong,
Then cut a ſlice. *Dryden's Fables.*

2. To ſave the *bacon,* is a phraſe for preſerving one's ſelf from being unhurt; borrowed from the care of houſewives in the country, where they have ſeldom any other proviſion in the houſe than dried bacon, to ſecure it from the marching ſoldiers.

What frightens you thus? my good ſon! ſays the prieſt;
You murder'd, are ſorry, and have been confeſt.
O father! my ſorrow will ſcarce ſave my *bacon;*
For 'twas not that I murder'd, but that I was taken. *Prior.*

BACULO'METRY. *n. ſ.* [from *baculus,* Lat. and μέτρον.] The art of meaſuring diſtances by one or more ſtaves. *Dict.*

BAD. *adj.* [*quaad,* Dutch; compar. *worſe;* ſuperl. *worſt.*]

1. Ill; not good: a general word uſed in regard to phyſical or moral faults, either of men or things.

Moſt men have politicks enough to make, through violence, the beſt ſcheme of government a *bad* one. *Pope.*

2. Vitious; corrupt.

Thou may'ſt repent,
And one *bad* act, with many deeds well done,
May'ſt cover. *Milton's Paradiſe Loſt, b.* xi. *l.* 256.
Thus will the latter, as the former, world
Still tend from *bad* to worſe. *Milton's Parad. Loſt, b.* xii.
Our unhappy fates
Mix thee amongſt the *bad,* or make thee run
Too near the paths, which virtue bids thee ſhun. *Prior.*

3. Unfortunate; unhappy.

The ſun his annual courſe obliquely made,
Good days contracted, and enlarg'd the *bad.* *Dryden.*

4. Hurtful; unwholeſome.

Reading was *bad* for his eyes, writing made his head ake. *Add.*

5. Sick.

BAD. } The preterite of *bid.*
BADE. }

And, for an earneſt of greater honour,
He *bad* me, from him, call thee Thane of Cawder. *Macb.*

BADGE. *n. ſ.* [A word of uncertain etymology; derived by *Junius* from *bode* or *bade,* a meſſenger; and ſuppoſed to be corrupted from *badage,* the credential of a meſſenger: but taken by *Skinner* and *Minſhew* from *bagghe,* Dut. a jewel, or *bague,* a ring, Fr.]

1. A mark or cognizance worn to ſhew the relation of the wearer to any perſon or thing.

But on his breaſt a bloody croſs he bore,
The dear remembrance of his dying lord;
For whoſe ſweet ſake that glorious *badge* he wore. *Spenſer.*

The outward ſplendour of his office, is the *badge* and token of that glorious and ſacred character which he inwardly bears. *Atterbury's Sermons.*

2. A token by which one is known.

A ſavage tygreſs on her helmet lies;
The famous *badge* Clarinda us'd to bear. *Fairfax, b.* ii.

3. The mark of any thing.

There appears much joy in him; even ſo much, that joy could not ſhew itſelf modeſt enough, without a *badge* of bitterneſs. *Shakeſp. Much ado about Nothing.*

Sweet mercy is nobility's true *badge.* *Shakeſ. Tit. Andron.*

Let him not bear the *badges* of a wreck,
Nor beg with a blue table on his back. *Dryden's Perſius.*

To BADGE. *v. a.* [from the noun.] To mark as with a badge.

Your royal father's murder'd.——
—— Oh, by whom?——
Thoſe of his chamber, as it ſeem'd, had don't;
Their hands and faces were all *badg'd* with blood,
So were their daggers. *Shakeſp. Macbeth.*

BADGER. *n. ſ.* [*bedour,* Fr.] An animal that earths in the ground, uſed to be hunted.

That a brock, or *badger,* hath legs of one ſide ſhorter than the other, is very generally received not only by theoriſts and unexperienced believers, but moſt who behold them daily. *Brown's Vulgar Errours, b.* iii.

BADGER LEGGED. *adj.* [from *badger* and *legged.*] Having legs of an unequal length, as the badger is ſuppoſed to have.

His body crooked all over, big-bellied, *badger legged,* and his complexion ſwarthy. *L'Eſtrange.*

BA'DGER. *n. ſ.* [perhaps from the Latin *bajulus,* a carrier; but, by *Junius,* derived from the *badger,* a creature who ſtows up his proviſion.] One that buys corn and victuals in one place, and carries it unto another. *Cowel.*

BA'DLY. *adv.* [from *bad.*] In a bad manner; not well.

How goes the day with us? Oh tell me, Hubert.—
Badly, I fear. How fares your majeſty? *Shak. King John.*

BA'DNESS. *n. ſ.* [from *bad.*] Want of good qualities, either natural or moral.

It was not your brother's evil diſpoſition made him ſeek his death; but a provoking merit, ſet awork by a reprovable *badneſs* in himſelf. *Shakeſp. King Lear.*

There is one convenience in this city, which makes ſome amends for the *badneſs* of the pavement. *Addiſon on Italy.*

I did not ſee how the *badneſs* of the weather could be the king's fault. *Addiſon. Freeholder.*

To BA'FFLE. *v. a.* [*beffler,* Fr.]

1. To elude.

They made a ſhift to think themſelves guiltleſs, in ſpite of all their ſins; to break the precept, and at the ſame time to *baffle* the curſe. *South.*

He hath deſerved to have the grace withdrawn, which he hath ſo long *baffled* and defied. *Atterbury.*

2. To confound; to defeat with ſome confuſion, as by perplexing or amuſing; to *baffle* is ſometimes leſs than to *conquer.*

Mezen-

Etruria lost,
He brings to Turnus' aid his *baffled* host. *Dryden's Æneid.*

When the mind has brought itself to close thinking, it may go on roundly. Every abstruse problem, every intricate question will not *baffle*, discourage, or break it. *Locke.*

3. To crush; to bring to nothing.

A foreign potentate trembles at a war with the English nation, ready to employ against him such revenues as shall *baffle* his designs upon their country. *Addison. Freeholder*, N° 20.

BA'FFLE. *n. s.* [from the verb.] A defeat.

It is the skill of the disputant that keeps off a *baffle*. *South.*

The authors having missed of their aims, are fain to retreat with frustration and a *baffle*. *South.*

BA'FFLER. *n. s.* [from *baffle.*] He that puts to confusion, or defeats.

Experience, that great *baffler* of speculation, assures us the thing is too possible, and brings, in all ages, matter of fact to confute our suppositions. *Government of the Tongue*, § 2.

BAG. *n. s.* [belȝe, Sax. from whence perhaps by dropping, as is usual, the harsh consonant, came *bege*, *bage*, *bag*.]

1. A sack, or pouch, to put any thing in, as money, corn.

Cousin, away for England; haste before,
And, ere our coming, see thou shake the *bags*
Of hoarding abbots; their imprison'd angels
Set thou at liberty. *Shakesp. King John.*

What is it that opens thy mouth in praises? Is it that thy *bags* and thy barns are full? *South.*

Those waters were inclosed within the earth as in a *bag*. *Burnet's Theory of the Earth.*

Once, we confess, beneath the patriot's cloak,
From the crack'd *bag* the dropping guinea spoke. *Pope.*

2. That part of animals in which some particular juices are contained, as the poison of vipers.

The swelling poison of the several sects,
Which, wanting vent, the nation's health infects,
Shall burst its *bag*. *Dryden.*

Sing on, sing on, for I can ne'er be cloy'd;
So may thy cows their burden'd *bags* distend. *Dryden.*

3. An ornamental purse of silk tied to men's hair.

We saw a young fellow riding towards us full gallop, with a bob wig and black silken *bag* tied to it. *Addison. Spectator.*

4. A term used to signify different quantities of certain commodities; as a *bag* of pepper; a *bag* of hops.

To BAG. *v. a.* [from the noun.]

1. To put into a bag.

Accordingly he drain'd those marshy grounds,
And *bagg'd* them in a blue cloud. *Dryden's King Arthur.*

Hops ought not to be *bagged* up hot. *Mortimer's Husbandry.*

2. To load with a bag.

Like a bee *bagg'd* with his honey'd venom,
He brings it to your hive. *Dryden's Don Sebastian.*

To BAG. *v. n.* To swell like a full bag.

The skin seemed much contracted, yet it *bagged*, and had a porringer full of matter in it. *Wiseman's Surgery.*

Two kids that in the valley stray'd,
I found by chance, and to my fold convey'd:
They drain two *bagging* udders every day. *Dryden's Virgil.*

BA'GATELLE. *n. s.* [*bagatelle*, Fr.] A trifle; a thing of no importance.

Heaps of hair rings and cypher'd seals;
Rich trifles, serious *bagatelles*. *Prior.*

BA'GGAGE. *n. s.* [from *bag*, *bagage*, Fr.]

1. The furniture and utensils of an army.

The army was an hundred and seventy thousand footmen, and twelve thousand horsemen, beside the *baggage*. *Judith*, vii. 2.

Riches are the *baggage* of virtue; they cannot be spared, nor left behind, but they hinder the march. *Bacon.*

They were probably always in readiness, and carried among the *baggage* of the army. *Addison's Remarks on Italy.*

2. The goods that are to be carried away, as *bag* and *baggage*.

Dolabella designed, when his affairs grew desperate in Egypt, to pack up *bag* and *baggage*, and sail for Italy. *Arbuth. on Coins.*

3. A worthless woman; in French *bagasse*; so called, because such women follow camps.

A spark of indignation did rise in her, not to suffer such a *baggage* to win away any thing of hers. *Sidney.*

When this *baggage* meets with a man who has vanity to credit relations, she turns him to account. *Spectat.* N° 205.

BA'GNIO. *n. s.* [*bagno*, Ital. a bath.] A house for bathing, sweating, and otherwise cleansing the body.

I have known two instances of malignant fevers produced by the hot air of a *bagnio*. *Arbuthnot on Air.*

BA'GPIPE. *n. s.* [from *bag* and *pipe*; the wind being received in a bag.] A musical instrument, consisting of a leathern bag, which blows up like a foot-ball, by means of a port vent or little tube fixed to it, and stopped by a valve; and three pipes or flutes, the first called the great pipe or drone, and the second the little one; which pass the wind out only at the bottom; the third has a reed, and is plaid on by compressing the bag under the arm, when full; and opening or stopping the holes, which are eight, with the fingers. The *bagpipe* takes in the compass of three octaves. *Chambers.*

No banners but shirts, with some bad *bagpipes* instead of drum and fife. *Sidney, b.* i.

He heard a *bagpipe*, and saw a general animated with the sound. *Addison. Freeholder*, N° 27.

BAGPI'PER. *n. s.* [from *bagpipe.*] One that plays on a bagpipe.

Some that will evermore peep thro' their eyes,
And laugh, like parrots, at a *bagpiper*. *Shak. M. of Venice.*

BAGUE'TTE. *n. s.* [Fr. a term of architecture.] A little round moulding, less than an astragal; sometimes carved and enriched.

To BAIGNE. *v. a.* [*bagner*, Fr.] To drench; to soak: a word out of use.

The women forslow not to *baigne* them, unless they plead their heels, with a worse perfume than Jugurth found in the dungeon. *Carew's Survey of Cornwal.*

BAIL. *n. s.* [of this word the etymologists give many derivations; it seems to come from the French *bailler*, to put into the hand; to deliver up, as a man delivers himself up in surety.]

Bail is the freeing or setting at liberty one arrested or imprisoned upon action either civil or criminal, under security taken for his appearance. There is both common and special *bail*; *common bail* is in actions of small prejudice, or slight proof, called common, because any sureties in that case are taken: whereas, upon causes of greater weight, or apparent speciality, *special bail* or surety must be taken. There is a difference between *bail* and mainprise; for he that is mainprised, is at large, until the day of his appearance: but where a man is bailed, he is always accounted by the law to be in their ward and custody for the time: and they may, if they will, keep him in ward or in prison at that time, or otherwise at their will. *Cowel.*

Worry'd with debts, and past all hopes of *bail*,
The unpity'd wretch lies rotting in a jail. *Roscommon.*

And bribe with presents, or when presents fail,
They send their prostituted wives for *bail*. *Dryden.*

To BAIL. *v. a.* [from the noun.]

1. To give bail for another.

Let me be their bail—
They shall be ready at your highness' will,
To answer their suspicion——
Thou shalt not *bail* them. *Shakesp. Titus Andronicus.*

2. To admit to bail.

When they had *bailed* the twelve bishops, who were in the Tower, the house of commons, in great indignation, caused them immediately again to be recommitted to the Tower. *Clarendon.*

BA'ILABLE. *adj.* [from *bail.*] That may be set at liberty by bail or sureties.

BA'ILIFF. *n. s.* [a word of doubtful etymology in itself, but borrowed by us from *baillie*, Fr.]

1. A subordinate officer.

Lausanne is under the canton of Berne, and governed by a *bailiff* sent them every three years from the senate of Berne. *Addison on Italy.*

2. An officer whose business it is to execute arrests.

It many times happeneth, that, by the under-sheriffs and their *bailiffs*, the owner hath incurred the forfeiture, before he cometh to the knowledge of the process that runneth against him. *Bacon.*

A *bailiff*, by mistake, seized you for a debtor, and kept you the whole evening in a spunging-house. *Swift.*

Swift as a bard the *bailiff* leaves behind. *Pope.*

3. An under-steward of a manor.

BA'ILIWICK. *n. s.* [of *baillie*, Fr. and pic, Sax.] The place of the jurisdiction of a bailiff within his hundred, or the lord's franchise. It is that liberty which is exempted from the sheriff of the county, over which the lord of the liberty appointeth a bailiff. *Cowel.*

A proper officer is to walk up and down his *bailiwick*. *Spenser on Ireland.*

There issued writs to the sheriffs, to return the names of the several land-owners in their several *bailiwicks*. *Hale's Origin of Mankind.*

To BAIT. *v. a.* [baтan, Sax. *baitzen*, Germ.]

1. To put meat upon a hook, in some place, to tempt fish or other animals.

Oh, cunning enemy, that to catch a saint,
With saints dost *bait* thy hook! most dangerous
Is that temptation that doth goad us on
To sin in loving virtue. *Shakesp. Measure for Measure.*

Let's be revenged on him; let's appoint him a meeting, give him a show of comfort in his suit, and lead him on with a fine *baited* delay, till he hath pawned his horses to mine host of the garter. *Shakesp. Merry Wives of Windsor.*

Many sorts of fishes feed upon insects, as is well known to anglers, who *bait* their hooks with them. *Ray.*

How are the sex improv'd in am'rous arts!
What new-found snares they *bait* for human hearts! *Gay.*

2. To give meat to one's self, or horses, on the road.

What so strong,
But wanting rest, will also want of might?
The sun, that measures heaven all day long,
At night doth *bait* his steeds the ocean waves among. *F. Q.*

To Bait. *v. a.* [from *battre*, Fr. to beat.] To attack with violence; to set dogs upon.

Who seeming sorely chaffed at his band,
As chained bear, whom cruel dogs do *bait*,
With idle force did fain them to withstand. *Fairy Queen.*
I will not yield
To kiss the ground before young Malcolm's feet;
And so be *baited* with the rabble's curse. *Shak. Macbeth.*

To Bait. *v. n.* To stop at any place for refreshment; perhaps this word is more properly *bate*; to *abate* speed.

But our desires, tyrannical extorsion
Doth force us there to set our chief delightfulness,
Where but a *baiting* place is all our portion. *Sidney.*
As one who on his journey *baits* at noon,
Tho' bent on speed: so here the archangel paus'd. *Par. Lost.*

In all our journey from London to his house, we did not so much as *bait* at a whig inn. *Addison. Spectat.* N° 126.

To Bait. *v. n.* [*as an hawk.*] To clap the wings; to make an offer of flying; to flutter.

All plum'd like estridges, that with the wind
Baited like eagles having lately bath'd;
Glittering in golden coats like images. *Shakesp. Henry* IV.
Hood my unman'd blood *baiting* in my cheeks
With thy black mantle; till strange love, grown bold,
Thinks true love acted simple modesty. *Shak. Rom. and Jul.*
Another way I have to man my haggard,
To make her come, and know her keepers call;
That is, to watch her as we watch these kites,
That *bait* and beat, and will not be obedient.
Shakesp. Taming of the Shrew.

Bait. *n. s.* [from the verb.]

1. Meat set to allure fish, or other animals, to a snare.

The pleasant'st angling is to see the fish
Cut with her golden oars the silver stream,
And greedily devour the treacherous *bait*.
Shakesp. Much ado about Nothing.

2. A temptation; an enticement.

And that same glorious beauty's idle boast,
Is but a *bait* such wretches to beguile. *Spens. sonnet* xli.

Taketh therewith the souls of men, as with certain *baits*.
Hooker, b. v. § 35.

Sweet words I grant, *baits* and allurements sweet
But greatest hopes of greatest crosses meet. *Fairfax, b.* ii.
Fruit, like that
Which grew in paradise, the *bait* of Eve
Us'd by the tempter. *Milton's Par. Lost, b.* x. *l.* 551.
Secure from foolish pride's affected state,
And specious flattery's more pernicious *bait*. *Roscommon.*
Her head was bare,
But for her native ornament of hair,
Which in a simple knot was ty'd above:
Sweet negligence! unheeded *bait* of love! *Dryden's Fab.*
Grant that others could with equal glory,
Look down on pleasures, and the *baits* of sense. *Add. Cato.*

3. A refreshment on a journey.

Baize. *n. s.* A kind of coarse open cloth stuff, having a long nap; sometimes frized on one side, and sometimes not frized, according to the uses it is intended for. This stuff is without wale, being wrought on a loom with two treddles, like flannel. *Chambers.*

To Bake. *v. a.* participle passive, *baked*, or *baken*. [bæcan, Sax. *becken*, Germ. supposed by *Wachter* to come from *bec*, which, in the Phrygian language, signified *bread*.]

1. To heat any thing in a close place; generally in an oven.

He will take thereof, and warm himself; yea, he kindleth it, and *baketh* bread. *Isaiah*, xliv. 15.

The difference of prices of bread proceeded from their delicacy in bread, and perhaps something in their manner of *baking*. *Arbuthnot on Coins.*

2. To harden in the fire.

The work of the fire is a kind of *baking*; and whatsoever the fire *baketh*, time doth in some degree dissolve. *Bacon.*

3. To harden with heat.

With vehement suns
When dusty summer *bakes* the crumbling clods,
How pleasant is't, beneath the twisted arch,
To ply the sweet carouse! *Philips.*
The sun with flaming arrows pierc'd the flood,
And, darting to the bottom, *bak'd* the mud. *Dryden.*

To Bake. *v. n.*

1. To do the work of baking.

I keep his house, and I wash, wring, brew, *bake*, scour, dress meat, and make the beds, and do all myself.
Shakesp. Merry Wives of Windsor.

2. To be heated or baked.

Fillet of a fenny snake,
In the cauldron boil and *bake*. *Shakesp. Macbeth.*

Baked *Meats.* Meats dressed by the oven.

There be some houses, wherein sweetmeats will relent, and *baked meats* will mould, more than others. *Bacon's Nat. Hist.*

Ba'kehouse. *n. s.* [from *bake* and *house*.] A place for baking bread.

I have marked a willingness in the Italian artizans, to distribute the kitchen, pantry, and *bakehouse*, under ground. *Wotton.*

Ba'ken. The *participle* from *to bake*.

There was a cake *baken* on the coals, and a cruse of water at his head. 1 *Kings*, xix. 6.

Ba'ker. *n. s.* [from *to bake*.] He whose trade is to bake.

In life and health, every man must proceed upon trust, there being no knowing the intention of the cook or *baker*. *South.*

Ba'lance. *n. s.* [*balance*, Fr. *bilanx*, Lat.]

1. One of the six simple powers in mechanicks, used principally for determining the difference of weight in heavy bodies. It is of several forms. *Chambers.*

2. A pair of scales.

A balance of power, either without or within a state, is best conceived by considering what the nature of a *balance* is. It supposes three things; first, the part which is held, together with the hand that holds it; and then the two scales, with whatever is weighed therein. *Swift.*

For when on ground the burden'd *balance* lies,
The empty part is lifted up the higher. *Sir John Davies.*

3. A metaphorical *balance*, or the mind employed in comparing one thing with another.

I have in equal *balance* justly weighed,
What wrong our arms may do, what wrongs we suffer:
Griefs heavier than our offences. *Shakesp. Henry* IV.

4. The act of comparing two things, as by the *balance*.

Comfort arises not from others being miserable, but from this inference upon the *balance*, that we suffer only the lot of nature. *L'Estrange's Fables.*

Upon a fair *balance* of the advantages on either side, it will appear, that the rules of the gospel are more powerful means of conviction than such message. *Atterbury.*

5. The overplus of weight; that quantity by which, of two things weighed together, one exceeds the other.

Care being taken, that the exportation exceed in value the importation; and then the *balance* of trade must of necessity be returned in coin or bullion. *Bacon's Adv. to Sir G. Villiers.*

6. That which is wanting to make two parts of an account even; as, he stated the account with his correspondent, and paid the *balance*.

7. Equipoise; as *balance* of power. See the second sense.

Love, hope, and joy, fair pleasure's smiling train,
Hate, fear, and grief, the family of pain;
These mixed with art, and to due bounds confin'd,
Make and maintain the *balance* of the mind. *Pope.*

8. The beating part of a watch.

It is but supposing that all watches, whilst the *balance* beats, think; and it is sufficiently proved, that my watch thought all last night. *Locke.*

9. In astronomy. One of the twelve signs of the zodiack, commonly called *Libra*.

To Ba'lance. *v. a.* [*valancer*, Fr.]

1. To weigh in a balance, either real or figurative; to compare by the balance.

If men would but *balance* the good and the evil of things, they would not venture soul and body for a little dirty interest. *L'Estrange's Fables.*

2. To regulate the weight in a balance.

Heav'n that hath plac'd this island to give law,
To *balance* Europe, and her states to awe. *Waller.*

3. To counterpoise; to weigh equal to.

The attraction of the glass is *balanced*, and rendered ineffectual by the contrary attraction of the liquor. *Newton's Opt.*

4. To regulate an account, by stating it on both sides.

Judging is, *balancing* an account, and determining on which side the odds lie. *Locke.*

5. To pay that which is wanting to make the two parts of an account equal.

Give him leave
To *balance* the account of Blenheim's day. *Prior.*

Though I am very well satisfied, that it is not in my power to *balance* accounts with my Maker, I am resolved, however, to turn all my endeavours that way. *Addison. Spectator.*

To Ba'lance. *v. n.* To hesitate; to fluctuate between equal motives, as a balance plays when charged with equal weights.

Were the satisfaction of lust, and the joys of heaven, offered at any one's present possession, he would not *balance*, or err in the determination of his choice. *Locke.*

Since there is nothing that can offend, I see not why you should *balance* a moment about printing it. *Atterbury to Pope.*

Ba'lancer. *n. s.* [from *balance*.] The person that weighs any thing.

Ba'lass *Ruby. n. s.* [*balas*, Fr. supposed to be an Indian term.] A kind of ruby.

Balass ruby is of a crimson colour, with a cast of purple, and seems best to answer the description of the ancients.
Woodward on Fossils.

To Balbu'cinate. *v. n.* [from *balbutio*, Lat.] To stammer in speaking. *Dict.*

To Balbu'tiate. *v. n.* The same with *balbucinate*. *Dict.*

Balco'ny. *n. s.* [*balcon*, Fr. *balcone*, Ital.] A frame of iron, wood, or stone, before the window of a room.

Then pleaſure came, who, liking not the faſhion,
Began to make *balconies*, terraces,
Till ſhe had weaken'd all by alteration. *Herbert.*

When dirty waters from *balconies* drop,
And dext'rous damſels twirl the ſprinkling mop. *Gay.*

Bald. *adj.* [*bal*, Welch.]

1. Without hair.

Neither ſhall men make themſelves *bald* for them. *Jer.* xvi. 6.

I find it remarked by Marchetti, that the cauſe of baldneſs in men is the dryneſs of the brain, and its ſhrinking from the ſkull; he having obſerved, that in *bald* perſons, under the *bald* part, there was a vacuity between the ſkull and the brain. *Ray.*

He ſhould imitate Cæſar, who, becauſe his head was *bald*, covered that defect with laurels. *Addiſon. Spect.* N° 232.

2. Without natural covering.

Under an oak, whoſe boughs were moſs'd with age,
And high top *bald* with dry antiquity. *Shakeſp. As you like it.*

3. Without the uſual covering.

He is ſet at the upper end o' th' table; but they ſtand *bald* before him. *Shakeſp. Coriolanus.*

4. Unadorned; inelegant.

Hobbes, in the preface to his own *bald* tranſlation of the Ilias, begins the praiſe of Homer when he ſhould have ended it. *Dryden's Fables, Preface.*

And that, though labour'd, line muſt *bald* appear,
That brings ungrateful muſick to the ear. *Creech.*

5. Stripped; naked; without dignity; without value; bare.

What ſhould the people do with theſe *bald* tribunes?
On whom depending, their obedience fails
To th' greater bench. *Shakeſp. Coriolanus.*

6. *Bald* was uſed by the northern nations, to ſignify the ſame as *audax*, bold; and is ſtill in uſe. So *Baldwin*, and by inverſion *Winbald*, is *bold conqueror*; *Ethelbald*, *nobly bold*; *Eadbald*, *happily bold*; which are of the ſame import as *Thraſeas*, *Thraſymachus*, and *Thraſybulus*, &c. *Gibſon's Camden.*

Ba'ldachin. *n. ſ.* [*baldachino*, Ital.] A piece of architecture, in form of a canopy, ſupported with columns, and ſerving as a covering to an altar. It properly ſignifies a rich ſilk, *du cange*, and was a canopy carried over the hoſt. *Build. Dict.*

Ba'lderdash. *n. ſ.* [probably of balb, Sax. bold, and *daſh*, to mingle.] Any thing jumbled together without judgment; rude mixture; a confuſed diſcourſe.

To **Ba'lderdash.** *v. a.* [from the noun.] To mix or adulterate any liquor.

Ba'ldly. *adv.* [from *bald.*] Nakedly; meanly; inelegantly.

Ba'ldmony. *n. ſ.* The ſame with Gentian; which ſee.

Ba'ldness. *n. ſ.* [from *bald.*]

1. The want of hair.
2. The loſs of hair.

Which happen'd on the ſkin to light,
And there corrupting to a wound,
Spreads leproſy and *baldneſs* round. *Swift.*

3. Meanneſs of writing; inelegance.

Ba'ldrick. *n. ſ.* [of uncertain etymology.]

1. A girdle. By ſome *Dictionaries* it is explained a *bracelet*; but I have not found it in that ſenſe.

Athwart his breaſt a *baldrick* brave he ware,
That ſhin'd like twinkling ſtars, with ſtones moſt precious rare. *Fairy Queen, b.* i.

A radiant *baldrick*, o'er his ſhoulders ty'd,
Suſtain'd the ſword, that glitter'd at his ſide. *Pope.*

2. The zodiack.

That like the twins of Jove, they ſeem'd in ſight,
Which deck the *baldrick* of the heavens bright. *Spenſer.*

Bale. *n. ſ.* [*balle*, Fr.] A bundle or parcel of goods packed up for carriage.

One hired an aſs in the dog-days, to carry certain *bales* of goods to ſuch a town. *L'Eſtrange.*

It is part of the *bales* in which bohea tea was brought over from China. *Woodward on Foſſils.*

Bale. *n. ſ.* [bæl, Sax. *bale*, Dan. *bal*, *bol*, Icelandiſh.] Miſery; calamity.

She look'd about, and ſeeing one in mail,
Armed to point, ſought back to turn again;
For light ſhe hated as the deadly *bale*. *Fairy Queen, b.* i.

To **Bale.** *v. a.* A word uſed by the ſailors, who bid *bale* out the water; that is, *lave* it out, by way of diſtinction from pumping. *Skinner.*

To **Bale.** *v. n.* [*emballer*, Fr. *imballare*, Ital.] To make up into a bale.

Ba'leful. *adj.* [from *bale.*]

1. Full of miſery; full of grief; ſorrowful; ſad; woful.

Ah! luckleſs babe, born under cruel ſtar,
And in dead parents *baleful* aſhes bred. *Fairy Queen, b.* i.

But when I feel the bitter *baleful* ſmart,
Which her fair eyes unwares do work in me,
I think that I a new Pandora ſee. *Spenſer, ſonnet* xxiv.

Round he throws his *baleful* eyes,
That witneſs'd huge affliction and diſmay,
Mix'd with obdurate pride and ſtedfaſt hate. *Par. Loſt, b.* i.

2. Full of miſchief; deſtructive.

But when he ſaw his threat'ning was but vain,
He turn'd about, and ſearch'd his *baleful* books again. *F. Q.*

Boiling choler chokes,
By ſight of theſe, our *baleful* enemies. *Shakeſp. Henry* VI.

Unſeen, unfelt, the firy ſerpent ſkims
Betwixt her linen and her naked limbs;
His *baleful* breath inſpiring, as he glides. *Dryden's Æneid.*

Happy Ièrne, whoſe moſt wholeſome air
Poiſons envenom'd ſpiders, and forbids
The *baleful* toad, and vipers from her ſhore. *Philips.*

Ba'lefully. *adv.* [from *baleful.*] Sorrowfully; miſchievouſly.

Balk. *n. ſ.* [*balk*, Dut. and Germ.] A great beam, ſuch as is uſed in building; a rafter over an outhouſe or barn.

Balk. *n. ſ.* [derived by *Skinner* from *valicare*, Ital. to paſs over.] A ridge of land left unploughed between the furrows, or at the end of the field.

To **Balk.** *v. a.* [See the noun.]

1. To diſappoint; to fruſtrate.

Another thing in the grammar ſchools I ſee no uſe of, unleſs it be to *balk* young lads in the way to learning languages. *Locke.*

Every one has a deſire to keep up the vigour of his faculties, and not to *balk* his underſtanding by what is too hard for it. *Locke.*

But one may *balk* this good intent,
And take things otherwiſe than meant. *Prior.*

The prices muſt have been high; for a people ſo rich would not *balk* their fancy. *Arbuthnot on Coins.*

Balk'd of his prey, the yelling monſter flies,
And fills the city with his hideous cries. *Pope's Odyſſey.*

Is there a variance? enter but his door,
Balk'd are the courts, and conteſt is no more. *Pope.*

2. To miſs any thing.

By griſly Pluto he doth ſwear,
He rent his clothes, and tore his hair;
And as he runneth here and there,
An acorn cup he greeteth;
Which ſoon he taketh by the ſtalk,
About his head he lets it walk,
Nor doth he any creature *balk*,
But lays on all he meeteth. *Drayt. Nymphid.*

3. To omit, or refuſe any thing.

This was looked for at your hand, and this was *balkt*. *Shakeſp. Twelfth Night.*

4. To heap, as on a ridge. This, or ſomething like this, ſeems to be intended here.

Ten thouſand bold Scots, three and twenty knights,
Balk'd in their own blood, did Sir Walter ſee
On Holmedon's plains. *Shakeſp. Henry* IV.

Ba'lkers. *n. ſ.* [In fiſhery.] Men who ſtand on a cliff, or high place on the ſhore, and give a ſign to the men in the fiſhing-boats, which way the paſſage or ſhole of herrings is. *Cowel.*

The pilchards are purſued by a bigger fiſh, called a pluſher, who leapeth above water, and bewrayeth them to the *balker*. *Carew's Survey of Cornwal.*

Ball. *n. ſ.* [*bol*, Dan. *bol.* Dut.]

Bel, diminutively *Belin*, the ſun, or Apollo of the Celtæ, was called by the ancient Gauls *Abellio*. Whatever was round, and in particular the head, was called by the ancients either *Bâl*, or *Bel*, and likewiſe *Bôl* and *Biil*. Among the modern Perſians, the head is called *Pole*; and the Flemings ſtill call the head *Bolle*. Πόλος is the head or poll, and πολεῖν, is to turn. Βῶλος likewiſe ſignifies a round ball, whence *bowl*, and *bell*, and *ball*, which the Welch term *bêl*. By the Scotch alſo the head is named *bhêl*; whence the Engliſh *bill* is derived, ſignifying the beak of a bird. Figuratively, the Phrygians and Thurians, by βαλλὴν underſtood a king. Hence alſo, in the Syriack dialects, βαάλ, βήλ, and likewiſe Βῶλ, ſignifies lord, and by this name alſo the ſun; and, in ſome dialects, Ἦλ and Ἶλ, whence Ἴλος, and Ἥλιος, Fήλιος, and Βήλιος, and alſo in the Celtick diminutive way of expreſſion, Ἕλενος, Fέλενος, and Βέλινος, ſignified the ſun; and Ἑλένη, Fελένη, and Βελένη, the moon. Among the Teutonicks, *hol* and *heil* have the ſame meaning; whence the adjective *holig*, or *heilig*, is derived, and ſignifies divine or holy; and the aſpiration being changed into *ſ*, the Romans form their *Sol*. *Baxter.*

1. Any thing made in a round form.

The worms with many feet, which round themſelves into *balls* under logs of timber, but not in the timber. *Bacon.*

Nor arms they wear, nor ſwords and bucklers wield,
But whirl from leathern ſtrings huge *balls* of lead. *Dryden.*

Like a *ball* of ſnow tumbling down a hill, he gathered ſtrength as he paſſed. *Howel's Vocal Foreſt.*

Still unripen'd in the dewy mines,
Within the *ball* a trembling water ſhines,
That through the chryſtal darts. *Addiſon's Rem. on Italy.*

Such of thoſe corpuſcles as happened to combine into one maſs, formed the metallick and mineral *balls*, or nodules, which we find. *Woodward's Natural Hiſtory.*

2. A round thing to play with, either with the hand or foot, or a racket.

Balls to the ſtars, and thralls to fortune's reign,
Turn'd from themſelves, infected with their cage,
Where death is fear'd, and life is held with pain. *Sidney.*

Thoſe I have ſeen play at *ball*, grow extremely earneſt who ſhould have the *ball*. *Sidney.*

3. A ſmall round thing, with ſome particular mark, by which votes are given, or lots caſt.

Let lots decide it.
For ev'ry number'd captive put a *ball*
Into an urn; three only black be there,
The reſt, all white, are ſafe. *Dryden's Don Sebaſtian.*

Minos, the ſtrict inquiſitor, appears;
Round in his urn the blended *balls* he rowls;
Abſolves the juſt, and dooms the guilty ſouls. *Dryden.*

4. A globe; as, the *ball* of the earth.

Julius and Antony, thoſe lords of all,
Low at her feet preſent the conquer'd *ball*. *Granville.*

Ye gods, what juſtice rules the *ball*?
Freedom and arts together fall. *Pope.*

5. A globe borne as an enſign of ſovereignty.

Hear the tragedy of a young man, that by right ought to hold the *ball* of a kingdom; but, by fortune, is made himſelf a ball, toſſed from miſery to miſery, and from place to place. *Bacon's Henry VII.*

6. Any part of the body that approaches to roundneſs; as the lower and ſwelling part of the thumb, the apple of the eye.

Be ſubject to no ſight but mine; inviſible
To every eye *ball* elſe. *Shakeſp. Tempeſt.*

To make a ſtern countenance, let your brow bend ſo, that that it may almoſt touch the *ball* of the eye. *Peacham.*

7. The parchment ſpread over a hollow piece of wood, ſtuffed with hair or wool, which the printers dip in ink, to ſpread it on the letters.

BALL. *n. ſ.* [*bal*, Fr. from *ballare*, low Lat. from βαλλίζειν, to dance.] An entertainment of dancing, at which the preparations are made at the expence of ſome particular perſon.

If golden ſconces hang not on the walls,
To light the coſtly ſuppers and the *balls*. *Dryden.*

He would make no extraordinary figure at a *ball*; but I can aſſure the ladies, for their conſolation, that he has writ better verſes on the ſex than any man. *Swift.*

BA'LLAD. *n. ſ.* [*balade*, Fr.] A ſong.

Ballad once ſignified a ſolemn and ſacred ſong, as well as trivial, when Solomon's Song was called the *ballad* of *ballads*; but now it is applied to nothing but trifling verſe. *Watts.*

An' I have not *ballads* made on you all, and ſung to filthy tunes, may a cup of ſack be my poiſon. *Shakeſp. Henry IV.*

Like the ſweet *ballad*, this amuſing lay
Too long detains the lover on his way. *Gay's Trivia.*

To BA'LLAD. *v. n.* [from the noun.] To make or ſing ballads.

Saucy lictors
Will catch at us like ſtrumpets, and ſcall'd rhimers
Ballad us out o' tune. *Shakeſp. Antony and Cleopatra.*

BA'LLAD-SINGER. *n. ſ.* [from *ballad* and *ſing*.] One whoſe employment it is to ſing ballads in the ſtreets.

No ſooner 'gan he raiſe his tuneful ſong,
But lads and laſſes round about him throng.
Not *ballad-ſinger*, plac'd above the crowd,
Sings with a note ſo ſhrilling, ſweet and loud. *Gay.*

BA'LLAST. *n. ſ.* [*ballaſte*, Dutch.]

1. Something put at the bottom of the ſhip to keep it ſteady to the center of gravity.

There muſt be ſome middle counſellors to keep things ſteady; for, without that *ballaſt*, the ſhip will roul too much. *Bacon's Eſſays.*

As for the aſcent of it, this may be eaſily contrived, if there be ſome great weight at the bottom of the ſhip, being part of its *ballaſt*; which, by ſome cord within, may be looſened from it. *Wilkins's Mathematical Magick.*

As when empty barks or billows float,
With ſandy *ballaſt* ſailors trim the boat;
So bees bear gravel ſtones, whoſe poiſing weight
Steers through the whiſtling winds their ſteddy flight. *Dryd.*

2. That which is uſed to make any thing ſteady.

Why ſhould he ſink where nothing ſeem'd to preſs?
His lading little, and his *ballaſt* leſs. *Swift.*

To BA'LLAST. *v. a.* [from the noun.]

1. To put weight at the bottom of a ſhip, in order to keep her ſteady.

If this ark be ſo *ballaſted*, as to be of equal weight with the like magnitude of water, it will be moveable. *Wilkins's Mathematical Magick.*

2. To keep any thing ſteady.

Whilſt thus to *ballaſt* love, I thought,
And ſo more ſteddily t' have gone,
I ſaw, I had love's pinnace overfraught. *Donne.*

Now you have given me virtue for my guide,
And with true honour *ballaſted* my pride. *Dryden's Aureng.*

BALLE'TTE. *n. ſ.* [*ballette*, Fr.] A dance in which ſome hiſtory is repreſented.

BA'LLIARDS. *n. ſ.* [from *ball* and *yard*, or ſtick to puſh it with.] A play at which a ball is driven by the end of a ſtick; now corruptly called *billiards*.

With dice, with cards, with *balliards*, far unfit,
With ſhuttlecocks miſſeeming manly wit. *Hubberd's Tale.*

BA'LLISTER. See BALUSTRE.

BALLO'N. }
BALLO'ON. } *n. ſ.* [*ballon*, Fr.]

1. A large round ſhort-necked veſſel uſed in chymiſtry.
2. In architecture; a ball or globe placed on the top of a pillar.
3. In fireworks; a ball of paſteboard, ſtuffed with combuſtible matter, which, when fired, mounts to a conſiderable height in the air, and then burſts into bright ſparks of fire, reſembling ſtars.

BA'LLOT. *n. ſ.* [*ballote*, Fr.]

1. A little ball or ticket uſed in giving votes, being put privately into a box or urn.
2. The act of voting by ballot.

To BA'LLOT. *v. n.* [*balloter*, Fr.] To chooſe by ballot, that is, by putting little balls or tickets, with particular marks, privately in a box; by counting which it is known what is the reſult of the poll, without any diſcovery by whom each vote was given.

No competition arriving to a ſufficient number of balls, they fell to *ballot* ſome others. *Wotton.*

Giving their votes by *balloting*, they lie under no awe. *Swift.*

BALLOTA'TION. *n. ſ.* [from *ballot*.] The act of voting by ballot.

The election is intricate and curious, conſiſting of ten ſeveral *ballotations*. *Wotton.*

BALM. *n. ſ.* [*baume*, Fr. *balſamum*, Lat.]

1. The ſap or juice of a ſhrub, remarkably odoriferous.

Balm trickles through the bleeding veins
Of happy ſhrubs, in Idumean plains. *Dryden's Virgil.*

2. Any valuable or fragrant ointment.

Thy place is filled, thy ſceptre wrung from thee;
Thy *balm* waſh'd off wherewith thou waſt anointed. *Shakeſp. Henry VI.*

3. Any thing that ſooths or mitigates pain.

You were conducted to a gentle bath,
And *balms* apply'd to you. *Shakeſp. Macbeth.*

Your praiſe's argument, *balm* of your age;
Deareſt and beſt. *Shakeſp. King Lear.*

BALM. }
BALM *Mint.* } *n. ſ.* [*meliſſa*, Lat.] The name of a plant.

It is a verticillate plant, with a labiated flower, conſiſting of one leaf, whoſe upper lip is roundiſh, upright, and divided into two; but the under lip, into three parts: out of the flower-cup riſes the pointal, attended, as it were, with four embryos; theſe afterwards turn to ſo many ſeeds, which are roundiſh, and incloſed in the flower-cup; to theſe notes may be added, the flowers are produced from the wings of the leaves, but are not whorled round the ſtalks. The ſpecies are, 1. Garden *balm*. 2. Garden *balm*, with yellow variegated flowers. 3. Stinking Roman *balm*, with ſofter hairy leaves. The firſt of theſe ſorts is cultivated in gardens for medicinal and culinary uſe: it is propagated by parting the roots either in ſpring or autumn. When they are firſt planted, if the ſeaſon proves dry, you muſt carefully water them until they have taken root. *Millar.*

BALM *of Gilead.*

1. The juice drawn from the balſam tree, by making inciſions in its bark. Its colour is firſt white, ſoon after green; but when it comes to be old, it is of the colour of honey. The ſmell of it is agreeable, and very penetrating; the taſte of it bitter, ſharp and aſtringent. As little iſſues from the plant by inciſion, the *balm* ſold by the merchants, is made of the wood and green branches of the tree, diſtilled by fire, which is generally adulterated with turpentine. *Calmet.*

It ſeems moſt likely to me, that the zori of Gilead, which we render in our Engliſh bible by the word *balm*, was not the ſame with the balſam of Mecca, but only a better ſort of turpentine, then in uſe for the cure of wounds and other diſeaſes. *Prideaux's Connection.*

2. A plant remarkable for the ſtrong balſamick ſcent, which its leaves emit, upon being bruiſed; whence ſome have ſuppoſed, erroneouſly, that the *balm of Gilead* was taken from this plant. *Millar.*

To BALM. *v. a.* [from *balm*.]

1. To anoint with balm.

Balm his foul head with warm diſtilled waters,
And burn ſweet wood. *Shakeſp. Taming of the Shrew.*

2. To ſooth; to mitigate; to aſſuage.

Oppreſt nature ſleeps:
This reſt might yet have *balm'd* thy ſenſes,
Which ſtand in hard cure. *Shakeſp. King Lear.*

BA'LMY. *adj.* [from *balm*.]

1. Having the qualities of balm.

Soft on the flow'ry herb I found me laid,
In *balmy* ſweat; which with his beams the ſun
Soon dry'd. *Milton's Paradiſe Loſt, b. viii.*

2. Producing balm.
3. Soothing; ſoft; mild.

Come, Deſdemona, 'tis the ſoldier's life
To have their *balmy* ſlumbers wak'd with ſtrife. *Shak. Othello.*

Such viſions hourly paſs before my ſight,
Which from my eyes their *balmy* ſlumbers fright. *Dryden.*

4. Fragrant; odoriferous.

Thoſe rich perfumes which, from the happy ſhore,
The winds upon their *balmy* winds convey'd,
Whoſe guilty ſweetneſs firſt the world betray'd. *Dryden.*

First Eurus to the rising morn is sent,
The regions of the *balmy* continent. *Dryden's Ovid.*

5. Mitigating; assuasive.

Oh *balmy* breath, that dost almost persuade
Justice to break her sword! *Shakesp. Othello.*

BA'LNEARY. *n. s.* [*balnearium*, Lat.] A bathing-room.

The *balnearies*, and bathing-places, he exposeth unto the summer setting. *Brown's Vulgar Errours, b.* vi. *c.* 7.

BALNEA'TION. *n. s.* [from *balneum*, Lat. a bath.] The act of bathing.

As the head may be disturbed by the skin, it may the same way be relieved, as is observable in *balneations*, and fomentations of that part. *Brown's Vulgar Errours, b.* ii. *c.* 6.

BA'LNEATORY. *adj.* [*balneatorius*, Lat.] Belonging to a bath or stove.

BA'LOTADE. *n. s.* The leap of an horse, so that when his fore-feet are in the air, he shews nothing but the shoes of his hinder-feet, without yerking out. A *balotade* differs from a capriole; for when a horse works at caprioles, he yerks out his hinder legs with all his force. *Farrier's Dict.*

B'ALSAM. *n. s.* [*balsamum*, Lat.] Ointment; unguent; an unctuous application thicker than oil, and softer than salve.

Christ's blood's our *balsam*; if that cure us here,
Him, when our judge, we shall not find severe. *Denham.*

BALSAM *Apple.* [*momordica*, Lat.] An annual Indian plant.

The flower consists of one leaf is of the expanded bell-shaped kind, but so deeply cut, as to appear composed of five distinct leaves: the flowers are some male, or barren; others female, growing upon the top of the embryo, which is afterwards changed into a fruit, which is fleshy, and sometimes more or less tapering and hollow, and, when ripe, usually bursts, and casts forth the seeds with an elasticity; which seeds are wrapped up in a membranous covering, and are, for the most part, indented on the edges. *Millar.*

BALSAM *Tree.*

This is a shrub which scarce grows taller than the pomegranate tree; it shoots out abundance of long slender branches, with a few small rounding leaves, always green; the wood of it is gummy, and of a reddish colour; the blossoms are like small stars, white, and very fragrant; whence spring out little pointed pods, inclosing a fruit like an almond, called carpobalsamum, as the wood is called xylobalsamum, and the juice opobalsamum; which see. This tree is cultivated in Arabia and Judea; but it is forbid to be sown or multiplied without the permission of the grand signior. *Calmet. Chambers.*

BALSA'MICAL. } *adj.* [from *balsam.*] Having the qualities of
BALSA'MICK. } balsam; unctuous; mitigating; soft; mild; oily.

If there be a wound in my leg, the vital energy of my soul thrusts out the *balsamical* humour of my blood to heal it. *Hale's Origin of Mankind.*

The aliment of such as have fresh wounds ought to be such as keeps the humours from putrefaction, and renders them oily and *balsamick.* *Arbuthnot on Diet.*

BA'LUSTER. *n. s.* [according to *du Cange*, from *balaustrium*, low Lat. a bathing place.] A small column or pilaster, from an inch and three quarters to four inches square or diameter. Their dimensions and forms are various; they are frequently adorned with mouldings; they are placed with rails on stairs, and in the fronts of galleries in churches.

This should first have been planched over, and railed about with *balusters.* *Carew's Survey of Cornwal.*

BA'LUSTRADE. *n. s.* [from *baluster.*] An assemblage of one or more rows of little turned pillars, called balusters, fixed upon a terras, or the top of a building, for separating one part from another.

BAM, BEAM, being initials in the name of any place, usually imply it to have been woody; from the Saxon beam, which we use in the same sense to this day. *Gibson's Camden.*

BA'MBOO. *n. s.* An Indian plant of the reed kind. It has several shoots, much larger than our ordinary reeds, which are knotty, and separated from space to space by joints. They are said by some, but by mistake, to contain sugar; the *bamboo* being much larger than the sugar-cane. The leaves grow out of each knot, and are prickly. They are four or five inches long, and an inch in breadth, somewhat pointed, and ribbed through the whole length with green and sharp fibres. Its flowers grow in ears, like those of wheat.

To BAMBO'OZLE. *v. a.* [a cant word not used in pure or in grave writings.] To deceive; to impose upon; to confound.

After Nick had *bamboozled* about the money, John called for counters. *Arbuthnot's John Bull.*

BAMBO'OZLER. *n. s.* [from *bamboozle.*] A tricking fellow; a cheat.

There are a set of fellows they call banterers and *bamboozlers*, that play such tricks. *Arbuthnot's John Bull.*

BAN. *n. s.* [*ban*, Teut. a publick proclamation, as of proscription, interdiction, excommunication, publick sale.]

1. Publick notice given of any thing, whereby any thing is publickly commanded or forbidden. This word we use especially in the publishing matrimonial contracts in the church, before marriage, to the end that if any man can say against the intention of the parties, either in respect of kindred or otherwise, they may take their exception in time. And, in the canon law, *banna sunt proclamationes sponsi & sponsæ in ecclesiis fieri soliti.* *Cowel.*

I bar it in the interest of my wife;
'Tis she is subcontracted to this lord,
And I her husband contradict your *bans.* *Shakesp. King Lear.*
Our *bans* thrice bid! and for our wedding-day
To draw her neck into the *bans.* *Hudibras.*

2. A curse; excommunication.

My kerchief bought! then press'd, then forc'd away! *Gay.*
In th' interim, spare for no trepans
Thou mixture rank of midnight weeds collected,
With Hecate's *ban* thrice blasted, thrice infected. *Hamlet.*

A great oversight it was of St. Peter, that he did not accurse Nero, whereby the pope might have got all; yet what need of such a *ban*, since friar Vincent could tell Atasalipa, that kingdoms were the pope's. *Raleigh's Essays.*

3. Interdiction.

Much more to taste it, under *ban* to touch. *Parad Lost.*

4. *Ban of the Empire*; a publick censure by which the privileges of any German prince are suspended.

He proceeded so far by treaty, that he was proferred to have the imperial *ban* taken off Altapinus, upon submission *Howel.*

To BAN. *v. a.* [*bannen*, Dut. to curse.] To curse; to execrate.

Shall we think that it *baneth* the work which they leave behind them, or taketh away the use thereof. *Hooker, b.* v.

It is uncertain whether this word, in the foregoing sense, is to be deduced from *ban*, to curse, or *bane*, to poison.

In thy closet pent up, rue my shame,
And *ban* our enemies, both mine and thine. *Shakesp. H.* VI.

Before these Moors went a Numidian priest, bellowing out charms, and casting scrowls of paper on each side, wherein he cursed and *banned* the Christians. *Knolles's Hist. of the Turks.*

BANA'NA *Tree.* See PLANTAIN; of which it is a species.

BAND. *n. s.* [*bende*, Dut. band, Saxon.]

1. A tye; a bandage; that by which one thing is joined to another.

You shall find the *band*, that seems to tie their friendship together, will be the very strangler of their amity. *Shakesp. Antony and Cleopatra.*

2. A chain by which any animal is kept in restraint. This is now usually spelt, less properly, *bond.*

So wild a beast, so tame ytaught to be,
And buxom to his *bands*, is joy to see. *Hubberd's Tale.*
Since you deny him ent'rance, he demands
His wife, whom cruelly you hold in *bands.* *Dryd. Aurengz.*

3. Any means of union or connexion between persons.

Here's eight that must take hands,
To join in Hymen's *bands.* *Shakesp. As you like it.*

4. Something worn about the neck; a neckcloth. It is now restrained to a neckcloth of particular form worn by clergymen, lawyers, and students in colleges.

For his mind I do not care,
That's a toy that I could spare:
Let his title be but great,
His cloaths rich, and *band* sit neat. *Ben Johnson's Underwoods.*

He took his present lodging at the mansion-house of a taylor's widow, who washes and can clear-starch his *bands.* *Addison.*

5. Any thing bound round another.

In old statues of stone in cellars, the feet of them being bound with leaden *bands*, it appeared that the lead did swell. *Bacon.*

6. A company of persons joined together in any common design.

And, good my lord of Somerset, unite
Your troops of horsemen with his *bands* of foot.
Shakesp. Henry VI *p.* i.
We few, we happy few, we *band* of brothers. *Sh. H.* V.
The queen in white array before her *band*,
Saluting took her rival by the hand. *Dryden's Fables.*

On a sudden, methought this select *band* sprang forward, with a resolution to climb the ascent, and follow the call of that heavenly musick. *Tatler*, N° 81.

Strait the three *bands* prepare in arms to join,
Each *band* the number of the sacred Nine. *Pope.*

7. In architecture. Any flat low member or moulding, called also fascia, face, or plinth.

To BAND. *v. a.* [from *band.*]

1. To unite together into one body or troop.

The bishop, and the duke of Glo'ster's men,
Have fill'd their pockets full of pebble stones,
And *banding* themselves in contrary parts,
Do pelt at one another's pates. *Shakesp. Henry* VI. *p.* i.

Some of the boys *banded* themselves as for the major, and others for the king; who, after six days skirmishing, at last made a composition, and departed. *Carew's Survey of Cornwal.*

To live exempt
From heav'n's high jurisdiction, in new league
Banded against his throne. *Milton's Par. Lost, b.* ii.

2. To bind over with a band.

And by his mother stood an infant lover,
With wings unfledg'd, his eyes were *banded* over. *Dryden.*

Bands *of a saddle*, are two pieces of iron nailed upon the bows of the saddle, to hold the bows in the right situation.

Ba'ndage. *n. s.* [*bandage*, Fr.]

1. Something bound over another.

Zeal too had a place among the rest, with a *bandage* over her eyes; though one would not have expected to have seen her represented in snow. *Addison. Freeholder*, N° 27.

Cords were fastened by hooks to my *bandages*, which the workmen had girt round my neck. *Gulliver's Travels.*

2. It is used, in surgery, for the fillet or roller wrapped over a wounded member; and, sometimes, for the act or practice of applying *bandages*.

Bandbox. *n. s.* [from *band* and *box*.] A slight box used for bands and other things of small weight.

My friends are surprized to find two *bandboxes* among my books, till I let them see that they are lined with deep erudition. *Addison. Spectator*, N° 85.

With empty *bandbox* she delights to range,
And feigns a distant errand from the 'Change. *Gay's Trivia.*

Ba'ndelet. *n. s.* [*bandelet*, Fr. In architecture.] Any little band, flat moulding, or fillet.

Ba'ndit. *n. s.* [*bandito*, Ital.] A man outlawed.

No savage fierce, *bandit*, or mountaineer,
Will dare to soil her virgin purity. *Milton's Poems.*
No *bandit* fierce, no tyrant mad with pride,
No cavern'd hermit, rests self satisfy'd. *Pope's Essay on Man.*

Bandi'tto. *n. s.* in the plural *banditti*. [*bandito*, Ital.]

A Roman sworder, and *banditto* slave,
Murder'd sweet Tully. *Shakesp. Henry* VI. *p.* ii.

Ba'ndog. *n. s.* [from *ban* or *band*, and *dog*. The original of this word is very doubtful. *Caius, de canibus Britannicis*, derives it from *band*, that is, *a dog chained up*. *Skinner* inclines to deduce it from *bana*, a *murderer*. May it not come from *ban* a *curse*, as we say a *curst cur*; or rather from *baund*, swelled or large, a *Danish* word; from whence, in some counties, they call a great nut a *ban-nut*.] A kind of large dog.

The time of night when Troy was set on fire,
The time when screech-owls cry, and *bandogs* howl.
Shakesp. Henry VI. *p.* ii.
Or privy, or pert, if any bin,
We have great *bandogs* will tear their skin. *Spens. Pastorals.*

Ba'ndoleers. *n s.* [*bandouliers*, Fr.] Small wooden cases covered with leather, each of them containing powder that is a sufficient charge for a musket.

Ba'ndrol. *n. s.* [*banderol*, Fr.] A little flag or streamer; the little fringed silk flag that hangs on a trumpet.

Ba'ndy. *n. s.* [from *bander*, Fr.] A club turned round at bottom for striking a ball at play.

To Ba'ndy. *v. a.* [probably from *bandy*, the instrument with which they strike balls at play, which being crooked, is named from the term *bander un arc*, to string or bend a bow.]

1. To beat to and fro, or from one to another.

They do cunningly, from one hand to another, *bandy* the service like a tennis-ball. *Spenser's Ireland.*

And like a ball *bandy'd* 'twixt pride and wit,
Rather than yield, both sides the prize will quit. *Denham.*
What, from the tropicks, can the earth repel?
What vigorous arm, what repercussive blow,
Bandies the mighty globe still to and fro? *Blackmore.*

2. To exchange; to give and take reciprocally.

Do you *bandy* looks with me, you rascal? *Shakesp. K. Lear.*
'Tis not in thee
To grudge my pleasures, to cut off my train,
To *bandy* hasty words. *Shakesp. King Lear.*

3. To agitate; to toss about.

This hath been so *bandied* amongst us, that one can hardly miss books of this kind. *Locke.*

Ever since men have been united into governments, the endeavours after universal monarchy have been *bandied* among them. *Swift.*

Let not obvious and known truths, or some of the most plain and certain propositions, be *bandied* about in a disputation. *Watts's Improvement of the Mind.*

To Ba'ndy. *v. n.* To contend, as at some game, in which each strives to drive the ball his own way.

No simple man that sees
This factious *bandying* of their favourites,
But that he doth presage some ill event. *Shakesp. Henry* VI.
A valiant son in law thou shalt enjoy:
One fit to *bandy* with thy lawless sons,
To ruffle in the commonwealth. *Shakesp. Tit. Andron.*
Could set up grandee against grandee,
To squander time away, and *bandy*,
Make lords and commoners lay sieges
To one another's privileges. *Hudibras.*

After all the *bandying* attempts of resolution, it is as much a question as ever. *Glanville's Scepsis, c.* iv.

Ba'ndyleg. *n. s.* [from *bander*, Fr.] A crooked leg.

He tells aloud your greatest failing,
Nor makes a scruple to expose
Your *bandyleg*, or crooked nose. *Swift.*

Ba'ndylegged. *adj.* [from *bandyleg*.] Having crooked legs.

The Ethiopians had an one-eyed *bandylegged* prince; such a person would have made but an odd figure. *Collier on Duelling.*

BANE. *n. s.* [bana, Sax. a murderer.]

1. Poison.

Begone, or else let me. 'Tis *bane* to draw
The same air with thee. *Ben Johnson's Catiline.*
All good to me becomes
Bane; and in heav'n much worse would be my state.
Milton's Par. Lost, *b.* ix. *l.* 122.
They, with speed,
Their course through thickest constellations held,
Spreading their *bane*. *Milton's Par. Lost*, *b.* x. *l.* 412.
Thus, am I doubly armed; my death and life,
My *bane* and antidote, are both before me:
This, in a moment, brings me to an end;
But that informs me I shall never die. *Addison's Cato.*

2. That which destroys; mischief; ruin.

Insolency must be represt, or it will be the *bane* of the Christian religion. *Hooker*, *b.* ii. § 7.

I will not be afraid of death and *bane*,
Till Birnam forest come to Dunsinane. *Shakesp. Macbeth.*
Suffices that to me strength is my *bane*,
And proves the source of all my miseries. *Milton's S. Agon.*
So entertain'd those odorous sweets the fiend,
Who came their *bane*. *Milton's Paradise Lost*, *b.* iv. *l.* 167.
Who can omit the Gracchi, who declare
The Scipios' worth, those thunderbolts of war,
The double *bane* of Carthage? *Dryden, Æneid* vi.

False religion is, in its nature, the greatest *bane* and destruction to government in the world. *South.*

To Bane. *v. a.* [from the noun.] To poison.

What if my house be troubled with a rat,
And I be pleas'd to give ten thousand ducats
To have it *ban'd*. *Shakesp. Merchant of Venice.*

Ba'neful. *adj.* [from *bane* and *full*.]

1. Poisonous.

For voyaging to learn the direful art,
To taint with deadly drugs the barbed dart;
Observant of the gods, and sternly just,
Ilus refus'd t' impart the *baneful* trust. *Pope's Odyssey*, *b.* i.

2. Destructive.

The silver eagle too is sent before,
Which I do hope will prove to them as *baneful*,
As thou conceiv'st it to the commonwealth. *B. Johns. Catil.*
The nightly wolf is *baneful* to the fold,
Storms to the wheat, to buds the bitter cold. *Dryden's Virgil.*

Ba'nefulness. *n. s.* [from *baneful*.] Poisonousness; destructiveness.

B'anewort. *n. s.* [from *bane* and *wort*.] A plant, the same with *deadly nightshade*. See Nightshade.

To Bang. *v. a.* [*vengolen*, Dutch.]

1. To beat; to thump; to cudgel: a low and familiar word.

One receiving from them some affronts, met with them handsomely, and *banged* them to good purpose. *Howel's V. For.*

He having got some iron out of the earth, put it into his servants hands to fence with, and *bang* one another. *Locke.*

Formerly I was to be *banged*, because I was too strong, and now, because I am too weak to resist; I am to be brought down, when too rich, and oppressed, when too poor. *Arbuth. J. Bull.*

2. To handle roughly; to treat with violence in general.

The desperate tempest hath so *bang'd* the Turks,
That their designment halts. *Shakesp. Othello.*

You should accost her with jests fire-new from the mint; you should have *banged* the youth into dumbness. *Shakesp. Twelfth Night.*

Bang. *n. s.* [from the verb.] A blow; a thump; a stroke: a low word.

I am a bachelor.—That's to say, they are fools that marry; you'll bear me a *bang* for that. *Shakesp. Julius Cæsar.*

With many a stiff twack, many a *bang*,
Hard crabtree and old iron rang. *Hudibras, cant.* ii.

I heard several *bangs* or buffets, as I thought, given to the eagle that held the ring of my box in his beak. *Gulliv. Travels.*

To BA'NISH. *v. a.* [*banir*, Fr. *banio*, low Lat. probably from *ban*, Teut. an outlawry, or proscription.]

1. To condemn to leave his own country.

Oh, fare thee well!
Those evils thou repeat'st upon thyself,
Have *banish'd* me from Scotland. *Shakesp. Macbeth.*

2. To drive away.

It is for wicked men only to dread God, and to endeavour to *banish* the thoughts of him out of their minds. *Tillotson.*

Successless all her soft caresses prove,
To *banish* from his breast his country's love. *Pope's Odyss.*

Ba'nisher. *n. s.* [from *banish*.] He that forces another from his own country.

In mere spite,
To be full quit of those my *banishers*,
Stand I before thee here. *Shakesp. Coriolanus.*

Ba'nishment. *n. s.* [*bannissement*, Fr.]

1. The act of banishing another; as, he secured himself by the *banishment* of his enemies.

2. The

2. The ſtate of being baniſhed; exile.

Now go we in content
To liberty, and not to *baniſhment*. *Shakeſp. As you like it.*
Round the wide world in *baniſhment* we roam,
Forc'd from our pleaſing fields and native home. *Dryden.*

BANK. *n. ſ.* [banc, Saxon.]

1. The earth riſing on each ſide of a water. We ſay, properly, the *ſhore* of the *ſea*, and the *banks* of a *river*, *brook*, or ſmall water.

Have you not made an univerſal ſhout,
That Tyber trembled underneath his *bank*. *Shak. Jul. Cæſ.*
Richmond, in Devonſhire, ſent out a boat
Unto the ſhore, to aſk thoſe on the *banks*,
If they were his aſſiſtants. *Shakeſp. Richard* III.
A brook whoſe ſtream ſo great, ſo good,
Was lov'd, was honour'd as a flood:
Whoſe *banks* the Muſes dwelt upon *Craſhaw.*
'Tis happy when our ſtreams of knowledge flow,
To fill their *banks*, but not to overthrow. *Denham.*
O early loſt! what tears the river ſhed,
When the ſad pomp along his *banks* was led! *Pope.*

2. Any heap of earth piled up.

They beſieged him in Abel of Bethmaachah, and they caſt up a *bank* againſt the city; and it ſtood in the trench. *Samuel*, xx. 15.

3. [from *banc*, Fr. a bench.] A ſeat or bench of rowers.

Plac'd on your *banks*, the luſty Trojans ſweep
Neptune's ſmooth face, and cleave the yielding deep. *Waller.*
Mean time the king with gifts a veſſel ſtores,
Supplies the *banks* with twenty choſen oars. *Dryd. Homer.*

That *banks* of oars were not in the ſame plain, but raiſed above one another, is evident from deſcriptions of ancient ſhips. *Arbuthnot on Coins.*

4. A place where money is laid up to be called for occaſionally.

Let it be no *bank*, or common ſtock, but every man be maſter of his own money. Not that I altogether miſlike *banks*, but they will hardly be brooked in regard of certain ſuſpicions. *Bacon's Eſſays.*

This maſs of treaſure you ſhould now reduce;
But you your ſtore have hoarded in ſome *bank*. *Denham.*

Their pardons and indulgences, and giving men a ſhare in ſaints merits, out of the common *bank* and treaſury of the church, which the pope has the ſole cuſtody of. *South.*

5. The company of perſons concerned in managing a bank.

To BANK. *v. a.* [from the noun.]

1. To lay up money in a bank.
2. To incloſe with banks.

Amid the cliffs
And burning ſands, that *bank* the ſhrubby vales. *Thomſon.*

BA'NK-BILL. *n. ſ.* [from *bank* and *bill*] A note for money laid up in a bank, at the ſight of which the money is paid.

Let three hundred pounds be paid her out of my ready money, or *bank-bills*. *Swift's Laſt Will.*

BA'NKER. *n. ſ.* [from *bank*.] One that trafficks in money; one that keeps or manages a bank.

Whole droves of lenders croud the *banker*'s doors,
To call in money. *Dryden's Spaniſh Friar.*
By powerful charms of gold and ſilver led,
The Lombard *bankers* and the change to waſte. *Dryden.*

BA'NKRUPCY. *n. ſ.* [from *bankrupt*.]

1. The ſtate of a man broken, or bankrupt.
2. The act of declaring one's ſelf bankrupt; as, he ſilenced the clamours of his creditors by a ſudden *bankrupcy*.

BA'NKRUPT. *adj.* [*banqueroute*, Fr. *bancorupto*, Ital.] In debt beyond the power of payment.

The king's grown *bankrupt*, like a broken man. *Shakeſp. Richard* III.

Sir, if you ſpend word for word with me,
I ſhall make your wit *bankrupt*. *Shak. Two Gent. of Verona.*

BA'NKRUPT. *n. ſ.* A man in debt beyond the power of payment.

Perkin gathered together a power, neither in number nor in hardineſs contemptible; but, in their fortunes, to be feared; being *bankrupts*, and many of them felons. *Bacon's Henry* VII.

It is with wicked men as with a *bankrupt*: when his creditors are loud and clamorous, and ſpeak big, he giveth them many good words. *Calamy.*

In vain at court the *bankrupt* pleads his cauſe;
His thankleſs country leaves him to her laws. *Pope.*

To BA'NKRUPT. *v. a.* To break; to diſable one from ſatisfying his creditors.

We caſt off the care of all future thirſt, becauſe we are already *bankrupted*. *Hammond's Fundamentals.*

BA'NNER. *n. ſ.* [*banniere*, Fr. *banair*, Welch.]

1. A flag; a ſtandard; a military enſign.

From France there comes a power,
Who already have ſecret ſeize
In ſome of our beſt ports, and are at point
To ſhew their open *banner*. *Shakeſp. King Lear.*
All in a moment through the gloom were ſeen
Ten thouſand *banners* riſe into the air,
With orient colours waving. *Milton's Par. Loſt, b.* i.

He ſaid no more;
But left his ſiſter and his queen behind,
And wav'd his royal *banner* in the wind. *Dryden.*
Fir'd with ſuch motives, you do well to join
With Cato's foes, and follow Cæſar's *banners*. *Addiſon's Cato.*

2. A ſtreamer borne at the end of a lance, or elſewhere.

BA'NNERET. *n. ſ.* [from *banner*.] A knight made in the field, with the ceremony of cutting off the point of his ſtandard, and making it a banner. They are next to barons in dignity; and were anciently called by ſummons to parliament. *Blount.*

A gentleman told king Henry, that Sir Richard Croftes, made *banneret* at Stoke, was a wiſe man; the king anſwered, he doubted not that, but marvelled how a fool could know. *Cambden's Remains.*

BA'NNEROL, more properly BANDEROL. *n. ſ.* [from *banderole*, Fr.] A little flag or ſtreamer.

King Oswald had a *bannerol* of gold and purple ſet over his tomb. *Camden's Remains.*

BA'NNIAN. *n. ſ.* A man's undreſs, or morning-gown; ſuch as is worn by the *Bannians* in the Eaſt Indies.

BA'NNOCK. *n. ſ.* A kind of oaten or peaſe meal cake, mixed with water, and baked upon an iron plate over the fire; uſed in the northern counties, and in Scotland.

BA'NQUET. *n. ſ.* [*banquet*, Fr. *banchetto*, Ital. *vanqueto*, Span.] A feaſt.

If a faſting day come, he hath on that day a *banquet* to make. *Hooker, b.* v. § 41.

In his commendations I am fed;
It is a *banquet* to me. *Shakeſp. Macbeth.*

You cannot have a perfect palace, except you have two ſeveral ſides; a ſide for the *banquet*, and a ſide for the houſhold; the one for feaſts and triumphs, and the other for dwelling. *Bacon's Eſſays.*

Shall the companions make a *banquet* of him? Shall they part him among the merchants? *Job*, xli. 6.

At that taſted fruit,
The ſun, as from Thyeſtean *banquet*, turn'd
His courſe intended. *Milton's Paradiſe Loſt, b.* x. *l.* 688.
That dares prefer the toils of Hercules
To dalliance, *banquets*, and ignoble eaſe. *Dryden's Juvenal.*

To BA'NQUET. *v. a.* [from the noun.] To treat any one with feaſts.

Welcome his friends,
Viſit his countrymen, and *banquet* them. *Shakeſp. Taming of the Shrew.*

They were *banqueted* by the way, and the nearer they approached, the more encreaſed the nobility. *Sir J. Hayward.*

To BA'NQUET. *v. n.* To feaſt; to fare daintily.

The mind ſhall *banquet*, tho' the body pine:
Fat paunches make lean pates, and dainty bits
Make rich the ribs, but banker out the wits. *Shakeſp. Love's Labour Loſt.*

So long as his innocence is his repaſt, he feaſts and *banquets* upon bread and water. *South.*

I purpos'd to unbend the evening hours,
And *banquet* private in the women's bow'rs. *Prior.*

BA'NQUETER. *n. ſ.* [from *banquet*.]

1. A feaſter; one that lives deliciouſly.
2. He that makes feaſts.

BA'NQUET-HOUSE. } *n. ſ.* [from *banquet* and *houſe*.] A
BA'NQUETING-HOUSE. } houſe where banquets are kept.

In a *banqueting-houſe*, among certain pleaſant trees, the table was ſet near to an excellent water-work. *Sidney.*

But at the walk's end behold, how rais'd on high
A *banquet-houſe* ſalutes the ſouthern ſky. *Dryden's Juvenal.*

BANQUETTE. *n. ſ.* [Fr. in fortification.] A ſmall bank at the foot of the parapet, for the ſoldiers to mount upon when they fire.

BA'NSTICLE. *n. ſ.* A ſmall fiſh, called alſo a ſtickleback.

To BANTER. *v. a.* [a barbarous word, without etymology, unleſs it be derived from *badiner*, Fr.] To play upon; to rally; to turn to ridicule; to ridicule.

The magiſtrate took it that he *bantered* him, and bad an officer take him into cuſtody. *L'Eſtrange.*

It is no new thing for innocent ſimplicity to be the ſubject of *bantering* drolls. *L'Eſtrange.*

Could Alcinous' gueſts withold
From ſcorn or rage? Shall we, cries one, permit
His leud romances, and his *bant'ring* wit? *Tate's Juvenal.*

BA'NTER. *n. ſ.* [from the verb.] Ridicule; raillery.

This humour, let it look never ſo ſilly, as it paſſes many times for frolick and *banter*, is one of the moſt pernicious ſnares in human life. *L'Eſtrange.*

Metaphyſicks are ſo neceſſary to a diſtinct conception, ſolid judgment, and juſt reaſoning on many ſubjects, that thoſe who ridicule it, will be ſuppoſed to make their wit and *banter* a refuge and excuſe for their own lazineſs. *Watts's Logick.*

BA'NTERER. *n. ſ.* [from *banter*.] One that banters; a droll.

What opinion have theſe religious *banterers* of the divine power? or what have they to ſay for this mockery and contempt? *L'Eſtrange.*

BA'NTLING. *n. ſ.* [if it has any etymology, it is perhaps corrupted from the old word *bairn, bairnling*, a little child.] A little child: a low word.

If the object of their love
Chance by Lucina's aid to prove,
They ſeldom let the *bantling* roar,
In baſket, at a neighbour's door. *Prior.*

BA'PTISM. *n. ſ.* [*baptiſmus*, Lat. βαπτισμὸς.]

1. An external ablution of the body, with a certain form of words, which operates and denotes an internal ablution or waſhing of the ſoul from original ſin. *Ayliffe's Parergon.*

Baptiſm is given by water, and that preſcript form of words which the church of Chriſt doth uſe. *Hooker, b.* iv. § 1.

To his great *baptiſm* flock'd,
With awe, the regions round, and with them came
From Nazareth the ſon of Joſeph deem'd,
Unmarkt, unknown. *Paradiſe Regained, b.* i. *l.* 21.

2. *Baptiſm* is often taken in Scripture for ſufferings.

I have a *baptiſm* to be baptized with, and how am I ſtraitened till it be accompliſhed? *Luke*, xii. 15.

BAPTI'SMAL. *adj.* [from *baptiſm.*] Of or pertaining to baptiſm.

When we undertake the *baptiſmal* vow, and enter on their new life, it would be apt to diſcourage us. *Hammond.*

BA'PTIST. *n. ſ.* [*baptiſte*, Fr. βαπτιστὴς.] He that adminiſters baptiſm.

Him the *Baptiſt* ſoon
Deſcry'd, divinely warn'd, and witneſs bore
As to his worthier—— *Parad. Regained, b.* i. *l.* 25.

BA'PTISTERY. *n. ſ.* [*baptiſterium*, Lat.] The place where the ſacrament of baptiſm is adminiſtred.

The great church, *baptiſtery*, and leaning tower, are well worth ſeeing. *Addiſon on Italy.*

To BAPTI'ZE. *v. a.* [*baptiſer*, Fr. from βαπτίζω.] To chriſten; to adminiſter the ſacrament of baptiſm.

He to them ſhall leave in charge,
To teach all nations what of him they learn'd,
And his ſalvation; them who ſhall believe,
Baptizing in the profluent ſtream, the ſign
Of waſhing them from guilt of ſin, to life
Pure, and in mind prepar'd, if ſo befal,
For death, like that which the Redeemer dy'd.
Milton's Paradiſe Loſt.

Let us reflect that we are chriſtians; that we are called by the name of the Son of God, and *baptized* into an irreconcileable enmity with ſin, the world, and the devil. *Rogers.*

BAPTI'ZER. *n. ſ.* [from *to baptize.*] One that chriſtens; one that adminiſters baptiſm.

BAR. *n. ſ.* [*barre*, Fr.]

1. A piece of wood, iron, or other matter, laid croſs a paſſage to hinder entrance.

And he made the middle *bar* to ſhoot through the boards from the one end to the other. *Exodus*, xxxvi. 33.

2. A bolt; a piece of iron or wood faſtened to a door, and entering into the poſt or wall to hold it.

The fiſh-gate did the ſons of Haſſenaah build, who alſo laid the beams thereof, and ſet up the doors thereof, the locks thereof, and the *bars* thereof. *Nehem.* iii. 3.

3. Any obſtacle which hinders or obſtructs.

I brake up for it my decreed place, and ſet *bars* and doors, and ſaid, hitherto ſhalt thou come, and no farther.
Job, xxxviii. 10.

And had his heir ſurviv'd him in due courſe,
What limits, England, hadſt thou found? what *bar?*
What world could have reſiſted? *Daniel's Civil War.*

Hard, thou know'ſt it, to exclude
Spiritual ſubſtance with corporeal *bar*. *Parad. Loſt, b.* iv.

Muſt I new *bars* to my own joy create,
Refuſe myſelf, what I had forc'd from fate? *Dryd. Aureng.*

Fatal accidents have ſet
A moſt unhappy *bar* between your friendſhip.
Rowe's Ambitious Stepmother.

4. A rock, or bank of ſand, at the entrance of a harbour or river, which ſhips cannot ſail over at low water.

5. Any thing uſed for prevention.

Leſt examination ſhould hinder and lett your proceedings, behold, for a *bar* againſt that impediment, one opinion newly added. *Hooker, Preface.*

Which Salique land the French unjuſtly gloze to be
The founder of this law, and female *bar*. *Shakeſp. Hen.* V.

6. The place where cauſes of law are tried, or where criminals are judged; ſo called from the *bar* placed to hinder crouds from incommoding the court.

The great duke
Came to the *bar*, where, to his accuſations,
He pleaded ſtill not guilty. *Shakeſp. Henry* VIII.

Some at the *bar* with ſubtlety defend,
Or on the bench the knotty laws untye. *Dryd. Juvenal.*

7. An incloſed place in a tavern or coffeehouſe, where the houſekeeper ſits and receives reckonings.

I was under ſome apprehenſion that they would appeal to me; and therefore laid down my penny at the *bar*, and made the beſt of my way. *Addiſon. Spectator*, N° 403.

8. In law. A peremptory exception againſt a demand or plea brought by the defendant in an action, that deſtroys the action of the plaintiff for ever. It is divided into a *bar* to common intent, and a *bar* ſpecial: a *bar* to a common intent, is an ordinary or general *bar*, that diſables the declaration or plea of the plaintiff: a *bar* ſpecial, is that which is more than ordinary, and falls out in the caſe in hand, upon ſome ſpecial circumſtance of the fact. *Cowel.*

Baſtardy is laid in *bar* of ſomething that is principally commenced. *Ayliffe's Parergon.*

9. Any thing by which the compages or ſtructure is held together.

I went down to the bottoms of the mountains: the earth, with her *bars*, was about me for ever. *Jonah*, ii. 6.

10. Any thing which is laid acroſs another, as *bars* in heraldry.

11. *Bar of gold* or *ſilver*, is a lump or wedge from the mines, melted down into a ſort of mould, and never wrought.

12. *Bars of a horſe.* The upper part of the gums between the tusks and grinders, which bears no teeth, and to which the bit is applied, and, by its friction, the horſe governed.

13. *Bars, in muſick*, are ſtrokes drawn perpendicularly acroſs the lines of a piece of muſick; uſed to regulate the beating or meaſure of muſical time.

BAR SHOT. *n. ſ.* Two half bullets joined together by an iron bar; uſed in ſea engagements for cutting down the maſts and rigging.

To BAR. *v. a.* [from the noun.]

1. To faſten or ſhut any thing with a bolt, or bar.

My duty cannot ſuffer
T' obey in all your daughter's hard commands;
Though their injunction be to *bar* my doors,
And let this tyrannous night take hold upon you.
Shakeſp. King Lear.

When you *bar* the window-ſhutters of your lady's bedchamber at nights, leave open the ſaſhes to let in the air.
Swift's Directions to the Chambermaid.

2. To hinder; to obſtruct.

When law can do no right,
Let it be lawful, that law *bar* no wrong. *Shakeſp. K. Lear.*

3. To prevent.

The houſes of the country were all ſcattered, and yet not ſo far off as that it *barred* mutual ſuccour. *Sidney, b.* i.

Doth it not ſeem a thing very probable, that God doth purpoſely add, Do after my judgments; as giving thereby to underſtand, that his meaning in the former ſentence was but to *bar* ſimilitude in ſuch things as were repugnant to his ordinances, laws, and ſtatutes? *Hooker.*

4. To ſhut out from.

Hath he ſet bounds between their love and me?
I am their mother; who ſhall *bar* them from me?
Shakeſp. Richard III.

Our hope of Italy not only loſt,
But ſhut from ev'ry ſhore, and *barr'd* from ev'ry coaſt. *Dryd.*

5. To exclude from a claim.

God hath abridged it, by *barring* us from ſome things of themſelves indifferent. *Hooker, b.* ii. § 4.

Give my voice on Richard's ſide,
To *bar* my maſter's heirs in true deſcent!
God knows I will not. *Shakeſp. Richard* III.

His civil acts do bind and *bar* them all;
And as from Adam, all corruption take,
So, if the father's crime be capital,
In all the blood, law doth corruption make. *Sir J. Davies.*

It was thought ſufficient not only to exclude them from that benefit, but to *bar* them from their money. *Clarendon.*

If he is qualified, why is he *barred* the profit, when he only performs the conditions? *Collier on Pride.*

6. To prohibit.

For though the law of arms doth *bar*
The uſe of venom'd ſhot in war. *Hudibras.*

What is a greater pedant than a mere man of the town? *Bar* him the playhouſes, and you ſtrike him dumb. *Addiſon.*

7. To except; to make an exception.

Well, we ſhall ſee your bearing.—
—Nay, but I *bar* to-night; you ſhall not gage me
By what we do to-night. *Shakeſp. Merchant of Venice.*

8. In law. To hinder the proceſs of a ſuit.

But buff and belt men never know theſe cares;
No time, nor trick of law, their action *bars:*
Their cauſe they to an eaſier iſſue put. *Dryden's Juvenal.*

From ſuch delays as conduce to the finding out of truth, a criminal cauſe ought not to be *barred*. *Ayliffe's Parergon.*

If a biſhop be a party to a ſuit, and excommunicates his adverſary, ſuch excommunication ſhall not diſable or *bar* his adverſary. *Ayliffe's Parergon.*

9. To *bar* a vein.

This is an operation performed upon the veins of the legs of a horſe, and other parts, with intent to ſtop the malignant humours. It is done by opening the ſkin above it, diſengaging it, and tying it both above and below, and ſtriking between two ligatures.

BARB. *n. s.* [*barba*, a beard, Lat.]
1. Any thing that grows in the place of the beard.
The barbel, so called by reason of his *barb* or wattels at his mouth, under his chaps. *Walton's Angler.*
2. The points that stand backward in an arrow, or fishing-hook, to hinder them from being extracted.
Nor less the Spartan fear'd, before he found
The shining *barb* appear above the wound. *Pope's Iliad.*
3. The armour for horses.
Their horses were naked, without any *barbs*; for albeit many brought *barbs*, few regarded to put them on. *Hayward.*

BARB. *n. s.* [contracted from *Barbary*.] A Barbary horse.
These horses are brought from Barbary; they are commonly of a slender light size, and very lean and thin, usually chosen for stallions. *Barbs*, as it is said, may die, but never grow old; the vigour and mettle of *barbs* never cease, but with their life. *Farrier's Dict.*

To BARB. *v. a.* [from the noun.]
1. To shave; to dress out the beard.
Shave the head, and tie the beard, and say it was the desire of the penitent to be so *barbed* before his death. *Shakesp. Measure for Measure.*
2. To furnish horses with armour.
A warriour train
That like a deluge pour'd upon the plain;
On *barbed* steeds they rode in proud array,
Thick as the college of the bees in May. *Dryden's Fables.*
3. To jag arrows with hooks.
The twanging bows
Send showers of shafts, that on their *barbed* points
Alternate ruin bear. *Philips.*

BA'RBACAN. *n. s.* [*barbacane*, Fr. *barbacana*, Span.]
1. A fortification placed before the walls of a town.
Within the *barbacan* a porter sate,
Day and night duly keeping watch and ward:
Nor wight, nor word mote pass out of the gate,
But in good order, and with due regard. *Fairy Queen.*
2. A fortress at the end of a bridge.
3. An opening in the wall through which the guns are levelled.

BARBADOES *Cherry.* [*malphigia*, Lat.]
It has a small quinquefid calix, of one leaf, having bifid segments; the flower consists of five leaves, in form of a rose, having several stamina collected in form of a tube; the ovary, in the bottom of the flower-cup, becomes a globular, fleshy, soft fruit; in which is a single capsule, containing three stony winged nuts. In the West Indies, it rises to be fifteen or sixteen feet high, where it produces great quantities of a pleasant tart fruit; propagated in gardens there, but in Europe it is a curiosity. *Millar.*

BA'RBA'DOES *Tar.* A bituminous substance, differing little from the petroleum floating on several springs in England and Scotland. *Woodward's Method of Fossils.*

BARBA'RIAN. *n. s.* [*barbarus*, Lat. It seems to have signified at first only *foreign*, or a *foreigner*; but, in time, implied some degree of wildness or cruelty.]
1. A man uncivilized; untaught; a savage.
Proud Greece, all nations else *barbarians* held,
Boasting, her learning all the world excell'd. *Denham.*
There were not different gods among the Greeks and *barbarians*. *Stillingfleet's Defence of Disc. on Romish Idolatry.*
But with descending show'rs of brimstone fir'd,
The wild *barbarian* in the storm expir'd. *Addison.*
2. A foreigner.
I would they were *barbarians*, as they are,
Though in Rome litter'd. *Shakesp. Coriolanus.*
3. A brutal monster; a man without pity: a term of reproach.
Thou fell *barbarian*!
What had he done? what could provoke thy madness
To assassinate so great, so brave a man! *A. Philips D. Mot.*

BARBA'RIAN. *adj.* Belonging to barbarians; savage.
Some felt the silent stroke of mould'ring age,
Barbarian blindness. *Pope's Epistles.*

BARBA'RICK. *adj.* [*barbaricus*, Lat.] Foreign; far-fetched.
The gorgeous East, with richest hand,
Show'rs on her kings *barbarick* pearl and gold. *Par. Lost.*
The eastern front was glorious to behold,
With diamond flaming, and *barbarick* gold. *Pope.*

BA'RBARISM. *n. s.* [*barbarismus*, Lat.]
1. A form of speech contrary to the purity and exactness of any language.
The language is as near approaching to it, as our modern *barbarism* will allow; which is all that can be expected from any now extant. *Dryden's Juvenal, Dedication.*
2. Ignorance of arts; want of learning.
I have for *barbarism* spoke more
Than for that angel knowledge you can say.
Shakesp. Love's Labour Lost.
The genius of Raphael having succeeded to the times of *barbarism* and ignorance, the knowledge of painting is now arrived to perfection. *Dryd. Dufresnoy, Preface.*
3. Brutality; savageness of manners; incivility.
Moderation ought to be had in tempering and managing the Irish, to bring them from their delight of licentious *barbarism* unto the love of goodness and civility. *Spenser's State of Irel.*
Divers great monarchies have risen from *barbarism* to civility, and fallen again to ruin. *Sir J. Davies on Ireland.*
4. Cruelty; barbarity; unpitying hardness of heart.
They must per force have melted,
And *barbarism* itself have pity'd him. *Shakesp. Richard II.*

BARBA'RITY. *n. s.* [from *barbarous*.]
1. Savageness; incivility.
2. Cruelty; inhumanity.
And they did treat him with all the rudeness, reproach, and *barbarity* imaginable. *Clarendon, b.* viii.
3. Barbarism; impurity of speech.
Next Petrarch followed, and in him we see
What rhime improv'd in all its height, can be
At best a pleasing sound, and sweet *barbarity*. *Dryden.*
Latin often expresses that in one word, which either the *barbarity* or narrowness of modern tongues cannot supply in more. *Dryden.*
Affected refinements, which ended by degrees in many *barbarities*, before the Goths had invaded Italy. *Swift.*

BA'RBAROUS. *adj.* [*barbare*, Fr. βάρβαρος.]
1. Stranger to civility; savage; uncivilized.
What need I say more to you? What ear is so *barbarous*, but hath heard of Amphialus? *Sidney.*
The doubtful damsel dare not yet commit
Her single person to their *barbarous* truth. *Fairy Q. b.* i.
Thou art a Roman; be not *barbarous*. *Shakesp. T. Andron.*
And he left governour, Philip, for his country a Phrygian, and for manners more *barbarous* than he that set him there. *2 Macc.* v. 22.
A *barbarous* country must be broken by war, before it be capable of government; and when subdued, if it be not well planted, it will eftsoons return to barbarism. *Davies on Ireland.*
2. Ignorant; unacquainted with arts.
They who restored painting in Germany, not having those reliques of antiquity, retained that *barbarous* manner. *Dryden.*
3. Cruel; inhuman.
By their *barbarous* usage, he died within a few days, to the grief of all that knew him. *Clarendon, b.* viii.

BA'RBAROUSLY. *adv.* [from *barbarous*.]
1. Ignorantly; without knowledge or arts.
2. In a manner contrary to the rules of speech.
We *barbarously* call them blest,
Whilst swelling coffers break their owner's rest. *Stepney.*
3. Cruelly; inhumanly.
But yet you *barbarously* murder'd him. *Dryd. Span. Friar.*
She wishes it may prosper; but her mother used one of her nieces very *barbarously*. *Spectator*, N° 483.

BA'RBAROUSNESS. *n. s.* [from *barbarous*.]
1. Incivility of manners.
Excellencies of musick and poetry are grown to be little more, but the one fiddling, and the other rhiming; and are indeed very worthy of the ignorance of the friar, and the *barbarousness* of the Goths. *Temple.*
2. Impurity of language.
It is also much degenerated and impaired, as touching the pureness of speech; being overgrown with *barbarousness*. *Brerewood on Languages.*
3. Cruelty.
The *barbarousness* of the trial, and the persuasives of the clergy, prevailed to antiquate it. *Hale's Common Law of Engl.*

To BA'RBECUE. *v. a.* A term used in the West-Indies for dressing a hog whole; which, being split to the backbone, is laid flat upon a large gridiron, raised about two foot above a charcoal fire, with which it is surrounded.
Oldfield, with more than harpy throat endu'd,
Cries, send me, gods, a whole hog *barbecu'd*. *Pope.*

BA'RBECUE. *n. s.* A hog drest whole, in the West Indian manner.

BA'RBED. *participial adj.* [from *to barb*.]
1. Furnished with armour.
His glittering armour he will command to rust,
His *barbed* steeds to stables. *Shakesp. Richard II.*
2. Bearded; jagged with hooks or points.
If I conjecture right, no drizzling show'r,
But rattling storm of arrows *barb'd* with fire.
Milton's Par. Lost, b. vi. *l.* 544.

BA'RBEL. *n. s.* [from *barb*.]
1. A kind of fish found in rivers, large and strong, but coarse.
The *barbel* is so called, by reason of the barb or wattels at his mouth, or under his chaps. *Walton's Angler.*
2. Knots of superfluous flesh growing up in the channels of the mouth of a horse. *Farrier's Dict.*

BA'RBER. *n. s.* [from *to barb*.] A man who shaves the beard.
His chamber being stived with friends or suitors, he gave his legs, arms, and breasts to his servants to dress; his head and face to his *barber*; his eyes to his letters, and his ears to petitioners. *Wotton.*
With those thy boist'rous locks, no worthy match
For valour to assail
But by the *barber*'s razor best subdu'd. *Milton's Samf. Agon.*

What syſtem, Dick, has right averr'd
The cauſe, why woman has no beard?
In points like theſe we muſt agree;
Our *barber* knows as much as we. *Prior.*

To BA'RBER. *v. a.* [from the noun.] To dreſs out; to powder.

Our courteous Antony,
Whom ne'er the word of No, woman heard ſpeak,
Being *barber'd* ten times o'er, goes to the feaſt.
Shakeſp. Antony and Cleopatra.

BARBER-CHIRURGEON. *n. ſ.* A man who joins the practice of ſurgery to the barber's trade; ſuch as were all ſurgeons formerly, but now it is uſed only for a low practiſer of ſurgery.

He put himſelf into *barber-chirurgeons* hands, who, by unfit applications, rarified the tumour. *Wiſeman's Surgery.*

BARBER-MONGER. *n. ſ.* A word of reproach in *Shakeſpeare*, which ſeems to ſignify a fop; a man decked out by his barber.

Draw, you rogue; for though it be night, the moon ſhines; I'll make a ſop of the moonſhine of you; you whoreſon, cullionly, *barber-monger*, draw. *Shakeſp. King Lear.*

BA'RBERRY. *n. ſ.* [*berberis*, Lat.] Pipperidge buſh.

It is ſet with ſharp prickles; the leaves are long, and ſerrated on the edges; the flowers conſiſt of ſix leaves, which expand in form of a roſe, and are of a yellow colour; the fruit is long, of an acid taſte, and, for the moſt part, of a red colour, and grows in cluſters; the bark of the tree is whitiſh. The ſpecies are, 1. The common *barberry*. 2. *Barberry* without ſtones. The firſt of theſe ſorts is very common in England, and often planted for hedges. *Millar.*

Barberry is a plant that bears a fruit very uſeful in houſewifery; that which beareth its fruit without ſtones is counted beſt. *Mortimer's Husbandry.*

BARD. *n. ſ.* [*bardd*, Welch.] A poet.

There is amongſt the Iriſh a kind of people called *bards*, which are to them inſtead of poets; whoſe profeſſion is to ſet forth the praiſes or diſpraiſes of men in their poems or rhimes; the which are had in high regard and eſtimation among them. *Spenſer on Ireland.*

And many *bards* that to the trembling chord,
Can tune their timely voices cunningly. *Fairy Queen, b.* i.

The *bard* who firſt adorn'd our native tongue,
Tun'd to his Britiſh lyre this ancient ſong,
Which Homer might without a bluſh rehearſe. *Dryden.*

BARE. *adj.* [bare, Sax. *bar*, Dan.]

1. Naked; without covering.

The trees are *bare* and naked, which uſe both to cloath and houſe the kern. *Spenſer on Ireland.*

Then ſtretch'd her arms t' embrace the body *bare*;
Her claſping hands incloſe but empty air. *Dryden.*

In the old Roman ſtatues, theſe two parts were always *bare*, and expoſed to view, as much as our hands and face at preſent. *Addiſon's Travels.*

2. Uncovered in reſpect.

Though the lords uſed to be covered whilſt the commons were *bare*, yet the commons would not be *bare* before the Scottiſh commiſſioners; and ſo none were covered. *Clarendon.*

3. Unadorned; plain; ſimple; without ornament.

Yet was their manners then but *bare* and plain;
For th' antique world exceſs and pride did hate. *Fairy Q.*

4. Detected; without concealment.

Theſe falſe pretexts and varniſh'd colours failing,
Bare in thy guilt, how foul muſt thou appear?
Milton's Sampſon Agoniſtes, l. 901.

5. Poor; without plenty.

Were it for the glory of God, that the clergy ſhould be left as *bare* as the apoſtles, when they had neither ſtaff nor ſcrip; God would, I hope, endue them with the ſelf-ſame affection. *Hooker, Preface.*

Even from a *bare* treaſury, my ſucceſs has been contrary to that of Mr. Cowley. *Dryden's Epiſtles, Dedication.*

6. Mere.

It was a *bare* petition of a ſtate
To one whom they had puniſh'd. *Shakeſp. Coriolanus.*

You have an exchequer of words, and no other treaſure for your followers; for it appears, by their bare liveries, that they live by your *bare* words. *Shakeſp. Two Gent. of Verona.*

Nor are men prevailed upon by *bare* words, only through a defect of knowledge; but carried, with theſe puffs of wind, contrary to knowledge. *South.*

7. Threadbare; much worn; as, *bare* liveries, in the laſt quotation from *Shakeſpeare.*

8. Not united with any thing elſe.

A deſire to draw all things to the determination of *bare* and naked Scripture, hath cauſed much pains to be taken in abating the credit of man. *Hooker, b.* ii. § 7.

That which offendeth us, is the great diſgrace which they offer unto our cuſtom of *bare* reading the word of God. *Hooker.*

9. Sometimes it has *of* before the thing taken away.

Tempt not the brave and needy to deſpair;
For, tho' your violence ſhould leave them *bare*
Of gold and ſilver, ſwords and darts remain. *Dryden's Juv.*

Making a law to reduce intereſt, will not raiſe the price of land; it will only leave the country *barer of* money. *Locke.*

To BARE. *v. a.* [from the adjective.] To ſtrip; to make bare or naked.

The turtle on the *bared* branch,
Laments the wounds that death did launch. *Spenſer.*

There is a fabulous narration, that an herb groweth in the likeneſs of a lamb, and feedeth upon the graſs, in ſuch ſort as it will *bare* the graſs round about. *Bacon's Natural Hiſtory.*

Eriphyle here he found
Baring her breaſt, yet bleeding with the wound. *Dryden.*

He *bar'd* an ancient oak of all her boughs:
Then on a riſing ground the trunks he plac'd. *Dryden.*

For virtue, when I point the pen,
Bare the mean heart that lurks beneath a ſtar;
Can there be wanting to defend her cauſe,
Lights of the church, or guardians of the laws? *Pope.*

BARE, or BORE. The *preterite* of *to bear*. See To BEAR.

BA'REBONE. *n. ſ.* [from *bare* and *bone*.] Lean, ſo that the bones appear.

Here comes lean Jack, here comes *barebone*; how long is it ago, Jack, ſince thou ſaweſt thy own knee? *Shakeſp. Hen.* IV.

BAREFACED. *adj.* [from *bare* and *face*.]

1. With the face naked; not maſked.

Your French crowns have no hair at all, and then you will play *barefaced*. *Shakeſp. Midſummer's Night's Dream.*

2. Shameleſs; unreſerved; without concealment; without diſguiſe.

The animoſities encreaſed, and the parties appeared *barefaced* againſt each other. *Clarendon, b.* viii.

It is moſt certain, that *barefaced* bawdry is the pooreſt pretence to wit imaginable. *Dryden.*

BAREFA'CEDLY. *adv.* [from *barefaced*.] Openly; ſhamefully without diſguiſe.

Though only ſome profligate wretches own it too *barefacedly*, yet, perhaps, we ſhould hear more, did not fear tie people' tongues. *Locke.*

BAREFA'CEDNESS. *n. ſ.* [from *barefaced*.] Effrontery; aſſurance; audaciouſneſs.

BA'REFOOT. *adj.* [from *bare* and *foot*.] Without ſhoes.

She muſt have a huſband;
I muſt dance *barefoot* on her wedding day. *Shakeſp*

Going to find a *barefoot* brother out,
One of our order. *Shakeſp. Romeo and Juliet.*

Ambitious love hath ſo in me offended,
That *barefoot* plod I the cold ground upon
With ſainted vow. *Shakeſpeare*

Envoys deſcribe this holy man, with his Alcaydes about him, ſtanding *barefoot*, bowing to the earth. *Addiſon.*

BAREFO'OTED. *adj.* Without ſhoes.

He himſelf, with a rope about his neck, *barefooted*, came to offer himſelf to the diſcretion of Leonatus *Sidney, b.* ii.

BA'REGNAWN. *adj.* [from *bare* and *gnawn*.] Eaten bare.

Know my name is loſt;
By treaſon's tooth *baregnawn* and cankerbit. *Shak. K Lear.*

BA'REHEADED. *adj.* [from *bare* and *head*.] Uncovered in reſpect.

He, *bareheaded*, lower than his proud ſteed's neck,
Beſpoke them thus. *Shakeſp. Richard* II.

Next, before the chariot, went two men *bareheaded*. *Bacon.*

The victor knight had laid his helm aſide,
Bareheaded, popularly low he bow'd. *Dryden's Fables.*

BA'RELY. *adv.* [from *bare*.]

1. Nakedly.

2. Merely; only; without any thing more.

The external adminiſtration of his word is as well by reading *barely* the Scripture, as by explaining the ſame. *Hooker.*

The duke of Lancaſter is dead;
And living too, for now his ſon is duke—
——*Barely* in title, not in revenue. *Shakeſp. Richard* II.

He *barely* nam'd the ſtreet, promis'd the wine;
But his kind wife gave me the very ſign. *Donne.*

Where the balance of trade *barely* pays for commodities with commodities, there money muſt be ſent, or elſe the debts cannot be paid. *Locke.*

BA'RENESS. *n. ſ.* [from *bare*.]

1. Nakedneſs.

So you ſerve us,
Till we ſerve you; but when you have our roſes,
You barely leave our thorns to prick ourſelves,
And mock us with our *bareneſs*. *Shak All's well that ends well.*

2. Leanneſs.

For their poverty, I know not where they had that; and for their *bareneſs*, they never learned that of me. *Shak. Hen.* IV.

3. Poverty.

Were it ſtript of its privileges, and made as like the primitive church for its *bareneſs* as its purity, it could legally want all ſuch privileges. *South.*

4. Meanneſs of clothes.

BA'RGAIN. *n. ſ.* [*bargen*, Welch; *bargaigne*, Fr.]

1. A contract or agreement concerning the ſale of ſomething.

What is marriage but a very *bargain*? wherein is ſought alliance, or portion, or reputation, with ſome deſire of iſſue; and not the faithful nuptial union of man and wife. *Bacon.*

No more can be due to me,
Than at the *bargain* made was meant. *Donne.*

2. The thing bought or sold.

Give me but my price for the other two, and you shall even have that into the *bargain.* *L'Estrange.*

He who is at the charge of a tutor at home, may give his son a more genteel carriage, with greater learning into the *bargain,* than any at school can do. *Locke.*

3. Stipulation.

There was a difference between courtesies received from their master and the duke; for that the duke's might have ends of utility and *bargain*; whereas their master's could not. *Bacon's Henry* VII.

4. An unexpected reply, tending to obscenity.

Where sold he *bargains,* whipstitch? *Dryden's Macflecknoe.*

As to *bargains,* few of them seem to be excellent, because they all terminate in one single point. *Swift.*

No maid at court is less asham'd,
Howe'er for selling *bargains* fam'd. *Swift.*

5. An event; an upshot: a low sense.

I am sorry for thy misfortune; however we must make the best of a bad *bargain:* thou art in jeopardy, that is certain. *Arbuthnot's History of J. Bull.*

6. In law.

Bargain and sale is a contract or agreement made for manours, lands, &c. also the transferring the property of them from the bargainer to the bargainee. *Cowel.*

To BA'RGAIN. *v. n.* [from the noun.] To make a contract for the sale or purchase of any thing; often with *for.*

Henry is able to enrich his queen;
And not to seek a queen to make him rich.
So worthless peasants *bargain for* their wives,
As market men for oxen, sheep, or horse. *Shakesp. Hen.* VI.

For those that are like to be in plenty, they may be *bargained for* upon the ground. *Bacon's Nat. Hist.* N° 675.

The thrifty state will *bargain* ere they fight. *Dryden.*

It is possible the great duke may *bargain for* the republick of Lucca, by the help of his great treasures. *Addison on Italy.*

BARGAINEE'. *n. s.* [from *bargain.*] He or she that accepts a bargain.

BA'RGAINER. *n. s.* [from *bargain.*] The person who profers, or makes a bargain.

BARGE. *n. s.* [*bargie,* Dut. from *barga,* low Lat.]

1. A boat for pleasure.

The *barge* she sat in, like a burnish'd throne,
Burnt on the water. *Shakesp. Antony and Cleopatra.*

It was consulted, when I had taken my *barge,* and gone ashore, that my ship should have set sail and left me there. *Raleigh's Essays.*

Plac'd in the gilded *barge,*
Proud with the burden of so sweet a charge;
With painted oars the youths begin to sweep
Neptune's smooth face. *Waller.*

2. A boat for burden.

BA'RGER. *n. s.* [from *barge.*] The manager of a barge.

Howsoever, many wafarers make themselves glee, by putting the inhabitants in mind of this privilege; who again, especially the women, like the Campellians in the north, and the London *bargers,* forslow not to baigne them. *Carew's Survey of Cornwal.*

BARK. *n. s.* [*barck,* Dan.]

1. The rind or covering of a tree.

Trees last according to the strength and quantity of their sap and juice; being well munited by their *bark* against the injuries of the air. *Bacon's Nat. Hist.* N° 583.

Wand'ring in the dark,
Physicians for the tree have found the *bark.* *Dryden.*

2. A small ship. [from *barca,* low Lat.]

Things, I say, being in this state, it came to pass, that the duke of Parma must have flown, if he would have come into England; for he could neither get *bark* nor mariner to put to sea. *Bacon on the War with Spain.*

It was that fatal and perfidious *bark,*
Built in th' eclipse, and rigg'd with curses dark,
That sunk so low that sacred head of thine. *Milton.*

Who to a woman trusts his peace of mind,
Trusts a frail *bark* with a tempestuous wind. *Granville.*

To BARK. *v. n.* [beorcan, Saxon.]

1. To make the noise which a dog makes, when he threatens or pursues.

Sent before my time
Into this breathing world, scarce half made up,
And that so lamely and unfashionably,
That dogs *bark* at me. *Shakesp. Richard* III.

Why do your dogs *bark* so? be there bears i' th' town? *Shakesp. Merry Wives of Windsor.*

In vain the herdman calls him back again;
The dogs stand off afar, and *bark* in vain. *Cowley.*

2. To clamour at; to pursue with reproaches.

Vile is the vengeance on the ashes cold,
And envy base, to *bark* at sleeping fame. *Fairy Queen, b.* ii. *cant.* viii.

You dare patronage
The envious *barking* of your saucy tongue,
Against my lord the duke of Somerset! *Shakesp. Henry* VI.

To BARK. *v. a.* [from the noun.] To strip trees of their bark.

The severest penalties ought to be put upon *barking* any tree that is not felled. *Temple.*

These trees, after they are *barked,* and cut into shape, are tumbled down from the mountains into the stream. *Addison's Remarks on Italy.*

BARK-BARED. *adj.* [from *bark* and *bare.*] Stripped of the bark.

Excorticated and *bark-bared* trees may be preserved, by nourishing up a shoot from the foot, or below the stripped place, cutting the body of the tree sloping off a little above the shoot, and it will quickly heal, and be covered with bark. *Mortimer's Art of Husbandry.*

BA'RKER. *n. s.* [from *bark.*]

1. One that barks or clamours.

What hath he done more than a base cur? barked and made a noise? had a fool or two to spit in his mouth? But they are rather enemies of my fame than me, these *barkers.* *Ben. Johnson's Discovery.*

2. [from *bark* of trees.] One that is employed in stripping trees.

BA'RKY. *adj.* [from *bark.*] Consisting of bark; containing bark.

Ivy so enrings the *barky* fingers of the elm. *Shakesp. Merry Wives of Windsor.*

BA'RLEY. *n. s.* [derived by *Junius* from בר.]

It hath a thick spike; the calyx, husk, awn, and flower, are like those of wheat or rye, but the awns are rough; the seed is swelling in the middle, and, for the most part, ends in a sharp point, to which the husks are closely united. The species are, 1. Common long-eared *barley.* 2. Winter or square *barley,* by some called *big.* 3. Sprat *barley,* or battledoor *barley.* All these sorts of *barley* are sown in the spring of the year, in a dry time. In some very dry light land, the *barley* is sown early in March; but in strong clayey soils it is not sown till April. The square *barley,* or *big,* is chiefly cultivated in the north of England, and in Scotland; and is hardier than the other sorts. Where *barley* is sown upon new broken up land, the usual method is to plough up the land in March, and let it lie fallow until June; at which time it is ploughed again, and sown with turneps, which are eaten by sheep in winter, by whose dung the land is greatly improved; and then, in March following, the ground is ploughed again, and sown with *barley.* *Millar.*

Barley is emollient, moistening, and expectorating; *barley* was chosen by Hippocrates as proper food in inflammatory distempers. *Arbuthnot on Aliments.*

BA'RLEYBRAKE. *n. s.* A kind of rural play.

By neighbours prais'd she went abroad thereby,
At *barleybrake* her sweet swift feet to try. *Sidney.*

BARLEY BROTH. *n. s.* [from *barley* and *broth.*] A low word, sometimes used for strong beer.

Can sodden water,
A drench for surreyn'd jades, their *barley broth,*
Decoct their cold blood to such valiant heat? *Shak. Hen.* V.

BARLEY CORN. *n. s.* [from *barley* and *corn.*] A grain of barley; the beginning of our measure of length; the third part of an inch.

A long, long journey, choak'd with brakes and thorns,
Ill measur'd by ten thousand *barley corns.* *Tickell.*

BARLEY MOW. *n. s.* [from *barley* and *mow.*] The place where reaped barley is stowed up.

Whenever by yon *barley mow* I pass,
Before my eyes will trip the tidy lass. *Gay's Pastorals.*

BARM. *n. s.* [*burm,* Welch; beorm, Sax.] Yeast; the ferment put into drink to make it work, and into bread, to lighten and swell it.

Are you not he
That sometimes make the drink to bear no *barm,*
Mislead light wand'rers, laughing at their harm? *Shakespear.*

You may try the force of imagination, upon staying the working of beer when the *barm* is put into it. *Bacon's Nat. History,* N° 992.

BA'RMY. *adj.* [from *barm.*] Containing barm.

Their jovial nights in frolicks and in play
They pass, to drive the tedious hours away;
And their cold stomachs with crown'd goblets cheer,
Of windy cider, and of *barmy* bear. *Dryden's Virgil.*

BARN. *n. s.* [bern, Sax.] A place or house for laying up any sort of grain, hay, or straw, &c.

In vain the *barns* expect their promis'd load,
Nor *barns* at home, nor reeks are heap'd abroad. *Dryden.*

I took notice of the make of several *barns* here: after having laid a frame of wood, they place, at the four corners of it, four blocks, in such a shape as neither mice nor vermin can creep up. *Addison on Italy.*

BA'RNACLE. *n. s.* [probably of bearn, Sax. a child, and aac, Sax. an oak.]

1. A

1. A bird like a goose, fabulously supposed to grow on trees.

Surely it is beyond even an atheist's credulity and impudence, to affirm that the first men might grow upon trees, as the story goes about *barnacles*; or perhaps might be the lice of some vast prodigious animals, whose species is now extinct. *Bentley's Sermons.*

And from the most refin'd of saints,
As naturally grow miscreants,
As *barnacles* turn solan geese
In th' islands of the Orcades. *Hudibras, p.* iii. *c.* ii.

2. An instrument made commonly of iron for the use of farriers, to hold a horse by the nose, to hinder him from struggling when any incision is made. *Farrier's Dict.*

BARO'METER. *n. s.* [from βάρος, weight, and μέτρον, measure.] A machine for measuring the weight of the atmosphere, and the variations in it, in order chiefly to determine the changes of the weather. It differs from the baroscope, which only shews that the air is heavier at one time than another, without specifying the difference. The *barometer* is founded upon the Torricellian experiment, so called from Torricelli the inventor of it, at Florence, in 1643; which is a glass tube filled with mercury, horizontally sealed at one end; the other open and immerged in a bason of stagnant mercury; so that, as the weight of the atmosphere diminishes, the mercury in the tube will descend, and, as it encreases, the mercury will ascend; the column of mercury suspended in the tube, being always equal to the weight of the incumbent atmosphere. Many attempts have been made to render the changes in the *barometer* more sensible, in order to measure the atmosphere more accurately; and hence arose a great number of *barometers*, of different structures. Dr. Halley observes, in the *Philosophical Transactions*, that in calm weather, when the air is inclined to rain, the mercury is commonly low; in serene good settled weather, high. On great winds, though unaccompanied with rain, the mercury is lowest of all, with regard to the point of the compass the wind blows on. The greatest heights of the mercury are on easterly and north-easterly winds, *cæteris paribus*. After great storms of wind, when the mercury has been low, it rises again very fast. In calm frosty weather, it stands high. The more northerly places find greater alterations than the more southern; and within the tropicks, and near them, there is little or no variation of the height of the mercury. The rising of the mercury forebodes fair weather after foul, and an easterly or north-easterly wind; its falling portends southerly or westerly winds, or both. In a storm, the mercury beginning to rise, is a pretty sure sign that it begins to abate. But there are frequently great changes in the air, without any perceptible alteration in the *barometer*. The alterations of the weight of the air, are generally allowed to be the cause of those in the *barometer*; but philosophers cannot easily determine whence those alterations rise in the atmosphere.

The measuring the heights of mountains, and finding the elevation of places above the level of the sea, hath been much promoted by barometrical experiments, founded upon that essential property of the air, its gravity or pressure. As the column of mercury in the *barometer* is counterpoised by a column of air of equal weight, so whatever causes make the air heavier or lighter, the pressure of it will be thereby encreased or lessened, and of consequence the mercury will rise or fall. Again, the air is condensed or expanded, in proportion to the weight or force that presses it. Hence it is, that the higher from the sea, in the midland countries, the mercury descends the lower; because the air becomes more rarified and lighter, and it falls lowest upon the tops of the highest mountains. *Harris.*

Gravity is another property of air, whereby it counterpoises a column of mercury from twenty-seven inches and one half to thirty and one half, the gravity of the atmosphere varying one tenth, which are its utmost limits; so that the exact specifick gravity of the air cannot be determined when the *barometer* stands at thirty inches, with a moderate heat of the weather. *Arbuthnot on Air.*

BAROME'TRICAL. *adj.* [from *barometer.*] Relating to the barometer.

He is very accurate in making *barometrical* and thermometrical instruments. *Derham's Physico-Theology.*

BA'RON. *n. s.* [The etymology of this word is very uncertain. *Baro*, among the Romans, signified a brave warriour, or a brutal man; and, from the first of these significations, *Menage* derives *baron*, as a term of military dignity. Others suppose it originally to signify only a man; in which sense *baron*, or *varon*, is still used by the Spaniards; and, to confirm this conjecture, our law yet uses *baron* and *femme*, husband and wife. Others deduce it from *ber*, an old Gaulish word, signifying commander; others from the Hebrew בר, of the same import. Some think it a contraction of *par homme*, or *peer*, which seems least probable.]

1. A degree of nobility next to a viscount. It may be probably thought, that anciently, in England, all those were called *barons*, that had such signiories as we now call *court barons*. And it is said, that, after the conquest, all such came to the parliament, and sat as nobles in the upper house. But when, by experience, it appeared, that the parliament was too much crouded with such multitudes, it became a custom, that none should come, but such as the king, for their extraordinary wisdom or quality, thought good to call by writ; which writ ran *hac vice tantum*. After that, men, seeing that this state of nobility was but casual, and depending merely on the prince's pleasure, obtained of the king letters patent of this dignity to them and their heirs male: and these were called *barons* by letters patent, or by creation; whose posterity are now those *barons* that are called lords of the parliament; of which kind the king may create more at his pleasure. It is nevertheless thought, that there are yet *barons* by writ, as well as *barons* by letters patent, and that they may be discerned by their titles; the *barons* by writ being those, that to the title of lord have their own surnames annexed; whereas the *barons* by letters patent, are named by their baronies. These *barons* which were first by writ, may now justly also be called *barons* by prescription; for that they have continued *barons*, in themselves and their ancestors, beyond the memory of man. There are also *barons* by tenure, as the bishops of the land, who, by virtue of baronies annexed to their bishopricks, have always had place in the upper house of parliament, and are called lords spiritual.

2. *Baron* is an officer, as *barons* of the exchequer to the king: of these the principal is called lord chief *baron*, and the three others are his assistants, between the king and his subjects, in causes of justice, belonging to the exchequer.

3. There are also *barons* of the cinque ports; two to each of the seven towns, Hastings, Winchelsea, Rye, Rumney, Hithe, Dover, and Sandwich, that have places in the lower house of parliament. *Cowel.*

They that bear
The cloth of state above, are four *barons*
Of the cinque ports. *Shakesp. Henry* VIII.

4. *Baron* is used for the husband in relation to his wife. *Cowel.*

5. A *baron* of beef is when the two sirloins are not cut asunder, but joined together by the end of the backbone. *Dict.*

BA'RONAGE. *n. s.* [from *baron.*]

1. The body of barons and peers.

His charters of the liberties of England, and of the forest, were hardly, and with difficulty, gained by his *baronage* at Staines, *A. D.* 1215. *Hale's Common Law of England.*

2. The dignity of a baron.

3. The land which gives title to a baron.

BA'RONESS. *n. s.* [*baronessa*, Ital. *baronissa*, Lat.] A baron's lady.

BA'RONET. *n. s.* [of *baron* and *et*, diminutive termination.] The lowest degree of honour that is hereditary; it is below a baron and above a knight; and has the precedency of all other knights, except the knights of the garter. It was first founded by king James I. *A. D.* 1611. *Cowel.* But it appears by the following passage, that the term was in use before, though in another sense.

King Edward III. being bearded and crossed by the clergy, they being too strong for him, so as he could not order and reform things, was advised to direct out his writs to certain gentlemen of the best abilities, entitling them therein barons in the next parliament. By which means he had so many barons in his parliament, as were able to weigh down the clergy; which barons were not afterwards lords, but *baronets*, as sundry of them do yet retain the name. *Spenser on Ireland.*

BA'RONY. *n. s.* [*baronnie*, Fr. beoꞃny, Sax.] That honour or lordship that gives title to a baron. Such are not only the fees of temporal barons, but of bishops also. *Cowel.*

BA'ROSCOPE. *n. s.* [βάρος and σκοπέω.] An instrument to shew the weight of the atmosphere. See BAROMETER.

If there was always a calm, the equilibrium could only be changed by the contents; where the winds are not variable, the alterations of the *baroscope* are very small. *Arbuth. on Air.*

BA'RRACAN. *n. s.* [*bouracan*, or *barracan*, Fr.] A strong thick kind of camelot.

BA'RRACK. *n. s.* [*barracca*, Span.]

1. Little cabins made by the Spanish fishermen on the sea shore; or little lodges for soldiers in a camp.

2. It is generally taken among us for buildings to lodge soldiers.

BA'RRATOR. *n. s.* [from *barat*, old Fr. from which is still retained *barateur*, a cheat.] A wrangler, and encourager of law suits.

Will it not reflect as much on thy character, Nic, to turn *barrator* in thy old days, a stirrer up of quarrels amongst thy neighbours. *Arbuthnot's History of J. Bull.*

BA'RRATRY. *n. s.* [from *barrator.*] The practice or crime of a barrator; foul practice in law.

'Tis arrant *barratry*, that bears
Point blank an action 'gainst our laws. *Hudibras.*

BA'RREL. *n. s.* [*baril*, Welch.]

1. A round wooden vessel to be stopped close.

It hath been observed by one of the ancients, that an empty *barrel* knocked upon with the finger, giveth a diapason to the sound of the like *barrel* full. *Bacon's Nat. History*, N° 186.

Trembling to approach
The little *barrel*, which he fears to broach. *Dryden's Persius.*

2. A particular measure in liquids. A *barrel* of wine is thirty one gallons and a half; of ale, thirty two gallons; of beer, thirty six gallons, and of beer vinegar, thirty four gallons.

3. In dry measure. A *barrel* of Essex butter contains one hundred

and

and ſix pounds; of Suffolk butter, two hundred and fifty ſix. A *barrel* of herrings ſhould contain thirty two gallons wine meaſure, holding uſually a thouſand herrings.

Several colleges, inſtead of limiting their rents to a certain ſum, prevailed with their tenants to pay the price of ſo many *barrels* of corn, as the market went. *Swift.*

4. Any thing hollow, as the *barrel* of a gun; that part which holds the ſhot.

Take the *barrel* of a long gun perfectly bored, ſet it upright with the breech upon the ground, and take a bullet exactly fit for it; then if you ſuck at the mouth of the *barrel* ever ſo gently, the bullet will come up ſo forcibly, that it will hazard the ſtriking out your teeth. *Digby on Bodies.*

5. A cylinder; frequently that cylinder about which any thing is wound.

Your ſtring and bow muſt be accommodated to your drill; if too weak, it will not carry about the *barrel.* *Moxon's Mechanical Exerciſes.*

6. *Barrel of the ear*, is a cavity behind the tympanum, covered with a fine membrane. *Dict.*

To BA'RREL. *v. a.* [from the noun.] To put any thing in a barrel for preſervation.

I would have their beef beforehand *barrelled*, which may be uſed as it is needed. *Spenſer on Ireland.*

Barrel up earth, and ſow ſome ſeed in it, and put it in the bottom of a pond. *Bacon's Nat. Hiſt.* Nº 531.

BA'RREL-BELLIED. *adj.* [from *barrel* and *belly.*] Having a large belly.

Dauntleſs at empty noiſes; lofty neck'd,
Sharp headed, *barrel-belly'd*, broadly back'd. *Dryd. Virgil.*

BA'RREN. *adj.* [bane, Sax. naked; properly applied to trees or ground unfruitful.]

1. Without the quality of producing its kind; not prolifick; applied to animals.

They hail'd him father to a line of kings.
Upon my head they plac'd a fruitleſs crown,
And put a *barren* ſceptre in my gripe,
No ſon of mine ſucceeding. *Shakeſp. Macbeth.*

There ſhall not be male or female *barren* among you, or among your cattle. *Deuter.* vii. 14.

2. Unfruitful; not fertile; ſterile.

The ſituation of this city is pleaſant, but the water is naught, and the ground *barren.* *2 Kings*, ii. 19.

Telemachus is far from exalting the nature of his country; he confeſſes it to be *barren.* *Pope's Odyſſey, b.* iv. *notes.*

From his far excurſion thro' the wilds
Of *barren* ether, faithful to his time,
They ſee the blazing wonder riſe anew. *Thomſon's Summer.*

3. Not copious; ſcanty.

Some ſchemes will appear *barren* of hints and matter, but prove to be fruitful. *Swift.*

4. Unmeaning; uninventive; dull.

There be of them that will make themſelves laugh, to ſet on ſome quantity of *barren* ſpectators to laugh too. *Shakeſpeare.*

BA'RRENLY. *adv.* [from *barren.*] Unfruitfully.

BA'RRENNESS. *n. ſ.* [from *barren.*]

1. Want of offspring; want of the power of procreation.

I pray'd for children, and thought *barrenneſs*
In wedlock a reproach. *Milton's Agoniſtes, l.* 350.

No more be mention'd then of violence
Againſt ourſelves; and wilful *barrenneſs*,
That cuts us off from hope. *Milton's Par. Loſt, b.* x.

2. Unfruitfulneſs; ſterility; infertility.

Within the ſelf ſame hamlet, lands have divers degrees of value, through the diverſity of their fertility or *barrenneſs.* *Bacon on Alienations.*

3. Want of invention; want of the power of producing any thing new.

The adventures of Ulyſſes are imitated in the Æneis; though the accidents are not the ſame, which would have argued him of a total *barrenneſs* of invention. *Dryden's Fables, Preface.*

4. Want of matter.

The importunity of our adverſaries hath conſtrained us longer to dwell than the *barrenneſs* of ſo poor a cauſe could have ſeemed either to require or to admit. *Hooker, b.* v. § 22.

5. In theology: aridity; want of emotion or ſenſibility.

The greateſt ſaints ſometimes are fervent, and ſometimes feel a *barrenneſs* of devotion. *Taylor's Guide to Devotion.*

BA'RRENWORT. *n. ſ.* [*epimedium*, Lat.] The name of a plant.

The ſtalks are divided into three branches, each ſuſtaining three leaves, ſhaped like ivy; the calyx conſiſts of four leaves; the flower, of four petals, hollow, and expanded in form of a croſs; the pointal of the flower becomes a pod with one cell, having two valves, in which are contained round flat ſeeds. *Millar.*

BA'RRFUL. *adj.* [from *bar* and *full.*] Full of obſtructions.

A *barrful* ſtrife!
Whoe'er I woo, myſelf would be his wife. *Shak. Tw. Night.*

BARRICA'DE. *n. ſ.* [*barricade*, Fr.]

1. A fortification made in haſte, of trees, earth, waggons, or any thing elſe, to keep off an attack.

2. Any ſtop; bar; obſtruction.

There muſt be ſuch a *barricade*, as would greatly annoy, or rather abſolutely ſtop, the currents of the atmoſphere. *Derham's Phyſico-Theology.*

To BARRICA'DE. *v. a.* [*barricader*, Fr.] To ſtop up a paſſage.

A new vulcano continually diſcharging that matter, which being till then *barricaded* up, and impriſoned in the bowels of the earth, was the occaſion of very great and frequent calamities. *Woodward's Natural Hiſtory.*

Now all the pavement ſounds with trampling feet,
And the mixt hurry *barricades* the ſtreet,
Entangled here, the waggon's lengthen'd team. *Gay.*

BARRICA'DO. *n. ſ.* [*barricada*, Span.] A fortification; a bar; any thing fixed to hinder entrance.

The acceſs of the town was only by a neck of land, between the ſea on the one part, and the harbour water, or inner ſea on the other; fortified clean over with a ſtrong rampier and *barricado.* *Bacon's War with Spain.*

To BARRICADO. *v. a.* [from the noun.] To fortify; to bar; to ſtop up.

Faſt we found, faſt ſhut
The diſmal gates, and *barricado'd* ſtrong! *Paradiſe Loſt.*

He had not time to *barricado* the doors; ſo that the enemy entered. *Clarendon, b.* viii.

The truth of cauſes we find ſo obliterated, that it ſeems almoſt *barricadoed* from any intellectual approach. *Harvey on Conſumptions.*

BA'RRIER. *n. ſ.* [*barriere*, Fr. It is ſometimes pronounced with the accent on the laſt ſyllable, but it is placed more properly on the firſt.]

1. A barricade; an entrenchment.

Safe in the love of heav'n an ocean flows
Around our realm, a *barrier* from the foes. *Pope's Odyſſey.*

2. A fortification, or ſtrong place, as on the frontiers of a country.

The queen is under the obligation of being guarantee of the Dutch having poſſeſſion of the ſaid *barrier*, and the revenues thereof, before a peace. *Swift.*

3. A ſtop; an obſtruction.

If you value yourſelf as a man of learning, you are building a moſt unpaſſable *barrier* againſt all improvement. *Watts's Improvement of the Mind.*

4. A bar to mark the limits of any place.

For juſts, and tourneys, and *barriers*, the glories of them are chiefly in the chariots, wherein the challengers make their entries. *Bacon's Eſſays.*

Pris'ners to the pillar bound,
At either *barrier* plac'd; nor, captives made,
Be freed, or arm'd anew. *Dryden's Fables.*

5. A boundary.

But wave whate'er to Cadmus may belong,
And fix, O muſe, the *barrier* of thy ſong,
At Oedipus. *Pope's Statius.*

How inſtinct varies in the groveling ſwine,
Compar'd, half-reas'ning elephant! with thine:
'Twixt that and reaſon, what a nice *barrier!*
For ever ſep'rate, yet for ever near. *Pope's Eſſay on Man.*

BA'RRISTER. *n. ſ.* [from *bar.*] A perſon qualified to plead the cauſes of clients in the courts of juſtice, called an advocate or licentiate in other countries and courts. *Barriſters*, now uſually denominated counſellors at law, were formerly obliged to ſtudy eight years before they were paſſed, now only ſeven, and ſometimes fewer. Outer *barriſters* are pleaders without the bar, to diſtinguiſh them from inner *barriſters*; ſuch are the benchers, or thoſe who have been readers, the council of the king, queen, and princes, who are admitted to plead within the bar. *Blount. Chambers.*

BA'RROW. *n. ſ.* [bepepe, Sax. ſuppoſed by *Skinner* to come from *bear.*] Any kind of carriage moved by the hand, as a *hand-barrow*; a frame of boards, with handles at each end, carried between two men; a *wheelbarrow*, that which one man puſhes forward, by raiſing it upon one wheel.

Have I lived to be carried in a baſket, like a *barrow* of butcher's offal, and to be thrown into the Thames? *Shakeſp. Merry Wives of Windſor.*

No *barrow*'s wheel
Shall mark thy ſtocking with a miry trace. *Gay's Trivia.*

BA'RROW. *n. ſ.* [bepg, Saxon.] A hog; whence *barrow* greaſe, or hog's lard.

BARROW, whether in the beginning or end of names of places, ſignifies a grove; from beappe, which the Saxons uſed in the ſame ſenſe. *Gibſon's Camden.*

BARROW is likewiſe uſed in Cornwal for a hillock, under which, in old times, bodies have been buried.

To BA'RTER. *v. n.* [*baratter*, Fr. to trick in traffick; from *barat*, craft, fraud.] To traffick by exchanging one commodity for another, in oppoſition to purchaſing with money.

As if they ſcorn'd to trade and *barter*,
By giving or by taking quarter. *Hudibras, p.* iii. *c.* i.

A man has not every thing growing upon his ſoil, and therefore is willing to *barter* with his neighbour. *Collier.*

To BA'RTER. *v. a.*

1. To give any thing in exchange for ſomething elſe.

For him was I exchang'd and ransom'd;
But with a baser man of arms by far,
Once, in contempt, they would have *barter'd* me.
Shakesp. Henry VI. *p.* i.

Then as thou wilt dispose the rest,
To those who, at the market rate,
Can *barter* honour for estate. *Prior.*

I see nothing left us, but to truck and *barter* our goods, like the wild Indians, with each other. *Swift.*

2. Sometimes it is used with the particle *away* before the thing given.

If they will *barter away* their time, methinks they should at least have some ease in exchange. *Decay of Piety.*

He also *bartered away* plums that would have rotted in a week, for nuts that would last good for his eating a whole year. *Locke.*

BA'RTER. *n. s.* [from the verb.] The act or practice of trafficking by exchange of commodities; sometimes the thing given in exchange.

From England they may be furnished with such things as they may want, and, in exchange or *barter*, send other things, with which they may abound. *Bacon's Advice to Villiers.*

He who corrupteth English with foreign words, is as wise as ladies that change plate for china; for which, I think, the laudable traffick of old cloaths is much the fairest *barter*.
Felton on the Classicks.

BA'RTERER. *n. s.* [from *barter.*] He that trafficks by exchange of commodities.

BA'RTERY. *n. s.* [from *barter.*] Exchange of commodities.

It is a received opinion, that, in most ancient ages, there was only *bartery* or change of commodities amongst most nations. *Camden's Remains.*

BA'RTRAM. *n. s.* A plant; the same with *pellitory*; which see.

BA'RTON. *n. s.* The demesne lands of a manour; the manour-house itself; and sometimes the out-houses. *Blount.*

BASE. *adj.* [*bas*, Fr. *basso*, Ital. *baxo*, Span. *bassus*, low Latin; βάσις.]

1. Mean; vile; worthless.

The harvest white plumb is a *base* plumb, and the white date plumb are no very good plumbs. *Bacon's Natural Hist.*

Pyreicus was only famous for counterfeiting all *base* things, as earthen pitchers, a scullery; whereupon he was surnamed Rupographus. *Peacham.*

2. Of mean spirit; disingenuous; illiberal; ungenerous; low; without dignity of sentiment.

Since the perfections are such in the party I love, as the feeling of them cannot come unto any unnoble heart; shall that heart, lifted up to such a height, be counted *base?* *Sidney.*

It is *base* in his adversaries thus to dwell upon the excesses of a passion. *Atterbury.*

I might be *base* enough to suspect, that you acted like some philosopher, who writ much better upon virtue than he practised it. *Swift.*

3. Of low station; of mean account; without dignity of rank; without honour.

If the lords and chief men degenerate, what shall be hoped of the peasants and *baser* people? *Spenser on Ireland.*

If that rebellion
Came like itself, in *base* and abject routs,
You reverend father, and these noble lords,
Had not been here. *Shakesp. Henry* IV. *p.* ii.

It could not else be, I should prove so *base*,
To sue and be denied such common grace. *Shak. Timon.*

And I will yet be more vile than this, and will be *base* in mine own sight. 2 *Sam.* vi. 22.

Insurrections of *base* people are commonly more furious in their beginnings. *Bacon's Henry* VII.

He whose mind
Is virtuous, is alone of noble kind;
Though poor in fortune, of celestial race,
And he commits the crime who calls him *base*. *Dryden.*

4. Base-born; born out of wedlock, and by consequence of no honourable birth.

Why bastard? wherefore *base?*
When my dimensions are as well compact
As honest madam's issue. *Shakesp. King Lear.*

This young lord lost his life with his father in the field, and with them a *base* son. *Camden's Remains.*

5. Applied to metals: without value; it is used in this sense of all metal except gold and silver.

A guinea is pure gold, if it has nothing but gold in it, without any alloy or *baser* metal. *Watts's Logick.*

6. Applied to sounds, deep; grave. It is more frequently written *bass*, though the comparative *baser* seems to require *base*.

In pipes, the lower the note holes be, and the further from the mouth of the pipe, the more *base* sound they yield.
Bacon's Natural History, N° 178.

BASE-BORN. *adj.* Born out of wedlock.

But see thy *base-born* child, thy babe of shame,
Who, left by thee, upon our parish came. *Gay.*

BASE-COURT. *n. s.* Lower court; not the chief court that leads to the house.

My lord, in the *base-court* he doth attend,
To speak with you. *Shakesp. Richard* II.

BASE-MINDED. *adj.* Mean spirited; worthless.

It signifieth, as it seemeth, no more than abject, *base-minded*, false hearted, coward, or nidget. *Camden's Remains.*

BASE-VIOL. *n. s.* [usually written *bass viol.*] An instrument which is used in concerts for the base sound.

At the very first grin he cast every human feature out of his countenance; at the second, he became the head of a *base-viol.*
Addison. Spectator, N° 174.

BASE. *n. s.* [*bas*, Fr. *basis*, Lat.]

1. The bottom of any thing; commonly used for the lower part of a building, or column.

What if it tempt thee tow'rd the flood, my lord?
Or to the dreadful summit of the cliff,
That beetles o'er his *base* into the sea. *Shakesp. Hamlet.*

Firm Dorick pillars found your solid *base*;
The fair Corinthian crowns the higher space. *Dryden.*

Columns of polish'd marble firmly set
On golden *bases*, are his legs and feet. *Prior.*

2. The pedestal of a statue.

Men of weak abilities in great place, are like little statues set on great *bases*, made the less by their advancement. *Bacon.*

Mercury was patron of flocks, and the ancients placed a ram at the *base* of his images. *Broome's Notes on the Odyssey.*

3. That part of any ornament which hangs down, as housings.

Phalantus was all in white, having his *bases* and caparison embroidered. *Sidney.*

4. The broad part of any body; as the bottom of a cone.

5. Stockings, or perhaps the armour for the legs, from *bas*, Fr.

Nor shall it e'er be said that wight,
With gauntlet blue and *bases* white,
And round blunt truncheon by his side,
So great a man at arms defy'd. *Hudibras.*

6. The place from which racers or tilters run; the bottom of the field.

He said; to their appointed *base* they went;
With beating heart th' expecting sign receive,
And, starting all at once, the barrier leave. *Dryden's Virg.*

7. The string that gives a base sound.

At thy well sharpen'd thumb, from shore to shore,
The trebles squeak for fear, the *bases* roar. *Dryden's Mackfl.*

8. An old rustick play; written by *Skinner*, bays.

He with two striplings (lads, more like to run
The country *base*, than to commit such slaughter)
Made good the passage. *Shakesp. Cymbeline.*

To BASE. *v. a.* [*basier*, Fr.] To embase; to make less valuable by admixture of meaner metals.

I am doubtful whether men have sufficiently refined metals, which we cannot *base*; as, whether iron, brass, and tin be refined to the height? *Bacon's Natural History*, N° 849.

BA'SELY. *adv.* [from *base.*]

1. In a base manner; meanly; dishonourably.

The king is not himself, but *basely* led
By flatterers. *Shakesp. Richard* II.

A lieutenant *basely* gave it up, as soon as Essex in his passage demanded it. *Clarendon.*

With broken vows his fame he will not stain,
With conquest *basely* bought, and with inglorious gain.
Dryden.

2. In bastardy.

These two Mitylene brethren, *basely* born, crept out of a small galliot unto the majesty of great kings.
Knolles's History of the Turks.

BA'SENESS. *n. s.* [from *base.*]

1. Meanness; vileness; badness.

Such is the power of that sweet passion,
That it all sordid *baseness* doth expel. *Spens. Hymn on Love.*

When a man's folly must be spread open before the angels, and all his *baseness* ript up before those pure spirits, this will be a double hell. *South.*

Your soul's above the *baseness* of distrust:
Nothing but love could make you so unjust. *Dryd. Aureng.*

2. Vileness of metal.

We alleged the fraudulent obtaining and executing his patent, the *baseness* of his metal, and the prodigious sum to be coined. *Swift.*

3. Bastardy.

Why brand they us
With base? with *baseness?* bastardy? *Shakesp. King Lear.*

4. Deepness of sound.

The just and measured proportion of the air percussed towards the *baseness* or trebleness of tones, is one of the greatest secrets in the contemplation of sounds. *Bacon's Nat. History.*

To BASH. *v. n.* [probably from *base.*] To be ashamed; to be confounded with shame.

His countenance was bold, and *bash'd* not
For Guyon's looks, but scornful eye-glance at him shot.
Fairy Queen, b. ii. *c.* iv.

BASHA'W. *n. s.* [sometimes written *bassa.*] A title of honour and command among the Turks; the viceroy of a province; the general of an army.

The Turks made an expedition into Persia; and because of the straits of the mountains, the *bashaw* consulted which way they should get in. *Bacon's Apophthegms.*

BA'SHFUL. *adj.* [This word, with all those of the same race, are of uncertain etymology. *Skinner* imagines them derived from *base*, or mean; *Minshew*, from *verbaesen*, Dut. to strike with astonishment; *Junius*, from βάσις, which he finds in *Hesychius* to signify shame. The conjecture of *Minshew* seems most probable.]

1. Modest; shamefaced.

I never tempted her with word too large;
But, as a brother to his sister, shew'd
Bashful sincerity, and comely love. *Shakesp. M. ado about N.*

2. Sheepish; vitiously modest.

He looked with an almost *bashful* kind of modesty, as if he feared the eyes of man. *Sidney.*

Hence, *bashful* cunning!
And prompt me plain and holy innocence. *Shakesp. Tempest.*

Our authour, anxious for his fame to night,
And *bashful* in his first attempt to write,
Lies cautiously obscure. *Addison's Drummer, Prologue.*

BA'SHFULLY. *adv.* [from *bashful.*] Timorously; modestly.

BA'SHFULNESS. *n. s.* [from *bashful.*]

1. Modesty, as shewn in outward appearance.

Philoclea a little mused how to cut the thread even, with eyes, cheeks and lips, whereof each sang their part, to make up the harmony of *bashfulness.* *Sidney.*

Such looks, such *bashfulness* might well adorn
The cheeks of youths that are more nobly born. *Dryden.*

2. Vitious or rustick shame.

For fear had bequeathed his room to his kinsman *bashfulness*, to teach him good manners. *Sidney, b.* i.

There are others who have not altogether so much of this foolish *bashfulness*, and who ask every one's opinion. *Dryden.*

BA'SIL. *n. s.* [*ocymum*, Lat.] The name of a plant.

This plant hath a labiated flower of one leaf, whose crest is upright, roundish, notched, and larger than the beard, which is generally curled, or gently cut. Out of the flower cup rises the pointal, attended by four embryos, that become so many seeds inclosed in a husk, which was before the flower cup; the husk is divided into two lips, the upper one growing upright, and is split into two; but the under one is cut into several parts. The species are eight; 1. Common *basil.* 2. Common *basil*, with dark green leaves, and white flowers. 3. Lesser *basil*, with narrow serrated leaves. 4. The least *basil*, commonly called *bush-basil*, &c. These annual plants are propagated from seeds in March, upon a moderate hot bed. In August they perfect their seeds. The first sort is prescribed in medicine; but the fourth is most esteemed for its beauty and scent. *Millar.*

BA'SIL. *n. s.* The angle to which the edge of a joiner's tool is ground away.

BA'SIL. *n. s.* The skin of a sheep tanned. *Dict.*

To BA'SIL. *v. a.* To grind the edge of a tool to an angle.

These chissels are not ground to such a basil as the joiners chissels on one of the sides, but are *basiled* away on both the flat sides; so that the edge lies between both the sides in the middle of the tool. *Moxon's Mechanical Exercises.*

BASI'LICA. *n. s.* [βασιλικὴ.] The middle vein of the arm so called, by way of pre-eminence. It is likewise attributed to many medicines for the same reason. *Quincy.*

BASI'LICAL. } *adj.* [from *basilica.* See BASILICA.] Belonging
BASI'LICK. } to the basilick vein.

These aneurisms following always upon bleeding the *basilick* vein, must be aneurisms of the humeral artery. *Sharp.*

BASILICK. *n. s.* [*basilique*, Fr. βασιλικὴ.] A large hall, having two ranges of pillars, and two isles or wings, with galleries over them. These *basilicks* were first made for the palaces of princes, and afterwards converted into courts of justice, and lastly into churches; whence a *basilick* is generally taken for a magnificent church, as the *basilick* of St. Peter at Rome.

BASI'LICON. *n. s.* [βασιλικὸν.] An ointment called also tetrapharmacon. *Quincy.*

I made incision into the cavity, and put a pledget of *basilicon* over it. *Wiseman's Surgery.*

BA'SILISK. *n. s.* [*basiliscus*, Lat. of βασιλίσκος, of βασιλεὺς, a king.]

1. A kind of serpent, called also a cockatrice, which is said to drive away all others by his hissing, and to kill by looking.

Make me not sighted like the *basilisk*;
I've look'd on thousands who have sped the better
By my regard, but kill'd none so. *Shakesp. Winter's Tale.*

The *basilisk* was a serpent not above three palms long, and differenced from other serpents by advancing his head, and some white marks or coronary spots upon the crown. *Brown's Vulgar Errours.*

2. A species of cannon or ordnance.

There we imitate and practise to make swifter motions than any you have: and to make them stronger and more violent than yours are; exceeding your greatest cannons and *basilisks.* *Bacon's New Atlantis.*

BA'SIN. *n. s.* [*bassin*, Fr. *bacile*, *bacino*, Ital. It is often written *bason*, but not according to etymology.]

1. A small vessel to hold water for washing, or other uses.

Let one attend him with a silver *basin*,
Full of rosewater, and bestrew'd with flowers.
Shakesp. Taming of the Shrew.

We have little wells for infusions, where the waters take the virtue quicker and better, than in vessels and *basins.* *Bacon.*

We behold a piece of silver in a *basin*, when water is put upon it, which we could not discover before, as under the verge thereof. *Brown's Vulgar Errours.*

2. A small pond.

On one side of the walk you see this hollow *basin*, with its several little plantations lying conveniently under the eye of the beholder. *Spectator*, N° 477.

3. A part of the sea inclosed in rocks, with a narrow entrance.

The jutting land two ample bays divides;
The spacious *basins* arching rocks inclose,
A sure defence from ev'ry storm that blows. *Pope's Odyssey.*

4. Any hollow place capacious of liquids.

If this rotation does the seas affect,
The rapid motion rather would eject
The stores, the low capacious caves contain,
And from its ample *basin* cast the main. *Blackmore's Creat.*

5. A dock for repairing and building ships.

6. In anatomy, a round cavity situated between the anterior ventricles of the brain.

7. A concave piece of metal by which glass grinders form their convex glasses.

8. A round shell or case of iron placed over a furnace, in which hatters mould the matter of a hat into form.

9. *Basins of a balance*; the same with the scales; one to hold the weight, the other the thing to be weighed.

BA'SIS. *n. s.* [*basis*, Lat.]

1. The foundation of any thing, as of a column or a building.

It must follow, that paradise, being raised to this height, must have the compass of the whole earth for a *basis* and foundation. *Raleigh's History of the World.*

Ascend my chariot, guide the rapid wheels
That shake heav'n's *basis.* *Milton's Paradise Lost, b.* vi.

In altar-wise a stately pile they rear;
The *basis* broad below, and top advanc'd in air. *Dryden.*

2. The lowest of the three principal parts of a column, which are the *basis*, *shaft*, and *capital.*

Upon our coming to the bottom, observing an English inscription upon the *basis*, we read it over several times.
Addison's Freeholder, N° 47.

3. That on which any thing is raised.

Such seems thy gentle height, made only proud
To be the *basis* of that pompous load,
Than which a nobler weight no mountain bears. *Denham.*

4. The pedestal.

How many times shall Cæsar bleed in sport,
That now on Pompey's *basis* lies along
No worthier than the dust? *Shakesp. Julius Cæsar.*

5. The groundwork or first principle of any thing.

Build me thy fortune upon the *basis* of valour.
Shakesp. Twelfth Night.

The friendships of the world are oft
Confederacies in vice, or leagues of pleasure;
Ours has severest virtue for its *basis.* *Addison's Cato.*

To BASK. *v. a.* [*backeren*, Dut. *Skinner.*] To warm by laying out in the heat; used almost always of animals.

And stretched out all the chimney's length,
Basks at the fire his hairy strength. *Milton.*

He was *basking* himself in the gleam of the sun. *L'Estrange.*

'Tis all thy business, business how to shun,
To *bask* thy naked body in the sun. *Dryden's Persius.*

To BASK. *v. n.* To lie in the warmth.

About him, and above, and round the wood,
The birds that haunt the borders of his flood;
That bath'd within, or *bask'd* upon his side,
To tuneful songs their narrow throats apply'd. *Dryden.*

Unlock'd, in covers let her freely run,
To range thy courts, and *bask* before the sun. *Tickell.*

Some in the fields of purest æther play,
And *bask* and whiten in the blaze of day. *Pope.*

BA'SKET. *n. s.* [*basged*, Welch; *bascauda*, Lat. *Barbara depictis venit bascauda Britannis.* Martial.] A vessel made of twigs, rushes, or splinters, or some other slender body interwoven.

Here is a *basket*; he may creep in, and throw foul linen upon him, as if going to bucking. *Shak. Merry Wives of Windsor.*

Thus while I sung, my sorrows I deceiv'd,
And bending osiers into *baskets* weav'd. *Dryden.*

Poor Peg was forced to go hawking and peddling; now and then carrying a *basket* of fish to the market. *Arbuth. J. Bull.*

BA'SKET-HILT. *n. s.* [from *basket* and *hilt.*] A hilt of a weapon so made as to contain the whole hand, and defend it from being wounded.

His puissant sword unto his side,
Near his undaunted heart, was ty'd:
With *basket-hilt*, that would hold broth,
And serve for fight and dinner both. *Hudibras, cant.* i.

Their beef they often in their murrions ſtew'd,
And in their *baſket hilts* their bev'rage brew'd.
King's Art of Cookery.

BA'SKET-WOMAN. *n. ſ.* [from *baſket* and *woman.*] A woman that plies at markets with a basket, ready to carry home any thing that is bought.

BASS. *adj.* [See BASE.] In muſick; grave; deep.

BASS-VIOL. See BASE-VIOL.

On the ſweep of the arch lies one of the Muſes, playing on a *baſs-viol.* *Dryden.*

BASS. *n. ſ.* [ſuppoſed by *Junius* to be derived, like *baſket*, from ſome Britiſh word ſignifying a *ruſh*; but perhaps more properly written *boſs*, from the French *boſſe.*] A mat uſed in churches.

Having woollen yarn, *baſs* mat, or ſuch like, to bind them withal. *Mortimer's Husbandry.*

BASS-RELIEF. *n. ſ.* [from *bas*, and *relief*, raiſed work, Fr.]

Sculpture, the figures of which do not ſtand out from the ground in their full proportion. *Felibien* diſtinguiſhes three kinds of *baſs-relief*; in the firſt, the front figures appear almoſt with the full relief; in the ſecond, they ſtand out no more than one half; and, in the third, much leſs, as in coins.

BA'SSA. See BASHAW.

BA'SSET. *n. ſ.* [*baſſet*, Fr.] A game at cards, invented at Venice.

Gameſters would no more blaſpheme; and lady Dabcheek's *baſſet* bank would be broke. *Dennis.*

BA'SSO RELIEVO. [Ital.] See BASS-RELIEF.

BASSO'N. } *n. ſ.* [*baſſon*, Fr.] A muſical inſtrument of the wind
BASSO'ON. } kind, blown with a reed, and furniſhed with eleven holes, which are ſtopped like other large flutes; its diameter at bottom is nine inches, and it ſerves for the baſs in concerts of hautboys, &c. *Trevoux.*

BA'SSOCK. *n. ſ.* The ſame with *baſs.*

BA'STARD. *n. ſ.* [*baſtardd*, Welch, of low birth; *baſtarde*, Fr.]

1. *Baſtard*, according to the civil and canon law, is a perſon born of a woman out of wedlock, or not married; ſo that, according to order of law, his father is not known. *Ayliffe.*

Him to the Lydian king Lycimnia bare,
And ſent her boaſted *baſtard* to the war. *Dryden.*

2. Any thing ſpurious or falſe.

It lies on you to ſpeak to th' people;
Not by your own inſtruction, but with words
But rooted in your tongue; *baſtards* and ſyllables
Of no allowance to your boſom's truth. *Shakeſp. Coriolanus.*

BA'STARD. *adj.* [from the noun.]

1. Begotten out of wedlock.

Peace is a very apoplexy, lethargy, inſenſible, a getter of more *baſtard* children than war's a deſtroyer of men. *Shakeſp. Coriolanus.*

2. Spurious; not genuine; ſuppoſititious; falſe; adulterate. In this ſenſe, any thing which bears ſome relation or reſemblance to another, is called ſpurious or *baſtard.*

You may partly hope that your father got you not, that you are not the Jew's daughter.—That were a kind of *baſtard* hope indeed. *Shakeſp. Merchant of Venice.*

Men who, under the diſguiſe of publick good, purſue their own deſigns of power, and ſuch *baſtard* honours as attend them. *Temple.*

BA'STARD *Cedar Tree.* [called *guazuma* in the Weſt Indies.]

The characters are; It hath a regular flower, conſiſting of five leaves, hollowed like a ſpoon at their baſe; but, at their tops, divided into two parts, like a fork. The flower cup conſiſts of three leaves, from whence ariſes the pointal, which afterwards becomes a roundiſh warted fruit, which has five cells, incloſing many ſeeds.

It grows plentifully in the low lands in Jamaica, where it riſes to the height of forty or fifty feet, and has a large trunk. The timber of this tree is cut into ſtaves, for caſes of all ſorts, and uſed for many other purpoſes. The fruit is eat by cattle, as it falls from the trees, and is eſteemed very good to fatten them; ſo that the planters often leave theſe trees ſtanding in their ſavannas, when they clear them from all other wood. *Millar.*

To BA'STARD. *v. a.* [from the noun.] To convict of being a baſtard; to ſtigmatize with baſtardy.

She lived to ſee her brother beheaded, and her two ſons depoſed from the crown, *baſtarded* in their blood, and cruelly murdered. *Bacon's Henry VII.*

To BA'STARDIZE. *v. a.* [from *baſtard.*]

1. To convict of being a baſtard.
2. To beget a baſtard.

I ſhould have been what I am, had the maidenlieſt ſtar in the firmament twinkled on my *baſtardizing.* *Shakeſp. King Lear.*

BA'STARDLY. *adv.* [from *baſtard.*] In the manner of a baſtard; ſpuriouſly.

Good ſeed degenerates, and oft obeys
The ſoil's diſeaſe, and into cockle ſtrays;
Let the mind's thoughts but be tranſplanted ſo
Into the body, and *baſtardly* they grow. *Donne.*

BA'STARDY. *n. ſ.* [from *baſtard.*] An unlawful ſtate of birth, which diſables the baſtard, both according to the laws of God and man, from ſucceeding to an inheritance. *Ayliffe's Parerg.*

Once ſhe ſlander'd me with *baſtardy*;
But whether I be true begot, or no,
That ſtill I lay upon my mother's head. *Shakeſp. K. John.*

In reſpect of the evil conſequents, the wife's adultery is worſe, as bringing *baſtardy* into a family. *Taylor's Holy Living.*

No more of *baſtardy* in heirs of crowns. *Pope's Epiſtles.*

To BASTE. *v. a.* participle paſſ. *baſted*, or *baſten.* [*baſtonner*, Fr. *Bazata*, in the Armorick dialect, ſignifies to ſtrike with a ſtick; from which perhaps *baſton* a ſtick, and all its derivatives, or collaterals, may be deduced.]

1. To beat with a ſtick.

Quoth ſhe, I grant it is in vain
For one's that *baſted* to feel pain,
Becauſe the pangs his bones endure,
Contribute nothing to the cure. *Hudibras.*

Tir'd with diſpute, and ſpeaking Latin,
As well as *baſting*, and bear bating. *Hudibras.*

Baſtings heavy, dry, obtuſe,
Only dulneſs can produce;
While a little gentle jerking
Sets the ſpirits all aworking. *Swift.*

2. To drip butter, or any thing elſe, upon meat as it turns upon the ſpit.

Sir, I think the meat wants what I have, a *baſting.* *Shakeſp. Romeo and Juliet.*

3. To moiſten meat on the ſpit by falling upon it.

The fat of roaſted mutton falling on the birds, will ſerve to *baſte* them, and ſo ſave time and butter. *Swift's Directions to the Cook.*

4. To ſew ſlightly. [*baſter*, Fr. to ſtitch.]

BASTINA'DE. } *n. ſ.* [*baſtonnade*, Fr.]
BASTINA'DO. }

1. The act of beating with a cudgel; the blow given with a cudgel.

But this courteſy was worſe than a *baſtinado* to Zelmane; ſo that again, with rageful eyes, ſhe bad him defend himſelf. *Sidney, b. ii.*

And all thoſe harſh and rugged ſounds
Of *baſtinados*, cuts and wounds. *Hudibras.*

2. It is ſometimes taken for a Turkiſh puniſhment of beating an offender on the ſoals of his feet.

To BASTINA'DE. } *v. a.* [from the noun; *baſtonner*, Fr.] To
To BASTINA'DO. } beat; to give the baſtinado.

Nick ſeized the longer end of the cudgel, and with it began to *baſtinado* old Lewis, who had ſlunk into a corner, waiting the event of the ſquabble. *Arbuthnot's Hiſtory of J. Bull.*

BA'STION. *n. ſ.* [*baſtion*, Fr.] A huge maſs of earth, uſually faced with ſods, ſometimes with brick, rarely with ſtone, ſtanding out from a rampart, of which it is a principal part, and was anciently called a bulwark. *Harris.*

Toward: but how? ay there's the queſtion;
Fierce the aſſault, unarm'd the *baſtion.* *Prior.*

BAT. *n. ſ.* [bat, Sax. This word ſeems to have given riſe to a great number of words in many languages; as, *battre*, Fr. to beat; *baton, battle, beat, batty*, and others. It probably ſignified a weapon that did execution by its weight, in oppoſition to a ſharp edge; whence *whirlbat* and *brickbat.*] A heavy ſtick or club.

A handſome *bat* he held,
On which he leaned, as one far in eld. *Hubberd's Tale.*

They were fried in arm chairs, and their bones broken with *bats.* *Hakewell on Providence.*

BAT. *n. ſ.* [the etymology unknown.] An animal having the body of a mouſe and the wings of a bird; not with feathers, but with a ſort of skin which is extended. It lays no eggs, but brings forth its young alive, and ſuckles them. It never grows tame, feeds upon flies, inſects, and fatty ſubſtances, ſuch as candles, oil, and cheeſe; and appears only in the ſummer evenings, when the weather is fine. *Calmet.*

When owls do cry,
On the *bat's* back I do fly. *Shakeſp. Tempeſt.*

But then grew reaſon dark; that fair ſtar no more
Could the fair forms of good and truth diſcern;
Bats they became who eagles were before;
And this they got by their deſire to learn. *Sir J. Davies.*

Some animals are placed in the middle betwixt two kinds, as *bats*, which have ſomething of birds and beaſts. *Locke.*

Where ſwallows in the winter ſeaſon keep,
And how the drowſy *bat* and dormouſe ſleep. *Gay.*

BAT-FOWLING. *n. ſ.* [from *bat* and *fowl.*] A particular manner of birdcatching in the night time, while they are at rooſt upon perches, trees, or hedges. They light torches or ſtraw, and then beat the buſhes; upon which the birds flying to the flames, are caught either with nets, or otherwiſe.

You would lift the moon out of her ſphere, if ſhe would continue in it five weeks without changing.—We ſhould ſo, and then go a *bat-fowling.* *Shakeſp. Tempeſt.*

Bodies lighted at night by fire, muſt have a brighter luſtre given them than by day; as ſacking of cities, *bat-fowling*, &c. *Peacham on Drawing.*

BA'TABLE. *adj.* [from *bate.*] Diſputable.

Batable ground seems to be the ground heretofore in question, whether it belonged to England or Scotland, lying between both kingdoms. *Cowel.*

BATCH. *n. s.* [from *bake.*]

1. The quantity of bread baked at a time.

The joiner puts the boards into ovens after the *batch* is drawn, or lays them in a warm stable. *Mortimer's Husbandry.*

2. Any quantity of any thing made at once, so as to have the same qualities.

Except he were of the same meal and *batch.* *Ben. Johnson.*

BA'TCHELOR. See BACHELOR.

BATE. *n. s.* [perhaps contracted from *debate.*] Strife; contention; as a *make-bate.*

To BATE. *v. a.* [contracted from *abate.*]

1. To lessen any thing; to retrench.

Shall I bend low, and in a bondman's key,
With *bated* breath, and whisp'ring humbleness,
Say this? *Shakesp. Merchant of Venice.*

Nor envious at the sight will I forbear
My plenteous bowl, nor *bate* my plenteous cheer. *Dryden.*

2. To sink the price.

When the landholder's rent falls, he must either *bate* the labourer's wages, or not employ, or not pay him. *Locke.*

3. To lessen a demand.

Bate me some, and I will pay you some, and, as most debtors do, promise you infinitely. *Shakesp. Henry* IV.

4. To cut off; to take away.

Bate but the last, and 'tis what I would say. *Dryd. Sp. Friar.*

To BATE. *v. n.*

1. To grow less.

Bardolph, am not I fallen away vilely since this last election? Do I not *bate?* do I not dwindle? Why, my skin hangs about me like an old lady's loose gown. *Shak. Hen.* IV.

2. To remit; with *of* before the thing.

Abate thy speed, and I will *bate of* mine. *Dryden.*

BATE seems to have been once the preterite of *bite*, as *Shakespeare* uses *biting faulchion*; unless, in the following lines, it may be rather deduced from *beat.*

Yet there the steel staid not, but inly *bate*
Deep in his flesh, and open'd wide a red flood gate. *F. Queen.*

BA'TEFUL. *adj.* [from *bate* and *full.*] Contentious.

He knew her haunt, and haunted in the same,
And taught his sheep her sheep in food to thwart;
Which soon as it did *bateful* question frame,
He might on knees confess his guilty part. *Sidney.*

BA'TEMENT. *n. s.* [from *abatement.*] Diminution; a term only used among artificers.

To abate, is to waste a piece of stuff; instead of asking how much was cut off, carpenters ask what *batement* that piece of stuff had. *Moxon's Mechanical Exercises.*

BATH. *n. s.* [bað, Saxon.]

1. A *bath* is either hot or cold, either of art or nature. Artificial *baths* have been in great esteem with the ancients, especially in complaints to be relieved by revulsion, as inveterate headaches, by opening the pores of the feet, and also in cutaneous cases. But the modern practice has greatest recourse to the natural *baths*; most of which abound with a mineral sulphur, as appears from their turning silver and copper blackish. The cold *baths* are the most convenient springs, or reservatories, of cold water to wash in, which the ancients had in great esteem; and the present age can produce abundance of noble cures performed by them. *Quincy.*

Why may not the cold *bath*, into which they plunged themselves, have had some share in their cure? *Addison. Spectator.*

2. A state in which great outward heat is applied to the body, for the mitigation of pain, or any other purpose.

In the height of this *bath*, when I was more than half stewed in grease like a Dutch dish, to be thrown into the Thames. *Shakespeare's Merry Wives of Windsor.*

Sleep, the birth of each day's life, sore labour's *bath*,
Balm of hurt minds. *Shakesp. Macbeth.*

3. In chymistry, it generally signifies a vessel of water, in which another is placed that requires a softer heat than the naked fire. *Balneum Mariæ* is a mistake, for *balneum maris*, a sea or water *bath.* A sand heat is sometimes called *balneum siccum*, or *cinereum.* *Quincy.*

We see that the water of things distilled in water, which they call the *bath*, differeth not much from the water of things distilled by fire. *Bacon's Natural History*, N° 684.

4. A sort of Hebrew measure, containing the tenth part of an homer, or seven gallons and four pints, as a measure for things liquid; and three pecks and three pints, as a measure for things dry. *Calmet.*

Ten acres of vineyard shall yield one *bath*, and the seed of an homer shall yield an ephah. *Isaiah*, v. 10.

To BATHE. *v. a.* [baðian, Saxon.]

1. To wash in a bath.

Others, on silver lakes and rivers, *bath'd*
Their downy breast. *Milton's Paradise Lost, b.* x. *l.* 437.

Chancing to *bathe* himself in the river Cydnus, through the excessive coldness of these waters, he fell sick, near unto death, for three days. *South.*

2. To supple or soften by the outward application of warm liquours.

Bathe them, and keep their bodies soluble the while by clysters, and lenitive boluses. *Wiseman's Surgery.*

I'll *bathe* your wounds in tears for my offence. *Dryden.*

3. To wash with any thing.

Phœnician Dido stood,
Fresh from her wound, her bosom *bath'd* in blood. *Dryden.*

Mars could in mutual blood the centaurs *bathe*,
And Jove himself give way to Cinthia's wrath. *Dryden.*

To BATHE. *v. n.* To be in the water, or in any thing resembling a bath.

Except they meant to *bathe* in reeking wounds,
I cannot tell. *Macbeth.*

The delighted spirit
To *bathe* in firy floods, or to reside
In thrilling regions of thick ribbed ice. *Sh. Meas. for Meas.*

The gallants dancing by the river side,
They *bathe* in summer, and in winter slide. *Waller.*

But *bathe*, and, in imperial robes array'd,
Pay due devotions. *Pope's Odyssey.*

BA'TING, or ABA'TING. *prep.* [from *bate*, or *abate.* This word, though a participle in itself, seems often used as a preposition.] Except.

The king, your brother, could not choose an advocate,
Whom I would sooner hear on any subject,
Bating that only one, his love, than you. *Rowe's R. Conv.*

If we consider children, we have little reason to think, that they bring many ideas with them, *bating*, perhaps, some faint ideas of hunger and thirst. *Locke.*

BA'TLET. *n. s.* [from *bat.*] A square piece of wood, with a handle, used in beating linen when taken out of the buck.

I remember the kissing of her *batlet*, and the cow's dugs that her pretty chopt hands had milked. *Shakesp. As you like it.*

BATO'ON. *n. s.* [*baston*, or *bâton*, Fr. formerly spelt *baston.*]

1. A staff or club.

We came close to the shore, and offered to land; but straightways we saw divers of the people with *bastons* in their hands, as it were, forbidding us to land. *Bacon's N. Atlantis.*

That does not make a man the worse,
Although his shoulders with *batoon*
Be claw'd and cudgell'd to some tune. *Hudibras.*

2. A truncheon or marshal's staff; a badge of military honour.

BA'TTAILLOUS. *adj.* [from *battaille*, Fr.] Having the appearance of a battle; warlike; with military appearance.

He started up, and did himself prepare
In sun bright arms and *battailous* array. *Fairfax, b.* i.

The French came foremost *battailous* and bold. *Fairf. b.* i.

A firy region, stretch'd
In *battailous* aspect, and nearer view
Bristled with upright beams innumerable
Of rigid spears, and helmets throng'd. *Paradise Lost, b.* vi.

BATTA'LIA. *n. s.* [*battaglia*, Ital.] The order of battle.

Next morning the king put his army into *battalia.* *Clarend.*

BATTA'LION. *n. s.* [*bataillon*, Fr.]

1. A division of an army; a troop; a body of forces. It is now confined to the infantry, and the number is uncertain, but generally from five to eight hundred men. Some regiments consist of one *battalion*, and others are divided into two, three or more.

When sorrows come, they come not single spies,
But in *battalions.* *Shakesp. Hamlet.*

In this *battalion* there were two officers, called Thersites and Pandarus. *Tatler*, N° 56.

The pierc'd *battalions* disunited fall,
In heaps on heaps: one fate o'erwhelms them all. *Pope.*

2. An army. This sense is not now in use.

Six or seven thousand is their utmost power.
—Why, our *battalion* trebles that account. *Shakesp. Rich.* III.

To BA'TTEN. *v. a.* [a word of doubtful etymology.]

1. To fatten, or make fat; to feed plenteously.

We drove afield,
Batt'ning our flock with the fresh dews of night. *Milton.*

2. To fertilize.

The meadows here, with *batt'ning* ooze enrich'd,
Give spirit to the grass; three cubits high
The jointed herbage shoots. *Philips.*

To BA'TTEN. *v. n.* To grow fat; to live in indulgence.

Follow your function, go and *batten* on cold bits. *Sh. Coriol.*

Burnish'd and *batt'ning* on their food, to show
The diligence of careful herds below. *Dryden's H. and P.*

The lazy glutton safe at home will keep,
Indulge his sloth, and *batten* on his sleep. *Dryden.*

As at full length the pamper'd monarch lay,
Batt'ning in ease, and slumb'ring life away. *Garth.*

Tway mice, full blythe and amicable,
Batten beside erle Robert's table. *Prior.*

While paddling ducks the standing lake desire,
Or *batt'ning* hogs roll in the sinking mire. *Gay's Pastorals.*

BA'TTEN. *n. s.* A word used only by workmen.

A *batten* is a scantling of wooden stuff, two, three or four inches broad, seldom above one thick, and the length unlimited. *Moxon's Mechanical Exercises.*

To BA'TTER. *v. a.* [*battre*, to beat, Fr.]
1. To beat; to beat down; frequently used of walls thrown down by artillery, or of the violence of engines of war.
To appoint *battering* rams against the gates, to cast a mount, and to build a fort. *Ezek.* xxi. 22.
These haughty words of hers
Have *batter'd* me like roaring cannon shot,
And made me almost yield upon my knees. *Shakesp. H.* VI.
Britannia there, the fort in vain
Had *batter'd* been with golden rain:
Thunder itself had fail'd to pass. *Waller.*
Be then, the naval stores, the nation's care,
New ships to build, and *batter'd* to repair. *Dryden.*
2. To wear with beating.
Crowds to the castle mounted up the street,
Batt'ring the pavement with their coursers feet. *Dryden.*
If you have a silver saucepan for the kitchen use, let me advise you to *batter* it well; this will shew constant good housekeeping. *Swift's Directions to the Cook.*
3. Applied to persons: to wear out with service.
The *batter'd* veteran strumpets here,
Pretend at least to bring a modest ear. *Southern.*
I am a poor old *battered* fellow, and I would willingly end my days in peace. *Arbuthnot's History of J. Bull.*
As the same dame, experienc'd in her trade,
By names of toasts retails each *batter'd* jade. *Pope.*

To BA'TTER. *v. n.* A word used only by workmen.
The side of a wall, or any timber, that bulges from its bottom or foundation, is said to *batter*. *Moxon's Mech. Exercises.*

BA'TTER. *n. s.* [from *to batter.*] A mixture of several ingredients beaten together with some liquour; so called from its being so much beaten.
One would have all things little, hence has try'd
Turkey poults fresh'd from th' egg in *batter* fry'd.
King's Art of Cookery.

BA'TTERER. *n. s.* [from *batter.*] He that batters.

BA'TTERY. *n. s.* [from *batter*, or *batterie*, Fr.]
1. The act of battering.
Strong wars they make, and cruel *battery* bend,
'Gainst fort of reason, it to overthrow. *Fairy Queen, b.* ii.
Earthly minds, like mud walls, resist the strongest *batteries.* *Locke.*
2. The instruments with which a town is battered, placed in order for action.
Where is best place to make our *batt'ry* next?——
——I think at the north gate. *Shakesp. Henry* VI.
It plants this reasoning and that argument, this consequence and that distinction, like so many intellectual *batteries*, till at length it forces a way and passage into the obstinate inclosed truth. *South.*
See, and revere th' artillery of heav'n,
Drawn by the gale, or by the tempest driv'n:
A dreadful fire the floating *batt'ries* make,
O'erturn the mountain, and the forest shake. *Blackmore.*
3. The frame, or raised work, upon which cannons are mounted.
4. In law, a violent striking of any man. In trespass for assault and *battery*, one may be found guilty of the assault, yet acquitted of the *battery*. There may therefore be assault without *battery*; but *battery* always implies an assault. *Chambers.*
Why does he suffer this rude knave now to knock him about the sconce with a dirty shovel, and will not tell him of his action and *battery*? *Shakesp. Hamlet.*
Sir, quo' the lawyer, not to flatter ye,
You have as good and fair a *battery*,
As heart can wish, and need not shame
The proudest man alive to claim. *Hudibras, p.* iii. *c.* iii.

BA'TTLE. *n. s.* [*bataille*, Fr.]
1. A fight; an encounter between opposite armies. We generally say a *battle* of many, and a *combat* of two.
The English army that divided was
Into two parts, is now conjoin'd in one;
And means to give you *battle* presently. *Shakesp. Henry* VI.
The *battle* done, and they within our power,
She'll never see his pardon. *Shakesp. King Lear.*
The race is not to the swift, nor the *battle* to the strong. *Eccles.* ix. 11.
So they joined *battle*, and the heathen being discomfited fled into the plain. 1 *Maccab.* iv. 14.
2. A body of forces, or division of an army.
The king divided his army into three *battles*; whereof the vanguard only, well strengthened with wings, came to fight. *Bacon's Henry* VII.
3. The main body, as distinct from the van and rear.
The earl of Angus led the avant-guard, himself followed with the *battle* a good distance behind, and after came the arrier. *Hayward.*
4. We say to join *battle*; to give *battle*.

To BA'TTLE. *v. n.* [*batailler*, Fr.] To join battle; to contend in fight.
'Tis ours by craft and by surprize to gain:
'Tis yours to meet in arms, and *battle* in the plain. *Prior.*
We daily receive accounts of ladies *battling* it on both sides. *Addison. Freeholder*, N° 23.
I own, he hates an action base,
His virtues *batt'ling* with his place. *Swift.*

BA'TTLE-ARRAY. *n. s.* [See BATTLE and ARRAY.] Array, or order of battle.
Two parties of fine women, placed in the opposite side boxes, seemed drawn up in *battle-array* one against another. *Addison.*

BA'TTLE-AXE. *n. s.* A weapon used anciently, probably the same with a *bill.*
Certain tinners, as they were working, found spear heads, *battle-axes*, and swords of copper, wrapped in linen clouts. *Carew's Survey of Cornwal.*

BA'TTLEDOOR. *n. s.* [so called from *door*, taken for a flat board, and *battle*, or *striking.*] An instrument with a handle and a flat blade, used in play to strike a ball, or shuttlecock.
Play-things, which are above their skill, as tops, gigs, *battledoors*, and the like, which are to be used with labour, should indeed be procured them. *Locke.*

BA'TTLEMENT. *n. s.* [generally supposed to be formed from *battle*, as the parts from whence a building is defended against assailants; perhaps only corrupted from *bâtiment*, Fr.] A wall raised round the top of a building, with embrasures, or interstices, to look through, to annoy an enemy.
He fix'd his head upon our *battlements.* *Shak. Macbeth.*
Thou shalt make a *battlement* for thy roof, that thou bring not blood upon thine house, if any man fall from thence. *Deut.* xxii. 8.
Through this we pass
Up to the highest *battlement*, from whence
The Trojans threw their darts. *Denham.*
Their standard planted on the *battlement*,
Despair and death among the soldiers sent. *Dryd. Aurengz.*
No, I shan't envy him, whoe'er he be,
That stands upon the *battlements* of state;
I'd rather be secure than great. *Norris.*
The weighty mallet deals resounding blows,
Till the proud *battlements* her tow'rs inclose. *Gay's Trivia.*

BA'TTY. *adj.* [from *bat.*] Belonging to a bat.
Till o'er their brows death counterfeiting sleep,
With leaden legs and *batty* wings doth creep.
Shakesp. Midsummer Night's Dream.

BA'VAROY. *n. s.* A kind of cloke, or surtout.
Let the loop'd *bavaroy* the fop embrace,
Or his deep cloke be spatter'd o'er with lace. *Gay's Trivia.*

BA'UBEE. *n. s.* A word used in Scotland, and the northern counties, for a halfpenny.
Tho' in the draw'rs of my japan bureau,
To lady Gripeall I the Cæsars show,
'Tis equal to her ladyship or me,
A copper Otho, or a Scotch *baubee.* *Bramst. Man of Taste.*

BA'VIN. *n. s.* [of uncertain derivation.] A stick like those bound up in faggots; a piece of waste wood.
He ambled up and down
With shallow jesters and rash *bavin* wits,
Soon kindled, and soon burnt. *Shakesp. Henry* IV.
For moulded to the life in clouts,
Th' have pick'd from dunghills thereabouts,
He's mounted on a hazel *bavin*,
A crop'd malignant baker gave him. *Hudibras, p.* iii. *c.* iii.
The smaller truncheons make billet, *bavin*, and coals. *Mortimer's Art of Husbandry.*

To BAULK. See BALK.

BA'WBLE. *n. s.* [*Baubellum*, in barbarous Latin, signified a jewel, or any thing valuable, but not necessary. *Omnia baubella sua dedit Othoni.* *Howden.* Probably from *beau*, Fr.] A gewgaw; a trifling piece of finery; a thing of more show than use; a trifle. It is in general, whether applied to persons or things, a term of contempt.
She haunts me in every place. I was on the sea bank with some Venetians, and thither comes the *bawble*, and falls me thus about my neck. *Shakesp. Othello.*
It is a paltry cap,
A custard coffin, a *bawble*, a silken pie. *Shak. Tam. Shrew.*
If, in our contest, we do not interchange useful notions, we shall traffick toys and *bawbles.* *Government of the Tongue.*
This shall be writ to fright the fry away,
Who draw their little *bawbles*, when they play. *Dryden.*
A lady's watch needs neither figures nor wheels;
'Tis enough that 'tis loaded with *bawbles* and seals. *Prior.*
Our author then, to please you in your way,
Presents you now a *bawble* of a play,
In gingling rhyme. *Granville.*
A prince, the moment he is crown'd,
Inherits every virtue round,
As emblems of the sov'reign pow'r;
Like other *bawbles* of the Tow'r. *Swift.*

BA'WBLING. *adj.* [from *bawble.*] Trifling; contemptible: a word not now in use, except in conversation.
A *bawbling* vessel was he captain of,
For shallow draught and bulk unprized;
With which such scathful grapple did he make,
With the most noble bottom of our fleet.
Shakesp. Twelfth Night.

BA'WCOCK. *n. s.* [perhaps from *beau*, or *baude*, and *cock.*] A familiar word, which seems to signify the same as *fine fellow.*

Why, how now, my *bawcock*? how dost thou, chuck? *Shakesp. Twelfth Night.*

BAWD. *n. s.* [*baude*, old Fr.] A procurer, or procuress; one that introduces men and women to each other, for the promotion of debauchery.

If your worship will take order for the drabs and the knaves, you need not to fear the *bawds.* *Shakesp. Measure for Meas.*

This commodity,
This *bawd*, this broker, this all changing word,
Hath drawn him from his own determin'd aid. *Sh. K. John.*

Our author calls colouring *lena sororis*, the *bawd* of her sister design; she dresses her up, she paints her, she procures for the design, and makes lovers for her. *Dryden's Dufresnoy.*

To BAWD. *v. n.* [from the noun.] To procure; to provide gallants with strumpets.

Leucippe is agent for the king's lust, and *bawds*, at the same time, for the whole court. *Addison. Spectator*, N° 266.

And in four months a batter'd harridan;
Now nothing's left, but wither'd, pale, and shrunk,
To *bawd* for others, and go shares with punk. *Swift.*

BA'WDILY. *adv.* [from *bawdy.*] Obscenely.

BA'WDINESS. *n. s.* [from *bawdy.*] Obscenenes.

BA'WDRICK. *n. s.* [See BALDRICK.] A belt.

Fresh garlands too, the virgin's temples crown'd;
The youth's gilt swords wore at their thighs, with silver *bawdricks* bound. *Chapman's Iliad, b.* xviii.

BA'WDRY. *n. s.* [contracted from *bawdery*, the practice of a bawd.]

1. A wicked practice of procuring and bringing whores and rogues together. *Ayliffe's Parergon.*

Cheating and *bawdry* go together in the world. *L'Estrange.*

2. Obscenity; unchaste language.

Pr'ythee, say on; he's for a jig, or a tale of *bawdry*, or he sleeps. *Shakesp. Hamlet.*

I have no salt: no *bawdry* he doth mean:
For witty, in his language, is obscene. *B. Johnson.*

It is most certain, that barefaced *bawdery* is the poorest pretence to wit imaginable. *Dryden.*

BA'WDY. *adj.* [from *bawd.*] Obscene; unchaste; generally aplied to language.

The *bawdy* wind that kisses all it meets,
Is hush'd within the hollow mine of earth,
And will not hear't. *Shakesp. Othello.*

Only they,
That come to hear a merry *bawdy* play,
Will be deceiv'd. *Shakesp. Henry* VIII. *Prologue.*

Not one poor *bawdy* jest shall dare appear;
For now the batter'd veteran strumpets here
Pretend at least to bring a modest ear. *Southern.*

BA'WDY-HOUSE. *n. s.* A house where traffick is made by wickedness and debauchery.

Has the pope lately shut up the *bawdy-houses*, or does he continue to lay a tax upon sin? *Dennis.*

To BAWL. *v. n.* [*balo*, Lat.]

1. To hoot; to cry with great vehemence, whether for joy or pain. A word always used in contempt.

They *bawl* for freedom in their senseless mood,
And still revolt, when truth would set them free. *Par. Reg.*

To cry the cause up heretofore,
And *bawl* the bishops out of door. *Hudibras.*

Through the thick shades th' eternal scribbler *bawls*,
And shakes the statues on their pedestals. *Dryd. Juvenal.*

From his lov'd home no lucre him can draw;
The senate's mad decrees he never saw;
Nor heard at *bawling* bars corrupted law. *Dryden.*

Loud menaces were heard, and foul disgrace,
And *bawling* infamy, in language base,
'Till sense was lost in sound, and silence fled the place. *Dryden's Fables.*

So on the tuneful Margarita's tongue
The list'ning nymphs, and ravish'd heroes hung;
But citts and fops the heav'n born musick blame,
And *bawl*, and hiss, and damn her into fame. *Smith on J. Philips.*

I have a race of orderly elderly people, who can *bawl* when I am deaf, and tread softly when I am only giddy and would sleep. *Swift.*

2. To cry as a froward child.

A little child was *bawling*, and an old woman chiding it. *L'Estrange's Fables.*

If they were never suffered to have what they cried for, they would never, with *bawling* and peevishness, contend for mastery. *Locke.*

My husband took him in, a dirty boy; it was the business of the servants to attend him, the rogue did *bawl* and make such a noise. *Arbuthnot's History of John Bull.*

To BAWL. *v. a.* To proclaim as a crier.

It grieved me, when I saw labours which had cost so much, *bawled* about by common hawkers. *Swift.*

BA'WREL. *n. s.* A kind of hawk. *Dict.*

BA'WSIN. *n. s.* A badger. *Dict.*

BAY. *adj.* [*badius*, Lat.]

A *bay* horse is what is inclining to a chesnut; and this colour is various, either a light *bay* or a dark *bay*, according as it is less or more deep. There are also coloured horses, that are called dappled *bays.* All *bay* horses are commonly called brown by the common people.

All *bay* horses have black manes, which distinguish them from the sorrel, that have red or white manes.

There are light *bays* and gilded *bays*, which are somewhat of a yellowish colour. The chesnut *bay* is that which comes nearest to the colour of the chesnut. *Farrier's Dict.*

I remember, my lord, you gave good words the other day of a *bay* courser I rode on. 'Tis yours because you liked it. *Shakesp. Timon.*

Poor Tom! proud of heart, to ride on a *bay* trotting horse over four inch'd bridges. *Shakesp. King Lear.*

His colour grey,
For beauty dappled, or the brightest *bay.* *Dryden's Virgil.*

BAY. *n. s.* [*baye*, Dutch.]

1. An opening into the land, where the water is shut in on all sides, except at the entrance.

A reverend Syracusan merchant,
Who put unluckily into this *bay.* *Shakesp. Comedy of Err.*

We have also some works in the midst of the sea, and some *bays* upon the shore for some works, wherein is required the air and vapour of the sea. *Bacon.*

Here in a royal bed the waters sleep,
When tir'd at sea, within this *bay* they creep. *Dryden.*

Some of you have already been driven to this *bay.* *Dryden's Epistle to the Whigs.*

Hail, sacred solitude! from this calm *bay*
I view the world's tempestuous sea. *Roscommon.*

2. A pond head raised to keep in store of water for driving a mill.

BAY. *n. s.* [*abboi*, Fr. signifies the last extremity; as, *Innocence est aux abboins.* Boileau. *Innocence is in the utmost distress.* It is taken from *abboi*, the barking of a dog at hand, and thence signified the condition of a stag when the hounds were almost upon him.] The state of any thing surrounded by enemies, and obliged to face them by an impossibility of escape.

This ship, for fifteen hours, sate like a stag among hounds at the *bay*, and was sieged and fought with, in turn, by fifteen great ships. *Bacon's War with Spain.*

Fair liberty pursu'd, and meant a prey
To lawless power, here turn'd, and stood at *bay.* *Denham.*

Nor flight was left, nor hopes to force his way;
Embolden'd by despair, he stood at *bay*;
Resolv'd on death, he dissipates his fears,
And bounds aloft against the pointed spears. *Dryden's Æneid.*

All, fir'd with noble emulation, strive;
And, with a storm of darts, to distance drive
The Trojan chief; who held at *bay*, from far
On his Vulcanian orb, sustain'd the war. *Dryden's Virgil.*

We have now, for ten years together, turned the whole force and expence of the war, where the enemy was best able to hold us at a *bay.* *Swift.*

He stands at *bay*,
And puts his last weak refuge in despair. *Thomson.*

BAY. *n. s.* In architecture, a term used to signify the magnitude of a building; as if a barn consists of a floor and two heads, where they lay corn, they call it a barn of two *bays.* These *bays* are from fourteen to twenty feet long, and floors, from ten to twelve broad, and usually twenty feet long, which is the breadth of the barn. *Builder's Dict.*

If this law hold in Vienna ten years, I'll rent the fairest house in it after threepence a *bay.* *Shakesp. Meas. for Meas.*

There may be kept one thousand bushels in each *bay*, there being sixteen *bays*, each eighteen foot long, about seventeen wide, or three hundred square feet in each *bay.* *Mortimer.*

BAY *Tree.* [*laurus*, Lat.] This tree hath a flower of one leaf, shaped like a funnel, and divided into four or five segments. The male flowers, which are produced on separate trees from the female, have eight stamina, which are branched into arms; the ovary of the female flowers becomes a berry, inclosing a single seed within an horny shell, which is covered with a skin. The species are, 1. The common *bay* with male flowers. 2. The common fruit bearing *bay tree.* 3. The gold striped *bay tree*, &c. The first and second sorts are old inhabitants of the English gardens; and as there are varieties obtained from the same seeds, they are promiscuously cultivated, and are not to be distinguished asunder until they have produced flowers. These plants are propagated either from seeds, or by laying down the tender branches, which will take root in one year's time. *Mill.*

I have seen the wicked in great power, and spreading himself like a green *bay tree.* *Psalm* xxxvii 35.

BAY. *n. s.* A poetical name for an honorary crown or garland, bestowed as a prize for any kind of victory or excellence.

Beneath his reign shall Eusden wear the *bays.* *Pope.*

To BAY. *v. n.* [*abboyer*, Fr.]

1. To bark as a dog at a thief, or at the game which he pursues.

And all the while she stood upon the ground,
The wakeful dogs did never cease to *bay.* *Fairy Queen, b.* i.

The

The hounds at nearer diſtance hoarſely *bay'd*;
The hunter cloſe purſu'd the viſionary maid;
She rent the heav'n with loud laments, imploring aid.
Dryden's Fables.

2. [from *bay*, an incloſed place.] To encompaſs about; to ſhut in.
We are at the ſtake,
And *bay'd* about with many enemies. *Shakeſp. Julius Cæſar.*

To Bay. *v. a.* To follow with barking; to bark at.
I was with Hercules and Cadmus once,
When in the wood of Crete they *bay'd* the bear
With hounds of Sparta. *Shakeſp. Midſum. Night's Dream.*
If he ſhould do ſo,
He leaves his back unarm'd, the French and Welch
Baying him at the heels. *Shak. Henry* IV.

Bay *Salt.* Salt made of ſea water, which receives its conſiſtence from the heat of the ſun, and is ſo called from its brown colour. The greateſt quantities of this ſalt are made in France, on the coaſt of Bretagne, Saintonge, &c. from the middle of May to the end of Auguſt, by letting the ſea water into ſquare pits or baſons, where its ſurface being ſtruck and agitated by the rays of the ſun, it thickens at firſt imperceptibly, and becomes covered over with a ſlight cruſt, which hardening by the continuance of the heat, is wholly converted into ſalt. The water in this condition is ſcalding hot, and the cryſtallization is perfected in eight, ten, or at moſt fifteen days. *Chamb.*

All eruptions of air, though ſmall and ſlight, give ſound, which we call crackling, puffing, ſpitting, &c. as in *bay ſalt* and bay leaves caſt into the fire. *Bacon's Nat. Hiſtory*, N° 123.

Bay *Window.* A window jutting outward, and therefore forming a kind of bay or hollow in the room.

It hath *bay windows* tranſparent as barricadoes.
Shakeſp. Twelfth Night.

Bay *Yarn.* A denomination ſometimes uſed promiſcuouſly with woollen yarn. *Chambers.*

Ba'yard. *n. ſ.* [from *bay.*] A bay horſe.

Ba'yonet. *n. ſ.* [*bayonette*, Fr.] A ſhort ſword or dagger fixed at the end of a muſket, by which the foot hold off the horſe.

One of the black ſpots is long and ſlender, and reſembles a dagger or *bayonet.* *Woodward on Foſſils.*

Bayze. See Baize.

BDE'LLIUM. *n. ſ.* [βδέλλιον; בדלה.] An aromatick gum brought from the Levant, uſed as a medicine and a perfume. *Bdellium* is mentioned both by the ancient naturaliſts and in ſcripture; but it is doubtful whether any of theſe be the ſame with the modern kind. *Chambers.*

This *bdellium* is a tree of the bigneſs of an olive, whereof Arabia hath great plenty, which yieldeth a certain gum, ſweet to ſmell to, but bitter in taſte, called alſo *bdellium.* The Hebrews take the loadſtone for *bdellium.* *Raleigh's Hiſtory.*

To BE. *v. n.* [This word is ſo remarkably irregular, that it is neceſſary to ſet down many of its terminations.
Preſent. *I am*, *thou art*, *he is*, *we are*, &c.
eom, eaꞃꞇ, iꞅ, aꞃon, Sax.
Preter. *I was*, *thou wert*, *he was*, *we were*, &c.
ƿæꞅ, ƿæꞃe, ƿaꞅ, ƿæꞃon, Sax.
The conjunctive mood.
I be, *thou beeſt*, *he be*, *we be*, &c.
beo, biꞅꞇ, beo, beon, Sax.]

1. To have ſome certain ſtate, condition, quality, or accident; as, the man *is* wiſe.
Seventy ſenators died
By their proſcriptions, Cicero *being* one. *Shakeſp. J. Cæſar.*
He hath to night *been* in unuſual pleaſure. *Macbeth.*
Be what thou hop'ſt to *be*, or what thou *art*,
Reſign to death, it *is* not worth enjoying. *Shakeſp. H.* VI.
Be but about
To ſay, ſhe's a goodly lady, and
The juſtice of your hearts will add thereto,
'Tis pity ſhe's not honeſt, honourable. *Shak. Winter's Tale.*

Let them ſhew the former things what they *be*, that we may conſider them. *Iſaiah*, xli. 22.
Therefore *be* ſure,
Thou, when the bridegroom with his feaſtful friends
Paſſes to bliſs at the mid hour of night,
Haſt gain'd thy entrance, virgin wiſe and pure. *Par. Reg.*

Is it not eaſy to diſcern what ſuch men would *be* at. *Stillingfl.*

To ſay a man has a clear idea of quantity, without knowing how great it *is*, *is* to ſay, he has the clear idea of the number of the ſands, who knows not how many they *be.* *Locke.*

2. It is the auxiliary verb by which the verb paſſive is formed.
The wine of life *is* drawn, and the meer lees
Is left this vault to brag of. *Shakeſp. Macbeth.*

3. To exiſt; to have exiſtence.
The times have *been*,
That when the brains were out the man would die. *Macbeth.*
Here ceaſe, ye pow'rs, and let your vengeance end,
Troy *is* no more, and can no more offend. *Dryden.*
All th' impoſſibilities, which poets
Count to extravagance of looſe deſcription,
Shall ſooner *be.* *Rowe's Ambitious Stepmother.*
To *be* contents his natural deſire;
He aſks no angel's wing, nor ſeraph's fire. *Pope's Eſſ. on M.*

4. To have ſomething by appointment or rule.

If all political power be derived only from Adam, and *be* to deſcend only to his ſucceſſive heirs, by the ordinance of God, and divine inſtitution, this is a right antecedent and paramount to all government. *Locke.*

BEACH. *n. ſ.* The ſhore; particularly that part that is daſhed by the waves; the ſtrand.
The fiſhermen, that walk upon the *beach*,
Appear like mice. *Shakeſp. King Lear.*
Deep to the rocks of hell, the gather'd *beach*
They faſten'd, and the mole immenſe wrought on,
Over the foaming deep. *Milton's Par. Loſt, b.* x. *l.* 299.

They find the waſhed amber further out upon the *beaches* and ſhores, where it has been longer expoſed. *Woodward on Foſſils.*

Be'ached. *adj.* [from *beach.*] Expoſed to the waves.
Timon hath made his everlaſting manſion
Upon the *beached* verge of the ſalt flood;
Which once a day, with his emboſſed froth,
The turbulent ſurge ſhall cover. *Shakeſp. Timon.*

Be'achy. *adj.* [from *beach.*] Having beaches.
Other times, to ſee
The *beachy* girdle of the ocean
Too wide for Neptune's hips. *Shakeſp. Henry* IV.

Be'acon. *n. ſ.* [beacon, Sax. from becn, a ſignal, and becnan, whence beckon, to make a ſignal.]

1. Something raiſed on an eminence, to be fired on the approach of an enemy, to alarm the country.
His blazing eyes, like two bright ſhining ſhields,
Did burn with wrath, and ſparkled living fire;
As two broad *beacons* ſet in open fields,
Send forth their flames. *Fairy Queen, b.* i.
Modeſt doubt is called
The *beacon* of the wiſe. *Shakeſp. Troilus and Creſſida.*

The king ſeemed to account of the deſigns of Perkin as a may-game; yet had given order for the watching of *beacons* upon the coaſts, and erecting more where they ſtood too thin. *Bacon's Henry* VII.
No flaming *beacons* caſt their blaze afar,
The dreadful ſignal of invaſive war. *Gay's Rural Sports*

2. Marks erected, or lights made in the night, to direct navigators in their courſes, and warm them from rocks, ſhallows and ſandbanks.

Bead. *n. ſ.* [beade, prayer, Saxon.]

1. Small globes or balls of glaſs or pearl, or other ſubſtance, ſtrung upon a thread, and uſed by the Romaniſts to count their prayers; from whence the phraſe to *tell beads*, or to be at one's *beads*, is to be at prayer.
That aged dame, the lady of the place,
Who all this while was buſy at her *beads.* *Fairy Q. b.* i.
Thy voice I ſeem in every hymn to hear,
With ev'ry *bead* I drop too ſoft a tear. *Pope's El. to Abel.*

2. Little balls worn about the neck for ornament.
With ſcarfs and fans, and double change of brav'ry,
With amber bracelets, *beads*, and all ſuch knav'ry.
Shakeſp. Taming of a Shrew.

3. Any globular bodies.
Thy ſpirit within thee hath been ſo at war,
That *beads* of ſweat have ſtood upon thy brow. *Sh. H.* IV.

Several yellow lumps of amber, almoſt like *beads*, with one ſide flat, had faſtened themſelves to the bottom. *Boyle.*

Bead *Tree.* [Azedarach.]

It hath pennated leaves like thoſe of the aſh; the flowers conſiſt of five leaves, which expand in form of a roſe; in the centre of the flower is a long fimbriated tube, containing the ſtyle; the fruit is roundiſh and fleſhy, containing a hard furrowed nut, divided into five cells, each containing one oblong broadiſh ſeed. The outſide pulp of the fruit in ſome countries is eaten; but the nut is, by religious perſons, bored through, and ſtrung as beads; whence it takes its name. It produces ripe fruits in Italy and Spain. *Millar.*

Be'adle. *n. ſ.* [bydel, Sax. a meſſenger; *bedeau*, Fr. *bedel*, Sp. *bedelle*, Dutch.]

1. A meſſenger or ſervitor belonging to a court. *Cowel.*

2. A petty officer in pariſhes, whoſe buſineſs it is to puniſh petty offenders.
A dog's obey'd in office.
Thou raſcal *beadle*, hold thy bloody hand:
Why doſt thou laſh that whore? *Shakeſp. King Lear.*

They ought to be taken care of in this condition, either by the *beadle* or the magiſtrate. *Spectator*, N° 130.
Their common loves, a lewd abandon'd pack,
The *beadle's* laſh ſtill flagrant on their back. *Prior.*

Be'adroll. *n. ſ.* [from *bead* and *roll.*] A catalogue of thoſe who are to be mentioned at prayers.

The king, for the better credit of his eſpials abroad, did uſe to have them curſed by name amongſt the *beadroll* of the king's enemies. *Bacon's Henry* VII.

Be'adsman. *n. ſ.* [from *bead* and *man.*] A man employed in praying, generally in praying for another.
An holy hoſpital,
In which ſeven *beadſmen*, that had vowed all
Their life to ſervice of high heaven's king. *Fairy Queen, b.* i.

In

In thy danger,
Commend thy grievance to my holy prayer;
For I will be thy *beadsman*, Valentine. *Sh. T. Gentl. of Ver.*

BE'AGLE. *n. ſ.* [*bigle*, Fr.] A ſmall hound with which hares are hunted.

The reſt were various huntings.
The graceful goddeſs was array'd in green;
About her feet were little *beagles* ſeen,
That watch'd with upward eyes the motions of their queen. *Dryden's Fables.*

To plains with well bred *beagles* we repair,
And trace the mazes of the circling hare. *Pope.*

BEAK. *n. ſ.* [*bec*, Fr. *pig*, Welch.]

1. The bill or horny mouth of a bird.

His royal bird
Prunes the immortal wing, and cloys his *beak*,
As when his god is pleas'd. *Shakeſp. Cymbeline.*

He ſaw the ravens with their horny *beaks*
Food to Elijah bringing. *Milton's Par. Regained, b.* ii.

The magpye, lighting on the ſtock,
Stood chatt'ring with inceſſant din,
And with her *beak* gave many a knock. *Swift.*

2. A piece of braſs like a beak, fixed at the head of the ancient gallies, with which they pierced their enemies.

With boiling pitch another, near at hand,
From friendly Sweden brought, the ſeams inſtops;
Which, well laid o'er, the ſalt ſea waves withſtand,
And ſhakes them from the riſing *beak* in drops. *Dryden.*

3. A beak is a little ſhoe, at the toe about an inch long, turned up and faſtened in upon the forepart of the hoof. *Farrier's D.*

4. Any thing ending in a point like a beak; as the ſpout of a cup; a prominence of land.

Cuddenbeak, from a well advanced promontory, which entitled it *beak*, taketh a proſpect of the river. *Carew's Survey.*

BE'AKED. *adj.* [from *beak.*] Having a beak; having the form of a beak.

And queſtion'd every guſt of rugged winds,
That blows from off each *beaked* promontory. *Milton.*

BE'AKER. *n. ſ.* [from *beak.*] A cup with a ſpout in the form of a bird's beak.

And into pikes and muſqueteers
Stampt *beakers*, cups and porringers. *Hudibras, cant.* ii.

With dulcet bev'rage this the *beaker* crown'd,
Fair in the midſt, with gilded cups around. *Pope's Odyſſey.*

BEAL. *n. ſ.* [*bolla*, Ital.] A whelk or pimple.

To BEAL. *v. n.* [from the noun.] To ripen; to gather matter, or come to a head, as a ſore does.

BEAM. *n. ſ.* [beam, Sax. a tree; ʒunnebeam, a ray of the ſun.]

1. The main piece of timber that ſupports the houſe.

A *beam* is the largeſt piece of wood in a building, which always lies croſs the building or the walls, ſerving to ſupport the principal rafters of the roof, and into which the feet of the principal rafters are framed. No building has leſs than two *beams*, one at each head. Into theſe, the girders of the garret floor are alſo framed; and if the building be of timber, the teazel-tenons of the poſts are framed. The proportions of *beams* in or near London, are fixed by act of parliament. A *beam* fifteen feet long, muſt be ſeven inches on each ſide its ſquare, and five on the other; if it be ſixteen feet long, one ſide muſt be eight inches, the other ſix; and ſo proportionable to their lengths. *Builder's Dict.*

The building of living creatures is like the building of a timber houſe; the walls and other parts have columns and *beams*, but the roof is tile, or lead, or ſtone. *Bacon's N. Hiſt.*

He heav'd, with more than human force, to move
A weighty ſtone, the labour of a team,
And rais'd from thence he reach'd the neighb'ring *beam*. *Dryd.*

2. Any large and long piece of timber: a *beam* muſt have more length than thickneſs, by which it is diſtinguiſhed from a block.

But Lycus, ſwifter,
Springs to the walls and leaves his foes behind,
And ſnatches at the *beam* he firſt can find. *Dryden's Æneid.*

3. That part of a balance, at the ends of which the ſcales are ſuſpended.

Poiſe the cauſe in juſtice' equal ſcales,
Whoſe *beam* ſtands ſure, whoſe rightful cauſe prevails. *Shakeſp. Henry* VI. *p.* ii.

If the length of the ſides in the balance, and the weights at the ends be both equal, the *beam* will be in a horizontal ſituation: but if either the weights alone be equal, or the diſtances alone, the *beam* will accordingly decline. *Wilk. Mathem. Mag.*

4. The horn of a ſtag.

And taught the woods to echo to the ſtream
His dreadful challenge, and his claſhing *beam*. *Denham.*

5. The pole of a chariot; that piece of wood which runs between the horſes.

Juturna heard, and ſeiz'd with mortal fear,
Forc'd from the *beam* her brother's charioteer. *Dryden.*

6. Among weavers, a cylindrical piece of wood belonging to the loom, on which the web is gradually rolled as it is wove.

The ſtaff of his ſpear was like a weaver's *beam*. 1 *Chr.* xi. 23.

7. The ray of light emitted from ſome luminous body, or received by the eye.

Let them preſent me death upon the wheel,
Or pile ten hills on the Tarpeian rock,
That the precipitation might downſtretch
Below the *beam* of ſight. *Shakeſp. Coriolanus.*

Pleaſing, yet cold, like Cynthia's ſilver *beam*. *Dryden.*

As heav'n's bleſt *beam* turns vinegar to ſour. *Pope.*

BEAM *of an anchor.* The ſtraight part or ſhank of an anchor, to which the hooks are faſtened.

BEAM *Compaſſes.* A wooden or braſs inſtrument, with ſliding ſockets, to carry ſeveral ſhifting points, in order to draw circles with very long radii; and uſeful in large projections, for drawing the furniture on wall dials. *Harris.*

To BEAM. *v. n.* [from the noun.] To emit rays or beams.

Each emanation of his fires
That *beams* on earth, each virtue he inſpires. *Pope.*

BEAM *Tree.* See WILDSERVICE, of which it is a ſpecies.

BE'AMY. *adj.* [from *beam.*]

1. Radiant; ſhining; emitting beams.

His double-biting axe, and *beamy* ſpear;
Each aſking a gigantick force to rear. *Dryden's Fables.*

All-ſeeing ſun!
Hide, hide in ſhameful night, thy *beamy* head. *Smith.*

2. Having horns or antlers.

Rouze from their deſert dens the briſtled rage
Of boars, and *beamy* ſtags in toils engage. *Dryden's Virgil.*

BEAN. *n. ſ.* [*faba*, Lat.]

It hath a papilionaceous flower, ſucceeded by a long pod, filled with large flat kidney-ſhaped ſeeds; the ſtalks are firm and hollow; the leaves grow by pairs, and are faſtened to a midrib. The ſpecies are, 1. The common garden *bean*. 2. The horſe *bean*. There are ſeveral varieties of the garden *beans*, differing either in colour or ſize. The principal ſorts which are cultivated in England, are the Mazagan, the ſmall Liſbon, the Spaniſh, the Tokay, the Sandwich, and Windſor *beans*. The Mazagan *bean* is brought from a ſettlement of the Portugueſe on the coaſt of Africa, of the ſame name; and is by far the beſt ſort to plant for an early crop, a great bearer, and alſo an excellent taſted *bean*. The broad Spaniſh, Tokay, Sandwich, and Windſor *beans* are for the latter crops. *Millar.*

His allowance of oats and *beans* for his horſe was greater than his journey required. *Swift.*

BEAN *Caper.* [*fabago.*]

The leaves of this plant are produced by pairs upon the ſame footſtalk, and the footſtalks grow oppoſite at the joints of the ſtalks; the cup of the flower conſiſts of five leaves; and the flowers have alſo five leaves, expanded like a roſe, with ſtamina ſurrounding the ſtyle, in the center of the flower cup. This ſtyle becomes a cylindrical fruit, five cornered, divided into five cells, each containing many flat ſeeds. *Millar.*

BEAN *Treſſel.* An herb.

To BEAR. *v. a.* pret. *I bore*, or *bare*; part. paſſ. *bore*, or *born*. [beoɲan, beɲan, Sax. *bairan*, Gothick. It is founded as *bare*, as the *are* in *care* and *dare.*]

1. This is a word uſed with ſuch latitude, that it is not eaſily explained.

We ſay to *bear* a burden, to *bear* ſorrow or reproach, to *bear* a name, to *bear* a grudge, to *bear* fruit, or to *bear* children. The word *bear* is uſed in very different ſenſes. *Watts's Logick.*

2. To carry as a burden.

They *bear* him upon the ſhoulder; they carry him and ſet him in his place. *Iſaiah*, xlvi. 7.

And Solomon had threeſcore and ten thouſand that *bare* burdens. 1 *Kings*, v. 15.

As an eagle ſtirreth up her neſt, fluttereth over her young, ſpreadeth abroad her wings, taketh them, *beareth* them on her wings. *Deuteronomy*, xxxii. 11.

We ſee ſome, who, we think, have *born* leſs of the burden, rewarded above ourſelves. *Decay of Piety.*

3. To convey or carry.

My meſſage to the ghoſt of Priam *bear*;
Tell him a new Achilles ſent thee there. *Dryden's Æneid.*

A gueſt like him, a Trojan gueſt before,
In ſhew of friendſhip, ſought the Spartan ſhore,
And raviſh'd Helen from her huſband *bore*. *Dryd.*

4. To carry as a mark of authority.

I do commit into your hand
Th' unſtained ſword that you have us'd to *bear*. *Shakeſp. Henry* IV. *p.* ii.

5. To carry as a mark of diſtinction.

He may not *bear* ſo fair and ſo noble an image of the divine glory, as the univerſe in its full ſyſtem. *Hale's Orig. of Mank.*

His pious brother, ſure the beſt
Who ever *bore* that name. *Dryden.*

The ſad ſpectators ſtiffen'd with their fears,
She ſees, and ſudden every limb ſhe ſmears;
Then each of ſavage beaſts the figure *bears*. *Garth.*

His ſupreme ſpirit or mind will *bear* its beſt reſemblance, when it repreſents the ſupreme infinite. *Cheyne's Phil. Prin.*

So we ſay, to *bear* arms in a coat.

6. To carry as in ſhow.

Look like the time; *bear* welcome in your eye,
Your hand, your tongue; look like the innocent flower,
But be the ſerpent under't. *Shakeſp. King Lear.*

7. To carry as in truſt.

He was a thief, and had the bag, and *bare* what was put therein. *John*, xii. 6.

8. To ſupport; to keep from falling.

Under colour of rooting out popery, the moſt effectual means to *bear* up the ſtate of religion may be removed, and ſo a way be made either for paganiſm, or for extreme barbariſm to enter. *Hooker, b.* iv. § 1.

And Samſon took hold of the two middle pillars, upon which the houſe ſtood, and on which it was *born* up. *Judges*, xvi. 29.

A religious hope does not only *bear* up the mind under her ſufferings, but makes her rejoice in them. *Addiſon. Spectat.*

Some power inviſible ſupports his ſoul,
And *bears* it up in all its wonted greatneſs. *Addiſon's Cato.*

9. To keep afloat.

The waters encreaſed, and *bare* up the ark, and it was lifted up above the earth. *Geneſis*, vii. 17.

10. To ſupport with proportionate ſtrength.

Animals that uſe a great deal of labour and exerciſe, have their ſolid parts more elaſtick and ſtrong; they can *bear*, and ought to have ſtronger food. *Arbuthnot on Aliments.*

11. To carry in the mind, as love, hate.

How did the open multitude reveal
The wond'rous love they *bear* him under hand!
Daniel's Civil War.

They *bare* great faith and obedience to the kings. *Bacon.*

Darah, the eldeſt *bears* a generous mind,
But to implacable revenge inclin'd. *Dryden's Aurengz.*

The coward *bore* the man immortal ſpite. *Dryden's Ovid.*

As for this gentleman, who is fond of her, ſhe *beareth* him an invincible hatred. *Swift.*

That inviolable love I *bear* to the land of my nativity, prevailed upon me to engage in ſo bold an attempt. *Swift.*

12. To endure, as pain, without ſinking.

It was not an enemy that reproached me, then I could have *born* it. *Pſalm* liv. 12.

13. To ſuffer; to undergo.

I have *born* chaſtiſements, I will not offend any more. *Job*, xxxiv. 31.

That which was torn of beaſts, I brought not unto thee, I *bare* the loſs of it; of my hand didſt thou require it. *Geneſis*, xxxi. 39.

14. To permit; to ſuffer without reſentment.

Not the gods, nor angry Jove will *bear*
Thy lawleſs wand'ring walks in upper air. *Dryd. Æneid.*

15. To be capable of; to admit.

To reject all orders of the church which men have eſtabliſhed, is to think worſe of the laws of men in this reſpect, than either the judgment of wiſe men alloweth, or the law of God itſelf will *bear*. *Hooker, b.* iii.

Being the ſon of one earl of Pembroke, and younger brother to another, who liberally ſupplied his expence, beyond what his annuity from his father would *bear*. *Clarendon.*

Give his thought either the ſame turn, if our tongue will *bear* it, or, if not, vary but the dreſs. *Dryden.*

Do not charge your coins with more uſes than they can *bear*. It is the method of ſuch as love any ſcience, to diſcover all others in it. *Addiſon on Medals.*

Had he not been eager to find miſtakes, he would not have ſtrained my words to ſuch a ſenſe as they will not *bear*. *Atterb.*

In all criminal caſes, the moſt favourable interpretation ſhould be put upon words that they poſſibly can *bear*. *Swift.*

16. To produce, as fruit.

There be ſome plants that *bear* no flower, and yet *bear* fruit: there be ſome that *bear* flowers, and no fruit: there be ſome that *bear* neither flowers nor fruit. *Bacon's Natural Hiſtory.*

They wing'd their flight aloft; then ſtooping low,
Perch'd on the double tree that *bears* the golden bough.
Dryden's Æneid.

Say, ſhepherd, ſay, in what glad ſoil appears
A wond'rous tree that ſacred monarchs *bears*. *Pope's Paſt.*

17. To bring forth, as a child.

The queen that *bore* thee,
Oftner upon her knees than on her feet,
Died every day ſhe liv'd. *Shakeſp. Macbeth.*

Ye know that my wife *bare* two ſons. *Geneſis*, xliv. 27.

What could that have done?
What could the muſe herſelf that Orpheus *bore*,
The muſe herſelf, for her enchanting ſon? *Milton.*

The ſame Æneas, whom fair Venus *bore*
To fam'd Anchiſes on th' Idean ſhore. *Dryden's Æneid.*

18. To give birth to.

Here dwelt the man divine whom Samos *bore*,
But now ſelf-baniſh'd from his native ſhore. *Dryden.*

19. To poſſeſs, as power or honour.

When vice prevails, and impious men *bear* ſway,
The poſt of honour is a private ſtation. *Addiſon's Cato.*

20. To gain; to win.

As it more concerns the Turk than Rhodes,
So may he with more facile queſtion *bear* it;
For that it ſtands not in ſuch warlike brace. *Shakeſp. Othello.*

Becauſe the Greek and Latin have ever *born* away the prerogative from all other tongues, they ſhall ſerve as touchſtones to make our trials by. *Camden.*

Some think to *bear* it by ſpeaking a great word, and being peremptory; and go on, and take by admittance that which they cannot make good. *Bacon.*

21. To maintain; to keep up.

He finds the pleaſure and credit of *bearing* a part in the converſation, and of hearing his reaſons approved. *Locke.*

22. To ſupport any thing good or bad.

I was carried on to obſerve, how they did *bear* their fortunes, and principally, how they did employ their times. *Bacon's Holy War.*

23. To exhibit.

Ye Trojan flames, your teſtimony *bear*,
What I perform'd and what I ſuffer'd there. *Dryden.*

24. To be anſwerable for.

If I bring him not unto thee, let me *bear* the blame for ever. *Geneſis*, xliii. 9.

O more than madmen! you yourſelves ſhall *bear*
The guilt of blood and ſacrilegious war. *Dryden.*

25. To ſupply.

What have you under your arm? Somewhat, that will *bear* your charges in your pilgrimage? *Dryden's Spaniſh Friar.*

26. To be the object of.

I'll be your father and your brother too;
Let me but *bear* your love, I'll bear your cares.
Shakeſp. Henry IV. *p.* ii.

27. To behave; to act in character.

Some good inſtruction give,
How I may *bear* me here. *Shakeſp. Tempeſt.*
Hath he *born* himſelf penitent in priſon?
Shakeſp. Meaſure for Meaſure.

28. To hold; to reſtrain.

Do you ſuppoſe the ſtate of this realm to be now ſo feeble, that it cannot *bear* off a greater blow than this? *Hayward.*

29. To impel; to urge; to puſh.

The reſidue were ſo diſordered as they could not conveniently fight or fly, and not only juſtled and *bore* down one another, but, in their confuſed tumbling back, brake a part of the avant-guard. *Sir J. Hayward.*

Contention, like a horſe
Full of high feeding, madly hath broke looſe,
And *bears* down all before him. *Shakeſp. Henry* IV. *p.* ii.

Their broken oars, and floating planks, withſtand
Their paſſage, while they labour to the land;
And ebbing tides *bear* back upon th' uncertain ſand.
Dryden's Æneid.

Now with a noiſeleſs gentle courſe
It keeps within the middle bed;
Anon it lifts aloft the head,
And *bears* down all before it with impetuous force. *Dryden.*

Truth is *born* down, atteſtations neglected, the teſtimony of ſober perſons deſpiſed. *Swift.*

The hopes of enjoying the abbey lands would ſoon *bear* down all conſiderations, and be an effectual incitement to their perverſion. *Swift.*

30. To conduct; to manage.

My hope is
So to *bear* through, and out, the conſulſhip,
As ſpite ſhall ne'er wound you, though it may me.
Ben. Johnſon's Catiline.

31. To preſs.

Cæſar doth *bear* me hard; but he loves Brutus.
Shakeſp. Julius Cæſar.

Though he *bear* me hard,
I yet muſt do him right. *Ben. Johnſon's Catiline.*

Theſe men *bear* hard upon the ſuſpected party, purſue her cloſe through all her windings. *Addiſon. Spectator*, N° 170.

32. To incite; to animate.

But confidence then *bore* thee on; ſecure
Either to meet no danger, or to find
Matter of glorious trial. *Milton's Par. Loſt, b.* i. *l.* 1175.

33. *To bear a body.* A colour is ſaid to *bear a body* in painting, when it is capable of being ground ſo fine, and mixing with the oil ſo entirely, as to ſeem only a very thick oil of the ſame colour.

34. *To bear date.* To carry the mark of the time when any thing was written.

35. *To bear a price.* To have a certain value.

36. *To bear in hand.* To amuſe with falſe pretences; to deceive.

Your daughter, whom ſhe *bore in hand* to love
With ſuch integrity, ſhe did confeſs,
Was as a ſcorpion to her ſight. *Shakeſp. Cymbeline.*

He griev'd,
That ſo his ſickneſs, age, and impotence,
Was falſely *born in hand*, ſends out arreſts
On Fortinbras. *Shakeſp. Hamlet.*

He repaired to Bruges, deſiring of the ſtates of Bruges, to enter

enter peaceably into their town, with a retinue fit for his eſtate; and *bearing* them *in hand*, that he was to communicate with them of divers matters of great importance, for their good. *Bacon's Henry* VII.

It is no wonder, that ſome would *bear* the world *in hand*, that the apoſtle's deſign and meaning is for preſbytery, though his words are for epiſcopacy. *South.*

37. *To bear off.* To carry away by force.

I will reſpect thee as a father, if
Thou *bear'ſt* my life *off* hence. *Shakeſp. Winter's Tale.*

The ſun views half the earth on either way,
And here brings on, and there *bears off* the day. *Creech.*

Give but the word, we'll ſnatch this damſel up,
And *bear* her *off*. *Addiſon's Cato.*

My ſoul grows deſperate.
I'll *bear* her *off*. *A. Philips's Diſtreſt Mother.*

38. *To bear out.* To ſupport; to maintain; to defend.

I hope your warrant will *bear out* the deed. *Shak. K. John.*

I can once or twice a quarter *bear out* a knave againſt an honeſt man. *Shakeſp. Henry* IV. *p.* ii.

Changes are never without danger, unleſs the prince be able to *bear out* his actions by power. *Sir J. Hayward.*

Quoth Sidrophel, I do not doubt
To find friends that will *bear* me *out*. *Hudibras.*

It is company only that can *bear* a man *out* in an ill thing. *South.*

I doubted whether that occaſion could *bear* me *out* in the confidence of giving your ladyſhip any further trouble. *Temple.*

To Bear. *v. n.*

1. To ſuffer pain.

Stranger, ceaſe thy care;
Wiſe is the ſoul; but man is born to *bear*:
Jove weighs affairs of earth in dubious ſcales,
And the good ſuffers while the bad prevails. *Pope's Odyſſey.*

2. To be patient.

I cannot, cannot *bear*; 'tis paſt, 'tis done;
Periſh this impious, this deteſted ſon. *Dryden's Fables.*

3. To be fruitful or prolifick.

A fruit tree hath been blown up almoſt by the roots, and ſet up again, and the next year *bear* exceedingly. *Bacon.*

Betwixt two ſeaſon comes th' auſpicious air,
This age to bloſſom, and the next to *bear*. *Dryden.*

Melons on beds of ice are taught to *bear*,
And, ſtrangers to the ſun, yet ripen here. *Granville.*

4. To take effect; to ſucceed.

Having pawned a full ſuit of cloaths for a ſum of money, which, my operator aſſured me, was the laſt he ſhould want to bring all our matters to *bear*. *Guardian*, Nº 166.

5. To act in character.

Inſtruct me
How I may formally in perſon *bear*,
Like a true friar. *Shakeſp. Meaſure for Meaſure.*

6. To tend; to be directed to any point.

The oily drops ſwimming on the ſpirit of wine, moved reſtleſly to and fro, ſometimes *bearing* up to one another, as if all were to unite into one body, and then falling off, and continuing to ſhift places. *Boyle.*

Never did men more joyfully obey,
Or ſooner underſtood the ſign to fly:
With ſuch alacrity they *bore* away. *Dryden's Annus Mirab.*

Whoſe navy like a ſtiff-ſtretch'd cord did ſhew,
Till he *bore* in, and bent them into flight. *Dryden.*

On this the hero fix'd an oak in ſight,
The mark to guide the mariners aright:
To *bear* with this, the ſeamen ſtretch their oars,
Then round the rock they ſteer, and ſeek the former ſhores. *Dryden's Æneid.*

In a convex mirrour, we view the figures and all other things, which *bear* out with more life and ſtrength than nature itſelf. *Dryden's Dufreſnoy.*

7. To act as an impellent, or as a reciprocal power; generally with the particles *upon* or *againſt*.

We were encounter'd by a mighty rock,
Which being violently *born upon*,
Our helpleſs ſhip was ſplitted in the midſt. *Shakeſpeare.*

Upon the tops of mountains, the air which *bears againſt* the reſtagnant quickſilver, is leſs preſſed. *Boyle.*

The ſides *bearing* one *againſt* the other, they could not lie ſo cloſe at the bottoms. *Burnet's Theory of the Earth.*

As a lion bounding in his way,
With force augmented *bears againſt* his prey,
Sideling to ſeize. *Dryden's Fables.*

Becauſe the operations to be performed by the teeth, require a conſiderable ſtrength in the inſtruments which move the lower jaw, nature hath provided this with ſtrong muſcles, to make it *bear* forcibly *againſt* the upper jaw. *Ray.*

The weight of the body doth *bear* moſt *upon* the knee-joints, in raiſing itſelf up, and moſt *upon* the muſcles of the thighs, in coming down. *Wilkins's Mathematical Magick.*

The waves of the ſea *bear* violently and rapidly *upon* ſome ſhores, the waters being pent up by the land. *Broome on the Odyſſey.*

8. To act upon.

Spinola, with his ſhot, did *bear upon* thoſe within, who appeared upon the walls. *Hayward.*

9. To be ſituated with reſpect to other places.

10. *To bear up.* To ſtand firm without falling.

So long as nature
Will *bear up* with this exerciſe, ſo long
I daily vow to uſe it. *Shakeſp. Winter's Tale.*

Perſons in diſtreſs may ſpeak of themſelves with dignity; it ſhews a greatneſs of ſoul, that they *bear up* againſt the ſtorms of fortune. *Broome's Notes on the Odyſſey.*

The conſciouſneſs of integrity, the ſenſe of a life ſpent in doing good, will enable a man to *bear up* under any change of circumſtances. *Atterbury.*

When our commanders and ſoldiers were raw and unexperienced, we loſt battles and towns; yet we *bore up* then, as the French do now; nor was there any thing deciſive in their ſucceſſes. *Swift.*

11. *To bear with.* To endure an unpleaſing thing.

They are content to *bear with* my abſence and folly. *Sidney.*

Though I muſt be content to *bear with* thoſe that ſay you are reverend grave men; yet they lie deadly, that tell you, you have good faces. *Shakeſp. Coriolanus.*

Look you lay home to him;
Tell him his pranks have been too broad to *bear with.* *Shakeſp. Hamlet.*

Bear with me then, if lawful what I aſk. *Paradiſe Loſt.*

BEAR. *n. ſ.* [bena, Saxon.]

1. A rough ſavage animal.

Every part of the body of theſe animals is covered with thick ſhaggy hair, of a dark brown colour, and their claws are hooked, which they uſe in climbing trees. They feed upon fruits, honey, bees, and fleſh. Some have falſely reported, that *bears* bring their young into the world ſhapeleſs, and that their dams lick them into form. The dams go no longer than thirty days, and generally produce five young ones. In the winter, they lie hid and aſleep, the male forty days, and the female four months; and ſo ſoundly for the firſt fourteen days, that blows will not wake them. In the ſleepy ſeaſon, they are ſaid to have no nouriſhment but from licking their feet; for it is certain they eat nothing, and, at the end of it, the males are very fat. This animal has naturally an hideous look, but when enraged it is terrible; and, as rough and ſtupid as it ſeems to be, it is capable of diſcipline; it leaps, dances, and plays a thouſand little tricks at the ſound of a trumpet. The fleſh of *bears* was much eſteemed by the ancients. They abound in Poland, Muſcovy, Lithuania, and the great foreſts in Germany; and alſo in the remote northern countries, where the ſpecies is white. *Calmet.*

Call hither to the ſtake my two brave *bears*,
Bid Saliſbury and Warwick come to me.—
—Are theſe thy *bears*? we'll bait thy *bears* to death,
And manacle the bearward in their chains. *Shak. Henry* VI.

Thou'dſt ſhun a *bear*;
But if thy flight lay tow'rd the roaring ſea,
Thou'dſt meet the *bear* i' th' mouth. *Shakeſp. King Lear.*

2. The name of two conſtellations, called the *greater* and *leſſer bear*; in the tail of the *leſſer bear*, is the pole ſtar.

E'en then when Troy was by the Greeks o'erthrown,
The *bear* oppos'd to bright Orion ſhone. *Creech.*

Bear-bind. *n. ſ.* A ſpecies of bindweed; which ſee.

Bear-fly. *n. ſ.* [from *bear* and *fly*.] An inſect.

There be of flies, caterpillars, canker-flies, and *bear-flies*. *Bacon's Natural Hiſtory.*

Bear-garden. *n. ſ.* [from *bear* and *garden.*]

1. A place in which bears are kept for ſport.

Hurrying me from the playhouſe, and the ſcenes there, to the *bear-garden*, to the apes, and aſſes, and tygers. *Stillingfl.*

I could not forbear going to a place of renown for the gallantry of Britons, namely to the *bear-garden*. *Spect.* Nº 436.

2. Any place of tumult or miſrule.

Bear-garden. *adj.* A word uſed in familiar or low phraſe for *rude* or *turbulent*; as, a *bear-garden fellow*; that is, a man rude enough to be a proper frequenter of the bear-garden. *Bear-garden ſport*, is uſed for groſs inelegant entertainment.

Bear's-breech. *n. ſ.* [*acanthus.*] The name of a plant.

The leaves are like thoſe of the thiſtle; the flowers labiated; the under lip of the flower is divided into three ſegments, which, in the beginning, is curled up in the form of a tube; in the place of the under lip are produced the ſtamina, which ſupport the pointals; the cup of the flowers is compoſed of prickly leaves, the upper part of which is bent over, like an arch, and ſupplies the defect of the upper lip of the flower; the fruit is of an oval form, divided in the middle into two cells, each containing one ſmooth ſeed. The ſpecies are, 1. The ſmooth-leaved garden *bear's-breech*. 2. The prickly *bear's-breech*. 3. The middle *bear's-breech*, with ſhort ſpines, &c. The firſt is uſed in medicine, and is ſuppoſed to be the *mollis acanthus* of Virgil. The leaves of this plant are cut upon the capitals of the Corinthian pillars, and were formerly in great eſteem with the Romans. They are eaſily propagated by paring the roots in February or March, or by the ſeeds ſown at the ſame time. *Millar.*

BEAR'S-EAR, or *Auricula*. [*auricula ursi*, Lat.] The name of a plant.

It hath a perennial root; the leaves are thicker and smoother than those of the primrose; the cup of the flower is shorter, so that the tube appears naked; the flower is shaped like a funnel; the upper part is expanded, and divided into five segments; this is succeeded by a globular seed-vessel, containing many small seeds; every year it produces vast quantities of new flowers, differing in shape, size, or colour; and there is likewise a great variety in the leaves of these plants. They flower in April, and ripen their seeds in June. *Millar.*

BEAR'S-EAR, or *Sanicle*. [*cortusa*, Lat.]

This plant hath a perennial root; the leaves are roundish, rough, and crenated on the edges, like those of ground ivy; the cup of the flower is small, and divided into six parts; the flowers are shaped, like a funnel, cut at the top into many segments, and disposed in an umbel; the fruit is roundish, terminating in a point, and is closely fixt in the cup, in which are contained many small angular seeds. We have but one species of this plant, which is nearly allied to the *auricula ursi*; but the flowers are not quite so large and fair. It loses its leaves in winter, but puts out new ones early in the spring; and, in April, it produces flowers, which are sometimes succeeded by seed pods; but it is very rare that they perfect their seeds with us. *Millar.*

BEAR'S-FOOT. *n. s.* See HELLEBORE, of which it is a species.

BEAR'S-WORT. *n. s.* An herb.

BEARD. *n. s.* [beaꝛb, Saxon.]

1. The hair that grows on the lips and chin.

Ere on thy chin the springing *beard* began
To spread a doubtful down, and promise man. *Prior.*

2. *Beard* is used for the face; as, to do any thing to a man's *beard*, is to do it in defiance, or to his face.

Rail'd at their covenant, and jeer'd
Their rev'rend parsons to my *beard*. *Hudibras.*

3. *Beard* is used to mark age or virility; as, he has a long *beard*, means he is old.

This ancient ruffian, Sir, whose life I have spared at suit of his grey *beard*. *Shakesp. K. Lear.*

Some thin remains of chastity appear'd,
Ev'n under Jove, but Jove without a *beard*. *Dryden.*

Would it not be an insufferable thing, for a professor to have his authority, of forty years standing, confirmed by general tradition, and a reverend *beard*, overturned by an upstart novelist? *Locke.*

4. Sharp prickles growing upon the ears of corn.

The ploughman lost his sweat, and the green corn
Hath rotted ere its youth attain'd a *beard*.
Shakesp. Midsummer Night's Dream.

A certain farmer complained, that the *beards* of his corn cut the reapers and threshers fingers. *L'Estrange.*

5. A barb on an arrow.

6. The *beard* or chuck of a horse, is that part which bears the curb of the bridle. *Farrier's Dict.*

To BEARD. *v. a.* [from *beard*.]

1. To take or pluck by the beard, in contempt or anger.

No man so potent breathes upon the ground,
But I will *beard* him. *Shakesp. Henry IV. p. i.*

2. To oppose to the face; to set at open defiance.

He, whensoever he should swerve from duty, may be able to *beard* him. *Spenser's State of Ireland.*

The design of utterly extirpating monarchy and episcopacy, the presbyterians alone begun, continued, and would have ended, if they had not been *bearded* by that new party, with whom they could not agree about dividing the spoil. *Swift.*

BE'ARDED. *adj.* [from *beard*.]

1. Having a beard.

Think every *bearded* fellow, that's but yok'd,
May draw with you. *Shakesp. Othello.*

Old prophecies foretel our fall at hand,
When *bearded* men in floating castles land. *Dryden.*

2. Having sharp prickles, as corn.

As when a field
Of Ceres, ripe for harvest, waving bends
Her *bearded* grove of ears, which way the wind
Sways them. *Milton's Paradise Lost, b. iv. l. 982.*

The fierce virago
Flew o'er the fields, nor hurt the *bearded* grain. *Dryden.*

3. Barbed or jagged.

Thou shouldst have pull'd the secret from my breast,
Torn out the *bearded* steel to give me rest. *Dryd. Aurengz.*

BE'ARDLESS. *adj.* [from *beard*.]

1. Without a beard.

There are extant some coins of Cunobelin, king of Essex and Middlesex, with a *beardless* image, inscribed *Cunobelin*.
Cambden's Remains.

2. Youthful.

And, as young striplings wheep the top for sport,
On the smooth pavement of an empty court,
The wooden engine flies and whirls about,
Admir'd with clamours of the *beardless* rout. *Dryden.*

BE'ARER. *n. s.* [from *to bear*.]

1. A carrier of any thing, who conveys any thing from one place or person to another.

He should the *bearers* put to sudden death,
Not shriving time allow'd. *Shakesp. Hamlet.*

Forgive the *bearer* of unhappy news;
Your alter'd father openly pursues
Your ruin. *Dryden's Aurengzebe.*

No gentleman sends a servant with a message, without endeavouring to put it into terms brought down to the capacity of the *bearer*. *Swift.*

2. One employed in carrying burthens.

And he set threescore and ten thousand of them to be *bearers* of burdens. *2 Chron. ii. 18.*

3. One who wears any thing.

O majesty!
When thou dost pinch thy *bearer*, thou dost sit
Like a rich armour worn in heat of day,
That scalds with safety. *Shakesp. Henry IV. p. ii.*

4. One who carries the body to the grave.

5. A tree that yields its produce.

This way of procuring autumnal roses, in some that are good *bearers*, will succeed. *Boyle.*

Reprune apricots and peaches, saving as much of the young likeliest shoots as are well placed; for the raw *bearers* commonly perish the new ones succeeding. *Evelyn's Kalendar.*

6. In architecture. A post or brick wall raised up between the ends of a piece of timber, to shorten its bearing; or to prevent its bearing with the whole weight at the ends only.

7. In heraldry. See SUPPORTER.

BE'ARHERD. *n. s.* [from *bear* and *herd*; as *shepherd*, from *sheep*.] A man that tends bears.

He that is more than a youth, is not for me; and he that is less than a man, I am not for him; therefore I will even take sixpence in earnest of the *bearherd*, and lead his apes into hell.
Shakesp. Much ado about Nothing.

BE'ARING. *n. s.* [from *bear*.]

1. The site or place of any thing with respect to something else.

But of this frame, the *bearings* and the ties,
The strong connections, nice dependencies,
Gradations just, has thy pervading soul
Look'd through? or can a part contain the whole? *Pope.*

2. Gesture; mien; behaviour.

That is Claudio; I know him by his *bearing*.
Shakesp. Much ado about Nothing.

3. In architecture. *Bearing* of a piece of timber, with carpenters, is the space either between the two fixt extremes thereof, or between one extreme and a post, brick-wall, &c. trimmed up between the ends, to shorten its *bearing*. *Builder's Dict.*

BE'ARWARD. *n. s.* [from *bear* and *ward*.] A keeper of bears.

We'll bait thy bears to death,
And manacle the *bearward* in their chains. *Shak. Henry VI.*

The bear is led after one manner, the multitude after another; the *bearward* leads but one brute, and the mountebank leads a thousand. *L'Estrange.*

BEAST. *n. s.* [*beste*, Fr. *bestia*, Lat.]

1. An animal distinguished from birds, insects, fishes, and man.

The man that once did sell the lion's skin,
While the *beast* liv'd, was kill'd with hunting him. *Shakesp.*

Beasts of chase are the buck, the doe, the fox, the martern, and the roe. *Beasts* of the forest are the hart, the hind, the hare, the boar, and the wolf. *Beasts* of warren are the hare and cony. *Cowel.*

2. An irrational animal, opposed to man; as man and *beast*.

I dare do all that may become a man;
Who dares do more, is none.——
——What *beast* was't then
That made you break this enterprize to me? *Macbeth.*

Medea's charms were there, Circean feasts,
With bowls that turn'd enamour'd youths to *beasts*. *Dryden.*

3. A brutal savage man, a man acting in any manner unworthy of a reasonable creature.

BE'ASTINGS. See BEESTINGS.

BE'ASTLINESS. *n. s.* [from *beastly*.] Brutality; practice of any kind contrary to the rules of humanity.

They held this land, and with their filthiness
Polluted this same gentle soil long time;
That their own mother loath'd their *beastliness*,
And 'gan abhor her brood's unkindly crime. *Fairy Queen.*

BE'ASTLY. *adj.* [from *beast*.]

1. Brutal; contrary to the nature and dignity of man. It is used commonly as a term of reproach.

Wouldst thou have thyself fall in the confusion of men, or remain a beast with beasts?—Ay—a *beastly* ambition. *Shakesp.*

You *beastly* knave, know you no reverence? *King Lear.*

With lewd, prophane, and *beastly* phrase,
To catch the world's loose laughter or vain gaze. *B. Johns.*

Vain idols,

It is commonly charged upon the gentlemen of the army, that the *beastly* vice of drinking to excess, hath been lately, from their example, restored among us. *Swift.*

2. Having the nature or form of beasts.

Beastly divinities, and droves of gods. *Prior.*

To BEAT. *v. a.* preter. *beat*, part. paſſ. *beat*, or *beaten*. [*battre*, French.]

1. To ſtrike; to knock; to lay blows upon.

So fight I, not as one that *beateth* the air. 1 *Cor.* ix. 26.

He rav'd with all the madneſs of deſpair;
He roar'd, he *beat* his breaſt, he tore his hair. *Dryden.*

2. To puniſh with ſtripes or blows.

They've choſe a conſul that will from them take
Their liberties; make them of no more voice
Than dogs, that are as often *beat* for barking,
And therefore kept to do ſo. *Shakeſp. Coriolanus.*

Miſtreſs Ford, good heart, is *beaten* black and blue, that you cannot ſee a white ſpot about her. *Shakeſp. M. Wives of Windſ.*

There is but one fault for which children ſhould be *beaten*; and that is obſtinacy or rebellion. *Locke.*

3. To ſtrike an inſtrument of muſick.

Bid them come forth and hear,
Or at their chamber door I'll *beat* the drum,
Till it cry, ſleep to death. *Shakeſp. King Lear.*

4. To break to powder, or comminute by blows.

The people gathered manna, and ground it in mills, or *beat* it in a mortar, and baked it. *Numbers*, xi. 8.

They did *beat* the gold into thin plates, and cut it into wires, to work it. *Exodus*, xxxix. 3.

They ſave the laborious work of *beating* of hemp, by making the axletree of the main wheel of their corn mills longer than ordinary, and placing of pins in them, to raiſe large hammers like thoſe uſed for paper and fulling mills, with which they *beat* moſt of their hemp. *Mortimer's Husbandry.*

Neſtor, we ſee, furniſhed the gold, and he *beat* it into leaves, ſo that he had occaſion to make uſe of his anvil and hammer. *Broome's Notes on the Odyſſey.*

5. To ſtrike buſhes or ground, or make a motion to rouze game.

It is ſtrange how long ſome men will lie in wait to ſpeak, and how many other matters they will *beat* over to come near it. *Bacon's Eſſays.*

When from the cave thou riſeſt with the day,
To *beat* the woods, and rouze the bounding prey. *Prior.*

Together let us *beat* this ample field,
Try what the open, what the covert yield. *Pope.*

6. To threſh; to drive the corn out of the huſk.

She gleaned in the field, and *beat* out that ſhe had gleaned. *Ruth*, ii. 17.

7. To mix things by long and frequent agitation.

By long *beating* the white of an egg, you may bring it into white curds. *Boyle.*

8. To batter with engines of war.

And he *beat* down the tower of Penuel, and ſlew the men of the city. *Judges*, viii. 17.

9. To daſh, as water, or bruſh as wind.

Beyond this flood a frozen continent
Lies dark and wild; *beat* with perpetual ſtorms
Of whirlwind and dire hail. *Milt. Paradiſe Loſt*, *b.* ii.

With tempeſts *beat*, and to the winds a ſcorn. *Roſcommon.*

While winds and ſtorms his lofty forehead *beat*,
The common fate of all that's high or great. *Denham.*

As when a lion in the midnight hours,
Beat by rude blaſts, and wet with wintry ſhow'rs,
Deſcends terrifick from the mountain's brow. *Pope.*

10. To tread a path.

While I this unexampled taſk eſſay,
Paſs awful gulfs, and *beat* my painful way,
Celeſtial dove, divine aſſiſtance bring. *Blackmore.*

11. To make a path by marking it with tracks.

He that will know the truth of things, muſt leave the common and *beaten* track. *Locke.*

12. To conquer; to ſubdue; to vanquiſh.

If Hercules and Lichas play at dice,
Which is the better man? The greater throw
May turn by fortune from the weaker hand:
So is Alcides *beaten* by his page. *Shakeſp. Merchant of Venice.*

You ſouls of geeſe,
That bear the ſhapes of men, how have you run
From ſlaves that apes would *beat?* *Shakeſp. Coriolanus.*

Five times, Marcius,
I have fought with thee, ſo often haſt thou *beat* me. *Shakeſp.*

I have diſcern'd the foe ſecurely lie,
Too proud to fear a *beaten* enemy. *Dryden's Indian Emp.*

The common people of Lucca are firmly perſuaded, that one Lucqueſe can *beat* five Florentines. *Addiſon on Italy.*

Pyrrhus, king of Epirus, joining his ſhips to thoſe of the Syracuſans, *beat* the Carthaginians at ſea. *Arbuthnot on Coins.*

13. To harraſs; to over-labour.

It is no point of wiſdom for a man to *beat* his brains, and ſpend his ſpirits about things impoſſible. *Hakewell on Providence.*

And as in priſons mean rogues beat
Hemp, for the ſervice of the great;
So Whacum *beat* his dirty brains
T' advance his maſter's fame and gains. *Hudibras.*

I know not why any one ſhould waſte his time, and *beat* his head about the Latin grammar, who does not intend to be a critick. *Locke.*

14. To lay, or preſs, as ſtanding corn by hard weather.

Her own ſhall bleſs her;
Her foes ſhake, like a field of *beaten* corn,
And hang their heads with ſorrow. *Shakeſp. Henry VIII.*

15. To depreſs; to cruſh by repeated oppoſition; uſually with the particle *down*.

Albeit a pardon was proclaimed, touching any ſpeech tending to treaſon, yet could not the boldneſs be *beaten down* either with that ſeverity, or with this lenity be abated. *Hayward.*

Our warriours propagating the French language, at the ſame time they are *beating down* their power. *Addiſon. Spect.* N° 165.

Such an unlook'd for ſtorm of ills falls on me,
It *beats down* all my ſtrength. *Addiſon's Cato.*

16. To drive by violence.

Twice have I ſally'd, and was twice *beat* back. *Dryden.*

He that proceeds upon other principles in his inquiry, does at leaſt poſt himſelf in a party, which he will not quit, till he be *beaten* out. *Locke.*

He cannot *beat* it out of his head, but that it was a cardinal who picked his pocket. *Addiſon. Freeholder*, N° 44.

The younger part of mankind might be *beat* off from the belief of the moſt important points even of natural religion, by the impudent jeſts of a profane wit. *Watts's Impr. of the Mind.*

17. To move with fluttering agitation.

Thrice have I *beat* the wing, and rid with night
About the world. *Dryden's State of Innocence.*

18. *To beat down.* To endeavour by treaty to leſſen the price demanded.

Surveys rich moveables with curious eye,
Beats down the price, and threatens ſtill to buy. *Dryden.*

She perſuaded him to truſt the renegado with the money he had brought over for their ranſom; as not queſtioning but he would *beat down* the terms of it. *Addiſon. Spectat.* N° 199.

19. *To beat down.* To ſink or leſſen the value.

Uſury *beats down* the price of land; for the employment of money is chiefly either merchandizing or purchaſing; and uſury way-lays both. *Bacon's Eſſays*, N° 42.

20. *To beat up.* To attack ſuddenly; to alarm.

They lay in that quiet poſture, without making the leaſt impreſſion upon the enemy, by *beating up* his quarters, which might eaſily have been done. *Clarendon, b.* viii.

Will. fancies he ſhould never have been the man he is, had not he broke windows, knocked down conſtables, and *beat up* a lewd woman's quarters, when he was a young fellow. *Addiſ.*

21. *To beat the hoof.* To walk; to go on foot.

To Beat. *v. n.*

1. To move in a pulſatory manner.

I would gladly underſtand the formation of a ſoul, and ſee it *beat* the firſt conſcious pulſe. *Collier on Thought.*

2. To daſh, as a flood or ſtorm.

This publick envy ſeemeth to *beat* chiefly upon miniſters. *Bacon's Eſſays*, N° 9.

Your brow, which does no fear of thunder know,
Sees rowling tempeſts vainly *beat* below. *Dryden.*

And one ſees many of the like hollow ſpaces worn in the bottoms of the rocks, as they are more or leſs able to reſiſt the impreſſions of the water that *beats* againſt them. *Addiſon.*

3. To knock at a door.

The men of the city beſet the houſe round about, and *beat* at the door, and ſpake to the maſter of the houſe. *Judg.* xix. 22.

4. To move with frequent repetitions of the ſame act or ſtroke.

No pulſe ſhall keep
His nat'ral progreſs, but ſurceaſe to *beat*. *Sh. Rom. and Jul.*

My temp'rate pulſe does regularly *beat*;
Feel, and be ſatisfy'd. *Dryden's Perſius, Sat.* iii.

A man's heart *beats*, and the blood circulates, which it is not in his power, by any thought or volition, to ſtop. *Locke.*

5. To throb; to be in agitation, as a ſore ſwelling.

A turn or two I'll walk,
To ſtill my *beating* mind. *Shakeſp. Tempeſt.*

6. To fluctuate; to be in agitation.

The tempeſt in my mind
Doth from my ſenſes take all feeling elſe,
Save what *beats* there. *Shakeſp. King Lear.*

7. To try different ways; to ſearch.

I am always *beating* about in my thoughts for ſomething that may turn to the benefit of my dear countrymen. *Addiſon. Guard.*

To find an honeſt man, I *beat* about,
And love him, court him, praiſe him in or out. *Pope.*

8. To act upon with violence.

The ſun *beat* upon the head of Jonah, that he fainted, and wiſhed in himſelf to die. *Jonah*, iv. 48.

9. To ſpeak frequently; to repeat; to enforce by repetition.

We are drawn on into a larger ſpeech, by reaſon of their ſo great earneſtneſs, who *beat* more and more upon theſe laſt alleged words. *Hooker, b.* ii. § 4.

How frequently and fervently doth the ſcripture *beat* upon this cauſe? *Hakewell on Providence.*

10. *To beat up*; as, to *beat up* for ſoldiers. The word *up* ſeems redundant.

Beat. *part. paſſive.* [from the verb.]

Like a rich veſſel *beat* by ſtorms to ſhore,
'Twere madneſs ſhould I venture out once more. *Dryden.*

BEAT. *n.ſ.* [from the verb.]

1. Stroke.

2. Manner of ſtriking.

Albeit the baſe and treble ſtrings of a viol be turned to an uniſon; yet the former will ſtill make a bigger or broader ſound than the latter, as making a broader *beat* upon the air. *Grew's Coſmologia Sacra, b.* ii. *c.* 2.

With a careleſs *beat*,
Struck out the mute creation at a heat. *Dryd. Hind and P.*

3. Manner of being ſtruck; as, the *beat* of the pulſe, or a drum.

BE'ATEN. *particip. adj.* [from *to beat.*]

What makes you, Sir, ſo late abroad,
Without a guide, and this no *beaten* road? *Dryd. W. of Bath.*

BE'ATER. *n.ſ.* [from *beat.*]

1. An inſtrument with which any thing is comminuted or mingled.

Beat all your mortar with a *beater* three or four times over, before you uſe it; for thereby you incorporate the ſand and lime well together. *Moxon's Mechanical Exerciſes.*

2. A perſon much given to blows.

The beſt ſchoolmaſter of our time, was the greateſt *beater.* *Aſcham's Schoolmaſter.*

BEATI'FICAL. } *adj.* [*beatificus*, low Lat. from *beatus*, happy.]
BEATI'FICK. } That which has the power of making happy, or compleating fruition; bliſsful. It is uſed only of heavenly fruition after death.

Admiring the riches of heav'n's pavement
Than ought divine or holy elſe, enjoy'd
In viſion *beatifick*. *Milton's Par. Loſt, b.* i. *l.* 684.

It is alſo their felicity to have no faith; for, enjoying the *beatifical* viſion in the fruition of the object of faith, they have received the full evacuation of it. *Brown's Vulgar Errours, b.* i.

We may contemplate upon the greatneſs and ſtrangeneſs of the *beatifick* viſion; how a created eye ſhould be ſo fortified, as to bear all thoſe glories, that ſtream from the fountain of uncreated light. *South.*

BEATI'FICALLY. *adv.* [from *beatifical.*] In ſuch a manner as to compleat happineſs.

Beatifically to behold the face of God in the fulneſs of wiſdom, righteouſneſs and peace, is bleſſedneſs no way incident unto the creatures beneath man. *Hakewell on Providence.*

BEATIFICA'TION. *n.ſ.* [from *beatifick.*] A term in the Romiſh church, diſtinguiſhed from canonization. *Beatification* is an acknowledgment made by the pope, that the perſon beatified is in heaven, and therefore may be reverenced as bleſſed; but is not a conceſſion of the honours due to ſaints, which are conferred by canonization.

To BEA'TIFY. *v. a.* [*beatifico*, Lat.]

1. To make happy; to bleſs with the completion of celeſtial enjoyment.

I wiſh I had the wings of an angel, to have aſcended into paradiſe, and to have beheld the forms of thoſe *beatified* ſpirits, from which I might have copied my archangel. *Dryden.*

The uſe of ſpiritual conference is unimaginable and unſpeakable, eſpecially if free and unreſtrained, bearing an image of that converſation which is among angels and *beatified* ſaints. *Hammond's Fundamentals.*

We ſhall know him to be the fulleſt good, the neareſt to us, and the moſt certain; and, conſequently, the moſt *beatifying* of all others. *Brown's Coſmologia Sacra, b.* iii. *c.* 4.

2. To ſettle the character of any perſon by a publick acknowledgment that he is received in heaven, though he is not inveſted with the dignity of a ſaint.

Over-againſt this church ſtands a large hoſpital, erected by a ſhoemaker, who has been *beatified*, though never ſainted. *Addiſon on Italy.*

BE'ATING. *n.ſ.* [from *beat.*] Correction; puniſhment by blows.

Playwright, convict of publick wrongs to men,
Takes private *beatings*, and begins again. *Ben. Johnſon.*

BEA'TITUDE. *n.ſ.* [*beatitudo*, Lat.]

1. Bleſſedneſs; felicity; happineſs: commonly uſed of the joys of heaven.

The end of that government, and of all man's aims, is agreed to be *beatitude*, that is, his being completely well. *Digby.*

This is the image and little repreſentation of heaven; it is *beatitude* in picture. *Taylor's Holy Living.*

He ſet out the felicity of his heaven, by the delights of ſenſe; ſlightly paſſing over the accompliſhment of the ſoul, and the *beatitude* of that part which earth and viſibilities too weakly affect. *Brown's Vulgar Errours, b.* i. *c.* 2.

2. A declaration of bleſſedneſs made by our Saviour to particular virtues.

BEAU. *n.ſ.* [*beau*, Fr. It is ſounded like *bo*, and has often the French plural *beaux.*] A man of dreſs; a man whoſe great care is to deck his perſon.

What, will not *beaux* attempt to pleaſe the fair? *Dryden.*

The water nymphs are too unkind
To Vill'roy; are the land nymphs ſo?
And fly they all, at once combin'd
To ſhame a general, and a *beau*? *Prior.*

You will become the delight of nine ladies in ten, and the envy of ninety-nine *beaux* in a hundred. *Swift's Direct. to Footm.*

BE'AVER. *n.ſ.* [*bievre*, Fr.]

1. An animal, otherwiſe named the *caſtor*, amphibious, and remarkable for his art in building his habitation; of which many wonderful accounts are delivered by travellers. His ſkin is very valuable on account of the fur.

The *beaver* being hunted, biteth off his ſtones, knowing that for them only his life is ſought. *Hakewell on Providence.*

They placed this invention upon the *beaver*, for the ſagacity and wiſdom of that animal; indeed from its artifice in building. *Brown's Vulgar Errours, c.* 4.

2. A hat of the beſt kind; ſo called from being made of the fur of beaver.

You ſee a ſmart rhetorician turning his hat, moulding it into different cocks, examining the lining and the button during his harangue: A deaf man would think he was cheapening a *beaver*, when he is talking of the fate of a nation. *Addiſon. Sp.*

The broker here his ſpacious *beaver* wears,
Upon his brow ſit jealouſies and cares. *Gay's Trivia.*

3. The part of a helmet that covers the face. [*baviere*, Fr.]

His dreadful hideous head
Cloſe couched on the *beaver*, ſeem'd to throw,
From flaming mouth, bright ſparkles firy red. *Fairy Queen.*

Big Mars ſeems bankrupt in their beggar'd hoſt,
And faintly through a ruſty *beaver* peeps. *Shakeſp. H.* V.

He was ſlain upon a courſe at tilt, the ſplinters of the ſtaff going in at his *beaver*. *Bacon's Eſſays*, Nº 36.

BE'AVERED. *adj.* [from *beaver.*] Covered with a beaver; wearing a beaver.

His *beaver'd* brow a birchen garland bears,
Dropping with infant's blood, and mother's tears:
All fleſh is humbled. *Pope's Dunciad.*

BEAU'ISH. *adj.* [from *beau.*] Befitting a beau; foppiſh.

BEAU'TEOUS. *adj.* [from *beauty.*] Fair; elegant in form; pleaſing to the ſight; beautiful. This word is chiefly poetical.

I can, Petrucio, help thee to a wife,
With wealth enough, and young, and *beauteous*.
Shakeſp. Taming of the Shrew.

Alas! not hoping to ſubdue,
I only to the flight aſpir'd;
To keep the *beauteous* foe in view,
Was all the glory I deſir'd. *Prior.*

BEAU'TEOUSLY. *adv.* [from *beauteous.*] In a beauteous manner; in a manner pleaſing to the ſight; beautifully.

Look upon pleaſures not upon that ſide that is next the ſun, or where they look *beauteouſly*; that is, as they come towards you to be enjoyed. *Taylor's Holy Living.*

BEAU'TEOUSNESS. *n.ſ.* [from *beauteous.*] The ſtate or quality of being beauteous; beauty.

From leſs virtue, and leſs *beauteouſneſs*,
The gentiles fram'd them gods and goddeſſes. *Donne.*

BEAU'TIFUL. *adj.* [from *beauty* and *full.*] Fair; having the qualities that conſtitute beauty.

He ſtole away and took by ſtrong hand all the *beautiful* women in his time. *Raleigh's Hiſt. of the World.*

The principal and moſt important parts of painting, is to know what is moſt *beautiful* in nature, and moſt proper for that art; that which is the moſt *beautiful*, is the moſt noble ſubject: ſo, in poetry, tragedy is more *beautiful* than comedy, becauſe the perſons are greater whom the poet inſtructs, and conſequently the inſtructions of more benefit to mankind. *Dryden's Dufreſnoy, Preface.*

Beautiful looks are rul'd by fickle minds,
And ſummer ſeas are turn'd by ſudden winds. *Prior.*

BEAU'TIFULLY. *adv.* [from *beautiful.*] In a beautiful manner.

No longer ſhall the boddice aptly lac'd,
From thy full boſom to thy ſlender waiſt,
That air and harmony of ſhape expreſs,
Fine by degrees, and *beautifully* leſs. *Prior.*

BEAU'TIFULNESS. *n.ſ.* [from *beautiful.*] The quality of being beautiful; beauty; excellence of form.

To BEAU'TIFY. *v. a.* [from *beauty.*] To adorn; to embelliſh; to deck; to grace; to add beauty to.

Never was ſorrow more ſweetly ſet forth, their faces ſeeming rather to *beautify* their ſorrow, than their ſorrow to cloud the beauty of their faces. *Hayward on Edward* VI.

Sufficeth not that we are brought to Rome,
To *beautify* thy triumphs and return,
Captive to thee and to thy Roman yoke. *Shakeſp. T. Andron.*

Theſe were not created to *beautify* the earth alone, but for the uſe of man and beaſt. *Raleigh's Hiſtory of the World.*

How all conſpire to grace
Th' extended earth, and *beautify* her face. *Blackmore's Creat.*

There is charity and juſtice; and the one ſerves to heighten and *beautify* the other. *Atterbury.*

To BEAU'TIFY. *v. n.* To grow beautiful; to advance in beauty.

It muſt be a proſpect pleaſing to God himſelf, to ſee his creation for ever *beautifying* in his eyes, and drawing nearer to him, by greater degrees of reſemblance. *Addiſon. Spectator.*

BEAU'TY. *n.ſ.* [*beauté*, Fr.]

1. That

1. That aſſemblage of graces, or proportion of parts, which pleaſes the eye.

Beauty conſiſts of a certain compoſition of colour and figure, cauſing delight in the beholder. *Locke.*

Your *beauty* was the cauſe of that effect,
Your *beauty*, that did haunt me in my ſleep.—
—If I thought that, I tell thee, homicide,
Theſe nails ſhould rend that *beauty* from my cheeks.
Shakeſp. Richard III.

Beauty is beſt in in a body that hath rather dignity of preſence than *beauty* of aſpect. The beautiful prove accompliſhed, but not of great ſpirit, and ſtudy for the moſt part rather behaviour than virtue. *Bacon.*

The beſt part of *beauty* is that which a picture cannot expreſs. *Bacon's Ornament. Ration.* N° 64.

Of the *beauty* of the eye I ſhall ſay little, leaving that to poets and orators; that it is a very pleaſant and lovely object to behold, if we conſider the figure, colours, ſplendour of it, is the leaſt I can ſay. *Ray on Creation.*

He view'd their twining branches with delight,
And prais'd the *beauty* of the pleaſing ſight. *Pope.*

2. A particular grace, feature, or ornament.

The ancient pieces are beautiful, becauſe they reſemble the *beauties* of nature; and nature will ever be beautiful, which reſembles thoſe *beauties* of antiquity. *Dryden's Dufreſnoy.*

Wherever you place a patch, you deſtroy a *beauty*. *Addiſon.*

3. Any thing more eminently excellent than the reſt of that with which it is united.

This gave me an occaſion of looking backward on ſome *beauties* of my author in his former books. *Dryd. Fab. Pref.*

With incredible pains have I endeavoured to copy the ſeveral *beauties* of the ancient and modern hiſtorians. *Arbuthnot.*

4. A beautiful perſon.

Remember that Pellean conquerour,
A youth, how all the *beauties* of the eaſt
He ſlightly view'd, and ſlightly overpaſs'd. *Paradiſe Loſt.*
What can thy ends, malicious *beauty*, be?
Can he, who kill'd thy brother, live for thee? *Dryden.*

To BEAU'TY. *v. a.* [from the noun.] To adorn; to beautify; to embelliſh.

The harlot's cheek, *beautied* with plaſt'ring art,
Is not more ugly to the thing that helps it,
Than is my deed to your moſt painted word. *Shak. Hamlet.*

BEAUTY-SPOT. *n. ſ.* [from *beauty* and *ſpot.*] A ſpot placed to direct the eye to ſomething elſe, or to heighten ſome beauty; a foil; a patch.

The filthineſs of ſwine makes them the *beauty-ſpot* of the animal creation. *Grew's Coſmologia Sacra, b.* iii. *c.* 2. § 49.

BECAFI'CO. *n. ſ.* [*becafigo*, Span.] A bird like a nightingale, feeding on figs and grapes; a fig-pecker. *Pineda.*

The robin-redbreaſt, till of late, had reſt,
And children ſacred held a martin's neſt;
Till *becaficos* ſold ſo dev'liſh dear,
To one that was, or would have been, a peer. *Pope.*

To BECA'LM. *v. a.* [from *calm.*]

1. To ſtill the elements.

The moon ſhone clear on the *becalmed* flood. *Dryden.*

2. To keep a ſhip from motion.

A man *becalmed* at ſea, out of ſight of land, in a fair day, may look on the ſun, or ſea, or ſhip, a whole hour, and perceive no motion. *Locke.*

3. To quiet the mind.

Soft whiſp'ring airs, and the lark's mattin ſong,
Then woo to muſing, and *becalm* the mind
Perplex'd with irkſome thoughts. *Philips.*
Baniſh his ſorrows, and *becalm* his ſoul
With eaſy dreams. *Addiſon's Cato.*

4. To *becalm* and to *calm* differ in this, that *to calm* is to ſtop motion, and *to becalm* is to with-hold from motion.

BECA'ME. The preterite of *become*; which ſee.

BECA'USE. *conjunct.* [from *by* and *cauſe.*]

1. For this reaſon that; on this account that; for this cauſe that.

How great ſoever the ſins of any perſon are, Chriſt died for him, *becauſe* he died for all; and he died for thoſe ſins, *becauſe* he died for all ſins; only he muſt reform. *Hammond's Fundam.*

Men do not ſo generally agree in the ſenſe of theſe as of the other, *becauſe* the intereſts, and luſts, and paſſions of men, are more concerned in the one than the other. *Tillotſ. Preface.*

2. It has, in ſome ſort, the force of a *prepoſition*; but, becauſe it is compounded of a noun, has *of* after it.

Infancy demands aliment, ſuch as lengthens fibres without breaking, *becauſe of* the ſtate of accretion. *Arbuth. on Aliments.*

To BECHA'NCE. *v. n.* [from *be* and *chance.*] To befal; to happen to: a word proper, but now in little uſe.

My ſons, God knows what has *bechanced* them.
Shakeſp. Henry VI. *p.* ii.
All happineſs *bechance* to thee at Milan.
Shakeſp. Two Gentlemen of Verona.

BE'CHICKS. *n. ſ.* [βηχικὰ, of βὴξ, a cough.] Medicines proper for relieving coughs. *Dict.*

To BECK. *v. a.* [beacn, Sax. *bec*, Fr. head.] To make a ſign with the head.

Bell, book, and candle, ſhall not drive me back,
When gold and ſilver *beck* me to come on. *Shakeſ. K. John.*
Oh, this falſe ſoul of Egypt, this gay charm,
Whoſe eye *beck'd* forth my wars, and called them home.
Shakeſp. Antony and Cleopatra.

BECK. *n. ſ.* [from the verb.]

1. A ſign with the head; a nod.

Haſte thee, nymph, and bring with thee
Quips, and cranks, and wanton wiles,
Nods, and *becks*, and wreathed ſmiles. *Milton.*

2. A nod of command.

Neither the luſty kind ſhewed any roughneſs, nor the eaſier any idleneſs; but ſtill like a well obeyed maſter, whoſe *beck* is enough for diſcipline. *Sidney, b.* ii.

Then forthwith to him takes a choſen band
Of ſpirits, likeſt to himſelf in guile,
To be at hand, and at his *beck* appear. *Milton's Par. Reg.*
The menial fair, that round her wait,
At Helen's *beck* prepare the room of ſtate. *Pope's Odyſſ. b.* iii.

To BE'CKON. *v. a.* [from *beck*, or beacn, Sax. a ſign.] To make a ſign to.

With her two crooked hands ſhe ſigns did make,
And *beckon'd* him. *Fairy Queen, b.* ii. *cant.* iv. *ſtanz.* 13.
It *beckons* you to go away with it,
As if it ſome impartment did deſire
To you alone. *Shakeſp. Hamlet.*
With this his diſtant friends he *beckons* near,
Provokes their duty, and prevents their fear. *Dryden.*

To BE'CKON. *v. n.* To make a ſign.

Alexander *beckoned* with the hand, and would have made his defence unto the people. *Acts*, xix. 33.

When he had raiſed my thoughts by thoſe tranſporting airs, he *beckoned* to me, and, by the waving of his hand, directed me to approach. *Addiſon. Spectator*, N° 159.

Sudden you mount! you *beckon* from the ſkies,
Clouds interpoſe, waves roar, and winds ariſe. *Pope.*

To BECLI'P. *v. a.* [of be clyppan, Sax.] To embrace. *Dict.*

To BECO'ME. *v. a.* pret. *I became*; comp. pret. *I have become.* [from *by* and *come.*]

1. To enter into ſome ſtate or condition, by a change from ſome other.

The Lord God breathed into his noſtrils the breath of life, and man *became* a living ſoul. *Gen.* ii. 7.

And unto the Jews I *became* a Jew, that I might gain the Jews. 1 *Cor.* ix. 20.

A ſmaller pear, grafted upon a ſtock that beareth a greater pear, will *become* great. *Bacon's Natural Hiſtory*, N° 453.

My voice thou oft haſt heard, and haſt not fear'd,
But ſtill rejoic'd; how is it now *become*
So dreadful to thee? *Milton's Paradiſe Loſt, b.* x. *l.* 120.
So the leaſt faults, if mix'd with faireſt dead,
Of future ill *become* the fatal ſeed. *Prior.*

2. *To become of.* To be the fate of; to be the end of; to be the final condition of. It is obſervable, that this word is never, or very ſeldom, uſed but with the interrogative *what.*

What is then *become of* ſo huge a multitude, as would have overſpread a great part of the continent? *Raleigh's Eſſays.*

Perplex'd with thoughts, *what* would *become*
Of me, and all mankind. *Milton's Par. Loſt, b.* xii. *l.* 275.

The firſt hints of the circulation of the blood were taken from a common perſon's wondering *what became of* all the blood which iſſued out of the heart. *Graunt's Bills of Mortality.*

What will *become of* me then? for when he is free, he will infallibly accuſe me. *Dryden's Spaniſh Friar.*

What became of this thoughtful buſy creature, when removed from this world, has amazed the vulgar, and puzzled the wiſe. *Rogers's Sermons.*

3. In the following paſſage, the phraſe, *where is he become*, is uſed for *what is become of him.*

I cannot joy, until I be reſolved
Where our right valiant father *is become.* *Shakeſp. Hen.* VI.

To BECO'ME. *v. a.* [from *be* or *by*, and cpemen, Sax. to pleaſe.]

1. Applied to perſons; to appear in a manner ſuitable to ſomething.

If I *become* not a cart as well as another man, a plague on my bringing up. *Shakeſp. Henry* IV. *p.* i.

Why would I be a queen? becauſe my face
Would wear the title with a better grace;
If I *became* it not, yet it would be
Part of your duty, then, to flatter me. *Dryd. Conq. of Gran.*

2. Applied to things; to be ſuitable to the perſon; to befit; to be congruous to the appearance, or character, or circumſtances, in ſuch a manner as to add grace; to be graceful.

She to her ſire made humble reverence,
And bowed low, that her right well *became*,
And added grace unto her excellence. *Fairy Queen, b.* i.
I would I had ſome flowers of the ſpring that might
Become your time of day; and your's, and your's,
That wear upon your virgin branches yet
Your maidenheads growing. *Shakeſp. Winter's Tale.*
Yet be ſad, good brothers;
For, to ſpeak truth, it very well *becomes* you. *Sh. Henry* IV.

Your dishonour
Mangles true judgment, and bereaves the state
Of that integrity, which should *become* it. *Shakesp. Coriol.*

Wicherly was of my opinion, or, rather, I of his: for it *becomes* me so to speak of so excellent a poet. *Dryd. Dufr. Pref.*

He utterly rejected their fables concerning their gods, as not *becoming* good men, much less those which were worshipped for gods. *Stillingfl. Def. of Disc. on Rom. Idolatry.*

BECO'MING. *particip. adj.* [from *become.*] That which pleases by an elegant propriety; graceful. It is sometimes used with the particle *of*; but generally without any government of the following words.

Of thee, kind boy, I ask no red and white
To make up my delight,
No odd *becoming* graces,
Black eyes, or little know not what, in faces. *Suckling.*

Their discourses are such as belong to their age, their calling, and their breeding; such as are *becoming of* them, and *of* them only. *Dryd. Fables, Preface.*

Yet some *becoming* boldness I may use;
I've well deserv'd, nor will he now refuse. *Dryd. Aurengz.*

Make their pupils repeat the action, that they may correct what is constrained in it, till it be perfected into an habitual and *becoming* easiness. *Locke.*

BECO'MING. *n. s.* [from *become.*] Behaviour: a word not now in use.

Sir, forgive me,
Since my *becomings* kill me, when they do not
Eye well to you. *Shakesp. Antony and Cleopatra.*

BECO'MINGLY. *adv.* [from *becoming.*] After a becoming or proper manner.

BECO'MINGNESS. *n. s.* [from *becoming.* See TO BECOME.] Decency; elegant congruity; propriety.

Nor is the majesty of the divine government greater in its extent, than the *becomingness* hereof is in its manner and form. *Grew's Cosmologia Sacra, b.* iii. *c.* I.

BED. *n. s.* [beb, Sax.]

1. Something made to sleep on.

Lying not erect, but hollow, which is in the making of the *bed*; or with the legs gathered up, which is in the posture of the body, is the more wholsome. *Bacon's Nat. Hist.* Nº 738.

Rigour now is gone to *bed*,
And advice with scrupulous head. *Milton.*

Those houses then were caves, or homely sheds,
With twining oziers fenc'd, and moss their *beds*. *Dryden.*

2. Lodging; the convenience of a place to sleep in.

On my knees I beg,
That you'll vouchsafe me, raiment, *bed*, and food.
Shakesp. King Lear.

3. Marriage.

George, the eldest son of this second *bed*, was, after the death of his father, by the singular care and affection of his mother, well brought up. *Clarendon.*

4. Bank of earth raised in a garden.

Herbs will be tenderer and fairer, if you take them out of *beds*, when they are newly come up, and remove them into pots, with better earth. *Bacon's Nat. Hist.* Nº 459.

5. The channel of a river, or any hollow.

So high as heav'd the tumid hills, so low
Down sunk a hollow bottom, broad, and deep,
Capacious *bed* of waters. *Milt. Par. Lost, b.* vii. *l.* 288.

The great magazine for all kinds of treasure is supposed to be the *bed* of the Tiber. We may be sure, when the Romans lay under the apprehensions of seeing their city sacked by a barbarous enemy, that they would take care to bestow such of their riches that way, as could best bear the water. *Addison.*

6. The place where any thing is generated, or reposited.

See hoary Albula's infected tide
O'er the warm *bed* of smoaking sulphur glide. *Addison.*

7. A layer; a stratum; a body spread over another.

I see no reason, but the surface of the land should be as regular as that of the water, in the first production of it; and the strata, or *beds* within, lie as even. *Burnet's Theory.*

8. *To bring to* BED. To deliver of a child. It is often used with the particle *of*; as, *she was brought to* bed of *a daughter.*

Ten months after Florimel happen'd to wed,
And was *brought* in a laudable manner *to bed.* *Prior.*

9. *To make the* BED. To put the bed in order after it has been used.

I keep his house, and I wash, wring, brew, bake, scour, dress meat, and *make the beds*, and do all myself.
Shakesp. Merry Wives of Windsor.

BED *of a Mortar.* [with gunners.] A solid piece of oak hollowed in the middle, to receive the breech and half the trunnions. *Dict.*

BED *of a great gun.* That thick plank which lies immediately under the piece, being, as it were, the body of the carriage. *Dict.*

To BED. *v. a.* [from the noun.]

1. To go to bed with.

They have married me:
I'll to the Tuscan wars, and never *bed* her.
Shakesp. All's well that ends well.

2. To be placed in bed.

She was publickly contracted, stated as a bride, and solemnly *bedded*; and, after she was laid, Maximilian's ambassadour put his leg, stript naked to the knee, between the espousal sheets.
Bacon's Henry VII.

3. To be made partaker of the bed.

There was a doubt ripped up, whether Arthur was *bedded* with his lady. *Bacon's Henry* VII.

4. To sow, or plant in earth.

Lay the turf with the grass-side downward, upon which lay some of your best mould to *bed* your quick in, and lay your quick upon it. *Mortimer's Husbandry.*

5. To lay in a place of rest, or security.

Let coarse bold hands, from slimy nest,
The *bedded* fish in banks outwrest. *Donne.*

A snake *bedded* himself under the threshold of a country-house. *L'Estrange's Fables.*

6. To lay in order; in strata.

And as the sleeping soldiers in th' alarm,
Your *bedded* hairs, like life in excrements,
Start up, and stand on end. *Shakesp. Hamlet.*

To BED. *v. n.* To cohabit.

If he be married, and *bed* with his wife, and afterwards relapse, he may possibly fancy that she infected him.
Wiseman's Surgery.

To BEDA'BBLE. *v. a.* [from *dabble.*] To wet; to besprinkle. It is generally applied to persons, in a sense including inconvenience.

Never so weary, never so in woe,
Bedabbled with the dew, and torn with briars,
I can no further crawl, no further go.
Shakesp. Midsummer Night's Dream.

To BEDA'GGLE. *v. a.* [from *daggle.*] To bemire; to soil cloaths, by letting them reach the dirt in walking.

To BEDA'SH. *v. a.* [from *dash.*] To bemire by throwing dirt; to bespatter; to wet with throwing water.

When thy warlike father, like a child,
Told the sad story of my father's death,
That all the standers by had wet their cheeks,
Like trees *bedash'd* with rain. *Shakesp. Richard* III.

To BEDA'WB. *v. a.* [from *dawb.*] To dawb over; to besmear; to soil, with spreading any viscous body over it.

A piteous coarse, a bloody piteous coarse,
Pale, pale as ashes, all *bedawb'd* in blood,
All in gore blood. *Shakesp. Romeo and Juliet.*

To BEDA'ZZLE. *v. a.* [from *dazzle.*] To make the sight dim by too much lustre.

My mistaken eyes,
That have been so *bedazzled* by the sun,
That every thing I look on seemeth green.
Shakesp. Taming of the Shrew.

BEDCHA'MBER. *n. s.* [from *bed* and *chamber.*] The chamber appropriated to rest.

They were brought to the king, abiding then in his *bedchamber.* *Hayward.*

He was now one of the *bedchamber* to the prince. *Clarendon.*

BEDCLO'ATHS. *n. s.* [from *bed* and *cloaths.* It has no *singular.*] Coverlets spread over a bed.

For he will be swine drunk, and, in his sleep, he does little harm, save to his *bedcloaths* about him.
Shakesp. All's well that ends well.

BE'DDER. } *n. s.* [from *bed.*] The nether-stone of an oil-
BEDE'TTER. } mill. *Dict.*

BE'DDING. *n. s.* [from *bed.*] The materials of a bed; a bed.

There be no inns where meet *bedding* may be had; so that his mantle serves him then for a bed. *Spenser's Ireland.*

First, with assiduous care from winter keep,
Well fother'd in the stalls, thy tender sheep;
Then spread with straw the *bedding* of thy fold,
With fern beneath, to fend the bitter cold. *Dryd. Georg.*

Arcite return'd, and, as in honour ty'd,
His foe with *bedding*, and with food supply'd. *Dryden.*

To BEDE'CK. *v. a.* [from *deck.*] To deck; to adorn; to grace.

Thou sham'st thy shape, thy love, thy wit,
And usest none in that true use indeed,
Which should *bedeck* thy shape, thy love, thy wit.
Shakesp. Romeo and Juliet.

Female it seems,
That so *bedeck'd*, ornate, and gay,
Comes this way. *Milton's Samf. Agonistes, l.* 710.

With ornamental drops *bedeck'd* I stood,
And writ my victory with my enemy's blood. *Norris.*

Now Ceres, in her prime,
Smiles fertile, and with ruddiest freight *bedeckt.* *Philips.*

BE'DEHOUSE. *n. s.* [from bebe, Sax. a prayer, and *house.*] An hospital or almshouse, where the poor people prayed for their founders and benefactors.

BEDE'TTER. See BEDDER.

To BEDE'W. *v. a.* [from *dew.*] To moisten gently, as with the fall of dew.

Bedew her pasture's grass with faithful English blood.
Shakesp. Richard II.

Let

Let all the tears that should *bedew* my herse,
Be drops of balm to sanctify thy head. *Shakesp. Hen.* IV.

The countess received a letter from him, whereunto all the while she was writing her answer, she *bedewed* the paper with her tears. *Wotton.*

What slender youth, *bedew'd* with liquid odours,
Courts thee on roses, in some pleasant cave? *Milton.*

Balm from a silver box distill'd around,
Shall all *bedew* the roots, and scent the sacred ground. *Dryd.*

He said: and falling tears his face *bedew*. *Dryd. Æneid.*

BE'DFELLOW. *n. s.* [from *bed* and *fellow.*] One that lies in the same bed.

He loves your people,
But tie him not to be their *bedfellow*. *Shakesp. Coriolanus.*

Misery acquaints a man with strange *bedfellows*. *Shakesp. Tempest.*

And how doth my cousin, your *bedfellow*?
And your fairest daughter, and mine? *Shakesp. Henry* IV.

Why doth the crown lie there upon his pillow,
Being so troublesom a *bedfellow*? *Shakesp. Henry* IV.

A man would as soon choose him for his *bedfellow* as his playfellow. *L'Estrange.*

What charming *bedfellows*, and companions for life, men choose out of such women? *Addison. Guardian*, N° 120.

To BEDI'GHT. *v. a.* [from *dight.*] To adorn; to dress; to set off.

A maiden fine *bedight* he hapt to love;
The maiden fine *bedight* his love retains,
And for the village he forsakes the plains. *Gay.*

To BEDI'M. *v. a.* [from *dim.*] To make dim; to obscure; to cloud; to darken.

I have *bedimm'd*
The noontide sun, call'd forth the mutinous winds,
And 'twixt the green sea and the azur'd vault
Set roaring war. *Shakesp. Tempest.*

To BEDI'ZEN. *v. a.* [from *dizen.*] To dress out.

BE'DLAM. *n. s.* [corrupted from *Bethlehem*, the name of a religious house in London, converted afterwards into an hospital for the mad and lunatick.]

1. A madhouse; a place appointed for the cure of lunacy.
2. A madman; a lunatick.

Let's follow the old earl, and get the *bedlam*
To lead him where he would; his roguish madness
Allows itself to any thing. *Shakesp. King Lear.*

BE'DLAM. *adj.* [from the noun.] Belonging to a madhouse; fit for a madhouse.

The country gives me proof and precedent
Of *bedlam* beggars, who, with roaring voices,
Strike in their numb'd and mortify'd bare arms,
Pins, wooden pricks. *Shakesp. King Lear.*

BE'DLAMITE. *n. s.* [from *bedlam.*] An inhabitant of Bedlam; a madman.

If wild ambition in thy bosom reign,
Alas! thou boast'st thy sober sense in vain;
In these poor *bedlamites* thyself survey. *Lewis's Miscel.*

BE'DMAKER. *n. s.* [from *bed* and *make.*] A person in the universities, whose office it is to make the beds, and clean the chambers.

I was deeply in love with my *bedmaker*, upon which I was rusticated for ever. *Spectator*, N° 598.

BE'DMATE. *n. s.* [from *bed* and *mate.*] A bedfellow; one that partakes of the same bed.

Had I so good occasion to lie long
As you, prince Paris, nought but heav'nly business
Should rob my *bedmate* of my company. *Shak. Tr. and Cress.*

BE'DMOULDING. / BE'DDING MOULDING. } *n. s.* [from *bed* and *mould.*] A term used by workmen, to signify those members in the cornice, which are placed below the coronet. *Builder's Dict.*

BE'DPOST. *n. s.* [from *bed* and *post.*] The post at the corner of the bed, which supports the canopy.

I came the next day prepared, and placed her in a clear light, her head leaning to a *bedpost*, another standing behind, holding it steady. *Wiseman's Surgery.*

BE'DPRESSER. *n. s.* [from *bed* and *press.*] A heavy lazy fellow.

This sanguine coward, this *bedpresser*, this horseback-breaker, this huge hill of flesh. *Shakesp. Henry* IV. *p.* i.

To BEDRA'GGLE. *v. a.* [from *be* and *draggle.*] To soil the cloaths, by suffering them, in walking, to reach the dirt.

Poor Patty Blount, no more be seen
Bedraggled in my walks so green. *Swift.*

To BEDRE'NCH. *v. a.* [from *be* and *drench.*] To drench; to soak; to saturate with moisture.

Far off from the mind of Bolingbroke
It is, such crimson tempest should *bedrench*
The fresh green lap of fair king Richard's land. *Shakesp. King Richard* III.

BE'DRID. *adj.* [from *bed* and *ride.*] Confined to the bed by age or sickness.

Norway, uncle of young Fontinbras,
Who, impotent and *bedrid*, scarcely hears
Of this his nephew's purpose. *Shakesp. Hamlet.*

Lies he not *bedrid*? and, again, does nothing,
But what he did being childish? *Shakesp. Winter's Tale.*

Now, as a myriad
Of ants durst th' emperor's lov'd snake invade:
The crawling galleys, seagulls, finny chips,
Might brave our pinnaces, our *bedrid* ships. *Donne.*

Hanging old men, who were *bedrid*, because they would not discover where their money was. *Clarendon, b.* viii.

Infirm persons, when they come to be so weak as to be fixed to their beds, hold out many years; some have lain *bedrid* twenty years. *Ray.*

BE'DRITE. *n. s.* [from *bed* and *rite.*] The privilege of the marriage bed.

Whose vows are, that no *bedrite* shall be paid
Till Hymen's torch be lighted. *Shakesp. Tempest.*

To BEDRO'P. *v. a.* [from *be* and *drop.*] To besprinkle; to mark with spots or drops; to speckle.

Not so thick swarm'd once the soil
Bedrop'd with blood of Gorgon. *Milt. Par. Lost, b.* x. *l.* 527.

Our plenteous streams a various race supply;
The silver eel in shining volumes roll'd,
The yellow carp, in scales *bedrop'd* with gold. *Pope's W. For.*

BE'DSTEAD. *n. s.* [from *bed* and *stead.*] The frame on which the bed is placed.

Chimnies with scorn rejecting smoak;
Stools, tables, chairs, and *bedsteads* broke. *Swift.*

BE'DSTRAW. *n. s.* [from *bed* and *straw.*] The straw laid under a bed to make it soft.

Fleas breed principally of straw or mats, where there hath been a little moisture; or the chamber or *bedstraw* kept close, and not aired. *Bacon's Nat. Hist.* N° 696.

BEDSWE'RVER. *n. s.* [from *bed* and *swerve.*] One that is false to the bed; one that ranges or swerves from one bed to another.

She's a *bedswerver*, even as bad as those,
That vulgars give bold'st titles to. *Shakesp. Winter's Tale.*

BE'DTIME. *n. s.* [from *bed* and *time.*] The hour of rest; sleeping time.

What masks, what dances shall we have,
To wear away this long age of three hours,
Between our after-supper and *bedtime*? *Shakesp. Midsummer Night's Dream.*

After evening repasts, till *bedtime*, their thoughts will be best taken up in the easy grounds of religion. *Milt. on Education.*

The scouring drunkard, if he does not fight
Before his *bedtime*, takes no rest that night. *Dryden's Juv.*

To BEDU'NG. *v. a.* [from *be* and *dung.*] To cover, or manure with dung.

To BEDU'ST. *v. a.* [from *be* and *dust.*] To sprinkle with dust.

BE'DWARD. *adv.* [from *bed* and *ward.*] Toward bed.

In heart
As merry, as when our nuptial day was done,
And tapers burnt to *bedward*. *Shakesp. Coriolanus.*

To BEDWA'RF. *v. a.* [from *be* and *dwarf.*] To make little; to hinder in growth; to stunt.

'Tis shrinking, not close weaving, that hath thus
In mind and body both *bedwarfed* us. *Donne.*

BE'DWORK. *n. s.* [from *bed* and *work.*] Work done in bed; work performed without toil of the hands.

The still and mental parts,
That do contrive how many hands shall strike,
When fulness call them on, and know, by measure
Of their observant toil, the enemy's weight;
Why this hath not a finger's dignity,
They call this *bedwork*, mapp'ry, closet war. *Shakesp. Troilus and Cressida.*

BEE. *n. s.* [beo, Saxon.]

1. The animal that makes honey, remarkable for its industry and art.

So work the honey *bees*,
Creatures that, by a ruling nature, teach
The art of order to a peopled kingdom. *Shakesp. Hen.* V.

From the Moorish camp,
There has been heard a distant humming noise,
Like *bees* disturb'd, and arming in their hives. *Dryden.*

A company of poor insects, whereof some are *bees*, delighted with flowers, and their sweetness; others beetles, delighted with other viands. *Locke.*

2. An industrious and careful person. This signification is only used in familiar language.

BEE-EATER. *n. s.* [from *bee* and *eat.*] A bird that feeds upon bees.

BEE-FLOWER. *n. s.* [from *bee* and *flower.*] A species of foolstones; which see. It grows upon dry places, and flowers in April. *Millar.*

BEE-GARDEN. *n. s.* [from *bee* and *garden.*] A place to set hives of bees in.

A convenient and necessary place ought to be made choice of, for your apiary, or *bee-garden*. *Mortimer's Husbandry.*

BEE-HIVE. *n. s.* [from *bee* and *hive.*] The case, or box, in which bees are kept.

BEE-MASTER. *n. s.* [from *bee* and *master.*] One that keeps bees.

They that are *bee-masters*, and have not care enough of them, must not expect to reap any considerable advantage by them. *Mortimer's Husbandry.*

BEECH. *n. s.* [bece, or boc, Saxon.]

This tree hath leaves somewhat resembling those of the hornbeam; the male flowers grow together in a round bunch, at remote distances from the fruit, which consists of two triangular nuts, inclosed in a rough hairy rind, divided into four parts. There is but one species of this tree at present known, except two varieties, with striped leaves. It will grow to a considerable stature, though the soil be stony and barren; as also, upon the declivities of mountains. The shade of this tree is very injurious to most sorts of plants, which grow near it; but is generally believed to be very salubrious to human bodies. The timber is of great use to turners and joiners. The mast is very good to fatten swine and deer; and affords a sweet oil, and has supported some families with bread. *Millar.*

Black was the forest, thick with *beech* it stood. *Dryden.*

Nor is that sprightly wildness in their notes,
Which, clear and vigorous, warbles from the *beech*.
Thomson's Spring.

BE'ECHEN. *adj.* [bucene, Sax.] Consisting of the wood of the beech; belonging to the beech.

With diligence he'll serve us when we dine,
And in plain *beechen* vessels fill our wine. *Dryden's Juv.*

BEEF. *n. s.* [*bœuf*, French.]

1. The flesh of black cattle prepared for food.

What say you to a piece of *beef* and mustard?
Shakesp. Taming of the Shrew.

The fat of roasted *beef* falling on the birds, will baste them. *Swift.*

2. An ox, bull, or cow, considered as fit for food. In this sense it has the plural *beeves*; the singular is seldom found.

A pound of man's flesh
Is not so estimable or profitable,
As flesh of muttons, *beeves*, or goats. *Shakesp. M. of Ven.*

Alcinoüs slew twelve sheep, eight white-tooth'd swine,
Two crook-haunch'd *beeves*. *Chapman's Odyssey.*

There was not any captain, but had credit for more victuals than we spent there; and yet they had of me fifty *beeves* among them. *Sir Walter Raleigh's Apology.*

On hides of *beeves*, before the palace gate,
Sad spoils of luxury! the suitors sate. *Pope's Odyssey.*

BEEF. *adj.* [from the substantive.] Consisting of the flesh of black cattle.

If you are employed in marketing, do not accept of a treat of a *beef* stake, and a pot of ale, from the butcher. *Swift.*

BEEF-EATER. *n. s.* [from *beef* and *eat*, because the commons is beef when on waiting.] A yeoman of the guard.

BE'EMOL. *n. s.* This word I have found only in the example, and know nothing of the etymology, unless it be a corruption of *bymodule*, from *by* and *modulus*, a note; that is, a note out of the regular order.

There be intervenient in the rise of eight, in tones, two *beemols*, or half notes; so as, if you divide the tones equally, the eight is but seven whole and equal notes. *Bacon's Nat. Hist.*

BEEN. [beon, Saxon.] The *participle preterite* of TO BE; which see.

BEER. *n. s.* [*bîr*, Welch.] Liquour made of malt and hops. It is distinguished from ale, either by being older or smaller.

Here's a pot of good double *beer*, neighbour, drink.
Shakesp. Henry VI. p. ii.

It were good to try clarifying with almonds in new *beer*.
Bacon's Natural History, N° 768.

Flow, Welsted! flow, like thine inspirer, *beer*;
Tho' stale, not ripe; tho' thin, yet never clear;
So sweetly mawkish, and so smoothly dull;
Heady, not strong; and foaming, tho' not full. *Pope.*

BE'ESTINGS. See BIESTINGS.

BEET. *n. s.* [*beta*, Lat.] The name of a plant.

It hath a thick, fleshy root; the flowers have no visible leaves, but many stamina, or threads, collected into a globe; the cup of the flower is divided into five segments; the seeds are covered with an hard outer coat, and grow two or three together in a bunch. The species are; 1. The common white *beet*. 2. The common green *beet*. 3. The common red *beet*. 4. The turnep-rooted red *beet*. 5. The great red *beet*. 6. The yellow *beet*. 7. The Swiss or Chard *beet*. The two first mentioned are preserved in gardens, for the use of their leaves in pot herbs. The other sorts are propagated for their roots, which are boiled as parsneps. The red *beet* is most commonly cultivated and used in garnishing dishes. The Swiss *beet* is by some much esteemed. *Millar.*

BE'ETLE. *n. s.* [bytel, Saxon.]

1. An insect distinguished by having hard cases or sheaths, under which he folds his wings.

They are as shards, and he their *beetle*. *Sh. Ant. and Cleop.*

The poor *beetle*, that we tread upon,
In corporal suff'rance finds a pang as great,
As when a giant dies. *Shakesp. Measure for Measure.*

Others come in place, sharp of sight, and too provident for that which concerned their own interest; but as blind as *beetles* in foreseeing this great and common danger.
Knolles's History of the Turks.

A grott there was with hoary moss o'ergrown,
The clasping ivies up the ruins creep,
And there the bat and drowsy *beetle* sleep. *Garth.*

The butterflies and *beetles* are such numerous tribes, that I believe, in our own native country alone, the species of each kind may amount to one hundred and fifty, or more. *Ray.*

2. A heavy mallet, or wooden hammer, with which wedges are driven.

If I do, fillip me with a three-man *beetle*. *Shakesp. Henry IV.*

When, by the help of wedges and *beetles*, an image is cleft out of the trunk of some well grown tree; yet, after all the skill of artificers to set forth such a divine block, it cannot, one moment, secure itself from being eaten by worms, or defiled by birds, or cut in pieces by axes. *Stillingfleet.*

To BE'ETLE. *v. n.* [from the noun.] To jut out; to hang over.

What if it tempt you tow'rd the flood, my lord?
Or to the dreadful summit of the cliff,
That *beetles* o'er his base into the sea. *Shakesp. Hamlet.*

Or where the hawk,
High in the *beetling* cliff, his airy builds. *Thomson's Spring.*

BEETLEBRO'WED. *adj.* [from *beetle* and *brow*.] Having prominent brows.

BEETLEHE'ADED. *adj.* [from *beetle* and *head*.] Loggerheaded; wooden headed; having a head stupid, like the head of a wooden beetle.

A whoreson, *beetleheaded*, flap-ear'd knave.
Shakesp Taming of the Shrew.

BE'ETLESTOCK. *n. s.* [from *beetle* and *stock*.] The handle of a beetle.

To crouch, to please, to be a *beetlestock*
Of thy great master. *Shakespeare.*

BE'ETRAVE. } See BEET.
BE'ET RADISH. }

BEEVES. *n. s.* [The *plural* of *beef*.] Black cattle; oxen.

One way, a band select from forage drives
A herd of *beeves*, fair oxen, and fair kine,
From a fat meadow ground. *Milton's Paradise Lost*, b. xi.

Others make good the paucity of their breed with the length and duration of their days; whereof there want not examples in animals uniparous: first, in bisulcous or cloven-hoofed, as camels and *beeves*; whereof there is above a million annually slain in England. *Brown's Vulgar Errours*, b. vi. c. 6.

Beeves, at his touch, at once to jelly turn,
And the huge boar is shrunk into an urn. *Pope's Dunciad.*

To BEFA'LL. *v. n.* [from *fall*. It *befell*, it *hath befallen*.]

1. To happen to: used generally of ill.

Let me know
The worst that may *befall* me in this case.
Shakesp. Midsummer Night's Dream.

Other doubt possesses me, lest harm
Befall thee, sever'd from me. *Milton's Parad. Lost*, b. ix.

This venerable person, who probably heard our Saviour's prophecy of the destruction of Jerusalem, drew his congregation out of those unparalleled calamities, which *befell* his countrymen. *Addison on the Christian Religion.*

This disgrace has *befallen* them, not because they deserved it, but because the people love new faces. *Addison's Freeholder.*

2. To happen to, as good.

Bion asked an envious man, that was very sad, what harm had befallen unto him, or what good had *befallen* unto another man? *Bacon's Apophthegms.*

No man can certainly conclude God's love or hatred to any person, from what *befalls* him in this world. *Tillotson.*

3. To happen; to come to pass.

But since th' affairs of men are still uncertain,
Let's reason with the worst that may *befall*. *Shak. J. Cæsar.*

I have reveal'd
This discord which *befell*, and was in heav'n
Among th' angelick pow'rs. *Milton's Parad. Lost*, b. vi.

4. It is used sometimes with *to* before the person to whom any thing happens.

Some great mischief hath *befall'n*
To that meek man. *Milton's Paradise Lost*, b. xi.

5. *To befall of.* To become of; to be the state or condition of: a phrase little used.

Do me the favour to dilate at full,
What hath *befall'n of* them, and thee, till now.
Shakespeare's Comedy of Errours.

To BEFI'T. *v. a.* [from *be* and *fit*.] To suit; to be suitable to; to become.

Blind is his love, and best *befits* the dark.
Shakesp. Romeo and Juliet.

Out of my sight, thou serpent!—That name best
Befits thee, with him leagu'd; thyself as false. *Parad. Lost.*

I will bring you where she sits,
Clad in splendour, as *befits*
Her deity. *Milton.*

Thou, what *befits* the new lord mayor,
Art anxiously inquisitive to know. *Dryden.*

To Befo'ol. *v. a.* [from *be* and *fool.*] To infatuate; to fool; to deprive of understanding; to lead into errour.

Men *befool* themselves infinitely, when, by venting a few sighs, they will needs persuade themselves that they have repented. *South.*

Jeroboam thought policy the best piety, though in nothing more *befooled*; the nature of sin being not only to defile, but to infatuate. *South.*

Befo're. *prep.* [biforan, Sax.]

1. Farther onward in place.

Their common practice was to look no further *before* them than the next line; whence it will follow, that they can drive to no certain point. *Dryden.*

2. In the front of; not behind.

Who shall go
Before them in a cloud, and pillar of fire:
By day a cloud, by night a pillar of fire,
To guide them in their journey, and remove
Behind them, while th' obdurate king pursues. *Par. Lost.*

3. In the presence of; noting authority or conquest.

Great queen of gathering clouds,
See, we fall *before* thee!
Prostrate we adore thee! *Dryden's Albion.*
The Alps and Pyreneans sink *before* him. *Addison's Cato.*

4. In the presence of; noting respect.

We see that blushing, and the casting down of the eyes both, are more when we come *before* many. *Bacon.*

They represent our poet betwixt a farmer and a courtier, when he drest himself in his best habit, to appear *before* his patron. *Dryden's Virgil, Dedication.*

5. In sight of.

Before the eyes of both our armies here,
Let us not wrangle. *Shakesp. Julius Cæsar.*

6. Under the cognizance of; noting jurisdiction.

If a suit be begun *before* an archdeacon, the ordinary may license the suit to an higher court. *Ayliffe's Parergon.*

7. In the power of; noting the right of choice.

Give us this evening; thou hast morn and night,
And all the year *before* thee, for delight. *Dryden.*

He hath put us in the hands of our own counsel. Life and death, prosperity and destruction, are *before* us. *Tillotson.*

8. By the impulse of something behind.

Her part, poor soul! seeming as burdened
With lesser weight, but not with lesser woe,
Was carried with more speed *before* the wind. *Sh. Com. of Err.*
Hurried by fate, he cries, and born *before*
A furious wind, we leave the faithful shore. *Dryden.*

9. Preceding in time.

Particular advantages it has before all the books which have appeared *before* it in this kind. *Dryden's Dufresnoy.*

10. In preference to.

We should but presume to determine which should be the fittest, till we see he hath chosen some one, which one we may then boldly say to be the fittest, because he hath taken it *before* the rest. *Hooker, b.* iii.

We think poverty to be infinitely desirable *before* the torments of covetousness. *Taylor's Holy Living.*

11. Prior to; nearer to any thing; as, the eldest son is *before* the younger in succession.

12. Superiour to; as, he is *before* his competitors both in right and power.

Before. *adv.*

1. Sooner than; earlier in time.

Heav'nly born,
Before the hills appear'd, or fountain flow'd,
Thou with eternal wisdom didst converse. *Par. Lost, b.* vii.
Before two months their orb with light adorn,
If heav'n allow me life, I will return. *Dryden's Fables.*

2. In time past.

Such a plenteous crop they bore
Of purest and well winnow'd grain,
As Britain never knew *before.* *Dryden.*

3. In some time lately past.

I shall resume somewhat which hath been *before* said, touching the question beforegoing. *Hale's Origin of Mankind.*

4. Previously to; in order to.

Before this elaborate treatise can become of use to my country, two points are necessary. *Swift.*

5. To this time; hitherto.

The peaceful cities of th' Ausonian shore,
Lull'd in their ease, and undisturb'd *before*,
Are all on fire. *Dryden's Æneid.*

6. Already.

You tell me, mother, what I knew *before*,
The Phrygian fleet is landed on the shore. *Dryden's Æneid.*

7. Farther onward in place.

Thou'rt so far *before*,
The swiftest wing of recompence is slow
To overtake. *Shakespeare.*

Befo'rehand. *adv.* [from *before* and *hand.*]

1. In a state of anticipation, or preoccupation; sometimes with the particle *with.*

Quoth Hudibras, I am *beforehand*
In that already, *with* your command. *Hudibras.*
Your soul has been *beforehand with* your body,
And drunk so deep a draught of promis'd bliss,
She slumbers o'er the cup. *Dryden's Don Sebastian.*

I have not room for many reflections; the last cited author has been *beforehand with* me, in its proper moral. *Addison.*

2. Previously; by way of preparation, or preliminary.

His profession is to deliver precepts necessary to eloquent speech; yet so, that they which receive them, may be taught *beforehand* the skill of speaking. *Hooker, b.* i.

It would be resisted by such as had *beforehand* resisted the general proofs of the gospel. *Atterbury.*

When the lawyers brought extravagant bills, Sir Roger used to bargain *beforehand*, to cut off a quarter of a yard in any part of the bill. *Arbuthnot's History of J. Bull.*

3. In a state of accumulation, or so as that more has been received than expended.

Stranger's house is at this time rich, and much *beforehand*; for it hath laid up revenue these thirty-seven years. *Bacon.*

4. At first; before any thing is done.

What is a man's contending with insuperable difficulties, but the rolling of Sisyphus's stone up the hill, which is soon *beforehand* to return upon him again? *L'Estrange's Fables.*

Befo'retime. *adv.* [from *before* and *time.*] Formerly; of old time.

Beforetime in Israel, when a man went to enquire of God, thus he spake. 1 *Sam.* ix. 9.

To Befo'rtune. *v. n.* [from *be* and *fortune.*] To happen to; to betide.

I give consent to go along with you;
Recking as little what betideth me,
As much I wish all good *befortune* you.
Shakesp. Two Gentlemen of Verona.

To Befo'ul. *v. a.* [from *be* and *foul.*] To make foul; to soil; to dirt.

To Befri'end. *v. a.* [from *be* and *friend.*] To favour; to be kind to; to countenance; to shew friendship to; to benefit.

If it will please Cæsar
To be so good to Cæsar, as to hear me,
I shall beseech him to *befriend* himself. *Shakesp. J. Cæsar.*
Now if your plots be ripe, you are *befriended*
With opportunity. *Denham's Sophy.*
See them embarked,
And tell me if the winds and seas *befriend* them. *Addison.*
Be thou the first true merit to *befriend*;
His praise is lost, who stays till all commend. *Pope.*
Brother-servants must always *befriend* one another. *Swift.*

To Befri'nge. *v. a.* [from *be* and *fringe.*] To decorate, as with fringes.

When I flatter, let my dirty leaves
Cloath spice, line trunks, or, flutt'ring in a rowe,
Befringe the rails of Bedlam and Soho. *Pope.*

To BEG. *v. n.* [beggeren, Germ.] To live upon alms; to live by asking relief of others.

I cannot dig; to *beg* I am ashamed. *Luke,* xvi. 3.

To Beg. *v. a.*

1. To ask; to seek by petition.

He went to Pilate, and *begged* the body. *Matth.* xxvii. 58.

2. To take any thing for granted, without evidence or proof.

We have not *begged* any principles or suppositions, for the proof of this; but taking that common ground, which both Moses and all antiquity present. *Burnet's Theory of the Earth.*

To Bege't. *v. a.* I *begot*, or *begat*; I have *begotten*, or *begot.* [begetan, Saxon; to obtain. See To GET.]

1. To generate; to procreate; to become the father of children.

But first come the hours, which were *begot*
In Jove's sweet paradise, of day and night,
Which do the seasons of the year allot. *Spenser's Epithal.*
I talk of dreams,
Which are the children of an idle brain,
Begot of nothing but vain phantasy. *Shakesp. Romeo and Jul.*

Who hath *begotten* me these, seeing I have lost my children, and am desolate. *Isaiah,* xlix. 21.

'Twas he the noble Claudian race *begat.* *Dryden's Æneid.*
Love is *begot* by fancy, bred
By ignorance, by expectation fed. *Granville.*

2. To produce, as effects.

If to have done the thing you gave in charge,
Beget you happiness, be happy then;
For it is done. *Shakesp. Richard* II.

My whole intention was to *beget*, in the minds of men, magnificent sentiments of God and his works. *Cheyne's Phil. Prin.*

3. To produce, as accidents.

Is it a time for story, when each minute
Begets a thousand dangers? *Denham's Sophy.*

4. It is sometimes used with *on*, or *upon*, before the mother.

Begot upon
His mother Martha by his father John. *Spectator.*

Bege'tter. *n. s.* [from *beget.*] He that procreates, or begets; the father.

For what their prowess gain'd, the law declares
Is to themselves alone, and to their heirs:
No share of that goes back to the *begetter*,
But if the son fights well, and plunders better,—— *Dryden.*

Men continue the race of mankind, commonly without the intention, and often against the consent and will of the *begetter*. *Locke.*

Be'ggar. *n. s.* [from *beg*. It is more properly written *begger*; but the common orthography is retained, because the derivatives all preserve the *a*.]

1. One who lives upon alms; one who has nothing but what is given him.

He raiseth up the poor out of the dust, and lifteth up the *beggar* from the dunghill, to set them among princes. *1 Samuel*, ii. 8.

We see the whole equipage of a *beggar* so drawn by Homer, as even to retain a nobleness and dignity. *Broome on the Odyssey.*

2. One who supplicates for any thing; a petitioner; for which, *beggar* is a harsh and contemptuous term.

What subjects will precarious kings regard?
A *beggar* speaks too softly to be heard. *Dryd. Conq of Gran.*

3. One who assumes what he does not prove.

These shameful *beggars* of principles, who give this precarious account of the original of things, assume to themselves to be men of reason. *Tillotson.*

To Be'ggar. *v. a.* [from the noun.]

1. To reduce to beggary; to impoverish.

Whose heavy hand hath bow'd you to the grave,
And *beggar'd* your's for ever. *Shakesp. Macbeth.*

They shall spoil the clothiers wool, and *beggar* the present spinners. *Graunt's Bills of Mortality.*

If the miser durst his farthings spare,
With heav'n, for twopence, cheaply wipes his score,
Lifts up his eyes, and hastes to *beggar* more. *Gay's Trivia.*

2. To deprive.

Necessity, of matter *beggar'd*,
Will nothing stick our persons to arraign
In ear and ear. *Shakesp. Hamlet.*

3. To exhaust.

For her person,
It *beggar'd* all description; she did lie
In her pavilion, cloth of gold, of tissue,
O'er-picturing Venus. *Shakesp. Antony and Cleopatra.*

Be'ggarliness. *n. s.* [from *beggarly*.] The state of being beggarly; meanness; poverty.

Be'ggarly. *adj.* [from *beggar*.] Mean; poor; indigent; in the condition of a beggar: used both of persons and things.

I ever will, though he do shake me off
To *beggarly* divorcement, love him dearly. *Shakesp. Othello.*

Who, that beheld such a bankrupt *beggarly* fellow as Cromwell entering the parliament house, with a thread bare torn cloak, and a greasy hat, could have suspected, that he should, by the murder of one king, and the banishment of another, ascend the throne? *South.*

The next town has the reputation of being extremely poor and *beggarly*. *Addison on Italy.*

Corusodes, by extreme parsimony, saved thirty-four pounds out of a *beggarly* fellowship. *Swift.*

Be'ggarly. *adv.* [from *beggar*.] Meanly; despicably; indigently.

Touching God himself, hath he revealed, that it is his delight to dwell *beggarly*? and that he taketh no pleasure to be worshipped, saving only in poor cottages? *Hooker*, *b.* v.

Be'ggary. *n. s.* [from *beggar*.] Indigence; poverty in the utmost degree.

On he brought me into so bare a house, that it was the picture of miserable happiness and rich *beggary*. *Sidney*, *b.* ii.

While I am a beggar, I will rail,
And say there is no sin, but to be rich:
And being rich, my virtue then shall be,
To say there is no vice, but *beggary*. *Shakesp. King John.*

We must become not only poor for the present, but reduced, by further mortgages, to a state of *beggary* for endless years to come. *Swift.*

To BEGI'N. *v. n.* I *began*, or *begun*; I have *begun*. [beʒinnan, Sax. from *be*, or *by to*, and ʒanʒan, ʒaan, or ʒan, to go.]

1. To enter upon something new: applied to persons.

Begin every day to repent; not that thou shouldst at all defer it; but all that is past ought to seem little to thee, seeing it is so in itself. *Begin* the next day with the same zeal, fear, and humility, as if thou hadst never *begun* before. *Taylor.*

I'll sing of heroes and of kings;
Begin my muse. *Cowley.*

2. To commence any action or state; to do the first act, or first part of an act; to make the first step from not doing to doing.

They *began* at the ancient men which were before the house. *Ezekiel*, ix. 6.

Of these no more you hear him speak;
He now *begins* upon the Greek:
These rang'd and show'd, shall, in their turns,
Remain obscure as in their urns. *Prior.*

Beginning from the rural gods, his hand
Was lib'ral to the pow'rs of high command. *Dryden's Fab.*

Rapt into future times, the bard *begun*,
A virgin shall conceive. *Pope's Messiah.*

3. To enter upon existence; as, the world *began*; the practice *began*.

4. To have its original.

And thus the hard and stubborn race of man,
From animated rock and flint *began*. *Blackmore.*

From Nimrod first the savage chase *began*;
A mighty hunter, and his game was man. *Pope.*

5. To take rise.

Judgment must *begin* at the house of God. *1 Pet.* iv. 17.

The song *begun* from Jove. *Dryden.*

All *began*,
All ends in love of God, and love of man. *Pope.*

6. To come into act.

Now and then a sigh he stole,
And tears *began* to flow. *Dryden.*

To Begin. *v. a.*

1. To do the first act of any thing; to pass from not doing to doing, by the first act.

Ye nymphs of Solyma, *begin* the song. *Pope's Messiah.*

They have been awaked, by these awful scenes, to *begin* religion; and, afterwards, their virtue has improved itself into more refined principles, by divine grace. *Watts.*

2. To trace from any thing as the first ground.

The apostle *begins* our knowledge in the creatures, which leads us to the knowledge of God. *Locke.*

3. *To begin with.* To enter upon; to fall to work upon.

A lesson which requires so much time to learn, had need be early *begun with*. *Government of the Tongue.*

Begi'nner. *n. s.* [from *begin*.]

1. He that gives the first cause, or original, to any thing.

Thus heaping crime on crime, and grief on grief,
To loss of love adjoining loss of friend,
I meant to purge both with a third mischief,
And, in my woe's *beginner*, it to end. *Fairy Queen*, *b.* ii.

Socrates maketh Ignatius, the bishop of Antioch in Syria, the first *beginner* thereof, even under the apostles themselves. *Hook.*

2. An unexperienced attempter; one in his rudiments; a young practitioner.

Palladius, behaving himself nothing like a *beginner*, brought the honour to the Iberian side. *Sidney*, *b.* i.

They are, to *beginners*, an easy and familiar introduction; a mighty augmentation of all virtue and knowledge in such as are entered before. *Hooker*, *b.* v. §. 37.

I have taken a list of several hundred words in a sermon of a new *beginner*, which not one hearer could possibly understand. *Swift.*

Begi'nning. *n. s.* [from *begin*.]

1. The first original or cause.

Wherever we place the *beginning* of motion, whether from the head or the heart, the body moves and acts by a consent of all its parts. *Swift.*

2. The entrance into act, or being.

Also in the day of your gladness, and in your solemn days, and in the *beginnings* of your months, you shall blow the trumpets over your burnt offering. *Numbers*, x. 10.

Youth, what man's age is like to be, doth show;
We may our end by our *beginning* know. *Denham.*

3. The state in which any thing first is.

By viewing nature, nature's handmaid, art
Makes mighty things from small *beginnings* grow:
Thus fishes first to shipping did impart,
Their tail the rudder, and their head the prow. *Dryden.*

4. The rudiments, or first grounds or materials.

The understanding is passive; and whether or not it will have these *beginnings*, and materials of knowledge, is not in its own power. *Locke.*

5. The first part of any thing.

The causes and designs of an action, are the *beginning*; the effects of these causes, and the difficulties that are met with in the execution of these designs, are the middle; and the unravelling and resolution of these difficulties, are the end. *Pope on Epick Poetry.*

To Begi'rd. *v. a.* I *begirt*, or *begirded*; I have *begirt*. [from *be* and *gird*.]

1. To bind with a girdle.

Or should she confident,
As sitting queen ador'd on beauty's throne,
Descend, with all her winning charms *begirt*,
T' enamour. *Milton's Paradise Lost*, *b.* ii. *l.* 213.

2. To surround; to encircle; to encompass.

Begird th' almighty throne,
Beseeching, or besieging. *Milton's Paradise Lost*, *b.* v. *l.* 868.

At home surrounded by a servile croud,
Prompt to abuse, and in detraction loud:
Abroad *begirt* with men, and swords, and spears;
His very state acknowledging his fears. *Prior.*

3. To shut in with a siege; to beleaguer; to block up.

It was so closely *begirt* before the king's march into the west, that the council humbly desired his majesty, that he would relieve it. *Clarendon*, *b.* viii.

To

To BEGI'RT. *v. a.* [This is, I think, only a corruption of *begird*; perhaps by the printer.] To begird. See BEGIRD.

And, Lentulus, *begirt* you Pompey's houfe,
To feize his fons alive; for they are they
Muft make our peace with him. *Ben. Johnfon's Catiline.*

BE'GLERBEG. *n. f.* [Turkifh.] The chief governour of a province among the Turks.

To BEGNA'W. *v. a.* [from *be* and *gnaw.*] To bite; to eat away; to corrode; to nibble.

His horfe is ftark fpoiled with the ftaggers, *begnawn* with the bots, waid in the back, and fhoulder fhotten. *Shakefp. Taming of the Shrew.*

The worm of confcience ftill *begnaw* thy foul. *Shakefp. Richard III.*

BEGO'NE. *interject.* [only a coalition of the words *be gone.*] Go away; hence; hafte away

Begone! the goddefs cries, with ftern difdain;
Begone! nor dare the hallow'd ftream to ftain.
She fled, for ever banifh'd from the train. *Addifon.*

BEGO'T.
BEGO'TTEN. } The *participle paffive* of the verb *beget.*

Remember that thou waft *begot* of them. *Ecclus,* vii. 28.

The firft he met, Antiphates the brave,
But bafe *begotten* on a Theban flave. *Dryden's Æneid.*

To BEGRE'ASE. *v. a.* [from *be* and *greafe.*] To foil or dawb with unctuous or fat matter.

To BEGRI'ME. *v. a.* [from *be* and *grime.* See GRIME and GRIM.] To foil with dirt deep impreffed; to foil in fuch a manner that the natural hue cannot eafily be recovered.

Her name, that was as frefh
As Dian's vifage, is now *begrim'd,* and black
As my own face. *Shakefp. Othello.*

To BEGUI'LE. *v. a.* [from *be* and *guile.*]

1. To impofe upon; to delude; to cheat.

This I fay, left any man fhould *beguile* you with enticing words. *Coloff.* ii. 4.

The ferpent me *beguil'd,* and I did eat! *Milton's Paradife Loft, b.* x.

Whofoever fees a man, who would have *beguiled,* and impofed upon him, by making him believe a lie, he may truly fay, that is the man who would have ruined me. *South.*

2. To deceive; to evade.

Is wretchednefs depriv'd that benefit,
To end itfelf by death? 'Twas yet fome comfort,
When mifery could *beguile* the tyrant's rage,
And fruftrate his proud will. *Shakefp. King Lear.*

3. To deceive pleafingly; to amufe.

With thefe fometimes fhe doth her time *beguile;*
Thefe do by fits her phantafy poffefs. *Sir J. Davies.*

Sweet leave me here a while;
My fpirits grow dull, and fain I would *beguile*
The tedious day with fleep. *Hamlet.*

BEGU'N. The *participle paffive* of *begin.*

But thou bright morning ftar, thou rifing fun,
Which in thefe latter times haft brought to light
Thofe myfteries, that, fince the world *begun,*
Lay hid in darknefs and eternal night. *Sir J. Davies.*

BEHA'LF. *n. f.* [This word *Skinner* derives from *half,* and interprets it, *for my half*; as, *for my part.* It feems to me rather corrupted from *behoof,* profit; the pronunciation degenerating eafily to *behafe*; which, in imitation of other words fo founded, was written, by thofe who knew not the etymology, *behalf.*]

1. Favour; caufe.

He was in confidence with thofe who defigned the deftruction of Strafford; againft whom he had contracted fome prejudice, in the *behalf* of his nation. *Clarendon, b.* viii.

Were but my heart as naked to thy view,
Marcus would fee it bleed in his *behalf.* *Addifon's Cato.*

Never was any nation bleffed with more frequent interpofitions of divine providence in its *behalf.* *Atterbury.*

2. Vindication; fupport.

He might, in his prefence, defy all Arcadian knights, in the *behalf* of his miftrefs's beauty. *Sidney.*

Left the fiend,
Or in *behalf* of man, or to invade
Vacant poffeffion, fome new trouble raife. *Paradife Loft.*

Others believe, that, by the two Fortunes, were meant profperity or affliction; and produce, in their *behalf,* an ancient monument. *Addifon's Remarks on Italy.*

To BEHA'VE. *v. a.* [from *be* and *have.*]

1. To carry; to conduct: ufed almoft always with the reciprocal pronoun.

We *behaved* not *ourfelves* diforderly among you. *2 Theffal.* iii. 7.

Manifeft figns came from heaven, unto thofe that *behaved themfelves* manfully. *2 Macc.* ii. 21.

To their wills wedded, to their errours flaves,
No man, like them, they think, *himfelf behaves.* *Denham.*

We fo live, and fo act, as if we were fecure of the final iffue and event of things, however we may *behave ourfelves.* *Atterbury.*

2. It feems formerly to have had the fenfe of, to govern; to fubdue; to difcipline: but this is not now ufed.

But who his limbs with labours, and his mind
Behaves with cares, cannot fo eafy mifs. *Fairy Queen, b.* ii.

With fuch fober and unnoted paffion,
He did *behave* his anger ere 'twas fpent,
As if he had but prov'd an argument. *Shakefp. Timon.*

To BEHAVE. *v. n.* To act; to conduct one's felf. It is taken either in a good or a bad fenfe; as, he *behaved* well or ill.

BEHA'VIOUR. *n. f.* [from *behave.*]

1. Manner of behaving one's felf, whether good or bad; manners.

Mopfa, curious in any thing but her own good *behaviour,* followed Zelmane. *Sidney.*

2. External appearance.

And he changed his *behaviour* before them, and feigned himfelf mad in their hands. *1 Sam* xxi. 13.

3. Gefture; manner of action, adapted to particular occafions.

Well witneffing the moft fubmiffive *behaviour,* that a thralled heart could exprefs. *Sidney.*

When we make profeffion of our faith, we ftand; when we acknowledge our fins, or feek unto God for favour, we fall down; becaufe the gefture of conftancy becometh us beft in the one, in the other the *behaviour* of humility. *Hooker, b.* v.

One man fees how much another man is a fool, when he dedicates his *behaviour* to love. *Shakefp. Much ado about Noth.*

4. Elegance of manners; gracefulnefs.

He marked, in Dora's dancing, good grace and handfome *behaviour.* *Sidney, b.* i.

The beautiful prove accomplifhed, but not of great fpirit; and ftudy, for the moft part, rather *behaviour* than virtue. *Bacon's Ornam. Rational.* N° 63.

He who advifeth the philofopher, altogether devoted to the Mufes, fometimes to offer facrifice to the altars of the Graces, thought knowledge imperfect without *behaviour.* *Wotton.*

5. Conduct; general practice; courfe of life.

To him, who hath a profpect of the ftate that attends men after this life, depending on their *behaviour* here, the meafures of good and evil are changed. *Locke.*

6. *To be upon one's behaviour.* A familiar phrafe, noting fuch a ftate as requires great caution; a ftate in which a failure in behaviour will have bad confequences.

Tyrants themfelves *are upon their behaviour* to a fuperiour power. *L'Eftrange's Fables.*

To BEHE'AD. *v. a.* [from *be* and *head.*] To deprive of the head; to kill by cutting off the head.

See a reverend Syracufan merchant
Beheaded publickly. *Shakefp. Romeo and Juliet.*

His *beheading* he underwent with all chriftian magnanimity. *Clarendon, b.* vii.

On each fide they fly,
By chains connext, and, with deftructive fweep,
Behead whole troops at once. *Philips.*

Mary, queen of the Scots, was *beheaded* in the reign of queen Elizabeth. *Addifon on Italy.*

BEHE'LD. *particip. paffive,* from *behold*; which fee.

All hail! ye virgin daughters of the main!
Ye ftreams, beyond my hopes *beheld* again! *Pope's Odyffey.*

BE'HEMOTH. *n. f.* *Behemoth,* in Hebrew, fignifies beafts in general, particularly the larger kind, fit for fervice. But Job fpeaks of an animal, which he calls *behemoth,* and defcribes its particular properties at large, in *chap.* xl. 15. *Bochart* has taken much care to make it appear to be the *hippopotamus,* or river-horfe. *Sanctius* thinks it is an ox. The Fathers fuppofe the devil to be meant by it. But we agree with the generality of interpreters, in their opinion, that it is the elephant. *Calmet.*

Behold now *behemoth,* which I made with thee; he eateth grafs as an ox. *Job,* xl. 15.

Behold! in plaited mail
Behemoth rears his head. *Thomfon's Summer, l.* 695.

BE'HEN.
BEN. } *n. f.* Valerian roots. Alfo a fruit refembling the tamarifk, from which perfumers extract an oil. *Dict.*

BEHE'ST. *n. f.* [from *be* and *heft*; hæſ, Saxon.] Command; precept; mandate.

Her tender youth had obediently lived under her parents *behefts,* without framing, out of her own will, the forechoofing of any thing. *Sidney, b.* ii.

Such joy he had their ftubborn hearts to quell,
And fturdy courage tame with dreadful awe,
That his *beheft* they fear'd as proud tyrant's law. *Fairy Q.*

I, meffenger from everlafting Jove,
In his great name thus his *beheft* do tell. *Fairfax, b.* i. *ft.* 17.

To vifit oft thofe happy tribes,
On high *behefts* his angels to and fro
Pafs'd frequent. *Milton's Paradife Loft, b.* vi. *l.* 153.

Reign thou in hell, thy kingdom; let me ferve
In heav'n God ever bleft, and his divine
Behefts obey, worthieft to be obey'd! *Paradife Loft, b.* vi.

To BEHI'GHT. *v. a.* pret. *behot,* part. *behight.* [from hatan, to promife, Sax.]

1. To promife.

Sir Guyon, mindful of his vow yplight,
Up roſe from drowſy couch, and him addreſt,
Unto the journey which he had *behight*.
Fairy Queen, b. ii. *cant.* ii.

2. To entruſt; to commit.
That moſt glorious houſe that gliſt'reth bright,
Whereof the keys are to thy hand *behight*
By wiſe Fidelia. *Fairy Queen, b.* i. *cant.* x. *ſtanz.* 50.

3. Perhaps to call; to name; *bight* being often put, in old authors, for *named*, or *was named*.

BEHI'ND. *prep.* [hindan, Saxon.]

1. At the back of another.
Acomates haſted with two hundred harquebuſiers, which he had cauſed his horſemen to take *behind* them upon their horſes. *Knolles's Hiſtory of the Turks.*

2. On the back part; not before.
She came in the preſs *behind*, and touched. *Mark*, v. 27.

3. Towards the back.
The Benjamites looked *behind* them. *Judges*, xx. 40.

4. Following another.
Her huſband went with her, weeping *behind* her. 2*Sam.*iii. 16.

5. Remaining after the departure of ſomething elſe.
He left *behind* him, myſelf, and a ſiſter, both born in one hour. *Shakeſp. Twelfth Night.*
Piety and virtue are not only delightful for the preſent, but they leave peace and contentment *behind* them. *Tillotſon.*

6. Remaining after the death of thoſe to whom it belonged.
What he gave me to publiſh, was but a ſmall part of what he left *behind* him. *Pope's Letters.*

7. At a diſtance from ſomething going before.
Such is the ſwiftneſs of your mind,
That, like the earth's, it leaves our ſenſe *behind*. *Dryden.*

8. Inferiour to another; having the poſteriour place with regard to excellence.
After the overthrow of this firſt houſe of God, a ſecond was erected; but with ſo great odds, that they wept, which beheld how much this latter came *behind* it. *Hooker, b.* 5. § 1.

9. On the other ſide of ſomething.
From light retir'd, *behind* his daughter's bed,
He, for approaching ſleep, compos'd his head. *Dryden.*

BEHI'ND. *adv.*

1. Out of ſight; not yet produced to view; remaining.
We cannot be ſure, that we have all the particulars before us; and that there is no evidence *behind*, and yet unſeen, which may caſt the probability on the other ſide. *Locke.*

2. Moſt of the former ſenſes may become *adverbial*, by ſuppreſſing the *accuſative caſe*; as, I left my money *behind*, or *behind me*.

BEHI'NDHAND. *adv.* [from *behind* and *hand*.]

1. In a ſtate in which rents or profits, or any advantage, is anticipated; ſo that leſs is to be received, or more performed, than the natural or juſt proportion.
Your trade would ſuffer, if your being *behindhand* has made the natural uſe ſo high, that your tradeſman cannot live upon his labour. *Locke.*

2. Not upon equal terms, with regard to forwardneſs. In this ſenſe, it is followed by *with*.
Conſider, whether it is not better to be half a year *behindhand with* the faſhionable part of the world, than to ſtrain beyond his circumſtances. *Spectator*, Nº 488.

3. *Shakeſpeare* uſes it as an *adjective*, but licentiouſly, for backward; tardy.
And theſe thy offices,
So rarely kind, are as interpreters
Of my *behindhand* ſlackneſs. *Shakeſp. Winter's Tale.*

To BEHO'LD. *v. a.* pret. *I beheld*, *I have beheld*, or *beholden*. [behealdan, Saxon.] To view; to ſee; to look upon.
Son of man, *behold* with thine eyes, and hear with thine ears. *Ezek.* xl. 4.
When ſome young Theſſalians, on horſeback, were *beheld* afar off, while their horſes watered, while their heads were depreſſed, they were conceived by the ſpectators to be one animal. *Brown's Vulgar Errours, b.* i. *c.* 4.
Man looks aloft, and, with erected eyes,
Beholds his own hereditary ſkies. *Dryden.*
At this, the former tale again he told,
With thund'ring tone, and dreadful to *behold*. *Dryden's Fab.*

BEHO'LD. *interject.* [from the verb.] See; lo: a word by which attention is excited, or admiration noted.
Behold! I am with thee, and will keep thee. *Gen.* xxviii. 15.
When out of hope, *behold* her! not far off,
Such as I ſaw her in my dream, adorn'd
With what all earth or heaven could beſtow,
To make her amiable. *Milton's Paradiſe Loſt, b.* viii. *l.* 481.

BEHO'LDEN. *particip. adj.* [*gehouden*, Dutch; that is, held in obligation. It is very corruptly written *beholding*.] Obliged; bound in gratitude; with the particle *to*.
Horns, which ſuch as you are fain to be *beholden to* your wives for. *Shakeſp. As you like it.*
Little are we *beholden to* your love,
And little looked for at your helping hands. *Shakeſp. R.* III.
I found you next; in reſpect of bond both of near alliance, and particularly of communication in ſtudies: wherein I muſt acknowledge myſelf *beholden to* you. *Bacon's Eſſays.*
I think myſelf mightily *beholden to* you for the reprehenſion you then gave us. *Addiſon. Guardian*, Nº 109.
We, who ſee men under the awe of juſtice, cannot conceive, what ſavage creatures they would be without it; and how much *beholden* we are *to* that wiſe contrivance. *Atterbury.*

BEHO'LDER. *n. ſ.* [from *behold*.] Spectator; he that looks upon any thing.
Was this the face,
That, like the ſun, did make *beholders* wink? *Shakeſp. R.* II.
Theſe beaſts among
Beholders rude, and ſhallow to diſcern
Half what in thee is fair, one man except,
Who ſees thee? *Milton's Paradiſe Loſt, b.* ix. *l.* 543.
Things of wonder give no leſs delight
To the wiſe Maker's, than *beholder's* ſight. *Denham.*
The juſtling chiefs in rude encounters join,
Each fair *beholder* trembling for her knight. *Granville.*
The charitable foundations in the church of Rome, exceed all the demands of charity, and raiſe envy, rather than compaſſion, in the breaſts of *beholders*. *Atterbury.*

BEHO'LDING. *adj.* [corrupted from *beholden*.] Obliged. See BEHOLDEN.
Becauſe I would not be *beholding* to fortune for any part of the victory, I deſcended. *Sidney, b.* ii.

BEHO'LDING. *n. ſ.* Obligation.
Love to virtue, and not to any particular *beholdings*, hath expreſſed this my teſtimony. *Carew's Survey of Cornwal.*

BEHO'LDINGNESS. *n. ſ.* [from *beholding*, miſtaken for *beholden*.] The ſtate of being obliged.
The king invited us to his court, ſo as I muſt acknowledge a *beholdingneſs* unto him. *Sidney, b.* ii.
In this my debt I ſeem'd loth to confeſs,
In that I ſhunn'd *beholdingneſs*. *Donne.*

BEHO'OF. *n. ſ.* [from *behoove*.] That which behooves; that which is advantageous; profit; advantage.
Her majeſty may alter any thing of thoſe laws, that may be more both for her own *behoof*, and for the good of the people. *Spenſer on Ireland.*
No mean recompence it brings
To your *behoof*: if I that region loſt,
All uſurpation thence expell'd, reduce
To her original darkneſs, and your ſway. *Milton.*
Wer't thou ſome ſtar, which, from the ruin'd roof
Of ſhak'd Olympus, by miſchance didſt fall;
Which careful Jove, in nature's true *behoof*,
Took up, and in fit place did reinſtate. *Milton.*
Becauſe it was for the *behoof* of the animal, that, upon any ſudden accident, it might be awakened, there were no ſhuts or ſtopples made for the ears. *Ray on the Creation.*
It would be of no *behoof*, for the ſettling of government, unleſs there were a way taught, how to know the perſon to whom belonged this power and dominion. *Locke.*

To BEHO'OVE. *v. n.* [behofan, Saxon; *it is a duty*.] To be fit; to be meet; either with reſpect to duty, neceſſity, or convenience. It is uſed only imperſonally with *it*.
For better examination of their quality, *it behooveth* the very foundation and root, the higheſt wellſpring and fountain of them, to be diſcovered. *Hooker, b.* i. § 1.
He did ſo prudently temper his paſſions, as that none of them made him wanting in the offices of life, which *it behooved*, or became him to perform. *Atterbury.*
But ſhould you lure the monarch of the brook,
Behooves you then to ply your fineſt art. *Thomſon's Spring.*

BEHO'OVEFUL. *adj.* [from *behoof*.] Uſeful; profitable; advantageous. This word is ſomewhat antiquated.
It is very *behooveful* in this country of Ireland, where there are waſte deſerts full of graſs, that the ſame ſhould be eaten down. *Spenſer on Ireland.*
Laws are many times full of imperfections; and that which is ſuppoſed *behooveful* unto men, proveth oftentimes moſt pernicious. *Hooker, b.* iv. §. 14.
Madam, we have culled ſuch neceſſaries
As are *behooveful* for our ſtate tomorrow. *Sh. Rom. and Jul.*
It may be moſt *behooveful* for princes, in matters of grace, to tranſact the ſame publickly: ſo it is as requiſite, in matters of judgment, puniſhment, and cenſure, that the ſame be tranſacted privately. *Clarendon.*

BEHO'OVEFULLY. *adv.* [from *behooveful*.] Profitably; uſefully.
Tell us of more weighty diſlikes than theſe, and that may more *behoovefully* import the reformation. *Spenſer on Ireland.*

BEHO'T. [*preterite*, as it ſeems, of *behight*, to promiſe.]
With ſharp intended ſting ſo rude him ſmote,
That to the earth him drove as ſtriken dead,
Ne living wight would have him life *behot*. *Fairy Q. b.* i.

To BEHO'WL. *v. a.* [from *be* and *howl*.]

1. To howl at.
Now the hungry lion roars,
And the wolf *behowls* the moon. *Shakeſp. Midſum. N. Dr.*

2. Perhaps, to howl over, or lament clamorouſly.

BE'ING. *particip.* [from *be*.]

Thoſe,

Those, who have their hope in another life, look upon themselves as *being* on their passage through this. *Atterbury.*

BE'ING. *n. s.* [from *be.*]

1. Existence; opposed to nonentity.

Of him all things have both received their first *being*, and their continuance to be that which they are. *Hooker, b.* v.

Yet is not God the author of her ill,
Though author of her *being*, and being there. *Davies.*

There is none but he,
Whose *being* I do fear: and under him
My genius is rebuked. *Shakesp. Macbeth.*

Thee, Father, first they sung, omnipotent,
Immutable, immortal, infinite,
Eternal king! Thee, author of all *being*,
Fountain of light! *Milton's Par. Lost, b.* iii. *l.* 374.

Merciful and gracious, thou gavest us *being*, raising us from nothing to be an excellent creation. *Taylor's Guide to Devotion.*

Consider every thing as not yet in *being*; then examine, if it must needs have been at all, or what other ways it might have been. *Bentley.*

2. A particular state or condition.

Those happy spirits, which ordain'd by fate
For future *being*, and new bodies wait. *Dryden's Æneid.*

Heav'n from all creatures hides the book of fate;
From brutes what men, from men what spirits know;
Or who could suffer *being* here below? *Pope's Essay on Man.*

3. The person existing.

Ah, fair, yet false; ah, *being* form'd to cheat,
By seeming kindness, mixt with deep deceit. *Dryden.*

It is folly to seek the approbation of any *being*, besides the supreme; because no other *being* can make a right judgment of us, and because we can procure no considerable advantage from the approbation of any other *being*. *Addison. Spectator.*

As now your own, our *beings* were of old,
And once inclos'd in woman's beauteous mold. *Pope.*

BE'ING. *conjunct.* [from *be.*] Since. *Dict.*

BE IT SO. A phrase of anticipation, *suppose it be so*; or of permission, *let it be so.*

My gracious duke,
Be't so she will not here, before your grace,
Consent to marry with Demetrius;
I beg the ancient privilege of Athens. *Sh. Midf. N. Dream.*

To BELA'BOUR. *v. a.* [from *be* and *labour.*] To beat; to thump: a word in low speech.

What several madnesses in men appear:
Orestes runs from fancy'd furies here;
Ajax *belabours* there an harmless ox,
And thinks that Agamemnon feels the knocks. *Dryden, jun.*

He sees virago Nell *belabour*,
With his own staff, his peaceful neighbour. *Swift.*

To BELA'CE. *v. a.* [Sea term.] To fasten; as to *belace* a rope. *D.*

BE'LAMIE. *n. s.* [*bel amie*, Fr.] A friend; an intimate. This word is out of use.

Wise Socrates
Pour'd out his life, and last philosophy,
To the fair Critias, his dearest *belamie*. *Fairy Q. b.* ii. *c.* vii.

BE'LAMOUR. *n. s.* [*bel amour*, Fr.] Gallant; consort; paramour: obsolete.

Lo, lo, how brave she decks her bounteous bow'r,
With silken curtains, and gold coverlets,
Therein to shrowd her sumptuous *belamour*. *Fairy Q. b.* ii.

BELA'TED. *adj.* [from *be* and *late.*] Benighted; out of doors late at night.

Fairy elves,
Whose midnight revels, by a forest side,
Or fountain, some *belated* peasant sees,
Or dreams he sees. *Milton's Paradise Lost, b.* i. *l.* 781.

Or near Fleetditch's oozy brinks,
Belated, seems on watch to lie. *Swift.*

To BELA'Y. *v. a.* [from *be* and *lay*; as, to *waylay*, to lie in wait, to lay wait for.]

1. To block up; to stop the passage.

The speedy horse all passages *belay*,
And spur their smoaking steeds to cross their way. *Dryden.*

2. To place in ambush.

'Gainst such strong castles needeth greater might,
Than those small forces ye were wont *belay*. *Spens. sonn.* xiv.

To BELAY *a rope.* [Sea term.] To splice; to mend a rope, by laying one end over another.

To BELCH. *v. n.* [bealcan, Saxon.]

1. To eject the wind from the stomach; to eruct.

The waters boil, and, *belching* from below,
Black sands as from a forceful engine throw. *Dryden's Virg.*

The symptoms are, a sour smell in their fæces, *belchings*, and distensions of the bowels. *Arbuthnot on Aliments.*

2. To issue out by eructation.

A triple pile of plumes his crest adorn'd,
On which with *belching* flames Chimæra burn'd. *Dryden.*

To BELCH. *v. a.* To throw out from the stomach; to eject from any hollow place. It is a word implying coarseness; hatefulness; or horrour.

They are all but stomachs, and we all but food;
They eat us hungerly, and, when they're full,
They'll *belch* us. *Shakespeare.*

The bitterness of it I now *belch* from my heart. *Sh. Cymbel.*

Immediate in a flame,
But soon obscur'd with smoke, all heav'n appear'd,
From those deep-throated engines *belch'd*. *Parad. Lost, b.* vi.

The gates that now
Stood open wide, *belching* outrageous flame
Far into chaos, since the fiend pass'd through. *Parad. Lost.*

Rough as their savage lords who rang'd the wood,
And, fat with acorns, *belch'd* their windy food. *Dryden.*

There *belcht* the mingl'd streams of wine and blood,
And human flesh, his indigested food. *Pope's Odyssey, b.* ix.

When I an am'rous kiss design'd,
I *belch'd* an hurricane of wind. *Swift.*

BELCH. *n. s.* [from the verb.]

1. The act of eructation.

2. A cant term for malt liquour.

A sudden reformation would follow, among all sorts of people; porters would no longer be drunk with *belch*. *Dennis.*

BELDA'M. *n. s.* [*belle dame*, which, in old French, signified probably an old woman, as *belle age*, old age.]

1. An old woman; generally a term of contempt, marking the last degree of old age, with all its faults and miseries.

Then sing of secret things that came to pass,
When *beldam* nature in her cradle was. *Milton.*

2. A hag.

Why, how now, Hecat, you look angerly?—
—Have I not reason, *beldams*, as you are?
Saucy and overbold? *Shakesp. Macbeth.*

The resty sieve wagg'd ne'er the more;
I wept for woe, the testy *beldam* swore. *Dryden.*

To BELE'AGUER. *v. a.* [*beleggeren*, Dutch.] To besiege; to block up a place; to lie before a town.

Their business, which they carry on, is the general concernment of the Trojan camp, then *beleaguer'd* by Turnus and the Latins. *Dryden's Dufresnoy, Preface.*

Against *beleaguer'd* heav'n the giants move:
Hills pil'd on hills, on mountains mountains lie,
To make their mad approaches to the sky. *Dryden. Ovid.*

BELE'AGURER. *n. s.* [from *beleaguer.*] One that besieges a place.

BELEMNI'TES. *n. s.* [from βέλος, a dart or arrow, because of its resemblance to the point of an arrow.] Arrowhead, or fingerstone, of a whitish and sometimes a gold colour.

BELFLO'WER. *n. s.* [from *bell* and *flower*, because of the shape of its flower; in Latin *campanula.*] A plant.

The flower consists of one leaf, shaped like a bell, and, before it is blown, is of a pentagonal figure; and, when fully opened, cut into five segments at the top. The seed vessel is divided into three cells, each having a hole at the bottom, by which the seed is emitted. There is a vast number of the species of this plant. 1. The tallest pyramidal *belflower*. 2. The blue peach-leaved *belflower*. 3. The white peach-leaved *belflower*. 4. Garden *belflower*, with oblong leaves and flowers; commonly called *Canterbury bells*. 5. Canary *belflower*, with orrach leaves and a tuberose root. 6. Blue *belflower*, with edible roots, commonly called *rampions*. 7. Venus looking-glass *belflower*, &c. The first sort is commonly cultivated to adorn chimnies, halls, &c. in summer. It produces sometimes twelve branches, four or five feet high, with large beautiful flowers, almost the whole length of the stalks. The peach-leaved *belflowers* are very hardy, and may be planted in open beds or borders, where they will flower very strong. The *Canterbury bells* are biennial. The *Canary belflower* is one of the most beautiful plants of the greenhouse, yielding its flowers in December, January, and February. The *rampion* is propagated for its root, which was formerly in greater esteem in England than at present. The sorts of *Venus looking-glass* are annual plants. *Millar.*

BELFO'UNDER. *n. s.* [from *bell* and *found.*] He whose trade it is to found or cast bells.

Those that make recorders know this, and likewise *belfounders*, in fitting the tune of their bells. *Bacon's Natural Hist.*

BE'LFRY. *n. s.* [*Beffroy*, in French, is a tower; which was perhaps the true word, till those, who knew not its original, corrupted it to *belfry*, because bells were in it.] The place where the bells are rung.

Fetch the leathern bucket that hangs in the *belfry*; that is curiously painted before, and will make a figure. *Gay's What d' ye call it.*

BELGA'RD. *n. s.* [*belle egard*, Fr.] A soft glance; a kind regard: an old word, now wholly disused.

Upon her eyelids many graces sat,
Under the shadow of her even brows,
Working *belgards*, and amorous retreats. *Fairy Q. b.* ii. *c.* iii.

To BELI'E. *v. a.* [from *be* and *lie.*]

1. To counterfeit; to feign; to mimick.

Which durst, with horses hoofs that beat the ground,
And martial brass, *belie* the thunder's sound. *Dryden.*

The shape of man, and imitated beast
The walk, the words, the gesture could supply,
The habit mimick, and the mien *belie*. *Dryden's Fables.*

2. To give the lie to; to charge with falſehood.

Sure there is none but fears a future ſtate;
And when the moſt obdurate ſwear they do not,
Their trembling hearts *belie* their boaſtful tongues. *Dryden.*

Paint, patches, jewels laid aſide,
At night aſtronomers agree,
The evening has the day *belied*,
And Phyllis is ſome forty-three. *Prior.*

3. To calumniate; to raiſe falſe reports of any man.

'Tis ſlander, whoſe breath
Rides on the poſting winds, and doth *belie*
All corners of the world. *Shakeſp. Cymbeline.*

Thou doſt *belie* him, Piercy, thou *belieſt* him;
He never did encounter with Glendower. *Shakeſp. Hen.* IV.

4. To give a falſe repreſentation of any thing.

Uncle, for heav'n's ſake, comfortable words.—
—Should I do ſo, I ſhould *belie* my thoughts. *Shakeſp. R.* II.

Tuſcan Valerus by force o'ercame,
And not *belied* his mighty father's name. *Dryden's Æneid.*

In the diſpute whate'er I ſaid,
My heart was by my tongue *belied*;
And in my looks you might have read,
How much I argu'd on your ſide. *Prior.*

BELI'EF. *n. ſ.* [from *believe.*]

1. Credit given to ſomething which we know not of ourſelves, on account of the authority by which it is delivered.

Thoſe comforts that ſhall never ceaſe,
Future in hope, but preſent in *belief.* *Wotton.*

Faith is a firm *belief* of the whole word of God, of his goſpel, commands, threats, and promiſes. *Wake's Prep. for Death.*

2. The theological virtue of faith, or firm confidence of the truths of religion.

No man can attain *belief* by the bare contemplation of heaven and earth; for that they neither are ſufficient to give us as much as the leaſt ſpark of light concerning the very principal myſteries of our faith. *Hooker, b.* v. §. 22.

3. Religion; the body of tenets held by the profeſſors of faith.

In the heat of general perſecution, whereunto chriſtian *belief* was ſubject upon the firſt promulgation, it much confirmed the weaker minds, when relation was made how God had been glorified through the ſufferings of martyrs. *Hooker, b.* v.

4. Perſuaſion; opinion.

He can, I know, but doubt to think he will;
Yet hope would fain ſubſcribe, and tempts *belief.* *Milton.*

All treaties are grounded upon the *belief*, that ſtates will be found in their honour and obſervance of treaties. *Temple.*

5. The thing believed; the object of belief.

Superſtitious prophecies are not only the *belief* of fools, but the talk ſometimes of wiſe men. *Bacon.*

6. Creed; a form containing the articles of faith.

BELI'EVABLE. *adj.* [from *believe.*] Credible; that which may be credited or believed.

To BELI'EVE. *v. a.* [ȝelyꝼan, Saxon.]

1. To credit upon the authority of another, or from ſome other reaſon than our perſonal knowledge.

A propoſition, which they are perſuaded, but do not know to be true, it is not ſeeing, but *believing.* *Locke.*

Ten thouſand things there are, which we *believe* merely upon the authority or credit of thoſe who have ſpoken or written of them. *Watts's Logick.*

2. To put confidence in the veracity of any one.

The people may hear when I ſpeak with thee, and *believe* thee for ever. *Exodus*, xix. 9.

To BELIEVE. *v. n.*

1. To have a firm perſuaſion of any thing.

They may *believe* that the Lord God of their fathers, the God of Abraham, the God of Iſaac, and the God of Jacob, hath appeared unto thee. *Geneſis*, xlv.

2. To exerciſe the theological virtue of faith.

Now God be prais'd, that, to *believing* ſouls,
Gives light in darkneſs, comfort in deſpair. *Shakeſp. H.* VI.

For with the heart man *believeth* unto righteouſneſs, and with the mouth confeſſion is made unto ſalvation. *Romans*, x. 10.

3. With the particle *in*; to hold as an object of faith.

Believe in the Lord your God, ſo ſhall you be eſtabliſhed. *2 Chron.* xx. 20.

4. With the particle *upon*; to truſt; to place full confidence in; to reſt upon with faith.

To them gave he power to become the ſons of God, even to them that *believe on* his name. *John*, i. 12.

5. *I believe*, is ſometimes uſed as a way of ſlightly noting ſome want of certainty or exactneſs.

Though they are, *I believe*, as high as moſt ſteeples in England, yet a perſon, in his drink, fell down, without any other hurt than the breaking of an arm. *Addiſon on Italy.*

BELI'EVER. *n. ſ.* [from *believe.*]

1. He that believes, or gives credit.

Diſcipline began to enter into conflict with churches, which, in extremity, had been *believers* of it. *Hooker, Pref.*

2. A profeſſour of chriſtianity.

Infidels themſelves did diſcern in matters of life, when *believers* did well, when otherwiſe. *Hooker, b.* 2. §. 2.

If he which writeth, do that which is forcible, how ſhould he which readeth, be thought to do that, which, in itſelf, is of no force to work belief, and to ſave *believers?* *Hooker, b.* v.

Myſteries held by us have no power, pomp, or wealth, but have been maintained by the univerſal body of true *believers*, from the days of the apoſtles, and will be to the reſurrection; neither will the gates of hell prevail againſt them. *Swift.*

BELI'EVINGLY. *adv.* [from *to believe.*] After a believing manner.

BELI'KE. *adv.* [from *like*, as *by likelihood.*]

1. Probably; likely; perhaps.

There came out of the ſame woods a horrible foul bear, which fearing, *belike*, while the lion was preſent, came furiouſly towards the place where I was. *Sidney.*

Belike fortune was afraid to lay her treaſures, where they ſhould be ſtained with ſo many perfections. *Sidney.*

Lord Angelo, *belike*, thinking me remiſs in my office, awakens me with this unwonted putting on. *Shakeſp. M. for Meaſ.*

Joſephus affirmeth, that one of them remained even in his time; meaning, *belike*, ſome ruin or foundation thereof. *Raleigh's Hiſtory of the World.*

2. It is ſometimes uſed in a ſenſe of irony; as, *we are to ſuppoſe.*

We think, *belike*, that he will accept what the meaneſt of them would diſdain. *Hooker, b.* viii. § 15.

God appointed the ſea to one of them, and the land to the other, becauſe they were ſo great, that the ſea could not hold them both; for elſe, *belike*, if the ſea had been large enough, we might have gone a fiſhing for elephants. *Brerew. on Languages.*

BELI'VE. *adv.* [bılıve, Sax. probably from bı and lıꝼe, in the ſenſe of vivacity; ſpeed; quickneſs.] Speedily; quickly: a word out of uſe.

By that ſame way the direful dames do drive
Their mournful chariot, fill'd with ruſty blood,
And down to Pluto's houſe are come *belive.* *Fairy Q. b.* i.

BELL. *n. ſ.* [bel, Saxon; ſuppoſed, by *Skinner*, to come from *pelvis*, Lat. a baſin. See BALL.]

1. A veſſel, or hollow body of caſt metal, formed to make a noiſe by the act of a clapper, hammer, or ſome other inſtrument ſtriking againſt it. *Bells* are always in the towers of churches, to call the congregation together.

Your flock, aſſembled by the *bell*,
Encircled you, to hear, with rev'rence. *Shakeſp. Henry* IV.

Get thee gone, and dig my grave thyſelf,
And bid the merry *bells* ring to thy ear,
That thou art crowned, not that I am dead. *Shakeſp. H.* IV.

Four *bells* admit twenty four changes in ringing, and five *bells* one hundred and twenty. *Holder's Elements of Speech.*

He has no one neceſſary attention to any thing, but the *bell*, which calls to prayers twice a day. *Addiſon. Spect.* N° 264.

2. It is uſed for any thing in the form of a *bell*, as the cups of flowers.

Where the bee ſucks, there ſuck I,
In a cowſlip's *bell* I lie. *Shakeſp. Tempeſt.*

The humming bees that hunt the golden dew,
In ſummer's heat on tops of lilies feed,
And creep within their *bells* to ſuck the balmy ſeed. *Dryden.*

3. A ſmall hollow globe of metal perforated, and containing in it a ſolid ball; which, when it is ſhaken by bounding againſt the ſides, gives a ſound.

As the ox hath his yoke, the horſe his curb, and the faulcon his *bells*, ſo hath man his deſire. *Shakeſp. As you like it.*

4. *To bear the bell.* To be the firſt, from the wether, that carries a *bell* among the ſheep, or the firſt horſe of a drove that has *bells* on his collar.

5. The Italians have carried away the *bell* from all other nations, as may appear both by their books and works. *Hakewell on Providence.*

To ſhake the bells. A phraſe, in *Shakeſpeare*, taken from the *bells* of a hawk.

Neither the king, nor he that loves him beſt,
The proudeſt he that holds up Lancaſter,
Dares ſtir a wing, if Warwick *ſhakes his bells. Shakeſp. H.* VI.

To BELL. *v. n.* [from the noun.] To grow in buds or flowers, in the form of a bell.

Hops, in the beginning of Auguſt, *bell*, and are ſometimes ripe. *Mortimer's Huſbandry.*

BELL-FASHIONED. *adj.* [from *bell* and *faſhion.*] Having the form of a bell.

The thorn apple riſes with a ſtrong round ſtalk, having large *bell-faſhioned* flowers at the joints. *Mortimer's Art of Husbandry.*

BELLE. *n. ſ.* [*beau*, *belle*, Fr.] A young lady.

What motive could compel
A well-bred lord t' aſſault a gentle *belle*;
O ſay, what ſtranger cauſe yet unexplor'd,
Could make a gentle *belle* reject a lord? *Pope's R. of the Lock.*

BELLES LETTRES. n. ſ. [Fr.] Polite literature. It has no *ſingular.*

The exactneſs of the other, is to admit of ſomething like diſcourſe, eſpecially in what regards the *belles lettres.* *Tatler.*

BE'LLIBONE. *n. ſ.* [from *bellus*, beautiful, and *bonus*, good, Lat. *belle & bonne*, Fr.] A woman excelling both in beauty and goodneſs. A word now out of uſe.

Pan may be proud, that ever he begot
Such a *bellibone*,
And Syrinx rejoice, that ever was her lot
To bear ſuch a one. *Spenſer's Paſtorals.*

Belli'gerous. *adj.* [*belliger*, Lat.] Waging war. *Dict.*

Be'lling. *n. ſ.* A hunting term, ſpoken of a roe, when ſhe makes a noiſe in rutting time. *Dict.*

Belli'potent. *adj.* [*bellipotens*, Lat.] Puiſſant; mighty in war. *Dict.*

To Be'llow. *v. n.* [bellan, Saxon.]

1. To make a noiſe as a bull.

Jupiter became a bull, and *bellow'd*; the green Neptune
A ram, and bleated. *Shakeſp. Winter's Tale.*

What bull dares *bellow*, or what ſheep dares bleat
Within the lion's den? *Dryden's Spaniſh Friar.*

But now, the huſband of a herd muſt be
Thy mate, and *bellowing* ſons thy progeny. *Dryden.*

2. To make any violent outcry.

He faſten'd on my neck, and *bellow'd* out,
As he'd burſt heav'n. *Shakeſp. King Lear.*

3. To vociferate; to clamour. In this ſenſe, it is a word of contempt.

The dull fat captain, with a hound's deep throat,
Would *bellow* out a laugh in a baſe note. *Dryd. Perſ. ſat.* v.

This gentleman is accuſtomed to roar and *bellow* ſo terribly loud, that he frightens us. *Tatler*, Nº 54.

4. To roar as the ſea in a ſtorm; or as the wind; to make any continued noiſe, that may cauſe terrour.

Till, at the laſt, he heard a dreadful ſound,
Which through the wood loud *bellowing* did rebound.
Fairy Queen, b. i. *cant.* 7. *ſtanz.* 7.

The riſing rivers float the nether ground;
And rocks the *bellowing* voice of boiling ſeas rebound. *Dryd.*

Be'llows. *n. ſ.* [bılız, Sax. perhaps it is corrupted from *bellies*, the wind being contained in the hollow, or *belly*. It has no *ſingular*; for we uſually ſay *a pair of bellows*; but *Dryden* has uſed *bellows* as a *ſingular*.]

1. The inſtrument uſed to blow the fire.

Since ſighs into my inward furnace turned,
For *bellows* ſerve to kindle more the fire. *Sidney.*

One, with great *bellows*, gather'd filling air,
And, with forc'd wind, the fuel did inflame. *Fairy Q. b.* ii.

The ſmith prepares his hammer for the ſtroke,
While the lung'd *bellows* hiſſing fire provoke. *Dryden's Juv.*

The lungs, as *bellows*, ſupply a force of breath; and the *aſpera arteria* is as the noſe of *bellows*, to collect and convey the breath. *Holder's Elements of Speech.*

2. In the following paſſage, it is *ſingular*.

Thou neither, like a *bellows*, ſwell'ſt thy face,
As if thou wert to blow the burning maſs
Of melting ore. *Dryden's Perſius, ſat.* v.

Be'lluine. *adj.* [*belluinus*, Lat.] Beaſtly; belonging to a beaſt; ſavage; brutal.

If human actions were not to be judged, men would have no advantage over beaſts. At this rate, the animal and *belluine* life would be the beſt. *Atterbury's Preface to his Sermons.*

BE'LLY. *n. ſ.* [*balg*, Dutch; *bol, bola*, Welch.]

1. That part of the human body which reaches from the breaſt to the thighs, containing the bowels.

The body's members
Rebell'd againſt the *belly*; thus accus'd it;—
That only like a gulf it did remain,
Still cupboarding the viand, never bearing
Like labour with the reſt. *Shakeſp. Coriolanus.*

2. In beaſts, it is uſed, in general, for that part of the body next the ground.

And the Lord ſaid unto the ſerpent, upon thy *belly* ſhalt thou go, and duſt ſhalt thou eat all the days of thy life. *Gen.* iii. 14.

3. The womb; in this ſenſe, it is commonly uſed ludicrouſly or familiarly.

I ſhall anſwer that better, than you can the getting up of the negro's *belly*: the Moor is with child by you.
Shakeſp. Merchant of Venice.

The ſecret is grown too big for the pretence, like Mrs. Primly's big *belly*. *Congreve's Way of the World.*

4. That part of man which requires food, in oppoſition to the *back*, or that which demands cloaths.

They were content with a licentious and idle life, wherein they might fill their *bellies* by ſpoil, rather than by labour.
Sir J. Hayward.

Whoſe god is their *belly*. *Phil.* iii. 19.

He that ſows his grain upon marble, will have many a hungry *belly* before harveſt. *Arbuthnot's Hiſtory of J. Bull.*

5. The part of any thing that ſwells out into a larger capacity.

Fortune ſometimes turneth the handle of the bottle, which is eaſy to be taken hold of; and, after, the *belly*, which is hard to graſp. *Bacon's Ornament. Ration.*

An Iriſh harp hath the concave, or *belly*, not along the ſtrings, but at the end of the ſtrings. *Bacon's Nat. Hiſtory*, Nº 146.

6. Any place in which ſomething is incloſed.

Out of the *belly* of hell cried I, and thou heardſt my voice.
Jonah, ii. 2.

To Be'lly. *v. n.* [from the noun.] To ſwell into a larger capacity; to hang out; to bulge out.

Thus by degrees day waſtes, ſigns ceaſe to riſe,
For *bellying* earth, ſtill riſing up, denies
Their light a paſſage, and confines our eyes.
Creech's Manilius.

The pow'r appeas'd, with winds ſuffic'd the ſail,
The *bellying* canvas ſtrutted with the gale. *Dryden's Fables.*

Loud ratt'ling ſhakes the mountains and the plain,
Heav'n *bellies* downwards, and deſcends in rain. *Dryden.*

'Midſt theſe diſports, forget they not to drench
Themſelves with *bellying* goblets. *Philips.*

Be'llyache. *n. ſ.* [from *belly* and *ache.*] The colick; or pain in the bowels.

Be'llybound. *adj.* [from *belly* and *bound.*] Diſeaſed, ſo as to be coſtive, and ſhrunk in the belly.

Be'lly-fretting. *n. ſ.* [from *belly* and *fret.*]

1. [With farriers.] The chafing of a horſe's belly with the foregirt.

2. A great pain in a horſe's belly, cauſed by worms. *Dict.*

Be'llyful. *n. ſ.* [from *belly* and *full.*] As much food as fills the belly, or ſatisfies the appetite.

Be'llygod. *n. ſ.* [from *belly* and *god.*] A glutton; one who makes a god of his belly.

What infinite waſte they made this way, the only ſtory of Apicus, a famous *bellygod*, may ſuffice to ſhew.
Hakewell on Providence.

Be'lly-pinched. *adj.* [from *belly* and *pinch.*] Starved.

This night, wherein the cubdrawn bear would couch,
The lion, and the *belly-pinched* wolf,
Keep their furr dry; unbonnetted he runs. *Shakeſp. K. Lear.*

Be'llyroll. *n. ſ.* [from *belly* and *roll.*] A roll ſo called, as it ſeems, from entering into the hollows.

They have two ſmall harrows that they clap on each ſide of the ridge, and ſo they harrow right up and down, and roll it with a *bellyroll*, that goes between the ridges, when they have ſown it. *Mortimer's Husbandry.*

Be'lly-timber. *n. ſ.* [from *belly* and *timber.*] Food; materials to ſupport the belly.

Where *belly-timber*, above ground
Or under, was not to be found. *Hudibras, cant.* i.

The ſtrength of every other member
Is founded on your *belly-timber.* *Prior.*

Be'lly-worm. *n. ſ.* [from *belly* and *worm.*] A worm that breeds in the belly.

Be'lman. *n. ſ.* [from *bell* and *man.*] He whoſe buſineſs it is to proclaim any thing in towns, and to gain attention by ringing his bell.

It was the owl that ſhriek'd, the fatal *belman*
Which gives the ſtern'ſt good night. *Shakeſp. Macbeth.*

Where Titian's glowing paint the canvas warm'd,
Now hangs the *belman's* ſong, and paſted here
The colour'd prints of Overton appear. *Gay's Trivia.*

The *belman* of each pariſh, as he goes his circuit, cries out every night, Paſt twelve o' clock. *Swift.*

Be'lmetal. *n. ſ.* [from *bell* and *metal.*] The metal of which bells are made; being a mixture of five parts copper with one of pewter.

Belmetal has copper one thouſand pounds, tin from three hundred to two hundred pounds, braſs one hundred and fifty pounds. *Bacon's Phyſical Remains.*

Colours which ariſe on *belmetal*, when melted and poured on the ground, in open air, like the colours of water bubbles, are changed by viewing them at divers obliquities. *Newton's Opt.*

To Belo'ck. *v. a.* [from *be* and *lock.*] To faſten, as with a lock.

This is the hand, with which a vow'd contract
Was faſt *belock'd* in thine. *Shakeſp. Meaſure for Meaſure.*

Be'lomancy. *n. ſ.* [from βέλος and μαντεία.]

Belomancy, or divination by arrows, hath been in requeſt with Scythians, Alans, Germans, with the Africans and Turks of Algier. *Brown's Vulgar Errours, b.* v. *c.* 22.

To Belo'ng. *v. n.* [*belangen*, Dutch.]

1. To be the property of.

To light on a part of a field *belonging* to Boaz. *Ruth*, ii. 3.

2. To be the province or buſineſs of.

There is no need of any ſuch redreſs;
Or if there were, it not *belongs* to you. *Shakeſp. Hen.* IV.

The declaration of theſe latent philoſophers *belongs* to another paper. *Boyle.*

To Jove the care of heav'n and earth *belongs*. *Dryd. Virg.*

3. To adhere, or be appendent to.

He went into a deſart *belonging* to Bethſaida. *Luke*, ix. 10.

4. To have relation to.

To whom *belongeſt* thou? whence art thou? 1 *Sam.* xxx. 13.

5. To be the quality or attributes of.

The faculties *belonging* to the ſupreme ſpirit, are unlimited and boundleſs, fitted and deſigned for infinite objects.
Cheyne's Philoſophical Principles.

6. To be referred to.

He careth for things that *belong* to the Lord. 1 *Cor.* vii. 32.

Belo'ved. *participle.* [from *belove*, derived of *love.* It is obſervable,

ſervable, that, though the *participle* be of very frequent uſe, the *verb* is ſeldom or never admitted; as we ſay, you are much *beloved* by me, but not, I *belove* you.] Loved; dear.

I think, it is not meet,
Mark Anthony, ſo well *belov'd* of Cæſar,
Should outlive Cæſar. *Shakeſp. Julius Cæſar.*

In likeneſs of a dove
The ſpirit deſcended, while the father's voice
From heav'n pronounc'd him his *beloved* ſon.
Milton's Paradiſe Regained, b. i. *l.* 32.

BELO'W. *prep.* [from *be* and *low.*]

1. Under in place; not ſo high.

He'll beat Aufidius' head *below* his knee,
And tread upon his neck. *Shakeſp. Macbeth.*

2. Inferiour in dignity.

The noble Venetians think themſelves equal at leaſt to the electors of the empire, and but one degree *below* kings. *Addiſon on Italy.*

3. Inferiour in excellence.

His Idylliums of Theocritus are as much *below* his Manilius, as the fields are below the ſtars. *Felton on the Claſſicks.*

4. Unworthy of; unbefitting.

'Tis much *below* me on his throne to ſit;
But when I do, you ſhall petition it. *Dryden's Indian Emp.*

BELO'W. *adv.*

1. In the lower place; in the place neareſt the center.

To men ſtanding *below* on the ground, thoſe that be on the top of Paul's, ſeem much leſs than they are, and cannot be known; but, to men above, thoſe *below* ſeem nothing ſo much leſſened, and may be known. *Bacon's Nat. Hiſtory,* N° 205.

The upper regions of the air perceive the collection of the matter of the tempeſts and winds before the air here *below*; and therefore the obſcuring of the ſmaller ſtars, is a ſign of tempeſt following. *Bacon's Natural Hiſtory,* N° 818.

His ſultry heat infects the ſky;
The ground *below* is parch'd, the heav'ns above us fry. *Dryd.*

This ſaid, he led them up the mountain's brow,
And ſhews them all the ſhining fields *below.* *Dryden.*

2. On earth; in oppoſition to *heaven.*

And let no tears from erring pity flow,
For one that's bleſs'd above, immortaliz'd *below.*
Smith, To the Memory of J. Philips.

The faireſt child of Jove,
Below for ever ſought, and bleſs'd above. *Prior.*

3. In hell; in the regions of the dead; oppoſed to *heaven* and *earth.*

The gladſome ghoſts in circling troops attend,
Delight to hover near; and long to know
What bus'neſs brought him to the realms *below.* *Dryd. Æn.*

When ſuff'ring ſaints aloft in beams ſhall glow,
And proſp'rous traitors gnaſh their teeth *below.* *Tickell.*

To BELO'WT. *v. a.* [from *be* and *lowt,* a word of contempt.] To treat with opprobrious language; to call names.

Sieur Gaulard, when he heard a gentleman report, that, at a ſupper, they had not only good cheer, but alſo ſavoury epigrams, and fine anagrams, returning home, rated and *belowted* his cook, as an ignorant ſcullion, that never dreſſed him either epigrams or anagrams. *Camden's Remains.*

BELSWA'GGER. *n. ſ.* A cant word for a whoremaſter.

You are a charitable *belſwagger*; my wife cried out fire, and you called out for engines. *Dryden's Spaniſh Friar.*

BELT. *n. ſ.* [belt, Sax. *baltheus,* Lat.] A girdle; a cincture in which a ſword, or ſome weapon, is commonly hung.

He cannot buckle his diſtemper'd cauſe
Within the *belt* of rule. *Shakeſp. Macbeth.*

Ajax ſlew himſelf with the ſword given him by Hector, and Hector was dragged about the walls of Troy by the *belt* given him by Ajax. *South.*

Then ſnatch'd the ſhining *belt,* with gold inlaid;
The *belt* Eurytion's artful hands had made. *Dryden's Æneid.*

BELWE'THER. *n. ſ.* [from *bell* and *wether.*] A ſheep which leads the flock with a bell on his neck.

The fox will ſerve my ſheep to gather,
And drive to follow after their *belwether.* *Spenſ. Hub. Tale.*

To offer to get your living by the copulation of cattle; to be a bawd to a *belwether.* *Shakeſp. As you like it.*

The flock of ſheep, and *belwether,* thinking to break into another's paſture, and being to paſs over another bridge, juſtled till both fell into the ditch. *Howel's England's Tears.*

To BELY'. See BELIE.

To BEMA'D. *v. a.* [from *be* and *mad.*] To make mad; to turn the brain.

Making juſt report
Of how unnatural and *bemadding* ſorrow,
The king hath cauſe to plain. *Shakeſp. King Lear.*

To BEMI'RE. *v. a.* [from *be* and *mire.*] To drag, or incumber in the mire; to ſoil by paſſing through dirty places.

Away they rode in homely ſort,
Their journey long, their money ſhort,
The loving couple well *bemir'd*;
The horſe and both the riders tir'd. *Swift.*

To BEMO'AN. *v. a.* [from *to moan.*] To lament; to bewail; to expreſs ſorrow for.

He falls, he fills the houſe with heavy groans,
Implores their pity, and his pain *bemoans.* *Dryden's Æneid.*

The gods themſelves the ruin'd ſeats *bemoan,*
And blame the miſchiefs that themſelves have done.
Addiſon's Remarks on Italy.

BEMO'ANER. *n. ſ.* [from the verb.] A lamenter; the perſon that laments.

To BEMO'IL. *v. a.* [*be* and *moil,* from *mouiller,* Fr.] To bedraggle; to bemire; to encumber with dirt and mire.

Thou ſhouldſt have heard in how miry a place, how ſhe was *bemoiled,* how he left her with the horſe upon her. *Shakeſp.*

To BEMO'NSTER. *v. a.* [from *be* and *monſter.*] To make monſtrous.

Thou chang'd, and ſelf-converted thing! for ſhame,
Bemonſter not thy feature. *Shakeſp. King Lear.*

BEMU'SED. *adj.* [from *to muſe.*] Overcome with muſing; dreaming: a word of contempt.

Is there a parſon much *bemus'd* in beer,
A maudlin poeteſs, a rhiming peer? *Pope's Epiſtles.*

BEN. See BEHEN.

BENCH. *n. ſ.* [benc, Sax. *banc,* Fr.]

1. A ſeat, diſtinguiſhed from a *ſtool* by its greater length.

The ſeats and *benches* ſhone of ivory,
An hundred nymphs ſat ſide by ſide about. *Spenſ. Viſ. of Bellay.*

All Rome is pleas'd, when Statius will rehearſe,
And longing crouds expect the promis'd verſe;
His lofty numbers, with ſo great a guſt,
They hear, and ſwallow with ſuch eager luſt:
But while the common ſuffrage crown'd his cauſe,
And broke the *benches* with their loud applauſe,
His muſe had ſtarv'd, had not a piece unread,
And by a player bought, ſupply'd her bread. *Dryd. Juvenal.*

2. A ſeat of juſtice; the ſeat where judges ſit.

A ſon ſet your decrees at naught:
To pluck down juſtice from your awful *bench*;
To trip the courſe of law, and blunt the ſword
That guards the peace and ſafety of your perſon.
Shakeſp. Henry IV. *p.* ii.

Cyriac, whoſe grandſire on the royal *bench*
Of Britiſh Themis, with no mean applauſe,
Pronounc'd, and in his volumes taught our laws,
Which others at their bar ſo often wrench. *Milton.*

3. The perſons ſitting on a *bench*; as, the whole *bench* voted the ſame.

Fools to popular praiſe aſpire,
Of publick ſpeeches, which worſe fools admire;
While, from both *benches,* with redoubl'd ſounds,
Th' applauſe of lords and commoners abounds. *Dryd. Virg.*

To BENCH. *v. a.* [from the noun.]

1. To furniſh with benches.

'Twas *bench'd* with turf, and, goodly to be ſeen,
The thick young graſs aroſe in freſher green. *Dryden's Fab.*

2. To ſeat upon a bench.

His cupbearer, whom I from meaner form
Have *bench'd,* and rear'd to worſhip. *Shakeſp. Winter's Tale.*

BE'NCHER. *n. ſ.* [from *bench.*] Thoſe gentlemen of the inns of court are called *benchers,* who have been readers; they being admitted to plead within the bar, are alſo called inner barriſters. The *benchers,* being the ſeniors of the houſe, are intruſted with its government and direction, and out of them is a treaſurer yearly choſen. *Blount. Chambers.*

I was taking a walk in the gardens of Lincoln's-Inn, a favour that is indulged me by ſeveral *benchers,* who are grown old with me. *Tatler,* N° 100.

To BEND. *v. a.* pret. *bended,* or *bent*; part. paſſ. *bended,* or *bent.* [benban, Saxon; *bander,* Fr. as *Skinner* thinks, from *pandare,* Lat.]

1. To make crooked; to crook; to inflect.

The rainbow compaſſeth the heaven with a glorious circle, and the hands of the Moſt High hath *bended* it. *Ecclus,* xliii. 12.

They *bend* their bows, they whirl their ſlings around:
Heaps of ſpent arrows fall, and ſtrew the ground;
And helms, and ſhields, and rattling arms reſound.
Dryden's Æneid.

2. To direct to a certain point.

Octavius, and Mark Anthony,
Came down upon us with a mighty power,
Bending their expedition tow'rd Philippi. *Shakeſp. J. Cæſar.*

Why doſt thou *bend* thy eyes upon the earth,
And ſtart ſo often, when thou ſitt'ſt alone. *Shakeſp.*

Your gracious eyes upon this labour *bend.* *Fairfax, b.* i.

To that ſweet region was our voyage *bent,*
When winds, and ev'ry warring element,
Diſturb'd our courſe. *Dryden's Virgil.*

Then, with a ruſhing ſound, th' aſſembly *bend*
Diverſe their ſteps: the rival rout aſcend
The royal dome. *Pope's Odyſſey, b.* ii. *l.* 295.

3. To apply.

Men will not *bend* their wits to examine, whether things, wherewith they have been accuſtomed, be good or evil. *Hooker.*

He is within, with two right reverend fathers,
Divinely *bent* to meditation. *Shakeſp. Richard* III.

When

When he fell into the gout, he was no longer able to *bend* his mind or thoughts to any publick business. *Temple.*

4. To put any thing in order for use; a metaphor taken from bending the bow.

I'm settled, and *bend* up
Each corporal agent to this terrible feat. *Shakesp. King Lear.*

As a fowler was *bending* his net, a blackbird asked him what he was doing. *L'Estrange, fab.* xcvi.

5. To incline.

But when to mischief mortals *bend* their will,
How soon they find fit instruments of ill? *Pope's R. of the L.*

6. To subdue; to make submissive; as, war and famine will *bend* our enemies.

7. *To bend the brow.* To knit the brow; to frown.

Some have been seen to bite their pen, scratch their head, *bend their brows,* bite their lips, beat the board, and tear their paper. *Camden's Remains.*

To Bend. *v. n.*

1. To be incurvated.

2. To lean or jut over.

There is a cliff, whose high and *bending* head
Looks fearfully on the confined deep. *Shakesp.*

Earth seems
Far stretch'd around, to meet the *bending* sphere. *Thomson.*

3. To resolve; to determine.

Not so, for once, indulg'd they sweep the main,
Deaf to the call, or, hearing, hear in vain;
But, *bent* on mischief, bear the waves before. *Dryd. Fables.*

While good, and anxious for his friend,
He's still severely *bent* against himself;
Renouncing sleep, and rest, and food, and ease. *Addis. Cato.*

A state of slavery, which they are *bent* upon with so much eagerness and obstinacy. *Addison. Freeholder.*

He is every where *bent* on instruction, and avoids all manner of digressions. *Addison's Essay on the Georgicks.*

4. To be submissive; to bow.

The sons of them that afflicted thee, shall come *bending* unto thee. *Isaiah,* lx. 14.

Bend. *n. s.* [from *to bend.*]

1. Flexure; incurvation.

'Tis true, this god did shake;
His coward lips did from their colour fly;
And that same eye, whose *bend* doth awe the world,
Did lose its lustre. *Shakesp. Julius Cæsar.*

2. The crooked timbers which make the ribs or sides of a ship. *Skinner.*

3. With heralds. One of the eight honourable ordinaries, containing a fifth when uncharged; but when charged, a third part of the escutcheon. It is made by two lines, drawn thwartways from the dexter chief to the sinister base point. *Harris.*

Be'ndable. *adj.* [from *bend.*] That may be incurvated; that may be inclined.

Be'nder. *n. s.* [from *to bend.*]

1. The person who bends.

2. The instrument with which any thing is bent.

These bows, being somewhat like the long bows in use amongst us, were bent only by a man's immediate strength, without the help of any *bender,* or rack, that are used to others. *Wilkins's Mathematical Magick.*

Be'ndwith. *n. s.* An herb. *Dict.*

Bene'aped. *adj.* [from *neap.*] A ship is said to be *beneaped,* when the water does not flow high enough to bring her off the ground, over a bar, or out of a dock. *Dict.*

Bene'ath. *prep.* [beneop, Sax. beneden, Dutch.]

1. Under; lower in place.

Their woolly fleeces, as the rites requir'd,
He laid *beneath* him, and to rest retir'd. *Dryden, Æn.* vii.

Ages to come might Ormond's picture know;
And palms for thee *beneath* his laurels grow. *Prior.*

2. Under, as overborn or overwhelmed by some pressure.

Our country sinks *beneath* the yoke;
It weeps, it bleeds, and each new day a gash
Is added to her wounds. *Shakesp. Macbeth.*

And oft on rocks their tender wings they tear,
And sink *beneath* the burdens which they bear. *Dryden's Virg.*

3. Lower in rank, excellence, or dignity.

We have reason then to be persuaded, that there are far more species of creatures above us, than there are *beneath.* *Locke.*

4. Unworthy of; unbeseeming; not equal to.

He will do nothing that is *beneath* his high station, nor omit doing any thing which becomes it. *Atterbury.*

Bene'ath. *adv.*

1. In a lower place; under.

I destroyed the Amorite before them; I destroyed his fruits from above, and his roots from *beneath.* *Amos,* ii. 9.

The earth which you take from *beneath,* will be barren and unfruitful. *Mortimer's Art of Husbandry.*

2. Below, as opposed to *heaven.*

Any thing that is in heaven above, or that is in the earth *beneath.* *Exodus,* xx. 4.

Be'nedict. *adj.* [*benedictus,* Lat.] Having mild and salubrious qualities: an old physical term.

It is not a small thing won in physick, if you can make rhubarb, and other medicines that are *benedict,* as strong purgers as those that are not without some malignity. *Bacon's N. Hist.*

Benedi'ction. *n. s.* [*benedictio,* Lat.]

1. Blessing; a decretory pronunciation of happiness.

A sov'reign shame so bows him; his unkindness,
That stript her from his *benediction,* turn'd her
To foreign casualties, gave her dear rights
To his doghearted daughters. *Shakesp. King Lear.*

From him will raise
A mighty nation; and upon him show'r
His *benediction* so, that, in his seed,
All nations shall be blest. *Milton's Par. Lost, b.* xii. *l.* 125.

2. The advantage conferred by blessing.

Prosperity is the blessing of the Old Testament; adversity is the blessing of the New; which carrieth the greater *benediction,* and the clearer revelation of God's favour. *Bacon's Essays.*

3. Acknowledgments for blessings received; thanks.

Could he less expect
Than glory and *benediction,* that is, thanks? *Parad. Reg.*

Such ingenious and industrious persons are delighted in searching out natural rarities; reflecting upon the Creator of them his due praises and *benedictions.* *Ray on the Creation.*

4. The form of instituting an abbot.

What consecration is to a bishop, that *benediction* is to an abbot; but in a different way: for a bishop is not properly such, till consecration; but an abbot, being elected and confirmed, is properly such before *benediction.* *Ayliffe's Parergon.*

Benefa'ction. *n. s.* [from *benefacio,* Lat.]

1. The act of conferring a benefit.

2. The benefit conferred; which is the more usual sense.

One part of the *benefactions,* was the expression of a generous and grateful mind. *Atterbury.*

Benefa'ctor. *n. s.* [from *benefacio,* Lat.] He that confers a benefit; frequently he that contributes to some publick charity.

Then swell with pride, and must be titled gods,
Great *benefactors* of mankind, deliverers,
Worshipp'd with temple, priest, and sacrifice.
Milton's Paradise Regained, b. iii. *l.* 82.

From that preface he took his hint, though he had the baseness not to acknowledge his *benefactor.* *Dryden's Fables, Pref.*

I cannot but look upon the writer as my *benefactor,* if he conveys to me an improvement of my understanding. *Addison. Freeholder,* N° 40.

Whoever makes ill returns to his *benefactor,* must needs be a common enemy to mankind. *Swift's Gulliver's Travels.*

Benefa'ctress. *n. s.* [from *benefactor.*] A woman who confers a benefit.

Be'nefice. *n. s.* [from *beneficium,* Lat.] Advantage conferred on another. This word is generally taken for all ecclesiastical livings, be they dignities or others. *Cowel.*

And of the priest eftsoons 'gan to enquire,
How to a *benefice* he might aspire. *Spenser's Hubb. Tale.*

Much to himself he thought, but little spoke,
And, undepriv'd, his *benefice* forsook. *Dryden's Fables.*

Be'neficed. *adj.* [from *benefice.*] Possessed of a benefice, or church preferment.

The usual rate between the *beneficed* man and the religious person, was one moiety of the benefice. *Ayliffe's Parergon.*

Bene'ficence. *n. s.* [from *beneficent.*] The practice of doing good; active goodness.

You could not extend your *beneficence* to so many persons; yet you have lost as few days as that excellent emperour. *Dryden's Juvenal, Dedicat.*

Love and charity extends our *beneficence* to the miseries of our brethren. *Rogers.*

Bene'ficent. *adj.* [from *beneficus, beneficentior,* Lat.] Kind; doing good. It differs from *benign,* as the act from the disposition; *beneficence* being kindness, or *benignity,* exerted in action.

Such a creature could not have his origination from any less than the most wise and *beneficent* being, the great God. *Hale's Origin of Mankind.*

But Phœbus, thou, to man *beneficent,*
Delight'st in building cities. *Prior.*

Benefi'cial. *adj.* [from *beneficium,* Lat.]

1. Advantageous; conferring benefits; profitable; useful; with *to* before the person benefited.

Not that any thing is made to be *beneficial to* him, but all things for him, to shew beneficence and grace in them. *Hooker, b.* i. § 8.

This supposition grants the opinion to conduce to order in the world, and consequently to be very *beneficial to* mankind. *Tillotson, sermon* i.

The war, which would have been most *beneficial to* us, and destructive to the enemy, was neglected. *Swift.*

Are the present revolutions in circular orbs, more *beneficial* than the other would be? *Bentley's Sermons.*

2. Helpful; medicinal.

In the first access of such a disease, any deobstruent, without much acrimony, is *beneficial.* *Arbuthnot on Diet.*

Benefi'cial. *n. s.* An old word for a benefice.

For

For that the groundwork is, and end of all,
How to obtain a *beneficial.* *Spenser's Hubberd's Tale.*

BENEFI'CIALLY. *adv.* [from *beneficial.*] Advantageously; profitably; helpfully.

BENEFI'CIALNESS. *n. s.* [from *beneficial.*] Usefulness; profit; helpfulness.

Though the knowledge of these objects be commendable for their contentation and curiosity, yet they do not commend their knowledge to us, upon the account of their usefulness and *beneficialness.* *Hale's Origin of Mankind.*

BENEFI'CIARY. *adj.* [from *benefice.*] Holding something in subordination to another; having a dependent and secondary possession, without sovereign power.

The duke of Parma was tempted by no less promise, than to be made a feudatory, or *beneficiary* king of England, under the seignory in chief of the pope. *Bacon's War with Spain.*

BENEFI'CIARY. *n. s.* He that is in possession of a benefice.

A benefice is either said to be a benefice with the cure of souls, or otherwise. In the first case, if it be annexed to another benefice, the *beneficiary* is obliged to serve the parish church in his own proper person. *Ayliffe's Parergon.*

BE'NEFIT. *n. s.* [*beneficium*, Lat.]

1. A kindness; a favour conferred; an act of love.

When noble *benefits* shall prove
Not well dispos'd, the mind grown once corrupt,
They turn to vicious forms. *Shakesp. Henry* VIII.

Bless the Lord, O my soul, and forget not all his *benefits.* *Psalm* ciii. 2.

As many as offer'd life,
Neglect not, and the *benefit* embrace
By faith, not void of works. *Paradise Lost, b.* xii. *l.* 426.

2. Advantage; profit; use.

The creature abateth his strength for the *benefit* of such as put their trust in thee. *Wisdom,* xvi. 24.

3. In law.

Benefit of clergy is an ancient liberty of the church, when a priest, or one within orders, is arraigned of felony before a secular judge, he may pray his clergy; that is, pray to be delivered to his ordinary, to purge himself of the offence objected to him: and this might be done in case of murder. The ancient law, in this point of *clergy,* is much altered; for clerks are no more delivered to their ordinaries to be purged, but now every man, though not within orders, is put to read at the bar, being found guilty, and convicted of such felony as this *benefit* is granted for; and so burnt in the hand, and set free for the first time, if the ordinary's commissioner, or deputy, standing by, do say, *Legit ut clericus*; or, otherwise, suffereth death for his transgression. *Cowel.*

To BE'NEFIT. *v. a.* [from the noun.] To do good to; to advantage.

What course I mean to hold,
Shall nothing *benefit* your knowledge. *Shakesp. Wint. Tale.*

He was so far from *benefiting* trade, that he did it a great injury, and brought Rome in danger of a famine. *Arbuthnot.*

To BE'NEFIT. *v. n.* To gain advantage.

To tell you therefore what I have *benefited* herein, among old renowned authors, I shall spare. *Milton on Education.*

BENE'MPT. *adj.* [See NEMPT.] Appointed; marked out; an obsolete word.

Much greater gifts for Guerdon thou shalt gain,
Than kid or cosset, which I thee *benempt*;
Then up, I say. *Spenser's Pastorals.*

To BENE'T. *v. a.* [from *net.*] To ensnare; to surround as with toils.

Being thus *benetted* round with villains,
Ere I could mark the prologue, to my bane,
They had begun the play. *Shakesp. Hamlet.*

BENE'VOLENCE. *n. s.* [*benevolentia*, Lat.]

1. Disposition to do good; kindness; charity; good will.

Grasp the whole worlds of reason, life, and sense,
In one close system of *benevolence.* *Pope's Essay on Man.*

2. The good done; the charity given.

3. A kind of tax.

This tax, called a *benevolence*, was devised by Edward IV. for which he sustained much envy. It was abolished by Richard III. *Bacon's Henry* VII.

BENE'VOLENT. *adj.* [*benevolens, benevolentia*, Lat.] Kind; having good will, or kind inclinations.

Thou good old man, *benevolent* as wise. *Pope's Odyssey.*

Nature all
Is blooming and *benevolent* like thee. *Thomson.*

BENE'VOLENTNESS. *n. s.* The same with *benevolence.*

BENGA'L. *n. s.* [from *Bengal* in the East Indies.] A sort of thin slight stuff, made of silk and hair, for womens apparel.

BE'NJAMIN. *n. s.* [*Benzoin.*] The name of a tree.

From a calyx, which consists of four leaves, are produced three small flowers, which have an oblong tube; the upper part, which is expanded, is divided into eight segments; between which are several short threads, and, in the middle of the tube, is the ovarium, which becomes a fruit. It was brought from Virginia into England, and is propagated by laying down the tender branches in the spring of the year. *Millar.*

BE'NJAMIN. *n. s.* A gum. See BENZOIN.

To BENI'GHT. *v. a.* [from *night.*]

1. To involve in darkness; to embarrass by want of light; to bring on night.

He that has light within his own breast,
May sit i' th' centre, and enjoy bright day;
But he that hides a dark soul, and foul thoughts,
Benighted walks under the mid-day sun;
Himself is his own dungeon. *Milton.*

Those bright stars that did adorn our hemisphere, as those dark shades that did *benight* it, vanish. *Boyle.*

But what so long in vain, and yet unknown
By poor mankind's *benighted* wit, is sought,
Shall in this age to Britain first be shown. *Dryd. Ann. Mir.*

A storm begins, the raging waves run high,
The clouds look heavy, and *benight* the sky. *Garth's Ovid.*

The miserable race of men, that live
Benighted half the year, benumm'd with frosts
Under the polar Bear. *Philips.*

2. To surprise with the coming on of night.

Being *benighted*, the sight of a candle I saw a good way off, directed me to a young shepherd's house. *Sidney, b.* i.

Or some *benighted* angel, in his way,
Might ease his wings; and, seeing heav'n appear
In its best work of mercy, think it there. *Dryden.*

BENI'GN. *adj.* [*benignus*, Lat. It is pronounced without the *g*, as if written *benine*; but the *g* is preserved in *benignity.*]

1. Kind; generous; liberal; actually good. See BENEFICENT.

This turn hath made amends! Thou hast fulfill'd
Thy words, Creator bounteous and *benign!*
Giver of all things fair. *Milton's Parad. Lost, b.* viii. *l.* 492.

So shall the world go on,
To good malignant, to bad men *benign.* *Par. Lost, b.* xii.

We owe more to heav'n than to the sword,
The wish'd return of so *benign* a lord. *Waller.*

What heaven bestows upon the earth, in kind influences and *benign* aspects, is paid it back again in sacrifice and adoration. *South.*

They who delight in the suffering of inferiour creatures, will not be very compassionate or *benign.* *Locke.*

Diff'rent are thy names,
As thy kind hand has founded many cities,
Or dealt *benign* thy various gifts to men. *Prior.*

2. Wholesome; not malignant.

These salts are of a *benign* mild nature, in healthy persons; but, in others, retain their original qualities, which they discover in cachexies. *Arbuthnot on Aliments.*

BENIGN *Disease*, is when all the usual symptoms appear in the small pox, or any acute disease, favourably, and without any irregularities, or unexpected changes. *Quincy.*

BENI'GNESS. *n. s.* [from *benign.*] The same with *benignity.*

BENI'GNITY. *n. s.* [from *benign.*]

1. Graciousness; goodness; actual kindness.

He which useth the benefit of any special *benignity*, may enjoy it with good conscience. *Hooker, b.* v. § 9.

The king was desirous to establish peace rather by *benignity* than blood. *Hayward.*

It is true, that his mercy will forgive offenders, or his *benignity* co-operate to their conversions. *Brown's Vulgar Errours.*

Although he enjoys the good that is done him, he is unconcerned to value the *benignity* of him that does it. *South.*

2. Salubrity; wholesome quality; friendliness to vital nature.

Bones receive a quicker agglutination in sanguine than in cholerick bodies, by reason of the *benignity* of the serum, which sendeth out better matter for a callus. *Wiseman's Surgery.*

BENI'GNLY. *adv.* [from *benign.*] Favourably; kindly; graciously.

'Tis amazement more than love,
Which her radiant eyes do move;
If less splendour wait on thine,
Yet they so *benignly* shine,
I would turn my dazled sight
To behold their milder light. *Waller.*

Oh truly good, and truly great!
For glorious as he rose, *benignly* so he set. *Prior.*

BE'NISON. *n. s.* [*benir*, to bless; *benissons*, Fr.] Blessing; benediction.

We have no such daughter; nor shall ever see
That face of hers again; therefore, begone
Without our grace, our love, our *benison.* *Shakesp. K. Lear.*

Unmuffle, ye fair stars, and thou, fair moon,
That wont'st to love the traveller's *benison.* *Milton.*

BE'NNET. *n. s.* An herb; the same with *avens*, which see.

BENT. *n. s.* [from the verb *to bend.*]

1. The state of being bent; a state of flexure; curvity.

Strike gently, and hold your rod at a *bent* a little while. *Walton's Angler.*

2. Degree of flexure.

There are divers subtle inquiries concerning the strength required to the bending of them; the force they have in the discharge, according to the several *bents*; and the strength required to be in the string of them. *Wilkins's Mathematical Magick.*

3. De-

3. Declivity.

A mountain ſtood,
Threat'ning from high, and overlook'd the wood.
Beneath the lowring brow, and on a *bent*,
The temple ſtood of Mars armipotent. *Dryd. Pal. and Arc.*

4. Utmoſt power, as of a bent bow.

Then let thy love be younger than thyſelf,
Or thy affection cannot hold the *bent*. *Shakeſp. Tw. Night.*

We both obey;
And here give up ourſelves, in the full *bent*,
To lay our ſervice freely at your feet. *Shakeſp. Hamlet.*

5. Application of the mind; ſtrain of the mental powers.

The underſtanding ſhould be brought to the knotty parts of knowledge, that try the ſtrength of thought, and a full *bent* of the mind, by inſenſible degrees. *Locke.*

6. Inclination; diſpoſition towards ſomething.

O who does know the *bent* of womens fantaſy!
Fairy Queen, b. i. *cant.* iv. *ſtanz.* 24.

To your own *bents* diſpoſe you; you'll be found,
Be you beneath the ſky. *Shakeſp. Winter's Tale.*

He knew the ſtrong *bent* of the country towards the houſe of York. *Bacon's Henry* VII.

Soon inclin'd t' admit delight,
The *bent* of nature! *Milton's Par. Loſt, b.* xi. *l.* 597.

The golden age was firſt; when man, yet new,
No rule but uncorrupted reaſon knew;
And, with a native *bent*, did good purſue. *Dryden. Ovid.*

Let there be the ſame propenſity and *bent* of will to religion, and there will be the ſame ſedulity and indefatigable induſtry. *South.*

'Tis odds but the ſcale turns at laſt on nature's ſide, and the evidence of one or two ſenſes gives way to the united *bent* and tendency of all the five. *Atterbury.*

7. Determination; fixed purpoſe.

Their unbelief we may not impute unto inſufficiency in the mean which is uſed, but to the wilful *bent* of their obſtinate hearts againſt it. *Hooker, b.* v. § 22.

Yet we ſaw them forced to give way to the *bent*, and current humour of the people, in favour of their ancient and lawful government. *Temple.*

8. Turn of the temper, or diſpoſition; ſhape, or faſhion, ſuperinduced by art.

Not a courtier,
Although they wear their faces to the *bent*
Of the king's look, but hath a heart that is
Glad at the thing they ſcoul at. *Shakeſp. Cymbeline.*

Two of them hath the very *bent* of honour.
Shakeſp. Much ado about Nothing.

Then thy ſtreight rule ſet virtue in my ſight,
The crooked line reforming by the right;
My reaſon took the *bent* of thy command,
Was form'd and poliſh'd by thy ſkilful hand. *Dryden's Perſ.*

9. Tendency; flexion; particular direction.

The exerciſing the underſtanding, in the ſeveral ways of reaſoning, teacheth the mind ſuppleneſs, to apply itſelf more dexterouſly to *bents* and turns of the matter, in all its reſearches. *Locke.*

10. A ſtalk of graſs, called *bent-graſs*.

His ſpear, a *bent* both ſtiff and ſtrong,
And well near of two inches long;
The pile was of a horſe-fly's tongue,
Whoſe ſharpneſs naught reverſed. *Drayt. Nymphid.*

Then the flowers of the vines; it is a little duſt, like the duſt of a *bent*, which grows upon the cluſter, in the firſt coming forth. *Bacon's Eſſays.*

June is drawn in a mantle of dark graſs-green, upon his head a garland of *bents*, kingcups, and maidenhair.
Peacham on Drawing.

BE'NTING *Time.* [from *bent.*] The time when pigeons feed on bents before peas are ripe.

Bare *benting times*, and moulting months, may come,
When, lagging late, they cannot reach their home.
Dryden's Hind and Panther.

To BENU'M. *v. a.* [benumen, Saxon.]

1. To make torpid; to take away the ſenſation and uſe of any part by cold, or by ſome obſtruction.

So ſtings a ſnake that to the fire is brought,
Which harmleſs lay with cold *benumm'd* before.
Fairfax, b. ii. *ſtanz.* 85.

The winds blow moiſt and keen, which bids us ſeek
Some better ſhroud, ſome better warmth, to cheriſh
Our limbs *benumm'd*. *Milton's Paradiſe Loſt, b.* x. *l.* 1069.

My ſinews ſlacken, and an icy ſtiffneſs
Benums my blood. *Denham's Sophy.*

It ſeizes upon the vitals, and *benums* the ſenſes; and where there is no ſenſe, there can be no pain. *South.*

Will they be the leſs dangerous, when warmth ſhall bring them to themſelves, becauſe they were once frozen and *benummed* with cold? *L'Eſtrange, fab.* ix.

2. To ſtupify.

Theſe accents were her laſt: the creeping death
Benumm'd her ſenſes firſt, then ſtopp'd her breath. *Dryden.*

BENZO'IN. *n. ſ.* A medicinal kind of reſin imported from the Eaſt Indies, and vulgarly called *benjamin*. It is procured by making an inciſion in a tree, whoſe leaves reſemble thoſe of the lemon tree. It is of a yellowiſh colour, an agreeable ſcent, it melts eaſily, and is of three ſorts. The firſt, which is eſteemed the beſt, comes from Siam, and is called *amygdaloides*, being interſperſed with white ſpots, reſembling broken almonds. The ſecond is black, and very odoriferous; it drops from young trees, and comes from Sumatra. The third is alſo black, but leſs odoriferous, and is found in Java and Sumatra. *Trevoux. Chambers.*

The liquor we have diſtilled from *benzoin*, is ſubject to frequent viciſſitudes of fluidity and firmneſs. *Boyle.*

BENZOIN *Tree.* See BENJAMIN *Tree.*

To BEPA'INT. *v. a.* [from *paint.*] To cover with paint.

Thou know'ſt, the maſk of night is on my face,
Elſe would a maiden bluſh *bepaint* my cheek.
Shakeſp. Romeo and Juliet.

To BEPI'NCH. *v. a.* [from *pinch.*] To mark with pinches.

In their ſides, arms, ſhoulders, all *bepincht*,
Ran thick the weals, red with blood, ready to ſtart out.
Chapman's Iliad.

To BEPI'SS. *v. a.* [from *piſs.*] To wet with urine.

One cauſed, at a feaſt, a bagpipe to be played, which made the knight *bepiſs* himſelf, to the great diverſion of all then preſent, as well as confuſion of himſelf. *Derham's Phyſico-Theol.*

To BEQUE'ATH. *v. a.* [cpiþ, Sax. a will.] To leave by will to another.

She had never been diſinherited of that goodly portion, which nature had ſo liberally *bequeathed* to her. *Sidney.*

Let's chooſe executors, and talk of wills;
And yet not ſo—for what can we *bequeath*,
Save our depoſed bodies to the ground? *Shakeſp. Richard* II.

My father *bequeath'd* me by will but a poor thouſand crowns.
Shakeſp. As you like it.

Methinks this age ſeems reſolved to *bequeath* poſterity ſomewhat to remember it. *Glanville's Sceſſis, c.* 21.

For you, whom beſt I love and value moſt,
But to your ſervice I *bequeath* my ghoſt. *Dryden's Fables.*

BEQUE'ATHMENT. *n. ſ.* [from *bequeath.*] A legacy. *Dict.*

BEQU'EST. *n. ſ.* [from *bequeath.*] Something left by will; a legacy.

He claimed the crown to himſelf; pretending an adoption, or *bequeſt*, of the kingdom unto him by the Confeſſor.
Hale's Common Law of England.

To BERA'TTLE. *v. a.* [from *rattle.*] To rattle off; to make a noiſe at in contempt.

Theſe are now the faſhion, and ſo *berattle* the common ſtage, ſo they call them, that many, wearing rapiers, are afraid of gooſequills, and dare ſcarce come thither. *Shakeſp. Hamlet.*

BE'RBERRY. *n. ſ.* [*berberis*, ſometimes written *barberry*, which ſee.] A berry of a ſharp taſte, uſed for pickles.

Some never ripen to be ſweet, as tamarinds, *berberries*, crabs, ſloes, &c. *Bacon's Natural Hiſtory,* Nº 644.

To BERE'AVE. *v. n.* preter. *I bereaved*, or *bereft*. [beɲeoɼian, Saxon.]

1. To ſtrip of; to deprive of. It has generally the particle *of* before the thing taken away.

Madam, you have *bereft* me *of* all words,
Only my blood ſpeaks to you in my veins. *Shakeſp. M. of V.*

That when thou com'ſt to kneel at Henry's feet,
Thou may'ſt *bereave* him *of* his wits with wonder.
Shakeſp. Henry VI. *p.* i.

There was never a prince *bereaved of* his dependences by his council, except there hath been either an overgreatneſs in one counſellor. *Bacon's Eſſays.*

The ſacred prieſts with ready knives *bereave*
The beaſts *of* life. *Dryden's Æneid.*

To deprive us of metals, is to make us mere ſavages; it is to *bereave* us *of* all arts and ſciences, *of* hiſtory and letters, nay *of* revealed religion too, that ineſtimable favour of heaven.
Bentley's Sermons.

2. Sometimes it is uſed without *of*.

Bereave me not,
Whereon I live! thy gentle looks, thy aid,
Thy counſel, in this uttermoſt diſtreſs. *Parad. Loſt, b.* x.

3. To take away from.

All your intereſt in thoſe territories
Is utterly *bereft* you, all is loſt. *Shakeſp. Henry* VI. *p.* ii.

BERE'AVEMENT. *n. ſ.* [from *bereave.*] Deprivation. *Dict.*

BERE'FT. *part. paſſ.* of *bereave.*

The chief of either ſide, *bereft* of life,
Or yielded to the foe, concludes the ſtrife. *Dryden's Fab.*

BERG. See BURROW.

BE'RGAMOT. *n. ſ.* [*bergamotte*, Fr.]

1. A ſort of pear, commonly called *burgamot*. See PEAR.
2. A ſort of eſſence, or perfume, drawn from a fruit produced by ingrafting a lemon tree on a bergamot pear ſtock.
3. A ſort of ſnuff, which is only clean tobacco, with a little of the eſſence rubbed into it.

BE'RGMASTER. *n. ſ.* [from beɲᵹ, Sax. and *maſter.*] The bailiff, or chief officer, among the Derbyſhire miners.

BE'RGMOTE. *n. s.* [of beɲᵹ, a mountain, and mote, a meeting, Saxon.] A court held upon a hill for deciding controversies among the Derbyshire miners. *Blount.*

To BERHY'ME. *v. a.* [from *rhyme.*] To celebrate in rhyme, or verses: a word of contempt.

Now is he for the numbers that Petrarch flow'd in: Laura to his lady was but a kitchen wench; marry, she had a better love to *berhyme* her. *Shakesp. Romeo and Juliet.*

I sought no homage from the race that write;
I kept, like Asian monarchs, from their sight:
Poems I heeded, now *berhymed* so long,
No more than thou, great George! a birthday song. *Pope.*

BERLI'N. *n. s.* [from *Berlin*, the city where they were first made.] A coach of a particular form.

Beware of Latin authors all!
Nor think your verses sterling,
Though with a golden pen you scrawl,
And scribble in a *berlin*. *Swift.*

BERME. *n. s.* [Fr. In fortification.] A space of ground three, four, or five feet wide, left without between the foot of the rampart and the side of the mote, to prevent the earth from falling down into the mote; and sometimes it is palisadoed. *Harris.*

To BERO'B. *v. a.* [from *rob.*] To rob; to plunder; to wrong any, by taking away something from him by stealth or violence.

She said, ah dearest lord! what evil star
On you hath frown'd, and pour'd his influence bad,
That of yourself you thus *berobbed* are. *Fairy Queen, b.* viii.

BE'RRY. *n. s.* [beɲıᵹ, Sax. from beɲan, to bear.] Any small fruit, with many seeds or small stones.

She smote the ground, the which straight forth did yield
A fruitful olive tree, with *berries* spread,
That all the gods admir'd. *Spens. Muiopotmos.*

The strawberry grows underneath the nettle,
And wholesome *berries* thrive and ripen best,
Neighbour'd by fruit of basest quality. *Shakesp. Henry* V.

To BE'RRY. *v. n.* [from the noun.] To bear berries.

BE'RRY-BEARING *Cedar.* [*cedrus baccifera.*]

The leaves are squamose, somewhat like those of the cypress. The katkins, or male flowers, are produced at remote distances from the fruit on the same tree. The fruit is a berry, inclosing three hard seeds in each. The species are, 1. The yellow *berry-bearing cedar*. 2. The Phœnician *cedar*. These trees are propagated by sowing their berries, which are brought from the Streights, in boxes of light sandy earth; but they are at present very rare, and only to be found in some curious old collections. The wood is of great use in the Levant, is large timber, and may be thought the shittim-wood mentioned in the Scripture, of which many of the ornaments to the famous temple of Solomon were made. It is accounted excellent for carving, and esteemed equal almost to any sort of timber for its durableness. *Millar.*

BE'RRY-BEARING *Orach.* See MULBERRY BLIGHT.

BERT, is the same with our *bright*; in the Latin, *illustris* and *clarus*. So *Ecbert*, *eternally famous*, or *bright*; *Sigbert*, *famous conquerour*. And she who was termed by the Germans *Bertha*, was by the Greeks called *Eudoxia*, as is observed by *Lintprandus*. Of the same sort were these, *Phædrus*, *Epiphanius*, *Photius*, *Lampridius*, *Fulgentius*, *Illustrius*. *Gibson's Camden.*

BERTH. *n. s.* [with sailors.] See BIRTH.

BE'RTRAM. *n. s.* [*pyrethrum*, Lat.] A sort of herb, called also *bastard pellitory*.

BE'RYL. *n. s.* [*beryllus*, Lat.] A kind of precious stone.

May thy billows roul ashore
The *beryl* and the golden ore. *Milton.*

The *beryl* of our lapidaries is only a fine sort of cornelian, of a more deep bright red, sometimes with a cast of yellow, and more transparent than the common cornelian. *Woodward's Method of Fossils.*

To BESCRE'EN. *v. a.* [from *screen.*] To cover with a screen; to shelter; to conceal.

What man art thou, that thus *bescreen'd* in night,
So stumblest on my counsel? *Shakesp. Romeo and Juliet.*

To BESE'ECH. *v. a.* pret. I *besought*, I have *besought*. [from ꞃecan, Sax. *versoeken*, Dutch.]

1. To entreat; to supplicate; to implore; sometimes before a person.

I *beseech* you, Sir, pardon me; it is only a letter from my brother, that I have not all over-read. *Shakesp. King Lear.*

I *beseech* thee for my son Onesimus, whom I have begotten in my bonds. *Philemon*, 10.

I, in the anguish of my heart, *beseech* you
To quit the dreadful purpose of your soul. *Addison's Cato.*

2. To beg; to ask; before a thing.

But Eve fell humble, and *besought*
His peace, and thus proceeded in her plaint. *Par. Lost, b.* x.

Before I come to them, I *beseech* your patience, whilst I speak something to ourselves here present. *Sprat.*

To BESE'EM. *v. n.* [*beziemen*, Dutch.] To become; to be fit; to be decent for.

What form of speech, or behaviour, *beseemeth* us in our prayers to Almighty God? *Hooker, b.* v. § 34.

This oversight
Beseems thee not, in whom such virtues spring.
Fairfax, b. i. *stanz.* 78.

Verona's ancient citizens
Cast by their brave *beseeming* ornaments.
Shakesp. Romeo and Juliet.

What thoughts he had, *beseems* not me to say;
Though some surmise he went to fast and pray. *Dryden.*

BESE'EN. *particip.* [from *besie. Skinner.* This word I have only found in *Spenser.*] Adapted; adjusted; becoming.

Forth came that ancient lord and aged queen,
Armed in antique robes down to the ground,
And sad habiliments, right well *beseen*. *Fairy Queen, b.* i.

To BESE'T. *v. a.* pret. I *beset*; I have *beset*. [beꞅıttan, Sax.]

1. To besiege; to hem in; to inclose, as with a siege.

Follow him that's fled;
The thicket is *beset*, he cannot 'scape. *Shakesp. T. G. of Ver.*

Now, Cæsar, let thy troops *beset* our gates,
And barr each avenue———
Cato shall open to himself a passage. *Addison's Cato.*

I know thou look'st on me, as on a wretch
Beset with ills, and cover'd with misfortunes. *Addis. Cato.*

2. To embarrass; to perplex; to entangle without any means of escape.

Now, daughter Sylvia, you are hard *beset*.
Shakesp. Two Gentlemen of Verona.

Thus Adam, sore *beset*, reply'd. *Milton's Par. Lost, b.* x.

Sure, or I read her visage much amiss,
Or grief *besets* her hard. *Rowe's Jane Shore.*

We be in this world *beset* with sundry uneasinesses, distracted with different desires. *Locke.*

3. To waylay; to surround.

Draw forth thy weapon; we're *beset* with thieves;
Rescue thy mistress. *Shakesp. Taming of the Shrew.*

The only righteous in a world perverse,
And therefore hated, therefore so *beset*
With foes, for daring single to be just. *Paradise Lost, b.* xi.

True fortitude I take to be the quiet possession of a man's self, and an undisturbed doing his duty, whatever evil *besets*, or danger lies in his way. *Locke.*

4. To fall upon; to harrass.

But they him spying, both with greedy force
At once upon him ran, and him *beset*
With strokes of mortal steel. *Fairy Queen, b.* ii. *cant.* ii.

To BESHRE'W. *v. a.* [The original of this word is somewhat obscure; as it evidently implies *to wish ill*, some derive it from *beschryen*, Germ. to enchant. *Topsel*, in his *Book of Animals*, deduces it from the *shrew mouse*, an animal, says he, so poisonous, that its bite is a severe curse. A *shrew* likewise signifies a scolding woman; but its origin is not known.]

1. To wish a curse to.

Nay, quoth the cock; but I *beshrew* us both,
If I believe a saint upon his oath. *Dryden's Fables.*

2. To happen ill to.

Beshrew thee, cousin, which did'st lead me forth
Of that sweet way I was in to despair. *Shakesp. Richard* II.

Now much *beshrew* my manners, and my pride,
If Hermia meant to say Lysander lied. *Shakesp.*

BESI'DE. } *prep.* [from *be* and *side.*]
BESI'DES. }

1. At the side of another; near.

Beside the hearse a fruitful palmtree grows,
Ennobled since by this great funeral. *Fairfax, b.* iii. *st.* 72.

He caused me to sit down *beside* him. *Bacon's N. Atlantis.*

At his right hand, Victory
Sat eagle-wing'd: *beside* him hung his bow. *Par. Lost, b.* vi.

Fair Lavinia fled the fire
Before the gods, and stood *beside* her sire. *Dryden's Æneid.*

Fair is the kingcup that in meadow blows;
Fair is the daisy that *beside* her grows. *Gay's Pastorals.*

Now under hanging mountains,
Beside the falls of fountains,
Unheard, unknown,
He makes his moan. *Pope's St. Cæcilia.*

2. Over and above.

Doubtless, in man there is a nature found,
Beside the senses, and above them far. *Sir J. Davies.*

In brutes, *besides* the exercise of sensitive perception and imagination, there are lodged instincts antecedent to their imaginative faculty. *Hale's Origin of Mankind.*

We may be sure there were great numbers of wise and learned men, *beside* those whose names are in the christian records, who took care to examine our Saviour's history.
Addison on the Christian Religion.

Precepts of morality, *besides* the natural corruption of our tempers, are abstracted from ideas of sense.
Addison's Essay on the Georgicks.

3. Not according to, though not contrary; as we say, some things are *beside* nature, some are *contrary* to nature.

The Stoicks did hold a necessary connexion of causes; but they believed, that God doth act *præter & contra naturam*, be-

side and against nature. *Bramhall against Hobbes.*

To say a thing is a chance, as it relates to second causes, signifies no more, than that there are some events *beside* the knowledge, purpose, expectation, and power of second causes. *South.*

Providence often disposes of things by a method *beside*, and above the discoveries of man's reason. *South.*

It is *beside* my present business to enlarge upon this speculation. *Locke.*

4. Out of; in a state of deviating from.

You are too wilful blame,
And, since your coming here, have done
Enough to put him quite *besides* his patience. *Shakesp. H. IV.*

Of vagabonds we say,
That they are ne'er *beside* their way. *Hudibras, cant.* i.

These may serve as landmarks, to shew what lies in the direct way of truth, or is quite *besides* it. *Locke.*

5. Before a reciprocal pronoun, out of; as, *beside himself*; out of the order of rational beings; out of his wits.

They be carried *besides themselves*, to whom the dignity of publick prayer doth not discover somewhat more fitness in men of gravity, than in children. *Hooker, b.* ii. § 31.

Only be patient, till we have appeas'd
The multitude, *beside themselves* with fear. *Shakesp. J. Cæs.*

Festus said with a loud voice, Paul, thou art *beside thyself*: much learning doth make thee mad. *Acts*, xxvi. 24.

BESIDE. } *adv.*
BESIDES. }

1. More than that; over and above.

If Cassio do remain,
He hath a daily beauty in his life,
That makes me ugly; and, *besides*, the Moor
May unfold me to him; there stand I in peril. *Othello.*

Besides, you know not, while you here attend,
Th' unworthy fate of your unhappy friend. *Dryden's Æn.*

That man that doth not know those things, which are of necessity for him to know, is but an ignorant man, whatever he may know *besides*. *Tillotson, serm.* i.

Some wondered, that the Turk never attacks this treasury. But, *besides*, that he has attempted it formerly with no success, it is certain the Venetians keep too watchful an eye. *Addison's Remarks on Italy.*

2. Not in this number; beyond this class; not included here.

And the men said unto Lot, hast thou here any *besides*? *Genesis*, xix. 12.

Outlaws and robbers, who break with all the world *besides*, must keep faith among themselves. *Locke.*

All that we feel of it, begins and ends
In the small circle of our foes or friends;
To all *beside* as much an empty shade,
An Eugene living, as a Cæsar dead. *Pope's Essay on Man.*

And dead, as living, 'tis our author's pride
Still to charm those who charm the world *beside*. *Pope.*

BESI'DERY. *n. s.* A species of pear, which see.

To BESI'EGE. *v. a.* [from *siege.*] To beleaguer; to lay siege to; to beset with armed forces; to endeavour to win a town or fortress, by surrounding it with an army, and forcing the defendants, either by violence or famine, to give admission.

And he shall *besiege* thee in all thy gates, until thy high and fenced walls come down. *Deut.* xxviii. 52.

The queen, with all the northern earls and lords,
Intend here to *besiege* you in your castle. *Shakesp. Henry* VI.

BESI'EGER. *n. s.* [from *besiege.*] One employed in a siege.

There is hardly a town taken, in the common forms, where the *besiegers* have not the worse of the bargain. *Swift.*

To BESLU'BBER. *v. a.* [from *slubber.*] To dawb; to smear.

He persuaded us to tickle our noses with speargrass, and make them bleed; and then *beslubber* our garments with it, and swear it was the blood of true men. *Shakesp. Henry* IV.

To BESME'AR. *v. a.* [from *smear.*]

1. To bedawb; to overspread with something that sticks on.

He lay as in a dream of deep delight,
Besmear'd with precious balm, whose virtuous might
Did heal his wounds. *Fairy Queen, b.* i. *cant.* ii.

That face of his I do remember well;
Yet when I saw it last, it was *besmear'd*
As black as Vulcan. *Shakesp. Twelfth Night.*

First Moloch! horrid king! *besmear'd* with blood
Of human sacrifice, and parents tears. *Paradise Lost, b.* i.

Her fainting hand let fall the sword, *besmear'd*
With blood. *Sir J. Denham.*

Her gushing blood the pavement all *besmear'd*. *Dryden.*

2. To soil; to foul.

My honour would not let ingratitude
So much *besmear* it. *Shakesp. Merchant of Venice.*

To BESMI'RCH. *v. a.* To soil; to discolour.

Perhaps he loves you now,
And now no soil of cautel doth *besmirch*
The virtue of his will. *Shakesp. Hamlet.*

Our gayness, and our gilt, are all *besmirch'd*
With rainy marching in the painful field. *Shakesp. Henry* V.

To BESMO'KE. *v. a.* [from *smoke.*]

1. To foul with smoke.

2. To harden or dry in smoke.

To BESMU'T. *v. a.* [from *smut.*] To blacken with smoke or soot.

BE'SOM. *n. s.* [beſm, beſma, Saxon.] An instrument to sweep with.

Bacon commended an old man that sold *besoms*: a proud young fellow came to him for a *besom* upon trust; the old man said, borrow of thy back and belly, they will never ask thee again; I shall dun thee every day. *Bacon's Apophthegms.*

I will sweep it with the *besom* of destruction, saith the Lord of hosts. *Isaiah*, xiv. 22.

To BESO'RT. *v. a.* [from *sort.*] To suit; to fit; to become.

Such men as may *besort* your age,
And know themselves and you. *Shakesp. King Lear.*

BESO'RT. *n. s.* [from the verb.] Company; attendance; train.

I crave fit disposition for my wife,
With such accommodation and *besort*,
As levels with her breeding. *Shakesp. Othello.*

To BESO'T. *v. a.* [from *sot.*]

1. To infatuate; to stupify; to dull; to take away the senses.

Swinish gluttony
Ne'er looks to heav'n amidst his gorgeous feast,
But, with *besotted* base ingratitude,
Crams and blasphemes his feeder. *Milton.*

Or fools *besotted* with their crimes,
That know not how to shift betimes. *Hudibras, p.* iii. *c.* ii.

He is *besotted*, and has lost his reason; and what then can there be for religion to take hold of him by. *South.*

2. To make to doat.

Paris, you speak
Like one *besotted* on your sweet delights.
Shakesp. Troilus and Cressida.

Trust not thy beauty; but restore the prize,
Which he, *besotted* on that face and eyes,
Would rend from us. *Dryden's Fables.*

BESO'UGHT. [*part. passive* of *beseech*; which see.]

Hasten to appease
Th' incensed Father, and th' incensed Son,
While pardon may be found, in time *besought*.
Milt. Paradise Lost, b. v. *l.* 848.

To BESPA'NGLE. *v. a.* [from *spangle.*] To adorn with spangles; to besprinkle with something shining.

Not Berenice's locks first rose so bright,
The heav'ns *bespangling* with dishevell'd light. *Pope.*

To BESPA'TTER. *v. a.* [from *spatter.*] To soil by throwing filth; to spot or sprinkle with dirt or water.

Those who will not take vice into their bosoms, shall yet have it *bespatter* their faces. *Government of the Tongue*, § 5.

His weapons are the same which women and children use; a pin to scratch, and a squirt to *bespatter*. *Swift, lett.* lxix.

Fair Britain, in the monarch blest,
Whom never faction could *bespatter*. *Swift.*

To BESPA'WL. *v. a.* [from *spawl.*] To dawb with spittle.

To BESPE'AK. *v. a.* I *bespoke*, or *bespake*; I have *bespoke*, or *bespoken*. [from *speak.*]

1. To order, or entreat any thing beforehand, or against a future time.

If you will marry, make your loves to me;
My lady is *bespoke*. *Shakesp. King Lear.*

Here is the cap your worship did *bespeak*.
Shakesp. Taming of the Shrew.

When Baboon came to Strutt's estate, his tradesmen waited upon him, to *bespeak* his custom. *Arbuthnot's Hist. of J. Bull.*

A heavy writer was to be encouraged, and accordingly many thousand copies were *bespoke*. *Swift.*

2. To make way by a previous apology.

My preface looks as if I were afraid of my reader, by so tedious a *bespeaking* of him. *Dryden.*

3. To forebode; to tell something beforehand.

Thy started fears *bespoke* dangers, and formed ominous prognosticks, in order to scare the allies. *Swift, Examin.* N° 45.

4. To speak to; to address. This sense is chiefly poetical.

With hearty words her knight she 'gan to chear,
And, in her modest manner, thus *bespake*,
Dear knight. *Fairy Queen, b.* i. *cant.* i. *stanz.* 8.

At length with indignation thus he broke
His awful silence, and the powers *bespoke*. *Dryden.*

Then staring on her with a ghastly look,
And hollow voice, he thus the queen *bespoke*. *Dryden.*

5. To betoken; to shew.

When the abbot of St. Martin was born, he had so little of the figure of a man, that it *bespoke* him rather a monster. *Locke.*

He has dispatch'd me hence,
With orders that *bespeak* a mind compos'd. *Addison's Cato.*

BESPE'AKER. *n. s.* [from *bespeak.*] He that bespeaks any thing.

They mean not with love to the *bespeaker* of the work, but delight in the work itself. *Wotton's Architecture.*

To BESPE'CKLE. *v. a.* [from *speckle.*] To mark with speckles, or spots.

To BESPE'W. *v. a.* [from *spew.*] To dawb with spew or vomit.

To BESPI'CE. *v. a.* [from *spice.*] To season with spices.

Thou might'st *bespice* a cup
To give mine enemy a lasting wink. *Shakesp. Winter's Tale.*

To Bespi'T. *v. a.* I *bespat*, or *bespit*; I have *bespit*, or *bespitten.* [from *spit.*] To dawb with spittle.

Bespo'ke. [*irreg. particip.* from *bespeak*; which see.]

To Bespo'T. *v. a.* [from *spot.*] To mark with spots.

Mildew rests on the wheat, *bespotting* the stalks with a different colour from the natural. *Mortimer's Husbandry.*

To Bespre'ad. *v. a.* [from *spread.*] To spread over; to cover over.

His nuptial bed,
With curious needles wrought, and painted flowers *bespread.* *Dryden.*

The globe is equally *bespread*; so that no place wants proper inhabitants. *Derham's Physico-Theology.*

To Bespri'nkle. *v. a.* [from *sprinkle.*] To sprinkle over; to scatter over.

He indeed, imitating the father poet, whose life he had also written, hath *besprinkled* his work with many fabulosities. *Brown's Vulgar Errours, b.* i. *c.* 8.

A purple flood
Flows from the trunk, that welters in the blood:
The bed *besprinkles*, and bedews the ground. *Dryden.*

To Bespu'tter. *v. a.* [from *sputter.*] To sputter over something; to dawb any thing by sputtering, or throwing out spittle upon it.

Best. *adj.* the *superlative* from *good.* [bet, betena, betst, good, better, best, Saxon.]

1. Most good; that which has good qualities in the highest degree.

And he will take your fields, even the *best* of them, and give them to his servants. 1 *Samuel*, viii. 14.

When the *best* things are not possible, the best may be made of those that are. *Hooker, b.* v. § 9.

When he is *best*, he is a little more than a man; and when he is worst, he is a little better than a beast. *Shakesp. M. of Ven.*

I think it a good argument to say, the infinitely wise God hath made it so: and therefore it is *best.* But it is too much confidence of our own wisdom, to say, I think it *best*, and therefore God hath made it so. *Locke.*

An evil intention perverts the *best* actions, and makes them sins. *Addison. Spectator*, N° 213.

2. *The best.* The utmost power; the strongest endeavour; the most; the highest perfection.

I profess not talking: only this,
Let each man do his *best.* *Shakesp. Henry* IV. *p.* i.

The duke did his *best* to come down. *Bacon's War with Sp.*

He does this to the *best* of his power. *Locke.*

My friend, said he, our sport is at the *best.* *Addis. Ovid.*

3. *To make the best.* To carry to its greatest perfection; to improve to the utmost.

Let there be freedom to carry their commodities where they may *make the best* of them, except there be some special cause of caution. *Bacon.*

His father left him an hundred drachmas; Alnaschar, in order to *make the best* of it, laid it out in glasses. *Addison. Spect.*

We set sail, and *made the best* of our way, till we were forced, by contrary winds, into St. Remo. *Addison on Italy.*

Best. *adv.* [from *well.*] In the highest degree of goodness.

He shall dwell in that place where he shall choose in one of thy gates, where it liketh him *best.* *Deut.* xxiii. 16.

Best is sometimes used in composition.

These latter *best-be-trust-spies* had some of them further instructions, to draw off the best friends and servants of Perkin, by making remonstrances to them, how weakly his enterprize and hopes were built. *Bacon's Henry* VII.

By this law of loving even our enemies, the christian religion discovers itself to be the most generous and *bestnatured* institution that ever was in the world. *Tillotson, sermon* v.

To Besta'in. *v. a.* [from *stain.*] To mark with stains; to spot.

We will not line his thin *bestained* cloke
With our pure honours. *Shakesp. King John.*

To Beste'ad. *v. a.* I *bested*; I have *bested.* [from *stead.*]

1. To profit.

Hence vain deluding joys,
The brood of folly, without father bred,
How little you *bestead*,
Or fill the fixed mind with all your toys. *Milton.*

2. To treat; to accommodate.

And they shall pass through it hardly *bestead*, and hungry. *Isaiah*, viii. 21.

Be'stial. *adj.* [from *beast.*]

1. Belonging to a beast, or to the class of beasts.

His wild disorder'd walk, his haggard eyes,
Did all the *bestial* citizens surprize. *Dryden's Hind and P.*

2. Having the qualities of beasts; brutal; below the dignity of reason or humanity; carnal.

I have lost the immortal part of myself, and what remains is *bestial.* *Shakesp. Othello.*

Moreover, urge his hateful luxury,
And *bestial* appetite, in change of lust. *Shakesp. Rich.* III.

For those, the race of Israel oft forsook
Their living strength, and, unfrequented, left
His righteous altar, bowing lowly down
To *bestial* gods. *Milton's Paradise Lost, b.* i. *l.* 435.

The things promised are not gross and carnal, such as may court and gratify the most *bestial* part of us. *Decay of Piety.*

Bestia'lity. *n. s.* [from *bestial.*] The quality of beasts; degeneracy from human nature.

What can be a greater absurdity, than to affirm *bestiality* to be the essence of humanity, and darkness the center of light? *Arbuthnot and Pope's Mart. Scriblerus.*

Be'stially. *adv.* [from *bestial.*] Brutally; in a manner below humanity.

To Besti'ck. *v. a.* preter. I *bestuck*, I have *bestuck.* [from *stick.*] To stick over with any thing; to mark any thing by infixing points or spots here and there.

Truth shall retire,
Bestuck with sland'rous darts; and works of faith
Rarely be found. *Milt. Par. Lost, b.* xii. *l.* 536.

To Besti'r. *v. a.* [from *stir.*]

1. To put into vigorous action. It is seldom used otherwise than with the reciprocal pronoun.

As when men wont to watch
On duty, sleeping found by whom they dread,
Rouze and *bestir themselves* ere well awake. *Milton.*

Bestirs her then, and from each tender stalk
Whatever earth, all-bearing mother, yields,
She gathers. *Par. Lost, b.* v.

But, as a dog that turns the spit,
Bestirs himself, and plies his feet
To climb the wheel, but all in vain,
His own weight brings him down again. *Hudibras, p.* ii. *c.* iii.

What aileth them, that they must needs *bestir themselves* to get in air, to maintain the creature's life? *Ray on Creation.*

2. It is used by *Shakespeare* with a common word.

I am scarce in breath, my lord.—No marvel you have so *bestirred* your valour, you cowardly rascal! *Shakesp. King Lear.*

To BESTO'W. *v. a.* [*besteden*, Dutch.]

1. To give; to confer upon.

All men would willingly have yielded him praise; but his nature was such as to *bestow* it upon himself, before any could give it. *Sidney.*

All the dedicate things of the house of the Lord did they *bestow* upon Baalim. 2 *Chron.* xxiv. 7.

Sir Julius Cæsar had, in his office, the disposition of the six clarks places; which he had *bestowed* to such persons as he thought fit. *Clarendon.*

2. To give as charity.

Our Saviour doth plainly witness, that there should not be as much as a cup of cold water *bestowed* for his sake, without reward. *Hooker, b.* ii. § 8.

And though he was unsatisfied in getting,
Which was a sin; yet in *bestowing*, madam,
He was most princely. *Shakesp. Henry* VIII.

Spain to your gift alone her Indies owes;
For what the pow'rful takes not, he *bestows.* *Dryden.*

You always exceed expectations: as if yours was not your own, but to *bestow* on wanting merit. *Dryden's Fables, Ded.*

3. To give in marriage.

Good rev'rend father, make my person yours;
And tell me how you would *bestow* yourself. *Shakesp.*

I could have *bestowed* her upon a fine gentleman, who extremely admired her. *Tatler*, N° 75.

4. To give as a present.

Pure oil and incense on the fire they throw,
And fat of victims which his friends *bestow.* *Dryden.*

5. To apply.

The sea was not the duke of Marlborough's element; otherwise the whole force of the war would infallibly have been *bestowed* there. *Swift.*

6. To lay out upon.

And thou shalt *bestow* that money for whatsoever thy soul lusteth after, for oxen, for sheep, or for wine. *Deut.* xiv. 26.

7. To lay up; to stow; to place.

And when he came to the tower, he took them from their hand, and *bestowed* them in the house. 2 *Kings*, v. 24.

Besto'wer. *n. s.* [from *bestow.*] Giver; he that confers any thing; disposer.

They all agree in making one supreme God; and that there are several beings that are to be worshipped under him; some as the *bestowers* of thrones, but subordinate to the Supreme. *Stillingfl.*

Bestra'ught. *particip.* [Of this *participle* I have not found the *verb*; by analogy we may derive it from *bestract*; perhaps it is corrupted from *distraught.*] Distracted; mad; out of one's senses; out of one's wits.

Ask Marian, the fat alewife, if she knew me not. What! I am not *bestraught.* *Shakesp. Tam. the Shrew.*

To Bestre'w. *v. a.* particip. pass. *bestrewed*, or *bestrown.* [from *strew.*] To sprinkle over.

So thick *bestrown*,
Abject and lost lay these, covering the flood. *Par. Lost, b.* i.

To Bestri'de. *v. a.* I *bestrid*; I have *bestrid*, or *bestridden.* [from *stride.*]

1. To stride over any thing; to have any thing between one's legs.

Why

Why, man, he doth *bestride* the narrow world
Like a colossus. *Shakesp. Julius Cæsar.*
Make him *bestride* the ocean, and mankind
Ask his consent, to use the sea and wind. *Waller.*

2. To step over.

That I see thee here,
Thou noble thing! more dances my rapt heart,
Than when I first my wedded mistress saw
Bestride my threshold. *Shakesp. Coriolanus.*

3. It is often used of riding.

He *bestrides* the lazy pacing clouds,
And sails upon the bosom of the air. *Shakesp. Rom. and Jul.*
That horse, that thou so often hast *bestrid:*
That horse, that I so carefully have dress'd. *Shakesp. R.* II.
Venetians do not more uncouthly ride,
Than did their lubber state mankind *bestride.* *Dryden.*
The bounding steed you pompously *bestride*,
Shares with his lord the pleasure and the pride. *Pope.*

4. It is used sometimes of a man standing over something which he defends.

He *bestrid*
An o'erpress'd Roman, and i' th' consul's view
Slew three opposers: Tarquin's self he met,
And struck him on his knee. *Shakesp. Coriolanus.*
Let us rather
Hold fast the mortal sword; and, like good men,
Bestride our downfaln birthdom. *Shakesp. Macbeth.*

If thou see me down in the battle, and *bestride* me, so; 'tis a point of friendship. *Shakesp. Henry* IV. *p.* i.

He doth *bestride* a bleeding land,
Gasping for life, under great Bolingbroke. *Shak. Henry* IV.

To Bestu'd. *v. a.* [from *stud.*] To adorn with studs, or shining prominences.

Th' unsought diamonds
Would so emblaze the forehead of the deep,
And so *bestud* with stars, that they below
Would grow inur'd to light. *Milton.*

BET. *n. s.* [pebbian, to wager; peb, a wager, Sax. from which the etymologists derive *bet.* I should rather imagine it to come from betan, to mend, encrease, or *better*, as a *bet* encreases the original wager.] A wager; something laid to be won upon certain conditions.

The hoary fool, who many days
Has struggl'd with continu'd sorrow,
Renews his hope, and blindly lays
The desp'rate *bet* upon tomorrow. *Prior.*
His pride was in piquette,
Newmarket fame, and judgment at a *bet.* *Pope.*

To Bet. *v. a.* [from the noun.] To wager; to stake at a wager.

He drew a good bow: and dead? John of Gaunt loved him well, and *betted* much upon his head. *Shakesp. Henry* IV. *p.* ii.

He flies the court for want of clothes,
Cries out 'gainst cocking, since he cannot *bet.* *B. Johnson.*
The god, unhappily engag'd,
Complain'd, and sigh'd, and cry'd, and fretted,
Lost ev'ry earthly thing he *betted.* *Prior.*

Bet. The old *preterite* of *beat.*

He staid for a better hour, till the hammer had wrought and *bet* the party more pliant. *Bacon's Henry* VII.

To Beta'ke. *v. a.* preter. I *betook*; part. pass. *betaken.* [from *take.*]

1. To take; to seize: an obsolete sense.

Then to his hands that writ he did *betake*,
Which he disclosing read. *Fairy Queen, b.* i. *c.* xii. *st.* 25.

2. To have recourse to; with the reciprocal pronoun.

The adverse party *betaking itself* to such practices as men embrace, when they behold things brought to desperate extremities. *Hooker, b.* iv. § 14.

Thou tyrant!
Do not repent these things; for they are heavier
Than all thy woes can stir: therefore *betake thee*
To nothing but despair. *Shakesp. Winter's Tale.*
The rest, in imitation, to like arms
Betook them, and the neighb'ring hills up tore.
Milton's Paradise Lost, b. vi. *l.* 663.

3. To apply; with the reciprocal pronoun.

With ease such fond chimeras we pursue,
As fancy frames for fancy to subdue:
But when *ourselves* to action we *betake*,
It shuns the mint, like gold that chymists make. *Dryden.*

As my observations have been the light whereby I have hitherto steer'd my course, so I here *betake myself* to them again. *Woodward's Natural History.*

4. To move; to remove.

Soft she withdrew; and, like a wood nymph light,
Oread or Dryad, or of Delia's train,
Betook her to the groves. *Milton's Paradise Lost, b.* ix. *l.* 389.
They both *betook them* several ways;
Both to destroy. *Milton's Paradise Lost, b.* x. *l.* 610.

To Bete'em. *v. a.* [from *teem.*] To bring forth; to bestow; to give.

So would I, said th' enchanter, glad and fain
Beteem to you his sword, you to defend;
But that this weapon's pow'r I well have kend,
To be contrary to the work that ye intend. *Fairy Q. b.* ii.
Belike for want of rain; which I could well
Beteem them from the tempest of mine eyes.
Shakesp. Midsummer Night's Dream.

To Bethi'nk. *v. a.* I *bethought*; I have *bethought.* [from *think.*] To recal to reflection; to bring back to consideration, or recollection. It is generally used with the reciprocal pronoun, and *of* before the subject of thought.

They were sooner in danger than they could almost *bethink themselves of* change. *Sidney, b.* ii.

I have *bethought me of* another fault. *Shak. Meas. for M.*

I, better *bethinking myself*, and misliking his determination, gave him this order. *Raleigh's Essays.*

He himself,
Insatiable of glory, had lost all:
Yet *of* another plea *bethought him* soon. *Parad. Regained.*

The nets were laid, yet the birds could never *bethink themselves*, till hamper'd, and past recovery. *L'Estrange.*

Cherippus, then in time *yourself bethink*,
And what your rags will yield by auction sink. *Dryden.*

A little consideration may allay his heat, and make him *bethink himself*, whether this attempt be worth the venture. *Locke.*

BE'THLEHEM. *n. s.* [See BEDLAM.] An hospital for lunaticks.

Be'thlehemite. *n. s.* [See Bedlamite.] A lunatick; an inhabitant of a madhouse.

Betho'ught. *particip.* [from *bethink*; which see.]

To Bethra'l. *v. a.* [from *thrall.*] To enslave; to conquer; to bring into subjection.

Ne let that wicked woman 'scape away,
For she it is that did my lord *bethral.* *Shakesp. King John.*

To Bethu'mp. *v. a.* [from *thump.*] To beat; to lay blows upon: a ludicrous word.

I was never so *bethumpt* with words,
Since first I call'd my brother's father dad. *Shak. King John.*

To Beti'de. *v. n.* pret. *It betided*, or *betid*; part. pass. *betid.* [from tid, Sax. See Tide.]

1. To happen to; to befal; to bechance; whether good or bad.

Said he then to the Palmer, reverend sire,
What great misfortune hath *betid* this knight? *Fairy Queen.*
But say, if our deliverer up to heav'n
Must reascend, what will *betide* the few,
His faithful, left among th' unfaithful herd,
The enemies of truth? *Milton's Paradise Lost, b.* xii. *l.* 480.

2. Sometimes it has *to.*

Neither know I,
What is *betid to* Cloten; but remain
Perplext in all. *Shakesp. Cymbeline.*

3. To come to pass; to fall out; to happen.

She, when her turn was come her tale to tell,
Told of a strange adventure that *betided*,
Betwixt the fox and th' ape by him misguided. *Spens. Hubb.*
In winter's tedious nights, sit by the fire
With good old folks, and let them tell thee tales
Of woful ages, long ago *betid.* *Shakesp. Richard* II.
Let me hear from thee by letters,
Of thy success in love; and what news else
Betideth here in absence of thy friend. *Sh. Two Gent. of Ver.*

4. To become.

If he were dead, what would *betide* of thee? *Sh. Rich.* III.

Beti'me. } *adv.* [from *by* and *time*; that is, by the proper
Beti'mes. } time.]

1. Seasonably; early.

Send succours, lords, and stop the rage *betime.*
Shakesp. Henry VI. *p.* ii.
To measure life, learn thou *betimes*, and know
Toward solid good what leads the nearest way. *Par. Reg.*

2. Soon; before long time has passed.

Whiles they are weak, *betimes* with them contend;
For when they once to perfect strength do grow,
Strong wars they make. *Fairy Queen, b.* ii. *c.* iv. *st.* 34.
He tires *betimes*, that spurs too fast *betimes.* *Sh. Rich.* II.

There be some have an over early ripeness in their years, which fadeth *betimes:* these are first, such as have brittle wits, the edge whereof is soon turned. *Bacon's Essays.*

Remember thy Creator in the days of thy youth; that is, enter upon a religious course *betimes.* *Tillotson, sermon* i.

Short is the date, alas! of modern rhymes;
And 'tis but just to let them live *betimes.* *Pope's Essay on Crit.*

3. Early in the day.

He that drinks all night, and is hanged *betimes* in the morning, may sleep the sounder next day. *Sh. Measure for Measure.*

They rose *betimes* in the morning, and offered sacrifice.
1 *Macc.* iv. 52.

Be'tle. } *n. s.* An Indian plant, called water pepper. *Dict.*
Be'tre. }

To Beto'ken. *v. a.* [from *token.*]

1. To signify; to mark; to represent.

We know not wherefore churches should be the worse, if, at this

this time, when they are delivered into God's own possession, ceremonies fit to *betoken* such intents, and to accompany such actions, be usual. *Hooker, b.* v. § 12.

2. To foreshew; to presignify.

The kindling azure, and the mountain's brow,
Illum'd with fluid gold, his near approach
Betoken glad. *Thomson's Summer, l.* 80.

BE'TONY. *n. s.* [*betonica*, Lat.] A plant.

The leaves are green, rough, and crenated on the edges: the flowers are disposed in a spike; the upper crest of the flower is advanced, and divided into two segments; the beard, or lower part of the flower, is divided into three, and the middle segment is bifid; each flower is, for the most part, succeeded by four naked seeds. The species are, 1. Common or wood *betony*. 2. *Betony*, with a white flower. 3. Greater Danish *betony*. The first is very common in woods and shady places, and is greatly esteemed as a vulnerary herb. *Millar.*

BETO'OK. [*irreg. pret.* from *betake*; which see.]

To BETO'SS. *v. a.* [from *toss*.] To disturb; to agitate; to put into violent motion.

What said my man, when my *betossed* soul
Did not attend him as we rode? *Shakesp. Romeo and Juliet.*

To BETRA'Y. *v. a.* [*trahir*, Fr.]

1. To give into the hands of enemies by treachery, or breach of trust.

If ye be come to *betray* me to mine enemies, seeing there is no wrong in mine hands, the God of our fathers look thereon, and rebuke it. 1 *Chron.* xii. 17.

Jesus said unto them, the Son of man shall be *betrayed* into the hands of men. *Matt.* xvii. 22.

For fear is nothing else but a *betraying* of the succours which reason offereth. *Wisdom*, xvii. 12.

He was not to be won, either by promise or reward, to *betray* the city. *Knolles's History of the Turks.*

2. To discover that which has been entrusted to secrecy.

3. To make known something that were better concealed.

Be swift to hear, but be cautious of your tongue, lest you *betray* your ignorance. *Watts's Improvement of the Mind.*

4. To make liable to fall into something inconvenient.

His abilities created in him great confidence; and this was like enough to *betray* him to great errours, and many enemies. *King Charles.*

The bright genius is ready to be so forward, as often *betrays* itself into great errours in judgment. *Watts.*

5. To show; to discover; in a neutral sense.

The Veian and the Gabian tow'rs shall fall,
And one promiscuous ruin cover all;
Nor, after length of years, a stone *betray*
The place where once the very ruins lay. *Addison on Italy.*

BETRA'YER. *n. s.* [from *betray*.] He that betrays; a traitor.

The wise man doth so say of fear, that it is a *betrayer* of the forces of reasonable understanding. *Hooker, b.* v. § 3.

You cast down your courage through fear, the *betrayer* of all succours which reason can afford. *Sir J. Hayward.*

They are only a few *betrayers* of their country; they are to purchase coin, perhaps, at half price, and vend it among us to the ruin of the publick. *Swift.*

To BETRI'M. *v. a.* [from *trim*.] To deck; to dress; to grace; to adorn; to embellish; to beautify; to decorate.

Thy banks with pionied and tulip'd brims,
Which spungy April at thy hest *betrims*,
To make cold nymphs chaste crowns. *Shakesp. Tempest.*

To BETRO'TH. *v. a.* [from *troth*; *betrowen*, Dutch.]

1. To contract to any one, in order to marriage; to affiance.

He, in the first flower of my freshest age,
Betrothed me unto the only heir
Of a most mighty king, most rich and sage. *Fairy Q. b.* i.

To her, my lord,
Was I *betrothed*, ere I Hermia saw. *Shakesp. Midsum. N. Dr.*

By soul's publick promise she
Was sold then, and *betroth'd* to Victory. *Cowley's Davideis.*

2. To unite any one to another by promise of marriage.

And what man is there that hath *betrothed* a wife, and hath not taken her? let him go and return unto his house. *Deut.* xx. 7.

3. To nominate to a bishoprick, in order to consecration.

If any person be consecrated a bishop to that church, whereunto he was not before *betrothed*, he shall not receive the habit of consecration, as not being canonically promoted. *Ayliffe.*

To BETRU'ST. *v. a.* [from *trust*.] To entrust; to put into the power of another, in confidence of fidelity.

Betrust him with all the good, which our own capacity will allow us, or his sufficiency encourage us to hope for, either in this life, or that to come. *Grew's Cosmologia Sacra, b.* iii. *c.* 5.

Whatsoever you would *betrust* to your memory, let it be disposed in a proper method. *Watts's Improvement of the Mind.*

BE'TTER. *adj.* The *comparative* of *good*. [bet, *good*, betera, *better*, Sax.] Having good qualities in a greater degree than something else. See GOOD.

He has a horse *better* than the Neapolitan's; a *better* bad habit of frowning than the count Palatine. *Shakesp. Merchant of Venice.*

I have seen *better* faces in my time,
Than stand on any shoulders that I see
Before me at this instant. *Shakesp. King Lear.*

Having a desire to depart, and be with Christ; which is far *better*. *Phil.* i. 23.

The BETTER.

1. The superiority; the advantage; with the particle *of* before him, or that, over which the advantage is gained.

The Corinthians that morning, as the days before, had *the better*. *Sidney, b.* ii.

The voyage of Drake and Hawkins was unfortunate; yet, in such sort, as doth not break our prescription, to have had *the better of* the Spaniards. *Bacon's War with Spain.*

Dionysius, his countryman, in an epistle to Pompey, after an express comparison, affords him *the better of* Thucydides. *Brown's Vulgar Errours, b.* i. *c.* 8.

You think fit
To get *the better of* me, and you shall;
Since you will have it so—I will be yours. *Southerne.*

The gentleman had always so much *the better of* the satyrist, that the persons touched did not know where to fix their resentment. *Prior, Preface to his Poems.*

2. Improvement; as, *for the better*, so as to improve it.

If I have altered him any where *for the better*, I must at the same time acknowledge, that I could have done nothing without him. *Dryden's Fab. Preface.*

BE'TTER. *adv.* [comparative of *well*.] Well, in a greater degree.

Then it was *better* with me than now. *Hos.* vii.

Better a mechanick rule were stretched or broken, than a great beauty were omitted. *Dryd. Virg. Dedication.*

The *better* to understand the extent of our knowledge, one thing is to be observed. *Locke.*

He that would know the idea of infinity, cannot do *better*, than by considering to what infinity is attributed. *Locke.*

To BE'TTER *v. a.* [from the noun]

1. To improve; to meliorate.

The very cause of his taking upon him our nature, was to *better* the quality, and to advance the condition thereof. *Hooker, b.* viii. § 54.

He is furnished with my opinion, which is *bettered* with his own learning. *Shakesp. Merchant of Venice.*

Heir to all his lands and goods,
Which I have *better'd*, rather than decreas'd. *Shakesp. Taming of the Shrew.*

But Jonathan, to whom both hearts were known,
With well-tim'd zeal, and with an artful care,
Restor'd, and *better'd* soon, the nice affair. *Cowley's David.*

The church of England, the purest and best reformed church in the world; so well reformed, that it will be found easier to alter than to *better* its constitution. *South.*

The Romans took pains to hew out a passage for these lakes, to discharge themselves, for the *bettering* of the air. *Addison.*

2. To surpass; to exceed.

The works of nature do always aim at that which cannot be *bettered*. *Hooker, b.* i. § 5.

He hath born himself beyond the promise of his age; he hath, indeed, better *bettered* expectation, than you must expect of me to tell you. *Shakesp. Much ado about Nothing.*

What you do
Still *betters* what is done; when you speak sweet,
I'd have you do it ever. *Shakesp. Winter's Tale.*

3. To advance.

The king thought his honour would suffer, during a treaty, to *better* a party. *Bacon's Henry* VII.

BE'TTER. *n. s.* [from the adjective.] Superiour in goodness.

Their *betters* would be hardly found, if they did not live among men, but in a wilderness by themselves. *Hooker, b.* i.

The courtesy of nations allows you my *better*, in that you are the first-born. *Shakesp. As you like it.*

That ye thus hospitably live,
Is mighty grateful to your *betters*,
And makes e'en gods themselves your debtors. *Prior.*

I have some gold and silver by me, and shall be able to make a shift, when many of my *betters* are starving. *Swift.*

BE'TTOR. *n. s.* [from *to bet*.] One that lays betts or wagers.

I observed a stranger among them, of a genteeler behaviour than ordinary; but notwithstanding he was a very fair *bettor*, nobody would take him up. *Addison. Spectator*, N° 126.

BE'TTY. *n. s.* [probably a cant word, without etymology.] An instrument to break open doors.

Record the stratagems, the arduous exploits, and the nocturnal scalades of needy heroes, describing the powerful *betty*, or the artful picklock. *Arbuthnot's History of J. Bull.*

BETWE'EN. *prep.* [betweonan, betwinan, Saxon; from the original word twa, *two*.]

1. In the intermediate space.

What modes
Of smell the headlong lioness *between*,
And hound sagacious on the tainted green? *Pope.*

2. From

2. From one to another; noting intercourse.

He should think himself unhappy, if things should go so *between* them, as he should not be able to acquit himself of ingratitude towards them both. *Bacon's Henry* VII.

3. Belonging to two in partnership.

I ask, whether Castor and Pollux, with only one soul *between* them, which thinks and perceives in one what the other is never conscious of, are not two distinct persons? *Locke.*

4. Bearing relation to two.

If there be any discord or suits *between* them and any of the family, they are compounded and appeased. *Bacon's Atlantis.*

Friendship requires, that it be *between* two at least; and there can be no friendship where there are not two friends. *South.*

5. In separation, or distinction of one from the other.

Their natural constitutions put so wide a difference *between* some men, that art would never master. *Locke.*

Children quickly distinguish *between* what is required of them, and what not. *Locke.*

6. *Between* is properly used of two, and *among* of more; but perhaps this accuracy is not always preserved.

BETWI'XT. *prep.* [betpẏx, Saxon. It has the same signification with *between*, and is indifferently used for it.]

1. In the midst of two.

Hard by, a cottage chimney smokes,
From *betwixt* two aged oaks. *Milton.*

Methinks, like two black storms on either hand,
Our Spanish army and your Indians stand;
This only place *betwixt* the clouds is clear. *Dryd. Ind. Emp.*

If contradicting interests could be mixt,
Nature herself has cast a bar *betwixt*. *Dryden's Aurengzebe.*

2. From one to another.

Five years since there was some speech of marriage
Betwixt myself and her. *Shakesp. Measure for Measure.*

BE'VEL. } *n. s.* In masonry and joinery, a kind of square, one
BE'VIL. } leg of which is frequently crooked, according to the sweep of an arch or vault. It is moveable on a point or centre, and so may be set to any angle. An angle that is not square, is called a *bevil angle*, whether it be more obtuse, or more acute, than a right angle. *Builder's Dict.*

Their houses are very ill built, their walls *bevil*, without one right angle in any apartment. *Swift's Gulliver's Travels.*

To BE'VEL. *v. a.* [from the noun.] To cut to a bevel angle.

These rabbets are ground square; but the rabbets on the groundsel are *bevelled* downwards, that rain may the freelier fall off. *Moxon's Mechanical Exercises.*

BE'VER. See BEAVER.

BE'VERAGE. *n. s.* [from *bevere*, to drink, Ital.]

1. Drink; liquour to be drank in general.

I am his cupbearer;
If from me he have wholesome *beverage*,
Account me not your servant. *Shakesp. Winter's Tale.*

Grains, pulses, and all sorts of fruits, either bread or *beverage*, may be made almost of all. *Brown's Vulgar Errours, b.* iii.

A pleasant *beverage* he prepar'd before,
Of wine and honey mix'd. *Dryden's Fables.*

The coarse lean gravel on the mountain sides,
Scarce dewy *bev'rage* for the bees provides. *Dryden's Virgil.*

2. *Beverage*, or water cyder, is made by putting the mure into a fat, adding water, as you desire it stronger or smaller. The water should stand forty eight hours on it, before you press it; when it is pressed, turn it up immediately. *Mortimer's Husb.*

3. A treat upon wearing a new suit of cloaths.

4. A treat at first coming into a prison, called also *garnish*.

BE'VY. *n. s.* [*beva*, Ital.]

1. A flock of birds.

2. A company; an assembly.

And in the midst thereof, upon the floor,
A lovely *bevy* of fair ladies sat,
Courted of many a jolly paramour. *Fairy Queen, b.* ii. *c.* ix.

They on the plain
Long had not walk'd, when, from the tents, behold
A *bevy* of fair women. *Milton's Paradise Lost, b.* xi. *l.* 582.

Nor rode the nymph alone,
Around a *bevy* of bright damsels shone. *Pope's Odyssey.*

To BEWA'IL. *v. a.* [from *wail.*] To bemoan; to lament; to express sorrow for.

In this city he
Hath widow'd and unchilded many a one,
Which to this hour *bewail* the injury. *Shakesp. Coriolanus.*

Thy ambition,
Thou scarlet sin, robb'd this *bewailing* land
Of noble Buckingham, my father in law. *Shakesp. H.* VIII.

Yet wiser Ennius gave command to all
His friends, not to *bewail* his funeral. *Sir J. Denham.*

I cannot but *bewail*, as in their first principles, the miseries and calamities of our children. *Addison. Spectator,* N° 127.

To BEWA'RE. *v. n.* [from *be* and *ware*, or *wary*; that is, cautious: thus, in an old treatise, I have found, *be ye ware*. See WARY. Ᵹepaɲian, Saxon; *warer*, Danish.]

1. To regard with caution; to be suspicious of danger from: generally the particle *of* goes before the thing which excites caution.

You must *beware of* drawing or painting clouds, winds, and thunder, towards the bottom of your piece. *Dryden's Dufresn.*

Every one ought to be very careful to *beware* what he admits for a principle. *Locke.*

Warn'd by the sylph, oh, pious maid, *beware!*
This to disclose is all thy guardian can;
Beware of all, but most *beware of* man. *Pope's Rape of the L.*

2. It is observable, that it is only used in such forms of speech as admit the word *be*: thus we say, *he may beware, let him beware, he will beware*; but not, *he did beware*, or *he has been ware.*

To BEWE'EP. *v. a.* [from *weep.*] To weep over or upon; to bedew with tears.

Old fond eyes,
Beweep this cause again; I'll pluck ye out,
And cast you, with the waters that you lose,
To temper clay. *Shakesp. King Lear.*

Larded all with sweet flowers,
Which *bewept* to the grave did go,
With true love showers. *Shakesp. Hamlet.*

To BEWE'T. *v. a.* [from *wet.*] To wet; to moisten; to bedew; to water.

His napkin, with his true tears all *bewet*,
Can do no service on her sorrowful cheeks.
Shakesp. Titus Andronicus.

To BEWI'LDER. *v. a.* [from *wild.*] To lose in pathless places; to confound for want of a plain road; to perplex; to entangle; to puzzle.

We parted thus; I homeward sped my way,
Bewilder'd in the wood till dawn of day. *Dryden's Fables.*

We no solution of our question find;
Your words *bewilder*, not direct the mind. *Blackmore.*

Our understanding traces 'em in vain,
Lost and *bewilder'd* in the fruitless search. *Addison's Cato.*

It is good sometimes to lose and *bewilder* ourselves in such studies. *Watts's Improvement of the Mind.*

To BEWI'TCH. *v. a.* [from *witch.*]

1. To injure by witchcraft, or fascination, or charms.

Look how I am *bewitch'd*; behold, mine arm
Is like a blasted sapling wither'd up. *Shakesp. Richard* III.

I have forsworn his company hourly this twenty year, and yet I am *bewitched* with the rogue's company. If the rascal has not given me medicines to make me love him, I'll be hang'd. *Shakesp. Henry* IV.

My flocks are free from love, yet look so thin;
What magick has *bewitch'd* the woolly dams,
And what ill eyes beheld the tender lambs? *Dryden's Virgil.*

2. To charm; to please to such a degree, as to take away the power of resistance.

Doth even beauty beautify,
And most *bewitch* the wretched eye. *Sidney, b.* ii.

The charms of poetry our souls *bewitch*;
The curse of writing is an endless itch. *Dryden's Juvenal.*

I do not know, by the character that is given of her works, whether it is not for the benefit of mankind that they were lost; they were filled with such *bewitching* tenderness and rapture, that it might have been dangerous to have given them a reading. *Addison. Spectator,* N° 223.

BEWI'TCHERY. *n. s.* [from *bewitch.*] Fascination; charm; resistless prevalence.

There is a certain *bewitchery*, or fascination in words, which makes them operate with a force beyond what we can give an account of. *South.*

BEWI'TCHMENT. *n. s.* [from *bewitch.*] Fascination; power of charming.

I will counterfeit the *bewitchment* of some popular man, and give it bountifully to the desirers. *Shakesp. Coriolanus.*

To BEWRA'Y. *v. a.* [pneᵹan, bepneᵹan, Saxon.]

1. To betray; to discover perfidiously.

Fair feeling words he wisely 'gan display,
And, for her humour fitting purpose, fain
To tempt the cause itself for to *bewray*. *Fairy Queen, b.* i.

2. To shew; to make visible: this word is now little in use.

She saw a pretty blush in Philodea's cheeks *bewray* a modest discontentment. *Sidney.*

Men do sometimes *bewray* that by deeds, which to confess they are hardly drawn. *Hooker, b.* i. § 7.

Next look on him that seems for counsel fit,
Whose silver locks *bewray* his store of days. *Fairfax, b.* iii.

BEWRA'YER. *n. s.* [from *bewray.*] Betrayer; discoverer; divulger.

When a friend is turned into an enemy, and a *bewrayer* of secrets, the world is just enough to accuse the perfidiousness of the friend. *Addison. Spectator,* N° 225.

BEYO'ND. *prep.* [beᵹeonꝺ, beᵹeonꝺan, Saxon.]

1. Before; at a distance not yet reached.

What's fame? a fancy'd life in others breath,
A thing *beyond* us, ev'n before our death
Just what you hear, you have. *Pope's Essay on Man.*

2. On the farther side of.

Neither is it *beyond* the sea, that thou shouldst say, who shall go over the sea for us, and bring it unto us. *Deut.* xxx. 13.

Now

Now we are on land, we are but between death and life; for we are *beyond* the old world and the new. *Bacon's New Atlantis.*

We cannot think men *beyond* sea will part with their money for nothing. *Locke.*

3. Farther onward than.

He that sees a dark and shady grove,
Stays not, but looks *beyond* it on the sky. *Herbert.*

4. Past; out of the reach of.

Beyond the infinite and boundless reach
Of mercy, if thou did'st this deed of death,
Art thou damn'd, Hubert. *Shakesp. King John.*

Yet these declare
Thy goodness *beyond* thought, and pow'r divine.
Milton's Paradise Lost, b. v. *l.* 158.

The just, wise, and good God, neither does, nor can require of man any thing that is impossible, or naturally *beyond* his power to do. *South.*

Consider the situation of our earth; it is placed so conveniently, that plants flourish, and animals live; this is matter of fact, and *beyond* all dispute. *Bentley's Sermons.*

5. Above; exceeding to a greater degree than.

Timotheus was a man both in power, riches, parentage, goodness, and love of his people, *beyond* any of the great men of my country. *Sidney.*

One thing, in this enormous accident, is, I must confess, to me *beyond* all wonder. *Wotton.*

To his expences, *beyond* his income, add debauchery, idleness, and quarrels amongst his servants, whereby his manufactures are disturbed, and his business neglected. *Locke.*

As far as they carry conviction to any man's understanding, my labour may be of use: *beyond* the evidence it carries with it, I advise him not to follow any man's interpretation. *Locke.*

6. Above in excellence.

His satires are incomparably *beyond* Juvenal's; if to laugh and rally, is to be preferred to railing and declaiming. *Dryden.*

7. Remote from; not within the sphere of.

With equal mind, what happens, let us bear;
Nor joy, nor grieve too much for things *beyond* our care.
Dryden's Fables.

8. *To go beyond*, is to deceive; to circumvent.

She made earnest benefit of his jest, forcing him to do her such services, as were both cumbersome and costly; while he still thought he *went beyond* her, because his heart did not commit the idolatry. *Sidney.*

That no man *go beyond*, and defraud his brother in any matter. 1 *Thess.* iv. 6.

BE'ZEL. } *n. s.* That part of a ring in which the stone is
BE'ZIL. } fixed.

BE'ZOAR. *n. s.* [from *pa*, against, and *zahar*, poison, Persick.] A medicinal stone, formerly in high esteem as an antidote, and brought from the East Indies, where it is said to be found in the dung of an animal of the goat kind, called *pazan*; the stone being formed in its belly, and growing to the size of an acorn, and sometimes to that of a pigeon's egg. Were the real virtues of this stone answereable to its reputed ones, it were doubtless a panacea. Indeed its rarity, and the peculiar manner of its formation, which is now supposed to be fabulous, have perhaps contributed as much to its reputation as its intrinsick worth. At present, it begins to be discarded in the practice of medicine, as of no efficacy at all. There are also some occidental *bezoars* brought from Peru, which are reckoned inferiour to the oriental. The name of this stone is also applied to several chymical compositions, designed for antidotes, or counter-poisons; as mineral, solar, and jovial *bezoars*. *Savary. Chambers.*

BEZOA'RDICK. *adj.* [from *bezoar.*] Medicines compounded with *bezoar.*

The *bezoardicks* are necessary to promote sweat, and drive forth the putrefied particles. *Floyer on the Humours.*

BIA'NGULATED. } *adj.* [from *binus* and *angulus*, Lat.] Having
BIA'NGULOUS. } corners or angles. *Dict.*

BI'AS. *n. s.* [*biais*, Fr. said to come from *bihay*, an old Gaulish word, signifying *cross*, or *thwart.*]

1. The weight lodged on one side of a bowl, which turns it from the strait line.

Madam, we'll play at bowls——
——'Twill make me think the world is full of rubs,
And that my fortune runs against the *bias*. *Shakesp. R.* II.

2. Any thing which turns a man to a particular course; or gives the direction to his measures.

You have been mistook:
But nature to her *bias* drew in that. *Shakesp. Twelfth Night.*

This is that boasted *bias* of thy mind,
By which one way to dulness 'tis inclin'd. *Dryden's Mackfl.*

Morality influences mens lives, and gives a *bias* to all their actions. *Locke.*

Wit and humour, that expose vice and folly, furnish useful diversions. Raillery, under such regulations, unbends the mind from severer contemplations, without throwing it off from its proper *bias*.
Addison's Freeholder, N° 45.

Thus nature gives us, let it check our pride,
The virtue nearest to our vice ally'd;
Reason the *bias* turns to good or ill. *Pope's Essay on Man.*

3. Propension; inclination.

As for the religion of our poet, he seems to have some little *bias* towards the opinions of Wickliff. *Dryd. Fab. Preface.*

To BI'AS. *v. a.* [from the noun.] To incline to some side; to balance one way; to prejudice.

Were I in no more danger to be misled by ignorance, than I am to be *biassed* by interest, I might give a very perfect account. *Locke.*

A desire leaning to either side, *biasses* the judgment strangely; by indifference for every thing but truth, you will be excited to examine. *Watts's Improvement of the Mind.*

BI'AS. *adv.* It seems to be used *adverbially* in the following passage, conformably to the French, *mettre une chose de biais*, to give any thing a wrong interpretation.

Every action that hath gone before,
Whereof we have record, trial did draw
Bias and thwart, not answering the aim.
Shakesp. Troilus and Cressida.

BIB. *n. s.* A small piece of linen put upon the breasts of children, over their cloaths.

I would fain know, why it should not be as noble a task, to write upon a *bib* and hanging-sleeves, as on the *bulla* and *prætexta*. *Addison on ancient Medals.*

To BIB. *v. n.* [*bibo*, Lat.] To tipple; to sip; to drink frequently.

He playeth with *bibbing* mother Meroë, as though she were so named, because she would drink mere wine without water. *Camden.*

To appease a froward child, they gave him drink as often as he cried; so that he was constantly *bibbing*, and drank more in twenty four hours than I did. *Locke.*

BIBA'CIOUS. *adj.* [*bibax*, Lat.] Much addicted to drinking. *D.*

BIBA'CITY. *n. s.* [*bibacitas*, Lat.] The quality of drinking much.

BI'BBER. *n. s.* [from *to bib.*] A tippler; a man that drinks often.

BI'BLE. *n. s.* [from βιβλίον, a book; called, by way of excellence, *The Book.*] The sacred volume in which are contained the revelations of God.

If we pass from the apostolic to the next ages of the church, the primitive christians looked on their *bibles* as their most important treasure. *Government of the Tongue*, § 3.

We must take heed how we accustom ourselves to a slight and irreverent use of the name of God, and of the phrases and expressions of the holy *bible*, which ought not to be applied upon every slight occasion. *Tillotson, sermon* i.

In questions of natural religion, we should confirm and improve, or connect our reasonings, by the divine assistance of the *bible*. *Watts's Logick.*

BIBLIO'GRAPHER. *n. s.* [from βιβλὸς, and γράφω, to write.] A writer of books; a transcriber. *Dict.*

BIBLIOTHE'CAL. *adj.* [from *bibliotheca*, Lat.] Belonging to a library. *Dict.*

BI'BULOUS. *adj.* [*bibulus*, Lat.] That which has the quality of drinking moisture; spungy.

Strow'd *bibulous* above, I see the sands,
The pebbly gravel next, and guttur'd rocks. *Thomson.*

BICA'PSULAR. *adj.* [*bicapsularis*, Lat.] A plant whose seed vessel is divided into two parts.

BICE. *n. s.* The name of a colour used in painting. It is either green or blue.

Take green *bice*, and order it as you do your blue *bice*, you may diaper upon it with the water of deep green. *Peacham.*

BICI'PITAL. } *adj.* [*biceps*, *bicipitis*, Lat.]
BICI'PITOUS. }

1. Having two heads.

While men believe *bicipitous* conformation in any species, they admit a gemination of principal parts. *Brown's Vulg. Err.*

2. It is applied to one of the muscles of the arm.

A piece of flesh is exchanged from the *bicipital* muscle of either party's arm. *Brown's Vulgar Errours, b.* ii. *c.* 3.

To BI'CKER. *v. n.* [*bicre*, Welsh, a contest.]

1. To skirmish; to fight without a set battle; to fight off and on.

They fell to such a *bickering*, that he got a halting, and lost his picture. *Sidney.*

In thy face
I see thy fury; if I longer stay,
We shall begin our ancient *bickerings*. *Shakesp. Henry* VI.

2. To quiver; to play backward and forward.

And from about him fierce effusion rowl'd
Of smoke, and *bickering* flame, and sparkles dire.
Milton's Paradise Lost, b. vi. *l.* 674.

An icy gale, oft shifting o'er the pool,
Breathes a blue film, and, in its mid career,
Arrests the *bickering* stream. *Thomson's Winter, l.* 730.

BI'CKERER. *n. s.* [from the verb.] A skirmisher.

BI'CKERN. *n. s.* [apparently corrupted from *beakiron.*] An iron ending in a point.

A blackſmith's anvil is ſometimes made with a pike, or *bickern*, or beakiron, at one end. *Moxon's Mechan. Exerciſes.*

BICO'RNE. }
BICO'RNOUS. } *adj.* [*bicornis*, Lat.] Having two horns.

We ſhould be too critical, to queſtion the letter Y, or *bicornous* element of Pythagoras; that is, the making of the horns equal. *Brown's Vulgar Errours, b.* v. *c.* 19.

BICO'RPORAL. *adj.* [*bicorpor*, Lat.] Having two bodies.

To BID. *v. a.* pret. I *bid*, *bad*, *bade*, I have *bid*, or *bidden.* [biddan, Saxon.]

1. To deſire; to aſk; to call; to invite.

I am *bid* forth to ſupper, Jeſſica;
There are my keys. *Shakeſp. Merchant of Venice.*

Go ye into the highways, and, as many as you ſhall find, *bid* to the marriage. *Matt.* xxii. 9.

We ought, when we are *bidden* to great feaſts and meetings, to be prepared beforehand. *Hakewell on Providence.*

2. To command; to order; before things or perſons.

Saint Withold footed thrice the wold,
He met the nightmare, and her name told,
Bid her alight, and her troth plight. *Shakeſp. King Lear.*

He chid the ſiſters,
When firſt they put the name of king upon me,
And *bade* them ſpeak to him. *Shakeſp. Macbeth.*

Haſte to the houſe of ſleep, and *bid* the god,
Who rules the nightly viſions with a nod,
Prepare a dream. *Dryden's Fables.*

Curſe on the tongue that *bids* this general joy.
—Can they be friends of Antony, who revel
When Antony's in danger? *Dryd. All for Love.*

Thames heard the numbers, as he flow'd along,
And *bade* his willows learn the moving ſong. *Pope.*

Acquire a government over your ideas, that they may come when they are called, and depart when they are *bidden.* *Watts's Logick.*

3. To offer; to propoſe; as, to *bid* a price.

Come, and be true.—
—Thou *bidſt* me to my loſs: for true to thee,
Were to prove falſe. *Shakeſp. Cymbeline.*

When a man is reſolute to keep his ſins while he lives, and yet unwilling to relinquiſh all hope, he will embrace that profeſſion, which *bids* faireſt to the reconciling thoſe ſo diſtant intereſts. *Decay of Piety.*

As when the goddeſſes came down of old,
With gifts, their young Dardanian judge they try'd,
And each *bade* high to win him to their ſide. *Granville.*

To give intereſt a ſhare in friendſhip, is to ſell it by inch of candle; he that *bids* moſt ſhall have it: and when it is mercenary, there is no depending on it. *Collier on Friendſhip.*

4. To proclaim; to offer; or to make known by ſome publick voice.

Our bans thrice *bid!* and for our wedding day
My kerchief bought! then preſs'd, then forc'd away.
Gay's What d'ye call it.

5. To pronounce; to declare.

You are retir'd,
As if you were a feaſted one, and not
The hoſteſs of the meeting; pray you, *bid*
Theſe unknown friends to's welcome. *Shakeſp. Wint. Tale.*

Divers of them, as we paſſed by them, put their arms a little abroad; which is their geſture, when they *bid* any welcome. *Bacon's New Atlantis.*

How, Didius, ſhall a Roman, ſore repuls'd,
Greet your arrival to this diſtant iſle?
How *bid* you welcome to theſe ſhatter'd legions? *A. Philips.*

6. To denounce.

Thyſelf and Oxford, with five thouſand men,
Shall croſs the ſeas, and *bid* falſe Edward battle.
Shakeſp. Henry VI. *p.* iii.

She *bid* war to all that durſt ſupply
The place of thoſe her cruelty made die. *Waller.*

The captive cannibal, oppreſt with chains,
Yet braves his foes, reviles, provokes, diſdains;
Of nature fierce, untameable, and proud,
He *bids* defiance to the gaping croud,
And ſpent at laſt, and ſpeechleſs as he lies,
With fiery glances mocks their rage, and dies. *Granville.*

7. To pray. See BEAD.

If there come any unto you, and bring not this doctrine, receive him not into your houſe, neither *bid* him God ſpeed. 2 *John*, 10.

When they deſired him to tarry longer with them, he conſented not, but *bade* them farewel. *Acts*, xviii. 21.

By ſome haycock, or ſome ſhady thorn,
He *bids* his beads both even ſong and morn. *Dryd. W. of B.*

BI'DALE. *n. ſ.* [from *bid* and *ale.*] An invitation of friends to drink at a poor man's houſe, and there to contribute charity. *Dict.*

BI'DDEN. *part. paſſ.* [from *to bid.*]

1. Invited.

There were two of our company *bidden* to a feaſt of the family. *Bacon.*

Madam, the *bidden* gueſts are come. *A. Philips.*

2. Commanded.

'Tis theſe that early taint the female ſoul,
Inſtruct the eyes of young coquettes to roll,
Teach infants cheeks a *bidden* bluſh to know,
And little hearts to flutter at a beau. *Pope's R. of the Lock.*

BI'DDER. *n. ſ.* [from *to bid.*] One who offers or propoſes a price.

He looked upon ſeveral dreſſes which hung there, and expoſed to the purchaſe of the beſt *bidder.* *Addiſon. Spectator.*

BI'DDING. *n. ſ.* [from *bid.*] Command; order.

How, ſay'ſt thou, that Macduff denies his perſon
At our great *bidding?* *Shakeſp. Macbeth.*

At his ſecond *bidding*, darkneſs fled,
Light ſhone, and order from diſorder ſprung.
Milton's Parad. Loſt, b. iii. *l.* 712.

To BIDE. *v. a.* [bidan, Sax.] To endure; to ſuffer.

Poor naked wretches, whereſoe'er you are,
That *bide* the pelting of this pitileſs ſtorm. *Shakeſp. K. Lear.*

The wary Dutch this gathering ſtorm foreſaw,
And durſt not *bide* it on the Engliſh coaſt. *Dryd. Ann. Mir.*

To BIDE. *v. n.*

1. To dwell; to live; to inhabit.

All knees to thee ſhall bow, of them that *bide*
In heav'n, or earth, or under earth in hell. *Par. Loſt, b.* iii.

2. To remain in a place.

Safe in a ditch he *bides*,
With twenty trenched gaſhes on his head;
The leaſt a death to nature. *Shakeſp. Macbeth.*

3. To continue in a ſtate.

And they alſo, if they *bide* not ſtill in unbelief, ſhall be graffed in. *Romans*, xi. 23.

4. It has probably all the ſignifications of the word *abide*; which ſee: but it being grown ſomewhat obſolete, the examples of its various meanings are not eaſily found.

BIDE'NTAL. *adj.* [*bidens*, Lat.] Having two teeth.

Ill management of forks is not to be helped, when they are only *bidental.* *Swift.*

BI'DING. *n. ſ.* [from *bide.*] Reſidence; habitation.

At Antwerp has my conſtant *biding* been. *Rowe's J. Sh.*

BIE'NNIAL. *adj.* [*biennis*, Lat.] Of the continuance of two years.

Then why ſhould ſome be very long lived, others only annual or *biennial?* *Ray on the Creation.*

BIER. *n. ſ.* [from *to bear*, as *feretrum*, in Latin, from *fero.*] A carriage, or frame of wood, on which the dead are carried to the grave.

And now the prey of fowls he lies,
Nor wail'd of friends, nor laid on groaning *bier.* *Fairy Q.*

They bore him barefaced on the *bier*,
And on his grave remains many a tear. *Shakeſp. Hamlet.*

He muſt not float upon his wat'ry *bier*,
Unwept. *Milton.*

Griefs always green, a houſhold ſtill in tears:
Sad pomps, a threſhold throng'd with daily *biers*,
And liveries of black. *Dryden's Juvenal, ſat.* x.

Make as if you hanged yourſelf, they will convey your body out of priſon in a *bier.* *Arbuthnot's J. Bull.*

BI'ESTINGS. *n. ſ.* [bẏyꞇınꝫ, Saxon.] The firſt milk given by a cow after calving, which is very thick.

And twice beſides, her *bieſtings* never fail
To ſtore the dairy with a brimming pale. *Dryden's Virgil.*

BIFA'RIOUS. *adj.* [*bifarius*, Lat.] Twofold; what may be underſtood two ways. *Dict.*

BI'FEROUS. *adj.* [*biferens*, Lat.] Bearing fruit twice a year.

BI'FID. }
BI'FIDATED. } *adj.* [*bifidus*, Lat. a botanical term.] Divided in two; ſplit in two; opening with a cleft.

BIFO'LD. *adj* [from *binus*, Lat. and *fold.*] Twofold; double.

If beauty have a ſoul, this is not ſhe;
If ſouls guide vows, if vows are ſanctimony,
If ſanctimony be the gods delight,
If there be rule in unity itſelf,
This is not ſhe; O madneſs of diſcourſe!
That cauſe ſets up with and againſt thyſelf!
Bifold authority. *Shakeſp. Troilus and Creſſida.*

BIFO'RMED. *adj.* [*biformis*, Lat.] Compounded of two forms, or bodies.

BIFU'RCATED. *adj.* [from *binus*, two, and *furca*, a fork, Lat.] Shooting out, by a diviſion, into two heads.

A ſmall white piece, *bifurcated*, or branching into two, and finely reticulated all over. *Woodward on Foſſils.*

BIFURCA'TION. *n. ſ.* [from *binus* and *furca*, Lat.] Diviſion into two; opening into two parts.

The firſt catachreſtical and far derived ſimilitude, it holds with man; that is, in a *bifurcation*, or diviſion of the root into two parts. *Brown's Vulgar Errours, b.* ii. *c.* 6.

BIG. *adj.* [This word is of uncertain, or unknown etymology; *Junius* derives it from βαγαῖος; *Skinner*, from *bug*, which, in *Daniſh*, ſignifies the belly.]

1. Great in bulk; large.

Both in addition and diviſion, either of ſpace or duration, when the idea under conſideration becomes very *big*, or very ſmall,

ſmall, its preciſe bulk becomes very obſcure and confuſed. *Locke.*

A troubled ocean, to a man who ſails in it, is, I think, the *biggeſt* object that he can ſee in motion. *Spectator*, Nº 489.

Then commerce brought into the publick walk
The buſy merchant, the *big* warehouſe built. *Thomſon.*

2. Teeming; pregnant; great with young; with the particle *with.*

A bear *big with* young hath ſeldom been ſeen. *Bacon.*

Lately on yonder ſwelling buſh,
Big with many a common roſe,
This early bud began to bluſh. *Waller.*

3. Sometimes with *of*; but rarely.

His gentle lady,
Big of this gentleman, our theam, deceas'd
As he was born. *Shakeſp. Cymbeline.*

4. Full of ſomething; and deſirous, or about, to give it vent.

The great, th' important day,
Big with the fate of Cato and of Rome. *Addiſon's Cato.*

Now *big with* knowledge of approaching woes,
The prince of augurs, Halithreſes, roſe. *Pope's Odyſſey.*

5. Diſtended; ſwoln; ready to burſt; uſed often of the effects of paſſion, as grief, rage.

Thy heart is *big*; get thee apart, and weep. *Shakeſp. Julius Cæſar.*

6. Great in air and mien; proud; ſwelling; tumid; haughty; ſurly.

How elſe, ſaid he, but with a good bold face,
And with *big* words, and with a ſtately pace. *Hub. Tale.*

To the meaner man, or unknown in the court, ſeem ſomewhat ſolemn, coy, *big*, and dangerous of look, talk, and anſwer. *Aſcham's Schoolmaſter.*

If you had but looked *big*, and ſpit at him, he'd have run. *Shakeſp. Winter's Tale.*

Or does the man i' th' moon look *big*,
Or wear a huger perriwig,
Than our own native lunaticks. *Hudibras, p.* ii. *cant.* iii.

Of governments that once made ſuch a noiſe, and looked ſo *big* in the eyes of mankind, as being founded upon the deepeſt counſels, and the ſtrongeſt force; nothing remains of them but a name. *South.*

In his moſt proſperous ſeaſon, he fell under the reproach of being a man of *big* looks, and of a mean and abject ſpirit. *Clarendon.*

Thou thyſelf, thus inſolent in ſtate,
Art but perhaps ſome country magiſtrate,
Whoſe power extends no farther than to ſpeak
Big on the bench, and ſcanty weights to break. *Dryden.*

To grant *big* Thraſo valour, Phormio ſenſe,
Should indignation give, at leaſt offence. *Garth.*

7. Great in ſpirit; lofty; brave.

What art thou? have not I
An arm as big as thine? a heart as *big*?
Thy words, I grant, are *bigger*: for I wear not
My dagger in my mouth. *Shakeſp. Cymbeline.*

BI'GAMIST. *n. ſ.* [*bigamius*, low Lat.] One that has committed bigamy. See BIGAMY.

By the papal canons, a clergyman, that has a wife, cannot have an eccleſiaſtical benefice; much leſs can a *bigamiſt* have ſuch a benefice, according to that law. *Ayliffe's Parergon.*

BI'GAMY. *n. ſ.* [*bigamia*, low Latin.]

1. The crime of having two wives at once.

A beauty-waining and diſtreſſed widow
Seduc'd the pitch and height of all his thoughts,
To baſe declenſion, and loath'd *bigamy*. *Shakeſp. Richard* III.

Randal determined to commence a ſuit againſt Martin, for *bigamy* and inceſt. *Arbuthnot and Pope's Martinus Scriblerus.*

2. In the canon law. The marriage of a ſecond wife, or of a widow, or a woman already debauched; which, in the church of Rome, were conſidered as bringing a man under ſome incapacities for eccleſiaſtical offices.

BIGBE'LLIED. *adj.* [from *big* and *belly.*] Pregnant; with child; great with young.

When we have laught to ſee the ſails conceive,
And grow *bigbellied* with the wanton wind. *Shakeſp. Midſummer Night's Dream.*

Children, and *bigbellied* women require antidotes ſomewhat more grateful to the palate. *Harvey on the Plague.*

So many well ſhaped innocent virgins are blocked up, and waddling up and down like *bigbellied* women. *Addiſon. Spect.*

We purſued our march, to the terrour of the market people, and the miſcarriage of half a dozen *bigbellied* women. *Addiſon's Freeholder.*

BI'GGIN. *n. ſ.* [*beguin*, Fr.] A child's cap.

Sleep now!
Yet not ſo ſound, and half ſo deeply ſweet,
As he, whoſe brow with homely *biggin* bound,
Snores out the watch of night. *Shakeſp. Henry* IV. *p.* ii.

BIGHT. *n. ſ.* It is explained by *Skinner*, the circumference of a coil of rope.

BI'GLY. *adv.* [from *big.*] Tumidly; haughtily; with a bluſtering manner.

Would'ſt thou not rather chooſe a ſmall renown,
To be the may'r of ſome poor paltry town;
Bigly to look, and barb'rouſly to ſpeak;
To pound falſe weights, and ſcanty meaſures break? *Dryden's Juvenal, ſat.* x.

BI'GNESS. *n. ſ.* [from *big.*]

1. Bulk; greatneſs of quantity.

If panicum be laid below, and about the bottom of a root, it will cauſe the root to grow to an exceſſive *bigneſs*. *Bacon.*

People were ſurpriſed at the *bigneſs*, and uncouth deformity of the camel. *L'Eſtrange's Fables.*

The brain of man, in reſpect of his body, is much larger than in any other animal's; exceeding in *bigneſs* three oxens brains. *Ray on the Creation.*

2. Size; whether greater or ſmaller.

Several ſorts of rays make vibrations of ſeveral *bigneſſes*, which, according to their *bigneſſes*, excite ſenſations of ſeveral colours; and the air, according to their *bigneſſes*, excites ſenſations of ſeveral ſounds. *Newton's Opticks.*

BI'GOT. *n. ſ.* [The etymology of this word is unknown; but it is ſuppoſed, by *Camden* and others, to take its riſe from ſome occaſional phraſe.] A man devoted to a certain party; prejudiced in favour of certain opinions; a blind zealot. It is uſed often with *to* before the object of zeal; as, a *bigot to* the Carteſian tenets.

Religious ſpite, and pious ſpleen bred firſt
This quarrel, which ſo long the *bigots* nurſt. *Tate. Juvenal.*

In philoſophy and religion, the *bigots* of all parties are generally the moſt poſitive. *Watts's Improvement of the Mind.*

BI'GOTED. *adj.* [from *bigot.*] Blindly prepoſſeſſed in favour of ſomething; irrationally zealous; with *to.*

Bigotted to this idol, we diſclaim
Reſt, health, and eaſe, for nothing but a name. *Garth.*

Preſbyterian merit, during the reign of that weak, *bigotted*, and ill adviſed prince, will eaſily be computed. *Swift.*

BI'GOTRY. *n. ſ.* [from *bigot.*]

1. Blind zeal; prejudice; unreaſonable warmth in favour of party or opinions; with the particle *to.*

Were it not for a *bigotry to* our own tenets, we could hardly imagine, that ſo many abſurd, wicked, and bloody principles, ſhould pretend to ſupport themſelves by the goſpel. *Watts.*

2. The practice or tenet of a bigot.

Our ſilence makes our adverſaries think we perſiſt in thoſe *bigotries*, which all good and ſenſible men deſpiſe. *Pope.*

BI'GSWOLN. *adj.* [from *big* and *ſwoln.*] Turgid; ready to burſt.

Might my *bigſwoln* heart
Vent all its griefs, and give a looſe to ſorrow. *Addiſ. Cato.*

BI'G-UDDERED. *adj.* [from *big* and *udder.*] Having large udders; having dugs ſwelled with milk.

Now driv'n before him, through the arching rock,
Came, tumbling heaps on heaps, th' unnumber'd flock,
Big-udder'd ews, and goats of female kind. *Pope's Odyſſey.*

BI'LANDER. *n. ſ.* [*belandre*, Fr.] A ſmall veſſel of about eighty tons burden, uſed for the carriage of goods. It is a kind of hoy, manageable by four or five men, and has maſts and ſails after the manner of a hoy. They are uſed chiefly in Holland, as being particularly fit for the canals. *Savary. Trevoux.*

Like *bilanders* to creep
Along the coaſt, and land in view to keep. *Dryden.*

BI'LBERRY. *n. ſ.* [from bılıᵹ, Sax. a bladder, and *berry*; according to *Skinner.*] The ſame with *whortleberry*; which ſee.

Cricket, to Windſor chimneys ſhalt thou leap;
There pinch the maids as blue as *bilberries*. *Shakeſp. Merry Wives of Windſor.*

BI'LBO. *n. ſ.* [corrupted from *Bilboa*, where the beſt weapons are made.] A rapier; a ſword.

To be compaſſed like a good *bilbo*, in the circumference of a peck, hilt to point, heel to head. *Shakeſp. M. W. of Windſor.*

BI'LBOES. *n. ſ.* A ſort of ſtocks, or wooden ſheckles for the feet, uſed for puniſhing offenders at ſea.

Methought I lay,
Worſe than the mutines, in the *bilboes*. *Shakeſp. Hamlet.*

BILE. *n. ſ.* [*bilis*, Lat.] A thick, yellow, bitter liquour, ſeparated in the liver, collected in the gall-bladder, and diſcharged into the lower end of the duodenum, or beginning of the jejunum, by the common duct. Its uſe is to ſheathe or blunt the acids of the chyle; becauſe they, being entangled with its ſulphurs, thicken it ſo, that it cannot be ſufficiently diluted by the ſuccus pancreaticus, to enter the lacteal veſſels. *Quincy.*

In its progreſſion, ſoon the labour'd chyle
Receives the confluent rills of bitter *bile*;
Which, by the liver ſever'd from the blood,
And ſtriving through the gall-pipe, here unload
Their yellow ſtreams. *Blackmore.*

BILE. *n. ſ.* [bile, Sax. perhaps from *bilis*, Lat. This is generally ſpelt *boil*; but, I think, leſs properly.] A ſore angry ſwelling.

But yet thou art my fleſh, my blood, my daughter;
Or, rather, a diſeaſe that's in my fleſh;
Thou art a *bile* in my corrupted blood. *Shakeſp. King Lear.*

Thoſe *biles* did run—ſay ſo—did not the general run? were not that a botchy ſore? *Shakeſp. Troilus and Creſſida.*

A furun-

A furunculus is a painful tubercle, with a broad basis, arising in a cone. It is generally called a *bile*, and, in it its state, is accompanied with inflammation, pulsation, and tension.
Wiseman's Surgery.

BILGE *in a ship.* The compass or breadth of the ship's bottom. *Skinner.*

To BILGE. *v. n.* [from the noun.] To spring a leak; to let in water, by striking upon a rock: a sea term. *Skinner.*

BI'LIARY. *adj.* [from *bilis*, Lat.] Belonging to the bile.

Voracious animals, and such as do not chew, have a great quantity of gall; and some of them have the *biliary* duct inserted into the pylorus. *Arbuthnot on Aliments.*

BI'LINGSGATE. *n. s.* [A cant word, borrowed from *Bilingsgate* in London, a place where there is always a croud of low people, and frequent brawls and foul language.] Ribaldry; foul language.

There stript, fair rhet'rick languish'd on the ground,
And shameful *bilingsgate* her robes adorn. *Dunciad, b.* iv.

BILI'NGUOUS. *adj.* [*bilinguis*, Lat.] Having, or speaking two tongues.

BI'LIOUS. *adj.* [from *bilis*, Lat.] Consisting of bile; partaking of bile.

Why *bilious* juice a golden light puts on,
And floods of chyle in silver currents run. *Garth.*

When the taste of the mouth is bitter, it is a sign of redundance of a *bilious* alkali. *Arbuthnot on Aliments.*

To BILK. *v. a.* [derived by Mr. *Lye* from the Gothick, *bilaican.*] To cheat; to defraud, by running in debt, and avoiding payment.

Bilk'd stationers for yeomen stood prepar'd. *Dryden.*
What comedy, what farce can more delight,
Than grinning hunger, and the pleasing sight
Of your *bilk'd* hopes? *Dryden's Juvenal, sat.* v.

BILL *n. s.* [bile, Sax. See BALL.] The beak of a fowl.

Their *bills* were thwarted crossways at the end, and, with these, they would cut an apple in two at one snap.
Carew's Survey of Cornwal.

It may be tried, whether birds may not be made to have greater or longer *bills*, or greater and longer talons.
Bacon's Natural History, N° 757.

In his *bill*
An olive leaf he brings, pacifick sign! *Paradise Lost, b.* xi.
No crowing cock does there his wings display,
Nor with his horny *bill* provoke the day. *Dryden's Fables.*

BILL. *n. s.* [bille, Sax. ꞇpibille, a two edged axe.]

1. A kind of hatchet with a hooked point, used in country work, as a *hedging bill*; so called from its resemblance in form to the beak of a bird of prey.

Standing troops are servants armed, who use the lance and sword, as other servants do the sickle, or the *bill*, at the command of those who entertain them. *Temple.*

2. A kind of weapon anciently carried by the foot; a battle axe.

Yea distaff women manage rusty *bills*;
Against thy seat both young and old rebel. *Shakesp. R.* II.

BILL. *n. s.* [*billet*, French.]

1. A written paper of any kind.

He does receive
Particular addition from the *bill*
That writes them all alike. *Shakesp. Macbeth.*

2. An account of money.

Ordinary expence ought to be limited by a man's estate, and ordered to the best, that the *bills* may be less than the estimation abroad. *Bacon's Essays.*

3. A law presented to the parliament, not yet made an act.

No new laws can be made, nor old laws abrogated or altered, but by parliament; where *bills* are prepared, and presented to the two houses. *Bacon's Advice to Villiers.*

How now, for mitigation of this *bill*,
Urg'd by the commons? Doth his majesty
Incline to it, or no? *Shakesp. Henry* V.

4 An act of parliament.

There will be no way left for me to tell you, that I remember you, and that I love you; but that one, which needs no open warrant, or secret conveyance; which no *bills* can preclude, or no kings prevent. *Atterbury to Pope.*

5. A physician's prescription.

Like him that took the doctor's *bill*,
And swallow'd it instead o' th' pill. *Hudibras, p.* i. *cant.* ii.
The medicine was prepar'd according to the *bill*.
L'Estrange, fab. 183.
Let them, but under your superiours, kill,
When doctors first have sign'd the bloody *bill*. *Dryden.*

6. An advertisement.

And in despair, their empty pit to fill,
Set up some foreign monster in a *bill*. *Dryden.*

7. In law.

1. An obligation, but without condition or forfeiture for nonpayment. 2. A declaration in writing, that expresseth either the grief and the wrong, that the complainant hath suffered by the party complained of; or else some fault, that the party complained of, hath committed against some law. This *bill* is sometimes offered to justices errants in the general assizes; but most to the lord chancellor. It containeth the fact complained of, the damages thereby suffered, and petition of process against the defendant for redress. *Cowel.*

The fourth thing very maturely to be consulted by the jury, is, what influence their finding the *bill* may have upon the kingdom. *Swift.*

8. *A bill of mortality.* An account of the numbers that have died in any district.

Most who took in the weekly *bills of mortality*, made little other use of them, than to look at the foot, how the burials encreased or decreased. *Graunt's Bills of Mortality.*

So liv'd our sires, ere doctors learn'd to kill,
And multiply'd with theirs the weekly *bill*. *Dryden.*

9. *A bill of fare.* An account of the season, of provisions, or of the dishes at a feast.

It may seem somewhat difficult to make out the *bills of fare* for some of the forementioned suppers. *Arbuthnot on Coins.*

10. *A bill of exchange.* A note ordering the payment of a sum of money in one place, to some person assigned by the drawer or remitter, in consideration of the value paid to him in another place.

The comfortable sentences are our *bills of exchange*, upon the credit of which we lay our cares down, and receive provisions.
Taylor's Rule of living holy.

All that a *bill of exchange* can do, is to direct to whom money is due, or taken up upon credit, in a foreign country, shall be paid. *Locke.*

To BILL. *v. n.* [from *bill*, a beak.] To caress, as doves by joining bills; to be fond.

Doves, they say, will *bill*, after their pecking, and their murmuring. *Ben Johnson's Catiline.*

Still amorous, and fond, and *billing*,
Like Philip and Mary on a shilling. *Hudibras, p.* iii. *c.* i.
They *bill*, they tread; Alcyone compress'd,
Seven days sits brooding on her floating nest. *Dryden.*
He that bears th' artillery of Jove,
The strong pounc'd eagle, and the *billing* dove. *Dryden.*

To BILL. *v. a.* [from *bill*, a writing.] To publish by an advertisement: a cant word.

His masterpiece was a composition that he *billed* about under the name of a sovereign antidote. *L'Estrange.*

BI'LLET. *n. s.* [*billet*, French.]

1. A small paper; a note.

When he found this little *billet*, in which was only written, *Remember Cæsar*, he was exceedingly confounded. *Clarendon.*

2. A ticket directing soldiers at what house to lodge.

3. *Billet doux*, or a soft *billet*; a love letter.

'Twas then, Belinda! if report say true,
Thy eyes first open'd on a *billet doux*. *Pope's Rape of the L.*
Bawds and pimps will be carrying about *billet doux*.
Arbuthnot and Pope's Martinus Scriblerus.

4. A small log of wood for the chimney.

Let us then calculate, when the bulk of a faggot or *billet*, is dilated and rarified to the degree of fire, how vast a place it must take up. *Digby on Bodies.*

Their *billet* at the fire was found. *Prior.*

To BI'LLET. *v. a.* [from the noun.]

1. To direct a soldier by a ticket, or note, where he is to lodge.

Retire thee; go where thou art *billeted*:
Away, I say. *Shakesp. Othello.*

2. To quarter soldiers.

They remembered him of charging the kingdom, by *billeting* soldiers. *Raleigh's History of the World.*

The counties throughout the kingdom were so incensed, and their affections poisoned, that they refused to suffer the soldiers to be *billeted* upon them. *Clarendon.*

BI'LLIARDS. *n. s. without a singular.* [*billard*, Fr. of which that language has no etymology; and therefore they probably derived from England both the play and the name; which is corrupted from *balyards*; yards or sticks with which a ball is driven along a table. Thus *Spenser*:

Balyards much unfit,
And shuttlecocks misseeming manly wit. *Hubb. Tale.*]

A game at which a ball is forced against another on a table.

Let it alone; let's to *billiards*. *Shakesp. Antony and Cleop.*
Even nose and cheek, withal,
Smooth as is the *billiard* ball. *Ben. Johnson's Underwoods.*

Some are forced to bound or fly upwards, almost like ivory balls meeting on a *billiard* table. *Boyle.*

When the ball obeys the stroke of a *billiard* stick, it is not any action of the ball, but bare passion. *Locke.*

BI'LLOW. *n. s.* [*bilge*, Germ. *bolg*, Dan. probably of the same original with bılıᵹ, Sax. a bladder.] A wave swoln, and hollow.

From whence the river Dee, as silver cleen,
His tumbling *billows* roll with gentle rore. *Fairy Queen, b.* i.

Billows sink by degrees, even when the wind is down that first stirred them. *Wotton.*

Chasing Nereus with his trident throws
The *billows* from the bottom. *Sir J. Denham.*
But when loud *billows* lash the sounding shore,
The hoarse rough verse should like the torrent roar. *Pope.*

To

To Bi'llow. *v. n.* [from the noun.] To ſwell, or roll, as a wave.

The *billowing* ſnow, and violence of the ſhow'r,
That from the hills diſperſe their dreadful ſtore,
And o'er the vales collected ruin pour. *Prior.*

Bi'llowy. *adj.* [from *billow.*] Swelling; turgid; wavy.

And whitening down the moſſy-tinctur'd ſtream,
Deſcends the *billowy* foam. *Thomſon's Spring, l.* 380.

Bin. *n. ſ.* [binne, Sax.] A place where bread, or corn, or wine, is repoſited.

The moſt convenient way of picking hops, is into a long ſquare frame of wood, called a *bin.* *Mortimer's Husbandry.*

As when from rooting in a *bin*,
All pouder'd o'er from tail to chin,
A lively maggot ſallies out,
You know him by his hazel ſnout. *Swift.*

Bi'nary. *adj.* [from *binus*, Lat.] Two; dual; double.

Bi'nary *Arithmetick.* A method of computation propoſed by Mr. Leibnitz, in which, in lieu of the ten figures in the common arithmetick, and the progreſſion from ten to ten, he has only two figures, and uſes the ſimple progreſſion from two to two. This method appears to be the ſame with that uſed Chineſe four thouſand years ago. *Chambers.*

To BIND. *v. a.* pret. *I bound*; particip. paſſ. *bound*, or *bounden.* [bindan, Saxon.]

1. To confine with bonds; to enchain.

Wilt thou play with him as with a bird? or wilt thou *bind* him for thy maidens? *Job*, xli. 5.

2. To gird; to enwrap; to involve.

Who hath *bound* the waters in a garment. *Prov.* xxx. 4.

3. To faſten to any thing.

Thou ſhalt *bind* this line of ſcarlet thread in the window, which thou didſt let us down by. *Joſhua*, ii. 18.

Keep my commandments, and live: and my law, as the apple of thine eye. *Bind* them upon thy fingers, write them upon the table of thine heart. *Prov.* vii. 3, 4.

4. To faſten together.

Gather ye together firſt the tares, and *bind* them in bundles, to burn them. *Matt.* xiii. 20.

5. To cover a wound with dreſſings and bandages.

When he ſaw him, he had compaſſion on him, and went to him, and *bound* up his wounds. *Luke*, x. 34.

Having filled up the bared cranium with our dreſſings, we *bound* up the wound. *Wiſeman's Surgery.*

6. To compel; to conſtrain.

Thoſe canons, or imperial conſtitutions, which have not been received here, do not *bind.* *Hale's Common Law of Engl.*

7. To oblige by ſtipulation, or oath.

If a man vow a vow, or ſwear an oath to *bind* his ſoul with a bond, he ſhall not break his word. *Numbers*, xxx. 2.

Swear by the ſolemn oath, that *binds* the gods. *Pope.*

8. To oblige by duty or law.

Though I am *bound* to every act of duty,
I am not *bound* to that, all ſlaves are free to. *Shakeſp. Othello.*

Duties expreſsly required in the plain language of Scripture, ought to *bind* our conſciences more than thoſe which are but dubiouſly inferred. *Watts's Improvement of the Mind.*

9. To oblige by kindneſs.

10. To confine; to hinder.

Now I'm cabin'd, cribb'd, confin'd, *bound* in
To ſaucy doubts and fears. *Shakeſp. Macbeth.*

You will ſooner, by imagination, *bind* a bird from ſinging, than from eating or flying. *Bacon's Natural Hiſt.* N° 989.

Though paſſion be the moſt obvious and general, yet it is not the only cauſe that *binds* up the underſtanding, and confines it, for the time, to one object, from which it will not be taken off. *Locke.*

In ſuch a diſmal place,
Where joy ne'er enters, which the ſun ne'er cheers,
Bound in with darkneſs, overſpread with damps. *Dryden.*

11. To hinder the flux of the bowels; to make coſtive.

Rhubarb hath manifeſtly in it parts of contrary operations; parts that purge, and parts that *bind* the body. *Bacon.*

The whey of milk doth looſe, the milk doth *bind.* *Herbert.*

12. To reſtrain.

The more we are *bound* up to an exact narration, we want more life, and fire, to animate and inform the ſtory. *Felton.*

13. *To bind a book.* To put it in a cover.

Was ever book, containing ſuch vile matter,
So fairly *bound?* *Shakeſp. Romeo and Juliet.*

Thoſe who could never read the grammar,
When my dear volumes touch the hammer,
May think books beſt, as richeſt *bound.* *Prior.*

14. *To bind to.* To oblige to ſerve ſome one.

If ſtill thou do'ſt retain
The ſame ill habits, the ſame follies too,
Still thou art *bound to* vice, and ſtill a ſlave. *Dryden's Perſ.*

15. *To bind to.* To contract with any body.

Art thou *bound to* a wife? ſeek not to be looſed. 1 *Cor.* vii.

16. *To bind over.* To oblige to make appearance.

Sir Roger was ſtaggered with the reports concerning this woman, and would have *bound her over* to the country ſeſſions. *Addiſon. Spectator*, N° 117.

To Bind. *v. n.*

1. To contract the parts together; to grow ſtiff and hard.

If the land riſe full of clots, and if it is a *binding* land, you muſt make it fine by harrowing of it. *Mortimer's Husbandry.*

2. To make coſtive.

3. To be obligatory.

The promiſes and bargains for truck, between a Swiſs and an Indian, in the woods of America, are *binding* to them, though they are perfectly in a ſtate of nature, in reference to one another. *Locke.*

Bind. *n. ſ.* A ſpecies of hops.

The two beſt ſorts are the white and the grey *bind*; the latter is a large ſquare hop, and more hardy. *Mortimer.*

Bi'nder. *n. ſ.* [from *to bind.*]

1. A man whoſe trade it is to bind books.

2. A man that binds ſheaves.

Three *binders* ſtood, and took the handfuls reapt
From boys that gather'd quickly up. *Chapman's Iliads.*

A man, with a *binder*, may reap an acre of wheat in a day, if it ſtand well. *Mortimer's Husbandry.*

3. A fillet; a ſhred cut to bind with.

Upon that I laid a double cloth, of ſuch length and breadth as might ſerve to encompaſs the fractured member; which I cut from each end to the middle, into three *binders.* *Wiſeman.*

Bi'nding. *n. ſ.* [from *bind.*] A bandage.

This beloved young woman began to take off the *binding* of his eyes. *Tattler*, N° 55.

Bi'ndweed. *n. ſ.* [*convolvulus*, Lat.] The name of a plant.

It hath, for the moſt part, trailing ſtalks; the leaves grow alternately on the branches; the flower conſiſts of one leaf, ſhaped like a bell, whoſe mouth is widely expanded; the ovary becomes a roundiſh membraneous fruit, wrapped up within the flower cup; and is generally divided into three cells, each containing one angular ſeed. The ſpecies are thirty ſix. 1. The common white great *bindweed*, vulgarly called *bearbind.* 2. Leſſer field *bindweed*, with a roſe coloured flower, vulgarly called *gravelbind.* 3. Common ſea *bindweed*, with round leaves. 4. Great American *bindweed*, with ſpacious yellow ſweet ſcented flowers, commonly called *Spaniſh arbour vine*, or *Spaniſh woodbine.* 5. White and yellow Spaniſh potatoes. 6. Red Spaniſh potatoes. 7. The jalap, &c. The firſt of theſe ſpecies is a very troubleſome weed in gardens; and the ſecond ſort is ſtill a worſe weed than the former. The third ſort is found upon gravelly or ſandy ſhores, where the ſalt water overflows: this is a ſtrong purge, and, as ſuch, is often uſed in medicine. The fourth ſort is common in the hot parts of America, and is planted to cover arbours and ſeats: one of theſe plants will grow to the length of ſixty or an hundred feet, and produce great quantities of ſide branches, and large fragrant yellow flowers, ſucceeded by three large angular ſeeds. The two kinds of potatoes are much cultivated in the Weſt Indies, for food; and, from the roots, a drink is made, called *mobby*, ſtronger or weaker: it is a ſprightly liquour, but not ſubject to fly into the head; nor will it keep beyond four or five days. Theſe roots have been brought from America, and are cultivated in Spain and Portugal; but, in general, they are not ſo well liked as the common potato, being too ſweet and luſcious. The jalap, whoſe root has been long uſed in medicine, is a native of the province of Italapa, about two days journey from La Vera Cruz. *Millar.*

Bindweed is of two ſorts, the larger and the ſmaller; the firſt ſort flowers in September, and the laſt in June and July. *Mortimer's Husbandry.*

Bi'nocle. *n. ſ.* [from *binus* and *oculus.*] A kind of dioptrick teleſcope, fitted ſo with two tubes joining together in one, as that a diſtant object may be ſeen with both eyes together. *Harris.*

Bino'cular. *adj.* [from *binus* and *oculus*, Lat.] Having two eyes.

Moſt animals are *binocular*, ſpiders, for the moſt part, octonocular, and ſome ſenocular. *Derham's Phyſico-Theology.*

Bino'mial *Root.* [in algebra.] A root compoſed of only two parts or members, connected with the ſigns *plus* or *minus.* *Harris.*

Bino'minous. *adj.* [from *binus* and *nomen*, Lat.] Having two names.

Bio'grapher. *n. ſ.* [βίος and γράφω.] A writer of lives; a relator not of the hiſtory of nations, but of the actions of particular perſons.

Our Grubſtreet *biographers* watch for the death of a great man, like ſo many undertakers, on purpoſe to make a penny of him. *Addiſon. Freeholder*, N° 35.

Bio'graphy. *n. ſ.* [βίος and γράφω.]

In writing the lives of men, which is called *biography*, ſome authors place every thing in the preciſe order of time when it occurred. *Watts's Logick.*

Bi'ovac. } Bi'hovac. } Bi'vouac. } *n. ſ.* [Fr. from *wey wach*, a double guard, Germ. in war.] A guard at night performed by the whole army; which, either at a ſiege, or lying before an enemy, every evening draws out from its tents or huts, and continues all night in arms before its lines or camp, to prevent any ſurpriſe. *To raiſe the biovac*, is to return the army to their tents at break of day. *Trevoux. Harris.*

Bi'parous. *adj.* [from *binus* and *pario*, Lat.] Bringing forth two at a birth.

Bi'partite. *adj.* [from *binus* and *partior*, Lat.] Having two correſpondent parts; divided into two.

Biparti'tion. *n. ſ.* [from *bipartite*.] The act of dividing into two; or of making two correſpondent parts.

Bi'ped. *n. ſ.* [*bipes*, Lat.] An animal with two feet.

No ſerpent, or fiſhes oviparous, have any ſtones at all; neither *biped* nor quadruped oviparous, have any exteriourly. *Brown's Vulgar Errours, b.* iii. *c.* 4.

Bi'pedal. *adj.* [*bipedalis*, Lat.] Two feet in length; or having two feet.

Bipe'nnated. *adj.* [from *binus* and *penna*, Lat.] Having two wings.

All *bipennated* inſects have poiſes joined to the body. *Derham's Phyſico-Theology.*

Bipe'talous. *adj.* [of *bis*, Lat. and πέταλον.] A flower conſiſting of two leaves. *Dict.*

Bi'quadrate. } *n. ſ.* [in algebra.] The fourth power, ariſing
Biquadra'tick. } from the multiplication of a ſquare number, or quantity by itſelf. *Harris.*

BIRCH *Tree.* [birc, Sax. *betula*, Lat.]

The leaves are like thoſe of the poplar; the ſhoots are very ſlender and weak; the katkins are produced at remote diſtances from the fruits, on the ſame tree; the fruit becomes a little ſquamoſe cone; the ſeeds are winged, and the tree caſts its outer rind every year. This tree is propagated by ſuckers, which may be tranſplanted either in October or February; it delights in a poor ſoil. The timber of this tree is uſed to make chairs, &c. It is alſo planted for hop poles, hoops, &c. and it is often uſed to make brooms. *Millar.*

Bi'rchen. *adj.* [from *birch.*] Made of birch.

His beaver'd brow a *birchen* garland bears. *Dunciad, b.* iv.

BIRD. *n. ſ.* [bird, or brid, a chicken, Saxon.] A general term for the feathered kind; a fowl. In common talk, *fowl* is uſed for the larger, and *bird* for the ſmaller kind of feathered animals.

The poor wren,
The moſt diminutive of *birds*, will fight,
Her young ones in her neſt, againſt the owl. *Macbeth.*

Sh' had all the regal makings of a queen;
As holy oil, Edward confeſſor's crown,
The rod and *bird* of peace, and all ſuch emblems,
Laid nobly on her. *Shakeſp. Henry* VIII.

The *bird* of Jove, ſtoop'd from his airy tour,
Two *birds* of gayeſt plume before him drove.
Milton's Paradiſe Loſt, b. xi. *l.* 186.

Hence men and beaſts the breath of life obtain,
And *birds* of air, and monſters of the main. *Dryden's Æn.*

There are ſome *birds* that are inhabitants of the water, whoſe blood is cold as fiſhes, and their fleſh is ſo like in taſte, that the ſcrupulous are allowed them on fiſh days. *Locke.*

Some ſquire perhaps you take delight to rack,
Who viſits with a gun, preſents with *birds*. *Pope.*

To Bird. *v. n.* [from the noun.] To catch birds.

I do invite you tomorrow morning to my houſe, to breakfaſt; after, we'll a *birding* together. *Shakeſp. M. W. of Windſ.*

Bi'rdbolt. *n. ſ.* [from *bird* and *bolt*, or *arrow*.] A ſmall ſhot, or arrow, to be ſhot at birds.

To be generous, guiltleſs, and of free diſpoſition, is to take thoſe things for *birdbolts*, that you deem cannon bullets. *Shakeſp. Twelfth Night.*

Bi'rdcage. *n. ſ.* [from *bird* and *cage*. See Cage.]

Birdcages taught him the pulley, and tops the centrifugal force. *Arbuthnot and Pope's Martinus Scriblerus.*

Bi'rdcatcher. *n. ſ.* [from *bird* and *catch*.] One that makes it his employment to take birds.

A poor lark entered into a miſerable expoſtulation with a *birdcatcher*, that had taken her in his net. *L'Eſtrange.*

Bi'rder. *n. ſ.* [from *bird*.] A birdcatcher.

Bi'rding piece. *n. ſ.* [from *bird* and *piece*.] A fowling piece; a gun to ſhoot birds with.

I'll creep up into the chimney.—There they always uſe to diſcharge their *birding pieces*; creep into the kill hole. *Shakeſp. Merry Wives of Windſor.*

Bi'rdlime. *n. ſ.* [from *bird* and *lime*.] A glutinous ſubſtance, which is ſpread upon twigs, by which the birds that light upon them are entangled.

Birdlime is made of the bark of holly, boiled for ten or twelve hours; and when the green coat is ſeparated from the other, they cover it up for a fortnight, in a moiſt place, and pound it into a tough paſte, that no fibres of the wood be left; then it is waſhed in a running ſtream, till no motes appear, and put up to ferment for four or five days, and ſcummed as often as any thing ariſes, and then laid up for uſe; at which time they incorporate with it a third part of nut oil, over the fire. The *birdlime* brought from Damaſcus is ſuppoſed to be made of ſebeſtens, the kernels being frequently found in it; but this will not endure the froſt or wet. That brought from Spain is of an ill ſmell; but the bark of our lantone, or wayfaring ſhrub, will make very good *birdlime*. *Chambers.*

Holly is of ſo viſcous a juice, as they make *birdlime* of the bark of it. *Bacon's Natural Hiſtory*, N° 592.

With ſtores of gather'd glue, contrive
To ſtop the vents and crannies of their hive;
Not *birdlime*, or Idean pitch, produce
A more tenacious maſs of clammy juice. *Dryden's Virgil.*

I'm enſnar'd;
Heav'ns *birdlime* wraps me round, and glues my wings.
Dryden's King Arthur.

The woodpecker, and other birds of this kind, becauſe they prey upon flies which they catch with their tongue, have a couple of bags filled with a viſcous humour, as if it were a natural *birdlime*, or liquid glue. *Grew's Coſmologia Sacra, b.* i. *c.* 5.

Bi'rdman. *n. ſ.* [from *bird* and *man*.] A birdcatcher; a fowler.

As a fowler was bending his net, a blackbird aſked him what he was doing; why, ſays he, I am laying the foundations of a city; and ſo the *birdman* drew out of ſight. *L'Eſtrange.*

Bi'rdseye. *n. ſ.* [*Adonis*, Lat.] The name of a plant.

The leaves are like fennel or chamomile; the flowers conſiſt of many leaves, which are expanded in form of a roſe; the ſeeds are collected into oblong heads. The ſpecies are, 1. The common red *birds eye*. 2. The long leaved yellow *birds eye*, &c. The firſt ſort is ſown in open borders, as an annual flower plant. The yellow ſort is uncommon in England. *Millar.*

Bi'rdsfoot. [*ornithopodium*, Lat.] The name of a plant.

It has a papilionaceous flower; the ovary, which riſes out of the flower cup, afterwards becomes a pod, ſometimes diſtinguiſhed into bells by tranſverſe partitions, full of ſeeds, for the moſt part roundiſh; the leaves grow by threes, but have two wings, or little leaves, at the origin of their foot ſtalks. The ſpecies are, 1. The talleſt hairy *birdsfoot* trefoil, with a glomerated flower. 2. Upright hoary *birdsfoot* trefoil, &c. The firſt of theſe plants is, by ſome, ſuppoſed to be the *cytiſis* of Virgil; it dies to the ground with us every winter, and riſes again the ſucceeding ſpring; and, when the roots are ſtrong, the ſhoots will riſe to four or five feet high, and produce flowers in great plenty; if it be cut while young, the cows are very fond of it, but horſes will not eat it, unleſs they are very hungry. *Millar.*

Bi'rdsnest. *n. ſ.* An herb. *Dict.*

Bi'rdstongue. *n. ſ.* An herb. *Dict.*

Bi'rgander. *n. ſ.* A fowl of the gooſe kind. *Dict.*

Birt. *n. ſ.* A fiſh; the ſame with the *turbot*; which ſee.

BIRTH. *n. ſ.* [beorþ, Sax.]

1. The act of coming into life.

But thou art fair, and, at thy *birth*, dear boy,
Nature and fortune join'd to make thee great. *Shakeſp. K. J.*

In Spain, our ſprings like old mens children be,
Decay'd and wither'd from their infancy;
No kindly ſhowers fall on our barren earth,
To hatch the ſeaſons in a timely *birth*. *Dryden.*

2. Extraction; lineage.

Moſt virtuous virgin, born of heav'nly *birth*. *Fairy Q.*

All truth I ſhall relate: nor firſt can I
Myſelf to be of Grecian *birth* deny. *Sir J. Denham.*

3. Rank which is inherited by deſcent.

He doth object, I am too great of *birth*.
Shakeſp. Merry Wives of Windſor.

Be juſt in all you ſay, and all you do;
Whatever be your *birth*, you're ſure to be
A peer of the firſt magnitude to me. *Dryden's Juvenal.*

4. The condition, or circumſtances, in which any man is born.

High in his chariot then Haleſus came,
A foe by *birth* to Troy's unhappy name. *Dryden's Virgil.*

5. Thing born; production.

The people fear me; for they do obſerve
Unfather'd heirs and loathly *births* of nature. *Shakeſp. H.* IV.

That poets are far rarer *births* than kings,
Your nobleſt father prov'd. *Ben. Johnſon's Epigrams.*

Who of themſelves
Abhor to join: and, by imprudence mix'd,
Produce prodigious *births*, of body, or mind.
Milton's Paradiſe Loſt, b. xi. *l.* 687.

She, for this many thouſand years,
Seems to have practis'd with much care,
To frame the race of woman fair;
Yet never could a perfect *birth*
Produce before, to grace the earth. *Waller.*

His eldeſt *birth*
Flies, mark'd by heav'n, a fugitive o'er earth. *Prior.*

The vallies ſmile, and, with their flow'ry face,
And wealthy *births*, confeſs the flood's embrace. *Blackmore.*

Others hatch their eggs, and tend the *birth*, till it is able to ſhift for itſelf. *Addiſon. Spectator*, N° 120.

6. The act of bringing forth.

That fair Syrian ſhepherdeſs,
Who after years of barrenneſs,
The highly favour'd Joſeph bore
To him that ſerv'd for her before;

And at her next *birth*, much like thee,
Through pangs fled to felicity. *Milton.*

7. The ſeamen call a due or proper diſtance between ſhips lying at an anchor, or under ſail, a *birth*. Alſo the proper place aboard for a meſs to put their cheſts, *&c.* is called the *birth* of that meſs. Alſo a convenient place to moor a ſhip in, is called a *birth*. *Harris.*

BI'RTHDAY. *n. ſ.* [from *birth* and *day*.]

1. The day on which any one is born.

Orient light,
Exhaling firſt from darkneſs, they beheld
Birthday of heaven and earth. *Milton's Paradiſe Loſt, b.* vii.

2. The day of the year in which any one was born, annually obſerved.

This is my *birthday*; as this very day
Was Caſſius born. *Shakeſp. Julius Cæſar.*

They tell me, 'tis my *birthday*, and I'll keep it
With double pomp of ſadneſs:
'Tis what the day deſerves, which gave me breath. *Dryden.*

Your country dames,
Whoſe cloaths returning *birthday* claims. *Prior.*

BI'RTHDOM. *n. ſ.* [This is erroneouſly, I think, printed in *Shakeſpeare*, *birthdoom*. It is derived from *birth* and *dom*. See DOM; as *kingdom*, *dukedom*.] Privilege of birth.

Let us rather
Hold faſt the mortal ſword; and, like good men,
Beſtride our downfaln *birthdom*. *Shakeſp. Macbeth.*

BI'RTHNIGHT. *n. ſ.* [from *birth* and *night*.]

1. The night in which any one is born.

Th' angelick ſong in Bethlehem field,
On thy *birthnight*, that ſung the Saviour born. *Par. Regain.*

2. The night annually kept in memory of any one's birth.

A youth more glitt'ring than a *birthnight* beau. *Pope.*

BI'RTHPLACE. *n. ſ.* [from *birth* and *place*.] Place where any one is born.

My *birthplace* have I and my lovers left;
This enemy's town I'll enter. *Shakeſp. Coriolanus.*

A degree of ſtupidity beyond even what we have been ever charged with, upon the ſcore of our *birthplace* and climate. *Swift's Addreſs to Parliament.*

BI'RTHRIGHT. *n. ſ.* [from *birth* and *right*.] The rights and privileges to which a man is born; the right of the firſt born.

Thy blood and virtue
Contend for empire in thee, and thy goodneſs
Shares with thy *birthright*. *Shakeſp. All's well that ends well.*

And haſt been found
By merit, more than *birthright*, Son of God.
Milton's Parad. Loſt, b. iii. *l.* 308.

I lov'd her firſt, I cannot quit the claim,
But will preſerve the *birthright* of my paſſion. *Otway's Orph.*

While no baſeneſs in this breaſt I find,
I have not loſt the *birthright* of my mind. *Dryden's Aurengz.*

To ſay, that liberty and property are the *birthright* of the Engliſh nation, but that if a prince invades them by illegal methods, we muſt upon no pretence reſiſt, is to confound governments. *Addiſon's Whig Examiner.*

BIRTHSTRA'NGLED. *adj.* [from *birth* and *ſtrangle*.] Strangled or ſuffocated in being born.

Finger of *birthſtrangl'd* babe,
Ditch deliver'd by a drab. *Shakeſp. Macbeth.*

BI'RTHWORT. *n. ſ.* [from *birth* and *wort*; I ſuppoſe from a quality of haſtening delivery. *Ariſtolochia*, Lat.] The name of a plant.

The ſtalks are flexible; the leaves are placed alternately on the branches; the flowers conſiſt of one leaf, are of an anomalous figure, hollowed like a pipe, and ſhaped like a tongue, generally hooked; the flower cup turns to a membraneous, oval ſhaped fruit, divided into five cells, and full of flat ſeeds. The ſpecies are, 1. The round rooted *birthwort*. 2. The climbing *birthwort*. 3. Spaniſh *birthwort*, &c. The firſt and ſecond are ſometimes uſed in medicine, and are eaſily propagated by parting their roots. *Millar.*

BI'SCOTIN. *n. ſ.* [French.] A confection made of flour, ſugar, marmalade, eggs, *&c.*

BI'SCUIT. *n. ſ.* [from *bis*, twice, Lat. and *cuit*, baked, Fr.]

1. A kind of hard dry bread, made to be carried to ſea; it is baked for long voyages four times.

The *biſcuit* alſo in the ſhips, eſpecially in the Spaniſh gallies, was grown hoary, and unwholeſome. *Knolles's Hiſtory of the Turks.*

Many have been cured by abſtinence from drink, eating dry *biſcuit*, which creates no thirſt, and ſtrong frictions four or five times a day. *Arbuthnot on Diet.*

2. A compoſition of fine flour, almonds, and ſugar, made by the confectioners.

To BISE'CT. *v. a.* [from *binus* and *ſeco*, to cut, Lat.] To divide into two parts.

The rational horizon *biſecteth* the globe into two equal parts. *Brown's Vulgar Errours, b.* vi. *c.* 5.

BISE'CTION. *n. ſ.* [from the verb.] A geometrical term, ſignifying the diviſion of any quantity into two equal parts.

BI'SHOP. *n. ſ.* [from *epiſcopus*, Lat. the Saxons formed bıſcop, which was afterwards ſoftened into *biſhop*.] One of the head order of the clergy.

A *biſhop* is an overſeer, or ſuperintendant, of religious matters in the chriſtian church. *Ayliffe's Parergon.*

You ſhall find him well accompany'd
With reverend fathers, and well learned *biſhops*.
Shakeſp. Richard III.

Their zealous ſuperſtition thinks, or pretends, they cannot do God a greater ſervice, than to deſtroy the primitive, apoſtolical, and anciently univerſal government of the church by *biſhops*. *K. Charles.*

In caſe a *biſhop* ſhould commit treaſon and felony, and forfeit his eſtate, with his life, the lands of his biſhoprick remain ſtill in the church. *South.*

On the word *biſhop*, in French *evéque*, I would obſerve, that there is no natural connexion between the ſacred office and the letters or ſound; for *evéque*, and *biſhop*, ſignify the ſame office, though there is not one letter alike in them. *Watts's Logick.*

BI'SHOP. *n. ſ.* A cant word for a mixture of wine, oranges, and ſugar.

Fine oranges,
Well roaſted, with ſugar and wine in a cup,
They'll make a ſweet *biſhop*, when gentle folks ſup. *Swift.*

To BI'SHOP. *v. a.* [from the noun.] To confirm; to admit ſolemnly into the church.

They are prophane, imperfect, oh! too bad,
Except confirm'd and *biſhoped* by thee. *Donne.*

BI'SHOPRICK. *n. ſ.* [bıſcopꞃıce, Saxon.] The dioceſe of a biſhop; the diſtrict over which the juriſdiction of a biſhop extends.

It will be fit, that, by the king's ſupreme power in cauſes eccleſiaſtical, they be ſubordinate under ſome biſhop, and *biſhoprick*, of this realm. *Bacon's Advice to Villiers.*

A virtuous woman ſhould reject marriage, as a good man does a *biſhoprick*; but I would adviſe neither to perſiſt in refuſing. *Addiſon. Spectator*, N° 89.

Thoſe paſtors had epiſcopal ordination, poſſeſſed preferments in the church, and were ſometimes promoted to *biſhopricks* themſelves. *Swift on the Sentiments of a Church of E. man.*

BI'SHOPSWEED. [*Ammi*, Lat.] The name of a plant.

This is an umbelliferous weed, with ſmall ſtriated ſeeds; the petals of the flowers are unequal, and ſhaped like a heart. The ſeeds of the greater *biſhopsweed* are uſed in medicine, and ſhould be ſown in an open ſituation, early in the ſpring. *Mill.*

BISK. *n. ſ.* [*biſque*, Fr.] Soup; broth made by boiling ſeveral ſorts of fleſh.

A prince, who in a foreſt rides aſtray,
And, weary, to ſome cottage finds the way,
Talks of no pyramids, or fowl, or *biſks* of fiſh,
But hungry ſups his cream ſerv'd up in earthen diſh.
King's Art of Cookery.

BI'SKET. See BISCUIT.

BI'SMUTH. *n. ſ.* The ſame as *marcaſite*; it properly ſignifies a hard, white, brittle, mineral ſubſtance, of a metalline nature, found at Miſnia; though ſuppoſed to be only a recrementitious matter thrown off in the formation of tin, as unfit to enter its compoſition. There are ſome, however, who eſteem it a metal *ſui generis*; though it uſually contains ſome ſilver. There is an artificial *biſmuth* made, for the ſhops, of tin. *Quincy.*

BI'SSEXTILE. *n. ſ.* [from *bis*, and *ſextilis*, Lat.] Leap year; the year in which the day, ariſing from ſix odd hours in each year, is intercalated.

The year of the ſun conſiſteth of three hundred and ſixty five days and ſix hours, wanting eleven minutes; which ſix hours omitted, will, in time, deprave the compute; and this was the occaſion of *biſſextile*, or leap year. *Brown's Vulgar Errours, b.* iv. *c.* 12.

Towards the latter end of February is the *biſſextile* or intercalar day; called *biſſextile*, becauſe the ſixth of the calends of March is twice repeated. *Holder on Time.*

BI'SSON. *adj.* [derived by *Skinner* from *by* and *ſin*.] Blind.

But who, oh! who hath ſeen the mobled queen,
Run barefoot up and down, threat'ning the flames
With *biſſon* rheum. *Shakeſp. Hamlet.*

What harm can your *biſſon* conſpectuities glean out of this character. *Shakeſp. Coriolanus.*

BI'STRE. *n. ſ.* [French.] A colour made of chimney ſoot boiled, and then diluted with water; uſed by painters in waſhing their deſigns. *Trevoux.*

BI'STORT. *n. ſ.* [*biſtorta*, Lat.] The name of a plant called alſo *ſnakeweed*; which ſee.

BI'STOURY. *n. ſ.* [*biſtouri*, Fr.] A ſurgeon's inſtrument uſed in making inciſions, of which there are three ſorts; the blade of the firſt turns like that of a lancet; but the ſtraight *biſtoury* has the blade fixed in the handle; the crooked *biſtoury* is ſhaped like a half moon, having the edge on the inſide. *Chambers.*

BISU'LCOUS. *adj.* [*biſulcus*, Lat.] Clovenfooted.

For the ſwine, although multiparous, yet being *biſulcous*, and only clovenhoofed, are farrowed with open eyes, as other *biſulcous* animals. *Brown's Vulgar Errours, b.* iii. *c.* 26.

BIT. *n. ſ.* [bıꞇol, Saxon.] Signifies the whole machine of all the iron appurtenances of a bridle, as the bit-mouth, the branches, the curb, the fevil holes, the tranchefil, and the crofs chains; but fometimes it is ufed to fignify only the bit-mouth in particular. *Farrier's Dict.*

They light from their horfes, pulling off their *bits*, that they might fomething refrefh their mouths upon the grafs. *Sidney.*

We have ftrict ftatutes, and moft biting laws,
The needful *bits* and curbs of headftrong fteeds.
Shakesp. Meafure for Meafure.

He hath the *bit* faft between his teeth, and away he runs. *Stillingfleet.*

Unus'd to the reftraint
Of curbs and *bits*, and fleeter than the winds. *Addif. Cato.*

BIT. *n. f.* [from *bite.*]

1. As much meat as is put into the mouth at once.

How many prodigal *bits* have flaves and peafants
This night englutted? *Shakefp. Timon of Athens.*

Follow your function, go and batten on cold *bits*. *Shakefp.*

The mice found it troublefome to be ftill climbing the oak for every *bit* they put in their bellies. *L'Eftrange.*

By this the boiling kettle had prepar'd,
And to the table fent the fmoaking lard,
A fav'ry *bit*, that ferv'd to relifh wine. *Dryden's Fables.*

John was the darling; he had all the good *bits*, was crammed with good pullet, chicken, and capon. *Arbuthnot's J. Bull.*

2. A fmall piece of any thing.

Then clap four flices of pilafter on't,
That, lac'd with *bits* of ruftick, makes a front. *Pope.*

He bought at thoufands, what with better wit
You purchafe as you want, and *bit* by *bit*. *Pope's Epiftles.*

His majefty has power to grant a patent for ftamping round *bits* of copper, to every fubject he hath. *Swift.*

3. A Spanifh Weft Indian filver coin, valued at fevenpence halfpenny.

4. *A bit the better or worfe.* In the fmalleft degree.

There are few that know all the tricks of thefe lawyers; for aught I can fee, your cafe is not a *bit* clearer than it was feven years ago. *Arbuthnot's Hiftory of J. Bull.*

To BIT. *v. a.* [from the noun.] To put the bridle upon a horfe.

BITCH. *n. f.* [bicce, Saxon.]

1. The female of the canine kind; as the wolf, the dog, the fox, the otter.

And at his feet a *bitch* wolf fuck did yield
To two young babes. *Spenf. Vifion of Bellay.*

I have been credibly informed, that a *bitch* will nurfe, play with, and be fond of young foxes, as much as, and in place of her puppies. *Locke.*

2. A name of reproach for a woman.

John had not run a madding fo long, had it not been for an extravagant *bitch* of a wife. *Arbuthnot's Hiftory of J. Bull.*

To BITE. *v. a.* pret. I *bit*; part. paff. I have *bit*, or *bitten*. [bitan, Saxon.]

1. To crufh, or pierce with the teeth.

My very enemy's dog,
Though he had *bit* me, fhould have ftood that night
Againft my fire. *Shakefp. King Lear.*

Such fmiling rogues as thefe,
Like rats, oft *bite* the holy cords in twain,
Too intricate t' unloofe. *Shakefp. King Lear.*

Thefe are the youths that thunder at a playhoufe, and fight for *bitten* apples. *Shakefp. Henry VIII.*

He falls; his arms upon his body found,
And with his bloody teeth he *bites* the ground. *Dryden.*

There was lately a young gentleman *bit* to the bone, who has now indeed recovered. *Tatler, N° 62.*

Their foul mouths have not opened their lips without a falfity; though they have fhowed their teeth as if they would *bite* off my nofe. *Arbuthnot and Pope's Martinus Scriblerus.*

2. To give pain by cold.

Here feel we the icy phang,
And churlifh chiding of the winter's wind;
Which when it *bites* and blows upon my body,
Ev'n till I fhrink with cold, I fmile. *Shakefp. As you like it.*

Full fifty years harnefs'd in rugged fteel,
I have endur'd the *biting* winter's blaft,
And the feverer heats of parching fummer.
Rowe's Ambitious Stepmother.

3. To hurt or pain with reproach.

Each poet with a diff'rent talent writes;
One praifes, one inftructs, another *bites*. *Rofcommon.*

4. To cut; to wound.

I've feen the day, with my good *biting* faulchion,
I would have made them fkip. *Shakefp. King Lear.*

5. To make the mouth fmart with an acrid tafte.

It may be the firft water will have more of the fcent, as more fragrant; and the fecond more of the tafte, as more bitter, or *biting*. *Bacon's Natural Hiftory, N° 21.*

6. To cheat; to trick; to defraud: a low phrafe.

Afleep and naked as an Indian lay,
An honeft factor ftole a gem away:
He pledg'd it to the knight; the knight had wit,
So kept the diamond, and the rogue was *bit*. *Pope.*

If you had allowed half the fine gentlemen to have converfed with you, they would have been ftrangely *bit*, while they thought only to fall in love with a fair lady. *Pope's Letters.*

BITE. *n. f.* [from the verb.]

1. The feizure of any thing by the teeth.

Does he think he can endure the everlafting burnings, or arm himfelf againft the *bites* of the never dying worm? *South.*

Nor dogdays parching heat, that fplits the rocks,
Are half fo harmful as the greedy flocks;
Their venom'd *bite*, and fcars indented on the ftocks.
Dryden's Virgil's Georgicks, b. ii. l. 522.

2. The act of a fifh that takes the bait.

I have known a very good fifher angle diligently four or fix hours for a river carp, and not have a *bite*. *Walton's Angler.*

3. A cheat; a trick; a fraud; in low and vulgar language.

Let a man be ne'er fo wife,
He may be caught with fober lies;
For take it in its proper light,
'Tis juft what coxcombs call a *bite*. *Swift.*

4. A fharper; one who commits frauds.

BI'TER. *n. f.* [from *bite.*]

1. He that bites.

Great barkers are no *biters*. *Camden's Remains.*

2. A fifh apt to take the bait.

He is fo bold, that he will invade one of his own kind, and you may therefore eafily believe him to be a bold *biter*. *Walton.*

3. A tricker; a deceiver.

A *biter* is one who tells you a thing, you have no reafon to difbelieve in itfelf, and perhaps has given you, before he bit you, no reafon to difbelieve it for his faying it; and, if you give him credit, laughs in your face, and triumphs that he has deceived you. He is one who thinks you a fool, becaufe you do not think him a knave. *Spectator, N° 504.*

BI'TTACLE. *n. f.* A frame of timber in the fteerage of a fhip, where the compafs is placed. *Dict.*

BI'TTEN. *particip. paff.* [from *to bite*; which fee.]

BI'TTER. *adj.* [biтep, Saxon.]

1. Having a hot, acrid, biting tafte, like wormwood.

Bitter things are apt rather to kill than engender putrefaction. *Bacon's Nat. Hift. N° 696.*

Though a man in a fever fhould, from fugar, have a *bitter* tafte, which, at another time, produces a fweet one; yet the idea of *bitter* in that man's mind, would be as clear and diftinct from the idea of fweet, as if he had tafted only gall. *Locke.*

2. Sharp; cruel; fevere.

Friends now faft fworn,
Unfeparable, fhall within this hour,
On a diffenfion of a doit, break out
To *bittereft* enmity. *Shakefp. Coriolanus.*

Hufbands, love your wives, and be not *bitter* againft them. *Coloff. iii. 19.*

The word of God, inftead of a *bitter*, teaches us a charitable zeal. *Sprat.*

3. Calamitous; miferable.

Noble friends and fellows, whom to leave
Is only *bitter* to him, only dying;
Go with me, like good angels, to my end. *Shakefp. H. VIII.*

A dire induction am I witnefs to;
And will to France, hoping, the confequence
Will prove as *bitter*, black, and tragical. *Shakefp. Rich. III.*

Tell him, that if I bear my *bitter* fate,
'Tis to behold his vengeance for my fon. *Dryden's Æneis.*

4. Painful; inclement.

And fhun the *bitter* confequence: for know,
The day thou eat'ft thereof, my fole command
Tranfgreft, inevitably thou fhalt die. *Paradife Loft, b. viii.*

The fowl the borders fly,
And fhun the *bitter* blaft, and wheel about the fky. *Dryden.*

5. Sharp; reproachful; fatirical.

Go with me,
And, in the breath of *bitter* words, let's fmother
My damned fon. *Shakefp. Richard III.*

6. Mournful; afflicted.

Wherefore is light given unto him that is in mifery, and life unto the *bitter* in foul? *Job, iii. 20.*

7. In any manner, unpleafing or hurtful.

Bitter is an equivocal word; there is *bitter* wormwood, there are *bitter* words, there are *bitter* enemies, and a *bitter* cold morning. *Watts's Logick.*

BI'TTERGOURD. *n. f.* [*colocynthis*, Lat.] The name of a plant.

It is, in all refpects, like the gourd, excepting the leaves of the plant being deeply jagged, and the fruit being exceffively bitter, and not eatable. There are feveral varieties of this plant, which are very common in divers parts of the Eaft and Weft Indies. *Millar.*

BI'TTERLY. *adv.* [from *bitter.*]

1. With a bitter tafte.

2. In a bitter manner; forrowfully; calamitoufly.

I fo lively acted with my tears,
That my poor miftrefs, moved therewithal,
Wept *bitterly*. *Shakefp. Two Gentlemen of Verona.*

Bitterly haſt thou paid, and ſtill art paying
That rigid ſcore. *Milton's Agoniſtes, l.* 432.

3. Sharply; ſeverely.

His behaviour is not to cenſure *bitterly* the errours of their zeal. *Sprat.*

BI'TTERN. *n. ſ.* [*butour*, Fr.] A bird with long legs, and a long bill, which feeds upon fiſh; remarkable for the noiſe which he makes, uſually called *bumping*. See BITTOUR.

The poor fiſh have enemies enough, beſides ſuch unnatural fiſhermen as otters, the cormorant, and the *bittern*. *Walton.*

So that ſcarce
The *bittern* knows his time, with bill ingulpht,
To ſhake the ſounding marſh. *Thomſon's Spring.*

BI'TTERN. *n. ſ.* [from *bitter.*] A very bitter liquour, which drains off in making of common ſalt, and uſed in the preparation of Epſom ſalt. *Quincy.*

BI'TTERNESS. *n. ſ.* [from *bitter.*]

1. A bitter taſte.

The idea of whiteneſs, or *bitterneſs*, is in the mind, exactly anſwering that power which is in any body to produce it there. *Locke.*

2. Malice; grudge; hatred; implacability.

The *bitterneſs* and animoſity between the chief commanders was ſuch, that a great part of the army was marched. *Clarend.*

3. Sharpneſs; ſeverity of temper.

His ſorrows have ſo overwhelm'd his wits,
Shall we be thus afflicted in his wreaks,
His fits, his frenzy, and his *bitterneſs?* *Shakeſp. Tit. Andr.*

Pierpoint and Crew appeared now to have contracted more *bitterneſs* and ſourneſs than formerly, and were more reſerved towards the king's commiſſioners. *Clarendon, b.* viii.

4. Satire; piquancy; keenneſs of reproach.

Some think their wits have been aſleep, except they dart out ſomewhat piquant, and to the quick: men ought to find the difference between ſaltneſs and *bitterneſs*. *Bacon, Eſſay* 33.

5. Sorrow; vexation; affliction.

There appears much joy in him, even ſo much, that joy could not ſhew itſelf modeſt enough, without a badge of *bitterneſs*. *Shakeſp. Much ado about Nothing.*

They ſhall mourn for him, as one mourneth for his only ſon, and ſhall be in *bitterneſs* for him, as one that is in *bitterneſs* for his firſtborn. *Zech.* xii. 10.

Moſt purſue the pleaſures, as they call them, of their natures, which begin in ſin, are carried on with danger, and end in *bitterneſs*. *Wake's Preparation for Death.*

I oft, in *bitterneſs* of ſoul, deplor'd
My abſent daughter, and my dearer lord. *Pope's Odyſſey.*

BI'TTERSWEET. *n. ſ.* [from *bitter* and *ſweet.*] The name of an apple, which has a compound taſte of ſweet and bitter.

It is but a *bitterſweet* at beſt, and the fine colours of the ſerpent do by no means make amends for the ſmart and poiſon of his ſting. *South.*

When I expreſs the taſte of an apple, which we call the *bitterſweet*, none can miſtake what I mean. *Watts's Logick.*

BI'TTERVETCH. *n. ſ.* [*orobus*, Lat.]

This plant hath a papilionaceous flower, out of whoſe empalement riſes the pointal, wrapt up in the membrane, which becomes a round pod, full of oval ſhaped ſeeds; two leaves, joined together, grow upon a rib that terminates in a point. *Millar.*

BI'TTOUR. *n. ſ.* [*butour*, Fr.] The name of a bird, commonly called the *bittern*; [See BITTERN.] but perhaps as properly *bittour*.

Then to the waters brink ſhe laid her head;
And, as a *bittour* bumps within a reed,
To thee alone, O lake, ſhe ſaid, I tell. *Dryden's W. of Bath.*

BITU'ME. *n. ſ.* [from *bitumen.*] Bitumen. See BITUMEN.

Mix with theſe
Idæan pitch, quick ſulphur, ſilver's ſpume,
Sea onion, hellebore, and black *bitume*. *May's Virgil.*

BITU'MEN. *n. ſ.* [Lat.] A fat unctuous matter dug out of the earth, or ſcummed off lakes, as the Aſphaltis in Judæa, of various kinds; ſome ſo hard as to be uſed for coals; others ſo glutinous as to ſerve for mortar. *Savary.*

It is reported, that *bitumen* mingled with lime, and put under water, will make, as it were, an artificial rock, the ſubſtance becometh ſo hard. *Bacon's Nat. Hiſtory,* N° 783.

The fabrick ſeem'd a work of riſing ground,
With ſulphur and *bitumen* caſt between. *Dryden's Fables.*

Bitumen is a body that readily takes fire, yields an oil, and is ſoluble in water. *Woodward's Method of Foſſils.*

BITU'MINOUS. *adj.* [from *bitumen.*] Having the nature and qualities of bitumen; compounded of bitumen.

Naphtha, which was the *bituminous* mortar uſed in the walls of Babylon, grows to an entire and very hard matter, like a ſtone. *Bacon's Phyſical Remains.*

The fruitage fair to ſight, like that which grew
Near that *bituminous* lake, where Sodom flam'd.
Milton's Par. Loſt, b. x. *l.* 562.

BIVA'LVE. *adj.* [from *binus* and *valvæ*, Lat.] Having two valves or ſhutters; a term uſed of thoſe fiſh that have two ſhells, as oyſters; and of thoſe plants whoſe ſeed pods open their whole length, to diſcharge their ſeeds, as peas.

In the cavity lies looſe the ſhell of ſome ſort of *bivalve*, larger than could be introduced in at either of thoſe holes. *Woodward on Foſſils.*

BIVA'LVULAR. *adj.* [from *bivalve.*] Having two valves. *Dict.*

BI'XWORT. *n. ſ.* An herb. *Dict.*

BI'ZANTINE. *n. ſ.* [more properly ſpelt *byzantine*; from *Byzantium.*] A great piece of gold valued at fifteen pound, which the king offereth upon high feſtival days; it is yet called a *bizantine*, which anciently was apiece of gold coined by the emperours of Conſtantinople. *Camden's Remains.*

To BLAB. *v. a.* [*blabberen*, Dutch.]

1. To tell what ought to be kept ſecret; it uſually implies rather thoughtleſſneſs than treachery; but may be uſed in either ſenſe.

The gaudy, *blabbing*, and remorſeful day,
Is crept into the boſom of the ſea. *Shakeſp. Henry* VI.

Thy dues be done, and none left out,
Ere the *blabbing* eaſtern ſcout
The nice morn on the Indian ſteep,
From her cabin'd loophole peep. *Milton.*

Nature has made man's breaſt no windores,
To publiſh what he does within doors;
Nor what dark ſecrets there inhabit,
Unleſs his own raſh folly *blab* it. *Hudibras, p.* ii. *c.* ii.

Sorrow nor joy can be diſguis'd by art,
Our foreheads *blab* the ſecrets of our heart. *Dryden's Juv.*

It is unlawful to give any kind of religious worſhip to a creature; but the very *indices* of the fathers cannot eſcape the *index expurgatorius*, for *blabbing* ſo great a truth. *Stillingfleet.*

Nor whiſper to the tattling reeds
The blackeſt of all female deeds;
Nor *blab* it on the lonely rocks,
Where echo ſits, and liſt'ning mocks. *Swift.*

2. To tell; in a good ſenſe.

That delightful engine of her thoughts,
That *blabb'd* them with ſuch pleaſing eloquence,
Is torn from forth that pretty hollow cage.
Shakeſp. Titus Andronicus.

To BLAB. *v. n.* To tattle; to tell tales.

Your mute I'll be;
When my tongue *blabs*, then let mine eyes not ſee.
Shakeſp. Twelfth Night.

BLAB. *n. ſ.* [from the verb.] A teltale; a thoughtleſs babbler; a treacherous betrayer of ſecrets.

The ſecret man heareth many confeſſions; for who will open himſelf to a *blab*, or babbler? *Bacon, Eſſay* 6.

To have reveal'd
Secrets of man, the ſecrets of a friend,
Contempt and ſcorn of all, to be excluded
All friendſhip, and avoided as a *blab*. *Milton's Agoniſtes.*

Whoever ſhews me a very inquiſitive body, I'll ſhew him a *blab*, and one that ſhall make privacy as publick as a proclamation. *L'Eſtrange.*

I ſhould have certainly gone about ſhewing my letters, under the charge of ſecrecy, to every *blab* of my acquaintance. *Swift's Letters.*

BLA'BBER. *n. ſ.* [from *blab.*] A tattler; a teltale.

To BLA'BBER. *v. n.* To whiſtle to a horſe. *Skinner.*

BLA'BBERLIPPED. *Skinner.* See BLOBBERLIPPED.

BLACK. *adj.* [blac, Saxon.]

1. Of the colour of night.

In the twilight in the evening, in the *black* and dark night. *Prov.* vii. 9.

By Ariſtotle it ſeems to be implied, in theſe problems which enquire why the ſun makes man *black*, and not the fire, why it whitens wax, yet blacks the ſkin. *Brown's Vulgar Errours.*

2. Dark.

The heaven was *black* with clouds and wind, and there was a great rain. 1 *Kings,* xviii. 45.

3. Cloudy of countenance; ſullen.

She hath abated me of half my train;
Look'd *black* upon me. *Shakeſp. King Lear.*

4. Horrible; wicked; atrocious.

Either my country never muſt be freed,
Or I conſenting to ſo *black* a deed. *Dryden's Indian Emp.*

5. Diſmal; mournful.

A dire induction am I witneſs to;
And will to France, hoping, the conſequence,
Will prove as bitter, *black*, and tragical. *Shakeſp. Rich.* III.

6. *Black and blue.* The colour of a bruiſe; a ſtripe.

Miſtreſs Ford, good heart, is beaten *black and blue*, that you cannot ſee a white ſpot about her. *Merry Wives of Windſor.*

And, wing'd with ſpeed and fury, flew
To reſcue knight from *black and blue*. *Hudibras, cant.* ii.

BLACK-BROWED. *adj.* [from *black* and *brow.*] Having black eyebrows; gloomy; diſmal; threatening.

Come, gentle night; come, loving, *black-brow'd* night,
Give me my Romeo. *Shakeſp. Romeo and Juliet.*

Thus when a *black-brow'd* guſt begins to riſe,
White foam at firſt on the curl'd ocean fries,
Then roars the main, the billows mount the ſkies.
Dryden, Æneid vii. *l.* 736.

BLACK-BRYONY. *n. ſ.* [*tamnus*, Lat.] The name of a plant.

It is male and female in different plants; the flowers of the male plant conſiſt of one leaf, and are bell ſhaped; but theſe are barren; the embryos are produced on the female plants, which become oval berries, including roundiſh ſeeds. Theſe plants have no claſper, as the white bryony hath. The ſpecies are, 1. The common *black-bryony*. 2. *Black-bryony* of Crete, with a trifid leaf, *&c.* The firſt is rarely cultivated in gardens, but grows wild under hedges, and is gathered for medicinal uſe. It may be eaſily propagated by ſowing the ſeeds, ſoon after they are ripe, under the ſhelter of buſhes; where, in the ſpring, the plants will come up, and ſpread their branches over the buſhes. *Millar.*

BLACK-CATTLE. Oxen; bulls; and cows.

The other part of the grazier's buſineſs is what we call *black-cattle*, producing hides, tallow, and beef, for exportation. *Swift.*

BLACK-EARTH. *n. ſ.* It is every where obvious on the ſurface of the ground, and what we call mould. *Woodw. on Foſſils.*

BLACK-GUARD. *adj.* [from *black* and *guard.*] A cant word amongſt the vulgar; by which is implied a dirty fellow; of the meaneſt kind.

Let a *black-guard* boy be always about the houſe, to ſend on your errands, and go to market for you on rainy days. *Swift.*

BLACK-LEAD. *n. ſ.* [from *black* and *lead.*] A mineral found in the lead-mines, much uſed for pencils; it is not fuſible, or not without a very great heat.

You muſt firſt get your *black-lead* ſharpened finely, and put faſt into quills, for your rude and firſt draught. *Peacham.*

BLACK-MAIL. *n. ſ.* A certain rate of money, corn, cattle, or other conſideration, paid to men allied with robbers, to be by them protected from the danger of ſuch as uſually rob or ſteal. *Cowel.*

BLACK-PUDDING. *n. ſ.* [from *black* and *pudding.*] A kind of food made of blood and grain.

Through they were lin'd with many a piece
Of ammunition bread and cheeſe,
And fat *black-puddings*, proper food
For warriours that delight in blood. *Hudibras, p.* i. *cant.* i.

BLACK-ROD. *n. ſ.* [from *black* and *rod.*] The uſher belonging to the order of the garter; ſo called from the *black rod* he carries in his hand. He is of the king's chamber, and likewiſe uſher of the parliament. *Cowel.*

BLACK. *n. ſ.* [from the adjective.]

1. A black colour.

Black is the badge of hell,
The hue of dungeons, and the ſcowl of night.
Shakeſp. Love's Labour Loſt.

For the production of *black*, the corpuſcles muſt be leſs than any of thoſe which exhibit colours. *Newton's Opticks.*

2. Mourning.

Riſe, wretched widow, riſe; nor, undeplor'd,
Permit my ghoſt to paſs the Stygian ford:
But riſe, prepar'd in *black*, to mourn thy periſh'd lord.
Dryden's Fables.

3. A blackamoor.

4. That part of the eye which is black.

It ſuffices that it be in every part of the air, which is as big as the *black* or ſight of the eye. *Digby.*

To BLACK. *v. a.* [from the noun.] To make black; to blacken.

Blacking over the paper with ink, not only the ink would be quickly dried up, but the paper, that I could not burn before, would be quickly ſet on fire. *Boyle on Colours.*

Then in his fury *black'd* the raven o'er,
And bid him prate in his white plumes no more.
Addiſon's Ovid's Metamorph. b. ii.

BLA'CKAMOOR. *n. ſ.* [from *black* and *Moor.*] A man by nature of a black complexion; a negro.

They are no more afraid of a *blackamoor*, or a lion, than of a nurſe, or a cat. *Locke on Education,* § 115.

BLA'CKBERRIED *Heath.* [*empetrum*, Lat.] The name of a plant.

It hath leaves like thoſe of the heath; the flowers are male and female, which grow in different parts of the ſame plant; the male flowers have no petals; the female are ſucceeded by blackberries, in each of which are contained three or four hard ſeeds. This little ſhrub grows wild upon the mountains in Staffordſhire, Devonſhire, and Yorkſhire. *Millar.*

BLA'CKBERRY *Buſh. n. ſ.* A ſpecies of bramble; which ſee.

BLA'CKBERRY. *n. ſ.* The fruit of the blackberry buſh.

The policy of theſe crafty ſneering raſcals, that ſtale old mouſe eaten cheeſe Neſtor, and that ſame dogfox Ulyſſes, is not proved worth a *blackberry*. *Shakeſp. Troilus and Creſſida.*

Then ſad he ſung the children in the wood;
How *blackberries* they pluck'd in deſarts wild,
And fearleſs at the glittering faulchion ſmil'd. *Gay's Paſt.*

BLA'CKBIRD. *n. ſ.* [from *black* and *bird.*] The name of a bird.

Of ſinging birds, they have linnets, goldfinches, *blackbirds*, thruſhes, and divers others. *Carew's Survey of Cornwal.*

A ſchoolboy ran unto't, and thought
The crib was down, the *blackbird* caught. *Swift.*

To BLA'CKEN. *v. a.* [from *black.*]

1. To make of a black colour.

Bleſs'd by aſpiring winds, he finds the ſtrand
Blacken'd by crouds. *Prior.*
While the long fun'rals *blacken* all the way. *Pope.*

2. To darken.

That little cloud that appear'd at firſt to Elijah's ſervant, no bigger than a man's hand, but preſently after grew, and ſpread, and *blackened* the face of the whole heaven. *South.*

3. To defame; or make infamous.

Let us *blacken* him what we can, ſaid that miſcreant Harriſon, of the bleſſed king, upon the wording and drawing up his charge againſt his approaching trial. *South.*

The morals *blacken'd*, when the writings 'ſcape
The libell'd perſon, and the pictur'd ſhape. *Pope.*

To BLA'CKEN. *v. n.* To grow black.

The hollow ſound
Sung in the leaves, the foreſt ſhook around,
Air *blacken'd*, roll'd the thunder, groan'd the ground. *Dryden.*

BLA'CKISH. *adj.* [from *black.*] Somewhat black.

Part of it all the year continues in the form of a *blackiſh* oil. *Boyle.*

BLA'CKMOOR. *n. ſ.* [ftom *black* and *Moor.*] A negro.

The land of Chus makes no part of Africa; nor is it the habitation of *blackmoors*; but the country of Arabia, eſpecially the happy and ſtony. *Brown's Vulgar Errours, b.* vi. *c.* 11.

More to weſt
The realm of Bacchus to the *blackmoor* ſea. *Par. Reg. b.* iv.

BLA'CKNESS. *n. ſ.* [from *black.*]

1. Black colour.

Blackneſs is only a diſpoſition to abſorb, or ſtifle, without reflection, moſt of the rays of every ſort that fall on the bodies. *Locke's Elements of Natural Philoſophy, c.* ii.

There would emerge one or more very black ſpots, and, within thoſe, other ſpots of an intenſer *blackneſs*. *Newt. Opt.*

His tongue, his prating tongue, had chang'd him quite,
To ſooty *blackneſs* from the pureſt white. *Addiſon's Ovid.*

2. Darkneſs.

His faults in him ſeem as the ſpots of heav'n,
More fiery by night's *blackneſs*. *Shakeſp. Ant. and Cleopatra.*

BLA'CKSMITH. *n. ſ.* [from *black* and *ſmith.*] A ſmith that works in iron; ſo called from being very ſmutty.

The *blackſmith* may forge what he pleaſes. *Howel's E. Tears.*

Shut up thy doors with bars and bolts; it will be impoſſible for the *blackſmith* to make them ſo faſt, but a cat and a whoremaſter will find a way through them. *Spectator,* N° 205.

BLA'CKTAIL. *n. ſ.* [from *black* and *tail.*] A fiſh; a kind of perch, by ſome called *ruffs*, or *popes*. See POPE. *Dict.*

BLA'CKTHORN. *n. ſ.* [from *black* and *thorn.*] The ſame with the ſloe. See PLUM, of which it is a ſpecies.

BLA'DDER. *n. ſ.* [blæðꝺne, Saxon; *blader*, Dutch.]

1. That veſſel in the body which contains the urine.

The *bladder* ſhould be made of a membranous ſubſtance, and extremely dilatable for receiving and containing the urine, till an opportunity of emptying it. *Ray on the Creation.*

2. It is often filled with wind, to which alluſions are frequently made.

That huge great body which the giant bore,
Was vanquiſh'd quite, and of that monſtrous maſs
Was nothing left, but like an empty *bladder* was. *Fairy Q.*

A *bladder* but moderately filled with air, and ſtrongly tied, being held near the fire, grew exceeding turgid and hard; but afterwards being brought nearer to the fire, it ſuddenly broke, with ſo loud a noiſe as made us for a while after almoſt deaf. *Boyle.*

3. It is uſual for thoſe that learn to ſwim, to ſupport themſelves with blown bladders.

I have ventur'd,
Like little wanton boys, that ſwim on *bladders*,
Theſe many ſummers, in a ſea of glory;
But far beyond my depth: my highblown pride
At length broke under me. *Shakeſp. Henry* VIII.

4. A bliſter; a puſtule.

BLA'DDER-NUT. *n. ſ.* [*ſtaphylodendron*, Lat.] A plant.

The flower conſiſts of ſeveral leaves, which are placed circularly, and expand in form of a roſe; out of whoſe many headed flower cup riſes the pointal, which becomes a membranaceous fruit, ſomewhat like the inflated bladder of fiſhes, and divided into two or three cells, containing ſeeds in form of a ſcull. The ſpecies are, 1. The common wild *bladder-nut*. 2. Three leaved Virginian *bladder-nut*. 3. *Bladder-nut*, with ſingle ſhining leaves. 4. *Bladder-nut*, with narrow bay leaves. 5. Three leaved American *bladder-nut*, with cut leaves. The firſt of theſe trees is found wild in the woods, and other ſhady places, in the northern parts of England. The ſecond ſort is a native of America, but is ſo hardy as to endure the ſevereſt cold of our climate, in the open air. Both theſe kinds may be propagated, by ſowing their ſeeds early in the ſpring. They will commonly grow in England to the height of twelve or fourteen feet. *Mill.*

BLA'DDER-SENA. *n. ſ.* [*colutea*, Lat.] The name of a plant.

It hath a papilionaceous flower, ſucceeded by pods, reſembling the inflated bladder of fiſhes, in which are contained ſeveral kidney ſhaped ſeeds. The ſpecies are five. Theſe ſhrubs grow to the height of eight or ten feet; and, among flowering trees,

trees, the oddness of their flowers and pods will make a pretty variety. *Millar.*

BLADE. *n. s.* [blæð, bleð, Sax. *bled*, Fr.] The spire of grass before it grows to seed; the green shoots of corn which rise from the seed. This seems to me the primitive signification of the word *blade*; from which, I believe, the *blade* of a sword was first named, because of its similitude in shape; and, from the *blade* of a sword, that of other weapons or tools.

There is hardly found a plant that yieldeth a red juice in the *blade* or ear, except it be the tree that beareth *sanguis draconis.* *Bacon.*

Sends in his feeding flocks betimes, t' invade
The rising bulk of the luxuriant *blade.* *Dryden's Georg.*

If we were able to dive into her secret recesses, we should find that the smallest *blade* of grass, or most contemptible weed, has its particular use. *Swift on the Faculties of the Mind.*

Hung on every spray, on every *blade*
Of grass, the myriad dewdrops twinkle round. *Thomson.*

BLADE. *n. s.* [*blatte*, Germ. *blad*, Dutch.]

1. The sharp or striking part of a weapon or instrument, distinct from the handle. It is usually taken for a weapon, and so called probably from the likeness of a sword *blade* to a *blade* of grass.

He fought all round about, his thirsty *blade*
To bathe in blood of faithless enemy. *Fairy Queen, b.* i.

She knew the virtue of her *blade*, nor would
Pollute her sabre with ignoble blood. *Dryden's Hind and P.*

Be his this sword, whose *blade* of brass displays
A ruddy gleam; whose hilt a silver blaze. *Pope.*

2. A brisk man, either fierce or gay, called so in contempt. So we say *mettle* for *courage.*

You'll find yourself mistaken, Sir, if you'll take upon you to judge of these *blades* by their garbs, looks, and outward appearance. *L'Estrange.*

Then turning about to the hangman, he said,
Dispatch me, I pri'thee, this troublesome *blade.* *Prior.*

BLADE *of the Shoulder.* } *n. s.* The bone called by anatomists the
BLA'DEBONE. } scapula, or scapular bone.

He fell most furiously on the broiled relicks of a shoulder of mutton, commonly called a *bladebone.* *Pope.*

To BLADE. *v. a.* [from the noun.] To furnish, or fit with a blade.

BLA'DED. *adj.* [from *blade.*] Having blades or spires.

Her silver visage in the wat'ry glass,
Decking with liquid pearl the *bladed* grass.
Shakesp. Midsummer Night's Dream.

As where the lightning runs along the ground,
Nor *bladed* grass, nor bearded corn succeeds,
But scales of scurf and putrefaction breeds. *Dryden.*

BLAIN. *n. s.* [bleȝene, Sax. *bleyne*, Dutch.] A pustule; a botch; a blister.

Itches, *blains*,
Sow all th' Athenian bosoms, and the crop
Be general leprosy. *Shakesp. Timon.*

Botches and *blains* must all his flesh imboss,
And all his people. *Milton's Par. Lost, b.* xii. *l.* 180.

Whene'er I hear a rival nam'd,
I feel my body all inflam'd;
Which breaking out in boils and *blains*,
With yellow filth my linen stains. *Swift.*

BLA'MABLE. *adj.* [from *blame.*] Culpable; faulty.

Virtue is placed between two extremes, which are on both sides equally *blamable.* *Dryden's Dufresnoy.*

BLA'MABLENESS. *n. s.* [from *blamable.*] Fault; the state of being liable to blame.

BLA'MABLY. *adv.* [from *blamable.*] Culpable; in a manner liable to censure.

A process may be carried on against a person, that is maliciously or *blamably* absent, even to a definitive sentence. *Ayliffe.*

To BLAME. *v. a.* [*blâmer*, Fr.]

1. To censure; to charge with a fault: it generally implies a slight censure.

Our pow'r
Shall do a court'sy to our wrath, which men
May *blame*, but not controul. *Shakesp. King Lear.*

Porphyrius, you too far did tempt your fate;
'Tis true, your duty to me it became;
But praising that, I must your conduct *blame.*
Dryden's Tyrannick Love.

Each finding, like a friend,
Something to *blame*, and something to commend. *Pope.*

2. To *blame* has usually the particle *for* before the fault.

The reader must not *blame* me *for* making use here, all along of the word sentiment. *Locke.*

3. Sometimes, but rarely, *of.*

Tomoreus he *blam'd of* inconsiderate rashness, for that he would busy himself in matters not belonging to his vocation.
Knolles's History of the Turks.

BLAME. *n. s.* [from the verb.]

1. Fault; imputation of a fault.

In arms, the praise of success is shared amongst many; yet the *blame* of misadventures is charged upon one.
Sir J. Hayward.

They lay the *blame* on the poor little ones, sometimes passionately enough, to divert it from themselves. *Locke.*

2. Crime; that which produces or deserves censure.

Who would not judge us to be discharged of all *blame*, which are confest to have no great fault, even by their very word and testimony, in whose eyes no fault of ours hath ever hitherto been accustomed to seem small. *Hooker, b.* v. § 27.

I unspeak mine own detraction; here abjure
The taints and *blames* I laid upon myself,
For strangers to my nature. *Shakesp. Macbeth.*

3. Hurt.

Therewith upon his crest,
With rigour so outrageous he smit,
That a large share it hew'd out of the rest,
And glancing down his shield, from *blame* him fairly blest.
Fairy Queen, b. i. *cant.* ii. *stanz.* 18.

4. There is a peculiar structure of this word, in which it is not very evident whether it be a *noun* or a verb; but I conceive it to be the *noun.* *To blame*, in French, *à tort.*

You were *to blame*, I must be plain with you,
To part so slightly with your wife's first gift.
Shakesp. Merchant of Venice.

I do not ask whether they were mistaken; but, on supposition they were not, whether they were *to blame* in the manner.
Stillingfleet.

Now we should hold them much *to blame*,
If they went back before they came. *Prior.*

BLA'MEFUL. *adj.* [from *blame* and *full.*] Criminal; guilty; meriting blame.

Is not the causer of these timeless deaths,
As *blameful* as the executioner? *Shakesp. Richard* III.

Bluntwitted lord, ignoble in demeanour,
If ever lady wrong'd her lord so much,
Thy mother took into her *blameful* bed
Some stern untutor'd churl. *Shakesp. Henry* VI. *p.* ii.

BLA'MELESS. *adj.* [from *blame.*]

1. Guiltless; innocent; exempt from censure or blame.

She found out the righteous, and preserved him *blameless* unto God. *Wisdom*, x. 5.

The flames ascend on either altar clear,
While thus the *blameless* maid address'd her pray'r. *Dryden.*

Such a lessening of our coin will deprive great numbers of *blameless* men, of a fifth part of their estates. *Locke.*

2. Sometimes it is used with *of.*

We will be *blameless of* this thine oath. *Joshua*, ii. 17.

BLA'MELESLY. *adv.* [from *blameless.*] Innocently; without crime.

It is the wilful opposing explicit articles, and not the not believing them when not revealed, or not with that conviction, against which he cannot *blamelesly*, without pertinacy, hold out, that will bring danger of ruin on any. *Hammond's Fundamentals.*

BLA'MELESNESS. *n. s.* [from *blameless.*] Innocence; exemption from censure.

Having resolved, with him in Homer, that all is chargeable on Jupiter and fate, they infer, with him, the *blamelesness* of the inferiour agent. *Hammond's Fundamentals.*

BLA'MER. *n. s.* [from *blame.*] One that blames or finds fault; a censurer.

In me you've hallowed a pagan muse,
And denizon'd a stranger, who, mistaught
By *blamers* of the times they marr'd, hath sought
Virtues in corners. *Donne.*

BLAMEWO'RTHY. *adj.* [from *blame* and *worthy.*] Culpable; blameable; worthy of blame or censure.

Although the same should be *blameworthy*, yet this age hath reasonably well forborn to incur the danger of any such blame.
Hooker, b. v. § 12.

To BLANCH. *v. a.* [*blanchir*, Fr.]

1. To whiten; to change from some other colour to white.

You can behold such sights,
And keep the natural ruby of your cheeks,
When mine is *blanch'd* with fear. *Shakesp. Macbeth.*

A way of whiting wax cheaply may be of use; and we have set down the practice of tradesmen who *blanch* it. *Boyle.*

And sin's black dye seems *blanch'd* by age to virtue.
Dryden's Spanish Friar.

2. To strip or peel such things as have husks.

Their suppers may be bisket, raisins of the sun, and a few *blanched* almonds. *Wiseman's Surgery.*

3. To obliterate; to wash out; to balk; to pass over.

The judges thought it dangerous to admit ifs and ands, to qualify treason; whereby every one might express his malice, and *blanch* his danger. *Bacon's Henry* VII.

You are not transported in an action that warms the blood and is appearing holy, to *blanch*, or take for admitted, the point of lawfulness. *Bacon's Holy War.*

To BLANCH. *v. n.* To evade; to shift; to speak soft.

Optimi consiliarii mortui; books will speak plain, when counsellors *blanch.* *Bacon.*

BLA'NCHER. *n. s.* [from *blanch.*] A whitener. *Dict.*

BLAND. *adj.* [*blandus*, Lat.] Soft; mild; gentle.

In her face excuſe
Came prologue; and apology too prompt;
Which, with *bland* words at will, ſhe thus addreſs'd.
Milton's Par. Loſt, b. ix. *l.* 855.

An even calm
Perpetual reign'd, ſave what the zephyrs *bland*
Breath'd o'er the blue expanſe. *Thomſon's Spring.*

To BLA'NDISH. *v. a.* [*blandior*, Lat.] To ſmooth; to ſoften. I have met with this word in no other paſſage.

Muſt'ring all her wiles,
With *blandiſh'd* parleys, feminine aſſaults,
Tongue-batteries, ſhe ſurceas'd not day nor night,
To ſtorm me over-watch'd, and weary'd out.
Milton's Agoniſtes, l. 402.

BLA'NDISHMENT. *n. ſ.* [from *blandiſh*; *blanditiæ*, Lat.]

1. Act of fondneſs; expreſſion of tenderneſs by geſture.

The little babe up in his arms he hent,
Who, with ſweet pleaſure and bold *blandiſhment*,
'Gan ſmile. *Fairy Queen, b.* ii. *c.* ii. *ſtanz.* 1.

Each bird and beaſt, behold
Approaching two and two; theſe cow'ring low
With *blandiſhment*. *Milt. Paradiſe Loſt, b.* viii. *l.* 351.

2. Soft words; kind ſpeeches.

He was both well and fair ſpoken, and would uſe ſtrange ſweetneſs and *blandiſhment* of words, where he deſired to effect or perſuade any thing that he took to heart. *Bacon's H.* VII.

3. Kind treatment; careſs.

Him Dido now with *blandiſhment* detains;
But I ſuſpect the town where Juno reigns. *Dryden's Virgil.*

In order to bring thoſe infidels within the wide circle of whiggiſh community, neither *blandiſhments* nor promiſes are omitted. *Swift's Examiner*, N° 47.

BLANK. *adj.* [*blanc*, Fr. derived by *Menage* from *Albianus*, thus: *Albianus, albianicus, bianicus, biancus, bianco, blanicus, blancus, blanc*; by others, from *blanc*, which, in Daniſh, ſignifies *ſhining*; in conformity to which, the Germans have *blancker*, to *ſhine*; the Saxons, blæcan; and the Engliſh, *bleach*, to *whiten*.]

1. White.

To the *blank* moon
Her office they preſcrib'd: to th' other five
Their planetary motions. *Parad. Loſt, b.* x. *l.* 656.

2. Without writing; unwritten; empty of all marks.

Our ſubſtitutes at home ſhall have *blank* charters,
Whereto, when they know that men are rich,
They ſhall ſubſcribe them for large ſums of gold.
Shakeſp. Richard II.

Upon the debtor ſide, I find innumerable articles; but, upon the creditor ſide, little more than *blank* paper. *Addiſon. Spectat.*

3. Confuſed; cruſhed; diſpirited; ſubdued; depreſſed.

There without ſuch boaſt, or ſign of joy,
Solicitous and *blank*, he thus began. *Par. Regained, b.* ii.

Adam ſoon as he heard
The fatal treſpaſs done by Eve, amaz'd,
Aſtonied ſtood, and *blank*, while horrour chill
Ran through his veins, and all his joints relax'd.
Milton's Paradiſe Loſt, b. ix. *l.* 888.

But now no face divine contentment wears;
'Tis all *blank* ſadneſs, or continual fears. *Pope.*

4. Without rhime; where the rhime is *blanched*, or miſſed.

The lady ſhall ſay her mind freely, or the *blank* verſe ſhall halt for it. *Shakeſp. Hamlet.*

Long have your ears been fill'd with tragick parts;
Blood and *blank* verſe have harden'd all your hearts.
Addiſon's Drummer, Prologue.

Our *blank* verſe, where there is no rhime to ſupport the expreſſion, is extremely difficult to ſuch as are not maſters in the tongue. *Addiſon's Remarks on Italy.*

BLANK. *n. ſ.* [from the adjective.]

1. A void ſpace.

I cannot write a paper full as I uſed to do; and yet I will not forgive a *blank* of half an inch from you. *Swift.*

2. A lot, by which nothing is gained; which has no prize marked upon it.

If you have heard your general talk of Rome,
And of his friends there, it is lots to *blanks*
My name hath touch'd your ears. *Shakeſp. Coriolanus.*

In fortune's lottery lies
A heap of *blanks*, like this, for one ſmall prize. *Dryden.*

The world the coward will deſpiſe,
When life's a *blank*, who pulls not for a prize. *Dryden.*

3. A paper from which the writing is effaced.

She has left him
The *blank* of what he was;
I tell thee, eunuch, ſhe has quite unmann'd him. *Dryden.*

4. A paper unwritten; any thing without marks or characters.

For him, I think not on him; for his thoughts,
Would they were *blanks*, rather than fill'd with me.
Shakeſp. Twelfth Night.

Omiſſion to do what is neceſſary,
Seals a commiſſion to a *blank* of danger. *Shakeſp. Tr. and Cr.*

For the book of knowledge fair,
Preſented with an univerſal *blank*
Of nature's works, to me expung'd and ras'd. *Par. Loſt.*

A life ſo ſpent is one great *blank*, which, though not blotted with ſin, is yet without any characters of grace or virtue.
Rogers, ſerm. xii.

5. The point to which an arrow is directed; ſo called, becauſe, to be more viſible, it was marked with white.

Slander,
Whoſe whiſper o'er the world's diameter,
As level as the cannon to his *blank*,
Tranſports its poiſon'd ſhot. *Shakeſp. Hamlet.*

6. Aim; ſhot.

The harlot king
Is quite beyond my aim; out of the *blank*
And level of my brain. *Shakeſp. Winter's Tale.*

I have ſpoken for you all my beſt,
And ſtood within the *blank* of his diſpleaſure,
For my free ſpeech. *Shakeſp. Othello.*

7. Object to which any thing is directed.

See better, Lear, and let me ſtill remain
The true *blank* of thine. *Shakeſp. King Lear.*

To BLANK. *v. a.* [from *blank*; *blanchir*, Fr.]

1. To damp; to confuſe; to diſpirit.

Each oppoſite, that *blanks* the face of joy,
Meet what I would have well, and it deſtroy. *Shakeſp. Haml.*

Dagon muſt ſtoop, and ſhall ere long receive
Such a diſcomfit, as ſhall quite deſpoil him
Of all theſe boaſted trophies won on me,
And with confuſion *blank* his worſhippers. *Milton's Agoniſt.*

If the atheiſt, when he dies, ſhould find that his ſoul remains, how will this man be amazed and *blanked*? *Tillotſon.*

2. To efface; to annul.

All former purpoſes were *blanked*, the governour at a bay, and all that charge loſt and cancelled. *Spenſer on Ireland.*

BLA'NKET. *n. ſ.* [*blanchette*, Fr.]

1. An woollen cover, ſoft, and looſely woven, ſpread commonly upon a bed, over the linen ſheet, for the procurement of warmth.

Nor heav'n peep through the *blanket* of the dark,
To cry, hold! hold! *Shakeſp. King Lear.*

The abilities of man muſt fall ſhort on one ſide or other, like too ſcanty a *blanket* when you are abed; if you pull it upon your ſhoulders, you leave your feet bare; if you thruſt it down upon your feet, your ſhoulders are uncovered. *Temple.*

Himſelf among the ſtoried chiefs he ſpies,
As from the *blanket* high in air he flies. *Pope's Dunciad.*

2. A kind of pear, ſometimes written *blanquet*. See PEAR.

To BLA'NKET. *v. a.* [from the noun.]

1. To cover with a blanket.

My face I'll grime with filth;
Blanket my loins; tie all my hair in knots. *Sh. King Lear.*

2. To toſs in a blanket, by way of penalty or contempt.

Ah, oh! he cry'd, what ſtreet, what lane, but knows
Our purgings, pumpings, *blanketings*, and blows? *Pope.*

BLA'NKLY. *adv.* [from *blank*.] In a blank manner; with whiteneſs; with paleneſs; with confuſion.

To BLARE. *v. n.* [*blaren*, Dutch.] To bellow; to roar. *Skinn.*

To BLASPHE'ME. *v. a.* [*blaſphemo*, low Lat.]

1. To ſpeak in terms of impious irreverence of God.

2. To ſpeak evil of.

The trueſt iſſue of thy throne,
By his own interdiction ſtands accurs'd,
And does *blaſpheme* his breed. *Shakeſ. Macbeth.*

Thoſe who from our labours heap their board,
Blaſpheme their feeder, and forget their lord. *Pope's Odyſſey.*

To BLASPHE'ME. *v. n.* To ſpeak blaſphemy.

Liver of *blaſpheming* Jew,
Gall of goat, and ſlips of yew. *Shakeſp. Macbeth.*

I puniſhed them oft in every ſynagogue, and compelled them to *blaſpheme*. *Acts*, xxvi. 11.

BLASPHE'MER. *n. ſ.* [from *blaſpheme*.] A wretch that ſpeaks of God in impious and irreverent terms.

Who was before a *blaſphemer*, and a perſecutor, and injurious. 1 *Tim.* i. 13.

Even that *blaſphemer* himſelf would inwardly reverence him, as he in his heart really deſpiſes him for his cowardly baſe ſilence. *South.*

Deny the curſt *blaſphemer*'s tongue to rage,
And turn God's fury from an impious age. *Tickell.*

Should each *blaſphemer* quite eſcape the rod,
Becauſe the inſult's not to man, but God. *Pope.*

BLA'SPHEMOUS. *adj.* [from *blaſpheme*. It is uſually ſpoken with the accent on the firſt ſyllable, but uſed by *Milton* with it on the ſecond.] Impiouſly irreverent with regard to God.

O man, take heed how thou the gods do move,
To cauſe full wrath, which thou canſt not reſiſt;
Blaſphemous words the ſpeaker vain do prove. *Sidney, b.* ii

And dar'ſt thou to the Son of God propound,
To worſhip thee accurſt; now more accurſt
For this attempt, bolder than that on Eve,
And more *blaſphemous*? *Milton's Paradiſe Regained, b.* iii.

A man can hardly paſs the ſtreets, without having his ears grated with ſuch horrid and *blaſphemous* oaths and curſes. *Tillot.*

That any thing that wears the name of a chriſtian, or but of man,

man, should venture to own such a villainous, impudent, and *blasphemous* assertion in the face of the world, as this! *South.*

Bla'sphemously. *adv.* [from *blaspheme.*] Impiously; with wicked irreverence.

Where is the right use of his reason, while he would *blasphemously* set up to controul the commands of the Almighty? *Swift.*

Bla'sphemy. *n. s.* [from *blaspheme.*]

Blasphemy, strictly and properly, is an offering of some indignity, or injury, unto God himself, either by words or writing. *Ayliffe's Parergon.*

But that my heart's on future mischief set,
I would speak *blasphemy*, ere bid you fly;
But fly you must. *Shakesp. Henry* VI. *p.* ii.

Intrinsick goodness consists in accordance, and sin in contrariety, to the secret will of God; or else God could not be defined good, so far as his thoughts and secrets, but only superficially good, as far as he is pleased to reveal himself, which is perfect *blasphemy* to imagine. *Hammond's Fundamentals.*

BLAST. *n. s.* [from blæst, Saxon; *blasen*, Germ. to blow.]

1. A gust, or puff of wind.

They that stand high, have many *blasts* to shake them;
And, if they fall, they dash themselves to pieces.
Shakesp. Richard III.

Welcome, then,
Thou unsubstantial air, that I embrace;
The wretch that thou hast blown unto the worst,
Owes nothing to thy *blasts*. *Shakesp. King Lear.*

Perhaps thy fortune doth controul the winds,
Doth loose or bind their *blasts* in secret cave. *Fairfax, b.* i.

Three ships were hurry'd by the southern *blast*,
And on the secret shelves with fury cast. *Dryden's Æneid.*

2. The sound made by blowing any instrument of wind musick.

In peace there's nothing so becomes a man,
As modest stilness and humility;
But when the *blast* of war blows in our ears,
Then imitate the action of the tyger. *Shakesp. Henry* V.

He blew his trumpet—the angelick *blast*
Fill'd all the regions. *Milt. Par. Lost, b.* xi. *l.* 76.

The Veline fountains, and sulphureous Nar,
Shake at the baleful *blast*, the signal of the war. *Dryden's Æn.*

Whether there be two different goddesses called Fame, or one goddess sounding two different trumpets, it is certain, villainy has as good a title to a blast from the proper trumpet, as virtue has from the former. *Swift.*

3. The stroke of a malignant planet; the infection of any thing pestilential.

By the *blast* of God they perish. *Job*, iv. 9.

To Blast. *v. a.* [from the noun.]

1. To strike with some sudden plague or calamity.

You nimble lightnings, dart your blinding flames
Into her scornful eyes! infect her beauty,
You fensuck'd fogs, drawn by the powerful sun,
To fall and *blast* her pride. *Shakesp. King Lear.*

Oh! Portius, is there not some chosen curse,
Some hidden thunder in the store of heaven,
Red with uncommon wrath, to *blast* the man,
Who owes his greatness to his country's ruin. *Addison. Cato.*

2. To make to wither.

Upon this *blasted* heath you stop our way. *Macbeth.*

And behold seven thin ears, and *blasted* with the eastwind sprung up after them. *Gen.* xli. 6.

She that like lightning shin'd, while her face lasted,
The oak now resembles, which lightning had *blasted*.
Waller.

To his green years your censures you would suit,
Not *blast* that blossom, but expect the fruit. *Dryden.*

Agony unmix'd, incessant gall
Corroding every thought, and *blasting* all
Love's paradise. *Thomson's Spring, l.* 1075.

3. To injure; to invalidate.

He shews himself either very weak, if he will take my word, when he thinks I deserve no credit; or very malicious, if he knows I deserve credit, and yet goes about to *blast* it.
Stillingfleet's Defence of Discourses on Romish Idolatry.

4. To cut off; to hinder from coming to maturity.

This commerce, Jeshophat king of Juda endeavoured to renew; but his enterprize was *blasted* by the destruction of vessels in the harbour. *Arbuthnot on Coins.*

5. To confound; to strike with terrour.

Trumpeters,
With brazen din, *blast* you the city's ears;
Make mingle with your ratt'ling tabourines.
Shakesp. Antony and Cleopatra.

Bla'stment. *n. s.* [from *blast.*] Blast; sudden stroke of infection.

In the morn, and liquid dew of youth,
Contagious *blastments* are most imminent. *Shakesp. Hamlet.*

Bla'tant. *adj.* [*blatttant*, Fr.] Bellowing as a calf.

You learn'd this language from the *blatant* beast. *Dryden.*

To Bla'tter. *v. n.* [from *blatero*, Lat.] To roar; to make a senseless noise. It is a word not now used.

She rode at peace, through his only pains and excellent endurance, however envy list to *blatter* against him. *Spens. Irel.*

Blattera'tion. *n. s.* [*blateratio*, Lat.] Noise; senseless roar.

Blay. *n. s.* A small white river fish; called also a *bleak*, which see.

BLAZE. *n. s.* [blaʃe, a torch, Saxon.]

1. A flame; the light of the flame: *blaze* implies more the light than the heat.

They are in a most warlike preparation, and hope to come upon them in the heat of their division.—The main *blaze* of it is past; but a small thing would make it flame again.
Shakesp. Coriolanus.

Thy throne is darkness in th' abyss of light,
A *blaze* of glory that forbids the sight. *Dryden's Hind and P.*

What groans of men shall fill the martial field!
How fierce a *blaze* his flaming pile shall yield!
What fun'ral pomp shall floating Tiber see! *Dryden's Æn.*

2. Publication; wide diffusion of report.

For what is glory but the *blaze* of fame;
The people's praise, if always praise unmixt?
Milton's Paradise Lost, b. iii. *l.* 47.

3. *Blaze* is a white mark upon a horse, descending from the forehead almost to the nose. *Farrier's Dict.*

To Blaze. *v. n.* [from the noun.]

1. To flame; to shew the light of the flame.

Thus you may long live an happy instrument for your king and country; you shall not be a meteor, or a *blazing* star, but *stella fixa*; happy here, and more happy hereafter.
Bacon's Advice to Villiers.

The third fair morn now *blaz'd* upon the main,
Then glossy smooth lay all the liquid plain. *Pope's Odyssey.*

2. To be conspicuous.

To Blaze. *v. a.*

1. To publish; to make known; to spread far and wide.

The noise of this fight, and issue thereof, being *blazed* by the country people to some noblemen thereabouts, they came thither. *Sidney, b.* ii.

My words, in hopes to *blaze* a stedfast mind,
This marble chose, as of like temper known. *Sidney.*

Thou shalt live, till we can find a time
To *blaze* your marriage, reconcile your friends,
Beg pardon of thy prince, and call thee back.
Shakesp. Romeo and Juliet.

When beggars die, there are no comets seen;
The heav'ns themselves *blaze* forth the death of princes.
Shakesp. Julius Cæsar.

But he went out, and began to publish it much, and to *blaze* abroad the matter. *Mark*, i. 45.

Such musick worthiest were to *blaze*
The peerless height of her immortal praise,
Whose lustre leads us. *Milton.*

Far beyond
The sons of Anak, famous now and *blaz'd*,
Fearless of danger, like a petty god
I walk'd about. *Milton's Agonistes, l.* 527.

Whose follies, *blaz'd* about, to all are known,
And are a secret to himself alone. *Granville.*

But, mortals, know, 'tis still our greatest pride
To *blaze* those virtues, which the good would hide. *Pope.*

2. To blazon; to give an account of ensigns armorial in proper terms. This is not now used.

This, in ancient times, was called a fierce; and you should then have *blazed* it thus: he bears a fierce, sable, between two fierces, or. *Peacham on Drawing.*

3. To inflame; to fire. This is not a proper use.

Pall'd thy *blazed* youth
Becomes assuag'd, and doth beg the alms
Of palsied eld. *Shakesp. Measure for Measure.*

Bla'zer. *n. s.* [from *blaze.*] One that spreads reports.

Utterers of secrets he from thence debarr'd,
Babblers of folly, and *blazers* of crime;
His larum-bell might loud and wide be heard,
When cause requir'd, but never out of time;
Early and late it rung, at evening and at prime. *Fairy Queen.*

To Bla'zon. *v. a.* [*blasonner*, Fr.]

1. To explain, in proper terms, the figures on ensigns armorial.

King Edward gave to them the coat of arms, which I am not herald enough to *blazon* into English. *Addison. Guardian.*

2. To deck; to embellish; to adorn.

Then *blazons* in dread smiles her hideous form;
So lightning gilds the unrelenting storm. *Garth's Dispensat.*

3. To display; to set to show.

O thou goddess,
Thou divine nature! how thyself thou *blazon'st*
In these two princely boys! they are as gentle
As zephyrs blowing below the violet,
Not wagging his sweet head. *Shakesp. Cymbeline.*

4. To celebrate; to set out.

One that excels the quirk of *blazoning* pens,
And, in terrestrial vesture of creation,
Does bear all excellency. *Shakesp. Othello.*

5. To blaze about; to make publick.

What's

What's this but libelling against the senate,
And *blazoning* our injustice every where? *Shakesp. Tit. Andr.*

BLA'ZON. *n. s.* [from the verb.]

1. The art of drawing or explaining coats of arms.

Proceed unto beasts that are given in arms, and teach me what I ought to observe in their *blazon.* *Peacham.*

2. Show; divulgation; publication.

But this eternal *blazon* must not be
To ears of flesh and blood. *Shakesp. Hamlet.*

3. Celebration; proclamation of some quality.

I am a gentleman.—I'll be sworn thou art;
Thy tongue, thy face, thy limbs, action, and spirit,
Do give thee five-fold *blazon.* *Shakesp. Twelfth Night.*

Men con over their pedigrees, and obtrude the *blazon* of their exploits upon the company. *Collier on Pride.*

BLA'ZONRY. *n. s.* [from *blazon.*] The art of blazoning.

Give me certain rules as to the principles of *blazonry.* *Peacham on Drawing.*

To BLEACH. *v a.* [*bleechen*, Germ.] To whiten; commonly to whiten by exposure to the open air.

When turtles tread, and rooks and daws;
And maidens *bleach* their summer smocks.
Shakesp. Love's Labour Lost.

Should I not seek
The clemency of some more temp'rate clime,
To purge my gloom; and, by the sun refin'd,
Bask in his beams, and *bleach* me in the wind? *Dryden.*

For there are various penances enjoin'd;
And some are hung to *bleach* upon the wind;
Some plung'd in waters. *Dryden's Æneid.*

To BLEACH. *v. n.* To grow white; to grow white in the open air.

The white sheet *bleaching* in the open field. *Sh. W. Tale.*

On every nerve
The deadly winter seizes; shuts up sense;
Lays him along the snows, a stiffen'd corse,
Stretch'd out, and *bleaching* in the northern blast. *Thomson.*

BLEAK. *adj.* [blac, blæc, Saxon.]

1. Pale.

2. Cold; chill.

Intreat the north
To make his *bleak* winds kiss my parched lips,
And comfort me with cold. *Shakesp. King John.*

The goddess that in rural shrine
Dwell'st here with Pan, or Sylvan, by blest song
Forbidding every *bleak* unkindly fog
To touch the prosperous growth of this tall wood. *Milton.*

Her desolation presents us with nothing but *bleak* and barren prospects. *Addison. Spectator,* N° 477.

Say, will ye bless the *bleak* Atlantick shore,
Or bid the furious Gaul be rude no more. *Pope.*

BLEAK. *n. s.* [from his white or *bleak* colour.] A small river fish.

The *bleak*, or freshwater sprat, is ever in motion, and therefore called by some the river swallow. His back is of a pleasant, sad sea water green; his belly white and shining like the mountain snow. *Bleaks* are excellent meat, and in best season in August. *Walton's Angler.*

BLE'AKNESS. *n. s.* [from *bleak.*] Coldness; chilness.

The inhabitants of Nova Zembla go naked, without complaining of the *bleakness* of the air in which they are born; as the armies of the northern nations keep the field all winter. *Addison. Guardian,* N° 102.

BLE'AKY. *adj.* [from *bleak.*] Bleak; cold; chill.

On shrubs they browze, and, on the *bleaky* top
Of rugged hills, the thorny bramble crop. *Dryden.*

BLEAR. *adj.* [*blaer*, a blister, Dutch.]

1. Dim with rheum or water; sore with rheum.

It is an ancient tradition, that *blear* eyes affect sound eyes. *Bacon's Natural History,* N° 923.

It is no more in the power of calumny to blast the dignity of an honest man, than of the *blear* eyed owl to cast scandal on the sun. *L'Estrange.*

His *blear* eyes ran in gutters to his chin;
His beard was stubble, and his cheeks were thin. *Dryden.*

When thou shalt see the *blear* ey'd fathers teach
Their sons this harsh and mouldy sort of speech. *Dryden.*

2. Dim; obscure in general; or that which makes dimness.

Thus I hurl
My dazling spells into the spungy air,
Of power to cheat the eye with *blear* illusion,
And give it false presentments. *Milton.*

To BLEAR. *v. a.* [from the adjective.]

1. To make the eyes watry, or sore with rheum.

All tongues speak of him, and the *bleared* sights
Are spectacled to see him. *Shakesp. Coriolanus.*

The Dardanian wives,
With *bleared* visages, come forth to view
Th' issue of th' exploit. *Shakesp. Merchant of Venice.*

When I was young, I, like a lazy fool,
Would *blear* my eyes with oil, to stay from school;
Averse to pains. *Dryden's Persius, sat.* iii.

2. To dim the eyes.

BLE

This may stand for a pretty superficial argument, to *blear* our eyes, and lull us asleep in security. *Raleigh's Essays.*

BLE'AREDNESS. *n. s.* [from *bleared.*] The state of being bleared, or dimmed with rheum.

The defluxion falling upon the edges of the eyelids, makes a *blearedness.* *Wiseman's Surgery.*

To BLEAT. *v. n.* [blætan, Sax.] To cry as a sheep.

We were as twinn'd lambs, that did frisk i' th' sun,
And *bleat* the one at th' other. *Shakesp. Winter's Tale.*

You may as well use question with the wolf,
Why he hath made the ewe *bleat* for the lamb.
Shakesp. Merchant of Venice.

While on sweet grass her *bleating* charge does lie,
Our happy lover feeds upon her eye. *Roscommon.*

What bull dares bellow, or what sheep dares *bleat*
Within the lion's den? *Dryden's Spanish Friar.*

BLEAT. *n. s.* [from the verb.] The cry of a sheep or lamb.

Set in my ship, mine ear reach'd, where we rod,
The bellowing of oxen, and the *bleat*
Of fleecy sheep. *Chapman's Odyssey, b.* xii.

The rivers and their hills around,
With lowings, and with dying *bleats* resound. *Dryden.*

BLEB. *n. s.* [*blaen*, to swell, Germ.] A blister. *Skinner.*

BLED. *particip.* [from *to bleed.*]

To BLEED. *v. n.* pret. I *bled*; I have *bled.* [bledan, Saxon.]

1. To lose blood; to run with blood.

I *bleed* inwardly for my lord. *Shakesp. Timon.*

Bleed, bleed, poor country!
Great tyranny, lay thou thy basis sure;
For goodness dare not check thee! *Shakesp. Macbeth.*

Many, upon the seeing of others *bleed*, or strangled, or tortured, themselves are ready to faint, as if they *bled.* *Bacon's Nat. History,* N° 795.

2. To die a violent death.

The lamb thy riot dooms to *bleed* today;
Had he thy reason, would he skip and play? *Pope.*

3. To drop, as blood. It is applied to any thing that drops from some body, as blood from an animal.

For me the balm shall *bleed*, and amber flow,
The coral redden, and the ruby glow. *Pope's Winds. Forest.*

To BLEED. *v. a.* To let blood; to take blood from.

That from a patriot of distinguish'd note,
Have *bled*, and purg'd me to a simple vote. *Pope.*

BLEIT. } *adj.* Bashful. It is used in Scotland, and the border-
BLATE. } ing counties.

To BLE'MISH. *v. a.* [from *blame, Junius*; from *blême*, white, Fr. *Skinner.*]

1. To mark with any deformity.

Likelier that my outward face might have been disguised, than that the face of so excellent a mind could have been thus *blemished.* *Sidney.*

2. To defame; to tarnish, with respect to reputation.

Not that my verse would *blemish* all the fair;
But yet if some be bad, 'tis wisdom to beware. *Dryden.*

Those, who, by concerted defamations, endeavour to *blemish* his character, incur the complicated guilt of slander and perjury. *Addison. Freeholder.*

BLE'MISH. *n. s.* [from the verb.]

1. A mark of deformity; a scar; a diminution of beauty.

As he hath caused a *blemish* in a man, so shall it be done to him again. *Lev.* xxiv. 20.

Open it such a distance off from the eyelid, that you divide not that; for, in so doing, you will leave a remediless *blemish.* *Wiseman's Surgery.*

2. Reproach; disgrace; imputation.

Live thou, and to thy mother dead attest,
That clear she died from *blemish* criminal. *Fairy Queen, b.* ii.

That you have been earnest, should be no *blemish* or discredit at all unto you. *Hooker, Preface.*

And if we shall neglect to propagate these blessed dispositions, what others can undertake it, without some *blemish* to us? some reflection on our negligence? *Sprat.*

None more industriously publish the *blemishes* of an extraordinary reputation, than such as lie open to the same censures; raising applause to themselves, for resembling a person of an exalted reputation, though in the blamable parts of his character. *Addison. Spectator,* N° 256.

3. A soil; turpitude; taint; deformity.

First shall virtue be vice, and beauty be counted a *blemish*,
Ere that I leave with song of praise her praise to solemnize.
Sidney, b. i.

Is conformity with Rome a *blemish* unto the church of England, and unto churches abroad an ornament? *Hooder, b.* iv. §. 6.

Not a hair perish'd:
On their sustaining garments not a *blemish*,
But fresher than before. *Shakesp. Tempest.*

Evadne's husband 'tis a fault
To love, a *blemish* to my thought. *Waller's M. Trag.*

That your duty may no *blemish* take,
I will myself your father's captive make. *Dryd. Indian Emp.*

Such a mirth as this is capable of making a beauty, as well as a *blemish*, the subject of derision. *Addison. Spect.* N° 291.

To Blench. *v. n.* To shrink; to start back; to fly off.

I'll observe his looks;
I'll tent him to the quick; if he but *blench*,
I know my course. *Shakesp. Hamlet.*

Patience herself, what goddess ere she be,
Doth lesser *blench* at sufferance than I do. *Shakesp. Tr. and Cr.*

Hold you ever to our special drift;
Though sometimes you do *blench* from this to that,
As cause doth minister. *Shakep. Merry Wives of Windsor.*

To Blench. *v. a.* To hinder; to obstruct.

The rebels besieged them, winning the even ground on the top, by carrying up great trusses of hay before them, to *blench* the defendants sight, and dead their shot. *Carew's Survey.*

To BLEND. *v. a.* preter. I *blended*; anciently, *blent*. [blendan, Saxon.]

1. To mingle together.

'Tis beauty truly *blent*, whose red and white
Nature's own sweet and cunning hand hath laid on. *Shakesp. Twelfth Night.*

The mistion taught by the ancients is too slight or gross; for bodies, mixed according to their hypothesis, would not appear such to the acute eyes of a lynx, who would discern the elements, if they were no otherwise mingled, than but *blended*, but not united. *Boyle.*

He had his calmer influence, and his mien
Did love and majesty together *blend.* *Dryden.*

The grave, where even the great find rest,
And *blended* lie th' oppressor and th' oppress'd. *Pope.*

2. To confound.

The moon should wander from her beaten way, the times and seasons of the year *blend* themselves by disordered and confused mixture. *Hooker, b.* i. § 3.

3. To pollute; to spoil; to corrupt. This signification was anciently much in use, but is now wholly obsolete.

Which when he saw, he burnt with jealous fire;
The eye of reason was with rage *yblent*. *Fairy Queen, b.* ii.

Regard of worldly muck doth foully *blend*,
And low abase the high heroick spirit. *Fairy Queen, b.* ii.

The whilst thy kingdom from thy head is rent,
And thy throne royal with dishonour *blent*. *Spens. Hubb.*

Ble'nder. *n. s.* [from *to blend.*] The person that mingles.

Blent. The obsolete *participle* of *blend*. See Blend.

To BLESS. *v. a.* [bletsian, Saxon.]

1. To make happy; to prosper.

The quality of mercy is not strain'd;
It droppeth as the gentle rain of heaven
Upon the place beneath. It is twice *bless'd*;
It *blesseth* him that gives, and him that takes. *Merch. of Ven.*

Had I but died an hour before this chance,
I had liv'd a *blessed* time: for, from this instant,
There's nothing. *Shakesp. Macbeth.*

This kingdom enjoyed the greatest calm, and the fullest measure of felicity, that any people, in any age for so long time together, have been *blessed* with. *Clarendon.*

Happy this isle, which such a hero *blest*;
What virtue dwells not in his loyal breast? *Waller.*

In vain with folding arms the youth assay'd
To stop her flight, and strain the flying shade;
But she return'd no more, to *bless* his longing eyes. *Dryden.*

O hospitable Jove! we thus invoke,
Bless to both nations this auspicious hour. *Dryden's Æn.*

2. To wish happiness to another; to pronounce a blessing upon him.

And this is the blessing wherewith Moses the man of God *blessed* the children of Israel, before his death. *Deut.* xxxiii. 1.

3. To praise; to glorify for benefits received; to celebrate.

Unto us there is one only guide of all agents natural, and he both the creator and worker of all in all, alone to be *blessed*, adored, and honoured by all for ever. *Hooker, b.* i. § 3.

But *bless'd* be that great pow'r, that hath us bless'd
With longer life than earth and heav'n can have. *Davies.*

4. It seems, in one place of *Spenser*, to signify the same as *to wave*; *to brandish*; *to flourish*.

Whom when the prince to battle new addrest,
And threat'ning high his dreadful stroke did see,
His sparkling blade about his head he *blest*,
And smote off quite his right leg by the knee. *Fairy Q. b.* i.

Ble'ssed. *particip. adj.* [from *to bless.*] Happy; enjoying heavenly felicity.

Ble'ssed *Thistle*. [*cnicus*, Lat.] The name of a plant.

The characters are; It hath flosculous flowers; consisting of many florets, which are multifid, and stand upon the embryo; these florets are inclosed in a scaly cup, surrounded with leaves. The species are, 1. The *blessed thistle*. 2. The yellow distaff *thistle*. The *blessed thistle* is cultivated in gardens for the herb, which is dried and preserved for medicinal uses; but of late years it hath been less used than formerly. *Millar.*

Ble'ssedly. *adv.* [from *blessed.*] Happily.

This accident of Clitophon's taking had so *blessedly* procured their meeting. *Sidney, b.* i.

Ble'ssedness. *n. s.* [from *blessed.*]

1. Happiness; felicity.

Many times have I, leaning to yonder palm, admired the *blessedness* of it, that it could bear love without the sense of pain. *Sidney.*

His overthrow heap'd happiness upon him;
For then, and not till then, he felt himself,
And found the *blessedness* of being little. *Shakesp. Hen.* VIII.

2. Sanctity.

Earthlier happy is the rose distill'd,
Than that, which, withering on the virgin thorn,
Grows, lives, and dies in single *blessedness*. *Shakesp. Midsummer Night's Dream.*

3. Heavenly felicity.

It is such an one, as, being begun in grace, passes into glory, *blessedness*, and immortality. *South.*

4. Divine favour.

Ble'sser. *n. s.* [from *bless.*] He that blesses, or gives a blessing; he that makes any thing prosper.

When thou receivest praise, take it indifferently, and return it to God, as the giver of the gift, or the *blesser* of the action. *Taylor's Holy Living.*

Ble'ssing. *n. s.* [from *bless.*]

1. Benediction; a prayer by which happiness is implored for any one.

2. A declaration by which happiness is promised in a prophetick and authoritative manner.

The person that is called, kneeleth down before the chair, and the father layeth his hand upon his head, or her head, and giveth the *blessing*. *Bacon's New Atlantis.*

3. Any of the means of happiness; a gift; an advantage; a benefit.

Nor are his *blessings* to his banks confin'd,
But free, and common, as the sea and wind. *Denham.*

Political jealousy is very reasonable in persons persuaded of the excellency of their constitution, who believe that they derive from it the most valuable *blessings* of society. *Addison.*

A just and wise magistrate is a *blessing* as extensive as the community to which he belongs: a *blessing* which includes all other *blessings* whatsoever, that relate to this life. *Atterbury.*

4. Divine favour.

My pretty cousin,
Blessing upon you! *Shakesp. Macbeth.*

I had most need of *blessing*, and amen,
Stuck in my throat. *Shakesp. Macbeth.*

Honour thy father and mother, both in word and deed, that a *blessing* may come upon thee from them. *Ecclus*, iii. 8.

He shall receive the *blessing* from the Lord. *Psalm* xxix. 5.

5. The Hebrews, under this name, often understand the presents which friends make to one another; in all probability, because they are generally attended with *blessings* and compliments both from those who give, and those who receive. *Calmet.*

And Jacob said, receive my present at my hand; take, I pray thee, my *blessing* that is brought to thee. *Gen.* xxxiii. 10.

Blest. *particip. adj.* [from *bless.*]

Peace to thy gentle shade, and endless rest!
Blest in thy genius, in thy love too *blest!* *Pope.*

Blew. The *preterite* from *blow*; which see.

The rest fled into a strong tower, where, seeing no remedy, they desperately *blew* up themselves, with a great part of the castle, with gunpowder. *Knolles's History of the Turks.*

Bleyme. *n. s.* An inflammation in the foot of a horse, proceeding from bruised blood, between the sole and the bone. *Farrier's Dict.*

Blight. *n. s.* [The etymology unknown.]

1. Mildew; according to *Skinner*; but it seems taken by most writers, in a general sense, for any cause of the failure of fruits.

I complained to the oldest and best gardeners, who often fell into the same misfortune, and esteemed it some *blight* of the spring. *Temple.*

2. Any thing nipping, or blasting.

When you come to the proof once, the first *blight* of frost shall most infallibly strip you of all your glory. *L'Estrange.*

To Blight. *v. a.* [from the noun.]

1. To corrupt with mildew.

This vapour bears up along with it any noxious mineral steams; it then blasts vegetables, *blights* corn and fruit, and is sometimes injurious even to men. *Woodward's Natural Hist.*

2. In general, to blast; to hinder from fertility.

My country neighbours do not find it impossible to think of a lame horse they have, or their *blighted* corn, till they have run over in their minds all beings. *Locke.*

But lest harsh care the lover's peace destroy,
And roughly *blight* the tender buds of joy,
Let reason teach. *Lyttleton.*

BLIND. *adj.* [blind, Saxon.]

1. Without sight; deprived of the sense of seeing; dark.

The *blind* man that governs his steps by feeling, in defect of eyes, receives advertisement of remote things through a staff. *Digby on the Soul.*

Those

Those other two equall'd with me in fate,
So were I equall'd with them in renown!
Blind Thamyris, and *blind* Mæonides;
And Tiresias, and Phineus, prophets old. *Par. Lost, b.* iii.

2. Intellectually dark; unable to judge; ignorant; with *to* before that which is unseen.

All authors *to* their own defects are *blind*;
Hadst thou, but Janus like, a face behind,
To see the people, what splay mouths they make;
To mark their fingers, pointed at thy back. *Dryden's Pers.*

3. Sometimes *of*.

Blind of the future, and by rage misled,
He pulls his crimes upon his people's head. *Dryden's Fab.*

4. Unseen; out of the publick view; private; generally with some tendency to some contempt or censure.

To grievous and scandalous inconveniencies they make themselves subject, with whom any *blind* or secret corner is judged a fit house of common prayer. *Hooker, b.* v. § 25.

5. Not easily discernible; hard to find; dark; obscure; unseen.

There be also *blind* fires under stone, which flame not out; but oil being poured upon them, they flame out. *Bacon.*

Where else
Shall I inform my unacquainted feet
In the *blind* mazes of this tangl'd wood? *Milton.*

How have we wander'd a long dismal night,
Led through *blind* paths by each deluding light. *Roscommon.*

Part creeping underground, their journey *blind*,
And climbing from below, their fellows meet. *Dryden.*

So mariners mistake the promis'd gust,
And, with full sails, on the *blind* rocks are lost. *Dryden.*

A postern door, yet unobserv'd and free,
Join'd by the length of a *blind* gallery,
To the king's closet bed. *Dryden's Æneid.*

6. *Blind Vessels.* [with chymists.] Such as have no opening but on one side.

To Blind. *v. a.* [from the noun.]

1. To make blind; to deprive of sight.

You nimble lightnings, dart your *blinding* flames
Into her scornful eyes! *Shakesp. King Lear.*

Of whose hand have I received any bribe to *blind* mine eyes therewith? and I will restore it. 1 *Sam.* xii. 3.

A blind guide is certainly a great mischief; but a guide that *blinds* those whom he should lead, is undoubtedly a much greater. *South.*

2. To darken; to obscure to the eye.

So whirl the seas, such darkness *blinds* the sky,
That the black night receives a deeper dye. *Dryden's Fab.*

3. To obscure to the understanding.

The state of the controversy between us he endeavoured, with all his art, to *blind* and confound. *Stillingfleet.*

Blind. *n. s.*

1. Something to hinder the sight.

Hardly any thing in our conversation is pure and genuine; civility casts a *blind* over the duty, under some customary words. *L'Estrange.*

2. Something to mislead the eye, or the understanding.

These discourses set an opposition between his commands and decrees; making the one a *blind* for the execution of the other. *Decay of Piety.*

To Bli'ndfold. *v. a.* [from *blind* and *fold.*] To hinder from seeing, by blinding the eyes.

When they had *blindfolded* him, they struck him on the face. *Luke,* xxii. 64.

Bli'ndfold. *adj.* [from the verb.] Having the eyes covered.

And oft himself he chanc'd to hurt unwares,
Whilst reason, blent through passion, nought descried,
But, as a *blindfold* bull, at random fares,
And where he hits, nought knows, and where he hurts, nought cares. *Fairy Queen, b.* ii. *c.* iv. *stanz.* 7.

Who *blindfold* walks upon a river's brim,
When he should see, has he deserv'd to swim? *Dryden.*

When lots are shuffled together, or a man *blindfold* casts a dye, what reason can he have to presume, that he shall draw a white stone rather than a black? *South.*

They will look into the state of the nation with their own eyes, and be no longer led *blindfold* by a male legislature. *Addison. Freeholder,* N° 32.

Bli'ndly. *adv.* [from *blind.*]

1. Without sight.

2. Implicitely; without examination.

The old king, after a long debate,
By his imperious mistress *blindly* led,
Has given Cydaria to Orbellan's bed. *Dryd. Indian Emp.*

How ready zeal for interest and party, is to charge atheism on those, who will not, without examining, submit, and *blindly* swallow their nonsense. *Locke.*

2. Without judgment or direction.

How seas, and earth, and air, and active flame,
Fell through the mighty void; and, in their fall,
Were *blindly* gather'd in this goodly ball. *Dryden's Silenus.*

Bli'ndman's buff. *n. s.* A play in which some one is to have his eyes covered, and hunt out the rest of the company.

Disguis'd in all the mask of night,
We left our champion on his flight:
At *blindman's buff* to grope his way,
In equal fear of night and day. *Hudibras, p.* iii. *c.* ii.

He imagines I shut my eyes again; but surely he fancies I play at *blindman's buff* with him; for he thinks I never have my eyes open. *Stillingfleet's Defence of Disc. on Romish Idolatry.*

Bli'ndness. *n. s.* [from *blind.*]

1. Want of sight.

Nor can we call it choice, when what we chuse,
Folly and *blindness* only could refuse. *Denham.*

2. Ignorance; intellectual darkness.

All the rest as born of savage brood,
But with base thoughts are into *blindness* led,
And kept from looking on the lightsome day. *Spenser.*

Whensoever we would proceed beyond these simple ideas, we fall presently into darkness and difficulties, and can discover nothing farther but our own *blindness* and ignorance. *Locke.*

Bli'ndside. *n. s.* [from *blind* and *side.*] Weakness; foible; weak part.

He is too great a lover of himself; but this is one of his *blindsides*; and the best of men, I fear, are not without them. *Swift's Wonderful Wonder of Wonders.*

Bli'ndworm. *n. s.* [from *blind* and *worm.*] A small viper, the least of our English serpents, but venemous.

You spotted snakes, with double tongue,
Thorny hedgehogs, be not seen;
Newts and *blindworms*, do no wrong;
Come not near our fairy queen. *Shakesp. Mid. N. Dr.*

The greater slow worm, called also the *blindworm*, is commonly thought to be blind, because of the littleness of his eyes. *Grew's Musæum.*

To BLINK. *v. n.* [*blincken*, Danish.]

1. To wink, or twinkle with the eyes.

So politick, as if one eye
Upon the other were a spy;
That to trepan the one to think
The other blind, both strove to *blink*. *Hudibras, p.* iii. *c.* ii.

2. To see obscurely.

What's here! the portrait of a *blinking* idiot.
Shakesp. Merchant of Venice.

Sweet and lovely well,
Shew me thy chink, to *blink* through with mine eyne.
Shakesp. Midsummer Night's Dream.

His figure such as might his soul proclaim;
One eye was *blinking*, and one leg was lame. *Pope's Iliad.*

Bli'nkard. *n. s.* [from *blink.*]

1. One that has bad eyes.

2. Something twinkling.

In some parts we see many glorious and eminent stars, in others few of any remarkable greatness, and, in some, none but *blinkards*, and obscure ones. *Hakewell on Providence.*

BLISS. *n. s.* [bliʃʃe, Sax. from bliðaʃian, to rejoice.]

1. The highest degree of happiness; blessedness; felicity; generally used of the happiness of blessed souls.

A mighty Saviour hath witnessed of himself, I am the way; the way that leadeth us from misery into *bliss*. *Hooker, b.* i.

Dim sadness did not spare
That time celestial visages; yet, mix'd
With pity, violated not their *bliss*. *Par. Lost, b.* x. *l.* 23.

With me
All my redeem'd may dwell, in joy and *bliss*. *Par. Lost, b.* xi.

2. Felicity in general.

Condition, circumstance is not the thing;
Bliss is the same in subject or in king. *Pope.*

Bli'ssful. *adj.* [from *bliss* and *full.*] Full of joy; happy in the highest degree.

Yet swimming in that sea of *blissful* joy,
He nought forgot. *Fairy Queen, b.* i. *c.* i. *stan.* 41.

The two saddest ingredients in hell, are deprivation of the *blissful* vision, and confusion of face. *Hammond.*

Reaping immortal fruits of joy and love,
Uninterrupted joy, unrival'd love,
In *blissful* solitude. *Milton's Paradise Lost, b.* iii. *l.* 89.

First in the fields I try the silvan strains,
Nor *blush* to sport in Windsor's *blissful* plains. *Pope.*

Bli'ssfully. *adv.* [from *blissful.*] Happily.

Bli'ssfulness. *n. s.* [from *blissful.*] Happiness; fulness of joy.

To Bli'ssom. *v. n.* To caterwaul; to be lustful. *Dict.*

BLI'STER. *n. s.* [*bluyster*, Dutch.]

1. A pustule formed by raising the cuticle from the cutis, and filled with serous blood.

In this state she gallops, night by night,
O'er ladies lips, who strait on kisses dream,
Which oft the angry mob with *blisters* plagues,
Because their breaths with sweetmeats tainted are.
Shakesp. Romeo and Juliet.

I found a great *blister* drawn by the garlick, but had it cut, which run a good deal of water, but filled again by next night. *Temple.*

2. Any swelling made by the separation of a film or skin from the other parts.

 Upon

Upon the leaves there riſeth a tumour like a *bliſter*. *Bacon.*

To BLI'STER. *v. n.* [from the noun.] To riſe in bliſters.

If I prove honeymouth, let my tongue *bliſter*,
And never to my red look'd anger be
The trumpet any more. *Shakeſp. Winter's Tale.*

Embrace thy knees with loathing hands,
Which *bliſter* when they touch thee. *Dryden's Don Sebaſt.*

To BLI'STER. *v. a.*

1. To raiſe bliſters by ſome hurt, as a burn, or rubbing.

Look, here comes one, a gentlewoman of mine,
Who falling in the flames of her own youth,
Hath *bliſter'd* her report. *Shakeſp. Meaſure for Meaſure.*

2. To raiſe bliſters with a medical intention.

I *bliſtered* the legs and thighs; but was too late, he died howling. *Wiſeman's Surgery.*

BLITHE. *adj.* [bliðe, Saxon.] Gay; airy; merry; joyous; ſprightly; mirthful.

We have always one eye fixed upon the countenance of our enemies; and, according to the *blithe* or heavy aſpect thereof, our other eye ſheweth ſome other ſuitable token either of diſlike or approbation. *Hooker, b.* iv. § 9.

Then ſigh not ſo, but let them go,
And be you *blithe* and bonny. *Shakeſp. M. ado about Noth.*

For that fair female troop thou ſaw'ſt, that ſeem'd
Of goddeſſes, ſo *blithe*, ſo ſmooth, ſo gay;
Yet empty of all good. *Milton's Paradiſe Loſt, b.* xi.

To whom the wily adder, *blithe* and glad:
Empreſs! the way is ready, and not long. *Par. Loſt, b.* ix.

And the milkmaid ſingeth *blithe*,
And the mower whets his ſcythe. *Milton.*

Should he return, that troop ſo *blithe* and bold,
Precipitant in fear, would wing their flight. *Pope.*

BLI'THLY. *adv.* [from *blithe.*] In a blithe manner.

BLI'THNESS. } *n. ſ.* [from *blithe.*] The quality of being
BLI'THSOMNESS. } blithe.

BLI'THSOME. *adj.* [from *blithe.*] Gay; cheerful.

Froſty blaſts deface
The *blithſome* year: trees of their ſhrivell'd fruits
Are widow'd. *Philips.*

To BLOAT. *v. a.* [probably from *blow.*] To ſwell, or make turgid with wind.

His rude eſſays
Encourage him, and *bloat* him up with praiſe,
That he may get more bulk before he dies. *Dryden.*

The ſtrutting petticoat ſmooths all diſtinctions, levels the mother with the daughter. I cannot but be troubled to ſee ſo many well-ſhaped innocent virgins *bloated* up, and waddling up and down like bigbellied women. *Addiſon. Spectator.*

To BLOAT. *v. n.* To grow turgid.

If a perſon of a firm conſtitution begins to *bloat*, from being warm grows cold, his fibres grow weak. *Arbuthnot.*

BLO'ATEDNESS. *n. ſ.* [from *bloat.*] Turgidneſs; ſwelling; tumour.

Laſſitude, lazineſs, *bloatedneſs*, and ſcorbutical ſpots, are ſymptoms of weak fibres. *Arbuthnot on Aliments.*

BLO'BBER. *n. ſ.* [from *blob.*] A word uſed in ſome counties for a bubble.

There ſwimmeth alſo in the ſea a round ſlimy ſubſtance, called a *blobber*, reputed noiſome to the fiſh. *Carew.*

BLO'BBERLIP. *n. ſ.* [from *blob*, or *blobber*, and *lip.*] A thick lip.

They make a wit of their inſipid friend,
His *blobberlips* and beetlebrows commend. *Dryden's Juvenal.*

BLO'BLIPPED. } *adj.* Having ſwelled or thick lips.
BLO'BBERLIPPED. }

A *bloblipped* ſhell, which ſeemeth to be a kind of muſſel. *Grew's Muſæum.*

His perſon deformed to the higheſt degree; flat noſed, and *blobberlipped.* *L'Eſtrange.*

BLOCK. *n. ſ.* [*block*, Dutch; *bloc*, Fr.]

1. A heavy piece of timber, rather thick than long.

2. A maſs of matter.

Homer's apotheoſis conſiſts of a groupe of figures, cut in the ſame *block* of marble, and riſing one above another. *Addiſon.*

3. A maſſy body.

Small cauſes are ſufficient to make a man uneaſy, when great ones are not in the way: for want of a *block*, he will ſtumble at a ſtraw. *Swift's Thoughts on various Subjects.*

4. A rude piece of timber; in contempt.

When, by the help of wedges and beetles, an image is cleft out of the trunk of ſome tree, yet, after all the ſkill of artificers to ſet forth ſuch a divine *block*, it cannot one moment ſecure itſelf from being eaten by worms. *Stillingfleet.*

5. The piece of wood on which hats are formed.

He wears his faith but as the faſhion of his hat; it ever changes with the next *block.* *Shakeſp. Much ado about Nothing.*

6. The wood on which criminals are beheaded.

Some guard theſe traitors to the *block* of death,
Treaſon's true bed, and yielder up of breath. *Shakeſp. H. IV.*

At the inſtant of his death, having a long beard, after his head was upon the *block*, he gently drew his beard aſide, and ſaid, this hath not offended the king. *Bacon's Apophthegms.*

I'll drag him thence,
Even from the holy altar to the *block.* *Dryden's W. of B.*

7. An obſtruction; a ſtop.

Can he ever dream, that the ſuffering for righteouſneſs ſake is our felicity, when he ſees us run ſo from it, that no crime is *block* enough in our way, to ſtop our flight? *Decay of Piety.*

8. A ſea term for a pully.

9. A blockhead; a fellow remarkable for ſtupidity.

The country is a deſert, where the good
Gain'd, inhabits not; born's not underſtood;
There men become beaſts, and prone to all evils;
In cities, *blocks.* *Donne.*

What tongueleſs *blocks* were they, would they not ſpeak?
Shakeſp. Richard III.

To BLOCK. *v. a.* [*bloquer*, Fr.] To ſhut up; to incloſe, ſo as to hinder egreſs.

The ſtates about them ſhould neither by encreaſe of dominion, nor by *blocking* of trade, have it in their power to hurt or annoy. *Bacon's War with Spain.*

Recommend it to the governour of Abingdon, to ſend ſome troops to *block* it up, from infeſting the great road. *Clarendon.*

They *block* the caſtle kept by Bertram;
But now they cry, down with the palace, fire it. *Dryden.*

The abbot raiſes an army, and *blocks* up the town on the ſide that faces his dominions. *Addiſon on Italy.*

BLOCK-HOUSE. *n. ſ.* [from *block* and *houſe.*] A fortreſs built to obſtruct or block up a paſs.

His entrance is guarded with *block-houſes*, and that on the town's ſide fortified with ordnance. *Carew's Survey of Cornw.*

Rocheſter water reacheth far within the land, and is under the protection of ſome *block-houſes.* *Raleigh's Eſſays.*

BLOCK-TIN. *n. ſ.* [from *block* and *tin.*] So the tradeſmen call that which is moſt pure or unmixed, and as yet unwrought. *Boyle.*

BLOCKA'DE. *n. ſ.* [from *block.*] A ſiege carried on by ſhutting up the place.

The enemy was neceſſitated wholly to abandon the *blockade* of Olivenza. *Tatler, N°* 51.

Round the goddeſs roll
Broad hats and hoods, and caps, a ſable ſhoal;
Thick, and more thick, the black *blockade* extends. *Pope.*

To BLOCKA'DE. *v. a.* [from the noun.] To ſhut up.

Huge bales of Britiſh cloth *blockade* the door,
A hundred oxen at your levee roar. *Pope.*

BLO'CKHEAD. *n. ſ.* [from *block* and *head.*] A ſtupid fellow; a dolt; a man without parts.

Your wit will not ſo ſoon out as another man's will; it is ſtrongly wedged up in a *blockhead.* *Shakeſp. Coriolanus.*

We idly ſit like ſtupid *blockheads*,
Our hands committed to our pockets. *Hudibras, p.* iii. *c.* ii.

A *blockhead* rubs his thoughtleſs ſkull,
And thanks his ſtars he was not born a fool. *Pope.*

BLO'CKHEADED. *adj.* [from *blockhead.*] Stupid; dull.

Says a *blockheaded* boy, theſe are villainous creatures.
L'Eſtrange's Fables.

BLO'CKISH. *adj.* [from *block.*] Stupid; dull.

Make a lott'ry,
And, by decree, let *blockiſh* Ajax draw
The ſort to fight with Hector. *Shakeſp. Troilus and Creſſ.*

BLO'CKISHLY. *adv.* [from *blockiſh.*] In a ſtupid manner.

BLO'CKISHNESS. *n. ſ.* [from *blockiſh.*] Stupidity.

BLO'MARY. *n. ſ.* The firſt forge in the iron mills, through which the metal paſſes, after it has been firſt melted from the mine. *Dict.*

BLO'NKET. *n. ſ.* [I ſuppoſe for *blanket.*]

Our *blonket* livery's been all too ſad
For thilke ſame ſeaſon, when all is yclad
With pleaſance. *Spenſer's Paſtorals.*

BLOOD. *n. ſ.* [blod, Saxon.]

1. The red liquour that circulates in the bodies of animals.

But fleſh with the life thereof, which is the *blood* thereof, ſhall you not eat. *Gen.* ix. 4.

2. Child; progeny.

We'll no more meet, no more ſee one another:
But yet thou art my fleſh, my *blood*, my daughter.
Shakeſp. King Lear.

3. Family; kindred.

As many and as well born *bloods* as thoſe,
Stand in his face, to contradict his claim. *Shakeſp. K. John.*

O! what an happineſs is it to find
A friend of our own *blood*, a brother kind. *Waller.*

According to the common law of England, in adminiſtrations, the whole *blood* ought to be preferred to the half *blood.* *Ayliffe's Parergon.*

4. Deſcent; lineage.

Epithets of flattery, deſerved by few of them; and not running in a *blood*, like the perpetual gentleneſs of the Ormond family. *Dryden's Fab. Dedication.*

5. Blood royal; royal lineage.

They will almoſt
Give us a prince o' th' *blood*, a ſon of Priam,
In change of him. *Shakeſp. Troilus and Creſſida.*

6. Birth; high extraction.

I am a gentleman of *blood* and breeding. *Shakeſp. K. Lear.*

7. Mur-

7. Murder; violent death.

It will have blood; they say, *blood* will have blood. *Shakesp. Macbeth.*

The voice of thy brother's *blood* crieth unto me from the ground. *Gen.* iv. 10.

8. Life.

When wicked men have slain a righteous person in his own house, upon his bed, shall I not therefore now require his *blood* at your hand? 2 *Sam.* iv. 11.

9. *For blood.* Though his blood or life was at stake: a low phrase.

A crow lay battering upon a muscle, and could not, *for his blood*, break the shell to come at the fish. *L'Estrange.*

10. The carnal part of man.

Flesh and *blood* hath not revealed it unto thee, but my father which is in heaven. *Matt.* xvi. 17.

11. Temper of mind; state of the passions.

Will you, great sir, that glory blot,
In cold *blood*, which you gain'd in hot? *Hudibras.*

12. Hot spark; man of fire.

The news put divers young *bloods* into such a fury, as the English ambassadors were not, without peril, to be outraged. *Bacon's Henry* VII.

13. The juice of any thing.

He washed his garments in wine, and his cloaths in the *blood* of grapes. *Gen.* xlix. 11.

To Blood. *v. a.* [from the noun.]

1. To stain with blood.

When the faculties intellectual are in vigour, not drenched, or, as it were, *blooded* by the affections. *Bacon's Apophth.*

Then all approach the slain with vast surprise,
And, scarce secure, reach out their spears afar,
And *blood* their points, to prove their partnership in war. *Dryden's Fables.*

He was *blooded* up to his elbows by a couple of Moors, whom he had been butchering with his own imperial hands. *Addison.*

2. To enter; to enure to blood, as a hound.

Fairer than fairest, let none ever say,
That ye were *blooded* in a yielded prey. *Spenser, sonn.* xx.

3. To blood, is sometimes to let blood medically.

4. To heat; to exasperate.

By this means, matters grew more exasperate; the auxiliary forces of French and English were much *blooded* one against another. *Bacon's Henry* VII.

Blood-boltered. *adj.* [from *blood* and *bolter.*] Blood-sprinkled.

The *blood-bolter'd* Banquo smiles upon me. *Macbeth.*

Blood-hot. *adj.* [from *blood* and *hot.*] Hot in the same degree with blood.

A good piece of bread first to be eaten, will gain time to warm the beer *blood-hot*, which then he may drink safely. *Locke.*

To Blood-let. *v. a.* [from *blood* and *let.*] To bleed; to open a vein medicinally.

The chyle is not perfectly assimilated into blood, by its circulation through the lungs, as is known by experiments of *blood-letting.* *Arbuthnot on Aliments.*

Blood-letter. *n. s.* [from *blood-let.*] A phlebotomist; one that takes away blood medically.

This mischief happening to aneurisms, proceedeth from the ignorance of the *blood-letter*, who, not considering the errour committed in letting blood, binds up the arm carelessly. *Wiseman's Surgery.*

Blood-stone. *n. s.* [from *blood* and *stone.*] The name of a stone.

There is a stone, which they call the *blood-stone*, which, worn, is thought to be good for them that bleed at the nose; which, no doubt, is by astriction, and cooling of the spirits. *Bacon.*

The *blood-stone* is green, spotted with a bright blood-red. *Woodward on Fossils.*

Blood-thirsty. *adj.* [from *blood* and *thirst.*] Desirous to shed blood.

And high advancing his *blood-thirsty* blade,
Struck one of those deformed heads. *Fairy Queen, b.* i.

The image of God the *blood-thirsty* have not; for God is charity and mercy itself. *Raleigh's History.*

Blood-vessel. *n. s.* [from *blood* and *vessel.*] A vessel appropriated by nature to the conveyance of the blood.

The skins of the forehead were extremely tough and thick, and had not in them any *blood-vessel*, that we were able to discover. *Addison. Spectator*, N° 275.

Blo'odflower. *n. s.* [*hæmanthus*, Lat.] A plant.

This plant was originally brought from the Cape of Good Hope, and has been many years preserved in the curious gardens in Holland, where they now have many sorts; but in England it is still very rare. *Millar.*

Bloodgui'ltiness. *n. s.* [from *blood* and *guilty.*] Murder; the crime of shedding blood.

And were there rightful cause of difference,
Yet were't not better, fair it to accord,
Than with *bloodguiltiness* to heap offence,
And mortal vengeance join to crime abhorr'd. *Fairy Q. b.* ii.

Blo'odhound. *n. s.* [from *blood* and *hound.*] A hound that follows by the scent, and seizes with great fierceness.

Hear this, hear this, thou tribune of the people:
Thou zealous, publick *bloodhound*, hear, and melt. *Dryden.*

Where are these rav'ning *bloodhounds*, that pursue
In a full cry, gaping to swallow me? *Southerne's Inn. Adult.*

A *bloodhound* will follow the tract of the person he pursues, and all hounds the particular game they have in chace. *Arbuthnot on Aliments.*

And though the villain 'scape a while, he feels
Slow vengeance, like a *bloodhound*, at his heels. *Swift.*

Blo'odily. *adv.* [from *bloody.*] With disposition to shed blood; cruelly.

I told the pursuivant,
As too triumphing, how mine enemies,
To-day at Pomfret, *bloodily* were butcher'd. *Shakesp. R.* III.

This day, the poet, *bloodily* inclin'd,
Has made me die, full sore against my mind. *Dryden.*

Blo'odiness. *n. s.* [from *bloody.*] The state of being bloody.

It will manifest itself by its *bloodiness*; yet sometimes the scull is so thin as not to admit of any. *Sharp's Surgery.*

Blo'odless. *adj.* [from *blood.*]

1. Without blood; dead.

He cheer'd my sorrows, and, for sums of gold,
The *bloodless* carcase of my Hector sold. *Dryden's Æneid.*

2. Without slaughter.

War brings ruin where it should amend;
But beauty, with a *bloodless* conquest, finds
A welcome sov'reignty in rudest minds. *Waller.*

Blo'odshed. *n. s.* [from *blood* and *shed.*]

1. The crime of blood, or murder.

Full many mischiefs follow cruel wrath;
Abhorred *bloodshed*, and tumultuous strife,
Unmanly murder, and unthrifty scath. *Fairy Queen, b.* i.

All murders past do stand excus'd in this;
And this so sole, and so unmatchable,
Shall prove a deadly *bloodshed* but a jest,
Exampled by this heinous spectacle. *Shakesp. King John.*

A man, under the transports of a vehement rage, passes a different judgment upon murder and *bloodshed*, from what he does when his revenge is over. *South.*

2. Slaughter.

So by him Cæsar got the victory,
Through great *bloodshed*, and many a sad assay. *Fairy Q. b.* ii.

Of wars and *bloodshed*, and of dire events,
I could with greater certainty foretel. *Dryden's Tyran. Love.*

Blo'odshedder. *n. s.* [from *bloodshed.*] Murderer.

He that taketh away his neighbour's living, slayeth him: and he that defraudeth the labourer of his hire, is a *bloodshedder.* *Ecclus*, xxxiv. 22.

Blo'odshot. } *adj.* [from *blood* and *shot.*] Filled with
Bloodsho'tten. } blood bursting from its proper vessels.

And that the winds their bellowing throats would try,
When redd'ning clouds reflect his *bloodshot* eye. *Garth.*

Blo'odsucker. *n. s.* [from *blood* and *suck.*]

1. A leech; a fly; any thing that sucks blood.

2. A cruel man; a murderer.

God keep the prince from all the pack of you;
A knot you are of damned *bloodsuckers.* *Shakesp. Rich.* III.

The nobility cried out upon him, that he was a *bloodsucker*, a murderer, and a parricide. *Hayward.*

Blo'ody. *adj.* [from *blood.*]

1. Stained with blood.

2. Cruel; murderous; applied either to men or facts.

By continual martial exercises, without blood, she made them perfect in that *bloody* art. *Sidney, b.* ii.

False of heart, light of ear, *bloody* of hand. *Shakesp. K. Lear.*

I grant him *bloody*,
Luxurious, avaricious, false, deceitful. *Shakesp. Macbeth.*

Thou *bloodier* villain,
Than terms can give thee out. *Shakesp. Macbeth.*

Alas! why gnaw you so your nether lip?
Some *bloody* passion shakes your very frame;
These are portents: but yet I hope, I hope,
They do not point on me. *Shakesp. Othello.*

The *bloody* fact
Will be aveng'd; and th' other's faith approv'd,
Lose no reward; though here thou see him die,
Rolling in dust and gore. *Milton's Paradise Lost, b.* xi. *l.* 457.

The *bloodiest* vengeance which she could pursue,
Would be a trifle to my loss of you. *Dryden's Indian Emp.*

Proud Nimrod first the *bloody* chace began,
A mighty hunter, and his prey was man. *Pope's W. Forest.*

Bloody-flux. See Flux.

Cold, by retarding the motion of the blood, and suppressing perspiration, produces giddiness, sleepiness, pains in the bowels, loosenesses, *bloody-fluxes.* *Arbuthnot on Air.*

Bloody-minded. *adj.* [from *bloody* and *mind.*] Cruel; inclined to bloodshed.

I think you'll make me mad: truth has been at my tongue's end this half hour, and I have not the power to bring it out, for fear of this *bloody-minded* colonel. *Dryden's Spanish Friar.*

BLOOM. *n. s.* [*blum*, Germ. *bloem*, Dutch.]

1. A blossom; the flower which precedes the fruit.

How nature paints her colours, how the bee
Sits on the *bloom*, extracting liquid sweet. *Par. Lost, b.* v.
A medlar tree was planted by;
The spreading branches made a goodly show,
And full of opening *blooms* was ev'ry bough. *Dryden.*
Haste to yonder woodbine bow'rs;
The turf with rural dainties shall be crown'd,
While opening *blooms* diffuse their sweets around. *Pope.*

2. The state of immaturity; the state of any thing improving, and ripening to higher perfection.
Were I no queen, did you my beauty weigh,
My youth in *bloom*, your age in its decay. *Dryden's Aurengz.*

3. The blue colour upon plums and grapes newly gathered.

4. [In the iron works.] A piece of iron wrought into a mass, two feet square.

To Bloom. *v. n.* [from the noun.]

1. To bring or yield blossoms.

The rod of Aaron for the house of Levi was budded, and brought forth buds, and *bloomed* blossoms, and yielded almonds. *Numb.* xvii. 8.

It is a common experience, that if you do not pull off some blossoms the first time a tree *bloometh*, it will blossom itself to death. *Bacon's Natural Hist.* N° 449.

2. To produce, as blossoms.

Rites and customs, now superstitious, when the strength of virtuous, devout, or charitable affection *bloomed* them, no man could justly have condemned as evil. *Hooker, b.* v. § 3.

3. To be in a state of youth and improvement.
Beauty, frail flow'r, that ev'ry season fears,
Blooms in thy colours for a thousand years. *Pope's Epistles.*
O greatly bless'd with every *blooming* grace!
With equal steps the paths of glory trace. *Pope's Odyss. b.* i.

Blo'omy. *adj.* [from *bloom.*] Full of blooms; flowery.
O nightingale! that on yon *bloomy* spray
Warblest at eve, when all the woods are still. *Milton.*
Departing spring could only stay to shed
Her *bloomy* beauties on the genial bed,
But left the manly summer in her stead. } *Dryden.*
Hear how the birds, on ev'ry *bloomy* spray,
With joyous musick wake the dawning day. *Pope.*

Blore. *n. s.* [from *blow.*] Act of blowing; blast.
Out rusht, with an unmeasur'd roar,
Those two winds, tumbling clouds in heaps; ushers to either's *blore.* *Chapman's Iliads.*

BLO'SSOM. *n. s.* [blosme, Sax.] The flower that grows on any plant, previous to the seed or fruit. We generally call those flowers *blossoms*, which are not much regarded in themselves, but as a token of some following production.
Cold news for me:
Thus are my *blossoms* blasted in the bud,
And caterpillars eat my leaves away. *Shakesp. Henry* IV.
Merrily, merrily shall I live now,
Under the *blossom* that hangs on the bough. *Shakesp. Tempest.*

The pulling off many of the *blossoms* of a fruit tree, doth make the fruit fairer. *Bacon's Natural History,* N° 449.
To his green years your censure you would suit,
Not blast the *blossom*, but expect the fruit. *Dryden.*
Sweeter than spring,
Thou sole surviving *blossom* from the root,
That nourish'd up my fortune. *Thomson's Autumn.*

To Blo'ssom. *v. n.* [from the noun.] To put forth blossoms.
This is the state of man: to day he puts forth
The tender leaves of hope; tomorrow *blossoms*,
And bears his blushing honours thick upon him. *Sh. H.* VIII.

Although the figtree shall not *blossom*, neither shall fruit be in the vines, yet I will rejoice in the Lord. *Habb.* iii. 17.

The want of rain at *blossoming* time, often occasions the dropping off of the blossoms, for want of sap. *Mortimer.*

To BLOT. *v. a.* [from *blottir*, Fr. to hide.]

1. To obliterate; to make writing invisible, by covering it with ink.
You that are king,
Have caus'd him, by new act of parliament,
To *blot* out me, and put his own son in. *Shakesp. Henry* VI.
Ev'n copious Dryden wanted, or forgot,
The last and greatest art, the art to *blot.* *Pope.*

A man of the most understanding will find it impossible to make the best use of it, while he writes in constraint, perpetually softening, correcting, or *blotting* out expressions. *Swift.*

2. To efface; to erase.
O Bertran, oh! no more my foe, but brother:
One act like this *blots* out a thousand crimes. *Dryden.*

These simple ideas, offered to the mind, the understanding can no more refuse, nor alter, nor *blot* out, than a mirrour can refuse, alter, or obliterate, the images which the objects produce. *Locke.*

3. To make black spots on a paper; to blur.

Heads overfull of matter, be like pens over full of ink, which will sooner *blot*, than make any fair letter at all. *Ascham's Schoolmaster.*
O sweet Portia!
Here are a few of the unpleasant'st words
That ever *blotted* paper. *Shakesp. Merchant of Venice.*

4. To disgrace; to disfigure.
Unknit that threat'ning unkind brow;
It *blots* thy beauty, as frost bites the meads,
Confounds thy fame. *Shakesp. Taming of the Shrew.*
My guilt thy growing virtues did defame;
My blackness *blotted* thy unblemish'd name. *Dryden's Æn.*
For mercy's sake, restrain thy hand,
Blot not thy innocence with guiltless blood. *Rowe.*

5. To darken.
He sung how earth *blots* the moon's gilded wane,
Whilst foolish men beat sounding brass in vain. *Cowley.*

Blot. *n. s.* [from the verb.]

1. An obliteration of something written.
Let flames on your unlucky papers prey,
Your wars, your loves, your praises, be forgot,
And make of all an universal *blot.* *Dryden's Juven. sat.* vii.

2. A blur; a spot upon paper.

3. A spot in reputation; a stain; a disgrace; a reproach.
Make known,
It is no vicious *blot*, murder, or foulness,
That hath depriv'd me. *Shakesp. King Lear.*

A lie is a foul *blot* in a man; yet it is continually in the mouth of the untaught. *Ecclus*, xx. 24.

A disappointed hope, a *blot* of honour, a strain of conscience, an unfortunate love, will serve the turn. *Temple.*

4. [At backgammon.] When a single man lies open to be taken up; whence to hit a *blot.*

He is too great a master of his art, to make a *blot* which may so easily be hit. *Dryden's Dedication, Æneid.*

Blotch. *n. s.* [from *blot.*] A spot or pustule upon the skin.

Spots and *blotches*, of several colours and figures, straggling over the body; some are red, others yellow, livid, or black. *Harvey on Consumptions.*

To Blote. *v. a.* To smoke, or dry by the smoke; as *bloted* herrings, or red herrings.

BLOW. *n. s.* [*blowe*, Dutch.]

1. A stroke.
A most poor man, made tame to fortune's *blows*,
Who, by the art of known and feeling sorrows,
Am pregnant to good pity. *Shakesp. King Lear.*
A woman's tongue,
That gives not half so great a *blow* to th' ear,
As will a chesnut. *Shakesp. Taming of the Shrew.*

Words of great contempt, commonly finding a return of equal scorn, *blows* were fastened upon the most pragmatical of the crew. *Clarendon.*

2. The fatal stroke; the stroke of death.
Assuage your thirst of blood, and strike the *blow.* *Dryd.*

3. A single action; a sudden event.

Every year they gain a victory, and a town; but if they are once defeated, they lose a province at a *blow.* *Dryden.*

4. The act of a fly, by which she lodges eggs in flesh.
I much fear, lest with the *blows* of flies,
His brass inflicted wounds are fill'd. *Chapman's Iliads.*

To Blow. *v. n.* pret. *blew*; particip. pass. *blown.* [blapan, Sax.]

1. To move with a current of air.

At his sight the mountains are shaken, and at his will the south wind *bloweth.* *Ecclus*, xliii. 16.

Fruits, for long keeping, gather before they are full ripe, and in a dry day, towards noon, and when the wind *bloweth* not south; and when the moon is in decrease. *Bacon's Nat. Hist.*
By the fragrant winds that *blow*
O'er th' Elysian flow'rs. *Pope's St. Cæcilia.*

2. This word is used sometimes impersonally with *it.*

It blew a terrible tempest at sea once, and there was one seaman praying. *L'Estrange.*

If *it blows* a happy gale, we must set up all our sails, though it sometimes happens, that our natural heat is more powerful than our care and correctness. *Dryden's Dufresnoy.*

3. To pant; to puff; to be breathless.

Here's Mrs. Page at the door, sweating and *blowing*, and looking wildly. *Shakesp. Merry Wives of Windsor.*
Each aking nerve refuse the lance to throw,
And each spent courser at the chariot *blow.* *Pope's Iliad.*

4. To breathe.

Says the satyr, if you have gotten a trick of *blowing* hot and cold out of the same mouth, I've e'en done with ye. *L'Estrange.*

5. To sound by being blown.
Nor with less dread the loud
Ethereal trumpet from on high 'gan *blow.* *Par. Lost, b.* vi.
There let the prating organ *blow*,
To the full-voic'd quire below. *Milton.*

6. To sound, or play musically by wind.

When ye *blow* an alarm, then the camps that lie on the east parts shall go forward. *Numb.* x. 5.

7. *To blow over.* To pass away without effect.

Storms, though they *blow over* divers times, yet may fall at last. *Bacon's Essays,* N° 16.
When the storm is *blown over*,
How blest is the swain,
Who begins to discover
An end of his pain. *Granville.*

But

But those clouds being now happily *blown over*, and our sun clearly shining out again, I have recovered the relapse. *Denham.*

8. *To blow up.* To fly into the air by the force of gunpowder.

On the next day, some of the enemy's magazines *blew up*; and it is thought they were destroyed on purpose by some of their men. *Tatler*, N° 59.

To Blow. *v. a.*

1. To drive by the force of the wind.

Though you unty the winds,
Though bladed corn be lodg'd, and trees *blown* down,
Though castles topple on their warders heads. *Macbeth.*

Fair daughter, *blow* away those mists and clouds,
And let thy eyes shine forth in their full lustre. *Denham.*

These primitive heirs of the christian church, could not so easily *blow* off the doctrine of passive obedience. *South.*

2. To inflame with wind.

I have created the smith that *bloweth* the coals in the fire. *Isaiah*, liv. 16.

3. To swell; to puff into size.

No *blown* ambition doth our arms incite,
But love, dear love, and our ag'd father's right. *King Lear.*

4. To form by blowing them into shape.

Spherical bubbles, that boys sometimes *blow* with water, to which soap hath given a tenacity. *Boyle.*

5. To sound an instrument of wind musick.

Where the bright seraphim, in burning row,
Their loud uplifted angel trumpets *blow*. *Milton.*

6. To warm with the breath.

When isicles hang by the wall,
And Dick the shepherd *blows* his nail,
And Tom bears logs into the hall,
And milk comes frozen home in pail. *Shak. L. Lab. Lost.*

7. To spread by report.

But never was there man of his degree,
So much esteem'd, so well belov'd as he:
So gentle of condition was he known,
That through the court his courtesy was *blown*. *Dryden.*

8. *To blow out.* To extinguish by wind or the breath.

Your breath first kindled the dead coal of war,
And brought in matter, that should feed this fire:
And now 'tis far too huge to be *blown out*,
With that same weak wind which enkindled it. *Sh. K. John.*

Moon, slip behind some cloud, some tempest, rise,
And *blow out* all the stars that light the skies. *Dryden.*

9. *To blow up.* To raise or swell with breath.

A plague of sighing and grief! it *blows* a man *up* like a bladder. *Shakesp. Henry* IV. *p.* i.

Blown up with the conceit of his merit, he did not think he had received good measure from the king. *Bacon's Hen.* VII.

Before we had exhausted the receiver, the bladder appeared as full as if *blown up* with a quill. *Boyle.*

It was my breath that *blew* this tempest *up*,
Upon your stubborn usage of the pope. *Shakesp. K. John.*

His presence soon *blows up* the unkindly fight,
And his loud guns speak thick like angry men. *Dryden.*

An empty bladder gravitates no more than when *blown up*, but somewhat less; yet descends more easily, because with less resistance. *Grew's Cosmologia Sacra*, *b.* ii. *c.* 6.

When the mind finds herself very much inflamed with devotion, she is too much inclined to think that it is *blown up* with something divine within herself. *Addis. Spect.* N° 201.

10. *To blow up.* To destroy with gunpowder; to raise into the air.

The captains hoping, by a mine, to gain the city, approached with soldiers ready to enter upon *blowing up* of the mine. *Knolles's History of the Turks.*

Their chief *blown up* in air, not waves, expir'd,
To which his pride presum'd to give the law. *Dryden.*

Not far from the said well, *blowing up* a rock, he formerly observed some of these. *Woodward on Fossils.*

11. To infect with the eggs of flies.

I would no more endure
This wooden slavery, than I would suffer
The flesh-fly *blow* my mouth. *Shakesp. Tempest.*

Rather at Nilus' mud
Lay me stark naked, and let the water flies
Blow me into abhorring. *Shakesp. Antony and Cleopatra.*

12. *To blow upon.* To make stale.

I am wonderfully pleased, when I meet with any passage in an old Greek or Latin author, that is not *blown upon*, and which I have never met with in any quotation. *Addison.*

He will whisper an intrigue that is not yet *blown upon* by common fame. *Addison. Spectator*, N° 105.

To Blow. *v. n.* [blopan, Saxon.] To bloom; to blossom.

We lose the prime to mark how spring
Our tended plants, how *blows* the citron grove,
What drops the myrrh, and what the balmy reed.
Milton's Paradise Lost, *b.* v. *l.* 22.

This royal fair
Shall, when the blossom of her beauty's *blown*,
See her great brother on the British throne. *Waller.*

Fair is the kingcup that in meadow *blows*,
Fair is the daisy that beside her grows. *Gay's Pastorals.*

For thee Idume's spicy forests *blow*,
And seeds of gold in Ophir's mountains glow. *Pope.*

Blo'wer. *n. s.* [from *blow.*] A melter of tin.

Add his care and cost in buying wood, and in fetching the same to the blowing-house, together with the *blowers*, two or three months extreme and encreasing labour. *Carew's Survey.*

Blown. The *participle passive* of *blow.*

All the sparks of virtue, which nature had kindled in them, were so *blown* to give forth their uttermost heat, that justly it may be affirmed, they inflamed the affections of all that knew them. *Sidney*, *b.* ii.

The trumpets sleep, while cheerful horns are *blown*,
And arms employ'd on birds and beasts alone. *Pope.*

Blo'wpoint. *n. s.* A child's play.

Shortly boys shall not play
At spancounter or *blowpoint*, but shall pay
Toll to some courtier. *Donne.*

Blowth. *n. s.* [from *blow.*] Bloom, or blossom.

Ambition and covetousness being but green, and newly grown up, the seeds and effects were as yet but potential, and in the *blowth* and bud. *Raleigh's History of the World.*

Blowze. *n. s.* A ruddy fat-faced wench.

Blo'wzy. *adj.* [from *blowze.*] Sun burnt; high coloured.

BLU'BBER. *n. s.* [See Blob.] The part of a whale that contains the oil.

To Blu'bber. *v. n.* [from the noun.] To weep in such a manner as to swell the cheeks.

Even so lies she,
Blubb'ring and weeping, weeping and *blubb'ring.*
Shakesp. Romeo and Juliet.

A thief came to a boy that was *blubbering* by the side of a well, and asked what he cried for. *L'Estrange.*

Soon as Glumdalclitch miss'd her pleasing care,
She wept, she *blubber'd*, and she tore her hair. *Swift.*

To Blu'bber. *v. a.* To swell the cheeks with weeping.

Fair streams represent unto me my *blubbered* face; let tears procure your stay. *Sidney.*

The wild wood gods arrived in the place,
There find the virgin doleful, desolate,
With ruffled raiment, and fair *blubber'd* face,
As her outrageous foe had left her late. *Fairy Queen*, *b.* i.

Tir'd with the search, not finding what she seeks,
With cruel blows she pounds her *blubber'd* cheeks. *Dryden.*

Blu'bbered. *particip. adj.* [from *to blubber.*] Swelled; big; applied commonly to the lip.

Thou sing with him, thou booby! never pipe
Was so profan'd, to touch that *blubber'd* lip. *Dryden.*

Blu'dgeon. *n. s.* A short stick, with one end loaded, used as an offensive weapon.

BLUE. *adj.* [blæp, Sax. *bleu*, Fr.] One of the seven original colours.

There's gold, and here,
My *bluest* veins to kiss; a hand that kings
Have lipt. *Shakesp. Antony and Cleopatra.*

Where fires thou find'st unrak'd, and hearths unswept,
There pinch the maids as *blue* as bilberry.
Shakesp. Merry Wives of Windsor.

O coward conscience! how dost thou afflict me?
The lights burn *blue*—Is it not dead midnight?
Cold fearful drops stand on my trembling flesh.
Shakesp. Richard III.

Why does one climate, and one soil endue
The blushing poppy with a crimson hue;
Yet leave the lily pale, and tinge the violet *blue*? *Prior.*

There was scarce any other colour sensible, besides red and *blue*; only the *blues*, and principally the second *blue*, inclined a little to green. *Newton's Opticks.*

Bluebo'ttle. *n. s.* [from *blue* and *bottle.*]

1. A flower of the bell shape; a species of *bottleflower*; which see.

If you put *bluebottles*, or other blue flowers, into an ant-hill, they will be stained with red; because the ants thrust their stings, and instil into them their stinging liquour. *Ray.*

2. A fly with a large blue belly.

Say, sire of insects, mighty Sol,
A fly upon the chariot-pole
Cries out, what *bluebottle* alive
Did ever with such fury drive? *Prior.*

Blue-eyed. *adj.* [from *blue* and *eye.*] Having blue eyes.

Rise then, fair *blue-ey'd* maid, rise and discover
Thy silver brow, and meet thy golden lover. *Crashaw.*

Nor to the temple was she gone, to move,
With prayers, the *blue-ey'd* progeny of Jove. *Dryden.*

Blueha'ired. *adj.* [from *blue* and *hair.*] Having blue hair.

This place,
The greatest and the best of all the main,
He quarters to his *bluehair'd* deities. *Milton's Par. Regain.*

Blu'ely. *adv.* [from *blue.*] With a blue colour.

This 'squire he drop'd his pen full soon,
While as the light burnt *bluely*. *Swift.*

Blu'eness. *n. s.* [from *blue.*] The quality of being blue.

In a moment our liquour may be deprived of its *blueness*, and restored to it again, by the affusion of a few drops of liquours. *Boyle on Colours.*

Bluff. *adj.* Big; surly; blustering.

Like those whom stature did to crowns prefer,
Black-brow'd and *bluff*, like Homer's Jupiter. *Dryden.*

Blu'ish. *adj.* [from *blue.*] Blue in a small degree.

Side sleeves and skirts, round underborne, with a *bluish* tinsel. *Shakesp. Much ado about Nothing.*

At last, as far as I could cast my eyes
Upon the sea, somewhat, methought, did rise
Like *bluish* mists. *Dryden's Indian Emperour.*

Here, in full light, the russet plains extend,
There wrapt in clouds the *bluish* hills ascend. *Pope.*

Blu'ishness. *n. s.* [from *blue.*] A small degree of blue colour.

I could make, with crude copper, a solution without the *bluishness*, that is wont to accompany its vulgar solutions. *Boyle.*

To BLU'NDER. *v. n.* [*blunderen*, Dutch; perhaps from *blind.*]

1. To mistake grosly; to err very widely; to mistake stupidly. It is a word implying contempt.

It is one thing to forget matter of fact, and another to *blunder* upon the reason of it. *L'Estrange.*

The grandees and giants in knowledge, who laughed at all besides themselves, as barbarous and insignificant, yet *blundered*, and stumbled, about their grand and principal concern. *South.*

2. To flounder; to stumble.

He who now to sense, now nonsense leaning,
Means not, but *blunders* round about a meaning. *Pope.*

To Blunder. *v. a.* To mix foolishly or blindly.

He seems to understand no difference between titles of respect and acts of worship; between expressions of esteem and devotion; between religious and civil worship: for he *blunders* and confounds all these together; and whatever proves one, he thinks, proves all the rest. *Stillingfleet.*

Blu'nder. *n. s.* [from the verb.] A gross or shameful mistake.

It was the advice of Schomberg to an historian, that he should avoid being particular in the drawing up of an army, and other circumstances in the day of battle; for that he had observed notorious *blunders* and absurdities committed by writers not conversant in the art of war. *Addison. Freeholder.*

It is our own ignorance that makes us charge those works of the Almighty, as defects or *blunders*, as ill-contrived or ill-made. *Derham's Physico-Theology.*

Blu'nderbuss. *n. s.* [from *blunder.*] A gun that is charged with many bullets, so that, without any exact aim, there is a chance of hitting the mark.

There are *blunderbusses* in every loop-hole, that go off of their own accord, at the squeaking of a fiddle. *Dryden.*

Blu'nderer. *n. s.* [from *blunder.*] A man apt to commit blunders; a blockhead.

Another sort of judges will decide in favour of an authour, or will pronounce him a mere *blunderer*, according to the company they have kept. *Watts's Improvement of the Mind.*

Blu'nderhead. *n. s.* [from *blunder* and *head.*] A stupid fellow.

At the rate of this thick-skulled *blunderhead*, every plow-jobber shall take upon him to read upon divinity. *L'Estrange.*

BLUNT. *adj.* [etymology uncertain.]

1. Dull on the edge or point; not sharp.

If the iron be *blunt*, and he do not whet the edge, then must he put to more strength. *Ecclef.* x. 10.

Thanks to that beauty, which can give an edge to the *bluntest* swords. *Sidney, b.* i.

2. Dull in understanding; not quick.

Valentine being gone, I'll quickly cross,
By some sly trick, *blunt* Thurio's dull proceeding.
Shakesp. Two Gentlemen of Verona.

Whitehead, a grave divine, was of a *blunt* stoical nature; one day the queen happened to say, I like thee the better, because thou livest unmarried. He answered; Madam, I like you the worse. *Bacon's Apophthegms.*

3. Rough; not delicate; not civil.

The mayor of the town came to seize them in a *blunt* manner, alleging a warrant to stop them. *Wotton.*

'Tis not enough your counsel still be true;
Blunt truths more mischief than nice falsehoods do. *Pope.*

4. Abrupt; not elegant.

To use too many circumstances, ere one come to the matter, is wearisome; to use none at all, is *blunt*. *Bacon.*

5. Hard to penetrate. This use is improper.

I find my heart hardened and *blunt* to new impressions; it will scarce receive or retain affections of yesterday.
Pope, Lett. lxxxiii. *to Swift.*

To Blunt. *v. a.* [from the noun.]

1. To dull the edge or point.

So sicken waining moons too near the sun,
And *blunt* their crescents on the edge of day. *Dryden.*

Earthly limbs, and gross allay,
Blunt not the beams of heav'n, and edge of day. *Dryden.*

He had such things to urge against our marriage,
As, now declar'd, would *blunt* my sword in battle,
And dastardize my courage. *Dryden's Don Sebastian.*

2. To repress, or weaken any appetite, desire, or power of the mind.

Blunt not his love;
Nor loose the good advantage of his grace,
By seeming cold. *Shakesp. Henry* IV. *p.* 2.

Blu'ntly. *adv.* [from *blunt.*]

1. In a blunt manner; without sharpness.

2. Coarsely; plainly; roughly.

I can keep honest counsels, marr a curious tale in telling it, and deliver a plain message *bluntly*. *Shakesp. King Lear.*

A man of honest blood,
Who to his wife, before the time assign'd
For childbirth came, thus *bluntly* spoke his mind. *Dryden.*

Blu'ntness. *n. s.* [from *blunt.*]

1. Want of edge or point; dulness; obtuseness; want of sharpness.

The crafty boy, that had full oft essay'd
To pierce my stubborn and resisting breast,
But still the *bluntness* of his darts betray'd. *Suckling.*

2. Coarseness; roughness of manners; rude sincerity.

His silence grew wit, his *bluntness* integrity, his beastly ignorance, virtuous simplicity. *Sidney, b.* i.

Manage disputes with civility; whence some readers will be assisted to discern a difference betwixt *bluntness* of speech and strength of reason. *Boyle.*

False friends, his deadliest foes, could find no way,
But shows of honest *bluntness* to betray. *Dryd. H. and Pan.*

Blu'ntwitted. *adj.* [from *blunt* and *wit.*] Dull; stupid.

Bluntwitted lord, ignoble in demeanour. *Shakesp. H.* VI.

BLUR. *n. s.* [*borra*, Span. a blot. *Skinn.*] A blot; a stain; a spot.

Man, once fallen, was nothing but a great *blur*; a total universal pollution. *South.*

To Blur. *v. a.* [from the noun.]

1. To blot; to efface; to obscure.

Such an act,
That *blurs* the grace and blush of modesty,
Calls virtue hypocrite. *Shakesp. King Lear.*

Long is it since I saw him;
But time hath nothing *blurr'd* those lines of favour,
Which then he wore. *Shakesp. Cymbeline.*

Concerning innate principles, I desire these men to say, whether they can, or cannot, by education and custom, be *blurred* and blotted out. *Locke.*

2. To blot; to stain.

Sarcasms may eclipse thine own,
But cannot *blur* my lost renown. *Hudibras, p.* i. *cant.* iii.

To Blurt. *v. a.* [without etymology.] To speak inadvertently; to let fly without thinking.

Others cast out bloody and deadly speeches at random, and cannot hold, but *blurt* out those words, which afterwards they are forced to eat. *Hakewell on Providence.*

They had some belief of a Deity, which they, upon surprizal, thus *blurt* out. *Government of the Tongue,* § 5.

To BLUSH. *v. n.* [*blosen*, Dutch.]

1. To betray shame or confusion, by a red colour in the cheek.

I have mark'd
A thousand *blushing* apparitions
To start into her face; a thousand innocent shames,
In angel whiteness, bear away these blushes.
Shakesp. Much ado about Nothing.

Pale and bloodless,
Being all descended to the lab'ring heart,
Which with the heart there cools, and ne'er returneth
To *blush* and beautify the cheek again. *Shakesp. Henry* VI.

I will go wash:
And when my face is fair, you shall perceive
Whether I *blush*, or no. *Shakesp. Cymbeline.*

All these things are graceful in a friend's mouth, which are *blushing* in a man's own. *Bacon, Essay* 28.

Shame causeth *blushing*; *blushing* is the resort of the blood to the face; although *blushing* will be seen in the whole breast, yet that is but in passage to the face. *Bacon's Nat. History.*

Blush then, but *blush* for your destructive silence,
That tears your soul. *Smith's Phædr. and Hippolitus.*

2. To carry a red colour, or any soft and bright colour.

To day he puts forth
The tender leaves of hope; tomorrow blossoms,
And bears his *blushing* honours thick upon him. *Sh. H.* VI.

Along those *blushing* borders, bright with dew. *Thomson.*

3. It has *at* before the cause of shame.

He whin'd, and roar'd away your victory,
That pages *blush'd at* him; and men of heart
Look'd wond'ring at each other. *Shakesp. Coriolanus.*

You have not yet lost all your natural modesty, but *blush at* your vices. *Calamy's Sermons.*

Blush. *n. s.* [from the verb.]

1. The colour in the cheeks, raised by shame or confusion.

The virgin's wish, without her fears, impart,
Excuse the *blush*, and pour out all the heart. *Pope.*

2. A red or purple colour.

But here the roses *blush* so rare,
Here the mornings smile so fair,
As if neither cloud, nor wind,
But would be courteous, would be kind. *Crashaw.*

3. Sudden

3. Sudden appearance; a signification that seems barbarous, yet used by good writers.

All purely identical propositions, obviously and at first *blush*, appear to contain no certain instruction in them. *Locke.*

BLU'SHY. *adj.* [from *blush.*] Having the colour of a blush.

Blossoms of trees, that are white, are commonly inodorate; those of apples, crabs, and peaches, are *blushy*, and smell sweet. *Bacon's Natural Hist.* N° 507.

Stratonica entering, moved a *blushy* colour in his face; but, deserting him, he relapsed into the same paleness and languour. *Harvey on Consumptions.*

To BLU'STER. *v. n.* [supposed from *blast.*]

1. To roar as a storm; to be violent and loud.

Earth his uncouth mother was,
And *blust'ring* Æolus his boasted fire. *Spenser.*
So now he storms with many a sturdy stoure;
So now his *blust'ring* blast each coast doth scour. *Spenser.*

2. To bully; to puff; to swagger; to be tumultuous.

My heart's too big to bear this, says a *blustering* fellow; I'll destroy myself. Sir, says the gentleman, here's a dagger at your service; so the humour went off. *L'Estrange.*

Either he must sink to a downright confession, or else he must huff and *bluster*, till perhaps he raise a counter-storm. *Government of the Tongue.*

Virgil had the majesty of a lawful prince, and Statius only the *blustering* of a tyrant. *Dryden's Spanish Friar, Dedication.*

There let him reign the jailor of the wind;
With hoarse commands his breathing subjects call,
And boast and *bluster* in his empty hall. *Dryden's Æneid.*

BLU'STER. *n. s.* [from the verb.]

1. Roar; noise; tumult.

The skies look grimly,
And threaten present *blusters*. *Shakesp. Twelfth Night.*
To the winds they set
Their corners; when with *bluster* to confound
Sea, air, and shore. *Milton's Paradise Lost, b.* x. *l.* 665.
So, by the brazen trumpet's *bluster*,
Troops of all tongues and nations muster. *Swift.*

2. Boast; boisterousness; turbulence; fury.

Spare thy Athenian cradle, and those kin,
Which in the *bluster* of thy wrath must fall
With those that have offended. *Shakesp. Timon.*

A coward makes a great deal more *bluster* than a man of honour. *L'Estrange.*

BLU'STERER. *n. s.* [from *bluster.*] A swaggerer; a bully; a tumultuous noisy fellow.

BLU'STROUS. *adj.* [from *bluster.*] Tumultuous; noisy.

The ancient heroes were illustrious
For being benign, and not *blustrous.* *Hudibras, p.* i. *c.* iii.

BMI. *n. s.* A note in musick.

Gamut I am, the ground of all accord,
Bmi, Bianca, take him for thy lord. *Shakesp. Tam. Shrew.*

BO. *interj.* A word of terrour; from *Bo*, an old northern captain, of such fame, that his name was used to terrify the enemy. *Temple.*

BOAR. *n. s.* [baɲ, Saxon; *beer*, Dutch.] The male swine.

To fly the *boar*, before the *boar* pursues,
Were to incense the *boar* to follow us. *Shakesp. Rich.* III.
She sped the *boar* away;
His eyeballs glare with fire, suffus'd with blood;
His neck shuts up a thickest thorny wood;
His bristled back a trench impal'd appears. *Dryden's Fables.*

BO'AR-SPEAR. *n. s.* [from *boar* and *spear.*] A spear used in hunting the boar.

And in her hand a sharp *boar-spear* she held,
And at her back a bow and quiver gay,
Stuff'd with steel-headed darts. *Fairy Queen, b.* i. *c.* iii.
Echion threw the first, but miss'd his mark,
And struck his *boar-spear* on a maple bark. *Dryden's Ovid.*

BOARD. *n. s.* [*baurd*, Goth. bɲæd, Saxon.]

1. A piece of wood of more length and breadth than thickness.

With the saw they have sundred trees in *boards* and planks. *Raleigh's Essays.*

Every house has a *board* over the door, whereon is written the number, sex, and quality of the persons living in it. *Temple.*

Go now, go trust the wind's uncertain breath,
Remov'd four fingers from approaching death;
Or seven at most, when thickest is the *board.* *Dryden's Juv.*

2. A table. [from *burdd*, Welch.]

Soon after which, three hundred lords he slew,
Of British blood, all sitting at his *board.* *Fairy Queen, b.* ii.
In bed he slept not, for my urging it;
At *board* he fed not, for my urging it. *Shakesp. Com. of Err.*
I'll follow thee in fun'ral flames; when dead,
My ghost shall thee attend at *board* and bed. *Sir J. Denham.*

Cleopatra made Antony a supper, which was sumptuous and royal; howbeit there was no extraordinary service upon the *board.* *Hakewell on Providence.*

May ev'ry god his friendly aid afford;
Pan guard thy flock, and Ceres bless thy *board.* *Prior.*

3. Entertainment; food.

4. A table at which a council or court is held.

Both better acquainted with affairs, than any other who sat then at that *board.* *Clarendon.*

5. An assembly seated at a table; a court of jurisdiction.

I wish the king would be pleased sometimes to be present at that *board*; it adds a majesty to it. *Bacon's Advice to Villiers.*

6. The deck or floor of a ship; *on board* signifies in a ship.

Now *board* to *board* the rival vessels row,
The billows lave the skies, and ocean groans below. *Dryd.*

Our captain thought his ship in so great danger, that he confessed himself to a capuchin, who was *on board.* *Addison.*

He ordered his men to arm long poles with sharp hooks, wherewith they took hold of the tackling, which held the mainyard to the mast of their enemy's ship; then, rowing their own ship, they cut the tackling, and brought the mainyard by the *board.* *Arbuthnot on Coins.*

To BOARD. *v. a.* [from the noun.]

1. To enter a ship by force; the same as to storm, used of a city.

I *boarded* the king's ship: now on the beak,
Now in the waste, the deck, in every cabin,
I flam'd amazement. *Shakesp. Tempest.*
Yet not inclin'd the English ship to *board*,
More on his guns relies than on his sword,
From whence a fatal volley we receiv'd;
It miss'd the duke; but his great heart it griev'd. *Waller.*
Arm, arm, she cry'd, and let our Tyrians *board*
With our's his fleet, and carry fire and sword. *Denham.*

2. To attack, or make the first attempt upon a man; *aborder quelqu'un*, Fr.

Whom thus at gaze, the Palmer 'gan to *board*
With goodly reason, and thus fair bespake. *Fairy Q. b.* ii.
Away, I do beseech you, both away;
I'll *board* him presently. *Shakesp. Hamlet.*

Sure, unless he knew some strain in me, that I knew not myself, he would never have *boarded* me in this fury. *Shakespeare.*

They learn what associates and correspondents they had, and how far every one is engaged, and what new ones they meant afterwards to try or *board.* *Bacon's Henry* VII.

3. To lay or pave with boards.

Having thus *boarded* the whole room, the edges of some boards lie higher than the next board; therefore they peruse the whole floor; and, where they find any irregularities, plane them off. *Moxon's Mechanical Exercises.*

To BOARD. *v. n.* To live in a house, where a certain rate is paid for eating.

That we might not part,
As we at first did *board* with thee,
Now thou wouldst taste our misery. *Herbert.*

We are several of us, gentlemen and ladies, who *board* in the same house; and, after dinner, one of our company stands up, and reads your paper to us all. *Spectator*, N° 961.

To BOARD. *v. a.* To place as a boarder in another's house.

BOARD-WAGES. *n. s.* [from *board* and *wages.*] Wages allowed to servants to keep themselves in victuals.

What more than madness reigns,
When one short sitting many hundreds drains,
And not enough is left him, to supply
Board-wages, or a footman's livery? *Dryden's Juv. sat.* i.

BO'ARDER. *n. s.* [from *board.*] A tabler; one that eats with another at a settled rate.

BO'ARDING-SCHOOL. *n. s.* [from *board* and *school.*] A school where the scholars live with the teacher.

A blockhead, with melodious voice,
In *boarding-schools* can have his choice. *Swift.*

BO'ARISH. *adj.* [from *boar.*] Swinish; brutal, cruel.

I would not see thy cruel nails
Pluck out his poor old eyes; nor thy fierce sister,
In his anointed flesh stick *boarish* phangs. *Shakesp. K. Lear.*

To BOAST. *v. n.* [*bôst*, Welch.]

1. To brag; to display one's own worth, or actions, in great words; to talk ostentatiously; with *of.*

For I know the forwardness of your mind, for which I *boast of* you to them of Macedonia. 2 *Cor.* ix. 2.

2. Sometimes it is used with *in.*

Some surgeons I have met, carrying bones about in their pockets, *boasting in* that which was their shame. *Wiseman.*

3. To exalt one's self.

Thus with your mouth you have *boasted* against me, and multiplied your words against me. *Ezek.* xxxv. 13.

To BOAST. *v. a.*

1. To brag of; to display with ostentatious language.

For if I have *boasted* any thing to him of you, I am not ashamed. 2 *Cor.* vii. 14.

If they vouchsafed to give god the praise of his goodness; yet they did it only, in order to *boast* the interest they had in him. *Atterbury.*

2. To magnify; to exalt.

They that trust in their wealth, and *boast* themselves *in* the multitude of their riches. *Psalm* xlix. 6.

Confounded be all them that serve graven images, that *boast* themselves *of* idols. *Psalm* xcvii. 7.

BOAST. *n. s.* [from the verb.]

1. A cause of boasting; an occasion of pride; the thing boasted.

 Not

Not Tyro, nor Mycene, match her name,
Nor great Alcmena, the proud *boasts* of fame. *Pope's Odyss.*

2. An expression of ostentation; a proud speech.

Thou that makest thy *boast* of the law, through breaking the law dishonourest thou God? *Rom.* ii. 23.

The world is more apt to find fault than to commend; the *boast* will probably be censured, when the great action that occasioned it, is forgotten. *Spectator*, N° 255.

BO'ASTER. *n. s.* [from *boast.*] A bragger; a man that vaunts any thing ostentatiously.

Complaints the more candid and judicious of the chymists themselves are wont to make of those *boasters*, that confidently pretend, that they have extracted the salt or sulphur of quicksilver, when they have disguised it by additaments, wherewith it resembles the concretes. *Boyle.*

No more delays, vain *boaster!* but begin;
I prophesy beforehand I shall win:
I'll teach you how to brag another time. *Dryden's Virgil.*

He the proud *boasters* sent, with stern assault,
Down to the realms of night. *Philips.*

BO'ASTFUL. *adj.* [from *boast* and *full.*] Ostentatious; inclined to brag.

Boastful, and rough, your first son is a 'squire;
The next a tradesman, meek, and much a liar. *Pope.*

BO'ASTINGLY. *adv.* [from *boasting.*] Ostentatiously.

We look on it as a pitch of impiety, *boastingly* to avow our sins; and it deserves to be considered, whether this kind of confessing them, have not some affinity with it. *Decay of Piety.*

BOAT. *n. s.* [bat, Saxon.]

1. A vessel to pass the water in. It is usually distinguished from other vessels, by being smaller and uncovered, and commonly moved by rowing.

I do not think that any one nation, the Syrian excepted, to whom the knowledge of the ark came, did find out at once the device of either ship or *boat*, in which they durst venture themselves upon the seas. *Raleigh's Essays.*

An effeminate scoundrel multitude!
Whose utmost daring is to cross the Nile,
In painted *boats*, to fright the crocodile. *Tate. Juv. sat.* xv.

2. A ship of a small size; as, a *passage boat*, *pacquet boat*, *advice boat*, *fly boat.*

BOA'TION. *n. s.* [from *boare*, Lat.] Roar; noise; loud sound.

In Messina insurrection, the guns were heard from thence as far as Augusta and Syracuse, about an hundred Italian miles. These distances being, in a short time, in loud *boations.* *Derham's Physico-Theology.*

BO'ATMAN. } *n. s.* [from *boat* and *man.*] He that manages a
BO'ATSMAN. } boat.

Boatsmen through the crystal water show,
To wond'ring passengers, the walls below. *Dryden.*

That booby Phaon only was unkind,
An ill-bred *boatman*, rough as waves and wind. *Prior.*

BO'ATSWAIN. *n. s.* [from *boat* and *swain.*] An officer on board a ship, who has charge of all her rigging, ropes, cables, anchors, sails, flags, colours, pendants, &c. He also takes care of the long-boat and its furniture, and steers her either by himself or his mate. He calls out the several gangs and companies to the execution of their watches, works, and spells; and he is also a kind of provost marshal, seizes, and punishes all offenders, that are sentenced by the captain, or court martial of the whole fleet. *Harris.*

Sometimes the meanest *boatswain* may help to preserve the ship from sinking. *Howel's Pre-eminence of Parliament.*

To BOB. *v. a.* [of uncertain etymology; *Skinner* deduces it from *bobo*, foolish, Span.]

1. To cut. *Junius.*

2. To beat; to drub; to bang.

Those bastard Britons, whom our fathers
Have in their own land beaten, *bobb'd*, and thump'd.
Shakesp. Richard III.

3 To cheat; to gain by fraud.

I have *bobbed* his brain more than he has beat my bones.
Shakesp. Troilus and Cressida.

Live, Rodorigo!
He calls me to a restitution large,
Of gold and jewels, that I *bobb'd* from him,
As gifts to Desdemona. *Shakesp. Othello.*

Here we have been worrying one another, who should have the booty, till this cursed fox has *bobbed* us both on't. *L'Estr.*

To BOB. *v. n.* To play backward and forward; to play loosely against any thing.

And sometimes lurk I in a gossip's bowl,
In very likeness of a roasted crab;
And when she drinks, against her lips I *bob*,
And on her wither'd dewlap pour the ale. *Midsum. N. Dr.*

They comb, and then they order ev'ry hair;
A birthday jewel *bobbing* at their ear. *Dryd. Persius, sat.* i.

You may tell her,
I'm rich in jewels, rings, and *bobbing* pearls,
Pluck'd from Moors ears. *Dryden's Spanish Friar.*

BOB. *n. s.* [from the verb neuter.]

1. Something that hangs so as to play loosely; generally an ornament at the ear; a pendant; an ear-ring.

The gaudy gossip, when she's set agog,
In jewels drest, and at each ear a *bob.* *Dryd. Juv. sat.* vi.

2. The word repeated at the end of a stanza.

To bed, to bed, will be the *bob* of the song. *L'Estrange.*

3. A blow.

I am sharply taunted, yea, sometimes with pinches, nips, and *bobs.* *Ascham's Schoolmaster.*

BO'BBIN. *n. s.* [*bobine*, Fr. from *bombyx*, Lat.] A small pin of wood, with a notch, to wind the thread about, when women weave lace.

The things you follow, and make songs on now, should be sent to knit, or sit down to *bobbins*, or bone-lace. *Tatler.*

BO'BBINWORK. *n. s.* [from *bobbin* and *work.*] Work woven with bobbins.

Not netted nor woven with warp and woof, but after the manner of *bobbinwork.* *Grew's Musæum.*

BO'BCHERRY. *n. s.* [from *bob* and *cherry.*] A play among children, in which the cherry is hung so as to bob against the mouth.

Bobcherry teaches at once two noble virtues, patience and constancy; the first, in adhering to the pursuit of one end; the latter, in bearing a disappointment. *Arb. and Pop. M. Scr.*

BO'BTAIL. [from *bob*, in the sense of *cut.*] Cut tail; short tail.

Avaunt, you curs!
Be thy mouth or black or white,
Or *bobtail* like, or trundle tail,
Tom will make him weep and wail. *Shakesp. King Lear.*

BO'BTAILED. *adj.* [from *bobtail.*] Having a tail cut, or short.

There was a *bobtailed* cur cried in a gazette, and one that found him, brought him home to his master. *L'Estrange.*

B'OBWIG. *n. s.* [from *bob* and *wig.*] A short wig.

A young fellow riding towards us full gallop, with a *bobwig* and a black silken bag tied to it, stopt short at the coach, to ask us how far the judges were behind. *Spectator*, N° 129.

BO'CASINE. *n. s.* A sort of linen cloth; a fine buckram. *Dict.*

BO'CKELET. } *n. s.* A kind of long-winged hawk. *Dict.*
BO'CKERET. }

To BODE. *v. a.* [bodian, Sax.] To portend; to be the omen of. It is used in a sense of either good or bad.

This *bodes* some strange eruption to our state. *Hamlet.*

By this design, you have opposed their false policy, with true and great wisdom; what they *boded* would be a mischief to us, you are providing, shall be one of our principal strengths. *Sprat's Sermons.*

It happen'd once, a *boding* prodigy!
A swarm of bees that cut the liquid sky,
Upon the topmost branch in clouds alight. *Dryden's Æneid.*

If firy red his glowing globe descends,
High winds and furious tempests he portends:
But if his cheeks are swoln with livid blue,
He *bodes* wet weather by his watry hue. *Dryden's Georg.*

To BODE. *v. n.* To be an omen; to foreshew.

Sir, give me leave to say, whatever now
The omen prove, it *boded* well to you. *Dryden's Aurengz.*

BO'DEMENT. *n. s.* [from *bode.*] Portent; omen; prognostick.

This foolish, dreaming, superstitious girl
Makes all these *bodements.* *Shakesp. Troilus and Cressida.*

Macbeth shall never vanquisht be, until
Great Birnam wood to Dunsinane's high hill
Shall come against him ——
——— That will never be:
Sweet *bodements*, good. *Shakesp. Macbeth.*

To BODGE. *v. n.* [a word in *Shakespeare*, which is perhaps corrupted from *boggle.*] To boggle; to stop; to fail.

With this we charg'd again; but out! alas,
We *bodg'd* again; as I have seen a swan,
With bootless labour, swim against the tide. *Shakesp. H.* VI.

BO'DICE. *n. s.* [from *bodies.*] Stays; a waistcoat quilted with whalebone, worn by women.

Her *bodice* halfway she unlac'd,
About his arms she slily cast
The silken band, and held him fast. *Prior.*

This consideration should keep ignorant nurses and *bodice* makers from meddling. *Locke on Education*, § 11.

BO'DILESS. *adj.* [from *body.*] Incorporeal; without a body.

Which *bodiless* and immaterial are,
And can be only lodg'd within our minds. *Davies.*

This is the very coinage of your brain,
This *bodiless* creation ecstasy
Is very cunning in. *Shakesp. Hamlet.*

These are but shadows,
Phantoms *bodiless* and vain,
Empty visions of the brain. *Swift.*

BO'DILY. *adj.* [from *body.*]

1. Corporeal; containing body.

What resemblance could wood or stone bear to a spirit void of all sensible qualities, and *bodily* dimensions? *South.*

2. Relating to the body, not the mind.

Of such as resorted to our Saviour Christ, being present on earth, there came not any unto him with better success, for the benefit of their souls everlasting happiness, than they whose *bodily* necessities gave occasion of seeking relief. *Hooker, b.* v.

Virtue

Virtue atones for *bodily* defects; beauty is nothing worth, without a mind. *L'Estrange.*

As clearness of the *bodily* eye doth dispose it for a quicker sight, so doth freedom from lust and passion, dispose us for the most perfect acts of reason. *Tillotson.*

I would not have children much beaten for their faults, because I would not have them think *bodily* pain the greatest punishment. *Locke on Education*, § 115.

3. Real; actual.

Whatever hath been thought on in this state,
That could be brought to *bodily* act, ere Rome
Had circumvention? *Shakesp. Coriolanus.*

BO'DILY. *adv.* Corporeally; united with matter.

It is his human nature, in which the godhead dwells *bodily*, that is advanced to these honours, and to this empire. *Watts.*

BO'DKIN. *n. s.* [*boddiken*, or small body, *Skinner.*]

1. An instrument with a small blade and sharp point, used to bore holes.

Each of them had *bodkins* in their hands, wherewith continually they pricked him. *Sidney's Arcadia.*

2. An instrument to draw a thread or ribbond through a loop.

Or plung'd in lakes of bitter washes lie,
Or wedg'd whole ages in a *bodkin*'s eye. *Pope's R. of the L.*

3. An instrument to dress the hair.

You took constant care
The *bodkin*, comb, and essence to prepare:
For this your locks in paper-durance bound. *Pope.*

BO'DY. *n. s.* [bodiȝ, Saxon; it originally signified the height or stature of a man.]

1. The material substance of an animal, opposed to the immaterial soul.

All the valiant men arose, and went all night, and took the *body* of Saul, and the *bodies* of his sons, from the wall. 1 *Sam.* xxxi. 12.

Take no thought for your life, what ye shall eat, or what ye shall drink; nor yet for your *body*, what ye shall put on. *Matt.* vi. 25.

By custom, practice, and patience, all difficulties and hardships, whether of *body* or of fortune, are made easy to us. *L'Estrange.*

2. Matter; opposed to spirit.

3. A person; a human being; whence *somebody*, and *nobody*.

Surely, a wise *body*'s part it were not, to put out his fire, because his foolish neighbour, from whom he borrowed wherewith to kindle it, might say, were it not for me, thou wouldst freeze. *Hooker, b.* iv. § 9.

A deflowred maid!
And by an eminent *body*, that enforc'd
The law against it! *Shakesp. Measure for Measure.*

'Tis a passing shame,
That I, unworthy *body* as I am,
Should censure thus one lovely gentleman. *Sh. Two G. of Ver.*

No *body* seeth me; what need I to fear? the Most High will not remember my sins. *Ecclus*, xxiii. 18.

All civility and reason obliged every *body* to submit. *Clarend.*

Good may be drawn out of evil, and a *body's* life may be saved, without having any obligation to his preserver. *L'Estr.*

4. Reality; opposed to representation.

A shadow of things to come; but the *body* is of Christ. *Coloss.*

5. A collective mass; a joint power.

There is in the knowledge both of God and man this certainty, that life and death have divided between them the whole *body* of mankind. *Hooker, b.* v. § 49.

There were so many disaffected persons of the nobility, that there might a *body* start up for the king. *Clarendon, b.* viii.

When these pigmies pretend to form themselves into a *body*, it is time for us, who are men of figure, to look about us. *Addison. Guardian*, N° 108.

6. The main army; the battle; distinct from the wings, van and rear.

The van of the king's army was led by the general and Wilmot; in the *body* was the king and the prince; and the rear consisted of one thousand foot, commanded under colonel Thelwell. *Clarendon, b.* viii.

7. A corporation; a number of men united by some common tye.

I shall now mention a particular, wherein your whole *body* will be certainly against me, and the laity, almost to a man, on my side. *Swift.*

Nothing was more common, than to hear that reverend *body* charged with what is inconsistent, despised for their poverty, and hated for their riches. *Swift.*

8. The outward condition.

I verily, as absent in *body*, have judged. 1 *Cor.* v. 3.

9. The main part; the bulk; as, the *body*, or hull, of a ship; the *body* of a coach; the *body* of a church; the *body*, or trunk, of a man; the *body*, or trunk, of a tree.

Thence sent rich merchandizes by boat to Babylon, from whence, by the *body* of Euphrates, as far as it bended westward, and, afterward, by a branch thereof. *Raleigh's History.*

This city has navigable rivers, that run up into the *body* of Italy, by which they might supply many countries with fish. *Addison's Remarks on Italy.*

10. A substance.

Even a metalline *body*, and therefore much more a vegetable or animal, may, by fire, be turned into water. *Boyle.*

11. [In geometry.] Any solid figure.

12. A pandect; a general collection; as, a *body* of the civil law; a *body* of divinity.

13. Strength; as, wine of a good *body*.

BODY-CLOATHS. *n. s.* [from *body* and *cloaths.*] Cloathing for horses that are dieted.

However it be, I am informed, that several asses are kept in *body-cloaths*, and sweated every morning upon the heath. *Addison. Spectator*, N° 173.

To BO'DY. *v. a.* [from the noun.] To produce in some form.

As imagination *bodies* forth
The forms of things unknown, the poet's pen
Turns them to shape. *Shakesp. Midsummer Night's Dream.*

BOG. *n. s.* [*bog*, soft, Irish.] A marish; a morass; a ground too soft to bear the weight of the body.

Through fire and through flame, through ford and whirlpool, o'er *bog* and quagmire. *Shakesp. King Lear.*

A gulf profound! as that Serbonian *bog*,
Betwixt Damiata and Mount Casius old. *Par. Lost, b.* ii.

He walks upon *bogs* and whirlpools; wheresoever he treads, he sinks. *South.*

Learn from so great a wit, a land of *bogs*
With ditches fenc'd, a heaven fat with fogs. *Dryden.*

He is drawn, by a sort of *ignis fatuus*, into *bogs* and mire, almost every day of his life. *Watts's Improvement of the Mind.*

BOG-TROTTER. *n. s.* [from *bog* and *trot.*] One that lives in a boggy country.

To BO'GGLE. *v. n.* [from *bogil*, Dutch, a spectre; a bugbear; a phantom.]

1. To start; to fly back; to fear to come forward.

You *boggle* shrewdly; every feather starts you.
Shakesp. All's well that ends well.

We start and *boggle* at every unusual appearance, and cannot endure the sight of the bugbear. *Glanville's Scepsis, c.* 16.

Nature, that rude, and in her first essay,
Stood *boggling* at the roughness of the way;
Us'd to the road, unknowing to return,
Goes boldly on, and loves the path when worn. *Dryden.*

2. To hesitate; to be in doubt.

And never *boggle* to restore
The members you deliver o'er,
Upon demand. *Hudibras, p.* iii. *c.* i.

The well-shaped changeling is a man that has a rational soul, say you. Make the ears a little longer, and more pointed, and the nose a little flatter than ordinary, and then you begin to *boggle*. *Locke.*

3. To play fast and loose; to dissemble.

When summoned to his last end, it was no time for him to *boggle* with the world. *Howel's Vocal Forest.*

BO'GGLER. *n. s.* [from *boggle.*] A doubter; a timorous man.

You have been a *boggler* ever. *Shakesp. Ant. and Cleop.*

BO'GGY. *adj.* [from *bog.*] Marshy; swampy.

Their country was very narrow, low, and *boggy*, and, by great industry and expences, defended from the sea. *Arbuthnot.*

BO'GHOUSE. *n. s.* [from *bog* and *house.*] A house of office.

BOHE'A. *n. s.* [an Indian word.] A species of tea, of higher colour, and more astringent taste, than green tea.

Coarse pewter, appearing to consist chiefly of lead, is part of the bales in which *bohea* tea was brought from China. *Woodw.*

As some frail cup of China's fairest mold,
The tumults of the boiling *bohea* braves,
And holds secure the coffee's sable waves. *Tickell.*

She went from op'ra, park, assembly, play,
To morning walks, and pray'rs three hours a day;
To part her time 'twixt reading and *bohea*,
To muse, and spill her solitary tea. *Pope.*

To BOIL. *v. n.* [*bouiller*, Fr. *bullio*, Lat.]

1. To be agitated by heat; to fluctuate with heat.

He saw there *boil* the firy whirlpools. *Chapman's Odyssey.*

Suppose the earth removed, and placed nearer to the sun, in the orbit of Mercury, there the whole ocean would *boil* with extremity of heat. *Bentley.*

2. To be hot; to be fervent, or effervescent.

That strength with which my *boiling* youth was fraught,
When in the vale of Balasor I fought. *Dryden's Aurengzebe.*

Well I knew,
What perils youthful ardour would pursue,
That *boiling* blood would carry thee too far. *Dryden's Æn.*

3. To move with an agitation like that of boiling water.

Then headlong shoots beneath the dashing tide,
The trembling fins the *boiling* waves divide. *Gay.*

In the dubious point, where, with the pool,
Is mixt the trembling stream, or where it *boils*
Around the stone. *Thomson's Spring.*

4. To be in hot liquour, in order to be made tender by the heat.

Fillet of a fenny snake,
In the cauldron *boil* and bake. *Shakesp. Macbeth.*

5. To cook by boiling.

If you live in a rich family, roasting and *boiling* are below the

the dignity of your office, and which it becomes you to be ignorant of. *Swift's Directions to the Cook.*

6. *To boil over.* To run over the veſſel with heat.

A few ſoft words and a kiſs, and the good man melts; ſee how nature works and *boils over* in him. *Congreve's Old Batchel.*

This hollow was a vaſt cauldron, filled with melted matter, which, as it *boiled over* in any part, ran down the ſides of the mountain. *Addiſon on Italy.*

To Boil. *v. a.* To heat, by putting into boiling water; to ſeeth.

To try whether ſeeds be old or new, the ſenſe cannot inform; but if you *boil* them in water, the new ſeeds will ſprout ſooner. *Bacon's Natural Hiſtory.*

In eggs *boiled* and roaſted, into which the water entereth not at all, there is ſcarce any difference to be diſcerned. *Bacon.*

Boil. *n. ſ.* See Bile.

Bo'ilary. *n. ſ.* [from *to boil.*] A place at the ſalt-works where the ſalt is boiled.

Bo'iler. *n. ſ.* [from *boil.*]

1. The perſon that boils any thing.

That ſuch alterations of terreſtrial matter are not impoſſible, ſeems evident from that notable practice of the *boilers* of ſaltpetre. *Boyle.*

2. The veſſel in which any thing is boiled.

This coffee-room is much frequented; and there are generally ſeveral pots and *boilers* before the fire. *Woodward.*

BOISTEROUS. *adj.* [*byſter*, furious, Dutch.]

1. Violent; loud; roaring; ſtormy.

By a divine inſtinct, men's minds miſtruſt
Enſuing danger; as by proof we ſee
The waters ſwell before a *boiſterous* ſtorm. *Shakeſp. R.* III.

As when loud winds a well-grown oak would rend
Up by the roots, this way and that they bend
His reeling trunk, and with a *boiſt'rous* ſound
Scatter his leaves, and ſtrew them on the ground. *Waller.*

2. Turbulent; tumultuous; furious.

Spirit of peace,
Wherefore do you ſo ill tranſlate yourſelf
Out of the ſpeech of peace, that bears ſuch grace,
Into the harſh and *boiſt'rous* tongue of war? *Shakeſp. H.* IV.

His ſweetneſs won a more regard
Unto his place, than all the *boiſt'rous* moods
That ignorant greatneſs practiſeth. *Ben. Johnſon's Catiline.*

God, into the hands of their deliverer,
Puts invincible might,
To quell the mighty of the earth, th' oppreſſor,
The brute and *boiſt'rous* force of violent men. *Milton.*

Still muſt I beg thee not to name Sempronius:
Lucia; I like not that loud *boiſterous* man. *Addiſon's Cato.*

3. Unwieldy.

His *boiſterous* club, ſo buried in the ground,
He could not rearen up again ſo light,
But that the knight him at avantage found. *Fairy Q. b.* i.

4. It is uſed by *Woodward* of heat.

When the ſun hath gained a greater ſtrength, the heat becomes too powerful and *boiſterous* for them. *Natural Hiſtory.*

Bo'isterously. *adv.* [from *boiſterous.*] Violently; tumultuouſly.

A ſceptre ſnatch'd, with an unruly hand,
Muſt be as *boiſterouſly* maintain'd, as gain'd. *Sh. King John.*

Thoſe are all remains of the univerſal deluge, when the water of the ocean, being *boiſterouſly* turned out upon the earth, bore along with it all moveable bodies. *Woodward's N. Hiſt.*

Another faculty of the intellect comes *boiſterouſly* in, and wakes me from ſo pleaſing a dream. *Swift's Letters.*

Bo'isterousness. *n. ſ.* [from *boiſterous.*] The ſtate or quality of being boiſterous; tumultuouſneſs; turbulence.

Bo'lary. *adj.* [from *bole.*] Partaking of the nature of bole, or clay.

A weak and inanimate kind of loadſtone, with a few magnetical lines, but chiefly conſiſting of a *bolary* and clammy ſubſtance. *Brown's Vulgar Errours, b.* ii. *c.* 3.

BOLD. *adj.* [balꝺ, Saxon.]

1. Daring; brave; ſtout; courageous; magnanimous; fearleſs; intrepid.

The wicked flee when no man purſueth; but the righteous are *bold* as a lion. *Prov.* xxviii. 1.

I have ſeen the councils of a noble country grow *bold*, or timorous, according to the fits of his good or ill health that managed them. *Temple.*

2. Executed with ſpirit, and without mean caution.

Theſe, nervous, *bold*; thoſe, languid and remiſs. *Roſcom.*

The cathedral church is a very *bold* work, and a maſterpiece in Gothick architecture. *Addiſon on Italy.*

3. Confident; not ſcrupulous; not timorous.

We were *bold* in our God to ſpeak unto you the goſpel of God with much contention. 1 *Theſſ.* ii. 2.

I can be *bold* to ſay, that this age is adorned with ſome men of that judgment, that they could open new and undiſcovered ways to knowledge. *Locke.*

4. Impudent; rude.

In thy proſperity he will be as thyſelf, and will be *bold* over thy ſervants. If thou be brought low, he will be againſt thee. *Ecclus*, vi. 11.

5. Licentious; ſuch as ſhew great liberty of fiction.

Which no *bold* tales of Gods or monſters ſwell,
But human paſſions, ſuch as with us dwell. *Waller.*

6. Standing out to the view; ſtriking to the eye.

Catechreſes and hyperboles are to be uſed judiciouſly, and placed in poetry, as heightenings and ſhadows are in painting, to make the figures *bolder*, and cauſe it to ſtand off to ſight. *Dryden's State of Innocence, Preface.*

7. Open; ſmooth; even; level: a ſailor's term.

Her dominions lie ſcattered, and have *bold* acceſſible coaſts. *Howel's Vocal Foreſt.*

8. *To make bold.* To take freedoms: a phraſe not grammatical, though common. *To be bold* is better; as, *I was bold to ſpeak.*

I have *made bold* to ſend to your wife;
My ſuit is, that ſhe will to Deſdemona
Procure me ſome acceſs. *Shakeſp. Othello.*

Making ſo *bold*,
My fears forgetting manners, to unſeal
Their grand commiſſion. *Shakeſp. Hamlet.*

And were y' as good as George a Green,
I ſhall *make bold* to turn agen. *Hudibras, p.* ii. *c.* ii.

I durſt not *make* thus *bold* with Ovid, leſt ſome future Milbourn ſhould ariſe. *Dryden's Fables, Preface.*

Some men have the fortune to be eſteemed wits, only for *making bold* to ſcoff at theſe things, which the greateſt part of mankind reverence. *Tillotſon.*

To Bo'lden. *v. a.* [from *bold.*] To make bold; to give confidence.

Quick inventers, and fair ready ſpeakers, being *boldened* with their preſent abilities, to ſay more, and perchance better too, at the ſudden, for that preſent, than any other can do, uſe leſs help of diligence and ſtudy. *Aſcham's Schoolmaſter.*

I am much too vent'rous,
In tempting of your patience; but am *bolden'd*
Under your promis'd pardon. *Shakeſp. Henry* VIII.

Bo'ldface. *n. ſ.* [from *bold* and *face.*] Impudence; ſaucineſs; a term of reproach and reprehenſion.

How now, *boldface!* cries an old trot; ſirrah, we eat our own hens, I'd have you to know; and what you eat, you ſteal. *L'Eſtrange.*

Bo'ldfaced. *adj.* [from *bold* and *face.*] Impudent.

I have ſeen thoſe ſillieſt of creatures; and, ſeeing their rare works, I have ſeen enough to confute all the *boldfaced* atheiſts of this age. *Bramhall againſt Hobbes.*

Bo'ldly. *adv.* [from *bold.*]

1. In a bold manner; with courage; with ſpirit.

Thus we may *boldly* ſpeak, being ſtrengthened with the example of ſo reverend a prelate. *Hooker, b.* v. § 19.

I ſpeak to ſubjects, and a ſubject ſpeaks,
Stirr'd up by heav'n thus *boldly* for his king. *Shakeſp. R.* III.

2. It may perhaps be ſometimes uſed in a bad ſenſe, for *impudently.*

Bo'ldness. *n. ſ.* [from *bold.*]

1. Courage; bravery; intrepidity; ſpirit; fortitude; magnanimity; daringneſs.

Her horſe ſhe rid ſo, as might ſhew a fearful *boldneſs*, daring to do that, which ſhe knew not how to do. *Sidney, b.* ii.

2. Exemption from caution, and ſcrupulous nicety.

The *boldneſs* of the figures is to be hidden, ſometimes by the addreſs of the poet, that they may work their effect upon the mind. *Dryden's State of Innocence, Preface.*

3. Freedom; liberty.

Great is my *boldneſs* of ſpeech toward you; great is my glorying in you. 2 *Cor.* vii. 4.

4. Confident truſt in God..

Our fear excludeth not that *boldneſs* which becometh ſaints. *Hooker, b.* v. § 47.

We have *boldneſs* and acceſs with confidence, by the faith of him. *Epheſ.* iii. 12.

Having therefore *boldneſs* to enter into the holieſt by the blood of Jeſus. *Heb.* x. 19.

5. Aſſurance; freedom from fear.

Wonderful is the caſe of *boldneſs* in civil buſineſs; what firſt? *Boldneſs.* What ſecond, and third? *Boldneſs.* And yet *boldneſs* is a child of ignorance and baſeneſs, far inferiour to other parts. *Bacon's Eſſays*, N° 12.

Sure if the guilt were theirs, they could not charge thee
With ſuch a gallant *boldneſs:* if 'twere thine,
Thou couldſt not hear't with ſuch a ſilent ſcorn. *Denham.*

His diſtance, though it does not inſtruct him to think wiſer than other princes, yet it helps him to ſpeak with more *boldneſs* what he thinks. *Temple.*

Boldneſs is the power to ſpeak or do what we intend, before others, without fear or diſorder. *Locke.*

6. Impudence.

That moderation, which uſeth to ſuppreſs *boldneſs*, and to make them conquer that ſuffer. *Hooker, Dedication.*

BOLE. *n. ſ.*

1. The body or trunk of a tree.

All fell upon the high-hair'd oaks, and down their curled brows
Fell buſtling to the earth; and up went all the *boles* and boughs. *Chapman's Iliads.*

But

But when the ſmoother *bole* from knots is free,
We make a deep inciſion in the tree. *Dryden's Virgil, Georg.*
View well this tree, the queen of all the grove;
How vaſt her *bole*, how wide her arms are ſpread;
How high above the reſt ſhe ſhoots her head! *Dryden.*

2. A kind of earth.

Bole Armeniack is an aſtringent earth, which takes its name from Armenia, the country from which we have it. *Woodward.*

3. A meaſure of corn, containing ſix buſhels.

Of good barley put eight *boles*, that is, about ſix Engliſh quarters, in a ſtone trough. *Mortimer.*

BO'LIS. *n. ſ.* [Lat.]

Bolis is a great firy ball, ſwiftly hurried through the air, and generally drawing a tail after it. Ariſtotle calls it *capra*. There have often been immenſe balls of this kind. *Muſchenbrock.*

BOLL. *n. ſ.* A round ſtalk or ſtem; as, a *boll* of flax.

To BOLL. *v. n.* [from the noun.] To riſe in a ſtalk.

And the flax and the barley was ſmitten: for the barley was in the ear, and the flax was *bolled*. *Exodus*, ix. 31.

BO'LSTER. *n. ſ.* [bolꝼꞇne, Sax. *bolſter*, Dutch.]

1. Something laid on the bed, to raiſe and ſupport the head; commonly a bag filled with down or feathers.

Perhaps ſome cold bank is her *bolſter* now,
Or 'gainſt the rugged bark of ſome broad elm,
Leans her unpillow'd head. *Milton.*
This arm ſhall be a *bolſter* for thy head;
I'll fetch clean ſtraw to make a ſoldier's bed. *Gay.*

2. A pad, or quilt, to hinder any preſſure, or fill up any vacuity.

Up goes her hand, and off ſhe ſlips
The *bolſters* that ſupply her hips. *Swift.*

3. A pad, or compreſs, to be laid on a wound.

The bandage is the girt, which hath a *bolſter* in the middle, and the ends tacked firmly together. *Wiſeman's Surgery.*

4. In horſemanſhip.

The *bolſters* of a ſaddle are thoſe parts raiſed upon the bows, to hold the rider's thigh. *Farrier's Dict.*

To BO'LSTER. *v. a.* [from the noun.]

1. To ſupport the head with a bolſter.
2. To afford a bed to.

Mortal eyes do ſee them *bolſter*,
More than their own. *Shakeſp. Othello.*

3. To hold wounds together with a compreſs.

The practice of *bolſtering* the cheeks forward, does little ſervice to the wound, and is very uneaſy to the patient. *Sharp.*

4. To ſupport; to hold up; to maintain. This is now an expreſſion ſomewhat coarſe and obſolete.

We may be made wiſer by the publick perſuaſions grafted in men's minds, ſo they be uſed to further the truth, not to *bolſter* errour. *Hooker, b.* iii. § 4.

The lawyer ſets his tongue to ſale for the *bolſtering* out of unjuſt cauſes. *Hakewell on Providence.*

It was the way of many to *bolſter* up their crazy, doating conſciences with confidences. *South.*

BOLT. *n. ſ.* [*boult*, Dutch; βολὶς.]

1. An arrow; a dart ſhot from a croſsbow.

Yet mark'd I where the *bolt* of Cupid fell;
It fell upon a little weſtern flower;
Before milk white, now purple with love's wound.
Shakeſp. Midſummer Night's Dream.
The blunted *bolt* againſt the nymph he dreſt;
But, with the ſharp, transfix'd Apollo's breaſt. *Dryden.*

2. Lightning; a thunderbolt.

Sing'd with the flames, and with the *bolts* transfix'd,
With native earth your blood the monſters mix'd. *Dryden.*

3. *Bolt upright*; that is, upright as an arrow.

Bruſh-iron, native or from the mine, conſiſteth of long ſtriæ, about the thickneſs of a ſmall knitting needle, *bolt upright*, like the briſtles of a ſtiff bruſh. *Grew's Muſæum.*

As I ſtood *bolt upright* upon one end, one of the ladies burſt out. *Addiſon. Spectator*, N° 90.

4. The bar of a door, ſo called from being ſtrait like an arrow; we now ſay, *ſhoot the bolt*, when we ſpeak of faſtening or opening a door.

'Tis not in thee, to oppoſe the *bolt*
Againſt my coming in. *Shakeſp. King Lear.*

5. An iron to faſten the legs of a priſoner.

Away with him to priſon; lay *bolts* enough upon him.
Shakeſp. Meaſure for Meaſure.

6. A ſpot or ſtain. See BLOOD-BOLTERED.

That ſupernal judge, that ſtirs good thoughts
In my breaſt, of ſtrong authority,
To look into the *bolts* and ſtains of right. *Shakeſp. K. John.*

To BOLT. *v. a.* [from the noun.]

1. To ſhut or faſten with a bolt.

The *bolted* gates flew open at the blaſt;
The ſtorm ruſh'd in, and Arcite ſtood aghaſt. *Dryden.*

2. To blurt out, or throw out precipitantly.

I hate when vice can *bolt* her arguments,
And virtue has no tongue to check her pride. *Milton.*

3. To faſten, as a bolt or pin; to pin; to keep together.

That I could reach the axel, where the pins are,
Which *bolt* this frame; that I might pull them out. *B. Johnſ.*

4. To fetter; to ſhackle.

It is great
To do that thing that ends all other deeds,
Which ſhackles accidents, and *bolts* up change.
Shakeſp. Antony and Cleopatra.

5. To ſift; or ſeparate the parts of any thing with a ſieve. [*bluter*, Fr.]

Saying, he now had *boulted* all the flour,
And that it was a groom of baſe degree,
Which of my love was partner. *Fairy Queen, b.* ii. *c.* 4.

In the *bolting* and ſifting of fourteen years of power and favour, all that came out could not be pure meal. *Wotton.*

I cannot *bolt* this matter to the bran,
As Bradwardin and holy Auſtin can. *Dryden's Fables.*

6. To examine by ſifting; to try out; to lay open.

It would be well *bolted* out, whether great refractions may not be made upon reflections, as well as upon direct beams.
Bacon's Natural Hiſtory, N° 762.

The judge, or jury, or parties, or the council, or attornies, propounding occaſional queſtions, beats and *bolts* out the truth much better than when the witneſs delivers only a formal ſeries.
Hale's Hiſtory of the Common Law.

Time and nature will *bolt* out the truth of things, through all diſguiſes. *L'Eſtrange.*

7. To purify; to purge.

The fanned ſnow
That's *bolted* by the northern blaſt twice o'er. *Winter's Tale.*

To BOLT. *v. n.* To ſpring out with ſpeed and ſuddenneſs; to ſtart out with the quickneſs of an arrow.

This Puck ſeems but a dreaming dolt,
Still walking like a ragged colt,
And oft out of a buſh doth *bolt*,
Of purpoſe to deceive us. *Drayton's Nymphid.*

They erected a fort, and from thence they *bolted* like beaſts of the foreſt, ſometimes into the foreſt, ſometimes into the woods and faſtneſſes, and ſometimes back again to their den.
Bacon's War with Spain.

As the houſe was all in a flame, out *bolts* a mouſe from the ruins, to ſave herſelf. *L'Eſtrange.*

I have reflected on thoſe men, who, from time to time, have ſhot themſelves into the world. I have ſeen many ſucceſſions of them; ſome *bolting* out upon the ſtage with vaſt applauſe, and others hiſſed off. *Dryden.*

The birds to foreign ſeats repair'd,
And beaſts, that *bolted* out, and ſaw the foreſt bar'd. *Dryd.*

BOLT-ROPE. *n. ſ.* [from *bolt* and *rope*.] The rope on which the ſail of a ſhip is ſewed and faſtened. *Sea Dict.*

BO'LTER. *n. ſ.* [from the verb.] A ſieve to ſeparate meal from bran or huſks; or to ſeparate finer from coarſer parts.

Theſe hakes, and divers others of the fore-cited, are taken with threads, and ſome of them with the *bolter*, which is a ſpiller of a bigger ſize. *Carew's Survey of Cornwal.*

Dowlas, filthy dowlas: I have given them away to bakers wives, and they have made *bolters* of them. *Shakeſp. Henry* IV.

With a good ſtrong chopping-knife mince the two capons, bones and all, as ſmall as ordinary minced meat; put them into a large neat *bolter*. *Bacon's Natural Hiſt.* N° 46.

When ſuperciliouſly he ſifts
Through coarſeſt *bolter* others gifts. *Hudibras, p.* i. *c.* iii.

BO'LTHEAD. *n. ſ.* A long ſtrait-necked glaſs veſſel, for chymical diſtillations, called alſo a *matraſs*, or *receiver*.

This ſpirit abounds in ſalt, which may be ſeparted, by putting the liquour into a *bolthead*, with a long and narrow neck.
Boyle's Sceptical Chymiſtry.

BO'LTING-HOUSE. *n. ſ.* [from *bolt* and *houſe*.] The place where meal is ſifted.

The jade is returned as white, and as powdered, as if ſhe had been at work in a *bolting-houſe*. *Dennis's Letters.*

BO'LTSPRIT. } *n. ſ.* A maſt running out at the head of a ſhip,
BO'WSPRIT. } not ſtanding upright, but aſlope. The but-end of it is generally ſet againſt the foot of the foremaſt; ſo that they are a ſtay to one another. The length without board is ſufficient to let its ſails hang clear of all incumbrances. If the *boltſprit* fail in bad weather, the foremaſt cannot hold long after. *Bowſprit* is perhaps the right ſpelling. *Sea Dictionary.*

Sometimes I'd divide,
And burn in many places; on the topmaſt,
The yards, and *boltſprit*, would I flame diſtinctly. *Sh. Temp.*

BO'LUS. *n. ſ.* [βῶλος.] A form of medicine, in which the ingredients are made up into a ſoft maſs, larger than pills, to be ſwallowed at once.

Keep their bodies ſoluble the while by clyſters, lenitive *boluſes* of caſſia and manna, with ſyrup of violets. *Wiſeman.*

By poets we are well aſſur'd,
That love, alas! can ne'er be cur'd;
A complicated heap of ills,
Deſpiſing *boluſes* and pills. *Swift.*

BOMB. *n. ſ.* [*bombus*, Lat.]

1. A loud noiſe.

There was an upper chamber, which being thought weak, was ſupported by a pillar of iron, of the bigneſs of one's arm in the midſt; which, if you had ſtruck, would make a little flat noise in the room, but a great *bomb* in the chamber beneath. *Bacon's Natural Hist.* Nº 151.

2. A hollow iron ball, or shell, filled with gunpowder, and furnished with a vent for a fusee, or wooden tube, filled with combustible matter; to be thrown out from a mortar, which had its name from the noise it makes. The fusee, being set on fire, burns slowly till it reach the gunpowder, which goes off at once, bursting the shell to pieces with incredible violence; whence the use of *bombs* in besieging towns. The largest are about eighteen inches in diameter. By whom they were invented, is not known, and the time is uncertain, some fixing it to 1588, and others to 1495. *Chambers.*

The loud cannon missive iron pours,
And in the slaught'ring *bomb* Gradivus roars. *Rowe.*

To BOMB. *v. a.* [from the noun.] To fall upon with bombs; to bombard.

Our king thus trembles at Namur,
Whilst Villeroy, who ne'er afraid is,
To Bruxelles marches on secure,
To *bomb* the monks, and scare the ladies. *Prior.*

BOMB-CHEST. *n. s.* [from *bomb* and *chest.*] A kind of chest filled usually with bombs, and sometimes only with gunpowder, placed under ground, to tear and blow it up in the air, with those who stand on it. They are now much disused. *Chambers.*

BOMB-KETCH. } *n. s.* A kind of ship, strongly built, to bear
BOMB-VESSEL. } the shock of a mortar, when bombs are to be fired into a town.

Nor could an ordinary fleet, with *bomb-vessels*, hope to succeed against a place that has in its arsenal gallies and men of war. *Addison on Italy.*

BO'MBARD. *n. s.* [*bombardus*, Lat.] A great gun; a cannon: it is a word now obsolete.

They planted in divers places twelve great *bombards*, wherewith they threw huge stones into the air, which, falling down into the city, might break down the houses. *Knolles's History.*

To BOMBA'RD. *v. a.* [from the noun.] To attack with bombs.

A medal is struck on the English failing in their attempts on Dunkirk, when they endeavoured to blow up a fort, and *bombard* the town. *Addison on ancient Medals.*

BOMBARDI'ER. *n. s.* [from *bombard.*] The engineer whose employment it is to shoot bombs.

The *bombardier* tosses his balls sometimes into the midst of a city, with a design to fill all around him with terrour and combustion. *Tatler*, Nº 88.

BOMBA'RDMENT. *n. s.* [from *bombard.*] An attack made upon any city, by throwing bombs into it.

Genoa is not yet secure from a *bombardment*, though it is not so exposed as formerly. *Addison on Italy.*

BO'MBASIN. *n. s.* [*bombasin*, Fr.. from *bombycinus*, silken, Lat.] A slight silken stuff, for mourning.

BO'MBAST. *n. s.* [This word seems to be derived from *Bombastius*, one of the names of Paracelsus; a man remarkable for sounding professions, and unintelligible language.] Fustian; big words, without meaning.

Not pedants motley tongue, soldiers *bombast*,
Mountebanks drug-tongue, nor the terms of law,
Are strong enough preparatives to draw
Me to hear this. *Donne.*

Are all the flights of heroick poetry to be concluded *bombast*, unnatural, and mere madness, because they are not affected with their excellencies? *Dryden's State of Innocence, Preface.*

BO'MBAST. *adj.* [from the substantive.] High sounding; of big sound without meaning.

He, as loving his own pride and purpose,
Evades them with a *bombast* circumstance,
Horribly stuff'd with epithets of war. *Shakesp. Othello.*

BOMBILA'TION. *n. s.* [from *bombus*, Lat.] Sound; noise; report.

How to abate the vigour, or silence the *bombilation* of guns, a way is said to be by borax and butter, mixt in a due proportion, which will almost take off the report, and also the force of the charge. *Brown's Vulgar Errours, b.* ii. *c.* 5.

BOMBY'CINOUS. *adj.* [*bombycinus*, Lat.] Silken; made of silk. *D.*

BONA ROBA. n. s. [Ital. a fine gown.] A whore.

We knew where the *bona robas* were. *Shakesp. Henry* IV.

BONA'SUS. n. s. [Lat.] A kind of buffalo, or wild bull.

BONCHRE'TIEN. n. s. [French.] A species of pear, so called, probably, from the name of a gardener. See PEAR.

BOND. *n. s.* [bonb, Sax. *bound*; it is written indifferently, in many of its senses, *bond*, or *band.* See BAND.]

1. Cords, or chains, with which any one is bound.

There left me, and my man, both bound together;
Till, gnawing with my teeth my *bonds* asunder,
I gain'd my freedom. *Shakesp. Comedy of Errours.*

2. Ligament that holds any thing together.

Let any one send his contemplation to the extremities of the universe, and see, what conceivable hoops, what *bond* he can imagine to hold this mass of matter in so close a pressure together. *Locke.*

3. Union; connexion.

Observe, in working up the walls, that no side of the house, nor any part of the walls, be wrought up three feet above the other, before the next adjoining wall be wrought up to it, so that they may be all joined together, and make a good *bond.* *Mortimer's Husbandry.*

4. Chains; imprisonment; captivity.

Whom I perceived to have nothing laid to his charge, worthy of death, or of *bonds.* *Acts*, xxiii. 29.

5. Cement of union; cause of union; link of connexion.

Wedding is great Juno's crown;
O blessed *bond* of board and bed! *Shakesp. As you like it.*

Love cools, brothers divide, and the *bond* is cracked 'twixt son and father. *Shakesp. King Lear.*

6. A writing of obligation to pay a sum, or perform a contract.

Go with me to a notary, seal me there
Your single *bond.* *Shakesp. Merchant of Venice.*

What if I ne'er consent to make you mine;
My father's promise ties me not to time;
And *bonds* without a date, they say are void. *Dryden.*

7. Obligation; law by which any man is obliged.

Unhappy that I am! I cannot heave
My heart into my mouth: I love your majesty
According to my *bond*, no more nor less. *Shakesp. K. Lear.*

Take which you please, it dissolves the *bonds* of government and obedience. *Locke.*

BOND. *adj.* [from *bind*, perhaps for *bound*; from ᵹebonben, Saxon.] Captive; in a servile state.

Whether we be Jews or Gentiles, whether we be *bond* or free. 1 *Cor.* xii. 13.

BO'NDAGE. *n. s.* [from *bond.*] Captivity; imprisonment; state of restraint.

You only have overthrown me, and in my *bondage* consists my glory. *Sidney, b.* ii.

Say, gentle princess, would you not suppose
Your *bondage* happy, to be made a queen?—
—To be a queen in *bondage*, is more vile
Than is a slave in base servility. *Shakesp. Henry* VI. *p.* i.

Our cage
We make a choir, as doth the prison'd bird,
And sing our *bondage* freely. *Shakesp. Cymbeline.*

He must resolve by no means to be enslaved, and brought under the *bondage* of observing oaths, which ought to vanish, when they stand in competition with eating or drinking, or taking money. *South.*

The king, when he design'd you for my guard,
Resolv'd he would not make my *bondage* hard. *Dryden.*

If she has a struggle for honour, she is in a *bondage* to love; which gives the story its turn that way. *Pope; notes on Iliad.*

BO'NDMAID. *n. s.* [from *bond*, captive, and *maid.*] A woman slave.

Good sister, wrong me not, nor wrong yourself,
To make a *bondmaid* and a slave of me. *Shakesp. T. Shrew.*

BO'NDMAN. *n. s.* [from *bond* and *man.*] A man slave.

Amongst the Romans, in making of a *bondman* free, was it not wondered wherefore so great ado should be made; the master to present his slave in some court, to take him by the hand, and not only to say, in the hearing of the publick magistrate, I will that this man become free; but, after those solemn words uttered, to strike him on the cheek, to turn him round, the hair of his head to be shaved off, the magistrate to touch him thrice with a rod; in the end, a cap and a white garment given him. *Hooker, b.* iv. § 1.

O freedom! first delight of human kind;
Not that which *bondmen* from their masters find. *Dryden.*

BONDSE'RVANT. *n. s.* [from *bond* and *servant.*] A slave; a servant without the liberty of quitting his master.

And if thy brother, that dwelleth by thee, be waxen poor, and be sold unto thee; thou shalt not compel him to serve as a *bondservant.* *Lev.* xxv. 39.

BONDSE'RVICE. *n. s.* [from *bond* and *service.*] The condition of a bondservant; slavery.

Upon those did Solomon levy a tribute of *bondservice.* 1 *Kings*, ix. 21.

BO'NDSLAVE. *n. s.* [from *bond* and *slave.*] A man in slavery; a slave.

Love enjoined such diligence, that no apprentice, no, no *bondslave*, could ever be, by fear, more ready at all commandments, than that young princess was. *Sidney, b.* ii.

All her ornaments are taken away; of a freewoman she is become a *bondslave.* 1 *Mac.* ii. 11.

Commonly the *bondslave* is fed by his lord, but here the lord was fed by his *bondslave.* *Sir J. Davies on Ireland.*

BO'NDSMAN. *n. s.* [from *bond* and *man.*]

1. A slave.

Carnal greedy people, without such a precept, would have no mercy upon their poor *bondsmen* and beasts. *Derh. Ph. Theol.*

2. A person bound, or giving security for another.

BO'NDSWOMAN. *n. s.* [from *bond* and *woman.*] A woman slave.

My lords, the senators
Are sold for slaves, and their wives for *bondswomen.*
Ben. Johnson's Catiline.

BONE.

BONE. *n. s.* [ban, Saxon.]

1. The solid parts of the body of an animal are made up of hard fibres, tied one to another by small transverse fibres, as those of the muscles. In a fœtus they are porous, soft, and easily discerned. As their pores fill with a substance of their own nature, so they increase, harden, and grow close to one another. They are all spongy, and full of little cells, or are of a considerable firm thickness, with a large cavity, except the teeth; and where they are articulated, they are covered with a thin and strong membrane, called the periosteum. Each bone is much bigger at its extremity than in the middle, that the articulations might be firm, and the *bones* not easily put out of joint. But, because the middle of the *bone* should be strong, to sustain its alloted weight, and resist accidents, the fibres are there more closely compacted together, supporting one another; and the *bone* is made hollow, and consequently not so easily broken, as it must have been, had it been solid and smaller. *Quincy.*

Thy *bones* are marrowless, thy blood is cold. *Macbeth.*

There was lately a young gentleman bit to the *bone*. *Tatler.*

2. A fragment of meat; a bone with as much flesh as adheres to it.

Like Æsop's hounds, contending for the *bone*,
Each pleaded right, and would be lord alone. *Dryden.*

3. *To be upon the bones.* To attack.

Puss had a month's mind *to be upon the bones* of him, but was not willing to pick a quarrel. *L'Estrange.*

4. *To make no bones.* To make no scruple; a metaphor taken from a dog, who readily swallows meat that has no bones.

5. BONES. A sort of bobbins, made of trotter bones, for weaving bonelace.

6. BONES. Dice.

But then my study was to cog the dice,
And dext'rously to throw the lucky sice:
To shun ames ace that swept my stakes away;
And watch the box, for fear they should convey
False *bones*, and put upon me in the play. *Dryden's Pers.*

To BONE. *v. a.* [from the noun.] To take out the bones from the flesh.

BO'NELACE. *n. s.* [from *bone* and *lace*; the bobbins with which lace is woven being frequently made of bones.] Flaxen lace, such as women wear on their linen.

The things you follow, and make songs on now, should be sent to knit, or sit down to bobbins or *bonelace*. *Tatler.*

We destroy the symmetry of the human figure, and foolishly contrive to call off the eye from great and real beauties, to childish gewgaw ribbands and *bonelace*. *Spectator*, N° 99.

BO'NELESS. *adj.* [from *bone*.] Without bones.

I would, while it was smiling in my face,
Have pluckt my nipple from his *boneless* gums,
And dasht the brains out. *Shakesp. King Lear.*

To BO'NESET. *v. n.* [from *bone* and *set*.] To restore a bone out of joint to its place; or join a bone broken to the other part.

A fractured leg set in the country by one pretending to *bonesetting*. *Wiseman's Surgery.*

BO'NESETTER. *n. s.* [from *boneset*.] A chirurgeon; one who particularly professes the art of restoring broken or luxated bones.

At present my desire is only to have a good *bonesetter*. *Denham's Sophy.*

BO'NFIRE. *n. s.* [from *bon*, good, Fr. and *fire*.] A fire made for some publick cause of triumph or exultation.

Ring ye the bells to make it wear away,
And *bonfires* make all day. *Spenser's Epithalamium.*

How came so many *bonfires* to be made in queen Mary's days? Why, she had abused and deceived her people. *South.*

Full soon by *bonfire*, and by bell,
We learnt our liege was passing well. *Gay.*

BO'NGRACE. *n. s.* [*bonne grace*, Fr.] A forehead-cloth, or covering for the forehead. *Skinner.*

I have seen her beset all over with emeralds and pearls, ranged in rows about her cawl, her peruke, her *bongrace*, and chaplet. *Hakewell on Providence.*

BO'NNET. *n. s.* [*bonet*, Fr.] A covering for the head; a hat; a cap.

Go to them with this *bonnet* in thy hand,
And thus far having stretch'd it, here be with them,
Thy knee bussing the stones; for, in such business,
Action is eloquence. *Shakesp. Coriolanus.*

They had not probably the ceremony of veiling the *bonnet* in their salutations; for, in medals, they still have it on their heads. *Addison on ancient Medals.*

BO'NNET. [In fortification.] A kind of little ravelin, without any ditch, having a parapet three feet high, anciently placed before the points of the saliant angles of the glacis; being pallisadoed round: of late also used before the angles of bastions, and the points of ravelins.

BO'NNET *à prestre*, or priest's cap, is an outwork, having at the head three saliant angles, and two inwards. It differs from the double tenaille, because its sides, instead of being parallel, grow narrow at the gorge, and open wider at the front.

BO'NNETS. [In the sea language.] Small sails set on the courses on the mizzen, mainsail, and foresail of a ship, when these are too narrow or shallow to cloath the mast, or in order to make more way in calm weather. *Chambers.*

BO'NNILY. *adv.* [from *bonny*.] Gayly; handsomely; plumply.

BO'NNINESS. *n. s.* [from *bonny*.] Gayety; handsomeness; plumpness.

BO'NNY. *adj.* [from *bon*, *bonne*, Fr. It is a word now almost confined to the Scottish dialect.]

1. Handsome; beautiful.

Match to match I have encounter'd him,
And made a prey for carrion kites and crows,
Ev'n of the *bonny* beast he lov'd so well. *Shakesp. Henry VI.*
Thus wail'd the louts in melancholy strain,
Till *bonny* Susan sped across the plain. *Gay's Pastorals.*

2. Gay; merry; frolicksome; cheerful; blithe.

Then sigh not so, but let them go,
And be you blithe and *bonny*. *Shakesp. Much ado about N.*

3. It seems to be generally used in conversation for *plump*.

BONNY-CLABBER. *n. s.* A word used in some counties for sour buttermilk.

We scorn, for want of talk, to jabber,
Of parties o'er our *bonny-clabber*;
Nor are we studious to enquire,
Who votes for manours, who for hire. *Swift.*

BO'NUM MAGNUM. n. s. See PLUM; of which it is a species.

BO'NY. *adj.* [from *bone*.]

1. Consisting of bones.

At the end of this hole is a membrane, fastened to a round *bony* limb, and stretched like the head of a drum; and therefore, by anatomists, called *tympanum*. *Ray on the Creation.*

2. Full of bones.

BO'OBY. *n. s.* [a word of no certain etymology; *Henshaw* thinks it a corruption of *bull-beef* ridiculously; *Skinner* imagines it to be derived from *bobo*, foolish, Span. *Junius* finds *bowbard* to be an old Scottish word for a *coward*, a *contemptible fellow*; from which he naturally deduces *booby*; but the original of *bowbard* is not known.] A dull, heavy, stupid fellow; a lubber.

But one exception to this fact we find,
That *booby* Phaon only was unkind,
An ill-bred boatman, rough as waves and wind. *Prior.*
Young master next must rise to fill him wine,
And starve himself to see the *booby* dine. *King.*

BOOK. *n. s.* [boc, Sax. supposed from *boc*, a beech; because they wrote on beechen boards, as *liber* in Latin, from the rind of a tree.]

1. A volume in which we read or write.

See a *book* of prayer in his hand;
True ornaments to know a holy man. *Shakesp. Richard III.*
Receive the sentence of the law for sins,
Such as by God's *book* are adjudg'd to death. *Shakesp. Henry IV.*

But in the coffin that had the *books*, they were found as fresh as if they had been but newly written; being written on parchment, and covered over with watch candles of wax. *Bacon.*

Books are a sort of dumb teachers; they cannot answer sudden questions, or explain present doubts: this is properly the work of a living instructor. *Watts.*

2. A particular part of a work.

The first *book* we divide into sections; whereof the first is these chapters past. *Burnet's Theory of the Earth.*

3. The register in which a trader keeps an account of his debts.

This life
Is nobler than attending for a check;
Prouder, than rustling in unpaid for silk:
Such gain the cap of him that makes them fine,
Yet keeps his *book* uncross'd. *Shakesp. Cymbeline.*

4. *In books.* In kind remembrance.

I was so much *in his books*, that, at his decease, he left me the lamp by which he used to write his lucubrations. *Addison.*

5. *Without book.* By memory; by repetition; without reading.

Sermons read they abhor in the church; but sermons *without book*, sermons which spend their life in their birth, and may have publick audience but once. *Hooker, b. v. § 21.*

To BOOK. *v. a.* [from the noun.] To register in a book.

I beseech your grace, let it be *booked* with the rest of this day's deeds; or I will have it in a particular ballad else, with mine own picture on the top of it. *Shakesp. Henry IV. p. ii.*

He made wilful murder high treason; he caused the marchers to *book* their men, for whom they should make answer. *Davies on Ireland.*

BOOK-KEEPING. *n. s.* [from *book* and *keep*.] The art of keeping accounts, or recording the transactions of a man's affairs, in such a manner, that at any time he may thereby know the true state of the whole, or any part, of his affairs, with clearness and expedition. *Harris.*

BO'OKBINDER. *n. s.* [from *book* and *bind*.] A man whose profession it is to bind books.

BO'OKFUL. *adj.* [from *book* and *full*.] Full of notions gleaned from books; crouded with undigested knowledge.

The

The *bookful* blockhead, ignorantly read,
With loads of learned lumber in his head,
With his own tongue ſtill edifies his ears,
And always liſt'ning to himſelf appears. *Pope's Eſſ. on Crit.*

Bo'OKISH. *adj.* [from *book.*] Given to books; acquainted only with books. It is generally uſed contemptuouſly.

I'll make him yield the crown,
Whoſe *bookiſh* rule hath pull'd fair England down.
Shakeſp. Henry VI. *p.* ii.

I'm not *bookiſh*, yet I can read waiting gentlewomen in the 'ſcape. *Shakeſp. Winter's Tale.*

Xantippe follows the example of her nameſake; being married to a *bookiſh* man, who has no knowledge of the world.
Spectator, N° 482.

Bo'OKISHNESS. *n. ſ.* [from *bookiſh.*] Much application to books; over-ſtudiouſneſs.

BOOKLE'ARNED. *adj.* [from *book* and *learned.*] Verſed in books, or literature: a term implying ſome ſlight contempt.

Whate'er theſe *booklearn'd* blockheads ſay,
Solon's the veri'ſt fool in all the play. *Dryden's Perſius.*

He will quote paſſages out of Plato and Pindar, at his own table, to ſome *booklearned* companion, without bluſhing. *Swift.*

BOOKLE'ARNING. *n. ſ.* [from *book* and *learning.*] Skill in literature; acquaintance with books; a term of ſome contempt.

They might talk of *booklearning* what they would; but, for his part, he never ſaw more unſeaty fellows than great clerks.
Sidney.

Neither does it ſo much require *booklearning* and ſcholarſhip, as good natural ſenſe, to diſtinguiſh true and falſe, and to diſcern what is well proved, and what is not. *Burnet's Th. Earth.*

Bo'OKMAN. *n. ſ.* [from *book* and *man.*] A man whoſe profeſſion is the ſtudy of books.

This civil war of wits were much better us'd
On Navarre and his *bookmen*; for here 'tis abus'd.
Shakeſp. Love's Labour Loſt.

Bo'OKMATE. *n. ſ.* [from *book* and *mate.*] Schoolfellow.

This Armado is a Spaniard that keeps here in court,
A phantaſm, a monarch, and one that makes ſport
To the prince and his *bookmates*. *Shakeſp. Love's Labour Loſt.*

Bo'OKSELLER. *n. ſ.* [from *book* and *ſell.*] He whoſe profeſſion it is to ſell books.

He went to the *bookſeller*, and told him in anger, he had ſold a book in which there was falſe divinity.
Walton's Life of Biſhop Saunderſon.

Bo'OKWORM. *n. ſ.* [from *book* and *worm.*]

1. A worm or mite that eats holes in books, chiefly when damp.

My lion, like a moth or *bookworm*, feeds upon nothing but paper, and I ſhall beg of them to diet him with wholeſome and ſubſtantial food. *Guardian*, N° 114.

2. A ſtudent too cloſely given to books; a reader without judgment.

Among thoſe venerable galleries and ſolitary ſcenes of the univerſity, I wanted but a black gown, and a ſalary, to be as mere a *bookworm* as any there. *Pope's Letters.*

Bo'OLY. *n. ſ.* [an Iriſh term.]

All the Tartarians, and the people about the Caſpian ſea, which are naturally Scythians, live in herds; being the very ſame that the Iriſh *boolies* are, driving their cattle continually with them, and feeding only on their milk and white meats.
Spenſer's Ireland.

BOOM. *n. ſ.* [from *boom*, a tree, Dutch.]

1. [In ſea language.] A long pole uſed to ſpread out the clue of the ſtudding ſail; and ſometimes the clues of the mainſail and foreſail are boomed out.

2. Apole with buſhes or baſkets, ſet up as a mark to ſhew the ſailors how to ſteer in the channel, when a country is overflown.
Sea Dict.

3. A bar of wood laid croſs a harbour, to keep off the enemy.

As his heroick worth ſtruck envy dumb,
Who took the Dutchman, and who cut the *boom*. *Dryden.*

To BOOM. *v. n.* [from the noun. A ſea term.] To ruſh with violence; as a ſhip is ſaid to come *booming*, when ſhe makes all the ſail ſhe can.

Forſook by thee, in vain I ſought thy aid,
When *booming* billows clos'd above my head. *Pope's Odyſſ.*

BOON. *n. ſ.* [from bene, Sax. a petition.] A gift; a grant; a benefaction; a preſent.

Vouchſafe me for my meed but one fair look:
A ſmaller *boon* than this I cannot beg,
And leſs than this, I'm ſure, you cannot give.
Shakeſp. Two Gentlemen of Verona.

That courtier, who obtained a *boon* of the emperour, that he might every morning whiſper him in the ear, and ſay nothing, aſked no unprofitable ſuit for himſelf. *Bacon.*

The bluſt'ring fool has ſatisfy'd his will;
His *boon* is giv'n; his knight has gain'd the day,
But loſt the prize. *Dryden's Fables.*

What rhetorick didſt thou uſe,
To gain this mighty *boon*? ſhe pities me! *Addiſon's Cato.*

BOON. *adj.* [*bon*, Fr.] Gay; merry; as, a *boon* companion.

Satiate at length,
And heighten'd as with wine, jocund and *boon*,
Thus to herſelf ſhe pleaſingly began. *Parad. Loſt*, *b.* ix.

I know the infirmity of our family; we are apt to play the *boon* companion, and throw our money away in our cups.
Arbuthnot's Hiſt. of J. Bull.

BOOR. *n. ſ.* [*beer*, Dutch; ᵹebuꞃe, Sax.] A ploughman; a country fellow; a lout; a clown.

The bare ſenſe of a calamity is called grumbling; and if a man does but make a face upon the *boor*, he is preſently a malecontent. *L'Eſtrange.*

He may live as well as a *boor* of Holland, whoſe cares of growing ſtill richer waſte his life. *Temple.*

To one well-born, th' affront is worſe and more,
When he's abus'd and baffl'd by a *boor*. *Dryden.*

Bo'ORISH. *adj.* [from *boor.*] Clowniſh; ruſtick; untaught; uncivilized.

Therefore, you clown, abandon, which is in the vulgar, leave the ſociety, which, in the *booriſh*, is, company of this female. *Shakeſp. As you like it.*

Bo'ORISHLY. *adv.* [from *booriſh.*] In a booriſh manner; after a clowniſh manner.

Bo'ORISHNESS. *n. ſ.* [from *booriſh.*] Clowniſhneſs; ruſticity; coarſeneſs of manners.

BOOSE. *n. ſ.* [boꞅıᵹ, Sax.] A ſtall for a cow or an ox.

To BOOT. *v. a.* [*baten*, to profit, Dutch; boꞇ, in Saxon, is recompence, repentance, or fine paid by way of expiation; boꞇan is, to repent, or to compenſate; as,

He ıꞅ pıꞅ ꝥ bıꞇ and boꞇe,
Anꝺ beꞇ bıvoꞃen ꝺome.]

1. To profit; to advantage.

It ſhall not *boot* them, who derogate from reading, to excuſe it, when they ſee no other remedy; as if their intent were only to deny, that aliens and ſtrangers from the family of God are won, or that belief doth uſe to be wrought at the firſt in them, without ſermons. *Hooker*, *b.* v. § 22.

For what I have, I need not to repeat;
And what I want, it *boots* not to complain. *Shakeſp. R.* II.

If we ſhun
The purpos'd end, or here lie fixed all,
What *boots* it us theſe wars to have begun. *Fairfax*, *b.* i.

What *boots* the regal circle on his head,
That long behind he trails his pompous robe? *Pope.*

2. To enrich; to benefit.

And I will *boot* thee with what gift beſide,
That modeſty can beg. *Shakeſp. Ant. and Cleopatra.*

BOOT. *n. ſ.* [from the verb.]

1. Profit; gain; advantage.

My gravity,
Wherein, let no man hear me, I take pride,
Could I, with *boot*, change for an idle plume,
Which the air beats for vain. *Shakeſp. Meaſure for Meaſ.*

2. *To boot.* With advantage; over and above.

Canſt thou, O partial ſleep, give thy repoſe
To the wet ſeaboy, in an hour ſo rude:
And, in the calmeſt and the ſtilleſt night,
With all appliances, and means *to boot*,
Deny it to a king? *Shakeſp. Henry* IV. *p.* ii.

Man is God's image; but a poor man is
Chriſt's ſtamp *to boot*: both images regard. *Herbert.*

He might have his mind and manners formed, and he be inſtructed *to boot* in ſeveral ſciences. *Locke.*

3. It ſeems, in the following lines, uſed for *booty*, or plunder.

Others, like ſoldiers, armed in their ſtings,
Make *boot* upon the ſummer's velvet buds. *Shakeſp. Henry* V.

BOOT. *n. ſ.* [*bottas*, Armorick; *botes*, a ſhoe, Welch; *botte*, French.]

1. A covering for the leg, uſed by horſemen.

That my leg is too long—
—No; that it is too little.—
—I'll wear a *boot*, to make it ſomewhat rounder.
Shakeſp. Two Gentlemen of Verona.

Shew'd him his room, where he muſt lodge that night,
Pull'd off his *boots*, and took away the light. *Milton.*

Biſhop Wilkins ſays, he does not queſtion, but it will be as uſual for a man to call for his wings, when he is going a journey, as it is now to call for his *boots*. *Addiſon. Guardian.*

2. A kind of rack for the leg, formerly uſed in Scotland for torturing criminals.

BOOT *of a Coach.* The ſpace between the coachman and the coach.

To BOOT. *v. a.* [from the noun.] To put on boots.

Boot, *boot*, Maſter Shallow; I know the young king is ſick for me: let us take any man's horſes. *Shakeſp. Henry* IV. *p.* ii.

BOOT-HOSE. *n. ſ.* [from *boot* and *hoſe.*] Stockings to ſerve for boots; ſpatterdaſhes.

His lacquey with a linen ſtock on one leg, and a *boot-hoſe* on the other, gartered with a red and blue liſt.
Shakeſp. Taming of the Shrew.

BOOT-TREE. *n. ſ.* [from *boot* and *tree.*] Two pieces of wood, ſhaped like a leg, to be driven into boots, for ſtretching and widening them.

Bo'OTCATCHER. *n. ſ.* [from *boot* and *catch.*] The perſon whoſe buſineſs at an inn is to pull off the boots of paſſengers.

The oftler and the *bootcatcher* ought to partake. *Swift.*

Bo'oted. *adj.* [from *boot.*] In boots; in a horfeman's habit.

A *booted* judge fhall fit to try his caufe,
Not by the ftatute, but by martial laws. *Dryden's Juvenal.*

Booth. *n. f.* [*boed*, Dutch; *bwth*, Welch.] A houfe built of boards, or boughs, to be ufed for a fhort time.

The clothiers found means to have all the queft made of the northern men, fuch as had their *booths* ftanding in the fair. *Camden's Remains.*

Much mifchief will be done at Bartholomew fair, by the fall of a *booth*. *Swift's Predictions.*

Bo'otless. *adj.* [from *boot.*]

1. Ufelefs; unprofitable; unavailing; without advantage.

When thofe accurfed meffengers of hell
Came to their wicked man, and 'gan tell
Their *bootlefs* pains, and ill fucceeding night. *Fairy Q. b.* i.

God did not fuffer him, being defirous of the light of wifdom, with *bootlefs* expence of travel, to wander in darknefs. *Hooker, b.* i. *p.* 36.

Bootlefs fpeed,
When cowardice purfues, and valour flies. *Shakefpeare.*
Let him alone;
I'll follow him no more with *bootlefs* pray'rs:
He feeks my life. *Shakefp. Merchant of Venice.*

2. Without fuccefs; perhaps without booty; *Shakefpeare* having, in another place, ufed the word *boot* for *booty*.

Thrice from the banks of Wye,
And fandy bottom'd Severn, have I fent
Him *bootlefs* home, and weatherbeaten back. *Shakefp. H.* IV.

Bo'oty. *n. f.* [*buyt*, Dutch; *butin*, Fr.]

1. Plunder; pillage; fpoils gained from the enemy.

One way a band felect from forage drives
A herd of beeves, fair oxen, and fair kine,
Their *booty*. *Milton's Paradife Loft, b.* xi. *l.* 650.

His confcience is the hue and cry that purfues him; and when he reckons that he has gotten a *booty*, he has only caught a Tartar. *L'Eftrange.*

For, fhould you to extortion be inclin'd,
Your cruel guilt will little *booty* find. *Dryden's Juv. fat.* viii.

2. Things gotten by robbery.

If I had a mind to be honeft, I fee, fortune would not fuffer me; fhe drops *booties* in my mouth. *Shakefp. Winter's Tale.*

3. *To play booty.* To play difhoneftly, with an intent to lofe. The French ufe, *Je fuis botte*, when they mean to fay, *I will not go.*

We underftand what we ought to do; but when we deliberate, we *play booty* againft ourfelves: our confciences direct us one way, our corruptions hurry us another. *L'Eftrange.*

I have fet this argument in the beft light, that the ladies may not think I *write booty*. *Dryden.*

Bope'ep. *n. f.* [from *bo* and *peep.*] To look out, and draw back as if frighted, or with the purpofe to fright fome other.

Then they for fudden joy did weep,
And I for forrow fung,
That fuch a king fhould play *bopeep*,
And go the fools among. *Shakefp. King Lear.*

Rivers,
That ferve inftead of peaceful barriers,
To part th' engagements of their warriours,
Where both from fide to fide may fkip,
And only encounter at *bopeep*. *Hudibras, p.* iii. *c.* iii.

There the devil plays at *bopeep*, puts out his horns to do mifchief, then fhrinks them back for fafety. *Dryden's Span. Friar.*

BORA'CHIO. n. f. [*borracho*, Span.] A drunkard.

How you ftink of wine! D' ye think my niece will ever endure fuch a *borachio!* you're an abfolute *borachio*. *Congreve's Way of the World.*

Bo'rable. *adj.* [from *bore.*] That may be bored.

Bo'rage. *n. f.* [from *borago*, Lat.] A plant.

The leaves are broad and rough; the flowers confift of one leaf; are of a wheel fhape, and divided into five fegments, almoft to the bottom, which end in fharp points, like a ftar; the apices, in the middle of the flower, are fharp-pointed, and adhere together; the feeds are rough, and appear like a viper's head. This plant is often ufed in the kitchen, and for a cool tankard in the fummer time; and the flowers are ufed in medicinal cordials. *Millar.*

BO'RAMEZ. n. f. The Scythian lamb, generally known by the name of *Agnus Scythicus.*

Much wonder is made of the *boramez*, that ftrange plant-animal, or vegetable lamb of Tartary, which wolves delight to feed on; which hath the fhape of a lamb, affordeth a bloody juice upon breaking, and liveth while the plants be confumed about it. *Brown's Vulgar Errours, b.* iii. *c.* 27.

BO'RAX. n. f. [*borax*, low Latin.] An artificial falt, prepared from fal armoniac, nitre, calcined tartar, fea falt, and alum, diffolved in wine. It is principally ufed to folder metals, and fometimes an uterine ingredient in medicine. *Quincy.*

Bo'rdel. *n. f.* [*bordeel*, Teut. *bordel*, Armorick.] A brothel; a bawdyhoufe.

Making even his own houfe a ftews, a *bordel*, and a fchool of lewdnefs, to inftil vice into the unwary years of his poor children. *South.*

BO'RDER. *n. f.* [*bord*, Germ. *bord*, Fr.]

1. The outer part or edge of any thing.

They have, of Paris work, looking-glaffes, bordered with broad *borders* of cryftal, and great counterfeit precious ftones. *Bacon's Natural Hift.* N° 960.

The light muft ftrike on the middle, and extend its greateft clearnefs on the principal figures; diminifhing by degrees, as it comes nearer and nearer to the *borders*. *Dryden's Dufrefnoy.*

2. The march or edge of a country; the confine.

If a prince keep his refidence on the *border* of his dominions, the remote parts will rebel; but if he make the centre his feat, he fhall eafily keep them in obedience. *Spenfer.*

3. The outer part of a garment, generally adorned with needlework, or ornaments.

4. A bank raifed round a garden, and fet with flowers; a narrow rank of herbs or flowers.

There he arriving, round about doth fly
From bed to bed, from one to other *border*,
And takes furvey, with curious bufy eye,
Of every flower and herb there fet in order. *Spenfer's Muiop.*

All with a *border* of rich fruit trees crown'd,
Whofe loaded branches hide the lofty mound:
Such various ways the fpacious alleys lead,
My doubtful mufe knows not what path to tread. *Waller.*

To Bo'rder. *v. n.* [from the noun.]

1. To confine upon; to touch fomething elfe at the fide or edge.

It *bordereth* upon the province of Croatia, which, in time paft, was continual wars with the Turks garrifons. *Knolles's Hiftory of the Turks.*

Virtue and Honour had their temples *bordering* on each other, and are fometimes both on the fame coin. *Addifon.*

2. To approach nearly to.

All wit, which *borders* upon profanenefs, and makes bold with thofe things to which the greateft reverence is due, deferves to be branded with folly. *Tillotfon.*

To Bo'rder. *v. a.*

1. To adorn with a border of ornaments.

2. To reach; to touch; to confine upon.

Sheba and Raamah are thofe parts of Arabia, which *border* the fea called the Perfian gulf. *Raleigh's Hiftory.*

Bo'rderer. *n. f.* [from *border.*] He that dwells on the borders, extreme parts, or confines.

They of thofe marches, gracious fovereign!
Shall be a wall fufficient to defend
Our inland from the pilfering *borderers*. *Shakefp. Henry* V.

An ordinary horfe will carry two facks of fand; and, of fuch, the *borderers* on the fea do beftow fixty, at leaft in every acre; but moft hufbands double that number. *Carew's Survey.*

The eafieft to be drawn
To our fociety, and to aid the war:
The rather for their feat, being next *bord'rers*
On Italy; and that they abound with horfe. *B. Johnf. Catil.*

The king of Scots in perfon, with Perkin in his company, entered with a great army, though it chiefly confifted of *borderers*, being raifed fomewhat fuddenly. *Bacon's Henry* VII.

Volga's ftream
Sends oppofite, in fhaggy armour clad,
Her *borderers*; on mutual flaughter bent,
They rend their countries. *Philips.*

To Bo'rdrage. *v. n.* [from *border.*] To plunder the borders.

Long time in peace his realm eftablifhed,
Yet oft annoy'd with fundry *bordragings*
Of neighbour Scots, and foreign fcatterlings. *Fairy Q. b.* ii.

To BORE. *v. a.* [boɲian, Sax.] To pierce in a hole.

I'll believe as foon,
This whole earth may be *bor'd*; and that the moon
May through the centre creep. *Shakep. Midfum. Night's Dr.*

Mulberries will be fairer, if you *bore* the trunk of the tree through, and thruft, into the places *bored*, wedges of fome hot trees. *Bacon's Natural Hift.* N° 456.

Take the barrel of a long gun, perfectly *bored*, and fet it upright, and take a bullet exactly fit for it; and then if you fuck at the mouth of the barrel never fo gently, the bullet will come up fo forcibly, that it will hazard the ftriking out your teeth. *Digby on Bodies.*

But Capys, and the graver fort, thought fit
The Greeks fufpected prefent to commit
To feas or flames; at leaft, to fearch and *bore*
The fides, and what that fpace contains t'explore. *Denham.*

Thefe diminutive caterpillars are able, by degrees, to pierce or *bore* their way into a tree, with very fmall holes; which, after they are fully entered, grow together. *Ray.*

Confider, reader, what fatigues I've known,
What riots feen, what buftling crouds I *bor'd*,
How oft I crofs'd where carts and coaches roar'd. *Gay.*

To Bore. *v. n.*

1. To make a hole.

A man may make an inftrument to *bore* a hole an inch wide, or half an inch, and fo lefs; not to *bore* a hole of a foot. *Wilkins's Mathematical Magick.*

2. To pufh forward towards a certain point.

Thoſe milk paps,
That through the window lawn *bore* at men's eyes,
Are not within the leaf of pity writ. *Shakeſp. Timon.*

Nor ſouthward to the raining regions run;
But *boring* to the weſt, and hov'ring there,
With gaping mouths they draw prolifick air. *Dryden.*

To **Bore.** *v. n.* [with farriers.] Is when a horſe carries his noſe near the ground. *Dict.*

Bore. *n. ſ.* [from the verb.]

1. The hole made by boring.

Into hollow engines long and round,
Thick ramm'd, at th' other *bore* with touch of fire
Dilated, and infuriate. *Milton's Paradiſe Loſt, b.* vi.

We took a cylindrical pipe of glaſs, whoſe *bore* was about a quarter of an inch in diameter. *Boyle.*

2. The inſtrument with which a hole is bored.

So ſhall that hole be fit for the file, or ſquare *bore*, if the curioſity of your propoſed work cannot allow it to paſs without filing. *Moxon's Mechanical Exerciſes.*

3. The ſize of any hole.

Our careful monarch ſtands in perſon by,
This new-caſt cannon's firmneſs to explore;
The ſtrength of big-corn'd powder loves to try,
And ball and cartridge ſorts for every *bore*. *Dryden.*

It will beſt appear in the *bores* of wind inſtruments; therefore cauſe pipes to be made with a ſingle, double, and ſo on, to a ſextuple *bore*; and mark what tone every one giveth. *Bacon.*

Bore. The *preterite* of *bear*.

The father *bore* it with undaunted ſoul,
Like one who durſt his deſtiny controul;
Yet with becoming grief he *bore* his part,
Reſign'd his ſon, but not reſign'd his heart. *Dryden.*

'Twas my fate
To kill my father, and pollute his bed,
By marrying her who *bore* me. *Dryden and Lee's OEdipus.*

Bo'real. *adj.* [*borealis*, Lat.] Northern.

Crete's ample fields diminiſh to our eye;
Before the *boreal* blaſts the veſſels fly. *Pope's Odyſſey.*

Bo'reas. *n. ſ.* [Lat.] The north wind.

Boreas, and Cærias, and Argeſtas loud,
And Thraſcias, rend the woods, and ſeas up-turn.
Milton's Paradiſe Loſt, b. x. *l.* 699.

Bo'ree. *n. ſ.* A kind of dance.

Dick could neatly dance a jig,
But Tom was beſt at *borees*. *Swift.*

Bo'rer. *n. ſ.* [from *bore*.] A piercer; an inſtrument to make holes with.

The maſter-bricklayer muſt try all the foundations, with a *borer*, ſuch as well-diggers uſe, to try what ground they have. *Moxon's Mechanical Exerciſes.*

Born. The *participle paſſive* of *bear*.

Their charge was always *born* by the queen, and duly paid out of the exchequer. *Bacon.*

The great men were enabled to oppreſs their inferiours; and their followers were *born* out and countenanced in wicked actions. *Sir John Davies on Ireland.*

Upon ſome occaſions, Clodius may be bold and inſolent, *born* away by his paſſion. *Swift.*

To be **Born.** *v. n. paſſ.* [derived from the word to *bear*, in the ſenſe of *bringing forth*; as, my mother *bore* me twenty years ago; or, I was *born* twenty years ago.]

1. To come into life.

When we are *born*, we cry, that we are come
To this great ſtage of fools. *Shakeſp. King Lear.*

Nor nature's law with fruitleſs ſorrow mourn,
But die, O mortal man! for thou waſt *born*. *Prior.*

All that are *born* into the world, are ſurrounded with bodies, that perpetually and diverſly affect them. *Locke.*

2. It is uſually ſpoken with regard to circumſtances; as, he was *born* a prince; he was *born* to empire; he was *born* for greatneſs; that is, formed at the birth.

The ſtranger that dwelleth with you, ſhall be unto you as one *born* among you, and thou ſhalt love him as thyſelf. *Levit.* xix. 34.

Yet man is *born* unto trouble, as the ſparks fly upward. *Job*, v. 7.

A friend loveth at all times, and a brother is *born* for adverſity. *Prov.* xvii. 17.

The new *born* babe by nurſes overlaid. *Dryden.*

Either of you knights may well deſerve
A princeſs *born*; and ſuch is ſhe you ſerve. *Dryden's Fab.*

Two riſing creſts his royal head adorn;
Born from a god, himſelf to godhead *born*. *Dryden's Æn.*

Both muſt alike from heav'n derive their light;
Theſe *born* to judge, as well as thoſe to write. *Pope.*

For all mankind alike require their grace;
All *born* to want; a miſerable race! *Pope's Odyſſey.*

I was *born* to a good eſtate, although it now turneth to little account. *Swift's Story of an injured Lady.*

Their lands are let to lords, who never deſigned to be tenants, naturally murmur at the payment of rents, as a ſubſerviency they were not *born* to. *Swift.*

3. It has uſually the particle *of* before the mother.

Be bloody, bold, and reſolute, laugh to ſcorn
The pow'r of man; for none *of* woman *born*
Shall harm Macbeth. *Shakeſp. Macbeth.*

I being *born of* my father's firſt wife, and ſhe *of* his third, ſhe converſes with me rather like a daughter than a ſiſter. *Tatler.*

Bo'rough. *n. ſ.* [bophoe, Saxon.]

1. It ſignified anciently a ſurety, or a man bound for others.

A *borough*, as I here uſe it, and as the old laws ſtill uſe, is not a borough town, that is, a franchiſed town; but a main pledge of an hundred free perſons, therefore called a free *borough*, or, as you ſay, *francplegium*. For *borth*, in old Saxon, ſignifieth a pledge or ſurety; and yet it is ſo uſed with us in ſome ſpeeches, as Chaucer ſaith, *St. John to Borch*; that is, for aſſurance and warranty. *Spenſer's Ireland.*

2. A town with a corporation.

Bo'rough *Engliſh*, is a cuſtomary deſcent of lands or tenements, whereby, in all places where this cuſtom holds, lands and tenements deſcend to the youngeſt ſon; or, if the owner have no iſſue, to his youngeſt brother. *Cowel.*

Bo'rrel. *n. ſ.* [it is explained by *Junius* without etymology.] A mean fellow.

Siker thou ſpeak'ſt like a lewd ſorrel,
Of heaven, to deemen ſo:
Howbe I am but rude and *borrel*,
Yet nearer ways I know. *Spenſer's Paſt.*

To **BO'RROW.** *v. a.* [*borgen*, Dutch; bopgian, Saxon.]

1. To take ſomething from another upon credit.

He *borrowed* a box of the ear of the Engliſhman, and ſwore he would pay him again when he was able. *Shakeſp. Merchant of Venice.*

We have *borrowed* money for the king's tribute, and that upon our lands and vineyards. *Neh.* v. 4.

2. To aſk of another the uſe of ſomething for a time.

Then he ſaid, go, *borrow* thee veſſels abroad of all thy neighbours. 2 *Kings*, iv. 3.

Where darkneſs and ſurprize made conqueſt cheap!
Where virtue *borrowed* the arms of chance,
And ſtruck a random blow! *Dryden's Span. Friar.*

3. To take ſomething of another.

A *borrow'd* title haſt thou bought too dear;
Why didſt thou tell me that thou wert a king? *Sh. H.* IV.

They may *borrow* ſomething of inſtruction even from their paſt guilt. *Decay of Piety.*

I was engaged in the tranſlation of Virgil, from whom I have *borrowed* only two months. *Dryden's Dufreſn.*

Theſe verbal ſigns they ſometimes *borrow* from others, and ſometimes make themſelves; as one may obſerve among the new names children give to things. *Locke.*

Some perſons of bright parts have narrow remembrance; for having riches of their own, they are not ſolicitous to *borrow*. *Watts's Improvement of the Mind.*

4. To uſe as one's own, though not belonging to one.

Unkind and cruel, to deceive your ſon
In *borrow'd* ſhapes, and his embrace to ſhun. *Dryden's Æn.*

Bo'rrow. *n. ſ.* [from the verb.] The thing borrowed.

Yet of your royal preſence I'll adventure
The *borrow* of a week. *Shakeſp. Winter's Tale.*

Bo'rrower. *n. ſ.* [from *borrow*.]

1. He that borrows; he that takes money upon truſt.

His talk is of nothing but of his poverty, for fear belike leſt I ſhould have proved a young *borrower*. *Sidney, b.* ii.

Neither a *borrower* nor a lender be;
For loan oft loſes both itſelf and friend,
And borrowing dulls the edge of huſbandry. *Hamlet.*

Go not, my horſe, the better;
I muſt become a *borrower* of the night
For a dark hour or twain. *Shakeſp. Macbeth.*

But you invert the cov'nants of her truſt,
And harſhly deal, like an ill *borrower*,
With that which you receiv'd on other terms. *Milton.*

2. He that takes what is another's, and uſes it as his own.

Some ſay, that I am a great *borrower*; however, none of my creditors have challenged me for it. *Pope.*

Bo'scage. *n. ſ.* [*boſcage*, Fr.] Wood, or woodlands; repreſentation of woods.

We bent our courſe thither, where we ſaw the appearance of land; and, the next day, we might plainly diſcern that it was a land flat to our ſight, and full of *boſcage*, which made it ſhew the more dark. *Bacon's N. Atlantis.*

Chearful paintings in feaſting and banqueting rooms; graver ſtories in galleries; landſkips and *boſcage*, and ſuch wild works, in open terraces, or ſummer-houſes. *Wotton.*

Bo'sky. *adj.* [*boſque*, Fr.] Woody.

And with each end of thy blue bow do'ſt crown
My *boſky* acres, and my unſhrub'd down. *Shakeſp. Tempeſt.*

I know each land, and every alley green,
Dingle, or buſhy dell, of this wild wood,
And every *boſky* bourn from ſide to ſide. *Milton.*

BO'SOM. *n. ſ.* [boſme, boſom, Saxon.]

1. The embrace of the arms holding any thing to the breaſt.

2. The breaſt; the heart.

Our good old friend,
Lay comforts to your *boſom*; and beſtow
Your needful counſel to our buſineſſes. *Shakeſp. King Lear.*

3. The incloſure.

Unto laws thus made and received by a whole church, they which live within the *boſom* of that church, muſt not think it a matter indifferent, either to yield, or not to yield, obedience. *Hooker, b.* ii.

4. The folds of the dreſs that cover the breaſt.

Put now thy hand into thy *boſom*; and he put his hand into his *boſom*: and when he took it out, behold his hand was leprous as ſnow. *Exodus*, iv. 6.

5. The tender affections; kindneſs; favour.

Whoſe age has charms in it, whoſe title more,
To pluck the common *boſoms* on his ſide. *Shakeſp. K. Lear.*

To whom the great Creator thus reply'd:
O Son, in whom my ſoul hath chief delight;
Son of my *boſom*, Son who art alone
My word, my wiſdom, and effectual might. *Par. Loſt, b.* iii.

6. Inclination; deſire.

If you can pace your wiſdom
In that good path that I could wiſh it go,
You ſhall have your *boſom* on this wretch.
Shakeſp. Meaſure for Meaſure.

BOSOM, in compoſition, implies intimacy; confidence; a fondneſs.

No more that thane of Cawder ſhall deceive
Our *boſom-int'reſt*; go, pronounce his death. *Macbeth.*

This Antonio,
Being the *boſom-lover* of my lord,
Muſt needs be like my lord. *Shakeſp. Merchant of Venice.*

Thoſe domeſtick traitors, *boſom-thieves*,
Whom cuſtom hath call'd wives; the readieſt helps
To betray the heady huſbands, rob the eaſy.
Ben. Johnſon's Catiline.

He ſent for his *boſom-friends*, with whom he moſt confidently conſulted, and ſhewed the paper to them; the contents whereof he could not conceive. *Clarendon.*

The fourth privilege of friendſhip is that which is here ſpecified in the text, a communication of ſecrets. A *boſom-ſecret*, and a *boſom-friend*, are uſually put together. *South.*

She who was a *boſom-friend* of her royal miſtreſs, he calls an inſolent woman, the worſt of her ſex. *Addiſon's Whig Exam.*

To BO'SOM. *v. a.* [from the noun.]

1. To incloſe in the boſom.

Boſom up my counſel;
You'll find it wholeſome. *Shakeſp. Henry* VIII.

I do not think my ſiſter ſo to ſeek,
Or ſo unprincipl'd in virtue's book,
And the ſweet peace that *boſoms* goodneſs ever. *Milton.*

2. To conceal in privacy.

The groves, the fountains, and the flow'rs,
That open now their choiceſt *boſom'd* ſmells,
Reſerv'd for night, and kept for thee in ſtore. *Par. Loſt, b.* v.

Towers and battlements it ſees,
Boſom'd high in tufted trees,
Where perhaps ſome beauty lies,
The cynoſure of neighbouring eyes. *Milton.*

To happy convents, *boſom'd* deep in vines,
Where ſlumber abbots, purple as their wines. *Pope.*

BO'SON. *n. ſ.* [corrupted from *boatſwain.*]

The barks upon the billows ride,
The maſter will not ſtay;
The merry *boſon* from his ſide
His whiſtle takes, to check and chide
The ling'ring lad's delay. *Dryden's Albion.*

BOSS. *n. ſ.* [*boſſe*, Fr.]

1. A ſtud; an ornament raiſed above the reſt of the work; a ſhining prominence.

What ſignifies beauty, ſtrength, youth, fortune, embroidered furniture, or gaudy *boſſes*? *L'Eſtrange.*

This ivory was intended for the *boſſes* of a bridle, was laid up for a prince, and a woman of Caria or Mæonia dyed it.
Pope's Notes on Iliad.

2. The part riſing in the midſt of any thing.

He runneth upon him, even on his neck, upon the thick *boſſes* of his bucklers. *Job*, xv. 26.

3. A thick body of any kind.

A *boſs* made of wood, with an iron hook, to hang on the laths, or on a ladder, in which the labourer puts the mortar at the britches of the tiles. *Moxon's Mechanical Exerciſes.*

If a cloſe appulſe be made by the lips, then is framed M; if by the *boſs* of the tongue to the palate, near the throat, then K.
Holder's Elements of Speech.

BO'SSAGE. *n. ſ.* [in architecture.]

1. Any ſtone that has a projecture, and is laid in a place in a building, to be afterwards carved.

2. Ruſtick work, which conſiſts of ſtones, which ſeem to advance beyond the naked of a building, by reaſon of indentures or channels left in the joinings: theſe are chiefly in the corners of edifices, and called ruſtick quoins. *Builder's Dict.*

BO'SVEL. *n. ſ.* A ſpecies of *crowfoot*; which ſee.

BOTA'NICAL. } *adj.* [from βοτάνη, an herb.] Relating to herbs;
BOTA'NICK. } ſkilled in herbs.

Some *botanical* criticks tell us, the poets have not rightly followed the traditions of antiquity, in metamorphoſing the ſiſters of Phaeton into poplars. *Addiſon on Italy.*

BO'TANIST. *n. ſ.* [from *botany.*] One ſkilled in plants; one who ſtudies the various ſpecies of plants.

The uliginous lacteous matter, taken notice of by that diligent *botaniſt*, was only a collection of corals. *Woodward.*

Then ſpring the living herbs, beyond the power
Of *botaniſt* to number up their tribes. *Thomſon's Spring.*

BOTANO'LOGY. *n. ſ.* [βοτανολογία.] A diſcourſe upon plants. *D.*

BO'TANY. *n. ſ.* [from βοτάνη, an herb.] The ſcience of plants; that part of natural hiſtory which relates to vegetables.

BOTA'RGO. n. ſ. [*botarga*, Span.] A reliſhing ſort of food, made of the roes of the mullet fiſh; much uſed on the coaſts of the Mediterranean, as an incentive to drink. *Chambers.*

BOTCH. *n. ſ.* [*bozza*, pronounced *botza*, Ital.]

1. A ſwelling, or eruptive diſcoloration of the ſkin.

Time, which rots all, and makes *botches* pox,
And, plodding on, muſt make a calf an ox,
Hath made a lawyer. *Donne.*

Botches and blains muſt all his fleſh imboſs,
And all his people. *Milton's Paradiſe Loſt, b.* xii. *l.* 180.

It proves far more incommodious, which, if it were propelled in boils, *botches*, or ulcers, as in the ſcurvy, would rather conduce to health. *Harvey on Conſumptions.*

2. A part in any work ill finiſhed, ſo as to appear worſe than the reſt.

With him,
To leave no rubs or *botches* in the work,
Fleance, his ſon, muſt embrace the fate. *Shakeſp. Macbeth.*

3. An adſcititious, adventitious part clumſily added.

If both thoſe words are not notorious *botches*, I am much deceived; though the French tranſlator thinks otherways.
Dryden's Dedication, Æneid.

A comma ne'er could claim
A place in any Britiſh name;
Yet, making here a perfect *botch*,
Thruſts your poor vowel from his notch. *Swift.*

To BOTCH. *v. a.* [from the noun.]

1. To mend or patch cloaths clumſily.

Their coats, from *botching* newly brought, are torn. *Dryden.*

2. To mend any thing awkwardly.

To *botch* up what th' had torn and rent,
Religion and the government. *Hudibras, p.* iii. *c.* ii.

3. To put together unſuitably, or unſkilfully; to make up of unſuitable pieces.

Go with me to my houſe,
And hear thou there, how many fruitleſs pranks
This ruffian hath *botch'd* up, that thou thereby
May ſmile at this. *Shakeſp. Twelfth Night.*

Her ſpeech is nothing,
Yet the unſhaped uſe of it doth move
The hearers to collection; they aim at it,
And *botch* the words up fit to their own thoughts. *Hamlet.*

For treaſon *botch'd* in rhyme will be thy bane;
Rhime is the rock on which thou art to wreck. *Dryden.*

4. To mark with botches.

Young Hylas, *botch'd* with ſtains too foul to name,
In cradle here renews his youthful frame. *Garth's Diſpenſ.*

BO'TCHER. *n. ſ.* [from *botch.*] A mender of old cloaths; the ſame to a taylor as a cobler to a ſhoemaker.

He was a *botcher's* prentice in Paris, from whence he was whipt for getting the ſheriff's fool with child.
Shakeſp. All's well that ends well.

Botchers left old cloaths in the lurch,
And fell to turn and patch the church. *Hudibras, c.* ii.

BO'TCHY. *adj.* [from *botch.*] Marked with botches.

And thoſe boils did run—ſay ſo—Did not the general run?
Were not that a *botchy* ſore? *Shakeſp. Troilus and Creſſ.*

BOTE. *n. ſ.* [bote, Sax. a word now out of uſe.]

1. A compenſation or amends for a man ſlain, which is bound to another. *Cowel.*

2. It was uſed for any payment.

BOTH. *adj.* [baτu, baτþa, Sax.] The two; as well the one as the other. *Et l'un & l'autre*, Fr. It is uſed only of two.

And the next day, *both* morning and afternoon, he was kept by our party. *Sidney, b.* ii.

Moſes and the prophets, Chriſt and his apoſtles, were in their times all preachers of God's truth; ſome by word, ſome by writing; ſome by *both*. *Hooker, b.* v. § 19.

Which of them ſhall I take?
Both? one? or neither? neither can be enjoy'd,
If *both* remain alive. *Shakeſp. King Lear.*

Two lovers cannot ſhare a ſingle bed;
As therefore *both* are equal in degree,
The lot of *both* he left to deſtiny. *Dryden's Fables.*

A Venus and a Helen have been ſeen,
Both perjur'd wives, the goddeſs and the queen. *Granville.*

BOTH. *conj.* [from the adjective.] As well: it has the conjunction *and* to correſpond with it.

Both the boy was worthy to be prais'd,
And Stimichon has often made me long,
To hear, like him, ſo ſoft, ſo ſweet a ſong. *Dryden's Paſt.*

Bo'TRYOID. *adj.* [βοτρυοειδής.] Having the form of a bunch of grapes.

The outſide is thick ſet with *botryoid* effloreſcencies, or ſmall knobs, yellow, bluiſh, and purple; all of a ſhining metallick hue. *Woodward of Foſſils.*

Bots. *n. ſ.* [*without a ſingular.*] A ſpecies of ſmall worms in the entrails of horſes; anſwering, perhaps, to the *aſcarides* in human bodies.

Peaſe and beans are as dank here as a dog, and that is the next way to give poor jades the *bots:* this houſe is turned upſide down ſince Robin the oſtler died. *Shakeſp. Henry* IV. *p.* i.

BOTTLE. *n. ſ.* [*bouteille*, Fr.]

1. A ſmall veſſel of glaſs, or other matter, with a narrow mouth, to put liquour in.

The ſhepherd's homely curds,
His cold thin drink out of his leather *bottle*,
Is far beyond a prince's delicates. *Shakeſp. Henry* VI. *p.* iii.

Many have a manner, after other men's ſpeech, to ſhake their heads. A great officer would ſay, it was as men ſhake a *bottle*, to ſee if there was any wit in their heads, or no. *Bacon.*

Then if thy ale in glaſs thou wouldſt confine,
Let thy clean *bottle* be entirely dry. *King's Molly of Mount.*

He threw into the enemy's ſhips earthen *bottles* filled with ſerpents, which put the crew in diſorder, and made them fly. *Arbuthnot on Coins.*

2. A quantity of wine uſually put into a bottle; a quart.

Sir, you ſhall ſtay, and take t'other *bottle*. *Spect.* N° 462.

3. A quantity of hay or graſs bundled up.

Methinks I have a great deſire to a *bottle* of hay; good hay, ſweet hay, hath no fellow. *Shakeſp. Midſum. Night's Dream.*

But I ſhould wither in one day, and paſs
To a lock of hay, that am a *bottle* of graſs. *Donne.*

To Bo'ttle. *v. a.* [from the noun.] To incloſe in bottles.

You may have it a moſt excellent cyder royal, to drink or to *bottle*. *Mortimer's Husbandry.*

When a hogſhead of wine is to be *bottled* off, waſh your bottles immediately before you begin; but be ſure not to drain them. *Swift's Directions to the Butler.*

Bo'ttle is often compounded with other words; as, *bottle-friend*, a drinking friend; *bottle-companion*.

Sam, who is a very good *bottle-companion*, has been the diverſion of his friends. *Addiſon. Spect.* N° 89.

Bo'ttleflower. *n. ſ.* [*cyanus*, Lat.] A plant.

It hath a ſquamoſe hairy calyx; the diſk of the flower is almoſt plain, but the outer florets, round the borders, are large, tubulous, and deeply cut in; theſe outer florets are always barren; but the inner florets have a ſingle naked ſeed ſucceeding each. The ſpecies are, 1. The greater broad-leaved *blue-bottle*, commonly called *globe-flower*. 2. The greater narrow-leaved *blue bottle*, or *globe-flower*. 3. The purple *ſweet ſultan*. 4. *Corn-bottle*, with a white flower. The firſt and ſecond ſorts are abiding plants, which increaſe greatly by their creeping roots. The *ſweet ſultans* will begin to flower, and continue till the froſt prevents them. The *corn-bottles* were alſo annuals, which, for the diverſity of their flowers, were propagated in gardens; but of late years they are almoſt excluded. *Millar.*

Bo'ttlescrew. *n. ſ.* [from *bottle* and *ſcrew*.] A ſcrew to pull out the cork.

A good butler always breaks off the point of his *bottleſcrew* in two days, by trying which is hardeſt, the point of the ſcrew, or the neck of the bottle. *Swift.*

BO'TTOM. *n. ſ.* [botm, Saxon; *bodem*, Germ.]

1. The loweſt part of any thing.

2. The ground under the water.

Shallow brooks that flow'd ſo clear,
The *bottom* did the top appear. *Dryden.*

3. The foundation; the ground-work.

On this ſuppoſition my reaſonings proceed, and cannot be affected by objections which are far from being built on the ſame *bottom*. *Atterbury.*

4. A dale; a valley; a low ground.

In the purlieus ſtands a ſheep-cote,
Weſt of this place; down in the neighbour *bottom*. *Shakeſp. As you like it.*

On both the ſhores of that fruitful *bottom*, which I have before mentioned, are ſtill to be ſeen the marks of ancient edifices. *Addiſon on Italy.*

Equal convexity could never be ſeen: the inhabitants of ſuch an earth could have only the proſpect of a little circular plane, which would appear to have an acclivity on all ſides; ſo that every man would fancy himſelf the loweſt, and that he always dwelt and moved in a *bottom*. *Bentley.*

5. The part moſt remote from the view; the deepeſt part.

His propoſals and arguments ſhould with freedom be examined to the *bottom*, that, if there be any miſtake in them, no body may be miſled by his reputation. *Locke.*

6. Bound; limit.

But there's no *bottom*, none,
In my voluptuouſneſs. *Shakeſp. Macbeth.*

*

7. The utmoſt extent or profundity of any man's capacity, whether deep or ſhallow.

As I return, I will fetch off theſe juſtices: I do ſee the *bottom* of Juſtice Shallow: how ſubject we old men are to the vice of lying! *Shakeſp Henry* IV. *p.* ii.

8. The laſt reſort; the remoteſt cauſe; firſt motion.

He wrote many things which are not publiſhed in his name; and was at the *bottom* of many excellent counſels, in which he did not appear. *Addiſon.*

9. A ſhip; a veſſel for navigation.

A bawbling veſſel was he captain of,
With which, ſuch ſcathful grapple did he make
With the moſt noble *bottom* of our fleet. *Shakeſp. T. Night.*

My ventures are not in one *bottom* truſted;
Nor to one place. *Shakeſp. Merchant of Venice.*

We have memory, not of one ſhip that ever returned, and but of thirteen perſons only, at ſeveral times, that choſe to return in our *bottoms*. *Bacon's New Atlantis.*

He's a fooliſh ſeaman,
That when his ſhip is ſinking, will not
Unlade his hopes into another *bottom*. *Denham's Sophy.*

He puts to ſea upon his own *bottom*; holds the ſtern himſelf; and now, if ever, we may expect new diſcoveries. *Norris.*

He ſpreads his canvas, with his pole he ſteers,
The freights of flitting ghoſts in his thin *bottom* bears. *Dryd.*

10. A chance; an adventure; or ſecurity.

He began to ſay, that himſelf and the prince were too much to venture in one *bottom*. *Clarendon, b.* viii.

We are embarked with them on the ſame *bottom*, and muſt be partakers of their happineſs or miſery. *Spect.* N° 273.

11. A ball of thread wound up together.

This whole argument will be like *bottoms* of thread, cloſe wound up. *Bacon's War with Spain.*

The ſilkworms finiſh their *bottoms* in about fifteen days. *Mortimer's Husbandry.*

Each Chriſtmas they accounts did clear,
And wound their *bottom* round the year. *Prior.*

12. Bottom *of a lane.* The loweſt end.

13. Bottom *of beer.* The grounds, or dregs.

To Bo'ttom. *v. a.* [from the noun.]

1. To build upon; to fix upon as a ſupport.

They may have ſomething of obſcurity, as being *bottomed* upon, and fetched from the true nature of the things. *Hale.*

Pride has a very ſtrong foundation in the mind; it is *bottomed* upon ſelf-love. *Collier on Pride.*

The grounds upon which we *bottom* our reaſoning, are but a part; ſomething is left out, which ſhould go into the reckoning. *Locke.*

Every action is ſuppoſed to be *bottomed* upon ſome principle. *Atterbury.*

2. To wind upon ſomething; to twiſt thread round ſomething.

Therefore, as you unwind your love for him,
Leſt it ſhould ravel, and be good to none,
You muſt provide to *bottom* it on me. *Shakeſp. T. G. of Ver.*

To Bo'ttom. *v. n.* To reſt upon as its ſupport.

Find out upon what foundation any propoſition, advanced, *bottoms*; and obſerve the intermediate ideas, by which it is joined to that foundation upon which it is erected. *Locke.*

Bo'ttomed. *adj.* [from *bottom.*] Having a bottom; it is uſually compounded.

There being prepared a number of *flat-bottomed* boats, to tranſport the land-forces, under the wing and protection of the great navy. *Bacon's War with Spain.*

Bo'ttomless. *adj.* [from *bottom.*] Without a bottom; fathomleſs.

Wickedneſs may well be compared to a *bottomleſs* pit, into which it is eaſier to keep one's ſelf from falling, than, being fallen, to give one's ſelf any ſtay from falling infinitely. *Sidney.*

Is not my ſorrow deep, having no bottom?
Then be my paſſions *bottomleſs* with them. *Shakeſp. T. Andr.*

Him the Almighty pow'r
Hurl'd headlong, flaming from th' etherial ſky,
To *bottomleſs* perdition. *Milton's Par. Loſt, b.* i. *l.* 47.

Bo'ttomry. *n. ſ.* [in navigation and commerce.] The act of borrowing money on a ſhip's bottom; that is, by engaging the veſſel for the repayment of it, ſo as that, if the ſhip miſcarry, the lender loſes the money advanced; but, if it arrives ſafe at the end of the voyage, he is to repay the money lent, with a certain premium or intereſt agreed on; and this on pain of forfeiting the ſhip. *Harris.*

BOUCHET. *n. ſ.* [French.] A ſort of pear. *Dict.*

Boud. *n. ſ.* An inſect which breeds in malt; called alſo a *weevil*. *Dict.*

To Bouge. *v. n.* [*bouge*, Fr.] To ſwell out.

Bough. *n. ſ.* [boᵹ, Saxon; the *gh* is mute.] An arm or large ſhoot of a tree, bigger than a branch, yet not always diſtinguiſhed from it.

He ſaw a vine-labourer, that, finding a *bough* broken, took a branch of the ſame *bough*, and tied it about the place broken. *Sidney, b.* ii.

Their lord and patron loud did him proclaim,
And at his feet their laurel *boughs* did throw. *Fairy Q. b.* i.

From the *bough*
She gave him of that fair enticing fruit. *Parad. Lost, b.* ix.
As the dove's flight did guide Æneas, now
May thine conduct me to the golden *bough*. *Denham.*
Under some fav'rite myrtle's shady *boughs*,
They speak their passions in repeated vows. *Roscommon.*
See how, on every *bough*, the birds express,
In their sweet notes, their happiness. *Dryden's Indian Emp.*
'Twas all her joy the rip'ning fruits to tend,
And see the *boughs* with happy burdens bend. *Pope.*

BOUGHT. preter. of *to buy*; which see.

BOUGHT. *n. s.* [from *to bow*.]

1. A twist; a link; a knot.
His huge long tail wound up in hundred folds,
Whose wreathed *boughts* whenever he unfolds,
And thick entangled knots adown does slack. *Fairy Q. b.* i.
Immortal verse,
Such as the meeting soul may pierce
In notes, with many a winding *bought*
Of linked sweetness, long drawn out. *Milton.*

2. A flexure.
The flexure of the joints is not the same in elephants as in other quadrupeds, but nearer unto those of a man; the *bought* of the fore-legs not directly backward, but laterally, and somewhat inward. *Brown's Vulgar Errours, b.* iii. *c.* i.

BOUILLON. *n. s.* [French.] Broath; soup; any thing made to be supped: a term used in cookery.

BO'ULDER *Walls.* [in architecture.] Walls built of round flints or pebbles, laid in a strong mortar; used where the sea has a beach cast up, or where there are plenty of flints. *Builder's Dict.*

To BOULT. *v. a.* See To BOLT.

To BOUNCE. *v. n.* [a word formed, says *Skinner*, from the sound.]

1. To fall or fly against any thing with great force, so as to rebound.
The fright awaken'd Arcite with a start,
Against his bosom *bounc'd* his heaving heart. *Dryden.*
Just as I was putting out my light, another *bounces* as hard as he can knock. *Swift's Bickerstaff detected.*

2. To spring; to make a sudden leap.
High nonsense is like beer in a bottle, which has, in reality, no strength and spirit, but frets, and flies, and *bounces*, and imitates the passions of a much nobler liquour. *Add. Whig Exam.*
Rous'd by the noise,
And musical clatter,
They *bounce* from their nest,
No longer will tarry. *Swift.*
Out *bounc'd* the mastiff of the triple head;
Away the hare with double swiftness fled. *Swift.*

3. To boast; to bully: a sense used only in familiar speech.

4. To be bold, or strong.
Forsooth the *bouncing* Amazon,
Your buskin'd mistress, and your warriour love,
To Theseus must be wedded. *Shakesp. Midsum. Night's Dr.*

BOUNCE. *n. s.* [from the verb.]

1. A strong sudden blow.
The *bounce* burst ope the door; the scornful fair
Relentless look'd, and saw him beat his quiv'ring feet in air. *Dryden.*

2. A sudden crack or noise.
What cannoneer begot this lusty blood?
He speaks plain cannon fire, and smoke, and *bounce*;
He gives the bastinado with his tongue. *Shakesp. K. John.*
Two hazel-nuts I threw into the flame,
And to each nut I gave a sweetheart's name;
This with the loudest *bounce* me sore amaz'd,
That in a flame of brightest colour blaz'd. *Gay.*

3. A boast; a threat; in low language.

BO'UNCER. *n. s.* [from *bounce*.] A boaster; a bully; an empty threatner.

BOUND. *n. s.* [from *bind*.]

1. A limit; a boundary; that by which any thing is terminated.
Illimitable ocean! without *bound*;
Without dimension; where length, breadth, and height,
And time, and place, are lost. *Paradise Lost, b.* ii. *l.* 892.
Those vast Scythian regions were separated by the common natural *bounds*, of rivers, lakes, mountains, woods, or marshes. *Temple.*
Indus and Ganges, our wide empire's *bounds*,
Swell their dy'd currents with their natives wounds. *Dryden.*
Through all th' infernal *bounds*,
Which flaming Phlegethon surrounds,
Sad Orpheus sought his consort lost. *Pope's St. Cæcilia.*

2. A limit by which any excursion is restrained.
Hath he set *bounds* between their love and me?
I am their mother, who shall bar me from them. *Rich.* III.
Stronger and fiercer by restraint he roars,
And knows no *bound*, but makes his pow'r his shores. *Denh.*
Any *bounds* made with body, even adamantine walls, are far from putting a stop to the mind, in its farther progress in space. *Locke.*

3. [from *to bound, v. n.*] A leap; a jump; a spring.
Do but note a wild and wanton herd,
Or race of youthful and unhandled colts,
Fetching mad *bounds*, bellowing, and neighing loud.
Shakesp. Merchant of Venice.
The horses started with a sudden *bound*,
And flung the reins and chariot to the ground. *Addis. Ovid.*
Dext'rous he 'scapes the coach with nimble *bounds*,
Whilst ev'ry honest tongue stop thief resounds. *Gay.*

4. A rebound; the leap of something flying back by the force of the blow.
These inward disgusts are but the first *bound* of this ball of contention. *Decay of Piety.*

To BOUND. *v. a.* [from the noun.]

1. To limit; to terminate.
A lofty tow'r, and strong on every side,
With treble walls, which Phlegethon surrounds,
Whose firy flood the burning empire *bounds*. *Dryden's Æn.*

2. To restrain; to confine.
Take but degree away, untune that string,
The *bounded* waters
Would lift their bosoms higher than the shores,
And make a sop of all this solid globe. *Shakesp. Tr. and Cr.*

To BOUND. *v. n.* [*bondir*, Fr.]

1. To jump; to spring; to move forward by leaps.
My mother's blood
Runs on the dexter cheek, and this sinister
Bounds in my sire's. *Shakesp. Troilus and Cressida.*
Torrismond appear'd,
Gave me his hand, and led me lightly o'er,
Leaping and *bounding* on the billows heads. *Dryden.*
Before his lord the ready spaniel *bounds*,
Panting with hope, he tries the furrow'd grounds. *Pope.*
When sudden through the woods a *bounding* stag
Rush'd headlong down, and plung'd amidst the river. *Rowe.*
Warbling to the vary'd strain, advance
Two sprightly youths, to form the *bounding* dance. *Pope.*

2. To rebound; to fly back by repercussion.
Mark then a *bounding* valour in our English,
That being dead, like to the bullets grazing,
Breaks out into a second course of mischief. *Shakesp. H.* V.

To BOUND. *v. a.* To make to bound.
If I might buffet for any love, or *bound* my horse for her favours, I would lay on like a butcher, and sit like a jackanapes, never off. *Shakesp. Henry* V.
If love, ambitious, sought a match of birth,
Whose veins *bound* richer blood than lady Blanch. *Rich.* III.

BOUND. *participle passive* of *bind*.
Nay, said Pamela, none shall take that office from myself, being so much *bound* as I am for my education. *Sidney, b.* ii.
This is Antonio,
To whom I am so infinitely *bound*.—
—You should in all sense be much *bound* to him;
For, as I hear, he was much *bound* for you. *Merch. of Ven.*
The gentleman is learn'd, a most rare speaker,
To nature none more *bound*. *Shakesp. Henry* VIII.
The bishops of Hungary, being wonderfully rich, were *bound* to keep great numbers of horsemen, which they used to bring into the field. *Knolles's History of the Turks.*
They summoned the governour to deliver it to them, or else they would not leave one stone upon another. To which the governour made no other reply, than that he was not *bound* to repair it; but, however, he would, by God's help, keep the ground afterwards. *Clarendon, b.* viii.

BOUND. *adj.* [a word of doubtful etymology.] Destined; intending to come to any place.
His be that care, whom most it doth concern,
Said he; but whither with such hasty flight
Art thou now *bound*? for well might I discern
Great cause, that carries thee so swift and light. *Fairy Q. b.* ii.
To be *bound* for a port one desires extremely, and sail to it, with a fair gale, is very pleasant. *Temple.*
Willing we sought your shores, and hither *bound*,
The port so long desir'd, at length we found. *Dryden.*

BO'UNDARY. *n. s.* [from *bound*.] Limit; bound.
He suffers the confluence and clamours of the people to pass all *boundaries* of laws, and reverence to his authority. *K. Charles.*
Sensation and reflection are the *boundaries* of our thoughts; beyond which the mind, whatever efforts it would make, is not able to advance. *Locke.*
Great part of our sins consist in the irregularities attending the ordinary pursuits of life; so that our reformation must appear, by pursuing them within the *boundaries* of duty. *Rogers.*

BO'UNDEN. *participle passive* of *bind*.
Hereafter, in a better world than this,
I shall desire more love and knowledge of you.—
—I rest much *bounden* to you: fare you well. *Shakesp.*
We also most humbly besought him to accept of us as his true servants, by as just a right as ever men on earth were *bounden*. *Bacon's New Atlantis.*
To be careful for a provision of all necessaries for ourselves, and those who depend on us, is a *bounden* duty. *Rogers.*

BO'UNDING-STONE. } *n. s.* A stone to play with.
BOUND-STONE.

I am past a boy;
A sceptre's but a play-thing, and a globe
A bigger *bounding-stone*. *Dryden's Don Sebastian.*

BO'UNDLESNESS. *n. s.* [from *boundless*.] Exemption from limits.

God has corrected the *boundlessness* of his voluptuous desires, by stinting his capacities. *South.*

BO'UNDLESS. *adj.* [from *bound*.] Unlimited; unconfined; immeasurable; illimitable.

Beyond the infinite and *boundless* reach
Of mercy, if thou didst this deed of death,
Art thou damn'd, Hubert. *Shakesp. King John.*

Heav'n has of right all victory design'd;
Whence *boundless* power dwells in a will confin'd. *Dryden.*

Man seems as *boundless* in his desires, as God is in his being; and therefore nothing but God himself can satisfy him. *South.*

Though we make duration *boundless* as it is, we cannot extend it beyond all being. God fills eternity, and it is hard to find a reason, why any one should doubt that he fills immensity. *Locke.*

Some guide the course of wand'ring orbs on high,
Or roll the planets through the *boundless* sky. *Pope.*

BO'UNTEOUS. *adj.* [from *bounty*.] Liberal; kind; generous; munificent; beneficent: a word used chiefly in poetry for *bountiful*.

Every one,
According to the gift, which *bounteous* nature
Hath in him inclos'd. *Shakesp. Macbeth.*

Her soul abhorring avarice,
Bounteous; but almost *bounteous* to a vice. *Dryden.*

BO'UNTEOUSLY. *adv.* [from *bounteous*.] Liberally; generously; largely.

He *bounteously* bestow'd unenvy'd good
On me. *Dryden's State of Innocence.*

BO'UNTEOUSNESS. *n. s.* [from *bounteous*.] Munificence; liberality; kindness.

He filleth all things living with *bounteousness*. *Psalms.*

BO'UNTIFUL. *adj.* [from *bounty* and *full*.]

1. Liberal; generous; munificent.

As *bountiful* as mines of India. *Shakesp. Henry* IV. *p.* i.

If you will be rich, you must live frugal; if you will be popular, you must be *bountiful*. *Taylor's Rule of living holy.*

I am obliged to return my thanks to many, who, without considering the man, have been *bountiful* to the poet. *Dryden.*

God, the *bountiful* authour of our being. *Locke.*

2. It has *of* before the thing given, and *to* before the person receiving.

Our king spares nothing, to give them the share of that felicity, *of* which he is so *bountiful to* his kingdom. *Dryden's Dufr.*

BO'UNTIFULLY. *adv.* [from *bountiful*.] Liberally; in a bountiful manner; largely.

And now thy alms is giv'n,
And thy poor starv'ling *bountifully* fed. *Donne.*

It is affirmed, that it never raineth in Egypt; the river *bountifully* requiting it in its inundation. *Brown's Vulgar Errours.*

BO'UNTIFULNESS. *n. s.* [from *bountiful*.] The quality of being bountiful; generosity.

Enriched to all *bountifulness*. 2 *Cor.* ix. 11.

BO'UNTIHEAD. } *n. s.* [from *bounty* and *head*, or *hood*. See
BO'UNTIHEDE. } HOOD.] Goodness; virtue. It is now
BO'UNTIHOOD. } wholly out of use.

This goodly frame of temperance,
Formerly grounded, and fast settled
On firm foundation of true *bountihead*. *Fairy Q. b.* ii.

How shall frail pen, with fear disparaged,
Conceive such sovereign glory, and great *bountihood*? *F. Q.*

BO'UNTY. *n. s.* [*bonté*, Fr.]

1. Generosity; liberality; munificence.

We do not so far magnify her exceeding *bounty*, as to affirm, that she bringeth into the world the sons of men, adorned with gorgeous attire. *Hooker, b.* iii. § 4.

If you knew to whom you shew this honour,
I know you would be prouder of the work,
Than customary *bounty* can enforce you. *Shakesp.*

Such moderation with thy *bounty* join,
That thou may'st nothing give, that is not thine. *Denham.*

Those godlike men, to wanting virtue kind,
Bounty well plac'd preferr'd, and well design'd,
To all their titles. *Dryden's Juv. sat.* v.

2. It seems distinguished from charity, as a *present* from an *alms*; being used, when persons, not absolutely necessitous, receive gifts; or when gifts are given by great persons.

Tell a miser of *bounty* to a friend, or mercy to the poor, and he will not understand it. *South.*

Her majesty did not see this assembly so proper to excite charity and compassion; though I question not but her royal *bounty* will extend itself to them. *Addison. Guardian*, N° 105.

To BO'URGEON. *v. n.* [*bourgeonner*, Fr.] To sprout; to shoot into branches; to put forth buds.

Long may the dew of heaven distil upon them, to make them *bourgeon*, and propagate among themselves. *Howel.*

O that I had the fruitful heads of Hydra,
That one might *bourgeon* where another fell!
Still would I give thee work! *Dryden's Don Sebastian.*

BOURN. *n. s.* [*borne*, Fr.]

1. A bound; a limit.

Bourn, bound of land, tilth, vineyard, none. *Sh. Tempest.*

That undiscover'd country, from whose *bourn*
No traveller e'er returns. *Shakesp. Hamlet.*

False,
As dice are to be wish'd, by one that fixes
No *bourn* 'twixt his and mine. *Shakesp. Winter's Tale.*

I know each lane, and every alley green,
And every bosky *bourn* from side to side. *Milton.*

2. [from burn, Saxon.] A brook; a torrent: whence many towns, seated near brooks, have names ending in *bourn*. It is not now used in either sense; though the second continues in the Scottish dialect.

Ne swelling Neptune, ne loud thund'ring Jove,
Can change my cheer, or make me ever mourn;
My little boat can safely pass this perilous *bourn*. *Fairy Q.*

To BOUSE. *v. n.* [*buysen*, Dut.] To drink lavishly; to tope.

As he rode, he somewhat still did eat,
And in his hand did bear a *bousing* can,
Of which he sipt. *Fairy Queen, b.* iii. *c.* iv.

BO'USY. *adj.* [from *bouse*.] Drunken.

The guests upon the day appointed came,
Each *bousy* farmer, with his simp'ring dame. *King.*

With a long legend of romantick things,
Which in his cups the *bousy* poet sings. *Dryden's Juv. sat.* x.

BOUT. *n. s.* [*botta*, Ital.] A turn; as much of an action as is performed at one time, without interruption; a single part of any action carried on by successive intervals.

The play began: Pas durst not Cosma chace;
But did intend next *bout* with her to meet. *Sidney.*

Ladies, that have your feet
Unplagu'd with corns, we'll have a *bout*. *Shakesp.*

When in your motion you are hot,
As make your *bouts* more violent to that end,
He calls for drink. *Shakesp. Hamlet.*

If he chance to 'scape this dismal *bout*,
The former legatees are blotted out. *Dryden's Juv. sat.* xii.

A weasel seized a bat; the bat begged for life: says the weasel, I give no quarter to birds: says the bat, I am a mouse; look on my body: so she got off for that *bout*. *L'Estrange.*

We'll see when 'tis enough,
Or if it wants the nice concluding *bout*. *King.*

BOUTEFEU. n. s. [French.] An incendiary; one who kindles feuds and discontents.

Animated by a base fellow, called John à Chamber, a very *boutefeu*, who bore much sway among the vulgar, they entered into open rebellion. *Bacon's Henry* VII.

Nor could ever any order be obtained impartially to punish the known *boutefeus*, and open incendiaries. *King Charles.*

Besides the herd of *boutefeus*,
We set on work without the house. *Hudibras.*

BO'UTISALE. *n. s.* [I suppose from *bouty*, or *booty*, and *sale*.] A sale at a cheap rate; as booty or plunder is commonly sold.

To speak nothing of the great *boutisale* of colleges and chantries. *Sir J. Hayward.*

BOUTS RIMEZ. [French.] The last words or rhimes of a number of verses given to be filled up.

To BOW. *v. a.* [buȝen, Saxon.]

1. To bend, or inflect.

A threepence *bow'd*, would hire me,
Old as I am, to queen it. *Shakesp. Henry* VIII.

Orpheus, with his lute, made trees,
And the mountain tops, that freeze,
Bow themselves when he did sing. *Shakesp. Henry* VIII.

Some *bow* the vines, which bury'd in the plain,
Their tops in distant arches rise again. *Dryden's Virgil.*

The mind has not been made obedient to discipline, when at first it was most tender, and most easy to be *bowed*. *Locke.*

2. To bend the body in token of respect or submission.

They came to meet him, and *bowed* themselves to the ground before him. 2 *Kings*, ii. 15.

Is it to *bow* down his head as a bulrush, and to spread sackcloth and ashes under him? wilt thou call this a fast, and an acceptable day to the Lord? *Isaiah*, lviii. 5.

3. To bend, or incline, in condescension.

Let it not grieve thee to *bow* down thine ear to the poor, and give him a friendly answer. *Ecclus*, iv. 8.

4. To depress; to crush.

Are you so gospell'd,
To pray for this good man, and for his issue,
Whose heavy hand hath *bow'd* you to the grave,
And beggar'd yours for ever. *Shakesp. Macbeth.*

Now wasting years my former strength confound,
And added woes may *bow* me to the ground. *Pope.*

To BOW. *v. n.*

1. To bend; to suffer flexure.
2. To make a reverence.

Rather let my head
Stoop to the block, than these knees *bow* to any,
Save to the God of heav'n, and to my king. *Shakesp. H. VI.*

This is the great idol to which the world *bows*; to this we pay our devoutest homage. *Decay of Piety.*

Admir'd, ador'd by all the circling crowd,
For wheresoe'er she turn'd her face, they *bow'd*. *Dryden.*

3. To stoop.

The people *bowed* down upon their knees, to drink water. *Judges*, vii. 6.

4. To sink under pressure.

They stoop, they *bow* down together; they could not deliver the burden. *Isaiah*, xlvi. 2.

Bow. *n. s.* [from the verb. It is pronounced, like the verb, as *now*, *how*.] An act of reverence or submission, by bending the body.

Some clergy too she wou'd allow,
Nor quarrel'd at their awkward *bow*. *Swift.*

Bow. *n. s.* [pronounced as *grow*, *no*, *lo*, without any regard to the *w*.]

1. An instrument of war, made by holding wood or metal bent with a string, which, by its spring, shoots arrows with great force.

Take, I pray thee, thy weapons, thy quiver and thy *bow*, and go out to the field, and take me some venison. *Gen.* xxvii. 3.

The white faith of hist'ry cannot show,
That e'er the musket yet could beat the *bow*. *Alleyne's Henry* VII.

Twining woody haunts, or the tough yew
To *bows* strong-straining. *Thomson's Autumn.*

2. A rainbow.

I do set my *bow* in the cloud, and it shall be for a token of a covenant between me and the earth. *Gen.* ix. 13.

3. The instrument with which string-instruments are struck.

Their instruments were various in their kind;
Some for the *bow*, and some for breathing wind:
The sawtry, pipe, and hautboy's noisy band,
And the soft lute trembling beneath the touching hand. *Dryden's Fables.*

4. The doubling of a string in a slip-knot.

Make a knot, and let the second knot be with a *bow*. *Wiseman's Surgery.*

5. A yoke.

As the ox hath his *bow*, Sir, the horse his curb, and the faulcon his bells, so man hath his desire. *Shakesp. As you like it.*

6. Bow *of a saddle.* The *bows of a saddle* are two pieces of wood laid archwise, to receive the upper part of a horse's back, to give the saddle its due form, and to keep it tight. *Farrier's D.*

7. Bow *of a ship.* That part of her which begins at the loof, and compassing ends of the stern, and ends at the sternmost parts of the forecastle. If a ship hath a broad bow, they call it a *bold bow*; if a narrow thin bow, they say she hath a *lean bow*. The piece of ordnance that lies in this place, is called the *bowpiece*; and the anchors that hang here, are called her *great* and *little bowers*.

8. Bow is also a mathematical instrument, made of wood, formerly used by seamen in taking the sun's altitude.

9. Bow is likewise a beam of wood or brass, with three long screws, that direct a lath of wood or steel to any arch; used commonly to draw draughts of ships, projections of the sphere, or wherever it is requisite to draw long arches. *Harris.*

Bow-bearer. *n. s.* [from *bow* and *bear*.] An under-officer of the forest. *Cowel.*

Bow-bent. *adj.* [from *bow* and *bent*.] Crooked.

A sibyl old, *bow-bent* with crooked age,
That far events full wisely could presage. *Milton.*

Bow-hand. *n. s.* [from *bow* and *hand*.] The hand that draws the bow.

Surely he shoots wide on the *bow-hand*, and very far from the mark. *Spenser's Ireland.*

Bow-legged. *adj.* [from *bow* and *leg*.] Having crooked legs.

Bow-shot. *n. s.* [from *bow* and *shot*.] The space which an arrow may pass in its flight from the bow.

Though he were not then a *bow-shot* off, and made haste; yet, by that time he was come, the thing was no longer to be seen. *Boyle's Spring of the Air.*

To Bo'wel. *v. a.* [from the noun.] To pierce the bowels.

But to the *bowell'd* cavern darting deep
The mineral kinds confess thy mighty power. *Thomson.*

BO'WELS. *n. s.* [*boyaux*, Fr.]

1. Intestines; the vessels and organs within the body.

He smote him therewith in the fifth rib, and shed out his *bowels*. 2 *Sam.* xx. 10.

2. The inner parts of any thing.

Had we no quarrel else to Rome, but that
Thou art thence banish'd, we would muster all
From twelve to seventy; and pouring war
Into the *bowels* of ungrateful Rome,
Like a bold flood appear. *Shakesp. Coriolanus.*

His soldiers spying his undaunted spirit,
A Talbot! Talbot! cried out amain,
And rush'd into the *bowels* of the battle. *Shakesp. Henry* VI.

As he saw drops of water distilling from the rock, by following the veins, he has made himself two or three fountains in the *bowels* of the mountain. *Addison on Italy.*

3. Tenderness; compassion.

He had no other consideration of money, than for the support of his lustre; and whilst he could do that, he cared not for money; having no *bowels* in the point of running in debt, or borrowing all he could. *Clarendon.*

4. This word seldom has a *singular*, except in writers of anatomy.

Bo'wer. *n. s.* [from *bough* or *branch*, or from the verb *to bow* or *bend*.]

1. An arbour; a sheltered place covered with green trees, twined and bent.

But, O sad virgin, that thy power
Might raise Musæus from his *bower*. *Milton.*

To Gods appealing, when I reach their *bow'rs*
With loud complaints, they answer me in show'rs. *Waller.*

Refresh'd, they wait them to the *bow'r* of state,
Where, circl'd with his peers, Atrides sat. *Pope.*

2. It seems to signify, in *Spenser*, a blow; a stroke: *bourrer*, Fr. to fall upon.

His rawbone arms, whose mighty brawned *bowers*
Were wont to rive steel plates, and helmets hew,
Were clean consum'd, and all his vital powers
Decay'd. *Spenser's Fairy Queen, b.* i. *cant.* viii. *stanz.* 41.

Bo'wer. *n. s.* [from the *bow* of a ship.] Anchors so called. See Bow.

To Bo'wer. *v. a.* [from the noun.] To embower; to inclose.

Thou didst *bower* the spirit,
In mortal paradise of such sweet flesh. *Shakesp.*

Bo'wery. *adj.* [from *bower*.] Full of bowers.

Landskips how gay the *bow'ry* grotto yields,
Which thought creates, and lavish fancy builds. *Tickell.*

Snatch'd through the verdant maze, the hurried eye
Distracted wanders: now the *bowery* walk
Of covert close, where scarce a speck of day
Falls on the lengthen'd gloom, protracted sweeps. *Thomson.*

To Bowge. See To Bouge.

BOWL. *n. s.* [*buelin*, Welch; which signifies, according to *Junius*, any thing made of horn, as drinking cups anciently were. It is pronounced *bole*.]

1. A vessel to hold liquids, rather wide than deep; distinguished from a cup, which is rather deep than wide.

Give me a *bowl* of wine;
I have not that alacrity of spirit,
Nor cheer of mind, that I was wont to have. *Richard* III.

If a piece of iron be fastened on the side of a *bowl* of water, a loadstone, in a boat of cork, will presently make into it. *Brown's Vulgar Errours, b.* ii. *c.* iii.

The sacred priests, with ready knives, bereave
The beasts of life, and in full *bowls* receive
The streaming blood. *Dryden's Æneid.*

While the bright Sein, t' exalt the soul,
With sparkling plenty crowns the *bowl*,
And wit and social mirth inspires. *Fenton to Lord Gower.*

2. The hollow part of any thing.

If you are allowed a large silver spoon for the kitchen, let half the *bowl* of it be worn out with continual scraping. *Swift's Directions to the Cook.*

3. A basin, or fountain.

But the main matter is so to convey the water, as it never stay either in the *bowl* or in the cistern. *Bacon's Essays.*

BOWL. *n. s.* [*boule*, Fr. It is pronounced as *cow*, *howl*.] A round mass, which may be rolled along the ground.

Like to a *bowl* upon a subtle ground,
I've tumbl'd past the throw. *Shakesp. Coriolanus.*

How finely dost thou times and seasons spin!
And make a twist checker'd with night and day!
Which, as it lengthens, winds, and winds us in,
As *bowls* go on, but turning all the way. *Herbert.*

Like him, who would lodge a *bowl* upon a precipice, either my praise falls back, or stays not on the top, but rowls over. *Dryden's Juvenal, Dedication.*

Men may make a game at *bowls* in the summer, and a game at whisk in the winter. *Dennis's Letters.*

Though that piece of wood, which is now a *bowl*, may be made square, yet, if roundness be taken away, it is no longer a *bowl*. *Watts's Logick.*

To Bowl. *v. a.* [from the noun.]

1. To play at bowls.

2. To throw bowls at any thing.

Alas! I had rather be set quick i' th' earth,
And *bowl'd* to death with turnips. *Merry W. of Windsor.*

Bo'wlder-stones. *n. s.* Lumps or fragments of stones or marble, broke from the adjacent cliffs, rounded by being tumbled to and again by the action of the water; whence their name. *Woodward on Fossils.*

Bo'wler. *n. s.* [from *bowl*.] He that plays at bowls.

Bo'wline. } *n. s.* [sea term.] A rope fastened to the middle
Bo'wling. } part of the outside of a sail; it is fastened in three or four parts of the sail, called the *bowling bridle*. The use of the *bowling* is to make the sails stand sharp or close to a wind. *Harr.*

BO'WLING-GREEN. *n. s.* [from *bowl* and *green.*] A level piece of ground, kept smooth for bowlers.

A bowl equally poised, and thrown upon a plain *bowling-green*, will run necessarily in a direct line. *Bentley.*

BO'WMAN. *n. s.* [from *bow* and *man.*] An archer; he that shoots with a bow.

The whole city shall flee, for the noise of the horsemen and *bowmen.* *Jerem.* iv. 29.

BO'WSPRIT. *n. s.* [from the *bow* of the ship.] This word is generally spelt *boltsprit*; which see.

To BO'WSSEN. *v. a.* [probably of the same original with *bouse*, but found in no other passage.] To drench; to soak.

The water fell into a close walled plot; upon this wall was the frantick person set, and from thence tumbled headlong into the pond; where a strong fellow tossed him up and down, until the patient, by foregoing his strength, had somewhat forgot his fury: but if there appeared small amendment, he was *bowssened* again and again, while there remained in him any hope of life, for recovery. *Carew's Survey of Cornwal.*

BO'WSTRING. *n. s.* [from *bow* and *string.*] The string by which the bow is kept bent.

He hath twice or thrice cut Cupid's *bowstring*, and the little hangman dare not shoot at him. *Shakesp. Much ado about Noth.*

Sound will be conveyed to the ear, by striking upon a *bowstring*, if the horn of the bow be held to the ear. *Bacon.*

BO'WYER. *n. s.* [from *bow.*]

1. An archer; one that uses the bow.

Call for vengeance from the *bowyer* king. *Dryden.*

2. One whose trade is to make bows.

BOX. *n. s.* [box, Saxon; *buxus*, Lat.] A tree.

The characters are; The leaves are pennated, and evergreen; it hath male flowers, that are produced at remote distances from the fruit, on the same tree; the fruit is shaped like a porridge-pot inverted, and is divided into three cells, containing two seeds in each, which, when ripe, are cast forth by the elasticity of the vessels. The species are; 1. The *box-tree.* 2. The narrow-leaved *box-tree.* 3. Striped *box.* 4. The golden edged *box-tree.* 5. The dwarf *box.* 6. The dwarf striped *box.* 7. The silver edged *box.* On Boxhill, near Darking in Surrey, were formerly many large trees of this kind; but, of late years, their number is pretty much decreased; yet some remain of a considerable bigness. The wood is very useful for engravers and mathematical instrument-makers; being so hard, close, and ponderous, as to sink in water. *Millar.*

Box, there are two sorts of it; the dwarf *box*, and a taller sort, that grows to a considerable height. The dwarf *box* is very good for borders, and is easily kept in order, with one clipping in the year. It will increase of slips set in March, or about Bartholomew-tide, and may be raised of layers and suckers, and will prosper on the declivity of cold, dry, barren, chalky hills, where nothing else will grow. *Mortimer.*

BOX. *n. s.* [box, Sax. *buyste*, Germ.]

1. A case made of wood, or other matter, to hold any thing. It is distinguished from *chest*, as the *less* from the *greater.* It is supposed to have its name from the *box* wood.

A perfect magnet, though but in an ivory *box*, will, through the *box*, send forth his embracing virtue to a beloved needle. *Sidney, b.* ii.

About his shelves
A beggarly account of empty *boxes.* *Shakesp. Rom. and Jul.*

This head is to open a most wide voracious mouth, which shall take in letters and papers. There will be under it a *box*, of which the key will be kept in my custody, to receive such papers as are dropped into it. *Addison. Guard.* N° 98.

This casket India's glowing gems unlocks,
And all Arabia breathes from yonder *box.* *Pope.*

2. The case of the mariners compass.

3. The chest into which money given is put.

So many more, so every one was used,
That to give largely to the *box* refused. *Spenser.*

4. The seats in the playhouse, where the ladies are placed.

'Tis left to you, the *boxes* and the pit
Are sovereign judges of this sort of wit. *Dryden.*

She glares in balls, front *boxes*, and the ring,
A vain, unquiet, glittering, wretched thing. *Pope.*

To BOX. *v. a.* [from the noun.] To inclose in a box.

Box'd in a chair, the beau impatient sits,
While spouts run clatt'ring o'er the roof by fits. *Swift.*

BOX. *n. s.* [*bock*, a cheek, Welch.] A blow on the head given with the hand.

For the *box* o' th' ear that the prince gave you, he gave it like a rude prince. *Shakesp. Henry* IV.

If one should take my hand perforce, and give another a *box* on the ear with it, the law punisheth the other. *Bramhall against Hobbes.*

There may happen concussions of the brain from a *box* on the ear. *Wiseman's Surgery.*

Olphis, the fisherman, received a *box* on the ear from Thestylis. *Addison. Spectator,* N° 233.

To BOX. *v. n.* [from the noun.] To fight with the fist.

The ass very fairly looked on, till they had *boxed* themselves a-weary, and then left them fairly in the lurch. *L'Estrange.*

A leopard is like a cat; he *boxes* with his forefeet, as a cat doth her kitlins. *Grew.*

The fighting with a man's shadow consists in brandishing two sticks, loaden with plugs of lead; this gives a man all the pleasure of *boxing*, without the blows. *Spectat.* N° 115.

He hath had six duels, and four and twenty *boxing* matches, in defence of his majesty's title. *Spectator,* N° 629.

To BOX. *v. a.* To strike with the fist.

BO'XEN. *adj.* [from *box.*]

1. Made of box.

The young gentlemen learned, before all other things, to design upon tablets of *boxen* wood. *Dryden's Dufresnoy.*

As lads and lasses stood around,
To hear my *boxen* hautboy sound. *Gay's Pastorals.*

2. Resembling box.

Her faded cheeks are chang'd to *boxen* hue,
And in her eyes the tears are ever new. *Dryden.*

BO'XER. *n. s.* [from *box.*] A man who fights with his fist.

BOY. *n. s.* [*bub*, Germ. the etymology is not agreed on.]

1. A male child; not a girl.

2. One in the state of adolescence; older than an infant, yet not arrived at puberty or manhood.

Speak thou, *boy*;
Perhaps thy childishness will move him more
Than can our reasons. *Shakesp. Coriolanus.*

Sometimes forgotten things, long cast behind,
Rush forward in the brain, and come to mind:
The nurse's legends are for truths receiv'd,
And the man dreams but what the *boy* believ'd. *Dryden.*

3. A word of contempt for young men, as noting their immaturity.

Men of worth and parts will not easily admit the familiarity of *boys*, who yet need the care of a tutor. *Locke.*

The pale *boy* senator yet tingling stands,
And holds his breeches close with both his hands. *Pope.*

To BOY. *v. n.* [from the noun.] To act apishly, or like a boy.

Anthony
Shall be brought drunken forth, and I shall see
Some squeaking Cleopatra *boy* my greatness,
I' th' posture of a whore. *Shakesp. Antony and Cleopatra.*

BO'YHOOD. *n. s.* [from *boy.*] The state of a boy; the part of life in which we are boys.

If you should look at him, in his *boyhood*, through the magnifying end of a perspective, and, in his manhood, through the other, it would be impossible to spy any difference; the same air, the same strut. *Swift.*

BO'YISH. *adj.* [from *boy.*]

1. Belonging to a boy.

I ran it through, e'en from my *boyish* days,
To th' very moment that he bade me tell it. *Shakesp. Othello.*

2. Childish; trifling.

This unheard sauciness, and *boyish* troops,
The king doth smile at, and is well prepar'd
To whip this dwarfish war, these pigmy arms. *Sh. K. John.*

Young men take up some English poet for their model, and imitate him, without knowing wherein he is defective, where he is *boyish* and trifling. *Dryden.*

BO'YISHLY. *adv.* [from *boyish.*] Childishly; triflingly.

BO'YISHNESS. *n. s.* [from *boyish.*] Childishness; trivialness.

BO'YISM. *n. s.* [from *boy.*] Puerility; childishness.

He had complained he was farther off, by being so near, and a thousand such *boyisms*, which Chaucer rejected as below the subject. *Dryden's Fab. Preface.*

BP. An abbreviation of bishop.

BRA'BBLE. *n. s.* [*brabbelen*, Dutch.] A clamorous contest; a squabble; a broil.

Here in the streets, desperate in shame and state,
In private *brabble* did we apprehend him. *Shakesp. T. Night.*

To BRA'BBLE. *v. n.* [from the noun.] To clamour; to contest noisily.

BRA'BBLER. *n. s.* [from *brabble.*] A clamorous, quarrelsome, noisy fellow.

To BRACE. *v. a.* [*embrasser*, Fr.]

1. To bind; to tie close with bandages.

The women of China, by *bracing* and binding them from their infancy, have very little feet. *Locke.*

2. To intend; to make tense; to strain up.

The tympanum is not capable of tension that way, in such a manner as a drum is *braced.* *Holder's Elements of Speech.*

The diminution of the force of the pressure of the external air, in *bracing* the fibres, must create a debility in muscular motion. *Arbuthnot on Air.*

BRACE. *n. s.* [from the verb.]

1. Cincture; bandage.

2. That which holds any thing tight.

The little bones of the ear-drum do the same office in straining and relaxing it, as the *braces* of the war drum do in that. *Derham's Physico-Theology.*

3. BRACE. [in architecture.] Is a piece of timber framed in with bevil joints, used to keep the building from swerving either way. *Builder's Dict.*

4. BRACES. [a sea term.] Ropes belonging to all the yards, ex-

cept the mizen. They have a pendant seized to the yard-arm, two *braces* to each yard; and, at the end of the pendant, a block is seized, through which the rope called the *brace* is reeved. The *braces* serve to square and traverse the yards. *Sea Dict.*

5. BRACES *of a coach.* Thick straps of leather on which it hangs.

6. Harness.

7. BRACE. [in printing.] A crooked line inclosing a passage, which ought to be taken together, and not separately; as in a triplet.

Charge Venus to command her son,
Wherever else she lets him rove,
To shun my house, and field, and grove;
Peace cannot dwell with hate or love. *Prior.*

8. Warlike preparation; from *bracing* the armour; as we say, *girded* for the battle.

As it more concerns the Turk than Rhodes,
So may he with more facile question bear it;
For that it stands not in such warlike *brace*,
But altogether lacks th' abilities
That Rhodes is dress'd in. *Shakesp. Othello.*

9. Tension; tightness.

The most frequent cause of deafness is the laxness of the tympanum, when it has lost its *brace* or tension. *Holder.*

BRACE. *n. s.* [of uncertain etymology.]

1. A pair; a couple. It is not *braces*, but *brace*, in the *plural.*

Down from a hill the beasts that reign in woods,
First hunter then, pursu'd a gentle *brace*,
Goodliest of all the forest, hart and hind. *Par. Lost, b.* xi.
Ten *brace* and more of greyhounds, snowy fair,
And tall as stags, ran loose, and cours'd around his chair. *Dryden's Fables.*

2. It is used generally in conversation as a sportsman's word.

He is said, this summer, to have shot with his own hands fifty *brace* of pheasants. *Addison. Freeholder*, N° 36.

3. It is applied to men in contempt.

But you, my *brace* of lords, were I so minded,
I here could pluck his highness' frown upon you. *Sh. Tempest.*

BRA'CELET. *n. s.* [*bracelet*, Fr.]

1. An ornament for the arms.

Both his hands were cut off, being known to have worn *bracelets* of gold about his wrists. *Sir J. Hayward.*

Tie about our tawny wrists
Bracelets of the fairy twists. *Ben. Johnson's Fairy Prince.*

A very ingenious lady used to wear, in rings and *bracelets*, store of those gems. *Boyle.*

2. A piece of defensive armour for the arm.

BRA'CER. *n. s.* [from *brace.*] A cincture; a bandage.

When they affect the belly, they may be restrained by a *bracer*, without much trouble. *Wiseman's Surgery.*

BRACH. *n. s.* [*braque*, Fr.] A bitch hound.

Truth's a dog must to kennel; he must be whipped out, when the lady *brach* may stand by the fire, and stink. *Shakesp.*

BRA'CHIAL. *adj.* [from *brachium*, an arm, Lat.] Belonging to the arm.

BRACHY'GRAPHY. *n. s.* [βραχὺς, short, and γράφω, to write.] The art or practice of writing in a short compass.

All the certainty of those high pretenders, bating what they have of the first principles, and the word of God, may be circumscribed by as small a circle as the creed, when *brachygraphy* had confined it within the compass of a penny. *Glanville.*

BRACK. *n. s.* [from *break.*] A breach; a broken part.

The place was but weak, and the *bracks* fair; but the defendants, by resolution, supplied all the defects. *Hayward.*

Let them compare my work with what is taught in the schools, and if they find in theirs many *bracks* and short ends, which cannot be spun into an even piece, and, in mine, a fair coherence throughout, I shall promise myself an acquiescence. *Digby on the Soul, Dedicat.*

BRA'CKET. *n. s.* A piece of wood fixed for the support of something.

Let your shelves be laid upon *brackets*, being about two feet wide, and edged with a small lath. *Mortimer.*

BRA'CKISH. *adj.* [*brack*, Dutch.] Salt; somewhat salt: it is used particularly of the water of the sea.

Pits upon the sea shore turn into fresh water, by percolation of the salt through the sand: but it is farther noted, after a time, the water in such pits will become *brackish* again. *Bacon.*

When I had gain'd the brow and top,
A lake of *brackish* waters on the ground,
Was all I found. *Herbert.*

The wise contriver, on his end intent,
Mix'd them with salt, and season'd all the sea.
What other cause could this effect produce?
The *brackish* tincture through the main diffuse? *Blackmore.*

BRA'CKISHNESS. *n. s.* [from *brackish.*] Saltness.

All the artificial strainings, hitherto discovered, leave a *brackishness* in salt water, that makes it unfit for animal uses. *Cheyne's Philosophical Principles.*

BRAD, being an initial, signifies *broad, spacious*, from the Saxon bꞃab, and the Gothick *braid.* *Gibson's Camden*

BRAD. *n. s.* A sort of nail to floor rooms with. They are about the size of a tenpenny nail, but have not their heads made with a shoulder over their shank, as other nails, but are made pretty thick towards the upper end, that the very top may be driven into, and buried in the board they nail down; so that the tops of these *brads* will not catch the thrums of the mops, when the floor is washing. *Moxon's Mechanical Exercises.*

To BRAG. *v. n.* [*braggeren*, Dutch.]

1. To boast; to display ostentatiously; to tell boastful stories.

Thou coward! art thou *bragging* to the stars?
Telling the bushes that thou look'st for wars,
And wilt not come? *Shakesp. Midsum. Night's Dream.*

Mark me, with what violence she first loved the Moor, but for *bragging*, and telling her fantastical lies. *Shakesp. Othello.*

In *bragging* out some of their private tenets, as if they were the received established doctrine of the church of England. *Sanderson's Pax Ecclesiæ.*

The rebels were grown so strong there, that they intended then, as they already *bragged*, to come over, and make this the seat of war. *Clarendon.*

Mrs. Bull's condition was looked upon as desperate by all the men of art; but there were those that *bragged* they had an infallible ointment. *Arbuthnot's Hist. of J. Bull.*

2. It has *of* before the thing boasted.

Knowledge being the only thing *whereof* we poor old men can *brag*, we cannot make it known but by utterance. *Sidney.*

Verona *brags of* him,
To be a virtuous and well govern'd youth. *Shakesp.*

Ev'ry busy little scribbler now,
Swells with the praises which he gives himself,
And taking sanctuary in the croud,
Brags of his impudence, and scorns to mend. *Roscommon.*

3. *On* is used, but improperly.

Yet lo! in me what authors have to *brag on*,
Reduc'd at last to hiss in my own dragon. *Pope's Dunciad.*

BRAG. *n. s.* [from the verb.]

1. A boast; a proud expression.

A kind of conquest
Cæsar made here; but made not here his *brag*
Of came, and saw, and overcame. *Shakesp. Cymbeline.*

It was such a new thing for the Spaniards to receive so little hurt, upon dealing with the English, as Avellaneda made great *brags* of it, for no greater matter than the waiting upon the English afar off. *Bacon's War with Spain.*

2. The thing boasted.

Beauty is nature's *brag*, and must be shewn
In courts, at feasts, and high solemnities,
Where most may wonder. *Milton.*

BRAGGADO'CIO. *n. s.* [from *brag.*] A puffing, swelling, boasting fellow.

The world abounds in terrible fanfarons, in the masque of men of honour; but these *braggadocios* are easy to be detected. *L'Estrange.*

By the plot, you may guess much of the characters of the persons; a *braggadocio* captain, a parasite, and a lady of pleasure. *Dryden.*

BRA'GGART. *adj.* [from *brag.*] Boastful; vainly ostentatious.

Shall I, none's slave, of high-born or rais'd men
Fear frowns; and my mistress, truth, betray thee
To th' huffing, *braggart*, puft nobility? *Donne.*

BRA'GGART. *n. s.* [from *brag.*] A boaster.

Who knows himself a *braggart*,
Let him fear this; for it will come to pass,
That every *braggart* shall be found an ass.
Shakesp. All's well that ends well.

BRA'GGER. *n. s.* [from *brag.*] A boaster; an ostentatious fellow.

Such as have had opportunity to sound these *braggers* thoroughly, by having sometimes endured the penance of their sottish company, have found them, in converse, empty and insipid. *South.*

BRA'GLESS. *adj.* [from *brag.*] Without a boast; without ostentation.

The bruit is, Hector's slain, and by Achilles.——
——If it is so, *bragless* let it be,
Great Hector was as good a man as he. *Shak. Tr. and Cress.*

BRA'GLY. *adv.* [from *brag.*] Finely; so as it may be bragged

Seest not thilk hawthorn stud,
How *bragly* it begins to bud,
And utter his tender head?
Flora now calleth forth each flower,
And bids make ready Maia's bower. *Spenser's Past.*

To BRAID. *v. a.* [bꞃæban, Saxon.] To weave together.

Close the serpent sly,
Insinuating, wove with gordian twine
His *braided* train, and of his fatal guile
Gave proof unheeded. *Milton's Par. Lost, b.* iv. *l.* 347.

Osier wands, lying loosely, may each of them be easily dissociated from the rest; but when *braided* into a basket, they cohere strongly. *Boyle.*

A ribband did the *braided* tresses bind,
The rest was loose, and wanton'd in the wind. *Dryden.*

Since in *braided* gold her foot is bound,
And a long trailing manteau sweeps the ground,
Her shoe disdains the street. *Gay's Trivia.*

BRAID. *n. s.* [from the verb.] A texture; a knot, or complication of something woven together.

Listen where thou art sitting,
Under the glossy, cool, translucent wave,
In twisted *braids* of lillies knitting
The loose train of thy amber-dropping hair. *Milton.*

No longer shall thy comely traces break
In flowing ringlets on thy snowy neck,
Or sit behind thy head, an ample round,
In graceful *braids*, with various ribbon bound. *Prior.*

BRAID. *adj.* [To *brede*, in *Chaucer*, is to *deceive.*] An old word, which seems to signify *deceitful.*

Since Frenchmen are so *braid*,
Marry 'em that will. I'll live and die a maid.
Shakesp. All's well that ends well.

BRAILS. *n. s.* [Sea term.] Small ropes reeved through blocks, which are seized on either side the ties, a little off upon the yard; so that they come down before the sails of a ship, and are fastened at the skirt of the sail to the crengles. Their use is, when the sail is furled across, to hale up its bunt, that it may the more readily be taken up or let fall. *Harris.*

BRAIN. *n. s.* [bꞃæȝen, Sax. *breyne*, Dutch.]

1. That collection of vessels and organs in the head, from which sense and motion arise.

The *brain* is divided into *cerebrum* and *cerebellum*. *Cerebrum* is that part of the *brain*, which possesses all the upper and forepart of the *cranium*, being separated from the *cerebellum* by the second process of the *dura mater*, under which the *cerebellum* is situated. The substance of the *brain* is distinguished into outer and inner; the former is called *corticalis*, *cinerea*, or *glandulosa*; the latter, *medullaris*, *alba*, or *nervea*. *Cheselden.*

If I be served such another trick, I'll have my *brains* ta'en out, and buttered, and give them to a dog for a new year's gift. *Shakesp. Merry Wives of Windsor.*

That man proportionably hath the largest *brain*, I did, I confess, somewhat doubt, and conceived it might have failed in birds, especially such as having little bodies, have yet large cranies, and seem to contain much *brain*, as snipes and woodcocks; but, upon trial, I find it very true. *Brown's Vulgar Errours.*

2. That part in which the understanding is placed; therefore taken for the understanding.

The force they are under is a real force, and that of their fate but an imaginary conceived one; the one but in their *brains*, the other on their shoulders. *Hammond's Fundamentals.*

A man is first a geometrician in his *brain*, before he be such in his hand. *Hale's Origin of Mankind.*

3. Sometimes the affections.

My son Edgar! had he a hand to write this, a heart and *brain* to breed it in? *Shakesp. King Lear.*

To BRAIN. *v. a.* [from the noun.] To dash out the brains; to kill by beating out the brains.

Why, as I told thee, 'tis a custom with him i' th' afternoon to sleep; there thou may'st *brain* him. *Shakesp. Tempest.*

Outlaws of nature,
Fit to be shot and *brain'd*, without a process,
To stop infection; that's their proper death. *Dryden.*

Next seiz'd two wretches more, and headlong cast,
Brain'd on the rock, his second dire repast. *Pope's Odyssey.*

BRA'INISH. *adj.* [from *brain.*] Hotheaded; furious; as, *cerebrosus* in Latin.

In his lawless fit,
Behind the arras hearing something stir,
He whips his rapier out, and cries, a rat!
And, in his *brainish* apprehension, kills
The unseen good old man. *Shakesp. Hamlet.*

BRA'INLESS. *adj.* [from *brain.*] Silly; thoughtless; witless.

Some *brainless* men have, by great travel and labour, brought to pass, that the church is now ashamed of nothing more than of saints. *Hooker, b.* v. § 20.

If the dull *brainless* Ajax come safe off,
We'll dress him up in voices. *Shakesp. Troilus and Cressida.*

The *brainless* stripling, who, expell'd the town,
Damn'd the stiff college, and pedantick gown,
Aw'd by thy name, is dumb. *Tickell.*

BRA'INPAN. *n. s.* [from *brain* and *pan.*] The skull containing the brains.

With those huge bellows in his hands, he blows
New fire into my head: my *brainpan* glows. *Dryden.*

BRA'INSICK. *adj.* [from *brain* and *sick.*] Diseased in the understanding; addleheaded; giddy; thoughtless.

Nor once deject the courage of our minds,
Because Cassandra's mad; her *brainsick* raptures
Cannot distaste the goodness of a quarrel. *Troilus and Cress.*

They were *brainsick* men, who could neither endure the government of their king, nor yet thankfully receive the authours of their deliverance. *Knolles's History of the Turks.*

BRA'INSICKLY. *adv.* [from *brainsick.*] Weakly; headily.

Why, worthy thane,
You do unbend your noble strength to think
So *brainsickly* of things. *Shakesp. Macbeth.*

BRA'INSICKNESS. *n. s.* [from *brainsick.*] Indiscretion; giddiness.

BRAIT. *n. s.* A term used by jewellers for a rough diamond. *D.*

BRAKE. The *preterite* of *break.*

He thought it sufficient to correct the multitude with sharp words, and *brake* out into this cholerick speech. *Knolles's Hist.*

BRAKE. *n. s.* [of uncertain etymology.] A thicket of brambles, or of thorns.

A dog of this town used daily to fetch meat, and to carry the same unto a blind mastiff, that lay in a *brake* without the town. *Carew's Survey of Cornwal.*

If I'm traduc'd by tongues, which neither know
My faculties nor person; let me say,
'Tis but the fate of place, and the rough *brake*
That virtue must go through. *Shakesp. Henry* VIII.

In every bush and *brake*, where hap may find
The serpent sleeping. *Milton's Par. Lost, b.* ix. *l.* 160.

Full little thought of him the gentle knight,
Who, flying death, had there conceal'd his flight;
In *brakes* and brambles hid, and shunning mortal sight.
Dryden's Fables.

BRAKE. *n. s.*

1. An instrument for dressing hemp or flax.
2. The handle of a ship's pump.
3. A baker's kneading trough.
4. A sharp bit or snaffle for horses. *Dict.*

BRA'KY. *adj.* [from *brake.*] Thorny; prickly; rough.

Redeem arts from their rough and *braky* seats, where they lie hid and overgrown with thorns, to a pure, open light, where they may take the eye, and may be taken by the hand.
Ben. Johnson's Discovery.

BRA'MBLE. *n. s.* [bꞃemlaꞅ, Sax. *rubus*, Lat.]

1. This plant hath a flower consisting of five leaves, which are placed circularly, and expand in form of a rose; the flower-cup is divided into five parts, containing many stamina, or chives, in the bosom of the flower; in the centre of which rises the pointal, which afterwards becomes the fruit, consisting of many protuberances, and full of juice. The species are; 1. The common *bramble*, or blackberry bush. 2. The dewberry bush, or lesser *bramble*. 3. The common greater *bramble* bush, with white fruit. 4. The greater *bramble* bush, with a beautiful striped leaf. 5. The raspberry bush, or hindberry. 6. The raspberry bush, with white fruit. 7. The raspberry bush, with late red fruit. 8. The raspberry bush, without thorns. 9. The Virginian raspberry bush, with black fruit. The first and second sorts are very common in hedges, and upon dry banks, in most parts of England, and are rarely cultivated in gardens. The third sort was found by Mr. Jacob Bobart in a hedge, not far from Oxford. The fourth sort is a variety of the common *bramble*, differing therefrom only in having striped leaves. The raspberry bush is also very common in divers woods, in the northern counties of England; but is cultivated in all curious gardens, for the sake of its fruit. All these plants are easily propagated by suckers, which they send from the roots in great plenty. The best time to take them off, and transplant them, is in October. *Millar.*

2. It is taken, in popular language, for any rough prickly shrub.

The bush my bed, the *bramble* was my bow'r,
The woods can witness many a woful store. *Spenser's Past.*

There is a man haunts the forest, that abuses our young plants with carving Rosalind on their barks; hangs odes upon hawthorns, and elegies on *brambles*; all, forsooth, deifying the name of Rosalind. *Shakesp. As you like it.*

Content with food, which nature freely bred,
On wildings and on strawberries they fed:
Cornels and *bramble* berries gave the rest,
And falling acorns furnish'd out a feast. *Dryden's Ovid.*

Thy younglings, Cuddy, are but just awake,
No thrustles shrill the *bramble* bush forsake. *Gay's Past.*

BRA'MBLING. *n. s.* A bird, called also a *mountain chaffinch. Dict.*

BRAN. *n. s.* [*brenna*, Ital.] The husks of corn ground; the refuse of the sieve.

From me do back receive the flow'r of all,
And leave me but the *bran*. *Shakesp. Coriolanus.*

The citizens were driven to great distress for want of victuals; bread they made of the coarsest *bran*, moulded in cloaths; for otherwise it would not cleave together. *Hayward.*

In the sifting of fourteen years of power and favour, all that came out, could not be pure meal, but must have, among it, a certain mixture of padar and *bran*, in this lower age of human fragility. *Wotton.*

I cannot bolt this matter to the *bran*,
As Bradwardin and holy Austin can. *Dryden's Fables.*

Then water him, and, drinking what he can,
Encourage him to thirst again with *bran*. *Dryden's Virgil.*

BRANCH. *n. s.* [*branche*, Fr.]

1. The shoot of a tree from one of the main boughs. See BOUGH.

Why grow the *branches*, when the root is gone?
Why wither not the leaves that want their sap? *Shakesp.*

2. Any member or part of the whole; any distinct article; any section or subdivision.

Your

Your oaths are paſt, and now ſubſcribe your names,
That his own hand may ſtrike his honour down,
That violates the ſmalleſt *branch* herein.
Shakeſp. Love's Labour Loſt.

The belief of this was of ſpecial importance, to confirm our hopes of another life, on which ſo many *branches* of chriſtian piety does immediately depend. *Hammond's Fundamentals.*

In the ſeveral *branches* of juſtice and charity, comprehended in thoſe general rules, of loving our neighbour as ourſelves, and of doing to others as we would have them do to us, there is nothing but what is moſt fit and reaſonable. *Tillotſon.*

This precept will oblige us to perform our duty, according to the nature of the various *branches* of it. *Rogers.*

3. Any part that ſhoots out from the reſt.

And ſix *branches* ſhall come out of the ſides of it; three *branches* of the candleſtick out of the one ſide, and three *branches* of the candleſtick out of the other ſide. *Exod.* xxv. 32.

His blood, which diſperſeth itſelf by the *branches* of veins, may be reſembled to waters carried by brooks. *Raleigh's Hiſt.*

4. A ſmaller river running into, or proceeding from a larger.

If, from a main river, any *branch* be ſeparated and divided, then, where that *branch* doth firſt bound itſelf with new banks, there is that part of the river where the *branch* forſaketh the main ſtream, called the head of the river. *Raleigh's Hiſtory.*

5. Any part of a family deſcending in a collateral line.

His father, a younger *branch* of the ancient ſtock planted in Somerſetſhire, took to wife the widow. *Carew's Survey.*

6. The offspring; the deſcendant.

Great Anthony! Spain's well-beſeeming pride,
Thou mighty *branch* of emperours and kings! *Craſhaw.*

7. The antlers or ſhoots of a ſtag's horn.

8. The *branches* of a bridle are two pieces of bended iron, that bear the bit-mouth, the chains, and the curb, in the interval between the one and the other. *Farrier's Dict.*

9. [In architecture.] The arches of Gothick vaults; which arches tranſverſing from one angle to another, diagonal ways, form a croſs between the other arches, which make the ſides of the ſquare, of which the arches are diagonals. *Harris.*

To Branch. *v. n.* [from the noun.]

1. To ſpread in branches.

They were trained together in their childhoods, and there rooted betwixt them ſuch an affection, which cannot chooſe but *branch* now. *Shakeſp. Winter's Tale.*

The cauſe of ſcattering the boughs, is the haſty breaking forth of the ſap; and therefore thoſe trees riſe not in a body of any height, but *branch* near the ground. The cauſe of the Pyramis, is the keeping in of the ſap, long before it *branch*, and the ſpending of it, when it beginneth to *branch* by equal degrees. *Bacon's Natural Hiſt.* N° 588.

Plant it round with ſhade
Of laurel, ever-green, and *branching* plain. *Milt. Agoniſtes.*

Straight as a line in beauteous order ſtood,
Of oaks unſhorn a venerable wood;
Freſh was the graſs beneath, and ev'ry tree
At diſtance planted, in a due degree,
Their *branching* arms in air, with equal ſpace,
Stretch'd to their neighbours with a long embrace. *Dryden.*

One ſees her thighs transform'd, another views
Her arms ſhot out, and *branching* into boughs. *Addiſon. Ovid.*

2. To ſpread into ſeparate and diſtinct parts and ſubdiviſions.

The Alps at the one end, and the long range of Appenines that paſſes through the body of it, *branch* out, on all ſides, into ſeveral different diviſions. *Addiſon on Italy.*

If we would weigh, and keep in our minds, what it is we are conſidering, that would beſt inſtruct us when we ſhould, or ſhould not, *branch* into farther diſtinctions. *Locke.*

3. To ſpeak diffuſively, or with the diſtinction of the parts of a diſcourſe.

I have known a woman *branch* out into a long diſſertation upon the edging of a petticoat. *Spectator*, N° 247.

4. To have horns ſhooting out into antlers.

The ſwift ſtag from under ground
Bore up his *branching* head. *Milton's Par. Loſt, b.* vii. *l.* 470.

To Branch. *v. a.*

1. To divide as into branches.

The ſpirit of things animate are all continued within themſelves, and are *branched* in canals, as blood is; and the ſpirits have not only branches, but certain cells or ſeats, where the principal ſpirits do reſide. *Bacon's Natural Hiſt.*

2. To adorn with needlework, repreſenting flowers and ſprigs.

In robe of lily white ſhe was array'd,
That from her ſhoulder to her heel down raught,
The train whereof looſe far behind her ſtray'd,
Branch'd with gold and pearl, moſt richly wrought.
Spenſer's Fairy Queen, b. ii. *cant.* 9.

Bra'ncher. *n. ſ.* [from *branch.*]

1. One that ſhoots out into branches.

If their child be not ſuch a ſpeedy ſpreader and *brancher*, like the vine, yet he may yield, with a little longer expectation, as uſeful and more ſober fruit than the other. *Wotton.*

2. In falconry, a young hawk. [*branchier*, Fr.]

I enlarge my diſcourſe to the obſervation of the eires, the *brancher*, and the two ſorts of lentners. *Walton's Angler.*

Bra'nchiness. *n. ſ.* [from *branchy.*] Fulneſs of branches.

Bra'nchless. *adj.* [from *branch.*]

1. Without ſhoots or boughs

2. Without any valuable product; naked.

If I loſe mine honour,
I loſe myſelf; better I were not yours,
Than yours ſo *branchleſs.* *Shakeſp. Antony and Cleopatra.*

Bra'nchy. *adj.* [from *branch.*] Full of branches; ſpreading.

Trees on trees o'erthrown,
Fall crackling round him, and the foreſts groan;
Sudden full twenty on the plain are ſtrow'd,
And lopp'd, and lighten'd of their *branchy* load. *Pope.*

What carriage can bear away all the various, rude, and unwieldy loppings of a *branchy* tree at once? *Watts.*

BRAND. *n. ſ.* [bnanb, Saxon.]

1. A ſtick lighted, or fit to be lighted in the fire.

Have I caught thee?
He that parts us ſhall bring a *brand* from heav'n,
And fire us hence. *Shakeſp. King Lear.*

Take it, ſhe ſaid, and when your needs require,
This little *brand* will ſerve to light your fire. *Dryden's Fab.*

If, with double diligence they labour to retrieve the hours they have loſt, they ſhall be ſaved; though this is a ſervice of great difficulty, and like a *brand* plucked out of the fire. *Rogers.*

2. A ſword, in old language. [*brandar*, Runick.]

They looking back, all the eaſtern ſide beheld
Of paradiſe, ſo late their happy ſeat!
Wav'd over by that flaming *brand*; the gate
With dreadful faces throng'd, and fiery arms.
Milton's Paradiſe Loſt, b. xii. *l.* 643.

3. A thunderbolt.

The fire omnipotent prepares the *brand*,
By Vulcan wrought, and arms his potent hand;
Then flaming hurls it. *Granville.*

4. A mark made by burning a criminal with a hot iron, to note him as infamous.

Clerks convict ſhould be burned in the hand, both becauſe they might taſte of ſome corporal puniſhment, and that they might carry a *brand* of infamy. *Bacon's Hen.* VII.

The rules of good and evil are inverted, and a *brand* of infamy paſſes for a badge of honour. *L'Eſtrange.*

Where did his wit on learning fix a *brand*,
And rail at arts he did not underſtand? *Dryden's Macfleckno.*

To Brand. *v. a.* [*branden*, Dutch.] To mark with a brand, or note of infamy.

Have I liv'd thus long a wife, a true one,
Never yet *branded* with ſuſpicion? *Shakeſp. Henry* VIII.

The king was after *branded*, by Perkin's proclamation, for an execrable breaker of the rights of holy church. *Bacon.*

Brand not their actions with ſo foul a name;
Pity, at leaſt, what we are forc'd to blame. *Dryden.*

Ha! dare not for thy life, I charge thee, dare not
To *brand* the ſpotleſs virtue of my prince. *Rowe.*

Our Punick faith
Is infamous, and *branded* to a proverb. *Addiſon's Cato.*

The ſpreader of the pardons anſwered him an eaſier way, by *branding* him with hereſy. *Atterbury.*

Bra'ndgoose. *n. ſ.* A kind of wild fowl, leſs than a common gooſe, having its breaſt and wings of a dark colour. *Dict.*

To Bra'ndish. *v. a.* [from *brand*, a ſword.]

1. To wave, or ſhake, or flouriſh, as a weapon.

Brave Macbeth,
Diſdaining fortune, with his *brandiſh'd* ſteel,
Like valour's minion, carved out his paſſage. *Shakeſp.*

He ſaid, and *brandiſhing* at once his blade,
With eager pace purſu'd the flaming ſhade. *Dryden.*

Let me march their leader, not their prince;
And, at the head of your renown'd Cydonians,
Brandiſh this fam'd ſword. *Smith's Phædr. and Hippol.*

2. To play with; to flouriſh.

He, who ſhall employ all the force of his reaſon, only in *brandiſhing* of ſyllogiſms, will diſcover very little. *Locke.*

Bra'ndling. *n. ſ.* The name for a particular worm.

The dew-worm, which ſome alſo call the lob-worm, and the *brandling*, are the chief. *Walton's Angler.*

Bra'ndy. *n. ſ.* [contracted from *brandewine*, or *burnt wine.*] A ſtrong liquour diſtilled from wine.

If he travels the country, and lodgeth at inns, every dram of *brandy* extraordinary that you drink, raiſeth his character.
Swift's Directions to the Footman.

Bra'ndy-wine. The ſame with *brandy.*

It has been a common ſaying, A hair of the ſame dog; and thought, that *brandy-wine* is a common relief to ſuch. *Wiſeman.*

BRA'NGLE. *n. ſ.* [uncertainly derived.] Squabble; wrangle.

The payment of tythes in this kingdom, is ſubject to many frauds, *brangles*, and other difficulties, not only from papiſts and diſſenters, but even from thoſe who profeſs themſelves proteſtants. *Swift.*

To Bra'ngle. *v. n.* [from the noun.] To wrangle; to ſquabble.

When polite converſing ſhall be improved, company will be no no longer pestered with dull story-tellers, nor *brangling* disputers. *Swift's Introduct. to genteel Conversation.*

BRA'NGLEMENT. *n. s.* [from *brangle.*] The same with *brangle.*

BRANK. *n. s.* Buckwheat, or *brank*, is a grain very useful and advantageous in dry barren lands. *Mortimer.*

BRA'NNY. *adj.* [from *bran.*] Having the appearance of bran.

It became serpiginous, and was, when I saw it, covered with white *branny* scales. *Wiseman.*

BRA'SIER. *n. s.* [from *brass.*]

1. A manufacturer that works in brass.

There is a fellow somewhat near the door, he should be a *brasier* by his face. *Shakesp. Henry* VIII.

Brasiers that turn andirons, pots, kettles, &c. have their lathe made different from the common turners lathe. *Moxon.*

2. A pan to hold coals. [probably from *embraser*, Fr.]

It is thought they had no chimneys, but were warmed with coals on *brasiers*. *Arbuthnot on Coins.*

BRASI'L. } *n. s.* An American wood, commonly supposed to have
BRAZI'L. } been thus denominated, because first brought from Brasil: though Huet shews it had been known by that name, many years before the discovery of that country; and the best sort comes from Fernambuc. The tree ordinarily grows in dry barren rocky places, is very thick and large, usually crooked and knotty; its flowers, which are of a beautiful red, exhale an agreeable smell, which strengthens the brain. The bark is so thick, that when the trunk is peeled, which might before be equal in circumference to the body of a man, it is reduced to that of his leg. The wood is heavy, and so dry, that it scarce raises any smoke. It is used by turners, and takes a good polish; but chiefly in dying, though it gives but a spurious red. *Chamb.*

BRASS. *n. s.* [bꞃaꞅ, Sax. *prês*, Welch.]

1. A yellow metal, made by mixing copper with lapis calaminaris. It is used, in popular language, for any kind of metal in which copper has a part.

Brass is made of copper and calaminaris. *Bacon.*

Men's evil manners live in *brass*, their virtues
We write in water. *Shakesp. Henry* VIII.

Let others mold the running mass
Of metals, and inform the breathing *brass.* *Dryden.*

2. Impudence.

BRA'SSINESS. *n. s.* [from *brassy.*] An appearance like brass; some quality of brass.

BRA'SSY. *adj.* [from *brass.*]

1. Partaking of brass.

The part in which they lie, is near black, with some sparks of a *brassy* pyrites in it. *Woodward.*

2. Hard as brass.

Losses,
Enough to press a royal merchant down,
And pluck commiseration of his state
From *brassy* bosoms, and rough hearts of flint. *Shakesp.*

3. Impudent.

BRAST. *particip. adj.* [from *burst.*] Burst; broken.

There creature never past,
That back returned without heavenly grace,
But dreadful furies which their chains have *brast*,
And damned sprights sent forth to make ill men agast.
Fairy Queen, b. v. *c.* v. *stanz.* 31.

BRAT. *n. s.* [Its etymology is uncertain; bꞃatt, in Saxon, signifies a blanket; from which, perhaps, the modern signification may have come.]

1. A child, so called in contempt.

He leads them like a thing
Made by some other deity than nature,
That shapes man better; and they follow him,
Against us *brats*, with no less confidence,
Than boys pursuing summer butterflies. *Shakesp. Coriolanus.*

This *brat* is none of mine:
Hence with it, and, together with the dame,
Commit them to the fire. *Shakesp. Winter's Tale.*

The friends, that got the *brats*, were poison'd too;
In this sad case what could our vermin do? *Roscommon.*

Jupiter summoned all the birds and beasts before him, with their *brats* and little ones, to see which of them had the prettiest children. *L'Estrange.*

I shall live to see the invisible lady, to whom I was obliged, and whom I never beheld, since she was a *brat* in hanging-sleeves. *Swift.*

I give command to kill or save,
Can grant ten thousand pounds a year,
And make a beggar's *brat* a peer. *Swift.*

2. The progeny; the offspring.

The two late conspiracies were the *brats* and offspring of two contrary factions. *South.*

BRAVA'DO. *n. s.* [from *bravada*, Span.] A boast; a brag.

Spain, to make good the *bravado*,
Names it the invincible armado. *Anonymous.*

BRAVE. *adj.* [*brave*, Fr.]

1. Courageous; daring; bold; generous; high-spirited.

An Egyptian soothsayer made Antonius believe, that his genius, which otherways was *brave* and confident, was, in the presence of Octavius Cæsar, poor and cowardly. *Bacon.*

From armed foes to bring a royal prize,
Shows your *brave* heart victorious as your eyes. *Waller.*

2. Gallant; having a noble mien; lofty; graceful.

I'll prove the prettier fellow of the two,
And wear my dagger with a *braver* grace. *Shakesp.*

3. Magnificent; grand.

Rings put upon his fingers,
And *brave* attendants near him, when he wakes;
Would not the beggar then forget himself? *Shakesp.*

But whosoe'er it was nature design'd
First a *brave* place, and then as *brave* a mind. *Denham.*

4. Excellent; noble: it is an indeterminate word, used to express the superabundance of any valuable quality in men or things.

Let not old age disgrace my high desire,
O heavenly soul, in human shape contain'd;
Old wood inflam'd doth yield the *bravest* fire,
When younger doth in smoke his virtue spend. *Sidney.*

If there be iron-ore, and mills, iron is a *brave* commodity where wood aboundeth. *Bacon.*

If a statesman has not this science, he must be subject to a *braver* man than himself, whose province it is to direct all his actions to this end. *Digby on the Soul, Dedication.*

BRAVE. *n. s.* [*brave*, Fr.]

1. A hector; a man daring beyond decency or discretion.

Hot *braves*, like thee, may fight, but know not well
To manage this, the last great stake. *Dryden.*

Morat's too insolent, too much a *brave*,
His courage to his envy is a slave. *Dryden's Aurengz.*

2. A boast; a challenge; a defiance.

There end thy *brave*, and turn thy face in peace;
We grant thou canst outscold us. *Shakesp. King John.*

To BRAVE. *v. a.* [from the noun.]

1. To defy; to challenge; to set at defiance.

He upbraids Iago, that he made him
Brave me upon the watch. *Shakesp. Othello.*

My nobles leave me, and my state is *brav'd*,
Ev'n at my gates, with ranks of foreign powers. *Shakesp.*

The ills of love, not those of fate I fear;
These I can *brave*, but those I cannot bear. *Dryden.*

Like a rock unmov'd, a rock that *braves*
The raging tempest, and the rising waves. *Dryden's Æneid.*

2. To carry a boasting appearance of.

Both particular persons and factions are apt enough to flatter themselves, or, at least, to *brave* that which they believe not.
Bacon's Essays, Nº 16.

BRA'VELY. *adv.* [from *brave.*] In a brave manner; courageously; gallantly; splendidly.

Martin Swart, with his Germans, performed *bravely.* *Bacon.*

No fire, nor foe, nor fate, nor night,
The Trojan hero did affright,
Who *bravely* twice renew'd the fight. *Denham.*

Your valour *bravely* did th' assault sustain,
And fill'd the moats and ditches with the slain. *Dryden*

BRA'VERY. *n. s.* [from *brave.*]

1. Courage; magnanimity; generosity; gallantry.

Certainly it denotes no great *bravery* of mind, to do that out of a desire of fame, which we could not be prompted to by a generous passion for the glory of him that made us.
Spectator, Nº 255.

Juba, to all the *bravery* of a hero,
Adds softest love, and more than female sweetness. *Addison.*

2. Splendour; magnificence.

Where all the *bravery* that eye may see,
And all the happiness that heart desire,
Is to be found. *Spenser's Hubberd's Tale.*

3. Show; ostentation.

Let princes choose ministers more sensible of duty than of rising, and such as love business rather upon conscience than upon *bravery.* *Bacon's Essays*, Nº 37.

4. Bravado; boast.

Never could man, with more unmanlike *bravery*, use his tongue to her disgrace, which lately had sung sonnets of her praises. *Sidney's Arcadia.*

For a *bravery* upon this occasion of power, they crowned their new king in the cathedral church of Dublin. *Bacon.*

There are those that make it a point of *bravery*, to bid defiance to the oracles of divine revelation. *L'Estrange.*

BRA'VO. *n. s.* [*bravo*, Ital.] A man who murders for hire.

For boldness, like the *bravoes* and banditti, is seldom employed, but upon desperate services. *Government of the Tongue.*

No *bravoes* here profess the bloody trade,
Nor is the church the murd'rer's refuge made. *Gay's Trivia.*

To BRAWL. *v. n.* [*brouiller*, or *brauler*, Fr.]

1. To quarrel noisily and indecently.

She troubled was, alas! that it might be,
With tedious *brawlings* of her parents dear. *Sidney.*

Here comes a man of comfort, whose advice
Hath often still'd my *brawling* discontent. *Shakesp.*

How now, Sir John! what, are you *brawling* here?
Does this become your place, your time, your business?
Shakesp. Henry IV. *p.* ii.

Their batt'ring cannon charged to the mouths,
Till their foul-fearing clamours have *brawl'd* down
The flinty ribs of this contemptuous city. *Shakesp. K. John.*

In council she gives licence to her tongue
Loquacious, *brawling*, ever in the wrong. *Dryden's Fables.*

Leave all noisy contests, all immodest clamours, *brawling* language, and especially all personal scandal and scurrility to the meanest part of the vulgar world. *Watts.*

2. To speak loud and indecently.

His divisions, as the times do *brawl*,
Are in three heads; one pow'r against the French,
And one against Glendower. *Shakesp. Henry* IV. *p.* ii.

3. To make a noise.

As he lay along
Under an oak, whose antique root peeps out
Upon the brook that *brawls* along this wood. *Shakesp.*

BRAWL. *n. s.* [from the verb.] Quarrel; noise; scurrility.

He findeth, that controversies thereby are made but *brawls*; and therefore wisheth, that, in some lawful assembly of churches, all these strifes may be decided. *Hooker, Preface.*

Never since that middle summer's spring
Met we on hill, in dale, forest, or mead,
But with thy *brawls* thou hast disturb'd our sport.
Shakesp. Midsummer Night's Dream.

That bonum is an animal,
Made good with stout polemick *brawl.* *Hudibras.*

BRA'WLER. *n. s.* [from *brawl.*] A wrangler; a quarrelsome, noisy fellow.

An advocate may incur the censure of the court, for being a *brawler* in court, on purpose to lengthen out the cause. *Ayliffe.*

BRAWN. *n. s.* [of uncertain etymology.]

1. The fleshy or musculous part of the body.

The *brawn* of the arm must appear full, shadowed on one side, then shew the wrist-bone thereof. *Peacham.*

But most their looks on the black monarch bend,
His rising muscles and his *brawn* commend;
His double biting ax, and beamy spear,
Each asking a gigantick force to rear. *Dryden's Fables.*

2. The arm, so called from its being musculous.

I'll hide my silver beard in a gold beaver,
And in my vantbrace put this wither'd *brawn.* *Shakesp.*

I had purpose
Once more to hew thy target from thy *brawn.* *Shakesp.*

3. Bulk; muscular strength.

Thy boist'rous hands are then of use, when I,
With this directing head, those hands apply;
Brawn without brain is thine. *Dryden's Fables.*

4. The flesh of a boar.

The best age for the boar is from two years to five years old, at which time it is best to geld him, or sell him for *brawn.* *Mortimer.*

5. A boar.

BRA'WNER. *n. s.* [from *brawn.*] A boar killed for the table.

At Christmas time be careful of your fame,
See the old tenant's table be the same;
Then if you would send up the *brawner* head,
Sweet rosemary and bays around it spread. *King.*

BRA'WNINESS. *n. s.* [from *brawny.*] Strength; hardness.

This *brawniness* and insensibility of mind, is the best armour we can have against the common evils and accidents of life. *Locke.*

BRA'WNY. *adj.* [from *brawn.*] Musculous; fleshy; bulky; of great muscles and strength.

The *brawny* fool, who did his vigour boast,
In that presuming confidence was lost. *Dryden's Juven.*

The native energy
Turns all into the substance of the tree,
Starves and destroys the fruit, is only made
For *brawny* bulk, and for a barren shade. *Dryden's Virgil.*

To BRAY. *v. a.* [bꞃacan, Sax. *braier*, Fr.] To pound; or grind small.

I'll burst him; I will *bray*
His bones as in a mortar. *Chapman's Iliads.*

Except you would *bray* christendom in a mortar, and mould it into a new paste, there is no possibility of a holy war. *Bacon.*

To BRAY. *v. n.* [*broire*, Fr. *barrio*, Lat.]

1. To make a noise as an ass.

Laugh, and they
Return it louder than an ass can *bray.* *Dryden's Juvenal.*

2. To make an offensive or disagreeable noise.

What, shall our feast be kept with slaughter'd men?
Shall *braying* trumpets, and loud churlish drums,
Clamours of hell, be measures to our pomp? *Shakesp.*

Arms on armour clashing, *bray'd*
Horrible discord. *Milton's Paradise Lost, b.* vi. *l.* 209.

'Agad if he should hear the lion roar, he'd cudgel him into an ass, and to his primitive *braying.* *Congreve's Old Batchelor.*

BRAY. *n. s.* [from the verb.] Noise; sound.

Boist'rous untun'd drums,
And harsh resounding trumpets dreadful *bray.* *Shakesp.*

BRA'YER. *n. s.* [from *bray.*]

1. One that brays like an ass

Hold! cry'd the queen; a cat-call each shall win;
Equal your merits, equal is your din!
But that this well-disputed game may end,
Sound forth, my *brayers!* and the welkin rend. *Pope.*

2. [With printers; from *to bray*, or *beat.*] An instrument to temper the ink.

To BRAZE. *v. a.* [from *brass.*]

1. To solder with brass.

If the nut be not to be cast in brass, but only hath a worm *brazed* into it, this niceness is not so absolutely necessary, because that worm is first turned up, and bowed into the grooves of the spindle, and you may try that before it is *brazed* in the nut. *Moxon's Mechanical Exercises.*

2. To harden to impudence.

I have so often blushed to acknowledge him, that now I am *brazed* to it. *Shakesp. King Lear.*

If damned custom hath not *braz'd* it so,
That it is proof and bulwark against sense. *Shakesp. Hamlet.*

BRA'ZEN. *adj.* [from *brass.*]

1. Made of brass.

Get also a small pair of *brazen* compasses, and a fine ruler, for taking the distance. *Peacham.*

A bough his *brazen* helmet did sustain;
His heavier arms lay scatter'd on the plain. *Dryden's Æn.*

2. Proceeding from brass: a poetical use.

Trumpeters
With *brazen* din blast you the city's ear,
Make mingle with your rattling tabourines. *Shakesp.*

3. Impudent.

To BRA'ZEN. *v. n.* To be impudent; to bully.

When I used to reprimand him for his tricks, he would talk saucily, lye, and *brazen* it out, as if he had done nothing amiss. *Arbuthnot's Hist. of J. Bull.*

BRA'ZENFACE. *n. s.* [from *brazen* and *face.*] An impudent wretch.

You do, if you suspect me in any dishonesty.——Well said, *brazenface*; hold it out. *Shakesp. Merry Wives of Winds.*

BRA'ZENFACED. *adj.* [from *brazenface.*] Impudent; shameless.

What a *brazenfaced* varlet art thou, to deny thou knowest me? Is it two days ago, since I tript up thy heels, and beat thee before the king? *Shakesp. King Lear.*

Quick-witted, *brazenfac'd*, with fluent tongues,
Patient of labours, and dissembling wrongs. *Dryden.*

BRA'ZENNESS. *n. s.* [from *brazen.*]

1. Appearing like brass.

2. Impudence.

BRA'ZIER. *n. s.* See BRASIER.

The halfpence and farthings in England, if you should sell them to the *brazier*, you would not lose above a penny in a shilling. *Swift's Draper's Letters.*

BREACH. *n. s.* [from *break*; *breche*, Fr.]

1. The act of breaking any thing.

This tempest
Dashing the garment of this peace, aboded
The sudden *breach* on't. *Shakesp. Henry* VIII.

2. The state of being broken.

O you kind gods!
Cure this great *breach* in his abused nature. *Shakesp.*

3. A gap in a fortification made by a battery.

The wall was blown up in two places; by which *breach* the Turks seeking to have entered, made bloody fight. *Knolles.*

Till mad with rage upon the *breach* he fir'd,
Slew fiends and foes, and in the smoke retir'd. *Dryden.*

4. The violation of a law or contract.

That oath would sure contain them greatly, or the *breach* of it bring them to shorter vengeance. *Spenser's Ireland.*

What are those *breaches* of the law of nature and nations, which do forfeit all right in a nation to govern? *Bacon.*

Breach of duty towards our neighbours, still involves in it a *breach* of duty towards God. *South.*

The laws of the gospel are the only standing rules of morality; and the penalties affixed by God to the *breach* of those laws, the only guards that can effectually restrain men within the true bounds of decency and virtue. *Rogers.*

5. The opening in a coast.

But th' heedful boatman strongly forth did stretch
His brawny arms, and all his body strain,
That th' utmost sandy *breach* they shortly fetch,
While the dread danger does behind remain. *Fairy Queen.*

6. Difference; quarrel; separation of kindness.

It would have been long before the jealousies and *breaches* between the armies, would have been composed. *Clarendon.*

7. Infraction; injury.

This *breach* upon his kingly power was without a precedent. *Clarendon.*

BREAD. *n. s.* [bꞃeoꝺ, Saxon.]

1. Food made of ground corn.

Mankind have found the means to make them into *bread*, which is the lightest and properest aliment for human bodies. *Arbuthnot on Aliments.*

Bread that decaying man with strength supplies,
And gen'rous wine, which thoughtful sorrow flies. *Pope.*

2. Food in general, such as nature requires; to *get bread*, implies, to get sufficient for support without luxury.

In the sweat of thy face shalt thou eat *bread*. *Gen.* iii. 19.

If these pretenders were not supported by the simplicity of the inquisitive fools, the trade would not find them *bread*. *L'Estrange.*

This dowager on whom my tale I found,
A simple sober life in patience led,
And had but just enough to buy her *bread*. *Dryden.*

When I submit to such indignities,
Make me a citizen, a senator of Rome;
To sell my country, with my voice, for *bread*. *Philips.*

I neither have been bred a scholar, a soldier, nor to any kind of business; this creates uneasiness in my mind, fearing I shall in time want *bread*. *Spectator*, N° 203.

3. Support of life at large.

God is pleased to try our patience by the ingratitude of those, who, having eaten of our *bread*, have lift up themselves against us. *King Charles.*

But sometimes virtue starves, while vice is fed;
What then? Is the reward of virtue *bread*? *Pope.*

BREAD-CHIPPER. *n. s.* [from *bread* and *chip.*] One that chips bread; a baker's servant.

No abuse, Hal, on my honour; no abuse.——Not to dispraise me, and call me pander, and *bread-chipper*, and I know not what? *Shakesp. Henry* IV. *p.* ii.

BREAD-CORN. *n. s.* [from *bread* and *corn.*] Corn of which bread is made.

There was not one drop of beer in the town; the bread, and *bread-corn*, sufficed not for six days. *Hayward.*

When it is ripe, they gather it, and, bruising it among *bread-corn*, they put it up into a vessel, and keep it as food for their slaves. *Broome's Notes on the Odyssey, b.* viii.

BREAD-ROOM. *n. s.* [In a ship.] A part of the hold separated by a bulk-head from the rest, where the bread and bisket for the men are kept. *Sea Dict.*

BREADTH. *n. s.* [from bꝛab, broad, Saxon.] The measure of any plain superficies from side to side.

There is in Ticinum, in Italy, a church that hath windows only from above: it is in length an hundred feet, in *breadth* twenty, and in height near fifty; having a door in the midst. *Bacon's Nat. Hist.* N° 794.

The river Ganges, according unto later relations, if not in length, yet in *breadth* and depth, may be granted to excel it. *Brown's Vulgar Errours, b.* vi. *c.* 7.

Then all approach the slain with vast surprize,
Admire on what a *breadth* of earth he lies. *Dryden.*

In our Gothick cathedrals, the narrowness of the arch makes it rise in height; the lowness opens it in *breadth*. *Addison.*

To BREAK. *v. a.* pret. I *broke*, or *brake*; part. pass. *broke*, or *broken.* [bꝛecan, Saxon.]

1. To part by violence.

When I *brake* the five loaves among five thousand, how many baskets of fragments took ye up? *Mark*, viii. 19.

Let us *break* their bands asunder, and cast away their cords from us. *Psalm* ii. 3.

See, said the sire, how soon 'tis done;
Then took and *broke* them one by one:
So strong you'll be in friendship ty'd;
So quickly *broke*, if you divide. *Swift.*

2. To burst, or open by force.

Moses tells us, that the fountains of the earth were *broke* open, or clove asunder. *Burnet's Theory.*

3. To pierce; to divide, as light divides darkness.

By a dim winking lamp, which feebly *broke*
The gloomy vapours, he lay stretch'd along. *Dryden.*

4. To destroy by violence.

This is the fabrick, which, when God *breaketh* down, none can build up again. *Burnet's Theory.*

5. To overcome; to surmount.

Into my hand he forc'd the tempting gold,
While I with modest struggling *broke* his hold. *Gay.*

6. To batter; to make breaches or gaps in.

I'd give bay Curtal, and his furniture,
My mouth no more were *broken* than these boys,
And writ as little beard. *Shakesp. All's well that ends well.*

7. To crush or destroy the strength of the body.

O father abbot!
An old man, *broken* with the storms of state,
Is come to lay his weary bones among ye;
Give him a little earth for charity. *Shakesp. Henry* VIII.

The breaking of that parliament
Broke him; as that dishonest victory
At Chæronea, fatal to liberty,
Kill'd with report that old man eloquent. *Milton.*

Have not some of his vices weakened his body, and *broke* his health? have not others dissipated his estate, and reduced him to want? *Tillotson.*

8. To sink or appal the spirit.

I'll brave her to her face;
I'll give my anger its free course against her:
Thou shalt see, Phœnix, how I'll *break* her pride. *Philips.*

9. To subdue.

Why, then, thou can'st not *break* her to the lute.—
—Why, no; for she hath broke the lute to me. *Shakesp. Taming the Shrew.*

Behold young Juba, the Numidian prince,
With how much care he forms himself to glory,
And *breaks* the fierceness of his native temper. *Addison's Cato.*

10. To crush; to disable; to incapacitate.

The defeat of that day at Cropredy was much greater than it then appeared to be; and it even *broke* the heart of his army. *Clarendon.*

Your hopes without are vanish'd into smoke;
Your captains taken, and your armies *broke*. *Dryden.*

11. To weaken the mind.

Opprest nature sleeps:
This rest might yet have balm'd thy *broken* senses,
Which, if conveniency will not allow,
Stand in hard cure. *Shakesp. King Lear.*

If any dabler in poetry dares venture upon the experiment, he will only *break* his brains. *Felton on the Classicks.*

12. To tame; to train to obedience.

What boots it to *break* a colt, and to let him streight run loose at random? *Spenser's State of Ireland.*

So fed before he's *broke*, he'll bear
Too great a stomach patiently to feel
The lashing whip, or chew the curbing steel. *May's Virgil.*

That hot-mouth'd beast that bears against the curb,
Hard to be *broken* even by lawful kings. *Dryden.*

No sports but what belong to war they know,
To *break* the stubborn colt, to bend the bow. *Dryden.*

Virtues like these,
Make human nature shine, reform the soul,
And *break* our fierce barbarians into men. *Addison's Cato.*

13. To make bankrupt.

For this few know themselves: for merchants *broke*,
View their estate with discontent and pain. *Davies.*

The king's grown bankrupt, like a *broken* man. *Shakesp.*

With arts like these, rich Matho, when he speaks,
Attracts all fees, and little lawyers *breaks*. *Dryden.*

A command or call to be liberal, all of a sudden impoverishes the rich, *breaks* the merchant, and shuts up every private man's exchequer. *South.*

14. To crack or open the skin, so as that the blood comes.

She could have run and waddled all about; even the day before she *broke* her brow; and then my husband took up the child. *Shakesp. Romeo and Juliet.*

Weak soul! and blindly to destruction led:
She break her heart! she'll sooner *break* your head. *Dryden.*

15. To violate a contract or promise.

Lovers *break* not hours,
Unless it be to come before their time. *Shakesp. T. G. of Ver.*

Pardon this fault, and, by my soul I swear,
I never more will *break* an oath with thee. *Shakesp.*

Did not our worthies of the house,
Before they *broke* the peace, *break* vows? *Hudibras.*

16. To infringe a law.

Unhappy man! to *break* the pious laws
Of nature, pleading in his children's cause. *Dryden.*

17. To intercept; to hinder the effect of.

Break their talk, mistress, quickly; my kinsman shall speak for himself. *Shakesp. Merry Wives of Windsor.*

Spirit of wine, mingled with common water, yet so as if the first fall be *broken*, by means of a sop, or otherwise, it stayeth above. *Bacon's Physical Remains.*

Think not my sense of virtue is so small;
I'll rather leap down first, and *break* your fall. *Dryden.*

As one condemn'd to leap a precipice,
Who sees before his eyes the depth below,
Stops short, and looks about for some kind shrub,
To *break* his dreadful fall. *Dryden's Spanish Friar.*

She held my hand, the destin'd blow to *break*,
Then from her rosy lips began to speak. *Dryden.*

18. To interrupt.

Some solitary cloister will I choose,
Coarse my attire, and short shall be my sleep,
Broke by the melancholy midnight bell. *Dryden's Sp. Friar.*

The father was so moved, that he could only command his voice, *broke* with sighs and sobbings, so far as to bid her proceed. *Addison. Spectator*, N° 164.

The poor shade shiv'ring stands, and must not *break*
His painful silence, till the mortal speak. *Tickell.*

Sometimes in *broken* words he sigh'd his care,
Look'd pale, and tumbled when he view'd the fair. *Gay.*

19. To separate company.

Did not Paul and Barnabas dispute with that vehemence, that they were forced to *break* company? *Atterbury.*

20. To dissolve any union.

It is great folly, as well as injustice, to *break* off so noble a relation. *Collier of Friendship.*

21. To reform; with *of*.

The French were not quite *broken of* it, until some time after they became christians. *Grew's Cosmologia Sacra, b.* iii. *c.* 6.

22. To open ſomething new; to propound ſomething by an overture.

When any new thing ſhall be propounded, no counſellor ſhould ſuddenly deliver any poſitive opinion, but only hear it, and, at the moſt, but to *break* it, at firſt, that it may be the better underſtood at the next meeting. *Bacon.*

I, who much deſir'd to know
Of whence ſhe was, yet fearful how to *break*
My mind, adventur'd humbly thus to ſpeak. *Dryden's Fab.*

23. *To break the back.* To ſtrain or diſlocate the vertebræ with too heavy burdens.

I'd rather crack my ſinews, *break my back*,
Than you ſhould ſuch diſhonour undergo. *Shakeſp. Tempeſt.*

24. *To break the back.* To diſable one's fortune.

O, many
Have *broke their backs*, with laying manors on 'em,
For this great journey. *Shakeſp. Henry* VIII.

25. *To break a deer.* To cut it up at table.
26. *To break faſt.* To eat the firſt time in the day.
27. *To break ground.* To plow.

When the price of corn falleth, men generally give over ſurplus tillage, and *break no more ground* than will ſerve to ſupply their own turn. *Carew's Survey of Cornwal.*

The huſbandman muſt firſt *break the land*, before it be made capable of good ſeed. *Sir J. Davies on Ireland.*

28. *To break ground.* To open trenches.
29. *To break the heart.* To deſtroy with grief.

Good my lord, enter here.——
—Will't *break my heart?*——
I'd rather *break mine own.* *Shakeſp. King Lear.*

Should not all relations bear a part?
It were enough to *break a ſingle heart.* *Dryden.*

30. *To break a jeſt.* To utter a jeſt unexpected.
31. *To break the neck.* To lux, or put out the neck joints.

I had as lief thou didſt *break his neck*, as his fingers. *Shakeſp.*

32. *To break off.* To put a ſudden ſtop.
33. *To break off.* To preclude by ſome obſtacle ſuddenly interpoſed.

To check the ſtarts and ſallies of the ſoul,
And *break off* all its commerce with the tongue. *Addiſon.*

34. *To break up.* To diſſolve; to put a ſudden end to.

Who cannot reſt till he good fellows find;
He *breaks up* houſe, turns out of doors his mind. *Herbert.*

He threatened, that the tradeſmen would beat out his teeth, if he did not retire immediately, and *break up* the meeting. *Arbuthnot's Hiſtory of J. Bull.*

35. *To break up.* To open; to lay open.

The ſhells being thus lodged amongſt this mineral matter, when this comes now to be *broke up*, it exhibits impreſſions of the ſhells. *Woodward on Foſſils.*

36. *To break up.* To ſeparate or diſband.

After taking the ſtrong city of Belgrade, Solyman returning to Conſtantinople, *broke up* his army, and there lay ſtill the whole year following. *Knolles's Hiſtory of the Turks.*

37. *To break upon the wheel.* To puniſh by ſtretching a criminal upon the wheel, and breaking his bones with bats.
38. *To break wind.* To give vent to wind in the body.

To Break. *v. n.*

1. To part in two.

Give ſorrow words, the grief that does not ſpeak,
Whiſpers the o'erfraught heart, and bids it *break.* *Shakeſp.*

2. To burſt.

The clouds are ſtill above; and, while I ſpeak,
A ſecond deluge o'er our heads may *break.* *Dryden.*

The Roman camp
Hangs o'er us black and threatning, like a ſtorm
Juſt *breaking* on our heads. *Dryden's All for Love.*

3. To burſt by daſhing, as waves on a rock.

He could compare the confuſion of a multitude to that tumult in the Icarian ſea, daſhing and *breaking* among its crowd of iſlands. *Pope's Eſſay on Homer.*

At laſt a falling billow ſtops his breath,
Breaks o'er his head, and whelms him underneath. *Dryden.*

4. To break as a ſwelling; to open, and diſcharge matter.

Some hidden abſceſs in the meſentery, *breaking* ſome few days after, was diſcovered to be an apoſteme. *Harvey.*

Aſk one who hath ſubdued his natural rage, how he likes the change, and undoubtedly he will tell you, that it is no leſs happy than the eaſe of a *broken* impoſtume, after the painful gathering and filling of it. *Decay of Piety.*

5. To open as the morning.

The day *breaks* not, it is my heart,
Becauſe that I and you muſt part.
Stay, or elſe my joys will die,
And periſh in their infancy. *Donne.*

When a man thinks of any thing in the darkneſs of the night, whatever deep impreſſions it may make in his mind, they are apt to vaniſh as ſoon as the day *breaks* about him. *Addiſon. Spectator*, N° 465.

6. To burſt forth; to exclaim.

Every man,
After the hideous ſtorm that follow'd, was
A thing inſpir'd; and, not conſulting, *broke*
Into a general prophecy. *Shakeſp. Henry* VIII.

7. To become bankrupt.

I did mean, indeed, to pay you with this; which, if, like an ill venture, it come unluckily home, I *break*, and you, my gentle creditors, loſe. *Shakeſp. Henry* IV. *p.* ii. *Epilogue.*

He that puts all upon adventures, doth oftentimes *break*, and come to poverty. *Bacon's Eſſays*, N° 35.

Cutler ſaw tenants *break*, and houſes fall,
For very want he could not build a wall. *Pope.*

8. To decline in health and ſtrength.

Yet thus, methinks, I hear them ſpeak;
See how the dean begins to *break*:
Poor gentleman! he droops apace. *Swift.*

9. To iſſue out with vehemence.

Whoſe wounds, yet freſh, with bloody hands he ſtrook,
While from his breaſt the dreadful accents *broke.* *Pope.*

10. To make way with ſome kind of ſuddeneſs, impetuoſity, or violence.

Calamities may be neareſt at hand, and readieſt to *break* in ſuddenly upon us, which we, in regard of times or circumſtances, may imagine to be fartheſt off. *Hooker, b.* v. § 41.

The three mighty men *broke* through the hoſt of the Philiſtines. 2 *Sam.* xxiii. 16.

They came into Judah, and *brake* into it. 2 *Chron.* xxi. 17.

Or who ſhut up the ſea within doors, when it *brake* forth, as if it had iſſued out of the womb? *Job*, xxxviii. 8.

This, this is he; ſoftly awhile,
Let us not *break* in upon him. *Milton's Agoniſtes, l.* 115.

He reſolved, that Balfour ſhould uſe his utmoſt endeavour to *break* through with his whole body of horſe. *Clarendon, b.* viii.

When the channel of a river is overcharged with water, more than it can deliver, it neceſſarily *breaks* over the banks, to make itſelf room. *Hale's Origin of Mankind.*

Sometimes his anger *breaks* through all diſguiſes,
And ſpares not gods nor men. *Denham's Sophy.*

Till through thoſe clouds the ſun of knowledge *brake*,
And Europe from her lethargy did wake. *Denham.*

Oh! could'ſt thou *break* through fate's ſevere decree,
A new Marcellus ſhall ariſe in thee. *Dryden's Æneid.*

At length I've acted my ſevereſt part;
I feel the woman *breaking* in upon me,
And melt about my heart, my tears will flow. *Addiſon's Cato.*

How does the luſtre of our father's actions,
Through the dark cloud of ills that cover him,
Break out, and burn with more triumphant blaze! *Addiſon.*

And yet, methinks, a beam of light *breaks* in,
On my departing ſoul. *Addiſon's Cato.*

There are not wanting ſome, who, ſtruck with the uſefulneſs of theſe charities, *break* through all the difficulties and obſtructions that now lie in the way towards advancing them. *Atterbury.*

Almighty pow'r, by whoſe moſt wiſe command,
Helpleſs, forlorn, uncertain here I ſtand;
Take this faint glimmering of thyſelf away,
Or *break* into my ſoul with perfect day! *Arbuthnot.*

Heav'n its ſparkling portals wide diſplay,
And *break* upon thee in a flood of day! *Pope's Meſſiah.*

I muſt pay her the laſt duty of friendſhip wherever ſhe is, though I *break* through the whole plan of life which I have formed in my mind. *Swift's Letters.*

11. To come to an explanation.

But perceiving this great alteration in his friend, he thought fit to *break* with him thereof. *Sidney, b.* i.

Stay with me awhile;
I am to *break* with thee of ſome affairs,
That touch me near. *Shakeſp. Two Gentlemen of Verona.*

Break with them, gentle love,
About the drawing as many of their huſbands
Into the plot, as can; if not, to rid 'em,
That'll be the eaſier practice. *B. Johnſon's Catiline.*

12. To fall out; to be friends no longer.

Be not afraid to *break*
With murd'rers, and traitors, for the ſaving
A life ſo near and neceſſary to you,
As is your country's. *B. Johnſon's Catiline.*

To *break* upon the ſcore of danger or expence, is to be mean and narrow-ſpirited. *Collier on Friendſhip.*

Sighing, he ſays, we muſt certainly *break*,
And my cruel unkindneſs compels him to ſpeak. *Prior.*

13. *To break from.* To ſeparate from with ſome vehemence.

How didſt thou ſcorn life's meaner charms,
Thou who cou'dſt *break from* Laura's arms? *Roſcommon.*

Thus radiant *from* the circling crowd he *broke*;
And thus with manly modeſty he ſpoke. *Dryden's Virgil.*

This cuſtom makes bigots and ſcepticks; and thoſe that *break from* it, are in danger of hereſy. *Locke.*

14. *To break in.* To enter unexpectedly, without proper preparation.

The doctor is a pedant, that, with a deep voice, and a magiſterial air, *breaks in* upon converſation, and drives down all before him. *Addiſon on Italy.*

15. To

15. *To break.* To discard.

When I see a great officer *broke*, a change made in the court, or the ministry, and this under the most gracious princess that ever reigned. *Swift.*

16. *To break loose.* To escape from captivity.

Who would not, finding way, *break loose* from hell,
And boldly venture to whatever place,
Farthest from pain? *Milton's Par. Lost, b.* iv. *l.* 889.

17. *To break loose.* To shake off restraint.

If we deal falsely in covenant with God, and *break loose* from all our engagements to him, we release God from all the promises he has made to us. *Tillotson.*

18. *To break off.* To desist suddenly.

Do not peremptorily *break off*, in any business, in a fit of anger; but howsoever you shew bitterness, do not act any thing that is not revocable. *Bacon.*

Pius Quintus, at the very time when that memorable victory was won by the Christians at Lepanto, being then hearing of causes in consistory, *broke off* suddenly, and said to those about him, it is now more time we should give thanks to God. *Bacon.*

When you begin to consider, whether you may safely take one draught more, let that be accounted a sign late enough to *break off*. *Taylor's Rule of living holy.*

19. *To break off from.* To part from with violence.

I must *from* this enchanting queen *break off*. *Shakesp.*

20. *To break out.* To discover itself in sudden effects.

Let not one spark of filthy lustful fire
Break out, that may her sacred peace molest. *Spenser.*

They smother and keep down the flame of the mischief, so as it may not *break out* in their time of government; what comes afterwards, they care not. *Spenser's Ireland.*

Such a deal of wonder is *broken out* within this hour, that ballad-makers cannot be able to express it. *Shakesp.*

As fire *breaks out* of flint by percussion, so wisdom and truth issueth out of the agitation of argument. *Howel.*

Fully ripe, his swelling fate *breaks out*,
And hurries him to mighty mischiefs on. *Dryden.*

All turn'd their sides, and to each other spoke;
I saw their words *break out* in fire and smoke. *Dryden.*

Like a ball of fire, the further thrown,
Still with a greater blaze she shone,
And her bright soul *broke out* on ev'ry side. *Dryden.*

There can be no greater labour, than to be always dissembling; there being so many ways by which a smothered truth is apt to blaze, and *break out*. *South.*

They are men of concealed fire, that doth not *break out* in the ordinary circumstances of life. *Addison on the War.*

A violent fever *broke out* in the place, which swept away great multitudes. *Addison. Spectator,* N° 164.

21. *To break out.* To have eruptions from the body, as pustules or sores.

22. *To break out.* To become dissolute.

He *broke* not *out* into his great excesses, while he was restrained by the counsels and authority of Seneca. *Dryden.*

23. *To break up.* To cease; to intermit.

It is credibly affirmed, that, upon that very day, when the river first riseth, great plagues in Cairo use suddenly to *break up*. *Bacon's Natural Hist.* N° 743.

24. *To break up.* To dissolve itself.

These, and the like conceits, when men have cleared their understanding, by the light of experience, will scatter and *break up*, like mist. *Bacon's Nat. Hist.* N° 124.

The speedy depredation of air upon watery moisture, and version of the same into air, appeareth in nothing more visible, than the sudden discharge or vanishing of a little cloud of breath, or vapour, from glass, or any polished body; for the mistiness scattereth, and *breaketh up* suddenly. *Bacon.*

But, ere he came near it, the pillar and cross of light *brake up*, and cast itself abroad, as it were, into a firmament of many stars. *Bacon's New Atlantis.*

What we obtain by conversation, is oftentimes lost again, as soon as the company *breaks up*, or, at least, when the day vanishes. *Watts.*

25 *To break up.* To begin holidays; to be dismissed from business.

Our army is dispers'd already:
Like youthful steers unyok'd, they took their course
East, west, north, south: or, like a school *broke up*,
Each hurries tow'rds his home and sporting-place. *Shakesp.*

26. *To break with.* To part friendship with any.

There is a slave whom we have put in prison,
Reports, the Volscians, with two several powers,
Are entered in the Roman territories.—
—Go see this rumourer whipt. It cannot be,
The Volscians dare *break with* us. *Shakesp. Coriolanus.*

Can there be any thing of friendship in snares, hooks, and trapans? Whosoever *breaks with* his friend upon such terms, has enough to warrant him in so doing, both before God and and man. *South.*

Invent some apt pretence,
To *break with* Bertran. *Dryden's Spanish Friar.*

27. It is to be observed of this extensive and perplexed *verb*, that, in all its significations, whether *active* or *neutral*, it has some reference to its primitive meaning, by implying either detriment, suddenness, or violence.

BREAK. *n. s.* [from the verb.]

1. State of being broken; opening.

From the *break* of day until noon, the roaring of the cannon never ceased. *Knolles's Hist. of the Turks.*

For now, and since first *break* of day, the fiend,
Mere serpent in appearance, forth was come. *Parad. Lost.*

They must be drawn from far, and without *breaks*, to avoid the multiplicity of lines. *Dryden's Dufresnoy.*

The sight of it would be quite lost, did it not sometimes discover itself through the *breaks* and openings of the woods that grow about it. *Addison.*

2. A pause; an interruption.

3. A line drawn, noting that the sense is suspended.

All modern trash is
Set forth with num'rous *breaks* and dashes. *Swift.*

BRE'AKER. *n. s.* [from *break.*]

1. He that breaks any thing.

Cardinal, I'll be no *breaker* of the law. *Shakesp. H.* IV.

If the churches were not employed to be places to hear God's law, there would be need of them, to be prisons for the *breakers* of the laws of men. *South.*

2. A wave broken by rocks or sandbanks.

To BRE'AKFAST. *v. n.* [from *break* and *fast.*] To eat the first meal in the day.

As soon as Phœbus' rays inspect us,
First, Sir, I read, and then I *breakfast*. *Prior.*

BRE'AKFAST. *n. s.* [from the verb.]

1. The first meal in the day.

The duke was at *breakfast*, the last of his repasts in this world. *Wotton.*

2. The thing eaten at the first meal.

Hope is a good *breakfast*, but it is a bad supper. *Bacon.*

A good piece of bread would be often the best *breakfast* for my young master. *Locke.*

3. A meal, or food in general.

Had I been seized by a hungry lion,
I would have been a *breakfast* to the beast. *Shakesp.*

I lay me down to gasp my latest breath,
The wolves will get a *breakfast* by my death,
Yet scarce enough their hunger to supply. *Dryden.*

BRE'AKNECK. *n. s.* [from *break* and *neck.*] A fall in which the neck is broken; a steep place endangering the neck.

I must
Forsake the court; to do't or no, is certain
To me a *breakneck*. *Shakesp. Winter's Tale.*

BRE'AKPROMISE. *n. s.* [from *break* and *promise.*] One that makes a practice of breaking his promise.

I will think you the most atheistical *breakpromise*, and the most hollow lover. *Shakesp. As you like it.*

BRE'AKVOW. *n. s.* [from *break* and *vow.*] He that practises the breach of vows.

That daily *breakvow*, he that wins of all,
Of kings, of beggars, old men, young men, maids.
Shakesp. King John.

BREAM. *n. s.* [*brame*, Fr.] The name of a fish.

The *bream* being at full growth, is a large fish; he will breed both in rivers and ponds, but loves best to live in ponds. He is, by *Gesner*, taken to be more elegant than wholsome. He is long in growing, but breeds exceedingly in a water that pleases him, and, in many ponds, so fast as to overstock them, and starve the other fish. He is very broad, with a forked tail, and his scales set in excellent order. He hath large eyes, and a narrow sucking mouth, two sets of teeth, and a lozing bone, to help his grinders. The male is observed to have two large melts, and the female two large bags of eggs or spawn. *Walton's Angler.*

A broad *bream*, to please some curious taste,
While yet alive in boiling water cast,
Vex'd with unwonted heat, boils, flings about. *Waller.*

BREAST. *n. s.* [bneoꞅꞇ, Saxon.]

1. The middle part of the human body, between the neck and the belly.

2. The dugs or teats of women which contain the milk.

The substance of the breasts is composed of a great number of glands, of an oval figure, which lie in a great quantity of fat. Their excretory ducts, as they approach the nipple, join and unite together, till at last they form seven, eight, or more, small pipes, called *tubuli lactiferi*, which have several cross canals, by which they communicate with one another, that if any of them be stopped, the milk, which was brought to it, might not stagnate, but pass through by the other pipes, which all terminate in the extremity of the nipple. They have arteries and veins from the subclavian and intercostal. They have nerves from the vertebral pairs, and from the sixth pair of the brain. Their use is to separate the milk for the nourishment of the fœtus. The tubes, which compose the glands of the *breast* in maids, like a sphincter muscle, contract so closely, that no part of the blood can enter them; but when the womb grows big with a fœtus, and compresses the descending trunk of the great artery, the blood flows in a greater quantity, and with a greater force, through the arteries of the *breasts*, and forces a passage into their glands, which, being at first narrow, admits only of a thin water; but growing wider by degrees, as the womb grows bigger, the glands receive a thick serum, and, after birth, they run with a thick milk; because that blood, which before did flow to the fœtus, and, for three or four days afterwards, by the uterus, beginning then to stop, does more dilate the mamillary glands. *Quincy.*

They pluck the fatherless from the *breast*. *Job*, xxiv. 9.

3. The part of a beast that is under the neck, between the forelegs.

4. The heart; the conscience; the disposition of the mind.

Needless was written law, where none opprest;
The law of man was written in his *breast*. *Dryden's Ovid.*

5. The passions; the regard.

Margarita first possess'd,
If I remember well, my *breast*. *Cowley.*

To BREAST. *v. a.* [from the noun.] To meet in front; to oppose breast to breast.

The threaden sails
Draw the huge bottoms through the furrow'd sea,
Breasting the lofty surge. *Shakesp. Henry* V.

BRE'ASTBONE. *n. s.* [from *breast* and *bone.*] The bone of the breast; the sternum.

The belly shall be eminent by shadowing the flank, and under the *breastbone*. *Peacham.*

BRE'ASTCASKET. *n. s.* [from *breast* and *casket.*] With mariners. The largest and longest caskets, which are a sort of strings placed in the middle of the yard.

BRE'ASTFAST. *n. s.* [from *breast* and *fast.*] In a ship. A rope fastened to some part of her forward on, to hold her head to a warp, or the like. *Harris.*

BRE'ASTHIGH. *adj.* [from *breast* and *high.*] Up to the breast.

The river itself gave way unto her, so that she was straight *breasthigh*. *Sidney.*

Lay madam Partlet basking in the sun,
Breasthigh in sand. *Dryden's Fables.*

BRE'ASTHOOKS. *n. s.* [from *breast* and *hook.*] With shipwrights. The compassing timbers before, that help to strengthen the stem, and all the forepart of the ship. *Harris.*

BRE'ASTKNOT. *n. s.* [from *breast* and *knot.*] A knot or bunch of ribbands worn by women on the breast.

Our ladies have still faces, and our men hearts, why may we not hope for the same atchievements from the influence of this *breastknot?* *Addison. Freeholder*, N° 11.

BRE'ASTPLATE. *n. s.* [from *breast* and *plate.*] Armour for the breast.

What stronger *breastplate* than a heart untainted?
Thrice is he arm'd, that hath his quarrel just. *Shakesp.*

'Gainst shield, helm, *breastplate*, and, instead of those,
Five sharp smooth stones from the next brook he chose. *Cowley.*

This venerable champion will come into the field, armed only with a pocket-pistol, before his old rusty *breastplate* could be scoured, and his cracked headpiece mended. *Swift.*

BRE'ASTPLOUGH. *n. s.* [from *breast* and *plough.*] A plough used for paring turf, driven by the breast.

The *breastplough*, which a man shoves before him. *Mortim.*

BRE'ASTROPES. *n. s.* [from *breast* and *rope.*] In a ship. Those ropes which fasten the yards to the parrels, and, with the parrels, hold the yards fast to the mast. *Harris.*

BRE'ASTWORK. *n. s.* [from *breast* and *work.*] Works thrown up as high as the breast of the defendants; the same with *parapet*.

Sir John Astley cast up *breastworks*, and made a redoubt for the defence of his men. *Clarendon*, *b.* viii.

BREATH. *n. s.* [bꞃæð, Saxon.]

1. The air drawn in and ejected out of the body by living animals.

Whither are they vanish'd?
Into the air: and what seem'd corporal
Melted, as *breath* into the wind. *Shakesp. King Lear.*

2. Life.

No man has more contempt than I of *breath*;
But whence hast thou the pow'r to give me death? *Dryden.*

3. The state or power of breathing freely; opposed to the condition in which a man is breathless and spent.

At other times, he casts to sue the chace
Of swift wild beasts, or run on foot a race,
T' enlarge his *breath*, large breath in arms most needful,
Or else, by wrestling, to wax strong and heedful. *Spenser.*

What is your difference? speak.—
—I am scarce in *breath*, my lord. *Shakesp. King Lear.*

Spaniard, take *breath*; some respite I'll afford;
My cause is more advantage than your sword. *Dryden.*

Our swords so wholly did the fates employ,
That they, at length, grew weary to destroy;
Refus'd the work we brought, and out of *breath*,
Made sorrow and despair attend for death. *Dryden's Aureng.*

4. Respiration; the power of breathing.

Rest, that gives all men life, gave him his death,
And too much breathing put him out of *breath*. *Milton.*

5. Respite; pause; relaxation.

Give me some *breath*; some little pause, dear lord,
Before I positively speak. *Shakesp. Richard* III.

6. Breeze; moving air.

Vent all thy passion, and I'll stand its shock,
Calm and unruffled as a summer's sea,
When not a *breath* of wind flies o'er its surface. *Addis. Cato.*

7. A single act; an instant.

You menace me, and court me in a *breath*,
Your Cupid looks as dreadfully as death. *Dryden.*

BRE'ATHABLE. *adj.* [from *breath.*] That may be breathed; as, *breathable* air.

To BREATHE. *v. n.* [from *breath.*]

1. To draw in and throw out the air by the lungs.

Safe return'd, the race of glory past,
New to his friends embrace, had *breath'd* his last. *Pope.*

2. To live.

Let him *breathe*, between the heav'ns and earth,
A private man in Athens. *Shakesp. Antony and Cleopatra.*

3. To take breath; to rest.

He presently followed the victory so hot upon the Scots, that he suffered them not to *breathe*, or gather themselves together again. *Spenser's State of Ireland.*

Three times they *breath'd*, and three times did they drink,
Upon agreement. *Shakesp. Henry* IV. *p.* i.

When France had *breath'd*, after intestine broils,
And peace and conquest crown'd her foreign toils. *Roscomm.*

4. To pass by breathing.

Shall I not then be stifled in the vault,
To whose foul mouth no healthsome air *breathes* in,
And there be strangl'd ere my Romeo comes? *Shakesp.*

To BREATHE. *v. a.*

1. To inspire, or inhale into one's own body, and eject or expire out of it.

They wish to live,
Their pains and poverty desire to bear,
To view the light of heav'n, and *breathe* the vital air. *Dryd.*

They here began to *breathe* a most delicious kind of æther, and saw all the fields about them covered with a kind of purple light. *Tatler*, N° 81.

2. To inject by breathing.

He *breathed* into us the breath of life, a vital active spirit; whose motions, he expects, should own the dignity of its original. *Decay of Piety.*

I would be young, be handsome, be belov'd,
Could I but *breathe* myself into Adrastus. *Dryden.*

3. To expire; to eject by breathing.

She is called, by ancient authours, the tenth muse; and, by Plutarch, is compared to Caius, the son of Vulcan, who *breathed* out nothing but flame. *Spectator*, N° 223.

4. To exercise; to keep in breath.

Thy greyhounds are as swift as *breathed* stags. *Shakesp.*

5. To inspire; to move or actuate by breath.

The artful youth proceed to form the quire;
They *breathe* the flute, or strike the vocal wire. *Prior.*

6. To exhale; to send out as breath.

His altar *breathes*
Ambrosial odours, and ambrosial flow'rs. *Milton's Par. Lost.*

7. To utter privately.

I have tow'rd heaven *breath'd* a secret vow,
To live in prayer and contemplation. *Shakesp. Mer. of Ven.*

8. To give air or vent to.

The ready cure to cool the raging pain,
Is underneath the foot to *breathe* a vein. *Dryden's Virgil.*

BRE'ATHER. *n. s.* [from *breathe.*]

1. One that breathes, or lives.

She shows a body rather than a life,
A statue than a *breather*. *Shakesp. Antony and Cleopatra.*

I will chide no *breather* in the world but myself. *Shakesp.*

2. One that utters any thing.

No particular scandal once can touch,
But it confounds the *breather*. *Shakesp. Meas. for Measure.*

3. Inspirer; one that animates or infuses by inspiration.

The *breather* of all life does now expire:
His milder father summons him away. *Norris.*

BRE'ATHING. *n. s.* [from *breathe.*]

1. Aspiration; secret prayer.

While to high heav'n his pious *breathings* turn'd,
Weeping he hop'd, and sacrificing mourn'd. *Prior.*

2. Breathing place; vent.

The warmth distends the chinks, and makes
New *breathings*, whence new nourishment she takes. *Dryd.*

BRE'ATHLESS. *adj.* [from *breath.*]

1. Out of breath; spent with labour.

Well knew
The prince, with patience and sufferance sly,
So hasty heat soon cooled to subdue;
Tho' when he *breathless* wax, that battle 'gan renew. *Fairy Q.*

I remember when the fight was done,
When I was dry with rage, and extreme toil,

Breathless, and faint, leaning upon my sword,
Came there a certain lord. *Shakesp. Henry* IV. *p.* i.
Many so strained themselves in their race, that they fell down *breathless* and dead. *Hayward.*
Breathless and tir'd, is all my fury spent,
Or does my glutted spleen at length relent? *Dryden's Æn.*

2. Dead.
Kneeling before this ruin of sweet life,
And breathing to this *breathless* excellence,
The incense of a vow, a holy vow. *Shakesp. King John.*
Yielding to the sentence, *breathless* thou
And pale shalt lie, as what thou buriest now. *Prior.*

BRED. *particip. pass.* [from *to breed.*]
Their malice was *bred* in them, and their cogitation would never be changed. *Wisdom*, xii. 10.

BREDE. *n. s.* See BRAID.
In a curious *brede* of needle-work, one colour falls away by such just degrees, and another rises so insensibly, that we see the variety, without being able to distinguish the total vanishing of the one, from the first appearance of the other. *Addison.*

BREECH. *n. s.* [supposed from bꞃæcan, Sax.]
1. The lower part of the body; the back part.
When the king's pardon was offered by a herauld, a lewd boy turned towards him his naked *breech*, and used words suitable to that gesture. *Hayward.*
The storks devour snakes and other serpents; which when they begin to creep out at their *breethes*, they will presently clap them close to a wall, to keep them in. *Grew's Musæum.*
2. Breeches.
Ah! that thy father had been so resolv'd!—
—That you might still have worn the petticoat,
And ne'er have stoln the *breech* from Lancaster. *Shakespeare.*
3. The hinder part of a piece of ordnance.
So cannons, when they mount vast pitches,
Are tumbl'd back upon their *breeches*. *Anonym.*

To BREECH. *v. a.* [from the noun.]
1. To put into breeches.
2. To fit any thing with a breech; as, to *breech* a gun.

BRE'ECHES. *n. s.* [bꞃæc, Sax. from *bracca*, an old Gaulish word; so that *Skinner* imagines the name of the part covered with *breeches*, to be derived from that of the garment. In this sense it has no *singular*.]
1. The garment worn by men over the lower part of the body.
Petrachio is coming in a new hat and an old jerkin, and a pair of old *breeches*, thrice turned. *Shakesp. Taming the Shrew.*
Rough satires, sly remarks, ill-natur'd speeches,
Are always aim'd at poets that wear *breeches*. *Prior.*
Give him a single coat to make, he'd do't;
A vest, or *breeches*, singly; but the brute
Cou'd ne'er contrive all three to make a suit.
King's Art of Cookery.
2. To wear the *breeches*, is, to usurp the authority of the husbands.
The wife of Xanthus was proud and domineering, as if her fortune, and her extraction, had entitled her to the *breeches*.
L'Estrange.

To BREED. *v. a.* preter. I *bred*, I have *bred*. [bꞃæban, Sax.]
1. To procreate; to generate; to produce more of the species.
None fiercer in Numidia *bred*,
With Carthage were in triumph led. *Roscommon.*
2. To occasion; to cause; to produce.
Thereat he roared for exceeding pain,
That, to have heard, great horrour would have *bred*. *F. Q.*
Our own hearts we know, but we are not certain what hope the rites and orders of our church have *bred* in the hearts of others. *Hooker, b.* iv.
What hurt ill company, and overmuch liberty, *breedeth* in youth! *Ascham's Schoolmaster.*
Intemperance and lust *breed* infirmities and diseases, which, being propagated, spoil the strain of a nation. *Tillotson.*
3. To contrive; to hatch; to plot.
My son Edgar! had he a hand to write this! a heart and brain to *breed* it in! *Shakesp. King Lear.*
4. To produce from one's self.
Children would *breed* their teeth with much less danger.
Locke on Education.
5. To give birth to; to be the native place.
Mr. Harding, and the worthiest divine christendom hath *bred* for the space of some hundreds of years, were brought up together in the same university. *Hooker.*
Hail, foreign wonder!
Whom, certain, these rough shades did never *breed*. *Milton.*
6. To educate; to qualify by education.
Whoe'er thou art, whose forward years are bent
On state-affairs to guide the government;
Hear first what Socrates of old has said
To the lov'd youth, whom he at Athens *bred*. *Dryden.*
To *breed* up the son to common sense,
Is evermore the parent's least expence. *Dryden's Juvenal.*
And left the pillagers, to rapine *bred*,
Without controul, to strip and spoil the dead. *Dryden.*
His farm may not remove his children too far from him, or the trade he *breeds* them up in. *Locke.*
7. To bring up; to take care of from infancy.
Bred up in grief, can pleasure be our theme?
Our endless anguish, does not nature claim?
Reason and sorrow are to us the same. *Prior.*
Ah, wretched me! by fates averse decreed
To bring thee forth with pain, with care to *breed*. *Dryden.*

To BREED. *v. n.*
1. To bring young.
Lucina, it seems, was *breeding*, and she did nothing but entertain the company with a discourse upon the difficulty of reckoning to a day. *Spectator*, N° 431.
2. To encrease by new production.
But could youth last, and love still *breed*,
Had joys no date, and age no need;
Then these delights my mind might move
To live with thee, and be thy love. *Raleigh.*
3. To be produced; to have birth.
Where they most *breed* and haunt, I have observ'd,
The air is delicate. *Shakesp. King Lear.*
There is a worm that *breedeth* in old snow, and dieth soon after it cometh out of the snow. *Bacon's Nat. Hist.* N° 696.
The caterpillar is one of the most general of worms, and *breedeth* of dew and leaves. *Bacon.*
It hath been the general tradition and belief, that maggots and flies *breed* in putrefied carcases. *Bentley.*
4. To raise a breed.
In the choice of swine, choose such to *breed* of as are of long large bodies. *Mortimer.*

BREED. *n. s.* [from the verb.]
1. A cast; a kind; a subdivision of species.
I bring you witnesses,
Twice fifteen thousand hearts of England's *breed*. *Shakesp.*
The horses were young and handsome, and of the best *breed* in the north. *Shakesp. Henry* VIII.
Walled towns, stored arsenals, and ordnance; all this is but a sheep in a lion's skin, except the *breed* and disposition of the people be stout and warlike. *Bacon's Essays*, N° 30.
Infectious streams of crowding sins began,
And through the spurious *breed* and guilty nation ran.
Roscommon.
Rode fair Ascanius on a firy steed,
Queen Dido's gift, and of the Tyrian *breed*. *Dryden.*
A cousin of his last wife's was proposed; but John would have no more of the *breed*. *Arbuthnot's Hist. of J. Bull.*
2. Progeny; offspring.
If thou wilt lend this money, lend it not
As to thy friend; for when did friendship take
A *breed* of barren metal of his friend? *Shakesp. Mer. of Ven.*
3. A number produced at once; a hatch.
She lays them in the sand, where they lie till they are hatched; sometimes above an hundred at a *breed*. *Grew's Musæum.*

BRE'EDBATE. *n. s.* [from *breed* and *bate.*] One that breeds quarrels; an incendiary.
An honest, willing, kind fellow, as ever servant shall come in house withal; and, I warrant you, no teltale, nor no *breedbate*. *Shakesp. Merry Wives of Windsor.*

BRE'EDER. *n. s.* [from *breed.*]
1. That which produces any thing.
Time is the nurse and *breeder* of all good. *Shakesp.*
2. The person which brings up another.
Time was, when Italy and Rome have been the best *breeders* and bringers up of the worthiest men. *Ascham's Schoolmaster.*
3. A female that is prolifick.
Get thee to a nunnery; why wouldst thou be a *breeder* of sinners? *Shakesp. Hamlet.*
Here is the babe, as loathsome as a toad,
Amongst the fairest *breeders* of our time. *Shakesp. Tit. Andr.*
Let there be an hundred persons in London, and as many in the country, we say, that if there be sixty of them *breeders* in London, there are more than sixty in the country. *Graunt.*
Yet if a friend a night or two should need her,
He'd recommend her as a special *breeder*. *Pope.*
4. One that takes care to raise a breed.
The *breeders* of English cattle turned much to dairy, or else kept their cattle to six or seven years old. *Temple.*

BRE'EDING. *n. s.* [from *breed.*]
1. Education; instruction; qualifications.
She had her *breeding* at my father's charge,
A poor physician's daughter. *Shakesp. All's well that ends well.*
I am a gentleman of blood and *breeding*. *Shakesp. K. Lear.*
I hope to see it a piece of none of the meanest *breeding*, to be acquainted with the laws of nature. *Glanville's Scepsis, Pref.*
2. Manners; knowledge of ceremony.
As men of *breeding*, sometimes men of wit,
T' avoid great errours, must the less commit. *Pope.*
The Graces from the court did next provide
Breeding, and wit, and air, and decent pride. *Swift.*
3. Nurture; care to bring up from the infant state.
Why was my *breeding* order'd and prescrib'd,
As of a person separate to God,
Design'd for great exploits. *Milton's Agonistes, l.* 30.

BREESE. *n. s.* [bꞃıoꞅa, Saxon.] A stinging fly; the gadfly.

The

The learned write, the inſect *breeſe*
Is but the mongrel prince of bees. *Hudibras.*

A fierce loud buzzing *breeſe*, their ſtings draw blood,
And drive the cattle gadding through the wood;
Seiz'd with unuſual pains, they loudly cry;
Tanagrus haſtens thence, and leaves his channels dry. *Dryd.*

BREEZE. *n. ſ.* [*brezza*, Ital.] A gentle gale; a ſoft wind.

We find, that theſe hotteſt regions of the world, ſeated under the equinoctial line, or near it, are ſo refreſhed with a daily gale of eaſterly wind, which the Spaniards call *breeze*, that doth ever more blow ſtrongeſt in the heat of the day. *Raleigh.*

From land a gentle *breeze* aroſe by night,
Serenely ſhone the ſtars, the moon was light,
And the ſea trembled with her ſilver light. } *Dryden.*

Gradual ſinks the *breeze*
Into a perfect calm: that not a breath
Is heard to quiver through the cloſing wood. *Thomſon.*

BRE'EZY. *adj.* [from *breeze.*] Fanned with gales.

The ſeer, while zephyrs curl the ſwelling deep,
Baſks on the *breezy* ſhore, in grateful ſleep,
His oozy limbs. *Pope's Odyſſey, b.* iii. *l.* 545.

BRE'HON. *n. ſ.* An Iriſh word.

In the caſe of murder, the *brehon*, that is, their judge, will compound between the murderer and the party murdered, which proſecute the action, that the malefactor ſhall give unto them, or to the child or wife of him that is ſlain, a recompence, which they call an eriach. *Spenſer's State of Ireland.*

BREME. *adj.* [from bꞃemman, Sax. to rage or fume.] Cruel; ſharp; ſevere.

And when the ſhining ſun laugheth once,
You deemen the ſpring come at once:
But eft, when you count, you freed from fear,
Comes the *breme* winter, with chamfred brows,
Full of wrinkles, and froſty furrows. *Spenſer's Paſtorals.*

BRENT. *adj.* [from bꞃennan, Sax. to burn.] Burnt.

What flames, quoth he, when I thee preſent ſee
In danger rather to be drent than *brent*? *Fairy Queen, b.* ii.

BREST. *n. ſ.* [In architecture.] That member of a column, called alſo the *torus*, or *tore*.

BREST *Summers.* The pieces in the outward parts of any timber building, and in the middle floors, into which the girders are framed. *Harris.*

BRET. *n. ſ.* A fiſh of the turbut kind, called alſo *burt* or *brut*. *Dict.*

BRE'THREN. *n. ſ.* [The *plural* of *brother.*] See BROTHER.

All theſe ſects are *brethren* to each other in faction, ignorance, iniquity, perverſeneſs, pride. *Swift.*

BREVE. *n. ſ.* [In muſick.] A note or character of time, equivalent to two meaſures or minims. *Harris.*

BRE'VIARY. *n. ſ.* [*breviaire*, Fr. *breviarium*, Lat.]

1. An abridgment; an epitome; a compendium.

Creſconius, an African biſhop, has given us an abridgment, or *breviary* thereof. *Ayliffe's Parergon.*

2. The book containing the daily ſervice of the church of Rome.

BRE'VIAT. *n. ſ.* [from *brevis*, *brevio*, Lat.] A ſhort compendium.

It is obvious for the ſhalloweſt diſcourſer to infer, that the whole counſel of God, as far as it is incumbent for man to know, is compriſed in that one *breviat* of evangelical truth. *Decay of Piety.*

BRE'VIATURE. *n. ſ.* [from *brevio*, Lat.] An abbreviation.

BREVI'ER. *n. ſ.* A particular ſize of letter uſed in printing; ſo called, probably, from being originally uſed in printing a *breviary*; as,

Nor love thy life, nor hate, but what thou liv'ſt,
Live well, how long or ſhort, permit to heav'n. *Milton.*

BRE'VITY. *n. ſ.* [*brevitas*, Lat.] Conciſeneſs; ſhortneſs; contraction into few words.

Virgil, ſtudying *brevity*, and having the command of his own language, could bring thoſe words into a narrow compaſs, which a tranſlator cannot render without circumlocutions. *Dryden.*

To BREW. *v. a.* [*brouwen*, Dutch; *brawen*, German; bꞃiƿan, Saxon.]

1. To make liquours by mixing ſeveral ingredients.

We have drinks alſo *brewed* with ſeveral herbs, and roots, and ſpices. *Bacon.*

Mercy guard me!
Hence with thy *brew'd* enchantments, foul deceiver. *Milton.*

2. To prepare by mixing things together.

Here's neither ruſh nor ſhrub to bear off any weather at all, and another ſtorm *brewing*. *Shakeſp. Tempeſt.*

Take away theſe chalices; go, *brew* me a pottle of ſack finely. *Shakeſp. Merry Wives of Windſor.*

Or *brew* fierce tempeſts on the watry main,
Or o'er the globe diſtil the kindly rain. *Pope's R. of the L.*

3. To contrive; to plot.

I found it to be the moſt malicious and frantick ſurmiſe, and the moſt contrary to his nature, that, I think, had ever been *brewed* from the beginning of the world, howſoever countenanced by a libellous pamphlet of a fugitive phyſician, even in print. *Wotton.*

To BREW. *v. n.* To perform the office of a brewer.

I keep his houſe, and waſh, wring, *brew*, bake, ſcour, dreſs meat, and make the beds, and do all myſelf. *Shakeſp.*

BREW. *n. ſ.* [from the verb.] Manner of brewing; or thing brewed.

Trial would be made of the like *brew* with potato roots, or burr roots, or the pith of artichokes, which are nouriſhing meats. *Bacon's Natural Hiſtory*, N° 47.

BRE'WAGE. *n. ſ.* [from *brew.*] Mixture of various things.

Go, brew me a pottle of ſack finely.
——With eggs, Sir?——
—Simple of itſelf: I'll no pullet-ſperm in my *brewage.*
Shakeſp. Merry Wives of Windſor.

BRE'WER. *n. ſ.* [from *brew.*] A man whoſe profeſſion it is to make beer.

When *brewers* marr their malt with water. *Sh. King Lear.*

Men every day eat and drink, though I think no man can demonſtrate out of Euclid or Apollonius, that his baker, or *brewer*, or cook, has not conveyed poiſon into his meat or drink. *Tillotſon.*

BRE'WHOUSE. *n. ſ.* [from *brew* and *houſe.*] A houſe appropriated to brewing.

In our *brewhouſes*, bakehouſes, and kitchens, are made divers drinks, breads, and meats. *Bacon's New Atlantis.*

BRE'WING. *n. ſ.* [from *brew.*] Quantity of liquour brewed.

A *brewing* of new beer, ſet by old beer, maketh it work again. *Bacon's Natural Hiſtory*, N° 314.

BRE'WIS. *n. ſ.* A piece of bread ſoaked in boiling fat pottage, made of ſalted meat.

BRI'AR. *n. ſ.* See BRIER.

BRIBE. *n. ſ.* [*Bribe*, in French, originally ſignifies a piece of bread, and is applied to any piece taken from the reſt; it is therefore likely, that a *bribe* originally ſignified, among us, a ſhare of any thing unjuſtly got.] A reward given to pervert the judgment, or corrupt the conduct.

You have condemn'd and noted Lucius Pella,
For taking *bribes* here of the Sardians. *Shakeſp. Julius Cæſar.*

Nor leſs may Jupiter to gold aſcribe,
When he turn'd himſelf into a *bribe.* *Waller.*

If a man be covetous, profits or *bribes* may put him to the teſt. *L'Eſtrange.*

There's joy when to wild will you laws preſcribe,
When you bid fortune carry back her *bribe.* *Dryden.*

To BRIBE. *v. a.* [from the noun.] To gain by bribes; to give bribes, rewards, or hire, to bad purpoſes. It is ſeldom, and not properly, uſed in a good ſenſe.

How pow'rful are chaſte vows! the wind and tide
You *brib'd* to combat on the Engliſh ſide. *Dryden.*

BRI'BER. *n. ſ.* [from *bribe.*] One that pays for corrupt practices.

Affection is ſtill a *briber* of the judgment; and it is hard for a man to admit a reaſon againſt the thing he loves; or to confeſs the force of an argument againſt an intereſt. *South.*

BRI'BERY. *n. ſ.* [from *bribe.*] The crime of taking rewards for bad practices.

There was a law made by the Romans, againſt the *bribery* and extortion of the governours of provinces: before, ſays Cicero, the governours did bribe and extort as much as was ſufficient for themſelves; but now they bribe and extort as much as may be enough not only for themſelves, but for judges, jurors, and magiſtrates. *Bacon.*

No *bribery* of courts, or cabals of factions, or advantages of fortune, can remove him from the ſolid foundations of honour and fidelity. *Dryden's Aurengz. Preface.*

BRICK. *n. ſ.* [*brick*, Dutch; *brique*, Fr. according to *Menage*, from *imbrex*, Lat. whence *brica.*]

1. A maſs of burnt clay, ſquared for the uſe of builders.

For whatſoever doth ſo alter a body, as it returneth not again to that it was, may be called *alteratio major*; as coals made of wood, or *bricks* of earth. *Bacon's Natural Hiſtory.*

They generally gain enough by the rubbiſh and *bricks*, which the preſent architects value much beyond thoſe of a modern make, to defray the charges of their ſearch. *Addiſon.*

But ſpread, my ſons, your glory thin or thick,
On paſſive paper, or on ſolid *brick.* *Pope's Dunciad.*

2. A loaf ſhaped like a brick.

To BRICK. *v. a.* [from the noun.] To lay with bricks.

The ſexton comes to know where he is to be laid, and whether his grave is to be plain or *bricked.* *Swift.*

BRI'CKBAT. *n. ſ.* [from *brick* and *bat.*] A piece of brick.

Earthen bottles, filled with hot water, do provoke in bed a ſweat more daintily than *brickbats* hot. *Bacon's Natural Hiſt.*

BRI'CKCLAY. *n. ſ.* [from *brick* and *clay.*] Clay uſed for making brick.

I have obſerved it only in pits wrought for tile and *brickclay.* *Woodward on Foſſils.*

BRI'CKDUST. *n. ſ.* [from *brick* and *duſt.*] Duſt made by pounding bricks.

This ingenious authour, being thus ſharp ſet, got together a convenient quantity of *brickduſt*, and diſpoſed of it into ſeveral papers. *Spectator*, N° 283.

BRI'CKEARTH. *n. ſ.* [from *brick* and *earth.*] Earth uſed in making bricks.

They grow very well both on the hazelly *brickearths*, and on gravel. *Mortimer.*

BRICK-KILN. *n. ſ.* [from *brick* and *kiln.*] A kiln; a place to burn bricks.

Like the Iſraelites in the *brick-kilns*, they multiplied the more for their oppreſſion. *Decay of Piety.*

BRI'CKLAYER. *n. ſ.* [from *brick* and *lay.*] A man whoſe trade it is to build with bricks; a brick-maſon.

The elder of them, being put to nurſe,
And ignorant of his birth and parentage,
Became a *bricklayer*, when he came to age. *Shakeſp. H.* VI.
If you had liv'd, Sir,
Time enough to have been interpreter
To Babel's *bricklayers*, ſure the tow'r had ſtood. *Donne.*

BRI'CKMAKER. *n. ſ.* [from *brick* and *make.*] One whoſe trade it is to make bricks.

They are common in clay-pits; but the *brickmakers* pick them out of the clay. *Woodward on Foſſils.*

BRI'DAL. *adj.* [from *bride.*] Belonging to a wedding; nuptial; connubial.

Our wedding chear to a ſad fun'ral feaſt,
Our ſolemn hymns to ſullen dirges change,
Our *bridal* flowers ſerve for a buried corſe. *Shakeſp.*
Come, I will bring thee to thy *bridal* chamber. *Shakeſp.*
The amorous bird of night
Sung ſpouſal, and bid haſte the ev'ning ſtar,
On his hill-top to light the *bridal* lamp. *Parad. Loſt, b.* viii.
Your ill-meaning politician lords,
Under pretence of *bridal* friends and gueſts,
Appointed to await me thirty ſpies. *Milton's Agoniſt. l.* 1195.
When to my arms thou brought'ſt thy virgin love,
Fair angels ſung our *bridal* hymn above. *Dryden.*
With all the pomp of woe, and ſorrow's pride!
Oh, early loſt! oh, fitter to be led
In chearful ſplendour to the *bridal* bed! *Walſh.*
For her the ſpouſe prepares the *bridal* ring,
For her white virgins hymenæals ſing. *Pope's Eloiſa to Abel.*

BRI'DAL. *n. ſ.* The nuptial feſtival.

Nay, we muſt think, men are not gods;
Nor of them look for ſuch obſervance always,
As fits the *bridal*. *Shakeſp. Othello.*
Sweet day, ſo cool, ſo calm, ſo bright,
The *bridal* of the earth and ſky,
Sweet dews ſhall weep thy fall to-night;
For thou muſt die. *Herbert.*
In death's dark bow'rs our *bridals* we will keep,
And his cold hand
Shall draw the curtain when we go to ſleep. *Dryden.*

BRIDE. *n. ſ.* [bryd, Saxon; *brudur*, in Runick, ſignifies a beautiful woman.] A woman new married.

Help me mine own love's praiſes to reſound,
Ne let the fame of any be envy'd;
So Orpheus did for his own *bride*. *Spenſer's Epithalamium.*
The day approach'd, when fortune ſhould decide
Th' important enterprize, and give the *bride*. *Dryden's Fab.*
Theſe are tributes due from pious *brides*,
From a chaſte matron, and a virtuous wife. *Smith's Phædr.*

BRI'DEBED. *n. ſ.* [from *bride* and *bed.*] Marriage-bed.

Now until the break of day,
Through this houſe each fairy ſtray;
To the beſt *bridebed* will we,
Which by us ſhall bleſſed be. *Shakeſp. Midſum. Night's Dr.*
Would David's ſon, religious, juſt, and brave,
To the firſt *bridebed* of the world receive
A foreigner, a heathen, and a ſlave? *Prior.*

BRI'DECAKE. *n. ſ.* [from *bride* and *cake.*] A cake diſtributed to the gueſts at the wedding.

With the phant'ſies of hey-troll,
Troll about the bridal bowl,
And divide the broad *bridecake*
Round about the bride's ſtake. *Ben. Johnſon's Underwoods.*

The writer, reſolved to try his fortune, faſted all day, and, that he might be ſure of dreaming upon ſomething at night, procured an handſome ſlice of *bridecake*, which he placed very conveniently under his pillow. *Spectator*, N° 597.

BRI'DEGROOM. *n. ſ.* [from *bride* and *groom.*] A new married man.

As are thoſe dulcet ſounds in break of day,
That creep into the dreaming *bridegroom's* ear,
And ſummon him to marriage. *Shakeſp. Merch. of Venice.*
Why, happy *bridegroom!*
Why doſt thou ſteal ſo ſoon away to bed? *Dryden.*

BRI'DEMEN. } *n. ſ.* The attendants on the bride and bridegroom.
BRI'DEMAIDS. }

BRI'DESTAKE. *n. ſ.* [from *bride* and *ſtake.*] It ſeems to be a poſt ſet in the ground, to dance round, like a maypole.

And divide the broad bridecake,
Round about the *brideſtake*. *Ben. Johnſon's Underwoods.*

BRI'DEWELL. *n. ſ.* [The palace built by St. *Bride's*, or *Bridget's well*, was turned into a workhouſe.] A houſe of correction.

He would contribute more to reformation than all the workhouſes and *Bridewells* in Europe. *Spectator*, N° 157.

3

B R I

BRIDGE. *n. ſ.* [brıcg, Saxon.]

1. A building raiſed over water for the convenience of paſſage.

What need the *bridge* much broader than the flood?
Shakeſp. Much ado about Nothing.
And proud Araxes, whom no *bridge* could bind. *Dryden.*

2. The upper part of the noſe.

The raiſing gently the *bridge* of the noſe, doth prevent the deformity of a ſaddle noſe. *Bacon's Natural Hiſtory*, N° 28.

3. The ſupporter of the ſtrings in ſtringed inſtruments of muſick.

To BRIDGE. *v. a.* [from the noun.] To raiſe a bridge over any place.

Came to the ſea; and over Helleſpont
Bridging his way, Europe with Aſia join'd. *Par. Loſt, b.* x.

BRI'DLE. *n. ſ.* [*bride*, Fr.]

1. The headſtall and reins by which a horſe is reſtrained and governed.

Creeping and crying, till they ſeiz'd at laſt
His courſer's *bridle*, and his feet embrac'd. *Dryden's Fables.*

2. A reſtraint; a curb; a check.

The king reſolved to put that place, which ſome men fancied to be a *bridle* upon the city, into the hands of ſuch a man as he might rely upon. *Clarendon.*

A bright genius often betrays itſelf into many errours, without a continual *bridle* on the tongue. *Watts.*

To BRI'DLE. *v. a.* [from the noun.]

1. To reſtrain, or guide by a bridle.

I *bridle* in my ſtruggling muſe with pain,
That longs to launch into a bolder ſtrain. *Addiſon.*

2. To put a bridle on any thing.

The queen of beauty ſtop'd her *bridled* doves;
Approv'd the little labour of the Loves. *Prior.*

3. To reſtrain; to govern.

The diſpoſition of theſe things is committed to them, whom law may at all times *bridle*, and ſuperiour power controul.
Hooker, b. v. § 9.

With a ſtrong, and yet a gentle hand,
You *bridle* faction, and our hearts command. *Waller.*

To BRI'DLE. *v. n.* To hold up the head.

BRI'DLEHAND. *n. ſ.* [from *bridle* and *hand.*] The hand which holds the bridle in riding.

In the turning, one might perceive the *bridlehand* ſomething gently ſtir; but, indeed, ſo gently, as it did rather diſtil virtue than uſe violence. *Sidney, b.* ii.

The heat of ſummer put his blood into a ferment, which affected his *bridlehand* with great pain. *Wiſeman's Surgery.*

BRIEF. *adj.* [*brevis*, Lat. *brief*, Fr.]

1. Short; conciſe. It is now ſeldom uſed but of words.

A play there is, my lord, ſome ten words long,
Which is as *brief* as I have known a play;
But by ten words, my lord, it is too long,
Which makes it tedious. *Shakeſp. Midſum. Night's Dream.*
I will be mild and gentle in my words.—
—And *brief*, good mother, for I am in haſte. *Shakeſp. R.* III.
I muſt begin with rudiments of art,
To teach you gamut in a *briefer* ſort,
More pleaſant, pretty, and effectual. *Shakeſp. Tam. Shrew.*
They nothing doubt prevailing, and to make it *brief* wars.
Shakeſp. Coriolanus.

The *brief* ſtile is that which expreſſeth much in little.
Ben. Johnſon's Diſcovery.

If I had quoted more words, I had quoted more profaneneſs; and therefore Mr. Congreve has reaſon to thank me for being *brief*. *Collier's View of the Stage.*

2. Contracted; narrow.

The ſhrine of Venus, or ſtraight pight Minerva,
Poſtures beyond *brief* nature. *Shakeſp. Cymbeline.*

BRIEF. *n. ſ.* [*brief*, Dutch, a letter.]

1. A writing of any kind.

There is a *brief*, how many ſports are ripe:
Make choice of which your highneſs will ſee firſt. *Shakeſp.*

The apoſtolical letters are of a twofold kind and difference, *viz.* ſome are called *briefs*, becauſe they are compriſed in a ſhort and compendious way of writing. *Ayliffe's Parergon.*

2. A ſhort extract, or epitome.

But how you muſt begin this enterprize,
I will your highneſs thus in *brief* adviſe. *Fairy Queen, b.* ii.

I doubt not but I ſhall make it plain, as far as a ſum or *brief* can make a cauſe plain. *Bacon's Holy War.*

The *brief* of this tranſaction is, theſe ſprings that ariſe here, are impregnated with vitriol. *Woodward on Foſſils.*

3. In law.

A writ whereby a man is ſummoned to anſwer to any action; or it is any precept of the king in writing, iſſuing out of any court, whereby he commands any thing to be done. *Cowel.*

4. The writing given the pleaders, containing the caſe.

The *brief* with weighty crimes was charg'd,
On which the pleader much enlarg'd. *Swift.*

5. Letters patent, giving licence to a charitable collection for any publick or private loſs.

6. [In muſick.] A meaſure of quantity, which contains two ſtrokes down in beating time, and as many up. *Harris.*

BRI'EFLY. *adv.* [from *brief.*] Conciſely; in few words.

I will

I will ſpeak in that manner which the ſubject requires; that is, probably, and moderately, and *briefly*. *Bacon.*

The modeſt queen a while, with downcaſt eyes,
Ponder'd the ſpeech; then *briefly* thus replies. *Dryden.*

BRI'EFNESS. *n. ſ.* [from *brief.*] Conciſeneſs; ſhortneſs.

They excel in grandity and gravity, in ſmoothneſs and propriety, in quickneſs and *briefneſs*. *Camden's Remains.*

BRI'ER. *n. ſ.* [bꞃæꞃ, Sax.] A plant.

The ſweet and the wild ſorts are both ſpecies of the *roſe*; which ſee.

What ſubtle hole is this,
Whoſe mouth is cover'd with rude growing *briers*? *Shakeſp.*

Then thrice under a *brier* doth creep,
Which at both ends was rooted deep,
And over it three times doth leap;
Her magick much availing. *Drayton's Nymphid.*

BRI'ERY. *adj.* [from *brier.*] Rough; thorny; full of briers.

BRIG, and poſſibly alſo BRIX, is derived from the Saxon bꞃicᵹ, a bridge; which, to this day, in the northern counties, is called a *brigg*, and not a *bridge*. *Gibſon's Camden.*

BRIGA'DE. *n. ſ.* [*brigade*, Fr. It is now generally pronounced with the accent on the laſt ſyllable.] A diviſion of forces; a body of men, conſiſting of ſeveral ſquadrons of horſe, or battalions of foot.

Or fronted *brigades* form. *Paradiſe Loſt*, *b.* ii.

Here the Bavarian duke his *brigades* leads,
Gallant in arms, and gaudy to behold. *Philips.*

BRIGA'DE *Major*. An officer appointed by the brigadier to aſſiſt him in the management and ordering of his brigade; and he there acts as as a major general does in an army. *Harris.*

BRIGADI'ER *General*. An officer who commands a brigade of horſe or foot in an army; next in order below a major general.

BRI'GAND. *n. ſ.* [*brigand*, Fr.] A robber; one that belongs to a band of robbers.

There might be a rout of ſuch barbarous theeviſh *brigands* in ſome rocks; but it was a degeneration from the nature of man, a political creature. *Bramhal againſt Hobbes.*

BRI'GANDINE. } *n. ſ.* [from *brigand.*]
BRI'GANTINE. }

1. A light veſſel; ſuch as has been formerly uſed by corſairs or pirates.

Like as a a warlike *brigandine*, apply'd
To fight, lays forth her threatful pikes afore
The engines, which in them ſad death do hide. *Spenſer.*

Scarce five years are paſt,
Since in your *brigantine* you ſail'd to ſee
The Adriatick wedded. *Otway's Venice Preſerved.*

The conſul obliged him to deliver up his fleet, and reſtore the ſhips, reſerving only to himſelf two *brigantines*. *Arbuthnot.*

2. A coat of mail.

Then put on all thy gorgeous arms, thy helmet
And *brigandine* of braſs, thy broad habergeon,
Vantbraſs, and greves. *Milton's Agoniſtes*, *l.* 1119.

BRIGHT. *adj.* [beoꞃꞇ, Saxon.]

1. Shining; glittering; full of light.

Through a cloud
Drawn round about thee like a radiant ſhrine,
Dark, with exceſſive *bright*, thy ſkirts appear. *Par. L. b.* iii.

Then ſhook the ſacred ſhrine, and ſudden light
Sprung through the vaulted roof, and made the temple *bright*. *Dryden.*

2. Clear; evident.

He muſt not proceed too ſwiftly, that he may with more eaſe, with *brighter* evidence, and with ſurer ſucceſs, draw the learner on. *Watts's Improvement of the Mind.*

3. Illuſtrious; as, a *bright* reign, a *bright* action.

4. Witty; acute; ſubtle; as a *bright* genius.

To BRI'GHTEN. *v. a.* [from *bright.*]

1. To make bright; to make to ſhine.

The purple morning riſing with the year,
Salutes the ſpring, as her celeſtial eyes
Adorn the world, and *brighten* all the ſkies. *Dryden.*

2. To make luminous by light from without.

An ecſtaſy, that mothers only feel,
Plays round my heart, and *brightens* up my ſorrow,
Like gleams of ſunſhine in a louring ſky. *Philips's D. Moth.*

3. To make gay, or alert.

Hope elevates, and joy
Brightens his creſt. *Milton's Paradiſe Loſt*, *b.* ix. *l.* 634.

4. To make illuſtrious.

The preſent queen would *brighten* her character, if ſhe would exert her authority to inſtil virtues into her people. *Swift.*

Yet time ennobles, or degrades each line;
It *brighten'd* Craggs's, and may darken thine. *Pope.*

5. To make acute, or witty.

To BRI'GHTEN. *v. n.* To grow bright; to clear up; as, *the ſky brightens*.

BRI'GHTLY. *adv.* [from *bright.*] Splendidly; with luſtre.

Safely I ſlept, till *brightly* dawning ſhone
The morn conſpicuous on her golden throne. *Pope.*

BRI'GHTNESS. *n. ſ.* [from *bright.*]

1. Luſtre; ſplendour; glitter.

The blazing *brightneſs* of her beauty's beam,
And glorious light of her ſun-ſhining face,
To tell, were as to ſtrive againſt the ſtream. *Fairy Q. b.* i.

A ſword, by long lying ſtill, will contract a ruſt, which ſhall deface its *brightneſs*. *South.*

Vex'd with the preſent moment's heavy gloom,
Why ſeek we *brightneſs* from the years to come? *Prior.*

2. Acuteneſs.

The *brightneſs* of his parts, the ſolidity of his judgment, and the candour and generoſity of his temper, diſtinguiſhed him in an age of great politeneſs. *Prior.*

BRI'LLIANCY. *n. ſ.* [from *brilliant.*] Luſtre; ſplendour.

BRI'LLIANT. *adj.* [*brillant*, Fr.] Shining; ſparkling; ſplendid; full of luſtre.

So have I ſeen in larder dark
Of veal a lucid loin,
Replete with many a *brilliant* ſpark,
As wiſe philoſophers remark,
At once both ſtink and ſhine. *Dorſet.*

BRI'LLIANT. *n. ſ.* A diamond of the fineſt cut, formed into angles, ſo as to refract the light, and ſhine more.

In deference to his virtues, I forbear
To ſhew you what the reſt in orders were;
This *brilliant* is ſo ſpotleſs and ſo bright,
He needs not foil, but ſhines by his own proper light. *Dryd.*

BRI'LLIANTNESS. *n. ſ.* [from *brilliant.*] Splendour; luſtre.

BRILLS. *n. ſ.* The hair on the eyelids of a horſe. *Dict.*

BRIM. *n. ſ.* [*brim*, Icelandiſh.]

1. The edge of any thing.

His hat being in the form of a turban, daintily made, the locks of his hair came down about the *brims* of it. *Bacon.*

2. The upper edge of any veſſel.

To make the coming hours o'erflow with joy,
And pleaſure down the *brim*. *Shakeſp. All's well that ends well.*

How my head in ointment ſwims!
How my cup o'erlooks her *brims*! *Craſhaw.*

So when with crackling flames a cauldron fries,
The bubbling waters from the bottom riſe,
Above the *brims* they force their firy way. *Dryden's Æn.*

Thus in a baſon drop a ſhilling,
Then fill the veſſel to the *brim*,
You ſhall obſerve, as you are filling,
The pond'rous metal ſeems to ſwim. *Swift.*

3. The top of any liquour.

The feet of the prieſts that bare the ark, were dipped in the *brim* of the water. *Joſh.* iii. 15.

4. The bank of a fountain.

It told me it was Cynthia's own,
Within whoſe cheerful *brims*
That curious nymph had oft been known
To bathe her ſnowy limbs. *Drayton.*

To BRIM. *v. a.* [from the noun.] To fill to the top.

May thy *brimmed* waves, for this,
Their full tribute never miſs,
From a thouſand rills. *Milton.*

This ſaid, a double wreath Evander twin'd;
And poplars black and white his temples bind:
Then *brims* his ample bowl; with like deſign
The reſt invoke the gods, with ſprinkled wine. *Dryden.*

To BRIM. *v. n.* To be full to the brim.

Now horrid frays
Commence, the *brimming* glaſſes now are hurl'd
With dire intent. *Philips.*

BRI'MFUL. *adj.* [from *brim* and *full.*] Full to the top; overcharged.

Meaſure my caſe, how by thy beauty's filling,
With ſeed of woes my heart *brimful* is charg'd. *Sidney, b.* i.

We have try'd the utmoſt of our friends;
Our legions are *brimful*, our cauſe is ripe. *Shakeſp. J. Cæſ.*

Her *brimful* eyes, that ready ſtood,
And only wanted will to weep a flood,
Releas'd their watry ſtore. *Dryden's Fables.*

The good old king at parting wrung my hand,
His eyes *brimful* of tears; then ſighing, cry'd,
Prithee, be careful of my ſon. *Addiſon's Cato.*

BRI'MFULNESS. *n. ſ.* [from *brimful.*] Fulneſs to the top.

The Scot, on his unfurniſh'd kingdom,
Came pouring like a tide into a breach,
With ample and *brimfulneſs* of his force. *Shakeſp. Hen.* V.

BRI'MMER. *n. ſ.* [from *brim.*] A bowl full to the top.

When healths go round, and kindly *brimmers* flow,
Till the freſh garlands on their foreheads glow. *Dryden.*

BRI'MMING. *adj.* [from *brim.*] Full to the brim.

And twice beſides her beeſtings never fail,
To ſtore the dairy with a *brimming* pail. *Dryden.*

BRI'MSTONE. *n. ſ.* [corrupted from *brin* or *brenſtone*, that is, firy ſtone.] Sulphur. See SULPHUR.

From his infernal furnace forth he threw
Huge flames, that dimmed all the heaven's light,
Enroll'd in duſkiſh ſmoke and *brimſtone* blue. *Fairy Q. b.* i.

This vapour is generally ſuppoſed to be ſulphureous, though I can ſee no reaſon for ſuch a ſuppoſition: I put a whole bundle of of lighted *brimstone* matches to the smoke, they all went out in an instant. *Addison on Italy.*

Bri'mstony. *adj.* [from *brimstone.*] Full of brimstone; containing sulphur; sulphureous.

Bri'nded. *adj.* [*brin*, Fr. a branch.] Streaked; tabby; marked with branches.

Thrice the *brinded* cat hath mew'd. *Shakesp. Macbeth.*
She tam'd the *brinded* lioness,
And spotted mountain pard. *Milton.*
My *brinded* heifer to the stake I lay;
Two thriving calves she suckles twice a day. *Dryden.*

Bri'ndle. *n. s.* [from *brinded.*] The state of being brinded.
A natural *brindle.* *Clarissa.*

Bri'ndled. *adj.* [from *brindle.*] Brinded; streaked.

The boar, my sisters! aim the fatal dart,
And strike the *brindled* monster to the heart. *Addison's Ovid.*

BRINE. *n. s.*

1. Water impregnated with salt.

The encreasing of the weight of water, will encrease its power of bearing; as we see *brine*, when it is salt enough, will bear an egg. *Bacon's Nat. History*, N° 790.

Dissolve the sheeps dung in water, and add to it as much salt as will make it a strong *brine*, in this liquour, to steep your corn. *Mortimer.*

2. The sea.

All, but mariners,
Plung'd in the foaming *brine*, did quit the vessel,
Then all afire with me. *Shakesp. Tempest.*
The air was calm, and, on the level *brine*,
Sleek Panope, with all her sisters, play'd. *Milton.*
As when two adverse winds
Engage with horrid shock, the ruffled *brine*
Roars stormy. *Philips.*

3. Tears.

What a deal of *brine*
Hath wash'd thy sallow cheeks for Rosaline! *Shakesp.*

Bri'nepit. *n. s.* [from *brine* and *pit.*] Pit of salt water.

Then I lov'd thee,
And shew'd thee all the qualities o' th' isle,
The fresh springs, *brinepits*, barren place, and fertile. *Shakesp. Tempest.*

To **BRING.** *v. a.* [bpingan, Sax. preter. I *brought*; part. pass. *brought*; bpohr, Sax.]

1. To fetch from another place; distinguished from to *carry*, or convey, to another place.

I was the chief that rais'd him to the crown,
And I'll be chief to *bring* him down again. *Shakesp. H.* VI.

And as she was going to fetch it, he called to her, and said, *Bring* me, I pray thee, a morsel of bread in thy hand. *1 Kings*, xvii. 11.

A registry of lands may furnish easy securities of money, that shall be *brought* over by strangers. *Temple.*

2. To convey in one's own hand; not to send by another.

And if my wish'd alliance please your king,
Tell him he should not send the peace, but *bring.* *Dryden.*

3. To produce; to procure.

There is nothing will *bring* you more honour, and more ease, than to do what right in justice you may. *Bacon.*

4. To cause to come.

He protests he loves you,
And needs no other suitor, but his liking
To *bring* you in again. *Shakesp. Othello.*

There is but one God, who made heaven and earth, and sea and winds; but the folly and madness of mankind *brought* in the images of gods. *Stillingfleet.*

The fountains of the great deep being broke open, so as a general destruction and devastation was *brought* upon the earth, and all things in it. *Burnet's Theory.*

Bring back gently their wandering minds, by going before them in the train they should pursue, without any rebuke. *Locke.*

The great question, which, in all ages, has disturbed mankind, and *brought* on them those mischiefs. *Locke.*

5. To introduce.

Since he could not have a seat among them himself, he would *bring* in one, who had more merit. *Tatler*, N° 81.

6. To reduce; to recal.

Nathan's fable had so good an effect, as to *bring* the man after God's own heart to a right sense of his guilt. *Spect.* N° 83.

7. To attract; to draw along.

In distillation, the water ascends difficultly, and *brings* over with it some part of the oil of vitriol. *Newton's Opticks.*

8. To put into any particular state or circumstances, to make liable to any thing.

Having got the way of reasoning, which that study necessarily *brings* the mind to, they might be able to transfer it to other parts of knowledge, as they shall have occasion. *Locke.*

The question for *bringing* the king to justice was immediately put, and carried without any opposition, that I can find. *Swift's Presbyterian Plea.*

9. To conduct.

A due consideration of the vanities of the world, will naturally *bring* us to the contempt of it; and the contempt of the world will as certainly *bring* us home to ourselves. *L'Estrange.*

The understanding should be *brought* to the difficult and knotty parts of knowledge, by insensible degrees. *Locke.*

10. To recal; to summons.

But those, and more than I to mind can *bring*,
Menalcas has not yet forgot to sing. *Dryden.*

11. To induce; to prevail upon.

The nature of the things, contained in those words, would not suffer him to think otherwise, how, or whensoever, he is *brought* to reflect on them. *Locke.*

It seems so preposterous a thing to men, to make themselves unhappy in order to happiness, that they do not easily *bring* themselves to it. *Locke.*

Profitable employments would be no less a diversion than any of the idle sports in fashion, if men could but be *brought* to delight in them. *Locke.*

12. *To bring about.* [See About.] To bring to pass; to effect.

This he conceives not hard to *bring about*,
If all of you would join to help him out. *Dryden's Ind. Emp.*

This turn of mind threw off the oppositions of envy and competition; it enabled him to gain the most vain and impracticable into his designs, and to *bring about* several great events, for the advantage of the publick. *Addison's Freeholder.*

13. *To bring forth.* To give birth to; to produce.

The good queen,
For she is good, hath *brought* you *forth* a daughter:
Here 'tis; commends it to your blessing. *Shakesp.*
More wonderful
Than that which, by creation, first *brought forth*
Light out of darkness! *Paradise Lost, b.* xii. *l.* 472.
Bewail thy falsehood, and the pious works
It hath *brought forth*, to make thee memorable
Among illustrious women, faithful wives. *Milton's Agonist.*
Bellona leads thee to thy lover's hand,
Another queen *brings forth* another brand,
To burn with foreign fires her native land! *Dryden, Æneid* vii. *l.* 444.

Idleness and luxury *bring forth* poverty and want; and this tempts men to injustice; and that causeth enmity and animosity. *Tillotson.*

The value of land is raised, when it is fitted to *bring forth* a greater quantity of any valuable product. *Locke.*

14. *To bring forth.* To bring to light.

The thing that is hid, *bringeth* he *forth* to light. *Job*, xxviii. 11.

15. *To bring in.* To reduce.

Send over into that realm such a strong power of men, as should perforce *bring in* all that rebellious rout, and loose people. *Spenser on Ireland.*

16. *To bring in.* To afford gain.

The sole measure of all his courtesies is, what return they will make him, and what revenue they will *bring* him *in.* *South.*

Trade *brought* us *in* plenty and riches. *Locke.*

17. *To bring in.* To introduce.

Entertain no long discourse with any; but, if you can, *bring in* something to season it with religion. *Taylor.*

The fruitfulness of Italy and the like, are not *brought in* by force, but naturally rise out of the argument. *Addison.*

Quotations are best *brought in*, to confirm some opinion controverted. *Swift.*

18. *To bring off.* To clear; to procure to be acquitted; to cause to escape.

I trusted to my head, that has betrayed me; and I found fault with my legs, that would otherwise have *brought* me *off.* *L'Estrange.*

Set a kite upon the bench, and it is forty to one he'll *bring off* a crow at the bar. *L'Estrange.*

The best way to avoid this imputation, and to *bring off* the credit of our understanding, is to be truly religious. *Tillotson.*

19. *To bring on.* To engage in action.

If there be any that would reign, and take up all the time, let him find means to take them off, and *bring* others *on.* *Bacon, Essay* 36.

20. *To bring over.* To convert; to draw to a new party.

This liberty should be made use of upon few occasions, of small importance, and only with a view of *bringing over* his own side, another time, to something of greater and more publick moment. *Swift on the Sentiments of a Ch. of Engl. man.*

The protestant clergy will find it, perhaps, no difficult matter to *bring* great numbers *over* to the church. *Swift.*

21. *To bring out.* To exhibit; to shew.

If I make not this cheat *bring out* another, and the shearers prove sheep, let me be unrolled. *Shakesp. Winter's Tale.*

Which he could *bring out*, where he had,
And what he bought them for, and paid. *Hudibras.*
These shake his soul, and, as they boldly press,
Bring out his crimes, and force him to confess. *Dryden.*

Another way made use of, to find the weight of the denarii, was by the weight of Greek coins; but those experiments *bring out* the denarius heavier. *Arbuthnot.*

22. *To bring under.* To subdue; to repress.

That sharp course which you have set down, for the *bringing* under

under of those rebels of Ulster, and preparing a way for their perpetual reformation. *Spenser's Ireland.*

To say, that the more capable, or the better deserver, hath such right to govern, as he may compulsorily *bring under* the less worthy, is idle. *Bacon's Holy War.*

23. *To bring up.* To educate; to instruct; to form.

The well *bringing up* of the people, serves as a most sure bond to hold them. *Sidney, b.* i.

He that takes upon him the charge of *bringing up* young men, especially young gentlemen, should have something more in him than Latin. *Locke.*

They frequently conversed with this lovely virgin, who had been *brought up* by her father in the same course of knowledge. *Addison. Guardian*, Nº 167.

24. *To bring up.* To bring into practice.

Several obliging deferences, condescensions, and submissions, with many outward forms and ceremonies, were first of all *brought up* among the politer part of mankind, who lived in courts and cities. *Spectator*, Nº 119.

25. *To bring up.* To cause to advance.

Bring up your army; but, I think, you'll find,
They've not prepar'd for us. *Shakesp. Coriolanus.*

BRI'NGER. *n. s.* [from *bring.*] The person that brings any thing.

Yet the first *bringer* of unwelcome news
Hath but a losing office: and his tongue
Sounds ever after as a sullen bell,
Remember'd tolling a dead friend. *Shakesp. Henry* IV. *p.* ii.

Best you see safe the *bringer*
Out of the host: I must attend mine office. *Shakesp.*

BRI'NGER UP. Instructor; educator.

Italy and Rome have been breeders and *bringers up* of the worthiest men. *Ascham's Schoolmaster.*

BRI'NISH. *adj.* [from *brine.*] Having the taste of brine; salt.

Nero would be tainted with remorse
To hear and see her plaints, her *brinish* tears. *Shakesp.*

For now I stand, as one upon a rock,
Environ'd with a wilderness of sea,
Who marks the waxing tide grow wave by wave;
Expecting ever when some envious surge
Will, in his *brinish* bowels, swallow him. *Shakesp. T. Andr.*

BRI'NISHNESS. *n. s.* [from *brinish.*] Saltness; tendency to saltness.

BRINK. *n. s.* [*brink*, Danish.] The edge of any place, as of a precipice or a river.

Th' amazed flames stand gather'd in a heap,
And from the precipice's *brink* retire,
Afraid to venture on so large a leap. *Dryden's Ann. Mirab.*

We stand therefore on the *brinks* and confines of those states at the day of doom. *Atterbury.*

So have I seen, from Severn's *brink*,
A flock of geese jump down together;
Swim where the bird of Jove wou'd sink,
And, swimming, never wet a feather. *Swift.*

BRI'NY. *adj.* [from *brine.*] Salt.

He, who first the passage try'd,
In harden'd oak his heart did hide;
Or his, at least, in hollow wood,
Who tempted first the *briny* flood. *Dryden.*

Then, *briny* seas, and tasteful springs, farewel,
Where fountain nymphs, confus'd with Nereïds, dwell.
Addison's Remarks on Italy.

A muriatick or *briny* taste seems to be produced by a mixture of an acid and alkaline salt; for spirit of salt, and salt of tartar, mixed, produce a salt like sea salt. *Arbuthnot on Aliments.*

BRI'ONY. See BRYONY.

BRISK. *adj.* [*brusque*, Fr.]

1. Lively; vivacious; gay; sprightly; applied to men.

Pr'ythee, die, and set me free,
Or else be
Kind and *brisk*, and gay like me. *Sir J. Denham.*

A creeping young fellow, that had committed matrimony with a *brisk* gamesome lass, was so altered in a few days, that he was liker a sceleton than a living man. *L'Estrange.*

Why shou'd all honour then be ta'en
From lower parts, to load the brain:
When other limbs we plainly see,
Each in his way, as *brisk* as he? *Prior.*

2. Powerful; spirituous.

Our nature here is not unlike our wine;
Some sorts, when old, continue *brisk* and fine. *Denham.*

Under ground, the rude Riphæan race
Mimick *brisk* cyder, with the brake's product wild,
Sloes pounded, hips, and servis' harshest juice. *Philips.*

It must needs be some exteriour cause, and the *brisk* acting of some objects without me, whose efficacy I cannot resist. *Locke.*

3. Vivid; bright.

Objects appeared much darker, because my instrument was overcharged; had it magnified thirty or twenty five times, it would have made the object appear more *brisk* and pleasant. *Newton's Opticks.*

To BRISK UP. *v. n.* To come up briskly.

BRI'SKET. *n. s.* [*brichet*, Fr.] The breast of an animal.

See that none of the wool be wanting, that their gums be red, teeth white and even, and the *brisket* skin red. *Mortimer.*

BRI'SKLY. *adv.* [from *brisk.*] Actively; vigorously.

We have seen the air in the bladder suddenly expand itself so much, and so *briskly*, that it manifestly lifted up some light bodies that leaned upon it. *Boyle.*

I could plainly perceive the creature to suck in many of the most minute animalcula, that were swimming *briskly* about in the water. *Ray on the Creation.*

BRI'SKNESS. *n. s.* [from *brisk.*]

1. Liveliness; vigour; quickness.

Some remains of corruption, though they do not conquer and extinguish, yet will slacken and allay the vigour and *briskness* of the renewed principle. *South.*

2. Gayety.

But the most distinguishing part of his character seems to me, to be his *briskness*, his jollity, and his good humour. *Dryd.*

BRI'STLE. *n. s.* [bɲıȷτl, Sax.] The stiff hair of swine.

I will not open my lips so wide as a *bristle* may enter. *Shakesp.*

He is covered with hair, and not, as the boar, with *bristles*, which probably spend more upon the same matter which, in other creatures, makes the horns; for *bristles* seem to be nothing else but a horn split into a multitude of little ones. *Grew.*

Two boars whom love to battle draws,
With rising *bristles*, and with frothy jaws,
Their adverse breasts with tusks oblique they wound. *Dryd.*

To BRI'STLE. *v. a.* [from the noun.] To erect in bristles.

Now for the bare-pickt bone of majesty,
Doth dogged war *bristle* his angry crest,
And snarleth in the gentle eyes of peace. *Shakesp. K. John.*

Which makes him plume himself, and *bristle* up
The crest of youth against your dignity. *Shakesp. H.* IV.

To BRI'STLE. *v. n.* To stand erect as bristles.

Be it ounce, or cat, or bear,
Pard, or boar with *bristled* hair,
In thy eye that shall appear,
When thou wak'st, it is thy dear. *Shakesp. Midsum. N. Dr.*

Stood Theodore surpriz'd in deadly fright,
With chatt'ring teeth, and *bristling* hair upright;
Yet arm'd with inborn worth. *Dryden's Fables.*

Thy hair so *bristles* with unmanly fears,
As fields of corn that rise in bearded ears. *Dryden's Persius.*

To BRISTLE *a thread.* To fix a bristle to it.

BRI'STLY. *adj.* [from *bristle.*] Thick set with bristles.

The leaves of the black mulberry are somewhat *bristly*, which may help to preserve the dew. *Bacon's Natural Hist.*

If the eye were so acute as to rival the finest microscope, the sight of our own selves would affright us; the smoothest skin would be beset all over with rugged scales and *bristly* hairs. *Bentley.*

Thus mastful beech the *bristly* chesnut bears,
And the wild ash is white with bloomy pears. *Dryden's Virg.*

The careful master of the swine,
Forth hasted he to tend his *bristly* care. *Pope's Odyss. b.* xiv.

BRI'STOL STONE. A kind of soft diamond found in a rock near the city of Bristol.

Of this kind of crystal are the better and larger sort of *Bristol stones*, and the Kerry stones of Ireland. *Woodward.*

BRIT. *n. s.* The name of a fish.

The pilchards were wont to pursue the *brit*, upon which they feed, into the havens. *Carew's Survey of Cornwal.*

To BRITE. } *v. n.* Barley, wheat, or hops, are said to *brite*,
To BRIGHT. } when they grow over-ripe. *Dict.*

BRI'TTLE. *adj.* [bɲıττan, Saxon.] Fragile; apt to break; not tough.

The wood of vines is very durable; though no tree hath the twigs, while they are green, so *brittle*, yet the wood dried is extremely tough. *Bacon's Natural Hist.* Nº 622.

From earth all came, to earth must all return,
Frail as the cord, and *brittle* as the urn. *Prior.*

Of airy pomp, and fleeting joys,
What does the busy world conclude at best,
But *brittle* goods, that break like glass? *Granville.*

If the stone is *brittle*, it will often crumble, and pass in the form of gravel. *Arbuthnot on Diet.*

BRI'TTLENESS. *n. s.* [from *brittle.*] Aptness to break; fragility.

A wit quick without brightness, sharp without *brittleness*. *Ascham's Schoolmaster.*

Artificers, in the tempering of steel, by holding it but a minute or two longer or lesser in the flame, give it very differing tempers, as to *brittleness* or toughness. *Boyle.*

BRIZE. *n. s.* The gadfly.

A *brize*, a scorned little creature,
Through his fair hide his angry sting did threaten. *Spenser.*

BROACH. *n. s.* [*broche*, Fr.]

1. A spit.

He was taken into service in his court, to a base office in his kitchen; so that he turned a *broach*, that had worn a crown. *Bacon's Henry* VII.

Whose offered entrails shall his crime reproach,
And drip their fatness from the hazle *broach*. *Dryden's Virgil.*

2. A musical instrument, the sounds of which are made by turning round a handle. *Dict.*

3. [With hunters.] A start of the head of a young stag, growing sharp like the end of a spit. *Dict.*

To BROACH. *v. a.* [from the noun.]

1. To spit; to pierce as with a spit.

As by a low but loving likelihood,
Were now the general of our gracious empress,
As in good time he may, from Ireland coming,
Bringing rebellion *broached* on his sword. *Shakesp. Henry* V.

He felled men as one would mow hay, and sometimes *broached* a great number of them upon his pike, as one would carry little birds spitted upon a stick. *Hakewell on Providence.*

2. To pierce a vessel in order to draw the liquour; to tap.

3. To open any store.

I will notably provide, that you shall want neither weapons, victuals, nor aid; I will open the old armouries, I will *broach* my store, and bring forth my stores. *Knolles's History.*

4. To give out, or utter any thing.

This errour, that Pison was Ganges, was first *broached* by Josephus. *Raleigh.*

Those who were the chief instruments of raising the noise, made use of those very opinions themselves had *broached*, for arguments to prove, that the change of ministers was dangerous. *Swift's Examiner*, N° 45.

5. To let out any thing.

And now the field of death, the lists,
Were enter'd by antagonists,
And blood was ready to be *broach'd*,
When Hudibras in haste approach'd. *Hudibras, cant.* ii.

BRO'ACHER. *n. s.* [from *broach.*]

1. A spit.

The youth approach'd the fire, and, as it burn'd,
On five sharp *broachers* rank'd, the roast they turn'd;
These morsels stay'd their stomachs. *Dryden.*

2. An opener, or utterer of any thing; the first authour.

There is much pride and vanity in the affectation of being the first *broacher* of an heretical opinion. *L'Estrange.*

Numerous parties denominate themselves, not from the grand Authour and Finisher of our faith, but from the first *broacher* of their idolized opinions. *Decay of Piety.*

This opinion is commonly, but falsely, ascribed to Aristotle, not as its first *broacher*, but as its ablest patron. *Cheyne.*

BROAD. *adj.* [bnab, Saxon.]

1. Wide; extended in breadth; distinguished from length.

The weeds that his *broad* spreading leaves did shelter,
Are pull'd up root and all by Bolingbroke. *Shakesp. R.* II.

The top may be justly said to grow *broader*, as the bottom narrower. *Temple.*

Of all your knowledge this vain fruit you have,
To walk with eyes *broad* open to your grave. *Dryden.*

So lofty was the pile, a Parthian bow,
With vigour drawn, must send the shaft below,
The bottom was full twenty fathom *broad*. *Dryden's Fables.*

He launch'd the firy bolt from pole to pole,
Broad burst the lightnings, deep the thunders roll. *Pope.*

As cloath'd in cloudy storm,
Weak, wan, and *broad*, he skirts the southern sky. *Thomson.*

2. Large.

To keep him at a distance from falsehood and cunning, which has always a *broad* mixture of falsehood; this is the fittest preparation of a child for wisdom. *Locke.*

3. Clear; open.

In mean time he, with cunning to conceal
All thought of this from others, himself bore
In *broad* house, with the wooers us before. *Chapman's Odyss.*

It no longer seeks the shelter of night and darkness, but appears in the *broadest* light. *Decay of Piety.*

If children were left alone in the dark, they would be no more afraid than in *broad* sunshine. *Locke.*

4. Gross; coarse.

The reeve and the miller are distinguished from each other, as much as the lady prioress and the *broad* speaking gap-toothed wife of Bath. *Dryden's Fables, Pref.*

Love made him doubt his *broad* barbarian sound;
By love, his want of words and wit he found. *Dryden.*

If open vice be what you drive at,
A name so *broad* will ne'er connive at. *Dryden's Albion.*

The *broadest* mirth unfeeling folly wears,
Less pleasing far than virtue's very tears. *Pope.*

Room for my lord! three jockeys in his train;
Six huntsmen with a shout precede his chair;
He grins, and looks *broad* nonsense with a stare. *Pope.*

5. Obscene; fulsom; tending to obscenity.

As chaste and modest as he is esteemed, it cannot be denied, but in some places he is *broad* and fulsome. *Dryden's Juv. Ded.*

Though, now arraign'd, he read with some delight;
Because he seems to chew the cud again,
When his *broad* comment makes the text too plain. *Dryden.*

6. Bold; not delicate; not reserved.

Who can speak *broader* than he that has no house to put his head in? Such may rail against great buildings. *Shakesp.*

From *broad* words, and 'cause he fail'd
His presence at the tyrant's feast, I hear,
Macduff lives in disgrace. *Shakesp. Macbeth.*

BROAD *as long.* Equal upon the whole.

The mobile are still for levelling; that is to say, for advancing themselves: for it is as *broad as long*, whether they rise to others, or bring others down to them. *L'Estrange.*

BROAD-CLOTH. *n. s.* [from *broad* and *cloth.*] A fine kind of cloath.

Thus, a wise taylor is not pinching;
But turns at ev'ry seam an inch in:
Or else, be sure, your *broad-cloth* breeches
Will ne'er be smooth, nor hold their stitches. *Swift.*

BROAD-EYED. *adj.* [from *broad* and *eye.*] Having a wide survey.

In despite of *broad-ey'd* watchful day,
I would into thy bosom pour my thoughts:
But, ah! I will not. *Shakesp. King John.*

BROAD-LEAVED. *adj.* [from *broad* and *leaf.*] Having broad leaves.

Narrow and *broad-leaved* cyprus-grass of the same sort. *Woodward on Fossils.*

To BRO'ADEN. *v. n.* [from *broad.*] To grow broad. I know not whether this word occurs, but in the following passage.

Low walks the sun, and *broadens* by degrees,
Just o'er the verge of day. *Thomson's Summer, l.* 1605.

BRO'ADLY. *adv.* [from *broad.*] In a broad manner.

BRO'ADNESS. *n. s.* [from *broad.*]

1. Breadth; extent from side to side.

2. Coarseness; fulsomness.

I have used the cleanest metaphor I could find, to palliate the *broadness* of the meaning. *Dryden.*

BRO'ADSHOULDERED. *adj.* [from *broad* and *shoulder.*] Having a large space between the shoulders.

Big-bon'd, and large of limbs, with sinews strong,
Broadshouldered, and his arms were round and long. *Dryden.*

I am a tall, *broadshouldered*, impudent, black fellow; and, as I thought, every way qualified for a rich widow. *Spectator.*

BRO'ADSIDE. *n. s.* [from *broad* and *side.*]

1. The side of a ship, distinct from the head or stern.

From vaster hopes than this he seem'd to fall,
That durst attempt the British admiral:
From her *broadsides* a ruder flame is thrown,
Than from the firy chariot of the sun. *Waller.*

2. The volly of shot fired at once from the side of a ship.

3. [In printing.] A sheet of paper containing one large page.

BRO'ADSWORD. *n. s.* [from *broad* and *sword.*] A cutting sword, with a broad blade.

He, in fighting a duel, was run through the thigh with a *broadsword*. *Wiseman.*

BRO'ADWISE. *adv.* [from *broad* and *wise.*] According to the direction of the breadth.

If one should, with his hand, thrust a piece of iron *broadwise* against the flat cieling of his chamber, the iron would not fall as long as the force of the hand perseveres to press against it. *Boyle.*

BROCA'DE. *n. s.* [*brocado*, Span.] A silken stuff, variegated with colours of gold or silver.

I have the conveniency of buying and importing rich *brocades*. *Spectator*, N° 288.

Or stain her honour, or her new *brocade*,
Forget her pray'rs, or miss a masquerade. *Pope.*

BROCA'DED. *adj.* [from *brocade.*]

1. Drest in brocade.

2. Woven in the manner of a brocade.

Should you the rich *brocaded* suit unfold,
Where rising flow'rs grow stiff with frosted gold. *Gay.*

BRO'CAGE. *n. s.* [from *broke.*]

1. The gain gotten by promoting bargains.

Yet sure his honesty
Got him small gains, but shameless flattery,
And filthy *brocage*, and unseemly shifts,
And borrow base, and some good ladies gifts. *Spenser.*

2. The hire given for any unlawful office.

As for the politick and wholesome laws, they were interpreted to be but *brocage* of an usurer, thereby to woo and win the hearts of the people. *Bacon's Henry* VII.

3. The trade of dealing in old things.

Poor poet ape, that would be thought our chief,
Whose works are e'en the frippery of wit,
From *brocage* is become so bold a thief,
As we, the rob'd, leave rage, and pity it. *Ben. Johnson.*

So much as the quantity of money is lessened, so much must the share of every one that has a right to this money be the less, whether he be landholder, for his goods, or labourer, for his hire, or merchant, for his *brocage*. *Locke.*

BRO'CCOLI. *n. s.* [Ital.] See CABBAGE; of which it is a species.

Content with little, I can piddle here,
On *broccoli* and mutton round the year;
But ancient friends, tho' poor or out of play,
That touch my bell, I cannot turn away. *Pope.*

To BROCHE. See To BROACH.

So Geoffry of Boullion, at one draught of his bow, ſhooting againſt David's tower in Jeruſalem, *broched* three feetleſs birds. *Camden's Remains.*

BROCK. *n. ſ.* [bɲoc, Saxon.] A badger.

BRO'CKET. *n. ſ.* A red deer, two years old.

BROGUE. *n. ſ.* [*brog*, Iriſh.]

1. A kind of ſhoe.

I thought he ſlept; and put
My clouted *brogues* from off my feet, whoſe rudeneſs
Anſwer'd my ſteps too loud. *Shakeſp. Cymbeline.*

Sometimes it is given out, that we muſt either take three halfpence, or eat our *brogues*. *Swift.*

2. A cant word for a corrupt dialect, or manner of pronunciation.

To BRO'IDER. *v. a.* [*brodir*, Fr.] To adorn with figures of needle-work.

A robe and a *broidered* coat, and a girdle. *Exodus*, xxviii. 4.

Infant Albion lay
In mantles *broider'd* o'er with gorgeous pride. *Tickell.*

BRO'IDERY. *n. ſ.* [from *broider*.] Embroidery; flower-work; additional ornaments wrought upon cloath.

The golden *broidery* tender Milkah wove,
The breaſt to Kenna ſacred, and to love,
Lie rent and mangled. *Tickell.*

BROIL. *n. ſ.* [*brouiller*, Fr.] A tumult; a quarrel.

Say to the king thy knowledge of the *broil*,
As thou didſt leave it. *Shakeſp. Macbeth.*

He has ſent the ſword both of civil *broils*, and publick war, amongſt us. *Wake.*

Rude were their revels, and obſcene their joys,
The *broils* of drunkards, and the luſt of boys. *Granville.*

To BROIL. *v. a.* [*bruler*, Fr.] To dreſs or cook by laying on the coals, or before the fire.

Some ſtrip the ſkin, ſome portion out the ſpoil,
Some on the fire the reeking entrails *broil*. *Dryden's Æneid.*

To BROIL. *v. n.* To be in the heat.

Where have you been *broiling*?—
——Among the croud i' th' abbey, where a finger
Could not be wedg'd in more. *Shakeſp. Henry* VIII.

Long ere now all the planets and comets had been *broiling* in the ſun, had the world laſted from all eternity. *Cheyne.*

To BROKE. *v. n.* [of uncertain etymology. *Skinner* ſeems inclined to derive it from *to break*, becauſe *broken* men turn factors or *brokers*. *Caſanbon*, from πράττειν. *Skinner* thinks, again, that it may be contracted from *procurer*. Mr. *Lye* more probably deduces it from bɲuccan, Sax. to be buſy.] To tranſact buſineſs for others, or by others. It is uſed generally in reproach.

He does, indeed,
And *brokes* with all that can, in ſuch a ſuit,
Corrupt the tender honour of a maid. *Shakeſp.*

The gains of bargains are of a more doubtful nature, when men ſhould wait upon other's neceſſity; *broke* by ſervants and inſtruments to draw them on. *Bacon.*

BRO'KING. *particip. adj.* In the broker's hands.

Redeem from *broking* pawn the blemiſh'd crown,
Wipe off the duſt that hides our ſceptre's gilt. *Shakeſp.*

BRO'KEN. [*particip. paſſ.* of *break*.]

Preſerve men's wits from being *broken* with the very bent of ſo long attention. *Hooker.*

BRO'KEN MEAT. Fragments; meat that has been cut.

Get three or four chairwomen to attend you conſtantly in the kitchen, whom you pay at ſmall charges; only with the *broken meat*, a few coals, and all the cinders. *Swift.*

BRO'KENHEARTED. *adj.* [from *broken* and *heart*.] Having the ſpirits cruſhed by grief or fear.

He hath ſent me to bind up the *brokenhearted*. *Iſa.* lxi. 1.

BRO'KENLY. *adv.* [from *broken*.] Without any regular ſeries.

Sir Richard Hopkins hath done ſomewhat of this kind, but *brokenly* and glancingly; intending chiefly a diſcourſe of his own voyage. *Hakewell on Providence.*

BRO'KER. *n. ſ.* [from *to broke*.]

1. A factor; one that does buſineſs for another; one that makes bargains for another.

Brokers, who, having no ſtock of their own, ſet up and trade with that of other men; buying here, and ſelling there, and commonly abuſing both ſides, to make out a little paultry gain. *Temple.*

Some South-ſea *broker*, from the city,
Will purchaſe me, the more's the pity;
Lay all my fine plantations waſte,
To fit them to his vulgar taſte. *Swift.*

2. One who deals in old houſhold goods.

3. A pimp; a match-maker.

A goodly *broker*!
Dare you preſume to harbour wanton lines?
To whiſper and conſpire againſt my youth? *Shakeſp.*

In chuſing for yourſelf, you ſhew'd your judgment;
Which being ſhallow, you ſhall give me leave
To play the *broker* in mine own behalf. *Shakeſp. Henry* VI.

BRO'KERAGE. *n. ſ.* [from *broker*.] The pay or reward of a broker. See BROCAGE.

BRO'NCHOCELE. *n. ſ.* [βρογχοκήλη.] A tumour of that part of the aſpera arteria, called the *bronchus*. *Quincy.*

BRO'NCHIAL. } *adj.* [βρόγχος.] Belonging to the throat.
BRO'NCHICK. }

Inflammation of the lungs may happen either in the *bronchial* or pulmonary veſſels, and may ſoon be communicated from one to the other, when the inflammation affects both the lobes. *Arbuthnot on Diet.*

BRONCHO'TOMY. *n. ſ.* [βρόγχος and τέμνω.] That operation which opens the windpipe by inciſion, to prevent ſuffocation in a quinſey. *Quincy.*

The operation of *bronchotomy* is an inciſion made into the aſpera arteria, to make way for the air into the lungs, when reſpiration is obſtructed by any tumour compreſſing the larynx. *Sharp's Surgery.*

BROND. *n. ſ.* See BRAND.

Fooliſh old man, ſaid then, the pagan wroth,
That weeneſt words or charms may force withſtond,
Soon ſhalt thou ſee, and then believe for troth,
That I can carve with this enchanted *brond*. *Fairy Q. b.* ii.

BRONTO'LOGY. *n. ſ.* [βροντη and λογία.] A diſſertation upon thunder. *Dict.*

BRONZE. *n. ſ.* [*bronze*, Fr.]

1. Braſs.

Imbrown'd with native *bronze*, lo! Henley ſtands,
Tuning his voice, and balancing his hands. *Pope's Dunc.*

2. A medal.

I view with anger and diſdain,
How little gives thee joy or pain;
A print, a *bronze*, a flower, a root,
A ſhell, a butterfly can do't. *Prior.*

BROOCH. *n. ſ.* [*broke*, Dutch.]

1. A jewel; an ornament of jewels.

Ay, marry, our chains and our jewels.—
Your *brooches*, pearls, and owches. *Shakeſp. Henry* IV. *p.* ii.

Richly ſuited, but unſeaſonable; juſt like the *brooch* and the toothpick, which we wear not now. *Shakeſp.*

I know him well; he is the *brooch*, indeed,
And gem of all the nation. *Shakeſp. Hamlet.*

2. [With painters.] A painting all of one colour. *Dict.*

To BROOCH. *v. a.* [from the noun.] To adorn with jewels.

Not th' imperious ſhew
Of the full-fortun'd Cæſar, ever ſhall
Be *brooch'd* with me. *Shakeſp. Antony and Cleopatra.*

To BROOD. *v. n.* [bɲædan, Saxon.]

1. To ſit on eggs; to hatch them.

Thou from the firſt
Waſt preſent, and, with mighty wings outſpread,
Dove-like ſat'ſt *brooding* on the vaſt abyſs,
And mad'ſt it pregnant. *Milton's Par. Loſt, b.* i. *l.* 21.

Here nature ſpreads her fruitful ſweetneſs round,
Breathes on the air, and *broods* upon the ground. *Dryden.*

2. To cover chickens under the wing.

Exalted hence, and drunk with ſecret joy,
Their young ſucceſſion all their cares employ;
They breed, they *brood*, inſtruct and educate,
And make proviſion for the future ſtate. *Dryden's Virgil.*

Find out ſome uncouth cell,
Where *brooding* darkneſs ſpreads his jealous wings,
And the night raven ſings. *Milton.*

3. To watch, or conſider any thing anxiouſly.

Defraud their clients, and, to lucre ſold,
Sit *brooding* on unprofitable gold,
Who dare not give. *Dryden's Æneid.*

As rejoicing miſers
Brood o'er their precious ſtores of ſecret gold. *Smith's Phædr.*

4. To mature any thing by care.

It was the opinion of Clinias, as if there were ever amongſt nations a *brooding* of a war, and that there is no ſure league but impuiſſance to do hurt. *Bacon's War with Spain.*

To BROOD. *v. a.* To cheriſh by care; to hatch.

Of crouds afraid, yet anxious when alone,
You'll ſit and *brood* your ſorrows on a throne. *Dryden.*

BROOD. *n. ſ.* [from the verb.]

1. Offspring; progeny.

The heavenly father keep his *brood*
From foul infection of ſo great a vice. *Fairfax, b.* i.

With terrours, and with clamours compaſs'd round,
Of mine own *brood*, that on my bowels feed. *Par. L. b.* ii.

Or any other of that heav'nly *brood*,
Let down in cloudy throne to do the world ſome good. *Milton.*

Ælian diſcourſes of ſtorks, and their affection toward their *brood*, whom they inſtruct to fly. *Brown's Vulgar Errours.*

2. Generation.

Have you forgotten Libya's burning waſtes,
Its barren rocks, parch'd earth, and hills of ſand,
Its tainted air, and all its *broods* of poiſon? *Addiſon's Cato.*

3. A hatch; the number hatched at once.

I was wonderfully pleaſed to ſee the different workings of inſtinct in a hen followed by a *brood* of ducks. *Spect.* N° 121.

4. Something brought forth; a production.

Such things become the hatch and *brood* of time. *Shakesp.*

5. The act of covering the eggs.

Something's in his soul,
O'er which his melancholy sits on *brood*;
And I doubt the hatch and the disclose
Will be some danger. *Shakesp. Hamlet.*

BRO'ODY. *adj.* [from *brood.*] In a state of sitting on the eggs; inclined to sit.

The common hen, all the while she is *broody*, sits, and leads her chickens, and uses a voice which we call clocking. *Ray.*

BROOK. *n. s.* [bꞃoc, or bꞃoca, Saxon.] A running water, less than a river; a rivulet.

A substitute shines brightly as a king,
Until a king be by; and then his state
Empties itself, as doth an inland *brook*
Into the main of waters. *Shakesp. Merchant of Venice.*

Or many grateful altars I would rear,
Of grassy turf; and pile up every stone,
Of lustre, from the *brook*; in memory,
Of monument to ages. *Milton's Par. Lost, b.* xi. *l.* 325.

And to Cephisus' *brook* their way pursue:
The stream was troubled, but the ford they knew. *Dryden.*

Springs make little rivulets; those united, make *brooks*; and those coming together, make rivers, which empty themselves into the sea. *Locke.*

To BROOK. *v. a.* [bꞃucan, Sax.] To bear; to endure; to support.

Even they, which *brook* it worst, that men should tell them of their duties, when they are told the same by a law, think very well and reasonably of it. *Hooker, b.* i.

A thousand more mischances than this one,
Have learn'd me to *brook* this patiently. *Shakesp. T. G. of Ver.*

How use doth breed a habit in a man!
This shadowy desart, unfrequented woods,
I better *brook* than flourishing peopl'd towns. *Shakesp.*

Heav'n, the seat of bliss,
Brooks not the works of violence, and war. *Par. Lost, b.* vi.

Most men can much rather *brook* their being reputed knaves, than for their honesty be accounted fools. *South.*

Restraint thou wilt not *brook*; but think it hard,
Your prudence is not trusted as your guard. *Dryden.*

To BROOK. *v. n.* To endure; to be content.

He, in these wars, had flatly refused his aid; because he could not *brook*, that the worthy prince Plangus was, by his chosen Tiridates, preferred before him. *Sidney's Arcadia.*

BRO'OKLIME. *n. s.* [*becabunga*, Lat.] A sort of water speedwell; very common in ditches.

BROOM. *n. s.* [bꞃom, Saxon.]

1. This tree hath a papilionaceous flower, whose pointal, which rises from the flower-cup, afterward becomes a short, roundish, swelling pod, containing, for the most part, one kidney-shaped seed in each. *Millar.*

Ev'n humble *broom*, and osiers, have their use,
And shade for sheep, and food for flocks, produce. *Dryden.*

2. A besom; so called from the matter of which it is made.

Not a mouse
Shall disturb this hallow'd house;
I am sent with *broom* before,
To sweep the dust behind the door. *Sh. Midsum. Night's Dr.*

If they came into the best apartment, to set any thing in order, they were saluted with a *broom*. *Arbuthnot's John Bull.*

BRO'OMLAND. *n. s.* [*broom* and *land.*] Land that bears broom.

I have known sheep cured of the rot, when they have not been far gone with it, only by being put into *broomlands*. *Mortimer's Husbandry.*

BRO'OMSTAFF. *n. s.* [from *broom* and *staff.*] The staff to which the *broom* is bound; the handle of a besom.

They fell on; I made good my place; at length they came to the *broomstaff* with me; I defied 'em still. *Shakesp. H.* VIII.

From the age,
That children tread this worldly stage,
Broomstaff, or poker, they bestride,
And round the parlour love to ride. *Prior.*

Sir Roger pointed at something behind the door, which I found to be an old *broomstaff*. *Spectator*, N° 117.

BRO'OMY. *adj.* [from *broom.*] Full of broom.

If it grow mossy or *broomy*, which these lands are inclined to, then break it up again, and order it as you did before, laying of it down again from the wheat-stubble. *Mortimer.*

The youth with *broomy* stumps began to trace
The kennel edge, where wheels had worn the place. *Swift.*

BROTH. *n. s.* [bꞃoð, Sax.] Liquour in which flesh is boiled.

You may make the *broth* for two days, and take the one half every day. *Bacon's Physical Remains.*

Instead of light desserts, and luscious froth,
Our authour treats to-night with Spartan *broth*. *Southerne.*

If a nurse, after being sucked dry, eats *broth*, the infant will suck the *broth* almost unaltered. *Arbuthnot on Aliments.*

BRO'THEL.
BRO'THELHOUSE. } *n. s.* [*bordel*, Fr.] A house of lewd entertainment; a bawdyhouse.

Perchance
I saw him enter such a house of sale,
Videlicet, a *brothel*. *Shakesp. Hamlet.*

Then courts of kings were held in high renown,
Ere made the common *brothels* of the town:
There, virgins honourable vows receiv'd,
But chaste as maids in monasteries liv'd. *Dryden's. W. of B.*

From its old ruins *brothelhouses* rise,
Scenes of lewd loves, and of polluted joys. *Dryden's Mackfl.*

The libertine retires to the stews, and to the *brothel*. *Rogers.*

BRO'THER. *n. s.* [bꞃoðeꞃ, bꞃoðoꞃ, Saxon.] Plural, *brothers*, or *brethren*.

1. One born of the same father and mother.

Be sad, good *brothers*;
Sorrow so royally in you appears,
That I will deeply put the fashion on. *Shakesp. Hen.* IV.

Whilst kin their kin, *brother* the *brother* foils,
Like ensigns all, against like ensigns bend. *Daniel.*

T' whom Michael! thus, he also mov'd, reply'd:
These two are *brethren*, Adam, and to come
Out of thy loins. *Milton's Paradise Lost, b.* xi. *l.* 454.

Comparing two men, in reference to one common parent, it is very easy to form the ideas of *brothers*. *Locke.*

2. Any one closely united.

We few, we happy few, we band of *brothers*;
For he, to day that sheds his blood with me,
Shall be my *brother*: *Shakesp. Henry* V.

3. Any one resembling another in manner, form, or profession.

He also that is slothful in his work, is *brother* to him that is a great waster. *Prov.* xviii. 9.

4. *Brother* is used, in theological language, for man in general.

BRO'THERHOOD. *n. s.* [from *brother* and *hood.*]

1. The state or quality of being a brother.

This deep disgrace of *brotherhood*
Touches me deeper than you can imagine. *Shakesp. R.* II.
Finds *brotherhood* in thee no sharper spur? *Shakesp. R.* II.

So it be a right to govern, whether you call it supreme fatherhood, or supreme *brotherhood*, will be all one, provided we know who has it. *Locke.*

2. An association of men for any purpose; a fraternity.

There was a fraternity of men at arms, called the *brotherhood* of St. George, erected by parliament, consisting of thirteen the most noble and worthy persons. *Davies on Ireland.*

3. A class of men of the same kind.

He was sometimes so engaged among the wheels, that not above half the poet appeared; at other times, he became as conspicuous as any of the *brotherhood*. *Addison. Guardian.*

BRO'THERLY. *adj.* [from *brother.*] Natural; such as becomes or beseems a brother.

He was a priest, and looked for a priest's reward; which was our *brotherly* love, and the good of our souls and bodies. *Bacon.*

Though more our money than our cause,
Their *brotherly* assistance draws. *Denham.*

They would not go before the laws, but follow them; obeying their superiours, and embracing one another in *brotherly* piety and concord. *Addison's Freeholder*, N° 33.

BRO'THERLY. *adv.* After the manner of a brother; with kindness and affection.

I speak but *brotherly* of him; but should I anatomize him to thee as he is, I must blush and weep, and thou look pale and wonder. *Shakesp. As you like it.*

BROUGHT. [*participle passive* of *bring.*]

The Turks, possessed with a needless fear, forsook the walls, and could not, by any persuasions or threats of the captains, be *brought* on again to the assault. *Knolles's History.*

The instances *brought* by our authour are but slender proofs. *Locke.*

BROW. *n. s.* [bꞃopa, Saxon.]

1. The arch of hair over the eye.

'Tis now the hour which all to rest allow,
And sleep sits heavy upon every *brow*. *Dryden's Ind. Emp.*

2. The forehead.

She could have run, and waddled about;
For even the day before she broke her *brow*. *Shakesp.*

So we some antique hero's strength,
Learn by his launce's weight and length;
As these vast beams express the beast,
Whose shady *brows* alive they drest. *Waller.*

3. The general air of the countenance.

Then call them to our presence, face to face,
And frowning *brow* to *brow*. *Shakesp. Richard* II.

Though all things foul would bear the *brows* of grace,
Yet grace must look still so. *Shakesp. Macbeth.*

4. The edge of any high place.

The earl, nothing dismayed, came forwards that day unto a little village, called Stoke, and there encamped that night, upon the *brow* or hanging of a hill. *Bacon's Henry* VII.

On the *brow* of the hill beyond that city, they were somewhat perplexed by espying the French embassador, with the king's coach, and others, attending him. *Wotton.*

Them with fire, and hostile arms,
Fearless assault; and, to the *brow* of heav'n
Pursuing, drive them out from God and bliss. *Par. L. b.* vi.

To BROW. *v. a.* [from the noun.] To bound; to limit; to be at the edge of.

Tending

Tending my flocks hard by i' th' hilly crofts,
That *brow* this bottom glad. *Milton.*

To BRO'WBEAT. *v. a.* [from *brow* and *beat.*] To depress with severe brows, and stern or lofty looks.

It is not for a magistrate to frown upon, and *browbeat* those who are hearty and exact in their ministry; and, with a grave, insignificant nod, to call a resolved zeal, want of prudence. *South.*

What man will voluntarily expose himself to the imperious *browbeatings* and scorns of great men? *L'Estrange.*

Count Tariff endeavoured to *browbeat* the plaintiff, while he was speaking; but though he was not so imprudent as the count, he was every whit as sturdy. *Addison.*

I will not be *browbeaten* by the supercilious looks of my adversaries, who now stand cheek by jowl by your worship. *Arbuthnot and Pope's Mart. Scriblerus.*

BRO'WBOUND. *adj.* [from *brow* and *bound.*] Crowned; having the head encircled with a diadem.

In that day's feats,
He prov'd the best man i' th' field, and, for his meed,
Was *browbound* with the oak. *Shakesp. Coriolanus.*

BRO'WSICK. *adj.* [from *brow* and *sick.*] Dejected; hanging the head.

But yet a gracious influence from you,
May alter nature in our *browsick* crew. *Suckling.*

BROWN. *adj.* [bꞃun, Saxon.] The name of a colour, compounded of black and any other colour.

Brown, in High Dutch, is called *braun*; in the Netherlands, *bruyn*; in French, *coleur brune*; in Italian, *bruno*; in Greek, ὀρφνινω αἴθοψ, from the colour of the Ethiopians; for αἴθω is to burn, and ὤψ, a face; for that blackness or swarthiness in their faces, is procured through heat. In Latin it is called *fuscus*, *quasi* φῶς σκιᾶται, that is, from darkening or overshadowing the light; or of φώσκειν, which is to burn or scorch. *Peacham.*

I like the new tire within excellently, if the hair were a little *browner.* *Shakesp. Much ado about Nothing.*

From whence high Ithaca overlooks the floods,
Brown with o'ercharging shades and pendent woods. *Pope.*

Long untravell'd heaths,
With desolation *brown*, he wanders waste. *Thomson.*

BRO'WNBILL. *n. s.* [from *brown* and *bill.*] The ancient weapon of the English foot; why it is called *brown*, I have not discovered; but we now say *brown musket* from it.

And *brownbills*, levied in the city,
Made bills to pass the grand committee. *Hudibras.*

BRO'WNISH. *adj.* [from *brown.*] Somewhat brown.

A *brownish* grey iron-stone, lying in thin strata, is poor, but runs freely. *Woodward on Fossils.*

BRO'WNNESS. *n. s.* [from *brown.*] A brown colour.

She would confess the contention in her own mind, between that lovely, indeed most lovely, *brownness* of Musidorus's face, and this colour of mine. *Sidney, b.* ii.

BRO'WNSTUDY. *n. s.* [from *brown* and *study.*] Gloomy meditations; study in which we direct our thoughts to no certain point.

They live retired, and then they doze away their time in drowsiness and *brownstudies*; or, if brisk and active, they lay themselves out wholly in making common places. *Norris.*

To BROWSE. *v. a.* [*brouser*, Fr.] To eat branches, or shrubs.

And being down, is trod in the durt
Of cattle, and *broused*, and sorely hurt. *Spenser's Pastorals.*

Thy palate then did deign
The roughest berry on the rudest hedge:
Yea, like the stag, when snow the pasture sheets,
The barks of trees thou *browsedst.* *Shakesp. Ant. and Cleop.*

To BROWSE. *v. n.* To feed: it is used with the particle *on.*

They have scared away two of my best sheep; if any where I have them, 'tis by the sea-side, *browsing on* ivy. *Shakesp.*

A goat, hard pressed, took sanctuary in a vineyard; so soon as he thought the danger over, he fell presently a *browsing upon* the leaves. *L'Estrange.*

Could eat the tender plant, and, by degrees,
Browse on the shrubs, and crop the budding trees. *Blackm.*

The Greeks were the descendants of savages, ignorant of agriculture, and *browsing on* herbage, like cattle. *Arbuthnot.*

BROWSE. *n. s.* [from the verb.] Branches, or shrubs, fit for the food of goats, or other animals.

The greedy lioness the wolf pursues,
The wolf the kid, the wanton kid the *browse.* *Dryden.*

On that cloud-piercing hill,
Plinlimmon, from afar the traveller kens,
Astonish'd, how the goats their shrubby *browse*
Gnaw pendent. *Philips.*

To BRUISE. *v. a.* [*briser*, Fr.] To crush or mangle with the heavy blow of something not edged or pointed; to crush by any weight; to beat into gross powder; to beat together coarsely.

Fellows in arms, and my most loving friends,
Bruis'd underneath the yoke of tyranny. *Shakesp. R.* III.

And fix far deeper in his head their stings,
Than temporal death shall *bruise* the victor's heel,
Or theirs whom he redeems. *Par. Lost, b.* xii *l.* 433.

As in old chaos heav'n with earth confus'd,
And stars with rocks together crush'd and *bruis'd.* *Waller.*

They beat their breasts with many a *bruising* blow,
Till they turn'd livid, and corrupt the snow. *Dryden's Fab.*

BRUISE. *n. s.* [from the verb.] A hurt with something blunt and heavy.

One arm'd with metal, th' other with wood,
This fit for *bruise*, and that for blood. *Hudibras.*

I since have labour'd
To bind the *bruises* of a civil war;
And stop the issues of their wasting blood. *Dryden.*

BRU'ISEWORT. *n. s.* An herb; the same with COMFREY; which see.

BRUIT. *n. s.* [*bruit*, Fr.] Rumour; noise; report.

Wherewith a *bruit* ran from one to the other, that the king was slain. *Sidney, b.* ii.

Upon some *bruits* he apprehended a fear, which moved him to send to Sir William Herbert to remain his friend. *Hayw.*

I am not
One that rejoices in the common wreck,
As common *bruit* doth put it. *Shakesp. Timon.*

To BRUIT. *v. a.* [from the noun.] To report; to noise abroad; to rumour. Neither the verb nor the noun are now much in use.

His death,
Being *bruited* once, took fire and heat away
From the best temper'd courage in his troops. *Shak. Hen.* V.

It was *bruited*, that I meant nothing less than to go to Guiana. *Raleigh's Essays.*

BRU'MAL. *adj.* [*brumalis*, Lat.] Belonging to the winter.

About the *brumal* solstice, it hath been observed, even unto a proverb, that the sea is calm, and the winds do cease, till the young ones are excluded, and forsake their nests. *Brown's Vulgar Errours, b.* iii. *c.* 10.

BRUN, BRAN, BROWN, BOURN, BURN, are all derived from the Sax. boꞃn, bouꞃn, bꞃunna, buꞃna; all signifying a river or brook. *Gibson's Camden.*

BRUNE'TT. *n. s.* [*brunette*, Fr.] A woman with a brown complexion.

Your fair women therefore thought of this fashion, to insult the olives and the *brunettes.* *Addison. Guardian,* N° 109.

BRU'NION. *n. s.* [*brugnon*, Fr.] A sort of fruit between a plum and a peach. *Trevoux.*

BRUNT. *n. s.* [*brunst*, Dutch.]

1. Shock; violence.

Erona chose rather to bide the *brunt* of war, than venture him. *Sidney, b.* ii.

God, who caus'd a fountain, at thy pray'r,
From the dry ground to spring, thy thirst t' allay
After the *brunt* of battle. *Milton's Agonistes, l.* 581.

Faithful ministers are to stand and endure the *brunt*: a common soldier may fly, when it is the duty of him that holds the standard to die upon the place. *South.*

2. Blow; stroke.

A wicked ambush, which lay hidden long
In the close covert of her guileful eyen,
Thence breaking forth, did thick about me throng,
Too feeble I t' abide the *brunt* so strong. *Spenser's Sonnets.*

The friendly rug preserv'd the ground,
And headlong knight, from bruise or wound,
Like featherbed betwixt a wall,
An heavy *brunt* of cannon-ball. *Hudibras.*

BRUSH. *n. s.* [*brosse*, Fr. from *bruscus*, Lat.]

1. An instrument to clean any thing, by rubbing off the dirt or soil. It is generally made of bristles set in wood.

2. It is used for the larger and stronger pencils used by painters.

Whence comes all this rage of wit? this arming all the pencils and *brushes* of the town against me? *Stillingfleet.*

With a small *brush* you must smear the glue well upon the joint of each piece. *Moxon's Mechanical Exercises.*

3. A rude assault; a shock; rough treatment; which, by the same metaphor, we call a *scouring.*

Let grow thy sinews till their knots be strong,
And tempt not yet the *brushes* of the war. *Shakesp.*

It could not be possible, that, upon so little a *brush* as Waller had sustained, he could not be able to follow and disturb the king. *Clarendon, b.* viii.

Else when we put it to the push,
They had not giv'n us such a *brush.* *Hudibras.*

To BRUSH. *v. a.* [from the noun.]

1. To sweep or rub with a brush.

If he be not in love with some woman, there is no believing old signs; he *brushes* his hat o' morning; what should that bode? *Shakesp. Much ado about Nothing.*

2. To strike with quickness, as in brushing.

The wrathful beast about him turned light,
And him so rudely passing by, did *brush*
With his long tail, that horse and man to ground did rush.
Spenser's Fairy Queen, b. i. *cant.* ii. *stanz.* 16.

Has Somnus *brush'd* thy eyelids with his rod? *Dryden.*

His son Cupavo *brush'd* the briny flood,
Upon his stern a brawny centaur stood. *Dryden's Æneid.*

High

High o'er the billows flew the massy load,
And near the ship came thund'ring on the flood,
It almost *brush'd* the helm. *Pope's Odyssey, b.* ix.

3. To paint with a brush.

You have commissioned me to paint your shop, and I have done my best to *brush* you up like your neighbours. *Pope.*

4. To carry away, by an act like that of brushing.

And from the boughs *brush* off the evil dew,
And heal the harms of thwarting thunder blew. *Milton.*

The receptacle of waters, into which the mouths of all rivers must empty themselves, ought to have so spacious a surface, that as much water may be continually *brushed* off by the winds, and exhaled by the sun, as, besides what falls again, is brought into it by all the rivers. *Bentley.*

5. To move as the brush.

A thousand nights have *brush'd* their balmy wings
Over these eyes. *Dryden's Don Sebastian.*

To Brush. *v. n.*

1. To move with haste: a ludicrous word, applied to men.

Nor wept his fate, nor cast a pitying eye,
Nor took him down, but *brush'd* regardless by. *Dryden.*

The French had gather'd all their force,
And William met them in their way;
Yet off they *brush'd*, both foot and horse. *Prior.*

2. To fly over; to skim lightly.

Nor love is always of a vicious kind,
But oft to virtuous acts inflames the mind,
Awakes the sleepy vigour of the soul,
And, *brushing* o'er, adds motion to the pool. *Dryden's Fab.*

Bru'sher. *n. s.* [from *brush.*] He that uses a brush.

Sir Henry Wotton used to say, that criticks were like *brushers* of noblemens cloaths. *Bacon's Apophthegms.*

Bru'shwood. *n. s.* [from *brush* and *wood.* I know not whether it may not be corrupted from *browsewood.*] Rough, low, close, shrubby thickets; small wood fit for fire.

It smokes, and then with trembling breath she blows,
Till in a cheerful blaze the flames arose.
With *brushwood*, and with chips, she strengthens these,
And adds at last the boughs of rotten trees. *Dryden's Fab.*

Bru'shy. *adj.* [from *brush.*] Rough or shaggy, like a brush.

I suspected, that it might have proceeded from some small unheeded drop of blood, wiped off by the *brushy* substance of the nerve, from the knife wherewith it was cut. *Boyle.*

To Bru'stle. *v. n.* [bnaʃtlan, Saxon.] To crackle; to make a small noise. *Skinner.*

Bru'tal. *adj.* [*brutal*, Fr. from *brute.*]

1. That which belongs to a brute; that which we have in common with brutes.

There is no opposing *brutal* force to the stratagems of human reason. *L'Estrange.*

2. Savage; cruel; inhuman.

The *brutal* bus'ness of the war
Is manag'd by thy dreadful servants' care. *Dryden.*

Bruta'lity. *n. s.* [*brutalité*, Fr.] Savageness; churlishness; inhumanity.

Courage, in an ill-bred man, has the air, and escapes not the opinion of *brutality.* *Locke.*

To Brut'alize. *v. n.* [*brutaliser*, Fr.] To grow brutal or savage.

Upon being carried to the Cape of Good Hope, he mixed, in a kind of transport, with his countrymen, *brutalized* with them in their habit and manners, and would never again return to his foreign acquaintance. *Addison's Freeholder.*

To Bruta'lize. *v. a.* To make brutal or savage.

Bru'tally. *adv.* [from *brutal.*] Churlishly; inhumanly; cruelly.

Mrs. Bull aimed a knife at John, though John threw a bottle at her head, very *brutally* indeed. *Arbuthnot.*

BRUTE. *adj.* [*brutus*, Lat.]

1. Senseless; unconscious.

Nor yet are we so low and base as their atheism would depress us; not walking statues of clay, not the sons of *brute* earth, whose final inheritance is death and corruption. *Bentl.*

2. Savage; irrational; ferine.

Even *brute* animals make use of this artificial way of making divers motions, to have several significations to call, warn, chide, cherish, threaten. *Holder's Elements of Speech.*

In the promulgation of the Mosaick law, if so much as a *brute* beast touched the mountain, it was to be struck through with a dart. *South.*

3. Bestial; in common with beasts.

Then to subdue, and quell, through all the earth,
Brute violence, and proud tyrannick pow'r. *Par. Regained.*

4. Rough; ferocious; uncivilized.

The *brute* philosopher, who ne'er has prov'd
The joy of loving, or of being lov'd. *Pope.*

Brute. *n. s.* [from the adjective.] A brute creature; a creature without reason; a savage.

What may this mean? Language of man pronounc'd
By tongue of *brute*, and human sense express'd? *Par. Lost.*
To judgment he proceeded, on th' accurs'd
Serpent, tho' *brute*; unable to transfer
The guilt on him, who made him instrument
Of mischief. *Milton's Paradise Lost, b.* x. *l.* 165.

Brutes may be considered as either, aerial, terrestrial, aquatick, or amphibious. I call those aerial, which have wings, wherewith they can support themselves in the air; terrestrial are those, whose only place of rest is upon the earth; aquatick are those, whose constant abode is upon the water. *Locke.*

To those three present impulses, of sense, memory, and instinct, most, if not all, the sagacities of *brutes* may be reduced. *Hale's Origin of Mankind.*

Heav'n from all creatures hides the book of fate;
All but the page prescrib'd, this present state;
From *brutes* what men, from men what spirits know;
Or who could suffer being here below? *Pope's Ess. on Man.*

To Brute. *v. a.* [written ill for *bruit.*] To report.

This, once *bruted* through the army, filled them all with heaviness. *Knolles's History of the Turks.*

Bru'teness. *n. s.* [from *brute.*] Brutality; a word not now used.

Thou dotard vile,
That with thy *bruteness* shend'st thy comely age. *Fairy Q.*

To Bru'tify. *v. a.* [from *brute.*] To make a man a brute.

O thou salacious woman! am I then *brutified?* Ay; feel it here; I sprout, I bud, I blossom, I am ripe horn mad. *Congreve's Old Batchelor.*

Bru'tish. *adj.* [from *brute.*]

1. Bestial; resembling a beast.

Osiris, Isis, Orus, and their train,
With monstrous shapes and sorceries abus'd
Fanatick Egypt, and her priests, to seek
Their wand'ring gods disguis'd in *brutish* forms. *Par. Lost.*

2. Having the qualities of a brute; rough; savage; ferocious.

Brutes, and *brutish* men, are commonly more able to bear pain, than others. *Grew's Cosmologia Sacra, b.* ii. *c.* 6.

3. Gross; carnal.

For thou thyself hast been a libertine,
As sensual as the *brutish* sting itself. *Shakesp. As you like it.*

After he has slept himself into some use of himself, by much ado he staggers to his table again, and there acts over the same *brutish* scene. *South.*

4. Ignorant; untaught; uncivilized.

They were not so *brutish*, that they could be ignorant to call upon the name of God. *Hooker, b.* v. § 35.

Bru'tishly. *adv.* [from *brutish.*] In the manner of a brute; of a savage and unnatural man.

I am not so diffident of myself, as *brutishly* to submit to any man's dictates. *K. Charles.*

For a man to found a confident practice upon a disputable principle, is *brutishly* to outrun his reason. *South.*

Bru'tishness. *n. s.* [from *brutish.*] Brutality; savageness; insensibility.

All other courage, besides that, is not true valour, but *brutishness.* *Sprat.*

Bry'ony. *n. s.* [*bryonia*, Lat.] A plant.

It has a climbing stalk, with spines; the leaves are like those of the vine; the flowers consist of one leaf, which is expanded at the top, and divided into five parts, and, in the female plants, succeeded by round berries, growing on footstalks; the flowers of the male plants have five apices in each, but are barren. The species are, 1. The common white *bryony.* 2. Smooth African *bryony*, with deep cut leaves, and yellow flowers, &c. The first sort grows upon dry banks, under hedges, in many parts of England; but may be cultivated in a garden for use, by sowing the berries in the spring of the year, in a dry poor soil. The roots of this plant have been formerly cut into a human shape, and carried about the country, and shewn as mandrakes. *Mill.*

Bub. *n. s.* [a cant word.] Strong malt liquour.

Or if it be his fate to meet
With folks who have more wealth than wit,
He loves cheap port, and double *bub*,
And settles in the humdrum club. *Prior.*

BUBBLE. *n. s.* [*bobbel*, Dutch.]

1. A small bladder of water; a film of water filled with wind.

Bubbles are in the form of a hemisphere; air within, and a little skin of water without: and it seemeth somewhat strange, that the air should rise so swiftly, while it is in the water, and, when it cometh to the top, should be stayed by so weak a cover as that of the *bubble* is. *Bacon's Natural History,* N° 24.

The colours of *bubbles*, with which children play, are various, and change their situation variously, without any respect to confine or shadow. *Newton's Opticks.*

2. Any thing which wants solidity and firmness; any thing that is more specious than real.

The earl of Lincoln was induced to participate, not lightly upon the strength of the proceedings there, which was but a *bubble*, but upon letters from the lady Margaret. *Bacon.*

Then a soldier,
Seeking the *bubble*, reputation,
Even in the cannon's mouth. *Shakesp. As you like it.*

War, he sung, is toil and trouble,
Honour but an empty *bubble*,
Fighting still, and still destroying. *Dryden.*

3. A cheat; a false show.
The nation then too late will find;
Directors promises but wind,
South-sea at best a mighty *bubble*. *Swift.*
4. The person cheated.
Cease, dearest mother, cease to chide;
Gany's a cheat, and I'm a *bubble*;
Yet why this great excess of trouble. *Prior.*
He has been my *bubble* these twenty years, and, to my certain knowledge, understands no more of his own affairs, than a child in swaddling clothes. *Arbuthnot's Hist. of J. Bull.*

To BU'BBLE. *v. n.* [from the noun.] To rise in bubbles.
Alas! a crimson river of warm blood,
Like to a *bubbling* fountain stirr'd with wind,
Doth rise and fall. *Shakesp. Titus Andronicus.*
Adder's fork, and blindworm's sting,
Lizard's leg, and owlet's wing:
For a charm of pow'rful trouble,
Like a hellbroth boil and *bubble*. *Shakesp. Macbeth.*
Still *bubble* on, and pour forth blood and tears. *Dryden.*
2. To run with a gentle noise.
For thee the *bubbling* springs appear'd to mourn,
And whispering pines made vows for thy return. *Dryden.*
The same spring suffers at some times a very manifest remission of its heat: at others, as manifest an increase of it; yea, sometimes to that excess, as to make it boil and *bubble* with extreme heat. *Woodward's Nat. Hist.*
Not *bubbling* fountains to the thirsty swain,
Not show'rs to larks, or sunshine to the bee,
Are half so charming as thy sight to me. *Pope.*

To BU'BBLE. *v. a.* To cheat: a cant word.
He tells me, with great passion, that she has *bubbled* him out of his youth; and that she has drilled him on to five and fifty. *Addison. Spectator*, N° 89.
Charles Mather could not *bubble* a young beau better with a toy. *Arbuthnot's Hist. of J. Bull.*

BU'BBLER. *n. s.* [from *bubble.*] A cheat.
What words can suffice to express, how infinitely I esteem you, above all the great ones in this part of the world; above all the Jews, jobbers, and *bubblers*. *Digby to Pope.*

BU'BBY. *n. s.* A woman's breast.
Foh! say they, to see a handsome, brisk, genteel, young fellow, so much governed by a doating old woman; why don't you go and suck the *bubby*? *Arbuthnot's John Bull.*

BU'BO. *n. s.* [Lat. from βουβὼν, the groin.] That part of the groin from the bending of the thigh to the scrotum; and therefore all tumours in that part are called *buboes*. *Quincy.*
I suppurated it after the manner of a *bubo*, opened it, and endeavoured detersion. *Wiseman's Surgery.*

BUBONOCE'LE. *n. s.* [Lat. from βουβὼν, the groin, and κήλη, a rupture.] A particular kind of rupture, when the intestines break down into the groin. *Quincy.*
When the intestine, or omentum, falls through the rings of the abdominal muscles into the groin, it is called *hernia inguinalis*, or, if into the scrotum, *scrotalis*: these two, though the first only is properly so called, are known by the name of *bubonocele*. *Sharp's Surgery.*

BUCANI'ERS. *n. s.* A cant word for the privateers, or pirates, of America.

BUCCELLA'TION. *n. s.* [*buccella*, a mouthful, Lat.] In some chymical authours, signifies a dividing into large pieces. *Harris.*

BUCK. *n. s.* [*bauche*, Germ. suds, or lye.]
1. The liquour in which cloaths are washed.
Buck? I would I could wash myself of the *buck*: I warrant you, buck, and of the season too it shall appear. *Shakesp.*
2. The cloaths washed in the liquour.
Of late, not able to travel with her furred pack, she washes *bucks* here at home. *Shakesp. Henry* VI. *p.* ii.

BUCK. *n. s.* [*bwch*, Welch; *bock*, Dutch; *bouc*, Fr.] The male of the fallow deer; the male of rabbets, and other animals.
Bucks, goats, and the like, are said to be tripping or saliant, that is, going or leaping. *Peacham.*

To BUCK. *v. a.* [from the noun.] To wash clothes.
Here is a basket; he may creep in here, and throw foul linen upon him, as if it were going to *bucking*. *Shakesp.*

To BUCK. *v. n.* [from the noun.] To copulate as bucks and does.
The chief time of setting traps, is in their *bucking* time. *Mortimer.*

BU'CKBASKET. *n. s.* The basket in which cloaths are carried to the wash.
They conveyed me into a *buckbasket*; rammed me in with foul shirts, foul stockings, and greasy napkins. *Shakesp.*

BU'CKBEAN. *n. s.* [*bocksboonen*, Dutch.] A plant; a sort of *trefoil.*
The bitter nauseous plants, as centaury, *buckbane*, gentian, of which tea may be made, or wines by infusion. *Floyer.*

BU'CKET. *n. s.* [*baquet*, Fr.]
1. The vessel in which water is drawn out of a well.
Now is this golden crown like a deep well,
That owes two *buckets*, filling one another;
The emptier ever dancing in the air,
The other down unseen, and full of water. *Shakesp. R.* II.
Is the sea ever likely to be evaporated by the sun, or to be emptied with *buckets*? *Bentley.*
2. The vessels in which water is carried, particularly to quench a fire.
Now streets grow throng'd, and, busy as by day,
Some run for *buckets* to the hallow'd quire;
Some cut the pipes, and some the engines play;
And some, more bold, mount ladders to the fire. *Dryden.*
The porringers, that in a row
Hung high, and made a glitt'ring show,
To a less noble substance chang'd,
Were now but leathern *buckets* rang'd. *Swift.*

BU'CKLE. *n. s.* [*bwccl*, Welch, and the same in the Armorick; *boucle*, Fr.]
1. A link of metal, with a tongue or catch made to fasten one thing to another.
Fair lined slippers for the cold,
With *buckles* of the purest gold. *Shakesp.*
The chlamys was a sort of short cloak tied with a *buckle*, commonly to the right shoulder. *Arbuthnot on Coins.*
Three seal-rings; which after, melted down,
Form'd a vast *buckle* for his widow's gown. *Pope.*
2. The state of the hair crisped and curled, by being kept long in the same state.
The greatest beau was dressed in a flaxen periwig; the wearer of it goes in his own hair at home, and lets his wig lie in *buckle* for a whole half year. *Spectator*, N° 129.
That live-long wig, which Gorgon' self might own,
Eternal *buckle* takes in Parian stone. *Pope.*

To BU'CKLE. *v. a.* [from the noun.]
1. To fasten with a buckle.
Like saphire, pearl, in rich embroidery,
Buckled below fair knighthood's bending knee. *Shakesp.*
France, whose armour conscience *buckl'd* on,
Whom zeal and charity brought to the field. *Shakesp.*
Thus, ever, when I *buckle* on my helmet,
Thy fears afflict thee. *Philips.*
When you carry your master's riding-coat, wrap your own in it, and *buckle* them up close with a strap. *Swift.*
2. To prepare to do any thing: the metaphor is taken from *buckling* on the armour.
The Saracen, this hearing, rose amain,
And catching up in haste his three square shield,
And shining helmet, soon him *buckled* to the field. *Fairy Q.*
3. To join in battle.
The Lord Gray, captain of the men at arms, was forbidden to charge, until the foot of the avantguard were *buckled* with them in front. *Hayward.*
4. To confine.
How brief the life of man
Runs his erring pilgrimage!
That the stretching of a span
Buckles in his sum of age. *Shakesp. As you like it.*

To BU'CKLE. *v. n.* [*bucken*, Germ.]
1. To bend; to bow.
As the wretch, whose fever-weaken'd joints,
Like strengthless hinges, *buckle* under life,
Impatient of his fit, breaks like a fire
Out of his keeper's arms. *Shakesp. Henry* IV. *p.* ii.
Now a covetous old crafty knave,
At dead of night, shall raise his son, and cry,
Turn out, you rogue! how like a beast you lie;
Go *buckle* to the law. *Dryden.*
2. *To buckle to.* To apply to; to attend. See *active*, second sense.
This is to be done in children, by trying them, when they are by laziness unbent, or by avocation bent another way, and endeavouring to make them *buckle to* the thing proposed. *Locke.*
3. *To buckle with.* To engage with; to encounter.
For single combat, thou shalt *buckle with* me. *Shakesp.*
Yet thou, they say, for marriage dost provide;
Is this an age to *buckle with* a bride? *Dryden's Juv. sat.* vi.

BU'CKLER. *n. s.* [*bwccled*, Welch; *bouclier*, Fr.] A shield; a defensive weapon buckled on the arm.
He took my arms, and, while I forc'd my way,
Through troops of foes, which did our passage stay;
My *buckler* o'er my aged father cast,
Still fighting, still defending as I past. *Dryden's Aurengzebe.*
This medal compliments the emperour in the same sense as the old Romans did their dictator Fabius, when they called him the *buckler* of Rome. *Addison on ancient Medals.*

To BU'CKLER. *v. a.* [from the noun.] To support; to defend.
Fear not, sweet wench, they shall not touch thee, Kate;
I'll *buckler* thee against a million. *Shakesp. Tam. the Shrew.*
Can Oxford, that did ever fence the right,
Now *buckler* falshood with a pedigree? *Shakesp. Henry* VI.

BU'CKLER-THORN. *n. s. Christ's-thorn.*

BU'CKMAST. *n. s.* The fruit or mast of the beech tree.

BU'CKRAM. *n. s.* [*bougran*, Fr.] A sort of strong linen cloth, stiffened with gum, used by taylors and staymakers.
I have peppered two of them; two, I am sure, I have paid, two rogues in *buckram* suits. *Shakesp. Henry* IV.

BU'CKRAMS. *n. s.* The same with *wild garlick.* See GARLICK.

BU'CKSHORN PLANTAIN. *n. s.* [*coronopus*, Lat. from the form of the leaf.] A plant.

It agrees in flower and fruit with the plantain; but its leaves are deeply cut in on the edges; whereas the leaves of the plantain are either entire, or but slightly indented. The species are four; 1. Garden *buckshorn plantain*, or hartshorn, &c. The first species, though entitled a garden plant, yet is found wild upon most commons, and barren heaths; where, from the poorness of the soil, it appears to be very different from the garden kind, as being little more than a fourth part so large. This species was formerly cultivated in gardens as a salad herb, but, at present, is little regarded, and wholly disused. *Miller.*

BU'CKTHORN. *n. s.* [*rhamnus*, Lat. supposed to be so called from bucc, Sax. the belly.]

It hath a funnel-shaped flower, consisting of one leaf, divided toward the top into four or five segments; out of the flower-cup rises the pointal, which becomes a soft roundish berry, very full of juice, inclosing four hard seeds. The species are, Common purging *buckthorn*. 2. Lesser purging *buckthorn*. 3. *Buckthorn*, with long spines, and a white bark of Montpelier. The first of these trees is very common in hedges; the berries of which are used in medicine, particularly for making a syrup, which was formerly in great use; though, of late, other sorts of berries have either been mixed with those of the *buckthorn*, or wholly substituted in their place; which mixture hath spoiled the syrup, and rendered it less esteemed. The *buckthorn* berries may be distinguished whether they are right or not, by opening them, and observing the number of seeds in each; for these have commonly four. The second sort is less common in England. Both these sorts may be propagated, by laying down their tender branches in autumn. The first sort will grow to the height of eighteen or twenty feet; the second sort seldom rises above eight feet high. They may also be propagated by seeds. *Miller.*

BU'CKWHEAT. *n. s.* [*buckweitz*, Germ. *fagopyrum*, Lat.]

The flowers grow in a spike, or branched from the wings of the leaves; the cup of the flower is divided into five parts, and resembles the petals of a flower; the seeds are black, and three cornered. The species are, 1. Common upright *buckwheat*. 2. Common creeping *buckwheat*. The first is cultivated in England, and is a great improvement to dry barren lands. The second grows wild, and is seldom cultivated. *Miller.*

BUCO'LICK. *adj.* [βουκολικα, from βουκολος, a cowherd.] Pastoral.

BUD. *n. s.* [*bouton*, Fr.] The first shoot of a plant; a gem.

Be as thou wast wont to be;
See as thou wast wont to see:
Dian's *bud* o'er Cupid's flower
Hath such force and blessed power. *Shakesp. Mids. N. Dr.*

Writers say, as the most forward *bud*
Is eaten by the canker ere it blow,
Even so by love the young and tender wit
Is turn'd to folly, blasting in the *bud*,
Losing his verdure even in the prime. *Shakesp. T. G. of Ver.*

When you the flow'rs for Chloe twine,
Why do you to her garland join,
The meanest *bud* that falls from mine? *Prior.*

Insects wound the tender *buds*, with a long hollow trunk, and deposit an egg in the hole, with a sharp corroding liquour, that causeth a swelling in the leaf, and closeth the orifice. *Bentley.*

To BUD. *v. n.* [from the noun.]

1. To put forth young shoots, or gems.

Bud forth as a rose growing by the brook of the field. *Ecclus*, xxxix. 13.

There the fruit, that was to be gathered from such a conflux, quickly *budded* out. *Clarendon*, *b.* ii.

Heav'n gave him all at once, then snatch'd away,
Ere mortals all his beauties could survey;
Just like the flow'r that *buds* and withers in a day. *Dryd.*

Tho' lab'ring yokes on their own necks they fear'd,
And felt for *budding* horns on their smooth foreheads rear'd. *Dryden's Silenus.*

2. To be in the bloom, or growing.

Young *budding* virgin, fair and fresh and sweet,
Whither away, or where is thy abode? *Shakesp.*

To BUD. *v. a.* To inoculate; to graff by inserting a bud into the rind of another tree.

Of apricocks, the largest masculine is much improved by *budding* upon a peach stock. *Temple.*

To BUDGE. *v. n.* [*bouger*, Fr.] To stir; to move off the place: a low word.

All your prisoners
In the lime grove, which weatherfends your cell,
They cannot *budge* till your release. *Shakesp. Tempest.*

The mouse ne'er shun'd the cat, as they did *budge*
From rascals worse than they. *Shakesp. Coriolanus.*

I thought th' hadst scorn'd to *budge*
For fear. *Hudibras, cant.* ii.

BUDGE. *adj.* [of uncertain etymology.] Surly; stiff; formal.

O foolishness of men! that lend their ears
To those *budge* doctors of the stoicks. *Milton.*

BUDGE. *n. s.* The dressed skin or fur of lambs. *Dict.*

BU'DGER. *n. s.* [from the verb.] One that moves or stirs from his place.

Let the first *budger* die the other's slave,
And the gods doom him after. *Shakesp. Coriolanus.*

BU'DGET. *n. s.* [*bogette*, Fr.]

1. A bag, such as may be easily carried.

If tinkers may have leave to live,
And bear the sowskin *budget*;
Then my account I well may give,
And in the stocks avouch it. *Shakesp. Winter's Tale.*

Sir Robert Clifford, in whose bosom, or *budget*, most of Perkin's secrets were laid up, was come into England. *Bacon.*

His *budget* with corruptions cramm'd,
The contributions of the damn'd. *Swift.*

2. It is used for a store, or stock.

It was nature, in fine, that brought off the cat, when the fox's whole *budget* of inventions failed him. *L'Estrange.*

BUFF. *n. s.* [from *buffalo.*]

1. A sort of leather prepared from the skin of the buffalo; used for waist belts, pouches, &c.

A ropy chain of rheums, a visage rough,
Deform'd, unfeatur'd, and a skin of *buff*. *Dryden's Juvenal.*

2. The skins of elks and oxen dressed in oil, and prepared after the same manner as that of the buffalo.

3. A military coat made of thick leather, so that a blow cannot easily pierce it.

A fiend, a fury, pitiless and rough,
A wolf, nay worse, a fellow all in *buff*. *Shakesp.*

To BUFF. *v. a.* [*buffe*, Fr.] To strike: it is a word not in use.

There was a shock,
To have *buff'd* out the blood
From ought but a block. *Ben. Johnson's Underwoods.*

BU'FFALO. *n. s.* [Ital.] A kind of wild ox.

Become th' unworthy browse
Of *buffaloes*, salt goats, and hungry cows. *Dryden's Virgil.*

BU'FFET. *n. s.* [*buffetto*, Ital.] A blow with the fist; a box on the ear.

O, I could divide myself, and go to *buffets*, for moving such a dish of skimmed milk with so honourable an action. *Shakesp.*

A man that fortune's *buffets* and rewards
Hast ta'en with equal thanks. *Shakesp. Hamlet.*

Go, baffl'd coward, lest I run upon thee,
And with one *buffet* lay thy structure low. *Milton's Agonist.*

Round his hollow temples, and his ears,
His buckler beats; the son of Neptune, stunn'd
With these repeated *buffets*, quits the ground. *Dryden.*

BUFFE'T. *n. s.* [*buffette*, Fr.] A kind of cupboard; or set of shelves, where plate is set out to shew, in a room of entertainment.

The rich *buffet* well-colour'd serpents grace,
And gaping Triton's spew to wash your face. *Pope.*

To BU'FFET. *v. n.* [from the noun.] To strike with the hand; to box; to beat.

Why, woman, your husband is in his old lunes again; he so *buffets* himself on the forehead, crying, peer out, peer out! that any madness I ever yet beheld, seemed but tameness. *Shakesp.*

Our ears are cudgell'd; not a word of his
But *buffets* better than a fist of France. *Shakesp. K. John.*

The torrent roar'd, and we did *buffet* it
With lusty sinews; throwing it aside. *Shakesp. Jul. Cæsar.*

Instantly I plung'd into the sea,
And, *buffeting* the billows to her rescue,
Redeem'd her life with half the loss of mine. *Otway.*

To BU'FFET. *v. n.* To play a boxing-match.

If I might *buffet* for my love, I could lay on like a butcher. *Shakesp. Henry* V.

BU'FFETER. *n. s.* [from *buffet.*] A boxer; one that buffets.

BU'FFLE. *n. s.* [*beuffle*, Fr.] The same with *buffalo*; a wild ox.

To BU'FFLE. *v. n.* [from the noun.] To puzzle; to be at a loss.

This was the utter ruin of that poor, angry, *buffling*, well-meaning mortal, Pistorides, who lies equally under the contempt of both parties. *Swift.*

BU'FFLEHEADED. *adj.* [from *buffle* and *head.*] A man with a large head, like a buffalo; dull; stupid; foolish.

BUFFO'ON. *n. s.* [*buffon*, Fr.]

1. A man whose profession is to make sport, by low jests and antick postures; a jackpudding.

No prince would think himself greatly honoured, to have his proclamation canvassed on a publick stage, and become the sport of *buffoons*. *Watts.*

2. A man that practises indecent raillery.

It is the nature of drolls and *buffoons*, to be insolent to those that will bear it, and slavish to others. *L'Estrange.*

The bold *buffoon*, whene'er they trade the green,
Their motion mimicks, but with gest obscene. *Garth.*

BUFFO'ONERY. *n. s.* [from *buffoon.*]

1. The practice or art of a buffoon.

Courage, in an ill-bred man, has the air, and escapes not the opinion of brutality; learning becomes pedantry, and wit *buffoonery*. *Lock on Education.*

2. Low jests; ridiculous pranks; scurrile mirth. *Dryden* places the accent, improperly, on the first syllable.

Where publick ministers encourage *buffoonery*, it is no wonder

der if buffoons ſet up for publick miniſters. *L'Eſtrange.*

And whilſt it laſts, let *buffoonery* ſucceed,
To make us laugh; for never was more need. *Dryden.*

BUG. *n. ſ.* A ſtinking inſect bred in old houſhold ſtuff. In the following paſſage, wings are erroneouſly aſcribed to it.

Yet let me flap this *bug* with gilded wings,
This painted child of dirt, which ſtinks and ſtings. *Pope.*

BUG. } *n. ſ.* [It is derived by ſome from *big*, by others from
BU'GBEAR. } *pug*; *bug*, in Welch, has the ſame meaning.] A frightful object; a walking ſpectre, imagined to be ſeen; generally now uſed for a falſe terrour to frighten babes.

Each trembling leaf and whiſtling wind they hear,
As ghaſtly *bug* their hair on end does rear,
Yet both do ſtrive their fearfulneſs to feign. *Fairy Q. b.* ii.

Sir, ſpare your threats;
The *bug* which you would fright me with, I ſeek. *Shakeſp.*

Haſt not ſlept to-night? would he not, naughty man, let it ſleep? a *bugbear* take him. *Shakeſp. Troilus and Creſſida.*

We have a horrour for uncouth monſters; but, upon cuſtom and experience, all theſe *bugs* grow familiar and eaſy to us. *L'Eſtrange.*

Such *bugbear* thoughts, once got into the tender minds of children, ſink deep, ſo as not eaſily, if ever, to be got out again. *Locke.*

To the world, no *bugbear* is ſo great,
As want of figure, and a ſmall eſtate. *Pope.*

BU'GGINESS. *n. ſ.* [from *buggy*.] Being infected with bugs.

BU'GGY. *adj.* [from *bug*.] Abounding with bugs.

BU'GLE. } *n. ſ.* [from buᵹen, Sax. to bend, *Skinner*; from
BU'GLEHORN. } *bucala*, Lat. a heifer, *Junius*; from *bugle*, the bonaſus. *Lye*.] A hunting horn.

Then took that ſquire an horny *bugle* ſmall,
Which hung adown his ſide in twiſted gold,
And taſſels gay. *Fairy Queen, b.* i. *c.* viii. *ſtanz.* 3.

That I will have a recheate winded in my forehead, or hang my *bugle* in an inviſible baldrick, all women ſhall pardon me. *Shakeſp. Much ado about Nothing.*

He gave his *buglehorn* a blaſt,
That through the woodland echo'd far and wide. *Tickell.*

BU'GLE. *n. ſ.* A ſhining bead of black glaſs.

Bugle bracelets, necklace amber,
Perfume for a lady's chamber. *Shakeſp. Winter's Tale.*

'Tis not your inky brows, your black ſilk hair,
Your *bugle* eyeballs, nor your cheek of cream,
That can entame my ſpirits to your worſhip. *Shakeſp.*

BU'GLE. *n. ſ.* [from *bugula*, Lat.] A plant.

It hath a flower conſiſting of one leaf, divided into three parts; out of the flower-cup ariſes the pointal, fixed like a nail, attended by four embryos, which become ſo many oblong ſeeds, ſhut up in a huſk; the flowers are placed in whorles round the ſtalk. The ſpecies are, 1. Common *bugle*. 2. The greateſt *bugle* of the Alps. 3. Hairy eaſtern *bugle*, with an inverted blue flower, ſpotted with white. 4. Eaſtern *bugle*, with a purpliſh violet coloured flower, &c. The firſt and ſecond ſorts grow wild in moiſt woods and meadows, and continue in flower from May to September. The *bugle* is greatly eſteemed as a vulnerary herb, and is uſed both externally and internally. They are very hardy plants, and propagate greatly by their trailing ſtalks. *Miller.*

BU'GLE. *n. ſ.* A ſort of wild ox. *Philips's World of Words.*

BU'GLOSS. [from *bugloſſum*, Lat.] The herb ox-tongue.

The flowers are ſmall and tubulous, divided at the top into five obtuſe ſegments, and are expanded in a round form; the ſeeds are like the head of a viper. They may be cultivated by ſowing their ſeeds in the ſpring; its flowers are uſed in medicinal cordials. *Miller.*

To BUILD. *v. a.* preter. I *built*, I have *built*. [*bilden*, Dutch.]

1. To raiſe from the ground; to make a fabrick, or an edifice.

Thus ſaith the Lord, thou ſhalt not *build* me an houſe to dwell in. *Hooker, b.* ii. § 6.

When uſurers tell their gold in the field,
And whores and bawds do churches *build*. *Shakeſp.*

When the head-dreſs was *built* up in a couple of cones and ſpires, which ſtood ſo exceſſively high on the ſide of the head, that a woman, who was but a pigmy without her head-dreſs, appeared like a coloſſus upon putting it on. *Spectator*, N° 98.

To *build*, to plant, whatever you intend,
To rear the column, or the arch to bend. *Pope.*

2. To raiſe any thing on a ſupport or foundation.

Love *built* on beauty, ſoon as beauty, dies;
Chooſe this face, chang'd by no deformities. *Donne.*

I would endeavour to deſtroy thoſe curious, but groundleſs ſtructures, that men have *built* up of opinions alone. *Boyle.*

To BUILD. *v. n.* To depend on; to reſt on.

By a man's authority, we here underſtand the force which his word hath for the aſſurance of another's mind, that *buildeth* upon it. *Hooker.*

Some *build* rather upon the abuſing of others, and putting tricks upon them, than upon ſoundneſs of their own proceedings. *Bacon's Eſſays*, N° 23.

Even thoſe who had not taſted of your favours, yet *built* ſo much on the fame of your beneficence, that they bemoaned the loſs of their expectations. *Dryden's Fables, Dedication.*

This is certainly a much ſurer way, than to *build* on the interpretations of an authour, who does not conſider how the ancients uſed to think. *Addiſon on ancient Medals.*

BUI'LDER. *n. ſ.* [from *build*.] He that builds; an architect.

But fore-accounting oft makes *builders* miſs;
They found, they felt, they had no leaſe of bliſs. *Sidney.*

When they, which had ſeen the beauty of the firſt temple built by Solomon, beheld how far it excelled the ſecond, which had not *builders* of like abilities, the tears of their grieved eyes the prophets endeavoured, with comforts, to wipe away. *Hooker, b.* v. § 14.

Mark'd out for ſuch an uſe, as if 'twere meant
T' invite the *builder*, and his choice prevent. *Denham.*

Her wings with lengthen'd honour let her ſpread,
And, by her greatneſs, ſhew her *builder*'s fame. *Prior.*

BUI'LDING. *n. ſ.* [from *build*.] A fabrick; an edifice.

Thy ſumptuous *buildings*, and thy wife's attire,
Have coſt a maſs of publick treaſury. *Shakeſp. Henry* VI.

View not this ſpire by meaſure giv'n
To *buildings* rais'd by common hands:
That fabrick riſes high as heav'n,
Whoſe baſis on devotion ſtands. *Prior.*

Among the great variety of ancient coins which I ſaw at Rome, I could not but take particular notice of ſuch as relate to any of the *buildings* or ſtatues that are ſtill extant. *Addiſon.*

BUILT. *n. ſ.* [from *build*.] The form; the ſtructure.

As is the *built*, ſo different is the fight;
Their mounting ſhot is on our ſails deſign'd;
Deep in their hulls our deadly bullets light,
And through the yielding planks a paſſage find. *Dryden.*

There is hardly any country, which has ſo little ſhipping as Ireland; the reaſon muſt be, the ſcarcity of timber proper for this *built*. *Temple.*

BULB. *n. ſ.* [*bulbus*, Lat.] A round body, or root.

Take up your early autumnal tulips, and *bulbs*, if you will remove them. *Evelyn's Kalend.*

If we conſider the *bulb*, or ball of the eye, the exteriour membrane, or coat thereof, is made thick, tough, or ſtrong, that it is a very hard matter to make a rupture in it. *Ray.*

BULBA'CEOUS. *adj.* [*bulbaceus*, Lat.] The ſame with *bulbous*. *D.*

BU'LBOUS. *adj.* [from *bulb*.] Containing bulbs; conſiſting of bulbs.

There are of roots, *bulbous* roots, fibrous roots, and hirſute roots. And I take it, in the *bulbous*, the ſap haſteneth moſt to the air and ſun. *Bacon's Nat. Hiſtory*, N° 616.

Set up your traps for vermin, eſpecially amongſt your *bulbous* roots. *Evelyn's Kalendar.*

There leaves, after they are ſwelled out, like a *bulbous* root, to make the bottle, bend inward, or come again cloſe to the ſtalk. *Ray on the Creation.*

The beginning of the internal jugulars have a *bulbous* cavity. *Ray on the Creation.*

To BULGE. *v. n.* [It was originally written *bilge*; *bilge* was the lower part of the ſhip, where it ſwelled out; from bılıᵹ, Sax. a bladder.]

1. To take in water; to founder.

Thrice round the ſhip was toſt,
Then *bulg'd* at once, and in the deep was loſt. *Dryden.*

2. To jut out.

The ſide, or part of the ſide of a wall, or any timber that *bulges* from its bottom or foundation, is ſaid to batter, or hang over the foundation. *Moxon's Mechanical Exerciſes.*

BU'LIMY. *n. ſ.* [βουλιμία, from βοῦς, an ox, and λιμὸς, hunger.] An enormous appetite, attended with fainting, and coldneſs of the extremities. *Dict.*

BULK. *n. ſ.* [*bulcke*, Dutch, the breaſt, or largeſt part of a man.]

1. Magnitude; ſize; quantity.

Againſt theſe forces there were prepared near one hundred ſhips; not ſo great of *bulk* indeed, but of a more nimble motion, and more ſerviceable. *Bacon's War with Spain.*

The Spaniards and Portugueſe have ſhips of great *bulk*, but fitter for the merchant than the man of war; for burden than for battle. *Raleigh's Eſſays.*

Though an animal arrives at its full growth, at a certain age, perhaps it never comes to its full *bulk* till the laſt period of life. *Arbuthnot on Aliments.*

2. Greatneſs; largeneſs.

Things, or objects, cannot enter into the mind, as they ſubſiſt in themſelves, and, by their own natural *bulk*, paſs into the apprehenſion; but they are taken in by their ideas. *South.*

3. The groſs; the majority.

Thoſe very points, in which theſe wiſe men diſagreed from the *bulk* of the people, are points in which they agreed with the received doctrines of our nature. *Addiſon. Freeholder*, N° 51.

Change in property, through the *bulk* of a nation, makes ſlow marches, and its due power always attends it. *Swift.*

The *bulk* of the debt muſt be leſſened gradually. *Swift.*

4. Main fabrick.

He rais'd a ſigh, ſo piteous and profound,
That it did ſeem to ſhatter all his *bulk*,
And end his being. *Shakeſp. King Lear*

5. The

5. The main part of a ship's cargo; as, to *break bulk*, is to open the cargo.

BULK. *n. s.* [from *bielcke*, Dan. a beam.] A part of a building jutting out.

Here stand behind this *bulk*. Straight will he come:
Wear thy good rapier bare, and put it home. *Shakesp. Othello.*

The keeper coming up, found Jack with no life in him; he took down the body, and laid it on a *bulk*, and brought out the rope to the company. *Arbuthnot's History of John Bull.*

BU'LKHEAD. *n. s.* A partition made across a ship, with boards, whereby one part is divided from another. *Harris.*

BU'LKINESS. *n. s.* [from *bulky.*] Greatness of stature, or size.

Wheat, or any other grain, cannot serve instead of money, because of its *bulkiness*, and too quick change of its quantity. *Locke.*

BU'LKY. *adj.* [from *bulk.*] Of great size or stature.

Latreus, the *bulkiest* of the double race,
Whom the spoil'd arms of slain Halesus grace. *Dryden.*

Huge Telephus, a formidable page,
Cries vengeance; and Orestes' *bulky* rage,
Unsatisfy'd with margins closely writ,
Foams o'er the covers. *Dryden's Juvenal, sat.* i.

The manner of sea engagements, which was to bore and sink the enemy's ships with the rostra, gave *bulky* and high ships a great advantage. *Arbuthnot on Coins.*

BULL. *n. s.* [*bulle*, Dutch.]

1. The male of black cattle; the male to a cow.

A proper gentlewoman, Sir, and a kinswoman of my master's.—Even such kin as the parish heifers are to the town *bull*. *Shakesp. Henry* IV. *p.* ii.

Bulls are more crisp upon the forehead than cows. *Bacon.*

Best age to go to *bull*, or calve, we hold,
Begins at four, and ends at ten years old. *May's Virgil.*

The nobler herds,
Where round the lordly *bull*, in rural ease,
They ruminating lie. *Thomson's Summer, l.* 920.

2. In the scriptural sense, an enemy powerful, fierce, and violent.

Many *bulls* have compassed me: strong *bulls* of Bashan have beset me round. *Psalm* xxii. 12.

3. One of the twelve signs of the zodiack.

At last from Aries rolls the bounteous sun,
And the bright *Bull* receives him. *Thomson's Spring.*

4. A letter published by the pope.

A *bull* is letters called apostolick by the canonists, strengthened with a leaden seal, and containing in them the decrees and commandments of the pope or bishop of Rome. *Ayliffe.*

There was another sort of ornament wore by the young nobility, called *bullæ*; round, or of the figure of a heart, hung about their necks like diamond crosses. Those *bullæ* came afterwards to be hung to the diplomas of the emperours and popes, from whence they had the name of *bulls*. *Arbuthnot.*

It was not till after a fresh *bull* of Leo's had declared how inflexible the court of Rome was in the point of abuses. *Atterb.*

5. A blunder; a contradiction.

I confess it is what the English call a *bull*, in the expression, though the sense be manifest enough. *Pope's Letters.*

BULL, in composition, generally notes the large size of any thing, as *bull-head*, *bulrush*, *bull-trout*; and is therefore only an inclusive particle, without much reference to its original signification.

BULL-BAITING. *n. s.* [from *bull* and *bait.*] The sport of baiting bulls with dogs.

What am I the wiser for knowing that Trajan was in the fifth year of his tribuneship, when he entertained the people with a horse-race or *bull-baiting?* *Addison on ancient Medals.*

BULL-BEEF. *n. s.* [from *bull* and *beef.*] Coarse beef; the flesh of bulls.

They want their porridge and their fat *bull-beeves*. *Shakesp.*

BULL-BEGGAR. *n. s.* [This word probably came from the insolence of those who begged, or raised money by the pope's bull.] Something terrible; something to fright children with.

These fulminations from the Vatican were turned into ridicule; and, as they were called *bull-beggars*, they were used as words of scorn and contempt. *Ayliffe's Parergon.*

BULL-CALF. *n. s.* [from *bull* and *calf.*] A he-calf; used for a stupid fellow: a term of reproach.

And, Falstaff, you carried your guts away as nimbly, and roared for mercy, and still ran and roared, as ever I heard *bull-calf*. *Shakesp. Henry* IV.

BULL-DOG. *n. s.* [from *bull* and *dog.*] A dog of a particular form, remarkable for his courage. He is used in baiting the bull; and this species is so peculiar to Britain, that they are said to degenerate when they are carried to other countries.

All the harmless part of him is no more than that of a *bull-dog*; they are tame no longer than they are not offended. *Addison. Spectator*, N° 438.

BULL-FINCH. *n. s.* A small bird, that has neither song nor whistle of its own, yet is very apt to learn, if taught by the mouth. *Philips's World of Words.*

The blackbird whistles from the thorny brake,
The mellow *bull-finch* answers from the groves. *Thomson.*

BULL-FLY. }
BULL-BEE. } *n. s.* An Insect. *Philips's World of Words.*

BULL-HEAD. *n. s.* [from *bull* and *head.*]

1. A stupid fellow; a blockhead.

2. The name of a fish.

The miller's thumb, or *bull-head*, is a fish of no pleasing shape; it has a head big and flat, much greater than suitable to its body; a mouth very wide, and usually gaping; he is without teeth, but his lips are very rough, much like a file; he hath two fins near to his gills, which are roundish or crested; two fins under his belly, two on the back, one below the vent, and the fin of his tail is round. Nature hath painted the body of this fish with whitish, blackish, brownish spots. They are usually full of spawn all the summer, which swells their vents in the form of a dug. The *bull-head* begins to spawn in April; in winter we know no more what becomes of them than of eels or swallows. *Walton's Angler.*

3. A little black water vermin. *Philips's World of Words.*

BULL-TROUT. *n. s.* A kind of trout.

There is, in Northumberland, a trout called a *bull-trout*, of a much greater length and bigness than any in these southern parts. *Walton's Angler.*

BULL-WEED. *n. s.* The same with *knapweed*; which see.

BULL-WORT, or BISHOPS-WEED. *n. s.* [*ammi*, Lat.] An umbelliferous plant with small striated seeds; the petals of the flowers are unequal, and shaped like a heart. Its seeds are used in medicine. *Miller.*

BU'LLACE. *n. s.* A wild sour plum. See PLUM.

In October, and the beginning of November, come services, medlars, *bullaces*; roses cut or removed, to come late; holy-oaks, and such like. *Bacon's Essays*, N° 47.

BU'LLET. *n. s.* [*boulet*, Fr.] A round ball of metal, usually shot out of guns.

As when the devilish ironengine wrought
In deepest hell, and fram'd by furies skill,
With windy nitre and quick sulphur fraught,
And ramm'd with *bullet* round, ordain'd to kill. *Fairy Q. b.* i.

Giaffer, their leader, desperately fighting amongst the foremost of the janizaries, was at once shot with two *bullets*, and slain. *Knolles's History of the Turks.*

And as the built, so different is the fight;
Their mounting shot is on our sails design'd:
Deep in their hulls our deadly *bullets* light,
And through the yielding planks a passage find. *Dryden.*

BU'LLION. *n. s.* [*billon*, Fr.] Gold or silver in the lump; unwrought; uncoined.

The balance of trade must of necessity be returned in coin or *bullion*. *Bacon's Advice to Villiers.*

A second multitude,
With wond'rous art, found out the massy ore,
Severing each kind, and scumm'd the *bullion* dross. *Milton's Paradise Lost.*

Bullion is silver, whose workmanship has no value. And thus foreign coin hath no value here for its stamp, and our coin is *bullion* in foreign dominions. *Locke.*

In every vessel there is stowage for immense treasures, when the cargo is pure *bullion*. *Addison on the State of the War.*

BULLI'TION. *n. s.* [from *bullio*, Lat.] The act or state of boiling.

There is to be observed in these dissolutions, which will not easily incorporate, what the effects are, as the *bullition*; the precipitation to the bottom; the ejaculation towards the top; the suspension in the midst; and the like. *Bacon's Physical Rem.*

BU'LLOCK. *n. s.* [from *bull.*] A young bull.

Why, that's spoken like an honest drover: so they sell *bullocks*. *Shakesp. Much ado about Nothing.*

Some drive the herds; here the fierce *bullock* scorns
Th' appointed way, and runs with threat'ning horns. *Cowley.*

Until the transportation of cattle into England was prohibited, the quickest trade of ready money here was driven by the sale of young *bullocks*. *Temple.*

BU'LLY. *n. s.* [*Skinner* derives this word from *burly*, as a corruption in the pronunciation; which is very probably right: or from *bulky*, or *bull-eyed*; which are less probable. May it not come from *bull*, the pope's letter, implying the insolence of those who came invested with authority from the papal court?] A noisy, blustering, quarrelling fellow: it is generally taken for a man that has only the apperance of courage.

Mine host of the garter.—What says my *bully* rock? Speak scholarly and wisely. *Shakesp. Merry Wives of Windsor.*

All on a sudden the doors flew open, and in comes a crew of roaring *bullies*, with their wenches, their dogs, and their bottles. *L'Estrange's Fables.*

'Tis so ridic'lous, but so true withal,
A *bully* cannot sleep without a brawl. *Dryden's Juv. sat.* iii.

A scolding hero is, at the worst, a more tolerable character than a *bully* in petticoats. *Addison's Freeholder*, N° 38.

The little man is a *bully* in his nature, but, when he grows cholerick, I confine him till his wrath is over. *Addison. Spect.*

To BU'LLY. *v. a.* [from the noun.] To overbear with noise or menaces.

Prentices, parish clerks, and hectors meet,
He that is drunk, or *bully'd*, pays the treat. *King's Cookery.*

To BU'LLY. *v. n.* To be noisy and quarrelsome.

BU'LRUSH. *n. s.* [from *bull* and *rush.*] A large rush, such as grows

grows in rivers, without knots; though *Dryden* has given it the epithet *knotty*, confounding it, probably, with the reed.

To make fine cages for the nightingale,
And baskets of *bulrushes*, was my wont. *Spenser.*

All my praises are as but a *bulrush* cast upon a stream; they are born up by the strength of the current. *Dryden.*

The edges were with bending osiers crown'd;
The *knotty bulrush* next in order stood,
And all within of reeds a trembling wood. *Dryden's Fables.*

BU'LWARK. *n. s.* [*bolwercke*, Dutch; probably only from its strength and largeness.]

1. A fortification; a citadel.

But him the squire made quickly to retreat,
Encountering fierce with single sword in hand,
And 'twixt him and his lord did like a *bulwark* stand.
Spenser's Fairy Queen, b. i. *cant.* viii. *stanz.* 12.

Who oft repair
Their earthen *bulwarks* 'gainst the ocean flood. *Fairfax, b.* i.

Taking away needless *bulwarks*, divers were demolished upon the sea coasts. *Hayward.*

We have *bulwarks* round us;
Within our walls are troops enur'd to toil. *Addison's Cato.*

Our naval strength is a general *bulwark* to the British nation. *Addison's Freeholder*, N° 42.

2. A security.

Some making the wars their *bulwark*, that have before gored the gentle bosom of peace with pillage and robbery. *Shakesp.*

To BU'LWARK. *v. a.* [from the noun.] To fortify; to strengthen with bulwarks.

And yet no *bulwark'd* town, or distant coast,
Preserves the beauteous youth from being seen. *Addison.*

BUM. *n. s.* [*bomme*, Dutch.]

1. The buttocks; the part on which we sit.

The wisest aunt telling the saddest tale,
Sometime for threefoot stool mistaketh me,
Then slip I from her *bum*, down topples she. *Shakesp.*

This said, he gently rais'd the knight,
And set him on his *bum* upright. *Hudibras.*

From dusty shops neglected authours come,
Martyrs of pies, and relicks of the *bum*. *Dryden's Mackfl.*

The learned Sydenham does not doubt,
But profound thought will bring the gout;
And that with *bum* on couch we lie,
Because our reason's soar'd too high. *W—n.*

2. It is used, in composition, for any thing mean or low, as *bumbailiff.*

BUMBA'ILIFF. *n. s.* [from *bum* and *bailiff.*] A bailiff of the meanest kind; one that is employed in arrests.

Go, Sir Andrew, scout me for him at the corner of the orchard, like a *bumbailiff.* *Shakesp. Twelfth Night.*

BU'MBARD. *n. s.* [wrong written for *bombard*; which see.] A great gun; a great barrel.

Yond same black cloud, yond huge one looks
Like a foul *bumbard*, that would shed his liquour.
Shakesp. Tempest.

BU'MBAST. *n. s.* [falsely written for *bombast*; the etymology of which I am now very doubtful of; *bombast* and *bombasine* being mentioned, with great probability, by *Junius*, as coming from *boom*, a tree, and *sein*, silk; the silk or cotton of a tree.]

1. A cloth made by sewing one stuff upon another; patchwork.

The usual *bumbast* of black bits sewed into ermine, our English women are made to think very fine. *Grew.*

2. Linen stuffed with cotton; stuffing.

We have received your letters full of love,
And, in our maiden council, rated them
As courtship, pleasant jest, and courtesy,
As *bumbast*, and as lining to the time. *Shakesp.*

BUMP. *n. s.* [perhaps from *bum*, as being prominent.] A swelling; a protuberance.

It had upon its brow a *bump* as big as a young cockrel's stone; a perilous knock, and it cried bitterly. *Shakesp. Rom. and Jul.*

Not though his teeth are beaten out, his eyes
Hang by a string, in *bumps* his forehead rise. *Dryden's Juv.*

To BUMP. *v. a.* [from *bombus*, Lat.] To make a loud noise, or bomb. [See BOMB.] It is applied, I think, only to the bittern.

Then to the water's brink she laid her head,
And as a bittour *bumps* within a reed,
To thee alone, O lake, she said——— *Dryden.*

BU'MPER. *n. s.* [from *bump.*] A cup filled till the liquour swells over the brims.

Places his delight
All day in plying *bumpers*, and at night
Reels to the bawds. *Dryden's Juv. sat.* viii.

BU'MPKIN. *n. s.* [This word is of uncertain etymology; *Henshaw* derives it from *pumpkin*, a kind of worthless gourd, or melon. This seems harsh. *Bump* is used amongst us for a knob, or lump; may not *bumpkin* be much the same with *clodpate*, *loggerhead*, *block*, and *blockhead.*] An awkward heavy rustick; a country lout.

The poor *bumpkin*, that had never seen nor heard of such delights before, blessed herself at the change of her condition. *L'Estrange's Fables.*

A heavy *bumpkin*, taught with daily care,
Can never dance three steps with a becoming air. *Dryden.*

In his white cloak the magistrate appears,
The country *bumpkin* the same liv'ry wears. *Dryden.*

It was a favour to admit them to breeding; they might be ignorant *bumpkins* and clowns, if they pleased. *Locke.*

BU'MPKINLY. *adj.* [from *bumpkin.*] Having the manners or appearance of a clown; clownish.

He is a simple, blundering, and yet conceited fellow, who, aiming at description, and the rustick wonderful, gives an air of *bumpkinly* romance to all he tells. *Clarissa.*

BUNCH. *n. s.* [*buncker*, Danish, the crags of the mountains.]

1. A hard lump; a knob.

They will carry their treasures upon the *bunches* of camels, to a people that shall not profit them. *Josh.* xxx. 6.

He felt the ground, which he had wont to find even and soft, to be grown hard with little round balls or *bunches*, like hard boiled eggs. *Boyle.*

2. A cluster; many of the same kind growing together.

Vines, with clust'ring *bunches* growing. *Shakesp. Tempest.*

Titian said, that he knew no better rule for the distribution of the lights and shadows, than his observations drawn from a *bunch* of grapes. *Dryden's Dufresnoy.*

For thee, large *bunches* load the bending vine,
And the last blessings of the year are thine. *Dryden.*

3. A number of things tied together.

And on his arms a *bunch* of keys he bore. *Fairy Q. b.* i.

All? I know not what ye call all; but if I fought not with fifty of them, I am a *bunch* of radish. *Shakesp. Henry* IV. *p.* i.

Ancient Janus, with his double face,
And *bunch* of keys, the porter of the place. *Dryden.*

The mother's *bunch* of keys, or any thing they cannot hurt themselves with, serves to divert little children. *Locke.*

4. Any thing bound into a knot.

Upon the top of all his lofty crest,
A *bunch* of hairs discolour'd diversly,
With sprinkled pearl and gold full richly drest. *Fairy Q. b.* i.

To BUNCH. *v. n.* [from the noun.] To swell out in a bunch; to grow out in protuberances.

It has the resemblance of a large champignon before it is opened, *bunching* out into a large round knob at one end.
Woodward on Fossils.

BUNCHBA'CKED. *adj.* [from *bunch* and *back.*] Having bunches on the back.

The day shall come, that thou shalt wish for me,
To help thee curse this pois'nous *bunchback'd* toad. *Shakesp.*

BU'NCHINESS. *n. s.* [from *bunchy.*] The quality of being bunchy, or growing in bunches.

BU'NCHY. *adj.* [from *bunch.*] Growing into bunches; knotty.

He is more especially distinguished from other birds, by his *bunchy* tail, and the shortness of his legs. *Grew's Musæum.*

BU'NDLE. *n. s.* [bynble, Sax. from bynb.]

1. A number of things bound together.

As to the *bundles* of petitions in parliament, they were, for the most part, petitions of private persons. *Hale's Law of Engl.*

Try, lads, can you this *bundle* break;
Then bids the youngest of the six
Take up a well-bound heap of sticks. *Swift.*

In the north, they bind them up in small *bundles*, and make small ricks of them. *Mortimer's Husbandry.*

2. A roll; any thing rolled up cylindrically.

She carried a great *bundle* of Flanders lace under her arm; but finding herself overloaden, she dropped the good man, and brought away the *bundle.* *Spectator*, N° 499.

To BU'NDLE. *v. a.* [from the noun.] To tie in a bundle; to tie together; with *up.*

We ought to put things together, as well as we can, *doctrinæ causâ*; but, after all, several things will not be *bundled up* together, under our terms and ways of speaking. *Locke.*

See how the double nation lies,
Like a rich coat with skirts of frize;
As if a man, in making posies,
Should *bundle* thistles *up* with roses. *Swift.*

BUNG. *n. s.* [*bing*, Welch.] A stopple for a barrel.

After three nights are expired, the next morning pull out the *bung* stick, or plug. *Mortimer.*

To BUNG. *v. a.* [from the noun.] To stop; to close up.

BU'NGHOLE. *n. s.* [from *bung* and *hole.*] The hole at which the barrel is filled, and which is afterward stopped up.

Why may not imagination trace the noble dust of Alexander, till he find it stopping a *bunghole.* *Shakesp.*

To BU'NGLE. *v. n.* [See BUNGLER.] To perform clumsily.

When men want light,
They make but *bungling* work. *Dryden's Spanish Friar.*

Letters to me are not seldom opened, and then sealed in a *bungling* manner before they come to my hands. *Swift to Pope.*

To BU'NGLE. *v. a.* To botch; to manage clumsily; to conduct awkwardly.

Other devils, that suggest by-treasons
Do botch and *bungle* up damnation,
With patches, colours, and with forms being fetcht
From glist'ring semblances of piety. *Shakesp. Henry* V.

They make lame miſchief, though they mean it well:
Their int'reſt is not finely drawn, and hid,
But ſeams are coarſely *bungled* up, and ſeen. *Dryden's D. Seb.*

Bu'ngle. *n. ſ.* [from the verb.] A botch; an awkwardneſs; an inaccuracy; a clumſy performance.

Errours and *bungles* are committed, when the matter is inapt or contumacious. *Ray on the Creation.*

Bu'ngler. *n. ſ.* [*bwngler*, Welch; *q. bôn y glér*, i. e. the laſt or loweſt of the profeſſion. *Davies.*] A bad workman; a clumſy performer; a man without ſkill.

Painters, at the firſt, were ſuch *bunglers*, and ſo rude, that, when they drew a cow or a hog, they were fain to write over the head what it was; otherwiſe the beholder knew not what to make of it. *Peacham on Drawing.*

Hard features every *bungler* can command;
To draw true beauty ſhews a maſter's hand. *Dryden.*
A *bungler* thus, who ſcarce the nail can hit,
With driving wrong will make the pannel ſplit. *Swift.*

Bu'nglingly. *adv.* [from *bungling.*] Clumſily; awkwardly.

To denominate them monſters, they muſt have had ſome ſyſtem of parts, compounded of ſolids and fluids, that executed, though but *bunglingly*, their peculiar functions. *Bentley.*

Bunn. *n. ſ.* [*bunelo*, Span.] A kind of ſweet bread.

Thy ſongs are ſweeter to mine ear,
Than to the thirſty cattle rivers clear;
Or winter porridge to the lab'ring youth,
Or *bunns* and ſugar to the damſel's tooth. *Gay's Paſtorals.*

Bunt. *n. ſ.* [corrupted, as *Skinner* thinks, from *bent.*] A ſwelling part; an increaſing cavity.

The Wear is a frith, reaching ſlopewiſe through the ooze, from the land to low water mark, and having in it a *bunt* or cod, with an eye-hook, where the fiſh entering, upon the coming back with the ebb, are ſtopped from iſſuing out again, forſaken by the water, and left dry on the ooze. *Carew.*

To **Bunt.** *v. n.* [from the noun.] To ſwell out, as the ſail *bunts* out.

Bu'nter. *n. ſ.* A cant word for a woman who picks up rags about the ſtreet; and uſed, by way of contempt, for any low vulgar woman.

Bu'nting. *n. ſ.* The name of a bird.

Then my dial goes not true; I took this lark for a *bunting*. *Shakeſp. All's well that ends well.*

BUOY. *n. ſ.* [*boüe*, or *boye*, Fr. *boya*, Span.] A piece of cork or wood floating on the water, tied to a weight at the bottom.

The fiſhermen, that walk upon the beach,
Appear like mice; and yond tall anchoring bark
Diminiſh'd to her cock; her cock a *buoy*,
Almoſt too ſmall for ſight. *Shakeſp. King Lear.*
Like *buoys*, that never ſink into the flood,
On learning's ſurface we but lie and nod. *Pope's Dunciad.*

To **Buoy.** *v. a.* [from the noun. The *u* is mute in both.] To keep afloat; to bear up by ſpecifick lightneſs.

All art is uſed to ſink epiſcopacy, and launch preſbytery in England; which was lately *buoyed* up in Scotland, by the like artifice of a covenant. *K. Charles.*

The water which riſes out of the abyſs, for the ſupply of ſprings and rivers, would not have ſtopped at the ſurface of the earth, but marched directly up into the atmoſphere, wherever there was heat enough in the air to continue its aſcent, and *buoy* it up. *Woodward's Nat. Hiſt.*

To **Buoy.** *v. n.* To float.

Riſing merit will *buoy* up at laſt. *Pope's Eſſay on Crit.*

Buo'yancy. *n. ſ.* [from *buoyant.*] The quality of floating.

All the winged tribes owe their flight and *buoyancy* to it. *Derham's Phyſico-Theology.*

Buo'yant. *adj.* [from *buoy.*] Floating; light; that which will not ſink.

I ſwom with the tide, and the water under me was *buoyant*. *Dryden.*

His once ſo vivid nerves,
So full of *buoyant* ſpirit, now no more
Inſpire the courſe. *Thomſon's Autumn, l.* 455.

Bur, Bour, Bor, come from the Sax. buꞃ, an inner-chamber, or place of ſhade and retirement. *Gibſon's Camden.*

Bur. *n. ſ.* [*bourre*, Fr. is *down*; the *bur* being filled with a ſoft *tomentum*, or down.] A rough head of a plant, which ſticks to the hair or cloaths.

Nothing teems,
But hateful docks, rough thiſtles, keckſies, *burs*,
Loſing both beauty and utility. *Shakeſp. Henry* V.
Hang off, thou cat, thou *bur*; vile thing, let looſe;
Or I will ſhake thee from me like a ſerpent. *Shakeſp.*

Dependents and ſuitors are always the *burs*, and ſometimes the briers of favourites. *Wotton.*

Whither betake her
From the chill dew, amongſt rude *burs* and thiſtles. *Milton.*
And where the vales with violets once were crown'd,
Now knotty *burs* and thorns diſgrace the ground. *Dryden.*

A fellow ſtuck like a *bur*, that there was no ſhaking him off. *Arbuthnot's Hiſt. of J. Bull.*

Bu'rbot. *n. ſ.* A fiſh full of prickles. *Dict.*

Bu'rdelais. *n. ſ.* A ſort of grape. See **Vine.**

BU'RDEN. *n. ſ.* [byꞃðen, Sax. and therefore properly written *burthen.* It is ſuppoſed to come from *burdo*, Lat. a mule, as *onus* from ὄνος, an aſs.]

1. A load; ſomething to be carried.

Camels have their provender
Only for bearing *burdens*, and ſore blows
For ſinking under them. *Shakeſp. Coriolanus.*

It is of uſe in lading of ſhips, and may help to ſhew what *burden* in the ſeveral kinds they will bear. *Bacon's Phyſ. Rem.*

2. Something grievous or wearisome.

Couldſt thou ſupport
That *burden*, heavier than the earth to bear? *Par. Loſt, b.* x.

None of the things they are to learn, ſhould ever be made a *burden* to them, or impoſed on them as a taſk. *Locke.*

Deaf, giddy, helpleſs, left alone,
To all my friends a *burden* grown. *Swift.*

3. A birth: now obſolete.

Thou hadſt a wife once, called Æmilia,
That bore thee at a *burden* two fair ſons. *Shakeſp.*

4. The verſe repeated in a ſong.

At ev'ry cloſe ſhe made, th' attending throng
Reply'd, and bore the *burden* of the ſong. *Dryden's Fab.*

5. The quantity that a ſhip will carry; or the capacity of a ſhip.

To **Bu'rden.** *v. a.* [from the noun.] To load; to incumber.

Burden not thyſelf above thy power. *Ecclus*, xiii. 2.

I mean not that other men be eaſed, and you *burdened*. *Cor.* viii. 13.

Bu'rdener. *n. ſ.* [from *burden.*] A loader; an oppreſſour.

Bu'rdenous. *adj.* [from *burden.*]

1. Grievous; oppreſſive; wearisome.

Make no jeſt of that which hath ſo earneſtly pierced me through, nor let that be light to thee, which to me is ſo *burdenous*. *Sidney, b.* i.

2. Uſeleſs.

To what can I be uſeful, wherein ſerve,
But to ſit idle on the houſhold hearth,
A *burd'nous* drone; to viſitants a gaze. *Milton's Agoniſtes.*

Bu'rdensome. *adj.* [from *burden.*] Grievous; troubleſome to be born.

His leiſure told him, that his time was come,
And lack of load made his life *burdenſome.* *Milton.*
Could I but live till *burdenſome* they prove,
My life would be immortal as my love. *Dryden's Ind. Emp.*

Aſſiſtances always attending us, upon the eaſy condition of our prayers, and by which the moſt *burdenſome* duty will become light and eaſy. *Rogers.*

Bu'rdensomeness. *n. ſ.* [from *burdenſome.*] Weight; heavineſs; uneaſineſs to be born.

Bu'rdock. *n. ſ.* See **Dock.**

Bureau'. *n. ſ.* [*bureau*, Fr.] A cheſt of drawers. It is pronounced as if it were ſpelt *buro.*

For not the deſk with ſilver nails,
Nor *bureau* of expence,
Nor ſtandiſh well japan'd, avails
To writing of good ſenſe. *Swift.*

Burg. *n. ſ.* See **Burrow.**

Bu'rgage. *n. ſ.* [from *burg*, or *burrow.*] A tenure proper to cities and towns, whereby men of cities or burrows hold their lands or tenements of the king, or other lord, for a certain yearly rent. *Cowel.*

The groſs of the borough is ſurveyed together in the beginning of the county; but there are ſome other particular *burgages* thereof, mentioned under the titles of particular mens poſſeſſions. *Hale's Origin of Mankind.*

Bu'rgamot. *n. ſ.* [*bergamotte*, Fr.] A ſpecies of pear.

Bu'rganet. / Bu'rgonet. *n. ſ.* [from *bourginote*, Fr.] A kind of helmet.

Upon his head his gliſtering *burganet*,
The which was wrought by wonderous device,
And curiouſly engraven, he did fit. *Spenſer's Muiopotmos.*
This day I'll wear aloft my *burgonet*,
Ev'n to affright thee with the view thereof. *Shakeſp. H.* VI.
The demy Atlas of this earth, the arm
And *burgonet* of man. *Shakeſp. Antony and Cleopatra.*

I was page to a footman, carrying after him his pike and *burganet*. *Hakewell on Providence.*

BURGEO'IS. *n. ſ.* [*bourgeois*, Fr.]

1. A citizen; a burgeſs.

It is a republick itſelf, under the protection of the eight ancient cantons. There are in it an hundred *burgeois*, and about a thouſand ſouls. *Addiſon on Italy.*

2. A type of a particular ſort, probably ſo called from him who firſt uſed it; as,

Laugh where we muſt, be candid where we can,
But vindicate the ways of God to man. *Pope.*

Bu'rgess. *n. ſ.* [*bourgeois*, Fr.]

1. A citizen; a freeman of a city, or corporate town.
2. A repreſentative of a town corporate.

The whole caſe was diſperſed by the knights of ſhires, and *burgeſſes* of towns, through all the veins of the land. *Wotton.*

BURGH. *n. ſ.* [See **Burrow.**] A corporate town or burrow.

Many towns in Cornwal, when they were firſt allowed to

 ſend

send burgesses to the parliament, bore another proportion to London than now; for several of these *burghs* send two burgesses, whereas London itself sends but four. *Graunt.*

BU'RGHER. *n. s.* [from *burgh.*] One who has a right to certain privileges in this or that place. *Locke.*

It irks me, the poor dappled fools,
Being native *burghers* of this desart city,
Should in their own confines, with forked heads,
Have their round haunches gor'd. *Shakesp. As you like it.*

After the multitude of the common people was dismissed, and the chief of the *burghers* sent for, the imperious letter was read before the knights of the order, and the better sort of citizens. *Knolles's History of the Turks.*

BU'RGHERSHIP. *n. s.* [from *burgher.*] The privilege of a burgher.

BU'RGHMASTER. See BURGOMASTER.

BU'RGLAR. *n. s.* [See BURGLARY.] The crime of housebreaking.

BU'RGLARY. *n. s.* [from *burg*, a house, and *larron*, a thief.] In the natural signification of the word, is nothing but the robbing of a house: but as it is a term of art, our common lawyers restrain it to robbing a house by night, or breaking in with an intent to rob, or do some other felony. The like offence committed by day, they call house-robbing, by a peculiar name. *Cowel.*

What say you, father? *Burglary* is but a venial sin among soldiers. *Dryden's Spanish Friar.*

BU'RGOMASTER. *n. s.* [from *burg* and *master.*] One employed in the government of a city.

They chuse their councils and *burgomasters* out of the burgeois, as in the other governments of Switzerland. *Addison.*

BURH, is a tower; and from that, a defence or protection; so *Cwenburh* is a woman ready to assist; *Cuthbur*, eminent for assistance. *Gibson's Camden.*

BU'RIAL. *n. s.* [from *to bury.*]

1. The act of burying; sepulture; interment.

Nor would we deign him *burial* of his men. *Shakesp.*

See my wealthy Andrew dock'd in sand,
Vailing her high top lower than her ribs,
To kiss her *burial.* *Shakesp. Merchant of Venice.*

Your body I sought, and had I found
Design'd for *burial* in your native ground. *Dryden's Æneid.*

2. The act of placing any thing under earth or water.

We have great lakes, both salt and fresh; we use them for *burials* of some natural bodies: for we find a difference of things buried in earth, and things buried in water. *Bacon.*

3. The church service for funerals.

The office of the church is performed by the parish priest, at the time of his interment, if not prohibited unto persons excommunicated, and laying violent hands on themselves, by a rubrick of the *burial* service. *Ayliffe's Parergon.*

BU'RIER. *n. s.* [from *bury.*] He that buries; he that performs the act of interment.

Let one spirit of the firstborn Cain
Reign in all bosoms, that, each heart being set
On bloody courses, the rude scene may end,
And darkness be the *burier* of the dead. *Shakesp. Henry IV.*

BU'RINE. *n. s.* [French.] A graving tool; a graver.

Wit is like the graver's *burine* upon copper, or the corrodings of aquafortis, which engrave and indent the characters, that they can never be defaced. *Government of the Tongue.*

BU'RLACE. *n. s.* [corruptly written for *burdelais.*] A sort of grape. See VINE.

To BURL. *v. a.* To dress cloth as fullers do. *Dict.*

BURLE'SQUE. *adj.* [Fr. from *burlare*, Ital. to jest.] Jocular; tending to raise laughter, by unnatural or unsuitable language or images.

Homer, in his character of Vulcan and Thersites, in his story of Mars and Venus, in his behaviour of Irus, and in other passages, has been observed to have lapsed into the *burlesque* character, and to have departed from that serious air, which seems essential to the magnificence of an epick poem. *Addison. Spectator*, Nº 279.

BURLE'SQUE. *n. s.* Ludicrous language, or ideas; ridicule.

When a man lays out a twelvemonth on the spots in the sun, however noble his speculations may be, they are very apt to fall into *burlesque.* *Addison on ancient Medals.*

To BURLE'SQUE. *v. a.* [from the adjective.] To turn to ridicule.

Would Homer apply the epithet divine to a modern swineherd? if not, it is an evidence, that Eumeus was a man of consequence; otherwise Homer would *burlesque* his own poetry. *Broome's Notes on the Odyssey.*

BU'RLINESS. *n. s.* [from *burly.*] Bulk; bluster.

BU'RLY. *adj.* [*Junius* has no etymology; *Skinner* imagines it to come from *boorlike*, clownish.] Great of stature; great of size; bulky; tumid.

Steel, if thou turn thine edge, or cut not out the *burly* boned clown in chines of beef, ere thou sleep in thy sheath, I beseech Jove on my knees, thou may'st be turned into hobnails. *Shakesp. Henry VI. p. ii.*

It was the orator's own *burly* way of nonsense. *Cowley.*

Away with all your Carthaginian state,
Let vanquish'd Hannibal without doors wait,
Too *burly* and too big to pass my narrow gate. } *Dryden.*

Her husband, it seems, being a very *burly* man, she thought it would be less trouble for her to bring away little Cupid. *Addison. Spectator*, Nº 499.

To BURN. *v. a.* [bernan, Saxon.]

1. To consume with fire.

That where she fed his amorous desires
With soft complaints, and felt his hottest fires,
There other flames might waste his earthly part,
And *burn* his limbs, where love had *burn'd* his heart. *Dryden.*

O that I could but weep, to vent my passion!
But this dry sorrow *burns* up all my tears. *Dryden's Sp. Fr.*

A fleshy excrescence, becoming exceeding hard, is supposed to demand extirpation, by *burning* away the induration, or amputating. *Sharp's Surgery.*

2. To wound or hurt with fire or heat.

Hand for hand, foot for foot, *burning* for *burning*, wound for wound, stripe for stripe. *Exodus*, xxi. 25.

To BURN. *v. n.*

1. To be on fire; to be kindled.

The barge she sat in, like a burnish'd throne,
Burnt on the water. *Shakesp. Antony and Cleopatra.*

O coward conscience! how dost thou afflict me?
The light *burns* blue — Is it not dead midnight?
Cold trembling drops stand on my trembling flesh. *Shakesp.*

Oh! prince, oh! wherefore *burn* your eyes? and why
Is your sweet temper turn'd to fury? *Rowe's Royal Convert.*

2. To be inflamed with passion.

When I *burnt* in desire to question them further, they made themselves air, into which they vanished. *Shakesp. Macbeth.*

Tranio, I *burn*, I pine, I perish Tranio,
If I atchieve not this young modest girl. *Shakesp.*

3. To act as fire.

These things sting him
So venomously, that *burning* shame detains him
From his Cordelia. *Shakesp. King Lear.*

In Raleigh mark their every glory mix'd;
Raleigh, the scourge of Spain! whose breast with all
The sage, the patriot, and the hero *burn'd.* *Thomson.*

4. To be hot

I had a glimpse of him; but he shot by me
Like a young hound upon a *burning* scent. *Dryden's Sp. Fr.*

BURN. *n. s.* [from the verb.] A hurt caused by fire.

We see the phlegm of vitriol is a very effectual remedy against *burns.* *Boyle.*

BU'RNER. *n. s.* [from *burn.*] A person that burns any thing.

BU'RNET. *n. s.* [*pimpinella*, Lat.] The name of a plant.

The common *burnet* is found wild in great plenty upon dry chalky hills; yet is often cultivated in gardens for medicinal uses. *Millar.*

The even mead that erst brought sweetly forth
The freckled cowslip, *burnet*, and green clover. *Shakesp.*

BU'RNING. *n. s.* [from *burn.*] Fire; flame; state of inflammation.

The mind surely, of itself, can feel none of the *burnings* of a fever. *South.*

In liquid *burnings*, or on dry to dwell,
Is all the sad variety of hell. *Dryden's State of Innocence.*

BU'RNING-GLASS. *n. s.* [from *burning* and *glass.*] A glass which collects the rays of the sun into a narrow compass, and so increases their force.

The appetite of her eye did seem to scorch me up like a *burning-glass.* *Shakesp. Merry Wives of Windsor.*

Love is of the nature of a *burning-glass*, which, kept still in one place, fireth; changed often, it doth nothing. *Suckling.*

O diadem, thou centre of ambition,
Where all its different lines are reconciled,
As if thou wert the *burning-glass* of glory. *Dryden and Lee.*

To BU'RNISH. *v. a.* [*burnir*, Fr.] To polish; to give a gloss to.

The barge she sat in, like a *burnish'd* throne,
Burnt on the water. *Shakesp Antony and Cleopatra.*

Mislike me not for my complexion,
The shadow'd livery of the *burnish'd* sun,
To whom I am a neighbour, and near bred. *Shakesp.*

Make a plate of them, and *burnish* it as they do iron. *Bacon.*

The frame of *burnish'd* steel, that cast a glare
From far, and seem'd to thaw the freezing air. *Dryden.*

To BU'RNISH. *v. n.* To grow bright or glossy.

I've seen a snake in human form,
All stain'd with infamy and vice,
Leap from the dunghill in a trice,
Burnish, and make a gawdy show,
Become a gen'ral, peer, and beau. *Swift.*

To BU'RNISH. *v. n.* [of uncertain etymology.] To grow; to spread out.

This they could do, while Saturn fill'd the throne,
Ere Juno *burnish'd*, or young Jove was grown. *Dryden's Juv. sat.* xiii.

To shoot, and spread, and *burnish* into man. *Dryden.*

Mrs.

Mrs. Primly's great belly; ſhe may lace it down before, but it *burniſhes* on her lips. *Congreve's Way of the World.*

BU'RNISHER. *n. ſ.* [from *burniſh.*]

1. The perſon that burniſhes or poliſhes.
2. The tool with which bookbinders give a gloſs to the leaves of books; it is commonly a dog's tooth ſet in a ſtick.

BURNT. [*particip. paſſ.* of *burn.*]

I find it very difficult to know,
Who, to refreſh th' attendants to a grave,
Burnt claret firſt, or Naples biſket gave. *King's Cookery.*

BURR. *n. ſ.* [See BUR.] The lobe or lap of the ear. *Dict.*

BURR *Pump.* [In a ſhip.] A pump by the ſide of a ſhip, into which a ſtaff ſeven or eight foot long is put; having a burr or knob of wood at the end, which is drawn up by a rope faſtened to the middle of it, called alſo a *bilge pump.* *Harris.*

BU'RRAS *Pipe.* [With ſurgeons.] An inſtrument or veſſel uſed to keep corroding powders in, as vitriol, precipitate. *Harris.*

BU'RREL. *n. ſ.* A ſort of pear, otherwiſe called the *red butter pear*, from its ſmooth, delicious, and ſoft pulp, which is ripe in the end of September. *Phillips's World of Words.*

BU'RREL *Fly.* [from *bourreler*, Fr. to execute; to torture.] An inſect, called alſo *oxfly*, *gadbee*, or *breeze.* *Dict.*

BU'RREL *Shot.* [from *bourreler*, to execute, Fr. and *ſhot.*] In gunnery. Small bullets, nails, ſtones, pieces of old iron, *&c.* put into caſes, to be diſcharged out of the ordnance; a ſort of caſe-ſhot. *Harris.*

BU'RROCK. *n. ſ.* A ſmall wear or dam, where wheels are laid in a river for catching of fiſh. *Phillips's World of Words.*

BU'RROW, BERG, BURG, BURGH. *n. ſ.* [derived from the Saxon buꞃᵹ, býꞃᵹ, a city, tower, or caſtle. *Gibſon's Camden.*]

1. A corporate town, that is not a city, but ſuch as ſends burgeſſes to the parliament. All places that, in former days, were called *borough*, were ſuch as were fenced or fortified. *Cowel.*

King of England ſhalt thou be proclaim'd
In ev'ry *burrow*, as we paſs along. *Shakeſp. Henry* VI. *p.* iii.

Poſſeſſion of land was the original right of election among the commons; and *burrows* were entitled to ſit, as they were poſſeſſed of certain tracts. *Temple.*

2. The holes made in the ground by conies.

When they ſhall ſee his creſt up again, and the man in blood, they will out of their *burrows*, like conies after rain, and revel all with him. *Shakeſp. Coriolanus.*

To BU'RROW. *v. n.* [from the noun.] To make holes in the ground; to mine, as conies or rabbits.

Some ſtrew ſand among their corn, which, they ſay, prevents mice and rats *burrowing* in it; becauſe of its falling into their ears. *Mortimer.*

Little ſinuſes would often form, and *burrow* underneath. *Sharp's Surgery.*

BU'RSAR. *n. ſ.* [*burſarius*, Lat.]

1. The treaſurer of a college.
2. Students ſent as exhibitioners to the univerſities in Scotland by each preſbytery, from whom they have a ſmall yearly allowance for four years.

BURSE. *n. ſ.* [*bourſe*, Fr. *burſa*, Lat. a purſe; or from *byrſa*, Lat. the exchange of Carthage.] An exchange where merchants meet, and ſhops are kept; ſo called, becauſe the ſign of the purſe was anciently ſet over ſuch a place; whence the Exchange in the Strand was termed Britain's Burſe by James I. *Phillips.*

To BURST. *v. n.* I *burſt*; I have *burſt*, or *burſten.* [buꞃſtan, Saxon.]

1. To break, or fly open.

So ſhall thy barns be filled with plenty, and thy preſſes ſhall *burſt* out with new wine. *Prov.* iii. 10.

2. To fly aſunder.

Yet am I thankful; if my heart were great,
'Twould *burſt* at this. *Shakeſp. All's well that ends well.*

3. To break away; to ſpring.

You *burſt*, ah cruel! from my arms,
And ſwiftly ſhoot along the mall,
Or ſoftly glide by the canal. *Pope.*

4. To come ſuddenly.

A reſolved villain,
Whoſe bowels ſuddenly *burſt* out; the king
Yet ſpeaks, and, peradventure, may recover. *Shakeſp.*

If the worlds
In worlds incloſ'd, ſhou'd on his ſenſes *burſt*,
He wou'd abhorrent turn. *Thomſon's Summer, l.* 310.

5. To come by violence.

Well didſt thou, Richard, to ſuppreſs thy voice;
For had the paſſions of thy heart *burſt* out,
I fear, we ſhould have ſeen decypher'd there
More ranc'rous ſpight. *Shakeſp. Henry* VI. *p.* i.

Where is the notable paſſage over the river Euphrates, *burſting* out by the vallies of the mountain Antitaurus; from whence the plains of Meſopotamia, then part of the Perſian kingdom, begin to open themſelves. *Knolles's Hiſtory of the Turks.*

Young ſpring protrudes the *burſting* gems. *Thomſon.*

6. To begin an action violently.

She *burſt* into tears, and wrung her hands. *Arbuthnot.*

To BURST. *v. a.* To break ſuddenly; to make a quick and violent diſruption.

My breaſt I'll *burſt* with ſtraining of my courage,
And from my ſhoulders crack my arms aſunder,
But I will chaſtiſe this high-minded ſtrumpet. *Shakeſp.*

He faſten'd on my neck, and bellow'd out,
As if he would *burſt* heav'n. *Shakeſp. King Lear.*

Moſes ſaith alſo, the fountains of the great abyſs were *burſt* aſunder, to make the deluge; and what means this abyſs, and the burſting of it, if reſtrained to Judea? what appearance is there of this diſruption there? *Burnet's Theory.*

If the juices of an animal body were, ſo as by the mixture of the oppoſites, to cauſe an ebullition, they would *burſt* the veſſels. *Arbuthnot on Aliments.*

BURST. *n. ſ.* [from the verb.] A ſudden diſruption; a ſudden and violent action of any kind.

Since I was man,
Such ſheets of fire, ſuch *burſt* of horrid thunder,
Such groans of roaring wind and rain, I never
Remember to have heard. *Shakeſp. King Lear.*

Down they came, and drew
The whole roof after them, with *burſt* of thunder,
Upon the heads of all. *Milton's Agoniſtes, l.* 1650.

Impriſon'd fire, in the cloſe dungeons pent,
Roar to get looſe, and ſtruggle for a vent,
Eating their way, and undermining all,
Till with a mighty *burſt* whole mountains fall. *Addiſon.*

BURST. } *participial adj.* [from *burſt.*] Diſeaſed with a her-
BU'RSTEN. } nia, or rupture.

BU'RSTENESS. *n. ſ.* [from *burſt.*] A rupture, or hernia.

BU'RSTWORT. *n. ſ.* [from *burſt* and *wort*; *herniaria*, Lat.] An herb good againſt ruptures. *Dict.*

BURT. *n. ſ.* A flat fiſh of the turbot kind.

To BU'RTHEN. *v. a.* }
BU'RTHEN. *n. ſ.* } See BURDEN.

Sacred to ridicule his whole life long,
And the ſad *burthen* of ſome merry ſong. *Pope.*

BU'RTON. *n. ſ.* [In a ſhip.] A ſmall tackle to be faſtened any where at pleaſure, conſiſting of two ſingle pullies, for hoiſting ſmall things in or out. *Phillips's World of Words.*

BU'RY. } *n. ſ.* [from buꞃᵹ, Sax.] A dwelling-place; a termina-
BE'RY. } tion ſtill added to the names of ſeveral places; as, *Aldermanbury*, St. *Edmund's bury.* *Phillips's World of Words.*

BU'RY. *n. ſ.* [corrupted from *borough.*]

It is his nature to dig himſelf *buries*, as the coney doth; which he doth with very great celerity. *Grew.*

To BU'RY. *v. a.* [býꞃıᵹean, Saxon.]

1. To inter; to put into a grave.

When he lies along,
After your way his tale pronounc'd, ſhall *bury*
His reaſons with his body. *Shakeſp. Coriolanus.*

2. To inter, with the rites and ceremonies of ſepulture.

Slave, thou haſt ſlain me!
If ever thou wilt thrive, *bury* my body. *Shakeſp. King Lear.*

If you have kindneſs left, there ſee me laid;
To *bury* decently the injur'd maid,
Is all the favour. *Waller.*

3. To conceal; to hide.

This is the way to make the city flat,
And *bury* all, which yet diſtinctly ranges,
In heaps and piles of ruin. *Shakeſp. Coriolanus.*

4. To place one thing within another.

A tearing groan did break
The name of Antony; it was divided
Between her heart and lips; ſhe render'd life,
Thy name ſo *bury'd* in her. *Shakeſp. Antony and Cleopatra.*

BU'RYING-PLACE. *n. ſ.* A place appointed for the ſepulture of dead bodies.

The place was formerly a church-yard, and has ſtill ſeveral marks in it of graves and *burying-places.* *Spectator*, N° 110.

BUSH. *n. ſ.* [*bois*, Fr.]

1. A thick ſhrub.

Eft through the thick they heard one rudely ruſh,
With noiſe whereof, he, from his lofty ſteed,
Down fell to ground, and crept into a *buſh*,
To hide his coward head from dying dread. *Fairy Q. b.* ii.

The poller, and exactor of fees, juſtifies the reſemblance of the courts of juſtice to the *buſh*, whereunto while the ſheep flies for defence from the weather, he is ſure to loſe part of the fleece. *Bacon's Eſſays*, N° 47.

Her heart was that ſtrange *buſh*, whoſe ſacred fire,
Religion did not conſume, but inſpire
Such piety, ſo chaſte uſe of God's day,
That what we turn to feaſt, ſhe turn'd to pray. *Donne.*

With ſuch a care,
As roſes from their ſtalks we tear,
When we would ſtill prefer them new,
And freſh as on the *buſh* they grew. *Waller.*

The ſacred ground
Shall weeds and pois'nous plants refuſe to bear;
Each common *buſh* ſhall Syrian roſes wear. *Dryden's Virg.*

2. A bough of a tree fixed up at a door, to ſhew that liquours are ſold there.

If it be true, that good wine needs no *buſh*, 'tis true that a good play needs no epilogue. *Shakeſp. As you like it.*

To BUSH. *v. n.* [from the noun.] To grow thick.

The roſes *buſhing* round
About her glow'd; half ſtooping to ſupport
Each flow'r of tender ſtalk. *Milton's Par. Loſt, b.* ix.

A guſhing fountain broke
Around it, and above, for ever green,
The *buſhing* alders form'd a ſhady ſcene. *Pope's Odyſſey.*

BU'SHEL. *n. ſ.* [*boiſſeau*, Fr. *buſſellus*, low Lat.]

1. A meaſure containing eight gallons; a ſtrike.

His reaſons are as two grains of wheat hid in two *buſhels* of chaff; you ſhall ſeek all day ere you find them; and when you have them, they are not worth the ſearch. *Shakeſp.*

2. It is uſed, in common language, indefinitely for a large quantity.

The worthies of antiquity bought the rareſt pictures with *buſhels* of gold, without counting the weight or the number of pieces. *Dryden's Dufreſnoy.*

3. *Buſhels of a cart-wheel.* Irons within the hole of the nave, to preſerve it from wearing. [from *bouche*, Fr. a mouth.] *Dict.*

BU'SHINESS. *n. ſ.* [from *buſhy.*] The quality of being buſhy.

BU'SHMENT. *n. ſ.* [from *buſh.*] A thicket; a cluſter of buſhes.

Princes thought how they might diſcharge the earth of woods, briars, *buſhments*, and waters, to make it more habitable and fertile. *Raleigh's Hiſtory of the World.*

BU'SHY. *adj.* [from *buſh.*]

1. Thick; full of ſmall branches, not high.

The gentle ſhepherd ſat beſide a ſpring,
All in the ſhadow of a *buſhy* brier. *Spenſer's Paſtorals.*

Generally the cutting away of boughs and ſuckers at the root and body, doth make trees grow high; and, contrariwiſe, the polling and cutting of the top, make them ſpread and grow *buſhy*. *Bacon's Nat. Hiſtory*, N° 424.

2. Thick like a buſh.

Statues of this god, with a thick *buſhy* beard, are ſtill many of them extant in Rome. *Addiſon on Italy.*

3. Full of buſhes.

The kids with pleaſure browſe the *buſhy* plain;
The ſhow'rs are grateful to the ſwelling grain. *Dryden.*

BU'SILESS. *adj.* [from *buſy.*] At leiſure; without buſineſs; unemployed.

Theſe ſweet thoughts do even refreſh my labour,
Moſt *buſileſs* when I do it. *Shakeſp.*

BU'SILY. *adv.* [from *buſy.*] With an air of importance; with an air of hurry; actively; importunately.

Or if too *buſily* they will enquire
Into a victory, which we diſdain,
Then let them know, the Belgians did retire,
Before the patron ſaint of injur'd Spain. *Dryden.*

BU'SINESS. *n. ſ.* [from *buſy.*]

1. Employment; multiplicity of affairs.

Muſt *buſineſs* thee from hence remove?
Oh! that's the worſt diſeaſe of love. *Donne.*

2. An affair. In this ſenſe it has the *plural.*

Beſtow
Your needful counſel to our *buſineſſes*,
Which crave the inſtant uſe. *Shakeſp. King Lear.*

3. The ſubject of buſineſs; the affair or object that engages the care.

You are ſo much the *buſineſs* of our ſouls, that while you are in ſight, we can neither look nor think on any elſe; there are no eyes for other beauties. *Dryden.*

The great *buſineſs* of the ſenſes, being to take notice of what hurts or advantages the body. *Locke.*

4. Serious engagement, in oppoſition to trivial tranſactions.

I never knew one, who made it his *buſineſs* to laſh the faults of other writers, that was not guilty of greater himſelf. *Addiſ.*

He had *buſineſs* enough upon his hands, and was only a poet by accident. *Prior's Preface.*

When diverſion is made the *buſineſs* and ſtudy of life, though the actions choſen be in themſelves innocent, the exceſs will render them criminal. *Rogers.*

5. Right of action.

What *buſineſs* has a tortoiſe among the clouds? *L'Eſtrange.*

6. A point; a matter of queſtion; ſomething to be examined or conſidered.

Fitneſs to govern, is a perplexed *buſineſs*; ſome men, ſome nations, excel in the one ability, ſome in the other. *Bacon.*

7. Something to be tranſacted.

They were far from the Zidonians, and had no *buſineſs* with any one. *Judges*, xviii. 7.

8. Something required to be done.

To thoſe people that dwell under or near the equator, this ſpring would be moſt peſtilent; as for thoſe countries that are nearer the poles, in which number are our own, and the moſt conſiderable nations of the world, a perpetual ſpring will not do their *buſineſs*; they muſt have longer days, a nearer approach of the ſun. *Bentley.*

9. *To do one's buſineſs.* To kill, deſtroy, or ruin him.

BUSK. *n. ſ.* [*buſque*, Fr.] A piece of ſteel or whalebone, worn by women to ſtrengthen their ſtays.

Off with that happy *buſk*, which I envy,
That ſtill can be, and ſtill can ſtand ſo nigh. *Donne.*

BU'SKIN. *n. ſ.* [*broſeken*, Dutch.]

1. A kind of half boot; a ſhoe which comes to the midleg.

The foot was dreſſed in a ſhort pair of crimſon velvet *buſkins*; in ſome places open, to ſhew the fairneſs of the ſkin. *Sidney.*

Sometimes Diana he her takes to be,
But miſſeth bow, and ſhafts, and *buskins* to her knee. *Spenſer's Fairy Queen, b.* i. *cant.* vi. *ſtanz.* 16.

There is a kind of ruſticity in all thoſe pompous verſes; ſomewhat of a holiday ſhepherd ſtrutting in his country *buſkins*. *Dryden.*

2. A kind of high ſhoe wore by the ancient actors of tragedy, to raiſe their ſtature.

Great Fletcher never treads in *buskins* here,
Nor greater Johnſon dares in ſocks appear. *Dryden.*
In her beſt light the comick Muſe appears,
When ſhe, with borrow'd pride the *buskin* wears. *Smith.*

BU'SKINED. *adj.* [from *buskin.*] Dreſſed in buſkins.

Or what, though rare, of later age,
Ennobl'd hath the *buskin'd* ſtage? *Milton.*
Here, arm'd with ſilver bows, in early dawn,
Her *buskin'd* virgins trac'd the dewy lawn. *Pope.*

BU'SKY. *adj.* [written more properly by *Milton*, *bosky.* See BOSKY.] Woody; ſhaded with woods; overgrown with trees.

How bloodily the ſun begins to peer
Above yon *busky* hill! *Shakeſp. Henry* IV. *p.* i.

BUSS. *n. ſ.* [*bus*, the mouth, Iriſh; *baiſer*, Fr.]

1. A kiſs; a ſalute with the lips.

Thou doſt give me flattering *buſſes.*—By my troth, I kiſs thee with a moſt conſtant heart. *Shakeſp. Henry* IV. *p.* ii.

Some ſquire perhaps you take delight to rack,
Who viſits with a gun, preſents with birds,
Then gives a ſmacking *buſs.* *Pope.*

2. A boat for fiſhing. [*buſſe*, German.]

If the king would enter towards building ſuch a number of boats and *buſſes*, as each company could eaſily manage, it would be an encouragement both of honour and advantage. *Temple.*

To BUSS. *v. a.* [from the noun.] To kiſs; to ſalute with the lips.

Yonder walls, that partly front your town,
Yond towers, whoſe wanton tops do *buſs* the clouds,
Muſt kiſs their feet. *Shakeſp. Troilus and Creſſida.*

Go to them with this bonnet in thy hand,
Thy knee *buſſing* the ſtones; for, in ſuch buſineſs,
Action is eloquence. *Shakeſp. Coriolanus.*

BUST. *n. ſ.* [*buſto*, Ital.] A ſtatue repreſenting a man to his breaſt.

Agrippa, or Caligula, is a common coin, but a very extraordinary *buſt*; and a Tiberius, a rare coin, but a common *buſt.* *Addiſon on Italy.*

Ambition ſigh'd: ſhe found it vain to truſt
The faithleſs column, and the crumbling *buſt.* *Pope.*

BU'STARD. *n. ſ.* [*biſtarde*, Fr.] A wild turkey.

His ſacrifices were phenicopters, peacocks, *buſtards*, turkeys, pheaſants; and all theſe were daily offered. *Hakewell.*

To BU'STLE. *v. n.* [of uncertain etymology; perhaps from *buſy.*] To be buſy; to ſtir; to be active.

Come, *buſtle*, *buſtle*—capariſon my horſe. *Shakeſp. R.* III.
God take king Edward to his mercy,
And leave the world for me to *buſtle* in. *Shakeſp. Rich.* III.

Sir Henry Vane was a buſy and *buſtling* man, who had credit enough to do his buſineſs in all places. *Clarendon, b.* ii.

A poor abject worm,
That crawl'd awhile upon a *buſtling* world,
And now am trampled to my duſt again. *Southerne's Oroonoko.*

Ye ſov'reign lords, who ſit like gods in ſtate,
Awing the world, and *buſtling* to be great! *Granville.*

BU'STLE. *n. ſ.* [from the verb.] A tumult; a hurry; a combuſtion.

Wiſdom's ſelf
Oft ſeeks to ſweet retired ſolitude;
She plumes her feathers, and lets grow her wings,
That, in the various *buſtle* of reſort,
Were all too ruffl'd. *Milton.*

This is the creature that pretends to knowledge, and that makes ſuch a noiſe and *buſtle* for opinions. *Glanville's Scepſis.*

Such a doctrine made a ſtrange *buſtle* and diſturbance in the world, which then ſat warm and eaſy in a free enjoyment of their luſts. *South.*

If the Count had given them a pot of ale after it, all would have been well, without any of this *buſtle.* *Spectator*, N° 481.

BU'STLER. *n. ſ.* [from *buſtle.*] An active ſtirring man.

BU'SY. *adj.* [byrgian, Sax. It is pronounced as *biſſy.*]

1. Employed with earneſtneſs.

My miſtreſs ſends you word, that ſhe is *buſy*, and cannot come. *Shakeſp. Taming the Shr.*

The chriſtians, ſometimes valiantly receiving the enemy, and ſometimes charging them again, repulſed the proud enemy, ſtill *buſy* with them. *Knolles's Hiſtory of the Turks.*

2. Bustling; active; meddling.

The next thing which she waking looks upon,
On meddling monkey, or on *busy* ape,
She shall pursue it with the soul of love. *Shakesp.*

This *busy* pow'r is working day and night;
For when the outward senses rest do take,
A thousand dreams, fantastical and light,
With flutt'ring wings, do keep her still awake. *Davies.*

The coming spring would first appear,
And all this place with roses strow,
If *busy* feet would let them grow. *Waller.*

All written since that time, seem to have little more than events we are glad to know, or the controversy of opinions, wherein the *busy* world has been so much employed. *Temple.*

Religious motives and instincts are so *busy* in the heart of every reasonable creature, that no man would hope to govern a society, without regard to those principles. *Addison. Freeholder.*

To Bu'sy. *v. a.* [from the noun.] To employ; to engage; to make or keep busy.

He in great passion all this while did dwell,
More *busying* his quick eyes her face to view,
Than his dull ears to hear what she did tell. *Fairy Queen, b.* i.

The pleasure which I took at my friend's pleasure herein, idly *busied* me thus to express the same. *Carew's Survey.*

My Harry,
Be it thy course to *busy* giddy minds
With foreign quarrels. *Shakesp. Henry* IV. *p.* ii.

While they were *busied* to lay the foundations, their buildings were overthrown by an earthquake, and many thousands of the Jews were overwhelmed. *Raleigh's History.*

The points which *busied* the devotion of the first ages, and the curiosity of the later. *Decay of Piety.*

The ideas it is *busied* about, should be natural and congenial ones, which it had in itself. *Locke.*

The learning and disputes of the schools have been much *busied* about genus and species. *Locke.*

For the rest, it must be owned, he does not *busy* himself, by entering deep into any party, but rather spends his time in acts of hospitality. *Swift.*

Bu'sybody. *n. s.* [from *busy* and *body.*] A vain, meddling, fantastical person.

Going from house to house, tatlers and *busybodies*, are the canker and rust of idleness, as idleness is the rust of time. *Taylor's Holy Living.*

Busybodies and intermeddlers are a dangerous sort of people to have to do withal. *L'Estrange.*

She is well acquainted with all the favourite servants, *busybodies*, dependants, and poor relations of all persons of condition in the whole town. *Spectator,* N° 437.

BUT. *conjunct.* [bute, butan, Saxon.]

1. Except.

An emission of immateriate virtues we are a little doubtful to propound, it is so prodigious: *but* that it is so constantly avouched by many. *Bacon.*

Who can it be, ye gods! *but* perjur'd Lycon?
Who can inspire such storms of rage, *but* Lycon?
Where has my sword left one so black, *but* Lycon?
Smith's Phædra and Hippolitus.

Your poem hath been printed, and we have no objection *but* the obscurity of several passages, by our ignorance in facts and persons. *Swift.*

2. Yet; nevertheless. It sometimes only enforces *yet.*

Then let him speak, and any that shall stand without, shall hear his voice plainly; *but* yet made extreme sharp and exile, like the voice of puppets: and yet the articulate sounds of the words will not be confounded. *Bacon's Nat. Hist.* N° 155.

Our wants are many, and grievous to be born, *but* quite of another kind. *Swift.*

3. The particle which introduces the minor of a syllogism; now.

If there be a liberty and possibility for a man to kill himself today, then it is not absolutely necessary that he shall live till tomorrow; *but* there is such a liberty, therefore no such necessity. *Bramhall against Hobbes.*

God will one time or another make a difference between the good and the evil. *But* there is little or no difference made in this world: therefore there must be another world, wherein this difference shall be made. *Watts's Logick, Introduct.*

4. Only; nothing more than.

If my offence be of mortal kind,
That not my service, past or present sorrows,
Can ransom me into his love again;
But to know so, must be my benefit. *Shakesp. Othello.*

And *but* infirmity,
Which waits upon worn times, hath something seiz'd
His wish'd ability, he had himself
The lands and waters measur'd. *Shakesp. Winter's Tale.*

What nymph soe'er his voice *but* hears,
Will be my rival, though she have *but* ears. *Ben. Johnson.*

No, Aurengzebe, you merit all my heart,
And I'm too noble *but* to give a part. *Dryden.*

Did *but* men consider the true notion of God, he would appear to be full of goodness. *Tillotson.*

If we do *but* put virtue and vice in equal circumstances, the advantages of ease and pleasure will be found to be on the side of religion. *Tillotson.*

The mischiefs or harms that come by play, inadvertency, or ignorance, are not at all, or *but* very gently, to be taken notice of. *Locke on Education.*

If a reader examines Horace's art of poetry, he will find *but* very few precepts in it, which he may not meet with in Aristotle. *Addison. Spectator.*

Prepar'd I stand: he was *but* born to try
The lot of man, to suffer and to die. *Pope's Odyssey.*

5. Than.

The full moon was no sooner up, and shining in all its brightness, *but* he privately opened the gate of paradise. *Guardian,* N° 167.

6. But that; without this consequence that.

Frosts that constrain the ground,
Do seldom their usurping power withdraw,
But raging floods pursue their hasty hand. *Dryden.*

7. Otherwise than that.

It cannot be *but* nature hath some director, of infinite power, to guide her in all her ways. *Hooker, b.* i. § 3.

Who shall believe,
But you misuse the reverence of your place? *Shakesp.*

8. Not otherwise than.

A genius so elevated and unconfined as Mr. Cowley's, was *but* necessary to make Pindar speak English. *Dryden.*

9. By any other means than.

Out of that will I cause those of Cyprus to mutiny: whose qualification shall come into no true taste again, *but* by transplanting of Cassio. *Shakesp. Othello.*

10. If it were not for this; if this were not.

Believe me, I had rather have lost my purse
Full of cruzades. And *but* my noble Moor
Is true of mind, and made of no such baseness,
As jealous creatures are, it were enough
To put him to ill-thinking. *Shakesp. Othello.*

I here do give thee that with all my heart,
Which, *but* thou hast already, with all my heart
I would keep from thee. *Shakesp. Othello.*

11. However; howbeit.

I do not doubt but I have been to blame;
But, to pursue the end for which I came,
Unite your subjects first, then let us go,
And pour their common rage upon the foe. *Dryden.*

12. It is used after *no doubt*, *no question*, and such words, and signifies the same with *that.* It sometimes is joined with *that.*

They made no account, *but that* the navy should be absolutely master of the seas. *Bacon's War with Spain.*

I fancied to myself a kind of ease in the change of the paroxysm; never suspecting *but that* the humour would have wasted itself. *Dryden.*

There is no question *but* the king of Spain will reform most of the abuses. *Addison on Italy.*

13. That. This seems no proper sense in this place.

It is not therefore impossible, *but* I may alter the complexion of my play, to restore myself into the good graces of my fair criticks. *Dryden's Aurengzebe, Preface.*

14. Otherwise than.

I should sin
To think *but* nobly of my grandmother. *Shakesp. Tempest.*

15. Even; not longer ago than.

Beroe *but* now I left; whom, pin'd with pain,
Her age and anguish from these rites detain. *Dryden.*

It is evident, in the instance I gave *but* now, the consciousness went along. *Locke.*

16. A particle by which the meaning of the foregoing sentence is bounded or restrained.

Thus fights Ulysses, thus his fame extends,
A formidable man, *but* to his friends. *Dryden.*

17. An objective particle; yet it may be objected.

But yet, madam———
I do not like *but* yet; it does allay
The good precedence; fie upon *but* yet!
But yet is as a jaylour, to bring forth
Some monstrous malefactor. *Shakesp. Antony and Cleopatra.*

Must the heart then have been formed and constituted, before the blood was in being? *But* here again, the substance of the heart itself is most certainly made and nourished by the blood, which is conveyed to it by the coronary arteries. *Bentl.*

18. But for; without; had not this been.

Rash man! forbear, *but* for some unbelief,
My joy had been as fatal as my grief. *Waller.*

Her head was bare,
But for her native ornament of hair,
Which in a simple knot was ty'd above. *Dryden's Fables.*

When the fair boy receiv'd the gift of right,
And, *but* for mischief, you had dy'd for spight. *Dryden.*

BUT. *n. s.* [*bout*, French.] A boundary.

But, if I ask you what I mean by that word, you will answer, I mean this or that thing, you cannot tell which; but if I join it with the words in construction and sense, as, but I will not, a but of wine, *but* and boundary, the ram will but, shoot at but, the meaning of it will be as ready to you as any other word. *Holder's Elements of Speech.*

BUT. *n. s.* [In sea language.] The end of any plank which joins to another on the outside of a ship, under water. *Harris.*

BUT-END. *n. s.* [from *but* and *end.*] The blunt end of any thing; the end upon which it rests.

The reserve of foot galled their foot with several vollies, and then fell on them with the *but-ends* of their muskets. *Clarendon.*

Thy weapon was a good one when I wielded it, but the *but-end* remains in my hands. *Arbuthnot's John Bull.*

Some of the soldiers accordingly pushed them forwards with the *but-ends* of their pikes, into my reach. *Gulliver's Travels.*

BU'TCHER. *n. s.* [*boucher*, Fr.]

1. One that kills animals to sell their flesh.

The shepherd and the *butcher* both may look upon one sheep with pleasing conceits. *Sidney.*

Hence he learnt the *butcher*'s guile,
How to cut your throat, and smile;
Like a *butcher* doom'd for life,
In his mouth to wear his knife. *Swift.*

2. One that is delighted with blood.

Honour and renown are bestowed on conquerours, who, for the most part, are but the great *butchers* of mankind. *Locke.*

To BU'TCHER. *v. a.* [from the noun.] To kill; to murder.

In suff'ring thus thy brother to be slaughter'd,
Thou shewest the naked pathway to thy life,
Teaching stern murder how to *butcher* thee. *Shakesp. R.* II.
Uncharitably with me have you dealt,
And shamefully by you my hopes are *butcher'd.* *Shakesp.*

The poison and the dagger are at hand to *butcher* a hero, when the poet wants brains to save him. *Dryden's Don Sebast.*

BUTCHERS-BROOM, or KNEEHOLLY. *n. s.* [*ruscus*, Lat.]

The flower-cup consists of one leaf, cut into several divivisions, out of which is produced a globular bell-shaped flower, consisting also of one leaf, in the center of which rises the pointal, which afterwards becomes a soft roundish fruit, in which are inclosed one or two hard seeds. It is very common in the woods, in divers parts of England, and is rarely cultivated in gardens. The roots are sometimes used in medicine, and the green shoots are cut and bound into bundles, and sold to the butchers, who use it as besoms to sweep their blocks; from whence it had the name of *butchers-broom.* *Millar.*

BU'TCHERLINESS. *n. s.* [from *butcherly.*] In a butcherly manner.

BU'TCHERLY. *adj.* [from *butcher.*] Cruel; bloody; barbarous.

There is a way, which, brought into schools, would take away this *butcherly* fear in making of Latin. *Ascham's Schoolm.*

What stratagems, how fell, how *butcherly*,
This deadly quarrel daily doth beget! *Shakesp. Henry* VI.

BU'TCHERY. *n. s.* [from *butcher.*]

1. The trade of a butcher.

Yet this man, so ignorant in modern *butchery*, has cut up half an hundred heroes, and quartered five or six miserable lovers, in every tragedy he has written. *Pope.*

2. Murder; cruelty; slaughter.

If thou delight to view thy heinous deeds,
Behold this pattern of thy *butcheries.* *Shakesp. Rich.* III.

The *butchery*, and the breach of hospitality, is represented in this fable under the mask of friendship. *L'Estrange.*

Can he a son to soft remorse incite,
Whom goals, and blood, and *butchery* delight? *Dryden.*

3. The place where blood is shed.

This is no place, this house is but a *butchery*;
Abhor it, fear it, do not enter it. *Shakesp. As you like it.*

BU'TLER. *n. s.* [*bouteiller*, Fr. *boteler*, or *botiller*, old English, from *bottle*; he that is employed in the care of bottling liquours.] A servant in a family employed in furnishing the table.

Butlers forget to bring up their beer time enough. *Swift.*

BU'TLERAGE. *n. s.* [from *butler.*] The duty upon wines imported, claimed by the king's butler.

Those ordinary finances are casual or uncertain, as be the escheats, the customs, *butlerage*, and impost. *Bacon.*

BU'TLERSHIP. *n. s.* [from *butler.*] The office of a butler.

BU'TMENT. *n. s.* [*aboutement*, Fr.] That part of the arch which joins it to the upright pier.

The supporters or *butments* of the said arch cannot suffer so much violence, as in the precedent flat posture. *Wotton.*

BUTT. *n. s.* [*but*, Fr.]

1. The place on which the mark to be shot at is placed.

He calls on Bacchus, and propounds the prize;
The groom his fellow groom at *butts* defies,
And bends his bow, and levels with his eyes. } *Dryd.*

2. The point at which the endeavour is directed.

Be not afraid though you do see me weapon'd;
Here is my journey's end; here is my *butt*,
The very sea-mark of my journey's end. *Shakesp. Othello.*

3. The object of aim; the thing against which any attack is directed.

The papists were the most common-place, and the *butt* against whom all the arrows were directed. *Clarendon.*

4. A man upon whom the company break their jests.

I played a sentence or two at my *butt*, which I thought very smart, when my ill genius suggested to him such a reply as got all the laughter on his side. *Spectator*, N° 175.

5. A stroke given in fencing.

If disputes arise
Among the champions for the prize;
To prove who gave the fairer *butt*,
John shews the chalk on Robert's coat. *Prior.*

BUTT. *n. s.* [butt, Saxon.] A vessel; a barrel containing one hundred and twenty six gallons of wine; a butt contains one hundred and eight gallons of beer; and from fifteen to twenty two hundred weight, is a butt of currans.

I escaped upon a *butt* of sack, which the sailors heaved overboard. *Shakesp. Tempest.*

To BUTT. *v. a.* [*botten*, Dutch.] To strike with the head.

Come, leave your tears: a brief farewel: the beast
With many heads *butts* me away. *Shakesp. Coriolanus.*

Nor wars are seen,
Unless, upon the green,
Two harmless lambs are *butting* one the other. *Wotton.*

A snow-white steer, before thy altar led,
Butts with his threat'ning brows, and bellowing stands. *Dryden's Æneid.*

A ram will *butt* with his head, though he be brought up tame, and never saw that manner of fighting. *Ray on the Cr.*

BU'TTER. *n. s.* [buttere, Sax. *butyrum*, Lat.]

1. An unctuous substance made by agitating the cream of milk, till the oil separates from the whey.

And he took *butter* and milk, and the calf which he had dressed, and set before them. *Gen.* xviii. 8.

2. *Butter of antimony.* A chymical preparation, made by uniting the acid spirits of sublimate corrosive with regulus of antimony. It is a great caustick. *Harris.*

3. *Butter of tin*, is made with tin and sublimate corrosive. This preparation continually emits fumes. *Harris.*

To BU'TTER. *v. a.* [from the noun.]

1. To smear, or oil with butter.

'Twas her brother, that, in pure kindness to his horse, *buttered* his hay. *Shakesp. King Lear.*

Words *butter* no parsnips. *L'Estrange.*

2. To encrease the stakes every throw, or every game: a cant term among gamesters.

It is a fine simile in one of Mr. Congreve's prologues, which compares a writer to a *buttering* gamester, that stakes all his winning upon one cast; so that if he loses the last throw, he is sure to be undone. *Addison. Freeholder*, N° 40.

BU'TTERBUMP. *n. s.* A fowl; the same with *bittourn.*

BU'TTERBUR. *n. s.* [*petasites*, Lat.]

It is a plant with a flosculous flower, consisting of many florets, divided into many parts, sitting on the embryo, and continued in a cylindrical empalement, divided also into many parts; the embryo becomes afterwards a seed furnished with down, and the flowers appear before the leaves. It is used in medicine, and grows wild in great plenty by the sides of ditches. *Millar.*

BU'TTERFLOWER. *n. s.* A yellow flower, with which the fields abound in the month of May.

Let weeds, instead of *butterflow'rs*, appear,
And meads, instead of daisies, hemlock bear. *Gay.*

BU'TTERFLY. *n. s.* [buttenflege, Saxon.] A beautiful insect, so named because it first appears at the beginning of the season for butter.

Eftsoons that damsel, by her heav'nly might,
She turned into a winged *butterfly*,
In the wide air to make her wand'ring flight. *Spenser.*

Tell old tales, and laugh
At gilded *butterflies*; and hear poor rogues
Talk of court news. *Shakesp. King Lear.*

And so befel, that as he cast his eye
Among the colworts on a *butterfly*,
He saw false Reynard. *Dryden's Fables.*

That which seems to be a powder upon the wings of a *butterfly*, is an innumerable company of extreme small feathers, not to be discerned without a microscope. *Grew.*

BU'TTERIS. *n. s.* An instrument of steel set in a wooden handle, used in paring the foot, or cutting the hoof of a horse. *Farr. D.*

BU'TTERMILK. *n. s.* [from *butter* and *milk.*] The whey that is separated from the cream when butter is made.

A young man, who was fallen into an ulcerous consumption, devoted himself to *buttermilk*, by which sole diet he recovered. *Harvey on Consumptions.*

The scurvy of mariners is cured by acids; as ripe fruits, lemons, oranges, *buttermilk*; and alkaline spirits hurt them. *Arbuthnot on Diet.*

BU'TTERPRINT. *n. s.* [from *butter* and *print.*] A piece of carved wood, used to mark butter.

A *butterprint*, in which were engraven figures of all sorts and sizes, applied to the lump of butter, left on it the figure. *Locke.*

BU'TTERTOOTH. *n. s.* [from *butter* and *tooth.*] The great broad foreteeth.

BU'TTERWOMAN. *n. s.* [from *butter* and *woman.*] A woman that sells butter.

Tongue,

Tongue, I must put you into a *butterwoman's* mouth, and buy myself another of Bajazet's mute, if you prattle me into these perils. *Shakesp. All's well that ends well.*

BU'TTERWORT. *n. s.* A plant; the same with *sanicle.*

BU'TTERY. *adj.* [from *butter.*] Having the appearance or qualities of butter.

Nothing more convertible into hot cholerick humours, than its *buttery* parts. *Harvey on Consumptions.*

The best oils, thickened by cold, have a white colour; and milk itself has its whiteness from the caseous fibres, and its *buttery* oil. *Floyer on the Humours.*

BU'TTERY. *n. s.* [from *butter*; or, according to *Skinner*, from *bouter*, Fr. to place or lay up.] The room where provisions are laid up.

Go, sirrah, take them to the *buttery*,
And give them friendly welcome every one. *Shakesp.*

All that need a cool and fresh temper, as cellars, pantries, and *butteries*, to the north. *Wotton.*

My guts ne'er suffer'd from a college-cook,
My name ne'er enter'd in a *buttery* book.
Brampston's Man of Taste.

BU'TTOCK. *n. s.* [supposed, by *Skinner*, to come from *aboutir*, Fr. inserted by *Junius* without etymology.] The rump; the part near the tail.

It is like a barber's chair that fits all the *buttocks*. *Shakesp.*

Such as were not able to stay themselves, should be holden up by others of more strength, riding behind them upon the *buttocks* of the horse. *Knolles's History of the Turks.*

The tail of a fox was never made for the *buttocks* of an ape. *L'Estrange's Fables.*

BU'TTON. *n. s.* [*bottwn*, Welch; *bouton*, Fr.]

1. A catch, or small ball, by which the dress of man is fastened.

Pray you, undo this *button*. *Shakesp. King Lear.*

I mention those ornaments, because, of the simplicity of the shape, want of ornaments, *buttons*, loops, gold and silver lace, they must have been cheaper than ours. *Arbuthnot on Coins.*

2. Any knob or ball fastened to a smaller body.

We fastened to the upper marble certain wires, and a *button*. *Boyle.*

Fair from its humble bed I rear'd this flow'r,
Suckled and chear'd, with air, and sun and show'r;
Soft on the paper ruff its leaves I spread,
Bright with the gilded *button* tipt its head. *Pope's Dunciad.*

3. The bud of a plant.

The canker galls the infants of the spring,
Too oft before their *buttons* be disclos'd. *Shakesp. Hamlet.*

BU'TTON. *n. s.* The sea urchin, which is a kind of crabfish that has prickles instead of feet. *Ainsworth.*

To BU'TTON. *v. a.* [from the noun.]

1. To dress; to cloath.

One whose hard heart is *button'd* up with steel. *Shakesp.*

He gave his legs, arm, and breast, to his ordinary servant, to *button* and dress him. *Wotton.*

2. To fasten with buttons.

BU'TTONHOLE. *n. s.* [from *button* and *hole.*] The loop in which the button of the cloaths is caught.

Let me take you a *buttonhole* lower. *Shakesp. Love's Lab. L.*

I'll please the maids of honour, if I can:
Without black velvet breeches, what is man?
I will my skill in *buttonholes* display,
And brag, how oft I shift me ev'ry day. *Bramst. M. of Taste.*

BU'TTRESS. *n. s.* [from *aboutir*, Fr.]

1. A prop; a wall built to support another wall.

No jutting frize,
Buttress, nor coigne of vantage, but this bird,
Hath made his pendant bed, and procreant cradle. *Shakesp.*

Fruit trees, set upon a wall against the sun, between elbows or *buttresses* of stone, ripen more than upon a plain wall. *Bacon.*

But we inhabit a weak city here,
Which *buttresses* and props but scarcely bear. *Dryden's Juv.*

2. A prop; a support.

It will concern us to examine the force of this plea, which our adversaries are still setting up against us, as the ground pillar and *buttress* of the good old cause of nonconformity. *South.*

To BU'TTRESS. *v. a.* [from the noun.] To prop; to support.

BU'TWINK. *n. s.* The name of a bird. *Dict.*

BUTYRA'CEOUS. *adj.* [*butyrum*, Lat. butter.] Having the qualities of butter.

Chyle has the same principles as milk; a viscidity from the caseous parts, and an oiliness from the *butyraceous* parts. *Floyer on the Humours.*

BU'TYROUS. *adj.* [*butyrum*, Lat.] Having the properties of butter.

Its oily red part is from the *butyrous* parts of chyle. *Floyer.*

BU'XOM. *adj.* [bucrum, Sax. from bugan, to bend. It originally signified *obedient*, as *John de Trevisa*, a clergyman, tells his patron, that he is *obedient and* buxom *to all his commands*. In an old form of marriage used before the Reformation, the bride promised to be *obedient and* buxom *in bed and at board*; from which expression, not well understood, its present meaning seems to be derived.]

1. Obedient; obsequious.

He did tread down, and disgrace all the English, and set up and countenance the Irish; thinking thereby to make them more tractable and *buxom* to his government. *Spenser's Ireland.*

He, with broad sails,
Winnow'd the *buxom* air. *Milton.*

2. Gay; lively; brisk.

I'm born
Again a fresh child of the *buxom* morn,
Heir of the sun's first beams. *Crashaw.*

Zephyr, with Aurora playing,
As he met her once a maying,
Fill'd her with thee, a daughter fair,
So *buxom*, blithe, and debonnair. *Milton.*

Sturdy swains,
In clean array, for rustick dance prepare,
Mixt with the *buxom* damsels, hand in hand,
They frisk and bound. *Philips.*

3. Wanton; jolly.

Almighty Jove descends, and pours
Into his *buxom* bride his fruitful show'rs. *Dryden's Virgil.*

She feign'd the rites of Bacchus! cry'd aloud,
And to the *buxom* god the virgin vow'd. *Dryden's Æneid.*

BU'XOMLY. *adv.* [from *buxom.*] Wantonly; amorously.

BU'XOMNESS. *n. s.* [from *buxom.*] Wantonness; amorousness.

To BUY. *v. a.* preter. I *bought*; I have *bought*. [bicgean, Sax.]

1. To purchase; to acquire by paying a price; to obtain for money, or something equivalent; to gain by sale, not gift or theft.

They must *buy* up no corn growing within twelve miles of Geneva, that so the filling of their magazines may not prejudice their market. *Addison on Italy.*

2. To procure some advantage by something that deserves it, or at some price.

I have *bought*
Golden opinions from all sorts of people. *Shakesp. Macbeth.*

Pent to linger
But with a grain a day, I would not *buy*
Their mercy at the price of one fair word. *Shakesp. Coriol.*

Pleasure with praise, and danger they would *buy*,
And with a foe that would not only fly. *Denham.*

3. To manage by money.

You, and all the kings of christendom,
Are led so grosly by this meddling priest,
Dreading the curse that money may *buy* out. *Shakesp. K. J.*

What pitiful things are power, rhetorick, or riches, when they would terrify, dissuade, or *buy* off conscience? *South.*

To BUY. *v. n.* To treat about a purchase.

I will *buy* with you, sell with you, talk with you, walk with you, and so following. *Shakesp. Merchant of Venice.*

BU'YER. *n. s.* [from *to buy.*] He that buys; a purchaser.

When a piece of art is set before us, let the first caution be, not to ask who made it, lest the fame of the authour do captivate the fancy of the *buyer*. *Wotton's Architecture.*

To BUZZ. *v. n.* [*bizzen*, Teut. to growl. *Junius.*]

1. To hum; to make a noise like bees, flies, or wasps.

And all the chamber filled was with flies,
Which *buzzed* all about, and made such sound,
That they encumber'd all men's ears and eyes,
Like many swarms of bees assembled round. *Fairy Q. b.* ii.

There be more wasps, that *buzz* about his nose,
Will make this sting the sooner. *Shakesp. Henry* VIII.

Herewith arose a *buzzing* noise among them, as if it had been the rustling sound of the sea afar off. *Hayward.*

For still the flowers ready stand,
One *buzzes* round about,
One lights, one tastes, gets in, gets out. *Suckling.*

What though no bees around your cradle flew,
Nor on your lips distill'd their golden dew;
Yet have we oft' discover'd, in their stead,
A swarm of drones that *buzz'd* about your head. *Pope.*

We join, like flies and wasps, in *buzzing* about wit. *Swift.*

2. To whisper; to prate.

There is such confusion in my pow'rs,
As after some oration fairly spoke
By a beloved prince, there doth appear
Among the *buzzing* multitude. *Shakesp. Merch. of Venice.*

To BUZZ. *v. a.* To whisper; to spread secretly.

Where doth the world thrust forth a vanity,
That is not quickly *buzz'd* into his ears? *Shakesp. Rich.* II.

I will *buzz* abroad such prophecies,
That Edward shall be fearful of his life. *Shakesp. Hen.* VI.

Did you not hear
A *buzzing* of a separation
Between the king and Catherine? *Shakesp. Henry* VIII.

They might *buzz* and whisper it one to another, and, tacitely withdrawing from the presence of the apostles, they then lift their voices, and noise it about the city. *Bentley.*

BUZZ. *n. s.* [from the verb.] A hum; a whisper; a talk.

The hive of a city or kingdom, is in best condition, when there is least noise or *buzz* in it. *Bacon's Apophthegms.*

Where I found the whole outward room in a *buzz* of politicks. *Addison. Spectator,* N° 403.

BU'ZZARD.

BU'ZZARD. *n. s.* [*busard*, Fr.]

1. A degenerate or mean species of hawk.

More pity that the eagle should be maw'd,
While kites and *buzzards* prey at liberty. *Shakesp. R.* III.
The noble *buzzard* ever pleas'd me best;
Of small renown, 'tis true: for, not to lie,
We call him but a hawk by courtesy. *Dryden's Hind and P.*

2. A blockhead; a dunce.

Those blind *buzzards*, who, in late years, of wilful maliciousness, would neither learn themselves, nor could teach others any thing at all. *Ascham's Schoolmaster.*

BU'ZZER. *n. s.* [from *buzz.*] A secret whisperer.

Her brother is in secret come from France,
And wants not *buzzers* to infest his ear
With petulant speeches of his father's death. *Shak. Hamlet.*

BY. *prep.* [bi, biᵹ, Saxon.]

1. It notes the agent.

The Moor is with child *by* you, Launcelot. *Shak. Hen.* VI.

The grammar of a language is sometimes to be carefully studied *by* a grown man. *Locke.*

2. It notes the instrument, and is always used after a verb neuter, where *with* would be put after an active; as, he was killed *with* a sword; he died *by* a sword.

But *by* Pelides' arms when Hector fell,
He chose Æneas, and he chose as well. *Dryden, Æn.* vi.

3. It notes the cause of any event.

This fight had the more weight with him, as *by* good luck not above two of that venerable body were fallen asleep. *Addison. Freeholder.*

4. It notes the means by which any thing is performed.

You must think, if we give you any thing, we hope to gain *by* you. *Shakesp. Coriolanus.*

Happier! had it suffic'd him to have known
Good *by* itself, and evil not at all. *Parad. Lost, b.* xi. *l.* 89.

The heart knows that *by* itself, which nothing in the world besides can give it any knowledge of. *South.*

We obtain the knowledge of a multitude of propositions *by* sensation and reflection. *Watts's Logick.*

5. It shews the manner of an action.

I have not patience; she consumes the time
In idle talk, and owns her false belief:
Seize her *by* force, and bear her hence unheard.
Dryden's Don Sebastian.

By chance, within a neighbouring brook,
He saw his branching horns, and alter'd look. *Addison.*

6. It has a signification, noting the method in which any successive action is performed, with regard to time or quantity.

The best for you, is to re-examine the cause, and to try it even point *by* point, argument *by* argument, with all the exactness you can. *Hooker, Preface.*

We are not to stay all together, but to come by him where he stands, *by* ones, *by* twos, and *by* threes. *Shakesp. Coriolanus.*

He calleth them forth *by* one, and *by* one, by the name, as he pleaseth, though seldom the order be inverted. *Bacon.*

The captains were obliged to break that piece of ordnance, and so *by* pieces to carry it away, that the enemy should not get so great a spoil. *Knolles's History of the Turks.*

Common prudence would direct me to take them all out, and examine them one *by* one. *Boyle.*

Others will soon take pattern and encouragement by your building; and so house *by* house, street *by* street, there will at last be finished a magnificent city. *Sprat.*

Explor'd her, limb *by* limb, and fear'd to find
So rude a gripe had left a livid mark behind. *Dryden's Fab.*

Thus year *by* year they pass, and day *by* day,
Till once, 'twas on the morn of chearful May,
The young Æmilia——— *Dryden's Fab.*

I'll gaze for ever on thy god like father,
Transplanting one *by* one into my life,
His bright perfections, till I shine like him. *Addison's Cato.*

Let the blows be *by* pauses laid on. *Locke.*

7. It notes the quantity had at one time.

Bullion will sell *by* the ounce for six shillings and fivepence unclipped money. *Locke.*

What we take daily *by* pounds, is at least of as much importance as of what we take seldom, and only *by* grains and spoonfuls. *Arbuthnot on Aliments, Preface.*

The North, *by* myriads, pours her mighty sons;
Great nurse of Goths, of Alans, and of Huns. *Pope.*

8. At, or in; noting place.

We see the great effects of battles *by* sea; the battle of Actium decided the empire of the world. *Bacon's Essays.*

Arms, and the man, I sing, who, forc'd *by* fate,
Expell'd, and exil'd, left the Trojan shore;
Long labours both *by* sea and land he bore. *Dryden's Æn.*

I would have fought *by* land, where I was stronger:
You hinder'd it; yet, when I fought at sea,
Forsook me fighting. *Dryden's All for Love.*

9. According to; noting permission.

It is lawful, both *by* the laws of nature and nations, and *by* the law divine, which is the perfection of the other two. *Bacon's Holy War.*

10. According to; noting proof.

The present, or like, system of the world cannot possibly have been eternal, *by* the first proposition; and, without God, it could not naturally, nor fortuitously, emerge out of a chaos, *by* the third proposition. *Bentley.*

The faculty, or desire, being infinite, *by* the preceding proposition, may contain, or receive both these. *Cheyne.*

11. After; according to; noting imitation or conformity.

The gospel gives us such laws, as every man, that understands himself, would chuse to live *by*. *Tillotson.*

In the divisions I have made, I have endeavoured, the best I could, to govern myself *by* the diversity of matter. *Locke.*

This ship, by good luck, fell into their hands at last, and served as a model to build others *by*. *Arbuthnot on Coins.*

12. From; noting judgment or token.

Thus, *by* the musick, we may know,
When noble wits a hunting go,
Through groves that on Parnassus grow. } *Waller.*

By what he has done, before the war in which he was engaged, we may expect what he will do after a peace. *Dryden.*

The son of Hercules he justly seems,
By his broad shoulders and gigantick limbs. *Dryden.*

Who's that stranger? *By* his warlike port,
His fierce demeanour, and erected look,
He's of no vulgar note. *Dryden's All for Love.*

Judge the event
By what has pass'd. *Dryden's Spanish Friar.*

The punishment is not to be measured *by* the greatness or smallness of the matter, but *by* the opposition it carries, and stands in, to that respect and submission that is due to the father. *Locke*

By your description of the town, I imagine it to lie under some great enchantment. *Pope's Letters.*

By what I have always heard and read, I take the strength of a nation— *Swift.*

13. It notes the sum of the difference between two things compared.

Meantime she stands provided of a Laius,
More young and vigorous too *by* twenty springs. *Dryden.*

Her brother Rivers,
Ere this, lies shorter *by* the head at Pomfret.
Rowe's Jane Shore.

By giving the denomination to less quantities of silver *by* one twentieth, you take from them their due. *Locke.*

14. It notes co-operation, or cohabitation.

By her he had two children at one birth. *Shakesp. Hen.* VI.

15. For; noting continuance of time. This sense is not now in use.

Ferdinand and Isabella recovered the kingdom of Granada from the Moors; having been in possession thereof *by* the space of seven hundred years. *Bacon's Henry* VII.

16. As soon as; not later than; noting time.

By this, the sons of Constantine which fled,
Ambrise and Uther, did ripe years attain. *Fairy Q. b.* ii.

Hector, *by* the fifth hour of the sun,
Will, with a trumpet, 'twixt our tents and Troy,
Tomorrow morning call some knight to arms.
Shakesp. Troilus and Cressida.

He err'd not; for, *by* this, the heav'nly bands
Down from a sky of jasper lighted now
In paradise. *Milton's Paradise Lost, b.* x. *l.* 208.

These have their course to finish round the earth
By morrow ev'ning. *Paradise Lost, b.* iv. *l.* 662.

The angelick guards ascended, mute and sad
For man: for, of his state *by* this they knew. *Par. L. b.* x.

By that time a siege is carried on two or three days, I am altogether lost and bewildered in it. *Addison. Spect.* N° 165.

By this time, the very foundation was removed. *Swift.*

By the beginning of the fourth century from the building of Rome, the tribunes proceeded so far, as to accuse and fine the consuls. *Swift.*

17. Beside; noting passage.

Many beautiful places standing along the sea-shore, make the town appear much longer than it is, to those that sail *by* it. *Addison on Italy.*

18. Beside; near to; in presence; noting proximity of place.

So thou may'st say, the king lies *by* a beggar, if a beggar dwell near him; or the church stands *by* thy tabour, if thy tabour stand *by* the church. *Shakesp. Twelfth Night.*

Here he comes himself;
If he be worth any man's good voice,
That good man sit down *by* him. *Ben. Johnson's Catiline.*

A spacious plain, whereon
Were tents of various hue: *by* some, were herds
Of cattle grazing. *Milton's Paradise Lost, b.* xi. *l.* 557.

Stay *by* me; thou art resolute and faithful;
I have employment worthy of thy arm. *Dryden's D. Sebast.*

19. Before *himself*, *herself*, or *themselves*, it notes the absence of all others.

Sitting in some place, *by himself*, let him translate into English his former lesson. *Ascham's Schoolmaster*

Solyman resolved to assault the breach, after he had, *by himself*

ſelf, in a melancholy mood, walked up and down in his tent. *Knolles's Hiſt. of the Turks.*

I know not whether he will annex his diſcourſe to his appendix, or publiſh it *by itſelf*, or at all. *Boyle's Spring of the Air.*

He will imagine, that the king, and his miniſters, ſat down, and made them *by themſelves*, and then ſent them to their allies, to ſign. *Swift.*

More pleas'd to keep it, till their friends could come,
Then eat the ſweeteſt *by themſelves* at home. *Pope.*

20. It is the ſolemn form of ſwearing.

His godhead I invoke, *by* him I ſwear. *Dryden's Fab.*

21. At hand.

He kept then ſome of the ſpirit *by* him, to verify what he believes. *Boyle.*

The merchant is not forced to keep ſo much money *by* him, as in other places, where they have not ſuch a ſupply. *Locke.*

22. It is uſed in forms of adjuring, or obteſting.

Which, O! avert *by* yon etherial light,
Which I have loſt for this eternal night;
Or if, by dearer ties, you may be won,
By your dead ſire, and *by* your living ſon. *Dryden's Æn.*

Now *by* your joys on earth, your hopes in heav'n,
O ſpare this great, this good, this aged king! *Dryden.*

O, cruel youth!
By all the pain that wrings my tortur'd ſoul!
By all the dear deceitful hopes you gave me,
O, ceaſe! at leaſt, once more delude my ſorrows.
Smith's Phædrus and Hippolita.

23. It ſignifies ſpecification and particularity.

Upbraiding heav'n, from whence his lineage came,
And cruel calls the gods, and cruel thee, *by* name. *Dryden.*

24. By proxy of; noting ſubſtitution.

The gods were ſaid to feaſt with Ethiopians; that is, they were preſent with them *by* their ſtatues. *Broome, notes on Odyſſ.*

25. In the ſame direction with.

They are alſo ſtriated, or furrowed, *by* the length, and the ſides curiouſly punched, or pricked. *Grew.*

By. *adv.*

1. Near; at a ſmall diſtance.

And in it lies, the god of ſleep;
And, ſnorting *by*,
We may deſcry
The monſters of the deep. *Dryden's Albion.*

2. Beſide; paſſing.

I did hear
The galloping of horſe. Who was't came *by*? *Shakeſp. Macbeth.*

3. In preſence.

The ſame words in my lady Philoclea's mouth, as from one woman to another, ſo as there was no other body *by*, might have had a better grace. *Sidney.*

I'll not be *by*, the while, my lieges, farewel:
What will become hereof, there's none can tell.
Shakeſp. Richard III.

There while I ſing, if gentle youth be *by*,
That tunes my lute, and winds the ſtrings ſo high. *Waller.*

Pris'ners and witneſſes were waiting *by*;
Theſe had been taught to ſwear, and thoſe to die.
Roſcommon.

You have put a principle into him, which will influence his actions, when you are not *by*. *Locke.*

By and by. In a ſhort time.

He overtook Amphialus, who had been ſtaid here, and *by and by* called him to fight with him. *Sidney.*

The noble knight alighted *by and by*,
From lofty ſteed, and bad the lady ſtay,
To ſee what end of fight ſhould him befall that day.
Spenſer's Fairy Queen, b. i. cant. viii. ſtanz. 2.

In the temple, *by and by*, with us,
Theſe couples ſhall eternally be knit.
Shakeſp. Midſummer's Night's Dream.

O how this ſpring of love reſembleth
Th' uncertain glory of an April day;
Which now ſhews all the beauty of the ſun,
And *by and by* a cloud takes all away.
Shakeſp. Two Gentlemen of Verona.

Now a ſenſible man, *by and by* a fool, and preſently a beaſt.
Shakeſp. Othello.

By. *n. ſ.* [from the prepoſition.] Something not the direct and immediate object of regard.

In this inſtance, there is, upon the *by*, to be noted, the percolation of the verjuice through the wood.
Bacon's Natural Hiſtory, N° 79.

This wolf was forced to make bold, ever and anon, with a ſheep in private, by the *by*. *L'Eſtrange.*

Hence we may underſtand, to add that upon the *by*, that it is not neceſſary. *Boyle.*

So, while my lov'd revenge is full and high,
I'll give you back your kingdom by the *by*.
Dryden's Conqueſt of Granada.

By, in compoſition, implies ſomething out of the direct way; and, conſequently, ſome obſcurity, as a *by-road*; ſomething irregular, as a *by-end*; or ſomething collateral, as a *by-concernment*; or private, as a *by-law*. This compoſition is uſed at pleaſure, and will be underſtood by the examples following.

By-coffeehouse. *n. ſ.* A coffeehouſe in an obſcure place.

I afterwards entered a *by-coffeehouſe*, that ſtood at the upper end of a narrow lane, where I met with a nonjuror.
Addiſon. Spectator, N° 403.

By-concernment. *n. ſ.* An affair which is not the main buneſs.

Our plays, beſides the main deſign, have under-plots, or *by-concernments*, or leſs conſiderable perſons and intrigues, which are carried on with the motion of the main plot.
Dryden on Dramatick Poetry.

By-dependence. *n. ſ.* An appendage; ſomething accidentally depending on another.

Theſe,
And your three motives to the battle, with
I know not how much more, ſhould be demanded;
And all the other *by-dependences*,
From chance to chance. *Shakeſp. Cymbeline.*

By-design. *n. ſ.* An incidental purpoſe.

And if ſhe miſs the mouſe-trap lines,
They'll ſerve for other *by-deſigns*,
And make an artiſt underſtand,
To copy out her ſeal or hand;
Or find void places in the paper,
To ſteal in ſomething to entrap her. *Hudibras, p. iii. c. iii.*

By-end. *n. ſ.* Private intereſt; ſecret advantage.

All people that worſhip for fear, profit, or ſome other *by-end*, fall within the intendement of this fable. *L'Eſtrange.*

By-gone. *adj.* [a Scotch word.] Paſt.

Tell him, you're ſure
All in Bohemia's well: this ſatisfaction
The *by-gone* day proclaim'd. *Shakeſp. Winter's Tale.*

As we have a conceit of motion coming, as well as *bygone*; ſo have we of time, which dependeth thereupon.
Grew's Coſmologia Sacra, b. ii. c. iii.

By-interest. *n. ſ.* Intereſt diſtinct from that of the publick.

Various factions and parties, all aiming at *by-intereſt*, without any ſincere regard to the publick good. *Atterbury.*

By-law. *n. ſ.*

By-laws are orders made in court-leets, or court-barons, by common aſſent, for the good of thoſe that make them, farther than the publick law binds. *Cowel.*

There was alſo a law, to reſtrain the *by-laws* and ordinances of corporations. *Bacon's Henry VII.*

In the beginning of this record is inſerted the law or inſtitution; to which are added two *by-laws*, as a comment upon the general law. *Addiſon. Spectator, N° 608.*

By-matter. *n. ſ.* Something incidental.

I knew one, that, when he wrote a letter, he would put that which was moſt material into the poſtſcript, as if it had been a *by-matter*. *Bacon's Eſſays, N° 23.*

By-name. *n. ſ.* A nickname; name of reproach, or accidental appellation.

Robert, eldeſt ſon to the Conquerour, uſed ſhort hoſe, and thereupon was *by-named* Court-hoſe, and ſhewed firſt the uſe of them to the Engliſh. *Camden's Remains.*

By-past. *adj.* Paſt; a term of the Scotch dialect.

Wars, peſtilences, and diſeaſes, have not been fewer for theſe three hundred years *by-paſt*, than ever they have been ſince we have had records. *Cheyne's Philoſophical Principles.*

By-path. *n. ſ.* A private or obſcure path.

Heav'n knows, my ſon,
By what *by-paths*, and indirect crooked ways,
I got this crown. *Shakeſp. Henry IV. p. ii.*

By-respect. *n. ſ.* Private end or view.

It may be, that ſome, upon *by-reſpects*, find ſomewhat friendly uſage in uſance, at ſome of their hands.
Carew's Survey of Cornwal.

The archbiſhops and biſhops, next under the king, have the government of the church: be not you the mean to prefer any to thoſe places, for any *by-reſpects*, but only for their learning, gravity, and worth. *Bacon's Advice to Villiers.*

Auguſtus, who was not altogether ſo good as he was wiſe, had ſome *by-reſpects* in the enacting of this law; for to do any thing for nothing, was not his maxim.
Dryden's Juvenal, Dedication.

By-road. *n. ſ.* An obſcure unfrequented path.

Through ſlipp'ry *by-roads*, dark and deep,
They often climb, and often creep. *Swift.*

By-room. *n. ſ.* A private room within another.

I pr'ythee, do thou ſtand in ſome *by-room*, while I queſtion my puny drawer to what end he gave the ſugar.
Shakeſp. Henry IV. p. i.

By-speech. *n. ſ.* An incidental or caſual ſpeech, not directly relating to the point.

When they come to allege what word and what law they meant, their common ordinary practice is to quote *by-ſpeeches* in ſome hiſtorical narration or other, and to uſe them as if they were written in moſt exact form of law. *Hooker, b. iii. § 4.*

By-stander. *n. ſ.* A looker one; one unconcerned.

She

She broke her feathers againſt the frame of the picture, and, falling to the ground upon it, was taken up by the *by-ſtanders*. *L'Eſtrange's Fables.*

The *by-ſtanders* aſked him, why he ran away, his bread being weight? That was more than I knew, ſays he. *Locke.*

BY-STREET. *n. ſ.* An obſcure ſtreet.

The broker here his ſpacious beaver wears,
Upon his brow ſit jealouſies and cares;
Bent on ſome mortgage, to avoid reproach,
He ſeeks *by-ſtreets*, and ſaves th' expenſive coach.
Gay's Trivia.

BY-VIEW. *n. ſ.* Private ſelf-intereſted purpoſe.

No *by-views* of his own ſhall miſlead him. *Atterbury.*

BY-WALK. *n. ſ.* A private walk; not the main road.

All which he moves afterwards in *by-walks*, or under-plots, as diverſions to the main deſign, leſt it ſhould grow tedious; though they are ſtill naturally joined. *Dryden.*

The chief avenue ought to be the moſt ample and noble; but there ſhould be *by-walks*, to retire into ſometimes, for eaſe and refreſhment. *Broome's Notes on the Odyſſey.*

BY-WAY. *n. ſ.* A private and obſcure way.

Night ſtealths are commonly driven in *by-ways*, and by blind fords, unuſed of any but ſuch like. *Spenſer on Ireland.*

Other *by-ways* he himſelf betook,
Where never foot of living wight did tread.
Spenſer's Fairy Queen, b. i. *cant.* vii. *ſtanz.* 50.

Wholly abſtain, or wed: thy beauteous Lord
Allows thee choice of paths; take no *by-ways*,
But gladly welcome what he doth afford;
Not grudging that thy luſt hath bounds and ſtays. *Herbert.*

A ſervant, or a favourite, if he be in want, and no other apparent cauſe of eſteem, is commonly thought but a *by-way* to cloſe corruption. *Bacon's Eſſays,* Nº 11.

This is wonderfully diverting to the underſtanding, thus to receive a precept, that enters, as it were, through a *by-way*, and to apprehend an idea that draws a whole train after it.
Addiſon's Eſſay on the Georgicks.

BY-WEST. Weſtward; to the weſt of.

Whereupon grew that by-word, uſed by the Iriſh, that they dwelt *by-weſt* the law, which dwelt beyond the river of the Barrow. *Sir John Davies on Ireland.*

BY-WORD. *n. ſ.* A ſaying; a proverb.

Duke of York, be king;
And baſhful Henry be depoſed; whoſe cowardice
Hath made us *by-words* to our enemies.
Shakeſp. Henry VI. *p.* iii.

I knew a wiſe man, that had it for a *by-word*, when he ſaw men haſten to a concluſion, Stay a little, that we may make an end the ſooner. *Bacon's Eſſays,* Nº 26.

We are become a *by-word* among the nations for our ridiculous feuds and animoſities. *Addiſon's Freeholder,* Nº 50.

It will be his lot often, to look ſingular, in looſe and licentious times, and to become a *by-word* and a reproach, on that account, among the men of wit and pleaſure. *Atterbury.*

BY'ASS. *n. ſ.* See BIAS.

Every inordinate luſt is a falſe *byaſs* upon men's underſtandings, which naturally draws towards atheiſm. *Tillotſon.*

BYE, BEE, come immediately from the Saxon, bẏ, bẏnᵹ, *i. e.* a dwelling. *Gibſon's Camden.*

BY'ZANTINE. See BIZANTINE.

C.

C, The third letter of the alphabet, has two ſounds; one like *k*, as, *call*, *clock*, *craft*, *coal*, *companion*, *cuneiform*; the other as *s*, as, *Cæſar*, *ceſſation*, *cinder*. It ſounds like *k* before *a*, *o*, *u*, or a conſonant; and like *s*, before *e*, *i*, and *y*.

CAB. *n. ſ.* [קַב.] A Hebrew meaſure, containing about three pints Engliſh, or the eighteenth part of the ephah.

CABA'L. *n. ſ.* [*cabale*, Fr. קבלה, tradition.]

1. The ſecret ſcience of the Hebrew rabbins.
2. A body of men united in ſome cloſe deſign. A *cabal* differs from a *party*, as *few* from *many*.

She often interpoſed her royal authority, to break the *cabals* which were forming againſt her firſt miniſters. *Addiſon.*

3. Intrigue.

When each, by curs'd *cabals* of women, ſtrove,
To draw th' indulgent king to partial love. *Dryden's Aureng.*

To CABA'L. *v. n.* [*cabaler*, Fr.] To form cloſe intrigues; to intrigue; to unite in ſmall parties.

His mournful friends, ſummon'd to take their leaves,
Are throng'd about his couch, and ſit in council:
What thoſe *caballing* captains may deſign,
I muſt prevent, by being firſt in action. *Dryden's D. Sebaſt.*

CA'BALIST. *n. ſ.* [from *cabal.*] One ſkilled in the traditions of the Hebrews.

Then Jove thus ſpake: With care and pain
We form'd this name, renown'd in rhime,
Not thine, immortal Neufgermain!
Coſt ſtudious *cabaliſts* more time. *Swift.*

CABALLI'STICAL. } *adj.* [from *cabal.*] Something that has an
CABALLI'STICK. } occult meaning.

The letters are *caballiſtical*, and carry more in them than it is proper for the world to be acquainted with. *Addiſon. Spect.*

He taught him to repeat two *caballiſtick* words, in pronouncing of which the whole ſecret conſiſted. *Spectator*, Nº 578.

CABA'LLER. *n. ſ.* [from *cabal.*] He that engages in cloſe deſigns; an intriguer.

Factious and rich, bold at the council board,
But cautious in the field, he ſhun'd the ſword;
A cloſe *caballer*, and tongue-valiant lord. } *Dryden.*

CABA'LLINE. *adj.* [*caballinus*, Lat.] Belonging to a horſe; as, *caballine* aloes, or horſe aloes.

CA'BARET. n. ſ. [French.] A tavern.

Suppoſe this ſervant paſſing by ſome *cabaret*, or tennis-court, where his comrades were drinking or playing, ſhould ſtay with them, and drink or play away his money. *Bramhall againſt Hobbes.*

CA'BBAGE. *n. ſ.* [*cabus*, Fr. *braſſica*, Lat.] A plant.

The leaves are large, fleſhy, and of a glaucous colour; the flowers conſiſt of four leaves, which are ſucceeded by long taper pods, containing ſeveral round acrid ſeeds. The ſpecies are, 1. The common white *cabbage*. 2. The red *cabbage*. 3. The Ruſſian *cabbage*. 4. The flat-ſided *cabbage*. 5. The ſugar loaf *cabbage*. 6. The early Batterſea *cabbage*. 7. The white Savoy *cabbage*. 8. The green Savoy *cabbage*. 9. The *boorcole*. 10. The green *broccoli*. 11. The Italian *broccoli*. 12. The turnep-rooted *cabbage*. 13. The *cauliflower*. 14. The turnep *cabbage*. 15. Curled *colewort*. 16. The muſk *cabbage*. 17. Branching tree *cabbage*, from the ſea coaſt. 18. Brown *broccoli*. 19. Common *colewort*. 20. Perennial Alpine *colewort*. 21. Perfoliated wild *cabbage*, with a white flower. 22. Perfoliated *cabbage*, with a purple flower. The common white, red, flat, and long-ſided *cabbages*, are chiefly cultivated for winter uſe; the ſeeds of which muſt be ſown in the middle of March, in beds of good freſh earth. The Ruſſian *cabbage* was formerly in much greater eſteem than at preſent, and is rarely brought to the market. The early Batterſea and ſugar-loaf *cabbages*, are called Michaelmas *cabbages*; the ſeaſon for ſowing them is in the middle of July, in an open ſpot of ground. The Savoy *cabbages* are propagated for winter uſe, as being generally eſteemed the better, when pinched by froſt. The *boorcole* is never eaten till the froſt has rendered it tender. The turnep *cabbage* was formerly more cultivated in England than at preſent; and ſome eſteem this kind for ſoups, but it is generally too ſtrong, and ſeldom good, except in hard winters. The curled *colewort* is more generally eſteemed, and is fit for uſe after Chriſtmas, and continues good until April. The muſk *cabbage* has, through negligence, been almoſt loſt in England, though, for eating, it is one of the beſt kinds we have; for it is always looſer, and the leaves more criſp and tender, and has a moſt agreeable muſky ſcent when cut. It will be fit for uſe in October, November, and December. The branching ſea *cabbage* is found wild in England, and on the ſea coaſt, and is ſometimes gathered by the poor inhabitants in the ſpring, and eaten; but it is apt to be ſtrong and bitter. The brown *broccoli* is by many eſteemed, though it does not deſerve a place in the kitchen garden, where the Roman *broccoli* can be obtained, which is much ſweeter, and will continue longer in ſeaſon. The Roman *broccoli* has large heads, which appear in the center of the plants like cluſters of buds. The heads ſhould be cut before they run up to ſeed, with about four or five inches of the ſtems; the ſkin of theſe ſtems ſhould be ſtripped off, before they are boiled; they will eat very tender, and little inferiour to aſparagus. The common *colewort* is now almoſt loſt near London, where their markets are uſually ſupplied with *cabbage* or Savoy plants inſtead of them; which, being tenderer and more delicate, are better worth cultivating. The perennial Alpine *colewort* is alſo little cultivated at preſent. The other two ſorts of wild *cabbage* are varieties fit for a botanick garden, but are plants of no uſe. The *cauliflowers* have, of late years, been ſo far improved in England, as to exceed, in goodneſs and magnitude, what are produced in moſt parts of Europe; and, by the ſkill of the gardeners, are continued for ſeveral months together; but the moſt common ſeaſon for them is in May, June, and July. *Miller.*

Cole, *cabbage*, and coleworts, which are ſoft and demulcent, without any acidity; the jelly, or juice, of red *cabbage*, baked in an oven, and mixed with honey, is an excellent pectoral. *Arbuthnot on Aliments.*

To CA'BBAGE. *v. a.* [a cant word among taylors.] To ſteal in cutting clothes.

Your taylor, inſtead of ſhreads, *cabbages* whole yards of cloth. *Arbuthnot's Hiſtory of J. Bull.*

CA'BBAGE TREE. *n. ſ.* A ſpecies of *palm-tree*; which ſee.

It is very common in the Caribee iſlands, where it grows to a prodigious height. The leaves of this tree envelope each other, ſo that thoſe which are incloſed, being deprived of the air, are blanched; which is the part the inhabitants cut for plaits for hats, &c. and the genuine, or young ſhoots, are pickled, and ſent into England by the name of cabbage; but whenever this part is cut out, the trees are deſtroyed; nor do they riſe again from the old roots; ſo that there are very few trees left remaining near plantations, except for ornament; for their ſtems being exceeding ſtraight, and their leaves being produced very regularly at top, will afford a moſt beautiful proſpect; for which reaſon, the planters generally ſpare two or three of them near their habitations. *Miller.*

CA'BBAGE-WORM. *n. ſ.* An inſect.

CA'BIN. *n. ſ.* [*cabane*, Fr. *chabin*, Welch, a cottage.]

1. A ſmall room.

So long in ſecret *cabin* there he held
Her captive to his ſenſual deſire,
Till that with timely fruit her belly ſwell'd,
And bore a boy unto a ſavage ſire. *Fairy Queen, b.* i. *c.* vi.

2. A ſmall chamber in a ſhip.

Give thanks you have lived ſo long, and make yourſelf ready, in your *cabin*, for the miſchance of the hour, if it ſo happen. *Shakeſp. Tempeſt.*

Men may not expect the uſe of many *cabins*, and ſafety at once, in the ſea ſervice. *Raleigh's Eſſays.*

The cheſsboard, we ſay, is in the ſame place it was, if it remain in the ſame part of the *cabin*, though, perhaps, the ſhip it is in, ſails all the while. *Locke.*

3. A cottage, or ſmall houſe.

Come from marble bow'rs, many times the gay harbour of anguiſh,
Unto a ſilly *cabin*, though weak, yet ſtronger againſt woes. *Sidney, b.* i.

Neither ſhould that odious cuſtom be allowed, of flaying off the green ſurface of the ground, to cover their *cabins*, or make up their ditches. *Swift.*

4. A tent.

Some of green boughs their ſlender *cabins* frame,
Some lodged were Tortoſa's ſtreets about. *Fairfax, b. i.*

To CA'BIN. *v. n.* [from the noun.] To live in a cabin.

I'll make you feed on berries and on roots,
And feed on curds and whey, and ſuck the goat,
And *cabin* in a cave. *Shakeſp. Titus Andronicus.*

To CA'BIN. *v. a.* To confine in a cabin.

Fleance is 'ſcap'd:
Then comes my fit again; I had elſe been perfect;
Whole as the marble, ſounded as the rock;
As broad and gen'ral as the caſing air;
But now I'm *cabin'd*, cribb'd, confin'd, bound in,
To ſaucy doubts and fear. *Shakeſp. Macbeth.*

CA'BINED. *adj.* [from *cabin.*] Belonging to a cabin.

The nice morn, on the Indian ſteep,
From her *cabin'd* loophole peep. *Milton.*

CA'BINET. *n. ſ.* [*cabinet*, Fr.]

1. A ſet of boxes or drawers for curioſities; a private box.

At both corners of the farther ſide, by way of return, let there be two delicate or rich *cabinets*, daintily paved, richly hanged, glazed with cryſtaline glaſs, and a rich cupola in the midſt, and all other elegancy that may be thought on. *Bacon's Eſſays.*

Who ſees a ſoul in ſuch a body ſet,
Might love the treaſure for the *cabinet*. *Ben. Johnſon.*
In vain the workman ſhew'd his wit,
With rings and hinges counterfeit,
To make it ſeem, in this diſguiſe,
A *cabinet* to vulgar eyes. *Swift.*

2. Any place in which things of value are hidden.

Thy breaſt hath ever been the *cabinet*,
Where I have lock'd my ſecrets. *Denham's Sophy.*

We cannot diſcourſe of the ſecret, but by deſcribing our duty; but ſo much duty muſt needs open a *cabinet* of myſteries. *Taylor's Worthy Communicant.*

3. A private room in which conſultations are held.

You began in the *cabinet* what you afterwards practiſed in the camp. *Dryden.*

4. In *Spenſer* it ſeems to ſignify a hut, or houſe.

Hearken awhile in thy green *cabinet*,
The lawrel ſong of careful Colinet. *Spenſer's Paſtorals.*

CA'BINET-COUNCIL. *n. ſ.* A council held in a private manner, with unuſual privacy and confidence.

The doctrine of Italy, and practice of France, in ſome kings times, hath introduced *cabinet-councils*. *Bacon's Eſſays.*

From the higheſt to the loweſt it is univerſally read; from the *cabinet-council* to the nurſery. *Gay to Swift.*

CA'BINET-MAKER. *n. ſ.* [from *cabinet* and *make.*] One that makes ſmall nice work in wood.

The root of an old white thorn will make very fine boxes and combs; ſo that they would be of great uſe for the *cabinet-makers*, as well as the turners, and others. *Mortimer.*

CA'BLE. *n. ſ.* [*cabl*, Welch; *cabel*, Dutch.] The great rope of a ſhip to which the anchor is faſtened.

What though the maſt be now blown overboard,
The *cable* broke, the holding anchor loſt,
And half our ſailors ſwallow'd in the flood,
Yet lives our pilot ſtill? *Shakeſp. Henry VI. p. iii.*

True it is, that the length of the *cable* is the life of the ſhip in all extremities; and the reaſon is, becauſe it makes ſo many bendings and waves, as the ſhip, riding at that length, is not able to ſtretch it; and nothing breaks that is not ſtretched. *Raleigh's Eſſays.*

The *cables* crack, the ſailors fearful cries
Aſcend; and ſable night involves the ſkies. *Dryden's Virg.*

CA'BURNS. *n. ſ.* Small ropes uſed in ſhips. *Dict.*

CA'CAO. See CHOCOLATENUT.

CACHE'CTICAL. } *adj.* [from *cachexy.*] Having an ill habit of
CACHE'CTICK. } body; ſhewing an ill habit.

Young and florid blood, rather than vapid and *cahectical*. *Arbuthnot on Air.*

The crude chyle ſwims in the blood, and appears as milk in the blood, let out of ſome perſons who are generally *cachectick*. *Floyer on the Humours.*

CACHE'XY. *n. ſ.* [καχεξία.] A general word to expreſs a great variety of ſymptoms; moſt commonly it denotes ſuch a diſtemperature of the humours, as hinders nutrition, and weakens the vital and animal functions, proceeding from weakneſs of the fibres, and an abuſe of the non-naturals, and often from ſevere acute diſtempers. *Arbuthnot on Diet.*

CACHINNA'TION. *n. ſ.* [*cachinnatio*, Lat.] A loud laughter. *D.*

CA'CKEREL. *n. ſ.* A fiſh, ſaid to make thoſe who eat it laxative.

To CA'CKLE. *v. n.* [*kaeckelen*, Dutch.]

1. To make a noiſe as a gooſe.

The nightingale, if ſhe ſhould ſing by day,
When every gooſe is *cackling*, would be thought
No better a muſician than the wren. *Shakeſp. M. of Venice.*
Gooſe, if I had you upon Sarum plain,
I'd drive thee *cackling* home to Camelot. *Shakeſp. K. Lear.*
Or rob the Roman geeſe of all their glories,
And ſave the ſtate, by *cackling* to the tories. *Pope.*

2. Sometimes it is uſed for the noiſe of a hen.

Now to my ſtory I return again:
The trembling widow, and her daughters twain,
This woful *cackling* cry, with horrour heard,
Of thoſe diſtracted damſels in the yard. *Dryden's Fab.*

3. To laugh; to giggle.

Then Nic. grinned, *cackled*, and laughed, till he was like to kill himſelf, and ſeemed to be ſo pleaſed, that he fell a friſking and dancing about the room. *Arbuthnot's J. Bull.*

CA'CKLE. *n. ſ.* [from the verb.] The voice of a gooſe or fowl.

The ſilver gooſe before the ſhining gate
There flew, and, by her *cackle*, ſav'd the ſtate. *Dryden.*

CAC'KLER. *n. ſ.* [from *cackle.*]

1. A fowl that cackles.

2. A teltale; a tatler.

CACOCHY'MICAL. } *adj.* [from *cacochymy.*] Having the humours
CACOCHY'MICK. } corrupted.

It will prove very advantageous, if only *cacochymick*, to clarify his blood with a laxative. *Harvey on Conſumptions.*

If the body be *cacochymical*, the tumours are apt to degenerate into very venomous and malignant abſceſſes. *Wiſeman.*

The ancient writers diſtinguiſhed putrid fevers, by putrefaction of blood, choler, melancholy, and phlegm; and this is to be explained by an effervescence happening in a particular *cacochymical* blood. *Floyer on the Humours.*

CACOCHY'MY. *n. ſ.* [κακοχυμία.] A depravation of the humours from a ſound ſtate, to what the phyſicians call by a general name of a *cacochymy*. Spots, and diſcolourations of the ſkin, are ſigns of weak fibres; for the lateral veſſels, which lie out of the road of circulation, let groſs humours paſs, which could not, if the veſſels had their due degree of ſtricture. *Arbuthnot on Aliments.*

Strong beer, a liquour that attributes the better half of its ill qualities to the hops, conſiſting of an acrimonious firy nature, ſets the blood, upon the leaſt *cacochymy*, into an orgaſmus, by an ill ferment. *Harvey on Conſumptions.*

CACO'PHONY. *n. ſ.* [κακοφωνία.] A bad ſound of words.

To CACU'MINATE. *v. a.* [*cacumino*, Lat.] To make ſharp or pyramidal. *Dict.*

CADA'VEROUS. *adj.* [*cadaver*, Lat.] Having the appearance of a dead carcaſs; having the qualities of a dead carcaſs.

In vain do they ſcruple to approach the dead, who livingly are *cadaverous*, for fear of any outward pollution, whoſe temper pollutes themſelves. *Brown's Vulgar Errours, b.* ix. *c.* 10.

The urine, long detained in the bladder, as well as glaſs, will grow red, fœtid, *cadaverous*, and alkaline. The caſe is the ſame with the ſtagnant waters of hydropical perſons. *Arbuthnot on Aliments.*

CA'DDIS. *n. ſ.*

1. A kind of tape or ribbon.

He hath ribbons of all the colours of the rainbow; inkles, *caddiſes*, cambricks, lawns; why, he ſings them over as if they were gods and goddeſſes. *Shakeſp. Winter's Tale.*

2. A kind of worm or grub found in a caſe of ſtraw.

He eſpecially loves the mayfly, which is bred of the codworm, or *caddis*; and theſe make the trout bold and luſty. *Walton's Angler.*

CADE. *n. ſ.* [It is deduced, by *Skinner*, from *cadeler*, Fr. an old word, which ſignifies to breed up tenderly.] Tame; ſoft; delicate; as a *cade* lamb, a lamb bred at home.

To CADE. *v. a.* [from the noun.] To breed up in ſoftneſs.

CADE. *n. ſ.* [*cadus*, Lat.] A barrel.

We John Cade, ſo termed of our ſuppoſed father.——Or rather of ſtealing a *cade* of herrings. *Shakeſp. Henry VI. p. ii.*

Soon as thy liquour from the narrow cells
Of cloſe preſs'd huſks is freed, thou muſt refrain
Thy thirſty ſoul; let none perſuade to broach
Thy thick, unwholſome, undigeſted *cades*. *Philips.*

CADE-WORM. *n. ſ.* The ſame with *caddis*.

CA'DENCE. } *n. ſ.* [*cadence*, Fr.]
CA'DENCY. }

1. Fall; ſtate of ſinking; decline.

Now was the ſun in weſtern *cadence* low
From noon; and gentle airs, due at their hours,
To fan the earth, now wak'd. *Paradiſe Loſt, b.* x. *l.* 92.

2. The fall of the voice.

The ſliding, in the cloſe or *cadence*, hath an agreement with the figure in rhetorick, which they call *præter expectatum*; for there is a pleaſure even in being deceived. *Bacon's Nat. Hiſt.*

There be words not made with lungs,
Sententious ſhow'rs! O! let them fall,
Their *cadence* is rhetorical. *Craſhaw.*

3. The flow of verſes, or periods.

The words, the verſification, and all the other elegancies of ſound, as *cadences*, and turns of words upon the thought, perform exactly the ſame office both in dramatick and epick poetry. *Dryden's Dufreſnoy.*

The *cadency* of one line muſt be a rule to that of the next; as the ſound of the former muſt ſlide gently into that which follows. *Dryden.*

4. The tone or ſound.

Hollow rocks retain
The ſound of bluſt'ring winds, which all night long

Had rous'd the ſea, now with horſe *cadence* lull
Sea-faring men, o'erwatch'd. *Paradiſe Loſt, b.* ii. *l.* 287.

He hath a confuſed remembrance of words ſince he left the univerſity; he hath loſt half their meaning, and puts them together with no regard, except to their *cadence*. *Swift.*

5. In horſemanſhip.

Cadence is an equal meaſure or proportion, which a horſe obſerves in all his motions, when he is thoroughly managed. *Farrier's Dict.*

CA'DENT. *adj.* [*cadens*, Lat.] Falling down.

CADE'T. *n. ſ.* [*cadet*, Fr. pronounced *cadé*.]

1. The younger brother.

2. The youngeſt brother.

Joſeph was the youngeſt of the twelve, and David the eleventh ſon, and the *cadet* of Jeſſe. *Brown's Vulgar Errours.*

3. A voluntier in the army, who ſerves in expectation of a commiſſion.

CA'DEW. *n. ſ.* A ſtraw worm. See CADDIS. *Dict.*

CA'DGER. *n. ſ.* A huckſter; one who brings butter, eggs, and poultry, from the country to market.

CA'DI. n. ſ. A magiſtrate among the Turks, whoſe office ſeems to anſwer to that of a juſtice of peace.

CADI'LLACK. *n. ſ.* A ſort of pear; which ſee.

CÆCIAS. n. ſ. [Lat.] A wind from the north.

Now, from the north,
Boreas and *Cæcias* and Argeſtes loud
And Thraſcias rend the woods, and ſeas upturn.
Milton's Paradiſe Loſt, b. x. *l.* 699.

CÆSA'REAN. See CESARIAN.

CÆSURA. n. ſ. [Lat.] A figure in poetry, by which a ſhort ſyllable after a complete foot is made long.

CAFTAN. n. ſ. [Perſick.] A Perſian veſt or garment.

CAG. *n. ſ.* A barrel or wooden veſſel, containing four or five gallons.

CAGE. *n. ſ.* [*cage*, Fr. from *cavea*, Lat.]

1. An incloſure of twigs or wire, in which birds are kept.

See whether a *cage* can pleaſe a bird? or whether a dog grow not fiercer with tying? *Sidney.*

He taught me how to know a man in love; in which *cage* of ruſhes, I am ſure, you are not a priſoner. *Shakeſp. As you like it.*

Though ſlaves, like birds that ſing not in a *cage*,
They loſt their genius, and poetick rage;
Homers again and Pindars may be found,
And his great actions with their numbers crown'd. *Waller.*

And parrots, imitating human tongue,
And ſinging birds in ſilver *cages* hung;
And ev'ry fragrant flow'r, and od'rous green,
Were ſorted well, with lumps of amber laid between.
Dryden's Fables.

A man recurs to our fancy, by remembering his garment, a beaſt, bird, or fiſh, by the *cage*, or court-yard, or ciſtern, wherein it was kept. *Watts's Improvement of the Mind.*

The reaſon why ſo few marriages are happy, is, becauſe young ladies ſpend their time in making nets, not in making *cages*. *Swift's Thoughts on various Subjects.*

2. A place for wild beaſts, incloſed with paliſadoes.

3. A priſon for petty malefactors.

To CAGE. *v. a.* [from the noun.] To incloſe in a cage.

He ſwoln, and pamper'd with high fare,
Sits down, and ſnorts, *cag'd* in his baſket-chair. *Donne.*

CA'IMAN. n. ſ. The American name of a crocodile.

To CAJO'LE. *v. a.* [*cageoller*, Fr.] To flatter; to ſooth; to coax: a low word.

Thought he, 'tis no mean part of civil
State-prudence, to *cajole* the devil. *Hudibras, cant.* ii. *p.* iii.

The one affronts him, while the other *cajoles* and pities him; takes up his quarrel, ſhakes his head at it, claſps his hand upon his breaſt, and then proteſts and proteſts. *L'Eſtrange.*

CAJO'LER. *n. ſ.* [from *cajole*.] A flatterer; a wheedler.

CAJO'LERY. *n. ſ.* [*cajolerie*, Fr.] Flattery.

CA'ISSON. n. ſ. [French.] A cheſt of bombs or powder, laid in the enemy's way, to be fired at their approach.

CA'ITIFF. *n. ſ.* [*cattivo*, Ital. a ſlave; whence it came to ſignify a bad man, with ſome implication of meanneſs; as *knave* in Engliſh, and *fur* in Latin; ſo certainly does ſlavery deſtroy virtue.

Ἥμισυ τῆς ἀρετῆς ἀποαίνυται δούλιον ἦμαρ. *Homer.*

A ſlave and a ſcoundrel are ſignified by the ſame words in many languages.] A mean villain; a deſpicable knave.

Vile *caitiff*, vaſſal of dread and deſpair,
Unworthy of the common breathed air;
Why liveſt thou, dead dog, a longer day,
And doſt not unto death thyſelf prepare? *Fairy Queen, b.* ii.

'Tis not impoſſible
But one, the wicked'ſt *caitiff* on the ground,
May ſeem as ſhy, as grave, as juſt, as abſolute,
As Angelo. *Shakeſp. Meaſure for Meaſure.*

The wretched *caitiff*, all alone,
As he believ'd, began to moan,
And tell his ſtory to himſelf. *Hudibras, p.* iii. *c.* iii.

CAKE. *n. ſ.* [*cuch*, Teutonick.]

1. A kind of delicate bread.

You muſt be ſeeing chriſtnings? do you look for ale and *cakes* here, you rude raſcals? *Shakeſp. Henry* VIII.

My *cake* is dough, but I'll in among the reſt,
Out of hope of all, but my ſhare of the feaſt.
Shakeſp. Taming of the Shrew.

The diſmal day was come, the prieſts prepare
Their leaven'd *cakes*, and fillets for my hair. *Dryden's Æn.*

2. Any thing of a form rather flat than high; by which it is ſometimes diſtinguiſhed from a loaf.

There is a *cake* that groweth upon the ſide of a dead tree, that hath gotten no name, but it is large and of a cheſnut colour, and hard and pithy. *Bacon's Nat. Hiſt.* N° 552.

Then when the fleecy ſkies new cloath the wood,
And *cakes* of ruſtling ice come rolling down the flood.
Dryden's Virgil, Georg. i. *l.* 418.

To CAKE. *v. n.* [from the noun.] To harden, as dough in the oven.

This burning matter, as it ſunk very leiſurely, had time to *cake* together, and form the bottom, which covers the mouth of that dreadful vault that lies underneath it. *Addiſon on Italy.*

This is that very Mab,
That plats the manes of horſes in the night,
And *cakes* the elflocks in foul ſluttiſh hairs,
Which, once entangl'd, much misfortune bodes. *Shakeſp.*

He rins'd the wound,
And waſh'd away the ſtrings and clotted blood,
That *cak'd* within. *Addiſon.*

CALABA'SH *Tree.*

It hath a flower conſiſting of one leaf, divided at the brim into ſeveral parts; from whoſe cup riſes the pointal, in the hinder part of the flower; which afterwards becomes a fleſhy fruit, having an hard ſhell. They riſe to the height of twenty-five or thirty feet in the Weſt Indies, where they grow naturally in woods, and the ſavannas. The ſhells are uſed by the negroes for cups, as alſo for making inſtruments of muſick, by making a hole in the ſhell, and putting in ſmall ſtones, with which they make a ſort of rattle. *Miller.*

CALAMA'NCO. *n. ſ.* [a word derived, probably by ſome accident, from *calamancus*, Lat. which, in the middle ages, ſignified a hat.] A kind of woollen ſtuff.

He was of a bulk and ſtature larger than ordinary, had a red coat, flung open to ſhew a *calamanco* waiſtcoat. *Tatler*, N° 96.

CA'LAMINE, or *Lapis Calaminaris. n. ſ.* A kind of foſſile bituminous earth, which, being mixed with copper, changes it into braſs; it is dug in barren rocky ground, and is often found in lead mines, or has lead mixed with it. It is uſed as an abſorbent and drier, in outward medicinal applications, but is ſeldom given inwardly.

We muſt not omit thoſe, which, though not of ſo much beauty, yet are of greater uſe, *viz.* loadſtones, whetſtones of all kinds, limeſtones, *calamine*, or *lapis calaminaris*. *Locke.*

CA'LAMINT. *n. ſ.* [*calamintha*, Lat.] The name of a plant.

It hath a long tubulous flower, which opens at the top into two lips; the upper lip is roundiſh, and divided into two ſegments: theſe flowers are produced from the joints of the ſtalks, at the footſtalks of the leaves, in bunches, upon pretty long pedicles, or footſtalks. This plant grows wild, and is uſed in medicine. *Miller.*

CALA'MITOUS. *adj.* [*calamitoſus*, Lat.]

1. Miſerable; involved in diſtreſs; oppreſſed with infelicity; unhappy; wretched; applied to men.

This is a gracious proviſion God Almighty hath made in favour of the neceſſitous and *calamitous*; the ſtate of ſome, in this life, being ſo extremely wretched and deplorable, if compared with others. *Calamy.*

2. Full of miſery; diſtreſſful; applied to external circumſtances.

What *calamitous* effects the air of this city wrought upon us the laſt year, you may read in my diſcourſe of the plague.
Harvey on Conſumptions.

Strict neceſſity
Subdues me, and *calamitous* conſtraint!
Leſt on my head both ſin and puniſhment,
However inſupportable, be all
Devolv'd. *Milton's Paradiſe Loſt, b.* x. *l.* 132.

Much rather I ſhall chuſe
To live the pooreſt in my tribe, than richeſt,
And be in that *calamitous* priſon left. *Milton's Agoniſtes.*

In this ſad and *calamitous* condition, deliverance from an oppreſſour would have even revived them. *South.*

CALA'MITOUSNESS. *n. ſ.* [from *calamitous*.] Miſery; diſtreſs.

CALA'MITY. *n. ſ.* [*calamitas*, Lat.] Misfortune; cauſe of miſery; diſtreſs.

Another ill accident is drought, and the ſpindling of the corn, which with us is rare, but in hotter countries common; inſomuch as the word *calamity* was firſt derived from *calamus*, when the corn could not get out of the ſtalk. *Bacon's Nat. Hiſt.*

Which infinite *calamity* ſhall cauſe
To human life, and houſhold peace confound. *Par. L. b.* x.

From adverse shores in safety let her hear
Foreign *calamity*, and distant war;
Of which, great heav'n, let her no portion bear. *Prior.*

CA'LAMUS. *n. s.* [Lat.] A sort of reed or sweet scented wood, mentioned in scripture with the other ingredients of the sacred perfumes. It is a knotty root, reddish without, and white within, which puts forth long and narrow leaves, and brought from the Indies. The prophets speak of it as a foreign commodity of great value. These sweet reeds have no smell when they are green, but when they are dry only. Their form differs not from other reeds, and their smell is perceived upon entering the marshes. *Calmet.*

Take thou also unto thee principal spices of pure myrrh, of sweet cinnamon, and of sweet *calamus*. *Exodus*, xxx. 23.

CALA'SH. *n. s.* [*caleche*, Fr.] A small carriage of pleasure.

Daniel, a sprightly swain, that us'd to slash
The vig'rous steeds, that drew his lord's *calash*. *King's Mully of Mountown.*

The ancients used *calashes*, the figures of several of them being to be seen on ancient monuments. They are very simple, light, and drove by the traveller himself. *Arbuthnot on Coins.*

CA'LCEATED. *adj.* [*calceatus*, Lat.] Shod; fitted with shoes.

CALCEDO'NIUS. *n. s.* [Lat.] A kind of precious stone.

Calcedonius is of the agat kind, and of a misty grey, clouded with blue, or with purple. *Woodward on Fossils.*

To CA'LCINATE. See To CALCINE.

CALCINA'TION. *n. s.* [from *calcine*; *calcination*, Fr.] Such a management of bodies by fire, as renders them reducible to powder; wherefore it is called chymical pulverization. This is the next degree of the power of fire beyond that of fusion; for when fusion is longer continued, not only the more subtile particles of the body itself fly off, but the particles of fire likewise insinuate themselves in such multitudes, and are so blended through its whole substance, that the fluidity, first caused by the fire, can no longer subsist. From this union arises a third kind of body, which, being very porous and brittle, is easily reduced to powder; for, the fire having penetrated everywhere into the pores of the body, the particles are both hindered from mutual contact, and divided into minute atoms. *Quincy.*

Divers residences of bodies are wont to be thrown away, as soon as the distillation or *calcination* of the body that yielded them is ended. *Boyle.*

This may be effected, but not without a *calcination*, or reducing it by art into a subtile powder. *Brown's Vulgar Err.*

CALCI'NATORY. *n. s.* [from *calcinate*.] A vessel used in calcination.

To CALCI'NE. *v. a.* [*calciner*, Fr. from *calx*, Lat.]

1. To burn in the fire to a calx, or friable substance. See CALCINATION.

In hardening, by baking without melting, the heat hath these degrees; first, it indurateth, then maketh fragile, and, lastly, it doth *calcinate*. *Bacon's Nat. Hist.* N° 87.

The solids seem to be earth, bound together with some oil; for if a bone be *calcined*, so as the least force will crumble it, being immersed in oil, it will grow firm again. *Arbuthnot on Aliments.*

2. To burn up.

Firy disputes that union have *calcin'd*,
Almost as many minds as men we find. *Denham.*

To CALCI'NE. *v. n.* To become a calx by heat.

This crystal is a pellucid fissile stone, clear as water, and without colour, enduring a red heat without losing its transparency, and, in a very strong heat, *calcining* without fusion. *Newton's Opticks.*

To CA'LCULATE. *v. a.* [*calculer*, Fr. from *calculus*, Lat. a little stone or bead, used in operations of numbers.]

1. To compute; to reckon.

2. To compute the situation of the planets at any certain time.

A cunning man did *calculate* my birth,
And told me, that by water I should die. *Shakesp. Hen.* VI.

Why all these fires, why all these gliding ghosts,
Why old men fools, and children *calculate*,
Why all those things change from their ordinance? *Shakesp. Julius Cæsar.*

Who were there then in the world, to observe the births of those first men, and *calculate* their nativities, as they sprawled out of ditches? *Bentley.*

3. To adjust; to project for any certain end.

The reasonableness of religion clearly appears, as it tends so directly to the happiness of men, and is, upon all accounts, *calculated* for our benefit. *Tillotson.*

CALCULA'TION. *n. s.* [from *calculate*.]

1. A practice, or manner of reckoning; the art of numbering.

Cypher, that great friend to *calculation*; or rather, which changeth *calculation*, into easy computation. *Holder on Time.*

2. A reckoning; the result of arithmetical operation.

If then their *calculation* be true; for so they reckon. *Hooker.*

Being different from *calculations* of the ancients, their observations confirm not ours. *Brown's Vulgar Errours.*

CALCULA'TOR. *n. s.* [from *calculate*.] A computer; a reckoner.

CA'LCULATORY. *adj.* [from *calculate*.] Belonging to calculation.

CA'LCULE. *n. s.* [*calculus*, Lat.] Reckoning; compute.

The general *calcule*, which was made in the last perambulation, exceeded eight millions. *Howel's Vocal Forest.*

CA'LCULOSE. } *adj.* [from *calculus*, Lat.] Stony; gritty.
CA'LCULOUS. }

The volatile salt of urine will coagulate spirits of wine; and thus, perhaps, the stones, or *calculose* concretions in the kidney or bladder, may be produced. *Brown's Vulgar Err.*

I have found, by opening the kidneys of a *calculous* person, that the stone is formed earlier than I have suggested. *Sharp.*

CA'LCULUS. *n. s.* [Latin.] The stone in the bladder.

CA'LDRON. *n. s.* [*chauldron*, Fr. from *calidus*, Lat.] A pot; boiler; a kettle.

In the midst of all
There placed was a *caldron* wide and tall,
Upon a mighty furnace, burning hot. *Fairy Queen, b.* ii.

Some strip the skin, some portion out the spoil;
The limbs, yet trembling, in the *caldrons* boil;
Some on the fire the reeking entrails broil. *Dryden's Æn.*

In the late eruptions, this great hollow was like a vast *caldron*, filled with glowing and melted matter, which, as it boiled over in any part, ran down the sides of the mountain. *Addison's Remarks on Italy.*

CALECHE. See CALASH.

CALEFA'CTION. *n. s.* [from *calefacio*, Lat.]

1. The act of heating any thing.

2. The state of being heated.

CALEFA'CTIVE. *adj.* [from *calefacio*, Lat.] That which makes any thing hot; heating.

CALEFA'CTORY. *adj.* [from *calefacio*, Lat.] That which heats.

To CA'LEFY. *v. n.* [*calesio*, Latin.] To grow hot; to be heated.

Crystal will *calefy* unto electricity; that is, a power to attract straws, or light bodies, and convert the needle, freely placed. *Brown's Vulgar Errours, b.* ii *c.* 1.

CA'LENDAR. *n. s.* [*calendarium*, Lat.] A register of the year, in which the months, and stated times, are marked, as festivals and holidays.

What hath this day deserv'd? what hath it done,
That it in golden letter should be set
Among the high tides, in the *calendar*? *Shakesp. K. John.*

We compute from *calendars* differing from one another; the compute of the one anticipating that of the other. *Brown's Vulgar Errours, b.* iv. *c.* 12.

Curs'd be the day when first I did appear;
Let it be blotted from the *calendar*,
Lest it pollute the month. *Dryden's Fab.*

To CA'LENDER. *v. a.* [*calendrer*, Fr. *Skinner*.] To dress cloth; to lay the nap of cloth smooth.

CA'LENDER. *n. s.* [from the verb.] A hot press; a press in which clothiers smooth their cloth.

CA'LENDRER. *n. s.* [from *calender*.] The person who calenders.

CA'LENDS. *n. s.* [*calendæ*, Lat. It has no *singular*.] The first day of every month among the Romans.

CA'LENTURE. *n. s.* [from *caleo*, Lat.] A distemper peculiar to sailors, in hot climates; wherein they imagine the sea to be green fields, and will throw themselves into it, if not restrained. *Quincy.*

And for that lethargy was there no cure,
But to be cast into a *calenture*. *Denham.*

So, by a *calenture* misled,
The mariner with rapture sees,
On the smooth ocean's azure bed,
Enamell'd fields, and verdant trees;
With eager haste, he longs to rove
In that fantastick scene, and thinks
It must be some enchanted grove;
And in he leaps, and down he sinks. *Swift.*

CALF. *n. s.* *calves* in the *plural*. [cealf, Saxon; *kalf*, Dutch.]

1. The young of a cow.

The colt hath about four years of growth; and so the fawn, and so the *calf*. *Bacon's Nat. Hist.* N° 759.

Acosta tells us of a fowl in Peru, called condores, which will, of themselves, kill and eat up a whole *calf* at a time. *Wilkins's Mathematical Magick.*

Ah! Blouzelind, I love thee more by half,
Than does their fawns, or cows the new-fall'n *calf*. *Gay.*

2. *Calves* of the lips, mentioned by Hosea, signify sacrifices of praise and prayers, which the captives of Babylon addressed to God, being no longer in a condition to offer sacrifices in his temple. *Calmet.*

Take with you words, and turn to the Lord, and say unto him, Take away all iniquity, and receive us graciously: so will we render the *calves* of our lips. *Hosea*, xiv. 2.

3. The thick, plump, bulbous part of the leg. [*kalf*, Dutch.]

Into her legs I'd have love's issues fall,
And all her *calf* into a gouty small. *Suckling.*

The *calf* of that leg blistered. *Wiseman's Surgery.*

CA'LIBER. *n. s.* [*calibre*, Fr.] The bore; the diameter of the barrel of a gun; the diameter of a bullet.

CA'LICE. *n. s.* [*calix*, Lat.] A cup; a chalice.

There is a natural analogy between the ablution of the body

and

and the purification of the soul; between eating the holy bread and drinking the sacred *calice*, and a participation of the body and blood of Christ. *Taylor.*

CA'LICO. *n. s.* [from *Calecut* in India.] An Indian stuff made of cotton; sometimes stained with gay and beautiful colours.

I wear the hoop petticoat, and am all in *calicoes*, when the finest are in silks. *Addison. Spect.* N° 293.

CA'LID. *adj.* [*calidus*, Lat.] Hot; burning; fervent.

CALI'DITY. *n. s.* [from *calid.*] Heat.

Ice will dissolve in any way of heat; for it will dissolve with fire, it will colliquate in water, or warm oil; nor doth it only submit unto an actual heat, but not endure the potential *calidity* of many waters. *Brown's Vulgar Errours, b.* ii. *c.* 1.

CA'LIF. } *n. s.* [*khalifa*, Arab. an heir or successor.] A title as-
CA'LIPH. } sumed by the successors of Mahomet among the Saracens, who were vested with absolute power in affairs, both religious and civil.

CALIGA'TION. *n. s.* [from *caligo*, Lat. to be dark.] Darkness; cloudiness.

Instead of a diminution, or imperfect vision, in the mole, we affirm an abolition, or total privation; instead of *caligation*, or dimness, we conclude a cecity, or blindness. *Brown's Vulg. Err.*

CALI'GINOUS. *adj.* [*caliginosus*, Lat.] Obscure; dim; full of darkness.

CALI'GINOUSNESS. *n. s.* [from *caliginous.*] Darkness; obscurity.

CA'LIGRAPHY. *n. s.* [καλλιγραφία.] Beautiful writing.

This language is incapable of *caligraphy*. *Prideaux's Conn.*

CA'LIPERS. See CALLIPERS.

CA'LIVER. *n. s.* [from *caliber.*] A handgun; a harquebuse; an old musket.

Come, manage me your *caliver*. *Shakesp. Henry* IV. *p.* ii.

CA'LIX. *n. s.* [Latin.] A cup; a word used in botany; as, the *calix* of a flower.

To CALK. *v. a.* [from *calage*, Fr. hemp, with which leaks are stopped; or from cæle, Sax. the keel. *Skinner.*] To stop the leaks of a ship.

There is a great errour committed in the manner of *calking* his majesty's ships; which being done with rotten oakum, is the cause they are leaky. *Raleigh's Essays.*

So here some pick out bullets from the side;
Some drive old oakum through each seam and rift;
Their left-hand does the *calking* iron guide,
The rattling mallet with the left they lift. *Dryden.*

CA'LKER. *n. s.* [from *calk.*] The workman that stops the leaks of a ship.

The ancients of Gebal, and the wise men thereof, were in thee thy *calkers*; all the ships of the sea, with their mariners, were in thee to occupy thy merchandize. *Ezek.* xxvii. 9.

CA'LKING. *n. s.* A term in painting, used where the backside is covered with black lead, or red chalk, and the lines traced through on a waxed plate, wall, or other matter, by passing lightly over each stroke of the design with a point, which leaves an impression of the colour on the plate or wall. *Chambers.*

To CALL. *v. a.* [*calo*, Lat. *kalder*, Danish.]

1. To name; to denominate.

And God *called* the light day, and the darkness he *called* night. *Gen.* i. 5.

2. To summon, or invite, to or from any place, thing, or person.

Be not amazed, *call* all your senses to you, defend my reputation, or bid farewel to your good life for ever. *Shakesp. Merry Wives of Windsor.*

Why came not the slave back to me, when I *called* him? *Shakesp. King Lear.*

Are you *call'd* forth from out a world of men,
To slay the innocent? *Shakesp. Richard* III.

Lodronius, that famous captain, was *called* up, and told by his servants, that the general was fled. *Knolles's Hist.*

Or *call* up him, that left half told
The story of Cambuscan bold. *Milton.*

Drunkenness *calls* off the watchmen from their towers; and then evils proceed from a loose heart, and an untied tongue. *Taylor's Holy Living.*

The soul makes use of her memory, to *call* to mind what she is to treat of. *Duppa's Rules to Devotion.*

Such fine employments our whole days divide,
The salutations of the morning tide
Call up the sun; those ended, to the hall
We wait the patron, hear the lawyers bawl. *Dryden.*

Then, by consent, abstain from further spoils,
Call off the dogs, and gather up the spoils. *Addison.*

By the pleasures of the imagination or fancy, I mean such as arise from visible objects, when we *call* up their ideas into our minds by paintings, statues, or descriptions. *Addison. Spectator.*

Why dost thou *call* my sorrows up afresh!
My father's name brings tears into my eyes. *Addis. Cato.*

I am *called* off from publick dissertations, by a domestick affair of great importance. *Tatler,* N° 50.

Æschylus has a tragedy, entitled *Persæ*, in which the shade of Darius is *called* up. *Broome's Notes on the Odyssey.*

The passions *call* away the thoughts, with incessant importunity, toward the object that excited them. *Watts.*

3. To convoke; to summon together.

Now *call* we our high court of parliament. *Shakesp.*

The king being informed of much that had passed that night, sent to the lord mayor to *call* a common council immediately. *Clarendon.*

4. To summon judicially.

The king had sent for the earl to return home, where he should be *called* to account for all his miscarriages. *Clarendon.*

Once a day, especially in the early years of life and study, *call* yourselves to an account, what new ideas, what new proposition or truth, you have gained. *Watts.*

5. To summon by command.

In that day did the Lord God of hosts *call* to weeping, and to mourning, and to baldness, and to girding with sackcloth. *Isaiah*, xxii. 12.

6. In the theological sense, to inspire with ardours of piety; or to summon into the church.

Paul a servant of Jesus Christ, *called* to be an apostle, separated unto the gospel of God. *Rom.* i. 1.

7. To invoke; to appeal to.

I *call* God for a record upon my soul, that, to spare you, I came not as yet unto Corinth. 2 *Cor.* i. 23.

When that lord perplexed their counsels and designs, with inconvenient objections in law, the authority of the lord Manchester, who had trod the same paths, was still *called* upon. *Clarendon.*

8. To proclaim; to publish.

Nor ballad-singer, plac'd above the croud,
Sings with a note so shrilling, sweet, and loud,
Nor parish-clerk, who *calls* the psalm so clear. *Gay.*

9. To make a short visit.

And, as you go, *call* on my brother Quintus,
And pray him, with the tribunes, to come to me. *Ben. Johnson's Catiline.*

He ordered her to *call* at his house once a week, which she did for some time after, when he heard no more of her. *Temple.*

That I might begin as near the fountain-head as possible, I first of all *called* in at St. James's. *Addison. Spect.* N° 403.

We *called* in at Morge, where there is an artificial port. *Addison on Italy.*

10. To excite; to put in action; to bring into view.

He swells with angry pride,
And *calls* forth all his spots on every side. *Cowley.*

See Dionysius Homer's thoughts refine,
And *call* new beauties forth from ev'ry line. *Pope.*

11. To stigmatize with some opprobrious denomination.

Deafness unqualifies men for all company, except friends; whom I can *call* names, if they do not speak loud enough. *Swift to Pope.*

12. *To call back.* To revoke; to retract.

He also is wise, and will bring evil, and will not *call back* his words; but will arise against the house of the evil doers, and against the help of them that work iniquity. *Isaiah*, xxxi. 2.

13. *To call for.* To demand; to require; to claim.

Madam, his majesty doth *call for* you,
And *for* your grace, and you, my noble lord. *Shakesp.*

You see, how men of merit are sought after; the undeserver may sleep, when the man of action is *called for*. *Shakesp.*

Among them he a spirit of phrensy sent,
Who hurt their minds,
And urg'd you on, with mad desire,
To *call* in haste *for* their destroyer. *Milton's Agonistes.*

For master, or *for* servant, here to *call*,
Was all alike, where only two were all. *Dryden's Fab.*

He commits every sin that his appetite *calls for*, or perhaps his constitution or fortune can bear. *Rogers.*

14. *To call in.* To resume money at interest.

Horace describes an old usurer, as so charmed with the pleasures of a country life, that, in order to make a purchase, he *called in* all his money; but what was the event of it? why, in a very few days after, he put it out again. *Addison. Spectator.*

15. *To call in.* To resume any thing that is in other hands.

If clipped money be *called in* all at once, and stopped from passing by weight, I fear it will stop trade, and put our affairs all at a stand. *Locke.*

Neither is any thing more cruel and oppressive in the French government, than their practice of *calling in* their money, after they have sunk it very low, and then coining it anew, at a higher value. *Swift.*

16. *To call in.* To summon together; to invite.

The heat is past, follow me no farther now;
Call in the pow'rs, good cousin, Westmoreland. *Shakesp.*

He fears my subjects loyalty,
And now must *call in* strangers. *Denham's Sophy.*

17. *To call on.* To solicite for a favour, or a debt.

I would be loth to pay him before his day; what need I be so forward with him, that *calls* not *on* me? *Shakesp. Henry* IV.

18. *To call on.* To repeat solemnly.

Thrice *call upon* my name, thrice beat your breast,
And hail me thrice to everlasting rest. *Dryden.*

The Athenians, when they lost any men at sea, went to the shores,

ſhores, and, calling thrice on their names, raiſed a cenotaph, or empty monument, to their memories. *Broome on the Odyſſ.*

19. *To call over.* To read aloud a liſt or muſter-roll.

20. *To call out.* To challenge; to ſummon to fight.

When their ſov'reign's quarrel *calls* 'em *out*,
His foes to mortal combat they defy. *Dryden's Virgil.*

21. *To call upon.* To implore; to pray to.

Call upon me in the day of trouble; I will deliver thee, and thou ſhalt glorify me. *Pſalm* i. 15.

CALL. *n. ſ.* [from the verb.]

1. A vocal addreſs.

But would you ſing, and rival Orpheus' ſtrain,
The wond'ring foreſts ſoon ſhould dance again:
The moving mountains hear the pow'rful *call*,
And headlong ſtreams hang liſt'ning in their fall. *Pope.*

2. Requiſition.

It may be feared, whether our nobility would contentedly ſuffer themſelves to be always at the *call*, and to ſtand to the ſentence of a number of mean perſons. *Hooker, Preface.*

But death comes not at *call*; juſtice divine
Mends not her ſloweſt pace, for pray'rs or cries. *Par. Loſt.*

3. Divine vocation; ſummons to true religion.

Yet he at length, time to himſelf beſt known,
Rememb'ring Abraham, by ſome wond'rous *call*,
May bring them back repentant and ſincere. *Par. Regained.*

St. Paul himſelf believed he did well, and that he had a *call* to it, when he perſecuted the chriſtians, whom he confidently thought in the wrong: but yet it was he, and not they, who were miſtaken. *Locke.*

4. A ſummons from heaven; an impulſe.

How juſtly then will impious mortals fall,
Whoſe pride would ſoar to heav'n without a *call?* *Roſcomm.*
Thoſe who to empire by dark paths aſpire,
Still plead a *call* to what they moſt deſire. *Dryden.*

5. Authority; command.

Oh! Sir, I wiſh he were within my *call*, or your's. *Denh.*

6. A demand; a claim.

Dependence is a perpetual *call* upon humanity, and a greater incitement to tenderneſs and pity, than any other motive whatſoever. *Addiſon. Spectator*, N° 181.

7. An inſtrument to call birds.

For thoſe birds or beaſts were made from ſuch pipes or *calls*, as may expreſs the ſeveral tones of thoſe creatures, which are repreſented. *Wilkins's Mathemat. Magick.*

8. Calling; vocation; employment.

Now, through the land, his cure of ſouls he ſtretch'd,
And, like a primitive apoſtle, preach'd:
Still chearful, ever conſtant to his *call*;
By many follow'd, lov'd by moſt, admir'd by all. *Dryden.*

9. A nomination.

Upon the ſixteenth was held the ſerjeants feaſt at Ely place, there being nine ſerjeants of that *call.* *Bacon's Henry* VII.

CA'LLAT. } *n. ſ.* A trull.
CA'LLET. }

He call'd her whore; a beggar, in his drink,
Could not have laid ſuch terms upon his *callet.* *Shakeſp.*

CA'LLING. *n. ſ.* [from *call.*]

1. Vocation; profeſſion; trade.

If God has interwoven ſuch a pleaſure with our ordinary *calling*, how much ſuperiour muſt that be, which ariſes from the ſurvey of a pious life? Surely, as much as chriſtianity is nobler than a trade. *South.*

We find ourſelves obliged to go on in honeſt induſtry in our *callings.* *Rogers.*

I cannot forbear warning you againſt endeavouring at wit in your ſermons; becauſe many of your *calling* have made themſelves ridiculous by attempting it. *Swift.*

I left no *calling* for this idle trade,
No duty broke, no father diſobey'd. *Pope.*

2. Proper ſtation, or employment.

The Gauls found the Roman ſenators ready to die with honour in their *callings.* *Swift.*

3. Claſs of perſons united by the ſame employment or profeſſion.

It may be a caution to all chriſtian churches and magiſtrates, not to impoſe celibacy on whole *callings*, and great multitudes of men or women, who cannot be ſuppoſable to have the gift of continence. *Hammond.*

4. Divine vocation; invitation or impulſe to the true religion.

St. Peter was ignorant of the *calling* of the Gentiles. *Hakewell on Providence.*

CA'LLIPERS. *n. ſ.* [of this word I know not the etymology, nor does any thing more probable occur, than that, perhaps, the word is corrupted from *clippers*, inſtruments with which any thing is *clipped*, incloſed or embraced.] Compaſſes with bowed ſhanks.

Callipers meaſure the diſtance of any round, cylindrick, conical body, either in their extremity, or any part leſs than the extreme; ſo that, when workmen uſe them, they open the two points to their deſcribed width, and turn ſo much ſtuff off the intended place, till the two points of the *callipers* fit juſt over their work. *Moxon's Mechanical Exerciſes.*

CALLO'SITY. *n. ſ.* [*calloſité*, Fr.] A kind of ſwelling without pain, like that of the ſkin, by hard labour; and therefore, when wounds, or the edges of ulcers, grow ſo, they are ſaid to be callous. *Quincy.*

The ſurgeon ought to vary the diet of his patient, as he finds the fibres looſen too much, are too flaccid, and produce funguſes, or as they harden and produce *calloſities*; in the firſt caſe, wine and ſpirituous liquours are uſeful, in the laſt hurtful. *Arbuthnot on Diet.*

CA'LLOUS. *adj.* [*callus*, Lat.]

1. Indurated; hardned; having the pores ſhut up.

In progreſs of time, the ulcers became ſinuous and *callous*, with induration of the glands. *Wiſeman's Surgery.*

2. Hardned; inſenſible.

Licentiouſneſs has ſo long paſſed for ſharpneſs of wit, and greatneſs of mind, that the conſcience is grown *callous. L'Eſtr.*

The wretch is drench'd too deep,
His ſoul is ſtupid, and his heart aſleep:
Fatten'd in vice, ſo *callous* and ſo groſs,
He ſins, and ſees not, ſenſeleſs of his loſs. *Dryden's Perſius.*

CA'LLOUSNESS. *n. ſ.* [from *callous.*]

1. Hardneſs; induration of the fibres.

The oftner we uſe the organs of touching, the more of theſe ſcales are formed, and the ſkin becomes the thicker, and ſo a *callouſneſs* grows upon it. *Cheyne's Philoſoph. Principles.*

2. Inſenſibility.

If they let go their hope of everlaſting life with willingneſs, and entertain final perdition with exultation, ought they not to be eſteemed deſtitute of common ſenſe, and abandoned to a *callouſneſs* and numbneſs of ſoul? *Bentley.*

CA'LLOW. *adj.* Unfledged; naked; without feathers.

Burſting with kindly rapture, forth diſclos'd
Their *callow* young. *Paradiſe Loſt, b.* vii. *l.* 420.
Then as an eagle, who, with pious care,
Was beating widely on the wing for prey,
To her now ſilent airy does repair,
And finds her *callow* infants forc'd away. *Dryden.*
How in ſmall flights they know to try their young,
And teach the *callow* child her parent's ſong. *Prior.*

CA'LLUS. *n. ſ.* [Latin.]

1. An induration of the fibres.

2. The hard ſubſtance by which broken bones are united.

CALM. *adj.* [*calme*, Fr. *kalm*, Dutch.]

1. Quiet; ſerene; not ſtormy; not tempeſtuous; applied to the elements.

Calm was the day, and, through the trembling air,
Sweet breathing Zephyrus did ſoftly play
A gentle ſpirit, that lightly did allay
Hot Titan's beams, which then did gliſter fair. *Spenſer.*

2. Undiſturb'd; unruffled; applied to the paſſions.

It is no ways congruous, that God ſhould be frightning men into truth, who were made to be wrought upon by *calm* evidence, and gentle methods of perſuaſion. *Atterbury.*

The queen her ſpeech with *calm* attention hears,
Her eyes reſtrain the ſilver-ſtreaming tears. *Pope's Odyſſey:*

CALM. *n. ſ.*

1. Serenity; ſtillneſs; freedom from violent motion.

It ſeemeth moſt agreeable to reaſon, that the waters rather ſtood in a quiet *calm*, than that they moved with any raging or overbearing violence. *Raleigh's Hiſtory of the World.*

Every pilot
Can ſteer the ſhip in *calms*; but he performs
The ſkilful part, can manage it in ſtorms. *Denham's Sophy.*
Nor God alone in the ſtill *calm* we find,
He mounts the ſtorm, and walks upon the wind. *Pope.*

2. Freedom from diſturbance; quiet; repoſe; applied to the paſſions.

Great and ſtrange *calms* uſually portend the moſt violent ſtorms: and therefore, ſince ſtorms and *calms* do always follow one another, certainly, of the two, it is much more eligible to have the ſtorm firſt, and the *calm* afterwards: ſince a *calm* before a ſtorm is commonly a peace of a man's own making; but a *calm* after a ſtorm, a peace of God's. *South.*

To CALM. *v. a.* [from the noun.]

1. To ſtill; to quiet.

Neptune we find buſy in the beginning of the Æneis, to *calm* the tempeſt raiſed by Æolus. *Dryden.*

2. To pacify; to appeaſe.

Jeſus, whoſe bare word checked the ſea, as much exerts himſelf in ſilencing the tempeſts, and *calming* the inteſtine ſtorms within our breaſts. *Decay of Piety.*

Thoſe paſſions, which ſeem ſomewhat *calmed*, may be entirely laid aſleep, and never more awakened. *Atterbury.*

He will'd to ſtay,
The ſacred rites and hecatombs to pay,
And *calm* Minerva's wrath. *Pope's Odyſſey, b.* iii. *l.* 175.

CA'LMER. *n. ſ.* [from *calm.*] The perſon or thing which has the power of giving quiet.

Angling was, after tedious ſtudy, a reſt to his mind, a cheerer of his ſpirits, a diverter of ſadneſs, a *calmer* of unquiet thoughts, a moderator of paſſions, a procurer of contentedneſs. *Walton.*

CA'LMLY. *adv.* [from *calm.*]

1. Without ſtorms, or violence; ſerenity.

In nature, things move violently to their place, and *calmly* in their place; ſo virtue in ambition is violent, in authority ſetled and calm. *Bacon's Eſſays*, Nº 11.

His curled brows
Frown on the gentle ſtream, which *calmly* flows. *Denham.*

2. Without paſſions; quietly.

The nymph did like the ſcene appear,
Serenely pleaſant, *calmly* fair;
Soft fell her words, as flew the air. *Prior.*

CA'LMNESS. *n. ſ.* [from *calm.*]

1. Tranquillity; ſerenity.

While the ſteep horrid roughneſs of the wood
Strives with the gentle *calmneſs* of the flood. *Denham.*

2. Mildneſs; freedom from paſſion.

I've been i' th' market-place, and, Sir, 'tis fit
You have ſtrong party, or defend yourſelf
By *calmneſs*, or by abſence: all's in anger. *Shakeſp. Coriol.*

I beg the grace,
You would lay by thoſe terrours of your face;
Till *calmneſs* to your eyes you firſt reſtore,
I am afraid, and I can beg no more. *Dryden's Conq. of Gran.*

CA'LMY. *adj.* [from *calm.*] Calm; peaceful.

And now they nigh approached to the ſted,
Where as thoſe mermaides dwelt: it was a ſtill
And *calmy* bay, on th' one ſide ſheltered
With the broad ſhadow of an hoary hill. *Fairy Queen, b.* ii.

CA'LOMEL. *n ſ.* [*calomelas*, a chymical word.] Mercury ſix times ſublimed.

He repeated lenient purgatives with *calomel*, once in three or four days. *Wiſeman's Surgery.*

CALORI'FICK. *adj.* [*calorificus*, Lat.] That which has the quality of producing heat; heating.

Calorifick principle is either excited within the heated body, or transferred to it, through any medium, from ſome other. Silver will grow hotter than the liquour it contains.
Grew's Coſmologia Sacra, b. i. *c.* 2. § 9.

CALO'TTE. n. ſ. [French.]

1. A cap or coif, worn as an eccleſiaſtical ornament in France.

2. [In architecture.] A round cavity or depreſſure, in form of a cap or cup, lathed and plaiſtered, uſed to diminiſh the riſe or elevation of a moderate chapel, cabinet, alcove, *&c.* *Harris.*

CALO'YERS. n. ſ. [καλὸς] Monks of the Greek church.

CA'LTROPS. *n. ſ.* [colꞇꞃæppe, Saxon.]

1. An inſtrument made with three ſpikes, ſo that which way ſoever it falls to the ground, one of them points upright, to wound horſes feet.

The ground about was thick ſown with *caltrops*, which very much incommoded the ſhoeleſs Moors.
Dr. Addiſon's Account of Tangiers.

2. A plant.

It is very common in the South of France, Spain, and Italy, where it grows among corn, and on moſt of the arable land, and is very troubleſome to the feet of cattle; for the fruit being armed with ſtrong prickles, run into the feet of the cattle, which walk over the land. This is certainly the plant which is mentioned in Virgil's Georgick, under the name of *tribulus*.
Miller.

To CALVE. *v. n.* [from *calf.*]

1. To bring a calf; ſpoken of a cow.

When ſhe has *calv'd*, then ſet the dam aſide,
And for the tender progeny provide. *Dryden's Virgil.*

2. It is uſed metaphorically for any act of bringing forth; and ſometimes of men, by way of reproach.

I would they were barbarians, as they are,
Though in Rome litter'd; not Romans: as they are not;
Though *calved* in the porch o' th' capitol. *Shakeſp. Coriolan.*

The graſſy clods now *calv'd*, now half appear'd
The tawny lion, pawing to get free
His hinder parts. *Paradiſe Loſt, b.* vii. *l.* 463.

CALVES-SNOUT. See SNAPDRAGON.

CALVI'LLE. n. ſ. [French.] A ſort of apple. See APPLE.

To CALU'MNIATE. *v. n.* [*calumnior*, Lat.] To accuſe falſely; to charge without juſt ground.

Beauty, wit, high birth, deſert in ſervice,
Love, friendſhip, charity, are ſubject all
To envious and *calumniating* time. *Shakeſp. Tr. and Creſſ.*

He mixes truth with falſehood, and has not forgotten the old rule of *calumniating* ſtrongly, that ſomething may remain.
Dryden's Fables, Preface.

Do I *calumniate*! thou ungrateful Vanoc!—
Perfidious prince!—Is it a calumny
To ſay, that Gwendolen betroth'd to Yver,
Was by her father firſt aſſur'd to Valens? *A. Philips, Brit.*

To CALU'MNIATE. *v. a.* To ſlander.

One trade or art, even thoſe that ſhould be the moſt liberal, ſhall make it their buſineſs to diſdain and *calumniate* another.
Sprat.

CALUMNIA'TION. *n. ſ.* [from *calumniate.*] That which we call *calumniation*, is a malicious and falſe repreſentation of an enemy's words or actions, to an offenſive purpoſe. *Ayliffe.*

CALUMNI'ATOR. *n. ſ.* [from *calumniate.*] A forger of accuſation; a ſlanderer.

He that would live clear of the envy and hatred of potent *calumniators*, muſt lay his finger upon his mouth, and keep his hand out of the ink-pot. *L'Eſtrange.*

At the ſame time that Virgil was celebrated by Gallus, we know that Bavius and Mævius were his declared foes and *calumniators*. *Addiſon. Spectator.*

CALU'MNIOUS. *adj.* [from *calumny.*] Slanderous; falſely reproachful.

Virtue itſelf 'ſcapes not *calumnious* ſtrokes. *Shakeſp. Haml.*

With *calumnious* art
Of counterfeited truth, thus held their ears. *Par. L. b.* v.

CA'LUMNY. *n. ſ.* [*calumnia*, Lat.] Slander; falſe charge; groundleſs accuſation.

Be thou as chaſte as ice, as pure as ſnow,
Thou ſhalt not eſcape *calumny*. *Shakeſp. Hamlet.*

It is a very hard *calumny* upon our ſoil or climate, to affirm, that ſo excellent a fruit will not grow here. *Temple.*

CALX. n. ſ. [Latin.] Any thing that is rendered reducible to powder by burning.

Gold, that is more denſe than lead, reſiſts peremptorily all the dividing power of fire; and will not at all be reduced into a *calx*, or lime, by ſuch operation as reduces lead into it.
Digby on Bodies.

CA'LYCLE. *n. ſ.* [*calyculus*, Lat.] A ſmall bud of a plant. *Dict.*

CAMA'IEU. *n. ſ.* [from *camachuia*, which name is given by the orientals to the onyx, when, in preparing it, they find another colour.]

1. A ſtone with various figures and repreſentations of landſkips, formed by nature.

2. [In painting.] A term uſed where there is only one colour, and where the lights and ſhadows are of gold, wrought on a golden or azure ground. This kind of work is chiefly uſed to repreſent baſſo relievos. *Chambers.*

CA'MBER. *n. ſ.* [See CAMBERING.] A term among workmen.

Camber, a piece of timber cut arching, ſo as a weight conſiderable being ſet upon it, it may, in length of time, be induced to a ſtraight. *Moxon's Mechanical Exerciſes.*

CA'MBERING. *n. ſ.* A word mentioned by *Skinner*, as peculiar to ſhipbuilders, who ſay, that a place is *cambering*, when they mean arched. [from *chambré*, French.]

CA'MBRICK. *n. ſ.* [from *Cambray*, a city in Flanders, where it was principally made.] A kind of fine linen, uſed for ruffles, womens ſleeves and caps.

He hath ribbons of all the colours of the rainbow; inkles, caddiſes, *cambricks*, and lawns. *Shakeſp. Winter's Tale.*

Rebecca had, by the uſe of a looking-glaſs, and by the further uſe of certain attire, made of *cambrick*, upon her head, attained to an evil art. *Tatler*, Nº 110.

Confed'rate in the cheat, they draw the throng,
And *cambrick* handkerchiefs reward the ſong. *Gay's Trivia.*

CAME. The *preterite* of *to come*.

Till all the pack *came* up, and ev'ry hound
Tore the ſad huntſman, grov'ling on the ground. *Addiſon.*

CA'MEL. *n. ſ.* [*camelus*, Lat.] An animal very common in Arabia, Judea, and the neighbouring countries. One ſort is large, and full of fleſh, and fit to carry burdens of a thouſand pounds weight, having one bunch upon its back. Another have two bunches upon their backs, like a natural ſaddle, and are fit either for burdens, or men to ride on. A third kind is leaner, and of a ſmaller ſize, called dromedaries, becauſe of their ſwiftneſs; which are generally uſed for riding by men of quality. See DROMEDARY.

Camels have large ſolid feeet, but not hard; in the ſpring, their hair falls entirely off, in leſs than three days time, when the flies are extremely uneaſy to them. *Camels*, it is ſaid, will continue ten or twelve days without eating or drinking, and keep water a long time in their ſtomach, for their refreſhment. It is reported, that nature has furniſhed them, for this purpoſe, with a very large ventricle, with many bags cloſed within the coats of it, round about it, for reſerving the water. But the Jeſuits in China, where they diſſected ſeveral *camels*, found no ſuch bags. When a *camel* is upon a journey, his maſter follows him, ſinging and whiſtling; and the louder he ſings, the better the *camel* goes. The fleſh of *camels* is ſerved up at the beſt tables, among the Arabians, Perſians, and other eaſtern nations; but the uſe of it was forbid the Hebrews, they being ranked by Moſes among the unclean creatures, *Deut.* xiv. 7. *Calmet.*

Patient of thirſt and toil,
Son of the deſart! even the *camel* feels,
Shot through his wither'd heart, the firy blaſt. *Thomſon.*

CAME'LOPARD. *n. ſ.* [from *camelus* and *pardus*, Lat.] An Abyſſinian animal, taller than an elephant, but not ſo thick. He is ſo named, becauſe he has a neck and head like a camel; he is ſpotted like a pard, but his ſpots are white upon a red ground. The Italians call him *giaraffa*. *Trevoux.*

CA'MELOT. } *n. ſ.* [from *camel.*] A kind of ſtuff originally made
CA'MLET. } by a mixture of ſilk and camels hair; it is now made with wool and ſilk.

This habit was not of camels ſkin, nor any courſe texture of its hair, but rather ſome finer weave of *camelot*, grograin, or the like; in as much as theſe ſtuffs are ſuppoſed to be made of the hair of that animal. *Brown's Vulgar Errours.*

Mean-

Meantime the paſtor ſhears their hoary beards,
And eaſes, of their hair, the loaden herds:
Their *camelots* warm in tents the ſoldier hold,
And ſhield the ſhiv'ring mariner from cold. *Dryden's Virgil.*

CAME'RA OBSCURA. [Latin.] An optical machine uſed in a darkened chamber, ſo that the light coming only through a double convex glaſs, objects expoſed to daylight, and oppoſite to the glaſs, are repreſented inverted upon any white matter placed in the focus of the glaſs. *Martin.*

CA'MERADE. *n. ſ.* [from *camera*, a chamber, Lat.] One that lodges in the ſame chamber; a boſom companion. By corruption we now uſe *comrade.*

Camerades with him, and confederates in his worthy deſign, *Rymer's Tragedies of laſt Age.*

CA'MERATED. *adj.* [*cameratus*, Lat.] Arched; roofed ſlopewiſe.

CAMERA'TION. *adj.* [*cameratio*, Lat.] A vaulting or arching.

CAMISA'DO. *n. ſ.* [*camiſa*, a ſhirt, Ital. *camiſium*, low Lat.] An attack made by ſoldiers in the dark; on which occaſion they put their ſhirts outward, to be ſeen by each other.

They had appointed the ſame night, whoſe darkneſs would have encreaſed the fear, to have given a *camiſado* upon the Engliſh. *Hayward.*

CA'MISATED. *adj.* [from *camiſa*, a ſhirt.] Dreſſed with the ſhirt outward.

CA'MLET. See CAMELOT.

He had on him a gown with wide ſleeves, of a kind of water *camlet*, of an excellent azure colour. *Bacon.*

CA'MMOCK. *n. ſ.* [cammoc, Saxon.] An herb; the ſame with *petty whin*, or *reſtharrow.*

Its flower is papilionaceous, and ſucceeded by a ſwelling pod, ſometimes long, and ſometimes ſhort, which is bivalve, and filled with kidney-ſhaped ſeeds.

There are many ſpecies of this plant, of which four ſorts grow wild in England; and that called the *prickly reſtharrow*, with purple flowers, is uſed in medicine. The roots of this plant ſpread far under ground, and are ſo tough, that, in ploughing, it often ſtops the oxen. *Miller.*

CAMO'YS. *adj.* [*camus*, Fr.] Flat; level; depreſſed. It is only uſed of the noſe.

Many Spaniards, of the race of Barbary Moors, though after frequent commixture, have not worn out the *camoys* noſe unto this day. *Brown's Vulgar Errours, b.* vi. *c.* 10.

CAMP. *n. ſ.* [*camp*, Fr. camp, Sax. from *campus*, Lat.] The order of tents, placed by armies when they keep the field. We uſe the phraſe *to pitch a camp*, to encamp.

From *camp* to *camp*, through the foul womb of night,
The hum of either army ſtilly ſounds. *Shakeſp. Hen.* V.
Next, to ſecure our *camp*, and naval pow'rs,
Raiſe an embattel'd wall, with lofty tow'rs. *Pope's Iliad.*

To CAMP. *v. a.* [from the noun.] To encamp; to lodge in tents, for hoſtile purpoſes.

Had our great palace the capacity
To *camp* this hoſt, we would all ſup together. *Shakeſp.*

CAMP-FIGHT. *n. ſ.* An old word for *combat.*

For their trial by *camp-fight*, the accuſer was, with the peril of his own body, to prove the accuſed guilty; and, by offering him his glove or gantlet, to challenge him to this trial. *Hakewell.*

CAMPA'IGN. } *n. ſ.* [*campaigne*, French; *campania*, Ital.]
CAMPA'NIA. }

1. A large, open, level tract of ground, without hills.

The contrary of all this happens in countries thinly inhabited, and eſpecially in vaſt *campanias*, where there are few cities, beſides what grow by the reſidence of kings. *Temple.*

Thoſe grateful groves, that ſhade the plain,
Wher Tiber rolls majeſtick to the main,
And fattens, as he runs, the fair *campaign.* *Garth's Ovid.*

2. The time for which any army keeps the field, without entering into quarters.

This might have haſtened his march, which would have made a fair concluſion of the *campaign.* *Clarendon.*

An iliad riſing out of one *campaign.* *Addiſon.*

CAMPA'NIFORM. *adj.* [of *campana*, a bell, and *forma*, Lat.] A term uſed of flowers, which are in the ſhape of a bell. *Harris.*

CAMPA'NULATE. *adj.* The ſame with *campaniform.*

CAMPE'STRAL. *adj.* [*campeſtris*, Lat.] Growing in fields.

The mountain beech is the whiteſt; but the *campeſtral*, or wild beech, is of a blacker colour, and more durable. *Mortimer's Husbandry.*

CA'MPHIRE TREE. *n. ſ.* [*camphora*, Lat.]

It hath leaves like thoſe of the pear tree, but full of ribs, which grow alternately on the branches; the flowers conſiſt of one leaf, divided into five or ſix ſegments; the fruit is ſhaped like a nut, the ſhell tender, and the kernel bifid. There are two ſorts of this tree; one is a native of the iſle of Borneo, from which the beſt *camphire* is taken, which is ſuppoſed to be a natural exſudation from the tree, produced in ſuch places where the bark of the tree has been wounded or cut. The other ſort is a native of Japan, which Dr. Kempfer deſcribes to be a kind of bay, bearing black or purple berries, and from whence the inhabitants prepare their *camphire*, by making a ſimple decoction of the root and wood of this tree, cut into ſmall pieces; but this ſort of *camphire* is, in value, eighty or an hundred times leſs than the true Bornean *camphire.* *Miller.*

CA'MPHORATE. *adj.* [from *camphora*, Lat.] Impregnated with camphire.

By ſhaking the ſaline and *camphorate* liquours together, we eaſily confounded them into one high coloured liquour. *Boyle.*

CA'MPION. *n. ſ.* [*lychnis*, Lat.] A plant.

The leaves are whole, and grow oppoſite by pairs upon the ſtalks; the cup of the flower is whole, and either tubulous or ſwelling; the flower conſiſts of five leaves, which expand in form of a clove gilliflower, and are generally heart ſhaped; the ovary, which riſes in the centre of the calyx, becomes a conical fruit, which is wrapt up in the flower cup, and has commonly one cell, filled with ſeeds, which are roundiſh, angular, and kidney-ſhaped. *Miller.*

CA'MUS. *n. ſ.* [probably from *camiſa*, Lat.] A thin dreſs, mentioned by *Spenſer.*

And was yclad, for heat of ſcorching air,
All in ſilken *camus*, lilly white,
Purfled upon with many a folded plight. *Fairy Queen, b.* ii.

CAN. *n. ſ.* [canne, Sax.] A cup; generally a cup made of metal, or ſome other matter than earth.

I hate it as an unfill'd *can.* *Shakeſp. Twelfth Night.*

One tree, the coco, affordeth ſtuff for houſing, cloathing, ſhipping, meat, drink, and *can.* *Grew's Coſmologia Sacra.*

His empty *can*, with ears half worn away,
Was hung on high, to boaſt the triumph of the day. *Dryden.*

CAN. *v. n.* [*konnen*, Dutch. It is ſometimes, though rarely, uſed alone; but is in conſtant uſe as an expreſſion of the potential mood; as, I *can* do, thou *canſt* do, I *could* do, thou *couldeſt* do. It has no other terminations.]

1. To be able; to have power.

In place there is licence to do good and evil, whereof the latter is a curſe; for, in evil, the beſt condition is not to will; the ſecond not to *can.* *Bacon's Eſſays,* N° 11.

O, there's the wonder!
Mecænas and Agrippa, who *can* moſt
With Cæſar, are his foes. His wife Octavia,
Driv'n from his houſe, ſollicits her revenge,
And Dolabella, who was once his friend.
Dryden's All for Love.

He *can* away with no company, whoſe diſcourſe goes beyond what claret and diſſoluteneſs inſpires. *Locke.*

2. It expreſſes the potential mood; as, I *can* do it.

If ſhe *can* make me bleſt? She only *can*:
Empire, and wealth, and all ſhe brings beſide,
Are but the train and trappings of her love. *Dryden.*

3. It is diſtinguiſhed from *may*, as *power* from *permiſſion*; I *can* do it; it is in my power: I *may* do it; it is allowed me: but, in poetry, they are confounded.

4. *Can* is uſed of the perſon with the *verb active*, where *may* is uſed; of the thing, with the *verb paſſive*; as, I *can* do it; it *may* be done.

CANA'ILLE. *n. ſ.* [French.] The loweſt people; the dregs; the lees; the offſcouring of the people: a French term of reproach.

CANA'L. *n. ſ.* [*canalis*, Lat.]

1. A baſon of water in a garden.

The walks and long *canals* reply. *Pope.*

2. Any tract or courſe of water made by art; as the *canals* in Holland.

3. [In anatomy.] A conduit or paſſage through which any of the juices of the body flow.

CA'NAL-COAL. *n. ſ.* A fine kind of coal, dug up in England.

Even our *canal-coal* nearly equals the foreign jet. *Woodward on Foſſils.*

CANALI'CULATED. *adj.* [from *canaliculatus*, Lat.] Channelled; made like a pipe or gutter. *Dict.*

CANA'RY. *n. ſ.* [from the *Canary* iſlands.] Wine brought from the Canaries; ſack.

I will to my honeſt knight Falſtaff, and drink *canary* with him.——I think I ſhall drink in pipe wine firſt with him; I'll make him dance. *Shakeſp. Merry Wives of Windſor.*

To CANA'RY. *v. a.* A cant word, which ſeems to ſignify to frolick.

Maſter, will you win your love with a French brawl?——How mean'ſt thou, brawling in French?——No, my compleat maſter; but to jigg off a tune at the tongue's end, *canary* to it with your feet, humour it with turning up your eyelids. *Shakeſp. Love's Labour Loſt.*

CANA'RY BIRD. An excellent ſinging bird, of a green colour, formerly bred in the Canaries, and nowhere elſe, but now bred in ſeveral parts of Europe, particularly Germany.

Of ſinging birds, they have linnets, goldfinches, ruddocks, *canary birds*, blackbirds, thruſhes, and divers other. *Carew's Survey of Cornwal.*

To CA'NCEL. *v. a.* [*canceller*, Fr. from *cancellis notare*, to mark with croſs lines.]

1. To croſs a writing.

2. To efface; to obliterate in general.

Now welcome night, thou night ſo long expected,
That long day's labour doth at laſt defray,

And all my cares which cruel love collected,
Has summ'd in one, and *cancelled* for aye. *Spenser.*

Know then, I here forget all former griefs,
Cancel all grudge; repeal thee home again.
Shakesp. Two Gentlemen of Verona.

Thou whom avenging pow'rs obey,
Cancel my debt, too great to pay,
Before the sad accounting day. *Roscommon.*

I pass the bills, my lords,
For *cancelling* your debts. *Southerne's Spartan Dame.*

CA'NCELLATED. *particip. adj.* [from *cancel.*] Cross-barred, marked with lines crossing each other.

The tail of the castor is almost bald, though the beast is very hairy; and *cancellated*, with some resemblance to the scales of fishes. *Grew's Musæum.*

CANCELLA'TION. *n. s.* [from *cancel.*] According to Bartolus, is an expunging or wiping out of the contents of an instrument, by two lines drawn in the manner of a cross. *Ayliffe's Parerg.*

CA'NCER. *n. s.* [*cancer*, Lat.]

1. A crabfish.
2. The sign of the summer solstice.

When now no more th' alternate twins are fir'd,
And *Cancer* reddens with the solar blaze,
Short is the doubtful empire of the night *Thomson.*

3. A virulent swelling, or sore, not to be cured.

Any of these three may degenerate into a schirrus, and that schirrus into a *cancer.* *Wiseman.*

As when a *cancer* on the body feeds,
And gradual death from limb to limb proceeds;
So does the chilness to each vital part,
Spread by degrees, and creeps into the heart. *Addison's Ovid.*

To CA'NCERATE. *v. n.* [from *cancer.*] To grow cancerous; to become a cancer.

But striking his fist upon the point of a nail in the wall, his hand *cancerated*, he fell into a fever, and soon after died on't. *L'Estrange's Fables.*

CANCERA'TION. *n. s.* [from *cancerate.*] A growing cancerous.

CA'NCEROUS. *n. s.* [from *cancer.*] Having the virulence and qualities of a cancer.

How they are to be treated when they are strumous, schirrhous, or *cancerous*, you may see in their proper places. *Wisem.*

CA'NCEROUSNESS. *n. s.* [from *cancerous.*] The state of being cancerous.

CA'NCRINE. *adj.* [from *cancer.*] Having the qualities of a crab.

CA'NDENT. *adj.* [*candens*, Lat.] Hot; in the highest degree of heat, next to fusion.

If a wire be heated only at one end, according as that end is cooled upward or downward, it respectively requires a verticity, as we have declared in wires totally *candent.*
Brown's Vulgar Errours, b. ii. *c.* 2.

CA'NDICANT. *adj.* [*candicans*, Lat.] Growing white; whitish. *Dict.*

CA'NDID. *adj.* [*candidus*, Lat.]

1. White. This sense is very rare.

The box receives all black: but, pour'd from thence,
The stones came *candid* forth, the hue of innocence. *Dryd.*

2. Without malice; without deceit; fair; open; ingenuous.

The import of the discourse will, for the most part, if there be no designed fallacy, sufficiently lead *candid* and intelligent readers into the true meaning of it. *Locke.*

A *candid* judge will read each piece of wit,
With the same spirit that its authour writ. *Pope.*

CA'NDIDATE. *n. s.* [*candidatus*, Lat.] A competitor; one that solicites, or proposes himself for something of advancement.

So many *candidates* there stand for wit,
A place at court is scarce so hard to get. *Anonymous.*

One would be surprised to see so many *candidates* for glory.
Addison. Spect. N° 256.

2. It has generally *for* before the thing sought.

What could thus high thy rash ambition raise?
Art thou, fond youth, a *candidate for* praise? *Pope.*

3. Sometimes *of.*

Thy firstfruits of poesy were giv'n,
To make thyself a welcome inmate there,
While yet a young probationer,
And *candidate of* heav'n. *Dryden.*

CA'NDIDLY. *adv.* [from *candid.*] Fairly; without trick; without malice; ingenuously.

We have often desired, they would deal *candidly* with us; for if the matter stuck only there, we would propose, that every man should swear, that he is a member of the church of Ireland. *Swift.*

CA'NDIDNESS. *n. s.* [from *candid.*] Ingenuity; openness of temper; purity of mind.

It presently sees the guilt of a sinful action; and, on the other side, observes the *candidness* of a man's very principles, and the sincerity of his intentions. *South.*

To CA'NDIFY. *v. a.* [*candifico*, Lat.] To make white; to whiten. *Dict.*

CA'NDLE. *n. s.* [*candela*, Lat.]

1. A light made of wax or tallow, surrounding a wick of flax or cotton.

Here burns my *candle* out, ay, here it dies,
Which, while it lasted, gave King Henry light. *Shakesp.*

We see that wax *candles* last longer than tallow *candles*, because wax is more firm and hard. *Bacon's Nat. History.*

Take a child, and, setting a *candle* before him, he shall find his pupil to contract very much, to exclude the light, with the brightness whereof it would otherwise be dazzled. *Ray.*

2. Light, or luminary.

By these bless'd *candles* of the night,
Had you been there, I think you would have begg'd
The ring of me, to give the worthy doctor.
Shakesp. Merchant of Venice.

CA'NDLEBERRY TREE. See SWEET-WILLOW; of which it is a species.

CANDLEHO'LDER. *n. s.* [from *candle* and *hold.*]

1. He that holds the candle.
2. He that remotely assists.

Let wantons, light of heart,
Tickle the senseless rushes with their heels;
For I am proverb'd with a grandsire phrase,
To be a *candleholder*, and look on. *Shakesp.*

CA'NDLELIGHT. *n. s.* [from *candle* and *light.*] The light of a candle.

In darkness, *candlelight* may serve to guide men's steps, which, to use in the day, were madness. *Hooker, b.* ii. § 4.

Before the day was done, her work she sped,
And never went by *candlelight* to bed. *Dryden's Fab.*

The boding owl
Steals from her private cell by night,
And flies about the *candlelight.* *Swift.*

Such as are adapted to meals, will indifferently serve for dinners or suppers, only distinguishing between daylight and *candlelight.* *Swift's Introduct. to genteel Conversation.*

2. The necessary candles for use.

I shall find him coals and *candlelight.* *Molineux to Locke.*

CA'NDLEMAS. *n. s.* [from *candle* and *mass.*] The feast of the purification of the Blessed Virgin, which was formerly celebrated with many lights in churches.

The harvest dinners are held by every wealthy man, or, as we term it, by every good liver, between Michaelmas and *Candlemas.* *Carew's Survey of Cornwal.*

There is a general tradition in most parts of Europe, that inferreth the coldness of the succeeding winter, upon shining of the sun upon *Candlemas* day. *Brown's Vulgar Errours.*

Come *Candlemas* nine years ago she dy'd,
And now lies bury'd by the yew-tree side. *Gay.*

CA'NDLESTICK. *n. s.* [from *candle* and *stick.*] The instrument that holds candles.

The horsemen sit like fixed *candlesticks*,
With torch-staves in their hands; and their poor jades
Lob down their heads, dropping the hide and hips.
Shakesp. Henry V.

These countries were once christian, and members of the church, and where the golden *candlesticks* did stand. *Bacon.*

I know a friend, who has converted the essays of a man of quality, into a kind of fringe for his *candlesticks.* *Addison.*

CA'NDLESTUFF. *n. s.* [from *candle* and *stuff.*] Kitchen stuff; grease; tallow.

But then you will say, that their vapour can last but a short time; to that it may be answered, that, by the help of oil, and wax, and other *candlestuff*, the flame may continue, and the wick not burn. *Bacon's Nat. Hist.* N° 774.

CANDLEWA'STER. *n. s.* [from *candle* and *waste.*] That which consumes candles; a spendthrift.

Patch grief with proverbs, make misfortune drunk
With *candlewasters.* *Shakesp. Much ado about Nothing.*

CA'NDOCK. *n. s.* A weed that grows in rivers.

Let them dry six or twelve months, both to kill the waterweeds, as water-lilies, *candocks*, reate, and bulrushes, and also, that as these die for want of water, so grass may grow on the pond's bottom. *Walton's Angler.*

CA'NDOUR. *n. s.* [*candor*, Lat.] Sweetness of temper; purity of mind; openness; ingenuity; kindness.

He should have so much of a natural *candour* and sweetness, mixed with all the improvement of learning, as might convey knowledge with a sort of gentle insinuation. *Watts.*

To CA'NDY. *v. a.* [probably from *candare*, a word used in later times, for to *whiten.*]

1. To conserve with sugar, in such a manner as that the sugar lies in flakes, or breaks into tangles.

Should the poor be flatter'd?
No, let the *candy'd* tongue lick absurd pomp,
And crook the pregnant hinges of the knee,
Where thrift may follow fawning. *Shakesp. Hamlet.*

They have in Turky confections like to *candied* conserves, made of sugar and lemons, or sugar and citrons, or sugar and violets, and some other flowers, and some mixture of amber. *Bacon.*

With *candy'd* plantanes, and the juicy pine,
On choicest melons and sweet grapes they dine. *Waller.*

2. To form into congelations.

Will the cold brook,
Candied with ice, cawdle thy morning toast,
To cure thy o'er-night's surfeit? *Shakesp. Timon.*

3. To incrust with congelations.

Since when those frosts that winter brings,
Which *candy* every green,
Renew us like the teeming springs,
And we thus fresh are seen. *Drayton.*

To CA'NDY. *v. n.* To grow congealed.

CA'NDY *Lion's foot.* [*catanance*, Lat.] A plant.

The cup of the flower is squamose; the florets round the margin are much longer than those in the middle of the flower; the seeds are wrapt up in a leafy or downy substance within the cup, or outer covering. This plant begins to flower in May, and continues till August or September. *Miller.*

CANE. *n. s.* [*canna*, Lat.]

1. A kind of strong reed, of which walking staffs are made; a walking staff. See REED.

The king thrust the captain from him with his *cane*; whereupon he took his leave, and went home. *Harvey.*

If the poker be out of the way, or broken, stir the fire with your master's *cane*. *Swift.*

2. The plant which yields the sugar.

This cane or reed grows plentifully both in the East and West Indies. Other reeds have their skin hard and dry, and their pulp void of juice; but the skin of the sugar *cane* is soft, and the spongy matter or pith it contains very juicy. It usually grows four or five feet high, and about half an inch in diameter; though some have been mentioned in the island of Tabago twenty four feet high. The stem or stalk is divided by knots a foot and a half apart. At the top it puts forth a number of long green tufted leaves, from the middle of which arise the flower and the seed. There are likewise leaves springing out from each knot; but these usually fall as the *cane* rises. The ground fit for sugar *canes* is light, soft, and spongy, lying on a descent proper to carry off the water, and well turned to the sun. They usually plant them in pieces cut a foot and a half below the top of the flower, and they are ordinarily ripe in ten months, though sometimes not till fifteen; at which time they are found quite full of a white succulent marrow, whence is expressed the liquour of which sugar is made. When ripe, they are cut, their leaves cleared off, and they are carried in bundles to the mills, which consist of three wooden rollers, covered with steel plates. *Chambers.*

And the sweet liquour on the *cane* bestow,
From which prepar'd the luscious sugars flow. *Blackmore.*

3. A lance; a dart made of cane; whence the Spanish *inego de cannas.*

Abenamar, thy youth these sports has known,
Of which thy age is now spectator grown;
Judge like thou sitt'st, to praise or to arraign,
The flying skirmish of the darted *cane*. *Dryden's Conq. of Gr.*

4. A reed.

Food may be afforded to bees, by small *canes* or troughs conveyed into their hives. *Mortimer's Husbandry.*

To CANE. *v. a.* [from the noun.] To beat with a walking staff.

CANI'CULAR. *adj.* [*canicularis*, Lat.] Belonging to the dog-star; as, *canicular* or dog-days.

In regard to different latitudes unto some, the *canicular* days are in the winter; as unto such as are under the equinoctial line; for, unto them, it ariseth, when the sun is about the tropick of Cancer, which season unto them is winter.
Brown's Vulgar Errours, b. iv. *c.* 12.

CANI'NE. *adj.* [*caninus*, Lat.]

1. Having the properties of a dog.

A third kind of women are made up of *canine* particles: these are scolds, who imitate the animals out of which they were taken, always busy and barking, and snarl at every one that comes in their way. *Addison. Spectator*, N° 209.

2. *Canine* hunger, in medicine, is an appetite which cannot be satisfied.

It may occasion an exorbitant appetite of usual things, which they will take in such quantities, till they vomit them up like dogs, from whence it is called *canine*. *Arbuthnot on Aliments.*

CA'NISTER. *n. s.* [*canistrum*, Lat.]

1. A small basket.

My lovely care,
Take the presents, which the nymphs prepare:
White lilies in full *canisters* they bring,
With all the glories of the purple spring. *Dryden's Virg.*

2. A small vessel in which any thing, such as tea or coffee, is laid up.

CA'NKER. *n. s.* [*cancer*, Lat. It seems to have the same meaning and original with *cancer*, but to be accidentally written with a *k*, when it denotes bad qualities in a less degree; or, *canker* might come from *chancre*, Fr. and *cancer* from the Latin.]

1. A worm that preys upon, and destroys fruits.

And loathful idleness he doth detest,
The *canker* worm of every gentle breast. *Spenser.*

That which the locust hath left, hath the *canker* worm eaten. *Joel*, i. 4.

A huffing, shining, flatt'ring, cringing coward,
A *canker* worm of peace, was rais'd above him. *Otway.*

2. A fly that preys upon fruits.

There be of flies, caterpillars, *canker* flies, and bear flies. *Walton's Angler.*

3. Any thing that corrupts or consumes.

Yet writers say, as in the sweetest bud
The eating *canker* dwells; so eating love
Inhabits in the finest wits of all. *Shakesp. Two G. of Verona.*

It is the *canker* and ruin of many men's estates, which, in process of time, breeds a publick poverty. *Bacon.*

Sacrilege may prove an eating *canker*, and a consuming moth, in the estate that we leave them. *Atterbury.*

No longer live the *cankers* of my court;
All to your several states with speed resort;
Waste in wild riot what your land allows,
There ply the early feast, and late carouse. *Pope.*

4. A kind of wild worthless rose.

To put down Richard, that sweet lovely rose,
And plant this thorn, this *canker* Bolingbroke. *Shakesp.*

Draw a cherry with the leaf, the shaft of a steeple, a single or *canker* rose. *Peacham.*

5. An eating or corroding humour.

I am not glad, that such a sore of time
Should seek a plaister by a contemn'd revolt,
And heal th' inveterate *canker* of one wound,
By making many. *Shakesp. King John.*

6. Corrosion; virulence.

As with age his body uglier grows,
So his mind with *cankers*. *Shakesp. Tempest.*

7. A disease in trees. *Dict.*

To CA'NKER. *v. n.* [from the noun.] To grow corrupt.

That cunning architect of *canker'd* guile,
Whom princes late displeasure left in bands,
For falsed letters, and suborned wile. *Fairy Queen, b.* ii. *c.* i.

I will lift the down trod Mortimer
As high i' th' air as this unthankful king,
As this ingrate and *canker'd* Bolingbroke. *Shakesp. Hen.* IV.

Silvering will sully and *canker* more than gilding; which, if it might be corrected with a little mixture of gold, will be profitable. *Bacon's Physical Remains.*

Or what the cross dire looking planet smite,
Or hurtful worm with *canker'd* venom bite. *Milton.*

To some new clime, or to thy native sky,
Oh! friendless and forsaken virtue, fly:
The Indian air is deadly to thee grown;
Deceit and *canker'd* malice rule thy throne. *Dryden's Auren.*

Let envious jealousy, and *canker'd* spight
Produce my actions to severest light,
And tax my open day, or secret night. } *Prior.*

To CA'NKER. *v. a.*

1. To corrupt; to corrode.

Restore to God his due in tithe and time:
A tithe purloin'd, *cankers* the whole estate. *Herbert.*

2. To infect; to pollute.

An honest man will enjoy himself better in a moderate fortune, that is gained with honour and reputation, than in an overgrown estate, that is *cankered* with the acquisitions of rapine and exaction. *Addison. Spectator*, N° 469.

CA'NKERBIT. *particip. adj.* [from *canker* and *bit*.] Bitten with an envenomed tooth.

Know thy name is lost;
By treason's tooth baregnawn and *cankerbit*. *Shakesp. K. Lear.*

CA'NNABINE. *adj.* [*cannabinus*, Lat.] Hempen. *Dict.*

CA'NNIBAL. *n. s.* An anthropophagite; a man-eater.

The *cannibals* themselves eat no man's flesh, of those that die of themselves, but of such as are slain. *Bacon's Nat. Hist.*

They were little better than *cannibals*, who do hunt one another; and he that hath most strength and swiftness, doth eat and devour all his fellows. *Davies on Ireland.*

It was my bent to speak,
Of the *cannibals* that each other eat;
The anthropophagi, and men whose heads
Did grow beneath their shoulders. *Shakesp. Othello.*

The captive *cannibal*, opprest with chains,
Yet braves his foes, reviles, provokes, disdains;
Of nature fierce, untameable, and proud,
He bids defiance to the gaping croud;
And spent at last, and speechless as he lies,
With firy glances mocks their rage, and dies. *Granville.*

If an eleventh commandment had been given, Thou shalt not eat human flesh; would not these *cannibals* have esteemed it more difficult than all the rest? *Bentley.*

CA'NNIBALLY. *adv.* [from *cannibal.*] In the manner of a cannibal.

Before Corioli, he scotcht him and notcht him like a carbanado.—Had he been *cannibally* given, he might have broiled, and eaten him too. *Shakesp. Coriolanus.*

CA'NNIPERS. *n. s.* [corrupted from *callipers*; which see.]

The square is taken by a pair of *cannipers*, or two rulers clapped to the side of a tree, measuring the distance between them. *Mortimer's Husbandry.*

CA'NNON. *n. s.* [*cannon*, Fr. from *canna*, Lat. a pipe, meaning a large tube.]
1. A great gun for battery.
2. A gun larger than can be managed by the hand. They are of so many sizes, that they decrease in the bore from a ball of forty-eight pounds to a ball of five ounces.

As *cannons* overcharg'd with double cracks,
So they redoubled strokes upon the foe. *Shakesp. Macbeth.*

He had left all the *cannon* he had taken; and now he sent all his great *cannon* to a garrison. *Clarendon.*

The making, or price, of these gunpowder instruments, is extremely expensive, as may be easily judged by the weight of their materials; a whole *cannon* weighing commonly eight thousand pounds; a half *cannon*, five thousand; a culverin, four thousand five hundred; a demi-culverin, three thousand; which, whether it be in iron or brass, must needs be very costly. *Wilkins's Mathematical Magick.*

CANNON-BALL. } *n. s.* [from *cannon*, *ball*, *bullet*, and *shot*.]
CANNON-BULLET. } The balls which are shot from great
CANNON-SHOT. } guns.

He reckons those for wounds that are made by bullets, although it be a *cannon-shot*. *Wiseman's Surgery.*

Let a *cannon-bullet* pass through a room, it must strike successively the two sides of the room. *Locke.*

To CANNONA'DE. *v. n.* [from *cannon*.] To play the great guns; to batter or attack with great guns.

Both armies *cannonaded* all the ensuing day. *Tatler*, N° 63.

To CANNONA'DE. *v. a.* To fire upon the enemy with cannon.

CANNONI'ER. *n. s.* [from *cannon*.] The engineer that manages the cannon.

Give me the cups:
And let the kettle to the trumpets speak,
The trumpets to the *cannonier* without,
The cannons to the heav'ns, the heav'ns to earth. *Shakesp.*

A third was a most excellent *cannonier*, whose good skill did much endamage the forces of the king. *Hayward.*

CA'NNOT. A word compounded of *can* and *not*.

I *cannot* but believe many a child can tell twenty, long before he has any idea of infinity at all. *Locke.*

CANO'A. } *n. s.* A boat made by cutting the trunk of a tree in-
CA'NOE. } to a hollow vessel.

Others made rafts of wood, and others devised the boat of one tree, called the *canoa*, which the Gauls, upon the river Roan, used in assisting the transportation of Hannibal's army. *Raleigh's Essays.*

They maintained a war against Semiramis, in which they had four thousand monoxyla, or *canoes*, of one piece of timber. *Arbuthnot on Coins.*

CA'NON. *n. s.* [κανὼν.]
1. A rule; a law.

The truth is, they are rules and *canons* of that law, which is written in all mens hearts; the church had for ever, no less than now, stood bound to observe them, whether the apostle had mentioned them, or no. *Hooker, b.* iii. § 4.

His books are almost the very *canon* to judge both doctrine and discipline by. *Hooker, Pref.*

Religious *canons*, civil laws are cruel,
Then what should war be? *Shakesp. Timon.*

Canons in logick are such as these: every part of a division, singly taken, must contain less than the whole; and a definition must be peculiar and proper to the thing defined. *Watts's Logick.*

2. The laws made by ecclesiastical councils.

Canon law is that law, which is made and ordained in a general council, or provincial synod of the church. *Ayliffe.*

These were looked on as lapsed persons, and great severities of penance were prescribed them, as appears by the *canons* of Ancyra, and many others. *Stillingfleet.*

3. The books of Holy Scripture; or the great rule.

Canon also denotes those books of Scripture, which are received as inspired and canonical, to distinguish them from either profane, apocryphal, or disputed books. Thus we say, that *Genesis* is part of the sacred *canon* of the Scripture. *Ayliffe.*

4. A dignitary in cathedral churches.

For deans and *canons*, or prebends, of cathedral churches, in their first institution, they were of great use in the church; they were to be of counsel with the bishop for his revenue, and for his government in causes ecclesiastical. *Bacon.*

Swift much admires the place and air,
And longs to be a *canon* there.
A *canon!* that's a place too mean:
No, doctor, you shall be a dean,
Two dozen *canons* round your stall,
And you the tyrant o'er them all. *Swift.*

5. *Canons Regular.* Such as are placed in monasteries. *Ayliffe.*
6. *Canons Secular.* Lay canons, who have been, as a mark of honour, admitted into some chapters.
7. [Among chirurgeons.] An instrument used in sewing up wounds. *Dict.*
8. A large sort of printing letter, probably so called from being first used in printing a book of canons; or perhaps from its size, and therefore properly written *cannon.*

CA'NON BIT. *n. s.* That part of the bit let into the horse's mouth.

A goodly person, and could manage fair,
His stubborn steed with *canonbit*,
Who under him did trample as the air. *Fairy Queen, b.* i.

CA'NONESS. *n. s.* [*canonissa*, low Lat.]

There are also, in popish countries, women which they call secular *canonesses*, living after the example of secular canons. *Ayliffe's Parergon.*

CANO'NICAL. *adj.* [*canonicus*, low Lat.]
1. According to the canon.
2. Constituting the canon.

Publick readings there are of books and writings, not *canonical*, whereby the church doth also preach, or openly make known the doctrine of virtuous conversation. *Hooker, b.* v.

No such book was found amongst those *canonical* scriptures. *Raleigh's History of the World.*

3. Regular; stated; fixed by ecclesiastical laws.

Seven times in a day do I praise thee, said David; from this definite number some ages of the church took their pattern for their *canonical* hours. *Taylor.*

4. Spiritual; ecclesiastical; relating to the church.

York anciently had a metropolitan jurisdiction over all the bishops of Scotland, from whom they had their consecration, and to whom they swore *canonical* obedience. *Ayliffe.*

CANO'NICALLY. *adv.* [from *canonical.*] In a manner agreeable to the canon.

It is a known story of the friar, who, on a fasting day, bids his capon be carp, and then very *canonically* eat it. *Government of the Tongue.*

CANO'NICALNESS. *n. s.* [from *canonical.*] The quality of being canonical.

CA'NONIST. *n. s.* [from *canon.*] A man versed in the ecclesiastical laws; a professour of the canon law.

John Fisher, bishop of Rochester, when the king would have translated him from that poor bishoprick, he refused, saying, he would not forsake his poor little old wife; thinking of the fifteenth canon of the Nicene council, and that of the *canonists*, *Matrimonium inter episcopum & ecclesiam esse contractum, &c.* *Camden's Remains.*

Of whose strange crimes no *canonist* can tell,
In what commandment's large contents they dwell. *Pope.*

CANONIZA'TION. *n. s.* [from *canonize.*] The act of declaring any man a saint.

It is very suspicious, that the interests of particular families, or churches, have too great a sway in their *canonizations.* *Addison on Italy.*

To CA'NONIZE. *v. a.* [from *canon*, to put into the canon, or rule for observing festivals.] To declare any man a saint.

The king, desirous to bring into the house of Lancaster celestial honour, became suitor to pope Julius, to *canonize* king Henry VI. for a saint. *Bacon's Henry* VII.

By those hymns all shall approve
Us *canoniz'd* for love. *Donne.*

They have a pope too, who hath the chief care of religion, and of *canonizing* whom he thinks fit, and thence have the honour of saints. *Stillingfleet.*

CA'NONRY. } *n. s.* [from *canon.*] An ecclesiastical benefice in
CA'NONSHIP. } some cathedral or collegiate church, which has a prebend, or a stated allowance out of the revenues of such church, commonly annexed to it. *Ayliffe's Parergon.*

CA'NOPIED. *adj.* [from *canopy.*] Covered with a canopy.

I sat me down to watch upon a bank,
With ivy *canopy'd*, and interwove
With flaunting honeysuckle. *Milton.*

CA'NOPY. *n. s.* [*canopeum*, low Lat.] A covering of state over a throne or bed; a covering spread over the head.

She is there brought unto a paled green,
And placed under a stately *canopy*,
The warlike feats of both those knights to see. *Fairy Queen.*

Now spread the night her spangled *canopy*,
And summon'd every restless eye to sleep. *Fairfax.*

Nor will the raging fever's fire abate,
With golden *canopies*, and beds of state. *Dryden.*

To CA'NOPY. *v. a.* [from the noun.] To cover with a canopy.

The birch, the myrtle, and the bay,
Like friends did all embrace;
And their large branches did display,
To *canopy* the place. *Dryden.*

CANO'ROUS. *adj.* [*canorus*, Lat.] Musical; tuneful.

Birds that are most *canorous*, and whose notes we most commend, are of little throats, and short. *Brown's Vulgar Errours.*

CANT. *n. s.* [probably from *cantus*, Lat. implying the odd tone of voice used by vagrants; but imagined by some to be corrupted from *quaint.*]
1. A corrupt dialect used by beggars and vagabonds.
2. A particular form of speaking peculiar to some certain class or body of men.

I write not always in the proper terms of navigation, land service, or in the *cant* of any profession. *Dryden.*

If we would trace out the original of that flagrant and avowed impiety, which has prevailed among us for some years, we should find, that it owes its rise to that *cant* and hypocrisy, which

which had taken possession of the people's minds in the times of the great rebellion. *Addison. Freeholder*, N° 37.

Astrologers, with an old paltry *cant*, and a few pot-hooks for planets, to amuse the vulgar, have too long been suffered to abuse the world. *Swift's Predictions for the Year* 1701.

A few general rules, with a certain *cant* of words, has sometimes set up an illiterate heavy writer, for a most judicious and formidable critick. *Addison. Spectator*, N° 291.

3. A whining pretension to goodness, in formal and affected terms.

Of promise prodigal, while pow'r you want,
And preaching in the self-denying *cant*. *Dryden's Aurengz.*

4. Barbarous jargon.

The affectation of some late authours, to introduce and multiply *cant* words, is the most ruinous corruption in any language. *Swift.*

5. Auction.

Numbers of these tenants, or their descendants, are now offering to sell their leases by *cant*, even those which were for lives. *Swift.*

To CANT. *v. n.* [from the noun.] To talk in the jargon of particular professions, or in any kind of formal affected language, or with a peculiar and studied tone of voice.

Men *cant* endlessly about *materia* and *forma*; hunt chimeras by rules of art, or dress up ignorance in words of bulk or sound, which may stop up the mouth of enquiry. *Glanville's Scepsis Scientifica.*

That uncouth affected garb of speech, or *canting* language rather, if I may so call it, which they have of late taken up, is the signal distinction and characteristical note of that, which, in that their new language, they call the godly party. *Sanderson.*

The busy, subtile serpents of the law,
Did first my mind from true obedience draw;
While I did limits to the king prescribe,
And took for oracles that *canting* tribe. *Roscommon.*

Unskill'd in schemes by planets to foreshow,
Like *canting* rascals, how the wars will go. *Dryden's Juven.*

CANTA'LIVER. See CANTILIVER.

CANTA'TA. n. s. [Ital.] A song.

CANTA'TION. *n. s.* [from *canto*, Lat.] The act of singing.

CA'NTER. *n. s.* [from *cant.*] A term of reproach for hypocrites, who talk formally of religion, without obeying it.

CANTERBURY BELLS. See BELFLOWER.

CANTERBURY GALLOP. [In horsemanship.] The hard gallop of an ambling horse, commonly called a canter; and probably derived from the monks riding to Canterbury on easy ambling horses.

CANTHA'RIDES. n. s. [Latin.] Spanish flies; used to raise blisters.

The flies, *cantharides*, are bred of a worm, or caterpillar, but peculiar to certain fruit trees; as are the fig tree, the pine tree, and the wild brier; all which bear sweet fruit, and fruit that hath a kind of secret biting or sharpness: for the fig hath a milk in it, that is sweet and corrosive; the pine apple hath a kernel that is strong and abstersive. *Bacon's Nat. History.*

CA'NTHUS. n. s. [Latin.] The corner of the eye. The internal is called the greater, and the external the lesser *canthus*. *Quincy.*

A gentlewoman was seized with an inflammation and tumour in the great *canthus*, or angle of her eye. *Wiseman.*

CA'NTICLE. *n. s.* [from *canto*, Lat.] A song; used generally for a song in scripture.

This right of estate, in some nations, is yet more significantly expressed by Moses in his *canticles*, in the person of God to the Jews. *Bacon's Holy War.*

CANTI'LIVERS. *n. s.* Pieces of wood framed into the front or other sides of an house, to sustain the molding and eaves over it. *Moxon's Mechanical Exercises.*

CA'NTLE. *n. s.* [*kant*, Dutch, a corner; *eschantillon*, Fr. a piece.] A piece with corners. *Skinner.*

See how this river comes, me crankling in,
And cuts me from the best of all my land,
A huge halfmoon, a monstrous *cantle* out. *Shakesp. H. IV.*

To CA'NTLE. *v. a.* [from the noun.] To cut in pieces.

For four times talking, if one piece thou take,
That must be *cantled*, and the judge go snack. *Dryden's Juv.*

CA'NTLET. *n. s.* [from *cantle.*] A piece; a fragment.

Raging with high disdain, repeats his blows;
Nor shield, nor armour can their force oppose;
Huge *cantlets* of his buckler strew the ground,
And no defence in his bor'd arms is found. *Dryden.*

CA'NTO. n. s. [Ital.] A book, or section of a poem.

Why, what would you do?———
—Make a willow cabbin at your gate,
And call upon my soul within the house;
Write loyal *cantos* of contemned love. *Shakesp. Tw. Night.*

CA'NTON. *n. s.* [from κανθὸς, the corner of the eye; and hence came the *cantons* of the Switzers. It is the reward of a prince given to an earl. *Peacham.*]

1. A small parcel or division of land.

Only that little *canton* of land, called the English pale, containing four small shires, did maintain a bordering war with the Irish, and retain the form of English government. *Davies.*

2. A small community, or clan.

The same is the case of rovers by land; such, as yet, are some *cantons* in Arabia, and some petty kings of the mountains, adjacent to straits and ways. *Bacon's Holy War.*

To CA'NTON. *v. a.* [from the noun.] To divide into little parts.

Families shall quit all subjection to him, and *canton* his empire into less governments for themselves. *Locke.*

It would certainly be for the good of mankind, to have all the mighty empires and monarchies of the world *cantoned* out into petty states and principalities. *Addison on Italy.*

The late king of Spain, reckoning it an indignity to have his territories *cantoned* out into parcels by other princes, during his own life, and without his consent, rather chose to bequeath the monarchy entire to a younger son of France. *Swift.*

They *canton* out to themselves a little province in the intellectual world, where they fancy the light shines, and all the rest is in darkness. *Watts's Improvement of the Mind.*

To CA'NTONIZE. *v. a.* [from *canton.*] To parcel out into small divisions.

Thus was all Ireland *cantonized* among ten persons of the English nation. *Davies on Ireland.*

The whole forest was in a manner *cantonized* amongst a very few in number, of whom some had regal right. *Howel.*

CA'NTRED. *n. s.* The same in Wales as an *hundred* in England. For *cantre*, in the British language, signifieth an hundred. *Cowel.*

The king regrants to him all that province, reserving only the city of Dublin, and the *cantreds* next adjoining, with the maritime towns. *Davies on Ireland.*

CA'NVASS. *n. s.* [*canevas*, Fr. *cannabis*, Lat. hemp.] A kind of cloth woven for several uses, as sails, painting cloths, tents.

The master commanded forthwith to set on all the *canvass* they could, and fly homeward. *Sidney.*

And eke the pens that did his pinions bind,
Were like main yards with flying *canvass* lin'd. *Fairy Q. b.* i.

Their *canvass* castles up they quickly rear,
And build a city in an hour's space. *Fairfax, b.* ii.

Where-e'er thy navy spreads her *canvass* wings,
Homage to thee, and peace to all she brings. *Waller.*

With such kind passion hastes the prince to fight,
And spreads his flying *canvass* to the Sound;
Him whom no danger, were he there, could fright;
Now absent, every little noise can wound. *Dryden.*

Thou, Kneller, long with noble pride,
The foremost of thy art, hast vy'd
With nature in a generous strife,
And touch'd the *canvass* into life. *Addison.*

To CA'NVASS. *v. a.* [*Skinner* derives it from *cannabasser*, Fr. to beat hemp; which being a very laborious employment, it is used to signify, to search diligently into.]

1. To sift; to examine.

I have made careful search on all hands, and *canvassed* the matter with all possible diligence. *Woodward.*

2. To debate; to controvert.

The curs discovered a raw hide in the bottom of a river, and laid their heads together how to come at it: they *canvassed* the matter one way and t'other, and concluded, that the way to get it, was to drink their way to it. *L'Estrange.*

To CA'NVASS. *v. n.* To sollicite.

This crime of *canvassing*, or solliciting for church preferment, is, by the canon law, called simony. *Ayliffe's Parergon.*

CA'NY. *adj.* [from *cane.*]

1. Full of canes.
2. Consisting of canes.

But in his way lights on the barren plains
Of Sericana, where Chineses drive,
With sails and wind, their *cany* wagons light. *Parad. Lost.*

CA'NZONET. *n. s.* [*canzonetta*, Ital.] A little song.

Vecchi was most pleasing of all others, for his conceit and variety, as well his madrigals as *canzonets*. *Peacham.*

CAP. *n. s.* [*cap*, Welch; *cæppe*, Sax. *cappe*, Germ. *cappe*, Fr. *cappa*, Ital. *capa*, Span. *kappe*, Dan. and Dutch; *caput*, a head, Latin.]

1. The garment that covers the head.

Here is the *cap* your worship did bespeak.—
Why, this was moulded on a porringer,
A velvet dish. *Shakesp. Taming the Shrew.*

I have ever held my *cap* off to thy fortune.—
—Thou hast serv'd me with much faith. *Shakesp.*

First, lolling, sloth in woollen *cap*,
Taking her after-dinner nap. *Swift.*

The *cap*, the whip, the masculine attire,
For which they roughen to the sense. *Thomson's Autumn.*

2. The ensign of the cardinalate.

Henry the fifth did sometimes prophesy,
If once he came to be a cardinal,
He'd make his *cap* coequal with the crown. *Shakesp. H. VI.*

3. The topmost; the highest.

Thou art the *cap* of all the fools alive. *Shakesp. Timon.*

4. A reverence made by uncovering the head.

They

They more and leſs, came in with *cap* and knee,
Met him in boroughs, cities, villages. *Shakeſp. Henry* IV.

Should the want of a *cap* or a cringe ſo mortally diſcompoſe him, as we find afterwards it did. *L'Eſtrange.*

5. A veſſel made like a cap.

It is obſerved, that a barrel or *cap*, whoſe cavity will contain eight cubical feet of air, will not ſerve a diver above a quarter of an hour. *Wilkins.*

6. *Cap of a great gun.* A piece of lead laid over the touch-hole, to preſerve the prime.

7. *Cap of maintenance.* One of the regalia carried before the king at the coronation.

To Cap. *v. a.* [from the noun.]

1. To cover on the top.

The bones next the joint are *capped* with a ſmooth cartilaginous ſubſtance, ſerving both to ſtrength and motion. *Derham.*

2. To ſnatch off the cap.

If one, by another occaſion, take any thing from another, as boys ſometimes uſe to *cap* one another, the ſame is ſtraight felony. *Spenſer on Ireland.*

3. *To cap verſes.* To name alternately verſes beginning with a particular letter; to name alternately.

Where Henderſon, and th' other maſſes,
Were ſent to *cap* texts, and put caſes. *Hudibras.*

Sure it is a pitiful pretence to ingenuity, that can be thus kept up, there being little need of any other faculty but memory, to be able to *cap* texts. *Government of the Tongue,* § 3.

There is an author of ours, whom I would deſire him to read, before he ventures at *capping* characters. *Atterbury.*

Cap *à pè.*
Cap *à piè.* } [*cap à piè*, Fr.] From head to foot; all over.

A figure like your father,
Arm'd at all points exactly, *cap à pè*,
Appears before them, and, with ſolemn march,
Goes ſlow and ſtately by them. *Shakeſp. Hamlet.*

There for the two contending knights he ſent,
Arm'd *cap à piè*, with rev'rence low they bent;
He ſmil'd on both. *Dryden's Fables.*

A woodlouſe,
That folds up itſelf in itſelf for a houſe,
As round as a ball, without head, without tail,
Incloſ'd *cap à pè* in a ſtrong coat of mail. *Swift.*

Cap-paper. A ſort of coarſe browniſh paper.

Having, for trial ſake, filtred it through *cap-paper*, there remained in the filtre a powder. *Boyle.*

Capabi'lity. *n. ſ.* [from *capable.*] Capacity; the quality of being capable.

CA'PABLE. *adj.* [*capable*, Fr.]

1. Endued with powers equal to any particular thing.

To ſay, that the more *capable*, or the better deſerver, hath ſuch right to govern, as he may compulſorily bring under the leſs worthy, is idle. *Bacon.*

When we conſider ſo much of that ſpace, as is equal to, or *capable* to receive a body of any aſſigned dimenſions. *Locke.*

When you hear any perſon give his judgment, conſider with yourſelf whether he be a *capable* judge. *Watts.*

2. Intelligent; able to underſtand.

Look you, how pale he glares;
His form and cauſe conjoined, preaching to ſtones,
Would make them *capable.* *Shakeſp. Hamlet.*

3. Capacious; able to receive or underſtand.

I am much bound to God, that he hath endued you with one *capable* of the beſt inſtructions. *Digby.*

4. Suſceptible.

The ſoul, immortal ſubſtance, to remain,
Conſcious of joy, and *capable* of pain. *Prior.*

5. Qualified for; without any natural impediment.

There is no man that believes the goodneſs of God, but muſt be inclined to think, that he hath made ſome things for as long a duration as they are *capable* of. *Tillotſon.*

6. Qualified for; without legal impediment.

Of my land,
Loyal and natural boy! I'll work the means
To make thee *capable.* *Shakeſp. King Lear.*

7. It has the particle *of* before a noun.

What ſecret ſprings their eager paſſions move,
How *capable of* death for injur'd love. *Dryden's Virgil.*

8. Hollow. This ſenſe is not now in uſe.

Lean but upon a ruſh,
The cicatrice, and *capable* impreſſure,
Thy palm ſome moments keeps. *Shakeſp. As you like it.*

Ca'pableness. *n. ſ.* [from *capable.*] The quality or ſtate of being capable; knowledge; underſtanding; power of mind.

CAPA'CIOUS. *adj.* [*capax*, Lat.]

1. Wide; large; able to hold much.

Beneath th' inceſſant weeping of thoſe drains,
I ſee the rocky Siphons ſtretch'd immenſe,
The mighty reſervoirs of harden'd chalk,
Or ſtiff compacted clay, *capacious* found. *Thomſon's Autumn.*

2. Extenſive; equal to much knowledge, or great deſign.

There are ſome perſons of a good genius, and a *capacious* mind, who write and ſpeak very obſcurely. *Watts.*

Capa'ciousness. *n. ſ.* [from *capacious.*] The power of holding or receiving; largeneſs.

A concave meaſure, of known and denominate capacity, ſerves to meaſure the *capaciouſneſs* of any other veſſel. In like manner, to a given weight, the weight of all other bodies may be reduced, and ſo found out. *Holder on Time.*

To Capa'citate. *v. a.* [from *capacity.*] To make capable; to enable; to qualify.

By this inſtruction we may be *capacitated* to obſerve thoſe errours. *Dryden.*

Theſe ſort of men were ſycophants only, and were endued with arts of life, to *capacitate* them for the converſation of the rich and great. *Tatler,* N° 56.

Capa'city. *n. ſ.* [*capacité*, Fr.]

1. The power of holding or containing any thing.

Had our palace the *capacity*
To camp this hoſt, we would all ſup together. *Shakeſp.*

Notwithſtanding thy *capacity*
Receiveth as the ſea, nought enters there,
Of what validity and pitch ſoe'er,
But falls into abatement and low price. *Shakeſp. Tw. Night.*

For they that moſt and greateſt things embrace,
Enlarge thereby their mind's *capacity*,
As ſtreams enlarg'd, enlarge the channel's ſpace. *Davies.*

Space, conſidered in length, breadth, and thickneſs, I think, may be called *capacity.* *Locke.*

2. The force or power of the mind.

No intellectual creature in the world, is able, by *capacity*, to do that which nature doth without *capacity* and knowledge. *Hooker, b.* i. § 3.

In ſpiritual natures, ſo much as there is of deſire, ſo much there is alſo of *capacity* to receive. I do not ſay, there is always a *capacity* to receive the very thing they deſire; for that may be impoſſible. *South.*

An heroick poem requires the accompliſhment of ſome extraordinary undertaking; which requires the ſtrength and vigour of the body, the duty of a ſoldier, and the *capacity* and prudence of a general. *Dryden's Juv. Dedication.*

3. Power; ability.

Since the world's wide frame does not include
A cauſe with ſuch *capacities* endu'd,
Some other cauſe o'er nature muſt preſide. *Blackmore.*

4. Room; ſpace.

There remained, in the *capacity* of the exhauſted cylinder, ſtore of little rooms, or ſpaces, empty or devoid of air. *Boyle.*

5. State; condition; character.

A miraculous revolution, reducing many from the head of a triumphant rebellion, to their old condition of maſons, ſmiths, and carpenters; that, in this *capacity*, they might repair what, as colonels and captains, they had ruined and defaced. *South.*

You deſire my thoughts as a friend, and not as a member of parliament; they are the ſame in both *capacities.* *Swift.*

CAPA'RISON. *n. ſ.* [*caparazon*, a great cloke, Span.] A horſe-cloth, or a ſort of cover for a horſe, which is ſpread over his furniture. *Farrier's Dict.*

Tilting furniture, emblazon'd ſhields,
Impreſſes quaint, *capariſons*, and ſteeds,
Baſes, and tinſel trappings, gorgeous knights,
At jouſt, and tournament. *Paradiſe Loſt, b.* ix. *l.* 31.

Some wore a breaſtplate, and a light juppon;
Their horſes cloath'd with rich *capariſon.* *Dryden's Fab.*

To Capa'rison. *v. a.* [from the noun.]

1. To dreſs in capariſons.

At his command,
The ſteeds, *capariſon'd* with purple, ſtand;
With golden trappings, glorious to behold,
And champ betwixt their teeth the foaming gold. *Dryden.*

2. To dreſs pompouſly; in a ludicrous ſenſe.

Don't you think, though I am *capariſoned* like a man, I have a doublet and hoſe in my diſpoſition? *Shakeſp. As you like it.*

Cape. *n. ſ.* [*cape*, Fr.]

1. Headland; promontory.

What from the *cape* can you diſcern at ſea?—
—Nothing at all; it is a high wrought flood. *Shakeſp. Oth.*

The parting ſun,
Beyond the earth's green *cape*, and verdant iſles,
Heſperean ſets; my ſignal to depart. *Parad. Loſt, b.* viii.

The Romans made war upon the Tarentines, and obliged them by treaty not to ſail beyond the *cape.* *Arbuthnot on Coins.*

2. The neck-piece of a cloke.

He was cloathed in a robe of fine black cloth, with wide ſleeves and *cape.* *Bacon.*

CA'PER. *n. ſ.* [from *caper*, Latin, a goat.] A leap; a jump; a ſkip.

We that are true lovers, run into ſtrange *capers*; but as all is mortal in nature, ſo is all nature in love mortal in folly. *Shakeſp. As you like it.*

Flimnap, the treaſurer, is allowed to cut a *caper* on the ſtrait rope, at leaſt an inch higher than any other lord in the whole empire. *Swift's Gulliver's Travels.*

Ca'per. *n. ſ.* [*capparis*, Lat.] An acid pickle. See Caper-bush.

We invent new ſauces and pickles, which reſemble the animal

2

animal ferment in taste and virtue, as mangoes, olives, and capers. *Floyer on the Humours.*

CA'PER BUSH. *n. s.* [*capparis*, Lat.]

Its flower consists of four leaves, which are expanded in form of a rose; the fruit is fleshy, and shaped like a pear; in which are contained many roundish seeds. This plant grows in the South of France, in Spain and in Italy, upon old walls and buildings; and the buds of the flowers, before they are open, are pickled for eating. *Miller.*

To CA'PER. *v. n.* [from the noun.]

1. To dance frolicksomely.

The truth is, I am only old in judgment; and he that will *caper* with me for a thousand marks, let him lend me the money, and have at him. *Shakesp. Henry* IV. *p.* ii.

2. To skip for merriment.

Our master
Cap'ring to eye her. *Shakesp. Tempest.*

His nimble hand's instinct then taught each string
A *cap'ring* cheerfulness, and made them sing
To their own dance. *Crashaw.*

The family tript it about, and *caper'd*, like hailstones bounding from a marble floor. *Arbuthnot's John Bull.*

3. To dance; spoken in contempt.

The stage would need no force, nor song, nor dance,
Nor *capering* monsieur from active France. *Rowe.*

CA'PERER. *n. s.* [from *caper.*] A dancer; in contempt.

The tumbler's gambols some delight afford;
No less the nimble *caperer* on the cord:
But these are still insipid stuff to thee,
Coop'd in a ship, and toss'd upon the sea. *Dryden's Juv.*

CA'PIAS. n. s. [Lat.] A writ of two sorts, one before judgment, called *capias ad respondendum*, in an action personal, if the sheriff, upon the first writ of distress, return that he has no effects in his jurisdiction. The other is a writ of execution after judgment. *Cowel.*

CAPILLA'CEOUS. *adj.* The same with *capillary.*

CAPI'LLAMENT. *n. s.* [*capillamentum*, Lat.] Those small threads or hairs which grow up in the middle of a flower, and adorned with little herbs at the top, are called *capillaments.* *Quincy.*

CA'PILLARY. *adj.* [from *capillus*, hair, Lat.]

1. Resembling hairs; small; minute; applied to plants.

Capillary, or *capillaceous* plants, are such as have no main stalk or stem, but grow to the ground, as hairs on the head; and which bear their seeds in little tufts or protuberances on the backside of their leaves. *Quincy.*

Our common hyssop is not the least of vegetables, nor observed to grow upon walls; but rather, as Lemnius well conceiveth, some kind of *capillaries*, which are very small plants, and only grow upon walls and stony places. *Brown's Vulgar Errours, b.* vi. *c.* 7.

2. Applied to vessels of the body. Small; as the ramifications of the arteries. *Quincy.*

Ten *capillary* arteries in some parts of the body, as in the brain, are not equal to one hair; and the smallest lymphatick vessels are an hundred times smaller than the smallest *capillary* artery. *Arbuthnot on Aliments.*

CAPILLA'TION. *n. s.* [from *capillus*, Lat.] A vessel like a hair; a small ramification of vessels.

Nor is the humour contained in smaller veins, or obscurer *capillations*, but in a vesicle. *Brown's Vulgar Errours, b.* iii.

CA'PITAL. *adj.* [*capitalis*, Lat.]

1. Relating to the head.

Needs must the serpent now his *capital* bruise
Expect with mortal pain. *Paradise Lost, b.* xii. *l.* 383.

2. Criminal in the highest degree, so as to touch life.

Edmund, I arrest thee
On *capital* treason. *Shakesp. King Lear.*

Several cases deserve greater punishment than many crimes that are *capital* among us. *Swift.*

3. That which affects life.

In *capital* causes, wherein but one man's life is in question, the evidence ought to be clear; much more in a judgment upon a war, which is *capital* to thousands. *Bacon.*

4. Chief; principal.

I will, out of that infinite number, reckon but some that are most *capital*, and commonly occurrent both in the life and conditions of private men. *Spenser on Ireland.*

As to swerve in the least points, is errour; so the *capital* enemies thereof God hateth, as his deadly foes, aliens, and, without repentance, children of endless perdition. *Hooker.*

They are employed by me, and do, in themselves, tend to confirm the truth of a *capital* article in religion. *Atterbury.*

5. Chief; metropolitan.

This had been
Perhaps thy *capital* seat, from whence had spread
All generations; and had hither come,
From all the ends of th' earth, to celebrate
And reverence thee, their great progenitor. *Par. Lost, b.* xi.

6. Applied to letters; large; such as are written at the beginnings or heads of books.

Our most considerable actions are always present, like *capital* letters to an aged and dim eye. *Taylor's Rule of Living holy.*

The first whereof is written in *capital* letters, without chapters or verses. *Grew's Cosmologia Sacra.*

7. *Capital Stock.* The principal or original stock of a trading company.

CA'PITAL. *n. s.* [from the adjective.]

1. The upper part of a pillar.

You see the volute of the Ionick, the foliage of the Corinthian, and the uovali of the Dorick, mixed, without any regularity, on the same *capital.* *Addison on Italy.*

2. The chief city of a nation or kingdom.

CA'PITALLY. *adv.* [from *capital.*] In a capital manner.

CAPITA'TION. *n. s.* [from *caput*, the head, Lat.] Numeration by heads.

He suffered also for not performing the commandment of God, concerning *capitation*; that, when the people were numbered, for every head they should pay unto God a shekel. *Brown's Vulgar Errours, b.* vii. *c.* 11.

CA'PITE. n. s. [from *caput*, *capitis*, Lat.]

A tenure which holdeth immediately of the king, as of his crown, be it by knight's service or socage, and not as of any honour, castle, or manour: and therefore it is otherwise called a tenure, that holdeth merely of the king, because, as the crown is a corporation and seigniory in gross, as the common lawyers term it, so the king that possesseth the crown, is, in account of law, perpetually king, and never in his minority, nor ever dieth. *Cowel.*

CAPI'TULAR. *n. s.* [from *capitulum*, Lat. an ecclesiastical chapter.]

1. A body of the statutes of a chapter.

That this practice continued to the time of Charlemain, appears by a constitution in his *capitular.* *Taylor.*

2. A member of a chapter.

Canonists do agree, that the chapter makes decrees and statutes, which shall bind the chapter itself, and all its members or *capitulars.* *Ayliffe's Parergon.*

To CAPI'TULATE. *v. n.* [from *capitulum*, Lat.]

1. To draw up any thing in heads or articles.

Percy, Northumberland,
The archbishop of York, Douglas, and Mortimer,
Capitulate against us, and are up. *Shakesp. Henry* IV. *p.* i.

2. To yield, or surrender up, on certain stipulations.

The king took it for a great indignity, that thieves should offer to *capitulate* with him as enemies. *Hayward.*

I still pursued, and, about two o' clock this afternoon, she thought fit to *capitulate.* *Spectator*, N° 566.

CAPITULA'TION. *n. s.* [from *capitulate.*] Stipulation; terms; conditions.

It was not a complete conquest, but rather a dedition upon terms and *capitulations*, agreed between the conquerour and the conquered; wherein, usually, the yielding party secured to themselves their law and religion. *Hale.*

CAPI'VI TREE. *n. s.* [*copaiba*, Lat.]

It hath a flower consisting of five leaves, which expand in form of a rose; the pointal is fixed in the centre of the flower, which afterwards becomes a pod, containing one or two seeds, which are surrounded with a pulp of a yellow colour. This tree grows near a village called Ayapel, in the province of Antiochi, in the Spanish West Indies, about ten days journey from Carthagena. There are great numbers of these trees in the woods about this village, which grow to the height of sixty feet; some of them do not yield any of the balsam; those that do, are distinguished by a ridge, which runs along their trunks. These trees are wounded in their centre, and they apply vessels to the wounded part, to receive the balsam, which will all flow out in a short time. One of these trees will yield five or six gallons of balsam. *Miller.*

CA'PON. *n. s.* [*capo*, Lat.] A castrated cock.

In good roast beef my landlord sticks his knife;
The *capon* fat delights his dainty wife. *Gay's Pastorals.*

CAPONNI'ERE. n. s. [Fr. a term in fortification.] A covered lodgment, of about four or five feet broad, encompassed with a little parapet of about two feet high, serving to support planks laden with earth. This lodgment contains fifteen or twenty soldiers, and is usually placed at the extremity of the counterscarp, having little embrasures made in them, through which they fire. *Harris.*

CAPO'T. n. s. [French.] Is when one party wins all the tricks of cards at the game of picquet.

To CAPO'T. *v. a.* [from the noun.] When one party has won all the tricks of cards at picquet, he is said to have *capotted* his antagonist.

CAPO'UCH. *n. s.* [*capuce*, French] A monk's hood. *Dict.*

CA'PPER. *n. s.* [from *cap.*] One who makes or sells caps.

CAPRE'OLATE. *adj.* [from *capreolus*, a tendril of a vine, Lat.] Such plants as turn, wind, and creep along the ground, by means of their tendrils, as gourds, melons, and cucumbers, are termed, in botany, *capreolate* plants. *Harris.*

CAPRI'CE. } *n. s.* [*caprice*, Fr. *capricho*, Span.] Freak;
CAPRI'CHIO. } fancy; whim; sudden change of humour.

It is a pleasant spectacle to behold the shifts, windings, and unexpected *caprichios* of distressed nature, when pursued by a close and well managed experiment. *Glanville's Scepsis, Pref.*

Heav'n's great view is one, and that the whole;
That counterworks each folly and *caprice*,
That disappoints th' effect of ev'ry vice. *Pope.*

If there be a single spot more barren, or more distant from the church, the rector or vicar may be obliged, by the *caprice* or pique of the bishop, to build, under pain of sequestration. *Swift.*

Their passions move in lower spheres,
Where'er *caprice* or folly steers. *Swift.*

All the various machines and utensils would now and then play odd pranks and *caprices*, quite contrary to their proper structures, and design of the artificers. *Bentley.*

CAPRI'CIOUS. *adj.* [*capricieux*, Fr.] Whimsical; fanciful; humoursome.

CAPRI'CIOUSLY. *adv.* [from *capricious.*] Whimsically; in a manner depending wholly upon fancy.

CAPRI'CIOUSNESS. *n. s.* [from *capricious.*] The quality of being led by caprice, humour, whimsicalness.

A subject ought to suppose, that there are reasons, although he be not apprised of them; otherwise he must tax his prince of *capriciousness*, inconstancy, or ill design. *Swift.*

CA'PRICORN. *n. s.* [*capricornus*, Lat.] One of the signs of the zodiack; the winter solstice.

Let the longest night in *Capricorn* be of fifteen hours, the day consequently must be of nine. *Notes to Creech's Manilius.*

CAPRIO'LE. n. s. [French. In horsemanship.] *Caprioles* are leaps *firma à firma*, or such as a horse makes in one and the same place, without advancing forwards, and in such a manner, that when he is in the air, and height of his leap, he yerks or strikes out with his hinder legs, even and near. A *capriole* is the most difficult of all the high manage, or raised airs. It is different from the *croupade* in this, that the horse does not show his shoes; and from a *balotade*, in that he does not yerk out in a *balotade*. *Farrier's Dict.*

CA'PSTAN. *n. s.* [corruptly called *capstern*; *cabestan*, Fr.] A cylinder, with levers to wind up any great weight, particularly to raise the anchors.

The weighing of anchors by the *capstan*, is also new. *Raleigh's Essays.*

No more behold thee turn my watch's key,
As seamen at a *capstan* anchors weigh. *Swift.*

CA'PSULAR. } CA'PSULARY. } *adj.* [*capsula*, Lat.] Hollow like a chest.

It ascendeth not directly unto the throat, but ascending first into a *capsulary* reception of the breast-bone, it ascendeth again into the neck. *Brown's Vulgar Errours.*

CA'PSULATE. } CA'PSULATED. } *adj.* [*capsula*, Lat.] Inclosed, or in a box.

Seeds, such as are corrupted and stale, will swim; and this agreeth unto the seeds of plants locked up and *capsulated* in their husks. *Brown's Vulgar Errours, b.* iv. *c.* vi.

The heart lies immured, or *capsulated*, in a cartilage, which includes the heart, as the skull doth the brain. *Derham.*

CA'PTAIN. *n. s.* [*capitain*, Fr.]

1. A chief commander.

Dismay'd not this
Our *captains*, Macbeth and Banquo? *Shakesp. Macbeth.*

2. The commander of a company in a regiment.

A *captain!* these villains will make the name of *captain* as odious as the word occupy; therefore *captains* had need look to it. *Shakesp. Henry* IV. *p.* ii.

The grim *captain*, in a surly tone,
Cries out, pack up, ye rascals, and be gone. *Dryden*

3. The chief commander of a ship.

The Rhodian *captain*, relying on his knowledge, and the lightness of his vessel, passed, in open day, through all the guards. *Arbuthnot on Coins.*

4. It was anciently written *capitain.*

And evermore their cruel *capitain*
Sought with his rascal routs t' inclose them round. *Fairy Q.*

5. *Captain General.* The general or commander in chief of an army.

6. *Captain Lieutenant.* The commanding officer of the colonel's troop or company, in every regiment. He commands as youngest captain.

CA'PTAINRY. *n. s.* [from *captain.*] The power over a certain district; the chieftainship.

There should be no rewards taken for *captainries* of counties, nor no shares of bishopricks for nominating of bishops. *Spenser on Ireland.*

CA'PTAINSHIP. *n. s.* [from *captain.*]

1. The rank, quality, or post of a captain.

The lieutenant of the colonel's company might well pretend to the next vacant *captainship* in the same regiment. *Wotton.*

2. The condition or post of a chief commander.

Therefore so please thee to return with us,
And of our Athens, thine and ours, to take
The *captainship*. *Shakesp. Timon.*

3. The chieftainship of a clan, or government of a certain district.

To diminish the Irish lords, he did abolish their pretended and usurped *captainships*. *Davies on Ireland.*

CAPTA'TION. *n. s.* [from *capto*, Lat.] The practice of catching favour or applause; courtship; flattery.

I am content my heart should be discovered, without any of those dresses, or popular *captations*, which some men use in their speeches. *King Charles.*

CA'PTION. *n. s.* [from *capio*, Lat. to take.] The act of taking any person by a judicial process.

CA'PTIOUS. *adj.* [*captieux*, Fr. *captiosus*, Lat.]

1. Given to cavils; eager to object.

If he shew a forwardness to be reasoning about things, take care, that nobody check this inclination, or mislead it by *captious* or fallacious ways of talking with him. *Locke.*

2. Insidious; ensnaring.

She taught him likewise how to avoid sundry *captious* and tempting questions, which were like to be asked of him. *Bacon.*

CA'PTIOUSLY. *adv.* [from *captious.*] In a captious manner; with an inclination to object.

Use your words as *captiously* as you can, in your arguing on one side, and apply distinctions on the other. *Locke.*

CA'PTIOUSNESS. *n. s.* [from *captious.*] Inclination to find fault; inclination to object; peevishness.

Captiousness is a fault opposite to civility; it often produces misbecoming and provoking expressions and carriage. *Locke.*

To CA'PTIVATE. *v. a.* [*captiver*, Fr. *captivo*, Lat.]

1. To take prisoner; to bring into bondage.

How ill beseeming is it in thy sex,
To triumph like an Amazonian trull,
Upon their woes, whom fortune *captivates?* *Shakesp. H.* VI.

That hast by tyranny these many years
Wasted our country, slain our citizens,
And sent our sons and husbands *captivate*. *Shakesp. Henry* VI.

He deserves to be a slave, that is content to have the rational sovereignty of his soul, and the liberty of his will, so *captivated*. *K. Charles.*

They stand firm, keep out the enemy, truth, that would *captivate* or disturb them. *Locke.*

2. To charm; to overpower with excellence; to subdue.

Wisdom enters the last, and so *captivates* him with her appearance, that he gives himself up to her. *Addison. Guardian.*

3. To enslave; with *to*.

They lay a trap for themselves, and *captivate* their understandings *to* mistake, falsehood and errour. *Locke.*

CAPTIVA'TION. *n. s.* [from *captivate.*] The act of taking one captive.

CA'PTIVE. *n. s.* [*captif*, Fr. *captivus*, Lat.]

1. One taken in war; a prisoner to an enemy.

You have the *captives*,
Who were the opposites of this day's strife. *Shak. K. Lear.*

This is no other than that forced respect a *captive* pays to his conquerour, a slave to his lord. *Rogers.*

Free from shame
Thy *captives*: I ensure the penal claim. *Pope's Odyssey.*

2. It is used with *to* before the captor.

If thou say Antony lives, 'tis well,
Or friends with Cæsar, or not *captive to* him. *Shakesp.*

My mother, who the royal sceptre sway'd,
Was *captive to* the cruel victor made. *Dryden.*

3. One charmed, or ensnared by beauty or excellence.

My woman's heart
Grossly grew *captive to* his honey words. *Shak. Richard* III.

CA'PTIVE. *adj.* [*captivus*, Lat.] Made prisoner in war; kept in bondage or confinement.

But fate forbids; the Stygian floods oppose,
And with nine circling streams the *captive* souls inclose. *Dryden, Æn.* vi.

To CA'PTIVE. *v. a.* [from the noun. It was used formerly with the accent on the last syllable, but now it is on the first.] To take prisoner; to bring into a condition of servitude.

But being all defeated save a few,
Rather than fly, or be *captiv'd*, herself she slew. *Fairy Q. b.* ii.

Oft leavest them to hostile sword
Of heathen and profane, their carcasses
To dogs and fowls a prey, or else *captiv'd*. *Milton's Agonist.*

What further fear of danger can there be?
Beauty, which *captives* all things, sets me free. *Dryden.*

Still lay the god: the nymph surpriz'd,
Yet, mistress of herself, devis'd,
How she the vagrant might inthral,
And *captive* him, who *captives* all. *Prior.*

CAPTI'VITY. *n. s.* [*captivité*, Fr. *captivitas*, low Lat.]

1. Subjection by the fate of war; bondage; servitude to enemies.

This is the serjeant,
Who, like a good and hardy soldier, fought
'Gainst my *captivity*. *Shakesp. King Lear.*

There in *captivity* he lets them dwell
The space of seventy years; then brings them back;
Rememb'ring mercy. *Paradise Lost, b.* xii. *l.* 344.

The name of Ormond will be more celebrated in his *captivity*, than in his greatest triumphs. *Dryden's Fab. Dedicat.*

2. Slavery; servitude.

For men to be tied, and led by authority, as it were with a kind

kind of *captivity* of judgment; and though there be reason to the contrary, not to listen unto it. *Hooker.*

The apostle tells us, there is a way of bringing every thought into *captivity* to the obedience of Christ. *Decay of Piety.*

When love's well timed, 'tis not a fault to love
The strong, the brave, the virtuous, and the wise,
Sink in the soft *captivity* together. *Addison's Cato.*

CA'PTOR. *n. s.* [from *capio*, to take, Lat.] He that takes a prisoner, or a prize.

CA'PTURE. *n. s.* [*capture*, Fr. *captura*, Lat.]

1. The act or practice of taking any thing.

The great sagacity, and many artifices used by birds, in the investigation and *capture* of their prey. *Derham's Phys. Theol.*

2. The thing taken; a prize.

CAPU'CHED. *adj.* [from *capuce*, Fr. a hood.] Covered over as with a hood.

They are differently cucullated and *capuched* upon the head and back, and, in the cicada, the eyes are more prominent. *Brown's Vulgar Errours, b.* iv. *c.* iii.

CAPUCHI'N. *n. s.* A female garment, consisting of a cloak and hood, made in imitation of the dress of capuchin monks; whence its name is derived.

CAR, CHAR, in the names of places, seem to have relation to the British *caer*, a city. *Gibson's Camden.*

CAR. *n. s.* [*car*, Welch; *karre*, Dut. cræt, Sax. *carrus*, Lat.]

1. A small carriage of burden, usually drawn by one horse or two.

When a lady comes in a coach to our shops, it must be followed by a *car* loaded with Mr. Wood's money. *Swift.*

2. In poetical language, a chariot; a chariot of war, or triumph.

Henry is dead, and never shall revive:
Upon a wooden coffin we attend,
And death's dishonourable victory,
We with our stately presence glorify,
Like captives bound to a triumphant *car*. *Shakesp. Hen.* VI.

Wilt thou aspire to guide the heav'nly *car*,
And with thy daring folly burn the world. *Shakesp.*

And the gilded *car* of day,
His glowing axle doth allay
In the steep Atlantick stream. *Milton.*

See, where he comes, the darling of the war!
See millions crouding round the gilded *car*! *Prior.*

3. The Charles's wain, or Bear; a constellation.

Ev'ry fixt and ev'ry wand'ring star,
The Pleiads, Hyads, and the Northern *Car*. *Dryden.*

CA'RABINE. } *n. s.* [*carabine*, Fr.] A small sort of fire-arm,
CA'RBINE. } shorter than a fusil, and carrying a ball of twenty-four in the pound, hung by the light horse at a belt over the left shoulder. It is a kind of medium between the pistol and the musket, having its barrel two foot and a half long.

CARABINI'ER. *n. s.* [from *carabine*.] A sort of light horse carrying longer carabines than the rest, and used sometimes on foot. *Chambers.*

CA'RACK. *n. s.* [*caraca*, Spanish.] A large ship of burden; the same with those which are now called *galleons*.

In which river, the greatest *carack* of Portugal may ride afloat ten miles within the forts. *Raleigh.*

The bigger whale like some huge *carack* lay,
Which wanteth sea-room with her foes to play. *Waller.*

CA'RACOLE. *n. s.* [*caracole*, Fr. from *caracol*, Span. a snail.] An oblique tread, traced out in semi-rounds, changing from one hand to another, without observing a regular ground.

When the horse advance to charge in battle, they ride sometimes in *caracoles*, to amuse the enemy, and put them in doubt, whether they are about to charge them in the front or in the flank. *Farrier's Dict.*

To CA'RACOLE. *v. n.* [from the noun.] To move in caracoles.

CA'RAT. } *n. s.* [*carat*, Fr.]
CA'RACT. }

1. A weight of four grains, with which diamonds are weighed.
2. A manner of expressing the fineness of gold.

A mark, being an ounce Troy, is divided into twenty-four equal parts, called *caracts*, and each *caract* into four grains; by this weight is distinguished the different fineness of their gold; for, if to the finest of gold be put two *caracts* of alloy, both making, when cold, but an ounce, or twenty-four *caracts*, then this gold is said to be twenty-two *caracts* fine. *Cocker.*

Thou best of gold, art worst of gold;
Other, less fine in *carat*, is more precious. *Shakesp. H.* IV.

CA'RAVAN. *n. s.* [*caravanne*, Fr. from the Arabick.] A troop or body of merchants or pilgrims, as they travel in the East.

Set forth
Their airy *caravan*, high over seas
Flying, and over lands, with mutual wing
Easing their flight. *Milton's Par. Lost, b.* vii. *c.* 428.

When Joseph, and the Blessed Virgin Mother, had lost their most holy Son, they sought him in the retinues of their kindred, and the *caravans* of the Galilæan pilgrims. *Taylor.*

CARAVA'NSARY. *n. s.* [from *caravan*.] A house built in the Eastern countries for the reception of travellers.

The inns which receive the caravans in Persia, and the Eastern countries, are called by the name of *caravansaries*. *Spectator*, N° 289.

The spacious mansion, like a Turkish *caravansary*, entertains the vagabond with only bare lodging. *Pope's Letters.*

CA'RAVEL. } *n. s.* [*caravela*, Span.] A light, round, old fashion-
CA'RVEL. } ed ship, with a square poop, formerly used in Spain and Portugal.

CA'RAWAY. *n. s.* [*carui*, Lat.] A plant.

This plant hath winged leaves, cut into small segments, and placed opposite on the stalks, having no footstalk; the petals of the flowers are bifid, and shaped like a heart; the seeds are long, slender, smooth, and furrowed. It is sometimes found wild in rich moist pastures, especially in Holland and Lincolnshire. The seeds are used in medicine, and likewise in the confectionary. *Miller.*

CARBONA'DO. *n. s.* [*carbonnade*, Fr. from *carbo*, a coal, Lat.] Meat cut cross, to be broiled upon the coals.

If I come in his way willingly, let him make a *carbonado* of me. *Shakesp. Henry* IV.

To CARBONA'DO. *v. a.* [from the noun.] To cut, or hack.

Draw, you rogue, or I'll so *carbonado*
Your shanks. *Shakesp. King Lear.*

CA'RBUNCLE. *n. s.* [*carbunculus*, Lat. a little coal.]

1. A jewel shining in the dark, like a lighted coal or candle.

A *carbuncle* entire, as big as thou art,
Were not so rich a jewel. *Shakesp. Coriolanus.*

His head
Crested aloft, and *carbuncle* his eyes,
With burnish'd neck of verdant gold. *Par. Lost, b.* ix.

It is commonly related, and believed, that a *carbuncle* does shine in the dark like a burning coal; from whence it hath its name. *Wilkins's Mathematical Magick.*

Carbuncle is a stone of the ruby kind, of a rich blood-red colour. *Woodward.*

2. Red spots or pimples breaking out upon the face or body.

It was a pestilent fever, but there followed no *carbuncle*, no purple or livid spots, or the like, the mass of the blood not being tainted. *Bacon's Henry* VII.

Red blisters, rising on their paps, appear,
And flaming *carbuncles*, and noisome sweat. *Dryden.*

CA'RBUNCLED. *adj.* [from *carbuncle*.]

1. Set with carbuncles.

He gave thee, friend,
An armour all of gold; it was a king's.—
—He has deserv'd it, were it *carbuncled*
Like holy Phœbus' car. *Shakesp. Antony and Cleopatra.*

2. Spotted; deformed with carbuncles.

CARBU'NCULAR. *adj.* [from *carbuncle*.] Belonging to a carbuncle; red like a carbuncle.

CARBUNCULA'TION. *n. s.* [*carbunculatio*, Lat.] The blasting of the young buds of trees or plants, either by excessive heat or excessive cold. *Harris.*

CA'RCANET. *n. s.* [*carcan*, Fr.] A chain or collar of jewels.

Say, that I linger'd with you at your shop,
To see the making of her *carcanet*. *Shak. Comedy of Errours.*

I have seen her beset and bedeckt all over with emeralds and pearls, and a *carcanet* about her neck. *Hakewell on Providence.*

CA'RCASS. *n. s.* [*carquasse*, Fr.]

1. A dead body of any animal.

To blot the honour of the dead,
And with foul cowardice his *carcass* shame,
Whose living hands immortaliz'd his name. *Fairy Q. b.* ii.

Where cattle pastur'd late, now scatter'd lies,
With *carcasses* and arms, th' insanguin'd field,
Deserted. *Milton's Par. Lost, b.* xi. *l.* 654.

If a man visits his sick friend, in hope of legacy, he is a vulture, and only waits for the *carcass*. *Taylor.*

The scaly nations of the sea profound,
Like shipwreck'd *carcasses*, are driv'n aground. *Dryden.*

2. Body; in a ludicrous sense.

Today how many would have given their honours,
To've sav'd their *carcasses*? *Shakesp. Cymbeline.*

He that finds himself in any distress, either of *carcass* or of fortune, should deliberate upon the matter, before he prays for a change. *L'Estrange.*

3. The decayed parts of any thing; the ruins; the remains.

A rotten *carcass* of a boat, not rigg'd,
Nor tackle, sail, nor mast. *Shakesp. Tempest.*

4. The main parts, naked, without completion or ornament; as the walls of a house.

What could be thought a sufficient motive to have had an eternal *carcass* of an universe, wherein the materials and positions of it were eternally laid together? *Hale's Origin of Mank.*

5. [In gunnery.] A kind of bomb usually oblong, consisting of a shell or case, sometimes of iron, with holes, more commonly of a coarse strong stuff, pitched over, and girt with iron hoops, filled with combustibles, and thrown from a mortar. *Harris.*

CA'RCELAGE. *n. s.* [from *carcer*, Lat.] Prison fees. *Dict.*

CARCINO'MA. *n. s.* [from καρκίνος, a crab.] A particular ulcer, called a cancer, very difficult to cure. A disorder likewise in the horny coat of the eye, is thus called by some writers. *Quincy.*

CARCINO'MATOUS. *adj.* [from *carcinoma*.] Cancerous; tending to a cancer.

CARD. *n. ſ.* [*carte*, Fr. *charta*, Lat.]

1. A paper painted with figures, uſed in games of chance or ſkill.

A vengeance on your crafty wither'd hide!
Yet I have fac'd it with a *card* of ten.
Shakeſp. Taming of the Shrew.

There all is marr'd, there lies a cooling *card*. *Shakeſp.*

Soon as ſhe ſpreads her hand, th' aerial guard
Deſcend, and ſit on each important *card*;
Firſt, Ariel perch'd upon a matadore. *Pope.*

2. The paper on which the winds are marked under the mariner's needle.

Upon his *cards* and compaſs firms his eye,
The maſters of his long experiment. *Fairy Queen, b.* ii.

The very points they blow;
All the quarters that they know,
I' th' ſhipman's *card*. *Shakeſp. Macbeth.*

How abſolute the knave is? we muſt ſpeak by the *card*, or equivocation will undo us. *Shakeſp. Hamlet.*

On life's vaſt ocean diverſely we ſail,
Reaſon the *card*, but paſſion is the gale. *Pope.*

3. [*kaarde*, Dutch.] The inſtrument with which wool is combed, or comminuted, or laid over for ſpinning.

To CARD. *v. a.* [from the noun.] To comb, or comminute wool with a piece of wood, thick ſet with crooked wires.

The while their wives do ſit
Beſide them, *carding* wool. *May's Virgil's Georgicks.*

Go, *card* and ſpin,
And leave the buſineſs of the war to men. *Dryden.*

To CARD. *v. n.* To game; to play much at cards; as, a *carding* wife.

CARDAMO'MUM. *n. ſ.* [Latin.] A medicinal ſeed, of the aromatick kind, contained in pods, and brought from the Eaſt Indies. *Chambers.*

CA'RDER. *n. ſ.* [from *card.*]

1. One that cards wool.

The clothiers all have put off
The ſpinſters, *carders*, fullers, weavers. *Shakeſp. Henry* VIII.

2. One that plays much at cards.

CARDI'ACAL. } *adj.* [καρδία, the heart.] Cordial; having the
CA'RDIACK. } quality of invigorating.

CA'RDIALGY. *n. ſ.* [from καρδία, the heart, and ἄλγος, pain.] The heart-burn; a pain ſuppoſed to be felt in the heart, but more properly in the ſtomach, which ſometimes riſes all along from thence up to the œſophagus, occaſioned by ſome acrimonious matter. *Quincy.*

CA'RDINAL. *adj.* [*cardinalis*, Lat.] Principal; chief.

The diviſions of the year in frequent uſe with aſtronomers, according to the *cardinal* interſections of the zodiack; that is, the two equinoctials, and both the ſolſtitial points.
Brown's Vulgar Errours, b. vi. *c.* 3.

His *cardinal* perfection was induſtry. *Clarendon.*

CA'RDINAL. *n. ſ.* One of the chief governours of the Romiſh church, by whom the pope is elected out of their own number, which contains ſix biſhops, fifty prieſts, and fourteen deacons, who conſtitute the ſacred college, and are choſen by the pope.

A *cardinal* is ſo ſtiled, becauſe ſerviceable to the apoſtolick ſee, as an axle or hinge on which the whole government of the church turns; or as they have, from the pope's grant, the hinge and government of all the affairs of the Romiſh church.
Ayliffe's Parergon.

You hold a fair aſſembly;
You are a churchman, or, I'll tell you, *cardinal*,
I ſhould judge now unhappily. *Shakeſp. Henry* VIII.

CARDINAL'S FLOWER. *n. ſ.* [*rapuntium*, Lat.]

The flower conſiſts of one leaf, of an anomalous figure, hollowed like a pipe, channelled, and divided into many parts, in the ſhape of a tongue, defended by a covering, which infolds the pointal; when the flowers decay, the flower-cup turns to a fruit, divided into three cells, full of ſmall ſeeds, which adhere to a placenta, divided into three parts. The ſpecies are, 1 Greater rampions, with a crimſon ſpiked flower, commonly called the ſcarlet *cardinal's flower*. 2. The blue *cardinal's flower*. The firſt ſort is greatly prized for the beauty of its rich crimſon flowers, exceeding all flowers in deepneſs. *Miller.*

CA'RDINALATE. } *n. ſ.* [from *cardinal.*] The office and rank
CA'RDINALSHIP. } of a cardinal.

An ingenious cavalier, hearing that an old friend of his was advanced to a *cardinalate*, went to congratulate his eminence upon his new honour. *L'Eſtrange.*

CARDMA'KER. *n. ſ.* [from *card* and *make.*] A maker of cards.

Am not I Chriſtophero Sly, by occupation a *cardmaker?*
Shakeſp. Taming of the Shrew.

CA'RDMATCH. *n. ſ.* [from *card* and *match.*] A match made by dipping pieces of card in melted ſulphur.

Take care, that thoſe may not make the moſt noiſe who have the leaſt to ſell; which is very obſervable in the venders of *cardmatches*. *Addiſon. Spectator*, N° 251.

CA'RDUUS. See THISTLE.

CARE. *n. ſ.* [cape, Saxon.]

1. Solicitude; anxiety; perturbation of mind; concern.

Or, if I would take care, that *care* ſhould be,
For wit that ſcorn'd the world, and liv'd like me. *Dryden.*

Nor ſullen diſcontent, nor anxious *care*,
Ev'n though brought thither, could inhabit there. *Dryden.*

It will raiſe in your ſoul the greateſt *care* of fulfilling the divine will. *Wake's Preparation for Death.*

2. Caution.

Well, ſweet Jack, have a *care* of thyſelf. *Shakeſp. H.* IV.

The fooliſh virgins had taken no *care* for a further ſupply, after the oil, which was at firſt put into their lamps, was ſpent, as the wiſe had done. *Tillotſon.*

Begone! the prieſt expects you at the altar.—
But, tyrant, have a *care*, I come not thither.
A. Philips's Diſtreſt Mother.

3. Regard; charge; heed in order to protection and preſervation.

You come in ſuch a time,
As if propitious fortune took a *care*
To ſwell my tide of joys to their full height. *Dryden.*

If we believe that there is a God, that takes *care* of us, and we be careful to pleaſe him, this cannot but be a mighty comfort to us. *Tillotſon.*

4. It is a looſe and vague word, implying attention or inclination, in any degree more or leſs.

We take *care* to flatter ourſelves with imaginary ſcenes and proſpects of future happineſs. *Atterbury.*

5. The object of care, of caution, or of love.

O my poor kingdom, ſick with civil blows!
When that my care could not with-hold thy riots,
What wilt thou do, when riot is thy *care?* *Shakeſp. H.* IV.

Fluſh'd were his cheeks, and glowing were his eyes:
Is ſhe thy *care?* is ſhe thy *care?* he cries. *Dryden.*

Your ſafety, more than mine, was then my *care:*
Leſt of the guide bereft, the rudder loſt,
Your ſhip ſhould run againſt the rocky coaſt. *Dryden.*

The wily fox,
Who lately filch'd the turkey's callow *care*. *Gay's Trivia.*

None taught the trees a nobler race to bear,
Or more improv'd the vegetable *care*. *Pope.*

To CARE. *v. n.* [from the noun.]

1. To be anxious or ſolicitous; to be in concern about any thing.

She *cared* not what pain ſhe put her body to, ſince the better part, her mind, was laid under ſo much agony. *Sidney, b.* ii.

As the Germans, both in language and manners, differed from the Hungarians, ſo were they always at variance with them; and therefore much *cared* not, though they were by him ſubdued. *Knolles's Hiſtory of the Turks.*

Well, on my terms thou wilt not be my heir;
If thou *car'ſt* little, leſs ſhall be my care. *Dryden's Perſius.*

2. To be inclined; to be diſpoſed; with *for* or *to.*

Not *caring to* obſerve the wind,
Or the new ſea explore. *Waller.*

The remarks are introduced by a compliment to the works of an authour, who, I am ſure, would not *care for* being praiſed at the expence of another's reputation. *Addiſon. Guardian.*

Having been now acquainted, the two ſexes did not *care to* part. *Addiſon.*

Great maſters in painting never *care for* drawing people in the faſhion. *Spectator*, N° 129.

3. To be affected with; to have regard to; with *for.*

You dote on her that *cares* not *for* your love.
Shakeſp. Two Gentlemen of Verona.

There was an ape that had twins; ſhe doted upon one of them, and did not much *care for* t'other. *L'Eſtrange.*

Where few are rich, few *care for* it; where many are ſo, many deſire it. *Temple.*

CA'RECRAZED. *adj.* [from *care* and *craze.*] Broken with care and ſolicitude.

Theſe both put off, a poor petitioner,
A *carecraz'd* mother of a many children. *Shakeſp. Rich.* III.

To CARE'EN. *v. a.* [*cariner*, Fr. from *carina*, Lat.] A term in the ſea language. To lay a veſſel on one ſide, to caulk, ſtop up leaks, refit, or trim the other ſide. *Chambers.*

To CARE'EN. *v. n.* To be in the ſtate of careening.

CARE'ER. *n. ſ.* [*carriere*, Fr.]

1. The ground on which a race is run.

They had run themſelves too far out of breath, to go back again the ſame *career*. *Sidney, b.* ii.

2. A courſe; a race.

What rein can hold licentious wickedneſs,
When down the hill he holds his fierce *career?* *Shakeſp.*

3. Full ſpeed; ſwift motion.

It is related of certain Indians, that they are able, when a horſe is running in his full *career*, to ſtand upright on his back.
Wilkins's Mathematical Magick.

Practiſe them now to curb the turning ſteed,
Mocking the foe; now to his rapid ſpeed
To give the rein, and, in the full *career*,
To draw the certain ſword, or ſend the pointed ſpear. *Prior.*

4. Courſe of action; uninterrupted procedure.

Shall quips and ſentences, and theſe paper bullets of the brain, awe a man from the *career* of his humour?
Shakeſp. Much ado about Nothing.

The heir of a blasted family has rose up, and promised fair, and yet, at length, a cross event has certainly met and stopt him in the *career* of his fortune. *South.*

Knights in knightly deeds should persevere,
And still continue what at first they were;
Continue, and proceed in honour's fair *career.* *Dryden.*

To CARE'ER. *v. n.* [from the noun.] Running with swift motion.

With eyes, the wheels
Of beryl, and *careering* fires between. *Parad. Lost, b.* vi.

CA'REFUL. *adj.* [from *care* and *full.*]

1. Anxious; solicitous; full of concern.

Martha, thou art *careful*, and troubled about many things. *Luke,* x. 41.

Welcome, thou pleasing slumber;
A while embrace me in thy leaden arms,
And charm my *careful* thoughts. *Denham's Sophy.*

2. Provident; diligent; cautious; with *of* or *for.*

Behold, thou hast been *careful for* us with all this care; what is to be done for thee? *2 Kings,* iv. 13.

To cure their mad ambition, they were sent
To rule a distant province, each alone:
What could a *careful* father more have done? *Dryden.*

3. Watchful; with *of.*

It concerns us to be *careful of* our conversations. *Ray.*

4. Subject to perturbations; exposed to troubles; full of anxiety; full of solicitude.

By him that rais'd me to this *careful* height,
From that contented hap, which I enjoy'd. *Shakesp. Richard* III.

CA'REFULLY. *adv.* [from *careful.*]

1. In a manner that shews care.

Envy, how *carefully* does it look? how meager and ill-complexion'd? *Collier.*

2. Heedfully; watchfully; vigilantly; attentively.

You come most *carefully* upon your hour. *Shakesp. Hamlet.*

By considering him so *carefully* as I did before my attempt, I have made some faint resemblance of him. *Dryden.*

All of them, therefore, studiously cherished the memory of their honourable extraction, and *carefully* preserved the evidences of it. *Atterbury.*

CA'REFULNESS. *n. s.* [from *careful.*] Vigilance; heedfulness; caution.

The death of Selymus was, with all *carefulness*, concealed by Ferhates. *Knolles's History of the Turks.*

CA'RELESLY. *adv.* [from *careless.*] Negligently; inattentively; without care; heedlesly.

There he him found all *carelesly* display'd,
In secret shadow from the sunny ray. *Fairy Queen, b.* ii.

Not content to see,
That others write as *carelesly* as he. *Waller.*

CA'RELESNESS. *n. s.* [from *careless.*] Heedlesness; inattention; negligence; absence of care; manner; void of care.

For Coriolanus, neither to care whether they love or hate him, manifests the true knowledge he has in their disposition, and, out of his noble *carelesness*, lets them plainly see it. *Shakesp. Coriolanus.*

Who, in the other extreme, only doth
Call a rough *carelesness* good fashion;
Whose cloak his spurs tear, or whom he spits on,
He cares not. *Donne.*

It makes us to walk warily, and tread sure, for fear of our enemies; and that is better, than to be flattered into pride and *carelesness.* *Taylor's Rule of living holy.*

The ignorance or *carelesness* of the servants can hardly leave the master disappointed. *Temple.*

I who at sometimes spend, at others spare,
Divided between *carelesness* and care. *Pope.*

CA'RELESS. *adj.* [from *care.*]

1. Without care; without solicitude; unconcerned; negligent; inattentive; heedless; regardless; thoughtless; neglectful; unheeding; unthinking; unmindful; with *of* or *about.*

Knowing that if the worst befal them, they shall lose nothing but themselves; *whereof* they seem very *careless.* *Spenser's Irel.*

Nor lose the good advantage of his grace,
By seeming cold, or *careless of* his will. *Shakesp. Henry* IV.

A woman the more curious she is about her face, is commonly the more *careless* about her house. *Ben. Johnson.*

A father, unnaturally *careless of* his child, sells or gives him to another man. *Locke.*

2. Cheerful; undisturbed.

Thus wisely *careless*, innocently gay,
Cheerful he play'd. *Pope.*

In my cheerful morn of life,
When nurs'd by *careless* solitude I liv'd,
And sung of nature with unceasing joy,
Pleas'd have I wander'd through your rough domain. *Thomson's Autumn, l.* 5.

3. Unheeded; thoughtless; unconsidered.

The freedom of saying as many *careless* things as other people, without being so severely remarked upon. *Pope.*

4. Unmoved by; unconcerned at.

Careless of thunder from the clouds that break,
My only omens from your looks I take. *Granville.*

To CARE'SS. *v. a.* [*caresser*, Fr. from *carus*, Lat.] To endear; to fondle; to treat with kindness.

If I can feast, and please, and *caress* my mind with the pleasures of worthy speculations, or virtuous practices, let greatness and malice vex and abridge me, if they can. *South.*

CARE'SS. *n. s.* [from the verb.] An act of endearment; an expression of tenderness.

He, she knew, would intermix
Grateful digressions, and solve high dispute
With conjugal *caresses.* *Paradise Lost, b.* viii. *l.* 54.

There are some men who seem to have brutal minds wrapt up in human shapes; their very *caresses* are crude and importune. *L'Estrange.*

After his successour had publickly owned himself a Roman catholick, he began with his first *caresses* to the church party. *Swift.*

CA'RET. *n. s.* [*caret*, Lat. there is wanting.] A note which shews where something interlined should be read.

CA'RGASON. *n. s.* [*cargaçon*, Spanish.] A cargo.

My body is a *cargason* of ill humours. *Howel's Letters.*

CA'RGO. *n. s.* [*charge*, Fr.] The lading of a ship; the merchandise or wares contained and conveyed in a ship.

In the hurry of the shipwreck, Simonides was the only man that appeared unconcerned, notwithstanding that his whole fortune was at stake in the *cargo.* *L'Estrange.*

A ship, whose *cargo* was no less than a whole world, that carried the fortune and hopes of all posterity. *Burnet's Theory.*

This gentleman was then a young adventurer in the republick of letters, and just fitted out for the university with a good *cargo* of Latin and Greek. *Addison. Spectator,* N° 494.

CA'RICOUS *Tumour.* [from *carica*, a fig, Lat.] A swelling in the form of a fig.

CA'RIES. *n. s.* [Latin.] That rottenness which is peculiar to a bone. *Quincy.*

Fistulas of a long continuance, are, for the most part, accompanied with ulcerations of the gland, and *caries* in the bone. *Wiseman's Surgery.*

CARIO'SITY. *n. s.* [from *carious.*] Rottenness.

This being too general, taking in all *cariosity* and ulcers of the bones. *Wiseman's Surgery.*

CA'RIOUS. *adj.* [*cariosus*, Lat.] Rotten.

I discovered the blood to arise by a *carious* tooth. *Wiseman.*

CARK. *n. s.* [ceaꞃc, Saxon.] Care; anxiety; solicitude; concern; heedfulness. This word is now obsolete.

And Klaius taking for his youngling *cark*,
Lest greedy eyes to them might challenge lay,
Busy with oker did their shoulders mark. *Sidney.*

Down did lay
His heavy head, devoid of careful *cark.* *Fairy Queen, b.* i.

To CARK. *v. n.* [ceaꞃcan, Saxon.] To be careful; to be solicitous; to be anxious. It is now very little used, and always in an ill sense.

I do find what a blessing is chanced to my life, from such muddy abundance of *carking* agonies, to states which still be adherent. *Sidney, b.* i.

What can be vainer, than to lavish out our lives in the search of trifles, and to lie *carking* for the unprofitable goods of this world? *L'Estrange.*

Nothing can supersede our own *carkings* and contrivances for ourselves, but the assurance that God cares for us. *Decay of Piety.*

CARLE. *n. s.* [ceoꞃl, Saxon.] A mean, rude, rough, brutal man. We now use *churl.*

The *carle* beheld, and saw his guest
Would safe depart, for all his subtile sleight. *Fairy Q. b.* i.

Answer, thou *carle*, and judge this riddle right,
I'll frankly own thee for a cunning wight. *Gay's Pastorals.*

The editor was a covetous *carle*, and would have his pearls of the highest price. *Bentley.*

CA'RLINE THISTLE. [*carlina*, Lat.] A plant; placed in the catalogue of simples in the college dispensatory, but rarely ordered in medicine. *Miller.*

CA'RLINGS. *n. s.* [In a ship.] Timbers lying fore and aft, along from one beam to another; on these the ledges rest, on which the planks of the deck are made fast. *Harris.*

CA'RMAN. *n. s.* [from *car* and *man.*] A man whose employment it is to drive cars.

If the strong cane support thy walking hand,
Chairmen no longer shall the wall command;
E'en sturdy *carmen* shall thy nod obey,
And rattling coaches stop to make thee way. *Gay's Trivia.*

CA'RMELITE. *n. s.* [*carmelite*, Fr.] A sort of pear; which see.

CARMI'NATIVE. *adj.* [supposed to be so called, as having *vim carminis*, the power of a charm.]

Carminatives are such things as dilute and relax at the same time, because wind occasions a spasm, or convulsion in some parts. Whatever promotes insensible perspiration, is *carminative*; for wind is perspirable matter retained in the body. *Arbuthnot on Aliments.*

Carminative and dieuretick
Will damp all passion sympathetick. *Swift.*

CA'RMINE. *n. s.* A bright red or crimson colour, bordering on purple, used by painters in miniature. It is the most valuable product of the cochineal mastick, and of an excessive price. *Chambers.*

CA'RNAGE. *n. s.* [*carnage*, Fr. from *caro*, *carnis*, Lat.]
1. Slaughter; havock; massacre.
He brought the king's forces upon them rather as to *carnage* than to fight, insomuch as without any great loss or danger to themselves, the greatest part of the seditious were slain. *Hayw.*
2. Heaps of flesh.
Such a scent I draw
Of *carnage*, prey innumerable! and taste
The savour of death from all things there that live. *Milton.*
His ample maw, with human *carnage* fill'd,
A milky deluge next the giant swill'd. *Pope's Odyssey.*

CA'RNAL. *adj.* [*carnal*, Fr. *carnalis*, low Lat.]
1. Fleshly; not spiritual.
Thou dost justly require us, to submit our understandings to thine, and deny our *carnal* reason, in order to thy sacred mysteries and commands. *King Charles.*
From that pretence
Spiritual laws by *carnal* pow'r shall force
On every conscience. *Milton's Paradise Lost, b.* xii. *l.* 521.
Not such in *carnal* pleasure: for which cause,
Among the beasts no meat for thee was found. *Parad. Lost.*
A glorious apparition! had not doubt,
And *carnal* fear, that day dim'd Adam's eye. *Par. Lost, b.* xi.
He perceives plainly, that his appetite to spiritual things abates, in proportion as his sensual appetite is indulged and encouraged; and that *carnal* desires kill not only the desire, but even the power of tasting purer delights. *Atterbury.*
2. Lustful; lecherous; libidinous.
This *carnal* cur
Preys on the issue of his mother's body. *Shak. R.* III.

CARNA'LITY. *n. s.* [from *carnal.*]
1. Fleshly lust; compliance with carnal desires.
If godly, why do they wallow and sleep in all the *carnalities* of the world, under pretence of christian liberty? *South.*
2. Grossness of mind.
He did not institute this way of worship, but because of the *carnality* of their hearts, and the proneness of that people to idolatry. *Tillotson.*

CA'RNALLY. *adv.* [from *carnal.*] According to the flesh; not spiritually.
Where they found men in diet, attire, furniture of house, or any other way observers of civility and decent order, such they reproved, as being *carnally* and earthly minded. *Hooker, Preface.*
In the sacrament we do not receive Christ *carnally*, but we receive him spiritually; and that of itself is a conjugation of blessings and spiritual graces. *Taylor's Worthy Communicant.*

CA'RNALNESS. *n. s.* The same with *carnality.* *Dict.*

CARNA'TION. *n. s.* [*carnes*, Lat.] The name of the natural flesh colour; from whence perhaps the flower is named; the name of a flower. See CLOVEGILLIFLOWER.
And lo the wretch! whose vile, whose insect lust
Laid this gay daughter of the spring in dust:
O punish him! or to th' Elysian shades
Dismiss my soul, where no *carnation* fades. *Pope.*

CARNE'LION. *n. s.* A precious stone.
The common *carnelion* has its name from its flesh colour; which is, in some of these stones, paler, when it is called the female *carnelion*; in others deeper, called the male. *Woodward.*

CARNE'OUS. *adj.* [*carneus*, Lat.] Fleshy.
I have observed in a calf, the umbilical vessels to terminate in certain bodies, divided into a multitude of *carneous* papillæ. *Ray on the Creation.*

To CARNI'FY. *v. n.* [from *caro*, *carnis*, Lat.] To breed flesh; to turn nutriment into flesh.
At the same time I think, I deliberate, I purpose, I command: in inferiour faculties, I walk, I see, I hear, I digest, I sanguify, I *carnify*. *Hale's Origin of Mankind.*

CA'RNIVAL. *n. s.* [*carnaval*, Fr.] The feast held in the popish countries before Lent.
The whole year is but one mad *carnival*, and we are voluptuous not so much upon desire or appetite, as by way of exploit and bravery. *Decay of Piety.*

CARNI'VOROUS. *adj.* [from *carnis* and *voro.*] Flesh-eating; that of which flesh is the proper food.
In birds there is no mastication or comminution of the meat in the mouth; but in such as are not *carnivorous*, it is immediately swallowed into the crop or crow. *Ray on the Creation.*
Man is by his frame, as well as his appetite, a *carnivorous* animal. *Arbuthnot on Aliments.*

CARNO'SITY. *n. s.* [*carnosité*, Fr.] Fleshy excrescences.
By this method, and by this course of diet, with sudorificks, the ulcers are healed, and that *carnosity* resolved. *Wiseman.*

CA'RNOUS. *adj.* [from *caro*, *carnis*, Lat.] Fleshy.
The first or outward part is a thick and *carnous* covering, like that of a walnut; the second, a dry and flosculous coat, commonly called mace. *Brown's Vulgar Errours, b.* ii. *c.* 6.
The muscle whereby he is enabled to draw himself together, the academists describe to be a distinct *carnous* muscle, extended to the ear. *Ray on the Creation.*

CA'ROB, or *St. John's Bread.* [*siliqua*, Lat.] A plant.
It hath a petalous flower, having many stamina, which grow from the divisions of the flower-cup; in the centre of which rises the pointal, which afterward becomes a fruit or pod, which is plain and fleshy, containing several roundish plain seeds. This tree is very common in Spain, and in some parts of Italy, as also in the Levant, where it grows in the hedges, and produces a great quantity of long, flat, brown-coloured pods, which are thick, mealy, and of a sweetish taste. These pods are many times eaten by the poorer sort of inhabitants. *Miller.*

CARO'CHE. *n. s.* [from *carosse*, Fr.] A coach; a carriage of pleasure. It is used in the comedy of *Albumazar*, but now it is obsolete.

CA'ROL. *n. s.* [*carola*, Ital. from *choreola*, Lat.]
1. A song of joy and exultation.
And let the Graces dance unto the rest,
For they can do it best:
The whiles the maidens do their *carol* sing,
To which the woods shall answer, and their echo ring.
Spenser's Epithalamium.
Even in the old testament, if you listen to David's harp, you shall hear as many herse-like airs as *carols*. *Bacon.*
Oppos'd to her, on t' other side advance
The costly feast, the *carol*, and the dance,
Minstrels and musick, poetry and play,
And balls by night, and tournaments by day. *Dryden's Fab.*
2. A song of devotion.
No night is now with hymn or *carol* blest. *Shakesp.*
They gladly thither haste; and, by a choir
Of squadron'd angels, hear his *carol* sung. *Par. Lost, b.* xii.
3. A song in general.
The *carol* they began that hour,
How that a life was but a flower,
In the spring time. *Shakesp. As you like it.*

To CA'ROL. *v. n.* [*carolare*, Ital.] To sing; to warble; to sing in joy and festivity.
Hark, how the cheerful birds do chant their lays,
And *carol* of love's praise. *Spenser's Epithalamium.*
This done, she sung, and *caroll'd* out so clear,
That men and angels might rejoice to hear. *Dryden.*
Hov'ring swans their throats releas'd
From native silence, *carol* sounds harmonious. *Prior.*

To CA'ROL. *v. a.* To praise; to celebrate.
She with precious viol'd liquours heals,
For which the shepherds at their festivals,
Carol her goodness loud in rustick lays. *Milton.*

CA'ROTID. *adj.* [*carotides*, Lat.] Two arteries which arise out of the ascending trunk of the aorta, near where the subclavian arteries arise.
The *carotid*, vertebral, and splenick arteries, are not only variously contorted, but also here and there dilated, to moderate the motion of the blood; so the veins are also variously dilated. *Ray on the Creation.*

CARO'USAL. *n. s.* [from *carouse*. It seems more properly pronounced with the accent upon the second syllable; but *Dryden* accents it on the first.] A festival.
This game, these *carousals* Ascanius taught,
And building Alba to the Latins brought. *Dryden's Æn.*

To CARO'USE. *v. n.* [*carousser*, Fr. from *gar ausz*, all out, Germ.] To drink; to quaff; to drink largely.
He calls for wine: a health, quoth he, as if
H'ad been aboard *carousing* to his mates
After a storm. *Shakesp. Taming of the Shrew.*
Learn with how little life may be preserved,
In gold and myrrh they need not to *carouse*. *Raleigh.*
Now hats fly off, and youths *carouse*,
Healths first go round, and then the house,
The brides came thick and thick. *Suckling.*
Under the shadow of friendly boughs
They sit *carousing*, where their liquour grows. *Waller.*

To CARO'USE. *v. a.* To drink.
Now my sick fool, Roderigo,
Whom love hath turn'd almost the wrong side out,
To Desdemona hath tonight *carous'd*
Potations pottle deep. *Shakesp. Othello.*
Our cheerful guests *carouse* the sparkling tears
Of the rich grape, whilst musick charms their ears. *Denham.*

CARO'USE. *n. s.* [from the verb.]
1. A drinking match.
Waste in wild riot what your land allows,
There ply the early feast, and late *carouse*. *Pope's Odyssey.*
2. A hearty dose of liquour.
He had so many eyes watching over him, as he could not drink a full *carouse* of sack; but the state was advertised thereof within few hours after. *Davies on Ireland.*
Please you, we may contrive this afternoon,
And quaff *carouses* to our mistress' health. *Shakesp.*

CARO'USER. *n. s.* [from *carouse.*] A drinker; a toper.
The bold *carouser*, and advent'ring dame,
Nor fear the fever, nor refuse the flame;

Safe

Safe in his skill from all constraint set free,
But conscious shame, remorse, and piety. *Granville.*

CARP. *n. s.* [*carpe*, Fr.] A pond fish.

A friend of mine stored a pond of three or four acres with *carps* and tench. *Hale's Origin of Mankind.*

To CARP. *v. n.* [*carpo*, Lat.] To censure; to cavil; to find fault; with *at* before the thing or person censured.

Tertullian, even often through discontentment, *carpeth* injuriously *at* them, as though they did it even when they were free from such meaning. *Hooker, b.* iv. § 7.

This your all licens'd fool
Does hourly *carp* and quarrel, breaking forth
In rank and not to be endured riots. *Shakesp. King Lear.*

No, not a tooth or nail to scratch,
And *at* my actions *carp* or catch. *Herbert.*

When I spoke,
My honest homely words were *carp'd*, and censur'd,
For want of courtly stile. *Dryden's Don Sebastian.*

CA'RPENTER. *n. s.* [*charpentier*, Fr.] An artificer in wood; a builder of houses and ships. He is distinguished from a joiner, as the carpenter performs larger and stronger work.

This work performed with advisement good,
Godfrey his *carpenters*, and men of skill,
In all the camp, sent to an aged wood. *Fairfax, b.* iii.

In building Hiero's great ship, there were three hundred *carpenters* employed for a year together. *Wilkins's Dædalus.*

In burden'd vessels, first with speedy care,
His plenteous stores do season'd timbers send,
Thither the brawny *carpenters* repair,
And, as the surgeons of maim'd ships, attend. *Dryden.*

CA'RPENTRY. *n. s.* [from *carpenter.*] The trade or art of a carpenter.

It had been more proper for me to have introduced *carpentry* before joinery, because necessity did doubtless compel our forefathers to use the conveniency of the first, rather than the extravagancy of the last. *Moxon's Mechanical Exercises.*

CA'RPER. *n. s.* [from *to carp.*] A caviller; a censorious man.

I have not these weeds,
By putting on the cunning of a *carper*. *Shakesp. Timon.*

CA'RPET. *n. s.* [*karpet*, Dutch.]

1. A covering of various colours, spread upon floors or tables.

Be the Jacks fair within, the Jills fair without, *carpets* laid, and every thing in order. *Shakesp. Taming of the Shrew.*

Against the wall, in the middle of the halfpace, is a chair placed before him, with a table and *carpet* before it. *Bacon.*

2. Ground variegated with flowers, and level and smooth.

Go signify as much, while here we march
Upon the grassy *carpet* of this plain. *Shakesp. Richard* III.

The *carpet* ground shall be with leaves o'erspread,
And boughs shall weave a cov'ring for your head. *Dryden.*

3. Any thing variegated.

The whole dry land is, for the most part, covered over with a lovely *carpet* of green grass, and other herbs. *Ray.*

4. *Carpet* is used, proverbially, for a state of ease and luxury; as, a *carpet* knight, a knight that has never known the field, and has recommended himself only at table.

He is knight, dubbed with unhacked rapier, and on *carpet* consideration. *Shakesp. Twelfth Night.*

5. To be on the *carpet*, [*sur le tapis*, Fr.] is the subject of consideration; an affair in hand.

To CA'RPET. *v. a.* [from the noun.] To spread with carpets.

We found him in a fair chamber, richly hanged and *carpeted* under foot, without any degrees to the state; he was set upon a low throne, richly adorned, and a rich cloth of state over his head, of blue sattin embroidered. *Bacon's New Atlantis.*

The dry land surface we find every where almost naturally *carpeted* over with grass, and other agreeable wholesome plants. *Derham's Physico-Theology.*

CA'RPING. *particip. adj.* [from *to carp.*] Captious; censorious.

No *carping* critick interrupts his praise,
No rival strives, but for a second place. *Granville.*

Lay aside therefore a *carping* spirit, and read even an adversary with an honest design to find out his true meaning: do not snatch at little lapses, and appearances of mistake. *Watts.*

CA'RPINGLY. *adv.* [from *carping.*] Captiously; censoriously.

We derive out of the Latin at second hand by the French, and make good English, as in these adverbs, *carpingly*, currently, actively, colourably. *Camden's Remains.*

CA'RPMEALS. *n. s.* A kind of coarse cloth made in the North of England. *Phillips's World of Words.*

CA'RPUS. *n. s.* [Latin.] The wrist, so named by anatomists, which is made up of eight little bones, of different figures and thickness, placed in two ranks, four in each rank. They are strongly tied together by the ligaments which come from the radius, and by the annulary ligament. *Quincy.*

I found one of the bones of the *carpus* lying loose in the wound. *Wiseman's Surgery.*

CA'RRACK. See CARACK.

CA'RRAT. See CARAT.

CARRA'WAY. See CARAWAY.

Nay, you shall see mine orchard, where, in an arbour, we will eat a last year's pippin of my own grafting, with a dish of *carraways*, and so forth; come, cousin, silence, and then to bed. *Shakesp. Henry* IV. *p.* ii.

CA'RRIAGE. *n. s.* [*cariage*, Fr. baggage; from *carry.*]

1. The act of carrying or transporting, or bearing any thing.

The unequal agitation of the winds, though material to the *carriage* of sounds farther or less way, yet do not confound the articulation. *Bacon's Natural Hist.* Nº 193.

If it seem so strange to move this obelisk for so little space, what may we think of the *carriage* of it out of Egypt? *Wilkins's Mathematical Magick.*

2. Conquest; acquisition.

Solyman resolved to besiege Vienna, in good hope, that, by the *carriage* away of that, the other cities would, without resistance, be yielded. *Knolles's History of the Turks.*

3. Vehicle; that in which any thing is carried.

What horse or *carriage* can take up and bear away all the loppings of a branchy tree at once? *Watts.*

4. The frame upon which cannon is carried.

He commanded the great ordnance to be laid upon *carriages*, which before lay bound in great unwieldy timber, with rings fastened thereto, and could not handsomely be removed to or fro. *Knolles's History of the Turks.*

5. Behaviour; personal manners.

Before his eyes he did cast a mist, by his own insinuation, and by the *carriage* of his youth, that expressed a natural princely behaviour. *Bacon's Henry* VII.

Though in my face there's no affected frown,
Nor in my *carriage* a feign'd niceness shown,
I keep my honour still without a stain. *Dryden.*

Let them have ever so learned lectures of breeding, that which will most influence their *carriage*, will be the company they converse with, and the fashion of those about them. *Locke.*

6. Conduct; measures; practices.

You may hurt yourself; nay, utterly
Grow from the king's acquaintance by this *carriage*. *Shakesp. Henry* VIII.

He advised the new governour to have so much discretion in his *carriage*, that there might be no notice taken in the exercise of his religion. *Clarendon, b.* viii.

7. Management; manner of transacting.

The manner of *carriage* of the business, was as if there had been secret inquisition upon him. *Bacon's Henry* VII.

CA'RRIER. *n. s.* [from *to carry.*]

1. One who carries something.

You must distinguish between the motion of the air, which is but a *vehiculum causæ*, a *carrier* of the sounds, and the sounds conveyed. *Bacon's Nat. Hist.* Nº 125.

For winds, when homeward they return, will drive
The loaded *carriers* from their evening hive. *Dryden.*

2. One whose profession or trade is to carry goods for others.

I have rather made it my choice to transcribe all, than to venture the loss of my originals by post or *carrier*. *Pierce's Lett.*

The roads are crouded with *carriers*, laden with rich manufactures. *Swift.*

3. A messenger; one who carries a message.

The welcome news is in the letter found;
The *carrier*'s not commission'd to expound;
It speaks itself. *Dryden's Religio Laici.*

4. The name of a species of pigeons, so called from the reported practice of some nations, who send them with letters tied to their necks, which they carry to the place where they were bred, however remote.

There are tame and wild pigeons, and of tame there are croppers, *carriers*, runts. *Walton's Angler.*

CA'RRION. *n. s.* [*charogne*, Fr.]

1. The carcase of something not proper for food.

They did eat the dead *carrions*, and one another soon after; insomuch that the very carcases they scraped out of their graves. *Spenser on Ireland.*

It is I,
That, lying by the violet in the sun,
Do, as the *carrion* does, not as the flower. *Shakesp.*

This foul deed shall smell above the earth,
With *carrion* men groaning for burial. *Shakesp. J. Cæsar.*

You'll ask me why I rather chuse to have
A weight of *carrion* flesh, than to receive
Three thousand ducats. *Shakesp. Measure for Measure.*

Ravens are seen in flocks where a *carrion* lies, and wolves in herds to run down a deer. *Temple.*

Sheep, oxen, horses fall; and heap'd on high,
The diff'ring species in confusion lie,
Till, warn'd by frequent ills, the way they found,
To lodge their lothsome *carrion* under ground. *Dryden.*

Criticks, as they are birds of prey, have ever a natural inclination to *carrion*. *Pope.*

2. A name of reproach for a worthless woman.

Shall we send that foolish *carrion*, Mrs. Quickly, to him, and excuse his throwing into the water. *Shakesp. Merry Wives of Windsor.*

3. Any flesh so corrupted as not to be fit for food.

Not all that pride that makes thee swell,
As big as thou dost blown up veal;

Nor all thy tricks and slights to cheat,
Sell all thy *carrion* for good meat. *Hudibras.*

The wolves will get a breakfast by my death,
Yet scarce enough their hunger to supply,
For love has made me *carrion* ere I die. *Dryden.*

CA'RRION. *adj.* [from the subst.] Relating to carcases; feeding upon carcases.

Match to match I have encounter'd him,
And made a prey for *carrion* kites and crows,
Ev'n of the bonny beasts he lov'd so well. *Shakesp. H.* VI.

The charity of our death-bed visits from one another, is much at a rate with that of a *carrion* crow to a sheep; we smell a carcase. *L'Estrange.*

CA'RROT. *n. s.* [*carote*, Fr. *daucus*, Lat.]

It hath a fleshy root; the leaves are divided into narrow segments; the petals of the flower are unequal, and shaped like a heart; the umbel, when ripe, is hollowed and contracted, appearing somewhat like a bird's nest; the seeds are hairy, and in shape of lice. The species are; 1. Common wild *carrot.* 2. Dwarf wild *carrot*, with broader leaves. 3. Dark red-rooted garden *carrot.* 4. The orange coloured *carrot.* 5. The white *carrot.* The first grows wild upon arable land, and is seldom cultivated. This is the particular sort which should be used in medicine, and for which the druggists commonly sell the seeds of the garden *carrot.* The third and fourth sorts are commonly cultivated for the kitchen; as is the fifth sort, though not so common in England. The white is generally preferred for the sweetest. But, in order to preserve *carrots* for use all the winter and spring, about the beginning of November, when the green leaves are decayed, dig them up, and lay them in sand in a dry place, where the frost cannot come to them. *Miller.*

Carrots, though garden roots, yet they do well in the fields for seed, though the land for them should rather be digged than plowed. *Mortimer.*

His spouse orders the sack to be immediately opened, and greedily pulls out of it half a dozen bunches of *carrots.* *Dennis.*

CA'RROTINESS. *n. s.* [from *carroty.*] Redness of hair.

CA'RROTY. *adj.* [from *carrot.*] Spoken of red hair, on account of its resemblance in colour to carrots.

CA'RROWS. *n. s.* [an Irish word.]

The *carrows* are a kind of people that wander up and down to gentlemens houses, living only upon cards and dice; who, though they have little or nothing of their own, yet will they play for much money. *Spenser on Ireland.*

To CA'RRY. *v. a.* [*charier*, Fr. from *currus*, Lat. See CAR.]

1. To convey *from* a place; opposed to *bring*, or convey *to* a place.

When he dieth, he shall *carry* nothing away. *Ps.* xlix. 18.

And devout men *carried* Stephen to his burial. *Acts*, viii. 2.

I mean to *carry* her away this evening, by the help of these two soldiers. *Dryden's Spanish Friar.*

As in a hive's vimineous dome,
Ten thousand bees enjoy their home;
Each does her studious action vary,
To go and come, to fetch and *carry.* *Prior.*

They exposed their goods with the price marked upon them, then retired; the merchants came, left the price which they would give upon the goods, and likewise retired; the Seres returning, *carried* off either their goods or money, as they liked best. *Arbuthnot on Coins.*

2. To transport.

They began to *carry* about in beds those that were sick. *Mark*, vi. 55.

The species of audibles seem to be *carried* more manifestly through the air, than the species of visibles. *Bacon's Nat. Hist.*

Where many great ordnance are shot off together, the sound will be *carried*, at the least, twenty miles upon the land. *Bacon.*

3. To bear; to have about one.

Do not take out bones like surgeons I have met with, who *carry* them about in their pockets. *Wiseman's Surgery.*

4. To take; to have with one.

If the ideas of liberty and volition were *carried* along with us in our minds, a great part of the difficulties that perplex men's thoughts would be easier resolved. *Locke.*

I have listened with my utmost attention for half an hour to an oratour, without being able to *carry* away one single sentence out of a whole sermon. *Swift.*

5. To convey by force.

Go, *carry* Sir John Falstaff to the Fleet;
Take all his company along with him. *Shakesp. Henry* IV.

6. To effect any thing.

There are some vain persons, that whatsoever goeth alone, or moveth upon greater means, if they have never so little hand in it, they think it is they that *carry* it. *Bacon.*

Oft-times we lose the occasion of *carrying* a business well thoroughly by our too much haste. *Ben. Johnson's Discovery.*

These advantages will be of no effect, unless we improve them to words, in the *carrying* of our main point. *Addison.*

7. To gain in competition.

And hardly shall I *carry* out my side,
Her husband being alive. *Shakesp. King Lear.*

How many stand for consulships?—Three, they say; but it is thought of every one Coriolanus will *carry* it. *Shakesp.*

I see not yet how many of these six reasons can be fairly avoided; and yet if any of them hold good, it is enough to *carry* the cause. *Saunderson.*

The latter still enjoying his place, and continuing a joint commissioner of the treasury, still opposed, and commonly *carried* away every thing against him. *Clarendon.*

8. To gain after resistance.

The count wooes your daughter,
Lays down his wanton siege before her beauty;
Resolves to *carry* her; let her consent,
As we'll direct her now, 'tis best to bear it. *Shakesp.*

What a fortune does the thick lips owe,
If he can *carry* her thus? *Shakesp. Othello.*

The town was distressed, and ready for an assault, which, if it had been given, would have cost much blood; but yet the town would have been *carried* in the end. *Bacon's Henry* VII.

9. To prevail; with *it.* [*le porter*, Fr.]

Are you all resolved to give your voices?
But that's no matter; the greater part *carries it.* *Shakesp.*

By these, and the like arts, they promised themselves, that they should easily *carry it*; so that they entertained the house all the morning with other debates. *Clarendon.*

If the numerousness of a train must *carry it*, virtue may go follow Astræa, and vice only will be worth the courting. *Glanv.*

Children, who live together, often strive for mastery, whose wills shall *carry it* over the rest. *Locke.*

In pleasures and pains, the present is apt to *carry it*, and those at a distance have the disadvantage in the comparison. *Locke.*

10. To bear out; to face through; to outface.

If a man *carries it* off, there is so much money saved; and if he be detected, there will be something pleasant in the frolick. *L'Estrange.*

11. To preserve external appearance.

My niece is already in the belief that he's mad; we may *carry it* thus for our pleasure, and his penance. *Shak. T. Night.*

12. To manage; to transact.

The senate is generally as numerous as our house of commons; and yet *carries* its resolutions so privately, that they are seldom known. *Addison's Remarks on Italy.*

13. To behave; to conduct; with the reciprocal pronoun.

Neglect not also the examples of those that have *carried themselves* ill in the same place. *Bacon.*

He attended the king into Scotland, where he did *carry himself* with much singular sweetness and temper. *Wotton.*

He *carried himself* so insolently in the house, and out of the house, to all persons, that he became odious. *Clarendon.*

14. To bring forward; to advance in any progress.

It is not to be imagined how far constancy will *carry* a man; however, it is better walking slowly in a rugged way, than to break a leg and be a cripple. *Locke.*

This plain natural way, without grammar, can *carry* them to a great degree of elegancy and politeness in their language. *Locke on Education*, § 168.

There is no vice which mankind *carries* to such wild extremes, as that of avarice. *Swift.*

15. To urge; to bear on with some kind of external impulse.

Men are strongly *carried* out to, and hardly took off from, the practice of vice. *South.*

He that the world, or flesh, or devil, can *carry* away from the profession of an obedience to Christ, is no son of the faithful Abraham. *Hammond's Practical Catechism.*

Ill nature, passion, and revenge, will *carry* them too far in punishing others; and therefore God hath certainly appointed government to restrain the partiality and violence of men. *Locke.*

16. To bear; to have; to obtain.

In some vegetables, we see something that *carries* a kind of analogy to sense; they contract their leaves against the cold; they open them to the favourable heat. *Hale's Origin of Mank.*

17. To exhibit to show; to display on the outside; to set to view.

The aspect of every one in the family *carries* so much satisfaction, that it appears he knows his happy lot. *Addison. Spect.*

18. To imply; to import.

It *carries* too great an imputation of ignorance, lightness or folly, for men to quit and renounce their former tenets, presently upon the offer of an argument, which they cannot immediately answer. *Locke.*

19. To contain.

He thought it *carried* something of argument in it, to prove that doctrine. *Watts's Improvement of the Mind.*

20. To have annexed; to have any thing joined.

There was a righteous and a searching law, directly forbidding such practices; and they knew that it *carried* with it the divine stamp. *South.*

There are many expressions, which *carry* with them to my mind no clear ideas. *Locke.*

The obvious portions of extension, that affect our senses, *carry* with them into the mind the idea of finite. *Locke.*

21. To convey or bear any thing united or adhering, by communication of motion.

We see also manifestly, that sounds are *carried* with wind; and

and therefore ſounds will be heard further with the wind than againſt the wind. *Bacon's Natural Hiſtory*, Nº 125.

22. To move or continue any thing in a certain direction.

His chimney is *carried* up through the whole rock, ſo that you ſee the ſky through it, notwithſtanding the rooms lie very deep. *Addiſon on Italy.*

23. To puſh on ideas in a train.

Manethes, that wrote of the Egyptians, hath *carried* up their government to an incredible diſtance. *Hale's Origin of Mank.*

24. To receive; to endure.

Some have in readineſs ſo many odd ſtories, as there is nothing but they can wrap it into a tale, to make others *carry* it with more pleaſure. *Bacon, Eſſay* 23.

25. To ſupport; to ſuſtain.

Carry camomile, or wild thyme, or the green ſtrawberry, upon ſticks, as you do hops upon poles. *Bacon's Nat. Hiſtory.*

26. To bear, as trees.

Set them a reaſonable depth, and they will *carry* more ſhoots upon the ſtem. *Bacon's Natural Hiſtory*, Nº 425.

27. To fetch and bring, as dogs.

Young whelps learn eaſily to *carry*; young popinjays learn quickly to ſpeak. *Aſcham's Schoolmaſter.*

28. *To carry off.* To kill.

Old Parr lived to one hundred and fifty three years of age, and might have gone further, if the change of air had not *carried* him *off*. *Temple.*

29. *To carry on.* To promote; to help forward.

It *carries on* the ſame deſign that is promoted by authours of a graver turn, and only does it in another manner. *Addiſon.*

30. *To carry on.* To continue; to advance from one ſtage to another.

By the adminiſtration of grace, begun by our Bleſſed Saviour, *carried on* by his diſciples, and to be completed by their ſucceſſours to the world's end, all types that darkened this faith, are enlightned. *Sprat.*

Æneas's ſettlement in Italy was *carried on* through all the oppoſitions in his way to it, both by ſea and land. *Addiſon.*

31. *To carry on.* To proſecute; not to let ceaſe.

France will not conſent to furniſh us with money ſufficient to *carry on* the war. *Temple.*

32. *To carry through.* To ſupport; to keep from failing, or being conquered.

That grace will *carry* us, if we do not wilfully betray our ſuccours, victoriouſly *through* all difficulties. *Hammond.*

To Ca'rry. *v. n.*

1. A hare is ſaid, by hunters, to *carry*, when ſhe runs on rotten ground, or on froſt, and it ſticks to her feet.

2. A horſe is ſaid to *carry well*, when his neck is arched, and he holds his head high; but when his neck is ſhort, and ill ſhaped, and he lowers his head, he is ſaid to *carry low*.

3. *To carry it high.* To be proud.

Ca'rry-tale. *n. ſ.* [from *carry* and *tale*.] A talebearer.

Some *carry-tale*, ſome pleaſeman, ſome ſlight zany,
Told our intents before. *Shakeſp. Love's Labour Loſt.*

CART. *n. ſ.* See Car. [cꞃæt, cꞃat, Sax.]

1. A carriage in general.

The Scythians are deſcribed by Herodotus to lodge always in *carts*, and to feed upon the milk of mares. *Temple.*

Triptolemus, ſo ſung the Nine,
Strew'd plenty from his *cart* divine. *Dryden.*

2. A wheel-carriage, uſed commonly for luggage.

Now while my friend, juſt ready to depart,
Was packing all his goods in one poor *cart*,
He ſtopp'd a little—— *Dryden's Juvenal.*

3. A ſmall carriage with two wheels, uſed by huſbandmen, diſtinguiſhed from a *waggon*, which has four wheels.

Alas! what weights are theſe that load my heart!
I am as dull as winter-ſtarved ſheep,
Tir'd as a jade in overloaden *cart*. *Sidney.*

4. The vehicle in which criminals are carried to execution.

The ſquire, whoſe good grace was to open the ſcene,
Now fitted the halter, now travers'd the *cart*,
And often took leave, but was loth to depart. *Prior.*

To Cart. *v. a.* [from the noun.] To expoſe in a cart by way of puniſhment.

Democritus ne'er laugh'd ſo loud,
To ſee bawds *carted* through the croud. *Hudibras.*

No woman led a better life:
She to intrigues was e'en hard-hearted;
She chuckl'd when a bawd was *carted*;
And thought the nation ne'er would thrive,
Till all the whores were burnt alive. *Prior.*

To Cart. *v. n.* To uſe carts for carriage.

Oxen are not ſo good for draught, where you have occaſion to *cart* much, but for winter ploughing. *Mortimer.*

Cart-horse. *n. ſ.* [from *cart* and *horſe*.] A coarſe unwieldy horſe, fit only for the cart.

It was determined, that theſe ſick and wounded ſoldiers ſhould be carried upon the *cart-horſes*. *Knolles.*

Cart-jade. *n. ſ.* [from *cart* and *jade*.] A vile horſe, fit only for the cart.

He came out with all his clowns, horſed upon ſuch *cart-jades*, ſo furniſhed, I thought if that were thrift, I wiſhed none of my friends or ſubjects ever to thrive. *Sidney, b. ii.*

Cart-load. *n. ſ.* [from *cart* and *load*.]

1. A quantity of any thing piled on a cart.

A *cart-load* of carrots appeared of darker colour, when looked upon where the points were obverted to the eye, than where the ſides were ſo. *Boyle.*

Let Wood and his accomplices travel about a country with *cart-loads* of their ware, and ſee who will take it. *Swift.*

2. A quantity ſufficient to load a cart.

Cart-way. *n. ſ.* [from *cart* and *way*.] A way through which a carriage may conveniently travel.

Where your woods are large, it is beſt to have a *cart-way* along the middle of them. *Mortimer's Huſbandry.*

CARTE BLANCHE. [French.] A blank paper; a paper to be filled up with ſuch conditions as the perſon to whom it is ſent thinks proper.

Ca'rtel. *n. ſ.* [*cartel*, Fr. *cartello*, Ital.] A writing containing, for the moſt part, ſtipulations between enemies.

As this diſcord among the ſiſterhood is likely to engage them in a long and lingring war, it is the more neceſſary that there ſhould be a *cartel* ſettled among them. *Addiſon's Freeholder.*

Ca'rter. *n. ſ.* [from *cart*.] The man who drives a cart, or whoſe trade it is to drive a cart.

If he love her not,
Let me be no aſſiſtant for a ſtate,
But keep a farm, and *carters*. *Shakeſp. Hamlet.*

The divine goodneſs never fails, provided that, according to the advice of Hercules to the *carter*, we put our own ſhoulders to the work. *L'Eſtrange.*

The criminals are ſeiz'd upon the place:
Carter and hoſt confronted face to face. *Dryden.*

It is the prudence of a *carter* to put bells upon his horſes, to make them carry their burdens cheerfully. *Dryden's Dufreſnoy.*

CA'RTILAGE. *n. ſ.* [*cartilago*, Lat.] A ſmooth and ſolid body, ſofter than a bone, but harder than a ligament. In it are no cavities or cells for containing of marrow; nor is it covered over with any membrane to make it ſenſible, as the bones are. The *cartilages* have a natural elaſticity, by which, if they are forced from their natural figure or ſituation, they return to it of themſelves, as ſoon as that force is taken away. *Quincy.*

Thoſe canals, by degrees, are aboliſhed, and grow ſolid; ſeveral of them united, grow a membrane; theſe membranes further conſolidated, become *cartilages*, and *cartilages* bones. *Arbuthnot on Aliments.*

Cartilagi'neous. } *n. ſ.* [from *cartilage*.] Conſiſting of car-
Cartila'ginous. } tilages.

By what artifice the *cartilagineous* kind of fiſhes poiſe themſelves, aſcend and deſcend at pleaſure, and continue in what depth of water they liſt, is as yet unknown. *Ray.*

The larynx gives paſſage to the breath, and, as the breath paſſeth through the rimula, makes a vibration of thoſe *cartilaginous* bodies, which forms that breath into a vocal ſound or voice. *Holder's Elements of Speech.*

Carto'on. *n. ſ.* [*cartone*, Ital.] A painting or drawing upon large paper.

It is with a vulgar idea that the world beholds the *cartoons* of Raphael, and every one feels his ſhare of pleaſure and entertainment. *Watts's Logick.*

Carto'uch. *n. ſ.* [*cartouche*, Fr.] A caſe of wood three inches thick at the bottom, girt round with marlin, and holding forty-eight musket balls, and ſix or eight iron balls of a pound weight. It is fired out of a hobit or ſmall mortar, and is proper for defending a paſs. *Harris.*

Ca'rtrage. } *n. ſ.* [*cartouche*, Fr.] A caſe of paper or parch-
Ca'rtridge. } ment filled with gunpowder, uſed for the greater expedition in charging guns.

Our careful monarch ſtands in perſon by,
His new-caſt cannons firmneſs to explore;
The ſtrength of big-corn'd powder loves to try,
And ball and *cartrage* ſorts for every bore. *Dryden.*

Ca'rtrut. *n. ſ.* [from *cart* and *rut*; *route*, a way.] The track made by a cart wheel.

Ca'rtulary. *n. ſ.* [from *charta*, paper, Lat.] A place where papers or records are kept.

Ca'rtwright. *n. ſ.* [from *cart* and *wright*.] A maker of carts.

After local names, the moſt names have been derived from occupations or profeſſions; as, Taylor, Potter, Smith, *Cartwright*. *Camden's Remains.*

To CARVE. *v. a.* [ceoꞃꝼan, Sax. *kerven*, Dutch.]

1. To cut wood, or ſtone, or other matter, into elegant forms.

Taking the very refuſe among thoſe which ſerved to no uſe, he hath *carved* it diligently when he had nothing elſe to do. *Wiſdom*, xiii. 13.

Had Democrates really *carved* mount Athos into a ſtatue of Alexander the Great, and had the memory of the fact been obliterated by ſome accident, who could afterwards have proved it impoſſible, but that it might caſually have been? *Bentley.*

2. To cut meat at the table.

3. To make any thing by carving or cutting.

Yet fearing idleneſs, the nurſe of ill,
In ſculpture exercis'd his happy ſkill;

And *carv'd* in iv'ry such a maid so fair,
As nature could not with his art compare,
Were she to work. *Dryden.*

4. To engrave.

O Rosalind! these trees shall be my books,
And in their barks my thoughts I'll character;
That every eye, which in this forest looks,
Shall see thy virtue witness'd every where.
Run, run, Orlando, *carve* on every tree,
The fair, the chaste, the unexpressive she. *Shakesp.*

5. To chuse one's own part.

He had been a keeper of his flocks, both from the violence of robbers and his own soldiers; who could easily have *carved* themselves their own food. *South.*

How dares sinful dust and ashes invade the prerogative of providence, and *carve* out to himself the seasons and issues of life and death? *South.*

The labourer's share, being seldom more than a bare subsistence, never allows that body of men opportunity to struggle with the richer, unless when some common and great distress emboldens them to *carve* to their wants. *Locke.*

6. To cut; to hew.

Or they will buy his sheep forth of the cote,
Or they will *carve* the shepherd's throat. *Spenser's Pastorals.*
Brave Macbeth, with his brandish'd steel,
Like valour's minion, *carved* out his passage. *Shakesp.*

To CARVE. *v. n.*

1. To exercise the trade of a sculptor.
2. To perform at table the office of supplying the company from the dishes.

I do mean to make love to Ford's wife; I spy entertainment in her; she discourses, she *carves*, she gives the leer of invitation. *Shakesp. Merry Wives of Windsor.*

Well then, things handsomely were serv'd;
My mistress for the strangers *carv'd.* *Prior.*

CA'RVEL. *n. s.* [See CARAVEL.] A small ship.

I gave them order, if they found any Indians there, to send in the little fly-boat, or the *carvel*, into the river; for, with our great ships, we durst not approach the coast. *Raleigh.*

CA'RVER. *n. s.* [from *carve.*]

1. A sculptor.

All arts and artists Perseus could command,
Who sold for hire, or wrought for better fame,
The master painters and the *carvers* came. *Dryden.*

2. He that cuts up the meat at the table.

Meanwhile thy indignation yet to raise,
The *carver*, dancing round each dish, surveys
With flying knife, and, as his art directs,
With proper gestures ev'ry fowl dissects. *Dryden.*

3. He that chooses for himself.

In this kind, to come in braving arms,
Be his own *carver*, and cut out his way,
To find out right with wrongs it may not be. *Shak. R.* II.

We are not the *carvers* of our own fortunes. *L'Estrange.*

CA'RVING. *n. s.* [from *carve.*] Sculpture; figures carved.

They can no more last like the ancients, than excellent *carvings* in wood, like those in marble and brass. *Temple.*

The lids are ivy, grapes in clusters lurk
Beneath the *carving* of the curious work. *Dryden's Virgil.*

CARU'NCLE. *n. s.* [*caruncula*, Lat.] A small protuberance of flesh, either natural or morbid.

Caruncles are a sort of loose flesh, arising in the urethra by the erosion made by virulent acid matter. *Wiseman.*

CARYATES. } *n. s.* [from *Carya*, a city taken by the Greeks,
CARYA'TIDES. } who led away the women captives; and, to perpetuate their slavery, represented them in buildings as charged with burdens.] An order of columns or pilasters under the figures of women, dressed in long robes, serving to support entablatures. *Chambers.*

CASCA'DE. *n. s.* [*cascade*, Fr. *cascata*, Ital. from *cascare*, a low word, to fall] A cataract; a water-fall.

Rivers diverted from their native course,
And bound with chains of artificial force,
From large *cascades* in pleasing tumult roll'd,
Or rose through figur'd stone, or breathing gold. *Prior.*

The most enlivening part of all is the river Teverone, which throws itself down a precipice, and falls by several *cascades*, from one rock to another, till it gains the bottom of the valley. *Addison on Italy.*

CASE. *n. s.* [*caisse*, Fr. a box.]

1. Something that covers or contains any thing else; a covering; a box; a sheath.

O cleave, my sides!
Heart, once be stronger than thy continent,
Crack thy frail *case*. *Shakesp. Antony and Cleopatra.*
Each thought was visible that roll'd within,
As through a crystal *case* the figur'd hours are seen. *Dryden.*

Other caterpillars produced maggots, that immediately made themselves up in *cases*. *Ray on the Creation.*

The body is but a *case* to this vehicle. *Broome on the Odyssey.*

Just then Clarissa drew, with tempting grace,
A two-edg'd weapon from her shining *case*. *Pope.*

2. The outer part of a house or building.

The *case* of the holy house is nobly designed, and executed by great masters. *Addison on Italy.*

3. A building unfurnished.

He had a purpose likewise to raise, in the university, a fair *case* for such monuments, and to furnish it with other choice collections from all parts of his own charge. *Wotton.*

CASE-KNIFE. *n. s.* [from *case* and *knife.*] A large kitchen knife.

The king always acts with a great *case-knife* stuck in his girdle, which the lady snatches from him in the struggle, and so defends herself. *Addison's Remarks on Italy.*

CASE-SHOT. *n. s.* [from *case* and *shot.*] Bullets inclosed in a case.

In each seven small brass and leather guns, charged with *case-shot*. *Clarendon, b.* viii.

CASE. *n. s.* [*casus*, Lat.]

1. Condition with regard to outward circumstances.

Unworthy wretch, quoth he, of so great grace,
How dare I think such glory to attain?
These that have it attain'd, were in like *case*,
Quoth he, as wretched, and liv'd in like pain. *Fairy Queen.*
Question your royal thoughts, make the *case* yours;
Be now a father, and propose a son. *Shakesp. Henry* IV. *p.* ii.
Some knew the face,
And all had heard the much lamented *case*. *Dryden.*

These were the circumstances under which the Corinthians then were, and the argument which the apostle advances, is intended to reach their particular *case*. *Atterbury.*

My youth may be made, as it never fails in executions, a *case* of compassion. *Pope's Preface to his Works.*

2. State of things.

He saith, that if there can be found such an inequality between man and man, as there is between man and beast, or between soul and body, it investeth a right of government, which seemeth rather an impossible *case*, than an untrue sentence. *Bacon's Holy War.*

Here was the *case*; an army of English, wasted and tired with a long winter's siege, engaged an army of a greater number than themselves, fresh and in vigour. *Bacon.*

I can but be a slave where-ever I am; so that taken or not taken, 'tis all a *case* to me. *L'Estrange.*

They are excellent in order to certain ends; he hath no need to use them, as the *case* now stands, being provided for with the provision of an angel. *Taylor's Holy Living.*

Your parents did not produce you much into the world, whereby you have fewer ill impressions; but they failed, as is generally the *case*, in too much neglecting to cultivate your mind. *Swift.*

3. In physick; state of the body.

It was well; for we had rather met with calms and contrary winds, than any tempests; for our sick were many, and in very ill *case*. *Bacon.*

Chalybeate water seems to be a proper remedy in hypochondriacal *cases*. *Arbuthnot on Aliments.*

4. In ludicrous language, condition with regard to leanness, or health.

Thou liest, most ignorant monster, I am in *case* to justle a constable. *Shakesp. Tempest.*

Pray have but patience till then, and when I am in little better *case*, I'll throw myself in the very mouth of you. *L'Estr.*

Quoth Ralph, I should not, if I were
In *case* for action, now be here. *Hudibras, p.* i. *cant.* iii.
For if the sire be faint, or out of *case*,
He will be copy'd in his famish'd race. *Dryden's Virgil.*
The priest was pretty well in *case*,
And shew'd some humour in his face;
Look'd with an easy careless mien,
A perfect stranger to the spleen. *Swift.*

5. Contingence.

The atheist, in case things should fall out contrary to his belief or expectation, hath made no provision for this *case*; if, contrary to his confidence, it should prove in the issue that there is a God, the man is lost and undone for ever. *Tillotson.*

6. Question relating to particular persons or things.

Well do I find each man most wise in his own *case*. *Sidney.*

It is strange, that the ancient fathers should not appeal to this judge, in all *cases*, it being so short and expedite a way for the ending of controversies. *Tillotson.*

7. Representation of any fact or question.

If he be not apt to beat over matters, and to call up one thing, to prove and illustrate another, let him study the lawyers *cases*: so every defect of the mind may have a special receipt. *Bacon, Essay* 51.

8. The variation of nouns.

The several changes which the noun undergoes in the Latin and Greek tongues, in the several numbers, are called *cases*, and are designed to express the several views or relations under which the mind considers things with regard to one another; and the variation of the noun for this purpose is called declension. *Clark's Latin Grammar.*

9. *In case.* [*nel caso*, Ital.] If it should happen; upon the supposition that: a form of speech now little used.

For

For *in case* it be certain, hard it cannot be for them to shew us where we shall find it; that we may say these were the orders of the apostles. *Hooker, b.* iii.

A sure retreat to his forces, *in case* they should have an ill day, or unlucky chance in the field. *Bacon's Henry* VII.

This would be the accomplishment of their common felicity, *in case*, either by their evil destiny or advice, they suffered not the occasion to be lost. *Hayward.*

To CASE. *v. a.* [from the noun.]

1. To put in a case or cover.

Case ye, *case* ye; on with your vizours; there's money of the king's coming down the hill. *Shakesp. Henry* IV. *p.* i.

The cry went once for thee,
And still it might, and yet it may again,
If thou would'st not entomb thyself alive,
And *case* thy reputation in a tent. *Shakesp. Troil. and Cress.*

On whose luxuriant herbage, half conceal'd,
Like a fall'n cedar, far diffus'd his train,
Cas'd in green scales, the crocodile extends. *Thomson.*

2. To cover as a case.

Then comes my fit again, I had else been perfect;
As broad, and gen'ral, as the *casing* air,
To saucy doubts and fears. *Shakesp. Macbeth.*

3. To cover on the outside with materials different from the inside.

Then they began to *case* their houses with marble. *Arbuthnot on Coins.*

4. To strip off the covering; to take off the skin.

We'll make you some sport with the fox ere we *case* him. *Shakesp. All's well that ends well.*

To CASE. *v. n.* To put cases; to contrive representations of facts.

They fell presently to reasoning and *casing* upon the matter with him, and laying distinctions before him. *L'Estrange.*

To CASEHA'RDEN. *v. a.* [from *case* and *harden.*] To harden on the outside.

The manner of *casehardening* is thus: Take cow horn or hoof, dry it thoroughly in an oven, then beat it to powder; put about the same quantity of bay salt to it, and mingle them together with stale chamberlye, or else white wine vinegar. Lay some of this mixture upon loam, and cover your iron all over with it; then wrap the loam about all, and lay it upon the hearth of the forge to dry and harden. Put it into the fire, and blow up the coals to it, till the whole lump have just a blood-red heat. *Moxon's Mechanical Exercises.*

CA'SEMATE. *n. s.* [from *casa armata*, Ital. *casamata*, Span. a vault formerly made to separate the platforms of the lower and upper batteries.]

1. [In fortification.] A kind of vault or arch of stone-work, in that part of the flank of a bastion next the curtin, somewhat retired or drawn back towards the capital of the bastion, serving, as a battery, to defend the face of the opposite bastion, and the moat or ditch. *Chambers.*

2. The well, with its several subterraneous branches, dug in the passage of the bastion, till the miner is heard at work, and air given to the mine. *Harris.*

CA'SEMENT. *n. s.* [*casamento*, Ital.] A window opening upon hinges.

Why, then may you have a *casement* of the great chamber window, where we play, open, and the moon may shine in at the *casement*. *Shakesp. Midsummer Night's Dream.*

Here in this world they do much knowledge read,
And are the *casements* which admit most light. *Davies.*

They, waken'd with the noise, did fly
From inward room to window eye,
And gently op'ning lid, the *casement*,
Look'd out, but yet with some amazement. *Hudibras.*

There is as much difference between the clear representations of the understanding then, and the obscure discoveries that it makes now, as there is between the prospect of a *casement* and a key-hole. *South.*

CA'SEOUS. *adj.* [*caseus*, Lat.] Resembling cheese; cheesy.

Its fibrous parts are from the *caseous* parts of the chyle. *Floyer on Humours.*

CA'SERN. *n. s.* [*caserne*, Fr.] A little room or lodgement erected between the rampart and the houses of fortified towns, to serve as apartments or lodgings for the soldiers of the garrison, with beds. *Harris.*

CA'SEWORM. *n. s.* [from *case* and *worm.*] A grub that makes itself a case.

Cadises, or *caseworms*, are to be found in this nation, in several distinct counties, and in several little brooks. *Floyer.*

CASH. *n. s.* [*caisse*, Fr. a chest.] Money; properly ready money; money in the chest, or at hand.

A thief, bent to unhoard the *cash*
Of some rich burgher. *Paradise Lost, b.* ii. *l.* 188.

He is at an end of all his *cash*; he has both his law and his daily bread now upon trust. *Arbuthnot's John Bull.*

He sent the thief, that stole the *cash*, away,
And punish'd him that put it in his way. *Pope.*

CA'SH-KEEPER. *n. s.* [from *cash* and *keep.*] A man entrusted with the money.

Dispensator was properly a *cash-keeper*, or privy-purse. *Arbuthnot on Coins.*

CA'SHEWNUT. *n. s.* A tree.

The cup of the flower, which is produced at the extremity of a footstalk, is oblong and quinquefid; the flower consists of one leaf, which is divided into five long narrow segments; in the bottom of the calyx is the ovary, which becomes a soft pear-shaped fruit; upon the apex of which grows a vessel, in which is contained one kidney-shaped seed. This tree is very common in Jamaica and Barbadoes, where it grows very large, but in England will rarely stand through our winters. The inhabitants of the West Indies plant them from branches taken from the old trees; which, with them, take root very well, and in two years time produce fruits. *Miller.*

CASHI'ER. *n. s.* [from *cash.*] He that has charge of the money.

If a steward or *cashier* be suffered to run on, without bringing him to a reckoning, such a sottish forbearance will teach him to shuffle. *South.*

A Venetian, finding his son's expences grow very high, ordered his *cashier* to let him have no more money than what he should count when he received it. *Locke.*

Flight of *cashiers*, or mobs, he'll never mind;
And knows no losses, while the muse is kind. *Pope.*

To CASHI'ER. *v. a.* [*casser*, Fr. *cassare*, Lat.]

1. To discard; to dismiss from a post, or a society, with reproach.

Does 't not go well? Cassio hath beaten thee,
And thou by that small hurt hast *cashier'd* Cassio. *Shakesp.*

Seconds in factions many times prove principals; but many times also they prove cyphers, and are *cashiered*. *Bacon.*

If I had omitted what he said, his thoughts and words being thus *cashiered* in my hands, he had no longer been Lucretius. *Dryden.*

They have already *cashiered* several of their followers as mutineers. *Addison's Freeholder.*

The ruling rogue, who dreads to be *cashier'd*,
Contrives, as he is hated, to be fear'd. *Swift.*

2. It seems, in the following passages, to signify the same as to annul; to vacate; which is sufficiently agreeable to the derivation.

If we should find a father corrupting his son, or a mother her daughter, we must charge this upon a peculiar anomaly and baseness of nature; if the name of nature may be allowed to that which seems to be utter *cashiering* of it, and deviation from, and a contradiction to, the common principles of humanity. *South.*

Some, out of an overfondness of that darling invention, *cashier*, or at least endeavour to invalidate, all other arguments, and forbid us to hearken to those proofs, as weak or fallacious. *Locke.*

CASK. *n. s.* [*casque*, Fr. *cadus*, Lat.]

1. A barrel; a wooden vessel to stop up liquour or provisions.

The patient turning himself abed, it makes a fluctuating kind of noise, like the rumbling of water in a *cask*. *Harvey.*

Perhaps tomorrow he may change his wine,
And drink old sparkling Alban, or Setine,
Whose title, and whose age, with mould o'ergrown,
The good old *cask* for ever keeps unknown. *Dryden.*

2. It has *cask* in a kind of plural sense, to signify the commodity or provision of casks.

Great inconveniencies grow by the bad *cask* being commonly so ill seasoned and conditioned, as that a great part of the beer is ever lost and cast away. *Raleigh.*

CASK. } *n. s.* [*casque*, Fr. *cassis*, Lat.] A helmet; armour for
CASQUE. } the head: a poetical word.

Let thy blows, doubly redoubled,
Fall like amazing thunder on the *casque*
Of thy pernicious enemy. *Shakesp. Richard* II.

And these
Sling weighty stones, when from afar they fight;
Their *casques* are cork, a covering thick and light. *Dryden.*

What are his aims? why does he load with darts
His trembling hands, and crush beneath a *cask*
His wrinkled brows? *Addison's Cato.*

CA'SKET. *n. s.* [a diminutive of *caisse*, a chest, Fr. *casse*, *cassette.*] A small box or chest for jewels, or things of particular value.

O ignorant poor man! what dost thou bear,
Lock'd up within the *casket* of thy breast?
What jewels, and what riches hast thou there?
What heav'nly treasure in so weak a chest? *Davies.*

They found him dead, and cast into the streets,
An empty *casket*, where the jewel, life,
By some damn'd hand was robb'd, and ta'en away. *Shakesp.*

Mine eye hath found that sad sepulchral rock,
That was the *casket* of heav'n's richest store. *Milton.*

That had by chance pack'd up his choicest treasure
In one dear *casket*, and sav'd only that. *Otway's Ven. Preserv.*

This *casket* India's glowing gems unlocks,
And all Arabia breathes from yonder box. *Pope.*

To CA'SKET. *v. a.* [from the noun.] To put in a casket.

I have writ my letters, *casketed* my treasure, and given order for our horses. *Shakesp. All's well that ends well.*

CASSAMUNA'IR. *n. s.* An aromatick vegetable, being a species of *galangal*, brought from the East, and highly valued as a nervous and stomachick simple. *Quincy.*

To CA'SSATE. *v. a.* [*casser*, Fr. *cassare*, low Lat.] To vacate; to invalidate; to make void; to nullify.

This opinion supersedes and *cassates* the best medium we have. *Ray on the Creation.*

CASSA'TION. *n. s.* [*cassatio*, Lat.] A making null or void. *D.*

CA'SSAVI. } *n. s.* An American plant.
CA'SSADA. }

It has a short spreading bell-shaped flower, consisting of one leaf, cut into several parts, whose pointal afterwards becomes a roundish fruit, composed of three cells joined together, each containing one oblong seed. To these notes should be added, male flowers having no pointal, and which, growing round the female flower, fall off, and are never fruitful. The species are six: 1. The common *cassavi*, or *cassada*. 2. The most prickly *cassavi*, with a chaste tree leaf. 3. Tree-like less prickly *cassavi*, with white flowers growing in umbels, and a stinging wolfsbane leaf. 4. Shrubby *cassavi*, without prickles, and smooth leaves, which are less divided, &c. The first sort is cultivated in all the warm parts of America, where the root, after being divested of its milky juice, is ground to flour, and then made into cakes of bread. Of this there are two sorts. The most common has purplish stalks, with the veins and leaves of a purplish colour; but the stalks of the other are green, and the leaves of a lighter green. The last sort is not venomous, even when the roots are fresh and full of juice; which the negroes frequently dig up, roast, and eat, like potatoes, without any ill effects. The *cassada* is propagated by cuttings, about fifteen or sixteen inches long, taken from those plants whose roots are grown to maturity. These cuttings are planted by the Americans in their rainy seasons, a foot or fourteen inches deep in the ground; and the land in which they are placed, must be well wrought. When the cuttings have taken root, they require no farther care than to be kept clear from weeds; and, in about eight or nine months, when grown to maturity, in good ground they will be as large as the calf of a man's leg, but commonly equal to the size of good parsneps. *Miller.*

CA'SSAWARE. See CASSIOWARY.

CA'SSIA. *n. s.* A sweet spice mentioned by *Moses*, *Exod.* xxx. 24. as an ingredient in the composition of the holy oil, which was to be made use of in the consecration of the sacred vessels of the tabernacle. This aromatick is said to be the bark of a tree very like cinamon, and grows in the Indies without being cultivated. *Calmet.*

All thy garments smell of myrrh, aloes, and *cassia*. *Ps.* xlv. 8.

CA'SSIA. *n. s.* The name of a tree.

It hath a cylindrical, long, taper, or flat pod, divided into many cells by transverse diaphragms; in each of which is contained one hard seed, lodged, for the most part, in a clammy black substance, which is purgative. The flowers have five leaves, disposed orbicularly. The species are nine; 1. The American *cassia*, with roundish pointed leaves. 2. The purging *cassia*, or pudding pipe tree, &c. Many of these plants will flower the second year, and some of them will produce ripe seeds with us. The second sort grows to be a very large tree, not only in Alexandria, but also in the West Indies. This is what produces the purging *cassia* of the shops. *Miller.*

CA'SSIDONY, or *Stickadore*. *n. s.* [*stoechas*, Latin.] The name of a plant.

CA'SSIOWARY. *n. s.* A large bird of prey in the East Indies.

Have a clear idea of the relation of dam and chick, between the two *cassiowaries* in St. James's Park. *Locke.*

CA'SSOCK. *n. s.* [*casaque*, Fr.] A close garment; now generally that which clergymen wear under their gowns.

Half of the which dare not shake the snow from off their *cassocks*, lest they shake themselves to pieces. *Shakesp. All's well that ends well.*

His scanty salary compelled him to run deep in debt for a new gown and *cassock*, and now and then forced him to write some paper of wit or humour, or preach a sermon for ten shillings, to supply his necessities. *Swift.*

CA'SSWEED. *n. s.* A common weed, otherwise called *shepherd's pouch*.

To CAST. *v. a.* preter. *cast*; particip. pass. *cast*. [*kaster*, Danish.]

1. To throw with the hand.

I rather chuse to endure the wounds of those darts, which envy *casteth* at novelty, than to go on safely and sleepily in the easy ways of ancient mistakings. *Raleigh's Hist. of the World.*

They had compassed in his host, and *cast* darts at the people from morning till evening. 1 *Macc.* vii. 80.

Then *cast* thy sword away,
And yield thee to my mercy, or I strike. *Dryden and Lee.*

2. To throw away, as useless or noxious.

Old Capulet, and Montague,
Have made Verona's ancient citizens
Cast by their grave beseeming ornaments. *Shakesp.*

I have bought
Golden opinion from all sort of people,
Which would be worn now in their newest gloss,
Not *cast* aside so soon. *Shakesp. Macbeth.*

When men, presuming themselves to be the only masters of right reason, *cast* by the votes and opinions of the rest of mankind, as not worthy of reckoning. *Locke.*

3. To throw dice, or lots.

And Joshua *cast* lots for them in Shiloh. *Josh.* xviii. 10.

4. To throw from a high place.

Bear him to the rock Tarpeian, and from thence
Into destruction *cast* him. *Shakesp. Coriolanus.*

5. To throw in wrestling.

And I think, being too strong for him, though he took my legs sometime, yet I made a shift to *cast* him. *Shakesp. Macbeth.*

6. To throw as a net or snare.

I speak for your own profit, not that I may *cast* a snare upon you. 1 *Cor.* vii. 35.

7. To drop; to let fall.

They let down the boat into the sea, as though they would have *cast* anchor. *Acts*, xxvii. 30.

8. To expose.

His friends contend to embalm his body, his enemies, that they may *cast* it to the dogs. *Pope's Essay on Homer.*

9. To drive by violence of weather.

Howbeit we must be *cast* upon a certain island. *Acts*, xxvii. 26.

What length of lands, what ocean have you pass'd,
What storms sustain'd, and on what shore been *cast*? *Dryd.*

10. To build by throwing up earth; to raise.

And shooting in the earth, *casts* up a mount of clay.
Spenser's Fairy Queen, b. i. c. viii. stanz. 9.

The king of Assyria shall not come into this city, nor shoot an arrow there, nor come before it with shield, nor *cast* a bank against it. 2 *Kings*, xix. 32.

At length Barbarossa having *cast* up his trenches, landed fifty-four pieces of artillery for battery. *Knolles's History.*

Earth-worms will come forth, and moles will *cast* up more, and fleas bite more, against rain. *Bacon's Nat. History.*

11. To put into any certain state.

Jesus had heard that John was *cast* into prison. *Matt.* iv. 12.

At thy rebuke both the chariot and horse are *cast* into a dead sleep. *Psalm* lxxvi. 6.

12. To condemn in a trial.

But oh, that treacherous breast! to whom weak you
Did trust our counsels, and we both may rue,
Having his falsehood found too late, 'twas he
That made me *cast* you guilty, and you me. *Donne.*

We take up with the most incompetent witnesses, nay, often suborn our own surmises and jealousies, that we may be sure to *cast* the unhappy criminal. *Governm. of the Tongue*, § 6.

He could not, in this forlorn case, have made use of the very last plea of a *cast* criminal; nor so much as have cried, Mercy! Lord, mercy! *South.*

There then we met; both try'd, and both were *cast*,
And this irrevocable sentence past. *Dryden's Theod. and Hon.*

13. To condemn in a law-suit. [from *caster*, Fr.]

The northern men were agreed, and, in effect, all the other, to *cast* our London escheatour. *Camden's Remains.*

Were the case referred to any competent judge, they would inevitably be *cast*. *Decay of Piety.*

14. To defeat.

No martial project to surprise,
Can ever be attempted twice;
Nor *cast* design serve afterwards,
As gamesters tear their losing cards. *Hudibras, p.* iii. *c.* iii.

15. To cashier.

You are but now *cast* in his mood, a punishment more in policy than in malice; even so as one would beat his offenceless dog, to affright an imperious lion. *Shakesp. Othello.*

16. To leave behind in a race.

In short, so swift your judgments turn and wind,
You *cast* our fleetest wits a mile behind. *Dryden.*

17. To shed; to let fall; to lay aside; to moult.

Our chariot lost her wheels, their points our spears,
The bird of conquest her chief feather *cast*. *Fairfax, b.* iii.

Of plants some are green all winter, others *cast* their leaves. *Bacon's Natural History*, N° 592.

The *casting* of the skin is, by the ancients, compared to the breaking curd of the secundine, or cawl, but not rightly; for that were to make every *casting* of the skin a new birth: and besides, the secundine is but a general cover, not shaped according to the parts, but the skin is shaped according to the parts. The creatures that *cast* the skin, are the snake, the viper, the grashopper, the lizzard, the silkworm, &c. *Bacon's Natural History*, N° 732.

O fertile head, which ev'ry year
Could such a crop of wonders bear!
Which might it never have been *cast*,
Each year's growth added to the last,
These lofty branches had supply'd
The earth's bold sons prodigious pride. *Waller.*

The waving harvest bends beneath his blast,
The forest shakes, the groves their honours *cast*. *Dryden.*

From hence, my lord, and love, I thus conclude,
That though my homely ancestors were rude,
Mean as I am, yet may I have the grace
To make you father of a generous race:

And noble then am I, when I begin,
In virtue cloath'd, to *cast* the rags of sin. *Dryden's W. of B.*

The ladies have been in a kind of moulting season, having *cast* great quantities of ribbon and cambrick, and reduced the human figure to the beautiful globular form. *Addison. Spectator.*

18. To lay aside, as fit to be worn no longer.

So may *cast* poets write; there's no pretension
To argue loss of wit, from loss of pension. *Dryden's D. Seb.*

He has ever been of opinion, that giving *cast* clothes to be worn by valets, has a very ill effect upon little minds. *Addison.*

19. To have abortions; to bring forth before the time.

Thy ews and thy she-goats have not *cast* their young, and the rams of thy flock have I not eaten. *Gen.* xxxi. 38.

20. To overweigh; to make to preponderate; to decide by overballancing.

Which being inclined, not constrained, contain within themselves the *casting* act, and a power to command the conclusion. *Brown's Vulgar Errours, b.* iv. *c.* 13.

How much interest *casts* the balance in cases dubious. *South.*

Life and death are equal in themselves,
That which could *cast* the balance, is thy falshood. *Dryden.*

Not many years ago, it so happened, that a cobler had the *casting* vote for the life of a criminal, which he very graciously gave on the merciful side. *Addison on Italy.*

Suppose your eyes sent equal rays
Upon two distant pots of ale,
In this sad state, your doubtful choice
Would never have the *casting* voice. *Prior.*

21. To compute; to reckon; to calculate.

Hearts, tongues, figure, scribes, bards, poets, cannot
Think, speak, *cast*, write, sing, number, ho!
His love to Antony. *Shakesp. Antony and Cleopatra.*

Here is now the smith's note for shoeing and plow-irons.—
Let it be *cast* and paid. *Shakesp. Henry* IV. *p.* ii.

You *cast* th' event of war, my noble lord,
And summ'd th' account of chance, before you said,
Let us make head. *Shakesp. Henry* IV. *p.* ii.

The best way to represent to life the manifold use of friendship, is to *cast* and see how many things there are, which a man cannot do himself. *Bacon's Essays.*

I have lately been *casting* in my thoughts the several unhappinesses of life, and comparing the infelicities of old age to those of infancy. *Addison. Spectator,* N° 131.

22. To contrive; to plan out.

The cloister facing the South, is covered with vines, and would have been proper for an orange-house; and had, I doubt not, been *cast* for that purpose, if this piece of gardening had been then in as much vogue as it is now. *Temple.*

23. To judge; to consider in order to judgment.

If thou couldst, doctor, *cast*
The water of my land, find her disease,
And purge it to a sound and pristine health,
I would applaud thee to the very echo,
That should applaud again. *Shakesp. Macbeth.*

Peace, brother, be not over exquisite
To *cast* the fashion of uncertain evils. *Milton.*

24. To fix the parts in a play.

Our parts in the other world will be new *cast*, and mankind will be there ranged in different stations of superiority. *Addison. Spectator,* N° 219.

25. To glance; to direct the eye.

Zelmanes's languishing countenance, with crossed arms, and sometimes *cast* up eyes, she thought to have an excellent grace. *Sidney, b.* ii.

As he past along,
How earnestly he *cast* his eyes upon me. *Shakesp. H.* VIII.

Begin, auspicious boy, to *cast* about
Thy infant eyes, and, with a smile, thy mother single out. *Dryden's Virgil, Past.* iv.

Far eastward *cast* thine eye, from whence the sun,
And orient science, at a birth begun. *Pope's Dunciad.*

He then led me to the rock, and, placing me on the top of it, *Cast* thy eyes eastward, said he, and tell me what thou seest. *Addison. Spectator,* N° 159.

26. To found; to form by running in a mould.

When any such curious work of silver is to be *cast*, as requires that the impression of hairs, or very slender lines, be taken off by the metal, it is not enough, that the silver be barely melted; but it must be kept a considerable while in a strong fusion. *Boyle.*

How to build ships, and dreadful ordnance *cast*,
Instruct the artist. *Waller.*

The father's grief restrain'd his art;
He twice essay'd to *cast* his son in gold,
Twice from his hands he dropp'd the forming mould. *Dryden, Æneid* vi.

27. To melt metal into figures.

Yon' croud, he might reflect, yon' joyful croud
With restless rage would pull my statue down,
And *cast* the brass anew to his renown. *Prior.*

This was but as a refiner's fire, to purge out the dross, and then *cast* the mass again into a new mould. *Burnet's Theory.*

28. To model; to form.

We may take a quarter of a mile for the common measure of the depth of the sea, if it were *cast* into a channel of an equal depth every where. *Burnet's Theory of the Earth.*

Under this influence, derived from mathematical studies, some have been tempted to *cast* all their logical, their metaphysical, and their theological and moral learning into this method. *Watts's Logick.*

29. To communicate by reflection or emanation.

So bright a splendour, so divine a grace,
The glorious Daphnis *casts* on his illustrious race. *Dryden.*

We may happen to find a fairer light *cast* over the same scriptures, and see reason to alter our sentiments even in some points of moment. *Watts's Improvement of the Mind.*

30. To yield, or give up, without reserve or condition.

The reason of mankind cannot suggest any solid ground of satisfaction, but in making God our friend, and in carrying a conscience so clear, as may encourage us, with confidence, to *cast* ourselves upon him. *South.*

31. To inflict.

The world is apt to *cast* great blame on those who have an indifferency for opinions, especially in religion. *Locke.*

32. *To cast away.* To shipwreck.

Sir Francis Drake, and John Thomas, meeting with a storm, it thrust John Thomas upon the islands to the South, where he was *cast away.* *Raleigh's Essays.*

His father Philip had, by like mishap, been like to have been *cast away* upon the coast of England. *Knolles's History.*

With pity mov'd, for others *cast away*
On rocks of hope and fears. *Roscommon.*

But now our fears tempestuous grow,
And *cast* our hopes *away*;
Whilst you, regardless of our woe,
Sit careless at a play. *Dorset.*

33. *To cast away.* To lavish; to waste in profusion; to turn to no use.

They that want means to nourish children, will abstain from marriage; or, which is all one, they *cast away* their bodies upon rich old women. *Raleigh's Essays.*

France, hast thou yet more blood to *cast away*?
Say, shall the current of our right run on? *Shakesp. K. J.*

He might be silent, and not *cast away*
His sentences in vain. *Ben. Johnson's Catiline.*

O Marcia, O my sister, still there's hope!
Our father will not *cast away* a life,
So needful to us all, and to his country. *Addison's Cato.*

34. *To cast away.* To ruin.

It is no impossible thing for states, by an oversight in some one act or treaty between them and their potent opposites, utterly to *cast away* themselves for ever. *Hooker, b.* iii. § 10.

35. *To cast down.* To deject; to depress the mind.

We're not the first,
Who, with best meaning, have incurr'd the worst;
For thee, oppressed king, I am *cast down*;
Myself could else outfrown false fortune's frown. *Shakesp. King Lear.*

The best way will be to let him see you are much *cast down*, and afflicted, for the ill opinion he entertains of you. *Addison. Spectator,* N° 171.

36. *To cast off.* To discard; to put away.

The prince will, in the perfectness of time,
Cast off his followers. *Shakesp. Henry* IV. *p.* ii.

He led me on to mightiest deeds,
But now hath *cast* me *off*, as never known. *Milt. Agonistes.*

How! not call him father? I see preferment alters a man strangely; this may serve me for an use of instruction, to *cast off* my father, when I am great. *Dryden's Spanish Friar.*

I long to clasp that haughty maid,
And bend her stubborn virtue to my passion:
When I have gone thus far, I'd *cast* her *off*. *Addison's Cato.*

37. *To cast off.* To reject.

It is not to be imagined, that a whole society of men should publickly and professedly disown, and *cast off* a rule, which they could not but be infallibly certain was a law. *Locke.*

38. *To cast off.* To disburden one's self of.

All conspired in one to *cast off* their subjection to the crown of England. *Spenser's State of Ireland.*

This maketh them, through an unweariable desire of receiving instruction, to *cast off* the care of those very affairs, which do most concern their estate. *Hooker, Preface.*

The true reason why any man is an atheist, is because he is a wicked man: religion would curb him in his lusts; and therefore he *casts* it *off*, and puts all the scorn upon it he can. *Tillotson, Serm.* ii.

Company, in any action, gives credit and countenance to the agent; and so much as the sinner gets of this, so much he *casts off* of shame. *South.*

We see they never fail to exert themselves, and to *cast off* the oppression, when they feel the weight of it. *Addison.*

39. *To cast off.* To leave behind.

Away he scours cross the fields, *casts off* the dogs, and gains a wood; but, pressing through a thicket, the bushes held him by

by the horns, till the hounds came in, and plucked him down.
L'Estrange, Fab. xliii.

40. *To cast off.* [hunting term.] To let go, or set free; as, to *cast off* the dogs.

41. *To cast out.* To reject; to turn out of doors.
Thy brat hath been *cast out*, like to itself, no father owning it. *Shakesp. Winter's Tale.*

42. *To cast out.* To vent; to speak; with some intimation of negligence or vehemence.
Why dost thou *cast out* such ungenerous terms
Against the lords and sovereigns of the world? *Add. Cato.*

43. *To cast up.* To compute; to calculate.
Some writers, in *casting up* the goods most desirable in life, have given them this rank, health, beauty, and riches. *Temple.*
A man who designs to build, is very exact, as he supposes, in *casting up* the cost beforehand; but, generally speaking, he is mistaken in his account. *Dryden's Fab. Preface.*

44. *To cast up.* To vomit.
Thou, beastly feeder, art so full of him,
That thou provok'st thyself to *cast* him *up*. *Shakesp. H.* IV.
Their villainy goes against my weak stomach, and therefore I must *cast* it *up*. *Shakesp. Henry* V.
O, that in time Rome did not *cast*
Her errours *up*, this fortune to prevent. *Ben. Johnson's Catil.*
Thy foolish errour find;
Cast up the poison that infects thy mind. *Dryden.*

To Cast. *v. n.*

1. To contrive; to turn the thoughts.
Then closely as he might, he *cast* to leave
The court, not asking any pass or leave. *Spenser.*
From that day forth, I *cast* in careful mind,
To seek her out with labour and long time. *Fairy Q. b.* i.
We have three that bend themselves, looking into the experiments of their fellows, and *cast* about how to draw out of them things of use and practice for man's life and knowledge. *Bacon's New Atlantis.*
But first he *casts* to change his proper shape;
Which else might work him danger or delay. *Par. L. b.* iii.
As a fox, with hot pursuit
Chas'd through a warren, *cast* about
To save his credit. *Hudibras, p.* ii. *cant.* iii.
All events, called casual, among inanimate bodies, are mechanically produced according to the determinate figures, textures, and motions of those bodies, which are not conscious of their own operations, nor contrive and *cast* about how to bring such events to pass. *Bentley.*
This way and that I *cast* to save my friends,
Till one resolve my varying counsel ends. *Pope's Odyssey.*

2. To admit of a form, by casting or melting.
It comes at the first fusion into a mass that is immediately malleable, and will not run thin, so as to *cast* and mould, unless mixed with poorer ore, or cinders. *Woodward on Fossils.*

3. To warp; to grow out of form.
Stuff is said to *cast* or warp, when, by its own drought, or moisture of the air, or other accident, it alters its flatness and straightness. *Moxon's Mechanical Exercises.*

Cast. *n. s.* [from the verb.]

1. The act of casting or throwing; a throw.
So when a sort of lusty shepherds throw
The bar by turns, and none the rest outgo
So far, but that the rest are measuring *casts*,
Their emulation and their pastime lasts. *Waller.*
Yet all these dreadful deeds, this deadly fray,
A *cast* of dreadful dust will soon allay. *Dryden's Virgil.*

2. The thing thrown.
Some harrow their ground over, and sow wheat or rye on it with a broad *cast*; some only with a single *cast*, and some with a double. *Mortimer.*

3. State of any thing cast or thrown.
In his own instance of casting ambs-ace, though it partake more of contingency than of freedom; supposing the positure of the party's hand, who did throw the dice; supposing the figure of the table, and of the dice themselves; supposing the measure of force applied, and supposing all other things which did concur to the production of that *cast*, to be the very same they were, there is no doubt but, in this case, the *cast* is necessary. *Bramhall's Answer to Hobbes.*
Plato compares life to a game at tables; there what *cast* we shall have is not in our power, but to manage it well, that is. *Norris.*

4. The space through which any thing is thrown.
And he was withdrawn from them about a stone's *cast*, and kneeled down and prayed. *Luke,* xxii. 41.

5. A stroke; a touch.
We have them all with one voice for giving him a *cast* of their court prophecy. *South.*
Another *cast* of their politicks, was that of endeavouring to impeach an innocent lady, for her faithful and diligent service of the queen. *Swift's Examiner,* N° 19.
This was a *cast* of Wood's politicks; for his information was wholly false and groundless, which he knew very well. *Swift.*

6. Motion of the eye.
Pity causeth sometimes tears, and a flexion or *cast* of the eye aside; for pity is but grief in another's behalf; the *cast* of the eye is a gesture of aversion, or lothness, to behold the object of pity. *Bacon's Natural History.*
If any man desires to look on this doctrine of gravity, let him turn the first *cast* of his eyes on what we have said of fire. *Digby on the Soul.*
There held in holy passion still,
Forget thyself to marble, till,
With a sad leaden downward *cast*,
Thou fix them on the earth as fast. *Milton.*
They are the best epitomes in the world, and let you see, with one *cast* of an eye, the substance of above an hundred pages. *Addison on ancient Medals.*

7. The throw of dice.

8. Chance from the cast of dice.
Were it good,
To set the exact wealth of all our states
All at one *cast*; to set so rich a main
On the nice hazard of some doubtful hour? *Shakesp. H.* IV.
In the last war, has it not sometimes been an even *cast*, whether the army should march this way or that way? *South.*

9. Venture from throwing dice.
When you have brought them to the very last *cast*, they will offer to come to you, and submit themselves. *Spenser on Ireland.*
With better grace an ancient chief may yield
The long contended honours of the field,
Than venture all his fortune at a *cast*,
And fight, like Hannibal, to lose at last. *Dryden.*
Will you turn recreant at the last *cast*? you must along. *Dryden's Spanish Friar.*

10. A mould; a form.
The whole would have been an heroick poem, but in another *cast* and figure, than any that ever had been written before. *Prior.*

11. A shade; or tendency to any colour.
A flaky mass, grey, with a *cast* of green, in which the talky matter makes the greatest part of the mass. *Woodward.*
The qualities of blood in a healthy state are to be florid, the red part congealing, and the serum ought to be without any greenish *cast*. *Arbuthnot on Aliments.*

12. Exteriour appearance.
The native hue of resolution
Is sicklied o'er with the pale *cast* of thought. *Shakesp. Hamlet.*
New names, new dressings, and the modern *cast*,
Some scenes, some persons alter'd, and outfac'd
The world. *Sir J. Denham.*

13. Manner; air; mien.
Pretty conceptions, fine metaphors, glittering expressions, and something of a neat *cast* of verse, are properly the dress, gems, or loose ornaments of poetry. *Pope's Letters.*
Neglect not the little figures and turns on the words, nor sometimes the very *cast* of the periods; neither omit or confound any rites or customs of antiquity. *Pope's Ess. on Homer.*

14. A flight; a number of hawks dismissed from the fist.
A *cast* of merlins there was besides, which, flying of a gallant height over certain bushes, would beat the birds that rose, down unto the bushes, as falcons will do wild fowl over a river. *Sidney, b.* ii.

Ca'stanet. *n. s.* [*castaneta*, Sp.] Small shells of ivory, or hard wood, which dancers rattle in their hands.
If there had been words enow between them, to have expressed provocation, they had gone together by the ears like a pair of *castanets*. *Congreve's Way of the World.*

Ca'staway. *n. s.* [from *cast* and *away*.] A person lost, or abandoned by providence.
Neither given any leave to search in particular who are the heirs of the kingdom of God, who *castaways*. *Hooker, b.* v.
Lest that by any means, when I have preached to others, I myself should be a *castaway*. 1 *Cor.* ix. 27.

Ca'staway. *adj.* [from the subst.] Useless; of no value.
We only prize, pamper, and exalt this vassal and slave of death, or only remember, at our *castaway* leisure, the imprisoned immortal soul. *Raleigh's History.*

Ca'sted. The *participle preterite* of *cast*, but improperly, and found perhaps only in the following passage.
When the mind is quicken'd, out of doubt,
The organs, though defunct and dead before,
Break up their drowsy grave, and newly move
With *casted* slough and fresh legerity. *Shakesp. Henry* V.

Ca'stellain. *n. s.* [*castellano*, Span.] The captain, governour, or constable of a castle.

Ca'stellany. *n. s.* [from *castle*.] The manour or lordship belonging to a castle; the extent of its land and jurisdiction. *Phillips's World of Words.*

Ca'stellated. *adj.* [from *castle*.] Inclosed within a building, as a fountain or cistern *castellated*. *Dict.*

Ca'ster. *n. s.* [from *to cast*.]

1. A thrower; he that casts.
If, with this throw, the strongest *caster* vye,
Still, further still, I bid the discus fly. *Pope's Odyssey.*

2. A calculator; a man that calculates fortunes.

 Did

Did any of them set up for a *caster* of fortunate figures, what might he not get by his predictions? *Addison. Spect.* N° 191.

To CA'STIGATE. *v. a.* [*castigo*, Lat.] To chastise; to chasten; to correct; to punish.

If thou didst put this sour cold habit on,
To *castigate* thy pride, 'twere well. *Shakesp. Timon.*

CASTIGA'TION. *n. s.* [from *to castigate.*]

1. Penance; discipline.

This hand of yours requires
A sequester from liberty; fasting and prayer,
With *castigation*, exercise devout. *Shakesp. Othello.*

2. Punishment; correction.

The ancients had these conjectures touching these floods and conflagrations, so as to frame them into an hypothesis for the *castigation* of the excesses of generation. *Hale's Orig. of Mank.*

3. Emendation.

Their *castigations* were accompanied with encouragements; which care was taken, to keep me from looking upon as mere compliments. *Boyle's Seraphick Love.*

CA'STIGATORY. *adj.* [from *castigate.*] Punitive, in order to amendment.

There were other ends of penalties inflicted, either probatory, *castigatory*, or exemplary. *Bramhall against Hobbes.*

CA'STING-NET. *n. s.* [from *casting* and *net.*] A net to be thrown into the water.

Casting-nets did rivers bottoms sweep. *May's Virgil.*

CA'STLE. *n. s.* [*castellum*, Lat.]

1. A strong house, fortified against assaults.

The *castle* of Macduff I will surprise. *Shakesp. Macbeth.*
To forfeit all your goods, lands, tenements,
And *castles.* *Shakesp. Henry VIII.*

2. CASTLES *in the air.* [*chateaux d'Espagne*, Fr.] Projects without reality.

These were but like *castles in the air*, and in men's fancies vainly imagined. *Raleigh's History of the World.*

CASTLE SOAP. *n. s.* [I suppose corrupted from *Castile soap.*] A kind of soap.

I have a letter from a soap-boiler, desiring me to write upon the present duties on *Castle soap.* *Addison. Spectator*, N° 488.

CASTLED. *adj.* [from *castle.*] Furnished with castles.

The horses neighing by the wind is blown,
And *castled* elephants o'erlook the town. *Dryden's Aurengz.*

CA'STLEWARD. *n. s.* [from *castle* and *ward.*]

An imposition laid upon such of the king's subjects, as dwell within a certain compass of any castle, toward the maintenance of such as watch and ward the castle. *Cowel.*

CA'STLING. *n. s.* [from *cast.*] An abortive.

We should rather rely upon the urine of a *castling's* bladder, a resolution of crabs eyes, or a second distillation of urine, as Helmont hath commended. *Brown's Vulgar Errours.*

CA'STOR, CHESTER, are derived from the Sax. ceaster, a city, town, or castle; and that from the Latin *castrum*; the Saxons chusing to fix in such places of strength and figure, as the Romans had before built or fortified. *Gibson's Camden.*

CA'STOR. *n. s.* [*castor*, Lat.]

1. A beaver. See BEAVER.
2. A fine hat made of the furr of a beaver.

CA'STOR and POLLUX. [In meteorology.] A firy meteor, which, at sea, appears sometimes sticking to a part of the ship, in form of one, two, or even three or four balls. When one is seen alone, it is more properly called Helena, which portends the severest part of the storm to be yet behind; two are denominated *Castor* and *Pollux*, and sometimes Tyndarides, which portend a cessation of the storm. *Chambers.*

CASTO'REUM. *n. s.* [from *castor.* In pharmacy.] A liquid matter inclosed in bags or purses, near the anus of the castor, falsely taken for his testicles. These bags are about the bigness of a goose's egg, and found indifferently in males and females; when taken off, the matter dries and condenses, so as to be reduced to a powder, which is oily, of a sharp bitter taste, and a strong disagreeable smell, and used to fortify the head and nervous parts. *Chambers.*

CASTRAMETA'TION. *n. s.* [from *castrametor*, Lat.] The art or practice of encamping.

To CA'STRATE. *v. a.* [*castro*, Lat.]

1. To geld.
2. To take away the obscene parts of a writing.

CASTRA'TION. *n. s.* [from *castrate.*] The act of gelding.

The largest needle should be used, in taking up the spermatick vessels in *castration.* *Sharp's Surgery.*

CA'STERIL. } *n. s.* A kind of hawk.
CA'STREL. }

CASTRE'NSIAN. *adj.* [*castrensis*, Lat.] Belonging to a camp. *D.*

CA'SUAL. *adj.* [*casuel*, Fr. from *casus*, Lat.] Accidental; arising from chance; depending upon chance; not certain.

The revenue of Ireland, both certain and *casual*, did not rise unto ten thousand pounds. *Davies on Ireland.*

That which seemeth most *casual* and subject to fortune, is yet disposed by the ordinance of God. *Raleigh's History.*

Whether found, where *casual* fire
Had wasted woods, on mountain, or in vale
Down to the veins of earth. *Paradise Lost, b.* xi. *l.* 566.

The commissioners entertained themselves by the fire-side, in general and *casual* discourses. *Clarendon, b.* viii.

Most of our rarities have been found out by *casual* emergency, and have been the works of time and chance, rather than of philosophy. *Glanville's Scepsis, c.* 21.

The expences of some of them always exceed their certain annual income; but seldom their *casual* supplies. I call them *casual*, in compliance with the common form. *Atterbury.*

CA'SUALLY. *adv.* [from *casual.*] Accidentally; without design, or set purpose.

Go, bid my woman
Search for a jewel, that too *casually*
Hath left mine arm. *Shakesp. Cymbeline.*

Wool new shorn, laid *casually* upon a vessel of verjuice, had drunk up the verjuice, though the vessel was without any flaw. *Bacon's Natural Hist.* N° 79.

I should have acquainted my judge with one advantage, and which I now *casually* remember. *Dryden's Virgil, Dedication.*

CA'SUALNESS. *n. s.* [from *casual.*] Accidentalness.

CA'SUALTY. *n. s.* [from *casual.*]

1. Accident; a thing happening by chance, not design.

With more patience men endure the losses that befall them by mere *casualty*, than the damages which they sustain by injustice. *Raleigh's Essays.*

That Octavius Cæsar should shift his camp that night that it happened to be took by the enemy, was a mere *casualty*; yet it preserved a person, who lived to establish a total alteration of government in the imperial city of the world. *South.*

2. Chance that produces unnatural death.

Builds in the weather on the outward wall,
Ev'n in the force and road of *casualty.*
Shakesp. Merchant of Venice.

It is observed in particular nations, that, within the space of two or three hundred years, notwithstanding all *casualties*, the number of men doubles. *Burnet's Theory of the Earth.*

We find one *casualty* in our bills, of which, though there be daily talk, there is little effect. *Graunt's Bills of Mortality.*

CA'SUIST. *n. s.* [*casuiste*, Fr. from *casus*, Lat.] One that studies and settles cases of conscience.

The judgment of any *casuist*, or learned divine, concerning the state of a man's soul, is not sufficient to give him confidence. *South.*

You can scarce see a bench of porters without two or three *casuists* in it, that will settle you the rights of princes.
Addison. Freeholder, N° 53.

Who shall decide, when doctors disagree,
And soundest *casuists* doubt, like you and me? *Pope.*

CASUI'STICAL. *adj.* [from *casuist.*] Relating to cases of conscience; containing the doctrine relating to cases.

What arguments they have to beguile poor, simple, unstable souls with, I know not; but surely the practical, *casuistical*, that is, the principal, vital part of their religion savours very little of spirituality. *South.*

CA'SUISTRY. *n. s.* [from *casuist.*] The science of a casuist; the doctrine of cases of conscience.

Concession would not pass for good *casuistry* in these ages.
Pope's Odyssey, Notes.

Morality, by her false guardians drawn,
Chicane in furs, and *casuistry* in lawn. *Pope's Dunciad.*

CAT. *n. s.* [*katz*, Teuton. *chat*, Fr.] A domestick animal that catches mice, commonly reckoned by naturalists the lowest order of the leonine species.

'Twas you incens'd the rabble:
Cats, that can judge as fitly of his worth,
As I can of those mysteries, which heav'n
Will not have earth to know. *Shakesp. Coriolanus.*

Thrice the brinded *cat* hath mew'd. *Shakesp. Macbeth.*

A *cat*, as she beholds the light, draws the ball of her eye small and long, being covered over with a green skin, and dilates it at pleasure. *Peacham on Drawing.*

CAT. *n. s.* A sort of ship.

CAT *in the pan.* [imagined by some to be rightly written *Catipan*, as coming from *Catipani*, revolted governours. An unknown correspondent imagines, very naturally, that it is corrupted from *Cate in the pan.*]

There is a cunning which we, in England, call the turning of the *cat in the pan*; which is, when that which a man says to another, he lays it as if another had said it to him. *Bacon.*

CAT *o' nine tails.* A whip with nine lashes, used for the punishment of crimes.

You dread reformers of an impious age,
You awful *cat o' nine tails* to the stage,
This once be just, and in our cause engage.
Prologue to Vanbrugh's False Friend.

CATACHRE'SIS. *n. s.* [κατάχρησις, abuse.] It is, in rhetorick, the abuse of a trope, when the words are too far wrested from their native signification, or when one word is abusively put for another, for want of the proper word; as, *a voice* beautiful *to the ear.* *Smith's Rhetorick.*

CATACHRE'STICAL. *adj.* [from *catachresis.*] Contrary to proper use; forced; far fetched.

A

A *catachreſtical* and far derived ſimilitude it holds with men, that is, in a bifurcation. *Brown's Vulgar Errours.*

CA'TACLYSM. *n. ſ.* [κατακλυσμός.] A deluge; an inundation; uſed generally for the univerſal deluge.

The opinion that held theſe *cataclyſms* and empyroſes univerſal, was ſuch, as held, that it put a total conſummation unto things in this lower world. *Hale's Origin of Mankind.*

CA'TACOMBS. *n. ſ.* [from κατὰ and κύμβος, a hollow or cavity.] Subterraneous cavities for the burial of the dead; of which there are a great number about three miles from Rome, ſuppoſed to be the caves and cells where the primitive chriſtians hid and aſſembled themſelves, and where they interred the martyrs, which are accordingly viſited with devotion. But, anciently, the word *catacomb* was only underſtood of the tombs of St. Peter and St. Paul; and Mr. Monro, in the *Philoſophical Tranſactions*, ſuppoſes the *catacombs* to have been originally the ſepulchres of the firſt Romans. Places like theſe might afford convenient reſortments to the primitive chriſtians, but could never be built by them. *Chambers.*

CATAGMA'TICK. *adj.* [κάταγμα, a fracture.] That which has the quality of conſolidating the parts.

I put on a *catagmatick* emplaſter, and, by the uſe of a laced glove, ſcattered the pituitous ſwelling, and ſtrengthened it. *Wiſeman's Surgery.*

CATALE'PSIS. *n. ſ.* [κατάληψις.] A lighter ſpecies of the apoplexy, or epilepſy.

There is a diſeaſe called a *catalepſis*, wherein the patient is ſuddenly ſeized without ſenſe or motion, and remains in the ſame poſture in which the diſeaſe ſeizeth him. *Arbuthnot.*

CA'TALOGUE. *n. ſ.* [κατάλογος.] An enumeration of particulars; a liſt; a regiſter of things one by one.

In the *catalogue* ye go for men,
As hounds, and greyhounds, mungrels, ſpaniels, curs,
Showghes, water rugs, and demy wolves, are cleped
All by the name of dogs. *Shakeſp. Macbeth.*

Make a *catalogue* of all the proſperous ſacrilegious perſons, and I believe they will be repeated much ſooner than the alphabet. *South.*

I was in the library of manuſcripts belonging to St. Laurence, of which there is a printed *catalogue*; I looked into the Virgil which diſputes its antiquity with that of the Vatican. *Addiſon's Remarks on Italy.*

The bright Tygete, and the ſhining Bears,
With all the ſailors *catalogue* of ſtars. *Addiſon's Ovid.*

CATAMO'UNTAIN. *n. ſ.* [from *cat* and *mountain.*] A fierce animal, reſembling a cat.

The black prince of Monomotapa, by whoſe ſide were ſeen the glaring *catamountain*, and the quill-darting porcupine. *Arbuthnot and Pope's Mart. Scriblerus.*

CA'TAPHRACT. *n. ſ.* [*cataphracta*, Lat.] A horſeman in complete armour.

On each ſide went armed guards,
Both horſe and foot before him and behind,
Archers and ſlingers, *cataphracts* and ſpears. *Milt. Agoniſt.*

CA'TAPLASM. *n. ſ.* [κατάπλασμα.] A poultice; a ſoft and moiſt application.

I bought an unction of a mountebank,
So mortal, that but dip a knife in it,
Where it draws blood, no *cataplaſm* ſo rare,
Collected from all ſimples that have virtue
Under the moon, can ſave. *Shakeſp. Hamlet.*

Warm *cataplaſms* diſcuſs, but ſcalding hot may confirm the tumour. *Arbuthnot on Aliments.*

CA'TAPULT. *n. ſ.* [*catapulta*, Lat.] An engine uſed anciently to throw ſtones.

The baliſta violently ſhot great ſtones and quarrels, as alſo the *catapults*. *Camden's Remains.*

CA'TARACT. *n. ſ.* [καταῤῥάκτης.] A fall of water from on high; a ſhoot of water; a caſcade.

Blow, winds, and crack your cheeks; rage, blow!
You *cataracts* and hurricanes, ſpout,
Till you have drench'd our ſteeples, drown'd the cocks. *Shakeſp. King Lear.*

What if all
Her ſtores were open'd, and this firmament
Of hell ſhould ſpout her *cataracts* of fire?
Impendent horrours! *Milton's Par. Loſt, b.* ii. *l.* 170.

No ſooner he, with them of man and beaſt
Select for life, ſhall in the ark be lodg'd,
And ſhelter'd round; but all the *cataracts*
Of heav'n ſet open, on the earth ſhall pour
Rain, day and night. *Milton's Par. Loſt, b.* xi. *l.* 824.

Torrents and loud impetuous *cataracts*,
Through roads abrupt, and rude unfaſhion'd tracts,
Run down the lofty mountain's channel'd ſides,
And to the vale convey their foaming tides. *Blackmore.*

CA'TARACT. [In medicine.] A ſuffuſion of the eye, when little clouds, motes, and flies, ſeem to float about in the air; when confirmed, the pupil of the eye is either wholly, or in part, covered, and ſhut up with a little thin ſkin, ſo that the light has no admittance. *Quincy.*

Saladine hath a yellow milk, which hath likewiſe much acrimony; for it cleanſeth the eyes: it is good alſo for *cataracts*. *Bacon's Natural Hiſtory*, N° 639.

CATA'RRH. *n. ſ.* [καταῤῥέω, *defluo.*] A defluxion of a ſharp ſerum from the glands about the head and throat, generally occaſioned by a diminution of inſenſible perſpiration, or cold, wherein what ſhould paſs by the ſkin, ouzes out upon thoſe glands, and occaſions irritations. The cauſes are, whatſoever occaſions too great a quantity of ſerum in the body; whatſoever hinders the diſcharge by urine, and the pores of the ſkin. *Quincy.*

All fev'rous kinds,
Convulſions, epilepſies, fierce *catarrhs*. *Par. Loſt, b.* xi.

Neither was the body then ſubject to die by piecemeal, and languiſh under coughs, *catarrhs*, or conſumptions. *South.*

CATA'RRHAL. } *adj.* [from *catarrh.*] Relating to a catarrh;
CATA'RRHOUS. } proceeding from a catarrh.

The *catarrhal* fever requires evacuations. *Floyer.*

Old age attended with a glutinous, cold, *catarrhous*, leucophlegmatick conſtitution. *Arbuthnot on Diet.*

CATA'STROPHE. *n. ſ.* [καταστροφή.]

1. The change or revolution, which produces the concluſion or final event of a dramatick piece.

Pat!—He comes like the *cataſtrophe* of the old comedy. *Shakeſp. King Lear.*

That philoſopher declares for tragedies, whoſe *cataſtrophes* are unhappy, with relation to the principal characters. *Dennis.*

2. A final event; a concluſion generally unhappy.

Here was a mighty revolution, the moſt horrible and portentuous *cataſtrophe* that nature ever yet ſaw; an elegant and habitable earth quite ſhattered. *Woodward's Nat. Hiſt.*

CA'TCAL. *n. ſ.* [from *cat* and *call.*] A ſqueaking inſtrument, uſed in the playhouſe to condemn plays.

A young lady, at the theatre, conceived a paſſion for a notorious rake that headed a party of *catcals*. *Spectator*, N° 602.

Three *catcals* be the bribe
Of him, whoſe chatt'ring ſhames the monkey tribe. *Pope.*

To CATCH. *v. a.* preter. I *catched*, or *caught*; I have *catched* or *caught.* [*ketſen*, Dutch.]

1. To lay hold on with the hand; intimating the ſuddenneſs of the action.

And when he aroſe againſt me, I *caught* him by his beard, and ſmote him, and ſlew him. 1 *Sam.* xvii. 35.

2. To ſtop any thing flying; to receive any thing in the paſſage.

Others, to *catch* the breeze of breathing air,
To Tuſculum or Algido repair;
Or in moiſt Tivoli's retirement find
A cooling ſhade. *Addiſon on Italy.*

3. To ſeize any thing by purſuit.

I ſaw him run after a gilded butterfly, and, when he *caught* it, he let it go again; and after it again; and over and over he comes, and up again; and *caught* it again. *Shakeſp. Coriolan.*

4. To ſtop any thing.

A ſhepherd diverted himſelf with toſſing up eggs, and *catching* them again. *Spectator*, N° 160.

5. To enſnare; to intangle in a ſnare; to hold in a trap.

And they ſent unto him certain of the Phariſees and of the Herodians, to *catch* him in his words. *Mar.* xii. 13.

Theſe artificial methods of reaſoning are more adapted to *catch* and entangle the mind, than to inſtruct and inform the underſtanding. *Locke.*

6. To receive ſuddenly.

The curling ſmoke mounts heavy from the fires,
At length it *catches* flame, and in a blaze expires. *Dryden.*

But ſtopp'd for fear, thus violently driv'n,
The ſparks ſhould *catch* his axletree of heav'n. *Dryden.*

7. To faſten ſuddenly upon; to ſeize.

The mule went under the thick boughs of a great oak, and his head *caught* hold of the oak. 2 *Sam.* xviii. 19.

Would they, like Benhadad's embaſſadours, *catch* hold of every amicable expreſſion? *Decay of Piety.*

8. To ſeize unexpectedly.

To *catch* ſomething out of his mouth, that they might accuſe him. *Luke*, xi. 54.

9. To ſeize eagerly.

They have *caught* up every thing greedily, with that buſy minute curioſity, and unſatisfactory inquiſitiveneſs, which Seneca calls the diſeaſe of the Greeks. *Eſſay on Homer.*

10. To pleaſe; to ſeize the affections; to charm.

For I am young, a novice in the trade,
The fool of love, unpractis'd to perſuade,
And wanting the ſoothing arts that *catch* the fair,
But, caught myſelf, lie ſtruggling in the ſnare. *Dryden.*

I've perus'd her well;
Beauty and honour in her are ſo mingled,
That they have *caught* the king. *Shakeſp. Henry* VIII.

11. To receive any contagion or diſeaſe.

I cannot name the diſeaſe, and it is *caught*
Of you that yet are well. *Shakeſp. Winter's Tale.*

Thoſe meaſles,
Which we diſdain ſhould tetter us, yet ſeek
The very way to *catch* them. *Shakeſp. Coriolanus.*

In

In ſooth I know not why I am ſo ſad:
It wearies me; you ſay it wearies you;
But how I *caught* it, found it, or came by it,
I am to learn. *Shakeſp. Merchant of Venice.*

The ſofteſt of our Britiſh ladies expoſe their necks and arms to the open air, which the men could not do, without *catching* cold, for want of being accuſtomed to it. *Addiſon. Guardian.*

Or call the winds through long arcades to roar,
Proud to *catch* cold at a Venetian door. *Pope.*

12. *To catch at.* To endeavour ſuddenly to lay hold on.

Saucy lictors
Will *catch at* us like ſtrumpets, and ſcald rhimers
Ballad us out of tune. *Shakeſp. Antony and Cleopatra.*

Make them *catch at* all opportunities of ſubverting the ſtate. *Addiſon's State of the War.*

To Catch. *v. n.* To be contagious; to ſpread infection.

'Tis time to give them phyſick, their diſeaſes
Are grown ſo *catching.* *Shakeſp. Henry* VIII.

Sickneſs is *catching*; oh, were favour ſo!
Your's would I catch, fair Hermia, ere I go. *Shakeſp.*

Conſidering it with all its malignity and *catching* nature, it may be enumerated with the worſt of epidemicks. *Harvey.*

When the yellow hair in flame ſhould fall,
The *catching* fire might burn the golden cawl. *Dryden.*

The palace of Deiphobus aſcends
In ſmoaky flames, and *catches* on his friends. *Dryden.*

Does the ſedition *catch* from man to man,
And run among the ranks? *Addiſon's Cato.*

Catch. *n. ſ.* [from the verb.]

1. Seizure; the act of ſeizing any thing that flies, or hides.

And ſurely taught by his open eye,
His eye, that ev'n did mark her trodden graſs,
That ſhe would fain the *catch* of Strephon fly. *Sidney.*

2. The act of taking quickly from another.

Several quires, placed one over againſt another, and taking the voice by *catches* anthem-wiſe, give great pleaſure. *Bacon.*

3. A ſong ſung in ſucceſſion, where one catches it from another.

This is the tune of our *catch,* plaid by the picture of nobody. *Shakeſp. Tempeſt.*

Far be from thence the glutton paraſite,
Singing his drunken *catches* all the night. *Dryden, jun.*

The meat was ſerv'd, the bowls were crown'd,
Catches were ſung, and healths went round. *Prior.*

4. Watch; the poſture of ſeizing.

Both of them lay upon the *catch* for a great action; it is no wonder therefore, that they were often engaged on one ſubject. *Addiſon on ancient Medals.*

5. An advantage taken; hold laid on.

All which notions are but ignorant *catches* of a few things, which are moſt obvious to men's obſervations. *Bacon.*

The motion is but a *catch* of the wit upon a few inſtances; as the manner is in the philoſophy received. *Bacon.*

Fate of empires, and the fall of kings,
Should turn on flying hours, and *catch* of moments. *Dryden.*

6. The thing caught; profit; advantage.

Hector ſhall have a great *catch,* if he knock out either of your brains; he were as good crack a fuſty nut with no kernel. *Shakeſp. Troilus and Creſſida.*

7. A ſnatch; a ſhort interval of action.

It has been writ by *catches,* with many intervals. *Locke.*

8. A taint; a ſlight contagion.

We retain a *catch* of thoſe pretty ſtories, and our awakened imagination ſmiles in the recollection. *Glanville's Sceþſis, c.* 3.

9. Any thing that catches and holds, as a hook.

10. A ſmall ſwift ſailing ſhip.

Ca'tcher. *n. ſ.* [from *catch.*]

1. He that catches.

2. That in which any thing is caught.

Scallops will move ſo ſtrongly, as oftentimes to leap out of the *catcher* wherein they are caught. *Grew's Muſæum.*

Ca'tchfly. *n. ſ.* [from *catch* and *fly.*] A plant; a ſpecies of *campion*; which ſee.

Ca'tchpoll. *n. ſ.* [from *catch* and *poll.*] A ſerjeant; a bumbailiff.

Though now it be uſed as a word of contempt, yet, in ancient times, it ſeems to have been uſed without reproach, for ſuch as we now call ſerjeants of the mace, or any other that uſes to arreſt men upon any cauſe. *Cowel.*

They call all temporal buſineſſes underſheriffries, as if they were but matters for underſheriffs and *catchpolls*; though many times thoſe underſheriffries do more good than their high ſpeculations. *Bacon's Eſſays.*

Another monſter,
Sullen of aſpect, by the vulgar call'd
A *catchpoll,* whoſe polluted hands the gods,
With force incredible and magick charms,
Erſt have endu'd, if he his ample palm
Should haply on ill fated ſhoulder lay
Of debtor. *Philips.*

Ca'tchword. *n. ſ.* [from *catch* and *word.* With printers.] The word at the corner of the page under the laſt line, which is repeated at the top of the next page.

Catechе'tical. *adj.* [from κατηχέω.] Conſiſting of queſtions and anſwers.

Socrates introduced a *catechetical* method of arguing; he would aſk his adverſary queſtion upon queſtion, till he convinced him out of his own mouth, that his opinions were wrong. *Addiſon. Spectator,* N° 238.

Catechе'tically. *adv.* [from *catechetical.*] In the way of queſtion and anſwer.

To Ca'techise. *v. a.* [κατηχέω.]

1. To inſtruct by aſking queſtions, and correcting the anſwers.

I will *catechiſe* the world for him; that is, make queſtions, and bid them anſwer. *Shakeſp. Othello.*

Had thoſe three thouſand ſouls been *catechiſed* by our modern caſuiſts, we had ſeen a wide difference. *Decay of Piety.*

2. To queſtion; to interrogate; to examine; to try by interrogatories.

Why then I ſuck my teeth, and *catechiſe*
My piked man of countries. *Shakeſp. King John.*

There flies about a ſtrange report,
Of ſome expreſs arriv'd at court;
I'm ſtopp'd by all the fools I meet,
And *catechis'd* in ev'ry ſtreet. *Swift.*

Ca'techiser. *n. ſ.* [from *to catechiſe.*] One who catechizes.

Ca'techism. *n. ſ.* [from κατηχίζω.] A form of inſtruction by means of queſtions and anſwers, concerning religion.

Ways of teaching there have been ſundry always uſual in God's church; for the firſt introduction of youth to the knowledge of God, the Jews even till this day have their *catechiſms.* *Hooker, b.* v. § 19.

He had no *catechiſm* but the creation, needed no ſtudy but reflection, and read no book but the volume of the world. *South.*

Ca'techist. *n. ſ.* [κατηχιστής.] One whoſe charge is to inſtruct by queſtions, or to queſtion the uninſtructed concerning religion.

None of years and knowledge was admitted, who had not been inſtructed by the *catechiſt* in this foundation, which the *catechiſt* received from the biſhop. *Hammond's Fundamentals.*

Catechu'men. *n. ſ.* [κατηχούμενος.] One who is yet in the firſt rudiments of chriſtianity; the loweſt order of chriſtians in the primitive church.

The prayers of the church did not begin in St. Auſtin's time, till the *catechumens* were diſmiſſed. *Stillingfleet.*

Catechume'nical. *adj.* [from *catechumen.*] Belonging to the catechumens. *Dict.*

Catego'rical. *adj.* [from *category.*] Abſolute; adequate; poſitive; equal to the thing to be expreſſed.

The king's commiſſioners deſired to know whether the parliament's commiſſioners did believe, that biſhops were unlawful? To which they could never obtain a *categorical* anſwer. *Clarendon, b.* viii.

A ſingle propoſition, which is alſo *categorical,* may be divided again into ſimple and complex. *Watts's Logick.*

Catego'rically. *adv.* [from *categorical.*] Poſitively; expreſly.

I dare affirm, and that *categorically,* in all parts where-ever trade is great, and continues ſo, that trade muſt be nationally profitable. *Child's Diſcourſe of Trade.*

Ca'tegory. *n. ſ.* [κατηγορία.] A claſs; a rank; an order of ideas; a predicament.

The abſolute infinitude, in a manner, quite changes the nature of beings, and exalts them into a different *category.* *Cheyne.*

Catena'rian. *adj.* [from *catena,* Lat.] Relating to a chain; reſembling a chain.

In geometry, the *catenarian* curve is formed by a rope or chain hanging freely between two points of ſuſpenſion. *Harris.*

The back is bent after the manner of the *catenarian* curve, by which it obtains that curvature that is ſafeſt for the included marrow. *Cheyne's Philoſophical Principles.*

To Ca'tenate. *v. a.* [from *catena,* Lat.] To chain. *Dict.*

Catena'tion. *n. ſ.* [from *catena,* Lat.] Link; regular connexion.

Which *catenation,* or conſerving union, whenever his pleaſure ſhall divide, let go, or ſeparate, they ſhall fall from their exiſtence. *Brown's Vulgar Errours.*

To Ca'ter. *v. n.* [from *cates.*] To provide food; to buy in victuals.

He that doth the ravens feed,
Yea providently *caters* for the ſparrow,
Be comfort to my age. *Shakeſp. As you like it.*

Ca'ter. *n. ſ.* [from the verb.] Provider; collector of proviſions, or victuals.

The oyſters dredged in this Lyner, find a welcomer acceptance, where the taſte is *cater* for the ſtomach, than thoſe of the Tamar. *Carew's Survey of Cornwal.*

Ca'ter. *n. ſ.* [*quatre,* Fr.] The four of cards and dice.

Ca'ter-cousin. *n. ſ.* A corruption of *quatre-couſin,* from the ridiculouſneſs of calling couſin or relation to ſo remote a degree.

His maſter and he, ſaving your worſhip's reverence, are ſcarce *cater-couſins.* *Shakeſp. Merchant of Venice.*

Poetry and reaſon, how come theſe to be *cater-couſins?* *Rymer's Tragedies of the laſt Age.*

CA'TERER. *n. s.* [from *cater.*] One employed to select and buy in provisions for the family; the providore or purveyor.

Let no scent offensive the chamber infest;
Let fancy, not cost, prepare all our dishes;
Let the *caterer* mind the taste of each guest,
And the cook in his dressing comply with their wishes.
Ben. Johnson's Tavern Academy.

He made the greedy ravens to be Elias's *caterers*, and bring him food. *King Charles.*

Seldom shall one see in cities or courts that athletick vigour, which is seen in poor houses, where nature is their cook, and necessity their *caterer.* *South.*

CA'TERESS. *n. s.* [from *cater.*] A woman employed to cater, or provide victuals.

Impostor! do not charge innocent nature,
As if she would her children should be riotous
With her abundance? she, good *cateress*,
Means her provision only to the good. *Milton.*

CATERPI'LLAR. *n. s.* [This word *Skinner* and *Minshew* are inclined to derive from *chatte peluse*, a weasel; it seems easily deducible from *cates*, food, and *piller*, Fr. to rob; the animal that eats up the fruits of the earth.] A worm which, when it gets wings, is sustained by leaves and fruits.

The *caterpillar* breedeth of dew and leaves; for we see infinite *caterpillars* breed upon trees and hedges, by which the leaves of the trees or hedges are consumed. *Bacon.*

Auster is drawn with a pot pouring forth water, with which descend grasshoppers, *caterpillars*, and creatures bred by moisture. *Peacham on Drawing.*

CATERPI'LLAR. *n. s.* [*scorpioides*, Lat.] The name of a plant.

It hath a papilionaceous flower, out of whose empalement rises the pointal, which afterwards becomes a jointed pod, convoluted like a snail or caterpillar. *Miller.*

To CATERWA'UL. *v. n.* [from *cat.*]

1. To make a noise as cats in rutting time.
2. To make any offensive or odious noise.

What a *caterwauling* do you keep here? If my lady has not called up her steward Malvolio, and bid him turn you out of doors, never trust me. *Shakesp. Twelfth Night.*

Was no dispute between
The *caterwauling* bretheren? *Hudibras, p.* i. *c.* iii.

CATES. *n. s.* [of uncertain etymology; *Skinner* imagines it may be corrupted from *delicate*; which is not likely, because *Junius* observes, that the Dutch have *kater* in the same sense with our *cater.* It has no *singular.*] Viands; food; dish of meat; generally employed to signify nice and luxurious food.

The fair acceptance, Sir, creates
The entertainment perfect, not the *cates.* *Ben Johnson.*

O wasteful riot, never well content
With low priz'd fare; hunger ambitious
Of *cates* by land and sea far fetcht and sent. *Raleigh.*

Alas, how simple to these *cates*,
Was that crude apple, that diverted Eve! *Par. Lost, b.* ii.

They by th' alluring odour drawn, in haste
Fly to the dulcet *cates*, and crouding sip
Their palatable bane. *Philips.*

With costly *cates* she stain'd her frugal board,
Then with ill-gotten wealth she bought a lord. *Arbuthnot.*

CA'TFISH. *n. s.* The name of a sea-fish in the West Indies; so called from its round head and large glaring eyes, by which they are discovered in hollow rocks. *Philips's World of Words.*

CA'THARPINGS. *n. s.* Small ropes in a ship, running in little blocks from one side of the shrouds to the other, near the deck; they belong only to the main shrouds; and their use is to force the shrouds tight, for the ease and safety of the masts, when the ship rolls. *Harris.*

CATHA'RTICAL. } *adj.* [καθαρτικός.] Purging medicines. The
CATHA'RTICK. } vermicular or peristaltick motion of the guts continually helps on their contents, from the pylorus to the rectum; and every irritation either quickens that motion in its natural order, or occasions some little inversions in it. In both, what but slightly adheres to the coats, will be loosened, and they will be more agitated, and thus rendered more fluid. By this only it is manifest, how a *cathartic* hastens and increases the discharges by stool; but where the force of the stimulus is great, all the appendages of the bowels, and all the viscera in the abdomen, will be twitched; by which a great deal will be drained back into the intestines, and made a part of what they discharge. *Quincy.*

Quicksilver precipitated either with gold, or without addition, into a powder, is wont to be strongly enough *cathartical*, though the chymists have not yet proved, that either gold or mercury hath any salt at all, much less any that is purgative. *Boyle's Sceptical Chymistry.*

Lustrations and *cathartick*s of the mind were sought for, and all endeavour used to calm and regulate the fury of the passions. *Decay of Piety.*

The piercing causticks ply their spiteful pow'r,
Emeticks ranch, and keen *cathartick*s scour. *Garth.*

Plato has called mathematical demonstrations the *cathartick*s or purgatives of the soul. *Addison. Spectator,* N° 507.

CATHA'RTICALNESS. *n. s.* [from *cathartical.*] Purging quality.

CA'THEAD. *n. s.* A kind of fossil.

These nodules, with leaves in them, called *catheads*, seem to consist of a sort of iron stone, not unlike that which is found in the rocks near Whitehaven in Cumberland, where they call them catscaups. *Woodward on Fossils.*

CA'THEAD. *n. s.* [In a ship.] A piece of timber with two shivers at one end, having a rope and a block, to which is fastened a great iron hook, to trice up the anchor from the hawse to the top of the forecastle. *Sea Dict.*

CATHE'DRAL. *adj.* [from *cathedra*, Lat. a chair of authority; an episcopal see.]

1. Episcopal; containing the see of a bishop.

A *cathedral* church is that wherein there are two or more persons, with a bishop at the head of them, that do make as it were one body politick. *Ayliffe's Parergon.*

Methought I sat in seat of majesty,
In the *cathedral* church of Westminster. *Shakesp. Henry* VI.

2. Belonging to an episcopal church.

His constant and regular assisting at the *cathedral* service was never interrupted by the sharpness of weather. *Locke.*

3. In low phrase, antique; venerable; old. This seems to be the meaning in the following lines.

Here aged trees *cathedral* walks compose,
And mount the hill in venerable rows;
There the green infants in their beds are laid. *Pope.*

CATHE'DRAL. *n. s.* The head church of a diocese.

There is nothing in Leghorn so extraordinary as the *cathedral*, which a man may view with pleasure, after he has seen St. Peter's. *Addison on Italy.*

CA'THERINE PEAR. See PEAR.

For streaks of red were mingled there,
Such as are on a *Catherine pear*,
The side that's next the sun. *Suckling.*

CATHE'TER. *n. s.* [καθετήρ.] A hollow and somewhat crooked instrument, to thrust into the bladder, to assist in bringing away the urine, when the passage is stopped by a stone or gravel.

A large clyster, suddenly injected, hath frequently forced the urine out of the bladder; but if it fail, a *catheter* must help you. *Wiseman's Surgery.*

CA'THOLES. *n. s.* [In a ship.] Two little holes astern above the gun-room ports, to bring in a cable or hawser through them to the capstain, when there is occasion to heave the ship astern. *Sea Dict.*

CATHO'LICISM. *n. s.* [from *catholick.*] Adherence to the catholick church.

CA'THOLICK. *adj.* [*catholique*, Fr. καθόλικος.] Universal or general.

1. The church of Jesus Christ is called *catholick*, because it extends throughout the world, and is not limited by time.
2. Some truths are said to be *catholick*, because they are received by all the faithful.
3. *Catholick* is often set in opposition to heretick or sectary, and to schismatick.
4. *Catholick*, or canonical epistles, are seven in number; that of St. James, two of St. Peter, three of St. John, and that of St. Jude. They are called *catholick*, because they are directed to all the faithful, and not to any particular church; and canonical, because they contain excellent rules of faith and morality. *Calmet.*

Doubtless the success of those your great and *catholick* endeavours will promote the empire of man over nature, and bring plentiful accession of glory to your nation. *Glanville's Scepsis.*

Those systems undertake to give an account of the formation of the universe, by mechanical hypotheses of matter, moved either uncertainly, or according to some *catholick* laws. *Ray.*

CATHO'LICON. *n. s.* [from *catholick*; καθόλικον ἴαμα.] An universal medicine.

Preservation against that sin, is the contemplation of the last judgment. This is indeed a *catholicon* against all; but we find it particularly applied by St. Paul to judging and despising our brethren. *Government of the Tongue.*

CA'TKINS. *n. s.* [*kattekens*, Dutch. In botany.] An assemblage of imperfect flowers hanging from trees, in manner of a rope or cat's tail; serving as male blossoms, or flowers of the trees, by which they are produced. *Chambers.*

CA'TLIKE. *adj.* [from *cat* and *like*.] Like a cat.

A lioness, with udders all drawn dry,
Lay couching head on ground, with *catlike* watch.
Shakesp. As you like it.

CA'TLING. *n. s.*

1. A dismembring knife, used by surgeons. *Harris.*
2. It seems to be used by *Shakespeare* for catgut; the materials of fiddle strings.

What musick there will be in him after Hector has knocked out his brains, I know not. But, I am sure, none; unless the fidler Apollo get his sinews to make *catlings* of. *Tr. and Cress.*

3. The down or moss growing about walnut trees, resembling the hair of a cat. *Harris.*

CA'TMINT. *n. s.* [*cataria*, Lat.] The name of a plant.

The leaves are like those of the nettle or betony, for the most part hoary, and of a strong scent. The flowers are collected into a thick spike; the crest of the flower is broad and bifid;

and

and the lip divided into three ſegments. It grows wild, and is uſed in medicine. *Miller.*

CATO'PTRICAL. *adj.* [from *catoptricks.*] Relating to catoptricks, or viſion by reflection.

A *catoptrical* or dioptrical heat is ſuperiour to any, vitrifying the hardeſt ſubſtances. *Arbuthnot on Air.*

CATO'PTRICKS. *n. ſ.* [κάτοπτρον, a looking glaſs.] That part of opticks which treats of viſion by reflection.

CA'TPIPE. *n. ſ.* [from *cat* and *pipe.*] The ſame with *catcal*; an inſtrument that makes a ſqueaking noiſe.

Some ſongſters can no more ſing in any chamber but their own, than ſome clerks can read in any book but their own; put them out of their road once, and they are mere *catpipes* and dunces. *L'Eſtrange.*

CAT'S-EYE. A ſtone.

Cat's-eye is of a gliſtering grey, interchanged with a ſtraw colour. *Woodward on Foſſils.*

CAT'S-FOOT. *n. ſ.* An herb; the ſame with *alehoof*, or *ground-ivy*; which ſee.

CAT'S-HEAD. *n. ſ.* A kind of apple.

Cat's-head, by ſome called the go-no-further, is a very large apple, and a good bearer. *Mortimer's Huſbandry.*

CA'TSILVER. *n. ſ.* A kind of foſſile.

Catſilver is compoſed of plates that are generally plain and parallel, and that are flexible and elaſtick; and is of three ſorts, the yellow or golden, the white or ſilvery, and the black. *Woodward on Foſſils.*

CAT'S-TAIL. *n. ſ.*

1. A long round ſubſtance, that grows in winter upon nut-trees, pines, &c.
2. A kind of reed which bears a ſpike like the tail of a cat. *Phillips's World of Words.*

CA'TSUP. *n. ſ.* A kind of pickle, made from muſhrooms.

And, for our home-bred Britiſh cheer,
Botargo, *catſup*, and cavier. *Swift.*

CA'TTLE. *n. ſ.* [a word of very common uſe, but of doubtful or unknown etymology. It is derived by *Skinner*, *Menage*, and *Spelman*, from *capitalia*, *quæ ad caput pertinent*; perſonal goods: in which ſenſe *chattels* is yet uſed in our law. *Mandeville* uſes *catele* for *price.*]

1. Beaſts of paſture; not wild nor domeſtick.

Make poor men's *cattle* break their necks. *Shakeſp. T. Andr.*

And God made the beaſt of the earth after his kind, and *cattle* after their kind, and every thing that creepeth upon the earth after his kind. *Gen.* i. 25.

2. It is uſed in reproach of human beings.

Boys and women are for the moſt part *cattle* of this colour. *Shakeſp. As you like it.*

CAVALCA'DE. *n. ſ.* [Fr. from *cavallo*, a horſe, Ital.] A proceſſion on horſeback.

Your *cavalcade* the fair ſpectators view,
From their high ſtandings, yet look up to you:
From your brave train each ſingles out a ray,
And longs to date a conqueſt from your day. *Dryden.*

How muſt the heart of the old man rejoice, when he ſaw ſuch a numerous *cavalcade* of his own raiſing? *Addiſon. Spect.*

CAVALI'ER. *n. ſ.* [*cavalier*, Fr.]

1. A horſeman; a knight.
2. A gay ſprightly military man.

For who is he, whoſe chin is but enrich'd
With one appearing hair, that will not follow
Theſe cull'd and choice drawn *cavaliers* to France?
Shakeſp. Henry VIII.

3. The appellation of the party of king Charles the firſt.

Each party grows proud of that appellation, which their adverſaries at firſt intend as a reproach: of this ſort were the Guelfs and Gibelines, Hugenots, and *Cavaliers*. *Swift.*

CAVALI'ER. *adj.* [from the ſubſt.]

1. Gay; ſprightly; warlike.
2. Generous; brave.

The people are naturally not valiant, and not much *cavalier*. Now it is the nature of cowards to hurt, where they can receive none. *Suckling.*

3. Diſdainful; haughty.

CAVALI'ERLY. *adv.* [from *cavalier.*] Haughtily; arrogantly; diſdainfully.

CA'VALRY. *n. ſ.* [*cavalerie*, Fr.] Horſe troops; bodies of men furniſhed with horſes for war.

If a ſtate run moſt to gentlemen, and the huſbandmen and plowmen be but as their workfolks, you may have a good *cavalry*, but never good ſtable bands of foot. *Bacon's Henry* VII.

Their *cavalry*, in the battle of Blenheim, could not ſuſtain the ſhock of the Britiſh horſe. *Addiſon on the State of the War.*

To CA'VATE. *v. a.* [*cavo*, Lat.] To hollow out; to dig into a hollow.

CAVA'ZION. *n. ſ.* [from *cavo*, Lat. In architecture.] The hollowing or underdigging of the earth for cellarage; allowed to be the ſixth part of the height of the whole building. *Phillips's World of Words.*

CA'UDEBECK. *n. ſ.* A ſort of light hats, ſo called from a town in France where they were firſt made. *Phillips's World of Words.*

CA'UDLE. *n. ſ.* [*chaudeau*, Fr.] A mixture of wine and other ingredients, given to women in childbed, and ſick perſons.

Ye ſhall have a hempen *caudle* then, and the help of a hatchet. *Shakeſp. Henry* VI. *p.* ii.

He had good broths, *caudle*, and ſuch like; and I believe he did drink ſome wine. *Wiſeman's Surgery.*

To CA'UDLE. *v. a.* [from the noun.] To make caudle; to mix as caudle.

Will the cold brook,
Candied with ice, *caudle* thy morning taſte,
To cure thy o'ernight's ſurfeit? *Shakeſp. Timon.*

CAVE. *n. ſ.* [*cave*, Fr. *cavea*, Lat.]

1. A cavern; a den; a hole entering horizontally under the ground; a habitation in the earth.

The wrathful ſkies
Gallow the very wand'rers of the dark,
And make them keep their *caves*. *Shakeſp. King Lear.*

Bid him bring his power
Before ſun-riſing, leſt his ſon George fall
Into the blind *cave* of eternal night. *Shakeſp. Richard* III.

They did ſquare, and carve, and poliſh their ſtone and marble works, even in the very *cave* of the quarry. *Wotton.*

Through this a *cave* was dug with vaſt expence,
The work it ſeem'd of ſome ſuſpicious prince. *Dryden.*

2. A hollow; any hollow place.

The object of ſight doth ſtrike upon the pupil of the eye directly; whereas the *cave* of the eye doth hold off the ſound a little. *Bacon's Natural Hiſtory*, Nº 272.

To CAVE. *v. n.* [from the noun.] To dwell in a cave.

It may be heard at court, that ſuch as we
Cave here, haunt here, are outlaws, and in time
May make ſome ſtronger head. *Shakeſp. Cymbeline.*

CAVE'AT. *n. ſ.* [*caveat*, Lat. *let him beware.*]

A *caveat* is an intimation given to ſome ordinary or eccleſiaſtical judge by the act of man, notifying to him, that he ought to beware how he acts in ſuch or ſuch an affair. *Ayliffe.*

The chiefeſt *caveat* in reformation muſt be to keep out the Scots. *Spenſer on Ireland.*

I am in danger of commencing poet, perhaps laureat; pray deſire Mr. Rowe to enter a *caveat*. *Trumball to Pope.*

CA'VERN. *n. ſ.* [*caverna*, Lat.] A hollow place in the ground.

Where wilt thou find a *cavern* dark enough
To maſk thy monſtrous viſage? *Shakeſp. Julius Cæſar.*

Monſters of the foaming deep,
From the deep ooze, and gelid *cavern* rous'd,
They flounce and tremble in unwieldy joy. *Thomſon.*

CA'VERNED. *adj.* [from *cavern.*]

1. Full of caverns; hollow; excavated.

Embattled troops, with flowing banners, paſs
Through flow'ry meads, delighted; nor diſtruſt
The ſmiling ſurface; whilſt the *cavern'd* ground
Burſts fatal, and involves the hopes of war
In firy whirles. *Philips.*

High at his head from out the *cavern'd* rock,
In living rills a guſhing fountain broke. *Pope's Odyſſey.*

2. Inhabiting a cavern.

No bandit fierce, no tyrant mad with pride,
No *cavern'd* hermit, reſt ſelf-ſatisfy'd. *Pope's Eſſay on Man.*

CA'VERNOUS. *adj.* [from *cavern.*] Full of caverns.

No great damages are done by earthquakes, except only in thoſe countries which are mountainous, and conſequently ſtony and *cavernous* underneath. *Woodward's Nat. Hiſtory.*

CAVE'SSON. *n. ſ.* [Fr. In horſemanſhip.]

A ſort of noſeband, ſometimes made of iron, and ſometimes of leather or wood; ſometimes flat, and ſometimes hollow or twiſted; which is put upon the noſe of a horſe, to forward the ſuppling and breaking of him.

An iron *caveſſon* ſaves and ſpares the mouths of young horſes when they are broken; for, by the help of it, they are accuſtomed to obey the hand, and to bend the neck and ſhoulders, without hurting their mouths, or ſpoiling their bars with the bit. *Farrier's Dict.*

CAUF. *n. ſ.* A cheſt with holes on the top, to keep fiſh alive in the water. *Phillips's World of Words.*

CAUGHT. *particip. paſſ.* [from *to catch*; which ſee.]

CAVIA'RE. *n. ſ.* [the etymology uncertain, unleſs it come from *garum*, Lat. ſauce, or pickle, made of fiſh ſalted.]

The eggs of a ſturgeon being ſalted, and made up into a maſs, were firſt brought from Conſtantinople by the Italians, and called *caviare*. *Grew's Muſæum.*

CAVI'ER. *n. ſ.* A corruption of *caviare*. See CATSUP.

To CA'VIL. *v. n.* [*caviller*, Fr. *cavillari*, Lat.] To raiſe captious and frivolous objections.

I'll give thrice ſo much land
To any well deſerving friend;
But, in the way of bargain, mark ye me,
I'll *cavil* on the ninth part of a hair. *Shakeſp. Henry* IV.

My lord, you do not well, in obſtinacy
To *cavil* in the courſe of this contract. *Shakeſp. Henry* VI.

He *cavils* firſt at the poet's inſiſting ſo much upon the effects of Achilles's rage. *Pope's Notes on the Iliad.*

To CA'VIL. *v. a.* To receive or treat with objections.

Thou didst accept them: wilt thou enjoy the good,
Then *cavil* the conditions? *Paradise Lost, b.* x. *l.* 579.

CA'VIL. *n. s.* [from the verb.] False or frivolous objections.

Wiser men consider how subject the best things have been unto *cavil*, when wits, possessed with disdain, have set them up as their mark to shoot at. *Hooker, b.* v. § 4.

Several divines, in order to answer the *cavils* of those adversaries to truth and morality, began to find out farther explanations. *Swift.*

CAVILLA'TION. *n. s.* [from *cavil.*] The disposition to make captious objection; the practice of objecting.

I might add so much concerning the large odds between the case of the eldest churches, in regard of heathens, and ours, in respect of the church of Rome, that very *cavillation* itself should be satisfied. *Hooker, b.* iv. § 7.

CA'VILLER. *n. s.* [*cavillator*, Lat.] A man fond of making objections; an unfair adversary; a captious disputant.

The candour which Horace shews, is that which distinguishes a critick from a *caviller*; he declares, that he is not offended at those little faults, which may be imputed to inadvertency. *Addison. Guardian*, N° 110.

There is, I grant, room still left for a *caviller* to misrepresent my meaning. *Atterbury's Pref. to his Sermons.*

CA'VILLINGLY. *adv.* [from *cavilling.*] In a cavilling manner.

CA'VILLOUS. *adj.* [from *cavil.*] Full of objections.

Those persons are said to be *cavillous* and unfaithful advocates, by whose fraud and iniquity justice is destroyed. *Ayliffe.*

CA'VIN. n. s. [French.] In the military art it signifies a natural hollow, fit to cover a body of troops, and consequently facilitate their approach to a place. *Dict.*

CA'VITY. *n. s.* [*cavitas*, Latin.] Hollowness; hollow; hollow place.

The vowels are made by a free passage of breath, vocalized through the *cavity* of the mouth; the said *cavity* being differently shaped by the postures of the throat, tongue, and lips. *Holder's Elements of Speech.*

There is nothing to be left void in a firm building; even the *cavities* ought not to be filled with rubbish, which is of a perishing kind. *Dryden's Dedication to Æneid.*

Materials packed together with wonderful art in the several *cavities* of the scull. *Addison. Spectator*, N° 275.

An instrument with a small *cavity*, like a small spoon, dipt in oil, may fetch out the stone. *Arbuthnot on Diet.*

If the atmosphere was reduced into water, it would not make an orb above thirty two feet deep, which would soon be swallowed up by the *cavity* of the sea, and the depressed parts of the earth. *Bentley.*

CAUK. *n. s.* It denotes a coarse talky spar. *Woodward.*

CA'UKY. *adj.* [from *cauk.*] A white, opaque, *cauky* spar, shot or pointed. *Woodward on Fossils.*

CAUL. *n. s.* [of uncertain etymology.]

1. The net in which women inclose their hair; the hinder part of a woman's cap.

Ne spared they to strip her naked all,
Then when they had despoil'd her tire and *caul*,
Such as she was, their eyes might her behold. *Fairy Q. b.* i.

Her head with ringlets of her hair is crown'd,
And in a golden *caul* the curls are bound. *Dryden's Æneid.*

2. Any kind of small net.

An Indian mantle of feathers, and the feathers wrought into a *caul* of packthread. *Grew's Musæum.*

3. The omentum; the integument in which the guts are inclosed.

The *caul* serves for the warming the lower belly, like an apron or piece of woollen cloth. Hence a certain gladiatour, whose *caul* Galen cut out, was so liable to suffer cold, that he kept his belly constantly covered with wool. *Ray on the Creation.*

The beast they then divide, and disunite
The ribs and limbs, observant of the rite:
On these, in double *cauls* involv'd with art,
The choicest morsels lay. *Pope's Odyssey, b.* iii. *l.* 585.

CAULI'FEROUS. *adj.* [from *caulis*, a stalk, and *fero*, to bear, Lat.] A term in botany for such plants as have a true stalk, which a great many have not.

CAULI'FLOWER. *n. s.* [from *caulis*, Lat. the stalk of a plant.] A species of *cabbage*; which see.

Towards the end of the month, earth up your winter plants and salad herbs; and plant forth your *cauliflowers* and cabbage, which were sown in August. *Evelyn's Kalendar.*

To CAULK. See To CALK.

To CAUPO'NATE. *v. n.* [*caupono*, Lat.] To keep a victualling-house; to sell wine or victuals. *Dict.*

CAU'SABLE. *adj.* [from *causo*, low Lat.] That which may be caused, or effected by a cause.

That may be miraculously effected in one, which is naturally *causable* in another. *Brown's Vulgar Errours, b.* iii. *c.* 21.

CAU'SAL. *adj.* [*causalis*, low Lat.] Relating to causes; implying or containing causes.

Every motion owning a dependence on prerequired motors, we can have no true knowledge of any, except we would distinctly pry into the whole method of *causal* concatenations. *Glanville's Scepsis Scientifica, c.* 35.

Causal propositions are, where two propositions are joined by *causal* particles; as, houses were not built, *that* they might be destroyed; Rehoboam was unhappy, *because* he followed evil counsel. *Watts's Logick.*

CAUSA'LITY. *n. s.* [*causalitas*, low Latin.] The agency of a cause; the quality of causing.

As he created all things, so is he beyond and in them all, in his very essence, as being the soul of their *causalities*, and the essential cause of their existences. *Brown's Vulgar Errours.*

By an unadvised transiliency from the effect to the remotest cause, we observe not the connection, through the interposal of more immediate *causalities*. *Glanville's Scepsis, c.* 14.

CA'USALLY. *adv.* [from *causal.*] According to the order or series of causes.

Thus may it more be *causally* made out, what Hippocrates affirmeth. *Brown's Vulgar Errours.*

CAUSA'TION. *n. s.* [from *causo*, low Lat.] The act or power of causing.

Thus doth he sometimes delude us in the conceits of stars and meteors, besides their allowable actions, ascribing effects thereunto of independent *causation*. *Brown's Vulgar Errours.*

CA'USATIVE. *adj.* [a term in grammar.] That expresses a cause or reason.

CA'USATOR. *n. s.* [from *causo*, low Lat.] A causer; an authour of any effect.

Demonstratively understanding the simplicity of perfection, and the invisible condition of the first *causator*, it was out of the power of earth, or the areopagy of hell, to work them from it. *Brown's Vulgar Errours, b.* i. *c.* 10.

CAUSE. *n. s.* [*causa*, Lat.]

1. That which produces or effects any thing; the efficient.

The wise and learned amongst the very heathens themselves, have all acknowledged some first *cause*, whereupon originally the being of all things dependeth; neither have they otherwise spoken of that *cause*, than as an agent, which, knowing what and why it worketh, observeth, in working, a most exact order or law. *Hooker, b.* i. §2.

Butterflies, and other flies, revive easily when they seem dead, being brought to the sun or fire; the *cause* whereof is the diffusion of the vital spirit, and the dilating of it by a little heat. *Bacon's Natural History*, N° 697.

Cause is a substance exerting its power into act, to make one thing begin to be. *Locke.*

2. The reason; motive to any thing.

The rest shall bear some other fight,
As *cause* will be obey'd. *Shakesp. Macbeth.*

So great, so constant, and so general a practice, must needs have not only a *cause*, but also a great, a constant, and a general *cause*, every way commensurate to such an effect. *South.*

Thus, royal sir! to see you landed here,
Was *cause* enough of triumph for a year. *Dryden.*

Æneas wond'ring stood: then ask'd the *cause*,
Which to the stream the crouding people draws. *Dryden.*

Even he,
Lamenting that there had been *cause* of enmity,
Will often wish fate had ordain'd you friends.
Rowe's Ambitious Stepmother.

3. Cause of debate; subject of litigation.

O madness of discourse!
That *cause* sets up with and against thyself!
Bifold authority. *Shakesp. Troilus and Cressida.*

Hear the *causes* between your brethren, and judge righteously between every man and his brother, and the stranger that is with him. *Deut.* i. 16.

4. Side; party; ground or principle of action or opposition.

Ere to thy *cause*, and thee, my heart inclin'd,
Or love to party had seduc'd my mind. *Tickell.*

To CAUSE. *v. a.* [from the noun.] To effect as an agent; to produce.

She weeping ask'd, in these her blooming years,
What unforeseen misfortune *caus'd* her care
To loath her life, and languish in despair. *Dryden's Fables.*

Things that move so swift, as not to affect the senses distinctly, and so *cause* not any train of ideas in the mind, are not perceived to move. *Locke.*

CAU'SELESLY. *adv.* [from *causeless.*] Without cause; without reason.

Human laws are not to be broken with scandal, nor at all without reason; for he that does it *causelesly*, is a despiser of the law, and undervalues its authority. *Taylor's Holy Living.*

CAU'SELESS. *adj.* [from *cause.*]

1. Without cause; original to itself.

Reach th' Almighty's sacred throne,
And make his *causeless* pow'r, the cause of all things, known.
Blackmore's Creation.

2. Without just ground or motive.

Yet is my truth yplight,
And love avow'd to other lady late,
That, to remove the same, I have no might;
To change love *causeless*, is reproach to warlike knight.
Spenser's Fairy Queen, b. ii. *cant.* vii. *stanz.* 50.

And me and mine, threats not with war but death;
Thus *cauſeleſs* hatred endleſs is uneath. *Fairfax, b.* iv

The *cauſeleſs* diſlike, which others have conceived, is no ſufficient reaſon for us to forbear in any place. *Hooker, b.* v.

As women yet who apprehend
Some ſudden cauſe of *cauſeleſs* fear,
Although that ſeeming cauſe take end,
A ſhaking through their limbs they find. *Waller.*

Alas! my fears are *cauſeleſs* and ungrounded,
Fantaſtick dreams, and melancholy fumes. *Denham's Sophy.*

Ca'user. *n. ſ.* [from *cauſe.*] He that cauſes; the agent by which an effect is produced.

Is not the *cauſer* of theſe timeleſs deaths,
As blameful as the executioner? *Shakeſp. Richard* III.

Ca'usey. } *n. ſ.* [*chauſſée*, Fr. This word, by a falſe notion of
Ca'useway. } its etymology, has been lately written *cauſeway.*] A way raiſed and paved; a way raiſed above the reſt of the ground.

To Shuppim the lot came forth weſtward by the *cauſey*. *1 Chron.* xxvi. 16.

Th' other way Satan went down,
The *cauſeway* to hell-gate. *Paradiſe Loſt, b.* x. *l.* 415.

But that broad *cauſeway* will direct your way,
And you may reach the town by noon of day. *Dryden.*

Whoſe *cauſeway* parts the vale with ſhady rows;
Whoſe ſeats the weary traveller repoſe. *Pope.*

Ca'ustical. } *adj.* [καυςικὸς.] Medicaments which, by their
Ca'ustick. } violent activity and heat, deſtroy the texture of the part to which they are applied, and eat it away, or burn it into an eſchar, which they do by the extreme minuteneſs, aſperity, and quantity of motion, that, like thoſe of fire itſelf, deſtroy the texture of the ſolids themſelves, and change what they are applied to, into a ſubſtance like burnt fleſh; which, in a little time, with detergent dreſſing, falls quite off, and leaves a vacuity in the part. *Quincy.*

If extirpation be ſafe, the beſt way will be by *cauſtical* medicines or eſcaroticks. *Wiſeman's Surgery.*

I propoſed eradicating by eſcaroticks, and began with a *cauſtick* ſtone. *Wiſeman's Surgery.*

Air too hot, cold and moiſt, abounding perhaps with *cauſtick*, aſtringent, and coagulating particles. *Arbuthnot.*

Ca'ustick. *n. ſ.* A cauſtick or burning application.

It was a tenderneſs to mankind, that introduced corroſives and *cauſticks*, which are indeed but artificial fires. *Temple.*

The piercing *cauſticks* ply their ſpiteful pow'r,
Emeticks ranch, and keen cathárticks ſcour. *Garth.*

CA'UTEL. *n. ſ.* [*cautela*, Lat.] Caution; ſcruple; a word diſuſed.

Perhaps he loves you now;
And now no ſoil of *cautel* doth beſmerch
The virtue of his will. *Shakeſp. Hamlet.*

Ca'utelous. *adj.* [*cauteleux*, Fr.]

1. Cautious; wary; provident.

Palladio doth wiſh, like a *cautelous* artiſan, that the inward walls might bear ſome good ſhare in the burden. *Wotton.*

2. Wily; cunning; treacherous.

Of themſelves, for the moſt part, they are ſo *cautelous* and wily headed, eſpecially being men of ſo ſmall experience and practice in law matters, that you would wonder whence they borrow ſuch ſubtilties and ſly ſhifts. *Spenſer on Ireland.*

Your ſon
Will or exceed the common, or be caught
With *cautelous* baits and practice. *Shakeſp. Coriolanus.*

Ca'utelously. *adv.* [from *cautelous.*] Cunningly; ſlily; treacherouſly; cautiouſly; warily.

The Jews, not undoubtedly reſolved of the ſciatica ſide of Jacob, do *cauteloúſly*, in their diet, abſtain from both. *Brown's Vulgar Errours, b.* vii. *c.* 1.

All pretorian courts, if any of the parties be laid aſleep, under pretence of a retirement, and the other party doth *cautelouſly* get the ſtart and advantage, yet they will ſet back all things *in ſtatu quo prius.* *Bacon's War with Spain.*

Cauteriza'tion. *n. ſ.* [from *cauterize.*] The act of burning fleſh with hot irons, or cauſtick medicaments.

They require, after *cauterization*, no ſuch bandage, as that thereby you need to fear interception of the ſpirits. *Wiſeman.*

To Ca'uterize. *v. a.* [*cauteriſer*, Fr.] To burn with the cautery.

For each true word a bliſter, and each falſe,
Be *cauterizing* to the root o' th' tongue,
Conſuming it with ſpeaking. *Shakeſp. Timon.*

No marvel though cantharides have ſuch a corroſive and *cauterizing* quality; for there is not one other of the inſecta, but is bred of a duller matter. *Bacon's Natural Hiſtory.*

The deſign of the cautery is to prevent the canal from cloſing; but the operators confeſs, that, in perſons *cauterized*, the tears trickle down ever after. *Sharp's Surgery.*

CA'UTERY. *n. ſ.* [καίω, *uro.*]

Cautery is either actual or potential; the firſt is burning by a hot iron, and the latter with cauſtick medicines. The actual *cautery* is generally uſed to ſtop mortification, by burning the dead parts to the quick; or to ſtop the effuſion of blood, by ſearing up the veſſels. *Quincy.*

In heat of fight it will be neceſſary to have your actual *cautery* always ready; for that will ſecure the bleeding arteries in a moment. *Wiſeman's Surgery.*

CA'UTION. *n. ſ.* [*caution*, Fr. *cautio*, Lat.]

1. Prudence, as it reſpects danger; foreſight; provident care; warineſs.

2. Security for.

Such conditions, and *cautions* of the condition, as might aſſure the people with as much aſſurance as worldly matters bear. *Sidney.*

The Cedar, upon this new acqueſt, gave him part of Baccharia for *caution* for his diſburſements. *Howel's Vocal Foreſt.*

The parliament would yet give his majeſty ſufficient *caution* that the war ſhould be proſecuted. *Clarendon.*

He that objects any crime, ought to give *caution* by the means of ſureties, that he will perſevere in the proſecution of ſuch crimes. *Ayliffe's Parergon.*

3. Proviſion or ſecurity againſt; direction.

In deſpite of all the rules and *cautions* of government, the moſt dangerous and mortal of vices will come off. *L'Eſtrange.*

4. Proviſionary precept.

Attention to the forementioned ſymptoms affords the beſt *cautions* and rules of diet, by way of prevention. *Arbuthnot.*

5. Warning.

To Ca'ution. *v. a.* [from the noun.] To warn; to give notice of a danger.

How ſhall our thought avoid the various ſnare?
Or wiſdom to our *caution'd* ſoul declare
The diff'rent ſhapes thou pleaſeſt to employ,
When bent to hurt, and certain to deſtroy? *Prior.*

You *caution'd* me againſt their charms,
But never gave me equal arms;
Your leſſons found the weakeſt part,
Aim'd at the head, but reach'd the heart. *Swift.*

Ca'utionary. *adj.* [from *caution.*] Given as a pledge, or in ſecurity.

I am made the *cautionary* pledge,
The gage and hoſtage of your keeping it. *Southerne.*

Is there no ſecurity for the iſland of Britain? Has the enemy no *cautionary* towns and ſea-ports, to give us for ſecuring trade? *Swift.*

Ca'utious. *adj.* [from *cautus*, Lat.] Wary; watchful.

Be *cautious* of him; for he is ſometimes an inconſtant lovers becauſe he hath a great advantage. *Swift.*

Ca'utiously. *adv.* [from *cautious.*] In an attentive, wary manner.

They know how fickle common lovers are:
Their oaths and vows are *cautiouſly* believ'd;
For few there are but have been once deceiv'd. *Dryden.*

Ca'utiousness. *n. ſ.* [from *cautious.*] Watchfulneſs; vigilance; circumſpection; provident care; prudence with reſpect to danger.

I could not but approve their generous conſtancy and *cautiouſneſs.* *K. Charles.*

We ſhould always act with great *cautiouſneſs* and circumſpection, in points where it is not impoſſible that we may be deceived. *Addiſon. Spectator*, N° 399.

To Caw. *v. n.* [taken from the ſound.] To cry as the rook, raven, or crow.

Ruſſet-pated choughs, many in ſort,
Riſing and *cawing* at the gun's report. *Shakeſp.*

There is a walk of aged elms, ſo very high, that the rooks and crows upon the tops ſeem to be *cawing* in another region. *Addiſon. Spectator*, N° 110.

The rook, who high amid the boughs
In early ſpring, his airy city builds,
And ceaſeleſs *caws.* *Thomſon's Spring.*

Ca'yman. *n. ſ.* The American name for the alligator or crocodile.

To CEASE. *v. n.* [*ceſſer*, Fr. *ceſſo*, Lat.]

1. To leave off; to ſtop; to give over; to deſiſt.

The lives of all, who *ceaſe* from combat, ſpare;
My brother's be your moſt peculiar care. *Drdyen's Aureng.*

2. To fail; to be extinct.

The poor man ſhall never *ceaſe* out of the land. *Deut.* xv. 11.

The ſoul being removed, the faculties and operations of life, ſenſe and intellection *ceaſe* from that *moles corporea*, and are no longer in it. *Hale's Origin of Mankind.*

3. To be at an end.

But now the wonder *ceaſes*, ſince I ſee
She kept them only, Tityrus, for thee. *Dryden's Virgil's Paſt.*

4. To reſt.

The miniſters of Chriſt have *ceaſed* from their labours. *Sprat.*

To Cease. *v. a.* To put a ſtop to; to put an end to.

Haſte you to lord Timon;
Importune him for monies; be not *ceas'd*
With ſlight denial. *Shakeſp. Timon.*

You may ſooner, by imagination, quicken or ſlack a motion, than raiſe or *ceaſe* it; as it is eaſier to make a dog go ſlower, than

than to make him ſtand ſtill. *Bacon's Natural Hiſt.* Nº 990.

Ceaſe then this impious rage. *Paradiſe Loſt*, *b.* v. *l.* 845.

But he her fears to *ceaſe*,
Sent down the meek-ey'd peace. *Milton.*

The diſcord is compleat, nor can they *ceaſe*
The dire debate, nor yet command the peace. *Dryden.*

CEASE. *n. ſ.* [from the verb.] Extinction; failure.

The *ceaſe* of majeſty
Dies not alone, but, like a gulph, withdraws
What's near it, with it. *Shakeſp. Hamlet.*

CE'ASELESS. *adj.* [from *ceaſe*.] Inceſſant; perpetual; continual; without pauſe; without ſtop; without end.

My guiltleſs blood muſt quench the *ceaſeleſs* fire,
On which my endleſs tears were bootleſs ſpent. *Fairfax.*

All theſe, with *ceaſeleſs* praiſe his works behold,
Both day and night. *Paradiſe Loſt*, *b.* iv. *l.* 679.

Like an oak
That ſtands ſecure, though all the winds employ
Their *ceaſeleſs* roar, and only ſheds its leaves,
Or maſt, which the revolving ſpring reſtores. *Philips.*

CE'CITY. *n. ſ.* [*cæcitas*, Lat.] Blindneſs; privation of ſight.

They are not blind, nor yet diſtinctly ſee; there is in them no *cecity*, yet more than a cecutiency; they have ſight enough to diſcern the light, though not perhaps to diſtinguiſh objects or colours. *Brown's Vulgar Errours.*

CECU'TIENCY. *n. ſ.* [*cæcutio*, Lat.] Tendency to blindneſs; cloudineſs of ſight.

There is in them no cecity, yet more than a *cecutiency*. *Brown's Vulgar Errours*, *b.* iii. *c.* 18.

CE'DAR. *n. ſ.* [*cedrus*, Lat.] A tree.

It is evergreen; the leaves are much narrower than thoſe of the pine-tree, and many of them produced out of one tubercle, reſembling a painter's pencil; it hath male flowers, or katkins, produced at remote diſtances from the fruit on the ſame tree. The ſeeds are produced in large cones, ſquamoſe and turbinated. The extenſion of the branches is very regular in *cedar* trees; the ends of the ſhoots declining, and thereby ſhewing their upper ſurface, which is conſtantly cloathed with green leaves, ſo regularly as to appear at a diſtance like a green carpet, and, in waving about, make an agreeable proſpect. It is ſurpriſing that this tree has not been more cultivated in England; for it would be a great ornament to barren bleak mountains, even in Scotland, where few other trees would grow; it being a native of Mount Libanus, where the ſnow continues moſt part of the year. What we find in Scripture, of the lofty *cedars*, is no ways applicable to the ſtature of this tree; for we find by thoſe now growing in England, and by the teſtimony of travellers, that have ſeen thoſe few remaining trees on Mount Libanus, they are not inclined to grow very lofty, but extend their branches very far; to which the alluſion, made by the Pſalmiſt, agrees very well, when, deſcribing the flouriſhing ſtate of a people, he ſays, *they ſhall ſpread their branches like the cedar tree.* Maundrel, in his Travels, ſays, he meaſured one of the largeſt *cedars* on Mount Libanus, and found it to be twelve yards ſix inches in circumference, and ſound, and thirty ſeven yards in the ſpread of its boughs. At about five or ſix yards from the ground, it was divided into five limbs, each of which was equal to a great tree. The wood of this famous tree is accounted proof againſt the putrefaction of animal bodies. The ſaw duſt is thought to be one of the ſecrets uſed by the mountebanks, who pretend to have the embalming myſtery. This wood is alſo ſaid to yield an oil, which is famous for preſerving books and writings, and the wood is thought by my lord Bacon to continue above a thouſand years ſound. It is alſo recorded, that, in the temple of Apollo, at Utica, there was found timber of near two thouſand years old; and the ſtatue of the goddeſs, in the famous Epheſian temple, was ſaid to be of this material, as well as the timber work of that glorious ſtructure. This ſort of timber is very dry, and ſubject to ſplit; nor does it well endure to be faſtened with nails; therefore pins of the ſame wood are much preferable. *Miller.*

I muſt yield my body to the earth:
Thus yields the *cedar* to the axe's edge,
Whoſe arms gave ſhelter to the princely eagle;
Under whoſe ſhade the ramping lion ſlept,
Whoſe top branch overpeer'd Jove's ſpreading tree,
And kept low ſhrubs from winter's pow'rful wind.
Shakeſp. Henry VI. *p.* iii.

CE'DRINE. *adj.* [*cedrinus*, Lat.] Of or belonging to the cedar tree.

To CEIL. *v. a.* [*cælo*, Lat.] To overlay, or cover the inner roof of a building.

And the greater houſe he *ceiled* with fir-tree, which he overlaid with fine gold. 2 *Chron.* iii. 5.

How will he, from his houſe *ceiled* with cedar, be content with his Saviour's lot, not to have where to lay his head? *Decay of Piety.*

CE'ILING. *n. ſ.* [from *ceil*.] The inner roof.

Varniſh makes *ceilings* not only ſhine, but laſt. *Bacon.*

And now the thicken'd ſky
Like a dark *ceiling* ſtood; down ruſh'd the rain
Impetuous. *Milton's Paradiſe Loſt*, *b.* xi. *l.* 743.

So when the ſun by day, or moon by night,
Strike on the poliſh'd braſs their trembling light,
The glitt'ring ſpecies here and there divide,
And caſt their dubious beams from ſide to ſide:
Now on the walls, now on the pavement play,
And to the *ceiling* flaſh the glaring day. *Dryden's Æneid.*

CE'LANDINE, (*greater.*) [*chelidonium*, Lat.] A plant.

The cup of the flower conſiſts of two leaves, which ſoon fall away; the flower has four leaves, that are expanded in form of a croſs. It grows wild, and is uſed in medicine. *Miller.*

CE'LANDINE, (*the leſſer*, or *Pilewort.*) [*chelidonium minus*, Lat.]

It hath a gramoſe or granuloſe root; the leaves are roundiſh; the flower ſtalks trail upon the ground; the cup of the flower conſiſts of three leaves. *Miller.*

CE'LATURE. *n. ſ.* [*cælatura*, Lat.] The art of engraving or cutting in metals.

To CE'LEBRATE. *v. a.* [*celebro*, Lat.]

1. To praiſe; to commend; to give praiſe to; to make famous.

The ſongs of Sion were pſalms and pieces of poetry, that adored or *celebrated* the Supreme Being. *Addiſon. Spectator.*

I would have him read over the *celebrated* works of antiquity, which have ſtood the teſt of ſo many different ages. *Addiſon.*

2. To diſtinguiſh by ſolemn rites; to perform ſolemnly.

He ſlew all them that were gone to *celebrate* the ſabbath. 2 *Maccab.* v. 26.

On the feaſt day, the father cometh forth, after divine ſervice, into a large room, where the feaſt is *celebrated*. *Bacon.*

3. To mention in a ſet or ſolemn manner, whether of joy or ſorrow.

This pauſe of pow'r, 'tis Ireland's hour to mourn;
While England *celebrates* your ſafe return. *Dryden.*

CELEBRA'TION. *n. ſ.* [from *celebrate*.]

1. Solemn performance; ſolemn remembrance.

He laboured to drive ſorrow from her, and to haſten the *celebration* of their marriage. *Sidney.*

He ſhall conceal it,
While you are willing it ſhall come to note;
What time we will our *celebration* keep,
According to my birth. *Shakeſp. Twelfth Night.*

During the *celebration* of this holy ſacrament, you attend earneſtly to what is done by the prieſt. *Taylor.*

2. Praiſe; renown; memorial.

No more ſhall be added in this place, his memory deſerving a particular *celebration*, than that his learning, piety and virtue, have been attained by few. *Clarendon.*

Some of the ancients may be thought ſometimes to have uſed a leſs number of letters, by the *celebration* of thoſe who have added to their alphabet. *Holder's Elements of Speech.*

CELE'BRIOUS. *adj.* [*celeber*, Lat.] Famous; renowned; noted.

The Jews, Jeruſalem, and the Temple, having been always ſo *celebrious*; yet when, after their captivities, they were deſpoiled of their glory, even then, the Aſſyrians, Greeks, and Romans, honoured, with ſacrifices, the moſt high God, whom that nation worſhipped. *Grew's Coſmologia Sacra.*

CELE'BRIOUSLY. *adv.* [from *celebrious.*] In a famous manner.

CELE'BRIOUSNESS. *n. ſ.* [from *celebrious.*] Renown; fame.

CELE'BRITY. *n. ſ.* [*celebritas*, Lat.] Celebration; fame.

The manner of her receiving, and the *celebrity* of the marriage, were performed with great magnificence. *Bacon.*

CELE'RIACK. *n. ſ.* A ſpecies of parſley; it is alſo called *turnep-rooted celery.*

CELE'RITY. *n. ſ.* [*celeritas*, Lat.] Swiftneſs; ſpeed; velocity.

We very well ſee in them, who thus plead, a wonderful *celerity* of diſcourſe; for, perceiving at the firſt but only ſome cauſe of ſuſpicion, and fear leſt it ſhould be evil, they are preſently, in one and the ſelf-ſame breath, reſolved, that what beginning ſoever it had, there is no poſſibility it ſhould be good. *Hooker.*

His former cuſtom and practice was ever full of forwardneſs and *celerity*, to make head againſt them. *Bacon's Henry* VII.

Thus, with imagin'd wings, our ſwift ſcene flies,
In motion with no leſs *celerity*
Than that of thought. *Shakeſp. Henry* V.

Three things concur to make a percuſſion great; the bigneſs, the denſity, and the *celerity* of the body moved. *Digby.*

Whatever encreaſeth the denſity of the blood, even without encreaſing its *celerity*, heats, becauſe a denſer body is hotter than a rarer. *Arbuthnot on Aliments.*

CE'LERY. *n. ſ.* A ſpecies of *parſley*; which ſee.

CELE'STIAL. *adj.* [*celeſtis*, Lat.]

1. Heavenly; relating to the ſuperiour regions.

There ſtay, until the twelve *celeſtial* ſigns
Have brought about their annual reckoning.
Shakeſp. Love's Labour Loſt.

The ancients commonly applied *celeſtial* deſcriptions of other climes to their own. *Brown's Vulgar Errours*, *b.* iv. *c.* 12.

2. Heavenly; relating to the bleſſed ſtate.

Play that ſad note
I nam'd my knell; whilſt I ſit meditating
On that *celeſtial* harmony I go to. *Shakeſp. Henry* VIII.

3. Heavenly, with reſpect to excellence.

Canſt thou pretend deſire, whom zeal inflam'd
To worſhip, and a pow'r *celeſtial* nam'd? *Dryden.*

Telemachus, his bloomy face
Glowing *celeſtial* ſweet, with godlike grace. *Pope's Odyſſey.*

CELE'STIAL. *n. ſ.* [from the adj.] An inhabitant of heaven.

Thus affable and mild, the prince precedes,
And to the dome th' unknown *celeſtial* leads. *Pope's Odyſſey.*

CELE'STIALLY. *adv.* [from *celeſtial.*] In a heavenly manner.

To CELE'STIFY. *v. a.* [from *celeſtis,* Lat.] To give ſomething of heavenly nature to any thing.

We ſhould affirm, that all things were in all things, that heaven were but earth terreſtrified, and earth but heaven *celeſtified,* or that each part above had influence upon its affinity below. *Brown's Vulgar Errours.*

CE'LIACK. *adj.* [κοιλία, the belly.] Relating to the lower belly.

The blood moving ſlowly through the *celiack* and meſenterick arteries, produce complaints. *Arbuthnot on Aliments.*

CE'LIBACY. *n. ſ.* [from *cœlebs,* Latin.] Single life; unmarried ſtate.

I can attribute their numbers to nothing but their frequent marriages; for they look on *celibacy* as an accurſed ſtate, and generally are married before twenty. *Spectator,* N° 495.

By teaching them how to carry themſelves in their relations of huſbands and wives, parents and children, they have, without queſtion, adorned the goſpel, glorified God, and benefited man, much more than they could have done in the devouteſt and ſtricteſt *celibacy.* *Atterbury.*

CE'LIBATE. *n. ſ.* [*cœlibatus,* Lat.] Single life.

Where polygamy is forbidden, the males oblige themſelves to *celibate,* and then multiplication is hindered. *Graunt.*

CELL. *n. ſ.* [*cella,* Lat.]

1. A ſmall cavity or hollow place.

The brain contains ten thouſand *cells,*
In each ſome active fancy dwells. *Prior.*

How theſe for ever, though a monarch reign,
Their ſep'rate *cells* and properties maintain. *Pope.*

2. The cave or little habitation of a religious perſon.

Beſides, ſhe did intend confeſſion
At Patrick's *cell* this even; and there ſhe was not. *Shakeſp.*

Then did religion in a lazy *cell,*
In empty, airy contemplations dwell. *Denham.*

3. A ſmall and cloſe apartment in a priſon.

4. Any ſmall place of reſidence.

Mine eyes he cloſ'd, but open left the *cell*
Of fancy, my internal ſight. *Par. Loſt, b.* viii. *l.* 460.

5. Little bags or bladders, where fluids, or matter of different ſorts are lodged; common both to animals and plants. *Quincy.*

CE'LLAR. *n. ſ.* [*cella,* Lat.] A place under ground, where ſtores are repoſited.

If this fellow had lived in the time of Cato, he would, for his puniſhment, have been confined to the bottom of a *cellar* during his life. *Peacham on Drawing.*

CE'LLARAGE. *n. ſ.* [from *cellar.*] The part of the building which makes the cellars.

Come on, you hear this fellow in the *cellarage.* *Shakeſp.*

Take care alſo, that it be well watered and wooded; that it have a good aſcent to it, which makes a houſe wholeſome, and gives opportunity for *cellarage.* *Mortimer's Huſbandry.*

CE'LLARIST. *n. ſ.* [*cellarius,* Lat.] The butler in a religious houſe. *Dict.*

CE'LLULAR. *adj.* [*cellula,* Lat.] Conſiſting of little cells or cavities.

The urine, inſinuating itſelf amongſt the neighbouring muſcles, and *cellular* membranes, deſtroyed four. *Sharp's Surgery.*

CE'LSITUDE. *n. ſ.* [*celſitudo,* Lat.] Height. *Dict.*

CE'MENT. *n ſ.* [*cæmentum,* Lat.]

1. The matter with which two bodies are made to cohere; as, mortar or glue.

Your temples burned in their *cement,* and your franchiſes confined into an augre's bore. *Shak. Coriol.*

There is a *cement* compounded of flower, whites of eggs, and ſtones powdered, that becometh hard as marble. *Bacon.*

You may ſee divers pebbles, and a cruſt of *cement* or ſtone between them, as hard as the pebbles themſelves. *Bacon.*

The foundation was made of rough ſtone, joined together with a moſt firm *cement;* upon this was laid another layer, conſiſting of ſmall ſtones and *cement.* *Arbuthnot on Coins.*

2. Bond of union in friendſhip.

Let not the piece of virtue which is ſet
Betwixt us, as the *cement* of our love,
To keep it builded, be the ram to batter.
Shakeſp. Antony and Cleopatra.

What *cement* ſhould unite heaven and earth, light and darkneſs? *Glanville's Scepſis, c.* iv.

Look over the whole creation, and you ſhall ſee, that the band or *cement,* that holds together all the parts of this great and glorious fabrick, is gratitude. *South.*

To CEME'NT. *v. a.* [from the noun.] To unite by means of ſomething interpoſed.

But how the fear of us
May *cement* their diviſions, and bind up
The petty difference, we yet not know. *Shak. Ant. and Cl.*

Liquid bodies have nothing to *cement* them; they are all looſe and incoherent, and in a perpetual flux: even an heap of ſand, or fine powder, will ſuffer no hollowneſs within them, though they be dry ſubſtances. *Burnet's Theory of the Earth.*

Edgar
Cemented all the long contending powers. *Philips.*

Love with white lead *cements* his wings;
White lead was ſent us to repair
Two brighteſt, brittleſt earthly things,
A lady's face, and china ware. *Swift.*

To CEME'NT. *v. n.* To come into conjunction; to cohere.

When a wound is recent, and the parts of it are divided by a ſharp inſtrument, they will, if held in cloſe contact for ſome time, reunite by inoſculation, and *cement* like one branch of a tree ingrafted on another. *Sharp's Surgery.*

CEMENTA'TION. *n. ſ.* [from *cement.*] The act of cementing, or uniting with cement.

CE'METERY. *n. ſ.* [κοιμητήριον.] A place where the dead are repoſited.

The ſouls of the dead appear frequently in *cemeteries,* and hover about the places where their bodies are buried, as ſtill hankering about their old brutal pleaſures, and deſiring again to enter the body. *Addiſon. Spectator,* N° 90.

CEN, and CIN, denote *kinsfolk;* ſo *Cinulph* is a help to his kindred; *Cinehelm,* a protector of his kinsfolk; *Cinburg,* the defence of his kindred; *Cinric,* powerful in kindred.
Gibſon's Camden.

CE'NATORY. *adj.* [from *ceno,* to ſup, Lat.] Relating to ſupper.

The Romans waſhed, were anointed, and wore a *cenatory* garment; and the ſame was practiſed by the Jews.
Brown's Vulgar Errours.

CENOBI'TICAL. *adj.* [κοινὸς and βίος.] Living in community.

They have multitudes of religious orders, black and gray, eremitical and *cenobitical,* and nuns. *Stillingfleet.*

CE'NOTAPH. *n. ſ.* [κενὸς and τάφος.] A monument for one buried elſewhere.

Priam, to whom the ſtory was unknown,
As dead, deplor'd his metamorphos'd ſon;
A *cenotaph* his name and title kept,
And Hector round the tomb with all his brothers wept.
Dryden's Fables.

The Athenians, when they loſt any men at ſea, raiſed a *cenotaph,* or empty monument. *Notes on Odyſſey.*

CENSE. *n. ſ.* [*cenſus,* Lat.] Publick rates.

We ſee what floods of treaſure have flowed into Europe by that action; ſo that the *cenſe,* or rates of Chriſtendom, are raiſed ſince ten times, yea twenty times told. *Bacon.*

To CENSE. *v. a.* [*encenſer,* Fr.] To perfume with odours.

The Salii ſing, and *cenſe* his altars round
With Saban ſmoke, their heads with poplar bound. *Dryden.*

Grineus was near, and caſt a furious look
On the ſide-altar, *cens'd* with ſacred ſmoke,
And bright with flaming fires. *Dryden.*

CE'NSER. *n. ſ.* [*encenſoir,* Fr.] The pan or veſſel in which incenſe is burned.

Here's ſnip, and nip, and cut, and ſliſh, and ſluſh,
Like to a *cenſer* in a barber's ſhop.
Shakeſp. Taming of the Shrew.

Antoninus gave piety in his money, like a lady with a *cenſer* before an altar. *Peacham on Drawing.*

Of incenſe clouds,
Fuming from golden *cenſers,* hid the mount. *Par. Loſt, b.* vii.

CE'NSOR. *n. ſ.* [*cenſor,* Lat.]

1. An officer of Rome, who had the power of correcting manners.

2. One who is given to cenſure and exprobation.

Ill-natur'd *cenſors* of the preſent age,
And fond of all the follies of the paſt. *Roſcommon.*

The moſt ſevere *cenſor* cannot but be pleaſed with the prodigality of his wit, though, at the ſame time, he could have wiſhed, that the maſter of it had been a better manager. *Dryd.*

CENSO'RIAN. *adj.* [from *cenſor.*] Relating to the cenſor.

As the chancery had the pretorian power for equity, ſo the ſtar-chamber had the *cenſorian* power for offences under the degree of capital. *Bacon's Henry* VII.

CENSO'RIOUS. *adj.* [from *cenſor.*]

1. Addicted to cenſure; ſevere; full of invectives.

Do not too many believe no religion to be pure, but what is intemperately rigid? no zeal to be ſpiritual, but what is *cenſorious,* or vindicative? *Sprat.*

O! let my preſence make my travels light,
And potent Venus ſhall exalt my name
Above the rumours of *cenſorious* fame. *Prior.*

2. Sometimes it has *of* before the object of reproach.

A dogmatical ſpirit inclines a man to be *cenſorious of* his neighbours. *Watts's Improvement of the Mind.*

3. Sometimes *on.*

He treated all his inferiours of the clergy with a moſt ſanctified pride; was rigorouſly and univerſally *cenſorious upon* all his brethren of the gown. *Swift.*

CENSO'RIOUSLY. *adv.* [from *cenſorious.*] In a ſevere reflecting manner.

CENSO'RIOUSNESS. *n. ſ* [from *cenſorious.*] Diſpoſition to reproach; habit of reproaching.

Sourneſs of diſpoſition, and rudeneſs of behaviour, *cenſoriouſneſs* and ſiniſter interpretation of things, all croſs and diſtaſteful humours, render the converſation of men grievous and uneaſy to one another. *Tillotſon.*

CE'NSORSHIP. *n. ſ.* [from *cenſor.*]

1. The office of a cenſor.
2. The time in which the office of cenſor is born.

It was brought to Rome in the *cenſorſhip* of Claudius. *Brown's Vulgar Errours, b.* iii. *c.* 12.

CE'NSURABLE. *adj.* [from *cenſure.*] Worthy of cenſure; blameable; culpable.

A ſmall miſtake may leave upon the mind the laſting memory of having been taunted for ſomething *cenſurable. Locke.*

CE'NSURABLENESS. *n. ſ.* [from *cenſurable.*] Blamableneſs; liable to be cenſured.

CE'NSURE. *n. ſ.* [*cenſura*, Latin.]

1. Blame; reprimand; reproach.

Enough for half the greateſt of theſe days,
To 'ſcape my *cenſure*, not expect my praiſe. *Pope.*

2. Judgment; opinion.

Madam, and you, my ſiſter, will you go
To give your *cenſures* in this weighty buſineſs? *Shakeſp. Richard* III.

3. Judicial ſentence.

To you, lord governour,
Remains the *cenſure* of this helliſh villain. *Shakeſp. Othello.*

4. A ſpiritual puniſhment inflicted by ſome eccleſiaſtical judge. *Ayliffe's Parergon.*

Upon the unſucceſsfulneſs of milder medicaments, uſe that ſtronger phyſick, the *cenſures* of the church. *Hammond.*

To CE'NSURE. *v. a.* [*cenſurer*, Fr.]

1. To blame; to brand publickly.

The like *cenſurings* and deſpiſings have embittered the ſpirits, and whetted both the tongues and pens of learned men one againſt another. *Sanderſon.*

2. To condemn by a judicial ſentence.

CE'NSURER. *n. ſ.* [from *cenſure.*] He that blames; he that reproaches.

We muſt not ſtint
Our neceſſary actions, in the fear
To cope malicious *cenſurers. Shakeſp. Henry* VIII.

A ſtateſman, who is poſſeſt of real merit, ſhould look upon his political *cenſurers* with the ſame neglect, that a good writer regards his criticks. *Addiſon, Freeholder,* Nº 17.

CENT. *n. ſ.* [*centum*, Lat. a hundred.] A hundred; as, five *per cent*, that is, five in the hundred.

CE'NTAUR. *n. ſ.* [*centaurus*, Lat.]

1. A poetical being, ſuppoſed to be compounded of a man and a horſe.

Down from the waſte they are *centaurs*, though women all above. *Shakeſp. King Lear.*

The idea of a *centaur* has no more falſehood in it, than the name *centaur. Locke.*

Feats, Theſſalian *centaurs* never knew,
And their repeated wonders ſhake the dome. *Thomſon.*

2. The archer in the zodiack.

The chearleſs empire of the ſky,
To Capricorn, the *Centaur* archer yields. *Thomſon.*

CE'NTAURY, *(greater.)* [*centaurium majus*, Lat.] A plant.

It is one of the *plantæ capitulæ*, or of thoſe plants whoſe flowers are collected into a head, as the thiſtle, and hath a perennial root; its leaves are without ſpines, and are ſawed on the edges; the cup of the flower is ſquamoſe, but hath no ſpines; the florets are large and ſpacious. One of the ſpecies, having cut leaves, is uſed in medicine. *Miller.*

CE'NTAURY, *(leſſer.)* [*centaurium minus*, Lat.]

The leaves grow by pairs, oppoſite to each other; the flowers conſiſt of one leaf, funnel ſhaped, and divided into five acute ſegments; they grow on the tops of the ſtalks in cluſters; the ſeed veſſel is of a cylindrick form, and is divided into two cells, wherein many ſmall ſeeds are contained. It grows wild, and is uſed in medicine. *Miller.*

Add pounded galls, and roſes dry,
And with Cecropian thyme ſtrong ſcented *centaury. Dryden.*

CE'NTENARY. *n ſ.* [*centenarius*, Lat.] The number of a hundred.

In every *centenary* of years from the creation, ſome ſmall abatement ſhould have been made. *Hakewell on Providence.*

CENTE'SIMAL. *n. ſ.* [*centeſimus*, Latin.] Hundredth; the next ſtep of progreſſion after decimal in the arithmetick of fractions.

The neglect of a few *centeſimals* in the ſide of the cube, would bring it to an equality with the cube of a foot. *Arbuthnot on Coins.*

CENTIFO'LIOUS. *adj.* [from *centum* and *folium*, Lat.] Having an hundred leaves.

CE'NTIPEDE. *n. ſ.* [from *centum* and *pes.*] A poiſonous inſect in the Weſt Indies, commonly called by the Engliſh *forty legs.*

CE'NTO. *n. ſ.* [*cento*, Lat.] A compoſition formed by joining ſcrapes from other authours.

It is quilted, as it were, out of ſhreds of divers poets, ſuch as ſcholars call a *cento. Camden's Remains.*

If any man think the poem a *cento*, our poet will but have done the ſame in jeſt which Boileau did in earneſt. *Advertiſement to Pope's Dunciad.*

CE'NTRAL. *adj.* [from *centre.*] Relating to the centre; containing the centre.

There is now, and was then, a ſpace or cavity in the *central* parts of it; ſo large as to give reception to that mighty maſs of water. *Woodward's Natural Hiſtory.*

Umbriel, a duſky melancholy ſprite,
Down to the *central* earth, his proper ſcene,
Repairs. *Pope's Rape of the Lock.*

CE'NTRALLY. *adv.* [from *central.*] With regard to the centre.

Though one of the feet moſt commonly bears the weight, yet we ſee that the whole weight reſts *centrally* upon it. *Dryden's Dufreſnoy.*

CE'NTRE. *n. ſ.* [*centrum*, Lat.] The middle; that which is equally diſtant from all extremities.

The heav'ns themſelves, the planets, and this *centre*,
Obſerve degree, priority, and place. *Shakeſp. Troilus and Creſſida.*

If we frame an image of a round body all of fire, the flame proceeding from it, would diffuſe itſelf every way; ſo that the ſource, ſerving for the *centre* there, would be round about an huge ſphere of fire and light. *Digby on Bodies.*

To CE'NTRE. *v. a.* [from the noun.] To place on a centre; to fix as on a centre.

One foot he *centred*, and the other turn'd
Round through the vaſt profundity obſcure. *Milton's Paradiſe Loſt, b.* vii. *l.* 228.

By thy each look, and thought, and care, 'tis ſhown,
Thy joys are *centred* all in me alone. *Prior.*

He may take a range all the world over, and draw in all that wide air and circumference of ſin and vice, and *centre* it in his own breaſt. *South.*

O impudent, regardful of thy own,
Whoſe thoughts are *centred* on thyſelf alone! *Dryden.*

To CE'NTRE. *v. n.*

1. To reſt on; to repoſe on; as bodies when they gain an equilibrium; to meet in a point, as lines in a centre.

Where there is no viſible truth wherein to *centre*, errour is as wide as men's fancies, and may wander to eternity. *Decay of Piety.*

What hopes you had in Diomede, lay down;
Our hopes muſt *centre* on ourſelves alone. *Dryden's Æneid.*

The common acknowledgments of the body will at length *centre* in him, who appears ſincerely to aim at the common benefit. *Atterbury.*

It was atteſted by the viſible *centring* of all the old prophecies in the perſon of Chriſt, and by the completion of theſe prophecies ſince, which he himſelf uttered. *Atterbury.*

2. To be placed in the midſt or centre.

As God in heav'n
Is centre, yet extends to all; ſo thou,
Centring, receiv'ſt from all thoſe orbs. *Par. Loſt, b.* ix.

CE'NTRICK. *adj.* [from *centre.*] Placed in the centre.

Some that have deeper digg'd in mine than I,
Say, where his *centrick* happineſs doth lie. *Donne.*

CENTRI'FUGAL. *adj.* [from *centrum* and *fugio*, Lat.] Having the quality acquired by bodies in motion, of receding from the centre.

They deſcribed an hyperbola, by changing the centripetal into a *centrifugal* force. *Cheyne's Philoſophical Principles.*

CENTRI'PETAL. *adj.* [from *centrum* and *peto*, Lat.] Having a tendency to the center; having gravity.

The direction of the force, whereby the planets revolve in their orbits, is towards their centres; and this force may be very properly called attractive, in reſpect of the central body, and *centripetal*, in reſpect of the revolving body. *Cheyne.*

CE'NTRY. } See SENTINEL.
SE'NTRY. }

The thoughtleſs wits ſhall frequent forfeits pay,
Who 'gainſt the *centry*'s box diſcharge their tea. *Gay.*

CE'NTUPLE. *adj.* [*centuplex*, Lat.] An hundred fold.

To CENTU'PLICATE. *v. a.* [*centuplicatum*, of *centum* and *plico*, Lat.] To make a hundred fold; to repeat a hundred times. *D.*

To CENTU'RIATE. *v. a.* [*centurio*, Lat.] To divide into hundreds.

CENTURIA'TOR. *n. ſ.* [from *century.*] A name given to hiſtorians, who diſtinguiſh times by centuries; which is generally the method of eccleſiaſtical hiſtory.

The *centuriators* of Magdeburg were the firſt that diſcovered this grand impoſture. *Ayliffe's Parergon.*

CENTU'RION. *n. ſ.* [*centurio*, Latin.] A military officer among the Romans, who commanded an hundred men.

Have an army ready, ſay you?—A moſt royal one. The *centurions*, and their charges, diſtinctly billeted already in the entertainment, and to be on foot at an hour's warning. *Shakeſp. Coriolanus.*

CE'NTURY. *n. ſ.* [*centuria*, Lat.]

1. A hundred; uſually employed to ſpecify time; as, the ſecond *century.*

The nature of eternity is ſuch, that, though our joys, after ſome

ſome *centuries* of years, may ſeem to have grown older, by having been enjoyed ſo many ages, yet will they really ſtill continue new. *Boyle.*

And now time's whiter ſeries is begun,
Which in ſoft *centuries* ſhall ſmoothly run. *Dryden.*

The liſts of biſhops are filled with greater numbers than one would expect; but the ſucceſſion was quick in the three firſt *centuries*, becauſe the biſhop very often ended in the martyr. *Addiſon on the Chriſtian Religion.*

2. It is ſometimes uſed ſimply for a hundred.

Romulus, as you may read, did divide the Romans into tribes, and the tribes into *centuries* or hundreds. *Spenſer.*

When
With wild woodleaves and weeds I have ſtrew'd his grave,
And on it ſaid a *century* of pray'rs,
Such as I can, twice o'er, I'll weep and ſigh. *Shakeſp. Cymb.*

CEOL. An initial in the names of men, which ſignifies a ſhip or veſſel, ſuch as thoſe that the Saxons landed in. *Gibſon's Camden.*

Ce'phalalgy. *n. ſ.* [κεφαλαλγία.] The headach. *Dict.*

Cepha'lick. *adj.* [κεφαλὴ.] That which is medicinal to the head.

Cephalick medicines are all ſuch as attenuate the blood, ſo as to make it circulate eaſily through the capillary veſſels of the brain. *Arbuthnot on Aliments.*

I dreſſed him up with ſoft folded linen, dipped in a *cephalick* balſam. *Wiſeman.*

CERA'STES. n. ſ. [κεράστης.] A ſerpent having horns, or ſuppoſed to have them.

Scorpion, and aſp, and amphiſbena dire,
Ceraſtes horn'd, hydrus, and elops drear. *Par. Loſt, b.* x.

Ce'rate. *n. ſ.* [*cera*, Lat. wax.] A medicine made of wax, which, with oil, or ſome ſofter ſubſtance, makes a conſiſtence ſofter than a plaiſter. *Quincy.*

Ce'rated. *adj.* [*ceratus*, Lat.] Waxed; covered with wax.

To CERE. *v. a.* [from *cera*, Lat. wax.] To wax.

You ought to pierce the ſkin with a needle, and ſtrong brown thread, *cered* about half an inch from the edges of the lips. *Wiſeman.*

Ce'rebel. *n ſ.* [*cerebellum*, Lat.] Part of the brain.

In the head of man, the baſe of the brain and *cerebel*, yea, of the whole ſcull, is ſet parallel to the horizon. *Derham.*

Ce'recloth. *n. ſ.* [from *cere* and *cloth.*] Cloth ſmeared over with glutinous matter, uſed to wounds and bruiſes.

The ancient Egyptian mummies were ſhrowded in a number of folds of linen, beſmeared with gums, in manner of *cerecloth.* *Bacon.*

Ce'rement. *n. ſ.* [from *cera*, Lat. wax.] Cloaths dipped in melted wax, with which dead bodies were infolded when they were embalmed.

Let me not burſt in ignorance, but tell,
Why canonized bones, hearſed in earth,
Have burſt their *cerements?* *Shakeſp. Hamlet.*

Ceremo'nial. *adj.* [from *ceremony.*]

1. Relating to ceremony, or outward rite.

What mockery will it be,
To want the bridegroom, when the prieſt attends,
To ſpeak the *ceremonial* rites of marriage?
Shakeſp. Taming of the Shrew.

We are to carry it from the hand to the heart, to improve a *ceremonial* nicety into a ſubſtantial duty, and the modes of civility into the realities of religion. *South.*

Chriſt did take away that external *ceremonial* worſhip that was among the Jews. *Stillingfleet.*

2. Formal; obſervant of old forms.

Oh monſtrous, ſuperſtitious puritan,
Of refin'd manners, yet *ceremonial* man,
That when thou meet'ſt one, with enquiring eyes
Doſt ſearch, and, like a needy broker, prize
The ſilk and gold he wears. *Donne.*

With dumb pride, and a ſet formal face,
He moves in the dull *ceremonial* track,
With Jove's embroider'd coat upon his back. *Dryden.*

Ceremo'nial. *n. ſ.* [from *ceremony.*]

1. Outward form; external rite.

The only condition that could make it prudent for the clergy, to alter the *ceremonial*, or any indifferent part, would be a reſolution in the legiſlature to prevent new ſects. *Swift.*

2. The order for rites and forms in the Romiſh church.

Ceremo'nialness. *n. ſ.* [from *ceremonial.*] The quality of being ceremonial; over much uſe of ceremony.

Ceremo'nious. *adj.* [from *ceremony.*]

1. Conſiſting of outward rites.

Under a different oeconomy of religion, God was more tender of the ſhell and *ceremonious* part of his worſhip. *South.*

2. Full of ceremony; awful.

O, the ſacrifice,
How *ceremonious*, ſolemn, and unearthly,
It was i' th' offering! *Shakeſp. Winter's Tale.*

3. Attentive to the outward rites of religion.

You are too ſenſeleſs obſtinate, my lord;
Too *ceremonious*, and traditional. *Shakeſp. Richard* III.

4. Civil; according to the ſtrict rules of civility; formally reſpectful.

They have a ſet of *ceremonious* phraſes, that run through all ranks and degrees among them. *Addiſon. Guard.* N° 104.

5. Obſervant of the rules of civility.

Then let us take a *ceremonious* leave,
And loving farewel of our ſeveral friends. *Shakeſp. R.* III.

6. Civil and formal to a fault.

The old caitiff was grown ſo *ceremonious*, as he would needs accompany me ſome miles in my way. *Sidney, b.* ii.

Ceremo'niously. *adv.* [from *ceremonious.*] In a ceremonious manner; formally; reſpectful.

Ceremoniouſly let us prepare
Some welcome for the miſtreſs of the houſe.
Shakeſp. Two Gentlemen of Verona.

Ceremo'niousness. *n. ſ.* [from *ceremonious.*] Fondneſs of ceremony; uſing too much ceremony.

CE'REMONY. *n. ſ.* [*ceremonia*, Lat.]

1. Outward rite; external form in religion.

Bring her up to the high altar, that ſhe may
The ſacred *ceremonies* partake. *Spenſer's Epithalamium.*

He is ſuperſtitious grown of late,
Quite from the main opinion he held once
Of fantaſy, of dreams, and *ceremonies.* *Shakeſp. J. Cæſar.*

Diſrobe the images,
If you find them deck'd with *ceremony.* *Shakeſp. J. Cæſar.*

2. Forms of civility.

The ſauce to meat is *ceremony*;
Meeting were bare without it. *Shakeſp. Macbeth.*

Not to uſe *ceremonies* at all, is to teach others not to uſe them again, and ſo diminiſh reſpect to himſelf. *Bacon.*

3. Outward forms of ſtate.

What art thou, thou idle *ceremony?*
What kind of god art thou, that ſuffer'ſt more
Of mortal grief, than do thy worſhippers?
Art thou aught elſe but place, degree, and form?
Shakeſp. Henry V.

A coarſer place,
Where pomp and *ceremonies* enter'd not,
Where greatneſs was ſhut out, and bigneſs well forgot.
Dryden's Fables.

Ce'rote. *n. ſ.* The ſame with *cerate*; which ſee.

In thoſe which are critical, a *cerote* of oil of olives, with white wax, hath hitherto ſerved my purpoſe. *Wiſeman.*

CE'RTAIN. *adj.* [*certus*, Lat.]

1. Sure; indubitable; unqueſtionable; undoubted; that which cannot be queſtioned, or denied.

This it is equally *certain* of, whether theſe ideas be more or leſs general. *Locke.*

Thoſe things are *certain* among men, which cannot be denied, without obſtinacy and folly. *Tillotſon.*

2. Reſolved; determined.

However I with thee have fix'd my lot,
Certain to undergo like doom of death,
Conſort with thee. *Milton's Par. Loſt, b.* ix. *l.* 953.

3. In an indefinite ſenſe, ſome; as, a *certain* man told me this.

How bad ſoever this faſhion may juſtly be accounted, *certain* of the ſame countrymen do paſs far beyond it. *Carew's Survey.*

I got them in my country's ſervice, when
Some *certain* of your brethren roar'd, and ran
From noiſe of our own drums. *Shakeſp. Coriolanus.*

Let there be *certain* leather bags made of ſeveral bigneſſes, which, for the matter of them, ſhould be tractable. *Wilkins.*

4. Undoubting; put paſt doubt.

This form before Alcyone preſent,
To make her *certain* of the ſad event. *Dryden.*

Ce'rtainly. *adv.* [from *certain.*]

1. Indubitably; without queſtion; without doubt.

Certainly he that, by thoſe legal means, cannot be ſecured, can be much leſs ſo by any private attempt. *Decay of Piety.*

What preciſe collection of ſimple ideas, modeſty or frugality ſtand for, in another's uſe, is not ſo *certainly* known. *Locke.*

2. Without fail.

Ce'rtainness. *n. ſ.* [from *certain.*] The ſame with *certainty.*

Ce'rtainty. *n. ſ.* [from *certain.*]

1. Exemption from doubt.

Certainty is the perception of the agreement or diſagreement of our ideas. *Locke.*

2. That which is real and fixed.

Doubting things go ill, often hurts more
Than to be ſure they do; for *certainties*
Or are paſt remedies, or timely knowing,
The remedy then born. *Shakeſp. Cymbeline.*

Ce'rtes. *adv.* [*certes*, Fr.] Certainly; in truth; in ſooth: an old word.

Certes, Sir Knight, ye've been too much to blame,
Thus for to blot the honour of the dead,
And with foul cowardice his carcaſe ſhame,
Whoſe living hands immortaliz'd his name. *Fairy Q. b.* ii.

For, *certes*, theſe are people of the iſland. *Shakeſp. Tempeſt.*

Certes, our authours are to blame. *Hudibras.*

CERTI'FICATE. *n. s.* [*certificat*, low Lat. he certifies.]
1. A writing made in any court, to give notice to another court of any thing done therein. *Cowel.*
2. Any testimony.
A *certificate* of poverty is as good as a protection. *L'Estr.*
I can bring *certificates*, that I behave myself soberly before company. *Addison. Spectator*, Nº 577.

To CE'RTIFY. *v. a.* [*certifier*, Fr.]
1. To give certain information of.
The English embassadours returned out of Flanders from Maximilian, and *certified* the king, that he was not to hope for any aid from him. *Bacon's Henry* VII.
This is designed to *certify* those things that are confirmed of God's favour. *Hammond's Fundamentals.*
2. It has *of* before the thing told.

CERTIORA'RI. *n. s.* [Latin.] A writ issuing out of the chancery, to call up the records of a cause therein depending, that justice may be done; upon complaint made by bill, that the party, who seeks the said writ, hath received hard dealing in the said court. *Cowel.*

CE'RTITUDE. *n. s.* [*certitudo*, Lat.] Certainty; freedom from doubt.
They thought at first they dream'd; for 'twas offence
With them, to question *certitude* of sense. *Dryden.*
There can be no *majus* and *minus* in the *certitude* we have of things, whether by mathematick demonstration, or any other way of consequence. *Grew's Cosmologia Sacra*, *b.* ii. *c.* iv. § 2.

CERVI'CAL. *adj.* [*cervicalis*, Lat.] Belonging to the neck.
The aorta bending a little upwards, sends forth the *cervical* and axillary arteries; the rest turning down again, forms the descending trunk. *Cheyne's Philosophical Principles.*

CERU'LEAN. }
CERU'LEOUS. } *adj.* [*cœruleus*, Lat.] Blue; sky coloured.
It afforded a solution, with, now and then, a light touch of sky colour, but nothing near so high as the *ceruleous* tincture of silver. *Boyle.*
From thee the saphire solid ether takes,
Its hue *cerulean.* *Thomson's Summer.*

CERULI'FICK. *adj.* [from *ceruleous.*] Having the power to produce a blue colour.
The several species of rays, as the rubifick, *cerulifick*, and others are separated one from another. *Grew's Cosmol. Sacra.*

CERU'MEN. *n. s.* [Latin.] The wax or excrement of the ear.

CE'RUSE. *n. s.* [*cerussa*, Lat.] White lead.
A preparation of lead with vinegar, which is of a white colour; whence many other things, resembling it in that particular, are by chymists called *ceruse*, as the *ceruse* of antimony, and the like. *Quincy.*

CESA'RIAN. *adj.* [from *Cæsar.*]
The *Cesarian* section is cutting a child out of the womb either dead or alive, when it cannot otherwise be delivered. Which circumstance, it is said, first gave the name of *Cæsar* to the Roman family so called. *Quincy.*

CESS. *n. s.* [probably corrupted from *cense*; See CENSE; though imagined by *Junius* to be derived from *saisire*, to seize.]
1. A levy made upon the inhabitants of a place, rated according to their property.
The like *cess* is also charged upon the country sometimes for victualling the soldiers, when they lie in garrison. *Spenser.*
2. The act of laying rates.
3. [from *cesse*, Fr.] It seems to have been used by *Shakespeare* for bounds, or limits.
I pr'ythee, Tom, beat Cutts's saddle, put a few flocks in the point; the poor jade is wrung in the withers out of all *cess*. *Shakesp. Henry* IV. *p.* i.

To CESS. *v. a.* [from the noun.] To rate; to lay charge on.
We are to consider how much land there is in all Ulster, that, according to the quantity thereof, we may *cess* the said rent, and allowance issuing thereout. *Spenser on Ireland.*

CESSA'TION. *n. s.* [*cessatio*, Lat.]
1. A stop; a rest; a vacation.
The day was yearly observed for a festival, by *cessation* from labour, and by resorting to church. *Hayward.*
True piety, without *cessation* tost
By theories, the practick part is lost. *Denham.*
There had been a mighty confusion of things, an interruption and perturbation of the ordinary course, and a *cessation* and suspension of the laws of nature. *Woodward's Nat. Hist.*
The rising of a parliament is a kind of *cessation* from politicks. *Addison. Freeholder*, Nº 55.
The serum, which is mixed with an alkali, being poured out to that which is mixed with an acid, raiseth an effervescence; at the *cessation* of which, the salts of which the acid was composed, will be regenerated. *Arbuthnot on Aliments.*
2. A pause of hostility, without peace.
When the succours of the poor protestants in Ireland were diverted, I was intreated to get them some respite, by a *cessation.* *K. Charles.*

CESSA'VIT. *n. s.* [Latin.]
A writ that lies upon this general ground, that the person, against whom it is brought, hath, for two years, omitted to perform such service, or pay such rent, as he is obliged by his tenure, and hath not, upon his land or tenement, sufficient goods or chattels to be distrained. *Cowel.*

CESSIBI'LITY. *n. s.* [from *cedo*, *cessum*, Latin.] The quality of receding, or giving way, without resistance.
If the subject strucken be of a proportionate *cessibility*, it seems to dull and deaden the stroke; whereas if the thing strucken be hard, the stroke seems to lose no force, but to work a greater effect. *Digby on the Soul.*

CE'SSIBLE. *adj.* [from *cedo*, *cessum*, Lat.] Easy to give way.
If the parts of the strucken body be so easily *cessible*, as without difficulty the stroke can divide them, then it enters into such a body, till it has spent its force. *Digby on the Soul.*

CE'SSION. *n. s.* [*cession*, Fr. *cessio*, Lat.]
1. Retreat; the act of giving way.
Sound is not produced without some resistance either in the air or the body percussed; for if there be a mere yielding or *cession*, it produceth no sound. *Bacon's Nat. Hist.* Nº 125.
2. Resignation; the act of yielding up or quitting to another.
A parity in their council would make and secure the best peace they can with France, by a *cession* of Flanders to that crown, in exchange for other provinces. *Temple.*

CE'SSIONARY. *adj.* [from *cession.*] As a *cessionary* bankrupt, one who has delivered up all his effects. *Martin.*

CE'SSMENT. *n. s.* [from *cess.*] An assessment or tax. *Dict.*

CE'SSOR. *n. s.* [from *cesso*, Lat.]
In law, he that ceaseth or neglecteth so long to perform a duty belonging to him, as that by his cess, or cessing, he incurreth the danger of law, and hath, or may have, the writ cessavit brought against him. Where it is said the tenant cesseth, such phrase is to be understood, as if it were said, the tenant cesseth to do that which he ought, or is bound to do by his land or tenement. *Cowel.*

CE'STUS. *n. s.* [Latin.] The girdle of Venus.
Venus, without any ornament but her own beauties, not so much as her own *cestus.* *Addison. Spectator*, Nº 425.

CETA'CEOUS. *adj.* [from *cete*, whales, Lat.] Of the whale kind.
Such fishes as have lungs or respiration, are not without the wezzon, as whales and *cetaceous* animals. *Brown's Vulg. Err.*
He hath created variety of these *cetaceous* fishes, which converse chiefly in the northern seas, whose whole body being encompassed round with a copious fat or blubber, it is enabled to abide the greatest cold of the sea-water. *Ray on the Creation.*

C FAUT. A note in the scale of musick.
Gamut I am, the ground of all accord,
A re, to plead Hortensio's passion;
B mi Bianca, take him for thy lord,
C faut, that loves with all affection.
Shakesp. Taming of the Shrew.

CH has, in words purely English, or fully naturalized, the sound of *tch*; a peculiar pronunciation, which it is hard to describe in words. In some words derived from the French, it has the sound of *sh*, as *chaise*; and, in some derived from the Greek, the sound of *k*, as *cholerick*.

CHACE. See CHASE.

CHAD. *n. s.* A sort of fish.
Of round fish there are brit, sprat, whiting, *chad*, eels, congar, millet. *Carew's Survey of Cornwal.*

To CHAFE. *v. a.* [*echauffer*, Fr.]
1. To warm with rubbing.
They laid him upon some of their garments, and fell to rub and *chafe* him, till they brought him to recover both breath, the servant, and warmth, the companion of living. *Sidney.*
At last, recovering heart, he does begin
To rub her temples, and to *chafe* her skin. *Fairy Q. b.* i.
Soft, and more soft, at ev'ry touch it grew;
Like pliant wax, when *chafing* hands reduce
The former mass to form, and frame to use. *Dryden.*
2. To heat.
Have I not heard the sea, puff'd up with winds,
Rage like an angry boar, *chafed* with sweat? *Shakesp.*
3. To perfume.
Lilies more white than snow,
New fall'n from heav'n, with violets mix'd, did grow;
Whose scent so *chaf'd* the neighbour air, that you
Would surely swear Arabick spices grew. *Suckling.*
4. To make angry.
Her intercession *chaf'd* him so,
When she for thy repeal was suppliant,
That to close prison he commanded her. *Shakesp.*
An offer of pardon more *chafed* the rage of those, who were resolved to live or die together. *Sir John Hayward.*
For all that he was inwardly *chafed* with the heat of youth and indignation, against his own people as well as the Rhodians, he moderated himself betwixt his own rage, and the offence of his soldiers. *Knolles's History of the Turks.*
This *chaf'd* the boar, his nostrils flames expire,
And his red eyeballs roll with living fire. *Dryden.*

To CHAFE. *v. n.*
1. To rage; to fret; to fume; to rave; to boil.
Therewith he 'gan full terribly to roar,
And *chaf'd* at that indignity right sore. *Spenser's Hub. Tale.*

My

My husband will not rejoice so much at the abuse of Falstaff, as he will *chafe* at the doctor's marrying my daughter.
Shakesp. Merry Wives of Windsor.

Be lion mettled, proud, and take no care,
Who *chafes*, who frets, or where conspirers are.
Shakesp. Macbeth.

How did they fume, and stamp, and roar, and *chafe*,
And swear; not Addison himself was safe. *Pope.*

2. To fret against any thing.

Once upon a raw and gusty day,
The troubled Tyber *chafing* with his shores. *Shakesp. J. Cæs.*
The murmuring surge,
That on th' unnumber'd idle pebbles *chafes*,
Cannot be heard so high. *Shakesp. King Lear.*

CHAFE. *n. s.* [from the verb.] A heat; a rage; a fury; a passion; a fume; a pett; a fret; a storm.

When Sir Thomas More was speaker of the parliament, with his wisdom and eloquence, he so crossed a purpose of cardinal Wolsey's, that the cardinal, in a *chafe*, sent for him to Whitehall. *Camden's Remains.*

At this the knight grew high in *chafe*,
And staring furiously on Ralph,
He trembled. *Hudibras, p.* ii. *c.* ii.

CHAFE-WAX. *n. s.* An officer belonging to the lord high chancellor, who fits the wax for the sealing of writs. *Harris.*

CHA'FER. *n. s.* [ceaꝼoꞃ, Sax. *kever*, Dutch.] An insect; a sort of yellow beetle.

CHA'FERY. *n. s.* A forge in an iron mill, where the iron is wrought into complete bars, and brought to perfection.
Phillips's World of Words.

CHAFF. *n. s.* [ceaꝼ, Sax. *kaf*, Dutch.]

1. The husks of corn that are separated by threshing and winnowing.

We shall be winnow'd with so rough a wind,
That ev'n our corn shall seem as light as *chaff*,
And good from bad find no partition. *Shakesp. Henry* IV.
Pleasure with instruction should be join'd;
So take the corn, and leave the *chaff* behind. *Dryden.*

He set before him a sack of wheat, as it had been just threshed out of the sheaf; he then bid him pick out the *chaff* from among the corn, and lay it aside by itself. *Spectator*, N° 291.

2. It is used for any thing worthless.

To CHA'FFER. *v. n.* [*kauffen*, Germ. to buy.] To treat about a bargain; to haggle; to bargain.

Nor rode himself to Paul's, the publick fair,
To *chaffer* for preferments with his gold,
Where bishopricks and sinecures are sold. *Dryden's Fables.*

The *chaffering* with dissenters, and dodging about this or t'other ceremony, is but like opening a few wickets, and leaving them a-jar. *Swift.*

In disputes with chairmen, when your master sends you to *chaffer* with them, take pity, and tell your master that they will not take a farthing less. *Swift.*

To CHA'FFER. *v. a.* [The active sense is obsolete.]

1. To buy.

He *chaffer'd* chairs in which churchmen were set,
And breach of laws to privy farm did let. *Spenser.*

2. To exchange.

Approaching nigh, he never staid to greet,
Ne *chaffer* words, proud courage to provoke. *Fairy Queen.*

CHA'FFERER. *n. s.* [from *chaffer.*] A buyer; bargainer; purchaser.

CHA'FFERN. *n. s.* [from *eschauffer*, Fr. to heat.] A vessel for heating water. *Dict.*

CHA'FFERY. *n. s.* [from *chaffer.*] Traffick; the practice of buying and selling.

The third is, merchandize and *chaffery*, that is, buying and selling. *Spenser's State of Ireland.*

CHA'FFINCH. *n. s.* [from *chaff* and *finch.*] A bird so called, because it delights in chaff, and is by some much admired for its song. *Phillips's World of Words.*

The *chaffinch*, and other small birds, are injurious to some fruits. *Mortimer's Husbandry.*

CHA'FFLESS. *adj.* [from *chaff.*] Without chaff.

The love I bear him,
Made me to fan you thus; but the gods made you,
Unlike all others, *chaffless*. *Shakesp. Cymbeline.*

CHA'FFWEED. *n. s.* [*gnaphalium*, Lat.] An herb; the same with *cudweed*; which see.

CHA'FFY. *adj.* [from *chaff.*] Like chaff; full of chaff; light.

If the straws be light and *chaffy*, and held at a reasonable distance, they will not rise unto the middle. *Brown's Vulgar Err.*

CHA'FINGDISH. *n. s.* [from *chafe* and *dish.*] A vessel to make any thing hot in; a portable grate for coals.

Make proof of the incorporation of silver and tin in equal quantities, whether it will endure the ordinary fire which belongeth to *chafingdishes*, posnets, and such other silver vessels.
Bacon's Physical Remains.

CHAGRI'N. *n. s.* [*chagrine*, Fr.] Ill humour; vexation; fretfulness; peevishness. It is pronounced *shagreen.*

Hear me, and touch Belinda with *chagrin*;
That single act gives half the world the spleen. *Pope.*

I grieve with the old, for so many additional inconveniencies and *chagrins*, more than their small remain of life seemed destined to undergo. *Pope's Letters.*

To CHAGRI'N. *v. a.* [*chagriner*, Fr.] To vex; to put out of temper; to teaze; to make uneasy.

CHAIN. *n. s.* [*chaine*, Fr.]

1. A series of links fastened one within another.

And Pharaoh took off his ring, and put it upon Joseph's hand, and put a gold *chain* about his neck. *Gen.* xli. 42.

2. A bond; a manacle; a fetter; something with which prisoners are bound.

Still in constraint your suff'ring sex remains,
Or bound in formal, or in real *chains*. *Pope.*

3. A line of links with which land is measured.

A surveyour may as soon, with his *chain*, measure out infinite space, as a philosopher, by the quickest flight of mind, reach it, or, by thinking, comprehend it. *Locke.*

4. A series linked together.

Those so mistake the Christian religion, as to think it is only a *chain* of fatal decrees, to deny all liberty of man's choice toward good or evil. *Hammond.*

As there is pleasure in the right exercise of any faculty, so especially in that of right reasoning; which is still the greater, by how much the consequences are more clear, and the *chains* of them more long. *Burnet's Theory of the Earth.*

To CHAIN. *v. a.* [from the noun.]

1. To fasten or link with a chain.

They repeal daily any wholesome act established against the rich, and provide more piercing statutes daily to *chain* up and restrain the poor. *Shakesp. Coriolanus.*

The mariners he *chained* in his own galleys for slaves.
Knolles's History of the Turks.

Or, march'd I *chain'd* behind the hostile car,
The victor's pastime, and the sport of war? *Prior.*
They, with joint force oppression *chaining*, set
Imperial justice at the helm. *Thomson.*

2. To bring into slavery.

This world, 'tis true,
Was made for Cæsar, but for Titus too:
And which more blest? who *chain'd* his country, say,
Or he, whose virtue sigh'd to lose a day? *Pope.*

3. To put on a chain.

The admiral seeing the mouth of the haven *chained*, and the castles full of ordnance, and strongly manned, durst not attempt to enter. *Knolles's History of the Turks.*

4. To unite.

O Warwick, I do bend my knee with thine,
And in this vow do *chain* my soul with thine.
Shakesp. Henry VI: *p.* iii.

CHA'INPUMP. *n. s.* [from *chain* and *pump.*] A pump used in large English vessels, which is double, so that one rises as the other falls. It yields a great quantity of water, works easily, and is easily mended, but takes up a great deal of room, and makes a disagreeable noise. *Chambers.*

It is not long since the striking of the topmast, a wonderful great ease to great ships both at sea and in harbour, hath been devised, together with the *chainpump*, which takes up twice as much water as the ordinary did; and we have lately added the bonnet and the drabble. *Raleigh's Essays.*

CHA'INSHOT. *n. s.* [from *chain* and *shot.*] Two bullets or half bullets, fastened together by a chain, which, when they fly open, cut away whatever is before them.

In sea fights oftentimes, a buttock, the brawn of the thigh, and the calf of the leg, are torn off by the *chainshot*, and splinters. *Wiseman's Surgery.*

CHA'INWORK. *n. s.* [from *chain* and *work.*] Work with open spaces like the links of a chain.

Nets of chequerwork, and wreaths of *chainwork*, for the chapiters which were upon the tops of the pillars. 1 *Kings*, vii. 17.

CHAIR. *n. s.* [*chair*, Fr.]

1. A moveable seat.

Whether thou choose Cervantes' serious air,
Or laugh and shake in Rab'lais' easy *chair*,
Or praise the court, or magnify mankind,
Or thy griev'd country's copper chains unbind. *Pope.*

If a *chair* be defined a seat for a single person, with a back belonging to it, then a stool is a seat for a single person, without a back. *Watts's Logick.*

2. A seat of justice, or of authority.

He makes for England, here to claim the crown.—
—Is the *chair* empty? Is the sword unsway'd?
Is the king dead? *Shakesp. Richard* III.

If thou be that princely eagle's bird,
Show thy descent by gazing 'gainst the sun;
For *chair* and dukedom, throne and kingdom, say;
Either that's thine, or else thou wert not his.
Shakesp. Henry VI. *p.* iii.

The honour'd gods
Keep Rome in safety, and the *chairs* of justice
Supply with worthy men. *Shakesp. Coriolanus.*

The committee of the commons appointed Mr. Pym to take the *chair*. *Clarendon.*

Her

Her grace ſat down to reſt a while,
In a rich *chair* of ſtate. *Shakeſp. Henry* VIII.

In this high temple, on a *chair* of ſtate,
The ſeat of audience, old Latinus ſate. *Dryden's Æneid.*

3. A vehicle born by men; a ſedan.

Think what an equipage thou haſt in air,
And view with ſcorn two pages and a *chair*. *Pope.*

CHA'IRMAN. *n. ſ.* [from *chair* and *man*.]

1. The preſident of an aſſembly.

In theſe aſſemblies generally one perſon is choſen *chairman* or moderator, to keep the ſeveral ſpeakers to the rules of order. *Watts's Improvement of the Mind.*

2. One whoſe trade it is to carry a chair.

One elbows him, one juſtles in the ſhole,
A rafter breaks his head, or *chairman*'s pole. *Dryden.*

Troy *chairmen* bore the wooden ſteed,
Pregnant with Greeks, impatient to be freed;
Thoſe bully Greeks, who, as the moderns do,
Inſtead of paying *chairmen*, run them through. *Swift.*

CHAISE. *n. ſ.* [*chaiſe*, Fr.] A carriage of pleaſure drawn by one horſe.

Inſtead of the chariot he might have ſaid the *chaiſe* of government; for a *chaiſe* is driven by the perſon that ſits in it. *Addiſon's Whig Examiner.*

CHALCO'GRAPHER. *n. ſ.* [χαλκογράφος, of χαλκὸς, braſs, and γράφω, to write or engrave.] An engraver in braſs.

CHALCO'GRAPHY. *n. ſ.* [χαλκογραφία.] Engraving in braſs.

CHA'LDER. }
CHA'LDRON. } *n. ſ.* A dry Engliſh meaſure of coals, conſiſting of thirty ſix buſhels heaped up, according to the ſealed buſhel kept at Guildhall, London. The
CHA'UDRON. }
chauldron ſhould weigh two thouſand pounds. *Chambers.*

CHA'LICE. *n. ſ.* [calic, Sax. *calice*, Fr. *calix*, Lat.]

1. A cup; a bowl.

When in your motion you are hot,
And, that he calls for drink, I'll have prepar'd him
A *chalice* for the nonce. *Shakeſp. Hamlet.*

2. It is generally uſed for a cup uſed in acts of worſhip.

All the church at that time did not think emblematical figures unlawful ornaments of cups or *chalices*. *Stillingfleet.*

CHA'LICED. *adj.* [from *calix*, Lat. the cup of a flower.] Having a cell or cup; applied by *Shakeſpeare* to a flower, but now obſolete.

Hark, hark! the lark at heav'n's gate ſings,
And Phœbus 'gins ariſe,
His ſteeds to water at theſe ſprings,
On *chalic'd* flowers that lies. *Shakeſp. Cymbeline.*

CHALK. *n. ſ.* [cealc; cealcſtan, Sax. *calck*, Welch.]

Chalk is a white foſſile, uſually reckoned a ſtone, but by ſome ranked among the boles. It is uſed in medicine as an abſorbent, and is celebrated for curing the heartburn. *Chambers.*

He maketh all the ſtones of the altar as *chalk* ſtones, that are beaten in ſunder. *Iſaiah*, xxvii. 9.

Chalk is of two ſorts; the hard, dry, ſtrong *chalk*, which is beſt for lime; and a ſoft, unctuous *chalk*, which is beſt for lands, becauſe it eaſily diſſolves with rain and froſt. *Mortimer.*

With *chalk* I firſt deſcribe a circle here,
Where theſe ethereal ſpirits muſt appear. *Dryden.*

To CHALK. *v. a.* [from the noun.]

1. To rub with chalk.

2. To manure with chalk.

Land that is *chalked*, if it is not well dunged, will receive but little benefit from a ſecond *chalking*. *Mortimer.*

3. To mark or trace out as with chalk.

Being not propt by anceſtry, whoſe grace
Chalks ſucceſſours their way. *Shakeſp. Henry* VIII.

His own mind *chalked* out to him the juſt proportions and meaſures of behaviour to his fellow creatures. *South.*

With theſe helps I might at leaſt have *chalked* out a way for others, to amend my errours in a like deſign. *Dryden.*

The time falls within the compaſs here *chalked* out by nature, very punctually. *Woodward's Natural Hiſtory.*

CHALK-CUTTER. *n. ſ.* [from *chalk* and *cut*.] A man that digs chalk.

Shells, by the ſeamen called chalk eggs, are dug up commonly in the *chalk-pits*, where the *chalk-cutters* drive a great trade with them. *Woodward.*

CHALK-PIT. *n. ſ.* [from *chalk* and *pit*.] A pit in which chalk is dug. See CHALK-CUTTER.

CHA'LKY. *adj.* [from *chalk*.]

1. Conſiſting of chalk; white with chalk.

As far as I could ken the *chalky* cliffs,
When from thy ſhore the tempeſt beats us back,
I ſtood upon the hatches in the ſtorm. *Shakeſp. Henry* VI.

That bellowing beats on Dover's *chalky* cliff. *Rowe's Royal Convert.*

2. Impregnated with chalk.

Chalky water towards the top of earth is too fretting. *Bacon.*

To CHA'LLENGE. *v. a.* [*chalenger*, Fr.]

1. To call another to anſwer for an offence by combat.

The prince of Wales ſtept forth before the king,
And, nephew, *challeng'd* you to ſingle fight. *Shakeſp. H.* IV.

2. To call to a conteſt.

Thus form'd for ſpeed, he *challenges* the wind,
And leaves the Scythian arrow far behind;
He ſcours along the field with looſen'd reins. *Dryden.*

I *challenge* any man to make any pretence to power by right of fatherhood, either intelligible or poſſible. *Locke.*

3. To accuſe.

Were the grac'd perſon of our Banquo preſent,
Whom I may rather *challenge* for unkindneſs. *Shak. Macbeth.*

4. In law; to object to the impartiality of any one. [See the noun.]

Though only twelve are ſworn, yet twenty four are to be returned, to ſupply the defects or want of appearance of thoſe that are *challenged* off, or make default. *Hale's Common Law.*

5. To claim as due.

The utter diſturbance of that divine order, whereby the preeminence of chiefeſt acceptation is by the beſt things worthily *challenged*. *Hooker, b.* i. § 7.

Which of you, ſhall we ſay, doth love us moſt?
That we our largeſt bounty may extend,
Where nature doth with merit *challenge*. *Shakeſp. K. Lear.*

And ſo much duty as my mother ſhew'd
To you, preferring you before her father;
So much I *challenge*, that I may profeſs
Due to the moor, my lord. *Shakeſp. Othello.*

Had you not been their father, theſe white flakes
Did *challenge* pity of them. *Shakeſp. K. Lear.*

So when a tyger ſucks the bullocks blood,
A famiſh'd lion, iſſuing from the wood,
Roars loudly fierce, and *challenges* the food. *Dryden's Fables.*

Haſt thou yet drawn o'er young Juba?
That ſtill would recommend thee more to Cæſar,
And *challenge* better terms. *Addiſon's Cato.*

6. To call any one to the performance of conditions.

I will now *challenge* you of your promiſe, to give me certain rules as to the principles of blazonry. *Peacham on Drawing.*

CHA'LLENGE. *n. ſ.* [from the verb.]

1. A ſummons to combat.

I never in my life
Did hear a *challenge* urg'd more modeſtly. *Shakeſp. H.* IV.

2. A demand of ſomething as due.

There muſt be no *challenge* of ſuperiority, or diſcountenancing of freedom. *Collier of Friendſhip.*

3. In law. An exception taken either againſt perſons or things; perſons, as in aſſize to the jurors, or any one or more of them, by the priſoner at the bar. *Challenge* made to the jurours, is either made to the array, or to the polls: *challenge* made to the array is, when the whole number is excepted againſt, as partially empannelled: *challenge* to or by the poll, is when ſome one or more are excepted againſt, as not indifferent: *challenge* to the jurours is divided into *challenge* principal, and *challenge* for cauſe: *challenge* principal is that which the law allows without cauſe alleged, or farther examination; as a priſoner at the bar, arraigned upon felony, may peremptorily challenge to the number of twenty, one after another, of the jury empannelled upon him, alleging no cauſe. *Cowel.*

You are mine enemy, I make my *challenge*,
You ſhall not be my judge. *Shakeſp. Henry* VIII.

CHA'LLENGER. *n. ſ.* [from *challenge*.]

1. One that defies or ſummons another to combat.

Young man, have you challenged Charles the wreſtler?—No, fair princeſs; he is the general *challenger*. *Shakeſp. As you like it.*

Death was denounc'd;
He took the ſummons, void of fear,
And unconcernedly caſt his eyes around,
As if to find and dare the grieſly *challenger*. *Dryden.*

2. One that claims ſuperiority.

Whoſe worth
Stood *challenger* on mount of all the age,
For her perfections. *Shakeſp. Hamlet.*

3. A claimant; one that requires ſomething as of right.

Earneſt *challengers* there are of trial, by ſome publick diſputation. *Hooker, Preface.*

CHALY'BEATE. *adj.* [from *chalybs*, Lat. ſteel.] Impregnated with iron or ſteel; having the qualities of ſteel.

The diet ought to ſtrengthen the ſolids, allowing ſpices and wine, and the uſe of *chalybeate* waters. *Arbuthnot on Diet.*

CHAMA'DE. *n. ſ.* [French.] The beat of the drum which declares a ſurrender.

Several French battalions made a ſhew of reſiſtance; but, upon our preparing to fill up a little foſſé, in order to attack them, they beat the *chamade*, and ſent us charte blanche. *Addiſon. Spectator*, N° 165.

CHA'MBER. *n. ſ.* [*chambre*, Fr. *camera*, Lat. *ſiambr*, Welch.]

1. An apartment in a houſe; generally uſed for thoſe appropriated to lodging.

Welcome, ſweet prince, to London, to your *chamber*. *Shakeſp. Richard* III.

Bid

Bid them come forth, and hear me,
Or at their *chamber* door I'll beat the drum,
Till it cry ſleep to death. *Shakeſp. King Lear.*
When we have mark'd with blood thoſe ſleepy two,
Of his own *chamber.* *Shakeſp. Hamlet.*

A natural cave in a rock may have ſomething not much unlike to parlours or *chambers.* *Bentley.*

2. Any retired room.

The dark caves of death, and *chambers* of the grave. *Prior.*

3. Any cavity or hollow.

Petit has, from an examination of the figure of the eye, argued againſt the poſſibility of a film's exiſtence in the poſteriour *chamber.* *Sharp.*

4. A court of juſtice.

In the Imperial *chamber* this vulgar anſwer is not admitted, *viz.* I do not believe it, as the matter is propounded and alleged. *Ayliffe's Parergon.*

5. The hollow part of a gun where the charge is lodged.

6. A ſpecies of great gun.

Names given them, as cannons, demi-cannons, *chambers,* arquebuſe, muſket, &c. *Camden's Remains.*

7. The cavity where the powder is lodged in a mine.

To CHA'MBER. *v. n.* [from the noun.]

1. To be wanton; to intrigue.

Let us walk honeſtly as in the day, not in rioting and drunkenneſs, not in *chambering* and wantonneſs. *Rom.* xiii. 13.

2. To reſide as in a chamber.

The beſt blood *chamber'd* in his boſom. *Shakeſp. Rich.* II.

CHA'MBERER. *n. ſ.* [from *chamber.*] A man of intrigue.

I have not thoſe ſoft parts of converſation,
That *chamberers* have. *Shakeſp. Othello.*

CHA'MBERFELLOW. *n. ſ.* [from *chamber* and *fellow.*] One that lies in the ſame chamber.

It is my fortune to have a *chamberfellow,* with whom I agree very well in many ſentiments. *Spectator,* N° 286.

CHA'MBERLAIN. *n. ſ.* [from *chamber.*]

1. Lord great chamberlain of England is the ſixth officer of the crown; a conſiderable part of his function is at a coronation; to him belongs the proviſion of every thing in the houſe of lords; he diſpoſes of the ſword of ſtate; under him are the gentleman uſher of the black rod, yeomen uſhers, and door-keepers. To this office the duke of Ancaſter makes an hereditary claim. *Chambers.*

2. Lord chamberlain of the houſhold has the overſight of all officers belonging to the king's chambers, except the precinct of the bedchamber. *Chambers.*

Humbly complaining to her deity,
Got my lord *chamberlain* his liberty. *Shakeſp. Rich.* II.

He was made lord ſteward, that the ſtaff of *chamberlain* might be put into the hands of his brother. *Clarendon.*

A patriot is a fool in every age,
Whom all lord *chamberlains* allow the ſtage. *Pope.*

3. A ſervant who has the care of the chambers.

Think'ſt thou,
That the bleak air, thy boiſterous *chamberlain,*
Will put thy ſhirt on warm? *Shakeſp. Timon.*
When Duncan is aſleep, his two *chamberlains*
We will with wine and waſſel convince. *Shakeſp. Macbeth.*
He ſerv'd at firſt Æmilia's *chamberlain.* *Dryden's Fables.*

4. A receiver of rents and revenues; as, *chamberlain* of the exchequer, of Cheſter, of the city of London. *Chambers.*

CHA'MBERLAINSHIP. *n. ſ.* [from *chamberlain.*] The office of a chamberlain.

CHA'MBERMAID. *n. ſ.* [from *chamber* and *maid.*] A maid whoſe buſineſs is to dreſs a lady, and wait in her chamber.

Men will not hiſs,
The *chambermaid* was named Ciſs. *Ben. Johnſon.*
Some coarſe country wench, almoſt decay'd,
Trudges to town, and firſt turns *chambermaid.* *Pope.*

When he doubted whether a word were intelligible or no, he uſed to conſult one of his lady's *chambermaids.* *Swift.*

If theſe nurſes ever preſume to entertain the girls with the common follies practiſed by *chambermaids* among us, they are publickly whipped. *Swift's Gulliver's Travels.*

To CHA'MBLET. *v. a.* [from *camelot.* See CAMELOT.] To vary; to variegate.

Some have the veins more varied and *chambleted;* as oak, whereof wainſcot is made. *Bacon's Natural Hiſtory.*

CHA'MBREL *of a Horſe.* The joint or bending of the upper part of the hinder leg. *Farrier's Dict.*

CHAME'LEON. *n. ſ.* [χαμαίλεων.]

The *chameleon* has four feet, and on each foot three claws. Its tail is long; with this, as well as with its feet, it faſtens itſelf to the branches of trees. Its tail is flat, its noſe long, and made in an obtuſe point; its back is ſharp, its ſkin plaited, and jagged like a ſaw from the neck to the laſt joint of the tail, and upon its head it has ſomething like a comb; like a fiſh, it has no neck. Some have aſſerted, that it lives only upon air; but it has been obſerved to feed on flies, catched with its tongue, which is about ten inches long, and three thick; made of white fleſh, round, but flat at the end; or hollow and open, reſembling an elephant's trunk. It alſo ſhrinks, and grows longer. This animal is ſaid to aſſume the colour of thoſe things to which it is applied; but our modern obſervers aſſure us, that its natural colour, when at reſt and in the ſhade, is a bluiſh grey; though ſome are yellow, and others green, but both of a ſmaller kind. When it is expoſed to the ſun, the grey changes into a darker grey, inclining to a dun colour, and its parts, which have leaſt of the light upon them, are changed into ſpots of different colours. The grain of its ſkin, when the light doth not ſhine upon it, is like cloth mixed with many colours. Sometimes when it is handled, it ſeems to be ſpeckled with dark ſpots, inclining to green. If it be put upon a black hat, it appears to be of a violet colour; and ſometimes if it be wrapped up in linen, when it is taken off, it is white; but it changes colour only in ſome parts of the body. *Calmet.*

A *chameleon* is a creature about the bigneſs of an ordinary lizard; his head unproportionably big, and his eyes great; he moveth his head without writhing of his neck, which is inflexible, as a hog doth; his back crooked, his ſkin ſpotted with little tumours, leſs eminent nearer the belly; his tail ſlender and long; on each foot he hath five fingers, three on the outſide, and two on the inſide; his tongue of a marvellous length in reſpect of his body, and hollow at the end, which he will launch out to prey upon flies; of colour green, and of a duſky yellow, brighter and whiter towards the belly; yet ſpotted with blue, white, and red. *Bacon's Natural Hiſtory,* N° 360.

I can add colours ev'n to the *chameleon;*
Change ſhapes with Proteus, for advantage. *Shakeſp. Hen* VI.

One part devours the other, and leaves not ſo much as a mouthful of that popular air, which the *chameleons* gaſp after. *Decay of Piety.*

The thin *chameleon,* fed with air, receives
The colour of the thing to which he cleaves. *Dryden.*

To CHA'MFER. *v. a.* [*chambrer,* Fr.] To channel; to make furrows or gutters upon a column.

CHA'MFER. } *n. ſ.* [from *to chamfer.*] A ſmall furrow or gut-
CHA'MFRET. } ter on a column.

CHA'MLET. *n. ſ.* [See CAMELOT.]

To make a *chamlet,* draw five lines, waved overthwart, if your diapering conſiſt of a double line. *Peacham on Drawing.*

CHA'MOIS. *n. ſ.* [*chamois,* Fr.] An animal of the goat kind, whoſe ſkin is made into ſoft leather, called among us *ſhammy.*

Theſe are the beaſts which you ſhall eat; the ox, the ſheep, and wild ox, and the *chamois.* *Deut.* xiv. 5.

CHA'MOMILE. *n. ſ.* [χαμαιμῆλον.] The name of an odoriferous plant.

It hath a fibroſe root; the cup of the flower is ſquamoſe, which expands, and appears like many leaves; the flowers are radicated; the petals of the flower are white, and the diſh yellow; the leaves are cut into five ſegments. This plant was formerly in great requeſt for making green walks, and is ſtill cultivated in phyſick gardens for medicinal uſe, though it grows wild in great plenty. *Miller.*

Cool violets, and orpine growing ſtill,
Embathed balm, and cheerful galingale,
Freſh coſtmary, and breathful *chamomile,*
Dull poppy, and drink-quick'ning ſetuale. *Spenſer's Muiop.*

For though the *chamomile,* the more it is trodden on the faſter it grows; yet youth, the more it is waſted, the ſooner it wears. *Shakeſp. Henry* IV. *p.* i.

Watery liquours force it, as diſtilled waters with diureticks, poſſet drink with *chamomile* flowers. *Floyer on the Humours.*

To CHAMP. *v. a.* [*champayer,* Fr.]

1. To bite with a frequent action of the teeth.

Coffee and opium are taken down, tobacco but in ſmoke, and betle is but *champed* in the mouth with a little lime. *Bacon.*

The fiend reply'd not, overcome with rage;
But, like a proud ſteed rein'd, went haughty on,
Champing his iron curb. *Paradiſe Loſt, b.* iv. *l.* 857.
At his command,
The ſteeds capariſon'd with purple ſtand,
And *champ* betwixt their teeth the foaming gold. *Dryden.*

2. To devour.

A tobacco pipe happened to break in my mouth, and the pieces left ſuch a delicious roughneſs on my tongue, that I *champed* up the remaining part. *Spectator,* N° 431.

To CHAMP. *v. n.* To perform frequently the action of biting.

Muttering and *champing,* as though his cud had troubled him, he gave occaſion to Muſidorus to come near him. *Sidney.*

They began to repent of that they had done, and irefully to *champ* upon the bit they had taken into their mouths. *Hooker.*

His jaws did not anſwer equally to one another; but by his frequent motion and *champing* with them, it was evident they were neither luxated nor fractured. *Wiſeman.*

CHA'MPAIGN. *n. ſ.* [*campagne,* Fr.] A flat open country.

In the abuſes of the cuſtoms, meſeems, you have a fair *champaign* laid open to you, in which you may at large ſtretch out your diſcourſe. *Spenſer's State of Ireland.*

Of all theſe bounds,
With ſhadowy foreſts and with *champaigns* rich'd,
We make thee lady. *Shakeſp. King Lear.*

If two bordering princes have their territory meeting on an open *champaign,* the more mighty will continually ſeek occaſion to to extend his limits unto the further border thereof. *Raleigh.*

Sir John Norris maintained a retreat without diſarray, by the ſpace of ſome miles, part of the way *champaign*, unto the city of Gaunt, with leſs loſs of men than the enemy. *Bacon.*

From his ſide two rivers flow'd,
Th' one winding, th' other ſtraight, and left between
Fair *champaign*, with leſs rivers interveen'd. *Paradiſe Reg.*

CHA'MPERTORS. *n. ſ.* [from *champerty*. In law.] Such as move ſuits, or cauſe them to be moved, either by their own or others procurement, and purſue, at their proper coſts, to have part of the land in conteſt, or part of the gains. *Cowel.*

CHA'MPERTY. *n. ſ.* [*champart*, Fr. In law.] A maintenance of any man in his ſuit while depending, upon condition to have part of the thing when it is recovered. *Cowel.*

CHAMPI'GNON. *n. ſ.* [*champignon*, Fr.] A kind of muſhroom.

He viler friends with doubtful muſhrooms treats,
Secure for you, himſelf *champignons* eats. *Dryden.*

It has the reſemblance of a large *champignon* before it is opened, branching out into a large round knob at one end. *Woodward on Foſſils.*

CHA'MPION. *n. ſ.* [*champion*, Fr. *campio*, low Lat.]

1. A man who undertakes a cauſe in ſingle combat.

In many armies, if the matter ſhould be tried by duel between two *champions*, the victory would go on the one ſide. *Bacon's Coll. of Good and Evil.*

For hot, cold, moiſt, and dry, four *champions* fierce,
Strive here for maſt'ry, and to battle bring
Their embryon atoms. *Par. Loſt, b.* ii. *l.* 898.

O light of Trojans, and ſupport of Troy,
Thy father's *champion*, and thy country's joy! *Dryden.*

At length the adverſe admirals appear,
The two bold *champions* of each country's right. *Dryden.*

2. A hero; a ſtout warriour.

A ſtouter *champion* never handled ſword. *Shakeſp. H.* VI.

This makes you incapable of conviction, and they applaud themſelves as zealous *champions* for truth, when indeed they are contending for errour. *Locke.*

3. In law.

In our common law, *champion* is taken no leſs for him that trieth the combat in his own caſe, than for him that fighteth in the caſe of another. *Cowel.*

To CHA'MPION. *v. a.* [from the noun.] To challenge to the combat.

The ſeed of Banquo, kings!
Rather than ſo, come, fate, into the liſt,
And *champion* me to th' utterance. *Shakeſp. Macbeth.*

CHANCE. *n. ſ.* [*chance*, Fr.]

1. Fortune; the cauſe of fortuitous events.

As th' unthought accident is guilty
Of what we wildly do, ſo we profeſs
Ourſelves to be the ſlaves of *chance*, and flies
Of every wind that blows. *Shakeſp. Winter's Tale.*

The only man of all that *chance* could bring,
To meet my arms, was worth the conquering. *Dryden.*

Chance is but a mere name, and really nothing in itſelf; a conception of our minds, and only a compendious way of ſpeaking, whereby we would expreſs, that ſuch effects as are commonly attributed to *chance*, were verily produced by their true and proper cauſes, but without their deſign to produce them. *Bentley.*

2. Fortune; the act of fortune, or chance.

Theſe things are commonly not obſerved, but left to take their *chance*. *Bacon's Eſſays.*

3. Accident; caſual occurrence; fortuitous event.

To ſay a thing is a *chance* or caſualty, as it relates to ſecond cauſes, is not profaneneſs, but a great truth; as ſignifying no more, than that there are ſome events beſides the knowledge and power of ſecond agents. *South.*

The beauty I beheld, has ſtruck me dead;
Unknowingly ſhe ſtrikes, and kills by *chance*;
Poiſon is in her eyes, and death in ev'ry glance. *Dryden.*

All nature is but art, unknown to thee;
All *chance* direction, which thou canſt not ſee. *Pope.*

4. Event; ſucceſs; luck.

Now we'll together, and the *chance* of goodneſs
Be like our warranted quarrel! *Shakeſp. Macbeth.*

5. Misfortune; unlucky accident.

You were us'd
To ſay, extremity was the trier of ſpirits,
That common *chances* common men could bear. *Shakeſp. Coriolanus.*

6. Poſſibility of any occurrence.

A *chance*, but chance may lead, where I may meet
Some wand'ring ſpirit of heav'n, by fountain ſide,
Or in thick ſhade retir'd. *Paradiſe Loſt, b.* iv. *l.* 530.

Then your ladyſhip might have a *chance* to eſcape this addreſs. *Swift.*

CHANCE. *adj.* [It is ſeldom uſed but in compoſition.] Happening by chance.

Now ſhould they part, malicious tongues would ſay,
They met like *chance* companions on the way. *Dryden's Hind and Panther.*

I would not take the gift,
Which, like a toy dropt from the hands of fortune,
Lay for the next *chance* comer. *Dryden and Lee's OEdipus.*

To CHANCE. *v. n.* [from the noun.] To happen; to fall out; to fortune.

Think what a chance thou *chanceſt* on; but think;——
Thou haſt thy miſtreſs ſtill. *Shakeſp. Cymbeline.*

How *chance* thou art not with the prince thy brother?
Shakeſp. Henry IV. *p.* ii.

Ay, Caſca, tell us what hath *chanc'd* today,
That Cæſar looks ſo ſad. *Shakeſp. Julius Cæſar.*

He *chanced* upon divers of the Turks victuallers, whom he eaſily took. *Knolles's Hiſtory of the Turks.*

I choſe the ſafer ſea, and *chanc'd* to find
A river's mouth impervious to the wind. *Pope's Odyſſey.*

CHANCE-MEDLEY. *n. ſ.* [from *chance* and *medley*. In law.]

The caſual ſlaughter of a man, not altogether without the fault of the ſlayer, when ignorance or negligence is joined with the chance; as if a man lop trees by an highway-ſide, by which many uſually travel, and caſt down a bough, not giving warning to take heed thereof, by which bough one paſſing by is ſlain: in this caſe he offends, becauſe he gave no warning, that the party might have taken heed to himſelf. *Cowel.*

If ſuch an one ſhould have the ill hap, at any time, to ſtrike a man dead with a ſmart ſaying, it ought, in all reaſon and conſcience, to be judged but a *chancemedley*. *South.*

CHA'NCEABLE. *adj.* [from *chance*.] Accidental.

The trial thereof was cut off by the *chanceable* coming thither of the king of Iberia. *Sidney, b.* ii.

CHA'NCEL. *n. ſ.* [from *cancelli*, Lat. lettices, with which the chancel was incloſed.] The eaſtern part of the church, in which the altar is placed.

Whether it be allowable or no, that the miniſter ſhould ſay ſervice in the *chancel*. *Hooker, b.* v. § 30.

The *chancel* of this church is vaulted with a ſingle ſtone of four feet in thickneſs, and an hundred and fourteen in circumference. *Addiſon's Remarks on Italy.*

CHA'NCELLOR. *n. ſ.* [*cancellarius*, Lat. *chancelier*, Fr. from *cancellare*, *literas vel ſcriptum linea per medium ducta damnare*, and ſeemeth of itſelf likewiſe to be derived *à cancellis*, which ſignify all one with κιγκλὶς, a lettice; that is, a thing made of wood or iron bars, laid croſsways one over another, ſo that a man may ſee through them in and out. It may be thought that judgment ſeats were compaſſed in with bars, to defend the judges and other officers from the preſs of the multitude, and yet not to hinder any man's view.]

Quæſitus regni tibi cancellarius *Angli,*
Primus ſolliciti mente petendus erit.
Hic eſt, qui regni leges cancellat iniquas,
Et mandata pii principis æqua facit.
Verſes of *Nigel de Wetekre* to the biſhop of Ely, chancellor to Richard I.

1. *Cancellarius*, at the firſt, ſignified the regiſters or actuaries in court; *grapharios*, *ſcil. qui conſcribendis & excipiendis judicum actis dant operam.* But this name is greatly advanced, and not only in other kingdoms but in this, is given to him that is the chief judge in cauſes of property; for the *chancellor* hath power to moderate and temper the written law, and ſubjecteth himſelf only to the law of nature and conſcience. *Cowel.*

Turn out, you rogue, how like a beaſt you lie:
Go, buckle to the law: Is this an hour
To ſtretch your limbs? you'll ne'er be *chancellor*. *Dryd. jun.*

Ariſtides was a perſon of the ſtricteſt juſtice, and beſt acquainted with the laws, as well as forms of their government; ſo that he was in a manner *chancellor* of Athens. *Swift.*

2. **CHANCELLOR** *in the Eccleſiaſtical Court.* A biſhop's lawyer; a man trained up in the civil and canon law, to direct the biſhops in matters of judgment, relating as well to criminal as to civil affairs in the church. *Ayliffe's Parergon.*

3. **CHANCELLOR** *of a Cathedral.* A dignitary, whoſe office it is to ſuperintend the regular exerciſe of devotion.

4. **CHANCELLOR** *of the Exchequer.* An officer who ſits in that court, and in the exchequer chamber, and, with the reſt of the court, ordereth things to the king's beſt benefit. He has power, with others, to compound for forfeitures on penal ſtatutes, bonds and recognizances entered into by the king. He has great authority in managing the royal revenue, and in matters of firſt-fruits. The court of equity is in the exchequer chamber, and is held before the lord treaſurer, *chancellor*, and barons, as that of common law before the barons only. *Cowel. Chamb.*

5. **CHANCELLOR** *of an Univerſity.* The principal magiſtrate, who, at Oxford, holds his office during life, but, at Cambridge, he may be elected every three years.

6. **CHANCELLOR** *of the Order of the Garter*, and other military orders, is an officer who ſeals the commiſſions and mandates of the chapter and aſſembly of the knights, keeps the regiſter of their deliberations, and delivers their acts under the ſeal of the order. *Chambers.*

CHA'NCELLORSHIP. *n. ſ.* The office of chancellor.

The next Sunday after he gave up his *chancellorſhip* of England, he came himſelf to his wife's pew, and uſed the uſual words of his gentleman-uſher, Madam, my lord is gone. *Camd.*

CHA'NCERY. *n. f.* [from *chancellor*; probably *chancellery*; then ſhortened.] The court of equity and conſcience, moderating the rigour of other courts, that are tied to the letter of the law; whereof the lord chancellor of England is the chief judge, or the lord keeper of the great ſeal. *Cowel.*

The contumacy and contempt of the party muſt be ſignified in the court of *chancery*, by the biſhops letters under the ſeal epiſcopal. *Ayliffe's Parergon.*

CHA'NCRE. *n. f.* [*chancre*, Fr.] An ulcer uſually ariſing from venereal maladies.

It is poſſible he was not well cured, and would have relapſed with a *chancre*. *Wiſeman.*

CHA'NCROUS. *adj.* [from *chancre*.] Having the qualities of a chancre; ulcerous.

You may think I am too ſtrict in giving ſo many internals in the cure of ſo ſmall an ulcer as a chancre, or rather a *chancrous* callus. *Wiſeman.*

CHANDELI'ER. *n. f.* [*chandelier*, Fr.] A branch for candles.

CHA'NDLER. *n. f.* [*chandelier*, Fr.] An artiſan whoſe trade it is to make candles, or a perſon who ſells them.

The ſack that thou haſt drunken me, would have bought me lights as good cheap at the deareſt *chandlers* in Europe. *Shakeſp. Henry* IV. *p.* i.

But whether black or lighter dies are worn,
The *chandler*'s baſket, on his ſhoulder born,
With tallow ſpots thy coat. *Gay's Trivia.*

CHA'NFRIN. *n. f.* [old French.] The forepart of the head of a horſe, which extends from under the ears, along the interval between the eyebrows, down to his noſe. *Farrier's Dict.*

To CHANGE. *v. a.* [*changer*, Fr. *cambio*, Lat.]

1. To put one thing in the place of another.

He that cannot look into his own eſtate, had need chooſe well whom he employeth, and *change* them often; for new are more timorous, and leſs ſubtile. *Bacon's Eſſays.*

2. To reſign any thing for the ſake of another, with *for* before the thing taken or received.

Perſons grown up in the belief of any religion, cannot *change* that *for* another, without applying their underſtanding duly to conſider and compare both. *South.*

The French and we ſtill change; but here's the curſe,
They *change for* better, and we *change for* worſe.
Dryden's Spaniſh Friar, Prologue.

3. To diſcount a larger piece of money into ſeveral ſmaller.

A ſhopkeeper might be able to *change* a guinea, or a moidore, when a cuſtomer comes for a crown's worth of goods. *Swift's Intelligencer*, N° 19.

4. To give and take reciprocally, with the particle *with* before the perſon to whom we give, and from whom we take.

To ſecure thy content, look upon thoſe thouſands, *with* whom thou wouldſt not, for any intereſt, *change* thy fortune and condition. *Taylor's Rule of Living Holy.*

5. To alter.

Thou ſhalt not ſee me bluſh,
Nor *change* my countenance for this arreſt;
A heart unſpotted is not eaſily daunted. *Shakeſp. Henry* VI.

Whatſoever is brought upon thee, take chearfully, and be patient when thou art *changed* to a low eſtate. *Ecclus*, ii. 4.

For the elements were *changed* in themſelves by a kind of harmony, like as in a pſaltery notes *change* the name of the tune, and yet are always ſounds. *Wiſdom*, xix. 18.

6. To mend the diſpoſition or mind.

I would ſhe were in heaven, ſo ſhe could
Intreat ſome pow'r to *change* this curriſh Jew.
Shakeſp. Merchant of Venice.

7. *To change a horſe*, or *to change hand*, is to turn or bear the horſe's head from one hand to the other, from the left to the right, or from the right to the left. *Farrier's Dict.*

To CHANGE. *v. n.*

1. To undergo change; to ſuffer alteration; as, his fortune may ſoon *change*, though he is now ſo ſecure.

One Julia, that his *changing* thought forgot,
Would better fit his chamber. *Shakeſp. Two Gent. of Verona.*

2. To change, as the moon; to begin a new monthly revolution.

I am weary of this moon; would he would *change*.
Shakeſp. Midſummer Night's Dream.

CHANGE. *n. f.* [from the verb.]

1. An alteration of the ſtate of any thing.

Since I ſaw you laſt,
There is a *change* upon you. *Shakeſp. Antony and Cleopatra.*

2. A ſucceſſion of one thing in the place of another.

O wond'rous *changes* of a fatal ſcene,
Still varying to the laſt! *Dryden.*

Nothing can cure this part of ill breeding, but *change* and variety of company, and that of perſons above us. *Locke.*

Empires by various turns ſhall riſe and ſet;
While thy abandon'd tribes ſhall only know
A diff'rent maſter, and a *change* of time. *Prior.*

Hear how Timotheus' various lays ſurprize,
And bid alternate paſſions fall and riſe!
While, at each *change*, the ſon of Libyan Jove
Now burns with glory, and then melts with love. *Pope.*

3. The time of the moon in which it begins a new monthly revolution.

Take ſeeds or roots, and ſet ſome of them immediately after the *change*, and others of the ſame kind immediately after the full. *Bacon's Nat. Hiſtory*, N° 893.

4. Novelty.

The hearts
Of all his people ſhall revolt from him,
And kiſs the lips of unacquainted *change*. *Shakeſp. K. John.*

Our fathers did, for *change*, to France repair,
And they, for *change*, will try our Engliſh air.
Dryden's Spaniſh Friar, Prologue.

5. In ringing; an alteration of the order in which a ſet of bells is ſounded.

Four bells admit twenty-four *changes* in ringing, and five bells one hundred and twenty. *Holder's Elements of Speech.*

Eaſy it may be to contrive new poſtures, and ring other *changes* upon the ſame bells. *Norris.*

6. That which makes a variety; that which may be uſed for another of the ſame kind.

I will now put forth a riddle unto you; if you can find it out, then I will give you thirty ſheets, and thirty *change* of garments. *Judges*, xiv. 12.

7. Small money, which may be given for larger pieces.

Wood buys up our old halfpence, and from thence the preſent want of *change* ariſes; but ſuppoſing not one farthing of *change* in the nation, five and twenty thouſand pounds would be ſufficient. *Swift.*

CHA'NGEABLE. *adj.* [from *change*.]

1. Subject to change; fickle; inconſtant.

A ſteady mind will admit ſteady methods and counſels; but there is no meaſure to be taken of a *changeable* humour. *L'Eſtrange.*

As I am a man, I muſt be *changeable*; and ſometimes the graveſt of us all are ſo, even upon ridiculous accidents.
Dryden's Aurengzebe, Preface.

2. Poſſible to be changed.

The fibrous or vaſcular parts of vegetables ſeem ſcarce *changeable* in the alimentary duct. *Arbuthnot on Aliments.*

3. Having the quality of exhibiting different appearances.

Now the taylor make thy doublet of *changeable* taffata; for thy mind is a very opal. *Shakeſp. Twelfth Night.*

CHA'NGEABLENESS. *n. f.* [from *changeable*.]

1. Inconſtancy; fickleneſs.

At length he betrothed himſelf to one worthy to be liked, if any worthineſs might excuſe ſo unworthy a *changeableneſs*. *Sidney*, *b.* ii.

There is no temper of mind more unmanly than that *changeableneſs* with which we are too juſtly branded by all our neighbours. *Addiſon. Freeholder*, N° 25.

2. Suſceptibility of change.

If how long they are to continue in force, be no where expreſſed, then have we no light to direct our judgment concerning the *changeableneſs* or immutability of them, but conſidering the nature and quality of ſuch laws. *Hooker*, *b.* iii. § 10.

CHA'NGEABLY. *adv.* [from *changeable*.] Inconſtantly.

CHA'NGEFUL. *adj.* [from *change* and *full*.] Full of change; inconſtant; uncertain; mutable; ſubject to variation; fickle.

Unſound plots, and *changeful* orders, are daily deviſed for her good, yet never effectually proſecuted or performed.
Spenſer on Ireland.

Britain, *changeful* as a child at play,
Now calls in princes, and now turns away. *Pope.*

CHA'NGELING. *n. f.* [from *change*; the word ariſes from an odd ſuperſtitious opinion, that the fairies ſteal away children, and put others that are ugly and ſtupid in their places.]

1. A child left or taken in the place of another.

And her baſe elfin breed there for thee left;
Such, men do *changelings* call, ſo chang'd by fairies theft.
Spenſer's Fairy Queen, *b.* i. *c.* x. *ſtanz.* 65.

She, as her attendant, hath
A lovely boy ſtol'n from an Indian king;
She never had ſo ſweet a *changeling*.
Shakeſp. Midſummer Night's Dream.

2. An ideot; a fool; a natural.

Changelings and fools of heav'n, and thence ſhut out,
Wildly we roam in diſcontent about. *Dryden's Tyrr. Love.*

Would any one be a *changeling*, becauſe he is leſs determined by wiſe conſiderations than a wiſe man? *Locke.*

3. One apt to change; a waverer.

'Twas not long
Before from world to world they ſwung;
As they had turn'd from ſide to ſide,
And as they *changelings* liv'd, they died. *Hudibras.*

CHA'NGER. *n. f.* [from *change*.] One that is employed in changing or diſcounting money.

CHA'NNEL. *n. f.* [*canal*, Fr. *canalis*, Lat.]

1. The hollow bed of running waters.

It is not ſo eaſy, now that things are grown into an habit, and have their certain courſe, to change the *channel*, and turn their ſtreams another way. *Spenſer's State of Ireland.*

Draw them to Tyber's bank, and weep your tears
Into the *channel*, till the loweſt ſtream
Do kiſs the moſt exalted ſhores of all. *Shakeſp. J. Cæſar.*

So th' injur'd ſea, which, from her wonted courſe,
To gain ſome acres, avarice did force;
If the new banks, neglected once, decay,
No longer will from her old *channel* ſtay. *Waller.*

Had not the ſaid ſtrata been diſlocated, ſome of them elevated, and others depreſſed, there would have been no cavity or *channel* to give reception to the water of the ſea. *Woodward.*

The tops of mountains and hills will be continually waſhed down by the rains, and the *channels* of rivers abraded by the ſtreams. *Bentley.*

2. Any cavity drawn longways.

Complaint and hot deſires, the lover's hell,
And ſcalding tears, that wore a *channel* where they fell. *Dryden's Fables.*

3. A ſtrait or narrow ſea, between two countries; as the Britiſh *Channel* between Britain and France; St. George's *Channel* between Britain and Ireland.

4. A gutter or furrow of a pillar.

To CHA'NNEL. *v. a.* [from the noun.] To cut any thing in channels.

No more ſhall trenching war *channel* her fields,
Nor bruiſe her flowrets with the armed hoofs
Of hoſtile paces. *Shakeſp. Henry* IV. *p.* i.

The body of this column is perpetually *channelled*, like a thick plaited gown. *Wotton's Architecture.*

Torrents, and loud impetuous cataracts,
Roll down the lofty mountain's *channel'd* ſides,
And to the vale convey their foaming tides. *Blackmore.*

To CHANT. *v. a.* [*chanter*, Fr.]

1. To ſing.

Wherein the chearful birds of ſundry kind
Do *chant* ſweet muſick. *Fairy Queen, b.* i. *c.* vii.

2. To celebrate by ſong.

The poets *chant* it in the theatres, the ſhepherds in the mountains. *Bramhall.*

3. To ſing in the cathedral ſervice.

To CHANT. *v. n.* To ſing; to make melody with the voice.

They *chant* to the ſound of the viol, and invent to themſelves inſtruments of muſick. *Amos*, vi. 7.

Heav'n heard his ſong, and haſten'd his relief;
And chang'd to ſnowy plumes his hoary hair,
And wing'd his flight, to *chant* aloft in air. *Dryden.*

CHANT. *n. ſ.* [from the verb.] Song; melody.

A pleaſant grove,
With *chant* of tuneful birds reſounding loud.
Milton's Paradiſe Loſt, b. ii. *l.* 290.

CHA'NTER. *n. ſ.* [from *chant.*] A ſinger; a ſongſter.

You curious *chanters* of the wood,
That warble forth dame Nature's lays. *Wotton.*

Jove's etherial lays, reſiſtleſs fire,
The *chanter's* ſoul, and raptur'd ſong inſpire,
Inſtinct divine! nor blame ſevere his choice,
Warbling the Grecian woes with harp and voice. *Pope.*

CHA'NTICLEER. *n. ſ.* [from *chanter* and *clair*, Fr.] The name given to the cock, from the clearneſs and loudneſs of his crow.

And chearful *chanticleer*, with his note ſhrill,
Had warned once, that Phœbus' firy car
In haſte was climbing up the eaſtern hill. *Fairy Queen, b.* i.

Hark, hark, I hear
The ſtrain of ſtrutting *chanticleer*. *Shakeſp. Tempeſt.*

Stay, the chearful *chanticleer*
Tells you that the time is near. *Ben. Johnſon's Maſk.*

Theſe verſes were mentioned by Chaucer, in the deſcription of the ſudden ſtir, and panical fear, when *Chanticleer* the cock was carried away by Reynold the fox. *Camden's Remains.*

Within this homeſtead liv'd without a peer,
For crowing loud, the noble *chanticleer*. *Dryden's Fab.*

CHA'NTRESS. *n. ſ.* [from *chant.*] A woman ſinger.

Sweet bird, that ſhun'ſt the noiſe of folly,
Moſt muſical, moſt melancholy,
Thee, *chantreſs* of the woods among,
I woo to hear thy even-ſong. *Milton.*

CHA'NTRY. *n ſ.* [from *chant.*]

Chantry is a church or chapel endowed with lands, or other yearly revenue, for the maintenance of one or more prieſts, daily to ſing maſs for the ſouls of the donors, and ſuch others as they appoint. *Cowel.*

Now go with me, and with this holy man,
Into the *chantry* by; to thoſe before him,
And, underneath that conſecrated roof,
Plight me the full aſſurance of your faith. *Shakeſp. T. Night.*

CHA'OS. *n. ſ.* [*chaos*, Lat. χάος.]

1. The maſs of matter ſuppoſed to be in confuſion before it was divided by the creation into its proper claſſes and elements.

The whole univerſe would have been a confuſed *chaos*, without beauty or order. *Bentley.*

2. Confuſion; irregular mixture.

Had I followed the worſt, I could not have brought church and ſtate to ſuch a *chaos* of confuſions, as ſome have done. *K. Charles.*

Their reaſon ſleeps, but mimick fancy wakes,
Supplies her parts, and wild ideas takes
From words and things, ill ſorted, and miſjoin'd,
The anarchy of thought, and *chaos* of the mind. *Dryden.*

3. Any thing where the parts are undiſtinguiſhed.

We ſhall have nothing but darkneſs and a *chaos* within, whatever order and light there be in things without us. *Locke.*

Pleas'd with a work, where nothing's juſt or fit,
One glaring *chaos* and wild heap of wit. *Pope.*

CHAO'TICK. *adj.* [from *chaos.*] Reſembling chaos; confuſed.

When the terraqueous globe was in a *chaotick* ſtate, and the earthy particles ſubſided, then thoſe ſeveral beds were, in all probability, repoſited in the earth. *Derham's Phyſico-Theology.*

To CHAP. *v. a.* [*kappen*, Dutch, to cut. This word ſeems originally the ſame with *chop*; nor were they probably diſtinguiſhed at firſt, otherwiſe than by accident; but they have now a meaning ſomething different, though referable to the ſame original ſenſe.] To break into *hiatus*, or gapings.

It alſo weakened more and more the arch of the earth, drying it immoderately, and *chapping* it in ſundry places. *Burnet's Theory of the Earth.*

Then would unbalanc'd heat licentious reign,
Crack the dry hill, and *chap* the ruſſet plain. *Blackmore.*

CHAP. *n. ſ.* [from the verb.] A cleft; an aperture; an opening; a gaping; a chink.

What moiſture the heat of the ſummer ſucks out of the earth, it is repaid in the rains of the next winter; and what *chaps* are made in it, are filled up again. *Burnet's Theory.*

CHAP. *n. ſ.* [This is not often uſed, except by anatomiſts, in the *ſingular.*] The upper or under part of a beaſt's mouth.

Froth fills his *chaps*, he ſends a grunting ſound,
And part he churns, and part befoams the ground. *Dryden.*

The nether *chap* in the male ſkeleton is half an inch broader than in the female, as being made to accommodate a bigger muſcle for the motion of the teeth. *Grew's Muſæum.*

CHAPE. *n. ſ.* [*chappe*, Fr.]

1. The catch of any thing by which it is held in its place; as the hook of a ſcabbard by which it ſticks in the belt; the point by which a buckle is held to the back ſtrap.

This is Monſieur Parolles, that had the whole theory of the war in the knot of his ſcarf, and the practice in the *chape* of his dagger. *Shakeſp. All's well that ends well.*

2. A braſs or ſilver tip or caſe, that ſtrenghtens the end of the ſcabbard of a ſword. *Phillips's World of Words.*

CHA'PEL. *n. ſ.* [*capella*, Lat.]

A *chapel* is of two ſorts, either adjoining to a church, as a parcel of the ſame, which men of worth build, or elſe ſeparate from the mother church, where the pariſh is wide, and is commonly called a *chapel* of eaſe, becauſe it is built for the eaſe of one or more pariſhioners, that dwell too far from the church, and is ſerved by ſome inferiour curate, provided for at the charge of the rector, or of ſuch as have benefit by it, as the compoſition or cuſtom is. *Cowel.*

She went in among thoſe few trees, ſo cloſed in the tops together, as they might ſeem a little *chapel*. *Sidney.*

Will you diſpatch us here under this tree, or ſhall we go with you to your *chapel?* *Shakeſp. As you like it.*

Where truth erecteth her church, he helps errour to rear up a *chapel* hard by. *Howel's Vocal Foreſt.*

A *chapel* will I build with large endowment. *Dryden.*

A free *chapel* is ſuch as is founded by the king of England. *Ayliffe's Parergon.*

CHA'PELESS. *adj.* [from *chape.*] Without a chape.

An old ruſty ſword, with a broken hilt, and *chapeleſs*, with two broken points. *Shakeſp. Taming of the Shrew.*

CHAPE'LLANY. *n. ſ.* [from *chapel.*]

A *chapellany* is uſually ſaid to be that which does not ſubſiſt of itſelf, but is built and founded within ſome other church, and is dependent thereon. *Ayliffe's Parergon.*

CHA'PELRY. *n. ſ.* [from *chapel.*] The juriſdiction or bounds of a chapel.

CHA'PERON. n. ſ. [French.] A kind of hood or cap worn by the knights of the garter in their habits.

I will omit the honourable habiliments, as robes of ſtate, parliament robes, *chaperons*, and caps of ſtate. *Camden.*

CHA'PFALN. *adj.* [from *chap* and *faln.*] Having the mouth ſhrunk.

A *chapfaln* beaver looſely hanging by
The cloven helm. *Dryden's Juv. ſat.* 10.

CHA'PITER. *n. ſ.* [*chapiteau*, Fr.] The upper part or capital of a pillar.

He overlaid your *chapiters* and your fillets with gold. *Exodus*, xxxvi. 38.

CHA'PLAIN. *n. ſ.* [*capellanus*, Latin.] He that performs divine ſervice in a chapel, and attends the king, or other perſon, for the inſtruction of him and his family, to read prayers, and preach. *Cowel.*

Wiſhing me to permit
John de la Court, my *chaplain*, a choice hour,
To hear from him a matter of ſome moment. *Shakeſp.*

Chaplain, away! thy prieſthood ſaves thy life.
Shakeſp. Henry VI. *p.* iii.

A chief

A chief governour can never fail of ſome worthleſs illiterate *chaplain*, fond of a title and precedence. *Swift.*

CHA'PLAINSHIP. *n. ſ.* [from *chaplain.*]
1. The office or buſineſs of a chaplain.
2. The poſſeſſion or revenue of a chapel.

CHA'PLESS. *adj.* [from *chap.*] Without any fleſh about the mouth.

Now my lady Worm's *chapleſs*, and knocked about the muzzard with a ſexton's ſpade. *Shakeſp. Hamlet.*

Shut me nightly in a charnel-houſe,
With reeky ſhanks and yellow *chapleſs* bones.
Shakeſp. Romeo and Juliet.

CHA'PLET. *n. ſ.* [*chapelet*, Fr.]
1. A garland or wreath to be worn about the head.

Upon old hyems' chin, and icy crown,
An od'rous *chaplet* of ſweet ſummer's buds,
Is, as in mockery, ſet. *Shakeſp. Midſum. Night's Dream.*

I ſtrangely long to know,
Whether they nobler *chaplets* wear,
Thoſe that their miſtreſs' ſcorn did bear,
Or thoſe that were us'd kindly. *Suckling.*

All the quire was grac'd
With *chaplets* green, upon their foreheads plac'd. *Dryden.*

The winding ivy *chaplet* to invade,
And folded fern, that your fair forehead ſhade. *Dryden.*

They with joyful nimble wing,
Flew dutifully back again,
And made an humble *chaplet* for the king. *Swift.*

2. A ſtring of beads uſed in the Romiſh church for keeping an account of the number rehearſed of pater noſters and ave marias. A different ſort of *chaplets* is alſo uſed by the Mahometans.
3. [In architecture.] A little moulding carved into round beads, pearls, or olives.
4. [In horſemanſhip.] A couple of ſtirrup leathers, mounted each of them with a ſtirrup, and joining at top in a ſort of leather buckle, which is called the head of the *chaplet*, by which they are faſtened to the pummel of a ſaddle, after they have been adjuſted to the length and bearing of the rider. They are made uſe of both to avoid the trouble of taking up or letting down the ſtirrups, every time a perſon mounts on a different horſe and ſaddle, and to ſupply the want of academy ſaddles, which have no ſtirrups to them. *Farrier's Dict.*
5. A tuft of feathers on the peacock's head.

CHA'PMAN. *n. ſ.* [ceapman, Sax.] A cheapner; one that offers as a purchaſer.

Fair Diomede, you do as *chapmen* do,
Diſpraiſe the thing that you intend to buy.
Shakeſp. Troilus and Creſſida.

Yet have they ſeen the maps, and bought 'em too,
And underſtand 'em as moſt *chapmen* do. *Ben. Johnſon.*

There was a collection of certain rare manuſcripts, exquiſitely written in Arabick; theſe were upon ſale to the Jeſuits at Antwerp, liquouriſh *chapmen* of ſuch wares. *Wotton.*

He dreſſed two, and carried them to Samos, as the likelieſt place for a *chapman*. *L'Eſtrange.*

Their *chapmen* they betray,
Their ſhops are dens, the buyer is their prey. *Dryden.*

CHAPS. *n ſ.* [from *chap.*]
1. The mouth of a beaſt of prey.

So on the downs we ſee
A haſten'd hare from greedy greyhound go,
And paſt all hope, his *chaps* to fruſtrate ſo. *Sidney.*

Open your mouth; this will ſhake your ſhaking, I can tell you, and that ſoundly; you cannot tell who's your friend; open your *chaps* again. *Shakeſp. Tempeſt.*

Their whelps at home expect the promis'd food,
And long to temper their dry *chaps* in blood. *Dryden.*

2. It is uſed in contempt for the mouth of a man.

CHAPT. } *particip. paſſ.* [from *to chap.*]
CHA'PPED. }

Like a table upon which you may run your finger without rubs, and your nail cannot find a joint; not horrid, rough, wrinkled, gaping, or *chapt*. *Ben. Johnſon's Diſcovery.*

Cooling ointment made,
Which on their ſun-burnt cheeks and their *chapt* ſkins they laid. *Dryden's Fab.*

CHA'PTER. *n. ſ.* [*chapitre*, Fr. from *capitulum*, Lat.]
1. A diviſion of a book.

The firſt book we divide into three ſections; whereof the firſt is theſe three *chapters*. *Burnet's Theory of the Earth.*

If theſe mighty men at *chapter* and verſe, can produce then no ſcripture to overthrow our church ceremonies, I will undertake to produce ſcripture enough to warrant them. *South.*

2. From hence comes the proverbial phraſe, *to the end of the chapter*; throughout; to the end.

Money does all things; for it gives and it takes away, it makes honeſt men and knaves, fools and philoſophers; and ſo forward, *mutatis mutandis, to the end of the chapter. L'Eſtrange.*

3. *Chapter*, from *capitulum*, ſignifieth, in our common law, as in the canon law, whence it is borrowed, an aſſembly of the clergy of a cathedral or collegiate church. *Cowel.*

The abbot takes the advice and conſent of his *chapter*, before he enters on any matters of importance. *Addiſon on Italy.*

4. The place in which aſſemblies of the clergy are held.

Though the canonical conſtitution does not ſtrictly require it to be made in the cathedral, yet it matters not where it be made, either in the choir or *chapter* houſe. *Ayliffe's Parergon.*

5. The place where delinquents receive diſcipline and correction. *Ayliffe's Parergon.*
6. A decretal epiſtle. *Ayliffe's Parergon.*

CHA'PTREL. *n. ſ.* [probably from *chapiter.*] The capitals of pillars, or pillaſters, which ſupport arches, commonly called impoſts.

Let the keyſtone break without the arch, ſo much as you project over the jaums with the *chaptrels*. *Moxon's Mechanical Exerciſes.*

CHAR. *n. ſ.* [of uncertain derivation.] A fiſh found only in Winander meer in Lancaſhire.

To CHAR. *v. a.* [See CHARCOAL.] To burn wood to a black cinder.

Spraywood, in *charring*, parts frequently into various cracks. *Woodward on Foſſils.*

CHAR. *n. ſ.* [cyppe, work, Sax. *Lye.* It is derived by *Skinner*, either from *charge*, Fr. buſineſs, or cape, Sax. care, or *keeren*, Dutch, to ſweep.] Work done by the day; a ſingle job or taſk.

But a meer woman, and commanded
By ſuch poor paſſion, as the maid that milks,
And does the meaneſt *chars*. *Shakeſp. Antony and Cleopatra.*

Harveſt done, to *char* work did aſpire;
Meat, drink, and twopence, were her daily hire. *Dryden.*

To CHAR. *v. n.* [from the noun.] To work at others houſes by the day, without being a hired ſervant.

CHA'R-WOMAN. *n. ſ.* [from *char* and *woman.*] A woman hired accidentally for odd work, or ſingle days.

Get three or four *char-women* to attend you conſtantly in the kitchen, whom you pay only with the broken meat, a few coals, and all the cinders. *Swift's Directions to the Cook.*

CHA'RACTER. *n ſ.* [*character*, Lat. χαρακτὴρ.]
1. A mark; a ſtamp; a repreſentation.

In outward alſo her reſembling leſs
His image, who made both; and leſs expreſſing
The *character* of that dominion giv'n
O'er other creatures. *Paradiſe Loſt, b.* viii. *l.* 542.

2. A letter uſed in writing or printing.

But his neat cookery!——
He cut our roots in *characters*. *Shakeſp. Cymbeline.*

The purpoſe is perſpicuous even as ſubſtance,
Whoſe groſſneſs little *characters* ſum up.
Shakeſp. Troilus and Creſſida.

It were much to be wiſhed, that there were throughout the world but one ſort of *character* for each letter, to expreſs it to the eye; and that exactly proportioned to the natural alphabet formed in the mouth. *Holder's Elements of Speech.*

3. The hand or manner of writing.

I found the letter thrown in at the caſement of my cloſet.—
You know the *character* to be your brother's. *Shak. King Lear.*

4. A repreſentation of any man as to his perſonal qualities.

Each drew fair *characters*, yet none
Of theſe they feign'd, excels their own. *Denham.*

5. An account of any thing as good or bad.

This ſubterraneous paſſage is much mended, ſince Seneca gave ſo bad a *character* of it. *Addiſon on Italy.*

6. The perſon with his aſſemblage of qualities.

In a tragedy, or epick poem, the hero of the piece muſt be advanced foremoſt to the view of the reader or ſpectator; he muſt outſhine the reſt of all the *characters*; he muſt appear the prince of them, like the ſun in the Copernican ſyſtem, encompaſſed with the leſs noble planets. *Dryden's Dufreſnoy.*

Homer has excelled all the heroick poets that ever wrote, in the multitude and variety of his *characters*; every god that is admitted into his poem, acts a part which would have been ſuitable to no other deity. *Addiſon. Spectator*, Nº 273.

7. Perſonal qualities; particular conſtitution of the mind.

Nothing ſo true as what you once let fall,
Moſt women have no *characters* at all. *Pope.*

8. Adventitious qualities impreſſed by a poſt or office.

The chief honour of the magiſtrate conſiſts in maintaining the dignity of his *character* by ſuitable actions. *Atterbury.*

To CHA'RACTER. *v. a.* [from the noun.] To inſcribe; to engrave.

Theſe few precepts in thy memory
See thou *character*. *Shakeſp. Hamlet.*

Shew me one ſcar *character'd* on thy ſkin. *Shakeſp. H. VI.*

O Roſalind! theſe trees ſhall be my books,
And in their barks my thoughts I'll *character*.
Shakeſp. As you like it.

CHARACTERI'STICAL. } *adj.* [from *characterize.*] That which
CHARACTERI'STICK. } conſtitutes the character, or marks the peculiar properties of any perſon or thing.

There are ſeveral others that I take to have been likewiſe ſuch, to which yet I have not ventured to prefix that *characteriſtick* diſtinction. *Woodward on Foſſils.*

The ſhining quality of an epick hero, his magnanimity, his conſtancy, his patience, his piety, or whatever *characteriſtical* virtue his poet gives him, raiſes our admiration. *Dryden.*

CHARACTERI'STICALNESS. *n. ſ.* [from *characteriſtical.*] The quality of being peculiar to a character.

CHARACTERI'STICK. *n. ſ.* That which conſtitutes the character; that which diſtinguiſhes any thing or perſon from others.

I ſhall here endeavour to ſhew, how this vaſt invention exerts itſelf, in a manner ſuperiour to that of any poet, as it is the great and peculiar *characteriſtick* which diſtinguiſhes him from all others. *Pope's Eſſay on Homer.*

CHARACTERISTICK *of a Logarithm.* The ſame with the *index* or *exponent.*

To CHA'RACTERIZE. *v. a.* [from *character.*]

1. To give a character or an account of the perſonal qualities of any man.

It is ſome commendation, that we have avoided publickly to *characterize* any perſon, without long experience. *Swift.*

2. To engrave, or imprint.

They may be called anticipations, prenotions, or ſentiments *characterized* and engraven in the ſoul, born with it, and growing up with it. *Hale's Origin of Mankind.*

3. To mark with a particular ſtamp or token.

There are faces not only individual, but gentilitious and national; European, Aſiatick, Chineſe, African, and Grecian faces are *characterized.* *Arbuthnot on Air.*

CHA'RACTERLESS. *adj.* [from *character.*] Without a character.

When water drops have worn the ſtones of Troy,
And blind oblivion ſwallowed cities up,
And mighty ſtates *characterleſs* are grated,
To duſty nothing. *Shakeſp. Troilus aud Creſſida.*

CHA'RACTERY. *n. ſ.* [from *character.*] Impreſſion; mark; diſtinction.

Fairies uſe flowers for their *charactery.*
Shakeſp. Merry Wives of Windſor.

All my engagements I will conſtrue to thee,
All the *charactery* of my ſad brows. *Shakeſp. Julius Cæſar.*

CHA'RCOAL. *n. ſ.* [imagined by *Skinner* to be derived from *char*, buſineſs; but, by Mr. *Lye*, from *to chark*, to burn.] Coal made by burning wood under turf. It is uſed in preparing metals.

Seacoal laſts longer than *charcoal*; and *charcoal* of roots, being coaled into great pieces, laſts longer than ordinary *charcoal.* *Bacon's Natural Hiſtory,* N° 779.

Love is a fire that burns and ſparkles,
In men as nat'rally as in *charcoals*,
Which ſooty chymiſts ſtop in holes,
When out of wood they extract coals. *Hudibras.*

Is there, who, lock'd from ink and paper, ſcrawls
With deſp'rate *charcoal* round his darken'd walls? *Pope.*

CHARD. *n. ſ.* [*charde*, Fr.]

1. *Chards* of artichokes are the leaves of fair artichoke plants, tied and wrapped up all over but the top, in ſtraw, during the autumn and winter; this makes them grow white, and loſe ſome of their bitterneſs. *Chambers.*

2. *Chards* of beet, are plants of white beet tranſplanted, producing great tops, which, in the midſt, have a large white, thick, downy, and cotton-like main ſhoot, which is the true *chard.* *Mortimer.*

To CHARGE. *v. a.* [*charger*, Fr. *caricare*, Ital. from *carrus*, Lat.]

1. To entruſt; to commiſſion for a certain purpoſe. It has *with* before the thing entruſted.

And the captain of the guard *charged* Joſeph *with* them, and he ſerved them. *Geneſis*, xl. 4.

What you have *charged* me *with*, that I have done.
Shakeſp. King Lear.

2. To impute as a debt, with *on* before the debtor.

My father's, mother's, brother's death, I pardon:
That's ſomewhat ſure; a mighty ſum of murder,
Of innocent and kindred blood ſtruck off,
My prayers and penance ſhall diſcount for theſe,
And beg of heav'n to *charge* the bill *on* me. *Dryden.*

It is not barely the ploughman's pains, the reaper's and threſher's toil, and the baker's ſweat, is to be counted into the bread we eat; the plough, mill, oven, or any other utenſils, muſt all be *charged on* the account of labour. *Locke.*

3. To impute; with *on* before the perſon to whom any thing is imputed.

No more accuſe thy pen, but *charge* the crime
On native ſloth, and negligence of time. *Dryden.*

It is eaſy to account for the difficulties he *charges on* the peripatetick doctrine. *Locke.*

Perverſe mankind! whoſe wills, created free,
Charge all their woes *on* abſolute decree;
All to the dooming gods their guilt tranſlate,
And follies are miſcall'd the crimes of fate. *Pope.*

We *charge* that *upon* neceſſity, which was really deſired and choſen. *Watts's Logick.*

4. To impoſe as a taſk. It has *with* before the thing impoſed.

The goſpel *chargeth* us *with* piety towards God, and juſtice and charity to men, and temperance and chaſtity in reference to ourſelves. *Tillotſon.*

5. To accuſe; to cenſure.

Speaking thus to you, I am ſo far from *charging* you as guilty in this matter, that I can ſincerely ſay, I believe the exhortation wholly needleſs. *Wake's Preparation for Death.*

6. To accuſe. It has *with* before the crime.

And his angels he *charged with* folly. *Job*, iv. 18.

7. To challenge.

The prieſt ſhall *charge* her by an oath. *Numb.* v. 19.

Thou canſt not, cardinal, deviſe a name
So ſlight, unworthy, and ridiculous,
To *charge* me to an anſwer as the pope. *Shakeſp. K. John.*

8. To command.

I may not ſuffer you to viſit them;
The king hath ſtrictly *charg'd* the contrary. *Shakeſp. R.* III.

Why doſt thou turn thy face? I *charge* thee, anſwer
To what I ſhall enquire. *Dryden and Lee's OEdipus.*

I *charge* thee, ſtand,
And tell thy name and buſineſs in the land. *Dryden.*

9. To fall upon; to attack; to make an onſet.

With his prepared ſword he *charges* home
My unprovided body, lanc'd my arm. *Shakeſp. King Lear.*

The Grecians rally, and their pow'rs unite;
With fury *charge* us, and renew the fight. *Dryden.*

Like your heroes of antiquity, he *charges* in iron, and ſeems to deſpiſe all ornament, but intrinſick merit. *Granville.*

10. To burden; to load.

Here's the ſmell of blood ſtill; all the perfumes of Arabia will not ſweeten this little hand. Oh! oh! oh!——What a ſigh is there? the heart is ſorely *charged.* *Shakeſp. Macbeth.*

When often urg'd, unwilling to be great,
Your country calls you from your lov'd retreat,
And ſends to ſenates, *charg'd* with common care,
Which none more ſhuns, and none can better bear. *Dryden.*

Like meat ſwallowed down for pleaſure and greedineſs, which only *charges* the ſtomach, or fumes into the brain. *Temple.*

A fault in the ordinary method of education, is the *charging* of childrens memories with rules and precepts. *Locke.*

11. To fill.

It is pity the obeliſks in Rome had not been *charged* with ſeveral parts of the Egyptian hiſtories, inſtead of hieroglyphicks. *Addiſon on Italy.*

12. To load a gun with powder and bullets.

CHARGE. *n. ſ.* [from the verb.]

1. Care; truſt; cuſtody.

One of the Turks laid down letters upon a ſtone, ſaying, that in them was contained that they had in *charge.*
Knolles's Hiſt. of the Turks.

A hard diviſion, when the harmleſs ſheep
Muſt leave their lambs to hungry wolves in *charge.* *Fairfax.*

He enquired many things, as well concerning the princes which had the *charge* of the city, whether they were in hope to defend the ſame. *Knolles's Hiſtory of the Turks.*

2. Precept; mandate; command.

Saul might even lawfully have offered to God thoſe reſerved ſpoils, had not the Lord, in that particular caſe, given ſpecial *charge* to the contrary. *Hooker, b.* v. § 17.

It is not for nothing, that St. Paul giveth *charge* to beware of philoſophy; that is to ſay, ſuch knowledge as men by natural reaſon attain unto. *Hooker, b.* iii. § 8.

The leaders having *charge* from you to ſtand,
Will not go off until they hear you ſpeak. *Shakeſp. H.* IV.

He, who requires
From us no other ſervice than to keep
This one, this eaſy *charge*, of all the trees
In paradiſe, that bear delicious fruit
So various, not to taſte that only tree
Of knowledge, planted by the tree of life. *Par. Loſt, b.* iv.

3. Commiſſion; truſt conferred; office.

If large poſſeſſions, pompous titles, honourable *charges*, and profitable commiſſions, could have made this proud man happy, there would have been nothing wanting to his eſtabliſhment.
L'Eſtrange.

Go firſt the maſter of thy herds to find
True to his *charge* a loyal ſwain and kind. *Pope.*

4. It had anciently ſometimes *over* before the thing committed to truſt.

I gave my brother *charge over* Jeruſalem; for he was a faithful man, and feared God above many. *Nehemiah*, vii. 2.

5. It has *of* before the ſubject of command or truſt.

Haſt thou eaten of the tree,
Whereof I gave thee *charge* thou ſhould'ſt not eat?
Milton's Paradiſe Loſt, b. x. *l.* 123.

6. It has *upon* before the perſon charged.

He loves God with all his heart, that is, with that degree of love, which is the higheſt point of our duty, and of God's *charge upon* us. *Taylor's Rule of Living Holy.*

7. Accuſation; imputation.

We need not lay new matter to his *charge*:
What you have ſeen him do, and heard him ſpeak,
Beating your officers, curſing yourſelves. *Shakeſp. Coriolan.*

Theſe very men are continually reproaching the clergy, and laying

laying to their *charge* the pride, the avarice, the luxury, the ignorance, and superstition of popish times. *Swift.*

8. The person or thing entrusted to care or management.

Why hast thou, Satan, broke the bounds prescrib'd
To thy transgressions, and disturb'd the *charge*
Of others? *Milton's Paradise Lost, b.* iv. *l.* 879.

More had he said, but, fearful of her stay,
The starry guardian drove his *charge* away,
To some fresh pasture. *Dryden.*

Our guardian angel saw them where they sate
Above the palace of our slumb'ring king;
He sigh'd, abandoning his *charge* to fate. *Dryden.*

This part should be the governour's principal care; that an habitual gracefulness and politeness, in all his carriage, may be settled in his *charge*, as much as may be, before he goes out of his hands. *Locke.*

9. An exhortation of a judge to a jury.

10. Expence; cost.

Being long since made weary with the huge *charge*, which you have laid upon us, and with the strong endurance of so many complaints. *Spenser on Ireland.*

Their *charge* was always born by the queen, and duly paid out of the exchequer. *Bacon's Advice to Villiers.*

Witness this army of such mass and *charge*,
Led by a delicate and tender prince. *Shakesp. Hamlet.*

He liv'd as kings retire, though more at large,
From publick business, yet of equal *charge*. *Dryden.*

11. It is, in later times, commonly used in the plural, *charges*.

A man ought warily to begin *charges*, which, once begun, will continue. *Bacon's Essays.*

Ne'er put yourself to *charges*, to complain
Of wrong, which heretofore you did sustain. *Dryden.*

The last pope was at considerable *charges*, to make a little kind of harbour in this place. *Addison on Italy.*

12. Onset.

And giving a *charge* upon their enemies, like lions, they slew eleven thousand footmen, and sixteen hundred horsemen, and put all the others to flight. 2 *Macc.* xi. 11.

Honourable retreats are no ways inferiour to brave *charges*; as having less of fortune, more of discipline, and as much of valour. *Bacon's War with Spain.*

13. The signal to fall upon enemies.

Our author seems to sound a *charge*, and begins like the clangour of a trumpet. *Dryden.*

14. The posture of a weapon fitted for the attack or combat.

Their neighing coursers, daring of the spur,
Their armed staves in *charge*, their beavers down.
Shakesp. Henry IV. *p.* ii.

15. The quantity of powder and ball put into a gun.

16. Among farriers.

Charge is a preparation, or a sort of ointment, of the consistence of a thick decoction, which is applied to the shoulder-splaits, inflammations, and sprains of horses.

A *charge* is of a middle nature, between an ointment and a plaister, or between a plaister and a cataplasm. *Farrier's Dict.*

17. In heraldry.

The *charge* is that which is born upon the colour, except it be a coat divided only by partition. *Peacham.*

CHA'RGEABLE. *adj.* [from *charge.*]

1. Expensive; costly.

Divers bulwarks were demolished upon the sea coasts, in peace *chargeable*, and little serviceable in war. *Hayward.*

Neither did we eat any man's bread for nought, but wrought with labour and travel night and day, that we might not be *chargeable* to any of you. 2 *Thess.* iii. 9.

There was another accident of the same nature on the Sicilian side, much more pleasant, but less *chargeable*; for it cost nothing but wit. *Wotton.*

Considering the *chargeable* methods of their education, their numerous issue, and small income, it is next to a miracle, that no more of their children should want. *Atterbury.*

2. Imputable, as a debt or crime.

Nothing can be a reasonable ground of despising a man, but some fault or other *chargeable* upon him. *South.*

3. Subject to charge or accusation; accusable.

Your papers would be *chargeable* with something worse than indelicacy; they would be immoral. *Spectator*, Nº 286.

CHA'RGEABLENESS. *n. s.* [from *chargeable.*] Expence; cost; costliness.

That which most deters me from such trials, is not their *chargeableness*, but their unsatisfactoriness, though they should succeed. *Boyle.*

CHA'RGEABLY. *adv.* [from *chargeable.*] Expensively; at great cost.

He procured it not with his money, but by his wisdom; not *chargeably* bought by him, but liberally given by others by his means. *Ascham's Schoolmaster.*

CHA'RGER. *n. s.* [from *charge.*] A large dish.

All the tributes land and sea affords,
Heap'd in great *chargers*, load our sumptuous boards.
Denham.

This golden *charger*, snatch'd from burning Troy,
Anchises did in sacrifice employ. *Dryden's Æneid.*

Ev'n Lamb himself, at the most solemn feast,
Might have some *chargers* not exactly dress'd.
King's Art of Cookery.

Nor dare they close their eyes,
Void of a bulky *charger* near their lips,
With which in often interrupted sleep,
Their frying blood compels to irrigate
Their dry furr'd tongues. *Philips.*

CHA'RILY. *adv.* [from *chary.*] Warily; frugally.

CHA'RINESS. *n. s.* [from *chary.*] Caution; nicety; scrupulousness.

I will consent to act any villainy against him, that may not sully the *chariness* of our honesty. *Shak. Merry W. of Windsor.*

CHA'RIOT. *n. s.* [*car-rhod*, Welch, a wheeled car; for it is known the Britons fought in such; *charriot*, Fr. *carretta*, Ital.]

1. A carriage of pleasure, or state.

Thy grand captain Antony
Shall set thee on triumphant *chariots*, and
Put garlands on thy head. *Shakesp. Antony and Cleopatra.*

He skims the liquid plains,
High on his *chariot*, and with loosen'd reins,
Majestick moves along. *Dryden's Æneid.*

2. A car in which men of arms were anciently placed.

3. A lighter kind of coach with only back seats.

To CHA'RIOT. *v. a.* [from the noun.] To convey in a chariot. This word is rarely used.

An angel all in flames ascended
As in a firy column *charioting*
His godlike presence. *Milton's Agonistes.*

CHARIOTE'ER. *n. s.* [from *chariot.*] He that drives the chariot. It is used only in speaking of military chariots, and those in the ancient publick games.

The gasping *charioteer* beneath the wheel
Of his own car. *Dryden's Fables.*

The burning chariot, and the *charioteer*,
In bright Boötes and his wane appear. *Addison on Italy.*

Show us the youthful handsome *charioteer*,
Firm in his seat, and running his career. *Prior.*

CHARIOT RACE. *n. s.* [from *chariot* and *race.*] A sport anciently used, where chariots were driven for the prize, as now horses run.

There is a wonderful vigour and spirit in the description of the horse and *chariotrace*. *Addison on the Georgicks.*

CHA'RITABLE. *adj.* [*charitable*, Fr. from *charité.*]

1. Kind in giving alms; liberal to the poor.

He that hinders a *charitable* person from giving alms to a poor man, is tied to restitution, if he hindered him by fraud or violence. *Taylor's Holy Living.*

Shortly thou wilt behold me poor, and kneeling
Before thy *charitable* door for bread. *Rowe's Jane Shore.*

How shall we then wish, that it might be allowed us to live over our lives again, in order to fill every minute of them with *charitable* offices! *Atterbury.*

Health to himself, and to his infants bread
The lab'rer bears: what his hard heart denies,
His *charitable* vanity supplies. *Pope.*

2. Kind in judging of others; disposed to tenderness; benevolent.

How had you been my friends else? Why have you that *charitable* title from thousands, did you not chiefly belong to my heart? *Shakesp. Timon.*

Of a politick sermon that had no divinity, the king said to bishop Andrews, Call you this a sermon? The bishop answered; By a *charitable* construction it may be a sermon. *Bacon.*

CHA'RITABLY. *adv.* [from *charity.*]

1. Kindly; liberally; with inclination to help the poor.

2. Benevolently; without malignity.

Nothing will more enable us to bear our cross patiently, injuries *charitably*, and the labour of religion comfortably.
Taylor's Guide to Devotion.

'Tis best sometimes your censure to restrain,
And *charitably* let the dull be vain. *Pope's Essay on Criticism.*

CHA'RITY. *n. s.* [*charité*, Fr. *charitas*, Lat.]

1. Tenderness; kindness; love.

By thee,
Founded in reason, loyal, just, and pure,
Relations dear, and all the *charities*
Of father, son, and brother, first were known.
Milton's Paradise Lost, b. iv. *l.* 756.

2. Goodwill; benevolence; disposition to think well of others.

My errours, I hope, are only those of *charity* to mankind, and such as my own *charity* has caused me to commit, that of others may more easily excuse. *Dryden's Religio Laici, Preface.*

3. The theological virtue of universal love.

Concerning *charity*, the final object whereof is that incomprehensible beauty which shineth in the countenance of Christ, the Son of the living God. *Hooker, b.* i. *p.* 38.

Peace, peace, for shame, if not for *charity*.—
—Urge neither *charity* nor shame to me;
Uncharitably with me have you dealt. *Shakesp. Richard* III.

Only

Only add
Deeds to thy knowledge anſwerable, add faith;
Add virtue, patience, temperance, add love,
By name to come call'd *charity*, the ſoul
Of all the reſt. *Milton's Paradiſe Loſt, b.* xii. *l.* 584.

Faith believes the revelations of God; hope expects his promiſes; *charity* loves his excellencies and mercies. *Taylor.*

But laſting *charity*'s more ample ſway,
Nor bound by time, nor ſubject to decay,
In happy triumph ſhall for ever live. *Prior.*

Charity, or a love of God, which works by a love of our neighbour, is greater than faith or hope. *Atterbury.*

4. Liberality to the poor.

The heathen poet, in commending the *charity* of Dido to the Trojans, ſpoke like a chriſtian. *Dryden's Fables, Dedicat.*

5. Alms; relief given to the poor.

We muſt incline to the king; I will look for him, and privily relieve him; go you and maintain talk with the duke, that my *charity* be not of him perceived. *Shakeſp. K. Lear.*

The ant did well to reprove the graſshopper for her ſlothfulneſs; but ſhe did ill then to refuſe her a *charity* in her diſtreſs. *L'Eſtrange.*

To CHARK. *v. a.* To burn to a black cinder, as wood is burned to make charcoal.

Exceſs, either with an apoplexy, knocks a man on the head, or, with a fever, like fire in a ſtrong-water ſhop, burns him down to the ground; or if it flames not out, *charks* him to a coal. *Grew's Coſmologia Sacra, b.* iii. *c.* v. § 10.

CHA'RLATAN. *n. ſ.* [*charlatan*, Fr. *ciarlatano*, Ital. from *ciarlare*, to chatter.] A quack; a mountebank; an empirick.

Saltimbanchoes, quackſalvers, and *charlatans*, deceive them in lower degrees. *Brown's Vulgar Errours. b.* i. *c.* 3.

For *charlatans* can do no good,
Until they're mounted in a crowd. *Hudibras.*

CHARLATA'NICAL. *adj.* [from *charlatan.*] Quackiſh; ignorant.

A cowardly ſoldier, and a *charlatanical* doctor, are the principal ſubjects of comedy. *Cowley, Preface.*

CHA'RLATANRY. *n. ſ.* [from *charlatan.*] Wheedling; deceit; cheating with fair words.

CHARLES's-WAIN. *n. ſ.* The northern conſtellation, called the Bear.

There are ſeven ſtars in Urſa minor, and in *Charles's-wain*, or Plauſtrum of Urſa major, ſeven. *Brown's Vulgar Errours.*

CHA'RLOCK. *n. ſ.* A weed growing among the corn with a yellow flower. It is a ſpecies of Mithridate muſtard.

CHARM. *n. ſ.* [*charme*, Fr. *carmen*, Latin.]

1. Words, or philtres, or characters, imagined to have ſome occult or unintelligible power.

I never knew a woman ſo dote upon a man; ſurely I think you have *charms.*——Not I, I aſſure thee; ſetting the attraction of my good parts aſide, I have no other *charms.* *Shakeſp. Merry Wives of Windſor.*

There have been ever uſed, either barbarous words, of no ſenſe, leſt they ſhould diſturb the imagination, or words of ſimilitude, that may ſecond and feed the imagination: and this was ever as well in heathen *charms*, as in *charms* of later times. *Bacon's Natural Hiſtory*, N° 948.

Alcyone he names amidſt his pray'rs,
Names as a *charm* againſt the waves and wind,
Moſt in his mouth, and ever in his mind. *Dryden.*

Antæus could, by magick *charms*,
Recover ſtrength, whene'er he fell. *Swift.*

2. Something of power to ſubdue oppoſition, and gain the affections.

Well ſounding verſes are the *charm* we uſe,
Heroick thoughts and virtue to infuſe. *Roſcommon.*

But what avail her unexhauſted ſtores,
Her blooming mountains and her ſunny ſhores,
With all the gifts that heaven and earth impart,
The ſmiles of nature, and the *charms* of art,
While proud oppreſſion in her vallies reigns,
And tyranny uſurps her happy plains? *Addiſon.*

To CHARM. *v. a.* [from the noun.]

1. To fortify with charms againſt evil.

Let fall thy blade on vulnerable creſts,
I bear a *charmed* life, which muſt not yield
To one of woman born. *Shakeſp. Macbeth.*

2. To make powerful by charms.

Arcadia was the *charmed* circle, where all his ſpirits for ever ſhould be enchanted. *Sidney, b.* ii.

3. To ſubdue by ſome ſecret power; to amaze.

I, in mine own woe *charm'd*,
Could not find death, where I did hear him groan;
Nor feel him where he ſtruck. *Shakeſp. Cymbeline.*

4. To ſubdue the mind by pleaſure.

'Tis your graces
That from my muteſt conſcience to my tongue,
Charms this report out. *Shakeſp. Cymbeline.*

Amoret! my lovely foe,
Tell me where thy ſtrength does lie:
Where the pow'r that *charms* us ſo,
In thy ſoul, or in thy eye? *Waller.*

CHA'RMER. *n. ſ.* [from *charm.*] One that has the power of charms, or enchantments.

That handkerchief
Did an Egyptian to my mother give;
She was a *charmer*, and could almoſt read
The thoughts of people. *Shakeſp. Othello.*

The paſſion you pretended,
Was only to obtain;
But when the charm is ended,
The *charmer* you diſdain. *Dryden's Sp. Friar.*

CHA'RMING. *particip. adj.* [from *charm.*] Pleaſing in the higheſt degree.

For ever all goodneſs will be *charming*, for ever all wickedneſs will be moſt odious. *Sprat.*

O *charming* youth! in the firſt op'ning page,
So many graces in ſo green an age. *Dryden.*

CHA'RMINGLY. *adv.* [from *charming.*] In ſuch a manner as to pleaſe exceedingly.

She ſmiled very *charmingly*, and diſcovered as fine a ſet of teeth as ever eye beheld. *Addiſon's Freeholder*, N° 11.

CHA'RMINGNESS. *n. ſ.* [from *charming.*] The power of pleaſing.

CHA'RNEL. *adj.* [*charnel*, Fr.] Containing fleſh, or carcaſes.

Such are thoſe thick and gloomy ſhadows damp
Oft found in *charnel* vaults, and ſepulchres,
Ling'ring and ſitting by a new-made grave. *Milton.*

CHA'RNEL-HOUSE. *n. ſ.* [*charnier*, Fr. from *caro, carnis*, Latin.] The place under churches where the bones of the dead are repoſited.

If *charnel-houſes* and our graves muſt ſend
Thoſe, that we bury, back; our monuments
Shall be the maws of kites. *Shakeſp. Macbeth.*

When they were in thoſe *charnel-houſes*, every one was placed in order, and a black pillar or coffin ſet by him. *Taylor.*

CHART. *n. ſ.* [*charta*, Lat.] A delineation or map of coaſts, for the uſe of ſailors. It is diſtinguiſhed from a *map*, by repreſenting only the coaſts.

The Portugueſe, when they had doubled the Cape of Good-Hope, found ſkilful pilates, uſing aſtronomical inſtruments, geographical *charts*, and compaſſes. *Arbuthnot on Coins.*

CHA'RTER. *n. ſ.* [*charta*, Latin.]

1. A *charter* is a written evidence of things done between man and man. *Charters* are divided into *charters* of the king, and *charters* of private perſons. *Charters* of the king are thoſe, whereby the king paſſeth any grant to any perſon or more, or to any body politick: as a *charter* of exemption, that no man ſhall be empannelled on a jury; *charter* of pardon, whereby a man is forgiven a felony, or other offence. *Cowel.*

If you deny it, let the danger light
Upon your *charter*, and your city's freedom.
Shakeſp. Merchant of Venice.

Here was that *charter* ſeal'd, wherein the crown
All marks of arbitrary power lays down. *Denham.*

She ſhakes the rubbiſh from her mounting brow,
And ſeems to have renew'd her *charter*'s date,
Which heav'n will to the death of time allow. *Dryden.*

2. Any writing beſtowing privileges or rights.

It is not to be wondered, that the great *charter* whereby God beſtowed the whole earth upon Adam, and confirmed it unto the ſons of Noah, being as brief in word as large in effect, hath bred much quarrel of interpretation. *Raleigh's Eſſays.*

God renewed this *charter* of man's ſovereignty over the creatures. *South.*

3. Privilege; immunity; exemption.

I muſt have liberty,
Withal as large a *charter* as the wind,
To blow on whom I pleaſe; for ſo fools have;
And they that are moſt gauled with my folly,
They moſt muſt laugh. *Shakeſp. As you like it.*

My mother,
Who has a *charter* to extol her blood,
When ſhe does praiſe me, grieves me. *Shakeſp. Coriolanus.*

CHARTER-PARTY. *n. ſ.* [*chartre partie*, Fr.] A paper relating to a contract, of which each party has a copy.

Charter-parties, or contracts, made even upon the high ſea, touching things that are not in their own nature maritime, belong not to the admiral's juriſdiction. *Hale's Common Law of England.*

CHA'RTERED. *adj.* [from *charter.*] Inveſted with privileges by charter; privileged.

When he ſpeaks,
The air, a *charter'd* libertine, is ſtill. *Shakeſp. Henry V.*

CHA'RY. *adj.* [from *care.*] Careful; cautious; wary; frugal.

Over his kindred he held a wary and *chary* care, which bountifully was expreſſed, when occaſion ſo required. *Carew's Survey of Cornwal.*

The *charieſt* maid is prodigal enough,
If ſhe unmaſk her beauty to the moon. *Shakeſpeare.*

To CHASE. *v. a.* [*chaſſer*, Fr.]

1. To hunt.

2. To purſue as an enemy.

And Abimelech *chaſed* him, and he fled before him. *Jud.* ix. 40.

3. To follow as a thing desirable.
4. To drive.
Thus *chased* by their brother's endless malice, from prince to prince, and from place to place, they, for their safety, fled at last to the city of Bisennis. *Knolles's Hist. of the Turks.*
When the following morn had *chas'd* away
The flying stars, and light restor'd the day. *Dryden.*

To CHASE *Metals.* See To ENCHASE.

CHASE. *n. s.* [from the verb.]
1. Hunting; pursuit of any thing as game.
Whilst he was hast'ning, in the *chase*, it seems,
Of this fair couple, meets he on the way
The father of this seeming lady. *Shakesp. Winter's Tale.*
There is no *chase* more pleasant, methinks, than to drive a thought, by good conduct, from one end of the world to another, and never to lose sight of it till it fall into eternity. *Burnet's Theory of the Earth.*
2. Fitness to be hunted, appropriation to *chase* or sport.
Concerning the beasts of *chase*, whereof the buck is the first, he is called the first year a fawn. *Shakesp. Love's L. Lost.*
A maid I am, and of thy virgin train;
Oh! let me still that spotless name retain,
Frequent the forests, thy chaste will obey,
And only make the beasts of *chase* my prey. *Dryden.*
3. Pursuit of an enemy, or of something noxious.
The admiral, with such ships only as could suddenly be put in readiness, made forth towards them; insomuch as of one hundred ships, there came scarce thirty to work: howbeit, with them, and such as came daily in, we set upon them, and gave them *chase*. *Bacon.*
One day, upon the sudden, he sallied out upon them with certain troops of horsemen, with such violence, that, at the first onset, he overthrew them, and, having them in *chase*, did speedy execution. *Knolles's Hist. of the Turks.*
They seek that joy, which us'd to glow,
Expanded on the hero's face;
When the thick squadrons prest the foe,
And William led the glorious *chase*. *Prior.*
4. Pursuit of something as desirable.
Yet this mad *chase* of fame, by few pursu'd,
Has drawn destruction on the multitude. *Dryden's Juvenal.*
5. Hunting match.
Tell him, h'ath made a match with such a wrangler,
That all the courts of France will be disturb'd
With *chases*. *Shakesp. Henry V.*
6. The game hunted.
She, seeing the towering of her pursued *chase*, went circling about, rising so with the less sense of rising. *Sidney, b.* ii.
Hold, Warwick: seek thee out some other *chase*,
For I myself must put this deer to death. *Shakesp. Henry* VI.
Honour's the noblest *chase*; pursue that game,
And recompence the loss of love with fame. *Granville.*
7. Open ground stored with such beasts as are hunted.
A receptacle for deer and game, of a middle nature between a forest and a park; being commonly less than a forest, and not endued with so many liberties; and yet of a larger compass, and stored with greater diversity of game than a park. A *chase* differs from a forest in this, because it may be in the hands of a subject, which a forest, in its proper nature, cannot; and from a park, in that it is not inclosed, and hath not only a larger compass, and more store of game, but likewise more keepers and overseers. *Cowel.*
He and his lady both are at the lodge,
Upon the northside of this pleasant *chase*. *Shakesp. Tit. And.*
8. *The* CHASE *of a gun*, is the whole bore or length of a piece, taken withinside. *Chambers.*

CHASE-GUN. *n. s.* [from *chase* and *gun.*] Guns in the forepart of the ship, fired upon those that are pursued.
Mean time the Belgians tack upon our rear,
And raking *chase-guns* through our stern they send. *Dryden.*

CHA'SER. *n. s.* [from *chase.*] Hunter; pursuer; driver.
Then began
A stop i' th' *chaser*, a retire; anon
A rout, confusion thick. *Shakesp. Cymbeline.*
So fast he flies, that his reviewing eye
Has lost the *chasers*, and his ear the cry. *Denham.*
Stretch'd on the lawn, his second hope survey,
At once the *chaser*, and at once the prey.
Lo Rufus tugging at the deadly dart,
Bleeds in the forest like a wounded hart. *Pope.*

CHASM. *n. s.* [χάσμα.]
1. A breach unclosed; a cleft; a gape; an opening.
In all that visible corporeal world, we see no *chasms* or gaps. *Locke.*
The water of this orb communicates with that of the ocean, by means of certain hiatuses or *chasms* passing betwixt it and the bottom of the ocean. *Woodward's Nat. Hist.*
The ground adust her riv'n mouth disparts,
Horrible *chasm!* profound. *Philips.*
2. A place unfilled; a vacuity.
Some lazy ages, lost in ease,
No action leave to busy chronicles;
Such, whose supine felicity but makes,
In story *chasms*, in epochas mistakes. *Dryden.*

CHASSELAS. n. s. [French.] A sort of grape. See VINE.

CHASTE. *adj.* [*chaste*, Fr. *castus*, Lat.]
1. Pure from all commerce of sexes; as a *chaste* virgin.
2. With respect to language; pure; uncorrupt; not mixed with barbarous phrases.
3. Without obscenity.
Among words which signify the same principal ideas, some are clean and decent, others unclean; some *chaste*, others obscene. *Watts's Logick.*
4. True to the marriage bed.
Love your children, be discreet, *chaste*, keepers at home. *Titus*, ii. 5.

CHASTE-TREE. *n. s.* [*vitex*, Lat.]
The flower consists of one leaf, with two lips; the forepart is tubulose, from whose flower-cup rises the pointal, which becomes an almost spherical fruit, divided into four cells. The leaves are fingered like those of hemp. This tree will grow to be eight or ten feet high, and produce their spikes of flowers at the extremity of every strong shoot in autumn. *Miller.*

To CHA'STEN. *v. a.* [*chastier*, Fr. *castigo*, Lat.] To correct; to punish; to mortify.
Chasten thy son while there is hope, and let not thy soul spare for his crying. *Prov.* xix. 18.
I follow thee, safe guide! the path
Thou lead'st me; and to the hand of heav'n submit,
However *chast'ning*. *Milton's Par. Lost, b.* xi. *l.* 373.
Some feel the rod,
And own, like us, the father's *chast'ning* hand. *Rowe's Royal Convert.*
From our lost pursuit she wills to hide
Her close decrees, and *chasten* human pride. *Prior.*

To CHASTI'SE. *v. a.* [*castigo*, Lat. antiently accented on the first syllable, now on the last.]
1. To punish; to correct by punishment; to afflict for faults.
My breast I'll burst with straining of my courage,
But I will *chastise* this high minded strumpet. *Sha. Hen.* VI.
I am glad to see the vanity or envy of the canting chymists thus discovered and *chastised*. *Boyle's Sceptical Chymist.*
How seldom is the world affrighted or *chastised* with signs or prodigies, earthquakes or inundations, famines or plagues? *Grew's Cosmologia Sacra.*
Like you, commission'd to *chastise* and bless,
He must avenge the world, and give it peace. *Prior.*
2. To reduce to order, or obedience.
Hie thee hither,
That I may pour my spirits in thine ear,
And *chastise*, with the valour of my tongue,
All that impedes thee. *Shakesp. King Lear.*
Know, Sir, that I
Will not wait pinion'd at your master's court,
Nor once be *chastis'd* with the sober eye
Of dull Octavia. *Shakesp. Antony and Cleopatra.*
The gay social sense
By decency *chastis'd*. *Thomson.*

CHASTI'SEMENT. *n. s.* [*chastiment*, Fr.] Correction; punishment. These words are all commonly, though not always, used of domestick or parental punishment.
Shall I so much dishonour my fair stars,
On equal terms to give him *chastisement?* *Shakesp. R.* II.
He held the *chastisement* of one which molested the see of Rome, pleasing to God. *Raleigh's Essays.*
For seven years what can a child be guilty of, but lying, or ill-natur'd tricks; the repeated commission of which shall bring him to the *chastisement* of the rod. *Locke.*
He receives a fit of sickness as the kind *chastisement* and discipline of his heavenly father, to wean his affections from the world. *Bentley.*

CHA'STITY. *n. s.* [*castitas*, Lat.]
1. Purity of the body.
Who can be bound by any solemn vow,
To force a spotless virgin's *chastity?* *Shakesp. Henry* VI.
Chastity is either abstinence or continence: abstinence is that of virgins or widows; continence of married persons: chaste marriages are honourable and pleasing to God. *Taylor's Rule of Living Holy.*
Ev'n here where frozen *chastity* retires,
Love finds an altar for forbidden fires. *Pope.*
2. Freedom from obscenity.
There is not *chastity* enough in language,
Without offence to utter them. *Sh. Much ado about Nothing.*
3. Freedom from bad mixture of any kind.

CHASTI'SER. *n. s.* [from *chastise.*] The person that chastises; a punisher; a corrector.

CHA'STLY. *adv.* [from *chaste.*] Without incontinence; purely; without contamination.
You should not pass here: no, though it were as virtuous to lie as to live *chastely*. *Shakesp. Coriolanus.*
Make first a song of joy and love,
Which *chastely* flame in royal eyes. *Wotton.*

Succeſſion of a long deſcent,
Which *chaſtly* in the channels ran,
And from our demi-gods began. *Dryden.*

CHA'STNESS. *n. ſ.* [from *chaſte.*] Chaſtity; purity.

To CHAT. *v. n.* [from *caqueter*, Fr. *Skinner*; perhaps from *a-chat*, purchaſe or cheapening, on account of the prate naturally produced in a bargain; or only, as it is moſt likely, contracted from *chatter.*] To prate; to talk idly; to prattle; to cackle; to chatter; to converſe at eaſe.

Thus *chatten* the people in their ſteads,
Ylike as a monſter of many heads. *Spenſer's Paſtorals.*

Becauſe that I familiarly ſometimes,
Do uſe you for my fool, and *chat* with you,
Your saucineſs will jeſt upon my love.
Shakeſp. Comedy of Errours.

All tongues ſpeak of him, and the bleared ſights
Are ſpectacled to ſee him. Your prattling nurſe
Into a rapture lets her baby cry,
While ſhe *chats* him. *Shakeſp. Coriolanus.*

The ſhepherds on the lawn
Sat ſimply *chatting* in a ruſtick row. *Milton.*

With much goodwill the motion was embrac'd,
To *chat* a while on their adventures paſs'd. *Dryden.*

CHAT. *n. ſ.* [from the verb.] Idle talk; prate; ſlight or negligent tattle.

Lords that can prate
As amply and unneceſſarily,
As this Gonzalo, I myſelf would make
A chough of as deep *chat.* *Shakeſp. Tempeſt.*

The time between before the fire they ſat,
And ſhorten'd the delay by pleaſing *chat.* *Drdyen.*

The leaſt is no inconſiderable good, but ſuch as he confeſſes is far greater than the tickling of his palate with a glaſs of wine, or the idle *chat* of a ſoaking club. *Locke.*

Snuff, or the fan, ſupplies each pauſe of *chat*,
With ſinging, laughing, ogling, and all that. *Pope.*

CHAT. *n. ſ.* The keys of trees are called *chats*, as aſh *chats.*

CHA'TELLANY. *n. ſ.* [*châtelenie*, Fr.] The diſtrict under the dominion of a caſtle.

Here are about twenty towns and forts of great importance, with their *chatellanies* and dependencies. *Dryden.*

CHA'TTEL. *n. ſ.* [See CATTLE.] Any moveable poſſeſſion: a term now ſcarce uſed but in forms of law.

Nay, look not big, nor ſtamp, nor ſtare, nor fret;
I will be maſter of what is mine own;
She is my goods, my *chattels.* *Shakeſp. Taming of the Shrew.*

Honour's a leaſe for lives to come,
And cannot be extended from
The legal tenant: 'tis a *chattle*
Not to be forfeited in battle. *Hudibras, p.* i. *c.* iii.

To CHA'TTER. *v. n.* [*caqueter*, Fr.]

1. To make a noiſe as a pie, or other unharmonious bird.

Nightingales ſeldom ſing, the pie ſtill *chattereth.* *Sidney.*

So doth the cuckow, when the mavis ſings,
Begin his witleſs note apace to *chatter.* *Spenſer's Sonnets.*

There was a crow ſat *chattering* upon the back of a ſheep; Well, ſirrah, ſays the ſheep, you durſt not have done this to a dog. *L'Eſtrange.*

Your birds of knowledge, that in duſky air
Chatter futurity. *Dryden and Lee's OEdipus.*

2. To make a noiſe by colliſion of the teeth.

Stood Theodore ſurpriz'd in deadly fright,
With *chatt'ring* teeth, and briſtling hair upright. *Dryden.*

Dip but your toes into cold water,
Their correſpondent teeth will *chatter.* *Prior.*

3. To talk idly or careleſly.

Suffer no hour to paſs away in a lazy idleneſs, an impertinent *chattering*, or uſeleſs trifles. *Watts's Logick.*

CHA'TTER. *n. ſ.* [from the verb.]

1. Noiſe like that of a pie or monkey.

The mimick ape began his *chatter*,
How evil tongues his life beſpatter. *Swift.*

2. Idle prate.

CHA'TTERER. *n. ſ.* [from *chatter.*] An idle talker; a pratler.

CHA'TWOOD. *n. ſ.* Little ſticks; fuel.

CHA'VENDER. *n. ſ.* [*Cheveſne*, Fr.] The chub; a fiſh.

Theſe are a choice bait for the chub, or *chavender*, or indeed any great fiſh. *Walton's Angler.*

CHAUMONTE'LLE. *n. ſ.* [Fr.] A ſort of pear; which ſee.

To CHAW. *v. a.* [*kawen*, Germ.] To champ between the teeth; to maſticate; to chew.

I home returning, fraught with foul deſpight,
And *chawing* vengeance all the way I went. *Fairy Q. b.* ii.

They come to us, but us love draws;
He ſwallows us, and never *chaws*;
He is the tyrant pike, and we the fry. *Donne.*

Whether he found any uſe of *chawing* little ſponges, dipt in oil, in his mouth, when he was perfectly under water, and at a diſtance from his engine. *Boyle.*

The man who laught but once to ſee an aſs
Mumbling to make the croſs-grain'd thiſtles paſs,
Might laugh again, to ſee a jury *chaw*
The prickles of unpalatable law. *Dryden.*

CHAW. *n. ſ.* [from the verb.] The chap; the upper or under part of a beaſt's mouth.

I will turn thee back, and put hooks into thy *chaws*, and will bring thee forth and all thine army. *Ezek.* xxxviii. 4.

CHA'WDRON. *n. ſ.* Entrails.

Add thereto a tyger's *chawdron*,
For the ingredients of our cauldron. *Shakeſp. Macbeth.*

CHEAP. *adj.* [ceapan, Sax. *koopen*, Dutch, to buy.]

1. To be had at a low rate; purchaſed for a ſmall price.

Where there are a great many ſellers to a few buyers, there the thing to be ſold will be *cheap.* On the other ſide, raiſe up a great many buyers for a few ſellers, and the ſame thing will immediately turn dear. *Locke.*

2. Of ſmall value; eaſy to be had; not reſpected.

The goodneſs, that is *cheap* in beauty, makes
Beauty brief in goodneſs. *Shakeſp. Meaſure for Meaſure.*

Had I ſo laviſh of my preſence been,
So common hackney'd in the eyes of men,
So ſtale and *cheap* to vulgar company. *Shakeſp. Henry* IV.

He that is too much in any thing, ſo that he giveth another occaſion of ſociety, maketh himſelf *cheap.* *Bacon.*

May your ſick fame ſtill languiſh till it die,
And you grow *cheap* in every ſubject's eye. *Dryden.*

The uſual titles of diſtinction, which belong to us, are turned into terms of deriſion and reproach, and every way is taken by profane men, towards rendering us *cheap* and contemptible. *Atterbury.*

CHEAP. *n. ſ.* [*cheping* is an old word for *market*; whence *Eaſt-cheap*, *Cheapſide.*] Market; purchaſe; bargain; as good *cheap*; [*a bon marche*, Fr.]

The ſame wine that comes out of Candia, which we pay ſo dear for now a days, in that good world was very good *cheap.* *Sidney, b.* ii.

It is many a man's caſe to tire himſelf out with hunting after that abroad, which he carries about him all the while, and may have it better *cheap* at home. *L'Eſtrange.*

Some few inſulting cowards, who love to vapour good *cheap*, may trample on thoſe who give leaſt reſiſtance. *Decay of Piety.*

To CHE'APEN. *v. a.* [ceapan, Sax. to buy.]

1. To attempt to purchaſe; to bid for any thing; to aſk the price of any commodity.

Rich ſhe ſhall be, that's certain; wiſe, or I'll none; virtuous, or I'll never *cheapen* her; fair, or I'll never look on her.
Shakeſp. Much ado about Nothing.

The firſt he *cheapened* was a Jupiter, which would have come at a very eaſy rate. *L'Eſtrange.*

So in a morning, without bodice,
Slipt ſometimes out to Mrs. Thody's,
To *cheapen* tea. *Prior.*

To ſhops in crouds the daggled females fly,
Pretend to *cheapen* goods, but nothing buy. *Swift.*

2. To leſſen value.

My hopes purſue a brighter diadem.
Can any brighter than the Roman be?
I find my profer'd love has *cheapen'd* me. *Dryd. Tyrr. Love.*

CHE'APLY. *adv.* [from *cheap.*] At a ſmall price; at a low rate.

By theſe I ſee
So great a day as this is *cheaply* bought. *Shakeſp. Macbeth.*

Blood, rapines, maſſacres, were *cheaply* bought,
So mighty recompence your beauty brought. *Dryden.*

CHE'APNESS. *n. ſ.* [from *cheap.*] Lowneſs of price.

Ancient ſtatutes incite merchant ſtrangers to bring in commodities; having for end *cheapneſs.* *Bacon's Henry* VII.

The diſcredit which is grown upon this kingdom, has been the great diſcouragement to other nations to tranſplant themſelves hither, and prevailed farther than all the invitations which the *cheapneſs* and plenty of the country has made them. *Temple.*

CHEAR. See CHEER.

To CHEAT. *v. a.* [of uncertain derivation; probably from *acheter*, Fr. to purchaſe, alluding to the tricks uſed in making bargains. See the noun.]

1. To defraud; to impoſe upon; to trick. It is uſed commonly of low cunning.

It is a dangerous commerce, where an honeſt man is ſure at firſt of being *cheated*; and he recovers not his loſſes, but by learning to *cheat* others. *Dryden.*

There are a ſort of people who find that the moſt effectual way to *cheat* the people, is always to pretend to infallible cures. *Tillotſon, Preface.*

2. It has *of* before the thing taken away by fraud.

I that am curtail'd by this fair proportion,
Cheated of feature by diſſembling nature,
Deform'd, unfiniſh'd. *Shakeſp. Richard* III.

CHEAT. *n. ſ.* [from the verb. Some think abbreviated from *eſcheat*, becauſe many fraudulent meaſures being taken by the lords of manours in procuring eſcheats, *cheat* the abridgment was brought to convey a bad meaning.]

1. A fraud; a trick; an impoſture.

The pretence of publick good is a *cheat* that will ever paſs, though ſo abuſed by ill men, that I wonder the good do not grow aſhamed to uſe it. *Temple.*

Emp'rick politicians use deceit,
Hide what they give, and cure but by a *cheat*. *Dryden.*
When I consider life, 'tis all a *cheat*;
Yet, fool'd with hope, men favour the deceit.
Trust on, and think tomorrow will repay;
Tomorrow's falser than the former day;
Lyes worse; and while it says, we shall be blest,
With some new joys cuts off what we possest. *Dryden.*

2. A person guilty of fraud.
Dissimulation can be no further useful than it is concealed; for as much as no man will trust a known *cheat*. *South.*
Like that notorious *cheat*, vast sums I give,
Only that you may keep me while I live. *Dryden's Cleomenes.*

CHE'ATER. *n. s.* [from *cheat.*] One that practises fraud.
I will be *cheater* to them both, and they shall be exchequers to me. [It is here for escheater.] *Shakesp. M. W. of W.*
They say this town is full of couzenage,
As nimble jugglers that deceive the eye;
Disguised *cheaters*, prating mountebanks,
And many such like libertines of sin. *Shakesp. Comedy of Err.*
He is no swaggerer, hostess; a tame *cheater* i' faith.——
Cheater, call you him? I will bar no honest man my house, nor no *cheater*. *Shakesp. Henry* IV. *p.* ii.
All sorts of injurious persons, the sacrilegious, the detainers of tithes, *cheaters* of mens inheritances, false witnesses and accusers. *Taylor's Rule of Living Holy.*

To CHECK. *v. a.* [from the French *echecs*, chess; from whence we use, at that game, the term *checkmate*, when we stop our adversary from carrying on his play any farther.]

1. To repress; to curb.
Reserve thy state; with better judgment *check*
This hideous rashness. *Shakesp. K. Lear.*
How fames may be sown and raised, how they may be spread and multiplied, and how they may be *checked* and laid dead. *Bacon's Essays.*
I hate when vice can bolt her arguments,
And virtue has no tongue to *check* her pride. *Milton.*
He who sat at a table, richly and deliciously furnished, but with a sword hanging over his head by one single thread or hair, surely had enough to *check* his appetite. *South.*

2. To reprove; to chide.
Richard, with his eye brimful of tears,
Then *check'd* and rated by Northumberland,
Did speak these words, now prov'd a prophecy. *Shakesp.*
His fault is much, and the good king his master
Will *check* him for't. *Shakesp. King Lear.*

3. To compare a bank note or other bill, with the correspondent cipher.

4. To control by a counter reckoning.

To CHECK. *v. n.*

1. To stop; to make a stop; with *at*.
With what wing the stanyel *checks at* it. *Shakesp.*
He must observe their mood on whom he jests,
The quality of the persons, and the time;
And, like the haggard, *check at* every feather
That comes before his eye. *Shakesp. Hamlet.*
The mind, once jaded by an attempt above its power, either is disabled for the future, or else *checks at* any vigorous undertaking ever after. *Locke.*

2. To clash; to interfere.
If love *check* once with business, it troubleth mens fortunes. *Bacon's Essays.*
I'll avoid his presence;
It *checks* too strong upon me. *Dryden's All for Love.*

CHECK. *n. s.* [from the verb.]

1. Repressure; stop; rebuff.
I do know, the state,
However this may gall him with some *check*,
Cannot with safety cast him. *Shakesp. Othello.*
Rebellion in this land shall lose his sway,
Meeting the *check* of such another day. *Shakesp. Henry* IV.
We see, also, that kings that have been fortunate conquerors in their first years, must have some *check* or arrest in their fortunes. *Bacon's Essay.*
God hath of late years manifested himself in a very dreadful manner, as if it were on purpose to give a *check* to this insolent impiety. *Tillotson.*
It was this viceroy's zeal, which gave a remarkable *check* to the first progress of christianity. *Addison. Freeholder,* N° 32.
God put it into the heart of one of our princes, to give a *check* to that sacrilege, which had been but too much winked at. *Atterbury.*
The great struggle with his passions is in the first *check*. *Rogers.*

2. Restraint; curb; government.
They who come to maintain their own breach of faith, the *check* of their consciences much breaketh their spirit. *Hayw.*
The impetuosity of the new officer's nature needed some restraint and *check*, for some time, to his immoderate pretences and appetite of power. *Clarendon.*
Some free from rhyme or reason, rule or *check*,
Break Priscian's head, and Pegasus's neck. *Pope.*
While such men are in trust, who have no *check* from within, nor any views but towards their interest. *Swift.*

3. A reproof; a slight.
Oh! this life
Is nobler than attending for a *check*;
Richer than doing nothing for a bauble. *Shakesp. Cymbeline.*

4. A dislike; a sudden disgust; something that stops the progress.
Say I should wed her, would not my wise subjects
Take *check*, and think it strange? perhaps revolt? *Dryden.*

5. In falconry, is when a hawk forsakes her proper game to follow rooks, pies, or other birds that cross her in her flight. *Chambers.*
A young woman is a hawk upon her wings; and if she be handsome, she is the more subject to go out on *check*. *Suckling.*
When whistled from the fist,
Some falcon stoops at what her eye design'd,
And with her eagerness, the quary miss'd,
Streight flies at *check*, and clips it down the wind. *Dryden.*

6. The person checking; the cause of restraint; a stop.
He was unhappily too much used as a *check* upon the lord Coventry. *Clarendon.*
A satyrical poet is the *check* of the laymen on bad priests. *Dryden's Fables, Preface.*
The letters have the natural production by several *checks* or stops, or, as they are usually called, articulations of the breath or voice. *Holder's Elements of Speech.*

7. The correspondent cipher of a bank bill.

8. A term used in the game of chess, when one party obliges the other either to move or guard his king.

9. *Clerk of the* CHECK, in the king's houshold, has the check and controulment of the yeomen of the guard, and all the ushers belonging to the royal family.

10. *Clerk of the* CHECK, in the king's navy at Plymouth, is also the name of an officer invested with like powers. *Chambers.*

To CHE'CKER. } *v. a.* [from *echecs*, chess, Fr.] To variegate or
To CHE'QUER. } diversify, in the manner of a chess-board, with alternate colours, or with darker and brighter parts.
The grey-ey'd morn smiles on the frowning night,
Check'ring the eastern clouds with streaks of light. *Shakesp. Romeo and Juliet.*
The green leaves quiver with the cooling wind,
And make a *chequer'd* shadow on the ground. *Shakesp.*
As the snake roll'd in the flow'ry bank,
With shining *checker'd* slough doth sting a child,
That for the beauty thinks it excellent. *Shakesp. Hen.* VI.
The wealthy spring yet never bore
That sweet, nor dainty flower,
That damask'd not the *checker'd* floor
Of Cynthia's summer bower. *Drayton's Cynthia.*
Many a youth and many a maid,
Dancing in the *checker'd* shade. *Milton.*
In the chess-board, the use of each chess-man is determined only within that *chequered* piece of wood. *Locke.*
In our present condition, which is a middle state, our minds are, as it were, *chequered* with truth and falsehood. *Addison.*
The ocean intermixing with the land, so as to *checker* it into earth and water. *Woodward's Natural History.*
Here waving groves a *checker'd* scene display,
And part admit, and part exclude the day. *Pope.*

CHE'CKER. } Work varied alternately as to its colours or
CHECKER-WORK. } materials.
Nets of *checker-work* and wreaths of chain-work for the chapiters which were upon the top of the pillars. 1 *Kings*, vii. 17.

CHE'CKMATE. *n. s.* [*echec et mat*, Fr.] The movement on the chess-board, that kills the opposite men, or hinders them from moving.
Love they him called, that gave me the *checkmate*,
But better might they have behote him hate. *Spenser.*

CHE'CKROLL. *n. s.* [from *check* and *roll.*] A roll or book, containing the names of such as are attendants on, and in pay to great personages, as their houshold servants. It is otherwise called the *chequer-roll*. *Cowel.*
Not daring to extend this law further than to the king's servants in *checkroll*, lest it should have been too harsh to the gentlemen and other commons of the kingdom. *Bacon's Hen.* VII.

CHEEK. *n. s.* [ceac, Saxon.]

1. The side of the face below the eye.
And now and then an ample tear trill'd down
Her delicate *cheek*. *Shakesp. King Lear.*
Her beauty hangs upon the *cheek* of night,
Like a rich jewel in an Æthiop's ear. *Shakesp. Rom. and Jul.*
I shall survey and spy
Death in thy *cheeks*, and darkness in thy eye. *Donne.*
Daughter of the rose, whose *cheeks* unite
The diff'ring titles of the red and white,
Who heaven's alternate beauty well display
The blush of morning and the milky way. *Dryden.*

2. A general name among mechanicks for almost all those pieces of their machines and instruments that are double, and perfectly alike. *Chambers.*

CHE'EKBONE. *n. s.* [from *cheek* and *bone.*]

I cut afterwards into the tumour, and felt the slug: it lay partly under the os jugale, or *cheekbone*. *Wiseman.*

CHE'EKTOOTH. *n. s.* [from *cheek* and *tooth.*] The hinder tooth or tusk.

He hath the *cheekteeth* of a great lion. *Joel*, i. 6.

CHEER. *n. s.* [*chere*, Fr. entertainment; *cara*, Sp. the countenance. It seems to have, in English, some relation to both these senses.]

1. Entertainment; provisions served at a feast.

But though my cates be mean, take them in good part;
Better *cheer* you may have, but not with better heart.
Shakesp. Comedy of Errours.

His will was never determined to any pursuit of good *cheer*, poignant sauces, and delicious wines. *Locke.*

2. Invitation to gaiety.

My royal lord,
You do not give the *cheer*; the feast is sold
That is not often vouched, while 'tis making
'Tis given with welcome. *Shakesp. Macbeth.*

3. Gaiety; jollity.

I have not that alacrity of spirit,
Nor *cheer* of mind, that I was wont to have. *Shakesp. R.* III.

4. Air of the countenance.

Right faithful true he was in deed and word,
But of his *cheer* did seem too solemn sad.
Nothing did he dread, but ever was ydrad. *Spens. Fairy Q.*
Which publick death, receiv'd with such a *cheer*,
As not a sigh, a look, a shrink bewrays
The least felt touch of a degenerous fear,
Gave life to envy, to his courage praise. *Daniel's Civil W.*
He ended; and his words their drooping *cheer*
Enlighten'd, and their languish'd hope reviv'd. *Milton.*
At length appear
Her grisly brethren stretch'd upon the bier:
Pale at the sudden sight, she chang'd her *cheer*.
Dryden's Fables.

5. Perhaps temper of mind in general.

Then were they all of good *cheer*, and they also took some meat. *Acts*, xxvii. 36.

To CHEER. *v. a.* [from the noun.]

1. To incite; to encourage; to inspirit.

He complained in vain, that he was betrayed: yet, for all that, he was nothing discouraged, but *cheered* up the footmen. *Knolles's History of the Turks.*

He *cheer'd* the dogs to follow her who fled,
And vow'd revenge on her devoted head. *Dryden's Fables.*

2. To comfort; to console.

I died, ere I could lend thee aid;
But *cheer* thy heart, and be thou not dismay'd.
Shakesp. Richard III.
Displeas'd at what, not suffering, they had seen,
They went to *cheer* the faction of the green. *Dryden.*

3. To gladden.

Hark! a glad voice the lonely desert *cheers*;
Prepare the way, a god, a god appears. *Pope's Messiah.*
The sacred sun, above the waters rais'd,
Thro' heaven's eternal brazen portals blaz'd,
And wide o'er earth diffus'd his *cheering* ray. *Pope.*

To CHEER. *v. n.* To grow gay or gladsome.

At sight of thee my gloomy soul *cheers* up;
My hopes revive, and gladness dawns within me.
A. Philips's Distrest Mother.

CHE'ERER. *n. s.* [from *to cheer.*] Gladner; giver of gaiety.

To thee alone be praise,
From whom our joy descends,
Thou *cheerer* of our days. *Wotton.*

Angling was, after tedious study, a rest to his mind, a *cheerer* of his spirits, a diverter of sadness, a calmer of unquiet thoughts. *Walton's Angler.*

Saffron is the safest and most simple cordial, the greatest reviver of the heart, and *cheerer* of the spirits. *Temple.*

Prime *cheerer*, light,
Of all material beings first and best. *Thomson's Summer.*

CHE'ERFUL. *adj.* [from *cheer* and *full.*]

1. Gay; full of life; full of mirth.

The *cheerful* birds of sundry kind
Do chaunt sweet music to delight his mind. *Fairy Q. b.* ii.

2. Having an appearance of gaiety.

A merry heart maketh a *cheerful* countenance: but by sorrow of the heart the spirit is broken. *Prov.* xv. 13.

CHE'ERFULLY. *adv.* [from *cheerful.*] Without dejection; with willingness; with gaiety.

Pluck up thy spirits, look *cheerfully* upon me.
Shakesp. Taming of the Shrew.
To their known stations *cheerfully* they go. *Dryden.*

Doctrine is that which must prepare men for discipline; and men never go on so *cheerfully*, as when they see where they go. *South.*

May the man
That *cheerfully* recounts the female's praise,
Find equal love, and love's untainted sweets
Enjoy with honour. *Philips.*

CHE'ERFULNESS. *n. s.* [from *cheerful.*]

1. Freedom from dejection; alacrity.

With what resolution and *cheerfulness*, with what courage and patience did vast numbers of all sorts of people, in the first ages of christianity, encounter all the rage and malice of the world, and embrace torments and death? *Tillotson.*

2. Freedom from gloominess.

I remember, then I marvelled to see her receive my commandments with sighs, and yet do them with *cheerfulness*.
Sidney, b. ii.

CHE'ERLESS. *adj.* [from *cheer.*] Without gaiety, comfort, or gladness.

For since mine eye your joyous sight did miss,
My cheerful day is turn'd to *cheerless* night. *Fairy Q. b.* i.
On a bank, beside a willow,
Heav'n her cov'ring, earth her pillow,
Sad Amynta sigh'd alone,
From the *cheerless* dawn of morning
Till the dews of night returning. *Dryden.*
Cheerless towns, far distant, never bless'd. *Thomson.*

CHE'ERLY. *adj.* [from *cheer.*]

1. Gay; cheerful.

They are useful to mankind, in affording them convenient situations of houses and villages, reflecting the benign and cherishing sun beams, and so rendering their habitations both more comfortable and more *cheerly* in winter. *Ray on Creation.*

Under heavy arms the youth of Rome
Their long laborious marches overcome;
Cheerly their tedious travels undergo. *Dryden's Virgil.*

2. Not gloomy.

CHE'ERLY. *adv.* [from *cheer.*] Cheerfully.

In God's name, *cheerly* on, courageous friends,
To reap the harvest of perpetual peace,
By this one bloody trial of sharp war. *Shakesp. Richard* III.
Oft listening how the hounds and horn
Cheerly rouse the slumb'ring morn. *Milton.*

CHE'ERY. *adj.* [from *cheer.*] Gay; sprightly; having the power to make gay.

Come, let us hie, and quaff a *cheery* bowl;
Let cider new wash sorrow from thy soul. *Gay's Pastorals.*

CHEESE. *n. s.* [*caseus*, Lat. cyse, Saxon.] A kind of food made by pressing the curd of coagulated milk, and suffering the mass to dry.

I will rather trust a Fleming with my butter, parson Hugh the Welchman with my *cheese*, than my wife with herself.
Shakesp. Merry Wives of Windsor.

CHE'ESECAKE. *n. s.* [from *cheese* and *cake.*] A cake made of soft curds, sugar and butter.

Effeminate he sat, and quiet;
Strange product of a *cheesecake* diet. *Prior.*
Where many a man at variance with his wife,
With soft'ning mead and *cheesecake* ends the strife.
King's Art of Cookery.

CHE'ESEMONGER. *n. s.* [from *cheese* and *monger.*] One who deals in cheese.

A true owl of London,
That gives out he is undone,
Being a *cheesemonger*,
By trusting. *Ben Johnson's Owls.*

CHE'ESEPRESS. *n. s.* [from *cheese* and *press.*] The press in which the curds are pressed.

The cleanly *cheesepress* she could never turn,
Her aukward fist did ne'er employ the churn. *Gay's Past.*

CHE'ESEVAT. *n. s.* [from *cheese* and *vat.*] The woodencase in which the curds are confined when they are pressed into cheese.

His sense occasions the careless rustick to judge the sun no bigger than a *cheesevat*. *Glanville's Scepsis, c.* 10.

CHE'ESY. *adj.* [from *cheese.*] Having the nature or form of cheese.

Acids mixed with them precipitate a tophaceous chalky matter, but not a *cheesy* substance. *Arbuthnot on Aliments.*

CHE'LY. *n. s.* [*chela*, Lat.] The claw of a shell fish.

It happeneth often, I confess, that a lobster hath the *chely*, or great claw, of one side longer than the other.
Brown's Vulgar Errours, b. iii. *c.* 5.

CHEMISTRY. See CHYMISTRY.

CHEQUER. See CHECKER.

To CHE'RISH. *v. a.* [*cherir*, Fr.] To support and forward with encouragement, help, and protection; to shelter; to nurse up.

Whenever Buckingham doth turn his hate
Upon your grace, and not with duteous love
Doth *cherish* you and yours, God punish me
With hate in those where I expect most love. *Shak. R.* III.
I would I were thy bird.——
—— —— Sweet, so would I;
But I should kill thee with too much *cherishing*.
Shakesp. Romeo and Juliet.
What doth *cherish* weeds but gentle air? *Shakesp. H.* VI.

Magistrates have always thought themselves concerned to *cherish* religion, and to maintain in the minds of men the belief of a God and another life. *Tillotson.*

But old god Saturn, which doth all devour,
Doth *cheriſh* her, and ſtill augments her might. *Davies.*

He that knowingly commits an ill, has the upbraidings of his own conſcience; thoſe who act by error, have its *cheriſhings* and encouragements to confirm and animate them. *Decay of Piety.*

CHE'RISHER. *n. ſ.* [from *cheriſh.*] An encourager; a ſupporter.

One of their greateſt praiſes it is to be the maintainers and *cheriſhers* of a regular devotion, a reverend worſhip, a true and decent piety. *Sprat's Serm.*

CHE'RISHMENT. *n. ſ.* [from *cheriſh.*] Encouragement; ſupport; comfort. It is now obſolete.

The one lives, her age's ornament,
That with rich bounty and dear *cheriſhment*,
Supports the praiſe of noble poeſie.
Spenſer's Tears of the Muſes.

CHE'RRY. *n. ſ.*
CHE'RRY-TREE. *n. ſ.* } [*ceriſe*, Fr. *ceraſus*, Lat.]

The tree hath large ſhining leaves: the fruit grows on long pedicles, and is roundiſh or heart-ſhaped: the ſtone is ſhort, tumid, and roundiſh. The ſpecies are; 1. The common red or garden cherry. 2. Large Spaniſh cherry. 3. The red heart cherry. 4. The white heart cherry. 5. The bleeding heart cherry. 6. The black heart cherry. 7. The May cherry. 8. The black cherry, or mazard. 9. The archduke cherry. 10. The yellow Spaniſh cherry. 11. The Flanders cluſter cherry. 12. The carnation cherry. 13. The large black cherry. 14. The bird cherry. 15. The red bird or Corniſh cherry. 16. The largeſt double flowered cherry. 17. The double flowered cherry. 18. The common wild cherry. 19. The wild northern Engliſh cherry, with late ripe fruit. 20. The ſhock or perfumed cherry. 21. The cherrytree with ſtriped leaves. And many other ſorts of cherries; as the amber cherry, lukeward, corone, Gaſcoigne, and the morello, which is chiefly planted for preſerving.

This fruit was brought out of Pontus at the time of the Mithridatick victory, by Lucullus, in the year of Rome 680; and was brought into Britain about 120 years afterwards, which was *An. Dom.* 55; and was ſoon after ſpread through moſt parts of Europe. It is generally eſteemed for its earlineſs, being of the firſt tree-fruits that appears to welcome in the fruit-ſeaſon. *Miller.*

Some devils aſk but the parings of one's nail, a pin, a nut, a *cherry* ſtone; but ſhe, more covetous, would have a chain. *Shakeſ. Com. of Errors.*

July I would have drawn in a jacket of light-yellow eating *cherries*, with his face and boſom ſun-burnt. *Peacham.*

All this done by a little ſpark of life, which, in its firſt appearance, might be incloſed in the hollow of a *cherry* ſtone. *Hale's Orig. of Mankind.*

All the ideas of all the ſenſible qualities of a *cherry* come into my mind by ſenſation. *Locke.*

CHE'RRY. *adj.* [from the ſubſtantive.] Reſembling a *cherry* in colour.

Shore's wife hath a pretty foot,
A *cherry* lip, a paſſing pleaſing tongue. *Shakeſ. Rich.* III.

CHE'RRY BAY. See LAUREL.

CHE'RRYCHEEKED. *adj.* [from *cherry* and *cheek.*] Having ruddy cheeks.

I warrant them *cherrycheek'd* country girls. *Cong. Old Bat.*

CHE'RRYPIT. *n. ſ.* [from *cherry* and *pit.*] A child's play, in which they throw cherry ſtones into a ſmall hole.

What! man, 'tis not for gravity to play at *cherrypit*. *Shakeſp. Twelfth Night.*

CHERSONE'SE. *n. ſ.* [χερσόνησος.] A peninſula; a tract of land almoſt ſurrounded by the ſea, but joined to the continent by a narrow neck or iſthmus.

CHERT. *n. ſ.* [from *quartz*, Germ.] A kind of flint.

Flint is moſt commonly found in form of nodules; but 'tis ſometimes found in thin ſtratæ, when 'tis called *chert.* *Woodw.*

CHE'RUB. *n. ſ.* [כרב *plur.* כרבים] It is ſometimes written in the plural, improperly, cherubims.]

A celeſtial ſpirit, which, in the hierarchy, is placed next in order to the ſeraphim. All the ſeveral deſcriptions which the Scripture gives us of *cherubim*, differ from one another; as they are deſcribed in the ſhapes of men, eagles, oxen, lions, and in a compoſition of all theſe figures put together. The hieroglyphical repreſentations in the embroidery upon the curtains of the Tabernacle, were called by Moſes, *Exod.* xxvi. 1. *cherubim* of cunning work. *Calmet.*

The roof o' th' chamber
With gold *cherubims* is fretted. *Shakeſp. Cymbeline.*

Heav'n's *cherubin* hors'd,
Upon the ſightleſs courſers of the air,
Shall blow the horrid deed in ev'ry eye,
That tears ſhall drown the wind. *Shakeſp. Macbeth.*

Some *cherub* finiſhes what you begun,
And to a miracle improves a tune. *Prior.*

CHERU'BICK. *adj.* [from *cherub.*] Angelick; relating to the cherubim.

Thy words
Attentive, and with more delighted ear,
Divine inſtructor! I have heard, than when
Cherubick ſongs by night from neighb'ring hills
Aerial muſick ſend. *Milton's Paradiſe Loſt, b.* v. *l.* 547.

And on the eaſt ſide of the garden place,
Where entrance up from Eden eaſieſt climbs,
Cherubick watch. *Milton's Paradiſe Loſt, b.* xi. *l.* 120.

CHE'RUBIN. *adj.* [from *cherub.*] Angelical.

This fell whore of thine,
Hath in her more deſtruction than thy ſword,
For all her *cherubin* look. *Shakeſp. Timon.*

CHE'RVIL. *n. ſ.* [*chærophyllum*, Lat.] It is an umbelliferous plant, whoſe leaves are divided into many ſegments: the petals of the flower are bifid and heart-ſhaped; and each flower is ſucceeded by two long ſeeds, not furrowed. The ſpecies are; 1. Garden *chervil.* 2. Wild perennial *chervil*, or cow-weed. The firſt of theſe ſpecies is cultivated for ſallads. *Miller.*

To CHE'RUP. *v. n.* [from *cheer*; perhaps from *cheer up*; corrupted to *cherip.*] To chirp; to uſe a cheerful voice.

The birds
Frame to thy ſong their cheerful *cheriping*;
Or hold their peace for ſhame of thy ſweet lays. *Spenſ. Paſt.*

CHE'SLIP. *n. ſ.* A ſmall vermin, that lies under ſtones or tiles. *Skinner.*

CHESS. *n. ſ.* [*echec*, Fr.] A nice and abſtruſe game, in which two ſets of men are moved in oppoſition to each other.

This game the Perſian magi did invent,
The force of Eaſtern wiſdom to expreſs;
From thence to buſy Europeans ſent,
And ſtyl'd by modern Lombards penſive *cheſs.* *Denham.*

So have I ſeen a king on *cheſs*,
(His rooks and knights withdrawn,
His queen and biſhops in diſtreſs)
Shifting about, grow leſs and leſs,
With here and there a pawn. *Dryden.*

CHE'SS-APPLE. *n. ſ.* See WILD SERVICE, of which it is a ſpecies.

CHE'SS-BOARD. *n. ſ.* [from *cheſs* and *board.*] The board or table on which the game of cheſs is plaid.

And cards are dealt, and *cheſsboards* brought,
To eaſe the pain of coward thought. *Prior.*

CHE'SS-MAN. *n. ſ.* [from *cheſs* and *man.*] A puppet for cheſs.

A company of *cheſsmen*, ſtanding on the ſame ſquares of the cheſsboard where we left them: we ſay, they are all in the ſame place, or unmoved. *Locke.*

CHE'SS-PLAYER. *n. ſ.* [from *cheſs* and *player.*] A gameſter at cheſs.

Thus like a ſkilful *cheſsplayer*, by little and little, he draws out his men, and makes his pawns of uſe to his greater perſons. *Dryden on Dramatick Poeſy.*

CHE'SSOM.

The tender *cheſſom* and mellow earth is the beſt, being mere mould, between the two extremes of clay and ſand; eſpecially if it be not loomy and binding. *Bacon's Nat. Hiſt.* N°. 665.

CHEST. *n. ſ.* [cyſt, Sax. *ciſta*, Lat.]

1. A box of wood or other materials, in which things are laid up.

He will ſeek there, on my word: neither preſs, *cheſt*, trunk, well, vault, but he hath an abſtract for the remembrance of ſuch places. *Shakeſp. Merry Wives of Windſor.*

But more have been by avarice oppreſt,
And heaps of money crowded in the *cheſt.* *Dryd. Juv. Sat.*

2. A CHEST *of Drawers.* A caſe with boxes or drawers.

3. The trunk of the body, or cavity from the ſhoulders to the belly.

Such as have round faces, or broad *cheſts*, or ſhoulders, have ſeldom or never long necks. *Brown's Vul. Err. b.* vii. *c.* 14.

He deſcribes another by the largeneſs of his *cheſt*, and breadth of his ſhoulders. *Pope's Notes on the Iliad.*

To CHEST. *v. a.* [from the noun.] To repoſite in a cheſt; to hoard.

CHEST-FOUNDERING. *n. ſ.* A diſeaſe in horſes. It comes near to a pleuriſy, or peripneumony, in a human body. *Far. Dict.*

CHE'STED. *adj.* [from *cheſt.*] Having a cheſt; as broad-cheſted, narrow-cheſted.

CHE'STER. See CASTOR.

CHE'STNUT. *n. ſ.*
CHE'STNUT-TREE. *n. ſ.* } [*chaſtaigne*, Fr. *caſtanea*, Lat.]

1. The tree hath katkins, which are placed at remote diſtances from the fruit, on the ſame tree. The outer coat of the fruit is very rough, and has two or three nuts included in each huſk or covering. This tree was formerly in greater plenty, as may be proved by the old buildings in London, which were, for the moſt part, of this timber; which is equal in value to the beſt oak, and, for many purpoſes, far exceeds it, particularly for making veſſels for liquors; it having a property, when once thoroughly ſeaſoned, to maintain its bulk conſtantly, and is not ſubject to ſhrink or ſwell, like other timber. *Miller.*

2. The fruit of the cheſtnut-tree.

A woman's tongue,
That gives not half ſo great a blow to th' ear,
As will a *cheſtnut* in a farmer's fire. *Shakeſ. Tam. of the Shrew.*

October has a baſket of ſervices, medlars and *cheſtnuts*, and fruits that ripen at the latter time. *Peacham on Drawing.*

3. The name of a brown colour.

His

His hair is of a good colour ———
——An excellent colour: your *cheſtnut* was ever the only colour *Shakeſp. As you like it.*

Merab's long hair was gloſſy *cheſtnut* brown. *Cowl. Dav.*

CHE'TON. *n. ſ.* See PLUM, of which it is a ſpecies.

CHEVALI'ER. *n. ſ.* [*chevalier*, Fr.] A knight; a gallant ſtrong man.

Renowned Talbot doth expect my aid;
And I am lowted by a traitor villain,
And cannot help the noble *chevalier*. *Shakeſ. Hen.* VI. *p.* 1.

CHEVA'UX de Friſe. *n. ſ.* [Fr. The ſingular *Cheval de Friſe* is ſeldom uſed.] The Frieſland horſe, which is a piece of timber, larger or ſmaller, and traverſed with wooden ſpikes, pointed with iron, five or ſix feet long; uſed in defending a paſſage, ſtopping a breach, or making a retrenchment to ſtop the cavalry. It is alſo called a turnpike, or tourniquet. *Chambers.*

CHE'VEN. *n. ſ.* [*cheveſne*, Fr.] A river fiſh; the ſame with chub.

CHE'VERIL. *n. ſ.* [*cheverau*, Fr.] A kid; kidleather.

A ſentence is but a *cheveril* glove to a good wit: how quickly the wrong ſide may be turned outward. *Shakeſp. Twelf. Night.*

Which gifts the capacity
Of your ſoft *cheveril* conſcience would receive,
If you might pleaſe to ſtretch it. *Shakeſpeare's Henry* VII.

O, here's a wit of *cheveril*, that ſtretches from an inch narrow to an ell broad. *Shakeſpeare's Romeo and Juliet.*

CHE'VISANCE. *n. ſ.* [*cheviſance*, Fr.] Enterprize; atchievement; A word now not in uſe.

Fortune, the foe of famous *cheviſance*,
Seldom, ſaid Guyon, yields to virtue's aid,
But in her way throws miſchief and miſchance.
Fairy Queen, b. ii. *cant.* 9. *ſtan.* 8.

CHE'VRON. *n. ſ.* [French.] One of the honourable ordinaries in heraldry. It repreſents two rafters of a houſe, ſet up as they ought to ſtand. *Harris.*

To CHEW. *v. a.* [ceopyan, Sax. *kauwen*, Dutch. It is very frequently pronounced *chaw*, and perhaps properly.]

1. To grind with the teeth; to maſticate.

If little faults, proceeding on diſtemper,
Shall not be wink'd at, how ſhall we ſtretch our eye,
When capital crimes, *chew'd*, ſwallow'd, and digeſted,
Appear before us. *Shakeſpeare's Henry* V.

Pacing through the foreſt,
Chewing the food of ſweet and bitter fancy. *Sh. As you like it.*

This pious cheat, that never ſuck'd the blood,
Nor *chew'd* the fleſh of lambs. *Dryden's Fables.*

The vales
Deſcending gently, where the lowing herd
Chews verd'rous paſture. *Philips.*

By *chewing*, ſolid aliment is divided into ſmall parts: in a human body, there is no other inſtrument to perform this action but the teeth. By the action of *chewing*, the ſpittle and mucus are ſqueezed from the glands, and mixed with the aliment; which action, if it be long continued, will turn the aliment into a ſort of chyle. *Arbuthnot on Aliments.*

2. To meditate; or ruminate in the thoughts.

While the fierce monk does at his trial ſtand,
He *chews* revenge, abjuring his offence:
Guile in his tongue, and murder in his hand,
He ſtabs his judge, to prove his innocence. *Prior.*

3. To taſte without ſwallowing.

Heav'n's in my mouth,
As if I did but only *chew* its name. *Shakeſp. Meaſ. for Meaſ.*

Some books are to be taſted, others to be ſwallowed, and ſome few to be *chewed* and digeſted: that is, ſome books are to be read only in parts; others to be read, but not curiouſly; and ſome few to be read wholly, with diligence and attention. *Bacon, Eſſay* 51.

To CHEW. *v. n.* To champ upon; to ruminate.

I will with patience hear, and find a time;
'Till then, my noble friend, *chew* upon this. *Shak. Jul. Cæſ.*

Inculcate the doctrine of diſobedience, and then leave the multitude to *chew* upon't. *L'Eſtrange, Fab.* 67.

Old politicians *chew* on wiſdom paſt,
And blunder on in buſineſs to the laſt. *Pope's Epiſt.* 1. *l.* 244.

CHICA'NE. *n. ſ.* [*chicane*, Fr. derived by *Menage* from the Spaniſh word *chico*, little.]

1. The art of protracting a conteſt by petty objection and artifice.

The general part of the civil law concerns not the *chicane* of private caſes, but the affairs and intercourſe of civilized nations, grounded upon the principles of reaſon. *Locke on Educ.*

His attornies have hardly one trick left; they are at an end of all their *chicane*. *Arbuthnot's Hiſtory of John Bull.*

2. Artifice in general. This ſenſe is only in familiar language.

Unwilling then in arms to meet,
He ſtrove to lengthen the campaign,
And ſave his forces by *chicane*. *Prior.*

To CHICA'NE. *v. n.* [*chicaner*, Fr.] To prolong a conteſt by tricks.

CHICA'NER. *n. ſ.* [*chicaneur*, Fr.] A petty ſophiſter; a trifling diſputant; a wrangler.

This is the only way to diſtinguiſh the two moſt different things I know in the world, a logical *chicaner* from a man of reaſon. *Locke on Human Underſtanding, S.* 3.

CHICA'NERY. *n. ſ.* [*chicanerie*, Fr.] Sophiſtry; mean arts of wrangle.

His anger at his ill ſucceſs, cauſed him to deſtroy the greateſt part of theſe reports; and only to preſerve ſuch as diſcovered moſt of the *chicanery* and futility of the practice. *Arbuthnot and Pope's Mart. Scrib.*

CHICHES. *n. ſ.* See CHICKPEAS.

CHI'CHLING VETCH. *n. ſ.* [*lathyrus*, Lat.] The plants of this ſpecies produce abundance of flowers, which are very ornamental in baſons or pots of flowers to place in chimnies, and other parts of large rooms. In Germany they are cultivated, and eaten as peas, though neither ſo tender nor well taſted. *Miller.*

CHICK. *n. ſ.* }
CHICKEN. *n. ſ.* } [cicen, Sax. *kiecken*, Dut.]

1. The young of a bird, particularly of a hen, or ſmall bird.

All my pretty ones?
What, all my pretty *chickens*, and their dam,
At one fell ſwoop! *Shakeſpear's Macbeth.*

For when the ſhell is broke, out comes a *chick*. *Davies.*

While it is a *chick*, and hath no ſpurs, nor cannot hurt, nor yet hath ſeen the like motion, yet he readily practiſeth it. *Hale's Origin of Mankind.*

Ev'n ſince ſhe was a ſe'n-night old, they ſay,
Was chaſte and humble to her dying day;
Nor *chick*, nor hen, was known to diſobey. *Dryd. Fables.*

Having the notion that one laid the egg out of which the other was hatched, I have a clear idea of the relation of dam and *chick*. *Locke.*

On rainy days alone I dine,
Upon a *chick* and pint of wine:
On rainy days I dine alone,
And pick my *chicken* to the bone. *Swift's Miſcellanies.*

2. A word of tenderneſs.

My Ariel, *chick*,
This is thy charge. *Shakeſpeare's Tempeſt.*

3. A term for a young girl.

Then, Chloe, ſtill go on to prate
Of thirty-ſix and thirty-eight;
Purſue your trade of ſcandal-picking,
Your hints, that Stella is no *chicken*. *Swift.*

CHI'CKENHEARTED. *adj.* [from *chicken* and *heart.*] Cowardly; timorous; fearful.

Now we ſet up for tilting in the pit,
Where 'tis agreed by bullies, *chickenhearted*,
To fright the ladies firſt, and then be parted. *Prol to Sp. Fr.*

The CHI'CKENPOX. *n. ſ.* An exanthematous diſtemper, ſo called from its being of no very great danger.

CHI'CKLING. *n. ſ.* [from *chick.*] A ſmall chicken.

CHI'CKPEAS. *n. ſ.* [from *chick* and *pea.*]

It hath a papilionaceous flower, ſucceeded by ſhort ſwelling pods, like the inflated bladder of a fiſh: the ſeeds are ſhaped like a ram's head. It is ſeldom cultivated in England, where peas will do well, which are much preferable. *Miller.*

CHI'CKWEED. *n. ſ.* [*chick* and *weed.*] The name of a plant.

Green mint, or *chickweed*, are common applications, and of good uſe, in all the hard ſwellings of the breaſt, occaſioned by milk. *Wiſeman of Tumours.*

To CHIDE. *v. a.* preter. *chid* or *chode*, part. *chid* or *chidden.* [cidan, Sax.]

1. To reprove; to check; to correct with words: applied to perſons.

Chide him for faults, and do it reverently,
When you perceive his blood inclin'd to mirth. *Sh. Hen.* VI.

If he do ſet
The very wings of reaſon to his heels,
And fly like *chidden* Mercury from Jove. *Sh. Troil. & Creſ.*

Thoſe, that do teach your babes,
Do it with gentle means, and eaſy taſks;
He might have *chid* me ſo: for, in good faith,
I am a child to chiding. *Shakeſpeare's Othello.*

Scylla wept,
And *chid* her barking waves into attention. *Milton.*

Above the waves as Neptune ſhew'd his face,
To *chide* the winds, and ſave the Trojan race. *Waller.*

You look, as if yon ſtern philoſopher
Had juſt now *chid* you. *Addiſon's Cato.*

If any woman of better faſhion in the pariſh happened to be abſent from church, they were ſure of a viſit from him, to *chide* and to dine with her. *Swift.*

2. To drive away with reproof.

Margaret my queen, and Clifford too,
Have *chid* me from the battle. *Shakeſpeare's Henry* VI.

3. To blame; to reproach: applied to things.

Winds murmur'd through the leaves your long delay,
And fountains, o'er the pebbles, *chid* your ſtay. *Dryden.*

I *chid* the folly of my thoughtleſs haſte;
For, the work perfected, the joy was paſt. *Prior.*

To CHIDE, *v. n.*

1. To clamour; to ſcold.

What had he to do to *chide* at me. *Shakesp. As you like it.*

Next morn, betimes, the bride was missing:
The mother scream'd, the father *chid*,
Where can this idle wench be hid? *Swift.*

2. To quarrel with.

The business of the state does him offence,
And he does *chide* with you. *Shakespeare's Othello.*

3. To make a noise.

My duty,
As doth a rock against the *chiding* flood,
Should the approach of this wild river break,
And stand unshaken yours. *Shakespear's Henry* VIII.

CHI'DER. *n. s.* [from *chide.*] A rebuker; a reprover.

Not her that chides, sir, at any hand, I pray.—
I love no chiders, sir. *Shakesp. Taming of the Shrew.*

CHIEF. *adj.* [*chef*, the head, Fr.]

1. Principal; most eminent; above the rest in any respect.

These were the *chief* of the officers that were over Solomon's works. 1 *Kings* ix. 23.

The hand of the princes and rulers hath been *chief* in this trespass. *Ezra* ix. 2.

Your country, *chief* in arms, abroad defend;
At home, with morals, arts, and laws amend. *Pope's Epist.*

2. Eminent; extraordinary.

A froward man soweth strife, and a whisperer separateth *chief* friends *Proverbs* xvi. 28.

3. Capital; of the first order; that to which other parts are inferior, or subordinate.

I came to have a good general view of the apostle's main purpose in writing the epistle, and the *chief* branches of his discourse wherein he prosecuted it. *Locke's Pref. to St. Paul's Ep.*

4. It is used by some writers in the superlative degree; but, I think, improperly: the comparative is never found.

We beseech you, bend you to remain
Here in the cheer and comfort of our eye,
Our *chiefest* courtier, cousin, and our son. *Shakesp. Hamlet.*
Doeg an Edomite, the *chiefest* of the herdmen. 1 *Sa* xxi. 7.

He sometimes denied admission to the *chiefest* officers of the army. *Clarendon, b.* viii.

CHIEF. *n. s.* [from the adjective.]

1. A commander; a leader.

Is pain to them
Less pain, less to be fled? or thou than they
Less hardy to endure? couragious *chief!*
The first in flight from pain. *Milton's Paradise Lost, b.* iv.

After or before were never known
Such *chiefs*; as each an army seem'd alone. *Dryden's Fab.*

A wit's a feather, and a *chief* a rod;
An honest man's the noblest work of God. *Pope's Ess. on Man.*

A prudent *chief* not always must display
His pow'rs in equal ranks, and fair array;
But with th' occasion and the place comply,
Conceal his force, nay seem sometimes to fly. *Po. Ess. Crit.*

2. In CHIEF, in law. *In capite*, without a superior lord.

All sums demandable, either for licence of alienation to be made of lands holden in *chief*, or for the pardon of any such alienation already made without licence, have been stayed in the way to the hanaper. *Bacon's Off. Alienations.*

I shall be proud to hold my dependance on you in *chief*, as I do part of my small fortune in Wiltshire. *Dryd. Ded. to Cleom.*

3. In Spenser it seems to signify somewhat like atchievement; a mark of distinction.

Where be the nosegays that she dight for thee?
The coloured chaplets wrought with a *chief*,
The knottish rush-rings, and gilt rosemary. *Spens. Past.*

4. In heraldry.

The *chief* is so called of the French word *chef*, the head or upper part: this possesses the upper third part of the escutcheon. *Peacham on Drawing.*

CHI'EFLESS. *adj.* [from *chief.*] Without a head; without a leader.

And *chiefless* armies doz'd out the campaign,
And navies yawn'd for orders on the main. *Dunciad, b.* iv.

CHI'EFLY. *adv.* [from *chief.*] Principally; eminently; more than common.

Any man who will seriously consider the nature of an epic poem, what actions it describes, and what persons they are *chiefly* whom it informs, will find it a work full of difficulty. *Dryden's Juven. Preface.*

Those parts of the kingdom, where the number and estates of the dissenters *chiefly* lay. *Swift.*

CHI'EFRIE. *n. s.* [from *chief.*] A small rent paid to the lord Paramount.

They shall be well able to live upon those lands, to yield her majesty reasonable *chiefrie*, and also give a competent maintenance unto the garrisons. *Spenser's Ireland.*

Would the reserved rent at this day be any more than a small *chiefrie*. *Swift.*

CHI'EFTAN. *n. s.* [from *chief*, *n. s.* captain.]

1. A leader; a commander.

That forc'd their *chieftain*, for his safety's sake,
(Their *chieftain* Humber named was aright)
Unto the mighty stream him to betake,
Where he an end of battle and of life did make. *Fairy Qu.*

2. The head of a clan.

It broke, and absolutely subdued all the lords and *chieftains* of the Irishry. *Davies on Ireland.*

CHIE'VANCE. *n. s.* [probably from *achevance*, Fr. purchase.] Traffick, in which money is extorted; as discount. Now obsolete.

There were good laws against usury, the bastard use of money; and against unlawful *chievances* and exchanges, which is bastard usury. *Bacon's Henry* VII.

CHILBLA'IN. *n. s.* [from *chil'*, cold, and *blain*; so that Temple seems mistaken in his etymology, or has written it wrong to serve a purpose.] Sores made by frost.

I remembered the cure of *childblanes* when I was a boy, (which may be called the children's gout) by burning at the fire. *Temple.*

CHILD. *n. s.* in the plural CHILDREN. [cild, Sax.]

1. An infant, or very young person.

In age, to wish for youth is full as vain,
As for a youth to turn a *child* again. *Denham.*

We should no more be kinder to one *child* than to another, than we are tender of one eye more than of the other *L'Estr.*

The young lad must not be ventured abroad at eight or ten, for fear of what may happen to the tender *child*; though he then runs ten times less risque than at sixteen. *Locke.*

The stroak of death is nothing: *children* endure it, and the greatest cowards find it no pain. *Wake's Prep for Death.*

2. One in the line of filiation, opposed to the parent.

Where *children* have been exposed, or taken away young, and afterwards have approached to their parents presence, the parents, though they have not known them, have had a secret joy, or other alteration thereupon. *Bacon's Nat. Hist.* N°. 239.

I shall see
The winged vengeance overtake such *children*. *Shakes. K. L.*

So unexhausted her perfections were,
That for more *children*, she had more to spare. *Dryden.*

He in a fruitful wife's embraces old,
A long increase of *children's children* told. *Add. Ovid's Met.*

3. In the language of scripture.

One weak in knowledge. *Isa.* x. 19. 1 *Cor.* xiii. 11.
Such as are young in grace. 1 *John*, ii. 13.
Such as are humble and docile. *Matt.* xvii. 3, 4.

The descendants of a man, how remote soever, are called *children*; as the *children* of Edom, the *children* of Israel.

The *children* of light, the *children* of darkness; who follow light, who remain in darkness.

The elect, the blessed, are also called the *children* of God.

How is he numbered among the *children* of God, and his lot is among the saints! *Wisdom*, v. 5.

In the New Testament, believers are commonly called *children* of God.

Ye are all the *children* of God, by faith in Jesus Christ. *Gal.* iii. 26. *Calmet.*

4. A girl child.

Mercy on's, a bearne! a very pretty bearne!
A boy, or *child*, I wonder! *Shakespeare's Winter's Tale.*

5. Any thing, the product or effect of another.

Macduff, this noble passion,
Child of integrity, hath from my soul
Wip'd the black scruples. *Shakespeare's Macbeth.*

6. *To be with* CHILD. To be pregnant.

If it must stand still, let wives with *child*,
Pray that their burthen may not fall this day,
Lest that their hopes prodigiously be crost. *Shakesp. K. John.*

To CHILD. *v. n.* [from the noun.] To bring children.

The spring, the summer,
The *childing* autumn, angry winter change
Their wonted liveries. *Shakesp. Midsummer Night Dream.*

As to *childing* women, young vigorous people, after irregularities of diet, in such it begins with hæmorrhages. *Arbuthnot.*

CHI'LDBEARING, participial substantive. [from *child* and *bear.*] The act of bearing children.

To thee,
Pains only in *childbearing* were foretold,
And, bringing forth, soon recompens'd with joy,
Fruit of thy womb. *Milton's Paradise Lost, b.* x. *l.* 1051.

The timorous and irresolute Sylvia has demurred 'till she is past *childbearing*. *Addison's Spectat.* N°. 89.

CHI'LDBED. *n. s.* [from *child* and *bed.*] The state of a woman bringing a child, or being in labour.

The funerals of prince Arthur, and of queen Elizabeth, who died in *childbed* in the Tower. *Bacon's Henry* VII.

Pure, as when wash'd from spot of *childbed* stain. *Par. Reg.*

Yet these, tho' poor, the pain of *childbed* bear. *Dryd. Juv.*

Let no one be actually married, 'till she hath the *childbed* pillows. *Spect.* N°. 606.

Women in *childbed* are in the case of persons wounded. *Arbuthnot on Diet.*

CHI'LDBIRTH. *n. s.* [from *child* and *birth.*] Travail; labour; the time of bringing forth; the act of bringing forth.

The

The mother of Pyrocles, shortly after her *childbirth*, died. *Sidney, b.* ii.

A kernel void of any taste, but not so of virtue, especially for women travailling in *childbirth*. *Carew's Survey of Cornwall.*

In the whole sex of women, God hath decreed the sharpest pains of *childbirth*; to shew, that there is no state exempt from sorrow. *Taylor's Holy Living.*

He to his wife, before the time assign'd
For *childbirth* came, thus bluntly spoke his mind. *Dryden.*

CHI'LDED. *adj.* [from *child.*] Furnished with a child.

How light and portable my pain seems now,
When that which makes me bend, makes the king bow;
He *childed* as I father'd. *Shakespeare's King Lear.*

CHI'LDERMAS DAY. [from *child* and *mass.*]

The day of the week, throughout the year, answering to the day on which the feast of the holy Innocents is solemnized, which weak and superstitious persons think an unlucky day.

So you talk not of hares, or such uncouth things; for that proves as ominous to the fisherman, as the beginning of a voyage on the day when *childermas day* fell, doth to the mariner. *Carew's Survey of Cornwall.*

CHI'LDHOOD. *n. s.* [from *child*, cilbhab, Sax.]

1. The state of infants; or, according to some, the time in which we are children.

Now I have stain'd the *childhood* of our joy
With blood, remov'd but little from our own. *Sh. R. & J.*

The sons of lords and gentlemen should be trained up in learning from their *childhoods*. *Spenser on Ireland.*

Seldom have I ceas'd to eye
Thy infancy, thy *childhood*, and thy youth. *Milt. Pa. Reg.*

The same authority that the actions of a man have with us in our *childhood*, the same, in every period of life, has the practice of all whom we regard as our superiours. *Rogers's Ser.*

2. The time of life between infancy and puberty.

Infancy and *childhood* demand thin, copious, nourishing aliment. *Arbuthnot on Aliments.*

3. The properties of a child.

Their love in early infancy began,
And rose as *childhood* ripen'd into man. *Dryden's Fables.*

CHI'LDISH. *adj.* [from *child.*]

1. Having the qualities of a child; trifling; ignorant; simple.

Learning hath its infancy, when it is but beginning and almost *childish*: then its youth, when it is luxuriant and juvenile. *Bacon's Essay*, 58.

2. Becoming only children; trivial; puerile.

Musidorus being elder by three or four years, by the difference there was taken away the occasion of *childish* contentions. *Sidney, b.* ii.

The lion's whelps she saw how he did bear,
And lull in rugged arms withouten *childish* fear. *Fairy Qu.*

When I was yet a child, no *childish* play
To me was pleasing; all my mind was set
Serious to learn and know. *Paradise Regained, b.* I.

The fathers looked on the worship of images as the most silly and *childish* thing in the world. *Stillingfleet's Defence.*

One that hath newly learn'd to speak and go,
Loves *childish* plays. *Roscommon.*

They have spoiled the beauty of the walls with abundance of *childish* sentences, that consist often in a jingle of words. *Addison on Italy.*

By conversation the *childish* humours of their younger days might be worn out. *Arbuthnot's History of J. Bull.*

CHI'LDISHLY. *adv.* [from *childish.*] In a childish trifling way; like a child.

Together with his fame their infamy was spread, who had so rashly and *childishly* ejected him. *Hooker's Preface.*

It is a thick misty error, supported by some men of excellent judgment in their own professions, but *childishly* unskilful in any thing besides. *Hayward on Edward* VI.

CHI'LDISHNESS. *n. s.* [from *childish.*]

1. Puerility; triflingness.

The actions of *childishness*, and unfashionable carriage, time and age will of itself be sure to reform. *Locke.*

Nothing in the world could give a truer idea of the superstition, credulity, and *childishness* of the Roman catholick religion. *Addison on Italy.*

2. Harmlessness.

Speak thou, boy;
Perhaps thy *childishness* will move him more
Than can our reasons. *Shakespear's Coriolanus.*

CHI'LDLESS. *adj.* [from *child.*] Without children; without offspring.

As thy sword hath made women *childless*, so shall thy mother be *childless* among women. 1 *Samuel*, xv. 33.

A man shall see the noblest works and foundations have proceeded from *childless* men; which have sought to express the images of their minds, where those of their bodies have failed: so the care of posterity is most in them that have no posterity. *Bacon's Essay*, 7.

Childless thou art, *childless* remain: so death
Shall be deceiv'd his glut. *Milton's Paradise Lost, b.* x. *l.* 989.

She can give you the reason why such a one died *childless*. *Spectator*, N°. 403.

CHI'LDLIKE. *adj.* [from *child* and *like.*] Becoming or beseeming a child.

Who can owe no less than *childlike* obedience to her that hath more than motherly care. *Hooker, b.* v. *s.* 8.

I thought the remnant of mine age
Should have been cherish'd by her *childlike* duty. *Shakespeare.*

CHI'LIAD. *n. s.* [from χιλιάς.] A thousand; a collection or sum containing a thousand.

We make cycles and periods of years; as decads, centuries, *chiliads*, &c. for the use of computation in history. *Holder.*

CHILIA'EDRON. *n. s.* [from χιλια.] A figure of a thousand sides.

In a man, who speaks of a *chiliaedron*, or a body of a thousand sides, the idea of the figure may be very confused, though that of the number be very distinct. *Locke.*

CHILIFA'CTVE. *adj.* [from *chile.*] That which makes chile.

Whether this be not effected by some way of corrosion, rather than any proper digestion, *chilifactive* mutation, or alimental conversion. *Brown's Vulgar Errors, b.* iii. *c.* 23.

CHILIFA'CTORY. *adj.* [from *chile.*] That which has the quality of making chile.

We should rather rely upon a *chilifactory* menstruum, or digestive preparation drawn from species or individuals, whose stomachs peculiarly dissolve lapideous bodies. *Brown's Vul. Er.*

CHILIFICA'TION. *n s.* [from *chile.*] The act of making chile.

Nor will we affirm that iron is indigested in the stomach of the Ostriche; but we suspect this effect to proceed not from any liquid reduction, or tendence to *chylification*, by the power of natural heat. *Brown's Vulgar Errors, b.* iii. *c.* 22.

CHILL. *adj* [cele, Sax.]

1. Cold; that which is cold to the touch.

And all my plants I save from nightly ill,
Of noisom winds, and blasting vapours *chill*. *Milton.*

2. Cold; having the sensation of cold; shivering with cold.

My heart, and my *chill* veins, now freezing with despair. *Rowe's Royal Convert.*

3. Depressed; dejected; discouraged.

CHILL. *n. s.* [from the adjective.] Chilness; cold.

I very well know one to have a sort of *chill* about his præcordia and head. *Derham's Physico-Theology.*

To CHILL. *v. a.* [from the adjective.]

1. To make cold.

Age has not yet
So shrunk my sinews, or so *chill'd* my veins,
But conscious virtue in my breast remains. *Dryd. Aurengzeb.*

Heat burns his rise, frost *chills* his setting beams,
And vex the world with opposite extremes. *Creech's Manil.*

Each changing season does its poison bring;
Rheums *chill* the winter, agues blast the spring. *Prior.*

Now no more the drum
Provokes to arms; or trumpet's clangor shrill
Affrights the wives, or *chills* the virgin's blood. *Philips.*

2. To depress; to deject; to discourage.

Every thought on God *chills* the gaiety of his spirits, and awakens terrors, which he cannot bear. *Rogers's Sermons.*

3. To blast with cold.

The fruits perish on the ground,
Or soon decay, by snows immod'rate *chill'd*,
By winds are blasted, or by lightning kill'd. *Blackm. Creat.*

CHI'LLINESS. *n. s.* [from *chilly.*] A sensation of shivering cold.

If the patient survives three days, the acuteness of the pain abates, and a *chilliness* or shivering affects the body. *Arbuthnot.*

CHI'LLY. *adj.* [from *chill.*] Somewhat cold.

A *chilly* sweat bedews
My shudd'ring limbs. *Philips.*

CHI'LNESS. *n. s.* [from *chill.*] Coldness; want of warmth.

If you come out of the sun suddenly into a shade, there followeth a *chilness* or shivering in all the body. *Bac. Nat. Hist.*

This, while he thinks, he lifts aloft his dart,
A gen'rous *chilness* seizes ev'ry part,
The veins pour back the blood, and fortify the heart. *Dryd.*

CHIMB. *n. s.* [*kime*, Dut.] The end of a barrel or tub.

CHIME. *n. s.* [The original of this word is doubtful. *Junius* and *Minshew* suppose it corrupted from *cimbal*; *Skinner* from *gamme*, or *gamut*; *Henshaw* from *chiamare*, to *call*, because the *chime* calls to church. Perhaps it is only softened from *chirme*, or *churme*, an old word for the sound of many voices, or instruments making a noise together.]

1. The consonant or harmonick sound of many correspondent instruments.

Hang our shaggy thighs with bells;
That, as we do strike a tune,
In our dance, shall make a *chime*. *Ben Johnson's Fairy Pr.*

The sound
Of instruments, that made melodious *chime*,
Was heard, of harp and organ. *Milton's Paradise Lost, b.* xi.

Love virtue, she alone is free;
She can teach you how to climb
Higher than the sphery *chime*. *Milton.*

2. The

2. The correſpondence of ſound.
Love firſt invented verſe, and form'd the rhime,
The motion meaſur'd, harmoniz'd the *chime*. *Dryden's Fab.*

3. The ſound of bells, not rung by ropes, but ſtruck with hammers. In this ſenſe it is always uſed in the plural, *chimes*.
We have heard the *chimes* at midnight. *Shakeſp. Henry* IV.

4. The correſpondence of proportion or relation.
The conceptions of things are placed in their ſeveral degrees of ſimilitude; as in ſeveral proportions, one to another: in which harmonious *chimes*, the voice of reaſon is often drowned. *Grew's Coſmol. b.* ii. *c.* 6. *ſ* 51.

To CHIME. *v. n.* [from the noun.]

1. To ſound in harmony or conſonance.
To make the rough recital aptly *chime*,
Or bring the ſum of Gallia's loſs to rhime,
'Tis mighty hard. *Prior.*

2. To correſpond in relation or proportion.
Father and ſon, huſband and wife, and ſuch other correlative terms, do belong one to another; and, through cuſtom, do readily *chime*, and anſwer one another, in people's memories. *Locke.*

3. To agree; to fall in with.
He not only ſat quietly and heard his father railed at, but often *chimed* in with the diſcourſe. *Arbuth. Hiſt. of J. Bull.*

4. To ſuit with; to agree.
Any ſect, whoſe reaſonings, interpretation, and language, I have been uſed to, will, of courſe, make all *chime* that way; and make another, and perhaps the genuine meaning of the author, ſeem harſh, ſtrange and uncouth to me. *Locke.*

5. To jingle; to clatter.
But with the meaner tribe I'm forc'd to *chime*,
And, wanting ſtrength to riſe, deſcend to rhime. *Smith.*

To CHIME. *v. a.* To move, or ſtrike, or ſound harmonically, or with juſt conſonancy.
With lifted arms they order ev'ry blow,
And *chime* their ſounding hammers in a row:
With labour'd anvils Ætna groans below. *Dryd. Georg.*

2. To ſtrike a bell with a hammer.

CHIME'RA, *n. ſ.* [*Chimæra*, Lat.] A vain and wild fancy, as remote from reality as the exiſtence of the poetical chimera, a monſter feigned to have the head of a lion, the belly of a goat, and the tail of a dragon.
In ſhort, the force of dreams is of a piece,
Chimeras all; and more abſurd, or leſs. *Dryden's Fables.*
No body joins the voice of a ſheep with the ſhape of a horſe, to be the complex ideas of any real ſubſtances, unleſs he has a mind to fill his head with *chimeras*, and his diſcourſe with unintelligible words. *Locke.*

CHIME'RICAL. *adj.* [from *chimera.*] Imaginary; fanciful; wildly, vainly, or fantaſtically conceived; fantaſtick.
Notwithſtanding the fineneſs of this allegory may attone for it in ſome meaſure, I cannot think that perſons of ſuch a *chimerical* exiſtence are proper actors in an epic poem. *Spectat.*

CHIME'RICALLY. *adv.* [from *chimerical.*] Vainly; wildly; fantaſtically.

CHI'MINAGE. *n. ſ.* [from *chimin*, an old law word for a road.] A toll for paſſage through a foreſt. *Cowel.*

CHI'MNEY. *n. ſ.* [*cheminée*, French.]

1. The paſſage through which the ſmoke aſcends from the fire in the houſe.
Chimnies, with ſcorn, rejecting ſmoke. *Swift.*

2. The turret raiſed above the roof of the houſe, for conveyance of the ſmoke.
The night has been unruly: where we lay,
Our *chimnies* were blown down. *Shakeſp. Macbeth.*

3. The fireplace.
The *chimney*
Is ſouth the chamber; and the chimneypiece,
Chaſte Dian bathing. *Shakeſp. Cymbeline.*
The fire which the Chaldeans worſhipped for a god, is crept into every man's *chimney*. *Raleigh's Hiſt. b.* i. *c.* 68.
Low offices, which ſome neighbours hardly think it worth ſtirring from their *chimney* ſides to obtain. *Swift on Sac. Teſt.*

CHIMNEY-CORNER. *n. ſ.* [from *chimney* and *corner.*] The fireſide; the ſeat on each end of the firegrate; uſually noted in proverbial language for being the place of idlers.
Yet ſome old men
Tell ſtories of you in their *chimney-corner*. *Denh. Sophy.*

CHI'MNEYPIECE. *n. ſ.* [from *chimney* and *piece.*] The ornamental piece of wood, or ſtone, that is ſet round the fireplace.
Poliſh and brighten the marble hearths and *chimneypieces* with a clout dipt in greaſe; nothing maketh them ſhine ſo well. *Swift's Directions to the Houſemaid.*

CHI'MNEYSWEEPER. *n. ſ.* [from *chimney* and *ſweeper.*]

1. One whoſe trade it is to clean foul chimnies of ſoot.
To look like her, are *chimneyſweepers* black:
And ſince her time are colliers counted bright. *Shakeſp.*
The little *chimneyſweeper* ſkulks along,
And marks with ſooty ſtains the heedleſs throng. *Gay's Triv.*
Even lying Ned the *chimneyſweeper* of Savoy, and Tom the Portugal duſtman, put in their claims. *Arb. Hiſt. of J. Bull.*

2. It is uſed proverbially for one of a mean and vile occupation.
Golden lads and girls, all muſt,
As *chimneyſweepers*, come to duſt. *Shakeſp. Cymbeline.*

CHIN. *n. ſ.* [cinne, Sax. *kinn*, Germ.] The part of the face beneath the under lip.
But all the words I could get of her, was wrying her waiſt, and thruſting out her *chin*. *Sidney.*
With his amazonian *chin* he drove
The briſtled lips before him. *Shakeſp. Coriolanus.*
He rais'd his hardy head, which ſunk again,
And, ſinking on his boſom, knock'd his *chin*. *Dryd. Fables.*

CHI'NA. *n. ſ.* [from *China*, the country where it is made.] China ware; porcelain; a ſpecies of veſſels made in China, dimly tranſparent, partaking of the qualities of earth and glaſs. They are made by mingling two kinds of earth, of which one eaſily vitrifies; the other reſiſts a very ſtrong heat: when the vitrifiable earth is melted into glaſs, they are completely burnt.
Spleen, vapours, or ſmall pox, above them all,
And miſtreſs of herſelf, tho' *china* fall. *Pope's Epiſt.* ii.
After ſupper, carry your plate and *china* together in the ſame baſket. *Swift's Directions to the Butler.*

CHI'NA-ORANGE. *n. ſ.* [from *China* and *orange.*] The ſweet orange; ſuppoſed originally of China.
Not many years has the *China-orange* been propagated in Portugal and Spain. *Mortimer's Art of Huſbandry.*

CHI'NA-ROOT. *n. ſ.* [from *China* and *root.*] A medicinal root, brought originally from China.

CHI'NCOUGH. *n. ſ.* [perhaps more properly *kincough*, from *kincken*, to pant, Dut. and *cough.*] A violent and convulſive cough, to which children are ſubject.
I have obſerved a *chincough*, complicated with an intermitting fever. *Flo.er on the Humours.*

CHINE. *n. ſ.* [*eſchine*, Fr. *ſchiena*, Ital. *ſpina*, Lat. *cein*, Arm.]

1. The part of the back, in which the ſpine or backbone is found.
She ſtrake him ſuch a blow upon his *chine*, that ſhe opened all his body. *Sidney, b.* i.
He preſents her with the tuſky head,
And *chine*, with riſing briſtles roughly ſpread. *Dryd. Fables.*

2. A piece of the back of an animal.
Cut out the burly boned clown in *chines* of beef ere thou ſleep. *Shakeſp. Henry* IV. *p.* 2.
He had killed eight fat hogs for this ſeaſon, and he had dealt about his *chines* very liberally amongſt his neighbours. *Spectat.*

To CHINE. *v. a.* [from the noun.] To cut into chines.
He that in his line did *chine* the long rib'd Apennine. *Dry.*

CHINK. *n. ſ.* [cinan, to gape, Sax.] A ſmall aperture longwiſe; an opening or gap between the parts of any thing.
Pyramus and Thiſby did talk through the *chink* of a wall.
Shakeſp. Midſummer Night's Dream.
Plagues alſo have been raiſed by anointing the *chinks* of doors, and the like. *Bacon's Nat. Hiſt.* N°. 916.
Though birds have no epiglottis, yet they ſo contract the *chink* of their larinx, as to prevent the admiſſion of wet or dry indigeſted. *Brown's Vulgar Errors.*
In vain ſhe ſearch'd each cranny of the houſe,
Each gaping *chink*, impervious to a mouſe. *Swift.*
Other inventions, falſe and abſurd, that are like ſo many *chinks* and holes to diſcover the rottenneſs of the whole fabrick. *South.*

To CHINK. *v. a.* [derived by *Skinner* from the ſound.] To ſhake ſo as to make a ſound.
He *chinks* his purſe, and takes his ſeat of ſtate:
With ready quills the dedicators wait. *Pope's Dunciad, b.* ii.

To CHINK. *v. n.* To ſound by ſtriking each other.
Lord Strutt's money ſhines as bright, and *chinks* as well, as 'ſquire South's. *Arbuthnot's Hiſt. of J. Bull.*
When not a guinea *chink'd* on Martin's boards,
And Atwill's ſelf was drain'd of all his hoards. *Swift.*

CHI'NKY. *adj.* [from *chink.*] Full of holes; gaping; opening into narrow clefts.
But plaiſter thou the *chinky* hives with clay. *Dryd. Virg. Geo.*
Grimalkin, to domeſtick vermin ſworn
An everlaſting foe, with watchful eye
Lies nightly brooding o'er a *chinky* gap,
Protending her fell claws, to thoughtleſs mice
Sure ruin. *Philips's Poems.*

CHINTS. *n. ſ.* Cloath of cotton made in India, and printed with colours.
Let a charming *chints*, and Bruſſels lace,
Wrap my cold limbs, and ſhade my lifeleſs face. *Pope's Ep.*

CHI'OPPINE. *n. ſ.* [from *chapin*, Span.] A high ſhoe, formerly worn by ladies.
Your ladyſhip is nearer heaven than when I ſaw you laſt, by the altitude of a *chioppine*. *Shakeſp. Hamlet.*
The woman was a giganteſs, and yet walked always in *chioppines*. *Cowley.*

CHIP, CHEAP, CHIPPING, in the names of places, imply a market; from the Sax. cyppan ceapan, to buy. *Gibſon's Cam.*

To CHIP. *v. a.* [probably corrupted from *chop.*] To cut into ſmall pieces; to diminiſh, by cutting away a little at a time.
To return to our ſtatue in the block of marble, we ſee it ſometimes

ſometimes only begun to be *chipped*; ſometimes rough hewn, and juſt ſketched into an human figure. *Addiſ. Spectat.*

The critick ſtrikes out all that is not juſt;
And 'tis ev'n ſo the butler *chips* his cruſt. *King's Cookery.*

Induſtry
Taught him to *chip* the wood, and hew the ſtone. *Thomſ.*

CHIP. *n. ſ.* [from the verb.]

1. A ſmall piece taken off by a cutting inſtrument.

Cucumbers do extremely affect moiſture, and over-drink themſelves, which chaff or *chips* forbiddeth. *Bacon's Nat. Hiſt.*

That *chip* made the iron ſwim, not by any natural power. *Taylor's Worthy Communicant.*

The ſtraw was laid below;
Of *chips* and ſerewood was the ſecond row. *Dryd. Fables.*

2. A ſmall piece, however made.

The manganeſe lies in the vein in lumps wrecked, in an irregular manner, among clay, coarſe ſpar, and *chips* of ſtone. *Woodward on Foſſils.*

CHI'PPING. *n. ſ.* [from *to chip.*] A fragment cut off.

They dung their land with the *chippings* of a ſort of ſoft ſtone. *Mortimer's Husbandry.*

The *chippings* and filings of theſe jewels, could they be preſerved, are of more value than the whole maſs of ordinary authors. *Felton on the Claſſicks.*

CHIRA'GRICAL. *adj.* [*chiragra*, Lat.] Having the gout in the hand; ſubject to the gout in the hand.

Chiragrical perſons do ſuffer in the finger as well as in the reſt, and ſometimes firſt of all. *Brown's Vulgar Errors, b.* iv. *c.* 5.

CHIRO'GRAPHER. *n. ſ.* [χεὶρ, the hand, γράφω, to write.] He that exerciſes or profeſſes the act or buſineſs of writing.

Thus paſſeth it from this office to the *chirographer's*, to be engroſſed. *Bacon's Office of Alienation.*

CHIRO'GRAPHIST. *n. ſ.* [See CHIROGRAPHER.] This word is uſed in the following paſſage, I think improperly, for one that tells fortunes, by examining the hand: the true word is *chiroſophiſt*, or *chiromancer.*

Let the phiſiognomiſts examine his features; let the *chirographiſts* behold his palm; but, above all, let us conſult for the calculation of his nativity. *Arbuth. and Pope's Mart. Scrib.*

CHIRO'GRAPHY. *n. ſ.* [See CHIROGRAPHER.] The art of writing.

CHIRO'MANCER. *n. ſ.* [See CHIROMANCY.] One that foretells future events by inſpecting the hand.

The middle ſort, who have not much to ſpare,
To *chiromancers'* cheaper art repair,
Who clap the pretty palm, to make the lines more fair. *Dryden's Juvenal, ſat.* vi.

CHI'ROMANCY. *n. ſ.* [χεὶρ, the hand, and μάντις, a prophet.] The art of foretelling the events of life, by inſpecting the hand.

There is not much conſiderable in that doctrine of *chiromancy* that ſpots in the top of the nails, do ſignify things paſt; in the middle, things preſent; and at the bottom, events to come. *Brown's Vulgar Errours, b.* v. *c.* 22.

To CHIRP. *v. n.* [perhaps contracted from *cheer up.* The Dutch have *circken.*] To make a cheerful noiſe; as birds, when they call without ſinging.

She *chirping* ran, he peeping flew away,
'Till hard by them both he and ſhe did ſtay. *Sidney.*

Came he right now to ſing a raven's note;
And thinks he, that the *chirping* of a wren
Can chaſe away the firſt conceived ſound. *Shak. Hen.* VI.

No *chirping* lark the welkin ſheen invokes. *Gay's Paſt.*

The careful hen
Calls all her *chirping* family around. *Thomſon's Spring.*

To CHIRP. *v. a.* [This ſeems apparently corrupted from *cheer up.*] To make cheerful.

Let no ſober bigot here think it a ſin,
To puſh on the *chirping* and moderate bottle. *Johnſ. Tav. Ac.*

Sir Balaam now, he lives like other folks;
He takes his *chirping* pint, he cracks his jokes. *Pope.*

CHIRP. [from the verb.] The voice of birds or inſects.

Winds over us whiſper'd, flocks by us did bleat,
And *chirp* went the graſhopper under our feet. *Spectat.*

CHI'RPER. *n. ſ.* [from *chirp.*] One that chirps; one that is chearful.

To CHIRRE. *v. n.* [ceopᵹan, Sax.] See CHURME.

To coo as a pigeon. *Junius.*

CHIRU'RGEON. *n. ſ.* [χειρȣργὸς, from χεὶρ, the hand, and ἔργον, work.] One that cures ailments, not by internal medicines, but outward applications. It is now generally pronounced, and by many written, *ſurgeon.*

When a man's wounds ceaſe to ſmart, only becauſe he has loſt his feeling, they are nevertheleſs mortal, for his not ſeeing his need of a *chirurgeon.* *South's Sermons.*

CHIRU'RGERY. *n. ſ.* [from *chirurgeon.*] The art of curing by external applications.

Gynecia having ſkill in *chirurgery*, an art in thoſe days much eſteemed. *Sidney, b.* i.

Nature could do nothing in her caſe without the help of *chirurgery*, in drying up the luxurious fleſh, and making way to pull out the rotten bones. *Wiſeman.*

CHIRU'RGICAL. } *adj.* See CHIRURGEON.
CHIRU'RGICK. }

1. Having qualities uſeful in outward applications to hurts.

As to the *chirurgical* or phyſical virtues of wax, it is reckoned a mean between hot and cold. *Mortim. Husbandry.*

2. Relating to the manual part of healing.

3. Manual in general, conſiſting in operations of the hand. This ſenſe, though the firſt, according to etymology, is now ſcarce found.

The *chirurgical* or manual, doth refer to the making inſtruments, and exerciſing particular experiments. *Wilkins.*

CHI'SEL. *n. ſ.* [*ciſeau*, Fr. of *ſciſſum*, Lat.] An inſtrument with which wood or ſtone is pared away.

What fine *chiſel*
Could ever yet cut breath? Let no man mock me,
For I will kiſs her. *Shakeſp. Winter's Tale.*

There is ſuch a ſeeming ſoftneſs in the limbs, as if not a *chiſel* had hewed them out of ſtone, but a pencil had drawn and ſtroaked them in oil. *Wotton's Architecture.*

Imperfect ſhapes: in marble ſuch are ſeen,
When the rude *chiſel* does the man begin. *Dryden.*

To CHI'SEL. *v. a.* [from the noun.] To cut with a chiſel.

CHIT. *n. ſ.* [according to Dr. Hickes, from *kind*, Germ. child; perhaps from *chico*, little, Span.]

1. A child; a baby. Generally uſed of young perſons in contempt.

Theſe will appear ſuch *chits* in ſtory,
'Twill turn all politicks to jeſt. *Anonymous.*

2. The ſhoot of corn from the end of the grain. A cant term with maltſters.

Barley, couched four days, will begin to ſhew the *chit* or ſprit at the root-end. *Mortimer's Husbandry*

3. A freckle, [from chick-peaſe.] In this ſenſe it is ſeldom uſed.

To CHIT. *v. n.* [from the noun.] To ſprout; to ſhoot at the end of the grain.

I have known barley *chit* in ſeven hours after it had been thrown forth. *Mortimer's Husbandry.*

CHI'TCHAT. *n. ſ.* [corrupted by reduplication from *chat.*] Prattle; idle prate; idle talk. A word only uſed in ludicrous converſation.

I am a member of a female ſociety, who call ourſelves the *chitchat* club. *Spectat.* N°. 560.

CHI'TTERLINGS. *n. ſ.* without ſingular. [from *ſchyterlingh*, Dut. *Minſhew*; from *kutteln*, Germ. *Skinner.*] The guts; the bowels. *Skinner.*

CHI'TTY. *adj.* [from *chit.*] Childiſh; like a baby.

CHI'VALROUS. *adj.* [from *chivalry.*] Relating to chivalry, or errant knighthood; knightly; warlike; adventurous; daring. A word now out of uſe.

And noble minds of yore allied were
In brave purſuit of *chivalrous* empriſe. *Fairy Queen, b.* i.

CHI'VALRY. *n. ſ.* [*chevalerie*, Fr. knighthood, from *cheval*, a horſe; as *eques* in Latin.]

1. Knighthood; a military dignity.

There be now, for martial encouragement, ſome degrees and orders of *chivalry*; which, nevertheleſs, are conferred promiſcuouſly upon ſoldiers and no ſoldiers. *Bacon's Eſſay*, 30.

2. The qualifications of a knight; as valour; dexterity in arms.

Thou haſt ſlain
The flow'r of Europe for his *chivalry.* *Shakeſp. Henry* VI.

I may ſpeak it to my ſhame,
I have a truant been to *chivalry.* *Shakeſp. Hen.* IV. *part* i.

3. The general ſyſtem of knighthood.

Solemnly he ſwore,
That by the faith which knights to knighthood bore,
And whate'er elſe to *chivalry* belongs,
He would not ceaſe 'till he reveng'd their wrongs. *Dryd. Fab.*

4. An adventure; an exploit.

They four doing acts more dangerous, though leſs famous, becauſe they were but private *chivalries.* *Sidney, b.* ii.

5. The body or order of knights.

And by his light
Did all the *chivalry* of England move
To do brave acts. *Shakeſp. Henry* IV. *part* ii.

6. In law.

Servitium militare, of the French, *chevalier*; a tenure of land by knights ſervice. There is no land but is holden mediately or immediately of the crown, by ſome ſervice or other; and therefore are all our freeholds, that are to us and our heirs, called *feuda*, fees, as proceeding from the benefit of the king. As the king gave to the nobles large poſſeſſions for this or that rent and ſervice, ſo they parcelled out their lands, ſo received for rents and ſervices as they thought good: and thoſe ſervices are by Littleton divided into *chivalry* and ſocage. The one is martial and military; the other, clowniſh and ruſtick. *Chivalry*, therefore, is a tenure of ſervice, whereby the tenant is bound to perform ſome noble or military office unto his lord, and is of two ſorts; either regal, that is, ſuch as may hold only of the king; or ſuch as may alſo hold of a common perſon as well as of the king. That which may hold only of the king is properly called ſergeantry, and is again divided into grand or petit, *i. e.* great or ſmall. *Chivalry* that may

may hold of a common person, as well as of the king, is called scutagium. *Cowel.*

7. It ought properly to be written *chevalry*. It is a word not much used, but in old poems or romances.

CHI'VES. *n. s.* [*cive*, Fr. *Skinner.*]

1. The threads or filaments rising in flowers, with seeds at the end.

The masculine or prolifick seed contained in the *chives*, or apices of the stamina. *Ray on the Creation.*

2. A species of small onion. *Skinner.*

CHLORO'SIS. *n. s.* [from χλωρὸς, green.] The green-sickness.

To CHOAK. See CHOKE.

CHO'COLATE. *n. s.* [*chocolate*, Span.]

1. The nut of the cacao-tree.

The tree hath a rose flower, of a great number of petals, from whose empalement arises the pointal, being a tube cut into many parts, which becomes a fruit shaped somewhat like a cucumber, and deeply furrowed, in which are contained several seeds, collected into an oblong heap, and slit down, somewhat like almonds. It is a native of America, and is found in great plenty in several places between the Tropicks, and grows wild. See COCOA. *Miller.*

2. The cake or mass, made by grinding the kernel of the cacao-nut with other substances, to be dissolved in hot water.

The Spaniards were the first who brought *chocolate* into use in Europe, to promote the consumption of their cacao-nuts, achiot, and other drugs, which their West Indies furnish, and which enter the composition of *chocolate*. *Chambers.*

3. The liquor, made by a solution of chocolate in hot water.

Chocolate is certainly much the best of these three exotick liquors: its oil seems to be both rich, alimentary, and anodyne. *Arbuthnot on Aliments.*

In fumes of burning *chocolate* shall glow,
And tremble at the sea that froths below! *Pope.*

CHO'COLATE-HOUSE. *n. s.* [*chocolate* and *house.*] A house where company is entertained with chocolate.

Ever since that time, Lisander has been twice a day at the *chocolate-house*. *Tatler*, N°. 54.

CHODE. [the old preterite, from *chide*.] See CHIDE.

And Jacob was wroth, and *chode* with Laban. *Gen.* xxxi.

CHOICE. *n. s.* [*choix*, French.]

1. The act of choosing; determination between different things proposed; election.

If you oblige me suddenly to chuse,
The *choice* is made; for I must both refuse. *Dryd. Ind. Emp.*
Soft elocution doth thy style renown,
Gentle or sharp, according to thy *choice*,
To laugh at follies, or to lash at vice. *Dryd. Pers. sat.* v.

2. The power of choosing; election.

Choice there is not, unless the thing which we take to be so in our power, that we might have refused it. If fire consume the stable, it chooseth not so to do, because the nature thereof is such that it can do no other. *Hooker, b.* i. *s.* 7.

There's no liberty like the freedom of having it at my own *choice*, whether I will live to the world, or to myself. *L'Estr.*

To talk of compelling a man to be good, is a contradiction; for where there is force, there can be no *choice*. Whereas all moral goodness consisteth in the elective act of the understanding will. *Grew's Cosmol. b.* iii. *c.* 2. *s.* 23.

Whether he will remove his contemplation from one idea to another, is many times in his *choice*. *Locke.*

3. Care in choosing; curiosity of distinction.

Julius Cæsar did write a collection of apophthegms: it is pity his book is lost; for I imagine they were collected with judgment and *choice*. *Bacon's Apophthegms.*

4. The thing chosen; the thing taken or approved, in preference to others.

Your *choice* is not so rich in birth as beauty:
That you might well enjoy her. *Shakesp. Winter's Tale.*
Take to thee, from among the cherubim,
Thy *choice* of flaming warriors. *Milton's Par. Lost, b.* xi.
Now Mars, she said, let fame exalt her voice;
Nor let thy conquests only be her *choice*. *Prior.*

5. The best part of any thing, that is more properly the object of choice.

The *choice* and flower of all things profitable in other books, the psalms do both more briefly contain, and more movingly also express. *Hooker, b* v. *s.* 37.

Thou art a mighty prince: in the *choice* of our sepulchres bury thy dead. *Gen.* xxiii. 6.

Their riders, the flow'r and *choice*
Of many provinces, from bound to bound. *Milt. Par. Reg.*

6. Several things proposed at once, as objects of judgment and election.

A braver *choice* of dauntless spirits,
Did never float upon the swelling tide. *Shakesp. K. John.*

7. *To make* CHOICE *of*. To choose; to take from several things proposed.

Wisdom, of what herself approves, makes *choice*,
Nor is led captive by the common voice. *Denham.*

CHOICE. *adj.* [*choisi*, French.]

1. Select; of extraordinary value.

After having set before the king the *choicest* of wines and fruits, told him the best part of his entertainment was to come. *Guardian*, N°. 167.

Thus in a sea of folly toss'd,
My *choicest* hours of life are lost. *Swift.*

2. Chary; frugal; careful. Used of persons.

He that is *choice* of his time, will also be *choice* of his company, and *choice* of his actions. *Taylor's Holy Living.*

CHO'ICELESS. *adj.* [from *choice.*] Without the power of choosing; without right of choice; not free.

Neither the weight of the matter, of which the cylinder is made, nor the round voluble form of it, are any more imputable to that dead *choiceless* creature, than the first motion of it was supposed to be; and, therefore, it cannot be a fit resemblance to shew the reconcileableness of fate with choice. *Hammond on Fundamentals.*

CHO'ICELY. *adv.* [from *choice.*]

1. Curiously; with exact choice.

A band of men,
Collected *choicely* from each county some. *Shakesp. Hen.* IV.

2. Valuably; excellently.

It is certain it is *choicely* good. *Walton's Angler.*

CHO'ICENESS. *n. s.* [from *choice.*] Nicety; particular value.

Carry into the shade such auriculas, seedlings or plants, as are for their *choiceness* reserved in pots. *Evelyn's Kalendar.*

CHOIR. *n. s.* [*chorus*, Latin.]

1. An assembly or band of singers.

They now assist the *choir*
Of angels, who their songs admire. *Waller.*

2. The singers in divine worship.

The *choir*,
With all the choicest musick of the kingdom,
Together sung *Te Deum*. *Shakesp. Henry* VIII.

3. The part of the church where the choristers or singers are placed.

The lords and ladies, having brought the queen
To a prepar'd place in the *choir*, fell off
At distance from her. *Shakesp. Henry* VIII.

To CHOKE. *v. a.* [aceocan, Sax. from ceoca, the *cheek* or *mouth*. According to *Minshew*, from חנק; from whence, probably, the Spanish, *ahogar*.]

1. To suffocate; to kill by stopping the passage of respiration.

But when to my good lord I prove untrue,
I'll *choke* myself. *Shakesp. Cymbeline.*
While you thunder'd, clouds of dust did *choke*
Contending troops. *Waller.*

2. To stop up; to obstruct; to block up a passage.

Men troop'd up to the king's capacious court,
Whose portico's were *chok'd* with the resort. *Chapm. Odyssey.*

They are at a continual expence to cleanse the ports, and keep them from being *choked* up, by the help of several engines. *Addison on Italy.*

While prayers and tears his destin'd progress stay,
And crowds of mourners *choke* their sov'reign's way. *Tickell.*

3. To hinder by obstruction.

As two spent swimmers, that do cling together,
And *choke* their art. *Shakesp. Macbeth.*
She cannot lose her perfect pow'r to see,
Tho' mists and clouds do *choke* her window-light. *Davies.*

It seemeth the fire is so *choked*, as not to be able to remove the stone. *Bacon's Nat. Hist.* N°. 361.

You must make the mould big enough to contain the whole fruit, when it is grown to the greatest; for else you will *choke* the spreading of the fruit. *Bacon's Nat. Hist.*

The fire, which *chok'd* in ashes lay,
A load too heavy for his soul to move,
Was upward blown below, and brush'd away by love. *Dryd.*

4. To suppress.

And yet we ventur'd; for the gain propos'd
Chok'd the respect of likely peril fear'd. *Shakesp. Hen.* IV.
Confess thee freely of thy sin:
For to deny each article with oath,
Cannot remove nor *choke* the strong conception
That I do groan withal. *Shakesp. Othello.*

5. To overpower; to suppress.

And that which fell among thorns are they, which, when they have heard, go forth, and are *choked* with cares, and riches, and pleasures of this life, and bring no fruit to perfection. *Luke*, viii. 14.

No fruitful crop the sickly fields return;
But oats and darnel *choke* the rising corn. *Dryden's Past.*

CHOKE. *n. s.* [from the verb.] The filamentous or capillary part of an artichoke. A cant word.

CHOKE-PEAR. *n. s.* [from *choke* and *pear.*]

1. A rough, harsh, unpalatable pear.

2. Any aspersion or sarcasm, by which another is put to silence. A low term.

Pardon me for going so low as to talk of giving *choke-pears*. *Clarissa.*

A CHO'KER. *n. s.* [from *choke.*]

1. One that chokes or suffocates another.

2. One that puts another to silence.

3. Any thing that cannot be answered.

CHO'KY. *adj.* [from *choke.*] That which has the power of suffocation.

CHO'LAGOGUES. *n. s.* [χόλος, *bile.*] Medicines which have the power of purging bile or choler.

CHO'LER. *n. s.* [*cholera*, Lat. from χολή.]

1. The bile.

Marcilius Ficimus increases these proportions, adding two more of pure *choler*. *Wotton on Education.*

There would be a main defect, if such a feeding animal, and so subject unto diseases from bilious causes, should want a proper conveyance for *choler*. *Brown's Vulgar Errours.*

2. The humour, which, by its super-abundance, is supposed to produce irascibility.

It engenders *choler*, planteth anger;
And better 'twere that both of us did fast,
Since, of ourselves, ourselves are cholerick,
Than feed it with such over-roasted flesh. *Sh. Tam. of Shrew.*

3. Anger; rage.

Put him to *choler* straight: he hath been used
Ever to conquer, and to have his word
Off contradiction. *Shakesp. Coriolanus.*

He, methinks, is no great scholar,
Who can mistake desire for *choler*. *Prior.*

CHO'LERICK. *adj.* [*cholericus*, Latin.]

1. Abounding with choler.

Our two great poets being so different in their tempers, the one *cholerick* and sanguine, the other phlegmatick and melancholick. *Dryden's Fables, Pref.*

2. Angry; irascible: of persons.

Bull, in the main, was an honest plain-dealing fellow, *cholerick*, bold, and of a very unconstant temper. *Arb. J. Bull.*

3. Angry; offensive: of words or actions.

There came in *cholerick* haste towards me about seven or eight knights. *Sidney, b.* ii.

Becanus threatneth all that read him, using his confident, or rather *cholerick* speech. *Raleigh's Hist. of the World.*

CHO'LERICKNESS. *n. s.* [from *cholerick.*] Anger; irascibility; peevishness.

To CHOOSE. *v. a.* I chose, I have chosen or chose. [*choisir*, Fr. ceoran, Sax. *kiesen*, Germ.]

1. To take by way of preference of several things offered; not to reject.

Did I *choose* him out of all the tribes of Israel to be my priest. 1 *Sam.* ii. 28.

I may neither *choose* whom I would, nor refuse whom I dislike. *Shakesp. Merchant of Venice.*

If he should offer to *choose*, and *choose* the right casket, you should refuse to perform your father's will, if you should refuse to accept him. *Shakesp. Merchant of Venice.*

2. To take; not to refuse.

Let us *choose* to us judgment; let us know among ourselves what is good. *Job*, xxxiv. 4.

The will has still so much freedom left as to enable it to *choose* any act in its kind good; as also to refuse any act in its kind evil. *South's Sermons.*

3. To select; to pick out of a number.

Choose you a man for you, and let him come down to me. 1 *Sa.* xvii. 8.

How much less shall I answer him, and *choose* out my words to reason with him? *Job*, ix. 14.

4. To elect for eternal happiness; to predestinate to life. A term of theologians.

To CHOOSE. *v. n.* To have the power of choice between different things. It is generally joined with a negative, and signifies must necessarily be.

Without the influence of the Deity supporting things, their utter annihilation could not *choose* but follow. *Hooker, b.* v.

Knaves abroad,
Who having by their own importunate suit,
Convinced or supplied them, they cannot *choose*
But they must blab. *Shakesp. Othello.*

When a favourite shall be raised upon the foundation of merit, then can he not *choose* but prosper. *Bacon's Adv. to Vill.*

Threw down a golden apple in her way;
For all her haste, she could not *choose* but stay. *Dryden.*

Those who are persuaded that they shall continue for ever, cannot *choose* but aspire after a happiness commensurate to their duration. *Tillotson.*

CHO'OSER. *n. s.* [from *choose.*] He that has the power or office of choosing; elector.

Come all into this nut, quoth she;
Come closely in, be rul'd by me;
Each one may here a *chooser* be,
For room you need not wrestle. *Drayton's Nymphid.*

In all things to deal with other men, as if I might be my own *chooser*. *Hammond's Pract. Catechism.*

This generality is not sufficient to make a good *chooser*, without a more particular contraction of his judgment. *Wott.*

To CHOP. *v. a.* [*kappen*, Dut. *couper*, French.]

1. To cut with a quick blow.

What shall we do, if we perceive
Lord Hastings will not yield to our complots?
——*Chop* off his head, man. *Shakesp. Rich.* III.

Within these three days his head is to be *chopt* off. *Shakesp.*

And where the cleaver *chops* the heifer's spoil,
Thy breathing nostril hold. *Gay's Trivia.*

2. To devour eagerly, with *up*.

You are for making a hasty meal, and for *chopping up* your entertainment, like an hungry clown. *Dryd. Span. Fryar.*

Upon the opening of his mouth he drops his breakfast, which the fox presently *chopp'd up*. *L'Estrange's Fables.*

3. To mince; to cut into small pieces.

They break their bones, and *chop* them in pieces, as for the pot. *Mic.* iii. 3.

Some grannaries are made with clay, mixed with hair, *chopped* straw, mulch, and such like. *Mortimer's Husbandry.*

By dividing of them into chapters and verses, they are so *chopped* and minced, and stand so broken and divided, that the common people take the verses usually for different aphorisms. *Locke's Preface to St. Paul's Epistles.*

4. To break into chinks.

I remember the cow's dugs, that her pretty *chopt* hands had milked. *Shakes As you like it.*

To CHOP. *v. n.*

1. To do any thing with a quick and unexpected motion, like that of a blow: as we say, the wind *chops* about, that is changes suddenly.

If the body repercussing be near, and yet not so near as to make a concurrent echoe, it *choppeth* with you upon the sudden. *Bacon's Nat. Hist.* N°. 248.

Out of greediness to get both, he *chops* at the shadow, and loses the substance. *L'Estrange, Fab.* 6.

2. To light or happen upon a thing suddenly, with *upon*.

To CHOP. *v. a.* [ceapan, Sax. *koopen*, Dut. to buy.]

1. To purchase generally by way of truck; to give one thing for another.

The *chopping* of bargains, when a man buys, not to hold, but to sell again grindeth upon the seller and the buyer. *Bacon.*

2. To put one thing in the place of another.

Sets up communities and senses,
To *chop* and change intelligencies. *Hudib. p.* iii. *cant.* 3.

Affirm the Trigons *chopp'd* and chang'd,
The watry with the fiery rang'd. *Hudib. p.* ii *cant.* 3.

We go on *chopping* and changing our friends, as well as our horses. *L'Estrange.*

3. To bandy; to altercate; to return one thing or word for another.

Let not the council at the bar *chop* with the judge, nor wind himself into the handling of the cause a-new, after the judge hath declared his sentence. *Bacon, Essay* 57.

You'll never leave off your *chopping* of logick, 'till your skin is turned over your ears for prating. *L'Estrange's Fables.*

CHOP. *n. s.* [from the verb.]

1. A piece chopped off. See CHIP.

Sir William Capel compounded for sixteen hundred pounds, yet Empson would have cut another *chop* out of him, if the king had not died. *Bacon's Henry* VII.

2. A small piece of meat, commonly of mutton.

Old Cross condemns all persons to be fops,
That can't regale themselves with mutton *chops*. *King's Cook.*

3. A crack, or cleft.

An infusion in water will make wood to swell; as we see in the filling of the *chops* of bowls, by laying them in water. *Bacon's Natural History*, N° 80.

CHOP-HOUSE. *n. s.* [*chop* and *house.*] A mean house of entertainment, where provision ready dressed is sold.

I lost my place at the *chop-house*, where every man eats in publick a mess of broth, or chop of meat, in silence. *Spectat.*

CHO'PIN. *n. s.* [French.]

1. A French liquid measure, containing nearly a pint of Winchester.

2. A term used in Scotland for a quart, of wine measure.

CHO'PPING. participial, *adj.* [In this sense, of uncertain etymology.] An epithet frequently applied to infants, by way of ludicrous commendation: imagined by *Skinner* to signify *lusty*, from caŗ, Sax. by others to mean a child that would bring money at a market. Perhaps a greedy, hungry child, likely to live.

Both Jack Freeman and Ned Wild,
Would own the fair and *chopping* child. *Fenton.*

CHOPPING-BLOCK. *n. s.* [*chop* and *block.*] A log of wood, on which any thing is laid to be cut in pieces.

The strait smooth elms are good for axel-trees, boards, *chopping-blocks*. *Mortimer's Husbandry.*

CHOPPING-KNIFE. *n. s.* [*chop* and *knife.*] A knife with which cooks mince their meat.

Here comes Dametas, with a sword by his side, a forrest-bill on his neck, and a *chopping-knife* under his girdle. *Sidney.*

CHO'PPY. *adj.* [from *chop.*] Full of holes, clefts, or cracks.

You seem to understand me,
By each at once her *choppy* finger laying
Upon her skinny lips. *Shakesp. Macbeth.*

CHOPS. *n. s.* without a singular. [corrupted probably from CHAPS, which see.]

1. The mouth of a beast.

So soon as my *chops* begin to walk, yours must be walking too, for company. *L'Estrange's Fab.*

2. The mouth of a man, used in contempt.

He ne'er shook hands, nor bid farewel to him,
'Till he unseam'd him from the nape to th' *chops*. *Shakes.*

3. The mouth of any thing in familiar language; as of a river; of a smith's vice.

CHO'RAL. *adj.* [from *chorus*, Lat.]

1. Belonging to or composing a choir or concert.

Choral symphonies. *Milton.*

2. Singing in a choir.

And *choral* seraphs sung the second day. *Amhurst.*

CHORD. *n. s.* [*chorda*, Lat. When it signifies a rope or string in general, it is written *cord*: when its primitive signification is preserved, the *h* is retained.]

1. The string of a musical instrument.

Who mov'd
Their stops and *chords*, was seen; his volant touch
Instinct thro' all proportions, low and high,
Fied, and pursu'd transverse the resonant fugue. *Milt. P. L.*

2. In geometry a right line, which joins the two ends of any arch of a circle.

To CHORD. *v. a.* [from the noun.] To furnish with strings or chords; to string.

What passion cannot musick raise and quell?
When Jubal struck the *chorded* shell,
His list'ning brethren stood around. *Dryden.*

CHORDE'E. *n. s.* [from *chorda*, Lat.] A contraction of the frœnum.

CHO'RION. *n. s.* [χωρεῖν, to contain.] The outward membrane that enwraps the fœtus.

CHO'RISTER. *n. s.* [from *chorus.*]

1. A singer in cathedrals; usually a singer of the lower order; a singing boy.

2. A singer in a concert. This sense is, for the most part, confined to poetry.

And let the roaring organs loudly play
The praises of the Lord in lively notes;
The whiles, with hollow throats,
The *choristers* the joyous anthem sing. *Spenser's Epithal.*

The new-born phœnix takes his way;
Of airy *choristers* a numerous train
Attend his progress. *Dryden.*

The musical voices and accents of the aerial *choristers*. *Ray.*

CHORO'GRAPHER. *n. s.* [from χώρα, a region, and γράφω, to describe.] He that describes particular regions or countries.

CHOROGRA'PHICAL. *adj.* [See CHOROGRAPHER.] Descriptive of particular regions or countries; laying down the boundaries of countries.

I have added a *chorographical* description of this terrestrial paradise. *Raleigh's Hist. of the World.*

CHOROGRA'PHICALLY. *adv.* [from *chorographical.*] In a chorographical manner; according to the rule of chorography; in a manner descriptive of particular regions.

CHORO'GRAPHY. *n. s.* [See CHOROGRAPHER.] The art or practice of describing particular regions, or laying down the limits and boundaries of particular provinces. It is less in its object than geography, and greater than topography.

CHO'RUS. *n. s.* [*chorus*, Latin.]

1. A number of singers; a concert.

The Grecian tragedy was at first nothing but a *chorus* of singers; afterwards one actor was introduced. *Dryden.*

Never did a more full and unspotted *chorus* of human creatures join together in a hymn of devotion. *Addis. Guardian.*

In praise so just let every voice be join'd,
And fill the gen'ral *chorus* of mankind! *Pope's Ess. Crit.*

2. The persons who are supposed to behold what passes in the acts of a tragedy, and sing their sentiments between the acts.

For supply,
Admit me *chorus* to this history. *Shakesp. Henry V. Prol.*

3. The song between the acts of a tragedy.

4. Verses of a song in which the company join the singer.

CHOSE. [the preter tense, from *To choose.*]

Our sovereign here above the rest might stand,
And here be *chose* again to rule the land. *Dryden.*

CHO'SEN. [the participle passive, from *To choose.*]

If king Lewis vouchsafe to furnish us
With some few bands of *chosen* soldiers,
I'll undertake to land them on our coast. *Shakesp. Hen. VI.*

CHOUGH. *n. s.* [ceo, Sax. *choucas*, Fr.] A bird which frequents the rocks by the sea side, like a jackdaw, but bigger. *Hanmer.*

In birds, kites and kestrels have a resemblance with hawks, crows with ravens, daws and *choughs*. *Bacon's Nat. Hist.*

To crows the like impartial grace affords,
And *choughs* and daws, and such republick birds. *Dryden.*

CHOULE. *n. s.* [commonly pronounced and written *jowl.*] The crop of a bird.

The *choule* or crop, adhering unto the lower side of the bill, and so descending by the throat, is a bag or sachel. *Br. Vul. Er.*

To CHOUSE. *v. a.* [The original of this word is much doubted by *Skinner*, who tries to deduce it from the French *gosser*, to laugh at; or *joncher*, to wheedle; and from the Teutonick *kosen*, to prattle. It is perhaps a fortuitous and cant word, without etymology.]

1. To cheat; to trick; to impose upon.

Freedom and zeal have *chous'd* you o'er and o'er;
Pray give us leave to bubble you once more. *Dryd. Pr. to Alb.*

From London they came, silly people to *chouse*,
Their lands and their faces unknown. *Swift.*

2. It has *of* before the thing taken away by fraud.

When geese and pullen are seduc'd,
And sows *of* sucking pigs are *chous'd*. *Hud part* ii. *cant.* 3.

A CHOUSE. *n. s.* [from the verb. This word is derived by *Henshaw* from *kiaus*, or *chiaus*, a messenger of the Turkish court; who, says he, is little better than a *fool.*]

1. A bubble; a tool; a man fit to be cheated.

A sottish *chouse*,
Who, when a thief has robb'd his house,
Applies himself to cunning men. *Hudib. part* iii. *cant.* 3.

2. A trick or sham.

To CHO'WTER. *v. n.* To grumble or mutter like a froward child. *Philips.*

CHRISM. *n. s.* [χρίσμα, an ointment.] Unguent; or unction: it is only applied to sacred ceremonies.

One act never to be repeated, is not the thing that Christ's eternal priesthood, denoted especially by his unction or *chrism*, refers to. *Hammond's Pract. Catech.*

CHRI'SOM. *n. s.* [See CHRISM.] A child that dies within a month after its birth. So called from the chrisom-cloath, a cloath anointed with holy unguent, which the children anciently wore till they were christened.

When the convulsions were but few, the number of *chrisoms* and infants was greater. *Graunt's Bills of Mortality.*

To CHRI'STEN. *adj.* [cÿrıꞅꞇnıan, Sax.]

1. To baptize; to initiate into christianity by water.

2. To name; to denominate.

Where such evils as these reign, *christen* the thing what you will, it can be no better than a mock millenium. *Burnet.*

CHRI'STENDOM. *n. s.* [from *Christ* and *dom.*] The collective body of christianity; the regions of which the inhabitants profess the christian religion.

What hath been done, the parts of *Christendom* most afflicted can best testify. *Hooker, b.* iv. *s.* 14.

An older and a better soldier, none
That *Christendom* gives out. *Shakesp.*

His computation is universally received over all *Christendom.* *Holder on Time.*

CHRI'STENING. *n. s.* [from the verb.] The ceremony of the first initiation into christianity.

The queen was with great solemnity crowned at Westminster, about two years after the marriage; like an old *christening*, that had staid long for godfathers. *Bacon's H.* VII.

We shall insert the causes, why the account of *christenings* hath been neglected more than that of burials. *Graunt's B. M.*

The day of the *christening* being come, the house was filled with gossips. *Arbuth. and Pope's Mart. Scriblerus.*

CHRI'STIAN. *n. s.* [*Christianus*, Lat.] A professor of the religion of Christ.

We *christians* have certainly the best and the holiest, the wisest and most reasonable religion in the world. *Tillotson.*

CHRI'STIAN. *adj.* Professing the religion of Christ.

I'll not be made a soft and dull-ey'd fool,
To shake the head, relent, and sigh, and yield
To *christian* intercessors. *Shakesp. Merchant of Venice.*

CHRISTIAN-NAME. *n. s.* The name given at the font, distinct from the Gentilitious name, or surname.

CHRI'STIANISM. *n. s.* [*christianismus*, Lat.]

1. The christian religion.

2. The nations professing christianity.

CHRISTIA'NITY. *n. s.* [*chretienté*, French.] The religion of christians.

God doth will that couples, which are married, both infidels, if either party be converted unto *christianity*, this should not make separation. *Hooker, b.* 2. *s.* 5.

Every one, who lives in the habitual practice of any voluntary sin, cuts himself off from *christianity*. *Addis. on Ch. Rel.*

To CHRI'STIANIZE. *v. a.* [from *christian.*] To make christian; to convert to christianity.

The principles of platonick philosophy, as it is now *christianized*. *Dryden's Juv. Dedicat.*

CHRI'STIANLY. *adv.* [from *christian.*] Like a christian; as becomes one who professes the holy religion of Christ.

CHRI'STMAS. *n. s.* [from *Christ* and *mass.*] The day on which the nativity of our blessed Saviour is celebrated, by the particular service of the church.

A CHRISTMAS-BOX. *n. s.* [from *christmas* and *box.*] A box in which little presents are collected at Christmas.

When time comes round, a *Christmas-box* they bear,
And one day makes them rich for all the year. *Gay's Trivia.*

CHRISTMAS-FLOWER. *n. s.* See HELLEBORE.

CHRIST'S-THORN. *n. s.* [So called, as *Skinner* fancies, because the thorns have some likeness to a cross.]

It hath long sharp spines: the flower has five leaves, in form of of a rose: out of the flower-cup, which is divided into several segments, rises the pointal, which becomes a fruit, shaped like a bonnet, having a shell almost globular, which is divided into three cells, in each of which is contained a roundish seed. This is by many persons supposed to be the plant from which our Saviour's crown of thorns was composed. *Miller.*

CHROMA'TICK. *adj.* [χρῶμα, colour.]

1. Relating to colour.

I am now come to the third part of painting, which is called the *chromatick*, or colouring. *Dryden's Dufresnoy.*

2. Relating to a certain species of antient music, now unknown.

It was observed he never touched his lyre in such a truly *chromatick* and enharmonick manner, as upon that occasion. *Arbuth. and Pope's Mart. Scriblerus.*

CHRO'NICAL. } *adj.* [from χρόνος, time.]
CHRO'NICK. }

A *chronical* distemper is of length; as dropsies, Asthma's, and the like. *Quincy.*

Of diseases some are *chronical*, and of long duration; as quartane agues, scurvy, &c. wherein we defer the cure unto more advantageous seasons. *Brown's Vulgar Errours.*

The lady's use of all these excellencies is to divert the old man, when he is out of the pangs of a *chronical* distemper. *Spectat.* N°. 449.

CHRO'NICLE. *n. s.* [*chronique*, Fr. from χρόνος, time.]

1. A register or account of events in order of time.

No more yet of this;
For 'tis a *chronicle* of day by day,
Not a relation for a breakfast. *Shakesp. Tempest.*

2. A history.

You lean too confidently on those Irish *chronicles*, which are most fabulous and forged. *Spenser on Ireland.*

If from the field I should return once more,
I and my sword will earn my *chronicle*. *Shak. Ant. and Cleop.*

I'm traduc'd by tongues, which neither knows
My faculties nor person, yet will be
The *chronicles* of my doing. *Shakesp. Henry* VIII.

I give up to historians the generals and heroes which crowd their annals, together with those which you are to produce for the British *chronicle*. *Dryden.*

To CHRO'NICLE. *v. a.* [from the noun.]

1. To record in chronicle, or history.

This to rehearse, should rather be to *chronicle* times than to search into reformation of abuses in that realm. *Spens. Irel.*

2. To register; to record.

For now the devil, that told me I did well,
Says that this deed is *chronicled* in hell. *Shakesp. Rich.* III.

Love is your master; for he masters you:
And he that is so yoked by a fool,
Methinks, should not be *chronicled* for wise. *Shakesp.*

I shall be the jest of the town; nay, in two days I expect to be *chronicled* in ditty, and sung in woful ballad. *Cong. Old Bat.*

CHRO'NICLER. *n. s.* [from *chronicle.*]

1. A writer of chronicles; a recorder of events in order of time.

Here gathering *chroniclers*, and by them stand
Giddy fantastick poets of each land. *Donne.*

2. A historian; one that keeps up the memory of things past.

I do herein rely upon these bards, or Irish *chroniclers*. *Spens.*

This custom was held by the druids and bards of our antient Britons, and of latter times by the Irish *chroniclers*, called rimers. *Raleigh's Hist. of the World.*

CHRO'NOGRAM. *n. s.* [χρόνος, time, and γράφω, to write.] An inscription including the date of any action.

Of this kind the following is an example:
Gloria lausque *Deo*, sæ*CL*or*VM* in sæc*V*la sunt.

A *chronogrammatical* verse, which includes not only this year 1660, but numerical letters enough to reach above a thousand years further, until the year 2867. *Howel's Parley.*

CHRONOGRAMMA'TICAL. *adj.* [from *chronogram*] Belonging to a chronogram. See the last example.

CHRONOGRA'MMATIST. *n. s.* [from *chronogram*] A writer of chronograms.

There are foreign universities, where, as you praise a man in England for being an excellent philosopher or poet, it is an ordinary character to be a great *chronogrammatist*. *Addison.*

CHRONO'LOGER. *n. s.* [χρόνος, time, and λόγος, doctrine] He that studies or explains the science of computing past time, or of ranging past events according to their proper years.

Chronologers differ among themselves about most great epocha's. *Holder on Time.*

CHRONOLO'GICAL. *adj.* [from *chronology.*] Relating to the doctrine of time.

Thus much touching the *chronological* account of some times and things past, without confining myself to the exactness of years. *Hale's Origin of Mankind.*

CHRONOLO'GICALLY. *adv.* [from *chronological.*] In a chronological manner; according to the laws or rules of chronology; according to the exact series of time.

CHRONO'LOGIST. *n. s.* [See CHRONOLOGER.] One that studies or explains time; one that ranges past events according to the order of time; a chronologer.

According to these *chronologists*, the prophecy of the Rabin that the world should last but six thousand years, has been long disproved. *Brown's Vulgar Errours.*

All that learn d noise and dust of the *chronologist* is wholly to be avoided. *Locke on Education.*

CHRONO'LOGY. *n. s.* [χρόνος, time, and λόγος, doctrine.] The science of computing and adjusting the periods of time; as the revolution of the sun and moon; and of computing time past, and referring each event to the proper year.

And the measure of the year not being so perfectly known to the ancients, rendered it very difficult for them to transmit a true *chronology* to succeeding ages. *Holder on Time.*

Where I allude to the customs of the Greeks, I believe I may be justified by the strictest *chronology*; though a poet is not obliged to the rules that confine an historian. *Prior.*

A CHRONO'METER. *n. s.* [χρόνος and μέτρον.] An instrument for the exact mensuration of time.

According to observation made with a pendulum *chronometer*, a bullet, at its first discharge, flies five hundred and ten yards in five half seconds. *Derham's Physico-Theology.*

CHRY'SALIS. *n. s.* [from χρυσός, gold, because of the golden colour in the nymphæ of some insects.]

A term used by some naturalists for aurelia, or the first apparent change of the maggot of any species of insects. *Chamb.*

CHRY'SOLITE. *n. s.* [χρυσός, gold, and λίθος, a stone.]

A precious stone of a dusky green, with a cast of yellow. *Woodward's Meth. Foss.*

Such another world,
Of one intire and perfect *chrysolite*,
I'd not have sold her for. *Shakesp. Othello.*

If metal, part seem'd gold, part silver clear:
If stone, carbuncle most, or *chrysolite*. *Milt. Par. Lost, b.* iii.

CHRYSO'PRASUS. *n. s.* [χρυσός, gold, and *prasinus*, green] A precious stone of a yellow colour, approaching to green.

The ninth a topaz, the tenth a *chrysoprasus*. *Rev.* xxi. 20.

CHUB. *n. s.* [from *cop*, a great head, *Skinner.*] A river fish. The chevin.

The *chub* is in prime from Midmay to Candlemas, but best in winter. He is full of small bones: he eats waterish; not firm, but limp and tasteless: nevertheless, he may be so dressed as to make him very good meat. *Walton's Angler.*

CHU'BBED. *adj.* [from *chub.*] Big-headed like a chub.

To CHUCK. *v. n.* [A word probably formed in imitation of the sound that it expresses; or perhaps corrupted from *chick.*]

To make a noise like a hen, when she calls her chickens.

To CHUCK. *v. a.*

1. To call as a hen calls her young.

Then crowing, clapp'd his wings, th' appointed call,
To *chuck* his wives together in the hall. *Dryden's Fables.*

2. To give a gentle blow under the chin, so as to make the mouth strike together.

Come, *chuck* the infant under the chin, force a smile, and cry, ay, the boy takes after his mother's relations. *Cong. O. B.*

CHUCK. *n. s* [from the verb.]

1. The voice of a hen.

He made the *chuck* four or five times, that people use to make to chickens when they call them. *Temple.*

2. A word of endearment, corrupted from chicken or chick.

Come, your promise.——What promise, *chuck? Sh. Othello.*

3. A sudden small noise.

CHUCK-FARTHING. *n. s.* [*chuck* and *farthing.*] A play, at which the money falls with a chuck into the hole beneath.

He lost his money at *chuck-farthing*, shuffle-cap, and all-fours. *Arbuthnot's History of John Bull.*

To CHU'CKLE. *v. n.* [*schaecken*, Dut.] To laugh vehemently; to laugh convulsively.

What tale shall I to my old father tell?
'Twill make him *chuckle* thou'rt bestow'd so well. *Dryd.*

She to intrigues was e'en hard hearted;
She *chuckl'd* when a bawd was carted. *Prior.*

To CHU'CKLE. *v. a.* [from *chuck.*]

1. To call as a hen.

I am not far from the women's apartment, I am sure; and if these birds are within distance, here's that will *chuckle* 'em together. *Dryden's Don Sebastian.*

2. To cocker; to fondle.

Your confessor, that parcel of holy guts and garbidge; he must *chuckle* you, and moan you. *Dryden's Spanish Fryar.*

CHU'ET. *n. s.* [probably from *To chew.*] An old word, as it seems, for forced meat.

As for *chuets*, which are likewise minced meat, instead of butter and fat, it were good to moisten them partly with cream, or almond or pistacho milk. *Bacon's Nat. Hist.* N°. 54.

CHUFF. *n. s.* [A word of uncertain derivation; perhaps corrupted from *chub*, or derived from *kwf*, Welsh, a stock.] A coarse, fat-headed, blunt clown.

Hang ye, gorbellied knaves, are you undone? No, ye fat *chuffs*, I would your store were here. *Shakes. Henry* IV.

A less generous *chuff* than this in the fable, would have hugged his bags to the last. *L'Estrange.*

CHU'FFILY. *adv.* [from *chuffy.*] Surlily; stomachfully.

John answered *chuffily*. *Clarissa.*

CHU'FFINESS. *n. s.* [from *chuffy*] Clownishness; surliness.

CHU'FFY. *adj.* [from *chuff.*] Blunt; surly; fat.

CHUM. *n. s.* [*chom*, Armorick, to live together.] A chamber fellow; a term used in the universities.

CHUMP *n. s.* A thick heavy piece of wood, less than a block.

When one is battered to shivers, they can quickly, of a *chump* of wood, accommodate themselves with another. *Moxon's Mech. Exer.*

CHURCH. *n. s.* [cẏrce, Sax. κυριακή.]

1. The collective body of christians, usually termed the catholick church.

The *church* being a supernatural society, doth differ from natural societies in this; that the persons unto whom we associate ourselves in the one, are men, simply considered as men; but they to whom we be joined in the other, are God, angels, and holy men. *Hooker, b.* i. *p.* 45.

2. The body of christians adhering to one particular opinion, or form of worship.

The *church* is a religious assembly, or the large fair building where they meet; and sometimes the same word means a synod of bishops, or of presbyters; and in some places it is the pope and a general council. *Watts's Logick.*

3. The place which christians consecrate to the worship of God.

That *churches* were consecrated unto none but the Lord only, the very general name chiefly doth sufficiently shew: *church* doth signify no other thing than the Lord's house. *Hook.*

Tho' you unty the winds, and let them fight
Against the *churches.* *Shakesp. Macbeth.*

4. It is used frequently in conjunction with other words; as *church-member*, the member of a church; *church-power*, spiritual or ecclesiastical authority.

To CHURCH. *v. a.* [from the noun.] To perform with any one the office of returning thanks in the church, after any signal deliverance, as from the danger of childbirth.

CHURCH-ALE. *n. s.* [from *church* and *ale.*] A wake, or feast, commemoratory of the dedication of the church.

For the *church-ale*, two young men of the parish are yearly chosen to be wardens, who make collection among the parishioners of what provision it pleaseth them to bestow. *Carew.*

CHURCH-ATTIRE. *n. s.* The habit in which men officiate at divine service.

These and such like were their discourses, touching that *church-attire*, which with us for the most part is used in publick prayer. *Hooker, b.* v. *s.* 29.

CHURCH-AUTHORITY. *n. s.* Ecclesiastical power; spiritual jurisdiction.

In this point of *church-authority*, I have sifted all the little scraps alleged. *Atterbury.*

CHURCH-BURIAL. *n. s.* Burial according to the rites of the church.

The bishop has the care of seeing that all christians, after their deaths, be not denied *church-burial*, according to the usage and custom of the place. *Ayliffe's Parergon.*

CHURCH-FOUNDER *n. s.* He that builds or endows a church.

Whether emperors or bishops in those days were *church-founders*, the solemn dedication of churches they thought not to be a work in itself either vain or superstitious. *Hooker.*

CHURCHMAN. *n. s.* [*church* and *man.*]

1. An ecclesiastic; a clergyman; one that ministers in sacred things.

If any thing be offered to you touching the church and *churchmen*, or church-government, rely not only upon yourself. *Bacon's Advice to Villers.*

A very difficult work to do, to reform and reduce a church into order, that had been so long neglected, and that was so ill filled by many weak and more wilful *churchmen.* *Clarend.*

Patience in want, and poverty of mind,
These marks of church and *churchmen* he design'd,
And living taught, and dying left behind. *Dryden's Fables.*

2. An adherent to the church of England.

CHURCH-WARDENS. *n. s.* [See WARDEN.] Are officers yearly chosen, by the consent of the minister and parishioners, according to the custom of each place, to look to the church, church-yard, and such things as belong to both; and to observe the behaviour of the parishioners, for such faults as appertain to the jurisdiction or censure of the ecclesiastical court. They are a kind of corporation, enabled by law to sue for any thing belonging to their church, or poor of their parish. *Cowel.*

There should likewise *church-wardens*, of the gravest men in the parish, be appointed, as they be here in England. *Spens.*

Our *church-wardens*
Feast on the silver, and give us the farthings. *Gay.*

CHURCHYARD. *n. s.* The ground adjoining to the church, in which the dead are buried; a cemetery.

I am almost afraid to stand alone
Here in the *churchyard*, yet I will adventure. *Shakespeare.*

In *churchyards*, where they bury much, the earth will consume the corps in far shorter time than other earth will. *Bacon.*

No place so sacred from such fops is barr'd;
Nor is Paul's church more safe than Paul's *churchyard.* *Pope.*

CHURL. *n. s.* [ceorl, Sax. *carl*, in German, is strong; rusticks being always observed to be strong bodied.]

1. A rustick; a countryman; a labourer.

One of the baser sort, which they call *churls*, being reproved for his oath, answered confidently, that his lord commanded him. *Spenser's State of Ireland.*

Churl, upon thy eyes I throw
All the pow'r this charm doth owe. *Shak. Mids. Night's Dr.*

From this light cause th' infernal maid prepares
The country *churls* to mischief, hate, and wars. *Dryd. Æn.*

2. A rude, surly, ill-bred man.

A *churl's* courtesy rarely comes, but either for gain or falshood. *Sidney, b.* ii.

3. A miser; a niggard; a selfish or greedy wretch.

Poison, I see, hath been his timeless end!
O *churl*, drink all, and leave no friendly drop
To help me after. *Shakesp. Romeo and Juliet.*

CHU'RLISH. *adj.* [from *churl.*]

1. Rude; brutal; harsh; austere; sour; merciless; unkind; uncivil.

A sea of melting pearl, which some call tears,
Those at her father's *churlish* feet she tender'd. *Shakesp.*

The interruption of their *churlish* drums
Cuts off more circumstance: they are at hand
To parly, or to fight. *Shakesp. King John.*

A lion in love with a lass, desired her father's consent. The answer was *churlish* enough, He'd never marry his daughter to a brute. *L'Estrange's Fables.*

He the pursuit of *churlish* beasts,
Preferr'd to sleeping on her breasts. *Waller.*

2. Selfish; avaritious.

The man was *churlish* and evil in his doings. 1 *Sa.* xxv. 3.

This sullen *churlish* thief,
Had all his mind plac'd upon Mully's beef. *King's M. of M.*

3. [Of things.] Unpliant; cross-grained; unmanageable; harsh; not yielding.

If there be emission of spirit, the body of the metal will be hard and *churlish.* *Bacon's Nat. Hist.* N°. 326.

The Cornish men were become, like metal often fired and quenched, *churlish*, and that would sooner break than bow. *Bacon's Henry* VII.

In the hundreds of Essex they have a very *churlish* blue clay. *Mortimer's Husbandry.*

4. Intractable; vexatious.

Will you again unknit
This *churlish* knot of all abhorred war. *Shakesp. Henry* IV.

Spain found the war so *churlish* and longsome, as they found they should consume themselves in an endless war. *Bacon.*

Spreads a path clear as the day,
Where no *churlish* rub says nay. *Crashaw.*

CHU'RLISHLY. *adv.* [from *churlish.*] Rudely; brutally.

To the oak, now regnant, the olive did *churlishly* put over the son for a reward of the service of his sire. *Howel's Voc. For.*

CHU'RLISHNESS. *n. s.* [from *churlish*; cẏрlıсneууe, Saxon.] Brutality; ruggedness of manner.

Better is the *churlishness* of a man than a courteous woman. *Ecclus.* xlii. 14.

In the *churlishness* of fortune, a poor honest man suffers in this world. *L'Estrange.*

CHURME. *n. s.* [more properly *chirm*, from the Saxon cẏrme, a clamour or noise; as *to chirre* is to coo as a turtle.] A confused sound; a noise.

He was conveyed to the Tower with the *churme* of a thousand taunts and reproaches. *Bacon's Henry* VII.

A CHURN. *n s.* [properly *chern*, from *kern*, Dut. cerene, Sax.] The vessel in which the butter is, by long and violent agitation, coagulated and separated from the serous parts of the milk.

Her aukward fist did ne'er employ the *churn.* *Gay's Past.*

To CHURN. *v. a.* [*kernen*, Dutch.]

1. To agitate or shake any thing by a violent motion.

Perchance he spoke not; but
Like a full acorn'd boar, a *churning* on,
Cried Oh. *Shakesp.*

Froth fills his chaps, he sends a grunting sound,
And part he *churns*, and part befoams the ground. *Dryden.*

Churn'd in his teeth, the foamy venom rose. *Ad. Ov. Met.*

The mechanism of nature, in converting our aliment, consists in mixing with it animal juices, and, in the action of the solid parts, *churning* them together. *Arbuthnot on Aliments.*

2. To make butter by agitating the milk.

The *churning* of milk bringeth forth butter. *Prov.* xxx. 33.

You may try the force of imagination, upon staying the coming of butter after the *churning.* *Bacon's Nat. Hist.*

CHU'RRWORM. *n. s.* [from cẏrran, Sax.] An insect that turns about nimbly; called also a fancricket. *Skinner. Philips.*

To CHUSE. See To CHOOSE.

CHYLA'CEOUS. *adj.* [from *chyle.*] Belonging to chyle; consisting of chyle.

When the spirits of the chyle have half fermented the *chylaceous* mass, it has the state of drink, not ripened by fermentation. *Floyer on the Humours.*

CHYLE. *n. s.* [χυλός.] The white juice formed in the stomach by digestion of the aliment, and afterwards changed into blood.

This powerful ferment, mingling with the parts,
The leven'd maſs to milky *chyle* converts. *Blackm. Creation.*

The *chyle* itſelf cannot paſs through the ſmalleſt veſſels. *Arbuthnot on Aliments.*

CHYLIFA'CTION. *n. ſ.* [from *chyle.*] The act or proceſs of making chyle in the body.

Drinking exceſſively during the time of *chylifaction*, ſtops perſpiration. *Arbuthnot on Aliments.*

CHYLIFA'CTIVE. *adj.* [from *chylus* and *facio*, to make, Lat.] Having the power of making chyle.

CHYLOPOE'TICK. *adj.* [χύλος and ποιέω.] Having the power, or the office, of forming chyle.

According to the force of the *chylopoetick* organs, more or leſs chyle may be extracted from the ſame food. *Arbuthnot.*

CHY'LOUS. *adj.* [from *chyle.*] Conſiſting of chyle; partaking of chyle.

Milk is the *chylous* part of an animal, already prepared. *Arb.*

CHY'MICAL. } *adj.* [*chymicus*, Latin.]
CHY'MICK. }

1. Made by chymiſtry.

I'm tir'd with waiting for this *chymick* gold,
Which fools us young, and beggars us when old. *Dryden.*

The medicines are ranged in boxes, according to their diſtinct natures, whether *chymical* or Galenical preparations. *Watts's Improvement of Mind, p. i. c. 17.*

2. Relating to chymiſtry.

Methinks already, from this *chymick* flame,
I ſee a city of more precious mold. *Dryd. Ann. Mirab.*

With *chymic* art exalts the min'ral pow'rs,
And draws the aromatick ſouls of flow'rs. *Pope's Windſ. For.*

CHY'MICALLY. *adv.* [from *chymical.*] In a chymical manner.

CHY'MIST. *n. ſ.* [See CHY'MISTRY.] A profeſſor of chymiſtry; a philoſopher by fire.

The ſtarving *chymiſt*, in his golden views
Supremely bleſt. *Pope's Eſſay on Man, Epiſt.* ii.

CHY'MISTRY. *n. ſ.* [derived by ſome from χυμός, juice, or χύω, to melt; by others from an oriental word, *kema*, black. According to the etymology, it is written with *y* or *e*.]

An art whereby ſenſible bodies contained in veſſels, or capable of being contained therein, are ſo changed, by means of certain inſtruments, and principally fire, that their ſeveral powers and virtues are thereby diſcovered, with a view to philoſophy, or medicine. *Boerhaave.*

Operations of *chymiſtry* fall ſhort of vital force: no chymiſt can make milk or blood of graſs. *Arbuthnot on Aliment.*

CIBA'RIOUS. *adj.* [*cibarius*, Lat. from *cibus*, food.] Relating to food; uſeful for food; edible.

CI'BOL. *n. ſ.* [*ciboule*, Fr.] A ſmall ſort of onion uſed in ſallads. See ONION. This word is common in the Scotch dialect; but the *l* is not pronounced.

Ciboules, or ſcallions, are a kind of degenerate onions. *Mort.*

CI'CATRICE. } *n. ſ.* [*cicatrix*, Latin.]
CI'CATRIX. }

1. The ſcar remaining after a wound.

One captain Spurio with his *cicatrice*, an emblem of war, here on his ſiniſter cheek. *Shakeſp. All's well that ends well.*

2. A mark; an impreſſure: ſo uſed by Shakeſpeare leſs properly.

Lean but upon a ruſh
The *cicatrice* and capable impreſſure
Thy palm ſome moment keeps. *Shakeſp. As you like it.*

CICATRISANT. *n. ſ.* [from *cicatrice.*] An application that induces a cicatrice.

CICATRISIVE. *adj.* [from *cicatrice.*] Having the qualities proper to induce a cicatrice.

CICATRIZA'TION. *n. ſ.* [from *cicatrice.*]

1. The act of healing the wound.

A vein burſted, or corroded in the lungs, is looked upon to be for the moſt part incurable, becauſe of the continual motion and coughing of the lungs, tearing the gap wider, and hindering the conglutination and *cicatrization* of the vein. *Harvey on Conſumptions.*

2. The ſtate of being healed, or ſkinned over.

To CI'CATRIZE. *v. a.* [from *cicatrix.*]

1. To apply ſuch medicines to wounds, or ulcers, as heal and ſkin them over. *Quincy.*

2. To heal and induce the ſkin over a ſore.

We incarned, and in a few days *cicatrized* it with a ſmooth cicatrix. *Wiſeman on Tumours.*

CI'CELY. *n. ſ.* A ſort of herb. See SWEET CICELY.

CICHORA'CEOUS. *adj.* [from *cichorium*, Lat.] Having the qualities of ſuccory.

Diureticks plentifully evacuate the ſalt ſerum; as all acid diureticks, and the teſtaceous and bitter *cichoraceous* plants. *Floyer on the Humours.*

To CI'CURATE. *v. a.* [*cicuro*, Lat.] To tame; to reclaim from wildneſs; to make tame and tractable.

After carnal converſation poiſons may yet retain ſome portion of their natures; yet are ſo refracted, *cicurated*, and ſubdued, as not to make good their deſtructive malignities. *Brown's Vulgar Errours, b. 7. c. 18.*

CICURA'TION. *n. ſ.* [from *circurate.*] The act of taming or reclaiming from wildneſs.

This holds not only in domeſtick and manſuete birds; for then it might be the effect of *cicuration* or inſtitution; but in the wild. *Ray on the Creation.*

CI'DER. *n. ſ.* [*cidre*, Fr. *ſidra*, Ital. *ſicera*, Lat. σικέρα, .שכר]

1. All kind of ſtrong liquors, except wine. This ſenſe is now wholly obſolete.

2. Liquor made of the juice of fruits preſſed.

We had alſo drink, wholſome and good wine of the grape, a kind of *cider* made of a fruit of that country; a wonderful pleaſing and refreſhing drink. *Bacon's New Atlant.*

3. The juice of apples expreſſed and fermented.

To the utmoſt bounds of this
Wide univerſe Silurian *cider* born,
Shall pleaſe all taſtes, and triumph o'er the vine. *Philips.*

CI'DERIST. *n. ſ.* [from *cider.*] A maker of cider.

When the *ciderists* have taken care for the beſt fruit, and ordered them after the beſt manner they could, yet hath their cider generally proved pale, ſharp, and ill taſted. *Mortimer.*

CI'DERKIN. *n. ſ.* [from *cider.*]

A low word uſed for the liquor made of the murk or groſs matter of apples, after the cider is preſſed out, and a convenient quantity of boiled water added to it; the whole infuſing for about forty-eight hours. *Philips's World of Words.*

Ciderkin is made for common drinking, and ſupplies the place of ſmall beer. *Mortimer.*

CIELING. *n. ſ.* See CEILING.

CIERGE. *n. ſ.* [French.] A candle carried in proceſſions.

CI'LIARY. *adj.* [*cilium*, Lat.] Belonging to the eyelids.

The *ciliary* proceſſes, or rather the ligaments, obſerved in the inſide of the ſclerotick tunicles of the eye, do ſerve inſtead of a muſcle, by the contraction, to alter the figure of the eye. *Ray on Creation.*

CILI'CIOUS. *adj.* [from *cilicium*, hair-cloth, Lat.] Made of hair.

A garment of camel's hair; that is, made of ſome texture of that hair, a coarſe garment, a *cilicious* or ſackcloth habit, ſuitable to the auſterity of his life. *Brown's Vulgar Errours.*

CI'MA. See CYMATIUM.

CIMA'R. See SIMAR.

CIME'LIARCH. *n. ſ.* [from κειμηλιαρχης.] The chief keeper of plate, veſtments, and things of value belonging to a church; a church-warden. *Dict.*

CI'METER. *n. ſ.* [*cimitarra*, Span. and Portug. from *chimeteir*, Turkiſh. *Bluteau's Portugueſe Dictionary.*] A ſort of ſword uſed by the Turks; ſhort; heavy; and recurvated, or bent backward. This word is ſometimes erroneouſly ſpelt *ſcimitar*, and *ſcymeter*; as in the following examples.

By this *ſcimitar*,
That ſlew the ſophy and a Perſian prince,
That won three fields of ſultan Solyman. *Shak. Mer. of Ven.*

Our armours now may ruſt, our idle *ſcymiters*
Hang by our ſides for ornament, not uſe. *Dryd. Don Sebaſt.*

CI'NCTURE. *n. ſ.* [*cinctura*, Latin.]

1. Something worn round the body.

Now happy he, whoſe cloak and *cincture*
Hold out this tempeſt. *Shakeſp. King John.*

Columbus found th' American, ſo girt
With feather'd *cincture*, naked elſe, and wild. *Milt. Pa. Loſt.*

He binds the ſacred *cincture* round his breaſt. *Pope's Odyſſ.*

2. An incloſure.

The court and priſon being within the *cincture* of one wall. *Bacon's Henry VII.*

3. [In architecture.] A ring or liſt at the top and bottom of the ſhaft of a column; ſeparating the ſhaft at one end from the baſe, at the other from the capital. It is ſuppoſed to be in imitation of the girths or ferrils anciently uſed, to ſtrengthen and preſerve the primitive wood-columns. *Chambers.*

CI'NDER. *n. ſ.* [*ceindre*, Fr. from *cineres*, Latin.]

1. A maſs ignited and quenched, without being reduced to aſhes.

I ſhould make very forges of my cheeks,
That would to *cinders* burn up modeſty,
Did but I ſpeak thy deeds. *Shakeſp. Othello.*

There is in ſmiths *cinders*, by ſome adheſion of iron, ſometimes to be found a magnetical operation. *Brown's Vul. Err.*

So ſnow on Ætna does unmelted lie,
Whoſe rolling flames and ſcatter'd *cinders* fly. *Waller.*

2. A hot coal that has ceaſed to flame.

If from adown the hopeful chops
The fat upon a *cinder* drops,
To ſtinking ſmoke it turns the flame. *Swift.*

CINDER-WENCH. } *n. ſ.* [*cinder* and *woman.*] A woman whoſe trade is to rake in heaps of aſhes for cinders.
CINDER-WOMAN. }

'Tis under ſo much naſty rubbiſh laid,
To find it out's the *cinder-woman's* trade. *Eſſay on Satire.*

She had above five hundred ſuits of fine cloaths, and yet went abroad like a *cinder-wench*. *Arbuth. Hiſt. of John Bull.*

In the black form of *cinder-wench* ſhe came,
When love, the hour, the place had baniſh'd ſhame. *Gay.*

CINERA'TION. *n. ſ.* [from *cineres*, Lat.] The reduction of any thing by fire to aſhes. A term of chymiſtry.

CINERI'TIOUS. *adj.* [*cinericius*, Lat.] Having the form or state of ashes.

The nerves arise from the glands of the *cineritious* part of the brain, and are terminated in all the parts of the body. *Cheyne's Philosophical Principles.*

CINE'RULENT. *adj.* [from *cineres*, Lat.] Full of ashes. *Dict.*

CI'NGLE. *n. s.* [from *cingulum*, Lat.] A girth for a horse. *Dict.*

CI'NNABAR. *n. s.* [*cinnabaris*, Latin.] Cinnabar is native or factitious: the factitious cinnabar is called vermilion.

Cinnabar is the ore out of which quicksilver is drawn, and consists partly of a mercurial, and partly of a sulphureo-ochreous matter. *Woodward's Meth. Foss.*

The particles of mercury uniting with the particles of sulphur, compose *cinnabar*. *Newt. Opt.*

CINNABAR *of Antimony*, is made of mercury, sulphur, and crude antimony.

CI'NNAMON. *n. s.* [*cinnamomum*, Lat.] The fragrant bark of a low tree in the island of Ceylon, possessed by the Dutch, in the East Indies. Its leaves resemble those of the olive, both as to substance and colour. The fruit resembles an acorn or olive, and has neither the smell nor taste of the bark. When boiled in water, it yields an oil, which, as it cools and hardens, becomes as firm and white as tallow; the smell of which is agreeable in candles. The trees are chiefly propagated by a sort of pigeons which feed on the fruit, and, carrying it to their young, drop it where it takes root. Cinnamon is chiefly used in medicine as an astringent. The cinnamon of the ancients was different from ours. *Chambers.*

Let Araby extol her happy coast,
Her *cinnamon* and sweet amomum boast. *Dryden's Fables.*

CINNAMON *Water* is made by distilling the bark, first infused in barley water, in spirit of wine or white wine. *Chambers.*

CINQUE. *n. s.* [Fr.] A Five. It is used in games alone; but is often compounded with other words.

CINQUE-FOIL. *n. s.* [*cinque feuille*, Fr.] A kind of five leaved clover.

CINQUE-PACE. *n. s.* [*cinque pas*, Fr.] A kind of grave dance.

Wooing, wedding, and repenting is a Scotch jig, a measure, and a *cinque pace*. The first suit is hot and hasty, like a Scotch jig, and full as fantastical; the wedding, mannerly and modest, as a measure, full of state and gravity; and then comes repentance, and, with his bad legs, falls into the *cinque pace* faster and faster, 'till he sinks into his grave. *Shakesp.*

CINQUE-PORTS. *n. s.* [*cinque ports*, Fr.]

Those havens that lie towards France, and therefore have been thought by our kings to be such as ought most vigilantly to be observed against invasion. In which respect, the places where they are have a special governour or keeper, called by his office Lord Warden of the *cinque ports*; and divers privileges granted to them, as a particular jurisdiction, their warden having the authority of an admiral among them, and sending out writs in his own name. The *cinque ports* are Dover, Sandwich, Rye, Hastings, Winchelsea, Rumney, and Hithe; some of which, as the number exceeds five, must either be added to the first institution by some later grant, or accounted as appendants to some of the rest. *Cowel.*

They, that bear
The cloth of state above her, are four barons
Of the *cinque ports*. *Shakesp. Henry VIII.*

CINQUE-SPOTTED. *adj.* Having five spots.

On her left breast
A mole, *cinque spotted*, like the crimson drops
I' th' bottom of a cowslip. *Shakesp. Cymbeline.*

CI'ON. *n. s.* [*sion*, or *scion*, French.]

1. A sprout; a shoot from a plant.

We have reason to cool our raging motions, our carnal stings, our unbitted lusts; whereof I take this that you call love, to be a sect or *cion*. *Shakesp. Othello.*

The stately Caledonian oak, newly settled in his triumphant throne, begirt with *cions* of his own royal stem. *Howel's Vocal Forest.*

2. The shoot engrafted or inserted on a stock.

The *cion* over-ruleth the stock quite; and the stock is but passive only, and giveth aliment, but no motion to the graft. *Bacon's Natural History*, N°. 421.

CI'PHER. *n. s.* [*chifre*, Fr. *zifra*, Ital. *cifra*, low Lat. from an oriental root.]

1. An arithmetical character, by which some number is noted; a figure.

2. An arithmetical mark, which, standing for nothing itself, increases the value of the other figures.

Mine were the very *cipher* of a function,
To find the faults, whose fine stands in record,
And let go by the actor. *Shakesp. Measure for Measure.*

If the people be somewhat in the election, you cannot make them nulls or *ciphers* in the privation or translation. *Bac.*

As, in accounts, *ciphers* and figures pass for real sums, so names pass for things. *South's Sermons.*

3. An intertexture of letters engraved usually on boxes or plate.

Troy flam'd in burnish'd gold; and o'er the throne,
Arms and the man in golden *ciphers* shone. *Pop. Temp. of F.*

Some mingling stir the melted tar, and some
Deep on the new-shorn vagrant's heaving side,
To stamp the master's *cipher*, ready stand. *Thoms. Summer.*

4. A character in general.

In succeeding times this wisdom began to be written in *ciphers* and characters, and letters bearing the form of creatures. *Raleigh's History of the World.*

5. A secret or occult manner of writing, or the key to it.

This book, as long liv'd as the elements,
In *cipher* writ, or new made idioms. *Donne.*

He was pleased to command me to stay at London, to send and receive all his letters; and I was furnished with mine several *ciphers*, in order to it. *Denham's Dedication.*

To CI'PHER. *v. n.* [from the noun.]

To practice arithmetick.

You have been bred to business; you can *cipher*: I wonder you never used your pen and ink. *Arbuth. Hist. of J. Bull.*

To CIPHER. *v. a.* To write in occult characters.

He frequented sermons, and penned notes: his notes he *ciphered* with Greek characters. *Hayward on Edward VI.*

To CI'RCINATE. *v. a.* [*circino*, Lat.] To make a circle; to compass round, or turn round. *Bailey.*

CIRCINA'TION. *n. s.* [*circinatio*, Lat.] An orbicular motion; a turning round; a measuring with the compasses. *Bailey.*

CI'RCLE. *n. s.* [*circulus*, Latin.]

1. A line continued 'till it ends where it begun, having all its parts equidistant from a common center.

Any thing, that moves round about in a *circle*, in less time than our ideas are wont to succeed one another in our minds, is not perceived to move; but seems to be a perfect intire *circle* of that matter, or colour, and not a part of a *circle* in motion. *Locke.*

Then a deeper still,
In *circle* following *circle*, gathers round
To close the face of things. *Thomson's Summer.*

2. The space included in a circular line.

3. A round body; an orb.

It is he that sitteth upon the *circle* of the earth. *Is.* xi. 22.

4. Compass; inclosure.

A great magician,
Obscured in the *circle* of the forest. *Shakes. As you like it.*

5. An assembly surrounding the principal person.

To have a box where eunuchs sing,
And, foremost in the *circle*, eye a king. *Pope's Hor. Ep.* i.

6. A company; an assembly.

I will call over to him the whole *circle* of beauties that are disposed among the boxes. *Addison's Guardian*, N°. 10.

Ever since that time, Lisander visits in every *circle*. *Tatler.*

7. Any series ending as it begins, and perpetually repeated.

There be divers fruit-trees in the hot countries, which have blossoms and young fruit, and young fruit and ripe fruit, almost all the year, succeeding one another; but this *circle* of ripening cannot be but in succulent plants, and hot countries. *Bacon's Natural History*, N°. 581.

Thus in a *circle* runs the peasant's pain,
And the year rolls within itself again. *Dryd. Virg. Geor.*

8. An inconclusive form of argument, in which the foregoing proposition is proved by the following, and the following proposition inferred from the foregoing.

That heavy bodies descend by gravity; and again, that gravity is a quality whereby an heavy body descends, is an impertinent *circle*, and teacheth nothing. *Glanv. Sceps. c.* 20.

That fallacy called a *circle*, is when one of the premisses in a syllogism is questioned and opposed, and we intend to prove it by the conclusion. *Watts's Logick.*

9. Circumlocution; indirect form of words.

Has he given the lye
In *circle* or oblique, or semicircle,
Or direct parallel? You must challenge him. *Flet. Q. of Cor.*

10. CIRCLES *of the German Empire.* Such provinces and principalities as have a right to be present at diets. They are in number ten. *Trevoux.*

To CI'RCLE. *v. a.* [from the noun.]

1. To move round any thing.

The lords that were appointed to *circle* the hill, had some days before planted themselves in places convenient. *Bacon.*

Another Cynthia her new journey runs,
And other planets *circle* other suns. *Pope's Dunciad, b.* iii.

2. To inclose; to surround.

What stern ungentle hands
Have lopp'd and hew'd, and made thy body bare
Of her two branches, those sweet ornaments,
Whose *circling* shadows kings have sought to sleep in. *Shak.*

While these fond arms, thus *circling* you, may prove
More heavy chains than those of hopeless love. *Prior.*

Unseen, he glided thro' the joyous crowd,
With darkness *circled*, and an ambient cloud. *Pope's Odyss.*

3. *To* CIRCLE *in.* To confine; to keep together.

We term those things dry which have a consistence within themselves, and which, to enjoy a determinate figure, do not require the stop or hindrance of another body to limit and *circle* them *in*. *Digby on Bodies.*

To CI'RCLE. *v. n.* To move circularly; to end where it begins.

The

The well fraught bowl
Circles inceſſant; whilſt the humble cell
With quavering laugh, and rural jeſts, reſounds. *Philips.*
Now the *circling* years diſcloſe
The day predeſtin'd to reward his woes. *Pope's Odyſſ.*

CI'RCLED. *adj.* [from *circle.*] Having the form of a circle; round.
Th' inconſtant moon,
That monthly changes in her *circled* orb. *Shakeſp. R. and J.*

CI'RCLET. *n. ſ.* [from *circle.*] A circle; an orb.
Then take repaſt, 'till Heſperus diſplay'd
His golden *circlet* in the weſtern ſhade. *Pope's Odyſſ.*

CI'RCLING. *participial adj.* [from *To circle.*] Having the form of a circle; circular; round.
Round he ſurveys, and well might, where he ſtood
So high above the *circling* canopy
Of night's extended ſhade. *Milton's Paradiſe Loſt, b.* iii.

CI'RCUIT. *n. ſ.* [*circuit*, Fr. *circuitus*, Latin.]
1. The act of moving round any thing.
The circuits, in former times, went but round about the pale; as the *circuit* of the cynoſura about the pole. *Davies.*
There are four moons alſo perpetually rolling round the planet Jupiter, and carried along with him in his periodical *circuit* round the ſun. *Watts's Improvement.*
2. The ſpace incloſed in a circle.
He led me up
A woody mountain, whoſe high top was plain
A *circuit* wide inclos'd. *Milton's Paradiſe Loſt, b.* viii.
3. Space; extent; meaſured by travelling round.
He attributeth unto it ſmallneſs, in reſpect of *circuit.* *Hooker, b.* v. *ſ.* 19.
The lake of Bolſena is reckoned one and twenty miles in *circuit.* *Addiſon on Italy.*
4. A ring; a diadem; that by which any thing is incircled.
And this fell tempeſt ſhall not ceaſe to rage,
Until the golden *circuit* on my head
Do calm the fury of this mad-brain'd flaw. *Shakeſp. Hen.* VI.
5. The viſitations of the judges for holding aſſiſes.
6. The tract of country viſited by the judges.
7. CIRCUIT *of Action.* In law, is a longer courſe of proceeding to recover the thing ſued for than is needful. *Cowel.*

To CI'RCUIT. *v. n.* [from the noun.] To move circularly.
Pining with equinoctial heat, unleſs
The cordial cup perpetual motion keep,
Quick *circuiting.* *Philips.*

CIRCUITE'ER. *n. ſ.* [from *circuit.*] One that travels a circuit.
Like your fellow *circuiteer* the ſun: you travel the round of the earth, and behold all the iniquities under the heavens. *Pope.*

CIRCUI'TION. *n. ſ.* [*circuitio*, Lat.]
1. The act of going round any thing.
2. Compaſs; maze of argument; comprehenſion.
To apprehend by what degrees they lean to things in ſhow, though not indeed repugnant one to another, requireth more ſharpneſs of wit, more intricate *circuitions* of diſcourſe, and depth of judgment, than common ability doth yield. *Hooker.*

CI'RCULAR. *adj.* [*circularis*, Latin.]
1. Round, like a circle; circumſcribed by a circle.
The frame thereof ſeem'd partly *circular*,
And part triangular. *Fairy Queen, b.* ii.
He firſt inclos'd for liſts a level ground;
The form was *circular.* *Dryd. Fables.*
Nero's port, compoſed of huge moles running round it, in a kind of *circular* figure. *Addiſon's Remarks on Italy.*
2. Succeſſive in order; always returning.
From whence th' innumerable race of things,
By *circular* ſucceſſive order ſprings. *Roſcommon.*
3. Vulgar; mean; circumforaneous.
Had Virgil been a *circular* poet, and cloſely adhered to hiſtory, how could the Romans have had Dido? *Dennis.*
4. CIRCULAR *Letter.* A letter directed to ſeveral perſons, who have the ſame intereſt in ſome common affair; as in the convocation of aſſemblies.
5. CIRCULAR *Lines.* Such ſtrait lines as are divided from the diviſions made in the arch of a circle; as the lines of ſines, tangents, and ſecants on the plain ſcale and ſector.
6. CIRCULAR *Sailing*, is that performed on the arch of a great circle.

CIRCULA'RITY. *n. ſ.* [from *circular.*] A circular form.
The heavens have no diverſity or difference, but a ſimplicity of parts, and equiformity in motion, continually ſucceeding each other; ſo that, from what point ſoever we compute, the account will be common unto the whole *circularity.* *Brown.*

CI'RCULARLY. *adj.* [from *circular.*]
1. In form of a circle.
The internal form of it conſiſts of ſeveral regions, involving one another like orbs about the ſame centre, or of the ſeveral elements caſt *circularly* about each other. *Burnet.*
2. With a circular motion.
Trade, which, like blood, ſhould *circularly* flow,
Stopp'd in their channels, found its freedom loſt. *Dryden.*
Every body moved *circularly* about any center, recede, or endeavour to recede, from that center of its motion. *Ray.*

To CI'RCULATE. *v. n.* [from *circulus.*] To move in a circle; to run round; to return to the place whence it departed in a conſtant courſe.
If our lives motions theirs muſt imitate,
Our knowledge, like our blood, muſt *circulate.* *Denham.*
Nature is a perpetual motion; and the work of the univerſe *circulates* without any interval or repoſe. *L'Eſtrange.*
In the civil wars, the money ſpent on both ſides was *circulated* at home; no publick debts contracted. *Swift.*

To CI'RCULATE. *v. a.* To put about.

CIRCULA'TION. *n. ſ.* [from *circulate.*]
1. Motion in a circle; a courſe in which the motion tends to the point from which it began.
What more obvious, one would think, than the *circulation* of the blood, unknown 'till the laſt age? *Burnet's Theory.*
As much blood paſſeth through the lungs as through all the reſt of the body: the *circulation* is quicker, and heat greater, and their texture extremely delicate. *Arbuthnot on Aliments.*
2. A ſeries in which the ſame order is always obſerved, and things always return to the ſame ſtate.
As for the ſins of peace, thou haſt brought upon us the miſeries of war; ſo for the ſins of war, thou ſeeſt fit to deny us the bleſſing of peace, and to keep us in a *circulation* of miſeries. *K. Charles.*
God, by the ordinary rule of nature, permits this continual *circulation* of human things. *Swift on Modern Education.*
3. A reciprocal interchange of meaning.
When the apoſtle ſaith of the Jews, that they crucified the Lord of glory; and when the ſon of man, being on earth, affirmeth that the ſon of man was in heaven at the ſame inſtant, there is in theſe two ſpeeches that mutual *circulation* before mentioned. *Hooker, b.* v. *ſ.* 53.

CI'RCULATORY. *n. ſ.* [from *circulate.*] A chymical veſſel, in which that which riſes from the veſſel on the fire, is collected and cooled in another fixed upon it, and falls down again.

CI'RCULATORY. *adj.* [from *circulate.*] Circulatory Letters are the ſame with CIRCULAR *Letters.*

CIRCUMA'MBIENCY. *n. ſ.* [from *circumambient.*] The act of encompaſſing.
Ice receiveth its figure according unto the ſurface whereof it concreteth, or the *circumambiency* which conformeth it. *Brown's Vulgar Errours, b.* ii. *c.* 1.

CIRCUMA'MBIENT. *adj.* [*circum* and *ambio*, Latin.] Surrounding; encompaſſing; incloſing.
The *circumambient* coldneſs towards the ſides of the veſſel, like the ſecond region, cooling and condenſing of it. *Wilkins.*

To CIRCUMA'MBULATE. *v. n.* [from *circum* and *ambulo*, Lat.] To walk round about. *Dict.*

To CIRCUMCI'SE. *v. a.* [*circumcido*, Latin.] To cut the prepuce or foreſkin, according to the law given to the Jews.
They came to *circumciſe* the children. *Luke* i. 59.
One is alarmed at the induſtry of the whigs, in aiming to ſtrengthen their routed party by a reinforcement from the *circumciſed.* *Swift's Examiner*, N°. 47.

CIRCUMCI'SION. *n. ſ.* [from *circumciſe.*] The rite or act of cutting off the foreſkin.
They left a race behind
Like to themſelves, diſtinguiſhable ſcarce
From Gentiles, but by *circumciſion* vain. *Milt. Par. Reg.*

To CIRCUMDU'CT. *v. a.* [*circumduco*, Lat.] To contravene; to nullify.
Acts of judicature may be cancelled and *circumducted* by the will and direction of the judge; as alſo by the conſent of the parties litigant, before the judge has pronounced and given ſentence. *Ayliffe's Parergon.*

CIRCUMDU'CTION. *n. ſ.* [from *circumduct.*]
1. Nullification; cancellation.
The citation may be circumducted, though the defendant ſhould not appear; and the defendant muſt be cited, as a *circumduction* requires. *Ayliffe's Parergon.*
2. A leading about.

CIRCU'MFERENCE. *n. ſ.* [*circumferentia*, Latin.]
1. The periphery; the line including and ſurrounding any thing.
Extend thus far thy bounds,
This be thy juſt *circumference*, O world! *Milton's Par. Loſt.*
Becauſe the hero is the center of the main action, all the lines from the *circumference* tend to him alone. *Dryd. Dufreſ.*
A coal of fire, moved nimbly in the *circumference* of a circle, makes the whole *circumference* appear like a circle of fire. *Newton's Opticks.*
2. The ſpace incloſed in a circle.
So was his will
Pronounc'd among the gods, and by an oath,
That ſhook heav'n's whole *circumference*, confirm'd. *Milton.*
He firſt inclos'd for liſts a level ground,
The whole *circumference* a mile around. *Dryden's Fables.*
3. The external part of an orbicular body.
The bubble, being looked on by the light of the clouds reflected from it, ſeemed red at its apparent *circumference.* If the clouds were viewed through it, the colour at its *circumference* would be blue. *Newton's Opticks.*
4. An orb; a circle; any thing circular or orbicular.

His pond'rous shield, large and round,
Behind him cast; the broad *circumference*
Hung on his shoulders like the moon. *Milton's Par. Lost.*

To CIRCU'MFERENCE. *v. a.* [from the noun.] To include in a circular space.

Nor is the vigour of this great body included only in itself, or *circumferenced* by its surface; but diffused at indeterminate distances. *Brown's Vulgar Errours, b.* ii. *c.* 2.

CIRCUMFERE'NTOR. *n. s.* [from *circumfero*, Lat. to carry about.] An instrument used in surveying, for measuring angles, consisting of a brass circle, an index with sights, and a compass, and mounted on a staff, with a ball and socket. *Chambers.*

CI'RCUMFLEX. *n. s.* [*circumflexus*, Lat.] An accent used to regulate the pronunciation of syllables, including or participating the acute and grave.

The *circumflex* keeps the voice in a middle tune, and therefore in the Latin is compounded of both the other. *Holder.*

CIRCU'MFLUENCE. *n. s.* [from *circumfluent.*] An inclosure of waters.

CIRCU'MFLUENT. *adj.* [*circumfluens*, Lat.] Flowing round any thing.

I rule the Paphian race,
Whose bounds the deep *circumfluent* waves embrace;
A duteous people, and industrious isle. *Pope's Odyss.*

CIRCU'MFLUOUS. *adj.* [*circumfluus*, Lat.] Environing with waters.

He the world
Built on *circumfluous* waters calm, in wide
Crystalline ocean. *Milton's Paradise Lost, b.* vii. *l.* 269.
Laertes' son girt with *circumfluous* tides. *Pope's Odyss.*

CIRCUMFORA'NEOUS. *adj.* [*circumforaneus*, Lat.] Wandering from house to house. As a *circumforaneous* fidler; one that plays at doors.

To CIRCUMFU'SE. *v. a.* [*circumfusus*, Lat.] To pour round; to spread every way.

Men see better, when their eyes are against the sun, or candle, if they put their hand before their eye. The glaring sun, or candle, weakens the eye; whereas the light *circumfused*, is enough for the perception. *Bacon's Nat. History.*

His army, *circumfus'd* on either wing. *Milt. Par. Lost.*
Earth, with her nether ocean, *circumfus'd*
Their pleasant dwelling-house. *Milton's Paradise Lost.*
This nymph the god Cephisus had abus'd,
With all his winding waters *circumfus'd.* *Addis. Ov. Met.*

CIRCUMFU'SILE. *adj.* [*circum* and *fusilis*, Lat.] That which may be poured or spread round any thing.

Artist divine, whose skilful hands infold
The victim's horn with *circumfusile* gold. *Pope's Odyss.*

CIRCUMFU'SION. *n. s.* [from *circumfuse.*] The act of spreading round; the state of being poured round.

To CIRCU'MGYRATE. *v. a.* [*circum* and *gyrus*, Lat.] To roll round.

All the glands of the body be congeries of various sorts of vessels, curled, *circumgyrated*, and complicated together. *Ray on Creation.*

CIRCUMGYRA'TION. *n. s.* [from *circumgyrate.*] The act of running round.

The sun turns round his own axis in twenty-five days, which arises from his first being put into such a *circumgyration.* *Cheyne's Philosophical Prin.*

CIRCUMJA'CENT. *adj.* [*circumjacens*, Lat.] Lying round any thing; bordering on every side.

CIRCUMINCE'SSION. *n. s.* [from *circum* and *incedo*, Lat.] A term used by the school-divines to express the existence of three divine persons in one another, in the mystery of the trinity. *Chambers.*

CIRCUMI'TION. *n. s.* [from *circumeo*, *circumitum*, Latin.] The act of going round. *Dict.*

CIRCUMLIGA'TION. *n. s.* [*circumligo*, Latin.]
1. The act of binding round.
2. The bond with which any thing is encompassed.

CIRCUMLOCU'TION. *n. s.* [*circumlocutio*, Latin.]
1. A circuit or compass of words; periphrasis.

Virgil, studying brevity, could bring these words into a narrow compass, which a translator cannot render without *circumlocutions.* *Dryden.*

I much prefer the plain Billingsgate way of calling names, because it would save abundance of time, lost by *circumlocution.* *Swift's Miscellanies.*

2. The use of indirect expressions.

These people are not to be dealt withal, but by a train of mystery and *circumlocution.* *L'Estrange.*

CIRCUMMU'RED. *adj.* [*circum* and *murus*, Lat.] Walled round; encompassed with a wall.

He hath a garden *circummur'd* with bricks. *Shakesp.*

CIRCUMNA'VIGABLE. *adj.* [from *circumnavigate.*] That which may be sailed round.

The being of Antipodes, the habitableness of the torrid zone, and the rendering the whole terraqueous globe *circumnavigable.* *Ray on the Creation.*

To CIRCUMNA'VIGATE. *v. a.* [*circum* and *navigo*, Lat.] To sail round.

CIRCUMNAVIGA'TION. *n. s.* [from *circumnavigate.*] The act of sailing round.

What he says concerning the *circumnavigation* of Africa, from the straits of Gibraltar to the Red Sea, is very remarkable. *Arbuthnot on Coins.*

CIRCUMPLICA'TION. *n. s.* [*circumplico*, Lat.]
1. The act of enwrapping on every side.
2. The state of being enwrapped.

CIRCUMPO'LAR. *adj.* [from *circum* and *polar.*] Stars near the North pole, which move round it, and never set in the Northern latitudes, are said to be *circumpolar stars.*

CIRCUMPOSI'TION. *n. s.* [from *circum* and *position.*] The act of placing any thing circularly.

Now is your season for *circumposition*, by tiles or baskets of earth. *Evelyn's Kalendar.*

CIRCUMRA'SION. *n. s.* [*circumrasio*, Latin.] The act of shaving or paring round. *Dict.*

CIRCUMROTA'TION. *n. s.* [*circum* and *roto*, Lat.]
1. The act of whirling round with a motion like that of a wheel. Circumvolution.
2. The state of being whirled round.

To CIRCUMSCRI'BE. *v. a.* [*circum* and *scribo*, Latin.]
1. To inclose in certain lines or boundaries.
2. To bound; to limit; to confine.

The good Andronicus,
With honour and with fortune is return'd;
From whence he *circumscribed* with his sword,
And brought to yoke th' enemies of Rome. *Shakesp. Tit. An.*
Therefore must his choice be *circumscrib'd*
Unto the voice and yielding of that body,
Whereof he's head. *Shakesp. Hamlet.*
And form'd the pow'rs of heav'n
Such as he pleas'd, and *circumscrib'd* their being! *Milton.*
The action great, yet *circumscrib'd* by time;
The words not forc'd, but sliding into rhime. *Dryden.*

We see that the external circumstances which do accompany mens acts, are those which do *circumscribe* and limit them. *Stillingfleet.*

You are above
The little forms which *circumscribe* your sex. *Southern.*

CIRCUMSCRI'PTION. *n. s.* [*circumscriptio*, Latin.]
1. Determination of particular form or magnitude.

In the *circumscription* of many leaves, flowers, fruits and seeds, nature affects a regular figure. *Ray on the Creation.*

2. Limitation; boundary; contraction; confinement.

I would not my unhoused free condition,
Put into *circumscription* and confine. *Shakesp. Othello.*

CIRCUMSCRI'PTIVE. *adj.* [from *circumscribe.*] Inclosing the superficies; marking the form or limits on the outside.

Stones regular, are distinguished by their external forms: such as is *circumscriptive*, or depending upon the whole stone, as in the eagle-stone; and this is properly called the figure. *Grew's Museum.*

CIRCUMSPE'CT. *adj.* [*circumspectum*, Lat.] Cautious; attentive to every thing; watchful on all sides.

None are for me,
That look into me with consid'rate eyes.
High-reaching Buckingham grows *circumspect.* *Shak. R.* III.

Men of their own nature *circumspect* and slow, but at the time discountenanced and discontent. *Haywood.*

The judicious doctor had been very watchful and *circumspect*, to keep himself from being imposed upon. *Boyle.*

CIRCUMSPE'CTION. *n. s.* [from *circumspect.*] Watchfulness on every side; cautious; general attention.

Observe the sudden growth of wickedness, from want of care and *circumspection* in the first impressions. *Clarendon.*

So saying, his proud step he scornful turn'd,
But with sly *circumspection.* *Milton's Paradise Lost, b.* iv.

CIRCUMSPE'CTIVE. *adj.* [*circumspicio*, *circumspectum*, Latin.] Looking round every way; attentive; vigilant; cautious.

No less alike the politick and wise,
All sly slow things, with *circumspective* eyes. *Pope's Essay.*

CIRCUMSPE'CTIVELY. *adv.* [from *circumspective.*] Cautiously; vigilantly; attentively; with watchfulness every way; watchfully.

CIRCUMSPE'CTLY. *adv.* [from *circumspect.*] With watchfulness every way; cautiously; watchfully; vigilantly.

Their authority weighs more with me than the concurrent suffrages of a thousand eyes, who never examined the thing so carefully and *circumspectly.* *Ray on the Creation.*

CIRCUMSPE'CTNESS. *n. s.* [from *circumspect.*] Caution; vigilance; watchfulness on every side.

Travel forces *circumspectness* on those abroad, who at home are nursed in security. *Wotton.*

CI'RCUMSTANCE. *n. s.* [*circumstantia*, Latin.]
1. Something appendant or relative to a fact: the same to a moral action as accident to a natural substance.

When men are ingenious in picking out *circumstances* of contempt, they do kindle their anger much. *Bacon's Essays.*

Our confessing or concealing persecuted truths, vary and change their very nature, according to different *circumstances* of time, place and persons. *South.*

2. The

2. The adjuncts of a fact, which make it more or less criminal; or make an accusation more or less probable.

Of these supposed crimes give me leave,
By *circumstance*, but to acquit myself. *Shakesp. Rich.* III.

3. Accident; something adventitious, which may be taken away without the annihilation of the principal thing considered.

Sense outside knows, the soul thro' all things sees:
Sense, *circumstance*; she doth the substance view. *Davies.*

4. Incident; event; generally of a minute or subordinate kind.

He defended Carlisle with very remarkable *circumstances* of courage, industry, and patience. *Clarendon, b.* viii.

The sculptor had in his thoughts the conqueror's weeping for new worlds, or some other the like *circumstance* in history. *Addison on Italy.*

The poet has gathered those *circumstances* which most terrify the imagination, and which really happen in the raging of a tempest. *Addison's Spectator*, N°. 489.

5. Condition; state of affairs. It is frequently used with respect to wealth or poverty; as good or ill *circumstances*.

None but a virtuous man can hope well in all *circumstances*. *Bacon's Ornam. Ration.*

We ought not to conclude, that if there be rational inhabitants in any of the planets, they must therefore have human nature, or be involved in the *circumstances* of our world. *Bentley.*

When men are easy in their *circumstances*, they are naturally enemies to innovations. *Addison's Freeholder*, N°. 42.

To CI'RCUMSTANCE. *v. a.* [from the noun.] To place in particular situation, or relation to the things.

To worthiest things,
Virtue, art, beauty, fortune, now I see,
Rareness or use, not nature, value brings,
And such as they are *circumstanc'd*, they be. *Donne.*

CI'RCUMSTANT. *adj.* [*circumstans*, Lat.] Surrounding; environing.

Its beams fly to visit the remotest parts of the world, and it gives motion to all *circumstant* bodies. *Digby on the Soul.*

CIRCUMSTA'NTIAL. *adj.* [*circumstantialis*, low Lat.]

1. Accidental; not essential.

This fierce abridgment
Hath to it *circumstantial* branches, which
Distinction should be rich in. *Shakesp. Cymbeline.*

This jurisdiction in the essentials of it, is as old as christianity; and those *circumstantial* additions of secular encouragement, christian princes thought necessary. *South's Sermons.*

Who would not prefer a religion that differs from our own in the *circumstantials*, before one that differs from it in the essentials. *Addison's Freeholder*, N°. 54.

2. Incidental; happening by chance; casual.

Virtue's but anguish, when 'tis several,
By occasion wak'd, and *circumstantial*. *Donne.*

3. Full of small events; particular; detailed.

He had been provoked by men's tedious and *circumstantial* recitals of their affairs, or by their multiplied questions about his own. *Prior's Dedication.*

CIRCUMSTANTIA'LITY. *n. s.* [from *circumstantial*.] The appendage of circumstances; the state of any thing as modified by circumstances.

CIRCUMSTA'NTIALLY. *adv.* [from *circumstantial*.]

1. Accordingly to circumstance; not essentially; accidentally.

Of the fancy and intellect, the powers are only *circumstantially* different. *Glanv. Sceps. c.* xiii.

2. Minutely; exactly; in every circumstance or particular.

Lucian agrees with Homer in every point *circumstantially*. *Broome's Notes on the Odyssey.*

To CIRCUMSTA'NTIATE. *v. a.* [from *circumstance*.]

1. To place in particular circumstances; to invest with particular accidents or adjuncts.

If the act were otherwise *circumstantiated*, it might will that freely, which now it wills freely. *Bramh. against Hobbs.*

2. To place in a particular condition, as with regard to power or wealth.

A number infinitely superior, and the best *circumstantiated* imaginable, are for the succession in the house of Hanover. *Swift's Miscellanies.*

To CIRCUMVA'LLATE. *v. a.* [*circumvallo*, Lat.] To inclose round with trenches or fortifications.

CIRCUMVALLA'TION. *n. s.* [from *circumvallate*, Lat.]

1. The art or act of casting up fortifications round a place.

When the czar first acquainted himself with mathematical learning, he practised all the rules of *circumvallation* and contravallation at the siege of a town in Livonia. *Watts's Logick.*

2. The fortification or trench thrown up round a place besieged.

This gave respite to finish those stupendious *circumvallations* and barricadoes, reared up by sea and land to begirt Petrina. *Howel's Vocal Forest.*

CIRCUMVE'CTION. *n. s.* [*circumvectio*, Latin.]

1. The act of carrying round.
2. The state of being carried round.

To CIRCUMVE'NT. *v. a.* [*circumvenio*, Lat.] To deceive; to cheat; to impose upon; to delude.

He fearing to be betrayed, or *circumvented* by his cruel brother, fled to Barbarossa. *Knolles's History of the Turks.*

As his malice is vigilant, he resteth not to *circumvent* the sons of the first deceived. *Brown's Vulgar Errours, b.* vii.

Should man
Fall *circumvented* thus by fraud. *Milton's Paradise Lost.*

Obstinately bent
To die undaunted, and to *circumvent*. *Dryden's Æn.* ii.

CIRCUMVE'NTION. *n. s.* [from *circumvent*.]

1. Fraud; imposture; cheat; delusion.

The inequality of the match between him and the subtlest of us, would quickly appear by a fatal *circumvention*: there must be a wisdom from above to over-reach this hellish wisdom. *South's Sermons.*

If he is in the city, he must avoid haranguing against *circumvention* in commerce. *Collier of Popularity.*

2. Prevention; pre-occupation: this sense is now out of use.

Whatever hath been thought on in this state,
That could be brought to bodily act, ere Rome
Had *circumvention*. *Shakesp. Coriolanus.*

To CIRCUMVE'ST. *v. a.* [*circumvestio*, Lat.] To cover round with a garment.

Who on this base the earth did'st firmly found,
And mad'st the deep to *circumvest* it round. *Wotton.*

CIRCUMVOLA'TION. *n. s.* [from *circumvolo*, Lat.] The act of flying round.

To CIRCUMVO'LVE. *v. a* [*circumvolvo*, Lat.] To roll round; to give a circular motion.

Could solid orbs be accommodated to phænomena, yet to ascribe each sphere an intelligence to *circumvolve* it, were unphilosophical. *Glanv. Sceps. c.* 20.

CIRCUMVOLU'TION. *n. s.* [*circumvolutus*, Lat.]

1. The act of rolling round.
2. The state of being rolled round.

The twisting of the guts is really either a *circumvolution*, or insertion of one part of the gut within the other. *Arbuthnot.*

3. The thing rolled round another.

Consider the obliquity or closeness of these *circumvolutions*; the nearer they are, the higher may be the instrument. *Wilk.*

CI'RCUS. } *n. s.* [*circus*, Latin.] An open space or area for
CI'RQUE. } sports, with seats round for the spectators.

A pleasant valley, like one of those *circuses*, which, in great cities somewhere, doth give a pleasant spectacle of running horses. *Sidney, b.* ii.

The one was about the *cirque* of Flora, the other upon the Tarpeian mountain. *Stillingfleet.*

See the *cirque* falls! th' unpillar'd temple nods;
Streets pav'd with heroes, Tyber choak'd with gods. *Pope.*

CIST. *n. s.* [*cista*, Latin.] A case; a tegument; commonly used in medicinal language for the coat or inclosure of a tumour.

CI'STED. *adj.* [from *cist*.] Inclosed in a cist, or bag.

CI'STERN. *n. s.* [*cisterna*, Latin.]

1. A receptacle of water for domestick uses.

'Tis not the rain that waters the whole earth, but that which falls into his own *cistern*, that must relieve him. *South.*

2. A reservoir; an inclosed fountain.

Had no part as kindly staid behind,
In the wide *cisterns* of the lakes confin'd;
Did not the springs and rivers drench the land,
Our globe would grow a wilderness of sand. *Blackmore.*

3. Any watry receptacle or repository.

So half my Egypt were submerg'd, and made
A *cistern* for scal'd snakes. *Shakes. Anthony and Cleopatra.*

But there's no bottom; none
In my voluptuousness: your wives, your daughters,
Your matrons and your maids, could not fill up
The *cistern* of my lust. *Shakesp. Macbeth.*

CISTUS. *n. s.* [Lat.] The name of a plant. The same with Rockrose.

CIT. *n. s.* [contracted from *citizen*.] An inhabitant of a city, in an ill sense. A pert low townsman; a pragmatical trader.

We bring you now to show what different things,
The *cits* or clowns are from the courts of kings. *Johnson.*

Study your race, or the soil of your family will dwindle into *cits* or squires, or run up into wits or madmen. *Tatler.*

Barnard, thou art a *cit*, with all thy worth;
But Bug and D—l, their honours, and so forth. *Pop. Hor.*

CI'TADEL. *n. s.* [*citadelle*, French.] A fortress; a castle, or place of arms in a city.

As he came to the crown by unjust means, as unjustly he kept it; by force of stranger soldiers in *citadels*, the nests of tyranny and murderers of liberty. *Sidney, b.* ii.

I'll to my charge, the *citadel*, repair. *Dryd. Aureng.*

CI'TAL. *n. s.* [from *cite*.]

1. Reproof; impeachment.

He made a blushing *cital* of himself,
And chid his truant youth. *Shakesp. Henry* IV. *P.* i.

2. Summons; citation; call into a court.
3. Quotation; citation.

CITA'TION. *n. s.* [*citatio*, Latin.]

The calling a person before the judge, for the sake of trying

trying the cause of action commenced against him. *Ayliffe.*

2. Quotation; the adduction of any passage from another author; or of another man's words.

3. The passage or words quoted; a quotation.

The letter-writter cannot read these *citations* without blushing, after the charge he hath advanced. *Atterb. Pref. Serm.*

View the principles of parties represented in their own authors, and not in the *citations* of those who would confute them. *Watts's Improvement on the Mind.*

4. Enumeration; mention.

These causes effect a consumption, endemick to this island: there remains a *citation* of such as may produce it in any country. *Harvey on Consumptions.*

CI'TATORY. *adj.* [from *To cite.*] Having the power or form of citation.

If a judge cite one to a place, to which he cannot come with safety, he may freely appeal, though an appeal be inhibited in the letters *citatory*. *Ayliffe's Parergon.*

To CITE. *v. a.* [*cito*, Latin.]

1. To summon to answer in a court.

He held a late court, to which
She oft' was *cited* by them, but appear'd not. *Sh. Hen.* VIII.

Forthwith the *cited* dead
Of all past ages, to the general doom
Shall hasten. *Milton's Paradise Lost, b.* iii. *l.* 327.

This power of *citing*, and dragging the defendant into court, was taken away. *Ayliffe's Parergon.*

2. To enjoin; to call upon another authoritatively; to direct; summon.

I speak to you, Sir Thurio;
For Valentine, I need not *cite* him to it. *Shakesp.*

This sad experience *cites* me to reveal,
And what I dictate is from what I feel. *Prior.*

3. To quote.

Demonstrations in scripture, may not otherwise be shewed than by *citing* them out of the scripture. *Hooker, b.* ii.

That passage of Plato, which I *cited* before. *Bacon.*

In banishment he wrote those verses, which I *cite* from his letter. *Dryden's Dedicat. to Æn.*

CI'TER. *n. s.* [from *cite.*]

1. One who cites into a court.

2. One who quotes; a quoter.

I must desire the *citer* henceforward to inform us of his editions too. *Atterbury.*

CITESS. *n. s.* [from *cit.*] A city woman. A word peculiar to *Dryden.*

Cits and *citesses* raise a joyful strain;
'Tis a good omen to begin a reign. *Dryd Albion and Alba.*

CI'THERN. *n. s.* [*cithara*, Latin.] A kind of harp; a musical instrument.

At what time the heathen had profaned it, even in that was it dedicated with songs and *citherns*, and harps and cymbals. *1 Mac.* iv. 54.

CI'TIZEN. *n. s.* [*civis*, Lat. *citoyen*, French.]

1. A freeman of a city; not a foreigner; not a slave.

All inhabitants within these walls are not properly *citizens*, but only such as are called freemen. *Raleigh's Hist. World.*

2. A townsman; a man of trade; not a gentleman.

When he speaks not like a *citizen*,
You find him like a soldier. *Shakespeare's Coriolanus.*

3. An inhabitant; a dweller in any place.

Far from noisy Rome, secure, he lives;
And one more *citizen* to Sibyl gives. *Dryden's Juvenal.*

CI'TIZEN. *adj.* [This is only in *Shakespeare.*] Having the qualities of a citizen; as cowardice, meanness.

So sick I am not, yet I am not well;
But not so *citizen* a wanton, as
To seem to die ere sick. *Shakespeare's Cymbeline.*

CI'TRINE. *adj.* [*citrinus*, Lat.] Lemon coloured; of a dark yellow.

The Butterfly, papilio major, has its wings painted with *citrine* and black, both in long streaks and spots. *Grew's Mus.*

By *citrine* urine of a thicker consistence, the saltness of phlegm is known. *Floyer on the Humours.*

CI'TRINE. *n. s.* [from *citrinus*, Latin.]

A species of crystal of an extremely pure, clear, and fine texture, generally free from flaws and blemishes. It is ever found in a long and slender column, irregularly hexangular, and terminated by an hexangular pyramid. It is from one to four or five inches in length. These crystals are of an extremely beautiful yellow, differing in degrees from that of a strong ochre colour to that of the peel of a lemon; and they have a very elegant brightness and transparence. This stone is very plentiful in the West Indies. Our jewellers have learned from the French and Italians to call it *citrine*; and often cut stones for rings out of it, which are generally mistaken for topazes. *Hill on Fossils.*

CITRON-TREE. *n. s.* [from *citrus*, Latin.]

It hath broad stiff leaves, like those of the laurel. The flowers consist of many leaves, expanded like a rose: the cup of the flower is slender and fleshy, and is divided into five segments at the top. The pistil becomes an oblong, thick, fleshy fruit, which is very full of juice, and contains several hard seeds. Genoa is the great nursery of Europe for these sorts of trees. One sort, with a pointed fruit, is in so great esteem, that the single fruits are sold at Florence for two shillings each. This fruit is not to be had in perfection in any part of Italy, but the plain between Pisa and Leghorn. *Miller.*

May the sun
With *citron* groves adorn a distant soil. *Addison.*

CITRON-WATER. *n. s.* Aqua vitæ, distilled with the rind of citrons.

Like *citron-waters* matrons cheeks inflame. *Pope.*

CI'TRUL. *n. s.* The same with *pumpion*, so named from its yellow colour.

CI'TY. *n. s.* [*cité*, French, *civitas*, Latin.]

1. A large collection of houses and inhabitants.

Men seek their safety from number better united, and from walls and other fortifications; the use whereof is to make the few a match for the many, and this is the original of *cities*. *Temple.*

City, in a strict and proper sense, means the houses inclosed within the walls: in a larger sense it reaches to all the suburbs. *Watts's Logick.*

2. In the English law.

A town corporate, that hath a bishop and a cathedral church. *Cowel.*

3. The inhabitants of a certain city, as distinguished from other subjects.

What is the *city* but the people?——
——True, the people are the *city*. *Shakesp. Coriolanus.*

I do suspect I have done some offence,
That seems disgracious in the *city's* eye. *Shakesp. Rich.* III.

CI'TY. *adj.*

1. Relating to the city.

His enforcement of the *city* wives. *Shakesp. Richard* III.

He, I accuse,
The *city* ports by this hath enter'd. *Shakesp. Coriolanus.*

2. Resembling the manners of the citizens.

Make not a *city* feast of it, to let the meat cool ere we can agree upon the first cut. *Shakespeare's Timon.*

CI'VET. *n. s.* [*civette*, Fr. *zibetta*, Arabic, signifying *scent.*] A perfume from the civet cat.

The *civet*, or *civet* cat, is a little animal, not unlike our cat, excepting that his snout is more pointed, his claws less dangerous, and his cry different. It is a native of the Indies, Peru, Brasil, Guinea. The perfume is formed like a kind of grease, or thick scum, in an aperture or bag under its tail, between the anus and pudendum. It is gathered from time to time, and abounds in proportion as the animal is fed. It is much used by perfumers and confectioners; but seldom prescribed in medicine. *Trevoux.*

Civet is of a baser birth than tar: the very uncleanly flux of a cat. *Shakespeare's As you like it.*

He rubs himself with *civet*: can you smell him out by that? *Shakespeare's Much ado about Nothing.*

Some putrefactions and excrements do yield excellent odours; as *civet* and musk, and, as some think, ambergrease. *Bacon's Natural History.*

CI'VICK. *adj.* [*civicus*, Latin.] Relating to civil honours or practises; not military.

With equal rays immortal Tully shone:
Behind, Rome's genius waits with *civick* crowns,
And the great father of his country owns. *Pop. Tem. of Fame.*

CI'VIL. *adj.* [*civilis*, Latin.]

1. Relating to the community; political; relating to the city or government.

God gave them laws of *civil* regimen, and would not permit their commonweal to be governed by any other laws than his own. *Hooker, b.* iii. *s.* 11.

Part such as appertain
To *civil* justice; part, religious rites
Of sacrifice. *Milton's Paradise Lost, b.* xii. *l.* 231.

But there is another unity, which would be most advantageous to our country; and that is your endeavour after a *civil*, a political union in the whole nation. *Sprat's Sermon.*

2. Relating to any man as a member of a community.

Break not your promise, unless it be unlawful or impossible; either out of your natural, or out of your *civil* power. *Taylor.*

3. Not in anarchy; not wild; not without rule or government.

For rudest minds with harmony were caught,
And *civil* life was by the muses taught. *Roscommon.*

4. Not foreign; intestine.

From a *civil* war, God of his mercy defend us, as that which is most desperate of all others. *Bacon to Villers.*

5. Not ecclesiastical; as, the ecclesiastical courts are controlled by the *civil.*

6. Not natural; as, a person banished or outlawed is said to suffer *civil*, though not natural death.

7. Not military; as, the *civil* magistrates authority is obstructed by war.

8. Not criminal; as, This is a *civil* process, not a criminal prosecution.

9. Civilised; not barbarous.

England was very rude and barbarous; for it is but even the other day since England grew *civil*. *Spenser on Ireland.*

10. Complaisant; civilised; gentle; well bred; elegant of manners; not rude; not brutal; not coarse.

I heard a mermaid, on a dolphin's back,
Uttering such dulcet and harmonious breath,
That the rude sea grew *civil* at her song. *Shakespeare.*

He was *civil* and well natured, never refusing to teach another. *Dryden's Dufresnoy.*

And fall these sayings from that gentle tongue,
Where *civil* speech and soft persuasion hung. *Prior.*

11. Grave; sober; not gay or shewy.

Thus night oft see me in thy pale career,
'Till *civil* suited morn appear. *Milton's Poems.*

12. Relating to the ancient consular or imperial government; as, *civil* law.

No woman had it; but a *civil* doctor. *Shak. Merch. of Ven.*

CIVI'LIAN. *n. s.* [*civilis*, Lat.] One that professes the knowledge of the old Roman law, and of general equity.

The professors of that law, called *civilians*, because the civil law is their guide, should not be discountenanced nor discouraged. *Bacon's Advice to Villers.*

A depending kingdom is a term of art, unknown to all ancient *civilians*, and writers upon government. *Swift.*

CIVILISA'TION. *n. s.* [from *civil.*]

A law, act of justice, or judgment, which renders a criminal process civil; which is performed by turning an information into an inquest, or the contrary. *Harris.*

CIVI'LITY. *n. s.* [from *civil.*]

1. Freedom from barbarity; the state of being civilised.

The English were at first as stout and warlike a people as ever the Irish; and yet are now brought unto that *civility*, that no nation in the world excelleth them in all goodly conversation, and all the studies of knowledge and humanity. *Spenser's State of Ireland.*

Divers great monarchies have risen from barbarism to *civility*, and fallen again to ruin. *Davies on Ireland.*

Wheresoe'er her conquering eagles fled,
Arts, learning, and *civility* were spread. *Denham's Poems.*

2. Politeness; complaisance; elegance of behaviour.

Art thou thus bolden'd, man, by thy distress;
Or else a rude despiser of good manners,
That in *civility* thou seem'st so empty? *Shak. As you like it.*

He, by his great *civility* and affability, wrought very much upon the people. *Clarendon, b.* viii.

I should be kept from a publication, did not what your *civility* calls a request, your greatness, command. *South.*

We, in point of *civility*, yield to others in our own houses. *Swift.*

3. Rule of decency; practise of politeness.

Love taught him shame; and shame, with love at strife,
Soon taught the sweet *civilities* of life. *Dryd. Cym. and Iphig.*

To CI'VILIZE. *v. a.* [from *civil.*] To reclaim from savageness and brutality; to instruct in the arts of regular life.

We send the graces and the muses forth,
To *civilize* and to instruct the North. *Waller.*

Musæus first, then Orpheus *civilize*
Mankind, and gave the world their deities. *Denham.*

Amongst those who are counted the *civilized* part of mankind, this original law of nature still takes place. *Locke.*

Osiris, or the Bacchus of the antients, is reported to have *civilized* the Indians, and reigned amongst them fifty-two years. *Arbuthnot on Coins.*

CI'VILIZER. *n. s.* [from *civilize.*] He that reclaims others from a wild and savage life; he that teaches the rules and customs of civility.

The *civilizers!*—the disturbers, say;—
The robbers, the corrupters of mankind!
Proud vagabonds! *Philips's Briton.*

CI'VILLY. *adv.* [from *civil.*]

1. In a manner relating to government, or to the rights or character of a member of a community; not naturally; not ecclesiastically; not criminally.

Men that are civil lead their lives after one common law; for that a multitude should, without harmony amongst themselves, concur in the doing of one thing; for this is *civilly* to live; or should manage community of life, it is not possible. *Hooker, b.* i. *p.* 46.

That accusation, which is publick, is either *civilly* commenced for the private satisfaction of the party injured; or else criminally, that is, for some publick punishment. *Ayliffe.*

2. Politely; complaisantly; gently; without rudeness; without brutality.

I will deal *civilly* with his poems: nothing ill is to be spoken of the dead. *Dryden's Preface to his Fables.*

I would have had Almeria and Osmyn parted *civilly*; as if it was not proper for lovers to do so. *Collier's View of the Stage.*

He thought them folks that lost their way,
And ask'd them *civilly* to stay. *Prior.*

3. Without gay or gaudy colours.

The chambers were handsome and cheerful, and furnished *civilly*. *Bacon's New Atlantis.*

CIZE. *n. s.* [perhaps from *incisa*, Lat. shaped or cut to a certain magnitude.] The quantity of any thing, with regard to its external form; often written *size.*

If no motion can alter bodies, that is, reduce them to some other *cize* or figure, then there is none of itself to give them the *cize* and figure which they have. *Grew's Cosmol. b.* i. *c.* 2.

CLACK. *n. s.* [*klatschen*, Germ. to rattle; to make a noise.]

1. Any thing that makes a lasting and importunate noise; generally used, in contempt, for the tongue.

But still his tongue ran on,
And with its everlasting *clack*,
Set all mens ears upon the rack. *Hudibras, Part* ii. *canto* 2.

Fancy flows in, and muse flies high;
He knows not when my *clack* will lie. *Prior.*

2. *The* CLACK *of a Mill.* A bell that rings when more corn is required to be put in.

Says John, just at the hopper will I stand,
And mark the *clack* how justly it will sound. *Betterton.*

To CLACK. *v. n.* [from the noun.]

1. To make a chinking noise.

2. To let the tongue run.

To CLACK. *v. a.* As to *clack wool*, is to cut off the sheep's mark, which makes it to weigh less, and so yield the less custom to the king. *Cowel.*

CLAD. *part. pret.* [This participle, which is now referred to *clothe*, seems originally to have belonged to *cleden*, or some such word, like *kleeden*, Dutch.] Clothed; invested; garbed.

He had *clad* himself with a new garment. 1 *Kings* xi. 29.

Beyond
The flow'ry dale of Sibma, *clad* with vine. *Milt. Par. Lost.*

But virtue too, as well as vice, is *clad*
In flesh and blood. *Waller.*

To her the weeping heav'ns become serene;
For her the ground is *clad* in cheerful green. *Dryden.*

The courtiers were all most magnificiently *clad.* *Swift.*

To CLAIM. *v. a.* [*clamer*, French.] To demand of right; to require authoritatively; not to beg or accept as favour, but to exact as due.

If only one man hath a divine right to obedience, no body can *claim* that obedience but he that can shew his right *Locke.*

We must know how the first ruler, from whom any one *claims*, came by his authority, before we can know who has a right to succeed him in it. *Locke.*

Poets have undoubted right to *claim*,
If not the greatest, the most lasting name. *Congreve.*

CLAIM. *n. s.* [from the verb.]

1. A demand of any thing, as due.

You, in the right of lady Blanch your wife,
May then make all the *claim* that Arthur did. *Shak. K. John.*

Forsworn thyself! The traitor's odious name
I first return, and then disprove thy *claim.* *Dryden.*

Will he not, therefore, of the two evils chuse the least, by submitting to a master, who hath no immediate *claim* upon him, rather than to another, who hath already revived several *claims* upon him? *Swift.*

2. A title to any privilege or possession in the hands of another.

Either there must have been but one sovereign over them all, or else every father of a family had been as good a prince, and had as good a *claim* to royalty as these. *Locke.*

3. In law.

A demand of any thing that is in the possession of another, or at the least out of his own: as *claim* by charter, *claim* by descent. *Cowel.*

4. The phrases are commonly to *make claim*, or to *lay claim.*

The king of Prussia *lays* in his *claim* for Neuf-Châtel, as he did for the principality of Orange. *Addison on Italy.*

If God, by his positive grant, gave dominion to any man, primogeniture can *lay* no *claim* to it, unless God so ordained. *Locke.*

CLA'IMABLE. *adj.* [from *claim.*] That which may be demanded as due.

CLA'IMANT. *n. s.* [from *claim.*] He that demands any thing as unjustly detained by another.

A CLA'IMER. *n. s.* [from *claim.*] He that makes a demand; he that requires any thing, as unjustly with-held from him.

CLAIR-OBSCURE. *n. s.* See CLARE-OBSCURE.

To CLA'MBER. *v. n.* [probably corrupted from *climb*; as *climber, clamber.*] To climb with difficulty; as with both hands and feet.

The kitchen malkin pins
Her richest lockram 'bout her reechy neck,
Clamb'ring the walls to eye him. *Shakespeare's Coriolanus.*

When you hear the drum,
Clamber not you up to the casements then. *Shakespeare.*

The men there do not without some difficulty *clamber* up the acclivities, dragging their kine with them. *Ray on the Creat.*

They were forced to *clamber* over so many rocks, and to tread upon the brink of so many precipices, that they were very often in danger of their lives. *Addison's Freeholder*, N°. 27.

To CLAMM. *v. a.* [in some provinces, to *cleam*, from clæmian, Sax. to glew together.] To clog with any glutinous matter.

A swarm of wasps got into a honey-pot, and there they cloyed

cloyed and *clammed* themselves, 'till there was no getting out again. *L'Estrange, Fab.* cxxvi.

The sprigs were all dawbed with lime, and the birds *clammed* and taken. *L'Estrange.*

CLA'MMINESS. *n. s.* [from *clammy.*] Viscosity; viscidity; tenacity; ropiness.

A greasy pipkin will spoil the *clamminess* of the glew. *Moxon.*

CLA'MMY. *adj.* [from *clamm.*] Viscous; glutinous; tenacious; adhesive; ropy.

Bodies *clammy* and cleaving, are such as have an appetite, at once, to follow another body, and to hold to themselves. *Bacon's Natural History*, N°. 293.

Neither the brain nor spirits can conserve motion: the former is of such a *clammy* consistence, it can no more retain it than a quagmire. *Glanv. Sceps.* c. 6.

Aghast he wak'd, and, starting from his bed,
Cold sweats, in *clammy* drops, his limbs o'erspread. *Dryden.*
I drop with *clammy* sweat. *Dryden's Fables.*
Joyful thou'lt see
The *clammy* surface all o'er strown with tribes
Of greedy insects. *Philips.*

There is an unctuous *clammy* vapour that arises from the stum of grapes, when they lie mashed together in the vat, which puts out a light, when dipped into it. *Addison on Italy.*

The continuance of the fever, *clammy* sweats, paleness, and at last a total cessation of pain, are signs of a gangrene and approaching death. *Arbuthnot on Diet.*

CLA'MOROUS. *adj.* [from *clamour.*] Vociferous; noisy; turbulent; loud.

It is no sufficient argument to say, that, in urging these ceremonies, none are so *clamorous* as Papists, and they whom Papists suborn. *Hooker, b.* iv. *sect.* 9.

He kiss'd her lips
With such a *clamorous* smack, that at the parting
All the church eccho'd. *Shakespeare's Taming of the Shrew.*
At my birth
The goats ran from the mountains, and the herds
Were strangely *clam'rous* in the frighted fields. *Shakespeare.*
With the *clam'rous* report of war,
Thus will I drown your exclamations. *Shakesp. Richard* III.
Then various elements against thee join'd,
In one more various animal combin'd,
And fram'd the *clam'rous* race of busy humankind. *Pope.*

A pamphlet that will settle the wavering, instruct the ignorant, and inflame the *clamorous.* *Swift.*

CLA'MOUR. *n. s.* [*clamor*, Latin.]

1. Outcry; noise; exclamation; vociferation.

Revoke thy doom,
Or whilst I can vent *clamour* from my throat,
I'll tell thee, thou do'st evil. *Shakesp. King Lear.*

The people grew then exorbitant in their *clamours* for justice. *King Charles.*

The Maid
Shall weep the fury of my love decay'd;
And weeping follow me, as thou do'st now,
With idle *clamours* of a broken vow. *Prior.*

2. It is used sometimes, but less fitly, of inanimate things.

Here the loud Arno's boist'rous *clamours* cease,
That with submissive murmurs glides in peace. *Addison.*

To CLA'MOUR. *v. n.* [from the noun.] To make outcries; to exclaim; to vociferate; to roar in turbulence.

The obscure bird *clamour'd* the live-long night. *Shakesp.*
Clamour your tongues, and not a word more. *Shakespeare.*

Let them not come in multitudes, or in a tribunitious manner; for that is to *clamour* counsels, not to inform them. *Bacon's Essay*, 21.

CLAMP. *n. s.* [*clamp*, French.]

1. A piece of wood joined to another, as an addition of strength.

2. A quantity of bricks.

To burn a *clamp* of brick of sixteen thousand, they allow seven ton of coals. *Mortimer's Husbandry.*

To CLAMP. *v. a.* [from the noun.]

When a piece of board is fitted with the grain to the end of another piece of board cross the grain, the first board is *clamped.* Thus the ends of tables are commonly *clamped*, to preserve them from warping. *Moxon's Mech. Exer.*

CLAN. *n. s.* [probably of Scottish original: *klaan*, in the Highlands, signifies *children.*]

1. A family; a race.

They around the flag
Of each his faction, in their several *clans*,
Swarm populous, un-number'd. *Milton's Paradise Lost, b.* ii.

Milton was the poetical son of Spenser, and Mr. Waller of Fairfax; for we have our lineal descents and *clans* as well as other families. *Dryden's Fables, Preface.*

2. A body or sect of persons, in a sense of contempt.

Patridge and the rest of his *clan* may hoot me for a cheat, if I fail in any single particular. *Swift's Predictions for* 1708.

CLA'NCULAR. *adj.* [*clancularius*, Latin.] Clandestine; secret; private; concealed; obscure; hidden.

Let us withdraw all supplies from our lusts, and not by any secret reserved affection give them *clancular* aids to maintain their rebellion. *Decay of Piety.*

CLANDE'STINE. [*adj. clandestinus*, Lat.] Secret; hidden; private; in an ill sense.

Tho' nitrous tempests, and *clandestine* death,
Fill'd the deep caves, and num'rous vaults beneath. *Blackm.*

CLANDE'STINELY. *adv.* [from *clandestine.*] Secretly; privately; in private; in secret.

There have been two printed papers *clandestinely* spread about, whereof no man is able to trace the original. *Swift.*

CLANG. *n. s.* [*clangor*, Lat.] A sharp, shrill noise.

With such a horrid *clang*
As on mount Sinai rang,
While the red fire and smould'ring clouds out brake. *Milton.*
An island, salt and bare,
The haunt of seals and orcs, and sea-mews *clang.* *Milton.*
What *clangs* were heard in German skies afar,
Of arms and armies rushing to the war. *Dryd. Virg. Georg.*
Guns, and trumpets *clang*, and solemn sound
Of drums, o'ercame their groans. *Philips.*

To CLANG. *v. n.* [*clango*, Lat.] To clatter; to make a loud shrill noise.

Have I not in a pitched battle heard
Loud 'larums, neighing steeds, and trumpets *clang.* *Shakesp.*
The Libyans clad in armour, lead
The dance; and *clanging* swords and shields they beat. *Prior.*

To CLANG. *v. a.* To strike together with a noise.

The fierce Curetes trod tumultuous
Their mystick dance, and *clang'd* their sounding arms;
Industrious with the warlike din to quell
Thy infant cries. *Prior.*

CLA'NGOUR. *n. s.* [*clangor*, Lat.] A loud shrill sound.

In death he cried,
Like to a dismal *clangour* heard from far,
Warwick, revenge my death. *Shakesp. Henry* VI. *P.* iii.
With joy they view the waving ensigns fly,
And hear the trumpet's *clangour* pierce the sky. *Dryd. Æn.*

CLA'NGOUS. *adj.* [from *clang.*] Making a clang.

We do not observe the cranes, and birds of long necks, have any musical, but harsh and *clangous* throats. *Brown.*

CLANK. *n. s.* [from *clang.*] A loud, shrill, sharp noise, made by the collision of hard and sonorous bodies.

They were joined by the melodious *clank* of marrow-bone and clever. *Spectator*, N°. 617.

To CLAP. *v. a.* [clappan, Sax. *klappen*, Dutch.]

1. To strike together with a quick motion, so as to make a noise by the collision.

Following the fliers,
With them he enters; who, upon the sudden,
Clapt to their gates. *Shakespeare's Coriolanus.*

Men shall *clap* their hands at him, and shall hiss him out of his place. *Job*, xxvii. 23.

Have you never seen a citizen, in a cold morning, *clapping* his sides, and walking before his shop? *Dryd. Spanish Fryar.*

He crowing *clapp'd* his wings, th' appointed call
To chuck his wives together in the hall. *Dryden's Fables.*
Each poet of the air her glory sings,
And round him the pleas'd audience *clap* their wings. *Dryd.*

He had just time to get in and *clap to* the door, to avoid the blow. *Locke on Education.*

In flow'ry wreaths the royal virgin drest
His bending horns, and kindly *clapt* his breast. *Addison.*
Glad of a quarrel, straight I *clap* the door,
Sir, let me see your works and you no more. *Pope's Epistles.*

2. To add one thing to another, implying the idea of something hasty, unexpected, or sudden.

As summer weareth out, they *clap* mouth to mouth, wing to wing, and leg to leg; and so, after a sweet singing, fall down into lakes. *Carew's Survey of Cornwall.*

This pink is one of Cupid's carriers: *clap* on more sails; pursue. *Shakespeare's Merry Wives of Windsor.*

Smooth temptations, like the sun, make a maiden lay by her veil and robe; which persecution, like the northern wind, made her hold fast, and *clap* close about her. *Taylor.*

If a man be highly commended, we think him sufficiently lessened, if we *clap* sin, or folly, or infirmity into his account. *Taylor's Rule of living holy.*

Razor-makers generally *clap* a small bar of Venice steel between two small bars of Flemish steel. *Moxon's Mech. Exer.*

The man *clapt* his fingers one day to his mouth, and blew upon them. *L'Estrange.*

His shield thrown by, to mitigate the smart,
He *clapp'd* his hand upon the wounded part. *Dryd. Æneid.*

If you leave some space empty for the air, then *clap* your hand upon the mouth of the vessel, and the fishes will contend to get uppermost in the water. *Ray on the Creation.*

It would be as absurd as to say, he *clapped* spurs to his horse at St. James's, and galloped away to the Hague. *Addison.*

By having their minds yet in their perfect freedom and indifferency, the likelier to pursue truth the better, having no biass yet *clapped* on to mislead them. *Locke.*

I have observed a certain chearfulness in as bad a system of features

features as ever was *clapped* together, which hath appeared lovely. *Addison's Spectator*, N°. 86.

Let all her ways be unconfin'd,
And *clap* your padlock on her mind. *Prior.*

Socrates or Alexander might have a fool's coat *clapt* upon them, and perhaps neither wisdom nor majesty would secure them from a sneer. *Watts's Improvement of the Mind.*

3. To do any thing with a sudden hasty motion, or unexpectedly.

We were dead asleep,
And, how we know not, all *clapt* under hatches. *Shakesp.*

He was no sooner entered into the town, but a scambling soldier *clapt* hold of his bridle, which he thought was in a begging or in a drunken fashion. *Wotton's Life of Duke of Buck.*

So much from the rest of his countrymen, and indeed from his whole species, that his friends would have *clapped* him into bedlam, and have begged his estate. *Spectator*, N°. 576.

Have you observ'd a sitting hare,
List'ning and fearful of the storm
Of horns and hounds, *clap* back her ear. *Prior.*

We will take our remedy at law, and *clap* an action upon you for old debts. *Arbuthnot's History of John Bull.*

4. To celebrate or praise by clapping the hands; to applaud.

I have often heard the stationer wishing for those hands to take off his melancholy bargain, which *clapped* its performance on the stage. *Dedication to Dryden's Spanish Fryar.*

5. To infect with a venereal poison. [See the noun.]

If the patient hath been formerly *clapt*, it will be the more difficult to cure him the second time, and worse the third. *Wiseman's Surgery.*

Let men and manners ev'ry dish adapt;
Who'd force his pepper where his guests are *clapt*? *King.*

6. *To* CLAP *up.* To complete suddenly, without much precaution.

No longer than we well could wash our hands,
To *clap* this royal bargain *up* of peace. *Shakes. King John.*
Was ever match *clapt up* so suddenly? *Shakespeare.*

A peace may be *clapped up* with that suddenness, that the forces, which are now in motion, may unexpectedly fall upon his skirts. *Howel's Vocal Forest.*

To CLAP. *v. n.*

1. To move nimbly with a noise.

Every door flew open
T' admit my entrance; and then *clapt* behind me,
To bar my going back. *Dryden's Cleomenes.*
A whirlwind rose, that, with a violent blast,
Shook all the dome: the doors around me *clapt*. *Dryden.*

2. To enter with alacrity and briskness upon any thing.

Come, a song.——
—Shall we *clap* into't roundly, without saying we are hoarse? *Shakespeare's As you like it.*

3. To strike the hands together in applause.

All the best men are ours; for 'tis ill hap
If they hold, when their ladies bid 'em *clap*. *Epilogue to Henry* VIII.

CLAP. *n. s.* [from the verb.]

1. A loud noise made by sudden collision.

Give the door such a *clap* as you go out, as will shake the whole room, and make every thing rattle in it. *Swift.*

2. A sudden or unexpected act or motion.

It is monstrous to me, that the South-sea should pay half their debts at one *clap*. *Swift's Letters.*

3. An explosion of thunder.

There shall be horrible *claps* of thunder, and flashes of lightning, voices and earthquakes. *Hakewill on Providence.*

The *clap* is past, and now the skies are clear. *Dryd. Juv.*

4. An act of applause.

The actors, in the midst of an innocent old play, are often startled in the midst of unexpected *claps* or hisses. *Addison.*

5. A venereal infection. [from *clapoir*, Fr.]

Time, that at last matures a *clap* to pox. *Pope's Sat.*

6. [With Falconers.] The nether part of the beak of a hawk.

CLA'PPER. *n. s.* [from *clap*.]

1. One who claps with his hands; an applauder.

2. The tongue of a bell.

He hath a heart as sound as a bell, and his tongue is the *clapper*; for what his heart thinks, his tongue speaks. *Shakes.*

I saw a young lady fall down the other day, and she much resembled an overturned bell without a *clapper*. *Addis. Guard.*

3. *The* CLA'PPER *of a Mill.* A piece of wood for shaking the hopper.

To CLAPPERCLA'W. *v. a.* [from *clap* and *claw*.] To tongue-beat; to scold.

Now they are *clapperclawing* one another, I'll go look on. *Shakespeare's Troilus and Cressida.*

They've always been at daggers-drawing,
And one another *clapperclawing*. *Hudibras, part* ii. *canto* 2.

CLA'RENCEUX, or CLA'RENCIEUX. *n. s.* The second king at arms: so named from the dutchy of *Clarence*.

CLARE-OBSCURE. *n. s.* [from *clarus*, bright, and *obscurus*, Lat.] Light and shade in painting.

As masters in the *clare-obscure*,
With various light your eyes allure;
A flaming yellow here they spread,
Draw off in blue, or charge in red;
Yet from these colours, oddly mix'd,
Your sight upon the whole is fix'd. *Prior.*

CLA'RET. *n. s.* [*clairet*, Fr.] French wine, of a clear pale-red colour.

Red and white wine are in a trice confounded into *claret*. *Boyle.*

The *claret* smooth, red as the lips we press
In sparkling fancy, while we drain the bowl. *Thoms. Autumn.*

CLA'RICORD. *n. s.* [from *clarus* and *chorda*, Latin.]

A musical instrument in form of a spinette, but more ancient. It has forty-nine or fifty keys, and seventy strings. *Chambers.*

CLARIFICA'TION. *n. s.* [from *clarify.*] The act of making any thing clear from impurities.

Liquors are, many of them, at the first, thick and troubled; as muste, wort, &c. but to know the means of accelerating *clarification*, we must first know the causes of *clarification*. *Bacon's Natural History*, N°. 301.

To CLA'RIFY. *v. a.* [*clarifier*, French.]

1. To purify or clear any liquor; to separate feculences or impurities.

The apothecaries *clarify* their syrups by whites of eggs, beaten with the juices which they would *clarify*; which whites of eggs gather all the dregs and grosser parts of the juice to them; and after, the syrup being set on the fire, the whites of eggs themselves harden, and are taken forth. *Bac. Nat. Hist.*

2. To brighten; to illuminate: this sense is rare.

The will was then ductile and pliant to all the motions of right reason: it met the dictates of a *clarified* understanding half way. *South's Sermons.*

The Christian religion is the only means that God has sanctified, to set fallen man upon his legs again, to *clarify* his reason, and to rectify his will. *South's Sermons.*

CLA'RION. *n. s.* [*clarin*, Span. from *clarus*, loud, Lat.] A trumpet; a wind-instrument of war.

And after, to his palace he them brings,
With shams, and trumpets, and with *clarions* sweet;
And all the way the joyous people sings. *Fairy Queen.*
Then strait commands, that at the warlike sound
Of trumpets loud, and *clarions*, be uprear'd
The mighty standard. *Milton's Paradise Lost, b.* i. *l.* 53.
Let fuller notes th' applauding world amaze,
And the loud *clarion* labour in your praise. *Pope.*

CLA'RITY. *n. s.* [*clarté*, French, *claritas*, Latin.] Brightness; splendour.

A light by abundant *clarity* invisible; an understanding which itself can only comprehend. *Sir Walter Raleigh.*

CLA'RY. *n. s.* An herb.

It hath a labiated flower of one leaf, whose upper lip is short and crested; but the under one is divided into three parts: the middle division is hollowed like a spoon. Out of the flower-cup arises the pointal, fixed like a nail to the hinder part of the flower, and attended with four embryo's, which turn to so many roundish seeds, inclosed in the cup of the flower. It grows wild on dry banks. *Miller.*

Plants that have circled leaves do all abound with moisture. The weakest kind of curling is roughness; as in *clary* and burr. *Bacon's Natural History*, N°. 651.

To CLASH. *v. n.* [*kletsen*, Dut. to make a noise.]

1. To make a noise by mutual collision; to strike one against another.

Three times, as of the *clashing* sound
Of arms, we heard. *Denham.*

Those few that should happen to *clash*, might rebound after the collision; or if they cohered, yet, by the real conflict with other atoms, might be separated again. *Bentley.*

How many candles may send out their light, without *clashing* upon one another; which argues the smallness of the parts of light, and the largeness of the interstices between particles of air and other bodies. *Cheyne's Phil. Prin.*

2. To act with opposite power, or contrary direction.

Neither was there any queen-mother who might *clash* with his counsellors for authority. *Bacon's Henry* VIII.

Those that will not be convinced what a help this is to the magistracy, would find it, if they should chance to *clash*. *South's Sermons.*

3. To contradict; oppose.

Wherever there are men, there will be *clashing* sometime or other; and a knock, or a contest, spoils all. *L'Estrange.*

The absurdity in this instance is obvious; and yet every time that *clashing* metaphors are put together, this fault is committed. *Spectator*, N°. 595.

To CLASH. *v. a.* To strike one thing against another, so as to produce a noise.

The nodding statue *clash'd* his arms,
And with a sullen sound and feeble cry,
Half sunk, and half pronounced the word of victory. *Dryd.*

CLASH. *n. s.* [from the verb.]

1. A noisy collision of two bodies.

The *clash* of arms and voice of men we hear. *Denham.*
He nobly seiz'd thee in the dire alarms
Of war and slaughter and the *clash* of arms. *Pope's Odyss.*

2. Opposition; contradiction.

Then from the *clashes* between popes and kings,
Debate, like sparks from flint's collision, springs. *Denham.*

In the very next line he reconciles the fathers and scripture, and shews there is no *clash* betwixt them. *Atterbury.*

A CLASP. *n. s.* [*chespe*, Dutch.]

1. A hook to hold any thing close; as a book, or garment.

The scorpion's claws here grasp a wide extent,
And here the crabs in lesser *clasps* are bent. *Addis. Ovid. Met.*

Hereupon he took me aside, and opening the *clasps* of the parchment cover, spoke, to my great surprize, in English. *Arbuthnot and Pope's Mart. Scrib.*

2. An embrace, in contempt.

Your fair daughter,
Transported with no worse nor better guard,
But with a knave of hire, a gondalier,
To the gross *clasps* of a lascivious Moor. *Shakesp. Othello.*

To CLASP. *v. a.* [from the noun.]

1. To shut with a clasp.

Sermons are the keys of the kingdom of heaven, and do open the scriptures; which being but read, remain, in comparison, still *clasped.* *Hooker, b.* v. *sect.* 22.

There Caxton slept, with Wynkin at his side,
One *clasp'd* in wood, and one in strong cow-hide. *Pope.*

2. To catch and hold by twining.

Direct
The *clasping* ivy where to climb. *Milton's Paradise Lost.*

3. To hold with the hands extended; to inclose between the hands.

Occasion turneth the handle of the bottle first to be received, and after the belly, which is hard to *clasp.* *Bacon's Ess.*

4. To embrace.

Thou art a slave, whom fortune's tender arm
With favour never *claspt*, but bred a dog. *Shakesp. Timon.*

Thy suppliant
I beg, and *clasp* thy knees. *Milton's Paradise Lost, b.* x.

He stoop'd below
The flying spear, and shun'd the promis'd blow;
Then creeping, *clasp'd* the hero's knees, and pray'd. *Dryd.*

Now, now he *clasps* her to his panting breast;
Now he devours her with his eager eyes. *Smith.*

5. To inclose.

Boys, with women's voices,
Strive to speak big, and *clasp* their female joints
In stiff unweildy arms against thy crown. *Shak. Richard* II.

CLA'SPER. *n. s.* [from *clasp.*] The tendrels or threads of creeping plants, by which they cling to other things for support.

The tendrels or *claspers* of plants are given only to such species as have weak and infirm stalks. *Ray on the Creation.*

CLASPKNIFE. *n. s.* [from *clasp* and *knife.*] A knife which folds into the handle.

CLASS. *n. s.* [from *classis*, Latin.]

1. A rank or order of persons.

Segrais has distinguished the readers of poetry, according to their capacity of judging, into three *classes. Dryd. Æn. Dedic.*

2. A number of boys learning the same lesson at the school.

We shall be seized away from this lower *class* in the school of knowledge, and our conversation shall be with angels and illuminated spirits. *Watts's Improvement of the Mind, p.* i.

3. A set of beings or things; a number ranged in distribution, under some common denomination.

Among this herd of politicians, any one sett make a very considerable *class* of men. *Addison's Freeholder*, N°. 53.

Whate'er of mungrel, no one *class* admits
A wit with dunces, and a dunce with wits. *Dunciad, b.* iv.

To CLASS. *v. a.* [from the noun.] To range according to some stated method of distribution; to range according to different ranks.

I considered that by the *classing* and methodizing such passages, I might instruct the reader. *Arbuthnot on Coins.*

CLA'SSICAL. }
CLA'SSICK. } *adj.* [*classicus*, Latin.]

1. Relating to antique authors; relating to literature.

Poetick fields encompass me around,
And still I seem to tread on *classick* ground. *Addison.*

With them the genius of *classick* learning dwelleth, and from them it is derived. *Felton on the Classicks.*

2. Of the first order or rank.

From this standard the value of the Roman weights and coins are deduced: in the settling of which I have followed Mr. Greaves, who may be justly reckoned a *classical* author on this subject. *Arbuthnot on Coins.*

CLA'SSICK. *n. s.* [*classicus*, Lat.] An author of the first rank: usually taken for ancient authors.

CLA'SSIS. n. s. [Latin.] Order; sort; body.

He had declared his opinion of that *classis* of men, and did all he could to hinder their growth. *Clarendon.*

To CLA'TTER. *v. n.* [clatrunge, a rattle, Saxon.]

1. To make a noise by knocking two sonorous bodies frequently together.

Now the sprightly trumpet, from afar,
Had rouz'd the neighing steeds to scour the fields,
While the fierce riders *clatter'd* on their shields. *Dryd. Æn.*

2. To utter a noise by being struck together.

All that night was heard an unwonted *clattering* of weapons, and of men running to and fro. *Knolles's History of the Turks.*

Down sunk the monster-bulk, and press'd the ground;
His arms and *clatt'ring* shield on the vast body sound. *Dryd.*

Their *clattering* arms with the fierce shocks resound,
Helmets and broken launces spread the ground. *Granville.*

3. To talk fast and idly.

Here is a great deal of good matter
Lost for lack of telling;
Now, siker, I see thou do'st but *clatter*;
Harm may come of melling. *Spenser's Pastorals.*

All those airy speculations, which bettered not men's manners, were only a noise and *clattering* of words. *Decay of Piety.*

To CLA'TTER. *v. a.*

1. To strike any thing so as to make it sound and rattle.

I only with an oaken staff will meet thee,
And raise such outcries on thy *clatter'd* iron,
That thou oft' shalt wish thyself at Gath. *Milton's Agonist.*

When all the bees are gone to settle,
You *clatter* still your brazen kettle. *Swift.*

2. To dispute, jar, or clamour. *Martin.* A low word.

A CLA'TTER. *n. s.* [from the verb.]

1. A rattling noise made by the frequent and quick collision of sonorous bodies. A *clatter* is a *clash* often repeated with great quickness, and seems to convey the idea of a sound sharper and shriller than *rattle.* [See the verb.]

I have seen a monkey overthrow all the dishes and plates in a kitchen, merely for the pleasure of seeing them tumble, and hearing the *clatter* they made in their fall. *Swift to Ld. Bolingb.*

2. It is used for any tumultuous and confused noise.

By this great *clatter*, one of greatest note
Seems bruited. *Shakespeare's Macbeth.*

Grow to be short,
Throw by your *clatter*,
And handle the matter. *Ben. Johnson's Under-woods.*

O Rourk's jolly boys
Ne'er dreamt of the matter,
'Till rous'd by the noise,
And musical *clatter.* *Swift.*

The jumbling particles of matter,
In chaos make not such a *clatter.* *Swift.*

CLA'VATED. *adj.* [*clavatus*, Lat.] Knobbed; set with knobs.

These appear plainly to have been *clavated* spikes of some kind of echinus ovarius. *Woodward on Fossils.*

CLA'UDENT. *adj.* [*claudens*, Lat.] Shutting; inclosing; confining. *Dict.*

To CLA'UDICATE. *v. n.* [*claudico*, Latin.] To halt; to limp. *Dict.*

CLAUDICA'TION. *n. s.* [from *claudicate.*] The act or habit of halting. *Dict.*

CLAVE. [the preterite of *cleave.*] See CLEAVE.

CLA'VELLATED. *adj.* [*clavellatus*, low Latin.] Made with burnt tartar. A chymical term. *Chambers.*

Air, transmitted through *clavellated* ashes into an exhausted receiver, loses weight as it passes through them. *Arbuthnot.*

CLA'VER. *n. s.* [clæfer pyrt, Sax.] This is now universally written *clover*, though not so properly. See CLOVER.

CLA'VICLE. *n. s.* [*clavicula*, Lat.] The collar bone.

Some quadrupeds can bring their fore feet unto their mouths; as most that have the *clavicles*, or collar bones. *Brown's Vulgar Errours.*

A girl was brought with angry wheals down her neck, towards the *clavicle.* *Wiseman's Surgery.*

CLAUSE. *n. s.* [*clausula*, Latin.]

1. A sentence; a single part of a discourse; a subdivision of a larger sentence; so much of a sentence as is to be construed together.

God may be glorified by obedience, and obeyed by performance of his will, although no special *clause* or sentence of scripture be in every such action set before men's eyes to warrant it. *Hooker, b.* ii. *sect.* 2.

2. An article, or particular stipulation.

The *clause* is untrue which they add, concerning the bishop. *Hooker, b.* iv. *sect.* 4.

When, after his death, they were sent both to Jews and Gentiles, we find not this *clause* in their commission. *South.*

CLA'USTRAL. *adj.* [from *claustrum*, Lat.] Relating to a cloyster, or religious house.

Claustral priors are such as preside over monasteries, next to the abbot or chief governour in such religious houses. *Ayliffe.*

CLA'USURE. *n. s.* [*clausura*, Lat.] Confinement; the act of shutting; the state of being shut.

In some monasteries the severity of the *clausure* is hard to be born. *Geddes.*

A CLAW. *n. s.* [clapan, Saxon.]

1. The foot of a beast or bird, armed with sharp nails; or the pincers or holders of a shell-fish.

I saw her range abroad to seek her food,
T' embrue her teeth and *claws* with lukewarm blood. *Spenser's Vis. of Bellay.*

What's justice to a man, or laws,
That never comes within their *claws?* *Hudibras, p.* ii.
He softens the harsh rigour of the laws,
Blunts their keen edge, and grinds their harpy *claws. Garth.*

2. Sometimes a hand, in contempt.

To CLAW. *v. a.* [clapan, Saxon.]

1. To tear with nails or claws.
Look, if the wither'd elder hath not his poll *claw'd* like a parrot. *Shakespeare's Henry* IV. *p.* ii.

2. To pull, as with the nails.
Adding to the former these many changes that have happened since, I am afraid we shall not so easily *claw* off that name. *South's Sermons.*

3. To tear or scratch in general.
But we must *claw* ourselves with shameful
And heathen stripes, by their example. *Hudibras, p.* ii.
They for their own opinions stand fast,
Only to have them *claw'd* and canvast. *Hudibras, p.* ii.

4. To scratch or tickle.
I must laugh when I am merry, and *claw* no man in his humour. *Shakespeare's Much ado about Nothing.*

5. To flatter: an obsolete sense. See CLAWBACK.

6. *To* CLAW *off*, or *away*. To scold; to rail at.
You thank the place where you found money; but the jade fortune is to be *clawed away* for't, if you should lose it. *L'Estr.*

CLA'WBACK. *n. s.* [from *claw* and *back.*] A flatterer; a sycophant; a wheedler. The pope's *clawbacks.* *Jewel.*

CLA'WED. *adj.* [from *claw.*] Furnished or armed with claws.
Among quadrupeds, of all the *clawed*, the lion is the strongest. *Grew's Cosmol. b.* ii. *c.* 8. *sect.* 6.

CLAY. *n. s.* [*clai*, Welsh; *kley*, Dutch.]

1. Unctuous and tenacious earth, such as will mould into a certain form.
Clays are earths firmly coherent, weighty and compact, stiff, viscid, and ductile to a great degree, while moist; smooth to the touch, not easily breaking between the fingers, nor readily diffusible in water; and, when mixed, not readily subsiding from it. *Hill on Fossils.*
Deep Acheron,
Whose troubled eddies, thick with ooze and *clay*,
Are whirl'd aloft. *Dryden's Æneid.*
Expose the *clay* to the rain, to drain it from salts, that the bricks may be more durable. *Woodward on Fossils.*
The sun, which softens wax, will harden *clay.* *Watts.*
Clover is the best way of improving *clays*, where manure is scarce. *Mortimer's Husbandry.*

2. In poetry, earth in general; the terrestrial element.
Why should our *clay*,
Over our spirits so much sway. *Donne.*

To CLAY. *v. a.* [from the noun.] To cover with clay; to manure with clay.
This manuring lasts fifty years: then the ground must be *clayed* again. *Mortimer's Husbandry.*

CLAY-COLD. *adj.* [*clay* and *cold.*] Lifeless; cold as the unanimated earth.
I wash'd his *clay-cold* corse with holy drops,
And saw him laid in hallow'd ground. *Rowe's Jane Shore.*

CLAY-PIT. *n. s.* [*clay* and *pit.*] A pit where clay is dug.
'Twas found in a *clay-pit.* *Woodward on Fossils.*

CLAYES. *n. s.* [*claye*, Fr. In fortification.] Wattles made with stakes interwove with osiers, to cover lodgments. *Chambers.*

CLA'YEY. *adj.* [from *clay.*] Consisting of clay; abounding with clay.
Some delight in a lax or sandy, some a heavy or *clayey* soil. *Derham's Physico-Theology.*

CLA'YISH. *adj.* [from *clay.*] Partaking of the nature of clay; containing particles of clay.
Small beer proves an unwholsom drink; perhaps, by being brewed with a thick, muddish, and *clayish* water, which the brewers covet. *Harvey on Consumptions.*

CLA'YMARL. *n. s.* [*clay* and *marl.*] A whitish, smooth, chalky clay.
Claymarl resembles clay, and is near a-kin to it; but is more fat, and sometimes mixed with chalk-stones. *Mortimer.*

CLEAN. *adj.* [*glan*, Welsh; clæne, Saxon.]

1. Free from dirt or filth.
Both his hands, most filthy feculent,
Above the water were on high extent,
And fain'd to wash themselves incessantly;
Yet nothing *cleaner* were for such intent,
But rather fouler. *Fairy Queen, b.* ii. *cant.* 7. *stan.* 61.
They make *clean* the outside of the cup and of the platter, but within they are full of extortion and excess. *Mat.* xxiii. 25.

2. Free from moral impurity; chaste; innocent; guiltless.

3. Elegant; neat; not unweildy; not encumbered with any thing useless or disproportioned.
The timber and wood are in some trees more *clean*, in some more knotty. *Bacon's Natural History.*
Yet thy waist is strait and *clean*,
As Cupid's shaft, or Hermes' rod. *Waller.*

4. Not foul with any loathsome disease; not leprous.
If the plague be somewhat dark, and spread not in the skin, the priest shall pronounce him *clean.* *Levit.* xiii. 6.

CLEAN. *adv.* Quite; perfectly; fully; completely. This sense is now little used.
Their actions have been *clean* contrary unto those before mentioned. *Hooker, b.* i. *sect.* 4.
Being seated, and domestick broils
Clean overblown. *Shakespeare's Richard* III.
A philosopher, pressed with the same objection, shapes an answer *clean* contrary. *Hakewell on Providence.*

To CLEAN. *v. a.* [from the adjective.] To free from dirt or filth.
Their tribes adjusted, *clean'd* their vig'rous wings,
And many a circle, many a short essay,
Wheel'd round and round. *Thomson's Autumn, l.* 865.

CLE'ANLILY. *adv.* [from *cleanly.*] In a cleanly manner.

CLE'ANLINESS. *n. s.* [from *cleanly.*]

1. Freedom from dirt or filth.
I shall speak nothing of the extent of this city, the *cleanliness* of its streets, nor the beauties of its piazza. *Addis. Italy.*

2. Neatness of dress; purity; the quality contrary to negligence and nastiness.
The mistress thought it either not to deserve, or not to need any exquisite decking, having no adorning but *cleanliness. Sidn.*
From whence the tender skin assumes
A sweetness above all perfumes;
From whence a *cleanliness* remains,
Incapable of outward stains. *Swift.*
Such *cleanliness* from head to heel;
No humours gross, or frowzy steams,
No noisome whiffs, or sweaty streams. *Swift.*

CLE'ANLY. *adj.* [from *clean.*]

1. Free from dirtiness; careful to avoid filth; pure in the person.
Next that shall mountain 'sparagus be laid,
Pull'd by some plain but *cleanly* country maid. *Dryden.*
An ant is a very *cleanly* insect, and throws out of her nest all the small remains of the corn on which she feeds. *Addison.*

2. That which makes cleanliness.
In our fantastick climes, the fair
With *cleanly* powder dry their hair. *Prior.*

3. Pure; innocent; immaculate.
Perhaps human nature meets few more sweetly relishing and *cleanly* joys, than those that derive from successful trials. *Glanv. Sceps. Preface.*

4. Nice; addressful; artful.
We can secure ourselves a retreat by some *cleanly* evasion. *L'Estrange's Fables.*

CLE'ANLY. *adv.* [from *clean.*]

1. Elegantly; neatly; without nastiness.
If I do grow great, I'll have sack, and live *cleanly* as a nobleman should. *Shakespeare's Henry* IV. *p.* i.

CLE'ANNESS. *n. s.* [from *clean.*]

1. Neatness; freedom from filth.

2. Easy exactness; justness; natural, unlaboured correctness.
He shewed no strength in shaking of his staff; but the fine *cleanness* of bearing it was delightful. *Sidney, b.* ii.
He minded only the clearness of his satyr, and the *cleanness* of expression. *Dryden's Juvenal's Dedication.*

3. Purity; innocence.
The *cleanness* and purity of one's mind is never better proved than in discovering its own faults at first view. *Pope.*

To CLEANSE. *v. a.* [clænȝian, Saxon.]

1. To free from filth or dirt, by washing or rubbing.
Cleanse the pale corps with a religious hand,
From the polluting weed and common sand. *Prior.*

2. To purify from guilt.
The blueness of a wound *cleanseth* away evil. *Prov.* xx. 30.
Not all her od'rous tears can *cleanse* her crime,
The plant alone deforms the happy clime. *Dryden's Ovid.*

3. To free from noxious tumours by purgation.
Can'st thou not minister to a mind diseas'd,
And with some sweet oblivious antidote,
Cleanse the stuff'd bosom of that perilous stuff
Which weighs upon the heart. *Shakespeare's Macbeth.*
This oil, combined with its own salt and sugar, makes it saponaceous and *cleansing*, by which quality it often helps digestion, and excites appetite. *Arbuthnot on Aliments.*

4. To free from leprosy.
Shew thyself to the priest, and offer for thy *cleansing* those things which Moses commanded. *Mark* i. 44.

5. To scour; to rid of all offensive things.
This river the Jews proffered the pope to *cleanse*, so they might have what they found. *Addison on Italy.*

A CLE'ANSER. *n. s.* [clænȝeꞃe, Sax.] That which has the quality of evacuating any foul humours; or digesting a sore; a detergent.
If there happens an imposthume, honey, and even honey of roses, taken inwardly, is a good *cleanser.* *Arbuth. on Alim.*

CLEAR. *adj.* [*clair*, Fr. *klaer*, Dut. *clarus*, Latin.]

1. Bright; transpicuous; pellucid; transparent; luminous; without opacity or cloudiness; not nebulous; not opacous; not dark.
The stream is so transparent, pure and *clear*,
That had the self-enamour'd youth gaz'd here,

He but the bottom, not his face had seen. *Denham.*

A tun about was ev'ry pillar there;
A polish'd mirrour shone not half so *clear.* *Dryden's Fables.*

2. Free from clouds; serene; as a *clear* day.
3. Without mixture; pure; unmingled.
4. Perspicuous; not obscure; not hard to be understood; not ambiguous.

We pretend to give a *clear* account how thunder and lightning is produced. *Temple.*

Many men reason exceeding *clear* and rightly, who know not how to make a syllogism. *Locke.*

5. Indisputable; evident; undeniable.

Remain'd to our almighty foe
Clear victory; to our part loss, and rout
Through all the empyrean. *Milton's Paradise Lost, b.* ii.

6. Apparent; manifest; not hid; not dark.

Unto God, who understandeth all their secret cogitations, they are *clear* and manifest. *Hooker, b.* iii *sect.* 1.

The pleasure of right reasoning is still the greater, by how much the consequences are more *clear*, and the chains of them more long. *Burnet's Theory of the Earth.*

7. Unspotted; guiltless; irreproachable.

Duncan has been so *clear* in his great office. *Shakespeare.*

Think that the *clearest* gods, who make them honours
Of mens impossibilities, have preserv'd thee. *Shak. K. Lear.*

Tho' the peripatetick philosophy has been most eminent in this way, yet other sects have not been wholly *clear* of it. *Locke.*

Statesman, yet friend to truth, in soul sincere,
In action faithful, and in honour *clear.* *Pope.*

8. Unprepossessed; not preoccupied; impartial.

Leucippe, of whom one look, in a *clear* judgment, would have been more acceptable than all her kindness, so prodigally bestowed. *Sidney, b.* ii.

9. Free from distress, prosecution, or imputed guilt.

The cruel corp'ral whisper'd in my ear,
Five pounds, if rightly tipt, would set me *clear.* *Gay.*

10. Free from deductions or incumbrances.

Hope, if the success happens to fail, is *clear* gains, as long as it lasts. *Collier against Despair.*

Whatever a foreigner, who purchases land here, gives for it, is so much every farthing *clear* gain to the nation; for that money comes *clear* in, without carrying out any thing for it. *Locke.*

I often wish'd that I had *clear*,
For life, six hundred pounds a year. *Swift.*

11. Unincumbered; without let or hindrance; vacant; unobstructed.

If he be so far beyond his health,
Methinks he should the sooner pay his debts,
And make a *clear* way to the gods. *Shakespeare's Timon.*

A post-boy winding his horn at us, my companion gave him two or three curses, and left the way *clear* for him. *Addis.*

A *clear* stage is left for Jupiter to display his omnipotence, and turn the fate of armies alone. *Pope's Essay on Homer.*

12. Out of debt.
13. Unintangled; at a safe distance from any danger or enemy.

Finding ourselves too slow of sail, we put on a compelled valour, and in the grapple I boarded them: on the instant they got *clear of* our ship. *Shakespeare's Hamlet.*

It requires care for a man with a double design to keep *clear of* clashing with his own reasonings. *L'Estrange.*

14. Canorous; sounding distinctly, plainly; articulately.

I much approved of my friend's insisting upon the qualifications of a good aspect and a *clear* voice. *Addison's Spectator.*

15. With *from*; free; guiltless.

I am *clear from* the blood of this woman. *Susan.* 46.

None is so fit to correct their faults, as he who is *clear from* any in his own writings. *Dryden's Juv. Dedication.*

16. Sometimes with *of*.

The air is *clearer of* gross and damp exhalations. *Temple.*

17. Used of persons. Distinguishing; judicious; intelligible: this is scarcely used but in conversation.

CLEAR. *adv.* Clean; quite; completely. A low word.

He put his mouth to her ear, and, under pretext of a whisper, bit it *clear* off. *L'Estrange, Fable* 98.

CLEAR. *n. s.* A term used by builders for the inside work of a house. *Dict.*

To CLEAR. *v. a.* [from the adjective.]

1. To make bright, by removing opacous bodies; to brighten.

Like Boreas in his race, when rushing forth,
He sweeps the skies, and *clears* the cloudy North. *Dryden.*

A favoury dish, a homely treat,
Where all is plain, where all is neat,
Clear up the cloudy foreheads of the great. *Dryden.*

2. To free from obscurity, perplexity, or ambiguity.

To *clear* up the several parts of this theory, I was willing to lay aside a great many other speculations. *Burnet's Theory.*

When, in the knot of the play, no other way is left for the discovery, then let a god descend, and *clear* the business to the audience. *Dryden's Æn. Dedication.*

By mystical terms and ambiguous phrases, he darkens what he should *clear* up. *Boyle's Sceps. Chym.*

Many knotty points there are,
Which all discuss, but few can *clear.* *Prior.*

3. To purge from the imputation of guilt; to justify; to vindicate; to defend: often with *from* before the thing.

Somerset was much *cleared* by the death of those who were executed, to make him appear faulty. *Sir John Hayward.*

To *clear* the Deity *from* the imputation of tyranny, injustice, and dissimulation, which none do throw upon God with more presumption than those who are the patrons of absolute necessity, is both comely and christian. *Bramh. against Hobbs.*

To *clear* herself,
For sending him no aid, she came from Egypt. *Dryden.*

I will appeal to the reader, and am sure he will *clear* me *from* partiality. *Dryden's Fables, Preface.*

How! wouldst thou *clear* rebellion? *Addis. Cato.*

Before you pray, *clear* your soul *from* all those sins, which you know to be displeasing to God. *Wake's Prepar. for Death.*

4. To cleanse, with *of*.

My hands are of your colour; but I shame
To wear a heart so white:
A little water *clears* us *of* this deed. *Shakesp. Macbeth.*

5. To discharge; to remove any incumbrance, or embarrassment.

A man digging in the ground did meet with a door, having a wall on each hand of it; from which having *cleared* the earth, he forced open the door. *Wilkins's Math. Magick.*

This one mighty sum has *clear'd* the debt. *Dryden.*

A statue lies hid in a block of marble; and the art of th statuary only *clears* away the superfluous matter, and removes the rubbish. *Addison's Spectator,* N°. 215.

Multitudes will furnish a double proportion towards the *clearing* of that expence. *Addison's Freeholder,* N°. 20.

6. To free from any thing offensive or noxious.

To *clear* the palace from the foe, succeed
The weary living, and revenge the dead. *Dryden's Æneis.*

It should be the skill and art of the teacher to *clear* their heads of all other thoughts, whilst they are learning of any thing. *Locke on Education.*

Augustus, to establish the dominion of the seas, rigged out a powerful navy to *clear* it of the pirates of Malta. *Arbuthnot.*

7. To clarify; as to *clear* liquors.
8. To gain without deduction.

He *clears* but two hundred thousand crowns a year, after having defrayed all the charges of working the salt. *Addison.*

9. To confer judgment or knowledge.

Our common prints would *clear* up their understandings, and animate their minds with virtue. *Addison's Spectator.*

10. *To* CLEAR *a ship*, at the custom-house, is to obtain the liberty of sailing, or of selling a cargo, by satisfying the customs.

To CLEAR. *v. n.*

1. To grow bright; to recover transparency.

So foul a sky *clears* not without a storm. *Shakes. K. John.*

2. Sometimes with *up.*

The mist, that hung about my mind, *clears up.* *Ad. Cato.*

Take heart, nor of the laws of fate complain;
Tho' now 'tis cloudy, 'twill *clear up* again. *Norris.*

Advise him to stay 'till the weather *clears up*, for you are afraid there will be rain. *Swift's Directions to the Groom.*

3. To be disengaged from incumbrances, distress, or entanglements.

He that *clears* at once, will relapse; for, finding himself out of straits, he will revert to his customs: but he that *cleareth* by degrees, induceth a habit of frugality, and gaineth as well upon his mind as upon his estate. *Bacon's Essays,* 29.

CLE'ARANCE. *n. s.* [from *clear.*] A certificate that a ship has been cleared at the customhouse.

CLE'ARER. *n. s.* [from *clear.*] Brightener; purifier; enlightener.

Gold is a wonderful *clearer* of the understanding: it dissipates every doubt and scruple in an instant. *Addison's Spectat.*

CLE'ARLY. *adv.* [from *clear.*]

1. Brightly; luminously.

Those mysteries of grace and salvation, which were but darkly disclosed unto them, have unto us more *clearly* shined. *Hooker, b.* iii. *sect.* 11.

2. Plainly; evidently; without obscurity or ambiguity.

Christianity first *clearly* proved this noble and important truth to the world. *Rogers.*

3. With discernment; acutely; without embarrassment, or perplexity of mind.

There is almost no man but sees *clearlier* and sharper the vices in a speaker than the virtues. *Ben Johnson's Discov.*

4. Without entanglement, or distraction of affairs.

He that doth not divide, will never enter into business; and he that divideth too much, will never come out of it *clearly.* *Bacon's Essays,* 26.

5. Without by-ends; without sinister views; honestly

When you are examining these matters, do not take into consideration any sensual or worldly interest; but deal *clearly* and impartially with yourselves. *Tillotson.*

6. Without deduction or cost.

7. Without reserve; without evasion; without subterfuge.

By a certain day they should *clearly* relinquish unto the king all their lands and possessions. *Davies on Ireland.*

CLE'ARNESS *n. s.* [from *clear.*]

1. Transparency; brightness.

It may be, percolation doth not only cause *clearness* and splendour, but sweetness of savour. *Bacon's Natural History.*

Glass in the furnace grows to a greater magnitude, and refines to a greater *clearness*, only as the breath within is more powerful, and the heat more intense.

2. Splendour; lustre.

Love, more clear than yourself, with the *clearness*, lays a night of sorrow upon me. *Sidney, b.* ii.

3. Distinctness; perspicuity.

If he chances to think right, he does not know how to convey his thoughts to another with *clearness* and perspicuity. *Addison's Spectator,* N°. 291.

CLEARSI'GHTED. *adj.* [*clear* and *sight.*] Perspicuous; discerning; judicious.

Clearsighted reason, wisdom's judgment leads;
And sense, her vassal, in her footsteps treads. *Denham.*

To CLE'ARSTARCH. *v. a.* [from *clear* and *starch.*] To stiffen with starch.

He took his present lodging at the mansion-house of a taylor's widow, who washes, and can *clearstarch* his bands. *Addis.*

To CLEAVE. *v. n.* pret. *I clave,* part. *cloven.* [cleoþan, Sax. *kleven,* Dutch.]

1. To adhere; to stick; to hold to.

The clarifying of liquors by adhesion, is effected when some *cleaving* body is mixed with the liquors, whereby the grosser part sticks to that *cleaving* body. *Bacon's Nat. History.*

Water, in small quantity, *cleaveth* to any thing that is solid. *Bacon's Natural History,* N°. 293.

When the dust groweth into hardness, and the clods *cleave* fast together. *Job,* xxxviii. 38.

The thin camelion, fed with air, receives
The colour of the thing to which he *cleaves.* *Dryd. Fables.*

2. To unite aptly; to fit.

New honours come upon him,
Like our strange garments, *cleave* not to their mould,
But with the aid of use. *Shakespeare's Macbeth.*

3. To unite in concord and interest.

The apostles did thus conform the Christians, according to the pattern of the Jews, and made them *cleave* the better. *Hooker, b.* iv. *sect.* 11.

If you shall *cleave* to my consent, when 'tis,
It shall make honour for you. *Shakespeare's Macbeth.*

The people would revolt, if they saw any of the French nation to *cleave* unto. *Knolles's History of the Turks.*

4. To be concomitant to; to join with.

We cannot imagine, that, in breeding or begetting faith, his grace doth *cleave* to the one, and utterly forsake the other. *Hooker, b.* v. *sect.* 22.

To CLEAVE. *v. a.* preterite, *I clove, I clave, I cleft;* part. pass. *cloven,* or *cleft.* [cleoþan, Sax. *klooven,* Dutch.]

1. To divide with violence; to split; to part forcibly into pieces.

And at their passing *cleave* th' Assyrian flood. *Milton.*

The fountains of it are said to have been *cloven,* or burst open. *Burnet's Theory of the Earth.*

The blessed minister his wings display'd,
And, like a shooting star, he *cleft* the night. *Dryden.*
Rais'd on her dusky wings, she *cleaves* the skies. *Dryden.*
Whom with such force he struck, he fell'd him down,
And *cleft* the circle of his golden crown. *Dryden's Fables.*

Or had the sun
Elected to the earth a nearer seat,
His beams had *cleft* the hill, the valley dry'd. *Blackmore.*

Where whole brigades one champion's arms o'erthrow,
And *cleave* a giant at a random blow. *Tickell.*

Not half so swift the trembling doves can fly,
When the fierce eagle *cleaves* the liquid sky. *Pope.*

2. To divide.

And every beast that parteth the hoof, and *cleaveth* the cleft into two claws. *Deutr.* xiv. 6.

To CLEAVE. *v. n.*

1. To part asunder.

Wars 'twixt you twain, would be
As if the world should *cleave,* and that slain men
Should solder up the rift. *Shakesp. Anthony and Cleopatra.*

The ground *clave* asunder that was under them. *Num.* xvi.

He cut the *cleaving* sky,
And in a moment vanish'd from her eye. *Pope's Odyssey.*

2. To suffer division.

It *cleaves* with a glossy polite substance, not plane, but with some little unevenness. *Newton's Opt.*

A CLE'AVER. *n. s.* [from *cleave.*]

1. A butcher's instrument to cut animals into joints.

You, gentlemen, keep a parcel of roaring bullies about me day and night, with huzza's and hunting-horns, and ringing the changes on butcher's *cleavers.* *Arbuth. Hist. of John Bull.*

Though arm'd with all thy *cleavers,* knives,
And axes made to hew down lives. *Hudibras, p.* iv. *cant.* 2.

2. A weed. Improperly written CLIVER, which see.

CLEES. *n. s.* The two parts of the foot of beasts which are cloven-footed. *Skinner.* It is a country word, and probably corrupted from *claws.*

CLEF. *n. s.* [from *clef,* key, Fr.] In musick, a mark at the beginning of the lines of a song, which shews the tone or key in which the piece is to begin. *Chambers.*

CLEFT. part. pass. [from *cleave.*] Divided; parted asunder.

Fat, with incense strew'd,
On the *cleft* wood. *Milton's Par. Lost, b.* xi. *l.* 440.

I never did on *cleft* Parnassus dream,
Nor taste the sacred Heliconian stream. *Dryden's Perseus.*

CLEFT. *n. s.* [from *cleave.*]

1. A space made by the separation of parts; a crack; a crevice.

The cascades seem to break through the *clefts* and cracks of rocks. *Addison's Guardian,* N°. 101.

The extremity of this cape has a long *cleft* in it, which was enlarged and cut into shape by Agrippa, who made this the great port for the Roman fleet. *Addison on Italy.*

The rest of it, being more gross and ponderous, does not move far; but lodges in the *clefts,* craggs, and sides of the rocks, near the bottoms of them. *Woodward's Nat. History.*

2. In farriery.

Clefts appear on the bought of the pasterns, and are caused by a sharp and malignant humour, which frets the skin; and it is accompanied with pain, and a noisom stench. *Farr. Dict.*

His horse it is the heralds west;
No, 'tis a mare, and hath a *cleft.* *B. Johnson's Under-woods.*

To CLE'FTGRAFT. *v. a.* [*cleft* and *graft.*] To engraft by cleaving the stock of a tree, and inserting a branch.

Filberts may be *cleftgrafted* on the common nut. *Mortimer.*

CLE'MENCY. *n. s.* [*clemence,* Fr. *clementia,* Lat.] Mercy; remission of severity; willingness to spare; tenderness in punishing.

I have stated the true notion of *clemency,* mercy, compassion, good-nature, humanity, or whatever else it may be called, so far as is consistent with wisdom. *Addison's Freeholder.*

CLE'MENT. *adj.* [*clemens,* Latin.] Mild; gentle; merciful; kind; tender; compassionate.

CLENCH. See CLINCH.

To CLEPE. *v. a.* [clypian, Saxon.] To call. Obsolete.

Three crabbed months had sowr'd themselves to death,
Ere I could make thee open thy white hand,
And *clepe* thyself my love. *Shakespeare's Winter's Tale.*

CLE'RGY. *n. s.* [*clerge,* Fr. *clerus,* Lat. κλῆρος, Greek.] The body of men set apart by due ordination for the service of God.

We hold that God's *clergy* are a state which hath been, and will be as long as there is a church upon earth, necessary, by the plain word of God himself; a state whereunto the rest of God's people must be subject, as touching things that appertain to their soul's health. *Hooker, b.* iii.

The convocation give a greater sum,
Than ever, at one time, the *clergy* yet
Did to his predecessors part withal. *Shakesp. Henry* V.

CLE'RGYMAN. *n. s.* [*clergy* and *man.*] A man in holy orders; a man set apart for ministration of holy things; not a laick.

How I have sped among the *clergymen,*
The sums I have collected shall express. *Shakesp. K. John.*

It seems to be in the power of a reasonable *clergyman* to make the most ignorant man comprehend his duty. *Swift.*

CLE'RICAL. *adj.* [*clericus,* Lat.] Relating to the clergy; as, a *clerical* man; a man in orders.

In *clericals* the keys are lined, and in colleges they use to line the table-men. *Bacon's Nat. History,* N°. 158.

Unless we may more properly read *clarichords.*

A CLERK. *n. s.* [clerc, Sax. *clericus,* Latin.]

1. A clergyman.

All persons were stiled *clerks* that served in the church of Christ, whether they were bishops, priests, or deacons. *Ayliffe.*

2. A scholar; a man of letters.

They might talk of book-learning what they would; but, for his part, he never saw more unfeaty fellows than great *clerks* were. *Sidney.*

The greatest *clerks* being not always the honestest, any more than the wisest men. *South.*

3. A man employed under another as a writer.

My lord Bassanio gave his ring away
Unto the judge; and then the boy, his *clerk,*
That took some pains in writing, he begg'd mine. *Shakesp.*

My friend was in doubt whether he should not exert the justice upon such a vagrant; but not having his *clerk* with him, who is a necessary counsellor, he let the thought drop. *Addis.*

4. A petty writer in publick offices: an officer of various kinds.

Take a just view, how many may remark
Who's now a lord, his grand-sire was a *clerk.* *Granville.*

It may seem difficult to make out the bills of fare for the suppers of Vitellius. I question not but an expert *clerk* of a kitchen can do it. *Arbuthnot.*

5. The layman who reads the responses to the congregation in the church, to direct the rest.

CLE'RKSHIP. *n. s.* [from *clerk*.]

1. Scholarship.
2. The office of a clerk of any kind.

He sold the *clerkship* of his parish, when it became vacant. *Swift's Miscellanies.*

CLEVE. CLIF. CLIVE. } In composition, at the beginning or end of the proper name of a place, denotes it to be situated on the side of a rock or hill; as *Cleveland, Clifton, Stancliff.*

CLE'VER. *adj.* [of no certain etymology.]

1. Dextrous; skilful.

It was the *cleverer* mockery of the two. *L'Estrange's Fables.*

I read Dyer's letter more for the stile than the news. The man has a *clever* pen, it must be owned. *Addison's Freeholder.*

2. Just; fit; proper; commodious.

I can't but think 'twould sound more *clever*,
To me, and to my heirs for ever. *Pope.*

3. Well-shaped; handsome.

She called him gundy-guts, and he called her lousy Peg, tho' the girl was a tight *clever* wench as any was. *Arbuthnot.*

4. This is a low word, scarcely ever used but in burlesque or conversation; and applied to any thing a man likes, without a settled meaning.

CLE'VERLY. *adv.* [from *clever*.] Dextrously; fitly; handsomely.

These would inveigle rats with th' scent,
And sometimes catch them with a snap,
As *cleverly* as th' ablest trap. *Hudibras, p.* ii. *canto* 1.

A rogue upon the highway may have as strong an arm, and take off a man's head as *cleverly* as the executioner. *South.*

CLE'VERNESS. *n. s.* [from *clever*.] Dexterity; skill; accomplishment.

CLEW. *n. s.* [clype, Sax. *klouwen*, Dutch.]

1. Thread wound upon a bottom; a ball of thread.

Eftsoons untwisting his deceitful *clew*;
He 'gan to weave a web of wicked guile. *Spens. Fairy Queen.*

While guided by some *clew* of heav'nly thread,
The perplex'd labyrinth we backward tread. *Roscommon.*

They see small *clews* draw vastest weights along,
Not in their bulk but in their order strong. *Dryden.*

2. A guide; a direction: because men direct themselves by a clew of thread in a labyrinth.

This alphabet must be your own *clew* to guide you. *Holder.*

Is there no way, no thought, no beam of light?
No *clew* to guide me thro' this gloomy maze,
To clear my honour, yet preserve my faith? *Smith.*

The reader knows not how to transport his thoughts over to the next particular, for want of some *clew*, or connecting idea, to lay hold of. *Watts's Logick, p.* iv. *c.* 2.

3. CLEW *of the sail of a Ship*, is the lower corner of it, which reaches down to that earing where the tackles and sheets are fastened. *Harris.*

To CLEW. *v. a.* [from *clew*, a sea-term.]

To Clew the Sails, is to raise them, in order to be furled, which is done by a rope fastened to the clew of a sail, called the clew-garnet. *Harris.*

To CLICK. *v. n.* [*clicken*, Dut. *cliqueter*, French.] To make a sharp, small, successive noise.

The solemn death-watch *click'd*, the hour she dy'd;
And shrilling crickets in the chimney cry'd. *Gay's Pastorals.*

CLI'CKER. *n. s.* [from *click*.] A low word for the servant of a salesman, who stands at the door to invite customers.

CLI'CKET. *n. s.* [from *click*.] The knocker of a door. *Skinner.*

CLI'ENT. *n. s.* [*cliens*, Latin.]

1. One who applies to an advocate for counsel and defence.

There is due from the judge to the advocate some commendation, where causes are well handled; for that upholds in the *client* the reputation of his counsel. *Bacon's Essays.*

Advocates must deal plainly with their *clients*, and tell the true state of their case. *Taylor's Rule of living holy.*

2. It may be perhaps sometimes used for a dependant in a more general sense.

I do think they are your friends and *clients*,
And fearful to disturb you. *Ben. Johnson's Catiline.*

CLI'ENTED. *particip. adj.* [from *client*.] Supplied with clients.

This due occasion of discouragement, the worst conditioned and least *cliented* petivoguers, do yet, under the sweet bait of revenge, convert to a more plentiful prosecution of actions. *Carew's Survey of Cornwal.*

CLIENTE'LE. *n. s.* [*clientela*, Lat.] The condition or office of a client. A word scarcely used.

There's Varus holds good quarters with him;
And, under the pretext of *clientele*,
Will be admitted. *Benj. Johnson's Catiline.*

CLI'ENTSHIP. *n. s.* [from *client*.] The condition of a client.

Patronage and *clientship* among the Romans always descended: the plebeian houses had recourse to the patrician line which had formerly protected them. *Dryd. Virg. Dedication.*

CLIFF. *n. s.* [*clivus*, Lat. clip, cliop, Saxon.]

1. A steep rock; a rock, according to *Skinner*, broken and craggy.

The Leucadians did use to precipitate a man from a high *cliff* into the sea. *Bacon's Nat. History*, N°. 886.

Mountaineers, that from Severus came,
And from the craggy *cliffs* of Tetrica. *Dryden's Æn.*

Where-ever 'tis so found scattered upon the shores, there is it as constantly found lodged in the *cliffs* thereabouts. *Woodw.*

2. The name of a character in musick. Properly CLEF.

CLIFT. *n. s.* The same with CLIFF, now disused.

Down he tumbled, like an aged tree,
High growing on the top of rocky *clift*. *Spens. Fairy Queen.*

CLIMA'CTER. *n. s.* [κλιμακτὴρ.] A certain space of time, or progression of years, which is supposed to end in a critical and dangerous time.

Elder times, settling their conceits upon *climacters*, differ from one another. *Brown's Vulgar Errours.*

CLIMACTE'RICK. CLIMACTE'RICAL. } *adj.* [from *climacter*.] Containing a certain number of years, at the end of which some great change is supposed to befal the body.

Certain observable years are supposed to be attended with some considerable change in the body; as the seventh year; the twenty-first, made up of three times seven; the forty-ninth, made up of seven times seven; the sixty-third, being nine times seven; and the eighty-first, which is nine times nine: which two last are called the grand *climactericks*. *Shakes.*

The numbers seven and nine, multiplied into themselves, do make up sixty-three, commonly esteemed the great *climacterical* of our lives. *Brown's Vulgar Errours, b.* iv. *c.* 12.

Your lordship being now arrived at your great *climacterique*, yet give no proof of the least decay of your excellent judgment and comprehension. *Dryden.*

My mother is something better, tho', at her advanced age, every day is a *climacterick*. *Pope.*

CLI'MATE. *n. s.* [κλίμα.]

1. A space upon the surface of the earth, measured from the equator to the polar circles; in each of which spaces the longest day is half an hour longer than in that nearer to the equator. From the polar circles to the poles climates are measured by the increase of a month.
2. In the common and popular sense, a region, or tract of land, differing from another by the temperature of the air.

Betwixt th' extremes, two happier *climates* hold
The temper that partakes of hot and cold. *Dryden's Ovid.*

On what new happy *climate* are we thrown? *Dryden.*

This talent of moving the passions cannot be of any great use in the northern *climates*. *Swift.*

To CLI'MATE. *v. n.* To inhabit. A word only in *Shakespeare.*

The blessed gods
Purge all infection from our air, whilst you
Do *climate* here. *Shakespeare's Winter's Tale.*

CLI'MATURE. *n. s.* The same with climate, and not in use.

Such harbingers preceding still the fates,
Have heav'n and earth together demonstrated
Unto our *climatures* and countrymen. *Shakespeare.*

CLI'MAX. *n. s.* [κλίμαξ.] Gradation; ascent: a figure in rhetorick, by which the sentence rises gradually; as Cicero says to Catiline, Thou do'st nothing, movest nothing, thinkest nothing; but I hear it, I see it, and perfectly understand it.

Choice between one excellency and another is difficult; and yet the conclusion, by a due *climax*, is evermore the best. *Dryden's Juv. Dedication.*

Some radiant Richmond every age has grac'd,
Still rising in a *climax*, 'till the last,
Surpassing all, is not to be surpast. *Granville.*

To CLIMB. *v. n.* pret. *clomb* or *climbed*; part. *clomb* or *climbed*. It is pronounced like *clime*. [climan, Sax. *klimmen*, Dutch.] To ascend up any place; to mount by means of some hold or footing. It implies labour and difficulty, and successive efforts.

You tempt the fury of my three attendants,
Lean famine, quartering steel, and *climbing* fire. *Shakesp.*

Things, at the worst, will cease; or else *climb* upward
To what they were before. *Shakesp. Macbeth.*

Jonathan *climbed* up upon his hands, and upon his feet. 1 *Sam.*

Thou, sun! of this great world both eye and soul,
Acknowledge him thy greater; sound his praise
In thy eternal course, both when thou *climb'st*,
And when high noon hast gain'd, and when thou fall'st. *Milton's Paradise Lost, b.* v. *l.* 174.

No rebel Titan's sacrilegious crime,
By heaping hills on hills, can thither *climb*. *Roscommon.*

Black vapours *climb* aloft, and cloud the day. *Dryden.*

What controuling cause
Makes waters, in contempt of nature's laws,
Climb up, and gain th' aspiring mountain's height. *Blackm.*

To CLIMB. *v. a.* To ascend.

When shall I come to th' top of that same hill?—
—You do *climb* up it now. Look, how we labour. *Shakesp.*

Is't not enough to break into my garden,
Climbing my walls, in spight of me the owner? *Shakesp.*

Thy arms pursue
Paths of renown, and *climb* ascents of fame. *Prior.*

Forlorn he must, and persecuted fly;
Climb the steep mountain, in the cavern lie. *Prior.*

CLI'MBER. *n. f.* [from *climb.*]

1. One that mounts or fcales any place or thing; a mounter; a rifer.

I wait not at the lawyer's gates,
Ne fhoulder *climbers* down the ftairs *Carew's Survey.*

2. A plant that creeps upon other fupports.

Ivy, briony, honey-fuckles, and other *climbers*, muft be dug up. *Mortimer.*

3. The name of a particular herb.

It hath a perennial fibrofe root: the leaves grow oppofite upon the ftalks. The flowers, moftly of four leaves, placed in form of a crofs, are naked, having no calyx: in the center of the flower are many hairy ftamina furrounding the pointal, which becomes a fruit; in which the feeds are gathered into a little head, ending in a kind of rough plume; whence it is called by the country people *old man's beard.* The fpecies are twelve, two of which grow wild. *Miller.*

CLIME. *n. f.* [contracted from *climate*, and therefore properly poetical.] Climate; region; tract of earth.

He can fpread thy name o'er land and feas,
Whatever *clime* the fun's bright circle warms. *Milt. Par. R.*

They apply the celeftial defcription of other *climes* unto their own. *Brown's Vulgar Errours, b.* iv. *c.* 12.

Of beauty fing, her fhining progrefs view,
From *clime* to *clime* the dazzling light purfue. *Granville.*

We fhall meet
In happier *climes*, and on a fafer fhore. *Addifon's Cato.*

Health to vigorous bodies, or fruitful feafons, in temperate *climes*, are common and familiar bleffings. *Atterbury's Sermons.*

To CLINCH. *v. a.* [clẏnga, Sax. to knock, *Junius. Clingo*, in Feftus, to encompafs, *Minfhew.*]

1. To hold in the hand with the fingers bent over it.

Simois rowls the bodies and the fhields
Of heroes, whofe difmember'd hands yet bear
The dart aloft, and *clinch* the pointed fpear. *Dryd. Virg. Æn.*

2. To contract or double the fingers.

Their talleft trees are about feven feet high, the tops whereof I could but juft reach with my fift *clinched.* *Swift.*

3. To bend the point of a nail in the other fide.

4. To confirm; to fix; as, *to clinch an argument.*

CLINCH. *n. f.* [from the verb.]

1. A word ufed in a double meaning; a pun; an ambiguity; a duplicity of meaning, with an identity of expreffion.

Such as they are, I hope they will prove, without a *clinch*, luciferous fearching after the nature of light. *Boyle.*

Pure *clinches* the fuburbian mufe affords,
And Panton waging harmlefs war with words. *Dryden.*
Here one poor word a hundred *clinches* makes. *Pope.*

2. That part of the cable which is faftened to the ring of the anchor.

CLI'NCHER. *n. f.* [from *clinch*] A cramp; a holdfaft; a piece of iron bent down to faften planks.

The wimbles for the work, Calypfo found;
With thofe he pierc'd 'em, and with *clinchers* bound. *Pope.*

To CLING. *v. n.* pret. *I clung*; part. *I have clung.* [*Klynger*, Danifh.]

1. To hang upon by twining round; to ftick to; to hold faft upon.

The broil long doubtful ftood;
As two fpent fwimmers that do *cling* together,
And choak their art. *Shakefpeare's Macbeth.*

Moft popular conful he is grown, methinks:
How the rout *cling* to him! *Benj. Johnfon's Catiline.*

The fontanel in his neck was defcried by the *clinging* of his hair to the plaifter. *Wifeman's Surgery.*

When they united and together *clung*,
When undiftinguifh'd in one heap they hung. *Blackmore.*

See in the circle, next Eliza plac'd,
Two babes of love, clofe *clinging* to her waift. *Pope.*

That they may the clofer *cling*,
Take your blue ribbon for a ftring. *Swift.*

2. To dry up; to confume; to wafte; to pine away. [Ꞓeclungen ꞇreop, a withered tree.]

If thou fpeak'ft falfe,
Upon the next tree fhalt thou hang alive,
'Till famine *cling* thee. *Shakefpeare's Macbeth.*

CLI'NGY. *adj.* [from *cling.*] Apt to cling; adhefive.

CLI'NICAL. } *adj.* [κλίνω, to lie down.] Thofe that keep their
CLI'NICK. } beds; thofe that are fick, paft hopes of recovery.

A *clinical convert*, one that is converted on his death-bed. This word occurs often in the works of *Taylor.*

To CLINK. *v. a.* [perhaps foftened from *clank*, or corrupted from *click.*] To ftrike fo as to make a fmall fharp noife.

Five years! a long leafe for the *clinking* of pewter. *Shakefp.*

To CLINK. *v. n.* To utter a fmall, fharp, interrupted noife.

The fever'd bars,
Submiffive, *clink* againft your brazen portals. *Prior.*

Underneath th' umbrella's oily fhed,
Safe thro' the wet on *clinking* pattens tread. *Gay's Trivia.*

CLINK. *n. f.* [from the verb.]

1. A fharp fucceffive noife; a knocking.

I heard the *clink* and fall of fwords. *Shakefp. Othello.*

2. It feems in *Spenfer* to have fome unufual fenfe.

Tho' creeping clofe, behind the wicket's *clink*,
Privily he peeped out thro' a chink. *Spenfer's Paftorals.*

CLI'NQUANT. *n. f.* [Fr.] Embroidery; fpangles; falfe glitter; tinfel finery.

To day the French,
All *clinquant*, all in gold, like heathen gods,
Shone down the Englifh. *Shakefp. Henry* VIII.

To CLIP. *v. a.* [clıppan, Saxon.]

1. To embrace, by throwing the arms round; to hug; to enfold in the arms.

He, that before fhunn'd her, to fhun fuch harms,
Now runs and takes her in his *clipping* arms. *Sidney.*

Here I *clip*
The anvil of my fword, and do conteft
Hotly, and nobly, with thy love. *Shakefp. Coriolanus.*

O nation, that thou couldft remove!
That Neptune's arms, who *clippeth* thee about. *Shakefp.*

Enter the city, *clip* your wives; your friends,
Tell them your feats. *Shakefpeare's Anthony and Cleopatra.*

The jades
That drag the tragick melancholy night,
Who with their drowfy, flow, and flagging wings,
Clip dead mens graves. *Shakefpeare's Henry* VI. *p.* ii.

The male refteth on the back of the female, *clipping* and embracing her with his legs about the neck and body. *Ray.*

2. To cut with fheers. [*Klipper*, Danifh; *klippen*, Dutch; apparently from the fame radical fenfe, fince fheers cut by inclofing and embracing.]

Your fheers come too late to *clip* the bird's wings, that already is flown away. *Sidney, b.* ii.

Then let him, that my love fhall blame,
Or *clip* love's wings, or quench love's flame. *Suckling.*

He *clips* hope's wings, whofe airy blifs
Much higher than fruition is. *Denham.*

But love had *clipp'd* his wings, and cut him fhort,
Confin'd within the purlieus of his court. *Dryden's Fables.*

If mankind had had wings, as perhaps fome extravagant atheift may think us deficient in that, all the world muft have confented to *clip* them. *Bentley.*

By this lock, this facred lock, I fwear,
Which never more fhall join its parted hair,
Clipp'd from the lovely head, where late it grew. *Pope.*

He fpent every day ten hours dozing, *clipping* papers, or darning his ftockings. *Swift.*

3. Sometimes with *off.*

We fhould then have as much feeling upon the *clipping off* a hair, as the cutting of a nerve. *Bentley's Sermons.*

4. It is particularly ufed of thofe who diminifh coin, by paring the edges.

This defign of new coinage, is juft of the nature of *clipping.* *Locke.*

5. To curtail; to cut fhort.

All my reports go with the modeft truth,
Nor more, nor *clipt*, but fo. *Shakefp. King Lear.*

Mrs. Mayorefs *clipp'd* the king's Englifh. *Addif. Spectator.*

Even in London, they *clip* their words after one manner about the court, another in the city, and a third in the fuburbs. *Swift.*

6. To confine; to hold; to contain.

Where is he living, *clipt* in with the fea,
Who calls me pupil? *Shakefpeare's Henry* IV. *p.* i.

To CLIP. *v. n.* A phrafe in falconry.

Some falcon ftoops at what her eye defign'd,
And with her eagernefs the quarry mifs'd,
Streight flies at check, and *clips* it down the wind. *Dryden.*

CLI'PPER. *n. f.* [from *clip.*] One that debafes coin by cutting.

It is no Englifh treafon to cut
French crowns, and to-morrow the king
Himfelf will be a *clipper.* *Shakefpear's Henry* V.

No coins pleafed fome medallifts more than thofe which had paffed through the hands of an old Roman *clipper.* *Addif.*

CLI'PPING. *n. f.* [from *clip.*] The part cut or clipped off.

Beings purely material, without fenfe, perception, or thought, as the *clippings* of our beards, and parings of our nails. *Locke.*

CLI'VER. *n. f.* An herb. More properly written *cleaver.*

It grows wild, the feeds fticking to the clothes of fuch as pafs by them. It is fometimes ufed in medicine. *Miller.*

A CLOAK. *n. f.* [lach, Saxon.]

1. The outer garment, with which the reft are covered.

You may bear it,
Under a *cloke* that is of any length. *Sh. Two Gent. of Verona.*

Their *clokes* were cloath of filver, mix'd with gold. *Dryd.*

All arguments will be as little able to prevail, as the wind did with the traveller to part with his *cloak*, which he held only the fafter. *Locke.*

Nimbly he rofe, and caft his garment down;
That inftant in his *cloak* I wrapt me round. *Pope's Odyffey.*

2. A concealment; a cover.

Not ufing your liberty for a *cloak* of malicioufnefs.
1 Pet. ii. 16.

To Cloak. *v. a.* [from the noun.]

1. To cover with a cloak.

2. To hide; to conceal.

Moſt heavenly fair, in deed and view,
She by creation was, 'till ſhe did fall;
Thenceforth ſhe ſought for helps to *cloak* her crimes withal.
Fairy Queen, b. ii. *cant.* 7. *ſtanz.* 45.

Clo'akbag. *n. ſ.* [from *cloak* and *bag.*] A portmanteau; a bag in which cloaths are carried.

Why do'ſt thou converſe with that trunk of humours, that ſtuffed *cloakbag* of guts. *Shakeſ. Henry* IV. *p.* i.

I have already fit
('Tis in my *cloakbag*) doublet, hat, hoſe, all
That anſwer to them. *Shakeſpeare's Cymbeline.*

CLOCK. *n. ſ.* [*clocc*, Welſh, from *clôch*, a bell, Welſh and Armorick; *cloche*, French.]

1. The inſtrument which, by a ſeries of mechanical movements, tells the hour by a ſtroke upon a bell.

If a man be in ſickneſs or pain, the time will ſeem longer without a *clock* or hour-glaſs than with it. *Bacon.*

The picture of Jerome uſually deſcribed at his ſtudy, is with a *clock* hanging by. *Brown's Vulgar Errours, b.* v. *c.* 17.

I told the *clocks*, and watch'd the waſting light. *Dryden.*

2. It is an uſual expreſſion to ſay, *What is it of the clock*, for *What hour is it?* Or *ten o'clock*, for *the tenth hour.*

What is't o'clock?——
——Upon the ſtroke of four. *Shakeſp. Richard* III.

Macicaus ſet forward about *ten o'clock* in the night, towards Andruſſa. *Knolles's Hiſtory of the Turks.*

About *nine of the clock* at night the king marched out of the North-port. *Clarendon, b.* viii.

3. The clock of a ſtocking; the flowers or inverted work about the ankle.

His ſtockings with ſilver *clocks* were raviſhed from him. *Swift on Modern Education.*

4. Clock is alſo the name of an inſect; a ſort of beetle. *Dict.*

Clo'ckmaker. *n. ſ.* [*clock* and *make.*] An artificer whoſe profeſſion is to make clocks.

This inequality has been diligently obſerved by ſeveral of our ingenious *clockmakers*, and equations been made and uſed by them. *Derham.*

Clo'ckwork. *n. ſ.* [*clock* and *work.*] Movements by weights or ſprings, like thoſe of a clock.

So if unprejudic'd you ſcan
The goings of this *clockwork*, man;
You find a hundred movements made
By fine devices in his head:
But 'tis the ſtomach's ſolid ſtroke,
That tells its being, what's a clock. *Prior.*

Within this hollow was Vulcan's ſhop, full of fire and *clockwork.* *Addiſon's Guardian*, N°. 103.

You look like a puppet moved by *clockwork.* *Arbuthnot.*

CLOD. *n. ſ.* [club, Sax. a little hillock; *klotte*, Dutch.]

1. A lump of earth or clay; ſuch a body of earth as cleaves or hangs together.

The earth that caſteth up from the plough a great *clod*, is not ſo good as that which caſteth up a ſmaller *clod.* *Bacon.*

I'll cut up, as plows
Do barren lands, and ſtrike together flints
And *clods*, th' ungrateful ſenate and the people. *B. Johnſon.*

Who ſmooths with harrows, or who pounds with rakes
The crumbling *clods.* *Dryden's Georg.*

2. A turf; the ground.

Byzantians boaſt, that on the *clod*,
Where once their ſultan's horſe has trod,
Grows neither graſs, nor ſhrub, nor tree. *Swift.*

3. Any thing vile, baſe, and earthy; as the body of man, compared to his ſoul.

And ye high heavens, the temple of the gods,
In which a thouſand torches, flaming bright,
Do burn, that to us wretched earthly *clods*,
In dreadful darkneſs, lend deſired light. *Spenſer's Epithalam.*

The ſpirit of man,
Which God inſpir'd, cannot together periſh
With this corporeal *clod.* *Milton's Paradiſe Loſt, b.* x.

How the purer ſpirit is united to this *clod*, is a knot too hard for our degraded intellects to untie. *Glanv. Sceſ. c.* 4.

In moral reflections there muſt be heat as well as dry reaſon, to inſpire this cold *clod* of clay, which we carry about with us. *Burnet's Theory, Preface.*

4. A dull, groſs, ſtupid fellow; a dolt.

The vulgar! a ſcarce animated *clod*,
Ne'er pleas'd with aught above 'em. *Dryden's Aurengzebe.*

To Clod. *v. n.* [from the noun.] To gather into concretions; to coagulate: for this we ſometimes uſe *clot.*

Let us go find the body, and from the ſtream,
With lavers pure, and cleanſing herbs, waſh off
The *clodded* gore. *Milton's Agon. l.* 1727.

To Clod. *v. a.* [from the noun.] To pelt with clods.

Clo'ddy. *adj.* [from *clod.*]

1. Conſiſting of earth or clods; earthy; muddy; miry; mean; groſs; baſe.

The glorious ſun,
Turning, with ſplendour of his precious eye,
The meagre *cloddy* earth to glittering gold. *Shakeſpeare.*

2. Full of clods unbroken.

Theſe lands they ſow always under furrow about Michaelmas, and leave it as *cloddy* as they can. *Mortimer's Huſbandry.*

Clo'dpate. *n. ſ.* [*clod* and *pate.*] A ſtupid fellow; a dolt; a thickſcull.

Clo'dpated. *adj.* [from *clodpate.*] Stupid; dull; doltiſh; thoughtleſs.

My *clodpated* relations ſpoiled the greateſt genius in the world, when they bred me a mechanick. *Arbuthnot.*

Clo'dpoll. *n. ſ.* [from *clod* and *poll.*] A thickſcull; a dolt; a blockhead.

This letter being ſo excellently ignorant, he will find that it comes from a *clodpoll.* *Shakeſp. Twelfth Night.*

To CLOG. *v. a.* [It is imagined by *Skinner* to come from *log*; by *Caſaubon* derived from κλοιὸς, a dog's collar, being thought to be firſt hung upon fierce dogs.]

1. To load with ſomething that may hinder motion; to encumber with ſhackles; to impede, by faſtening to the neck or leg a heavy piece of wood or iron.

If you find ſo much blood in his liver as will *clog* the foot of a flea, I'll eat the reſt of the anatomy. *Shak. Twelfth Night.*

Let a man wean himſelf from theſe worldly impediments, that here *clog* his ſoul's flight. *Digby on the Soul, Dedication.*

The wings of birds were *clog'd* with ice and ſnow. *Dryd.*

Fleſhly luſts do debaſe men's minds, and *clog* their ſpirits, make them groſs and foul, liſtleſs and unactive. *Tillotſon.*

Gums and pomatums ſhall his flight reſtrain,
While *clogg'd* he beats his ſilken wings in vain. *Pope.*

2. To hinder; to obſtruct.

The gutter'd rocks and congregated ſands,
Traitors enſteep'd to *clog* the guiltleſs keel. *Shakeſpeare.*

His majeſty's ſhips were not ſo over-peſtered and *clogged* with great ordnance as they are, whereof there is ſuperfluity. *Sir Walter Raleigh's Eſſays.*

3. To load; to burthen; to embarraſs.

Since thou haſt far to go, bear not along
The *clogging* burthen of a guilty ſoul. *Shakeſp. Richard* II.

You'll rue the time
That *clogs* me with this anſwer. *Shakeſp. Macbeth.*

They lanc'd a vein, and watch'd returning breath;
It came, but *clogg'd* with ſymptoms of his death. *Dryden.*

All the commodities that go up into the country, are *clogged* with impoſitions as ſoon as they leave Leghorn. *Addiſon.*

4. In the following paſſage it is improper.

Clocks and Jacks, though the ſcrews and teeth of the wheels and nuts be never ſo ſmooth, yet, if they be not oiled, will hardly move; though you *clog* them with never ſo much weight. *Ray on the Creation.*

To Clog. *v. n.*

1. To coaleſce; to adhere. In this ſenſe, perhaps, only corruptly uſed for *clod* or *clot.*

Move it ſometimes with a broom, that the ſeeds *clog* not together. *Evelyn's Kalendar.*

2. To be encumbered or impeded by ſome extrinſick matter.

In working through the bone, the teeth of the ſaw will begin to *clog.* *Sharp's Surgery.*

Clog. *n. ſ.* [from the verb.]

1. A load; a weight; any incumbrance hung upon any animal or thing to hinder motion.

I'm glad at ſoul I have no other child;
For thy eſcape would teach me tyranny,
To hang *clogs* on them. *Shakeſpeare's Othello.*

I did but prompt the age to quit their *clogs*,
By the known rules of ancient liberty. *Milt. Par. Reg.*

As a dog committed cloſe,
For ſome offence, by chance breaks looſe,
And quits his *clog*; but all in vain,
He ſtill draws after him his chain. *Hudibras.*

2. An incumbrance; a hindrance; an obſtruction; an impediment.

The wearineſs of the fleſh is an heavy *clog* to the will. *Hooker.*

They're our *clogs*, not their own: if a man be
Chain'd to a galley, yet the galley's free. *Donne.*

Their prince made no other ſtep than rejecting the pope's ſupremacy, as a *clog* upon his own power and paſſions. *Swift.*

Slavery is, of all things, the greateſt *clog* and obſtacle to ſpeculation. *Swift.*

3. A kind of additional ſhoe worn by women, to keep them from wet.

4. A wooden ſhoe.

In France the peaſantry goes barefoot; and the middle ſort, throughout all that kingdom, makes uſe of wooden *clogs.* *Harvey on Conſumptions.*

Clo'gginess. *n. ſ.* [from *cloggy.*] The ſtate of being clogged.

Clo'ggy. *adj.* [from *clog.*] That which has the power of clogging up.

By additaments of some such nature, some grosser and *cloggy* parts are retained; or else much subtilized, and otherwise altered. *Boyle's History of Firmness.*

CLO'ISTER. *n. s.* [clâs, Welsh; clauster, Sax. *closter*, Germ. *klooster*, Dut. *claustro*, Ital. *cloistre*, Fr. *claustrum*, Lat.]

1. A religious retirement; a monastery; a nunnery.

Nor in a secret *cloister* doth he keep
These virgin spirits, until their marriage-day. *Davies.*
Some solitary *cloister* will I choose,
And there with holy virgins live immur'd. *Dryd. Sp. Fryar.*

How could he have the leisure and retiredness of the *cloister*, to perform those acts of devotion. *Atterbury.*

2. A peristile; a piazza.

To CLO'ISTER. *v. a.* [from the noun.] To shut up in a religious house; to confine; to immure; to shut up from the world.

Cloister thee in some religious house. *Shakesp. Rich.* II.

They have by commandment, though in form of courtesy, *cloistered* us within these walls for three days. *Bacon.*

It was of the king's first acts to *cloister* the queen dowager in the nunnery of Bermondsey. *Bacon's Henry* VII.

Nature affords plenty of beauties, that no man need complain if the deformed are *cloistered* up. *Rymer's Tragedies.*

The gloom of *cloister'd* monks. *Thomson's Summer.*

CLO'ISTERAL. *adj.* [from *cloister*.] Solitary; retired; religiously recluse.

Upon this ground many *cloisteral* men of great learning and devotion, prefer contemplation before action. *Walton's Angler.*

CLO'ISTERED. *participial adj.* [from *cloister*.]

1. Solitary; inhabiting cloisters.

Ere the bat hath flown
His *cloister'd* flight, there shall be done
A deed of dreadful note. *Shakespeare's Macbeth.*

2. Built with peristiles or piazzas.

The Greeks and Romans had commonly two *cloistered* open courts, one serving for the women's side, and the other for the men. *Wotton's Architecture.*

CLO'ISTRESS. *n. s.* [from *cloister*.] A nun; a lady who has vowed religious retirement.

Like a *cloistress* she will veiled walk,
And water once a day her chamber round
With eye-offending brine. *Shakesp. Twelfth Night.*

CLOKE. *n. s.* See CLOAK.

CLOMB. [*pret.* of *To climb.*]

Ask to what end they *clomb* that tedious height. *Spenser.*
So *clomb* this first grand thief into God's fold. *Milton.*

To CLOOM. *v. a.* [corrupted from *cleam*, clæmian, Sax. which is still used in some provinces.] To close or shut with glutinous or viscous matter.

Rear the hive enough to let them in, and *cloom* up the skirts, all but the door. *Mortimer's Husbandry.*

To CLOSE. *v. a.* [*closa*, Armorick; *kluys*, Dutch; *clos*, French; *clausus*, Latin.]

1. To shut; to lay together.

Sleep instantly fell on me, call'd
By nature as in aid, and *clos'd* mine eyes. *Milt. Par. Lost.*
When the sad wife has *clos'd* her husband's eyes;
Lies the pale corps, not yet intirely dead? *Prior.*
I soon shall visit Hector, and the shades
Of my great ancestors. Cephisa, thou
Wilt lend a hand to *close* thy mistress' eyes. *Philips.*

2. To conclude; to end; to finish.

One frugal supper did our studies *close*. *Dryden's Pers. Sat.*

I *close* this with my earnest desires that you will seriously consider your estate. *Wake's Preparation for Death.*

Edward and Henry, now the boast of fame;
And virtuous Alfred, a more sacred name;
After a life of generous toils endur'd,
Clos'd their long glories with a sigh, to find
Th' unwilling gratitude of base mankind. *Pope's Ep. of Hor.*

3. To inclose; to confine; to reposite.

Every one
According to the gift which bounteous nature
Hath in him *clos'd*. *Shakespeare's Macbeth.*

4. To join; to unite fractures; to consolidate fissures.

The armourers accomplishing the knights,
With busy hammers *closing* rivets up. *Shakesp. Henry* V.

There being no winter yet to *close* up and unite its parts, and restore the earth to its former strength and compactness. *Burnet's Theory of the Earth.*

As soon as any publick rupture happens, it is immediately *closed up* by moderation and good offices. *Addison on Italy.*

All the traces drawn there are immediately *closed up*, as though you wrote them with your finger on the surface of a river. *Watts's Improvement of the Mind.*

To CLOSE. *v. n.*

1. To coalesce; to join its own parts together.

They, and all that appertained to them, went down alive into the pit, and the earth *closed* upon them. *Num.* xvi. 33.

In plants you may try the force of imagination upon the lighter sort of motions; as upon their *closing* and opening. *Bacon's Natural History*, N°. 991.

2. *To* CLOSE *upon.* To agree upon; to join in.

The jealousy of such a design in us, would induce France and Holland to *close upon* some measures between them to our disadvantage. *Temple.*

3. *To* CLOSE *with.* } To come to an agreement with; to
To CLOSE *in with.* } comply with; to unite with.

Intire cowardice makes thee wrong this virtuous gentlewoman, to *close with* us. *Shakespeare's Henry* IV. *p.* ii.

It would become me better, than to *close*
In terms of friendship *with* thine enemies. *Shak. Jul. Cæs.*

There was no such defect in man's understanding, but that it would *close with* the evidence. *South's Sermons.*

He took the time when Richard was depos'd,
And high and low *with* happy Harry *clos'd*. *Dryden.*

Pride is so unsociable a vice, that there is no *closing with* it. *Collier of Friendship.*

This spirit, poured upon iron, unites with the body, and lets go the water: the acid spirit is more attracted by the fixed body, and lets go the water, to *close with* the fixed body. *Newton's Opticks.*

Such a proof as would have been *closed with* certainly at the first, shall be set aside easily afterwards. *Atterbury.*

These governours bent all their thoughts and applications to *close in with* the people, who were now the stronger party. *Swift on the Dissentions in Athens and Rome.*

4. To grapple with in wrestling.

CLOSE. *n. s.* [from the verb.]

1. Any thing shut; without outlet.

The admirable effects of this distillation in *close*, which is like the wombs and matrices of living creatures. *Bacon.*

2. A small field inclosed.

I have a tree, which grows here in my *close*,
That mine own use invites me to cut down,
And shortly must I fell it. *Shakespeare's Timon.*

Certain hedgers dividing a *close*, chanced upon a great chest. *Carew's Survey of Cornwal.*

3. The manner of shutting.

The doors of plank were; their *close* exquisite,
Kept with a double key. *Chapman's Iliads, b.* ii.

4. The time of shutting up.

In the *close* of night,
Philomel begins her heav'nly lay. *Dryden.*

5. A grapple in wrestling.

The king went of purpose into the North, laying an open side unto Perkin, to make him come to the *close*, and so to trip up his heels, having made sure in Kent beforehand. *Bacon.*

Both fill'd with dust, but starting up, the third *close* they
had made,
Had not Achilles' self stood up. *Chapman's Iliads.*

6. A pause, or cessation, or rest.

The air, such pleasure loth to lose,
With thousand eccho's still prolongs each heav'nly *close*. *Milt.*
At ev'ry *close* she made, th' attending throng
Reply'd, and bore the burden of the song. *Dryden's Fables.*

7. A conclusion or end.

Speedy death,
The *close* of all my miseries, and the balm. *Milt. Agon.*
Thro' Syria, Persia, Greece she goes;
And takes the Romans in the *close*. *Prior.*

CLOSE. *adj.* [from the verb.]

1. Shut fast; so as to leave no part open; as a *close* box; a *close* house.

We suppose this bag to be tied *close* about, towards the window. *Wilkins.*

2. Without vent; without inlet; secret; private; not to be seen through.

Nor could his acts too *close* a vizard wear,
To 'scape their eyes whom guilt had taught to fear. *Dryden.*

3. Confined; stagnant; without ventilation.

If the rooms be low roofed, or full of windows and doors, the one maketh the air *close*, and not fresh; and the other maketh it exceeding unequal. *Bacon's Nat. History*, N°. 937.

4. Compact; solid; without interstices or vacuities.

The inward substance of the earth is of itself an uniform mass, *close* and compact. *Burnet's Theory of the Earth.*

The golden globe being put into a press, which was driven by the extreme force of skrews, the water made itself way thro' the pores of that very *close* metal. *Locke.*

5. Viscous; glutinous; not volatile.

This oil, which nourishes the lamp, is supposed of so *close* and tenacious a substance, that it may slowly evaporate. *Wilkins.*

6. Concise; brief; without exuberance or digression.

You lay your thoughts so *close* together, that were they *closer* they would be crouded, and even a due connection would be wanting. *Dryden's Juven. Dedication.*

Where the original is *close*, no version can reach it in the same compass. *Dryden.*

Read these instructive leaves, in which conspire
Fresnoy's *close* art and Dryden's native fire. *Pope.*

7. Immediate; without any intervening distance or space, whether of time or place.

Was I a man bred great as Rome herself,

Equal

Equal to all her titles! that could ſtand
Cloſe up with Atlas, and ſuſtain her name
As ſtrong as he doth heaven! *Ben. Johnſon's Catiline.*

We muſt lay aſide that lazy and fallacious method of cenſuring by the lump, and muſt bring things *cloſe* to the teſt of true or falſe. *Burnet's Theory of the Earth, Preface.*

Plant the ſpring crocus's *cloſe* to a wall. *Mort. Husbandry.*

Where'er my name I find;
Some dire misfortune follows *cloſe* behind. *Pope's El. to Abel.*

8. Approaching nearly; joined one to another.

Now ſit we *cloſe* about this taper here,
And call in queſtion our neceſſities. *Shakeſ. Julius Cæſar.*

9. Narrow; as a *cloſe* alley.

10. Admitting ſmall diſtance.

Short crooked ſwords in *cloſer* fight they wear. *Dryden.*

11. Undiſcovered; without any token by which one may be found.

Cloſe obſerve him for the ſake of mockery. *Cloſe*, in the name of jeſting! lie you there. *Shakeſ. Twelfth Night.*

12. Hidden; ſecret; not revealed.

A *cloſe* intent at laſt to ſhew me grace. *Spenſer.*

Some ſpagyriſts, that keep their beſt things *cloſe*, will do more to vindicate their art, or oppoſe their antagoniſts, than to gratify the curious, or benefit mankind. *Boyle.*

13. Having the quality of ſecrecy; truſty.

Conſtant you are,
But yet a woman; and for ſecreſy,
No lady *cloſer*. *Shakeſpeare's Henry IV. p. i.*

14. Having an appearance of concealment; cloudy; ſly.

That *cloſe* aſpect of his,
Does ſhew the mood of a much troubled breaſt. *Shakeſp.*

15. Without wandering; without deviation; attentive.

I diſcovered no way to keep our thoughts *cloſe* to their buſineſs, but by frequent attention getting the habit of attention. *Locke.*

16. Full to the point; home.

I am engaging in a large diſpute, where the arguments are not like to reach *cloſe* on either ſide. *Dryd. on Dram. Poeſy.*

17. Retired; ſolitary.

18. Secluded from communication; as *a cloſe priſoner*.

19. Applied to the weather, dark, cloudy, not clear.

CLOSE. *adv.* It is uſed ſometimes adverbially by itſelf; but more frequently in compoſition. As,

CLOSE-BANDED. *adj.* In cloſe order; thick ranged; or ſecretly leagued, which ſeems rather the meaning in this paſſage.

Nor in the houſe, with chamber ambuſhes
Cloſe-banded, durſt attack me. *Milton's Agon. l. 1121.*

CLOSE-BODIED. *adj.* Made to fit the body exactly.

If any clergy ſhall appear in any *cloſe-bodied* coat, they ſhall be ſuſpended. *Ayliffe's Parergon.*

CLOSE-HANDED. *adj.* Covetous.

Galba was very *cloſe-handed*: I have not read much of his liberalities. *Arbuthnot on Coins.*

CLOSE-PENT. *adj.* Shut cloſe; without vent.

Then in ſome *cloſe-pent* room it crept along,
And, ſmould'ring as it went, in ſilence fed. *Dryden.*

CLO'SELY. *adv.* [from *cloſe.*]

1. Without inlet or outlet.

Putting the mixture into a crucible *cloſely* luted at the top: *Boyle's Chym. Princ.*

2. Without much ſpace intervening; nearly.

My lord of Warwick, and my brother Gloſter,
Follow Fluellen *cloſely* at the heels. *Shakeſp. Henry V.*

If we look more *cloſely*, we ſhall find
Moſt have the ſeeds of judgment in their mind. *Pope.*

3. Secretly; ſlily.

A Spaniard, riding on the bay, ſent ſome *cloſely* into the village, in the dark of the night. *Carew's Surv. of Cornwal.*

4. Without deviation.

I hope I have tranſlated *cloſely* enough, and given them the ſame turn of verſe which they had in the original. *Dryden.*

CLO'SENESS. *n. ſ.* [from *cloſe.*]

1. The ſtate of being ſhut; or the quality of admitting to be ſhut without inlet or outlet.

In drums, the *cloſeneſs* round about that preſerveth the ſound, maketh the noiſe come forth of the drum-hole more loud, than if you ſhould ſtrike upon the like ſkin extended in the open air. *Bacon's Natural Hiſtory*, Nº. 142.

2. Narrowneſs; ſtraitneſs.

3. Want of air, or ventilation.

I took my leave, being half ſtifled by the *cloſeneſs* of the room. *Swift's Account of Partridge's Death.*

4. Compactneſs; ſolidity.

How could particles, ſo widely diſperſed, combine into that *cloſeneſs* of texture? *Bentley's Sermons.*

The haſte of the ſpirit to put forth, and the *cloſeneſs* of the bark cauſe prickles in boughs. *Bacon's Nat. Hiſtory*, Nº. 559.

5. Recluſeneſs; ſolitude; retirement.

I thus neglecting worldly ends, all dedicated
To *cloſeneſs*, and the bettering of my mind. *Shakeſp. Tempeſt.*

6. Secrecy; privacy.

To his confederates he was conſtant and juſt, but not open. Such was his enquiry, and ſuch his *cloſeneſs*, as they ſtood in the light towards him, and he ſtood in the dark towards them. *Bacon's Henry VII.*

A journey of much adventure had been not communicated with any of his majeſty's counſellors, being carried with great *cloſeneſs*, liker a buſineſs of love than ſtate. *Wotton.*

We riſe not againſt the piercing judgment of Auguſtus, nor the extreme caution or *cloſeneſs* of Tiberius. *Bacon's Eſſays.*

This prince was ſo very reſerved, that he would impart his ſecrets to no body: whereupon this *cloſeneſs* did a little periſh his underſtanding. *Collier of Friendſhip.*

7. Covetouſneſs; ſly avarice.

Irus judged, that while he could keep his poverty a ſecret, he ſhould not feel it: he improved this thought into an affectation of *cloſeneſs* and covetouſneſs. *Addiſon's Spectat.* Nº. 264.

8. Connection; dependance.

The actions and proceedings of wiſe men run in a much greater *cloſeneſs* and coherence with one another, than thus to drive at a caſual iſſue, brought under no forecaſt or deſign. *South's Sermons.*

CLO'SER. *n. ſ.* [from *cloſe.*] A finiſher; a concluder.

CLO'SESTOOL. *n. ſ.* [*cloſe* and *ſtool.*] A chamber implement.

A peſtle for his truncheon, led the van;
And his high helmet was a *cloſe-ſtool* pan. *Garth's Diſpenſ.*

CLO'SET. *n. ſ.* [from *cloſe.*]

1. A ſmall room of privacy and retirement.

The taper burneth in your *cloſet*. *Shakeſp. Julius Cæſar.*

He would make a ſtep into his *cloſet*, and after a ſhort prayer he was gone. *Wotton.*

2. A private repoſitory of curioſities and valuable things.

He ſhould have made himſelf a key, wherewith to open the *cloſet* of Minerva, where thoſe fair treaſures are to be found in all abundance. *Dryden's Dufreſnoy.*

He furniſhes her *cloſet* firſt, and fills
The crowded ſhelves with rarities of ſhells. *Dryd. Fables.*

To CLO'SET. *v. a.* [from the noun.]

1. To ſhut up, or conceal in a cloſet.

The heat
Of thy great love once ſpread, as in an urn,
Doth *cloſet* up itſelf. *Herbert.*

2. To take into a cloſet for a ſecret interview.

About this time began the project of *cloſeting*, where the principal gentlemen of the kingdom were privately catechiſed by his majeſty. *Swift.*

CLOSH. *n. ſ.* A diſtemper in the feet of cattle; called alſo the *founder*. *Dict.*

CLO'SURE. *n. ſ.* [from *cloſe.*]

1. The act of ſhutting up.

The chink was carefully cloſed up: upon which *cloſure* there appeared not any change. *Boyle's Spring of the Air.*

2. That by which any thing is cloſed or ſhut.

I admire your ſending your laſt to me quite open, without a ſeal, wafer, or any *cloſure* whatever. *Pope to Swift.*

3. The parts incloſing; incloſure.

O thou bloody priſon!
Within the guilty *cloſure* of thy walls
Richard the ſecond here was hack'd to death. *Sh. Rich. III.*

4. Concluſion; end.

We'll hand in hand all headlong caſt us down,
And make a mutual *cloſure* of our houſe. *Shak. Tit. Andron.*

CLOT. *n. ſ.* [probably, at firſt, the ſame with *clod*; but now always applied to different uſes.] Concretion; coagulation; grume.

The white of an egg, with ſpirit of wine, doth bake the egg into *clots*, as if it began to poch. *Bacon's Phyſ. Remarks.*

The opening itſelf was ſtopt with a *clot* of grumous blood. *Wiſeman's Surgery.*

To CLOT. *v. n.* [from the noun, or from *klotteren*, Dutch.]

1. To form clots, or clods; to hang together.

Huge unweildy bones, laſting remains
Of that gigantick race; which as he breaks
The *clotted* glebe, the plowman haply finds. *Philips.*

2. To concrete; to coagulate; to gather into concretions; as *clotted* milk, *clotted* blood.

Here mangled limbs, here brains and gore,
Lie *clotted*. *Philips.*

CLOTH. *n. ſ.* plural *cloths* or *clothes*. [clað, Saxon.]

1. Any thing woven for dreſs or covering, whether of animal or vegetable ſubſtance.

The Spaniards buy their linen *cloths* in that kingdom. *Swift.*

2. The piece of linnen ſpread upon a table.

Nor let, like Nævius, every error paſs,
The muſty wine, foul *cloth*, or greaſy glaſs. *Pope's Hor. Imit.*

3. The canvaſs on which pictures are delineated.

I anſwer you right painted *cloth*, from whence you have ſtudied your queſtions. *Shakeſp. As you like it.*

Who fears a ſentence, or an old man's ſaw,
Shall by a painted *cloth* be kept in awe. *Shak. Tarq. and Luc.*

This idea, which we may call the goddeſs of painting and of ſculpture, deſcends upon the marble and the *cloth*, and becomes the original of theſe arts. *Dryden's Pref. to Dufreſnoy.*

4. In the plural. Dreſs; habit; garment; veſture; veſt-

ments. Including whatever covering is worn on the body. In this sense always *clothes*. Pronounced *clo's*.

He with him brought Pryene, rich array'd
In Claribellae's *clothes*. *Spenser, b.* ii. *cant.* 4. *stanz.* 28.

Take up these *clothes* here, quickly: carry them to the laundress in Datchet-mead. *Shakesp. Merry Wives of Windsor.*

Strength grows more from the warmth of exercises than of *cloaths*. *Temple.*

5. The covering of a bed.

Gazing on her midnight foes,
She turn'd each way her frighted head,
Then sunk it deep beneath the *clothes*. *Prior.*

To CLOTHE. *v. a.* pret. I *clothed*, or *clad*; particip. I have *clothed*, or *clad*. [from *cloth*.]

1. To invest with garments; to cover with dress, from cold and injuries.

Care no more to *clothe* and eat. *Shakesp. Cymbeline.*

An inhabitant of Nova Zembla having lived in Denmark, where he was *clothed*, took the first opportunity of making his escape into nakedness. *Addison's Freeholder*, N°. 5.

The Britons in Cæsar's time painted their bodies, and *clothed* themselves with the skins of beasts. *Swift.*

With superior boon may your rich soil
Exuberant nature's better blessings pour
O'er every land, the naked nations *clothe*,
And be th' exhaustless granary of a world. *Thoms. Spring.*

2. To adorn with dress.

We *clothe* and adorn our bodies: indeed, too much time we bestow upon that. Our souls also are to be *clothed* with holy habits, and adorned with good works. *Ray on Creation.*

Embroider'd purple *clothes* the golden beds. *Pope's Statius.*

3. To invest; as with clothes.

They leave the shady realms of night,
And, *cloth'd* in bodies, breathe your upper light. *Dryden.*

Let both use the clearest language in which they can *clothe* their thoughts. *Watts's Improvement of the Mind, p.* i.

4. To furnish or provide with clothes.

CLO'THIER. *n. s.* [from *cloth*.] A maker of cloth.

The *clothiers* all, not able to maintain
The many to them 'longing, have put off
The spinsters, carders, fullers, weavers. *Shak. Hen.* VIII.

His commissioners should cause *clothiers* to take wool, paying only two parts of the price. *Hayward.*

They shall only spoil the *clothier's* wool, and beggar the present spinners, at best. *Graunt's Bills of Mort.*

CLO'THING. *n. s.* [from *To clothe*.] Dress; vesture; garments.

Thy bosom might receive my yielded spright,
And thine with it, in heav'n's pure *clothing* drest,
Through clearest skies might take united flight. *Fairfax.*

Your bread and *clothing*, and every necessary of life, entirely depend upon it. *Swift.*

CLOTHSHE'ARER. *n. s.* [from *cloth* and *shear*.] One who trims the cloth, and levels the nap.

My father is a poor man, and by his occupation a *clothshearer*. *Hakewill on Providence.*

CLO'TPOLL. *n. s* [from *clot* and *poll*.] Thickskull; blockhead.

What says the fellow, there? call the *clotpoll* back. *Shakes.*

2. Head, in scorn.

I have sent Clotens *clotpoll* down the stream,
In embassy to his mother. *Shakespeare's Cymbeline.*

To CLO'TTER. *v. n.* [*klotteren*, Dutch.] To concrete; to coagulate; to gather into lumps.

He dragg'd the trembling sire,
Slidd'ring thro' *clotter'd* blood and holy mire. *Dryd. Æn.*

CLO'TTY. *adj.* [from *clot*.] Full of clods; concreted; full of concretions.

The matter expectorated is thin, and mixt with thick, *clotty*, bluish streaks. *Harvey on Consumptions.*

Where land is *clotty*, and a shower of rain soaks through, you may make use of a roll to break it. *Mortimer's Husbandry.*

A CLOUD. *n. s.* [The derivation is not known. *Minshew* derives it from *claudo*, to shut; *Somner* from *clod*; *Casaubin* from ἀχλὺς, darkness; *Skinner* from *kladde*, Dutch, a spot.]

1. The dark collection of vapours in the air.

Now are the *clouds* that lower'd upon our house,
In the deep bosom of the ocean buried. *Shakes. Rich.* III.

As a mist is a multitude of small but solid globules, which therefore descend; so a vapour, and therefore a watry *cloud*, is nothing else but a congeries of very small and concave globules, which therefore ascend, to that height in which they are of equal weight with the air, where they remain suspended, 'till, by some motion in the air, being broken, they descend in solid drops; either small, as in a mist, or bigger, when many of them run together, as in rain. *Grew's Cosmol.*

Clouds are the greatest and most considerable of all the meteors, as furnishing water and plenty to the earth. They consist of very small drops of water, and are elevated a good distance above the surface of the earth; for a *cloud* is nothing but a mist flying high in the air, as a mist is nothing but a *cloud* here below. *Locke's Elem. Nat. Philos.*

How vapours, turn'd to *clouds*, obscure the sky;
And *clouds*, dissolv'd, the thirsty ground supply. *Roscommon.*

2. The veins, marks, or stains in stones, or other bodies.

3. Any state of obscurity or darkness.

Tho' poets may of inspiration boast,
Their rage, ill govern'd, in the *clouds* is lost. *Waller.*
How can I see the brave and young,
Fall in the *cloud* of war, and fall unsung? *Addison.*

4. Any thing that spreads wide; as a croud, a multitude.

The objection comes to no more than this, that amongst a *cloud* of witnesses, there was one of no very good reputation. *Atterbury.*

To CLOUD. *v. a.* [from the noun.]

1. To darken with clouds; to cover with clouds; to obscure.

What sullen fury *clouds* his scornful brow. *Pope's Statius.*

2. To obscure; to make less evident.

If men would not exhale vapours to *cloud* and darken the clearest truths, no man could miss his way to heaven for want of light. *Decay of Piety.*

3. To variegate with dark veins.

The handle smooth and plain,
Made of the *clouded* olive's easy grain. *Pope's Odyssey.*

To CLOUD. *v. n.* To grow cloudy; to grow dark with clouds.

CLO'UDBERRY. *n. s.* [from *cloud* and *berry*.] The name of a plant, called also *knotberry*.

It hath a perpetual flower: the fruit is composed of many acini, in form of the mulberry. This plant is found upon the tops of the highest hills in the North of England. *Miller.*

CLOUDCAPT. *adj.* [from *cloud* and *cap*.] Topped with clouds; touching the clouds.

The *cloudcapt* towers, the gorgeous palaces,
The solemn temples, the great globe itself,
Yea, all which it inherit, shall dissolve. *Shakesp. Tempest.*

CLOUDCOMPE'LLING. *adj.* [A word formed in imitation of νεφεληγέρετης, ill understood.] An epithet of Jupiter, by whom clouds were supposed to be collected.

Health to both kings, attended with a roar
Of cannons, eccho'd from th' affrighted shore;
With loud resemblance of his thunder, prove
Bacchus the seed of *cloudcompelling* Jove. *Waller.*
Supplicating move
Thy just complaint to *cloudcompelling* Jove. *Dryd. Homer.*

CLO'UDILY. *adv.* [from *cloudy*.]

1. With clouds; darkly.

2. Obscurely; not perspicuously.

Some had rather have good discipline delivered plainly, by way of precepts, than *cloudily* enwrapped in allegories. *Spenser.*

He was commanded to write so *cloudily* by Cornutus. *Dryd.*

CLO'UDINESS. *n. s.* [from *cloudy*.]

1. The state of being covered with clouds; darkness.

You have such a February face,
So full of frost, of storm and *cloudiness*. *Shakespeare.*

The situation of this island exposes it to a continual *cloudiness*, which in the summer renders the air cooler, and in the winter warm. *Harvey on Consumptions.*

2. Want of brightness.

I saw a cloudy Hungarian diamond made clearer by lying in a cold liquor; wherein, he affirmed, that upon keeping it longer, the stone would lose more of its *cloudiness*. *Boyle.*

CLO'UDLESS. *adj.* [from *cloud*.] Without clouds; clear; unclouded; bright; luminous; lightsome; pure; undarkened.

This Partridge soon shall view in *cloudless* skies,
When next he looks thro' Galilæo's eyes. *Pope.*

How many such there must be in the vast extent of space, a naked eye in a *cloudless* night may give us some faint glimpse. *Cheyne's Phil. Prin.*

CLO'UDY. *adj.* [from *cloud*.]

1. Covered with clouds; obscured with clouds; consisting of clouds.

As Moses entered into the tabernacle, the *cloudy* pillar descended, and stood at the door. *Exod.* xxxiii. 9.

2. Dark; obscure; not intelligible.

If you content yourself frequently with words instead of ideas, or with *cloudy* and confused notions of things, how impenetrable will that darkness be. *Watts's Improv. of the Mind.*

3. Gloomy of look; not open, nor cheerful.

So my storm-beaten heart likewise is cheer'd
With that sun-shine, when *cloudy* looks are clear'd. *Spenser.*
Witness my son, now in the shade of death,
Whose bright outshining beams thy *cloudy* wrath
Hath in eternal darkness folded up. *Shakesp. Richard* III.

4. Marked with spots or veins.

CLOVE. *n. s.* [the preterite of *cleave*.] See To CLEAVE.

CLOVE. *n. s.* [*clou*, Fr. a nail, from the similitude of a clove to a nail.]

1. A valuable spice brought from Ternate in the East Indies. It is the fruit or seed of a very large tree.

Clove seems to be the rudiment or beginning of a fruit growing upon clove-trees. *Brown's Vulgar Errours, b.* ii.

2. Some of the parts into which garlick separates, when the outer skin is torn off.

'Tis mortal sin an onion to devour;
Each *clove* of garlick is a sacred pow'r. *Tate's Juven. Sat.*

CLOVE-GILLYFLOWER. *n. s.* [from its smelling like *cloves*.] This

This plant hath an intire, oblong, cylindrical, ſmooth cup, which is indented at the top: the petals of the flower are narrow at bottom, and broad at top; and are, for the moſt part, cut about the edges. The ſeed-veſſel is of a cylindrical figure, containing many flat rough ſeeds. This genus may be divided into three claſſes: 1. The clove-gillyflower, or carnation. 2. The pink. 3. The ſweet William. The carnation, or clove-gillyflower, are diſtinguiſhed into four claſſes. The firſt, called flakes, having two colours only, and their ſtripes large, going quite through the leaves. The ſecond, called bizars, have flowers ſtriped, or variegated with three or four different colours. The third are piquettes: theſe flowers have always a white ground, and are ſpotted with ſcarlet, red, purple, or other colours. The fourth are called painted ladies: theſe have their petals of a red or purple colour on the upper ſide, and are white underneath. Of each of theſe claſſes there are numerous varieties. The true clove-gillyflower has been long in uſe for making a cordial ſyrup. There are two or three varieties commonly brought to the markets, which differ greatly in goodneſs; ſome having very little ſcent, when compared with the true ſort. The varieties of the pink are; the damaſk pink; white ſhock; ſcarlet, pheaſant-eyed pink, of which there are great varieties, both with ſingle and double flowers; old man's head; painted lady. Among the ſweet Williams are, 1. The broad-leaved ſweet William, with red flowers. 2. The broad-leaved ſweet William, with variegated flowers. 3. The double ſweet ſweet William, with red flowers, which burſt their pods. 4. The roſe-coloured double ſweet William. 5. The narrow-leaved ſweet William, called ſweet John. *Miller.*

CLO'VEN. part. pret. [from *cleave.*] See To CLEAVE.

There is Aufidius, liſt you what work he makes
Among your *cloven* army. *Shakeſp. Coriolanus.*

Now, heap'd high,
The *cloven* oaks and lofty pines do lie. *Waller.*

A chap-fallen beaver, looſely hanging by
The *cloven* helm, and arch of victory. *Dryd. Juv. Sat.* x.

CLOVEN-FOOTED. } *adj.* [*cloven* and *foot*, or *hoof.*] Having the
CLOVEN-HOOFED. } foot divided into two parts; not a round hoof; biſulcous.

There are the biſulcous or *cloven-hooft*; as camels and beavers. *Brown's Vulgar Errours.*

The *cloven-footed* fiend is baniſh'd from us. *Dryden.*

Great variety of water-fowl, both whole and *cloven-footed*, frequent the waters. *Ray on the Creation.*

CLO'VER. } *n. ſ.* [more properly *claver*, clæfeɲ, Saxon.]
CLOVER-GRASS. }

1. A ſpecies of TREFOIL, which ſee.

The even mead, that erſt brought ſweetly forth
The freckled cowſlip, burnet, and green *clover*. *Sh. Hen.* V.

Nature ſhall provide
Green graſs and fatt'ning *clover* for their fare. *Dryd. Virgil.*

Clover improves land, by the great quantity of cattle it maintains. *Mortimer's Huſbandry.*

My Blouzelinda is the blitheſt laſs,
Than primroſe ſweeter, or the *clover-graſs*. *Gay.*

2. *To live in* CLOVER, is to live luxuriouſly; clover being extremely delicious and fattening to cattle.

Well, Laureat, was the night in *clover* ſpent? *Ogle.*

CLO'VERED. *adj.* [from *clover.*] Covered with clover.

Flocks thick-nibbling thro' the *clover'd* vale. *Thom. Summ.*

CLOUGH. *n. ſ.* [clouȝh, Saxon.] The cleft of a hill; a cliff. In compoſition a hilly place.

CLOUGH. *n. ſ.* [in commerce.] An allowance of two pounds in every hundred weight for the turn of the ſcale, that the commodity may hold out weight when ſold by retail.

A CLOUT. *n. ſ.* [clut, Saxon.]

1. A cloth for any mean uſe.

His garment, nought but many ragged *clouts*,
With thorns together pinn'd, and patched was. *Spenſ. F. Q.*

A *clout* upon that head,
Where late the diadem ſtood. *Shakeſpeare's Hamlet.*

In pow'r of ſpittle and a *clout*,
When e'er he pleaſe to blot it out. *Swift.*

2. A patch on a ſhoe or coat.

3. Anciently, the mark of white cloth at which archers ſhot.

He drew a good bow: he ſhot a fine ſhoot: he would have clapt in the *clout* at twelve ſcore. *Shakeſp. Hen.* IV. *p.* ii.

4. An iron plate to keep an axle-tree from wearing.

To CLOUT. *v. a.* [from the noun.]

1. To patch; to mend coarſely.

I thought he ſlept, and put
My *clouted* brogues from off my feet, whoſe rudeneſs
Anſwer'd my ſteps too loud. *Shakeſp. Cymbeline.*

The dull ſwain
Treads on it daily with his *clouted* ſhoon. *Milton.*

2. To cover with a cloth.

Milk ſome unhappy ewe,
Whoſe *clouted* leg her hurt doth ſhew. *Spenſer's Paſtorals.*

3. To join awkwardly or coarſely together.

Many ſentences of one meaning be *clouted* up together. *Aſcham's Schoolmaſter.*

CLO'UTED. *participial adj.* Congealed; coagulated: corruptly uſed for *clotted.*

I've ſeen her ſkim the *clouted* cream,
And preſs from ſpongy curds the milky ſtream. *Gay's Paſt.*

CLO'UTERLY. *adj.* [probably by corruption from *louterly.*] Clumſy; awkward; as a *clouterly* fellow.

The ſingle wheel plough is a very *clouterly* ſort. *Mortimer.*

CLOWN. *n. ſ.* [imagined by *Skinner* and *Junius* to be contracted from *colonus.* It ſeems rather a Saxon word, corrupted from *lown*; *loen*, Dut. a word nearly of the ſame import.]

1. A ruſtick; a country fellow; a churl.

He came out with all his *clowns*, horſt upon cart-jades. *Sidney, b.* ii.

The *clowns*, a boiſt'rous, rude, ungovern'd crew,
With furious haſte to the loud ſummons flew. *Dryden's Æn.*

2. A coarſe ill-bred man.

In youth a coxcomb, and in age a *clown.* *Spectator.*

A country ſquire, repreſented with no other vice but that of being a *clown*, and having the provincial accent. *Swift.*

CLO'WNERY. *n. ſ.* [from *clown.*] Ill-breeding; churliſhneſs; rudeneſs; brutality.

The fool's conceit had both *clownery* and ill-nature. *L'Eſtr.*

CLO'WNISH. *adj.* [from *clown.*]

1. Conſiſting of ruſticks or clowns.

Young Silvia beats her breaſt, and cries aloud
For ſuccour from the *clowniſh* neighbourhood. *Dryd. Æn.*

2. Coarſe; rough; rugged.

But with his *clowniſh* hands their tender wings
He bruſheth off. *Spenſer's Fairy Queen, b.* i. *cant.* i.

3. Uncivil; ill-bred; ill-mannered.

What if we eſſay'd to ſteal
The *clowniſh* fool out of your father's court. *Shakeſpeare.*

4. Clumſy; ungainly.

With a grave look, in this odd equipage,
The *clowniſh* mimick traverſes the ſtage. *Prior.*

CLO'WNISHLY. *adv.* [from *clowniſh.*] Coarſely; rudely; brutally.

CLO'WNISHNESS. *n. ſ.* [from *clowniſh.*]

1. Ruſticity; coarſeneſs; unpoliſhed rudeneſs.

Even his Dorick dialect has an incomparable ſweetneſs in its *clowniſhneſs.* *Dryden.*

If the boy ſhould not make legs very gracefully, a dancing maſter will cure that defect, and wipe off that plainneſs which the a-la-mode people call *clowniſhneſs.* *Locke on Education.*

2. Incivility; brutality.

CLOWN'S MUSTARD. *n. ſ.* An herb. *Dict.*

To CLOY. *v. a.* [*enclouer*, Fr. To nail up; to ſtop up.]

1. To ſatiate; to ſate; to fill beyond deſire; to ſurfeit; to fill to loathing.

The length of thoſe ſpeeches had not *cloyed* Pyrocles, though he were very impatient of long deliberations. *Sidney.*

The very creed of Athanaſius, and that ſacred hymn of glory, are now reckoned as ſuperfluities, which we muſt in any caſe pare away, leſt we *cloy* God with too much ſervice. *Hooker, b.* v. *ſect.* 42.

Who can *cloy* the hungry edge of appetite,
By bare imagination of a feaſt? *Shakeſp. Richard* II.

Continually varying the ſame ſenſe, and taking up what he had more than enough inculcated before, he ſometimes *cloys* his readers inſtead of ſatisfying them. *Dryden.*

Whoſe little ſtore her well-taught mind does pleaſe,
Nor pinch'd with want, nor *cloy'd* with wanton eaſe. *Roſcom.*

Intemperance in eating and drinking, inſtead of delighting and ſatisfying nature, doth but load and *cloy* it. *Tillotſon.*

Settle, *cloy'd* with cuſtard and with praiſe,
Is gather'd to the dull of ancient days. *Pope's Dunciad.*

2. It ſeems to have, in the following paſſage, another ſenſe: perhaps to ſtrike the beak together.

His royal bird
Prunes the immortal wing, and *cloys* his beak,
As when his god is pleas'd. *Shakeſp. Cymbeline.*

3. To nail up guns, by ſtriking a ſpike into the touch-hole.

CLO'YLESS. *adj.* [from *cloy.*] That of which too much cannot be had; that which cannot cauſe ſatiety.

Epicurean cooks
Sharpen with *cloyleſs* ſauce his appetite. *Shak. Ant. and Cleop.*

CLO'YMENT. *n. ſ.* [from *cloy.*] Satiety; repletion beyond appetite.

Alas! their love may be call'd appetite:
No motion of the liver, but the palate;
That ſuffers ſurfeit, *cloyment*, and revolt. *Sh. Twelfth Night.*

CLUB. *n. ſ.* [*clwppa*, Welſh; *kluppel*, Dutch.]

1. A heavy ſtick; a ſtaff intended for offence.

He ſtrove his combred *club* to quit
Out of the earth. *Spenſer's Fairy Queen, b.* i. *cant.* 8.

As he pulled off his helmet, a butcher ſlew him with the ſtroak of a *club.* *Hayward.*

Arm'd with a knotty *club* another came. *Dryden's Æn.*

2. The name of one of the ſuits of cards.

The *clubs* black tyrant firſt her victim died,
Spite of his haughty mien and barb'rous pride. *Pope.*

3. [From cleoꝼan, to divide. *Skinner.*] The ſhot or dividend

dend of a reckoning, paid by the company in just proportions.

A fuddling couple sold ale: their humour was to drink drunk, upon their own liquor: they laid down their *club*, and this they called forcing a trade. *L'Estrange.*

4. An assembly of good fellows, meeting under certain conditions.

What right has any man to meet in factious *clubs* to vilify the government? *Dryden's Medal. Dedication.*

5. Concurrence; contribution; joint charge.

He's bound to vouch them for his own,
Tho' got b' implicite generation,
And general *club* of all the nation. *Hudibras, p.* ii. *cant.* 1.

To CLUB. *v. n.* [from the noun.]

1. To contribute to a common expence in settled proportions.
2. To join to one effect; to contribute separate powers to one end.

'Till grosser atoms, tumbling in the stream
Of fancy, madly met, and *club'd* into a dream. *Dryden.*

Every part of the body seems to *club* and contribute to the seed, else why should parents, born blind or deaf, sometimes generate children with the same imperfections. *Ray.*

Let sugar, wine, and cream together *club*,
To make that gentle viand, syllabub. *King.*

The owl, the raven, and the bat,
Club'd for a feather to his hat. *Swift.*

To CLUB. *v. a.* To pay to a common reckoning.

Plums and directors, Shylock and his wife,
Will *club* their testers now to take your life. *Pope's Horace.*

Fibres being distinct, and impregnated by distinct spirits, how should they *club* their particular informations into a common idea. *Collier on Thought.*

CLUBHE'ADED. *adj.* [*club* and *head.*] Having a thick head.

Small *clubheaded* anterinæ. *Derham's Physicotheology.*

CLUBLA'W. *n. s.* [*club* and *law.*] Regulation by force; the law of arms.

The enemies of our happy establishment seem to have recourse to the laudable method of *clublaw*, when they find all other means for enforcing the absurdity of their opinions to be ineffectual. *Addison's Freeholder*, N°. 50.

CLUBRO'OM. *n. s.* [*club* and *room.*] The room in which a club or company assembles.

These ladies resolved to give the pictures of their deceased husbands to the *clubroom*. *Addis. Spectator*, N°. 361.

To CLUCK. *v. n.* [*cloccian*, Welsh; *clochat*, Armorick; cloccan, Saxon; *klocken*, Dutch.] To call chickens; as a hen.

She, poor hen, fond of no second brood,
Has *cluck'd* thee to the wars. *Shakesp. Coriolanus.*

Ducklings, though hatched by a hen, if she brings them to a river, in they go, though the hen *clucks* and calls to keep them out. *Ray on the Creation.*

CLUMP. *n. s.* [formed from *lump.*] A shapeless piece of wood, or other matter, nearly equal in its dimensions.

CLUMPS. *n. s.* A numbscull. *Skinner.*

CLU'MSILY. *adv.* [from *clumsy.*] Awkwardly; without readiness; without nimbleness; without grace.

Upon the ground he walks very *clumsily* and ridiculously. *Ray on the Creation.*

This lofty humour is *clumsily* and inartificially managed, when affected. *Collier on Pride.*

CLU'MSINESS. *n. s.* [from *clumsy.*] Awkwardness; ungainliness; want of readiness, nimbleness, or dexterity.

The drudging part of life is chiefly owing to *clumsiness* and ignorance, which either wants proper tools, or skill to use them. *Collier on Fame.*

CLU'MSY. *adj.* [This word, omitted in the other etymologists, is rightly derived by *Bailey* from *lompsch*, Dutch, stupid. In English, *lump*, *clump*, *lumpish*, *clumpish*, *clumpishly*, *clumsily*, *clumsy.*] Awkward; heavy; artless; unhandy; without dexterity, readiness, or grace. It is used either of persons or actions, or things.

The matter ductile and sequacious, apt to be moulded into such shapes and machines, even by *clumsy* fingers. *Ray.*

But thou in *clumsy* verse, unlick'd, unpointed,
Hast shamefully defy'd. *Dryden.*

That *clumsy* outside of a porter,
How could it thus conceal a courtier? *Swift.*

CLUNG. The preterite and participle of *cling*.

To CLUNG. *v. n.* [clingan, Sax.] To dry as wood does, when it is laid up after it is cut. See To CLING.

CLUNG. *adj.* [clungu, Sax.[Wasted with leanness; shrunk up with cold.

CLU'STER. *n. s.* [clyster, Sax. *klister*, Dutch.]

1. A bunch; a number of things of the same kind growing or joined together.

Grapes will continue fresh and moist all winter, if you hang them *cluster* by *cluster* in the roof of a warm room. *Bacon.*

A swelling knot is rais'd;
Whence, in short space, itself the *cluster* shows,
And from earth's moisture, mixt with sun-beams, grows. *Denham.*

The saline corpuscles of one liquor do variously act upon the tinging corpuscles of another, so as to make many of them associate into a *cluster*, whereby two transparent liquors may compose a coloured one. *Newton's Opt.*

An elm was near, to whose embraces led,
The curling vine her swelling *clusters* spread. *Pope.*

2. A number of animals gathered together.

As bees
Pour forth their populous youth about the hive
In *clusters*. *Milton's Paradise Lost, b.* i. *l.* 771.

There with their clasping feet together clung,
And a long *cluster* from the laurel hung. *Dryden's Æn.*

3. A body of people collected: used in contempt.

We lov'd him; but like beasts
And coward nobles, gave way to your *clusters*,
Who did hoot him out o' th' city. *Shakesp. Coriolanus.*

My friend took his station among a *cluster* of mob, who were making themselves merry with their betters. *Addison.*

To CLU'STER. *v. n.* [from the noun.] To grow in bunches; to gather themselves into bunches, to congregate.

Forth flourish'd thick the *clustering* vine. *Milt. Par. Lost.*

Great father Bacchus to my song repair;
For *clustering* grapes are thy peculiar care. *Dryd. Virg. Geor.*

Or from the forest, falls the *cluster'd* snow,
Myriads of gems, that in the waving gleam
Gay-twinkle as they scatter. *Thomson's Winter, l.* 790.

To CLU'STER. *v. a.* To collect any thing into bodies.

CLUSTER-GRAPE. *n. s.* [from *cluster* and *grape.*]

The small black grape is by some called the currant, or *cluster-grape*; which I reckon the forwardest of the black sort. *Mortimer's Husbandry.*

CLU'STERY. *adj.* [from *cluster.*] Growing in clusters.

To CLUTCH. *v. a.* [Of uncertain etymology.]

1. To hold in the hand; to gripe; to grasp.

Is this a dagger I see before me,
The handle tow'rd my hand? Come, let me *clutch* thee. *Shakespeare's Macbeth.*

They,
Like moles within us, heave and cast about;
And, 'till they foot and *clutch* their prey,
They never cool. *Herbert.*

A man may set the poles together in his head, and *clutch* the whole globe at one intellectual grasp. *Collier on Thought.*

2. To contract; to double the hand, so as to seize and hold fast.

Not that I have the power to *clutch* my hand,
When his fair angels would salute my palm. *Shak. K. John.*

CLUTCH. *n. s.* [from the verb.]

1. The gripe; grasp; seizure.
2. Generally, in the plural, the paws, the talons.

It was the hard fortune of a cock to fall into the *clutches* of a cat. *L'Estrange, Fab.* ii.

3. Hands, in a sense of rapacity and cruelty.

Your greedy slav'ring to devour,
Before 'twas in your *clutches* pow'r. *Hudibras, p.* iii. *cant.* 2.

Set up the covenant on crutches,
'Gainst those who have us in their *clutches*. *Hudibras, p.* iii.

I must have great leisure, and little care of myself, if I ever more come near the *clutches* of such a giant. *Stillingfleet.*

A CLU'TTER. *n. s.* [See CLATTER.] A noise; a bustle; a busy tumult; a hurry; a clamour. A low word.

He saw what a *clutter* there was with huge, over-grown pots, pans, and spits. *L'Estrange, Fab.* 120.

The fav'rite child that just begins to prattle,
Is very humorsome, and makes great *clutter*,
'Till he has windows on his bread and butter. *King.*

Prithee, Tim, why all this *clutter*?
Why ever in these raging fits? *Swift.*

To CLU'TTER. *v. n.* [from the noun.] To make a noise, or bustle.

A CLY'STER. *n. s.* [κλυστὴρ.] An injection into the anus.

If nature relieves by a diarrhæa, without sinking the strength of the patient, it is not to be stopt, but promoted gently by emollient *clysters*. *Arbuthnot on Diet.*

To COACE'RVATE. *v. a.* [*coacervo*, Latin.] To heap up together.

The collocation of the spirits in bodies, whether the spirits be *coacervate* or diffused. *Bacon's Nat. History*, N°. 846.

COACERVA'TION. *n. s.* [from *coacervate.*] The act of heaping, or state of being heaped together.

The fixing of it is the equal spreading of the tangible parts, and the close *coacervation* of them. *Bacon's Nat. History.*

COACH. *n. s.* [*coche*, Fr. *kotczy*, among the Hungarians, by whom this vehicle is said to have been invented. *Minshew.*] A carriage of pleasure, or state, distinguished from a chariot by having seats fronting each other.

Basilius attended for her in a *coach*, to carry her abroad to see some sports. *Sidney, b.* ii.

A better would you fix?
Then give humility a *coach* and six. *Pope's Essay on Man.*

Suppose that last week my *coach* was within an inch of overturning

turning in a smooth even way, and drawn by very gentle horses. *Swift.*

To COACH. *v. a.* [from the noun.] To carry in a coach.

The needy poet sticks to all he meets,
Coach'd, carted, trod upon; now loose, now fast,
And carry'd off in some dog's tail at last. *Pope's Dunciad.*

COACH-BOX. *n. s.* [*coach* and *box.*] The seat on which the driver of the coach sits.

Her father had two coachmen: when one was in the *coach-box*, if the coach swung but the least to one side, she used to shriek. *Arbuthnot's History of John Bull.*

COACH-HIRE. *n. s.* Money paid for the use of a hired coach.

You exclaim as loud as those that praise,
For scraps and *coach-hire*, a young noble's plays. *Dryden.*

My expences in *coach-hire* make no small article. *Spectator.*

COACH-HOUSE. *n. s.* [*coach* and *house.*] The house in which the coach is kept from the weather.

Let him lie in the stable or the *coach-house*. *Swift.*

COACH-MAKER. *n. s.* [*coach* and *maker.*] The artificer whose trade is to make coaches.

Her chariot is an empty hazel-nut,
Made by the joyner, Squirrel, or old Grub,
Time out of mind, the fairies *coach-makers*. *Shakespeare.*

Take care of your wheels: get a new sett bought, and probably the *coach-maker* will consider you. *Swift.*

COACH-MAN. *n. s.* [*coach* and *man.*] The driver of a coach.

She commanded her trembling *coachman* to drive her chariot near the body of her king. *South.*

To COA'CT. *v. n.* [from *con* and *act.*] To act together; to act in concert.

But if I tell how these two did *coact*,
Shall I not lie in publishing a truth? *Shakespeare.*

COA'CTION. *n. s.* [*coactus*, Lat.] Compulsion; force, either restraining or impelling.

It had the passions in perfect subjection; and though its command over them was persuasive and political, yet it had the force of *coaction*, and despotical. *South's Sermons.*

COA'CTIVE. *adj.* [from *coact.*]

1. Having the force of restraining or impelling; compulsory; restrictive.

The Levitical priests in the old law, never arrogated unto themselves any temporal or *coactive* power. *Raleigh's Essays.*

2. Acting in concurrence. Obsolete.

Imagination,
With what's unreal thou *coactive* art. *Shakep. Winter's Tale.*

COADJU'MENT. *n. s.* [from *con* and *adjumentum*, Latin.] Mutual assistance. *Dict.*

COADJU'TANT. *n. s.* [from *con* and *adjuto.*] Helping; co-operating.

Thracius *coadjutant*, and the roar
Of fierce Euroclydon. *Philips.*

COADJU'TOR. *n. s.* [from *con* and *adjutor*, Latin.]

1. A fellow-helper; an assistant; an associate; one engaged in the assistance of another.

I should not succeed in a project, whereof I have had no hint from my predecessors the poets, or their seconds or *coadjutors* the criticks. *Dryden's Juv. Dedication.*

Away the friendly *coadjutor* flies. *Garth's Dispensary.*

A gownman of a different make,
Whom Pallas, once Vanessa's tutor,
Had fix'd on for her *coadjutor*. *Swift.*

2. In the canon law, one who is empowered or appointed to perform the duties of another.

A bishop that is unprofitable to his diocese ought to be deposed, and no *coadjutor* assigned him. *Ayliffes Parergon.*

COADJU'VANCY. *n. s.* [from *con* and *adjuvo*, Lat.] Help; concurrent help; contribution of help; co-operation.

Crystal is a mineral body, in the difference of stones, made of a lentous percolation of earth, drawn from the most pure and limpid juice thereof, owing to the coldness of the earth some concurrence and *coadjuvancy*, but not immediate determination and efficiency. *Brown's Vulgar Errours*, b ii.

COADUNI'TION. *n. s.* [from *con*, *ad*, *unitio*, Lat.] The conjunction of different substances into one mass.

Bodies seem to have an intrinsick principle of, or corruption from, the *coadunition* of particles endued with contrary qualities. *Hale's Origin of Mankind.*

To COAGME'NT. *v. a.* [from *con* and *agmen*, Lat.] To congregate or heap together. I have only found the participle in use.

Had the world been *coagmented* from that supposed fortuitous jumble, this hypothesis had been tolerable. *Glanv. Sceps. c.* 20.

COAGMENTA'TION. *n. s.* [from *coagment.*] Collection, or coacervation into one mass; union; conjunction.

The third part rests in the well joining, cementing, and *coagmentation* of words, when it is smooth, gentle, and sweet. *Benj. Johnson's Discoveries.*

COA'GULABLE. *adj.* [from *coagulate.*] That which is capable of concretion.

Stones that are rich in vitriol, being often drenched with rain-water, the liquor will then extract a fine and transparent substance, *coagulable* into vitriol. *Boyle's Scept. Chym.*

To COA'GULATE. *v. a.* [*coagulo*, Lat.] To force into concretions; as, by the affusion of some other substance, to turn milk.

Roasted in wrath and fire,
And thus o'ersized with *coagulate* gore. *Shakesp. Hamlet.*

Vivification ever consisteth in spirits attenuate, which the cold doth congeal and *coagulate*. *Bacon's Nat. History*, N°. 836.

Bitumen is found in lumps, or *coagulated* masses, in some springs. *Woodward's Natural History.*

The milk in the stomach of calves, which is *coagulated* by the runnet, is again dissolved and rendered fluid by the gall in the duodenum. *Arbuthnot on Aliments.*

To COA'GULATE. *v. n.* To run into concretions, or congelations.

Spirit of wine commixed with milk, a third part spirit of wine, and two parts milk, *coagulateth* little, but mingleth; and the spirit swims not above. *Bacon's Phys. Rem.*

About the third part of the oil olive, which was driven over into the receiver, did there *coagulate* into a whitish body, almost like butter. *Boyle's History of Fluidity.*

COAGULA'TION. *n. s.* [from *coagulate.*]

1. Concretion; congelation; the act of coagulating; the state of being coagulated.

2. The body formed by coagulation.

As the substance of *coagulations* is not merely saline, nothing dissolves them but what penetrates and relaxes at the same time. *Arbuthnot on Aliments.*

COA'GULATIVE. *adj.* [from *coagulate.*] That which has the power of causing concretion, or coagulation.

And to manifest yet further the *coagulative* power of them, we have sometimes in a minute arrested the fluidity of new milk, and turned it into a curdled substance, only by dexterously mingling with it a few drops of good oil of vitriol. *Boyle's History of Firmness.*

COAGULA'TOR. *n. s.* [from *coagulate.*] That which causes coagulation.

Coagulators of the humours are those things which expel the most fluid parts, as in the case of incrassating, or thickening; and by those things which suck up some of the fluid parts, as absorbents. *Arbuthnot on Diet.*

COAL. *n. s.* [col, Sax. *kol*, Germ. *kole*, Dut. *kul*, Danish.]

1. The common fossil fewel.

Coal is a black, sulphurous, inflammatory matter, dug out of the earth, serving for fewel. It is ranked among the minerals, and is common in Europe, though the English *coal* is of most repute. One species of pit-coal is called *cannel*, or *canole* coal, which is found in the northern counties; and is hard, glossy and light, apt to cleave into thin flakes, and, when kindled, yields a continual blaze 'till it be burnt out. *Chambers.*

Coals are solid, dry, opake, inflammable substances, found in large strata, splitting horizontally more easily than in any other direction; of a glossy hue, soft and friable, not fusible, but easily inflammable, and leaving a large residuum of ashes. *Hill on Fossils.*

But age, enforc'd, falls by her own consent;
As *coals* to ashes, when the spirit's spent. *Denham.*

We shall meet with the same mineral lodged in *coals*, that elsewhere we found in marle. *Woodward's Nat. History.*

2. The cinder of burnt wood, charcoal.

Whatsoever doth so alter a body, as it returneth not again to that it was, may be called alteratio major; as when cheese is made of curds, or *coals* of wood, or bricks of earth. *Bacon.*

3. Fire; any thing inflamed or ignited.

You are no surer, no,
Than is the *coal* of fire upon the ice,
Or hailstones in the sun. *Shakesp. Coriolanus.*

The rage of jealousy then fir'd his soul,
And his face kindled like a burning *coal*. *Dryd. Fables.*

You
Have blown this *coal* betwixt my lord and me. *Sh. H.* VIII.

To COAL. *v. n.* [from the noun.]

1. To burn wood to charcoal.

Add the tinner's care and cost, in buying the wood for this service, felling, framing, and piling it to be burnt; in fetching the same when it is *coaled*, through such far, foul, and cumbersome ways. *Carew's Survey of Cornwal.*

2. To delineate with a coal.

Marvailing, he *coaled* out rhimes upon the wall, near to the picture. *Camden's Remains.*

COAL-BLACK. *adj.* [*coal* and *black.*] Black in the highest degree; of the colour of a coal.

As burning Ætna, from his boiling stew,
Doth belch out flames, and rocks in pieces broke,
And ragged ribs of mountains molten new,
Enwrapt in *coal-black* clouds and filthy smoak. *Fairy Queen.*

Ethiopians and negroes become *coal-black* from fuliginous efflorescencies, and complectional tinctures. *Brown's Vul. Err.*

Coal-black his colour, but like jet it shone;
His legs and flowing tail were white alone. *Dryden.*

COAL-BOX. *n. s.* [*coal* and *box.*] A box to carry coals to the fire.

Leave a pail of dirty water, a *coal-box*, a bottle, a broom, and such other unsightly things. *Swift.*

COAL-MINE. *n. s.* [*coal* and *mine.*] A mine in which coals are dug; a coal-pit.

Springs are injurious to land, that flow from *coalmines.* *Mortimer's Husbandry.*

COAL-PIT. *n. s.* [from *coal* and *pit.*] A pit made in the earth, generally to a great depth, for digging coals.

A leaf of the polypody kind, found in the sinking of a *coalpit.* *Woodward on Fossils.*

COAL-STONE. *n. s.* [*coal* and *stone.*] A sort of cannel coal. See COAL.

Coal-stone flames easily, and burns freely; but holds and endures the fire much longer than coal. *Woodward on Fossils.*

COAL-WORK. *n. s.* [*coal* and *work.*] A coalery; a place where coals are found.

There is a vast treasure in the old English, from whence authors may draw constant supplies; as our officers make their surest remits from the *coal-works* and the mines. *Felton.*

CO'ALERY. *n. s.* [from *coal.*] A place where coals are dug.

Two fine stalactitæ were found hanging from a black stone, at a deserted vault in Benwell *coalery.* *Woodward on Fossils.*

To COALE'SCE. *v. n.* [*coalesco*, Latin.]

1. To unite in masses by a spontaneous approximation to each other.

When vapours are raised, they hinder not the transparency of the air, being divided into parts too small to cause any reflection in their superficies; but when they begin to *coalesce*, and constitute globules, those globules become of a convenient size to reflect some colours. *Newton's Opt.*

2. To grow together; to join.

COALE'SCENCE. *n. s.* [from *coalesce.*] The act of coalescing; concretion; union.

COALI'TION. *n. s.* [from *coalesco coalitum*, Latin.] Union in one mass or body; conjunction of separate parts in one whole.

The world's a mass of heterogeneous consistences, and every part thereof a *coalition* of distinguishable varieties. *Glanv. Sceps.*

In the first *coalition* of a people, their prospect is not great: they provide laws for their present exigence and convenience. *Hale's Common Law of England.*

'Tis necessary that these squandered atoms should convene and unite into great masses: without such a *coalition* the chaos must have reigned to all eternity. *Bentley.*

CO'ALY. *adj.* [from *coal.*] Containing coal.

Or *coaly* Tine, or ancient hallow'd Dee. *Milton.*

COAPTA'TION. *n. s.* [from *con* and *apto*, Lat.] The adjustment of parts to each other.

In a clock the hand is moved upon the dial, the bell is struck, and the other actions belonging to the engine are performed by virtue of the size, shape, bigness, and *coaptation* of the several parts. *Boyle's Scep. Chym.*

The same method makes both prose and verse beautiful, which consists in the judicious *coaptation* and ranging of the words. *Broome on the Odyssey.*

To COA'RCT. *v. a.* [*coarcto*, Latin.]

1. To straighten; to confine into a narrow compass.

2. To contract power.

If a man *coarcts* himself to the extremity of an act, he must blame and impute it to himself, that he has thus *coarcted* or straightened himself so far. *Ayliffe's Parergon.*

COARCTA'TION. *n. s.* [from *coarct.*]

1. Confinement; restraint to a narrow space.

The greatest winds, if they have no *coarctation*, or blow not hollow, give an interiour sound. *Bacon's Nat. History.*

2. Contraction of any space.

Straighten the artery never so much, provided the sides of it do not meet, the vessel will continue to beat below, or beyond the *coarctation.* *Ray on the Creation.*

3. Restraint of liberty.

Election is opposed not only to coaction, but also to *coarctation*, or determination to one. *Bramb. against Hobbs.*

COARSE. *adj.*

1. Not refined; not separated from impurities or baser parts.

I feel
Of what *coarse* metal ye are molded. *Shakesp. Henry VIII.*

2. Not soft or fine: used of cloath, of which the threads are large.

3. Rude; uncivil; rough of manners.

4. Gross; not delicate.

'Tis not the *coarser* tye of human law
That binds their peace. *Thomson's Spring.*

5. Inelegant; rude; unpolished.

Praise of Virgil is against myself, for presuming to copy, in my *coarse* English, his beautiful expressions. *Dryd. Æn.*

6. Unaccomplished; unfinished by art or education.

Practical rules may be useful to such as are remote from advice, and to *coarse* practitioners, which they are obliged to make use of. *Arbuthnot on Aliments.*

7. Mean; not nice; not elegant; vile.

Ill consort, and a *coarse* perfume,
Disgrace the delicacy of a feast. *Roscommon.*

A *coarse* and useless dunghill weed,
Fix'd to one spot, to rot just as it grows. *Otway's Orphan.*
From this *coarse* mixture of terrestrial parts,
Desire and fear by turns possess their hearts. *Dryden's Æn.*

CO'ARSELY. *adv.* [from *coarse.*]

1. Without fineness; without refinement.

2. Meanly; not elegantly.

John came neither eating nor drinking, but fared *coarsely* and poorly, according to the apparel he wore. *Br. Vul. Err.*

3. Rudely; not civilly.

The good cannot be too much honoured, nor the bad too *coarsely* used. *Dryden's Fables, Preface.*

4. Inelegantly.

Be pleased to accept the rudiments of Virgil's poetry, *coarsely* translated; but which yet retains some beauties of the author. *Dryden's Virgil, Dedication.*

CO'ARSENESS. *n. s.* [from *coarse.*]

1. Impurity; unrefined state.

First know the materials whereof the glass is made; then consider what the reason is of the *coarseness* or dearness. *Bacon.*

2. Roughness; want of fineness.

3. Grossness; want of delicacy.

'Tis with friends (pardon the *coarseness* of the illustration) as with dogs in couples; they should be of the same size. *L'Estrange, Fable 25.*

4. Roughness; rudeness of manners.

A base wild olive he remains;
The shrub the *coarseness* of the clown retains. *Garth's Ovid.*

5. Meanness; want of nicety.

Consider the penuriousness of the Hollanders, the *coarseness* of their food and raiment, and their little indulgences of pleasure. *Addison on the War.*

COAST. *n. s.* [*coste*, Fr. *costa*, Latin.]

1. The edge or margin of the land next the sea; the shore. It is not used for the banks of less waters.

He sees in English ships the Holland *coast.* *Dryden.*

2. It seems to be taken by *Newton* for side, like the French *coste.*

Some kind of virtue, lodged in some sides of the crystal, inclines and bends the rays towards the *coast*, of unusual refraction; otherwise the rays would not be refracted towards that *coast* rather than any other *coast*, both at their incidence and at their emergence, so as to emerge by a contrary situation of the *coast.* *Newton's Opt.*

3. *The* COAST *is clear.* A proverbial expression. The danger is over; the enemies have marched off.

Going out, and seeing that the *coast* was clear, Zelmane dismissed Musidorus. *Sidney.*

The royal spy, when now the *coast* was clear,
Sought not the garden, but retir'd unseen. *Dryden.*

To COAST. *v. n.* [from the noun.] To sail close by the coast; to sail within sight of land.

But steer my vessel with a steady hand,
And *coast* along the shore in sight of land. *Dryden's Virgil.*

The antients *coasted* only in their navigation, seldom taking the open sea. *Arbuthnot on Coins.*

To COAST. *v. a.* To sail by; to sail near to.

Nearchus, the admiral of Alexander, not knowing the compass, was fain to *coast* that shore. *Brown's Vulg. Errours.*

The greatest entertainment we found in *coasting* it, were the several prospects of woods, vineyards, meadows, and cornfields which lie on the borders of it. *Addison on Italy.*

CO'ASTER. *n. s.* [from *coast.*] He that sails timorously near the shore.

In our small skiff we must not launch too far;
We here but *coasters*, not discov'rers are. *Dryd. Tyran. Love.*

COAT. *n. s.* [*cotte*, Fr. *cotta*, Italian.]

1. The upper garment.

He was armed with a *coat* of mail, and the weight of the *coat* was five thousand shekels of brass. *1 Sam.* xvi. 5.

The *coat* of many colours they brought to their father, and said, this have we found: know now whether it be thy son's *coat* or no. *Gen.* xxxvii. 30.

2. Petticoat; the habit of a boy in his infancy; the lower part of a woman's dress.

A friend's younger son, a child in *coats*, was not easily brought to his book. *Locke.*

3. The habit or vesture, as demonstrative of the office.

For his intermeddling with arms, he is the more excuseable, because many of his *coat*, in those times, are not only martial directors, but commanders. *Howel's Vocal Forrest.*

Men of his *coat* should be minding their pray'rs,
And not among ladies, to give themselves airs. *Swift.*

4. The hair or fur of a beast; the covering of any animal.

He clad
Their nakedness with skins of beasts; or slain,
Or, as the snake, with youthful *coat* repaid;
And thought not much to clothe his enemies. *Milton.*

Give your horse some powder of brimstone in his oats, and it will make his *coat* lie fine. *Mortimer's Husbandry.*

You have given us milk
In luscious streams, and lent us your own *coat*
Against the winter's cold. *Thomson's Spring.*

2

5. Any

5. Any tegument; tunick; or covering.
The eye is defended with four *coats* or skins. *Peacham.*
The optick nerves have their medullary parts terminating in the brain, their teguments terminating in the *coats* of the eye. *Derham's Physico-Theology.*
Amber is a nodule, invested with a *coat*, called rock-amber. *Woodward on Fossils.*
6. That on which the ensigns armorial are portrayed.
The herald of love's mighty king,
In whose *coat* armour richly are display'd
All sorts of flowers the which on earth do spring. *Spenser.*
Cropp'd are the flower de-luces in your arms;
Of England's *coat* one half is cut away. *Shakesp. Hen. VI.*
At each trumpet was a banner bound,
Which, waving in the wind, display'd at large
Their master's *coat* of arms and knightly charge. *Dryden.*
To COAT. *v. a.* [from the noun.] To cover; to invest; to overspread: as, to *coat* a retort; to *coat* a ceiling.
To COAX. *v. a.* To wheedle; to flatter; to humour. A low word.
The nurse had changed her note; for she was then muzzling and *coaxing* the child; that's a good dear, says she. *L'Estrange.*
I *coax!* I wheedle! I'm above it. *Farquhar's Recr. Officer.*
COAXER. *n. s.* [from the verb.] A wheedler; a flatterer.
COB. A word often used in the composition of low terms; corrupted from cop, Sax. *kopf*, Germ. the head or top.
COB. *n. s.* A sort of sea-fowl; called also *sea-cob.* *Philips.*
CO'BALT. *n. s.* A marcasite frequent in Saxony.
Cobalt is plentifully impregnated with arsenick; contains copper and some silver. Being sublimed, the flores are of a blue colour: these German mineralists call zaffir. *Woodward.*
Cobalt is a dense, compact, and ponderous mineral, very bright and shining, and much resembling some of the antimonial ores. It is found in Germany, Saxony, Bohemia, and England; but ours is a poor kind. From *cobalt* are produced the three sorts of arsenick, white, yellow, and red; as also zaffre and smalt. *Hill on Fossils.*
To CO'BBLE. *v. a.* [*kobler*, Danish.]
1. To mend any thing coarsely: used generally of shoes.
If you be out, sir, I can mend you.—Why, sir, *cobble* you. *Shakesp. Julius Cæsar.*
They'll sit by th' fire, and presume to know
What's done i' th' capitol; making parties strong,
And feeble such as stand not in their liking,
Below their *cobbled* shoes. *Shakesp. Coriolanus.*
Many underlayers, when they could not live upon their trade, have raised themselves from *cobbling* to fluxing. *L'Estr.*
2. To do or make any thing clumsily, or unhandily.
Reject the nauseous praises of the times:
Give thy base poets back their *cobbled* rhimes. *Dryden.*
Believe not that the whole universe is mere bungling and blundering, nothing effected for any purpose or design, but all ill-favouredly *cobbled* and jumbled together. *Bentley.*
CO'BBLER. *n. s.* [from *cobble.*]
1. A mender of old shoes.
Not many years ago it happened that a *cobbler* had the casting vote for the life of a criminal. *Addison on Italy.*
2. A clumsy workman in general.
What trade are you?—
Truly, sir, in respect of a fine workman, I am but, as you would say, a *cobbler.* *Shakespeare's Julius Cæsar.*
3. In a kind of proverbial sense, any mean person.
Think you the great prerogative t' enjoy
Of doing ill, by virtue of that race;
As if what we esteem in *cobblers* base,
Would the high family of Brutus grace. *Dryd. Juv.*
CO'BIRONS. *n. s.* [*cob* and *iron.*] Irons with a knob at the upper end.
The implements of the kitchen; as spits, ranges, *cobirons*, and pots. *Bacon's Phys. Rem.*
COBI'SHOP. *n. s.* [*con* and *bishop.*] A coadjutant bishop.
Valerius, advanced in years, and a Grecian by birth, not qualified to preach in the Latin tongue, made use of Austin as a *cobishop*, for the benefit of the church of Hippo. *Ayliffe.*
CO'BNUT. *n. s.* [*cob* and *nut.*]
1. See HAZEL, of which it is a species.
2. A boy's game; the conquering nut.
CO'BSWAN. *n. s.* [*cob*, head, and *swan.*] The head or leading swan.
I'm not taken
With a *cobswan*, or a high-mounting bull,
As foolish Leda and Europa were. *Ben. Johnson's Catiline.*
CO'BWEB. *n. s.* [*kopweb*, Dutch.]
1. The web or net of a spider.
The luckless Clarion,
With violent swift flight, forth carried
Into the cursed *cobweb*, which his foe
Had framed for his final overthrow. *Spenser.*
Is supper ready, the house trimmed, rushes strewed, and *cobwebs* swept. *Shakesp. Taming of the Shrew.*
The spider went into the house of a burgher, and fell presently to her net-work of drawing *cobwebs* up and down. *L'Estrange's Fables.*
2. Any snare, or trap; implying insidiousness and weakness.
For he a rope of sand could twist,
As tough as learned Sorbonist;
And weave fine *cobwebs* fit for scull
That's empty, when the moon is full. *Hudibras, p. ii.*
Chronology at best is but a *cobweb* law, and he broke through it with his weight. *Dryden's Dedicat. ...n.*
Laws are like *cobwebs*, which may catch small flies; but let wasps and hornets break through. *Swift.*
CO'COA. *n. s.* See CACAO.
COCCI'FEROUS *adj.* [from κόκκος, and *fero*, Lat.] All plants or trees are so called that have berries. *Quincy.*
CO'CHINEAL. *n. s.* [*cochinilla*, Span. a woodlouse.]
An insect gathered upon the *opuntia*, and dried; from which a beautiful red colour is extracted. *Hill.*
CO'CHLEARY. *adj.* [from *cochlea*, Lat. a screw.] Screwform; in the form of a screw.
That at St. Dennis, near Paris, hath wreathy spires, and *cochleary* turnings about it, which agreeth with the description of the unicorn's horn in Ælian. *Brown's Vulgar Errours.*
CO'CHLEATED. *adj.* [from *cochlea*, Lat.] Of a screwed or turbinated form.
Two pieces of stone, struck forth of the cavity of the umbilici of shells, of the same sort with the foregoing: they are of a *cochleated* figure. *Woodward on Fossils.*
COCK. *n. s.* [cocc, Saxon; *coq*, French.]
1. The male to the hen; a domestick fowl, remarkable for his gallantry, pride, and courage.
Cocks have great combs and spurs; hens, little or none. *Bacon's Natural History*, N°. 85.
True *cocks* o' th' game,
That never ask for what, or whom, they fight;
But turn 'em out, and shew 'em but a foe,
Cry liberty, and that's a cause of quarrel. *Dryd. Span. Fryar.*
The careful hen
Calls all her chirping family around,
Fed and defended by the fearless *cock.* *Thomson's Spring.*
2. The male of any small birds.
He was confirmed in this by observing, that calves and philosophers, tygers and statesmen, *cock* sparrows and coquets, exactly resemble one another in the formation of the pineal gland. *Arbuth. and Pope's Mart. Scrib.*
3. The weathercock, that shews the direction of the wind by turning.
You cataracts and hurricanoes spout,
'Till you have drench'd our steeples, drown'd the *cocks!* *Shakespeare's King Lear.*
4. A spout to let out water at will, by turning the stop.
When every room
Hath blaz'd with lights, and bray'd with minstrelsy,
I have retir'd me to a wasteful *cock*,
And set mine eyes at flow. *Shakespeare's Timon.*
It were good there were a little *cock* made in the belly of the upper glass. *Bacon's Natural History*, N° 16.
Thus the small jett, which hasty hands unlock,
Spirts in the gard'ner's eyes who turns the *cock.* *Pope's Dunc.*
5. The notch of an arrow.
6. The part of the lock of a gun that strikes with the flint. [From *cocca*, Ital. the notch of an arrow. *Skinner.* Perhaps from the action, like that of a cock pecking.]
With hasty rage he snatch'd
His gunshot, that in holsters watch'd,
And bending *cock*, he levell'd full
Against th' outside of Talgol's skull. *Hudibras, p. i. cant. 2.*
A seven-shot gun carries powder and bullets for seven charges and discharges. Under the breech of the barrel is one box for the powder; a little before the lock another for the bullets; behind the *cock* a charger, which carries the powder from the box to a funnel at the further end of the lock. *Grew.*
7. A conquerour; a leader; a governing man.
Sir Andrew is grown the *cock* of the club since he left us. *Addison's Spectator*, N°. 130.
My schoolmaster call'd me a dunce and a fool;
But at cuffs I was always the *cock* of the school. *Swift.*
8. Cockcrowing; a note of the time in a morning.
We were carousing 'till the second *cock.* *Shakes. Macbeth.*
He begins at curfew, and goes 'till the first *cock.* *Shakesp.*
9. A cockboat; a small boat.
They take view of all sized *cocks*, barges, and fisherboats hovering on the coast. *Carew's Survey of Cornwal.*
The fishermen that walk upon the beach,
Appear like mice; and yond tall anchoring bark,
Diminish'd to her *cock*; her *cock*, a buoy,
Almost too small for sight. *Shakesp. King Lear.*
10. A small heap of hay. [Properly *cop.*]
As soon as the dew is off the ground spread the hay again, and turn it, that it may wither on the other side: then handle it, and, if you find it dry, make it up into *cocks.* *Mortimer.*
11. The form of a hat. [From the comb of the cock.]
You may see many a smart rhetorician turning his hat in

in his hands, moulding it into several different *cocks*. *Addison's Spectator*, Nº. 408.

12. The style or gnomon of a dial. *Chambers.*

13. The needle of a balance.

14. *Cock on the Hoop.* Triumphant; exulting.

Now I am a frisker, all men on me look;
What should I do but set *cock on the hoop?* *Camden's Remains.*

You'll make a mutiny among my guests!
You will set *cock a hoop!* *Shakesp. Romeo and Juliet.*

For Hudibras, who thought h' had won
The field, as certain as a gun,
And having routed the whole troop,
With victory was *cock a hoop.* *Hudibras, p.* i. *cant.* 3.

To Cock. *v a.* [from the noun.]

1. To set erect; to hold bolt upright, as a cock holds his head.

This is that muscle which performs the motion so often mentioned by the Latin poets, when they talk of a man's *cocking* his nose, or playing the rhinoceros. *Addison's Spect.*

Our Lightfoot barks, and *cocks* his ears;
O'er yonder stile see Lubberkin appears. *Gay's Pastorals.*

Dick would *cock* his nose in scorn,
But Tom was kind and loving. *Swift.*

2. To set up the hat with an air of petulance and pertness.

Dick, who thus long had passive sat,
Here strok'd his chin and *cock'd* his hat. *Prior.*

An alert young fellow *cock'd* his hat upon a friend of his who entered. *Addison's Spectator*, Nº. 403.

3. To mould the form of the hat.

4. To fix the cock of a gun ready for a discharge.

Some of them holding up their pistols *cocked*, near the door of the house, which they kept open. *Dryd. Dedicat. Æn.*

5. To raise hay in small heaps.

Sike mirth in May is meetest for to make,
Or summer shade, under the *cocked* hay. *Spenser's Pastorals.*

To Cock. *v. n.*

1. To strut; to hold up the head, and look big, or menacing, or pert.

Sir Fopling is a fool so nicely writ,
The ladies would mistake him for a wit;
And when he sings, talks loud, and *cocks*, would cry,
I vow, methinks, he's pretty company. *Dryden.*

Every one *cocks* and struts upon it, and pretends to overlook us. *Addison's Guardian*, Nº. 108.

2. To train or use fighting cocks.

Cries out 'gainst *cocking*, since he cannot bet. *B. Johnson.*

Cock, in composition, signifies small or little.

Cocka'de. *n. s.* [from *cock.*] A ribband worn in the hat.

A Co'ckatrice. *n. s.* [from *cock* and ατꝛεꝛ, Sax, a serpent.] A serpent supposed to rise from a cock's egg.

They will kill one another by the look, like *cockatrices.* *Shakespeare's Twelfth Night.*

This was the end of this little *cockatrice* of a king, that was able to destroy those that did not espy him first. *Bacon.*

This *cockatrice* is soonest crushed in the shell; but, if it grows, it turns to a serpent and a dragon. *Taylor.*

My wife! 'tis she, the very *cockatrice!* *Congr. Old Batchelor.*

Co'ckboat. *n. s.* [*cock* and *boat.*] A small boat belonging to a ship.

That invincible armada, which having not so much as fired a cottage of ours at land, nor taking a *cockboat* of ours at sea, wandered through the wilderness of the northern seas. *Bacon on the War with Spain.*

Did they, indeed, think it less dishonour to God to be like a brute, or a plant, or a *cockboat*, than to be like a man? *Stillingfleet's Defence of Disc. on Rom. Idolatry.*

Co'ckbroath. *n. s.* Broath made by boiling a cock.

Diet upon spoon-meats; as veal or *cockbroaths*, prepared with French barley. *Harvey on Consumptions.*

Cockcro'wing. *n. s.* [*cock* and *crow.*] The time at which cocks crow; the morning.

Ye know not when the master of the house cometh; at even, or at midnight, or at the *cockcrowing*, or in the morning. *Mar.* xiii. 35.

To Co'cker. *v. a.* [*coqueliner*, French.] To cade; to fondle; to indulge.

Most children's constitutions are spoiled by *cockering* and tenderness. *Locke on Education, sect.* 4.

He that will give his son sugar-plums to make him learn, does but authorize his love of pleasure, and *cocker* up that propensity which he ought to subdue. *Locke on Education, s.* 52.

Bred a fondling and an heiress;
Cocker'd by the servants round,
Was too good to touch the ground. *Swift.*

Co'cker. *n. s.* [from *cock.*] One who follows the sport of cockfighting.

Co'ckerel. *n. s.* [from *cock.*] A young cock.

Which of them first begins to crow?—
The old cock?—The *cockerel.* *Shakespeare's Tempest.*

What wilt thou be, young *cockerel*, when thy spurs
Are grown to sharpness? *Dryden's Cleomenes.*

Co'cket. *n. s.* [Of uncertain derivation.]

A seal belonging to the king's customhouse: likewise a scroll of parchment, sealed and delivered by the officers of the customhouse to merchants, as a warrant that their merchandize is entered. *Cowel.*

The greatest profit did arise by the *cocket* of hides; for wool and woolfells were ever of little value in this kingdom. *Davies.*

Co'ckfight. *n. s.* [*cock* and *fight.*] A battle or match of cocks.

In *cockfights*, to make one cock more hardy, and the other more cowardly. *Bacon's Natural History*, Nº. 990.

At the seasons of football and *cockfighting*, these little republicks reassume their national hatred to each other. *Addison.*

Co'ckhorse. [*cock* and *horse.*] On horseback; triumphant; exulting.

Alma, they strenuously maintain,
Sits *cockhorse* on her throne the brain. *Prior.*

CO'CKLE. *n. s.* [*coquille*, French.] A small testaceous fish.

It is a *cockle*, or a walnut-shell. *Shak. Tam. of Shrew.*

We may, I think, from the make of an oyster, or *cockle*, reasonably conclude, that it has not so many, nor so quick senses, as a man. *Locke.*

Three common *cockle* shells, out of gravel pits. *Woodward.*

Cockle-stairs. *n. s.* Winding or spiral stairs. *Chambers.*

Co'ckle. *n. s.* [coccel, Saxon.] A weed that grows in corn. The same with corn-rose; a species of Poppy.

In soothing them we nourish, 'gainst our senate,
The *cockle* of rebellion, insolence, sedition. *Shakespeare.*

Good seed degenerates, and oft' obeys
The soil's disease, and into *cockle* strays. *Donne.*

To Co'ckle. *v. a.* [from *cockle.*] To contract into wrinkles like the shell of a cockle.

Show'rs soon drench the camblet's *cockled* grain. *Gay.*

Co'ckled. *adj.* [from *cockle.*] Shelled; or perhaps cochleate, turbinated.

Love's feeling is more soft and sensible,
Than are the tender horns of *cockled* snails. *Shakespeare.*

Co'ckloft. *n. s.* [*cock* and *loft.*] The room over the garret, in which fowls are supposed to roost.

If the lowest floors already burn,
Cocklofts and garrets soon will take their turn. *Dryd. Juv.*

My garrets, or rather my *cocklofts* indeed, are very indifferently furnished; but they are rooms to lay lumber in. *Swift.*

Co'ckmaster. *n. s.* [*cock* and *master.*] One that breeds game cocks.

A *cockmaster* bought a patridge, and turned it among the fighting cocks. *L'Estrange.*

Co'ckmatch. *n. s.* [*cock* and *match.*] Cockfight for a prize.

At the same time that the heads of parties preserve towards one another an outward shew of good breeding, their tools will not so much as mingle together at a *cockmatch.* *Addison's Spectator*, Nº. 126.

Though quail-fighting is what is most taken notice of, they had doubtless *cockmatches* also. *Arbuth. and Pope's Mart. Scrib.*

Co'ckney. *n. s.* [A word of which the original is much controverted. The French use an expression, *Païs de cocaigne*, for a country of dainties.

Paris est pour un riche un Païs de cocaigne. *Boileau.*

Of this word they are not able to settle the original. It appears, whatever was its first ground, to be very ancient, being mentioned in an old Normanno-Saxon poem:

Far in see by west Spayng,
Is a lond ihote cocayng.

On which Dr. *Hickes* has this remark:

Nunc *coquin*, *coquine.* Quæ olim apud Gallas otio, gulæ & ventri deditos, *ignavum*, *ignavam*, *desidiosum*, *desidiosam*, *segnem* significabant. Hinc *urbanos* utpote à rusticis laboribus ad vitam sedentariam, & quasi desidiosam avocatos pagani nostri olim *cokaignes*, quod nunc scribitur *cockneys*, vocabant. Et poëta hic noster in monachos & moniales, ut segne genus hominum, qui desidiæ dediti, ventri indulgebant, & coquinæ amatores erant, malevolentissime invehitur, monasteria & monasticam vitam in descriptione terræ *cockaineæ*, parabolice perstringens.]

1. A native of London, by way of contempt.

So the *cockney* did to the eels, when she put them i' th' pasty alive. *Shakesp. King Lear.*

For who is such a *cockney* in his heart,
Proud of the plenty of the southern part,
To scorn that union, by which we may
Boast 'twas his countryman that writ this play. *Dorset.*

The *cockney*, travelling into the country, is surprized at many common practices of rural affairs. *Watts.*

2. Any effeminate, ignorant, low, mean, despicable citizen.

I am afraid this great lubber, the world, will prove a *cockney.* *Shakesp. Twelfth Night.*

Co'ckpit. *n. s.* [*cock* and *pit.*]

1. The area where cocks fight.

Can this *cockpit* hold
The vasty field of France? *Shakesp. Henry V.*

And now have I gained the *cockpit* of the western world, and academy of arms, for many years. *Howel's Vocal Forrest.*

2. A place on the lower deck of a man of war, where are subdivisions for the purser, the surgeon, and his mates. *Harris.*

Co'ckscomb. *n. ſ.* [*cock* and *comb.*] A plant. The ſame with Lonsewort, which ſee.

Co'ckshead. *n. ſ.* A plant, named alſo *ſainfoin.*

It hath a papilionaceous flower, out of whoſe empalement riſes the pointal; which afterwards becomes a creſted pod, ſometimes rough and full of ſeeds, ſhaped like a kidney. The flowers grow in a thick ſpike. It is an abiding plant, and eſteemed one of the beſt ſorts of fodder for cattle. *Miller.*

Co'ckshut. *n. ſ.* [from *cock* and *ſhut.*] The cloſe of the evening, at which time poultry go to rooſt.

Surrey and himſelf,
Much about *cockſhut* time, from troop to troop,
Went through the army. *Shakeſp. Richard* III.

Co'ckspur. *n. ſ.* [*cock* and *ſpur.*] Virginian hawthorn. A ſpecies of Medlar, which ſee.

Its large and beautiful flowers are produced in great bunches at the extremities of the branches; and its fruit, which is ripe in autumn, makes a fine appearance, growing in great cluſters; and is eſteemed good food for deer. *Miller.*

Co'cksure. [from *cock* and *ſure.*] Confidently certain; without fear or diffidence. A word of contempt.

We ſteal, as in a caſtle, *cockſure. Shakeſp. Henry* VI. *p.* i.

I thought myſelf *cockſure* of his horſe, which he readily promiſed me. *Pope's Letters.*

Cockswain. *n. ſ.* [coʒʒꝑaine, Saxon.] The officer who has the command of the cockboat. Corruptly Coxon.

Cockweed. *n. ſ.* [from *cock* and *weed.*] The name of a plant, called alſo Dittander, or *Pepperwort*, which ſee.

Cocoa. *n. ſ.* [*cacaotal*, Span. and therefore more properly written *cacao.*]

A ſpecies of palm-tree, cultivated in moſt of the inhabited parts of the Eaſt and Weſt Indies; but thought a native of the Maldives. It is one of the moſt uſeful trees to the inhabitants of America. The bark of the nut is made into cordage, and the ſhell into drinking bowls. The kernel of the nut affords them a wholeſome food, and the milk contained in the ſhell a cooling liquor. The leaves of the trees are uſed for thatching their houſes, and are alſo wrought into baſkets, and moſt other things that are made of oſiers in Europe. *Miller.*

The *cacao* or chocolate nut is a fruit of an oblong figure, much reſembling a large olive in ſize and ſhape. It is compoſed of a thin but hard and woody coat or ſkin, of a dark blackiſh colour; and of a dry kernel, filling up its whole cavity, fleſhy, dry, firm, and fattiſh to the touch, of a duſky colour, an agreeable ſmell, and a pleaſant and peculiar taſte. It was unknown to us 'till the diſcovery of America, where the natives not only drank the liquor made from the nuts, in the manner we do chocolate, but alſo uſed them as money. The tree is not very tall, but grows regularly, and is of a beautiful form, eſpecially when loaded with its fruit. Its ſtem is of the thickneſs of a man's leg, and but a few feet in height; its bark rough, and full of tubercles; and its leaves ſix or eight inches long, half as much in breadth, and pointed at the ends. The flowers ſtand on the branches, and even on the trunk of the tree, in cluſters, each having its own pedicle, an inch and ſometimes leſs in length: they are ſmall, of a yellowiſh colour, and are ſucceeded by the fruit, which is large and oblong, reſembling a cucumber, five, ſix, or eight inches in length, and three or four in thickneſs; and, when fully ripe, it is of a purple colour. Within the cavity of this fruit are lodged the *cocoa* nuts, uſually about thirty in number. This tree flowers twice or three times in the year, and ripens as many ſeries of fruits. *Hill's Hiſtory of the Mat. Medica.*

Amid' thoſe orchards of the ſun,
Give me to drain the *cocoa*'s milky bowl,
And from the palm to draw its freſhening wine. *Thomſon.*

Co'ctile. *adj.* [*coctilis*, Lat.] Made by baking, as a brick.

Co'ction. *n. ſ.* [*coctio*, Lat.] The act of boiling.

The diſeaſe is ſometimes attended with expectoration from the lungs, and that is taken off by a *coction* and reſolution of the feveriſh matter, or terminates in ſuppurations or a gangrene. *Arbuthnot on Diet.*

COD. } *n. ſ.* A ſea fiſh.
Co'dfish. }

COD. *n. ſ.* [coďďe, Saxon.] Any caſe or huſk in which ſeeds are lodged.

Thy corn thou there may'ſt ſafely ſow,
Where in full *cods* laſt year rich peaſe did grow. *May's Virg.*

They let peaſe lie in ſmall heaps as they are reaped, 'till they find the hawm and *cod* dry. *Motimer's Husbandry.*

To Cod. *v. n.* [from the noun.] To incloſe in a cod.

All *codded* grain being a deſtroyer of weeds, an improver of land, and a preparer of it for other crops. *Mort. Husband.*

Co'dders. *n. ſ.* [from *cod.*] Gatherers of peaſe. *Dict.*

Code. *n. ſ.* [*codex*, Latin.]

1. A book.
2. A book of the civil law.

We find in the Theodoſian and Juſtinian *code* the intereſt of trade very well provided for. *Arbuthnot on Coins.*

Indentures, cov'nants, articles they draw,
Large as the fields themſelves; and larger far
Than civil *codes* with all their gloſſes are. *Pope's Sat.*

Co'dicil. *n. ſ.* [*codicillus*, Latin.] An appendage to a will.

The man ſuſpects his lady's crying,
Was but to gain him to appoint her,
By *codicil*, a larger jointure. *Prior.*

Codi'lle. *n. ſ.* [*codille*, Fr. *codillo*, Span.] A term at ombre, when the game is won againſt the player.

She ſees, and trembles at th' approaching ill,
Juſt in the jaws of ruin, and *codille. Pope's Rape of the Lock.*

To CO'DLE. *v. a.* [*coquo coctulo*, Lat. *Skinner.*] To parboil; to ſoften by the heat of water.

Co'dling. *n. ſ.* [from *To codle.*] An apple generally codled, to be mixed with milk.

In July come gilliflowers of all varieties, early pears and plums in fruit, gennitings and *codlings. Bacon, Eſſay* 47.

Their entertainment at the height,
In cream and *codlings* rev'ling with delight. *King's Cookery.*

He let it lie all winter in a gravel walk, ſouth of a *codling* hedge. *Mortimer's Husbandry.*

A *codling*, e're it went his lip in,
Wou'd ſtrait become a golden pippin. *Swift.*

Coe'fficacy. *n. ſ.* [*con* and *efficacia*, Lat.] The power of ſeveral things acting together to produce an effect.

We cannot in general infer the efficacy of thoſe ſtars, or *coefficacy* particular in medications. *Brown's Vulgar Errours.*

Coeffi'ciency. *n. ſ.* [*con* and *efficio*, Latin.] Cooperation; the ſtate of acting together to ſome ſingle end.

The managing and carrying on of this work, by the ſpirits inſtrumental *coefficiency*, requires, that they be kept together, without diſtinction or diſſipation. *Glanville's Sceps. Scient.*

Coeffi'cient. *n. ſ.* [*con* and *efficiens*, Latin.]

1. That which unites its action with the action of another.
2. In algebra.

Such numbers, or given quantities, that are put before letters, or unknown quantities, into which letters they are ſuppoſed to be multiplied, and ſo do make a rectangle, or product with the letters; as $4a$, bx, cxx; where 4 is the coefficient of $4a$; b of bx, and c of cxx. *Chambers.*

3. In fluxions.

The *coefficient* of any generating term (in fluxions) is the quantity ariſing by the diviſion of that term, by the generated quantity. *Chambers.*

Co'eliack *Paſſion.* A diarrhæa, or flux, that ariſes from the indigeſtion or putrefaction of food in the ſtomach and bowels, whereby the aliment comes away little altered from what it was when eaten, or changed like corrupted ſtinking fleſh. *Quincy.*

Coe'mption. *n. ſ.* [*coemptio*, Lat.] The act of buying up the whole quantity of any thing.

Monopolies and *coemption* of wares for reſale, where they are not reſtrained, are great means to enrich. *Bacon's Eſſays.*

Coe'qual. *adj.* [from *con* and *equalis*, Lat.] Equal; being in the ſame ſtate with another.

Henry the fifth did ſometime prophecy,
If once he came to be a cardinal,
He'll make his cap *coequal* with the crown. *Shak. Hen.* VI.

Coequa'lity. *n. ſ.* [from *coequal.*] The ſtate of being equal.

To COE'RCE. *v. a.* [*coerceo*, Latin.] To reſtrain; to keep in order by force.

Puniſhments are manifold, that they may *coerce* this profligate ſort. *Ayliffe's Parergon.*

Coe'rcible. *adj.* [from *coerce.*]

1. That may be reſtrained.
2. That ought to be reſtrained.

Coe'rcion. *n. ſ.* [from *coerce.*] Penal reſtraint; check.

The *coercion* or execution of the ſentence in eccleſiaſtical courts, is only by excommunication of the perſon contumacious. *Hale's Hiſtory of the Common Law.*

Government has *coercion* and animadverſion upon ſuch as neglect their duty; without which coercive power, all government is toothleſs and precarious. *South's Sermons.*

Coe'rcive. *adj.* [from *coerce.*]

1. That which has the power of laying reſtraint.

All things on the ſurface ſpread, are bound
By their *coercive* vigour to the ground! *Blackmore.*

2. That which has the authority of reſtraining by puniſhment.

For miniſters to ſeek that themſelves might have *coercive* power over the church, would have been hardly conſtrued. *Hooker, Preface.*

The virtues of a magiſtrate or general, or a king, are prudence, counſel, active fortitude, *coercive* power, awful command, and the exerciſe of magnanimity, as well as juſtice. *Dryden's Juv. Dedication.*

Coesse'ntial. *adj.* [*con* and *eſſentia*, Latin.] Participating of the ſame eſſence.

The Lord our God is but one God, in which indiviſible unity we adore the father, as being altogether of himſelf; we glorify that conſubſtantial word which is the ſon; we bleſs and magnify that *coeſſential* ſpirit eternally proceeding from both, which is the holy ghoſt. *Hooker, b* v. *ſ.* 51.

Coessentia'lity. *n. s.* [from *coessential.*] Participation of the same essence.

Coeta'neous. *adj.* [*con* and *ætas*, Latin.]

1. Of the same age with another. Sometimes with *to.*

Eve was old as Adam, and Cain their son *coetaneous unto* both. *Brown's Vulgar Errours, b.* i. *c.* 3.

Every fault hath some penal effects, *coetaneous to* the act. *Government of the Tongue, s.* 6.

2. Sometimes *with.*

Through the body every member sustains another; and all are *coetaneous*, because none can subsist alone. *Bentley's Serm.*

Coete'rnal. *adj.* [*con* and *æternus*, Lat.] Equally eternal with another.

Or of the eternal *coeternal* beam! *Milton's Paradise Lost.*

Coete'rnally. *adv.* [from *coeternal.*] In a state of equal eternity with another.

Arius had already dishonoured his *coeternally* begotten son. *Hooker, b.* v. *s.* 52.

Coete'rnity. *n. s.* [from *coeternal.*] Having existence from eternity equal with another eternal being.

The eternity of the son's generation, and his *coeternity* and consubstantiality with the father, when he came down from heaven, and was incarnate. *Hammond's Fund.*

COE'VAL. *adj.* [*coævus*, Latin.]

1. Of the same age.

Even his teeth and white, like a young flock,
Coeval, and new shorn, from the clear brook
Recent. *Prior.*

2. Of the same age with another, followed by *with.*

This religion cannot pretend to be *coeval with* mankind. *Hale's Origin of Mankind.*

The monthly revolutions of the moon, or the diurnal of the earth upon its own axis, by the very hypothesis are *coequal with* the former. *Bentley's Sermons.*

Silence! *coeval with* eternity;
Thou wert, e're nature first began to be:
'Twas one vast nothing all, and all slept fast in thee. *Pope.*

3. Sometimes by *to.*

Although we had no monuments of religion ancienter than idolatry, we have no reason to conclude, that idolatrous religion was *coeval to* mankind. *Hale's Origin of Mankind.*

Coe'val. *n. s.* [from the adjective.] A contemporary.

As it were not enough to have outdone all your *coevals* in wit, you will excel them in good nature. *Pope.*

Coe'vous. *adj.* [*coævus*, Lat.] Of the same age.

Then it should not have been the first, as supposing some other thing *coevous* to it. *South's Sermons.*

To Coexi'st. *v. n.* [*con* and *existo*, Latin.]

1. To exist at the same time.

The three stars that *coexist* in heavenly constellations, are a multitude of stars. *Hale's Origin of Mankind.*

Of substances no one has any clear idea, farther than of certain simple ideas *coexisting* together. *Locke.*

2. Followed by *with.*

It is sufficient that we have the idea of the length of any regular periodical appearances, which we can in our minds apply to duration, *with* which the motion or appearance never *coexisted.* *Locke.*

Coexi'stence. *n. s.* [from *coexist.*]

1. Having existence at the same time with another.

The measuring of any duration, by some motion, depends not on the real *coexistence* of that thing to that motion, or any other periods of revolution. *Locke.*

2. More commonly followed by *with.*

We can demonstrate the being of God's eternal ideas, and their *coexistence with* him. *Grew's Cosmol. b.* ii. *c.* 4. *s.* 24.

Coexi'stent. *adj.* [from *coexist.*]

1. Having existence at the same time with another, with *to.*

To the measuring the duration of any thing by time, it is not requisite that that thing should be *coexistent to* the motion we measure by, or any other periodical revolution. *Locke.*

2. Sometimes *with.*

This proves no antecedent necessity, but *coexistent with* the act. *Bramb. Answer to Hobbs.*

Time is taken for so much of infinite duration as is *coexistent with* the motions of the great bodies of the universe. *Locke's Works.*

All that one point is either future or past, and no parts are *coexistent* or contemporary *with* it. *Bentley's Sermons.*

To Coexte'nd. *v. a.* [*con* and *extendo*, Lat.] To extend to the same space or duration with another.

Every motion is, in some sort, *coextended* with the body moved. *Grew's Cosmol. b.* ii. *c.* 1. *s.* 2.

Coexte'nsion. *n. s.* [from *coextend.*] The act or state of extending to the same space or duration with another.

And though it be a spirit, yet I find it is no inconvenience to have some analogy, at least of *coextension*, with my body. *Hale's Origin of Mankind.*

CO'FFEE. *n. s.* [It is originally Arabick, pronounced *caheu* by the Turks, and *cahuah* by the Arabs.] The tree is a species of Arabick Jessamine, which see.

It is found to succeed as well in the Caribbee islands as in their native place of growth: but whether the coffee produced in the West Indies will prove as good as that from Mocha in Arabia Felix, time will discover. The berry brought from the Levant is most esteemed; and the berry, when ripe, is found as hard as horn. *Miller.*

Coffee also denotes a drink prepared from the berries, very familiar in Europe for these eighty years, and among the Turks for one hundred and fifty. Some refer the invention of coffee to the Persians; from whom it was learned, in the fifteenth century, by a mufti of Aden, a city near the mouth of the Red Sea, where it soon came in vogue, and passed from thence to Mecca, and from Arabia Felix to Cairo. From Egypt the use of coffee advanced to Syria and Constantinople. Thevenot, the traveller, was the first who brought it into France; and a Greek servant, called Pasqua, brought into England by Mr. Daniel Edwards, a Turky merchant, in 1652, to make his coffee, first set up the profession of coffeeman, and introduced the drink among us; though some say Dr. Harvey had used it before. *Chambers.*

They have in Turky a drink called *coffee*, made of a berry of the same name, as black as soot, and of a strong scent, but not aromatical; which they take, beaten into powder, in water, as hot as they can drink it. This drink comforteth the brain and heart, and helpeth digestion. *Bacon.*

To part her time 'twixt reading and bohea,
Or o'er cold *coffee* trifle with the spoon. *Pope.*

Co'ffeehouse. *n. s.* [*coffee* and *house.*] A house of entertainment where coffee is sold, and the guests are supplied with news papers.

At ten, from *coffeehouse* or play,
Returning, finishes the day. *Prior.*

It is a point they do not concern themselves about, farther than perhaps as a subject in a *coffeehouse.* *Swift.*

Co'ffeeman. *n. s.* [*coffee* and *man.*] One that keeps a coffeehouse.

Consider your enemies the Lacedemonians; did ever you hear that they preferred a *coffeeman* to Agesilaus? *Addison.*

Co'ffeepot. *n. s.* [*coffee* and *pot.*] The covered pot in which coffee is boiled.

CO'FFER. *n. s.* [coffne, Saxon.]

1. A chest generally for keeping money.

Two iron *coffers* hung on either side,
With precious metal full as they could hold. *Fairy Queen.*

The lining of his *coffers* shall make coats
To deck our soldiers for these Irish wars. *Shakesp. Rich.* II.

If you destroy your governour that is wealthy, you must chuse another, who will fill his *coffers* out of what is left. *L'Estr.*

2. Treasure.

He would discharge it without any burthen to the queen's *coffers*, for honour sake. *Bacon's Advice to Villiers.*

3. [In architecture.] A square depressure in each interval between the modillions of the Corinthian cornice, usually filled with some enrichment. *Chambers.*

4. [In fortification.] A hollow lodgment across a dry moat, from six to seven foot deep, and from sixteen to eighteen broad; the upper part being made of pieces of timber, raised two foot above the level of the moat; which little elevation has hurdles laden with earth for its covering, and serves as a parapet with embrasures. *Chambers.*

To Co'ffer. *v. a.* [from the noun.] To treasure up in chests.

Treasure, as a war might draw forth, so a peace succeeding might *coffer* up. *Bacon's Henry* VII.

Co'fferer *of the King's Houshold. n. s.* A principal officer of his majesty's court, next under the comptroller, that, in the comptinghouse and elsewhere, hath a special oversight of other officers of the houshold, for their good demeanour in their offices. *Cowel.*

CO'FFIN. *n. s.* [*cofin*, French.]

1. The box or chest in which dead bodies are put into the ground. It is used both of wood and other matter.

He went as if he had been the *coffin* that carried himself to his sepulchre. *Sidney, b.* ii.

Not a flower sweet
On my black *coffin* let there be strown. *Sh. Twelfth Night.*

One fate they have,
The ship their *coffin*, and the sea their grave. *Waller.*

The joiner is fitting screws to your *coffin.* *Swift.*

2. A mould of paste for a pye.

3. A paper case, in form of a cone, used by grocers.

4. In farriery.

Coffin *of a horse*, is the whole hoof of the foot above the coronet, including the *coffin* bone. The *coffin* bone is a small spongy bone, inclosed in the midst of the hoof, and possessing the whole form of the foot. *Farrier's Dict.*

To Co'ffin. *v. a.* [from the noun.] To inclose in a coffin.

Would'st thou have laugh'd, had I come *coffin'd* home,
That weep'st to see me triumph? *Shakesp. Coriolanus.*

Let me lie
In prison, and here be *coffin'd*, when I die. *Donne.*

Co'ffinmaker. *n. s.* [*coffin* and *maker.*] One whose trade is to make coffins.

Where will be your sextons, *coffinmakers* and plummers? *Tatl.*

To COG. *v. a.* [A word of uncertain original, derived by *Skinner* from *coqueliner*, French.]

1. To flatter; to wheedle; to sooth by adulatory speeches.

I'll mountebank their loves,
Cog their hearts from them, and come home belov'd
Of all the trades in Rome. *Shakesp. Coriolanus.*

2. To obtrude by falsehood.

The outcry is, that I abuse his demonstration by a falsification, by *cogging* in the word. *Tillotson, Preface.*

I have *cogged* in the word to serve my turn. *Stillingfleet.*

Fustian tragedies, or insipid comedies, have, by concerted applauses, been *cogged* upon the town for masterpieces. *Dennis.*

3. *To* Cog *a die.* To secure it, so as to direct its fall: to falsify.

But then my study was to *cog* the dice,
And dext'rously to throw the lucky sice. *Dryden's Pers. Sat.*

For guineas in other men's breeches,
Your gamesters will palm and will *cog*. *Swift.*

Ye gallants of Newgate, whose fingers are nice
In diving in pockets, or *cogging* of dice. *Swift.*

To Cog. *v. n.* To lye; to wheedle.

Mrs. Ford, I cannot *cog*; I cannot prate, Mrs. Ford: now shall I sin in my wish. *Shakesp. Merry Wives of Windsor.*

COG. *n. s.* The tooth of a wheel, by which it acts upon another wheel.

To Cog. *v. a.* [from the noun.] To fix cogs in a wheel.

Co'gency. *n. s.* [from *cogent.*] Force; strength; power of compelling; conviction.

Maxims and axioms, principles of science, because they are self-evident, have been supposed innate; although nobody ever shewed the foundation of their clearness and *cogency*. *Locke.*

CO'GENT. *adj.* [*cogens*, Latin.] Forcible; resistless; convincing; powerful; having the power to compel conviction.

Such is the *cogent* force of nature. *Prior.*

They have contrived methods of deceit, one repugnant to another, to evade, if possible, this most *cogent* proof of a Deity. *Bentley.*

Co'gently. *adv.* [from *cogent.*] With resistless force; forcibly; so as to force conviction.

They forbid us to hearken to those proofs, as being weak or fallacious, which our own existence, and the sensible parts of the universe, offer so clearly and *cogently* to our thoughts. *Locke.*

Co'gger. *n. s.* [from *To cog.*] A flatterer; a wheedler.

Co'gglestone. *n. s.* [*cuogolo*, Ital.] A little stone; a small pebble. *Skinner.*

Co'gitable. *adj.* [from *cogito*, Lat.] That which may be thought on; what may be the subject of thought.

To CO'GITATE. *v. n.* [*cogito*, Lat.] To think. *Dict.*

Cogita'tion. *n. s.* [*cogitatio*, Latin.]

1. Thought; the act of thinking.

Having their *cogitations* darkened, and being strangers from the life of God, from the ignorance which is in them. *Hooker.*

A picture puts me in mind of a friend: the intention of the mind in seeing, is carried to the object represented, which is no more than simple *cogitation*, or apprehension of the person. *Stillingfleet's Defence of Disc. on Rom. Idol.*

This Descartes proves, that brutes have no *cogitation*, because they could never be brought to signify their thoughts by any artificial signs. *Ray on the Creation.*

These powers of *cogitation*, and volition and sensation, are neither inherent in matter as such, nor acquirable to matter by any motion and modification of it. *Bentley.*

2. Purpose; reflection previous to action.

The king, perceiving that his desires were intemperate, and his *cogitations* vast and irregular, began not to brook him well. *Bacon's Henry VII.*

3. Meditation.

On some great charge employ'd
He seem'd, or fixt in *cogitation* deep. *Milt. Paradise Lost.*

Co'gitative. *adj.* [from *cogito*, Latin.]

1. Having the power of thought and reflection.

If these powers of cogitation and sensation are neither inherent in matter, nor acquirable to matter, they proceed from some *cogitative* substance, which we call spirit and soul. *Bentley.*

2. Given to thought and deep meditation.

The earl had the closer and more reserved countenance, being by nature more *cogitative*. *Wotton.*

Cogna'tion. *n. s.* [*cognatio*, Latin.]

1. Kindred; descent from the same original.

Two vices I shall mention, as being of near *cognation* to ingratitude, pride and hard-heartedness, or want of compassion. *South's Sermons.*

Let the criticks tell me what certain sense they could put upon either of these four words, by their mere *cognation* with each other. *Watts's Improvement of the Mind.*

2. Relation; participation of the same nature.

He induceth us to ascribe effects unto causes of no *cognation*. *Brown's Vulgar Errours, b.* i. *c.* 11.

Cognise'e. *n. s.* [In law.] He to whom a fine in lands or tenements is acknowledged. *Cowel.*

Co'gnisour. *n. s.* [In law.] Is he that passeth or acknowledgeth a fine in lands or tenements to another. *Cowel.*

COGNI'TION. *n. s.* [*cognitio*, Latin.] Knowledge; complete conviction.

I will not be myself nor have *cognition*
Of what I feel: I am all patience. *Sh. Troil. and Cressida.*

God, as he created all things, so is he beyond and in them all, not only in power, as under his subjection, or in his presence, as in his *cognition*; but in their very essence, as in the soul of their casualties. *Brown's Vulgar Errours, b.* i. *c.* 2.

Co'gnitive. *adj.* [from *cognitus*, Latin.] Having the power of knowing.

Unless the understanding employ and exercise its *cognitive* or apprehensive power about these terms, there can be no actual apprehension of them. *South's Sermons.*

Co'gnizable. *adj.* [*cognoisable*, French.]

1. That falls under judicial notice.

2. Proper to be tried, judged, or examined.

Some are merely of ecclesiastical cognizance, others of a mixed nature, such as are *cognizable* both in the ecclesiastical and secular courts. *Ayliffe's Parergon.*

Co'gnizance. *n. s.* [*connoisance*, French.]

1. Judicial notice; trial; judicial authority.

It is worth the while, however, to consider how we may discountenance and prevent those evils which the law can take no *cognizance* of. *L'Estrange.*

Happiness or misery, in converse with others, depends upon things which human laws can take no *cognizance* of. *South.*

The moral crime is completed, and there are only circumstances wanting to work it up for the *cognizance* of the law. *Addison's Freeholder*, N°. 6.

2. A badge, by which any one is known.

And at the king's going away the earl's servants stood, in a seemly manner, in their livery coats, with *cognizances*, ranged on both sides, and made the king a bow. *Bacon's Henry VII.*

These were the proper *cognizances* and coat-arms of the tribes. *Brown's Vulgar Errours, b.* v. *c.* 10.

COGNO'MINAL. *adj.* [*cognomen*, Lat.] Having the same name.

Nor do those animals more resemble the creatures on earth, than they on earth the constellations which pass under animal names in heaven; nor the dogfish at sea much more make out the dog of the land, than his *cognominal* or namesake in the heavens. *Brown's Vulgar Errours, b.* iii. *c.* 24.

Cognomina'tion. *n. s.* [*cognomen*, Latin.]

1. A surname; the name of a family.

2. A name added from any accident or quality.

Pompey deserved the name great: Alexander, of the same *cognomination*, was generalissimo of Greece. *Brown's Vul. Err.*

COGNO'SCENCE. *n. s.* [*cognosco*, Latin.] Knowledge; the state or act of knowing. *Dict.*

Cogno'scible. *adj.* [*cognosco*, Latin.] That may be known; being the object of knowledge.

The same that is said for the redundance of matters intelligible and *cognoscible* in things natural, may be applied to things artificial. *Hale's Origin of Mankind.*

To COHA'BIT. *v. n.* [*cohabito*, Latin.]

1. To dwell with another in the same place.

The victorious Philistines were worsted by the captivated ark, which foraged their country more than a conquering army: they were not able to *cohabit* with that holy thing. *South's Sermons.*

2. To live together as husband and wife.

He knew her not to be his own wife, and yet had a design to *cohabit* with her as such. *Fiddes's Sermons.*

Coha'bitant. *n. s.* [from *cohabit.*] An inhabitant of the same place.

The oppressed Indians protest against that heaven where the Spaniards are to be their *cohabitants*. *Decay of Piety.*

Cohabita'tion. *n. s.* [from *cohabit.*]

1. The act or state of inhabiting the same place with another.

2. The state of living together as married persons.

Which defect, though it could not evacuate a marriage after *cohabitation*, and actual consummation, yet it was enough to make void a contract. *Bacon's Henry VII.*

Monsieur Brumars, at one hundred and two years, died for love of his wife, who was ninety-two at her death, after seventy years *cohabitation*. *Tatler*, N°. 56.

Cohe'ir. *n. s.* [*cohæres*, Lat.] One of several among whom an inheritance is divided.

Married persons, and widows and virgins, are all *coheirs* in the inheritance of Jesus, if they live within the laws of their estate. *Taylor's Holy Living.*

Cohe'iress. *n. s.* [from *coheir.*] A woman who has an equal share of an inheritance with other women.

To COHE'RE. *v. n.* [*cohæreo*, Latin.]

1. To stick together; to hold fast one to another, as parts of the same body.

Two pieces of marble, having their surface exactly plain, polite, and applied to each other in such a manner as to intercept the air, do *cohere* firmly together as one. *Woodward.*

We find that the force, whereby bodies *cohere*, is very much greater when they come to immediate contact, than when they are at ever so small a finite distance. *Cheyne's Phil. Prin.*

None

None want a place for all their center found,
Hung to the goddefs, and *coher'd* around;
Not clofer, orb in orb conglob'd, are feen
The buzzing bees about their dufky queen. *Pope's Dunciad.*

2. To be well connected; to follow regularly in the order of difcourfe.
3. To fuit; to fit; to be fitted to.
Had time *coher'd* with place, or place with wifhing. *Shakef.*
4. To agree.

COHE'RENCE. }
COHE'RENCY. } *n. f.* [*cohærentia*, Latin.]

1. That ftate of bodies in which their parts are joined together, from what caufe foever it proceeds, fo that they refift divulfion and feparation; nor can be feparated by the fame force by which they might be fimply moved, or being only laid upon one another, might be parted again. *Quincy.*

The weight or preffure of the air will not explain, nor can be a caufe of the *coherence* of the particles of air themfelves. *Locke.*

Matter is either fluid or folid; words that may comprehend the middle degrees between extreme fixednefs and *coherency*, and the moft rapid inteftine motion. *Bentley's Sermons.*

2. Connection; dependency; the relation of parts or things one to another.

It fhall be no trouble to find each controverfy's refting place, and the *coherence* it hath with things, either on which it dependeth, or which depend on it. *Hooker, Preface.*

Why between fermons and faith fhould there be ordinarily that *coherence*, which caufes have with their ufual effects? *Hooker.*

3. The texture of a difcourfe, by which one part follows another regularly and naturally.
4. Confiftency in reafoning, or relating, fo that one part of the difcourfe does not deftroy or contradict the reft.

Coherence of difcourfe, and a direct tendency of all the parts of it to the argument in hand, are moft eminently to be found in him. *Locke's Preface to St. Paul's Epiftles.*

COHE'RENT. *adj.* [*cohærens*, Latin.]

1. Sticking together, fo as to refift feparation.

By coagulating and diluting, that is, making their parts more or lefs *coherent*. *Arbuthnot on Aliments.*

Where all muft full, or not *coherent* be;
And all that rifes, rife in due degree. *Pope's Effay on Man.*

2. Suitable to fomething elfe; regularly adapted.

Inftruct my daughter,
That time and place, with this deceit fo lawful,
May prove *coherent*. *Shakefp. All's well that ends well.*

3. Confiftent; not contradictory to itfelf.

A *coherent* thinker, and a ftrict reafoner, is not to be made at once by a fet of rules. *Watts's Logick.*

COHE'SION. *n. f.* [from *cohere.*]

1. The act of fticking together.

Hard particles, heaped together, touch in a few points, and muft be feparable by lefs force than breaks a folid particle, whofe parts touch in all the fpace between them, without any pores or interftices to weaken their *cohefion*. *Newton's Opt.*

Solids and fluids differ in the degree of *cohefion*, which, being increafed, turns a fluid into a folid. *Arbuth. on Aliments.*

2. The ftate of union or infeparability.

What caufe of their *cohefion* can you find?
What props fupport, what chains the fabrick bind. *Blackm.*

3. Connection; dependence.

In their tender years, ideas that have no natural *cohefion*, come to be united in their heads. *Locke.*

COHE'SIVE. *adj.* [from *cohere.*] That has the power of fticking to another, and of refifting feparation.

COHE'SIVENESS. *n. f.* [from *cohefive.*] The quality of being cohefive; the quality of refifting feparation.

To COHI'BIT. *v. a.* [*cohibeo*, Lat.] To reftrain; to hinder. *Dict.*

To CO'HOBATE. *v. a.* To pour the diftilled liquor upon the remaining matter, and diftill it again.

The juices of an animal body are, as it were, *cohobated*, being excreted and admitted again into the blood with the frefh aliment. *Arbuthnot on Aliments.*

COHOBA'TION. *n. f.* [from *cohobate*] A returning any diftilled liquor again upon what it was drawn from, or upon frefh ingredients of the fame kind, to have it the more impregnated with their virtues. *Quincy.*

Cohobation is the pouring the liquor diftilled from any thing back upon the remaining matter, and diftilling it again. *Locke.*

This oil, dulcified by *cohobation* with an aromatized fpirit, is of ufe to reftore the digeftive faculty. *Grew's Mufæum.*

CO'HORT. *n. f.* [*cohors*, Latin.]

1. A troop of foldiers in the Roman armies, containing about five hundred foot.

The Romans levied as many *cohorts*, companies, and enfigns from hence as from any of their provinces. *Camden.*

2. In poetical language, a body of warriours.

Th' arch-angelic pow'r prepar'd
For fwift defcent; with him the *cohort* bright
Of watchful cherubim. *Milton's Paradife Loft, b.* xi. *l.* 127.

Here Churchill, not fo prompt
To vaunt as fight, his hardy *cohorts* join'd
With Eugene. *Philips's Blenheim.*

COHORTA'TION. *n. f.* [*cohortatio*, Latin.] Encouragement by words; incitement. *Dict.*

COIF. *n. f.* [*coeffe*, French, from *cofea*, for *cucufa*, low Latin.] The head-drefs; a lady's cap; the ferjeant's cap.

The judges of the four circuits in Wales, although they are not of the firft magnitude, nor need be of the degree of the *coif*, yet are they confiderable. *Bacon's Advice to Villiers.*

No lefs a man than a brother of the *coif* began his fuit, before he had been a twelvemonth at the Temple. *Addif. Spect.*

CO'IFED. *adj.* [from *coif.*] Wearing a coif.

CO'IFFURE. *n. f.* [*coeffure*, French.] Head-drefs.

I am highly pleafed with the *coiffure* now in fafhion, and think it fhews the good fenfe of the valuable part of the fex. *Addifon's Spectator*, N°. 98.

COIGNE. *n. f.* [An Irifh term, as it feems.]

Fitz Thomas of Defmond began that extortion of *coigne* and livery, and pay; that is, he and his army took horfe-meat and man's-meat, and money, at pleafure. *Davies on Irel.*

COIGNE. n. f. [French.]

1. A corner.
2. A wooden wedge ufed by printers.

To COIL. *v. a.* [*cueillir*, French.] To gather into a narrow compafs; as to coil a rope, to wind it in a ring.

The lurking particles of air fo expanding themfelves, muft neceffarily plump out the fides of the bladder, and fo keep them turgid, until the preffure of the air, that at firft *coiled* them, be re-admitted to do the fame thing again. *Boyle.*

COIL. *n. f.* [*kolleren*, Germ.]

1. Tumult; turmoil; buftle; ftir; hurry; confufion.

Who was fo firm, fo conftant, that this *coil*
Would not infect his reafon. *Shakefp. Tempeft.*
You, miftrefs, all this *coil* is 'long of you. *Shakefpeare.*
In that fleep of death what dreams may come,
When we have fhuffled off this mortal *coil*,
Muft give us paufe. *Shakefpeare's Hamlet.*

2. A rope wound into a ring.

COIN. *n. f.* [*coigne*, French.] A corner; any thing ftanding out angularly; a fquare brick cut diagonally; called often *quoin*, or *quine*.

No jutting frieze,
Buttrice, nor *coigne* of vantage, but this bird
Hath made his pendant bed. *Shakefpeare's Macbeth.*
See you yond' *coin* o' th' capitol, yond' corner ftone? *Shakef.*

COIN. *n. f.* [by fome imagined to come from *cuneus*, a wedge, becaufe metal is cut in wedges to be coined.]

1. Money ftamped with a legal impreffion.

He gave Dametas a good fum of gold in ready *coin*, which Menalcas had bequeathed. *Sidney, b.* i.

You have made
Your holy hat be ftamp'd on the king's *coin*. *Shak. H.* VIII.

I cannot tell how the poets will fucceed in the explication of *coins*, to which they are generally very great ftrangers. *Addif.*

She now contracts her vaft defign,
And all her triumphs fhrink into a *coin*. *Pope.*

2. Payment of any kind.

The lofs of prefent advantage to flefh and blood, is repaid in a nobler *coin*. *Hammond's Fundamentals.*

To COIN. *v. a.* [from the noun.]

1. To mint or ftamp metals for money.

They cannot touch me for *coining*: I am the king himfelf. *Shakefpeare's King Lear.*

They never put in practice a thing fo neceffary as *coined* money is. *Peacham of Antiquities.*

Tenants cannot *coin* rent juft at quarter-day, but muft gather it by degrees. *Locke.*

Can we be fure that this medal was really *coined* by an artificer, or is but a product of the foil from whence it was taken. *Bentley's Sermons.*

2. To make or forge any thing, in an ill fenfe.

My lungs
Coin words 'till their decay, againft thofe meafles,
Which we difdain fhould tetter us. *Shakefp. Coriolanus.*
Never *coin* a formal lye on't,
To make the knight o'ercome the giant. *Hudibras, p.* i.
Thofe motives induced Virgil to *coin* his fable. *Dryden.*
Some tale, fome new pretence, he daily *coin'd*,
To footh his fifter, and delude her mind. *Dryd. Virg. Æn.*
A term is *coined* to make the conveyance eafy. *Atterbury.*

CO'INAGE. *n. f.* [from *coin.*]

1. The act or practice of coining money.

The care of the *coinage* was committed to the inferior magiftrates; and I don't find that they had a publick trial as we folemnly practife in this country. *Arbuthnot.*

2. Coin; money; ftamped and legitimated metal.

This is conceived to be a *coinage* of fome Jews, in derifion of Chriftians, who firft began that portrait. *Brown.*

3. The charges of coining money.
4. Forgery; invention.

This is the very *coinage* of your brain;

This bodiless creation ecstacy
Is very cunning in. *Shakespeare's Hamlet.*

To COINCI'DE. *v. n.* [*coincido*, Latin.]

1. To fall upon the same point; to meet in the same point.

If the equator and ecliptick had *coincided*, it would have rendered the annual revolution of the earth quite useless. *Cheyne's Phil. Prin.*

2. To concur; to be consistent with.

The rules of right judgment, and of good ratiocination, often *coincide* with each other. *Watts's Logick.*

COI'NCIDENCE. *n. s.* [from *coincide.*]

1. The state of several bodies, or lines, falling upon the same point.

An universal equilibrium, arising from the *coincidence* of infinite centers, can never be naturally acquired. *Bentley's Serm.*

2. Concurrence; consistency; tendency of many things to the same end.

The very concurrence and *coincidence* of so many evidences that contribute to the proof, carries with it a great weight. *Hale's Origin of Mankind.*

3. It is followed by *with*.

The *coincidence* of the planes of this rotation *with* one another, and with the plane of the ecliptick, is very near the truth. *Cheyne's Phil. Prin.*

COI'NCIDENT. *adj.* [from *coincide.*]

1. Falling upon the same point.

These circles I viewed through a prism; and as I went from them, they came nearer and nearer together, and at length became *coincident*. *Newt. Opt.*

2. Concurrent; consistent; equivalent; tantamount.

Christianity teaches nothing but what is perfectly suitable to and *coincident* with the ruling principles of a virtuous and well inclined man. *South's Sermons.*

These words of our apostle are exactly *coincident* with that controverted passage in his discourse to the Athenians. *Bentley.*

COINDICA'TION. *n. s.* [from *con* and *indico*, Latin.] Many symptoms, betokening the same cause.

CO'INER. *n. s.* [from *coin.*]

1. A maker of money; a minter; a stamper of coin.

My father was I know not where
When I was stampt: some *coiner* with his tools
Made me a counterfeit. *Shakespeare's Cymbeline.*

It is easy to find designs that never entered into the thoughts of the sculptor or the *coiner*. *Addison on ancient Medals.*

There are only two patents referred to, both less advantageous to the *coiner* than this of Wood. *Swift.*

2. A counterfeiter of the king's stamp; a maker of base money.

3. An inventor.

Dionysius, a Greek *coiner* of etymologies, is commended by Athenæus. *Camden's Remains.*

To COJO'IN. *v. n.* [*conjungo*, Lat.] To join with another in the same office.

Thou may'st *cojoin* with something, and thou dost,
And that beyond commission. *Shakesp. Twelfth Night.*

CO'ISTRIL. *n. s.* A coward cock; a runaway.

He's a coward and a *coistril*, that will not drink to my niece. *Shakespeare's Twelfth Night.*

COIT. *n. s.* [*kote*, a die, Dutch.] A thing thrown at a certain mark. See QUOIT.

The time they wear out at *coits*, kayles, or the like idle exercises. *Carew's Survey of Cornwal.*

COI'TION. *n. s.* [*coitio*, Latin.]

1. Copulation; the act of generation.

I cannot but admire that philosophers should imagine frogs to fall from the clouds, considering how openly they act their *coition*, produce spawn, tadpoles and frogs. *Ray on Creation.*

He is not made productive of his kind, but by *coition* with a female. *Grew's Cosmol. b.* i. *s.* 25.

2. The act by which two bodies come together.

By Gilbertus this motion is termed *coition*, not made by any faculty attractive of one, but a syndrome and concourse of each. *Brown's Vulgar Errours, b.* ii. *c.* 3.

COKE. *n. s.* [Perhaps from *coquo*, *Skinner.*] Fewel made by burning pit-coal under earth, and quenching the cinders; as charcoal is made with wood. It is frequently used in drying malt.

CO'LANDER. *n. s.* [*colo*, to strain, Lat.] A sieve either of hair, twigs or metal, through which a mixture to be separated is poured, and which retains the thicker parts.

Take a thick woven osiar *colander*,
Through which the pressed wines are strained clear. *May.*

All the viscera of the body are but as so many *colanders* to separate several juices from the blood. *Ray on the Creation.*

The brains from nose and mouth, and either ear,
Came issuing forth, as through a *colander*
The curdled milk. *Dryden.*

COLA'TION. *n. s.* [from *colo*, Lat.] The art of filtering or straining.

CO'LATURE. *n. s.* [from *colo*, Latin.]

1. The art of straining; filtration.

2. The matter strained.

CO'LBERTINE. *n. s.* A kind of lace worn by women.

Go, hang out an old frisoneer gorget, with a yard of yellow *colbertine* again. *Congreve's Way of the World.*

CO'LCOTHAR. *n. s.* A term in chymistry.

Colcothar is the dry substance which remains after distillation, but commonly meant of the caput mortuum of vitriol. *Quincy.*

Colcothar, or vitriol burnt, though unto a redness, containing the fixed salt, will make good ink. *Brown's Vulg. Errours.*

COLD. *adj.* [colb, Saxon; *kalt*, German.]

1. Not hot; not warm; gelid; without warmth; without heat.

The diet in the state of manhood ought to be solid; and their chief drink water *cold*, because in such a state it has its own natural spirit. *Arbuthnot on Aliments.*

2. Chill; shivering; having sense of cold.

O noble English, that could entertain,
With half their force, the full power of France;
And let another half stand laughing by,
All out of work, and *cold* for action. *Shakes. Henry* V.

3. Having cold qualities; not volatile; not acrid.

Cold plants have a quicker perception of the heat of the sun than the hot herbs; as a *cold* hand will sooner find a little warmth than an hot. *Bacon's Natural History,* N°. 577.

4. Unaffected; frigid; without passion; without zeal; without concern; unactive; unconcerned.

There sprung up one kind of men, with whose zeal and forwardness the rest being compared, were thought to be marvellous *cold* and dull. *Hooker, Preface, s.* 8.

Infinite shall be made *cold* in religion, by your example, that never were hurt by reading books. *Ascham's Schoolmaster.*

Temp'rately proceed to what you would
Thus violently redress.——Sir, these *cold* ways,
That seem like prudent helps, are very poisonous. *Shakesp.*

New dated letters these,
Their *cold* intent, tenour and substance thus;
Here doth he wish his person, and his power,
The which he could not levy. *Shakesp. Henry* IV. *p.* ii.

We should not, when the blood was *cold*, have threatned
Our prisoners with the sword. *Shakespeare's Cymbeline.*

To see a world in flames, and an host of angels in the clouds, one must be much of a stoick to be a *cold* and unconcerned spectator. *Burnet's Preface to the Theory of the Earth.*

No drum or trumpet needs
T' inspire the coward, or to warm the *cold*,
His voice, his sole appearance, makes them bold. *Dryden.*

O, thou hast touch'd me with thy sacred theme,
And my *cold* heart is kindled at thy flame. *Rowe.*

A man must be of a very *cold* or degenerate temper, whose heart doth not burn within him in the midst of praise and adoration. *Addison's Freeholder,* N°. 49.

5. Unaffecting; unable to move the passions.

The rabble are pleased at the first entry of a disguise; but the jest grows *cold* even with them too, when it comes on in a second scene. *Addison's Remarks on Italy.*

6. Reserved; coy; not affectionate; not cordial; not friendly.

Let his knights have *colder* looks
Among you. *Shakespeare's King Lear.*

The commissioners grew more reserved and *colder* towards each other. *Clarendon, b.* viii.

7. Chaste.

You may
Convey your pleasures in a spacious plenty,
And yet seem *cold*, the time you may so hoodwink:
We've willing dames enough. *Shakespeare's Macbeth.*

8. Not welcome; not received with kindness or warmth of affection.

My master's suit will be but *cold*,
Since she respects my mistress' love. *Sh. Two Gent. of Verona.*

9. Not hasty; not violent.

10. Not affecting the scent strongly.

She made it good
At the hedge corner, in the *coldest* fault. *Shakespeare.*

11. Not having the scent strongly affected.

Smell this business with a sense as *cold*
As is a dead man's nose. *Shakespeare's Winter's Tale.*

COLD. *n. s.* [from the adjective.]

1. The cause of the sensation of cold; the privation of heat; the frigorifick power.

Fair lined slippers for the *cold*. *Shakespeare.*

Heat and *cold* are nature's two hands, whereby she chiefly worketh: and heat we have in readiness, in respect of the fire; but for *cold* we must stay 'till it cometh, or seek it in deep caves, or high mountains; and when all is done, we cannot obtain it in any great degree. *Bacon's Natural History,* N°. 69.

2. The sensation of cold; coldness; chilness.

When she saw her lord prepar'd to part,
A deadly *cold* ran shiv'ring to her heart. *Dryden's Fables.*

3. A disease caused by cold; the obstruction of perspiration.

What disease hast thou?——
A whorson *cold*, sir; a cough. *Shakesp. Henry* IV. *p.* 2.

Let no ungentle *cold* destroy
All taste we have of heav'nly joy. *Roscommon.*

Those rains, so covering the earth, might providentially contribute to the disruption of it, by stopping all the pores, and all evaporation, which would make the vapours within struggle violently, as we get a fever by a *cold*. *Burnet.*

Co'ldly. *adv.* [from *cold.*]

1. Without heat.

2. Without concern; indifferently; negligently; without warmth of temper or expression.

What England says, say briefly, gentle lord;
We *coldly* pause for thee. *Shakespeare's King John.*

Swift seem'd to wonder what he meant,
Nor would believe my lord had sent;
So never offer'd once to stir,
But *coldly* said, your servant, sir. *Swift.*

Co'ldness. *n. s.* [from *cold.*]

1. Want of heat; power of causing the sensation of cold.

He relates the excessive *coldness* of the water they met with in summer in that icy region, where they were forced to winter. *Boyle's Experiments.*

Such was the discord, which did first disperse
Form, order, beauty through the universe;
While driness moisture, *coldness* heat resists,
All that we have, and that we are subsists. *Denham.*

2. Unconcern; frigidity of temper; want of zeal; negligence; disregard.

Divisions of religion are not only the farthest spread, because in religion all men presume themselves interested; but they are also, for the most part, hotlier prosecuted: for as much as *coldness*, which, in other contentions, may be thought to proceed from moderation, is not in these so favourably construed. *Hooker, Dedicat.*

If upon reading the admired passages in such authors, he finds a *coldness* and indifference in his thoughts, he ought to conclude, that he himself wants the faculty of discovering them. *Addison's Spectator*, N°. 409.

It betrayed itself at first in a sort of indifference and carelessness in all her actions, and *coldness* to her best friends. *Arbuthnot's History of John Bull.*

3. Coyness; want of kindness; want of passion.

Unhappy youth! how will thy *coldness* raise
Tempests and storms in his afflicted bosom! *Addis. Cato.*

Let ev'ry tongue its various censures chuse,
Absolve with *coldness*, or with spite accuse. *Prior.*

4. Chastity; exemption from vehement desire.

The silver stream her virgin *coldness* keeps,
For ever murmurs, and for ever weeps. *Pope's Windf. For.*

COLE. *n. s.* [capl, Saxon.] A general name for all sorts of Cabbage, which see.

Co'leseed. *n. s.* [from *cole* and *seed.*]

Where land is rank, it is not good to sow wheat after a fallow; but *coleseed* or barley, or both, and then wheat. *Mortimer's Husbandry.*

Co'lewort. *n. s.* [caplpyrt, Sax.] See Cabbage, of which it is a species.

The decoction of *coleworts* is also commanded to bathe them. *Wiseman of an Erysipelas.*

Next took the *coleworts*, which her husband got
From his own ground (a small well-water'd spot);
She strip'd the stalks of all their leaves; the best
She cull'd, and then with handy care she dress'd. *Dryden.*

How turnips hide their swelling heads below,
And how the closing *coleworts* upwards grow. *Gay.*

Co'lick. *n. s.* [*colicus*, Latin.]

It strictly is a disorder of the colon; but loosely, any disorder of the stomach or bowels that is attended with pain. There are four sorts: 1. A bilious colick, which proceeds from an abundance of acrimony or choler irritating the bowels, so as to occasion continual gripes, and generally with a loosenefs; and this is best managed with lenitives and emollients. 2. A flatulent *colick*, which is pain in the bowels from flatus's and wind, which distend them into unequal and unnatural capacities; and this is managed with carminatives and moderate openers. 3. An hysterical *colick*, which arises from disorders of the womb, and is communicated by consent of parts to the bowels; and is to be treated with the ordinary hystericks. 4. A nervous *colick*, which is from convulsive spasms and contortions of the guts themselves, from some disorders of the spirits, or nervous fluid, in their component fibres; whereby their capacities are in many places streightened, and sometimes so as to occasion obstinate obstructions: this is best remedied by brisk catharticks, joined with opiates and emollient diluters. There is also a species of this distemper which is commonly called the stone *colick*, by consent of parts, from the irritation of the stone or gravel in the bladder or kidneys; and this is most commonly to be treated by nephriticks and oily diureticks, and is greatly assisted with the carminative turpentine clysters. *Quincy.*

Colicks of infants proceed from acidity, and the air in the aliment expanding itself, while the aliment ferments. *Arbuth.*

Co'lick. *adj.* Affecting the bowels.

Intestine stone, and ulcer, *colick* pangs. *Milton.*

To Colla'pse. *v. n.* [*collabor, collapsus*, Latin.] To fall together; to close so as that one side touches the other.

In consumptions and atrophy the liquids are exhausted, and the sides of the canals *collapse*; therefore the attrition is increased, and consequently the heat. *Arbuthnot on Diet.*

Colla'psion. *n. s.* [from *collapse.*]

1. The state of vessels closed.

2. The act of closing or collapsing.

CO'LLAR. *n. s.* [*collare*, Latin.]

1. A ring of metal put round the neck.

That's nothing, says the dog, but the fretting of my *collar*: nay, says the wolf, if there be a *collar* in the case, I know better things than to sell my liberty. *L'Estrange, Fab.* 68.

Ten brace and more of greyhounds,
With golden muzzles all their mouths were bound,
And *collars* of the same their neck surround. *Dryden's Fab.*

2. The part of the harness that is fastened about the horse's neck.

Her waggon-spokes made of long spinners legs,
The traces of the smallest spider's web,
The *collars* of the moonshine's watry beams. *Shakespeare.*

3. The part of the dress that surrounds the neck.

4. *To slip the* Collar. To get free; to escape; to disentangle himself from any engagement or difficulty.

When as the ape him heard so much to talk
Of labour, that did from his liking baulk,
He would have *slipt the collar* handsomely. *Hubberd's Tale.*

5. *A* Collar *of Brawn*, is the quantity bound up in one parcel.

Co'llar-bone. *n. s.* [from *collar* and *bone.*] The clavicle; the bones on each side of the neck.

A page riding behind the coach, fell down, bruised his face, and broke his right *collarbone*. *Wiseman's Surgery.*

To Co'llar. *v. a.* [from the noun.]

1. To seize by the collar; to take by the throat.

2. *To* Collar *beef*, or other meat; to roll it up, and bind it hard and close with a string or collar.

To COLLA'TE. *v. a.* [*confero collatum*, Latin.]

1. To compare one thing of the same kind with another.

Knowledge will be ever a wandering and indigested thing, if it be but a commixture of a few notions that are at hand and occur, and not excited from a sufficient number of instances, and those well *collated*. *Bacon's Natural History*, N°. 839.

They could not relinquish their Judaism, and embrace Christianity, without considering, weighing, and *collating* both religions. *South.*

2. To collate books; to examine if nothing be wanting.

3. With *to*. To place in an ecclesiastical benefice.

He thrust out the invader, and *collated* Amsdorf *to* the benefice: Luther performed the consecration. *Atterbury.*

If a patron shall neglect to present unto a benefice, that has been void above six months, the bishop may *collate* thereunto. *Ayliffe's Parergon.*

Colla'teral. *adj.* [*con* and *latus*, Latin.]

1. Side to side.

In his bright radiance and *collateral* light
Must I be comforted, not in his sphere. *Shakespeare.*

Thus saying, from his radiant seat he rose,
Of high *collateral* glory. *Milton's Paradise Lost, b.* x. *l.* 86.

2. Running parallel.

3. Diffused on either side.

But man by number is to manifest
His single imperfection; and beget
Like of his like, his image multiply'd;
In unity defective, which requires
Collateral love, and dearest amity. *Milton's Paradise Lost.*

4. In genealogy, those that stand in equal relation to some common ancestor.

The estate and inheritance of a person dying intestate, is, by right of devolution, according to the civil law, given to such as are allied to him *ex latere*, commonly stiled *collaterals*, if there be no ascendants or descendants surviving at the time of his death. *Ayliffe's Parergon.*

5. Not direct; not immediate.

They shall hear and judge 'twixt you and me,
If by direct or by *collateral* hand
They find us touch'd, we will our kingdom give
To you in satisfaction. *Shakespeare.*

6. Concurrent.

All the force of the motive lies entirely within itself: it receives no *collateral* strength from external considerations. *Atterbury's Sermons.*

Colla'terally. *adv.* [from *collateral.*]

1. Side by side.

These pullies may be multiplied according to sundry different situations, not only when they are subordinate, but also when they are placed *collaterally*. *Wilkins.*

2. Indirectly.

By asserting the scripture to be the canon of our faith, I have created two enemies: the papists more directly, because they have kept the scripture from us; and the fanaticks more *collaterally*,

collaterally, because they have assumed what amounts to an infallibility in the private spirit. *Dryden.*

3. In collateral relation.

COLLA'TION. *n. s.* [*collatio*, Latin.]

1. The act of conferring or bestowing; gift.

Neither are we to give thanks alone for the first *collation* of these benefits, but also for their preservation. *Ray on the Creat.*

2. Comparison of one copy, or one thing of the same kind, with another.

In the disquisition of truth, a ready fancy is of great use; provided that *collation* doth its office. *Grew's Cosmol. b.* 21.

I return you your Milton, which, upon *collation*, I find to be revised and augmented in several places. *Pope.*

3. In Law.

Collation is the bestowing of a benefice, by the bishop that hath it in his own gift or patronage; and differs from institution in this, that institution into a benefice is performed by the bishop at the presentation of another who is patron, or hath the patron's right for the time. *Cowel.*

Bishops should be placed by *collation* of the king under his letters patent, without any precedent election or confirmation ensuing. *Hayward.*

4. A repast.

COLLATI'TIOUS. *adj.* [*collatitius*, Lat.] Done by the contribution of many. *Dict.*

COLLA'TOR. *n. s.* [from *collate.*]

1. One that compares copies, or manuscripts.

To read the titles they give an editor, or *collator* of a manuscript, you would take him for the glory of letters. *Addison.*

2. One who presents to an ecclesiastical benefice.

A mandatory cannot interrupt an ordinary *collator*, 'till a month is expired from the day of presentation. *Ayliffe's Parerg.*

To COLLA'UD. *v. a.* [*collaudo*, Lat.] To join in praising. *Dict.*

CO'LLEAGUE. *n. s.* [*collega*, Lat.] A partner in office or employment. Anciently accented on the last syllable.

Easy it might be seen that I intend
Mercy *colleague* with justice, sending thee. *Milton's P. Lost.*

The regents, upon demise of the crown, would keep the peace without *colleagues*. *Swift.*

To COLLE'AGUE. *v. a.* [from the noun.] To unite with.

Colleagued with this dream of his advantage,
He hath not fail'd to pester us with message,
Importing the surrender of those lands. *Shakesp. Hamlet.*

To COLLE'CT. *v. a.* [*colligo collectum*, Latin.]

1. To gather together; to bring into one place.

'Tis memory alone that enriches the mind, by preserving what our labour and industry daily *collect*. *Watts.*

2. To draw many units, or numbers, into one sum.

Let a man *collect* into one sum as great a number as he pleases, this multitude, how great soever, lessens not one jot the power of adding to it. *Locke.*

3. To gain from observation.

The reverent care I bear unto my lord,
Made me *collect* these dangers in the duke. *Shak. Hen.* VI.

4. To infer as a consequence; to gather from premises.

How great the force of such an erroneous persuasion is, we may *collect* from our Saviour's premonition to his disciples. *Decay of Piety.*

They conclude they can have no idea of infinite space, because they can have no idea of infinite matter; which consequence, I conceive, is very ill *collected*. *Locke.*

5. *To* COLLECT *himself*. To recover from surprise; to gain command over his thoughts; to assemble his sentiments.

Be *collected*;
No more amazement. *Shakespeare's Tempest.*

Affrighted much,
I did in time *collect* myself, and thought
This was so, and no slumber. *Shakesp. Winter's Tale.*

Prosperity unexpected often maketh men careless and remiss; whereas they who receive a wound, become more vigilant and *collected*. *Hayward.*

CO'LLECT. *n. s.* [*collecta*, low Lat.] A short comprehensive prayer, used at the sacrament; any short prayer.

Then let your devotion be humbly to say over proper *collects*. *Taylor's Guide to Devotion.*

COLLECTA'NEOUS. *adj.* [*collectaneus*, Lat.] Gathered up together; collected; notes compiled from various books.

COLLE'CTIBLE. *adj.* [from *collect.*] That which may be gathered from the premises by just consequence.

Whether thereby be meant Euphrates, is not *collectible* from the following words. *Brown's Vulgar Errours, b.* vi. *c.* 8.

COLLE'CTION. *n. s.* [from *collect.*]

1. The act of gathering together.

2. An assemblage; the things gathered.

No perjur'd knight desires to quit thy arms,
Fairest *collection* of thy sex's charms. *Prior.*

The gallery is hung with a numerous *collection* of pictures. *Addison on Italy.*

3. The act of deducing consequences; ratiocination; discourse. This sense is now scarce in use.

If once we descend unto probable *collections*, we are then in the territory where free and arbitrary determinations, the territory where human laws take place. *Hooker, b.* i. *s.* 8.

4. A corollary; a consectary deduced from premises; deduction; consequence.

It should be a weak *collection*, if whereas we say, that when Christ had overcome the sharpness of death, he then opened the kingdom of Heaven to all believers; a thing in such sort affirmed with circumstance, were taken as insinuating an opposite denial before that circumstance be accomplished. *Hooker.*

This label
Is so from sense in hardness, that I can
Make no *collection* of it. *Shakespeare's Cymbeline.*

When she, from sundry arts, one skill doth draw;
Gath'ring from divers fights, one act of war;
From many cases like, one rule of law:
These her *collections*, not the senses are. *Davies.*

COLLECTI'TIOUS. *adj.* [*collectitius*, Lat.] Gathered up.

COLLE'CTIVE. *adj.* [from *collect*, *collectif*, French.]

1. Gathered into one mass; aggregated; accumulative.

A body *collective*, because it containeth a huge multitude. *Hooker, b.* iii. *sect.* 81.

The three forms of government differ only by the civil administration being in the hands of one or two, called kings, in a senate called the nobles, or in the people *collective* or representative, who may be called the commons. *Swift.*

The difference between a compound and a *collective* idea is, that a compound idea unites things of a different kind; but a *collective* idea, things of the same. *Watts's Logick.*

2. Employed in deducing consequences; argumentative.

Antiquity left unto us many falsities, controulable not only by critical and *collective* reason, but contrary observations. *Brown's Vulgar Errours, b.* i. *c.* 6.

3. [In grammar.] A collective noun is a word which expresses a multitude, though itself be singular; as a *company*; an *army*.

COLLE'CTIVELY. *adv.* [from *collective.*] In a general mass; in a body; not singly; not numbered by individuals; in the aggregate; accumulatively; taken together; in a state of combination or union.

Although we cannot be free from all sin *collectively*, in such sort that no part thereof shall be found inherent in us, yet distributively all great actual offences, as they offer themselves one by one, both may and ought to be by all means avoided. *Hooker, b.* v. *sect.* 48.

Singly and apart many of them are subject to exception, yet *collectively* they make up a good moral evidence. *Hale.*

The other part of the water was condensed at the surface of the earth, and sent forth *collectively* into standing springs and rivers. *Woodward's Natural History.*

COLLE'CTOR. *n. s.* [*collector*, Latin.]

1. A gatherer; he that collects scattered things together.

The grandfather might be the first *collector* of them into a body. *Hale's Common Law of England.*

Volumes, without any of the *collector's* own reflections. *Addison on Italy.*

2. A tax-gatherer; a man employed in levying duties, or tributes.

A great part of this treasure is now embezzled, lavished, and feasted away by *collectors*, and other officers. *Temple.*

The commissions of the revenue are disposed of, and the *collectors* are appointed by the commissioners. *Swift.*

COLLE'GATARY. *n. s.* [from *con* and *legatum*, a legacy, Latin.] In the civil law, a person to whom is left a legacy in common with one or more other persons. *Chambers.*

CO'LLEGE. *n. s.* [*collegium*, Latin.]

1. A community; a number of persons living by some common rules.

On barbed steeds they rode in proud array,
Thick as the *college* of the bees in May. *Dryden.*

2. A society of men set apart for learning or religion.

He is return'd with his opinions, which
Have satisfied the king for his divorce,
Gather'd from all the famous *colleges*
Almost in Christendom. *Shakespeare's Henry* VIII.

I would the *college* of the cardinals
Would chuse him pope, and carry him to Rome. *Sh. H.* VI.

This order or society is sometimes called Solomon's house, and sometimes the *college* of the six days work. *Bacon.*

3. The house in which the collegians reside.

Huldah the prophetess dwelt in Jerusalem in the *college*. *2 Kings* xxii. 14.

4. A college in foreign universities is a lecture read in publick.

COLLE'GIAL. *adj.* [from *college.*] Relating to a college; possessed by a college.

COLLE'GIAN. *n. s.* [from *college.*] An inhabitant of a college; a member of a college.

COLLE'GIATE. *adj.* [*collegiatus*, low Latin.]

1. Containing a college; instituted after the manner of a college.

I wish that yourselves did well consider how opposite certain of your positions are unto the state of *collegiate* societies, whereon the two universities consist. *Hooker, Pref. sect.* 8.

2. A *collegiate* church, was such as was built at a convenient distance from the cathedral church, wherein a number of presbyters were settled, and lived together in one congregation. *Ayliffe's Parergon.*

COLLE'GIATE. *n. s.* [from *college.*] A member of a college; a man bred in a college; an university man.

These are a kind of empiricks in poetry, who have got a receipt to please; and no *collegiate* like them, for purging the passions. *Rymer's Tragedies of the last Age.*

CO'LLET. *n. s.* [Fr. from *collum*, Lat. the neck.]

1. Anciently something that went about the neck: sometimes the neck.
2. That part of a ring in which the stone is set.
3. A term used by turners.

To COLLI'DE. *v. a.* [*collido*, Lat.] To strike against each other; to beat, to dash, to knock together.

Scintillations are not the accension of air upon collision, but inflammable effluencies from the bodies *collided.* *Brown.*

CO'LLIER. *n. s.* [from *coal.*]

1. A digger of coals; one that works in the coal pits.
2. A coal-merchant; a dealer in coals.

I knew a nobleman a great grasier, a great timberman, a great *collier*, and a great landman. *Bacon, Essay* 35.

3. A ship that carries coals.

CO'LLIERY. *n. s.* [from *collier.*]

1. The place where coals are dug.
2. The coal trade.

CO'LLIFLOWER. *n. s.* [from capl, Sax. cabbage, and *flower.*] See CAULIFLOWER and CABBAGE.

COLLIGA'TION. *n. s.* [*colligatio*, Lat.] A binding together.

These the midwife contriveth into a knot, whence that tortuosity or nodosity, the navel, occasioned by the *colligation* of vessels. *Brown's Vulgar Errours, b.* v. *c.* 5.

COLLIMA'TION. *n. s.* [from *collimo*, Lat.] The act of aiming at a mark; aim. *Dict.*

COLLINEA'TION. *n. s.* [*collineo*, Lat.] The act of aiming.

CO'LLIQUABLE. *adj.* [from *colliquate.*] Easily dissolved; liable to be melted.

The tender consistence renders it the more *colliquable* and consumptive. *Harvey on Consumptions.*

COLLI'QUAMENT. *n. s.* [from *colliquate.*] The substance to which any thing is reduced by being melted.

CO'LLIQUANT. *adj.* [from *colliquate.*] That which has the power of melting or dissolving.

To CO'LLIQUATE. *v. a.* [*colliqueo*, Latin.] To melt; to dissolve; to turn from solid to fluid.

The fire melted the glass, that made a great shew, after what was *colliquated* had been removed from the fire. *Boyle.*

The fat of the kidneys is apt to be *colliquated* through a great heat from within, and an ardent colliquative fever. *Harvey on Consumptions.*

COLLIQUA'TION. *n. s.* [*colliquatio*, Latin.]

The melting of any thing whatsoever by heat, more particularly such a temperament or disposition of the animal fluids as proceeds from a lax compages, and wherein they flow off through the secretory glands, and particularly through those of the skin, faster than they ought; which occasions fluxes of many kinds, but mostly profuse, greasy, clammy sweats. *Quincy.*

From them proceed arefaction, *colliquation*, concoction, maturation, and most effects of nature *Bacon's Nat. History.*

Any kind of universal diminution and *colliquation* of the body. *Harvey on Consumptions.*

COLLI'QUATIVE *adj.* [from *colliquate.*] Melting; dissolvent.

A *colliquative* fever is such as is attended with a diarrhæa, or profuse sweats, from too lax a contexture of the fluids. *Quincy.*

It is a consequent of a burning *colliquative* fever, whereby the humours, grease, fat, and flesh of the body are melted. *Harvey on Consumptions.*

COLLIQUEFA'CTION. *n. s.* [*colliquefacio*, Latin.] The act of melting together; reduction to one mass by fluxion in the fire.

After the incorporation of metals by simple *colliquefaction*, for the better discovering of the nature, and consents and dissents of metals, it would be tried by incorporating of their dissolutions. *Bacon's Physical Remarks.*

COLLI'SION. *n. s.* [from *collisio*, Latin.]

1. The act of striking two bodies together.

Or by *collision* of two bodies grind,
The air attrite to fire. *Milton's Paradise Lost, b.* x. *l.* 1072.

The devil sometimes borrowed fire from the altar to consume the votaries; and by the mutual *collision* of well-meant zeal, set even orthodox Christians in a flame. *Dec. of Piety.*

The flint and the steel you may move apart as long as you please; but it is the hitting and *collision* of them that must make them strike fire. *Bentley's Sermons.*

2. The state of being struck together; a clash.

Then from the clashes between popes and kings,
Debate, like sparks from flint's *collision*, springs. *Denham.*

To CO'LLOCATE. *v. a.* [*colloco*, Latin.] To place; to station.

If you desire to superinduce any virtue upon a person, take the creature in which that virtue is most eminent: of that creature take the parts wherein that virtue chiefly is *collocate.* *Bacon's Natural History.*

COLLOCA'TION. *n. s.* [*collocatio*, Latin.]

1. The act of placing; disposition.
2. The state of being placed.

In the *collocation* of the spirits in bodies, the *collocation* is equal or unequal; and the spirits are coacervate or diffused. *Bacon's Natural History,* N°. 846.

COLLOCU'TION. *n. s.* [*collocutio*, Latin.] Conference; conversation.

To COLLO'GUE. *v. n.* [probably from *colloquor*, Latin.] To wheedle; to flatter; to please with kind words. A low word.

CO'LLOP. *n. s.* [It is derived by *Minshew* from *coal* and *op*, a rasher broiled upon the coals; a carbonade.]

1. A small slice of meat.

Sweetbread and *collops* were with skewers prick'd
About the sides. *Dryd. Fables.*

A cook perhaps has mighty things profess'd;
Then sent up but two dishes nicely drest:
What signifies Scotch *collops* to a feast? *King's Cookery.*

2. A piece of any animal.

The lion is upon his death-bed: not an enemy that does not apply for a *collop* of him. *L'Estrange, Fable* 14. *Reflect.*

3. In burlesque language, a child.

Come, sir page,
Look on me with your welkin eye, sweet villain,
Most dear'st, my *collop.* *Shakespeare's Winter's Tale.*

Thou art a *collop* of my flesh,
And for thy sake I have shed many a tear. *Shak. Hen.* VI.

CO'LLOQUY. *n. s.* [*colloquium*, Latin.] Conference; conversation; alternate discourse; talk.

My earthly by his heav'nly over-power'd,
In that celestial *colloquy* sublime,
As with an object that excels the sense,
Dazzled, and spent, sunk down. *Milton's Paradise Lost.*

In retirement make frequent *colloquies*, or short discoursings, between God and thy own soul. *Taylor.*

CO'LLOW. *n. s.* [More properly *colly*, from *coal.*]

Collow is the word by which they denote black grime of burnt coals, or wood. *Woodward on Fossils.*

COLLU'CTANCY. *n. s.* [*colluctor*, Lat.] A tendency to contest; opposition of nature.

COLLUCTA'TION. *n. s.* [*colluctatio*, Lat.] Contest; struggle; contrariety; opposition; spite.

The thermæ, natural baths, or hot springs, do not owe their heat to any *colluctation* or effervescence of the minerals in them. *Woodward's Natural History.*

To COLLU'DE. *v. n.* [*colludo*, Lat.] To conspire in a fraud; to act in concert; to play into the hand of each other.

COLLU'SION. *n. s.* [*collusio*, Latin.]

Collusion is, in our common law, a deceitful agreement or compact between two or more, for the one part to bring an action against the other to some evil purpose; as to defraud a third of his right. *Cowel.*

By the ignorance of the merchants, or dishonesty of weavers, or the *collusion* of both, the ware was bad, and the price excessive. *Swift.*

COLLU'SIVE. *adj.* [from *collude.*] Fraudulently concerted. See COLLUSION.

COLLU'SIVELY. *adv.* [from *collusive*] In a manner fraudulently concerted.

COLLU'SORY. *adj.* [from *colludo*, Lat.] Carrying on a fraud by secret concert.

CO'LLY. *n. s.* [from *coal.*] The smut of coal.

Suppose thou saw her dressed in some old hirsute attire, out of fashion, coarse raiment, besmeared with soot, *colly*, perfumed with opopanax. *Burton on Melancholy.*

To CO'LLY. *v. a.* To grime with coal; to smut with coal.

Brief as the lightning in the *collied* night,
That, in a spleen, unfolds both heav'n and earth;
And, ere a man hath pow'r to say behold,
The jaws of darkness do devour it up. *Shakespeare.*

COLLY'RIUM. n. s. [Latin.] An ointment for the eyes.

CO'LMAR. n. s. [Fr.] A sort of PEAR, which see.

CO'LOGN *Earth. n. s.* Is a deep brown, very light bastard ochre, which, though generally esteemed an earth, is no pure native fossil; but contains more vegetable than mineral matter, and owes its origin to the remains of wood long buried in the earth. It is dug in France and Germany, particularly about Cologn, nor is England without it. *Hill on Fossils.*

CO'LON. *n. s.* [κῶλον.]

1. A point [:] used to mark a pause greater than that of a comma, and less than that of a period. Its use is not very exactly fixed, nor is it very necessary, being confounded by most with the semicolon. It was used before punctuation was refined, to mark almost any sense less than a period. To apply it properly, we should place it, perhaps, only where the sense is continued without dependence of grammar or construction; as, *I love him, I despise him: I have long ceased to trust, but shall never forbear to succour him.*
2. The greatest and widest of all the intestines, about eight or nine hands breadth long. It begins where the ilium ends, in the cavity of the os ilium on the right side; from thence ascending by the kidney, on the same side, it passes under the concave

concave side of the liver, to which it is sometimes tied, as likewise to the gall-bladder, which tinges it yellow in that place: then it runs under the bottom of the stomach to the spleen in the left side, to which it is also knit: from thence it turns down to the left kidney; and thence passing, in form of an S, it terminates at the upper part of the os sacrum, in the rectum. *Quincy.*

Now, by your cruelty hard bound,
I strain my guts, my *colon* wound. *Swift.*

The contents of the *colon* are of a sower, fetid, acid smell in rabbits. *Floyer on the Humours.*

COLONEL. *n. s.* [Of uncertain etymology. *Skinner* imagines it originally *colonialis*, the leader of a colony. *Minshew* deduces it from *colonna*, a pillar; as *patriæ columen*; *exercitus columen*. Each is plausible.] The chief commander of a regiment; a field officer of the highest rank, next to the general officers. It is now generally sounded with only two distinct syllables, *col'nel.*

The chiefest help must be the care of the *colonel*, that hath the government of all his garrison. *Spenser on Ireland.*

Captain or *colonel*, or knight in arms,
Whose chance on these defenceless doors may seize,
If deed of honour did thee ever please,
Guard them, and him within protect from harms. *Milton.*

CO'LONELSHIP. *n. s.* [from *colonel.*] The office or character of colonel.

While he continued a subaltern, he complained against the pride of colonels towards their officers; yet, in a few minutes after he had received his commission for a regiment, he confessed that *colonelship* was coming fast upon him. *Swift.*

To CO'LONISE. *v. a.* [from *colony.*] To plant with inhabitants; to settle with new planters; to plant with colonies.

There was never an hand drawn, that did double the rest of the habitable world, before this; for so a man may truly term it, if he shall put to account as well that that is, as that which may be hereafter, by the farther occupation and *colonizing* of those countries: and yet it cannot be affirmed, if one speak ingenuously, that it was the propagation of the Christian faith that was the adamant of that discovery, entry, and plantation; but gold and silver, and temporal profit and glory; so that what was first in God's providence, was but second in man's appetite and intention. *Bacon's Holy War.*

Druina hath advantage by acquest of islands, which she *colonizeth* and fortifieth daily. *Howel's Vocal Forest.*

COLONNA'DE. *n. s.* [from *colonna*, Ital. a column.]

1. A peristyle of a circular figure, or a series of columns, disposed in a circle, and insulated within side. *Builder's Dict.*

Here circling *colonnades* the ground inclose,
And here the marble statues breathe in rows. *Addis. on Italy.*

2. Any series or range of pillars.

For you my *colonnades* extend their wings. *Pope.*

CO'LONY. *n. s.* [*colonia*, Latin.]

1. A body of people drawn from the mother-country to inhabit some distant place.

To these new inhabitants and *colonies* he gave the same law under which they were born and bred. *Spenser on Ireland.*

Rooting out these two rebellious septs, he placed English *colonies* in their rooms. *Davies on Ireland.*

Osiris, or the Bacchus of the ancients, is reported to have civilized the Indians, planting *colonies* and building cities. *Arbuthnot on Coins.*

2. The country planted; a plantation.

The rising city, which from far you see,
Is Carthage; and a Trojan *colony*. *Dryd. Virg. Æn.*

CO'LOPHONY. *n. s.* [from *Colophon*, a city whence it came.] Rosin.

Of Venetian turpentine, slowly evaporating about a fourth or fifth part, the remaining substance suffered to cool, would afford me a coherent body, or a fine *colophony*. *Boyle.*

Turpentines and oils leave a *colophony*, upon the separation of their thinner oil. *Floyer on the Humours.*

COLOQUI'NTEDA. *n. s.* [*colocynthis*, Lat. κολοκυνθίς.] The fruit of a plant of the same name, brought from the Levant, about the bigness of a large orange, and often called bitter apple. Its colour is a sort of golden brown: its inside is full of kernels, which are to be taken out before it be used. Both the seed and pulp are intolerably bitter. It is a violent purgative, of considerable use in medicine. *Chambers.*

CO'LORATE. *adj.* [*coloratus*, Latin.] Coloured; died; marked or stained with some colour.

Had the tunicles and humours of the eye been *colorate*, many rays proceeding from visible objects would have been stopt. *Ray on the Creation.*

COLORA'TION. *n. s.* [*coloro*, Latin.]

1. The art or practice of colouring.

2. The state of being coloured.

Amongst curiosities I shall place *coloration*, though it be somewhat better; for beauty in flowers is their preheminence. *Bacon's Natural History*, Nº. 50.

COLORI'FICK. *adj.* [*colorificus*, Latin.] That which has the power of producing dies, tints, colours, or hues.

In this composition of white, the several rays do not suffer any change in their *colorifick* qualities by acting upon one another; but are only mixed, and by a mixture of their colours produce white. *Newton's Opt.*

COLO'SSE. } *n. s.* [*colossus*, Latin.] A statue of enormous
COLO'SSUS. } magnitude.

Not to mention the walls and palace of Babylon, the pyramids of Egypt, or *colosse* of Rhodes. *Temple.*

There huge *colossus* rose, with trophies crown'd,
And runick characters were grav'd around. *Pope.*

COLOSSE'AN. *adj.* [*colosseus*, Lat.] In form of a colossus; of the height and bigness of such a statue; giantlike.

CO'LOUR. *n. s.* [*color*, Latin.]

1. The appearance of bodies to the eye only; hue; die.

It is a vulgar idea of the *colours* of solid bodies, when we perceive them to be a red, or blue, or green tincture of the surface; but a philosophical idea, when we consider the various *colours* to be different sensations, excited in us by the refracted rays of light, reflected on our eyes in a different manner, according to the different size, or shape, or situation of the particles of which the surfaces of those bodies are composed. *Watts's Logick.*

Her hair shall be of what *colour* it please God. *Shakesp.*

For though our eyes can nought but *colours* see,
Yet *colours* give them not their pow'r of sight. *Davies.*

The lights of *colours* are more refrangible one than another in this order; red, orange, yellow, green, blue, indigo, deep violet. *Newton's Opt. Exp.* 7.

2. The freshness; or appearance of blood in the face.

My cheeks no longer did their *colour* boast. *Dryden.*

A sudden horror seiz'd his giddy head,
And his ears trickled, and his *colour* fled. *Dryden.*

3. The tint of the painter.

When each bold figure just begins to live,
The treach'rous *colours* the fair art betray,
And all the bright creation fades away. *Pope's Ess. Crit.*

4. The representation of any thing superficially examined.

Whose wisdom is only of this world, to put false *colours* upon things, to call good evil, and evil good, against the conviction of their own consciences. *Swift.*

5. Concealment; palliation; excuse; superficial cover.

It is no matter if I do halt; I have the wars for my *colour*, and my pension shall seem the more reasonable. *Sh. Hen.* IV.

Their sin admitted no *colour* or excuse. *King Charles.*

6. Appearance; pretence; false shew.

Under the *colour* of commending him,
I have access my own love to prefer. *Shakespeare.*

Merchants came to Rhodes with a great ship laded with corn, under the *colour* of the sale whereof they noted all that was done in the city. *Knolles's History of the Turks.*

7. Kind; species; character.

Boys and women are, for the most part, cattle of this *colour*. *Shakespeare's As you like it.*

8. In the plural, a standard; an ensign of war: they say the *colours* of the foot, and *standard* of horse.

He at Venice gave
His body to that pleasant country's earth,
And his pure soul unto his captain Christ,
Under whose *colours* he had fought so long. *Shak. Rich.* II.

Against all checks, rebukes, and manners,
I must advance the *colours* of my love,
And not retire. *Shakesp. Merry Wives of Windsor.*

The banks on both sides were filled with companies, passing all along the river under their *colours*, with trumpets sounding. *Knolles's History of the Turks.*

An author compares a ragged coin to a tattered *colours*. *Addis.*

To CO'LOUR. *v. a.* [*coloro*, Latin.]

1. To mark with some hue, or die.

The rays, to speak properly, are not *coloured*: in them there is nothing else than a certain power and disposition to stir up a sensation of this or that colour. *Newton's Opt.*

2. To palliate; to excuse; to dress in specious colours, or fair appearances.

I told him, that I would not favour or *colour* in any sort his former folly. *Raleigh's Essays.*

He *colours* the falshood of Æneas by an express command from Jupiter to forsake the queen. *Dryden's Dedic. Æn.*

3. To make plausible.

We have scarce heard of an insurrection that was not *coloured* with grievances of the highest kind, or countenanced by one or more branches of the legislature. *Addis. Freeholder.*

4. *To* COLOUR *a stranger's goods*, is when a freeman allows a foreigner to enter goods at the customhouse in his name; so that the foreigner pays but single duty, when he ought to pay double. *Phillips.*

To CO'LOUR. *v. n.* To blush. A low word, only used in conversation.

CO'LOURABLE. *adj.* [from *colour.*] Specious; plausible. It is now little used.

They have now a *colourable* pretence to withstand innovations, having accepted of other laws and rules already. *Spenser.*

They were glad to lay hold on so *colourable* a matter, and to traduce him as an author of suspicious innovation. *Hooker.*

Had I facrificed ecclefiaftical government and revenues to their covetoufnefs and ambition, they would have found no *colourable* neceffity of an army. *K. Charles.*

We hope the mercy of God will confider us unto fome mineration of our offences; yet had not the fincerity of our parents fo *colourable* expectations. *Brown's Vulgar Errours.*

CO'LOURABLY. *adv.* [from *colourable.*] Specioufly; plaufibly.

The procefs, howfoever *colourably* awarded, hath not hit the very mark whereat it was directed. *Bacon.*

CO'LOURED. *participial adj.* [from *colour.*] Streaked; diverfified with variety of hues.

The *coloured* are coarfer juiced, and therefore not fo well, and equally concocted. *Bacon's Nat. Hiftory.*

CO'LOURING. *n. f.* [from *colour.*] The part of the painter's art that teaches to lay on his colours with propriety and beauty.

From lines drawn true, our eye may trace
A foot, a knee, a hand, a face;
Yet if the *colouring* be not there,
At beft 'twill only not difpleafe. *Prior.*

CO'LOURIST. *n. f.* [from *colour.*] A painter who excels in giving the proper colours to his defigns.

Titian, Paul Veronefe, Van Dyck, and the reft of the good *colourifts*, have come neareft to nature. *Dryd. Dufrefnoy.*

CO'LOURLESS. *adj.* [from *colour.*] Without colour; not diftinguifhed by any hue; tranfparent.

Tranfparent fubftances, as glafs, water and air, when made very thin by being blown into bubbles, or otherways formed into plates, exhibit various colours, according to their various thinnefs; although, at a greater thicknefs, they appear very clear and *colourlefs.* *Newton's Opt.*

Pellucid *colourlefs* glafs or water, by being beaten into a powder or froth, do acquire a very intenfe whitenefs. *Bentley.*

COLT. *n. f.* [colt, Saxon.]

1. A young horfe: ufed commonly for the male offspring of a horfe, as *foal* for the female.

The *colt* hath about four years of growth, and fo the fawn, and fo the calf. *Bacon's Natural Hiftory*, N°. 759.

Like *colts* or unmanaged horfes, we ftart at dead bones and lifelefs blocks. *Taylor's Holy Living.*

No fports, but what belong to war, they know;
To break the ftubborn *colt*, to bend the bow. *Dryd. Æn.*

2. A young foolifh fellow.

Ay, that's a *colt*, indeed; for he doth nothing but talk of his horfe. *Shakefp. Merchant of Venice.*

To COLT. *v. n.* [from the noun.] To frifk; to be licentious; to run at large without rule; to riot; to frolick.

As foon as they were out of fight by themfelves, they fhook off their bridles, and began to *colt* anew more licentioufly than before. *Spenfer's State of Ireland.*

To COLT. *v. a.* To befool.

What a plague mean ye, to *colt* me thus? *Sh. Hen.* IV.

COLTS-FOOT. *n. f.* [from *colt* and *foot.*]

It hath a radiated flower, whofe difk confifts of many florets, but the crown compofed of many half florets: the embryoes are included in a multifid flowercup, which turns to downy feeds fixed in a bed. The fpecies are, 1. Common coltsfoot. 2. Round leaved fmooth colts-foot of the Alps. The firft common in watery places in England; the fecond grows wild upon the Alps: the flowers of this are purple, and thofe of the common fort yellow. *Miller.*

COLTS-TOOTH. *n. f.* [from *colt* and *tooth.*]

1. An imperfect or fuperfluous tooth in young horfes.

2. A love of youthful pleafure; a difpofition to the practices of youth.

Well faid, lord Sands;
Your *colts-tooth* is not caft yet?—
—No, my lord; nor fhall not, while I have a ftump. *Shak.*

CO'LTER. *n. f.* [culꞇoꞃ, Sax. *culter*, Lat.] The fharp iron of a plough that cuts the ground perpendicularly to the fhare.

CO'LTISH. *adj.* [from *colt.*] Having the tricks of a colt; wanton.

CO'LUBRINE. *adj.* [*colubrinus*, Latin.]

1. Relating to a ferpent.

2. Cunning; crafty.

CO'LUMBARY. *n. f.* [*columbarium*, Lat.] A dovecot; a pigeonhoufe.

The earth of *columbaries* or dovehoufes, is much defired in the artifice of faltpetre. *Brown's Vulgar Errours, b.* iii. *c.* 3.

CO'LUMBINE. *n. f.* [*columbina*, Latin.]

A plant with leaves like the meadow rue. the flowers are pendulous, and of an anomalous figure: the piftil of the flower becomes a membranaceous fruit, confifting of many pods, each containing many fhining black feeds. *Millar.*

Columbines are of feveral forts and colours. They flower in the end of May, when few other flowers fhew themfelves. *Mortimer's Hufbandry.*

CO'LUMBINE. *n. f.* [*columbinus*, Lat.] A kind of violet colour, or changeable dove colour. *Dict.*

CO'LUMN. *n. f.* [*columna*, Latin.]

1. A round pillar.

Some of the old Greek *columns*, and altars were brought from the ruins of Apollo's temple at Delos. *Peacham.*

Round broken *columns* clafping ivy twin'd. *Pope.*

2. Any body of certain dimenfions preffing vertically upon its bafe.

The whole weight of any *column* of the atmofphere, and likewife the fpecifick gravity of its bafes, are certainly known by many experiments. *Bentley's Sermons.*

3. [In the military art.] The long file or row of troops, or of baggage, of an army in its march. An army marches in one, two, three, or more columns, according as the ground will allow.

4. [With printers.] A column is half a page, when divided into two equal parts by a line paffing through the middle, from the top to the bottom; and, by feveral parallel lines, pages are often divided into three or more columns.

COLU'MNAR. } *adj.* [from *column.*] Formed in columns.
COLUMNA'RIAN. }

White *columnar* fpar, out of a ftone-pit. *Woodw. on Foffils.*

COLU'RES. *n. f.* [*coluri*, Latin; κόλουροι.]

Two great circles fuppofed to pafs through the poles of the world: one through the equinoctial points Aries and Libra; the other through the folftitial points, Cancer and Capricorn. They are called the equinoctial and folftitial *colures*, and divide the eclíptick into four equal parts. The points where they interfect the ecliptick are called the cardinal points. *Harris.*

Thrice the equinoctial line
He circled; four times crofs'd the car of night
From pole to pole, traverfing each *colure.* *Milton's Par. Loft.*

CO'LWORT. *n. f.* See COLEWORT.

CO'MA. *n. f.* [κῶμα.] A morbid difpofition to fleep; a lethargy.

COMA'RT. *n. f.*

By the fame *comart*,
And carriage of the articles defign'd,
His fell to Hamlet. *Shakefpeare's Hamlet.*

COMA'TE. *n. f.* [*con* and *mate.*] Companion.

My *comates* and brothers in exile. *Shakefp. As you like it.*

COMATO'SE. *adj.* [from *coma.*] Lethargick; fleepy to a difeafe.

Our beft caftor is from Ruffia; the great and principal ufe whereof, inwardly, is in hyfterical and *comatofe* cafes. *Grew's Mufæum.*

COMB in the end, and COMP in the beginning of names, feem to be derived from the Britifh *kum*, which fignifies a low fituation. *Gibfon's Camden.*

COMB, in *Cornifh*, fignifies a *valley*, and had the fame meaning anciently in the French tongue.

COMB. *n. f.* [camb, Saxon; *kam*, Dutch.]

1. An inftrument to feparate and adjuft the hair.

By fair Ligea's golden *comb*,
Wherewith fhe fits on diamond rocks,
Sleeking her foft alluring locks. *Milton.*

I made an inftrument in fafhion of a *comb*, whofe teeth, being in number fixteen, were about an inch and a half broad, and the intervals of the teeth about two inches wide. *Newton.*

2. The top or creft of a cock, fo called from its pectinated indentures.

Cocks have great *combs* and fpurs, hens little or none. *Bacon.*

High was his *comb*, and coral-red withal,
With dents embattl'd, like a caftle-wall. *Dryden.*

3. The cantons in which the bees lodge their honey. Perhaps from the fame word which makes the termination of towns, and fignifies *hollow* or *deep*.

This in affairs of ftate,
Employ'd at home, abides within the gate,
To fortify the *combs*, to build the wall,
To prop the ruins, left the fabrick fall. *Dryd. Virg. Georg.*

To COMB. *v. a.* [from the noun.]

1. To divide, and clean, and adjuft the hair with a comb.

Her care fhall be
To *comb* your noddle with a three-legg'd ftool. *Shakefpeare.*

Divers with us, that are grown grey, and yet would appear young, find means to make their hair black, by *combing* it, as they fay, with a leaden comb, or the like. *Bacon's Nat. Hift.*

She with ribbons tied
His tender neck, and *comb'd* his filken hide. *Dryden's Æn.*

There was a fort of engine, from which were extended twenty long poles, wherewith the man-mountain *combs* his head. *Swift.*

2. To lay any thing confifting of filaments fmooth, by drawing through narrow interftices; as, *to comb wool.*

COMB-BRUSH. *n. f.* [*comb* and *brufh.*] A brufh to clean combs.

COMB-MAKER. *n f.* [*comb* and *maker.*] One whofe trade is to make combs.

This wood is of ufe for the turner, engraver, carver, and *combmaker.* *Mortimer's Hufbandry.*

To CO'MBAT. *v. n.* [*combattre*, Fr.] To fight; generally in a duel, or hand to hand.

Pardon me, I will not *combat* in my fhirt. *Shakefpeare.*

To CO'MBAT. *v. a.* To oppofe; to fight.

Love yields at laft, thus *combated* by pride,
And fhe fubmits to be the Roman's bride. *Granville.*

CO'MBAT. *n. f.* [from the verb.] Conteft; battle; duel; ftrife;

strife; opposition generally between two; but sometimes it is used for battle.

Those regions were full both of cruel monsters and monstrous men; all which, by private *combats*, they delivered the countries of. *Sidney, b.* ii.

But, oh, the noble *combat* that, 'twixt joy and sorrow, was fought in Paulina! She had one eye declined for the loss of her husband, another elevated that the oracle was fulfilled. *Shakespeare's Winter's Tale.*

The *combat* now by courage must be try'd. *Dryden.*

CO'MBATANT. *n. s.* [*combattant*, French.]

1. He that fights with another; duellist; antagonist in arms.

So frown'd the mighty *combatants*, that hell
Grew darker at their frown. *Milton's Paradise Lost, b.* ii.

Who, single *combatant*,
Duel'd their armies rank'd in proud array,
Himself an army. *Milton's Agonistes, l.* 344.

He with his sword unsheath'd, on pain of life,
Commands both *combatants* to cease their strife. *Dryden.*

Like despairing *combatants* they strive against you, as if they had beheld unveiled the magical shield of Ariosto, which dazzled the beholders with too much brightness. *Dryden.*

2. A champion.

When any of those *combatants* strips his terms of ambiguity, I shall think him a champion for knowledge. *Locke.*

3. With *for* before the thing defended.

Men become *combatants for* those opinions. *Locke.*

CO'MBER. *n. s.* [from *comb.*] He whose trade it is to disentangle wool, and lay it smooth for the spinner.

CO'MBINATE. *adj.* [from *combine.*] Bethrothed; promised; settled by compact. A word of *Shakespeare.*

She lost a noble brother; with him the sinew of her fortune, her marriage dowry; with both, her *combinate* husband, this well seeming Angelo. *Shakesp. Measure for Measure.*

COMBINA'TION. *n. s.* [from *combine.*]

1. Union for some certain purpose; association; league. A combination is of private persons, a confederacy of states or sovereigns.

This cunning cardinal
The articles o' th' *combination* drew,
As himself pleas'd. *Shakespeare's Henry* VIII.

2. It is now generally used in an ill sense; but was formerly indifferent.

They aim to subdue all to their own will and power, under the disguises of holy *combinations*. *K. Charles.*

3. Union of bodies, or qualities; commixture; conjunction.

These natures, from the moment of their first *combination*, have been and are for ever inseparable. *Hooker, b.* v. *s.* 52.

Resolution of compound bodies by fire, does not so much enrich mankind as it divides the bodies; as upon the score of its making new compounds by new *combinations*. *Boyle.*

Ingratitude is always in *combination* with pride and hardheartedness. *South's Sermons.*

4. Copulation of ideas in the mind.

They never suffer any ideas to be joined in their understandings, in any other or stronger *combination* than what their own nature and correspondence give them. *Locke.*

5. COMBINATION is used in mathematicks, to denote the variation or alteration of any number of quantities, letters, sounds, or the like, in all the different manners possible. Thus the number of possible changes or *combinations* of the twenty-four letters of the alphabet, taken first two by two, then three by three, &c. amount to 1,391,724,288,887,252, 999,425,128,493,402,200. *Chambers.*

To COMBI'NE. *v. a.* [*combiner*, Fr. *binos jungere.*]

1. To join together.

Let us not then suspect our happy state,
As not secure to single or *combin'd*. *Milton's Paradise Lost.*

2. To link in union.

God, the best maker of all marriages,
Combine your hearts in one, your realms in one. *Shak. H.* V.

3. To agree; to accord; to settle by compact.

My heart's dear love is set on his fair daughter;
As mine on her's, so her's is set on mine,
And all *combin'd*, save what thou must *combine*
By holy marriage. *Shakespeare's Romeo and Juliet.*

4. To join words or ideas together; opposed to *analyse.*

To COMBI'NE. *v. n.*

1. To coalesce; to unite each with other. Used both of things and persons.

Honour and policy, like unsever'd friends
I' th' war, do grow together: grant that, and tell me
In peace what each of them by th' other loses,
That they *combine* not there? *Shakesp. Coriolanus.*

2. To unite in friendship or design.

Combine together 'gainst the enemy;
For these domestick and particular broils
Are not the question here. *Shakespeare's King Lear.*

You with your foes *combine*,
And seem your own destruction to design. *Dryd. Aurengz.*

CO'MBLESS. *adj.* [from *comb.*] Wanting a comb or crest.

What, is your crest a coxcomb?——
—A *combless* cock, so Kate will be my hen. *Shakespeare.*

COMBU'ST. *adj.* [from *cumburo*, *cumbustum*, Latin.]

When a planet is not above eight degrees and a half distant from the sun, either before or after him, it is said to be *combust*, or in *combustion*. *Harris.*

COMBU'STIBLE. *adj.* [*comburo combustum*, Lat.] Having the quality of catching fire; susceptible of fire.

Charcoals, made out of the wood of oxycedar, are white; because their vapours are rather sulphurous than of any other *combustible* substance. *Brown's Vulgar Errours, b.* vi. *c.* 12.

Sin is to the soul like fire to *combustible* matter, it assimilates before it destroys it. *South's Sermons.*

They are but strewed over with a little penitential ashes; and will, as soon as they meet with *combustible* matter, flame out. *Decay of Piety.*

The flame shall still remain;
Nor, 'till the fuel perish, can decay,
By nature form'd on things *combustible* to prey. *Dryden.*

COMBU'STIBLENESS. *n. s.* [from *combustible.*] Aptness to take fire.

COMBU'STION. *n. s.* [French.]

1. Conflagration; burning; consumption by fire.

The future *combustion* of the earth is to be ushered in and accompanied with all sorts of violent impressions upon nature. *Burnet's Theory of the Earth.*

2. Tumult; hurry; hubbub; bustle; hurly burly.

Mutual *combustions*, bloodsheds, and wastes may enforce them, through very faintness, after the experience of so endless miseries. *Hooker, b.* iv. *sect.* 14.

Prophecying, with accents terrible,
Of dire *combustion*, and confus'd events,
New-hatch'd to th' woeful time. *Shakespeare's Macbeth.*

Those long and cruel wars between the houses of York and Lancaster, brought all England into an horrible *combustion*. *Raleigh's Essays.*

How much more of pow'r,
Army against army, numberless, to raise
Dreadful *combustion* warring, and disturb,
Though not destroy, their happy native seat! *Milt. Pa. Lost.*

But say, from whence this new *combustion* springs? *Dryd.*

It moves in an inconceiveable fury and *combustion*, and at the same time with an exact regularity. *Addison's Guardian.*

To COME. *v. n.* pret. *came*, particip. *come.* [coman, Saxon; *komen*, Dut. *kommen*, German.]

1. To remove from a distant to a nearer place; to arrive. Oppose to *go.*

And troubled blood through his pale face was seen
To *come* and go, with tidings from the heart. *Fairy Queen.*

Cæsar will *come* forth to-day. *Shakesp. Julius Cæsar.*

Coming to look on you, thinking you dead,
I spake unto the crown as having sense. *Shakesp. Hen.* IV.

The colour of the king doth *come* and go,
Between his purpose and his conscience. *Shakesp. K. John.*

The Christians having stood almost all the day in order of battle, in the sight of the enemy, vainly expecting when he should *come* forth to give them battle, returned at night into their camp. *Knolles's History of the Turks.*

'Tis true that since the senate's succour *came*,
They grow more bold. *Dryden's Tyrannick Love.*

This Christian woman!
Ah! there the mischief *comes*. *Rowe's Royal Convert.*

2. To draw near; to advance towards.

By the pricking of my thumbs,
Something wicked this way *comes*. *Shakesp. Macbeth.*

3. To move in any manner towards another; implying the idea of being received by another, or of tending towards another. The word always respects the place to which the motion tends, not that place which it leaves; yet this meaning is sometimes almost evanescent and imperceptible.

I did hear
The galloping of horse: who was't *came* by? *Sh. Macbeth.*

Bid them cover the table, serve in the meat, and we will *come* in to dinner. *Shakesp. Merchant of Venice.*

As soon as the commandment *came* abroad, the children of Israel brought in abundance the first fruits. 2 *Chron.* xxxi. 5.

Knowledge is a thing of their own invention, or which they *come* to by fair reasoning. *Burnet's Theory of the Earth.*

It is impossible to *come* near your lordship at any time, without receiving some favour. *Congr. Dedic. to Old Batchelor.*

None may *come* in view, but such as are pertinent. *Locke.*

No perception of bodies, at a distance, may be accounted for by the motion of particles *coming* from them, and striking on our organs. *Locke.*

They take the colour of what is laid before them, and as soon lose and resign it to the next that happens to *come* in their way. *Locke.*

God has made the intellectual world harmonious and beautiful without us; but it will never *come* into our heads all at once. *Locke.*

4. To proceed; to issue.

Behold, my son, which *came* forth of my bowels, seeketh my life. 2 *Sa.* xvi. 11.

I came

I *came* forth from the father, and am come into the world. *Jo.* xvi. 28.

5. To advance from one ſtage or condition to another.

Truſt me, I am exceeding weary.——
—Is it *come* to that? I had thought wearineſs durſt not have attacked one of ſo high blood *Shakeſp. Henry* IV. *p.* ii.

Though he would after have turned his teeth upon Spain, yet he was taken order with before it *came* to that. *Bacon.*

Seditious tumults, and ſeditious fames, differ no more but as brother and ſiſter; eſpecially if it *come* to that, that the beſt actions of a ſtate are taken in ill ſenſe, and traduced. *Bacon, Eſſay* 16.

His ſoldiers had daily divers ſkirmiſhes with the Numidians, ſo that once the ſkirmiſh was like to *come* to a juſt battle. *Knolles's Hiſtory of the Turks.*

When it *came* to that once, they that had moſt fleſh wiſhed they had had leſs. *L'Eſtrange.*

Every new ſprung paſſion is a part of the action, except we conceive nothing to be action 'till the players *come* to blows. *Dryden on Dramatick Poetry.*

The force whereby bodies cohere is very much greater when they *come* to immediate contact, than when they are at ever ſo ſmall a finite diſtance. *Cheyne's Phil. Prin.*

6. To change condition either for better or worſe.

One ſaid to Ariſtippus, 'Tis a ſtrange thing why men ſhould rather give to the poor than to philoſophers. He anſwered, becauſe they think themſelves may ſooner *come* to be poor than to be philoſophers. *Bacon's Apophthegms.*

His ſons *come* to honour, and he knoweth it not. *Job* xiv. 21.

He being *come* to the eſtate, keeps on a very buſy family. *Locke.*

You were told your maſter had gone to a tavern, and *come* to ſome miſchance. *Swift.*

7. To attain any condition or character.

A ſerpent, e'er he *comes* to be a dragon,
Does eat a bat. *Benj. Johnſon's Catiline.*

How *came* the publican juſtified, but by a ſhort and humble prayer? *Duppa's Rules for Devotion.*

He wonder'd how ſhe *came* to know
What he had done, and meant to do. *Hudibras, p.* iii. *c.* I.

The teſtimony of conſcience, thus informed, *comes* to be ſo authentick, and ſo much to be relied upon. *South's Sermons.*

8. To become.

So *came* I a widow;
And never ſhall have length of life enough
To rain upon remembrance with mine eyes. *Shak. Hen.* IV.

When he returns from hunting,
I will not ſpeak with him; ſay I am ſick.
If you *come* ſlack of former ſervices,
You ſhall do well. *Shakeſpeare's King Lear.*

9. To arrive at ſome act or habit, or diſpoſition.

They would quickly *come* to have a natural abhorrence for that which they found made them ſlighted. *Locke.*

10. To change from one ſtate into another deſired; as the butter *comes* when the parts begin to ſeparate in the churn.

It is reported, that if you lay good ſtore of kernels of grapes about the root of a vine, it will make the vine *come* earlier, and proſper better. *Bacon's Natural Hiſtory,* N°. 35.

Then butter does refuſe to *come,*
And love proves croſs and humourſome. *Hudibras, p.* ii.

In the *coming* or ſprouting of malt, as it muſt not *come* too little, ſo it muſt not *come* too much. *Mort. Husbandry.*

11. To become preſent, and no longer future.

A time will *come,* when my maturer muſe,
In Cæſar's wars, a nobler theme ſhall chuſe. *Dryd. Virg. Geo.*

12. To become preſent; no longer abſent.

That's my joy
Not to have ſeen before; for nature now
Comes all at once, confounding my delight. *Dryd. K. Arth.*

Mean while the gods the dome of Vulcan throng,
Apollo *comes,* and Neptune *came* along. *Pope's Odyſſ. b.* viii.

Come then, my friend, my genius, *come* along,
Thou maſter of the poet and the ſong. *Pope's Eſſays.*

13. To happen; to fall out.

The duke of Cornwal, and Regan his dutcheſs, will be here with him this night.—
—How *comes* that? *Shakeſpeare's King Lear.*

Let me alone that I may ſpeak, and let *come* on me what will. *Job* xiii. 13.

14. To follow as a conſequence.

Thoſe that are kin to the king, never prick their finger but they ſay, there is ſome of the king's blood ſpilt. How *comes* that? ſays he, that takes upon him not to conceive: the anſwer is, I am the king's poor couſin, ſir. *Shakeſp. Henry* IV.

15. To ceaſe very lately from ſome act or ſtate; to have juſt done or ſuffered any thing.

David ſaid unto Uriah, *cameſt* thou not from thy journey? 2 *Sa.* xi. 10.

16. *To* COME *about.* To come to paſs; to fall out; to come into being. Probably from the French *venir a bout.*

And let me ſpeak to th' yet unknowing world,
How theſe things *came about.* *Shakeſpeare.*

That cherubim, which now appears as a God to a human ſoul, knows very well that the period will *come about* in eternity, when the human ſoul ſhall be as perfect as he himſelf now is. *Addiſon's Spectator,* N°. 3.

I conclude, however it *comes about,* that things are not as they ſhould be. *Swift.*

How *comes* it *about,* that, for above ſixty years, affairs have been placed in the hands of new men. *Swift.*

17. *To* COME *about.* To change; to come round.

The wind *came about,* and ſettled in the Weſt for many days. *Bacon's New Atlantis.*

On better thoughts, and my urg'd reaſons,
They are *come about,* and won to the true ſide. *B. Johnſon.*

18. *To* COME *again.* To return.

There came water thereout; and when he had drunk, his ſpirit *came again,* and he revived. *Judg.* xv. 19.

19. *To* COME *after.* To follow.

If any man will *come after* me, let him deny himſelf, and take up his croſs and follow me. *Mat* xvi. 24.

20. *To* COME *at.* To reach; to get within the reach of; to obtain; to gain.

Neither ſword nor ſceptre can *come at* conſcience; but it is above and beyond the reach of both. *Suckling.*

Cats will eat and deſtroy your marum, if they can *come at* it. *Evelyn's Kalendar.*

In order *to come at* a true knowledge of ourſelves, we ſhould conſider, on the other hand, how far we may deſerve praiſe. *Addiſon's Spectator,* N°. 399.

Nothing makes a woman more eſteemed by the oppoſite ſex than chaſtity, and we always prize thoſe moſt who are hardeſt *to come at.* *Addiſon's Spectator,* N°. 99.

21. *To* COME *by.* To obtain; to gain; to acquire.

Things moſt needful to preſerve this life, are moſt prompt and eaſy for all living creatures *to come by.* *Hooker, b.* 5. *ſ.* 22.

Love is like a child,
That longs for every thing that he can *come by.* *Shakeſpeare.*

Thy caſe
Shall be my precedent; as thou got'ſt Milan,
I'll *come by* Naples. *Shakeſpeare's Tempeſt.*

Are you not aſhamed to inforce a poor widow to ſo rough a courſe *to come by* her own. *Shakeſpeare's Henry* IV. *p.* ii.

The ointment wherewith this is done is made of divers ingredients, whereof the ſtrangeſt and hardeſt *to come by* is the moſs of a dead man unburied. *Bacon's Natural Hiſtory.*

And with that wicked lye
A letter they *came by,*
From our king's majeſty. *Denham.*

He tells a ſad ſtory, how hard it was for him *to come by* the book of Trigantius. *Stillingfl. Def. of Diſc. on Rom. Idols.*

Amidſt your train, this unſeen judge will wait,
Examine how you *came by* all your ſtate. *Dryd. Aurengzebe.*

22. *To* COME *in.* To enter.

What, are you there? *come in,* and give ſome help. *Shak.*

Yet the ſimple ideas, thus united in the ſame ſubject, are as perfectly diſtinct as thoſe that *come in* by different ſenſes. *Locke.*

23. *To* COME *in.* To comply; to yield; to hold out no longer.

If the arch-rebel Tyrone, in the time of theſe wars, ſhould offer to *come in,* and ſubmit himſelf to her majeſty, would you not have him received. *Spenſer on Ireland.*

24. *To* COME *in.* To arrive at a port, or place of rendezvous.

At what time our ſecond fleet, which kept the narrow ſeas, was *come in* and joined to our main fleet. *Bacon.*

There was the Plymouth ſquadron now *come in,*
Which in the Streights laſt winter was abroad. *Dryden.*

25. *To* COME *in.* To become modiſh; to be brought into uſe.

Then *came* rich cloaths and graceful action *in,*
Then inſtruments were taught more moving notes. *Roſcom.*

Silken garments did not *come in* 'till late, and the uſe of them in men was often reſtrained by law. *Arbuthnot on Coins.*

26. *To* COME *in.* To be an ingredient; to make part of a compoſition.

A generous contempt of that in which too many men place their happineſs, muſt *come in* to heighten his character. *Atterb.*

27. *To* COME *in for.* To be early enough to obtain: taken from hunting, where the dogs that are ſlow get nothing.

Shape and beauty, worth and education, wit and underſtanding, gentle nature and agreeable humour, honour and virtue, were *to come in for* their ſhare of ſuch contracts. *Temple.*

If thinking is eſſential to matter, ſtocks and ſtones will *come in for* their ſhare of privilege. *Collier on Thought.*

One who had i' the rear excluded been,
And cou'd not *for* a taſte o' th' fleſh *come in,*
Licks the ſolid earth. *Tate's Juv. Sat.* 15.

The reſt *came in for* ſubſidies, whereof they ſunk conſiderable ſums. *Swift.*

28. *To* COME *in to.* To join with; to bring help.

They marched to Wells, where the lord Audley, with whom their leaders had before ſecret intelligence, *came in to* them; and was by them, with great gladneſs and cries of joy, accepted as their general. *Bacon's Henry* VII.

29. *To* COME *in to.* To comply with; to agree to.

The

The fame of their virtues will make men ready *to come into* every thing that is done or designed for the publick good. *Atterbury's Sermons.*

30. *To* COME *near.* To approach; to resemble in excellence: a metaphor from races.

Whom you cannot equal or *come near* in doing, you would destroy or ruin with evil speaking. *Ben. Johnson's Discoveries.*

The whole atchieved with such admirable invention, that nothing ancient and modern seems *to come near* it. *Temple.*

31. *To* COME *of.* To proceed; as a descendant from ancestors.

Of Priam's royal race my mother *came.* *Dryden's Æn.*

Self-love is so natural an infirmity, that it makes us partial even to those that *come of* us, as well as ourselves. *L'Estrange.*

32. *To* COME *of.* To proceed; as effects from their causes.

Will you please, sir, be gone.
I told you what would *come of* this. *Shakesp. Winter's Tale.*

We see that the hiccough *comes of* fulness of meat, especially in children, which causeth an extension of the stomach. *Bacon's Natural History.*

What *came on't* at last but that, after the dogs had deserted, the wolves worried one part of the enemies. *L'Estrange.*

This *comes of* judging by the eye, without consulting the reason. *L'Estrange.*

My young master, whatever *comes on't*, must have a wife looked out for him by that time he is of age. *Locke.*

33. *To* COME *off.* To deviate; to depart from a rule or direction.

The figure of a bell partaketh of the pyramis, but yet *coming off* and dilating more suddenly. *Bacon's Nat. History.*

34. *To* COME *off.* To escape.

I knew the foul enchanter, though disguis'd,
Enter'd the very lime-twigs of his spells,
And yet *came off.* *Milton.*

How thou wilt here *come off*, surmounts my reach. *Milt.*

If, upon such a fair and full trial, he can *come off*, he is then clear and innocent. *South.*

Those that are in any signal danger implore his aid; and, if they *come off* safe, they call their deliverance a miracle. *Addison on Italy.*

35. *To* COME *off.* To end an affair; to be dismissed with our lot.

Oh, bravely *came* we *off*,
When with a volley of our needless shot,
After such bloody toil, we bid good-night. *Shakes. K. John.*

Ever since Spain and England have had any thing to debate one with the other, the English, upon all encounters, have *come off* with honour and the better. *Bacon on War with Spain.*

We must expect sometimes to *come off* by the worst, before we obtain the final conquest. *Calamy.*

He oft', in such attempts as these,
Came off with glory and success. *Hudibras, p. 1. cant. 1.*

36. *To* COME *off from.* To leave; to forbear.

To come off from these grave disquisitions, I would clear the point by one instance more. *Felton on the Classicks.*

37. *To* COME *on.* To advance; to make progress.

Of late, things seem *to come on* apace to their former state. *Bacon on the War with Spain.*

There was in the camp both strength and victual sufficient for the obtaining of the victory, if they would not protract the war until winter were *come on.* *Knolles's Hist. of the Turks.*

The sea *came on*, the south with mighty roar
Dispers'd and dash'd the rest upon the rocky shoar. *Dryden.*

So Travellers, who waste the day,
Noting at length the setting sun,
They mend their pace as night *comes on.* *Granville.*

38. *To* COME *on.* To advance to combat.

The great ordnance once discharged, the armies *came* fast *on*, and joined battle. *Knolles's History of the Turks.*

Rhymer, *come on*, and do the worst you can;
I fear not you, nor yet a better man. *Dryden.*

39. *To* COME *on.* To thrive; to grow big.

Come on, poor babe;
Some powerful spirit instruct the kites and ravens
To be thy nurses. *Shakespeare's Winter's Tale.*

It should seem by the experiments, both of the malt and of the roses, that they will *come* far faster *on* in water than in earth; for the nourishment is easier drawn out of water than out of earth. *Bacon's Natural History*, N°. 648.

40. *To* COME *over.* To repeat an act.

I saw him run after a gilded butterfly; and when he caught it, he let it go again, and after it again; and *over* and *over* he *comes*, and caught it again. *Shak. Coriolanus.*

41. *To* COME *over.* To revolt.

They are perpetually teizing their friends to *come over* to them. *Addison's Spectator*, N°. 185.

A man, in changing his side, not only makes himself hated by those he left, but is seldom heartily esteemed by those he *comes over* to. *Addison's Spectator*, N°. 162.

42. *To* COME *over.* To rise in distillation.

Perhaps also the phlegmatick liquor, that is wont to *come over* in this analysis, may, at least as to part of it, be produced by the operation of the fire. *Boyle.*

43. *To* COME *out.* To be made publick.

Before his book *came out*, I had undertaken the answer of several others. *Stillingfleet.*

I have been tedious; and, which is worse, it *comes out* from the first draught, and uncorrected. *Dryden.*

44. *To* COME *out.* To appear upon trial; to be discovered.

It is indeed *come out* at last, that we are to look on the saints as inferior deities. *Stillingfleet's Defence of Disc. on Rom. Idol.*

The weight of the denarius, or the seventh of a Roman ounce, *comes out* sixty-two grains and four sevenths. *Arbuthn.*

45. *To* COME *out with.* To give a vent to; to let fly.

Those great masters of chymical arcana must be provoked, before they will *come out with* them. *Boyle.*

46. *To* COME *to.* To consent or yield.

What is this, if my parson will not *come to*? *Swift.*

47. *To* COME *to.* To amount to.

The emperour imposed so great a custom upon all corn to be transported out of Sicily, that the very customs *came to* as much as both the price of the corn and the freight together. *Knolles's History of the Turks.*

You saucily pretend to know
More than your dividend *comes to.* *Hudibras, p. ii.*

Animals either feed upon vegetables immediately, or, which *comes to* the same at last, upon other animals which have fed upon them. *Woodward's Natural History.*

He pays not this tax immediately, yet his purse will find it by a greater want of money than that *comes to.* *Locke.*

48. *To* COME *to himself.* To recover his senses.

He falls into sweet ecstacy of joy, wherein I shall leave him 'till he *comes to himself.* *Temple.*

49. *To* COME *to pass.* To be effected; to fall out.

It *cometh*, we grant, many times *to pass* that the works of men being the same, their drifts and purpose therein are divers. *Hooker, b. v. sect. 14.*

How *comes* it *to pass*, that some liquors cannot pierce into or moisten some bodies, which are easily pervious to other liquors? *Boyle's History of Firmness.*

50. *To* COME *up.* To grow out of the ground.

Another ill accident is over-wet at sowing time, which with us breedeth much dearth, insomuch as the corn never *cometh up.* *Bacon's Natural History.*

Good intentions are at least the seeds of good actions, and every man ought to sow them, whether they *come up* or no. *Temple.*

51. *To* COME *up.* To make appearance.

If wars should mow them down never so fast, yet they may be suddenly supplied, and *come up* again. *Bacon.*

52. *To* COME *up.* To come into use, as *a fashion comes up.*

53. *To* COME *up to.* To amount to.

He prepares for a surrender, asserting that all these will not *come up to* near the quantity requisite. *Woodw. Nat. History.*

54. *To* COME *up to.* To rise to.

Whose ignorant credulity will not
Come up to th' truth. *Shakespeare's Winter's Tale.*

Considerations there are, that may make us, if not *come up to* the character of those who rejoice in tribulations, yet at least satisfy the duty of being patient. *Wake's Prep. for Death.*

The vestes byssinæ, which some ladies wore, must have been of such extraordinary price, that there is no stuff in our age *comes up to* it. *Arbuthnot on Coins.*

When the heart is full, it is angry at all words that cannot *come up to* it. *Swift.*

55. *To* COME *up with.* To overtake.

56. *To* COME *upon.* To invade; to attack.

Three hundred horse, and three thousand foot English, commanded by Sir John Norris, were charged by Parma, *coming upon* them with seven thousand horse. *Bacon.*

When old age *comes upon* him, it comes alone, bringing no other evil with it but itself. *South.*

COME. [participle of the verb.]

Thy words were heard, and I am *come* to thy words. *Dan.*

COME. A particle of exhortation; be quick; make no delay.

Come, let us make our father drink wine. *Gen.* xix. 32.

COME. A particle of reconciliation, or incitement to it.

Come, come, at all I laugh he laughs no doubt;
The only difference is, I dare laugh out. *Pope.*

COME. A kind of adverbial word for *when it shall come*; as, *come Wednesday*, when Wednesday shall come.

Come Candlemas, nine years ago she dy'd. *Gay.*

To COME. In futurity; not present; to happen hereafter.

It serveth to discover that which is hid, as well as to foretel that which is *to come.* *Bacon's Natural History.*

In times *to come*,
My waves shall wash the walls of mighty Rome. *Dryden.*

Taking a lease of land for years *to come*, at the rent of one hundred pounds. *Locke.*

COME. *n. s.* [from the verb.] A sprout: a cant term.

That the malt is sufficiently well dried, you may know both by the taste, and also by the falling off of the *come* or sprout. *Mortimer's Husbandry.*

COME'DIAN. *n. s.* [from *comedy.*]

1. A player or actor of comick parts.

2. A player in general; a stage-player; an actress or actor.

Melissarion, pretty honey-bee, when of a *comedian* she became a wealthy man's wife, would be saluted madam Pithias, or Prudence. *Camden's Remains.*

Comedians on the stage shew all their skill,
And after do as love and fortune will.

3. A writer of comedies.

Scaliger willeth us to admire Plautus as a *comedian*, but Terence as a pure and elegant speaker. *Peacham of Poetry.*

CO'MEDY. *n. s.* [*comedia*, Lat.] A dramatick representation of the lighter faults of mankind.

Your honour's players
Are come to play a pleasant *comedy*. *Shak. Tam. of the Shrew.*

A long, exact, and serious *comedy*,
In every scene some moral let it teach,
And, if it can, at once both please and preach. *Pope.*

CO'MELINESS. *n. s.* [from *comely*.] Grace; beauty; dignity.

A careless *comeliness* with comely care. *Sidney.*

The service of God hath not such perfection of grace and *comliness* as when the dignity of the place doth concur. *Hooker.*

They skilled not of the goodly ornaments of poetry, yet were sprinkled with some pretty flowers, which gave good grace and *comeliness*. *Spenser on Ireland.*

Hardly shall you meet with man or woman so aged or ill-favoured, but, if you will commend them for *comeliness*, nay and for youth too, shall take it well. *South.*

There is great pulchritude and *comeliness* of proportion in the leaves, flowers, and fruits of plants. *Ray on the Creation.*

A horseman's coat shall hide
Thy taper shape and *comeliness* of side. *Prior.*

CO'MELY. *adj.* [from *become*; or from cyeman, Sax. to please.]

1. Graceful; decent; having dignity or grandeur of mien or look. Comeliness seems to be that species of beauty which excites reverence rather than pleasure.

If the principal part of beauty is in decent motion, no marvel though persons in years seem many times more amiable; for no youth can be *comely* but by pardon, and considering the youth as to make up the comeliness. *Bacon, Essay* 44.

He that is *comely* when old and decrepit, surely was very beautiful when he was young. *South.*

Thou art a *comely*, young, and valiant knight. *Dryden.*

2. Used of things, decent; according to propriety.

Oh, what a world is this, when what is *comely*
Envenoms him that bears it! *Shakesp. As you like it.*

This is a happier and more *comely* time,
Than when these fellows ran about the streets,
Crying confusion. *Shakespeare's Coriolanus.*

CO'MELY. *adv.* [from the adjective.] Handsomely; gracefully.

To ride *comely*, to play at all weapons, to dance *comely*, be very necessary for a courtly gentleman. *Ascham's Schoolmaster.*

CO'MER. *n. s.* [from *come*.] One that comes.

Plants move upwards; but if the sap puts up too fast, it maketh a slender stalk, which will not support the weight; and therefore these are all swift and hasty *comers*. *Bacon.*

Time is like a fashionable host,
That slightly shakes his parting guest by th' hand;
But with his arms outstretch'd, as he would fly,
Grasps in the *comer*: welcome ever smiles,
And farewel goes out sighing. *Shak. Troilus and Cressida.*

Yourself, renowned prince, then stood as fair
As any *comer* I have look'd on yet,
For my affection. *Shakesp. Merchant of Venice.*

House and heart are open for a friend; the passage is easy, and not only admits, but even invites the *comer*. *South's Serm.*

It is natural to be kind to the last *comer*. *L'Estrange.*

Now leave those joys, unsuiting to thy age,
To a fresh *comer*, and resign the stage. *Dryden.*

The renowned champion of our lady of Loretto, and the miraculous translation of her chapel, about which he hath published a defiance to the world, and offers to prove it against all *comers*. *Stillingfleet.*

There it is not strange, that the mind should give itself up to the common opinion, or render itself to the first *comer*. *Locke.*

CO'MET. *n. s.* [*cometa*, Latin, a hairy star.]

A heavenly body in the planetary region appearing suddenly, and again disappearing; and, during the time of its appearance, moving through its proper orbit, like a planet. The orbits of *comets* are ellipses, having one of their foci in the center of the sun; and being very long and eccentrick, they become invisible, when in that part most remote from the sun. *Comets*, popularly called blazing stars, are distinguished from other stars by a long train or tail of light, always opposite to the sun: hence arises a popular division of comets into three kinds, *bearded*, *tailed*, and *haired* comets; though the division rather relates to the different circumstances of the same comet, than to the phænomena of the several. Thus when the comet is eastward of the sun, and moves from it, the comet is said to be bearded, *barbatus*, because the light marches before it. When the light is westward of the sun, the comet is said to be tailed, because the train follows it. When the comet and the sun are diametrically opposite, the earth being between them, the train is hid behind the body of the comet, excepting a little that appears around it, in form of a border of hair, hence called *crinitus*.

According to Sir Isaac Newton, the tail of a comet is a very thin slender vapour, emitted by the head or nucleus of the comet, ignited by their near neighbourhood to the sun, and this vapour is furnished by the atmosphere of the comet. The tails are of various lengths; and being produced in the perihelions of the comets, will go off along with their heads into remote regions, and there gradually vanish, 'till the comets return towards the sun. The vapours of comets being thus dilated, rarefied, and diffused through all the celestial regions, may probably, by little and little, by means of their own gravity, be attracted down to the planets, and become intermingled with their atmospheres. For the conservation of the water, and moisture of the planets, comets seem absolutely requisite; from whose condensed vapours and exhalations all that moisture which is spent in vegetations and putrefactions, and turned into dry earth, may be resupplied and recruited; for all vegetables grow and increase wholly from fluids; and, as to their greatest part, turn by putrefaction into earth again, an earthy slime being perpetually precipitated to the bottom of putrefying liquors. Hence the quantity of dry earth must continually increase, and the moisture of the globe decrease, and at last be quite evaporated, if it have not a continual supply from some part or other of the universe. And I suspect, adds Sir Isaac, that the spirit which makes the finest, subtilest, and best part of our air, and which is absolutely requisite for the life and being of all things, comes principally from the comets. On this principle there seems to be some foundation for the popular opinion of presages from comets; since the tail of a comet, thus intermingled with our atmosphere, may produce changes very sensible in animal and vegetable bodies.

The same great author has computed that the sun's heat, in the comet of 1680, was, to his heat with us at Midsummer, as twenty-eight thousand to one; and that the heat of the body of the comet, was near two thousand times as great as that of red-hot iron. He also calculates, that a globe of red-hot iron, of the dimensions of our earth, would scarce be cool in fifty thousand years. If then the comet be supposed to cool a hundred times as fast as red-hot iron, yet, since its heat was a thousand times greater, supposing it of the bigness of the earth, it would not be cool in a million of years. Hitherto no comet has threatened the earth with a nearer approach than that of 1680; for, by calculation, Dr. Halley found, on November 11, that comet was not above one semidiameter of the earth to the northward of the way of the earth; at which time, had the earth been in that part of its orbit, the comet would have had a parallax equal to that of the moon. What might have been the consequence of so near an appulse? a contact or shock of the celestial bodies? a deluge, Mr. Whiston says. Astronomers have been divided about the return of comets, and time and observation must determine the question. However, Dr. Halley has foretold the return of one in 1758, which formerly appeared in 1456. *Trevoux. Chambers.*

And wherefore gaze this goodly company,
As if they saw some wond'rous monument,
Some *comet*, or an unusual prodigy. *Shak. Tam. of the Shrew.*

Such his fell glances as the fatal light
Of staring *comets*. *Crashaw.*

I considered a *comet*, or, in the language of the vulgar, a blazing star, as a sky-rocket discharged by an hand that is almighty. *Addison's Guardian*, N°. 103.

Fierce meteors shoot their arbitrary light,
And *comets* march with lawless horrors bright. *Prior.*

CO'METARY. } *adj.* [from *comet*.] Relating to a comet.
COME'TICK. }

Refractions of light are in the planetary and *cometary* regions, as on our globe. *Cheyne's Phil. Prin.*

CO'MFIT. *n. s.* [*konfit*, Dutch. It should seem that both are formed by hasty pronunciation from *confect*.] A dry sweetmeat; any kind of fruit or root preserved with sugar, and dried.

By feeding me on beans and pease,
He crams in nasty crevices,
And turns to *comfits* by his arts,
To make me relish for desserts. *Hudibras, p.* iii. *cant.* i.

To CO'MFIT. *v. a.* [from the noun.] To preserve dry with sugar.

The fruit that does so quickly waste,
Men scarce can see it, much less taste,
Thou *comfitest* in streets to make it last. *Cowley.*

CO'MFITURE. *n. s.* [from *comfit*, or *confecture*.] Sweetmeat.

From country grass to *comfitures* of court,
Or city's quelque-choses, let not report
My mind transport. *Donne.*

To CO'MFORT. *v. a.* [*comforto*, low Latin. *Salvia comfortat nervos. Schol. Sal.*]

1. To strengthen; to enliven; to invigorate.

The evidence of God's own testimony, added unto the natural assent of reason, concerning the certainty of them, doth

doth not a little *comfort* and confirm the same. *Hooker, b. i.*

Light excelleth in *comforting* the spirits of men: light varied doth the same effect, with more novelty. This is the cause why precious stones *comfort*. *Bacon's Natural History*, N°. 960.

Some of the abbots had been guilty of *comforting* and assisting the rebels. *Ayliffe's Parergon.*

2. To console; to strengthen the mind under the pressure of calamity.

They bemoaned him, and *comforted* him over all the evil that the Lord had brought upon him. *Job*, xlii. 11.

Co'mfort. *n. s.* [from the verb.]

1. Support; assistance; countenance.

Poynings made a wild chace upon the wild Irish; where, in respect of the mountains and fastnesses, he did little good, which he would needs impute unto the *comfort* that the rebels should receive underhand from the earl of Kildare. *Bacon.*

The king did also appoint commissioners for the fining of all such as were of any value, and had any hand or partaking in the aid or *comfort* of Perkins, or the Cornishmen. *Bacon.*

2. Consolation; support under calamity or danger.

I will keep her ign'rant of her good,
To make her heavenly *comforts* of despair,
When it is least expected. *Shakesp. Measure for Measure.*

As they have no apprehension of those things, so they need no *comfort* against them. *Tillotson, Serm.* i.

3. That which gives consolation or support.

Your children were vexation to your youth,
But mine shall be a *comfort* to your age. *Shakesp. Rich.* III.

Co'mfortable. *adj.* [from *comfort.*]

1. Receiving comfort; susceptible of comfort.

For my sake be *comfortable*; hold death
A while at the arm's end. *Shakesp. As you like it.*

My lord leans wond'rously to discontent;
His *comfortable* temper has forsook him:
He is much out of health. *Shakespeare's Timon.*

What can promise him a *comfortable* appearance before his dreadful judge? *South.*

2. Dispensing comfort; having the power of giving comfort.

He had no brother, which though it be *comfortable* for kings to have, yet draweth the subjects eyes aside. *Bacon's Hen.* VII.

The lives of many miserable men were saved, and a *comfortable* provision made for their subsistence. *Dryd. Fab. Dedic.*

Co'mfortably. *adv.* [from *comfortable.*] In a comfortable manner; with comfort; without despair.

Upon view of the sincerity of that performance, hope *comfortably* and chearfully for God's performance. *Hammond.*

Co'mforter. *n. s.* [from *comfort.*]

1. One that administers consolation in misfortunes; one that strengthens and supports the mind in misery or danger.

This very prayer of Christ obtained angels to be sent him, as *comforters* in his agony. *Hooker, b.* v. *sect.* 48.

The heav'ns have blest you with a goodly son,
To be a *comforter* when he is gone. *Shakesp. Richard* III.

Nineveh is laid waste, who will bemoan her? whence shall I seek *comforters* for thee? *Neh.* iii. 7.

2. The title of the Third Person of the Holy Trinity; the Paraclete.

Co'mfortless. *adj.* [from *comfort.*] Without comfort; without any thing to allay misfortune: used of persons as well as things.

Yet shall not my death be *comfortless*, receiving it by your sentence. *Sidney, b.* ii.

Where was a cave, ywrought with wond'rous art,
Deep, dark, uneasy, doleful, *comfortless*. *Fairy Queen, b.* i.

News fitting to the night;
Black, fearful, *comfortless*, and horrible. *Shakesp. K. John.*

On thy feet thou stood'st at last,
Though *comfortless*, as when a father mourns
His children, all in view destroyed at once. *Milt. Par. Lost.*

That unsociable *comfortless* deafness had not quite tired me. *Swift.*

Co'mfrey. *n. s.* [*comfrie*, French.] A plant.

The flower consists of one leaf, shaped like a funnel, having an oblong tube, but shaped at the top like a pitcher: out of the flower-cup, which is deeply cut into five long narrow segments, rises the pointal, attended with four embryoes, which afterwards become so many seeds, in form somewhat like the head of a viper, which ripen in the flower-cup. It grows wild on the sides of banks and rivers, and is gathered for medicinal uses. *Miller.*

Co'mical. *adj.* [*comicus*, Latin.]

1. Raising mirth; merry; diverting.

The greatest resemblance of our author is in the familiar stile and pleasing way of relating *comical* adventures of that nature. *Dryden's Fables, Preface.*

Something so *comical* in the voice and gestures, that a man can hardly forbear being pleased. *Addison on Italy.*

2. Relating to comedy; befitting comedy.

That all might appear to be knit up in a *comical* conclusion, the duke's daughter was afterwards joined in marriage to the lord Lisle. *Hayward.*

They deny it to be tragical, because its catastrophe is a wedding, which hath ever been accounted *comical*. *Gay.*

Co'mically. *adv.* [from *comical.*]

1. In such a manner as raises mirth.

2. In a manner befitting comedy.

Co'micalness. *n. s.* [from *comical.*] The quality of being comical; the power of raising mirth.

CO'MICK. *adj.* [*comicus*, Lat. *comique*, French.]

1. Relating to comedy.

When I venture at the *comick* stile,
Thy scornful lady seems to mock my toil. *Waller.*

A *comick* subject loves an humble verse,
Thyestes scorns a low and *comick* stile;
Yet comedy sometimes may raise her voice. *Roscommon.*

Thy tragick muse gives smiles, thy *comick* sleep. *Dryden.*

2. Raising mirth.

Stately triumphs, mirthful *comick* shows,
Such as befit the pleasure. *Shakesp. Henry* VI. *p.* iii.

Co'ming. *n. s.* [from *To come.*]

1. The act of coming; approach.

Where art thou, Adam! wont with joy to meet
My *coming*, seen far off? *Milton's Paradise Lost, b.* x.

Sweet the *coming* on
Of grateful ev'ning mild. *Milton's Paradise Lost, b.* iv.

2. State of being come; arrival.

May't please you, noble madam, to withdraw
Into your private chamber; we shall give you
The full cause of our *coming*. *Shakesp. Henry* VIII.

Some people in America counted their years by the *coming* of certain birds amongst them at their certain seasons, and leaving them at others. *Locke.*

Coming-in. *n. s.* Revenue; income.

Here's a small trifle of wives, eleven widows and nine maids is a simple *coming-in* for one man. *Shakespeare.*

What are thy rents? what are thy *comings-in*?
O ceremony, shew me but thy worth:
What is thy toll, O adoration? *Shakesp. Henry* V.

Co'ming. *participial adj.* [from *come.*]

1. Fond; forward; ready to come.

Now will I be your Rosalind in a more *coming* on disposition; and ask me what you will, I will grant it. *Shakespeare.*

That very lapidary himself, with a *coming* stomach, and in the cock's place, would have made the cock's choice. *L'Estr.*

That he had been so affectionate a husband, was no ill argument to the *coming* dowager. *Dryd. Virg. Æn. Dedic.*

On morning wings, how active springs the mind,
How easy every labour it pursues,
How *coming* to the poet every muse! *Pope's Imit. of Horace.*

2. Future; to come.

Praise of great acts, he scatters as a seed,
Which may the like in *coming* ages breed. *Roscommon.*

Comi'tial. *adj.* [*comitia*, Lat. an assembly of the Romans.] Relating to the assemblies of the people of Rome.

Co'mity. *n. s.* [*comitas*, Latin.] Courtesy; civility; goodbreeding. *Dict.*

Co'mma. *n. s.* [κόμμα.]

1. The point which notes the distinction of clauses, and order of construction in the sentence, marked thus [,].

Comma's and points they set exactly right. *Pope.*

2. The ninth part of a tone, or the interval whereby a semitone or a perfect tone exceeds the imperfect tone. It is a term used only in theorical musick, to shew the exact proportions between concords. *Harris.*

To COMMA'ND. *v. a.* [*commander*, Fr. *mando*, Latin.]

1. To govern; to give orders to; to hold in subjection or obedience; contrary to obey.

Look, this feather,
Obeying with my wind when I do blow,
And yielding to another when it blows,
Commanded always by the greater gust;
Such is the lightness of you common men. *Shak. Hen.* VI.

Christ could *command* legions of angels to his rescue. *Decay of Piety.*

Should he, who was thy lord, *command* thee now,
With a harsh voice, and supercilious brow,
To servile duties. *Dryden's Pers. Sat.* 5.

2. To order; to direct to be done; contrary to prohibit: sometimes formerly with *of* before the person.

My conscience bids me ask, wherefore you have
Commanded of me these most pois'nous compounds. *Shakesp.*

We will sacrifice to the Lord our God, as he shall *command* us. *Ex.* viii. 27.

3. To have in power.

If the strong cane support thy walking hand,
Chairmen no longer shall the wall *command*. *Gay's Trivia.*

4. To overlook; to have so subject as that it may be seen or annoyed.

Up to the Eastern tower,
Whose height *commands* as subject all the vale,
To see the fight. *Shakespeare's Troilus and Cressida.*

His eye might there *command*, wherever stood
City, of old or modern fame; the seat
Of mightiest empire. *Milton's Paradise Lost, b.* xi. *l.* 385.

One

One ſide *commands* a view of the fineſt garden in the world. *Addiſon's Guardian*, Nº. 101.

To COMMA'ND. *v. n.* To have the ſupreme authority; to poſſeſs the chief power; to govern.

Thoſe two *commanding* powers of the ſoul, the underſtanding or the will. *South's Sermons.*

COMMA'ND. *n. ſ.* [from the verb.]

1. The right of commanding; power; ſupreme authority. It is uſed in military affairs, as magiſtracy or government in civil life; with *over*.

Take pity of your town and of your people,
While yet my ſoldiers are in my *command*. *Shakeſp. Hen.* V.

With lightning fill her awful hand,
And make the clouds ſeem all at her *command*. *Waller.*

He aſſumed an abſolute *command over* his readers. *Dryden.*

2. Cogent authority; deſpotiſm.

Thoſe he commands move only in *command*,
Nothing in love. *Shakeſp. Macbeth.*

Command and force may often create, but can never cure, an averſion; and whatever any one is brought to by compulſion, he will leave as ſoon as he can. *Locke on Education.*

3. The act of commanding; the mandate uttered; order.

Of this tree we may not taſte nor touch;
God ſo commanded, and left that *command*
Sole daughter of his voice. *Milton's Paradiſe Loſt, b.* ix.

As there is no prohibition of it, ſo no *command* for it. *Taylor.*

The captain gives *command*, the joyful train
Glide through the gloomy ſhade, and leave the main. *Dryd.*

4. The power of overlooking, or ſurveying any place.

The ſteepy ſtand,
Which overlooks the vale with wide *command*. *Dryd. Æn.*

COMMA'NDER. *n. ſ.* [from *command.*]

1. He that has the ſupreme authority; a general; a leader; a chief.

We'll do thee homage, and be rul'd by thee,
Love thee as our *commander* and our king. *Shakeſpeare.*

I have given him for a leader and *commander* to the people. *Iſ.* lv. 4.

The Romans, when *commanders* in war, ſpake to their army, and ſtyled them, My ſoldiers. *Bacon's Apophthegms.*

Charles, Henry, and Francis of France, often adventured rather as ſoldiers than as *commanders*. *Hayward.*

Sir Phelim O'neil appeared as their *commander* in chief. *Clar.*

Supreme *commander* both of ſea and land. *Waller.*

The heroick action of ſome great *commander*, enterpriſed for the common good, and honour of the Chriſtian cauſe. *Dryden's Juvenal, Dedication.*

Their great *commanders*, by credit in their armies, fell into the ſcales as a counterpoiſe to the people. *Swift.*

2. A paving beetle, or a very great wooden mallet, with an handle about three foot long, to uſe in both hands. *Moxon.*

3. An inſtrument of ſurgery.

The gloſſocomium, commonly called the *commander*, is of uſe in the moſt ſtrong tough bodies, and where the laxation hath been of long continuance. *Wiſeman's Surgery.*

COMMA'NDERY. *n. ſ.* [from *command.*] A body of the knights of Malta, belonging to the ſame nation.

COMMA'NDMENT. *n. ſ.* [*commandement*, French.]

1. Mandate; command; order; precept.

They plainly require ſome ſpecial *commandment* for that which is exacted at their hands. *Hooker, b.* iii. *ſect.* 7.

Say, you choſe him more after our *commandment*,
Than guided by your own affections. *Shakeſp. Coriolanus.*

By the eaſy *commandment* by God given to Adam, to forbear to feed thereon, it pleaſed God to make trial of his obedience. *Raleigh's Hiſtory of the World.*

2. Authority; coactive power.

I thought that all things had been ſavage here,
And therefore put I on the countenance
Of ſtern *commandment*. *Shakeſpeare's As you like it.*

3. By way of eminence, the precepts of the decalogue given by God to Moſes.

And he wrote upon the tables the words of the convenant and the ten *commandments*. *Exod.* xxxiv. 28.

COMMA'NDRESS. *n. ſ.* [from *commander.*] A woman veſted with ſupreme authority.

To preſcribe the order of doing in all things is a peculiar prerogative, which wiſdom hath, as queen or ſovereign *commandreſs*, over all other virtues. *Hooker, b* v. *ſect.* 8.

Be you *commandreſs* therefore, princeſs, queen
Of all our forces, be thy word a law. *Fairfax, b.* ii.

COMMATE'RIAL. *adj.* [from *con* and *materia.*] Conſiſting of the ſame matter with another thing.

The beaks in birds are *commaterial* with teeth. *Bacon.*

The body adjacent and ambient is not *commaterial*, but merely heterogeneal towards the body that is to be preſerved. *Bacon's Natural Hiſtory*, Nº. 171.

COMMATERIA'LITY. *n. ſ.* [from *commaterial.*] Reſemblance to ſomething in its matter.

CO'MMELINE. *n. ſ.* [*commelina*, Latin.] A plant.

The leaves are produced alternately, and ſurround the ſtalks at their baſe: the ſtalks trail upon the ground, and grow very branchy. At ſetting on of the branches, between the wing of the leaf and the ſtalk, is produced a flower of two leaves. From the upper part of the flower are produced three ſhort ſtamina, upon which are faſtened yellow apices, which reſemble the head of a muſhroom: in the under part of the flower are produced three other male ſtamina. The ovary is produced in the center of the flower, which is extended into a long intorted tube, and becomes an oblong fruit, divided into two cells, each containing one oblong ſeed. *Miller.*

COMME'MORABLE. *adj.* [from *commemorate.*] Deſerving to be mentioned with honour; worthy to be kept in remembrance.

To COMME'MORATE. *v. a.* [*con* and *memoro*, Latin.] To preſerve the memory by ſome publick act; to celebrate ſolemnly.

Such is the divine mercy, which we now *commemorate*; and if we *commemorate* it, we ſhall rejoice in the Lord. *Fiddes.*

COMMEMORA'TION. *n. ſ.* [from *commemorate.*] An act of publick celebration; ſolemnization of the memory of any thing.

But that which is daily offered in the church, is a daily *commemoration* of that one ſacrifice which was offered on the croſs. *Taylor's worthy Communicant.*

St. Auſtin believed that the martyrs, when the *commemorations* were made at their own ſepulchres, did join their prayers with the churches, in behalf of thoſe who there put up their ſupplications to God. *Stillingfleet's Def. of Diſc. on Rom. Idols.*

Commemoration was formerly made with thankſgiving, in honour of good men departed this world. *Ayliffe's Parergon.*

COMME'MORATIVE. *adj.* [from *commemorate.*] Tending to preſerve memory of any thing.

The annual offering of the Paſchal lamb was *commemorative* of that firſt Paſchal lamb. *Atterbury.*

To COMME'NCE. *v. n.* [*commencer*, French.]

1. To begin; to take beginning.

Why hath it given me earneſt of ſucceſs,
Commencing in a truth. *Shakeſpeare's Macbeth.*

Man, conſcious of his immortality, cannot be without concern for that ſtate that is to *commence* after this life. *Rogers.*

2. To take a new character.

If wit ſo much from ign'rance undergo,
Ah! let not learning too *commence* its foe! *Pope.*

To COMME'NCE. *v. a.* To begin; to make a beginning of; as *to commence a ſuit*.

COMME'NCEMENT. *n ſ.* [from *commence.*] Beginning; date.

The waters were gathered together into one place, the third day from the *commencement* of the creation. *Woodw. Nat. Hiſt.*

To COMME'ND. *v. a.* [*commendo*, Latin.]

1. To repreſent as worthy of notice, regard, or kindneſs; to recommend.

After Barbaroſſa was arrived, it was known how effectually the chief baſſa had *commended* him to Solyman. *Knolles's Hiſtory.*

Among the objects of knowledge, two eſpecially *commend* themſelves to our contemplation; the knowledge of God, and the knowledge of ourſelves. *Hale's Origin of Mankind.*

Vain-glory is a principle I ſhall *commend* to no man. *Decay of Piety.*

Theſe draw the chariot which Latinus ſends,
And the rich preſent to the prince *commends*. *Dryd. Æn.*

2. To deliver up with confidence.

To thee I do *commend* my watchful ſoul,
Ere I let fall the windows of mine eyes:
Sleeping and waking, O defend me ſtill. *Shakeſp. Rich.* III.

Father, into thy hands I *commend* my ſpirit. *Luke* xxiii. 46.

3. To praiſe; to mention with approbation.

Who is Silvia? What is ſhe,
That all our ſwains *commend* her?
Holy, fair, and wiſe is ſhe. *Shakeſpeare.*

Old men do moſt exceed in this point of folly, *commending* the days of their youth they ſcarce remembered, at leaſt well underſtood not. *Brown's Vulgar Errours.*

He lov'd my worthleſs rhymes; and, like a friend,
Would find out ſomething to *commend*. *Cowley.*

Hiſtorians *commend* Alexander for weeping when he read the actions of Achilles. *Dryden's Virg. Æn. Dedicat.*

Each finding, like a friend,
Something to blame, and ſomething to *commend*. *Pope.*

4. To mention by way of keeping in memory; to recommend to remembrance.

Signior Anthonio
Commends him to you.——
——Ere I ope his letter,
I pray you tell me how my good friend doth. *Sh. Mer. of Ven.*

COMME'ND. *n. ſ.* [from the verb.] Commendation: not now in uſe.

Tell her I ſend to her my kind *commends*:
Take ſpecial care my greetings be deliver'd. *Shak. Rich.* II.

COMME'NDABLE. *adj.* [from *commend.*] Laudable; worthy of praiſe. Anciently accented on the firſt ſyllable.

And power, unto itſelf moſt *commendable*,
Hath not a tomb ſo evident, as a chair
T'extol what it hath done. *Shakeſpeare's Coriolanus.*

Order and decent ceremonies in the church, are not only comely, but *commendable*. *Bacon's Advice to Villiers.*

Many

Many heroes, and most worthy persons, being sufficiently *commendable* from true and unquestionable merit, have received advancement from falshood. *Brown's Vulgar Errours.*

Britannia is not drawn, like other countries, in a soft peaceful posture; but is adorned with emblems, that mark out the military genius of her inhabitants. This is, I think, the only *commendable* quality that the old poets have touched upon in the description of our country. *Addison on ancient Medals.*

COMME'NDABLY. *adv.* [from *commendable.*] Laudably; in a manner worthy of commendation.

Of preachers the shire holdeth a number, all *commendably* labouring in their vocation. *Carew's Survey of Cornwal.*

COMME'NDAM. [*commenda*, low Latin.]

Commendam is a benefice, which, being void, is commended to the charge and care of some sufficient clerk to be supplied, until it be conveniently provided of a pastor. *Cowel.*

It had been once mentioned to him, that his peace should be made, if he would resign his bishoprick, and deanry of Westminster; for he had that in *commendam.* *Clarendon.*

COMME'NDATARY. *n. s.* [from *commendam.*] One who holds a living in commendam.

COMMENDA'TION. *n. s.* [from *commend.*]

1. Recommendation; favourable representation.

This jewel and my gold are your's, provided I have your *commendation* for my more free entertainment. *Shak. Cymbeline.*

The choice of them should be by the *commendation* of the great officers of the kingdom. *Bacon's Advice to Villiers.*

2. Praise; declaration of esteem.

His fame would not get so sweet and noble an air to fly in as in your breath, so could not you find a fitter subject of *commendation.* *Sidney, b.* ii.

Good-nature is the most godlike *commendation* of a man. *Dryden's Juvenal, Dedication.*

3. Message of love.

Mrs. Page has her hearty *commendations* to you too. *Shakesp.*

Hark you, Margaret,
No princely *commendations* to my king!———
———Such *commendations* as become a maid,
A virgin, and his servant, say to him. *Shakesp. Henry* VI.

COMME'NDATORY. *adj.* [from *commend.*] Favourably representative; containing praise.

It doth much add to a man's reputation, and is like perpetual letters *commendatory*, to have good forms: to attain them, it almost sufficeth not to despise them. *Bacon, Essay* 53.

We bestow the flourish of poetry on those *commendatory* conceits, which popularly set forth the eminency of this creature. *Brown's Vulgar Errours, b.* vi. *c.* 5.

If I can think that neither he nor you despise me, it is a greater honour to me, by far, than if all the house of lords writ *commendatory* verses upon me. *Pope.*

COMME'NDER. *n. s.* [from *commend.*] Praiser.

Such a concurrence of two extremes, by most of the same *commenders* and disprovers. *Wotton.*

COMMENSA'LITY. *n. s.* [from *commensalis*, Lat.] Fellowship of table; the custom of eating together.

They being enjoined and prohibited certain foods, thereby to avoid community with the Gentiles, upon promiscuous *commensality.* *Brown's Vulgar Errours, b.* iii. *c.* 25.

COMMENSURABI'LITY. *n. s.* [from *commensurable.*] Capacity of being compared with another, as to the measure; or of being measured by another. Thus an inch and a yard are commensurable, a yard containing a certain number of inches. The diameter and circumference of a circle are incommensurable, not being reduceable to any common measure. Proportion.

Some place the essence thereof in the proportion of parts, conceiving it to consist in a comely *commensurability* of the whole unto the parts, and the parts between themselves. *Brown.*

COMME'NSURABLE. *adj.* [*con* and *mensura*, Lat.] Reducible to some common measure; as a yard and a foot are measured by an inch.

COMME'NSURABLENESS. *n. s.* [from *commensurable.*] Commensurability; proportion.

There is no *commensurableness* between this object and a created understanding, yet there is a congruity and connaturality. *Hale's Origin of Mankind.*

To COMME'NSURATE. *v. a.* [*con* and *mensura*, Lat.] To reduce to some common measure.

That division is not natural, but artificial; and by agreement, as the aptest terms to *commensurate* the longitude of places. *Brown's Vulgar Errours, b.* vi. *c.* 7.

COMME'NSURATE. *adj.* [from the verb.]

1. Reducible to some common measure.

They permitted no intelligence between them, other than by the mediation of some organ equally *commensurate* to soul and body. *Government of the Tongue, s.* 1.

2. Equal; proportionable to each other.

Is our knowledge adequately *commensurate* with the nature of things? *Glanville's Sceps. c.* 2.

Those who are persuaded that they shall continue for ever, cannot chuse but aspire after a happiness *commensurate* to their duration. *Tillotson.*

Nothing *commensurate* to the desires of human nature, on which it could fix as its ultimate end, without being carried on with any farther desire. *Rogers's Sermons.*

Matter and gravity are always *commensurate.* *Bentley.*

COMME'NSURATELY. *adv.* [from *commensurate.*] With the capacity of measuring, or being measured by some other thing.

We are constrained to make the day serve to measure the year as well as we can, though not *commensurately* to each year; but by collecting the fraction of days in several years, 'till they amount to an even day. *Holder on Time.*

COMMENSURA'TION. *n. s.* [from *commensurate.*] Proportion; reduction of some things to some common measure.

A body over great, or over small, will not be thrown so far as a body of a middle size; so that, it seemeth, there must be a *commensuration* or proportion between the body moved and the force, to make it move well. *Bacon's Natural History.*

All fitness lies in a particular *commensuration*, or proportion of one thing to another. *South.*

To CO'MMENT. *v. n.* [*commentor*, Lat.] To annotate; to write notes upon an author; to expound; to explain; with *upon* before the thing explained.

Enter his chamber, view his lifeless corps,
And *comment* then *upon* his sudden death. *Shakes. Henry* VI.
Such are thy secrets, which my life makes good,
And *comments on* thee; for in ev'ry thing
Thy words do find me out, and parallels bring,
And in another make me understand. *Herbert.*

Criticks having first taken a liking to one of these poets, proceed to *comment on* him, and illustrate him. *Dryd. Juv. Ded.*

They have contented themselves only to *comment upon* those texts, and make the best copies they could after those originals. *Temple.*

Indeed I hate that any man should be idle, while I must translate and *comment.* *Pope.*

CO'MMENT. *n. s.* [from the verb.] Annotations on an author; notes; explanation; exposition; remarks.

In such a time as this, it is not meet
That every nice offence should bear its *comment.* *Shakesp.*
Forgive the *comment* that my passion made
Upon thy feature; for my rage was blind. *Shakes. K. John.*

All that is behind will be by way of *comment* on that part of the church of England's charity. *Hammond's Fundamentals.*

Adam came into the world a philosopher, which sufficiently appeared by his writing the nature of things upon their names: he could view essences in themselves, and read forms without the *comment* of their respective properties. *South's Sermons.*

All the volumes of philosophy,
With all their *comments*, never could invent
So politick an instrument. *Prior.*

Proper gestures, and vehement exertions of the voice, are a kind of *comment* to what he utters. *Addison's Spect.* N°. 407.

Still with itself compar'd, his text peruse;
And let your *comment* be the Mantuan muse. *Pope.*

CO'MMENTARY. *n. s.* [*commentarius*, Latin.]

1. An exposition; annotation; remark.

In religion, scripture is the best rule; and the church's universal practice, the best *commentary.* *King Charles.*

2. Memoir; narrative in familiar manner.

Vere, in a private *commentary* which he wrote of that service, testified that eight hundred were slain. *Bacon.*

They shew still the ruins of Cæsar's wall, that reached eighteen miles in length, as he has declared it in the first book of his *commentaries.* *Addison on Italy.*

COMMENTA'TOR. *n. s.* [from *comment.*] Expositor; annotator.

I have made such expositions of my authors, as no *commentator* will forgive me. *Dryden.*

Some of the *commentators* tell us, that Marsya was a lawyer who had lost his cause. *Addison on Italy.*

Galen's *commentator* tells us, that bitter substances engender choler, and burn the blood. *Arbuthnot on Aliments.*

You will have variety of *commentators* to explain the difficult passages to you. *Gay.*

No *commentator* can more slily pass
O'er a learn'd unintelligible place. *Pope.*

CO'MMENTER. *n. s.* [from *comment.*] One that writes comments; an explainer; an annotator.

Slily as any *commenter* goes by
Hard words or sense. *Donne.*

COMMENTI'TIOUS. *adj.* [*commentitius*, Lat.] Invented; fictitious; imaginary.

It is easy to draw a parallelism between that ancient and this modern nothing, and make good its resemblance to that *commentitious* inanity. *Glanville's Sceps. c.* 18.

CO'MMERCE. *n. s.* [*commercium*, Latin. It was anciently accented on the last syllable.] Intercourse; exchange of one thing for another; interchange of any thing; trade; traffick.

Places of publick resort being thus provided, our repair thither is especially for mutual conference, and, as it were, *commerce* to be had between God and us. *Hooker, b.* v. *s.* 17.

How could communities,
Degrees in schools, and brotherhoods in cities,

Peaceful *commerce* from dividable shores,
But by degree stand in authentick place? *Sh. Troil. and Cress.*
Instructed ships shall sail to quick *commerce*,
By which remotest regions are ally'd;
Which makes one city of the universe,
Where some may gain, and all may be supply'd. *Dryden.*

These people had not any *commerce* with the other known parts of the world *Tillotson.*

In any country, that hath *commerce* with the rest of the world, it is almost impossible now to be without the use of silver coin. *Locke.*

To COMME'RCE. *v. n.* [from the noun.] To hold intercourse with.

Come, but keep thy wonted state,
With even step and musing gait,
And looks *commercing* with the skies,
Thy rapt' soul sitting in thine eyes. *Milton.*

COMME'RCIAL. *adj.* [from *commerce.*] Relating to commerce or traffick.

CO'MMERE. n. s. [French] A common mother.

As peace should still her wheaten garland wear,
And stand a *commere* 'tween their amities. *Shakesp. Hamlet.*

To CO'MMIGRATE. *v. n.* [*con* and *migro*, Latin.] To remove in a body, or by consent, from one country to another

COMMIGRA'TION. *n. s* [from *commigrate*] A removal of a large body of people from one country to another.

Both the inhabitants of that and of our world lost all memory of their *commigration* hence. *Woodward's Nat. Hist.*

COMMINA'TION. *n. s.* [*comminatio*, Latin.]

1. A threat; a denunciation of punishment, or of vengeance.

Some parts of knowledge God has thought fit to seclude from us, to fence them not only by precept and *commination*, but with difficulty and impossibilities. *Decay of Piety.*

2. The recital of God's threatenings on stated days.

COMMI'NATORY. *adj.* [from *commination.*] Denunciatory; threatening.

To COMMI'NGLE. *v. a.* [*commisceo*, Latin.] To mix into one mass; to unite intimately; to mix; to blend.

Blest are those,
Whose blood and judgment are so well *commingled*,
That they are not a pipe for fortune's finger,
To sound what stop she please. *Shakespeare's Hamlet.*

To COMMI'NGLE. *v. n.* To unite with another thing.

Dissolutions of gum tragacanth and oil of sweet almonds do not *commingle*, the oil remaining on the top 'till they be stirred. *Bacon's Physical Rem.*

COMMINU'IBLE. *adj.* [from *comminute.*] Frangible; reducible to powder; susceptible of pulverisation.

The best diamonds are *comminuible* without it; and are so far from breaking hammers, that they submit unto pestillation, and resist not any ordinary pestle. *Browne's Vulgar Errours.*

To CO'MMINUTE. *v. a.* [*comminuo*, Latin.] To grind; to pulverise; to break into small parts.

Parchment, skins, and cloth drink in liquors, though themselves be intire bodies, and not *comminuted*, as sand and ashes. *Bacon's Natural History*, N°. 800.

COMMINU'TION. *n. s.* [from *comminute.*] The act of grinding into small parts; pulverisation.

Causes of fixation are the even spreading of the spirits and tangible parts, the closeness of the tangible parts, and the jejuneness or extreme *comminution* of spirits; of which the two first may be joined with a nature liquefiable. *Bacon.*

The jaw in men and animals furnished with grinders, hath an oblique or transverse motion, necessary for *comminution* of the meat. *Ray on the Creation.*

This smiting of the steel with the flint doth only make a *comminution*, and a very rapid whirling and melting of some particles; but that idea of flame is wholly in us. *Bentley.*

COMMI'SERABLE. *adj.* [from *commiserate.*] Worthy of compassion; pitiable; such as must excite sympathy or sorrow.

It is the sinfullest thing in the world to destitute a plantation once in forwardness: for, besides the dishonour, it is the guiltiness of blood of many *commiserable* persons. *Bacon's Ess.*

This was the end of this noble and *commiserable* person, Edward eldest son to the duke of Clarence. *Bacon's Hen.* VII.

To COMMI'SERATE. *v. a.* [*con* and *misereor*, Lat.] To pity; to look on with compassion; to compassionate.

Then we must those, who groan beneath the weight
Of age, disease, or want, *commiserate*. *Denham.*

We should *commiserate* our mutual ignorance, and endeavour to remove it. *Locke.*

COMMISERA'TION. *n. s.* [from *commiserate.*] Pity; compassion; tenderness, or concern for another's pains.

These poor seduced creatures, whom I can neither speak nor think of but with much *commiseration* and pity. *Hooker.*

Live, and hereafter say
A mad man's mercy bade thee run away.
——I do defy thy *commiseration*,
And apprehend thee for a felon here. *Shak. Rom. and Juliet.*

God knows with how much *commiseration*, and solicitous caution, I carried on that business, that I might neither encourage the rebels, nor discourage the Protestants. *K. Charles.*

She ended weeping; and her lovely plight
Immoveable, 'till peace obtain'd from fault
Acknowledg'd and deplor'd, in Adam wrought
Commiseration. *Milton's Paradise Lost, b.* x. *l.* 940.

From you their estate may expect effectual comfort, since there are none from whom it may not deserve *commiseration.* *Sprat's Sermons.*

No where fewer beggars appear to charm up *commiseration*, yet no where is there greater charity. *Graunt's Bills of Mort.*

I prevailed with myself to go and see him, partly out of *commiseration*, and partly out of curiosity. *Swift.*

CO'MMISSARY. *n. s.* [*commissarius*, low Latin.]

1. An officer made occasionally for a certain purpose; a delegate; a deputy.

2. It is a title of ecclesiastical jurisdiction, appertaining to such as exercises spiritual jurisdiction (at least so far as his commission permits) in places of the diocese so far distant from the chief city, as the chancellor cannot call the subjects. *Cowel.*

The *commissaries* of bishops have authority only in some certain place of the diocese, and in some certain causes of the jurisdiction limited to them by the bishop's commission. *Ayliffe.*

3. An officer who draws up lists of the numbers of an army, and regulates the procuration and conveyance of provision or ammunition.

But is it thus you English bards compose?
With Runick lays thus tag insipid prose?
And when you should your heroes deeds rehearse,
Give us a *commissary's* list in verse? *Prior.*

CO'MMISSARISHIP. *n. s.* [from *commissary.*] The office of a commissary.

A *commissariship* is not grantable for life, so as to bind the succeeding bishop, though it should be confirmed by the dean and chapter. *Ayliffe's Parergon.*

COMMI'SSION. *n. s.* [*commissio*, low Latin.]

1. The act of entrusting any thing.

2. A trust; a warrant by which any trust is held, or authority exercised.

Commission is the warrant, or letters patent, that all men exercising jurisdiction, either ordinary or extraordinary, have for their power. *Cowel.*

Omission to do what is necessary,
Seals a *commission* to a blank of danger. *Sh. Troil. and Cress.*

The subjects grief
Comes through *commissions*, which compel from each
The sixth part of his substance, to be levied
Without delay. *Shakespeare's Henry* VIII.

He led our powers;
Bore the *commission* of my place and person;
The which immediacy may well stand up,
And call itself your brother. *Shakesp. King Lear.*

He would have them fully acquainted with the nature and extent of their office, and so he joins *commission* with instruction: by one he conveys power, by the other knowledge. *South.*

3. A warrant by which a military officer is constituted.

Solyman, filled with the vain hope of the conquest of Persia, gave out his *commissions* into all parts of his empire, for the raising of a mighty army. *Knolles's Hist. of the Turks.*

I was made a colonel; though I gained my *commission* by the horse's virtues, having leapt over a six-bar gate. *Addis. Freeh.*

He for his son a gay *commission* buys,
Who drinks, whores, fights, and in a duel dies. *Pope.*

4. Charge; mandate; office; employment.

It was both a strange *commission*, and a strange obedience to a *commission*, for men, in the midst of their own blood, and being so furiously assailed, to hold their hands contrary to the laws of nature and necessity. *Bacon's War with Spain.*

Such *commission* from above
I have receiv'd, to answer thy desire
Of knowledge within bounds: beyond, abstain
To ask. *Milton's Paradise Lost.*

At his command the storms invade;
The winds by his *commission* blow;
'Till with a nod he bids them cease. *Dryden.*

He bore his great *commission* in his look;
But sweetly temper'd awe, and soften'd all he spoke. *Dryd.*

5. Act of committing a crime; perpetration. Sins of *commission* are distinguished in theology from sins of omission.

Every *commission* of sin introduces into the soul a certain degree of hardness. *South's Sermons.*

He indulges himself in the habit of known sin, whether *commission* of something which God hath forbidden, or the omission of something commanded. *Rogers's Sermons.*

6. A number of people joined in a trust or office.

7. The state of that which is intrusted to a number of joint officers; as *the broad seal was put into commission.*

8. [In commerce.] The order by which a factor trades for another person.

To COMMI'SSION. *v. a.* [from *commission.*] To empower; to appoint.

The peace polluted thus, a chosen band
He first *commissions* to the Latian land,
In threat'ning embassy. *Dryden's Æn. b.* vii. *l.* 648.

To COMMI'SSIONATE. *v. a.* [from *commission.*] To commission; to empower.

As he was thus sent by his father, so also were the apostles solemnly *commissionated* by him to preach to the Gentile world, who, with indefatigable industry and resolute sufferings, pursued the charge; and sure this is competent evidence, that the design was of the greatest and most weighty importance. *Decay of Piety.*

COMMI'SSIONER. *n. s.* [from *commission.*] One included in a warrant of authority.

A *commissioner* is one who hath commission, as letters patents, or other lawful warrant, to execute any publick office. *Cowel.*

One article they stood upon, which I with your *commissioners* have agreed upon. *Sidney.*

These *commissioners* came into England, with whom covenants were concluded. *Hayward.*

The archbishop was made one of the *commissioners* of the treasury. *Clarendon.*

Suppose itinerary *commissioners* to inspect, throughout the kingdom, into the conduct of men in office, with respect to morals and religion as well as abilities. *Swift.*

Like are their merits, like rewards they share,
That shines a consul, this *commissioner*. *Pope's Dunciad.*

COMMI'SSURE. *n. s.* [*commissura*, Latin.] Joint; a place where one part is joined to another.

All these inducements cannot countervail the inconvenience of disjointing the *commissures* with so many strokes of the chizel. *Wotton's Architecture.*

This animal is covered with a strong shell, jointed like armour by four transverse *commissures* in the middle of the body, connected by tough membranes. *Ray on the Creation.*

To COMMI'T. *v. a.* [*committo*, Latin.]

1. To intrust; to give in trust; to put into the hands of another.

It is not for your health thus to *commit*
Your weak condition to the raw, cold morning. *Shakesp.*

They who are desirous to *commit* to memory, might have ease. *2 Mac.* ii. 25.

2. To put in any place to be kept safe.

Is my muse controul'd
By servile awe? Born free, and not be bold!
At least I'll dig a hole within the ground,
And to the trusty earth *commit* the sound. *Dryd. Pers. Sat.*

3. To send to prison; to imprison.

Here comes the nobleman that *committed* the prince, for striking him about Bardolph. *Shakespeare's Henry* IV. *p.* ii.

They two were *committed*, at least restrained of their liberty. *Clarendon.*

So though my ankle she has quitted,
My heart continues still *committed*;
And, like a bail'd and main priz'd lover,
Although at large, I am bound over. *Hudibras, p.* ii.

4. To perpetrate; to do a fault; to be guilty of a crime.

Keep thy word justly; swear not; *commit* not with man's sworn spouse. *Shakespeare's King Lear.*

Letters out of Ulster gave him notice of the inhumane murders *committed* there upon a multitude of the Protestants. *Claren.*

A creeping young fellow *committed* matrimony with a brisk gamesome lass. *L'Estrange.*

'Tis policy
For son and father to take different sides;
Then lands and tenements *commit* no treason. *Dryden.*

COMMI'TMENT. *n. s.* [from *commit.*] Act of sending to prison; imprisonment.

It did not appear by any new examinations or *commitments*, that any other person of quality was discovered or appeached. *Bacon's Henry* VII.

They were glad to compound for his bare *commitment* to the Tower, whence he was within few days enlarged. *Clarendon.*

I have been considering, ever since my *commitment*, what it might be proper to deliver upon this occasion. *Swift.*

2. An order for sending to prison.

COMMI'TTEE. *n. s.* [from *commit.*]

Those to whom the consideration or ordering of any matter is referred, either by some court to whom it belongs, or by consent of parties. As in parliament, after a bill is read, it is either agreed to and passed, or not agreed to; or neither of these, but referred to the consideration of some appointed by the house, to examine it farther, who thereupon are called a *committee*. *Cowel.*

Manchester had orders to march thither, having a *committee* of the parliament with him, as there was another *committee* of the Scottish parliament always in that army; there being also now a *committee* of both kingdoms residing at London, for the carrying on the war. *Clarendon.*

All corners were filled with covenanters, confusion, *committee* men, and soldiers, serving each other to their ends of revenge, or power, or profit; and these *committee* men and soldiers were possest with this covenant. *Walton.*

COMMI'TTER. *n. s.* [from *commit.*] Perpetrator; he that commits.

Such an one makes a man not only a partaker of other men's sins, but a deriver of the whole guilt to himself; yet so as to leave the *committer* as full of guilt as before. *South.*

COMMI'TTIBLE. *adj.* [from *commit.*] Liable to be committed.

Besides the mistakes *committible* in the solary compute of years, the difference of chronology disturbs his computes. *Brown's Vulgar Errours, b* iv. *c.* 12.

To COMMI'X. *v. a.* [*commisceo*, Lat.] To mingle; to blend; to mix; to unite with things in one mass.

A dram of gold, dissolved in aqua regia, with a dram of copper in aqua fortis *commixed*, gave a great colour. *Bacon.*

I have written against the spontaneous generation of frogs in the clouds; or, on the earth, out of dust and rain-water *commixed*. *Ray on the Creation.*

It is manifest by this experiment, that the *commixed* impressions of all the colours do stir up and beget a sensation of white; that is, that whiteness is compounded of all the *colours*. *Newton's Opt.*

COMMI'XION. *n. s.* [from *commix.*] Mixture; incorporation of different ingredients.

Were thy *commixion* Greek and Trojan, so
That thou could'st say, this hand is Grecian all,
And this is Trojan. *Shakespeare's Troilus and Cressida.*

COMMI'XTION. *n. s.* [from *commix.*] Mixture; incorporation; union of various substances in one mass.

Some species there be of middle and participating natures, that is, of birds and beasts, as batts, and some few others, so confirmed and set together, that we cannot define the beginning or end of either; there being a *commixtion* of both in the whole, rather than adapation or cement of the one unto the other. *Brown's Vulgar Errours, b.* iii.

COMMI'XTURE. *n. s.* [from *commix.*]

1. The act of mingling; the state of being mingled; incorporation; union in one mass.

In the *commixture* of any thing that is more oily or sweet, such bodies are least apt to putrefy, the air working little upon them. *Bacon's Natural History*, N°. 350.

2. The mass formed by mingling different things; composition; compound.

Fair ladies, mask'd, are roses in the bud;
Or angels veil'd in clouds: are roses blown,
Dismask'd, their damask sweet *commixture* shewn. *Shakesp.*

My love and fear glew'd many friends to thee;
And now I fall, thy tough *commixtures* melt,
Impairing Henry, strength'ning misproud York. *Shakesp.*

There is scarcely any rising but by a *commixture* of good and evil arts. *Bacon, Essay* 15.

All the circumstances and respect of religion and state intermixed together in their *commixture*, will better become a royal history, or a council-table, than a single life. *Wotton.*

COMMO'DE. *n. s.* [French.] The head-dress of women.

Let them reflect how they would be affected, should they meet with a man on horseback, in his breeches and jack-boots, dressed up in a *commode* and a nightrail. *Spectat.* N°. 435.

She has contrived to shew her principles by the setting of her *commode*; so that it will be impossible for any woman that is disaffected to be in the fashion. *Addison's Freeholder*, N°. 8.

She, like some pensive statesman, walks demure,
And smiles, and hugs, to make destruction sure;
Or under high *commodes*, with looks erect,
Barefac'd devours, in gaudy colours deck'd. *Granville.*

COMMO'DIOUS. *adj.* [*commodus*, Latin.]

1. Convenient; suitable; accommodate to any purpose; fit; proper; free from hindrance or uneasiness.

Such a place cannot be *commodious* to live in; for being so near the moon, it had been too near the sun. *Raleigh's Hist.*

To that recess, *commodious* for surprize,
When purple light shall next suffuse the skies,
With me repair. *Pope's Odyss. b.* iv. *l.* 550.

2. Useful; suited to wants or necessities.

If they think we ought to prove the ceremonies *commodious*, they do greatly deceive themselves. *Hooker, b.* iv. *sect.* 4.

Bacchus was grown a proper young man, had found out the making of wine, and many things else *commodious* for mankind. *Raleigh's History of the World, b.* i. *c.* 6. *s.* 5.

The gods have done their part,
By sending this *commodious* plague. *Dryden's Oedipus.*

Maro's muse,
Thrice sacred muse, *commodious* precepts gives,
Instructive to the swains. *Phillips.*

COMMO'DIOUSLY. *adv.* [from *commodious.*]

1. Conveniently.

At the large foot of an old hollow tree,
In a deep cave seated *commodiously*,
There dwelt a good substantial country mouse. *Cowley.*

2. Without distress.

We need not fear
To pass *commodiously* this life, sustain'd

By him with many comforts, 'till we end
In duſt; our final reſt, and native home. *Milt. Par. Loſt.*

3. Suitably to a certain purpoſe
Wiſdom may have framed one and the ſame thing to ſerve *commodiouſly* for divers ends. *Hooker, b.* v. *ſect.* 42.
Galen, upon the conſideration of the body, challenges any one to find how the leaſt fibre might be more *commodiouſly* placed for uſe or comelineſs. *South's Sermons.*

COMMO'DIOUSNESS. *n. ſ.* [from *commodious.*] Convenience; advantage.
The place requireth many circumſtances; as the ſituation near the ſea, for the *commodiouſneſs* of an intercourſe with England. *Bacon.*
Of cities, the greatneſs and riches increaſe according to the *commodiouſneſs* of their ſituation in fertile countries, or upon rivers and havens. *Temple.*

COMMO'DITY. *n. ſ.* [*commoditas*, Latin]
1. Intereſt; advantage; profit.
They knew, that howſoever men may ſeek their own *commodity*, yet if this were done with injury unto others, it was not to be ſuffered. *Hooker, b.* v. *ſect.* 10.

Commodity, the biaſs of the world,
The world, which of itſelf is poiſed well,
'Till this advantage, this vile drawing biaſs,
This ſway of motion, this *commodity*,
Makes it take head from all indifferency,
From all direction, purpoſe, courſe, intent. *Shakeſ. K. John.*

After much debatement of the *commodities* or diſcommodities like to enſue, they concluded. *Hayward.*
2. Convenience of time or place.
There came into her head certain verſes, which, if ſhe had had preſent *commodity*, ſhe would have adjoined as a retraction to the other. *Sidney, b.* ii.
She demanded leave, not to loſe this long ſought for *commodity* of time, to eaſe her heart. *Sidney.*
Travellers turn out of the highway, drawn either by the *commodity* of a foot-path, or the delicacy or the freſhneſs of the fields. *Ben. Johnſon's Diſcov.*
3. Wares; merchandiſe; goods for traffick.

All my fortunes are at ſea;
Nor have I money, nor *commodity*
To raiſe a preſent ſum. *Shakeſp. Merchant of Venice.*

It had been difficult to make ſuch a mole where they had not ſo natural a *commodity* as the earth of Puzzuola, which immediately hardens in the water. *Addiſon's Remarks on Italy.*
Commodities are moveables, valuable by money, the common meaſure. *Locke.*
Of money in the commerce and traffick of mankind, the principal uſe is that of ſaving the commutation of more bulky *commodities*. *Arbuthnot on Coins.*

COMMO'DORE. *n. ſ.* [probably corrupted from the Spaniſh *comendador.*] The captain who commands a ſquadron of ſhips.

CO'MMON. *n. ſ.* [*communis*, Latin.]
1. Belonging equally to more than one.
Though life and ſenſe be *common* to man and brutes, and their operations in many things alike; yet by this form he lives the life of a man, and not of a brute, and hath the ſenſe of a man, and not of a brute. *Hale's Origin of Mankind.*
He who hath received damage, has, beſides the right of puniſhment *common* to him with other men, a particular right to ſeek reparation. *Locke.*
2. Having no poſſeſſor or owner.
Where no kindred are to be found, we ſee the poſſeſſion of a private man revert to the community, and ſo become again perfectly *common*, no body having a right to inherit them; nor can any one have a property in them, otherwiſe than in other things *common* by nature. *Locke.*
3. Vulgar; mean; not diſtinguiſhed by any excellence; often ſeen; eaſy to be had; of little value; not rare; not ſcarce.

Or as the man whom princes do advance,
Upon their gracious mercy-ſeat to ſit,
Doth *common* things, of courſe and circumſtance,
To the reports of *common* men commit. *Davies.*

4. Publick; general; ſerving the uſe of all.
He was adviſed by a parliament-man not to be ſtrict in reading all the *common* prayer, but make ſome variation. *Walt.*
I need not mention the old *common* ſhore of Rome, which ran from all parts of the town, with the current and violence of an ordinary river. *Addiſon on Italy.*
5. Of no rank; mean; without birth or deſcent.

Look, as I blow this feather from my face,
And as the air blows it to me again,
Such is the lightneſs of you *common* men. *Shak. Henry* VI.

Flying bullets now,
To execute his rage, appear too ſlow;
They miſs, or ſweep but *common* ſouls away,
For ſuch a loſs Opdam his life muſt pay. *Waller.*

6. Frequent; uſual; ordinary.
There is an evil which I have ſeen *common* among men. *Eccles.* vi. 1.
The Papiſts were the moſt *common* place, and the butt againſt whom all the arrows were directed. *Clarendon.*
Neither is it ſtrange that there ſhould be myſteries in divinity, as well as in the *commoneſt* operations in nature. *Swift.*
7. Proſtitute.
'Tis a ſtrange thing, the impudence of ſome women! was the word of a dame, who herſelf was *common.* *L'Eſtrange.*
Hipparchus was going to marry a *common* woman, but conſulted Philander upon the occaſion. *Spectator*, Nº. 475.
8. [In grammar.] Such verbs as ſignify both action and paſſion are called *common*; as *aſpernor*, *I deſpiſe*, or *am deſpiſed*; and alſo ſuch nouns as are both maſculine and feminine, as *parens.*

CO'MMON. *n. ſ* [from the adjective.] An open ground equally uſed by many perſons.

Then take we down his load, and turn him off,
Like to the empty aſs, to ſhake his ears,
And graze in *commons.* *Shakeſpeare's Julius Cæſar.*

Is not the ſeparate property of a thing the great cauſe of its endearment? Does any one reſpect a *common* as much as he does his garden? *South.*

CO'MMON. *adv.* [from the adjective.] Commonly; ordinarily.
I am more than *common* tall. *Shakeſp. As you like it.*

In CO'MMON.
1. Equally to be participated by a certain number.
By making an explicite conſent of every commoner neceſſary to any one's appropriating to himſelf any part of what is given *in common*, children or ſervants could not cut the meat which their father or maſter had provided for them *in common*, without aſſigning to every one his peculiar part. *Locke.*
2. Equally with another; indiſcriminately.
In a work of this nature it is impoſſible to avoid puerilities, it having that *in common* with dictionaries, and books of antiquities. *Arbuthnot on Coins.*

To CO'MMON. *v. n.* [from the noun.] To have a joint right with others in ſome common ground.

COMMON LAW contains thoſe cuſtoms and uſages which have, by long preſcription, obtained in this nation the force of laws. It is diſtinguiſhed from the ſtatute law, which owes its authority to acts of parliament.

COMMON PLEAS. The king's court now held in Weſtminſter-hall; but anciently moveable. *Gwin* obſerves, that 'till Henry III. granted the *magna charta* there were but two courts, the exchequer, and the king's bench, ſo called becauſe it followed the king; but upon the grant of that charter, the court of *common pleas* was erected, and ſettled at Weſtminſter. All civil cauſes, both real and perſonal, are, or were formerly, tried in this court, according to the ſtrict laws of the realm; and Forteſcue repreſents it as the only court for real cauſes. The chief judge is called the lord chief juſtice of the *common pleas*, and he is aſſiſted by three or four aſſociates, created by letters patent from the king. *Cowel.*

CO'MMONABLE. *adj.* [from *common.*] What is held in common.
Much good land might be gained from foreſts and chaſes, and from other *commonable* places, ſo as there be care taken that the poor commoners have no injury. *Bacon's Ad. to Villers.*

CO'MMONAGE. *n. ſ.* [from *common.*] The right of feeding on a common; the joint right of uſing any thing in common with others.

CO'MMONALTY. *n. ſ.* [*communauté*, French.]
1. The common people; the people of the lower rank.

Bid him ſtrive
To gain the love o' th' *commonalty*; the duke
Shall govern England. *Shakeſ. Henry* VIII.

There is in every ſtate, as we know, two portions of ſubjects; the nobles and the *commonalty.* *Bacon, Eſſay* 16.

The emmet joined in her popular tribes
Of *commonalty.* *Milton's Paradiſe Loſt, b.* vii. *l.* 489.

All gentlemen are almoſt obliged to it; and I know no reaſon we ſhould give that advantage to the *commonalty* of England, to be foremoſt in brave actions. *Dryd. Pref. to An. Mir.*
2. The bulk of mankind.
I myſelf too will uſe the ſecret acknowledgment of the *commonalty* bearing record of the God of Gods. *Hooker, b.* iii.

CO'MMONER. *n. ſ.* [from *common.*]
1. One of the common people; a man of low rank; of mean condition.

Doubt not
The *commoners*, for whom we ſtand, but they,
Upon their ancient malice, will forget. *Shakeſp. Coriolanus.*

His great men durſt not pay their court to him, 'till he had ſatiated his thirſt of blood by the death of ſome of his loyal *commoners.* *Addiſon's Freeholder*, Nº. 10.
2. A man not noble.

This *commoner* has worth and parts,
Is prais'd for arms, or lov'd for arts:
His head achs for a coronet;
And who is bleſs'd, that is not great? *Prior.*

3. A member of the houſe of commons.
4. One who has a joint right in common ground.
Much land might be gained from commonable places, ſo as there be care taken that the poor *commoners* have no injury. *Bacon's Advice to Villers.*

5. A student of the second rank at the university of Oxford; one that eats at the common table.

6. A prostitute.

Behold this ring,
Whose high respect, and rich validity,
Did lack a parallel: yet, for all that,
He gave it to a *commoner* o' th' camp. *Shakespeare*

COMMONI'TION. *n. s.* [*commonitio*, Latin.] Advice; warning; instruction.

CO'MMONLY. *adv.* [from *common.*] Frequently; usually; ordinarily.

This hand of your's requires
Much castigation, exercise devout;
For here's a strong and sweating devil here,
That *commonly* rebels. *Shakespeare's Othello.*

A great disease may change the frame of a body, though, if it lives to recover strength, it *commonly* returns to its natural constitution. *Temple.*

CO'MMONNESS. *n. s.* [from *common.*]

1. Equal participation among many.

Nor can the *commonness* of the guilt obviate the censure, there being nothing more frequent than for men to accuse their own faults in other persons. *Government of the Tongue, s.* 6.

2. Frequent occurrence; frequency.

Blot out that maxim, *res nolunt diu male administrari:* the *commonness* makes me not know who is the author; but sure he must be some modern. *Swift.*

To COMMONPLA'CE. *v. a.* To reduce to general heads.

I do not apprehend any difficulty in collecting and *commonplacing* an universal history from the whole body of historians. *Felton on the Classicks.*

COMMONPLACE-BOOK. *n. s.* A book in which things to be remembered are ranged under general heads.

I turned to my *commonplace-book*, and found his case under the word *coquette.* *Tatler*, N°. 107.

CO'MMONS. *n. s.*

1. The vulgar; the lower people; those who inherit no honours.

Little office
The hateful *commons* will perform for us;
Except, like curs, to tear us all in pieces. *Shakesp. Richard* II.
Hath he not pass'd the nobles and the *commons?* *Shakesp.*
These three to kings and chiefs their scenes display,
The rest before the ignoble *commons* play. *Dryden's Fables.*
The gods of greater nations dwell around,
And, on the right and left, the palace bound;
The *commons* where they can: the nobler sort,
With winding doors wide open, front the court. *Dryden.*

2. The lower house of parliament, by which the people are represented, and of which the members are chosen by the people.

My good lord,
How now for mitigation of this bill
Urg'd by the *commons?* Doth his majesty
Incline to it, or no? *Shakespeare's Henry* VI.

In the house of *commons* many gentlemen, unsatisfied of his guilt, durst not condemn him. *King Charles.*

3. Food; fare; diet: so called from colleges, where it is eaten in common.

He painted himself of a dove-colour, and took his *commons* with the pigeons. *L'Estrange.*

Mean while she quench'd her fury at the flood,
And with a lenten sallad cool'd her blood:
Their *commons*, though but coarse, were nothing scant;
Nor did their minds an equal banquet want. *Dryden.*
The doctor now obeys the summons,
Likes both his company and *commons*;
Displays his talent; sits 'till ten;
Next day invited, comes again. *Swift.*

COMMONWE'AL. } *n. s.* [from *common* and *weal*, or *wealth.*]
COMMONWE'ALTH. }

1. A polity; an established form of civil life.

Two foundations bear up publick societies; the one inclination, whereby all men desire sociable life; the other an order agreed upon, touching the manner of their union in living together: the latter is that which we call the law of a *commonweal.* *Hooker.*

It was impossible to make a *commonweal* in Ireland, without settling of all the estates and possessions throughout the kingdom. *Davies on Ireland.*

A continual parliament would but keep the *commonweal* in tune, by preserving laws in their vigour. *King Charles.*

There is no body in the *commonwealth* of learning who does not profess himself a lover of truth. *Locke.*

2. The publick; the general body of the people.

Such a prince,
So kind a father of the *commonweal.* *Shakesp. Henry* IV.

Their sons are well tutored by you: you are a good member of the *commonwealth.* *Shakespeare's Love's Labour Lost.*

3. A government in which the supreme power is lodged in the people; a republick.

Did he, or do yet any of them, imagine
The gods would sleep to such a Stygian practice,
Against that *commonwealth* which they have founded. *Johnson.*

Commonwealths were nothing more, in their original, but free cities; though sometimes, by force of orders and discipline, they have extended themselves into mighty dominions. *Temple.*

CO'MMORANCE. } *n. s.* [from *commorant.*] Dwelling; habitation; abode; residence.
CO'MMORANCY. }

The very quality, carriage, and place of *commorance* of witnesses, is by this means plainly and evidently set forth. *Hale's History of the Common Law of England.*

An archbishop, out of his diocese, becomes subject to the archbishop of the province where he has his abode and *commorancy.* *Ayliffe's Parergon.*

COMMORANT. *adj.* [*commorans*, Latin.] Resident; dwelling; inhabiting.

The abbot may demand and recover his monk, that is *commorant* and residing in another monastery. *Ayliffe's Parergon.*

COMMO'TION. *n. s.* [*commotio*, Latin.]

1. Tumult; disturbance; combustion; sedition; publick disorder; insurrection.

By flatt'ry he hath won the common hearts;
And when he'll please to make *commotion*,
'Tis to be fear'd they all will follow him. *Shakes. Henry* VI.

When ye shall hear of wars and *commotions*, be not terrified. *Luke* xxi. 9.

The Iliad consists of battles and a continual *commotion*; the Odyssey in patience and wisdom. *Broom's Notes on the Odyss.*

2. Perturbation; disorder of mind; heat; violence; agitation.

Some strange *commotion*
Is in his brain; he bites his lips, and starts. *Shak. Hen.* VIII.

He could not debate any thing without some *commotion*, when the argument was not of moment. *Clarendon.*

3. Disturbance; restlesness.

Sacrifices were offered when an earthquake happened, that he would allay the *commotions* of the water, and put an end to the earthquake. *Woodward's Natural History, p.* iii.

COMMO'TIONER. *n. s.* [from *commotion.*] One that causes commotions; a disturber of the peace. A word not in use.

The people more regarding *commotioners* than commissioners, flocked together, as clouds cluster against a storm. *Hayward.*

To COMMO'VE. *v. a.* [*commoveo*, Latin.] To disturb; to agitate; to put into a violent motion; to unsettle.

Strait the sands,
Commov'd around, in gathering eddies play. *Thoms. Summer.*

To CO'MMUNE. *v. n.* [*communico*, Lat.] To converse; to a together; to impart sentiments mutually.

So long as Guyon with her *communed*,
Unto the ground she cast her modest eye;
And ever and anon, with rosy red,
The bashful blood her snowy cheeks did dye. *Fairy Queen.*
I will *commune* with you of such things,
That want no ears but your's. *Shak. Measure for Measure.*

They would forbear open hostility, and resort unto him peaceably, that they might *commune* together as friends. *Hayw.*

Then *commune*, how that day they best may ply
Their growing work. *Milton's Paradise Lost, b.* ix. *l.* 201.

Ideas, as ranked under names, are those that, for the most part, men reason of within themselves, and always those which they *commune* about with others. *Locke.*

COMMUNICABI'LITY. *n. s.* [from *communicable.*] The quality of being communicated; capability to be imparted.

COMMU'NICABLE. *adj.* [from *communicate.*]

1. That which may become the common possession of more than one; with *to.*

Sith eternal life is *communicable unto* all, it behooveth that the word of God be so likewise. *Hooker, b.* v. *sect.* 20.

2. That which may be imparted, or recounted; with *to.*

Nor let thine own inventions hope
Things not reveal'd, which th' invisible king,
Only omniscient, hath suppress'd in night,
To none *communicable* in earth or heav'n. *Milton's Par. Lost.*
The happy place
Rather inflames thy torment, representing
Lost bliss, *to* thee no more *communicable.* *Milton's Par. Reg.*

COMMU'NICANT. *n. s.* [from *communicate.*] One who is present, as a worshipper, at the celebration of the Lord's Supper; one who participates of the blessed sacrament.

Communicants have ever used it; and we, by the form of the very utterance, do shew we use it as *communicants.* *Hooker.*

A constant frequenter of worship, and a never-failing monthly *communicant.* *Atterbury's Sermons.*

To COMMU'NICATE. *v. a.* [*communico*, Latin.]

1. To impart to others what is in our own power; to make others partakers; to confer a joint possession; to bestow.

Common benefits are to be *communicated* with all, but peculiar benefits with choice. *Bacon, Essay* 13.

Where God is worshipped, there he *communicates* his blessings and holy influences. *Taylor's Worthy Communicant.*

Which of the Grecian chiefs consorts with thee?
But Diomede desires my company,
And still *communicates* his praise with me. *Dryden's Fables.*

2. To reveal; to impart knowledge.

 I learned

I learned diligently, and do *communicate* wisdom liberally: I do not hide her riches. *Wisd.* vii. 13.

Charles the hardy would *communicate* his secrets with none; and least of all, those secrets which troubled him most. *Bacon.* He *communicated* those thoughts only with the lord Digby, the lord Colepeper, and the chancellor of the exchequer. *Clarendon, b.* viii.

3. It had anciently the preposition *with* before the person, to whom communication either of benefits or knowledge was made.

A journey of much adventure, which, to shew the strength of his privacy, had been before not *communicated with* any other. *Wotton.*

4. Now it has only *to.*

Let him, that is taught in the word, *communicate unto* him that teacheth. *Gal.* vi. 6.

His majesty frankly promised, that he could not, in any degree, *communicate to* any person the matter, before he had taken and *communicated to* them his own resolutions. *Clarendon.*

Those who speak in publick, are better heard when they discourse by a lively genius and ready memory, than when they read all they would *communicate to* their hearers. *Watts.*

To Commu'nicate. *v. n.*

1. To partake of the blessed sacrament.

The primitive Christians *communicated* every day. *Taylor.*

2. To have something in common with another; as, *the houses communicate*, there is a passage between them common to both, by which either may be entered from the other.

The whole body is nothing but a system of such canals, which all *communicate* with one another, mediately or immediately. *Arbuthnot on Aliments.*

Communica'tion. *n. s.* [from *communicate.*]

1. The act of imparting benefits or knowledge.

Both together serve completely for the reception and *communication* of learned knowledge. *Holder's Elements of Speech.*

2. Common boundary or inlet; passage or means, by which from one place there is a way without interruption to another.

The map shews the natural *communication* providence has formed between the rivers and lakes of a country at so great a distance from the sea. *Addison on Italy.*

The Euxine sea is conveniently situated for trade, by the *communication* it has both with Asia and Europe. *Arbuthnot.*

3. Interchange of knowledge; good intelligence between several persons.

Secrets may be carried so far, as to stop the *communication* necessary among all who have the management of affairs. *Swift.*

4. Conference; conversation.

Abner had *communication* with the elders of Israel, saying, ye sought for David in times past to be king over you: now then do it. 2 *Sam.* iii. 17.

The chief end of language, in *communication*, being to be understood, words serve not for that end, when any word does not excite in the hearers the same idea which it stands for in the mind of the speaker. *Locke.*

Commu'nicative. *adj.* [from *communicate.*] Inclined to make advantages common; liberal of benefits or knowledge; not close; not selfish.

We conceive them more than some envious and mercenary gardeners will thank us for; but they deserve not the name of that *communicative* and noble profession. *Evelyn's Kalendar.*

We think we have sufficiently paid for our want of prudence, and determine for the future to be less *communicative.* *Swift and Pope's Preface.*

Commu'nicativeness. *n. s.* [from *communicative.*] The quality of being communicative, of bestowing or imparting benefits or knowledge.

He is not only the most communicative of all beings, but he will also communicate himself in such measure as entirely to satisfy; otherwise some degrees of *communicativeness* would be wanting. *Norris.*

Commu'nion. *n. s.* [*communio*, Latin.[

1. Intercourse; fellowship; common possession; participation of something in common; interchange of transactions.

Consider, finally, the angels, as having with us that *communion* which the apostle to the Hebrews noteth; and in regard whereof, angels have not disdained to profess themselves our fellow servants. *Hooker, b.* i. *sect.* 4.

We are not, by ourselves, sufficient to furnish ourselves with competent stores for such a life as our nature doth desire; therefore we are naturally induced to seek *communion* and fellowship with others. *Hooker, b.* i. *sect.* 10.

The Israelites had never any *communion* or affairs with the Ethiopians. *Raleigh's History of the World.*

Thou, so pleas'd,
Can'st raise thy creature to what height thou wilt
Of union, or *communion*, deify'd. *Milton's Paradise Lost.*

We maintain *communion* with God himself, and are made in the same degree partakers of the Divine Nature. *Fiddes.*

2. The common or publick celebration of the Lord's Supper; the participation of the blessed sacrament.

They resolved, that the standing of the *communion* table in all churches should be altered. *Clarendon.*

Tertullian reporteth, that the picture of Christ was engraven upon the *communion* cup. *Peacham on Drawing.*

3. A common or publick act.

Men began publickly to call on the name of the Lord; that is, they served and praised God by *communion*, and in publick manner. *Raleigh's History of the World.*

4. Union in the common worship of any church.

Bare *communion* with a good church, can never alone make a good man; for, if it could, we should have no bad ones. *South's Sermons.*

Ingenuous men have lived and died in the *communion* of that church. *Stillingfleet.*

Commu'nity. *n. s.* [*communitas*, Latin.]

1 The commonwealth; the body politick.

How could *communities*,
Degrees in schools, and brotherhood in cities,
But by degree, stand in authentick place? *Sh. Troil. and Cress.*

Not in a single person only, but in a *community* or multitude of men. *Hammond's Fundamentals.*

This parable may be aptly enough expounded of the laws that secure a civil *community.* *L'Estrange.*

It is not designed for her own use, but for the whole *community.* *Addison's Guardian*, N°. 157.

The love of our country is impressed on our mind, for the preservation of the *community.* *Addison's Freeholder*, N°. 5.

He lives not for himself alone, but hath a regard in all his actions to the great *community.* *Atterbury.*

2. Common possession; the state contrary to property or appropriation.

This text is far from proving Adam sole proprietor, it is a confirmation of the original *community* of all things. *Locke.*

3. Frequency; commonness.

He was but, as the cuckow is in June,
Heard, not regarded; seen, but with such eyes,
As, sick and blunted with *community*,
Afford no extraordinary gaze. *Shakespeare.*

Commutabi'lity. *n. s.* [from *commutable.*] The quality of being capable of exchange.

Commu'table. *adj.* [from *commute.*] That may be exchanged for something else; that may be bought off, or ransomed.

Commuta'tion. *n. s.* [from *commute.*]

1. Change; alteration.

An innocent nature could hate nothing that was innocent: in a word, so great is the *commutation*, that the soul then hated only that which now only it loves, *i. e.* sin. *South's Sermons.*

2. Exchange; the act of giving one thing for another.

The whole universe is supported by giving and returning, by commerce and *commutation.* *South's Sermons.*

According to the present temper of mankind, it is absolutely necessary that there be some method and means of *commutation*, as that of money. *Ray on the Creation.*

The use of money in the commerce and traffick of mankind, is that of saving the *commutation* of more bulky commodities. *Arbuthnot on Coins.*

3. Ransom; the act of exchanging a corporal for a pecuniary punishment.

The law of God had allowed an evasion, that is, by way of *commutation* or redemption. *Brown's Vulgar Errours, b.* v.

Commu'tative. *adj.* [from *commute.*] Relative to exchange; as *commutative justice*, that honesty which is exercised in traffick, and which is contrary to fraud in bargains.

To COMMU'TE. *v. a.* [*commuto*, Latin.]

1. To exchange; to put one thing in the place of another; to give or receive one thing for another.

This will *commute* our tasks, exchange these pleasant and gainful ones, which God assigns, for those uneasy and fruitless ones we impose on ourselves. *Decay of Piety.*

2. To buy off, or ransom one obligation by another.

Some *commute* swearing for whoring; as if forbearance of the one were a dispensation for the other. *L'Estrange.*

To Commu'te. *v. n.* To attone; to bargain for exemption.

Those institutions which God designed for means to further men in holiness, they look upon as a privilege to serve instead of it, and to *commute* for it. *South's Sermons.*

Commu'tual. *adj.* [*con* and *mutual.*] Mutual; reciprocal: used only in poetry.

Love our hearts, and hymen did our hands,
Unite *commutual* in most sacred bands. *Shakespeare's Hamlet.*

There, with *commutual* zeal, we both had strove
In acts of dear benevolence and love;
Brothers in peace, not rivals in command. *Pope's Odyssey.*

CO'MPACT. *n. s.* [*pactum*, Latin.] A contract; an accord; an agreement; a mutual and settled appointment between two or more, to do or to forbear something.

I hope the king made peace with all of us;
And the *compact* is firm and true in me. *Shakesp. Rich.* III.

In the beginnings of speech there was an implicit *compact*, founded upon common consent, that such words, voices, or gestures, should be signs whereby they would express their thoughts. *South.*

To

To COMPA'CT. *v. a.* [*compingo compactum*, Latin.]
1. To join together with firmness; to unite closely; to consolidate.
Inform her full of my particular fears;
And thereto add such reasons of your own,
As may *compact* it more. *Shakespeare's King Lear.*
Nor are the nerves of his *compacted* strength
Stretch'd, and dissolv'd into unsinew'd length. *Denham.*
By what degrees this earth's *compacted* sphere
Was harden'd, woods, and rocks, and towns to bear. *Roscom.*
This disease is more dangerous as the solids are more strict and *compacted*, and consequently more so as people are advanced in age. *Arbuthnot on Diet.*
Now the bright sun *compacts* the precious stone,
Imparting radiant lustre, like his own. *Blackmore's Creation.*
2. To make out of something.
If he, *compact* of jars, grow musical,
We shall have shortly discord in the spheres. *Shakespeare.*
3. To league with.
Thou pernicious woman,
Compact with her that's gone, think'st thou thy oaths,
Though they would swear down each particular fact,
Were testimonies. *Shakesp. Measure for Measure.*
4. To join together; to bring into a system.
We see the world so *compacted*, that each thing preserveth other things, and also itself. *Hooker, b.* i. *s.* 9.
COMPA'CT. *adj.* [*compactus*, Latin.]
1. Firm; solid; close; dense; of firm texture.
Is not the density greater in free and open spaces, void of air and other grosser bodies, than within the pores of water, glass, crystal, gems, and other *compact* bodies. *Newton's Opt.*
Without attraction the dissevered particles of the chaos could never convene into such great *compact* masses as the planets. *Bentley.*
2. Brief; as *a compact discourse*.
COMPA'CTEDNESS. *n. s.* [from *compacted.*] Firmness; density;
Sticking or *compactedness*, being natural to density, requires some excess of gravity in proportion to the density, or some other outward violence, to break it. *Digby on Bodies.*
Those atoms are supposed infrangible, extremely compacted and hard; which *compactedness* and hardness is a demonstration, that nothing could be produced by them. *Cheyne.*
COMPA'CTLY. *adv.* [from *compact.*]
1. Closely; densely.
2. With neat joining; with good compacture.
COMPA'CTNESS. *n. s.* [from *compact.*] Firmness; closeness; density.
The rest, by reason of the *compactness* of terrestrial matter, cannot make its way to wells. *Woodw. Nat. History.*
COMPA'CTURE. *n. s.* [from *compact.*] Structure; manner in which any thing is joined together; compagination.
And over it a fair portcullis hong,
Which to the gate directly did incline,
With comely compass and *compacture* strong,
Neither unseemly short, nor yet exceeding long. *Fai. Queen.*
COMPA'GES. *n. s.* [Latin.] A system of many parts united.
The organs in animal bodies are only a regular *compages* of pipes and vessels, for the fluids to pass through. *Ray.*
COMPAGINA'TION. *n. s.* [*compago*, Latin.] Union; structure; junction; connexion; contexture.
The intire or broken *compagination* of the magnetical fabrick under it. *Brown's Vulgar Errours, b.* ii. *c.* 2.
CO'MPANABLENESS. *n. s.* [from *company.*] The quality of being a good companion; sociableness; a word not now in use.
His eyes full of merry simplicity, his words of hearty *companableness*. *Sidney, b.* ii.
COMPA'NION. *n. s.* [*compagnon*, French.] See COMPANY.
1. One with whom a man frequently converses, or with whom he shares his hours of relaxation. It differs from *friend*, as *acquaintance* from *confidence*.
How now, my lord, why do you keep alone?
Of sorriest fancies your *companions* make? *Shakes. Macbeth.*
Some friend is a *companion* at the table, and will not continue in the day of thy affliction. *Ecclus.* vi. 10.
With anxious doubts, with raging passions torn,
No sweet *companion* near, with whom to mourn. *Prior.*
2. A partner; an associate.
Epaphroditus, my brother and *companion* in labour, and fellow soldier. *Phil.* ii. 25.
3. A familiar term of contempt; a fellow.
I scorn you, scurvy *companion!* What? you poor, base, rascally, cheating, lack-linnen mate: away, you mouldy rogue, away. *Shakespeare's Henry* IV. *p.* ii.
It gives boldness to every petty *companion* to spread rumours to my defamation, in places where I cannot be present. *Raleigh's Essays.*
COMPA'NIONABLE. *adj.* [from *companion.*] Fit for good fellowship; social; agreeable.
He had a more *companionable* wit, and swayed more among the good fellows. *Clarendon, b.* viii.
COMPA'NIONABLY. *adv.* [from *companionable.*] In a companionable manner.

COMPA'NIONSHIP. *n. s.* [from *companion.*]
1. Company; train.
Alcibiades, and some twenty horse,
All of *companionship*. *Shakespeare's Timon.*
2. Fellowship; association.
If it be honour in your wars, to seem
The same you are not, which, for your best ends,
You call your policy; how is't less, or worse,
That it shall hold *companionship* in peace
With honour as in war. *Shakespeare's Coriolanus.*
CO'MPANY. *n. s.* [*compagnie*, French; either from *con* and *pagus*, one of the same town; or *con* and *panis*, one that eats of the same mess.]
1. Persons assembled together; a body of men.
Go, carry sir John Falstaff to the Fleet;
Take all his *company* along with him. *Shakesp. Henry* IV.
Honest *company*, I thank you all,
That have beheld me give away myself
To this most patient, sweet, and virtuous wife. *Shakesp.*
2. Persons assembled for the entertainment of each other; an assembly of pleasure.
A crowd is not *company*, and faces are but a gallery of pictures, where there is no love. *Bacon, Essay* 28.
3. Persons considered as assembled for conversation; or, as capable of conversation and mutual entertainment.
Monsieur Zulichem came to me among the rest of the good *company* of the town. *Temple.*
Knowledge of men and manners, the freedom of habitudes, and conversation with the best *company* of both sexes, is necessary. *Dryden.*
4. The state of a companion; the act of accompanying; conversation; fellowship.
It is more pleasant to enjoy the *company* of him that can speak such words, than by such words to be persuaded to follow solitariness. *Sidney.*
Nor will I wretched thee
In death forsake, but keep thee *company*. *Dryd. Fables.*
Abdallah grew by degrees so enamoured of her conversation, that he did not think he lived when he was not in *company* with his beloved Balsora. *Guardian*, N°. 167.
5. A number of persons united for the execution or performance of any thing; a band.
Shakespeare was an actor, when there were seven *companies* of players in the town together. *Dennis.*
6. Persons united in a joint trade or partnership.
7. A number of some particular rank or profession, united by some charter; a body corporate; a corporation.
This emperor seems to have been the first who incorporated the several trades of Rome into *companies*, with their particular privileges. *Arbuthnot on Coins.*
8. A subdivision of a regiment of foot; so many as are under one captain.
Every captain brought with him thrice so many in his *company*, as was expected. *Knolles's History of the Turks.*
9. *To bear* COMPANY. } To accompany; to associate with; to
To keep COMPANY. } be a companion to.
I do desire thee
To *bear* me *company*, and go with me. *Shakespeare.*
Those Indian wives are loving fools, and may do well to *keep company* with the Arrias and Portias of old Rome. *Dryd.*
Admitted to that equal sky,
His faithful dog shall *bear* him *company*. *Pope's Essay on Man.*
10. *To keep* COMPANY. To frequent houses of entertainment.
11. Sometimes in an ill sense.
Why should he call her whore? Who *keeps* her *company?* *Shakespeare's Othello.*
To CO'MPANY. *v. a.* [from the noun.] To accompany; to attend; to be companion to; to be associated with.
I am
The soldier that did *company* these three. *Shakes. Cymbeline.*
Thus, through what path soe'er of life we rove,
Rage *companies* our hate, and grief our love. *Prior.*
To CO'MPANY. *v. n.* To associate one's self with.
I wrote to you not to *company* with fornicators. 1 *Cor.* v. 9.
CO'MPARABLE. *adj.* [from *To compare.*] Worthy to be compared; of equal regard; worthy to contend for preference.
This present world affordeth not any thing *comparable* unto the publick duties of religion. *Hooker, b.* v. *sect.* 6.
A man *comparable* with any of the captains of that age, an excellent soldier both by sea and land. *Knolles's Hist. of the Turks.*
There is no blessing of life *comparable* to the enjoyment of a discreet and virtuous friend. *Addison's Spectator*, N°. 93.
CO'MPARABLY. *adv.* [from *comparable.*] In a manner worthy to be compared.
There could no form for such a royal use be *comparably* imagined, like that of the foresaid nation. *Wotton's Architect.*
COMPA'RATES. *n. s.* [from *compare.*] In logick, the two things compared to one another.
CO'MPARATIVE. *adj.* [*comparativus*, Latin.]
1. Estimated by comparison; not positive; not absolute.
Thou wert dignified enough,
Ev'n to the point of envy, if 'twere made

Comparative

Comparative for your virtues, to be stiled
The under hangman of his realm. *Shakesp. Cymbeline.*

There resteth the *comparative* that is, granted that it is either lawful or binding; yet whether other things be not to be preferred before the extirpation of heresies. *Bacon.*

The flower or blossom is a positive good; although the remove of it, to give place to the fruit, be a *comparative* good. *Bacon's Colours of Good and Evil.*

This bubble, by reason of its *comparative* levity to the fluid that incloses it, would necessarily ascend to the top. *Bentley.*

2. Having the power of comparing different things.

Beauty is not known by an eye or nose: it consists in a symmetry, and it is the *comparative* faculty which notes it. *Glanville's Scepsis Scientifica.*

3. [In grammar.] The comparative degree expresses more of any quantity in one thing than in another; as, *the right hand is the* stronger.

COMPA'RATIVELY. *adv.* [from *comparative.*] In a state of comparison; according to estimate made by comparison; not positively.

The good or evil, which is removed, may be esteemed good or evil *comparatively*, and not positively or simply. *Bacon.*

In this world whatever is called good is *comparatively* with other things of its kind, or with the evil mingled in its composition; so he is a good man that is better than men commonly are, or in whom the good qualities are more than the bad. *Temple.*

The vegetables being *comparatively* higher than the ordinary terrestrial matter of the globe, subsided last. *Woodward.*

But how few, *comparatively*, are the instances of this wise application! *Rogers.*

To COMPA'RE. *v. a.* [*comparo*, Latin.]

1. To make one thing the measure of another; to estimate the relative goodness or badness, or other qualities, of any one thing, by observing how it differs from something else.

I will hear Brutus speak.——
I will hear Cassius, and *compare* their reasons. *Shakespeare.*

They measuring themselves by themselves, and *comparing* themselves among themselves, are not wise. 2 *Cor.* x. 12.

No man can think it grievous, who considers the pleasure and sweetness of love, and the glorious victory of overcoming evil with good; and then *compares* these with the restless torment, and perpetual tumults, of a malicious and revengeful spirit. *Tillotson, Sermon* vi.

He that has got the ideas of numbers, and hath taken the pains to *compare* one, two, and three to six, cannot chuse but know they are equal. *Locke.*

Thus much of the wrong judgment men make of present and future pleasure and pain, when they are *compared* together, and so the absent considered as future. *Locke.*

2. It may be observed, that when the comparison intends only similitude or illustration by likeness, we use *to* before the thing brought for illustration; as, he *compared* anger *to* a fire.

Solon *compared* the people *unto* the sea, and orators and counsellors *to* the winds; for that the sea would be calm and quiet, if the winds did not trouble it. *Bacon's Apophthegms.*

3. When two persons or things are compared, to discover their relative proportion of any quality, *with* is used before the thing used as a measure.

Black Macbeth
Will seem as pure as snow, being *compar'd*
With my confineless harms. *Shakespeare's Macbeth.*

To *compare*
Small things *with* greatest. *Milton's Paradise Regained, b.* iv.

He carv'd in iv'ry such a maid so fair,
As nature could not *with* his art *compare.* *Dryden.*

If he *compares* this translation *with* the original, he will find that the three first stanzas are rendered almost word for word. *Addison's Spectator,* N°. 229.

4. *To compare* is, in *Spenser*, used after the Latin *comparo*, for to get; to procure; to obtain.

But, both from back and belly, still did spare
To fill his bags, and riches to *compare.* *Fairy Queen, b.* i.

COMPA'RE. *n. s.* [from the verb.]

1. The state of being compared; comparative estimate; comparison; possibility of entering into comparison.

There I the rarest things have seen,
Oh, things without *compare.* *Suckling.*

As their small galleys may not hold *compare*
With our tall ships. *Waller.*

Beyond *compare* the Son of God was seen
Most glorious. *Milton's Paradise Lost, b.* iii. *l.* 138.

2. Simile; similitude; illustration by comparison.

True swains in love shall in the world to come,
Approve their truths by Troilus; when their rhimes,
Full of protest, and oath, and big *compare,*
Want similies. *Shakespeare's Troilus and Cressida.*

COMPA'RISON. *n. s.* [*comparaison*, French.]

1. The act of comparing.

Natalis Comes, comparing his parts with those of a man, reckons his claws among them, which are much more like those of a lion: so easy it is to drive on the *comparison* too far, to make it good. *Grew's Musæum.*

Our author saves me the *comparison* with tragedy; for he says, that herein he is to imitate the tragick poet. *Dryden.*

2. The state of being compared.

If we will rightly estimate what we call good and evil, we shall find it lies much in *comparison.* *Locke.*

Objects near our view are apt to be thought greater than those of a larger size that are more remote; and so it is with pleasure and pain: the present is apt to carry it, and those at a distance have the disadvantage in the *comparison.* *Locke.*

3. A comparative estimate; proportion.

If men would live as religion requires, the world would be a most lovely and desireable place, in *comparison* of what now it is. *Tillotson, Sermon* iii.

One can scarce imagine how so plentiful a soil should become so miserably unpeopled, in *comparison* of what it once was. *Addison's Remarks on Italy.*

4. A simile in writing or speaking; an illustration by similitude.

As fair and as good a kind of hand in hand *comparison*, had been something too fair and too good for any lady in Britany. *Shakespeare's Cymbeline.*

5. [In grammar] The formation of an adjective through its various degrees of signification; as *strong, stronger, strongest.*

To COMPA'RT. *v. a.* [*compartir*, Fr. from *con* and *partior*, Lat.] To divide; to mark out a general design into its various parts and subdivisions.

I make haste to the casting and *comparting* of the whole work. *Wotton's Architecture.*

COMPA'RTIMENT. *n. s.* [*compartiment*, French.] A division of picture, or design.

The circumference is divided into twelve *compartiments*, each containing a complete picture. *Pope.*

COMPARTI'TION. *n. s.* [from *compart.*]

1. The act of comparting or dividing.

2. The parts marked out, or separated; a separate part.

Their temples and amphitheatres needed no *compartitions.* *Wotton's Architecture.*

COMPA'RTMENT. *n. s.* [*compartiment*, French.] Division; separate part of a design.

The square will make you ready for all manner of *compartments*, bases, pedestals, and buildings. *Peacham on Drawing.*

To CO'MPASS. *v. a.* [*compasser*, Fr. *compassare*, Ital. *passibus metiri*, Latin.]

1. To encircle; to environ; to surround; to inclose.

A darksome way,
That deep descended through the hollow ground,
And was with dread and horrour *compassed* around. *Fairy Q.*

I see thee *compass'd* with thy kingdom's peers,
That speak my salutation in their minds. *Shakesp. Macbeth.*

Now all the blessings
Of a glad father *compass* thee about! *Shakespeare's Tempest.*

The shady trees cover him with their shadow: the willows of the brook *compass* him about. *Job*, xl. 22.

Observe the crowds that *compass* him around. *Dryd. Virg.*

To dare that death, I will approach yet nigher;
Thus, wert thou *compassed* with circling fire. *Dryden.*

2. To walk round any thing.

Old Chorineus *compass'd* thrice the crew,
And dipp'd an olive-branch in holy dew,
Which thrice he sprinkl'd round. *Dryden's Æn.*

3. To beleaguer; to besiege; to block.

Thine enemies shall cast a trench about thee, and *compass* thee round, and keep thee in on every side. *Luke*, xix. 43.

4. To grasp; to inclose in the arms; to seize.

5. To obtain; to procure; to attain; to have in the power.

That which by wisdom he saw to be requisite for that people, was by as great wisdom *compassed.* *Hooker's Preface.*

His master being one of great regard,
In court to *compass* any suit not hard. *Hubbard's Tale.*

If I can check my erring love, I will;
If not, to *compass* her I'll use my skill. *Shakespeare.*

How can you hope to *compass* your designs,
And not dissemble them? *Denham's Sophy.*

The knowledge of what is good and what is evil, what ought and what ought not to be done, is a thing too large to be *compassed*, and too hard to be mastered, without brains and study, parts and contemplation. *South.*

He had a mind to make himself master of Weymouth, if he could *compass* it without engaging his army before it. *Claren.*

The church of Rome createth titular patriarchs of Constantinople and Alexandria; so loth is the pope to lose the remembrance of any title that he hath once *compassed.* *Brerewood.*

Invention is the first part, and absolutely necessary to them both; yet no rule ever was, or ever can be given, how to *compass* it. *Dryden's Dufresnoy.*

In ev'ry work regard the writer's end,
Since none can *compass* more than they intend. *Pope.*

6. [In law.] To take measures preparatory to any thing; as, *to compass the death of the king.*

CO'MPASS. *n. s.* [from the verb.]

1. Circle; round.

This

This day I breathed first; time is come round;
And where I did begin, there shall I end:
My life is run its *compass*. *Shakesp. Julius Cæsar.*

2. Extent; reach; grasp.

O, Juliet, I already know thy grief;
It strains me past the *compass* of my wits. *Shakespeare.*

That which is out of the *compass* of any man's power, is to that man impossible. *South's Sermons.*

How few there are may be justly bewailed, the *compass* of them extending but from the time of Hippocrates to that of Marcus Antoninus. *Temple.*

Animals in their generation are wiser than the sons of men; but their wisdom is confined to a few particulars, and lies in a very narrow *compass*. *Addison's Spectator*, N°. 120.

This author hath tried the force and *compass* of our language with much success. *Swift.*

3. Space; room; limits.

No less than the *compass* of twelve books is taken up in these. *Pope's Essay on Homer's Battles.*

The English are good confederates in an enterprize which may be dispatched in a short *compass* of time. *Addis. Freeholder.*

You have heard what hath been here done for the poor by the five hospitals and the workhouse, within the *compass* of one year, and towards the end of a long, expensive war. *Atterb.*

4. Enclosure; circumference.

And their mount Palatine,
Th' imperial palace, *compass* huge, and high
The structure. *Milton's Paradise Regained, b.* iv. *l.* 50.

Old Rome from such a race deriv'd her birth,
Which now on sev'n high hills triumphant reigns,
And in that *compass* all the world contains. *Dryd. Virg Geor.*

5. A departure from the right line; an indirect advance; as, *to fetch a compass round the camp.*

6. Moderate space; moderation; due limits.

Certain it is, that in two hundred years before (I speak within *compass*) no such commission had been executed in either of these provinces. *Davies on Ireland.*

Nothing is likelier to keep a man within *compass* than the having constantly before his eyes the state of his affairs, in a regular course of account. *Locke.*

7. The power of the voice to express the notes of musick.

You would sound me from my lowest note to the top of my *compass*. *Shakespeare's Hamlet.*

From harmony, from heavenly harmony,
This universal frame began:
From harmony to harmony,
Through all the *compass* of the notes it ran,
The diapason closing full in man. *Dryden.*

8. [This is rarely used in the singular.] The instrument with which circles are drawn.

If they be two, they are two so,
As stiff twin *compasses* are two:
Thy soul, the fixt foot, makes no show
To move; but doth, if th' other do. *Donne.*

In his hand
He took the golden *compasses*, prepar'd
In God's eternal store, to circumscribe
This universe, and all created things. *Milton's Parad. Lost.*

To fix one foot of their *compass* wherever they think fit, and extend the other to such terrible lengths, without describing any circumference at all, is to leave us and themselves in a very uncertain state. *Swift on Dissentions in Athens and Rome.*

9. The instrument composed of a needle and card, whereby mariners steer.

The breath of religion fills the sails, profit is the *compass* by which factious men steer their course. *King Charles.*

Rude as their ships was navigation then;
No useful *compass* or meridian known:
Coasting, they kept the land within their ken,
And knew no North but when the pole-star shone. *Dryden.*

With equal force the tempest blows by turns,
From ev'ry corner of the seamen's *compass*. *Row's J. Shore.*

He that first discovered the use of the *compass*, did more for the supplying and increase of useful commodities than those who built workhouses. *Locke.*

COMPASS-SAW. *n. s.*

The *compass-saw* should not have its teeth set, as other saws have; but the edge of it should be made so broad, and the back so thin, that it may easily follow the broad edge, without having its teeth set. Its office is to cut a round, or any other compass kerf; and therefore the edge must be made broad, and the back thin, that the back may have a wide kerf to turn in. *Moxon's Mechan. Exer.*

COMPA'SSION. *n. s.* [*compassion*, Fr. from *con* and *patior*, Lat.] Pity; commiseration; sorrow for the sufferings of others; painful sympathy.

Ye had *compassion* of me in my bonds. *Heb.* x. 34.

Their angry hands
My brothers hold, and vengeance these exact;
This pleads *compassion*, and repents the fact. *Dryd. Fables.*

The good-natured man is apt to be moved with *compassion* for those misfortunes or infirmities, which another would turn into ridicule. *Addison's Spectator*, N°. 169.

To COMPA'SSION. *v. a.* [from the noun.] To pity; to compassionate; to commiserate: a word scarcely used.

O, heavens! can you hear a good man groan,
And not relent, or not *compassion* him? *Shakes. Tit. Andron.*

COMPA'SSIONATE. *adj.* [from *compassion.*] Inclined to compassion; inclined to pity; merciful; tender; melting; soft; easily affected with sorrow by the misery of others.

There never was any heart truly great and generous, that was not also tender and *compassionate*. *South's Sermons.*

To COMPA'SSIONATE. *v. a.* [from the noun.] To pity; to commiserate.

Experience layeth princes torn estates before their eyes, and withal persuades them to *compassionate* themselves. *Raleigh.*

Compassionates my pains, and pities me!
What is compassion, when 'tis void of love? *Addison's Cato.*

COMPA'SSIONATELY. *adv.* [from *compassionate.*] Mercifully; tenderly.

The fines were assigned to the rebuilding St. Paul's, and thought therefore to be the more severely imposed, and the less *compassionately* reduced and excused. *Clarendon.*

COMPATE'RNITY. *n. s.* [*con* and *paternitas*, Latin.]

Gossipred, or *compaternity*, by the canon law, is a spiritual affinity; and a juror that was gossip to either of the parties might, in former times, have been challenged as not indifferent by our law. *Davies's State of Ireland.*

COMPATIBI'LITY. *n. s.* [from *compatible.*] Consistency; the power of co-existing with something else; agreement with any thing.

COMPA'TIBLE. *adj.* [corrupted, by an unskilful compliance with pronunciation, from *competible*, from *competo*, Latin, *to suit*, *to agree*. *Competible* is found in good writers, and ought always to be used.]

1. Suitable to; fit for; consistent with; not incongruous to.

The object of the will is such a good as is *compatible* to an intellectual nature. *Hale's Origin of Mankind.*

2. Consistent; agreeable.

Our poets have joined together such qualities as are by nature the most *compatible*; valour with anger, meekness with piety, and prudence with dissimulation. *Broome.*

COMPA'TIBLENESS. *n. s.* [from *compatible.*] Consistency; agreement with any thing.

COMPA'TIBLY. *adv.* [from *compatible.*] Fitly; suitably.

COMPA'TIENT. *adj.* [from *con* and *patior*, Latin.] Suffering together. *Dict.*

COMPA'TRIOT. *n. s.* [from *con* and *patria*, Lat.] One of the same country. *Dict.*

COMPE'ER. *n. s.* [*compar*, Latin.] Equal; companion; colleague; associate.

Sesostris,
That monarchs harness'd, to his chariot yok'd
Base servitude, and his dethron'd *compeers*
Lash'd furiously. *Philips.*

To COMPE'ER. *v. a.* [from the noun.] To be equal with; to mate.

In his own grace he doth exalt himself
More than in your advancement.
——In my right,
By me invested, he *compeers* the best. *Shakes. King Lear.*

To COMPE'L. *v. a.* [*compello*, Latin.]

1. To force to some act; to oblige; to constrain; to necessitate; to urge irresistibly.

You will *compel* me then to read the will? *Sh. Jul. Cæsar.*

The spinners, carders, fullers, *compell'd* by hunger,
And lack of other means, in desp'rate manner,
Daring th' event to the teeth, are all in uproar. *Shakesp.*

He refused, and said, I will not eat: but his servants, together with the woman, *compelled* him. *1 Sa.* xxvii. 23.

All these blessings could but enable, not *compel* us to be happy. *Clarendon.*

2. To take by force or violence; to ravish from; to seize. This signification is uncommon and harsh.

The subjects grief
Comes through commissions, which *compel* from each
The sixth part of his substance, to be levied
Without delay. *Shakespeare's Henry* VIII.

COMPE'LLABLE. *adj.* [from *compel.*] That may be forced.

COMPELLA'TION. *n. s.* [from *compello*, Latin.] The stile of address; the word of salutation.

The stile best fitted for all persons on all occasions to use, is the *compellation* of father, which our Saviour first taught. *Duppa's Rules of Devotion.*

The peculiar *compellation* of the kings in France, is by *sire*, which is nothing else but *father*. *Temple.*

COMPE'LLER. *n. s.* [from *compel.*] He that forces another.

CO'MPEND. *n. s.* [*compendium*, Latin.] Abridgment; summary; epitome; contraction; breviate.

Fix in memory the discourses, and abstract them into brief *compends*. *Watts's Improvement of the Mind, p.* i *c.* 17.

COMPENDIA'RIOUS. *adj.* [*compendiarius*, Latin.] Short; contracted; summary; abridged.

COMPENDIO'SITY. *n. ſ.* [from *compendious.*] Shortneſs; contracted brevity. *Dict.*

COMPE'NDIOUS. *adj.* [from *compendium.*] Short; ſummary; abridged; direct; comprehenſive; holding much in a narrow ſpace; near; by which time is ſaved, and circuition cut off.

They had learned more *compendious* and expeditious ways, whereby they ſhortened their labours, and ſo gained time. *Woodward's Natural Hiſtory.*

COMPE'NDIOUSLY. *adv.* [from *compendious.*] Shortly; in a ſhort method; ſummarily; in epitome.

By the apoſtles we have the ſubſtance of Chriſtian belief *compendiouſly* drawn into few and ſhort articles. *Hooker, b.* v.

The ſtate or condition of matter, before the world was a-making, is *compendiouſly* expreſſed by the word chaos. *Bentley.*

COMPE'NDIOUSNESS. *n. ſ.* [from *compendious.*] Shortneſs; brevity; comprehenſion in a narrow compaſs.

The inviting eaſineſs and *compendiouſneſs* of this aſſertion, ſhould dazzle the eyes. *Bentley's Sermons.*

COMPE'NDIUM. n. ſ. [Latin.] Abridgment; ſummary; breviate; abbreviature; that which holds much in a narrow room; the near way.

After we are grown well acquainted with a ſhort ſyſtem or *compendium* of a ſcience, which is written in the plaineſt and moſt ſimple manner, it is then proper to read a larger regular treatiſe on that ſubject. *Watts's Improvement of the Mind.*

COMPE'NSABLE. *adj.* [from *compenſate.*] That which may be recompenſed.

To COMPE'NSATE. *v. a.* [*compenſo*, Lat.] To recompenſe; to be equivalent to; to counterballance; to countervail; to make amends for.

The length of the night, and the dews thereof, do *compenſate* the heat of the day. *Bacon's Natural Hiſtory*, N°. 398.

The pleaſures of life do not *compenſate* the miſeries. *Prior.*

Nature to theſe, without profuſion kind,
The proper organs, proper pow'rs aſſign'd;
Each ſeeming want *compenſated* of courſe,
Here with degrees of ſwiftneſs, there of force. *Pope.*

COMPENSA'TION. *n. ſ.* [from *compenſate.*] Recompenſe; ſomething equivalent; amends.

Poynings, the better to make *compenſation* of his ſervice in the wars, called a parliament. *Bacon's Henry* VII.

All other debts may *compenſation* find;
But love is ſtrict, and will be paid in kind. *Dryd. Aurengz.*

COMPE'NSATIVE. *adj.* [from *compenſate.*] That which compenſates; that which countervails.

To COMPE'NSE. *v. a.* [*compenſo*, Latin.] To compenſate; to countervail; to be equivalent to; to counterballance; to recompenſe.

It ſeemeth, the weight of the quickſilver doth not *compenſe* the weight of a ſtone, more than the weight of the aqua-fortis. *Bacon's Nat. Hiſtory.*

The joys of the two marriages were *compenſed* with the mournings and funerals of prince Arthur. *Bacon's Henry* VII.

To COMPERE'NDINATE. *v. a.* [*comperendino*, Latin.] To delay.

COMPERENDINA'TION. *n. ſ.* [from *comperendinate*] Delay; dilatorineſs.

CO'MPETENCE. } *n. ſ.* [from *competent.*]
CO'MPETENCY. }

1. Such a quantity of any thing as is ſufficient, without ſuperfluity.

Something of ſpeech is to be indulged to common civility, more to intimacies and endearments, and a *competency* to thoſe recreative diſcourſes which maintain the chearfulneſs of ſociety. *Government of the Tongue.*

2. Such a fortune as, without exuberance, is equal to the neceſſities of life.

For *competence* of life I will allow you,
That lack of means enforce you not to evil. *Shak. Hen.* IV.

It is no mean happineſs to be ſeated in the mean: ſuperfluity comes ſooner by white hairs, but *competency* lives longer. *Shakeſpeare's Merchant of Venice.*

A diſcreet learned clergyman, with a *competency* fit for one of his education, may be an entertaining, an uſeful, and ſometimes a neceſſary companion. *Swift.*

Reaſon's whole pleaſure, all the joys of ſenſe,
Lie in three words, health, peace, and *competence.* *Pope.*

3. [In law] The power or capacity of a judge, or court, for taking cogniſance of an affair.

CO'MPETENT. *adj.* [*competens*, Latin.]

1. Suitable; fit; adequate; proportionate.

If there be any power in imagination, the diſtance muſt be *competent*, the medium not adverſe, and the body apt and proportionate *Bacon's Natural Hiſtory*, N°. 950.

The greateſt captain of the Engliſh brought rather a guard than a *competent* army to recover Ireland. *Davies on Ireland.*

2 Adapted to any purpoſe without defect or ſuperfluity.

To draw men from great exceſs, it is not amiſs, though we uſe them unto ſomewhat leſs than is *competent.* *Hooker.*

3. Reaſonable; moderate.

A *competent* number of the old being firſt read, the new ſhould ſucceed. *Hooker, b.* v. *ſect.* 40.

The clergy have gained ſome inſight into men and things, and a *competent* knowledge of the world. *Atterbury's Sermons.*

4. Qualified; fit.

Let us firſt conſider how *competent* we are for the office. *Government of the Tongue, ſect.* 6.

5. Conſiſtent with; incident to.

That is the privilege of the Infinite Author of things, who never ſlumbers nor ſleeps, but is not *competent* to any finite being. *Locke.*

CO'MPETENTLY. *adv.* [from *competent*]

1. Reaſonably; moderately; without ſuperfluity or want.

Some places require men *competently* endowed; but none think the appointment to be a duty of juſtice, bound to reſpect deſert. *Wotton.*

2. Adequately; properly.

I think it hath been *competently* proved. *Bentley.*

COMPE'TIBLE. *adj.* [from *competo*, Latin. For this word a corrupt orthography has introduced *compatible.*] Suitable to; conſiſtent with.

It is not *competible* with the grace of God ſo much as to incline any man to do evil. *Hammond on Fundamentals.*

Thoſe are properties not at all *competible* to body or matter, though of never ſo pure a mixture. *Glanville.*

COMPE'TIBLENESS. *n. ſ.* [from *competible.*] Suitableneſs; fitneſs.

COMPETI'TION. *n. ſ.* [from *con* and *petitio*, Latin.]

1. The act of endeavouring to gain what another endeavours to gain at the ſame time; rivalry; conteſt.

The ancient flames of diſcord and inteſtine wars, upon the *competition* of both houſes, would again return and revive. *Bacon's Henry* VII.

A portrait, with which one of Titian's could not come in *competition.* *Dryden's Dufreſnoy.*

Though what produces any degree of pleaſure, be in itſelf good, and what is apt to produce any degree of pain be evil, yet often we do not call it ſo, when it comes in *competition*: the degrees alſo of pleaſure and pain have a preference. *Locke.*

We ſhould be aſhamed to rival inferiours, and diſhonour our nature by ſo degrading a *competition.* *Rogers, Serm.* v.

2. Double claim; claim of more than one to one thing; anciently with *to.*

Competition to the crown there is none, nor can be. *Bacon.*

3. Now with *for.*

The prize of beauty was diſputed 'till you were ſeen; but now all pretenders have withdrawn their claims: there is no *competition* but *for* the ſecond place. *Dryden.*

COMPE'TITOR. *n. ſ.* [*con* and *petitor*, Latin.]

1. One that has a claim oppoſite to another's; a rival; with *for* before the thing claimed.

How furious and impatient they be,
And cannot brook *competitors* in love. *Shakeſp. Tit. Andron.*

Some undertake ſuits with purpoſe to let them fall, to gratify the *competitor.* *Bacon, Eſſay* 50.

Cicereius and Scipio were *competitors for* the office of prætor. *Tatler*, N°. 86.

He who truſts in God has the advantage in preſent felicity; and, when we take futurity into the account, ſtands alone, and is acknowledged to have no *competitor.* *Rogers, Serm.* 19.

2. It had formerly *of* before the thing claimed.

Selymes, king of Algiers, was in arms againſt his brother Mechemetes, *competitor of* the kingdom. *Knolles's Hiſtory.*

3. In *Shakeſpeare* it ſeems to ſignify only an opponent.

The Guilfords are in arms,
And every hour more *competitors*
Flock to the rebels. *Shakeſpeare's Richard* III.

COMPILA'TION. *n. ſ.* [from *compilo*, Latin.]

1. A collection from various authors.

2. An aſſemblage; a coacervation.

There is in it a ſmall vein filled with ſpar, probably ſince the time of the *compilation* of the maſs. *Woodward on Foſſils.*

To COMPI'LE. *v. a.* [*compilo*, Latin.]

1. To draw up from various authors; to collect into one body.

2. To write; to compoſe.

In poetry they *compile* the praiſes of virtuous men and actions, and ſatyrs againſt vice. *Temple.*

By the accounts which authors have left, they might learn that the face of ſea and land is the ſame that it was when thoſe accounts were *compiled.* *Woodward's Natural Hiſtory.*

The regard he had for his ſhield, had cauſed him formerly to *compile* a diſſertation concerning it. *Arbuthnot and Pope.*

3. To contain; to compriſe: not in uſe.

After ſo long a race as I have run
Through fairy-land, which thoſe ſix books *compile*,
Give leave to reſt me. *Spenſer, Sonnet* 80.

COMPI'LEMENT. *n. ſ.* [from *compile.*] Coacervation; the act of piling together; the act of heaping up.

I was encouraged to aſſay how I could build a man; for there is a moral as well as a natural or artificial *compilement*, and of better materials. *Wotton on Education.*

COMPI'LER. *n. ſ.* [from *compile.*] A collector; one who frames a compoſition from various authors.

Some draw experiments into titles and tables; those we call *compilers* *Bacon's New Atalantis.*

Some painful *compiler*, who will study old language, may inform the world that Robert earl of Oxford was high treasurer. *Swift.*

COMPLA'CENCE. } *n. s.* [*complacentia*, low Latin.]
COMPLA'CENCY. }

1. Pleasure; satisfaction; gratification.

I by conversing cannot these erect
From prone, nor in their ways *complacence* find. *Milton.*

When the supreme faculties move regularly, the inferior affections following, there arises a serenity and *complacency* upon the whole soul. *South.*

Diseases extremely lessen the *complacence* we have in all the good things of this life. *Atterbury's Sermons.*

Others proclaim the infirmities of a great man with satisfaction and *complacency*, if they discover none of the like in themselves. *Addison's Spectator*, N°. 256.

2. The cause of pleasure; joy.

O thou, in heav'n and earth the only peace
Found out for mankind under wrath! O thou,
My sole *complacence!* *Milton's Paradise Lost*, *b.* iii. *l.* 274.

3. Civility; complaisance; softness of manners.

They were not satisfied with their governour, and apprehensive of his rudeness and want of *complacency*. *Clarendon.*

His great humanity appeared in the benevolence of his aspect, the *complacency* of his behaviour, and the tone of his voice. *Addison's Freeholder*, N°. 39.

Complacency and truth, and manly sweetness,
Dwell ever on his tongue, and smooth his thoughts. *Addis.*
With mean *complacence* ne'er betray your trust,
Nor be so civil as to prove unjust. *Pope's Ess. Crit.*

COMPLA'CENT. *adj.* [*complacens*, Lat.] Civil; affable; soft; complaisant.

To COMPLA'IN. *v. n.* [*complaindre*, French.]

1. To mention with sorrow or resentment; to murmur; to lament. With *of* before the cause of sorrow.

Lord Hastings,
Humbly *complaining* to her deity,
Got my lord chamberlain his liberty. *Shakesp. Richard* III.

I will speak in the anguish of my spirit, I will *complain* in the bitterness of my soul. *Job*, vii. 11.

Shall I, like thee, on Friday night *complain?*
For on that day was Cœur de Lion slain. *Dryden's Fables.*

Do not all men *complain*, even these as well as others, *of* the great ignorance of mankind? *Burnet's Pref. to Theory of Earth.*

Thus accurs'd,
In midst of water I *complain of* thirst. *Dryden.*

2. Sometimes with *for* before the causal noun.

Wherefore doth a living man *complain*, a man *for* the punishment of his sins? *Lam.* iii. 39.

3. To inform against.

Now, master Shallow, you'll *complain of* me to the council? *Shakesp. Merry Wives of Windsor.*

To COMPLA'IN. *v. a.* [This sense is rare, and perhaps not very proper.] To lament; to bewail.

Gaufride, who couldst so well in rhime *complain*
The death of Richard, with an arrow slain. *Dryd. Fables.*

COMPLA'INANT. *n. s.* [from *complain.*] One who urges a suit, or commences a prosecution against another.

Congreve and this author are the most eager *complainants* of the dispute. *Collier's Defence.*

COMPLA'INER. *n. s.* [from *complain.*] One who complains; a murmurer; a lamenter.

St. Jude observes, that the murmurers and *complainers* are the same who speak swelling words. *Government of the Tongue.*

Philips is a *complainer*; and on this occasion I told lord Carteret, that *complainers* never succeed at court, though railers do. *Swift.*

COMPLA'INT. *n. s.* [*complainte*, French.]

1. Representation of pains or injuries; lamentation.

I cannot find any cause of *complaint*, that good laws have so much been wanting unto us, as we to them. *Hooker*, *Dedicat.*

As for me, is my *complaint* to man. *Job*, xxx. 4.

2. The cause or subject of complaint; grief.

The poverty of the clergy in England hath been the *complaint* of all who wish well to the church. *Swift.*

3. A malady; a disease.

One, in a *complaint* of his bowels, was let blood 'till he had scarce any left, and was perfectly cured. *Arbuthnot on Coins.*

4. Remonstrance against; information against.

Full of vexation, come I with *complaint*
Against my child. *Shakesp. Midsummer Night's Dream.*

Against the goddess these *complaints* he made. *Dryd. Æn.*

COMPLAISA'NCE. *n. s.* [*complaisance*, French.] Civility; desire of pleasing; act of adulation.

Her death is but in *complaisance* to her. *Dryden.*

You must also be industrious to discover the opinion of your enemies; for you may be assured, that they will give you no quarter, and allow nothing to *complaisance*. *Dryd. Dufresnoy.*

Fair Venus wept the sad disaster
Of having lost her fav'rite dove:
In *complaisance* poor Cupid mourn'd;
His grief reliev'd his mother's pain. *Prior.*

COMPLAISA'NT. *adj.* [*complaisant*, French.] Civil; desirous to please.

There are to whom my satire seems too bold;
Scarce to wise Peter *complaisant* enough,
And something said of Charters much too rough. *Pope.*

COMPLAISA'NTLY. *adv.* [from *complaisant.*] Civilly; with desire to please; ceremoniously.

In plenty starving, tantaliz'd in state,
And *complaisantly* help'd to all I hate;
Treated, caress'd, and tir'd, I take my leave. *Pope.*

COMPLAISA'NTNESS. *n. s.* [from *complaisant.*] Civility; compliance. *Dict.*

To COMPLA'NATE. } *v. a.* [from *planus*, Lat.] To level; to
To COMPLA'NE. } reduce to a flat and even surface.

The vertebræ of the neck and back-bone are made short and *complanated*, and firmly braced with muscles and tendons. *Derham's Physico-Theology.*

COMPLEA'T. See COMPLETE.

CO'MPLEMENT. *n. s.* [*complementum*, Latin.]

1. Perfection; fulness; completion; completement.

Our custom is both to place it in the front of our prayers as a guide, and to add it in the end of some principal limbs or parts, as a *complement* which fully perfecteth whatsoever may be defective in the rest. *Hooker*, *b.* v. *sect.* 35.

They as they feasted had their fill,
For a full *complement* of all their ill. *Hubberd's Tale.*

For a *complement* of these blessings, they were enjoyed by the protection of a king of the most harmless disposition, the most exemplary piety, the greatest sobriety, chastity, and mercy. *Clarendon.*

The sensible nature, in its *complement* and integrity, hath five exterior powers or faculties. *Hale's Origin of Mankind.*

2. Complete set; complete provision; the full quantity or number.

The god of love himself inhabits there, }
With all his rage, and dread, and grief and care; }
His *complement* of stores, and total war. *Prior.* }

3. Adscititious circumstances; appendages; parts not necessary, but ornamental.

If the case be such as permitteth not baptism, to have the decent *complements* of baptism, better it were to enjoy the body without his furniture than to wait for this, 'till the opportunity of that, for which we desire it, be lost. *Hooker*, *b.* v. *s.* 58.

These, which have lastly sprung up, for *complements*, rites, and ceremonies of church actions, are, in truth, for the greatest part, such silly things, that very easiness doth make them hard to be disputed of in serious manner. *Hooker*, *Dedication.*

A doleful case desires a doleful song,
Without vain art or curious *complements*. *Spenser.*

Garnish'd and deck'd in modest *complement*,
Not working with the ear, but with the eye. *Shak. Hen.* V.

4. [In geometry.] What remains of a quadrant of a circle, or of ninety degrees, after any certain arch hath been retrenched from it.

5. [In astronomy.] The distance of a star from the zenith.

6. CO'MPLEMENT *of the Curtain*, in fortification, that part in the interiour side of it which makes the demigorge.

7. *Arithmetical* COMPLEMENT *of a Logarithm*, is what the logarithm wants of 10,0000000. *Chambers.*

COMPLE'TE. *adj.* [*completus*, Latin.]

1. Perfect; full; without any defects.

With us the reading of scripture in the church is a part of our church liturgy, a special portion of the service which we do to God; and not an exercise to spend the time, when one doth wait for another coming, 'till the assembly of them that shall afterwards worship him be *complete*. *Hooker*, *b.* v. *s.* 19.

And ye are *complete* in him which is the head of all principality and power. *Col.* ii. 10.

Then marvel not, thou great and *complete* man,
That all the Greeks begin to worship Ajax. *Shakespeare.*

If any disposition should appear towards so good a work, the assistance of the legislative power would be necessary to make it more *complete*. *Swift.*

2. Finished; ended; concluded.

This course of vanity almost *complete*,
Tir'd in the field of life, I hope retreat. *Prior.*

To COMPLE'TE. *v. a* [from the noun.] To perfect; to finish.

In 1608, Mr. Sanderson was *completed* master of arts. *Walton's Life of Sanderson.*

To town he comes, *completes* the nation's hope,
And heads the bold train'd-bands, and burns a pope. *Pope.*

COMPLE'TELY. *adv.* [from *complete.*] Fully; perfectly.

Then tell us, how you can your bodies roll,
Through space of matter, so *completely* full? *Blackmore.*

Whatever person would aspire to be *completely* witty, smart, humorous and polite, must, by hard labour, be able to retain in his memory every single sentence contained in this work. *Swift's Introduction to Genteel Conversation.*

COMPLE'TEMENT. *n. s.* [from *completement*, French.] The act of completing.

Allow

Allow me to give you, from the best authors, the origin, the antiquity, the growth, the change, and the *completement* of satire among the Romans. *Dryden's Dedic. to Juvenal.*

COMPLE'TENESS. *n. s.* [from *complete.*] Perfection; the state of being complete.

I cannot allow their wisdom such a *completeness* and inerrability, as to exclude myself. *King Charles.*

These parts go to make up the *completeness* of any subject. *Watts's Logick.*

COMPLE'TION. *n. s.* [from *complete.*]

1. Accomplishment; act of fulfilling; state of being fulfilled.

There was a full entire harmony, and consent of all the divine predictions, receiving their *completion* in Christ. *South.*

2. Utmost height; perfect state.

He makes it the utmost *completion* of an ill character to bear a malevolence to the best men. *Pope's Notes on the Iliad.*

CO'MPLEX. *adj.* [*complexus*, Latin.] Composite; of many parts; not simple; including many particulars.

Ideas made up of several simple ones, I call *complex*; such as beauty, gratitude, a man, the universe; which though complicated of various simple ideas, or *complex* ideas made up of simple ones, yet are considered each by itself as one. *Locke.*

A secondary essential mode, called a property, sometimes goes toward making up the essence of a *complex* being. *Watts.*

With such perfection fram'd,
Is this *complex* stupendous scheme of things. *Thoms. Spring.*

CO'MPLEX. *n. s.* [from the adjective.] Complication; collection.

This parable of the wedding-supper comprehends in it the whole *complex* of all the blessings and privileges exhibited by the gospel. *South's Sermons.*

COMPLE'XEDNESS. *n. s.* [from *complex.*] Complication; involution of many particular parts in one integral; contrariety to simplicity; compound state or nature.

From the *complexedness* of these moral ideas, there follows another inconvenience, *viz.* that the mind cannot easily retain those precise combinations. *Locke.*

COMPLE'XION. *n. s.* [*complexio*, Latin.]

1. The inclosure or involution of one thing in another.

Though the terms of propositions may be complex, yet where the composition of the whole argument is thus plain, simple and regular, it is properly called a simple syllogism, since the *complexion* does not belong to the syllogistick form of it. *Watts's Logick.*

2. The colour of the external parts of any body.

Men judge by the *complexion* of the sky
The state and inclination of the day. *Shakesp. Rich.* II.

How sweetly dost thou minister to love,
That know love's grief by his *complexion!* *Shakespeare.*

What see you in those papers, that you lose
So much *complexion?* *Shakespeare's Henry* V.

He so takes on yonder, so rails against all married mankind, so curses all Eve's daughters, of what *complexion* soever. *Shak.*

Why doth not beauty then refine the wit,
And good *complexion* rectify the will? *Davies.*

Niceness, though it renders them insignificant to great purposes, yet it polishes their *complexion*, and makes their spirits seem more vigorous. *Collier on Pride.*

If I write on a black man, I run over all the eminent persons of that *complexion*. *Addison's Spectator*, Nº. 262.

3. The temperature of the body according to the various proportions of the four medical humours.

'Tis ill, though different your *complexions* are,
The family of heav'n for men should war. *Dryden's Fables.*

For from all tempers he could service draw,
The worth of each, with its allay, he knew;
And, as the confident of nature, saw
How she *complexions* did divide and brew. *Dryden.*

The methods of providence men of this *complexion* must be unfit for the contemplation of. *Burnet's Theory of the Earth.*

Let melancholy rule supreme,
Choler preside, or blood or phlegm,
It makes no diff'rence in the case,
Nor is *complexion* honour's place. *Swift.*

COMPLE'XIONAL. *adj.* [from *complexion.*] Depending on the complexion or temperament of the body.

Men and other animals receive different tinctures from *complexional* efflorescencies, and descend still lower as they partake of the fuliginous and denigrating humours. *Brown.*

Ignorance, where it proceeds from early or *complexional* prejudices, will not wholly exclude us from the favour of God. *Fiddes's Sermons.*

COMPLE'XIONALLY. *adv.* [from *complexion.*] By complexion.

An Indian king sent unto Alexander a fair woman, fed with poisons, either by converse or copulation *complexionally* to destroy him. *Brown's Vulgar Errours, b.* vii. *c.* 18.

COMPLE'XLY. *adv.* [from *complex.*] In a complex manner; not simply.

COMPLE'XNESS. *n. s.* [from *complex.*] The state of being complex.

COMPLE'XURE. *n. s.* [from *complex.*] The involution or complication of one thing with others.

COMPLI'ANCE. *n. s.* [from *comply.*]

1. The act of yielding to any desire or demand; accord; submission.

I am far from excusing that *compliance*, for plenary consent it was not, to his destruction. *King Charles.*

We are free from any necessary determination of our will to any particular action, and from a necessary *compliance* with our desire, set upon any particular, and then appearing preferable good. *Locke.*

Let the king meet *compliance* in your looks,
A free and ready yielding to your wishes. *Rowe.*

The actions to which the world solicits our *compliance* are sins, which forfeit eternal expectations. *Rogers.*

What *compliances* will remove dissention, while the liberty continues of professing what new opinions we please? *Swift.*

2. A disposition to yield to others; complaisance.

He was a man of few words, and of great *compliance*; and usually delivered that as his opinion, which he foresaw would be grateful to the king. *Clarendon, b.* viii.

COMPLI'ANT. *adj.* [from *comply.*]

1. Yielding; bending.

The *compliant* boughs
Yielded them. *Milton's Paradise Lost, b.* iv. *l.* 332.

2. Civil; complaisant.

To CO'MPLICATE. *v. a.* [*complico*, Latin.]

1. To entangle one with another; to join.

Though the particular actions of war are *complicate* in fact, yet they are separate and distinct in right. *Bacon.*

In case our offence against God hath been *complicated* with injury to men, we should make restitution. *Tillotson's Sermons.*

When the disease is *complicated* with other diseases, one must consider that which is most dangerous. *Arbuthnot on Diet.*

There are a multitude of human actions, which have so many *complicated* circumstances, aspects, and situations, with regard to time and place, persons and things, that it is impossible for any one to pass a right judgment concerning them, without entering into most of these circumstances. *Watts.*

2. To unite by involution of parts one in another.

Commotion in the parts may make them apply themselves one to another, or *complicate* and dispose them after the manner requisite to make them stick. *Boyle's History of Firmness.*

3. To form by complication; to form by the union of several parts into one integral.

Dreadful was the din
Of hissing through the hall! thick swarming now
With *complicated* monsters, head and tail. *Milt. Par. Lost.*

A man, an army, the universe, are *complicated* of various simple ideas, or complex ideas made up of simple ones. *Locke.*

CO'MPLICATE. *adj.* [from the verb.] Compounded of a multiplicity of parts.

What pleasure would felicitate his spirit, if he could grasp all in a survey; as a painter runs over a *complicate* piece wrought by Titian or Raphael. *Watts's Improv. of the Mind.*

CO'MPLICATENESS. *n. s.* [from *complicate.*] The state of being complicated; intricacy; perplexity.

There is great variety of intelligibles in the world, so much objected to our senses, and every several object is full of subdivided multiplicity and *complicateness*. *Hale's Origin of Mank.*

COMPLICA'TION. *n. s.* [from *complicate.*]

1. The act of involving one thing in another.

2. The state of being involved one in another.

All our grievances are either of body or of mind, or in *complications* of both. *L'Estrange.*

The notions of a confused knowledge are always full of perplexity and *complications*, and seldom in order. *Wilkins.*

3. The integral consisting of many things involved, perplexed, and united.

By admitting a *complication* of ideas, and taking too many things at once into one question, the mind is dazzled and bewildered. *Watts's Logick.*

CO'MPLICE. *n. s.* [Fr. from *complex*, an associate, low Latin.] One who is united with others in an ill design; an associate; a confederate; an accomplice.

To arms, victorious noble father,
To quell the rebels and their *complices*. *Shakesp. Henry* VI.

Justice was afterwards done upon the offenders, the principal being hanged and quartered in Smithfield; and divers of his chief *complices* executed in divers parts of the realm. *Hayw.*

The marquis prevailed with the king, that he might only turn his brother out of the garrison, after justice was done upon his *complices*. *Clarendon, b.* viii.

COMPLI'ER. *n. s.* [from *comply.*] A man of an easy temper; a man of ready compliance.

CO'MPLIMENT. *n. s.* [*compliment*, Fr.] An act, or expression of civility, usually understood to include some hypocrisy, and to mean less than it declares.

He observed few *compliments* in matter of arms, but such as proud anger did indite to him. *Sidney, b.* ii.

My servant, sir? 'Twas never merry world
Since lowly feigning was call'd *compliment*:
Y' are servant to the duke Orsino, youth. *Shakespeare.*

One whom the musick of his own vain tongue
Doth ravish, like inchanting harmony:
A man of *compliments*, whom right and wrong
Have chose as umpire of their meeting. *Shakespeare.*

What honour that,
But tedious waste of time, to sit and hear
So many hollow *compliments* and lies,
Outlandish flatteries? *Milton's Paradise Regain'd, b.* iv.

Virtue and religion, heaven and eternal happiness, are not trifles to be given up in a *compliment*, or sacrificed to a jest. *Rogers, Sermon* x.

To Co'MPLIMENT. *v. a.* [from the noun.] To sooth with acts or expressions of respect; to flatter; to praise.

It was not to *compliment* a society, so much above flattery and the regardless air of common applauses. *Glanv. Sceps. Pref.*

Monarchs should their inward soul disguise,
Dissemble and command, be false and wise;
By ignominious arts, for servile ends,
Should *compliment* their foes, and shun their friends. *Prior.*

The watchman gave so very great a thump at my door, that I awaked, and heard myself *complimented* with the usual salutation. *Tatler*, N°. 111.

She *compliments* Menelaus very handsomely, and says he wanted no accomplishment either of mind or body. *Pope.*

COMPLIME'NTAL *adj.* [from *compliment.*] Expressive of respect or civility; implying compliments.

I come to speak with Paris from the prince Troilus: I will make a *complimental* assault upon him. *Shak. Troil. and Cressida.*

Languages, for the most part, in terms of art and erudition, retain their original poverty, and rather grow rich and abundant in *complimental* phrases, and such froth. *Wotton.*

This falsehood of Ulysses is intirely *complimental* and officious. *Pope's Odyssey, Notes.*

COMPLIME'NTALLY. *adv.* [from *complimental.*] In the nature of a compliment; civilly; with artful or false civility.

This speech has been condemned as avaricious: Eustathius judges it spoken artfully and *complimentally. Broom on the Odyss.*

COMPLIME'NTER. *n. s.* [from *compliment.*] One given to compliments; a flatterer.

Co'MPLINE. *n. s.* [*compline*, Fr. *completinum*, low Lat.] The last act of worship at night, by which the service of the day is completed.

At morn and eve, besides their anthems sweet,
Their peny masses and their *complines* meet. *Hubb. Tale.*

To COMPLO'RE. *v. n.* [*comploro*, Lat.] To make lamentation together.

COMPLO'T. *n s.* [Fr. from *completum* for *complexum*, low Latin, *Menage.*] A confederacy in some secret crime; a plot; a conspiracy.

I cannot, my life, my brother, like but well
The purpose of the *complot* which ye tell. *Hubberd's Tale.*
I know their *complot* is to have my life. *Shak. Hen.* VI.

To COMPLO'T. *v. a.* [from the noun.] To form a plot; to conspire; to join in any secret design, generally criminal.

Nor ever by advised purpose meet,
To plot, contrive, or *complot* any ill. *Shakes. Richard* II.

A few lines after, we find them *complotting* together, and contriving a new scene of miseries to the Trojans. *Pope.*

COMPLO'TTER. *n. s.* [from *complot.*] A conspirator; one joined in a plot.

Jocasta too, no longer now my sister,
Is found *complotter* in the horrid deed. *Dryd. and Lee's Oedip.*

To COMPLY'. *v. n.* [*Skinner* derives it from the French *complaire*; but probably it comes from *complier*, to bend to. *Plier* is still in use.] To yield to; to be obsequious to; to accord with; to suit with. It has *with* before as well persons as things.

The rising sun *complys with* our weak sight,
First gilds the clouds, then shews his globe of light. *Waller.*

They did servilely *comply with* the people in worshipping God by sensible images and representations. *Tillotson.*

The truth of things will not *comply with* our conceits, and bend itself to our interest. *Tillotson.*

Remember I am she who sav'd your life,
Your loving, lawful, and *complying* wife. *Dryden.*

He made his wish *with* his estate *comply*,
Joyful to live, yet not afraid to die. *Prior.*

COMPO'NENT. *adj.* [*componens*, Latin.] That which constitutes the compound body.

The bigness of the *component* parts of natural bodies may be conjectured by their colours. *Newton's Opticks.*

To COMPO'RT. *v. n.* [*comporter*, Fr. from *porto*, Lat.] To agree; to suit. Followed by *with.*

Some piety's not good there, some vain disport
On this side sin, with that place may *comport. Donne.*

To be such does not *comport* with the nature of time. *Holder on Time.*

It is not every man's talent to distinguish aright how far our prudence may warrant our charity, and how far our charity may *comport* with our prudence. *L'Estrange.*

Children, in the things they do, if they *comport* with their age, find little difference, so they may be doing. *Locke.*

To COMPO'RT. *v. a.* To bear; to endure. This is a Gallick signification, not adopted among us.

The malecontented sort,
That never can the present state *comport*,
But would as often change as they change will. *Daniel.*

COMPO'RT. *n. s.* [from the verb] Behaviour; conduct; manner of acting and looking.

I shall account concerning the rules and manners of deportment in the receiving, our *comport* and conversation in and after it. *Taylor's Worthy Communicant.*

I know them well, and mark'd their rude *comport*;
In times of tempest they command alone,
And he but sits precarious on the throne. *Dryden's Fables.*

COMPO'RTABLE. *adj.* [from *comport.*] Consistent; not contradictory.

We cast the rules and cautions of this art into some *comportable* method. *Wotton's Architecture.*

COMPO'RTANCE. *n. s.* [from *comport.*] Behaviour; gesture of ceremony.

Goodly *comportance* each to other bear,
And entertain themselves with court'sies meet. *Fairy Queen.*

COMPO'RTMENT. *n. s.* [from *comport.*] Behaviour.

By her serious and devout *comportment* on these solemn occasions, she gives an example that is very often too much wanted. *Addison's Freeholder.*

To COMPO'SE. *v. a.* [*composer*, Fr. *compono*, Latin.]

1. To form a mass by joining different things together.

Zeal ought to be *composed* of the highest degrees of all pious affections. *Sprat.*

2. To place any thing in its proper form and method.

In a peaceful grave my corps *compose. Dryden's Æn.*

3. To dispose; to put in the proper state for any purpose.

The whole army seemed well *composed* to obtain that by their swords, which they could not by their pen. *Clarendon, b.* viii.

4. To put together a discourse or sentence.

Words so pleasing to God, as those which the son of God himself hath *composed*, were not possible for men to frame. *Hooker, b.* v. *sect.* 35.

5. To constitute by being parts of a whole.

Nor did Israel 'scape
Th' infection, when their borrow'd gold *compos'd*
The calf in Oreb. *Milton's Paradise Lost, b.* i. *l.* 483.

A few useful things, confounded with many trifles, fill their memories, and *compose* their intellectual possessions. *Watts.*

6. To calm; to quiet.

He would undertake the journey with him, by which all his fears would be *composed. Clarendon, b.* viii.

You, that had taught them to subdue their foes,
Cou'd order teach, and their high sp'rits *compose. Waller.*

Compose thy mind;
Nor frauds are here contriv'd, nor force design'd. *Dryden.*

He, having a full sway and command over the water, had power to still and *compose* it, as well as to move and disturb it. *Woodward's Natural History, p.* iii.

Yet to *compose* this midnight noise,
Go, freely search where-e'er you please. *Prior.*

7. To adjust the mind to any business, by freeing it from disturbance.

The mind being thus disquieted, may not be able easily to *compose* and settle itself to prayer. *Duppa's Rules for Devotion.*

We beseech thee to *compose* her thoughts, and preserve her reason, during her sickness. *Swift.*

8. To adjust; to settle; as, *to compose a difference.*

9. [With printers.] To arrange the letters; to put the letters in order in the forms.

10. [In musick.] To form a tune from the different musical notes.

COMPO'SED. *participial adj.* [from *compose.*] Calm; serious; even; sedate.

In Spain there is something still more serious and *composed* in the manner of the inhabitants. *Addison's Remarks on Italy.*

The Mantuan there in sober triumph sate,
Compos'd his posture, and his look sedate. *Pope.*

COMPO'SEDLY. *adv.* [from *composed.*] Calmly; seriously; sedately.

A man was walking before the door very *composedly* without a hat: one crying, Here is the fellow that killed the duke, every body asked which is he, the man without the hat very *composedly* answered, I am he. *Clarendon.*

COMPO'SEDNESS. *n. s.* [from *composed.*] Sedateness; calmness; tranquillity.

He that will think to any purpose, must have fixedness and *composedness* of humour, as well as smartness of parts. *Norris.*

COMPO'SER. *n. s.* [from *compose.*]

1. An author; a writer.

Now will be the right season of forming them to be able writers and *composers* in every excellent matter. *Milton.*

If the thoughts of such authors have nothing in them, they at least do no harm, and shew an honest industry and a good intention in the *composer. Addison's Freeholder*, N°. 40.

2. He that adapts the musick to words; he that forms a tune.

For compoſition I prefer next Ludovico, a moſt judicious and ſweet *compoſer*. *Peacham of Muſick.*

The *compoſer* has ſo expreſſed my ſenſe, where I intended to move the paſſions, that he ſeems to have been the poet as well as the *compoſer*. *Dryden's Albion and Albanius, Preface.*

COMPO'SITE. *adj.* [*compoſitus*, Latin.]

The *compoſite* order in architecture is the laſt of the five orders of columns; ſo named becauſe its capital is compoſed out of thoſe of the other orders; and it is alſo called the Roman and Italick order. *Harris.*

Some are of opinion, that the *compoſite* pillars of this arch were made in imitation of the pillars of Solomon's temple. *Addiſon's Remarks on Italy.*

COMPOSI'TION. *n. ſ.* [*compoſitio*, Latin.]

1. The act of forming an integral of various diſſimilar parts.

We have exact forms of *compoſition*, whereby they incorporate almoſt as they were natural ſimples. *Bacon's New Atlantis.*

In the time of the yncas reign in Peru, no *compoſition* was allowed by the laws to be uſed in point of medicine, but only ſimples proper to each diſeaſe. *Temple.*

2. The act of bringing ſimple ideas into complication, oppoſed to analyſis, or the ſeparation of complex notions.

The inveſtigation of difficult things, by the method of analyſis, ought ever to precede the method of *compoſition*. *Newt.*

3. A maſs formed by mingling different ingredients.

Heat and vivacity in age, is an excellent *compoſition* for buſineſs. *Bacon, Eſſay* 43.

Vaſt pillars of ſtone, caſed over with a *compoſition*, that looks the moſt like marble of any thing one can imagine. *Addiſon.*

Jove mix'd up all, and his beſt clay employ'd,
Then call'd the happy *compoſition* Floyd. *Swift.*

4. The ſtate of being compounded; union; conjunction; combination.

Contemplate things firſt in their own ſimple natures, and afterwards view them in *compoſition* with other things. *Watts.*

5. The arrangement of various figures in a picture.

The diſpoſition in a picture is an aſſembling of many parts: this is alſo called the *compoſition*, by which is meant the diſtribution and orderly placing of things, both in general and in particular. *Dryden's Dufreſnoy.*

6. Written work.

Writers are divided concerning the authority of the greater part of thoſe *compoſitions* that paſs in his name. *L'Eſtrange.*

That divine prayer has always been looked upon as a *compoſition* fit to have proceeded from the wiſeſt of men. *Addiſon.*

When I read rules of criticiſm, I enquire after the works of the author, and by that means diſcover what he likes in a *compoſition*. *Addiſon's Guardian*, N°. 115.

7. Adjuſtment; regulation.

A preacher in the invention of matter, election of words, *compoſition* of geſture, look, pronunciation, motion, uſeth all theſe faculties at once. *Benj. Johnſon's Diſcov.*

8. Compact; agreement; terms on which differences are ſettled.

To take away all ſuch mutual grievance, injuries and wrongs, there was no way but only by going upon *compoſition* and agreement amongſt themſelves. And again, all publick regiment, of what kind ſoever, ſeemeth evidently to have ariſen from deliberate advice, conſultation, and *compoſition* between men, judging it convenient and behoveful. *Hooker.*

Thus we are agreed;
I crave our *compoſition* may be written,
And ſeal'd between us. *Shakeſpeare's Anthony and Cleopatra.*

Their courage droops, and, hopeleſs now, they wiſh
For *compoſition* with th' unconquer'd fiſh. *Waller.*

9. The act of diſcharging a debt by paying part; the ſum paid.

10. Conſiſtency; congruity.

There is no *compoſition* in theſe news,
That gives them credit.———
—Indeed they are diſproportion'd. *Shakeſpeare's Othello.*

11. [In grammar.] The joining of two words together, or the prefixing a particle to another word, to augment, diminiſh, or change its ſignification.

12. A certain method of demonſtration in mathematicks, which is the reverſe of the analytical method, or of reſolution. It proceeds upon principles in themſelves ſelf-evident, on definitions, poſtulates and axioms, and a previouſly demonſtrated ſeries of propoſitions, ſtep by ſtep, 'till it gives a clear knowledge of the thing to be demonſtrated. This is called the ſynthetical method, and is uſed by Euclid in his Elements. *Harris.*

COMPO'SITIVE. *adj.* [from *compoſe*.] Compounded; or having the power of compounding. *Dict.*

COMPO'SITOR. *n. ſ.* [from *compoſe*.] He that ranges and adjuſts the types in printing; diſtinguiſhed from the preſſman, who makes the impreſſion upon paper.

CO'MPOST. *n. ſ.* [Fr. *compoſitum*, Lat.] A mixture of various ſubſtances for enriching the ground; manure.

We alſo have great variety of *compoſts* and ſoils, for the making of the earth fruitful. *Bacon's Atlantis.*

Avoid what is to come,
And do not ſpread the *compoſt* on the weeds,
To make them ranker. *Shakeſpeare's Hamlet.*

Water young planted ſhrubs, amomum eſpecially, which you can hardly refreſh too often, and it requires abundant *compoſt*. *Evelyn's Kalendar.*

There, as his dream foretold, a cart he found,
That carry'd *compoſt* forth to dung the ground. *Dryden.*

In vain the nurſling grove
Seems fair a while, cheriſh'd with foſter earth;
But when the alien *compoſt* is exhauſt,
Its native poverty again prevails. *Philips.*

To COMPO'ST. *v. a.* [from the noun.] To manure; to enrich with ſoil.

By removing into worſe earth, or forbearing to *compoſt* the earth, water-mint turneth into field-mint, and the colewort into rape. *Bacon's Natural Hiſtory*, N°. 518.

As for earth, it *compoſteth* itſelf; for I knew a garden that had a field poured upon it, and it did bear fruit excellently. *Bacon's Natural Hiſtory*, N°. 596.

COMPO'STURE. *n. ſ.* [from *compoſt*.] Soil; manure.

The earth's a thief,
That feeds and breeds by a *compoſture* ſtol'n
From gen'ral excrements. *Shakeſpeare's Timon.*

COMPO'SURE. *n. ſ.* [from *compoſe*.]

1. The act of compoſing or inditing.

Their own forms are not like to be ſo found, or comprehenſive of the nature of the duty, as forms of publick *compoſure*. *King Charles.*

2. Arrangement; combination; mixture; order.

Hence languages ariſe, when, by inſtitution and agreement, ſuch a *compoſure* of letters, *i. e.* ſuch a word, is intended to ſignify ſuch a certain thing. *Holder on Elements of Speech.*

From the various *compoſures* and combinations of theſe corpuſcles together, happen all the varieties of the bodies formed out of them. *Woodward's Natural Hiſtory.*

3. The form ariſing from the diſpoſition of the various parts.

In *compoſure* of his face,
Liv'd a fair, but manly grace. *Craſhaw.*

4. Frame; make; temperament.

To reel the ſtreets at noon, and ſtand the buffet
With ſlaves that ſmell of ſweat; ſay this becomes him:
As his *compoſure* muſt be rare indeed,
Whom theſe things cannot blemiſh. *Shakeſ. Ant. and Cleop.*

5. Diſpoſition; relative adjuſtment.

The duke of Buckingham ſprung, without any help, by a kind of congenial *compoſure*, to the likeneſs of our late ſovereign and maſter. *Wotton.*

6. Compoſition; framed diſcourſe.

Diſcourſes on ſuch occaſions are ſeldom the productions of leiſure, and ſhould be read with thoſe favourable allowances that are made to haſty *compoſures*. *Atterbury's Pref. to Sermons.*

In the *compoſures* of men, remember you are a man as well as they; and it is not their reaſon, but your own, that is given to guide you. *Watts's Improvement of the Mind.*

7. Sedateneſs; calmneſs; tranquillity.

To whom the virgin majeſty of Eve,
As one who loves, and ſome unkindneſs meets,
With ſweet auſtere *compoſure* thus reply'd. *Milt. Par. Loſt.*

The calmeſt and ſereneſt hours of life, when the paſſions of nature are all ſilent, and the mind enjoys its moſt perfect *compoſure*. *Watts's Logick.*

8. Agreement; compoſition; ſettlement of differences.

The treaty at Uxbridge gave the faireſt hopes of an happy *compoſure*. *King Charles.*

Van guard! to right and left the front unfold,
That all may ſee, who hate us, how we ſeek
Peace and *compoſure*. *Milton's Paradiſe Loſt, b.* vi. *l.* 560.

Things were not brought to an extremity where I left the ſtory: there ſeems yet to be room left for a *compoſure*; hereafter there may be only for pity. *Dryd. Pref. to Abſ. and Achit.*

COMPOTA'TION. *n. ſ.* [*compotatio*, Lat.] The act of drinking or tippling together.

Secrecy to words ſpoke under the roſe, only mean, in *compotation*, from the ancient cuſtom in ſympoſiack meetings, to wear chaplets of roſes. *Brown's Vulgar Errours.*

If thou wilt prolong
Dire *compotation*, forthwith reaſon quits
Her empire to confuſion and miſrule,
And vain debates; then twenty tongues at once
Conſpire in ſenſeleſs jargon; naught is heard
But din and various clamour, and mad rant. *Phillips.*

To COMPO'UND. *v. a.* [*compono*, Latin.]

1. To mingle many ingredients together in one maſs.

2. To form by uniting various parts.

Whoſoever *compoundeth* any like it, ſhall be cut off. *Ex.* xxx.

It will be difficult to evince, that nature does not make decompounded bodies; I mean, mingle together ſuch bodies as are already *compounded* of elementary, or rather of ſimple ones. *Boyle's Sceptical Chymiſt.*

The ideas, being each but one ſingle perception, are eaſier got than the more complex ones; and therefore are not liable to the uncertainty, which attends thoſe *compounded* ones. *Locke.*

3. To mingle in different poſitions; to combine.

We cannot have a ſingle image that did not enter through the

the sight; but we have the power of altering and *compounding* those images into all the varieties of picture. *Addis. Spectator.*

4. [In grammar.] To form one word from two or more words.

Where it and Tigris embrace each other under the city of Apamia, there do they agree of a joint and *compounded* name, and are called *Piso-Tigris.* *Raleigh's History of the World.*

5. To compose by being united.

Who'd be so mock'd with glory, as to live
But in a dream of friendship?
To have his pomp, and all what state *compounds*,
But only painted, like his varnish'd friends! *Shakes. Timon.*

6. To adjust a difference by some recession from the rigour of claims.

I would to God all strifes were well *compounded.* *Shakesp.*

If there be any discord or suits between any of the family, they are *compounded* and appeased. *Bacon's New Atlantis.*

7. To discharge a debt by paying only part.

Shall I, ye gods, he cries, my debts *compound?* *Gay.*

To COMPO'UND. *v. n.*

1. To come to terms of agreement by abating something of the first demand. It has *for* before the thing accepted or remitted.

They were, at last, glad to *compound for* his bare commitment to the Tower. *Clarendon.*

Pray but for half the virtues of this wife;
Compound for all the rest, with longer life. *Dryden.*

2. To bargain in the lump.

Here's a fellow will help you to-morrow: *compound* with him by the year. *Shakespeare's Measure for Measure.*

3. To come to terms.

Cornwal *compounded* to furnish ten oxen after Michaelmas for thirty pounds. *Carew's Survey of Cornwal.*

Once more I come to know of thee, king Harry,
If *for* thy ransom thou wilt now *compound*,
Before thy most assured overthrow? *Shakes. Henry V.*

Made all the royal stars recant,
Compound and take the covenant. *Hudibras, p.* ii. *cant.* 3.

But useless all, when he, despairing, found
Catullus then did with the winds *compound.* *Dryd. Juvenal.*

Paracelsus and his admirers have *compounded* with the Galenists, and brought a mixed use of chymical medicines into the present practice. *Temple.*

4. To determine. This is not in use.

We here deliver,
Subscribed by the consuls and patricians,
Together with the seal of the senate, what
We have *compounded* on. *Shakespeare's Coriolanus.*

CO'MPOUND. *adj.* [from the verb.]

1. Formed out of many ingredients; not single.

The ancient electrum had in it a fifth of silver to the gold, and made a *compound* metal, as fit for most uses as gold. *Bacon.*

Compound substances are made up of two or more simple substances. *Watts's Logick.*

2. [In grammar.] Composed of two or more words; not simple.

Those who are his greatest admirers, seem pleased with them as beauties; I speak of his *compound* epithets. *Pope.*

3. COMPOUND *or aggregated Flower*, in botany, is such as consists of many little flowers, concurring together to make up one whole one; each of which has its style and stamina, and adhering seed, and are all contained within one and the same calyx: such are the sunflower and dandelion. *Harris.*

CO'MPOUND. *n. s.* [from the verb.] The mass formed by the union of many ingredients.

For present use or profit, this is the rule: consider the price of the two simple bodies; consider again the dignity of the one above the other in use; then see if you can make a *compound*, that will save more in price than it will lose in dignity of the use. *Bacon's Physical Rem.*

As man is a *compound* and mixture of flesh, as well as spirit. *South's Sermons.*

Love, why do we one passion call?
When 'tis a *compound* of them all;
Where hot and cold, where sharp and sweet,
In all their equipages meet. *Swift.*

COMPO'UNDABLE. *adj.* [from *compound.*] Capable of being compounded.

COMPO'UNDER. *n. s.* [from *To compound.*]

1. One who endeavours to bring parties to terms of agreement.

Those softners, sweetners, *compounders*, and expedient-mongers, who shake their heads so strongly. *Swift.*

2. A mingler; one who mixes bodies.

To COMPREHE'ND. *v. a.* [*comprehendo*, Latin.]

1. To comprise; to include; to contain; to imply.

If there be any other commandment, it is briefly *comprehended* in this saying, namely, Thou shalt love thy neighbour as thyself. *Rom.* xiii. 9.

It would be ridiculous to grow old in the study of every necessary thing, in an art which *comprehends* so many several parts. *Dryden's Dufresnoy.*

2. To contain in the mind; to understand; to conceive.

Rome was not better by her Horace taught,
Than we are here to *comprehend* his thought. *Waller.*

'Tis unjust, that they who have not the least notion of heroic writing, should therefore condemn the pleasure which others receive from it, because they cannot *comprehend* it. *Dryd.*

COMPREHE'NSIBLE. *adj.* [*comprehensible*, Fren. *comprehensibilis*, Lat.] Intelligible; attainable by the mind; conceiveable by the understanding.

The horizon sets the bounds between the enlightened and dark parts of things, between what is and what is not *comprehensible* by us. *Locke.*

COMPREHE'NSIBLY. *adv.* [from *comprehensible.*] With great power of signification or understanding; significantly; with great extent of sense.

The words wisdom and righteousness are commonly used very *comprehensibly*, so as to signify all religion and virtue. *Tillot.*

COMPREHE'NSION. *n. s.* [*comprehensio*, Latin.]

1. The act or quality of comprising or containing; inclusion.

In the Old Testament there is a close *comprehension* of the New, in the New an open discovery of the Old. *Hooker, b.* v.

The *comprehension* of an idea regards all essential modes and properties of it; so body, in its *comprehension*, takes in solidity, figure, quantity, mobility. *Watts's Logick.*

2. Summary; epitome; compendium; abstract; abridgment in which much is comprised.

If we would draw a short abstract of human happiness, bring together all the various ingredients of it, and digest them into one prescription, we must at last fix on this wise and religious aphorism in my text, as the sum and *comprehension* of all. *Rogers, Sermon* 19.

3. Knowledge; capacity; power of the mind to admit and contain many ideas at once.

You give no proof of decay of your judgment, and *comprehension* of all things, within the compass of an human understanding. *Dryden.*

4. [In rhetorick.] A trope or figure, by which the name of a whole is put for a part, or that of a part for the whole, or a definite number for an indefinite. *Harris.*

COMPREHE'NSIVE. *adj.* [from *comprehend.*]

1. Having the power to comprehend or understand many things at once.

He must have been a man of a most wonderful *comprehensive* nature, because he has taken into the compass of his Canterbury tales the various manners and humours of the whole English nation in his age; not a single character has escaped him. *Dryden's Fables, Preface.*

His hand unstain'd, his uncorrupted heart,
His *comprehensive* head; all int'rests weigh'd,
All Europe sav'd, yet Britain not betray'd. *Pope's Epistles.*

2. Having the quality of comprising much; compendious; extensive.

So diffusive, so *comprehensive*, so catholick a grace is charity, that whatever time is the opportunity of any other virtue, that time is the opportunity of charity. *Sprat's Sermons.*

COMPREHE'NSIVELY. *adv.* [from *comprehensive.*] In a comprehensive manner.

COMPREHE'NSIVENESS. *n. s.* [from *comprehensive.*] The quality of including much in a few words or narrow compass.

Compare the beauty and *comprehensiveness* of legends on ancient coins. *Addison on Ancient Medals.*

To COMPRE'SS. *v. a.* [*compressus*, Latin.]

1. To force into a narrower compass; to squeeze together.

2. To embrace.

Her Neptune ey'd, with bloom of beauty blest,
And in his cave the yielding nymph *comprest.* *Pope's Odyss.*

There was in the island of Io a young girl *compressed* by a genius, who delighted to associate with the muses. *Pope.*

COMPR'ESS. *n. s.* [from the verb.] Bolsters of linen rags, by which surgeons suit their bandages for any particular part or purpose. *Quincy.*

I applied an intercipient about the ankle and upper part of the foot, and by *compress* and bandage dressed it up. *Wiseman.*

COMPRESSIBI'LITY. *n. s.* [from *compressible.*] The quality of being compressible; the quality of admitting to be brought by force into a narrower compass; as air may be compressed, but water can by no violence be reduced to less space than it naturally occupies.

COMPRE'SSIBLE. *adj.* [from *compress.*] Capable of being forced into a narrower compass; yielding to pressure, so as that one part is brought nearer to another.

Their being spiral particles, accounts for the elasticity of air; their being spherical particles, which gives free passage to any heterogeneous matter, accounts for air's being *compressible.* *Cheyne's Phil. Prin.*

COMPRE'SSIBLENESS. *n. s.* [from *compressible.*] Capability of being pressed close. *Dict.*

COMPRE'SSION. *n. s.* [*compressio*, Latin.] The act of bringing the parts of any body more near to each other by violence; the quality of admitting such an effort of force as may compel the body compressed into a narrower space.

Whensoever a solid body is pressed, there is an inward tumult in the parts thereof, seeking to deliver themselves from the *compression*; and this is the cause of all violent motion. *Bacon's Natural History*, N°. 9.

The

The powder in ſhot, being dilated into ſuch a flame as endureth not *compreſſion*, moveth likewiſe in round, the flame being in the nature of a liquid body, ſometimes recoiling. *Bacon's Natural Hiſtory.*

Tears are the effects of the *compreſſion* of the moiſture of the brain, upon dilatation of the ſpirits. *Bacon's Nat. Hiſt.*

He that ſhall find out an hypotheſis, by which water may be ſo rare, and yet not be capable of *compreſſion* by force, may doubtleſs, by the ſame hypotheſis, make gold and water, and all other bodies, as much rarer as he pleaſes; ſo that light may find a ready paſſage through tranſparent ſubſtances. *Newt.*

COMPRE'SSURE. *n. ſ.* [from *compreſs.*] The act or force of the body preſſing againſt another.

We tried whether heat would, notwithſtanding ſo forcible a *compreſſure*, dilate it. *Boyle's Spring of the Air.*

To COMPRI'NT. *v. n.* [*comprimere*, Latin.]

The word properly ſignifies to print together; but it is commonly taken, in law, for the deceitful printing of another's copy or book, to the prejudice of the rightful proprietor. *Philips's World of Words.*

To COMPRI'SE. *v. a.* [*comprendre compris*, French] To contain; to comprehend; to include.

The neceſſity of ſhortneſs cauſeth men to cut off impertinent diſcourſes, and to *compriſe* much matter in few words. *Hooker, b.* v. *ſect.* 32.

Do they not, under doctrine, comprehend the ſame that we intend by matters of faith? Do not they, under diſcipline, *compriſe* the regimen of the church? *Hooker, b.* iii. *ſ.* 3.

'Tis the polluted love that multiplies;
But friendſhip does two ſouls in one *compriſe*. *Roſcommon.*

COMPROBA'TION. *n. ſ.* [*comprobo*, Latin.] Proof; atteſtation.

That is only eſteemed a legal teſtimony which receives *comprobation* from the mouths of at leaſt two witneſſes. *Brown.*

CO'MPROMISE. *n. ſ.* [*compromiſſum*, Latin.]

1. *Compromiſe* is a mutual promiſe of two or more parties at difference, to refer the ending of their controverſies to the arbitrement or equity of one or more arbitrators. *Cowel.*

2. A compact or bargain, in which ſome conceſſions are made on each ſide.

Wars have not waſted it; for warr'd he hath not;
But baſely yielded, upon *compromiſe*,
That which his anceſtors atchiev'd with blows. *Sh. Rich.* II.

To CO'MPROMISE. *v. a.* [from the noun.]

1. To compound; to adjuſt a compact by mutual conceſſions; as, *they* compromiſed *the affair at a middle rate.*

2. In *Shakeſpeare* it means, unuſually, to accord; to agree.

Laban and himſelf were *compromis'd*,
That all the yearlings, which were ſtreak'd and pied,
Should fall as Jacob's hire. *Shakeſp. Merchant of Venice.*

COMPROMISSO'RIAL. *adj.* [from *compromiſe.*] Relating to a compromiſe.

COMPROVI'NCIAL. *n. ſ.* [from *con* and *provincial.*] Belonging to the ſame province.

At the conſecration of an archbiſhop, all his *comprovincials* ought to give their attendance. *Ayliffe's Parergon.*

COMPT. *n. ſ.* [*compte*, Fr. *computus*, Lat.] Account; computation; reckoning.

Your ſervants ever
Have theirs, themſelves, and what is theirs, in *compt*,
To make their audit at your highneſs' pleaſure,
Still to return your own. *Shakeſp. King John.*

To COMPT. *v. a.* [*compter*, French.] To compute; to number. We now uſe *To* COUNT, which ſee.

CO'MPTIBLE. *adj.* [from *compt.*] Accountable; reſponſible; ready to give account; ſubject; ſubmiſſive.

Good beauties, let me ſuſtain my ſcorn; I am very *comptible* even to the leaſt ſiniſter uſage. *Shakeſp.*

To COMPTRO'LL. *v. a.* [This word is written by ſome authors, who did not attend to the etymology, for *controll*; and ſome of its derivatives are written in the ſame manner.] To controll; to over-rule; to oppoſe.

COMPTRO'LLER. *n. ſ.* [from *comptroll.*] Director; ſupervíſor; ſuperior intendent; governour.

This night he makes a ſupper, and a great one,
To many lords and ladies:
I was ſpoke too, with Sir Henry Guilford,
This night to be *comptrollers*. *Shakeſ. Henry* VIII.

The *comptrollers* of vulgar opinions pretend to find out ſuch a ſimilitude in ſome kind of baboons. *Temple.*

My fates permit me not from hence to fly;
Nor he, the great *comptroller* of the ſky. *Dryden's Æneis.*

COMPTRO'LLERSHIP. *n. ſ.* [from *comptroller.*] Superintendence.

The gayle for ſtannery-cauſes is annexed to the *comptrollerſhip.* *Carew's Survey of Cornwal.*

COMPU'LSATIVELY. *adv.* [from *compulſatory.*] With force; by conſtraint. *Clariſſa.*

COMPU'LSATORY. *n. ſ.* [from *compulſor*, Latin.] Having the force of compelling; coactive.

Which is no other
But to recover from us by ſtrong hand,
And terms *compulſatory*, thoſe 'foreſaid lands
So by his father loſt. *Shakeſpeare's Hamlet.*

COMPU'LSION. *n. ſ.* [*compulſio*, Latin.]

1. The act of compelling to ſomething; force; violence of the agents.

If reaſons were as plenty as blackberries, I would give no man a reaſon on *compulſion.* *Shakeſpeare's Henry* IV. *p.* i.

Thoughts, whither have ye led me! with that ſweet
Compulſion thus tranſported. *Milton's Paradiſe Loſt, b.* ix.

Such ſweet *compulſion* doth in muſick lye,
To lull the daughters of neceſſity. *Milton.*

2. The ſtate of being compelled; violence ſuffered.

Compulſion is in an agent capable of volition, when the beginning or continuation of any action is contrary to the preference of his mind. *Locke.*

When the fierce foe hung on our broken rear,
With what *compulſion* and laborious flight
We ſunk thus low? *Milton's Paradiſe Loſt, b.* ii. *l.* 80.

This faculty is free from *compulſion*, and ſo ſpontaneous, and free from determination by the particular object. *Hale.*

Poſſibly there were others who aſſiſted Harold, partly out of fear and *compulſion.* *Hale on Common Law.*

COMPU'LSIVE. *adj.* [from *compulſer*, Fr. *compulſus*, Latin.] Having the power to compel; forcible.

The Danube, vaſt and deep,
Supreme of rivers, to the frightful brink,
Urg'd by *compulſive* arms, ſoon as they reach'd,
New terror chill'd their veins. *Philips.*

The clergy would be glad to recover their dues by a more ſhort and *compulſive* method. *Swift.*

COMPU'LSIVELY. *adv.* [from *compulſive.*] By force; by violence.

COMPU'LSIVENESS. *n. ſ.* [from *compulſive.*] Force; compulſion.

COMPU'LSORILY. *adv.* [from *compulſory.*] In a compulſory or forcible manner; by force; by violence.

To ſay that the better deſerver hath ſuch right to govern, as he may *compulſorily* bring under the leſs worthy, is idle. *Bac.*

COMPU'LSORY. *adj.* [*compulſoire*, French.] Having the power of neceſſitating or compelling.

He erreth in this, to think that actions, proceeding from fear, are properly *compulſory* actions; which, in truth, are not only voluntary, but free actions; neither compelled, nor ſo much as phyſically neceſſitated. *Bramh. againſt Hobbs.*

Kindly it would be taken to comply with a patent, although not *compulſory.* *Swift.*

COMPU'NCTION. *n. ſ.* [*componction*, Fr. from *pungo punctum*, to prick, Latin.]

1. The power of pricking; ſtimulation; irritation.

This is that acid and piercing ſpirit, which, with ſuch activity and *compunction*, invadeth the brains and noſtrils of thoſe that receive it. *Brown's Vulgar Errours, b.* vi. *c.* 12.

2. The ſtate of being pricked by the conſcience; repentance; contrition.

He acknowledged his diſloyalty to the king, with expreſſions of great *compunction.* *Clarendon.*

COMPU'NCTIOUS. *adj.* [from *compunction.*] Repentant; ſorrowful; tender.

Stop up th' acceſs and paſſage to remorſe,
That no *compunctious* viſitings of nature
Shake my fell purpoſe. *Shakeſpeare's Macbeth.*

COMPU'NCTIVE. *adj.* [from *compunction.*] Cauſing remorſe.

COMPURGA'TION. *n. ſ.* [*compurgatio*, Latin.] The practice of juſtifying any man's veracity by the teſtimony of another.

COMPURGA'TOR. *n. ſ.* [Latin.] One who bears his teſtimony to the credibility of another.

The next quarry, or chalk-pit, will give abundant atteſtation: theſe are ſo obvious, that I need not be far to ſeek for a *compurgator.* *Woodward's Natural Hiſtory.*

COMPU'TABLE. *adj.* [from *compute.*] Capable of being numbered or computed.

If, inſtead of twenty-four letters, there were twenty-four millions, as thoſe twenty-four millions are a finite number; ſo would all combinations thereof be finite, though not eaſily *computable* by arithmetick. *Hale's Origin of Mankind.*

COMPUTA'TION. *n. ſ.* [from *compute.*]

1. The act of reckoning; calculation.

My princely father
Then, by juſt *computation* of the time,
Found that the iſſue was not his. *Shakeſ. Richard* III.

2. The ſum collected or ſettled by calculation.

We paſs for women of fifty: many additional years are thrown into female *computations* of this nature. *Addiſ. Guardian.*

To COMPU'TE. *v. a.* [*computo*, Latin.] To reckon; to calculate; to number; to count.

Compute how much water would be requiſite to lay the earth under water. *Burnet's Theory of the Earth.*

Where they did *compute* by weeks, yet ſtill the year was meaſured by months. *Holder on Time.*

Alas! not dazzled with their noon-tide ray,
Compute the morn and ev'ning to the day;
The whole amount of that enormous fame,
A tale that blends their glory with their ſhame. *Pope.*

Compu'te. *n. s.* [*computus*, Lat.] Computation; calculation.

Compu'ter. *n. s.* [from *compute.*] Reckoner; accountant; calculator.

The kalendars of these *computers*, and the accounts of these days, are different. *Brown's Vulgar Errours, b.* vi. *c.* 4.

I have known some such ill *computers*, as to imagine the many millions in stocks so much real wealth. *Swift.*

Co'mputist. *n. s.* [*computiste*, Fr.] Calculator; one skilled in the art of numbers or computation.

The treasurer was a wise man, and a strict *computist*. *Wotton.*

We conceive we have a year in three hundred and sixty-five days exact: *computists* tell us, that we escape six hours. *Brown.*

Co'mrade. *n. s.* [*camerade*, Fr. from *camera*, a chamber, one that lodges in the same chamber, *contubernio fruitur.*]

1. One who dwells in the same house or chamber.

Rather I abjure all roofs, and chuse
To be a *comrade* with the wolf and owl. *Shakesp. K. Lear.*

2. A companion; a partner in any labour or danger.

He permitted them
To put out both thine eyes, and fetter'd send thee
Into the common prison, there to grind
Among the slaves and asses, thy *comrades*,
As good for nothing else. *Milton's Agonistes, l.* 1159.

A footman, being newly married, desired his *comrade* to tell him freely what the town said of it. *Swift.*

Con. A Latin inseparable preposition, which, at the beginning of words, signifies union or association; as *concourse*, a running together; to *convene*, to come together.

Con. [abbreviated from *contra*, against, Lat.] A cant word for one who is on the negative side of a question; as the *pros* and *cons*.

To CON. *v. a.* [connan, Sax. to know; as in *Chaucer*, *Old wymen connen mochil thinge*; that is, Old women have much knowledge.]

1. To know.

Of muses, Hobbinol, I *conne* no skill
Enough to me to paint out my unrest. *Spenser's Pastorals.*

2. To study; to commit to memory; to fix in the mind. It is a word now little in use, except in ludicrous language.

You are full of pretty answers: have you not been acquainted with goldsmiths wives, and *conn'd* them out of rings. *Shakespeare's As you like it.*

Here are your parts; and I am to intreat you to *con* them by to-morrow night. *Shakes. Midsummer Night's Dream.*

Our understanding cannot in this body arrive so clearly to the knowledge of God, and things invisible, as by orderly *conning* over the visible and inferior creatures. *Milton.*

Shew it him written; and, having the other also written in the paper, shew him that, after he has *conn'd* the first, and require it of him. *Holder's Elements of Speech.*

The books of which I'm chiefly fond,
Are such as you have whilom *conn'd*. *Prior.*

All this while John had *conn'd* over such a catalogue of hard words, as were enough to conjure up the devil. *Arbuthnot.*

3. *To* Con *thanks*; an old expression for *to thank*. It is the same with *sçavoir grè*.

I *con* him no thanks for't, in the nature he delivers it. *Shak.*

To CONCA'MERATE *v. a.* [*concamero*, Lat.] To arch over; to vault; to lay concave over.

Of the upper beak, an inch and a half consisteth of one *concamerated* bone, bended downwards, and toothed as the other. *Grew's Museum.*

Concamera'tion. *n. s.* [from *concamerate.*] Arch; vault.

What a romance is the story of those impossible *concamerations*, and feigned rotations of solid orbs? *Glanville's Sceps.*

To CONCA'TENATE. *v. a.* [from *catena*, Lat. a chain.] To link together; to unite in a successive order.

Concatena'tion *n. s.* [from *concatenate.*] A series of links; an uninterrupted unvariable succession.

The stoicks affirmed a fatal, unchangeable *concatenation* of causes, reaching even to the elicit acts of man's will. *South's Sermons.*

Concava'tion. *n. s.* [from *concave.*] The act of making concave.

CONCA'VE *adj.* [*concavus*, Latin.]

1. Hollow without angles; as, the inner surface of an eggshell, the inner curve of an arch: opposed to convex.

These great fragments falling hollow, inclosed under their *concave* surface a great deal of air. *Burnet's Theory of the Earth.*

2. Hollow.

Have you not made an universal shout,
That Tyber trembled underneath his banks,
To hear the replication of your sounds
Made in his *concave* shores? *Shakespeare's Julius Cæsar.*

For his verity in love, I do think him as *concave* as a covered goblet, or a worm-eaten nut. *Shakesp. As you like it.*

Conca'veness. *n. s.* [from *concave.*] Hollowness. *Dict.*

Conca'vity. *n. s.* [from *concave.*] Internal surface of a hollow spherical or spheroidical body.

They have taken the impresses of these shells with that exquisite niceness, that no metal, when melted and cast in a mould, can ever possibly represent the *concavity* of that mould with greater exactness than these flints do the *concavities* of the shells, wherein they were moulded. *Woodw. Natural History.*

Concavo-concave. *adj.* Concave or hollow on both sides.

Concavo-convex. *adj.* [from *concave* and *convex.*] Concave one way, and convex the other.

I procured therefore another *concavo-convex* plate of glass, ground on both sides to the same sphere with the former plate. *Newton's Opticks.*

A *concavo-convex* pentangular plate, part of a shell that belongs to the entrochus. *Woodward on Fossils.*

Co'ncavous. *adj.* [*concavus*, Latin.] Concave; hollow without angles.

Co'ncavously. *adv.* [from *concavous.*] With hollowness; in such a manner as discovers the internal surface of a hollow sphere.

The dolphin that carrieth Arion is *concavously* inverted, and hath its spine depressed. *Brown's Vulgar Errours, b* v.

To CONCE'AL. *v. a.* [*concelo*, Latin.] To hide; to keep secret; not to divulge; to cover; not to detect.

He oft' finds med'cine, who his grief imparts;
But double griefs afflict *concealing* hearts. *Fairy Queen, b.* i.

Come, Catesby, thou art sworn
As deeply to effect what we intend,
As closely to *conceal* what we impart. *Shakesp. Richard* III.

Ulysses himself adds, he was the most eloquent and the most silent of men: he knew that a word spoke never wrought so much good as a word *concealed*. *Broome's Notes on the Odyssey.*

There is but one way I know of conversing safely with all men, that is, not by *concealing* what we say or do, but by saying or doing nothing that deserves to be *concealed*. *Pope.*

Conce'alable. *adj.* [from *conceal*] Capable of being concealed; possible to be kept secret, or hid.

Returning a lye unto his Maker, and presuming to put off the searcher of hearts, he denied the omnisciency of God, whereunto there is nothing *concealable*. *Brown's Vulg. Errours.*

Conce'aledness. *n. s.* [from *conceal.*] The state of being concealed; privacy; obscurity. *Dict.*

Conce'aler. *n. s.* [from *conceal.*] He that conceals any thing.

They were to undergo the penalty of forgery, and the *concealer* of the crime was equally guilty.

Conce'alment. *n. s.* [from *conceal.*]

1. The act of hiding; secresy.

She never told her love;
But let *concealment*, like a worm in the bud,
Feed on her damask cheek. *Shakespeare's Twelfth Night.*

He is a worthy gentleman,
Exceedingly well read, and profited
In strange *concealments*. *Shakespeare's Henry* IV. *p.* i.

Though few own such sentiments, yet this *concealment* derives rather from the fear of man than of any Being above. *Glanville's Sceps. Preface.*

2. The state of being hid; privacy; delitescence.

A person of great abilities is zealous for the good of mankind, and as solicitous for the *concealment* as the performance of illustrious actions. *Addison's Freeholder*, N°. 33.

3. Hiding place; retreat; cover; shelter.

The choice of this holy name, as the most effectual *concealment* of a wicked design, supposes mankind satisfied that nothing but what is just is directed by the principles of it. *Rogers.*

The cleft tree
Offers its kind *concealment* to a few;
Their food its insects, and its moss their nests. *Thomson.*

To CONCE'DE. *v. a.* [*concedo*, Latin.] To yield; to admit; to grant; to let pass undisputed.

This must not be *conceded* without limitation. *Boyle.*

The atheist, if you do but *concede* to him that fortune may be an agent, doth presume himself safe and invulnerable. *Bentley's Sermons.*

CONCE'IT. *n. s.* [*concept*, French; *conceptus*, Latin.]

1. Conception; thought; idea; image in the mind.

Here the very shepherds have their fancies lifted to so high *conceits*, as the learned of other nations are content both to borrow their names and imitate their cunning. *Sidney.*

Impossible it was, that ever their will should change or incline to remit any part of their duty, without some object having force to avert their *conceit* from God. *Hooker, b.* i.

His grace looks chearfully and smooth this morning:
There's some *conceit*, or other, likes him well,
When that he bids good-morrow with such spirit. *Shakesp.*

In laughing there ever precedeth a *conceit* of somewhat ridiculous, and therefore it is proper to man. *Bacon's Nat. Hist.*

2. Understanding; readiness of apprehension.

How often, alas! did her eyes say unto me, that they loved? and yet, I not looking for such a matter, had not my *conceit* open to understand them. *Sidney, b.* ii.

The first kind of things appointed by laws humane, containeth whatsoever is good or evil, is notwithstanding more secret than that it can be discerned by every man's present *conceit*, without some deeper discourse and judgment. *Hooker, b.* i.

I shall be found of a quick *conceit* in judgment, and shall be admired. *Wisd.* viii. 11.

3. Opinion, generally in a ſenſe of contempt; fancy; imagination; fantaſtical notion.

I know not how *conceit* may rob
The treaſury of life, when life itſelf
Yields to the theft. *Shakeſpeare's King Lear.*

Strong *conceit*, like a new principle, carries all eaſily with it, when yet above common ſenſe. *Locke.*

Malbranche has an odd *conceit*,
As ever enter'd Frenchman's pate. *Prior.*

4. Opinion in a neutral ſenſe.

Seeſt thou a man wiſe in his own *conceit?* There is more hope of a fool than of him. *Prov.* xxvi. 12.

I ſhall not fail t' approve the fair *conceit*
The king hath of you. *Shakeſpeare's Henry* VIII.

5. A pleaſant fancy.

His wit is as thick as Tewkſbury muſtard: there is no more *conceit* in him than is in a mallet. *Shakeſp. Henry* IV. *p.* ii.

While he was on his way to the gibbet, a freak took him in the head to go off with a *conceit*. *L'Eſtrange.*

6. Sentiment, as diſtinguiſhed from imagery.

Some to *conceit* alone their works confine,
And glitt'ring thoughts ſtruck out at ev'ry line. *Pope.*

7. Fondneſs; favourable opinion; opinionative pride.

Since by a little ſtudying in learning, and great *conceit* of himſelf, he has loſt his religion; may he find it again by harder ſtudy under humbler truth. *Bentley.*

8. *Out of* Conceit *with.* No longer fond of.

Not that I dare aſſume to myſelf to have put him *out of conceit with* it, by having convinced him of the fantaſticalneſs of it. *Tillotſon, Preface.*

What hath chiefly put me *out of conceit with* this moving manner, is the frequent diſappointment. *Swift.*

To Conce'it. *v. a.* [from the noun.] To conceive; to imagine; to think; to believe.

One of two bad ways you muſt *conceit* me,
Either a coward, or a flatterer. *Shakeſ. Julius Cæſar.*

They looked for great matters at their hands, in a cauſe which they *conceited* to be for the liberty of the ſubject. *Bacon.*

He *conceits* himſelf to be ſtruck at, when he is not ſo much as thought of. *L'Eſtrange.*

The ſtrong, by *conceiting* themſelves weak, are thereby rendered as unactive, and conſequently as uſeleſs, as if they really were ſo. *South's Sermons.*

Conce'ited. *particip. adj.* [from *conceit.*]

1. Endowed with fancy.

He was of countenance amiable, of feature comely, active of body, well ſpoken, pleaſantly *conceited*, and ſharp of wit. *Knolles's Hiſtory of the Turks.*

2. Proud; fond of himſelf; opinionative; affected; fantaſtical.

There is another extreme in obſcure writers, which ſome empty *conceited* heads are apt to run into, out of a prodigality of words, and a want of ſenſe. *Felton on the Claſſicks.*

If you think me too *conceited*,
Or to paſſion quickly heated. *Swift.*

What you write of me, would make me more *conceited* than what I ſcribble myſelf. *Pope.*

3. With *of* before the object of conceit.

Every man is building a ſeveral way, impotently *conceited of* his own model and his own materials. *Dryden.*

If we conſider how vicious and corrupt the Athenians were, how *conceited of* their own wit, ſcience, and politeneſs. *Bentley.*

Conce'itedly. *adv.* [from *conceited*] Fancifully; whimſically.

Conceitedly dreſs her, and be aſſign'd
By you fit place for every flower and jewel;
Make her for love fit fuel. *Donne.*

Conce'itedness. *n. ſ.* [from *conceited.*] Pride; opinionativeneſs; fondneſs of himſelf.

When men think none worthy eſteem but ſuch as claim under their own pretences, partiality and *conceitedneſs* makes them give the pre-eminence. *Collier on Pride.*

Conce'itless. *adj.* [from *conceit.*] Stupid; without thought; dull of apprehenſion.

Think'ſt thou, I am ſo ſhallow, ſo *conceitleſs*,
To be ſeduced by thy flattery. *Shak. Two Gent. of Verona.*

Conce'ivable. *adj.* [from *conceive.*]

1. That may be imagined or thought.

If it were poſſible to contrive an invention, whereby any *conceivable* weight may be moved by any *conceivable* power with the ſame quickneſs by the hand, without other inſtrument, the works of nature would be too much ſubjected to art. *Wilkins's Math. Magick.*

2. That may be underſtood or believed.

The freezing of the words in the air in the Northern climes, is as *conceivable* as this ſtrange union. *Glanv. Scepſ. c.* 4.

It is not *conceivable* that it ſhould be indeed that very perſon, whoſe ſhape and voice it aſſumed. *Atterbury's Sermons.*

Conce'ivableness. *n. ſ.* [from *conceivable.*] The quality of being conceivable. *Dict.*

Conce'ivably. *adv.* [from *conceivable.*] In a conceivable or intelligible manner.

To CONCEIVE. *v. a.* [*concevoir*, Fr. *concipere*, Latin.]

1. To admit into the womb.

I was ſhapen in iniquity, and in ſin did my mother *conceive* me. *Pſalm* li. 5.

2. To form in the mind; to imagine.

Nebuchadnezzar hath *conceived* a purpoſe againſt you. *Jer.*

3. To comprehend; to underſtand. *He conceives the whole ſyſtem.*

This kiſs, if it durſt ſpeak,
Would ſtretch thy ſpirits up into the air:
Conceive, and fare thee well. *Shakeſpeare's King Lear.*

4. To think; to be of opinion.

If you compare my gentlemen with Sir John, you will hardly *conceive* him to have been bred in the ſame climate. *Sw.*

To Conce'ive. *v. n.*

1. To think; to have an idea of.

The griev'd commons
Hardly *conceive* of me: let it be nois'd,
That, through our interceſſion, this revokement
And pardon comes. *Shakeſpeare's Henry* VIII.

Conceive of things clearly and diſtinctly in their own natures; *conceive* of things completely in all their parts; *conceive* of things comprehenſively in all their properties and relations; *conceive* of things extenſively in all their kinds; *conceive* of things orderly, or in a proper method. *Watts's Logick.*

2. To become pregnant.

The flocks ſhould *conceive* when they came to drink. *Gen.*

The beauteous maid, whom he beheld, poſſeſs'd:
Conceiving as ſhe ſlept, her fruitful womb
Swell'd with the founder of immortal Rome. *Addiſon.*

Conce'iver. *n. ſ.* [from *conceive.*] One that underſtands or apprehends.

Though hereof prudent ſymbols and pious allegories be made by wiſer *conceivers*, yet common heads will fly unto ſuperſtitious applications. *Brown's Vulgar Errours, b.* 7. *c.* 1.

Conce'nt. *n. ſ.* [*concentus*, Latin.]

1. Concert of voices; harmony; concord of ſound.

It is to be conſidered, that whatſoever virtue is in numbers, for conducing to *concent* of notes, is rather to be aſcribed to the ante-number than to the entire number. *Bacon.*

2. Conſiſtency.

'Tis in *concent* to his own principles, which allow no merit, no intrinſick worth to accompany one ſtate more than another. *Atterbury.*

To CONCE'NTRATE. *v. a.* [*concentrer*, Fr. from *con* and *centrum*, Lat.] To drive into a narrow compaſs; to drive towards the center.

Spirit of vinegar, *concentrated* and reduced to its greateſt ſtrength, will coagulate the ſerum. *Arbuthnot on Aliments.*

Concentra'tion. *n. ſ.* [from *concentrate.*] Collection into a narrow ſpace round the center; compreſſion into a narrow compaſs.

All circular bodies, that receive a *concentration* of the light, muſt be ſhadowed in a circular manner *Peacham on Drawing.*

To Conce'ntre. *v. n.* [*concentrer*, Fr. from *con* and *centrum*, Latin.] To tend to one common centre; to have the ſame centre with ſomething elſe.

The bricks having firſt been formed in a circular mould, and then cut, before their burning, into four quarters or more, the ſides afterwards join ſo cloſely, and the points *concentre* ſo exactly, that the pillars appear one intire piece. *Wotton.*

All theſe are like ſo many lines drawn from ſeveral objects, that ſome way relate to him, and *concentre* in him. *Hale.*

To Conce'ntre. *v. a.* To emit towards one centre.

The having a part leſs to animate, will rather ſerve to *concentre* the ſpirits, and make them more active in the reſt. *Decay of Piety.*

In thee *concentring* all their precious beams
Of ſacred influence! *Milton's Paradiſe Loſt, b.* 9. *l.* 106.

Conce'ntrical. } *adj.* [*concentricus*, Lat.] Having one common centre.
Conce'ntrick. }

If, as in water ſtirr'd, more circles be
Produc'd by one, love ſuch additions take;
Thoſe, like ſo many ſpheres, but one heav'n make;
For they are all *concentrick* unto thee. *Donne.*

Any ſubſtance, pitched ſteddy upon two points, as on an axis, and moving about on that axis, alſo deſcribes a circle *concentrick* to the axis. *Moxon's Mech. Exer.*

If the cryſtalline humour had been *concentrical* to the ſclerodes, the eye would not have admitted a whole hemiſphere at one view. *Ray on the Creation.*

If a ſtone be thrown into ſtagnating water, the waves excited thereby continue ſome time to ariſe in the place where the ſtone fell into the water, and are propagated from thence into *concentrick* circles upon the ſurface of the water to great diſtances. *Newton's Opt.*

The manner of its concretion is by *concentrical* rings, like thoſe of an onion about the firſt kernel. *Arbuthnot on Diet.*

Circular revolutions in *concentrick* orbs about the ſun, or other central body, could in no wiſe be attained without the power of the Divine Arm. *Bentley's Sermons.*

Conce'ptacle. *n. ſ.* [*conceptaculum*, Lat.] That in which any thing is contained; a veſſel.

There

There is at this day resident, in that huge *conceptac'e*, water enough to effect such a deluge. *Woodward's Nat. Hist. Pref.*

CONCE'PTIBLE. *adj.* [from *concipio conceptum*, Latin.] That may be conceived; intelligible; capable to be understood.

Some of his attributes, and the manifestations thereof, are not only highly delectable to the intellective faculty, but are most suitable and easily *conceptible* by us, because apparent in his works. *Hale's Origin of Mankind.*

CONCE'PTION. *n. s.* [*conceptio*, Latin.]

1. The act of conceiving, or quickening with pregnancy.

I will greatly multiply thy sorrow, and thy *conception*; in sorrow thou shalt bring forth children. *Gen.* iii. 16.

Thy sorrow I will greatly multiply
By thy *conception*; children thou shalt bring
In sorrow forth. *Milton's Paradise Lost, b.* x. *l.* 194.

2. The state of being conceived.

Joy had the like *conception* in our eyes,
And at that instant, like a babe, sprung up. *Shakespeare.*

Our own productions flatter us: it is impossible not to be fond of them at the moment of their *conception*. *Dryd. Dufresn.*

3. Notion; idea; image in the mind.

As *conceptions* are the images or resemblances of things to the mind within itself, in the like manner are words or names the marks, tokens, or resemblances of those *conceptions* to the minds of them whom we converse with. *South's Sermons.*

Consult the acutest poets and speakers, and they will confess that their quickest, most admired *conceptions* were such as darted into their minds, like sudden flashes of lightning, they knew not how, nor whence; and not by any certain consequence, or dependence of one thought upon another, as it is in matters of ratiocination. *South's Sermons.*

To have right *conceptions* about them, we must bring our understandings to the inflexible natures and unalterable relations of things, and not endeavour to bring things to any preconceived notions of our own. *Locke.*

4. Sentiments; purpose.

Thou but remember'st me of my own *conception*. I have perceived a most faint neglect of late; which I have rather blamed as my own jealous curiosity, than as a very pretence and purpose of unkindness. *Shakespeare's King Lear.*

Please your highness, note
His dangerous *conception* in this point:
Not friended by his wish to your high person,
His will is most malignant, and it stretches
Beyond you to your friends. *Shakespeare's Henry* VIII.

5. Apprehension; knowledge.

And as if beasts conceiv'd what reason were,
And that *conception* should distinctly show
They should the name of reasonable bear;
For, without reason, none could reason know. *Davies.*

6. Conceit; sentiment; pointed thought.

He is too flatulent sometimes, and sometimes too dry; many times unequal, and almost always forced; and, besides, is full of *conceptions*, points of epigram, and witticisms; all which are not only below the dignity of heroic verse, but contrary to its nature. *Dryden's Juvenal, Dedication.*

CONCE'PTIOUS. *adj.* [*conceptum*, Latin.] Apt to conceive; fruitful; pregnant.

Common mother,
Ensear thy fertile and *conceptious* womb;
Let it no more bring out to ingrateful man. *Shakes. Timon.*

CONCE'PTIVE. *adj.* [*conceptum*, Latin.] Capable to conceive.

In hot climates, and where the uterine parts exceed in heat, by the coldness of this simple they may be reduced into a *conceptive* constitution. *Brown's Vulgar Errours, b.* vi. *c.* 7.

To CONCE'RN. *v. a.* [*concerner*, Fr. *concerno*, low Latin.]

1. To relate to; to belong to.

Exclude the use of natural reasoning about the sense of holy scripture, concerning the articles of our faith; and then, that the scripture doth *concern* the articles of our faith, who can assure us? *Hooker, b.* iii. *s.* 8.

Count Claudio may hear; for what I would speak of *concerns* him. *Shakespeare's Much ado about Nothing.*

Gracious things
Thou hast reveal'd; those chiefly which *concern*
Just Abraham, and his seed. *Milton's Paradise Lost, b.* xii.

This place *concerns* not at all the dominion of one brother over the other. *Locke.*

2. To affect with some passion; to touch nearly; to be of importance to.

I would not
The cause were known to them it most *concerns*. *Shakespear.*

Our wars with France have affected us in our most tender interests, and *concerned* us more than those with any other nation. *Addison on the State of the War.*

It much *concerns* them not to suffer the king to establish his authority on this side. *Addison's Remarks on Italy.*

The more the authority of any station in society is extended, the more it *concerns* publick happiness that it be committed to men fearing God. *Rogers's Sermons.*

3. To interest; to engage by interest.

I knew a young negroe who was sick of the small-pox: I found by enquiry, at a person's *concerned* for him, that the little tumours left whitish specks behind them. *Boyle on Colours.*

Above the rest two goddesses appear,
Concern'd for each: here Venus, Juno there. *Dryden's Æn.*

Providence, where it loves a nation, *concerns* itself to own and assert the interest of religion, by blasting the spoilers of religious persons and places. *South's Sermons.*

Whatever past actions it cannot reconcile, or appropriate to that present self by consciousness, it can be no more *concerned* in than if they had never been done. *Locke.*

They think themselves out of the reach of providence, and no longer *concerned* to solicit his favour. *Rogers, Sermon.* ii.

4. To disturb; to make uneasy.

In one compressing engine I shut a sparrow, without forcing any air in; and in an hour the bird began to pant, and be *concerned*, and in less than an hour and a half to be sick. *Derham.*

CONCE'RN. *n. s.* [from the verb.]

1. Business; affair; considered as relating to some one.

Let early care thy main *concerns* secure,
Things of less moment may delays endure. *Denham.*

This manner of exposing the private *concerns* of families, and sacrificing the secrets of the dead to the curiosity of the living, is one of those licentious practices, which might well deserve the animadversion of our government. *Addis. Freeholder.*

A heathen emperor said, if the gods were offended, it was their own *concern*, and they were able to vindicate themselves. *Swift.*

Religion is no trifling *concern*, to be performed in any careless and superficial manner. *Rogers, Sermon* xiii.

2. Interest; engagement.

No plots th' alarm to his retirements give;
'Tis all mankind's *concern* that he should live. *Dryden.*

When we speak of the conflagration of the world, these have no *concern* in the question. *Burnet's Theory of the Earth.*

3. Importance; moment.

Mysterious secrets of a high *concern*,
And weighty truths, solid convincing sense,
Explain'd by unaffected eloquence. *Roscommon.*

The mind is stunned and dazzled amidst that variety of objects: she cannot apply herself to those things which are of the utmost *concern* to her. *Addison's Spectator*, N°. 465.

4. Passion; affection; regard.

Ah, what *concerns* did both your souls divide!
Your honour gave us what your love deny'd. *Dryden.*
O Marcia, let me hope thy kind *concerns*,
And gentle wishes, follow me to battle! *Addison's Cato.*

Why all this *concern* for the poor? We want them not, as the country is now managed: where the plough has no work, one family can do the business of fifty. *Swift.*

CONCE'RNING. *prep.* [from *concern*: this word, originally a participle, has before a noun the force of a preposition.] Relating to; with relation to.

There is not any thing more subject to errour than the true judgment *concerning* the power and forces of an estate. *Bacon.*

The ancients had no higher recourse than to nature, as may appear by a discourse *concerning* this point in Strabo. *Brown.*

None can demonstrate that there is such an island as Jamaica, yet, upon testimony, I am free from all doubt *concerning* it. *Tillotson, Preface.*

CONCE'RNMENT. *n. s.* [from *concern*.]

1. The thing in which we are concerned or interested; affair; business; interest.

To mix with thy *concernments* I desist
Henceforth, nor too much disapprove my own. *Milt. Agon.*
This shews how useful you have been,
To bring the king's *concernments* in. *Hudibras, p.* iii. *cant.* 2.
Yet when we're sick, the doctor's fetcht in haste,
Leaving our great *concernment* to the last. *Denham.*

When my *concernment* takes up no more room or compass than myself, then, so long as I know where to breathe and to exist, I know also where to be happy. *South.*

He that is wise in the affairs and *concernments* of other men, but careless and negligent of his own, that man may be said to be busy, but he is not wise. *Tillotson.*

Our spiritual interests, and the great *concernments* of a future state, would doubtless recur often. *Atterbury.*

Propositions which extend only to the present life, are small, compared with those that have influence upon our everlasting *concernments*. *Watts's Improvement of the Mind.*

2. Relation; influence.

Sir, 'tis of near *concernment*, and imports
No less than the king's life and honour. *Denham's Sophy.*
He justly fears a peace with me would prove
Of ill *concernment* to his haughty love. *Dryd. Ind. Emperor.*

3. Intercourse; business.

The great *concernment* of men is with men, one amongst another. *Locke.*

4. Importance; moment.

I look upon experimental truths as matters of great *concernment* to mankind. *Boyle.*

5. Interposition; regard; meddling.

He married a daughter to the earl, without any other approbation

probation of her father, or *concernment* in it, than suffering him and her to come into his presence. *Clarendon.*

6. Passion; emotion of mind.

While they are so eager to destroy the fame of others, their ambition is manifest in their *concernment.* *Dryden.*

If it carry with it the notion of something extraordinary, if apprehension and *concernment* accompany it, the idea is likely to sink the deeper. *Locke.*

To CONCE'RT. *v. a.* [*concerter*, French, from *concertare*, Lat. to prepare themselves for some publick exhibition or performance, by private encounters among themselves.]

1. To settle any thing in private by mutual communication.
2. To settle; to contrive; to adjust.

Mark how already in his working brain
He forms the well-*concerted* scheme of mischief. *Rowe.*

Co'ncert. *n. s.* [from the verb.]

1. Communication of designs; establishment of measures among those who are engaged in the same affair.

All those discontents, how ruinous soever, have arisen from the want of a due communication and *concert.* *Swift.*

2. A symphony; many performers playing to the same tune.

Concerta'tion. *n. s.* [*concertatio*, Latin.] Strife; contention.

Conce'rtative. *adj.* [*concertativus*, Latin.] Contentious; quarrelsome; recriminating. *Dict.*

CONCE'SSION. *n. s.* [*concessio*, Latin.]

1. The act of granting or yielding.

The *concession* of these charters was in a parliamentary way. *Hale's Common Law of England.*

2. A grant; the thing yielded.

I still counted myself undiminished by my largest *concessions*, if by them I might gain the love of my people. *King Charles.*

When a lover becomes satisfied by small compliances, without further pursuits, then expect to find popular assemblies content with small *concessions.* *Swift.*

Conce'ssionary. *adj.* [from *concession.*] Given by indulgence or allowance.

Conce'ssively. *adv.* [from *concession.*] By way of concession; as yielding, not controverting by assumption.

Some have written rhetorically and *concessively*; not controverting, but assuming the question, which, taken as granted, advantaged the illation. *Brown's Vulgar Errours, b.* iii. *c.* 12.

Conch. *n. s.* [*concha*, Latin.] A shell; a sea-shell.

He furnishes her closet first, and fills
The crowded shelves with rarities of shells:
Adds orient pearls, which from the *conchs* he drew,
And all the sparkling stones of various hue. *Dryden's Fables.*

Co'nchoid. *n. s.* The name of a curve.

To CONCI'LIATE. *v. a.* [*concilio*, Lat.] To gain; to procure good will; to reconcile.

It was accounted a philtre, or plants that *conciliate* affection. *Brown's Vulgar Errours, b.* vi. *c.* 7.

Concilia'tion. *n. s.* [from *conciliate.*] The act of gaining or reconciling. *Dict.*

Concilia'tor. *n. s.* [from *conciliate.*] One that makes peace between others.

Conci'liatory. *adj.* [from *conciliate.*] Relating to reconciliation. *Dict.*

Conci'nnity. *n. s.* [from *concinnitas*, Latin.] Decency; fitness.

CONCI'NNOUS. *adj.* [*concinnus*, Latin.] Becoming; pleasant; agreeable.

CONCI'SE. *adj.* [*concisus*, cut, Latin.] Brief; short; broken into short periods.

The *concise* stile, which expresseth not enough, but leaves somewhat to be understood. *Ben. Johnson's Discoveries.*

Where the author is obscure, enlighten him; where he is too brief and *concise*, amplify a little, and set his notions in a fairer view. *Watts's Improvement of the Mind, p.* i. *c.* 4.

Conci'sely. *adv.* [from *concise.*] Briefly; shortly; in few words; in short sentences.

Ulysses here speaks very *concisely*, and he may seem to break abruptly into the subject. *Broome's Notes on the Odyssey, b.* vii.

Conci'seness. *n. s.* [from *concise.*] Brevity; shortness.

Giving more scope to Mezentius and Lausus, that version, which has more of the majesty of Virgil, has less of his *conciseness.* *Dryden.*

Conci'sion. *n. s.* [*concisum*, Latin.] Cutting off; excision; destruction.

Concita'tion. *n. s.* [*concitatio*, Latin.] The act of stirring up, or putting in motion.

The revelations of heaven are conceived by immediate illumination of the soul; whereas the deceiving spirit, by *concitation* of humours, produces conceited phantasmes. *Brown.*

Conclama'tion. *n. s.* [*conclamatio*, Latin.] An outcry or shout of many together. *Dict.*

Co'nclave. *n. s.* [*conclave*, Latin.]

1. A private apartment.
2. The room in which the cardinals meet; or the assembly of the cardinals.

I thank the holy *conclave* for their loves;
They've sent me such a man I would have wish'd for. *Shak.*

It was said of a cardinal, by reason of his apparent likelihood to step into St. Peter's chair, that in two *conclaves* he went in pope and came out again cardinal. *South's Sermons.*

3. A close assembly.

Forthwith a *conclave* of the godhead meets,
Where Juno in the shining senate sits. *Garth.*

To CONCLU'DE. *v. a.* [*concludo*, Latin.]

1. To shut.

The very person of Christ therefore, for ever and the selfsame, was only, touching bodily substance, *concluded* within the grave. *Hooker, b.* v. *s.* 52.

2. To include; to comprehend.

God hath *concluded* them all in unbelief, that he might have mercy upon all. *Romans*, xi. 32.

3. To collect by ratiocination.

The providences of God are promiscuously administred in this world; so that no man can *conclude* God's love or hatred to any person, by any thing that befals him. *Tillotson.*

4. To decide; to determine.

Youth, ere it sees the world, here studies rest;
And age, returning thence, *concludes* it best. *Dryden.*
But no frail man, however great or high,
Can be *concluded* blest before he die. *Addison's Ovid's Met.*

5. To end; to finish.

Is it concluded he shall be protector?
It is determin'd, not *concluded* yet;
But so it must be, if the king miscarry. *Shakesp. Rich.* III.

I will *conclude* this part with the speech of a counsellor of state. *Bacon.*

These are my theme, and how the war began,
And how *concluded* by the godlike man. *Dryden's Æn. b.* vii.

6. To oblige, as by the final determination.

If therefore they will appeal to revelation for their creation, they must be *concluded* by it. *Hale's Origin of Mankind.*

He never refused to be *concluded* by the authority of one legally summoned. *Atterbury.*

To Conclu'de. *v. n.*

1. To perform the last act of ratiocination; to collect the consequence; to determine.

For why should we the busy soul believe,
When boldly she *concludes* of that and this;
When of herself she can no judgment give,
Nor how, nor whence, nor where, nor what she is? *Davies.*

The blind man's relations import no necessity of *concluding*, that though black was the roughest of colours, therefore white should be the smoothest. *Boyle on Colours.*

There is something infamous in the very attempt: the world will *conclude* I had a guilty conscience. *Arbuth. Hist. of J. Bull.*

2. To settle opinion.

Can we *conclude* upon Luther's instability, as our author has done, because, in a single notion no way fundamental, an enemy writes that he had some doubtings? *Atterbury.*

I question not but your translation will do honour to our country; for I *conclude* of it already from those performances. *Addison to Pope.*

3. Finally to determine.

They humbly sue unto your excellence,
To have a goodly peace *concluded* of,
Between the realms of England and of France. *Shakespeare.*

4. To end.

And all around wore nuptial bonds, the ties
Of love's assurance, and a train of lies,
That, made in lust, *conclude* in perjuries. *Dryden's Fables.*

Conclu'dency. *n. s.* [from *concludent.*] Consequence; regular proof; logical deduction of reason.

Judgment concerning things to be known, or the neglect and *concludency* of them, ends in decision. *Hale.*

Conclu'dent. *adj.* [from *conclude.*] Decisive; ending in just and undeniable consequences.

Though these kind of arguments may seem more obscure, yet, upon a due consideration of them, they are highly consequential and *concludent* to my purpose. *Hale's Orig. of Mank.*

Conclu'sible. *adj.* [from *conclude.*] Determinable; certain by regular proof.

'Tis as certainly *conclusible* from God's prescience, that they will voluntarily do this, as that they will do it all. *Hammond.*

Conclu'sion. *n. s.* [from *conclude.*]

1. Determination; final decision.

Ways of peaceable *conclusion* there are but these two certain; the one a sentence of judicial decision, given by authority thereto appointed within ourselves; the other, the like kind of sentence given by a more universal authority. *Hooker.*

2. The collection from propositions premised; the consequence.

The *conclusion* of experience, from the time past to the time present, will not be sound and perfect. *Bacon's War with Spain.*

And marrying divers principles and grounds,
Out of their match a true *conclusion* brings. *Davies.*
Then doth the wit
Build fond *conclusions* on those idle grounds;
Then doth it fly the good, and ill pursue. *Davies.*
I only deal by rules of art,

Such

Such as are lawful, and judge by
Conclusions of astrology. *Hudibras, p.* ii. *cant.* iii.

It is of the nature of principles, to yield a *conclusion* different from themselves. *Tillotson, Preface.*

He granted him both the major and the minor; but denied him the *conclusion.* *Addison's Freeholder,* N°. 32.

3. The close; the last result of argumentative deduction.

Let us hear the *conclusion* of the whole matter, fear God and keep his commandments; for this is the whole duty of man. *Eccles.* xii. 13.

I have been reasoning, and in *conclusion* have thought it best to return to what fortune hath made my home. *Swift.*

4. The event of experiments.

Her physician tells me,
She has pursu'd *conclusions* infinite
Of easy ways to die. *Shakespeare's Anthony and Cleopatra.*

We practise likewise all *conclusions* of grafting and inoculating, as well of wild trees as fruit trees. *Bacon's New Atlant.*

5. The end; the upshot; the last part.

6. In *Shakespeare* it seems to signify silence; confinement of the thoughts.

Your wife Octavia, with her modest eyes
And still *conclusion*, shall acquire no honour,
Demuring upon me. *Shakespeare's Anthony and Cleopatra.*

CONCLU'SIVE. *adj.* [from *conclude.*]

1. Decisive; giving the last determination to the opinion.

The agreeing votes of both houses were not by any law or reason *conclusive* to my judgment. *King Charles.*

The last dictate of the understanding is not always absolute in itself, nor *conclusive* to the will, yet it produces no antecedent nor external necessity. *Bramh. Answer to Hobbs.*

They have secret reasons for what they seem to do, which, whatever they are, they must be equally *conclusive* for us as they were for them. *Rogers, Serm.* iv.

2. Regularly consequential.

Those that are not men of art, not knowing the true forms of syllogism, cannot know whether they are made in right and *conclusive* modes and figures. *Locke.*

CONCLU'SIVELY. *adv.* [from *conclusive.*] Decisively; with final determination.

This I speak only to desire Pollio and Eupolis not to speak peremptorily, or *conclusively*, touching the point of possibility, 'till they have heard me deduce the means of the execution. *Bacon's Holy War.*

CONCLU'SIVENESS. *n. s.* [from *conclusive.*] Power of determining the opinion; regular consequence.

Consideration of things to be known, of their several weights, *conclusiveness*, or evidence. *Hale's Orig. of Mankind.*

To CONCOA'GULATE. *v. a.* [from *con* and *coagulate.*] To curdle or congeal one thing with another.

The saline parts of those, upon their solution by the rain, may work upon those other substances, formerly *concoagulated* with them. *Boyle's Experiments.*

They do but coagulate themselves, without *concoagulating* with them any water. *Boyle's History of Firmness.*

CONCOAGULA'TION. *n. s.* [from *concoagulate.*] A coagulation by which different bodies are joined in one mass.

To CONCO'CT. *v. a.* [*concoquo*, Latin.]

1. To digest by the stomach, so as to turn food to nutriment.

The working of purging medicines cometh two or three hours after the medicines taken; for that the stomach first maketh a proof, whether it can *concoct* them. *Bac. Nat. Hist.*

Assuredly he was a man of a feeble stomach, unable to *concoct* any great fortune, prosperous or adverse. *Hayward.*

The vital functions are performed by general and constant laws; the food is *concocted*, the heart beats, the blood circulates, the lungs play. *Cheyne's Phil. Prin.*

The notions and sentiments of others judgment, as well as of our own memory makes our property: it does, as it were, *concoct* our intellectual food, and turns it into a part of our selves. *Watts's Improvement of the Mind, p.* i. *c.* 2.

2. To purify or sublime by heat; or heighten to perfection.

The small close-lurking minister of fate,
Whose high *concocted* venom through the veins
A rapid lightning darts. *Thomson's Summer.*

CONCO'CTION. *n. s.* [from *concoct.*] Digestion in the stomach; maturation by heat; the acceleration of any thing towards purity and perfection.

This hard rolling is between *concoction* and a simple maturation. *Bacon's Natural History,* N°. 324.

The constantest notion of *concoction* is, that it should signify the degrees of alteration of one body into another, from crudity to perfect *concoction*, which is the ultimity of that action or process. *Bacon's Natural History,* N°. 324.

He, though he knew not which soul spake,
Because both meant, both spake the same,
Might thence a new *concoction* take,
And part far purer than he came. *Donne.*

CONCO'LOUR. *adj.* [*concolor*, Latin.] Of one colour without variety.

In *concolour* animals, and such as are confined unto the same colour, we measure not their beauty thereby; for if a cow or blackbird grow white, we account it more pretty. *Brown.*

CONCO'MITANCE. } *n. s.* [from *concomitor*, Latin.] Subsistence
CONCO'MITANCY. } together with another thing.

The secondary action subsisteth not alone, but in *concomitancy* with the other; so the nostrils are useful for respiration and smelling, but the principal use is smelling. *Brown.*

To argue from a *concomitancy* to a causality, is not infallibly conclusive. *Glanville's Scep. c.* 23.

CONCO'MITANT. *adj.* [*concomitans*, Latin.] Conjoined with; concurrent with; coming and going with, as collateral, not causative, or consequential.

It is the spirit that furthereth the extension or dilatation of bodies, and it is ever *concomitant* with porosity and dryness. *Bacon's Natural History,* N°. 841.

It has pleased our wise Creator to annex to several objects, as also to several of our thoughts, a *concomitant* pleasure; and that in several objects, to several degrees. *Locke.*

CONCO'MITANT. *n. s.* Companion; person or thing collaterally connected.

These effects are from the local motion of the air, a *concomitant* of the sound, and not from the sound. *Bac. Nat. Hist.*

He made him the chief *concomitant* of his heir apparent and only son, in a journey of much adventure. *Wotton.*

In consumptions the preternatural *concomitants*, an universal heat of the body, a torminous diarrhæa, and hot distillations, have all a corrosive quality. *Harvey on Consumptions.*

The other *concomitant* of ingratitude is hard-heartedness, or want of compassion. *South's Sermons.*

Horrour stalks around,
Wild staring, and his sad *concomitant*,
Despair, of abject look. *Philips.*

Reproach is a *concomitant* to greatness, as satires and invectives were an essential part of a Roman triumph. *Addison.*

And for tobacco, who could bear it?
Filthy *concomitant* of claret! *Prior.*

Where antecedents, *concomitants* and consequents, causes and effects, signs and things signified, subjects and adjuncts, are necessarily connected with each other, we may infer. *Watts's Logick.*

CONCO'MITANTLY. *adv.* [from *concomitant.*] In company with others. *Dict.*

To CONCO'MITATE. *v. a.* [*concomitatus*, Lat.] To be collaterally connected with any thing; to come and go with another.

This simple bloody spectation of the lungs, is differenced from that which *concomitates* a pleurisy. *Harvey on Consumptions.*

CO'NCORD. *n. s.* [*concordia*, Latin.]

1. Agreement between persons or things; suitableness of one to another; peace; union; mutual kindness.

Had I power, I should
Pour the sweet milk of *concord* into hell,
Uproar the universal peace. *Shakespeare's Macbeth.*

What *concord* hath Christ with Belial? 2 *Cor.* vi. 15.

Kind *concord*, heavenly born! whose blissful reign
Holds this vast globe in one surrounding chain;
Soul of the world! *Tickell.*

2. A compact.

It appeareth by the *concord* made between Henry and Roderick the Irish king. *Davies on Ireland.*

3. Harmony; concent of sounds.

The man who hath not musick in himself,
Nor is not mov'd with *concord* of sweet sounds,
Is fit for treasons. *Shakesp. Merchant of Venice.*

4. Principal grammatical relation of one word to another.

Have those who have writ about declensions, *concords*, and syntaxes lost their labour? *Locke.*

CONCO'RDANCE. *n. s.* [*concordantia*, Latin.]

1. Agreement.

2. A book which shews in how many texts of scripture any word occurs.

I shall take it for an opportunity to tell you, how you are to rule the city out of a *concordance.* *South's Serm. Dedicat.*

Some of you turn over a *concordance*, and there, having the principal word, introduce as much of the verse as will serve your turn. *Swift.*

An old *concordance* bound long since. *Swift.*

3. A concord in grammar; one of the three chief relations in speech. It is not now in use in this sense.

After the three *concordances* learned, let the master read unto him the epistles of Cicero. *Askam's Schoolmaster.*

CONCO'RDANT. *adj.* [*concordans*, Lat.] Agreeable; agreeing; correspondent; harmonious.

Were every one employed in points *concordant* to their natures, professions, and arts, commonwealths would rise up of themselves. *Brown's Vulgar Errours, b.* i. *c.* 4.

CONCO'RDATE. *n. s.* [*concordat*, Fr. *concordatum*, Lat.] A compact; a convention.

How comes he to number the want of synods in the Gallican church among the grievances of that *concordate*, and as a mark of their slavery, since he reckons all convocations of the clergy in England to be useless and dangerous? *Swift.*

CONCO'RPORAL. *adj.* [from *concorporo*, Latin, to incorporate.] Of the same body. *Dict.*

To CONCO'RPORATE. *v. a.* [from *con* and *corpus.*] To unite in one mass or substance.

When we *concorporate* the sign with the signification, we conjoin the word with the spirit. *Taylor's Worthy Communicant.*

CONCORPORA'TION. *n. s.* [from *concorporate.*] Union in one mass; intimate mixture. *Dict.*

CO'NCOURSE. *n. s.* [*concursus*, Latin.]

1. The confluence of many persons or things to one place.

Do all the nightly guards,
The city's watches, with the people's fears,
The *concourse* of all good men, strike thee nothing? *B Johns.*

The coalition of the good frame of the universe was not the product of chance, or fortuitous *concourse* of particles of matter. *Hale's Origin of Mankind.*

Vain is his force, and vainer is his skill,
With such a *concourse* comes the flood of ill. *Dryden's Fables.*

2. The persons assembled.

The prince with wonder hears, from ev'ry part,
The noise and busy *concourse* of the mart. *Dryd. Virg. Æn.*

3. The point of junction or intersection of two bodies.

So soon as the upper glass is laid upon the lower, so as to touch it at one end, and to touch the drop at the other end, making, with the lower glass, an angle of about ten or fifteen minutes; the drop will begin to move towards the *concourse* of the glasses, and will continue to move with an accelerated motion, 'till it arrives at that *concourse* of the glasses. *Newton.*

CONCREMA'TION. *n. s.* [from *concremo*, Lat. to burn together.] The act of burning many things together. *Dict.*

CO'NCREMENT. *n. s.* [from *concresco*, Latin.] The mass formed by concretion; a collection of matter growing together.

There is the cohesion of the matter into a more loose consistency, like clay, and thereby it is prepared to the *concrement* of a pebble or flint. *Hale's Origin of Mankind.*

CONCRE'SCENCE. *n. s.* [from *concresco*, Lat.] The act or quality of growing by the union of separate particles.

Seeing it is neither a substance perfect, nor inchoate, how any other substance should thence take *concrescence* hath not been taught. *Raleigh's History of the World.*

To CONCRE'TE. *v. n.* [*concresco*, Latin.] To coalesce into one mass; to grow by the union and cohesion of parts.

The mineral or metallick matter, thus *concreting* with the crystalline, is equally diffused throughout the body of it. *Woodw.*

When any saline liquor is evaporated to a cuticle, and let cool, the salt *concretes* in regular figures; which argues that the particles of the salt, before they *concreted*, floated in the liquor at equal distances, in rank and file. *Newton.*

The blood of some who died of the plague, could not be made to *concrete*, by reason of the putrefaction already begun. *Arbuthnot on Aliments.*

To CONCRE'TE. *v. a.* To form by concretion; to form by the coalition of scattered particles.

That there are in our inferiour world divers bodies, that are *concreted* out of others, is beyond all dispute: we see it in the meteors. *Hale's Origin of Mankind.*

CO'NCRETE. *adj.* [from the verb.]

1. Formed by concretion; formed by coalition of separate particles into one mass.

The first *concrete* state, or consistent surface of the chaos, must be of the same figure as the last liquid state. *Burnet.*

2. In logick. Not abstract; applied to a subject.

A kind of mutual commutation there is, whereby those *concrete* names, God and man, when we speak of Christ, do take interchangeably one another's room; so that, for truth of speech, it skilleth not whether we say that the son of God hath created the world, and the son of man by his death hath saved it; or else that the son of man did create, and the son of God died to save the world. *Hooker, b. v. sect.* 53.

Concrete terms, while they express the quality, do also either express or imply, or refer to some subject to which it belongs; as white, round, long, broad, wise, mortal, living, dead: but these are not always noun adjectives in a grammatical sense; for a fool, a philosopher, and many other *concretes*, are substantives, as well as knavery, folly and philosophy, which are the abstract terms that belong to them. *Watts's Logick.*

CO'NCRETE. *n. s.* A mass formed by concretion; or union of various parts adhering to each other.

If gold itself be admitted, as it must be, for a porous *concrete*, the proportion of void to body, in the texture of common air, will be so much the greater. *Bentley's Sermons.*

CONCRE'TELY. *adv.* [from *concrete.*] In a manner including the subject with the predicate; not abstractly.

Sin considered not abstractedly for the mere act of obliquity, but *concretely*, with such a special dependance of it upon the will as serves to render the agent guilty. *Norris.*

CONCRE'TENESS. *n. s.* [from *concrete.*] Coagulation; collection of fluids into a solid mass. *Dict.*

CONCRE'TION. *n. s.* [from *concrete.*]

1. The act of concreting; coalition.

2. The mass formed by a coalition of separate particles.

Some plants upon the top of the sea, are supposed to grow of some *concretion* of slime from the water, where the sea stirreth little. *Bacon's Natural History*, N°. 568.

Heat, in general, doth not resolve and attenuate the juices of a human body; for too great heat will produce *concretions*. *Arbuthnot on Aliments.*

CO'NCRETIVE. *adj.* [from *concrete.*] Having the power to produce concretions; coagulative.

When wood and other bodies petrify, we do not ascribe their induration to cold, but unto salinous spirit, or *concretive* juices. *Brown's Vulgar Errours, b.* ii. *c.* 3.

CONCRE'TURE. *n. s.* [from *concrete.*] A mass formed by coagulation.

CONCU'BINAGE. *n. s.* [*concubinage*, Fr. *concubinatus*, Latin.] The act of living with a woman not married.

Adultery was punished with death by the ancient heathens: *concubinage* was permitted. *Broome's Notes on the Odyssey.*

CO'NCUBINE. *n. s.* [*concubina*, Lat.] A woman kept in fornication; a whore; a strumpet.

I know, I am too mean to be your queen;
And yet too good to be your *concubine*. *Shakesp. Henry* VI.

When his great friend was suitor to him to pardon an offender, he denied him: afterwards, when a *concubine* of his made the same suit, he granted it to her; and said, Such suits were to be granted to whores. *Bacon.*

He caused him to paint one of his *concubines*, called Campaspe, who had the greatest share in his affection. *Dryden's Dufresnoy.*

The wife, though a bright goddess, thus gives place
To mortal *concubines* of fresh embrace. *Granville.*

To CONCU'LCATE. *v. a.* [*conculco*, Latin.] To tread or trample under foot. *Dict.*

CONCULCA'TION. *n. s.* [*conculcatio*, Latin.] Trampling with the feet. *Dict.*

CONCU'PISCENCE. *n. s.* [*concupiscentia*, Latin.] Irregular desire; libidinous wish; lust; lechery.

We know even secret *concupiscence* to be sin, and are made fearful to offend, though it be but in a wandering cogitation. *Hooker, b.* i.

In our faces evident the signs
Of foul *concupiscence*; whence evil store,
Ev'n shame, the last of evils. *Milton's Paradise Lost, b.* ix.

Nor can they say, that the difference of climate inclines one nation to *concupiscence* and sensual pleasures, another to blood-thirstiness: it would discover great ignorance not to know, that a people has been over run with recently invented vice. *Bentley's Sermons.*

CONCU'PISCENT. *adj.* [*concupiscens*, Latin.] Libidinous; lecherous.

He would not, but by gift of my chaste body
To his *concupiscent* intemperate lust,
Release my brother! *Shakesp. Measure for Measure.*

CONCUPISCE'NTIAL. *adj.* [from *concupiscent.*] Relating to concupiscence. *Dict.*

CONCUPI'SCIBLE. *adj.* [*concupiscibilis*, Lat.] Impressing desire; eager; desirous; inclining to the pursuit or attainment of any thing.

The schools reduce all the passions to these two heads, the *concupiscible* and irascible appetite. *South's Sermons.*

To CONCU'R. *v. n.* [*concurro*, Latin.]

1. To meet in one point.

Though reason favour them, yet sense can hardly allow them; and, to satisfy, both these must *concur*. *Temple.*

2. To agree; to join in one action, or opinion.

Acts which shall be done by the greater part of my executors, shall be as valid and effectual as if all my executors had *concurred* in the same. *Swift's Last Will.*

3. It has *with* before the person with whom one agrees.

It is not evil simply to *concur with* the heathens, either in opinion or action; and that conformity with them is only then a disgrace, when we follow them in that they do amiss, or generally in that they do without reason. *Hooker, b.* iv.

4. It has *to* before the effect to which one concurs.

Their affections were known to *concur to* the most desperate counsels. *Clarendon.*

Extremes in nature equal good produce,
Extremes in man *concur to* general use. *Pope, Epist.* iii.

5. To be united with; to be conjoined.

To have an orthodox belief, and a true profession, *concurring* with a bad life, is only to deny Christ with a greater solemnity. *South's Sermons.*

Testimony is the argument; and, if fair probabilities of reason *concur* with it, this argument hath all the strength it can have. *Tillotson, Sermon* i.

6. To contribute to one common event with joint power.

When outward causes *concur*, the idle are soonest seized by this infection. *Collier on the Spleen.*

CONCU'RRENCE. } *n. s.* [from *concur.*]
CONCU'RRENCY. }

1. Union; association; conjunction.

We have no other measure but our own ideas, with the *concurrence* of other probable reasons, to persuade us. *Locke.*

2. Agreement;

2. Agreement; act of joining in any design, or measures.

Their *concurrence* in persuasion, about some material points belonging to the same polity, is not strange. *Hooker, Preface.*

The *concurrence* of the peers in that fury, can be imputed to the irreverence the judges were in. *Clarendon.*

Tarquin the proud was expelled by an universal *concurrence* of nobles and people. *Swift on the Dissent. in Athens and Rome.*

3. Combination of many agents or circumstances.

Struck with these great *concurrences* of things. *Crashaw.*

He views our behaviour in every *concurrence* of affairs, and sees us engage in all the possibilities of action. *Addis. Spectat.*

4. Assistance; help.

From these sublime images we collect the greatness of the work, and the necessity of the divine *concurrence* to it. *Rogers.*

5. Joint right; common claim.

A bishop might have officers, if there was a *concurrency* of jurisdiction between him and the archdeacon. *Ayliffe.*

CONCU'RRENT. *adj.* [from *concur.*]

1. Acting in conjunction; agreeing in the same act; contributing to the same event; concomitant in agency.

I join with these laws the personal presence of the king's son, as a *concurrent* cause of this reformation *Davies on Ireland.*

For without the *concurrent* consent of all these three parts of the legislature, no such law is or can be made. *Hale.*

All combin'd,
Your beauty, and my impotence of mind;
And his *concurrent* flame, that blew my fire;
For still our kindred souls had one desire. *Dryden's Fables.*

2. Conjoined; associate; concomitant.

There is no difference between the *concurrent* echo and the iterant, but the quickness or slowness of the return. *Bacon.*

CONCU'RRENT *n. s.* [from *concur.*] That which concurs; a contributory cause.

To all affairs of importance there are three necessary *concurrents*, without which they can never be dispatched; time, industry, and faculties. *Decay of Piety.*

CONCU'SSION. *n. s.* [*concussio*, Lat.] The act of shaking; agitation; tremefaction.

It is believed that great ringing of bells in populous cities, hath dissipated pestilent air; which may be from the *concussion* of the air. *Bacon's Natural History*, N°. 127.

There want not instances of such an universal *concussion* of the whole globe, as must needs imply an agitation of the whole abyss. *Woodward's Natural History, p.* iii.

The strong *concussion* on the heaving tide,
Roll'd back the vessel to the island's side. *Pope's Odyssey.*

CONCU'SSIVE. *adj.* [*concussus*, Latin.] Having the power or quality of shaking.

To CONDE'MN. *v. a.* [*condemno*, Latin.]

1. To find guilty; to doom to punishment; contrary to absolve.

My conscience hath a thousand several tongues,
And every tongue brings in a sev'ral tale,
And ev'ry tale *condemns* me for a villain. *Shakesp. Rich.* III.
Is he found guilty?——
——Yes truly, is he, and *condemn'd* upon't. *Sh. Hen.* VIII.

Considered as a judge, it *condemns* where it ought to absolve, and pronounces absolution where it ought to *condemn*. *Fiddes's Sermons.*

2. It has *to* before the punishment.

The son of man shall be betrayed unto the scribes, and they shall *condemn* him *to* death. *Mat.* xx. 18.

3. To censure; to blame; to declare criminal; contrary to approve.

Who then shall blame
His pester'd senses to recoil and start,
When all that is within him does *condemn*
Itself for being there? *Shakespeare's Macbeth.*

The poet who flourished in the scene, is *condemned* in the ruelle. *Dryden's Æn. Preface.*

He who was so unjust as to do his brother an injury, will scarce be so just as to *condemn* himself for it. *Locke.*

They who approve my conduct in this particular, are much more numerous than those who *condemn* it. *Spectator*, N°. 488.

4. To fine.

And the king of Egypt put him down at Jerusalem, and *condemned* the land in an hundred talents of silver. 2 *Chro.*

5. To show guilt by contrast.

The righteous that is dead shall *condemn* the ungodly which are living. *Wisd.* iv. 16.

CONDE'MNABLE. *adj.* [from *condemn.*] Blameable; culpable.

He commands to deface the print of a cauldron in ashes, which strictly to observe were *condemnable* superstition. *Brown.*

CONDEMNA'TION. *n. s.* [*condemnatio*, Latin.] The sentence by which any one is doomed to punishment; the act of condemning; the state of being condemned.

There is therefore now no *condemnation* to them. *Rom.* viii.

CONDE'MNATORY. *adj.* [from *condemn.*] Passing a sentence of condemnation, or of censure.

He that passes the first *condemnatory* sentence, is like the incendiary in a popular tumult, who is chargeable with all those disorders to which he gave rise. *Government of the Tongue.*

CONDE'MNER. *n. s.* [from *condemn.*] A blamer; a censurer; a censor.

Some few are the only refusers and *condemners* of this catholick practice. *Taylor's Worthy Communicant.*

CONDE'NSABLE. *adj* [from *condensate.*] That which is capable of condensation; that which can be drawn or compressed into a narrower compass.

This agent meets with resistance in the moveable, and not being in the utmost extremity of density, but *condensable* yet further, every resistance works something upon the mover to condense it. *Digby on the Soul.*

To CONDE'NSATE. *v. a.* [*condenso*, Latin.] To condense; to make thicker.

To CONDE'NSATE. *v. n.* To grow thicker.

CONDE'NSATE. *adj.* [*condensatus*, Latin.] Made thick; condensed; compressed into less space.

Water by nature is white; yea, thickened or *condensate*, most white, as it appeareth by the hail and snow. *Peacham.*

CONDENSA'TION. *n. s.* [from *condensate.*] The act of thickening any body, or making it more gross and weighty. Opposite to rarefaction.

If by natural arguments it may be proved, that water, by *condensation*, may become earth; the same reason teacheth, that earth, rarefied, may become water. *Raleigh's History.*

By water-glasses the account was not regular; for, from attenuation and *condensation*, the hours were shorter in hot weather than in cold. *Brown's Vulgar Errours, b.* v. *c.* 18.

The supply of its moisture is by rains and snow, and dews and *condensation* of vapours, and perhaps by subterraneous passages. *Bentley.*

To CONDE'NSE. *v. a.* [*condenso*, Latin.] To make any body more thick, close, and weighty; to drive or attract the parts of any body nearer to each other. Opposed to rarefy; to inspissate.

Moving in so high a sphere, he must needs, as the sun, raise many envious exhalations; which, *condensed* by a popular odium, were capable to cast a cloud upon the brightest merit. *King Charles.*

Some lead their youth abroad, while some *condense*
Their liquid store, and some in cells dispense. *Dryd. Virg.*

Such dense and solid strata arrest the ascending vapour, stop it at the surface of the earth, and collect and *condense* it there. *Woodward's Natural History, p.* iii.

To CONDE'NSE. *v. n.* To grow close and weighty; to withdraw its parts into a narrow compass.

The water falling from the upper parts of the cave, does presently there *condense* into little stones. *Boyle's Scept. Chym.*

All vapours, when they begin to *condense* and coalesce into small parcels, become first of that bigness whereby azure must be reflected, before they can constitute other colours. *Newton.*

CONDE'NSE. *adj.* [from the verb.] Thick; dense; condensated; close; massy; weighty.

They might be separated without consociating into the huge *condense* bodies of planets. *Bentley's Sermons.*

CONDE'NSER. *n. s.* [from *condense.*] A strong metalline vessel, wherein to crowd the air, by means of a syringe fastened thereto. *Quincy.*

CONDE'NSITY. *n. s.* [from *condense.*] The state of being condensed; condensation; denseness; density.

CO'NDERS. *n. s.* [*conduire*, French.]

Such as stand upon high places near the sea-coast, at the time of herring-fishing, to make signs to the fishers which way the shole of herrings passeth, which may better appear to such as stand upon some high cliff, by a kind of blue colour that the fish causeth in the water, than to those that be in the ships. These be likewise called *huers*, by likelihood of the French *huyer*, *exclamare*, and balkers. *Cowel.*

To CONDESCE'ND. *v. n.* [*condescendre*, Fr. from *descendo*, Latin.]

1. To depart from the privileges of superiority by a voluntary submission; to sink willingly to equal terms with inferiours; to sooth by familiarity.

This method carries a very humble and *condescending* air, when he that instructs seems to be the enquirer. *Watts.*

2. To consent to do more than mere justice can require.

Spain's mighty monarch,
In gracious clemency does *condescend*,
On these conditions, to become your friend. *Dryd. Ind. Em.*

He did not primarily intend to appoint this way; but *condescended* to it as most accommodate to their present state. *Tillotson, Sermon* 5.

3. To stoop; to bend; to yield; to submit; to become subject.

Can they think me so broken, so debas'd
With corporal servitude, that my mind ever
Will *condescend* to such absurd commands? *Milton.*

Nor shall my resolution
Disarm itself, nor *condescend* to parly
With foolish hopes. *Denham's Sophy.*

CONDESCE'NDENCE. *n. s.* [*condescendance*, French.] Voluntary submission to a state of equality with inferiours.

CONDESCE'NDINGLY. *adv.* [from *condescending.*] By way of voluntary humiliation; by way of kind concession.

We *condescendingly* made Luther's works umpires in the controversy. *Atterbury.*

CONDESCE'NSION. *n. s.* [from *condescend*] Voluntary humiliation; descent from superiority; voluntary submission to equality with inferiours.

It forbids pride and ambition, and vain glory; and commands humility and modesty, and *condescension* to others. *Tillots.*

Courtesy and *condescension* is an happy quality, which never fails to make its way into the good opinion, and into the very heart, and allays the envy which always attends a high station. *Atterbury's Sermons.*

Raphael, amidst his tenderness, shews such a dignity and *condescension* in all his behaviour, as are suitable to a superiour nature. *Addison's Spectator*, N°. 273.

CONDESCE'NSIVE. *adj.* [from *condescend.*] Courteous; willing to treat with inferiours on equal terms; not haughty; not arrogant.

CONDI'GN. *adj.* [*condignus*, Latin.] Worthy of a person; suitable; deserved; merited: it is always used of something deserved by crimes.

Unless it were a bloody murtherer,
I never gave them *condign* punishment. *Shakesp. Henry* VI.

Consider who is your friend, he that would have brought him to *condign* punishment, or he that has saved him. *Arbuthn.*

CONDI'GNESS. *n. s.* [from *condign.*] Suitableness; agreeableness to deserts. *Dict.*

CONDI'GNLY. *adv.* [from *condign.*] Deservedly; according to merit. *Dict.*

CO'NDIMENT. *n. s.* [*condimentum*, Latin.] Seasoning; sauce; that which excites the appetite by a pungent taste.

As for radish and the like, they are for *condiments*, and not for nourishment. *Bacon's Natural History.*

Many things are swallowed by animals rather for *condiment*, gust, or medicament, than any substantial nutriment. *Brown.*

CONDISCI'PLE. *n. s.* [*condiscipulus*, Lat.] A schoolfellow.

To CO'NDITE. *v. a.* [*condio*, Lat.] To pickle; to preserve by salts or aromaticks.

Much after the same manner as the sugar doth, in the *conditing* of pears, quinces, and the like. *Grew's Musæum.*

The most innocent of them are but like *condited* or pickled mushrooms, which, carefully corrected, may be harmless, but can never do good. *Taylor's Rule of living holy.*

CO'NDITEMENT. *n. s.* [from *condite.*] A composition of conserves, powders, and spices in the form of an electuary. *Dict.*

CONDI'TION. *n. s.* [*condition*, Fr. *conditio*, Latin.]

1. Quality; that by which any thing is denominated good or bad.

A rage, whose heat hath this *condition*,
That nothing can allay, nothing but blood. *Shakes. K. John.*

2. Attribute; accident; property.

The king is but a man: the violet smells, the element shews to him as to me: all his senses have but human *conditions*. *Shakespeare's Henry* V.

It seemed to us a *condition* and property of Divine Powers and Beings, to be hidden and unseen to others. *Bacon.*

They will be able to conserve their properties unchanged in passing through several mediums, which is another *condition* of the rays of light. *Newton's Opt.*

3. Natural quality of the mind; temper; temperament; complexion.

The child taketh most of his nature of the mother, besides speech, manners, and inclination, which are agreeable to the *conditions* of their mothers. *Spenser on Ireland.*

The best and soundest of his time hath been but rash: now must we look, from his age, to receive not alone the imperfections of long engrafted *condition*, but therewithal the unruly waywardness that infirm and cholerick years bring with them. *Shakespeare's King Lear.*

4. Moral quality; virtue, or vice.

Jupiter is hot and moist, temperate, modest, honest, adventurous, liberal, merciful, loving and faithful, that is, giving these inclinations; and therefore those ancient kings, beautified with these *conditions*, might be called there after Jupiter. *Raleigh's History of the World, b.* i. *c.* 6. *s.* 5.

Socrates espoused Xantippe only for her extreme ill *conditions*, above all of that sex. *South.*

5. State; circumstances.

To us all,
That feel the bruises of the days before,
And suffer the *condition* of these times
To lay an heavy and unequal hand
Upon our humours. *Shakespeare's Henry* IV.

It was not agreeable unto the *condition* of Paradise and state of innocence. *Brown's Vulgar Errours, b.* v. *c* 4.

Estimate the greatness of this mercy by the *condition* it finds the sinner in, when God vouchsafes it to them. *South's Serm.*

Did we perfectly know the state of our own *condition*, and what was most proper for us, we might have reason to conclude our prayers not heard, if not answered. *Wake's Preparation.*

This is a principle adapted to every passion and faculty of our nature, to every state and *condition* of our life. *Rogers.*

Some desponding people take the kingdom to be in no *condition* of encouraging so numerous a breed of beggars. *Swift.*

Condition, circumstance, is not the thing;
Bliss is the same in subject as in king. *Pope's Essay on Man.*

6. Rank.

I am, in my *condition*,
A prince, Miranda. *Shakespeare's Tempest.*

The king himself met with many entertainments, at the charge of particular men, which had been rarely practised 'till then by the persons of the best *condition*. *Clarendon.*

7. Stipulation; terms of compact.

Condition!
What *condition* can a treaty find
I' th' part that is at mercy? *Shakespeare's Coriolanus.*

I yield upon *conditions*.—We give none
To traitors: strike him down. *Ben. Johnson's Catiline.*

He could not defend it above ten days, and must then submit to the worst *conditions* the rebels were like to grant to his person, and to his religion. *Clarendon.*

Many are apt to believe remission of sins, but they believe it without the *condition* of repentance. *Taylor.*

Those barb'rous pirates willingly receive
Conditions, such as we are pleas'd to give. *Waller.*

Make our *conditions* with yon' captive king.—
Secure me but my solitary cell;
'Tis all I ask him. *Dryden's Don Sebastian.*

8. The writing in which the terms of agreement are comprised; compact; bond.

Go with me to a notary, seal me there
Your single bond; and in a merry sport,
If you repay me not on such a day,
In such a place, such sum or sums as are
Express'd in the *condition*, let the forfeit
Be nominated. *Shakespeare's Merchant of Venice.*

To CONDI'TION. *v. n.* [from the noun] To make terms; to stipulate.

It was *conditioned* between Saturn and Titan, that Saturn should put to death all his male children. *Raleigh's History.*

Small towns, which stand stiff, 'till great shot
Enforce them, by war's law, *condition* not. *Donne.*

'Tis one thing, I must confess, to *condition* for a good office, and another thing to do it gratis. *L'Estrange, Fab.* 137.

CONDI'TIONAL. *adj.* [from *condition.*]

1. By way of stipulation; not absolute; with limitations; on particular terms.

For the use we have his express commandment, for the effect his *conditional* promise; so that, without obedience to the one, there is of the other no assurance. *Hooker, b.* v. *s.* 57.

Many scriptures, though as to their formal terms they are absolute, yet as to their sense they are *conditional*. *South.*

This strict necessity they simple call;
Another sort there is *conditional*. *Dryden's Fables.*

2. In grammar and logick. Expressing some condition or supposition.

CONDI'TIONAL. *n. s.* [from the adjective.] A limitation. A word not now in use.

He said, if he were sure that young man were king Edward's son, he would never bear arms against him. This case seems hard, both in respect of the *conditional*, and in respect of the other words. *Bacon's Henry* VII.

CONDITIONA'LITY. *n. s.* [from *conditional.*] The quality of being conditional; limitation by certain terms.

And as this clear proposal of the promises may inspirit our endeavours, so is the *conditionality* most efficacious to necessitate and engage them. *Decay of Piety.*

CONDI'TIONALLY. *adv.* [from *conditional.*] With certain limitations; on particular terms; on certain stipulations.

I here intail
The crown to thee, and to thine heirs for ever;
Conditionally, that here thou take an oath
To cease this civil war. *Shakespeare's Henry* VI. *p.* iii.

A false apprehension understands that positively, which was but *conditionally* expressed. *Brown's Vulgar Errours, b.* vii.

We see large preferments tendered to him, but *conditionally*, upon his doing wicked offices: conscience shall here, according to its office, interpose and protest. *South.*

CONDI'TIONARY. *adj.* [from *condition.*] Stipulated.

Would God in mercy dispense with it as a *conditionary*, yet we could not be happy without it, as a natural qualification for heaven. *Norris.*

To CONDI'TIONATE. *v. a.* [from *condition.*] To make conditions for; to regulate by certain conditions.

That ivy ariseth but where it may be supported; we cannot ascribe the same unto any science therein, which suspends and *conditionates* its eruption. *Brown's Vulgar Errours, b.* iii.

CONDI'TIONATE. *adj.* [from the verb.] Established on certain terms or conditions.

That which is mistaken to be particular and absolute, duly understood, is general, but *conditionate*, and belongs to none, who shall not perform the condition? *Hammond.*

CONDI'TIONED. *adj.* [from *condition.*] Having qualities or properties good or bad.

The

The deareſt friend to me, the kindeſt man,
The beſt *condition'd*. *Shakeſpeare's Merchant of Venice.*

To CONDO'LE. *v. n.* [*condoleo*, Latin.] To lament with thoſe that are in misfortune; to expreſs concern for the miſeries of others. It has *with* before the perſon for whoſe misfortune we profeſs grief.

Your friends would have cauſe to rejoice, rather than *condole with* you. *Temple.*

I congratulate with the republick of beaſts upon this honour done to their king; and muſt *condole with* us poor mortals, who, by diſtance, are rendered incapable of paying our reſpects. *Addiſon's Guardian*, Nº. 118.

To CONDO'LE. *v. a.* To bewail with another.

I come not, Sampſon, to *condole* thy chance,
As theſe perhaps, yet wiſh it had not been,
Though for no friendly intent. *Milton's Agoniſtes, l.* 1076.

Why ſhould our poet petition Iſis for her ſafe delivery, and afterwards *condole* her miſcarriage. *Dryden.*

CONDO'LEMENT. *n. ſ.* [from *condole.*] Grief; ſorrow; mourning.

To perſevere
In obſtinate *condolement*, is a courſe
Of impious ſtubbornneſs, unmanly grief. *Shakeſp. Hamlet.*

CONDO'LENCE. *n. ſ.* [*condolance*, French.] The expreſſion of grief for the ſorrows of another; the civilities and meſſages of friends upon any loſs or misfortune.

The reader will excuſe this digreſſion, due by way of *condolence* to my worthy brethren. *Arbuth. Preface to J. Bull.*

A CONDO'LER. *n. ſ.* [from *condole.*] One that compliments another upon his misfortunes.

CONDONA'TION. *n. ſ.* [*condonatio*, Lat.] A pardoning; a forgiving. *Dict.*

To CONDU'CE. *v. n.* [*conduco*, Lat.] To promote an end; to contribute; to ſerve to ſome purpoſe. Followed by *to.*

The boring of holes in that kind of wood, and then laying it abroad, ſeemeth to *conduce* to make it ſhine. *Bac. Nat. Hiſt.*

The means and preparations that may *conduce* unto the enterprize. *Bacon's Holy War.*

Every man does love or hate things, according as he apprehends them to *conduce* to this end, or to contradict it. *Tillotſ.*

They may *conduce* to farther diſcoveries for compleating the theory of light. *Newton.*

To CONDU'CE. *v. a.* To conduct; to accompany in order to ſhew the way. In this ſenſe I have only found it in the following paſſage.

He was ſent to *conduce* hither the princeſs Henrietta-Maria. *Wotton.*

CONDU'CIBLE. *adj.* [*conducibilis*, Latin.] Having the power of conducing; having a tendency to promote or forward.

To both, the medium which is moſt propitious and *conducible*, is air. *Bacon's Natural Hiſtory*, Nº. 265.

Thoſe motions of generations and corruptions, and of the *conducibles* thereunto, are wiſely and admirably ordered and contemporated by the wiſe providence of the rector of all things. *Hale's Origin of Mankind.*

None of theſe magnetical experiments are ſufficient for a perpetual motion, though thoſe kind of qualities ſeem moſt *conducible* unto it. *Wilkins's Math. Magic.*

Our Saviour hath enjoined us a reaſonable ſervice: all his laws are in themſelves *conducible* to the temporal intereſt of them that obſerve them. *Bentley's Sermons.*

CONDU'CIBLENESS. *n. ſ.* [from *conducible.*] The quality of contributing to any end. *Dict.*

CONDU'CIVE. *adj.* [from *conduce.*] That which may contribute to any end; having the power of forwarding or promoting.

An action, however *conducive* to the good of our country, will be repreſented as prejudicial to it. *Addiſon's Freeholder.*

Thoſe proportions of the good things of this life, which are moſt conſiſtent with the intereſts of the ſoul, are alſo moſt *conducive* to our preſent felicity. *Rogers, Serm.* 2.

CONDU'CIVENESS. *n. ſ.* [from *conducive.*] The quality of conducing.

I mention ſome examples of the *conduciveneſs* of the ſmallneſs of a body's parts to its fluidity. *Boyle's Hiſt. of Fluidity.*

CO'NDUCT. *n. ſ.* [*conduit*, Fr. *con* and *ductus*, Latin.]

1. Management; economy.

Young men, in the *conduct* and manage of actions, embrace more than they can hold, ſtir more than they can quiet, and fly to the end without conſideration of the means. *Bacon.*

How void of reaſon are our hopes and fears!
What in the *conduct* of our life appears
So well deſign'd, ſo luckily begun,
But when we have our wiſh, we wiſh undone? *Dryd. Juv.*

2. The act of leading troops; the duty of a general.

Conduct of armies is a prince's art. *Waller.*

3. Convoy; eſcorte; guard.

I was aſhamed to aſk the king footmen and horſemen, and *conduct* for ſafeguard againſt our adverſaries. 1 *Eſdr.* viii. 51.

His majeſty,
Tend'ring my perſon's ſafety, hath appointed
This *conduct* to convey me to the Tower. *Shakeſ. Rich.* III.

4. The act of convoying or guarding.

Some three or four of you,
Go, give him courteous *conduct* to this place. *Shakeſpeare.*

5. A warrant by which a convoy is appointed, or ſafety is aſſured.

6. Behaviour; regular life.

Though all regard for reputation is not quite laid aſide, it is ſo low, that very few think virtue and *conduct* of abſolute neceſſity for preſerving it. *Swift.*

To CONDU'CT. *v. a.* [*conduire*, French.]

1. To lead; to direct; to accompany in order to ſhew the way.

I ſhall ſtrait *conduct* you to a hill ſide, where I will point you out the right path. *Milton on Education.*

O may thy pow'r, propitious ſtill to me,
Conduct my ſteps to find the fatal tree,
In this deep foreſt. *Dryden's Æn.*

2. To uſher, and to attend in civility.

Pray, receive them nobly, and *conduct* them
Into our preſence. *Shakeſpeare's Henry* VIII.

Aſcanius bids 'em be *conducted* in. *Dryden's Æn.*

3. To manage; as, *to conduct an affair.*

4. To head an army; to order troops.

CONDUCTI'TIOUS. *adj.* [*conductitius*, Latin.] Hired; employed for wages.

The perſons were neither titularies nor perpetual curates, but perſons intirely *conductitious* and removeable at pleaſure. *Ayliffe's Parergon.*

CONDU'CTOR. *n. ſ.* [from *conduct.*]

1. A leader; one who ſhews another the way by accompanying him.

Shame of change, and fear of future ill,
And zeal, the blind *conductor* of the will. *Dryden.*

2. A chief; a general.

Who is *conductor* of his people?—
As 'tis ſaid, the baſtard ſon of Glo'ſter. *Shakeſp. K. Lear.*

3. A manager; a director.

If he did not intirely project the union and regency, none will deny him to have been the chief *conductor* in both. *Addiſon.*

4. An inſtrument to put up into the bladder, to direct the knife in cutting for the ſtone. *Quincy.*

CONDU'CTRESS. *n. ſ.* [from *conduct.*] A woman that directs; directreſs.

CO'NDUIT. *n. ſ.* [*conduit*, French.]

1. A canal of pipes for the conveyance of waters; an aqueduct.

Water, in *conduit* pipes, can riſe no higher
Than the well-head from whence it firſt doth ſpring. *Davies.*

This face of mine is hid
In ſap conſuming winter's drizzled ſnow,
And all the *conduits* of my blood froze up. *Shakeſpeare.*

God is the fountain of honour; and the *conduit*, by which he conveys it to the ſons of men, are virtuous and generous practices. *South's Sermons.*

Theſe organs are the nerves which are the *conduits* to convey them from without, to their audience in the brain. *Locke.*

Wiſe nature likewiſe, they ſuppoſe,
Has drawn two *conduits* down our noſe. *Prior.*

2. The pipe or cock at which water is drawn.

I charge and command, that the *conduit* run nothing but claret wine. *Shakeſpeare's Henry* VI. *p.* ii.

CONDUPLICA'TION. *n. ſ.* [*conduplicatio*, Latin.] A doubling; a duplicate.

CONE. *n. ſ.* [κῶνος. Τȣ̃ κώνȣ βάσις κύκλος ἐςί, *Ariſtotle.*] A ſolid body, of which the baſe is a circle, and which ends in a point.

CO'NEY. See CONY.

To CONFA'BULATE. *v. n.* [*confabulo*, Lat.] To talk eaſily or careleſly together; to chat; to prattle.

CONFABULA'TION. *n. ſ.* [*confabulatio*, Lat.] Eaſy converſation; chearful and careleſs talk.

CONFA'BULATORY. *adj.* [from *confabulate.*] Belonging to talk or prattle.

CONFARREA'TION. *n. ſ.* [*confarreatio*, Lat. from *far corn.*] The ſolemnization of marriage by eating bread together.

By the ancient laws of Romulus, the wife was by *confarreation* joined to the huſband. *Ayliffe's Parergon.*

To CO'NFECT. *v. a.* [*confectus*, Latin.] To make up into ſweetmeats; to preſerve with ſugar. It ſeems now corrupted into *comfit.*

CO'NFECT. *n. ſ.* [from the verb.] A ſweetmeat.

CONFE'CTION. *n. ſ.* [*confectio*, Latin.]

1. A preparation of fruit, or juice of fruit, with ſugar; a ſweetmeat.

Haſt thou not learn'd me to preſerve? yea ſo,
That our great king himſelf doth woo me oft
For my *confections?* *Shakeſpeare's Cymbeline.*

They have in Turky and the Eaſt certain *confections*, which they call ſervets, which are like to candied conſerves, and are made of ſugar and lemons. *Bacon's Natural Hiſtory.*

He ſaw him devour fiſh and fleſh, ſwallow wines and ſpices, *confections* and fruits of numberleſs ſweets and flavours. *Addiſ.*

2. An aſſemblage of different ingredients; a compoſition; a mixture.

Of beſt things then, what world ſhall yield *confection*
To liken her? *Shakeſpeare.*

There will be a new *confection* of mould, which perhaps will alter the seed. *Bacon's Natural History*, N°. 528.

CONFE'CTIONARY. *n. s.* [from *confection*.] One whose trade is to make sweetmeats.

Myself,
Who had the world as my *confectionary*,
The mouths, the tongues, the eyes, the hearts of men
At duty, more than I could frame employments. *Shakesp.*

CONFE'CTIONER *n. s.* [from *confection*.] One whose trade is to make confections or sweetmeats.

Confectioners make much use of whites of eggs. *Boyle.*

CONFE'DERACY. *n. s.* [*confederation*, Fr. *fœdus*, Latin.] A league; a contract by which several persons or bodies of men engage to support each other; union; engagement; federal compact.

What *confederacy* have you with the traitors? *Sh. K. Lear.*

Judas sent them to Rome, to make a league of amity and *confederacy* with them. *1 Mac.* viii. 17.

Virgil has a whole *confederacy* against him, and I must endeavour to defend him. *Dryden's Virg. Æn. Dedication.*

The friendships of the world are oft
Confederacies in vice, or leagues of pleasure. *Addison.*

An avaricious man in office is in *confederacy* with the whole clan of his district, or dependance; which, in modern terms of art, is called to live and let live. *Swift's Examiner*, N°. 27.

To CONFE'DERATE. *v. a.* [*confederer*, French.] To join in a league; to unite; to ally.

They were secretly *confederated* with Charles's enemy. *Knolles's History of the Turks.*

To CONFE'DERATE. *v. n.* To league; to unite in a league.

By words men come to know one another's minds; by those they covenant and *confederate*. *South's Sermons.*

It is a *confederating* with him to whom the sacrifice is offered. *Atterbury.*

CONFE'DERATE. *adj.* [from the verb.] United in league.

For they have consulted together with one consent: they are *confederate* against thee. *Ps.* lxxxiii. 5.

All the swords
In Italy, and her *confederate* arms,
Could not have made this peace. *Shakespeare's Coriolanus.*

While the mind of man looketh upon second causes scattered, it may sometimes rest in them, and go no farther; but when it beholdeth the chain of them *confederate* and linked together, it must need fly to providence and deity. *Bacon.*

Oh race *confed'rate* into crimes, that prove
Triumphant o'er th' eluded rage of Jove! *Pope's Statius.*

In a *confederate* war, it ought to be considered which party has the deepest share in the quarrel. *Swift.*

CONFE'DERATE. *n. s.* [from the verb.] One who engages to support another; an ally.

Sir Edmond Courtney, and the haughty prelate,
With many more *confederates*, are in arms. *Sh. Richard* III.

We still have fresh recruits in store,
If our *confederates* can afford us more. *Dryden's Æn.*

CONFEDERA'TION. *n. s.* [*confederation*, French.] League; compact of mutual support; alliance.

The three princes enter into some strict league and *confederation* amongst themselves. *Bacon's Henry* VII.

Nor can those *confederations* or designs be durable, when subjects make bankrupt of their allegiance. *King Charles.*

To CONFE'R. *v. n.* [*confero*, Lat. *conferer*, French.] To discourse with another upon a stated subject; to ventilate any question by oral discussion; to converse solemnly; to talk gravely together; to compare sentiments.

You will hear us *confer* of this, and by an auricular assurance have your satisfaction. *Shakespeare's King Lear.*

Reading makes a full man, conference a ready man, and writing an exact man; and therefore, if a man write little, he had need have a great memory; if he *confer* little, he had need have a present wit; and if he read little, he had need have much cunning, to seem to know that he doth not. *Bacon.*

When they had commanded them to go aside out of the council, they *conferred* among themselves. *Acts*, iv. 15.

He was thought to *confer* with the lord Colepeper upon the subject; but had some particular thoughts, upon which he then *conferred* with nobody. *Clarendon*, *b.* viii.

The Christian princess in her tent *confers*
With fifty of your learn'd philosophers;
Whom with such eloquence she does persuade,
That they are captives to her reasons made. *Dryd. Tyr. Love.*

To CONFE'R. *v. a.*

1. To compare; to examine by comparison with other things of the same kind.

The words in the 8th verse, *conferred* with the same words in the 20th, make it manifest. *Raleigh's History of the World.*

If we *confer* these observations with others of the like nature, we may find cause to rectify the general opinion. *Boyle.*

Pliny *conferring* his authors, and comparing their works together, found those that went before transcribed by those that followed. *Brown's Vulgar Errours*, *b* i. *c* 6.

2. To give; to bestow; with *on* before him who receives the gift.

Rest to the limbs, and quiet I *confer*
On troubled minds. *Waller.*

The *conferring* this honour *upon* him would increase the credit he had. *Clarendon*, *b.* viii.

Coronation to a king, *confers* no royal authority *upon* him. *South.*

There is not the least intimation in scripture of this privilege *conferred upon* the Roman church. *Tillotson.*

Thou *conferrest* the benefits, and he receives them; the first produces love, and the last ingratitude. *Arbuth. Hist. of J. Bull.*

3. To contribute; to conduce. With *to*.

The closeness and compactness of the parts resting together, doth much *confer to* the strength of the union. *Glanv.*

CO'NFERENCE. *n. s.* [*conference*, French.]

1. The act of conversing on serious subjects; formal discourse; oral discussion of any question.

I shall grow skilful in country matters, if I have often *conference* with your servant. *Sidney*, *b.* ii.

Sometime they deliver it, whom privately zeal and piety moveth to be instructors of others by *conference*; sometime of them it is taught, whom the church hath called to the publick, either reading thereof, or interpreting. *Hooker*, *b.* v. *s.* 22.

What passion hangs these weights upon my tongue!
I cannot speak to her; yet she urg'd *conference*. *Shakespeare.*

2. An appointed meeting for discussing some point, by personal debate.

3. Comparison; examination of different things by comparison of each with other.

Our diligence must search out all helps and furtherances, which scriptures, councils, laws, and the mutual *conference* of all men's collections and observations may afford. *Hooker.*

The *conference* of these two places, containing so excellent a piece of learning as this, expressed by so worthy a wit as Tully's was, must needs bring on pleasure to him that maketh true account of learning. *Ascham's Schoolmaster.*

CONFE'RRER. *n. s.* [from *confer*.]

1. He that converses.
2. He that bestows.

To CONFE'SS. *v. a.* [*confesser*, Fr. *confiteor confessum*, Latin.]

1. To acknowledge a crime; to own a failure.

He doth in some sort confess it. If it be *confessed*, it is not redressed. *Shakespeare's Merry Wives of Windsor.*

Human faults with human grief *confess*;
'Tis thou art chang'd. *Prior.*

2. It has *of* before the thing confessed, when it is used reciprocally.

Confess thee freely *of* thy sin;
For to deny each article with oath,
Cannot remove nor choke the strong conception. *Sh. Othello.*

3. To disclose the state of the conscience to the priest, in order to repentance and pardon.

If our sin be only against God, yet to *confess* it to his minister may be of good use. *Wake's Preparation for Death.*

4. To hear the confession of a penitent, as a priest.

5. To own; to avow; to profess; not to deny.

Whosoever therefore shall *confess* me before men, him will I *confess* also before my father which is in heaven; but whosoever shall deny me before men, him will I also deny before my father which is in heaven. *Matt.* x. 32, 33.

6. To grant; not to dispute.

They may have a clear view of good, great and *confessed* good, without being concerned, if they can make up their happiness without it. *Locke.*

7. To shew; to prove; to attest.

Tall thriving trees *confess'd* the fruitful mold;
The red'ning apple ripens here to gold. *Pope's Odyssey*, *b.* vii.

8. It is used in a loose and unimportant sense by way of introduction, or as an affirmative form of speech.

I must *confess* I was most pleased with a beautiful prospect, that none of them have mentioned. *Addison on Italy.*

To CONFE'SS. *v. n.* To make confession; to disclose; to reveal; as, *he is gone to the priest to confess*.

CONFE'SSEDLY. *adv.* [from *confessed*.] Avowedly; indisputably.

Labour is *confessedly* a great part of the curse, and therefore no wonder if men fly from it. *South.*

Great genius's, like great ministers, though they are *confessedly* the first in the commonwealth of letters, must be envyed and calumniated. *Pope's Essay on Homer.*

CONFE'SSION. *n. s.* [from *confess*.]

1. The acknowledgment of a crime; the discovery of one's own guilt.

Your engaging me first in this adventure of the Moxa, and desiring the story of it from me, is like giving one the torture, and then asking his *confession*, which is hard usage. *Temple.*

2. The act of disburdening the conscience to a priest.

You will have little opportunity to practise such a *confession*, and should therefore supply the want of it by a due performance of it to God. *Wake's Preparation for Death.*

3. Profession; avowal.

Who, before Pontius Pilate, witnessed a good *confession*? *1 Tim.* vi. 13.

If

If there be one amongst the fair'st of Greece,
That loves his mistress more than in *confession*,
And dare avow her beauty and her worth,
In other arms than her's; to him this challenge. *Shakesp.*

4. A formulary in which the articles of faith are comprised.

CONFE'SSIONAL. *n. s.* [French.] The seat or box in which the confessor sits to hear the declarations of his penitents.

In one of the churches I saw a pulpit and *confessional*, very finely inlaid with lapis-lazuli. *Addison's Remarks on Italy.*

CONFE'SSIONARY. *n. s.* [*confessionaire*, Fr.] The confession-chair or seat, where the priest sits to hear confessions. *Dict.*

CO'NFESSOR. *n. s.* [*confesseur*, French.]

1. One who makes profession of his faith in the face of danger. He who dies for religion is a martyr; he who suffers for it is a confessor.

The doctrine in the thirty-nine articles is so orthodoxly settled, as cannot be questioned without danger to our religion, which hath been sealed with the blood of so many martyrs and *confessors*. *Bacon's Advice to Villiers.*

Was not this an excellent *confessor* at least, if not a martyr in this cause? *Stillingfleet.*

The patience and fortitude of a martyr or *confessor* lie concealed in the flourishing times of Christianity. *Addison's Spect.*

It was the assurance of a resurrection that gave patience to the *confessor*, and courage to the martyr. *Rogers, Sermon* viii.

2. He that hears confessions, and prescribes rules and measures of penitence.

See that Claudio
Be executed by nine to-morrow morning:
Bring him his *confessor*, let him be prepar'd;
For that's the utmost of his pilgrimage. *Shakespeare.*

If you find any sin that lies heavy upon you, disburthen yourself of it into the bosom of your *confessor*, who stands between God and you to pray for you. *Taylor.*

One must be trusted; and he thought her fit,
As passing prudent, and a parlous wit:
To this sagacious *confessor* he went,
And told her. *Dryden's Wife of Bath.*

3. He who confesses his crimes. *Dict.*

CONFE'ST. *adj.* [a poetical word for *confessed.*] Open; known; acknowledged; not concealed; not disputed.

But wherefore should I seek,
Since the perfidious author stands *confest?*
This villain has traduc'd me. *Rowe's Royal Convert.*

CONFE'STLY. *adv.* [from *confest.*] Undisputably; evidently; without doubt or concealment.

They address to that principle which is *confestly* predominant in our nature. *Decay of Piety.*

CONFI'CIENT. *adj.* [*conficiens*, Lat.] That causes or procures; effective. *Dict.*

CO'NFIDANT. *n. s.* [*confident*, French.] A person trusted with private affairs, commonly with affairs of love.

Martin composed his billet-doux, and intrusted it to his *confidant*. *Arbuthnot and Pope's Mart. Scriblerus.*

To CONFI'DE. *v. n.* [*confido*, Latin.] To trust in; to put trust in.

He alone won't betray, in whom none will *confide*. *Congr.*

CO'NFIDENCE. *n. s.* [*confidentia*, Latin.]

1. Firm belief of another's integrity or veracity; reliance.

Society is built upon trust, and trust upon *confidence* of one another's integrity. *South's Sermons.*

2. Trust in his own abilities or fortune; security; opposed to dejection or timidity.

Alas, my lord,
Your wisdom is consum'd in *confidence*:
Do not go forth to-day. *Shakespeare's Julius Cæsar.*

His times, being rather prosperous than calm, had raised his *confidence* by success. *Bacon's Henry* VII.

He had an ambition and vanity, and a *confidence* in himself, which sometimes intoxicated, and transported, and exposed him. *Clarendon.*

3. Vitious boldness; false opinion of his own excellencies; opposed to modesty.

These fervent reprehenders of things established by publick authority, are always confident and bold-spirited men; but their *confidence*, for the most part, riseth from too much credit given to their own wits, for which cause they are seldom free from errors. *Hooker, Dedication.*

4. Consciousness of innocence; honest boldness; firmness of integrity.

Be merciful unto them which have not the *confidence* of good works. 2 *Esd.* viii. 36.

Just *confidence*, and native righteousness,
And honour. *Milton's Paradise Lost, b.* ix. *l.* 1056.

5. Trust in the goodness of another.

Beloved, if our heart condemn us not, then have we *confidence* towards God. 1 *Jo.* iii. 21.

6. That which gives or causes confidence, boldness, or security.

CO'NFIDENT. *adj* [from *confide.*]

1. Assured beyond doubt.

He is so sure and *confident* of his particular election, as to resolve he can never fall. *Hammond on Fundamentals.*

I am *confident*, that very much may be done towards the improvement of philosophy. *Boyle*

2. Positive; affirmative; dogmatical.

3. Secure of success; without fear of miscarriage.

Both valiant, as men despising death; both *confident*, as unwonted to be overcome. *Sidney.*

Douglas, and the Hot-spur both together,
Are *confident* against the world in arms. *Shakesp. Hen.* IV

Be not *confident* in a plain way. *Ecclus.* xxxii. 21.

People forget how little they know, when they grow *confident* upon any present state of things. *South's Sermons.*

4. Without suspicion; trusting without limits.

He, true knight,
No lesser of her honour *confident*,
Than I did truly find her, stakes this ring. *Shak. Cymbeline.*

Rome, be as just and gracious unto me,
As I am *confident* and kind to thee. *Shakesp. Tit. and Andr.*

5. Bold to a vice; elated with false opinion of his own excellencies; impudent.

CO'NFIDENT. *n. s.* [from *confide.*] One trusted with secrets.

If ever it comes to this, that a man can say of his *confident*, he would have deceived me, he has said enough. *South.*

You love me for no other end,
But to become my *confident* and friend;
As such, I keep no secret from your sight. *Dryden's Aureng.*

CO'NFIDENTLY. *adv.* [from *confident.*]

1. Without doubt; without fear of miscarriage.

We shall not be ever the less likely to meet with success, if we do not expect it too *confidently*. *Atterbury's Sermons.*

2. With firm trust.

The maid becomes a youth; no more delay
Your vows, but look, and *confidently* pay. *Dryden.*

3. Without appearance of doubt; without suspecting any failure or deficiency; positively; dogmatically.

Many men least of all know what they themselves most *confidently* boast. *Ben. Johnson's Discoveries.*

It is strange how the ancients took up experiments upon credit, and yet did build great matters upon them: the observation of some of the best of them, delivered *confidently*, is, that a vessel filled with ashes will receive the like quantity of water as if it had been empty; but this is utterly untrue. *Bacon's Natural History*, N°. 34.

Every fool may believe, and pronounce *confidently*; but wise men will conclude firmly. *South.*

CO'NFIDENTNESS. *n. s.* [from *confident.*] Favourable opinion of one's own power; assurance. *Dict.*

CONFIGURA'TION. *n. s.* [*configuration*, French.]

1. The form of the various parts of any thing, as they are adapted to each other.

The different effects of fire and water, which we call heat and cold, result from the so differing *configuration* and agitation of their particles. *Glanville's Sceps. c.* 12.

No other account can be given of the different animal secretions, than the different *configuration* and action of the solid parts. *Arbuthnot on Aliments.*

There is no plastick virtue concerned in shaping them, but the *configurations* of the particles whereof they consist. *Woodw.*

2. The face of the horoscope, according to the aspects of the planets towards each other at any time.

To CONFI'GURE. *v. a.* [from *figura*, Latin.] To dispose into any form.

Mother earth brought forth legs, arms, and other members of the body, scattered and distinct, at their full growth; which coming together, cementing, and so *configuring* themselves into human shape, made lusty men. *Bentley's Sermons.*

CO'NFINE. *n. s.* [*confinis*, Lat. It had formerly the accent on the last syllable.] Common boundary; border; edge.

Here in these *confines* slily have I lurk'd,
To watch the waining of mine enemies. *Shakesp. Rich.* III.

You are old:
Nature in you stands on the very verge
Of her *confine*. *Shakespeare's King Lear.*

The *confines* of the river Niger, where the negroes are, are well watered. *Bacon's Natural History*, N°. 399.

'Twas ebbing darkness, past the noon of night,
And Posphor on the *confines* of the night. *Dryd. Fables.*

The idea of duration, equal to a revolution of the sun, is applicable to duration, where no motion was; as the idea of a foot, taken from bodies here, to distances beyond the *confines* of the world, where are no bodies. *Locke.*

CO'NFINE. *adj.* [*confinis*, Latin.] Bordering upon; beginning where the other ends; having one common boundary.

To CONFI'NE. *v. n.* To border upon; to touch on different territories.

Half lost, I seek
What readiest path leads where your gloomy bounds
Confine with heav'n. *Milton's Paradise Lost, b.* ii. *l.* 975.

Full in the midst of this created space,
Betwixt heav'n, earth, and skies, there stands a place
Confining on all three. *Dryden.*

To CONFI'NE. *v. a.* [*confiner*, Fr. *confinis*, Latin.]

1. To bound; to limit.

2. To shut up; to imprison; to immure; to restrain within certain limits.

I'll not over the threshold.———
———Fy, you *confine* yourself most unreasonably: come, you must go visit the good lady. *Shakespeare's Coriolanus.*

I had been
As broad and gen'ral as the casing air;
But now I'm cabbin'd, cribb'd, *confin'd*, bound in
To saucy doubts. *Shakespeare's Macbeth.*

3. To restrain; to tie up to.

He is to *confine* himself to the compass of numbers, and the slavery of rhime. *Dryden.*

CONFI'NELESS. *adj.* [from *confine.*] Boundless; unlimited; unbounded; without end.

Black Macbeth
Will seem as pure as snow, and the poor state
Esteem him as a lamb, being compar'd
With my *confineless* harms. *Shakespeare's Macbeth.*

CONFI'NEMENT. *n. s.* [from *confine.*] Imprisonment; incarceration; restraint of liberty.

Our hidden foes,
Now joyful from their long *confinement* rose. *Dryd Virgil.*

The mind hates restraint, and is apt to fancy itself under *confinement*, when the sight is pent up in a narrow compass. *Addison's Spectator*, N°. 412.

As to the numbers who are under this restraint, people do not seem so much surprised at the *confinement* of some as the liberty of others. *Addison's Freeholder*, N°. 16.

CONFI'NER. *n. s.* [from *confine.*]

1. A borderer; one that lives upon confines; one that inhabits the extreme parts of a country.

The senate hath stirr'd up the *confiners*. *Shakesp. Cymbeline.*

Happy *confiners* you of other lands,
That shift your soil. *Daniel's Civil War.*

2. A near neighbour.

Though gladness and grief be opposite in nature, yet they are such neighbours and *confiners* in art, that the least touch of a pencil will translate a crying into a laughing face. *Wotton.*

3. One which touches upon two different regions.

The participles or *confiners* between plants and living creatures, are such as have no local motion; such as oysters *Bacon.*

CONFI'NITY. *n. s.* [*confinitas*, Latin.] Nearness; neighbourhood. *Dict.*

To CONFI'RM. *v. a.* [*confirmo*, Latin.]

1. To put past doubt by new evidence.

The testimony of Christ was *confirmed* in you. 1 *Cor.* i. 6.

Whilst all the stars, that round her burn,
And all the planets in their turn,
Confirm the tidings as they roll,
And spread the truth from pole to pole. *Addison's Spectator.*

2. To settle; to establish either persons or things.

I *confirm* thee in the high priesthood, and appoint thee ruler. 1 *Mac.* xi. 57.

Confirm the crown to me and to mine heirs. *Sh. Henry* VI.

3. To fix; to radicate.

Fernelius never cured a *confirmed* pox without it. *Wiseman.*

4. To complete; to perfect.

He only liv'd but 'till he was a man;
The which no sooner had his prowess *confirm'd*,
But like a man he died. *Shakespeare's Macbeth.*

5. To strengthen by new solemnities or ties.

That treaty, so prejudicial, ought to have been remitted rather than *confirmed.* *Swift.*

6. To admit to the full privileges of a Christian, by imposition of hands.

Those which are thus *confirmed*, are thereby supposed to be fit for admission to the sacrament. *Hammond's Fundamentals.*

CONFI'RMABLE. *adj.* [from *confirm.*] That which is capable of incontestible evidence.

It may receive a spurious inmate, as is *confirmable* by many examples. *Brown's Vulgar Errours, b.* iii. *c.* 17.

CONFIRMA'TION. *n. s.* [from *confirm.*]

1. The act of establishing any thing or person; settlement; establishment.

Embrace and love this man.———
———With brother's love I do it.—
———And let heav'n
Witness how dear I hold this *confirmation!* *Shak. Hen.* VIII.

2. Evidence by which any thing is ascertained; additional proof.

A false report hath
Honour'd with *confirmation* your great judgment. *Shakesp.*

The sea-captains answered, that they would perform his command; and, in *confirmation* thereof, promised not to do any thing which beseemed not valiant men. *Knolles's History.*

3. Proof; convincing testimony.

Wanting frequent *confirmation* in a matter so confirmable, their affirmation carrieth but slow persuasion. *Brown.*

The arguments brought by Christ for the *confirmation* of his doctrine, were in themselves sufficient. *South's Sermons.*

4. An ecclesiastical rite.

What is prepared for in catechising, is, in the next place, performed by *confirmation*; a most profitable usage of the church, transcribed from the practice of the apostles, which consists in two parts: the child's undertaking, in his own name, every part of the baptismal vow, (having first approved himself to understand it); and to that purpose, that he may more solemnly enter this obligation, bringing some godfather with him, not now (as in baptism) as his procurator to undertake for him, but as a witness to testify his entering this obligation. *Hammond on Fundamentals.*

CONFIRMA'TOR. *n. s.* [from *confirmo*, Latin.] An attester; he that puts a matter past doubt.

There wants herein the definitive *confirmator*, and test of things uncertain, the sense of man. *Brown's Vulgar Errours.*

CONFI'RMATORY. *adj.* [from *confirm.*] Giving additional testimony; establishing with new force.

CONFI'RMEDNESS. *n. s.* [from *confirmed.*] Confirmed state; radication.

If the difficulty arise from the *confirmedness* of habit, every resistance, as it weakens the habit, abates the difficulty. *Decay of Piety.*

CONFI'RMER. *n. s.* [from *confirm.*] One that confirms; one that produces evidence or strength; an attester; an establisher.

Be these sad sighs *confirmers* of thy words?
Then speak again. *Shakespeare's King John.*

The oath of a lover is no stronger than the word of a tapster: they are both the *confirmers* of false reckonings. *Shak.*

CONFI'SCABLE. *adj.* [from *confiscate.*] Liable to forfeiture.

To CONFI'SCATE. *v. a.* [*confiscare*, *confisquer*, i. e. *in publicum addicere*, from *fiscus*, which originally signifieth a hamper, pannier, basket, or freil; but metonymically the emperor's treasure, because it was anciently kept in such hampers. *Cowel.*] To transfer private property to the prince or publick, by way of penalty for an offence.

It was judged that he should be banished, and his whole estate *confiscated* and seized, and his houses pulled down. *Bacon.*

Whatever fish the vulgar fry excel,
Belong to Cæsar, wheresoe'er they swim,
By their own worth *confiscated* to him. *Dryd. Juv. Sat.* iv.

CONFI'SCATE. *adj.* [from the verb.] Transferred to the publick as forfeit.

Thy lands and goods
Are, by the laws of Venice, *confiscate*
Unto the state of Venice. *Shakesp. Merchant of Venice.*

CONFISCA'TION. *n. s.* [from *confiscate.*] The act of transferring the forfeited goods of criminals to publick use.

It was in every man's eye, what great forfeitures and *confiscations* he had at that present to help himself. *Bacon's H.* VII.

CO'NFITENT. *n. s.* [*confitens*, Latin.] One confessing; one who confesses his faults.

A wide difference there is between a meer *confitent* and a true penitent. *Decay of Piety.*

CO'NFITURE. *n. s.* [French, from *confectura*, Latin.] A sweetmeat; a confection.

It is certain, that there be some houses wherein *confitures* and pies will gather mould more than in others. *Bacon.*

We contain a *confiture* house, where we make all sweetmeats, dry and moist, and divers pleasant wines. *Bacon.*

To CONFI'X. *v. a.* [*configo confixum*, Latin.] To fix down; to fasten.

As this is true,
Let me in safety raise me from my knees;
Or else, for ever be *confixed* here,
A marble monument! *Shakesp. Measure for Measure.*

CONFLA'GRANT. *adj.* [*conflagrans*, Latin.] Burning together; involved in a general fire.

Then raise
From the *conflagrant* mass, purg'd and refin'd,
New heav'ns, new earth. *Milton's Paradise Lost, b.* xii.

CONFLAGRA'TION. *n. s.* [*conflagratio*, Latin.]

1. A general fire spreading over a large space.

The opinion deriveth the complexion from the deviation of the sun, and the *conflagration* of all things under Phaeton. *Brown's Vulgar Errours, b.* vi. *c.* 10.

Next o'er the plains, where ripen'd harvests grow,
The running *conflagration* spreads below. *Addis. Ovid's Met.*

Mankind hath had a gradual increase, notwithstanding what floods and *conflagrations*, and the religious profession of celibacy, may have interrupted. *Bentley's Sermons.*

2. It is generally taken for the fire which shall consume this world at the consummation of things.

CONFLA'TION. *n. s.* [*conflatum*, Latin.]

1. The act of blowing many instruments together.

The sweetest and best harmony is, when every part or instrument is not heard by itself, but a *conflation* of them all. *Bacon's Natural History*, N°. 225.

2. A casting or melting of metal.

CONFLE'XURE. *n. s.* [*conflexura*, Latin.] A bending or turning.

To CONFLI'CT. *v. n.* [*confligo*, Lat.] To strive; to contest; to fight; to struggle; to contend; to encounter; to engage.

Bare

Bare unhoused trunks
To the *conflicting* elements exposed,
Answer meer nature. *Shakespeare's Timon.*

You shall hear under the earth a horrible thundering of fire and water *conflicting* together. *Bacon's Natural History.*

A man would be content to strive with himself, and *conflict* with great difficulties, in hopes of a mighty reward. *Tillotson.*

Lash'd into foam, the fierce *conflicting* brine
Seems o'er a thousand raging waves to burn. *Thoms. Winter.*

A CO'NFLICT. *n.s.* [*conflictus*, Latin.]

1. A violent collision, or opposition of two substances.

Pour dephlegmed spirit of vinegar upon salt of tartar, and there will be such a *conflict* or ebullition, as if there were scarce two more contrary bodies in nature. *Boyle's Scept. Chym.*

2. A combat; a fight between two. It is seldom used of a general battle.

The luckless *conflict* with the giant stout,
Wherein captiv'd, of life or death he stood in doubt.
Fairy Queen, b. i. *can.* 7. *stanz.* 26.

It is my father's face,
Whom in this *conflict* I unawares have kill'd. *Shak. H.* VI.

3. Contest; strife; contention.

There is a kind of merry war betwixt signior Benedick and her: they never meet but there's a skirmish of wit between them.—Alas! he gets nothing by that. In our last *conflict*, four of his five wits went halting off. *Shakespeare.*

4. Struggle; agony; pang.

No assurance touching victories can make present *conflicts* so sweet and easy, but nature will shun and shrink from them. *Hooker, b.* v. *sect.* 48.

If he attempt this great change, with what labour and *conflict* must he accomplish it? *Rogers's Sermon.*

He perceiv'd
Th' unequal *conflict* then, as angels look
On dying saints. *Thomson's Summer, l.* 1190.

CO'NFLUENCE. *n.s.* [*confluo*, Latin.]

1. The junction or union of several streams.

You see this *confluence*, this great flood of visiters. *Shakes.*

Nimrod, who usurped dominion over the rest, sat down in the very *confluence* of all those rivers which watered Paradise. *Raleigh's History of the World.*

Bagdet is beneath the *confluence* of Tigris and Euphrates. *Brerewood on Languages.*

In the veins innumerable little rivulets have their *confluence* into the great vein, the common channel of the blood. *Bentley.*

2. The act of crowding to a place.

You had found by experience the trouble of all men's *confluence*, and for all matters, to yourself. *Bacon's Adv. to Villiers.*

3. A concourse; a multitude crouded into one place.

This will draw a *confluence* of people from all parts of the country. *Temple.*

CO'NFLUENT. *adj.* [*confluens*, Lat.] Running one into another; meeting.

At length, to make their various currents one,
The congregated floods together run:
These *confluent* streams make some great river's head,
By stores still melting and descending fed. *Blackm. Creation.*

CO'NFLUX. *n.s.* [*confluxio*, Latin.]

1. The union of several currents; concourse.

He quickly, by the general *conflux* and concourse of the whole people, streightened his quarters. *Clarendon, b.* viii.

2. Crowd; multitude collected.

To the gates cast round thine eye, and see
What *conflux* issuing forth, or ent'ring in. *Milt. Par. Reg.*

CONFO'RM. *adj.* [*conformis*, Latin.] Assuming the same form; wearing the same form; resembling.

Variety of tunes doth dispose the spirits to variety of passions *conform* unto them. *Bacon's Natural History, b.* x.

To CONFO'RM. *v. a.* [*conformo*, Latin.] To reduce to the like appearance, shape, or manner with something else.

Then followed that most natural effect of *conforming* one's self to that which she did like. *Sidney, b.* ii.

The apostles did *conform* the Christians as much as might be, according to the pattern of the Jews. *Hooker, b.* iv. *s.* 11.

Demand of them wherefore they *conform* not themselves unto the order of the church? *Hooker, b.* iii.

To CONFO'RM. *v. n.* To comply with; to yield to.

Among mankind so few there are,
Who will *conform* to philosophick fare. *Dryden jun. Juv.*

CONFO'RMABLE. *adj.* [from *conform.*]

1. Having the same form; using the same manners; agreeing either in exterior or moral characters; similar; resembling.

The Gentiles were not made *conformable* unto the Jews, in that which was necessarily to cease at the coming of Christ. *Hooker, b.* iv. *sect.* 11.

2. It has sometimes *to* before that with which there is agreement.

He gives a reason *conformable to* the principles. *Arbuthnot.*

3. Sometimes *with.*

The fragments of Sappho give us a taste of her way of writing, perfectly *conformable with* that character we find of her. *Addison's Spectator*, N°. 223.

4. Agreeable; suitable; not opposite; consistent.

Nature is very consonant and *conformable to* herself. *Newton.*

The productions of a great genius, with many lapses, are preferable to the works of an inferiour author, scrupulously exact, and *conformable to* all the rules of correct writing. *Addison.*

5. Compliant; ready to follow directions; submissive; peaceable; obsequious.

I've been to you a true and humble wife,
At all time to your will *conformable*. *Shakespeare's Hen.* VIII.

For all the kingdoms of the earth to yield themselves willingly *conformable*, in whatever should be required, it was their duty. *Hooker, b.* iv. *sect.* 14.

Such spiritual delusions are reformed by a *conformable* devotion, and the well-tempered zeal of the true Christian spirit. *Stratt's Sermons.*

CONFO'RMABLY. *adv.* [from *conformable.*] With conformity; agreeably; suitably.

So a man observe the agreement of his own imaginations, and talk *conformably*, it is all certainty. *Locke.*

I have treated of the sex *conformably* to this definition. *Addis.*

CONFORMA'TION. *n.s.* [French; *conformatio*, Latin.]

1. The form of things as relating to each other; the particular texture, and consistence of the parts of a body, and their disposition to make a whole; as, *light of different colours is reflected from bodies according to their different* conformation.

Varieties are found in the different natural shapes of the mouth, and several *conformations* of the organs. *Holder's Elem.*

Where there happens to be such a structure and *conformation* of the earth, as that the fire may pass freely unto these spiracles, it then readily gets out. *Woodward's Nat. History.*

2. The act of producing suitableness, or conformity to any thing.

Virtue and vice, sin and holiness, and the *conformation* of our hearts and lives to the duties of true religion and morality, are things of more consequence than the furniture of understanding. *Watts.*

CONFO'RMIST. *n.s.* [from *conform.*] One that complies with the worship of the church of England; not a dissenter.

CONFO'RMITY. *n.s.* [from *conform.*]

1. Similitude; resemblance; the state of having the same character of manners or form.

By the knowledge of truth, and exercise of virtue, man, amongst the creatures of this world, aspireth to the greatest *conformity* with God. *Hooker, b.* i. *sect.* 5.

Judge not what is best
By pleasure, though to nature seeming meet;
Created as thou art to nobler end,
Holy and pure, *conformity* divine! *Milton's Paradise Lost.*

Space and duration have a great *conformity* in this, that they are justly reckoned amongst our simple ideas. *Locke.*

This metaphor would not have been so general, had there not been a *conformity* between the mental taste and the sensitive taste. *Addison's Spectator*, N°. 400.

2. It has in some authors *with* before the model to which the conformity is made.

The end of all religion is but to draw us to a *conformity with* God. *Decay of Piety.*

3. In some *to.*

We cannot be otherwise happy but by our *conformity to* God. *Tillotson.*

Conformity in building *to* other civil nations, hath disposed us to let our old wooden dark houses fall to decay. *Graunt.*

4. Consistency.

Many instances prove the *conformity* of the essay with the notions of Hippocrates. *Arbuthnot on Aliments.*

CONFORTA'TION. *n.s.* [from *conforto*, a low Latin word.] Collation of strength; corroboration.

For corroboration and *confortation*, take such bodies as are of astringent quality, without manifest cold. *Bacon's Nat. Hist.*

To CONFO'UND. *v. a.* [*confondre*, Fr. *confundo*, Latin.]

1. To mingle things so that their several forms or natures cannot be discerned.

Let us go down, and there *confound* their language, that they may not understand one another's speech. *Gen.* xi. 7.

2. To perplex; to compare or mention without due distinction.

A fluid body and a wetting liquor are wont, because they agree in many things, to be *confounded*. *Boyle's Hist. of Fluidity.*

They who strip not ideas from the marks men use for them, but *confound* them with words, must have endless dispute. *Locke.*

3. To disturb the apprehension by indistinct words or notions.

I am yet to think, that men find their simple ideas agree, though, in discourse, they *confound* one another with different names. *Locke.*

4. To throw into consternation; to perplex; to terrify; to amaze; to astonish; to stupify.

So spake the son of God; and Satan stood
A while as mute, *confounded* what to say. *Milt. Par. Reg.*

Now with furies surrounded,
Despairing, *confounded*,
He trembles, he glows,
Amidst Rhodope's snows. *Pope's St. Cecilia.*

5. To destroy; to overthrow.

Let

Let them be *confounded* in all their power and might, and let their strength be broken. *Dan.* xxi.

The gods *confound* thee! do'st thou hold there still? *Shak.*

Confo'unded. *particip. adj.* [from *confound.*] Hateful; detestable; enormous; odious: a low cant word.

A most *confounded* reason for his brutish conception. *Grew.*

Sir, I have heard another story,
He was a most *confounded* Tory;
And grew, or he is much bely'd,
Extremely dull before he dy'd. *Swift.*

Confo'undedly. *adv* [from *confounded.*] Hatefully; shamefully: a low or ludicrous word.

You are *confoundedly* given to squirting up and down, and chattering. *L'Estrange.*

Thy speculations begin to smell *confoundedly* of woods and meadows. *Addison's Spectator*, N°. 131.

Confo'under. *n. s.* [from *confound.*] He who disturbs, perplexes, terrifies, or destroys.

Confrate'rnity. *n. s.* [from *con* and *fraternitas*, Latin.] A brotherhood; a body of men united for some religious purpose.

We find three days appointed every year to be kept, and a *confraternity* established for that purpose with the laws of it. *Stillingfleet's Defence of the Discourse on Rom. Idol.*

Confrica'tion. *n. s.* [from *con* and *frico*, Lat.] The act of rubbing against any thing.

It hath been reported, that ivy hath grown out of a stag's horn; which they suppose did rather come from a *confrication* of the horn upon the ivy, than from the horn itself. *Bacon.*

To CONFRO'NT. *v. a.* [*confronter*, French.]

1. To stand against another in full view; to face.

He spoke, and then *confronts* the bull;
And on his ample forehead, aiming full,
The deadly stroke descended. *Dryden's Virg. Æn.*

2. To stand face to face, in opposition to another.

We began to lay his unkindness unto him: he seeing himself *confronted* by so many, went not to denial, but to justify his cruel falshood. *Sidney*, *b.* ii.

In these two things the East and West churches did interchangeably both *confront* the Jews and concur with them. *Hooker*, *b.* i. *sect.* 11.

Blood hath bought blood, and blows have answer'd blows,
Strength match'd with strength, and power *confronted* power. *Shakespeare's King John.*

Bellona's bridegroom, lapt in proof,
Confronted him with self comparisons,
Point against point rebellious, arm 'gainst arm. *Shak. Macb.*

3. To oppose one evidence to another in open court.

4. To compare one thing with another.

When I *confront* a medal with a verse, I only shew you the same design executed by different hands. *Addison on Medals.*

Confronta'tion. *n. s.* [French.] The act of bringing two evidences face to face.

To CONFU'SE. *v. a.* [*confusus*, Latin.]

1 To disorder; to disperse irregularly.

2. To mix, not separate.

3. To perplex, not distinguish; to obscure.

We may have a clear and distinct idea of the existence of many things, though our ideas of their intimate essences and causes are very *confused* and obscure. *Watts's Logick.*

4. To hurry the mind.

Confus'd and sadly she at length replies. *Pope's Statius.*

Confu'sedly. *adv.* [from *confused.*]

1. In a mixed mass; without separation.

These four nations are every where mixt in the Scriptures, because they dwelt *confusedly* together. *Raleigh's History.*

2. Indistinctly; one mingled with another.

Th' inner court with horror, noise and tears,
Confus'dly fill'd; the women's shrieks and cries
The arched vaults re-echo. *Denham.*

On mount Vesuvius next he fix'd his eyes,
And saw the smoaking tops *confus'dly* rise;
A hideous ruin! *Addison's Remarks on Italy.*

I viewed through a prism, and saw them most *confusedly* defined, so that I could not distinguish their smaller parts from one another. *Newton's Opt.*

Heroes and heroines shouts *confus'dly* rise,
And base and treble voices strike the skies. *Pope.*

3. Not clearly; not plainly.

He *confusedly* and obscurely delivered his opinion. *Clarendon.*

4. Tumultuously; hastily; not deliberately; not exactly.

The propriety of thoughts and words, which are the hidden beauties of a play, are but *confusedly* judged in the vehemence of action. *Dryden's Dedicat. to the Spanish Fryar.*

Confu'sedness. *n. s.* [from *confused.*] Want of distinctness; want of clearness.

Hitherunto these titles of honour carry a kind of *confusedness*, and rather betokened a successive office than an established dignity. *Carew's Survey of Cornwal.*

The cause of the *confusedness* of our notions, next to natural inability, is want of attention. *Norris.*

Confu'sion. *n. s.* [from *confuse*]

1 Irregular mixture; tumultuous medly; disorder.

God, only wise, to punish pride of wit,
Among men's wits hath this *confusion* wrought;
As the proud tow'r, whose points the clouds did hit,
By tongues *confusion* was to ruin brought. *Davies.*

2. Tumult.

God is not a god of sedition and *confusion*, but of order and of peace. *Hooker, Preface.*

This is a happier and more comely time,
Than when these fellows ran about the streets
Crying *confusion.* *Shakespeare's Coriolanus.*

3. Indistinct combination.

The *confusion* of two different ideas, which a customary connexion of them in their minds hath made to them almost one, fills their head with false views, and their reasonings with false consequences. *Locke.*

4. Overthrow; destruction.

The strength of their illusion,
Shall draw him in to his *confusion.* *Shakespeare's Macbeth.*

5. Astonishment; distraction of mind; hurry of ideas.

Confusion dwelt in ev'ry face,
And fear in ev'ry heart,
When waves on waves, and gulphs in gulphs,
O'ercame the pilot's art. *Spectator*, N°. 489.

Confu'table. *adj.* [from *confute.*] Possible to be disproved; possible to be shewn false.

At the last day, that inquisitor shall not present to God a bundle of calumnies, or *confutable* accusations; but will offer unto his omniscience a true list of our transgressions. *Brown.*

Confuta'tion. *n. s.* [*confutatio*, Latin.] The act of confuting; disproof.

To CONFU'TE. *v. a.* [*confuto*, Latin.] To convict of errour or falshood; to disprove.

He could on either side dispute;
Confute, change hands, and still *confute.* *Hudibras.*

For a man to doubt whether there be any hell, and thereupon to live as if there were none, but, when he dies, to find himself *confuted* in the flames, must be the height of woe. *South.*

CO'NGE. *n. s.* [*conge*, French.]

1. Act of reverence; bow; courtesy.

The captain salutes you with *conge* profound,
And your ladyship curt'sies half way to the ground. *Swift.*

2. Leave; farewel.

So, courteous *conge* both did give and take,
With right hands plighted, pledges of good will. *Fairy Qu.*

To Co'nge. *v. n.* [from the noun.] To take leave.

I have *congeed* with the duke, and done my adieu with his nearest. *Shakespeare's All's well that ends well.*

CO'NGE D'ELIRE is French; and signifies, in common law, the king's permission royal to a dean and chapter, in time of vacation, to chuse a bishop. The king, as sovereign patron of all archbishopricks, bishopricks, and other ecclesiastical benefices, had, in ancient times, the free appointment of all ecclesiastical dignities; investing them first *per baculum & annulum*, and afterwards by his letters patent. In process of time he made the election over to others, under certain forms and conditions; as, that they should, at every vacation, before they chuse, demand of the king a *congè d'elire*, that is, licence to proceed to election. *Cowel.*

A woman, when she has made her own choice, for form's sake, sends a *conge d'elire* to her friends. *Spectator*, N°. 475.

Co'nge. *n. s.* [In architecture.] A moulding in form of a quarter round, or a cavetto, which serves to separate two members from one another: such is that which joins the shaft of the column to the cincture *Chambers.*

To CONGE'AL. *v. a.* [*congelo*, Latin.]

1. To turn, by frost, from a fluid to a solid state.

What more miraculous thing may be told,
Than ice, which is *congeal'd* with senseless cold,
Should kindle fire by wonderful device? *Spenser.*

In whose capacious womb
A vapoury deluge lies, to snow *congealed.* *Thomson's Winter.*

2. To bind or fix, as by cold.

Oh, gentlemen, see! see, dead Henry's wounds
Open their *congeal'd* mouths, and bleed afresh. *Shak. R.* III.

Too much sadness hath *congeal'd* your blood. *Shakespeare.*

To Conge'al. *v. n.* To concrete; to gather into a mass by cold.

When water *congeals*, the surface of the ice is smooth and level, as the surface of the water was before. *Burnet's Theory.*

Conge'alment. *n. s.* [from *congeal.*] The clot formed by congelation; concretion.

Enter the city, clip your wives, your friends;
Tell them your feats, whilst they with joyful tears
Wash the *congealment* from your wounds. *Sh. Ant. and Cleop.*

Conge'lable. *adj.* [from *congeal.*] Susceptible of congelation; capable of losing its fluidity.

The consistencies of bodies are very divers: dense, rare, tangible, pneumatical, fixed, hard, soft, *congelable*, not *congelable*, liquefiable, not liquefiable. *Bacon*, N°. 839.

The chymists define salt, from some of its properties, to be a body fixable in the fire, and *congelable* again by cold into brittle glebes or crystals. *Arbuthnot on Aliments.*

Congela'tion.

CONGELA'TION. *n. ſ.* [from *congeal.*]

1. Act of turning fluids to ſolids.

The capillary tubes are obſtructed either by outward compreſſion or *congelation* of the fluid. *Arbuthnot on Aliments.*

There are *congelations* of the redundant water, precipitations, and many other operations. *Arbuthnot on Air.*

2. State of being congealed, or made ſolid.

Many waters and ſprings will never freeze; and many parts in rivers and lakes, where there are mineral erruptions, will ſtill perſiſt without *congelation.* *Brown's Vulgar Errours.*

CO'NGENER. *n. ſ.* [Latin.] Of the ſame kind or nature.

The cherry-tree has been often grafted on the laurel, to which it is a *congener.* *Miller.*

CONGE'NEROUS. *adj.* [*congener*, Latin.] Of the ſame kind; ariſing from the ſame original.

Thoſe bodies, being of a *congenerous* nature, do readily receive the impreſſions of their nature. *Brown's Vulgar Errours.*

From extreme and laſting colds proceeds a great run of apoplexies, and other *congenerous* diſeaſes. *Arbuthnot on Air.*

CONGE'NEROUSNESS. *n. ſ.* [from *congenerous.*] The quality of being from the ſame original; belonging to the ſame claſs. *Dict.*

CONGE'NIAL. *adj.* [*con* and *genius*, Lat.] Partaking of the ſame genius; kindred; cognate.

He ſprung, without any help, by a kind of *congenial* compoſure, as we may term it, to the likeneſs of our late ſovereign and maſter. *Wotton.*

You look with pleaſure on thoſe things which are ſomewhat *congenial*, and of a remote kindred to your own conceptions. *Dryden's Dedication of Juvenal.*

Smit with the love of ſiſter arts we came,
And met *congenial*, mingling flame with flame. *Pope's Epiſt.*

He acquires a courage, and ſtiffneſs of opinion, not at all *congenial* with him. *Swift on the Diſſentions in Athens and Rome.*

CONGENIA'LITY. *n. ſ.* [from *congenial.*] Participation of the ſame genius; cognation of mind.

CONGE'NIALNESS. *n. ſ.* [from *congenial.*] Cognation of mind.

CONGE'NITE. *adj.* [*congenitus*, Latin.] Of the ſame birth; born with another; connate; begotten together.

Many concluſions of moral and intellectual truths, ſeem, upon this account, to be *congenite* with us, connatural to us, and engraven in the very frame of the ſoul. *Hale's Origin.*

Did we learn an alphabet in our embryo-ſtate! And how comes it to paſs, that we are not aware of any ſuch *congenite* apprehenſions? *Glanville's Sceps. c.* 5.

CO'NGER. *n. ſ.* [*congrus*, Latin.] The ſea-eel.

Many fiſh, whoſe ſhape and nature are much like the eel, frequent both the ſea and freſh rivers; as the mighty *conger*, taken often in the Severn. *Walton's Angler.*

CONGE'RIES. *n. ſ.* [Latin.] A maſs of ſmall bodies heaped up together.

The air is nothing but a *congeries* or heap of ſmall, and, for the moſt part, of flexible particles, of ſeveral ſizes, and of all kinds of figures. *Boyle.*

To CONGE'ST. *v. a.* [*congero*, *congeſtum*, Lat.] To heap up; to gather together.

CONGE'STIBLE. *adj.* [from *congeſt.*] That may be heaped up. *Dict.*

CONGE'STION. *n. ſ.* [*congeſtio*, Latin.]

A collection of matter, as in abſceſſes and tumours. *Quincy.*

Congeſtion is then ſaid to be the cauſe of a tumour, when the growth of it is ſlow, and without pain. *Wiſeman.*

CO'NGIARY. *n. ſ.* [*congiarium*, from *congius*, a meaſure of corn, Lat.] A gift diſtributed to the Roman people or ſoldiery, originally in corn, afterwards in money.

We ſee on them the emperor and general officers, ſtanding as they diſtributed a *congiary* to the ſoldiers or people. *Addiſon.*

To CONGLA'CIATE. *v. n.* [*conglaciatus*, Latin.] To turn to ice.

No other doth properly *conglaciate* but water; for the determination of quickſilver is properly fixation, and that of milk coagulation. *Brown's Vulgar Errours, b.* ii. *c.* 1.

CONGLACIA'TION. *n. ſ.* [from *conglaciate.*] The ſtate of being changed, or act of changing into ice.

If cryſtal be a ſtone, it is concreted by a mineral ſpirit and lapidifical principles; for, while it remained in a fluid body, it was a ſubject very unfit for proper *conglaciation.* *Brown.*

To CO'NGLOBATE. *v. a.* [*conglobatus*, Latin.] To gather into a hard firm ball.

The teſticle, as is ſaid, is one large *conglobated* gland, conſiſting of ſoft fibres, all in one convolution. *Grew's Coſmol.*

CO'NGLOBATE. *adj.* [from the verb.] Moulded into a firm ball, of which the fibres are not diſtinctly viſible.

Fluids are ſeparated from the blood in the liver, and the other *conglobate* and conglomerate glands. *Cheyne's Phil. Prin.*

CO'NGLOBATELY. *adv.* [from *conglobate.*] In a ſpherical form. *Dict.*

CONGLOBA'TION. *n. ſ.* [from *conglobate.*] A round body; collection into a round maſs.

In this ſpawn are diſcerned many ſpecks, or little *conglobations*, which in time become black. *Brown's Vulgar Errours.*

To CONGLO'BE. *v. a.* [*conglobo*, Lat.] To gather into a round maſs; to conſolidate in a ball.

Then he founded, then *conglob'd*
Like things to like. *Milton's Paradiſe Loſt, b.* vii. *l.* 239.
For all their centre found,
Hung to the goddeſs, and coher'd around:
Not cloſer, orb in orb *conglob'd*, are ſeen
The buzzing bees about their duſky queen. *Pope's Dunciad.*

To CONGLO'BE. *v. n.* To coaleſce into a round maſs.

Thither they
Haſted with glad precipitance, up-roll'd
As drops on duſt *conglobing* from the dry. *Milton's Par. Loſt.*

To CONGLO'MERATE. *v. a.* [*conglomero*, Lat.] To gather into a ball, like a ball of thread; to inweave into a round maſs.

The liver is one great *conglomerated* gland, compoſed of innumerable ſmall glands, each of which conſiſteth of ſoft fibres, in a diſtinct or ſeparate convolution. *Grew's Coſmol.*

CONGLO'MERATE. *adj.* [from the verb.]

1. Gathered into a round ball, ſo as that the conſtituent parts and fibres are diſtinct.

Fluids are ſeparated in the liver, and the other conglobate and *conglomerate* glands. *Cheyne's Phil. Prin.*

2. Collected; twiſted together.

The beams of light, when they are multiplied and *conglomerate*, generate heat. *Bacon's Natural Hiſtory*, N°. 267.

CONGLOMERA'TION. *n. ſ.* [from *conglomerate.*]

1. Collection of matter into a looſe ball.

2. Intertexture; mixture.

The multiplication and *conglomeration* of ſounds doth generate rarefaction of the air. *Bacon's Natural Hiſtory.* N°. 267.

To CONGLU'TINATE. *v. a.* [*conglutino*, Latin.] To cement; to reunite; to heal wounds.

To CONGLU'TINATE. *v. n.* To coaleſce; to unite by the intervention of a callous.

CONGLUTINA'TION. *n. ſ.* [from *conglutinate.*] The act of uniting wounded bodies; reunion; healing.

The cauſe is a temperate *conglutination*; for both bodies are clammy and viſcous, and do bridle the deflux of humours to the hurts. *Bacon's Natural Hiſtory*, N°. 677.

To this elongation of the fibres is owing the union or *conglutination* of parts ſeparated by a wound. *Arbuth. on Aliments.*

CONGLU'TINATIVE. *adj.* [from *conglutinate.*] Having the power of uniting wounds.

CONGLUTINA'TOR. *n. ſ.* [from *conglutinate.*] That which has the power of uniting wounds.

The oſteocolla is recommended as a *conglutinator* of broken bones. *Woodward on Foſſils.*

CONGRA'TULANT. *adj.* [from *congratulate.*] Rejoicing in participation; expreſſing participation of another's joy.

Forth ruſh'd in haſte the great conſulting peers,
Rais'd from the dark divan, and with like joy
Congratulant approach'd him. *Milton's Paradiſe Loſt, b.* x.

To CONGRA'TULATE. *v. a.* [*gratulor*, Latin.]

1. To compliment upon any happy event; to expreſs joy for the good of another.

I *congratulate* our Engliſh tongue, that it has been enriched with words from all our neighbours. *Watts's Logick.*

2. It has ſometimes the accuſative caſe of the cauſe of joy, and *to* before the perſon.

An eccleſiaſtical union within yourſelves, I am rather ready to *congratulate to* you. *Spratt's Sermons.*

The ſubjects of England may *congratulate to* themſelves, that the nature of our government and the clemency of our king ſecure us. *Dryden's Preface to Aurengzebe.*

To CONGRA'TULATE. *v. n.* To rejoice in participation.

I cannot but, with much pleaſure, *congratulate* with my dear country, which hath outdone all Europe in advancing converſation. *Swift's Introduction to Genteel Converſation.*

CONGRATULA'TION. *n. ſ.* [from *congratulate.*]

1. The act of profeſſing joy for the happineſs or ſucceſs of another.

2. The form in which joy for the happineſs of another is profeſſed.

CONGRA'TULATORY. *adj.* [from *congratulate.*] Expreſſing joy for the good fortune of another.

To CONGRE'E. *v. n.* [from *gre*, French.] To agree; to accord; to join; to unite.

For government,
Put into parts, doth keep in one concent,
Congreeing in a full and natural cloſe. *Shakeſpeare's Henry* V.

To CONGRE'ET. *v. n.* [from *con* and *greet.*] To ſalute reciprocally.

My office hath ſo far prevail'd,
That face to face, and royal eye to eye,
You have *congreeted.* *Shakeſpeare's Henry* V.

To CO'NGREGATE. *v. a.* [*congrego*, Lat.] To collect together; to aſſemble; to bring into one place.

Any multitude of Chriſtian men *congregated*, may be termed by the name of a church. *Hooker, b.* iii. *ſect.* 1.

Theſe waters were afterwards *congregated*, and called the ſea. *Raleigh's Hiſtory of the World.*

Tempeſts

Tempests themselves, high seas, and howling winds,
The gutter'd rocks and *congregated* sands,
As having sense of beauty, do omit
Their mortal natures. *Shakespeare's Othello.*

The dry land, earth; and the great receptacle
Of *congregated* waters, he call'd seas;
And saw that it was good. *Milton's Paradise Lost, b.* vii.

Heat *congregates* homogeneal bodies, and separates heterogeneal ones. *Newton's Opt.*

Light, *congregated* by a burning glass, acts most upon sulphureous bodies, to turn them into fire. *Newton's Opt.*

To CO'NGREGATE. *v. n.* To assemble; to meet; to gather together.

He rails,
Ev'n there where merchants most do *congregate*,
On me, my bargains. *Shakespeare's Merchant of Venice.*

'Tis true, (as the old proverb doth relate)
Equals with equals often *congregate*. *Denham.*

CO'NGREGATE. *adj.* [from the verb.] Collected; compact.

Where the matter is most *congregate*, the cold is the greater. *Bacon's Natural History*, N°. 72.

CONGREGA'TION. *n. f.* [from *congregate.*]

1. A collection; a mass of various parts brought together.

This brave o'erhanging firmament appears no other thing to me, than a foul and pestilent *congregation* of vapours. *Shak.*

2. An assembly met to worship God in publick, and hear doctrine.

The words which the minister first pronounceth, the whole *congregation* shall repeat after him. *Hooker, b.* v. *sect.* 36.

The practice of those now-a-days that prefer houses before churches, and a conventicle before the *congregation*. *South's Sermons.*

If those preachers, who abound in epiphonema's, would look about them, they would find part of their *congregation* out of countenance, and the other asleep. *Swift.*

3. CONGREGATIONS *of Cardinals*, are assemblies distributed by the pope into several chambers, like our offices and courts. *Chambers.*

CONGREGA'TIONAL. *adj.* [from *congregation.*] Publick; pertaining to a congregation or assembly.

CO'NGRESS. *n. f.* [*congressus*, Latin.]

1. A meeting; a shock; a conflict.

Here Pallas urges on, and Lausus there;
Their *congress* in the field great Jove withstands,
Both doom'd to fall, but fall by greater hands. *Dryd. Æn.*

From these laws may be deduced the rules of the *congresses* and reflections of two bodies. *Cheyne's Phil. Prin.*

2. An appointed meeting for settlement of affairs between different nations.

CONGRE'SSIVE. *adj.* [from *congress.*] Meeting; encountering; coming together.

If it be understood of sexes conjoined, all plants are female; and if of disjoined, and *congressive* generation, there is no male or female in them. *Brown's Vulgar Errours, b.* ii. *c.* 6.

To CONGRU'E. *v. n.* [from *congruo*, Latin.] To agree; to be consistent with; to suit; to be agreeable to any purpose.

Our sovereign process imports at full,
By letters *congruing* to that effect,
The present death of Hamlet. *Shakespeare's Hamlet.*

CONGRU'ENCE. *n. f.* [*congruentia*, Latin.] Agreement; suitableness of one thing to another; consistency.

CONGRU'ENT. *adj.* [*congruens*, Latin.] Agreeing; correspondent.

These planes were so separated as to move upon a common side of the *congruent* squares, as an axis. *Cheyne's Phil. Prin.*

CONGRU'ITY. *n. f.* [from *congrue.*]

1. Suitableness; agreeableness.

Congruity of opinions to our natural constitution, is one great incentive to their reception. *Glanville.*

2. Fitness; pertinence.

A whole sentence may fail of its *congruity* by wanting one particle. *Sidney.*

3. Consequence of argument; reason; consistency.

With what *congruity* doth the church of Rome deny, that her enemies do at all appertain to the church of Christ? *Hook.*

4. [In geometry.] Figures or lines which exactly correspond, when laid over one another, are in congruity.

CO'NGRUMENT. *n. f.* [from *congrue.*] Fitness; adaptation.

The *congrument* and harmonious fitting of periods in a sentence, hath almost the fastening and force of knitting and connexion. *Ben. Johnson's Discov.*

CO'NGRUOUS. *adj.* [*congruus*, Latin.]

1. Agreeable to; consistent with.

The existence of God is so many ways manifest, and the obedience we owe him so *congruous* to the light of reason, that a great part of mankind give testimony to the law of nature. *Locke.*

2. Suitable to; accommodated to; proportionate or commensurate.

The faculty is infinite, the object infinite, and they infinitely *congruous* to one another. *Cheyne's Phil. Prin.*

3. Rational; fit.

Motives that address themselves to our reason, are fittest to be employed upon reasonable creatures: it is no ways *congruous*, that God should be always frightening men into an acknowledgment of the truth. *Atterbury.*

CO'NGRUOUSLY. *adv.* [from *congruous.*] Suitably; pertinently; consistently.

This conjecture is to be regarded, because, *congruously* unto it, one having warmed the bladder, found it then lighter than the opposite weight. *Boyle's Spring of the Air.*

CO'NICAL. } *adj.* [*conicus*, Latin.] Having the form of a
CO'NICK. } cone, or round pyramid.

Tow'ring firs in *conick* forms arise,
And with a pointed spear divide the skies. *Prior.*

A brown flint of a *conick* figure: the basis is oblong. *Woodw.*

They are *conical* vessels, with their bases towards the heart; and as they pass on, their diameters grow still less and less. *Arbuthnot on Aliments.*

CO'NICALLY. *adv.* [from *conical*] In form of a cone.

In a watering pot, shaped *conically*, or like a sugar loaf, filled with water, no liquor falls through the holes at the bottom, whilst the gardener keeps his thumb upon the orifice at the top. *Boyle's Spring of the Air.*

CO'NICALNESS. *n. f.* [from *conical.*] The state or quality of being conical.

CONICK *Section. n. f.* A curve line arising from the section of a cone by a plane.

CO'NICK *Sections.* } *n. f.* That part of geometry which considers
CO'NICKS. } the cone, and the curves arising from its sections.

To CONJE'CT. *v. n.* [*conjectum*, Lat.] To guess; to conjecture.

I intreat you then,
From one that but imperfectly *conjects*,
Your wisdom would not build yourself a trouble. *Shakesp.*

CONJE'CTOR. *n. f.* [from *conject*] A guesser; a conjecturer.

For so *conjectors* would obtrude,
And from thy painted skin conclude. *Swift.*

CONJE'CTURABLE. *adj.* [from *conjecture.*] Being the object of conjecture; possible to be guessed.

CONJE'CTURAL. *adj.* [from *conjecture.*] Depending on conjecture; said or done by guess.

They'll sit by th' fire, and presume to know
Who thrives, and who declines, side factions, and give out
Conjectural marriages. *Shakespeare's Coriolanus.*

Thou speak'st it falsely, as I love mine honour,
And mak'st *conjectural* fears to come into me. *Shakespeare.*

It were a matter of great profit, save that I doubt it is too *conjectural* to venture upon, if one could discern what corn, herbs, or fruits, are likely to be in plenty or scarcity. *Bacon.*

The two last words are not in Callimachus, and consequently the rest are only *conjectural*, and an erroneous addition. *Broom's Notes on the Odyssey.*

CONJECTURA'LITY. *n. f.* [from *conjectural.*] That which depends upon guess.

They have not recurred unto chronology, or the records of time, but taken themselves unto probabilities, and the *conjecturality* of philosophy. *Brown's Vulgar Errours, b.* vi. *c.* 1.

CONJE'CTURALLY. *adv.* [from *conjectural.*] By guess; by conjecture.

Whatsoever may be at any time out of Scripture, but probably and *conjecturally* surmised. *Hooker, b.* i.

CONJE'CTURE. *n. f.* [*conjectura*, Latin.]

1. Guess; imperfect knowledge; preponderation of opinion without proof.

In the casting of lots a man cannot, upon any ground of reason, bring the event of them so much as under *conjecture*. *South's Sermons.*

2. Idea; notion; conception: not now in use.

Now entertain *conjecture* of a time,
When creeping murmur, and the poring dark,
Fills the wide vessel of the universe. *Shakesp. Henry* V.

To CONJE'CTURE. *v. a.* [from the noun.] To guess; to judge by guess; to entertain an opinion upon bare probability.

When we look upon such things as equally may or may not be, human reason can then, at the best, but *conjecture* what will be. *South's Sermons.*

A CONJE'CTURER. *n. f.* [from *conjecture.*] A guesser; one who forms opinion without proof.

If we should believe very grave *conjecturers*, carnivorous animals now were not flesh devourers then. *Brown's Vul. Err.*

I shall leave the wise *conjecturers* to their own imaginations. *Addison, Spectator*, N°. 271.

CONI'FEROUS. *adj.* [*conus* and *fero*, Latin.]

Such trees, shrubs, or herbs are *coniferous* as bear a squamose scaly fruit, of a woody substance, and a figure approaching to that of a cone, in which there are many seeds; and when they are ripe, the several cells or partitions in the cone gape or open, and the seeds drop out. Of this kind are the fir, pine, beech, and the like. *Quincy.*

To CONJO'BBLE. *v. a.* [from *con*, together, and *jobbernol*, the head.] To concert; to settle; to discuss. A low cant word.

What would a body think of a minister that should *conjobble*

jobble matters of state with tumblers, and confer politicks with tinkers? *L'Estrange.*

To CONJO'IN. *v. a.* [*conjoindre*, Fr. *conjungo*, Latin.]

1. To unite; to consolidate into one.

Thou wrong'st Pirithous, and not him alone;
But, while I live, two friends *conjoin'd* in one. *Dryden.*

2. To unite in marriage.

If either of you know any inward impediment,
Why you should not be *conjoin'd*, I charge
You on your souls to utter it. *Shakesp. Much ado, &c.*

3. To associate; to connect.

Common and universal spirits convey the action of the remedy into the part, and *conjoin* the virtue of bodies far disjoined. *Brown's Vulgar Errours, b.* ii. *c.* 3.

Men of differing interests can be reconciled in one communion; at least, the designs of all can be *conjoined* in ligatures of the same reverence, and piety, and devotion. *Taylor.*

Let that which he learns next be nearly *conjoined* with what he knows already. *Locke.*

To CONJO'IN. *v. n.* To league; to unite.

This part of his
Conjoins with my disease, and helps to end me. *Sh. Henry* IV.

CONJO'INT. *adj.* [*conjoint*, Fr.] United; connected; associate.

CONJO'INT *Degrees.* [In musick.] Two notes which immediately follow each other in the order of the scale; as *ut* and *re*. *Dict.*

CONJO'INTLY. *adv.* [from *conjoint.*] In union; together; in association; jointly; not apart.

A gross and frequent error, commonly committed in the use of doubtful remedies, *conjointly* with those that are of approved virtues. *Brown's Vulgar Errours, b.* ii. *c.* 5.

The parts of the body separately, make known the passions of the soul, or else *conjointly* one with the other. *Dryden.*

CO'NISOR. See COGNISOR.

CO'NJUGAL. *adj.* [*conjugalis*, Lat.] Matrimonial; belonging to marriage; connubial.

Their *conjugal* affection still is ty'd,
And still the mournful race is multiply'd. *Dryd. Fables.*

I could not forbear commending the young woman for her *conjugal* affection, when I found that she had left the good man at home. *Spectator*, N°. 499.

He mark't the *conjugal* dispute;
Nell roar'd incessant, Dick sat mute. *Swift.*

CO'NJUGALLY. *adv.* [from *conjugal.*] Matrimonially; connubially.

To CO'NJUGATE. *v. a.* [*conjugo*, Latin.]

1. To join; to join in marriage; to unite.

Those drawing as well marriage as wardship, gave him both power and occasion to *conjugate* at pleasure the Norman and the Saxon houses. *Wotton.*

2. To inflect verbs; to decline verbs through their various terminations.

CO'NJUGATE. *n. s.* [*conjugatus*, Latin.] Agreeing in derivation with another word, and therefore generally resembling in signification.

His grammatical argument, grounded upon the derivation of spontaneous from *sponte*, weighs nothing: we have learned in logick, that *conjugates* are sometimes in name only, and not in deed. *Bramh. Answer to Hobbs.*

CO'NJUGATE *Diameter*, or *Axis*. [In geometry.] A right line bisecting the transverse diameter. *Chambers.*

CONJUGA'TION. *n. s.* [*conjugatio*, Latin.]

1. A couple; a pair.

The heart is so far from affording nerves unto other parts, that it receiveth very few itself from the sixth *conjugation* or pair of nerves. *Brown's Vulgar Errours, b.* iv. *c.* 4.

2. The act of uniting or compiling things together.

All the various mixtures and *conjugations* of atoms do beget nothing. *Bentley's Sermons.*

3. The form of inflecting verbs through their series of terminations.

Have those who have writ so much about declensions and *conjugations*, about concords and syntaxes, lost their labour, and been learned to no purpose? *Locke.*

4. Union; assemblage.

The supper of the Lord is the most sacred, mysterious, and useful *conjugation* of secret and holy things and duties. *Taylor.*

CONJU'NCT. *adj.* [*conjunctus*, Latin.] Conjoined; concurrent; united.

It pleas'd the king his master to strike at me,
When he, *conjunct* and flatt'ring his displeasure,
Tript me behind. *Shakespeare's King Lear.*

CONJU'NCTION. *n. s.* [*conjunctio*, Latin.]

1. Union; association; league.

With our small *conjunction* we should on,
To see how fortune is dispos'd to us. *Shakesp. Henry* IV.

He will unite the white rose and the red;
Smile, heaven, upon his fair *conjunction*,
That long hath frown'd upon their enmity. *Shak. Rich.* III.

The treaty gave abroad a reputation of a strict *conjunction* and amity between them. *Bacon's Henry* VII.

Man can effect no great matter by his personal strength, but as he acts in society and *conjunction* with others. *South.*

An invisible hand from heaven mingles hearts and souls by strange, secret, and unaccountable *conjunctions*. *South.*

2. The congress of two planets in the same degree of the zodiack, where they are supposed to have great power and influence.

God, neither by drawing waters from the deep, nor by any *conjunction* of the stars, should bury them under a second flood. *Raleigh's History of the World.*

Has not a poet more virtues and vices within his circle? Cannot he observe their influences in their oppositions and *conjunctions*, in their altitudes and depressions? He shall sooner find ink than nature exhausted. *Rymer's Tragedies of last Age.*

Pompey and Cæsar were two stars of such a magnitude, that their *conjunction* was as fatal as their opposition. *Swift.*

3. A word made use of to connect the clauses of a period together, and to signify the relation they have to one another. *Clarke's Latin Grammar.*

CONJU'NCTIVE. *adj.* [*conjunctivus*, Latin.]

1. Closely united: a sense not in use.

She's so *conjunctive* to my life and soul,
That as the star moves not but in his sphere,
I could not but by her. *Shakespeare's Henry* IV. *p.* i.

2. [In grammar.] The mood of a verb, used subsequently to a conjunction.

CONJU'NCTIVELY. *adv.* [from *conjunctive.*] In union; not apart.

These are good mediums *conjunctively* taken, that is, not one without the other. *Brown's Vulgar Errours, b.* iii. *c.* 9.

CONJU'NCTIVENESS. *n. s.* [from *conjunctive*] The quality of joining or uniting.

CONJU'NCTLY. *adv.* [from *conjunct.*] Jointly; together; not apart.

CONJU'NCTURE. *n. s.* [*conjoncture*, French.]

1. Combination of many circumstances, or causes.

I never met with a more unhappy *conjuncture* of affairs than in the business of that earl. *King Charles.*

Every virtue requires time and place, a proper object, and a fit *conjuncture* of circumstances. *Addison's Spectator*, N°. 257.

2. Occasion; critical time.

Such censures always attend such *conjunctures*, and find fault for what is not done, as with that which is done. *Clarendon.*

3. Mode of union; connection.

He is quick to perceive the motions of articulation, and *conjunctures* of letters in words. *Holder's Elements of Speech.*

4. Consistency.

I was willing to grant to presbytery what with reason it can pretend to, in a *conjuncture* with episcopacy. *King Charles.*

CONJURA'TION. *n. s.* [from *conjure.*]

1. The form or act of summoning another in some sacred name.

We charge you, in the name of God, take heed:
Under this *conjuration* speak, my lord. *Shakesp. Henry* V.

2. A magical form of words; an incantation; an enchantment.

Your *conjuration*, fair knight, is too strong for my poor spirit to disobey. *Sidney.*

What drugs, what charms,
What *conjuration*, and what mighty magick,
For such proceeding I am charg'd withal,
I won his daughter with? *Shakespeare's Othello.*

3. A plot; a conspiracy. *Dict.*

To CONJU'RE. *v. a.* [*conjuro*, Latin.]

1. To summon in a sacred name; to enjoin with the highest solemnity.

He concluded with sighs and tears to *conjure* them, that they would no more press him to consent to a thing so contrary to his reason. *Clarendon.*

The church may address her sons in the form St. Paul does the Philippians, when he *conjures* them to unity. *Dec. of Piety.*

I *conjure* you! Let him know,
Whate'er was done against him, Cato did it. *Addis. Cato.*

2. To conspire; to bind many by an oath to some common design. This sense is rare.

He in proud rebellious arms
Drew after him the third part of heav'n's sons,
Conjur'd against the highest. *Milton's Paradise Lost, b.* ii.

3. To influence by magick; to affect by enchantment; to charm

What black magician *conjures* up this fiend,
To stop devoted charitable deeds? *Shakesp. Richard* III.

What is he whose griefs
Bear such an emphasis? whose phrase of sorrow
Conjures the wand'ring stars, and makes them stand
Like wonder-wounded hearers? *Shakespeare's Hamlet.*

I thought their own fears, whose black arts first raised up those turbulent spirits, would force them to *conjure* them down again. *King Charles.*

You have *conjured* up persons that exist no where else but on old coins, and have made our passions and virtues visible. *Addison on Ancient Medals.*

4. It is to be observed, that when this word is used for *summon* or *conspire*, its accent is on the last syllable, *conjúre*; when for *charm*, on the first, *cónjure*.

To CO'NJURE. *v. n.* To practise charms or enchantments; to enchant.

My invocation is honest and fair; and in his mistress's name I *conjure* only but to raise up him. *Shakes. Rom. and Jul.*

Out of my door, you witch! you hag, you baggage, you poulcat, you runaway! Out, out, out; I'll *conjure* you, I'll fortunetell you. *Shakespeare's Merry Wives of Windsor.*

CO'NJURER. *n. s.* [from *conjure.*]

1. An enchanter; one that uses charms.

Good doctor Pinch, you are a *conjurer*;
Establish him in his true sense again. *Shak. Com. of Errours.*
Figures in the book
Of some dread *conjurer*, that would enforce nature. *Donne.*
Thus has he done you British consorts right,
Whose husbands, should they pry like mine to-night,
Would never find you in your conduct slipping,
Though they turn'd *conjurers* to take you tripping. *Addison.*

2. An impostor who pretends to secret arts; a cunning man.

From the account the loser brings,
The *conj'rer* knows who stole the things. *Prior.*

3. By way of irony; a man of shrewd conjecture; a man of sagacity.

Though ants are very knowing, I don't take them to be *conjurers*; and therefore they could not guess that I had put some corn in that room. *Addison, Guardian*, N°. 156.

CONJU'REMENT. *n. s.* [from *conjure.*] Serious injunction; solemn demand.

I should not be induced but by your earnest intreaties and serious *conjurements*. *Milton on Education.*

CONNA'SCENCE. *n. s.* [*con* and *nascor*, Latin.]

1. Common birth; production at the same time; community of birth.

2. The act of uniting or growing together: improperly.

Symphysis denotes a *connascence*, or growing together. *Wiseman's Surgery.*

CONNA'TE. *adj.* [from *con* and *natus*, Latin.] Born with another; being of the same birth.

Many, who deny all *connate* notions in the speculative intellect, do yet admit them in this. *South.*

Their dispositions to be reflected some at a greater, and others at a less thickness, of thin plates or bubbles, are *connate* with the rays, and immutable. *Newton's Opt.*

CONNA'TURAL. *adj.* [*con* and *natural.*]

1. Suitable to nature.

Whatever draws me on,
Or sympathy, or some *connat'ral* force,
Pow'rful at greatest distance to unite,
With secret amity. *Milton's Paradise Lost, b.* x. *l.* 246.

2. United with the being; connected by nature.

First, in man's mind we find an appetite
To learn and know the truth of ev'ry thing,
Which is *connatural*, and born with it. *Davies.*

These affections are *connatural* to us, and as we grow up so do they. *L'Estrange.*

3. Participation of the same nature.

Is there no way, besides
These painful passages, how we may come
To death, and mix with our *connatural* dust? *Milt. Pa. Lost.*

CONNATURA'LITY. *n. s.* [from *connatural.*] Participation of the same nature; natural inseparability.

There is a *connaturality* and congruity between that knowledge and those habits, and that future estate of the soul. *Hale.*

CONNA'TURALLY. *adv.* [from *connatural.*] By the act of nature; originally.

Some common notions seem *connaturally* engraven in the soul, antecedently to discussive ratiocination. *Hale.*

CONNA'TURALNESS. *n. s.* [from *connatural.*] Participation of the same nature; natural union.

Such is the *connaturalness* of our corruptions, except we looked for an account hereafter. *Pearson on the Creed.*

To CONNE'CT. *v. a.* [*connecto*, Latin.]

1. To join; to link; to unite; to conjoin; to fasten together.

The corpuscles that constitute the quicksilver will be so *connected* to one another, that, instead of a fluid body, they will appear in the form of a red powder. *Boyle.*

2. To unite by intervention, as a cement.

The natural order of the *connecting* ideas must direct the syllogisms, and a man must see the connection of each intermediate idea with those that it *connects*, before he can use it in a syllogism. *Locke.*

3. To join in a just series of thought, or regular construction of language; as, *the authour* connects *his reasons well.*

To CONNE'CT. *v. n.* To cohere; to have just relation to things precedent and subsequent. This is seldom used but in conversation.

CONNE'CTIVELY. *adv.* [from *connect.*] In conjunction; in union; jointly; conjointly; conjunctly.

The people's power is great and indisputable, whenever they can unite *connectively*, or by deputation, to exert it. *Swift.*

To CONNE'X. *v. a.* [*connexum*, Latin.] To join or link together; to fasten to each other.

Those birds who are taught some words or sentences, cannot *connex* their words or sentences in coherence with the matter which they signify. *Hale's Origin of Mankind.*

They fly,
By chains *connex'd*, and with destructive sweep
Behead whole troops at once. *Philips.*

CONNE'XION. *n. s.* [from *connex*, or *connexio*, Lat.]

1. Union; junction; the act of fastening together; the state of being fastened together.

My heart, which, by a secret harmony,
Still moves with thine, join'd in *connexion* sweet. *Milton.*

There must be a future state, where the eternal and inseparable *connexion* between virtue and happiness shall be manifested. *Atterbury's Sermons.*

2. Just relation to some thing precedent or subsequent; consequence of argumentation; coherence.

The contemplation of the human nature doth, by a necessary *connexion* and chain of causes, carry us up to the Deity. *Hale's Origin of Mankind.*

Each intermediate idea must be such as, in the whole chain, hath a visible *connexion* with those two it is placed between. *Locke.*

A conscious, wise, reflecting cause,
That can deliberate, means elect, and find
Their due *connexion* with the end design'd. *Blackm. Creation.*

CONNE'XIVE. *adj.* [from *connex.*] Having the force of connexion; conjunctive.

The predicate and subject are joined in a form of words by *connexive* particles. *Watts's Logick.*

CONNICTA'TION. *n. s.* [from *connicto*, Lat.] A winking. *Dict.*

CONNI'VANCE. *n. s.* [from *connive.*]

1. The act of winking: not in use.

2. Voluntary blindness; pretended ignorance; forbearance.

It is better to mitigate usury by declaration, than to suffer it to rage by *connivance*. *Bacon, Essay* 42.

Disobedience, having gained one degree of liberty, will demand another: every vice interprets a *connivance* an approbation. *South's Sermons.*

A *connivance* to admit half, will produce ruinous effects. *Swift's Address to Parliament.*

To CONNI'VE. *v. n.* [*conniveo*, Latin.]

1. To wink.

This artist is to teach them how to nod judiciously, to *connive* with either eye. *Spectator*, N°. 305.

2. To pretend blindness or ignorance; to forbear; to pass uncensured.

The licentiousness of inferiours, and the remissness of superiours, is such, that the one violates, and the other *connives*. *Decay of Piety.*

With whatever colours he persuades authority to *connive* at his own vices, he will desire its protection from the effects of other men's. *Rogers, Sermon* 16.

He thinks it a scandal to government to *connive* at such tracts as reject all revelation. *Swift.*

CONNOISSE'UR. n. s. [French.] A judge; a critick: it is often used of a pretended critick.

Your lesson learnt, you'll be secure
To get the name of *connoisseur*. *Swift.*

To CO'NNOTATE. *v. a.* [*con* and *nota*, Lat.] To designate something besides itself; to imply; to infer.

God's foreseeing doth not include or *connotate* predetermining, any more than I decree with my intellect. *Hammond.*

CONNOTA'TION. *n. s.* [from *connotate.*] Implication of something besides itself; inference; illation.

By reason of the co-existence of one thing with another, there ariseth a various relation or *connotation* between them. *Hale's Origin of Mankind.*

To CONNO'TE. *v. a.* [*con* and *nota*, Latin.] To imply; to betoken; to include.

Good, in the general notion of it, *connotes* also a certain suitableness of it to some other thing. *South's Sermons.*

CONNU'BIAL. *adj.* [*connubialis*, Latin.] Matrimonial; nuptial; pertaining to marriage; conjugal.

Should second love a pleasing flame inspire,
And the chaste queen *connubial* rites require. *Pope's Odyssey.*

CO'NOID. *n. s.* [κωνοειδής.] A figure partaking of a cone; approaching to the form of a cone.

The tympanum is not capable of tension as a drum: there remains another way, by drawing it at the center into a *conoid* form. *Holder's Elements of Speech.*

CONOI'DICAL. *adj.* [from *conoid.*] Approaching to a conick form, to the form of a round pyramid.

To CONQUA'SSATE. *v. a.* [*conquasso*, Latin.] To shake; to agitate.

Vomits do violently *conquassate* the lungs. *Harvey.*

CONQUASSA'TION. *n. s.* [from *conquassate.*] Agitation; concussion.

To CO'NQUER. *v. a.* [*conquerir*, Fr. *conquirere*, Latin.]

1. To gain by conquest; to over-run; to win.

They had *conquered* them, and brought them under tribute. I *Mac.* viii. 2.

'Twas fit,
Who *conquer'd* nature, should preside o'er wit. *Pope.*
We *conquer'd* France, but felt our captive's charms. *Pope.*

2. To overcome; to subdue; to vanquish.

Both tugging to be victors, breast to breast;
Yet neither conqueror, nor *conquer'd*. *Shakesp. Henry* VI.

Anna *conquers* but to save,
And governs but to bless. *Smith.*

3. To surmount; to overcome; as, *he conquered his reluctance.*

To Co'nquer. *v. n.* To get the victory; to overcome.

Put him to choler straight: he hath been used
Ever to *conquer*, and to have his word
Off contradiction. *Shakespeare's Coriolanus.*

Equal success had set these champions high,
And both resolv'd to *conquer*, or to die. *Waller.*

The logick of a *conquering* sword has no great propriety. *Decay of Piety.*

Co'nquerable. *adj.* [from *conquer.*] Possible to be overcome.

While the heap is small, and the particulars few, he will find it easy and *conquerable*. *South's Sermons.*

Co'nqueror. *n. s.* [from *conquer.*]

1. A man that has obtained a victory; a victor.

Bound with triumphant garlands will I come,
And lead thy daughter to a *conqueror's* bed. *Shakes. Rich.* III.

A critick that attacks authors in reputation, is as the slave who called out to the *conqueror*, *Remember, Sir, that you are a man.* *Addison's Guardian*, N°. 110.

2. One that subdues and ruins countries.

Deserving freedom more
Than those their *conquerors*, who leave behind
Nothing but ruin wheresoe'er they rove. *Milt. Parad. Reg.*

That tyrant god, that restless *conqueror*,
May quit his pleasure, to assert his pow'r. *Prior.*

Co'nquest. *n. s.* [*conqueste*, French.]

1. The act of conquering; subjection.

A perfect *conquest* of a country reduces all the people to the condition of subjects. *Davies on Ireland.*

2. Acquisition by victory; thing gained.

More willingly I mention air,
This our old *conquest*; than remember hell,
Our hated habitation. *Milton's Paradise Regained*, *b.* i.

3. Victory; success in arms.

I must yield my body to the earth,
And by my fall, the *conquest* to my foe. *Shakesp. Henry* VI.

I'll lead thy daughter to a conqueror's bed;
To whom I will retail my *conquest* won,
And she shall be sole victress. *Shakespeare's Richard* III.

Not to be o'ercome, was to do more
Than all the *conquests* former kings did gain. *Dryden.*

In joys of *conquest* he resigns his breath,
And, fill'd with England's glory, smiles in death. *Addison.*

CONSANGUI'NEOUS. *adj.* [*consanguineus*, Lat.] Near of kin; of the same blood; related by birth, not affined.

Am I not *consanguineous*? Am I not of her blood? *Shakesp.*

Consangui'nity. *n. s.* [*consanguinitas*, Latin.] Relation by blood; relation by descent from one common progenitor. Distinguished from *affinity*, or relation by marriage. Nearness of kin.

I've forgot my father;
I know no touch of *consanguinity*. *Shakes. Troil. and Cressida.*

There is the supreme and indissoluble *consanguinity* and society between men in general; of which the heathen poet, whom the apostle calls to witness, saith, We are all his generation. *Bacon's Holy War.*

The first original would subsist, though he outlived all terms of *consanguinity*, and became a stranger unto his progeny. *Brown's Vulgar Errours*, *b.* vi. *c.* 6.

Christ has condescended to a cognation and *consanguinity* with us. *South's Sermons.*

Consarcina'tion. *n. s.* [from *consarcino*, Latin, to piece.] The act of patching together. *Dict.*

CO'NSCIENCE. *n. s.* [*conscientia*, Latin.]

1. The knowledge or faculty by which we judge of the goodness or wickedness of ourselves.

When a people have no touch of *conscience*, no sense of their evil doings, it is bootless to think to restrain them. *Spenser.*

On earth,
Who against faith, and *conscience*, can be heard
Infallible? *Milton's Paradise Lost*, *b.* xii. *l.* 529.

Such a *conscience* has not been wanting to itself, in endeavouring to get the clearest information about the will of God. *South's Sermons.*

But why must those be thought to 'scape, that feel
Those rods of scorpions, and those whips of steel,
Which *conscience* shakes? *Dryden's Juv. Sat.* 13.

No courts created yet, nor cause was heard;
But all was safe, for *conscience* was their guard. *Dryd. Ovid.*

Conscience signifies that knowledge which a man hath of his own thoughts and actions; and, because if a man judgeth fairly of his actions, by comparing them with the law of God, his mind will approve or condemn him, this knowledge or *conscience* may be both an accuser and a judge. *Swift.*

2. Justice; the estimate of conscience; the determination of conscience; honesty.

This is thank-worthy, if a man, for *conscience* toward God, endure grief. 1 *Pet.* ii. 19.

Now is Cupid a child of *conscience*; he makes restitution. *Shakespeare's Merry Wives of Windsor.*

He had, against right and *conscience*, by shameful treachery, intruded himself into another man's kingdom in Africk. *Knolles's History of the Turks.*

What you require cannot, in *conscience*, be deferred beyond this time. *Milton.*

Her majesty is, without question, obliged in *conscience* to endeavour this by her authority, as much as by her practice. *Swift's Project for the Advancement of Religion.*

3. Consciousness; knowledge of our own thoughts or actions.

Merit, and good works, is the end of man's motion; and *conscience* of the same is the accomplishment of man's rest. *Bac.*

The reason why the simpler sort are moved with authority, is the *conscience* of their own ignorance. *Hooker*, *b.* ii. *s.* 6.

The sweetest cordial we receive at last,
Is *conscience* of our virtuous actions past. *Denham.*

Hector was in an absolute certainty of death, and depressed with the *conscience* of being in an ill cause. *Pope.*

4. Real sentiment; veracity; private thoughts.

Do'st thou in *conscience* think, tell me, Æmilia,
That there be women do abuse their husbands,
In such gross kind? *Shakespeare's Othello.*

They did in their *consciences* know, that he was not able to send them any part of it. *Clarendon*, *b.* viii.

5. Scruple; difficulty.

We must make a *conscience* in keeping the just laws of superiours. *Taylor's Holy Living.*

Why should not the one make as much *conscience* of betraying for gold, as the other of doing it for a crust. *L'Estr.*

Children are travellers newly arrived in a strange country; we should therefore make *conscience* not to mislead them. *Locke.*

6. In ludicrous language, reason; reasonableness.

Why do'st thou weep? Can'st thou the *conscience* lack,
To think I shall lack friends? *Shakespeare's Timon.*

Half a dozen fools are, in all *conscience*, as many as you should require. *Swift.*

Conscie'ntious. *adj.* [from *conscience.*] Scrupulous; exactly just; regulated by conscience.

Lead a life in so *conscientious* a probity, as in thought, word and deed to make good the character of an honest man. *L'Estr.*

Conscie'ntiously. *adv.* [from *conscientious.*] According to the direction of conscience.

More stress has been laid upon the strictness of law, than *conscientiously* did belong to it. *L'Estrange.*

There is the erroneous as well as the rightly informed conscience; and if the conscience happens to be deluded, sin does not therefore cease to be sin, because a man committed it *conscientiously*. *South's Sermons.*

Conscie'ntiousness. *n. s.* [from *conscientious.*] Exactness of justice; tenderness of conscience.

It will be a wonderful *conscientiousness* in them, if they will content themselves with less profit than they can make. *Locke.*

Co'nscionable. *adj.* [from *conscience.*] Reasonable; just; according to conscience.

A knave, very voluble; no farther *conscionable* than in putting on the meer form of civil and humane seeming. *Shak.*

Co'nscionableness. *n. s.* [from *conscionable.*] Equity; reasonableness. *Dict.*

Co'nscionably. *adv.* [from *conscionable.*] In a manner agreeable to conscience; reasonably; justly.

A prince must be used *conscionably* as well as a common person. *Taylor's Holy Living.*

Co'nscious. *adj.* [*conscius*, Latin.]

1. Endowed with the power of knowing one's own thoughts and actions.

Matter hath no life nor perception, and is not *conscious* of its own existence. *Bentley's Sermons.*

Among substances some are thinking or *conscious* beings, or have a power of thought. *Watts's Logick.*

2. Knowing from memory; having the knowledge of any thing without any new information.

The damsel then to Tancred sent,
Who *conscious* of th' occasion, fear'd th' event. *Dryden.*

3. Admitted to the knowledge of any thing; with *to.*

The rest stood trembling, struck with awe divine,
Æneas only *conscious to* the sign,
Presag'd th' event. *Dryden's Æn.*

Roses or honey cannot be thought to smell or taste their own sweetness, or an organ be *conscious to* its musick, or gunpowder to its flashing or noise. *Bentley's Sermons.*

4. Bearing witness by conscience to any thing.

The queen had been solicitous with the king on his behalf, being *conscious to* herself that he had been encouraged by her. *Clarendon*, *b.* viii.

Co'nsciously. *adv.* [from *conscious.*] With knowledge of one's own actions.

If these perceptions, with their consciousness, always remained in the mind, the same thinking thing would be always *consciously* present. *Locke.*

Co'nsciousness.

CONSCIOUSNESS. *n. s.* [from *conscious.*]

1. The perception of what passes in a man's own mind. *Locke.*

If spirit be without thinking, I have no idea of any thing left; therefore *consciousness* must be its essential attribute. *Watts.*

Such ideas, no doubt, they would have had, had not their *consciousness* to themselves, of their ignorance of them, kept them from so idle an attempt. *Locke.*

2. Internal sense of guilt, or innocence.

No man doubts of a Supreme Being, until, from the *consciousness* of his provocations, it become his interest there should be none. *Government of the Tongue, s.* 3.

An honest mind is not in the power of a dishonest: to break its peace, there must be some guilt or *consciousness*. *Pope.*

CO'NSCRIPT. *adj.* [from *conscribo*, Latin.] A term used in speaking of the Roman senators, who were called *Patres conscripti*, from their names being written in the register of the senate.

CONSCRI'PTION. *n. s.* [*conscriptio*, Latin.] An enrolling or registering. *Dict.*

To CO'NSECRATE. *v. a.* [*consecro*, Latin.]

1. To make sacred; to appropriate to sacred uses.

Enter into the holiest by the blood of Jesus, by a new and living way which he hath *consecrated* for us. *Heb.* x. 20.

The water *consecrate* for sacrifice,
Appears all black. *Waller.*

A bishop ought not to *consecrate* a church which the patron has built for filthy gain to himself, and not for true devotion. *Ayliffe's Parergon.*

2. To dedicate inviolably to some particular purpose, or person; with *to.*

He shall *consecrate unto* the Lord the days of his separation, and shall bring a lamb of the first year for a trespass offering. *Num.* vi. 12.

3. To canonize.

CO'NSECRATE. *adj.* [from the verb.] Consecrated; sacred; devoted; devote; dedicated.

Shouldst thou but hear I were licentious;
And that this body, *consecrate* to thee,
By ruffian lust should be contaminate. *Shak. Com. of Err.*

The cardinal standing before the choir, lets them know that they were assembled in that *consecrate* place to sing unto God. *Bacon's Henry* VII.

Into these secret shades, cry'd she,
How dar'st thou be so bold
To enter, *consecrate* to me;
Or touch this hallow'd mold? *Drayton's Queen of Cynth.*

CO'NSECRATER. *n. s.* [from *consecrate.*] One that performs the rites by which any thing is devoted to sacred purposes.

Whether it be not against the notion of a sacrament, that the *consecrater* alone should partake of it. *Atterbury.*

CONSECRA'TION. *n. s.* [from *consecrate.*]

1. A rite or ceremony of dedicating and devoting things or persons to the service of God, with an application of certain proper solemnities. *Ayliffe's Parergon.*

At the erection and *consecration* as well of the tabernacle as of the temple, it pleased the Almighty to give a sign. *Hooker.*

The *consecration* of his God is upon his head. *Num.* vi. 7.

We must know that *consecration* makes not a place sacred, but only solemnly declares it so: the gift of the owner to God makes it God's, and consequently sacred. *South.*

2. The act of declaring one holy by canonization.

The Roman calendar swells with new *consecrations* of saints. *Hale's Origin of Mankind.*

CO'NSECTARY. *adj.* [from *consectarius*, Lat.] Consequent; consequential; following by consequence.

From the inconsistent and contrary determinations thereof, *consectary* impieties and conclusions may arise. *Brown.*

CO'NSECTARY. *n. s.* [from the adjective.] Deduction from premises; consequence; corollary.

These propositions are *consectaries* drawn from the observations. *Woodward's Natural History.*

CONSECU'TION. *n. s.* [*consecutio*, Latin.]

1. Train of consequences; chain of deductions; concatenation of propositions.

Some *consecutions* are so intimately and evidently connexed to or found in the premises, that the conclusion is attained, and without any thing of ratiocinative progress. *Hale.*

2. Succession.

In a quick *consecution* of the colours, the impression of every colour remains in the sensorium. *Newton's Opt.*

3. In astronomy.

The month of *consecution*, or, as some term it, of progression, is the space between one conjunction of the moon with the sun unto another. *Brown's Vulgar Errours, b.* iv. *c.* 12.

CONSE'CUTIVE. *adj.* [*consecutif*, French.]

1. Following in train; uninterrupted; successive.

That obligation upon the lands did not come into disuse but by fifty *consecutive* years of exemption. *Arbuth. on Coins.*

2. Consequential; regularly succeeding.

This is seeming to comprehend only the actions of a man, *consecutive* to volition. *Locke.*

CONSE'CUTIVELY. *adv.* [from *consecutive.*] A term used in the school philosophy, in opposition to antecedently, and sometimes to effectively or causally. *Dict.*

To CONSE'MINATE. *v. a.* [*consemino*, Latin.] To sow different seeds together. *Dict.*

CONSE'NSION. *n. s.* [*consensio*, Latin.] Agreement; accord.

A great number of such living and thinking particles could not possibly, by their mutual contact, and pressing and striking, compose one greater individual animal, with one mind and understanding, and a vital *consension* of the whole body. *Bentley.*

CONSE'NT. *n. s.* [*consensus*, Latin.]

1. The act of yielding or consenting.

If you shall cleave to my *consent*, when 'tis,
It shall make honour for you. *Shakespeare's Macbeth.*

I am far from excusing or denying that compliance; for plenary *consent* it was not. *King Charles.*

When thou can'st truly call these virtues thine,
Be wise and free, by heav'n's *consent* and mine. *Dryd. Pers.*

2. Concord; agreement; accord; unity of opinion.

The fighting winds would stop there and admire,
Learning, *consent* and concord from his lyre. *Cowley's David.*

3. Coherence with; relation to; correspondence.

Demons found
In fire, air, flood, or under ground,
Whose power hath a true *consent*
With planet or with element. *Milton.*

4. Tendency to one point; joint operation.

Such is the world's great harmony that springs
From union, order, full *consent* of things. *Pope's Ess. on Man.*

5. In physick.

The perception one part has of another, by means of some fibres and nerves common to them both; and thus the stone in the bladder, by vellicating the fibres there, will effect and draw them so into spasms, as to affect the bowels in the same manner by the intermediation of nervous threads, and cause a colick; and extend their twiches sometimes to the stomach, and occasion vomitings. *Quincy.*

To CONSE'NT. *v. n.* [*consentio*, Latin.]

1. To be of the same mind; to agree.

2. To co-operate to the same end.

3. To yield; to give consent; to allow; to admit. With *to.*

Ye comets, scourge the bad revolting stars
That have *consented unto* Henry's death. *Shakes. Henry* VI.

In this we *consent unto* you, if ye will be as we be. *Genesis.*

Their num'rous thunder would awake
Dull earth, which does with heav'n *consent*
To all they wrote. *Waller.*

CONSENTA'NEOUS. *adj.* [*consentaneus*, Latin.] Agreeable to; consistent with.

In the picture of Abraham sacrificing his son, Isaac is described a little boy; which is not *consentaneous* unto the circumstance of the text. *Brown's Vulgar Errours, b.* v. *c.* 8.

It will cost no pains to bring you to the knowing, nor to the practice, it being very agreeable and *consentaneous* to every one's nature. *Hammond's Practical Catechism.*

CONSENTA'NEOUSLY. *adv.* [from *consentaneous.*] Agreeably; consistently; suitably.

Paracelsus did not always write so *consentaneously* to himself, that his opinions were confidently to be collected from every place of his writings, where he seems to express it. *Boyle.*

CONSENTA'NEOUSNESS. *n. s.* [from *consentaneous.*] Agreement; consistence. *Dict.*

CONSE'NTIENT. *adj.* [*consentiens*, Latin.] Agreeing; united in opinion; not differing in sentiment.

The authority due to the *consentient* judgment and practice of the universal church. *Oxford Reasons against the Covenant.*

CO'NSEQUENCE. *n. s.* [*consequentia*, Latin.]

1. That which follows from any cause or principle.

2. Event; effect of a cause.

Spirits that know
All mortal *consequences* have pronounc'd it. *Shakes. Macbeth.*
Shun the bitter *consequence*; for know,
The day thou eatest thereof, thou shalt die. *Milt. Pa. Lost.*

3. Proposition collected from the agreement of other previous propositions; deduction; conclusion.

It is no good *consequence*, that because reason aims at our being happy, therefore it forbids us all voluntary sufferings. *Decay of Piety.*

4. The last proposition of a syllogism; as, *what is commanded by our Saviour is our duty: prayer is commanded, therefore prayer is our duty.*

Can syllogism set things right?
No, majors soon with minors fight:
Or both in friendly consort join'd,
The *consequence* limps false behind. *Prior.*

5. Concatenation of causes and effects.

Sorrow being the natural and direct offer of sin, that which first brought sin into the world, must, by necessary *consequence*, bring in sorrow too. *South's Sermons.*

I felt
That I must after thee, with this thy son:
Such fatal *consequence* unites us three. *Milton's Paradise Lost.*

6. That which produces consequences; influence; tendency.

As

As it is aſſerted without any colour of ſcripture-proof, ſo it is of very ill *conſequence* to the ſuperſtructing of good life. *Hammond on Fundamentals.*

7. Importance; moment.

The inſtruments of darkneſs
Win us with honeſt trifles, to betray us
In deepeſt *conſequence.* *Shakeſpeare's Macbeth.*

The anger of Achilles was of ſuch *conſequence,* that it embroiled the kings of Greece. *Addiſon's Spectator,* N°. 267.

Their common people are ſunk in poverty, ignorance and cowardice; and of as little *conſequence* as women and children. *Swift's Preſbyterian Plea of Merit.*

CO'NSEQUENT. *adj.* [*conſequens,* Latin.]

1. Following by rational deduction.

2. Following as the effect of a cauſe. With *to.*

It was not a power poſſible to be inherited, becauſe the right was *conſequent to,* and built on, an act perfectly perſonal. *Locke.*

3. Sometimes with *upon.*

This ſatisfaction or diſſatisfaction, *conſequent upon* a man's acting ſuitably or unſuitably to conſcience, is a principle not eaſily to be worn out. *South's Sermons.*

CO'NSEQUENT. *n. ſ.*

1. Conſequence; that which follows from previous propoſitions by rational deduction.

Doth it follow that they, being not the people of God, are in nothing to be followed? This *conſequent* were good, if only the cuſtom of the people of God is to be obſerved. *Hooker.*

2. Effect; that which follows an acting cauſe.

They were ill paid; and they were ill governed, which is always a *conſequent* of ill payment. *Davies on Ireland.*

He could ſee *conſequents* yet dormant in their principles, and effects yet unborn. *South's Sermons.*

CONSEQUE'NTIAL. *adj.* [from *conſequent.*]

1. Produced by the neceſſary concatenation of effects to cauſes.

We ſometimes wrangle, when we ſhould debate;
A *conſequential* ill which freedom draws;
A bad effect, but from a noble cauſe. *Prior.*

2. Having the conſequences juſtly connected with the premiſes; concluſive.

Though theſe kind of arguments may ſeem obſcure; yet, upon a due conſideration of them, they are highly *conſequential,* and concludent to my purpoſe. *Hale's Origin of Mankind.*

CONSEQUE'NTIALLY. *adv.* [from *conſequential.*]

1. With juſt deduction of conſequences; with right connection of ideas.

No body writes a book without meaning ſomething, though he may not have the faculty of writing *conſequentially,* and expreſſing his meaning. *Addiſon's Whig Examiner.*

2. By conſequence; not immediately; eventually.

This relation is ſo neceſſary, that God himſelf cannot diſcharge a rational creature from it; although *conſequentially* indeed he may do ſo, by the annihilation of ſuch creatures. *South.*

3. In a regular ſeries.

Were a man a king in his dreams, and a beggar awake, and dreamt *conſequentially,* and in continued unbroken ſchemes, would he be in reality a king or a beggar? *Addiſon.*

CONSEQUE'NTIALNESS. *n. ſ.* [from *conſequential.*] Regular conſecution of diſcourſe. *Dict.*

CO'NSEQUENTLY. *adv.* [from *conſequent.*]

1. By conſequence; neceſſarily; inevitably; by the connection of effects to their cauſes.

In the moſt perfect poem a perfect idea was required, and *conſequently* all poets ought rather to imitate it. *Dryd. Dufreſn.*

The place of the ſeveral ſorts of terreſtrial matter, ſuſtained in the fluid, being contingent and uncertain, their intermixtures with each other are *conſequently* ſo. *Woodward.*

2. In conſequence; purſuantly.

There is *conſequently,* upon this diſtinguiſhing principle, an inward ſatisfaction or diſſatisfaction in the heart of every man, after good or evil. *South's Sermons.*

CO'NSEQUENTNESS. *n. ſ.* [from *conſequent.*] Regular connection of propoſitions; conſecution of diſcourſe.

Let them examine the *conſequentneſs* of the whole body of the doctrine I deliver. *Digby on the Soul, Dedication.*

CONSE'RVABLE. *adj.* [from *conſervo,* Latin, to keep.] Capable of being kept, or maintained.

CONSE'RVANCY. *n. ſ.* [from *conſervans,* Latin.] Courts held by the Lord Mayor of London for the preſervation of the fiſhery on the river Thames, are called *Courts of Conſervancy.*

CONSERVA'TION. *n. ſ.* [*conſervatio,* Latin.]

1. The act of preſerving; care to keep from periſhing; continuance; protection.

Though there do indeed happen ſome alterations in the globe, yet they are ſuch as tend rather to the benefit and *conſervation* of the earth, and its productions, than to the diſorder and deſtruction of both. *Woodward's Natural Hiſtory.*

2. Preſervation from corruption.

It is an enquiry of excellent uſe, to enquire of the means of preventing or ſtaying of putrefaction; for therein conſiſteth the means of *conſervation* of bodies. *Bacon's Nat. Hiſtory.*

CONSE'RVATIVE. *adj.* [from *conſervo,* Latin.] Having the power of oppoſing diminution or injury.

The ſpherical figure, as to all heavenly bodies, ſo it agreeth to light, as the moſt perfect and *conſervative* of all others. *Peacham.*

CONSERVA'TOR. *n. ſ.* [Latin.] Preſerver; one that has the care or office of keeping any thing from detriment, diminution, or extinction.

For that you declare that you have many ſick amongſt you, he was warned by the *conſervator* of the city, that he ſhould keep at a diſtance. *Bacon's New Atlantis.*

The lords of the ſecret council were likewiſe made *conſervators* of the peace of the two kingdoms, during the intervals of parliament. *Clarendon.*

Such individuals as are the ſingle *conſervators* of their own ſpecies. *Hale's Origin of Mankind.*

CONSE'RVATORY. *n. ſ.* [from *conſervo,* Latin.] A place where any thing is kept in a manner proper to its peculiar nature; as, fiſh in a pond, corn in a granary.

A *conſervatory* of ſnow and ice, ſuch as they uſe for delicacy to cool wine in ſummer. *Bacon's Natural Hiſtory,* N°. 70.

You may ſet your tender trees and plants, with the windows and doors of the greenhouſes and *conſervatories* open, for eight or ten days before April. *Evelyn's Kalendar.*

The water diſpenſed to the earth and atmoſphere by the great abyſs, that ſubterranean *conſervatory* is by that means reſtored back. *Woodward's Natural Hiſtory.*

CONSE'RVATORY. *adj.* Having a preſervative quality. *Dict.*

To CONSE'RVE. *v. a.* [*conſervo,* Latin.]

1. To preſerve without loſs or detriment.

Nothing was loſt out of theſe ſtores, ſince the part of *conſerving* what others have gained in knowledge is eaſy. *Temple.*

They will be able to *conſerve* their properties unchanged in paſſing through ſeveral mediums, which is another condition of the rays of light. *Newton's Opt.*

2. To candy or pickle fruit.

CONSE'RVE. *n. ſ.* [from the verb.]

1. A ſweetmeat made of the inſpiſſated juices of fruit, boiled with ſugar 'till they will harden and candy.

Will't pleaſe your honour, taſte of theſe *conſerves?* *Shak.*

They have in Turkey and the Eaſt certain confections, which they call ſervets, which are like to candied *conſerves,* and are made of ſugar and lemons. *Bacon's Natural Hiſtory.*

The more coſt they were at, and the more ſweets they beſtowed upon them, the more their *conſerves* ſtunk. *Dennis.*

2. A conſervatory or place in which any thing is kept. This ſenſe is unuſual.

Tuberoſes will not endure the wet of this ſeaſon, therefore ſet the pots into your *conſerve,* and keep them dry. *Evelyn.*

CONSE'RVER. *n. ſ.* [from *conſerve.*]

1. A layer up; a repoſiter; one that preſerves any thing from loſs or diminution.

He hath been moſt induſtrious, both collecter and *conſerver* of choice pieces in that kind. *Hayward on Edward* VI.

In the Eaſtern regions there ſeems to have been a general cuſtom of the prieſts having been the perpetual *conſervers* of knowledge and ſtory. *Temple.*

2. A preparer of conſerves.

CONSE'SSION. *n. ſ.* [*conſeſſio,* Latin.] A ſitting together. *Dict.*

CONSE'SSOR. *n. ſ.* [Latin.] One that ſits with others. *Dict.*

To CONSI'DER. *v. a.* [*conſidero,* Latin.]

1. To think upon with care; to ponder; to examine; to ſift; to ſtudy.

At our more *conſider'd* time we'll read,
Anſwer, and think upon this buſineſs. *Shakeſp. Hamlet.*

It is not poſſible to act otherwiſe, *conſidering* the weakneſs of our faculties. *Spectator,* N°. 465.

2. To take into the view; not to omit in the examination.

It ſeems neceſſary, in the choice of perſons for greater employments, to *conſider* their bodies as well as their minds, and ages and health as well as their abilities. *Temple.*

3. To have regard to; to reſpect; not to deſpiſe.

Let us *conſider* one another to provoke unto love, and to good works. *Heb.* x. 24.

4. A kind of interjection; a word whereby attention is ſummoned.

Conſider,
Thy life hath yet been private, moſt part ſpent
At home. *Milton's Paradiſe Regained, b.* iii. *l.* 229.

5. To requite; to reward one for his trouble.

Take away with thee the very ſervices thou haſt done, which, if I have not enough *conſidered,* to be more thankful to thee ſhall be my ſtudy. *Shakeſpeare's Winter's Tale.*

To CONSI'DER. *v. n.*

1. To think maturely; not to judge haſtily or raſhly.

None *conſidereth* in his heart, neither is there knowledge nor underſtanding. *Iſaiah* xliv. 1.

2. To deliberate; to work in the mind.

Widow, we will *conſider* of your ſuit;
And come ſome other time to know our mind. *Shak. H.*VI.

Such a treatiſe might be conſulted by Jurymen, before they *conſider* of their verdict. *Swift.*

3. To doubt; to heſitate.

Many maz'd *conſiderings* did throng,
And preſs'd in with this caution. *Shakeſpeare's Henry* VIII.

'Twas grief no more, or grief and rage were one
Within her soul; at last 'twas rage alone,
Which burning upwards, in succession dries
The tears that stood *considering* in her eyes. *Dryden's Fables.*

CONSI'DERABLE. *adj.* [from *consider.*]

1. Worthy of consideration; worthy of regard and attention.

Eternity is infinitely the most *considerable* duration. *Tillotson.*

It is *considerable* that some urns have had inscriptions on them, expressing that the lamps were burning. *Wilkins.*

2. Respectable; above neglect; deserving notice.

Men *considerable* in all worthy professions, eminent in many ways of life. *Sprat's Sermons.*

I am so *considerable* a man, that I cannot have less than forty shillings a year. *Addison's Freeholder*, N°. 1.

3. Important; valuable.

Christ, instead of applauding St. Peter's zeal, upbraided his absurdity that could think his mean aids *considerable* to him, who could command legions of angels to his rescue. *Dec. of Pi.*

In painting, not every action nor every person is *considerable* enough to enter into the cloth. *Dryden's Dufresnoy.*

Many can make themselves masters of as *considerable* estates as those who have the greatest portions of land. *Addison.*

4. More than a little. It has a middle signification between little and great.

Many had brought in very *considerable* sums of money. *Clarendon*, *b.* viii.

Those earthy particles, when they came to be collected, would constitute a body of a very *considerable* thickness and solidity. *Burnet's Theory of the Earth.*

CONSI'DERABLENESS. *n. s.* [from *considerable.*] Importance; dignity; moment; value; desert; a claim to notice.

We must not always measure the *considerableness* of things by their most obvious and immediate usefulness, but by their fitness to make or contribute to the discovery of things highly useful. *Boyle's Proemial Essay.*

Their most slight and trivial occurrences, by being theirs, they think to acquire a *considerableness*, and are forcibly imposed upon the company. *Government of the Tongue*, *s.* 9.

CONSI'DERABLY. *adv.* [from *considerable.*]

1. In a degree deserving notice, though not the highest.

And Europe still *considerably* gains,
Both by their good example and their pains. *Roscommon.*

2. With importance; importantly.

I desire no sort of favour so much, as that of serving you more *considerably* than I have been yet able to do. *Pope.*

CONSI'DERANCE. *n. s.* [from *consider.*] Consideration; reflection; sober thought.

After this cold *consid'rance*, sentence me;
And, as you are a king, speak in your state,
What I have done that misbecame my place. *Shak. H.* IV.

CONSI'DERATE. *adj.* [*consideratus*, Latin.]

1. Serious; given to consideration; prudent; not rash; not negligent.

I will converse with iron-witted fools,
And unrespective boys: none are for me,
That look into me with *consid'rate* eyes. *Shakesp. Rich.* III.

Æneas is patient, *considerate*, and careful of his people. *Dryden's Fables, Preface.*

I grant it to be in many cases certain, that it is such as a *considerate* man may prudently rely and proceed upon, and hath no just cause to doubt of. *Tillotson, Preface.*

The expediency in the present juncture, may appear to every *considerate* man. *Addison's Freeholder*, N°. 16.

2. Having respect to; regardful.

Though they will do nothing for virtue, yet they may be presumed more *considerate* of praise. *Decay of Piety.*

3. Moderate; not rigorous. This sense is much used in conversation.

CONSI'DERATELY. *adv.* [from *considerate.*] Calmly; coolly; prudently.

Circumstances are of such force, as they sway an ordinary judgment of a wise man, not fully and *considerately* pondering the matter. *Bacon's Colours of Good and Evil.*

CONSI'DERATENESS. *n. s.* [from *considerate.*] The quality of being considerate; prudence. *Dict.*

CONSIDERA'TION. *n. s.* [from *consider.*]

1. The act of considering; mental view; regard; notice.

As to present happiness and misery, when that alone comes in *consideration*, and the consequences are removed, a man never chuses amiss. *Locke.*

2. Mature thought; prudence; serious deliberation.

Let us think with *consideration*, and consider with acknowledging, and acknowledge with admiration. *Sidney.*

The breath no sooner left his father's body,
But that his wildness mortified in him;
Consideration, like an angel, came,
And whipt th' offending Adam out of him. *Shakesp. H.* V.

3. Contemplation; meditation upon any thing.

The love you bear to Mopsa hath brought you to the *consideration* of her virtues, and that *consideration* may have made you the more virtuous, and so the more worthy. *Sidney.*

4. Importance; claim to notice; worthiness of regard.

Lucan is the only author of *consideration* among the Latin poets, who was not explained for the use of the dauphin, because the whole Pharsalia would have been a satire upon the French form of government. *Addison's Freeholder*, N°. 40.

5. Equivalent; compensation.

We are provident enough not to part with any thing serviceable to our bodies under a good *consideration*, but make little account of our souls. *Ray on the Creation.*

Foreigners can never take our bills for payment, though they might pass as valuable *considerations* among your own people. *Locke.*

6. Motive of action; influence; ground of conduct.

He had been made general upon very partial, and not enough deliberated *considerations*. *Clarendon*, *b.* viii.

He was obliged, antecedent to all other *considerations*, to search an asylum. *Dryden's Virg. Æn. Dedication.*

The world cannot pardon your concealing it, on the same *consideration*. *Dryden's Juv. Dedication.*

7. Reason; ground of concluding.

Not led by any commandment, yet moved with such *considerations* as have been before set down. *Hooker*, *b.* v. *s.* 95.

Uses, not thought upon before, be reasonable causes of retaining that which other *considerations* did procure to be instituted. *Hooker*, *b.* v. *s.* 42.

8. [In law.] *Consideration* is the material cause of a contract, without which no contract bindeth. It is either expressed, as if a man bargain to give twenty shillings for a horse; or else implied, as when a man comes into an inn, and taking both meat and lodging for himself and his horse, without bargaining with the host, if he discharge not the house, the host may stay his horse. *Cowel.*

The *consideration*, in regard whereof the law forbiddeth these things, was not because those nations did use them. *Hook.*

CONSI'DERER. *n. s.* [from *consider.*] A man of reflection; a thinker.

A vain applause of wit for an impious jest, or of reason for a deep *considerer*. *Government of the Tongue.*

To CONSI'GN. *v. a.* [*consigno*, Latin.]

1. To give to another any thing, with the right to it, in a formal manner; to give into other hands; to transfer. Sometimes with *to*, sometimes *over to.*

Men, by free gift, *consign over* a place *to* the Divine Worship. *South.*

Must I pass
Again to nothing, when this vital breath
Ceasing, *consigns* me *o'er to* rest and death? *Prior.*

At the day of general account, good men are then to be *consigned over to* another state, a state of everlasting love and charity. *Atterbury.*

2. To appropriate; to quit for a certain purpose.

The French commander *consigned* it *to* the use for which it was intended by the donor. *Dryden's Fables, Dedication.*

3. To commit; to entrust.

The four evangelists *consigned to* writing that history. *Addis.*

Atrides, parting for the Trojan war,
Consign'd the youthful consort *to* his care. *Pope's Odyssey.*

To CONSI'GN. *v. n.*

1. To yield; to submit; to resign. This is not now in use.

Thou hast finish'd joy and moan;
All lovers young, all lovers must
Consign to thee, and come to dust. *Shakespeare's Cymbeline.*

2. To sign; to consent to. Obsolete.

A maid yet rosed over with the virgin crimson of modesty: it were, my lord, a hard condition for a maid to *consign* to. *Sh.*

CONSIGNA'TION. *n. s.* [from *consign.*]

1. The act of consigning; the act by which any thing is delivered up to another.

As the hope of salvation is a good disposition towards it, so is despair a certain *consignation* to eternal ruin. *Taylor.*

2. The act of signing.

If we find that we increase in duty, then we may look upon the tradition of the holy sacramental symbols as a direct *consignation* of pardon. *Taylor's Worthy Communicant.*

CONSI'GNMENT. *n. s.* [from *consign.*]

1. The act of consigning.

2. The writing by which any thing is consigned.

CONSI'MILAR. *adj.* [from *consimilis*, Latin.] Having one common resemblance. *Dict.*

To CONSI'ST. *v. n.* [*consisto*, Latin.]

1. To subsist; not to perish.

He is before all things, and by him all things *consist*. *Col.* i.

2. To continue fixed; without dissipation.

Flame doth not mingle with flame, as air doth with air, or water with water, but only remaineth contiguous; as it cometh to pass betwixt *consisting* bodies. *Bacon's Nat. History.*

It is against the nature of water, being a flexible and ponderous body, to *consist* and stay itself, and not fall to the lower parts about it. *Brerewood on Languages.*

3. To be comprised; to be contained.

I pretend not to tie the hands of artists, whose skill *consists* only in a certain manner which they have affected. *Dryden.*

A great beauty of letters does often *consist* in little passages of private conversation, and references to particular matters. *Walsh.*

4. To be composed.

The

The land would *consist* of plains and valleys, and mountains, according as the pieces of this ruin were placed and disposed. *Burnet's Theory of the Earth.*

5. To agree; not to oppose; not to contradict.

Necessity and election cannot *consist* together in the same act. *Bramhal against Hobbs.*

His majesty would be willing to consent to any thing that could *consist* with his conscience and honour. *Clarendon, b.* viii.

Nothing but what may easily *consist* with your plenty, your prosperity, is requested of you. *Sprat's Sermons.*

You could not help bestowing more than is *consisting* with the fortune of a private man, or with the will of any but an Alexander. *Dryden's Fables, Dedication.*

It cannot *consist* with the Divine Attributes, that the impious man's joys should, upon the whole, exceed those of the upright. *Atterbury.*

Health *consists* with temperance alone. *Pope's Ess. on Man.*

The only way of securing the constitution will be by lessening the power of domestick adversaries, as much as can *consist* with lenity. *Swift's Thoughts on the State of Affairs.*

CONSI'STENCE.
CONSI'STENCY. } *n. s.* [*consistentia*, low Latin.]

1. State with respect to material existence.

Water, being divided, maketh many circles, 'till it restore itself to the natural *consistence*. *Bacon's Natural History.*

The *consistencies* of bodies are very divers: dense, rare, tangible, pneumatical, volatile, fixed, determinate, indeterminate, hard, and soft. *Bacon's Natural History*, N°. 839.

There is the same necessity for the Divine influence and regimen to order and govern, conserve and keep together the universe in that *consistence* it hath received, as it was at first to give it, before it could receive it. *Hale's Origin of Mankind.*

I carried on my enquiries farther, to try whether this rising world, when formed and finished, would continue always the same, in the same form, structure, and *consistency*. *Burnet.*

2. Degree of denseness or rarity.

Let the expressed juices be boiled into the *consistence* of a syrup. *Arbuthnot on Aliments.*

3. Substance; form; make.

His friendship is of a noble make, and a lasting *consistency*. *South's Sermons.*

4. Agreement with itself, or with any other thing; congruity; uniformity.

That *consistency* of behaviour, whereby he inflexibly pursues those measures, which appear the most just and equitable. *Addison's Freeholder*, N°. 2.

5. A state of rest, in which things capable of growth or decrease continue for some time at a stand, without either; as the growth, *consistence*, and return of a tree. *Chambers.*

CONSI'STENT. *adj.* [*consistens*, Latin.]

1. Not contradictory; not opposed.

With reference to such a lord, to serve and to be free, are terms not *consistent* only, but equivalent. *South's Sermons.*

A great part of their politicks others do not think *consistent* with honour to practise. *Addison's Remarks on Italy.*

On their own axis as the planets run,
Yet make at once their circle round the sun;
So two *consistent* motions act the soul,
And one regards itself, and one the whole. *Pope's Essays.*

Shew me one that has it in his power
To act *consistent* with himself an hour. *Pope's Epist. of Hor.*

The fool *consistent*, and the false sincere;
Priests, princes, women, no dissemblers here. *Pope's Epist.*

2. Firm; not fluid.

The sand, contained within the shell, becoming solid and *consistent*, at the same time that of the stratum without it did. *Woodward's Natural History, p.* v.

CONSI'STENTLY. *adv.* [from *consistent.*] Without contradiction; agreeably.

The Phœnicians are of this character, and the poet describes them *consistently* with it: they are proud, idle, and effeminate. *Broom's Notes on the Odyssey, b.* vii.

CONSISTO'RIAL. *adj.* [from *consistory.*] Relating to the ecclesiastical court.

An official, or chancellor, has the same *consistorial* audience with the bishop himself that deputes him. *Ayliffe's Parergon.*

CO'NSISTORY. *n. s.* [*consistorium*, Latin.]

1. The place of justice in the court Christian. *Cowel.*

An offer was made, that, for every one minster, there should be two of the people to sit and give voice in the ecclesiastical *consistory*. *Hooker, Preface.*

Pius Quintus was then hearing of causes in *consistory*. *Bacon's Natural History*, N°. 98.

Christ himself, in that great *consistory*, shall deign to step down from his throne. *South's Sermons.*

2. The assembly of cardinals.

How far I've proceeded,
Or how far further shall, is warranted
By a commission from the *consistory*,
Yea the whole *consist'ry* of Rome. *Shakespeare's Hen.* VIII.

A late prelate, of remarkable zeal for the church, were religions to be tried by lives, would have lived down the pope and the whole *consistory*. *Atterbury.*

3. Any solemn assembly.

In mid air
To council summons all his mighty peers
Within thick clouds, and dark tenfold involv'd,
A gloomy *consistory*. *Milton's Paradise Regained, b.* i.

At Jove's assent the deities around,
In solemn state the *consistory* crown'd. *Pope's Statius.*

4. Place of residence.

My other self, my counsel's *consistory*, my oracle,
I, as a child, will go by thy direction. *Shakesp. Rich.* III.

CONSO'CIATE. *n. s.* [from *consocio*, Latin.] An accomplice; a confederate; a partner.

Patridge and Stanhope were condemned as *consociates* in the conspiracy of Somerset. *Hayward.*

To CONSO'CIATE. *v. a.* [*consocio*, Latin.]

1. To unite; to join.

Generally the best outward shapes are also the likeliest to be *consociated* with good inward faculties. *Wotton on Educat.*

2. To cement; to hold together.

The ancient philosophers always brought in a supernatural principle to unite and *consociate* the parts of the chaos. *Burnet.*

To CO'NSOCIATE. *v. n.* To coalesce; to unite.

If they cohered, yet by the next conflict with other atoms they might be separated again, without ever *consociating* into the huge condense bodies of planets. *Bentley's Sermons.*

CONSOCIA'TION. *n. s.* [from *consociate.*]

1. Alliance.

There is such a *consociation* of offices between the prince and whom his favour breeds, that they may help to sustain his power, as he their knowledge. *Ben. Johnson's Discoveries.*

2. Union; intimacy; companionship.

By so long and so various *consociation* with a prince, he had now gotten, as it were, two lives in his own fortune and greatness. *Wotton.*

CONSO'LABLE. *adj.* [from *console.*] That which admits comfort.

To CO'NSOLATE. *v. a.* [*consolor*, Latin.] To comfort; to console; to ease in misery.

I will be gone,
That pitiful rumour may report my flight,
To *consolate* thine ear. *Shakesp. All's well that ends well.*

What may somewhat *consolate* all men that honour virtue, we do not discover the latter scene of his misery in authors of antiquity. *Brown's Vulgar Errours, b.* vii. *c.* 17.

CONSOLA'TION. *n. s.* [*consolatio*, Latin.] Comfort; alleviation of misery; such alleviation as is produced by partial remedies.

We that were in the jaws of death, were now brought into a place where we found nothing but *consolations*. *Bacon.*

Against such cruelties,
With inward *consolations* recompens'd;
And oft supported so, as shall amaze
Their proudest persecutors. *Milton's Paradise Lost, b.* xii.

Let the righteous persevere with patience, supported with this *consolation*, that their labour shall not be in vain. *Rogers.*

CONSOLA'TOR. *n. s.* [Latin.] A comforter.

CONSO'LATORY. *n. s.* [from *consolate.*] A speech or writing containing topicks of comfort.

Consolatories writ
With studied argument, and much persuasion sought,
Lenient of grief and anxious thought. *Milton's Agonistes.*

CONSO'LATORY. *adj.* [from *consolate.*] Tending to give comfort.

To CONSO'LE. *v. a.* [*consolor*, Lat.] To comfort; to cheer; to free from the sense of misery.

Others the syren sisters compass round,
And empty heads *console* with empty sound. *Pope's Dunciad.*

CONSO'LE. *n. s.* [French.] In architecture, is a part or member projecting in manner of a bracket, or shoulder-piece, serving to support a cornice, bust, vase, beam, and frequently used as keys of arches. *Chambers.*

CONSO'LER. *n. s.* [from *console.*] One that gives comfort.

Pride once more appears upon the stage, as the great *consoler* of the miseries of man. *Comment. on Pope's Ess. on Man.*

CONSO'LIDANT. *adj.* [from *consolidate.*] That which has the quality of uniting wounds.

To CONSO'LIDATE. *v. a.* [*consolider*, Fr. *solidus*, Latin.]

1. To form into a compact and solid body; to harden; to unite into a solid mass.

The word may be rendered either he stretched, or he fixed and *consolidated* the earth above the waters. *Burnet's Theory.*

The effects of spirits in stopping hemorrhages, and *consolidating* the fibres, is well known to chirurgeons. *Arbuthnot.*

2. To combine or unite two parliamentary bills into one.

To CONSO'LIDATE. *v. n.* To grow firm, hard, or solid.

In hurts and ulcers in the head, dryness maketh them more apt to *consolidate*. *Bacon's Natural History*, N°. 785.

The sand, sparry, and flinty matter was then soft, and susceptible of any form in these shelly moulds; and it *consolidated*, and became hard afterwards. *Woodward's Nat. History.*

CONSOLIDA'TION. *n. s.* [from *consolidate.*]

1. The act of uniting into a solid mass.

The

The *consolidation* of the marble, and of the stone, did not fall out at random. *Woodward's Natural History.*

2. The annexing of one bill in parliament to another.

3. In law, it is used for the combining and uniting of two benefices in one. *Cowel.*

CONSO'LIDATIVE. *adj.* [from *consolidate.*] That which has the quality of healing wounds. *Dict.*

CO'NSONANCE. } *n. s.* [*consonance*, Fr. *consonans*, Latin.]
CO'NSONANCY. }

1. Accord of sound.

The two principal *consonances* that most ravish the ear, are, by the consent of all nature, the fifth and the octave. *Wotton.*

And winds and waters flow'd
In *consonance.* *Thomson's Spring.*

2. Consistency; congruence; agreeableness.

Such decisions held *consonancy* and congruity with resolutions and decisions of former times. *Hale's Law of England.*

I have thus largely set down this, to shew the perfect *consonancy* of our persecuted church to the doctrine of scripture and antiquity. *Hammond on Fundamentals.*

3. Agreement; concord; friendship. A sense now not used.

Let me conjure you by the rights of our fellowship, by the *consonancy* of our youth. *Shakespeare's Hamlet.*

CO'NSONANT. *adj.* [*consonans*, Lat.] Agreeable; according; consistent: followed by either *with* or *to.*

Were it *consonant unto* reason to divorce these two sentences, the former of which doth shew how the latter is restrained? *Hooker.*

That where much is given there shall be much required, is a thing *consonant with* natural equity. *Decay of Piety.*

Religion looks *consonant to* itself. *Decay of Piety.*

He discovers how *consonant* the account which Moses hath left, of the primitive earth, is *to* this from nature. *Woodward.*

CO'NSONANT. *n. s.* [*consonans*, Latin.] A letter which cannot be sounded, or but imperfectly, by itself.

In all vowels the passage of the mouth is open and free, without any appulse of an organ of speech to another: but in all *consonants* there is an appulse of the organs, sometimes (if you abstract the *consonants* from the vowels) wholly precluding all sound; and, in all of them, more or less checking and abetting it. *Holder's Elements of Speech.*

He considered these as they had a greater mixture of vowels or *consonants*, and accordingly employed them as the verse required a greater smoothness. *Pope's Essay on Homer.*

CO'NSONANTLY. *adv.* [from *consonant.*] Consistently; agreeably.

This as *consonantly* it preacheth, teacheth, and delivereth, as if but one tongue did speak for all. *Hooker, b.* v. *s.* 42.

Ourselves are formed according to that mind which frames things *consonantly* to their respective natures. *Glanv. Sceps. c.* 1.

If he will speak *consonantly* to himself, he must say that happened in the original constitution. *Tillotson.*

CO'NSONANTNESS. *n. s.* [from *consonant.*] Agreeableness; consistency. *Dict.*

CO'NSONOUS. *adj.* [*consonus*, Latin.] Agreeing in sound; symphonious.

CONSOPIA'TION. *n. s.* [from *consopio*, Latin.] The act of laying to sleep.

One of his maxims is, that a total abstinence from intemperance is no more philosophy than a total *consopiation* of the senses is repose. *Digby to Pope.*

CO'NSORT. *n. s.* [*consors*, Latin. It had anciently the accent on the latter syllable, but has it now on the former.]

1. Companion; partner; generally a partner of the bed; a wife or husband.

Male he created thee; but thy *consort*
Female for race: then bless'd mankind, and said,
Be fruitful, multiply, and fill the earth. *Milton's Par. Lost.*

Thy Bellona, who the *consort* came,
Not only to thy bed, but to thy fame. *Denham.*

He single chose to live, and shun'd to wed,
Well pleas'd to want a *consort* of his bed. *Dryden's Fables.*

His warlike amazon her host invades,
Th' imperial *consort* of the crown of Spades. *Pope.*

2. An assembly; a divan; a consultation.

In one *consort* there sat
Cruel revenge, and rancorous despite,
Disloyal treason, and heart-burning hate. *Fairy Queen, b.* ii.

3. A number of instruments playing together; a symphony. This is probably a mistake for *concert.*

A *consort* of musick in a banquet of wine, is as a signet of carbuncle set in gold. *Ecclus.* xxxii. 5.

4. Concurrence; union.

Take it singly, and it carries an air of levity; but, in *consort* with the rest, you see, has a meaning quite different. *Atterbury.*

To CONSO'RT. *v. n.* [from the noun.] To associate with; to unite with; to keep company with.

What will you do? Let's not *consort* with them. *Shakesp.*

Which of the Grecian chiefs *consorts* with thee? *Dryden.*

To CONSO'RT. *v. a.*

1. To join; to mix; to marry.

He, with his *consorted* Eve,
The story heard attentive. *Milton's Paradise Lost, b.* vii.

He begins to *consort* himself with men, and thinks himself one. *Locke on Education, sect* 213.

2. To accompany.

I'll meet with you upon the mart,
And afterward *consort* you 'till bed-time. *Shakespeare.*

CONSO'RTABLE. *adj.* [from *consort.*] To be compared with; to be ranked with; suitable.

He was *consortable* to Charles Brandon, under Henry VIII. who was equal to him. *Wotton.*

CONSO'RTION. *n s.* [*consortio*, Latin.] Partnership; fellowship; society. *Dict.*

CONSPE'CTABLE. *adj.* [from *conspectus*, Latin.] Easy to be seen. *Dict.*

CONSPECTU'ITY. *n. s.* [from *conspectus*, Latin] Sight; view; sense of seeing. This word is, I believe, peculiar to *Shakespeare*, and perhaps corrupt.

What harm can your bisson *conspectuities* glean out of this character? *Shakespeare's Coriolanus.*

CONSPE'RSION. *n. s.* [*conspersio*, Lat.] A sprinkling about. *Dict.*

CONSPICU'ITY. *n. s.* [from *conspicuous.*] Brightness; favourableness to the sight.

If this definition be clearer than the thing defined, midnight may vie for *conspicuity* with noon. *Glanv. Sceps. c.* 18.

CONSPI'CUOUS. [*conspicuus*, Latin.]

1. Obvious to the sight; seen at distance.

Or come I less *conspicuous?* Or what change
Absents thee? *Milton's Paradise Lost, b.* x. *l.* 107.

2. Eminent; famous; distinguished.

He attributed to each of them that virtue which he thought most *conspicuous* in them. *Dryden's Juven. Dedication.*

Thy father's merit points thee out to view,
And sets thee in the fairest point of light,
To make thy virtues or thy faults *conspicuous.* *Addis. Cato.*

The house of lords,
Conspicuous scene! *Pope's Epist. of Horace.*

CONSPI'CUOUSLY. *adv.* [from *conspicuous.*]

1. Obviously to the view.

These methods may be preserved *conspicuously*, and intirely distinct. *Watts's Logick, p.* iv. *c.* 1.

2. Eminently; famously; remarkably.

CONSPI'CUOUSNESS. *n. s.* [from *conspicuous*]

1. Exposure to the view; state of being visible at a distance.

Looked on with such a weak light, they appear well proportioned fabricks; yet they appear so but in that twilight, which is requisite to their *conspicuousness.* *Boyle's Proem. Essay.*

2. Eminence; fame; celebrity.

Their writings attract more readers by the author's *conspicuousness.* *Boyle on Colours.*

CONSPI'RACY. *n. s.* [*conspiratio*, Latin.]

1. A private agreement among several persons to commit some crime; a plot; a concerted treason.

O *conspiracy!*
Sham'st thou to shew thy dang'rous brow by night,
When evils are most free? *Shakespeare's Julius Cæsar.*

I had forgot that foul *conspiracy*
Of the beast Caliban, and his confed'rates,
Against my life. *Shakespeare's Tempest.*

When scarce he had escap'd the blow
Of faction and *conspiracy*,
Death did his promis'd hopes destroy. *Dryden.*

2. In law, an agreement of men to do any thing; always taken in the evil part. It is taken for a confederacy of two at the least, falsely to indict one, or to procure one to be indicted of felony. *Cowel.*

3. A concurrence; a general tendency of many causes to one event.

When the time now came that misery was ripe for him, there was a *conspiracy* in all heavenly and earthly things, to frame fit occasions to lead him unto it. *Sidney, b.* ii.

CONSPI'RANT. *adj.* [*conspirans*, Latin.] Conspiring; engaged in a conspiracy or plot; plotting.

Thou art a traitor,
Conspirant 'gainst this high illustrious prince. *Shak. K. Lear.*

CONSPIRA'TION. *n. s.* [*conspiratio*, Lat.] A plot. *Dict.*

CONSPI'RATOR. *n. s.* [from *conspiro*, Latin.] A man engaged in a plot; one who has secretly concerted with others commission of a crime; a plotter.

Achitophel is among the *conspirators* with Absalom. 2 *Sam.*

Stand back, thou manifest *conspirator*;
Thou that contriv'st to murder our dread lord. *Sh. Hen.* VI.

But let the bold *conspirator* beware;
For heav'n makes princes its peculiar care. *Dryd. Spa. Fryar.*

One put into his hand a note of the whole conspiracy against him, together with all the names of the *conspirators.* *South's Sermons.*

To CONSPI'RE. *v. n.* [*conspiro*, Latin.]

1. To concert a crime; to plot; to hatch secret treason.

Tell me what they deserve,
That do *conspire* my death with devilish plots
Of damned witchcraft? *Shakespeare's Richard* III.

What

What was it
That mov'd pale Cassius to *conspire?* *Shak. Ant. and Cleop.*

They took great indignation, and *conspired* against the king. *Bel.* 28.

Let the air be excluded; for that undermineth the body, and *conspireth* with the spirit of the body to dissolve it. *Bacon.*

There is in man a natural possibility to destroy the world; that is, to *conspire* to know no woman. *Brown's Vulgar Errours.*

The press, the pulpit, and the stage,
Conspire to censure and expose our age. *Roscommon.*

2. To agree together; as, *all things* conspire *to make him happy.*

CONSPI'RER. *n. s.* [from *conspire.*] A conspirator; a plotter.

Take no care,
Who chafes, who frets, and where *conspirers* are;
Macbeth shall never vanquish'd be. *Shakespeare's Macbeth.*

CONSPI'RING *Powers.* [In mechanicks.] All such as act in direction not opposite to one another. *Harris.*

CONSPURCA'TION. *n. s.* [from *conspurco*, Latin.] The act of defiling; defilement; pollution.

CO'NSTABLE. *n. s.* [*comes stabuli*, as it is supposed.]

1. Lord high *constable* is an ancient officer of the crown, long disused in England, but lately subsisting in France; where the *constable* commanded the mareschals, and was the first officer of the army. The function of the *constable* of England consisted in the care of the common peace of the land in deeds of arms, and in matters of war. To the court of the *constable* and marshal belonged the cognizance of contracts, deeds of arms without the realm, and combats and blasonry of arms within it. The first *constable* of England was created by the Conqueror, and the office continued hereditary 'till the thirteenth of Henry VIII. when it was laid aside, as being so powerful as to become troublesome to the king. From these mighty magistrates are derived the inferiour *constables* of hundreds and franchises; two of whom were ordained, in the thirteenth of Edward I. to be chosen in every hundred for the conservation of the peace, and view of armour. These are now called high *constables*, because continuance of time, and increase both of people and offences, have occasioned others in every town of like nature, but inferiour authority, called petty *constables*. Besides these, we have *constables* denominated from particular places; as *constable of the Tower*, *of Dover castle*, *of the castle of Carnarvon*; but these are properly *castellani*, or governours of castles. *Cowel. Chambers.*

When I came hither, I was lord high *constable*,
And duke of Buckingham; now poor Edward Bohun. *Shak.*

The knave *constable* had set me i' th' stocks, i' th' common stocks, for a witch. *Shakesp. Merry Wives of Windsor.*

The *constable* being a sober man, and known to be an enemy to those acts of sedition, went among them, to observe what they did. *Clarendon.*

2. *To over-run the* CONSTABLE. [Perhaps from *conte stable*, Fr. the settled, firm and stated account.] To spend more than what a man knows himself to be worth: a low phrase.

CO'NSTABLESHIP. *n. s.* [from *constable.*] The office of a constable.

This keepership is annexed to the *constableship* of the castle, and that granted out in lease. *Carew's Survey of Cornwal.*

CO'NSTANCY. *n. s.* [*constantia*, Latin.]

1. Immutability; perpetuity; unalterable continuance.

The laws of God himself no man will ever deny to be of a different constitution from the former, in respect of the one's *constancy*, and the mutability of the other. *Hooker, b.* i.

2. Consistency; unvaried state.

Incredible, that *constancy* in such a variety, such a multiplicity, should be the result of chance. *Ray on the Creation.*

3. Resolution; firmness; steadiness; unshaken determination.

In a small isle, amidst the widest seas,
Triumphant *constancy* has fix'd her seat;
In vain the syrens sing, the tempests beat. *Prior.*

4. Lasting affection; continuance of love, or friendship.

Constancy is such a stability and firmness of friendship, as overlooks and passes by lesser failures of kindness, and yet still retains the same habitual good-will to a friend. *South.*

5. Certainty; veracity; reality.

But all the story of the night told over,
More witnesseth than fancy's images,
And grows to something of great *constancy*,
But, however, strange and admirable. *Shakespeare.*

CO'NSTANT. *adj.* [*constans*, Latin.]

1. Firm; fixed; not fluid.

If you take highly rectified spirit of wine, and dephlegmed spirit of urine, and mix them, you may turn these two fluid liquors into a *constant* body. *Boyle's History of Firmness.*

2. Unvaried; unchanged; immutable; durable.

3. Firm; resolute; determined; immoveable; unshaken.

Some shrewd contents,
Now steal the colour from Bassanio's cheek:
Some dear friend dead; else nothing in the world
Could turn so much the constitution
Of any *constant* man. *Shakespeare's Merchant of Venice.*

4. Free from change of affection.

Both loving one fair maid, they yet remained *constant* friends. *Sidney, b.* ii.

5. Certain; not various; steady; firmly adherent.

Now, through the land, his care of souls he stretch'd;
And like a primitive apostle preach'd;
Still chearful, ever *constant* to his call;
By many follow'd, lov'd by most, admir'd by all. *Dryden.*

He shewed his firm adherence to religion as modelled by our national constitution, and was *constant* to its offices in devotion, both in publick and in his family. *Addison, Freeholder.*

CO'NSTANTLY. *adv.* [from *constant.*] Unvariably; perpetually; certainly; steadily.

It is strange that the fathers should never appeal; nay, that they should not *constantly* do it. *Tillotson.*

To CONSTE'LLATE. *v. n.* [*constellatus*, Latin.] To join lustre; to shine with one general light.

The several things which most engage our affections, do, in a transcendent manner, shine forth and *constellate* in God. *Boyle.*

To CONSTE'LLATE. *v. a.* To unite several shining bodies in one splendour.

These scattered perfections, which were divided among the several ranks of inferiour natures, were summed up and *constellated* in ours. *Glanv. Sceps. c.* 1.

CONSTELLA'TION. *n. s.* [from *constellate.*]

1. A cluster of fixed stars.

For the stars of heaven, and the *constellations* thereof, shall not give their light. *Is.* xiii. 10.

The earth, the air resounded,
The heav'ns and all the *constellations* rung. *Milt. Par. Lost.*

A *constellation* is but one;
Though 'tis a train of stars. *Dryden.*

2. An assemblage of splendours, or excellencies.

The condition is a *constellation* or conjuncture of all those gospel-graces, faith, hope, charity, self-denial, repentance, and the rest. *Hammond's Pract. Cat.*

CONSTERNA'TION. *n. s.* [from *consterno*, Latin.] Astonishment; amazement; alienation of mind by a surprise; surprise; wonder.

They find the same holy *consternation* upon themselves that Jacob did at Bethel, which he called the gate of heaven. *South.*

The natives, dubious whom
They must obey, in *consternation* wait,
'Till rigid conquest will pronounce their liege. *Philips.*

To CO'NSTIPATE. *v. a.* [from *constipo*, Latin.]

1. To croud together into a narrow room; to thicken; to condense.

Of cold, the property is to condense and *constipate*. *Bacon.*

It may, by amassing, cooling, and *constipating* of waters, turn them into rain. *Ray on the Creation.*

There might arise some vertiginous motions or whirlpools in the matter of the chaos, whereby the atoms might be thrust and crouded to the middle of those whirlpools, and there *constipate* one another into great solid globes. *Bentley.*

2. To stuff up, or stop by filling up the passages.

It is not probable that any aliment should have the quality of intirely *constipating* or shutting up the capillary vessels. *Arbuthnot on Aliments.*

3. To bind the belly; or make costive.

CONSTIPA'TION. *n. s.* [from *constipate.*]

1. The act of crouding any thing into less room; condensation.

This worketh by the detention of the spirits, and *constipation* of the tangible parts. *Bacon's Natural History*, N°. 341.

It requires either absolute fulness of matter, or a pretty close *constipation* and mutual contact of its particles. *Bentley.*

2. Stoppage; obstruction by plenitude.

The inactivity of the gall occasions a *constipation* of the belly. *Arbuthnot on Aliments.*

CONSTI'TUENT. *adj.* [*constituens*, Latin.] That which makes any thing what it is; necessary to existence; elemental; essential; that of which any thing consists.

Body, soul, and reason, are the three parts necessarily *constituent* of a man. *Dryden's Dufresnoy.*

All animals derived all the *constituent* matter of their bodies, successively, in all ages, out of this fund. *Woodw. Nat. Hist.*

It is impossible that the figures and sizes of its *constituent* particles, should be so justly adapted as to touch one another in every point. *Bentley's Sermons.*

CONSTI'TUENT. *n. s.*

1. The person or thing which constitutes or settles any thing in its peculiar state.

Their first composure and origination requires a higher and nobler *constituent* than chance. *Hale's Orig. of Mankind.*

2. That which is necessary to the subsistence of any thing.

The obstruction of the mesentery is a great impediment to nutrition; for the lymph in those glands is a necessary *constituent* of the aliment. *Arbuthnot on Aliments.*

3. He that deputes another.

To CO'NSTITUTE. *v. a.* [*constituo*, Latin.]

1. To give formal existence; to make any thing what it is; to produce.

Prudence is not only a moral but christian virtue, such as is necessary to the *constituting* of all others. *Decay of Piety.*

2. To erect; to establish.

We must obey laws appointed and *constituted* by lawful authority, not against the law of God. *Taylor's Holy Living.*

3. To depute; to appoint another to an office.

CO'NSTITUTER. *n. s.* [from *constitute.*] He that constitutes or appoints.

CONSTITU'TION. *n. s.* [from *constitute.*]

1. The act of constituting; enacting; deputing; establishing; producing.

2. State of being; particular texture of parts; natural qualities.

This is more beneficial to us than any other *constitution.* *Bentley's Sermons.*

This light being trajected through the parallel prisms, if it suffered any change by the refraction of one, it lost that impression by the contrary refraction of the other; and so, being restored to its pristine *constitution,* became of the same condition as at first. *Newton's Opt.*

3. Corporeal frame.

Amongst many bad effects of this oily *constitution,* there is one advantage; such who arrive to age, are not subject to stricture of fibres. *Arbuthnot on Aliments.*

4. Temper of body, with respect to health or disease.

If such men happen, by their native *constitutions,* to fall into the gout, either they mind it not at all, having no leisure to be sick, or they use it like a dog. *Temple.*

Beauty is nothing else but a just accord and mutual harmony of the members, animated by a healthful *constitution.* *Dryden's Dufresnoy.*

5. Temper of mind.

Dametas, according to the *constitution* of a dull head, thinks no better way to shew himself wise than by suspecting every thing in his way. *Sidney.*

Some dear friend dead; else nothing in the world
Could turn so much the *constitution*
Of any constant man. *Shakespeare's Merchant of Venice.*

He defended himself with undaunted courage, and less passion than was expected from his *constitution.* *Clarendon.*

6. Established form of government; system of laws and customs.

The Norman conqu'ring all by might,
Mixing our customs, and the form of right,
With foreign *constitutions* he had brought. *Daniel's Civ. War.*

7. Particular law; established usage; establishment; institution.

We lawfully may observe the positive *constitutions* of our own churches. *Hooker, b.* iv. *sect.* 5.

Constitution, properly speaking in the sense of the civil law, is that law which is made and ordained by some king or emperor; yet the canonists, by adding the word *sacred* to it, make it to signify the same as an ecclesiastical canon. *Ayliffe.*

CONSTITU'TIONAL. *adj.* [from *constitution.*]

1. Bred in the constitution; radical.

It is not probable any *constitutional* illness will be communicated with the small-pox by inoculation. *Sharpe's Surgery.*

2. Consistent with the constitution; legal.

CONSTITU'TIVE. *adj.* [from *constitute.*]

1. That which constitutes any thing what it is; elemental; essential; productive.

Although it be placed among the non-naturals, that is, such as neither naturally *constitutive,* nor merely destructive, do preserve or destroy. *Brown's Vulgar Errours, b.* iii. *c.* 9.

The very elements and *constitutive* parts of a schismatick, being the esteem of himself, and the contempt of others. *Decay of Piety.*

2. Having the power to enact or establish.

To CONSTRA'IN. *v. a.* [*constraindre,* Fr. *constringo,* Latin.]

1. To compel; to force to some action.

Thy sight, which should
Make our eyes flow with joy,
Constrains them weep. *Shakespeare's Coriolanus.*

2. To hinder by force; to restrain.

My sire in caves *constrains* the winds,
Can with a breath their clam'rous rage appease;
They fear his whistle, and forsake the seas. *Dryden.*

3. To necessitate.

The scars upon your honour, therefore, he
Does pity as *constrained* blemishes,
Nothing deserv'd. *Shakespeare's Anthony and Cleopatra.*

When to his lust Ægysthus gave the rein,
Did fate or we th' adult'rous act *constrain?* *Pope's Odyssey.*

4. To violate; to ravish.

Her spotless chastity,
Inhuman traitors, you *constrain'd* and forc'd. *Shak. Tit. And.*

5. To confine; to press.

How the strait stays the slender waste *constrain?* *Gay.*

CONSTRA'INABLE. *adj.* [from *constrain.*] Liable to constraint; obnoxious to compulsion.

Whereas men before stood bound in conscience to do as reason teacheth, they are now, by virtue of human law, *constrainable*; and, if they outwardly transgress, punishable. *Hooker.*

CONSTRA'INER. *n. s.* [from *constrain.*] He that constrains.

CONSTRA'INT. *n. s.* [*contrainte,* French.] Compulsion; compelling force; violence; act of over-ruling the desire; confinement.

I did suppose it should be on *constraint*;
But, heav'n be thank'd, it is but voluntary. *Shak. K. John.*

Like you a man; and hither led by fame,
Not by *constraint,* but by my choice, I came. *Dryd. In. Emp.*

The constant desire of happiness, and the *constraint* it puts upon us to act for it, no body, I think, accounts an abridgment of liberty. *Locke.*

To CONSTRI'CT. *v. a.* [*constringo constrictum,* Latin.]

1. To bind; to cramp; to confine into a narrow compass.

2. To contract; to cause to shrink.

Such things as *constrict* the fibres and strengthen the solid parts. *Arbuthnot on Diet.*

CONSTRI'CTION. *n. s.* [from *constrict.*] Contraction; compression.

The air which these receive into the lungs, may serve to render their bodies equiponderant to the water; and the *constriction* or dilatation of it, may probably assist them to ascend or descend in the water. *Ray on the Creation.*

CONSTRI'CTOR. *n. s.* [*constrictor,* Latin.] That which compresses or contracts.

He supposed the *constrictors* of the eye-lids must be strengthened in the supercilious. *Arbuth. and Pope's Mart Scrib.*

To CONSTRI'NGE. *v. a.* [*constringo,* Lat.] To compress; to contract; to bind.

The dreadful spout,
Which shipmen do the hurricano call,
Constring'd in mass by the almighty sun. *Sh. Tro. and Cress.*

Strong liquors, especially inflammatory spirits, intoxicate, *constringe,* harden the fibres, and coagulate the fluids. *Arbuth.*

CONSTRI'NGENT. *adj.* [*constringens,* Latin.] Having the quality of binding or compressing.

Try a deep well, or a conservatory of snow, where the cold may be more *constringent.* *Bacon's Natural History,* N°. 380.

It binds
Our strengthen'd bodies in a cold embrace
Constringent. *Thomson's Winter, l.* 700.

To CONSTRU'CT. *v. a.* [*constructus,* Lat.] To build; to form; to compile; to constitute.

Let there be an admiration of those divine attributes and prerogatives, for whose manifesting he was pleased to *construct* this vast fabrick. *Boyle's Usefulness of Natural Philosophy.*

CONSTRU'CTION. *n. s.* [*constructio,* Latin.]

1. The act of building, or piling up in a regular method.

2. The form of building; structure; conformation.

There's no art
To shew the mind's *construction* in the face. *Shak. Macbeth.*

The ways were made of several layers of flat stones and flint: the *construction* was a little various, according to the nature of the soil, or the materials which they found. *Arbuth.*

3. [In grammar.] The putting of words, duly chosen, together in such a manner as is proper to convey a complete sense. *Clarke's Latin Grammar.*

Some particles constantly, and others in certain *constructions,* have the sense of a whole sentence contained in them. *Locke.*

4. The act of arranging terms in the proper order, by disentangling transpositions; the act of interpreting; explanation.

This label, whose containing
Is so from sense in hardness, that I can
Make no collection of it, let him shew
His skill in the *construction.* *Shakespeare's Cymbeline.*

5. The sense; the meaning; interpretation.

In which sense although we judge the apostle's words to have been uttered, yet hereunto we do not require them to yield, that think any other *construction* more sound. *Hooker.*

He that would live at ease, should always put the best *construction* on business and conversation. *Collier on the Spleen.*

Religion, in its own nature, produces good will towards men, and puts the mildest *construction* upon every accident that befals them. *Spectator,* N°. 483.

6. Judgment; mental representation.

It cannot, therefore, unto reasonable *constructions* seem strange, or savour of singularity, that we have examined this point. *Brown's Vulgar Errours, b.* iv. *c.* 13.

7. The manner of describing a figure or problem in geometry.

8. CONSTRUCTION *of Equations,* in algebra, is the method of reducing a known equation into lines and figures, in order to a geometrical demonstration.

CONSTRU'CTURE. *n. s.* [from *construct.*] Pile; edifice; fabrick.

They shall the earth's *constructure* closely bind,
And to the center keep the parts confin'd. *Blackmore.*

To CO'NSTRUE. *v. a.* [*construo,* Latin.]

1. To range words in their natural order; to disentangle transposition.

I'll teach mine eyes with meek humility,
Love-learned letters to her eyes to read;

Which

Which her deep wit, that true heart's thought can spell,
Will soon conceive, and learn to *construe* well. *Spenser.*

Virgil is so very figurative, that he requires (I may almost say) a grammar apart to *construe* him. *Dryden.*

Thus we are put to *construe* and paraphrase our own words, to free ourselves either from the ignorance or malice of our adversaries. *Stillingfleet's Defence of Discourse on Roman Idol.*

2. To interpret; to explain; to shew the meaning.

I must crave that I be not so understood or *construed*, as if any such thing, by virtue thereof, could be done without the aid and assistance of God's most blessed spirit. *Hooker, b.* iii.

Construe the times to their necessities,
And you shall say, indeed, it is the time,
And not the king, that doth you injuries. *Shak. Hen.* IV.

When the word is *construed* into its idea, the double meaning vanishes. *Addison on Ancient Medals.*

To CO'NSTUPRATE. *v. a.* [*constupro*, Lat.] To violate; to debauch; to defile.

CONSTUPRA'TION. *n. s.* [from *constuprate.*] Violation; defilement.

CONSUBSTA'NTIAL. *adj.* [*consubstantialis*, Latin.]

1. Having the same essence or subsistence.

The Lord our God, is but one God: in which indivisible unity, notwithstanding we adore the Father, as being altogether of himself, we glorify that *consubstantial* word which is the Son; we bless and magnify that co-essential Spirit, eternally proceeding from both, which is the Holy Ghost. *Hooker, b.* v.

2. Being of the same kind or nature.

It continueth a body *consubstantial* with our bodies; a body of the same, both nature and measure, which it had on earth. *Hooker, b.* v. *s.* 54.

In their conceits the human nature of Christ was not *consubstantial* to ours, but of another kind. *Brerewood.*

CONSUBSTANTIA'LITY. *n. s.* [from *consubstantial.*] Existence of more than one, in the same substance.

The eternity of the Son's generation, and his co-eternity and *consubstantiality* with the Father, when he came down from heaven. *Hammond on Fundamentals.*

To CONSUBSTA'NTIATE. *v. a.* [from *con* and *substantia*, Lat.] To unite in one common substance or nature.

CONSUBSTANTIA'TION. *n. s.* [from *consubstantiate.*] The union of the body of our blessed Saviour with the sacramental element, according to the Lutherans.

In the point of *consubstantiation*, toward the latter end of his life, he changed his mind. *Atterbury.*

CO'NSUL. *n. s.* [*consul*, *consulendo*, Latin.]

1. The chief magistrate in the Roman republick.

Or never be so noble as a *consul*,
Nor yoke with him for tribune. *Shakespeare's Coriolanus.*

Consuls of mod'rate pow'r in calms were made;
When the Gauls came, one sole dictator sway'd. *Dryden.*

2. An officer commissioned in foreign parts to judge between the merchants of his nation, and protect their commerce.

CO'NSULAR. *adj.* [*consularis*, Latin.]

1. Relating to the consul.

The *consular* power had only the ornaments, without the force of the royal authority. *Spectator*, Nº. 287.

2. CONSULAR *Man.* One who had been consul.

Rise not the *consular* men, and left their places,
So soon as thou sat'st down? *Ben. Johnson's Catiline.*

CO'NSULATE. *n. s.* [*consulatus*, Latin.] The office of consul.

His name and *consulate* were effaced out of all publick registers and inscriptions. *Addison's Remarks on Italy.*

CO'NSULSHIP. *n. s.* [from *consul.*] The office of consul.

The patricians should do very ill,
To let the *consulship* be so defil'd. *Ben. Johnson's Catiline.*

The lovely boy, with his auspicious face,
Shall Pollio's *consulship* and triumph grace. *Dryden.*

To CONSU'LT. *v. n.* [*consulto*, Latin.] To take counsel together; to deliberate in common. It has *with* before the person admitted to consultation.

Every man,
After the hideous storm that follow'd, was
A thing inspir'd; and, not *consulting*, broke
Into a general prophecy, that this tempest,
Dashing the garment of this peace, aboded
The sudden breach on't. *Shakespeare's Henry* VIII.

A senate-house, wherein three hundred and twenty men sat *consulting* always for the people. 1 *Mac.* viii. 15.

Consult not *with* the slothful for any work. *Ecclus.* xxxvii.

He sent for his bosom friends, *with* whom he most confidently *consulted*, and shewed the paper to them, the contents whereof he could not conceive. *Clarendon.*

To CONSU'LT. *v. a.*

1. To ask advice of; as, *he* consulted *his friends.*

2. To regard; to act with view or respect to.

We are, in the first place, to *consult* the necessities of life, rather than matters of ornament and delight. *L'Estrange.*

The senate owes its gratitude to Cato,
Who with so great a soul *consults* its safety,
And guards our lives, while he neglects his own. *Add. Cato.*

3. To plan; to contrive.

Thou hast *consulted* shame to thy house, by cutting off many people. *Heb.* ii. 10.

Many things were there *consulted* for the future, yet nothing was positively resolved. *Clarendon, b.* viii.

4. To search into; to examine; as, *to* consult *an author.*

CO'NSULT. *n. s.* [from the verb. It is variously accented.]

1. The act of consulting.

Yourself in person head one chosen half,
And march t' oppress the faction in *consult*
With dying Dorax. *Dryden's Don Sebastian.*

2. The effect of consulting; determination.

He said, and rose the first; the council broke;
And all their grave *consults* dissolv'd in smoke. *Dryd. Fables.*

3. A council; a number of persons assembled in deliberation.

Divers meetings and *consults* of our whole number, to consider of the former labours. *Bacon.*

A *consult* of coquets below
Was call'd, to rig him out a beau. *Swift.*

CONSULTA'TION. *n. s.* [from *consult.*]

1. The act of consulting; secret deliberation.

The chief priests held a *consultation* with the elders and scribes. *Mark*, xv. 1.

2. A number of persons consulted together; a council.

A *consultation* was called, wherein he advised a salivation. *Wiseman of Abscesses.*

3. [In law.] *Consultatio* is a writ, whereby a cause, being formerly removed by prohibition from the ecclesiastical court, or court christian, to the king's court, is returned thither again: for the judges of the king's court, if, upon comparing the libel with the suggestion of the party, they do find the suggestion false, or not proved, and therefore the cause to be wrongfully called from the court christian; then, upon this *consultation* or deliberation, decree it to be returned again. *Cowel.*

CONSU'LTER. *n. s.* [from *consult.*] One that consults or asks council or intelligence.

There shall not be found among you a charmer, or a *consulter* with familiar spirits, or a wizard. *Deutr.* xviii. 11.

CONSU'MABLE. *adj.* [from *consume.*] Susceptible of destruction; possible to be wasted, spent, or destroyed.

It does truly agree in this common quality ascribed unto both, of being incombustible, and not *consumable* by fire; but yet there is this inconvenience, that it doth contract so much fuliginous matter from the earthy parts of the oil, though it was tried with some of the purest oil which is ordinary to be bought, that in a very few days it did choak and extinguish the flame. *Wilkins's Mathem. Magick.*

Our growing rich or poor depends only on, which is greater or less, our importation or exportation of *consumable* commodities. *Locke.*

To CONSU'ME. *v. a.* [*consumo*, Latin.] To waste; to spend; to destroy.

Where two raging fires meet together,
They do *consume* the thing that feeds their fury. *Shakespeare.*

Thou shalt carry much seed out into the field, and shalt gather but little in; for the locusts shall *consume* it. *Deut.* xxviii.

Thus in soft anguish she *consumes* the day,
Nor quits her deep retirement. *Thomson's Spring.*

To CONSU'ME. *v. n.* To waste away; to be exhausted.

These violent delights have violent ends,
And in their triumph die; like fire and powder,
Which, as they meet, *consume*. *Shakesp. Romeo and Juliet.*

CONSU'MER. *n. s.* [from *consume.*] One that spends, wastes, or destroys any thing.

Money may be considered as in the hands of the *consumer*, or of the merchant who buys the commodity, when made to export. *Locke.*

To CONSU'MMATE. *v. a.* [*consommer*, Fr. *consummare*, Lat.] To complete; to perfect; to finish; to end. Anciently accented on the first syllable.

Yourself, myself, and other lords, will pass
To *consummate* this business happily. *Shakesp. King John.*

There shall we *consummate* our spousal rites. *Shakespeare.*

The person was cunning enough to begin the deceit in the weaker, and the weaker sufficient to *consummate* the fraud in the stronger. *Brown's Vulgar Errours, b.* i. *c.* 1.

He had a mind to *consummate* the happiness of the day. *Tatl.*

CONSU'MMATE. *adj.* [from the verb.] Complete; perfect; finished; *omnibus numeris absolutus.*

I do but stay 'till your marriage be *consummate*. *Shakespeare.*

Earth, in her rich attire
Consummate, lovely smil'd. *Milton's Paradise Lost, b.* vii.

Gratian, among his maxims for raising a man to the most *consummate* greatness, advises to perform extraordinary actions, and to secure a good historian. *Addison, Freeholder*, Nº. 35.

If a man of perfect and *consummate* virtue falls into a misfortune, it raises our pity, but not our terrour. *Addis. Spectat.*

CONSUMMA'TION. *n. s.* [from *consummate.*]

1. Completion; perfection; end.

That just and regular process, which it must be supposed to take from its original to its *consummation*. *Addis. Spectator.*

2. The end of the present system of things; the end of the world.

From the first beginning of the world unto the last *consummation*

ſummation thereof, it neither hath been, nor can be otherwiſe. *Hooker, b.* ii. *ſect.* 4.

3. Death; end of life.

Ghoſt, unlaid, forbear thee!
Nothing ill come near thee!
Quiet *conſummation* have,
And renowned be thy grave! *Shakeſpeare's Cymbeline.*

CONSU'MPTION. *n. ſ.* [*conſumptio*, Latin.]

1. The act of conſuming; waſte; deſtruction.

In commodities the value riſes as its quantity is leſs and vent greater, which depends upon its being preferred in its *conſumption.* *Locke.*

Etna and Veſuvius have ſent forth flames for this two or three thouſand years, yet the mountains themſelves have not ſuffered any conſiderable diminution or *conſumption*; but are, at this day, the higheſt mountains in thoſe countries. *Woodw.*

2. The ſtate of waſting or periſhing.

3. [In phyſick.] A waſte of muſcular fleſh. It is frequently attended with a hectick fever, and is divided by phyſicians into ſeveral kinds, according to the variety of its cauſes. *Quincy.*

Conſumptions ſow
In hollow bones of man. *Shakeſpeare's Timon.*

The ſtoppage of women's courſes, if not ſuddenly looked to, ſets them into a *conſumption*, dropſy, or other diſeaſe. *Harvey on Conſumptions.*

CONSU'MPTIVE. *adj.* [from *conſume.*]

1. Deſtructive; waſting; exhauſting; having the quality of conſuming.

A long *conſumptive* war is more likely to break this grand alliance than diſable France. *Addiſon on the State of the War.*

2. Diſeaſed with a conſumption.

Nothing taints ſound lungs ſooner than inſpiring the breath of *conſumptive* lungs. *Harvey on Conſumptions.*

The lean, *conſumptive* wench, with coughs decay'd,
Is call'd a pretty, tight, and ſlender maid. *Dryden.*

By an exact regimen a *conſumptive* perſon may hold out for years. *Arbuthnot on Diet.*

CONSU'MPTIVENESS. *n. ſ.* [from *conſumptive.*] A tendency to a conſumption.

CONSU'TILE. *adj.* [*conſutilis*, Latin.] That is ſewed or ſtitched together. *Dict.*

To CONTA'BULATE. *v. a.* [*contabulo*, Latin.] To floor with boards.

CONTABULA'TION. *n. ſ.* [*contabulatio*, Latin.] A joining of boards together; a boarding a floor.

CO'NTACT. *n. ſ.* [*contactus*, Latin.] Touch; cloſe union; juncture of one body to another.

The Platoniſts hold, that the ſpirit of the lover doth paſs into the ſpirits of the perſon loved, which cauſeth the deſire of return into the body; whereupon followeth that appetite of *contact* and conjunction. *Bacon's Natural Hiſtory*, N°. 944.

When the light fell ſo obliquely on the air, which in other places was between them, as to be all reflected, it ſeemed in that place of *contact* to be wholly tranſmitted. *Newton's Opt.*

The air, by its immediate *contact*, may coagulate the blood which flows along the air-bladders. *Arbuthnot on Diet.*

CONTA'CTION. *n. ſ.* [*contactus*, Latin] The act of touching; a joining one body to another.

That deleterious it may be at ſome diſtance, and deſtructive without corporal *contaction*, there is no high improbability. *Brown's Vulgar Errours, b.* iii. *c.* 7.

CONTA'GION. *n. ſ.* [*contagio*, Latin.]

1. The emiſſion from body to body by which diſeaſes are communicated.

If we two be one, and thou play falſe,
I do digeſt the poiſon of thy fleſh,
Being ſtrumpeted by thy *contagion.* *Shakeſ. Com. of Errours.*

In infection and *contagion* from body to body, as the plague and the like, the infection is received many times by the body paſſive; but yet is, by the ſtrength and good diſpoſition thereof, repulſed. *Bacon.*

2. Infection; propagation of miſchief, or diſeaſe.

Nor will the goodneſs of intention excuſe the ſcandal and *contagion* of example. *King Charles.*

Down fell they,
And the dire hiſs renew'd, and the dire form
Catch'd by *contagion.* *Milton's Paradiſe Loſt, b.* x. *l.* 544.

3. Peſtilence; venomous emanations.

Will he ſteal out of his wholſome bed,
To dare the vile *contagion* of the night? *Shak. Jul. Cæſar.*

CONTA'GIOUS. *adj.* [from *contagio*, Latin.] Infectious; caught by approach; poiſonous; peſtilential.

The jades
That drag the tragick melancholly night,
From their miſty jaws
Breathe foul, *contagious* darkneſs in the air. *Shak. Hen.* VI.

We ſicken ſoon from her *contagious* care,
Grieve for her ſorrows, groan for her deſpair. *Prior.*

CONTA'GIOUSNESS. *n. ſ.* [from *contagious.*] The quality of being contagious.

To CONTA'IN. *v. a.* [*contineo*, Latin.]

1. To hold as a veſſel.

2. To compriſe; as a writing.

There are many other things which Jeſus did, the which, if they ſhould be written every one, I ſuppoſe that even the world itſelf could not *contain* the books that ſhould be written. *John*, xxi. 25.

Wherefore alſo it is *contained* in the ſcripture. 1 *Pet.* ii. 6.

3. To reſtrain; to with-hold; to keep within bounds.

All men ſhould be *contained* in duty ever after, without the terrour of warlike forces. *Spenſer on Ireland.*

I tell you, ſirs,
If you ſhould ſmile, he grows impatient.——
—Fear not, my lord, we can *contain* ourſelves. *Shakeſp.*

To CONTA'IN. *v. n.* To live in continence.

I felt the ardour of my paſſion increaſe, 'till I could no longer *contain.* *Arbuthnot and Pope.*

CONTA'INABLE. *adj.* [from *contain.*] Poſſible to be contained.

The air, *containable* within the cavity of the eolipile, amounted to eleven grains. *Boyle.*

To CONTA'MINATE. *v. a.* [*contamino*, Lat.] To defile; to pollute; to corrupt by baſe mixture.

Shall we now
Contaminate our fingers with baſe bribes? *Shak. Jul. Cæſar.*

A baſe pander holds the chamber-door,
Whilſt by a ſlave, no gentler than a dog,
His faireſt daughter is *contaminated.* *Shakeſp. Henry* V.

Do it not with poiſon; ſtrangle her in her bed,
Even in the bed ſhe hath *contaminated.* *Shakeſpeare's Othello.*

I quickly ſhed
Some of his baſtard-blood; and, in diſgrace,
Beſpoke him thus: *contaminated*, baſe,
And miſbegotten blood I ſpill of thine. *Shak. Hen.* VI. *p.* i.

Though it be neceſſitated, by its relation to fleſh, to a terreſtrial converſe; yet 'tis like the ſun, without *contaminating* its beams. *Glanv. Apol.*

He that lies with another man's wife, propagates children in another's family for him to keep, and *contaminates* the honour thereof as much as in him lies. *Ayliffe's Parergon.*

CONTA'MINATE. *adj.* [from the verb.] Polluted; defiled.

What if this body, conſecrate to thee,
By ruffian luſt ſhould be *contaminate?* *Shak. Com. of Err.*

CONTAMINA'TION. *n. ſ.* [from *contaminate.*] Pollution; defilement.

CONTE'MERATED. *adj.* [*contemeratus*, Latin.] Violated; polluted. *Dict.*

To CONTE'MN. *v. a.* [*contemno*, Latin] To deſpiſe; to ſcorn; to ſlight; to diſregard; to neglect; to defy.

Yet better thus, and known to be *contemned*,
Than ſtill *contemned* and flattered. *Shakeſpeare's King Lear.*

Pygmalion then the Tyrian ſceptre ſway'd;
One who *contemn'd* divine and human laws,
Then ſtrife enſu'd. *Dryden's Virgil's Æneid.*

CONTE'MNER. *n. ſ.* [from *contemn.*] One that contemns; a deſpiſer; a ſcorner.

He counſels him to perſecute innovators of worſhip, not only as *contemners* of the gods, but diſturbers of the ſtate. *South.*

To CONTE'MPER. *v. a.* [*contempero*, Latin.] To moderate; to reduce to a lower degree by mixing ſomething of oppoſite qualities.

The leaves qualify and *contemper* the heat, and hinder the evaporation of moiſture. *Ray on the Creation.*

CONTE'MPERAMENT. *n. ſ.* [from *contempero*, Latin] The degree of any quality.

There is nearly an equal *contemperament* of the warmth of our bodies to that of the hotteſt part of the atmoſphere. *Derh.*

To CONTE'MPERATE. *v. a.* [from *contemper.*] To diminiſh any quality by ſomething contrary; to moderate; to temper.

The mighty Nile and Niger do not only moiſten and *contemperate* the air, but refreſh and humectate the earth. *Brown.*

If blood abound, let it out, regulating the patient's diet, and *contemperating* the humours. *Wiſeman's Surgery.*

CONTEMPERA'TION. *n. ſ.* [from *contemperate.*]

1. The act of diminiſhing any quality by admixture of the contrary; the act of moderating or tempering.

The uſe of air, without which there is no continuation in life, is not nutrition, but the *contemperation* of fervour in the heart. *Brown's Vulgar Errours.*

2. Proportionate mixture; proportion.

There is not greater variety in men's faces, and in the *contemperations* of their natural humours, than there is in their phantaſies. *Hale's Origin of Mankind.*

To CONTE'MPLATE. *v. a.* [*contemplor*, Lat] To conſider with continued attention; to ſtudy; to meditate.

There is not much difficulty in confining the mind to *contemplate* what we have a great deſire to know. *Watts.*

To CONTE'MPLATE. *v. n.* To muſe; to think ſtudiouſly with long attention.

So many hours muſt I take my reſt;
So many hours muſt I *contemplate.* *Shakeſpeare's Henry* VI.

Sapor had an heaven of glaſs, which he trod upon, *contemplating* over the ſame as if he had been Jupiter. *Peacham.*

How can I conſider what belongs to myſelf, when I have been ſo long *contemplating* on you. *Dryd. Juv. Preface.*

CONTEMPLA'TION. *n. ſ.* [from *contemplate.*]

1. Meditation; ſtudious thought on any ſubject; continued attention.

How now, what ſerious *contemplation* are you in?
Shakeſpeare's King Lear.

Contemplation is keeping the idea, which is brought into the mind, for ſome time actually in view. *Locke.*

2. Holy meditation; a holy exerciſe of the ſoul, employed in attention to ſacred things.

I have breathed a ſecret vow,
To live in prayer and *contemplation*,
Only attended by Neriſſa here. *Shakeſp. Merch. of Venice.*

3. The faculty of ſtudy; oppoſed to the power of action.

There are two functions, *contemplation* and practice, according to that general diviſion of objects; ſome of which entertain our ſpeculation, others employ our actions. *South.*

CONTE'MPLATIVE. *adj.* [from *contemplate.*]

1. Given to thought or ſtudy; ſtudious; thoughtful.

Fixt and *contemplative* their looks,
Still turning over nature's books. *Denham.*

2. Employed in ſtudy; dedicated to ſtudy.

I am no courtier, nor verſed in ſtate affairs: my life hath rather been *contemplative* than active. *Bacon's Advice to Villiers.*

Contemplative men may be without the pleaſure of diſcovering the ſecrets of ſtate, and men of action are commonly without the pleaſure of tracing the ſecrets of divine art. *Grew's Coſmol.*

3. Having the power of thought or meditation.

So many kinds of creatures might be to exerciſe the *contemplative* faculty of man. *Ray on the Creation.*

CONTE'MPLATIVELY. *adv.* [from *contemplative.*] Thoughtfully; attentively; with deep attention.

CONTEMPLA'TOR. *n. ſ.* [Latin.] One employed in ſtudy; an enquirer after knowledge; a ſtudent.

In the Perſian tongue the word *magus* imports as much as a *contemplator* of divine and heavenly ſcience. *Raleigh's Hiſtory.*

The Platonick *contemplators* reject both theſe deſcriptions, founded upon parts and colours. *Brown's Vulgar Errours.*

CONTE'MPORARY. *adj.* [*contemporain*, French.]

1. Living in the ſame age; coetaneous.

Albert Durer was *contemporary* to Lucas. *Dryd. Dufreſnoy.*

2. Born at the ſame time.

A grove born with himſelf he ſees,
And loves his old *contemporary* trees. *Cowley.*

3. Exiſting at the ſame point of time.

It is impoſſible to make the ideas of yeſterday, to-day, and to-morrow, to be the ſame; or bring ages paſt and future together, and make them *contemporary*. *Locke.*

CONTE'MPORARY. *n. ſ.* One who lives at the ſame time with another.

All this in blooming youth you have atchiev'd;
Nor are your foil'd *contemporaries* griev'd. *Dryden.*

As he has been favourable to me, he will hear of his kindneſs from our *contemporaries*; for we are fallen into an age illiterate, cenſorious, and detracting. *Dryd. Juv. Preface.*

The active part of mankind, as they do moſt for the good of their *contemporaries*, very deſervedly gain the greateſt ſhare in their applauſes. *Addiſon's Freeholder*, Nº. 40.

To CONTE'MPORISE. *v. a.* [*con* and *tempus*, Latin.] To make contemporary; to place in the ſame age.

The indifferency of their exiſtences *contemporiſed* into our actions, admits a farther conſideration.
Brown's Vulgar Errours, b. i. *c.* 11.

CONTE'MPT. *n. ſ.* [*contemptus*, Latin.]

1. The act of deſpiſing others; ſlight regard; ſcorn.

It was neither in *contempt* nor pride that I did not bow. *Eſth.*

The ſhame of being miſerable,
Expoſes men to ſcorn and baſe *contempt*,
Even from their neareſt friends. *Denham.*

There is no action in the behaviour of one man towards another, of which human nature is more impatient than of *contempt*; it being a thing made up of theſe two ingredients, an undervaluing of a man, upon a belief of his utter uſeleſſneſs and inability, and a ſpiteful endeavour to engage the reſt of the world in the ſame belief and ſlight eſteem of him.
South's Sermons.

His friend ſmil'd ſcornful, and with proud *contempt*
Rejects as idle what his fellow dreamt. *Dryden's Fables.*

2. The ſtate of being deſpiſed; vileneſs.

The place was like to come unto *contempt*. 2 *Mac.* iii. 18.

CONTE'MPTIBLE. *adj.* [from *contempt.*]

1. Worthy of contempt; deſerving ſcorn.

No man truly knows himſelf, but he groweth daily more *contemptible* in his own eyes. *Taylor's Guide to Devotion.*

From no one vice exempt,
And moſt *contemptible* to ſhun contempt. *Pope's Epiſtles.*

2. Deſpiſed; ſcorned; neglected.

There is not ſo *contemptible* a plant or animal that does not confound the moſt enlarged underſtanding. *Locke.*

3. Scornful; apt to deſpiſe. This is no proper uſe.

If ſhe ſhould make tender of her love, 'tis very poſſible he'll ſcorn it; for the man hath a *contemptible* ſpirit. *Shakeſpeare.*

CONTE'MPTIBLENESS. *n. ſ.* [from *contemptible.*] The ſtate of being contemptible; the ſtate of being deſpiſed; meanneſs; vileneſs; baſeneſs; cheapneſs.

Who, by a ſteddy practice of virtue, comes to diſcern the *contemptibleneſs* of thoſe baits wherewith he allures us.
Decay of Piety.

CONTE'MPTIBLY. *adv.* [from *contemptible.*] Meanly; in a manner deſerving contempt.

Know'ſt thou not
Their language, and their ways? They alſo know,
And reaſon not *contemptibly*. *Milton's Paradiſe Loſt, b.* viii.

CONTE'MPTUOUS. *adj.* [from *contempt.*] Scornful; apt to deſpiſe; uſing words or actions of contempt; inſolent.

To neglect God all our lives, and know that we neglect him; to offend God voluntarily, and know that we offend him, caſting our hopes on the peace which we truſt to make at parting, is no other than a rebellious preſumption, and even a *contemptuous* laughing to ſcorn and deriding of God, his laws and precepts. *Raleigh's Hiſtory of the World.*

Some much averſe I found, and wond'rous harſh,
Contemptuous, proud, ſet on revenge and ſpite. *Milt. Agon.*

Rome, the proudeſt part of the heathen world, entertained the moſt *contemptuous* opinion of the Jews. *Atterbury.*

CONTE'MPTUOUSLY. *adv.* [from *contemptuous.*] With ſcorn; with deſpite; ſcornfully; deſpitefully.

I throw my name againſt the bruiſing ſtone,
Trampling *contemptuouſly* on thy diadem. *Shakeſpeare.*

The apoſtles and moſt eminent Chriſtians were poor, and uſed *contemptuouſly*. *Taylor's Holy Living.*

If he governs tyrannically in youth, he will be treated *contemptuouſly* in age; and the baſer his enemies, the more intolerable the affront. *L'Eſtrange, Fab.* 14. *Moral.*

A wiſe man would not ſpeak *contemptuouſly* of a prince, though out of his dominions. *Tillotſon.*

CONTE'MPTUOUSNESS. *n. ſ.* [from *contemptuous.*] Diſpoſition to contempt; inſolence. *Dict.*

To CONTE'ND. *v. n.* [*contendo*, Latin.]

1. To ſtrive; to ſtruggle in oppoſition.

Hector's forehead ſpit forth blood
At Grecian ſwords *contending*. *Shakeſpeare's Coriolanus.*

When he reads
Thy perſonal venture in the rebels fight,
His wonders and his praiſes do *contend*
Which ſhould be thine or his. *Shakeſpeare's Macbeth.*

Death and nature do *contend* about them,
Whether they live or die. *Shakeſpeare's Macbeth.*

Diſtreſs not the Moabites, neither *contend* with them in battle; for I will not give thee of their land. *Deutr.* ii. 9.

2. To vie; to act in emulation.

3. It has *for* before the ground or cauſe of contention.

You ſit above, and ſee vain men below
Contend for what you only can beſtow. *Dryden.*

The queſtion which our author would *contend for*, if he did not forget it, is what perſons have a right to be obeyed. *Locke.*

4. Sometimes *about.*

He will find that many things he fiercely *contended about* were trivial. *Decay of Piety.*

5. It has *with* before the opponent.

This battle fares like to the morning's war,
When dying clouds *contend with* growing light. *Sh. H.* VI.

If we conſider him as our maker, we cannot *contend with* him. *Temple.*

6. Sometimes *againſt.*

In ambitious ſtrength I did
Contend againſt thy valour. *Shakeſpeare's Coriolanus.*

To CONTE'ND. *v. a.* To diſpute any thing; to conteſt.

Their airy limbs in ſports they exerciſe,
And on the green *contend* the wreſtler's prize. *Dryd. Æneid.*

A time of war at length will come,
When Carthage ſhall *contend* the world with Rome. *Dryd.*

Thus low we lie,
Shut from this day and that *contended* ſky. *Dryden.*

CONTE'NDENT. *n. ſ.* [from *contend.*] Antagoniſt; opponent; champion; combatant.

In all notable changes and revolutions the *contendents* have been ſtill made a prey to the third party. *L'Eſtrange, Fab.* 15.

CONTE'NDER. *n. ſ.* [from *contend.*] Combatant; champion.

The *contenders* for it, look upon it as an undeniable truth. *Locke.*

Thoſe diſputes often ariſe in good earneſt, where the two *contenders* do really believe the different propoſitions which they ſupport. *Watts's Improvement of the Mind, p.* i. *c.* 10.

CONTE'NT. *adj.* [*contentus*, Latin.]

1. Satisfied ſo as not to repine; eaſy, though not highly pleaſed.

Born to the ſpacious empire of the Nine,
One wou'd have thought ſhe ſhou'd have been *content*,
To manage well that mighty government. *Dryden.*

Who is *content*, is happy. *Locke.*

A man is perfectly *content* with the ſtate he is in, when he is perfectly without any uneaſineſs. *Locke.*

Foe to loud praiſe, and friend to learned eaſe,
Content with ſcience in the vale of peace. *Pope's Epiſtles.*

2. Satisfied ſo as not to oppoſe.

Submit you to the people's voices,
Allow their officers, and be *content*
To ſuffer lawful cenſure. *Shakeſpeare's Coriolanus.*

To CONTE'NT. *v. a.* [from the adjective.]

1. To ſatisfy ſo as to ſtop complaint; not to offend; to appeaſe without plenary happineſs or complete gratification.

Content thyſelf with this much, and let this ſatisfy thee, that I love thee. *Sidney.*

It doth much *content* me
To hear him ſo inclin'd. *Shakeſpeare's Hamlet.*

If a man ſo temper his actions, as in ſome one of them he doth *content* every faction, the muſick of praiſe will be fuller. *Bac.*

Great minds do ſometimes *content* themſelves to threaten, when they could deſtroy. *Tillotſon, Preface.*

Do not *content* yourſelves with obſcure and confuſed ideas, where clearer are to be attained. *Watts's Logick.*

2. To pleaſe; to gratify.

Is the adder better than the eel,
Becauſe his painted ſkin *contents* the eye? *Shakeſpeare.*

CONTE'NT. *n. ſ.* [from the verb.]

1. Moderate happineſs; ſuch ſatisfaction as, though it does not fill up deſire, appeaſes complaint.

Nought's had, all's ſpent,
Where our deſire is got without *content*. *Shakeſp. Macbeth.*

One thought *content* the good to be enjoy'd;
This every little accident deſtroy'd. *Dryden.*

A wiſe *content* his even ſoul ſecur'd;
By want not ſhaken, nor by wealth allur'd. *Smith on Philips.*

2. Acquieſcence; ſatisfaction in a thing unexamined.

Others for language all their care expreſs,
And value books, as women men, for dreſs:
Their praiſe is ſtill—the ſtyle is excellent;
The ſenſe they humbly take upon *content*. *Pope's Epiſtles.*

3. [From *contentus*, contained.] That which is contained, or included in any thing.

Though my heart's *content* firm love doth bear,
Nothing of that ſhall from mine eyes appear. *Shakeſpeare.*

Scarcely any thing can be certainly determined of the particular *contents* of any ſingle maſs of ore by mere inſpection. *Woodward's Natural Hiſtory, p.* iv.

Theſe experiments are made on the blood of healthy animals: in a lax and weak habit ſuch a ſerum might afford other *contents*. *Arbuthnot on Aliments.*

4. The power of containing; extent; capacity.

This iſland had then fifteen hundred ſtrong ſhips, of great *content*. *Bacon.*

It were good to know the geometrical *content*, figure, and ſituation of all the lands of a kingdom, according to natural bounds. *Graunt's Bills of Mortality.*

5. That which is compriſed in a writing. In this ſenſe the plural only is in uſe.

I have a letter from her
Of ſuch *contents*, as you will wonder at. *Shakeſpeare.*

I ſhall prove theſe writings not counterfeits, but authentick, and the *contents* true, and worthy of a divine original. *Grew's Coſmol. b.* iv. *c.* 1. *ſ.* 1.

The *contents* of both books come before thoſe of the firſt book, in the thread of the ſtory. *Addiſon's Spectator*, N°. 267.

CONTENTA'TION. *n. ſ.* [from *content*.] Satisfaction; content.

I ſeek no better warrant than my own conſcience, nor no greater pleaſure than mine own *contentation*. *Sidney.*

The ſhield was not long after incruſted with a new ruſt, and is the ſame; a cut of which hath been engraved and exhibited, to the great *contentation* of the learned. *Arbu. and Pope.*

CONTE'NTED. *participial adj.* [from *content*.] Satisfied; at quiet; not repining; not demanding more; eaſy, though not plenarily happy.

Barbaroſſa, in hope by ſufferance to obtain another kingdom, ſeemed *contented* with the anſwer. *Knolles's Hiſtory.*

Dream not of other worlds,
Contented that thus far has been reveal'd,
Not of earth only, but of higheſt heav'n. *Milt. Par. Loſt.*

If he can deſcry
Some nobler foe approach, to him he calls,
And begs his fate, and then *contented* falls. *Denham.*

To diſtant lands Vertumnus never roves,
Like you, *contented* with his native groves. *Pope.*

CONTE'NTION. *n. ſ.* [*contentio*, Latin.]

1. Strife; debate; conteſt; quarrel; mutual oppoſition.

Can we with manners aſk what was the difference?
——Safely, I think; 'twas a *contention* in publick. *Shakeſp.*

But avoid fooliſh queſtions and genealogies, and *contentions* and ſtrivings. *Tit.* iii. 9.

Can they keep themſelves in a perpetual *contention* with their eaſe, their reaſon, and their God, and not endure a ſhort combat with a ſinful cuſtom. *Decay of Piety.*

The ancients made *contention* the principle that reigned in the chaos at firſt, and then love; the one to expreſs the diviſions, and the other the union of all parties in the middle and common bond. *Burnet's Theory of the Earth.*

2. Emulation; endeavour to excel.

Sons and brother at a ſtrife!
What is your quarrel? how began it firſt?
——No quarrel, but a ſweet *contention*. *Shakeſp. Hen.* VI.

3. Eagerneſs; zeal; ardour; vehemence of endeavour.

Your own earneſtneſs and *contention* to effect what you are about, will continually ſuggeſt to you ſeveral artifices. *Holder.*

This is an end, which, at firſt view, appears worthy our utmoſt *contention* to obtain. *Rogers.*

CONTE'NTIOUS. *adj.* [from *contend*] Quarrelſom; given to debate; perverſe; not peaceable.

Thou think'ſt much that this *contentious* ſtorm
Invades us to the ſkin. *Shakeſpeare's King Lear.*

There are certain *contentious* humours that are never to be pleaſed. *L'Eſtrange.*

Reſt made them idle, idleneſs made them curious, and curioſity *contentious*. *Decay of Piety.*

CONTE'NTIOUS *Juriſdiction.* [In law.] A court which has a power to judge and determine differences between contending parties. The lord chief juſtices, and judges, have a *contentious* juriſdiction; but the lords of the treaſury, and the commiſſioners of the cuſtoms, have none, being merely judges of accounts and tranſactions. *Chambers.*

CONTE'NTIOUSLY. *adv.* [from *contentious*.] Perverſely; quarrelſomely.

We ſhall not *contentiouſly* rejoin, or only to juſtify our own, but to applaud and confirm his maturer aſſertions. *Brown.*

CONTE'NTIOUSNESS. *n. ſ.* [from *contentious*.] Proneneſs to conteſt; perverſeneſs; turbulence; quarrelſomeneſs.

Do not *contentiouſneſs* and cruelty, and ſtudy of revenge, ſeldom fail of retaliation? *Bentley's Sermons.*

CONTE'NTLESS. *adj.* [from *content*.] Diſcontented; diſſatisfied; uneaſy.

Beſt ſtates, *contentleſs*,
Have a diſtracted and moſt wretched being,
Worſe than the worſt, content. *Shakeſpeare's Timon.*

CONTE'NTMENT. *n. ſ.* [from *content*, the verb.]

1. Acquieſcence without plenary ſatisfaction.

Such men's *contentment* muſt be wrought by ſtratagem: the uſual method of fare is not for them. *Hooker, b.* iv. *ſ.* 8.

Submiſſion is the only reaſoning between a creature and its Maker, and *contentment* in his will is the beſt remedy we can apply to misfortunes. *Temple.*

Contentment, without external honour, is humility; without the pleaſure of eating, temperance. *Grew's Coſmol.*

Some place the bliſs in action, ſome in eaſe,
Thoſe call it pleaſure, and *contentment* theſe. *Pope's Eſſays.*

But now no face divine *contentment* wears,
'Tis all blank ſadneſs, or continual tears. *Pope.*

2. Gratification.

At Paris the prince ſpent one whole day, to give his mind ſome *contentment* in viewing of a famous city. *Wotton.*

CONTE'RMINOUS. *adj.* [*conterminus*, Latin.] Bordering upon; touching at the boundaries.

This inſenſibly conformed ſo many of them, as were *conterminous* to the colonies and garriſons, to the Roman laws. *Hale's Law of England.*

CONTERRA'NEOUS. *adj.* [*conterraneus*, Lat.] Of the ſame country. *Dict.*

To CONTE'ST. *v. a.* [*conteſter*, Fr. probably from *contra teſtari*, Latin.] To diſpute; to controvert; to litigate; to call in queſtion.

'Tis evident, upon what account none have preſumed to *conteſt* the proportion of theſe ancient pieces. *Dryd. Dufreſn.*

To CONTE'ST. *v. n.* Followed by *with*.

1. To ſtrive; to contend.

The difficulty of an argument adds to the pleaſure of *conteſting with* it, when there are hopes of victory. *Burnet.*

2. To vie; to emulate.

I do *conteſt*
As hotly and as nobly *with* thy love,
As ever in ambitious ſtrength I did
Contend againſt thy valour. *Shakeſpeare's Coriolanus.*

Of man, who dares in pomp *with* Jove *conteſt*,
Unchang'd, immortal, and ſupremely bleſt? *Pope's Odyſſey.*

CONTE'ST. *n. ſ.* [from the verb.] Diſpute; difference; debate.

This of old no leſs *conteſts* did move,
Than when for Homer's birth ſev'n cities ſtrove. *Denham.*

A definition is the only way whereby the meaning of words can be known, without leaving room for *conteſt* about it. *Locke.*

Leave all noiſy *conteſts*, all immodeſt clamours, and brawling language. *Watts.*

CONTE'STABLE. *adj.* [from *conteſt*.] That may be conteſted; diſputable; controvertible.

CONTE'STABLENESS. *n. ſ.* [from *conteſtable*.] Poſſibility of conteſt. *Dict.*

CONTESTA'TION. *n. ſ.* [from *conteſt*.] The act of conteſting; debate; ſtrife.

Doors ſhut, viſits forbidden, and, which was worſe, divers *conteſtations*, even with the queen herſelf. *Wotton.*

After years ſpent in domeſtick, unſociable *conteſtations*, ſhe found means to withdraw. *Clarendon, b.* viii.

To

To CONTE'X. *v. a.* [*contexo*, Lat.] To weave together; to unite by interposition of parts.

The fluid body of quickfilver is *contexed* with the falts it carries up in fublimation. *Boyle.*

Co'NTEXT. *n. f.* [*contextus*, Latin.] The general feries of a difcourfe; the parts of the difcourfe that precede and follow the fentence quoted.

That chapter is really a reprefentation of one, which hath only the knowledge, not practice of his duty; as is manifeft from the *context*. *Hammond on Fundamentals.*

CONTE'XT. *adj.* [from *contex.*] Knit together; firm.

Hollow and thin, for lightnefs; but withal *context* and firm, for ftrength. *Derham's Phyfico-Theology.*

CONTE'XTURE. *n. f.* [from *contex.*] The difpofition of parts one amongft others; the compofition of any thing out of feparate parts; the fyftem; the conftitution; the manner in which any thing is woven or formed.

He was not of any delicate *contexture*; his limbs rather fturdy than dainty. *Wotton.*

Every fpecies, afterwards expreffed, was produced from that idea, forming that wonderful *contexture* of created beings. *Dryden's Dufrefnoy, Preface.*

Hence 'gan relax,
The ground's *contexture*; hence Tartarian dregs,
Sulphur, and nitrous fpume, enkindling fierce,
Bellow'd within their darkfome caves. *Philips.*

This apt, this wife *contexture* of the fea,
Makes it the fhips, driv'n by the winds, obey;
Whence hardy merchants fail from fhore to fhore. *Blackm.*

CONTIGNA'TION. *n. f.* [*contignatio*, Latin.]

1. A frame of beams or boards joined together.

We mean a porch, or cloifter, or the like, of one *contignation*, and not in ftoried buildings. *Wotton's Architecture.*

2. The act of framing or joining a fabrick.

CONTIGU'ITY. *n. f.* [from *contiguous.*] Actual contact; fituation in which two bodies or countries touch upon each other.

He defined magnetical attraction to be a natural imitation and difpofition conforming unto *contiguity*. *Brown, b.* ii.

The immediate *contiguity* of that convex were a real fpace. *Hale's Origin of Mankind.*

CONTI'GUOUS. *adj.* [*contiguus*, Latin.]

1. Meeting fo as to touch; bordering upon each other; not feparate.

Flame doth not mingle with flame as air doth with air, or water with water, but only remaineth *contiguous*, as it cometh to pafs betwixt confifting bodies. *Bacon's Nat. Hiftory*, N°. 31.

The loud mifrule
Of chaos far remov'd; left fierce extremes,
Contiguous, might diftemper the whole frame. *Milt. Pa. Loft.*

The Eaft and Weft
Upon the globe, a mathematick point
Only divides: thus happinefs and mifery,
And all extremes, are ftill *contiguous*. *Denham's Sophy.*

Diftinguifh them by the diminution of the lights and fhadows, joining the *contiguous* objects by the participation of their colours. *Dryden's Dufrefnoy.*

When I viewed it too near, the two halfs of the paper did not appear fully divided from one another, but feemed *contiguous* at one of their angles. *Newton's Opt.*

2. It has fometimes *with*.

Water, being *contiguous with* air, cooleth it, but moifteneth it not. *Bacon's Natural Hiftory*, N°. 865.

CONTI'GUOUSLY. *adv.* [from *contiguous.*] Without any intervening fpaces.

Thus difembroil'd, they take their proper place,
The next of kin *contiguoufly* embrace,
And foes are funder'd by a larger fpace. *Dryden's Ovid.*

CONTI'GUOUSNESS. *n. f.* [from *contiguous.*] Clofe connection; coherence. *Dict.*

Co'NTINENCE. } *n. f.* [*continentia*, Latin.]
Co'NTINENCY. }

1. Reftraint; command of one's felf.

He knew what to fay; he knew alfo when to leave off, a *continence* which is practifed by few writers. *Dryd. Fab. Pref.*

2. Chaftity in general.

Where is he?—
—In her chamber, making a fermon of *continency* to her,
and rails, and fwears, and rates. *Shak. Tam. of the Shrew.*

Suffer not difhonour to approach
Th' imperial feat; to virtue confecrate,
To juftice, *continence*, and nobility. *Shak. Titus Andronicus.*

3. Forbearance of lawful pleafure.

Content without lawful venery, is *continence*; without unlawful, chaftity. *Grew's Cofmol.*

4. Moderation in lawful pleafures.

Chaftity is either abftinence or *continence*: abftinence is that of virgins or widows; *continence*, of married perfons. *Taylor.*

5. Continuity; uninterrupted courfe.

Anfwers ought to be made before the fame judge, before whom the depofitions were produced, left the *continence* of the courfe fhould be divided; or, in other terms, left there fhould be a difcontinuance of the caufe. *Ayliffe's Parergon.*

CO'NTINENT. *adj.* [*continens*, Latin.]

1. Chafte; abftemious in lawful pleafures.

Life
Hath been as *continent*, as chafte, as true,
As I am now unhappy. *Shakefpeare's Winter's Tale.*

2. Reftrained; moderate; temperate.

I pray you, have a *continent* forbearance, 'till the fpeed of his rage goes flower. *Shakefpeare's King Lear.*

3. Continuous; connected.

The North-eaft part of Afia is, if not *continent* with the Weft fide of America, yet certainly it is the leaft disjoined by fea of all that coaft of Afia. *Brerewood on Languages.*

Co'NTINENT. *n. f.* [*continens*, Latin.]

1. Land not disjoined by the fea from other lands.

Whether this portion of the world were rent,
By the rude ocean, from the *continent*;
Or thus created, it was fure defign'd
To be the facred refuge of mankind. *Waller.*

The declivity of rivers will be fo much the lefs, and therefore the *continents* will be the lefs drained, and will gradually increafe in humidity. *Bentley's Sermons.*

2. That which contains any thing. This fenfe is perhaps only in *Shakefpeare*.

You fhall find in him the *continent* of what part a gentleman would fee. *Shakefpeare's Hamlet.*

O cleave my fides!
Heart, once be ftronger than thy *continent*,
Crack thy frail cafe. *Shakefp. Anthony and Cleopatra.*

Clofe pent-up guilts,
Rive your contending *continents*. *Shakefpeare's King Lear.*

To CONTI'NGE. *v. n.* [*contingo*, Lat.] To touch; to reach; to happen. *Dict.*

CONTI'NGENCE. } *n. f.* [from *contingent.*] The quality of being
CONTI'NGENCY. } fortuitous; accidental poffibility.

Their credulities affent unto any prognofticks, which, confidering the *contingency* in events, are only in the prefcience of God. *Brown's Vulgar Errours, b.* i. *c.* 3.

For once, O heav'n! unfold thy adamantine book;
If not thy firm, immutable decree,
At leaft the fecond page of great *contingency*,
Such as confifts with wills originally free. *Dryden.*

Ariftotle fays, we are not to build certain rules upon the *contingency* of human actions. *South's Sermons.*

CONTI'NGENT. *adj.* [*contingens*, Latin.] Falling out by chance; accidental; not determinable by any certain rule.

Hazard naturally implies in it, firft, fomething future; fecondly, fomething *contingent*. *South.*

I firft thoroughly informed myfelf in all material circumftances of it, in more places than one, that there might be nothing cafual or *contingent* in any one of thofe circumftances. *Woodward's Natural Hiftory.*

CONTI'NGENT. *n. f.*

1. A thing in the hands of chance.

By *contingents* we are to underftand thofe things which come to pafs without any human forecaft. *Grew's Cofmol. b.* iii. *c.* 2.

His underftanding could almoft pierce into future *contingents*, his conjectures improving even to prophecy. *South's Sermons.*

2. A proportion that falls to any perfon upon a divifion: thus, in time of war, each prince of Germany is to furnifh his *contingent* of men, money, and munition.

CONTI'NGENTLY. *adv.* [from *contingent.*] Accidentally; without any fettled rule.

It is digged out of the earth *contingently*, and indifferently, as the pyritæ and agates. *Woodward's Natural Hiftory, p.* iv.

CONTI'NGENTNESS. *n. f.* [from *contingent.*] Accidentalnefs.

CONTI'NUAL. *adj.* [*continuus*, Latin.]

1. Inceffant; proceeding without interruption; fucceffive without any fpace of time between. *Continual* is ufed of time, and *continuous* of place.

He that is of a merry heart, hath a *continual* feaft. *Prov.* 15.
'Tis all blank fadnefs, or *continual* tears. *Pope.*

2. [In law.] A *continual* claim is made from time to time, within every year and day, to land or other thing, which, in fome refpect, we cannot attain without danger. For example, if I be diffeifed of land, into which, though I have right into it, I dare not enter, for fear of beating; it behooveth me to hold on my right of entry to the beft opportunity of me and mine heir, by approaching as near it as I can, once every year as long as I live; and fo I fave the right of entry to my heir. *Cowel.*

CONTI'NUALLY. *adv.* [from *continual.*]

1. Without paufe; without interruption.

The drawing of the boughs into the infide of a room, where a fire is *continually* kept, hath been tried with grapes. *Bacon's Natural Hiftory*, N°. 405.

2. Without ceafing.

Why do not all animals *continually* increafe in bignefs, during the whole fpace of their lives? *Bentley's Sermons.*

CONTI'NUANCE. *n. f.* [from *continue.*]

1. Succeffion uninterrupted.

The brute immediately regards his own prefervation, or the *continuance* of his fpecies. *Addifon's Spectator*, N°. 120.

2. Permanence

2. Permanence in one ſtate.

Continuance of evil doth in itſelf increaſe evil. *Sidney.*

A chamber where a great fire is kept, though the fire be at one ſtay, yet with the *continuance* continually hath its heat increaſed. *Sidney, b.* ii.

Theſe Romiſh caſuiſts ſpeak peace to the conſciences of men, by ſuggeſting ſomething which ſhall ſatisfy their minds, notwithſtanding a known, avowed *continuance* in ſins. *South.*

3. Abode in a place.

4. Duration; laſtingneſs.

You either fear his humour, or my negligence, that you call in queſtion the *continuance* of his love. *Shak. Twelfth Night.*

Their duty depending upon fear, the one was of no greater *continuance* than the other. *Hayward.*

That pleaſure is not of greater *continuance*, which ariſes from the prejudice or malice of its hearers. *Addiſ. Freeholder.*

5. Perſeverance.

To them who, by patient *continuance* in well-doing, ſeek for glory, and honour, and immortality, eternal life. *Ro.* ii. 7.

6. Progreſſion of time.

In thy book all my members were written, which in *continuance* were faſhioned. *Pſ.* cxxxix. 16.

Conti'nuate. *adj.* [*continuatus*, Latin.]

1. Immediately united.

We are of him and in him, even as though our very fleſh and bones ſhould be made *continuate* with his. *Hooker, b.* v.

2. Uninterrupted; unbroken.

A moſt incomparable man breath'd, as it were,
To an untirable and *continuate* goodneſs. *Shakeſp. Timon.*

Continua'tion. *n. ſ.* [from *continuate.*] Protraction, or ſucceſſion uninterrupted.

Theſe things muſt needs be the works of providence, for the *continuation* of the ſpecies, and upholding the world. *Ray.*

The Roman poem is but the ſecond part of the Illias; a *continuation* of the ſame ſtory. *Dryd. Fables, Preface.*

Conti'nuative. *n. ſ.* [from *continuate.*] An expreſſion noting permanence or duration.

To theſe may be added *continuatives*; as Rome remains to this day, which includes at leaſt two propoſitions, *viz.* Rome was, and Rome is. *Watts's Logick.*

Continua'tor. *n. ſ.* [from *continuate.*] He that continues or keeps up the ſeries or ſucceſſion.

It ſeems injurious to providence to ordain a way of production which ſhould deſtroy the producer, or contrive the continuation of the ſpecies by the deſtruction of the *continuator.* *Brown's Vulgar Errours, b.* iii. *c.* 15.

To CONTI'NUE. *v. n.* [*continuer*, Fr. *continuo*, Latin.]

1. To remain in the ſame ſtate.

The multitude *continue* with me now three days, and have nothing to eat. *Mat.* xv. 32.

2. To laſt; to be durable.

Thy kingdom ſhall not *continue.* 1 *Sa.* xiii. 14.

For here have we no *continuing* city, but we ſeek one to come. *Heb.* xiii. 14.

3. To perſevere.

If ye *continue* in my word, then are ye my diſciples indeed. *Jo.* viii. 31.

To Conti'nue. *v. a.*

1. To protract, or repeat without interruption.

O *continue* thy loving kindneſs unto them. *Pſ.* xxxvi. 10.

2. To unite without a chaſm, or intervening ſubſtance.

The dark abyſs, whoſe boiling gulph
Tamely endur'd a bridge of wond'rous length,
From hell *continu'd* reaching th' utmoſt orb
Of this frail world. *Milton's Paradiſe Loſt, b.* ii. *l.* 1029.

Here Priam's ſon, Deiphobus, he found,
Whoſe face and limbs were one *continu'd* wound;
Diſhoneſt, with lop'd arms, the youth appears,
Spoil'd of his noſe, and ſhorten'd of his ears. *Dryd. Æn.*

Where any motion or ſucceſſion is ſo ſlow, as that it keeps not pace with the ideas in our minds, there the ſeries of a conſtant *continued* ſucceſſion is loſt; and we perceive it not but with certain gaps of reſt between. *Locke.*

You know how to make yourſelf happy, by only *continuing* ſuch a life as you have been long accuſtomed to lead. *Pope.*

Conti'nuedly. *adv.* [from *continued.*] Without interruption; without ceaſing.

By perſeverance, I do not underſtand a *continuedly* uniform, equal courſe of obedience, and ſuch as is not interrupted with the leaſt act of ſin. *Norris.*

Conti'nuer. *n. ſ.* [from *continue.*] Having the power of perſeverance.

I would my horſe had the ſpeed of your tongue, and ſo good a *continuer.* *Shakeſpeare's Much ado about Nothing.*

Continu'ity. *n. ſ.* [*continuitas*, Latin.]

1. Connection uninterrupted; coheſion; cloſe union.

It is certain, that in all bodies there is an appetite of union, and evitation of ſolution of *continuity.* *Bacon's Nat. Hiſtory.*

After the great lights there muſt be great ſhadows, which we call repoſes, becauſe in reality the ſight would be tired, if it were attracted by a *continuity* of glittering objects. *Dryd.*

It wraps itſelf about the flame, and by its *continuity* hinders any air or nitre from coming. *Addiſon's Remarks on Italy.*

2. In phyſick.

That texture or coheſion of the parts of an animal body, upon the deſtruction of which there is ſaid to be a ſolution of *continuity.* *Quincy.*

As in the natural body a wound or ſolution of *continuity* is worſe than a corrupt humour, ſo in the ſpiritual. *Bac. Eſſays.*

The ſolid parts may be contracted by diſſolving their *continuity*; for a fibre, cut through, contracts itſelf. *Arbuthnot.*

Conti'nuous. *adj.* [*continuus*, Latin.] Joined together without the intervention of any ſpace.

As the breadth of every ring is thus augmented, the dark intervals muſt be diminiſhed, until the neighbouring rings become *continuous*, and are blended. *Newton's Opt.*

To whoſe dread expanſe,
Continuous depth, and wond'rous length of courſe,
Our floods are rills. *Thomſon's Summer, l.* 835.

To CONTO'RT. *v. a.* [*contortus*, Latin.] To twiſt; to writhe.

The vertebral arteries are variouſly *contorted.* *Ray.*

Air ſeems to conſiſt of ſpires *contorted* into ſmall ſpheres, through the interſtices of which the particles of light may freely paſs. *Cheyne.*

Conto'rtion. *n. ſ.* [from *contort.*] Twiſt; wry motion; flexure.

Diſruption they would be in danger of, upon a great and ſudden ſtretch or *contortion.* *Ray on the Creation.*

How can ſhe acquire thoſe hundred graces and motions, and airs, the *contortions* of every muſcular motion in the face? *Swift.*

CONTOUR. n. ſ. [French.] The outline; the line by which any figure is defined or terminated.

Co'ntra. A Latin prepoſition uſed in compoſition, which ſignifies *againſt.*

CONTRA'BAND. *adj.* [*contrabando*, Ital. contrary to proclamation.] Prohibited; illegal; unlawful.

If there happen to be found an irreverent expreſſion, or a thought too wanton, in the cargo, let them be ſtaved or forfeited, like *contraband* goods. *Dryden's Fables, Preface.*

To Co'ntraband. *v. a.* [from the adjective.] To import goods prohibited.

To CONTRA'CT. *v. a.* [*contractus*, Latin.]

1. To draw together; to ſhorten.

Why love among the virtues is not known,
Is, that love *contracts* them all in one. *Donne.*

2. To bring two parties together; to make a bargain.

On him thy grace did liberty beſtow;
But firſt *contracted*, that, if ever found,
His head ſhould pay the forfeit. *Dryden's Fables.*

3. To betroth; to affiance.

The truth is, ſhe and I, long ſince *contracted*,
Are now ſo ſure that nothing can diſſolve us. *Shakeſpeare.*

She was a lady of the higheſt condition in that country, and *contracted* to a man of merit and quality. *Tatler,* N°. 58.

4. To procure; to bring; to incur; to draw; to get.

Of enemies he could not but *contract* good ſtore, while moving in ſo high a ſphere. *King Charles.*

He that but conceives a crime in thought,
Contracts the danger of an actual fault. *Dryden's Juv.*

Like friendly colours, found them both unite,
And each from each *contract* new ſtrength and light. *Pope.*

Such behaviour we *contract* by having much converſed with perſons of high ſtations. *Swift.*

5. To ſhorten; to abridge; to epitomiſe.

To Contra'ct. *v. n.*

1. To ſhrink up; to grow ſhort.

Whatever empties the veſſels, gives room to the fibres to *contract.* *Arbuthnot on Aliments.*

2. To bargain; as, *to* contract *for a quantity of proviſions.*

Contra'ct. *part. adj.* [from the verb.] Affianced; contracted.

Firſt was he *contract* to lady Lucy;
Your mother lives a witneſs to that vow. *Shakeſ. Rich.* III.

Co'ntract. *n. ſ.* [from the verb. Anciently accented on the firſt.]

1. An act whereby two parties are brought together; a bargain; a compact.

The agreement upon orders, by mutual *contract*, with the conſent to execute them by common ſtrength, they make the riſe of all civil governments. *Temple.*

Shall Ward draw *contracts* with a ſtateſman's ſkill?
Or Japhet pocket, like his grace, a will? *Pope.*

2. An act whereby a man and woman are betrothed to one another.

Touch'd you the baſtardy of Edward's children?—
—I did, with his *contract* with lady Lucy,
And his *contract* by deputy in France. *Shakeſ. Richard* III.

3. A writing in which the terms of a bargain are included.

Contra'ctedness. *n. ſ.* [from *contracted.*] The ſtate of being contracted; contraction. *Dict.*

Contractibi'lity. *n. ſ.* [from *contractible.*] Poſſibility of being contracted; quality of ſuffering contraction.

By

By this continual *contractibility* and dilatibility by different degrees of heat, the air is kept in a constant motion. *Arbuthn.*

CONTRA'CTIBLE. *adj.* [from *contract.*] Capable of contraction.

Small air-bladders, dilatable and *contractible*, are capable to be inflated by the admission of air, and to subside at the expulsion of it. *Arbuthnot on Aliments.*

CONTRA'CTIBLENESS. *n. s.* [from *contractible.*] The quality of suffering contraction. *Dict.*

CONTRA'CTILE. *adj.* [from *contract.*] Having the power of contraction, or of shortening itself.

The arteries are elastick tubes, endued with a *contractile* force, by which they squeeze and drive the blood still forward. *Arbuthnot on Aliments.*

CONTRA'CTION. *n. s.* [*contractio*, Latin.]

1. The act of contracting or shortening.

The main parts of the poem, such as the fable and sentiments, no translator can prejudice but by omissions or *contractions.* *Pope's Essay on Homer.*

2. The act of shrinking or shriveling.

Oil of vitriol will throw the stomach into involuntary *contractions.* *Arbuthnot on Aliments.*

3. The state of being contracted, or drawn into a narrow compass.

Some things induce a *contraction* in the nerves, placed in the mouth of the stomach, which is a great cause of appetite. *Bacon.*

Comparing the quantity of *contraction* and dilatation made by all the degrees of each colour, I found it greatest in the red. *Newton's Opt.*

4. [In grammar.] The reduction of two vowels or syllables to one.

5. Any thing in its state of abbreviation or contraction; as, *the writing is full of* contractions.

CONTRA'CTOR. *n. s.* [from *contract.*] One of the parties to a contract or bargain.

Let the measure of your affirmation or denial be the understanding of your *contractor*; for he that deceives the buyer or the seller by speaking what is true, in a sense not understood by the other, is a thief. *Taylor's Rule of Living Holy.*

All matches, friendships, and societies are dangerous and inconvenient, where the *contractors* are not equals. *L'Estrange.*

To CONTRADI'CT. *v. a.* [*contradico*, Latin.]

1. To oppose verbally; to assert the contrary to what has been asserted.

It is not lawful to *contradict* a point of history which is known to all the world, as to make Hannibal and Scipio contemporaries with Alexander. *Dryden's Dedication, Æn.*

2. To be contrary to; to repugn; to oppose.

No truth can *contradict* any truth. *Hooker, b.* ii. *sect.* 7.

I *contradict* your banes:
If you will marry, make your loves to me. *Shak. K. Lear.*

CONTRADI'CTER. *n. s.* [from *contradict.*] One that contradicts; one that opposes; an opposer.

If no *contradicter* appears herein, and the suit was only commenced against such as openly reproached him, in respect of his legitimacy, it will surely be good for the inheritance itself. *Ayliffe's Parergon.*

If a gentleman is a little sincere in his representations, he is sure to have a dozen *contradicters.* *Swift's View of Ireland.*

CONTRADI'CTION. *n. s.* [from *contradict.*]

1. Verbal opposition; controversial assertion.

That tongue,
Inspir'd with *contradiction*, durst oppose
A third part of the gods. *Milton's Paradise Lost, b.* vi.

2. Opposition.

Consider him that endureth such *contradiction* of sinners against himself, lest ye be wearied. *Heb.* xii. 3.

3. Inconsistency; incongruity in words or thoughts.

The apostle's advice to be angry and sin not, was a *contradiction* in their philosophy. *South's Sermons.*

If truth be once perceived, we do thereby also perceive whatsoever is false in *contradiction* to it. *Grew's Cosmol. b.* ii.

4. Contrariety, in thought or effect.

All *contradictions* grow in those minds, which neither absolutely climb the rock of virtue, nor freely sink into the sea of vanity. *Sidney, b.* ii.

Laws human must be made without *contradiction* unto any positive law in scripture. *Hooker, b.* iii. *s.* 9.

Can he make deathless death? That were
Strange *contradiction*, which to God himself
Impossible is held; as argument
Of weakness, not of pow'r. *Milton's Paradise Lost, b.* x.

CONTRADI'CTIOUS. *adj.* [from *contradict.*]

1. Filled with contradictions; inconsistent.

The rules of decency, of government, of justice itself, are so different in one place from what they are in another, so party-coloured and *contradictious*, that one would think the species of men altered according to their climates. *Collier.*

2. Inclined to contradict; given to cavil.

CONTRADI'CTIOUSNESS. *n. s.* [from *contradictious.*] Inconsistency; contrariety to itself.

This opinion was, for its absurdity and *contradictiousness*, unworthy of the contemplation and refined spirit of Plato. *Norris's Miscellanies.*

CONTRADI'CTORILY. *adv.* [from *contradictory.*] Inconsistently with himself; oppositely to others.

Such as have discoursed hereon, have so diversely, contrarily, or *contradictorily* delivered themselves, that no affirmative from thence can be reasonably deduced. *Brown's Vulg. Err.*

CONTRADI'CTORINESS. *n. s.* [from *contradictory.*] Opposition in the highest degree. *Dict.*

CONTRADI'CTORY. *adj.* [*contradictorius*, Latin.]

1. Opposite to; inconsistent with.

The Jews hold, that in case two rabbies should happen to contradict one another, they were yet bound to believe the *contradictory* assertions of both. *South's Sermons.*

The schemes of those gentlemen are most absurd, and *contradictory* to common sense. *Addison's Freeholder*, N°. 7.

2. [In logick.] That which is in the fullest opposition, where both the terms of one proposition are opposite to those of another.

CONTRADI'CTORY. *n. s.* A proposition which opposes another in all its terms; contrariety; inconsistency.

It is common with princes to will *contradictories*; for it is the solecism of power to think to command the end, and yet not to endure the means. *Bacon, Essay* 20.

To ascribe unto him a power of election, not to chuse this or that indifferently, is to make the same thing to be determined to one, and to be not determined to one, which are *contradictories.* *Bramh. Answer to Hobbs.*

CONTRADISTI'NCTION. *n. s.* [from *contradistinguish.*] Distinction by opposite qualities.

We must trace the soul in the ways of intellectual actions, whereby we may come to the distinct knowledge of what is meant by imagination, in *contradistinction* to some other powers. *Glanville's Sceps. c.* 13.

That there are such things as sins of infirmity, in *contradistinction* to those of presumption, is a truth not to be questioned. *South.*

To CONTRADISTI'NGUISH. *v. a.* [from *contra* and *distinguish.*] To distinguish not simply by differential but by opposite qualities.

The primary ideas we have peculiar to body, as *contradistinguished* to spirit, are the cohesion of solid, and consequently separable parts, and a power of communicating motion by impulse. *Locke.*

These are our complex ideas of soul and body, as *contradistinguished.* *Locke.*

CONTRAFI'SSURE. *n. s.* [from *contra* and *fissure.*]

Contusions, when great, do usually produce a fissure or crack of the scull, either in the same part where the blow was inflicted, and then it is called fissure; or in the contrary part, in which case it obtains the name of *contrafissure.* *Wiseman.*

To CONTRAI'NDICATE. *v. a.* [*contra* and *indico*, Lat.] To point out some peculiar or incidental symptom or method of cure, contrary to what the general tenour of the malady requires.

Vomits have their use in this malady; but the age and sex of the patient, or other urgent or *contraindicating* symptoms, must be observed. *Harvey on Consumptions.*

CONTRAINDICA'TION. *n. s.* [from *contraindicate.*] An indication or symptom, which forbids that to be done which the main scope of a disease points out at first. *Quincy.*

I endeavour to give the most simple idea of the distemper, and the proper diet, abstracting from the complications of the first, or the *contraindications* to the second. *Arbuth. on Aliments.*

CONTRAMU'RE. *n. s.* [*contremur*, French.] In fortification, is an out wall built about the main wall of a city. *Chambers.*

CONTRANI'TENCY. *n. s.* [from *contra* and *nitens*, Latin.] Reaction; a resistency against pressure. *Dict.*

CONTRAPOSI'TION. *n. s.* [from *contra* and *position.*]

1. A placing over against.

2. In logick. See CONVERSION.

CONTRAREGULA'RITY. *n. s.* [from *contra* and *regularity.*] Contrariety to rule.

It is not only its not promoting, but its opposing, or at least its natural aptness to oppose the greatest and best of ends; so that it is not so properly an irregularity as a *contraregularity.* *Norris.*

CONTRA'RIANT. *adj.* [*contrariant*, from *contrarier*, French.] Inconsistent; contradictory: a term of law.

The very depositions of witnesses themselves, being false, various, *contrariant*, single, inconcludent. *Ayliffe's Parergon.*

CO'NTRARIES. *n. s.* [from *contrary.*] In logick, propositions which destroy each other; but of which the falshood of one does not establish the truth of the other.

If two universals differ in quality, they are *contraries*; as, *every vine is a tree, no vine is a tree.* These can never be both true together, but they may be both false. *Watts's Logick.*

CONTRARI'ETY. *n. s.* [from *contrarietas*, Latin.]

1. Repugnance; opposition.

The will about one and the same thing may, in contrary respects,

respects, have contrary inclinations, and that without *contrariety*. *Hooker, b.* v. *sect.* 48.

It principally failed by late setting out, and by some *contrariety* of weather at sea. *Wotton.*

Their religion had more than negative *contrariety* to virtue. *Decay of Piety.*

There is a *contrariety* between those things that conscience inclines to, and those that entertain the senses. *South.*

There is nothing more common than *contrariety* of opinions; nothing more obvious than that one man wholly disbelieves what another only doubts of, and a third stedfastly believes and firmly adheres to. *Locke.*

2. Inconsistency; quality or position destructive of its opposite.

Making a *contrariety* the place of my memory, in her foulness I beheld Pamela's fairness, still looking on Mopsa, but thinking on Pamela. *Sidney.*

He which will perfectly recover a sick and restore a diseased body unto health, must not endeavour so much to bring it to a state of simple *contrariety*, as of fit proportion in *contrariety* unto those evils which are to be cured. *Hooker, b.* iv. *s.* 8.

He will be here, and yet he is not here;
How can these *contrarieties* agree? *Shakesp. Henry* IV. *p.* i.

These two interests are of that nature, that it is to be feared they cannot be divided; but they will also prove opposite, and not resting in a bare diversity, quickly rise into a *contrariety*. *South's Sermons.*

CONTRA'RILY. *adv.* [from *contrary.*]

1. In a manner contrary.

Many of them conspire to one and the same action, and all this *contrarily* to the laws of specifick gravity, in whatever posture the body be formed. *Ray on the Creation.*

2. Different ways; in different directions.

Though all men desire happiness, yet their wills carry them so *contrarily*, and consequently some of them to what is evil. *Locke.*

CONTRA'RINESS. *n. s.* [from *contrary.*] Contrariety; opposition. *Dict.*

CONTRA'RIOUS. *adj.* [from *contrary.*] Opposite; repugnant the one to the other.

God of our fathers, what is man!
That Thou towards him, with hand so various,
Or might I say *contrarious*,
Temper'st thy providence through his short course? *Milton.*

CONTRA'RIOUSLY. *adv.* [from *contrarious.*] Oppositely; contrarily.

Many things, having full reference
To one consent, may work *contrariously*. *Shakesp. Henry* V.

CONTRA'RIWISE. *adv.* [*contrary* and *wise.*] See WISE.

1. Conversely.

Divers medicines in greater quantity move stool, and in smaller urine; and so, *contrariwise*, some in greater quantity move urine, and in smaller stool. *Bacon's Natural History.*

Every thing that acts upon the fluids, must, at the same time, act upon the solids, and *contrariwise*. *Arbuth. on Alim.*

2. On the contrary.

The matter of faith is constant, the matter, *contrariwise*, of actions daily changeable. *Hooker, b.* iii. *s.* 10.

This request was never before made by any other lords; but, *contrariwise*, they were humble suiters to have the benefit and protection of the English laws. *Davies on Ireland.*

The sun may set and rise:
But we, *contrariwise*,
Sleep, after our short light,
One everlasting night. *Raleigh's History of the World.*

CO'NTRARY. *adj.* [*contrarius*, Latin.]

1. Opposite; contradictory; not simply different, or not alike, but repugnant, so that one destroys or obstructs the other.

Perhaps some thing, repugnant to her kind,
By strong antipathy the soul may kill;
But what can be *contrary* to the mind,
Which holds all contraries in concord still. *Davies.*

2. Inconsistent; disagreeing.

He that believes it, and yet lives *contrary* to it, knows that he hath no reason for what he does. *Tillotson, Serm.* v.

The various and *contrary* choices that men make in the world, do not argue that they do not at all pursue good; but that the same thing is not good to every man alike. *Locke.*

3. Adverse; in an opposite direction.

The ship was in the midst of the sea, tossed with the waves; for the wind was *contrary*. *Mat.* xiv. 24.

CO'NTRARY. *n. s.* [from the adjective.]

1. A thing of opposite qualities.

No *contraries* hold more antipathy,
Than I and such a knave. *Shakespeare's King Lear.*

He sung
Why *contraries* feed thunder in the cloud. *Cowley's Davideis.*

Honour should be concern'd in honour's cause;
That is not to be cur'd by *contraries*,
As bodies are, whose health is often drawn
From rankest poisons. *Southern's Oroonoko.*

2. A proposition contrary to some other; a fact contrary to the allegation.

The instances brought by our author are but slender proofs of a right to civil power and dominion in the first-born, and do rather shew the *contrary*. *Locke.*

3. *On the* CONTRARY. In opposition; on the other side.

He pleaded still not guilty;
The king's attorney, *on the contrary*,
Urg'd on examinations, proofs, confessions
Of diverse witnesses. *Shakespeare's Henry* VIII.

If justice stood on the side of the single person, it ought to give good men pleasure to see that right should take place; but when, *on the contrary*, the commonweal of a whole nation is overborn by private interest, what good man but must lament? *Swift.*

4. *To the* CONTRARY. To a contrary purpose; to an opposite intent.

They did it, not for want of instruction *to the contrary. Still.*

To CO'NTRARY. *v. a.* [*contrarier*, French.] To oppose; to thwart; to contradict.

When I came to court I was advised not to *contrary* the king. *Latimer.*

Finding in him the force of it, he would no further *contrary* it, but employ all his service to medicine it. *Sidney.*

CO'NTRAST. *n. s.* [*contraste*, Fr.] Opposition and dissimilitude of figures, by which one contributes to the visibility or effect of another.

To CO'NTRAST. *v. a.* [from the noun.]

1. To place in opposition, so that one figure shews another to advantage.

2. To shew another figure to advantage by its colour or situation.

The figures of the groups must not be all on a side, that is, with their face and bodies all turned the same way; but must *contrast* each other by their several positions. *Dryd. Dufresnoy.*

CONTRAVALLA'TION. *n. s.* [from *contra* and *vallo*, Latin.] The fortification thrown up, by the besiegers, round a city, to hinder the sallies of the garrison.

When the late czar of Muscovy first acquainted himself with mathematical learning, he practised all the rules of circumvallation and *contravallation* at the siege of a town in Livonia. *Watts's Logick.*

To CONTRAVE'NE. *v. a.* [*contra* and *venio*, Lat.] To oppose; to obstruct; to baffle.

CONTRAVE'NER. *n. s.* [from *contravene.*] He who opposes another.

CONTRAVE'NTION. *n. s.* [French.] Opposition.

Yet if Christianity did not lend its name to stand in the gap, and to employ or divert these humours, they must of necessity be spent in *contraventions* to the laws of the land. *Swift.*

CONTRAYE'RVA. *n. s.* [*contra*, against, and *yerva*, a name by which the Spaniards call black hellebore; and, perhaps, sometimes poison in general.] A species of birthwort growing in Jamaica, where it is much used as an alexipharmick. *Miller.*

CONTRECTA'TION. *n. s.* [*contrectatio*, Latin.] A touching or handling. *Dict.*

CONTRI'BUTARY. *adj.* [from *con* and *tributary.*] Paying tribute to the same sovereign.

Thus we are engaged in the objects of geometry and arithmetick; yea, the whole mathematicks must be *contributary*, and to them all nature pays a subsidy. *Glanville's Sceps. c.* 25.

To CONTRI'BUTE. *v. a.* [*contribuo*, Latin.] To give to some common stock; to advance towards some common design.

England *contributes* much more than any other of the allies. *Addison on the State of the War.*

His master *contributed* a great sum of money to the Jesuits church, which is not yet quite finished. *Addison on Italy.*

To CONTRI'BUTE. *v. n.* To bear a part; to have a share in any act or effect.

Whatever praises may be given to works of judgment, there is not even a single beauty in them to which the invention must not *contribute*. *Pope's Essay on Homer.*

CONTRIBU'TION. *n. s.* [from *contribute.*]

1. The act of promoting some design in conjunction with other persons.

2. That which is given by several hands for some common purpose.

It hath pleased them of Macedonia to make a certain *contribution* for the poor saints. *Rom.* xv. 26.

Beggars are now maintained by voluntary *contributions*. *Graunt's Bills of Mortality.*

3. That which is paid for the support of an army lying in a country.

The people 'twixt Philippi and this ground,
Do stand but in a forc'd affection;
For they have grudg'd us *contribution*. *Shakes. Jul. Cæsar.*

CONTRI'BUTIVE. *adj.* [from *contribute.*] That which has the power or quality of promoting any purpose in concurrence with other motives.

As the value of the promises renders them most proper incentives

centives to virtue, so the manner of proposing we shall find also highly *contributive* to the same end. *Decay of Piety.*

CONTRI'BUTOR. *n. s.* [from *contribute.*] One that bears a part in some common design; one that helps forward, or exerts his endeavours to some end, in conjunction with others.

I promis'd we would be *contributors*,
And bear his charge of wooing, whatsoe'er. *Shakespeare.*

A grand *contributor* to our dissentions is passion. *Dec. of Piety.*

Art thou a true lover of thy country? Zealous for its religious and civil liberties? And a chearful *contributor* to all those publick expences which have been thought necessary to secure them? *Atterbury.*

CONTRI'BUTORY. *adj.* [from *contribute.*] Promoting the same end; bringing assistance to some joint design, or increase to some common stock.

To CONTRI'STATE. *v. a.* [*contristo*, Latin.] To sadden; to make sorrowful; to make melancholy.

Blackness and darkness are but privatives, and therefore have little or no activity: somewhat they do *contristate*, but very little. *Bacon's Natural History*, N°. 73.

CONTRISTA'TION. *n. s.* [from *contristate.*] The act of making sad; the state of being made sad; sorrow; heaviness of heart; sadness; sorrowfulness; gloominess; grief; moan; mournfulness; trouble; discontent; melancholy.

Incense and nidorous smells, such as were of sacrifices, were thought to intoxicate the brain, and to dispose men to devotion; which they may do by a kind of sadness and *contristation* of the spirits, and partly also by heating and exalting them. *Bacon's Natural History*, N°. 932.

CONTRI'TE. *adj.* [*contritus*, Latin.]

1. Bruised; much worn.
2. Worn with sorrow; harrassed with the sense of guilt; penitent. In the books of divines *contrite* is sorrowful for sin, from the love of God and desire of pleasing him; and *attrite* is sorrowful for sin, from the fear of punishment.

I Richard's body have interred now;
And on it have bestow'd more *contrite* tears,
Than from it issu'd forced drops of blood. *Shak. Henry* V.

With tears
Wat'ring the ground, and with our sighs the air
Frequenting, sent from hearts *contrite*, in sign
Of sorrow unfeign'd, and humiliation meek. *Milt. Pa. Lost.*

The *contrite* sinner is restored to pardon, and, through faith in Christ, our repentance is intitled to salvation. *Rogers's Serm.*

CONTRI'TENESS. *n. s.* [from *contrite.*] Contrition; repentance. *Dict.*

CONTRI'TION. *n. s.* [from *contrite.*]

1. The act of grinding; or rubbing to powder.

Some of those coloured powders, which painters use, may have their colours a little changed, by being very elaborately and finely ground; where I see not what can be justly pretended for those changes, besides the breaking of their parts into less parts by that *contrition*. *Newton's Opt.*

2. Penitence; sorrow for sin: in the strict sense, the sorrow which arises from the desire to please God, distinguished from *attrition*, or imperfect repentance produced by dread of hell.

What is sorrow and *contrition* for sin? A being grieved with the conscience of sin, not only that we have thereby incurred such danger, but also that we have so unkindly grieved and provoked so good a God. *Hammond's Pract. Cat.*

Fruits of more pleasing savour, from thy seed
Sown with *contrition* in his heart, than those
Which, his own hand manuring, all the trees
Of paradise could have produc'd. *Milton's Paradise Lost.*

Your fasting, *contrition*, and mortification, when the church and state appoints, and that especially in times of greater riot and luxury. *Sprat's Sermons.*

My future days shall be one whole *contrition*;
A chapel will I build with large endowment,
Where every day an hundred aged men
Shall all hold up their wither'd hands to heav'n. *Dryden.*

CONTRI'VABLE. *adj.* [from *contrive.*] Possible to be planned by the mind; possible to be invented and adjusted.

It will hence appear how a perpetual motion may seem easily *contrivable.* *Wilkins's Dædalus.*

CONTRI'VANCE. *n. s.* [from *contrive.*]

1. The act of contriving; excogitation; the thing contrived.

There is no work impossible to these *contrivances*, but there may be as much acted by this art as can be fancied by imagination. *Wilkins's Math. Mag.*

Instructed, you'll explore
Divine *contrivance*, and a God adore. *Blackmore's Creation.*

2. Scheme; plan; disposition of parts or causes.

Our bodies are made according to the most curious artifice, and orderly *contrivance.* *Glanville's Sceps. c.* 7.

3. A conceit; a plot; an artifice.

Have I not manag'd my *contrivance* well,
To try your love, and make you doubt of mine? *Dryden.*

There might be a feint, a *contrivance* in the matter, to draw him into some secret ambush. *Atterbury's Sermons.*

To CONTRI'VE. *v. a.* [*controuver*, French.]

1. To plan out; to excogitate.

One that slept in the *contriving* lust, and waked to do it. *Shakespeare's King Lear.*

What more likely to *contrive* this admirable frame of the universe than infinite wisdom. *Tillotson.*

Our poet has always some beautiful design, which he first establishes, and then *contrives* the means which will naturally conduct him to his end. *Dryden.*

2. To wear away. Out of use.

Three ages, such as mortal men *contrive.* *Fairy Queen.*

To CONTRI'VE. *v. n.* To form or design; to plan; to scheme; to complot.

Please ye, we may *contrive* this afternoon,
And quaff carouses to our mistress' health. *Shakespeare.*

CONTRI'VEMENT. *n. s.* [from *contrive.*] Invention. *Dict.*

CONTRI'VER. *n. s.* [from *contrive.*] An inventer; one that plans a design; a schemer.

I, the mistress of your charms,
The close *contriver* of all harms,
Was never call'd to bear my part. *Shakespeare's Macbeth.*

Epeus, who the fraud's *contriver* was. *Denham.*

Plain loyalty, not built on hope,
I leave to your *contriver*, Pope:
None loves his king and country better,
Yet none was ever less their debtor. *Swift.*

Scenes of blood and desolation, I had painted as the common effects of those destructive machines; whereof, he said, some evil genius, enemy to mankind, must have been the first *contriver.* *Gulliv. Travels.*

CONTRO'L. *n. s.* [*controle*, that is, *contre role*, French.]

1. A register or account kept by another officer, that each may be examined by the other.
2. Check; restraint.

Let partial spirits still aloud complain,
Think themselves injur'd that they cannot reign;
And own no liberty, but where they may,
Without *control*, upon their fellows prey. *Waller.*

He shall feel a force upon himself from within, and from the *control* of his own principles, to engage him to do worthily. *South.*

If the sinner shall win so complete a victory over his conscience, that all those considerations shall be able to strike no terrour into his mind, lay no restraint upon his lusts, no *control* upon his appetites, he is certainly too strong for the means of grace. *South's Sermons.*

Speak, what Phœbus has inspir'd thy soul
For common good, and speak without *control.* *Dryd. Hom.*

3. Power; authority; superintendence.

The beasts, the fishes, and the winged fowls,
Are their male's subjects, and at their *controls.* *Shakespeare.*

To CONTRO'L. *v. a.* [from the noun.]

1. To keep under check by a counter reckoning.
2. To govern; to restrain; to subject.

Authority to convent, to *control*, to punish, as far as with excommunication, whomsoever they should think worthy. *Hooker, Preface.*

Give me a staff of honour for mine age;
But not a sceptre to *control* the world. *Shakes. Tit. Andron.*

Who shall *control* me for my works? *Ecclus.* v. 3.

I feel my virtue struggling in my soul;
But stronger passion does its pow'r *control.* *Dryd. Aurengz.*

O, dearest Andrew, says the humble droll,
Henceforth may I obey, and thou *control* *Prior.*

3. To overpower; to confute; as, *he* controlled *all the evidence of his adversary.*

As for the time while he was in the Tower, and the manner of his brother's death, and his own escape, she knew they were things that a very few could *control.* *Bacon's Henry* VII.

CONTRO'LLABLE. *adj.* [from *control.*] Subject to control; subject to command; subject to be over-ruled.

Passion is the drunkenness of the mind, and therefore, in its present workings, not *controllable* by reason. *South.*

CONTRO'LLER. *n. s.* [from *control.*] One that has the power of governing or restraining; a superintendent.

He does not calm his contumelious spirit,
Nor cease to be an arrogant *controller.* *Shakesp. Henry* VI.

The great *controller* of our fate,
Deign'd to be man, and liv'd in low estate. *Dryden.*

CONTRO'LLERSHIP. *n. s.* [from *controller.*] The office of a controller.

CONTRO'LMENT. *n. s.* [from *control.*]

1. The power or act of superintending or restraining; restraint; superintendence.

They made war and peace one with another, without *controlment.* *Davies on Ireland.*

2. Opposition; resistance; confutation.

Were it reason that we should suffer the same to pass without *controlment*, in that current meaning whereby every where it prevaileth. *Hooker, b.* iii. *sect.* 7.

Here have we war for war, and blood for blood,
Controlment for *controlment.* *Shakespeare's King John.*

CONTROVE'RSIAL. *adj.* [from *controversy.*] Relating to disputes; disputatious.

It

It happens in *controversial* discourses as it does in the assaulting of towns, where, if the ground be but firm whereon the batteries are erected, there is no farther enquiry of whom it is borrowed, nor whom it belongs to, so it affords but a fit rise for the present purpose. *Locke.*

CO'NTROVERSY. *n. s.* [*controversia*, Latin.]

1. Dispute; debate; agitation of contrary opinions: a dispute is commonly oral, and a controversy in writing.

How cometh it to pass that we are so rent with mutual contentions, and that the church is so much troubled? If men had been willing to learn, all these *controversies* might have died the very day they were first brought forth. *Hooker, b.* i.

Without *controversy* great is the mystery of godliness. 1 *Tim.*

Wild *controversy* then, which long had slept,
Into the press from ruin'd cloisters leapt. *Denham.*

This left no room for *controversy* about the title, nor for encroachment on the right of others. *Locke.*

2. A suit in law.

If there be a *controversy* between men, and they come unto judgment, that the judges may judge them, then they shall justify the righteous and condemn the wicked. *Deutr.* xxv. 1.

3. A quarrel.

The Lord hath a *controversy* with the nations. *Jer.* xxv. 31.

4. Opposition; enmity: this is an unusual sense.

The torrent roar'd, and we did buffet it
With lusty sinews; throwing it aside,
And stemming it with hearts of *controversy*. *Shak. Jul. Cæs.*

To CO'NTROVERT. *v. a.* [*controverto*, Lat.] To debate; to ventilate in opposite books; to dispute any thing in writing.

If any person shall think fit to *controvert* them, he may do it very safely for me. *Cheyne's Phil. Princ.*

CONTROVE'RTIBLE. *adj.* [from *controvert.*] Disputable; that may be the cause of controversy.

Discoursing of matters dubious, and many *controvertible* truths, we cannot without arrogancy intreat a credulity, or implore any farther assent than the probability of our reasons and verity of our experiments. *Brown's Vulgar Errours, b.* i.

CONTROVE'RTIST. *n. s.* [from *controvert.*] Disputant; a man versed or engaged in literary wars or disputations.

Who can think himself so considerable as not to dread this mighty man of demonstration, this prince of *controvertists*, this great lord and possessor of first principles. *Tillotson, Preface.*

CONTU'MACIOUS. *adj.* [*contumax*, Latin.] Obstinate; perverse; stubborn; inflexible.

He is in law said to be a *contumacious* person, who, on his appearance afterwards, departs the court without leave. *Ayliffe.*

There is another very efficacious method for subduing of the most obstinate *contumacious* sinner, and bringing him into the obedience of the faith of Christ. *Hammond's Fundamentals.*

CONTUMA'CIOUSLY. *adv.* [from *contumacious.*] Obstinately; stubbornly; inflexibly; perversely.

CONTUMA'CIOUSNESS. *n. s.* [from *contumacious.*] Obstinacy; perverseness; inflexibility; stubbornness.

From the description I have given of it, a judgment may be given of the difficulty and *contumaciousness* of cure. *Wiseman.*

CO'NTUMACY. *n. s.* [from *contumacia*, Latin.]

1. Obstinacy; perverseness; stubbornness; inflexibility.

Such acts
Of *contumacy* will provoke the Highest
To make death in us live. *Milton's Paradise Lost, b.* x.

2. [In law.] A wilful contempt and disobedience to any lawful summons or judicial order. *Ayliffe's Parergon.*

These certificates do only, in the generality, mention the party's *contumacies* and disobedience. *Ayliffe's Parergon.*

CONTUME'LIOUS. *adj.* [*contumeliosus*, Latin.]

1. Reproachful; rude; sarcastick; contemptuous.

With scoffs and scorns, and *contumelious* taunts,
In open market-place produc'd they me
To be a publick spectacle. *Shakespeare's Henry* VI. *p.* i.

In all the quarrels and tumults at Rome, though the people frequently proceeded to rude *contumelious* language, yet no blood was ever drawn in any popular commotions, 'till the time of the Gracchi. *Swift on the Dissent. in Athens and Rome.*

2. Inclined to utter reproach; brutal; rude.

There is yet another sort of *contumelious* persons, who, indeed, are not chargeable with that circumstance of ill employing their wit; for they use none in it. *Governm. of the Tongue.*

Giving our holy virgins to the stain
Of *contumelious*, beastly, madbrain'd war. *Shakesp. Timon.*

3. Productive of reproach; shameful; ignominious.

As it is in the highest degree injurious to them, so is it *contumelious* to him. *Decay of Piety.*

CONTUME'LIOUSLY. *adv.* [from *contumelious.*] Reproachfully; contemptuously; rudely.

The people are not wont to take so great offence, when they are excluded from honours and offices, as when their persons are *contumeliously* trodden upon. *Hooker, b.* i. *sect.* 10.

Fie, lords; that you, being supreme magistrates,
Thus *contumeliously* should break the peace. *Shakesp. Hen.* VI.

CONTUME'LIOUSNESS. *n. s.* [from *contumelious.*] Rudeness; reproach.

CO'NTUMELY. *n. s.* [*contumelia*, Latin.] Rudeness; contemptuousness; bitterness of language; reproach.

If the helm of chief government be in the hands of a few of the wealthiest, then laws, providing for continuance thereof, must make the punishment of *contumely* and wrong, offered unto any of the common sort, sharp and grievous, that so the evil may be prevented. *Hooker, b.* i. *sect.* 10.

Th' oppressor's wrong, the proud man's *contumely*,
The pang of despis'd love, the law's delay. *Shakesp. Hamlet.*

It was undervalued and depressed with some bitterness and *contumely*. *Clarendon, b.* viii.

Why should any man be troubled at the *contumelies* of those whose judgment deserves not to be valued? *Tillotson.*

Eternal *contumely* attend that guilty title which claims exemption from thought, and arrogates to its wearers the prerogative of brutes. *Addison's Guardian*, N°. 123.

To CONTU'SE. *v. a.* [*contusus*, Latin.]

1. To beat together; to bruise.

Of their roots, barks, and seeds, *contused* together, and mingled with other earth, and well watered with warm water, there came forth herbs much like the other. *Bacon's Nat. Hist.*

2. To bruise the flesh without a breach of the continuity.

The ligature *contuses* the lips in cutting them, so that they require to be digested before they can unite. *Wiseman's Surgery.*

CONTU'SION. *n. s.* [from *contusio.*]

1. The act of beating or bruising.

2. The state of being beaten or bruised.

Take a piece of glass, and reduce it to powder, it acquiring by *contusion* a multitude of minute surfaces, from a diaphanous, degenerates into a white body. *Boyle on Colours.*

3. A bruise; a compression of the fibres, distinguished from a wound.

That winter lion, who in rage forgets
Aged *contusions*, and all bruise of time. *Shakesp. Henry* VI.

The bones, in sharp colds, wax brittle; and all *contusions*, in hard weather, are more difficult to cure. *Bacon's Nat. History.*

CONVAL LILY. See LILY *of the* VALLEY.

CONVALE'SCENCE. } *n. s.* [from *convalesco*, Latin.] Renewal
CONVALE'SCENCY. } of health; recovery from a disease.

Being in a place out of the reach of any alarm, she recovered her spirits to a reasonable *convalescence*. *Clarendon, b.* viii.

CONVALE'SCENT. *adj.* [*convalescens*, Latin.] Recovering; returning to a state of health.

CONVE'NABLE. *adj.* [*convenable*, French.]

1. Consistent with; agreeable to; accordant to. Not now in use.

He is so meek, wise, and merciable,
And with his word his work is *convenable*. *Spenser's Past.*

2. That may be convened.

To CONVE'NE. *v. n.* [*convenio*, Latin.] To come together; to assemble; to associate; to unite.

The fire separates the aqueous parts from the others wherewith they were blended in the concrete, and brings them into the receiver, where they *convene* into a liquor. *Boyle.*

There are settled periods of their *convening*, or a liberty left to the prince for convoking the legislature. *Locke.*

In short-sighted men, whose eyes are too plump, the refraction being too great, the rays converge and *convene* in the eyes, before they come at the bottom. *Newton's Opt.*

To CONVE'NE. *v. a.*

1. To call together; to assemble; to convoke.

No man was better pleased with the *convening* of this parliament than myself. *King Charles.*

All the factious and schismatical people would frequently, as well in the night as the day, *convene* themselves by the sound of a bell. *Clarendon.*

And now th' almighty father of the gods
Convenes a council in the blest abodes. *Pope's Statius.*

2. To summon judicially.

By the papal canon law, clerks, in criminal and civil causes, cannot be *convened* before any but an ecclesiastical judge. *Ayliffe.*

CONVE'NIENCE. } *n. s.* [*convenientia*, Latin.]
CONVE'NIENCY. }

1. Fitness; propriety.

In things not commanded of God, yet lawful, because permitted, the question is, what light shall shew us the *conveniency* which one hath above another. *Hooker, b.* ii. *s.* 4.

2. Commodiousness; ease; freedom from difficulties.

A man putting all his pleasures into one, is like a traveller's putting all his goods into one jewel: the value is the same, and the *convenience* greater. *South's Sermons.*

Every man must want something for the *conveniency* of his life, for which he must be obliged to others. *Calamy's Serm.*

There is another *convenience* in this method, during your waiting. *Swift's Directions to the Footman.*

3. Cause of ease; accommodation.

If it have not such a *convenience*, voyages must be very uncomfortable. *Wilkins's Math. Magic.*

A man alters his mind as the work proceeds, and will have this or that *convenience* more, of which he had not thought when he began. *Dryden's Fables, Preface.*

There was a pair of ſpectacles, a pocket perſpective, and ſeveral other little *conveniencies*, I did not think myſelf bound in honour to diſcover. *Gulliver's Travels.*

3. Fitneſs of time or place.

Uſe no farther means;
But with all brief and plain *conveniency*,
Let me have judgment. *Shakeſpeare's Merchant of Venice.*

CONVE'NIENT. *adj.* [*conveniens*, Latin.]

1. Fit; ſuitable; proper; well adapted; commodious.

The leaſt and moſt trivial epiſodes, or under actions, are either neceſſary or *convenient*; either ſo neceſſary that without them the poem muſt be imperfect, or ſo *convenient* that no others can be imagined more ſuitable to the place in which they are. *Dryd. Dedication to the Æneid.*

Health itſelf is but a kind of temper, gotten and preſerved by a *convenient* mixture of contrarieties. *Arbuth. on Aliments.*

2. It has either *to* or *for* before the following noun: perhaps it ought generally to have *for* before perſons, and *to* before things.

Give me neither poverty nor riches, feed me with food *convenient for* me. *Prov.* xxx. 8.

There are ſome arts that are peculiarly *convenient to* ſome particular nations. *Tillotſon.*

CONVE'NIENTLY. *adv.* [from *convenient.*]

1. Commodiouſly; without difficulty.

I this morning know
Where we ſhall find him moſt *conveniently*. *Shakeſp Hamlet.*

2. Fitly; with proper adaptation of part to part, or of the whole to the effect propoſed.

It would be worth the experiment to inquire, whether or no a ſailing chariot might be more *conveniently* framed with moveable ſails, whoſe force may be impreſſed from their motion, equivalent to thoſe in a wind-mill. *Wilkins's Mat. Mag.*

CO'NVENT. *n. ſ.* [*conventus*, Latin.]

1. An aſſembly of religious perſons; a body of monks or nuns.

He came to Leiceſter;
Lodg'd in the abbey, where the reverend abbot,
With all his *convent*, honourably receiv'd him. *Sh. H.* VIII.

2. A religious houſe; an abbey; a monaſtery; a nunnery.

One ſeldom finds in Italy a ſpot of ground more agreeable than ordinary, that is not covered with a *convent*. *Addiſon.*

To CONVE'NT. *v. a.* [*convenio*, Latin.] To call before a judge or judicature.

He with his oath
By all probation will make up full clear,
Whenever he's *convented*. *Shakeſp. Meaſure for Meaſure.*

They ſent forth their precepts to attach men, and *convent* them before themſelves at private houſes. *Bacon's Henry* VII.

CO'NVENTICLE. *n. ſ.* [*conventiculum*, Latin.]

1. An aſſembly; a meeting.

They are commanded to abſtain from all *conventicles* of men whatſoever; even out of the church, to have nothing to do with publick buſineſs. *Ayliffe's Parergon.*

2. An aſſembly for worſhip. Generally uſed in an ill ſenſe, including hereſy or ſchiſm.

It behoveth, that the place where God ſhall be ſerved by the whole church be a publick place, for the avoiding of privy *conventicles*, which, covered with pretence of religion, may ſerve unto dangerous practices. *Hooker, b.* v. *ſect.* 12.

A ſort of men, who are content to be ſtiled of the church of England, who perhaps attend its ſervice in the morning, and go with their wives to a *conventicle* in the afternoon. *Swift.*

3. A ſecret aſſembly; an aſſembly where conſpiracies are formed.

Ay, all of you have laid your heads together,
(Myſelf had notice of your *conventicles*)
And all to make away my guiltleſs life. *Shakeſp. Henry* VI.

CONVE'NTICLER. *n. ſ.* [from *conventicle.*] One that ſupports or frequents private and unlawful aſſemblies.

Another crop is too like to follow; nay, I fear, it is unavoidable, if the *conventiclers* be permitted ſtill to ſcatter. *Dryd.*

CONVE'NTION. *n. ſ.* [*conventio*, Latin.]

1. The act of coming together; union; coalition; junction.

They are to be reckoned amongſt the moſt general affections of the *conventions*, or aſſociations of ſeveral particles of matter into bodies of any certain denomination. *Boyle.*

2. An aſſembly.

Publick *conventions* are liable to all the infirmities, follies, and vices of private men. *Swift.*

3. A contract; an agreement for a time, previous to a definitive treaty.

CONVE'NTIONAL. *adj.* [from *convention.*] Stipulated; agreed on by compact.

Conventional ſervices reſerved by tenures upon grants, made out of the crown or knights ſervice. *Hale's Com. Law of Engl.*

CONVE'NTIONARY. *adj.* [from *convention.*] Acting upon contract; ſettled by ſtipulations.

The ordinary covenants of moſt *conventionary* tenants are, to pay due capon and due harveſt journeys. *Carew's Survey.*

CONVE'NTUAL. *adj.* [*conventuel*, French.] Belonging to a convent; monaſtick.

Thoſe are called *conventual* priors that have the chief ruling power over a monaſtery. *Ayliffe's Parergon.*

CONVE'NTUAL. *n. ſ.* [from *convent.*] A monk; a nun; one that lives in a convent.

I have read a ſermon of a *conventual*, who laid it down, that Adam could not laugh before the fall. *Addiſon's Spectator.*

To CONVE'RGE. *v. n.* [*convergo*, Latin.] To tend to one point from different places.

Where the rays from all the points of any object meet again, after they have been made to *converge* by reflexion or refraction, there they will make a picture of the object upon a white body. *Newton's Opt.*

Enſweeping firſt
The lower ſkies, they all at once *converge*
High to the crown of heaven. *Thomſon's Autumn.*

CONVE'RGENT. } *adj.* [from *converge.*] Tending to one point
CONVE'RGING. } from different places.

CONVE'RGING *Series.* See SERIES.

CONVE'RSABLE. *adj.* [from *converſe.* It is ſometimes written *converſible*, but improperly; *converſant*, *converſation*, *converſable.*] Qualified for converſation; fit for company; well adapted to the reciprocal communication of thoughts; communicative.

That fire and levity which makes the young ones ſcarce *converſible*, when tempered by years, makes a gay old age. *Guardian*, Nº. 101.

CONVE'RSABLENESS. *n. ſ.* [from *converſable.*] The quality of being a pleaſing companion; fluency of talk.

CONVE'RSABLY. *adv.* [from *converſable.*] In a converſable manner; with the qualities of a pleaſing communicative companion.

CONVE'RSANT. *adj.* [*converſant*, French.]

1. Acquainted with; having a knowledge of any thing acquired by familiarity and habitude; familiar: with *in*.

The learning and ſkill which he had by being *converſant in* their books. *Hooker, b.* iii. *ſect.* 8.

Let them make ſome towns near to the mountain's ſide, where they may dwell together with neighbours, and be *converſant in* the view of the world. *Spenſer's State of Ireland.*

Thoſe who are *converſant in* both the tongues, I leave to make their own judgment of it. *Dryden's Dufreſnoy.*

He uſes the different dialects as one who had been *converſant* with them all. *Pope's Eſſay on Homer.*

2. Having intercourſe with any; acquainted; familiar by cohabitation or fellowſhip; cohabiting: with *among* or *with*.

All that Moſes commanded, Joſhua read before all the congregation of Iſrael, with the women, and the little ones, and the ſtrangers that were *converſant among* them. *Joſ.* viii. 35.

Never to be infected with delight,
Nor *converſant with* eaſe and idleneſs. *Shakeſp. King John.*

Old men who have loved young company, and been *converſant* continually *with* them, have been of long life. *Bacon.*

Gabriel, this day by proof thou ſhalt behold,
Thou, and all angels *converſant* on earth
With man, or men's affairs, how I begin
To verify that ſolemn meſſage. *Milton's Parad. Regained.*

To ſuch a one, an ordinary coffeehouſe-gleaner of the city is an arrant ſtateſman, and as much ſuperiour too, as a man *converſant about* Whitehall and the court is to an ordinary ſhopkeeper. *Locke.*

3. Relating to; having for its object; concerning: with *about*, formerly *in*.

The matters *wherein* church polity is *converſant*, are the publick religious duties of the church. *Hooker, b.* iii.

If any think education, becauſe it is *converſant about* children, to be but a private and domeſtick duty, he has been ignorantly bred himſelf. *Wotton on Education.*

Diſcretion, conſidered both as an accompliſhment and as a virtue, not only as is *converſant about* worldly affairs, but as regarding our whole exiſtence. *Addiſon, Spectator*, Nº. 226.

Indifference cannot but be criminal, when it is *converſant about* objects which are ſo far from being of an indifferent nature, that they are of the higheſt importance to ourſelves and our country. *Addiſon's Freeholder*, Nº. 13.

CONVERSA'TION. *n. ſ.* [*converſatio*, Latin.]

1. Familiar diſcourſe; chat; eaſy talk: oppoſed to a formal conference.

She went to Pamela's chamber, meaning to joy her thoughts with the ſweet *converſation* of her ſiſter. *Sidney, b.* ii.

What I mentioned ſome time ago in *converſation*, was not a new thought, juſt then ſtarted by accident or occaſion. *Swift.*

2. A particular act of diſcourſing upon any ſubject; as, *we had a long* converſation *on that queſtion.*

3. Commerce; intercourſe; familiarity.

The knowledge of men and manners, the freedom of habitudes, and *converſation* with the beſt company of both ſexes. *Dryden.*

His apparent, open guilt;
I mean his *converſation* with Shore's wife. *Shakeſ. Rich.* III.

4. Behaviour; manner of acting in common life.

Having your *converſation* honeſt among the Gentiles. 1 *Pet.*

CONVE'RSATIVE. *adj.* [from *converſe.*] Relating to publick life, and commerce with men; not contemplative.

Finding him little ſtudious and contemplative, ſhe choſe to endue him with *converſative* qualities of youth. *Wotton.*

To CONVE'RSE. *v. n.* [*converser*, Fr. *conversor*, Latin.]

1. To cohabit with; to hold intercourse with; to be a companion to: followed by *with*.

Men then come to be furnished with fewer or more simple ideas from without, according as the objects they *converse with* afford greater or less variety. *Locke.*

By approving the sentiments of a person *with* whom he *conversed*, in such particulars as were just, he won him over from those points in which he was mistaken. *Addis. Freeholder.*

For him who lonely loves
To seek the distant hills, and there *converse*
With nature. *Thomson's Summer, l.* 130.

2. To be acquainted with; to be familiar to.

I will *converse with* iron-witted fools,
And unrespective boys: none are for me,
That look into me with considerate eyes. *Shakes. Rich.* III.

3. To convey the thoughts reciprocally in talk.

Go therefore half this day, as friend with friend,
Converse with Adam. *Milton's Paradise Lost, b.* v. *l.* 230.
Much less can bird with beast, or fish with fowl,
So well *converse*. *Milton's Paradise Lost, b.* viii. *l.* 396.

4. To discourse familiarly upon any subject: with *on* before the thing.

We had *conversed* so often *on* that subject, and he had communicated his thoughts of it so fully to me, that I had not the least remaining difficulty. *Dryden's Dufresnoy.*

5. To have commerce with a different sex.

Being asked by some of her sex, in how long a time a woman might be allowed to pray to the gods, after having *conversed* with a man? If it were a husband, says she, the next day; if a stranger, never. *Guardian*, N°. 165.

Co'nverse. *n. s.* [from the verb. It is sometimes accented on the first syllable, sometimes on the last. *Pope* has used both: the first is more analogical.]

1. Conversation; manner of discoursing in familiar life.

His *converse* is a system fit,
Alone to fill up all her wit. *Swift.*
Gen'rous *converse*; a soul exempt from pride,
And love to praise with reason on his side. *Pope's Ess. on Crit.*
Form'd by thy *converse*, happily to steer
From grave to gay, from lively to severe. *Pope's Ess. on Man.*

2. Acquaintance; cohabitation; familiarity.

Though it be necessitated, by its relation to flesh, to a terrestrial *converse*; yet it is like the sun, without contaminating its beams. *Glanville's Apol.*

By such a free *converse* with persons of different sects, we shall find that there are persons of good sense and virtue, persons of piety and worth. *Watts's Improvement of the Mind.*

3. [In geometry.] A proposition is said to be the *converse* of another, when, after drawing a conclusion from something first proposed, we proceed to suppose what had been before concluded, and to draw from it what had been supposed. Thus, if two sides of a triangle be equal, the angles opposite to those sides are also equal: the *converse* of the proposition is, that if two angles of a triangle be equal, the sides opposite to those angles are also equal. *Chambers.*

Conve'rsely. *adv.* [from *converse.*] With change of order; in a contrary order; reciprocally.

Conve'rsion. *n. s.* [*conversio*, Latin.]

1. Change from one state into another; transmutation.

Artificial *conversion* of water into ice, is the work of a few hours; and this of air may be tried by a month's space. *Bacon.*

There are no such natural gradations, and *conversions* of one metal and mineral into another, in the earth, as many have fancied. *Woodward's Natural History.*

The *conversion* of the aliment into fat, is not properly nutrition. *Arbuthnot on Aliments.*

2. Change from rebrobation to grace, from a bad to a holy life.

3. Change from one religion to another.

They passed through Phenice and Samaria, declaring the *conversion* of the Gentiles. *Acts* xv. 4.

4. The interchange of terms in an argument; as, *no virtue is vice*; *no vice is virtue*. *Chambers.*

5. Conversion *of Equations*, in algebra, is the reducing of a fractional equation into an integral one.

Conve'rsive. *adj.* [from *converse.*] Conversable; sociable.

To CONVE'RT. *v. a.* [*converto*, Latin.]

1. To change into another substance; to transmute.

If the whole atmosphere was *converted* into water, it would make no more than eleven yards water about the earth. *Burnet.*

2. To change from one religion to another.

3. To turn from a bad to a good life.

He which *converteth* the sinner from the errour of his way, shall save a soul from death, and shall hide a multitude of sins. *Ja.* v. 20.

Then will I teach transgressors thy ways, and sinners shall be *converted* unto thee. *Ps.* li. 13.

4. To turn towards any point.

Crystal will calify into electricity, and *convert* the needle freely placed. *Brown's Vulgar Errours, b.* ii. *c.* 1.

5. To apply to any use; to appropriate.

The abundance of the sea shall be *converted* unto thee, the forces of the Gentiles shall come unto thee. *Is.* lx. 5.

He acquitted himself not like an honest man; for he *converted* the prizes to his own use. *Arbuthnot on Coins.*

6. To change one proposition into another, so that what was the subject of the first becomes the predicate of the second.

The papists cannot abide this proposition *converted*: all sin is a transgression of the law; but every transgression of the law is sin. The apostle therefore turns it for us: all unrighteousness, says he, is sin; but every transgression of the law is unrighteousness, says Austin, upon the place. *Hale.*

To Conve'rt. *v. n.* To undergo a change; to be transmuted.

The love of wicked friends *converts* to fear;
That fear, to hate. *Shakespeare's Richard* II.

Co'nvert. *n. s.* [from the verb.] A person converted from one opinion or one practice to another.

The Jesuits did not persuade the *converts* to lay aside the use of images. *Stillingfleet's Defence of Discourse on Rom. Idol.*

When Platonism prevailed, the *converts* to Christianity of that school, interpreted Holy Writ according to that philosophy. *Locke.*

Let us not imagine that the first *converts* only of Christianity were concerned to defend their religion. *Rogers, Sermon* ix.

Conve'rter. *n. s.* [from *convert.*] One that makes converts.

Convertibi'lity. *n. s.* [from *convertible.*] The quality of being possible to be converted.

Conve'rtible. *adj.* [from *convert.*]

1. Susceptible of change; transmutable; capable of transmutation.

Minerals are not *convertible* into another species, though of the same genus; nor are they reducible into another genus. *Harvey on Consumptions.*

The gall is not an alcali; but it is alcalescent, conceptible and *convertible* into a corrosive alcali. *Arbuthnot on Aliments.*

2. So much alike as that one may be used for the other.

Though it be not the real essence of any substance, it is the specifick essence, to which our name belongs, and is *convertible* with it. *Locke.*

Many, that call themselves Protestants, look upon our worship to be idolatrous as well as that of the Papists, and put prelacy and popery together, as terms *convertible*. *Swift.*

Conve'rtibly. *adv.* [from *convertible.*] Reciprocally; with interchange of terms.

There never was any person ungrateful, who was not also proud; nor, *convertibly*, any one proud, who was not equally ungrateful. *South's Sermons.*

Co'nvertite. *n. s.* [*converti*, French.] A convert; one converted from another opinion.

Since you are a gentle *convertite*,
My tongue shall hush again this storm of war. *Sh. K. John.*
Nor would I be a *convertite* so cold,
As not to tell it. *Donne.*

CO'NVEX. *adj.* [*convexus*, Latin.] Rising in a circular form; opposite to concave.

It is the duty of a painter, even in this also, to imitate the *convex* mirrour, and to place nothing which glares at the border of his picture. *Dryden's Dufresnoy.*

An orb or ball round its own axis whirl;
Will not the motion to a distance hurl
Whatever dust or sand you on it place,
And drops of water from its *convex* face? *Blackm. Creation.*

Co'nvex. *n. s.* A convex body; a body swelling externally into a circular form.

A comet draws a long extended blaze;
From East to West burns through th' ethereal frame,
And half heav'n's *convex* glitters with the flame. *Tickel.*

Conve'xed. *particip. adj.* [from *convex.*] Formed convex; protuberant in a circular form.

In their natural figure they are straight; nor have they their spine *convexed*, or more considerably embowed than either sharks, porposes, whales, and other cetaceous animals. *Brown's Vulgar Errours, b.* v. *c.* 2.

Conve'xedly. *adv.* [from *convexed*.] In a convex form.

They be drawn *convexedly* crooked in one piece; yet the dolphin, that carrieth Arion, is concavously inverted, and hath its spine depressed. *Brown's Vulgar Errours, b.* v. *c.* 2.

Conve'xity. *n. s.* [from *convex.*] Protuberance in a circular form.

Convex glasses supply the defect of plumpness in the eye, and, by increasing the refraction, make the rays converge sooner, so as to convene distinctly at the bottom of the eye, if the glass have a due degree of *convexity*. *Newton's Opt.*

If the eye were so piercing as to descry even opake and little objects a hundred leagues off, it would do us little service; it would be terminated by neighbouring hills and woods, or in the largest and evenest plain, by the very *convexity* of the earth. *Bentley.*

Conve'xly. *adv.* [from *convex.*] In a convex form.

Almost all, both blunt and sharp, are *convexly* conical, *i. e.* they are all along convex, not only *per ambitum*, but between both ends. *Grew's Musæum.*

Conve'xness. *n. s.* [from *convex.*] Spheroidical protuberance; convexity.

CONVEXO-CONCAVE. *adj.* Having the hollow on the inſide, correſponding to the external protuberance.

These are the phenomena of thick *convexo-concave* plates of glaſs, which are every where of the ſame thickneſs. *Newton.*

To CONVE'Y. *v. a.* [*conveho*, Latin.]

1. To carry; to tranſport from one place to another.

Let letters be given me to the governours beyond the river, that they may *convey* me over 'till I come into Judea. *Neh.* ii. 7.

I will *convey* them by ſea in floats, unto the place thou ſhalt appoint me. *1 Kings*, v. 9.

2. To hand from one to another.

A divine natural right could not be *conveyed* down, without any plain, natural, or divine rule concerning it. *Locke.*

3. To remove ſecretly.

There was one *conveyed* out of my houſe yeſterday in this baſket. *Shakeſpeare's Merry Wives of Windſor.*

4. To bring any thing, as an inſtrument of tranſmiſſion; to tranſmit.

Since there appears not to be any ideas in the mind, before the ſenſes have *conveyed* any in, I conceive that ideas in the underſtanding are coeval with ſenſation. *Locke.*

5. To transfer; to deliver to another.

Adam's property or private dominion could not *convey* any ſovereignty or rule to his heir, who, not having a right to inherit all his father's poſſeſſions, could not thereby come to have any ſovereignity over his brethren. *Locke.*

6. To impart, by means of ſomething.

What obſcured light the heav'ns did grant,
Did but *convey* unto our fearful minds
A doubtful warrant of immediate death. *Shak. Com. of Err.*

Men fill one another's heads with noiſe and ſounds, but *convey* not thereby their thoughts. *Locke.*

That which uſes to produce the idea, though *conveyed* in by the uſual organ, not being taken notice of, there follows no ſenſation. *Locke.*

Some ſingle imperceptible bodies muſt come from them to the eyes, and thereby *convey* to the brain ſome motion which produces thoſe ideas. *Locke.*

They give energy to our expreſſions, and *convey* our thoughts in more ardent and intenſe phraſes, than any in our own tongue. *Addiſon's Spectator*, Nº. 405.

7. To impart; to introduce.

Others *convey* themſelves into the mind by more ſenſes than one. *Locke.*

8. To manage with privacy.

I will *convey* the buſineſs as I ſhall find means, and acquaint you withal. *Shakeſpeare's King Lear.*

CONVE'YANCE. *n. ſ.* [from *convey.*]

1. The act of removing any thing.

Tell her, thou mad'ſt away her uncle Clarence,
Her uncle Rivers; ay, and for her ſake,
Mad'ſt quick *conveyance* with her good aunt Ann. *Sh. R.* III.

2. Way for carriage or tranſportation.

Following the river downward, there is *conveyance* into the countries named in the text. *Raleigh's Hiſtory of the World.*

Iron works ought to be confined to places, where there is no *conveyance* for timber to places of vent, ſo as to quit the coſt of the carriage. *Temple.*

3. The method of removing ſecretly from one place to another.

Your huſband's here at hand; bethink you of ſome *conveyance*: in the houſe you cannot hide him. *Shakeſpeare.*

4. The means or inſtrument by which any thing is conveyed.

We powt upon the morning, are unapt
To give or to forgive; but when we've
Stuff'd theſe pipes, and theſe *conveyances* of blood,
With wine and feeding, we have ſuppler ſouls. *Sh. Coriolan.*

5. Tranſmiſſion; delivery from one to another.

Our author has provided for the deſcending and *conveyance* down of Adam's monarchical power, or paternal dominion, to poſterity. *Locke.*

6. Act of transferring property; grant.

Doth not the act of the parent, in any lawful grant or *conveyance*, bind their heirs for ever thereunto? *Spenſ. on Ireland.*

7. Writing by which property is transferred.

The very *conveyances* of his lands will hardly lie in this box; and muſt the inheritor himſelf have no more? *Shakeſ. Hamlet.*

This begot a ſuit in the Chancery before the lord Coventry, who found the *conveyances* in law to be ſo firm, that in juſtice he muſt decree the land to the earl. *Clarendon*, *b.* viii.

8. Secret management; juggling artifice; private removal; ſecret ſubſtitution of one thing for another.

It cometh herein to paſs with men, unadviſedly fallen into error, as with them whoſe ſtate hath no ground to uphold it, but only the help which, by ſubtile *conveyance*, they draw out of caſual events, ariſing from day to day, 'till at length they be clean ſpent. *Hooker*, *b.* iii. *ſ.* 4.

Cloſe *conveyance*, and each practice ill
Of coſinage and knavery. *Spenſer's Hubberd's Tale.*

I am this day come to ſurvey the Tower;
Since Henry's death, I fear, there is *conveyance*. *Sh. H.* VI.

Can they not juggle, and with ſlight
Conveyance play with wrong and right. *Hudibras*, *p.* ii. *c.* 2.

CONVE'YANCER. *n. ſ.* [from *conveyance.*] A lawyer who draws writings by which property is transferred.

CONVE'YER. *n. ſ.* [from *convey.*] One who carries or tranſmits any thing from one place or perſon to another.

The *conveyers* of waters of theſe times content themſelves with one inch in ſix hundred feet. *Brerewood on Languages.*

Thoſe who ſtand before earthly princes, in the neareſt degree of approach, who are the diſpenſers of their favours, and *conveyers* of their will to others, do, on that very account, challenge high honours to themſelves. *Atterbury's Sermons.*

To CONVI'CT. *v. a.* [*convinco*, Latin.]

1. To prove guilty; to detect in guilt.

And they which heard it, being *convicted* by their own conſcience, went out one by one. *Jo.* viii. 9.

Things, that at the firſt ſhew ſeemed poſſible, by ripping up the performance of them, have been *convicted* of impoſſibility. *Bacon's Holy War.*

2. To confute; to diſcover to be falſe.

Although not only the reaſon of any head, but experience of every hand, may well *convict* it, yet will it not by divers be rejected. *Broun's Vulgar Errours*, *b.* ii. *c.* 6.

CONVI'CT. *adj.* [rather the *participle* of the verb.] Convicted; detected in guilt.

Before I be *convict* by courſe of law,
To threaten me with death is moſt unlawful. *Shak. R.* III.

By the civil law a perſon *convict*, or confeſſing his own crime, cannot appeal. *Ayliffe's Parergon.*

Convict a papiſt he, and I a poet. *Pope's Epiſt. of Hor.*

CO'NVICT. *n. ſ.* [from the verb.] A perſon caſt at the bar; one found guilty of the crime charged againſt him; a criminal detected at his trial.

On the ſcore of humanity, the civil law allows a certain ſpace of time both to the *convict* and to perſons confeſſing, in order to ſatisfy the judgment. *Ayliffe's Parergon.*

CONVI'CTION. *n. ſ.* [from *convict.*]

1. Detection of guilt, which is, in law, either when a man is outlawed, or appears and confeſſes, or elſe is found guilty by the inqueſt. *Cowel.*

The third beſt abſent is condemn'd,
Convict by flight, and rebel to all law;
Conviction to the ſerpent none belongs. *Milton's Par. Loſt.*

2. The act of convincing; confutation; the act of forcing others, by argument, to allow a poſition.

When therefore the apoſtle requireth hability to convict hereticks, can we think he judgeth it a thing unlawful, and not rather needful, to uſe the principal inſtrument of their *conviction*, the light of reaſon. *Hooker*, *b.* iii. *ſ.* 8.

The manner of his *conviction* was deſigned, not as a peculiar privilege to him; but as a ſtanding miracle, a laſting argument, for the *conviction* of others, to the very end of the world. *Atterbury's Sermons.*

Their wiſdom is only of this world, to put falſe colours upon things, to call good evil, and evil good, againſt the *conviction* of their own conſciences. *Swift.*

CONVI'CTIVE. *adj.* [from *convict.*] Having the power of convincing.

To CONVI'NCE. *v. a.* [*convinco*, Latin.]

1. To force another to acknowledge a conteſted poſition.

That which I have all this while been endeavouring to *convince* men of, and to perſuade them to, is no other but what God himſelf doth particularly recommend to us, as proper for human conſideration. *Tillotſon.*

But having ſhifted ev'ry form to 'ſcape,
Convinc'd of conqueſt, he reſum'd his ſhape. *Dryd. Virg.*

Hiſtory is all the light we have in many caſes, and we receive from it a great part of the uſeful truths we have, with a *convincing* evidence. *Locke.*

2. To convict; to prove guilty of.

To *convince* all that are ungodly among them, of all their ungodly deeds. *Jude* 15.

The diſcovery of a truth, formerly unknown, doth rather *convince* man of ignorance, than nature of errour. *Raleigh.*

O ſeek not to *convince* me of a crime,
Which I can ne'er repent, nor can you pardon. *Dryden.*

3. To evince; to prove; to manifeſt; to vindicate.

Your Italy contains none ſo accompliſhed a courtier, to *convince* the honour of my miſtreſs. *Shakeſpeare's Cymbeline.*

4. To overpower; to ſurmount. This ſenſe is now obſolete.

There are a crew of wretched ſouls
That ſtay his cure; their malady *convinces*
The great eſſay of art. *Shakeſpeare's Macbeth.*

Knaves be ſuch abroad,
Who having, by their own importunate ſuit,
Or voluntary dotage of ſome miſtreſs,
Convinc'd or ſuppled them, they cannot chuſe
But they muſt blab. *Shakeſpeare's Othello.*

When Duncan is aſleep, his two chamberlains
Will I, with wine and waſſel, ſo *convince*,
That memory, the warder of the brain,
Shall be a fume. *Shakeſpeare's Macbeth.*

CONVI'NCEMENT. *n. ſ.* [from *convince.*] Conviction.

If that be not *convincement* enough, let him weigh the other also. *Decay of Piety.*

CONVI'NCIBLE. *adj.* [from *convince.*]

1. Capable of conviction.
2. Capable of being evidently disproved, or detected.

Upon what uncertainties, and also *convincible* falsities, they often erected such emblems, we have elsewhere delivered. *Brown's Vulgar Errours, b.* iii. *c.* 9.

CONVI'NCINGLY. *adv.* [from *convince.*] In such a manner as to leave no room for doubt or dispute; so as to produce conviction.

This he did so particularly and *convincingly*, that those of the parliament were in great confusion. *Clarendon, b.* viii.

The resurrection is so *convincingly* attested by such persons, with such circumstances, that they who consider and weigh the testimony, at what distance soever they are placed, cannot entertain any more doubt of the resurrection than the crucifixion of Jesus. *Atterbury's Sermons.*

CONVI'NCINGNESS. *n. s.* [from *convincing.*] The power of convincing.

To CONVI'VE. *v. a.* [*convivo*, Latin.] To entertain; to feast. A word, I believe, not elsewhere used.

First, all you peers of Greece, go to my tent,
There in the full *convive* you. *Shakesp Troilus and Cressida.*

CONVI'VAL. } *adj.* [*convivalis*, Latin.] Relating to an entertainment; festal; social.
CONVI'VIAL. }

I was the first who set up festivals;
Not with high tastes our appetites did force,
But fill'd with conversation and discourse;
Which feasts, *convivial* meetings we did name. *Denham.*

CONU'NDRUM. *n. s.* A low jest; a quibble; a mean conceit: a cant word.

Mean time he smoaks, and laughs at merry tale,
Or pun ambiguous, or *conundrum* quaint. *Philips.*

To CO'NVOCATE. *v. a.* [*convoco*, Lat.] To call together; to summon to an assembly.

CONVOCA'TION. *n. s.* [*convocatio*, Latin.]

1. The act of calling to an assembly.

Diaphantus making a general *convocation*, spake to them in this manner. *Sidney.*

2. An assembly.

On the eighth day shall be an holy *convocation* unto you. *Lev.* xxiii. 20.

3 An assembly of the clergy for consultation upon matters ecclesiastical, in time of parliament; and as the parliament consists of two distinct houses, so does this; the one called the upper house, where the archbishops and bishops sit severally by themselves; the other the lower house, where all the rest of the clergy are represented by their deputies. *Cowel.*

I have made an offer to his majesty,
Upon our spiritual *convocation*,
As touching France, to give a greater sum
Than ever at one time the clergy yet
Did to his predecessors part withal. *Shakespeare's Henry* IV.

This is the declaration of our church about it, made by those who met in *convocation*. *Stillingfl. Def. of Disc. on Ro. Idol.*

To CONVO'KE. *v. a.* [*convoco*, Latin.] To call together; to summon to an assembly.

Assemblies exercise their legislature at the times that their constitution, or their own adjournment appoints, if there be no other way prescribed to *convoke* them. *Locke.*

When next the morning warms the purple East,
Convoke the peerage. *Pope's Odyssey, b.* i. *l.* 354.

The senate originally consisted all of nobles, the people being only *convoked* upon such occasions as fell into their cognizance. *Swift.*

To CONVO'LVE. *v. a.* [*convolvo*, Latin.] To roll together; to roll one part upon another.

He writh'd him to and fro *convolv'd*. *Milton.*

Us'd to milder scents, the tender race
By thousands tumble from their honey'd domes,
Convolv'd and agonizing in the dust. *Thomson's Autumn.*

CO'NVOLUTED. *part.* [of the verb I have found no example.] Twisted; rolled upon itself.

This differs from Muscovy-glass only in this, that the plates of that are flat and plain, whereas these are *convoluted* and inflected. *Woodward on Fossils.*

CONVOLU'TION. *n. s.* [*convolutio*, Latin.]

1. The act of rolling any thing upon itself; the state of being rolled upon itself.

Observe the *convolution* of the said fibres in all other glands, in the same or some other manner. *Grew's Cosmol. b.* i. *c.* 5.

A thousand secret, subtle pipes bestow,
From which, by num'rous *convolutions* wound,
Wrap'd with th' attending nerve, and twisted round. *Blackm.*

2. The state of rolling together in company.

And toss'd wide round,
O'er the calm sea, in *convolution* swift
The feather'd eddy floats. *Thomson's Autumn, l.* 845.

To CONVO'Y. *v. a.* [*convoyer*, Fr. from *conviare*, low Latin.] To accompany by land or sea for the sake of defence; as, *he was* convoyed *by ships of war.*

CO'NVOY. *n. s.* [from the verb. Anciently the accent was on the last syllable; it is now on the first.]

1. Attendance on the road by way of defence.

Sister, as the winds give benefit,
And *convoy* is assistant, do not sleep,
But let me hear from you. *Shakespeare's Hamlet.*

Such fellows will learn you by rote where services were done; at such a breach, at such a *convoy*. *Shakesp. Henry* V.

Had not God set peculiar value upon his temple, he would not have made himself his people's *convoy* to secure them in their passage to it. *South's Sermons.*

My soul grows hard, and cannot death endure,
Your *convoy* makes the dangerous way secure. *Dryd. Aureng.*

Convoy ships accompany their merchants 'till they may prosecute the voyage without danger. *Dryden's Pref. Dufresnoy.*

2. The act of attending as a defence.

Swift, as a sparkle of a glancing star,
I shoot from heav'n to give him safe *convoy*. *Milt. Par. Reg.*

CO'NUSANCE. *n. s.* [*conoisance*, French.] Cognisance; notice; knowledge. A law term.

To CONVU'LSE. *v. a.* [*convulsus*, Latin.] To give an irregular and involuntary motion to the parts of any body.

Follows the loosen'd, aggravated roar,
Enlarging, deepening, mingling, peal on peal,
Crush'd horrible, *convulsing* heaven and earth. *Thomf. Summ.*

CONVU'LSION. *n. s.* [*convulsio*, Latin.]

1. A *convulsion* is an involuntary contraction of the fibres and muscles, whereby the body and limbs are preternaturally distorted. *Quincy.*

If my hand be put into motion by a *convulsion*, the indifferency of that operative faculty is taken away. *Locke.*

2. Any irregular and violent motion; tumult; commotion; disturbance.

All have been subject to some concussions, and fallen under the same *convulsions* of state, by dissentions or invasions. *Temple.*

CONVU'LSIVE. *adj.* [*convulsif*, French.] That which produces involuntary motion; that which gives twiches or spasms.

They are irregular and *convulsive* motions, or strugglings of the spirits. *Hale's Origin of Mankind.*

Shew me the flying soul's *convulsive* strife,
And all the anguish of departing life. *Dryden's Aurengzebe.*

Her colour chang'd, her face was not the same,
And hollow groans from her deep spirit came:
Her hair stood up; *convulsive* rage possess'd
Her trembling limbs, and heav'd her lab'ring breast. *Dryd.*

In silence weep,
And thy *convulsive* sorrows inward keep. *Prior.*

CO'NY. *n. s.* [*kanin*, Germ. *connil* or *connin*, Fr. *cuniculus*, Latin.] A rabit; an animal that burroughs in the ground.

With a short-legg'd hen,
Lemons and wine for sauce; to these a *cony*
Is not to be despair'd of, for our money. *Ben. Johns. Epig.*

The husbandman suffers by hares and *conys*, which eat the corn, trees. *Mortimer's Husbandry.*

CONY-BOROUGH. *n. s.* A place where rabbits make their holes in the ground.

To CO'NYCATCH. *v. n.* To catch a cony, is, in the old cant of thieves, to cheat; to bite; to trick.

I have matter in my head against you, and against your *conycatching* rascals. *Shakesp. Merry Wives of Windsor.*

CO'NYCATCHER. *n. s.* A thief; a cheat; a sharper; a tricking fellow; a rascal. Now obsolete.

To COO. *v. n.* [from the sound.] To cry as a dove or pigeon.

The stock-dove only through the forest *cooes*,
Mournfully hoarse. *Thomson's Summer, l.* 610.

COOK. *n. s.* [*coquus*, Latin.] One whose profession is to dress and prepare victuals for the table.

One mistress Quickly, which is in the manner of his nurse, or his dry-nurse, or his *cook*, or his laundry, his washer, and his wringer. *Shakespeare's Merry Wives of Windsor.*

The new-born babe, by nurses overlaid,
And the *cook* caught within the raging fire he made. *Dryden.*

Their *cooks* could make artificial birds and fishes, in default of the real ones, and which exceeded them in the exquisiteness of the taste. *Arbuthnot on Coins.*

COOK-MAID. *n. s.* [*cook* and *maid.*] A maid that dresses provisions.

A friend of mine was lately complaining to me, that his wife had turned off one of the best *cook-maids* in England. *Addison's Freeholder*, Nº. 32.

COOK-ROOM. *n. s.* [*cook* and *room.*] A Room in which provisions are prepared for the ship's crew.

To COOK. *v. a.* [*coquo*, Latin.]

1. To prepare victuals for the table.

Who can but think, that had either of the crimes been *cooked* to their palates, they might have changed messes. *Decay of Piety.*

2. To prepare for any purpose.

Hanging is the word, Sir; if you be ready for that, you are well *cookt*. *Shakespeare's Cymbeline.*

CO'OKERY. *n. s.* [from *cook.*] The art of dressing victuals.

Some man's wit

Found

Found th' art of cook'ry to delight his sense:
More bodies are consum'd and kill'd with it,
Than with the sword, famine, or pestilence. *Davies.*
Ev'ry one to *cookery* pretends. *King's Art of Cookery.*
These are the ingredients of plants before they are prepared by *cookery*. *Arbuthnot on Aliments.*

COOL. *adj.* [*koelen*, Dutch.]
1. Somewhat cold; approaching to cold.
He set his leg in a pale-full, as hot as he could well endure it, renewing it as it grew *cool*. *Temple.*
2. Not zealous; not ardent; not angry; not fond; without passion.

COOL. *n. s.* Freedom from heat; soft and refreshing coldness.
But see, where Lucia, at her wonted hour,
Amid' the *cool* of yon high marble arch,
Enjoys the noon-day breeze. *Addison's Cato.*
Philander was enjoying the *cool* of the morning, among the dews that lay on every thing about him, and that gave the air a freshness. *Addison on Ancient Medals.*

To COOL. *v. a.* [*koelen*, Dutch.]
1. To make cool; to allay heat.
Snow they use in Naples instead of ice, because, as they say, it *cools* or congeals any liquor sooner. *Addison on Italy.*
Jelly of currants, or the jelly of any ripe subacid fruit, is *cooling*, and very agreeable to the stomach. *Arbuthnot on Diet.*
2. To quiet passion; to calm anger; to moderate zeal.
It is but as a body slight distemper'd,
Which to its former strength may be restor'd,
With good advice and little medicine;
My lord Northumberland will soon be *cool'd*. *Shak. H. IV.*
He will keep his jealousy to himself, and repine in private, because he will be apt to fear some ill effect it may produce in *cooling* your love to him. *Addison's Spectator*, N°. 171.
They tell us, that had they thought they had been fighting only other people's quarrels, perhaps it might have *cooled* their zeal. *Swift.*

To COOL. *v. n.*
1. To grow less hot.
2. To grow less warm with regard to passion or inclination.
My humour shall not *cool*; I will incense Ford to deal with poison; I will possess him with yellowness. *Sh. M. W. of W.*
You never *cool* while you read Homer. *Dryd. Fab. Preface.*
I'm impatient 'till it be done; I will not give myself liberty to think, lest I should *cool*. *Congreve's Old Batchelor.*

CO'OLER. *n. s.* [from *cool*.]
1. That which has the power of cooling the body.
Coolers are of two sorts; first, those which produce an immediate sense of cold, which are such as have their parts in less motion than those of the organs of feeling; and secondly, such as, by particular viscidity, or grossness of parts, give a greater consistence to the animal fluids than they had before, whereby they cannot move so fast, and therefore will have less of that intestine force on which their heat depends. The former are fruits, all acid liquors, and common water; and the latter are such as cucumbers, and all substances producing viscidity. *Quincy.*
In dogs or cats there appeared the same necessity for a *cooler* as in man. *Harvey on Consumptions.*
Acid things were used only as *coolers*. *Arbuthn. on Aliments.*
2. A vessel in which any thing is made cool.
Your first wort being thus boiled, lade off into one or more *coolers*, or cool-backs, in which leave the sullage behind, and let it run off fine. *Mortimer's Art of Husbandry.*

CO'OLLY. *adv.* [from *cool*.]
1. Without heat, or sharp cold.
She in the gelid caverns, woodbine wrought,
And fresh bedew'd with ever-spouting streams,
Sits *coolly* calm. *Thomson's Summer*, l. 455.
2. Without passion.
Motives that address themselves *coolly* to our reason, are fittest to be employed upon reasonable creatures. *Atterbury.*

CO'OLNESS. *n. s.* [from *cool*.]
1. Gentle cold; a soft or mild degree of cold.
This difference consisteth not in the heat or *coolness* of spirits; for cloves, and other spices, naptha and petroleum, have exceeding hot spirits, hotter a great deal than oil, wax, or tallow, but not inflamed. *Bacon's Natural History.*
The toad loveth shade and *coolness*. *Bacon's Nat. History.*
Yonder the harvest of cold months laid up,
Gives a fresh *coolness* to the royal cup;
There ice, like crystal, firm and never lost,
Tempers hot July with December's frost. *Waller.*
The sheep enjoy the *coolness* of the shade. *Dryd. Virg.*
2. Want of affection; disinclination.
They parted with such *coolness* towards each other, as if they scarce hoped to meet again. *Clarendon*, b. viii.
3. Freedom from passion.

COOM. *n. s.*
1. Soot that gathers over an oven's mouth. *Philips.*
2. That matter that works out of the wheels of carriages. *Bailey.*
3. It is used in Scotland for the useless dust which falls from large coals.

COOMB, or COMB. *n. s.* [*comble*, Fr. *cumulus*, Lat. a heap; *Skinner.*] A measure of corn containing four bushels. *Bailey.*

COOP. *n. s.* [*kuype*, Dutch.]
1. A barrel; a vessel for the preservation of liquids.
2. A cage; a penn for animals; as poultry or sheep.
When Gracchus was slain, the same day the chickens refused to eat out of the *coop*; and Claudius Pulcher underwent the like success, when he contemned the tripudiary augurations. *Brown's Vulgar Errours*, b. i. c. 11.
There were a great many crammed capons together in a *coop*. *L'Estrange.*

To COOP. *v. a.* [from the noun.] To shut up in a narrow compass; to confine; to cage; to imprison.
That pale, that white-fac'd shore,
Whose foot spurns back the ocean's roaring tides,
And *coops* from other lands her islanders. *Shakesp. K. John.*
The Englishmen did *coop* up the lord Ravenstein, that he stirred not; and likewise held in strait siege the maritime part of the town. *Bacon's Henry VII.*
In the taking of a town the poor escape better than the rich; for the one is let go, and the other is plundered and *cooped* up. *L'Estrange.*
Twice conquer'd cowards, now your shame is shown,
Coop'd up a second time within your town!
Who dare not issue forth in open field. *Dryden's Æneid.*
One world suffic'd not Alexander's mind;
Coop'd up, he seem'd in earth and seas confin'd. *Dry. Juv.*
Coop'd in a narrow isle, observing dreams
With flattering wizards. *Dryden's Juv. Sat.* 10.
The Trojans, *coop'd* within their walls so long,
Unbar their gates, and issue in a throng. *Dryden's Æneid.*
The contempt of all other knowledge, as if it were nothing in comparison of law or physick, of astrology or chymistry, *coops* the understanding up within narrow bounds, and hinders it from looking abroad into other provinces of the intellectual world. *Locke.*
They are *cooped* in close by the laws of their countries, and the strict guards of those whose interest it is to keep them ignorant, lest, knowing more, they should believe the less in them. *Locke.*
What! *coop* whole armies in our walls again. *Pope.*

COOPE'E. *n. s.* [*coupé*, French.] A motion in dancing.

A CO'OPER. *n. s.* [from *coop*.] One that makes coops or barrels.
Societies of artificers and tradesmen, belonging to some towns corporate, such as weavers and *coopers*, by virtue of their charters, pretend to privilege and jurisdiction. *Child.*

CO'OPERAGE. *n. s.* [from *cooper*.] The price paid for cooper's work.

To COO'PERATE. *v. n.* [*con* and *opera*, Latin.]
1. To labour jointly with another to the same end.
It puzzleth and perplexeth the conceits of many, that perhaps would otherwise *cooperate* with him, and makes a man walk almost alone to his own ends. *Bacon, Essay* 6.
By giving man a free will, he allows man that highest satisfaction and privilege of *cooperating* to his own felicity. *Boyle.*
2. To concur in producing the same effect.
His mercy will not forgive offenders, or his benignity *cooperate* to their conversions. *Brown's Vulgar Errours*, b. i. c. 2.
All these causes *cooperating*, must, at last, weaken their motion. *Cheyne's Phil. Prin.*
The special acts and impressions by which the Divine Spirit introduces this charge, and how far human liberty *cooperates* with it, are subjects beyond our reach and comprehension. *Rogers, Sermon* 14.

COOPERA'TION. *n. s.* [from *cooperate*.] The act of contributing or concurring to the same end.
We might work any effect without and against matter; and this not holpen by the *cooperation* of angels or spirits, but only by the unity and harmony of nature. *Bacon's Natural History.*

COO'PERATIVE. *adj.* [from *cooperate*.] Promoting the same end jointly.

COOPERA'TOR. *n. s.* [from *cooperate*.] He that, by joint endeavours, promotes the same end with others.

COOPTA'TION. *n. s.* [*coopto*, Latin.] Adoption; assumption.

COO'RDINATE. *adj.* [*con* and *ordinatus*, Latin.] Holding the same rank; not being subordinate. Thus shell-fish may be divided into two *coordinate* kinds, crustateous and testaceous; each of which is again divided into many species, *subordinate* to the kind, but *coordinate* to each other.
The word Analysis signifies the general and particular heads of a discourse, with their mutual connexions, both *coordinate* and subordinate, drawn out into one or more tables. *Watts.*

COO'RDINATELY. *adv.* [from *coordinate*.] In the same rank; in the same relation; without subordination.

COO'RDINATENESS. *n. s.* [from *coordinate*.] The state of being coordinate.

COORDINA'TION. *n. s.* [from *coordinate*.] The state of holding the same rank; of standing in the same relation to something higher; collateralness.
In this high court of parliament there is a rare *coordination* of

of power, a wholsome mixture betwixt monarchy, optimacy, and democracy. *Howel's Pre-eminence of Parliament.*

When these petty intrigues of a play are so ill ordered, that they have no coherence with the other, I must grant that Lysidius has reason to tax that want of due connexion; for *coordination* in a play is as dangerous and unnatural as in a state. *Dryden on Dramatick Poesy.*

Coot. *n. s.* [*maer-koet*, Dut. *cotee*, French.] A small black water-fowl, seen often in fens and marshes.

A lake, the haunt
Of *coots*, and of the fishing cormorant. *Dryden's Fables.*

COP. *n. s.* [*kop*, Dut. cop, Sax.] The head; the top of any thing; any thing rising to a head. As a *cop*, vulgarly *cock* of hay; a *cob-castle*, properly *cop-castle*, a small castle or house on a hill. A *cob* of cherrystones for *cop*, a pile of stones one laid upon another; a tuft on the head of birds.

Co'pal. *n. s.* The Mexican term for a gum.

Copa'rcenary. *n. s.* [from *coparcener.*] Joint succession to any inheritance.

In the descent to all the daughters in *coparcenary*, for want of sons, the chief house is allotted to the eldest daughter. *Hale's History of Common Law.*

COPA'RCENER. *n. s.* [from *con* and *particeps*, Lat.]

Coparceners are otherwise called parceners; and, in common law, are such as have equal portion in the inheritance of the ancestor. *Cowel.*

This great lordship was broken and divided, and partition made between the five daughters: in every of these portions, the *coparceners* severally exercised the same jurisdiction royal, which the earl marshal and his sons had used, in the whole province. *Davies on Ireland.*

Copa'rceny. *n. s.* [See COPARCENER.] An equal share of coparceners. *Philips's World of Words.*

COPA'RTNER. *n. s.* [*co* and *partner.*] One that has a share in some common stock or affair; one equally concerned; a sharer; a partaker; a partner.

Our faithful friends,
Th' associates and *copartners* of our loss. *Milt. Parad. Lost.*
Shall I to him make known
As yet my change, and give him to partake
Full happiness with me? Or rather not;
But keep the odds of knowledge in my pow'r,
Without *copartner?* *Milton's Paradise Lost, b.* ix. *l.* 825.
Rather by them
I gain'd what I have gain'd, and with them dwell
Copartner in these regions of the world. *Milt. Parad. Reg.*

Copa'rtnership. *n. s.* [from *copartner.*] The state of bearing an equal part, or possessing an equal share.

In case the father left only daughters, and no sons, the daughters equally succeeded to their father as in *copartnership.* *Hale's History of Common Law.*

Co'patain. *adj.* [from *cope.*] High raised; pointed. *Hanmer.*

Oh, fine villain! a silken doublet, a velvet hose, a scarlet cloke, and a *copatain* hat. *Shakespeare's Taming of the Shrew.*

Copa'yva. *n. s.* [It is sometimes written *capivi, copivi, capayva, copayva, cupayva, cupayba.*] A gum which distils from a tree in Brasil. It is much used in disorders of the urinary passages.

Cope. *n. s.* [See Cop.]

1. Any thing with which the head is covered.
2. A sacerdotal cloak, or vestment worn in sacred ministration.
3. Any thing which is spread over the head; as the concave of the skies; any archwork over a door.

All these things that are contained
Within this goodly *cope*, both most and least,
Their being have, and daily are increast. *Spenser.*
Over head the dismal hiss
Of fiery darts in flaming volleys flew;
And, flying, vaulted either host with fire;
So, under fiery *cope*, together rush'd
Both battles main. *Milton's Paradise Lost, b.* vi. *l.* 215.

The scholar believes there is no man under the *cope* of heaven, who is so knowing as his master. *Dryd. Dufresnoy.*

To Cope. *v. a.* [from the noun.]

1. To cover, as with a cope.

A very large bridge, that is all made of wood, and *coped* over head. *Addison on Italy.*

2. To reward; to give in return.

I and my friend
Have, by your wisdom, been this day acquitted
Of grievous penalties; in lieu whereof,
Three thousand ducats, due unto the Jew,
We freely *cope* your courteous pains withal. *Shakespeare.*

3. To contend with; to oppose.

Know my name is lost;
By treason's tooth bare gnawn, and canker bit;
Yet I am noble as the adversary I come to *cope.* *Sh. K. Lear.*

To Cope. *v. n.*

1. To contend; to struggle; to strive. It has *with* before the thing or person opposed.

In this sense it is a word of doubtful etymology. The conjecture of *Junius* derives it from *koopen*, to *buy*, or some other word of the same import; so that to *cope with*, signifies to *interchange blows*, or any thing else, with another.

Let our trains
March by us, that we may peruse the men
We should have *cop'd withal.* *Shakespeare's Henry* IV. *p.* ii.
It is likely thou wilt undertake
A thing, like death, to chide away this shame,
That *copes with* death itself, to 'scape from it. *Shakespeare.*
But Eve was Eve;
This far his over-match, who, self deceiv'd
And rash, beforehand had no better weigh'd
The strength he was to *cope with*, or his own. *Milt. P. R.*

They perfectly understood both the hares and the enemy they were to *cope withal.* *L'Estrange's Fables.*

On every plain,
Host *cop'd with* host, dire was the din of war. *Philips.*

Their generals have not been able to *cope with* the troops of Athens, which I have conducted. *Addison's Whig Examiner.*

If the mind apply itself first to easier subjects, and things near a-kin to what is already known; and then advance to the more remote and knotty parts of knowledge by slow degrees, it will be able, in this manner, to *cope with* great difficulties, and prevail over them with amazing and happy success. *Watts's Improvement of the Mind.*

2. To encounter; to interchange kindness or sentiments.

Thou fresh piece
Of excellent witchcraft, who of force must know
The royal fool thou *cop'st* with. *Shakesp. Winter's Tale.*
I will make him tell the tale anew;
Where, how, how oft, how long ago, and when
He hath, and is again to *cope* your wife. *Shakesp. Othello.*
Thou art e'en as just a man,
As e'er my conversation *coped* withal. *Shakespeare's Hamlet.*

Co'pel. See Coppel.

Co'pesmate. *n. s.* [perhaps for *cupsmate*, a companion in drinking, or one that dwells under the same *cope*, for house.] Companion; friend. An old word.

Ne ever staid in place, ne spake to wight,
'Till that the fox his *copesmate* he had found. *Hubberd's Tale.*

Co'pier. *n. s.* [from *copy.*]

1. One that copies; a transcriber.

A coin is in no danger of having its characters altered by *copiers* and transcribers. *Addison on Ancient Coins.*

2. One that imitates; a plagiary; an imitator.

Without invention a painter is but a *copier*, and a poet but a plagiary of others. *Dryden's Dufresnoy.*

Let the faint *copier*, on old Tyber's shore,
Nor mean the task, each breathing bust explore;
Line after line with painful patience trace,
This Roman grandeur, that Athenian grace. *Tickel.*

Co'ping. *n. s.* [from *cope.*] The upper tire of masonry which covers the wall.

All these were of costly stones, even from the foundation unto the *coping.* 1 *Kings*, vii. 9.

The *coping*, the modillions, or dentils, make a noble shew by their graceful projections. *Addison's Freeholder*, N°. 415.

CO'PIOUS. *adj.* [*copia*, Latin.]

1. Plentiful; abundant; exuberant; in great quantities.

This alcaline acrimony indicates the *copious* use of vinegar and acid fruits. *Arbuthnot on Aliments.*

The tender heart is peace,
And kindly pours its *copious* treasures forth
In various converse. *Thomson's Spring.*

2. Abounding in words or images; not barren; not confined; not concise.

Co'piously. *adv.* [from *copious.*]

1. Plentifully; abundantly; in great quantities.
2. At large; without brevity or conciseness; diffusely.

These several remains have been so *copiously* described by abundance of travellers, and other writers, that it is very difficult to make any new discoveries on so beaten a subject. *Addis.*

Co'piousness. *n. s.* [from *copious.*]

1. Plenty; abundance; great quantity; exuberance.
2. Diffusion; exuberance of stile.

The Roman orator endeavoured to imitate the *copiousness* of Homer, and the Latin poet made it his business to reach the conciseness of Demosthenes. *Dryden.*

Co'pist. *n. s.* [from *copy.*] A copyer; a transcriber; an imitator.

Co'pland. *n. s.* A piece of ground in which the land terminates with an acute angle. *Dict.*

Co'pped. *adj.* [from *cop.*] Rising to a top or head.

It was broad in its basis, and rose *copped* like a sugar-loaf. *Wiseman's Surgery.*

Co'ppel. *n. s.* [This word is variously spelt; as *copel, cupel, cuple,* and *cuppel*; but I cannot find its etymology.] An instrument used in chymistry in the form of a dish, made of ashes, well washed, to cleanse them from all their salt; or of bones thoroughly calcined. Its use is to try and purify gold and silver, which is done by mingling lead with the metal, and exposing it in the *coppel* to a violent fire a long while. The impurities of the metal will then be carried off in dross, which is called the litharge of gold and ſilver. The refiners call the *coppel* a teſt. *Harris.*

CO'PPER. *n. ſ.* [*koper*, Dut. *cuprum*, Latin.] One of the ſix primitive metals.

Copper is the moſt ductile and malleable metal, after gold and ſilver. Of a mixture of *copper* and lapis calaminaris is formed braſs; a compoſition of *copper* and tin makes bell-metal; and *copper* and braſs, melted in equal quantities, produces what the French call bronze, uſed for figures and ſtatues. *Chambers.*

Copper is heavier than iron or tin; but lighter than ſilver, lead, and gold. It is not unfrequently found native in a malleable ſtate, but in ſmall quantities. In the ſtate of ore it makes, according to its various admixtures, many very different appearances. The richer *copper* ores are found in many parts of Germany and Sweden; and we have ſome in England little inferior to the fineſt Swediſh. *Hill on Foſſils.*

Two veſſels of fine *copper*, precious as gold. *Ezra*, viii. 27.

CO'PPER. *n. ſ.* A veſſel made of copper; commonly uſed for a boiler larger than a moveable pot.

They boiled it in a *copper* to the half; then they poured it into earthen veſſels. *Bacon's Natural Hiſtory*, Nº. 848.

COPPER-NOSE. *n. ſ.* [*copper* and *noſe.*] A red noſe.

He having colour enough, and the other higher, is too flaming a praiſe for a good complexion: I had as lieve Helen's golden tongue had commended Troilus for a *copper-noſe*. *Shakeſpeare's Troilus and Creſſida.*

Gutta roſacea ariſeth in little hard tubercles, affecting the face all over with great itching, which, being ſcratched, looks red, and riſe in great welks, rendering the viſage fiery; and, in progreſs of time, make *copper-noſes*, as we generally expreſs them. *Wiſeman.*

COPPER-PLATE. *n. ſ.* A plate on which pictures are engraven for the neater impreſſion: diſtinguiſhed from a wooden cut.

COPPER-WORK. *n. ſ.* [*copper* and *work.*] A place where copper is worked or manufactured.

This ſort is like thoſe now wrought at the *copper-works*. *Woodward on Foſſils.*

CO'PPERAS. *n. ſ.* [*kopperooſe*, Dut. *couperouſe*, Fr. ſuppoſed to be found in copper mines only.] A name given to three ſorts of vitriol; the green, the bluiſh green, and the white, which are produced in the mines of Germany, Hungary, and other countries. But what is commonly ſold here for *copperas*, is an artificial vitriol, made of a kind of ſtones found on the ſea-ſhore in Eſſex, Hampſhire, and ſo weſtward, ordinarily called gold ſtones from their colour. They abound with iron, and are expoſed to the weather in beds above ground, and receive the rains and dews, which in time breaks and diſſolves the ſtones: the liquor that runs off is pumped into boilers, in which is firſt put old iron, which, in boiling, diſſolves. When the boiling is finiſhed, the liquor is drawn off into coolers, where it ſhoots into cryſtals of a fine green colour. This factitious *copperas*, in many reſpects, perfectly agrees with the native green vitriol of Germany; and is uſed in dying hats and cloths black, and in making ink. *Chambers. Hill.*

It may be queſtioned, whether, in this operation, the iron or *copperas* be tranſmuted, from the cognation of *copperas* with copper, and the iron remaining after converſion. *Brown.*

CO'PPERSMITH. *n. ſ.* [*copper* and *ſmith.*] One that manufactures copper.

Salmoneus, as the Grecian tale is,
Was a mad *copperſmith* of Elis;
Up at his forge by morning-peep. *Swift.*

CO'PPERWORM. *n. ſ.* [*teredo*, in Latin.]

1. A little worm in ſhips.
2. A moth that fretteth garments.
3. A worm breeding in one's hand. *Ainſworth.*

CO'PPERY. *adj.* [from *copper.*] Containing copper; made of copper.

Some ſprings of Hungary, highly impregnated with vitriolick ſalts, diſſolve the body of one metal, ſuppoſe iron, put into the ſpring, and depoſite, in lieu of the irony particles carried off, *coppery* particles brought with the water out of the neighbouring copper-mines. *Woodward on Foſſils.*

CO'PPICE. *n. ſ.* [*coupeaux*, Fr. from *couper*, to cut or lop. It is often written *copſe.*] Low woods cut at ſtated times for fuel; a place over-run with bruſhwood.

A land, each ſide whereof was boarded both with high timber trees, and *copſes* of far more humble growth. *Sidney.*

Upon the edge of yonder *coppice*,
A ſtand, where you may have the faireſt ſhoot. *Shakeſpeare.*

In *coppice* woods, if you leave ſtaddles too thick, they will run to buſhes and briars, and have little clean underwood. *Bacon's Henry VII.*

The willows and the hazel *copſes* green,
Shall now no more be ſeen,
Fanning their joyous leaves to their ſoft lays. *Milton.*

Raiſe trees in your ſeminaries and nurſeries, and you may tranſplant them for *coppice* ground, walks, or hedges. *Mortim.*

The rate of *coppice* lands will fall upon the diſcovery of coal-mines. *Locke.*

COPPLE-DUST. *n. ſ.* [probably for *coppel*, or *cupel duſt.*] Powder uſed in purifying metals, or the groſs parts ſeparated by the cupel.

It may be alſo tried by incorporating powder of ſteel, or *copple-duſt*, by pouncing into the quickſilver. *Bacon's Phyſ. Rem.*

COPPLE-STONES are lumps and fragments of ſtone or marble, broke from the adjacent cliffs, rounded by being bowled and tumbled to and again by the action of the water. *Woodward.*

CO'PPLED. *adj.* [from *cop.*] Riſing in a conick form; riſing to a point.

There is ſome difference in this ſhape, ſome being flatter on the top, others more *coppled*. *Woodward on Foſſils.*

COPSE. *n. ſ.* [abbreviated from *coppice.*] Short wood cut at a certain growth for fuel; a place overgrown with ſhort wood.

The Eaſt quarters of the ſhire are not deſtitute of *copſe* woods. *Carew's Survey of Cornwal.*

Oaks and brambles, if the *copſe* be burn'd,
Confounded lie, to the ſame aſhes turn'd. *Waller.*
But in what quarter of the *copſe* it lay,
His eye by certain level could ſurvey. *Dryden's Fables.*

To COPSE. *v. a.* [from the noun.] To preſerve underwoods.

The neglect of *copſing* wood cut down, hath been of very evil conſequence. *Swift's Addreſs to Parliament.*

CO'PULA. *n. ſ.* [Latin.] The word which unites the ſubject and predicate of a propoſition; as, *books* are *dear*.

The *copula* is the form of a propoſition; it repreſents the act of the mind, affirming or denying. *Watts's Logick.*

To CO'PULATE. *v. a.* [*copulo*, Latin.] To unite; to conjoin; to link together.

If the force of cuſtom, ſimple and ſeparate, be great, the force of cuſtom *copulate* and conjoined, and collegiate, is far greater. *Bacon, Eſſay* 40.

To CO'PULATE. *v. n.* To come together as different ſexes.

Not only the perſons ſo *copulating* are infected, but alſo their children. *Wiſeman's Surgery.*

COPULA'TION. *n. ſ.* [from *copulate.*] The congreſs or embrace of the two ſexes.

Sundry kinds, even of conjugal *copulation*, are prohibited as unhoneſt. *Hooker, b* iv. *ſect.* 11.

CO'PULATIVE. *adj.* [*copulativus*, Latin.] A term of grammar.

Copulative propoſitions are thoſe which have more ſubjects or predicates connected by affirmative or negative conjunctions; as, riches *and* honours are temptations to pride: Cæſar conquered the Gauls *and* the Britons: neither gold *nor* jewels will purchaſe immortality. *Watts's Logick.*

CO'PY. *n. ſ.* [*copie*, Fr. *copia*, low Latin. *Quod cuipiam facta eſt* copia *exſcribendi. Junius* much inclines, after his manner, to derive it from κόπος, labour; becauſe, ſays he, to copy another's writing is very painful and laborious.]

1. A tranſcript from the archetype or original.

If virtue's ſelf were loſt, we might
From your fair mind new *copies* write. *Waller.*

I have not the vanity to think my *copy* equal to the original. *Denham.*

He ſtept forth, not only the *copy* of God's hands, but alſo the *copy* of his perfections, a kind of image or repreſentation of the Deity in ſmall. *South's Sermons.*

The Romans having ſent to Athens, and the Greek cities of Italy, for the *copies* of the beſt laws, choſe ten legiſlators to put them into form. *Swift on the Diſſent. in Athens and Rome.*

2. An individual book; one of many books; as, *a good or fair* copy.

The very having of the books of God was a matter of no ſmall charge, as they could not be had otherwiſe than in written *copies*. *Hooker, b.* v. *ſect.* 22.

3. The autograph; the original; the archetype; that from which any thing is copied.

It was the *copy* of our conference:
In bed he ſlept not, for my urging it;
At board he fed not, for my urging it. *Shak. Com. of Err.*

Let him firſt learn to write, after a *copy*, all the letters in the vulgar alphabet. *Holder's Elements of Speech.*

The firſt of them I have forgotten, and cannot eaſily retrieve, becauſe the *copy* is at the preſs. *Dryden.*

4. An inſtrument by which any conveyance is made in law.

Thou know'ſt that Banquo and his Fleance lives;
But in them nature's *copy*'s not eternal. *Shakeſp. Macbeth.*

5. A picture drawn from another picture.

COPY-BOOK. *n. ſ.* [*copy* and *book.*] A book in which copies are written for learners to imitate.

CO'PY-HOLD. *n. ſ.* [*copy* and *hold.*] A tenure, for which the tenant hath nothing to ſhew but the copy of the rolls made by the ſteward of his lord's court: for the ſteward, as he enrolls other things done in the lord's court, ſo he regiſters ſuch tenants as are admitted in the court, to any parcel of land or tenement belonging to the manor; and the tranſcript of this is called the court-roll, the copy of which the tenant takes from him, and keeps as his only evidence. This is called a baſe tenure, becauſe it holds at the will of the lord; yet not ſimply, but according to the cuſtom of the manor: ſo that if a copy-holder break not the cuſtom of the manor, and thereby forfeit his tenure, he cannot be turned out at the lord's pleaſure. Theſe cuſtoms of manors vary in one point or other, almost in every manor. Some *copy-holds* are finable, and some certain: that which is finable, the lord rates at what fine or income he pleases, when the tenant is admitted into it: that which is certain is a kind of inheritance, and called in many places customary; because the tenant dying, and the hold being void, the next of blood paying the customary fine, as two shillings for an acre, or so, cannot be denied his admission. Some copy-holders have, by custom, the wood growing upon their own land, which by law they could not have. Some hold by the verge in ancient demesne; and though they hold by copy, yet are they, in account, a kind of freeholder: for, if such a one commit felony, the king hath *annum, diem*, and *vastum*, as in case of freehold. Some others hold by common tenure, called mere *copy-hold*; and they committing felony, their land escheats to the lord of the manor. *Cowel.*

If a customary tenant die, the widow shall have what the law calls her free bench in all his *copy-hold* lands. *Addis. Spectat.*

COPY-HOLDER. *n. s.* [from *copyhold.*] One that is possessed of land in copyhold.

To CO'PY. *v. a.* [from the noun.]

1. To transcribe; to write after an original.

He who hurts a harmless neighbour's peace,
Who loves a lie, lame slander helps about,
Who writes a libel, or who *copies* out. *Pope's Epistles.*

2. To imitate; to propose to imitation; to endeavour to resemble.

He that borrows other men's experience, with this design of *copying* it out, possesses himself of one of the greatest advantages. *Decay of Piety.*

Set the examples, and their souls inflame,
To *copy* out their great forefathers fame. *Dryd. K. Arthur.*
To *copy* her few nymphs aspir'd,
Her virtues fewer swains admir'd. *Swift.*

To CO'PY. *v. n.*

1. To do any thing in imitation of something else.

Some imagine, that whatsoever they find in the picture of a master, who has acquired reputation, must of necessity be excellent; and never fail, when they *copy*, to follow the bad as well as the good things. *Dryden's Dufresnoy.*

2. It has sometimes *from* before the thing imitated.

When a painter *copies from* the life, he has no privilege to alter features and lineaments, under pretence that his picture will look better. *Dryden.*

3. Sometimes *after.*

Several of our countrymen, and Mr. Dryden in particular, seem very often to have *copied after* it in their dramatick writings, and in their poems upon love. *Addison's Spectator.*

To COQUE'T. *v. a.* [from the noun.] To entertain with compliments and amorous tattle; to treat with an appearance of amorous tenderness.

You are *coquetting* a maid of honour, my lord looking on to see how the gamesters play, and I railing at you both. *Swift.*

To COQU'ET. *v. n.* To act the lover.

Phyllis, who but a month ago
Was marry'd to the Tunbridge beau,
I saw *coquetting* t'other night,
In publick, with that odious knight. *Swift.*

CO'QUETRY. *n. s.* [*coqueterie*, French.] Affectation of amorous advances; desire of attracting notice.

I was often in company with a couple of charming women, who had all the wit and beauty one could desire in female companions, without a dash of *coquetry*, that from time to time gave me a great many agreeable torments. *Addis. Spect.*

COQU'ETTE. *n. s.* [*coquette*, Fr. from *coquart*, a prattler.] A gay, airy girl; a girl who endeavours to attract notice.

The light *coquettes* in sylphs aloft repair,
And sport and flutter in the fields of air. *Pope's Ra. of Lock.*

A *coquette* and a tinder-box are sparkled. *Arbuthn. and Pope.*

CO'RACLE. *n. s.* [*cwrwgle*, Welsh, probably from *corium*, leather, Lat.] A boat used in Wales by fishers; made by drawing leather or oiled cloath upon a frame of wicker work.

CO'RAL. *n. s.* [*corallium*, Latin.]

1. Red *coral* is a plant of great hardness and stony nature, while growing in the water, as it has after long exposure to the air. The vulgar opinion, that *coral* is soft, while in the sea, proceeds from a soft and thin coat, of a crustaceous matter, covering it while it is growing, and which is taken off before it is packed up for use. This external bark is of a fungous spongy texture, of a yellowish or greenish colour, and is full of an acrid juice resembling milk. It covers every part of the plant, and is easily separated from the internal or stony part by friction, while it is moist; but adheres to it very firmly, if suffered to dry on it. The whole *coral* plant grows to a foot or more in height, and is variously ramified. It is thickest at the stem, and its branches grow gradually smaller to the extremities. It grows to stones, or any other solid substances, without a root, or without any way penetrating them, as plants do the earth. It has been doubted whether *coral* were properly a plant or not; but as it is found to grow, and take in its nourishment in the manner of plants, and to produce flowers and seeds, or at least a matter analogous to seeds, it properly belongs to the vegetable kingdom. The ancients ascribed great virtues to red *coral*; but now it is only used internally as an astringent and absorbent, with other medicines of the same intention. We hear of white *coral*, of which the ancients make no mention; and what is sold under this name is a species of the madrepora, another sea-plant. There is a black *coral* of the same stony substance with the red, and as glossy as the blackest marble; but what is sold in the shops under that name, is a plant of a different genus, and of a tough horny texture. *Hill's Materia Medica.*

In the sea, upon the south-west of Sicily, much *coral* is found. It is a submarine plant: it hath no leaves: it brancheth only when it is under water. It is soft, and green of colour; but being brought into the air, it becometh hard and shining red, as we see. *Bacon's Natural History*, N°. 780.

This gentleman, desirous to find the nature of *coral*, caused a man to go down a hundred fathom into the sea, with express orders to take notice whether it were hard or soft in the place where it groweth. *Brown's Vulgar Errours*, *b.* ii. *c.* 5.

He hears the crackling sound of *coral* woods,
And sees the secret source of subterranean floods. *Dryd. Virg.*

A turret was inclos'd
Within the wall, of alabaster white,
And crimson *coral*, for the queen of night,
Who takes in Sylvan sports her chaste delight. *Dryden.*

Or where's the sense, direct or moral,
That teeth are pearl, or lips are *coral?* *Prior.*

2. The piece of coral which children have about their necks, imagined to assist them in breeding teeth.

Her infant grandame's *coral* next it grew;
The bells she gingled. *Pope.*

CORAL-TREE. *n. s.* [*corallodendron*, Latin.]

It is a native of America, and produces very beautiful scarlet flowers; but never any seeds in the European gardens. *Miller.*

CO'RALLINE. *adj.* [*corallinus*, Latin.] Consisting of coral; approaching to coral.

At such time as the sea is agitated, it takes up into itself terrestrial matter of all kinds, and in particular the *coralline* matter, letting it fall again, as it becomes more quiet and calm. *Woodward on Fossils.*

CO'RALLINE. *n. s.* [from the adjective.]

Coralline is a sea-plant used in medicine; but much inferiour to the coral in hardness. It is naturally very ramose or branched, and forms a bunch of filaments two or three inches long, and each of them of the thickness of a small packthread, and jointed. They are sometimes greenish, sometimes yellowish, often redish, and frequently white. *Hill.*

In Falmouth there is a sort of sand, or rather *coralline*, that lies under the owse, which they are forced to remove before they can come to the bed of sand. *Mortimer's Husbandry.*

CO'RALLOID. } *adv.* [κοραλλοειδής.] Resembling coral.
CO'RALLOIDAL. }

Now that plants and ligneous bodies may indurate under water, without approachment of air, we have experiment in coralline, with many *coralloidal* concretions. *Brown.*

The pentadrous, columnar, *coralloid* bodies, that are composed of plates set lengthways of the body, and passing from the surface to the axis of it. *Woodward on Fossils.*

CORA'NT. *n. s.* [*courant*, French.] A nimble sprightly dance.

It is harder to dance a *corant* well than a jigg; so in conversation, even, easy, and agreeable, more than points of wit. *Temple.*

I would as soon believe a widow in great grief for her husband, because I saw her dance a *corant* about his coffin. *Walsh.*

CO'RBAN. *n. s.* [קרבן.] An alms-basket; a receptacle of charity; a gift; an alms.

They think to satisfy all obligations to duty by their *corban* of religion. *King Charles.*

Corban stands for an offering or gift made to God, or his temple. The Jews sometimes swore by *corban*, or the gifts offered unto God. If a man made all his fortune *corban*, or devoted it to God, he was forbidden to use it. If all that he was to give his wife, or his father and mother, was declared *corban*, he was no longer permitted to allow them necessary subsistence. Even debtors were permitted to defraud their creditors, by consecrating their debt to God. Our Saviour reproaches the Jews, in the Gospel, with these uncharitable and irreligious vows. By this word such persons were likewise meant as devoted themselves to the service of God and his temple. *Corban* signifies also the treasury of the temple, where the offerings, which were made in money, were deposited. *Calmet.*

CORBE. *adj.* [*courbe*, French.] Crooked.

For siker thy head very tottie is,
So thy *corbe* shoulder it leans amiss. *Spenser's Pastorals.*

CO'RBEILS. *n. s.* Little baskets used in fortification, filled with earth, and set upon the parapet, to shelter the men in firing upon the besiegers.

CO'RBEL. *n. s.* [In architecture.] The representation of a basket, sometimes placed on the heads of the caryatides.

CO'RBEL. } *n. s.*
CO'RBIL. }

10. A short piece of timber sticking out six or eight inches from a wall, sometimes placed for strength under the semi-girders of a platform.
2. A niche or hollow left in walls for figures or statues. *Chambers.*

CORD. *n. s.* [*cort*, Welsh; *chorda*, Latin; *corde*, French.]
1. A rope; a string composed of several strands or twists.

Such smiling rogues as these,
Like rats, oft bite the holy *cords* in twain,
Too intrinsicate t' unloose. *Shakespeare's King Lear.*

She let them down by a *cord* through the window. *Jos.* ii. 5.

Form'd of the finest complicated thread,
These num'rous *cords* are through the body spread. *Blackm.*

2. The cords extended in setting up tents, furnish several metaphors in scripture.

Thine eyes shall see Jerusalem a quiet habitation, a tabernacle that shall not be taken down; none of the stakes thereof shall ever be removed, neither shall any of the *cords* thereof be broken. *Isaiah*, xxxiii. 20.

3. A quantity of wood for fuel, supposed to be measured with a cord; a pile eight feet long, four high, and four broad.

CORD-MAKER. *n. s.* [*cord* and *make*] One whose trade is to make ropes; a ropemaker.

CORD-WOOD. *n. s.* [*cord* and *wood.*] Wood piled up for fuel, to be sold by the cord.

To CORD. *v. a.* [from the noun.] To bind with ropes; to fasten with cords; to close by a bandage.

CO'RDAGE. *n. s.* [from *cord.*] A quantity of cords; the ropes of a ship.

They fastened their ships to the ground, and rid at anchor with cables of iron chains, having neither canvas nor *cordage.* *Raleigh, Essay* 1.

Spain furnished a sort of rush called spartum, useful for *cordage* and other parts of shipping. *Arbuthnot on Coins.*

To the *cordage* glued
The sailor, and the pilot to the helm. *Thomson's Winter.*

CO'RDED. *adj.* [from *cord.*] Made of ropes.

This night he meaneth, with a *corded* ladder,
To climb celestial Silvia's chamber-window. *Shakespeare.*

CORDELI'ER. *n. s.* A Franciscan frier; so named from the cord which serves him for a cincture.

And who to assist but a grave *cordelier.* *Prior.*

CO'RDIAL. *n. s.* [from *cor*, the heart, Latin.]
1. A medicine that increases the force of the heart, or quickens the circulation.
2. Any medicine that increases strength.

A *cordial*, properly speaking, is not always what increaseth the force of the heart; for, by increasing that, the animal may be weakened, as in inflammatory diseases. Whatever increaseth the natural or animal strength, the force of moving the fluids and muscles, is a *cordial:* these are such substances as bring the serum of the blood into the properest condition for circulation and nutrition; as broths made of animal substances, milk, ripe fruits, and whatever is endued with a wholsome but not pungent taste. *Arbuthnot on Aliments.*

3. Any thing that comforts, gladdens, and exhilerates.

Then with some *cordials* seek for to appease
The inward languor of my wounded heart,
And then my body shall have shortly ease;
But such sweet *cordials* pass physicians art. *Spenser.*

Comfort, like *cordials* after death, comes late. *Dryden.*

Your warrior offspring that upheld the crown,
The scarlet honour of your peaceful gown,
Are the most pleasing objects I can find,
Charms to my sight, and *cordials* to my mind. *Dryden.*

CO'RDIAL. *adj.*
1. Reviving; invigorating; restorative.

It is a thing I make, which hath the king
Five times redeem'd from death: I do not know
What is more *cordial.* *Shakespeare's Cymbeline.*

He only took *cordial* waters, in which we infused sometimes purgatives. *Wiseman's Surgery.*

2. Sincere; hearty; proceeding from the heart; without hypocrisy.

Doctrines are infused among Christians, which are apt to obstruct or intercept the *cordial* superstructing of Christian life or renovation, where the foundation is duly laid. *Hammond.*

With looks of *cordial* love,
Hung over her enamour'd. *Milton.*

CORDIA'LITY. *n. s.* [from *cordial.*]
1. Relation to the heart.

That the antients had any such respect of *cordiality*, or reference unto the heart, will much be doubted. *Brown.*

2. Sincerity; freedom from hypocrisy.

CO'RDIALLY. *adv.* [from *cordial.*] Sincerely; heartily; without hypocrisy.

Where a strong inveterate love of sin has made any doctrine or proposition, wholly unsuitable to the heart, no argument or demonstration, no nor miracle whatsoever, shall be able to bring the heart *cordially* to close with and receive it. *South's Sermons.*

CO'RDINER. *n. s.* [*cordonnier*, French.] A shoemaker. It is so used in divers statutes. *Cowel.*

CO'RDON. *n. s.* [Fr.] In fortification, a row of stones jutting out before the rampart and the basis of the parapet. *Chambers.*

CO'RDWAIN. *n. s.* [*Cordovan* leather, from *Cordova* in Spain.] Spanish leather.

Her straight legs most bravely were embay'd
In golden buskins of costly *cordwain.* *Fairy Queen, b.* ii.

CORDWA'INER. *n. s.* [Uncertain whether from *Cordovan*, Spanish leather, or from *cord*, of which shoes were formerly made, and are now used in the Spanish West Indies. *Trevoux.*] A shoemaker.

CORE. *n. s.* [*cœur*, French; *cor*, Latin.]
1. The heart.

Give me that man
That is not passion's slave, and I will wear him
In my heart's *core*; ay, in my heart of heart. *Shak. Hamlet.*

2. The inner part of any thing.

In the *core* of the square she raised a tower of a furlong high. *Raleigh's History of the World.*

Dig out the *cores* below the surface. *Mortimer's Husbandry.*

They wasteful eat,
Through buds and bark, into the blacken'd *core.* *Thomson.*

3. The inner part of a fruit which contains the kernels.

It is reported that trees, watered perpetually with warm water, will make a fruit with little or no *core* or stone. *Bacon.*

4. The matter contained in a boil or sore.

Launce the sore,
And cut the head; for, 'till the *core* be found,
The secret vice is fed, and gathers ground. *Dryd. Virgil.*

5. It is used by *Bacon* for a body or collection [from *corps*, French, pronounced *core.*]

He was more doubtful of the raising of forces to resist the rebels, than of the resistance itself; for that he was in a *core* of people whose affections he suspected. *Bacon's Henry* VII.

CORIA'CEOUS. *adj.* [*coriaceus*, Latin.]
1. Consisting of leather.
2. Of a substance resembling leather.

A stronger projectile motion of the blood must occasion greater secretions and loss of liquid parts, and from thence perhaps spissitude and *coriaceous* concretions. *Arbuthnot on Alim.*

CORIA'NDER. *n. s.* [*coriandrum*, Latin.]

It hath a fibrose annual root: the lower leaves are broad, but the upper leaves are deeply cut into five segments: the petals of the flower are unequal, and shaped like an heart: the fruit is composed of two hemispherical, and sometimes spherical seeds. The species are, 1. Greater *coriander.* 2. Smaller testiculated *coriander.* The first is cultivated for the seeds, which are used in medicine: the second sort is seldom found. *Miller.*

Israel called the name thereof manna; and it was, like *coriander* seed, white. *Exod.* xiii. 31.

CO'RINTH. *n. s.* [from the city of that name in *Greece.*] A small fruit commonly called currant.

The chief riches of Zant consisteth in *corinths*, which the inhabitants have in great quantities. *Broom's Notes on the Odyss.*

CORI'NTHIAN *Order*, is generally reckoned the fourth, but by some the fifth, of the five orders of architecture; and is the most noble, rich, and delicate of them all. Vitruvius ascribes it to Callimachus, a Corinthian sculptor, who is said to have taken the hint by passing by the tomb of a young lady, over which a basket with some of her playthings had been placed by her nurse, and covered with a tile; the whole having been placed over a root of acanthus. As it sprung up, the branches encompassed the basket; but arriving at the tile, bent downwards under the corners of it, forming a kind of a volute. Hence Calimachus imitated the basket by the vase of his capital, the tile in the abacus, and the leaves in the volute. This story is treated as a fable by Villalpandus, who imagines the *Corinthian* capital to have taken its original from an order in the temple of Solomon, whose leaves were those of the palm-tree. This order is distinguished from the rest by several characters. The capital is adorned with two rows of leaves, between which little stalks arise, of which the sixteen volutes are formed, which support the abacus. *Harris.*

Behind these figures are large columns of the *Corinthian Order*, adorned with fruit and flowers. *Dryden.*

CORK. *n. s.* [*cortex*, Lat. *korck*, Dutch.

Hic dies, anno redeunte, festus
Corticem *astrictum pice dimovebit*
Amphoræ, fumum bibere institutæ
Consule Tullo. Hor.]

1. A glandiferous tree, in all respects like the ilex, excepting the bark, which, in the *cork* tree, is thick, spongy, and soft. *Miller.*

The *cork* tree grows near the Pyrenæan hills, and in several parts of Italy, and the North of New England. *Mortimer.*

2. The bark of the cork tree used for stopples, or burnt into Spanish black. It is taken off without injury to the tree.
3. A piece of cork cut for the stopple of a bottle or barrel.

I pr'ythee take the *cork* out of thy mouth, that I may drink thy tidings. *Shakespeare's As you like it.*

Be sure, nay very sure, thy *cork* be good;
Then future ages shall of Peggy tell,
That nymph that brew'd and bottled ale so well. *King.*

 Nor

Nor ſtop, for one bad *cork*, his butler's pay. *Pope.*

CORKING-PIN. *n. ſ.* A pin of the largeſt ſize.

When you put a clean pillow-caſe on your lady's pillow, be ſure to faſten it well with three *corking-pins*, that it may not fall off in the night. *Swift's Direct. to the Chambermaid.*

CO'RKY. *adj.* [from *cork.*] Conſiſting of cork.

Bind faſt his *corky* arms. *Shakeſpeare's King Lear.*

CO'RMORANT. *n. ſ.* [*cormoran*, Fr. from *corvus marinus*, Latin.]

1. A bird that preys upon fiſh. It is nearly of the bigneſs of a capon, with a wry bill and broad feet, black on his body, but greeniſh about his wings. He is eminently greedy and rapacious.

Let fame, that all hunt after in their lives,
Live regiſter'd upon our brazen tombs;
When, ſpight of *cormorant* devouring time,
Th' endeavour of this preſent breath may buy
That honour which ſhall 'bate his ſcythe's keen edge. *Shak.*

Thoſe called birds of prey, as the eagle, hawk, puttock, and *cormorant*. *Peacham on Drawing.*

Thence up he flew, and on the tree of life
Sat like a *cormorant*. *Milton's Paradiſe Loſt, b.* iv. *l.* 194.

Not far from thence is ſeen a lake, the haunt
Of coots, and of the fiſhing *cormorant*. *Dryden's Fables.*

2. A glutton.

CORN. *n. ſ.* [corn, Sax. *korn*, Germ. It is found in all the Teutonick dialects; as, in an old Runick rhyme,

Hagul er kaldaſtur corna.
Hail is the coldeſt grain.]

1. The ſeeds which grow in ears, not in pods; ſuch as are made into bread.

Except a *corn* of wheat fall into the ground, and die, it abideth alone. *John* xii. 25.

The people cry you mock'd them; and, of late,
When *corn* was given them gratis, you repin'd. *Sh. Coriolan.*

2. Grain yet unreaped, ſtanding in the field upon its ſtalk.

Why he was met even now,
Crown'd with rank fumiter and furrow-weeds,
Darnel, and all the idle weeds that grow
In our ſuſtaining *corn*. *Shakeſpeare's King Lear.*

Landing his men, he burnt the *corn* all thereabouts, which was now almoſt ripe. *Knolles's Hiſtory of the Turks.*

Still a murmur runs
Along the ſoft inclining fields of *corn*. *Thomſon's Autumn.*

3. Grain in the ear, yet unthreſhed.

Thou ſhalt come to thy grave in a full age, like as a ſhock of *corn* cometh in in his ſeaſon. *Job*, v. 26.

4. An excreſcence on the feet, hard and painful; probably ſo called from its form, though by ſome ſuppoſed to be denominated from its *corneous* or horny ſubſtance.

Ladies, that have your feet
Unplagu'd with *corns*, we'll have a bout with you. *Shakeſp.*

The man that makes his toe,
What he his heart ſhould make,
Shall of a *corn* cry woe,
And turn his ſleep to wake. *Shakeſpeare's King Lear.*

Even in men, aches and hurts and *corns* do engrieve either towards rain or towards froſt. *Bacon's Natural Hiſtory.*

The hardeſt part of the *corn* is uſually in the middle, thruſting itſelf in a nail; whence it has the Latin appellation of *clavis*. *Wiſeman's Surgery.*

He firſt that uſeful ſecret did explain,
That pricking *corns* foretold the gath'ring rain. *Gay's Paſt.*

It looks as there were regular accumulations and gatherings of humours, growing perhaps in ſome people as *corns*. *Arbuth.*

Thus Lamb, renown'd for cutting *corns*,
An offer'd fee from Radcliff ſcorns. *Swift.*

To CORN. *v. a.* [from the noun.]

1. To ſalt; to ſprinkle with ſalt. The word is ſo uſed, as *Skinner* obſerves, by the old Saxons.

2. To granulate.

CORN-FIELD. *n. ſ.* A field where corn is growing.

It was a lover and his laſs,
That o'er the green *corn-field* did paſs. *Shakeſ. As you like it.*

You may ſoon enjoy the gallant ſights of armies, encampments, and ſtandards waving over your brother's *cornfields*. *Pope.*

CORN-FLAG. *n. ſ.* [*corn* and *flag.*]

It hath a fleſhy double tuberoſe root: the leaves are like thoſe of the fleur-de-lys: the flower conſiſts of one leaf, ſhaped like a lily, open at the top, in two lips; the upper imbricated, the under divided into five ſegments: the ovary becomes an oblong fruit, divided into three cells, filled with roundiſh ſeeds wrapt up in a cover. *Miller* enumerates eleven ſpecies of this plant, ſome with red flowers, and ſome with white. It is a proper ornament for borders.

CORN-FLOOR. *n. ſ.* The floor where corn is ſtored.

Thou haſt loved a reward upon every *corn-floor*. *Hoſ.* ix. 1.

CORN-FLOWER. *n. ſ.* [from *corn* and *flower.*]

There be certain *corn-flowers*, which come ſeldom or never in other places, unleſs they be ſet, but only amongſt corn; as the blue-bottle, a kind of yellow marygold, wild poppy, and furmitory. *Bacon's Natural Hiſtory*, N°. 482.

Corn-flowers are of many ſorts: ſome of them flower in June and July, and others in Auguſt. The ſeeds ſhould be ſown in March: they require a good ſoil. *Mortimer's Husband.*

CORN-LAND. *n. ſ.* [*corn* and *land.*] Land appropriated to the production of grain.

Paſtures and meadows are of ſuch advantage to huſbandry, that many prefer them to *corn-lands*. *Mortimer's Husbandry.*

CORN-MASTER. *n. ſ.* [*corn* and *maſter.*] One that cultivates corn for ſale.

I knew a nobleman in England, that had the greateſt audits of any man in my time; a great graſier, a great ſheep-maſter, a great timberman, a great collier, a great *corn-maſter*, and a great leadman. *Bacon, Eſſay* 35.

CORN-MARIGOLD. *n. ſ.* [from *corn* and *marigold.*]

It hath an annual root: the cup of the flower is hemiſpherical and ſcaly: the flowers are radiated; the rays being, for the moſt part, of a yellow flower, and the ſeeds are furrowed. *Miller.*

CORN-MILL. *n. ſ.* [*corn* and *mill.*] A mill to grind corn into meal.

Save the more laborious work of beating of hemp, by making the axle-tree of the *corn-mills* longer than ordinary, and placing pins in it to raiſe large hammers. *Mort. Husband.*

CORN-PIPE. *n. ſ.* [from *corn* and *pipe.*] A pipe made by ſlitting the joint of a green ſtalk of corn.

Now the ſhrill *corn-pipes*, echoing loud to arms,
To rank and file reduce the ſtraggling ſwarms. *Tickel.*

CORN-ROCKET. *n. ſ.* [from *corn* and *rocket.*]

The flower conſiſts of four leaves, in form of a croſs: the pointal becomes a four-cornered fruit, reſembling a creſted club, divided into four cells, in which are contained roundiſh ſeeds with a beak. This plant grows wild in the warm parts of France and Spain. *Miller.*

CORN-ROSE. *n. ſ.* See POPPY, of which it is a ſpecies.

CORN-SALLAD. *n. ſ.* [from *corn* and *ſallad.*]

The leaves grow by pairs oppoſite on the branches, which are always divided into two parts, and appear at the top like an umbrella. The flower conſiſts of one leaf, cut into many ſegments, and ſucceeded by one naked ſeed, having no down adhering to it, in which it differs from the valerian. Some ſorts of it grow wild. *Miller.*

Corn-ſallad is an herb, whoſe top-leaves are a ſallet of themſelves. *Mortimer's Husbandry.*

CO'RNAGE. *n. ſ.* [from *corne*, Fr. *cornu*, Latin.] A tenure which obliges the landholder to give notice of an invaſion by blowing a horn.

CO'RNCHANDLER. *n. ſ.* [*corn* and *chandler.*] One that retails corn.

CO'RNCUTTER. *n. ſ.* [from *corn* and *cut.*] A man whoſe profeſſion is to extirpate corns from the foot.

The nail was not looſe, nor did ſeem to preſs into the fleſh; for there had been a *corncutter*, who had cleared it. *Wiſeman.*

I have known a *corncutter*, who, with a right education, would have been an excellent phyſician. *Spectator*, N°. 307.

CO'RNEL. } *n. ſ.* [*cornus*, Latin.] See CORNELIAN-
CORNELIAN-TREE. } CHERRY.

The *Cornel-tree* beareth the fruit commonly called the cornel or cornelian cherry, as well from the name of the tree as the cornelian ſtone, the colour whereof it ſomewhat repreſents. The fruit is good in the kitchen and conſervatory. The wood is very durable, and uſeful for wheelwork. *Mortim. Husbandry.*

Take a ſervice-tree, or a *cornelian-tree*, or an elder-tree, which we know have fruits of harſh and binding juice, and ſet them near a vine or fig-tree, and ſee whether the grapes or figs will not be the ſweeter. *Bacon's Natural Hiſtory*, N°. 485.

Mean time the goddeſs, in diſdain, beſtows
The maſt and acorn, brutal food! and ſtrows
The fruits of *cornel*, as they feaſt around. *Pope's Odyſſey.*

CO'RNEL. } *n. ſ.* [*cornus*, Latin.]
CORNELIAN-CHERRY. }

The flower-cup conſiſts of four ſmall rigid leaves, expanded in form of a croſs; from the center of which are produced many ſmall yellowiſh flowers, conſiſting of four leaves, diſpoſed in form of an umbrella: theſe flowers are ſucceeded by fruit, oblong or of a cylindrical form, ſomewhat like an olive, containing an hard ſtone, which is divided into two cells, each containing a ſingle ſeed. The ſpecies are ten, of which the *cornelian-cherry*, or male cornel-tree, is very common, being propagated for its fruit, which, by many people, is preſerved to make tarts: it is alſo uſed in medicine as an aſtringent and cooler. There is likewiſe an officinal preparation of this fruit, called *Rob de cornus*. Dogberry, or gattentree, is very common in hedges, and the fruit of this plant is often brought into the markets, and ſold for buckthornberries; but in this fruit is but one ſtone, and in the buckthorn four. The ſaſſafras ſort is a native of America; and its root is much uſed in England to make a tea, which is greatly commended by ſome againſt violent defluxions. Moſt of the other ſorts are brought from America, except what is commonly called the dwarf honeyſuckle, which grows wild on the high mountains in the northern counties; but is with difficulty preſerved in gardens. *Miller.*

On wildings and on ſtrawberries they fed;

Cornels

Cornels and brambleberries gave the reſt,
And falling acorns furniſh'd out a feaſt. *Dryden's Ovid.*

CORNE'LIAN-STONE. See CARNELIAN.

CO'RNEMUSE. n. ſ. [French.] A kind of ruſtick flute.

CO'RNEOUS. *adj.* [*corneus*, Latin.] Horny; of a ſubſtance reſembling horn.

Such as have *corneous* or horny eyes, as lobſters, and cruſtaceous animals, are generally dimſighted. *Brown's Vulg. Err.*

The various ſubmarine ſhrubs are of a *corneous* or ligneous conſtitution, conſiſting chiefly of a fibrous matter. *Woodward.*

CO'RNER. *n. ſ.* [*cornel*, Welſh; *cornier*, French.]

1. An angle; a place incloſed by two walls or lines, which would interſect each other, if drawn beyond the point where they meet.

2. A ſecret or remote place.

There's nothing I have done yet, o' my conſcience,
Deſerves a *corner*. *Shakeſpeare's Henry* VIII.

It is better to dwell in a *corner* of a houſe-top, than with a brawling woman and in a wide houſe. *Proverbs*, xxv. 24.

I am perſuaded that none of theſe things are hidden from him; for this thing was not done in a *corner*. *Acts*, xxvi. 26.

All the inhabitants, in every *corner* of the iſland, have been abſolutely reduced under his immediate ſubjection. *Davies.*

Thoſe vices, that lurk in the ſecret *corners* of the ſoul. *Addiſ.*

Your active ſearch
Leaves no cold wintry *corner* unexplor'd. *Thomſon's Spring.*

3. The extremities; the utmoſt limit: thus every corner is the whole or every part.

Might I but through my priſon, once a day,
Behold this maid, all *corners* elſe o' th' earth
Let liberty make uſe of. *Shakeſpeare's Tempeſt.*

I turn'd, and try'd each *corner* of my bed,
To find if ſleep were there; but ſleep was loſt. *Dryden.*

CORNER-STONE. *n. ſ.* [*corner* and *ſtone.*] The ſtone that unites the two walls at the corner; the principal ſtone.

See you yond' coin o'th' capitol, yond' *corner-ſtone?* *Shakeſp.*

A maſon was fitting a *corner-ſtone*. *Howel's Vocal Foreſt.*

CORNER-TEETH *of a Horſe*, are the four teeth which are placed between the middling teeth and the tuſhes; and are two above and two below, on each ſide of the jaw, which ſhoot forth when the horſe is four years and a half old. *Farrier's Dict.*

CO'RNERWISE. *adv.* [*corner* and *wiſe.*] Diagonally; with the corner in front.

CO'RNET. *n. ſ.* [*cornette*, French.]

1. A muſical inſtrument blown with the mouth: uſed anciently in war, probably in the cavalry.

Iſrael played before the Lord on pſalteries and on timbrels, and on *cornets*. 2 *Sa.* vi. 5.

Other wind inſtruments require a forcible breath; as trumpets, *cornets*, and hunters horns. *Bacon's Natural Hiſtory.*

Cornets and trumpets cannot reach his ear,
Under an actor's noſe, he's never near. *Dryden's Juvenal.*

2. A company or troop of horſe; perhaps as many as had a cornet belonging to them. This ſenſe is now diſuſed.

Theſe noblemen were appointed, with ſome *cornets* of horſe and bands of foot, to put themſelves beyond the hill where the rebels were encamped. *Bacon.*

Seventy great horſes lay dead in the field, and one *cornet* was taken. *Hayward.*

They diſcerned a body of five *cornets* of horſe very full, ſtanding in very good order to receive them. *Clarendon.*

3. The officer that bears the ſtandard of a troop.

4. CORNET *of a Horſe*, is the loweſt part of his paſtern that runs round the coffin, and is diſtinguiſhed by the hair that joins and covers the upper part of the hoof. *Farrier's Dict.*

5. A ſcarf anciently worn by doctors. *Dict.*

6. A head-dreſs. *Dict.*

7. *A* CORNET *of Paper*, is deſcribed by *Skinner* to be a cap of paper, made by retailers for ſmall wares.

CO'RNETTER. *n. ſ.* [from *cornet.*] A blower of the cornet.

So great was the rabble of trumpeters, *cornetters*, and other muſicians, that even Claudius himſelf might have heard them. *Hakewill on Providence.*

CO'RNICE. *n. ſ.* [*corniche*, French.] The higheſt projection of a wall or column.

The *cornice* of the Palazzo Farneſe, which makes ſo beautiful an effect below, when viewed more nearly, will be found not to have its juſt meaſures. *Dryden's Dufreſnoy.*

The walls were maſſy braſs, the *cornice* high
Blue metals crown'd, in colours of the ſky. *Pope's Odyſſey.*

CORNICE *Ring.* [In gunnery.] The next ring from the muzzle backwards. *Chambers.*

COR'NICLE. *n. ſ.* [from *cornu*, Latin.] A little horn.

There will be found, on either ſide, two black filaments, or membranous ſtrings, which extend unto the long and ſhorter *cornicle*, upon protruſion. *Brown's Vulgar Errours*, *b.* iii.

CORNI'CULATE. *adj.* [from *cornu*, Lat.] A term in botany.

Corniculate plants are ſuch as produce many diſtinct and horned pods; and *corniculate* flowers are ſuch hollow flowers as have on their upper part a kind of ſpur, or little horn. *Chamb.*

CORNI'FICK. *adj.* [from *cornu* and *facio*, Latin.] Productive of horns; making horns. *Dict.*

CORNI'GEROUS. *adj.* [*corniger*, Latin.] Horned; having horns.

Nature, in other *cornigerous* animals, hath placed the horns higher, and reclining; as in bucks. *Brown's Vulgar Errours.*

CORNU'COPIÆ. n. ſ. [Lat.] The horn of plenty; a horn topped with fruits and flowers in the hands of a goddeſs.

To CORNU'TE. *v. a.* [*cornutus*, Latin.] To beſtow horns; to cuckold.

CORNU'TED. *adj.* [*cornutus*, Latin.] Grafted with horns; horned; cuckolded.

CORNU'TO. *n. ſ.* [from *cornutus*, Latin.] A man horned; a cuckold.

The peaking *cornuto* her huſband, dwelling in a continual larum of jealouſy. *Shakeſpeare's Merry Wives of Windſor.*

CO'RNY. *adj.* [from *cornu*, horn, Latin.]

1. Strong or hard like horn; horny.

Up ſtood the *corny* reed,
Embattel'd in her field. *Milton's Paradiſe Loſt*, *b.* vii.

2. [from *corn.*] Producing grain or corn.

Tell me why the ant,
'Midſt Summer's plenty, thinks of Winter's want,
By conſtant journeys, careful to prepare
Her ſtores; and bringing home the *corny* ear. *Prior.*

CO'ROLLARY. *n. ſ.* [*corollarium*, Lat. from *corolla*; *finis coronat opus*; or from *corollair*, Fr. a ſurplus.]

1. The concluſion: a corollary ſeems to be a concluſion, whether following from the premiſes neceſſarily or not.

Now ſince we have conſidered the malignity of this ſin of detraction, it is but a natural *corollary*, that we enforce our vigilance againſt it. *Government of the Tongue.*

As a *corollary* to this preface, in which I have done juſtice to others, I owe ſomewhat to myſelf. *Dryden's Fab. Preface.*

2. Surplus.

Bring a *corollary*,
Rather than want. *Shakeſpeare's Tempeſt.*

CORO'NA. n. ſ. [Latin.] A large flat member of the cornice, ſo called becauſe it crowns the entablature and the whole order. It is called by workmen the drip. *Chambers.*

In a cornice the gola or cymatium of the *corona*, the coping, the modillions or dentelli, make a noble ſhew by their graceful projections. *Spectator*, N°. 415.

CO'RONAL. *n. ſ.* [*corona*, Latin.] A crown; a garland.

Crown ye god Bacchus with a *coronal*,
And Hymen alſo crown with wreaths of vine. *Spenſer.*

CO'RONAL. *adj.* Belonging to the top of the head.

A man of about forty-five years of age came to me, with a round tubercle between the ſagittal and *coronal* ſuture. *Wiſem.*

CO'RONARY. *adj.* [*coronarius*, Latin.]

1. Relating to a crown; ſeated on the top of the head like a crown.

The baſiliſk of older times was a proper kind of ſerpent, not above three palms long, as ſome account; and differenced from other ſerpents by advancing his head, and ſome white marks, or *coronary* ſpots upon the crown. *Brown's Vulg. Err.*

2. It is applied in anatomy to arteries, which are fancied to encompaſs the heart in the manner of a garland.

The ſubſtance of the heart itſelf is moſt certainly made and nouriſhed by the blood, which is conveyed to it by the *coronary* arteries. *Bentley's Sermons.*

CORONA'TION. *n. ſ.* [from *corona*, Latin.]

1. The act or ſolemnity of crowning a king.

Fortune ſmiling at her work therein, that a ſcaffold of execution ſhould grow a ſcaffold of *coronation*. *Sidney*, *b.* ii.

Willingly I came to Denmark,
To ſhew my duty in your *coronation*. *Shakeſpeare's Hamlet.*

A cough, ſir, which I caught with ringing in the king's affairs upon his *coronation* day. *Shakeſpeare's Henry* IV. *p.* ii.

Now empreſs fame had publiſh'd the renown
Of Sh——'s *coronation* through the town. *Dryden's Macfl.*

2. The pomp or aſſembly preſent at a coronation.

In penſive thought recal the fancy'd ſcene,
See *coronations* riſe on ev'ry green. *Pope.*

CO'RONER. *n. ſ.* [from *corona.*] An officer whoſe duty is to enquire, on the part of the king, how any violent death was occaſioned; for which purpoſe a jury of twelve perſons is impannelled.

Go thou and ſeek the *coroner*, and let him ſit o' my uncle; for he's in the third degree of drink; he's drowned. *Shakeſp.*

CO'RONET. *n. ſ.* [*coronetta*, Ital. the diminutive of *corona*, a crown.] An inferiour crown worn by the nobility. The coronet of a duke is adorned with ſtrawberry leaves; that of a marquis has leaves with pearls interpoſed; that of an earl raiſes the pearls above the leaves; that of a viſcount is ſurrounded with only pearls; that of a baron has only four pearls.

The reſt was drawn into a *coronet* of gold, richly ſet with pearl. *Sidney.*

In his livery
Walk'd crowns and *coronets*, realms and iſlands were
As plates dropt from his pocket. *Shak. Ant. and Cleopatra.*

All the reſt are counteſſes.
——Their *coronets* ſay ſo. *Shakeſpeare's Henry* VIII.

Under a *coronet* his flowing hair,
In curls, on either cheek play'd. *Milton's Paradise Lost.*
Nor could our nobles hope their bold attempt,
Who ruin'd crowns, would *coronets* exempt. *Dryden.*
Peers and dukes, and all their sweeping train,
And garters, stars, and *coronets* appear. *Pope's Ra. of Lock.*

CO'RPORAL. *n. s.* [corrupted from *caporal*, French.] The lowest officer of the infantry, whose office is to place and remove the sentinels.

The cruel *corp'ral* whisper'd in my ear,
Five pounds, if rightly tipt, would set me clear. *Gay.*

CO'RPORAL *of a Ship.* An officer that hath the charge of setting the watches and sentries, and relieving them; who sees that all the soldiers and sailors keep their arms neat and clean, and teaches them how to use them. He has a mate under him. *Harris.*

CO'RPORAL. *adj.* [*corporel*, Fr. *corpus*, Latin.]

1. Relating to the body; belonging to the body.

To relief of lazars and weak age,
Of indigent faint souls, past *corporal* toil,
A hundred alms-houses, right well supplied. *Shak. Hen. V.*
Render to me some *corporal* sign about her,
More evident than this. *Shakespeare's Cymbeline.*

That God hath been otherwise seen, with *corporal* eyes, exceedeth the small proportion of my understanding. *Raleigh.*

They enjoy greater sensual pleasures, and feel fewer *corporal* pains, and are utter strangers to all those anxious and tormenting thoughts, which perpetually haunt and disquiet mankind. *Atterbury.*

2. Material; not spiritual. In the present language, when *body* is used philosophically in opposition to spirit, the word *corporeal* is used, as a *corporeal* being; but otherwise *corporal*. *Corporeal* is having a body; *corporal* relating to the body. This distinction seems not ancient.

Whither are they vanish'd?
Into the air: and what seem'd *corporal*
Melted, as breath, into the wind. *Shakespeare's Macbeth.*
And from these *corporal* nutriments, perhaps,
Your bodies may at last turn all to spirit. *Milt. Par. Lost.*

CORPORA'LITY. *n. s.* [from *corporal.*] The quality of being embodied.

If this light be not spiritual, yet it approacheth nearest unto spirituality; and if it have any *corporality*, then, of all other, the most subtile and pure. *Raleigh's Hist. of the World.*

CO'RPORALLY. *adv.* [from *corporal.*] Bodily.

The sun is *corporally* conjoined with basiliscus. *Brown.*

CO'RPORATE. *adj.* [from *corpus*, Latin.] United in a body or community; enabled to act in legal processes as an individual.

Breaking forth like a sudden tempest, he over-run all Munster and Connaught, defacing and utterly subverting all *corporate* towns that were not strongly walled. *Spenser on Ireland.*

They answer in a joint and *corporate* voice,
That now they are at fall. *Shakespeare's Timon.*

The nobles of Athens being not at this time a *corporate* assembly, therefore the resentment of the commons was usually turned against particular persons. *Swift.*

CO'RPORATENESS. *n. s.* [from *corporate.*] The state of a body corporate; a community. *Dict.*

CORPORA'TION. *n. s.* [from *corpus*, Latin.]

A *corporation* is a body politick, authorized by the king's charter to have a common seal, one head officer or more, and members, able, by their common consent, to grant or receive, in law, any thing within the compass of their charter: even as one man may do by law all things, that by law he is not forbidden; and bindeth the successors, as a single man binds his executor or heir. *Cowel.*

Of angels we are not to consider only what they are, and do, in regard of their own being; but that also which concerneth them, as they are linked into a kind of *corporation* amongst themselves, and of society or fellowship with men. *Hooker, b. i. sect. 4.*

Of this we find some foot-steps in our law,
Which doth her root from God and nature take;
Ten thousand men she doth together draw,
And of them all one *corporation* make. *Davies.*

CO'RPORATURE. *n. s.* [from *corpus*, Latin.] The state of being embodied. *Dict.*

CORPO'REAL. *adj.* [*corporeus*, Latin.]

1. Having a body; not immaterial. See CORPORAL.

The swiftness of those circles attribute,
Though numberless, to his omnipotence,
That to *corporeal* substances could add
Speed almost spiritual. *Milton's Paradise Lost, b. viii.*

Having surveyed the image of God in the soul, we are not to omit those characters that God imprinted upon the body, as much as a spiritual substance could be pictured upon a *corporeal.* *South's Sermons.*

God being supposed to be a pure spirit, cannot be the object of any *corporeal* sense. *Tillotson.*

The course is finish'd which thy fates decreed,
And thou from thy *corporeal* prison freed. *Dryden's Fables.*
Fix thy *corporeal* and internal eye
On the young gnat, or new-engender'd fly. *Prior.*

2. It is used by *Swift* inaccurately for *corporal.*

I am not in a condition to make a true step even on Aimsbury Downs; and I declare, that a *corporeal* false step is worse than a political one. *Swift.*

CORPORE'ITY. *n. s.* [from *corporeus*, Latin.] Materiality; the quality of being embodied; the state of having a body; bodiliness.

Since philosophy affirmeth, that we are middle substances between the soul and the body, they must admit of some *corporeity* which supposeth weight or gravity. *Brown's Vulg. Err.*

It is the saying of divine Plato, that man is nature's horizon, dividing betwixt the upper hemisphere of immaterial intellects and this lower of *corporeity.* *Glanville's Sceps. c. iv.*

The one attributed *corporeity* to God, and the other shape and figure. *Stillingfleet.*

CORPORIFICA'TION. *n. s.* [from *corporify.*] The act of giving body or palpability.

To CORPO'RIFY. *v. a.* [from *corpus*, Lat.] To embody; to inspissate into body.

A certain spirituous substance, extracted out of it, is mistaken for the spirit of the world *corporified.* *Boyle's Scept. Chym.*

CORPS. } *n. s.* [*corps*, Fr. *corpus*, Latin.]
CORPSE. }

1. A body, in contempt.

Though plenteous, all too little seems
To stuff this man, this vast unhide-bound *corps.* *Milton.*
He looks as man was made, with face erect,
That scorns his brittle *corps*, and seems asham'd
He's not all spirit. *Dryden's Don Sebastian.*

2. A carcase; a dead body; a corse.

Not a friend greet
My poor *corps*, where my bones shall be thrown. *Shakesp.*
There was the murder'd *corps* in covert laid,
And violent death in thousand shapes display'd. *Dryd. Fables*
See where the *corps* of thy dead son approaches. *Addison.*

The *corpse* was laid out upon the floor by the emperor's command: he then bid every one light his flambeau, and stand about the dead body. *Addison's Guardian, N°. 99.*

3. A body of forces.

CO'RPULENCE. } *n. s.* [*corpulentia*, Latin.]
CO'RPULENCY. }

1. Bulkiness of body; fleshiness; fulness of flesh.

To what a cumbersome unwieldiness,
And burdenous *corpulence* my love had grown. *Donne.*

It is but one species of *corpulency*; for there may be bulk without fat, from the great quantity of muscular flesh, the case of robust people. *Arbuthnot on Aliments.*

2. Spissitude; grossness of matter.

The musculous flesh serves for the vibration of the tail, the heaviness and *corpulency* of the water requiring a great force to divide it. *Ray on the Creation.*

CO'RPULENT. *adj.* [*corpulentus*, Latin.] Fleshy; bulky; having great bodily bulk.

We say it is a fleshy stile, when there is much periphrases, and circuit of words; and when with more than enough, it grows fat and *corpulent.* *Ben. Johnson's Discoveries.*

Excess of nourishment is hurtful; for it maketh the child *corpulent*, and growing in breadth rather than in height. *Bacon.*

CO'RPUSCLE. *n. s.* [*corpusculum*, Lat.] A small body; a particle of matter; an atom; a little fragment.

It will add much to our satisfaction, if those *corpuscles* can be discovered with microscopes. *Newton's Opt.*

Who knows what are the figures of the little *corpuscles* that compose and distinguish different bodies? *Watts's Logick.*

CORPU'SCULAR. } *adj.* [from *corpusculum*, Lat.] Relating
CORPUSCULA'RIAN. } to bodies; comprising bodies. It is the distinguishing epithet of that philosophy which attempts the rational solution of all physical appearances by the action of one body upon another.

As to natural philosophy I do not expect to see any principles proposed, more comprehensive and intelligible than the *corpuscularian* or mechanical. *Boyle.*

This may be said, that the modern *corpuscularians* talk, in most things, more intelligibly than the peripateticks. *Bentley.*

The mechanical or *corpuscular* philosophy, though peradventure the eldest, as well as the best in the world, had lain dead for many ages in contempt and oblivion. *Bentl y's Serm.*

CO'RRACLE. See CORRICLE.

To CORRA'DE. *v. a* [*corrado*, Latin.] To rub off; to wear away by frequent rubbing; to scrape together.

CORRADIA'TION. *n. s.* [*con* and *radius*, Lat.] A conjunction of rays in one point.

The impression of colour worketh not but by a cone of direct beams, or right lines, whereof the basis is in the object, and the vertical point in the eye; so as there is a *corradiation*, and conjunction of beams. *Bacon's Natural History, N°. 277.*

To CORRE'CT. *v. a.* [*corrigo correctum*, Latin.]

1. To punish; to chastise; to discipline.

Sad accidents, and a state of affliction, is a school of virtue; it *corrects* levity, and interrupts the confidence of sinning. *Tayl.*

After

After he has once been *corrected* for a lie, you must be sure never after to pardon it in him. *Locke on Education.*

Children being to be restrained by the parents only in vicious things, a look or nod only ought to *correct* them, when they do amiss. *Locke on Education.*

2. To amend; to take away faults, in writings or life.

This is a defect in the first make of some men's minds, which can scarce ever be *corrected* afterwards, either by learning or age. *Burnet's Theory of the Earth, Preface.*

Correcting nature, from what actually she is in individuals, to what she ought to be, and what she was created. *Dryden.*

I writ, because it amused me; I *corrected*, because it was as pleasant to me to *correct* as to write. *Pope's Preface.*

The mind may cool, and be at leisure to attend to its domestick concern: to consider what habit wants to be *corrected*, and what inclination to be subdued. *Rogers's Sermons.*

3. To obviate the qualities of one ingredient by another, or by any method of preparation.

As in habitual gout or stone,
The only thing that can be done,
Is to *correct* your drink and diet,
And keep the inward foe in quiet. *Prior.*

In cases of acidity, water is the proper drink: its quality of relaxing may be *corrected* by boiling it with some animal substances; as ivory or hartshorn. *Arbuthnot on Aliments.*

4. To remark faults.

CORRE'CT. *adj.* [*correctus*, Latin.] Revised or finished with exactness; free from faults.

What verse can do, he has perform'd in this,
Which he presumes the most *correct* of his. *Dryd. Aur. Prol.*

Always use the most *correct* editions: various readings will be only troublesome where the sense and language is complete. *Felton on the Classicks.*

CORRE'CTION. *n. s.* [from *correct.*]

1. Punishment; discipline; chastisement; penalty.

Wilt thou, pupil like,
Take thy *correction* mildly, kiss the rod? *Shakesp. Rich.* II.

An offensive wife,
That hath enrag'd him on to offer strokes,
As he is striking, holds his infant up,
And hangs resolv'd *correction* in the arm
That was uprear'd to execution. *Shakesp. Henry* IV. *p.* ii.

We are all but children here under the great master of the family; and he is pleased, by hopes and fears, by mercies and *corrections*, to instruct us in virtue. *Watts.*

2. Alteration to a better state; the act of taking away faults; amendment.

Another poet, in another age, make take the same liberty with my writings; if, at least, they live long enough to deserve *correction*. *Dryden's Fables, Preface.*

3. That which is substituted in the place of any thing wrong.

Corrections or improvements should be adjoined, by way of note or commentary, in their proper places. *Watts.*

4. Reprehension; animadversion.

They proceed with judgment and ingenuity, establishing their assertions not only with great solidity, but submitting them also unto the *correction* of future discovery. *Brown.*

One fault was too great lenity to her servants, to whom she always gave good counsel, but often too gentle *correction*. *Arbuthnot's History of John Bull.*

5. Abatement of noxious qualities, by the addition of something contrary.

To make courts hot, ambitious, wholesome, do not take
A dram of country's dulness; do not add
Corrections, but as chymists purge the bad. *Donne.*

CORRE'CTIONER. *n. s.* [from *correction.*] One that has been in the house of correction; a jayl-bird. This seems to be the meaning in *Shakespeare.*

I will have you soundly swinged for this, you blue-bottle rogue! you filthy famished *correctioner*. *Shakesp. Henry* IV.

CORRE'CTIVE. *adj.* [from *correct.*] Having the power to alter or obviate any bad qualities.

Mulberries are pectoral, *corrective* of the bilious alcali. *Arbuthnot on Aliments.*

CORRE'CTIVE. *n. s.*

1. That which has the power of altering or obviating any thing amiss.

The hair, wool, feathers, and scales, which all animals of prey do swallow, are a seasonable and necessary *corrective*, to prevent their greediness from filling themselves with too succulent a food. *Ray on the Creation.*

Humanly speaking, and according to the method of the world, and the little *correctives* supplied by art and discipline, it seldom fails but an ill principle has its course, and nature makes good its blow. *South's Sermons.*

2. Limitation; restriction.

There seems to be such an instance in the regiment, which the human soul exerciseth in relation to the body, that with certain *correctives* and exceptions, may give some kind of explication or adumbration thereof. *Hale's Origin of Mankind.*

CORRE'CTLY. *adv.* [from *correct.*] Accurately; appositely; exactly; without faults.

There are ladies, without knowing what tenses and participles, adverbs and prepositions are, speak as properly and as *correctly* as most gentlemen who have been bred up in the ordinary methods of grammar schools. *Locke on Education.*

Such lays as neither ebb nor flow,
Correctly cold, and regularly low. *Pope's Essay on Criticism.*

CORRE'CTNESS. *n. s.* [from *correct.*] Accuracy; exactness; freedom from faults.

Too much labour often takes away the spirit, by adding to the polishing; so that there remains nothing but a dull *correctness*, a piece without any considerable faults, but with few beauties. *Dryden's Dufresnoy.*

The softness of the flesh, the delicacy of the shape, air and posture, and the *correctness* of design in this statue, are inexpressible. *Addison on Italy.*

Late, very late, *correctness* grew our care,
When the tir'd nation breath'd from civil war. *Pope.*

Those pieces have never before been printed from the true copies, or with any tolerable degree of *correctness*. *Swift.*

CORRE'CTOR. *n. s.* [from *correct.*]

1. He that amends, or alters, by punishment or animadversion.

How many does zeal urge rather to do justice on some sins, than to forbear all sin? How many rather to be *correctors* than practisers of religion. *Sprat's Sermons.*

With all his faults he sets up to be an universal reformer and *corrector* of abuses, and a remover of grievances. *Swift.*

2. He that revises any thing to free it from faults; as the *corrector* of the press, that amends the errours committed in printing.

I remember a person, who, by his style and literature, seems to have been the *corrector* of a hedge press in Little Britain, proceeding gradually to an author. *Swift.*

3. In medicine.

Such an ingredient in a composition, as guards against or abates the force of another; as the lixivial salts prevent the grievous vellications of resinous purges, by dividing their particles, and preventing their adhesion to the intestinal membranes, whereby they sometimes occasion intolerable gripings; and as spices and carminative seeds also assist in the easier operation of some cathartick, by dissipating collections of wind. In making a medicine, such a thing is called a *corrector* which destroys or diminishes a quality that it could not otherwise be dispensed with: thus turpentines are *correctors* of quicksilver, by destroying its fluxility, and making it capable of mixture; and thus rectified spirit of wine breaks off the points of some acids, so as to make them become safe and good remedies, which before were destructive. *Quincy.*

To CO'RRELATE. *v. n.* [from *con* and *relatus*, Latin.] To have a reciprocal relation, as father and son.

CO'RRELATE *n. s.* One that stands in the opposite relation.

It is one thing for a father to cease to be a father, by casting off his son; and another for him to cease to be so, by the death of his son: in this the relation is at an end, for want of a *correlate*. *South's Sermons.*

CORRE'LATIVE. *adj.* [*con* and *relativus*, Latin.] Having a reciprocal relation, so that the existence of one in a particular state depends upon the existence of another.

Father and son, husband and wife, and such other *correlative* terms, seem nearly to belong one to another. *South.*

Giving is a relative action, and so requires a *correlative* to answer it: giving, on one part, transfers no property, unless there be an accepting on the other. *South's Sermons.*

CORRE'LATIVENESS. *n. s.* [from *correlative.*] The state of being correlative.

CORRE'PTION. *n. s.* [*corripio correptum*, Latin.] Objurgation; chiding; reprehension; reproof.

If we must needs be talking of other people's faults, let it not be to defame, but to amend them, by converting our detraction and backbiting into admonition and fraternal *correption*. *Government of the Tongue, sect.* 6.

To CORRESPO'ND. *v. n.* [*con* and *respondeo*, Latin.]

1. To suit; to answer; to be proportionate; to be adequate to; to be adapted; to fit.

The days, if one be compared with another successively throughout the year, are found not to be equal, and will not justly *correspond* with any artificial or mechanical equal measures of time. *Holder on Time.*

Words being but empty sounds, any farther than they are signs of our ideas, we cannot but assent to them, as they *correspond* to those ideas we have, but no farther than that. *Locke.*

2. To keep up commerce with another by alternate letters.

CORRESPO'NDENCE. }
CORRESPO'NDENCY. } *n. s.* [from *correspond.*]

1. Relation; reciprocal adaptation of one thing to another.

Between the law of their heavenly operations, and the actions of men in this our state of mortality, such *correspondence* there is as maketh it expedient to know in some sort the one, for the others more perfect direction. *Hooker, b.* i.

Whatever we fancy, things keep their course; and their habitudes, *correspondencies*, and relations keep the same to one another. *Locke.*

2. Intercourse; reciprocal intelligence.

I had discovered those unlawful *correspondencies* they had used, and engagements they had made to embroil my kingdoms. *King Charles.*

Sure the villains hold a *correspondence*
With the enemy, and thus they would betray us. *Denham.*

It happens very oddly, that the pope and I should have the same thought much about the same time: my enemies will be apt to say, that we hold a *correspondence* together, and act by concert in this matter. *Addison's Guardian*, N°. 116.

3. Friendship; interchange of offices or civilities.

Let such military persons be assured, and well reputed of, rather than factious and popular; holding also good *correspondence* with the other great men in the state. *Bacon, Essay* 17.

CORRESPO'NDENT. *adj.* [from *correspond.*] Suitable; adapted; agreeable; answerable.

What good or evil is there under the sun, what action *correspondent* or repugnant unto the law which God hath imposed upon his creatures, but in or upon it God doth work, according to the law which himself hath eternally purposed to keep. *Hooker.*

And as five zones th' etherial regions bind,
Five *correspondent* are to earth assign'd. *Dryden's Ovid.*

CORRESPO'NDENT. *n. s.* One with whom intelligence or commerce is kept up by mutual messages or letters.

He was pleased to command me to send to him, and receive from him all his letters from and to all his *correspondents* at home and abroad. *Denham's Dedication.*

CORRESPO'NSIVE. *adj.* [from *correspond.*] Answerable; adapted to any thing.

Priam's six gates i' th' city, with massy staples,
And *corresponsive* and fulfilling bolts,
Sperre up the sons of Troy. *Shakesp. Troilus and Cressida.*

CO'RRIDOR. *n. s.* [French.]

1. [In fortification.] The covert way lying round the whole compass of the fortifications of a place.

2. [In architecture.] A gallery or long isle round about a building, leading to several chambers at a distance from each other. *Harris.*

There is something very noble in the amphitheatre, though the high wall and *corridors* that went round it are almost intirely ruined. *Addison on Italy.*

CORRI'GIBLE. *adj.* [from *corrigo*, Latin.]

1. That which may be altered or amended.

2. He who is a proper object of punishment; punishable.

He was taken up very short, and adjudged *corrigible* for such presumptuous language. *Howel's Vocal Forest.*

3. Corrective; having the power to correct.

Our bodies are our gardens, to the which our wills are gardeners; so that, if we will either have it steril with idleness, or manured with industry, the power and *corrigible* authority of this lies in our will. *Shakespeare's Othello.*

CORRI'VAL. *n. s.* [*con* and *rival.*] Rival; competitor.

They had governours commonly out of the two families of the Geraldines and Butlers, both adversaries and *corrivals* one against the other. *Spenser on Ireland.*

He that doth redeem her thence, might wear
Without *corrival* all her dignities. *Shakesp. Henry* IV. *p.* i.

CORRI'VALRY. *n. s.* [from *corrival.*] Competition; opposition

CORRO'BORANT. *adj.* [from *corroborate*] Having the power to give strength.

There be divers sorts of bracelets fit to comfort the spirits, and they be of three intentions, refrigerant, *corroborant*, and aperient. *Bacon's Natural History*, N°. 961.

To CORRO'BORATE. *v. a.* [*con* and *roboro*, Latin.]

1. To confirm; to establish.

Machiavel well noteth, though in an ill-favoured instance, there is no trusting to the force of nature, nor to the bravery of words, except it be *corroborate* by custom. *Bacon.*

2. To strengthen; to make strong.

To fortify imagination there be three ways; the authority whence the belief is derived, means to quicken and *corroborate* the imagination, and means to repeat it and refresh it. *Bacon.*

It was said that the prince himself had, by the sight of foreign courts, and observations on the different natures of people, and rules of government, much excited and awaked his spirits, and *corroborated* his judgment. *Wotton.*

As any limb well and duly exercised grows stronger, the nerves of the body are *corroborated* thereby. *Watts.*

CORROBORA'TION. *n. s.* [from *corroborate.*] The act of strengthening or confirming; confirmation by some additional security; addition of strength.

The lady herself procured a bull, for the better *corroboration* of the marriage. *Bacon's Henry* VII.

CORRO'BORATIVE. *adj.* [from *corroborate.*] Having the power of increasing strength.

In the cure of an ulcer, with a moist intemperies, as the heart is weakened by too much humidity, you are to mix *corroboratives* of an astringent faculty; and the ulcer also requireth to be dried. *Wiseman's Surgery.*

To CORRO'DE. *v. a.* [*corrodo*, Latin.] To eat away by degrees, as a menstruum; to prey upon; to consume; to wear away gradually.

Statesmen purge vice with vice, and may *corrode*
The bad with bad, a spider with a toad;
For so ill thralls not them, but they tame ill,
And make her do much good against her will. *Donne.*

We know that aqua-fortis *corroding* copper, which is it that gives the colour to verdigrease, is wont to reduce it to a green blue solution. *Boyle on Colours.*

The nature of mankind, left to itself, would soon have fallen into dissolution, without the incessant and *corroding* invasions of so long a time. *Hale's Origin of Mankind.*

Hannibal the Pyreneans past,
And steepy Alps, the mounds that nature cast,
And with *corroding* juices, as he went,
A passage through the living rock he rent. *Dryd. Juvenal.*

Fishes, which neither chew their meat nor grind it in their stomachs, do, by a dissolvent liquor there provided, *corrode* and reduce it into a chylus. *Ray on the Creation.*

The blood turning acrimonious, *corrodes* the vessels, producing almost all the diseases of the inflammatory kind. *Arbuth.*

Through the heart,
Should jealousy its venom once diffuse,
'Tis then delightful misery no more,
But agony unmixt, incessant gall,
Corroding every thought, and blasting all
Love's paradise. *Thomson's Spring, l.* 1075.

CORRO'DENT. *adj.* [from *corrode.*] Having the power of corroding or wasting any thing away.

CORRO'DIBLE. *adj.* [from *corrode*] Possible to be consumed or corroded.

Metals, although *corrodible* by waters, yet will not suffer a liquation from the powerfulest heat communicable unto that element. *Brown's Vulgar Errours, b.* ii. *c.* 1.

CO'RRODY. *n. s.* [from *corrodo*, Latin.] A defalcation from an allowance or salary for some other than the original purpose.

In those days even noble persons, and other meaner men, ordered *corrodies* and pensions to their chaplains and servants out of churches. *Ayliffe's Parergon.*

CORROSIBI'LITY. *n. s.* [from *corrosible.*] The quality of being corrosible; possibility to be consumed by a menstruum.

CORRO'SIBLE. *adj.* [from *corrode.*] Possible to be consumed by a menstruum.

CORRO'SIBLENESS. *n. s.* [from *corrosible.*] Susceptibility of corrosion. *Dict.*

CORRO'SION. *n. s.* [*corrodo*, Latin.] The power of eating or wearing away by degrees.

Corrosion is a particular species of dissolution of bodies, either by an acid, or a saline menstruum. It is almost wholly designed for the resolution of bodies most strongly compacted, as bones and metals; so that the menstruums here employed, have a considerable moment or force. These liquors, whether acid or urinous, are nothing but salts dissolved in a little phlegm; therefore these being solid, and consequently containing a considerable quantity of matter, do both attract one another more, and are also more attracted by the particles of the body to be dissolved; so when the more solid bodies are put into saline menstruums, the attraction is stronger than in other solutions; and the motion, which is always proportional to the attraction, is more violent: so that we may easily conceive, when the motion is in such a manner increased, it should drive the salts into the pores of the bodies, and open and loosen their cohesion, though ever so firm. *Quincy.*

If there be any medicine that purgeth, and hath neither of the first two manifest qualities, it is to be held suspected as a kind of poison; for that it worketh either by *corrosion*, or by a secret malignity and enmity to nature. *Bacon's Nat. History.*

That *corrosion* and dissolution of bodies, even the most solid and durable, which is vulgarly ascribed to the air, is caused merely by the action of water upon them; the air being so far from injuring and preying upon the bodies it environs, that it contributes to their security and preservation. *Woodw.*

CORROSIVE. *adj.* [from *corrodo*, Latin. It was anciently pronounced with the accent on the first syllable, now indifferently.]

1. Having the power of consuming or wearing away.

Gold, after it has been divided by *corrosive* liquors into invisible parts, yet may presently be precipitated, so as to appear again in its own form. *Grew's Cosmol. b.* i. *c.* 2. *s.* 12.

The sacred sons of vengeance, on whose course
Corrosive famine waits, and kills the year. *Thomson's Spring.*

2. Having the quality to fret or vex.

If the maintenance of ceremonies be a *corrosive* to such as oppugn them, undoubtedly to such as maintain them it can be no great pleasure, when they behold that which they reverence is oppugned. *Hooker, b.* iv. *sect.* 10.

CORROSIVE. *n. s.*

1. That which has the quality of wasting any thing away, as the flesh of an ulcer.

He meant his *corrosives* to apply,
And with strict diet tame his stubborn malady. *Fairy Queen.*

2. That which has the power of fretting, or of giving pain.

Such speeches savour not of God in him that useth them,

and

and unto virtuously disposed minds they are grievous *corrosives.* *Hooker, b.* v. *sect.* 33.

Away; though parting be a fretful *corrosive,*
It is applied to a deathful wound. *Shakesp. Henry* VI. *p.* i.

Care is no cure, but rather *corrosive,*
For things that are not to be remedied. *Shakesp. Henry* VI.

CORRO'SIVELY. *adv.* [from *corrosive.*]

1. Like a corrosive.

At first it tasted somewhat *corrosively.* *Boyle on Saltpetre.*

2. With the power of corrosion.

CORRO'SIVENESS. *n. s.* [from *corrosive.*] The quality of corroding or eating away; acrimony.

We do infuse, to what he meant for meat,
Corrosiveness, or intense cold or heat. *Donne.*

Saltpetre betrays upon the tongue no heat nor *corrosiveness* at all, but coldness, mixt with a somewhat languid relish retaining to bitterness. *Boyle.*

CO'RRUGANT. *adj.* [from *corrugate.*] Having the power of contracting into wrinkles.

To CO'RRUGATE. *v. a.* [*corrugo,* Latin.] To wrinkle or purse up; as the skin is drawn into wrinkles by cold, or any other cause. *Quincy.*

The cramp cometh of contraction of sinews: it cometh either by cold or dryness; for cold and dryness do both of them contract and *corrugate.* *Bacon's Natural History,* N°. 964.

CORRUGA'TION. *n. s.* [from *corrugate.*] Contraction into wrinkles.

The pain of the solid parts is the *corrugation* or violent agitation of fibres, when the spirits are irritated by sharp humours. *Floyer on the Humours.*

To CORRU'PT. *v. a.* [*corrumpo corruptus,* Latin.]

1. To turn from a sound to a putrescent state; to infect.

2. To deprave; to destroy integrity; to vitiate; to bribe.

I fear lest by any means, as the serpent beguiled Eve through his subtilty, so your minds should be *corrupted* from the simplicity that is in Christ. 2 *Cor* xi. 3.

Even what things they naturally know, in those very things, as hearts void of reason, they *corrupted* themselves. *Jude,* v. 10.

Evil communications *corrupt* good manners. 1 *Cor.* xv. 33.

All that have miscarried
By underhand, *corrupted,* foul injustice. *Shak. Richard* III.

I have heard it said, the fittest time to *corrupt* a man's wife, is when she's fallen out with her husband. *Shakesp. Coriolanus.*

But stay, I smell a man of middle earth;
With tryal fire touch me his finger-end;
If he be chaste, the flame will back descend,
And turn him to no pain; but if he start,
It is the flesh of a *corrupted* heart. *Shak. M. W. of Windsor.*

Language being the conduit whereby men convey their knowledge, he that makes an ill use of it, though he does not *corrupt* the fountains of knowledge, which are in things, yet he stops the pipes. *Locke.*

Hear the black trumpet through the world proclaim,
That not to be *corrupted* is the shame. *Pope.*

3. To spoil; to do mischief.

To CORRU'PT. *v. n.* To become putrid; to grow rotten; to putrefy.

The aptness or propension of air or water to *corrupt* or putrefy, no doubt, is to be found before it break forth into manifest effects of diseases, blasting, or the like. *Bacon.*

CORRU'PT. *adj.* [from *corrupt.*] Vitious; tainted with wickedness; without integrity.

Let no *corrupt* communication proceed out of your mouth, but that which is good to the use of edifying. *Eph.* iv. 29.

Corrupt, corrupt, and tainted in desire. *Sh. M. W. of Winds.*

These kind of knaves I know, which in this plainness
Harbour more craft, and more *corrupter* ends,
Than twenty silky ducking observants. *Shakes. King Lear.*

Some, who have been *corrupt* in their morals, have yet been infinitely solicitous to have their children piously brought up. *South's Sermons.*

CORRU'PTER. *n. s.* [from *corrupt.*] He that taints or vitiates; he that lessens purity or integrity.

What is here?
The scriptures of the loyal Leonatus,
All turn'd to heresy? Away, away,
Corrupters of my faith! *Shakespeare's Cymbeline.*

From the vanity of the Greeks, the *corrupters* of all truth, who, without all ground of certainty, vaunt their antiquity, came the errour first of all. *Raleigh's History of the World, b.* i.

Those great *corrupters* of Christianity, and indeed of natural religion, the Jesuits. *Addison's Freeholder,* N°. 6.

CORRUPTIBI'LITY. *n. s.* [from *corruptible.*] Possibility to be corrupted.

CORRU'PTIBLE. *adj.* [from *corrupt*]

1. Susceptible of destruction by natural decay, or without violence.

Our *corruptible* bodies could never live the life they shall live, were it not that they are joined with his body, which is incorruptible, and that his is in ours as a cause of immortality. *Hooker.*

It is a devouring corruption of the essential mixture, which consisting chiefly of an oily moisture, is *corruptible* through dissipation. *Harvey on Consumptions.*

The several parts of which the world consists, being in their nature *corruptible,* it is more than probable, that, in an infinite duration, this frame of things would long since have been dissolved. *Tillotson's Sermons.*

2. Susceptible of corruption; possible to be tainted or vitiated.

CORRU'PTIBLENESS. *n. s.* [from *corruptible.*] Susceptibility of corruption.

CORRU'PTIBLY. *adv.* [from *corruptible.*] In such a manner as to be corrupted, or vitiated.

It is too late; the life of all his blood
Is touch'd *corruptibly.* *Shakespeare's King Lear.*

CORRU'PTION. *n. s.* [*corruptio,* Lat.]

1. The principle by which bodies tend to the separation of their parts.

2. Wickedness; perversion of principles; loss of integrity.

Precepts of morality, besides the natural *corruption* of our tempers, which makes us averse to them, are so abstracted from ideas of sense, that they seldom get an opportunity for descriptions and images. *Addison's Essay on the Georgicks.*

Amidst *corruption,* luxury and rage,
Still leave some ancient virtue's to our age. *Pope.*

3. Putrescence.

The wise contriver, on his end intent,
Careful this fatal errour to prevent,
And keep the waters from *corruption* free,
Mix'd them with salt, and season'd all the sea. *Blackmore.*

4. Matter or *pus* in a sore.

5. The means by which any thing is vitiated; depravation.

After my death I wish no other herald,
No other speaker of my living actions,
To keep mine honour from *corruption,*
But such an honest chronicler as Griffith. *Shak. Hen.* VIII.

The region hath by conquest, and *corruption* of other languages, received new and differing names. *Raleigh's History.*

All those four kinds of *corruption* are very common in their language; for which reasons the Greek tongue is become much altered. *Brerewood on Languages.*

6. [In law.] An infection growing to a man attainted of felony or treason, and to his issue: for as he loseth all to the prince, or other lord of the fee, so his issue cannot be heir to him, or to any other ancestor, of whom they might have claimed by him; and if he were noble, or a gentleman, he and his children are made ignoble and ungentle, in respect of the father. *Cowel.*

CORRU'PTIVE. *adj.* [from *corrupt.*] Having the quality of tainting or vitiating.

Not resembling themselves according to seminal condition, yet carrying a settled habitude unto the *corruptive* originals. *Brown's Vulgar Errours, b.* ii. *c.* 6.

It should be endued with an acid ferment, or some *corruptive* quality, for so speedy a dissolution of the meat and preparation of the chyle. *Ray on the Creation.*

CORRU'PTLESS. *adj.* [from *corrupt.*] Insusceptible of corruption; undecaying.

All around
The borders, with *corruptless* myrrh are crown'd. *Dryden.*

CORRU'PTLY. *adv.* [from *corrupt.*]

1. With corruption; with taint; with vice; without integrity.

O, that estates, degrees, and offices,
Were not deriv'd *corruptly,* that clear honour
Were purchas'd by the merit of the wearer. *Shakespeare.*

We have dealt very *corruptly* against thee, and have not kept the commandments. *Neh.* i. 7.

2. Vitiously; improperly; contrary to purity.

We have *corruptly* contracted most names, both of men and places. *Camden's Remains.*

CORRU'PTNESS. *n. s.* [from *corrupt.*] The quality of corruption; putrescence; vice.

CO'RSAIR. *n. s.* [French.] A pirate; one who professes to seize merchants.

CORSE. *n. s.* [*corps,* French]

1. A body.

For he was strong, and of so mighty *corse,*
As ever wielded spear in warlike hand *Spenser, can.* iii.

2. A dead body; a carcase: a poetical word.

That from her body, full of filthy sin,
He reft her hateful head, without remorse;
A stream of coal-black blood forth gushed from her *corse.* *Fairy Queen, b.* i. *cant.* 1. *stan.* 24.

Set down the *corse*; or, by saint Paul,
I'll make a *corse* of him that disobeys. *Shakesp. Richard* III.

What may this mean?
That thou, dead *corse,* again, in complete steel,
Revisit'st thus the glimpses of the moon,
Making night hideous? *Shakespeare's Hamlet.*

Here lay him down, my friends,
Full in my sight, that I may view at leisure
The bloody *corse,* and count those glorious wounds. *Addison.*

You heard the groans,
Heard nightly plung'd, amid' the sullen waves,
The frequent *corse.* *Thomson's Summer, l.* 1035.

Co'RSELET. *n. s.* [*corselet*, French.] A light armour for the forepart of the body.

Some shirts of maile, some coats of plate put on,
Some don'd a cuirace, some a *corslet* bright. *Fairfax, b.* i.

They lash, they foin, they pass, they strive to bore
Their *corslets*, and their thinnest parts explore. *Dryd. Fab.*

But heroes, who o'ercome or die,
Have their hearts hung extremely high;
The strings of which, in battle's heat,
Against their very *cors'lets* beat. *Prior.*

CO'RTICAL. *adj.* [*cortex*, bark, Lat.] Barky; belonging to the outer part; belonging to the rind; outward.

Their last extremities form a little gland, (all these little glands together make the *cortical* part of the brain) terminating in two little vessels. *Cheyne's Phil. Prin.*

Co'RTICATED. *adj.* [from *corticatus*, Lat.] Resembling the bark of a tree.

This animal is a kind of lizard, a quadruped *corticated* and depilous; that is, without wool, fur, or hair. *Brown.*

Co'RTICOSE. *adj.* [from *corticosus*, Lat.] Full of bark. *Dict.*

CORVE'TTO. *n. s.* The curvet. See CURVET.

You must draw the horse in his career with his manage, and turn, doing the *corvetto* and leaping. *Peacham on Drawing.*

CORU'SCANT. *adj.* [*corusco*, Latin.] Glittering by flashes; flashing.

CORUSCA'TION. *n. s.* [*coruscatio*, Latin.] Flash; quick vibration of light.

We see that lightnings and *coruscations*, which are near at hand, yield no sound. *Bacon's Natural History*, Nº. 114.

We may learn that sulphureous steams abound in the bowels of the earth, and ferment with minerals, and sometimes take fire with a sudden *coruscation* and explosion. *Newton's Opt.*

How heat and moisture mingle in a mass,
Or belch in thunder, or in lightning blaze;
Why nimble *coruscations* strike the eye,
And bold tornado's bluster in the sky. *Garth's Dispensatory.*

CORY'MBIATED. *adj.* [*corymbus*, Latin.] Garnished with branches of berries. *Dict.*

CORYMBI'FEROUS. *adv.* [from *corymbus* and *fero*, Lat.] Bearing fruit or berries in bunches.

Corymbiferous plants are distinguished into such as have a radiate flower, as the sun-flower; and such as have a naked flower, as the hemp-agrimony, and mugwort: to which are added those a-kin hereunto, such as scabious, teasel, thistle, and the like. *Quincy.*

CORY'MBUS. *n. s.* [Latin.]

It in general signifies the top of any thing; but amongst the ancient botanists it was used to express the bunches or clusters of berries of ivy, or the like: amongst modern botanists it is used for a compounded discous flower, whose seeds are not pappous, or do not fly away in down; such are the flowers of daisies, and common marygold; and therefore Mr. *Ray* makes one genus of plants to be such as have a compound discous flower, without any downy wings to carry off their seeds. *Quincy.*

COSCI'NOMANCY. *n. s.* [from κόσκινον, a sieve, and μαντεία, divination.] The art of divination by means of a sieve. A very ancient practice mentioned by Theocritus, and still used in some parts of England, to find out persons unknown. *Chambers.*

COSE'CANT. *n. s.* [In geometry.] The secant of an arch, which is the complement of another to ninety degrees. *Harris.*

Co'SHERING. *n. s.* [Irish.]

Cosherings were visitations and progresses made by the lord and his followers among his tenants; wherein he did eat them (as the English proverb is) out of house and home. *Davies.*

Co'SIER. *n. s.* [from *couser*, old Fr. to sew.] A botcher. *Hanmer.*

Do you make an alehouse of my lady's house, that ye squeak out your *cosier* catches, without any mitigation or remorse of voice? *Shakespeare's Twelfth Night.*

Co'SINE. *n. s.* [In geometry.] The right sine of an arch, which is the complement of another to ninety degrees. *Harris.*

COSME'TICK. *adj.* [κοσμητικὸς.] Having the power of improving beauty; beautifying.

No better *cosmeticks* than a severe temperance and purity, modesty and humility, a gracious temper and calmness of spirit; no true beauty without the signatures of these graces in the very countenance. *Ray on the Creation.*

First, rob'd in white, the nymph intent adores,
With head uncover'd, the *cosmetick* pow'rs. *Pope.*

CO'SMICAL. *adj.* [κόσμος.]

1. Relating to the world.

2. Rising or setting with the sun; not acronychal.

The *cosmical* ascension of a star we term that, when it ariseth together with the sun, or in the same degree of the ecliptick wherein the sun abideth. *Brown's Vulgar Errours, b.* iv. *c.* 13.

Co'SMICALLY. *adv.* [from *cosmical.*] With the sun; not acronychally.

From the rising of this star, not *cosmically*, that is, with the sun, but heliacally, that is, its emersion from the rays of the sun, the ancients computed their canicular days. *Brown.*

Co'SMOGONY. *n. s.* [κόσμ☉, and γόνη.] The rise or birth of the world; the creation.

COSMO'GRAPHER. *n. s.* [κόσμ☉ and γράφω.] One who writes a description of the world; distinct from geographer, who describes the situation of particular countries.

Thus the antient *cosmographers* do place the division of the East and Western hemisphere; that is, the first term of longitude in the Canary or Fortunate Islands, conceiving these parts the extremest habitations westward. *Brown's Vulgar Errours.*

COSMOGRA'PHICAL. *adj.* [from *cosmography.*] Relating to the general description of the world.

COSMOGRA'PHICALLY. *adv.* [from *cosmographical.*] In a manner relating to the science by which the structure of the world is discovered and described.

This it doth more plainly upon the terrella, or spherical magnet, *cosmographically* set out with circles of the globe. *Brown's Vulgar Errours, b.* ii. *c.* 2.

COSMO'GRAPHY. *n. s.* [κόσμ☉ and γράφω.] The science of the general system or affections of the world, distinct from geography, which delivers the situation and boundaries of particular countries.

Here it might see the world without travel; it being a lesser scheme of the creation, nature contracted, a little *cosmography*, or map of the universe. *South's Sermons.*

COSMOPO'LITAN. } *n. s.* [κόσμ☉ and πολίτης.] A citizen of the
COSMOPO'LITE. } world; one who is at home in every place.

Co'SSET. *n. s.* A lamb brought up without the dam.

If thou wilt bewail my woful teen,
I shall thee give yond' *cosset* for thy pain. *Spenser's Past.*

COST. *n. s.* [*kost*, Dutch. As this word is found in the remotest Teutonick dialects, even in the islandick, it is not probably derived to us from the Latin *consto*; though it is not unlikely that the French *couster* comes from the Latin.]

1. The price of any thing.

2. Sumptuousness; luxury.

The city woman bears
The *cost* of princes on unworthy shoulders. *Shakespeare.*

Let foreign princes vainly boast
The rude effects of pride and *cost*
Of vaster fabricks, to which they
Contribute nothing but the pay. *Waller.*

3. Charge; expence.

While he found his daughter maintained without his *cost*, he was content to be deaf to any noise of infamy. *Sidney, b.* ii.

I shall never hold that man my friend,
Whose tongue shall ask me for one penny *cost*,
To ransom home revolted Mortimer. *Shakesp. Henry* IV.

Have we eaten at all of the king's *cost*? or hath he given us any gift? 2 *Sa.* xix. 42.

And wilt thou, O cruel boast!
Put poor nature to such *cost*?
O! 'twill undo our common mother,
To be at charge of such another. *Crashaw.*

It is strange to see any ecclesiastical pile, not by ecclesiastical *cost* and influence, rising above ground; especially in an age in which men's mouths are open against the church, but their hands shut towards it. *South's Sermons.*

He whose tale is best, and pleases most,
Should win his supper at our common *cost*. *Dryden's Fables.*

Fourteen thousand pounds are paid by Wood for the purchase of his patent: what were his other visible *costs* I know not; what his latent, is variously conjectured. *Swift.*

4. Loss; fine; detriment.

What they had fondly wished, proved afterwards to their *costs* over true. *Knolles's History of the Turks.*

To COST. *v. n. pret. cost*; *particip. cost.* [*couster*, French.] To be bought for; to be had at a price.

The dagger and poison are always in readiness; but to bring the action to extremity, and then recover all, will require the art of a writer, and *cost* him many a pang. *Dryden.*

Co'STAL. *adj.* [*costa*, Lat. a rib.] Belonging to the ribs.

Hereby are excluded all cetaceous and cartilaginous fishes, many pectinal, whose ribs are rectilineal; and many *costal*, which have their ribs embowed. *Brown's Vulgar Err.*

Co'STARD. *n. s.* [from *coster*, a head.]

1. A head.

Take him over the *costard* with the belt of thy sword.
Shakespeare's Richard III.

2. An apple round and bulky like the head.

Many country vicars are driven to shifts; and, if our greedy patrons hold us to such conditions, they will make us turn *costard* mongers, grasiers, or sell ale. *Burton on Melancholy.*

CO'STIVE. *adj.* [*constipatus*, Lat. *constipé*, French.]

1. Bound in the body; having the excretions obstructed.

When the passage of the gall becomes obstructed, the body grows *costive*, and the excrements of the belly white. *Brown.*

While faster than his *costive* brains indites,
Philo's quick hand in flowing letters writes;
His case appears to me like honest Teague's,
When he was run away with by his legs. *Prior.*

2. Close; unpermeable.

Clay in dry seasons is *costive*, hardening with the sun and wind, 'till unlocked by industry, so as to admit of the air and heavenly influences. *Mortimer's Husbandry.*

Co'stiveness. *n. s.* [from *costive.*] The state of the body in which excretion is obstructed.

Costiveness disperses malign putrid fumes out of the guts and mesentery into all parts of the body, occasioning head-aches, fevers, loss of appetite, and disturbance of concoction. *Harvey.*

Costiveness has ill effects, and is hard to be dealt with by physick; purging medicines rather increasing than removing the evil. *Locke on Education, sect.* 23.

Co'stliness. *n. s.* [from *costly.*] Sumptuousness; expensiveness.

Though not with curious *costliness*, yet with cleanly sufficiency it entertained me. *Sidney, b.* i.

Nor have the frugaller sons of fortune any reason to object the *costliness*; since they frequently pay dearer for less advantageous pleasures. *Glanville's Sceps. Preface.*

Co'stly. *adj.* [from *cost.*] Sumptuous; expensive; of a high price.

Costly thy habit as thy purse can buy,
But not exprest in fancy; rich, not gaudy;
For the apparel oft proclaims the man. *Shakesp. Hamlet.*

Leave for a while thy *costly* country-seat;
And to be great indeed, forget
The nauseous pleasures of the great. *Dryden.*

The chapel of St. Laurence will be perhaps the most *costly* piece of work on the face of the earth, when completed. *Addison's Remarks on Italy.*

He is here speaking of Paradise, which he represents as a most charming and delightful place; abounding with things not only useful and convenient, but even the most rare and valuable, the most *costly* and desireable. *Woodw. Nat. History.*

Co'stmary. *n. s.* [*costus*, Latin.] An herb whose flowers are naked, and of a yellow colour, growing in umbels on the top of the stalks: the leaves are intire, and crenated about the edges. *Miller.*

Co'strel. *n. s.* [supposed to be derived from *coster.*] A bottle. *Skinner.*

Cot.
Cote. } At the end of the names of places, come generally from the Saxon cot, a cottage.
Coat. *Gibson's Camden.*

COT. *n. s.* [cot, Sax. *cwt*, Welsh.] A small house; a cottage; a hut; a mean habitation.

What that usage meant,
Which in her *cot* she daily practised. *Fairy Queen, b.* ii. *c.* 6.

Besides his *cot*, his flocks, and bounds of feed,
Are now on sale; and at our sheep *cot* now,
By reason of his absence, there is nothing
That you will feed on. *Shakespeare's As you like it.*

Hezekiah made himself stalls for all manner of beasts, and *cots* for flocks. 2 *Chron.* xxxii. 28.

My feeble goats,
With pains I drive from their forsaken *cotes. Dryden's Virgil.*

A stately temple shoots within the skies:
The crotchets of their *cot* in columns rise;
The pavement, polish'd marble they behold;
The gates with sculpture grac'd, the spires and tiles of gold. *Dryden's Baucis and Philemon.*

As Jove vouchsaf'd on Ida's top, 'tis said,
At poor Philemon's *cot* to take a bed. *Fenton.*

Cot. *n. s.* An abridgment of *cotquean.*

Cota'ngent. *n. s.* [In geometry.] The tangent of an arch which is the complement of another to ninety degrees. *Harris.*

To Cote. *v. a.* This word, which I have found only in Chapman, seems to signify the same as *To leave behind, To over pass.*

Words her worth had prov'd with deeds,
Had more ground been allow'd the race, and *coted* far his steeds. *Chapman's Iliads.*

Cote'mporary. *adj.* [*con* and *tempus*, Latin.] Living at the same time; coetaneous; contemporary.

What would not, to a rational man, *cotemporary* with the first voucher, have appeared probable, is now used as certain, because several have since, from him, said it one after another. *Locke.*

Co'tland. *n. s.* [*cot* and *land.*] Land appendant to a cottage.

Co'tquean. *n. s.* [probably from *coquin*, French.] A man who busies himself with women's affairs.

Look to the bak'd meats, good Angelica;
Spare not for cost.——
——Go, go, you *cotquean*, go;
Get you to bed. *Shakespeare's Romeo and Juliet.*

A stateswoman is as ridiculous a creature as a *cotquean*: each of the sexes should keep within its particular bounds. *Addison's Freeholder*, N°. 38.

You have given us a lively picture of husbands hen-peck'd; but you have never touched upon one of the quite different character, and who goes by the name of *cotquean. Add. Spect.*

Co'ttage. *n. s.* [from *cot.*] A hut; a mean habitation; a cot; a little house.

The sea-coast shall be dwellings and *cottages* for shepherds, and folds for flocks. *Zeph.* ii. 6.

They were right glad to take some corner of a poor *cottage*, and there to serve God upon their knees. *Hooker, b.* iv. *s.* 2.

The self-same sun that shines upon his court,
Hides not his visage from our *cottage*, but
Looks on both alike. *Shakespeare's Winter's Tale.*

Let the women of noble birth and great fortunes nurse their children, look to the affairs of the house, visit poor *cottages*, and relieve their necessities. *Taylor's Holy Living.*

It is difficult for a peasant, bred up in the obscurities of a *cottage*, to fancy in his mind the unseen splendors of a court. *South's Sermons.*

Beneath our humble *cottage* let us haste,
And here, unenvied, rural dainties taste. *Pope's Odyssey.*

Co'ttager. *n. s.* [from *cottage.*]

1. One who lives in a hut or cottage.

Let us from our farms,
Call forth our *cottagers* to arms. *Swift.*

The most ignorant Irish *cottager* will not sell his cow for a groat. *Swift's Address to Parliament.*

2. A cottager, in law, is one that lives on the common, without paying rent, and without any land of his own.

The husbandmen and plowmen be but as their work-folks and labourers, or else mere *cottagers*, which are but housed beggars. *Bacon's Henry* VII.

The yeomenry, or middle people, of a condition between gentlemen and *cottagers*. *Bacon's Henry* VII.

Co'ttier. *n. s.* [from *cot.*] One who inhabits a cot. *Dict.*

CO'TTON. *n. s.* [named, according to *Skinner*, from the down that adheres to the *mala cotonea*, or *quince*, called by the Italians *cotogni*; whence *cottone*, Ital. *cotton*, French.] The down of the cotton-tree.

The pin ought to be as thick as a rowling-pin, and covered with *cotton*, that its hardness may not be offensive. *Wiseman.*

Co'tton. *n. s.* A plant.

The flower consists of one leaf, cut into several segments almost to the bottom, and is of the expanded bell shape: from the center rises a pyramidal hollow tube, adorned and loaded with chives: from the empalement shoots up the pointal, fixed like a nail in the bottom of the flower and of the tube, which is changed into a roundish fruit, divided into four or more seminal cells, gaping at the top, and inclosing seeds, covered over and wrapped within that soft ductile wool, commonly known by the name of cotton. The species are, 1. Hot or shrubby *cotton.* 2. The most excellent American *cotton*, with a greenish seed. 3. Annual shrubby *cotton*, of the island of Providence, with a large quinquefid vine-leaf. 4. The tree *cotton.* 5. Tree *cotton* with a yellow flower. The first sort is cultivated plentifully in Candia, Lemnos, Cyprus, Malta, Sicily, and at Naples; as also between Jerusalem and Damascus, from whence the cotton is brought annually into these northern parts of Europe. It is sown upon tilled grounds in the spring of the year, and cut down and reaped in harvest, as corn with us. This *cotton* is the wool which incloses or wraps up the seeds, and is contained in a kind of brown husk or seed-vessel growing upon this shrub. It is from this sort that the vast quantities of *cotton* are taken, which furnish our parts of the world. It is brought from the islands, where the natives take great care of its culture. There are several sorts of *cotton* sold, which differ according to the countries from whence they come, and the various preparations made of them. The first is the *cotton* in the wool; that is, that which comes from the shell, from which only we take the seed: those come from Cyprus, Smyrna, &c. The second is the *cotton* in the yarn: the second and third sorts are also annual: these are cultivated in the West Indies in great plenty. But the fourth and fifth sorts grow in Egypt: these abide many years, and often arrive to be trees of great magnitude, from which the inhabitants are annually furnished with great quantities of *cotton.* One of these trees has a purplish and the other a yellow flower, which is the only difference between them. *Miller.*

Co'tton. *n. s.* Cloath or stuff made of cotton.

To Co'tton. *v. n.*

1. To rise with a nap.

2. To cement; to unite with: a cant word.

A quarrel between you will end in one of you being turned off, in which case it will not be easy to *cotton* with another. *Swift's Directions to the Cook.*

To COUCH. *v. n.* [*coucher*, French.]

1. To lie down on a place of repose.

If I court more women, you'll *couch* with more men. *Shak.*

Doth not the gentleman
Deserve as full, as fortunate a bed,
As ever Beatrice shall *couch* upon. *Shakespeare.*

When love's fair goddess
Couch'd with her husband in his golden bed. *Dryden's Æn.*

2. To lie down on the knees, as a beast to rest.

Trees bent their heads to hear him sing his wrongs,
Fierce tygers *couch'd* around, and loll'd their fawning tongues. *Dryden's Virg. Geor. b.* iv. *l.* 41.

These when death

Comes like a rushing lion, *couch* like spaniels,
With lolling tongues, and tremble at the paw. *Dryden.*

3. To lye down in secret, or in ambush.

We'll *couch* i' th' castle-ditch, 'till we see the light of our fairies. *Shakespeare's Merry Wives of Windsor.*

The earl of Angus *couched* in a furrow, and was passed over for dead, until a horse was brought for his escape. *Hayward.*

4. To lye in a bed, or stratum.

Blessed of the Lord be his land for the dew, and for the deep that *coucheth* beneath. *Deutr.* xxxiii. 13.

5. To stoop; or bend down; to lower in fear, in pain, in respect.

To *couch* down between Issachar, is a strong ass *couching* down between two burdens. *Gen.* xlix. 14.

These *couchings*, and these lowly curtesies,
Might stir the blood of ordinary men. *Shakesp. Jul. Cæsar.*

To Couch. *v. a.*

1. To repose; to lay on a place of repose.

Where unbruised youth, with unstuff'd brain,
Doth *couch* his limbs, there golden sleep doth reign. *Shakesp.*

2. To lay down any thing in a bed, or stratum.

If the weather be warm, we immediately *couch* malt about a foot thick; but if a hotter season require it, we spread it on the floor much thinner. *Mortimer's Husbandry.*

The sea and the land make one globe; and the waters *couch* themselves, as close as may be, to the centre of this globe, in a spherical convexity. *Burnet's Theory of the Earth.*

3. To bed; to hide in another body.

It is at this day in use at Gaza, to *couch* potsherds, or vessels of earth, in their walls, to gather the wind from the top, and to pass it down in spouts into rooms. *Bacon's Nat. History.*

4. To involve; to include; to comprise.

But who will call those noble who deface,
By meaner acts, the glories of their race;
Whose only title to our father's fame,
Is *couch'd* in the dead letters of their name? *Dryden's Juv.*

That great argument for a future state, which St. Paul hath *couched* in the words I have read to you. *Atterbury's Sermons.*

5. To include secretly; to hide: with *under*.

The foundation of all parables is some analogy or similitude between the topical or allusive part of the parable and the thing *couched under* it, and intended by it. *South's Sermons.*

There is all this, and more, that lies naturally *couched under* this allegory. *L'Estrange, Fable* 3.

The true notion of the institution being lost, the tradition of the deluge, which was *couched under* it, was thereupon at length suspended and lost. *Woodward's Natural History.*

6. To lay close to another.

And over all, with brazen scales was arm'd,
Like plated coat of steel, so *couched* near,
That nought might pierce. *Fairy Queen, b.* i. *cant.* 11.

7. To fix the spear in the rest; in the posture of attack.

The knight 'gan fairly *couch* his steady spear,
And fiercely ran at him with rigorous might. *Fairy Queen.*

Before each van
Prick forth the aery knights, and *couch* their spears,
'Till thickest legions close. *Milton's Paradise Lost, b.* ii.

The former wav'd in air
His flaming sword, Æneas *couch'd* his spear. *Dryden's Æn.*

8. To depress the film that overspreads the pupil of the eye. This is improperly called *couching the eye*, for *couching the cataract*: with equal impropriety they sometimes speak of *couching the patient*.

Some artist, whose nice hand
Couches the cataracts, and clears his eyes,
And all at once a flood of glorious light
Comes rushing on his eyes. *Dennis.*

Whether the cataract be wasted by being separated from its vessels, I have never known positively, by dissecting one that had been *couched*. *Sharp.*

Couch. *n. s.* [from the verb.]

1. A seat of repose, on which it is common to lye down dressed.

So Satan fell; and straight a firy globe
Of angels on full sail of wing flew nigh,
Who on their plumy vans receiv'd him soft,
From his uneasy station, and upbore
As on a floating *couch* through the blithe air. *Milt. Par. Reg.*

To loll on *couches*, rich with citron steds,
And lay their guilty limbs in Tyrian beds. *Dryd. Virg. Geo.*

2. A bed; a place of repose.

Let not the royal bed of Denmark be
A *couch* for luxury and damned incest. *Shakesp. Hamlet.*

Dire was the tossing! deep the groans! despair
Tended the sick, busiest from *couch* to *couch*. *Milt. Pa. Lost.*

This gentle knight, inspir'd by jolly May,
Forsook his early *couch* at early day. *Dryden's Fables.*

O, ye immortal pow'rs that guard the just,
Watch round his *couch*, and soften his repose. *Addis. Cato.*

3. A layer, or stratum.

This heap is called by maltsters a *couch*, or bed of raw malt. *Mortimer's Husbandry.*

Co'uchant. *adj.* [*couchant*, Fr.] Lying down; squatting.

If a lion were the proper coat of Judah, yet were it not probably a lion rampant, but rather *couchant* or dormant. *Brown's Vulgar Errours, b.* v. *c.* 10.

As a tiger, who by chance hath spy'd,
In some purlieu, two gentle fawns at play,
Strait couches close; then rising, changes oft
His *couchant* watch. *Milton's Paradise Lost, b.* iv. *l.* 403.

COUCHEE. *n. s.* [French.] Bedtime; the time of visiting late at night.

None of her sylvan subjects made their court;
Levees and *couchees* pass'd without resort. *Dryden.*

Co'ucher. *n. s.* [from *couch.*] He that couches or depresses cataracts.

Co'uchfellow. *n. s.* [*couch* and *fellow.*] Bedfellow; companion.

I have grated upon my good friends for three reprieves for you, and your *couchfellow*, Nim; or else you had looked through the grate like a geminy of baboons. *Shakespeare.*

Co'uchgrass. *n. s.* A weed.

The *couchgrass*, for the first year, insensibly robs most plants in sandy grounds apt to graze. *Mortimer's Husbandry.*

COVE. *n. s.*

1. A small creek or bay.
2. A shelter; a cover.

CO'VENANT. *n. s.* [*convenant*, Fr. *conventum*, Latin.]

1. A contract; a stipulation.

He makes a *covenant* never to destroy
The earth again by flood; nor let the sea
Surpass his bounds. *Milton's Paradise Lost, b.* xi. *l.* 892.

The English make the ocean their abode,
Whose ready sails with ev'ry wind can fly,
And make a *cov'nant* with th' unconstant sky. *Waller.*

2. An agreement on certain terms; a compact.

A *covenant* is a mutual compact, as we now consider it, betwixt God and man; consisting of mercies on God's part, made over to man, and of conditions on man's part, required by God. *Hammond's Pract. Catech.*

Some men live as if they had made a *covenant* with hell: let divines, fathers, friends say what they will, they stop their ears against them. *L'Estrange.*

3. A writing containing the terms of agreement.

I shall but lend my diamond 'till your return; let there be *covenants* drawn between us. *Shakespeare's Cymbeline.*

To Co'venant. *v. n.* [from the noun.]

1. To bargain; to stipulate.

His lord used commonly so to *covenant* with him, which if at any time the tenant disliked, he might freely depart at his pleasure. *Spenser's State of Ireland.*

It had been *covenanted* between him and the king of England, that neither of them should treat of peace or truce with the French king. *Hayward on Edward* VI.

By words men come to know one another's minds; by these they *covenant* and confederate. *South's Sermons.*

Jupiter *covenanted* with him, that it should be hot or cold, wet or dry, calm or windy, as the tenant should direct. *L'Est.*

2. To agree with another on certain terms: with *for*.

They *covenanted* with him *for* thirty pieces of silver. *Mat.*

Pointing to a heap of sand,
For ev'ry grain to live a year demand;
But, ah! unmindful of th' effect of time,
Forgot to *covenant* for youth and prime. *Garth's Ovid.*

Covenante'e. *n. s.* [from *covenant.*] A party to a covenant; a stipulator; a bargainer.

Both of them were respective rites of their admission into the several covenants, and the *covenantees* become thereby entitled to the respective privileges. *Ayliffe's Parergon.*

Covena'nter. *n. s.* [from *covenant.*] One who takes a covenant. A word introduced in the civil wars.

The *covenanters* shall have no more assurance of mutual assistance each from other, after the taking of the covenant, than they had before. *Oxford Reasons against the Covenant.*

Co'venous. *adj.* [from *covin.*] Fraudulent; collusive; trickish.

I wish some means devised for the restraint of these inordinate and *covenous* leases of lands, holden in chief, for hundreds or thousands of years. *Bacon's Off. of Alienation.*

To CO'VER. *v. a.* [*couvrir*, French.]

1. To overspread any thing with something else.

The pastures are cloathed with flocks, the valleys also are *covered* over with corn. *Ps.* lxv. 13.

A man ought not to *cover* his head. 1 *Cor.* xi. 7.

Go to thy fellows, bid them *cover* the table, serve in the meat, and we will come in to dinner. *Shak. Merch. of Venice.*

2. To conceal under something laid over.

Or lead me to some solitary place,
And *cover* my retreat from human race. *Dryd. Virg. Geor.*

3. To hide by superficial appearances.

4. To overwhelm; to bury.

Raillery and wit serve only to *cover* nonsense with shame, when reason has first proved it to be mere nonsense. *Watts.*

5. To shelter; to conceal from harm.

Charity ſhall *cover* the multitude of ſins. *1 Pet.* iv. 8.

6. To incubate; to brood on.

Natural hiſtorians obſerve, that only the male birds have voices; that their ſongs begin a little before breeding-time, and end a little after; that whilſt the hen is *covering* her eggs, the male generally takes his ſtand upon a neighbouring bough within her hearing, and by that means amuſes and diverts her with his ſongs during the whole time of her ſitting. *Add. Spect.*

7. To copulate with a female.

8. To wear the hat, or garment of the head, as a mark of ſuperiority.

That king had conferred the honour of grandee upon him, which was of no other advantage or ſignification to him, than to be *covered* in the preſence of that king. *Dryd. Dedicat. Æn.*

Co'ver. *n. ſ.* [from the verb.]

1. Any thing that is laid over another.

The ſecundine is but a general *cover*, not ſhaped according to the parts, but the ſkin is ſhaped according to the parts. *Bacon's Natural Hiſtory*, N°. 732.

The fountains could be ſtrengthened no other way than by making a ſtrong *cover* or arch over them. *Burnet's Theory.*

Oreſtes' bulky rage,
Unſatisfy'd with margins cloſely writ,
Foams o'er the *covers*, and not finiſh'd yet. *Dryd. Juv. Sat.*

With your hand, or any other *cover*, you ſtop the veſſel, ſo as wholly to exclude the air. *Ray on the Creation.*

2. A concealment; a ſcreen; a veil; a ſuperficial appearance, under which ſomething is hidden.

The truth and reaſon of things may be artificially and effectually inſinuated, under the *cover* either of a real fact, or of a ſuppoſed one. *L'Eſtrange.*

As the ſpleen has great inconveniences, ſo the pretence of it is a handſome *cover* for imperfections. *Collier on the Spleen.*

3. Shelter; defence.

In the mean time, by being compelled to lodge in the field, which grew now to be very cold, whilſt his army was under *cover*, they might be forced to retire. *Clarendon, b.* viii.

Cover-shame. *n. ſ.* [*cover* and *ſhame.*] Some appearance uſed to conceal infamy.

Does he put on holy garments for a *cover-ſhame* of lewdneſs? *Dryden's Spaniſh Fryar.*

Co'vering. *n. ſ.* [from *cover.*] Dreſs; veſture; any thing ſpread over another.

The women took and ſpread a *covering over* the well's mouth. *2 Sam.* xvii. 19.

Bring ſome *covering* for this naked ſoul,
Whom I'll intreat to lead me. *Shakeſpeare's King Lear.*

Sometimes providence caſts things ſo, that truth and intereſt lie the ſame way; and when it is wrapt up in this *covering*, men can be content to follow it. *South.*

Then from the floor he rais'd a royal bed,
With *cov'rings* of Sidonian purple ſpread. *Dryden's Fables.*

Co'verlet. *n. ſ.* [*couvrelict*, French.] The outermoſt of the bedcloaths; that under which all the reſt are concealed.

Lay her in lillies and in violets,
And ſilken curtains over her diſplay,
And odour'd ſheets, and arras *coverlets. Spenſer's Epithal.*

With ſilken curtains and gold *coverlets*,
Therein to ſhrowd her ſumptuous Bellamoure. *Fairy Queen.*

This done, the hoſt produc'd the genial bed,
Which with no coſtly *coverlet* they ſpread. *Dryden's Fables.*

The difficulties I was in, for want of a houſe and bed, being forced to lie on the ground, wrapt up in my *coverlet*. *Gulliver's Travels.*

Co'vert. *n. ſ.* [from *cover, couvert*, French.]

1. A ſhelter; a defence.

Let mine outcaſts dwell with thee, Moab; be thou a *covert* to them from the face of the ſpoiler. *Iſaiah*, xvi. 4.

There ſhall be a tabernacle for a ſhadow in the day-time from the heat, and for a place of refuge, and for a *covert* from ſtorm and rain. *Iſ.* iv. 6.

They are by ſudden alarm, or watch-word, to be called out to their military motions, under ſky or *covert*, according to the ſeaſon, as was the Roman wont. *Milton on Education.*

It was the hour of night, when thus the Son
Commun'd in ſilent walk, then laid him down
Under the hoſpitable *covert* nigh
Of trees thick interwoven. *Milton's Paradiſe Loſt, b.* ii.

Now have a care your carnations catch not too much wet, therefore retire them to *covert*. *Evelyn's Kalendar.*

2. A thicket, or hiding place.

Tow'rds him I made; but he was 'ware of me,
And ſtole into the *covert* of the wood. *Shakeſ. Rom. and Jul.*

I ſhall be your faithful guide,
Through this gloomy *covert* wide. *Milton.*

Thence to the *coverts*, and the conſcious groves,
The ſcenes of his paſt triumphs and his loves. *Denham.*

Deep into ſome thick *covert* would I run,
Impenetrable to the ſtars or ſun. *Dryden's State of Innocence.*

The deer is lodg'd; I've track'd her to her *covert*:
Be ſure ye mind the word; and when I give it,
Ruſh in at once, and ſeize upon your prey. *Addiſ. Cato.*

Co'vert. *adj.* [*couvert*, French.]

1. Sheltered; not open; not expoſed.

You are, of either ſide the green, to plant a *covert* alley, upon carpenter's work, about twelve foot in height, by which you may go in ſhade into the garden. *Bacon, Eſſay* 47.

The fox is a beaſt alſo very prejudicial to the huſbandman, eſpecially in places that are near foreſt-woods and *covert* places. *Mortimer's Huſbandry.*

Together let us beat this ample field,
Try what the open, what the *covert* yield. *Pope's Eſſays.*

2. Secret; hidden; private; inſidious.

And let us preſently go ſit in council,
How *covert* matters may be beſt diſclos'd,
And open perils ſureſt anſwered. *Shakeſp. Julius Cæſar.*

By what beſt way,
Whether of open war, or *covert* guile,
We now debate. *Milton's Paradiſe Loſt, b.* ii. *l.* 41.

Co'vert. *adj.* [*couvert*, French.] The ſtate of a woman ſheltered by marriage under her huſband; as *covert* baron, feme *covert*.

Inſtead of her being under *covert* baron, to be under *covert* feme myſelf; to have my body diſabled, and my head fortified. *Dryden's Spaniſh Fryar.*

Covert-way. *n. ſ.* [from *covert* and *way.*]

It is, in fortification, a ſpace of ground level with the field, on the edge of the ditch, three or four fathom broad, ranging quite round the half moons, or other works toward the country. One of the greateſt difficulties in a ſiege is to make a lodgment on the *covert-way*, becauſe uſually the beſieged palliſade it along the middle, and undermine it on all ſides. It is ſometimes called the corridor, and ſometimes the counterſcarp, becauſe it is on the edge of the ſcarp. *Harris.*

Co'vertly. *adv.* [from *covert.*] Secretly; cloſely; in private; with privacy.

Yet ſtill Aragnol (ſo his foe was hight)
Lay lurking, *covertly* him to ſurpriſe. *Spenſer's Muiopotmos.*

How can'ſt thou croſs this marriage?
—Not honeſtly, my lord; but ſo *covertly*, that no diſhoneſty ſhall appear in me. *Shakeſp. Much ado about Nothing.*

Amongſt the poets, Perſius *covertly* ſtrikes at Nero; ſome of whoſe verſes he recites with ſcorn and indignation. *Dryden.*

Co'vertness. *n. ſ.* [from *covert.*] Secrecy; privacy. *Dict.*

Co'verture. *n. ſ.* [from *covert.*]

1. Shelter; defence; not expoſure.

It may be it is rather the ſhade, or other *coverture*, that they take liking in, than the virtue of the herb. *Bacon's Nat. Hiſt.*

He ſaw his guileful act
By Eve, though all unweeting, ſeconded
Upon her huſband; ſaw their ſhame that ſought
Vain *covertures*. *Milton's Paradiſe Loſt, b.* x. *l.* 337.

The winds being ſo fierce, and the weather ſo ſevere, as not to ſuffer any thing to proſper or thrive beyond the height of a ſhrub, in any of all thoſe iſlands, unleſs it be protected by walls; as in gardens, or other like *coverture*. *Woodward.*

2. In law.

The eſtate and condition of a married woman, who, by the laws of our realm, is in *poteſtate viri*, and therefore diſabled to contract with any, to the prejudice of herſelf or her huſband, without his allowance or confirmation. *Cowel.*

The infancy of king Edward VI. and the *coverture* of queen Mary, did, in fact, diſable them to accompliſh the conqueſt of Ireland. *Davies on Ireland.*

To CO'VET. *v. a.* [*convoiter*, French.]

1. To deſire inordinately; to deſire beyond due bounds.

If it be a ſin to *covet* honour,
I am the moſt offending man alive. *Shakeſpeare's Henry* V.

I am yet
Unknown to woman, never was forſworn,
Scarcely have *coveted* what was mine own,
At no time broke my faith. *Shakeſpeare's Macbeth.*

O father! can it be that ſouls ſublime,
Return to viſit our terreſtrial clime?
And that the gen'rous mind, releas'd by death,
Can *covet* lazy limbs and mortal breath? *Dryden's Æn.*

2. To deſire earneſtly.

But *covet* earneſtly the beſt gifts. *1 Cor.* xii. 31.

To Co'vet. *v. n.* To have a ſtrong deſire.

The love of money is the root of all evil, which while ſome *coveted after*, they have erred from the faith. *1 Tim.* vi.

Co'vetable. *adj.* [from *covet.*] To be wiſhed for; to be coveted. *Dict.*

Co'vetise. *n. ſ.* [*convoitiſe*, French.] Avarice; covetouſneſs of money.

Moſt wretched wight, whom nothing might ſuffice,
Whoſe greedy luſt did lack in greateſt ſtore;
Whoſe need had end, but no end *covetiſe*. *Fairy Queen, b.* i.

Co'vetous. *adj.* [*convoiteux*, French.]

1. Inordinately deſirous.

While cumber'd with my dropping cloaths I lay,
The cruel nation, *covetous* of prey,
Stain'd with my blood the unhoſpitable coaſt. *Dryden's Æn.*

2. Inordinately eager of money; avaricious.

An heart they have exercised with *covetous* practices.
2 Pet. ii. 14.

What he cannot help in his nature, you must not account a vice in him: you must in no ways say he is *covetous*. *Shakesp.*

Let never so much probability hang on one side of a *covetous* man's reasoning, and money on the other, it is easy to foresee which will outweigh. *Locke.*

3. Desirous; eager: in a good sense.

Sheba was never
More *covetous* of wisdom and fair virtue,
Than this fair soul shall be. *Shakespeare's Henry* VIII.

He that is envious or angry at a virtue that is not his own, at the perfection or excellency of his neighbour, is not *covetous* of the virtue, but of its reward and reputation, and then his intentions are polluted. *Taylor's Rule of Living Holy.*

Co'vetously. *adv.* [from *covetous.*] Avariciously; eagerly.

If he care not for't, he will supply us easily; if he *covetously* reserve it, how shall's get it? *Shakespeare.*

Co'vetousness. *n. s.* [from *covetous.*] Avarice; inordinate desire of money; eagerness of gain.

When workmen strive to do better than well,
They do confound their skill in *covetousness*. *Shakes. K. John.*

He that takes pains to serve the ends of *covetousness*, or ministers to another's lust, or keeps a shop of impurities or intemperance, is idle in the worst sense. *Taylor's Holy Living.*

Covetousness debaseth a man's spirit, and sinks it into the earth. *Tillotson.*

Co'vey. *n. s.* [*couvee*, French.]

1. A hatch; an old bird with her young ones.

2. A number of birds together.

A flight of wasps and *covey* of partridges went to a farmer, and begged a sup of him to quench their thirst. *L'Estrange.*

A *covey* of patridges springing in our front, put our infantry in disorder. *Addison's Freeholder*, N°. 3.

There would be no walking in a shady wood without springing a *covey* of toasts. *Addison's Guardian*, N°. 112.

COUGH. *n. s.* [*kuch*, Dutch.] A convulsion of the lungs, vellicated by some sharp serosity. It is pronounced *coff*.

In consumptions of the lungs, when nature cannot expel the *cough*, men fall into fluxes of the belly, and then they die. *Bacon's Natural History*, N°. 63.

For his dear sake long restless nights you bore,
While rattling *coughs* his heaving vessels tore. *Smith.*

To Cough. *v. n.* [*kuchen*, Dutch.] To have the lungs convulsed; to make a noise in endeavouring to evacuate the peccant matter from the lungs.

Thou didst drink
The stale of horses, and the gilded puddle
Which beasts would *cough* at. *Shakesp. Anth. and Cleopatra.*

Thou hast quarrelled with a man for *coughing* in the street, because he hath wakened thy dog that hath lain asleep in the sun. *Shakespeare's Romeo and Juliet.*

The first problem enquireth why a man doth *cough*, but not an ox or cow; whereas the contrary is often observed. *Brown.*

If any humour be discharged upon the lungs, they have a faculty of clearing themselves, and casting it up by *coughing*. *Ray on the Creation.*

There are who to my person pay their court,
I *cough* like Horace, and though lean, am short. *Pope's Ep.*

To Cough. *v. a.* To eject by a cough; to expectorate.

If the matter be to be discharged by expectoration, it must first pass into the substance of the lungs, then into the aspera arteria, or weasand, and from thence be *coughed* up, and spit out by the mouth. *Wiseman's Surgery.*

Co'ugher. *n. s.* [from *cough.*] One that coughs. *Dict.*

Co'vin. } *n. s.* A deceitful agreement between two or more,
Co'vine. } to the hurt of another. *Cowel.*

Co'ving. *n. s.* [from *cove.*] A term in building, used of houses that project over the ground-plot and the turned projecture arched with timber, lathed and plaistered. *Harris.*

Could. [the imperfect preterite of *can.* See Can.] Was able to; had power to.

And if I have done well, and as is fitting the story, it is that which I desired; but if slenderly and meanly, it is that which I *could* attain unto. *2 Mac.* xv. 38.

What if he did not all the ill he *could*?
Am I oblig'd by that t' assist his rapines,
And to maintain his murders? *Dryden's Spanish Fryar.*

Co'ulter. *n. s.* [*culter*, Latin.] The sharp iron of the plow which cuts the earth, perpendicular to the share.

The Israelites went down to sharpen every man his share, and his *coulter*, and his ax, and his mattock. *1 Sa.* xiii. 20.

Literature is the grindstone to sharpen the *coulters*, to whet their natural faculties. *Hammond on Fundamentals.*

The plough for stiff clays is long and broad, and the *coulter* long, and very little bending, with a very large wing. *Mortim.*

CO'UNCIL. *n. s.* [*concilium*, Latin.]

1. An assembly of persons met together in consultation.

The chief priests, and all the *council*, sought false witness. *Mat.* xxvi. 59.

In histories composed by politicians, they are for drawing up a perpetual scheme of causes and events, and preserving a constant correspondence between the camp and the *council* table. *Addison's Spectator*, N°. 170.

2. An assembly of divines to deliberate upon religion.

Some borrow all their religion from the fathers of the Christian church, or from their synods or *councils*. *Watts.*

3. Persons called together to be consulted on any occasion, or to give advice.

They being thus assembled, are more properly a *council* to the king, the great *council* of the kingdom, to advise his majesty in those things of weight and difficulty, which concern both the king and people, than a court. *Bacon's Adv. to Villiers.*

4. The body of privy counsellors.

Without the knowledge
Either of king or *council*, you made bold
To carry into Flanders the great seal. *Shakesp. Henry* VIII.

Council-board. *n. s.* [*council* and *board.*] Council-table; table where matters of state are deliberated.

He hath commanded,
To-morrow morning to the *council-board*,
He be convened. *Shakespeare's Henry* VIII.

When ship-money was transacted at the *council-board*, they looked upon it as a work of that power they were obliged to trust. *Clarendon.*

And Pallas, if she broke the laws,
Must yield her foe the stronger cause;
A shame to one so much ador'd
For wisdom at Jove's *council-board*. *Swift.*

CO'UNSEL. *n. s.* [*consilium*, Latin.]

1. Advice; direction.

Let me give thee *counsel*, that thou mayest save thine own life. *1 Kings*, i. 12.

There is as much difference between the *counsel* that a friend giveth, and that a man giveth himself, as there is between the *counsel* of a friend and of a flatterer. *Bacon, Essay* 28.

The best *counsel* he could give him was, to go to his parliament. *Clarendon, b.* viii.

2. Consultation; interchange of opinions.

They that lay wait for my soul, take *counsel* together. *Psalm* lxxi. 10.

I hold as little *counsel* with weak fear
As you, or any Scot that lives. *Shakespeare's Henry* IV.

3. Deliberation; examination of consequences.

They all confess therefore, in the working of that first cause, that *counsel* is used, reason followed, and a way observed. *Hooker, b.* i. *sect.* 2.

4. Prudence; art; machination.

O how comely is the wisdom of old men, and understanding and *counsel* to men of honour. *Ecclus.* xxv. 5.

There is no wisdom, nor understanding, nor *counsel* against the Lord. *Prov.* xxi. 30.

5. Secrecy; the secrets intrusted in consulting.

The players cannot keep *counsel*; they'll tell all. *Shakespeare.*

6. Scheme; purpose; design.

The *counsel* of the Lord standeth for ever, the thoughts of his heart to all generations. *Psal.* xxxiii. 11.

The Lord will bring to light the hidden things of darkness, and will make manifest the *counsels* of the heart. *1 Cor.* iv. 5.

7. Those that plead a cause; the counsellors. This seems only an abbreviature usual in conversation.

Your hand, a covenant; we will have these things set down by lawful *counsel*. *Shakespeare's Cymbeline.*

For the advocates and *counsel* that plead, patience and gravity of learning is an essential part of justice; and an overspeaking judge is no well tuned cymbal. *Bacon, Essay* 57.

What says my *counsel* learned in the law? *Pope.*

To Co'unsel. *v. a.* [*consilior*, Latin.]

1. To give advice or counsel to any person.

But say, Lucetta, now we are alone,
Would'st thou then *counsel* me to fall in love? *Shakespeare.*

Truth shall nurse her;
Holy and heav'nly thoughts still *counsel* her. *Shak. Hen.*VIII.

Ill fortune never crushed that man whom good fortune deceived not; I therefore have *counselled* my friends never to trust to her fairer side, though she seemed to make peace with them. *Ben. Johnson's Discoveries.*

He supports my poverty with his wealth, and I *counsel* and instruct him with my learning and experience. *Taylor.*

2. To advise any thing.

The less had been our shame,
The less his *counsell'd* crime which brands the Grecian name. *Dryden's Fables.*

Co'unsellable. *adj.* [from *counsel.*] Willing to receive and follow the advice or opinions of others.

Very few men of so great parts were more *counsellable* than he; so that he would seldom be in danger of great errours, if he would communicate his own thoughts to disquisition. *Clar.*

Co'unsellor. *n. s.* [from *counsel.*]

1. One that gives advice.

His mother was his *counsellor* to do wickedly. *2 Chr.* xxii. 3.

She would be a *counsellor* of good things, and a comfort in cares. *Wisd.* viii. 9.

Death of thy soul! Those linen cheeks of thine
Are *counsellors* to fear. *Shakespeare's Macbeth.*

2. Confidant; bosom friend.

In such green palaces the first kings reign'd,
Slept in their shades, and angels entertain'd;
With such old *counsellors* they did advise,
And by frequenting sacred groves grew wise. *Waller.*

3. One whose province is to deliberate and advise upon publick affairs.

You are a *counsellor*,
And by that virtue no man dare accuse you. *Shak. H.* VIII.

Of *counsellors* there are two sorts: the first, *consiliarii nati*, as I may term them; such are the prince of Wales, and others of the king's sons: but the ordinary sort of *counsellors* are such as the king, out of a due consideration of their worth and abilities, and, withal, of their fidelity to his person and to his crown, calleth to be of council with him, in his ordinary government. *Bacon's Advice to Villiers.*

4. One that is consulted in a case of law; a lawyer.

CO'UNSELLORSHIP. *n. s.* [from *counsellor.*] The office or post of a privy counsellor.

Of the great offices and officers of the kingdom, the most part are such as cannot well be severed from the *counsellorship*. *Bacon's Advice to Villiers.*

To COUNT. *v. a.* [*compter*, Fr. *computare*, Latin.]

1. To number; to tell.

Here through this grate I can *count* every one,
And view the Frenchmen. *Shakespeare's Henry* VI. *p.* i.

The vicious *count* their years; virtuous, their acts. *Johns.*

For the preferments of the world, he that would reckon up all the accidents that they depend upon, may as well undertake to *count* the sands, or to sum up infinity. *South's Sermons.*

When men in sickness ling'ring lie,
They *count* the tedious hours by months and years. *Dryden.*

Argos now rejoice, for Thebes lies low;
Thy slaughter'd sons now smile, and think they won,
When they can *count* more Theban ghosts than theirs. *Dryd.*

2. To preserve a reckoning.

Some people in America *counted* their years by the coming of certain birds amongst them at their certain seasons, and leaving them at others. *Locke.*

3. To reckon; to place to an account.

He believed in the Lord, and he *counted* it to him for righteousness. *Gen.* xv. 6.

Not barely the plowman's pains is to be *counted* into the bread we eat; the labour of those who broke the oxen, must all be charged on the account of labour. *Locke.*

4. To esteem; to account; to reckon; to consider as having a certain character, whether good or evil.

When once it comprehendeth any thing above this, as the differences of time, affirmations, negations, and contradictions in speech, we then *count* it to have some use of natural reason. *Hooker, b.* i. *sect.* 6.

Count not thine handmaid for a daughter of Belial. 1 *Sam.* i.

Nor shall I *count* it heinous to enjoy
The publick marks of honour and reward
Conferr'd upon me. *Milton's Agonist. l.* 991.

You would not wish to *count* this man a foe!
In friendship, and in hatred, obstinate. *Philips's Briton.*

5. To impute to; to charge to.

All th' impossibilities, which poets
Count to extravagance of loose description,
Shall sooner be. *Rowe's Ambitious Step-mother.*

To COUNT. *v. n.* To found an account or scheme: with *upon*.

I think it a great errour to *count upon* the genius of a nation as a standing argument in all ages. *Swift.*

COUNT. *n. s.* [*compte*, French; *computus*, Latin.]

1. Number.

That we up to your palaces may mount,
Of blessed saints for to increase the *count*. *Spenser's Epithal.*

By my *count*,
I was your mother much upon these years. *Sh. Ro. and Jul.*

2. Reckoning.

Since I saw you last,
There is a change upon you.
——Well, I know not
What *counts* hard fortune casts upon my face. *Shakespeare.*

COUNT. *n. s.* [*comte*, Fr. *comes*, Latin.] A title of foreign nobility; an earl.

CO'UNTABLE. *adj.* [from *count.*] That which may be numbered.

The evils which you desire to be recounted are very many, and almost *countable* with those which were hidden in the basket of Pandora. *Spenser's State of Ireland.*

CO'UNTENANCE. *n. s.* [*contenance*, French.]

1. The form of the face; the system of the features.

So spake our sire, and by his *count'nance* seem'd
Entering on studious thoughts abstruse. *Milton's Parad. Lost.*

To whom, with *count'nance* calm, and soul sedate,
Thus Turnus. *Dryden's Æn.*

2. Air; look.

Well, Suffolk, yet thou shalt not see me blush,
Nor change my *countenance* for this arrest:
A heart unspotted is not easily daunted. *Shakesp. Henry* VI.

3. Calmness of look; composure of face.

She smil'd severe; nor with a troubled look,
Or trembling hand, the fun'ral present took;
Ev'n kept her *count'nance*, when the lid remov'd,
Disclos'd the heart unfortunately lov'd. *Dryden's Fables.*

The two maxims of any great man at court are, always to keep his *countenance*, and never to keep his word. *Swift.*

4. Confidence of mien; aspect of assurance.

The night beginning to persuade some retiring place, the gentlewoman, even out of *countenance* before she began her speech, invited me to lodge that night with her father. *Sidney.*

We will not make your *countenance* to fall by the answer ye shall receive. *Bacon's New Atlantis.*

Their best friends were out of *countenance*, because they found that the imputations, which their enemies had laid upon them, were well grounded. *Clarendon, b.* viii.

Your examples will meet it at every turn, and put it out of *countenance* in every place; even in private corners it will soon lose confidence. *Sprat's Sermons.*

If the outward profession of religion and virtue were once in practice and *countenance* at court, a good treatment of the clergy would be the necessary consequence. *Swift.*

If those preachers would look about, they would find one part of their congregation out of *countenance*, and the other asleep. *Swift.*

It is a kind of ill manners to offer objections to a fine woman, and a man would be out of *countenance* that should gain the superiority in such a contest: a coquette logician may be rallied, but not contradicted. *Addison's Freeholder*, N°. 32.

It puts the learned in *countenance*, and gives them a place among the fashionable part of mankind. *Addison's Freeholder.*

5. Affection or ill-will, as it appears upon the face.

Yet the stout fairy, mongst the middest crowd,
Thought all their glory vain in knightly view,
And that great princess too, exceeding proud,
That to strange knight no better *countenance* allow'd. *Fa. Q.*

The king hath on him such a *countenance*,
As he had lost some province, and a region
Lov'd, as he loves himself. *Shakespeare's Winter's Tale.*

6. Patronage; appearance of favour; appearance on any side; support.

The church of Christ, which held that profession which had not the publick allowance and *countenance* of authority, could not so long use the exercise of Christian religion but in private. *Hooker, b.* v. *sect.* 11.

His majesty maintained an army here, to give strength and *countenance* to the civil magistrate. *Davies on Ireland.*

Now then, we'll use
His *countenance* for the battle; which being done,
Let her who would be rid of him, devise
His speedy taking off. *Shakespeare's King Lear.*

This is the magistrate's peculiar province, to give *countenance* to piety and virtue, and to rebuke vice and profaneness. *Atterb.*

7. Superficial appearance; show; resemblance.

The election being done, he made *countenance* of great discontent thereat. *Ascham's Schoolmaster.*

Oh, you blessed ministers above!
Keep me in patience, and with ripen'd time
Unfold the evil, which is here wrapt up
In *countenance*. *Shakespeare's Measure for Measure.*

Bianca's love
Made me exchange my state with Tranio,
While he did bear my *countenance* in the town. *Shakespeare.*

To CO'UNTENANCE. *v. a.* [from the noun.]

1. To support; to patronise; to vindicate.

Neither shalt thou *countenance* a poor man in his cause. *Exod.*

This conceit, though *countenanced* by learned men, is not made out either by experience or reason. *Brown's Vulg. Err.*

This national fault of being so very talkative, looks natural and graceful in one that has grey hairs to *countenance* it. *Addis.*

2. To make a shew of.

Each to these ladies love did *countenance*,
And to his mistress each himself strove to advance. *Fai. Qu.*

3. To act suitably to any thing; to keep up any appearance.

Malcolm! Banquo!
As from your graves rise up, and walk like sprights,
To *countenance* this horrour. *Shakespeare's Macbeth.*

4. To encourage; to appear in defence.

At the first descent on shore he was not immured with a wooden vessel, but he did *countenance* the landing in his long-boat. *Wotton.*

CO'UNTENANCER. *n. s.* [from *countenance.*] One that countenances or supports another.

CO'UNTER. *n. s.* [from *count.*]

1. A false piece of money used as a means of reckoning.

Though these half-pence are to be received as money in the Exchequer, yet in trade they are no better than *counters*. *Swift's Considerations on Wood's Coin.*

2. Money in contempt.

When Marcus Brutus grows so covetous,
To lock such rascal *counters* from his friends,
Be ready, gods! with all your thunder-bolts,
Dash him to pieces. *Shakespeare's Julius Cæsar.*

3. The form on which goods are viewed and money told in a shop.

A fine gaudy minx, that robs our *counters* every night; and then goes out, and spends it upon our cuckold-makers. *Dryden.*

In half-whipt muslin, needles useless lie;
And shuttle-cocks a-cross the *counter* fly:
These sports warm harmless. *Gay's Trivia.*

Sometimes you would see him behind his *counter* selling broad-cloth, sometimes measuring linen. *Arbuth. Hist. of J. B.*

Whether thy *counter* shine with sums untold,
And thy wide-grasping hand grows black with gold. *Swift.*

4. COUNTER *of a Horse*, is that part of a horse's forehand that lies between the shoulder and under the neck. *Farrier's Dict.*

CO'UNTER. *adv.* [*contre*, Fr. *contra*, Latin.]

1. Contrary to; in opposition to.

Shall we erect two wills in Gods, and make the will of his purpose and intention run *counter* to the will of his approbation? *South's Sermons.*

The profit of the merchant, and the gain of the kingdom, are so far from being always parallels, that frequently they run *counter* one to the other. *Child's Discourse on Trade.*

He thinks it brave, at his first setting out, to signalize himself in running *counter* to all the rules of virtue. *Locke.*

2. The wrong way.

How chearfully on the false trail they cry,
Oh, this is *counter*, you false Danish dogs. *Shakesp. Hamlet.*

3. Contrary ways.

A man whom I cannot deny, may oblige me to use persuasions to another, which, at the same time I am speaking, I may wish may not prevail on him: in this case, it is plain, the will and the desire run *counter*. *Locke.*

4. This word is often found in composition, and may be placed before any word used in a sense of opposition.

That design was no sooner known, but others of an opposite party were appointed to set a *counter*-petition on foot. *Clar.*

To COUNTERA'CT. *v. a.* [*counter* and *act.*] To hinder any thing from its effect by contrary agency.

In this case we can find no principle within him strong enough to *counteract* that principle, and to relieve him. *South.*

To COUNTERBA'LANCE. *v. a.* [*counter* and *balance.*] To weigh against; to act against with an opposite weight.

There was so much air drawn out of the vessel, that the remaining air was not able to *counterbalance* the mercurial cylinder. *Boyle.*

Few of Adam's children are not born with some biass, which it is the business of education either to take off, or *counterbalance*. *Locke.*

COUNTERBA'LANCE. *n. s.* [from the verb.] Opposite weight; equivalent power.

But peaceful kings, o'er martial people set,
Each others poize and *counterbalance* are. *Dryd. Ann. Mirab.*

Money is the *counterbalance* to all other things purchaseable by it, and lying, as it were, in the opposite scale of commerce. *Locke.*

To COUNTERBU'FF. *v. a.* [from *counter* and *buff.*] To impell in a direction opposite to the former impulse; to strike back.

The giddy ship, betwixt the winds and tides,
Forc'd back and forwards, in a circle rides,
Stunn'd with the diff'rent blows; then shoots amain,
'Till *counterbuff'd* she stops, and sleeps again. *Dryden.*

COUNTERBU'FF. *n. s.* [*counter* and *buff.*] A blow in a contrary direction; a stroke that produces a recoil.

He at the second gave him such a *counterbuff*, that, because Phalantus was not to be driven from the saddle, the saddle with broken girths was driven from the horse. *Sidney.*

Go, captain Stub, lead on, and show
What house you come of, by the blow
You give sir Quintin, and the cuff
You 'scape o' th' sandbags *counterbuff*. *Ben. Johnson.*

CO'UNTERCASTER. *n. s.* [from *counter*, for a false piece of money, and *caster.*] A word of contempt for an arithmetician; a book-keeper; a caster of accounts; a reckoner.

I, of whom his eyes had seen the proof
At Rhodes, at Cyprus, must be let and calm'd
By debtor and creditor, this *countercaster*. *Shakesp. Othello.*

CO'UNTERCHANGE. *n. s.* [*counter* and *change.*] Exchange; reciprocation.

She, like harmless lightning, throws her eye
On him, her brothers, me, her master, hitting
Each object with a joy. The *counterchange*
Is sev'rally in all. *Shakespeare's Cymbeline.*

To CO'UNTERCHANGE. *v. a.* To give and receive.

COUNTERCHA'RM. *n. s.* [*counter* and *charm.*] That by which a charm is dissolved; that which has the power of destroying the effects of a charm.

Now touch'd by *countercharms* they change again,
And stand majestick, and recall'd to men. *Pope's Odyssey.*

To COUNTERCHA'RM. *v. a.* [from *counter* and *charm.*] To destroy the effect of an enchantment.

Like a spell it was to keep us invulnerable, and so *countercharm* all our crimes, that they should only be active to please, not hurt us. *Decay of Piety.*

To COUNTERCHE'CK. *v. a.* [*counter* and *check.*] To oppose; to stop with sudden opposition.

COUNTERCHE'CK. *n. s.* [from the verb.] Stop; rebuke.

If again I said his beard was not well cut, he would say I lye: this is called the *countercheck* quarrelsome. *Shakespeare.*

To COUNTERDRA'W. *v. a.* [from *counter* and *draw.*] With painters, to copy a design or painting by means of a fine linen cloth, an oiled paper, or other transparent matter, whereon the strokes appearing through are traced with a pencil. *Chamb.*

COUNTERE'VIDENCE. *n. s.* [*counter* and *evidence.*] Testimony by which the deposition of some former witness is opposed.

Sense itself detects its more palpable deceits by a *counter-evidence*, and the more ordinary impostures seldom outlive the first experiments. *Glanville's Sceps. c.* 10.

We have little reason to question his testimony in this point, seeing it is backed by others of good credit, and all because there is no *counterevidence*, nor any witness that appears against it. *Burnet's Theory of the Earth.*

To CO'UNTERFEIT. *v. a.* [*contrefaire*, French.]

1. To copy with an intent to pass the copy for an original; to forge.

What art thou,
That *counterfeits* the person of a king? *Shakesp. Henry* IV.

It came into this priest's fancy to cause this lad to *counterfeit* and personate the second son of Edward IV. supposed to be murdered. *Bacon's Henry* VII.

There have been some that could *counterfeit* the distance of voices, which is a secondary object of hearing, in such sort, as when they stand fast by you, you would think the speech came from afar off in a fearful manner. *Bacon's Nat. History.*

Say, lovely dream, where could'st thou find
Shadows to *counterfeit* that face? *Waller.*

It happens, that not one single line or thought is contained in this imposture, although it appears that they who *counterfeited* me had heard of the true one. *Swift.*

2. To imitate; to copy; to resemble.

And, Oh, you mortal engines, whose rude throats
Th' immortal Jove's dread clamours *counterfeit*,
Farewel! *Shakespeare's Othello.*

O Eve! in evil hour thou did'st give ear
To that false worm, of whomsoever taught
To *counterfeit* man's voice. *Milton's Paradise Lost, b.* ix.

To *counterfeit*, is to put on the likeness and appearance of some real excellency: Bristol-stones would not pretend to be diamonds, if there never had been diamonds. *Tillotson's Serm.*

CO'UNTERFEIT. *adj.* [from the verb.]

1. That which is made in imitation of another, with intent to pass for the original; forged; fictitious.

I learn
Now of my own experience, not by talk,
How *counterfeit* a coin they are, who friends
Bear in their superscription; in prosperous days
They swarm, but in adverse withdraw their head. *Milton.*

General observations drawn from particulars, are the jewels of knowledge, comprehending great store in a little room; but they are therefore to be made with the greater care and caution, lest, if we take *counterfeit* for true, our shame be the greater, when our stock comes to a severe scrutiny. *Locke.*

2. Deceitful; hypocritical.

True friends appear less mov'd than *counterfeit*. *Roscomm.*

CO'UNTERFEIT. *n. s.* [from the verb.]

1. One who personates another; an impostor.

I am no *counterfeit*; to die is to be a *counterfeit*; for he is but the *counterfeit* of a man, who hath not the life of a man. *Shakespeare's Henry* IV. *p.* i.

This priest, being utterly unacquainted with the true person, according to whose pattern he should shape his *counterfeit*, yet could think it possible for him to instruct his player, either in gesture or fashions, or in recounting past matters of his life and education, or in fit answers to questions, any ways to come near the resemblance of him whom he was to represent. *Bacon.*

But trust me, child, I'm much inclin'd to fear
Some *counterfeit* in this your Jupiter. *Addison's Ovid. Metam.*

2. Something made in imitation of another, intended to pass for that which it resembles; a forgery.

My father was I know not where,
When I was stampt. Some coiner, with his tools,
Made me a *counterfeit*; yet my mother seem'd
The Dian of that time. *Shakespeare's Cymbeline.*

There would be no *counterfeits* but for the sake of something that is real; for though all pretenders seem to be what they really are not, yet they pretend to be something that really is. *Tillotson's Sermons.*

CO'UNTERFEITER. *n. s.* [from *counterfeit.*] A forger; one who contrives copies to pass for originals.

Henry the second altered the coin, which was corrupted by *counterfeiters*, to the great good of the commonwealth. *Camden.*

Co'UNTERFEITLY. *adv.* [from *counterfeit.*] Falsely; fictitiously; with forgery.

Since the wisdom of their choice is rather to have my cap than my heart, I will practise the insinuating nod, and be off to them most *counterfeitly.* *Shakespeare's Coriolanus.*

COUNTERFE'RMENT. *n. s.* [*counter* and *ferment.*] Ferment opposed to ferment.

What unnatural motions and *counterferments* must a medly of intemperance produce in the body! When I behold a fashionable table, I fancy I see innumerable distempers lurking in ambuscade among the dishes. *Addison's Spectator,* N°. 195.

COUNTERFE'SANCE. *n. s.* [*contrefaisance,* French.] The act of counterfeiting; forgery.

And his man Reynold, with fine *counterfesance,*
Supports his credit and his countenance. *Hubberd's Tale.*
Such is the face of falshood, such the sight
Of foul Duessa, when her borrow'd light
Is laid away, and *counterfesance* known. *Fairy Queen, b.* i.

Co'UNTERFORT. *n. s.* [from *counter* and *fort.*]

Counterforts, buttresses or spurs, are pillars serving to support walls or terrasses, subject to bulge, or be thrown down. *Chambers.*

COUNTERGA'GE. *n. s.* [from *counter* and *gage.*] In carpentry, a method used to measure the joints by transferring the breadth of a mortise to the place where the tenon is to be, in order to make them fit each other. *Chambers.*

COUNTERGUA'RD. *n. s.* [from *counter* and *guard.*] A small rampart with parapet and ditch, to cover some part of the body of the place. *Military Dict.*

COUNTERLI'GHT. *n. s.* [from *counter* and *light.*] A window or light opposite to any thing, which makes it appear to a disadvantage. *Chambers.*

To COUNTERMA'ND. *v. a.* [*contremander,* French.]

1. To order the contrary to what was ordered before; to contradict, annul, or repeal a command.

In states notoriously irreligious, a secret and irresistible power *countermands* their deepest projects, and smites their policies with frustration and a curse. *South's Sermons.*

Avicen *countermands* letting blood in cholerick bodies, because he esteems the blood a bridle of the gall. *Harvey.*

2. To oppose; to contradict the orders of another.

For us to alter any thing, is to lift up ourselves against God, and, as it were, to *countermand* him. *Hooker.*

COUNTERMA'ND. *n. s.* [*contrmand,* Fr.] Repeal of a former order.

Have you no *countermand* for Claudio yet,
But he must die to-morrow? *Shakes. Measure for Measure.*

To COUNTERMA'RCH. *v. n.* [*counter* and *march.*] To march backward; to march in indirect ways.

COUNTERMA'RCH. *n. s.* [from the verb.]

1. Retrocession; march backward; march in a different direction from the former.

How are such an infinite number of things placed with such order in the memory, notwithstanding the tumults, marches, and *countermarches* of the animal spirits? *Collier on Thought.*

2. Change of measures; alteration of conduct.

They make him do and undo, go forward and backwards by such *countermarches* and retractions, as we do not willingly impute to wisdom. *Burnet's Theory of the Earth.*

COUNTERMA'RK. *n. s.* [from *counter* and *mark.*]

1. A second or third mark put on a bale of goods belonging to several merchants, that it may not be opened but in the presence of them all.

2. The mark of the goldsmiths company, to shew the metal is standard, added to that of the artificer.

3. An artificial cavity made in the teeth of horses, that have outgrown their natural mark, to disguise their age.

4. A mark added to a medal a long time after it is struck, by which the curious know the several changes in value which they have undergone. *Chambers.*

To COUNTERMA'RK. *v. a.* [*counter* and *mark.*]

A horse is said to be *countermarked* when his corner-teeth are artificially made hollow, a false mark being made in the hollow place, in imitation of the eye of a bean, to conceal the horse's age. *Farrier's Dict.*

COUNTERMI'NE. *n. s.* [*counter* and *mine.*]

1. A well or hole sunk into the ground, from which a gallery or branch runs out under ground, to seek out the enemy's mine, and disappoint it. *Military Dict.*

After this they mined the walls, laid the powder, and rammed the mouths; but the citizens made a *countermine,* and thereinto they poured such a plenty of water, that the wet powder could not be fired. *Hayward.*

2. Means of opposition; means of counteraction.

He thinking himself contemned, knowing no *countermine* against contempt but terror, began to let nothing pass, which might bear the colour of a fault, without sharp punishment. *Sidney, b.* ii.

3. A stratagem by which any contrivance is defeated.

The matter being brought to a trial of skill, the *countermine* was only an act of self-preservation. *L'Estrange, Fab.* 37.

To COUNTERMI'NE. *v. a.* [from the noun.]

1. To delve a passage into an enemy's mine, by which the powder may evaporate without mischief.

2. To counterwork; to defeat by secret measures.

Thus infallibly it must be, if God do not miraculously *countermine* us, and do more for us than we can do against ourselves. *Decay of Piety.*

COUNTERMO'TION. *n. s.* [*counter* and *motion.*] Contrary motion; opposition of motion.

That resistance is a *countermotion,* or equivalent to one, is plain by this, that any body which is pressed, must needs press again on the body that presses it. *Digby on the Soul.*

If any of the returning spirits should happen to fall foul upon others which are outward bound, these *countermotions* would overset them, or occasion a later arrival. *Collier.*

COUNTERMU'RE. *n. s.* [*contremur,* French.] A wall built up behind another wall, to supply its place.

The great shot flying continually through the breach, did beat down houses; but the *countermure,* new built against the breach, standing upon a lower ground, it seldom touched. *Knolles's History of the Turks.*

COUNTERNA'TURAL. *adj.* [*counter* and *natural.*] Contrary to nature.

A consumption is a *counternatural* hectick extenuation of the body. *Harvey on Consumptions.*

COUNTERNO'ISE. *n. s.* [*counter* and *noise.*] A sound by which any other noise is overpowered.

They endeavoured, either by a constant succession of sensual delights, to charm and lull asleep, or else, by a *counternoise* of revellings and riotous excesses, to drown the softer whispers of their conscience. *Calamy's Sermons.*

COUNTERO'PENING. *n. s.* [*counter* and *opening.*] An aperture or vent on the contrary side.

A tent, plugging up the orifice, would make the matter recur to the part disposed to receive it, and mark the place for a *counteropening.* *Sharp's Surgery.*

COUNTERPA'CE. *n. s.* [*counter* and *pace.*] Contrary measure; attempts in opposition to any scheme.

When the least *counterpaces* are made to these resolutions, it will then be time enough for our malecontents. *Swift.*

Co'UNTERPANE. *n. s.* [*contrepoint,* French.] A coverlet for a bed, or any thing else woven in squares. It is sometimes written, according to etymology, *counterpoint.*

In ivory coffers I have stufft my crowns;
In cypress chests my arras *counterpanes.* *Shakespeare.*

COUNTERPA'RT. *n. s.* [*counter* and *part.*] The correspondent part; the part which answers to another, as the two papers of a contract; the part which fits another, as the *key* of a cipher.

In some things the laws of Normandy agreed with the laws of England; so that they seem to be, as it were, copies or *counterparts* one of another. *Hale's Common Law of England.*

An old fellow with a young wench, may pass for a *counterpart* of this fable. *L'Estrange, Fab.* 82.

Oh *counterpart*
Of our soft sex; well are you made our lords:
So bold, so great, so god-like are you form'd,
How can you love so silly things as women? *Dryd. K. Arth.*

He is to consider the thought of his author, and his words, and to find out the *counterpart* to each in another language. *Dryden.*

In the discovery the two different plots look like *counterparts* and copies of one another. *Addison's Spectator,* N°. 267.

COUNTERPLE'A. *n. s.* [from *counter* and *plea.*] In law, a replication: as if a stranger to the action begun, desire to be admitted to say what he can for the safeguard of his estate; that which the demandant allegeth against this request is called a *counterplea.* *Cowel.*

To COUNTERPLO'T. *v. a.* [*counter* and *plot.*] To oppose one machination by another; to obviate art by art.

COUNTERPLO'T. *n. s.* [from the verb.] An artifice opposed to an artifice.

The wolf here, that had a plot upon the kid, was confounded by a *counterplot* of the kid's upon the wolf; and such a *counterplot* it was too, as the wolf, with all his sagacity, was not able to smell out. *L'Estrange, Fab.* 174.

Co'UNTERPOINT. *n. s.* A coverlet woven in squares, commonly spoken *counterpain.* See COUNTERPANE.

To COUNTERPO'ISE. *v. a.* [*counter* and *poise.*]

1. To counterbalance; to be equi-ponderant to; to act against with equal weight.

Our spoil we have brought home,
Do more than *counterpoise* a full third part
The charges of the action. *Shakespeare's Coriolanus.*

The force and the distance of weights, *counterpoising* one another, ought to be reciprocal. *Digby on the Soul.*

2. To produce a contrary action by an equal weight.

The heaviness of these bodies must be *counterpoised* by a plummet, that may be fastened about the pulley to the axis. *Wilkins's Math. Magic.*

3. To act with equal power against any person or cause.

So many freeholders of English will be able to beard and to *counterpoise* the rest. *Spenser on Ireland.*

Co'unterpoise. *n. s.* [from *counter* and *poise.*]
1. Equiponderance; equivalence of weight; equal force in the opposite scale of the balance.

Take her by the hand,
And tell her she is thine; to whom I promise
A *counterpoise*, if not in thy estate,
A balance more replete. *Shakesp. All's well that ends well.*

Fastening that to our exact balance, we put a metalline *counterpoise* into the opposite scale. *Boyle's Spring of the Air.*

2. The state of being placed in the opposite scale of the balance.

Th' Eternal hung forth his golden scales,
Wherein all things created first he weigh'd,
The pendulous round earth, with balanc'd air
In *counterpoise*. *Milton's Paradise Lost, b.* iv. *l.* 999.

3. Equipollence; equivalence of power.

The second nobles are a *counterpoise* to the higher nobility, that they grow not too potent. *Bacon, Essay* 20.

Their generals, by their credit in the army, were, with the magistrates and other civil officers, a sort of *counterpoise* to the power of the people *Swift on the Dissent. in Athens and Rome.*

Counterpo'ison. *n. s.* [*counter* and *poison.*] Antidote; medicine by which the effects of poison are obviated.

Counterpoisons must be adapted to the cause; for example, in poison from sublimate corrosive, and arsenick. *Arbuthnot.*

Counterpre'ssure. *n. s.* [*counter* and *pressure.*] Opposite force; power acting in contrary directions.

Does it not all mechanick heads confound,
That troops of atoms from all parts around,
Of equal number, and of equal force,
Should to this single point direct their course;
That so the *counterpressure* ev'ry way,
Of equal vigour, might their motions stay,
And, by a steady poise, the whole in quiet lay? *Blackm.*

Counterpro'ject. *n. s.* [*counter* and *project.*] Correspondent part of a scheme.

A clear reason why they never sent any forces to Spain, and why the obligation not to enter into a treaty of peace with France, until that entire monarchy was yielded as a preliminary, was struck out of the *counterproject* by the Dutch. *Swift.*

To Counterpro've. *v. a.* [from *counter* and *prove.*] To take off a design in black lead, or red chalk, by passing it through the rolling-press with another piece of paper, both being moistened with a sponge. *Chambers.*

To COUNTERRO'L. *v. a.* [*counter* and *roll.* This is now generally written as it is spoken, *control.*] To preserve the power of detecting frauds by a counter account.

Counterro'lment. *n. s.* [from *counterrol.*] A counter account; controlment.

This present manner of exercising of this office, hath so many testimonies, interchangeable warrants, and *counterrolments*, whereof each, running through the hands, and resting in the power of so many several persons, is sufficient to argue and convince all manner of falshood. *Bacon.*

Co'unterscarp. *n. s.* [from *counter* and *scarp.*] In fortification, is that side of the ditch which is next the camp, or properly the talus that supports the earth of the covert-way; although by this term is often understood the whole covert-way, with its parapet and glacis; and so it is to be understood when it is said the enemy lodged themselves on the *counterscarp*. *Harris.*

To Countersi'gn. *v. a.* [from *counter* and *sign.*] To sign an order or patent of a superiour, in quality of secretary, to render the thing more authentick. Thus charters are signed by the king, and *countersigned* by a secretary of state, or lord chancellor. *Chambers.*

Counterte'nor. *n. s.* [from *counter* and *tenor.*] One of the mean or middle parts of musick; so called, as it were, opposite to the tenor. *Harris.*

I am deaf for two months together: this deafness unqualifies me for all company, except a few friends with *countertenor* voices. *Swift.*

Counterti'de. *n. s.* [*counter* and *tide.*] Contrary tide; fluctuations of the water.

Such were our *countertides* at land, and so
Presaging of the fatal blow,
In your prodigious ebb and flow. *Dryden.*

Counterti'me. *n. s.* [*counter* and *time*, *contretemps*, French.]
1. The defence or resistance of a horse, that intercepts his cadence, and the measure of his manage. *Farrier's Dict.*
2. Defence; opposition.

Let cheerfulness on happy fortune wait,
And give not thus the *countertime* to fate. *Dryd. Aurengz.*

Countertu'rn. *n. s.* [*counter* and *turn.*]

The catastasis, called by the Romans status, the height and full growth of the play, we may call properly the *counterturn*, which destroys that expectation, embroils the action in new difficulties, and leaves you far distant from that hope in which it found you. *Dryden on Dramatick Poesy.*

To COUNTERVA'IL. *v. a.* [*contra* and *valeo*, Latin.] To be equivalent to; to have equal force or value; to act against with equal power.

In some men there may be found such qualities as are able to *countervail* those exceptions which might be taken against them, and such men's authority is not lightly to be shaken off. *Hooker, b.* ii. *sect.* 7.

And therewithal he fiercely at him flew,
And with important outrage him assail'd;
Who, soon prepar'd to field, his sword forth drew,
And him with equal valour *countervail'd*. *Fairy Queen, b.* ii.

The outward streams, which descend, must be of so much force as to *countervail* all that weight, whereby the ascending side, in every one of these revolutions, does exceed the other; and though this may be effected by making the water-wheels larger, yet then the motion will be so slow, that the screw will not be able to supply the outward streams. *Wilkins's Dedalus.*

We are to compute, that, upon balancing the account, the profit at last will hardly *countervail* the inconveniencies that go along with it. *L'Estrange, Fable* 112.

Counterva'il. *n. s.* [from the verb.]
1. Equal weight; power or value sufficient to obviate any effect or objection.
2. That which has equal weight or value with something else.

Surely, the present pleasure of a sinful act is a poor *countervail* for the bitterness of the review, which begins where the action ends, and lasts for ever. *South's Sermons.*

Countervie'w. *n. s.* [*counter* and *view.*]
1. Opposition; a posture in which two persons front each other.

Mean while, ere thus was sin'd and judg'd on earth,
Within the gates of hell sat sin and death,
In *counterview*. *Milton's Paradise Lost, b.* x. *l.* 231.

2. Contrast; a position in which two dissimilar things illustrate each other.

I have drawn some lines of Linger's character, on purpose to place it in *counterview* or contrast with that of the other company. *Swift's Introduction to Genteel Conversation.*

To Counterwo'rk. *v. a.* [*counter* and *work.*] To counteract; to hinder any effect by contrary operations.

But heav'n's great view is one, and that the whole:
That *counterworks* each folly and caprice;
That disappoints th' effect of ev'ry vice. *Pope's Ess. on Man.*

Co'untess. *n. s.* [*comitissa*, Lat. *comtesse*, French.] The lady of an earl or count.

I take it, she that carries up the train,
Is that old noble lady, the dutchess of Norfolk.
—It is, and all the rest are *countesses*. *Shakes. Henry* VIII.

It is the peculiar happiness of the *countess* of Abingdon to have been so truly loved by you, while she was living; and so gratefully honoured after she was dead. *Dryden.*

Counting-house. *n s.* [*count* and *house.*] The room appropriated by traders to their books and accounts.

Men in trade seldom think of laying out money upon land, 'till their profit has brought them in more than their trade can well employ; and their idle bags, cumbering their *counting-houses*, put them upon emptying them. *Locke.*

Co'untless. *adj.* [from *count.*] Innumerable; without number; not to be reckoned.

Ay, tear for tear, and loving kiss for kiss,
Thy brother Marcus tenders on thy lips:
O, were the sum of these that I should pay
Countless and infinite, yet would I pay them. *Shakespeare.*

But oh, her mind, that orcus which includes
Legions of mischief, *countless* multitudes
Of former curses. *Donne.*

By one *countless* sum of woes opprest,
Hoary with cares, and ignorant of rest,
We find the vital springs relax'd and worn;
Thus, thro' the round of age, to childhood we return. *Prior.*

I see, I cry'd, his woes, a *countless* train;
I see his friends o'erwhelm'd beneath the main. *Pope's Odyss.*

The feats which, shining through the chearful land,
In *countless* numbers, blest Britannia sees. *Thoms. Autumn.*

CO'UNTRY. *n. s.* [*contrée*, Fr. *contrata*, low Latin; supposed to be contracted from *conterrata.*]
1. A tract of land; a region.

Send out more horses, skirre the *country* round,
Hang those that talk of fear. *Shakespeare's Macbeth.*

They require to be examined concerning the descriptions of those *countries* of which they would be informed. *Sprat.*

2. The parts of a region distant from cities or courts; rural parts.

I see them hurry from *country* to town, and then from the town back again into the *country*. *Spectator*, N°. 626.

3. The place which any man inhabits.
4. The place of one's birth; the native soil.

The king set on foot a reformation in the ornaments and advantages of our *country*. *Sprat.*

O, save my *country*, heav'n, shall be your last. *Pope.*

5. The inhabitants of any region.

All the *country*, in a general voice,
Cry'd hate upon him; all their prayers and love
Were set on Hereford. *Shakespeare's Henry* IV. *p.* ii.

Co'untry. *adj.* [This word is scarcely used but in composition.]

1. Ruſtick; rural; villatick.

Cannot a *country* wench know, that having received a ſhilling from one that owes her three, and a ſhilling alſo from another that owes her three, that the remaining debts in each of their hands are equal? *Locke.*

I never meant any other, than that Mr. Trot ſhould confine himſelf to *country* dances. *Spectator*, Nº. 308.

He comes no nearer to a poſitive, clear idea of a poſitive infinite, than the *country* fellow had of the water which was yet to paſs the channel of the river where he ſtood. *Locke.*

Talk but with *country* people, or young people, and you ſhall find that the notions they apply this name to, are ſo odd that nobody can imagine they were taught by a rational man. *Locke.*

The low mechanicks of a *country* town do ſomewhat outdo him. *Locke.*

Come, we'll e'en to our *country* ſeat repair,
The native home of innocence and love. *Norris.*

2. Remote from cities or courts, and of an intereſt oppoſite to that of courts.

A *country* gentleman, learning Latin in the univerſity, removes thence to his manſion-houſe. *Locke.*

3. Peculiar to a region or people.

She laughing the cruel tyrant to ſcorn, ſpake in her *country* language. 2 *Macabees*, vii. 27.

4. Rude; ignorant; untaught.

We make a *country* man dumb, whom we will not allow to ſpeak but by the rules of grammar. *Dryden's Dufreſnoy.*

CO'UNTRYMAN. *n. ſ.* [from *country* and *man*]

1. One born in the ſame country, or tract of ground. *Locke.*

See, who comes here?
My *countryman*; but yet I know him not. *Shakeſp. Macbeth.*

Horace, great bard, ſo fate ordain'd, aroſe;
And bold as were his *countrymen* in fight,
Snatch'd their fair actions from degrading proſe,
And ſet their battles in eternal light. *Prior.*

The Britiſh ſoldiers act with greater vigour under the conduct of one whom they do not conſider only as their leader, but as their *countryman*. *Addiſon on the State of the War.*

2. A ruſtick; one that inhabits the rural parts.

All that have buſineſs to the court, and all *countrymen* coming up to the city, leave their wives in the country. *Graunt.*

3. A farmer; a huſbandman.

A *countryman* took a boar in his corn. *L'Eſtrange.*

CO'UNTY. *n. ſ.* [*comté*, Fr. *comitatus*, Latin.]

1. A ſhire; that is, a circuit or portion of the realm, into which the whole land is divided, for the better government thereof, and the more eaſy adminiſtration of juſtice; ſo that there is no part of the kingdom, but what lieth within ſome *county*. Every *county* is governed by a yearly officer, called a ſheriff, who, among other duties belonging to his office, puts in execution all the commands and judgments of the king's courts. Of theſe counties four are termed county-palatines, as that of Lancaſter, Cheſter, Durham, and Ely. A county-palatine is a juriſdiction of ſo high a nature, that whereas all pleas, touching the life and the maiming of a man, called pleas of the crown, and ordinarily held in the king's name, and which cannot paſs in the name of any other; the chief governors of theſe, by ſpecial charter from the king, ſent out all writs in their own name, and did all things touching juſtice as abſolutely as the prince himſelf in other counties, only acknowledging him their ſuperior and ſovereign. But this power has, by a ſtatute in Henry VIII. his time, been much abridged. Beſides the above counties of both ſorts, there are likewiſe counties corporate, which are certain cities or ancient boroughs upon which our princes have thought good to beſtow extraordinary liberties. Of theſe London is one, York another, the city of Cheſter a third, and Canterbury a fourth. And to theſe may be added many more; as the county of the town of Kingſton upon Hull, the county of the town of Haverfordweſt, and the county of Litchfield. *County* is, in another ſignification, uſed for the county-court which the ſheriff keeps every month within his charge, either by himſelf or his deputy. Of theſe counties, one with another, there are reckoned thirty-ſeven in England, beſides twelve in Wales. *Cowel.*

Diſcharge your powers unto their ſeveral *counties*,
As we will ours. *Shakeſp. Henry* IV. *p.* ii.

He caught his death the laſt *county* ſeſſions, where he would go to ſee juſtice done to a poor widow-woman and her fatherleſs children. *Addiſon's Spectator*, Nº. 517.

2. An earldom.

3. A count; a lord: now wholly obſolete.

The gallant, young, and noble gentleman,
The *county* Paris. *Shakeſpeare's Romeo and Juliet.*

He made Hugh Lupus *county* palatine of Cheſter, and gave that earldom to him and his heirs, to hold the ſame *ita liberè ad gladium ſicut rex tenebat Angliam ad coronam.* *Davies.*

COUPE'E. n. ſ. [French.] A motion in dancing, when one leg is a little bent and ſuſpended from the ground, and with the other a motion is made forwards. *Chambers.*

CO'UPLE. *n. ſ.* [*couple*, Fr. *copula*, Latin.]

1. A chain or tye that holds dogs together.

I'll keep my ſtable-ſtand where
I lodge my wife; I'll go in *couples* with her,
Than when I feel and ſee no further truſt her. *Shakeſp.*

It is in ſome ſort with friends as it is with dogs in *couples*; they ſhould be of the ſame ſize and humour. *L'Eſtrange's Fab.*

2. Two; a brace.

He was taken up by a *couple* of ſhepherds, and by them brought to life again. *Sidney.*

A ſchoolmaſter, who ſhall teach my ſon and your's, I will provide; yea, though the three do coſt me a *couple* of hundred pounds. *Aſcham.*

A piece of chryſtal incloſed a *couple* of drops, which looked like water when they were ſhaken, though perhaps they are nothing but bubbles of air. *Addiſon's Remarks on Italy.*

By adding one to one, we have the complex idea of a *couple*. *Locke.*

3. A male and his female.

So ſhall all the *couples* three,
Ever true in loving be. *Shakeſpeare's Midſum. Night's Dream.*

Oh! alas!
I loſt a *couple*, that 'twixt heaven and earth
Might thus have ſtood, begetting wonder, as
You gracious *couple* do. *Shakeſpeare's Winter's Tale.*

I have read of a feigned commonwealth, where the married *couple* are permitted, before they contract, to ſee one another naked. *Bacon's New Atlantis.*

He ſaid: the careful *couple* join their tears,
And then invoke the gods with pious prayers. *Dryden.*

All ſucceeding generations of men are the progeny of one primitive *couple*. *Bentley's Sermons.*

To CO'UPLE. *v. a.* [*copulo*, Latin]

1. To chain together.

Huntſman, I charge thee, tender well my hounds;
Leech Merriman, the poor cur is imboſt;
And *couple* Clowder with the deep-mouth'd Brach. *Shakeſp.*

2. To join one to another.

What greater ills have the heaven's in ſtore,
To *couple* coming harms with ſorrow paſt. *Sidney, b.* ii.

And wherefoe'er we went, like Juno's ſwans,
Still we went *coupled* and inſeparable. *Shakeſ. As you like it.*

Put the taches into the loops, and *couple* the tent together, that it may be one. *Exod.* xxvi. 11.

They behold your chaſte converſation *coupled* with fear. 1 *Pet.* iii. 2.

Their concernments were ſo *coupled*, that if nature had not, yet their religions would have made them brothers. *South.*

That man makes a mean figure in the eyes of reaſon, who is meaſuring ſyllables and *coupling* rhimes, when he ſhould be mending his own ſoul, and ſecuring his own immortality. *Pope.*

3. To marry; to wed; to join in wedlock.

I ſhall rejoice to ſee you ſo *coupled*, as may be fit both for your honour and your ſatisfaction. *Sidney.*

I am juſt going to aſſiſt with the archbiſhop, in degrading a parſon who *couples* all our beggars, by which I ſhall make one happy man. *Swift.*

To CO'UPLE. *v. n.* To join in embraces.

The fountains of waters there being rare, divers ſorts of beaſts come from ſeveral parts to drink; and ſo being refreſhed, fall to *couple*, and many times with ſeveral kinds. *Bacon's Natural Hiſtory*, Nº. 77.

Thou with thy luſty crew,
Caſt wanton eyes on the daughters of men,
And *coupled* with them, and begot a race. *Milt. Parad. Reg.*

That great variety of brutes in Africa, is by reaſon of the meeting together of brutes of ſeveral ſpecies, and waters, and the promiſcuous *couplings* of males and females of ſeveral ſpecies. *Hale's Origin of Mankind.*

After this alliance,
Let tigers match with hinds, and wolves with ſheep,
And every creature *couple* with his foe. *Dryd. Span. Fryar.*

COUPLE-BEGGAR. *n. ſ.* [*couple* and *beggar.*] One that makes it his buſineſs to marry beggars to each other.

No *couple-beggar* in the land,
E'er join'd ſuch numbers hand in hand. *Swift.*

CO'UPLET. *n. ſ.* [French.]

1. Two verſes; a pair of rhimes.

Then would they caſt away their pipes, and, holding hand in hand, dance by the only cadence of their voices, which they would uſe in ſinging ſome ſhort *couplets*, whereto the one half beginning, the other half ſhould anſwer. *Sidney, b.* i.

Then at the laſt, an only *couplet* fraught
With ſome unmeaning thing they call a thought;
A needleſs Alexandrine ends the ſong,
That, like a wounded ſnake, drags its ſlow length along.
Pope's Eſſay on Criticiſm.

In Pope I cannot read a line,
But with a ſigh I wiſh it mine;
When he can in one *couplet* fix
More ſenſe than I can do in ſix,
It gives me ſuch a jealous fit,
I cry, pox take him and his wit. *Swift.*

2. A pair; as of doves.

Anon, as patient as the female dove,
E're that her golden *couplets* are diſclos'd,
His ſilence will ſit drooping. *Shakeſpeare's Hamlet.*

COURAGE. *n. ſ.* [*courage*, Fr. from *cor*, Latin.] Bravery; active fortitude; ſpirit of enterpriſe.

The king becoming graces,
Devotion, patience, *courage*, fortitude;
I have no reliſh of them. *Shakeſpeare's Macbeth.*

Their diſcipline
Now mingled with their *courage*. *Shakeſpeare's Cymbeline.*

Hope arms their *courage*: from their tow'rs they throw
Their darts with double force, and drive the foe. *Dryden.*

Courage, that grows from conſtitution, very often forſakes a man when he has occaſion for it; and when it is only a kind of inſtinct in the ſoul, it breaks out on all occaſions, without judgment or diſcretion. That *courage* which ariſes from the ſenſe of our duty, and from the fear of offending Him that made us, acts always in an uniform manner, and according to the dictates of right reaſon. *Addiſon's Guardian.*

Nothing but the want of common *courage* was the cauſe of their misfortunes. *Swift.*

COURA'GEOUS. *adj.* [from *courage*.] Brave; daring; bold; enterpriſing; adventurous; hardy; ſtout.

His is very *courageous* mad, about his throwing into the water. *Shakeſpeare's Merry Wives of Windſor.*

And he that is *courageous* among the mighty, ſhall flee away naked in that day. *Amos*, ii. 16.

Let us imitate the *courageous* example of St. Paul, who choſe then to magnify his office when ill men conſpired to leſſen it. *Atterbury's Sermons.*

COURA'GEOUSLY. *adv.* [from *courageous*.] Bravely; ſtoutly; boldly.

The king the next day preſented him battle upon the plain, the fields there being open and champaign: the earl *courageouſly* came down, and joined battle with him. *Bacon's H.* VII.

COURA'GEOUSNESS. *n. ſ.* [from *courageous*.] Bravery; boldneſs; ſpirit; courage.

Nicanor hearing of the manlineſs and the *courageouſneſs* that they had to fight for their country, durſt not try the matter by the ſword. 2 *Mac.* xiv. 18.

COURA'NT. } *n. ſ.* [*courante*, French.] See CORANT.
COU'RANTO. }

1. A nimble dance.

I'll like a maid the better, while I have a tooth in my head: why, he is able to lead her a *couranto*. *Shakeſpeare.*

2. Any thing that ſpreads quick, as a paper of news.

To COURB. *v. n.* [*courber*, French.] To bend; to bow; to ſtoop in ſupplication.

In the fatneſs of theſe purſy times,
Virtue itſelf of vice muſt pardon beg,
Yea, *courb* and woo, for leave to do it good. *Shak. Hamlet.*

CO'URIER. *n. ſ.* [*courier*, French.] A meſſenger ſent in haſte; an expreſs; a runner.

I met a *courier*, one mine ancient friend. *Shakeſp. Timon.*

This thing the wary baſſa well perceiving, for more aſſurance, by ſpeedy *couriers* advertiſed Solyman of the taking of Tauris, and of the enemy's purpoſe, requeſting him with all ſpeed to repair with his army to Tauris. *Knolles's Hiſtory.*

COURSE. *n. ſ.* [*courſe*, Fr. *curſus*, Latin.]

1. Race; career.

And ſome ſhe arms with ſinewy force,
And ſome with ſwiftneſs in the *courſe*. *Cowley.*

2. Paſſage from place to place; progreſs. To this may be referred *the courſe of a river*.

And when we had finiſhed our *courſe* from Tyre, we came to Ptolemais. *Acts* xxi. 7.

A light, by which the Argive ſquadron ſteers
Their ſilent *courſe* to Ilium's well known ſhore. *Denham.*

3. Tilt; act of running in the liſts.

But this hot knight was cooled with a fall, which, at the third *courſe*, he received of Phalantus. *Sidney.*

4. Ground on which a race is run.

5. Track or line in which a ſhip ſails, or any motion is performed.

6. Sail; means by which the courſe is performed.

To the *courſes* we have deviſed ſtudding-ſails, ſprit-ſails, and top-ſails. *Raleigh's Eſſays.*

7. Progreſs from one gradation to another.

If ſhe live long,
And in the end meet the old *courſe* of death,
Women will all turn monſters. *Shakeſpeare's King Lear.*

When the ſtate of the controverſy is plainly determined, it muſt not be altered by another diſputant in the *courſe* of the diſputation. *Watts.*

8. Order of ſucceſſion; as, *every one in his* courſe

If any man ſpeak in an unknown tongue, let it be by two, or at the moſt by three, and that by *courſe*; and let one interpret. 1 *Cor.* xiv. 27.

9. Stated and orderly method.

The duke cannot deny the *courſe* of law. *Shakeſpeare.*

If God, by his revealed declaration, firſt gave rule to any man, he, that will claim by that title, muſt have the ſame poſitive grant of God for his ſucceſſion; for, if it has not directed the *courſe* of its deſcent and conveyance, no body can ſucceed to this title of the firſt Ruler. *Locke.*

10. Series of ſucceſſive and methodical procedure.

The glands did reſolve during her *courſe* of phyſick, and ſhe continueth very well to this day. *Wiſeman's Surgery.*

11. The elements of an art exhibited and explained, in a methodical ſeries Hence our *courſes* of philoſophy, anatomy, chemiſtry, and mathematicks. *Chambers.*

12. Conduct; manner of proceeding.

Grittus perceiving the danger he was in, began to doubt with himſelf what *courſe* were beſt for him to take. *Knolles.*

That worthy deputy finding nothing but a common miſery, took the beſt *courſe* he poſſibly could to eſtabliſh a commonwealth in Ireland. *Davies on Ireland.*

He placed commiſſioners there, who governed it only in a *courſe* of diſcretion, part martial, part civil. *Davies on Ireland.*

Give willingly what I can take by force;
And know, obedience is your ſafeſt *courſe*. *Dryd. Aurengz.*

But if a right *courſe* be taken with children, there will not be ſo much need of common rewards and puniſhments. *Locke.*

'Tis time we ſhould decree
What *courſe* to take. *Addiſon's Cato.*

The ſenate obſerving how, in all contentions, they were forced to yield to the tribunes and people, thought it their wiſeſt *courſe* to give way alſo to time. *Swift.*

13. Method of life; train of actions.

A woman of ſo working a mind, and ſo vehement ſpirits, as it was happy ſhe took a good *courſe*; for otherwiſe it would have been terrible. *Sidney.*

His addiction was to *courſes* vain;
His companies unletter'd, rude and ſhallow;
His hours fill'd up with riots, banquets, ſports. *Shak. H.* V.

Men will ſay,
That beauteous Emma vagrant *courſes* took,
Her father's houſe and civil life forſook. *Prior.*

14. Natural bent; uncontrolled will.

It is beſt to leave nature to her *courſe*, who is the ſovereign phyſician in moſt diſeaſes. *Temple.*

So every ſervant took his *courſe*,
And, bad at firſt, they all grew worſe. *Prior.*

15. Catamenia.

The like happens upon the ſtoppage of women's *courſes*, which, if not ſuddenly looked to, ſets them undoubtedly into a conſumption, dropſy, or ſome other dangerous diſeaſe. *Harvey on Conſumptions.*

16. Orderly ſtructure.

The tongue defileth the whole body, and ſetteth on fire the *courſe* of nature. *James*, iii. 6.

17. [In architecture.] A continued range of ſtones, level or of the ſame height, throughout the whole length of the building, and not interrupted by any aperture. *Harris.*

18. Series of conſequences.

Senſe is of *courſe* annex'd to wealth and power;
No muſe is proof againſt a golden ſhow'r. *Garth.*

With a mind unprepoſſeſſed by doctors and commentators of any ſect, whoſe reaſonings, interpretation and language, which I have been uſed to, will of *courſe* make all chime that way; and make another, and perhaps the genuine meaning of the author, ſeem harſh, ſtrained, and uncouth to me. *Locke.*

19. Number of diſhes ſet on at once upon the table.

Worthy ſir, thou bleed'ſt:
Thy exerciſe hath been too violent
For a ſecond *courſe* of fight. *Shakeſpeare's Coriolanus.*

Then with a ſecond *courſe* the tables load,
And with full chargers offer to the god. *Dryden's Æn.*

You are not to waſh your hands 'till after you have ſent up your ſecond *courſe*. *Swift's Directions to the Cook.*

So quick retires each flying *courſe*, you'd ſwear
Sancho's dread doctor and his wand was there. *Pope.*

20. Regularity; ſettled rule.

Neither ſhall I be ſo far wanting to myſelf, as not to deſire a patent, granted of *courſe* to all uſeful projectors. *Swift.*

21. Empty form.

Men talk as if they believed in God, but they live as if they thought there was none; their vows and promiſes are no more than words of *courſe*. *L'Eſtrange, Fab.* 47.

To COURSE. *v. a.* [from the noun.]

1. To hunt; to purſue.

The big round tears
Cours'd one another down his innocent noſe
In piteous chaſe. *Shakeſpeare's As you like it.*

The king is hunting the deer; I am *courſing* myſelf. *Shakeſpeare's Love's Labour loſt.*

Where's the thane of Cawdor?
We *cours'd* him at the heels, and had a purpoſe
To be his purveyor. *Shakeſpeare's Macbeth.*

2. To purſue with dogs that hunt in view.

It would be tried alſo in flying of hawks, or in *courſing* of a deer, or hart, with greyhounds. *Bacon's Natural Hiſtory.*

I am continually ſtarting hares for you to *courſe*: we were certainly cut out for one another; for my temper quits an amour just where thine takes it up. *Congreve's Old Batchelor.*

3. To put to speed; to force to run.

When they have an appetite
To venery, let them not drink nor eat,
And *course* them oft, and tire them in the heat. *May's Virg.*

To COURSE. *v. n.* To run; to rove about.

Swift as quickfilver it *courses* through
The nat'ral gates and allies of the body. *Shakesp. Hamlet.*

The blood, before cold and settled, left the liver white and pale, which is the badge of pusillanimity and cowardice; but the sherris warms it, and makes it *course* from the inwards to the parts extreme. *Shakespeare's Henry* IV. *p.* ii.

She did so *course* o'er my exteriours, with such a greedy intention, that the appetite of her eye did seem to scorch me up like a burning glass. *Shakespeare's Merry Wives of Windsor.*

Ten brace and more of greyhounds, snowy fair,
And tall as stags, ran loose, and *cours'd* around his chair. *Dry.*

All, at once
Relapsing quick, as quickly re-ascend
And mix, and thwart, extinguish, and renew,
All ether *coursing* in a maze of light. *Thomson's Autumn.*

CO'URSER. *n. s.* [from *course*; *coursier*, French.]

1. A swift horse; a war horse: a word not used in prose.

So, proudly pricketh on his *courser* strong,
And Atin ay him pricks with spurs of shame and wrong.
Fairy Queen, b. ii. *cant.* 5. *stanz.* 38.

Then to his absent guest the king decreed
A pair of *coursers*, born of heav'nly breed;
Who from their nostrils breath'd etherial fire,
Whom Circe stole from her celestial sire. *Dryden's Æn.*

Th' impatient *courser* pants in every vein,
And, pawing, seems to beat the distant plain;
Hills, vales, and floods appear already cross'd,
And, e're he starts, a thousand steps are lost. *Pope.*

2. One who pursues the sport of coursing hares.

A leash is a leathern thong, by which a falconer holds his hawk, or a *courser* leads his greyhound. *Hanmer.*

COURT. *n. s.* [*cour*, Fr. *koert*, Dut. *curtis*, low Latin.]

1. The place where the prince resides; the palace.

Here do you keep a hundred knights and squires,
Men so disorderly, so debauch'd and bold,
That this our *court*, infected with their manners,
Shews like a riotous inn; Epicurism and lust,
Make it more like a tavern, or a brothel,
Than a grac'd palace. *Shakespeare's King Lear.*

It shall be an habitation of dragons, and a *court* for owls.
Isaiah, xxvi. 13.

His care and exactness, that every man should have his due, was such, that you would think he had never seen a *court*: the politeness and civility with which this justice was administred, would convince you he never had lived out of one.
Prior's Dedication.

A suppliant to your royal *court* I come. *Pope's Odyssey.*

2. The hall or chamber where justice is administred.

Are you acquainted with the difference
That holds this present question in the *court*? *Shakespeare.*

St. Paul being brought unto the highest *court* in Athens, to give an account of the doctrine he had preached, concerning Jesus and the resurrection, took occasion to imprint on those magistrates a future state. *Atterbury's Sermons.*

3. Open space before a house.

You must have, before you come to the front, three *courts*: a green *court* plain, with a wall about it; a second *court* of the same, but more garnished, with little turrets, or other embellishments upon the wall; and a third *court*, to square with the front, not to be built but inclosed with a naked wall. *Bacon, Essay* 46.

Suppose it were the king's bedchamber, yet the meanest man in the tragedy must come and dispatch his business, rather than in the lobby or *court* yard (which is fitter for him), for fear the stage should be cleared, and the scenes broken. *Dryd.*

4. A small opening inclosed with houses and paved with broad stones.

5. Persons who compose the retinue of a prince.

Their wisdom was so highly esteemed, that some of them were always employed to follow the *courts* of their kings, to advise them. *Temple.*

6. Persons who are assembled for the administration of justice.

7. Any jurisdiction, military, civil, or ecclesiastical.

If any noise or soldier you perceive
Near to the wall, by some apparent sign
Let us have knowledge at the *court* of guard. *Shak. H.* VI.

The archbishop
Of Canterbury, accompanied with other
Learned and reverend fathers of his order,
Held a late *court* at Dunstable. *Shakespeare's Henry* VIII.

I have at last met with the proceedings of the *court* baron, held in that behalf. *Spectator*, N°. 623.

8. The art of pleasing; the art of insinuation.

Hast thou been never base? Did love ne'er bend
Thy frailer virtue, to betray thy friend?
Flatter me, make thy *court*, and say it did;
Kings in a crowd would have their vices hid. *Dryd. Aureng.*

Some sort of people, placing a great part of their happiness in strong drink, are always forward to make *court* to my young master, by offering that which they love best themselves. *Locke, sect.* 18.

I have been considering why poets have such ill success in making their *court*, since they are allowed to be the greatest and best of all flatterers: the defect is, that they flatter only in print or in writing. *Swift to Gay.*

9. It is often used in composition in most of its senses.

To COURT. *v. a.* [from the noun.]

1. To woo; to solicit a woman to marriage.

Follow a shadow, it flies you;
Seem to fly it, it will pursue:
So *court* a mistress, she denies you;
Let her alone, she will *court* you. *Ben. Johnson's Forest.*

Fir'd with her love, and with ambition led,
The neighb'ring princes *court* her nuptial bed. *Dryden's Æn.*

Alas! Sempronius, wouldst thou talk of love
To Marcia, whilst her father's life's in danger?
Thou might'st as well *court* the pale trembling vestal,
While she beholds the holy flame expiring. *Addison's Cato.*

Ev'n now, when silent scorn is all they gain,
A thousand *court* you, though they *court* in vain. *Pope.*

2. To solicit; to seek.

Their own ease and satisfaction would quickly teach children to *court* commendation, and avoid doing what they found condemned. *Locke on Education, sect.* 59.

3. To flatter; to endeavour to please.

COURT-CHAPLAIN. *n. s.* [*court* and *chaplain.*] One who attends the king to celebrate the holy office.

The maids of honour have been fully convinced by a famous *court-chaplain.* *Swift.*

COURT-DAY. *n. s.* [*court* and *day.*] Day on which justice is solemnly administred.

The judge took time to deliberate, and the next *court-day* he spoke. *Arbuth. and Pope's Mart. Scrib.*

COURT-DRESSER. *n. s.* [*court* and *dresser.*] One that dresses the court, or persons of rank; a flatterer.

There are many ways of fallacy; such arts of giving colours, appearances and resemblances, by this *court-dresser*, fancy. *Locke.*

COURT-FAVOUR. *n. s.* Favours or benefits bestowed by princes.

We part with the blessings of both worlds for pleasures, *court-favours*, and commissions; and at last, when we have sold ourselves to our lusts, we grow sick of our bargain. *L'Est.*

COURT-HAND. *n. s.* [*court* and *hand.*] The hand or manner of writing used in records and judicial proceedings.

He can make obligations, and write *court-hand.* *Sh. H.* VI.

COURT-LADY. *n. s.* [*court* and *lady.*] A lady conversant or employed in court.

The same study, long continued, is as intolerable to them, as the appearing long in the same clothes or fashion is to a *court-lady.* *Locke.*

CO'URTEOUS. *adj.* [*courtois*, French.] Elegant of manners; polite; well-bred; full of acts of respect.

He hath deserved worthily of his country;
And this ascent is not by such easy degrees,
As those who have been supple and *courteous* to the people.
Shakespeare's Coriolanus.

They are one while *courteous*, civil, and obliging; but, within a small time after, are supercilious, sharp, troublesome, fierce, and exceptious. *South's Sermons.*

CO'URTEOUSLY. *adv.* [from *courteous.*] Respectfully; civilly; complaisantly.

He thought them to be gentlemen of much more worth than their habits bewrayed, yet he let them *courteously* pass. *Wotton.*

Whilst Christ was upon earth, he was not only easy of access, he did not only *courteously* receive all that addressed themselves to him, but also did not disdain himself to travel up and down the country. *Calamy's Sermons.*

He arrived at the coast of Alcinous, who, being prevailed upon by the glory of his name, entertained him *courteously*.
Broom's Notes on the Odyssey.

CO'URTEOUSNESS. *n. s.* [from *courteous.*] Civility; complaisance.

CO'URTESAN. } *n. s.* [*cortisana*, low Latin.] A woman of the
CO'URTEZAN. } town; a prostitute; a strumpet.

'Tis a brave night to cool a *courtezan.* *Shakes. King Lear.*

With them there are no stews, no dissolute houses, no *courtesans*, nor any thing of that kind; nay, they wonder, with detestation, at you in Europe, which permit such things. *Bacon's New Atlantis.*

The Corinthian is a column, lasciviously decked like a *courtesan.* *Wotton.*

Charixus, the brother of Sappho, in love with Rhodope the *courtezan*, spent his whole estate upon her. *Addison's Spectator.*

CO'URTESY. *n. s.* [*courtoisie*, Fr. *cortesia*, Italian.]

1. Elegance of manners; civility; complaisance.

Sir, you are very welcome to our house:

It

It muſt appear in other ways than words,
Therefore I ſcant this breathing *courteſy*. *Shak. Merch. of Ven.*

Who have ſeen his eſtate, his hoſpitality, his *courteſy* to ſtrangers. *Peacham.*

He, who was compounded of all the elements of affability and *courteſy* towards all kind of people, brought himſelf to a habit of neglect, and even of rudeneſs, towards the queen. *Clarendon.*

So gentle of condition was he known,
That through the court his *courteſy* was blown. *Dryd. Fab.*

2. An act of civility or reſpect.

Fair ſir, you ſpit on me laſt Wedneſday;
You ſpurn'd me ſuch a day; another time
You call'd me dog; and for theſe *courteſies*,
I'll lend you thus much money. *Shakeſ. Merchant of Venice.*

Repoſe you there, while I to the hard houſe
Return, and force their ſcanted *courteſy*. *Shakeſp. K. Lear.*

When I was laſt at Exeter,
The mayor in *courteſy* ſhew'd me the caſtle. *Shakeſ. R. III.*

Sound all the lofty inſtruments of war,
And by that muſick let us all embrace;
For heav'n to earth ſome of us never ſhall
A ſecond time do ſuch a *courteſy*. *Shakeſpeare's Henry IV.*

Other ſtates, aſſuredly, cannot be juſtly accuſed for not ſtaying for the firſt blow; or for not accepting Polyphemus's *courteſy*, to be the laſt that ſhall be eaten up. *Bacon.*

3. The reverence made by women.

Some country girl, ſcarce to a *court'ſy* bred,
Would I much rather than Cornelia wed;
If, ſupercilious, haughty, proud and vain,
She brought her father's triumphs in her train. *Dryd. Juven.*

The poor creature was as full of *courteſies* as if I had been her godmother: the truth on't is, I endeavoured to make her look ſomething Chriſtian-like. *Congreve's Old Batchelor.*

4. A tenure, not of right, but by the favour of others; as, *to hold upon* courteſy.

5. Courtesy *of England.* A tenure by which, if a man marry an inheritance, that is, a woman ſeiſed of land, and getteth a child of her that comes alive into the world, though both the child and his wife die forthwith; yet, if ſhe were in poſſeſſion, ſhall he keep the land during his life, and is called tenant *per legem Angliæ*, or by the *courteſy* of England. *Cowel.*

To Co'urtesy. *v. n.* [from the noun.]

1. To perform an act of reverence.

Toby approaches, and *court'ſies* there to me. *Shakeſpeare.*

The petty traffickers,
That *court'ſy* to them, do them reverence. *Shakeſpeare.*

2. To make a reverence in the manner of ladies.

If I ſhould meet her in my way,
We hardly *court'ſy* to each other. *Prior.*

Co'urtier. *n. ſ.* [from *court.*]

1. One that frequents or attends the courts of princes.

He hath been a *courtier*, he ſwears.———
If any man doubts that, let him put me to my purgation. I have trod a meaſure; I have flattered a lady; I have been politick with my friend, ſmooth with mine enemy; I have undone three taylors; I have had four quarrels, and like to have fought one. *Shakeſpeare's As you like it.*

You are a flattering boy; now, I ſee you'll be a *courtier*. *Shakeſpeare's Merry Wives of Windſor.*

You know I am no *courtier*, nor verſed in ſtate-affairs. *Bac.*

The principal figure in a picture, is like a king among his *courtiers*, who ought to dim the luſtre of all his attendants. *Dryden's Dufreſnoy.*

2. One that courts or ſolicits the favour of another.

What
Made thee, all honour'd honeſt Roman Brutus,
With the arm'd reſt, *courtiers* of beauteous freedom,
To drench the capitol? *Shakeſ. Anthony and Cleopatra.*

There was not among all our princes a greater *courtier* of the people than Richard the IIId. not out of fear, but wiſdom. *Suckling.*

Co'urtine. See CURTAIN.

Co'urtlike. *adj.* [*court* and *like.*] Elegant; polite.

Our Engliſh tongue is, I will not ſay as ſacred as the Hebrew, or as learned as the Greek, but as fluent as the Latin, as courteous as the Spaniſh, as *courtlike* as the French, and as amorous as the Italian. *Camden's Remains.*

Co'urtliness. *n. ſ.* [from *courtly.*] Elegance of manners; grace of mien; complaiſance; civility.

Co'urtly. *adj.* [from *court.*] Relating or retaining to the court; elegant; ſoft; flattering.

In our own time, (excuſe ſome *courtly* ſtrains)
No whiter page than Addiſon's remains. *Pope's Ep. of Hor.*

Co'urtly. *adv.* In the manner of courts; elegantly.

They can produce nothing ſo *courtly* writ, or which expreſſes ſo much the converſation of a gentleman, as ſir John Suckling. *Dryden on Dramatick Poetry.*

Co'urtship. *n. ſ.* [from *court.*]

1. The act of ſoliciting favour.

He paid his *courtſhip* with the croud,
As far as modeſt pride allow'd. *Swift.*

2. The ſolicitation of a woman to marriage.

Be merry, and employ your chiefeſt thoughts
To *courtſhip*, and ſuch fair oſtents of love,
As ſhall conveniently become you there. *Shak. Merch. of Ven.*

In tedious *courtſhip* we declare our pain,
And e're we kindneſs find, firſt meet diſdain. *Dryd. Ind. Emp.*

Every man in the time of *courtſhip*, and in the firſt entrance of marriage, puts on a behaviour like my correſpondent's holiday ſuit. *Addiſon's Guardian*, N°. 113.

3. Civility; elegance of manners.

My *courtſhip* to an univerſity,
My modeſty I give to ſoldiers bare;
My patience to a gameſter's ſhare. *Donne.*

CO'USIN. *n. ſ.* [*couſin*, Fr. *conſanguineus*, Lat.] Any one collaterally related more remotely than a brother or ſiſter.

Macbeth unſeam'd him from the nape to th' chops,
And fix'd his head upon our battlements.
—Oh, valiant *couſin!* worthy gentleman. *Shakeſ. Macbeth.*

Tybalt, my *couſin!* O, my brother's child!
Unhappy ſight! alas, the blood is ſpill'd
Of my dear kinſman. *Shakeſpeare's Romeo and Juliet.*

Thou art, great lord, my father's ſiſter's ſon,
And *couſin* german to great Priam's ſeed. *Sh. Troil. and Creſſ.*

2. A title given by the king to a nobleman, particularly to thoſe of the council.

COW. *n. ſ.* [in the plural, anciently *kine*, or *keen*, now commonly *cows*; cu, Sax. *koe*, Dutch.] The female of the bull; the horned animal with cloven feet, kept for her milk and calves.

We ſee that the horns of oxen and *cows*, for the moſt part, are larger than the bulls; which is cauſed by abundance of moiſture, which in the horns of the bull faileth. *Bacon.*

After the fever is diminiſhed, aſſes and goats milk may be neceſſary; yea, a diet of *cows* milk alone. *Wiſeman's Surgery.*

Then, leaving in the fields his grazing *cows*,
He ſought himſelf ſome hoſpitable houſe:
Good Creton entertain'd his godlike gueſt. *Dryden's Fables.*

To Cow. *v. a.* [from *coward*, by contraction.] To depreſs with fear; to oppreſs with habitual timidity.

Macduff was from his mother's womb
Untimely ripp'd.——
——Accurſed be that tongue that tells me ſo;
For it hath *cow'd* my better part of man. *Shakeſp. Macbeth.*

By reaſon of their frequent revolts they have drawn upon themſelves the preſſures of war ſo often, that it ſeems to have ſomewhat *cowed* their ſpirits. *Howel's Vocal Foreſt.*

For when men by their wives are *cow'd*,
Their horns of courſe are underſtood. *Hudibras*, *p.* ii. *c.* 2.

Cow-herd. *n. ſ.* [*cow* and hyrd, Sax. a keeper.] One whoſe occupation is to tend cows.

Cow-house. *n. ſ.* [*cow* and *houſe.*] The houſe in which kine are kept.

You muſt houſe your milch-cows, that you give hay to in your *cow-houſe* all night. *Mortimer.*

Cow-leech. *n. ſ.* [*cow* and *leech.*] One who profeſſes to cure diſtempered cows.

To Cow-leech. *v. n.* To profeſs to cure cows.

Though there are many pretenders to the art of farriering and *cow-leeching*, yet many of them are very ignorant, eſpecially in the country. *Mortimer's Husbandry.*

Cow-weed. *n. ſ.* [*cow* and *weed.*] A ſpecies of chervil; which ſee.

Cow-wheat. *n. ſ.* [from *cow* and *wheat.*]

The leaves of this plant grow oppoſite by pairs: the flower conſiſts of one leaf; is of an anomalous figure, and divided into two lips, the uppermoſt of which has a ſpur, but the under one is intire: the fruit is round, and divided into two cells, containing ſeeds reſembling grains of wheat. This plant is very common in woods, and ſhady places. *Miller.*

CO'WARD. *n. ſ.* [*couard*, Fr. of uncertain derivation.]

1. A poltron; a wretch whoſe predominant paſſion is fear.

Pyrocles did ſuch wonders, beyond belief, as was able to lead Muſidorus to courage, though he had been born a *coward*. *Sidney*, *b.* ii.

There was a ſoldier that vaunted, before Julius Cæſar, of the hurts he had received in his face. Cæſar knowing him to be but a *coward*, told him, You were beſt take heed, next time you run away, how you look back *Bacon*, *Apophth.* 188.

Some are brave one day, and *cowards* another, as great captains have often told me, from their own experience and obſervation. *Temple.*

A *coward* does not always eſcape with diſgrace, but ſometimes alſo he loſes his life. *South.*

What can ennoble ſots, and ſlaves, and *cowards?*
Alas! not all the blood of all the Howards. *Pope.*

Tremble ye not, Oh friends! and *cowards* fly,
Doom'd by the ſtern Telemachus to die! *Pope's Odyſſey.*

2. It is ſometimes uſed in the manner of an adjective.

Having more man than wit about me, I drew;
And rais'd the houſe with loud and *coward* cries. *Shakeſpeare.*

Invading fears repel my *coward* joy,
And ills foreſeen the preſent bliſs deſtroy. *Prior.*

Co'wardice.

Co'wardice. *n. ſ.* [from *coward.*] Fear; habitual timidity; puſillanimity; want of courage.

> Certes, ſir knight, ye been too much to blame,
> Thus for to blot the honour of the dead;
> And with foul *cowardice* his carcaſe ſhame,
> Whoſe living hands immortaliz'd his name. *Fairy Queen.*

Gallant and fearleſs courage will turn into a native and heroick valour, and make them hate the *cowardice* of doing wrong *Milton on Education.*

> None was diſgrac'd; for falling is no ſhame,
> And *cowardice* alone is loſs of fame;
> The vent'rous knight is from the ſaddle thrown,
> But 'tis the fault of fortune, not his own. *Dryden's Fables.*

This great, this holy, this terrible Being, is preſent to all our affections; ſees every treacherous inclination of our heart to deſert his ſervice; and treaſures up, againſt the day of his wrath, the ſecret *cowardice* which deters us from aſſerting his cauſe, which prevails on us to compliment the vices of the great, to applaud the libertine, and laugh with the prophane. *Rogers, Sermon* 4.

Co'wardliness. *n. ſ.* [from *cowardly.*] Timidity; cowardice.

Co'wardly. *adj.* [from *coward.*]

1. Fearful; timorous; puſillanimous.

An Egyptian ſoothſayer made Antonius believe that his genius, otherwiſe brave and confident, was in the preſence of Octavius poor and *cowardly. Bacon's Natural Hiſtory,* N°. 940.

Let all ſuch as can enlarge their conſciences like hell, and ſtyle a *cowardly* ſilence in Chriſt's cauſe diſcretion, know, that Chriſt will one day ſcorn them. *South's Sermons.*

2. Mean; befitting a coward.

> I do find it *cowardly*, and vile,
> For fear of what might fall, ſo to prevent
> The time of life. *Shakeſpeare's Julius Cæſar.*

Co'wardly. *adv.* In the manner of a coward; meanly; vilely.

He ſharply reproved them as men of no courage, who had moſt *cowardly* turned their backs upon their enemies. *Knolles.*

Co'wardship. *n. ſ.* [from *coward.*] The character or qualities of a coward; meanneſs: a word not now in uſe.

A very diſhoneſt paltry boy, and more a coward than a hare: his diſhoneſty appears in leaving his friend here in neceſſity, and denying him; and for his *cowardſhip*, aſk Fabian. *Shakeſpeare's Twelfth Night.*

To Co'wer. *v. n.* [*cwrrian*, Welſh; *courber*, Fr. or perhaps borrowed from the manner in which a *cow* ſinks on her knees.] To ſink by bending the knees; to ſtoop; to ſhrink.

Let the pail be put over the man's head above water, and then he *cower* down, and the pail be preſſed down with him. *Bacon's Natural Hiſtory,* N°. 155.

> The ſplitting rocks *cower'd* in the ſinking ſands,
> And would not daſh me with their ragged ſides. *Shakeſpeare.*
> As thus he ſpake, each bird and beaſt beheld,
> Approaching two and two; theſe *cow'ring* low
> With blandiſhment, each bird ſtoop'd on his wing. *Milton.*
> Our dame ſits *cow'ring* o'er a kitchen fire;
> I draw freſh air, and nature's works admire. *Dryden's Fables.*

Co'wish. *adj.* [from *To cow*, to awe.] Timorous; fearful; mean; puſillanimous; cowardly.

> It is the *cowiſh* terrour of his ſpirit,
> That dares not undertake: he'll not feel wrongs
> Which tie him to an anſwer. *Shakeſpeare's King Lear.*

Co'wkeeper. *n. ſ.* [*cow* and *keeper.*] One whoſe buſineſs is to keep cows.

The terms *cowkeeper* and hogherd, are not to be uſed in our poetry; but there are no finer words in the Greek language. *Broom's Notes on the Odyſſey.*

COWL. *n. ſ.* [cuȝle, Saxon; *cucullus*, Latin.]

1. A monk's hood.

You may imagine that Francis Cornfield did ſcratch his elbow, when he had ſweetly invented, to ſignify his name, ſaint Francis with his friery *cowl* in a cornfield. *Camden's Rem.*

> What differ more, you cry, than crown and *cowl?*
> I'll tell you, friend, a wiſe man and a fool. *Pope's Eſſays.*

2. A veſſel in which water is carried on a pole between two.

Cowl-staff. *n. ſ.* [*cowl* and *ſtaff.*] The ſtaff on which a veſſel is ſupported between two men.

> Mounting him upon a *cowl-ſtaff*,
> Which (toſſing him ſomething high)
> He apprehended to be Pegaſus. *Suckling.*

The way by a *cowl-ſtaff* is ſafer: the ſtaff muſt have a bunch in the middle, ſomewhat wedge-like, and covered with a ſoft bolſter. *Wiſeman.*

Co'wslip. *n. ſ.* [cuſlippe, Sax. as ſome think, from their reſemblance of ſcent to the breath of a cow; perhaps from growing much in paſture-grounds, and often meeting the *cow's lip.*]

Cowſlip is alſo called pagil, grows wild in the meadows, and is a ſpecies of Primrose, which ſee. *Miller.*

He might as well ſay, that a *cowſlip* is as white as a lily. *Sidney.*

> Where the bee ſucks, there ſuck I;
> In a *cowſlip's* bell I lie. *Shakeſpeare's Tempeſt.*
> Thy little ſons
> Permit to range the paſtures: gladly they
> Will mow the *cowſlip* poſies, faintly ſweet. *Philips.*

Cows-lungwort. *n. ſ.* See Mullen, of which it is a ſpecies. *Miller.*

Co'xcomb. *n. ſ.* [*cock* and *comb*, corrupted from *cock's comb.*]

1. The top of the head.

As the cockney did to the eels, when ſhe put them i' the paſty alive; ſhe rapt them o' th' *coxcombs* with a ſtick, and cried down, wantons, down. *Shakeſpeare's King Lear.*

2. The comb reſembling that of a cock, which licenſed fools wore formerly in their caps.

There take my *coxcomb*: why, this fellow has baniſhed two of his daughters, and did the third a bleſſing againſt his will: if thou follow him, thou muſt needs wear my *coxcomb. Shakeſ.*

3. A fop; a ſuperficial pretender to knowledge or accompliſhments.

> I ſent to her,
> By this ſame *coxcomb* that we have i' th' wind,
> Tokens and letters, which ſhe did reſend. *Shakeſpeare.*
> I ſcorn, quoth ſhe, thou *coxcomb* ſilly,
> Quarter or council from a foe. *Hudibras, p.* i. *cant.* iii.

It is a vanity common in the world, for every pretending *coxcomb* to make himſelf one of the party ſtill with his betters. *L'Eſtrange, Fable* 135.

They overflowed with ſmart repartees, and were only diſtinguiſhed from the intended wits by being called *coxcombs*, though they deſerved not ſo ſcandalous a name. *Dryd. Dufreſ.*

> Some are bewilder'd in the maze of ſchools,
> And ſome made *coxcombs*, nature meant but fools. *Pope.*

Coxco'mical. *adj.* [from *coxcomb.*] Foppiſh; conceited: a low word unworthy of uſe.

Becauſe, as he was a very natural writer, and they were without prejudice, without prepoſſeſſion, without affectation, and without the influence of *coxcomical*, ſenſeleſs cabal, they were at liberty to receive the impreſſions which things naturally made on their minds. *Dennis.*

COY. *adj.* [*coi*, French, from *quietus*, Latin.]

1. Modeſt; decent.

> Jaſon is as *coy* as is a maide;
> He loked piteouſly, but naught he ſaid. *Chaucer.*

2. Reſerved; not acceſſible; not eaſily condeſcending to familiarity.

> And vain delight ſhe ſaw he light did paſs,
> A foe of folly and immodeſt toy;
> Still ſolemn ſad, or ſtill diſdainful *coy.* *Fairy Queen, b.* ii.
> Like Phœbus ſung the no leſs am'rous boy;
> Like Daphne ſhe, as lovely and as *coy.* *Waller.*

At this ſeaſon every ſmile of the ſun, like the ſmile of a *coy* lady, is as dear as it is uncommon. *Pope.*

To Coy. *v. n.* [from the adjective.]

1. To behave with reſerve; to reject familiarity.

> What, *coying* it again!
> No more; but make me happy to my guſt,
> That is, without your ſtruggling. *Dryden's King Arthur.*
> Retire! I beg you, leave me.——
> ——Thus to *coy* it!
> With one who knows you too! *Rowe's Jane Shore.*

2. To make difficulty; not to condeſcend willingly.

> If he *coy'd*
> To hear Cominius ſpeak, I'll keep at home. *Shak. Coriolan.*

Co'yly. *adv.* [from *coy.*] With reſerve; with diſinclination to familiarity.

> This ſaid; his hand he *coyly* ſnatcht away
> From forth Antinous' hand. *Chapman's Odyſſey, b.* ii.

Co'yness. *n. ſ.* [from *coy.*] Reſerve; unwillingneſs to become familiar.

When the ſun hath warmed the earth and water, three or four male carps will follow a female; and ſhe putting on a ſeeming *coyneſs*, they force her through weeds and flags. *Walton.*

> When the kind nymph would *coyneſs* feign,
> And hides but to be found again. *Dryden.*

Co'ystrel. *n. ſ.* A ſpecies of degenerate hawk.

> One they might truſt, their common wrongs to wreak:
> The muſquet and the *coyſtrel* were too weak,
> Too fierce the falcon. *Dryden's Hind and Panther.*

Coz. *n. ſ.* A cant or familiar word, contracted from *couſin.*

> Be merry, *coz*; ſince ſudden ſorrow
> Serves to ſay thus, ſome good thing comes to-morrow. *Shak.*

To CO'ZEN. *v. a.* [*To coſe* is in the old Scotch dialect, as *Junius* obſerves, to chop or change; whence *cozen*, to cheat, becauſe in ſuch traffick there is commonly fraud.] To cheat; to trick; to defraud.

Let the queen pay never ſo fully, let the muſter-maſter view them never ſo diligently, let the deputy or general look to them never ſo exactly, yet they can *cozen* them all. *Spenſer.*

Goring loved no man ſo well but that he would *cozen* him, and then expoſe him to publick mirth for having been *cozen'd.* *Clarendon, b.* viii.

He that ſuffers a government to be abuſed by careleſſneſs or neglect, does the ſame thing with him that maliciouſly and corruptly ſets himſelf to *cozen* it. *L'Eſtrange, Fab.* 21. *Reflect.*

You

You are not obliged to a literal belief of what the poet ſays; but you are pleaſed with the image, without being *cozened* by the fiction. *Dryden.*

What if I pleaſe to lengthen out his date
A day, and take a pride to *cozen* fate. *Dryden's Aurengzebe.*

Children may be *cozened* into a knowledge of the letters, and be taught to read, without perceiving it to be any thing but a ſport. *Locke on Education.*

Co'zenage. *n. ſ.* [from *cozen.*] Fraud; deceit; artifice; fallacy; trick; cheat.

Wiſdom without honeſty is meer craft and *cozenage*, and therefore the reputation of honeſty muſt firſt be gotten, which cannot be but by living well: a good life is a main argument. *Ben. Johnſon's Diſcoveries.*

There's no ſuch thing as that we beauty call,
It is meer *cozenage* all;
For though ſome long ago
Lik'd certain colours mingl'd ſo and ſo,
That doth not tie me now from chuſing new. *Suckling.*

Imaginary appearances offer themſelves to our impatient minds, which entertain theſe counterfeits without the leaſt ſuſpicion of their *cozenage*. *Glanv. Scepſ. c.* 14.

Strange *coz'nage!* none would live paſt years again,
Yet all hope pleaſure in what yet remain;
And from the dregs of life, think to receive
What the firſt ſprightly running could not give. *Dryd. Aur.*

But all theſe are trifles, if we conſider the fraud and *cozenage* of trading men and ſhopkeepers. *Swift.*

Co'zener. *n. ſ.* [from *cozen.*] A cheater; a defrauder.

Indeed, ſir, there are *cozeners* abroad, and therefore it behoves men to be wary. *Shakeſpeare's Winter's Tale.*

CRAB. *n. ſ.* [crabba, Sax. *krabbe*, Dutch.]

1. A cruſtaceous fiſh.

Thoſe that caſt their ſhell are, the lobſter, the *crab*, the crawfiſh, the hodmandod or dodman, and the tortoiſe. The old ſhells are never found; ſo as it is like they ſcale off and crumble away by degrees. *Bacon's Nat. Hiſt.*

The fox catches *crab* fiſh with his tail, which Olaus Magnus ſaith he himſelf was an eye-witneſs of. *Derham.*

2. A wild apple; the tree that bears a wild apple.

Noble ſtock
Was graft with *crab*-tree ſlip, whoſe fruit thou art. *Shakeſp.*

Fetch me a dozen *crab*-tree ſtaves, and ſtrong ones: theſe are but ſwitches. *Shakeſpeare's Henry* VIII.

When roaſted *crabs* hiſs in the bowl,
Then nightly ſings the ſtaring owl. *Shakeſpeare.*

Imagine you ſee him laid forth, newly ſlain, upon a bier of *crab*-tree and oaken rods. *Peacham on Drawing.*

Let him tell why a graft, taking nouriſhment from a *crab* ſtock, ſhall have a fruit more noble than its nurſe and parent. *Taylor's Rule of Living Holy.*

3. A peeviſh moroſe perſon.

4. A wooden engine with three claws for launching of ſhips, or heaving them into the dock. *Philips.*

5. The ſign in the zodiack.

Then parts the Twins and *Crab*, the Dog divides,
And Argo's keel, that broke the frothy tides. *Creech's Manil.*

Crab. *adj.* It is uſed by way of contempt for any ſour or degenerate fruit; as, *a* crab *cherry*, *a* crab *plum.*

Better gleanings their worn ſoil can boaſt,
Than the *crab* vintage of the neighb'ring coaſt. *Dryden.*

Cra'bbed. *adj.* [from *crab.*]

1. Peeviſh; moroſe; cynical; ſour.

A man of years, yet freſh, as mote appear,
Of ſwarth complexion, and of *crabbed* hue,
That him full of melancholy did ſhew. *Fairy Queen, b.* ii.

O, ſhe is
Ten times more gentle, than her father's *crabbed*;
And he's compos'd of harſhneſs. *Shakeſpeare's Tempeſt.*

2. Harſh; unpleaſing.

That was when
Three *crabbed* months had ſour'd themſelves to death,
'Ere I could make thee open thy white hand,
And clepe thyſelf my love. *Shakeſpeare's Winter's Tale.*

How charming is divine philoſophy!
Not harſh and *crabbed*, as dull fools ſuppoſe,
But muſical as is Apollo's lute,
And a perpetual feaſt of nectar'd ſweets,
Where no crude ſurfeit reigns. *Milton.*

Lucretius had choſen a ſubject naturally *crabbed*. *Dryden.*

3. Difficult; perplexing.

Beſide, he was a ſhrewd philoſopher,
And had read ev'ry text and gloſs over;
Whate'er the *crabbed'ſt* author hath,
He underſtood b' implicit faith. *Hudibras, p.* i. *cant.* 1.

Your *crabbed* rogues that read Lucretius,
Are againſt gods, you know, and teach us,
The god makes not the poet. *Prior.*

Cra'bbedly. *adv.* [from *crabbed.*] Peeviſhly.

Cra'bbedness. *n. ſ.* [from *crabbed.*]

1. Sourneſs of taſte.

2. Sourneſs of countenance; aſperity of manners.

3. Difficulty.

Cra'ber. *n. ſ.*

The poor fiſh have enemies enough, beſide ſuch unnatural fiſhermen; as otters, the cormorant, and the *craber*, which ſome call the water-rat. *Walton's Angler.*

Crabs-eyes. *n. ſ.* They are whitiſh bodies, from the bigneſs of a pea to that of the largeſt horſe-bean, rounded on one ſide and depreſſed on the other, heavy, moderately hard, and without ſmell. They are not the eyes of any creature, nor do they belong to the crab; but are produced by the common crawfiſh: the large ſea crawfiſh alſo affords them; and the ſtones are bred in two ſeparate bags, one on each ſide of the ſtomach. In July, and part of June and Auguſt, when the creature caſts its ſhell, the ſtones are not found in their places. We have them from Holland, Muſcovy, Poland, Denmark, Sweden, and many other places. They are alkaline, abſorbent, and in ſome degree diuretick. *Hill's Mat. Med.*

Several perſons had, in vain, endeavoured to ſtore themſelves with *crabs-eyes*. *Boyle's Experiments.*

CRACK. *n. ſ.* [*kraeck*, Dutch.]

1. A ſudden diſruption, by which the parts are ſeparated but a little way from each other.

2. The chink, fiſſure, or vacuity made by diſruption; a narrow breach.

Contuſions, when great, do uſually produce a fiſſure or *crack* of the ſkull, either in the ſame part where the blow was inflicted, or in the contrary part. *Wiſeman.*

At length it would crack in many places; and thoſe *cracks*, as they dilated, would appear of a pretty good, but yet obſcure and dark ſky-colour. *Newton's Opt.*

3. The ſound of any body burſting or falling.

If I ſay ſooth, I muſt report, they were
As cannons overcharg'd with double *cracks. Shakeſ. Macbeth.*

Now day appears, and with the day the king,
Whoſe early care had robb'd him of his reſt:
Far off the *cracks* of falling houſes ring,
And ſhrieks of ſubjects pierce his tender breaſt. *Dryden.*

4. Any ſudden and quick ſound.

A fourth?—ſtart eye!
What will the line ſtretch out to th' *crack* of doom? *Shakeſ.*

Vulcan was employed in hammering out thunderbolts, that every now and then flew up from the anvil with dreadful *cracks* and flaſhes. *Addiſon's Guardian*, N°. 103.

5. Any breach, injury, or diminution; a flaw.

And let us, Paladour, though now our voices
Have got the manniſh *crack*, ſing him to th' ground. *Shakeſ.*

I cannot
Believe this *crack* to be in my dread miſtreſs,
So ſovereignly being honourable. *Shakeſp. Winter's Tale.*

6. Crazineſs of intellect.

7. A man crazed.

I have invented projects for raiſing millions, without burthening the ſubject; but cannot get the parliament to liſten to me, who look upon me as a *crack* and a projector. *Addiſ. Spect.*

8. A whore; in low language.

9. A boaſt.

Leaſings, backbitings, and vain-glorious *cracks*,
All thoſe againſt that fort did bend their batteries. *Spenſer.*

10. A boaſter. This is only in low phraſe.

To Crack. *v. a.* [*kraecken*, Dutch.]

1. To break into chinks; to divide the parts a little from each other.

Look to your pipes, and cover them with freſh and warm litter out of the ſtable, a good thickneſs, leſt the froſts *crack* them. *Mortimer.*

2. To break; to ſplit.

O, madam, my heart is *crack'd*, it's *crack'd*. *Shakeſpeare.*

Thou wilt quarrel with a man for *cracking* nuts, having no other reaſon but becauſe thou haſt haſel-eyes. *Sh. Rom. and Jul.*

Should ſome wild fig-tree take her native bent,
And heave below the gaudy monument,
Would *crack* the marble titles, and diſperſe
The characters of all the lying verſe. *Dryd. Juv. Sat.* 10.

Or as a lute, which in moiſt weather rings
Her knell alone, by *cracking* of her ſtrings. *Donne.*

Honour is like that glaſſy bubble,
That finds philoſophers ſuch trouble;
Whoſe leaſt part *crack'd*, the whole does fly,
And wits are crack'd to find out why. *Hudibras, p.* ii. *cant.* 2.

3. To do any thing with quickneſs or ſmartneſs.

Sir Balaam now, he lives like other folks;
He takes his chirping pint, he *cracks* his jokes. *Pope's Epiſt.*

4. To break or deſtroy any thing.

You'll *crack* a quart together! Ha, will you not? *Shakeſp.*

Love cools, friendſhip falls off, brothers divide: in cities, mutinies; in countries, diſcord; in palaces, treaſon; and the bond *cracked* 'twixt ſon and father. *Shakeſpeare's King Lear.*

5. To craze; to weaken the intellect.

I was ever of opinion, that the philoſophers ſtone, and an holy war, were but the rendezvous of *cracked* brains, that wore their feather in their heads. *Bacon's Holy War.*

He thought none poets 'till their brains were *crackt*. *Roſc.*

To Crack. *v. n.*

1. To burst; to open in chinks.

By misfortune it *cracked* in the cooling, whereby we were reduced to make use of one part, which was straight and intire. *Boyle's Spring of the Air.*

2. To fall to ruin.

The credit not only of banks, but of exchequers, *cracks* when little comes in, and much goes out. *Dryd. Dedic. Æn.*

3. To utter a loud and sudden sound.

I will board her, though she chide as loud
As thunder, when the clouds in autumn *crack*. *Shakespeare.*

4. To boast: with *of.*

To look like her, are chimney-sweepers black.
And since her time are colliers counted bright.
And Ethiops *of* their sweet complexion *crack*.
Dark needs no candles now, for dark is light. *Shakes.*

Crack-brained. *adj.* [*crack* and *brained.*] Crazy; without right reason.

We have sent you an answer to the ill-grounded sophisms of those *crack-brained* fellows. *Arbuth. and Pope's Mart. Scrib.*

Crack-hemp. *n. s.* [*crack* and *hemp.*] A wretch fated to the gallows; a crack-rope. *Furcifer.*

Come hither, *crack-hemp.*
———I hope I may chuse, sir.
—Come hither, you rogue:
What, have you forgot me? *Shakes. Taming of the Shrew.*

Crack-rope. *n. s.* [from *crack* and *rope.*] A fellow that deserves hanging.

Cra'cker. *n. s.* [from *crack.*]

1. A noisy boasting fellow.

What *cracker* is this same that deafs our ears
With this abundance of superfluous breath. *Shak. K. John.*

2. A quantity of gunpowder confined so as to burst with great noise.

The bladder, at its breaking, gave a great report, almost like a *cracker*. *Boyle's Spring of the Air.*

And when, for furious haste to run,
They durst not stay to fire a gun,
Have don't with bonfires, and at home
Made squibs and *crackers* overcome. *Hudibras, p.* iii. *c.* 3.
Then furious he begins his march,
Drives rattling o'er a brazen arch,
With squibs and *crackers* arm'd, to throw
Among the trembling crowd below. *Swift.*

To Cra'ckle. *v. n.* [from *crack.*] To make slight cracks; to make small and frequent noises; to decrepitate.

All these motions, which we saw,
Are but as ice, which *crackles* at a thaw. *Donne.*
I fear to try new love,
As boys to venture on the unknown ice
That *crackles* underneath them. *Dryden.*
Caught her dishevell'd hair and rich attire;
Her crown and jewels *crackled* in the fire. *Dryden's. Æneid.*

Marrow is a specifick in that scurvy which occasions a *crackling* of the bones; in which case marrow performs its natural function of moistening them. *Arbuthnot on Aliments.*

Cra'cknel. *n. s.* [from *crack.*] A hard brittle cake.

Albee my love he seek with daily sute,
His clownish gifts and curtesies I disdain,
His kids, his *cracknels*, and his early fruit. *Spenser's Past.*
Pay tributary *cracknels*, which he sells;
And with our offerings, help to raise his vails. *Dryd. Juv.*

CRA'DLE. *n. s.* [cnabel, Saxon.]

1. A moveable bed, on which children or sick persons are agitated with a smooth and equal motion, to make them sleep.

She had indeed, sir, a son for her *cradle*, e're she had a husband for her bed. *Shakespeare's King Lear.*

No jutting frieze,
Buttrice, nor coigne of vantage, but this bird,
Hath made his pendant bed and procreant *cradle*. *Shakesp.*
His birth, perhaps, some paltry village hides,
And sets his *cradle* out of fortune's way. *Dryd. Ann. Mirab.*

A child knows his nurse and his *cradle*, and by degrees the playthings of a little more advanced age. *Locke.*

The *cradle* and the tomb, alas! so nigh:
To live, is scarce distinguish'd from to die. *Prior.*
Me let the tender office long engage,
To rock the *cradle* of reposing age;
With lenient arts extend a mother's breath,
Make languor smile, and smooth the bed of death. *Pope.*

2. It is used for infancy, or the first part of life.

He knew them to be inclined altogether to war, and therefore wholly trained them up, even from their *cradles*, in arms and military exercises. *Spenser's State of Ireland.*

The new duke's daughter, her cousin, loves her; being ever, from their *cradles*, bred together. *Shakesp. As you like it.*

They should scarcely depart from a form of worship, in which they had been educated from their *cradle*. *Clarendon.*

3. [With surgeons.] A case for a broken bone, to keep off pressure.

4. [With shipwrights.] A frame of timber raised along the outside of a ship by the bulge, serving more securely and commodiously to help to launch her. *Harris.*

To Cra'dle. *v. a.* [from the substantive.] To lay in a cradle; to rock in a cradle.

He that hath been *cradled* in majesty, will not leave the throne to play with beggars. *Glanv. Apol.*

The tears steal from our eyes, when in the street
With some betrothed virgin's herse we meet;
Or infant's fun'ral from the cheated womb,
Convey'd to earth, and *cradled* in a tomb. *Dryden.*

He shall be *cradled* in my ancient shield, so famous through the universities. *Arbuthnot and Pope's Mart. Scriblerus.*

Cradle-cloaths. *n. s.* [from *cradle* and *cloaths.*] Bed-cloaths belonging to a cradle.

O could it be prov'd,
That some night-tripping fairy had exchang'd,
In *cradle-cloaths*, our children where they lay,
And call mine Piercy, his Plantagenet;
Then would I have his Harry, and he mine. *Shakes. H. IV.*

CRAFT. *n. s.* [cpæft, Sax. *creft*, in old Welsh.]

1. Manual art; trade.

I hear an objection, even from some well-meaning men, that these delightful *crafts* may be divers ways ill applied in a land. *Wotton's Architecture.*

2. Fraud; cunning; artifice.

Th' offence is holy, that she hath committed;
And this deceit loses the name of *craft*,
Of disobedience, or unduteous title. *Shakespeare.*

This gives us a full view of wonderful art and *craft*, in raising such a structure of power and iniquity. *Ayliffe's Parerg.*

3. Small sailing vessels.

To Craft. *v. n.* [from the noun.] To play tricks; to practise artifice. Now out of use.

You've made fair hands,
You and your crafts! You've *crafted* fair. *Shakes Coriolanus.*

Cra'ftily. *adv.* [from *crafty.*] Cunningly; artfully; with more art than honesty.

But that which most impaired his credit was the common report that he did, in all things, favour the Christians; and had, for that cause, *craftily* persuaded Solyman to take in hand the unfortunate Persian war. *Knolles's Hist. of the Turks.*

May he not *craftily* infer
The rules of friendship too severe,
Which chain him to a hated trust;
Which make him wretched to be just? *Prior.*

Cra'ftiness. *n. s.* [from *crafty.*] Cunning; stratagem.

He taketh the wise in their own *craftiness*. *Job*, v. 13.

Cra'ftsman. *n. s.* [*craft* and *man.*] An artificer; a manufacturer; a mechanick.

That her became, as polish'd ivory,
Which cunning *craftsman*'s hand hath overlaid
With fair vermillion. *Fairy Queen, b.* ii. *cant.* ix. *stan.* 41.
What reverence he did throw away on slaves;
Wooing poor *craftsmen* with the craft of smiles. *Shak. R. II.*

What a resemblance this advice carries to the oration of Demetrius to his fellow *craftsmen!* *Decay of Piety.*

Cra'ftsmaster. *n. s.* [*craft* and *master.*] A man skilled in his trade.

He is not his *craftsmaster*, he doth not do it right. *Shakesp.*

There is art in pride: a man might as soon learn a trade. Those who were not brought up to it, seldom prove their *craftsmaster*. *Collier on Pride.*

Cra'fty. *adj.* [from *craft.*] Cunning; artful; full of artifices; fraudulent; sly.

Nay, you may think my love was *crafty* love,
And call it cunning. *Shakespeare's King John.*

This oppression did, of force and necessity, make the Irish a *crafty* people; for such as are oppressed, and live in slavery, are ever put to their shifts. *Davies on Ireland.*

Before he came in sight, the *crafty* god
His wings dismiss'd, but still retain'd his rod. *Dryden.*

No body was ever so cunning as to conceal their being so; and every body is shy and distrustful of *crafty* men. *Locke.*

CRAG. *n. s.*

1. *Crag* is, in British, a rough steep rock; and is used in the same sense in the northern counties at this day. *Gibson's Camd.*

2. The rugged protuberances of rocks.

And as mount Etna vomits sulphur out,
With clifts of burning *crags*, and fire and smoke. *Fairfax.*
Who hath dispos'd, but thou, the winding way,
Where springs down from the steepy *crags* do beat. *Wotton.*

A lion spied a goat upon the *crag* of a high rock. *L'Estran.*

3. The neck.

They looken bigge, as bulls that been bate,
And bearen the *cragg* so stiff and so state. *Spenser's Past.*

4. The small end of a neck of mutton: a low word.

Cra'gged. *adj.* [from *crag.*] Full of inequalities and prominences.

On a huge hill,
Cragged and steep, truth stands. *Crashaw.*

Cra'ggedness. *n. s.* [from *cragged.*] Fulness of crags or prominent rocks.

4

That

That *craggedneſs* or ſteepneſs of that mountain, maketh many parts of it in a manner inacceſſible. *Brerewood.*

CRA'GGINESS. *n. ſ.* [from *craggy.*] The ſtate of being craggy.

CRA'GGY. *adj.* [from *crag.*] Rugged; full of prominences; rough to walk on, or climb.

That ſame wicked wight
His dwelling has low in an hollow cave,
Far underneath a *craggy* clift ypight,
Dark, doleful, dreary, like a greedy grave. *Fairy Queen, b.* i.

It was impoſſible to paſs up the woody and *craggy* hills, without the loſs of thoſe commanders. *Raleigh's Eſſays.*

Mountaineers that from Severus came,
And from the *craggy* cliffs of Tetrica. *Dryden's Æn. b.* viii.

The town and republick of St. Marino ſtands on the top of a very high and *craggy* mountain. *Addiſon on Italy.*

To CRAM. *v. a.* [cꞃamman, Saxon.]

1. To ſtuff; to fill with more than can conveniently be held.

As much love in rhime,
As would be *cramm'd* up in a ſheet of paper,
Writ on both ſides the leaf, margent and all. *Shakeſpeare.*

Being thus *crammed* in the baſket, a couple of Ford's knaves were called. *Shakeſp. Merry Wives of Windſor.*

Thou haſt ſpoke as if thy eldeſt ſon ſhould be a fool, whoſe ſkull Jove *cram* with brains. *Shakeſpeare's Twelfth Night.*

Cram not in people by ſending too faſt company after company; but ſo as the number may live well in the plantation, and not by ſurcharge be in penury. *Bacon, Eſſay* 34.

2. To fill with food beyond ſatiety.

You'd mollify a judge, would *cram* a ſquire;
Or elſe ſome ſmiles from court you may deſire. *King.*

I am ſure children would be freer from diſeaſes, if they were not *crammed* ſo much as they are by fond mothers, and were kept wholly from fleſh the firſt three years. *Locke.*

As a man may be eating all day, and, for want of digeſtion, is never nouriſhed; ſo theſe endleſs readers may *cram* themſelves in vain with intellectual food. *Watts's Improvement.*

But Annius, crafty ſeer,
Came *cramm'd* with capon, from where Pollio dines. *Dunciad.*

3. To thruſt in by force.

You *cram* theſe words into mine ears, againſt
The ſtomach of my ſenſe. *Shakeſpeare's Tempeſt.*

Huffer, quoth Hudibras, this ſword
Shall down thy falſe throat *cram* that word. *Hudibras, p.* ii.

Fate has *cramm'd* us all into one leaſe,
And that even now expiring. *Dryden's Cleomenes.*

In another printed paper it is roundly expreſſed, that he will *cram* his braſs down our throats. *Swift.*

To CRAM. *v. n.* To eat beyond ſatiety.

The godly dame, who fleſhly failings damns,
Scolds with her maid, or with her chaplain *crams.*
Pope's Epilogue to Jane Shore.

CRA'MBO. *n. ſ.* [a cant word, probably without etymology.] A play at which one gives a word, to which another finds a rhyme; a rhyme.

So Mævius, when he drain'd his ſkull
To celebrate ſome ſuburb trull,
His ſimiles in order ſet,
And ev'ry *crambo* he could get. *Swift.*

CRAMP. *n. ſ.* [*krampe*, Dut. *crampe*, French.]

1. A ſpaſm or contraction of the limbs, generally removed by warmth and rubbing.

For this, be ſure, to-night thou ſhalt have *cramp*,
Side-ſtitches that ſhall pen thy breath up. *Shakeſp. Tempeſt.*

In a retreat, he outruns any lacquey; marry, in coming on, he has the *cramp.* *Shakeſpeare's All's well that ends well.*

The *cramp*, no doubt, cometh of contraction of ſinews; which is manifeſt, in that it cometh either by cold or dryneſs.
Bacon's Natural Hiſtory, Nº. 964.

Hares, ſaid to live on hemlock, do not make good the tradition; and he that obſerves what vertigoes, *cramps*, and convulſions follow thereon, in theſe animals, will be of our belief. *Brown's Vulgar Errours, b.* iii. *c.* 27.

2. A reſtriction; a confinement; obſtruction; ſhackle.

A narrow fortune is a *cramp* to a great mind, and lays a man under incapacities of ſerving his friend. *L'Eſtrange.*

3. A piece of iron bent at each end, by which two bodies are held together.

To the uppermoſt of theſe there ſhould be faſtened a ſharp graple, or *cramp* of iron, which may be apt to take hold of any place where it lights. *Wilkins's Mathem. Magick.*

CRAMP. *adj.* Difficult; knotty: a low term.

To CRAMP. *v. a.* [from the noun.]

1. To pain with cramps or twiches.

When the contracted limbs were *cramp'd*, ev'n then
A wat'riſh humour ſwell'd, and coz'd again. *Dryden's Virgil.*

2. To reſtrain; to confine; to obſtruct; to hinder.

It is impoſſible to conceive the number of inconveniences that will enſue, if borrowing be *cramped.* *Bacon, Eſſay* 42.

There are few but find that ſome companies benumb and *cramp* them, ſo that in them they can neither ſpeak nor do any thing that is handſome. *Glanville's Scepſ. c.* 24.

He, who ſerves, has ſtill reſtraints of dread upon his ſpirits, which, even in the midſt of action, *cramps* and ties up his activity. *South's Sermons.*

Dr. Hammond loves to contract and *cramp* the ſenſe of prophecies. *Burnet's Theory of the Earth.*

The antiquaries are for *cramping* their ſubjects into as narrow a ſpace as they can, and for reducing the whole extent of a ſcience into a few general maxims. *Addiſon on Italy.*

Marius uſed all endeavours for depreſſing the nobles, and raiſing the people; particularly for *cramping* the former in their power of judicature. *Swift on the Diſſent. in Ath. and Rome.*

No more
Th' expanſive atmoſphere is *cramp'd* with cold,
But full of life, and vivifying ſoul. *Thomſon's Spring.*

3. To bind with crampirons.

CRAMP-FISH. *n. ſ.* [from *cramp* and *fiſh.*] The torpedo, which benumbs the hands of thoſe that touch it.

CRAMPIRON. *n. ſ.* [from *cramp* and *iron.*] See CRAMP, Senſe 3.

CRA'NAGE. *n. ſ.* [*cranagium*, low Latin.] A liberty to uſe a crane for drawing up wares from the veſſels, at any creek of the ſea or wharf, unto the land, and to make profit of it. It ſignifies alſo the money paid and taken for the ſame. *Cowel.*

CRANE. *n. ſ.* [cꞃan, Sax. *kraen*, Dutch.]

1. A bird with a long beak.

Like a *crane*, or a ſwallow, ſo did I chatter. *Iſ.* xlviii. 14.
That ſmall infantry warr'd on by *cranes.* *Milt. Par. Loſt.*

2. An inſtrument made with ropes, pullies, and hooks, by which great weights are raiſed.

In caſe the mould about it be ſo ponderous as not to be removed by any ordinary force, you may then raiſe it with a *crane.* *Mortimer's Art of Huſbandry.*

Then commerce brought into the publick walk
The buſy merchant, the big warehouſe built,
Rais'd the ſtrong *crane.* *Thomſon's Autumn.*

3. A ſiphon; a crooked pipe for drawing liquors out of a caſk.

CRANES-BILL. *n. ſ.* [from *crane* and *bill.*]

1. An herb.

The leaves are conjugate: the cup conſiſts of one leaf, divided into five parts, expanded in form of a ſtar: the flowers conſiſt of five leaves, ſomewhat reſembling a creſted or lipped flower, with ten ſtamina ſurrounding the ovary. The fruit is of a pentagonal figure, with a beak, containing five ſeed-veſſels, in each of which is one tailed ſeed, which, when ripe, is caſt forth by the twiſting of the beak. It is common in ſeveral parts of England, growing in almoſt any ſoil or ſituation. *Miller.*

2. A pair of pincers terminating in a point, uſed by ſurgeons.

CRA'NIUM. *n. ſ.* [Latin.] The ſkull.

In wounds made by contuſion, when the *cranium* is a little naked, you ought not preſently to croud in doſſils; for if that contuſed fleſh be well digeſted, the bone will incarn with the wound without much difficulty. *Wiſeman's Surgery.*

CRANK. *n. ſ.* [This word is perhaps a contraction of *craneneck*, to which it may bear ſome reſemblance, and is part of the inſtrument called a *crane.*]

1. A crank is the end of an iron axis turned ſquare down, and again turned ſquare to the firſt turning down; ſo that, on the laſt turning down, a leather thong is ſlipt to tread the treddle-wheel about. *Moxon's Mech. Exerciſes.*

2. Any bending or winding paſſage.

I ſend it through the rivers of your blood,
Even to the court, the heart; to th' ſeat o' th' brain;
And, through the *cranks* and offices of man,
The ſtrongeſt nerves, and ſmall inferiour veins,
From me receive that natural competency,
Whereby they live. *Shakeſpeare's Coriolanus.*

3. Any conceit formed by twiſting or changing, in any manner, the form or meaning of a word.

Haſte thee, nymph, and bring with thee
Jeſt and youthful jollity,
Quips and *cranks*, and wanton wiles,
Nods and becks, and wreathed ſmiles,
Such as hang on Hebe's cheek,
And love to live in dimple ſleek. *Milton.*

CRANK. *adj.* [from *onkranck*, Dutch. *Skinner.*]

1. Healthy; ſprightly: ſometimes corrupted to *cranky.*

They looken bigge, as bulls that been bate,
And bearen the cragg ſo ſtiff and ſo ſtate,
As cockle, on his dunghil crowing *cranke.* *Spenſer's Paſt.*

2. Among ſailors, a ſhip is ſaid to be *crank*, when, by the form of its bottom, or by being loaded too much above, it is liable to be overſet. [from *kranck*, Dut. ſick.]

To CRA'NKLE. *v. n.* [from *crank.*] To run in and out; to run in flexures and windings.

See how this river comes me *crankling* in,
And cuts me from the beſt of all my land,
A huge half-moon, a monſtrous cantle out. *Shak. Hen.* IV.

To CRA'NKLE. *v. a.* To break into unequal ſurfaces; to break into angles.

Old Vaga's ſtream,
Forc'd by the ſudden ſhock, her wonted track
Forſook, and drew her humid train aſlope,
Crankling her banks. *Philips.*

CRA'NKLES. *n. s.* [from the verb.] Inequalities; angular prominences.

CRA'NKNESS. *n. s.* [from *crank.*]
1. Health; vigour.
2. Disposition to overset.

CRA'NNIED. *adj.* [from *cranny.*] Full of chinks.

A wall it is, as I would have you think,
That had in it a *crannied* hole or chink. *Shakespeare.*

A very fair fruit, and not unlike a citron; but somewhat rougher chopt and *crannied*, vulgarly conceived the marks of Adam's teeth. *Brown's Vulgar Errours, b.* vii. *c.* 1.

CRA'NNY. *n. s.* [*cren*, Fr. *crena*, Latin.] A chink; a cleft; a fissure.

The eye of the understanding is like the eye of the sense; for as you may see great objects through small *crannies* or holes, so you may see great axioms of nature through small and contemptible instances. *Bacon's Natural History*, N°. 91.

And therefore beat, and laid about,
To find a *cranny* to creep out. *Hudibras, p.* iii. *cant.* 1.

In a firm building, even the cavities ought not to be filled with rubbish, but with brick or stone, fitted to the *crannies*. *Dryden's Dedication to the Æneid.*

Within the soaking of water and springs, with streams and currents in the veins and *crannies*. *Burnet's Theo. of the Earth.*

He skipped from room to room, ran up stairs and down stairs, from the kitchen to the garrets, and he peeped into every *cranny*. *Arbuthnot's History of John Bull.*

CRAPE. *n. s.* [*crepa*, low Latin.] A thin stuff, loosely woven, of which the dress of the clergy is sometimes made.

And proud Roxana, fir'd with jealous rage,
With fifty yards of *crape* shall sweep the stage. *Swift.*

Nor thou, lord Arthur, shall escape:
To thee I often call'd in vain,
Against that assassin in *crape*;
Yet thou could'st tamely see me slain. *Swift.*

'Tis from high life high characters are drawn;
A saint in *crape*, is twice a saint in lawn. *Pope, Epistle* i.

CRA'PULENCE. *n. s.* [*crapula*, a surfeit, Latin.] Drunkenness; sickness by intemperance. *Dict.*

CRA'PULOUS. *adj.* [*crapulosus*, Lat.] Drunken; intemperate; sick with intemperance. *Dict.*

To CRASH. *v. n.* [a word probably formed from the thing.]
1. To make a loud complicated noise, as of many things falling or breaking at once.

There shall be a great *crashing* from the hills. *Zeph.* i. 10.

When convulsions cleave the lab'ring earth,
Before the dismal yawn appears, the ground
Trembles and heaves, the nodding houses *crash*. *Smith.*

To CRASH. *v. a.* To break or bruise.

My master is the great rich Capulet; and if you be not of the house of Montague, I pray you come and *crash* a cup of wine. *Shakespeare's Romeo and Juliet.*

Mr. *Warburton* has it, *crush a cup of wine.*

To crash, says *Hanmer*, is to be merry: a *crash* being a word still used in some counties for a merry bout.

It is surely better to read *crack*. See CRACK.

CRASH. *n. s.* [from the verb.] A loud sudden mixed sound, as of many things broken at the same time.

Senseless Ilium,
Seeming to feel this blow, with flaming top
Stoops to his base; and, with a hideous *crash*,
Takes prisoner Pyrrhus' ear. *Shakespeare's Hamlet.*

Moralizing sat I by the hazard-table: I look'd upon the uncertainty of riches, the decay of beauty, and the *crash* of worlds, with as much contempt as ever Plato did. *Pope.*

CRA'SIS. *n. s.* [κρᾶσις.] Temperature; constitution arising from the various properties of humours.

The fancies of men are so immediately diversified by the individual *crasis*, that every man owns something wherein none is like him. *Glanville's Sceps. c.* 15.

A man may be naturally inclined to pride, lust, and anger, as these inclinations are founded in a peculiar *crasis*, and constitution of the blood and spirits. *South's Sermons.*

CRASS. *adj.* [*crassus*, Latin.] Gross; coarse; not thin; not comminuted; not subtle; not consisting of small parts.

Metals are intermixed with the common terrestrial matter, so as not to be discoverable by human industry; or, if discoverable, so diffused and scattered amongst the *crasser* and more unprofitable matter, that it would never be possible to separate and extract it. *Woodward's Natural History.*

CRA'SSITUDE. *n. s.* [*crassitudo*, Latin.] Grossness; coarseness; thickness.

They must be but thin, as a leaf, or a piece of paper or parchment; for if they have a greater *crassitude*, they will alter in their own body, though they spend not. *Bacon's Nat. Hist.*

The Dead Sea, which vomiteth up bitumen, is of that *crassitude*, as living bodies, bound hand and foot, cast into it, have been born up, and not sunk. *Bacon's Natural History.*

The terrestrial matter carried by rivers into the sea, is sustained therein partly by the greater *crassitude* and gravity of the sea-water, and partly by its constant agitation. *Woodward.*

CRASTINA'TION. *n. s.* [from *crastino*, Latin, to-morrow.] Delay. *Dict.*

CRATCH. *n. s.* [*creche*, French; *crates*, Latin.] The palisaded frame in which hay is put for cattle.

When being expelled out of Paradise, by reason of sin, thou wert held in the chains of death; I was inclosed in the virgin's womb, I was laid in the *cratch*, I was wrapped in swathling-cloaths. *Hakewill on Providence.*

CRAVA'T. *n. s.* [of uncertain etymology.] A neck-cloath; any thing worn about the neck.

Less delinquents have been scourg'd,
And hemp on wooden anvils forg'd;
Which others for *cravats* have worn
About their necks, and took a turn. *Hudibras, p.* iii. *cant.* 1.

The restrictives were applied, one over another, to her throat: then we put her on a *cravat*. *Wiseman's Surgery.*

To CRAVE. *v. a.* [cpapian, Saxon.]
1. To ask with earnestness; to ask with submission; to beg; to entreat.

What one petition is there found in the whole litany, whereof we shall ever be able at any time to say, that no man living needeth the grace or benefit therein *craved* at God's hands? *Hooker.*

As for my nobler friends, I *crave* their pardons;
But for the mutable rank-scented many,
Let them regard me as I do not flatter. *Shakesp. Coriolanus.*

The poor people not knowing where to hide themselves from the fury of their enemies, nor of whom to *crave* help, fled as men and women dismayed. *Knolles's Hist. of the Turks.*

I would *crave* leave here, under the word action, to comprehend the forbearance too of any action proposed. *Locke.*

Each ardent nymph the rising current *craves*,
Each shepherd's pray'r retards the parting waves. *Prior.*

2. To ask insatiably.

The subjects arm'd; the more their princes gave,
Th' advantage only took the more to *crave*. *Denham.*

Him dost thou mean, who, spite of all his store,
Is ever *craving*, and will still be poor?
Who cheats for halfpence; and who doffs his coat,
To save a farthing in a ferry-boat. *Dryden's Pers. Sat.* iv.

3. To long; to wish unreasonably.

Levity pushes us on from one vain desire to another, in a regular vicissitude and succession of *cravings* and satiety. *L'Estr.*

He is actually under the power of a temptation, and the sway of an impetuous lust; both hurrying him to satisfy the *cravings* of it, by some wicked action. *South's Sermons.*

4. To call for importunately.

Our good old friend,
Lay comforts to your bosom; and bestow
Your needful counsel to our businesses,
Which *crave* the instant use. *Shakespeare's King Lear.*

The antecedent concomitants and effects of such a constitution, are acids, taken in too great quantities; sour eructations, and a *craving* appetite, especially of terrestrial and absorbent substances. *Arbuthnot on Aliments.*

5. Sometimes with *for* before the thing sought.

Once one may *crave for* love,
But more would prove
This heart too little, that too great. *Suckling.*

CRA'VEN. *n. s.* [derived by *Skinner* from *crave*, as one that craves or begs his life: perhaps it comes originally from the noise made by a conquered cock.]
1. A cock conquered and dispirited.

What, is your crest a coxcomb?——
——A combless cock, so Kate will be my hen.
—No cock of mine; you crow too like a *craven*. *Shakesp.*

2. A coward; a recreant.

Upon his coward breast
A bloody cross, and on his *craven* crest
A bunch of hairs discolour'd diversly. *Fairy Queen, b.* i.

Is it fit this soldier keep his oath?—
—He is a *craven* and a villain else. *Shakespeare's Henry* V.

Whether it be
Bestial oblivion, or some *craven* scruple,
Of thinking too precisely on th' event;
A thought, which quarter'd, hath but one part wisdom,
And ever three parts coward. *Shakespeare's Hamlet.*

Yet if the innocent some mercy find
From cowardice, not ruth did that proceed;
His noble foes durst not his *craven* kind
Exasperate by such a bloody deed. *Fairfax, b.* i. *stan.* 88.

To CRA'VEN. *v. a.* [from the noun.] To make recreant or cowardly. *Hanmer.*

'Gainst self-slaughter
There is a prohibition so divine,
That *cravens* my weak hand. *Shakespeare's Cymbeline.*

CRA'VER. *n. s.* [from *crave.*] A weak-hearted spiritless fellow. It is used in *Clarissa.*

To CRAUNCH. *v. a.* [*schrantsen*, Dutch; whence the vulgar say more properly to *scraunch.*] To crush in the mouth. The word is used by *Swift.*

CRAW. *n. s.* [*kroe*, Danish.] The crop or first stomach of birds.

In birds there is no mastication, or comminution of the meat in the mouth; but in such as are not carnivorous, it is immediately swallowed into the crop or *craw*, or at least into a kind of ante-stomach, which I have observed in many, especially piscivorous birds. *Ray on the Creation.*

CRA'WFISH. *n. s.* [sometimes written *crayfish*, properly *crevice*; in French *ecrevisse.*] A small crustaceous fish found in brooks; the small lobster of fresh water.

Those that cast their shell are the lobster, the crab, the *crawfish*, the hodmandod or dodman, and the tortoise. *Bacon.*

Let me to crack live *crawfish* recommend. *Pope's Hor. Im.*

The common *crawfish*, and the large sea *crawfish*, both produce the stones called crabs-eyes. In part of June, in July, and part of August, this animal not only casts its shell, but its very stomach is also consumed and digested, by a new one growing in its place. *Hill on the Materia Medica.*

To CRAWL. *v. n.* [*krielen*, Dutch.]

1. To creep; to move with a slow motion; to move without rising from the ground, as a worm.

That *crawling* insect, who from mud began;
Warm'd by my beams, and kindled into man! *Dryd. Auren.*

The streams but just contain'd within their bounds,
By slow degrees into their channels *crawl*;
And earth increases as the waters fall. *Dryden.*

A worm finds what it searches after, only by feeling, as it *crawls* from one thing to another. *Grew's Cosmol. b.* ii. *c.* 8.

The vile worm, that yesterday began
To *crawl*; thy fellow-creature, abject man! *Prior.*

2. To move weakly, and slowly.

'Tis our first intent
To shake all cares and business from our age,
While we unburthen'd *crawl* tow'rd death. *Shakes. K. Lear.*

They like tall fellows crept out of the holes; and secretly *crawling* up the battered walls of the fort, got into it. *Knolles.*

A look so pale no quartane ever gave;
Thy dwindled legs seem *crawling* to a grave. *Dryd. Juvenal.*

He was hardly able to *crawl* about the room, far less to look after a troublesome business. *Arbuthn. History of John Bull.*

Man is a very worm by birth,
Vile reptile, weak and vain!
A while he *crawls* upon the earth,
Then shrinks to earth again. *Swift.*

It will be very necessary for the threadbare gownman, and every child who can *crawl*, to watch the fields at harvest-time. *Swift.*

3. To move about hated and despised.

Cranmer
Hath *crawl'd* into the favour of the king,
And is his oracle. *Shakespeare's Henry* VIII.

Reflect upon that litter of absurd opinions that *crawl* about the world, to the disgrace of reason. *South's Sermons.*

How will the condemned sinner then *crawl* forth, and appear in his filth and shame, before that undefiled tribunal? *South's Sermons.*

Behold a rev'rend sire, whom want of grace
Has made the father of a nameless race,
Crawl through the street, shov'd on, or rudely press'd
By his own sons, that pass him by unbless'd! *Pope, Epist.* i.

CRA'WLER. *n. s.* [from *crawl.*] A creeper; any thing that creeps.

CRA'YFISH. *n. s.* [See CRAWFISH.] The river lobster.

The cure of the muriatick and armoniack saltness requires to use slimy meats; as snails, tortoises, jellies, and *crayfishes.* *Floyer on the Humours.*

CRA'YON. *n. s.* [*crayon*, French.]

1. A kind of pencil; a roll of paste to draw lines with.

Let no day pass over you without drawing a line; that is to say, without working, without giving some strokes of the pencil or the *crayon.* *Dryden's Dufresnoy.*

2. A drawing or design done with a pencil or crayon.

To CRAZE. *v. a.* [*ecraser*, French, to break to pieces.]

1. To break; to crush; to weaken.

In this consideration the answer of Calvin unto Farrel, concerning the children of Popish parents, doth seem *crazed.* *Hook.*

Relent, sweet Hermia; and, Lysander, yield
Thy *crazed* title to my certain right. *Shakespeare.*

Then through the firey pillar, and the cloud,
God looking forth, will trouble all his host,
And *craze* their chariot-wheels. *Milton's Parad. Lost*, *b.* xii.

2. To powder.

The tin ore passeth to the *crazing* mill, which, between two grinding stones, bruiseth it to a fine sand. *Carew's Survey.*

3. To crack the brain; to impair the intellect.

I lov'd him, friend,
No father his son dearer: true, to tell thee,
That grief hath *craz'd* my wits. *Shakespeare's King Lear.*

Wickedness is a kind of voluntary frenzy, and a chosen distraction; and every sinner does wilder and more extravagant things than any man can do that is *crazed* and out of his wits, only with this sad difference, that he knows better what he does. *Tillotson.*

CRA'ZEDNESS. *n. s.* [from *crazed.*] Decrepitude; brokenness; diminution of intellect.

The nature, as of men that have sick bodies, so likewise of the people in the *crazedness* of their minds, possessed with dislike and discontentment at things present, is to imagine that any thing would help them. *Hooker, Preface.*

CRA'ZINESS. *n. s.* [from *crazy.*]

1. State of being crazy; imbecillity; weakness.

Touching other places, she may be said to hold them as one should do a wolf by the ears; nor will I speak now of the *craziness* of her title to many of them. *Howel's Vocal Forest.*

2. Weakness of intellect.

CRA'ZY. *adj.* [*ecrasé*, French.]

1. Broken; decrepit.

Come, my lord,
We will bestow you in some better place;
Fitter for sickness and for *crazy* age. *Shakesp. Henry* VI.

When people are *crazy*, and in disorder, it is natural for them to groan. *L'Estrange.*

2. Broken witted; shattered in the intellect.

The queen of night, whose large command
Rules all the sea and half the land,
And over moist and *crazy* brains,
In high spring-tides, at midnight reigns. *Hudibras, p.* iii.

3. Weak; feeble; shattered.

Physick can but mend our *crazy* state,
Patch an old building, not a new create. *Dryden's Fables.*

Were it possible that the near approaches of eternity, whether by a mature age, a *crazy* constitution, or a violent sickness, should amaze so many, had they truly considered. *Wake.*

CREAGHT. *n. s.* [an Irish word.]

In these fast places they kept their *creaghts*, or herds of cattle, living by the milk of the cow, without husbandry or tillage. *Davies on Ireland.*

To CREAK. *v. n.* [corrupt from *crack.*]

1. To make a harsh protracted noise.

Let not the *creaking* of shoes, nor the rustling of silks, betray thy poor heart to women. *Shakespeare's King Lear.*

No door there was th' unguarded house to keep,
On *creaking* hinges turn'd, to break his sleep. *Dryd. Fables.*

2. It is sometimes used of animals.

The *creaking* locusts with my voice conspire,
They fry'd with heat, and I with fierce desire. *Dryd. Virgil.*

CREAM. *n. s.* [*cremor*, Latin.]

1. The unctuous or oily part of milk, which, when it is cold, floats on the top, and is changed by the agitation of the churn into butter; the flower of milk.

It is not your inky brows, your black silk hair,
Your bugle eye-balls, nor your cheek of *cream*,
That can entame my spirits to your worship. *Shakespeare.*

I am as vigilant as a cat to steal *cream.* *Shakesp. Henry* IV.

Cream is matured and made to rise more speedily, by putting in cold water; which, as it seemeth, getteth down the whey. *Bacon's Natural History*, N°. 314.

How the drudging goblin swet,
To earn his *cream*-bowl duly set;
When in one night, ere glimpse of morn,
His shadowy flail hath thresh'd the corn. *Milton.*

Let your various *creams* incircled be
With swelling fruit, just ravish'd from the tree. *King.*

Milk, standing some time, naturally separates into an oily liquor called *cream*, and a thinner, blue, and more ponderous liquor called skimmed milk. *Arbuthnot on Aliments.*

2. It is used for the best part of any thing; as, *the* cream *of a jest.*

To CREAM. *v. n.* [from the noun.] To gather cream.

There are a sort of men, whose visages
Do *cream* and mantle like a standing pond;
And do a wilful stiffness entertain,
With purpose to be drest in an opinion
Of wisdom, gravity, profound conceit. *Shak. Merch. of Ven.*

To CREAM. *v. a.* [from the noun.]

1. To skim off the cream.

2. To take the flower and quintessence of any thing: so used somewhere by *Swift.*

CREAM-FACED. *adj.* [*cream* and *faced.*] Pale; coward-looking.

Thou *cream-fac'd* lown,
Where got'st thou that goose-look. *Shakespeare's Macbeth.*

CRE'AMY. *adj.* [from *cream.*] Full of cream; having the nature of cream.

CRE'ANCE. n. s. [French.] Is, in falconry, a fine small line, fastened to a hawk's leash when she is first lured.

CREASE. *n. s.* [from *creta*, Latin, chalk. *Skinner.*] A mark made by doubling any thing.

Men of great parts are unfortunate in business, because they go out of the common road: I once desired lord Bolingbroke to observe, that the clerks used an ivory knife, with a blunt edge, to divide paper, which cut it even, only requiring a strong hand; whereas a sharp penknife would go out of the *crease*, and disfigure the paper. *Swift.*

To CREASE. *v. a.* [from the noun.] To mark any thing by doubling it, so as to leave the impression.

To CREA'TE. *v. a.* [*creo*, Latin.]

1. To form out of nothing; to cauſe to exiſt.

In the beginning God *created* the heaven and the earth. *Gen.* i. 1.

We having but imperfect ideas of the operations of our minds, and much imperfecter yet of the operations of God, run into great difficulties about free *created* agents, which reaſon cannot well extricate itſelf out of. *Locke.*

2. To produce; to cauſe; to be the occaſion.

Now is the time of help: your eye in Scotland
Would *create* ſoldiers, and make women fight,
To doff their dire diſtreſſes. *Shakeſpeare's Macbeth.*

His abilities were prone to *create* in him great confidence of undertakings, and this was like enough to betray him to great errours and many enemies. *King Charles.*

They eclipſe the cleareſt truths, by difficulties of their own *creating*, or no man could miſs his way to heaven for want of light. *Decay of Piety.*

None knew, 'till guilt *created* fear,
What darts or poiſon'd arrows were. *Roſcommon.*

Muſt I new bars to my own joy *create*,
Refuſe myſelf what I had forc'd from fate? *Dryd. Aurengz.*

Long abſtinence is troubleſome to acid conſtitutions, by the uneaſineſs it *creates* in the ſtomach. *Arbuthnot on Aliments.*

3. To beget.

And the iſſue there *create*,
Ever ſhall be fortunate. *Shakeſp. Midſummer-Night's Dream.*

4. To inveſt with any new character.

Ariſe my knights of the battle: I *create* you
Companions to our perſon, and will fit you
With dignities becoming your eſtates. *Shakeſp. Cymbeline.*

5. To give any new qualities; to put any thing in a new ſtate.

The beſt Britiſh undertaker had but a proportion of three thouſand acres for himſelf, with power to *create* a manor, and hold a court-baron. *Davies on Ireland.*

CREA'TION. *n. ſ.* [from *create.*]

1. The act of creating or conferring exiſtence.

Conſider the immenſity of the Divine Love, expreſſed in all the emanations of his providence; in his *creation*, in his conſervation of us. *Taylor.*

2. The act of inveſting with new qualities or character; as, the *creation* of peers.

3. The things created; the univerſe.

As ſubjects then, the whole *creation* came;
And from their natures Adam them did name. *Denham.*

Such was the ſaint, who ſhone with ev'ry grace,
Reflecting, Moſes like, his maſter's face:
God ſaw his image lively was expreſs'd,
And his own work as his *creation* bleſs'd. *Dryden's Fables.*

Nor could the tender new *creation* bear
Th' exceſſive heats or coldneſs of the year. *Dryden's Virgil.*

In days of yore, no matter where or when,
Before the low *creation* ſwarm'd with men. *Parnel.*

4. Any thing produced, or cauſed.

Art thou not, fatal viſion, ſenſible
To feeling as to ſight? Or art thou but
A dagger of the mind, a falſe *creation*,
Proceeding from the heat-oppreſſed brain? *Shakeſ. Macbeth.*

CREA'TIVE. *adj.* [from *create.*]

1. Having the power to create.

2. Exerting the act of creation.

To trace the outgoings of the ancient of days in the firſt inſtance, and of his *creative* power, is a reſearch too great for mortal enquiry. *South's Sermons.*

But come, ye generous minds, in whoſe wide thought,
Of all his works, *creative* beauty burns
With warmeſt beam. *Thomſon's Spring.*

CREA'TOR. *n. ſ.* [*creator*, Latin.] The being that beſtows exiſtence.

Open, ye heavens, your living doors; let in
The great *creator*, from his work return'd
Magnificent; his ſix days work, a world. *Milt. Parad. Loſt.*

When you lie down, cloſe your eyes with a ſhort prayer, commit yourſelf into the hands of your faithful *creator*; and when you have done, truſt him with yourſelf, as you muſt do when you are dying. *Taylor's Guide to Devotion.*

CRE'ATURE. *n. ſ.* [*creatura*, low Latin.]

1. A being not ſelf-exiſtent, but created by the ſupreme power.

Were theſe perſons idolaters for the worſhip they did not give to the Creator, or for the worſhip they did give to his *creatures*. *Stillingfleet's Defence of Diſcourſe on Rom. Idol.*

2. Any thing created.

God's firſt *creature* was light. *Bacon's New Atlantis.*

Imperfect the world, and all the *creatures* in it, muſt be acknowledged in many reſpects to be. *Tillotſon, Sermon* i.

3. An animal not human.

The queen pretended ſatisfaction of her knowledge only
In killing *creatures* vile, as cats and dogs. *Shakeſ. Cymbeline.*

4. A general term for man.

Yet crime in her could never *creature* find;
But for his love, and for her own ſelf-ſake,
She wander'd had from one to other Ind. *Fairy Queen, b.* i.

Moſt curſed of all *creatures* under ſky,
Lo Tantalus, I here tormented lye. *Fairy Queen, b.* ii. *c.* 7.

Though he might burſt his lungs to call for help,
No *creature* would aſſiſt or pity him. *Roſcommon.*

5. A word of contempt for a human being.

Hence; home, you idle *creatures*, get you home;
Is this a holiday? *Shakeſpeare's Julius Cæſar.*

He would into the ſtews,
And from the common *creatures* pluck a glove,
And wear it as a favour. *Shakeſpeare's Richard* III.

I've heard that guilty *creatures*, at a play,
Have, by the very cunning of the ſcene,
Been ſtruck ſo to the ſoul, that preſently
They have proclaim'd their malefactions. *Shakeſp. Hamlet.*

Nor think to-night of thy ill-nature,
But of thy follies, idle *creature*. *Prior.*

A good poet no ſooner communicates his works, but it is imagined he is a vain young *creature*, given up to the ambition of fame. *Pope.*

6. A word of petty tenderneſs.

And then, ſir, would he gripe and wring my hand;
Cry, Oh ſweet *creature*, and then kiſs me hard. *Shakeſpeare.*

Ah, cruel *creature*, whom do'ſt thou deſpiſe?
The gods, to live in woods, have left the ſkies. *Dryd. Virg.*

Some young *creatures* have learnt their letters and ſyllables by having them paſted upon little tablets. *Watts.*

7. A perſon who owes his riſe or his fortune to another.

He ſent to colonel Maſſey to ſend him men, which he, being a *creature* of Eſſex's, refuſed. *Clarendon.*

The duke's *creature* he deſired to be eſteemed. *Clarendon.*

Great princes thus, when favourites they raiſe,
To juſtify their grace, their *creatures* praiſe. *Dryd. Aurengz.*

The deſign was diſcovered by a perſon whom every body knows to be the *creature* of a certain great man. *Swift.*

CRE'ATURELY. *adj.* [from *creature.*] Having the qualities of a creature.

The ſeveral parts of relatives, or *creaturely* infinites, may have finite proportions to one another. *Cheyne's Phil. Prin.*

CRE'BRITUDE. *n. ſ.* [from *creber*, frequent, Latin.] Frequentneſs. *Dict.*

CRE'BROUS. *adj.* [from *creber*, Latin.] Frequent. *Dict.*

CRE'DENCE. *n. ſ.* [from *credo*, Lat. *credence*, Norman Fr.]

1. Belief; credit.

Ne let it ſeem, that *credence* this exceeds;
For he that made the ſame was known right well,
To have done much more admirable deeds;
It Merlin was. *Fairy Queen, b.* i. *cant.* 7. *ſtan.* 36.

Love and wiſdom,
Approv'd ſo to your majeſty, may plead
For ample *credence*. *Shakeſpeare's All's well that ends well.*

They did not only underhand give out that this was the true earl, but the friar, finding ſome *credence* in the people, took boldneſs in the pulpit to declare as much. *Bacon's H.* VII.

2. That which gives a claim to credit or belief.

After they had delivered to the king their letters of *credence*, they were led to a chamber richly furniſhed. *Hayward.*

CREDE'NDA. n. ſ. [Latin.] Things to be believed; articles of faith; diſtinguiſhed in theology from *agenda*, or practical duties.

Theſe were the great articles and *credenda* of Chriſtianity, that ſo much ſtartled the world. *South's Sermons.*

CRE'DENT. *adj.* [*credens*, Latin.]

1. Believing; eaſy of belief.

Then weigh what loſs your honour may ſuſtain,
If with too *credent* ear you liſt' his ſongs. *Shakeſp. Hamlet.*

2. Having credit; not to be queſtioned.

My authority bears a *credent* bulk,
That no particular ſcandal once can touch,
But it confounds the breather. *Shakeſp. Meaſure for Meaſure.*

CREDE'NTIAL. *n. ſ.* [from *credens*, Latin.] That which gives a title to credit; the warrant upon which belief or authority is claimed.

A few perſons of an odious and deſpiſed country could not have filled the world with believers, had they not ſhown undoubted *credentials* from the Divine Perſon who ſent them on ſuch a meſſage. *Addiſon on the Chriſtian Religion.*

CREDIBI'LITY. *n. ſ.* [from *credible.*] Claim to credit; poſſibility of obtaining belief; probability.

The firſt of thoſe opinions I ſhall ſhew to be altogether incredible, and the latter to have all the *credibility* and evidence of which a thing of that nature is capable. *Tillotſon, Serm.* i.

Calculate the ſeveral degrees of *credibility* and conviction, by which the one evidence ſurpaſſeth the other. *Atterbury.*

CRE'DIBLE. *adj.* [*credibilis*, Latin.] Worthy of credit; deſerving of belief; having a juſt claim to belief.

The ground of credit is the credibility of things credited; and things are made *credible*, either by the known condition and quality of the utterer, or by the manifeſt likelihood of truth in themſelves. *Hooker, b.* ii. *ſ.* 4.

None can demonſtrate to me, that there is ſuch an iſland as Jamaica; yet, upon the teſtimony of *credible* perſons, I am free from doubt. *Tillotſon, Preface.*

CRE'DIBLENESS.

CRE'DIBLENESS. *n. s.* [from *credible.*] Credibility; worthiness of belief; just claim to belief.

The *credibleness* of a good part of these narratives has been confirmed to me by a practiser of physick in the East Indies. *Boyle's History of Firmness.*

CRE'DIBLY. *adv.* [from *credible.*] In a manner that claims belief.

This, with the loss of so few of the English as is scarce credible, being, as hath been rather confidently than *credibly* reported, but of one man, though not a few hurt. *Bacon.*

CRE'DIT. *n. s.* [*credit*, French.]

1. Belief.

When the people heard these words, they gave no *credit* unto them, nor received them. *1 Mac.* x. 46.

I may give *credit* to reports. *Addison's Spectator*, N°. 130.

Some secret truths, from learned pride conceal'd,
To maids alone and children are reveal'd:
What though no *credit* doubting wits may give,
The fair and innocent shall still believe. *Pope's Ra. of Lock.*

2. Honour; reputation.

I published, because I was told I might please such as it was a *credit* to please. *Pope.*

3. Esteem; good opinion.

There is no decaying merchant, or inward beggar, hath so many tricks to uphold the *credit* of their wealth, as these empty persons have to maintain the *credit* of their sufficiency. *Bacon.*

His learning, though a poet said it,
Before a play, would lose no *credit.* *Swift.*
Yes, while I live, no rich or noble knave,
Shall walk the world in *credit* to his grave. *Pope's Hor. b.* ii.

4. Faith; testimony.

We are contented to take this upon your *credit*, and to think it may be. *Hooker, b.* iv. *sect.* 12.

The things which we properly believe, be only such as are received upon the *credit* of divine testimony. *Hooker, b.* v.

The author would have done well to have left so great a paradox only to the *credit* of a single assertion. *Locke.*

5. Trust reposed.

Credit is nothing but the expectation of money, within some limited time. *Locke.*

6. Promise given.

They have never thought of violating the publick *credit*, or of alienating the revenues to other uses than to what they have been thus assigned. *Addison's Remarks on Italy.*

7. Influence; power not compulsive; interest.

She employed his uttermost *credit* to relieve us, which was as great as a beloved son with a mother. *Sidney.*

They sent him likewise a copy of their supplication to the king, and desired him to use his *credit* that a treaty might be entered into. *Clarendon, b.* ii.

Having *credit* enough with his master to provide for his own interest, he troubled not himself for that of other men. *Claren.*

To CRE'DIT. *v. a.* [*credo*, Latin.]

1. To believe.

Now I change my mind,
And partly *credit* things that do presage. *Shakesp. Jul. Cæs.*

To *credit* the unintelligibility both of this union and motion, we need no more than to consider it. *Glanv. Sceps. c.* 4.

2. To procure credit or honour to any thing.

May here her monument stand so,
To *credit* this rude age; and show
To future times, that even we
Some patterns did of virtue see. *Waller.*

It was not upon design to *credit* these papers, nor to compliment a society so much above flattery. *Glanv. Sceps. Pref.*

At present you *credit* the church as much by your government, as you did the school formerly by your wit. *South.*

3. To trust; to confide in.

4. To admit as a debtor.

CRE'DITABLE. *adj.* [from *credit.*]

1. Reputable; above contempt.

He settled him in a good *creditable* way of living, having procured him by his interest one of the best places of the country. *Arbuthnot's History of John Bull.*

2. Honourable; estimable.

The contemplation of things, that do not serve to promote our happiness, is but a more specious and ingenious sort of idleness, a more pardonable and *creditable* kind of ignorance. *Tillotson, Sermon* i.

CRE'DITABLENESS. *n. s.* [from *creditable.*] Reputation; estimation.

Among all these snares, there is none more entangling than the *creditableness* and repute of customary vices. *Decay of Piety.*

CRE'DITABLY. *adv.* [from *creditable.*] Reputably; without disgrace.

Many will chuse rather to neglect their duty safely and *creditably*, than to get a broken pate in the church's service, only to be rewarded with that which will break their hearts too. *South's Sermons.*

CRE'DITOR. *n. s.* [*creditor*, Latin.] He to whom a debt is owed; he that gives credit: correlative to *debtor.*

There came divers of Anthonio's *creditors* in my company to Venice, that swear he cannot chuse but break. *Shakespeare.*

I am so used to consider myself as *creditor* and debtor, that I often state my accounts after the same manner, with regard to heaven and my own soul. *Addison's Spectator*, N°. 549.

No man of honour, as that word is usually understood, did ever pretend that his honour obliged him to be chaste or temperate, to pay his *creditors*, to be useful to his country, to do good to mankind, to endeavour to be wise or learned, to regard his word, his promise, or his oath. *Swift.*

CREDU'LITY. *n. s.* [*credulité*, French; *credulitas*, Latin.] Easiness of belief; readiness of credit.

The poor Plangus, being subject to that only disadvantage of honest hearts, *credulity*, was persuaded by him. *Sidney.*

The prejudice of *credulity* may, in some measure, be cured by learning to set a high value on truth. *Watts's Logick.*

CRE'DULOUS. *adj.* [*credulus*, Latin.] Apt to believe; unsuspecting; easily deceived.

A *credulous* father, and a brother noble,
Whose nature is so far from doing harm,
That he suspects none. *Shakespeare's King Lear.*

CRE'DULOUSNESS. *n. s.* [from *credulous.*] Aptness to believe; credulity.

CREED. *n. s.* [from *credo*, the first word of the apostles creed.]

1. A form of words in which the articles of faith are comprehended.

The larger and fuller view of this foundation is set down in the *creeds* of the church. *Hammond on Fundamentals.*

Will they, who decry *creeds* and creedmakers, say that one who writes a treatise of morality ought not to make in it any collection of moral precepts? *Fiddes's Sermons.*

2. Any solemn profession of principles or opinion.

For me, my lords,
I love him not, nor fear him; there's my *creed.* *Shakesp.*

To CREEK. *v. a.* [See *To* CREAK.] To make a harsh noise.

Shall I stay here,
Creeking my shoes on the plain masonry. *Shakespeare.*

CREEK. *n. s.* [cpecca, Sax. *kreke*, Dutch.]

1. A prominence or jut in a winding coast.

As streams, which with their winding banks do play,
Stopp'd by their *creeks*, run softly through the plain. *Davies.*
They on the bank of Jordan, by a *creek*,
Where winds with reeds and osiers whisp'ring play,
Their unexpected loss and plaints outbreath'd. *Parad. Reg.*

2. A small port; a bay; a cove.

A law was made here to stop their passage in every port and *creek.* *Davies on Ireland.*

3. Any turn, or alley.

A back-friend, a shoulder-clapper; one that commands
The passages of alleys, *creeks*, and narrow lands. *Shakesp.*

CRE'EKY. *adj.* [from *creek.*] Full of creeks; unequal; winding.

Who, leaning on the belly of a pot,
Pour'd forth a water, whose outgushing flood
Ran bathing all the *creeky* shore a-flot,
Whereon the Trojan prince spilt Turnus' blood. *Spenser.*

To CREEP. *v. n.* [preter. *crept*; cpypan, Sax. *krepan*, Germ.]

1. To move with the belly to the ground without legs; as a worm.

Ye that walk
The earth, and stately tread, or lowly *creep!* *Milt. Pa. Lost.*
And every creeping thing that *creeps* the ground. *Milton.*

If they cannot distinguish *creeping* from flying, let them lay down Virgil, and take up Ovid de Ponto. *Dryd. Dedicat. Æn.*

2. To grow along the ground, or on other supports.

The grottos cool, with shady poplars crown'd,
And *creeping* vines on arbours weav'd around. *Dryden.*

3. To move forward without bounds or leaps; as insects.

4. To move slowly and feebly.

To-morrow, and to-morrow, and to-morrow,
Creeps in this petty pace from day to day,
To the last syllable of recorded time. *Shakesp. Macbeth.*
Why should a man
Sleep when he wakes, and *creep* into the jaundice
By being peevish? *Shakespeare's Merchant of Venice.*

He who *creeps* after plain, dull, common sense, is safe from committing absurdities; but can never reach the excellence of wit. *Dryden's Tyrannick Love.*

5. To move secretly and clandestinely.

I'll *creep* up into the chimney.——
—There they always use to discharge their birding-pieces: *creep* into the kiln-hole. *Shakesp. Merry Wives of Windsor.*

Whate'er you are,
That in this desart inaccessible,
Under the shade of melancholy boughs,
Lose and neglect the *creeping* hours of time. *Shakespeare.*

Of this sort are they which *creep* into houses, and lead captive silly women. *2 Tim.* iii. 6.

Thou makest darkness, and it is night wherein all the beasts of the forest do *creep* forth. *Psal.* civ. 20.

Now and then a work or two has *crept* in to keep his first design in countenance. *Atterbury.*

6. To move timorously without soaring, or venturing into dangers.

Paradise Lost is admirable; but am I therefore bound to maintain, that there are no flats amongst his elevations, when it is evident he *creeps* along sometimes for above an hundred lines together? *Dryden.*

We here took a little boat, to *creep* along the sea-shore as far as Genoa. *Addison's Remarks on Italy.*

7. To come unexpected; to steal forward unheard and unseen.

By those gifts of nature and fortune he *creeps*, nay he flies, into the favour of poor silly women. *Sidney, b.* ii.

It seems, the marriage of his brother's wife
Has *crept* too near his conscience.
——No, his conscience
Has *crept* too near another lady. *Shakespeare's Henry* VIII.

Necessity enforced them, after they grew full of people, to spread themselves, and *creep* out of Shinar, or Babylonia. *Raleigh's History.*

None pretends to know from how remote corners of those frozen mountains, some of those fierce nations first *crept* out. *Temple.*

It is not to be expected that every one should guard his understanding from being imposed on, by the sophistry which *creeps* into most of the books of argument. *Locke.*

8. To behave with servility; to fawn; to bend.

They were us'd to bend,
To send their smiles before them to Achilles,
To come as humbly as they us'd to *creep*
To holy altars. *Shakespeare's Troilus and Cressida.*

CRE'EPER. *n. s.* [from *creep.*]

1. A plant that supports itself by means of some stronger body.

Plants that put forth their sap hastily, have bodies not proportionable to their length; therefore they are winders or *creepers*; as ivy, briony, and woodbine. *Bacon's Nat. History.*

2. An iron used to slide along the grate in kitchens.

3. A kind of patten or clog worn by women.

CREE'PHOLE. *n. s.* [*creep* and *hole.*]

1. A hole into which any animal may creep to escape danger.

2. A subterfuge; an excuse.

CREE'PINGLY. *adv.* [from *creeping.*] Slowly; after the manner of a reptile.

The joy, which wrought into Pygmalion's mind, was even such as, by each degree of Zelmane's words, *creepingly* entered into Philoclea's. *Sidney, b.* ii.

CREMA'TION. *n. s.* [*crematio*, Latin.] A burning.

CRE'MOR. *n. s.* [Latin.] A milky substance; a soft liquor resembling cream.

The food is swallowed into the stomach, where, mingled with dissolvent juices, it is reduced into a chyle or *cremor. Ray.*

CRE'NATED. *adj.* [from *crena*, Latin.] Notched; indented.

The cells are prettily *crenated*, or notched quite round the edges; but not straited down to any depth. *Woodw. on Fossils.*

CRE'PANE. *n. s.* [With farriers.] An ulcer seated in the midst of the forepart of the foot, caused by a bilious, sharp, and biting humour that frets the skin, or by a hurt given by striking of the hinder feet. *Farrier's Dict.*

To CRE'PITATE. *v. n.* [*crepito*, Latin.] To make a small crackling noise.

CREPITA'TION. *n. s.* [from *crepitate.*] A small crackling noise.

CRE'PT. *particip.* [from *creep.*]

There are certain men *crept* in unawares. *Jude*, iv.

This fair vine, but that her arms surround
Her marry'd elm, had *crept* along the ground. *Pope.*

CREPU'SCULE. *n. s.* [*crepusculum*, Lat.] Twilight. *Dict.*

CREPU'SCULOUS. *adj.* [*crepusculum*, Latin.] Glimmering; in a state between light and darkness.

A close apprehension of the one, might perhaps afford a glimmering light and *crepusculous* glance of the other. *Brown.*

The beginnings of philosophy were in a *crepusculous* obscurity, and it is yet scarce past the dawn. *Glanv. Sceps. c.* 27.

CRE'SCENT. *adj.* [from *cresco*, Latin.] Increasing; growing; in a state of increase.

I have seen him in Britain: he was then of a *crescent* note. *Shakespeare's Cymbeline.*

With these in troop
Came Astoreth, whom the Phœnicians call'd
Astarte, queen of heaven, with *crescent* horns. *Milt. P. L.*

CRE'SCENT. *n. s.* [*crescens*, Lat.] The moon in her state of increase; any similitude of the moon increasing.

My pow'r's a *crescent*, and my auguring hope
Says it will come to th' full. *Shakesp. Anthony and Cleopatra.*

Or Bactrian sophy, from the horns
Of Turkish *crescent*, leaves all waste beyond
The realm of Aladule, in his retreat. *Milton's Parad. Lost.*

Jove in dusky clouds involves the skies,
And the faint *crescent* shoots by fits before their eyes. *Dryd.*

And two fair *crescents* of translucent horn,
The brows of all their young increase adorn. *Pope's Odyssey.*

CRE'SCIVE. *adv.* [from *cresco*, Latin.] Increasing; growing.

So the prince obscur'd his contemplation
Under the veil of wildness, which, no doubt,
Grew like the summer-grass, fastest by night,
Unseen, yet *crescive* in his faculty. *Shakesp. Henry* V.

CRESS. *n. s.* [perhaps from *cresco*, it being a quick grower.] An herb.

Its flower consists of four leaves, placed in form of a cross; the pointal arises from the center of the flower-cup, and becomes a roundish smooth fruit, divided into two cells, and furnished with seeds, generally smooth. It is cultivated as a sallad-herb, and chiefly esteemed in the Winter and Spring, being one of the warm kind. *Miller.*

His court with nettles and with *cresses* stor'd,
With soups unbought, and sallads, blest his board. *Pope.*

CRE'SSET. *n. s.* [*croissete*, Fr. because beacons had crosses anciently on their tops.] A great light set upon a beacon, lighthouse, or watch-tower. *Hanmer.* They still raise armies in Scotland by carrying about the fire-cross.

At my nativity
The front of heav'n was full of firy shapes,
Of burning *cressets.* *Shakespeare's Henry* IV. *p.* i.

From the arched roof,
Pendent by subtle magick, many a row
Of starry lamps, and blazing *cressets*, fed
With naphtha and asphaltus, yielded light
As from a sky. *Milton's Paradise Lost, b* i. *l.* 726.

CREST. *n. s.* [*crista*, Latin.]

1. The plume of feathers on the top of the ancient helmet.

His valour, shewn upon our *crests* to-day,
Hath taught us how to cherish such high deeds,
Ev'n in the bosom of our adversaries. *Shakesp. Henry* IV.

2. The comb of a cock.

Others, on ground
Walk'd firm; the *crested* cock, whose clarion sounds
The silent hours. *Milton's Paradise Lost, b.* vii. *l.* 442.

3. The ornament of the helmet in heraldry.

Of what esteem *crests* were, in the time of king Edward the third's reign, may appear by his giving an eagle, which he himself had formerly born, for a *crest* to William Montacute, earl of Salisbury. *Camden's Remains.*

The horn;
It was a *crest* ere thou wast born:
Thy father's father wore it. *Shakespeare's As you like it.*

4. Any tuft or ornament on the head; as some which the poets assign to serpents.

Their *crests* divide,
And, tow'ring o'er his head, in triumph ride. *Dryd. Virgil.*

5. Pride; spirit; fire; courage; loftiness of mien.

When horses should endure the bloody spur,
They fall their *crests.* *Shakespeare.*

CRE'STED. *adj.* [from *crest*; *cristatus*, Latin.]

1. Adorned with a plume or crest.

The bold Ascalonites,
Then grov'ling soil'd their *crested* helmets in the dust. *Milt.*

At this, for new replies he did not stay;
But lac'd his *crested* helm, and strode away. *Dryden.*

2. Wearing a comb.

The *crested* bird shall by experience know,
Jove made not him his master-piece below. *Dryden's Fables.*

CREST-FALLEN. *adj.* [*crest* and *fall.*] Dejected; sunk; dispirited; cowed; heartless; spiritless.

I warrant you, they would whip me with their fine wits, 'till I were as *crest-fallen* as a dried pear. *Sh. Mer. W. of Winds.*

They prolate their words in a whining kind of querulous tone, as if they were still complaining and *crest-fallen. Howel.*

CRE'STLESS. *adj.* [from *crest.*] Not dignified with coat-armour; not of any eminent family.

His grandfather was Lionel duke of Clarence,
Third son to the third Edward king of England,
Sprung *crestless* yeomen from so deep a root. *Shakespeare.*

CRETA'CEOUS. *adj.* [*creta*, chalk, Lat.] Abounding with chalk; having the qualities of chalk; chalky.

What gives the light, seems hard to say; whether it be the *cretaceous* salt, the nitrous salt, or some igneous particles. *Grew.*

Nor from the sable ground expect success,
Nor from *cretaceous*, stubborn and jejune. *Philips.*

CRETA'TED. *adj.* [*cretatus*, Latin.] Rubbed with chalk. *Dict.*

CRE'VICE. *n. s.* [from *crever*, Fr. *crepare*, Latin, to burst.] A crack; a cleft; a narrow opening.

I pried me through the *crevice* of a wall,
When for his hand he had his two sons heads. *Shakespeare.*

I thought it no breach of good-manners to peep at a *crevice*, and look in at people so well employed. *Addison's Spectator.*

CREW. *n. s.* [probably from cnub, Saxon.]

1. A company of people associated for any purpose; as *gallant crew*, for troops. *Chevy-chase.*

There a noble *crew*
Of lords and ladies stood on every side,
Which, with their presence fair, the place much beautify'd.
Fairy Queen, b. i. *cant.* 4. *stanz.* 7.

2. The company of a ship.

The anchors drop'd, his *crew* the vessels moor. *Dryd. Æn.*

3. It is now generally used in a bad sense.

One of the banish'd *crew*,
I fear, hath ventur'd from the deep, to raise
New troubles. *Milton's Paradise Lost, b.* iv. *l.* 573.

He with a *crew*, whom like ambition joins
With him, or under him to tyrannize,
Marching from Eden tow'rds the west, shall find
The plain. *Milton's Paradise Lost, b.* xii. *l.* 38.

The last was he, whose thunder slew
The Titan race, a rebel *crew*. *Addison.*

CREW. [the preterit of *crow*.]

CRE'WEL. *n. s.* [*klewel*, Dutch.] Yarn twisted and wound on a knot or ball.

Take silk or *crewel*, gold or silver thread, and make these fast at the bent of the hook. *Walton's Angler.*

CRIB. *n. s.* [cꞃybbe, Sax. *crib*, German.]

1. The rack or manger of a stable.

Let a beast be lord of beasts, and his *crib* shall stand at the king's messe. *Shakespeare's Hamlet.*

The steer and lion at one *crib* shall meet,
And harmless serpents lick the pilgrim's feet. *Pope.*

2. The stall or cabbin of an ox.

3. A small habitation; a cottage.

Why rather, sleep, liest thou in smokey *cribs*,
Upon uneasy pallets stretching thee,
Than in the perfum'd chambers of the great? *Shakespeare.*

To CRIB. *v. a.* [from the noun.] To shut up in a narrow habitation; to confine; to cage.

Now I'm cabbin'd, *cribb'd*, confin'd, bound in
To saucy doubts and fears. *Shakespeare's Macbeth.*

CRI'BBAGE. *n. s.* A game at cards.

CRI'BBLE. *n. s.* [*cribrum*, Latin.] A corn-sieve. *Dict.*

CRIBRA'TION. *n. s.* [*cribro*, Latin.] The act of sifting, or separating by a sieve.

CRICK. *n. s.*

1. [from *cricco*, Italian.] The noise of a door.

2. [from cꞃyce, Saxon, a stake.] A painful stiffness in the neck.

CRI'CKET. *n. s.* [*krekel*, from *kreken*, to make a noise, Dutch.]

1. An insect that squeaks or chirps about ovens and fireplaces.

Didst thou not hear a noise?——
—I heard the owl scream, and the *crickets* cry. *Shakes. Mach.*

Far from all resort of mirth,
Save the *cricket* on the hearth. *Milton.*

The solemn death-watch click'd the hour she dy'd,
And shrilling *crickets* in the chimney cry'd. *Gay's Pastorals.*

2. [from cꞃyce, Saxon, a stick.] A sport, at which the contenders drive a ball with sticks in opposition to each other.

The judge, to dance, his brother serjeant call;
The senator at *cricket* urge the ball. *Pope's Dunciad, b.* iv.

3. [from *kriechen*, Germ. to creep.] A low seat or stool.

CRI'ER. *n. s.* [from *cry*.] The officer whose business is to cry or make proclamation.

He openeth his mouth like a *crier*. *Ecclus.* xx. 15.

The *criers* command silence, and the whole multitude present stand in a suspence. *Brerewood on Languages.*

The *crier* calls aloud
Our old nobility of Trojan blood,
Who gape among the crowd for their precarious food. *Dry.*

CRIME. *n. s.* [*crimen*, Lat. *crime*, French.] An act contrary to right; an offence; a great fault; an act of wickedness.

High God be witness, that I guiltless am;
But if yourself, sir knight, ye guilty find,
Or wrapped be in loves of former dame,
With *crime* do not it cover, but disclose the same. *Fairy Qu.*

No *crime* was thine, if 'tis no *crime* to love. *Pope.*

CRI'MEFUL. *adj.* [from *crime* and *full*.] Wicked; criminal; faulty in a high degree; contrary to duty; contrary to virtue.

You proceeded not against these feats,
So *crimeful* and so capital in nature. *Shakespeare's Hamlet.*

CRI'MELESS. *adj.* [from *crime*.] Innocent; without crime.

My foes could not procure me any scathe,
So long as I am loyal, true, and *crimeless*. *Shakesp. Hen.* VI.

CRI'MINAL. *adj.* [from *crime*.]

1. Faulty; contrary to right; contrary to duty; contrary to law.

Live thou, and to thy mother dead attest,
That clear she died from blemish *criminal*. *Fairy Quen, b.* ii.

What we approve in our friend, we can hardly be induced to think *criminal* in ourselves. *Rogers, Serm.* iv.

2. Guilty; tainted with crime; not innocent.

The neglect of any of the relative duties, render us *criminal* in the sight of God. *Rogers's Sermons.*

3. Not civil; as a *criminal* prosecution.

CRI'MINAL. *n. s.* [from *crime*.]

1. A man accused.

Was ever *criminal* forbid to plead?
Curb your ill-manner'd zeal. *Dryden's Spanish Fryar.*

2. A man guilty of a crime.

All three persons, that had held chief place of authority in their countries; all three ruined, not by war, or by any other disaster, but by justice and sentence, as delinquents and *criminals*. *Bacon.*

CRI'MINALLY. *adv.* [from *criminal*.] Not innocently; wickedly; guiltily.

As our thoughts extend to all subjects, they may be *criminally* employed on all. *Rogers's Sermons.*

CRI'MINALNESS. *n. s.* [from *criminal*.] Guiltiness; want of innocence.

CRIMINA'TION. *n. s.* [*criminatio*, Latin.] The act of accusing; accusation; arraignment; charge.

CRI'MINATORY. *adj.* [from *crimina*, Latin.] Relating to accusation; accusing; censorious.

CRI'MINOUS. *adj.* [*criminosus*, Latin.] Wicked; iniquitous; enormously guilty.

The punishment that belongs to that great and *criminous* guilt, is the forfeiture of his right and claim to all mercies, which are made over to him by Christ. *Hammond on Fundam.*

CRI'MINOUSLY. *adv.* [from *criminous*.] Enormously; very wickedly.

Some particular duties of piety and charity, which were most *criminously* omitted before. *Hammond's Pract. Catech.*

CRI'MINOUSNESS. *n. s.* [from *criminous*.] Wickedness; guilt; crime.

I could never be convinced of any such *criminousness* in him, as willingly to expose his life to the stroke of justice and malice of his enemies. *King Charles.*

CRI'MOSIN. *adj.* [*crimosino*, Italian.] A species of red colour.

Upon her head a *crimosin* coronet,
With damask roses and daffadilies set,
Bay-leaves between,
And primroses green,
Embellish the white violet. *Spenser's Pastorals.*

CRIMP. *adj.* [from *crumble*, or *crimble*.]

1. Friable; brittle; easily crumbled; easily reduced to powder.

Now the fowler, warn'd
By these good omens, with swift early steps,
Treads the *crimp* earth, ranging through fields and glades. *Philips.*

2. Not consistent; not forcible: a low cant word.

The evidence is *crimp*; the witnesses swear backwards and forwards, and contradict themselves; and his tenants stick by him. *Arbuthnot's History of John Bull.*

To CRI'MPLE. *v. a.* [from *rumple*, *crumple*, *crimple*.] To contract; to corrugate; to cause to shrink or contract.

He passed the cautery through them, and accordingly *crimpled* them up. *Wiseman's Surgery.*

CRI'MSON. *n. s.* [*cremosino*, Italian.]

1. Red, somewhat darkened with blue.

As *crimson* seems to be little else than a very deep red, with an eye of blue; so some kinds of red seem to be little else than heightened yellow. *Boyle on Colours.*

2. Red in general.

Can you blame her then, being a maid yet rosed over with the virgin *crimson* of modesty, if she deny the appearance of a naked blind boy, in her naked seeing self? *Shakes. Henry* V.

Beauty's ensign yet
Is *crimson* in thy lips, and in thy cheeks. *Shakespeare.*

The *crimson* stream distain'd his arms around,
And the disdainful soul came rushing through the wound. *Dryden's Æneis.*

Why does the soil endue
The blushing poppy with a *crimson* hue? *Prior.*

To CRI'MSON. *v. a* [from the noun.]

1. To dye with crimson.

Pardon me, Julius.—Here wast thou bay'd, brave hart:
Here didst thou fall; and here thy hunters stand
Sign'd in thy spoil, and *crimson'd* in thy lethe. *Shakespeare.*

CRI'NCUM. *n. s.* [a cant word.] A cramp; a contraction; whimsy.

For jealousy is but a kind
Of clap and *crincum* of the mind. *Hudibras, p* iii. *cant.* 1.

CRINGE. *n. s.* [from the verb.] Bow; servile civility.

Let me be grateful; but let far from me
Be fawning *cringe*, and false dissembling looks. *Philips.*

To CRINGE. *v. a.* [from *kriechen*, German.] To draw together; to contract.

Whip him, fellows,
'Till, like a boy, you see him *cringe* his face,
And whine aloud for mercy. *Shakes. Anthony and Cleopatra.*

To CRINGE. *v. n. kriechen*, German.] To bow; to pay court with bows; to fawn; to flatter.

Flatterers have the flexor muscles so strong, that they are always bowing and *cringing*. *Arbuthnot.*

The *cringing* knave, who seeks a place
Without success, thus tells his case. *Swift.*

CRINI'GEROUS. *adj.* [*criniger*, Latin.] Hairy; overgrown with hair. *Dict.*

To CRI'NKLE. *v. n.* [from *krinckelen*, Dutch.] To go in and out; to run in flexures.

Unless some sweetness at the bottom lie,
Who cares for all the *crinkling* of the pye? *King's Cookery.*

To CRI'NKLE. *v. a.* To mould into inequalities.
CRI'NKLE. *n. f.* [from the verb.] A wrinkle; a finuofity.
CRI'NOSE. *adj.* [from *crinis*, Latin] Hairy. *Dict.*
CRINO'SITY. *n. f.* [from *crinofe.*] Hairynefs. *Dict.*
CRI'PPLE. *n. f.* [crypel, Sax. *krepel*, Dutch.] A lame man; one that has loft or never enjoyed the ufe of his limbs.

He, poor man, by your firft order died,
And that a winged Mercury did bear:
Some tardy *cripple* had the countermand,
That came too lag to fee him buried. *Shakefpeare's R III.*

I am a *cripple* in my limbs; but what decays are in my mind, the reader muft determine. *Dryden's Fables, Pref.*

Among the reft there was a lame *cripple* from his birth, whom Paul commanded to ftand upright on his feet. *Bentley.*

See the blind beggar dance, the *cripple* fing,
The fot a hero, lunatick a king. *Pope's Effay on Man.*

To CRI'PPLE. *v. a.* [from the noun.] To lame; to make lame; to deprive of the ufe of limbs.

Knots upon his gouty joints appear,
And chalk is in his *crippled* fingers found. *Dryden's Perf.*

Tettyx, the dancing-mafter, threw himfelf from the rock, but was *crippled* in the fall. *Addifon.*

CRI'PPLENESS. *n. f.* [from *cripple.*] Lamenefs; privation of the limbs. *Dict.*
CRI'SIS. *n. f.* [κρίσις.]
1. The point in which the difeafe kills, or changes to the better.

Wife leeches will not vain receipts obtrude;
Deaf to complaints, they wait upon the ill,
'Till fome fafe *crifis* authorize their fkill. *Dryden.*

2. The point of time at which any affair comes to the height.

This hour's the very *crifis* of your fate;
Your good or ill, your infamy or fame,
And all the colour of your life depends
On this important now. *Dryden's Spanifh Fryar.*

The undertaking, which I am now laying down, was entered upon in the very *crifis* of the late rebellion, when it was the duty of every Briton to contribute his utmoft affiftance to the government, in a manner fuitable to his ftation and abilities. *Addifon's Freeholder, N°. 55.*

CRISP. *adj.* [*crifpus*, Latin.]
1. Curled.

Bulls are more *crifp* on the forehead than cows. *Bacon.*
The Ethiopian black, flat nofed, and *crifp* haired. *Hale.*

2. Indented; winding.

You nymphs, call'd Naiads, of the winding brooks,
With your fedg'd crowns, and ever harmlefs looks,
Leave your *crifp* channels, and on this green land
Anfwer your fummons, Juno does command. *Shakef. Temp.*

3. Brittle; friable.

In frofty weather, mufick within doors foundeth better; which may be by reafon not of the difpofition of the air, but of the wood or ftring of the inftrument, which is made more *crifp*, and fo more porous and hollow. *Bacon's Natural Hift.*

To CRISP. *v. a.* [*crifpo*, Latin]
1. To curl; to contract into knots or curls.

Severn, affrighted with their bloody looks,
Ran fearfully among the trembling reeds,
And hid his *crifp'd* head in the hollow bank. *Shak. Hen. IV.*

Young I'd have him too,
Yet a man, with *crifped* hair,
Caft in thoufand fnares and rings,
For love's fingers, and his rings. *Ben. Johnfon's Underwoods.*

The hafty application of fpirits of wine is not only unfit for inflammations in general, but alfo *crifps* up the veffels of the dura mater and brain, and fometimes produces a gangrene. *Sharp's Surgery.*

2. To twift.

Along the *crifped* fhades and bow'rs,
Revels the fpruce and jocund fpring. *Milton.*

3. To indent; to run in and out.

From that faphine fount the *crifped* brooks,
Rolling on orient pearl and fands of gold,
Ran nectar, vifiting each plant. *Milton's Paradife Loft, b. iv.*

CRISPA'TION. *n. f.* [from *crifp.*]
1. The act of curling.
2. The ftate of being curled.

Some differ in the hair and feathers, both in the quantity, *crifpation*, and colours of them; as he-lions are hirfute, and have great manes; the fhe's are fmooth, like cats. *Bacon.*

CRI'SPING-PIN. *n. f.* [from *crifp.*] A curling-iron.

The changeable fuits of apparel, and the mantles, and the wimples, and the *crifping-pins.* *If.* iii. 22.

CRISPI'SULCANT. *adj.* [*crifpifulcans*, Latin.] Waved, or undulating; as lightning is reprefented. *Dict.*
CRI'SPNESS. *n. f.* [from *crifp.*] Curlednefs.
CRI'SPY. *adj.* [from *crifp.*] Curled.

So are thofe *crifpy* fnaky locks, oft known
To be the dowry of a fecond head. *Shakefp. Merch. of Ven.*

CRITE'RION. *n. f.* [κριτήριον.] A mark by which any thing is judged of, with regard to its goodnefs or badnefs.

Mutual agreement and endearments was the badge of primitive believers; but we may be known by the contrary *criterion.* *Glanv. Scepf. c. 27.*

We have here a fure infallible *criterion*, by which every man may difcover and find out the gracious or ungracious difpofition of his own heart. *South's Sermons.*

By what *criterion* do ye eat, d'ye think,
If this is priz'd for fweetnefs, that for ftink? *Pope's Hor.*

CRI'TICK. *n. f.* [κριτικός.]
1. A man fkilled in the art of judging of literature; a man able to diftinguifh the faults and beauties of writing.

This fettles truer ideas in men's minds of feveral things, whereof we read the names in ancient authors, than all the large and laborious arguments of *criticks.* *Locke.*

Criticks I faw, that other names deface,
And fix their own with labour in their place. *Pope.*

Where an author has many beauties confiftent with virtue, piety, and truth, let not little *criticks* exalt themfelves, and fhower down their ill-nature. *Watts.*

2. A cenfurer; a man apt to find fault.

My chief defign, next to feeing you, is to be a fevere *critick* on you and your neighbour. *Swift.*

CRI'TICK. *adj.* Critical; relating to criticifm; relating to the art of judging of literary performances.

Thence arts o'er all the northern world advance,
But *critick* learning flourifh'd moft in France. *Pope.*

CRI'TICK. *n f.*
1. A critical examination; critical remarks; animadverfions.

I fhould be glad if I could perfuade him to continue his good offices, and write fuch another *critick* on any thing of mine. *Dryden.*

I fhould as foon expect to fee a *critique* on the poefy of a ring, as on the infcription of a medal. *Addifon on Medals.*

2. Science of criticifm.

If ideas and words were diftinctly weighed, and duly confidered, they would afford us another fort of logick and *critick* than what we have been hitherto acquainted with. *Locke.*

What is every year of a wife man's life, but a cenfure and *critique* on the paft? *Pope.*

Not that my quill to *criticks* was confin'd,
My verfe gave ampler leffons to mankind. *Pope.*

To CRI'TICK. *v. n.* [from *critick.*] To play the critick; to criticife.

They do but trace over the paths that have been beaten by the antients; or comment, *critick*, and flourifh upon them. *Temple.*

CRI'TICAL. *adj.* [from *critick.*]
1. Exact; nicely judicious; accurate; diligent.

It is fubmitted to the judgment of more *critical* ears, to direct and determine what is graceful and what is not. *Holder.*

Virgil was fo *critical* in the rites of religion, that he would never have brought in fuch prayers as thefe, if they had not been agreeable to the Roman cuftoms. *Stillingfleet.*

2. Relating to criticifm; as, *he wrote a* critical *differtation on the laft play.*
3. Captious; inclined to find fault.

What wouldft thou write of me, if thou fhouldft praife me?—
—O, gentle lady, do not put me to't;
For I am nothing, if not *critical.* *Shakefpeare's Othello.*

4. [from *crifis.*] Comprifing the time at which a great event is determined.

The moon is fuppofed to be meafured by fevens, and the *critical* or decretory days to be dependent on that number. *Brown's Vulgar Errours, b. iv. c. 12.*

Opportunity is in refpect to time, in fome fenfe, as time is in refpect to eternity: it is the fmall moment, the exact point, the *critical* minute, on which every good work fo much depends. *Sprat's Sermons.*

The people cannot but refent to fee their apprehenfions of the power of France, in fo *critical* a juncture, wholly laid afide. *Swift.*

CRI'TICALLY. *adv.* [from *critical.*] In a critical manner; exactly; curioufly.

Difficult it is to underftand the purity of Englifh, and *critically* to difcern good writers from bad, and a proper ftile from a corrupt one. *Dryden.*

Thefe fhells which are digged up out of the earth, feveral hundreds of which I now keep by me, have been nicely and *critically* examined by very many learned men. *Woodward.*

CRI'TICALNESS. *n f.* [from *critical.*] Exactnefs; accuracy; nicety.
To CRI'TICISE. *v. n.* [from *critick.*]
1. To play the critick; to judge; to write remarks upon any performance of literature; to point out faults and beauties.

They who can *criticife* fo weakly, as to imagine I have done my worft, may be convinced, at their own coft, that I can write feverely with more eafe than I can gently. *Dryden.*

Know well each ancient's proper character,
Without all this at once before your eyes,
Cavil you may, but never *criticife.* *Pope's Effay on Criticifm.*

2. To animadvert upon as faulty.

Nor would I have his father look fo narrowly into thefe accounts,

counts, as to take occasion from thence to *criticise* on his expences. *Locke.*

To CRI'TICISE. *v. a.* [from *critick.*] To censure; to pass judgment upon.

Nor shall I look upon it as any breach of charity to *criticise* the author, so long as I keep clear of the person. *Addison.*

CRI'TICISM. *n. s.* [from *critick.*]

1. *Criticism*, as it was first instituted by Aristotle, was meant a standard of judging well. *Dryden's Innocence, Pref.*

2. Remark; animadversion; critical observations.

There is not a Greek or Latin critick who has not shewn, even in the stile of his *criticisms*, that he was a master of all the eloquence and delicacy of his native tongue. *Addis. Spect.*

To CROAK. *v. n.* [cpacezzan, Saxon; *crocare*, Italian; *crocitare*, Latin.]

1. To make a hoarse low noise, like a frog.

The subtle swallow flies about the brook,
And querulous frogs in muddy pools do *croak.* *May's Virgil.*
So when Jove's block descended from on high,
Loud thunder to its bottom shook the bog,
And the hoarse nation *croak'd. Pope's Dunciad, b.* i. *l.* 264.
Blood, stuff'd in skins, is British christians food;
And France robs marshes of the *croaking* brood. *Gay.*

2. To caw or cry as a raven or crow.

The raven himself not hoarse,
That *croaks* the fatal entrance of Duncan
Under my battlements. *Shakespeare's Macbeth.*
The hoarse raven, on the blasted bough,
By *croaking* from the left, presag'd the coming blow. *Dryd.*

At the same time the walk of elms, with the *croaking* of the ravens, looks exceeding solemn and venerable. *Addis. Spectat.*

3. It may be used in contempt for any disagreeable or offensive murmur.

Their understandings are but little instructed, when all their whole time and pains is laid out to still the *croaking* of their own bellies. *Locke.*

CROAK. *n. s.* from the verb.] The cry or voice of a frog or raven.

The swallow skims the river's watry face,
The frogs renew the *croaks* of their loquacious race. *Dryd.*
Was that a raven's *croak*, or my son's voice?
No matter which, I'll to the grave and hide me. *Lee's Oed.*

CRO'CEOUS. *adj.* [*croceus*, Latin.] Consisting of saffron; like saffron. *Dict.*

CROCITA'TION. *n. s.* [*crocitatio*, Latin.] The croaking of frogs or ravens. *Dict.*

CROCK. *n. s.* [*kruick*, Dutch.] A cup; any vessel made of earth.

CRO'CKERY. *n. s.* Earthen ware.

CRO'CODILE. *n. s.* [from κρόκ☉, saffron, and δειλων, fearing.]

An amphibious voracious animal, in shape resembling a lizard, and found in Egypt and the Indies. It is covered with very hard scales, which cannot, without great difficulty, be pierced; except under the belly, where the skin is tender. It has a wide throat, with several rows of teeth, sharp and separated, which enter one another. Though its four legs are very short, it runs with great swiftness; but does not easily turn itself. It is long lived, and is said to grow continually to its death; but this is not probable. Some are fifteen or eighteen cubits long. Its sight is very piercing upon the ground, but in the water it sees but dimly; and it is said to spend the four winter months under water. When its bowels are taken out, or it is wounded, it smells very agreeably. *Crocodiles* lay their eggs, resembling goose-eggs, sometimes amounting to sixty, on the sand near the waterside, covering them with the sand, that the heat of the sun may contribute to hatch them. The Ichneumon, or Indian rat, which is as large as a tame cat, is said to break the *crocodile's* eggs whenever it finds them; and also, that it gets into the very belly of this creature, while it is asleep with its throat open, gnaws its entrails, and kills it. *Calmet.*

Glo'ster's show
Beguiles him; as the mournful *crocodile*,
With sorrow, snares relenting passengers. *Shakesp. Hen.* VI.

Crocodiles were thought to be peculiar unto the Nile. *Brown.*

Cæsar will weep, the *crocodile* will weep. *Dryden.*
Enticing *crocodiles*, whose tears are death;
Syrens, that murder with enchanting breath. *Granville.*

Crocodile is also a little animal, otherwise called stinx, very much like the lizard, or small *crocodile.* It lives by land and water; has four short small legs, a very sharp muzzle, and a short small tail. It is pretty enough to look at, being covered all over with little scales of the colour of silver, intermixt with brown, and of a gold colour upon the back. It always remains little, and is found in Egypt near the Red Sea, in Lybia, and in the Indies. *Trevoux.*

CRO'CODILINE. *adj.* [*crocodilinus*, Lat.] Like a crocodile. *Dict.*

CRO'CUS. *n. s.*

The best place to plant the Spring *crocus's* is close to a wall, or on the edge of boarded borders round a garden, mingling the colour of those of a season together. The seed must be kept in the husk 'till sown, and a light rich ground should be chosen for them. They must not be placed too thick: they may be increased also by off-sets. *Mortimer's Husbandry.*

Fair handed Spring unbosoms every grace,
Throws out the snow-drop and the *crocus* first. *Thomson.*

CROFT. *n. s.* [cꞃoꝼt, Saxon.] A little close joining to a house, that is used for corn or pasture.

This have I learn'd,
Tending my flocks hard by, i' th' hilly *crofts*
That brow this bottom glade. *Milton.*

CROISA'DE. } *n. s.* [*croisade*, Fr. from *croix*, a cross.] A holy
CROISA'DO. } war; a war carried on against infidels under the banner of the cross.

See that he take the name of Urban, because a pope of that name did first institute the *croisado*; and, as with an holy trumpet, did stir up the voyage for the Holy Land. *Bacon.*

CRO'ISES. *n. s.*

1. Pilgrims who carry a cross.

2. Soldiers who fight against infidels under the banner of the cross.

CRONE. *n. s.* [cꞃone, Sax. according to *Verstegan*; *kronie*, Dut. according to *Skinner.*]

1. An old ewe.

2. In contempt, an old woman.

Take up the bastard,
Take't up, I say; give't to thy *crone. Shakes. Winter's Tale.*

The *crone* being in bed with him on the wedding-night, and finding his aversion, endeavours to win his affection by reason. *Dryden's Fables, Preface.*

CRO'NET. *n. s.* The hair which grows over the top of an horse's hoof.

CRO'NY. *n. s.* [a cant word.] An old acquaintance; a companion of long standing.

So when the Scots, your constant *cronies*,
Th' espousers of your cause and monies. *Hudibras, p.* iii.
To oblige your *crony* Swift,
Bring our dame a new year's gift. *Swift.*
Strange, an astrologer should die,
Without one wonder in the sky!
Not one of all his *crony* stars,
To pay their duty at his herse? *Swift.*

CROOK. *n. s.* [*croc*, French.]

1. Any crooked or bent instrument.

2. A sheephook.

He left his *crook*, he left his flocks,
And wand'ring through the lonely rocks,
He nourish'd endless woe. *Prior.*

3. Any thing bent; a meander.

There fall those saphire-colour'd brooks,
Which, conduit like, with curious *crooks*,
Sweet islands make in that sweet land. *Sidney, b.* ii.

To CROOK. *v. a.* [*crocher*, French.]

1. To bend; to turn into a hook.

It is highly probable, that this disease proceeds from a redundant acidity, because vinegar will soften and *crook* tender bones. *Arbuthnot on Diet.*

2. To pervert from rectitude; to divert from the original end.

Whatsoever affairs pass such a man's hands, he *crooketh* them to his own ends; which must needs be often eccentrick to the ends of his master or state. *Bacon, Essay* 24.

CRO'OKBACK. *n. s.* [*crook* and *back.*] A term of reproach for a man that has gibbous shoulders.

Ay, *crookback*, here I stand to answer thee,
Or any he the proudest of thy sort. *Shakespeare's Henry* VI.

CRO'OKBACKED. *adj.* Having bent shoulders.

A dwarf as well may for a giant pass,
As negroe for a swan; a *crookback'd* lass
Be call'd Europa. *Dryden's Juvenal, Sat.* 8.

There are millions of truths that a man is not, or may not think himself, concerned to know; as, whether our king Richard III. was *crookbacked* or no. *Locke.*

CROO'KED. *adj.* [*crocher*, French.]

1. Bent; not strait; curve.

A bell or a cannon may be heard beyond a hill, which intercepts the sight of the sounding body; and sounds are propagated as readily through *crooked* pipes as through straight ones. *Newton's Opt.*

Mathematicians say of a straight line, that it is as well an index of its own rectitude as of the obliquity of a *crooked* one. *Woodward's Natural History.*

2. Winding; oblique; anfractuous.

A man shall never want *crooked* paths to walk in, if he thinks that he is in the right way, where-ever he has the footsteps of others to follow. *Locke.*

Among the *crooked* lanes, on every hedge,
The glow-worm lights his gem. *Thomson's Summer.*

3. Perverse; untoward; without rectitude of mind; given to obliquity of conduct.

They have corrupted themselves: they are a perverse and *crooked* generation. *Deutr.* xxxii. 5.

Hence, heap of wrath; foul, indigested lump!
As *crooked* in thy manners as thy shape. *Shakesp. Henry* VI.

We were not born *crooked*; we learned those windings and turnings of the serpent. *South's Sermons.*

CROO'KEDLY. *adv.* [from *crooked.*]

1. Not in a strait line.
2. Untowardly; not compliantly.

If we walk perversely with God, he will walk *crookedly* towards us. *Taylor's Rule of Living Holy.*

CROO'KEDNESS. *n. s.* [from *crooked.*]

1. Deviation from straitness; curvity; the state of being inflected; inflection.

He that knoweth what is straight, doth even thereby discern what is crooked; because the absence of straightness, in bodies capable thereof, is *crookedness.* *Hooker.*

2. Deformity of a gibbous body.

When the heathens offered a sacrifice to their false gods, they would make a severe search to see if there were any *crookedness* or spot, any uncleanness or deformity, in their sacrifice. *Taylor's Worthy Communicant.*

CROP. *n. s.* [cnop, Saxon.] The craw of a bird; the first stomach into which her meat descends.

In birds there is no mastication or comminution of the meat in the mouth; but in such as are not carnivorous, it is immediately swallowed into the *crop* or craw. *Ray on the Creation.*

But flutt'ring there, they nestle near the throne,
And lodge in habitations not their own,
By their high *crops* and corny gizzards known. *Dryden.*

CRO'PFULL. *adj.* [*crop* and *full.*] Satiated; with a full belly.

He stretch'd out all the chimney's length,
Basks at the fire his hairy strength;
And, *crop-full*, out of door he flings,
'Ere the first cock his matin rings. *Milton.*

CRO'PSICK. *adj.* [*crop* and *sick.*] Sick with repletion; sick with excess and debauchery.

Strange odds! where *crop-sick* drunkards must engage
A hungry foe, and arm'd with sober rage. *Tate's Juv. Sat.*

CROP. *n. s.* [cnoppa, Saxon.]

1. The highest part or end of any thing; as the head of a tree, the ear of corn.
2. The harvest; the corn gathered off a field; the product of the field.

And this of all my harvest hope I have,
Nought reaped but a weedy *crop* of care. *Spenser's Past.*
Lab'ring the soil, and reaping plenteous *crop*,
Corn, wine, and oil. *Milton's Paradise Lost, b.* xii.
The fountain which from Helicon proceeds,
That sacred stream, should never water weeds,
Nor make the *crop* of thorns and thistles grow. *Roscommon.*

Nothing is more prejudicial to your *crop* than mowing of it too soon, because the sap is not fully come out of the root. *Mortimer's Husbandry.*

3. Any thing cut off.

Guiltless of steel, and from the razor free,
It falls a plenteous *crop* reserv'd for thee. *Dryden's Fables.*

To CROP. *v. a.* [from the noun.]

1. To cut off the ends of any thing; to mow; to reap; to lop.

Crop'd are the flower-de-luces in your arms;
Of England's coat, one half is cut away. *Shakes. Hen.* VI.
He, upon whose side
The fewest roses are *crop'd* from the tree,
Shall yield the other in the right opinion. *Shakes. Henry* VI.
All the budding honours on thy crest
I'll *crop*, to make a garland for my head. *Shakes. Henry* IV.

I will *crop* off from the top of his young twigs a tender one, and will plant it upon an high mountain and eminent. *Ezek.* xvii. 22.

There are some tears of trees, which are combed from the beards of goats; for when the goats bite and *crop* them, especially in the mornings, the dew being on, the tear cometh forth, and hangeth upon their beards. *Bacon's Natural History.*

O Fruit divine!
Sweet of thyself, but much more sweet thus *crop'd. Milton.*
Age, like ripe apples, on earth's bosom drops;
While force our youth, like fruits, untimely *crops. Denham.*
Death destroys
The parent's hopes, and *crops* the growing boys. *Creech.*
No more, my goats, shall I behold you climb
The steepy cliffs, or *crop* the flow'ry thyme! *Dryd. Virgil.*

To CROP. *v. n.* To yield harvest.

Royal wench!
She made great Cæsar lay his sword to-bed;
He plough'd her, and she *cropt. Shakesp. Anth. and Cleopatra.*

CRO'PPER. *n. s.* [from *crop.*] A kind of pigeon with a large crop.

There are several kinds of trouts, as there be tame and wild pigeons; and of tame there be *croppers*, carriers, runts. *Walton's Angler.*

CRO'SIER. *n. s.* [*croiser*, Fr. from *croix*, a cross.] The pastoral staff of a bishop, which has a cross upon it.

When prelates are great, there is also danger from them; as it was in the times of Anselmus and Thomas Becket, who, with their *crosiers*, did almost try it with the king's sword. *Bacon, Essay* 20.

Grievances there were, I must confess, and some incongruities in my civil government; wherein some say the *crosier*, some say the distaff, was too busy. *Howel's England's Tears.*

Her front erect with majesty she bore,
The *crosier* wielded, and the mitre wore. *Dryden.*

CRO'SLET. *n. s.* [*croisselet*, French.]

1. A small cross.

Then Una 'gan to ask, if aught he knew,
Or heard abroad, of that her champion true,
That in his armour bare a *croslet* red. *Fairy Queen, b.* i.
Here an unfinish'd di'mond *croslet* lay,
To which soft lovers adoration pay. *Gay's Fan.*

2. It seems to be used in the following passage, by mistake, for *corselet.*

The *croslet* some, and some the cuishes mould,
With silver plated, and with ductile gold. *Dryden's Æn.*

CROSS. *n. s.* [*croix*, Fr. *croce*, Ital. *crux*, Latin.]

1. One strait body laid at right angles over another; the instrument by which the Saviour of the world suffered death.

They make a little *cross* of a quill, longways of that part of the quill which hath the pith, and crossways of that piece of the quill without pith. *Bacon's Natural History,* N°. 494.

You are first to consider seriously the infinite love of your Saviour, who offered himself for you as a sacrifice upon the *cross.* *Taylor's Guide to the Penitent.*

2. The ensign of the Christian religion.

Her holy faith and Christian *cross* oppos'd
Against the Saxon gods. *Rowe.*

3. A monument with a cross upon it to excite devotion; such as were anciently set in market-places.

She doth stray about
By holy *crosses*, where she kneels and prays. *Shakespeare.*

4. A line drawn through another.
5. Any thing that thwarts or obstructs; misfortune; hindrance; vexation; opposition; misadventure; trial of patience.

Wishing unto me many *crosses* and mischances in my love, whensoever I should love. *Sidney, b.* i.

Then let us teach our trial patience,
Because it is a customary *cross.* *Shakespeare.*

Heaven prepares good men with *crosses*; but no ill can happen to a good man. *Ben. Johnson's Discoveries.*

A great estate hath great *crosses*, and a mean fortune hath but small ones. *Taylor's Rule of Living Holy.*

6. Money so called, because marked with a cross.

He was said to make soldiers spring up out of the very earth to follow him, though he had not a *cross* to pay them salary. *Howel's Vocal Forest.*

Whereas we cannot much lament our loss,
Who neither carry'd back nor brought one *cross.* *Dryden.*

7. *Cross and Pile*, a play with money; at which it is put to chance whether the side, which bears a cross, shall lie upward, or the other.

Whacum had neither *cross* nor *pile*;
His plunder was not worth the while. *Hudibras, p.* ii.

This I humbly conceive to be perfect boys play; *cross*, I win, and *pile*, you lose; or, what's yours is mine, and what's mine is my own. *Swift.*

CROSS. *adj.* [from the substantive.]

1. Transverse; falling a-thwart something else.

Whatsoever penumbra should be made in the circles by the *cross* refraction of the second prism, all that penumbra would be conspicuous in the right lines which touch those circles. *Newton's Opticks.*

The sun, in that space of time, by his annual contrary motion eastward, will be advanced near a degree of the ecliptick, *cross* to the motion of the equator. *Holder on Time.*

The ships must needs encounter, when they either advance towards one another in direct lines, or meet in the intersection of *cross* ones. *Bentley's Sermons.*

2. Oblique; lateral.

Was this a face,
To stand against the deep dread bolted thunder?
In the most terrible and nimble stroke
Of quick *cross* lightning? *Shakespeare's King Lear.*

3. Adverse; opposite.

Were both love's captives; but with fate so *cross*,
One must be happy by the other's loss. *Dryden's Aurengzebe.*
Cross to our interests, curbing sense and sin;
Oppress'd without, and undermin'd within,
It thrives through pain. *Dryden.*

It runs *cross* to the belief and apprehension of the rest of mankind; a difficulty, which a modest and good man is scarce able to encounter. *Atterbury's Sermons.*

4. Perverse; untractable.

When, through the *cross* circumstances of a man's temper or condition, the enjoyment of a pleasure would certainly expose him to a greater inconvenience, then religion bids him quit it. *South's Sermons.*

5. Peevish; fretful; ill-humoured.
Did ever any man upon the rack afflict himself, because he had received a *cross* answer from his mistress? *Taylor.*
All *cross* and distasteful humours, and whatever else may render the conversation of men grievous and uneasy to one another, must be shunned. *Tillotson, Sermon* 5.
6. Contrary; contradictory.
The mind brings all the ends of a long and various hypothesis together; sees how one part coheres with, and depends upon another; and so clears off all the appearing contrarieties and contradictions, that seemed to lie *cross* and uncouth, and to make the whole unintelligible. *South's Sermons.*
7. Contrary to wish; unfortunate.
We learn the great reasonableness of not only a contented, but also a thankful acquiescence in any condition, and under the *crossest* and severest passages of providence. *South's Sermons.*
I cannot, without some regret, behold the *cross* and unlucky issue of my design; for by my dislike of disputes, I am engaged in one. *Glanv.*
8. Interchanged.
Evarchus made a *cross* marriage also with Dorilaus's sister, and shortly left her with child of the famous Pyrocles. *Sidney.*
They had long conference, not only upon commerce, but upon *cross* marriages, to be had between the king's son and the archduke's daughter; and again, between the archduke's son and the king's daughter. *Bacon's Henry* VII.
Cross. *prep.*
1. A-thwart; so as to intersect any thing.
They were advertised, that the enemy had, in the woods before them, whereby they were to pass, cut down great trees *cross* the ways, so that their horse could not possibly pass that way. *Knolles's History of the Turks.*

Betwixt the midst and these, the gods assign'd
Two habitable seats of human kind;
And *cross* their limits cut a sloaping way,
Which the twelve signs in beauteous order sway. *Dryd. Virg.*
Cross his back, as in triumphant scorn,
The hope and pillar of the house was born. *Dryd. Fables.*

2. Over; from side to side.
A fox was taking a walk one night *cross* a village. *L'Estran.*
To Cross. *v. a.* [from the noun.]
1. To lay one body, or draw one line, a-thwart another.

This forc'd the stubborn'st, for the cause,
To *cross* the cudgels to the laws;
That what by breaking them't had gain'd,
By their support might be maintain'd. *Hudibras, p.* iii. *c.* 2.

The loxia, or cross-bill, whose bill is thick and strong, with the tips *crossing* one another, with great readiness breaks open fir-cones, apples, and other fruit, to come at their kernels; as if the *crossing* of the bill was designed for this service. *Derham's Physico-Theology.*
I shall most carefully observe, not to *cross* over, or deface the copy of your papers for the future, and only to mark in the margin. *Pope.*
A hunted hare treads back her mazes, and *crosses* and confounds her former track. *Watts.*
2. To sign with the cross.
3. To mark out; to cancel; as, *to* cross *an article.*
4. To pass over.
He conquered this proud Turk as far as the Hellespont, which he *crossed*, and made a visit to the Greek emperor at Constantinople. *Temple.*

We found the hero, for whose only sake
We sought the dark abodes, and *cross'd* the bitter lake. *Dry.*

5. To move laterally, obliquely, or a-thwart; not in opposition; not in the same line.

But he them spying, 'gan to turn aside,
For fear, as seem'd, or for some feined loss;
More greedy they of news, fast towards him do *cross.* *Spens.*

6. To thwart; to interpose obstruction; to embarrass; to obstruct; to hinder.
Still do I *cross* this wretch, whatso he taketh in hand. *Hooker.*

The king no longer could endure
Thus to be *cross'd* in what he did intend. *Daniel's Civ. War.*

He was so great an enemy to Digby and Colepeper, who were only present in debates of the war with the officers, that he *crossed* all they proposed. *Clarendon, b.* viii.

Bury'd in private, and so suddenly!
It *crosses* my design, which was t' allow
The rites of funeral fitting his degree. *Dryd. Span. Fryar.*
Swell'd with our late successes on the foe,
Which France and Holland wanted pow'r to *cross*,
We urge an unseen fate. *Dryden.*
The firm patriot there,
Though still by faction, vice, and fortune *crost*,
Shall find the generous labour was not lost. *Addison's Cato.*

7. To counteract.
Then their wills clash with their understandings, and their appetites *cross* their duty. *Locke.*
8. To contravene; to hinder by authority; to countermand.
No governour is suffered to go on with any one course, but upon the least information he is either stopped and *crossed*, or other courses appointed him from hence. *Spenser on Ireland.*
It may make my case dangerous, to *cross* this in the smallest. *Shakespeare's Measure for Measure.*
9. To contradict.
In all this there is not a syllable which any ways *crosseth* us. *Hooker, b.* ii. *sect.* 6.
It is certain, howsoever it *cross* the received opinion, that sounds may be created without air. *Bacon's Natural History.*
10. To debar; to preclude.

From his loins no hopeful branch shall spring,
To *cross* me from the golden time I look for. *Shakes. H.* VI.

To Cross. *v. n.*
1. To lye a-thwart another thing.
2. To be inconsistent.
Men's actions do not always *cross* with reason. *Sidney.*
Cross-bar-shot. *n. s.* A round shot, or great bullet, with a bar of iron put through it. *Harris.*
To Cross-examine. *v. a.* [*cross* and *examine.*] To try the faith of evidence by captious questions of the contrary party.
If we may but *cross-examine* and interrogate their actions against their words, these will soon confess the invalidity of their solemnest confessions. *Decay of Piety.*
The judges shall, as they think fit, interrogate or *cross-examine* the witnesses. *Spectator*, N°. 608.
Cro'ss staff. *n. s.* [from *cross* and *staff.*] An instrument commonly called the forestaff, used by seamen to take the meridian altitude of the sun or stars. *Harris.*
A Cro'ssbite. *n. s.* [*cross* and *bite.*] A deception; a cheat.
The fox, that trusted to his address and manage, without so much as dreaming of a *cross-bite* from so silly an animal, fell himself into the pit that he had digged for another. *L'Estr.*
To Cro'ssbite. *v. a.* [from the noun.] To contravene by deception.
No rhetorick must be spent against *cross-biting* a country evidence, and frighting him out of his senses. *Collier.*

That many knotty points there are,
Which all discuss, but few can clear;
As nature slily had thought fit,
For some by-ends, to *cross-bite* wit. *Prior.*

Cro'ssbow. *n. s.* [*cross* and *bow.*] A missive weapon formed by placing a bow a-thwart a stock.
Gentlemen suffer their beasts to run wild in their woods and waste ground, where they are hunted and killed with *cross-bows* and pieces, in the manner of deer. *Carew's S. of Cornwal.*
The master of the *cross-bows*, lord Rambures. *Sh. H.* V.
Cro'ssbowers. *n. s.* [from *cross-bow.*] A shooter with a cross-bow.
The French assisted themselves by land with the *crossbowers* of Genoa against the English. *Raleigh's Essays.*
Cro'ssgrained. *adj.* [*cross* and *grain.*]
1. Having the fibres transverse or irregular.
If the stuff proves *crossgrained* in any part of its length, then you must turn your stuff to plane it the contrary way, so far as it runs *cross-grained.* *Moxon's Mech. Exer.*
2. Perverse; troublesome; vexatious.

We find in sullen writs,
And *cross-grain'd* works of modern wits,
The wonder of the ignorant. *Hudibras, p.* i. *cant.* 1.

The spirit of contradiction, in a *cross-grained* woman, is incurable. *L'Estrange.*
She was none of your *cross-grained*, termagant, scolding jades, that one had as good be hanged as live in the house with. *Arbuthnot's History of John Bull.*

But wisdom, peevish and *cross-grain'd*,
Must be oppos'd, to be sustain'd. *Prior.*

Cro'ssly. *adv.* [from *cross.*]
1. A-thwart; so as to intersect something else.
2. Oppositely; adversely; in opposition to.
He that provides for this life, but takes no care for eternity, is wise for a moment, but a fool for ever; and acts as untowardly, and *crossly* to the reason of things, as can be imagined. *Tillotson's Sermons.*
3. Unfortunately.
Cro'ssness. *n. s.* [from *cross.*]
1. Transverseness; intersection.
2. Perverseness; peevishness.
The lighter sort of malignity turneth but to a *crossness*, or aptness to oppose; but the deeper sort, to envy, or mere mischief. *Bacon, Essay* 13.
I deny nothing, fit to be granted, out of *crossness* or humour. *King Charles.*
Who would have imagined, that the stiff *crossness* of a poor captive should ever have had the power to make Haman's seat so uneasy to him? *L'Estrange, Fab.* 38.
They help us to forget the *crossness* of men and things, compose our cares and our passions, and lay our disappointments asleep. *Collier of the Entertainment of Books.*
Cro'ssrow. *n. s.* [*cross* and *row.*] Alphabet; so named because a cross is placed at the beginning, to shew that the end of learning is piety.

He hearkens after prophecies and dreams,
And from the *crossrow* plucks the letter G;
And says a wizard told him, that by G
His issue disinherited should be. *Shakespeare's Richard* III.

CRO'SSWIND. *n. s.* [*cross* and *wind.*] Wind blowing from the right or left.

The least unhappy persons do, in so fickle and so tempestuous a sea, as we all find this world, meet with many more either *crosswinds* or stormy gusts than prosperous gales. *Boyle's Seraphick Love.*

CRO'SSWAY. *n. s.* [*cross* and *way.*] A small obscure path intersecting the chief road.

Damn'd spirits all,
That in *crossways* and floods have burial,
Already to their wormy beds are gone. *Shakespeare.*

CRO'SSWORT. *n. s.* [from *cross* and *wort.*]

It hath soft leaves, like the ladies bedstraw, from which it differs in the number of leaves, that are produced at every joint; which in this are only four, disposed in form of a cross. The rough or hairy *crosswort* is sometimes used in medicine, and is found wild on dry sandy banks. *Miller.*

CROTCH. *n. s.* [*croc*, French.] A hook.

There is a tradition of a dilemma, that Moreton used to raise the benevolence to higher rates; and some called it his fork, and some his *crotch.* *Bacon's Henry* VII.

CRO'TCHET. *n. s.* [*crochet*, French.]

1. [In musick.] One of the notes or characters of time, equal to half a minim, and double a quaver. *Chambers.*

As a good harper, stricken far in years,
Into whose cunning hands the gout doth fall,
All his old *crotchets* in his brain he bears,
But on his harp plays ill, or not at all. *Davies.*

2. A support; a piece of wood fitted into another to support a building.

A stately temple shoots within the skies,
The *crotchets* of their cot in columns rise. *Dryden.*

3. [In printing.] Hooks in which words are included [thus.]

4. A perverse conceit; an odd fancy.

All the devices and *crotchets* of new inventions, which crept into her, tended either to twich or enlarge the ivy. *Howel.*

The horse smelt him out, and presently a *crotchet* came in his head how he might countermine him. *L'Estrange, Fab.* 37.

To CROUCH. *v. n.* [*crochu*, crooked, French.]

1. To stoop low; to lye close to the ground; as the lion *crouches* to his master.

2. To fawn; to bend servilely; to stoop meanly.

Every one that is left in thine house, shall come and *crouch* to him for a piece of silver and a morsel of bread. 1 *Sa.* ii. 36.

At his heels,
Leasht in like hounds, should famine, sword and fire,
Crouch for employment. *Shakespeare's Henry* V.

They fawn and *crouch* to men of parts, whom they cannot ruin; quote them, when they are present; and, when they are absent, steal their jests. *Dryden's Aurengzebe, Pref.*

Too well the vigour of that arm they know;
They lick the dust, and *crouch* beneath their fatal foe. *Dryd.*
Your shameful story shall record of me,
The men all *crouch'd*, and left a woman free. *Dryd. In. Emp.*

CROUP. *n. s.* [*crouppe*, French.]

1. The rump of a fowl.

2. The buttocks of a horse.

CROUPA'DES. *n. s.* [from *croup.*] Are higher leaps than those of corvets, that keep the fore and hind quarters of the horse in an equal height, so that he trusses his legs under his belly without yerking, or shooting his shoes. *Farrier's Dict.*

CROW. *n. s.* [cnape, Saxon.]

1. A large black bird that feeds upon the carcasses of beasts.

The *crows* and choughs, that wing the midway air,
Shew scarce so gross as beetles. *Shakespeare's King Lear.*
To *crows* he like impartial grace affords,
And choughs and daws, and such republick birds. *Dryden.*

2. *To pluck a* CROW, is to be industrious or contentious about that which is of no value.

If you dispute, we must even *pluck a crow* about it. *L'Estrange, Fable* 7.

Resolve before we go,
That you and I must *pull a crow.* *Hudibras, p.* ii. *cant.* ii.

3. A piece of iron used as a lever; as the *Latins* called a hook *corvus.*

The *crow* is used as a lever to lift up the ends of great heavy timber, when either a bauk or a rowler is to be laid under it, and then they thrust the claws between the ground and the timber; and laying a bauk, or some such stuff, behind the *crow*, they draw the other end of the shank backwards, and so raise the timber. *Moxon's Mech. Exer.*

Get me an iron *crow*, and bring it straight
Unto my cell. *Shakespeare's Romeo and Juliet.*
Against the gate employ your *crows* of iron. *Southern.*

4. [From *crow.*] The voice of a cock, or the noise which he makes in his gaiety.

CRO'WFOOT. *n. s.* [from *crow* and *foot*; in Latin, *ranunculus.*]

The flower consists of several leaves, which expand in form of a rose, having a many-leaved empalement: out of the middle of the flower rises the pointal, which becomes a fruit, either round, cylindrical, or spiked; to the axis of which, as a placenta, adhere many naked seeds. The species are sixteen, of which eleven were brought originally from Turkey.

CRO'WFOOT. *n. s.* [from *crow* and *foot.*] A caltrop or piece of iron with four points, two, three, or four inches long; so that, whatever way it falls, one point is up. It is used in war for incommoding the cavalry. *Military Dict.*

To CROW. *preterit. I crew*, or *crowed*; *I have crowed. v. n.* [cnapan, Saxon.]

1. To make the noise which a cock makes in gaiety, or defiance.

But even then the morning cock *crew* loud. *Shakes. Ham.*

Diogenes called an ill physician, cock. Why? saith he. Diogenes answered, Because when you *crew*, men use to rise. *Bacon, Apophth.* 284.

That the lyon trembles at the *crowing* of the cock, king James, upon trial, found to be fabulous. *Hakewill.*

Within this homestead liv'd, without a peer
For *crowing* loud, the noble Chanticleer,
So hight her cock. *Dryden's Fables.*

2. To boast; to bully; to vapour; to bluster; to swagger.

CROWD. *n. s.* [cnuð, Saxon.]

1. A multitude confusedly pressed together.

2. A promiscuous medly, without order or distinction.

He could then compare the confusion of a multitude to that tumult he had observed in the Icarian sea, dashing and breaking among its *crowd* of islands. *Essay on Homer.*

3. The vulgar; the populace.

He went not with the *crowd* to see a shrine,
But fed us, by the way, with food divine. *Dryden's Fables.*

4. [from *crwth*, Welsh.] A fiddle.

His fiddle is your proper purchase,
Won in the service of the churches;
And by your doom must be allow'd
To be, or be no more, a *crowd.* *Hudibras, p.* i. *cant.* 2.

To CROWD. *v. a.* [from the noun.]

1. To fill with confused multitudes.

A mind which is ever *crowding* its memory with things which it learns, may cramp the invention itself. *Watts.*

2. To press close together.

The time misorder'd, doth in common sense
Crowd us and crush us to this monstrous form,
To hold our safety up. *Shakespeare's Henry* IV. *p.* ii.

It seems probable, that the sea doth still grow narrower from age to age, and sinks more within its channel and the bowels of the earth, according as it can make its way into all those subterraneous cavities, and *crowd* the air out of them. *Burnet's Theory of the Earth.*

As the mind itself is thought to take up no space, so its actions seem to require no time; but many of them seem to be *crowded* into an instant. *Locke.*

Then let us fill
This little interval, this pause of life,
With all the virtues we can *crowd* into it. *Addison's Cato.*

3. To incumber by multitudes.

How short is life! Why will vain courtiers toil,
And *crowd* a vainer monarch for a smile? *Granville.*

4. *To* CROWD *Sail.* [A sea phrase.] To spread wide the sails upon the yards.

To CROWD. *v. n.*

1. To swarm; to be numerous and confused.

They follow their undaunted king;
Crowd through their gates; and in the fields of light,
The shocking squadrons meet in mortal fight. *Dryd. Virgil.*

2. To thrust among a multitude.

A mighty man, had not some cunning sin,
Amidst so many virtues, *crowded* in. *Cowley's Davideis.*

CRO'WDER. *n. s.* [from *crowd.*] A fiddler.

Chevy-chase sung by a blind *crowder.* *Sidney.*

CRO'WKEEPER. *n. s.* [*crow* and *keep.*] A scarecrow. The following passage is controverted.

That fellow handles his bow like a *crowkeeper.* *Shakespeare.*

CROWN. *n. s.* [*couronne*, Fr. *kroone*, Dut. *corona*, Latin.]

1. The ornament of the head which denotes imperial and regal dignity.

If thou be a king, where is thy *crown?*——
—My *crown* is in my heart, not on my head:
My *crown* is call'd content;
A *crown* it is that seldom kings enjoy. *Shakesp. Henry* VI.

Look down, you gods,
And on this couple drop a blessed *crown.* *Shakesp. Tempest.*

I would the college of the cardinals
Would chuse him pope, and carry him to Rome,
And set the triple *crown* upon his head. *Shakesp. Henry* VI.

Edward put to death a citizen,
Only for saying, he would make his son
Heir to the *crown.* *Shakespeare's Richard* III.

2. A garland.

Receive a *crown* for thy well-ordering of the feast. *Ecclus.* xxxii. 2.

3. Reward

3. Reward; honorary distinction.

They do it to obtain a corruptible *crown*, but we an incorruptible. *1 Cor.* ix. 25.

Let merit *crowns*, and justice laurels give,
But let me happy by your pity live. *Dryden's Epistles.*

4. Regal power; royalty.

The succession of a *crown* in several countries, places it on different heads. *Locke.*

5. The top of the head.

If he awake,
From toe to *crown* he'll fill our skins with pinches;
Make us strange stuff. *Shakespeare's Tempest.*

While his head was working upon this thought, the toy took him in the *crown* to send for the songster. *L'Estrange.*

Behold! if fortune, or a mistress frowns,
Some plunge in business, others save their *crowns.* *Pope.*

6. The top of any thing; as, of a mountain.

Upon the *crown* o' th' cliff, what thing was that
Which parted from you? *Shakespeare's King Lear.*

Huge trunks of trees, fell'd from the steepy *crown*
Of the bare mountains, roll with ruin down. *Dryden's Æn.*

7. Part of the hat that covers the head.

I once opened a remarkable atheroma: it was about as big as the *crown* of a man's hat, and lay underneath the pectoral muscle. *Sharp's Surgery.*

8. A piece of money, anciently stamped with a crown; five shillings.

Trust not to your servants, who may mislead you, or misinform you, by which they may perhaps gain a few *crowns.* *Bacon's Advice to Villiers.*

But he that can eat beef, and feed on bread which is so brown,
May satisfy his appetite, and owe no man a *crown.* *Suckling.*

An ounce of silver, whether in pence, groats, or *crown*-pieces, stivers or ducatoons, or in bullion, is, and eternally will be, of equal value to any other ounce of silver. *Locke.*

9. Honour; ornament; decoration; excellence; dignity.

Much experience is the *crown* of old men. *Ecclus.* xxv. 6.

Therefore my brethren, dearly beloved, and longed for, my joy and *crown*, stand fast in the Lord. *Philip*, iv. 1.

10. Completion; accomplishment.

CROWN-IMPERIAL. *n. s.* [*corona imperialis*, Lat.] A plant.

The flowers consist of six leaves, are bell-shaped, and hang downwards: these are ranged, as it were, into a crown, above which appears a great bush of leaves. The pointal of the flower becomes an oblong fruit, winged, and divided into three cells, filled with flat seeds. It hath a coated root, furnished with fibres at the bottom. *Miller.*

To CROWN. *v. a.* [from the noun.]

1. To invest with the crown or regal ornament:

Had you not come upon your cue, my lord,
William lord Hastings had pronounc'd your part;
I mean your voice for *crowning* of the king. *Shakes. R.* III.

Her who fairest does appear,
Crown her queen of all the year. *Dryden's Indian Emperor.*

2. To cover, as with a crown.

Umbro, the priest, the proud Marrabians led,
And peaceful olives *crown'd* his hoary head. *Dryden's Æn.*

3. To dignify; to adorn; to make illustrious.

Thou hast made him a little lower than the angels, and hast *crowned* him with glory and honour. *Ps.* viii. 5.

She shall be, to the happiness of England,
An aged princess; many days shall see her,
And yet no day without a deed to *crown* it. *Shakes. H.*VIII.

4. To reward; to recompense.

Urge your success; deserve a lasting name,
She'll *crown* a grateful and a constant flame. *Roscommon.*

5. To complete; to perfect.

The lasting and *crowning* privilege, or rather property of friendship, is constancy. *South's Sermons.*

6. To terminate; to finish.

All these a milk-white honeycomb surround,
Which in the midst the country banquet *crown'd.* *Dryden.*

CRO'WNGLASS. *n. s.* The finest sort of window-glass.

CRO'WNPOST. *n. s.* A post, which, in some buildings, stands upright in the middle, between two principal rafters.

CRO'WNSCAB. *n. s.* A stinking filthy scab, that breeds round about the corners of a horse's hoof, and is a cancerous and painful sore. *Farrier's Dict.*

CRO'WNWHEEL. *n. s.* The upper wheel of a watch next the balance, which is driven by it.

CRO'WNWORKS. *n. s.* [In fortification.] Bulwarks advanced towards the field to gain some hill or rising ground. *Harris.*

CRO'WNET. *n. s.* [from *crown.*]

1. The same with *coronet.*

2. In the following passage it seems to signify chief end; last purpose; probably from *finis coronat opus.*

Oh, this false soul of Egypt! this gay charm!
Whose eye beck'd forth my wars, and call'd them home;
Whose bosom was my *crownet*, my chief end;
Like a right gipsy hath, at fast and loose,
Beguil'd me to the very heart of loss. *Shak. Ant. and Cleop.*

4

CRO'YLSTONE. *n. s.* Crystallized cauk. In this the crystals are small. *Woodward's Foss.*

CRU'CIAL. *adj.* [*crux crucis*, Latin.] Transverse; intersecting one another.

Whoever has seen the practice of the *crucial* incision, must be sensible of the false reasoning used in its favour. *Sharp.*

To CRU'CIATE. *v. a.* [*crucio*, Latin.] To torture; to torment; to excruciate.

CRU'CIBLE. *n. s.* [*crucibulum*, low Latin.] A chymist's melting pot, made of earth; so called, because they were formerly marked with a cross.

Take a quantity of good silver, and put it in a *crucible* or melting cruse, and set them on the fire, well covered round about with coals. *Peacham on Drawing.*

CRUCI'FEROUS. *adj.* [*crux* and *fero*, Latin.] Bearing the cross. *Dict.*

CRU'CIFIER. *n. s.* [from *crucify.*] He that inflicts the punishment of crucifixion.

Visible judgments were executed on Christ's *crucifiers.* *Hammond on Fundamentals.*

CRU'CIFIX. *n. s.* [*crucifixus*, Latin.] A representation in picture or statuary of our Lord's passion.

There stands at the upper end of it a large *crucifix*, very much esteemed. The figure of our Saviour represents him in his last agonies of death. *Addison on Italy.*

CRUCIFI'XION. *n. s.* [from *crucifixus*, Latin.] The punishment of nailing to a cross.

This earthquake, according to the opinion of many learned men, happened at our Saviour's *crucifixion.* *Addison on Italy.*

CRU'CIFORM. *adj.* [*crux* and *forma*, Latin.] Having the form of a cross.

To CRU'CIFY. *v. a.* [*crucifigo*, Latin.] To put to death by nailing the hands and feet to a cross set upright.

They *crucify* to themselves the son of God afresh, and put him to an open shame. *Hebr.* vi. 6.

But to the cross he nails thy enemies,
The law that is against thee, and the sins
Of all mankind, with him there *crucify'd.* *Milt. Par. Lost.*

CRUCI'GEROUS. *adj.* [*cruciger*, Latin.] Bearing the cross.

CRUD. *n. s.* [commonly written *curd.* See CURD.] A concretion of any liquid into hardness or stiffness; coagulation.

CRUDE. *adj.* [*crudus*, Latin.]

1. Raw; not subdued by fire.

2. Not changed by any process or preparation.

Common *crude* salt, barely dissolved in common *aqua fortis*, will give it power of working upon gold. *Boyle on Fluidity.*

Fermented liquors have quite different qualities from the plant itself; for no fruit, taken *crude*, has the intoxicating quality of wine. *Arbuthnot on Aliments.*

3. Harsh; unripe.

A juice so *crude* as cannot be ripened to the degree of nourishment. *Bacon's Natural History*, N°. 632.

4. Unconcocted; not well digested in the stomach.

While the body, to be converted and altered, is too strong for the efficient that should convert or alter it, whereby it resisteth and holdeth fast, in some degree, the first form or consistence, it is, all that while, *crude* and inconcoct; and the process is to be called crudity and inconcoction. *Bac. Nat. Hist.*

5. Not brought to perfection; unfinished; immature.

In a moment up they turned,
Wide the celestial soil; and saw beneath
Th' originals of nature, in their *crude*
Conception. *Milton's Paradise Lost, b.* vi. *l.* 511.

6. Having indigested notions.

Deep vers'd in books, and shallow in himself,
Crude, or intoxicate, collecting toys. *Milton's Paradise Reg.*

7. Indigested; not fully concocted in the intellect.

Others, whom meer ambition fires, and dole
Of provinces abroad, which they have feign'd
To their *crude* hopes, and I as amply promis'd. *B. Johnson.*

What peradventure may seem full to me, may appear very *crude* and maimed to a stranger. *Digby on the Soul, Dedicat.*

Absurd expressions, *crude* abortive thoughts,
All the lewd legions of exploded faults. *Roscommon.*

CRU'DELY. *adv.* [from *crude.*] Unripely; without due preparation.

Th' advice was true; but fear had seiz'd the most,
And all good counsel is on cowards lost:
The question *crudely* put, to shun delay,
'Twas carry'd by the major part to stay. *Dryden.*

CRU'DENESS. *n. s.* [from *crude.*] Unripeness; indigestion.

CRU'DITY. *n. s.* [from *crude.*] Indigestion; inconcoction.

They are very temperate, whereby they prevent indigestion and *crudities*, and consequently putrescence of humours. *Brown.*

A diet of viscid aliment creates flatulency and *crudities* in the stomach. *Arbuthnot.*

2. Unripeness; want of maturity.

To CRU'DLE. *v. a.* [a word of uncertain etymology.] To coagulate; to congeal.

I felt my *crudled* blood
Congeal with fear; my hair with horrour stood. *Dryd. Æn.*

The

The Gelons use it, when, for drink and food,
They mix their *crudled* milk with horses blood. *Dryd. Virg.*

CRU'DY. *adj.* [from *crud.*]
1. Concreted; coagulated.
His cruel wounds with *crudy* blood congeal'd,
They binden up so wisely as they may. *Fairy Queen, b.* i.
2. [from *crude.*] Raw; chill.
Sherris sack ascends into the brain; dries me there all the foolish, dull, and *crudy* vapours which environ it. *Shakespeare.*

CRU'EL. *adj.* [*cruel*, French; *crudelis*, Latin.]
1. Pleased with hurting others; inhuman; hard-hearted; without pity; without compassion; savage; barbarous; unrelenting.
If wolves had at thy gate howl'd that stern time,
Thou should'st have said, Go, porter, turn the key;
All *cruel's* else subscrib'd. *Shakespeare's King Lear.*
If thou art that *cruel* god, whose eyes
Delight in blood, and human sacrifice. *Dryden's Ind. Emp.*
2. [Of things.] Bloody; mischievous; destructive; causing pain.
Consider mine enemies; for they are many, and they hate me with *cruel* hatred. *Ps.* xxv. 19.
We beheld one of the *cruelest* fights between two knights, that ever hath adorned the most martial story. *Sidney, b.* ii.

CRU'ELLY. *adv.* [from *cruel.*] In a cruel manner; inhumanly; barbarously.
He relies upon a broken reed, that not only basely fails, but also *cruelly* pierces the hand that rests upon it. *South's Sermon.*
Since you deny him entrance, he demands
His wife, whom *cruelly* you hold in bands. *Dryd. Aurengz.*

CRU'ELNESS. *n. s.* [from *cruel.*] Inhumanity; cruelty.
But she more cruel, and more savage wild,
Than either lion or the lioness,
Shames not to be with guiltless blood defil'd;
She taketh glory in her *cruelness.* *Spenser, Sonnet* 20.

CRU'ELTY. *n. s.* [*cruauté*, French.] Inhumanity; savageness; barbarity.
The *cruelty* and envy of the people,
Permitted by our dastard nobles,
Have suffer'd me by the voice of slaves to be
Whoop'd out of Rome. *Shakespeare's Coriolanus.*
There were great changes in the world by the revolutions of empire, the *cruelties* of conquering, and the calamities of enslaved nations. *Temple.*

CRU'ENTATE. *adj.* [*cruentatus*, Latin.] Smeared with blood.
Atomical aporrheas pass from the *cruentate* cloth or weapon to the wound. *Glanv. Sceps. c.* 24.

CRU'ET. *n. s.* [*kruicke*, Dutch.] A vial for vinegar or oyl, with a stopple.
Within thy reach I set the vinegar!
And fill'd the *cruet* with the acid tide,
While pepper-water worms thy bait supply'd. *Swift.*

CRUISE. *n. s.* [*kruicke*, Dutch.] A small cup.
I have not a cake, but an handful of meal in a barrel, and a little oil in a *cruise.* 1 *Kings*, xvii. 12.
The train prepare a *cruise* of curious mold,
A *cruise* of fragrance, form'd of burnish'd gold. *Pope's Odyss.*

A CRUISE. *n. s.* [*croise*, Fr. from the original *cruisers*, who bore the cross, and plundered only infidels.] A voyage in search of plunder.

To CRUISE. *v. n.* [from the noun.] To rove over the sea in search of opportunities to plunder; to wander on the sea without any certain course.

CRU'ISER. *n. s.* [from *cruise.*] One that roves upon the sea in search of plunder.
Amongst the *cruisers* it was complained, that their surgeons were too active in amputating fractured members. *Wiseman.*

CRUM. } *n. s.* [cruma, Saxon; *kruyme*, Dutch; *krummel*,
CRUMB. } German.
1. The soft part of bread; not the crust.
Take of manchet about three ounces, the *crumb* only thin cut; and let it be boiled in milk 'till it grow to a pulp. *Bacon.*
2. A small particle or fragment of bread.
More familiar grown, the table *crums*
Attract his slender feet. *Thomson's Winter, l.* 255.

To CRU'MBLE. *v. a.* [from *crumb.*] To break into small pieces; to comminute.
Flesh is but the glass which holds the dust
That measures all our time, which also shall
Be *crumbled* into dust. *Herbert.*
He with his bare wand can unthread thy joints,
And *crumble* all thy sinews. *Milton.*
By frequent parcelling and subdividing of inheritances, in process of time they became so divided and *crumbled*, that there were few persons of able estates. *Hale's Com. Law of Eng.*
At the same time we were *crumbled* into various factions and parties, all aiming at by-interests, without any sincere regard for the publick good. *Atterbury's Sermons.*
The other bill leaves three hundred pounds a year to the mother church; which three hundred pounds, by another act passed some years ago, they can divide likewise, and *crumble* as low as their will and pleasure will dispose of them. *Swift.*

To CRU'MBLE. *v. n.* To fall into small pieces.
There is so hot a summer in my brain,
That all my bowels *crumble* up to dust. *Shakesp. King John.*
Nor is the profit small the peasant makes,
Who smooths with harrow, or who pounds with rakes,
The *crumbling* clods. *Dryden's Georg.*
Ambition sigh'd: she found it vain to trust
The faithless column, and the *crumbling* bust. *Pope's Epist.*
If the stone is brittle, it will often *crumble*, and pass in the form of gravel. *Arbuthnot on Diet.*
What house, when its materials *crumble*,
Must not inevitably tumble? *Swift.*
For the little land that remains, provision is made by the late act against popery, that it will daily *crumble* away. *Swift.*

CRU'MENAL. *n. s.* [from *crumena*, Latin.] A purse.
The fat ox, that woon ligye in the stall,
Is now fast stalled in her *crumenal.* *Spenser's Pastorals.*

CRU'MMY. *adj.* [from *crum.*] Soft.

CRUMP. *adj.* [cnump, Saxon; *krom*, Dutch; *krumm*, Germ.] Crooked in the back.
When the workman took measure of him, he was *crump* shouldered, and the right side higher than the left. *L'Estrange.*

To CRU'MPLE. *v. a.* [from *crump*; or corrupted from *rumple*, *rompelen*, Dutch.] To draw into wrinkles; to crush together in complications.
Sir Roger alighted from his horse, and exposing his palm to two or three that stood by him, they *crumpled* it into all shapes, and diligently scanned every wrinkle that could be made. *Addis.*

CRU'MPLING. *n. s.* A small degenerate apple.

To CRUNK. } *v. n.* To cry like a crane. *Dict.*
To CRU'NKLE. }

CRU'PPER. *n. s.* [from *croupe*, Fr. the buttocks of the horse.] That part of the horseman's furniture that reaches from the saddle to the tail.
Clitophon had received such a blow, that he had lost the reins of his horse, with his head well nigh touching the *crupper* of the horse. *Sidney.*
Where have you left the money that I gave you?
——Oh—sixpence, that I had a Wednesday last,
To pay the saddler for my mistress' *crupper.* *Shakespeare.*
Full oft the rivals met, and neither spar'd
His utmost force, and each forgot to ward:
The head of this was to the saddle bent,
The other backward to the *crupper* sent. *Dryden.*

CRU'RAL. *adj.* [from *crus cruris*, Latin.] Belonging to the leg.
The sharpness of the teeth, and the strength of the *crural* muscles in lions and tygers, are the cause of the great and habitual immorality of those animals. *Arbuthnot.*

CRUSA'DE. } *n. s.* See CROISADE.
CRUSA'DO. }
1. An expedition against the infidels.
2. A coin stamped with a cross.
Believe me, I had rather have lost my purse
Full of *crusadoes.* *Shakespeare's Othello.*

CRUSE. See CRUISE.

CRU'SET. *n. s.* A goldsmith's melting pot. *Philips.*

To CRUSH. *v. a.* [*ecraser*, French.]
1. To press between two opposite bodies; to squeeze.
You speak him far.——
——I don't extend him, sir: within himself
Crush him together, rather than unfold
His measure fully. *Shakespeare's Cymbeline.*
The ass thrust herself unto the wall, and *crushed* Balaam's foot against the wall. *Num.* xxii. 25.
Bacchus that first, from out the purple grape,
Crush'd the sweet poison of misused wine. *Milt. Par. Lost.*
I fought and fell like one, but death deceiv'd me:
I wanted weight of feeble Moors upon me,
To *crush* my soul out. *Dryden's Don Sebastian.*
2. To press with violence.
When loud winds from diff'rent quarters rush,
Vast clouds encount'ring, one another *crush.* *Waller.*
3. To overwhelm; to beat down.
Put in their hands thy bruising irons of wrath,
That they may *crush* down, with a heavy fall,
Th' usurping helmets of our adversaries! *Shakes. Rich.* III.
The sad weight of such ingratitude
Will *crush* me into earth.
Vain is the force of man, and heav'n's as vain,
To *crush* the pillars which the pile sustain. *Dryden's Æn.*
4. To subdue; to depress; to dispirit.
They use them to plague their enemies, or to oppress and *crush* some of their own too stubborn freeholders. *Spenser on Ireland.*
Mine emulation
Hath not that honour in't it had; for
I thought to *crush* him in an equal force,
True sword to sword. *Shakespeare's Coriolanus.*
This act
Shall bruise the head of Satan, *crush* his strength,
Defeating sin and death, his two main arms. *Milt. Pa. Lost.*
What can that man fear, who takes care to please a Being that is so able to *crush* all his adversaries? a Being that can

divert any misfortune from befalling him, or turn any such misfortune to his advantage? *Addison's Guardian*, N°. 107.

To CRUSH. *v. n.* To be condensed; to come in a close body.

Poverty, cold wind, and *crushing* rain,
Beat keen and heavy on thy tender years. *Thoms. Autumn.*

CRUSH. *n. s.* [from the verb.] A collision.

Thou shalt flourish in immortal youth,
Unhurt amidst the war of elements,
The wrecks of matter, and the *crush* of worlds. *Addis. Cato.*

CRUST. *n. s.* [*crusta*, Latin.]

1. Any shell, or external coat, by which any body is enveloped.

I have known the statue of an emperor quite hid under a *crust* of dross. *Addison on Ancient Medals.*

2. An incrustation; collection of matter into a hard body.

Were the river a confusion of never so many different bodies, if they had been all actually dissolved, they would at least have formed one continued *crust*; as we see the scorium of metals always gathers into a solid piece. *Addison on Italy.*

The viscuous *crust* stops the entry of the chyle into the lacteals. *Arbuthnot on Aliments.*

3. The case of a pye made of meal, and baked.

He was never suffered to go abroad, for fear of catching cold: when he should have been hunting down a buck, he was by his mother's side learning how to season it, or put it in *crust*. *Addison's Spectator*, N°. 462.

4. The outer hard part of bread.

Th' impenetrable *crust* thy teeth defies,
And petrify'd with age, securely lies. *Dryden's Juv. Sat.* v.

5. A waste piece of bread.

Y' are liberal now; but when your turn is sped,
You'll wish me choak'd with every *crust* of bread. *Dryden.*
Men will do tricks, like dogs, for *crusts*. *L'Estrange.*

To CRUST. *v. a.* [from the noun.]

1. To envelop; to cover with a hard case.

Why gave you me a monarch's soul,
And *crusted* it with base plebeian clay. *Dryd. Span. Fryar.*

Nor is it improbable but that, in process of time, the whole surface of it may be *crusted* over, as the islands enlarge themselves, and the banks close in upon them. *Addison on Italy.*

And now their legs, and breasts, and bodies stood
Crusted with bark, and hard'ning into wood. *Addison.*

In some, who have run up to men without education, we may observe many great qualities darkened and eclipsed; their minds are *crusted* over, like diamonds in the rock. *Felton.*

2. To foul with concretions.

If your master hath many musty, or very foul and *crusted* bottles, let those be the first you truck at the next alehouse. *Swift's Directions to the Butler.*

To CRUST. *v. n.* To gather or contract a crust; to gain a hard covering.

I contented myself with a plaister upon the place that was burnt, which *crusted* and healed in very few days. *Temple.*

CRUSTA'CEOUS. *adj.* [from *crusta*, Lat.] Shelly, with joints; not testaceous; not with one continued uninterrupted shell. Lobster is *crustaceous*, oyster testaceous.

It is true that there are some shells, such as those of lobsters, crabs, and others of *crustaceous* kinds, that are very rarely found at land. *Woodward's Natural History.*

CRUSTA'CEOUSNESS. *n. s.* [from *crustaceous.*] The quality of having jointed shells.

CRU'STILY. *adv.* [from *crusty.*] Peevishly; snappishly.

CRU'STINESS. *n. s.* [from *crusty.*]

1. The quality of a crust.
2. Peevishness; moroseness.

CRU'STY. *adj.* [from *crust.*]

1. Covered with a crust.

The egg itself deserves our notice: its parts within, and its *crusty* coat without, are admirably well fitted for the business of incubation. *Derham's Physico-Theology.*

2. Sturdy; morose; snappish: a low word.

CRUTCH. *n. s.* [*croccia*, Ital. *croce*, Fr. *crucke*, Germ.] A support used by cripples.

Ah, thus king Henry throws away his *crutch*,
Before his legs be firm to bear his body. *Shakesp. Hen.* VI.

Beauty doth varnish age, as if new born,
And gives the *crutch* the cradle's infancy. *Shakespeare.*

Hence, therefore, thou nice *crutch*:
A scaly gauntlet now, with joints of steel,
Must glove this hand. *Shakespeare's Henry* IV. *p.* ii.

On these new *crutches* let them learn to walk. *Dryd. Geor.*

This fair defect, this helpless aid call'd wife,
The bending *crutch* of a decrepit life. *Dryden.*

At best a *crutch* that lifts the weak along,
Supports the feeble, but retards the strong. *Smith.*

The dumb shall sing, the lame his *crutch* forego,
And leap exulting like the bounding roe. *Pope's Messiah.*

To CRUTCH. *v. a.* [from *crutch.*] To support on crutches as a cripple.

I hasten Og and Doeg to rehearse,
Two fools that *crutch* their feeble sense on verse. *Dryden.*

To CRY. *v. n.* [*crier*, French.]

1. To speak with vehemence and loudness.

Methought I heard a voice *cry*, sleep no more!
Macbeth, doth murther sleep! the innocent sleep! *Shakesp.*

While his falling tears the stream supply'd,
Thus mourning to his mother goddess *cry'd*. *Dryden's Virg.*

2. To call importunately.

I *cried*, by reason of mine affliction, unto the Lord, and he heard me. *Jon.* ii. 2.

3. To talk eagerly or incessantly; to repeat continually.

They be idle; therefore they *cry*, saying let us go. *Ex.* v. 8.

4. To proclaim; to make publick.

Go and *cry* in the ears of Jerusalem. *Jer.* ii. 2.

The Egyptians shall help in vain, and to no purpose; therefore have I *cried*, concerning this, their strength is to sit still. *Is.* xxx. 7.

5. To exclaim.

Yet let them look they glory not in mischief,
Nor build their evils on the graves of great men;
For then, my guiltless blood must *cry* against them. *Shakesp.*

What's the matter,
That in the several places of the city
You *cry* against the noble senate. *Shakespeare's Coriolanus.*

If dressing, mistressing, and compliment,
Take up thy day, the sun himself will *cry*
Against thee. *Herbert.*

Lysimachus having obtained the favour of seeing his ships and machines, surprised at the contrivance, *cried* out that they were built with more than human art. *Arbuthnot on Coins.*

6. To utter lamentations.

We came *crying* hither:
Thou know'st, the first time that we smell the air,
We wawle and *cry*. *Shakespeare's King Lear.*

Behold, my servants shall sing for joy of heart; but ye shall *cry* for sorrow of heart, and shall howl for vexation of spirit. *Is.* lxv. 14.

When any great evil has been upon philosophers, they certainly sigh and groan as pitifully, and *cry* out as loud, as other men. *Tillotson, Sermon* v.

7. To squall, as an infant.

Should some god tell me, that should I be born,
And *cry* again, his offer I should scorn. *Denham.*

Thus, in a starry night, fond children *cry*
For the rich spangles that adorn the sky. *Waller.*

He struggles for breath, and *cries* for aid;
Then helpless in his mother's lap is laid. *Dryden's Fables.*

The child certainly knows that the wormseed or mustardseed it refuses, is not the apple or sugar it *cries* for. *Locke.*

8. To weep; to shed tears.

Her who still weeps with spungy eyes,
And her who is dry cork, and never *cries*. *Donne.*

9. To utter an inarticulate voice, as an animal.

He giveth to the beast his food, and to the young ravens which *cry*. *Psalm*, cxlvii. 9.

The beasts of the field *cry* also unto thee. *Joel*, i. 20.

10. To yelp, as a hound on a scent.

Why, Belman is as good as he, my lord;
He *cried* upon it at the meerest loss;
Trust me, I take him for the better dog. *Shakespeare.*

To CRY. *v. a.* To proclaim publickly something lost or found, in order to its recovery or restitution.

She seeks, she sighs, but no where spies him:
Love is lost, and thus she *cries* him. *Crashaw.*

To CRY *down.* *v. a.*

1. To blame; to depreciate; to decry.

Bavius *cries down* an admirable treatise of philosophy, and says there's atheism in it. *Watts's Improvement, p.* i. *c.* 6.

Men of dissolute lives *cry down* religion, because they would not be under the restraints of it. *Tillotson, Sermon* ii.

2. To prohibit.

By all means *cry down* that unworthy course of late times, that they should pay money. *Bacon's Advice to Villiers.*

3. To overbear.

I'll to the king,
And from a mouth of honour quite *cry down*
This Ipswich fellow's insolence. *Shakespeare's Henry* VIII.

To CRY OUT. *v. n.*

1. To exclaim; to scream; to clamour.

They make the oppressed to cry; they *cry out* by reason of the arm of the mighty. *Job*, xxxv. 5.

With that Susanna cried with a loud voice, and the two elders *cried out* against her. *Sus.* xxiv.

2. To complain loudly.

We are ready to *cry out* of an unequal management, and to blame the Divine administration. *Atterbury's Sermons.*

3. To blame; to censure: with *of*, *against*, *upon*.

Are these things then necessities?
Then let us meet them like necessities;
And that same word even now *cries out* on us. *Shakespeare.*

Giddy censure
Will then *cry out of* Marcius: oh, if he
Had borne the business. *Shakespeare's Coriolanus.*

Behold, I *cry out of* wrong, but I am not heard. *Job*, xix. 7.

Cry out upon the ſtars for doing
Ill offices, to croſs their wooing. *Hudibras, p.* iii. *cant.* 1.

Epiphanius *cries out upon* it as rank idolatry, and deſtructive to their ſouls who did it. *Stillingfleet.*

Tumult, ſedition and rebellion, are things that the followers of that hypotheſis *cry out againſt.* *Locke.*

I find every ſect, as far as reaſon will help them, make uſe of it gladly; and where it fails them, they *cry out* it is matter of faith, and above reaſon. *Locke.*

4. To declare loud.
5. To be in labour.

What! is ſhe *crying out?*———
———So ſaid her woman; and that her ſuff'rance made
Each pang a death. *Shakeſpeare's Henry* VIII.

To CRY *up. v. a.*

1. To applaud; to exalt; to praiſe.

Inſtead of *crying up* all things which are brought from beyond ſea, let us advance the native commodities of our own kingdom. *Bacon's Advice to Villiers.*

The philoſopher deſervedly ſuſpected himſelf of vanity, when *cried up* by the multitude. *Glanville's Sceps. c.* 18.

The aſtrologer, if his predictions come to paſs, is *cried up* to the ſtars from whence he pretends to draw them. *South.*

They ſlight the ſtrongeſt arguments that can be brought for religion, and *cry up* very weak ones againſt it. *Tillotſon's Serm.*

He may, out of intereſt, as well as conviction, *cry up* that for ſacred, which, if once trampled on and profaned, he himſelf cannot be ſafe, nor ſecure. *Locke.*

Poets, like monarchs on an Eaſtern throne,
Confin'd by nothing but their will alone,
Here can *cry up*, and there as boldly blame,
And, as they pleaſe, give infamy or fame. *Walſh.*

Thoſe who are fond of continuing the war, *cry up* our conſtant ſucceſs at a moſt prodigious rate. *Swift.*

2. To raiſe the price by proclamation.

All the effect that I conceive was made by *crying up* the pieces of eight, was to bring in much more of that ſpecies, inſtead of others current here. *Temple.*

CRY. *n. ſ.* [*cri*, French.]

1. Lamentation; ſhriek; ſcream.

And all the firſt-born in the land of Egypt ſhall die, and there ſhall be a great *cry* throughout all the land. *Exod.* xi. 5.

2. Weeping; mourning.
3. Clamour; outcry.

Amazement ſeizes all; the general *cry*
Proclaims Laocoon juſtly doom'd to die. *Dryden's Virg. Æn.*

Theſe narrow and ſelfiſh views have ſo great an influence in this *cry*, that there are ſeveral of my fellow freeholders who fancy the church in danger upon the riſing of bank-ſtock. *Add.*

4. Exclamation of triumph or wonder, or any other paſſion.

In popiſh countries ſome impoſtor cries out, a miracle! a miracle! to confirm the deluded vulgar in their errours; and ſo the *cry* goes round, without examining into the cheat. *Swift.*

5. Proclamation.
6. The hawkers proclamation of wares to be ſold in the ſtreet; as, *the* cries *of London.*
7. Acclamation; popular favour.

The *cry* went once for thee,
And ſtill it might, and yet it may again. *Shakeſpeare.*

8. Voice; utterance; manner of vocal expreſſion.

Sounds alſo, beſides the diſtinct *cries* of birds and beaſts, are modified by diverſity of notes of different length, put together, which make that complex idea called tune. *Locke.*

9. Importunate call.

Pray not thou for this people, neither lift up *cry* nor prayer for them. *Jer.* vii. 13.

10. Yelping of dogs.

He ſcorns the dog, reſolves to try
The combat next; but if their *cry*
Invades again his trembling ear,
He ſtrait reſumes his wonted care. *Waller.*

11. Yell; inarticulate noiſe.

There ſhall be the noiſe of a *cry* from the fiſhgate, and an howling from the ſecond, and a great craſhing from the hills. *Zeph.* i. 10.

12. A pack of dogs.

About her middle round,
A *cry* of hell-hounds never ceaſing bark'd. *Milt. Par. Loſt.*

You common *cry* of curs, whoſe breath I hate
As reek o' th' rotten fens; whoſe loves I prize
As the dead carcaſſes of unburied men,
That do corrupt my air. *Shakeſpeare's Coriolanus.*

CRY'AL. *n. ſ.* The heron. *Ainſworth.*

CRY'ER. See CRIER.

CRY'ER. *n. ſ.* A kind of hawk called the falcon gentle, an enemy to pigeons, and very ſwift. *Ainſworth.*

CRY'PTICAL. } *adj.* [κρύπτω.] Hidden; ſecret; occult; pri-
CRY'PTICK. } vate; unknown; not divulged.

The ſtudents of nature, conſcious of her more *cryptick* ways of working, reſolve many ſtrange effects into the near efficiency of ſecond cauſes. *Glanville's Apology.*

Speakers, whoſe chief buſineſs is to amuſe or delight, do not confine themſelves to any natural order, but in a *cryptical* or hidden method adapt every thing to their ends. *Watts.*

CRY'PTICALLY. *adv.* [from *cryptical*] Occultly; ſecretly: perhaps in the following example, the author might have written *critically.*

We take the word acid in a familiar ſenſe, without *cryptically* diſtinguiſhing it from thoſe ſapors that are a-kin to it. *Boyle.*

CRYPTO'GRAPHY. *n. ſ.* [κρύπτω and γράφω.]

1. The act of writing ſecret characters.
2. Secret characters; cyphers.

CRYPTO'LOGY. *n. ſ.* [κρύπτω and λόγος.] Ænigmatical language.

CRY'STAL. *n. ſ.* [κρύσταλλος.]

1. *Cryſtals* are hard, pellucid, and naturally colourleſs bodies, of regularly angular figures, compoſed of ſimple, not filamentous plates, not flexile or elaſtick, giving fire with ſteel, not fermenting with acid menſtrua, and calcining in a ſtrong fire. There are many various ſpecies of it produced in different parts of the globe. *Hill on Foſſils.*

Iſland cryſtal bears a red heat without loſing its tranſparency, and in a very intenſe heat calcines without fuſion: ſteeped a day or two in water, it loſes its natural poliſh: rubbed on cloth, it attracts ſtraws, like amber. *Chambers.*

Iſland cryſtal is a genuine ſpar, of an extremely pure, clear, and fine texture, ſeldom either blemiſhed with flaws or ſpots, or ſtained with any other colour. It is always an oblique parallelopiped of ſix planes, and found from a quarter of an inch to three inches in diameter. It is moderately heavy, but very ſoft, and is eaſily ſerated with a pin. It very freely calcines into a pure, but opaque white. It is found in the iſland of Iceland, and in many parts of Germany and France. A remarkable property of this body, which has much employed the writers on opticks, is its double refraction; ſo that if it be laid over a black line, drawn on paper, two lines appear in the place of one, of the ſame colour and thickneſs, and running parallel to one another at a ſmall diſtance. *Hill.*

Water, as it ſeems, turneth into *cryſtal*; as is ſeen in divers caves, where the *cryſtal* hangs *in ſtillicidiis. Bacon's Phyſ. Rem.*

If *cryſtal* be a ſtone, it is not immediately concreted by the efficacy of cold, but rather by a mineral ſpirit. *Brown.*

Cryſtal is certainly known, and diſtinguiſhed by the degree of its diaphaneity and of its refraction, as alſo of its hardneſs, which are ever the ſame. *Woodward's Math. Foſſ.*

3. *Cryſtal* is alſo uſed for a factitious body caſt in the glaſs-houſes, called alſo *cryſtal* glaſs, which is carried to a degree of perfection beyond the common glaſs; though it comes far ſhort of the whiteneſs and vivacity of the natural *cryſtal. Chambers.*

4. *Cryſtals* [in chymiſtry] expreſs ſalts or other matters ſhot or congealed in manner of *cryſtal.* *Chambers.*

If the menſtruum be overcharged, within a ſhort time the metals will ſhoot into certain *cryſtals.* *Bacon.*

CRY'STAL. *adj.*

1. Conſiſting of cryſtal.

Then, Jupiter, thou king of Gods,
Thy *cryſtal* window ope, look out. *Shakeſpeare's Cymbeline.*

2. Bright; clear; tranſparent; lucid; pellucid.

In groves we live, and lie on moſſy beds
By *cryſtal* ſtreams, that murmur through the meads. *Dryden.*

CRY'STALLINE. *adj.* [*cryſtallinus*, Latin.]

1. Conſiſting of cryſtal.

Mount eagle to my palace *cryſtalline. Shakeſp. Cymbeline.*

We provided ourſelves with ſome ſmall receivers, blown of *cryſtalline* glaſs. *Boyle's Spring of the Air.*

2. Bright; clear; pellucid; tranſparent.

The clarifying of water is an experiment tending to the health; beſides the pleaſure of the eye, when water is *cryſtalline.* It is effected by caſting in and placing pebbles at the head of the current, that the water may ſtrain through them. *Bacon's Natural Hiſtory,* N°. 7.

He on the wings of cherub rode ſublime
On the *cryſtalline* ſky, in ſaphir thron'd
Illuſtrious far and wide. *Milton's Paradiſe Loſt, b.* vi.

CRY'STALLINE *Humour. n. ſ.* The ſecond humour of the eye, that lies immediately next to the aqueous behind the uvea, oppoſite to the papilla, nearer to the forepart than the backpart of the globe. It is the leaſt of the humours, but much more ſolid than any of them. Its figure, which is convex on both ſides, reſembles two unequal ſegments of ſpheres, of which the moſt convex is on its backſide, which makes a ſmall cavity in the glaſſy humour in which it lies. It is covered with a fine coat, called aranea.

The parts of the eye are made convex, and eſpecially the *cryſtalline humour*, which is of a lenticular figure, convex on both ſides. *Ray on the Creation.*

CRYSTALLIZA'TION. *n. ſ.* [from *cryſtallize.*] Congelation into cryſtals.

Such a combination of ſaline particles as reſembles the form of a cryſtal, variouſly modified, according to the nature and texture of the ſalts. The method is by diſſolving any ſaline body in water, and filtering it, to evaporate, 'till a film appear at the top, and then let it ſtand to ſhoot; and this it does

does by that attractive force which is in all bodies, and particularly in salt, by reason of its solidity: whereby, when the menstruum or fluid, in which such particles flow, is sated enough or evaporated, so that the saline particles are within each other's attractive powers, they draw one another more than they are drawn by the fluid, then will they run into crystals. And this is peculiar to those, that let them be ever so much divided and reduced into minute particles, yet, when they are formed into crystals, they each of them reassume their proper shapes; so that one might as easily divest them of their saltness, as of their figure. This being an immutable and perpetual law, by knowing the figure of the crystals, we may understand what the texture of the particles ought to be, which can form those crystals; and, on the other hand, by knowing the texture of the particles, may be determined the figure of the crystals. *Quincy.*

2. The mass formed by congelation or concretion.

All natural metallick and mineral *crystallizations* were effected by the water, which first brought the particles, whereof each consists, out from amongst the matter of the strata. *Woodward's Natural History, p.* i.

To CRY'STALLIZE. *v. a.* [from *crystal.*] To cause to congeal or concrete in crystals.

If you dissolve copper in *aqua fortis*, or spirit of nitre, you may, by *crystallizing* the solution, obtain a goodly blue. *Boyle's Scept. Chym.*

To CRY'STALLIZE. *v. n.* To coagulate; congeal; concrete; or shoot into crystals.

Recent urine will likewise *crystallize* by inspissation, and afford a salt neither acid nor alkaline. *Arbuthnot on Aliments.*

CUB. *n. s.* [of uncertain etymology.]

1. The young of a beast; generally of a bear or fox.

I would outstare the sternest eyes that look,
Pluck the young sucking *cubs* from the she-bear. *Shakespeare.*
This night, wherein the *cub*-drawn bear would couch,
The lion, and the belly pinched wolf,
Keep their fur dry. *Shakespeare's King Lear.*

In the eagle's destroying one fox's *cubs*, there's power executed with oppression. *L'Estrange, Fable* 72.

2. The young of a whale, perhaps of any viviparous fish.

Two mighty whales, which swelling seas had tost,
One as a mountain vast, and with her came
A *cub*, not much inferior to his dame. *Waller.*

3. In reproach or contempt, a young boy or girl.

O thou dissembling *cub!* what wilt thou be,
When time hath sow'd a grizzle on thy case?
Or will not else thy craft so quickly grow,
That thine own trip shall be thine overthrow? *Shakespeare.*

O most comical sight! a country squire, with the equipage of a wife and two daughters, came to Mr. Snipwel's shop last night; but, such two unlicked *cubs!* *Congreve.*

To CUB. *v. a.* [from the noun.] To bring forth: used of beasts, or of a woman in contempt.

Cub'd in a cabbin, on a mattress laid,
On a brown George with lousy swabbers fed;
Dead wine, that stinks of the Borrachio, sup
From a foul jack, or greasy mapple cup. *Dryden's Pers. Sat.*

CUBA'TION. *n. s.* [*cubatio*, Lat.] The act of lying down. *Dict.*

CU'BATORY. *adj.* [from *cubo*, Lat.] Recumbent. *Dict.*

CU'BATURE. *n. s.* [from *cube.*] The finding exactly the solid content of any proposed body. *Harris.*

CUBE. *n. s.* [from κύβος, a die.]

1. [In geometry.] A regular solid body, consisting of six square and equal faces or sides, and the angles all right, and therefore equal. *Chambers.*

2. [In arithmetick.] See CUBICK *Number.*

All the master planets move about the sun at several distances, as their common center, and with different velocities. This common law being observed in all of them, that the squares of the times of the revolutions are proportional to the *cubes* of their distances. *Grew's Cosmolog. b.* i. *c.* 2. *s.* 6.

CUBE *Root.* }
CU'BICK *Root.* } *n. s.* The origin of a cubick number; or a number, by whose multiplication into itself, and again into the product, any given number is formed: thus two is the cube-root of eight. *Chambers.*

CU'BEB. *n. s.* A small dried fruit resembling pepper, but somewhat longer, of a greyish-brown colour on the surface, and composed of a corrugated or wrinkled external bark, covering a single and thin friable shell or capsule, containing a single seed of a roundish figure, blackish on the surface, and white within. It has an aromatick, but not very strong smell, and is acrid and pungent to the taste, but less so than pepper. *Cubebs* are brought into Europe from the island of Java; but the plant, which produces them, is wholly unknown to us. They are warm and carminative; and the Indians steep them in wine, and esteem them provocatives to venery. *Hill.*

Aromaticks, as *cubebs*, cinnamon, and nutmegs, are usually put into crude poor wines, to give them more oily spirits. *Floyer on the Humours.*

CU'BICAL. }
CU'BICK. } *adj.* [from *cube.*]

1. Having the form or properties of a cube.

A close vessel, containing ten *cubical* feet of air, will not suffer a wax-candle of an ounce to burn in it above an hour before it be suffocated. *Wilkins's Math. Mag.*

It is above a hundred to one, against any particular throw, that you do not cast any given set of faces with four *cubical* dice; because there are so many several combinations of the six faces of four dice. *Bentley's Sermons.*

2. It is applied to numbers.

The number of four, multiplied into itself, produceth the square number of sixteen; and that again multiplied by four, produceth the *cubick* number of sixty-four. If we should suppose a multitude actually infinite, there must be infinite roots, and square and *cubick* numbers; yet, of necessity, the root is but the fourth part of the square, and the sixteenth part of the *cubick* number. *Hale's Origin of Mankind.*

The number of ten hath been as highly extolled, as containing even, odd, long and plain, quadrate and *cubical* numbers. *Brown's Vulgar Errours, b.* iv. *c.* 12.

CU'BICALNESS. *n. s.* [from *cubical.*] The state or quality of being cubical.

CUBI'CULARY. *adj.* [*cubiculum*, Latin.] Fitted for the posture of lying down.

Custom, by degrees, changed their *cubiculary* beds into discubitory, and introduced a fashion to go from the baths unto these. *Brown's Vulgar Errours, b.* v. *c.* 6.

CU'BIFORM. *adj.* [from *cube* and *form.*] Of the shape of a cube.

CU'BIT. *n. s.* [from *cubitus*, Latin.] A measure in use among the ancients; which was originally the distance from the elbow, bending inwards, to the extremity of the middle finger. This measure is the fourth part of a well proportioned man's stature. Some fix the Hebrew *cubit* at twenty inches and a half, Paris measure; and others at eighteen. *Calm.*

From the tip of the elbow to the end of the long finger, is half a yard and a quarter of the stature, and makes a *cubit*; the first measure we read of, the ark of Noah being framed and measured by *cubits.* *Holder on Time.*

Measur'd by *cubit*, length, and breadth, and height. *Milton's Paradise Lost, b.* xi.

The Jews used two sorts of *cubits*; the sacred, and the profane or common one. *Arbuthnot on Measures.*

When on the goddess first I cast my sight,
Scarce seem'd her stature of a *cubit* height. *Pope.*

CU'BITAL. *adj.* [*cubitalis*, Latin.] Containing only the length of a cubit.

The watchmen of Tyre might well be called pygmies, the towers of that city being so high, that, unto men below, they appeared in a *cubital* stature. *Brown's Vulgar Errours, b.* iv.

CU'CKINGSTOOL. *n. s.* An engine invented for the punishment of scolds and unquiet women, which, in ancient times, was called tumbrel. *Cowel.*

These mounted on a chair-curale,
Which moderns call a *cucking-stool*,
March proudly to the river's side. *Hudibras, p.* ii. *cant.* 2.

CU'CKOLD. *n. s.* [*cocu*, Fr. from *coukoo.*] One that is married to an adultress; one whose wife is false to his bed.

But for all the whole world; why, who would not make her husband a *cuckold*, to make him a monarch? I should venture purgatory for't. *Shakespeare's Othello.*

There have been,
Or I am much deceiv'd, *cuckolds* ere now;
And many a man there is, ev'n at this present,
Now while I speak this, holds his wife by th' arm,
That little thinks she has been sluic'd in's absence. *Shakesp.*

For though the law makes null th' adulterer's deed
Of lands, to her the *cuckold* may succeed. *Dryden's Juvenal.*

Ever since the reign of king Charles II. the alderman is made a *cuckold*, the deluded virgin is debauched, and adultery and fornication are committed behind the scenes. *Swift.*

To CU'CKOLD. *v. a.*

1. To corrupt a man's wife; to bring upon a man the reproach of having an adulterous wife; to rob a man of his wife's fidelity.

If thou canst *cuckold* him, thou do'st thyself a pleasure, and me a sport. *Shakespeare's Othello.*

2. To wrong a husband by unchastity.

But suffer not thy wife abroad to roam,
Nor strut in streets with amazonian pace;
For that's to *cuckold* thee before thy face. *Dryd. Juv. Sat.* 6.

CU'CKOLDLY. *adj.* [from *cuckold.*] Having the qualities of a cuckold; poor; mean; cowardly; sneaking.

Poor *cuckoldly* knave, I know him not: yet I wrong him to call him poor; they say the jealous knave hath masses of money. *Shakespeare's Merry Wives of Windsor.*

CU'CKOLDMAKER. *n. s.* [*cuckold* and *make.*] One that makes a practice of corrupting wives.

If I spared any that had a head to hit, either young or old, he or she, cuckold or *cuckoldmaker*, let me never hope to see a chine again. *Shakespeare's Henry* VIII.

One Hernando, *cuckoldmaker* of this city, contrived to steal her away. *Dryden's Spanish Fryar.*

CU'CKOLDOM. *n. s.* [from *cuckold.*]

1. The act of adultery.

She

She is thinking on nothing but her colonel, and conspiring *cuckoldom* against me. *Dryden's Spanish Fryar.*

2. The state of a cuckold.

It is a true saying, that the last man of the parish that knows of his *cuckoldom*, is himself. *Arbuthn. Hist. of J. Bull.*

CU'CKOO. *n. s.* [*cwccw*, Welsh; *cocu*, Fr. *kockock*, Dutch.]

1. A bird which appears in the Spring; and is said to suck the eggs of other birds, and lay her own to be hatched in their place; from which practice, it was usual to alarm a husband at the approach of an adulterer by calling *cuckoo*, which, by mistake, was in time applied to the husband. This bird is remarkable for the uniformity of his note, from which his name in most tongues seems to have been formed.

Finding Mopsa, like a *cuckoo* by a nightingale, alone with Pamela, I came in. *Sidney.*

The merry *cuckoo*, messenger of Spring,
His trumpet shrill hath thrice already sounded. *Spenser.*

The plainsong *cuckoo* gray,
Whose note full many a man doth mark,
And dares not answer, nay. *Shakespeare.*

Take heed, have open eye; for thieves doo foot by night:
Take heed ere Summer comes, or *cuckoo* birds affright. *Shak.*

I deduce,
From the first note the hollow *cuckoo* sings,
The symphony of Spring; and touch a theme
Unknown to fame, the passion of the grove. *Thoms. Spring.*

2. It is a name of contempt.

Why, what a rascal art thou then, to praise him so for running?——
—A horseback, ye *cuckoo*;——but a-foot, he will not budge a foot. *Shakespeare's Henry IV. p. i.*

CUCKOO-BUD. }
CUCKOO-FLOWER. } *n. s.* The name of a flower.

When daizies pied, and violets blue,
And *cuckoo-buds* of yellow hue,
Do paint the meadows much bedight. *Shakespeare.*

Nettles, *cuckoo-flowers*,
Darnel, and all the idle weeds that grow
In our sustaining *corn*. *Shakespeare's King Lear.*

CUCKOO-SPITTLE. *n. s.*

Cuckoo-spittle, or woodseare, is that spumous dew or exudation, or both, found upon plants, especially about the joints of lavender and rosemary; observeable with us about the latter end of May. *Brown's Vulgar Errours, b. v. c. 8.*

CU'CULLATE. }
CU'CULLATED. } *adj.* [*cucullatus*, hooded, Latin.]

1. Hooded; covered, as with a hood or cowl.
2. Having the resemblance or shape of a hood.

They are differently *cucullated*, and capuched upon the head and back. *Brown's Vulgar Errours, b. v. c. 3.*

CU'CUMBER. *n. s.* [*cucumis*, Latin.] The name of a plant, and also of the fruit of that plant.

It hath a flower consisting of one single leaf, bell-shaped, and expanded toward the top, and cut into many segments; of which some are male, or barren, having no embryo, but only a large style in the middle, charged with the *farina*: others are female, or fruitful, being fastened to an embryo, which is afterwards changed into a fleshy fruit, for the most part oblong and turbinated, which is divided into three or four cells, inclosing many oblong seeds. The species are, 1. The common cucumber. 2. The white cucumber. 3. The long Turky cucumber. The first of these kinds is the most common in the English gardens. The second sort, which is by far the better fruit, as being less watery, and containing sweet seeds, is the most common kind cultivated in Holland. The third sort is propagated for the uncommon length of its fruit, and also its having less water, and fewer seeds; but it is not so fruitful as the common kind, nor will it come so early. The common sort is cultivated in three different seasons; the first of which is on hot-beds, under garden-frames, for early fruit: the second is under bell or hand glasses, for the middle crop; and the third is in the common ground for a late crop, or to pickle. *Miller.*

How *cucumbers* along the surface creep,
With crooked bodies and with bellies deep. *Dryden's Virgil.*

CU'CUMBER WILD. See WILD CUCUMBER.

CUCURBITA'CEOUS. *adj.* [from *cucurbita*, Latin, a gourd.]

Cucurbitaceous plants are those which resemble a gourd; such as the pumpion and melon. *Chambers.*

CU'CURBITE. *n. s.* [*cucurbita*, Latin.] A chymical vessel, commonly called a *body*, made of earth or glass, in the shape of a gourd, and therefore called *cucurbite*. *Quincy.*

I have, for curiosity's sake, distilled quicksilver in a *cucurbite*, fitted with a capacious glass-head. *Boyle on Colours.*

Let common yellow sulphur be put into a *cucurbite* glass, upon which pour the strongest *aqua fortis*. *Mortimer's Husb.*

CUD. *n. s.* [cuδ, Saxon.] That food which is reposited in the first stomach in order to rumination, or to be chewed again.

Many times, when my master's cattle came hither to chew their *cud* in this fresh place, I might see the young bull testify his love. *Sidney.*

You range the pathless wood,
While on a flow'ry bank he chews the *cud*. *Dryden.*

CU'DDEN. }
CU'DDY. } *n. s.* [without etymology.] A clown; a stupid rustick; a low dolt: a low bad word.

The slavering *cudden*, propp'd upon his staff,
Stood ready gaping with a grinning laugh. *Dryden.*

To CU'DDLE. *v. n.* [a low word, I believe, without etymology.] To lye close; to squat.

Have you mark'd a partridge quake,
Viewing the tow'ring faulcon nigh?
She *cuddles* low behind the brake;
Nor would she stay, nor dares she fly. *Prior.*

CU'DGEL. *n. s.* [*kudse*, Dutch.]

1. A stick to strike with, lighter than a club, shorter than a pole.

Vine twigs, while they are green, are brittle; yet the wood, dried, is extreme tough; and was used by the captains of armies, amongst the Romans, for their *cudgels*. *Bacon's N. Hist.*

Do not provoke the rage of stones
And *cudgels* to thy hide and bones.
Tremble and vanish. *Hudibras, p. i. cant. 2.*

The ass was quickly given to understand, with a good *cudgel*, the difference betwixt the one playfellow and the other. *L'Estrange, Fab. 15.*

His surly officer ne'er fail'd to crack
His knotty *cudgel* on his tougher back. *Dryden's Juvenal.*

This, if well reflected on, would make people more wary in the use of the rod and the *cudgel*. *Locke.*

The wise Cornelius was convinced, that these, being polemical arts, could no more be learned alone than fencing or *cudgel*-playing. *Arbuthnot and Pope's Martinus Scriblerus.*

2. *To cross the* CUDGELS, is to yield, from the practice of cudgel-players to lay one over the other.

It is much better to give way than it would be to contend at first, and then either to *cross the cudgels*, or to be baffled in the conclusion. *L'Estrange.*

To CU'DGEL. *v. a.* [from the noun.]

1. To beat with a stick.

My lord, he speaks most vilely of you, like a foul-mouth'd man, as he is; and said he would *cudgel* you. *Shakesp. H. IV.*

The ass courting his master, just as the spaniel had done, instead of being stroked and made much of, is only rated off and *cudgelled* for all his courtship. *South's Sermons.*

Three duels he fought, thrice ventur'd his life;
Went home, and was *cudgell'd* again by his wife. *Swift.*

2. To beat in general.

Cudgel thy brains no more about it; for your dull ass will not mend his pace with beating. *Shakespeare's Hamlet.*

A good woman happened to pass by as a company of young fellows were *cudgelling* a wallnut-tree, and asked them what they did that for. *L'Estrange.*

CUDGEL-PROOF. *adj.* Able to resist a stick.

His doublet was of sturdy buff,
And though not sword, yet *cudgel-proof*. *Hudibras, p. i.*

CU'DWEED. *n. s.* [from *cud* and *weed*.] A plant.

It hath downy leaves: the cup of the flower is scaly, neither shining nor specious: the flowers are cut in form of a star. It is cultivated for medicinal use. *Miller.*

CUE. *n. s.* [*queue*, a tail, French.]

1. The tail or end of any thing; as, the long curl of a wig.
2. The last words of a speech which the player who is to answer catches, and regards as intimation to begin.

Pyramus, you begin: when you have spoken your speech, enter into that brake; and so every one according to his *cue*. *Shakespeare's Midsummer Night's Dream.*

3. A hint; an intimation; a short direction.

What's Hecuba to him, or he to Hecuba,
That he should weep for her? What would he do,
Had he the motive and the *cue* for passion
That I have? He would drown the stage with tears. *Shakesp.*

Let him know how many servants there are, of both sexes, who expect vails; and give them their *cue* to attend in two lines, as he leaves the house. *Swift.*

4. The part which any man is to play in his turn.

Hold your hands,
Both you of my inclining, and the rest:
Were it my *cue* to fight, I should have known it
Without a prompter. *Shakespeare's Othello.*

Neither is Otto here a much more taking gentleman: nothing appears in his *cue* to move pity, or any way make the audience of his party. *Rymer's Tragedies of the last Age.*

5. Humour; temper of mind: a low word.

CUE'RPO. *n. s.* [Spanish.] To be in *cuerpo*, is to be without the upper coat or cloke, so as to discover the true shape of the *cuerpo* or body.

Expos'd in *cuerpo* to their rage,
Without my arms and equipage. *Hudibras, p. iii. cant. 3.*

CUFF. *n. s.* [*zuffa*, a battle, *zuffare*, to fight, Italian.]

1. A blow with the fist; a box; a stroke.

The priest let fall the book,
And as he stoop'd again to take it up,

The mad-brain'd bridegroom took him such a *cuff*,
That down fell priest and book, and book and priest. *Shak.*

There was, for a while, no money bid for argument, unless the poet and the player went to *cuffs* in the question. *Shakespeare's Hamlet.*

He gave her a *cuff* on the ear, and she would prick him with her knitting needle. *Arbuthnot's History of John Bull.*

Their own sects, which now lie dormant, would be soon at *cuffs* again with each other about power and preferment. *Swift.*

2. It is used of birds that fight with their talons.

To CUFF. *v. n.* [from the noun.] To fight; to scuffle.

Clapping farces acted by the court,
While the peers *cuff*, to make the rabble sport. *Dryd. Juv.*

To CUFF. *v. a.*

1. To strike with the fist.

I'll after him again, and beat him.——
——Do, *cuff* him soundly; but never draw thy sword. *Shakes.*

Well, sir Joseph, at your intreaty; but were not you, my friend, abused and *cuffed*, and kicked? *Congreve's Old Batchelor.*

2. To strike with talons.

Those lazy owls, who, perch'd near fortune's top,
Sit only watchful with their heavy wings
To *cuff* down new-fledg'd virtues, that would rise
To nobler heights, and make the grove harmonious. *Otway.*

The dastard crow, that to the wood made wing,
With her loud kaws her craven kind does bring,
Who, safe in numbers, *cuff* the noble bird. *Dryden.*

They with their quills did all the hurt they cou'd,
And *cuff'd* the tender chickens from their food. *Dryden.*

3. To strike with wings. This seems improper.

Hov'ring about the coasts they make their moan,
And *cuff* the cliffs with pinions not their own. *Dryd. Æn.*

CUFF. *n. s.* [*coeffe*, French.] Part of the sleeve.

He railed at fops; and, instead of the common fashion, he would visit his mistress in a morning-gown, band, short *cuffs*, and a peaked beard. *Arbuthnot's History of John Bull.*

CU'INAGE. *n. s.* The making up of twine into such forms, as it is commonly framed into, for carriage to other places *Cowel.*

CUIRASS. *n. s.* [*cuirasse*, Fr. from *cuir*, leather; *coraccia*, Ital.] A breastplate.

The lance pursu'd the voice without delay,
And pierc'd his *cuirass*, with such fury sent,
And sign'd his bosom with a purple dint. *Dryden.*

CUIRA'SSIER. *n. s.* [from *cuirass.*] A man at arms; a soldier in armour.

The field all iron, cast a gleaming brown,
Nor wanted clouds of foot, nor on each horn
Cuirassiers, all in steel, for standing fight. *Milt. Parad. Reg.*

The picture of St. George, wherein he is described like a *cuirassier*, or horseman completely armed, is rather a symbolical image than any proper figure. *Brown's Vulgar Errours.*

CUISH. *n. s.* [*cuisse*, French.] The armour that covers the thighs.

I saw young Harry, with his beaver on,
His *cuishes* on his thighs, gallantly arm'd,
Rise from the ground like feather'd Mercury. *Shak. Hen.* IV.

The croslet some, and some the *cuishes* mould,
With silver plated, and with ductile gold. *Dryden's Æn.*

But what had our author to wound Æneas with at so critical a time? And how came the *cuishes* to be worse tempered than the rest of his armour? *Dryden's Virg. Æn. Dedicat.*

CU'LDEES. *n. s.* [*colidei*, Latin.] Monks in Scotland.

CU'LERAGE. *n. s.* The same plant with ARSE-SMART. *Ainsw.*

CU'LINARY. *adj.* [*culina*, Latin.] Relating to the kitchen; relating to the art of cookery.

Great weight may condense those vapours and exhalations, as soon as they shall at any time begin to ascend from the sun, and make them presently fall back again into him, and by that action increase his heat; much after the manner that, in our earth, the air increases the heat of a *culinary* fire. *Newton.*

To those, who, by reason of their northern exposition, will be still forced to be at the expence of *culinary* fires, it will reduce the price of their manufacture. *Arbuthnot.*

To CULL. *v. a.* [*cueillir*, French.] To select from others; to pick out of many.

The best of every thing they had, being *culled* out for themselves, if there were in their flocks any poor diseased thing not worth the keeping, they thought it good enough for the altar of God. *Hooker, b.* v. *sect.* 34.

Our engines shall be bent
Against the brows of this resisting town:
Call for our chiefest men of discipline,
To *cull* the plots of best advantage. *Shakesp. King John.*

Like the bee, *culling* from ev'ry flow'r,
Our thighs are packt with wax, our mouths with honey. *Sh.*

In this covert will we make our stand,
Culling the principal of all the deer. *Shakes. Hen.* VI. *p.* iii.

I do remember an apothecary
In tatter'd weeds, with overwhelming brows,
Culling of simples. *Shakespeare's Romeo and Juliet.*

Then in a moment fortune shall *cull* forth,
Out of one side, her happy minion. *Shakesp. King John.*

The choicest of the British, the Roman, Saxon, and Norman laws, being *culled*, as it were, this grand charter was extracted. *Howel's Parley of Beasts.*

When false flow'rs of rhetorick thou would'st *cull*,
Trust nature, do not labour to be dull. *Dryden.*

From his herd he *culls*,
For slaughter, four the fairest of his bulls. *Dryd. Virg. Geor.*

When the current pieces of the same denomination are of different weights, then the traders in money *cull* out the heavier, and melt them down with profit. *Locke.*

With humble duty and officious haste,
I'll *cull* the farthest mead for thy repast. *Prior.*

The various off'rings of the world appear:
From each she nicely *culls* with curious toil,
And decks the goddess with the glitt'ring spoil. *Pope.*

CU'LLER. *n. s.* [from *cull.*] One who picks or chooses.

CU'LLION. *n. s.* [*coglione*, a fool, Ital. perhaps from *scullion.* It seems to import meanness rather than folly.] A scoundrel; a mean wretch.

Such a one as leaves a gentleman,
And makes a god of such a *cullion.* *Shak. Tam. of the Shrew.*

Up to the breach, you dogs; avaunt, you *cullions.* *Shakes.*

CU'LLIONLY. *adj.* [from *cullion.*] Having the qualities of a cullion; mean; base.

I'll make a sop o' th' moonshine of you: you whorson, *cullionly*, barber-monger, draw. *Shakespeare's King Lear.*

CU'LLUMBINE. *n. s.* [more properly spelt COLUMBINE, which see.] The flowers of this plant are beautifully variegated with blue, purple, red, and white. *Miller.*

Her goodly bosom, like a strawberry-bed;
Her neck, like to a bunch of *cullumbines.* *Spenser's Sonnets.*

CU'LLY. *n. s.* [*coglione*, Ital. a fool.] A man deceived or imposed upon; as, by sharpers or a strumpet.

Why should you, whose mother wits
Are furnish'd with all perquisits,
B' allow'd to put all tricks upon
Our *cully* sex, and we use none? *Hudibras, p.* iii.

Yet the rich *cullies* may their boasting spare:
They purchase but sophisticated ware. *Dryden.*

He takes it in mighty dudgeon, because I won't let him make me over by deed as his lawful *cully.* *Arbuthnot.*

To CU'LLY. *v. a.* [from the noun] To befool; to cheat; to trick; to deceive; to impose upon.

CULMI'FEROUS. *adj.* [*culmus* and *fero*, Latin.]

Culmiferous plants are such as have a smooth jointed stalk, and usually hollow; and at each joint the stalk is wrapped about with single, narrow, long, sharp-pointed leaves, and their seeds are contained in chaffy husks. *Quincy.*

There are also several sorts of grasses, both of the Cyprus and *culmiferous* kinds; some with broader, others with narrower leaves. *Woodward on Fossils.*

The properest food of the vegetable kingdom is taken from the farinaceous or mealy seeds of some *culmiferous* plants; as oats, barley, wheat, rice, rye, maize, panic, millet. *Arbuthn.*

To CU'LMINATE. *v. n.* [*culmen*, Latin.] To be vertical; to be in the meridian.

Far and wide his eye commands:
For sight no obstacle found here, or shade,
But all sunshine; as when his beams at noon
Culminate from th' equator. *Milton's Paradise Lost, b.* iii.

CULMINA'TION. *n. s.* [from *culminate.*] The transit of a planet through the meridian.

CULPABI'LITY. *n. s.* [from *culpable.*] Blameableness.

CU'LPABLE. *adj.* [*culpabilis*, Latin]

1. Criminal.

Proceed no straiter 'gainst our uncle Glo'ster,
Than from true evidence of good esteem,
He be approv'd in practice *culpable.* *Shakesp. Henry* VI. *p.* ii.

2. Guilty.

These being perhaps *culpable* of this crime, or favourers of their friends. *Spenser's State of Ireland.*

3. Blameable; blameworthy.

The wisdom of God setteth before us in Scripture so many admirable patterns of virtue, and no one of them, without somewhat noted wherein they were *culpable*, to the end that to him alone it might always be acknowledged, *Thou only art holy, Thou only art just.* *Hooker's Preface.*

All such ignorance is voluntary, and therefore *culpable*; for as much as it was in every man's power to have prevented it. *South's Sermons.*

CU'LPABLENESS. *n. s.* [from *culpable.*] Blame; guilt.

CU'LPABLY. *adv.* [from *culpable.*] Blameably; criminally.

If we perform this duty pitifully and *culpably*, it is not to be expected we should communicate holily. *Taylor.*

CU'LPRIT. *n. s.* [about this word there is great dispute. It is used by the judge at criminal trials, who, when the prisoner declares himself not guilty, and puts himself upon his trial, answers; *Culprit, God send thee a good deliverance.* It is likely that it is a corruption of *Qu'il paroit, May it so appear*, the with v[illegible] of the judge being that the prisoner may be found innocent.] A man arraigned before his judge.

The knight appear'd, and silence they proclaim;
Then first the *culprit* answer'd to his name;
And, after forms of law, was last requir'd
To name the thing that woman most desir'd. *Dryden.*

An author is in the condition of a *culprit*; the publick are his judges: by allowing too much, and condescending too far, he may injure his own cause; and by pleading and asserting too boldly, he may displease the court. *Prior's Pref. to Solomon.*

CU'LTER. *n. s.* [*culter*, Latin.] The iron of the plow perpendicular to the sheare. It is commonly written *coulter.*

Her fallow lees
The darnel, hemlock, and rank fumitory,
Doth root upon; while that the *culter* rusts,
That should deracinate such savagery. *Shakespeare's Hen.* V.

To CU'LTIVATE. *v. a.* [*cultiver*, French.]

1. To forward or improve the product of the earth, by manual industry.

Those excellent seeds implanted in your birth, will, if *cultivated*, be most flourishing in production; and, as the soil is good, and no cost nor care wanting to improve it, we must entertain hopes of the richest harvest. *Felton on the Classicks.*

2. To improve; to meliorate.

Were we but less indulgent to our faults,
And patience had to *cultivate* our thoughts,
Our muse would flourish. *Waller.*

To make man mild and sociable to man,
To *cultivate* the wild licentious savage
With wisdom, discipline, and liberal arts,
Th' embellishments of life. *Addison's Cato.*

CULTIVA'TION. *n. s.* [from *cultivate.*]

1. The art or practice of improving soils, and forwarding or meliorating vegetables.

2. Improvement in general; promotion; melioration.

An innate light discovers the common notions of good and evil, which, by *cultivation* and improvement, may be advanced to higher and brighter discoveries. *South's Sermons.*

A foundation of good sense, and a *cultivation* of learning, are required to give a seasoning to retirement, and make us taste the blessing. *Dryden.*

CULTIVA'TOR. *n. s.* [from *cultivate.*] One who improves, promotes, or meliorates; or endeavours to forward any vegetable product, or any thing else capable of improvement.

It has been lately complained of, by some *cultivators* of clover-grass, that from a great quantity of the seed not any grass springs up. *Boyle's Unsuccessful Experiments.*

CU'LTURE. *n. s.* [*cultura*, Latin.]

1. The act of cultivation; the act of tilling the ground; tillage.

Give us seed unto our heart, and *culture* to our understanding, that there may come fruit of it. 2 *Esd* viii. 6.

These three last were slower than the ordinary wheat of itself, and this *culture* did rather retard than advance. *Bacon.*

The plough was not invented 'till after the deluge; the earth requiring little or no care or *culture*, but yielding its increase freely, and without labour and toil. *Woodward.*

Where grows?—Where grows it not? If vain our toil,
We ought to blame the *culture*, not the soil.
Fix'd to no spot is happiness sincere. *Pope's Essay on Man.*

They rose as vigorous as the sun;
Then to the *culture* of the willing glebe. *Thomson's Spring.*

2. Art of improvement and melioration.

One might wear any passion out of a family by *culture*, as skilful gardeners blot a colour out of a tulip that hurts its beauty. *Tatler*, N°. 75.

To CU'LTURE. *v. a.* [from the noun.] To cultivate; to manure; to till. It is used by *Thomson*, but without authority.

CU'LVER. *n. s.* [culpre, Saxon.] A pigeon. An old word.

Had he so done, he had him snatch'd away,
More light than *culver* in the faulcon's fist. *Fairy Queen.*

Whence, borne on liquid wing,
The sound *culver* shoots. *Thomson's Spring.*

CU'LVERIN. *n. s.* [*colouvrine*, French.] A species of ordnance.

A whole cannon requires, for every charge, forty pounds of powder, and a bullet of sixty-four pounds; a *culverin*, sixteen pounds of powder, and a bullet of nineteen pounds; a demi-*culverin*, nine pounds of powder, and a bullet of twelve pounds. *Wilkins's Math. Magic.*

Here a well-polish'd mall gives us the joy
To see our prince his matchless force employ:
No sooner has he touch'd the flying ball,
But 'tis already more than half the mall;
And such a fury from his arm't has got,
As from a smoaking *culverin* 'twere shot. *Waller.*

CU'LVERKEY. *n. s.* A species of flower.

Looking down the meadows I could see a girl cropping *culverkeys* and cowslips, to make garlands. *Walton's Angler.*

To CU'MBER. *v. a.* [*kommeren*, *komberen*, to disturb, Dutch.]

1. To embarrass; to entangle; to obstruct.

Why asks he, what avails him not in fight,
And would but *cumber*, and retard his flight,
In which his only excellence is plac'd!
You give him death, that intercept his haste. *Dryd. Fables.*

Hardly his head the plunging pilot rears,
Clog'd with his cloaths, and *cumber'd* with his years. *Dryd.*

The learning and mastery of a tongue, being uneasy and unpleasant enough in itself, should not be *cumbered* with any other difficulties, as is done in this way of proceeding. *Locke.*

2. To croud or load with something useless.

I come seeking fruit on this fig tree, and find none: cut it down, why *cumbereth* it the ground? *Lu.* xiii. 7.

Let it not *cumber* your better remembrance. *Shakesp. Timon.*

The multiplying variety of arguments, especially frivolous ones, is not only lost labour, but *cumbers* the memory to no purpose. *Locke.*

3. To involve in difficulties and dangers; to distress.

Domestick fury, and fierce civil strife,
Shall *cumber* all the parts of Italy. *Shakespeare's Jul. Cæsar.*

4. To busy; to distract with multiplicity of cares.

Martha was *cumbered* about much serving. *Luke*, x. 40.

5. To be troublesome in any place.

Doth the bramble *cumber* a garden? It makes the better hedge; where, if it chances to prick the owner, it will tear the thief. *Grew's Cosmol. b.* iii. *c.* 2. *sect.* 47.

CU'MBER. *n. s.* [*komber*, Dutch.] Vexation; embarrassment; obstruction; hindrance; disturbance; distress.

By the occasion thereof I was brought to as great *cumber* and danger, as lightly any might escape. *Sidney, b.* ii.

Thus fade thy helps, and thus thy *cumbers* spring. *Spenser.*

The greatest ships are least serviceable, go very deep in water, are of marvellous charge and fearful *cumber*. *Raleigh.*

CU'MBERSOME. *adj.* [from *cumber.*]

1. Troublesome; vexatious.

Thinking it too early, as long as they had any day, to break off so pleasing a company, with going to perform a *cumbersome* obedience. *Sidney, b.* ii.

2. Burthensome; embarrassing.

I was drawn in to write the first part by accident, and to write the second by some defects in the first: these are the *cumbersome* perquisites of authors. *Arbuthnot on Aliments.*

3. Unweildy; unmanageable.

Very long tubes are *cumbersome*, and scarce to be readily managed. *Newton's Opt.*

CU'MBERSOMELY. *adj.* [from *cumbersome.*] In a troublesome manner; in a manner that produces hindrance and vexation.

CU'MBERSOMENESS *n. s.* [from *cumbersome.*] Encumbrance; hindrance; obstruction.

CU'MBRANCE. *n. s.* [from *cumber.*] Burthen; hindrance; impediment.

Extol not riches then, the toil of fools,
The wise man's *cumbrance*, if not snare; more apt
To slacken virtue, and abate her edge,
Than prompt her to do aught may merit praise. *Milt. P. L.*

CU'MBROUS. *adj.* [from *cumber.*]

1. Troublesome; vexatious; disturbing.

A cloud of *cumbrous* gnats do him molest;
All striving to infix their feeble stings,
That from their noyance he no where can rest. *Fairy Queen.*

2. Oppressive; burthensome.

Henceforth I fly not death, nor would prolong
Life much! Bent rather, how I may be quit,
Fairest and easiest, of this *cumbrous* charge. *Milt. Par. Lost.*

Black was his count'nance in a little space;
For all the blood was gather'd in his face:
Help was at hand; they rear'd him from the ground,
And from his *cumbrous* arms his limbs unbound;
Then lanc'd a vein. *Dryden.*

Possession's load was grown so great,
He sunk beneath the *cumb'rous* weight. *Swift.*

3. Jumbled; obstructing each other.

Swift to their several quarters hasted then
The *cumb'rous* elements, earth, flood, air, fire. *Milt. P. Lost.*

CU'MFREY. *n. s.* A medicinal plant.

CU'MIN. *n. s.* [*cuminum*, Latin.] A plant.

The root is annual, the leaves like those of fenel: the seeds small, long, narrow, and crooked; two of which succeed each other's flower, as in other umbelliferous plants. The seeds of this plant are used in medicine, which are brought from the island of Malta, where it is cultivated; for it is too tender for our climate. *Miller.*

Rank-smelling rue, and *cumin*, good for eyes. *Spenser.*

To CU'MULATE. *v. a.* [*cumulo*, Latin.] To heap together.

A man that beholds the mighty shoals of shells, bedded and *cumulated* heap upon heap, amongst earth, will scarcely conceive which way these could ever live. *Woodward's Nat. Hist.*

CUMULA'TION. *n. s.* The act of heaping together. *Dict.*

CUNCTA'TION. *n. s.* [*cunctatio*, Latin.] Delay; procrastination; dilatoriness.

It is most certain, that the English made not their best improvements of these fortunate events; and that especially by two miserable errours, *cunctation* in prosecuting, and haste in departure. *Hayward.*

The swiftest animal, conjoined with a heavy body, implies

that

that common moral, *festina lentè*; and that celerity should always be contempered with *cunctation*. *Brown's Vulg. Errours.*

CUNCTATOR. *n. s.* [Latin.] One given to delay; a lingerer; an idler; a sluggard.

Others, being unwilling to discourage such *cunctators*, always keep them up in good hope, that, if they are not yet called, they may yet, with the thief, be brought in at the last hour. *Hammond on Fundamentals.*

To CUND. *v. n.* [from *kennen*, to know, Dutch.] To give notice: a provincial or obsolete word. See CONDER.

They are directed by a balker or huer on the cliff, who, discerning the course of the pilchard, *cundeth*, as they call it, the master of each boat. *Carew's Survey of Cornwal.*

CUNEAL. *adj.* [*cuneus*, Latin.] Relating to a wedge; having the form of a wedge.

CUNEA'TED. *adj.* [*cuneus*, Latin.] Made in form of a wedge.

CU'NEIFORM. *adj.* [from *cuneus* and *forma*, Latin.] Having the form of a wedge.

CUNEIFORM-BONES. *n. s.* The fourth, fifth, and sixth bones of the foot; thus called from their wedge-like shape, being large above and narrow below. *Dict.*

CU'NNER. *n. s.* A kind of fish less than an oyster, that sticks close to the rocks. *Ainsworth.*

CU'NNING. *adj.* [from connan, Sax. *konnen*, Dut. to know.]

1. Skilful; knowing; well instructed; learned.

Schoolmasters will I keep within my house,
Fit to instruct her youth.—To *cunning* men
I will be very kind; and liberal
To mine own children, in good bringing up. *Shakespeare.*

I do present you with a man of mine,
Cunning in musick and the mathematicks,
To instruct her fully in those sciences. *Shakespeare.*

Wherein is he good, but to taste sack and drink it? Wherein neat and cleanly, but to carve a capon and eat it? Wherein *cunning*, but in craft? Wherein crafty, but in villainy? Wherein villainous, but in all things? Wherein worthy, but in nothing. *Shakespeare's Henry* IV. *p.* i.

Send me now therefore a man *cunning* to work in gold, and in silver, and that can skill to cut and to grave. 2 *Chron.* ii. 7.

When Pedro does the lute command,
She guides the *cunning* artist's hand. *Prior.*

2. Peformed with skill; artful.

And over them Arachne high did lift
Her *cunning* web, and spread her subtile net,
Enwrapped in foul smoak, and clouds more black than jet.
Spenser's Fairy Queen, b. ii. *cant.* 7. *stan.* 28.

And there beside of marble stone was built
An altar, carv'd with *cunning* imagery;
On which true Christians blood was often spilt,
And holy martyrs often done to die. *Spenser's Fairy Queen.*

Once put out thy light,
Thou *cunning'st* pattern of excelling nature,
I know not where is that Promethean heat
That can thy light relumine. *Shakespeare's Othello.*

3. Artfully deceitful; sly; designing; trickish; full of fetches and stratagems; subtle; crafty; subdolous.

Men will leave truth and misery to such as love it; they are resolved to be *cunning*: let others run the hazard of being sincere. *South's Sermons.*

4. Acted with subtilty.

The more he protested, the more his father thought he dissembled, accounting his integrity to be but a *cunning* face of falshood. *Sidney, b.* ii.

CU'NNING. *n. s.* [cunninȝe, Saxon.]

1. Artifice; deceit; slyness; sleight; craft; subtilty; dissimulation; fraudulent dexterity.

What if I be not so much the poet, as even that miserable subject of his *cunning*, whereof you speak. *Sidney.*

We take *cunning* for a sinister or crooked wisdom; and certainly there is great difference between a cunning man and a wise man, not only in point of honesty, but in point of ability. *Bacon, Essay* 23.

These small wares and petty points of *cunning* are infinite, and it were a good deed to make a list of them; for nothing doth more hurt than that cunning men pass for wise. *Bacon.*

2. Art; skill; knowledge.

CU'NNINGLY. *adv.* [from *cunning*.] Artfully; slyly; subtily; by fraudulent contrivance; craftily.

Amongst other crimes of this nature, there was diligent enquiry made of such as had raised and dispersed a bruit and rumour, a little before the field fought, that the rebels had the day, and that the king's army was overthrown, and the king fled; whereby it was supposed, that many succours were *cunningly* put off and kept back. *Bacon's Henry* VII.

I must meet my danger, and destroy him first;
But *cunningly* and closely. *Denham's Sophy.*

When stock is high, they come between,
Making by second-hand their offers;
Then *cunningly* retire unseen,
With each a million in his coffers. *Swift.*

CU'NNINGMAN. *n. s.* [*cunning* and *man*.] A man who pretends to tell fortunes, or teach how to recover stolen goods.

He sent him for a strong detachment
Of beadle, constable, and watchmen,
T' attack the *cunningman*, for plunder
Committed falsly on his lumber. *Hudibras, p.* iii. *cant.* 1

CU'NNINGNESS. *n. s.* [from *cunning*.] Deceitfulness; slyness.

CUP. *n. s.* [cup, Sax. *kop*, Dut. *coupe*, French.]

1. A small vessel to drink in.

Thou shalt deliver Pharaoh's *cup* into his hand, after the former manner when thou wast his butler. *Genesis*, xi. 13.

Ye heav'nly pow'rs, that guard
The British isles, such dire events remove
Far from fair Albion; nor let civil broils
Ferment from social *cups*. *Philips.*

2. The liquor contained in the cup; the draught.

Which when the vile enchanteress perceiv'd,
How that my lord from her I would reprieve,
With *cup* thus charm'd, imparting she deceiv'd. *Fairy Queen.*

All friends shall taste
The wages of their virtue, and all foes
The *cups* of their deservings. *Shakespeare's King Lear.*

Wil't please your lordship, drink a *cup* of sack. *Shakesp.*

They that never had the use
Of the grape's surprising juice,
To the first delicious *cup*
All their reason render up. *Waller.*

The best, the dearest fav'rite of the sky,
Must taste that *cup*; for man is born to die. *Pope's Odyss.*

3. Social entertainment; merry bout, [in the plural.]

Then shall our names,
Familiar in their mouth as houshold words,
Be in their flowing *cups* freshly remember'd. *Shakes. H.* V.

Let us suppose that I were reasoning, as one friend with another, by the fireside, or in our *cups*, without care, without any great affection to either party. *Knolles's History of the Turks.*

It was near a miracle to see an old man silent, since talking is the disease of age; but amongst *cups*, makes fully a wonder. *Ben. Johnson's Discoveries.*

Marrying, or prostituting, as befel
Rape or adultery, where passing fair
Allur'd them: thence from *cups*, to civil broils! *Milton.*

Amidst his *cups* with fainting shiv'ring seiz'd,
His limbs disjointed, and all o'er diseas'd,
His hand refuses to sustain the bowl. *Dryden's Persius.*

4. Any thing hollow like a cup; as, the husk of an acorn, the bell of a flower.

A pyrites of the same colour and shape, placed in the cavity of another of an hemispherick figure, in much the same manner as an acorn in its *cup*. *Woodward on Fossils.*

5. CUP *and Can.* Familiar companions. The *can* is the large vessel, out of which the *cup* is filled, and to which it is a constant associate.

You boasting tell us where you din'd,
And how his lordship was so kind;
Swear he's a most facetious man;
That you and he are *cup and can*:
You travel with a heavy load,
And quite mistake preferment's road. *Swift.*

To CUP. *v. a.* [from the noun.]

1. To supply with cups: this sense is obsolete.

Plumpy Bacchus, with pink eyne,
In thy vats our cares be drown'd:
With thy grapes our hairs be crown'd!
Cup us, 'till the world go round. *Shakesp. Ant. and Cleopatra.*

2. To fix a glass-bell or cucurbite upon the skin, to draw the blood in scarification.

The clotted blood lies heavy on his heart,
Corrupts, and there remains in spite of art:
Nor breathing veins, nor *cupping* will prevail;
All outward remedies and inward fail. *Dryden's Fables.*

You have quartered all the foul language upon me, that could be raked out of the air of Billingsgate, without knowing who I am; or whether I deserve to be *cupped* and scarified at this rate. *Spectator*, N°. 595.

Blistering, *cupping*, and bleeding are seldom of use but to the idle and intemperate. *Addison's Spectator*, N°. 195.

Him the damn'd doctors and his friends immur'd;
They bled, they *cupp'd*, they purg'd; in short they cur'd. *Pope.*

CUPBE'ARER. *n. s.*

1. An officer of the king's houshold.

There is conveyed to Mr. Villiers an intimation of the king's pleasure to wait and to be sworn his servant, and shortly after his *cupbearer* at large; and the Summer following he was admitted in ordinary. *Wotton.*

2. An attendant to give wine at a feast.

This vine was said to be given to Tros, the father of Priam, by Jupiter, as a recompence for his carrying away his son Ganymede to be his *cupbearer*. *Notes on the Odyssey.*

CU'PBOARD. *n. s.* [cup and bord, a case or receptacle, Saxon.] A case with shelves, in which victuals or earthen ware is placed.

Some trees are best for planchers, as deal; some for tables, *cupboards*, and desks, as walnut. *Bacon's Natural History.*

Codrus

Codrus had but one bed; ſo ſhort to boot,
That his ſhort wife's ſhort legs hung dangling out:
His *cupboard*'s head ſix earthen pitchers grac'd,
Beneath them was his truſty tankard plac'd. *Dryden's Juv.*
Yet their wine and their victuals theſe curmudgeon-lubbards,
Lock up from my ſight, in cellars and *cupboards*. *Swift.*

To CU'PBOARD. *v. a.* [from the noun.] To treaſure in a cupboard; to hoard up.

The belly did remain
I' th' midſt o' th' body, idle and unactive,
Still *cupboarding* the viand, never bearing
Like labour with the reſt. *Shakeſpeare's Coriolanus.*

CUPI'DITY. *n. ſ.* [*cupiditas*, Latin.] Concupiſcence; unlawful or unreaſonable longing.

CU'POLA. n. ſ. [Italian.] A dome; the hemiſpherical ſummit of a building.

Nature ſeems to have deſigned the head as the *cupola* to the moſt glorious of her works; and when we load it with ſupernumerary ornaments, we deſtroy the ſymetry of the human figure. *Addiſon's Spectator*, Nº. 28.

CU'PPEL. See COPPEL.

There be other bodies fixed, which have little or no ſpirit; ſo as there is nothing to fly out, as we ſee in the ſtuff whereof *cuppels* are made, which they put into furnaces, upon which fire worketh not. *Bacon's Natural Hiſtory*, Nº. 799.

CU'PPER. *n. ſ.* [from *cup*.] One who applies cupping-glaſſes; a ſcarifier.

CUPPING-GLASS. *n. ſ.* [from *cup* and *glaſs*.] A glaſs uſed by ſcarifiers to draw out the blood by rarefying the air.

A bubo, in this caſe, ought to be drawn outward by *cupping-glaſſes*, and brought to ſuppuration. *Wiſeman's Surgery.*

CU'PREOUS. *adj.* [*cupreus*, Latin.] Coppery; conſiſting of copper.

Having, by the intervention of a little ſal armoniack, made copper inflammable, I took ſome ſmall grains, and put them under the wiek of a burning candle, whereby they were with the melted tallow ſo kindled, that the green, not blue, flame of the *cupreous* body did burn for a good while. *Boyle.*

CUR. *n. ſ.* [*korre*, Dutch. See CURTAL.]

1. A worthleſs degenerate dog.

How does your fallow greyhound, ſir?—
'Tis a good dog.——
—A *cur*, ſir.——
—Sir, he's a good dog, and a fair dog. *Shakeſpeare.*

Here's an old drudging *cur* turned off to ſhift for himſelf, for want of the very teeth and heels that he had loſt in his maſter's ſervice. *L'Eſtrange, Fable* 25.

A *cur* may bear
The name of tiger, lion, or whate'er
Denotes the nobleſt or the faireſt beaſt. *Dryden's Juvenal.*

2. A term of reproach for a man.

What would you have, ye *curs*,
That like not peace nor war? *Shakeſpeare's Coriolanus.*

This knight had occaſion to inquire the way to St. Anne's-lane; upon which the perſon, whom he ſpoke to, called him a young popiſh *cur*, and aſked him, who made Anne a ſaint. *Addiſon's Spectator*, Nº. 125.

CU'RABLE. *adj.* [from *cure*.] That admits a remedy; that may be healed.

A conſumption of the lungs, at the beginning, herein differs from all other *curable* diſeaſes, that it is not to be worn away by change of diet, or a chearful ſpirit. *Harvey on Conſump.*

A deſperate wound muſt ſkilful hands employ,
But thine is *curable* by Philip's boy. *Dryden's Juvenal's Sat.*

CU'RABLENESS. *n. ſ.* [from *curable*.] Poſſibility to be healed.

CU'RACY. *n. ſ.* [from *curate*.] Employment of a curate, diſtinct from a benefice; employment which a hired clergyman holds under the beneficiary.

They get into orders as ſoon as they can, and, if they be very fortunate, arrive in time to a *curacy* here in town. *Swift.*

CU'RATE. *n. ſ.* [*curator*, Latin.] A clergyman hired to perform the duties of another.

He ſpar'd no pains; for *curate* he had none;
Nor durſt he truſt another with his care. *Dryden's Fables.*

2. A pariſh prieſt.

I thought the Engliſh of *curate* had been an eccleſiaſtical hireling.——No ſuch matter; the proper import of the word ſignifies one who has the cure of ſouls. *Collier on Pride.*

CU'RATESHIP. *n. ſ.* [from *curate*.] The ſame with curacy.

CU'RATIVE. *adj.* [from *cure*.] Relating to the cure of diſeaſes; not preſervative.

The therapeutick or *curative* phyſick, we term that which reſtores the patient unto ſanity. *Brown's Vulgar Errours, b* iv.

There may be taken proper uſeful indications, both preſervative and *curative*, from the qualities of the air. *Arbuthnot.*

CURA'TOR. n. ſ. [Latin.] One that has the care and ſuperintendence of any thing.

The *curators* of Bedlam aſſure us, that ſome lunaticks are perſons of honour. *Swift.*

CURB. *n. ſ.* [*courber*, to bend, French.]

1. A curb is an iron chain, made faſt to the upper part of the branches of the bridle, in a hole called the eye, and running over the beard of the horſe. *Farrier's Dict.*

The ox hath his bow, the horſe his *curb*, and the faulcon his bells; ſo man hath his deſire. *Shakeſ. As you like it.*

So four fierce courſers, ſtarting to the race,
Scow'r through the plain, and lengthen ev'ry pace;
Nor reins, nor *curbs*, nor threat'ning cries they fear. *Dryd.*

2. Reſtraint; inhibition; oppoſition; hindrance.

The Roman ſtate, whoſe courſe will on
The way it takes, cracking ten thouſand *curbs*
Of more ſtrong links aſunder, than can ever
Appear in your impediment. *Shakeſpeare's Coriolanus.*

We remain
In ſtricteſt bondage, though thus far remov'd,
Under th' inevitable *curb*, reſerv'd
His captive multitude. *Milton's Paradiſe Loſt, b.* ii. *l.* 322.

By theſe men, religion, that ſhould be
The *curb*, is made the ſpur to tyranny. *Denham's Sophy.*

Even they who think us under no other tie to the true intereſt of our country, will allow this to be an effectual *curb* upon us. *Atterbury's Sermons.*

3. A curb is a hard and callous tumour, which runs along the inſide of a horſe's hoof; that is, on that part of the hoof that is oppoſite to the leg of the lame ſide. *Farrier's Dict.*

To CURB. *v. a.* [from the noun.]

1. To guide or reſtrain a horſe with a curb.

Part wield their arms, part *curb* the foaming ſteed. *Milt.*

2. To reſtrain; to inhibit; to check; to confine; to hold back.

Were not the laws planted amongſt them at the firſt, and had they not governours to *curb* and keep them ſtill in awe and obedience? *Spenſer on Ireland.*

Then thou, the mother of ſo ſweet a child,
Her falſe imagin'd loſs ceaſe to lament,
And wiſely learn to *curb* thy ſorrows wild. *Milton.*

If ſenſe and learning are ſuch unſociable imperious things, he ought to keep down the growth of his reaſon, and *curb* his intellectuals. *Collier on Pride.*

At this ſhe *curb'd* a groan, that elſe had come;
And pauſing, view'd the preſent in the tomb;
Then to the heart ador'd devoutly glew'd
Her lips, and raiſing it, her ſpeech renew'd. *Dryd. Fables.*

'Till force returns, his ardour we reſtrain,
And *curb* his warlike wiſh to croſs the main. *Dryden.*

Knowing when a muſe ſhould be indulged
In her full flight, and when ſhe ſhould be *curbed*. *Roſcommon.*

Some poor cottage on the mountain's brow,
Where pinching want muſt *curb* thy warm deſires,
And houſhold cares ſuppreſs thy genial fires. *Prior.*

Nature to all things fix'd the limits fit,
And wiſely *curb'd* proud man's pretending wit. *Pope.*

2. Sometimes with *from*; ſometimes with *of*.

Yet you are *curb'd from* that enlargement by
The conſequence of the crown. *Shakeſpeare's Cymbeline.*

CURD. *n. ſ.* [See CRUDLE.] The coagulation of milk; the concretion of the thicker parts of any liquor.

Milk of itſelf is ſuch a compound of cream, *curds*, and whey, as it is eaſily turned and diſſolved. *Bacon's Nat. Hiſtory.*

This night, at leaſt, with me forget your care;
Cheſnuts and *curds*, and cream ſhall be your fare. *Dryden.*

Let Sporus tremble.—What! that thing of ſilk!
Sporus, that mere white *curd* of aſs's milk? *Pope.*

To CURD. *v. a.* [from the noun.] To turn to curds; to cauſe to coagulate.

Maiden, does it *curd* thy blood,
To ſay I am thy mother? *Shakeſp. All's well that ends well.*

To CU'RDLE. *v. n.* [from *curd*.] To coagulate; to ſhoot together; to concrete.

Powder of mint, and powder of red roſes, keep the milk ſomewhat from turning or *curdling* in the ſtomach. *Bacon.*

Some to the houſe,
The fold, and dairy, hungry bend their flight,
Sip round the pail, or taſte the *curdling* cheeſe. *Thom. Sum.*

To CU'RDLE. *v. a.* To cauſe to coagulate; to force into concretions.

His changed powers at firſt themſelves not felt,
'Till *curdled* cold his courage 'gan t' aſſail. *Fairy Queen, b.* i.

Mixed with the ſixth part of a ſpoonful of milk, it burnt to the ſpace of one hundred pulſes, and the milk was *curdled*. *Bacon's Natural Hiſtory*, Nº. 366.

My ſoul is all the ſame,
Unmov'd with fear, and mov'd with martial fame;
But my chill blood is *curdled* in my veins,
And ſcarce the ſhadow of a man remains. *Dryden's Virgil.*

Ev'n now I fall a victim to thy wrongs;
Ev'n now a fatal draught works out my ſoul;
Ev'n now it *curdles* in my ſhrinking veins
The lazy blood, and freezes at my heart. *Smith.*

There is in the ſpirit of wine ſome acidity, by which brandy *curdles* milk. *Floyer.*

CU'RDY. *adj.* [from *curd*.] Coagulated; concreted; full of curds; curdled.

It differs from a vegetable emulsion, by coagulating into a *curdy* mass with acids. *Arbuthnot on Aliments.*

CURE. *n. s.* [*cura*, Latin.]

1. Remedy; restorative.

This league that we have made,
Will give her sadness very little *cure*.
Brother of England, how may we content
This widow lady? *Shakespeare's King John.*

Cold, hunger, prisons, ills without a *cure*,
All these he must, and guiltless oft, endure. *Dryden's Fables.*

Now we're ador'd, and the next hour displease;
At first your *cure*, and after your disease. *Granville.*

Horace advises the Romans to seek a seat in some remote part, by way of a *cure* for the corruption of their manners. *Sw.*

2. Act of healing.

I do *cures* to-day, and to-morrow. *Lu.* xiii. 32.

3. The benefice or employment of a curate or clergyman.

If his *cure* lies among the lawyers, let nothing be said against entangling property, spinning out causes, squeezing clients, and making the laws a greater grievance than those who break them. *Collier.*

To CURE. *v. a.* [*curo*, Latin.]

1. To heal; to restore to health; to remedy; to recover: with *of* before the disease. Used of patients or diseases.

The bones, in sharp colds, wax brittle; and therefore all contusions of bones, in hard weather, are more difficult to *cure*. *Bacon's Natural History*, N°. 688.

Here the poor Lover, that has long endur'd
Some proud nymph's scorn, of his fond passion's *cur'd*. *Waller.*

I never knew any man *cured of* inattention. *Swift.*

Hear what from love unpractis'd hearts endure,
From love, the sole disease thou canst not *cure*. *Pope.*

2. To prepare in any manner, so as to be preserved from corruption.

The beef would be so ill chosen, or so ill *cured*, as to stink many times before it came so far as Holland. *Temple.*

CU'RELESS. *adj.* [*cure* and *less*.] Without cure; without remedy.

Bootless are plaints, and *cureless* are my wounds;
No way to fly, nor strength to hold out flight. *Shak. H.* VI.

Repair thy wit, good youth, or it will fall
To *cureless* ruin. *Shakespeare's Merchant of Venice.*

If, said he,
Your grief alone is hard captivity,
For love of heav'n, with patience undergo
A *cureless* ill, since fate will have it so. *Dryden's Fables.*

CU'RER. *n. s.* [from *cure*.] A healer; a physician.

He is a curer of souls, and you a *curer* of bodies: if you should fight, you go against the hair of your professions *Shak.*

The indexterity and worse success of the most famous of our consumption *curers*, do evidently demonstrate their dimness in beholding its causes. *Harvey on Consumptions.*

CU'RFEW. *n. s.* [*couvre feu*, French.] An evening-peal, by which the conqueror willed, that every man should rake up his fire, and put out his light; so that in many places at this day, where a bell is customarily rung towards bed time, it is said to ring *curfew*. *Cowel.*

You whose pastime
Is to make midnight mushrooms, that rejoice
To hear the solemn *curfew*. *Shakespeare's Tempest.*

Oft on a plat of rising ground,
I hear the far off *curfew* sound,
Over some wide-water'd shoar,
Swinging slow with sullen roar. *Milton.*

2. A cover for a fire; a fireplate.

But now for pans, pots, *curfews*, counters and the like, the beauty will not be so much respected, so as the compound stuff is like to pass. *Bacon's Phys. Rem.*

CURIA'LITY. *n. s.* [from *curialis*, Latin.] The privileges, prerogatives, or perhaps retinue of a court.

The court and *curiality*. *Bacon's Advice to Villiers.*

CURIO'SITY. *n. s.* [from *curious*.]

1. Inquisitiveness; inclination to enquiry.

2. Nicety; delicacy.

When thou wast in thy gilt, and thy perfume, they mockt thee for too much *curiosity*; in thy rags thou knowest none, but art despised for the contrary. *Shakespeare's Timon.*

3. Accuracy; exactness.

Qualities are so weighed, that *curiosity* in neither can make choice of either's moiety. *Shakespeare's King Lear.*

Our eyes and senses, however armed or assisted, are too gross to discern the *curiosity* of the workmanship of nature. *Ray on the Creation.*

4. An act of curiosity; nice experiment.

There hath been practised also a *curiosity*, to set a tree upon the north-side of a wall, and, at a little height, to draw it through the wall, and spread it upon the south-side; conceiving that the root and lower part of the stock should enjoy the freshness of the shade, and the upper boughs and fruit, the comfort of the sun: but it sorted not. *Bacon's Nat. History.*

5. An object of curiosity; rarity.

We took a ramble together to see the *curiosities* of this great town. *Addison's Freeholder*, N°. 47.

CU'RIOUS. *adj.* [*curiosus*, Latin.]

1. Inquisitive; desirous of information; addicted to enquiry.

Be not *curious* in unnecessary matters; for more things are shewn unto thee than men understand. *Ecclus.* iii. 23.

Even then to them the spirit of lyes suggests,
That they were blind, because they saw not ill;
And breath'd into their uncorrupted breasts
A *curious* wish, which did corrupt their will. *Davies.*

2. Attentive to; diligent about: sometimes with *after*.

It is pity a gentleman so very *curious after* things that were elegant and beautiful, should not have been as curious as to their origin, their uses, and their natural history. *Woodward.*

3. Sometimes with *of*.

Then thus a senior of the place replies,
Well read, and *curious* of antiquities. *Dryden's Fables.*

4. Accurate; careful not to mistake.

'Till Arrianism had made it a matter of great sharpness and subtlety of wit to be a sound believing Christian, men were not *curious* what syllables or particles of speech they used. *Hook.*

5. Difficult to please; solicitous of perfection; not negligent; full of care.

A temperate person is not *curious* of fancies and deliciousness; he thinks not much, and speaks not often of meat and drink. *Taylour.*

6. Exact; nice; subtle.

Both these senses embrace their objects at greater distance, with more variety, and with a more *curious* discrimation, than the other sense. *Holder.*

7. Artful; not neglectful; not fortuitous.

A vaile obscur'd the sunshine of her eyes,
The rose within herself her sweetness closed;
Each ornament about her seemly lies,
By *curious* chance, or careless art, composed. *Fairfax, b.* ii.

8. Elegant; neat; laboured; finished.

Understanding to devise *curious* works, to work in gold. *Ex.*

9. Rigid; severe; rigorous.

For *curious* I cannot be with you,
Signior Baptista, of whom I hear so well. *Shakespeare.*

CU'RIOUSLY. *adv.* [from *curious*.]

1. Inquisitively; attentively; studiously.

At first I thought there had been no light reflected from the water in that place; but observing it more *curiously*, I saw within it several smaller round spots, which appeared much blacker and darker than the rest. *Newton's Opt.*

2. Elegantly; neatly.

Nor is it the having of wheels and springs, though never so *curiously* wrought, and artificially set, but the winding of them up, that must give motion to the watch. *South's Sermons.*

3. Artfully; exactly.

4. Captiously.

CURL. *n. s.* [from the verb.]

1. A ringlet of hair.

She appareled herself like a page, cutting off her hair, leaving nothing but the short *curls* to cover that noble head. *Sid.*

Just as in act he stood, in clouds enshrin'd,
Her hand she fasten'd on his hair behind;
Then backward by his yellow *curls* she drew
To him, and him alone confess'd in view. *Dryden's Fables.*

2. Undulation; wave; sinuosity; flexure.

Thus it happens, if the glass of the prisms be free from veins, and their sides be accurately plain and well polished, without those numberless waves or *curls*, which usually arise from the sand holes, a little smoothed in polishing with putty. *Newton's Opt. Prop.* ii. *Th.* 2.

To CURL. *v. a.* [*krollen*, Dut. cyrpan, Sax. *krille*, Dan.]

1. To turn the hair in ringlets.

What hast thou been?—
—A serving man, proud in heart and mind, that *curled* my hair, wore gloves in my cap, served the lust of my mistress's heart, and did the act of darkness with her. *Shakesp. K. Lear.*

2. To writhe; to twist.

3. To dress with curls.

If she first meet the *curled* Antony,
He'll make demand of her kiss. *Shakesp. Ant. and Cleopatra.*

Up the trees
Climbing, sat thicker than the snaky locks
That *curl'd* Megæra. *Milton's Paradise Lost, b.* x. *l.* 560.

4. To raise in waves, undulations, or sinuosities.

The visitation of the winds,
Who take the ruffian billows by the top,
Curling their monstrous heads. *Shakespeare's Henry* IV. *p.* ii.

Seas would be pools, without the brushing air
To *curl* the waves. *Dryden's Fables.*

To CURL. *v. n.*

1. To shrink into ringlets.

Those slender aerial bodies are separated and stretched out, which otherwise, by reason of their flexibleness and weight, would flag or *curl*. *Boyle's Spring of the Air.*

2. To rise in undulations.

To every nobler portion of the town,

The

The *curling* billows roul their restless tide;
In parties now they straggle up and down,
As armies, unoppos'd, for prey divide. *Dryden.*
While *curling* smoaks from village tops are seen. *Pope.*

3. To twist itself.

Then round her slender waist he *curl'd*,
And stamp'd an image of himself, a sov'reign of the world. *Dryden's Fables.*

CU'RLEW. *n. s.* [*courlieu*, French.]

1. A kind of water-fowl, with a large beak of a grey colour, with red and black spots.
2. A bird larger than a partridge, with longer legs. It runs very swiftly, and frequents the cornfields in Spain, in Sicily, and sometimes in France. *Trevoux.*

CURMU'DGEON. *n. s.* [It is a vitious manner of pronouncing *cœur mechant*, Fr. an unknown correspondent.] An avaritious churlish fellow; a miser; a niggard; a churl; a griper.

And when he has it in his claws,
He'll not be hide-bound to the cause;
Nor shalt thou find him a *curmudgeon*,
If thou dispatch it without grudging. *Hudibras, p.* iii. *c.* 2.
Both their wine and their victuals these *curmudgeon* lubbards
Lock up from my sight, in cellars and cupboards. *Swift.*

A man's way of living is commended, because he will give any rate for it; and a man will give any rate rather than pass for a poor wretch, or a penurious *curmudgeon*. *Locke.*

CU'RMUDGEONLY. *adj.* [from *curmudgeon.*] Avaricious; covetous; churlish; niggardly.

In a country where he that killed a hog invited the neighbourhood, a *curmudgeonly* fellow advised with his companions how he might save the charge. *L'Estrange.*

CU'RRANT. *n. s.*

1. The tree hath no prickles; the leaves are large: the flower consists of five leaves, placed in form of a rose: the ovary, which arises from the center of the flower-cup, becomes a globular fruit, produced in bunches.
2. A small dried grape, properly written *corinth.*

They butter'd *currants* on fat veal bestow'd,
And rumps of beef with virgin honey stew'd;
Insipid taste, old friend, to them who Paris know,
Where rocombole, shallot, and the rank garlick grow. *King.*

CU'RRENCY. *n. s.* [from *current.*]

1. Circulation; power of passing from hand to hand.

The *currency* of those half-pence would, in the universal opinion of our people, be utterly destructive to this kingdom. *Swift.*

2. General reception.
3. Fluency; readiness of utterance; easiness of pronunciation.
4. Continuance; constant flow; uninterrupted course.

The *currency* of time to establish a custom, ought to be with a *continuando* from the beginning to the end of the term prescribed. *Ayliffe's Parergon.*

5. General esteem; the rate at which any thing is vulgarly valued.

He that thinketh Spain to be some great over-match for this estate, assisted as it is, and, may be, is no good mintman, but takes greatness of kingdoms according to their bulk and *currency*, and not after intrinsick value. *Bacon's War with Spain.*

6. The papers stamped in the English colonies by authority, and passing for money.

CU'RRENT. *adj.* [*currens*, Latin.]

1. Circulatory; passing from hand to hand.

Shekels of silver, *current* money with the merchant. *Gen.*

That there was *current* money in Abraham's time is past doubt, though it is not sure that it was stampt; for he is said to be rich in cattle, in silver, and in gold. *Arbuthnot.*

2. Generally received; uncontradicted; authoritative.

Many strange bruits are received for *current*. *Sidney.*

Because such as openly reprove supposed disorders of state, are taken for principal friends to the common benefit of all, under this fair and plausible colour, whatsoever they utter passeth for good and *current*. *Hooker, b.* i.

I have collected the facts, with all possible impartiality, from the *current* histories of those times. *Swift.*

3. Common; general.

They have been trained up from their infancy in one set of notions, without ever hearing or knowing what other opinions are *current* among mankind. *Watts's Improvement.*

About three months ago we had a *current* report of the king of France's death. *Addison's Spectator.*

4. Popular; such as is established by vulgar estimation.

We are also to consider the difference between worth and merit, strictly taken; that is, a man's intrinsick; this, his *current* value; which is less or more, as men have occasion for him. *Grew's Cosmol. b.* ii. *c.* 7. *sect.* 34.

5. Fashionable; popular.

Oft leaving what is natural and fit,
The *current* folly proves our ready wit;
And authors think their reputation safe,
Which lives as long as fools are pleas'd to laugh. *Pope.*

6. Passable; such as may be allowed or admitted.

Fouler than heart can think thee, thou canst make
No excuse *current*, but to hang thyself. *Shakesp. Rich.* III.

7. What is now passing; what is at present in its course; as, *the* current *year.*

CU'RRENT. *n. s.*

1. A running stream.

The *current*, that with gentle murmur glides,
Thou know'st, being stopp'd, impatiently doth rage;
But his fair course is not hindered:
He makes sweet musick with th' enamel'd stones. *Shakesp.*

These inequalities will vanish in one place, and presently appear in another, and seem perfectly to move like waves, succeeding and destroying one another; save that their motion oftentimes seems to be quickest, as if in that vast sea they were carried on by a *current*, or at least by a tide. *Boyle.*

Heav'n her Eridanus no more shall boast,
Whose fame in thine, like lesser *currents* lost;
Thy nobler streams shall visit Jove's abodes,
To shine among the stars, and bathe the gods. *Denham.*
Not fabled Po more swells the poet's lays,
While through the sky his shining *current* strays. *Pope.*

2. [In navigation.] Currents are certain progressive motions of the water of the sea in several places, either quite down to the bottom, or to a certain determinate depth; by which a ship may happen to be carried more swiftly or retarded in her course, according to the direction of the current, with or against the way of the ship. *Harris.*

CU'RRENTLY. *adj.* [from *current.*]

1. In a constant motion.
2. Without opposition.

The very cause which maketh the simple and ignorant to think they even see how the word of God runneth *currently* on your side, is, that their minds are forestalled, and their conceits perverted beforehand. *Hooker, Preface.*

3. Popularly; fashionably; generally.
4. Without ceasing.

CU'RRENTNESS. *n. s.* [from *current.*]

1. Circulation.
2. General reception.
3. Easiness of pronunciation.

When substantialness combineth with delightfulness, and *currentness* with stayedness, how can the language sound other than most full of sweetness? *Camden's Remains.*

CU'RRIER *n. s.* [*coriarius*, Latin.] One who dresses and pares leather for those who make shoes, or other things.

A *currier* bought a bearskin of a huntsman, and laid him down ready money for it. *L'Estrange.*

Warn'd by frequent ills, the way they found
To lodge their loathsome carrion under ground;
For useless to the *currier* were their hides,
Nor could their tainted flesh with ocean tides
Be free'd from filth. *Dryden's Virg. Geor. b.* iii *l.* 833.

CU'RRISH. *adj.* [from *cur.*] Having the qualities of a degenerate dog; brutal; sour; quarrelsome; malignant; churlish; uncivil; untractable; impracticable.

Sweet speaking oft a *currish* heart reclaims. *Sidney, b.* ii.
No care of justice, nor no rule of reason,
No temperance, nor no regard of season,
Did thenceforth ever enter in his mind,
But cruelty, the sign of *currish* kind. *Hubberd's Tale.*
In fashions wayward, and in love unkind;
For Cupid deigns not wound a *currish* mind. *Fairfax, b.* iv.
I would she were in heaven, so she could
Entreat some pow'r to change this *currish* Jew. *Shakespeare.*

She says your dog was a cur; and tells you, *currish* thanks is good enough for such a present. *Shakes. Two Gent. of Verona.*

To CU'RRY. *v. a.* [*corium*, leather, Latin.]

1. To dress leather, by beating and rubbing it.
2. To beat; to drub; to thresh; to chastise.

A deep design in't to divide
The well affected that confide;
By setting brother against brother,
To claw and *curry* one another. *Hudibras, p.* i. *cant* 1.

I may expect her to take care of her family, and *curry* her hide in case of refusal. *Addison's Spectator*, N°. 211.

3. To rub a horse with a scratching instrument, so as to smooth his coat, and promote his flesh.

Frictions make the parts more fleshy and full; as we see both in men, and in the *currying* of horses: the cause is, for that they draw a greater quantity of spirits and blood to the parts. *Bacon.*

4. To scratch in kindness; to rub down with flattery; to tickle.

If I had a suit to master Shallow, I would humour his men; if to his men, I would *curry* with master Shallow. *Shakesp.*

5. *To* CURRY *Favour.* To become a favourite by petty officiousness, slight kindnesses, or flattery.

He judged them still over-abjectly to fawn upon the heathens, and to *curry* favour with infidels. *Hooker, b.* iv. *s.* 7.

This humour succeeded so with the puppy, that an ass would go the same way to work to *curry* favour for himself. *L'Estrange.*

CU'RRYCOMB. *n. ſ.* [from *curry* and *comb.*] An iron inſtrument uſed for currying horſes.

He has a clearer idea from a little print than from a long definition; and ſo he would have of *ſtrigil* and *ſiſtrum*, if, inſtead of a *currycomb* and cymbal, he could ſee ſtamped in the margin ſmall pictures of theſe inſtruments. *Locke.*

To CURSE. *v. a.* [cuꞃꞅian, Saxon.]

1. To wiſh evil to; to execrate; to devote.

Curſe me this people; for they are too mighty for me. *Num.*

After Solyman had looked upon the dead body, and bitterly *curſed* the ſame, he cauſed a great weight to be tied unto it, and ſo caſt unto the ſea. *Knolles's Hiſtory of the Turks.*

What, yet again! the third time haſt thou *curſt* me:
This imprecation was for Laius' death,
And thou haſt wiſhed me like him. *Dryd. and Lee's Oedipus.*

2. To miſchief; to afflict; to torment.

On impious realms and barb'rous kings impoſe
Thy plagues, and *curſe* 'em with ſuch ſons as thoſe. *Pope.*

To CURSE. *v. n.* To imprecate; to deny or affirm with imprecation of divine vengeance.

The ſilver about which thou *curſedſt*, and ſpeakeſt of alſo in my ears, behold the ſilver is with me. *Jud.* xvi. 2.

CURSE. *n. ſ.* [from the verb.]

1. Malediction; wiſh of evil to another.

Neither have I ſuffered my mouth to ſin, by wiſhing a *curſe* to his ſoul. *Job*, xxxi. 30.

I never went from your lordſhip but with a longing to return, or without a hearty *curſe* to him who invented ceremonies, and put me on the neceſſity of withdrawing. *Dryden.*

2. Affliction; torment; vexation.

Curſe on the ſtripling! how he apes his ſire!
Ambitiouſly ſententious! *Addiſon's Cato.*

CU'RSED. *participial adj.* [from *curſe.*]

1. Under a curſe; hateful; deteſtable; abominable; wicked.

Merciful pow'rs!
Reſtrain in me the *curſed* thoughts that nature
Gives way to in repoſe. *Shakeſpeare's Macbeth.*

2. Unholy; unſanctified; blaſted by a curſe.

Come lady, while heav'n lends us grace,
Let us fly this *curſed* place,
Leſt the ſorcerer us entice
With ſome other new device;
Not a waſte or needleſs ſound,
'Till we come to holier ground. *Milton.*

3. Vexatious; troubleſome.

This *curſed* quarrel be no more renew'd;
Be, as becomes a wife, obedient ſtill;
Though griev'd, yet ſubject to her huſband's will. *Dryden.*

One day, I think, in Paradiſe he liv'd;
Deſtin'd the next his journey to purſue,
Where wounding thorns and *curſed* thiſtles grew. *Prior.*

CU'RSEDLY. *adv.* [from *curſed.*] Miſerably; ſhamefully: a low cant word.

Satisfaction and reſtitution lies ſo *curſedly* hard on the gizzards of our publicans. *L'Eſtrange.*

Sure this is a nation that is *curſedly* afraid of being over-run with too much politeneſs, and cannot regain one great genius but at the expence of another. *Pope.*

CU'RSEDNESS. *n. ſ.* [from *curſed.*] The ſtate of being under a curſe.

CU'RSHIP. *n. ſ.* [from *cur.*] Dogſhip; meanneſs; ſcoundrelſhip.

How durſt he, I ſay, oppoſe thy *curſhip*,
'Gainſt arms, authority, and worſhip. *Hudibras, p.* i.

CU'RSITOR. *n. ſ.* [Latin.] An officer or clerk belonging to the Chancery, that makes out original writs. They are called clerks of courſe, in the oath of the clerks of Chancery. Of theſe there are twenty-four in number, which have certain ſhires allotted to each of them, into which they make out ſuch original writs as are required. They are a corporation among themſelves. *Cowel.*

Then is the recognition and value, ſigned with the handwriting of that juſtice, carried by the *curſitor* in Chancery for that ſhire where thoſe lands do lie, and by him is a writ of covenant thereupon drawn, and ingroſſed in parchment. *Bacon.*

CU'RSORARY. *adj.* [from *curſus*, Latin.] Curſory; haſty; careleſs. A word, I believe, only found in the following line.

I have but with a *curſorary* eye
O'erglanc'd the articles. *Shakeſpeare's Henry* V.

CU'RSORILY. *adv.* [from *curſory.*] Haſtily; without care; without ſolicitous attention.

This power, and no other, Luther diſowns, as any one that views the place but *curſorily* muſt needs ſee. *Atterbury.*

CU'RSORINESS. *n. ſ.* [from *curſory.*] Slight attention.

CU'RSORY. *adj.* [from *curſorius*, Latin.] Haſty; quick; inattentive; careleſs.

The firſt, upon a *curſory* and ſuperficial view, appeared like the head of another man. *Addiſon.*

CURST. *adj.* Froward; peeviſh; malignant; miſchievous; malicious; ſnarling.

Mr. Maſon, after his manner, was very merry with both parties, pleaſantly playing both with the ſhrewd touches of many *curſt* boys, and with the ſmall diſcretion of many lewd ſchoolmaſters. *Aſcham's Schoolmaſter.*

I pray you, though you mock me, gentlemen,
Let her not hurt me: I was never *curſt*;
I have no gift at all in ſhrewiſhneſs:
I am a right maid, for my cowardice;
Let her not ſtrike me. *Shakeſ. Midſummer Night's Dream.*

I'll go ſee if the bear be gone from the gentleman, and how much he hath eaten: they are never *curſt* but when they are hungry. *Shakeſpeare's Winter's Tale.*

Her only fault, and that is fault enough,
Is, that ſhe is intolerably *curſt*,
And ſhrewd and forward, ſo beyond all meaſure,
That, were my ſtate far worſer than it is,
I would not wed her for a mine of gold. *Shakeſpeare.*

Go, write in a martial hand; be *curſt* and brief. It is no matter how witty, ſo it be eloquent, and full of invention. *Sh.*

When I diſſuaded him from his intent,
And found him pight to do it with *curſt* ſpeech,
I threaten'd to diſcover him. *Shakeſpeare's King Lear.*

And though his mind
Be ne'er ſo *curſt*, his tongue is kind. *Craſhaw.*

CU'RSTNESS. *n. ſ.* [from *curſt.*] Peeviſhneſs; frowardneſs; malignity.

Then, noble partners,
Touch you the ſow'reſt points with ſweeteſt terms,
Nor *curſtneſs* grow to the matter. *Shakeſ. Ant. and Cleopat.*

Her mouth ſhe writh'd, her forehead taught to frown,
Her eyes to ſparkle fires to love unknown;
Her ſallow cheeks her envious mind did ſhew,
And ev'ry feature ſpoke aloud the *curſtneſs* of a ſhrew. *Dryd.*

CURT. *adj.* [from *curtus*, Latin.] Short.

To CU'RTAIL. *v. a.* [*curto*, Latin. It was anciently written *curtal*, which perhaps is more proper; but dogs that had their tails cut, being called *curtal* dogs, the word was vulgarly conceived to mean originally *to cut the tail*, and was in time written according to that notion.]

1. To cut off; to cut ſhort; to ſhorten.

I, that am *curtail'd* of all fair proportion,
Deform'd, unfiniſh'd, ſent before my time
Into this breathing world. *Shakeſpeare's Richard* III.

Then why ſhould we ourſelves abridge,
And *curtail* our own privilege? *Hudibras, p.* ii. *cant.* 2.

Scribblers ſend us over their traſh in proſe and verſe, with abominable *curtailings* and quaint moderniſms. *Swift.*

This general employ, and expence of their time, would as aſſuredly *curtail* and retrench the ordinary means of knowledge and erudition, as it would ſhorten the opportunities of vice. *Woodward.*

Perhaps this humour of ſpeaking no more than we muſt, has ſo miſerably *curtailed* ſome of our words; and, in familiar writings and converſations, they often loſe all but their firſt ſyllables. *Addiſon's Spectator*, N°. 135.

2. It has *of* before the thing cut off.

The count aſſured the court, that Fact his antagoniſt had taken a wrong name, having *curtailed* it *of* three letters; for that his name was not *Fact*, but *Faction*. *Addiſon.*

CU'RTAIL *Dog. n. ſ.* A dog whoſe tail is cut off, and who is therefore hindered in courſing. Perhaps this word may be the original of *cur*.

I, amazed, ran from her as a witch; and I think, if my breaſt had not been made of faith, and my heart of ſteel, ſhe had transformed me to a *curtail dog*, and made me turn i' th' wheel. *Shakeſpeare's Comedy of Errours.*

CU'RTAIN. *n. ſ.* [*cortina*, Latin.]

1. A cloath contracted or expanded at pleaſure, to admit or exclude the light; to conceal or diſcover any thing; to ſhade a bed; to darken a room.

Their *curtains* ought to be kept open, ſo as to renew the air. *Arbuthnot on Diet.*

So through white *curtains* ſhot a tim'rous ray,
And op'd thoſe eyes that muſt eclipſe the day. *Pope.*

Thy hand, great dulneſs! let's the *curtain* fall,
And univerſal darkneſs buries all. *Pope's Dunciad, b.* iii.

2. *To draw the* CURTAIN. To cloſe it ſo as to ſhut out the light, or conceal the object.

I muſt *draw a curtain* before the work for a while, and keep your patience a little in ſuſpence, 'till materials are prepared. *Burnet's Theory of the Earth.*

Once more I write to you, and this once will be the laſt: the *curtain* will ſoon be *drawn* between my friend and me, and nothing left but to wiſh you a long good night. *Pope.*

3. To open it ſo as to diſcern the object.

Had I forgot thee? Oh, come in, Æmilia:
Soft, by and by; let me the *curtains* draw.
Where art thou? What's the matter with thee now? *Shakeſ.*

So ſoon as the all-cheering ſun
Should in the fartheſt Eaſt begin to draw
The ſhady *curtain* from Aurora's bed. *Shakeſ. Rom. and Jul.*

Peace, the lovers are aſleep:

They,

They, ſweet turtles! folded lie
In the laſt knot that love could tie:
Let them ſleep, let them ſleep on,
'Till this ſtormy night be gone;
And th' eternal morrow dawn,
Then the *curtain* will be drawn,
And they waken with that light,
Whoſe day ſhall never ſleep in night. *Craſhaw.*

4. [In fortification.] That part of the wall or rampart that lies between two baſtions. *Military Dict.*

The governour, not diſcouraged, ſuddenly of timber and boards raiſed up a *curtain* twelve foot high, at the back of his ſoldiers. *Knolles's Hiſtory of the Turks.*

CURTAIN-LECTURE. *n. ſ.* [from *curtain* and *lecture.*] A reproof given by a wife to her huſband in bed.

What endleſs brawls by wives are bred!
The *curtain-lecture* makes a mournful bed. *Dryden's Juven.*

She ought to exert the authority of the *curtain-lecture*, and, if ſhe finds him of a rebellious diſpoſition, to tame him. *Addiſ.*

To CU'RTAIN. *v. a.* [from the noun.] To incloſe or accommodate with curtains.

Now o'er one half the world
Nature ſeems dead, and wicked dreams abuſe
The *curtain'd* ſleep. *Shakeſpeare's Macbeth.*

The wand'ring prince and Dido,
When with a happy ſtorm they were ſurpriz'd,
And *curtain'd* with a counſel-keeping cave. *Shakeſpeare.*

But in her temple's laſt receſs incloſ'd,
On dulneſs' lap th' anointed head repoſ'd:
Him cloſe ſhe *curtain'd* round with vapours blue,
And ſoft beſprinkled with cimmerian dew. *Pope's Dunciad.*

CU'RTATE *Diſtance. n. ſ.* [In aſtronomy.] The diſtance of a planet's place from the ſun, reduced to the ecleptick.

CURTA'TION. *n. ſ.* [from *curto*, to ſhorten, Latin.] The interval between a planet's diſtance from the ſun and the curtate diſtance. *Chambers.*

CU'RTELASSE. } See CUTLASS.
CU'RTELAX. }

CU'RTSY. See COURTESY.

CU'RVATED. *adj.* [*curvatus*, Latin.] Bent.

CURVA'TION. *n. ſ.* [*curvo*, Latin.] The act of bending or crooking.

CU'RVATURE. *n. ſ.* [from *curve.*] Crookedneſs; inflexion; manner of bending.

It is bent after the manner of the catenarian curve, by which it obtains that *curvature* that is ſafeſt for the included marrow. *Cheyne's Phil. Prin.*

Flaccid it was beyond the activity of the muſcle, and *curvature* of the officles, to give it a due tenſion. *Holder.*

CURVE. *adj.* [*curvus*, Latin.] Crooked; bent; inflected; not ſtreight.

Unleſs an intrinſick principle of gravity or attraction, may make it deſcribe a *curve* line about the attracting body. *Bentley.*

CURVE. *n. ſ.* Any thing bent; a flexure or crookedneſs of any particular form.

And as you lead it round, in artful *curve*,
With eye intentive mark the ſpringing game. *Thomſon.*

To CURVE. *v. a.* [*curvo*, Latin.] To bend; to crook; to inflect.

And the tongue is drawn back and *curved. Holder on Speech.*

To CU'RVET. *v. n.* [*corvettare*, Italian.]

1. To leap; to bound.

Cry, holla! to thy tongue, I pr'ythee: it *curvets* unſeaſonably. *Shakeſpeare's As you like it.*

Himſelf he on an earwig ſet,
Yet ſcarce he on his back could get,
So oft and high he did *curvet*,
'Ere he himſelf could ſettle. *Drayton's Nymphid.*

Seiz'd with unwonted pain, ſurpriz'd with fright,
The wounded ſteed *curvets*; and, rais'd upright,
Lights on his feet before: his hoofs behind
Spring up in air aloft, and laſh the wind. *Dryden's Æneis.*

2. To friſk; to be licentious.

CU'RVET. *n. ſ.* [from the verb.]

1. A leap; a bound.
2. A frolick; a prank.

CURVILI'NEAR. *adj.* [*curvus* and *linea*, Lat.]

1. Conſiſting of a crooked line.

The impulſe continually draws the celeſtial body from its rectilinear motion, and forces it into a *curvilinear* orbit; ſo that it muſt be repeated every minute of time. *Cheyne.*

2. Compoſed of crooked lines.

CU'RVITY. *n. ſ.* [from *curve.*] Crookedneſs.

The joined ends of that bone and the incus receding, make a more acute angle at that joynt, and give a greater *curvity* to the poſture of the officles. *Holder's Elements of Speech.*

CU'SHION. *n. ſ.* [*kuſſen*, Dutch; *couſſin*, French.]

1. A pillow for the ſeat; a ſoft pad placed upon a chair.

Call Claudius, and ſome other of my men;
I'll have them ſleep on *cuſhions* in my tent. *Shak. Jul. Cæſar.*

If you are learn'd,
Be not as common fools; if you are not,
Let them have *cuſhions* by you. *Shakeſpeare's Coriolanus.*

But e're they ſat, officious Baucis lays
Two *cuſhions* ſtuff'd with ſtraw, the ſeat to raiſe;
Coarſe, but the beſt ſhe had. *Dryden's Fables.*

An Eaſtern king put a judge to death for an iniquitous ſentence; and ordered his hide to be ſtuffed into a *cuſhion*, and placed upon the tribunal, for the ſon to ſit on. *Swift.*

CU'SHIONED. *adj.* [from *cuſhion.*] Seated on a cuſhion; ſupported by cuſhions.

Many, who are *cuſhioned* upon thrones, would have remained in obſcurity. *Diſſertation on Parties.*

CUSP. *n. ſ.* [*cuſpis*, Latin.] A term uſed to expreſs the points or horns of the moon, or other luminary. *Harris.*

CU'SPATED. } *adj.* [from *cuſpis*, Latin.] When the leaves
CU'SPIDATED. } of a flower end in a point. *Quincy.*

CU'STARD. *n. ſ.* [*cwſtard*, Welſh.] A kind of ſweetmeat made by boiling eggs with milk and ſugar, 'till the whole thickens into a maſs. It is a food much uſed in city feaſts.

He cram'd them 'till their guts did ake,
With cawdle, *cuſtard*, and plumb cake. *Hudibras, cant.* ii.

Now may'rs and ſhrieves all huſh'd and ſatiate lay;
Yet eat, in dreams, the *cuſtard* of the day. *Pope's Dunciad.*

CU'STODY. *n. ſ.* [*cuſtodia*, Latin.]

1. Impriſonment; reſtraint of liberty.

The council remonſtranced unto queen Elizabeth the conſpiracies againſt her life, and therefore they adviſed her, that ſhe ſhould go leſs abroad weakly attended, as ſhe uſed; but the queen anſwered, ſhe had rather be dead than put in *cuſtody*. *Bacon's Apophthegms.*

For us enſlav'd, is *cuſtody* ſevere,
And ſtripes, and arbitrary puniſhment
Inflicted? *Milton's Paradiſe Loſt, b.* ii. *l.* 335.

2. Care; guardianſhip; charge.

Under the *cuſtody* and charge of the ſons of Merari, ſhall be the boards of the tabernacle. *Num.* iii. 36.

We being ſtrangers here, how dar'ſt thou truſt
So great a charge from thine own *cuſtody*. *Shakeſpeare.*

An offence it were, raſhly to depart out of the city committed to their *cuſtody*. *Knolles's Hiſtory of the Turks.*

There is generally but one coin ſtampt upon the occaſion, which is made a preſent to the perſon who is celebrated on it: by this means the whole fame is in his own *cuſtody*. *Addiſon.*

3. Defence; preſervation; ſecurity.

There was prepared a fleet of thirty ſhips for the *cuſtody* of the narrow ſeas. *Bacon's War with Spain.*

CU'STOM. *n. ſ.* [*couſtume*, French.]

1. Habit; habitual practice.

Blood and deſtruction ſhall be ſo in uſe,
That mothers ſhall but ſmile, when they behold
Their infants quarter'd by the hands of war;
All pity choak'd with *cuſtom* of fell deeds. *Shak. Jul. Cæſar.*

Cuſtom, a greater power than nature, ſeldom fails to make them worſhip. *Locke.*

2. Faſhion; common way of acting.
3. Eſtabliſhed manner.

According to the *cuſtom* of the prieſt's office, his lot was to burn incenſe when he went into the temple of the Lord. *Luk.* i.

And the prieſts *cuſtom* with the people was, that when any man offered ſacrifice, the prieſt's ſervants came, while the fleſh was in, with a fleſh-hook of three teeth in his hands. 1 *Sa.* ii.

4. Practiſe of buying of certain perſons.

You ſay he is aſſiduous in his calling, and is he not grown rich by it? Let him have your *cuſtom*, but not your votes. *Add.*

5. Application from buyers; as, *this trader has good* cuſtom.
6. [In law.] A law or right, not written, which, being eſtabliſhed by long uſe, and the conſent of our anceſtors, has been, and is, daily practiſed. We cannot ſay that this or that is a *cuſtom*, except we can juſtify that it hath continued ſo one hundred years; yet, becauſe that is hard to prove, it is enough for the proof of a *cuſtom*, if two or more can depoſe that they heard their fathers ſay, that it was a *cuſtom* all their time; and that their fathers heard their fathers alſo ſay, that it was likewiſe a *cuſtom* in their time. If it is to be proved by record, the continuance of a hundred years will ſerve. *Cuſtom* is either general or particular: general, that which is current through England; particular is that which belongs to this or that county; as gavelkind to Kent, or this or that lordſhip, city, or town. *Cuſtom* differs from preſcription; for *cuſtom* is common to more, and preſcription is particular to this or that man: preſcription may be for a far ſhorter time than *cuſtom*. *Cowel.*
7. Tribute; tax paid for goods imported, or exported.

The reſidue of theſe ordinary finances be caſual or uncertain, as be the eſcheats and forfeitures, the *cuſtoms*, butlerage, and impoſts. *Bacon.*

Thoſe commodities may be diſperſed, after having paid the *cuſtoms*, in England. *Temple.*

Cuſtoms to ſteal is ſuch a trivial thing,
That 'tis their charter to defraud their king. *Dryden.*

Strabo tells you, that Britain bore heavy taxes, eſpecially the *cuſtoms* on the importation of the Gallick trade. *Arbuthnot.*

CU'STOMHOUSE. *n. ſ.* The houſe where the taxes upon goods imported or exported are collected.

Some *cuſtomhouſe* officers, birds of paſſage, and oppreſſive thrifty ſquires, are the only thriving people amongſt us. *Swift.*

CU'STOMABLE. *adj.* [from *cuſtom.*] Common; habitual; frequent.

CU'STOMABLENESS. *n. ſ.* [from *cuſtomable.*]

1. Frequency; habit.
2. Conformity to cuſtom.

CU'STOMABLY. *adv.* [from *cuſtomable.*] According to cuſtom.

Kingdoms have *cuſtomably* been carried away by right of ſucceſſion, according to proximity of blood. *Hayward.*

CU'STOMARILY. *adv.* [from *cuſtomary.*] Habitually; commonly.

To call God to witneſs truth, or a lye perhaps, or to appeal to him on every trivial occaſion, in common diſcourſe, *cuſtomarily* without any conſideration of what we ſay, is one of the higheſt indignities and affronts that can be offered him. *Ray on the Creation.*

CU'STOMARINESS. *n. ſ.* [from *cuſtomary.*] Frequency; commonneſs; frequent occurrence.

A vice, which, for its guilt, may juſtify the ſharpeſt, and for its *cuſtomarineſs* the frequenteſt invectives, which can be made againſt it. *Government of the Tongue, ſect.* 3.

CU'STOMARY. *adj.* [from *cuſtom.*]

1. Conformable to eſtabliſhed cuſtom; according to preſcription.

Pray you now, if it may ſtand with the tune of your voices, that I may be conſul: I have here the *cuſtomary* gown. *Shakeſ.*

Several ingenious perſons, whoſe aſſiſtance might be conducive to the advance of real and uſeful knowledge, lay under the prejudices of education and *cuſtomary* belief. *Glanv. Sceps.*

2. Habitual.

We ſhould carefully avoid the profane and irreverent uſe of God's name, by curſing, or *cuſtomary* ſwearing, and take heed of the neglect or contempt of his worſhip, or any thing belonging to it. *Tillotſon, Sermon* 5.

3. Uſual; wonted.

Ev'n now I met him
With *cuſtomary* compliment, when he,
Wafting his eyes to th' contrary, and falling
A lip of much contempt, ſpeeds from me. *Shakeſpeare.*

CU'STOMED. *adj.* [from *cuſtom.*] Uſual; common; that to which we are accuſtomed.

No nat'ral exhalation in the ſky,
No common wind, no *cuſtomed* event,
But they will pluck away its nat'ral cauſe,
And call them meteors, prodigies, and ſigns. *Shak. K. John.*

CU'STOMER. *n. ſ.* [from *cuſtom.*] One who frequents any place of ſale for the ſake of purchaſing.

One would think it Overdone's houſe; for here be many old *cuſtomers.* *Shakeſpeare's Meaſure for Meaſure.*

A wealthy poet takes more pains to hire
A flatt'ring audience, than poor tradeſmen do
To perſuade *cuſtomers* to buy their goods. *Roſcommon.*

Don't you hear how lord Strut has beſpoke his liveries at Lewis Baboon's ſhop? Don't you ſee how that old fox ſteals away your *cuſtomers,* and turns you out of your buſineſs every day. *Arbuthnot.*

Thoſe papers are grown a neceſſary part in coffeehouſe furniture, and may be read by *cuſtomers* of all ranks for curioſity or amuſement. *Swift's Project for the Advancem. of Religion.*

I ſhewed you a piece of black and white ſtuff, juſt ſent from the dyer, which you were pleaſed to approve of, and be my *cuſtomer* for. *Swift.*

2. A common women. This ſenſe is now obſolete.

I marry her!—What, a *cuſtomer?* Pr'ythee, bear ſome charity to my wit; do not think it ſo unwholſome. *Shakeſ. Othello.*

CU'STREL. *n. ſ.*

1. A buckler-bearer.
2. A veſſel for holding wine. *Ainſworth.*

To CUT. pret. *cut*; part. paſſ. *cut.* [probably from the French *couteau,* a knife.]

1. To penetrate with an edged inſtrument; to divide any continuity by a ſharp edge.

Ah, *cut* my lace aſunder,
That my great heart may have ſome ſcope to beat,
Or elſe I ſwoon with this dead killing news. *Shakeſ. R.* III.

And when two hearts were join'd by mutual love,
The ſword of juſtice *cuts* upon the knot,
And ſevers 'em for ever. *Dryden's Spaniſh Fryar.*

Some I have *cut* away with ſciſſars. *Wiſeman's Surgery.*

2. To hew.

Thy ſervants can ſkill to *cut* timber in Lebanon. 2 *Chro.* ii.

3. To carve; to make by ſculpture.

Why ſhould a man, whoſe blood is warm within,
Sit like his grandſire *cut* in alabaſter? *Shakeſpeare.*

The triumphal is, indeed, defaced by time; but the plan of it is neatly *cut* upon the wall of a neighbouring building. *Addiſon's Remarks on Italy.*

4. To form any thing by cutting.

And they did beat the gold into thin plates, and *cut* it into wires. *Ex.* xxxix. 3.

Before the whiſtling winds the veſſels fly,
With rapid ſwiftneſs *cut* the liquid way,
And reach Gereſtus at the point of day. *Pope's Odyſſey, b.* iii.

5. To pierce with any uneaſy ſenſation.

The man was *cut* to the heart with theſe conſolations. *Addiſ.*

6. To divide packs of cards.

Supine they in their heav'n remain,
Exempt from paſſion and from pain;
And frankly leave us, human elves,
To *cut* and ſhuffle for ourſelves. *Prior.*

We ſure in vain the cards condemn,
Ourſelves both *cut* and ſhuffled them. *Prior.*

Take a freſh pack, nor is it worth our grieving
Who *cuts* or ſhuffles with our dirty leaving. *Granville.*

7. To interſect; to croſs; as, one line *cuts* another at right angles.

8. *To* CUT *down.* To fell; to hew down.

All the timber whereof was *cut down* in the mountains of Cilicia. *Knolles's Hiſtory of the Turks.*

9. *To* CUT *down.* To excel; to overpower.

So great is his natural eloquence, that he *cuts down* the fineſt orator, and deſtroys the beſt contrived argument, as ſoon as ever he gets himſelf to be heard. *Addiſon's Count Tariff.*

10. *To* CUT *off.* To ſeparate from the other parts by cutting.

And they caught him, and *cut off* his thumbs. *Jud.* i. 6.

11. *To* CUT *off.* To deſtroy; to extirpate; to put to death untimely.

All Spain was firſt conquered by the Romans, and filled with colonies from them, which were ſtill increaſed, and the native Spaniards ſtill *cut off.* *Spenſer on Ireland.*

By whoſe fell working I was firſt advanc'd,
And by whoſe pow'r I well might lodge a fear
To be again diſplac'd; which to avoid,
I *cut* them *off.* *Shakeſpeare's Henry* IV. *p.* ii.

Were I king,
I ſhould *cut off* the nobles for their lands. *Shakeſp. Macbeth.*

This great commander was ſuddenly *cut off* by a fatal ſtroke, given him with a ſmall contemptible inſtrument. *Howel.*

Irenæus was likewiſe *cut off* by martyrdom. *Addiſon.*

Ill-fated prince! Too negligent of life!
Cut off in the freſh, ripening prime of manhood,
Even in the pride of life. *Philips's Diſtreſt Mother.*

12. *To* CUT *off.* To reſcind.

Fetch the will hither, and we ſhall determine
How to *cut off* ſome charge in legacies. *Shakeſ. Jul. Cæſ.*

He that *cuts off* twenty years of life,
Cuts off ſo many years of fearing death. *Shakeſp. Jul. Cæſ.*

Preſume not on thy God, whoe'er he be:
Thee he regards not, owns not, hath *cut off*
Quite from his people. *Milton's Agon. l.* 1156.

The propoſal of a recompence from men, *cuts off* the hopes of future rewards. *Smalridge.*

13. *To* CUT *off.* To intercept; to hinder from union or return.

The king of this iſland, a wiſe man and a great warrior, handled the matter ſo, as he *cut off* their land forces from their ſhips. *Bacon.*

His party was ſo much inferior to the enemy, that it would infallibly be *cut off.* *Clarendon, b.* viii.

14. *To* CUT *off.* To put an end to; to obviate.

To *cut off* contentions, commiſſioners were appointed to make certain the limits. *Hayward.*

To *cut off* all further mediation and interpoſition, the king conjured him to give over all thoughts of excuſe. *Clarendon.*

It may compoſe our unnatural feuds, and *cut off* frequent occaſions of brutal rage and intemperance. *Addiſ. Freeholder.*

15. *To* CUT *off.* To take away; to withold.

We are concerned to *cut off* all occaſion from thoſe who ſeek occaſion, that they may have whereof to accuſe us. *Rogers.*

16. *To* CUT *off.* To preclude.

Every one who lives in the practice of any voluntary ſin, actually *cuts* himſelf *off* from the benefits and profeſſion of Chriſtianity. *Addiſon.*

This only object of my real care,
Cut off from hope, abandon'd to deſpair,
In ſome few poſting fatal hours is hurl'd
From wealth, from pow'r, from love, and from the world. *Pr.*

Why ſhould thoſe who wait at altars be *cut off* from partaking in the general benefits of law, or of nature. *Swift.*

17. *To* CUT *off.* To interrupt; to ſilence.

It is no grace to a judge to ſhew quickneſs of conceit in *cutting off* evidence or counſel too ſhort. *Bacon, Eſſay* 57.

18. *To* CUT *off.* To apoſtrophiſe; to abbreviate.

No vowel can be *cut off* before another, when we cannot ſink the pronunciation of it. *Dryden's Dedicat. Æn.*

19. *To* CUT *out.* To ſhape; to form.

By the pattern of mine own thoughts I *cut out*
The purity of his. *Shakeſpeare's Winter's Tale.*

I, for my part, do not like images *cut out* in juniper, or other garden ſtuff: they be for children. *Bacon, Eſſay* 47.

There is a large table at Montmorancy *cut out* of the thickneſs of a vine-ſtock. *Temple.*

The antiquaries being but indifferent taylors, they wrangle prodigiously about the *cutting out* the toga. *Arbuthnot on Coins.*

They have a large forrest *cut out* into walks, extremely thick and gloomy. *Addison.*

20. *To* CUT *out.* To scheme; to contrive.

Having a most pernicious fire kindled within the very bowels of his own forest, he had work enough *cut* him *out* to extinguish it. *Howel.*

Every man had *cut out* a place for himself in his own thoughts: I could reckon up in our army two or three lord-treasurers. *Addison.*

21. *To* CUT *out.* To adapt.

You know I am not *cut out* for writing a treatise, nor have a genius to pen any thing exactly. *Rymer.*

22. *To* CUT *out.* To debar.

I am *cut out* from any thing but common acknowledgments, or common discourse. *Pope.*

23. *To* CUT *out.* To excel; to outdo.

24. *To* CUT *short.* To hinder from proceeding by sudden interruption.

Thus much he spoke, and more he would have said,
But the stern heroe turn'd aside his head,
And *cut* him *short.* *Dryden's Æneis.*

Achilles *cut* him *short*; and thus replied,
My worth allow'd in words, is in effect deny'd. *Dryden.*

25. *To* CUT *short.* To abridge; as, *the soldiers were* cut short *of their pay.*

26. *To* CUT *up.* To divide an animal into convenient pieces.

The boar's intemperance, and the note upon him afterwards, on the *cutting* him *up*, that he had no brains in his head, may be moralized into a sensual man. *L'Estrange.*

27. *To* CUT *up.* To eradicate.

Who *cut up* mallows by the bushes, and juniper-roots for their meat. *Job*, xxx. 4.

This doctrine *cuts up* all government by the roots. *Locke.*

To CUT. *v. n.*

1. To make its way by dividing obstructions.

When the teeth are ready to *cut*, the upper part is rubbed with hard substances, which infants, by a natural instinct, affect. *Arbuthnot.*

2. To perform the operation of lithotomy.

He saved the lives of thousands by his manner of *cutting* for the stone. *Pope.*

3. To interfere; as, a horse that *cuts.*

CUT. *part. adj.* Prepared for use: a metaphor from hewn timber.

Sets of phrases, *cut* and dry,
Evermore thy tongue supply. *Swift.*

CUT. *n. s.* [from the noun.]

1. The action of a sharp or edged instrument; the blow of an ax or sword.

2. The impression or separation of continuity, made by an edge or sharp instrument; distinguished from that made by perforation with a pointed instrument.

3. A wound made by cutting.

Sharp weapons, according to the force, *cut* into the bone many ways, which *cuts* are called *sedes*, and are reckoned among the fractures. *Wiseman's Surgery.*

4. A channel made by art.

This great *cut* or ditch Sesostris the rich king of Egypt, and long after him Ptolomeus Philadelphus, purposed to have made a great deal wider and deeper, and thereby to have let in the Red Sea into the Mediterranean, for the readier transportation of the Indian merchandise to Cairo and Alexandria. *Knolles's History of the Turks.*

5. A part cut off from the rest.

Suppose a board to be ten foot long, and one broad, one *cut* is reckoned so many foot. *Mortimer's Husbandry.*

6. A small particle; a shred.

It hath a number of short *cuts* or shreddings, which may be better called wishes than prayers. *Hooker, b.* v. *sect.* 27.

7. A lot cut off a stick.

My lady Zelmane and my daughter Mopsa may draw *cuts*, and the shortest *cut* speak first. *Sidney, b.* ii.

A man may as reasonably draw *cuts* for his tenets, and regulate his persuasion by the cast of a die. *Locke.*

8. A near passage, by which some angle is cut off.

The ignorant took heart to enter upon this great calling, and instead of their cutting their way to it through the knowledge of the tongues, the fathers and councils, they have taken another and a shorter *cut.* *South's Sermons.*

There is a shorter *cut*, an easier passage. *Decay of Piety.*

The evidence of my sense is simple and immediate, and therefore I have but a shorter *cut* thereby to the assent to the truth of the things so evidenced. *Hale's Origin of Mankind.*

But the gentleman would needs see me part of my way, and carry me a short *cut* through his own ground, which saved me half a mile's riding. *Swift's Examiner*, N°. 20.

9. A picture cut or carved upon a stamp of wood or copper, and impressed from it.

In this form, according to his description, he is set forth in the prints or *cuts* of martyrs by Cevallerius. *Brown.*

Madam Dacier, from some old *cuts* of Terence, fancies that the larva or persona of the Roman actors was not only a vizard for the face, but had false hair to it. *Addison on Italy.*

10. The stamp on which a picture is carved.

11. The act or practice of dividing a pack of cards.

How can the muse her aid impart,
Unskill'd in all the terms of art!
Or in harmonious numbers put
The deal, the shuffle, and the *cut.* *Swift.*

12. Fashion; form; shape; manner of cutting into shape.

Their cloths are after such a pagan *cut* too,
That, sure, they've worn out Christendom. *Shakes. H.* VIII.

His tawny beard was th' equal grace
Both of his wisdom and his face;
In *cut* and dye so like a tile,
A sudden view it would beguile. *Hudibras, p.* i. *cant.* 1.

They were so familiarly acquainted with him as to know the very *cut* of his beard. *Stillingfl. Def. of Disc on Rom. Idol.*

Children love breeches, not for their *cut* or ease, but because the having them is a mark or step towards manhood. *Locke.*

A third desires you to observe well the toga on such a reverse, and asks you whether you can in conscience believe the sleeve of it to be of the true Roman *cut.* *Addison.*

Sometimes an old fellow shall wear this or that sort of *cut* in his cloaths with great integrity. *Addison's Spectator*, N°. 264.

Wilt thou buy there some high heads of the newest *cut* for my daughter. *Arbuthnot's History of John Bull.*

13. It seems anciently to have signified a fool or cully.

Send her money, knight: if thou hast her not in the end, call me *cut.* *Shakespeare's Twelfth Night.*

14. CUT *and long tail.* A proverbial expression for men of all kinds.

He will maintain you like a gentlewoman.——
Ay, that I will, come *cut and long tail*, under the degree of a squire. *Shakespeare's Merry Wives of Windsor.*

A quintin he,
In honour of this bridaltee,
Hath challeng'd either wide countee:
Come *cut and long tail*; for there be
Six batchelors as bold as he. *Ben. Johnson's Underwood.*

CU'TANEOUS. *adj.* [from *cutis*, Latin.] Relating to the skin.

This serous, nutritious mass is more readily circulated into the *cutaneous* or remotest parts of the body. *Floyer on Humours.*

Some sorts of *cutaneous* eruptions are occasioned by feeding much on acid unripe fruits and farinaceous substances. *Arbuthn.*

CU'TICLE. *n. s.* [*cuticula*, Latin.]

1. The first and outermost covering of the body, commonly called the scarf-skin. This is that soft skin which rises in a blister upon any burning, or the application of a blistering-plaister. It sticks close to the surface of the true skin, to which it is also tied by the vessels which nourish it, though they are so small as not to be seen. When the scarf-skin is examined with a microscope, it appears to be made up of several lays of exceeding small scales, which cover one another more or less, according to the different thickness of the scarf-skin in the several parts of the body. *Quincy.*

In each of the very fingers there are bones and gristles, and ligaments and membranes, and muscles and tendons, and nerves and arteries, and veins and skin, and *cuticle* and nail. *Bentley's Sermons.*

2. A thin skin formed on the surface of any liquor.

When any saline liquor is evaporated to *cuticle*, and let cool, the salt concretes in regular figures; which argues that the particles of the salt, before they concreted, floated in the liquor at equal distances in rank and file. *Newton's Opt.*

CUTI'CULAR. *adj.* [from *cutis*, Latin.] Belonging to the skin.

CUTH, signifies knowledge or skill. So *Cuthwin* is a knowing conqueror; *Cuthred* a knowing counsellor; *Cuthbert*, famous for skill. Much of the same nature are Sophocles and Sophianus. *Gib. Camden.*

CU'TLASS. *n. s.* [*coutelas*, French. This word is written sometimes *cutlace*, sometimes *cuttleax*: in *Shakespeare*, *curtleaxe*; and in *Pope*, *cutlash*] A broad cutting sword: the word is much in use among the seamen.

Were't not better
That I did suit me all points like a man?
A gallant *curtleax* upon my thigh,
A boar-spear in my hand. *Shakespeare's As you like it.*

To the lodgments of his herd he run,
Where the fat porkets slept beneath the sun;
Of two his *cutlash* launch'd the spouting blood,
These quarter'd, sing'd, and fix'd on forks of wood. *Pope.*

CU'TLER. *n. s.* [*coutelier*, French.] One who makes or sells knives.

A paultry ring
That she did give, whose poesy was
For all the world like *cutler's* poetry
Upon a knife; love me, and leave me not. *Shakespeare.*

In a bye *cutler's* shop on Tower-hill he bought a tenpenny knife: so cheap was the instrument of this great attempt. *Wott.*

He chose no other instrument than an ordinary knife, which he bought of a common *cutler.* *Clarendon.*

CU'TPURSE. *n. s.* [*cut* and *purse.*] One who steals by the method

method of cutting purses: a common practice when men wore their purses at their girdles, as was once the custom. A thief; a robber.

To have an open ear, a quick eye, and a nimble hand, is necessary for a *cutpurse*. *Shakespeare's Winter's Tale.*

A vice of kings,
A *cutpurse* of the empire and the rule,
That from a shelf the precious diadem stole,
And put it in his pocket. *Shakespeare's Hamlet.*

Was there no felony, no bawd,
Cutpurse, nor burglary abroad? *Hudibras, p.* i. *cant.* 2.

If we could imagine a whole nation to be *cutpurses* and robbers, would there then be kept that square dealing and equity in such a monstrous den of thieves. *Bentley's Sermons.*

CU'TTER. *n. s.* [from *cut.*]

1. An agent or instrument that cuts any thing.
2. A nimble boat that cuts the water.
3. The teeth that cut the meat.

The molares, or grinders are behind, nearest the center of motion, because there is a greater strength or force required to chew the meat than to bite a piece; and the *cutters* before, that they may be ready to cut off a morsel from any solid food, to be transmitted to the grinders. *Ray on the Creation.*

4. An officer in the Exchequer that provides wood for the tallies, and cuts the sum paid upon them; and then casts the same into the court to be written upon. *Cowel.*

CUT-THROAT. *n. s.* [*cut* and *throat*] A ruffian; a murderer; a butcher of men; an assassin.

Will you then suffer these robbers, *cut-throats*, base people, gathered out of all the corners of Christendom, to waste your countries, spoil your cities, murder your people, and trouble all your seas? *Knolles's History of the Turks.*

Perhaps the *cut-throat* may rather take his copy from the Parisian massacre, one of the horridest instances of barbarous inhumanity that ever was known. *South's Sermons.*

The ruffian robbers by no justice aw'd,
And unpaid *cut-throat* soldiers are abroad;
Those venal souls, who, harden'd in each ill,
To save complaints and prosecution, kill. *Dryden's Juvenal.*

CUT-THROAT. *adj.* Cruel; inhuman; barbarous.

If to take above fifty in the hundred be extremity, this in truth can be none other than *cut-throat* and abominable dealing. *Carew's Survey of Cornwal.*

CU'TTING. *n. s.* [from *cut.*] A piece cut off; a chop.

The burning of the *cuttings* of vines, and casting them upon land, doth much good. *Bacon's Natural History*, N°. 667.

Many are propagated above ground by slips or *cuttings. Ray.*

CU'TTLE. *n. s.* A fish, which, when he is pursued by a fish of prey, throws out a black liquor, by which he darkens the water and escapes.

It is somewhat strange, that the blood of all birds and beasts, and fishes, should be of a red colour, and only the blood of the *cuttle* should be as black as ink. *Bacon's Nat. Hist.*

He that uses many words for the explaining any subject, doth, like the *cuttle* fish, hide himself for the most part in his own ink. *Ray on the Creation.*

CU'TTLE. *n. s.* [from *cuttle.*] A foul mouthed fellow; a fellow who blackens the character of others. *Hanmer.*

Away, you cutpurse rascal; you filthy bung, away: by this wine I'll thrust my knife in your mouldy chaps, if you play the saucy *cuttle* with me. *Shakespeare's Henry* IV. *p.* ii.

CY'CLE. *n. s.* [*cyclus*, Latin; κύκλος.]

1. A circle.
2. A round of time; a space in which the same revolutions begin again; a periodical space of time.

We do more commonly use these words, so as to stile a lesser space a *cycle*, and a greater by the name of period; and you may not improperly call the beginning of a large period the epocha thereof. *Holder on Time.*

3. A method, or account of a method continued 'till the same course begins again.

We thought we should not attempt an unacceptable work, if here we endeavoured to present our gardeners with a complete *cycle* of what is requisite to be done throughout every month of the year. *Evelyn's Kalendar.*

4. Imaginary orbs; a circle in the heavens.

How build, unbuild, contrive
To save appearances; how gird the sphere
With centrick and excentrick, scribl'd o'er
Cycle and epicycle, orb in orb! *Milton's Paradise Lost, b.* viii.

CY'CLOID. *n. s.* [from κυκλοειδής, of κύκλος and εἶδος, shape.] A geometrical curve, of which the genesis may be conceived by imagining a nail in the circumference of a wheel: the line which the nail describes in the air, while the wheel revolves in a right line, is the cycloid.

CYCLO'IDAL. *adj.* [from *cycloid.*] Relating to a cycloid; as the *cycloidal* space, is the space contained between the cycloid and its substance. *Chambers.*

CYCLOPÆDI'A. *n. s.* [κύκλος and παιδεία.] A circle of knowledge; a course of the sciences.

CY'GNET. *n. s.* [from *cycnus*, Latin.] A young swan.

I am the *cygnet* to this pale faint swan,
Who chaunts a doleful hymn to his own death. *Shak. K. John.*

So doth the swan her downy *cygnets* save,
Keeping them pris'ners underneath her wings. *Shak. H.* VI.

Cygnets, from grey, turn white. *Bacon's Natural History.*

Young *cygnets* are good meat, if fatted with oats; but fed with weeds, they taste fishy. *Mortimer's Husbandry.*

CY'LINDER. *n. s.* [κύλινδρον.] A body having two flat surfaces and one circular.

The quantity of water which every revolution does carry, according to any inclination of the *cylinder*, may be easily found. *Wilkins.*

The square will make you ready for all manner of compartments, bases, pedistals, plots, and buildings; your *cylinder* for vaulted turrets, and round buildings. *Peacham.*

CYLI'NDRICAL. } *adj.* [from *cylinder.*] Partaking of the na-
CYLI'NDRICK. } ture of a cylinder; having the form of a cylinder.

Minera ferri stalactitia, when several of the *cylindrick* striæ are contiguous, and grow together into one sheaf, is called brushiron ore. *Woodward's Natural History, p.* iv.

Obstructions must be most incident to such parts of the body where the circulation and the elastick fibres are both smallest, and those are glands, which are the extremities of arteries formed into *cylindrical* canals. *Arbuthnot on Aliments.*

CYMA'R. *n. s.* [properly written *simar.*] A slight covering; a scarf.

Her comely limbs composed with decent care,
Her body shaded with a slight *cymar*;
Her bosom to the view was only bare. *Dryden.*

CYMATIUM. n. s. [Lat. from κυμάτιον, a little wave.] A member of architecture, whereof one half is convex, and the other concave. There are two sorts, of which one is hollow below, as the other is above. *Harris.*

In a cornice the gola, or *cymatium* of the corona, the coping, the modillions, or dentelli, make a noble show by their graceful projections. *Spectator*, N°. 415.

CY'MBAL. *n. s.* [*cymbalum*, Latin.] A musical instrument.

The trumpets, sackbuts, psalteries and fifes,
Tabors and *cymbals*, and the shouting Romans,
Make the sun dance. *Shakespeare's Coriolanus.*

If mirth should fail, I'll busy her with cares,
Silence her clamorous voice with louder wars;
Trumpets and drums shall fright her from the throne,
As sounding *cymbals* aid the lab'ring moon. *Dryd. Aurengz.*

CYNA'NTHROPY. *n. s.* [κυων κυνὸς, and ἄνθρωπος.] A species of madness in which men have the qualities of dogs.

CYNEGE'TICKS. *n. s.* [κυνηγετικα.] The art of hunting; the art of training and hunting with dogs.

CY'NICAL. } *adj.* [κυνικὸς.] Having the qualities of a dog;
CY'NICK. } currish; brutal; snarling; satirical.

He doth believe that some new fangled wit (it is his *cynical* phrase) will some time or other find out his art. *Wilkins.*

CY'NICK. *n. s.* [κύνικος.] A philosopher of the snarling or currish sort; a follower of Diogenes; a rude man; a snarler; a misanthrope.

How vilely doth this *cynick* rhime?—
Get you hence, sirrah; saucy fellow, hence. *Shakespeare.*

CY'NOSURE. *n. s.* [from κυνόσουρα.] The star near the North-pole, by which sailors steer.

Towers and battlements it sees
Bosom'd high in tufted trees,
Where perhaps some beauty lies,
The *cynosure* of neighbouring eyes. *Milton.*

CY'ON. See CION.

Gather *cyons* for graffs before the buds sprout. *Evelyn.*

CYPRESS-TREE. [*cypressus*, Latin.]

Its leaves are squamose and flat: the male flowers, which are likewise squamose, grow at remote distances from the fruit on the same tree. The fruit is of a spherical form, and is composed of many woody tubercles, in which are contained hard angular seeds. *Miller.*

The *cypress* is a tall strait tree, produced with great difficulty. Its fruit is of no use: its leaves are bitter, and the very smell and shade of it are dangerous. Hence the Romans looked upon it to be a fatal tree, and made use of it at funerals, and in mournful ceremonies. The wood of the *cypress-tree* is always green, very heavy, of a good smell, and never either rots or is worm eaten. It is distinguished into male and female: the branches of the male are, as it were, horizontal; and those of the female are upright, which is therefore generally used for palissades of gardens, and to make pyramids. The fruit is round, of an olive colour, and as large as nuts when they are ripe, and it grows in separate places. The Latins call it *conus*, because of its figure. This fruit is composed of a kind of scales, in the clefts of which are hidden little seeds, flat and angular. This tree is common on mount Libanus. *Calmet.*

In ivory coffers I have stufft my crowns;
In *cypress* chests my arras counterpanes. *Shakespeare.*

He

He taketh the *cypreſs* and the oak, which he ſtrengtheneth for himſelf among the trees of the foreſt. *Iſ.* xliv. 14.

Poplars and alders ever quivering play'd,
And nodding *cypreſs* form'd a fragrant ſhade. *Pope's Odyſſ.*

2. Being anciently uſed in funerals, it is the emblem of mourning.

Poiſon be their drink,
Their ſweeteſt ſhade a grove of *cypreſs* trees. *Shak Hen.* VI.

CY'PRUS. *n. ſ.* [I ſuppoſe from the place where it was made; or corruptly from *cypreſs*, as being uſed in mourning.] A thin tranſparent black ſtuff.

Lawn as white as driven ſnow,
Cyprus black as e'er was crow. *Shakeſp. Winter's Tale.*

To one of your receiving,
Enough is ſhewn: a *cyprus*, not a boſom,
Hides my poor heart! *Shakeſpeare.*

CYST. } *n. ſ.* [κυςις.] A bag containing ſome morbid
CY'STIS. } matter.

In taking it out the *cyſtis* broke, and ſhewed itſelf by its matter to be a meliceris. *Wiſeman's Surgery.*

There may be a conſumption, with a purulent ſpitting, when the vomica is contained in a *cyſt* or bag; upon the breaking of which the patient is commonly ſuffocated. *Arbuthnot on Diet.*

CY'STICK. *adj.* [from *cyſt*, a bag.] Contained in a bag.

The bile is of two ſorts; the *cyſtick*, or that contained in the gall-bladder, which is a ſort of repoſitory for the gall; or the hepatick, or what flows immediately from the liver. *Arbuthnot on Aliments.*

CYSTO'TOMY. *n. ſ.* [κύςις and τέμνω.] The act or practice of opening incyſted tumours, or cutting the bag in which any morbid matter is contained.

CZAR. *n. ſ.* [A Sclavonian word, written more properly *tzar*.] The title of the emperour of Ruſſia.

CZARI'NA. *n. ſ.* [from *czar*.] The empreſs of Ruſſia.

D.

D, Is a consonant nearly approaching in sound to T, but formed by a stronger appulse of the tongue to the upper part of the mouth. The sound of D in *English* is uniform, and it is never mute.

DA CAPO. [Ital.] A term in musick, which signifying from the head or the beginning, means that the first part of the tune should be repeated at the conclusion.

To DAB. *v. a.* [*dauber*, Fr.] To strike gently with something soft or moist.

A sore should never be wiped by drawing a piece of tow or rag over it, but only by *dabbing* it with fine lint. *Sharp.*

A DAB. *n. s.* [from the verb.]

1. A small lump of any thing.
2. A blow with something moist or soft.
3. Something moist or slimy thrown upon one.
4. [In low language.] An artist; a man expert at something. This is not used in writing.
5. A kind of small flat fish.

Of flat fish there are rays, flowks, *dabs*, plaice. *Carew.*

DAB-CHICK. *n. s.* A chicken newly hatched; a chicken with its feathers not yet grown.

A *dab chick* waddles through the copse,
On feet and wings, and flies, and wades, and hops. *Pope.*

To DA'BBLE. *v. a.* [*dabbelen*, Dutch.] To smear; to daub; to spatter; to besprinkle; to wet.

Then came by
A shadow like an angel, with bright hair
Dabbled in blood. *Shakespeare's Richard* III.

I scarified, and *dabbled* the wound with oil of turpentine. *Wiseman's Surgery.*

Mean while the South, rising with *dabbled* wings,
A sable cloud athwart the welkin flings. *Swift.*

To DA'BBLE. *v. n.*

1. To play in water; to move in water or mud.

Neither will a spirit, that dwells with stars, *dabble* in this impurer mud. *Glanville's Apology.*

The little one complained of her legs, that she could neither swim nor *dabble* with them. *L'Estrange.*

But when he found the boys at play,
And saw them *dabbling* in their clay,
He stood behind a stall to lurk,
And mark the progress of their work. *Swift.*

2. To do any thing in a slight, superficial, or shallow manner; to tamper.

Shakespeare shall bear it company, and be put into your hands, as clear and as fair as it came out of them; though you, I think, have been *dabbling* here and there with the text, I have had no more reverence for the writer, and the printer, and left every thing standing just as I found it. *Pope.*

DA'BBLER. *n. s.* [from *dabble.*]

1. One that plays in water.
2. One that meddles without mastery; one that never goes to the bottom of an affair; a superficial meddler.

He dares not complain of the tooth-ach, lest our *dabblers* in politicks should be ready to swear against him for disaffection. *Swift's Intelligencer*, N°. 19.

DACE. *n. s.* [of uncertain derivation: in most provinces called *dare.*] A small river fish, resembling a roach, but less.

Let me live harmlesly, and near the brink
Of Trent or Avon have a dwelling place;
Where I may see my quill or cork down sink,
With eager bite of pearch, or bleak, or *dace. Walton's Angl.*

DA'CTYLE. *n. s.* [δάκτυλος, a finger.] A poetical foot consisting of one long syllable and two short, like the joints of a finger; as *candidus.*

DAD. }
DA'DDY. } *n. s.* [The child's way of expressing *father*. It is remarkable, that, in all parts of the world, the word for father, as first taught to children, is compounded of *a* and *t*, or the kindred letter *d* differently placed; as *tad*, Welsh; ἄττα, Greek; *atta*, Gothick; *tata*, Latin. *Mammas atque tatas habet Afra*, Mart.] Father.

I was never so bethumpt with words,
Since first I call'd my brother's father *dad. Shakes. K. John.*

His loving mother left him to my care;
Fine child, as like his *dad* as he could stare! *Gay.*

DÆ'DAL. *adj.* [*dædalus*, Latin.]

1. Various; variegated.
2. Skilful: this is not the true meaning, nor should be imitated.

Nor hath
The *dædal* hand of nature only pour'd
Her gifts of outward grace. *Philips.*

DA'FFODIL. }
DAFFODI'LLY. } *n. s.* [Supposed by *Skinner* to be cor-
DAFFODOWNDI'LLY. } rupted from *asphodelus.*

This plant hath a lily-flower, consisting of one leaf, which is bell-shaped, and cut into six segments, which incircle its middle like a crown; but the empalement, which commonly rises out of a membranous vagina, turns to an oblong or roundish fruit, which is triangular, and gapes in three parts; is divided into three cells, and full of roundish seeds. *Miller.*

Strew me the green ground with *daffodowndillies*,
And cowslips, and kingcups, and loved lilies. *Spenser.*

Bid Amaranthus all his beauty shed,
And *daffodillies* fill their cups with tears,
To strew the laureate herse where Lycid lies. *Milton.*

The daughters of the flood have search'd the mead
For violets pale, and cropp'd the poppy's head:
The short narcissus, and fair *daffodil*,
Pancies to please the sight, and cassia sweet to smell. *Dryden.*

To DAFT. *v. a.* [contracted from *do aft*; that is, to *throw back*, to *throw off.*] To toss aside; to put away with contempt; to throw away slightly.

Where is his son,
The nimble-footed mad-cap prince of Wales,
And his comrades, that *daft* the world aside,
And bid it pass? *Shakespeare's Henry* IV. *p.* i.

I would she had bestow'd this dotage on me: I would have *dafft* all other respects, and made her half myself. *Shakesp.*

DAG. *n. s.* [*dague*, French.]

1. A dagger.
2. A handgun; a pistol: so called from serving the purposes of a dagger, being carried secretly, and doing mischief suddenly.

To DAG. *v. a.* [from *daggle.*] To daggle; to bemire; to let fall in the water: a low word.

DA'GGER. *n. s.* [*dague*, French.]

1. A short sword; a poniard.

She ran to her son's *dagger*, and struck herself a mortal wound. *Sidney, b.* ii.

This sword a *dagger* had his page,
That was but little for his age;
And therefore waited on him so,
As dwarfs upon knights errant do. *Hudibras, p.* i. *cant.* 1.

He strikes himself with his *dagger*; but being interrupted by one of his friends, he stabs him, and breaks the *dagger* on one of his ribs. *Addison on Italy.*

2. [In fencing schools.] A blunt blade of iron with a basket hilt, used for defence.
3. [With printers.] The obelus; a mark of reference in form of a dagger; as [†].

DA'GGERSDRAWING. *n. s.* [*dagger* and *draw.*] The act of drawing daggers; approach to open violence.

They always are at *daggersdrawing*,
And one another clapperclawing. *Hudibras, p.* ii. *cant.* 2.

I have heard of a quarrel in a tavern, where all were at *daggersdrawing*, 'till one desired to know the subject of the quarrel. *Swift.*

To DA'GGLE. *v. a.* [from *dag*, dew; a word, according to Mr. *Lye*, derived from the Danish; according to *Skinner*, from ðaȝ, sprinkled, or ðeaȝan, to dip. They are probably all of the same root.] To dip negligently in mire or water; to bemire; to besprinkle.

To DA'GGLE. *v. n.* To be in the mire; to run through wet or dirt.

Nor like a puppy, *daggled* through the town,
To fetch and carry sing-song up and down. *Pope's Epistles.*

DA'GGLEDTAIL. *n. s.* [*daggle* and *tail.*] Bemired; dipped in the water or mud; bespattered.

The gentlemen of wit and pleasure are apt to be choaked at the sight of so many *daggledtail* parsons, that happen to fall in their way. *Swift.*

DAILY. *adj.* [ðaȝlic. Saxon.] Happening every day, or very frequently; done every day; quotidian.

Much are we bound to heaven
In *daily* thanks, that gave us ſuch a prince. *Shak. H. VIII.*

Ceaſe, man of woman born! to hope relief
From *daily* trouble, and continu'd grief. *Prior.*

DA'ILY. *adv.* Every day; very often.

Let that man with better ſenſe adviſe,
That of the world leaſt part to us is read;
And *daily* how through hardy enterprize,
Many great regions are diſcovered. *Fairy Queen, b.* ii.

I was ambitious to be acquainted with a man, with whom I converſed almoſt *daily*, for years together. *Dryd. Virg. Ded*

DA'INTILY. *adv.* [from *dainty.*].

1. Elegantly; delicately.

This ſame truth is a naked and open day-light, that doth not ſhew the maſks and mummeries, and triumphs of the world, half ſo ſtately and *daintily* as candle-light. *Bacon.*

2. Deliciouſly; pleaſantly.

There is no region on earth ſo *daintily* watered, with ſuch great navigable rivers. *Howel's Vocal Foreſt.*

Thoſe young ſuiters had been accuſtomed to nothing but to ſleep well, and fare *daintily*. *Broom's View of Epick Poems.*

DA'INTINESS. *n. ſ.* [from *dainty.*]

1. Delicacy; ſoftneſs.

What ſhould yet thy palate pleaſe?
Daintineſs and ſofter eaſe,
Sleeked limbs, and fineſt blood? *Ben. Johnſon's Foreſt.*

2. Elegance; nicety.

The duke exceeded in the *daintineſs* of his leg and foot, and the earl in the fine ſhape of his hands. *Wotton.*

3. Squeamiſhneſs; faſtidiouſneſs.

Of ſand, and lime, and clay, Vitruvius hath diſcourſed without any *daintineſs*. *Wotton's Architecture.*

DA'INTY. *adj.* [derived by *Skinner* from *dain*, an old French word for *delicate*; which yet I cannot find in dictionaries.]

1. Pleaſing to the palate; of exquiſite taſte; delicious.

They are all over watery; whereas an higher concoction is required for ſweetneſs, or pleaſure of taſte, and therefore all your *dainty* plumbs are a little dry. *Bacon's Natural Hiſtory.*

2. Delicate; of acute ſenſibility; nice; ſqueamiſh; ſoft; luxurious; tender.

This is the floweſt, yet the *daintieſt* ſenſe;
For ev'n the ears of ſuch as have no ſkill,
Perceive a diſcord, and conceive offence;
And knowing not what's good, yet find the ill. *Davies.*

They were a fine and *dainty* people; frugal and yet elegant, though not military. *Bacon's Holy War.*

3. Scrupulous; ceremonious.

Which of you all
Will now deny to dance? She that makes *dainty*,
I'll ſwear hath corns. *Shakeſpeare's Romeo and Juliet.*

Therefore to horſe;
And let us not be *dainty* of leave-taking,
But ſhift away. *Shakeſpeare's Macbeth.*

4. Elegant; tenderly languiſhingly, or effeminately beautiful.

My houſe, within the city,
Is richly furniſhed with plate and gold,
Baſons and ewers to lave her *dainty* hands. *Shakeſpeare.*

Why ſhould ye be ſo cruel to yourſelf,
And to thoſe *dainty* limbs, which nature lent
For gentle uſage, and ſoft delicacy? *Milton.*

5. Nice; affectedly fine: in contempt.

Your *dainty* ſpeakers have the curſe,
To plead bad cauſes down to worſe. *Prior.*

DA'INTY. *n. ſ.*

1. Something nice or delicate; a delicacy; ſomething of exquiſite taſte.

Be not deſirous of his *dainties*; for they are deceitful meat. *Prov.* xxiii. 3.

A worm breedeth in meal, of the ſhape of a large white maggot, which is given as a great *dainty* to nightingales. *Bacon.*

She then produc'd her dairy ſtore,
And unbought *dainties* of the poor. *Dryden.*

The ſhepherd ſwains, with ſure abundance bleſt,
In the fat flock, and rural *dainties*, feaſt. *Pope's Odyſſey.*

2. A word of fondneſs formerly in uſe.

Why, that's my *dainty*; I ſhall miſs thee:
But yet thou ſhalt have freedom. *Shakeſpeare's Tempeſt.*

There is a fortune coming
Towards you, *dainty*, that will take thee thus,
And ſet thee aloft. *Ben. Johnſon's Catiline.*

DAIRY. *n. ſ.* [from *dey*, an old word for milk. Mr. *Lye.*]

1. The occupation or art of making various kinds of food from milk.

Grounds were turned much in England from breeding, either to feeding or *dairy*; and this advanced the trade of Engliſh butter, which will be extremely beaten down, when Ireland turns to it too. *Temple.*

2. The place where milk is manufactured.

Theſe beauties will ſuſpect
That you have no more worth
Than the coarſe and country fairy,
That doth haunt the hearth or *dairy*. *Ben. Johnſon.*

What ſtores my *dairies* and my folds contain!
A thouſand lambs that wander on the plain. *Dryden's Virgil.*

She in pens his flocks will fold,
And then produce her *dairy* ſtore. *Dryden.*

3. Paſturage; milk farm; ground where milch cattle are kept.

Dairies, being well houſewived, are exceeding commodious. *Bacon's Advice to Villiers.*

Children, in *dairy* countries, do wax more tall than where they feed more upon bread and fleſh. *Bacon's Natural Hiſtory.*

DA'IRYMAID. *n. ſ.* [*dairy* and *maid.*] The woman ſervant whoſe buſineſs is to manage the milk.

The pooreſt of the ſex have ſtill an itch,
To know their fortunes, equal to the rich:
The *dairymaid* enquires if ſhe ſhall take
The truſty taylor, and the cook forſake. *Dryden's Juvenal.*

Come up quickly, or we ſhall conclude that thou art in love with one of ſir Roger's *dairymaids*. *Addiſon's Spectator.*

DA'ISY. *n. ſ.* [dæȝeſeaȝe, day's eye. *Chaucer.*] A Spring-flower.

It hath a perennial root: the ſtalks are naked, and never branch out: the cup of the flower is ſcaly and ſimple, divided into many ſegments to the foot-ſtalk. The flowers are radiated; and the heads, after the petals are fallen off, reſemble obtuſe cones. *Miller.*

When *daiſies* pied, and violets blue,
And lady ſmocks all over white,
And cuckow buds of yellow hue,
Do paint the meadows much bedight. *Shakeſpeare.*

Then ſing by turns, by turns the muſes ſing,
Now hawthorns bloſſom, now the *daiſies* ſpring;
Now leaves the trees, and flow'rs adorn the ground:
Begin, the vales ſhall ev'ry note rebound. *Pope's Spring.*

This will find thee picking of *daiſies*, or ſmelling to a lock of hay. *Addiſon's Spectator*, Nº. 131.

Fair-handed Spring unboſoms every grace;
The *daiſy*, primroſe, violet, darkly blaze. *Thomſon's Spring.*

DALE. *n. ſ.* [*dalei*, Gothick; *dal*, Dutch and German.] A low place between hills; a vale; a valley.

Long toſt with ſtorms, and bet with bitter winds,
High over hills, and low adown the *dale*,
She wandred many a wood and meaſur'd many a vale.
Fairy Queen, b. i. *cant.* 7. *ſtanz.* 28.

Before the downfal of the fairy ſtate
This *dale*, a pleaſing region, not unbleſt,
This *dale* poſſeſs'd they, and had ſtill poſſeſs'd. *Tickell.*

He ſteals along the lonely *dale*
In ſilent ſearch. *Thomſon's Spring, l.* 220.

DA'LLIANCE. *n. ſ.* [from *dally.*]

1. Interchange of careſſes; acts of fondneſs.

Look thou be true: do not give *dalliance*
Too much the rein: the ſtrongeſt oaths are ſtraw
To th' fire i' th' blood. *Shakeſpeare's Tempeſt.*

Nor gentle purpoſe, nor endearing ſmiles
Wanted; nor youthful *dalliance*, as beſeems
Fair couple, link'd in happy nuptial league,
Alone as they. *Milton's Paradiſe Loſt, b.* iv. *l.* 332.

I'll head my people;
Then think of *dalliance* when the danger's o'er:
My warlike ſpirits work now another way,
And my ſoul's tun'd to trumpets. *Dryden's Don Sebaſtian.*

2. Conjugal converſation.

The giant, ſelf-diſmayed with the ſound,
Where he with his Dueſſa *dalliance* found,
In haſte came ruſhing forth from inner bow'r. *Fairy Queen.*

That, not myſtick, where the ſapient king
Held *dalliance* with his fair Egyptian ſpouſe. *Milt. Par. Loſt.*

Since thou claim'ſt me for thy ſire,
And my fair ſon here ſhow'ſt me, the dear pledge
Of *dalliance* had with thee in heav'n, and joys
Then ſweet, now ſad to mention. *Milton's Paradiſe Loſt.*

3. Delay; procraſtination.

Nay, come, I pray you, ſir, give me the chain;
Both wind and tide ſtay for this gentleman;
And I, to blame, have held him here too long.—
—Good lord, you uſe this *dalliance* to excuſe
Your breach of promiſe. *Shakeſp. Comedy of Errours.*

DA'LLIER. *n. ſ.* [from *dally.*] A trifler; a fondler.

The daily *dalliers* with pleaſant words, with ſmiling countenances, and with wagers, purpoſed to be loſt, before they were purpoſed to be made. *Aſcham's Schoolmaſter.*

DA'LLOP. *n. ſ.* [of unknown etymology.] A tuft, or clump.

Of barley the fineſt and greeneſt ye find,
Leave ſtanding in *dallops* 'till time ye do bind. *Tuſſer.*

To DA'LLY. *v. n.* [*dollen*, Dutch, to trifle.]

1. To trifle; to play the fool; to amuſe one's ſelf with idle play; to loſe time in trifles.

Take up thy maſter:

If thou ſhouldſt *dally* half an hour, his life,
With thine, and all that offer to defend him,
Stand in aſſured loſs. *Shakeſpeare's King Lear.*

He left his cur, and laying hold
Upon his arms, with courage bold
Cried out, 'tis now no time to *daly*,
The enemy begin to rally. *Hudibras, p.* i. *cant.* 3.

We have trifled too long already: it is madneſs to *dally* any longer, when our ſouls are at ſtake. *Calamy's Sermons.*

One hundred thouſand pounds muſt be raiſed; for there is no *dallying* with hunger. *Swift.*

2. To exchange careſſes; to play the wanton; to fondle.

He is not lolling on a lewd love bed,
But on his knees at meditation;
Not *dallying* with a brace of courtezans,
But meditating with two deep divines. *Shakeſp. Rich.* III.

3. To ſport; to play; to frolick.

She her airie buildeth in the cedar's top,
And *dallies* with the wind, and ſcorns the ſun. *Shak. R.* III.

4. To delay.

They that would not be reformed by that correction, wherein he *dallied* with them, ſhall feel a judgment worthy of God. *Wiſd.* xii. 26.

To Da'lly. *v. a.* To put off; to delay; to amuſe 'till a proper opportunity.

He fully ſet down, after his wonted manner, to perform ſervice; not by the hazard of one ſet battle, but by *dallying* off the time with often ſkirmiſhes. *Knolles's Hiſtory.*

Dam. *n. ſ.* [from *dame*, which formerly ſignified mother. *Had Nero never been an emperour, ſhu'de never his* dame *have be ſlaine. Chaucer.*]

1. The mother: uſed of beaſts, or other animals not human.

The *dam* runs lowing up and down,
Looking the way her harmleſs young one went,
And can do nought but wail her darling loſs. *Shak. H.* VI.

Mother, ſays a ſick kite, give over lamentations, and let me have your prayers: alas, my child, ſays the *dam*, which of the gods ſhall I go to? *L'Eſtrange, Fab.* 17.

They bring but one morſel of meat at a time, and have not fewer, it may be, than ſeven or eight young in the neſt together, which, at the return of their *dams*, do all at once, with equal greedineſs, hold up their heads and gape. *Ray.*

2. A human mother: in contempt or deteſtation.

This brat is none of mine;
It is the iſſue of Polixena:
Hence with it, and, together with the *dam*,
Commit them to the fire. *Shakeſpeare's Winter's Tale.*

Dam. *n. ſ.* [*dam*, Dutch.] A mole or bank to confine water.

As when the ſea breaks o'er its bounds,
And overflows the level grounds,
Thoſe banks and *dams*, that like a ſkreen
Did keep it out, now keep it in. *Hudibras, p.* ii. *cant.* 2.

Not with ſo fierce a rage the foaming flood
Roars, when he finds his rapid courſe withſtood;
Bears down the *dams* with unreſiſted ſway,
And ſweeps the cattle and the cots away. *Dryden's Æneis.*

Let looſe the reins to all your wat'ry ſtore,
Bear down the *dams*, and open every door. *Dryden.*

The inſide of the *dam* muſt be very ſmooth and ſtreight; and if it is made very ſloping on each ſide, it is the better. *Mortimer's Husbandry.*

To DAM. *v. a.* [demman, fordemman, Saxon; *dammen*, Dut.]

1. To confine, or ſhut up water by moles or dams.

I'll have the current in this place *damm'd* up;
And here the ſmug and ſilver Trent ſhall run
In a new channel, fair and evenly. *Shakeſ. Hen.* VI. *p.* ii.

Home I would go,
But that my doors are hateful to my eyes,
Fill'd and *damm'd* up with gaping creditors,
Watchful as fowlers when their game will ſpring. *Otway.*

Boggy lands are fed by ſprings, pent by a weight of earth, that *dams* in the water, and cauſes it to ſpread in the ground, ſo far as the earth is ſoft. *Mortimer's Husbandry.*

'Tis you muſt drive that trouble from your ſoul;
As ſtreams, when *damm'd*, forget their ancient current,
And wond'ring at their banks in other channels flow. *Smith.*

2. It is uſed by *Shakeſpeare* of fire, and by *Milton* of light.

The more thou *damm'ſt* it up, the more it burns. *Shakeſp.*

Moon! if your influence be quite *damm'd* up
With black uſurping miſts, ſome gentle taper,
Though a ruſh-candle from the wicker hole
Of ſome clay habitation, viſit us
With thy long levell'd rule of ſtreaming light. *Milton.*

DA'MAGE. *n. ſ.* [*domage*, French.]

1. Miſchief; hurt; detriment.

Groſs errours and abſurdities many commit for want of a friend to tell them of them, to the great *damage* both of their fame and fortune. *Bacon, Eſſay* 28.

Such as were either ſent from thence, or raiſed here, did commonly do more hurt and *damage* to the Engliſh ſubjects than to the Iriſh enemies, by their continual ſeſs and extortion. *Davies on Ireland.*

He repulſed the enemy very much to their *damage. Clarend.*

2. Loſs; miſchief ſuffered.

His heart exalts him in the harm
Already done, to have diſpeopled heav'n,
My *damage* fondly deem'd! *Milton's Paradiſe Loſt, b.* vii.

3. The value of miſchief done.

They believed that they were not able, though they ſhould be willing to ſell all they have in Ireland, to pay the *damages* which had been ſuſtained by the war. *Clarendon.*

4. Reparation of damage; retribution.

The biſhop demanded reſtitution of the ſpoils taken by the Scots, or *damages* for the ſame. *Bacon's Henry* VII.

Tell me whether, upon exhibiting the ſeveral particulars which I have related to you, I may not ſue her for *damages* in a court of juſtice? *Addiſon's Guardian*, Nº. 97.

5. [In law.] Any hurt or hindrance that a man taketh in his eſtate. In the common law it particularly ſignifies a part of what the jurors be to inquire of; for, after verdict given of the principal cauſe, they are likewiſe aſked their conſciences touching coſts, which are the charges of ſuit, and *damages*, which contain the hindrance which the plaintiff or demandant hath ſuffered, by means of the wrong done him by the defendant or tenant. *Cowel.*

When the judge had awarded due *damages* to a perſon, into whoſe field a neighbour's oxen had broke, it is reported that he reverſed his own ſentence, when he heard that the oxen, which had done this miſchief, were his own. *Watts's Logick.*

To Da'mage. *v. a.* [from the noun.] To miſchief; to injure; to impair; to hurt; to harm.

I conſider time as an immenſe ocean, into which many noble authors are entirely ſwallowed up, many very much ſhattered and *damaged*, ſome quite disjointed and broken into pieces. *Addiſon's Spectator.* Nº. 223.

To Da'mage. *v. n.* To take damage, or be damaged.

Da'mageable. *adj.* [from *damage.*]

1. Suſceptible of hurt; as, *damageable* goods.

2. Miſchievous; pernicious.

Obſcene and immodeſt talk is offenſive to the purity of God, *damageable* and infectious to the innocence of our neighbours, and moſt pernicious to ourſelves. *Governm. of the Tongue.*

Da'mascene. *n. ſ.* [*damaſcenus*, from *Damaſcus.*] A ſmall black plum; a Damſon, as it is now ſpoken.

In April follow the cherry tree in bloſſom, the *damaſcene* and plum trees in bloſſom, and the white thorn in leaf. *Bacon.*

In fruits the white commonly is meaner, as in pear plums and *damaſcenes*; and the choiceſt plums are black. *Bacon.*

DA'MASK. *n. ſ.* [*damaſquin*, French; *damaſchino*, Ital. from *Damaſcus.*]

1. Linen or ſilk woven in a manner invented at *Damaſcus*, by which part riſes above the reſt in flowers, or other forms.

Wipe your ſhoes, for want of a clout, with a *damaſk* napkin. *Swift's Rules to Servants.*

2. It is uſed for red colour in *Fairfax*, from the damaſk roſe.

And for ſome deale perplexed was her ſpirit;
Her *damaſk* late, now chang'd to pureſt white. *Fairfax, b.* ii.

To Da'mask. *v. a.* [from the noun.]

1. To form flowers upon ſtuffs.

2. To variegate; to diverſify.

Around him dance the roſy hours,
And *damaſking* the ground with flow'rs,
With ambient ſweets perfume the morn. *Fenton.*

3. To adorn ſteel-work with figures.

Damask-plum. See Plum.

Damask rose. *n. ſ.* The roſe of Damaſcus; a red roſe. See Rose.

Damaſk-roſes have not been known in England above one hundred years, and now are ſo common. *Bacon's Nat. Hiſtory.*

No gradual bloom is wanting from the bud,
Nor broad carnations, nor gay ſpotted pinks,
Nor, ſhower'd from every buſh, the *damaſk-roſe*. *Thomſon.*

Da'maskening. *n. ſ.* [from *damaſquiner*, Fr.] The art or act of adorning iron or ſteel, by making inciſions, and filling them up with gold or ſilver wire: uſed in enriching the blades of ſwords, and locks of piſtols. *Chambers.*

DAME. *n. ſ.* [*dame*, French; *dama*, Spaniſh.]

1. A lady; the title of honour to women.

The word *dame* originally ſignified a miſtreſs of a family, who was a lady; and it is uſed ſtill in the Engliſh law to ſignify a lady: but in common uſe, now-a-days, it repreſents a farmer's wife, or a miſtreſs of a family of the lower rank in the country. *Watts's Logick.*

Bleſs you, fair *dame!* I am not to you known,
Though in your ſtate of honour I am perfect:
If you will take a homely man's advice,
Be not found here. *Shakeſpeare's Macbeth.*

Not all theſe lords do vex me half ſo much
As that proud *dame*, the lord protector's wife. *Shak. H.* VI.

Shut your mouth, *dame*,
Or with this paper I ſhall ſtop it;
Thou worſe than any thing. *Shakeſpeare's King Lear.*

Sov'reign of creatures, univerſal *dame!* *Milt. Par. Loſt.*

2. It is ſtill uſed in poetry for women of rank.

His

His father Faunus: a Laurentian *dame*
His mother, fair Marica was her name. *Dryden's Æneid.*
Who would not repeat that bliss,
And frequent sight of such a *dame*
Buy with the hazard of his fame? *Waller.*

3. Mistress of a low family.
They killed the poor cock; for, say they, if it were not for his waking our *dame*, she would not wake us. *L'Estrange.*

4. Woman in general.
We've willing *dames* enough; there cannot be
That vulture in you to devour so many,
As will to greatness dedicate themselves,
Finding it so inclin'd. *Shakespeare's Macbeth.*

DAMES-VIOLET. *n. s.*
The flower of this plant, called also queen's gillyflower, consists, for the most part, of four leaves, which expand in form of a cross: out of the flower-cup arises the pointal, which becomes a long, taper, cylindrical pod, divided into two cells by an intermediate partition, to which the imbricated valves adhere on both sides, and are furnished with oblong, cylindrical, or globular seeds. *Miller.*

To DAMN. *v. a.* [*damno*, Latin.]
1. To doom to eternal torments in a future state.
Not in the legions
Of horrid hell, can come a devil more *damn'd*
In evils to top Macbeth. *Shakespeare's Macbeth.*
It is most necessary, that the church, by doctrine and decree, do *damn* and send to hell for ever those facts and opinions. *Bacon, Essay* 3.

2. To procure or cause to be eternally condemned.
That which he continues ignorant of, having done the utmost lying in his power, that he might not be ignorant of it, shall not *damn* him. *South's Sermons.*

3. To condemn.
His own impartial thought
Will *damn*, and conscience will record the fault. *Dryd. Juv.*

4. To hoot or hiss any publick performance; to explode.
They *damn* themselves, nor will my muse descend
To clap with such who fools and knaves commend. *Dryden.*
For the great dons of wit,
Phœbus gives them full privilege alone
To *damn* all others, and cry up their own. *Dryd. Ind. Emp.*
You are so good a critick, that it is the greatest happiness of the modern poets that you do not hear their works; and next, that you are not so arrant a critick as to *damn* them, like the rest, without hearing. *Pope.*

DA'MNABLE. *adj.* [from *damn.*]
1. Deserving damnation; justly doomed to never-ending punishment.
It gives him occasion of labouring with greater earnestness elsewhere, to entangle unwary minds with the snares of his *damnable* opinion. *Hooker, b.* 5. *sect.* 42.
He's a creature unprepar'd, unmeet for death;
And, to transport him in the mind he is,
Were *damnable.* *Shakespeare's Measure for Measure.*
As he does not reckon every schism of a *damnable* nature, so he is far from closing with the new opinion of those who make it no crime. *Swift.*

2. It is sometimes indecently used in a low and ludicrous sense; odious; pernicious.
Oh thou *damnable* fellow! did not I pluck thee by the nose for thy speeches? *Shakespeare's Measure for Measure.*

DA'MNABLY. *adv.* [from *damnable.*]
1. In such a manner as to incur eternal punishment; so as to be excluded from mercy.
We will propose the question, whether those who hold the fundamentals of faith may deny Christ *damnably*, in respect of those consequences that arise from them? *South's Sermons.*

2. It is indecently used in a ludicrous sense; odiously; hatefully.
The more sweets they bestowed upon them, the more *damnably* their conserves stunk. *Dennis.*

DAMNA'TION. *n. s.* [from *damn.*] Exclusion from divine mercy; condemnation to eternal punishment.
He that hath been affrighted with the fears of hell, or remembers how often he hath been spared from an horrible *damnation*, will not be ready to strangle his brother for a trifle. *Taylor's Worthy Communicant.*
Now mince the sin,
And mollify *damnation* with a phrase:
Say you consented not to Sancho's death,
But barely not forbade it. *Dryden's Spanish Fryar.*

DA'MNATORY. *adj.* [from *damnatorius.*] Containing a sentence of condemnation.

DA'MNED. *part. adj.* [from *damn.*] Hateful; detestable; abhorred; abominable.
Let not the royal bed of Denmark be
A couch for luxury and *damned* incest. *Shakesp. Hamlet.*
But, oh, what *damned* minutes tells he o'er,
Who doats, yet doubts; suspects, yet strongly loves. *Shak.*
Dare not
To brand the spotless virtue of my prince
With falshoods of most base and *damn'd* contrivance. *Rowe.*

DA'MNIFIC. *adj.* [from *damnify.*] Procuring loss; mischievous.

To DA'MNIFY. *v. a.* [from *damnifico*, Latin.]
1. To endamage; to injure; to cause loss to any.
He, who has suffered the damage, has a right to demand in his own name, and he alone can remit satisfaction: the *damnified* person has the power of appropriating the goods or service of the offender, by right of self-preservation. *Locke.*

2. To hurt; to impair.
When now he saw himself so freshly rear,
As if late fight had nought him *damnify'd*,
He was dismay'd, and 'gan his fate to fear. *Fairy Queen.*

DA'MNINGNESS. *n. s.* [from *damning.*] Tendency to procure damnation.
He may vow never to return to those sins which he hath had such experience of, for the emptiness and *damningness* of them, and so think himself a complete penitent. *Hammond.*

DAMP. *adj.* [*dampe*, Dutch.]
1. Moist; inclining to wet; not completely dry; foggy.
She said no more: the trembling Trojans hear,
O'erspread with a *damp* sweat and holy fear. *Dryden's Æn.*

2. Dejected; sunk; depressed.
All these and more came flocking, but with looks
Downcast and *damp*; yet such wherein appear'd
Obscure some glimpse of joy. *Milton's Paradise Lost, b.* I.

A DAMP. *n. s.*
1. Fog; moist air; moisture.
Thus Adam to himself lamented loud,
Through the still night; not now, as ere man fell,
Wholsom and cool, and mild; but with black air
Accompany'd, with *damps* and dreadful gloom. *Milt. P. L.*
A rift there was, which from the mountain's height
Convey'd a glimmering and malignant light,
A breathing-place to draw the *damps* away,
A twilight of an intercepted day. *Dryden's Fables.*

2. A noxious vapour exhaled from the earth.
The heat of the sun in the hotter seasons, penetrating the exterior parts of the earth, excites those mineral exhalations in subterraneous caverns, which are called *damps*: these seldom happen but in the summer-time, when the hotter the weather is, the more frequent are the *damps.* *Woodward.*

3. Dejection; depression of spirit; cloud of the mind.
Adam, by this from the cold sudden *damp*
Recov'ring, and his scatter'd spirits return'd,
To Michael thus his humble words address'd. *Milt. P. Lost.*
His name struck ev'ry where so great a *damp*,
As Archimedes through the Roman camp. *Roscommon.*
Even now, while thus I stand blest in thy presence,
A secret *damp* of grief comes o'er my thoughts. *Add. Cato.*
An eternal state, he knows and confesses that he has made no provision for, that he is undone for ever: a prospect which is enough to cast a *damp* over his sprightliest hours. *Rogers, Sermon* 19.
This commendable resentment against me, strikes a *damp* upon that spirit in all ranks and corporations of men. *Swift.*

To DAMP. *v. a.* [from the noun.]
1. To wet; to moisten; to make humid.
2. To depress; to deject; to chill.
The very loss of one pleasure is enough to *damp* the relish of another. *L'Estrange, Fable* 38.
Dread of death hangs over the mere natural man, and, like the hand-writing on the wall, *damps* all his jollity. *Atterb.*
It would be enough to *damp* their warmth in such pursuits, if they could once reflect, that in such course they will be sure to run upon the very rock they mean to avoid. *Swift.*

3. To weaken; to abandon.
A soft body *dampeth* the sound much more than a hard. *Bacon's Natural History*, N°. 158.
Unless an age too late, or cold
Climate, or years, *damp* my intended wing
Depress'd. *Milton's Paradise Lost, b.* ix.

DA'MPISHNESS. *n. s.* [from *damp.*] Tendency to wetness; fogginess; moisture.
It hath been used by some with great success to make their walls thick; and to put a lay of chalk between the bricks, to take away all *dampishness.* *Bacon's Natural History*, N°. 937.

DA'MPNESS. *n. s.* [from *damp.*] Moisture; fogginess.
Nor need they fear the *dampness* of the sky
Should flag their wings, and hinder them to fly;
'Twas only water thrown on sails too dry. *Dryden.*
By stacks they often have very great loss, by the *dampness* of the ground, which rots and spoils it. *Mortimer's Husbandry.*

DA'MPY. *adj.* [from *damp.*] Dejected; gloomy; sorrowful.
The lords did dispel *dampy* thoughts, which the remembrance of his uncle might raise, by applying him with exercises and disports. *Hayward.*

DA'MSEL. *n. s.* [*damoiselle*, French.]
1. A young gentlewoman; a young woman of distinction: now only used in verse.
Kneeling, I my servant's smiles implore,
And one mad *damsel* dares dispute my pow'r. *Prior.*

2. An attendant of the better rank.

With her train of *damsels* she was gone
In shady walks, the scorching heat to shun. *Dryden's Fables.*

3. A wench; a country lass.

The clowns are whoremasters, and the *damsels* with child.
Gay's Preface to What d'ye call it.

DA'MSON. *n. s.* [corruptly from *damascene.*] A small black plum. See DAMASCENE.

My wife desir'd some *damsons*,
And made me climb with danger of my life. *Shak. H.* VI.

DAN. *n. s.* [from *dominus*, as now *don* in Spanish, and *donna*, Italian, from *domina.*] The old term of honour for men; as we now say *master*.

This whimpled, whining, purblind, wayward boy,
This signor Junio's giant dwarf, *dan* Cupid. *Shakespeare.*
Dick, if this story pleaseth thee,
Pray thank *dan* Pope, who told it me. *Prior's Alma.*

To DANCE. *v. n.* [*danser*, Fr. *danzar*, Span. as some think from *tanza*, Arabick, a dance; as *Junius*, who loves to derive from Greek, thinks, from δόνησις.]

1. To move in measure; to move with steps correspondent to the sound of instruments.

What say you to young Mr. Fenton? He capers, he *dances*, he has eyes of youth, he writes verses. *Sh. Mer. W. of Windf.*

To DANCE *Attendance. v. a.* To wait with suppleness and obsequiousness.

Men are sooner weary to *dance* attendance at the gates of foreign lords, than to tarry the good leisure of their own magistrates. *Raleigh's Essays.*

It upbraids you
To let your father's friend, for three long months,
Thus *dance* attendance for a word of audience. *Dryd. Cleom.*

To DANCE. *v. a.*

1. To make to dance; to put into a lively motion.

Thy grandsire lov'd thee well;
Many a time he *danc'd* thee on his knee. *Shak. Tit. Andron.*
That I see thee here,
Thou noble thing! more *dances* my rapt' heart,
Than when I first my wedded mistress saw
Bestride my threshold. *Shakespeare's Coriolanus.*

In pestilences the malignity of the infecting vapour *danceth* the principal spirits. *Bacon's Natural History*, N°. 333.

DANCE. *n. s.* [from the verb.] A motion of one or many in concert, regulated by musick.

Our *dance* of custom, round about the oak of Herne the hunter. *Shakespeare's Merry Wives of Windsor.*

The honourablest part of talk is to give the occasion, and again to moderate and pass to somewhat else; for then a man leads the *dance*. *Bacon, Essay* 33.

But you perhaps expect a modish feast,
With am'rous songs and wanton *dances* grac'd. *Dryd. Juv.*

DA'NCER. *n. s.* [from *dance.*] One that practises the art of dancing.

He at Philippi kept
His sword e'en like a *dancer*, while I strook
The lean and wrinkled Cassius. *Shakes. Ant. and Cleopatra.*
Musicians and *dancers!* take some truce
With these your pleasing labours; for great use
As much weariness as perfection brings. *Donne.*

The earl was so far from being a good *dancer*, that he was no graceful goer. *Wotton.*

It is a usual practice in these times for our funambulours, or *dancers* on the rope, to attempt somewhat like to flying. *Wilkins's Math. Magic.*

He, perfect *dancer!* climbs the rope,
And balances your fear and hope. *Prior.*
Nature, I thought, perform'd too mean a part,
Forming her movements to the rules of art;
And, vex'd, I found that the musician's hand
Had o'er the *dancer's* mind too great command. *Prior.*

DA'NCINGMASTER. *n. s* [*dance* and *master.*] One who teaches the art of dancing.

The apes were taught their ape's tricks by a *dancingmaster*. *L'Estrange.*

The legs of a *dancingmaster*, and the fingers of a musician, fall, as it were, naturally, without thought or pains, into regular and admirable motions. *Locke on Understanding, sect.* 4.

DA'NCINGSCHOOL. *n. s.* [*dancing* and *school.*] The school where the art of dancing is taught.

They bid us to the English *dancingschools*,
And teach lavolta's high, and swift couranto's;
Saying our grace is only in our heels. *Shakesp. Henry* V.

A certain Egyptian king endowed a *dancingschool* for the institution of apes of quality. *L'Estrange.*

DANDELI'ON. *n. s.* [*dent de lion*, French.] The name of a plant.

It agrees in all respects with the hawkweed, but only in its having a single naked stalk, with one flower upon the top. *Miller.*

For cowslips sweet, let *dandelions* spread;
For Blouzelinda, blithsome maid, is dead! *Gay's Pastorals.*

DA'NDIPRAT. *n. s.* [*dandin*, French.] A little fellow; an urchin: a word used sometimes in fondness, sometimes in contempt.

To DA'NDLE. *v. a.* [*dandelen*, Dutch.]

1. To shake a child on the knee, or in the hands, to please and quiet him.

Then shall ye suck, and shall be born upon her sides, and be *dandled* upon her knees. *Is.* lxvi. 12.

Thy little brethren, which, like fairy sprights,
Oft skip into our chamber those sweet nights,
And, kiss'd and *dandl'd* on thy father's knee,
Were brib'd next day to tell what they did see. *Donne.*
Courts are but superficial schools to *dandle* fools. *Wotton.*
Sporting the lion ramp'd, and in his paw
Dandled the kid. *Milton's Paradise Lost, b.* iv. *l.* 344.

Motion occasions sleep, as we find by the common use of rocking froward children in cradles, or *dandling* them in their nurses arms. *Temple.*

2. To fondle; to treat like a child.

Their child shall be advanc'd,
And be received for the emp'ror's heir;
And let the emperor *dandle* him for his own. *Sh. Tit. Andr.*

They have put me in a silk gown, and a gaudy fool's cap; and I am ashamed to be *dandled* thus, and cannot look in the glass without blushing, to see myself turned into such a little pretty master. *Addison's Guardian*, N°. 113.

3. To delay; to procrastinate; to protract by trifles.

Captains do so *dandle* their doings, and dally in the service to them committed, as if they would not have the enemy subdued. *Spenser on Ireland.*

DA'NDLER. *n. s.* [from *dandle.*] He that dandles or fondles children.

DA'NDRUFF. *n. s.* [often written *dendriff*, from tan, the itch, and drof, sordid, filthy.] Scabs in the head; scurf at the roots of the hair.

DA'NEWORT. *n. s.* A species of elder; called also dwarf-elder, or wallwort.

DA'NGER. *n. s.* [*danger*, Fr. of uncertain derivation. *Skinner* derives it from *damnum*, *Menage* from *angaria*, *Minshew* from θάνατος, death, to which *Junius* seems inclined.] Risque; hazard; peril.

They that sail on the sea, tell of the *danger*. *Ecclus.* xliii. 24.

Our craft is in *danger* to be set at nought. *Acts*, x. 27.

I dare pawn down my life for him, that he hath writ this to feel my affection to your honour, and to no other pretence of *danger*. *Shakespeare's King Lear.*

More *danger* now from man alone we find,
Than from the rocks, the billows, and the wind. *Waller.*

To DA'NGER. *v. a.* [from the noun.] To put in hazard; to endanger.

Pompey's son stands up
For the main soldier; whose quality going on,
The sides o' th' world may *danger*. *Shakes. Ant. and Cleopat.*

DA'NGERLESS. *adj.* [from *danger.*] Without hazard; without risque; exempt from danger.

He shewed no less magnanimity in *dangerless* despising, than others in dangerous affecting the multiplying of kingdoms. *Sid.*

DA'NGEROUS. *adj.* [from *danger.*] Hazardous; perillous; full of danger.

A man of an ill tongue is *dangerous* in his city. *Ecclus.* ix.

All men counsel me to take away thy life, likely to bring forth nothing but *dangerous* and wicked effects. *Sidney, b.* ii.

Already we have conquer'd half the war,
And the less *dangerous* part is left behind. *Dryd. Ann. Mirab.*

DA'NGEROUSLY. *adv.* [from *dangerous.*] Hazardously; perillously; with danger.

But for your son, believe it, oh, believe it,
Most *dang'rously* you have with him prevail'd,
If not most mortal to him. *Shakespeare's Coriolanus.*
A sort of naughty persons
Have practis'd *dangerously* against your state,
Dealing with witches and with conjurers. *Shak. Hen.* VI.

It is just with God to permit those, which think they stand so surely, to fall most *dangerously*. *Hammond on Fundamentals.*

Plutarch says Telesilla, a noble lady, being *dangerously* sick, was by the oracle advised to apply her mind to the muse and poetry. *Peacham on Poetry.*

If it were so; which but to think were pride,
My constant love would *dangerously* be tried. *Dryden.*

DA'NGEROUSNESS. *n. s.* [from *dangerous.*] Danger; hazard; peril.

I shall not need to mind you of judging of the *dangerousness* of diseases, by the nobleness of that part affected. *Boyle.*

To DA'NGLE. *v. n.* [from *hang*, according to *Skinner*; as *hang, hangle dangle.*] To hang loose and quivering.

Go, bind thou up yond *dangling* apricocks. *Shak. R.* II.

He'd rather on a gibbet *dangle*,
Than miss his dear delight to wrangle. *Hudibras, p.* iii.
Codrus had but one leg; so short to boot,
That his short wife's short legs hung *dangling* out. *Dryden.*
With *dangling* hands he strokes th' imperial robe,
And with a cuckold's air commands the globe. *Smith.*

But have you not with thought beheld
The sword hang *dangling* o'er the shield. *Prior.*

2. To hang upon any one; to be an humble, useless, harmless follower.

The presbyterians, and other fanaticks that *dangle* after them, are well inclined to pull down the present establishment. *Swift.*

DA'NGLER. *n. s.* [from *dangle.*] A man that hangs about women only to waste time.

A *dangler* is of neither sex. *Ralph's Miscel.*

DANK. *adj.* [from *tuncken*, Germ. *Skinner.*] Damp; humid; moist; wet.

He her the maiden sleeping found,
On the *dank* and dirty ground. *Shakesp. Midsf. Night's Dream.*

Yet oft they quit
The *dank*, and, rising on stiff pinions, tour
The mid aereal sky. *Milton's Paradise Lost, b.* vii. *l.* 440.

Through each thicket, *dank* or dry,
Like a black mist, low creeping, he held on
His midnight search. *Milton's Paradise Lost, b.* ix. *l.* 179.

Lawrence, of virtuous father, virtuous son,
Now that the fields are *dank*, and ways are mire,
Where shall we sometimes meet, and by the fire
Help waste a sullen day? *Milton's Paradise Regained.*

By the rushy-fringed bank,
Where grows the willow and the osier *dank*,
My sliding chariot stays. *Milton.*

Me, in my vow'd
Picture, the sacred wall declares t' have hung
My *dank* and dropping weeds
To the stern god of sea. *Milton.*

To wash the skins of beasts and fowls herewith, would keep them from growing *dank* in moist weather. *Grew.*

DA'NKISH. *adj.* Somewhat dank.

They bound me, bore me thence,
And in a dark and *dankish* vault at home,
There left me. *Shakespeare's Comedy of Errours.*

To DAP. *v. n.* [corrupted from *dip.*] To let fall gently into the water: a word, I believe, only used by anglers.

I have taught him how to catch a chub, by *dapping* with a grasshopper. *Walton's Angler.*

DAPA'TICAL. *adj.* [from *dapaticus*, Latin.] Sumptuous in cheer. *Bailey.*

DA'PPER. *adj.* [*dapper*, Dutch.] Little and active; lively without bulk. It is usually spoken in contempt.

And on the tawny sands and shelves,
Trip the pert fairies and the *dapper* elves. *Milton.*

A pert *dapper* spark of a magpye, fancied the birds would never be governed 'till himself should sit at the helm. *L'Estr.*

DA'PPERLING. *n. s.* [from *dapper.*] A dwarf; a dandiprat. *Ainsworth.*

DA'PPLE. *adj.* [from *apple*; as *pommelé.*] Marked with various colours; variegated; streaked; imbricated: it is used chiefly of animals.

My country neighbours do not find it impossible to think of a lame horse, 'till they have run over all beings that are, and then pitch on *dapple.* *Locke.*

To DA'PPLE. *v. a.* [from the adjective.] To streak; to vary; to diversify with colours.

Certes, said she, I wot not how he hight;
But under him a grey steed did he weild,
Whose sides with *dappled* circles were endight. *Fairy Queen.*

The gentle day
Dapples the drowsy east with spots of grey. *Shakespeare.*

Horses that are *dappled*, turn white; and old squirrels turn grisly. *Bacon's Natural History*, N°. 85.

The lark begins his flight,
From his watch-tower in the skies,
'Till the *dappled* dawn doth rise. *Milton.*

I chose
The *dappl'd* pink, and blushing rose,
To deck my charming Cloe's hair. *Prior.*

The gods, to curse Pamela with her pray'rs,
Gave the gilt coach and *dappled* Flanders mares. *Pope.*

DAR. } *n. s.* A fish found in the Severn. *Bailey.*
DART. }

To DARE. *v. n.* pret. *I durst*; part. *I have dared.* [ꝺeaꞃꞃan, Saxon; *derren*, Dutch] To have courage for any purpose; not to be afraid; to adventure; to be adventurous.

I say 'tis copper. *Dar'st* thou be as good as thy word now?
—Why, Hal, thou know'st, as thou art but a man, I *dare*; but as thou art a prince, I fear thee. *Shakesf. Henry* IV. *p.* i.

I *dare* do all that may become a man;
Who *dares* do more, is none. *Shakespeare's Macbeth.*

They are both hanged; and so would this be, if he *durst* steal any thing advent'rously. *Shakespeare's Henry* V.

Neither of them was of that temper as to *dare* any dangerous fact. *Haywood.*

The father bore it with undaunted soul,
Like one who *durst* his destiny controul. *Dryden.*

Deliberate and well-weighed courage knows both to be cautious and to *dare*, as occasion offers. *Dryden.*

We *dare* not build much upon such a notion or doctrine, 'till it be very fully examined. *Watts's Improv. of the Mind.*

To DARE. *v. a.* To challenge; to defy.

I never in my life
Did hear challenge urg'd more modestly,
Unless a brother should a brother *dare*
To gentle exercise and proof of arms. *Shakesp. Henry* IV.

Here she stands:
Take but possession of her with a touch;
I *dare* thee but to breathe upon my love. *Shakespeare.*

He had many days, in this proud manner, come half seas over; and sometimes passing further, came and lay at the mouth of the harbour, and, as it were, *daring* them to fight. *Knolles's History of the Turks.*

Masters of the arts of policy thought that they might even defy and *dare* providence to the face. *South.*

All cold, but in her breast, I will despise;
And *dare* all heat but that in Celia's eyes. *Roscommon.*

Time! I *dare* thee to discover
Such a youth, and such a lover. *Dryden.*

Presumptuous wretch! with mortal art to *dare*
Immortal power, and brave the thunderer. *Granville.*

To DARE *Larks.* To catch them by means of a looking-glass, which keeps them in amaze 'till caught; to amaze.

Shrimps are dipped up in shallow water with little round nets, not much unlike that which is used for *daring* larks. *Carew.*

As larks lie *dar'd* to shun the hobby's flight. *Dryden.*

DARE. *n. s.* [from the verb.] Defiance; challenge.

Sextus Pompeius
Hath given the *dare* to Cæsar, and commands
The empire of the sea. *Shakesp. Anthony and Cleopatra.*

DA'REFUL. *adj.* [*dare* and *full*] Full of defiance.

We might have met them *dareful*, beard to beard,
And beat them backward home. *Shakespeare's Macbeth.*

DA'RING. *adj.* [from *dare.*] Bold; adventurous; fearless; courageous; intrepid; brave; stout.

The last Georgick has indeed many metaphors, but not so *daring* as this; for human thoughts and passions may be more naturally ascribed to a bee than to an inanimate plant. *Addison's Essays on the Georgicks.*

The song too *daring*, and the theme too great. *Prior.*

Grieve not, O *daring* prince! that noble heart. *Pope.*

DA'RINGLY. *adv.* [from *daring.*] Boldly; courageously; fearlessly; impudently; outrageously.

Some of the great principles of religion are every day openly and *daringly* attacked from the press. *Atterbury.*

Your brother, fir'd with success,
Too *daringly* upon the foe did press. *Halifax.*

DA'RINGNESS. *n. s.* [from *daring.*] Boldness.

DARK. *adj.* [ꝺeoꞃc, Saxon.]

1. Not light; without light.

Fleance, his son, who keeps him company,
Must embrace the fate of that *dark* hour. *Shakesf. Macbeth.*

While we converse with her, we mark
No want of day, nor think it *dark.* *Waller.*

2. Not of a showy or vivid colour.

If the plague be somewhat *dark*, and the plague spread not in the skin, the priest shall pronounce him clean. 1 *Lev.* xiii. 6.

In Muscovy itself the generality of the people are more inclined to have *dark* coloured hair than flaxen. *Boyle.*

3. Blind; without the enjoyment of light.

Thou wretched daughter of a *dark* old man,
Conduct my weary steps. *Dryd. and Lee's Oedipus.*

4. Opake; not transparent.

5. Obscure; not perspicuous.

What may seem *dark* at the first, will afterwards be found more plain. *Hooker, b.* i. *sect.* 1.

Mean time we shall express our *darker* purpose. *Shakesp.*

6. Not enlightened by knowledge; ignorant.

The age, wherein he liv'd, was *dark*; but he
Could not want sight, who taught the world to see. *Denh.*

7. Gloomy; not chearful.

All men of *dark* tempers, according to their degree of melancholy or enthusiasm, may find convents fitted to their humours. *Addison on Italy.*

DARK. *n. s.*

1. Darkness; obscurity; want of light.

Come, thick night,
And pall thee in the dunnest smoke of hell,
That my keen knife see not the wound it makes;
Nor heav'n peep through the blanket of the *dark*,
To cry hold, hold! *Shakespeare's Macbeth.*

Cloud and ever-during *dark*
Surrounds me! from the chearful ways of men
Cut off. *Milton's Paradise Lost, b.* iii. *l.* 45.

Whereas seeing requires light, and a free medium, and a right line to the objects, we can hear in the *dark* immured, and by curve lines. *Holder's Elements of Speech.*

2. Obscurity; condition of one unknown.

All he says of himself is, that he is an obscure person; one, I suppose he means, that is in the *dark*, and thinks it proper to continue so. *Atterbury.*

3. Want of knowledge.
'Till we ourselves perceive by our own understandings, we are as much in the *dark*, and as void of knowledge, as before. *Locke.*

To DARK. *v. a.* [from the noun.] To darken; to obscure: obsolete.

Fair when her breast, like a rich laden bark
With precious merchandize, she forth doth lay:
Fair when that cloud of pride, which oft doth *dark*
Her goodly light, with smiles she drives away. *Spenser.*

To DA'RKEN. *v. a.* [from *dark.*]
1. To make dark; to deprive of light.

Black with surrounding forests then it stood,
That hung above, and *darken'd* all the flood. *Addison.*
Whether the *darken'd* room to muse invite,
Or whiten'd wall provoke the skew'r to write. *Pope.*

2. To cloud; to perplex.
Such was his wisdom, that his confidence did seldom *darken* his foresight, especially in things near hand. *Bacon's Hen.* VII.
3. To foul; to sully.
The lusts and passions of men do sully and *darken* their minds, even by a natural influence. *Tillotson, Serm.* 4.

To DA'RKEN. *v. n.* To grow dark.

DA'RKLING. [a participle, as it seems, from *darkle*, which yet I have never found.] Being in the dark; being without light: a word merely poetical.

O, wilt thou *darkling* leave me? do not so. *Shakespeare.*
Darkling stands
The varying shore o' th' world. *Shakesp. Ant. and Cleopatra.*
The wakeful bird
Sings *darkling*, and, in shadiest covert hid,
Tunes her nocturnal note. *Milton's Paradise Lost, b.* iii.
Darkling they mourn their fate, whom Circe's pow'r,
With words and wicked herbs, from human kind
Had alter'd, and in brutal shapes confin'd. *Dryden's Æn.*

DA'RKLY. *adv.* [from *dark.*] In a situation void of light; obscurely; blindly.

For well you know, and can record alone,
What fame to future times conveys but *darkly* down. *Dryd.*

DA'RKNESS. *n. s.* [from *dark.*]
1. Absence of light.
Darkness was upon the face of the deep. *Gen.* i. 2.
I go whence I shall not return, even to the land of *darkness* and the shadow of death. *Job*, x. 20.
2. Opakeness.
3. Obscurity.
4. Infernal gloom; wickedness.

The instruments of *darkness* tell us truths;
Win us with honest trifles, to betray us
In deepest consequence. *Shakespeare's Macbeth.*

All the light truth has, or can have, is from the clearness and validity of those proofs upon which it is received: to talk of any other light in the understanding, is to put ourselves in the dark, or in the power of the prince of *darkness*. *Locke.*
5. The empire of Satan, or the devil.
Who hath delivered us from the power of *darkness*, and translated us into the kingdom of his dear son. *Coloss.* i. 13.

DA'RKSOME. *adj.* [from *dark.*] Gloomy; obscure; not well enlightened; not luminous.

He brought him through a *darksome* narrow pass,
To a broad gate, all built of beaten gold. *Fairy Queen, b.* ii.
And her fair eyes, like stars that dimmed were
With *darksome* cloud, now shew their goodly beams. *Spenser.*

You must not look to have an image, or the like, in any thing that is lightsome; for even a face in iron, red-hot, will not be seen, the light confounding the small differences of lightsome and *darksome* which shew the figure. *Bacon's N. Hist.*

A *darksome* cloud of locusts, swarming down,
Must eat, and on the ground leave nothing green. *Milton.*
He here with us to be,
Forsook the courts of everlasting day,
And chose with us a *darksome* house of mortal clay. *Milton.*
Mistaken blessing, which old age they call,
'Tis a long, nasty, *darksome* hospital. *Dryden's Juvenal.*
The *darksome* pines that o'er yon' rocks reclin'd,
Wave high, and murmur to the hollow wind. *Pope.*

DA'RLING. *adj.* [ꝺeorling, Sax.] Favourite; dear; beloved; regarded with great kindness and tenderness.
'Tis not for a generous prince to countenance oppression and injustice, even in his most *darling* favourites. *L'Estrange.*
Have a care lest some beloved notion, or some *darling* science, too far prevail over your mind. *Watts's Improvement.*

DA'RLING. *n. s.* A favourite; one much beloved.

Young Ferdinand they suppose is drown'd,
And his and my lov'd *darling*. *Shakespeare's Tempest.*
In Thames, the ocean's *darling*, England's pride,
The pleasing emblem of his reign does glide. *Halifax.*

She immediately became the *darling* of the princess Sophia. *Addison's Freeholder*, N°. 21.

To DARN. *v. a.* [of uncertain original.] To mend holes by imitating the texture of the stuff.

Will she thy linen wash, or hosen *darn*? *Gay.*

He spent every day ten hours in his *closet*, in *darning* his stockings, which he performed to admiration. *Swift.*

DA'RNEL. *n. s.* A weed growing in the fields. See GRASS.

He was met ev'n now
Crown'd with rank fumiter and furrow-weeds,
With hardocks, hemlock, nettles, cuckoo flowers,
Darnel, and all the idle weeds that grow
In our sustaining corn. *Shakespeare's King Lear.*
Want ye corn for bread?
'Twas full of *darnel*; do you like the taste? *Shak. H.* VI.
No fruitful crop the sickly fields return;
But oats and *darnel* choak the rising corn. *Dryd. Pastorals.*

To DA'RRAIN. *v. a.* [This word is by *Junius* referred to *dare*: it seems to me more probably deducible from *arranger la battaille.*]
1. To prepare for battle; to range troops for battle.
The town-boys parted in twain, the one side calling themselves Pompeians, the other Cæsarians; and then *darraining* a kind of battle, but without arms, the Cæsarians got the over-hand. *Carew's Survey of Cornwal.*

Comes Warwick, backing of the duke of York:
Darrain your battle; for they are at hand. *Shak. Hen.* VI.

2. To apply to the fight.

Therewith they 'gan to hurlen greedily,
Redoubted battle ready to *darraine*. *Fairy Queen, b.* ii.

DART. *n. s.* [*dard*, French.]
1. A missile weapon thrown by the hand; a small lance.
Here one is wounded or slain with a piece of a rock or flint; there another with a *dart*, arrow, or lance. *Peacham.*

O'erwhelm'd with *darts*, which from afar they fling,
The weapons round his hollow temples ring. *Dryden's Æn.*

2. [In poetry.] Any missile weapon.

To DART. *v. a.* [from the noun.]
1. To throw offensively.

He whets his tusks, and turns, and dares the war;
Th' invaders *dart* their jav'lins from afar. *Dryden's Æn.*
Pan came, and ask'd what magick caus'd my smart;
Or what ill eyes malignant glances *dart*. *Pope.*

2. To throw; to emit; as the sun *darts* his beams on the earth.

To DART. *v. n.* To fly as a dart; to let fly with hostile intention.

Now, *darting* Parthia, art thou struck. *Sh. Ant. and Cleop.*

To DASH. *v. a.* [The etymology of this word, in any of its senses, is very doubtful.]
1. To throw any thing suddenly against something.
If you *dash* a stone against a stone in the bottom of the water, it maketh a sound. *Bacon's Natural History*, N°. 792.
A man that cuts himself, and tears his own flesh, and *dashes* his head against the stones, does not act so unreasonably as he. *Tillotson, Serm.* 1.
2. To break by collision.

They that stand high, have many blasts to shake them;
And, if they fall, they *dash* themselves to pieces. *Shakesp.*
David's throne shall be like a tree,
Spreading and overshad'wing all the earth;
Or as a stone, that shall to pieces *dash*
All monarchies besides throughout the world. *Milt. P. Reg.*

3. To throw water in flashes.
Dashing water on them may prove the best remedy. *Mortim.*
4. To bespatter; to besprinkle.

This tempest,
Dashing the garment of this peace, aboded
The sudden breach on't. *Shakespeare's Henry* VIII.

5. To agitate any liquid, so as to make the surface fly off.

At once the brushing oars and brazen prow
Dash up the sandy waves, and ope the depths below. *Dryd.*

6. To mingle; to change by some small admixture.

Hight Whacum, bred to *dash* and draw,
Not wine, but more unwholsome law. *Hudibras, p.* ii. *c.* 3.

I take care to *dash* the character with such particular circumstances as may prevent ill-natured applications. *Addison.*
Several revealed truths are *dashed* and adulterated with a mixture of fables and human inventions. *Spectator*, N°. 580.
7. To form or print in haste, carelessly.

Never was *dash'd* out, at one lucky hit,
A fool, so just a copy of a wit. *Pope's Dunciad, b.* ii. *l.* 43.

8. To obliterate; to blot; to cross out.
To *dash* over this with a line, will deface the whole copy extremely, and to a degree that, I fear, may displease you. *Pope.*
9. To confound; to make ashamed suddenly; to surprise with shame or fear.

His tongue
Dropp'd manna, and could make the worse appear
The better reason, to perplex and *dash*
Maturest counsels. *Milton's Paradise Lost, b.* ii. *l.* 114.
Yearly enjoin'd, some say, to undergo
This annual, humbling certain number'd days,
To *dash* their pride and joy for man seduc'd. *Milt. Pa. Lost.*
An unknown hand still check'd my forward joy,
Dash'd me with blushes. *Dryd. and Lee's Oedipus.*

To *dash* this cavil, read but the practice of Christian emperors. *South.*

Nothing

Nothing *daſhed* the confidence of the mule like the braying of the aſs, in the very interim while he was dilating upon his genealogy. *L'Eſtrange, Fab.* 18.

The nymph, when nothing could Narciſſus move,
Still *daſh'd* with bluſhes for her ſlighted love. *Add. Ov. Met.*

After they had ſufficiently blaſted him in his perſonal capacity, they found it an eaſy work to *daſh* and overthrow him in his political. *South's Sermons.*

Some ſtronger pow'r eludes our ſickly will;
Daſhes our riſing hope with certain ill. *Prior.*

Daſh the proud gameſter in his gilded car;
Bare the mean heart that lurks beneath a ſtar. *Pope.*

To Dash. *v. n.*

1. To fly off the ſurface.

If the veſſel be ſuddenly ſtopt in its motion, the liquor continues its motion, and *daſhes* over the ſides of the veſſel. *Cheyne.*

2. To fly in flaſhes with a loud noiſe.

On each hand the guſhing waters play,
And down the rough caſcade, while *daſhing*, fall. *Thomſon.*

3. To ruſh through water ſo as to make it fly.

Doeg, though without knowing how or why,
Spurr'd boldly on, and *daſh'd* through thick and thin,
Through ſenſe and nonſenſe, never out or in. *Dryden.*

A Dash. *n. ſ.* [from the verb.]

1. Colliſion.

By the touch ethereal rous'd,
The *daſh* of clouds, or irritating war,
Of fighting winds, while all is calm below
They furious ſpring. *Thomſon's Summer, l.* 1100.

2. Infuſion; ſomething mingled in a ſmall proportion.

There is nothing which one regards ſo much, with an eye of mirth and pity, as innocence, when it has in it a *daſh* of folly. *Addiſon's Spectator,* N°. 247.

3. A mark in writing; a line ——, to note a pauſe, or omiſſion.

He is afraid of letters and characters, of notes and *daſhes*, which, ſet together, do ſignify nothing. *Brown's Vulgar Err.*

In modern wit all printed traſh is
Set off with num'rous breaks and *daſhes*. *Swift.*

4. Stroke; blow.

Stand back, you lords, and give us leave awhile.
—— She takes upon her bravely at firſt *daſh*. *Shakeſp. H.* V.

Dash. *adv.* An expreſſion of the ſound of water daſhed.

Hark, hark, the waters fall;
And, with a murmuring ſound,
Daſh, daſh, upon the ground,
To gentle ſlumbers call. *Dryden's Indian Emperor.*

DA'STARD. *n. ſ.* abaſtꝛiga, Saxon.] A coward; a poltron; A man infamous for fear.

The cruelty and envy of the people,
Permitted by our *daſtard* nobles,
And ſuffer'd me by th' voice of ſlaves to be
Whoop'd out of Rome. *Shakeſpeare's Coriolanus.*

Who now my matchleſs valour dare oppoſe?
How long will Dares wait his *daſtard* foes. *Dryden's Æn.*

Daſtard and drunkard, mean and inſolent;
Tongue-valiant hero, vaunter of thy might,
In threats the foremoſt, but the laſt in fight. *Dryden.*

Such bug-bear thoughts, once got into the minds of children, make them *daſtards*, and afraid of the ſhadow of darkneſs ever after. *Locke on Education, ſect.* 138.

Curſe on their *daſtard* ſouls, they ſtand aſtoniſh'd. *Addiſ.*

To Da'stard. *v. a.* To terrify; to intimidate; to deſert with cowardice; to diſpirit.

I'm weary of this fleſh which holds us here,
And *daſtards* manly ſoul with hope and fear. *Dryd. Ind. Emp.*

To Da'stardise. *v. a.* [from *daſtard.*] To intimidate; to deject with cowardice; to diſpirit; to depreſs; to terrify; to make an habitual coward.

He had ſuch things to urge againſt our marriage,
As, now declar'd, would blunt my ſword in battle,
And *daſtardiſe* my courage. *Dryden's Don Sebaſtian.*

Da'stardly. *adj.* [from *daſtard.*] Cowardly; mean; timorous.

This way of brawl and clamour is ſo arrant a mark of a *daſtardly* wretch, that he does as good as call himſelf ſo that uſes it. *L'Eſtrange.*

Da'stardy. *n. ſ.* [from *daſtard.*] Cowardlineſs; timorouſneſs.

Da'tary. *n. ſ.* [from *date.*] An officer of the Chancery of Rome, through whoſe hands moſt benefices paſs. *Dict.*

DATE. *n. ſ.* [*datte*, Fr. from *datum*, Latin.]

1. The time at which a letter is written, marked at the end or the beginning.

2. The time at which any event happened.

3. The time ſtipulated when any thing ſhall be done.

His days and times are paſt,
And my reliance on his fracted *dates*
Has ſmit my credit. *Shakeſpeare's Timon.*

My father's promiſe ties me not to time;
And bonds, without a *date*, they ſay are void. *Dryden.*

4. End; concluſion.

What time would ſpare, from ſteel receives its *date*;
And monuments, like men, ſubmit to fate. *Pope.*

5. Duration; continuance.

Could the declining of this fate, O friend,
Our *date* to immortality extend? *Denham.*

Then raiſe,
From the conflagrant maſs, purg'd, and refin'd,
New heav'ns, new earth, ages of endleſs *date*,
Founded in righteouſneſs. *Milton's Paradiſe Loſt.*

6. [from *dactylus.*] The fruit of the date-tree.

Hold, take theſe keys, and fetch more ſpices, nurſe.
—— They call for *dates* and quinces in the paſtry. *Shakeſp.*

Date-tree. *n. ſ.* See Palm, of which it is a ſpecies.

To Date. *v. a.* [from the noun.] To note with the time at which any thing is written or done.

'Tis all one, in reſpect of eternal duration yet behind, whether we begin the world ſo many millions of ages ago, or *date* from the late æra of about ſix thouſand years. *Bentley's Sermons.*

To all their *dated* backs he turns you round;
Theſe Aldus printed, thoſe Du Süeil has bound. *Pope's Epiſt.*

Da'teless. *adj.* [from *date.*] Without any fixed term.

The fly-ſlow hours ſhall not determinate
The *dateleſs* limit of thy dear exile. *Shakeſpeare's Rich.* II.

Da'tive. *adj.* [*dativus*, Latin.]

1. [In grammar.] The epithet of the caſe that ſignifies the perſon to whom any thing is given.

2. [In law.] Thoſe are term'd *dative* executors who are appointed ſuch by the judge's decree; as adminiſtrators with us here in England. *Ayliffe's Parergon.*

To DAUB. *v. a.* [*dabben*, Dutch; *dauber*, French.]

1. To ſmear with ſomething adheſive.

She took for him an ark of bulruſhes, and *daubed* it with ſlime and with pitch. *Exod.* ii. 3.

2. To paint courſely.

Haſty *daubing* will but ſpoil the picture, and make it ſo unnatural as muſt want falſe light to ſet it off. *Otw Orph. Dedic.*

They ſnatched out of his hands a lame imperfect piece, rudely *daubed* over with too little reflection, and too much haſte. *Dryden's Dufreſnoy.*

If a picture is *daubed* with many bright and glaring colours, the vulgar admire it as an excellent piece. *Watts's Logick.*

3. To cover with ſomething ſpecious or ſtrong, ſomething that diſguiſes what it lies upon.

So ſmooth he *daub'd* his vice with ſhew of virtue,
He liv'd from all attainder of ſuſpect. *Shakeſpeare's R.* III.

4. To lay on any thing gaudily or oſtentatiouſly.

Since princes will have ſuch things, it is better they ſhould be graced with elegancy than *daubed* with coſt. *Bacon's Eſſays.*

Let him be *daub'd* with lace, live high, and whore;
Sometimes be louſy, but be never poor. *Dryden's Juvenal.*

5. To flatter groſsly.

Let every one, therefore, attend the ſentence of his conſcience; for, he may be ſure, it will not *daub* nor flatter. *South.*

To Daub. *v. n.* To play the hypocrite.

I cannot *daub* it further;
And yet I muſt. *Shakeſpeare's King Lear.*

A Da'uber. *n. ſ.* [from *daub.*] A coarſe low painter.

What they call'd his picture, had been drawn at length by the *daubers* of almoſt all nations, and ſtill unlike him. *Dryden.*

Parts of different ſpecies jumbled together, according to the mad imagination of the *dauber*, to cauſe laughter. *Dryden.*

A ſign-poſt *dauber* would diſdain to paint
The one-ey'd hero on his elephant. *Dryden's Juven. Sat.*

The treacherous tapſter, Thomas,
Hangs a new angel two doors from us,
As fine as *daubers* hands can make it. *Swift.*

Da'ubry. *n. ſ.* [from *daub.*] An old word for any thing artful.

She works by charms, by ſpells, and ſuch *daubry* as this is beyond our element. *Shakeſpeare's Merry Wives of Windſor.*

Da'uby. *adj.* [from *daub.*] Viſcous; glutinous; adheſive.

Not in vain th' induſtrious kind,
With *dauby* wax and flow'rs the chinks have lin'd. *Dryden.*

Some the gall'd ropes with *dauby* marling bind,
Or ſear-cloth maſts with ſtrong tarpawling coats. *Dryden.*

Da'ughter. *n. ſ.* [*dauhtar*, Gothick; ðohteꝛ, Saxon; *dotter*, Runick; *dohter*, German; *dochter*, Dutch.]

1. The female offspring of a man or woman.

Your wives, your *daughters*,
Your matrons, and your maids, could not fill up
The ciſtern of my luſt. *Shakeſpeare's Macbeth.*

Now Aurora, *daughter* of the dawn,
With roſy luſtre purpled o'er the lawn. *Pope's Hom. Odyſſey.*

2. A daughter in law, or ſon's wife.

3. A woman.

Jacob went out to ſee the *daughters* of the land. *Gen.* xxxiv.

4. [In poetry.] Any deſcendent.

5. The penitent of a confeſſor.

Are you at leiſure, holy father, now;
Or ſhall I come to you at evening maſs?
—— My leiſure ſerves me, penſive *daughter*, now. *Shakeſp.*

To DAUNT. *v. a.* [*domter*, French, *domitare*, Latin.] To discourage; to fright; to intimidate.

Fairfax, whose name in arms through Europe rings,
And fills all mouths with envy or with praise,
And all her jealous monarchs with amaze,
And rumours loud, which *daunt* remotest kings. *Milton.*

Where the rude ax, with heaved stroke,
Was never heard the nymphs to *daunt*,
Or fright them from their hallow'd haunt. *Milton.*

Some presences *daunt* and discourage us, when others raise us to a brisk assurance. *Glanville's Sceps. c.* 24.

DA'UNTLESS. *adj.* [from *daunt*.] Fearless; not dejected; not discouraged.

Grow great by your example, and put on
The *dauntless* spirit of resolution. *Shakespeare's King John.*

Dauntless he rose, and to the fight return'd:
With shame his glowing cheeks, his eyes with fury burn'd. *Dryden's Virgil's Æneid.*

He, not by wants or woes opprest,
Stems the bold torrent with a *dauntless* breast. *Dryden.*

The utmost weight of affliction from ministerial power and popular hatred, were almost worth bearing, for the glory of such a *dauntless* conduct as he has shewn under it. *Pope.*

DA'UNTLESSNESS. *n. s.* [from *dauntless*.] Fearlessness.

DAW. *n. s.* [supposed by *Skinner* so named from his note; by *Junius* to be corrupted from *dawl*; the German *tul*, and *dol*, in the Bavarian dialect, having the same signification.] The name of a bird.

I will wear my heart upon my sleeve,
For *daws* to peck it. *Shakespeare's Othello.*

If death do quench us quite, we have great wrong,
That *daws*, and trees, and rocks should last so long,
When we must in an instant pass to nought. *Davies.*

The loud *daw*, his throat displaying, draws
The whole assembly of his fellow *daws*. *Waller.*

DAWK. *n. s.* A cant word among the workmen for a hollow or incision in their stuff.

Observe if any hollow or *dawks* be in the length. *Moxon.*

To DAWK. *v. a.* To mark with an incision.

Should they apply that side of the tool the edge lies on, the swift coming about of the work would, where a small irregularity of stuff should happen, jobb the edge into the stuff, and so *dawk* it. *Moxon's Mech. Exer.*

To DAWN. *v. n.* [supposed by the etymologists to have been originally to *dayen*, or advance towards day.]

1. To grow luminous; to begin to grow light.

I have been troubled in my sleep this night;
But *dawning* day new comfort hath inspir'd. *Shak. Tit. Andr.*

As it began to *dawn*, towards the first day of the week, came Mary Magdalene to see the sepulchre. *Mat.* xxviii. 1.

All night I slept, oblivious of my pain;
Aurora *dawn'd*, and Phœbus shin'd in vain. *Pope's Odyssey.*

2. To glimmer obscurely.

A Romanist, from the very first *dawning* of any notions in his understanding, hath this principle constantly inculcated, viz. that he must believe as the church. *Locke.*

3. To begin, yet faintly; to give some promises of lustre or eminence.

While we behold such dauntless worth appear
In *dawning* youth, and souls so void of fear. *Dryden's Æn.*

Thy hand strikes out some free design,
When life awakes and *dawns* at every line. *Pope.*

DAWN. *n. s.* [from the verb.]

1. The time between the first appearance of light and the sun's rise, reckoned from the time that the sun comes within eighteen degrees of the horizon.

Then on to-morrow's *dawn* your care employ,
To search the land, and where the cities lie,
And what the men; but give this day to joy. *Dryden's Æn.*

2. Beginning; first rise.

These tender circumstances diffuse a *dawn* of serenity over the soul. *Pope.*

But such their guiltless passion was,
As in the *dawn* of time inform'd the heart
Of innocence, and undissembling truth. *Thomson's Summer.*

DAY. *n. s.* [dæᵹ, Saxon.]

1. The time between the rising and setting of the sun, called the artificial day.

Why stand ye here all the *day* idle? *Mat.* xx. 6.

Of night impatient, we demand the *day*;
The *day* arrives, then for the night we pray:
The night and *day* successive come and go,
Our lasting pains no interruption know. *Blackmore's Creation.*

Or object new
Casual discourse draws on, which intermits
Our *day*'s work. *Milton's Paradise Lost, b.* ix. *l.* 224.

2. The time from noon to noon, called the natural day.

How many hours bring about the *day?*
How many *days* will finish up the year? *Shakesp. Henry* VI.

3. Light; sunshine.

Let us walk honestly, as in the *day*; not in rioting and drunkenness. *Rom.* xiii. 13.

The West yet glimmers with some streaks of *day*:
Now spurs the lated traveller apace,
To gain the timely inn. *Shakespeare's Macbeth.*

Around the fields did nimble lightning play,
Which offer'd us by fits, and snatch'd the *day*:
'Midst this was heard the shrill and tender cry
Of well-pleas'd ghosts, which in the storm did fly. *Dryden.*

Yet are we able only to survey
Dawnings of beams, and promises of *day*. *Prior.*

4. Any time specified and distinguished from other time; an age; the time. In this sense it is generally plural.

After him reigned Gutheline his heir,
The justest man, and truest, in his *days*. *Fairy Queen, b.* ii.

I think, in these *days*, one honest man is obliged to acquaint another who are his friends. *Pope.*

We have, at this time of *day*, better and more certain means of information than they had. *Woodward's Nat. Hist.*

5. Life: in this sense it is commonly plural. *He never in his days broke his word*; that is, *in his whole life*.

6. The day of contest; the contest; the battle.

His name struck fear, his conduct won the *day*;
He came, he saw, he seiz'd the struggling prey. *Roscommon.*

The noble thanes do bravely in the war;
The *day* almost itself professes your's,
And little is to do. *Shakespeare's Macbeth.*

Would you th' advantage of the fight delay,
If, striking first, you were to win the *day?* *Dryden.*

7. An appointed or fixed time.

Or if my debtors do not keep their *day*,
Deny their hands, and then refuse to pay,
I must with patience all the terms attend. *Dryden's Juvenal.*

8. A day appointed for some commemoration.

The field of Agincourt,
Fought on the *day* of Crispin Crispianus. *Shakesp. Hen.* V.

9. From day to day; without certainty or continuance.

Bavaria hath been taught, that merit and service doth oblige the Spaniard but from *day* to *day*. *Bacon's War with Spain.*

TO-DAY. On this day.

To-day, if ye will hear his voice, harden not your hearts. *Ps.*

The past is all by death possest,
And frugal fate, that guards the rest,
By giving, bids us live *to-day*. *Fenton.*

DA'YBED. *n. s.* [*day* and *bed*.] A bed used for idleness and luxury in the daytime.

Calling my officers about me, in my branched velvet gown; having come down from a *daybed*, where I have left Olivia sleeping. *Shakespeare's Twelfth Night.*

DA'YBOOK. *n. s.* [from *day* and *book*.] A tradesman's journal; a book in which all the occurrences of the day are set down.

DA'YBREAK. *n. s.* [*day* and *break*.] The dawn; the first appearance of light.

I watch'd the early glories of her eyes,
As men for *daybreak* watch the Eastern skies. *Dryd. In. Emp.*

DAYLA'BOUR. *n. s.* [*day* and *labour*.] Labour by the day; labour divided into daily tasks.

Doth God exact *daylabour*, light deny'd,
I fondly ask. *Milton's Paradise Regained.*

Did either his legs or his arms fail him? No; but *daylabour* was but an hard and a dry kind of livelihood to a man, that could get an estate with two or three strokes of his pen. *South.*

DAYLA'BOURER. *n. s.* [from *daylabour*.] One that works by the day.

In one night, ere glimpse of morn,
His shadowy flail hath thresh'd the corn
That ten *daylabourers* could not end. *Milton.*

The *daylabourer*, in a country village, has commonly but a small pittance of courage. *Locke.*

DA'YLIGHT. *n. s.* [*day* and *light*.] The light of the day, as opposed to that of the morn, or a taper.

By this the drooping *daylight* 'gan to fade,
And yield his room to sad succeeding night. *Fairy Queen, b.* i.

Nay, then thou mock'st me: thou shalt buy this dear,
If ever I thy face by *daylight* see.
Now go thy way. *Shakesp. Midsummer-Night's Dream.*

They by *daylight* passing through the midst of the Turks fleet, safely recovered the haven, to the great joy of the besieged Christians. *Knolles's History of the Turks.*

He stands in *daylight*, and disdains to hide
An act, to which by honour he is ty'd. *Dryden.*

Will you murder a man in plain *daylight?* *Dryd. Sp. Fryar.*

Yet though rough bears in covert seek defence,
White foxes stay, with seeming innocence;
That crafty kind with *daylight* can dispense. *Dryden.*

If bodies be illuminated by the ordinary prismatick colours, they will appear neither of their own *daylight* colours, nor of the colour of the light cast on them, but of some middle colour between both. *Newton's Opt.*

DAY-LI'LY. *n. s.* The same with ASPHODEL, which see.

DA'YSMAN. *n. s.* [*day* and *man*.] An old word for umpire. *Ains.* Perhaps rather, surety.

For what art thou,
That mak'st thyself his *daysman*, to prolong
The vengeance prest? *Fairy Queen, b.* ii. *cant.* 8.

DA'YSPRING.

DA'YSPRING. *n. s.* [*day* and *spring*.] The rise of the day; the dawn; the first appearance of light.

So all ere *dayspring*, under conscious night,
Secret they finish'd, and in order set. *Milton's Parad. Lost.*
The breath of heav'n fresh-blowing, pure and sweet,
With *dayspring* born, here leave me to respire. *Milt. Agon.*

DA'YSTAR. *n. s.* [*day* and *star*.] The morning star.

I meant to make her fair, and free, and wise,
Of greatest blood, and yet more good than great:
I meant the *daystar* should not brighter rise,
Nor lend like influence from his lucent seat. *Ben. Johnson.*
Sunk though he be beneath the watry floor;
So sinks the *daystar* in the ocean bed,
And yet anon repairs his drooping head. *Milton.*

DA'YTIME. *n. s.* [*day* and *time*.] The time in which there is light, opposed to night.

In the *daytime* she sitteth in a watch-tower, and flieth most by night; that she mingleth things done with things not done, and that she is a terror to great cities. *Bacon, Essay* 60.

My ants never brought out their corn but in the night when the moon did shine, and kept it under ground in the *daytime*. *Addison's Guardian*, N° 156.

DA'YWORK. *n. s.* [*day* and *work*.] Work imposed by the day; day labour.

True labour in the vineyard of thy lord,
Ere prime thou hast th' imposed *daywork* done. *Fairfax.*

To DAZE. *v. a.* [ꝺƿæſ, Saxon.] To overpower with light; to strike with too strong lustre; to hinder the act of seeing by too much light suddenly introduced.

They smote the glistering armies as they stand,
With quiv'ring beams, which *daz'd* the wond'ring eye. *Fairfax, b.* i. *stan.* 73.
Poor human kind, all *daz'd* in open day,
Err after bliss, and blindly miss their way. *Dryden.*

DA'ZIED. *adj.* [rather *dasied*. See DASY.] Besprinkled with daisies.

Let us
Find out the prettiest *dazied* plot we can,
And make him a grave. *Shakespeare's Cymbeline.*

To DA'ZZLE. *v. a.* [See DAZE.]

1. To overpower with light; to hinder the action of the sight by sudden lustre.

Fears use, many times, to be represented in such an imaginary fashion, as they rather *dazzle* men's eyes than open them. *Bacon's War with Spain.*

How is it that some wits are interrupted;
That now they *dazzled* are, now clearly see? *Davies.*

The places that have either shining sentiments or manners, have no occasion for them: a *dazzling* expression rather damages them, and serves only to eclipse their beauty. *Pope.*

2. To strike or surprise with splendour.

Those heav'nly shapes
Will *dazzle* now this earthly, with their blaze
Insufferably bright. *Milton's Paradise Lost, b.* ix. *l.* 1083.
Ah, friend! to *dazzle* let the vain design;
To raise the thought, or touch the heart, be thine. *Pope.*

To DA'ZZLE. *v. n.* To be overpowered with light; to lose the power of sight.

Dazzle mine eyes? or do I see three suns? *Shak. Hen.* VI.
Come, boy, and go with me; thy sight is young,
And you shall read, when mine begins to *dazzle*. *Shakesp.*

An overlight maketh the eyes *dazzle*, insomuch as perpetual looking against the sun would cause blindness. *Bacon.*

Look, Dianet, for I dare not trust these eyes;
They dance in mists, and *dazzle* with surprise. *Dryd. Auren.*

DE'ACON. *n. s.* [*diaconus*, Latin.]

1. One of the lowest order of the clergy.

Likewise must the *deacons* be grave. 1 *Tim.* iii. 8.

The constitutions that the apostles made concerning *deacons* and widows, in those primitive times, are very importunely urged by the disciplinarians. *Bp. Sanderson's Judgment.*

2. [In Scotland.] An overseer of the poor.

3. And also the master of an incorporated company.

DE'ACONESS. *n. s.* [from *deacon*.] A female officer in the ancient church.

DE'ACONRY. } *n. s.* [from *deacon*.] The office or dignity of
DE'ACONSHIP. } a deacon.

DEAD. *adj.* [ꝺeaꝺ, Sax. *dood*, Dutch.]

1. Deprived of life; exanimated.

The queen, my lord, is *dead*:
——She should have died hereafter. *Shakesp. Macbeth.*

A brute or a man are another thing, when they are alive, from what they are when *dead*. *Hale's Origin of Mankind.*

She either from her hopeless lover fled,
Or with disdainful glances shot him *dead*. *Dryden.*

2. With *of* before the cause of death.

This Indian told them, that, mistaking their course, the crew, all except himself, were *dead of* hunger. *Arbuthnot.*

3. Without life; inanimate.

All, all but truth, drops *dead*-born from the press,
Like the last gazette, or the last address. *Pope, Dial.* ii.

4. Imitating death; senseless; motionless.

At thy rebuke, O God of Jacob, both the chariot and horse are cast into a *dead* sleep. *Ps.* lxxvi. 6.

Anointing of the forehead, neck, feet, and backbone, we know is used for procuring *dead* sleeps. *Bacon's Nat. History.*

5. Unactive; motionless.

The tin sold sometimes higher, and sometimes lower, according to the quick vent and abundance, or the *dead* sale and scarcety. *Carew's Survey of Cornwall.*

Nay, there's a time when ev'n the rolling year
Seems to stand still: *dead* calms are in the ocean,
When not a breath disturbs the drousy main. *Lee's Oedipus.*

They cannot bear the *dead* weight of unemployed time lying upon their hands, nor the uneasiness it is to do nothing at all. *Locke on Education, sect.* 207.

6. Empty; vacant.

This colour, nevertheless, often carries the mind away; yea, it deceiveth the sense; and it seemeth to the eye a shorter distance of way, if it be all *dead* and continued, than if it have trees or buildings, or any other marks whereby the eye may divide it. *Bacon's C l. of Good and Evil.*

Nought but a blank remains, and a *dead* void space,
A step of life, that promis'd such a race. *Dryden.*

7. Useless; unprofitable.

The commodities of the kingdom they took, though they lay *dead* upon their hands for want of vent. *Bacon's Hen.* VII.

Persuade a prince that he is irresistible, and he will take care not to let so glorious an attribute lie *dead* and useless by him. *Addison's Whig Examiner.*

8. Dull; gloomy; unemployed.

Travelling over the mountain Amanus, then covered with deep snow, they came in the *dead* Winter to Aleppo in Syria. *Knolles's History of the Turks.*

There is something unspeakably chearful in a spot of ground which is covered with trees, that smiles amidst all the rigours of Winter, and gives us a view of the most gay season in the midst of that which is the most *dead* and melancholy. *Add. Spect.*

9. Still; obscure.

Their flight was only deferred until they might cover their disorders by the *dead* darkness of the night. *Hayward.*

10. Having no resemblance of life.

At a second sitting, though I alter not the draught, I must touch the same features over again, and change the *dead* colouring of the whole. *Dryden's Fab. Preface.*

11. Obtuse; dull; not sprightly. Used of sounds.

We took a bell of about two inches in diameter at the bottom, which was supported, in the midst of the cavity of the receiver, by a bent stick, by reason of its spring against the opposite parts of the inside of the vessel; in which when it was closed up, we observed that the bell seemed to sound more *dead* than it did when just before it sounded in the open air. *Boyle's Spring of the Air.*

12. Dull; frigid; not animated; not affecting.

How cold and *dead* does a prayer appear, that is composed in the most elegant forms of speech, when it is not heightened by solemnity of phrase from the sacred writings. *Addis. Spect.*

13. Tasteless; vapid; spiritless: of liquors.

14. Uninhabited.

Somewhat is left under *dead* walls and dry ditches. *Arbuthn.*

15. Without the natural force or efficacy; as, *a* dead *fire*.

16. Without the power of vegetation; as, *a* dead *bough*.

17. [In theology.] The state of spiritual death, lying under the power of sin.

You hath he quickened, who were *dead* in trespasses and sins. *Ephes.* ii. 1.

The DEAD. *n. s.* Dead men.

Jove saw from high, with just disdain,
The *dead* inspir'd with vital life again. *Dryd. Æn. b.* vii.

The ancient Romans generally buried their *dead* near the great roads. *Addison's Remarks on Italy.*

That the *dead* shall rise and live again, is beyond the discovery of reason, and is purely a matter of faith. *Locke.*

The tow'ring bard had sung in nobler lays,
How the last trumpet wakes the lazy *dead*. *Smith.*

DEAD. *n. s.* Time in which there is remarkable stillness or gloom; as at midwinter, and midnight.

After this life, to hope for the favours of mercy then, is to expect an harvest in the *dead* of winter. *South's Sermons.*

In the *dead* of the night, when the men and their dogs were all fast asleep. *L'Estrange.*

At length, in *dead* of night, the ghost appears
Of her unhappy lord. *Dryden's Virg. Æn.*

To DEAD. *v. n.* [from the noun.] To lose force, of whatever kind.

So iron, as soon as it is out of the fire, *deadeth* straitways. *Bacon's Natural History*, N°. 774.

To DEAD. } *v. a.*
To DE'ADEN. }

1. To deprive of any kind of force or sensation.

That the sound may be extinguished or *deaded* by discharging the pent air, before it cometh to the mouth of the piece, and to the open air, is not probable. *Bacon's Nat. Hist.*

It is requisite that the tympanum be tense, and hard stretched,

ſtretched, otherwiſe the laxneſs of that membrane will certainly *d ad* and damp the ſound. *Holder's Elements of Speech.*

This motion would be quickly *deadened* by countermotions; and we ſhould not remember any thing, but 'till the next impreſſion. *Glanv. Sceps. c.* 6.

We will not oppoſe any thing to them that is hard and ſtubborn, but by a ſoft anſwer *deaden* their force by degrees. *Burnet's Theory of the Earth.*

Our dreams are great inſtances of that activity which is natural to the human ſoul, and which is not in the power of ſleep to *deaden* or abate. *Spectator*, Nº. 487.

Anodyne, or abaters of pain, are ſuch things as relax the tenſion of the affected nervous fibres, or deſtroy the particular acrimony which occaſions the pain, or what *deadens* the ſenſation of the brain by procuring ſleep. *Arbuthnot on Diet.*

2. To make vapid, or ſpiritleſs.

The beer and the wine, as well within water as above, have not been palled or *deaded* at all. *Bacon's Natural Hiſtory.*

DEAD-DOING. *participial adj.* [*dead* and *do.*] Deſtructive; killing; miſchievous; having the power to make dead.

Hold, O dear lord, your *dead-doing* hand;
Then loud he cry'd, I am your humble thrall. *Fai. Queen.*

They never care how many others
They kill, without regard of mothers,
Or wives or children, ſo they can
Make up ſome fierce, *dead-doing* man. *Hudibras, p.* i. *can.* 11.

DEAD-LIFT. *n. ſ.* [*dead* and *lift.*] Hopeleſs exigence.

And have no power at all, nor ſhift,
To help itſelf at a *dead-lift.* *Hudibras, p.* ii. *cant.* 2.

DE'ADLY. *adj.* [from *dead.*]

1. Deſtructive; mortal; murtherous.

She that herſelf will ſhiver and diſbranch
From her material ſap, perforce muſt wither,
And come to *deadly* uſe. *Shakeſpeare's King Lear.*

She then on Romeo calls,
As if that name,
Shot from the *deadly* level of a gun,
Did murther her. *Shakeſpeare's Romeo and Juliet.*

Dry mourning will decay more *deadly* bring,
As a North wind burns a too forward Spring;
Give ſorrow vent, and let the ſluices go. *Dryden's Aurengb.*

2. Mortal; implacable.

The Numidians, in number infinite, are *deadly* enemies unto the Turks. *Knolles's Hiſtory of the Turks.*

DE'ADLY *adv.*

1. In a manner reſembling the dead.

Like dumb ſtatues, or unbreathing ſtones,
Star'd each on other, and look'd *deadly* pale. *Shakeſp. R.* III.

Young Arcite heard, and up he ran with haſte,
And aſk'd him why he look'd ſo *deadly* wan. *Dryd. Fables.*

2. Mortally.

I will break Pharaoh's arms, and he ſhall groan before him with the groanings of a *deadly* wounded man. *Ez.* xxx. 24.

3. Implacably; irreconcileably; deſtructively.

4. It is ſometimes uſed in a ludicrous ſenſe, only to enforce the ſignification of a word.

Mettled ſchoolboys ſet to cuff,
Will not confeſs that they have done enough,
Though *deadly* weary. *Orrery.*

John had got an impreſſion, that Lewis was ſo *deadly* cunning a man, that he was afraid to venture himſelf alone with him. *Arbuthnot's Hiſtory of John Bull.*

DE'ADNESS. *n. ſ.* [from *dead.*]

1. Frigidity; want of warmth; want of ardour; want of affection.

His grace removes the defect of inclination, by taking of our natural *deadneſs* and diſaffection towards them. *Rogers.*

2. Weakneſs of the vital powers; languour; faintneſs; inactivity of the ſpirits.

Your gloomy eyes betray a *deadneſs*,
And inward languiſhing. *Dryd. and Lee's Oedipus.*

3. Vapidneſs of liquors; loſs of ſpirit.

Deadneſs or flatneſs in cyder is often occaſioned by the too free admiſſion of air into the veſſels. *Mortimer's Husbandry.*

DE'ADNETTLE. *n. ſ.* A weed; the ſame with archangel.

DEAD RECKONING. *n. ſ.* [a ſea-term.] That eſtimation or conjecture which the ſeamen make of the place where a ſhip is, by keeping an account of her way by the log, by knowing the courſe they have ſteered by the compaſs, and by rectifying all with allowance for drift or lee-way; ſo that this reckoning is without any obſervation of the ſun, moon, and ſtars, and is to be rectified as often as any good obſervation can be had.

DEAF. *adj.* [*doof*, Dutch.]

1. Wanting the ſenſe of hearing.

Come on my right hand, for this ear is *deaf. Shakeſpeare.*

Infected minds
To their *deaf* pillows will diſcharge their ſecrets. *Shak. Mac.*

The chief deſign here intended by this account of the natural alphabet, is to prepare a more eaſy and expedite way to inſtruct ſuch as are *deaf* and dumb, and dumb only by conſequence of their want of hearing. *Holder's Elem of Speech.*

If any ſins afflict our life
With that prime ill, a talking wife,
'Till death ſhall bring the kind relief,
We muſt be patient, or be *deaf.* *Prior.*

Thus you may ſtill be young to me,
While I can better hear than ſee:
Oh ne'er may fortune ſhew her ſpight,
To make me *deaf*, and mend my ſight. *Swift.*

2. It has *to* before the thing that ought to be heard.

I will be *deaf to* pleading and excuſes;
Nor tears, nor prayers ſhall purchaſe out abuſes. *Shakeſpeare.*

Oh, that men's ears ſhould be
To counſel *deaf*, but not *to* flattery! *Shakeſpeare's Timon.*

Whilſt virtue courts them; but, alas, in vain:
Fly from her kind embracing arms,
Deaf to her fondeſt call, blind to her greateſt charms. *Roſc.*

Not ſo, for once indulg'd, they ſweep the main;
Deaf to the call, or, hearing, hear in vain. *Dryden.*

Hope, too long with vain deluſion fed,
Deaf to the rumour of fallacious fame,
Gives to the roll of death his glorious name. *Pope's Odyſſey.*

3. Deprived of the power of hearing.

Deaf with the noiſe, I took my haſty flight:
No mortal courage can ſupport the fright. *Dryd. Ind. Emp.*

4. Obſcurely heard.

Nor ſilence is within, nor voice expreſs,
But a *deaf* noiſe of ſounds that never ceaſe;
Confus'd and chiding, like the hollow roar
Of tides, receding from th' inſulted ſhoar. *Dryden.*

The reſt were ſeiz'd with ſullen diſcontent,
And a *deaf* murmur through the ſquadrons went. *Dryden.*

To DEAF. *v. a.* To deprive of the power of hearing.

Hearing hath *deaf'd* our ſailors; and if they
Know how to hear, there's none know what to ſay. *Donne.*

A ſwarm of their aerial ſhapes appears,
And, flutt'ring round his temples, *deafs* his ears. *Dryd. Æn.*

To DE'AFEN. *v. a.* [from *deaf.*] To deprive of the power of hearing.

But Salius enters; and exclaiming loud,
For juſtice *deafens*, and diſturbs the crowd. *Dryden's Virgil.*

From ſhouting men, and horns, and dogs, he flies,
Deafen'd and ſtunn'd with their promiſcuous cries. *Addiſon.*

DE'AFLY. *adv.* [from *deaf.*]

1. Without ſenſe of ſounds.

2. Obſcurely to the ear.

DE'AFNESS. *n. ſ.* [from *deaf.*] Want of the power of hearing; want of ſenſe of ſounds.

Thoſe who are deaf and dumb, are dumb by conſequence from their *deafneſs.* *Holder's Elements of Speech.*

The Dunciad had never been writ, but at his requeſt, and for his *deafneſs*; for had he been able to converſe with me, do you think I had amuſed my time ſo ill? *Pope.*

2. Unwillingneſs to hear.

I found ſuch a *deafneſs*, that no declaration from the biſhops could take place. *King Charles.*

DEAL. *n. ſ.* [*deel*, Dutch.]

1. Part.

A great *deal* of that which had been, was now to be removed out of the church. *Hooker, b.* 4. *ſect.* 14.

2. Quantity; degree of more or leſs. It is a general word for expreſſing *much* joined with the word *great.*

When men's affections do frame their opinions, they are in defence of errour more earneſt a great *deal* than, for the moſt part, ſound believers in the maintainance of truth, apprehending according to the nature of that evidence which ſcripture yieldeth. *Hooker, Preface.*

There is, indeed, ſtore of matters, fitter and better a great *deal* for teachers to ſpend time and labour in. *Hooker, b.* iv.

To weep with them that weep, doth eaſe ſome *deal*;
But ſorrow, flouted at, is double death. *Shakeſ. Tit. Andron.*

What a *deal* of cold buſineſs doth a man miſpend the better part of life in! In ſcattering compliments, and tendering viſits. *Ben. Johnſon's Diſcoveries.*

The charge, ſome *deal* thee haply honour may,
That noble Dudone had while here he liv'd. *Fairfax, b.* v.

Poſſibly ſome never ſo much as doubted of the ſafety of their ſpiritual eſtate; and, if ſo, let them reſt aſſured, that they have ſo much the more reaſon a great *deal* to doubt of it. *South's Sermons.*

The author, who knew that ſuch a deſign as this could not be carried on without a great *deal* of artifice and ſophiſtry, has puzzled and perplexed his cauſe, by throwing his thoughts together in a ſtudied confuſion. *Addiſon's Freeholder*, Nº. 31.

3. The art or practice of dealing cards.

How can the muſe her aid ſupport,
Unſkill'd in all the terms of art!
Or in harmonious numbers put
The *deal*, the ſhuffle, and the cut. *Swift.*

4. [*deyl*, Dutch.] Firwood; the wood of pines.

I have alſo found, that a piece of *deal*, far thicker than one would eaſily imagine, being purpoſely interpoſed betwixt my eye, placed in a room; and the clearer daylight was not

only

only somewhat transparent, but appeared quite through a lovely red. *Boyle on Colours.*

To DEAL. *v. a.* [*deelen*, Dutch.]

1. To distribute; to dispose to different persons.

Deal thy bread to the hungry, and bring the poor that are cast out, to thy house. *Isa.* lviii. 7.

One with a broken truncheon *deals* his blows. *Dryd. Fab.*

The business of mankind in this life, being rather to act than to know, their portion of knowledge is *dealt* them accordingly. *Addison's Spectator*, N°. 237.

How Spain prepares her banners to unfold,
And Rome *deals* out her blessings and her gold. *Tickell.*

Had the philosophers and great men of antiquity been possessed of the art of printing, there is no question but they would have made an advantage of it, in *dealing* out their lectures to the publick. *Addison's Spectator*, N°. 184.

If you *deal* out great quantities of strong liquor to the mob, there will be many drunk. *Watts's Improvement of the Mind.*

2. To scatter; to throw about.

Keep me from the vengeance of thy darts,
Which Niobe's devoted issue felt,
When hissing through the skies, the feather'd deaths were *dealt*. *Dryden's Fables.*

3. To give gradually, or one after another.

The nightly mallet *deals* resounding blows,
'Till the proud battlements her tow'rs inclose. *Gay.*

His lifted arms around his head he throws,
And *deals*, in whistling air, his empty blows. *Dryd. Virgil.*

To DEAL. *v. n.*

1. To traffick; to transact business; to trade.

It is generally better to *deal* by speech than by letter; and by the mediation of a third, than by a man himself. *Bacon.*

This is to drive a wholesale trade, when all other petty merchants *deal* but for parcels. *Decay of Piety.*

They buy and sell, they *deal* and traffick. *South.*

2. To act between two persons; to intervene.

Sometimes he that *deals* between man and man, raiseth his own credit with both, by pretending greater interest than he hath in either. *Bacon, Essay* 55.

3. To behave well or ill in any transaction.

I doubt not, if he will *deal* clearly and impartially, but that he will acknowledge all this to be true. *Tillotson's Sermons.*

4. To act in any manner.

Two deep enemies,
Foes to my rest, and my sweet sleep's disturbers,
Are they that I would have thee *deal* upon. *Shakesp. R.* III.

5. *To* DEAL *by.* To treat well or ill.

Such an one *deals* not fairly *by* his own mind, nor conducts his own understanding aright. *Locke.*

6. *To* DEAL *in.* To have to do with; to be engaged in; to practise.

Suiters are so distasted with delays and abuses, that plain-dealing, in denying to *deal in* suits at first, is grown not only honourable, but also gracious. *Bacon, Essay* 59.

The Scripture forbids even the countenancing a poor man in his cause; which is a popular way of preventing justice, that some men have *dealt in*, though without that success which they proposed to themselves in it. *Atterbury's Sermons.*

Among all sets of authors, there are none who draw upon themselves more displeasure than those who *deal in* political matters. *Addison's Freeholder*, N°. 40.

True logick is not that noisy thing that *deals* all *in* dispute and wrangling, to which the former ages had debased and confined it. *Watts's Logick.*

7. *To* DEAL *with.* To treat in any manner; to use well or ill.

Neither can the Irish, nor yet the English lords, think themselves wronged, nor hardly *dealt with*, to have that which is none of their own given to them. *Spenser's Ireland.*

Who then shall guide
His people? Who defend? Will they not *deal*
Worse *with* his followers, than *with* him they *dealt? Milton.*

If a man would have his conscience *deal* clearly *with* him, he must *deal* severely *with* that. *South's Sermons.*

God did not only exercise this providence towards his own people, but he *dealt* thus also *with* other nations. *Tillotson.*

But I will *deal* the more civilly *with* his two poems, because nothing ill is to be spoken of the dead. *Dryd. Fab. Preface.*

You wrote to me with the freedom of a friend, *dealing* plainly *with* me in the matter of my own trifles. *Pope.*

Reflect on the merits of the cause, as well as of the men, who had been thus *dealt with* by their country. *Swift.*

8. *To* DEAL *with.* To contend with.

If she hated me, I should know what passion to *deal with*. *Sidney, b.* ii.

Gentlemen were commanded to remain in the country, to govern the people, easy to be *dealt with* whilst they stand in fear. *Hayward.*

Then you upbraid me; I am pleas'd to see
You're not so perfect, but can fail like me:
I have no God to *deal with*. *Dryden's Aurengzebe.*

To DEA'LBATE. *v. a.* [*dealbo*, Lat.] To whiten; to bleach.

DEALBA'TION. *n. s.* [*dealbatio*, Lat.] The act of bleaching or whitening; rendering things white, which were not so before: a word which is now almost grown into disuse.

All seed is white in viviparous animals, and such as have preparing vessels, wherein it receives a manifold *dealbation*. *Brown's Vulgar Errours, b.* vi. *c.* 10.

DE'ALER. *n. s.* [from *deal.*]

1. One that has to do with any thing.

I find it common with these small *dealers* in wit and learning, to give themselves a title from their first adventure. *Swift.*

2. A trader or trafficker.

Where fraud is permitted and connived at, the honest *dealer* is always undone, and the knave gets the advantage. *Gulliver's Travels.*

3. A person who deals the cards.

DE'ALING. *n. s.* [from *deal.*]

1. Practice; action.

What these are!
Whose own hard *dealings* teach them to suspect
The thoughts of others. *Shakespeare's Merchant of Venice.*

Concerning the *dealings* of men, who adminster government, and unto whom the execution of that law belongeth, they have their judge, who sitteth in heaven. *Hooker, b.* ii.

But this was neither one pope's fault, nor one prince's destiny: he must write a story of the empire, that means to tell of all their *dealings* in this kind. *Raleigh's Essays.*

2. Intercourse.

It were to be wished, that men would promote it to the happiness of one another, in all their private *dealings*, among those who lie more immediately within their influence. *Addis.*

3. Measure of treatment; rules by which one treats another.

God's gracious *dealings* with men, are the aids and auxiliaries necessary to us in the pursuit of piety. *Hammond's Fundam.*

4. Traffick; business.

The doctor must needs die rich; he had great *dealings* in his way for many years. *Swift's Bickerstaff detected.*

DEAMBULA'TION. *n. s.* [*deambulatio*, Latin.] The act of walking abroad.

DEA'MBULATORY. *adj.* [*deambulo*, Latin.] Relating to the practice of walking abroad.

DEAN. *n. s.* [*decanus*, Latin; *doyen*, French.]

From the Greek word δέκα; in English, ten; because he was anciently set over ten canons or prebendaries at least in some cathedral church. *Ayliffe's Parergon.*

As there are two foundations of cathedral churches in England, the old and the new, (the new are those which Henry VIII. upon suppression of abbeys, transformed from abbot or prior, and convent to dean and chapter) so there are two means of creating these *deans*; for those of the old foundation are brought to their dignity much like bishops, the king first sending out his *Congé d'elire* to the chapter, the chapter then chusing, the king yielding his royal assent, and the bishop confirming them, and giving his mandate to instal them. Those of the new foundation are, by a shorter course, installed by virtue of the king's letters patents, without either election or confirmation. This word is also applied to divers, that are chief of certain peculiar churches or chapels; as the *dean* of the king's chapel, the *dean* of the Arches, the *dean* of St. George's chapel at Windsor, and the *dean* of Bocking in Essex. *Cowel.*

The *dean* and canons, or prebends of cathedral churches, in their first institution, were of great use in the church: they were not only to be of counsel with the bishop for his revenue, but chiefly for his government in causes ecclesiastical. Use your best means to prefer such to those places who are fit for that purpose. *Bacon's Advice to Villiers.*

DE'ANERY. *n. s.* [from *dean.*]

1. The office of a dean.

When he could no longer keep the *deanery* of the chapel-royal, he made him his successor in that near attendance upon the king. *Clarendon.*

2. The revenue of a dean.

Put both deans in one; or, if that's too much trouble,
Instead of the deans, make the *dean'ry* double. *Swift.*

3. The house of a dean.

Take her by the hand, away with her to the *deanery*, and dispatch it quickly. *Shakespeare's Merry Wives of Windsor.*

DE'ANSHIP. *n. s.* [from *dean.*] The office and rank of a dean.

DEAR. *adj.* [ꝺeoꞃ, Saxon.]

1. Beloved; favourite; darling.

Your brother Glo'ster hates you.
—Oh, no, he loves me, and he holds me *dear*. *Shak. R.* III.

The *dear*, *dear* name she bathes in flowing tears,
Hangs o'er the tomb. *Addison's Ovid. Metam. b.* ii.

And the last joy was *dearer* than the rest. *Pope.*

2. Valuable; of a high price; costly.

What made directors cheat the South sea year?
To feed on ven'son when it sold so *dear*. *Pope.*

3. Scarce; not plentiful; as, *a dear year*.

4. It seems to be sometimes used in *Shakespeare* for *deer*; sad; hateful; grievous.

What foolish boldness brought thee to their mercies,
Whom

Whom thou in terms so bloody, and so *dear*,
Hast made thine enemies? *Shakespeare's Twelfth Night.*
Let us return,
And strain what other means is left unto us
In our *dear* peril. *Shakespeare's Timon.*
Some *dear* cause
Will in concealment wrap me up a-while:
When I am known aright, you shall not grieve
Lending me this acquaintance. *Shakespeare's King Lear.*
Would I had met my *dearest* foe in heav'n,
Or ever I had seen that day. *Shakespeare's Hamlet.*
Thy other banish'd son, with this *dear* sight
Struck pale and bloodless. *Shakespeare's Titus Andronicus.*

DEAR. *n. s.* A word of endearment.
That kiss
I carried from thee, *dear*; and my true lip
Hath virgin'd it e'er since. *Shakespeare's Coriolanus.*
Go, *dear*; each minute does new danger bring. *Dryden.*
See, my *dear*,
How lavish nature has adorn'd the year. *Dryden.*

DE'ARBOUGHT. *adj.* [*dear* and *bought.*] Purchased at an high price.
O fleeting joys
Of Paradise, *dearbought* with lasting woe. *Milton's Par. Lost.*
Such *dearbought* blessings happen ev'ry day,
Because we know not for what things to pray. *Dryd. Fables.*
Forget not what my ransom cost,
Nor let my *dearbought* soul be lost. *Roscommon.*

DE'ARLING. *n. s.* [now written *darling.*] Favourite.
They do feed on nectar, heavenly wise,
With Hercules and Hebe, and the rest
Of Venus's *dearlings*, through her bounty blest. *Spenser.*

DE'ARLY. *adv.* [from *dear.*]
1. With great fondness.
For the unquestionable virtues of her person and mind, he loved her *dearly*. *Wotton.*
2. At an high price.
It is rarely bought, and then also bought *dearly* enough with such a fine. *Bacon.*
Turnus shall *dearly* pay for faith forsworn;
And corps, and swords, and shields, on Tyber born. *Dryd.*
My father dotes, and let him still dote on;
He buys his mistress *dearly* with his throne. *Dryd. Aurengz.*

To DEARN. *v. a.* [ꝺẏꝛnan, Sax. to hide.] To mend cloaths. See DARN.

DE'ARNESS. *n. s.* [from *dear.*]
1. Fondness; kindness; love.
My brother, I think, he holds you well, and in *dearness* of heart hath holp to effect your ensuing marriage. *Shakespeare.*
The whole senate dedicated an altar to friendship, as to a goddess, in respect of the great *dearness* of friendship between them two. *Bacon, Essay* 28.
He who hates his neighbour mortally, and wisely too, must profess all the *dearness* and friendship, with readiness to serve him. *Sonth's Sermons.*
2. Scarcity; high price.
Landlords prohibit tenants from plowing, which is seen in the *dearness* of corn. *Swift.*

DE'ARNLY. *adv.* [ꝺeoꝛn, Sax.] Secretly; privately; unseen. Obsolete.
At last, as chanc'd them by a forrest side
To pass, for succour from the scorching ray,
They heard a rueful voice, that *dearnly* cry'd
With piercing shrieks. *Fairy Queen, b.* ii. *cant.* 1. *stan.* 35.

DEARTH. *n. s.* [from *dear.*]
1. Scarcity which makes food dear.
In times of *dearth* it drained much coin out of the kingdom, to furnish us with corn from foreign parts. *Bacon to Villiers.*
There have been terrible years *dearths* of corn, and every place is strewed with beggars; but *dearths* are common in better climates, and our evils here lie much deeper. *Swift.*
2. Want; need; famine.
Pity the *dearth* that I have pined in,
By longing for that food so long a time. *Shakespeare.*
Of every tree that in the garden grows,
Eat freely with glad heart; fear here no *dearth*. *Milt. P. L.*
3. Barrenness; sterility.
They have brought on themselves that *dearth* of plot, and narrowness of imagination, which may be observed in all their plays. *Dryden on Dramatick Poesy.*

To DEARTI'CULATE. *n. s.* [*de* and *articulus*, Latin.] To disjoint; to dismember. *Dict.*

DEATH. *n. s.* [ꝺeaꝥ, Saxon.]
1. The extinction of life; the departure of the soul from the body.
He is the mediator of the New Testament, that by means of *death*, for the redemption of the transgressions, they which are called might receive the promise of eternal inheritance. *Heb.* ix. 15.
They say there is divinity in odd numbers, either in nativity or *death*. *Shakes. Merry Wives of Windsor.*
Death, a necessary end,
Will come, when it will come. *Shakesp. Julius Cæsar.*
He must his acts reveal,
From the first moment of his vital breath,
To his last hour of unrepenting *death*. *Dryden's Æn. b.* 6.
2. Mortality; destruction.
How did you dare
To trade and traffick with Macbeth,
In riddles and affairs of death? *Shakespeare's Macbeth.*
3. The state of the dead.
In swinish sleep
Their drenched natures lie, as in a *death*. *Shakes. Macbeth.*
4. The manner of dying.
Thou shalt die the *deaths* of them that are slain in the midst of the seas. *Ez.* xxviii. 8.
5. The image of mortality represented by a skeleton.
I had rather be married to a *death*'s head, with a bone in his mouth, than to either of these. *Shakes. Merch. of Venice.*
If I gaze now, 'tis but to see
What manner of *death*'s head 'twill be,
When it is free
From that fresh upper skin;
The gazer's joy, and sin. *Suckling.*
6. Murder, the act of destroying life unlawfully.
As in manifesting the sweet influence of his mercy, on the severe stroke of his justice; so in this, not to suffer a man of *death* to live. *Bacon, Essay* 14.
7. Cause of death.
They cried out, and said, O thou man of God, there is *death* in the pot. 2 *Kings*, iv. 40.
He caught his *death* the last county-sessions, where he would go to see justice done to a poor widow woman. *Addis. Spectat.*
8. Destroyer.
All the endeavours Achilles used to meet with Hector, and be the *death* of him, is the intrigue which comprehends the battle of the last day. *Pope's View of Epic Poetry.*
9. [In poetry.] The instrument of death.
Deaths invisible come wing'd with fire;
They hear a dreadful noise, and straight expire. *Dry. In. Em.*
Sounded at once the bow; and swiftly flies
The feather'd *death*, and hisses through the skies. *Dryd. Æn.*
Oft, as in airy rings they skim the Heath,
The clam'rous plovers feel the leaden *death*. *Pope.*
10. [In theology.] Damnation; eternal torments.
We pray that God will keep us from all sin and wickedness, from our ghostly enemy, and from everlasting *death*. *Church Catechism.*

DEATH-BED. *n. s.* [*death* and *bed.*] The bed to which a man is confined by mortal sickness.
Sweet soul, take heed, take heed of perjury;
Thou art on thy *death-bed*. *Shakespeare's Othello.*
Thy *death-bed* is no lesser than the land,
Wherein thou liest in reputation sick. *Shakes. Richard* II.
These are such things as a man shall remember with joy upon his *death-bed*; such as shall chear and warm his heart, even in that last and bitter agony. *South's Sermons.*
Then round our *death-bed* ev'ry friend should run,
And joyous of our conquest early won. *Dryden's Fables.*
A *death-bed* figure is certainly the most humbling sight in the world. *Collier on the Value of Life.*
A *death-bed* repentance ought not indeed to be neglected, because it is the last thing that we can do. *Atterbury's Serm.*
Fame can never make us lie down contentedly on a *death-bed*. *Pope.*

DE'ATHFUL. *adj.* [*death* and *full.*] Full of slaughter; destructive; murderous.
Your cruelty was such, as you would spare his life for many *deathful* torments. *Sidney, b.* ii.
Time itself, under the *deathful* shade of whose wings all things wither, hath wasted that lively virtue of nature in man and beasts, and plants. *Raleigh's History of the World.*
Blood, death, and *deathful* deeds are in that noise,
Ruin, destruction at the utmost point. *Milton's Agonist.*
These eyes behold
The *deathful* scene; princes on princes roll'd. *Pope's Odyss.*

DE'ATHLESS. *adj.* [from *death.*] Immortal; neverdying; everlasting.
God hath only immortality, though angels and human souls be *deathless*. *Boyle.*
Their temples wreath'd with leaves, that still renew;
For *deathless* laurel is the victor's due. *Dryden.*
Faith and hope themselves shall die,
While *deathless* charity remains. *Prior.*

DE'ATHLIKE. *adj.* [*death* and *like.*] Resembling death; still; gloomy; motionless; placid; calm; peaceful; undisturbed; resembling either the horrours or the quietness of death.
Why dost thou let thy brave soul lie supprest
In *deathlike* slumbers, while thy dangers crave
A waking eye and hand? *Crashaw.*
A *deathlike* sleep!
A gentle wafting to immortal life! *Milton's Paradise Lost.*
On seas, on earth, and all that in them dwell,
A *deathlike* quiet and deep silence fell. *Waller.*

Black

Black melancholy fits, and round her throws
A *deathlike* slumber, and a dread repose. *Pope.*

DEATH'S-DOOR. [*death* and *door.*] A near approach to death; the gates of death, πύλαι ἅδε. It is now a low phrase.

I myself knew a person of great sanctity, who was afflicted to *death's-door* with a vomiting. *Taylor's Worthy Communicant.*

There was a poor young woman that had brought herself even to *death's-door* with grief for her sick husband. *L'Estrange.*

DE'ATHSMAN. *n. s.* [*death* and *man.*] Executioner; hangman; headsman; he that executes the sentence of death.

He's dead; I'm only sorry
He had no other *deathsman*. *Shakespeare's King Lear.*

As *deathsmen* you have rid this sweet young prince. *Shak.*

DE'ATHWATCH. *n. s.* [*death* and *watch.*] An insect that makes a tinkling noise like that of a watch, and is superstitiously imagined to prognosticate death.

The solemn *deathwatch* click'd the hour she dy'd. *Gay.*

We learn to presage approaching death in a family by ravens and little worms, which we therefore call a *deathwatch*. *Watts.*

To DEA'URATE. *v. a.* [*deauro*, Latin.] To gild, or cover with gold. *Dict.*

DEAURA'TION. *n. s.* [from *deaurate.*] The act of gilding.

DEBACCHA'TION. *n. s.* [*debacchatio*, Latin.] A raging; a madness. *Dict.*

To DEBA'RB. *adj.* [from *de* and *barba*, Latin.] To deprive of his beard. *Dict.*

To DEBA'RK *v. a.* [*debarquer*, Fr.] To disembark. *Dict.*

To DEBA'R. *v. a.* [from *bar.*] To exclude; to preclude; to shut out from any thing; to hinder.

The same boats and the same buildings are found in countries two thousand miles distant, *debarred* from all commerce by unpassable mountains, lakes and deserts. *Raleigh's Essays.*

Not so strictly hath our Lord impos'd
Labour, as to *debar* us when we need
Refreshment, whether food, or talk between,
Food of the mind. *Milton's Paradise Lost, b.* ix. *l.* 236.

Civility, intended to make us easy, is employed in laying chains and fetters upon us, in *debarring* us of our wishes, and in crossing our most reasonable desires. *Swift's Examiner.*

To DEBA'SE. *v. a.* [from *base.*]

1. To reduce from a higher to a lower state.

Homer intended to teach, that pleasure and sensuality *debase* men into beasts. *Notes on the Odyssey.*

As much as you raise silver, you *debase* gold; for they are in the condition of two things, put in opposite scales; as much as the one rises, the other falls. *Locke.*

2. To make mean; to degenerate; to sink into meanness; to make despicable.

It is a kind of taking God's name in vain, to *debase* religion with such frivolous disputes. *Hooker, b.* v. *sect.* 30.

A man of large possessions has not leisure to consider of every slight expence, and will not *debase* himself to the management of every trifle. *Dryden.*

Restraining others, yet himself not free;
Made impotent by pow'r, *debas'd* by dignity. *Dryden.*

3. To sink; to vitiate with meanness.

He ought to be careful of not letting his subject *debase* his style, and betray him into a meanness of expression. *Addison.*

4. To adulterate; to lessen in value by base admixtures.

He reformed the coin, which was much adulterated and *debased* in the times and troubles of king Stephen. *Hale.*

Words so *debas'd* and hard, no stone
Was hard enough to touch them on. *Hudibras, p.* i. *cant.* 1.

DEBA'SEMENT. *n. s.* [from *debase.*] The act of debasing or degrading.

It is a wretched *debasement* of that sprightly faculty, the tongue, thus to be made the interpreter to a goat or boar. *Government of the Tongue, sect.* 12.

DEBA'SER. *n. s.* [from *debase.*] He that debases; he that adulterates; he that degrades another; he that sinks the value of things, or destroys the dignity of persons.

DEBA'TABLE. *adj.* [from *debate.*] Disputable; that which is, or may be, subject to controversy.

The French requested, that the fishing of Tweede, the *debatable* ground, and the Scottish hostages, might be restored to the Scots. *Hayward.*

A DEBA'TE. *n. s.* [*debat*, French.]

1. A personal dispute; a controversy.

Another way that men ordinarily use, to force others to submit to their judgments, and receive their opinion in *debate*, is to require the adversary to admit what they allege as a proof, or to assign a better. *Locke.*

It is to diffuse a light over the understanding, in our enquiries after truth, and not to furnish the tongue with *debate* and controversy. *Watts's Logick.*

2. A quarrel; a contest.

Now, lords, if heav'n doth give successful end
To this *debate* that bleedeth at our doors,
We will our youth lead on to higher fields,
And draw no swords but what are sanctified. *Shak. H.* IV.

'Tis thine to ruin realms, o'erturn a state;
Betwixt the dearest friends to raise *debate*. *Dryden's Æn.*

To DEBA'TE. *v. a.* [*debatre*, French.] To controvert; to dispute; to contest.

Debate thy cause with thy neighbour himself, and discover not a secret to another. *Prov.* xxv. 9.

He could not *debate* any thing without some commotion, even when the argument was not of moment. *Clarendon.*

To DEBATE. *v. n.*

1. To deliberate.

Your sev'ral suits
Have been consider'd and *debated* on. *Shakesp. Henry* VI.

2. To dispute.

He presents that great soul *debating* upon the subject of life and death with his intimate friends. *Tatler,* Nº. 53.

DEBA'TEFUL. *adj.* [from *debate.*]

1. [Of persons.] Quarrelsome; contentious.

2. [Of things.] Contested; occasioning quarrels.

DEBA'TEMENT. *n. s.* [from *debate.*] Contest; controversy.

Without *debatement* further, more or less,
He should the bearers put to sudden death. *Shakesp. Hamlet.*

DEBA'TER. *n. s.* [from *debate.*] A disputant; a controvertist.

To DEBA'UCH. [*desbaucher*, Fr. *debacchari*, Latin.]

1. To corrupt; to vitiate.

This it is to counsel things that are unjust; first, to *debauch* a king to break his laws, and then to seek protection. *Dryden's Spanish Fryar.*

2. To corrupt with lewdness.

Here do you keep a hundred knights and squires,
Men so disorder'd, so *debauch'd* and bold,
That this our court, infected with their manners,
Shews like a riotous inn. *Shakespeare's King Lear.*

3. To corrupt by intemperance.

No man's reason did ever dictate to him, that it is reasonable for him to *debauch* himself by intemperance and brutish sensuality. *Tillotson, Sermon* 6.

DEBA'UCH. *n. s.* [from the verb.] A fit of intemperance; luxury; excess; lewdness.

He will for some time contain himself within the bounds of sobriety; 'till within a little while he recovers his former *debauch*, and is well again, and then his appetite returns. *Calamy.*

The first physicians by *debauch* were made;
Excess began, and sloth sustains the trade. *Dryden's Fables.*

DEBAUCHE'E. *n. s.* [from *desbauché*, French.] A lecher; a drunkard; a man given to intemperance.

Could we but prevail with the greatest *debauchees* amongst us to change their lives, we should find it no very hard matter to change their judgments. *South's Sermons.*

DEBA'UCHER. *n. s.* [from *debauch.*] One who seduces others to intemperance or lewdness; a corrupter.

DEBA'UCHERY. *n. s.* [from *debauch.*] The practice of excess; intemperance; lewdness.

Oppose vices by their contrary virtues, hypocrisy by sober piety, and *debauchery* by temperance. *Sprat's Sermons.*

These magistrates, instead of lessening enormities, occasion just twice as much *debauchery* as there would be without them. *Swift's Project for the Advancement of Religion.*

DEBA'UCHMENT. *n. s.* [from *debauch.*] The act of debauching or vitiating; corruption.

They told them ancient stories of the ravishment of chaste maidens, or the *debauchment* of nations, or the extreme poverty of learned persons. *Taylor's Rule of living holy.*

To DEBE'L. } *v. a.* [*debello*, Latin.] To conquer; to
To DEBE'LLATE. } overcome in war.

It doth notably set forth the consent of all nations and ages, in the approbation of the extirpating and *debellating* of giants, monsters, and foreign tyrants, not only as lawful, but as meritorious even of divine honour. *Bacon's Holy War.*

Him long of old
Thou didst *debel*, and down from heaven cast
With all his army. *Milton's Paradise Regained, b.* iv.

DEBELLA'TION. *n. s.* [from *debellatio*, Lat.] The act of conquering in war.

DEBE'NTURE. *n. s.* [*debentur*, Latin, from *debeo.*] A writ or note, by which a debt is claimed.

You modern wits, should each man bring his claim,
Have desperate *debentures* on your fame;
And little would be left you, I'm afraid,
If all your debts to Greece and Rome were paid. *Swift.*

DE'BILE. *adj.* [*debilis*, Lat.] Weak; feeble; languid; faint; without strength; imbecile; impotent.

I have not wash'd my nose that bled,
Or foil'd some *debile* wretch, which without note
There's many else have done. *Shakespeare's Coriolanus.*

To DEBI'LITATE. *v. a.* [*debilito*, Latin.] To weaken; to make faint; to enfeeble; to emasculate.

In the lust of the eye, the lust of the flesh, and the pride of life, they seemed as weakly to fail as their *debilitated* posterity ever after. *Brown's Vulgar Errours, b.* 1. *cant.* 1.

The spirits being rendered languid, are incapable of ventilating and purifying the blood, and *debilitated* in attracting nutriment for the parts. *Harvey on Consumptions.*

DEBILITA'TION. *n. s.* [from *debilitatio*, Lat.] The act of weakening.

The weakneſs cannot return any thing of ſtrength, honour, or ſafety to the head, but a *debilitation* and ruin. *K. Charles.*

DEBI'LITY. *n. ſ.* [*debilitas*, Latin.] Weakneſs; feebleneſs; languor; faintneſs; imbecillity.

Methinks I am partaker of thy paſſion,
And in thy caſe do glaſs mine own *debility*. *Sidney.*

Aliment too vaporous or perſpirable will ſubject it to the inconveniencies of too ſtrong a perſpiration, which are *debility*, faintings, and ſometimes ſudden death. *Arbuthn. on Alim.*

DEBONA'IR. *adj.* [*debonnaire*, Fr.] Elegant; civil; well-bred; gentle; complaiſant.

Crying, let be that lady *debonair*,
Thou recreant knight, and ſoon thyſelf prepare
To battle, if thou mean her love to gain. *Fairy Queen.*

He met her once a maying,
There on beds of violets blue,
And freſh blown roſes waſh'd in dew,
Fill'd her with thee, a daughter fair,
So buckſom, blithe, and *debonair*. *Milton.*

The nature of the one is *debonair* and accoſtable; of the other, retired and ſupercilious; the one quick and ſprightful, the other ſlow and ſaturnine. *Howel's Vocal Foreſt.*

And ſhe that was not only paſſing fair,
But was withal diſcreet and *debonair*,
Reſolv'd the paſſive doctrine to fulfil. *Dryden's Nun's Prieſt.*

DEBONA'IRLY. *adv.* [from *debonair.*] Elegantly; with a genteel air.

DEBT. *n. ſ.* [*debitum*, Latin; *dette*, French.]

1. That which one man owes to another.

There was one that died greatly in *debt*: well, ſays one, if he be gone, then he hath carried five hundred ducats of mine with him into the other world. *Bacon, Apophth.* 141.

The *debt* of ten thouſand talents, which the ſervant owed the king, was no ſlight ordinary ſum. *Duppa's Devotions.*

To this great loſs a ſea of tears is due;
But the whole *debt* not to be paid by you. *Waller.*

Above a thouſand pounds in *debt*,
Takes horſe, and in a mighty fret
Rides day and night. *Swift.*

2. That which any one is obliged to do or ſuffer.

Your ſon, my lord, has paid a ſoldier's *debt*;
He only liv'd but 'till he was a man,
But like a man he died. *Shakeſpeare's Macbeth.*

DE'BTED. *part.* [from *debt.* *To* DEBT is not found.] Indebted; obliged to.

Which do amount to three odd ducats more
Than I ſtand *debted* to this gentleman. *Shak. Com. of Errours.*

DE'BTOR. *n. ſ.* [*debitor*, Latin.]

1. He that owes ſomething to another.

I am *debtor* both to the Greeks and to the Barbarians, both to the wiſe and to the unwiſe. *Ro.* i. 14.

The caſe of *debtors* in Rome, for the firſt four centuries, was, after the ſet time for payment, no choice but either to pay, or be the creditor's ſlave. *Swift.*

2. One that owes money.

I'll bring your latter hazard back again,
And thankfully reſt *debtor* for the firſt. *Shak. Merch. of Ven.*

If he his ample palm
Should hap'ly on ill-fated ſhoulder lay
Of *debtor*, ſtrait his body, to the touch
Obſequious, as whilom knights were wont,
To ſome enchanted caſtle is convey'd. *Philips.*

There dy'd my father, no man's *debtor*;
And there I'll die, nor worſe, nor better. *Pope's Horace.*

3. One ſide of an account-book.

When I look upon the *debtor* ſide, I find ſuch innumerable articles, that I want arithmetick to caſt them up; but when I look upon the creditor ſide, I find little more than blank paper. *Addiſon's Spectator*, N°. 549.

DEBULLI'TION. *n. ſ.* [*debullitio*, Lat.] A bubbling or ſeething over. *Dict.*

DECACU'MINATED. *adj.* [*decacuminatus*, Latin.] Having the top cut off. *Dict.*

DE'CADE. *n. ſ.* [δέκα, Gr. *decas*, Latin.] The ſum of ten; a number containing ten.

Men were not only out in the number of ſome days, the latitude of a few years, but might be wide by whole olympiads, and divers *decades* of years. *Brown's Vulgar Errours.*

We make cycles and periods of years; as *decades*, centuries, and chiliads, chiefly for the uſe of computations in hiſtory, chronology, and aſtronomy. *Holder on Time.*

All rank'd by ten; whole *decades*, when they dine,
Muſt want a Trojan ſlave to pour the wine. *Pope's Iliad.*

DECA'DENCY. *n. ſ.* [*decadence*, French.] Decay; fall. *Dict.*

DE'CAGON. *n. ſ.* [from δέκα, ten, and γωνία, a corner.] A plain figure in geometry, having ten ſides and angles.

DE'CALOGUE. *n. ſ.* [δεκάλογος, Greek.] The ten commandments given by God to Moſes.

The commands of God are clearly revealed both in the *decalogue* and other parts of ſacred writ. *Hammond.*

To DECA'MP. *v. n.* [*decamper*, French.] To ſhift the camp; to move off.

DECA'MPMENT. *n. ſ.* [from *decamp.*] The act of ſhifting the camp.

To DECA'NT. *v. a.* [*decanto*, Lat. *decanter*, Fr.] To pour off gently by inclination.

Take *aqua fortis*, and diſſolve in it ordinary coined ſilver, and pour the coloured ſolution into twelve times as much fair water, and then *decant* or filtrate the mixture, that it may be very clear. *Boyle.*

They attend him daily as their chief,
Decant his wine, and carve his beef. *Swift.*

DECANTA'TION. *n. ſ.* [*decantation*, Fr.] The act of decanting or pouring off clear.

DECA'NTER. *n. ſ.* [from *decant.*] A glaſs veſſel made for pouring off liquor clear from the lees.

To DECA'PITATE. *v. a.* [*decapito*, Latin.] To behead.

To DECA'Y. *v. n.* [*decheoir*, Fr. from *de* and *cadere*, Latin.] To loſe excellence; to decline from the ſtate of perfection; to be gradually impaired.

The monarch oak
Three centuries grows, and three he ſtays
Supreme in ſtate, and in three more *decays*. *Dryden.*

The garlands fade, the vows are worn away;
So dies her love, and ſo my hopes *decay*. *Pope.*

To DE'CAY. *v. a.* To impair; to bring to decay.

Infirmity, that *decays* the wiſe, doth ever make better the fool. *Shakeſpeare's Twelfth Night.*

Cut off a ſtock of a tree, and lay that which you cut off to putrefy, to ſee whether it will *decay* the reſt of the ſtock. *Bacon's Natural Hiſtory*, N°. 995.

He was of a very ſmall and *decayed* fortune, and of no good education. *Clarendon.*

Decay'd by time and wars, they only prove
Their former beauty by your former love. *Dryden.*

In Spain our ſprings, like old men's children, be
Decay'd and wither'd from their infancy. *Dryd. Ind. Emp.*

It is ſo ordered, that almoſt every thing which corrupts the ſoul *decays* the body. *Addiſon's Guardian*, N°. 120.

DECA'Y. *n. ſ.* [from the verb.]

1. Decline from the ſtate of perfection; ſtate of diminution.

What comfort to this great *decay* may come,
Shall be applied. *Shakeſpeare's King Lear.*

She has been a fine lady, and paints and hides
Her *decays* very well. *Ben. Johnſon's Catiline.*

And thoſe *decays*, to ſpeak the naked truth,
Through the defects of age, were crimes of youth. *Denham.*

By reaſon of the tenacity of fluids, and attrition of their parts, and the weakneſs of elaſticity in ſolids, motion is much more apt to be loſt than got, and is always upon the *decay*. *Newt.*

Each may feel encreaſes and *decays*,
And ſee now clearer and now darker days. *Eſſay on Criticiſm.*

Taught half by reaſon, half by mere *decay*,
To welcome death, and calmly paſs away. *Pope.*

2. The effects of diminution; the marks of decay.

They think, that whatever is called old muſt have the *decay* of time upon it, and truth too were liable to mould and rottenneſs. *Locke.*

3. Declenſion from proſperity.

And if thy brother be waxen poor, and fallen in *decay* with thee, then thou ſhalt relieve him. *Levit.* xxv. 35.

I am the very man,
That, from your firſt of difference and *decay*,
Have follow'd your ſad ſteps. *Shakeſpeare's King Lear.*

DECA'YER. *n. ſ.* [from *decay.*] That which cauſes decay.

Your water is a ſore *decayer* of your whorſon dead body. *Shakeſpeare's Hamlet.*

DECE'ASE. *n. ſ.* [*deceſſus*, Lat.] Death; departure from life.

Lands are by human law, in ſome places, after the owner's *deceaſe*, divided unto all his children; in ſome, all deſcendeth to the eldeſt ſon. *Hooker, b.* i. *ſect.* 10.

To DECE'ASE. *v. n.* [*decedo*, Latin.] To die; to depart from life.

He tells us Arthur is *deceas'd* to-night. *Shakeſ. King John.*

You ſhall die
Twice now, where others, that mortality
In her fair arms holds, ſhall but once *deceaſe*. *Chapm. Odyſſ.*

His lateſt victories ſtill thickeſt came,
As, near the centre, motion doth increaſe:
'Till he, preſs'd down by his own weighty name,
Did, like the veſtal, under ſpoils *deceaſe*. *Dryden.*

DECE'IT. *n. ſ.* [*deceptio*, Latin.]

1. Fraud; a cheat; a fallacy; any practice by which falſhood is made to paſs for truth.

My lips ſhall not ſpeak wickedneſs, nor my tongue utter *deceit*. *Job*, xxvii. 4.

2. Stratagem; artifice.

His demand
Springs not from Edward's well-meant honeſt love,
But from *deceit*, bred by neceſſity. *Shakeſpeare's Henry* VI.

3. [In law.] A ſubtile wily ſhift or deviſe; all manner of craft, ſubtilty, guile, fraud, wilineſs, ſlightneſs, cunning, covin, colluſion, practice and offence, uſed to deceive another man by any means, which hath no other proper or particular name but offence. *Cowel.*

Dece'itful. *adj.* [*deceit* and *full.*] Fraudulent; full of deceit.

I grant him bloody,
Luxurious, avaricious, false, *deceitful*,
Sudden, malicious, smacking of ev'ry sin
That has a name. *Shakespeare's Macbeth.*

The lovely young Lavinia once had friends,
And fortune smil'd, *deceitful*, on her birth. *Thomson's Autumn.*

Dece'itfully. *adv.* [from *deceitful.*] Fraudulently; with deceit.

Exercise of form may be *deceitfully* dispatched of course. *Wotton.*

Dece'itfulness. *n. s.* [from *deceitful.*] The quality of being fraudulent; tendency to deceive.

The care of this world, and the *deceitfulness* of riches, choke the word, and he becometh unfruitful. *Mat.* xiii. 22.

Dece'ivable. *adj.* [from *deceive.*]

1. Subject to fraud; exposed to imposture.

Man was not only *deceivable* in his integrity, but the angels of light in all their clarity. *Brown's Vulgar Errours, b.* i. *c.* 1.

How would thou use me now, blind, and thereby
Deceivable, in most things as a child
Helpless; hence easily contemn'd and scorn'd,
And last neglected. *Milton's Agonistes, l.* 938.

2. Subject to produce errour; deceitful.

It is good to consider of deformity, not as a sign, which is more *deceivable*, but as a cause which seldom faileth of the effect. *Bacon's Essays.*

He received nothing but fair promises, which proved *deceivable.* *Hayward.*

O everfailing trust
In mortal strength! And oh, what not in man
Deceivable and vain? *Milton's Agonistes, l.* 348.

Dece'ivableness. *n. s.* [from *deceivable.*] Liableness to be deceived.

He that has a great patron, has the advantage of his negligence and *deceivableness.* *Government of the Tongue, s.* 8.

To DECE'IVE. *v. a.* [*decipio*, Latin.]

1. To cause to mistake; to bring into errour; to impose upon.

Some have been apt to be *deceived* into an opinion, that there was a natural or divine right of primogeniture to both estate and power. *Locke.*

2. To delude by stratagem.

3. To cut off from expectation.

The Turkish general, *deceived* of his expectation, withdrew his fleet twelve miles off. *Knolles's History of the Turks.*

I now believ'd
The happy day approach'd, nor are my hopes *deceiv'd. Dryd.*

4. To mock; to fail.

They rais'd a feeble cry with trembling notes,
But the weak voice *deceiv'd* their gasping throats. *Dryd. Æn.*

Dece'iver. *n. s.* [from *deceive.*] One that leads another into errour; a cheat.

Sigh no more, ladies, sigh no more;
Men were *deceivers* ever:
One foot in sea, and one on shore;
To one thing constant never. *Shak. Much ado about Nothing.*

As for his dismission out of France, they interpreted it not as if he were detected, or neglected for a counterfeit *deceiver.* *Bacon's Henry* VII.

Those voices, actions or gestures, which men have not by any compact agreed to make the instruments of conveying their thoughts one to another, are not the proper instruments of deceiving, so as to denominate the person using them a lyar or *deceiver.* *South's Sermons.*

It is to be admired how any *deceiver* can be so weak to foretel things near at hand, when a very few months must of necessity discover the imposture. *Swift's Predictions.*

Adieu, the heart-expanding bowl,
And all the kind *deceivers* of the soul. *Pope's Horace.*

Dece'mber. *n. s.* [*december*, Latin.] The last month of the year; but named *december*, or the *tenth* month, when the year began in March.

Men are April when they woo, and *December* when they wed. *Shakespeare's As you like it.*

What should we speak of,
When we are old as you? When we shall hear
The rain and wind beat dark *December. Shakesp. Cymbeline.*

Dece'mpedal. *adj.* [from *decempeda*, Latin.] Ten feet in length. *Dict.*

Dece'mvirate. *n. s.* [*decemviratus*, Lat.] The dignity and office of the ten governours of Rome, who were appointed to rule the commonwealth instead of consuls. Their authority subsisted only two years.

DE'CENCE. }
DE'CENCY. } *n. s.* [*decence*, French; *decet*, Latin.]

1. Propriety of form; proper formality; becoming ceremony.

Those thousand *decencies*, that daily flow
From all her words and actions. *Milton's Paradise Lost.*

In good works there may be goodness in the general; but *decence* and gracefulness can be only in the particulars in doing the good. *Sprat's Sermons.*

Were the offices of religion stript of all the external *decencies* of worship, they would not make a due impression on the minds of those who assist at them. *Atterbury's Sermons.*

She speaks, behaves, and acts just as she ought;
But never, never reached gen'rous thought:
Virtue she finds too painful an endeavour,
Content to dwell in *decencies* for ever. *Pope.*

2. Suitableness to character; propriety.

And must I own, she said, my secret smart?
What with more *decence* were in silence kept. *Dryden's Æn.*

The next consideration, immediately subsequent to the being of a thing, is what agrees or disagrees with that thing; what is suitable or unsuitable to it; and from this springs the notion of *decency* or indecency, that which becomes or misbecomes. *South's Sermons.*

Sentiments which raise laughter, can very seldom be admitted with any *decency* into an heroick poem. *Addis. Spectat.*

3. Modesty; not ribaldry; not obscenity.

Immodest words admit of no defence;
For want of *decency* is want of sense. *Roscommon.*

Dece'nnial. *adj.* [from *decennium*, Latin.] What continues for the space of ten years.

Decenno'val. }
Decenno'vary. } *adj.* [*decem* and *novem*, Latin.] Relating to the number nineteen.

Meton, of old, in the time of the Peloponesian war, constituted a *decennoval* circle, or of nineteen years; the same which we now call the golden number. *Holder on Time.*

Seven months are retrenched in this whole *decennovary* progress of the epacts, to reduce the accounts of her motion and place to those of the sun. *Holder on Time.*

De'cent. *adj.* [*decens*, Lat.] Becoming; fit; suitable.

Since there must be ornaments both in painting and poetry, if they are not necessary, they must at least be *decent*; that is, in their due place, and but moderately used. *Dryden.*

De'cently. *adv.* [from *decent.*] In a proper manner; with suitable behaviour; without meanness or ostentation.

They could not *decently* refuse assistance to a person, who had punished those who had insulted their relation. *Broome.*

2. Without immodesty.

Past hope of safety, 'twas his latest care,
Like falling Cæsar, *decently* to die. *Dryden's Ann. Mirab.*

He performs what friendship, justice, truth require;
What could he more, but *decently* retire? *Swift.*

Deceptibi'lity. *n. s.* [from *deceit.*] Liableness to be deceived.

Some errours are so fleshed in us, that they maintain their interest upon the *deceptibility* of our decayed natures. *Glanville.*

Dece'ptible. *adj.* [from *deceit.*] Liable to be deceived; open to imposture; subject to fraud.

The first and father cause of common errour, is the common infirmity of human nature; of whose *deceptible* condition, perhaps, there should not need any other eviction than the frequent errours we shall ourselves commit. *Brown.*

Dece'ption. *n. s.* [*deceptio*, Latin.]

1. The act or means of deceiving; cheat; fraud; fallacy.

Being thus divided from truth in themselves, they are yet farther removed by advenient *deception.* *Brown's Vulgar Err.*

All *deception* is a misapplying of those signs, which, by compact or institution, were made the means of mens signifying or conveying their thoughts. *South's Sermons.*

2. The state of being deceived.

Reason, not impossibly, may meet
Some specious object by the foe suborn'd,
And fall into *deception* unaware. *Milton's Paradise Lost.*

Dece'ptious. *adj.* [from *deceit.*] Deceitful; apt to deceive.

Yet there is a credence in my heart,
That doth invert th' attest of eyes and ears;
As if those organs had *deceptious* functions,
Created only to calumniate. *Shakespeare's Troil. and Cressida.*

Dece'ptive. *adj.* [from *deceit.*] Having the power of deceiving. *Dict.*

Dece'ptory. *adj.* [from *deceit.*] Containing means of deceit. *Dict.*

DECE'RPT. *adj.* [*decerptus*, Lat.] Diminished; taken off. *Dict.*

Dece'rptible. *adj.* [*decerpo*, Latin.] That may be taken off. *Dict.*

Dece'rption. *n. s.* [from *decerpt.*] The act of lessening, or taking off. *Dict.*

Decerta'tion. *n. s.* [*decertatio*, Latin.] A contention; a striving; a dispute. *Dict.*

Dece'ssion. *n. s.* [*decessio*, Latin.] A departure; a going away. *Dict.*

To Decha'rm. *v. a.* [*decharmer*, French.] To counteract a charm; to disinchant.

Notwithstanding the help of physick, he was suddenly cured by *decharming* the witchcraft. *Harvey on Consumptions.*

To DECI'DE. *v. a.* [*decido*, Latin.]

1. To fix the event of; to determine.

The day approach'd when fortune should *decide*
Th' important enterprize, and give the bride. *Dryd. Fables.*

2. To determine a question or dispute.

In council oft, and oft in battle tried,
Betwixt thy master and the world *decide.* *Granville.*

Who shall *decide*, when doctors disagree,
And soundest casuists doubt? *Pope.*

De'cidence. *n. s.* [*decido*, Latin.]
1. The quality of being shed, or of falling off.
2. The act of falling away.
Men observing the *decidence* of their horn, do fall upon the conceit that it annually rotteth away, and successively reneweth again. *Brown's Vulgar Errours, b.* iii. *c.* 7.

Deci'der. *n. s.* [from *decide.*]
1. One who determines causes.
I cannot think that a jester or a monkey, a droll or a puppet, can be proper judges or *deciders* of controversy. *Watts.*
It is said that the man is no ill *decider* in common cases of property, where party is out of the question. *Swift.*
2. One who determines quarrels.

DECI'DUOUS. *adj.* [*deciduus*, Latin.] Falling; not perennial; not lasting through the year.
In botany the perianthium, or calyx, is *deciduous* with the flower. *Quincy.*

Deci'duousness. *n. s.* [from *deciduous.*] Aptness to fall; quality of fading once a year. *Dict.*

De'cimal. *adj.* [*decimus*, Latin.] Numbered by ten; multiplied by ten.
In the way we take now to name numbers by millions of millions of millions, it is hard to go beyond eighteen, or, at most, four and twenty *decimal* progressions, without confusion. *Locke.*

To DE'CIMATE. *v. a.* [*decimus*, Latin.] To tithe; to take the tenth.

Decima'tion. *n. s.* [from *decimate.*]
1. A tithing; a selection of every tenth by lot or otherwise.
2. A selection by lot of every tenth soldier, in a general mutiny, for punishment.
By *decimation* and a tithed death,
Take thou the destin'd tenth. *Shakespeare's Timon.*
A *decimation* I will strictly make
Of all who my Charinus did forsake;
And of each legion each centurion shall die. *Dryden.*

To DECI'PHER. *v. a.* [*dechiffrer*, French.]
1. To explain that which is written in ciphers.
Zelmane, that had the same character in her heart, could easily *decipher* it; and therefore, to keep him the longer in speech, desired to know the conclusion of the matter, and how the honest Dametas was escaped. *Sidney.*
Assurance is writ in a private character, not to be read, nor understood, but by the conscience, to which the spirit of God has vouchsafed to *decipher* it. *South's Sermons.*
2. To write out; to mark down in characters.
Could I give you a lively representation of guilt and horrour on this hand, and paint out eternal wrath, and *decipher* eternal vengeance on the other, then might I shew you the condition of a sinner hearing himself denied by Christ. *South.*
Then were laws of necessity invented, that so every particular subject might find his principal pleasure, *deciphered* unto him, in the tables of his laws. *Locke.*
3. To stamp; to characterise; to mark.
You are both *decipher'd*
For villains mark'd with rape. *Shakespeare's Titus Andronicus.*
4. To unfold; to unravel; as, *to* decipher *a perplexed affair.*

Deci'pherer. *n. s.* [from *decipher.*] One who explains writings in cypher.

Deci'sion. *n. s.* [from *decide.*]
1. Determination of a difference.
Pleasure and revenge
Have ears more deaf than adders, to the voice
Of any true *decision.* *Shakespeare's Troilus and Cressida.*
The great number of the undertakers, the worth of some of them, and their zeal to bring the matter to a *decision*, are sure arguments of the dignity and importance of it. *Woodward.*
War is a direct appeal to God for the *decision* of some dispute, which can by no other means be possibly determined. *Atterbury's Sermons.*
2. Determination of an event.
The time approaches,
That will with due *decision* make us know
What we shall say we have, and what we owe. *Shak. Macb.*
Their arms are to the last *decision* bent,
And fortune labours with the vast event. *Dryden's Aurengz.*
3. It is used in Scotland for a narrative, or reports of the proceedings of the court of session there.

Deci'sive. *adj.* [from *decide.*]
1. Having the power of determining any difference.
Such a reflection, though it carries nothing perfectly *decisive* in it, yet creates a mighty confidence in his breast, and strengthens him much in his opinion. *Atterbury's Sermons.*
This they are ready to look upon as a determination on their side, and *decisive* of the controversy between vice and virtue. *Rogers's Sermons.*
2. Having the power of settling any event.
For on th' event,
Decisive of this bloody day, depends
The fate of kingdoms. *Philips.*

Deci'sively. *adv.* [from *decisive.*] In a conclusive manner.

Deci'siveness. *n. s.* [from *decisive.*] The power of terminating any difference, or settling an event.

Deci'sory. *adj.* [from *decide.*] Able to determine or decide.

To Deck. *v. a.* [*decken*, Dutch.]
1. To cover; to overspread.
Ye mists and exhalations, that now rise
From hill or steaming lake, dusky or grey,
'Till the sun paint your fleecy skirts with gold,
In honour to the world's great Author, rise!
Whether to *deck* with clouds th' uncolour'd sky,
Or wet the thirsty earth with falling showers,
Rising or falling, still advance his praise. *Milt. Par. Lost.*
2. To dress; to array.
Sweet ornament! that *decks* a thing divine. *Shakespeare.*
Long may'st thou live to wail thy children's loss,
And see another, as I see thee now,
Deck'd in thy rights, as thou art stall'd in mine. *Sh. R.* III.
She sets to work millions of spinning worms,
That in their green shops weave the smooth-hair'd silk,
To *deck* her sons. *Milton.*
3. To adorn; to embellish.
But direful, deadly black, both leaf and bloom,
Fit to adorn the head, and *deck* the dreary tomb. *Fai. Queen.*
Now the dew with spangles *deck'd* the ground,
A sweeter spot of earth was never found. *Dryden.*
The god shall to his vot'ries tell
Each conscious tear, each blushing grace,
That *deck'd* dear Eloisa's face. *Prior.*

Deck. *n. s.* [from the verb.]
1. The floor of a ship.
Her keel plows hell,
And *deck* knocks heaven. *B. Johnson.*
We have also raised our second *decks*, and given more vent thereby to our ordinance, trying on our nether overloop. *Ralei.*
If any, born and bred under *deck*, had no other information but what sense affords, he would be of opinion that the ship was as stable as a house. *Glanv. Sceps. c.* 11.
On high-rais'd *decks* the haughty Belgians ride,
Beneath whose shade our humble frigates go. *Dryden.*
Day to night they bring,
With hymns and peans, to the Bowyer king:
At sun-set to their ship they make return,
And snore secure on *decks* 'till rosy morn. *Dryden's Iliad.*
2. Pack of cards piled regularly on each other.
Besides gems, many other sorts of stones are regularly figured: the Amianthus, of parallel threads, as in the pile of velvet; and the Selenites, of parallel plates, as in a *deck* of cards. *Grew's Cosmol. b.* i. *c.* 2.

De'cker. *n. s.* [from *deck.*] A dresser; one that apparels or adorns; a coverer.

To DECLA'IM. *v. n.* [*declamo*, Latin.] To harangue; to speak to the passions; to rhetoricate; to speak set orations.
What are his mischiefs, consul? You *declaim*
Against his manners, and corrupt your own. *B. Johns. Cat.*
The splendid *declaimings* of novices and men of heat. *South.*
It is usual for masters to make their boys *declaim* on both sides of an argument. *Swift.*
Dress up all the virtues in the beauties of oratory, and *declaim* aloud on the praise of goodness. *Watts's Improvement.*

Decla'imer. *n. s.* [from *declaim.*] One who makes speeches with intent to move the passions.
Your Salamander is a perpetual *declaimer* against jealousy. *Addison's Spectator*, N°. 198.

Declama'tion. *n. s.* [*declamatio*, Latin.] A discourse addressed to the passions; an harangue; a set speech; a piece of rhetorick.
The cause why *declamations* prevail so greatly, is, for that men suffer themselves to be deluded. *Hooker, b.* i. *s.* 8.
Thou mayst forgive his anger, while thou makest use of the plainness of his *declamation.* *Taylor's Rule of living holy.*

Declama'tor. *n. s.* [Latin.] A declaimer; an orator; a rhetorician.
Who could, I say, hear this generous *declamator*, without being fired at his noble zeal. *Tatler*, N°. 56.

Decla'matory. *adj.* [*declamatorius*, Latin.]
1. Relating to the practice of declaiming; pertaining to declamation; treated in the manner of a rhetorician.
This a while suspended his interment, and became a *declamatory* theme amongst the religious men of that age. *Wotton.*
2. Appealing to the passions.
He has run himself into his own *declamatory* way, and almost forgotten that he was now setting up for a moral poet. *Dryden.*

Decla'rable. *adj.* [from *declare.*] Capable of proof.
This is *declarable* from the best writers. *Brown's Vulg. Err.*

Declara'tion. *n. s.* [from *declare.*]
1. A proclamation or affirmation; oral expression; publication.
His promises are nothing else but *declarations*, what God will do for the good of men. *Hooker, b.* i. *s.* 2.
Though wit and learning are certain and habitual perfections

tions of the mind, yet the *declaration* of them, which alone brings the repute, is subject to a thousand hazards. *South.*

There are no where so plain and full *declarations* of his mercy and love to the sons of men, as are made in the gospel. *Tillotson, Sermon* 5.

2. An explanation of something doubtful. Obsolete.

3. [In law.] Declaration (*declaratio*) is properly the shewing forth, or laying out, of an action personal in any suit, though it is used sometimes for both personal and real actions. *Cowel.*

DECLA'RATIVE. *adj.* [from *declare.*] Making declaration; explanatory.

The names of things should be always taken from something observably *declarative* of their form or nature. *Grew.*

2. Making proclamation.

To this we may add the *vox populi*, so *declarative* on the same side. *Swift's Examiner*, N°. 44.

DECLA'RATORILY. *adv.* [from *declaratory.*] In the form of a declaration; not promissively; not in a decretory form.

Andreas Alciatus the civilian, and Franciscus de Cordua, have both *declaratorily* confirmed the same. *Brown's Vulg. Err.*

DECLA'RATORY. *adj.* [from *declare.*] Affirmative; expressive; not decretory; not promissory.

These blessings are not only *declaratory* of the good pleasure and intention of God towards them, but likewise of the natural tendency of the thing. *Tillotson, Serm.* 4.

To DECLA'RE. *v. a.* [*declaro*, Latin.]

1. To clear; to free from obscurity.

To *declare* this a little, we must assume that the surfaces of such bodies are exactly smooth. *Boyle on Colours.*

2. To make known; to tell evidently and openly.

It hath been *declared* unto some of you, that there are contentions among you. 1 *Cor.* i. 11.

The sun by certain signs *declares*,
Both when the South projects a stormy day,
And when the clearing North will puff the clouds away.
Dryden's Virg. Geor. l. 620.

3. To publish; to proclaim.

Declare his glory among the heathens. 1 *Chron.* xvi. 24.

4. To shew in open view.

We are a considerable body, who, upon a proper occasion, would not fail to *declare* ourselves. *Addison.*

To DECLA'RE. *v. n.* To make a declaration; to proclaim some resolution or opinion, some favour or opposition.

The internal faculties of will and understanding, decreeing and *declaring* against them. *Taylor's Rule of living holy.*

God is said not to have left himself without witness in the world, there being something fixed in the nature of men that will be sure to testify and *declare* for him. *South's Sermons.*

Like fawning courtiers, for success they wait;
And then come smiling, and *declare* for fate. *Dryden.*

DECLA'REMENT. *n. s.* [from *declare.*] Discovery; declaration; testimony.

Crystal will calify into electricity; that is, a power to attract straws, or light bodies, and convert the needle freely placed, which is a *declarement* of very different parts. *Brown.*

DECLA'RER. *n. s.* [from *declare.*] A proclaimer; one that makes any thing known.

DECLE'NSION. *n. s.* [*declinatio*, Latin.]

1. Tendency from a greater to a less degree of excellence.

A beauty-waining and distressed widow,
Ev'n in the afternoon of her best days,
Seduc'd the pitch and height of all his thoughts
To base *declension*. *Shakespeare's Richard* III.

Take the picture of a man in the greenness and vivacity of his youth, and in the latter date and *declensions* of his drooping years, and you will scarce know it to belong to the same person. *South's Sermons.*

2. Declination; descent.

We may reasonably allow as much for the *declension* of the land from that place to the sea, as for the immediate height of the mountain. *Burnet's Theory of the Earth.*

3. Inflexion; manner of changing nouns.

Declension is only the variation or change of the termination of a noun, whilst it continues to signify the same thing. *Clarke's Latin Grammar.*

DECLI'NABLE. *adj.* [from *decline.*] Having variety of terminations; as, a *declinable* noun.

DECLINA'TION. *n. s.* [*declinatio*, Latin.]

1. Descent; change from a better to a worse state; decay.

The queen, hearing of the *declination* of a monarchy, took it so ill, as she would never after hear of his suit. *Bacon, Ess.* 23.

Hope waits upon the flow'ry prime;
And Summer, though it be less gay,
Yet is not look'd on as a time
Of *declination* or decay. *Waller.*

2. The act of bending down; as, a *declination* of the head.

3. Variation from rectitude; oblique motion; obliquity.

Supposing there were a *declination* of atoms, yet will it not effect what they intend; for then they do all decline, and so there will be no more concourse than if they did perpendicularly descend. *Ray on the Creation.*

This *declination* of atoms in their descent, was itself either necessary or voluntary. *Bentley.*

4. Varition from a fixed point.

There is no *declination* of latitude, nor variation of the elevation of the pole, notwithstanding what some have asserted. *Woodward's Natural History.*

5. [In navigation.] The variation of the needle from the true meridian of any place to the East or West.

6. [In astronomy.] The *declination* of a star we call its shortest distance from the equator. *Brown's Vulgar Errours, b.* i. *c.* 13.

7. [In grammar.] The declension or inflection of a noun through its various terminations.

8. DECLINATION *of a Plane* [in dialing], is an arch of the horizon, comprehended either between the plane and the prime vertical circle, if accounted from the East or West; or else between the meridian and the plane, if accounted from the North or South. *Harris.*

DECLINA'TOR. } *n. s.* [from *decline.*] An instrument in dial-
DECLI'NATORY. } ing, by which the declination, reclination, and inclination of planes are determined. *Chambers.*

There are several ways to know the several planes; but the readiest is by an instrument called a *declinatory*, fitted to the variation of your place. *Moxon's Mech. Exer.*

To DECLI'NE. *v. n.* [*declino*, Latin.]

1. To lean downward.

And then with kind embracements, tempting kisses,
And with *declining* head into his bosom,
Bid him shed tears, as being overjoy'd. *Shakespeare.*

2. To deviate; to run into obliquities.

Neither shalt thou speak in a cause to *decline* after many, to wrest judgment. *Ex.* xxiii. 2.

3. To shun; to avoid to do any thing.

4. To sink; to be impaired; to decay. Opposed to improvement or exaltation.

Sons at perfect age, and fathers *declining*, the father should be as a ward to the son. *Shakespeare's King Lear.*

They'll be by th' fire, and presume to know
What's done i' th' capitol; who's like to rise,
Who thrives, and who *declines*. *Shakespeare's Coriolanus.*

Sometimes nations will *decline* so low
From virtue, which is reason, that no wrong,
But justice, and some fatal curse annex'd,
Deprives them of their outward liberty. *Milton's Par. Lost.*

That empire must *decline*,
Whose chief support and sinews are of coin. *Waller.*

And nature, which all acts of life designs,
Not like ill poets, in the last *declines*. *Denham.*

Thus then my lov'd Euryalus appears;
He looks the prop of my *declining* years! *Dryden's Æn.*

Next that, is when autumnal warmth *declines*;
E'er heat is quite decay'd, or cold begun,
Or Capricorn admits the Winter sun. *Dryden's Virg. Georg.*

Faith and morality are *declined* among us. *Swift.*

God, in his wisdom, hath been pleased to load our *declining* years with many sufferings, with diseases, and decays of nature. *Swift.*

To DECLI'NE. *v. a.*

1. To bend downward; to bring down.

And now fair Phœbus 'gan *decline* in haste,
His weary waggon to the western vale. *Fairy Queen, b.* ii.

And leaves the semblance of a lover, fixt
In melancholy deep, with head *declin'd*,
And love-dejected eyes. *Thomson's Spring, l.* 1020.

2. To shun; to avoid; to refuse; to be cautious of.

He had wisely *declined* that argument, though in their common sermons they gave it. *Clarendon, b.* viii.

Since the muses do invoke my pow'r,
I shall no more *decline* that sacred bow'r,
Where Gloriana, their great mistress, lies. *Waller.*

Though I the business did *decline*,
Yet I contriv'd the whole design,
And sent them their petition. *Denham.*

If it should be said that these minute bodies are indissoluble, because it is their nature to be so, that would not be to render a reason of the thing proposed, but, in effect, to *decline* rendering any. *Boyle's History of Firmness.*

Could her mind have been captivated with the glories of this world, she had them all laid before her; but she generously *declined* them, because she saw the acceptance of them was inconsistent with religion. *Addison's Freeholder*, N°. 21.

Whatever they judged to be most agreeable, or disagreeable, they would pursue or *decline*. *Atterbury.*

3. To modify a word by various terminations; to inflect.

You *decline* musa, and construe Latin, by the help of a tutor, or with some English translation. *Watts's Improvement.*

DECLI'NE. *n. s.* [from the substantive.] The state of tendency to the worse; diminution; decay. Contrary to increase, improvement, or elevation.

Thy rise of fortune did I only wed;
From its *decline*, determin'd to recede. *Prior.*

Those fathers lived in the *decline* of literature. *Swift.*

DECLI'VITY. *n. s.* [*declivis*, Latin.] Inclination or obliquity reckoned downwards; gradual descent; not precipitous or perpendicular: the contrary to acclivity.

Rivers will not flow, unless upon *declivity*, and their

sources be raised above the earth's ordinary surface, so that they may run upon a descent. *Woodward's Nat. History.*

I found myself within my depth; and the *declivity* was so small, that I walked near a mile before I got to the shore. *Gulliver's Travels.*

DECLI'VOUS. *adj.* [*declivis*, Lat.] Gradually descending; not precipitous; not perpendicularly sinking: the contrary to acclivous; moderately steep.

To DECO'CT. *v. a.* [*decoquo decoctum*, Latin.]

1. To prepare by boiling for any use; to digest in hot water.
2. To digest by the heat of the stomach.

There she *decocts*, and doth the food prepare;
There she distributes it to ev'ry vein,
There she expels what she may fitly spare. *Davies.*

3. To boil in water, so as to draw the strength or virtue of any thing.

The longer malt or herbs are *decocted* in liquor, the clearer it is. *Bacon's Natural History*, N°. 308.

4. To boil up to a consistence; to strengthen or invigorate by boiling.

Can sodden water, their barley-broth,
Decoct their cold blood to such valiant heat. *Shakesp. H.* V.

DECO'CTIBLE. *adj.* [from *decoct.*] That which may be boiled, or prepared by boiling. *Dict.*

DECO'CTION. *n. s.* [*decoctum*, Latin.]

1. The act of boiling any thing, to extract its virtues.

In infusion the longer it is, the greater is the part of the gross body that goeth into the liquor; but in *decoction*, though more goeth forth, yet it either purgeth at the top, or settleth at the bottom. *Bacon's Natural History*, N°. 308.

2. A preparation made by boiling in water.

They distil their husbands land
In *decoctions*; and are mann'd
With ten emp'rics, in their chamber
Lying for the spirit of amber. *Ben. Johnson.*

If the plant be boiled in water, the strained liquor is called the *decoction* of the plant. *Arbuthnot on Aliments.*

DECO'CTURE. *n. s.* [from *decoct.*] A substance drawn by decoction.

DECOLLA'TION. *n. s.* [*decollatio*, Lat.] The act of beheading.

He, by a *decollation* of all hope, annihilated his mercy: this, by an immoderancy thereof, destroyed his justice. *Brown.*

DECOMPO'SITE. *adj.* [*decompositus*, Latin.] Compounded a second time; compounded with things already composite.

Decomposites of three metals, or more, are too long to inquire of, except there be some compositions of them already observed. *Bacon's Phys. Rem.*

DECOMPOSI'TION. *n. s.* [*decompositus*, Lat.] The act of compounding things already compounded.

We consider what happens in the compositions and *decompositions* of saline particles. *Boyle.*

To DECOMPO'UND. *v. a.* [*decompono*, Latin.] To compose of things already compounded; to compound a second time; to form by a second composition.

Nature herself doth in the bowels of the earth make *decompounded* bodies, as we see in vitriol, cinnabar, and even in sulphur itself. *Boyle's Scept. Chym.*

When a word stands for a very complex idea, that is compounded and *decompounded*, it is not easy for men to form and retain that idea exactly. *Locke.*

If the violet, blue and green, be intercepted, the remaining yellow, orange, and red, will compound upon the paper an orange; and then, if the intercepted colours be let pass, they will fall upon this compounded orange, and, together with it, *decompound* a white. *Newton's Opt.*

DECOMPO'UND. *adj.* [from the verb.] Composed of things or words already compounded; compounded a second time.

The pretended salts and sulphur are so far from being elementary parts extracted out of the body of mercury, that they are rather, to borrow a term of the grammarians, *decompound* bodies, made up of the whole metal and the menstruum, or other additaments employed to disguise it. *Boyle.*

No body should use any compound or *decompound* of the substantial verbs, but as they are read in the common conjugations. *Arbuthnot and Pope's Mart. Scrib.*

DE'CORAMENT. *n. s.* [from *decorate.*] Ornament; embellishment. *Dict.*

To DE'CORATE. *v. a.* [*decoro*, Latin.] To adorn; to embellish; to beautify.

DECORA'TION. *n. s.* [from *decorate.*] Ornament; embellishment; added beauty.

The ensigns of virtues contribute to the ornament of figures; such as the *decorations* belonging to the liberal arts, and to war. *Dryden's Dufresnoy.*

This helm and heavy buckler I can spare,
As only *decorations* of the war:
So Mars is arm'd for glory, not for need. *Dryden.*

DECORA'TOR. *n. s.* [from *decorate.*] An adorner; an embellisher. *Dict.*

DECO'ROUS. *adj.* [*decorus*, Latin.] Decent; suitable to a character; becoming; proper; befitting; seemly.

It is not so *decorous*, in respect of God, that he should immediately do all the meanest and triflingest things himself, without making use of any inferiour or subordinate minister. *Ray on the Creation.*

To DECO'RTICATE. *v. a.* [*decortico*, Latin.] To divest of the bark or husk; to husk; to peel; to strip.

Take great barley, dried and *decorticated*, after it is well washed, and boil it in water. *Arbuthnot on Coins.*

DECORTICA'TION. *n. s.* [from *decorticate.*] The act of stripping the bark or husk.

DECO'RUM. n. s. [Latin.] Decency; behaviour contrary to licentiousness, contrary to levity; seemliness.

If your master
Would have a queen his beggar, you must tell him,
That majesty, to keep *decorum*, must
No less beg than a kingdom. *Shakespeare's Ant. and Cleop.*

I am far from suspecting simplicity, which is bold to trespass in points of *decorum*. *Wotton.*

Beyond the fix'd and settled rules
Of vice and virtue in the schools,
The better sort should set before 'em
A grace, a manner, a *decorum*. *Prior.*

Gentlemen of the army should be, at least, obliged to external *decorum*: a profligate life and character should not be a means of advancement. *Swift.*

He kept with princes due *decorum*;
Yet never stood in awe before 'em. *Swift.*

To DECO'Y. *v. a.* [from *koey*, Dutch, a cage.] To lure into a cage; to intrap; to draw into a snare.

A fowler had taken a patridge, who offered to *decoy* her companions into the snare. *L'Estrange.*

Decoy'd by the fantastick blaze,
Now lost, and now renew'd, he sinks absorpt,
Rider and horse. *Thomson's Autumn, l.* 1165.

DECO'Y. *n. s.* [from the verb.] Allurement to mischiefs; temptation.

The devil could never have had such numbers, had he not used some as *decoys* to ensnare others. *Government of the Tongue.*

These exuberant productions of the earth became a continual *decoy* and snare: they only excited and fomented lusts. *Woodward's Natural History.*

An old dramdrinker is the devil's *decoy*. *Berkley.*

DECO'YDUCK. *n. s.* A duck that lures others.

There is likewise a sort of ducks, called *decoyducks*, that will bring whole flights of fowl to their retirements, where are conveniences made for catching them. *Mortimer's Husb.*

To DECRE'ASE. *v. n.* [*decresco*, Latin.] To grow less; to be diminished.

From the moon is the sign of feasts, a light that *decreaseth* in her perfection. *Eccluf.* xliii. 7.

Unto fifty years the heart annually increaseth the weight of one drachm; after which, in the same proportion, it *decreaseth*. *Brown's Vulgar Errours, b.* v. *c.* 20.

It is to be observed, that when the sun comes to his tropicks, days increase and *decrease* but a very little for a great while together. *Newton's Opt.*

To DECRE'ASE. *v. a.* To make less; to diminish.

He did dishonourable find
Those articles, which did our state *decrease*. *Daniel's C. War.*

Nor cherish'd they relations poor,
That might *decrease* their present store. *Prior.*

Heat increases the fluidity of tenacious liquids, as of oil, balsam, and honey; and thereby *decreases* their resistance. *Newt.*

DECRE'ASE. *n. s.* [from the verb.] The state of growing less; decay.

By weak'ning toil, and hoary age o'ercome,
See thy *decrease*, and hasten to thy tomb. *Prior.*

2. The wain; the time when the visible face of the moon grows less.

See in what time the seeds, set in the increase of the moon, come to a certain height, and how they differ from those that are set in the *decrease* of the moon. *Bacon's Natural History.*

To DECRE'E. *v n.* [*decretum*, Latin.] To make an edict; to appoint by edict; to establish by law; to determine; to resolve.

They shall see the end of the wise, and shall not understand what God in his counsel hath *decreed* of him. *Wisd.* iv.

Father eternal! Thine is to *decree*;
Mine, both in heav'n and earth, to do thy will.
Milton's Paradise Lost, b. x. *l.* 68.

Had heav'n *decreed* that I should life enjoy,
Heav'n had *decreed* to save unhappy Troy. *Dryden's Æn.*

To DECRE'E. *v. a.* To doom or assign by a decree.

Thou shalt also *decree* a thing, and it shall be established. *Job.*

The king their father,
On just and weighty reasons, has *decreed*
His sceptre to the younger. *Rowe's Ambitious Step-mother.*

DECRE'E. *n. s.* [*decretum*, Latin.]

1. An edict; a law.

If you deny me, fie upon your law!
There is no force in the *decrees* of Venice. *Shakespeare.*

There went a *decree* from Cæsar Augustus, that all the world should be taxed. *Luke* ii. 1.

Are

Are we condemn'd by fate's unjust *decree*,
No more our houses and our homes to see? *Dryden's Virg.*

The Supreme Being is sovereignly good; he rewards the just, and punishes the unjust: and the folly of man, and not the *decree* of heaven, is the cause of human calamity. *Broome.*

2. An established rule.

When he made a *decree* for the rain, and a way for the lightning of the thunder. *Job* xxviii. 26.

3. A determination of a suit, or litigated cause.

4. [In canon law.] An ordinance, which is enacted by the pope himself, by and with the advice of his cardinals in council assembled, without being consulted by any one thereon. *Ayliffe's Parergon.*

De'crement. *n. s.* [*decrementum*, Latin.] Decrease; the state of growing less; the quantity lost by decreasing.

Upon the tropick, and first descension from our solstice, we are scarce sensible of declination; but declining farther, our *decrement* accelerates: we set apace, and in our last days precipitate into our graves. *Brown's Vulgar Errours.*

Rocks, mountains, and the other elevations of the earth, suffer a continual *decrement*, and grow lower and lower. *Woodw.*

DECRE'PIT. *adj.* [*decrepitus*, Latin.] Wasted and worn out with age; in the last stage of decay.

Decrepit miser! base, ignoble wretch! *Shakesp. H.* VI.

These years were short of many mens lives in this *decrepit* age of the world, wherein many exceed fourscore, and some an hundred years. *Raleigh's History of the World.*

This pope is *decrepit*, and the bell goeth for him: take order that there be chosen a pope of fresh year. *Bacon's H. War.*

Decrepit superstition, and such as had their nativity in times beyond all history, are fresh in the observation of many heads. *Brown's Vulgar Errours.*

And from the North to call
Decrepit Winter. *Milton's Paradise Lost, b.* x. *l.* 655.

Who this observes, may in his body find
Decrepit age, but never in his mind. *Denham.*

Propp'd on his staff, and stooping as he goes,
A painted mitre shades his furrow'd brows;
The god, in the *decrepit* form array'd,
The gardens enter'd, and the fruits survey'd. *Pope.*

The charge of witchcraft inspires people with a malevolence towards those poor *decrepit* parts of our species, in whom human nature is defaced by infirmity and dotage. *Addis.*

To DECRE'PITATE. *v. a.* [*decrepo*, Latin.] To calcine salt till it has ceased to crackle in the fire.

So will it come to pass in a pot of salt, although *decrepitated*. *Brown's Vulgar Errours, b.* ii.

Decrepita'tion. *n. s.* [from *decrepitate.*] The crackling noise which salt makes, when put over the fire in a crucible. *Quincy.*

Decre'pitness. } *n. s.* [from *decrepit.*] The last stage of decay; the last effects of old age.
Decre'pitude. }

Mother earth, in this her barrenness and *decrepitness* of age, can procreate such swarms of curious engines. *Bentley's Serm.*

Decre'scent. *adj.* [from *decrescens*, Latin.] Growing less; being in a state of decrease.

De'cretal. *adj.* [*decretum*, Latin.] Appertaining to a decree; containing a decree.

A *decretal* epistle is that which the pope decrees either by himself, or else by the advice of his cardinals; and this must be on his being consulted by some particular person or persons thereon. *Ayliffe's Parergon.*

De'cretal. *n. s.* [from the adjective.]

1. A book of decrees or edicts; a body of laws.

The second room, whose walls
Were painted fair with memorable gests,
Of magistrates, of courts, of tribunals,
Of commonwealths, of states, of policy,
Of law, of judgments, and of *decretals*. *Fairy Queen, b.* ii.

2. The collection of the pope's decrees.

Traditions and *decretals* were made of equal force, and as authentical as the sacred charter itself. *Howel's Vocal Forrest.*

De'cretist. *n. s.* [from *decree.*] One that studies or professes the knowledge of the decretal.

The *decretists* had their rise and beginning under the reign of the emperor Frederick Barbarossa. *Ayliffe's Parergon.*

De'cretory. *adj.* [from *decree.*]

1. Judicial; definitive.

There are lenitives that friendship will apply, before it will be brought to the *decretory* rigours of a condemning sentence. *South's Sermons.*

2. Critical; in which there is some definitive event.

The motions of the moon, supposed to be measured by sevens, and the critical or *decretory* days, depend on that number. *Brown's Vulgar Errours, b.* iv. *c.* 12.

Decri'al. *n. s.* [from *decry.*] Clamorous censure; hasty or noisy condemnation; concurrence in censuring any thing.

To DECRY'. *v. a.* [*decrier*, French.] To censure; to blame clamorously; to clamour against.

Malice in criticks reigns so high,
That for small errours they whole plays *decry*. *Dryden.*

Those measures which are extolled by one half of the kingdom, are naturally *decryed* by the other. *Addison's Freeh.*

They applied themselves to lessen their authority, *decryed* them as hard and unnecessary restraints. *Rogers, Serm.* 17.

Quacks and impostors are still cautioning us to beware of counterfeits, and *decry* others cheats only to make more way for their own. *Swift.*

Decu'mbence. } *n. s.* [*decumbo*, Latin.] The act of lying down; the posture of lying down.
Decu'mbency. }

This must come to pass, if we hold opinion they lie not down, and enjoy no *decumbence* at all; for station is properly no rest, but one kind of motion. *Brown's Vulgar Errours, b.* iii.

Not considering the ancient manner of *decumbency*, he imputed this gesture of the beloved disciple unto rusticity, or an act of incivility. *Brown's Vulgar Errours, b.* v. *c.* 6.

Decu'mbiture. *n. s.* [from *decumbo*, Latin.]

1. The time at which a man takes to his bed in a disease.

2. [In astrology.] A scheme of the heavens erected for that time, by which the prognosticks of recovery or death are discovered.

If but a mile she travel out of town,
The planetary hour must first be known,
And lucky moment: if her eye but akes,
Or itches, its *decumbiture* she takes. *Dryden's Juv. Sat.* vi.

De'cuple. *adj.* [*decuplus*, Latin.] Tenfold; the same number ten times repeated.

Man's length, that is, a perpendicular from the vertex unto the sole of the foot, is *decuple* unto his profundity; that is, a direct line between the breast and the spine. *Brown's Vul. Err.*

Supposing there be a thousand sorts of insects in this island, if the same proportion holds between the insects of England and of the rest of the world, as between plants domestick and exotick, that is, near a *decuple*, the species of insects wil amount to ten thousand. *Ray on the Creation.*

Decu'rion. *n. s.* [*decurio*, Lat.] A commander over ten; an officer subordinate to the centurion.

He instituted *decurions* through both these colonies, that is, one over every ten families. *Temple.*

Decu'rsion. *n. s.* [*decursus*, Lat.] The act of running down.

What is decayed by that *decursion* of waters, is supplied by the terrene fœces which water brings. *Hale's Orig. of Mankind.*

Decurta'tion. *n. s.* [*decurtatio*, Latin.] The act of cutting short, or shortening.

To DECU'SSATE. *v. a.* [*decusso*, Latin.] To intersect at acute angles.

This it performs by the action of a notable muscle on each side, of a great length, having the form of the letter X, made up of many fibres, *decussating* one another longways. *Ray.*

Decussa'tion. *n. s.* [from *decussate.*] The act of crossing; state of being crossed at unequal angles.

Though there be *decussation* of the rays in the pupil of the eye, and so the image of the object in the retina, or bottom of the eye, be inverted; yet doth not the object appear inverted, but in its right or natural posture. *Ray on the Creation.*

To DEDE'CORATE. *v. a.* [*dedecoro*, Latin.] To disgrace; to bring a reproach upon. *Dict.*

Dedecora'tion. *n. s.* [from *dedecorate.*] The act of disgracing; disgrace. *Dict.*

Dede'corous. *adj.* [*dedecus*, Lat.] Disgraceful; reproachful; shameful. *Dict.*

Dedenti'tion. *n. s.* [*de* and *dentitio*, Lat.] Loss or shedding of the teeth.

Solon divided it into ten septenaries, because in every one thereof a man received some sensible mutation: in the first is *dedentition*, or falling of teeth. *Brown's Vulgar Errours, b.* iv.

To DE'DICATE. *v. a.* [*dedico*, Latin.]

1. To devote to some divine power; to consecrate and set apart to sacred uses.

A pleasant grove
Was shot up high, full of the stately tree
That *dedicated* is to olympick Jove,
And to his son Alcides, when as he
Gain'd in Nemea goodly victory. *Fairy Queen, b.* ii. *cant.* 5.

The princes offered for *dedicating* the altar, in the day that it was anointed. *Num.* vii. 10.

Warn'd by the seer, to her offended name
We rais'd, and *dedicate* this wond'rous frame. *Dryden's Æn.*

2. To appropriate solemnly to any person or purpose.

There cannot be
That vulture in you to devour so many,
As will to greatness *dedicate* themselves. *Shakesp. Macbeth.*

Ladies, a gen'ral welcome from his grace
Salutes you all: this night he *dedicates*
To fair content and you. *Shakespeare's Henry* VIII.

He went to learn the profession of a soldier, to which he had *dedicated* himself. *Clarendon.*

Bid her instant wed,
And quiet *dedicate* her remnant life
To the just duties of an humble wife. *Prior.*

3. To inscribe to a patron.

He compiled ten elegant books, and *dedicated* them to the lord Burghley. *Peacham on Poetry.*

DE'DICATE. *adj.* [from the verb.] Consecrate; devote; dedicated; appropriate.

Prayers from preserved souls,
From fasting maids, whose names are *dedicate*
To nothing temporal. *Shakespeare's Measure for Measure.*

This tenth part, or tithe, being thus assigned unto him, leaveth now to be of the nature of the other nine parts, which are given us for our worldly necessities, and becometh as a thing *dedicate* and appropriate unto God. *Spelman.*

DEDICA'TION. *n. s.* [*dedicatio*, Latin.]

1. The act of dedicating to any being or purpose; consecration; solemn appropriation.

It cannot be laid to many mens charge, that they have been so curious as to trouble bishops with placing the first stone in the churches; or so scrupulous as, after the erection of them, to make any great ado for their *dedication*. *Hooker, b.* v. *s.* 12.

Among publick solemnities there is none so glorious as that under the reign of king Solomon, at the *dedication* of the temple. *Addison's Freeholder*, No. 49.

2. A servile address to a patron.

Proud as Apollo on his forked hill,
Sat full blown Bufo, puff'd by ev'ry quill;
Fed by soft *dedication* all day long,
Horace and he went hand in hand in song. *Pope, Epist.* xi.

DEDICA'TOR. *n. s.* [from *dedicate.*] One who inscribes his work to a patron with compliment and servility.

Leave dang'rous truths to unsuccessful satyrs,
And flattery to fulsome *dedicators*. *Pope's Essay on Criticism.*

DE'DICATORY. *adj.* [from *dedicate.*] Composing a dedication; complimental; adulatory.

Thus I should begin my epistle, if it were a *dedicatory* one; but it is a friendly letter. *Pope.*

DEDI'TION. *n. s.* [*deditio*, Latin.] The act of yielding up any thing; surrendry.

It was not a complete conquest, but rather a *dedition* upon terms and capitulations agreed between the conqueror and the conquered. *Hale's History of the Common Law.*

To DEDU'CE. *v. a.* [*deduco*, Latin.]

1. To draw in a regular connected series, from one time or one event to another.

O goddess, say, shall I *deduce* my rhimes
From the dire nation in its early times! *Pope.*

2. To form a regular chain of consequential prepositions.

Reason is nothing but the faculty of *deducing* unknown truths from principles already known. *Locke.*

3. To lay down in regular order, so as that the following shall naturally rise from the foregoing.

Lend me your song, ye nightingales! Oh pour
The mazy-running soul of melody
Into my varied verse! while I *deduce*,
From the first note the hollow cuckoo sings,
The symphony of Spring. *Thomson's Spring, l.* 575.

DEDU'CEMENT. *n. s.* [from *deduce.*] The thing deduced; the collection of reason; consequential preposition.

Praise and prayer are his due worship, and the rest of those *deducements*, which I am confident are the remote effects of revelation. *Dryden's Pref. to Rel. Laici.*

DEDU'CIBLE. *adj.* [from *deduce.*] Collectible by reason; consequential; discoverable from principles laid down.

The condition, although *deducible* from many grounds, yet shall we evidence it but from few. *Brown's Vulgar Errours, b.* i.

The general character of the new earth is paradisaical, and the particular character that it hath no sea; and both are apparently *deducible* from its formation. *Burnet's Theo. of the Earth.*

So far, therefore, as conscience reports any thing agreeable to, or *deducible* from these, it is to be hearkened to. *South.*

All properties of a triangle depend on, and are *deducible* from, the complex idea of three lines, including a space. *Locke.*

DEDU'CIVE. *adj.* [from *deduce.*] Performing the act of deduction. *Dict.*

To DEDU'CT. *v. a.* [*deduco*, Latin.]

1. To substract; to take away; to cut off; to defalcate.

We *deduct* from the computation of our years, that part of our time which is spent in incogitancy of infancy. *Norris.*

2. To separate; to dispart; to divide. Now not in use.

Having yet, in his *deducted* spright,
Some sparks remaining of that heavenly fire. *Spenser.*

DEDU'CTION. *n. s.* [*deductio*, Lat.] Consequential collection; consequence; preposition drawn from principles premised.

Out of scripture such duties may be duduced, by some kind of consequence, as by long circuit of *deduction* it may be that even all truth, out of any truth, may be concluded. *Hooker.*

Set before you the moral law of God, with such *deductions* from it as our Saviour hath drawn, or our own reason, well informed, can make. *Duppa's Rules for Devotion.*

That by diversity of motions we should spell out things not resembled by them, we must attribute to some secret *deduction*; but what this *deduction* should be, or by what mediums this knowledge is advanced, is as dark as ignorance. *Glanv. Sceps.*

You have laid the experiments together in such a way, and made such *deductions* from them, as I have not hitherto met with. *Boyle's Scept. Chym.*

All cross and distasteful humours are either expresly, or by clear consequence and *deduction*, forbidden in the New Testament. *Tillotson, Sermon* 5.

A reflection so obvious, that natural instinct seems to have suggested it even to those who never much attended to *deductions* of reason. *Rogers, Serm.* 19.

2. That which is deducted; defalcation.

Bring then these blessings to a strict account;
Make fair *deductions*, see to what they mount. *Pope's Essays.*

DEDU'CTIVE. *adj.* [from *deduct.*] Deducible; that which is or may be deduced from a position premised.

DEDU'CTIVELY. *adv.* [from *deductive.*] Consequentially; by regular deduction; by a regular train of ratiocination.

There is scarce a popular errour passant in our days, which is not either directly expressed, or *deductively* contained in this work. *Brown's Vulgar Errours, b.* i. *c.* 8.

DEED. *n. s.* [dæd, Saxon; *daed*, Dutch.]

1. Action, whether good or bad; thing done.

From lowest place when virtuous things proceed,
The place is dignified by th' doer's *deed*. *Shakespeare.*

The monster nought reply'd; for words were vain,
And *deeds* could only *deeds* unjust maintain. *Dryden.*

The same had not consented to the counsel and *deed*. *Luke.*

We are not secluded from the expectation of reward for our charitable *deeds*. *Smalridge's Sermons.*

2. Exploit; performance.

I, on the other side,
Us'd no ambition to commend my *deeds*;
The *deeds* themselves, though mute, spoke loud the doer. *Milt.*

Thousands were there in darker fame that dwelt,
Whose *deeds* some nobler poem shall adorn. *Dryd. Ann. Mir.*

3. Power of action; agency.

Nor knew I not
To be with will and *deed* created free. *Milt. Paradise Lost.*

4. Act declaratory of an opinion.

They desire, with strange absurdity, that to the same senate it should belong to give full judgment in matter of excommunication, and to absolve whom it pleased them, clean contrary to their own former *deeds* and oaths. *Hooker's Preface.*

5. Written evidence of any legal act.

The solicitor gave an evidence for a *deed*, which was impeached to be fraudulent. *Bacon.*

He builds his house upon the sand, and writes the *deeds*, by which he holds his estate, upon the face of a river. *South.*

6. Fact; reality; the contrary to fiction: whence the word *indeed.*

O that, as oft I have at Athens seen
The stage arise, and the big clouds descend;
So now in very *deed* I might behold
The pond'rous earth, and all yon marble roof,
Meet like the hands of Jove. *Lee's Oedipus.*

DEE'DLESS. *adj.* [from *deed.*] Unactive; without action; without exploits.

Speaking in deeds, and *deedless* in his tongue. *Shakespeare.*

Instantly, he cry'd, your female discord end,
Ye *deedless* boasters! and the song attend. *Pope's Odyssey.*

To DEEM. *v. n.* part. *dempt*, or *deemed.* [*domgan*, Gothick; *doemen*, Dutch; ðeman, Saxon.] To judge; to conclude upon consideration; to think; to opine; to determine.

Here eke that famous golden apple grew,
For which th' Idean ladies disagreed,
'Till partial Paris *dempt* it Venus' due. *Fairy Queen, b.* ii.

Do me not dy,
Ne *deem* thy force by fortune's doom unjust,
That hath, maugre her spite, thus low me laid in dust.
Fairy Queen, b. ii. *cant.* 5. *stanz.* 12.

But they that skill not of so heavenly matter,
All that they know not, envy or admire,
Rather than envy, let them wonder at her,
But not to *deem* of her desert aspire. *Spenser, Sonnet* 84.

So natural is the union of religion with justice, that we may boldly *deem* there is neither, where both are not. *Hooker.*

He, who to be *deem'd*
A god, leap'd fondly into Ætna flames. *Milt. Parad. Lost.*

These blessings, friend, a deity bestow'd;
For never can I *deem* him less than god. *Dryd. Virg. Past.*

Nature disturb'd,
Is *deem'd* vindictive to have chang'd her course. *Thomson.*

DEEM. *n. s.* [from the verb.] Judgment; surmise; opinion. Not now in use.

Hear me, my love, be thou but true of heart.
—I true! how now? what wicked *deem* is this? *Shakespear.*

DEE'MSTER. *n. s.* [from *deem.*] A judge: a word yet in use in Jersey and the Isle of Man.

DEEP. *adj.* [ðeep, Saxon.]

1. Having length downwards; descending far; profound.

All trees in high and sandy grounds are to be set *deep*, and in watery grounds more shallow. *Bacon's Natural History.*

The gaping gulph low to the centre lies,
And twice as *deep* as earth is distant from the skies. *Dryden.*

2. Low in situation; not high.

3. Measured from the surface downward.

Mr. Halley, in diving deep into the sea in a diving vessel, found,

found, in a clear sun-shine day, that when he was sunk many fathoms *deep* into the water, the upper part of his hand, on which the sun shone directly, appeared of a red colour. *Newt.*

4. Entering far; piercing a great way.

This avarice
Strikes *deeper*; grows with more pernicious root. *Sh. Macb.*

For, even in that season of the year, the ways in that vale were very *deep*. *Clarendon, b.* viii.

Thou hast not strength such labours to sustain:
Drink hellebore, my boy! drink *deep*, and scour thy brain. *Dryden's Pers. Sat.*

5. Far from the outer part.

So the false spider, when her nets are spread,
Deep ambush'd in her silent den does lie. *Dryd. Ann. Mirab.*

6. Not superficial; not obvious.

If the matter be knotty, and the sense lies *deep*, the mind must stop and buckle to it, and stick upon it with labour and thought, and close contemplation. *Locke.*

7. Sagacious; penetrating; having the power to enter far into a subject.

Who hath not heard it spoken,
How *deep* you were within the books of heav'n! *Shakesp.*

The spirit of *deep* prophecy she hath. *Shakesp. Henry* VI.

He's meditating with two *deep* divines. *Shakesp. Rich.* III.

He in my ear
Vented much policy and projects *deep*
Of enemies, of aids, battles and leagues,
Plausible to the world, to me worth naught. *Milt. Par. Reg.*

I do not discover the helps which this great man of *deep* thought mentions. *Locke.*

8. Full of contrivance; politick; insiduous.

When I have most need to employ a friend,
Deep, hollow, treacherous, and full of guile,
Be he to me. *Shakespeare's Richard* III.

9. Grave; solemn.

O God! if my *deep* prayers cannot appease thee,
But thou wilt be aveng'd on my misdeeds,
Yet execute thy wrath on me alone. *Shakesp. Rich.* III.

Nor awful Phœbus was on Pindus heard
With *deeper* silence, or with more regard. *Dryden's Silenius.*

10. Dark coloured.

With *deeper* brown the grove was overspread. *Dryd. Fab.*

11. Having a great degree of stilness, or gloom, or sadness.

Their *deep* poverty abounded into the riches of their liberality. 2 *Cor.* viii. 2.

And the Lord God caused a *deep* sleep to fall upon Adam. *Gen.* ii. 21.

12. Bass; grave in sound.

The sounds made by buckets in a well, are *deeper* and fuller than if the like percussion were made in the open air. *Bacon's Natural History*, N°. 152.

Deep. *n. s.* [from the adjective.]

1. The sea; the main; the abyss of waters; the ocean.

Yet we did lift up our hearts and voices to God above, who sheweth his wonders in the *deep*. *Bacon's New Atlantis.*

What earth in her dark bowels could not keep
From greedy man, lies safer in the *deep*. *Waller.*

Whoe'er thou art, whom fortune brings to keep
These rites of Neptune, monarch of the *deep*. *Pope's Odyss.*

2. The most solemn or still part.

There want not many that do fear,
In *deep* of night, to walk by this Herne's oak. *Shakespeare.*

The *deep* of night is crept upon our talk. *Shak. Jul. Cæs.*

Virgin face divine,
Attracts the hapless youth through storms and waves,
Alone in *deep* of night. *Philips.*

To Deépen. *v. a.* [from *deep.*]

1. To make deep; to sink far below the surface.

The city of Rome would receive a great advantage from the undertaking, as it would raise the banks and *deepen* the bed of the Tiber. *Addison's Travels.*

2. To darken; to cloud; to make dark.

You must *deepen* your colours so, that the orpiment may be the highest. *Peacham on Drawing.*

3. To make sad or gloomy. See DEEP. *adj.*

Her gloomy presence saddens all the scene,
Shades ev'ry flow'r, and darkens ev'ry green,
Deepens the murmurs of the falling floods,
And breathes a browner horror on the woods. *Pope.*

Deep-mouthed. *adj.* [*deep* and *mouth.*] Having a hoarse and loud voice.

Huntsman, I charge thee, tender well my hounds;
And couple Clowder with the *deep-mouth'd* Brach. *Shakesp.*

Behold the English beach
Pales in the flood with men, with wives and boys,
Whose shouts and claps outvoice that *deep-mouth'd* sea. *Shak.*

Then toils for beasts, and lime for birds were found,
And *deep-mouth'd* dogs did forest walks surround. *Dryden.*

Hills, dales, and forests far behind remain,
While the warm scent draws on the *deep-mouth'd* train. *Gay.*

Deep-mu'sing. *adj.* [*deep* and *muse.*] Contemplative; lost in thought.

But he *deep-musing* o'er the mountains stray'd,
Through mazy thickets of the woodland shade. *Pope's Odyss.*

De'eply. *adj.* [from *deep.*]

1. To a great depth; far below the surface.

Fear is a passion that is most *deeply* rooted in our natures, and flows immediately from the principle of self-preservation. *Tillotson, Serm.* 1.

Those impressions were made when the brain was more susceptive of them: they have been *deeply* engraven at the proper season, and therefore they remain. *Watts's Improvement.*

2. With great study or sagacity; not superficially; not carelesly; profoundly.

3. Sorrowfully; solemnly; with a great degree of seriousness or sadness.

He sighed *deeply* in his spirit. *Mark* viii. 12.

Klockins so *deeply* hath sworn ne'er more to come
In bawdy-house, that he dares not go home. *Donne.*

Upon the deck our careful general stood,
And *deeply* mus'd on the succeeding day. *Dryd. Ann. Mirab.*

4. With a tendency to darkness of colour.

Having taken of the *deeply* red juice of buckthorn berries, I let it drop upon white paper. *Boyle on Colours.*

5. In a high degree.

To keep his promise with him, he had *deeply* offended both his nobles and people. *Bacon's Henry* VII.

De'epness. *n. s.* [from *deep.*] Entrance far below the surface; profundity; depth.

Cazzianer set forward with great toil, by reason of the *deepness* of the way and heaviness of the great ordnance. *Knolles's History of the Turks.*

Some fell upon stony places, and they withered, because they had no *deepness* of earth. *Matt.* xiii. 5.

Deer. *n. s.* [deoƿ, Saxon; *thier*, Teutonick; θὴρ, Greek.] That class of animals which is hunted for venison, containing many subordinate species.

You have beaten my men, killed my *deer*, and broke open my lodge. *Shakespeare's Merry Wives of Windsor.*

The pale that held my lovely *deer*. *Waller.*

To DEFA'CE. *v. a.* [*defaire*, French.] To destroy; to raze; to ruin; to disfigure.

Fatal this marriage,
Defacing monuments of conquer'd France,
Undoing all. *Shakespeare's Henry* VI. *p.* ii.

Pay him six thousand, and *deface* the bond. *Shakespeare.*

Whose statues, freezes, columns broken lie,
And, though *defac'd*, the wonder of the eye. *Dryden.*

One nobler wretch can only rise;
'Tis he whose fury shall *deface*
The stoick's image in this piece. *Prior.*

Defa'cement. *n. s.* [from *deface.*] Violation; injury; rasure; abolition; destruction.

But what is this image, and how is it defaced? The poor men of Lyons will tell you, that the image of God is purity; and the *defacement*, sin. *Bacon's Holy War.*

Defa'cer. *n. s.* [from *deface.*] Destroyer; abolisher; violater.

That foul *defacer* of God's handywork,
Thy womb let loose, to chase us to our graves. *Sh. R.* III.

Defa'ilance. *n. s.* [*defaillance*, French.] Failure; miscarriage: a word not in use.

The affections were the authors of that unhappy *defailance*. *Glanv. Sceps. c.* 2.

To DEFA'LCATE. *v. a.* [from *falx falcis*, a sickle; *defalquer*, French.] To cut off; to lop; to take away part of a pension or salary. It is generally used of money.

Defalca'tion. *n. s* [from *defalcate.*] Diminution; abatement; excision of any part of a customary allowance.

The tea table is set forth with its customary bill of fare, and without any *defalcation*. *Addison's Spectator*, N°. 487.

To Defa'lk. *v. a.* [See DEFALCATE.] To cut off; to lop away.

What he *defalks* from some insipid sin, is but to make some other more gustful. *Decay of Piety.*

Defama'tion. *n s.* [from *defame.*] The act of defaming or bringing infamy upon another; calumny; reproach; censure; detraction.

Defamation is the uttering of reproachful speeches, or contumelious language of any one, with an intent of raising an ill fame of the party thus reproached; and this extends to writing, as by *defamatory* libels; and also to deeds, as by reproachful postures, signs and gestures. *Ayliffe's Parergon.*

Be silent, and beware, if such you see;
'Tis *defamation* but to say, that's he *Dryden's Juv. Sat.*

Many dark and intricate motives there are to detraction and *defamation*, and many malicious spies are searching into the actions of a great man. *Addison's Spectator*, N°. 256.

Defa'matory. *adj.* [from *defame.*] Calumnious; tending to defame; unjustly censorious; libellous; falsely satirical.

The most eminent sin is the spreading of *defamatory* reports. *Government of the Tongue, sect.* 5.

Augustus, conscious to himself of many crimes, made an edict against lampoons and satyrs, and *defamatory* writings. *Dryden's Juv. Dedication.*

To DEFA'ME. *v. a.* [*de* and *fama*, Latin.] To make infa-

mous;

mous; to censure falsely in publick; to deprive of honour; to dishonour by reports; to libel; to calumniate; to destroy reputation by either acts or words.

I heard the *defaming* of many. *Jer.* xx. 10.

They live as if they professed Christianity merely in spight, to *defame* it. *Decay of Piety.*

My guilt thy growing virtues did *defame*;
My blackness blotted thy unblemish'd name. *Dryden's Æn.*

DEFA'ME. *n. s.* [from the verb.] Disgrace; dishonour.

Many doughty knights he in his days
Had done to death,
And hung their conquer'd arms for more *defame*
On gallowtrees. *Fairy Queen, b.* ii. *cant.* 5. *stan.* 26.

DEFA'MER. *n. s.* [from *defame.*] One that injures the reputation of another; a detracter; a calumniator.

It may be a useful trial of the patience of the defamed, yet the *defamer* has not the less crime. *Government of the Tongue.*

To DEFA'TIGATE. *v. a.* [*defatigo*, Latin.] To weary; to tire. *Dict.*

DEFATIGA'TION. *n. s.* [*defatigatio*, Latin.] Weariness; fatigue. *Dict.*

DEFA'ULT. *n. s.* [*defaut*, French.]

1. Omission of that which we ought to do; neglect.

2. Crime; failure; fault.

Sedition tumbled into England more by the *default* of governours than the peoples. *Haywood.*

We that know what 'tis to fast and pray,
Are penitent for your *default* to-day. *Shak. Com. of Errours.*

Let me not rashly call in doubt
Divine prediction: what if all foretold
Had been fulfill'd, but through mine own *default*,
Whom have I to complain of, but myself? *Milt. Agonistes.*

Partial judges we are of our own excellencies, and other mens *defaults*. *Swift.*

3. Defect; want.

In *default* of the king's pay, the forces were laid upon the subject. *Davies on Ireland.*

Cooks could make artificial birds and fishes, in *default* of the real ones. *Arbuthnot on Coins.*

4. [In law.] Non-appearance in court at a day assigned. *Cowel.*

To DEFA'ULT. *v. a.* [from the noun.] To fail in performing any contract or stipulation; to forfeit by breaking a contract.

DEFE'ASANCE. *n. s.* [*defaisance*, French.]

1. The act of annulling or abrogating any contract or stipulation.

2. *Defeasance* is a condition annexed to an act; as to an obligation, a recognisance, or statute, which performed by the obligee, or the cognizee, the act is disabled and made void, as if it had never been done. *Cowel.*

3. The writing in which a defeasance is contained.

4. A defeat; conquest; the act of conquering; the state of being conquered. Obsolete.

That hoary king, with all his train,
Being arrived, where that champion stout,
After his foe's *defeasance*, did remain,
Him goodly greets, and fair does entertain. *Fairy Queen.*

DEFE'ASIBLE. *adj.* [from *defaire*, Fr. to make void.] That which may be annulled or abrogated.

He came to the crown by a *defeasible* title, so was never well settled. *Davies on Ireland.*

DEFE'AT. *n. s.* [from *defaire*, French.]

1. The overthrow of an army.

End Marlb'rough's work, and finish the *defeat*. *Addison.*

2. Act of destruction; deprivation.

A king, upon whose life
A damn'd *defeat* was made. *Shakespeare's Hamlet.*

To DEFE'AT. *v. a.* [from the noun.]

1. To overthrow.

Ye gods, ye make the weak most strong;
Therein, ye gods, ye tyrants do *defeat*. *Shakes. Jul. Cæsar.*

They invaded Ireland, and were *defeated* by the lord Mountjoy. *Bacon on the War with Spain.*

2. To frustrate.

To his accusations
He pleaded still not guilty, and alleg'd
Many sharp reasons to *defeat* the law. *Shakes. Henry* VIII.

Death,
Then due by sentence when thou did'st transgress,
Defeated of his seizure, many days,
Giv'n thee of grace. *Milton's Paradise Lost, b.* i. *l.* 254.

Discover'd, and *defeated* of your prey,
You skulk'd. *Dryden's Virg. Past.* 3.

He finds himself naturally to dread a superior Being, that can *defeat* all his designs, and disappoint all his hopes. *Tillotson.*

3. To abolish.

DEFE'ATURE. *n. s.* [from *de* and *feature.*] Change of feature; alteration of countenance.

Grief hath chang'd me,
And careful hours, with time's deformed hand,
Hath written strange *defeatures* in my face. *Shakespeare.*

To DE'FECATE. *v. a.* [*defæco*, Latin.]

1. To purge liquors from lees or foulness; to purify; to cleanse.

I practised a way to *defecate* the dark and muddy oil of amber. *Boyle's History of Firmness.*

The blood is not sufficiently *defecated* or clarified, but remains muddy. *Harvey on Consumptions.*

Provide a brazen tube
Inflext; self-taught and voluntary flies
The *defecated* liquor, through the vent
Ascending; then, by downward tract convey'd,
Spouts into subject vessels, lovely clear. *Philips.*

2. To purify from any extraneous or noxious mixture; to clear; to brighten.

We *defecate* the notion from materiality, and abstract quantity, place, and all kind of corporeity from it. *Glanv. Sceps.*

We are puzzled with contradictions, which are no absurdities to *defecate* faculties. *Glanv. Sceps. c.* 13.

DE'FECATE. *adj.* [from the verb.] Purged from lees or foulness.

This liquor was very *defecate*, and of a pleasing golden colour. *Boyle's Spring of the Air.*

DEFECA'TION. *n. s.* [*defæcatio*, Latin.] Purification; the act of clearing or purifying.

The spleen and liver are obstructed in their offices of *defecation*, whence vicious and dreggish blood. *Harvey on Consum.*

DEFE'CT. *n. s.* [*defectus*, Latin.]

1. Want; absence of something necessary; insufficiency; the fault opposed to superfluity.

Errors have been corrected, and *defects* supplied. *Davies.*

Had this strange energy been less,
Defect had been as fatal as excess. *Blackmore's Creation.*

2. Failing; want.

Oft 'tis seen
Our mean secures us, and our mere *defects*
Prove our commodities. *Shakespeare's King Lear.*

3. A fault; mistake; error.

We had rather follow the perfections of them whom we like not, than in *defects* resemble them whom we love. *Hooker.*

You praise yourself,
By laying *defects* of judgment to me. *Shakes. Ant. and Cleop.*

Trust not yourself; but your *defects* to know,
Make use of ev'ry friend—and ev'ry foe. *Pope's Essay.*

4. Any natural imperfection; a blemish; a failure.

Men, through some *defect* in the organs, want words, yet fail not to express their universal ideas by signs. *Locke.*

To DEFE'CT. *v. n.* [from the noun.] To be deficient; to fall short of; to fail. Obsolete.

Some lost themselves in attempts above humanity, yet the enquiries of most *defected* by the way, and tired within the sober circumference of knowledge. *Brown's Vulgar Errours.*

DEFECTIBI'LITY. *n. s.* [from *defectible.*] The state of failing; deficiency; imperfection.

The corruption of things corruptible depends upon the intrinsecal *defectibility* of the connection or union of the parts of things corporeal, which is rooted in the very nature of the things. *Hale's Origin of Mankind.*

DEFE'CTIBLE. *adj.* [from *defect.*]

1. Imperfect; deficient; wanting.

The extraordinary persons, thus highly favoured, were for a great part of their lives in a *defectible* condition. *Hale.*

DEFE'CTION. *n. s.* [*defectio*, Latin.]

1. Want; failure.

2. A falling away; apostacy.

This *defection* and falling away from God was first found in angels, and afterwards in men. *Raleigh's History of the World.*

If we fall away after tasting of the good word of God, how criminal must such a *defection* be? *Atterbury's Sermons.*

But there is more evil owing to our original *defection* from God, and the foolish and evil dispositions that are found in fallen man. *Watts's Logick.*

3. An abandoning of a king, or state; revolt.

He was diverted and drawn from hence by the general *defection* of the whole realm. *Davies on Ireland.*

Neither can this be meant of evil governours or tyrants, but of some perverseness and *defection* in the very nation itself. *Bacon's Holy War.*

DEFE'CTIVE. *adj.* [from *defectivus*, Latin.]

1. Full of defects; imperfect; not sufficient; not adequate to the purpose.

It subjects them to all the diseases depending upon a *defective* projectile motion of the blood. *Arbuthnot on Aliments.*

It will very little help to cure my ignorance, that this is the best of four or five hypotheses proposed, which are all *defective*. *Locke.*

If it renders us perfect in one accomplishment, it generally leaves us *defective* in another. *Addison's Spectator*, N°. 255.

2. Faulty; vitious; blameable.

Our tragedy writers have been notoriously *defective* in giving proper sentiments to the persons they introduce. *Addis.*

DEFE'CTIVE or *deficient Nouns* [in grammar.] Indeclinable nouns, or such as want a number, or some particular case.

DEFE'CTIVE *Verb* [in grammar.] A verb which wants some of its tenses.

DEFE'CTIVENESS. *n. s.* [from *defective.*] Want; the state of being imperfect; faultiness.

The lowness often opens the building in breadth, or the *defectiveness* of some other particular makes any single part appear in perfection. *Addison's Remarks on Italy.*

DEFE'NCE. *n. s.* [*defensio*, Latin.]

1. Guard; protection; security.

Rehoboam dwelt in Jerusalem, and built cities for *defence* in Judah. *2 Chro.* ii. 5.

The Lord is your protection and strong stay, a *defence* from heat, and a cover from the sun. *Eccluf.* xxxiv. 16.

Be thou my strong rock for an house of *defence* to save me. *Ps.* xxxi. 2.

Against all this there seems to be no *defence*, but that of supporting one established form of doctrine and discipline. *Sw.*

2. Vindication; justification; apology.

Alexander beckoned with his hand, and would have made his *defence* unto the people. *Acts* xix. 33.

The youthful prince
With scorn replied, and made this bold *defence*. *Dryden.*

3. Prohibition: this is a sense merely French.

Severe *defences* may be made against wearing any linnen under a certain breadth. *Temple.*

4. Resistance.

5. [In law.] The defendant's reply after declaration produced.

6. [In fortification.] The part that flanks another work.

DEFE'NCELESS. *adj.* [from *defence.*]

1. Naked; unarmed; unguarded; not provided with defence; unprepared.

Captain or colonel, or knight in arms,
Whose chance on these *defenceless* doors may seize,
If deed of honour did thee ever please,
Guard them, and him within protect from harms. *Milton.*

My sister is not so *defenceless* left
As you imagine: she has a hidden strength
Which you remember not. *Milton.*

Ah me! that fear
Comes thund'ring back with dreadful revolution
On my *defenceless* head. *Milton's Paradise Lost, b.* x. *l.* 815.

On a slave disarm'd,
Defenceless, and submitted to my rage,
A base revenge is vengeance on myself. *Dryd. Don Sebast.*

2. Impotent; unable to make resistance.

Will such a multitude of men employ
Their strength against a weak *defenceless* boy? *Addis. Ovid.*

To DEFE'ND. *v. a.* [*defendo*, Latin; *defendre*, French.]

1. To stand in defence of; to protect; to support.

There arose, to *defend* Israel, Tola the son of Puah. *Judg.*

Deliver me from mine enemies, O my God: *defend* me from them that rise up against me. *Ps.* lix. 1.

Heav'n *defend* your souls, that you think
I will your serious and great business scant. *Shakesp. Othello.*

2. To vindicate; to uphold; to assert; to maintain.

The queen on the throne, by God's assistance, is able to *defend* herself against all her majesty's enemies and allies put together. *Swift's Remarks on the Barrier Treaty.*

3. To fortify; to secure.

And here th' access a gloomy grove *defends*,
And here th' unnavigable lake extends. *Dryden's Æneis.*

4. To prohibit; to forbid. [*defendre*, French.]

Where can you say, in any manner, age,
That ever God *defended* marriage? *Chaucer.*

O sons! like one of us, man is become
To know both good and evil, since his taste
Of that *defended* fruit. *Milton's Paradise Lost, b.* xi. *l.* 86.

The use of it is little practised, and in some places *defended* by customs or laws. *Temple.*

5. To maintain a place, or cause, against those that attack it.

DEFE'NDABLE. *adj.* [from *defend.*] That may be defended.

DEFE'NDANT. *adj.* [from *defendo*, Latin.] Defensive; fit for defence.

Line and new repair our towns of war
With men of courage, and with means *defendant*. *Shakesp.*

DEFE'NDANT. *n. s.* [from the adjective.]

1. He that defends against assailants.

Those high towers, out of which the Romans might more conveniently fight with the *defendants* on the wall, those also were broken by his engines. *Wilkins's Math. Mag.*

2. [In law.] The person accused or sued.

This is the day appointed for the combat,
And ready are th' appellant and *defendant*. *Shak. Henry* VI.

Plaintiff dog, and bear *defendant*. *Hudibras.*

DEFE'NDER. *n. s.* [*defensor*, Latin.]

1. One that defends; a champion.

You have the power still
To banish your *defenders*, 'till at length
Your ignorance deliver you,
As most abated captives, to some nation
That won you without blows. *Shakespeare's Coriolanus.*

Do'st thou not mourn our pow'r employ'd in vain,
And the *defenders* of our city slain? *Dryden.*

2. An asserter; a vindicator.

Undoubtedly there is no way so effectual to betray the truth, as to procure it a weak *defender*. *South's Sermons.*

3. [In law.] An advocate; one that defends another in a court of justice.

DEFENSA'TIVE. *n. s.* [from *defence.*]

1. Guard; defence.

A very unsafe *defensative* it is against the fury of the lion, and surely no better than virginity, or blood royal, which Pliny doth place in cock-broth. *Brown's Vulgar Errours, b.* iii.

If the bishop has no other *defensatives* but excommunication, no other power but that of the keys, he may surrender up his pastoral staff. *South's Sermons.*

2. [In surgery.] A bandage, plaister, or the like, used to secure a wound from outward violence.

DEFE'NSIBLE. *adj.* [from *defence.*] That may be defended.

A field,
Which nothing but the sound of Hotspur's name,
Did seem to make *defensible*. *Shakespeare's Henry* IV. *p.* ii.

They must make themselves *defensible*, both against the natives and against strangers. *Bacon's Advice to Villiers.*

Having often heard Venice represented as one of the most *defensible* cities in the world, I informed myself in what its strength consists. *Addison's Remarks on Italy.*

2. Justifiable; right; capable of vindication.

I conceive it very *defensible* to disarm an adversary, and disable him from doing mischief. *Collier.*

DEFE'NSIVE. *adj.* [*defensif*, Fr. from *defendens*, Latin.]

1. That serves to defend; proper for defence; not offensive.

He would not be persuaded by danger to offer any offence, but only to stand upon the best *defensive* guard he could. *Sidney.*

My unpreparedness for war, testifies for me, that I am set on the *defensive* part. *King Charles.*

Defensive arms lay by, as useless here,
Where massy balls the neighbouring rocks do tear. *Waller.*

2. In a state or posture of defence.

What stood, recoil'd,
Defensive scarce, or with pale fear surpriz'd,
Fled ignominious. *Milton.*

DEFE'NSIVE. *n. s.* [from the adjective.]

1. Safeguard.

Wars preventive upon just fears, are true *defensives*, as well as on actual invasions. *Bacon's War with Spain.*

2. State of defence.

His majesty, not at all dismayed, resolved to stand upon the *defensive* only. *Clarendon, b.* viii.

DEFE'NSIVELY. *adv.* [from *defensive.*] In a defensive manner.

DEFE'NST. *part. pass.* [from *defence.*] Defended. Obsolete.

Stout men of arms, and with their guide of power,
Like Troy's old town, *defenst* with Illion's tow'r. *Fairfax.*

To DEFE'R. *v. n.* [from *differo*, Latin.]

1. To put off; to delay to act.

He will not long *defer*
To vindicate the glory of his name
Against all competition, nor will long
Endure it. *Milton's Agonistes, l.* 473.

Inure thyself by times to the love and practice of good deeds; for the longer thou *deferest* to be acquainted with them, the less every day thou wilt find thyself disposed to them. *Atterb.*

2. To pay deference or regard to another's opinion.

To DEFE'R. *v. a.*

1. To withold; to delay.

Defer the promis'd boon, the goddess cries,
Celestial azure brightning in the eyes. *Pope's Odyssey, b.* i.

Neither is this a matter to be *deferred* 'till a more convenient time of peace and leisure. *Swift.*

2. To refer to; to leave to another's judgment and determination.

The commissioners *deferred* the matter unto the earl of Northumberland, who was the principal man of authority in those parts. *Bacon's Henry* VII.

DE'FERENCE. *n. s.* [*deference*, French.]

1. Regard; respect.

Virgil could have excelled Varius in tragedy, and Horace in lyric poetry, but out of *deference* to his friends he attempted neither. *Dryden's Juven. Dedicat.*

He may be convinced that he is in an error, by observing those persons, for whose wisdom and goodness he has the greatest *deference*, to be of a contrary sentiment. *Swift.*

2. Complaisance; condescension.

A natural roughness makes a man uncomplaisant to others; so that he has no *deference* for their inclinations, tempers, or conditions. *Locke.*

3. Submission.

Most of our fellow-subjects are guided either by the prejudice of education, or a *deference* to the judgment of those who, perhaps, in their own hearts, disapprove the opinions which they industriously spread among the multitude. *Addison.*

DE'FERENT. *adj.* [from *deferens*, of *defero*, Latin.] That carries up and down.

The figures of pipes or concaves, through which sounds

ſounds paſs, or of other bodies *deferent*, conduce to the variety and alteration of the ſound. *Bacon's Natural Hiſtory*, N°. 220.

DE'FERENT. *n. ſ.* [from the adjective.] That which carries; that which conveys.

It is certain, however it croſſes the received opinion, that ſounds may be created without air, though air be the moſt favourable *deferent* of ſounds. *Bacon's Natural Hiſtory.*

DE'FERENTS [in ſurgery.] Certain veſſels in the human body, appointed for the conveyance of humours from one place to another. *Chambers.*

DEFI'ANCE. *n. ſ.* [from *deffi*, French.]

1. A challenge; an invitation to fight.

The firey Tybalt, with his ſword prepar'd,
Which, as he breath'd *defiance* to my ears,
He ſwung about his head. *Shakeſpeare's Romeo and Juliet.*

Nor is it juſt to bring
A war, without a juſt *defiance* made. *Dryden's Ind. Emp.*

2. A challenge to make any impeachment good.

3. Expreſſion of abhorrence or contempt.

The Novatian hereſy was very apt to attract well meaning ſouls, who, ſeeing it bad ſuch expreſs *defiance* to apoſtacy, could not ſuſpect that it was itſelf any defection from the faith. *Decay of Piety.*

No body will ſo openly bid *defiance* to common ſenſe, as to affirm viſible and direct contradictions. *Locke.*

DEFI'CIENCE. } *n. ſ.* [from *deficio*, Latin.] Defect; fail-
DEFI'CIENCY. } ing; imperfection.

Scaliger, finding a defect in the reaſon of Ariſtotle, introduceth one of no leſs *deficiency* himſelf. *Brown's Vulgar Errours.*

Thou in thyſelf art perfect, and in thee
Is no *deficience* found. *Milton's Paradiſe Loſt, b.* viii. *l.* 415.

We ſhall find, in our own natures, too great evidence of intellectual *deficience*, and deplorable confeſſions of human ignorance. *Glanv. Scepſ. c.* 3.

What great *deficience* is it, if we come ſhort of others? *Sprat's Sermons.*

The characters of comedy and tragedy are never to be made perfect, but always to be drawn with ſome ſpecks of frailty and *deficience*, ſuch as they have been deſcribed to us in hiſtory. *Dryden's Dufreſnoy, Pref.*

2. Want; ſomething leſs than is neceſſary.

What is to be conſidered in this caſe, is chiefly, if there be a ſufficient fulneſs or *deficiency* of blood, for different methods are to be taken. *Arbuthnot on Diet.*

There is no burden laid upon our poſterity, nor any *deficiency* to be hereafter made up by ourſelves, which has been our caſe in ſo many other ſubſidies. *Addiſon's Freeholder.*

DEFI'CIENT. *adj.* [*deficiens*, from *deficio*, Latin.] Failing; wanting; defective; imperfect.

O woman! beſt are all things as the will
Of God ordain'd them: his creating hand
Nothing imperfect or *deficient* left. *Milton's Paradiſe Loſt.*

Figures are either ſimple or mixed: the ſimple be either circular or angular; and of circular, either complete, as circles, or *deficient*, as ovals. *Wotton's Architect.*

Neither Virgil nor Homer were *deficient* in any of the former beauties. *Dryden's Fab. Pref.*

Several views, poſtures, ſtands, turns, limitations and exceptions, and ſeveral other thoughts of the mind, for which we have either none, or very *deficient* names, are diligently to be ſtudied. *Locke.*

DEFI'CIENT *Verbs.* See DEFECTIVE *Verbs.*

DEFI'CIENT *Nouns.* See DEFECTIVE *Nouns.*

DEFI'CIENT *Numbers* [in arithmetick] are thoſe numbers whoſe parts, added together, make leſs than the integer, whoſe parts they are. *Chambers.*

DEFI'ER. *n. ſ.* [from *deffi*, French.] A challenger; a contemner; one that dares and defies.

Is it not then high time that the laws ſhould provide, by the moſt prudent and effectual means, to curb thoſe bold and inſolent *defiers* of heaven. *Tillotſon, Serm.* 3.

To DEFI'LE. *v. a.* [apulan, Sax. from *ful*, *foul.*]

1. To make foul or impure; to make naſty or filthy; to dirty.

There is a thing, Harry, known to many in our land by the name of pitch: this pitch, as ancient writers do report, doth *defile*. *Shakeſpeare's Henry* IV. *p.* i.

He is juſtly reckoned among the greateſt prelates of this age, however his character may be *defiled* by mean and dirty hands. *Swift's Letter concerning the Sacramental Teſt.*

2. To pollute; to make legally or ritually impure.

That which dieth of itſelf he ſhall not eat, to *defile* himſelf therewith. *Lev.* xxii. 8.

Neither ſhall he *defile* himſelf for his father. *Lev.* xxi. 11.

3. To corrupt chaſtity; to violate.

Ev'ry object his offence revil'd,
The huſband murder'd, and the wife *defil'd.* *Prior.*

4. To taint; to corrupt; to vitiate; to make guilty.

Forgetfulneſs of good turns, *defiling* of ſouls, adultery and ſhameleſs uncleanneſs. *Wiſd.* xiv. 26.

God requires rather that we ſhould die than *defile* ourſelves with impieties. *Stillingfleet.*

Let not any inſtances of ſin *defile* your requeſts. *Wake.*

To DEFI'LE. *v. n.* [*deffiler*, French] To march; to go off file by file.

DEFI'LE. *n. ſ.* [*deffile*, Fr. from *file*, a line of ſoldiers, which is derived from *filum*, a thread.] A narrow paſſage; a long narrow paſs; a lane.

There is in Oxford a narrow *defile*, to uſe the military term, where the partiſans uſed to encounter. *Addiſ. Spectator.*

DEFI'LEMENT. *n. ſ.* [from *defile.*] The ſtate of being defiled; the act of defiling; naſtineſs; pollution; corruption; defedation.

Luſt,
By unchaſte looks, looſe geſtures, and foul talk,
Lets in *defilement* to the inward parts. *Milton.*

The unchaſte are provoked to ſee their vice expoſed, and the chaſte cannot rake into ſuch filth without danger of *defilement.* *Spectator*, N°. 286.

DEFI'LER. *n. ſ.* [from *defile.*] One that defiles; a corrupter; a violater.

At the laſt tremendous day I ſhall hold forth in my arms my much wronged child, and call aloud for vengeance on her *defiler.* *Addiſon's Guardian*, N°. 128.

DEFI'NABLE. *adj.* [from *define.*]

1. That which may be defined; capable of definition.

The Supreme Nature we cannot otherwiſe define, than by ſaying it is infinite, as if infinite were *definable*, or infinity a ſubject for our narrow underſtanding. *Dryden.*

2. That which may be aſcertained.

Concerning the time of the end of the world, the queſtion is, whether that time be *definable* or no. *Burnet's Theory.*

To DEFI'NE. *v. a.* [*definio*, Lat. *definir*, French.]

1. To give the definition; to explain a thing by its qualities and circumſtances.

Whoſe loſs can'ſt thou mean,
That do'ſt ſo well their miſeries *define?* *Sidney, b.* ii.

Though *defining* be thought the proper way to make known the proper ſignification, yet there are ſome words that will not be *defined.* *Locke.*

2. To circumſcribe; to mark the limit; to bound.

When the rings, or ſome parts of them, appeared only black and white, they were very diſtinct and well *defined*, and the blackneſs ſeemed as intenſe as that of the central ſpot. *Newt.*

To DEFI'NE. *v. n.* To determine; to decide; to decree.

The unjuſt judge is the capital remover of landmarks, when he *defineth* amiſs of lands and properties. *Bacon, Eſſ.* 57.

DEFI'NER. *n. ſ.* [from *define.*] One that explains; one that deſcribes a thing by its qualities.

Your God, forſooth, is found
Incomprehenſible and infinite;
But is he therefore found? Vain ſearcher! no:
Let your imperfect definition ſhow,
That nothing you, the weak *definer*, know. *Prior.*

DE'FINITE. *adj.* [from *definitus*, Latin.]

1. Certain; limited; bounded.

Hither to your arbour divers times he repaired, and here, by your means, had the ſight of the goddeſs, who in a *definite* compaſs can ſet forth infinite beauty. *Sidney, b.* i.

2. Exact; preciſe.

Ideots, in this caſe of favour, would
Be wiſely *definite.* *Shakeſpeare's Cymbeline.*

In a charge of adultery, the accuſer ought to ſet forth, in the accuſatory libel or inquiſition, which ſucceeds in the place of accuſation, ſome certain and *definite* time. *Ayliffe's Parerg.*

DE'FINITE. *n ſ.* [from the adjective.] Thing explained or defined.

If theſe things are well conſidered, ſpecial baſtardy is nothing elſe but the definition of the general; and the general, again, is nothing elſe but a *definite* of the ſpecial. *Ayliffe.*

DE'FINITENESS. *n. ſ.* [from *definite.*] Certainty; limitedneſs. *Dict.*

DEFINI'TION. *n. ſ.* [*definitio*, Latin; *definition*, French.]

1. A ſhort deſcription of a thing by its properties.

I drew my *definition* of poetical wit from my particular conſideration of him; for propriety of thoughts and words are only to be found in him; and, where they are proper, they will be delightful. *Dryden.*

2. Deciſion; determination.

3. [In logick.] The explication of the eſſence of a thing by its kind and difference.

What is man? Not a reaſonable animal merely; for that is not an adequate and diſtinguiſhing *definition.* *Bentley's Serm.*

DEFI'NITIVE. *adj.* [*definitivus*, Latin.] Determinate; poſitive; expreſs.

Other authors write often dubiouſly, even in matters wherein is expected a ſtrict and *definitive* truth. *Brown's Vulg. Err.*

I make haſte to the caſting and comparting of the whole work, being indeed the very *definitive* ſum of this art, to diſtribute uſefully and gracefully a well choſen plot. *Wotton.*

DEFI'NITIVELY. *adv.* [from *definitive.*] Poſitively; deciſively; expreſly.

Definitively thus I anſwer you:
Your love deſerves my thanks; but my deſert,
Unmeritable, ſhuns your high requeſt. *Shakeſp. Rich.* III.

That

That Metheusalah was the longest lived, of all the children of Adam, we need not grant; nor is it *definitively* set down by Moses. *Brown's Vulgar Errours, b.* vi. *c.* 6.

Bellarmine saith, because we think that the body of Christ may be in many places at once, locally and visibly; therefore we say and hold, that the same body may be circumscriptively and *definitively* in more places at once. *Hall.*

DEFI'NITIVENESS. *n. s.* [from *definitive.*] Decisiveness. *Dict.*

DEFLAGRABI'LITY. *n. s.* [from *deflagro*, Latin.] Combustibility; the quality of taking fire, and burning totally away.

We have been forced to spend much more time than the opinion of the ready *deflagrability*, if I may so speak, of saltpetre did beforehand permit us to imagine. *Boyle on Saltpetre.*

DEFLA'GRABLE. *adj.* [from *deflagro*, Lat.] Having the quality of wasting away wholly in fire, without any remains.

Our chymical oils, supposing that they were exactly pure, yet they would be, as the best spirit of wine is, but the more inflammable and *deflagrable.* *Boyle's Scept. Chym.*

DEFLAGRA'TION. *n. s.* [*deflagratio*, Latin.]

A term frequently made use of in chymistry, for setting fire to several things in their preparation; as in making Æthiops with fire, with sal prunellæ, and many others. *Quincy.*

The true reason, therefore, why that paper is not burned by the flame that plays about it, seems to be, that the aqueous part of the spirit of wine, being imbibed by the paper, keeps it so moist, that the flame of the sulphureous parts of the same spirit cannot fasten on it; and therefore, when the *deflagration* is over, you shall always find the paper moist; and sometimes we have found it so moist, that the flame of a candle would not readily light it. *Boyle.*

To DEFLE'CT. *v. n.* [*deflecto*, Latin.] To turn aside; to deviate from a true course, or right line.

At some parts of the Azores the needle *deflecteth* not, but lieth in the true meridian: on the other side of the Azores, and this side of the Equator, the North point of the needle wheeleth to the West. *Brown's Vulgar Errours.*

Arising beyond the Equator, it maketh northward almost fifteen degrees; and *deflecting* after westward, without meanders, continueth a strait course about forty degrees. *Brown.*

For did not some from a strait course *deflect*,
They could not meet, they could no world erect. *Blackm.*

DEFLE'CTION. *n. s.* [from *deflecto*, Latin.]

1. Deviation; the act of turning aside.

Needles incline to the South on the other side of the Equator; and, at the very line or middle circle, stand without *deflection.* *Brown's Vulgar Errours, b.* 2. *c.* 2.

2. A turning aside, or out of the way.

3. [In navigation.] The departure of a ship from its true course.

DEFLE'XURE. *n. s.* [from *deflecto*, Latin.] A bending down; a turning aside, or out of the way. *Dict.*

DEFLORA'TION. *n. s.* [*defloration*, Fr. from *defloratus*, Lat.]

1. The act of deflouring; the taking away of a woman's virginity.

2. A selection of that which is most valuable.

The laws of Normandy are, in a great measure, the *defloration* of the English laws, and a transcript of them. *Hale.*

To DEFLO'UR. *v. a.* [*deflorer*, French.]

1. To ravish; to take away a woman's virginity.

As is the lust of an eunuch to *deflour* a virgin, so is he that executeth judgment with violence. *Ecclus.* xx. 4.

Now will I hence to seek my lovely Moor,
And let my spleenful sons this trull *deflour*. *Shakesp. Tit. And.*

2. To take away the beauty and grace of any thing.

How on a sudden lost,
Defac'd, *deflour'd*, and now to death devote! *Milt. Pa. Lost.*

If he died young, he died innocent, and before the sweetness of his soul was *defloured* and ravished from him, by the flames and follies of a froward age. *Taylor's Rule of living holy.*

DEFLO'URER. *n. s.* [from *deflour.*] A ravisher; one that takes away virginity.

I have often wondered, that those *deflourers* of innocence, though dead to all the sentiments of virtue and honour, are not restrained by humanity. *Addison's Guardian.*

DEFLU'OUS. *adj.* [*defluus*, Latin.]

1. That flows down.

2. That falls off.

DEFLU'XION. *n. s.* [*defluxio*, Latin.] A defluxion; a flowing down of humours.

We see that taking cold moveth looseness, by contraction of the skin and outward parts; and so doth cold likewise cause rheums and *defluxions* from the head. *Bacon's Natural History.*

DEFLY'. *adv.* [from *deft.*] Dexterously; skilfully. Obsolete. Properly *deftly*.

Lo, how finely the graces can it foot
To the instrument;
They dauncen *defly*, and singen soote,
In their merriment. *Spenser's Pastorals.*

DEFOEDA'TION. *n. s.* [from *defœdus*, Lat.] The act of making filthy; pollution.

What native, unextinguishable beauty must be impressed and instincted through the whole, which the *defœdation* of so many parts by a bad printer, and a worse editor, could not hinder from shining forth. *Bentley's Preface to Milton.*

DEFO'RCEMENT. *n. s.* [from *force.*] A with-holding of lands and tenements by force from the right owner.

To DEFO'RM. *v. a.* [*deformo*, Latin.]

1. To disfigure; to make ugly; to spoil the form of any thing.

I that am curtail'd of this fair proportion,
Cheated of feature by dissembling nature,
Deform'd, unfinish'd, sent before my time
Into this breathing world, scarce half made up. *Sh. R.* III.

Wintry blasts
Deform the year delightless. *Thomson's Winter.*

2. To dishonour; to make ungraceful.

Old men with dust *deform'd* their hoary hair. *Dryd. Fab.*

DEFO'RM. *adj.* [*deformis*, Latin.] Ugly; disfigured; of an irregular form.

I did proclaim,
That whoso kill'd that monster most *deform*,
Should have mine only daughter to his dame. *Fairy Queen.*

So spake the griesly terror; and in shape,
So speaking and so threatning, grew tenfold
More dreadful and *deform*. *Milton's Paradise Lost, b.* ii.

Sight so *deform*, what heart of rock could long
Dry-ey'd behold. *Milton's Paradise Lost, b.* xi. *l.* 494.

DEFORMA'TION. *n. s.* [*deformatio*, Latin.] A defacing; a disfiguring.

DEFO'RMEDLY. *adv.* [from *deform.*] In an ugly manner.

DEFO'RMEDNESS. *n. s.* [from *deformed.*] Ugliness; a disagreeable form.

DEFO'RMITY. *n. s.* [*deformitas*, Latin.]

1. Ugliness; ill-favouredness.

I, in this weak piping time of peace,
Have no delight to pass away the time,
Unless to spy my shadow in the sun,
And descant on mine own *deformity*. *Shakespeare's Rich.* III.

Proper *deformity* seems not in the fiend
So horrid as in woman. *Shakespeare's King Lear.*

Where sits *deformity* to mock my body,
To shape my legs of an unequal size;
To disproportion me in every part. *Shakesp. Henry* VI. *p.* iii.

Why should not man,
Retaining still divine similitude
In part, from such *deformities* be free,
And, for his maker's image sake, exempt? *Milt. Pa. Lost.*

2. Ridiculousness; the quality of something worthy to be laughed at.

In comedy there is somewhat more of the worse likeness to be taken, because it is often to produce laughter, which is occasioned by the sight of some *deformity*. *Dryd. Pref. Dufres.*

3. Irregularity; inordinateness.

No glory is more to be envied than that of due reforming either church or state, when *deformities* are such, that the perturbation and novelty are not like to exceed the benefit of reforming. *King Charles.*

4. Dishonour; disgrace.

DEFO'RSOR. *n. s.* [from *forceur*, French.] One that overcomes and casteth out by force. A law term. *Blount.*

To DEFRA'UD. *v. a.* [*defraudo*, Latin.] To rob or deprive by a wile or trick; to cheat; to cozen; to deceive; to beguile. With *of* before the thing taken by fraud.

That no man go beyond and *defraud* his brother in any matter, because that the Lord is the avenger of all such, as we also have forewarned you and testified. *Thes.* iv. 6.

My son, *defraud* not the poor *of* his living, and make not the needy eyes to wait long. *Ecclus.* iv. 1.

They seem, after a sort, even to mourn, as being injured and *defrauded of* their right, when places, not sanctified as they are, prevent them unnecessarily in that pre-eminence and honour. *Hooker, b.* v. *s.* 16.

Then they, who brothers better claim disown,
Expel their parents, and usurp the throne;
Defraud their clients, and, to lucre sold,
Sit brooding on unprofitable gold. *Dryden's Æn.* 6.

But now he seiz'd Briseis' heav'nly charms,
And *of* my valour's prize *defrauds* my arms. *Pope's Iliad.*

There is a portion of our lives which every wise man may justly reserve for his own particular use, without *defrauding* his native country. *Dryden's Dedicat. to King Arthur.*

DEFRA'UDER. *n. s.* [from *defraud.*] A deceiver; one that cheats.

The profligate in morals grow severe,
Defrauders just, and sycophants sincere. *Blackm. Creation.*

To DEFRA'Y. *v. a.* [*defrayer*, French.] To bear the charges of; to discharge expences.

He would, out of his own revenue, *defray* the charges belonging to the sacrifices. *2 Mac.* ix. 16.

It is easy, Ireneus, to lay a charge upon any town; but to foresee how the same may be answered and *defrayed*, is the chief part of good advisement. *Spenser's State of Ireland.*

It

It is long ſince any ſtranger arrived in this part, and therefore take ye no care; the ſtate will *defray* you all the time you ſtay; neither ſhall you ſtay one day the leſs for that. *Bacon.*

DEFRA'YER. *n. ſ.* [from *defray.*] One that diſcharges expences.

DEFRA'YMENT. *n. ſ.* [from *defray.*] The payment of expences.

DEFT. *adj.* [dæpt, Saxon.] Obſolete.

1. Neat; handſome; ſpruce.

2. Proper; fitting.

You go not the way to examine: you muſt call the watch that are their accuſers.——
—Yea, marry, that's the *defteſt* way. *Shak. Much ado about N.*

3. Ready; dexterous.

Loud fits of laughter ſeiz'd the gueſts, to ſee
The limping god ſo *deft* at his new miniſtry. *Dryd. Iliad.*
The wanton calf may ſkip with many a bound,
And my cur, Tray, play *defteſt* feats around. *Gay's Paſt.*

DE'FTLY. *adv.* [from *deft.*] Obſolete.

1. Neatly; dexterouſly.

2. In a ſkilful manner.

Come, high or low,
Thyſelf and office *deftly* ſhow. *Shakeſpeare's Macbeth.*
Young Colin Clout, a lad of peerly meed,
Full well could dance, and *deftly* tune the reed. *Gay's Paſt.*

DEFU'NCT. *adj.* [*defunctus*, Latin.]

1. Dead; deceaſed.

I therefore beg it not,
To pleaſe the palate of my appetite;
Nor to comply with heat, the young affects,
In me *defunct*, and proper ſatisfaction. *Shakeſp. Othello.*
Here entity and quiddity,
The ſouls of *defunct* bodies fly. *Hudibras.*

DEFU'NCT. *n. ſ.* [from the adjective.] One that is deceaſed; a dead man, or woman.

Nature doth abhor to make his couch
With the *defunct*, or ſleep upon the dead. *Shakeſ. Cymbeline.*

In many of theſe caſes the ſearchers are able to report the opinion of the phyſician who was with the patient, as they receive the ſame from the friends of the *defunct*. *Graunt.*

DEFU'NCTION. *n. ſ.* [from *defunct.*] Death.

Nor did the French poſſeſs the Salique land,
Until four hundred one and twenty years
After *defunction* of king Pharamond. *Shakeſpeare's Hen.* V.

To DEFY'. *v. a.* [*deffier*, Fr. from *de fide decedere*, or ſome like phraſe, to fall from allegiance to rebellion, contempt, or inſult.]

1. To call to combat; to challenge.

I once again
Defy thee to the trial of mortal fight. *Milton's Agoniſtes.*
Where ſeek retreat, now innocence is fled!
Safe in that guard, I durſt even hell *defy*;
Without it, tremble now, when heav'n is nigh. *Dryden.*
Agis, the Lycian, ſtepping forth with pride,
To ſingle fight the boldeſt foe *defy'd*. *Dryden's Æn.*

2. To treat with contempt; to ſlight.

I do know
As many fools that ſtand in better place,
Garniſh'd like him, that for a trickſy word
Defy the matter. *Shakeſpeare's Merchant of Venice.*

DEFY'. *n. ſ.* [from the verb.] A challenge; an invitation to fight.

At this the challenger, with fierce *defy*,
His trumpet ſounds; the challeng'd makes reply:
With clangour rings the field, reſounds the vaulted ſky. *Dryd.*

DEFY'ER. *n. ſ.* [from *defy.*] A challenger; one that invites to fight.

God may, ſome time or other, think it the concern of his juſtice, and providence too, to revenge the affronts put upon them by ſuch impudent *defyers* of both, as neither believe a God, nor ought to be believed by man. *South's Sermons.*

DEGE'NERACY. *n. ſ.* [from *degeneratio*, Latin.]

1. A departing from the virtue of our anceſtors.

2. A forſaking of that which is good.

'Tis true, we have contracted a great deal of weakneſs and impotency by our wilful *degeneracy* from goodneſs; but that grace, which the goſpel offers to us for our aſſiſtance, is ſufficient for us. *Tillotſon, Serm.* 6.

The ruin of a ſtate is generally preceded by an univerſal *degeneracy* of manners, and contempt of religion, which is entirely our caſe at preſent. *Swift.*

3. Meanneſs.

There is a kind of ſluggiſh reſignation, as well as poorneſs and *degeneracy* of ſpirit, in a ſtate of ſlavery. *Addiſon.*

To DEGE'NERATE. *v. n.* [*degenerare*, Lat. *degenerer*, Fr. *degenerar*, Spaniſh.]

1. To fall from the virtue of anceſtors.

2. To fall from a more noble to a baſe ſtate.

When wit tranſgreſſeth decency, it *degenerates* into inſolence and impiety. *Tillotſon, Sermon* 2.

3. To fall from its kind; to grow wild or baſe.

Moſt of thoſe fruits that uſe to be grafted, if they be ſet of kernels or ſtones, *degenerate*. *Bacon's Natural Hiſtory*, N°. 519.

DEGE'NERATE. *adv.* [from the verb.]

1. Unlike his anceſtors; fallen from the virtue and merit of his anceſtors.

Thou art like enough
To fight againſt me under Piercy's pay;
To dog his heels, and curt'ſy at his frowns,
To ſhow how much thou art *degenerate*. *Shakeſp. Hen.* IV.
Yet thou haſt greater cauſe to be
Aſham'd of them, than they of thee;
Degenerate from their ancient brood,
Since firſt the court allow'd them food. *Swift.*

2. Unworthy; baſe.

So all ſhall turn *degen'rate*, all deprav'd;
Juſtice and temperance, truth, and faith forgot!
One man except. *Milton's Paradiſe Loſt, b.* xi. *l.* 806.

When a man ſo far becomes *degenerate* as to quit the principles of human nature, and to be a noxious creature, there is commonly an injury done ſome perſon or other. *Locke.*

DEGE'NERATENESS. *n. ſ.* [from *degenerate.*] Degeneracy; a being grown wild; out of kind. *Dict.*

DEGENERA'TION. *n. ſ.* [from *degenerate.*]

1. A deviation from the virtue of one's anceſtors.

2. A falling from a more excellent ſtate to one of leſs worth.

3. The thing changed from its primitive ſtate.

In plants, wherein there is no diſtinction of ſexes, theſe tranſplantations are yet more obvious than they; as that of barley into oats, of wheat into darnell; and thoſe grains which generally ariſe among corn, as cockle, aracus, œgilops, and other *degenerations*. *Brown's Vulgar Errours, b.* iii. *c.* 17.

DEGE'NEROUS. *adj.* [from *degener*, Latin.]

1. Degenerated; fallen from the virtue and merit of his anceſtors.

2. Vile; baſe; infamous; unworthy.

Let not the tumultuary violence of ſome mens immoderate demands ever betray me to that *degenerous* and unmanly ſlavery, which ſhould make me ſtrengthen them by my conſent. *King Charles.*

Shame, inſtead of piety, reſtrains them from many baſe and *degenerous* practices. *South's Sermons.*

Degenerous paſſion, and for man too baſe,
It ſeats its empire in the female race;
There rages, and, to make his blow ſecure,
Puts flatt'ry on, until the aim be ſure. *Dryden's Juvenal.*

DEGE'NEROUSLY. *adv.* [from *degenerous.*] In a degenerate manner; baſely; meanly.

How wounding a ſpectacle is it to ſee our greateſt heroes, like Hercules at the diſtaff, thus *degenerouſly* employed? *Decay of Piety.*

DEGLUTI'TION. *n. ſ.* [*deglutition*, Fr. from *deglutio*, Lat.] The act or power of ſwallowing.

When the *deglutition* is totally aboliſhed, the patient may be nouriſhed by clyſters. *Arbuthnot on Diet.*

DEGRADA'TION. *n. ſ.* [*degradation*, French.]

1. A deprivation of an office or dignity.

The word *degradation* is commonly uſed to denote a deprivation and removing of a man from his degree. *Ayliffe's Par.*

2. Degeneracy; baſeneſs.

So deplorable is the *degradation* of our nature, that whereas before we bore the image of God, we now retain only the image of men. *South's Sermons.*

3. [In painting.] A term made uſe of to expreſs the leſſening and rendering confuſed the appearance of diſtant objects in a landſkip, ſo as they may appear there as they would do to an eye placed at that diſtance from them. *Dict.*

To DEGRA'DE. *v. a.* [*degrader*, French.]

1. To put one from his degree; to deprive him of his office, dignity, or title.

He ſhould
Be quite *degraded*, like a hedgeborn ſwain,
That doth preſume to boaſt of gentle blood. *Shak. Hen.*VI.

2. To leſſen; to diminiſh the value of.

Nor ſhalt thou, by deſcending to aſſume
Man's nature, leſſen or *degrade* thine own. *Milt. Par. Loſt.*
All higher knowledge in her preſence falls
Degraded. *Milton's Paradiſe Loſt, b.* viii. *l.* 551.

DEGRAVA'TION. *n. ſ.* [from *degravate*, of *degravo*, Lat.] The act of making heavy. *Dict.*

DEGRE'E. *n. ſ.* [*degré*, French, from *gradus*, Latin.]

1. Quality; rank; ſtation; place of dignity.

Surely men of low *degree* are vanity, and men of high *degree* are a lie: to be laid in the balance, they are altogether lighter than vanity. *Pſ.* lxii. 9.

It was my fortune, common to that age,
To love a lady fair, of great *degree*,
The which was born of noble parentage,
And ſet in higheſt ſeat of dignity. *Fairy Queen, b.* ii. *cant.* 4.

I embrace willingly the ancient received courſe and conveniency of that diſcipline, which teacheth inferior *degrees* and orders in the church of God. *Hooker's Dedication.*

Well

Well then, Coleville is your name; a knight is your *degree*, and your place the dale. *Shakespeare's Henry* IV. *p.* ii.

Degree being vizarded,
Th' unworthiest shews as fairly in the mask. *Shakespeare.*

This noble youth to madness lov'd a dame
Of high *degree*, Honoria was her name. *Dryden.*

Farmers in *degree*,
He a good husband, a good housewife she. *Dryden.*

But is no rank, no station, no *degree*,
From this contagious taint of sorrow free? *Prior.*

2. The state and condition in which a thing is.

The book of wisdom noteth *degrees* of idolatry, making that of worshipping petty and vile idols more gross than simply the worshipping of the creature. *Bacon's Holy War.*

3. A step or preparation to any thing.

Her first *degree* was by setting forth her beauties, truly in nature not to be misliked, but as much advanced to the eye as abased to the judgment by art. *Sidney, b.* ii.

Which sight the knowledge of myself might bring,
Which to true wisdom is the first *degree*. *Davies.*

4. Order of lineage; descent of family.

King Latinus, in the third *degree*,
Had Saturn author of his family. *Dryden's Æn. b.* vii. *l.* 72.

5. The orders or classes of the angels.

The several *degrees* of angels may probably have larger views, and be endowed with capacities able to set before them, as in one picture, all their past knowledge at once. *Locke.*

6. Measure; proportion.

If you come to separate them, and that all the parts are equally heard as loud as one another they will stun you to that *degree*, that you would fancy your ears were torn in pieces. *Dryden's Dufresnoy.*

Poesy
Admits of no *degrees*; but must be still
Sublimely good, or despicably ill. *Roscommon.*

7. [In geometry.] The three hundred and sixtieth part of the circumference of a circle. The space of one degree in the heavens is accounted to answer to sixty miles.

In minds and manners, twins oppos'd we see;
In the same sign, almost the same *degree*. *Dryden's Pers. Sat.*

To you who live in chill *degree*,
As map informs, of fifty-three. *Dryden's Epistles.*

8. [In arithmetick.] A *degree* consists of three figures, viz. of three places comprehending units, tens and hundreds; so three hundred and sixty-five is a *degree*. *Cocker's Arithmetick.*

9. The division of the lines upon several sorts of mathematical instruments.

10. [In musick.] The intervals of sounds, which are usually marked by little lines. *Dict.*

11. [In physick and chymistry.] The vehemence or slackness of the hot or cold quality of a plant, mineral, or other mixt body.

The second, third, and fourth *degrees* of heat are more easily introduced than the first: every one is both a preparative and a step to the next. *South's Sermons.*

By DEGRE'ES. *adv.* Gradually; by little and little.

Their bodies are exercised in all abilities both of doing and suffering, and their minds acquainted by *degrees* with danger. *Sidney, b.* ii.

Doth not this ethereal medium, in passing out of water, glass, crystal, and other compact and dense bodies, into empty spaces, grow denser and denser by *degrees*? *Newton's Opt.*

Exulting in triumph, now swell the bold notes;
In broken air, trembling, the wild musick floats;
'Till by *degrees* remote and small,
The strains decay,
And melt away,
In a dying, dying fall. *Pope's Cecilia.*

A person who is addicted to play or gaming, though he took but little delight in it at first, by *degrees* contracts a strong inclination towards it. *Spectator,* N°. 447.

DEGUSTA'TION. *n. s.* [*degustatio*, Latin.] A tasting. *Dict.*

To DEHO'RT. *v. a.* [*dehortor*, Latin.] To dissuade; to advise to the contrary.

One of the greatest sticklers for this fond opinion, severely *dehorted* all his followers from prostituting mathematical principles unto common apprehension or practice. *Wilkins.*

The author of this epistle, and the rest of the apostles, do every where vehemently and earnestly *dehort* us from unbelief: did they never read these dehortations? *Ward on Infidelity.*

DEHORTA'TION. *n. s.* [from *dehortor*, Latin.] Dissuasion; a counselling to the contrary.

The author of this epistle, and the rest of the apostles, do every where vehemently and earnestly dehort from unbelief, did they never read these *dehortations*. *Ward on Infidelity.*

DEHO'RTATORY. *adj.* [from *dehortor*, Latin.] Belonging to dissuasion.

DEHO'RTER. *n. s.* [from *dehort*.] A dissuader; an adviser to the contrary.

DE'ICIDE. *n. s.* [from *deus* and *cædo*, Latin.] The murder of God; the act of killing God. It is only used in speaking of the death of our blessed Saviour.

Explain how perfection suffer'd pain,
Almighty languish'd, and Eternal dy'd;
How by her patient victor death was slain,
And earth profan'd, yet bless'd with *deicide!* *Prior.*

To DEJE'CT. *v. a.* [*dejicio*, Latin.]

1. To cast down; to afflict; to grieve; to depress; to sink; to discourage, to crush.

Well, I am your theme; you have the start of me; I am *dejected*; ignorance itself is a plummet o'er me; use me as you will. *Shakespeare's Merry Wives of Windsor.*

The lowest, most *dejected* thing of fortune,
Stands still in esperance; lives not in fear! *Shakes. K. Lear.*

Nor think to die, *dejects* my lofty mind;
All that I dread is leaving you behind! *Pope's R. of the Lock.*

2. To change the form with grief; to make to look sad.

Eneas here beheld, of form divine,
A godlike youth in glitt'ring armour shine,
With great Marcellus keeping equal pace;
But gloomy were his eyes, *dejected* was his face. *Dryd. Æn.*

DEJE'CT. *adj.* [*dejectus*, Latin.] Cast down; afflicted; low-spirited.

I am of ladies most *deject* and wretched,
That suck'd the honey of his musick vows. *Shakes. Hamlet.*

DEJE'CTEDLY. *adv.* [from *deject*.] In a dejected manner; afflictedly.

No man in that passion doth look strongly, but *dejectedly*; and that repulsion from the eyes, diverteth the spirits, and gives heat more to the ears, and the parts by them. *Bacon's N. Hist.*

DEJE'CTEDNESS. *n. s.* [from *dejected*.] A being cast down; a lowness of spirits. *Dict.*

DEJE'CTION. *n. s.* [*dejection*, Fr. from *dejectio*, Lat.]

1. A lowness of spirits; melancholy.

What besides
Of sorrow, and *dejection*, and despair,
Our frailty can sustain, thy tidings bring,
Departure from this happy place. *Milton's Paradise Lost.*

Deserted and astonished, he sinks into utter *dejection*; and even hope itself is swallowed up in despair. *Rogers's Sermons.*

2. Weakness; inability.

The effects of such an alkalescent state, in any great degree, are thirst and a *dejection* of appetite, which putrid things occasion more than any other. *Arbuthnot on Aliments.*

3. [In medicine.] A going to stool.

The liver should continually separate the choler from the blood, and empty it into the intestines, where there is good use for it, not only to provoke *dejection*, but also to attenuate the chyle. *Ray on the Creation.*

DEJE'CTURE. *n. s.* [from *deject*.] The excrements.

A disease opposite to this spissitude is too great fluidity, the symptoms of which are excess of animal secretions; as of perspiration, sweat, urine, liquid *dejectures*, leanness, weakness, and thirst. *Arbuthnot on Aliments.*

DEJERA'TION. *n. s.* [from *dejero*, Lat.] A taking of a solemn oath. *Dict.*

DEIFICA'TION. *n. s.* [*deification*, French.] The act of deifying, or making a god.

DE'IFORM. *adj.* [from *deus* and *forma*, Latin.] Of a godlike form.

To DE'IFY. *v. a.* [*deifier*, Fr. of *deus* and *fio*, Latin.]

1. To make a god of; to adore as god; to transfer into the number of the divinities.

Daphnis, the fields delight, the shepherds love,
Renown'd on earth, and *deify'd* above. *Dryden.*

Even the seals which we have of Julius Cæsar, which we know to be antique, have the star of Venus over them, though they were all graven after his death, as a note that he was *deified*. *Dryden's Virg. Æn Dedicat.*

Persuade the covetous man not to *deify* his money, and the proud man not to adore himself. *South's Sermons.*

Half of thee
Is *deify'd* before thy death. *Prior.*

2. To praise excessively; to extol one as if he were a god.

He did again so extol and *deify* the pope, as made all that he had said in praise of his master and mistress seem temperate and passable. *Bacon's Henry* VIII.

To DEIGN. *v. n.* [from *daigner*, Fr. of *dignor*, Latin.] To vouchsafe; to think worthy.

Deign to descend now lower, and relate
What may no less perhaps avail us known. *Milt. Par. Lost.*

Oh *deign* to visit our forsaken seats,
The mossy fountains, and the green retreats. *Pope's Summer.*

To DEIGN. *v. a.* To grant; to permit; to allow.

Now Sweno, Norway's king, craves composition;
Nor would we *deign* him burial of his men,
'Till he disburs'd ten thousand dollars. *Shakesp. Macbeth.*

DE'IGNING. *n. s.* [from *deign*.] A vouchsafing; a thinking worthy.

To DEI'NTEGRATE. *v. a.* [from *de* and *integro*, Latin.] To take from the whole; to spoil; to diminish. *Dict.*

DEI'PAROUS. *adj.* [*deiparus*, Latin.] That brings forth a god; the epithet applied to the blessed Virgin. *Dict.*

DE'ISM. *n. s.* [*deisme*, French.] The opinion of those that only

only acknowledge one God, without the reception of any revealed religion.

Deiſm, or the principles of natural worſhip, are only the faint remnants or dying flames of revealed religion in the poſterity of Noah. *Dryden's Pref. to Rel. Laici.*

DE'IST. *n. ſ.* [*deiſte*, French.] A man who follows no particular religion, but only acknowledges the exiſtence of God, without any other article of faith.

The diſcourſe is in the ſecond epiſtle of St. Peter, the third chapter, where certain *deiſts*, as they ſeem to have been, laughed at the prophecy of the day of judgment. *Burnet.*

DEI'STICAL. *adj.* [from *deiſt.*] Belonging to the hereſy of the deiſts.

But this folly and weakneſs of trifling, inſtead of arguing, does not happen to fail only to the ſhare of Chriſtian writers, but to ſome who have taken the pen in hand to ſupport the *deiſtical* or antichriſtian ſcheme of our days. *Watts.*

DE'ITY. *n. ſ.* [*déité*, French, from *deitas*, Latin.]

1. Divinity; the nature and eſſence of God.]

Some things he doth as God, becauſe his *deity* alone is the ſpring from which they flow; ſome things as man, becauſe they iſſue from his meer human nature; ſome things jointly as both God and man, becauſe both natures concur as principles thereunto. *Hooker, b.* v. *ſ.* 53.

With what arms
We mean to hold, what antiently we claim
Of *deity*, or empire. *Milton's Paradiſe Loſt, b.* v. *l.* 724.

2. A fabulous god; a term applied to the heathen gods and goddeſſes.

Will you ſuffer a temple, how poorly built ſoever, but yet a temple of your *deity*, to be razed? *Sidney, b.* ii.

Heard you not what an humble ſuppliant
Lord Haſtings was to her for his delivery?
—Who humbly complaining to her *deity*,
Got my lord chamberlain his liberty. *Shakeſp. Richard* III.

Give the gods a thankful ſacrifice when it pleaſeth their *deities* to take the wife of a man from him. *Sh. Ant. and Cleop.*

3. The ſuppoſed divinity of a heathen god.

They on their former journey forward paſs,
In ways unknown, her wandering knight to ſeek;
With pains far paſſing that long wandering Greek,
That for his love refuſed *deity*. *Fairy Queen, b.* i. *cant.* 4.

By what reaſon could the ſame *deity* be denied unto Laurentia and Flora, which was given to Venus? *Raleigh.*

DELACERA'TION. *n. ſ.* [from *delacero*, Latin.] A tearing in pieces. *Dict.*

DELACRYMA'TION. *n. ſ.* [*delacrymatio*, Lat.] A falling down of the humours; the wateriſhneſs of the eyes, or a weeping much. *Dict.*

DELACTA'TION. *n. ſ.* [*delactatio*, Latin.] A weaning from the breaſt. *Dict.*

DELA'PSED. *adj.* [With phyſicians.] [from *delapſus*, Latin.] Bearing or falling down. It is uſed in ſpeaking of the womb, and the like. *Dict.*

To DELA'TE. *v. a.* [from *delatus*, Lat.] Carried; conveyed.

Try exactly the time wherein ſound is *delated*. *Bacon.*

DELA'TION. *n. ſ.* [*delatio*, Latin.]

1. A carrying; conveyance.

In *delation* of ſounds, the incloſure of them preſerveth them, and cauſeth them to be heard further. *Bacon's Nat. Hiſtory.*

It is certain, that the *delation* of light is in an inſtant. *Bacon.*

There is a plain *delation* of the ſound from the teeth to the inſtrument of hearing. *Bacon's Natural Hiſtory,* Nº. 149.

2. An accuſation; an impeachment.

DELA'TOR. *n. ſ.* [*delator*, Latin.] An accuſer; an informer.

Men have proved their own *delators*, and diſcovered their own moſt important ſecrets. *Government of the Tongue.*

No ſooner was that ſmall colony, wherewith the depopulated earth was to be replanted, come forth of the ark, but we meet with Cham, a *delator* to his own father, inviting his brethren to that execrable ſpectacle of their parent's nakedneſs. *Government of the Tongue, ſ.* 2.

To DELA'Y. *v. a.* [from *delayer*, French.]

1. To defer; to put off.

And when the people ſaw that Moſes *delayed* to come down out of the mount, the people gathered themſelves together unto Aaron. *Ex.* xxxii. 1.

2. To hinder; to fruſtrate.

She flies the town, and mixing with a throng
Of madding matrons, bears the bride along:
Wand'ring through woods and wilds, and devious ways,
And with theſe arts the Trojan match *delays*. *Dryden's Æn.*

Be mindful, goddeſs, of thy promiſe made!
Muſt ſad Ulyſſes ever be *delay'd*? *Pope's Odyſſey, b.* x.

To DELA'Y. *v. n.* To ſtop; to ceaſe from action.

There ſeem to be certain bounds to the quickneſs and ſlowneſs of the ſucceſſion of thoſe ideas one to another in our minds, beyond which they can neither *delay* nor haſten. *Locke.*

DELA'Y. *n. ſ.* [from the verb.] A deferring; procraſtination; lingering inactivity.

I have learn'd that fearful commenting
Is leaden ſervitor to dull *delay*;
Delay leads impotent and ſnail-pac'd beggary. *Shakeſ. R.* III.

The conduct of our lives, and the management of our great concerns, will not bear *delay*. *Locke.*

2. Stay; ſtop.

The keeper charm'd, the chief without *delay*
Paſs'd on, and took the irremediable way. *Dryden's Æn.* 6.

DELA'YER. *n. ſ.* [from *delay.*] One that defers; a putter off.

DELE'CTABLE. *adj.* [*delectabilis*, Latin.] Pleaſing; delightful.

Ev'ning now approach'd;
For we have alſo our ev'ning, and our morn;
We ours for change *delectable*, not need. *Milton's Par. Loſt.*

Thence, as thou know'ſt,
He brought thee into this delicious grove,
This garden; planted with the trees of God;
Delectable, both to behold and taſte! *Milton's Parad. Loſt.*

Some of his attributes, and the manifeſtations thereof, are not only highly *delectable* to the intellective faculty, but are ſuitably and eaſily conceptible by us, becauſe apparent in his works; as his goodneſs, beneficence, wiſdom and power. *Hale.*

The apple's outward form,
Delectable, the witleſs ſwain beguiles;
'Till that with writhen mouth, and ſpattering noiſe,
He taſtes the bitter morſel. *Phillips.*

DELE'CTABLENESS. *n. ſ.* [from *delectable.*] Delightfulneſs; pleaſantneſs.

DELE'CTABLY. *adv.* Delightfully; pleaſantly.

DELECTA'TION. *n. ſ.* [*delectatio*, Latin.] Pleaſure; delight.

To DE'LEGATE. *v. a.* [*delego*, Latin.]

1. To ſend away.

2. To ſend upon an embaſſy.

3. To intruſt; to commit to another's power and juriſdiction.

As God hath imprinted his authority in ſeveral parts upon ſeveral eſtates of men, as princes, parents, ſpiritual guides; ſo he hath alſo *delegated* and committed part of his care and providence unto them. *Taylor's Rule of living holy.*

We are to remember, that as God is the univerſal monarch of the world, ſo we have all the relation of fellow-ſubjects to him; and can pretend no farther juriſdiction over each other, than what he has *delegated* to us. *Decay of Piety.*

Why does he wake the correſpondent moon,
And fill her willing lamp with liquid light,
Commanding her, with *delegated* pow'rs,
To beautify the world, and bleſs the night? *Prior.*

4. To appoint judges to hear and determine a particular cauſe.

DE'LEGATE. *n. ſ.* [*delegatus*, Latin.]

1. A deputy; a commiſſioner; a vicar; any one that is ſent to act for, or repreſent another.

If after her
Any ſhall live, which dare true good prefer,
Every ſuch perſon is her *delegate*,
T' accompliſh that which ſhould have been her fate. *Donne.*

There muſt be ſevere exactors of accounts from their *delegates* and miniſters of juſtice. *Taylor's Rule of living holy.*

Let the young Auſtrian then her terrours bear;
Great as he is, her *delegate* in war. *Prior.*

Elect by Jove, his *delegate* of ſway,
With joyous pride the ſummons I'd obey. *Pope's Odyſſey.*

2. [In law.] *Delegates* are perſons delegated or appointed by the king's commiſſion to ſit, upon an appeal to him, in the court of Chancery. *Blount.*

DE'LEGATE. *adj.* [*delegatus*, Latin.] Deputed; ſent to act for, or repreſent another.

Princes in judgment, and their *delegate* judges, muſt judge the cauſes of all perſons uprightly and impartially. *Taylor.*

DE'LEGATES [*Court of*]. A court wherein all cauſes of appeal, by way of devolution from either of the archbiſhops, are decided. *Ayliffe's Parergon.*

DELEGA'TION. *n. ſ.* [*delegatio*, Latin.]

1. A ſending away.

2. A putting in commiſſion.

3. The aſſignment of a debt to another.

DELENI'FICAL. *adj.* [*delenificus*, Latin.] Having virtue to aſſwage, or eaſe pain. *Dict.*

To DELE'TE. *v. a.* [from *deleo*, Lat] To blot out. *Dict.*

DELETE'RIOUS. *adj.* [*deleterius*, Latin.] Deadly; deſtructive; of a poiſonous quality.

Many things, neither *deleterious* by ſubſtance or quality, are yet deſtructive by figure, or ſome occaſional activity. *Brown.*

DELE'TERY. *adj.* [from *deleterius*, Latin.] Deſtructive; deadly; poiſonous.

Nor doctor epidemick,
Though ſtor'd with *deletery* med'cines,
(Which whoſoever took is dead ſince)
E'er ſent ſo vaſt a colony
To both the under worlds as he. *Hudibras, p.* i. *cant.* 2.

DELE'TION. *n. ſ.* [*deletio*, Latin.]

1. Act of raſing or blotting out.

2. A deſtruction.

Indeed, if there be a total *deletion* of every perſon of the oppoſing

poſing party or country, then the victory is complete, becauſe none remains to call it in queſtion. *Hale's Co. Law of England.*

DELF. } *n. ſ.* [from delwan, Sax. to dig.]
DELFE. }

1. A mine; a quarry.

Yet could not ſuch mines, without great pains and charges, if at all, be wrought: the *delfs* would be ſo flown with waters, that no gins or machines could ſuffice to lay and keep them dry. *Ray on the Creation.*

2. Earthen ware; counterfeit China ware, made at *Delph.*

Thus barter honour for a piece of *delf*:
No, not for China's wide domain itſelf. *Smart.*

DELIBA'TION. *n. ſ.* [*delibatio*, Latin.] An eſſay; a taſte.

To DELI'BERATE. *v. n.* [*delibero*, Latin.] To think, in order to choice; to heſitate.

A conſcious, wiſe, reflecting cauſe,
Which freely moves, and acts by reaſon's laws;
That can *deliberate* means elect, and find
Their due connection with the end deſign'd. *Blackm. Creat.*

When love once pleads admiſſion to our hearts,
In ſpite of all the virtue we can boaſt,
The woman that *deliberates* is loſt. *Addiſon.*

DELI'BERATE. *adj.* [*deliberatus*, Latin.]

1. Circumſpect; wary; adviſed; diſcreet.
2. Slow; tedious; not ſudden.

Commonly therefore it is for virtuous conſiderations, that wiſdom ſo far prevaileth with men as to make them deſirous of ſlow and *deliberate* death, againſt the ſtream of their ſenſual inclination. *Hooker, b.* v. *ſ.* 46.

Echoes are ſome more ſudden, and chop again as ſoon as the voice is delivered; others are more *deliberate*, that is, give more ſpace between the voice and the echo, which is cauſed by the local nearneſs or diſtance. *Bacon's Natural Hiſtory.*

DELI'BERATELY. *adv.* [from *deliberate.*] Circumſpectly; adviſedly; warily.

He judges to a hair of little indecencies; knows better than any man what is not to be written; and never hazards himſelf ſo far as to fall; but plods on *deliberately*, and, as a grave man ought, is ſure to put his ſtaff before him. *Dryden.*

DELI'BERATENESS. *n. ſ.* [from *deliberate.*] Circumſpection; warineſs; coolneſs; caution.

They would not ſtay the ripening and ſeaſon of counſels, or fair production of acts, in the order, gravity, and *deliberateneſs* befitting a parliament. *King Charles.*

DELIBERA'TION. *n. ſ.* [*deliberatio*, Latin.] The act of deliberating; thought in order to choice.

If mankind had no power to avoid ill or chuſe good by free *deliberation*, it ſhould never be guilty of any thing that was done. *Hammond's Fundamentals.*

DELI'BERATIVE. *adj.* [*deliberativus*, Latin.] Pertaining to deliberation; apt to conſider.

DELI'BERATIVE. *n. ſ.* [from the adjective.] The diſcourſe in which a queſtion is deliberated.

In *deliberatives*, the point is, what is evil; and of good, what is greater; and of evil, what is leſs. *Bacon.*

DE'LICACY. *n. ſ.* [*delicateſſe*, French, of *deliciæ*, Latin.]

1. Daintineſs; fineneſs in eating.

On hoſpitable thoughts intent,
What choice to chuſe for *delicacy* beſt. *Milton's Parad. Loſt.*

2. Any thing highly pleaſing to the ſenſes.

Theſe *delicacies*,
I mean of taſte, ſight, ſmell, herbs, fruits and flow'rs,
Walks, and the melody of birds. *Milton's Paradiſe Loſt.*

3. Softneſs; feminine beauty.

She had never ſeen a man of a more goodly preſence, in whom ſtrong making took not away *delicacy*, nor beauty fierceneſs. *Sidney, b.* ii.

4. Nicety; minute accuracy.

Van Dyck has even excelled him in the *delicacy* of his colouring, and in his cabinet pieces. *Dryden's Dufreſnoy.*

5. Neatneſs; elegance of dreſs.
6. Politeneſs; gentleneſs of manners.
7. Indulgence; gentle treatment.

Perſons in thoſe poſts are uſually born of families noble and rich, and ſo derive a weakneſs of conſtitution from the eaſe and luxury of their anceſtors, and the *delicacy* of their own education. *Temple.*

8. Tenderneſs; ſcrupulouſneſs; mercifulneſs.
9. Weakneſs of conſtitution.

DE'LICATE. *adj.* [*delicat*, French.]

1. Fine; not coarſe; conſiſting of ſmall parts.

As much blood paſſeth through the lungs as through all the reſt of the body: the circulation is quicker, and heat greater, and their texture is extremely *delicate*. *Arbuthnot on Aliments.*

2. Beautiful; pleaſing to the eye.
3. Nice; pleaſing to the taſte; of an agreeable flavour.

The chuſing of a *delicate* before a more ordinary diſh, is to be done as other human actions are, in which there are no degrees and preciſe natural limits deſcribed. *Taylour.*

4. Dainty; deſirous of curious meats.
5. Choice; ſelect; excellent.
6. Polite; gentle of manners.
7. Soft; effeminate; unable to bear hardſhips.

Witneſs this army of ſuch maſs and charge,
Led by a *delicate* and tender prince. *Shakeſpeare's Hamlet.*

Tender and *delicate* perſons muſt needs be oft angry, they have ſo many things to trouble them, which more robuſt natures have little ſenſe of. *Bacon, Eſſay* 58.

8. Pure; clear.

Where they moſt breed and haunt, I have obſerv'd
The air is *delicate*. *Shakeſpeare's Macbeth.*

DE'LICATELY. *adv.* [from *delicate.*]

1. Beautifully.

Ladies, like variegated tulips, ſhow,
'Tis to their changes half their charms we owe;
Such happy ſpots the nice admirer take,
Fine by defect, and *delicately* weak. *Pope, Epiſt.* ii. *l.* 41.

2. Finely; not coarſely.
3. Daintily.

Eat not *delicately*, or nicely; that is, be not troubleſome to thyſelf or others in the choice of thy meats, or the delicacy of thy ſauces. *Taylor's Rule of living holy.*

4. Choicely.
5. Politely.
6. Effeminately.

DE'LICATENESS. *n. ſ.* [from *delicate.*] The ſtate of being delicate; tenderneſs; ſoftneſs; effeminacy.

The delicate woman among you would not adventure to ſet the ſole of her foot upon the ground, for *delicateneſs* and tenderneſs. *Deutr.* xxviii. 56.

DE'LICATES. *n. ſ.* [from *delicate.*] Niceties; rarities; that which is choice and dainty.

The ſhepherd's homely curds,
His cold thin drink, out of his leather bottle,
All which ſecure and ſweetly he enjoys,
Is far beyond a prince's *delicates*. *Shakeſpeare's Henry* VI.

They their appetites not only feed
With *delicates* of leaves and marſhy weed;
But with thy ſickle reap the rankeſt land,
And miniſter the blade with bounteous hand. *Dryd. Virgil.*

With abſtinence all *delicates* he ſees,
And can regale himſelf with toaſt and cheeſe *King's Cookery.*

DE'LICES. *n. ſ.* pl. [*deliciæ*, Latin.] Pleaſures. This word is merely French.

And now he has pour'd out his idle mind
In dainty *delices* and laviſh joys,
Having his warlike weapons caſt behind,
And flowers in pleaſures and vain pleaſing toys. *Fai. Queen.*

DELI'CIOUS. *adj.* [*delicieux*, French, from *de icatus*, Latin.]

1. Sweet; delicate; that affords delight; agreeable; charming; grateful to the ſenſe or mind.

It is highly probable, that upon Adam's diſobedience Almighty God chaſed him out of paradiſe, the faireſt and moſt *delicious* part of the earth, into ſome other the moſt barren and unpleaſant of all the whole globe. *Woodward's Nat. Hiſtory.*

In his laſt hours his eaſy wit diſplay;
Like the rich fruit he ſings, *delicious* in decay. *Swift.*

Still on that breaſt enamour'd let me lie,
Still drink *delicious* poiſon from thy eye. *Pope's El. to Abelard.*

DELI'CIOUSLY. *adv.* [from *delicious.*] Sweetly; pleaſantly; delightfully.

How much ſhe hath glorified herſelf and lived *deliciouſly*, ſo much torment and ſorrow give her. *Rev.* xviii. 7.

DELI'CIOUSNESS. *n. ſ.* [from *delicious.*] Delight; pleaſure; joy.

Let no man judge of himſelf, or of the bleſſings and efficacy of the ſacrament itſelf, by any ſenſible reliſh, by the guſt and *deliciouſneſs*, which he ſometimes perceives, and other times does not perceive. *Taylor's Worthy Communicant.*

DELIGA'TION. *n. ſ.* [*deligatio*, Latin.] A binding up.

The third intention is *deligation*, or retaining the parts ſo joined together. *Wiſeman's Surgery.*

DELI'GHT. *n. ſ.* [*delice*, Fr. from *delector*, Latin.]

1. Joy; content; ſatisfaction.

And Saul commanded his ſervants, ſaying, commune with David ſecretly, and ſay, behold the king hath *delight* in thee, and all his ſervants love thee; now therefore be the king's ſon-in-law. 1 *Sa.* xviii. 22.

2. That which gives delight.

Come, ſiſters, chear we up his ſprights,
And ſhew the beſt of our *delights*:
We'll charm the air to give a ſound,
While you perform your antick round. *Shakeſp. Macbeth.*

Titus Veſpaſian was not more the *delight* of human kind: the univerſal empire made him only known, and more powerful, but could not make him more beloved. *Dryd. Juv. Dedic.*

She was his care, his hope, and his *delight*;
Moſt in his thought, and ever in his ſight. *Dryden's Fables.*

To DELI'GHT. *v. a.* [*delector*, Latin.]

1. To pleaſe; to content; to ſatiſfy; to afford pleaſure.

Delight thyſelf alſo in the Lord, and he ſhall give thee the deſires of thine heart. *Pſ.* xxxvii. 4.

To

Poor insects, whereof some are bees, *delighted with* flowers, and their sweetness; others beetles, *delighted with* other kinds of viands. *Locke.*

He heard, he took, and pouring down his throat,
Delighted, swill'd the large luxurious draught. *Pope's Odyss.*

To Deli'ght. *v. n.* To have delight or pleasure in. It is followed by *in*.

Doth my lord, the king, *delight in* this thing? 2 *Sa.* xxiv.

Blessed is the man that feareth the Lord, that *delighteth* greatly *in* his commandments. *Psal.* cxii. 1.

Deli'ghtful. *adj.* [from *delight* and *full.*] Pleasant; charming; full of delight.

He was given to sparing in so immeasurable sort, that he did not only bar himself from the *delightful*, but almost from the necessary use thereof. *Sidney, b.* iv.

No Spring nor Summer on the mountain seen,
Smiles with gay fruits, or with *delightful* green. *Addison.*

Deli'ghtfully. *adv.* Pleasantly; charmingly; with delight.

O voice! once heard
Delightfully, increase and multiply;
Now death to hear! *Milton's Paradise L. ft.*

Deli'ghtfulness. *n. s.* [from *delight.*] Pleasure; comfort; satisfaction.

This indeed shews the excellency of the object, but doth not altogether take away the *delightfulness* of the knowledge. *Tillotson, Sermon* 1.

Deli'ghtsome. *adj.* [from *delight.*] Pleasant; delightful.

The words themselves being so ancient, the knitting of them so short and intricate, and the whole periods and compass of his speech so *delightsome* for the roundness, and so grave for the strangeness. *Spenser.*

God has furnished every one with the same means of exchanging hunger and thirst for *delightsome* vigour. *Grew's Cosm.*

Deli'ghtsomely. *adv.* [from *delightsome.*] Pleasantly; in a delightful manner.

Deli'ghtsomeness. *n. s.* [from *delightsome.*] Pleasantness; delightfulness.

To DELI'NEATE. *v. a.* [*delineo*, Latin.]

1. To draw the first draught of a thing; to design.

2. To paint in colours; to represent a true likeness in a picture.

The licentia pictoria is very large: with the same reason they may *delineate* old Nestor like Adonis, Hecuba with Helen's face, and Time with Absolon's head. *Brown's Vulg. Err.*

3. To describe; to set forth in a lively manner.

It followeth to *delineate* the region, in which God first planted his delightful garden. *Raleigh's History of the World.*

I have not here time to *delineate* to you the glories of God's heavenly kingdom; nor, indeed, could I tell you, if I had, what the happiness of that place and portion is. *Wake.*

Delinea'tion. *n. s.* [*delineatio*, Latin.] The first draught of a thing.

In the orthographical schemes there should be a true *delineation*, and the just dimensions of each face, and of what things belong to it. *Mortimer's Husbandry.*

Deli'niment. *n. s.* [*delinimentum*, Latin.] A mitigating, or asswaging. *Dict.*

DELI'NQUENCY. *n. s.* [*delinquentia*, Latin.] A fault; a failure in duty; a misdeed.

They never punish the greatest and most intolerable *delinquency* of the tumults, and their exciters. *King Charles.*

Can
Thy years determine like the age of man,
That thou should'st my *delinquencies* exquire,
And with variety of tortures tire? *Sandys's Paraphr. of Job.*

A delinquent ought to be cited in the place or jurisdiction where the *delinquency* was committed by him. *Ayliffe's Parerg.*

Deli'nquent. *n. s.* [from *delinquens*, Latin.] An offender; one that has committed a crime or fault.

Such an envious state,
That sooner will accuse the magistrate
Than the *delinquent*; and will rather grieve
The treason is not acted, than believe. *Ben. Johnson's Catil.*

All three ruined, not by war, or any other disaster, but by justice and sentence, as *delinquents* and criminals; all three famous writers. *Bacon's Holy War.*

He had, upon frivolous surmises, been sent for as a *delinquent*, and been brought upon his knees at the bar of both houses. *Dryden's Æn. Dedicat.*

To DE'LIQUATE. *v. n.* [*deliqueo*, Latin.] To melt; to be dissolved.

It will be resolved into a liquor very analogous to that which the chymists make of salt of tartar, left in moist cellars to *deliquate*. *Boyle's Chym. Princip.*

Such an ebullition as we see made by the mixture of some chymical liquors; as oil of vitriol, and *deliquated* salt of tartar. *Cudworth on the Creation.*

Deliqua'tion. *n. s.* [*deliquatio*, Latin.] A melting; a dissolving.

DELI'QUIUM. *n. s.* Latin. [a chymical term.] A distillation by the force of fire, or a dissolving any calcined matter, by hanging it up in moist cellars, into a lixivious humour. *Dict.*

Deli'rament. *n. s.* [*deliramentum*, Latin.] A doting or foolish idle story. *Dict.*

To DELI'RATE. *v. n.* [*deliro*, Latin.] To dote; to rave; to talk or act idly. *Dict.*

Delira'tion. *n. s.* [*deliratio*, Latin.] Dotage; folly; madness. *Dict.*

Deli'rious. *adj* [*delirius*, Latin.]

1. Light-headed; raving; doting.

The people about him said he had been for some hours *delirious*; but when I saw him he had his understanding as well as ever I knew. *Swift.*

On bed
Delirious flung, sleep from his pillow flies. *Thomson's Spring.*

DELI'RIUM. *n. s.* [Latin.] Alienation of mind; dotage.

Too great alacrity and promptness in answering, especially in persons naturally of another temper, is a sign of an approaching *delirium*; and in a feverish *delirium* there is a small inflammation of the brain. *Arbuthnot on Diet.*

Delitiga'tion. *n. s.* [from *delitigo*, Latin.] A striving; a chiding; a contending. *Dict.*

To DELI'VER. *v. a.* [*delivrer*, French.]

1. To give; to yield; to offer; to present.

In any case thou shalt *deliver* him the pledge again when the sun goeth down. *Deut.* xxiv. 1

Now therefore receive no more money of your acquaintance, but *deliver* it for the breaches of the house. 2 *Kings.*

Yet within three days shall Pharaoh lift up thine head, and restore thee unto thy place; and thou shalt *deliver* Pharaoh's cup into his hand, after the former manner, when thou wast his butler. *Gen.* xl. 13.

It was no wonder that they, who at such a time could be corrupted to frame and *deliver* such a petition, would not be reformed by such an answer. *Dryden's Æn. Dedicat.*

2. To cast away; to throw off.

Charm'd with that virtuous draught, th' exalted mind
All sense of woe *delivers* to the wind. *Pope's Odyssey, b.* iv.

3. To surrender; to put into one's hands.

And David said to him, canst thou bring me down to this company? And he said, swear unto me by God, that thou wilt neither kill me, nor *deliver* me into the hands of my master, and I will bring thee down to this company. 1 *Sa.*

They obeyed not thy commandments, wherefore thou hast *delivered* us for a spoil, and unto captivity. *Tob.* iii. 4.

4. To save; to rescue.

Deliver me, O my God, out of the hand of the wicked, out of the hand of the unrighteous and cruel man. *Ps.* lxxi. 4.

I was like to be apprehended for the witch of Brainford; but that my admirable dexterity of wit, counterfeiting the action of an old woman, *delivered* me. *Sh. M. W. of Windsor.*

Thus she the captive did *deliver*;
The captive thus gave up his quiver. *Prior.*

5. To speak; to tell; to relate; to utter; to pronounce.

A mirth-moving jest,
Which his fair tongue, conceit's expositor,
Delivers in such apt and gracious words,
That aged ears play truant at his tales. *Shakespeare.*

Tell me your highness' pleasure;
What from your grace I shall *deliver* to him. *Shakesp. R.* III.

I knew a clergyman, who appeared to *deliver* his sermon without looking into his notes. *Swift.*

6. To disburden a woman of a child.

On her fright and fears,
She is something before her time *deliver'd*. *Sh. Winter's Tale.*

Tully was long ere he could be *delivered* of a few verses, and those poor ones too. *Peacham on Poetry.*

To Deli'ver *over*. *v. a.*

1. To put into another's hands; to leave to the discretion of another.

Deliver me not *over* unto the will of mine enemies; for false witnesses are risen up against me, and such as breathe out cruelty. *Ps.* xxvii. 12.

The constables have *delivered* her *over* to me, and she shall have whipping enough, I warrant her. *Shakespeare's Hen.* IV.

2. To give from hand to hand; to transmit.

If a true account may be expected by future ages from the present, your lordship will be *delivered over* to posterity in a fairer character than I have given. *Dryden's Ded. to K. Arthur.*

To Deli'ver *up*. *v. a.*

1. To surrender; to give up.

He that spared not his own son, but *delivered* him *up* for us all, how shall he not, with him also, freely give us all thing? *Rom.* viii. 32.

Are the cities that I got with wounds,
Deliver'd up again with peaceful words? *Shakesp. Hen.* VI.

Happy having such a son,
That would *deliver up* his greatness so
Into the hand of justice. *Shakespeare's Henry* IV. *p.* ii.

Deli'verance. *n. s.* [*delivrance*, French.]

1. The act of delivering a thing to another.

2. The

2. The act of freeing from captivity, slavery, or any oppression; rescue.

He hath sent me to heal the broken-hearted, to preach *deliverance* to the captives, and recovering of sight to the blind, to set at liberty those that are bound. *Lu.* iv. 18.

O God, command *deliverances* for Jacob. *Ps.* xliv. 4.

Whate'er befalls, your life shall be my care;
One death, or one *deliv'rance* we will share. *Dryden's Æn.*

3. The act of speaking; utterance; pronunciation.

If seriously I may convey my thoughts
In this my light *deliverance*, I have spoke
With one that in her sex, her years profession,
Wisdom and constancy, hath amaz'd me more
Than I dare blame my weakness. *Sh. All's well that ends well.*

4. The act of bringing childdren.

Ne'er mother
Rejoic'd *deliverance* more. *Shakespeare's Cymbeline.*

People have a superstitious belief, that in the labour of women it helpeth to the easy *deliverance*. *Bacon's Natural History.*

Deli'verer. *n. s.* [from *deliver.*]

1. A saver; a rescuer; a preserver; a releaser.

It doth notably set forth the consent of all nations and ages, in the approbation of the extirpating and debellating of giants, monsters, and foreign tyrants, not only as lawful, but as meritorious even of divine honour; and this, although the *deliverer* came from the one end of the world unto the other. *Bacon's Holy War.*

By that seed
Is meant thy great *deliverer*, who shall bruise
The serpent's head. *Milton's Paradise Lost, b.* xii. *l.* 149.

Andrew Doria has a statue erected to him at the entrance of the doge's palace, with the glorious title of *deliverer* of the commonwealth; and one of his family another, that calls him its preserver. *Addison's Remarks on Italy.*

Him their *deliverer* Europe does confess,
All tongues extol him, all religions bless. *Halifax.*

She wishes for death, as a *deliverer* from pain. *Bolingbroke.*

2. A relater; one that communicates something by speech or writing.

Divers chymical experiments, delivered by sober authors, have been believed false, only because the menstruums, or other materials employed in the unsuccessful trials of them, were not as highly rectified, or otherwise as exquisitely depurated, as those that were used by the *deliverers* of those experiments. *Boyle.*

Deli'very. *n. s.* [from the verb.]

1. The act of delivering, or giving.

2. Release; rescue; saving.

He swore, with sobs,
That he would labour my *delivery*. *Shakesp. Richard* III.

3. A surrender; giving up.

After the *delivery* of your royal father's person into the hands of the army, I undertaking to the queen mother, that I would find some means to get access to him, she was pleased to send me. *Denham, Dedication.*

Nor did he in any degree contribute to the *delivery* of his house, which was at first imagined, because it was so ill, or not at all defended. *Clarendon, b.* viii.

4. Utterance; pronunciation; speech.

We alledge what the scriptures themselves do usually speak, for the saving force of the word of God, not with restraint to any certain kind of *delivery*, but howsoever the same shall chance to be made known. *Hooker, b.* v. *sect.* 22.

5. Use of the limbs; activity.

The earl was the taller, and much the stronger; but the duke had the neater limbs, and freer *delivery*. *Wotton.*

6. Childbirth.

Like as a woman with child, that draweth near the time of her *delivery*, is in pain, and crieth out. *Is.* xxvi. 7.

Dell. *n. s.* [from *dal*, Dutch.]

1. A pit; a valley; a hole in the ground; any cavity in the earth. Obsolete.

The while, the like same unhappy ewe,
Whose clouted leg her hurt doth shew,
Fell headlong into a *dell*. *Spenser's Pastorals.*

I know each lane, and every alley green,
Dingle, or bushy *dell* of this wild wood. *Milt. Parad. Lost.*

But, foes to sun-shine, most they took delight
In *dells* and dales, conceal'd from human sight. *Tickell.*

Delph. *n. s.* [from *Delft*, the name of the capital of Delftland.] A fine sort of earthen ware.

A supper worthy of herself;
Five nothings in five plates of *delph*. *Swift.*

De'ltoide. *adj.* [from *delta*, the fourth letter of the Greek alphabet; so called by reason of its resembling this letter.] An epithet applied to a triangular muscle arising from the clavicula, and from the process of the same, whose action is to raise the arm upward.

Cut still more of the *deltoid* muscle, and carry the arm backward. *Sharp's Surgery.*

Delu'dable. *adj.* [from *delude.*] Liable to be deceived; that is easily imposed on.

Not well understanding omniscience, he is not so ready to deceive himself as to falsify unto him whose cogitation is no ways *deludable*. *Brown's Vulgar Errours, b.* i.

To DELU'DE. *v. a.* [*deludo*, Latin.]

1. To beguile; to cheat; to deceive; to impose on.

O, give me leave, I have *deluded* you;
'Twas neither Charles, nor yet the duke I nam'd;
But Reignier, king of Naples, that prevail'd. *Shak. H.* VI.

Let not the Trojans, with a feign'd pretence
Of proffer'd peace, *delude* the Latian prince. *Dryden's Æn.*

2. To disappoint; to frustrate.

Delu'der. *n. s.* [from *delude.*]

1. A beguiler; a deceiver; an impostor; a cheat; a false pretender.

Say, flatterer, say, ah fair *deluder* speak;
Answer me this, ere yet my heart does break. *Granville.*

To DE'LVE. *v. a.* [ȝelfan, Sax. *delven*, Dut. perhaps from δέλφαξ, a hog. *Junius.*]

1. To dig; to open the ground with a spade.

It shall go hard
But I will *delve* one yard below the mines,
And blow them at the moon. *Shakespeare's Hamlet.*

Delve of convenient depth your thrashing floor;
With temper'd clay then fill and face it o'er. *Dryd. Georg.*

Besides, the filthy swine will oft invade
Thy firm inclosure, and with *delving* snout
The rooted forest undermine. *Philips.*

2. To fathom; to sift; to sound one's opinion.

What's his name and birth?
—I cannot *delve* him to the root: his father
Was call'd Sicillius. *Shakespeare's Cymbeline.*

De'lve. *n. s.* [from the verb.] A ditch; a pitfal; a den; a cave.

He by and by
His feeble feet directed to the cry;
Which to that shady *delve* him brought at last,
Where Mammon earst did sun his treasury. *Fairy Queen.*

Such a light and metall'd dance
Saw you never yet in France;
And by landmen, for the nonce,
That turn round like grindle-stones,
Which they dig out fro' the *delves*,
For their bairns bread, wives, and selves. *Ben. Johnson.*

A **Delve** *of Coals.* A certain quantity of coals dug in the mind or pit. *Dict.*

De'lver. *n. s.* [from *delve.*] A digger; one that opens the ground with a spade.

DE'LUGE. *n. s.* [*deluge*, French, from *diluvium*, Latin.]

1. A general inundation; a laying entirely under water.

The apostle doth plainly intimate, that the old world was subject to perish by a *deluge*, as this is subject to perish by conflagration. *Burnet's Theory of the Earth.*

2. An overflowing of the natural bounds of a river.

But if with bays and dams they strive to force
His channel to a new or narrow course,
No longer then within his banks he dwells,
First to a torrent, then a *deluge* swells. *Denham.*

3. Any sudden and resistless calamity.

To **De'luge.** *v. a.* [from the noun.]

1. To drown; to lay totally under water.

The restless flood the land would overflow,
By which the *delug'd* earth would useless grow. *Blackmore.*

Still the battering waves rush in
Implacable, 'till *delug'd* by the foam
The ship sinks, found'ring in the vast abyss. *Philips.*

2. To overwhelm; to cause to sink under the weight of any calamity.

At length corruption, like a general flood,
Shall *deluge* all. *Pope's Epist.* iii. *l.* 137.

Delu'sion. *n. s.* [*delusio*, Latin.]

1. A cheat; guile; deceit; treachery; fraud; collusion; falsehood.

2. A false representation; illusion; errour; a chimerical thought.

Who therefore seeks in these
True wisdom, finds her not, or by *delusion*. *Milt. Par. Reg.*

I waking, view'd with grief the rising sun,
And fondly mourn'd the dear *delusion* gone. *Prior.*

Delu'sive. *adj.* [from *delusus*, Latin.] Apt to deceive; beguiling; imposing on.

When, fir'd with passion, we attack the fair,
Delusive sighs and brittle vows we bear. *Prior.*

The happy whimsey you pursue,
'Till you at length believe it true;
Caught by your own *delusive* art,
You fancy first, and then assert. *Prior.*

While the base and groveling multitude of different nations, ranks and ages were listening to the *delusive* deities, those of a more erect aspect and exalted spirit separated themselves from the rest. *Tatler*, Nº. 81.

A vast variety of phænomena, and those many of them so *delusive*, that it is very hard to escape imposition and mistake. *Woodward's Natural History, p.* iv.

Delu'sory. *adj.* [from *deluſus*, Latin.] Apt to deceive.

This confidence is founded on no better foundation than a *deluſory* prejudice. *Glanv. Sceps. c.* 12.

De'magogue. *n. ſ.* [δημαγωγός.] A ringleader of the rabble; a populous and factious orator.

Who were the chief *demagogues* and patrons of tumults, to ſend for them, to flatter and embolden them. *King Charles.*

A plauſible, inſignificant word, in the mouth of an expert *demagogue*, is a dangerous and dreadful weapon. *South's Serm.*

Demoſthenes and Cicero, though each of them a leader, or, as the Greeks called it, a *demagogue*, in a popular ſtate, yet ſeem to differ in their practice upon this branch of their art. *Swift.*

Dema'in.
Deme'an. } *n. ſ.* [*domaine*, French.
Deme'sne.

That land which a man holds originally of himſelf, called *dominium* by the civilians, and oppoſed to *feodum* or fee, which ſignifies thoſe that are held of a ſuperior lord. It is ſometimes uſed alſo for a diſtinction between thoſe lands that the lord of the manor has in his own hands, or in the hands of his leſſee, demiſed or let upon a rent for a term of years or life, and ſuch other lands appertaining to the ſaid manor as belong to free or copyholders; although the copyhold belonging to any manor, according to many good lawyers, is alſo accounted *demeans*. *Philips.*

Having now provided
A gentleman of noble parentage,
Of fair *demeſns*, youthful, and nobly allied. *Shakeſpeare.*

That earldom indeed had a royal juriſdiction and ſeigniory, though the lands of that county in *demeſne* were poſſeſſed for the moſt part by the ancient inheritors. *Davies on Ireland.*

The defects in thoſe acts for planting foreſt-trees might be fully ſupplied, ſince they have hitherto been wholly ineffectual, except about the *demeſnes* of a few gentlemen; and even there, in general, very unſkilfully made, and thriving accordingly. *Swift.*

Dema'nd. *n. ſ.* [*demande*, French.]

1. A claim; a challenging; the aſking of any thing with authority.

This matter is by the decree of the watchers, and the *demand* by the word of the holy ones. *Dan.* iv. 17.

Giving vent, gives life and ſtrength to our appetites; and he that has the confidence to turn his wiſhes into *demands*, will be but a little way from thinking he ought to obtain them. *Locke.*

2. A queſtion; an interrogation.

3. The calling for a thing in order to purchaſe it.

My bookſeller tells me, the *demand* for thoſe my papers increaſes daily. *Addiſon's Spectator*, N°. 124.

4. [In law.] The aſking of what is due. It hath alſo a proper ſignification diſtinguiſhed from plaint; for all civil actions are purſued either by demands or plaints, and the purſuer is called demandant or plaintiff. There are two manners of *demands*, the one of deed, the other in law: in deed, as in every *præcipe*, there is expreſs demand: in law, as every entry in land-diſtreſs for rent, taking or ſeiſing of goods, and ſuch like acts, which may be done without any words, are *demands* in law. *Blount.*

To **DEMA'ND.** *v. a.* [*demander*, French.]

1. To claim; to aſk for with authority.

The pound of fleſh, which I *demand* of him,
Is dearly bought, 'tis mine, and I will have it. *Shakeſpeare.*

2. To queſtion; to interrogate.

And when Uriah was come unto him, David *demanded* of him how Joab did, and how the people did, and how the war proſpered. 2 *Sa.* xi. 7.

If any friend of Cæſar's *demand*, why Brutus roſe againſt Cæſar, this is my anſwer: Not that I loved Cæſar leſs, but that I loved Rome more. *Shakeſpeare's Julius Cæſar.*

Young one,
Inform us of thy fortunes; for, it ſeems,
They crave to be *demanded.* *Shakeſpeare's Cymbeline.*

The oracle of Apollo being *demanded*, when the war and miſery of Greece ſhould have an end, reply'd, When they would double the altar in Delos, which was of a cubick form. *Peacham on Geometry.*

3. [In law.] To proſecute in a real action.

Dema'ndable. *adj.* [from *demand.*] That may be demanded; requeſted; aſked for.

All ſums *demandable*, either for licence of alienation to be made of lands holden in chief, or for the pardon of any ſuch alienation, already made without licence, have been ſtayed in the way to the hanaper. *Bacon's Off. of Alienation.*

Dema'ndant. *n. ſ.* [from *demand.*] He who is actor or plaintiff in a real action, becauſe he demandeth lands. *Coke.*

One of the witneſſes depoſed, that dining on a Sunday with the *demandant*, whoſe wife had ſat below the ſquire's lady at church, ſhe the ſaid wife dropped ſome expreſſions, as if ſhe thought her huſband ought to be knighted. *Spectator.*

Dema'nder. *n. ſ.* [*demandeur*, French.]

1. One that requires a thing with authority.

2. One that aſks a civil queſtion.

3. One that aſks for a thing in order to purchaſe it.

They grow very faſt and fat, which alſo bettereth their taſte, and delivereth them to the *demanders* ready uſe at all ſeaſons. *Carew's Survey of Cornwal.*

4. A dunner; one that demands a debt.

Deme'an. *n. ſ.* [from *demener*, French.]

1. A mien; preſence; carriage; demeanour; deportment.

At his feet, with ſorrowful *demean*,
And deadly hue, an armed corſe did lie. *Fairy Queen, b.* ii.

To **DEME'AN.** *v. a.* [from *demener*, French.]

1. To behave; to carry one's ſelf.

Thoſe plain and legible lines of duty requiring us to *demean* ourſelves to God humbly and devoutly, to our governors obediently, and to our neighbours juſtly, and to ourſelves ſoberly and temperately. *South's Sermons.*

A man cannot doubt but that there is a God; and that, according as he *demeans* himſelf towards him, he will make him happy or miſerable for ever. *Tillotſon, Serm.* i.

Strephon had long perplex'd his brains,
How with ſo high a nymph he might
Demean himſelf the wedding-night. *Swift.*

2. To leſſen; to debaſe; to undervalue.

Now, out of doubt, Antipholis is mad;
Elſe he would never ſo *demean* himſelf. *Sh. Com. of Errours.*

Deme'anour. *n. ſ.* [*demener*, French.] Carriage; behaviour.

Of ſo inſupportable a pride he was, that where his deeds might well ſtir envy, his *demeanour* did rather breed diſdain. *Sidney, b.* ii.

Angels beſt like us, when we are moſt like unto them in all parts of decent *demeanour.* *Hooker, b.* i.

His geſtures fierce
He mark'd, and mad *demeanour*, then alone,
As he ſuppos'd, all unobſerv'd, unſeen. *Milton's Par. Loſt.*

To whom thus Eve, with ſad *demeanour* meek,
Ill worthy I, ſuch title ſhould belong
To me tranſgreſſor! *Milton's Paradiſe Loſt, b.* xi. *l.* 162.

He was of a courage not to be daunted, which was manifeſted in all his actions, eſpecially in his whole *deméanour* at the Iſle of Ree, both at the landing, and upon the retreat. *Clar.*

Deme'ans. *n. ſ.* pl. An eſtate in goods or lands; that which a man poſſeſſes in his own right.

To **DEME'NTATE.** *v. n.* [*demento*, Latin.] To grow mad.

Dementa'tion. *n. ſ.* [*dementatio*, Latin.] A being mad, or frantick.

Deme'rit. *n. ſ.* [*demérite*, Fr. from *demeritus*, of *demereor*, Latin.] The oppoſite to merit; ill-deſerving; what makes one worthy of blame or puniſhment.

They ſhould not be able once to ſtir, or to murmur, but it ſhould be known, and they ſhortened according to their *demerits.* *Spenſer on Ireland.*

Thou liv'ſt by me; to me thy breath reſign;
Mine is the merit, the *demerit* thine. *Dryden's Fables.*

Whatever they acquire by their induſtry or ingenuity, ſhould be ſecure, unleſs forfeited by any *demerit* or offence againſt the cuſtom of the family. *Temple.*

2. Anciently the ſame with merit; deſert.

'Tis yet to know,
Which when I know that boaſting is an honour,
I ſhall promulgate, I fetch my life and being
From men of royal ſiege; and my *demerits*
May ſpeak, unbonnetting, to as proud a fortune
As this that I have reach'd. *Shakeſpeare's Othello.*

To **Deme'rit.** *v. a.* [*demeriter*, French.] To deſerve blame or puniſhment.

Deme'rsed. *adj.* [from *demerſus*, of *demergo*, Latin.] Plunged; drowned. *Dict.*

Deme'rsion. *n. ſ.* [*demerſio*, Latin.]

1. A drowning.

2. [In chymiſtry.] The putting any medicine in a diſſolving liquor. *Dict.*

Deme'sne. See **Demain.**

DE'MI. *inſeparable particle.* [*demi*, Fr. *dimidium*, Latin.] Half; one of two equal parts. This word is only uſed in compoſition; as *demigod*, that is, half human, half divine.

Demi-cannon. *n. ſ.* [*demi* and *cannon.*]

Demi-cannon *Loweſt.* A great gun that carries a ball of thirty pounds weight and ſix inches diameter. The diameter of the bore is ſix inches two eighth parts. *Dict.*

Demi-cannon *Ordinary.* A great gun ſix inches four eights diameter in the bore, twelve foot long. It carries a ſhot ſix inches one ſixth diameter, and thirty-two pounds weight. *Dict.*

Demi-cannon *of the greateſt Size.* A gun ſix inches and ſix eighth parts diameter in the bore, twelve foot long. It carries a ball of ſix inches five eights diameter, and thirty-ſix pounds weight. *Dict.*

What! this a ſleeve? 'Tis like a *demi-cannon.* *Shakeſp.*

Ten

Ten engines, that shall be of equal force either to a cannon or *demi-cannon*, culverin or demi-culverin, may be framed at the same price that one of these will amount to. *Wilkins.*

DEMI-CULVERIN. *n. s.* [*demi* and *culverin.*]

DEMI-CULVERIN *of the lowest Size.* A gun four inches two eights diameter in the bore, and ten foot long. It carries a ball four inches diameter, and nine pounds weight. *Dict.*

DEMI-CULVERIN *Ordinary.* A gun four inches four eights diameter in the bore, ten foot long. It carries a ball four inches two eights diameter, and ten pounds eleven ounces weight.

DEMI-CULVERIN, *elder Sort.* A gun four inches and six eights diameter in the bore, ten foot one third in length. It carries a ball four inches four eight parts diameter, and twelve pounds eleven ounces weight. *Milit. Dict.*

They continue a perpetual volley of *demi-culverins.* *Raleigh.*

The army left two *demi-culverins*, and two other good guns. *Clarendon, b.* viii.

DEMI-DEVIL. *n. s.* [*demi* and *devil.*] Partaking of infernal nature; half a devil.

Will you, I pray, demand that *demi-devil*,
Why he hath thus ensnar'd my soul and body? *Shak. Othel.*

DEMI-GOD. *n. s.* [*demi* and *god.*] Partaking of divine nature; half a god; an hero produced by the cohabitation of divinities with mortals.

He took his leave of them, whose eyes bad him farewel with tears, making temples to him as to a *demi-god.* *Sidney.*

Be gods, or angels, *demi-gods.* *Milton's Paradise Lost.*

Transported *demi-gods* stood round,
And men grew heroes at the sound,
Enflam'd with glory's charms. *Pope's St. Cæcilia.*

Nay, half in heaven, except (what's mighty odd)
A fit of vapours clouds this *demi-god.* *Pope's Epist. of Hor.*

DEMI-LANCE. *n. s.* [*demi* and *lance.*] A light lance; a spear; a half-pike.

On their steel'd heads, their *demi-lances* wore
Small pennons, which their ladies colours bore. *Dryden.*
Light *demi-lances* from afar they throw,
Fasten'd with leathern thongs to gaul the foe. *Dryden's Æn.*

DEMI-MAN. *n. s.* [*demi* and *man.*] Half a man. A term of reproach.

We must adventure this battle, lest we perish by the complaints of this barking *demi-man.* *Knolles's History of the Turks.*

DEMI-WOLF. *n. s.* [*demi* and *wolf.*] Half a wolf; a mongrel dog between a dog and wolf. *Lycisca.*

Spaniels, curs,
Showghs, water-rugs, and *demi-wolves*, are cleped
All by the name of dogs. *Shakespeare's Macbeth.*

DEMI'SE. *n. s.* [from *demetre*, *demis*, *demise*, French.] Death; decease. It is seldom used but in formal and ceremonious language.

About a month before the *demise* of queen Anne, the author retired. *Swift.*

To DEMI'SE. *v. a.* [*demis*, *demise*, French.] To grant at one's death; to grant by will; to bequeath.

My executors shall not have power to *demise* my lands to be purchased. *Swift's Last Will.*

DEMI'SSION. *n. s.* [*demissio*, Latin.] Degradation; diminution of dignity; depression.

Inexorable rigour is worse than a lasche *demission* of sovereign authority. *L'Estrange.*

To DEMI'T. *v. a.* [*demitto*, Latin.] To depress; to hang down; to let fall. *Dict.*

When they are in their pride, that is, advancing their train, if they decline their neck to the ground, they presently *demit*, and let fall the same. *Brown's Vulgar Errours, b.* iii.

DEMO'CRACY. *n. s.* [δημοκρατία.] One of the three forms of government; that in which the sovereign power is neither lodged in one man, nor in the nobles, but in the collective body of the people.

While many of the servants, by industry and virtue, arrive at riches and esteem, then the nature of the government inclines to a *democracy.* *Temple.*

The majority having the whole power of the community, may employ all that power in making laws, and executing those laws; and there the form of the government is a perfect *democracy.* *Locke.*

DEMOCRA'TICAL. *adj.* [from *democracy.*] Pertaining to a popular government; popular.

They are still within the line of vulgarity, and are *democratical* enemies to truth. *Brown's Vulgar Errours, b.* i. *c.* 3.

As the government of England has a mixture of *democratical* in it, so the right of inventing political lyes, is partly in the people. *Arbuthnot.*

To DEMO'LISH. *v. a.* [*demolir*, French; *demolior*, Latin.]

1. To throw down buildings; to raze; to destroy.

I expected the fabrick of my book would long since have been *demolished*, and laid even with the ground. *Tillotson, Pref.*

Red lightning play'd along the firmament,
And their *demolish'd* works to pieces rent. *Dryden's Ovid.*

DEMO'LISHER. *n. s.* [from *demolish.*] One that throws down buildings; a destroyer; a layer waste.

DEMOLI'TION. *n. s.* [from *demolish.*] The act of overthrowing or demolishing buildings; destruction.

Two gentlemen should have the direction in the *demolition* of Dunkirk. *Swift.*

DE'MON. *n. s.* [*dæmon*, Latin; δαίμων.] A spirit; generally an evil spirit; a devil.

I felt him strike, and now I see him fly:
Curs'd *demon!* O for ever broken lie
Those fatal shafts, by which I inward bleed. *Prior.*

DEMONI'ACAL. } *adj.* [from *demon.*]
DEMO'NIACK. }

1. Belonging to the devil; devilish.

He, all unarm'd,
Shall chase thee with the terror of his voice
From thy *demoniack* holds, possession foul. *Milton's Par. Reg.*

2. Influenced by the devil; produced by diabolical possession.

Demoniack phrensy, moping melancholy. *Milt. Par. Lost.*

DEMO'NIACK. *n. s.* [from the adjective.] One possessed by the devil; one whose mind is disturbed and agitated by the power of wicked and unclean spirits.

Those lunaticks and *demoniacks* that were restored to their right mind, were such as sought after him, and believed in him. *Bentley's Sermons.*

DEMO'NIAN. *adj.* [from *demon.*] Devilish; of the nature of devils.

Demonian spirits now, from the element
Each of his reign allotted, rightlier called
Pow'rs of fire, air, water, and earth beneath. *Parad. Reg.*

DEMONO'CRACY. *n. s.* [δαίμων and κρατέω.] The power of the devil. *Dict.*

DEMONO'LATRY. *n. s.* [δαίμων and λατρεία.] The worship of the devil. *Dict.*

DEMONO'LOGY. *n. s.* [δαίμων and λόγος.] Discourse of the nature of devils. Thus king James entitled his book concerning witches.

DEMO'NSTRABLE. *adj.* [*demonstrabilis*, Lat.] That which may be proved beyond doubt or contradiction; that which may be made not only probable, but evident.

The grand articles of our belief are as *demonstrable* as geometry. *Glanv. Sceps. c.* 24.

DEMO'NSTRABLY. *adv.* [from *demonstrable.*] In such a manner as admits of certain proof; evidently; beyond possibility of contradiction.

He should have compelled his ministers to execute the law, in those cases that *demonstrably* concerned the publick peace. *Cl.*

To DEMO'NSTRATE. *v. a.* [*demonstro*, Latin.] To prove with the highest degree of certainty; to prove in such a manner as reduces the contrary position to evident absurdity.

We cannot *demonstrate* these things so, as to shew that the contrary often involves a contradiction. *Tillotson, Pref.*

DEMONSTRA'TION. *n. s.* [*demonstratio*, Latin.]

1. The highest degree of deducible or argumental evidence; the strongest degree of proof; such proof as not only evinces the position proved to be true, but shews the contrary position to be absurd and impossible.

What appeareth to be true by strong and invincible *demonstration*, such as wherein it is not by any way possible to be deceived, thereunto the mind doth necessarily assent. *Hooker.*

Where the agreement or disagreement of any thing is plainly and clearly perceived, it is called *demonstration.* *Locke.*

2. Indubitable evidence of the senses or reason.

Which way soever we turn ourselves, we are encountered with clear evidences and sensible *demonstrations* of a Deity. *Till.*

DEMO'NSTRATIVE. *adj.* [*demonstrativus*, Latin.]

1. Having the power of demonstration; invincibly conclusive; certain.

An argument necessary and *demonstrative*, is such as, being proposed unto any man, and understood, the man cannot chuse but inwardly yield. *Hooker, Pref.*

2. Having the power of expressing clearly and certainly.

Painting is necessary to all other arts, because of the need which they have of *demonstrative* figures, which often give more light to the understanding than the clearest discourses we can make. *Dryden's Dufresnoy.*

DEMO'NSTRATIVELY. *adv.* [from *demonstrative.*]

1. With evidence not to be opposed or doubted.

No man, in matters of this life, requires an assurance either of the good which he designs, or of the evil which he avoids, from arguments *demonstratively* certain. *South's Sermons.*

First, I *demonstratively* prove,
That feet were only made to move. *Prior.*

2. Clearly; plainly; with certain knowledge.

Demonstratively understanding the simplicity of perfection, it was not in the power of earth to work them from it. *Brown.*

DEMONSTRA'TOR. *n. s.* [from *demonstrate.*] One that proves; one that teaches; one that demonstrates.

DEMONSTRA'TORY. *adj.* [from *demonstrate.*] Having the tendency to demonstrate.

DEMU'LCENT.

DEMU'LCENT. *adj.* [*demulcens*, Latin.] Softening; mollifying; assuasive.

Pease, being deprived of any aromatick parts, are mild and *demulcent* in the highest degree; but being full of aerial particles, are flatulent, when dissolved by digestion. *Arbuthnot.*

To DEMU'R. *v. n.* [*demeurer*, French; *dimorare*, Italian; *demorari*, Latin.]

1. To delay a process in law by doubts and objections. See DEMURRER.

To this plea the plaintiff *demurred.* *Walton's Angler.*

2. To pause in uncertainty; to suspend determination; to hesitate; to delay the conclusion of an affair.

Upon this rub the English ambassadours thought fit to *demur*, and so sent into England to receive directions from the lords of the council. *Hayward.*

Running into demands, they expect from us a sudden resolution in things, wherein the devil of Delphos would *demur*. *Brown's Vulgar Errours, b.* i. *c.* 3.

He must be of a very sluggish or querulous humour, that shall *demur* upon setting out, or demand higher encouragements than the hope of heaven. *Decay of Piety.*

News of my death from rumour he receiv'd,
And what he wish'd, he easily believ'd;
But long *demurr'd*, though from my hand he knew
I liv'd, so loth he was to think it true. *Dryden's Aurengzebe.*

3. To doubt; to have scruples or difficulties; to deliberate.

There is something in our composition, that thinks and apprehends, and reflects and deliberates, determines and doubts, consents and denies; that wills and *demurs*, and resolves and chuses, and rejects. *Bentley.*

To DEMU'R. *v. a.* To doubt of.

The latter I *demur*; for in their looks
Much reason, and in their actions, oft appears. *Milt. P. L.*

DEMU'R. *n. s.* [from the verb.] Doubt; hesitation; suspense of opinion.

O progeny of heav'n, empyreal thrones!
With reason hath deep silence and *demur*
Seiz'd us, though undismay'd. *Milton's Paradise Lost, b.* ix.

Certainly the highest and dearest concerns of a temporal life are infinitely less valuable than those of an eternal; and consequently ought, without any *demur* at all, to be sacrificed to them, whensoever they come in competition with them. *South.*

All my *demurs* but double his attacks;
At last he whispers, Do, and we go snacks. *Pope's Epistles.*

DEMU'RE. *adj.* [*des mœurs*, French.]

1. Sober; decent.

Lo! two most lovely virgins came in place,
With countenance *demure*, and modest grace. *Fairy Queen.*

Come, pensive nun, devout and pure,
Sober, stedfast and *demure*. *Milton.*

2. Grave; affectedly modest: it is now generally taken in a sense of contempt.

After a *demure* travel of regard, I tell them I know my place, as I would they should do theirs. *Shakesp. Twelfth Night.*

There be many wise men, that have secret hearts and transparent countenances; yet this would be done with a *demure* abasing of your eye sometimes. *Bacon, Essay* 23.

A company of mice, peeping out of their holes, spied a cat, that lay and looked so *demure* as if there had been neither life nor soul in her. *L'Estrange.*

So cat, transform'd, sat gravely and *demure*,
'Till mouse appear'd, and thought himself secure. *Dryden.*

Jove sent and found, far in a country scene,
Truth, innocence, good-nature, look serene;
From which ingredients, first, the dext'rous boy
Pick'd the *demure*, the aukward, and the coy. *Swift.*

To DEMU'RE. *v. n.* [from the noun.] To look with an affected modesty.

Your wife Octavia, with her modest eyes,
And still conclusion, shall acquire no honour,
Demuring upon me. *Shakesp. Anthony and Cleopatra.*

DEMU'RELY. *adv.* [from *demure.*] With affected modesty; solemnly; with pretended gravity.

Put on a sober habit,
Talk with respect, and swear but now and then,
Wear prayer-books in my pocket, look *demurely*. *Shakesp.*

Esop's damsel, turned from a cat to a woman, sat very *demurely* at the board's end, 'till a mouse ran before her. *Bacon.*

Next stood hypocrisy with holy leer,
Soft smiling, and *demurely* looking down;
But hid the dagger underneath the gown. *Dryden's Fables.*

2. In the following line it is the same with solemnly. *Warb.*

Hark, how the drums *demurely* wake the sleepers! *Shakes.*

DEMU'RENESS. *n. s.* [from *demure.*]

1. Modesty; soberness; gravity of aspect.

Her eyes having in them such a cheerfulness, as nature seemed to smile in them; though her mouth and cheeks obeyed to that pretty *demureness*, which the more one marked, the more one would judge the poor soul apt to believe. *Sidney.*

2. Affected modesty; pretended gravity.

DEMU'RRAGE. *n. s.* [from *demur.*] An allowance made by merchants to masters of ships, for their stay in a port beyond the time appointed.

DEMU'RRER. *n. s.* [*demeurer*, French; i. e. *manere in aliquo loco vel morari.*] A kind of pause upon a point of difficulty in an action; for, in every action, the controversy consists either in the fact, or in the law: if in the fact, that is tried by the jury; if in law, then is the case plain to the judge, or so hard and rare, as it breedeth just doubt. I call that plain to the judge, wherein he is assured of the law; and in such case the judge, with his associates, proceeds to judgment without farther work. But when it is doubtful to him and his associates, then is there stay made, and a time taken, either for the court to think farther upon it, and to agree, if they can; or else for all the justices to meet together in the Chequer-chamber, and, upon hearing that which the serjeants can say of both parts, to advise, and set down as law, whatsoever they conclude firm, without farther remedy. *Cowel.*

A prohibition was granted, and hereunto there was a *demurrer*. *Ayliffe's Parergon.*

DEN. *n. s.* [ðen, Saxon.]

1. A cavern or hollow running horizontally, or with a small obliquity, under ground; distinct from a hole, which runs down perpendicularly.

They here dispersed, some in the air, some on the earth, some in the waters, some amongst the minerals, *dens* and caves under the earth. *Hooker, b.* i. *s.* 4.

2. The cave of a wild beast.

What, shall they seek the lion in his *den*,
And fright him there? *Shakespeare's King John.*

The tyrant's *den*, whose use, though lost to fame,
Was now th' apartment of the royal dame,
The cavern, only to her father known,
By him was to his darling daughter shown. *Dryden's Fables.*

'Tis then the shapeless bear his *den* forsakes;
In woods and fields a wild destruction makes. *Dryd. Virgil.*

3. *Den* may signify either a valley or a woody place; for the Saxon ðen imports both. *Gibson's Camden.*

DENA'Y. *n. s.* [a word formed between *deny* and *nay.*] Denial; refusal.

To her in haste, give her this jewel: say
My love can give no place, bide no *denay*. *Sh. Twel. Night.*

DENDRO'LOGY. *n. s.* [δένδρον and λόγος.] The natural history of trees.

DENI'ABLE. *adj.* [from *deny.*] That which may be denied; that to which one may refuse belief.

The negative authority is also *deniable* by reason. *Brown.*

DENI'AL. *n. s.* [from *deny.*]

1. Negation; the contrary to confession.

No man more impudent to deny, where proofs were not manifest; no man more ready to confess, with a repenting manner of aggravating his own evil, where *denial* would but make the fault fouler. *Sidney, b.* ii.

2. Refusal; the contrary to grant, allowance, or concession.

Here comes your father; never make *denial*:
I must and will have Catharine to my wife. *Shakespeare.*

The *denial* of landing, and hasty warning us away, troubled us much: on the other side, to find people so full of humanity, did comfort us. *Bacon's New Atlantis.*

He, at every fresh attempt, is repell'd
With faint *denials*, weaker than before. *Dryden's Ann. Mir.*

3. Abjuration; contrary to acknowledgment of adherence.

We may deny God in all those acts that are capable of being morally good or evil: those are the proper scenes, in which we act our confessions or *denials* of him. *South's Sermons.*

DENI'ER. *n. s.* [from *deny.*]

1. A contradictor; an opponent; one that holds the negative of a proposition.

By the word virtue the affirmer intends our whole duty to God and man, and the *denier* by the word virtue means only courage, or, at most, our duty towards our neighbour, without including the idea of the duty which we owe to God. *Watts's Logick, p.* i. *c.* 6. *s.* 3.

2. A disowner; one that does not own or acknowledge.

If it was so fearful when Christ looked his *denier* into repentance, what will it be when he shall look him into destruction. *South's Sermons.*

3. A refuser; one that refuses.

It may be I am esteemed by my *denier*: sufficient of myself to discharge my duty to God as a priest, though not to men as a prince. *King Charles.*

DENIE'R. *n. s.* [from *denarius*, Lat. It is pronounced as *deneer*, in two syllables.] A small denomination of French money; the twelfth part of a sous.

You will not pay for the glasses you have burst?
——No, not a *denier*. *Shakesp. Taming of the Shrew.*

To DE'NIGRATE. *v. a.* [*denigro*, Latin.] To blacken; to make black.

By suffering some impression from fire, bodies are casually or artificially *denigrated* in their natural complexion: thus are charcoals made black by an infection of their own suffitus. *Brown's Vulgar Errours, b.* vi. *c.* 12.

Hartshorn, and other white bodies, will be *denigrated* by heat; yet camphire would not at all lose its whiteness. *Boyle.*

DENIGRA'TION. *n. ſ.* [*denigratio*, Latin.] A blackening, or making black.

Theſe are the advenient and artificial ways of *denigration*, anſwerably whereto may be the natural progreſs. *Brown.*

In ſeveral inſtances of *denigration* the metals are worn off, or otherwiſe reduced into very minute parts. *Boyle.*

DENIZA'TION. *n. ſ.* [from *denizen*.] The act of infranchiſing, or making free.

That the mere Iriſh were reputed aliens appears by the charters of *denization*, which in all ages were purchaſed by them. *Davies on Ireland.*

DE'NIZEN. } *n. ſ.* [from *dinaſddyn*, a man of the city, or *di-*
DE'NISON. } *neſydd*, free of the city, Welſh.] A freeman; one infranchiſed.

Denizen is a Britiſh law term, which the Saxons and Angles found here, and retained. *Davies's Preface.*

Thus th' Almighty ſire began: ye gods,
Natives, or *denizens*, of bleſt abodes,
From whence theſe murmurs? *Dryden.*

A great many plants will hardly, with nurſing, be made to produce their ſeed out of their native ſoil; but corn, ſo neceſſary for all people, is fitted to grow and to feed as a free *deniſon* of the world. *Grew's Coſm. b.* iii. *c.* 2.

He ſummons ſtraight his *denizens* of air;
The lucid ſquadrons the ſails repair. *Pope's Rape of the Lock.*

To **DE'NIZEN.** *v. a.* [from the noun.] To infranchiſe; to make free.

Pride, luſt, covetize, being ſeveral
To theſe three places, yet all are in all;
Mingled thus, their iſſue is inceſtuous;
Falſhood is *denizen'd*, virtue is barbarous. *Donne.*

To **DENO'MINATE.** *v. a.* [*denomino*, Latin.] To name; to give a name to.

Their commendable purpoſe being not of every one underſtood, they have been in latter ages conſtrued as though they had ſuperſtitiouſly meant either that thoſe places, which were *denominated* of angels and ſaints, ſhould ſerve for the worſhip of ſo glorious creatures; or elſe thoſe glorified creatures for defence, protection, and patronage of ſuch places. *Hooker, b.* v.

Predeſtination is deſtructive to all that is eſtabliſhed among men, to all that is moſt precious, to human nature, to the two faculties that *denominate* us men, underſtanding and will; for what uſe can we have of our underſtandings, if we cannot do what we know to be our duty? And if we act not voluntarily, what exerciſe have we of our wills? *Hammond's Fundamentals.*

DENOMINA'TION. *n. ſ.* [*denominatio*, Latin.] A name given to a thing, which commonly marks ſome principal quality of it.

But is there any token, *denomination*, or monument of the Gauls yet remaining in Ireland, as there is of the Scythians? *Spenſer's State of Ireland.*

The liking or diſliking of the people gives the play the *denomination* of good or bad; but does not really make or conſtitute it ſuch. *Dryden's Defence of Dramatick Poeſy.*

Philoſophy, the great idol of the learned part of the Heathen world, has divided it into many ſects and *denominations*; as Stoicks, Peripateticks, Epicureans, and the like. *South.*

All men are ſinners: the moſt righteous among us muſt confeſs ourſelves to come under that *denomination*. *Rogers.*

DENO'MINATIVE. *adj.* [from *denominate*.]

1. That which gives a name; that which confers a diſtinct appellation.

2. That which obtains a diſtinct appellation. This would be more analogically *denominable*.

The leaſt *denominative* part of time is a minute, the greateſt integer being a year. *Cocker's Arithmetick.*

DENOMINA'TOR. *n. ſ.* [from *denominate*.] The giver of a name; the perſon or thing that cauſes an appellation.

Both the ſeas of one name ſhould have one common *denominator*. *Brown's Vulgar Errours.*

DENOMINA'TOR *of a Fraction*, is the number below the line, ſhewing the nature and quality of the parts which any integer is ſuppoſed to be divided into: thus in $\frac{6}{8}$, 8 the *denominator* ſhews you, that the integer is ſuppoſed to be divided into 8 parts, or half quarters; and the numerator 6 ſhews, that you take 6 of ſuch parts, *i. e.* three quarters of the whole. *Harris.*

When a ſingle broken number or fraction hath for its *denominator* a number conſiſting of an unit, in the firſt place towards the left hand, and nothing but cyphers from the unit towards the right hand, it is then more aptly and rightly called a decimal fraction. *Cocker's Arithmetick.*

Denominator of any proportion, is the quotient ariſing from the diviſion of the antecedent by the conſequent: thus 6 is the *denominator* of the proportion that 30 hath to 5, becauſe 5) 30 (6. This is alſo called the exponent of the proportion, or ratio. *Harris.*

DENOTA'TION. *n. ſ.* [*denotatio*, Latin.] The act of denoting.

To **DENO'TE.** *v. a.* [*denoto*, Latin.] To mark; to be a ſign of; to betoken; to ſhew by ſigns; as, a quick pulſe *denotes* a fever.

To **DENOU'NCE.** *v. a.* [*denuncio*, Latin; *denoncer*, French.]

1. To threaten by proclamation.

I *denounce* unto you this day, that ye ſhall ſurely periſh. *Deut.*

He of their wicked ways
Shall them admoniſh, *denouncing* wrath to come
On their impenitence. *Milton's Paradiſe Loſt, b.* xi. *l.* 815.

They impoſe their wild conjectures for laws upon others, and *denounce* war againſt all that receive them not. *Dec. of Piety.*

2. To threaten by ſome outward ſign or expreſſion.

He ended frowning, and his look *denounc'd*
Deſperate revenge, and battle dangerous
To leſs than gods. *Milton's Paradiſe Loſt, b.* ii. *l.* 106.

The ſea grew white; the rolling waves from far,
Like heralds, firſt *denounce* the watry war. *Dryden.*

3. To give information againſt.

Archdeacons ought to propoſe parts of the New Teſtament to be learned by heart by inferior clergymen, and *denounce* ſuch as are negligent. *Ayliffe's Parergon.*

DENOU'NCEMENT. *n. ſ.* [from *denounce*.] The act of proclaiming any menace; the proclamation of intended evil; denunciation.

Falſe is the reply of Cain upon the *denouncement* of his curſe, My iniquity is greater than can be forgiven. *Brown's Vu. Err.*

DENO'UNCER. *n. ſ.* [from *denounce*.] One that declares ſome menace.

Here comes the ſad *denouncer* of my fate,
To toll the mournful knell of ſeparation. *Dryden.*

DENSE. *adj.* [*denſus*, Latin.] Cloſe; compact; approaching to ſolidity; having ſmall interſtices between the conſtituent particles.

The cauſe of cold is the denſity of the body; for all *denſe* bodies are colder than moſt other bodies, as metals, ſtone, glaſs; and they are longer in heating than ſofter bodies. *Bacon.*

In the air the higher you go, the leſs it is compreſſed, and conſequently the leſs *denſe* it is; and ſo the upper part is exceedingly thinner than the lower part which we breathe. *Locke.*

To **DE'NSHIRE.** *v. a.* A barbarous term of huſbandry.

Burning of land, or burn-bating, is commonly called *denſhiring*, that is, *Devenſhiring* or *Denbighſhiring*, becauſe moſt uſed or firſt invented there. *Mortimer's Huſbandry.*

DE'NSITY. *n. ſ.* [*denſitas*, Latin.] Cloſeneſs; compactneſs; cloſe adheſion, or near approach of parts.

Whilſt the denſeſt of metals, gold, if foliated, is tranſparent, and all metals become tranſparent, if diſſolved in menſtruums or vitrified, the opacity of white metals ariſeth not from their *denſity* alone. *Newton's Opticks.*

The air within the veſſels being of a leſs *denſity*, the outward air would preſs their ſides together; and, being of a greater *denſity*, would expand them ſo as to endanger the life of the animal. *Arbuthnot on Aliments.*

DE'NTAL. *adj.* [*dentalis*, Latin.]

1. Belonging or relating to the teeth.

2. [In grammar.] Pronounced principally by the agency of the teeth.

The Hebrews have aſſigned which letters are labial, which *dental*, and which guttural. *Bacon's Natural Hiſtory*, Nº. 198.

The *dental* conſonants are eaſy, therefore let them be next; firſt the labio-*dentals*, as alſo the lingua-*dentals*. *Holder's Elem.*

DE'NTAL. *n. ſ.* A ſmall ſhell-fiſh.

Two ſmall black and ſhining pieces, ſeem, by the ſhape, to have been formed in the ſhell of a *dental*. *Woodward on Foſſils.*

DENTE'LLI. *n. ſ.* [Italian.] Modillons.

The modillons, or *dentelli*, make a noble ſhow by graceful projections. *Spectator*, Nº. 415.

DENTICULA'TION. *n. ſ.* [*denticulatus*, Latin.] The ſtate of being ſet with ſmall teeth.

He omits the *denticulation* of the edges of the bill, or thoſe ſmall oblique inciſions made for the better retention of the prey. *Grew's Muſæum.*

DENTI'CULATED. *adj.* [*denticulatus*, Latin.] Set with ſmall teeth.

DE'NTIFRICE. *n. ſ.* [*dens* and *frico*, Latin.] A powder made to ſcour the teeth.

Is this grey powder a good *dentifrice*? *Ben. Johnſ. Catil.*

The ſhells of all ſorts of ſhell-fiſh, being burnt, obtain a cauſtick nature: moſt of them, ſo ordered and powdered, make excellent *dentifrices*. *Grew's Muſæum.*

DENTI'TION. *n. ſ.* [*dentitio*, Latin.]

1. The act of breeding the teeth.

2. The time at which childrens teeth are bred.

To **DENU'DATE.** *v. a.* [*denudo*, Latin.] To diveſt; to ſtrip; to lay naked.

'Till he has *denudated* himſelf of all incumbrances, he is unqualified. *Decay of Piety.*

DENUDA'TION. *n. ſ.* [from *denudate*.] The act of ſtripping, or making naked.

To **DENU'DE.** *v. a.* [*denudo*, Lat.] To ſtrip; to make naked; to diveſt.

Not a treaty can be obtained, unleſs we would *denude* ourſelf of all force to defend us. *Clarendon, b.* vi.

If in Summer-time you *denude* a vine-branch of its leaves, the grapes will never come to maturity. *Ray on the Creation.*

The eye, with the skin of the eye-lid, is *denuded*, to shew the muscle. *Sharp's Surgery.*

DENUNCIA'TION. *n. s.* [*denunciatio*, Latin.] The act of denouncing; the proclamation of a threat; a publick menace.

In a *denunciation* or indiction of a war, the war is not confined to the place of the quarrel, but is left at large. *Bacon.*

Christ tells the Jews, that, if they believe not, they shall die in their sins: did they never read those *denunciations?* *Ward.*

Midst of these *denunciations*, and notwithstanding the warning before me, I commit myself to lasting durance. *Congreve.*

DENUNCIA'TOR. *n. s.* [from *denuncio*, Latin.]

1. He that proclaims any threat.

2. He that lays an information against another.

The *denunciator* does not make himself a party in judgment, as the accuser does. *Ayliffe's Parergon.*

To DENY'. *v. a.* [*denier*, French; *denego*, Latin.]

1. To contradict an accusation; not to confess.

Sarah *denied*, saying, I laughed not; for she was afraid. *Gen.*

2. To refuse; not to grant.

My young boy
Hath an aspect of intercession, which
Great nature cries—*deny* not. *Shakesp. Coriolanus.*
Ah, charming fair, said I,
How long can you my bliss and your's *deny?* *Dryden.*

3. To abnegate; to disown.

It shall be therefore a witness unto you, lest you *deny* your God. *Josh.* xxiv. 27.

4. To renounce; to disregard; to treat as foreign or not belonging to one.

The best sign and fruit of *denying* ourselves, is mercy to others. *Sprat's Sermons.*

When St. Paul says, if in this life only we have hope in Christ, we are of all men most miserable: he considers Christians as *denying* themselves in the pleasures of this world, for the sake of Christ. *Atterbury's Sermons, Pref.*

To DEOBSTRU'CT. *v. a.* [*deobstruo*, Latin.] To clear from impediments; to free from such things as hinder a passage.

It is a singular good wound-herb, useful for *deobstructing* the pores of the body *More's Antidote against Atheism.*

Such as carry off the fæces and mucus, *deobstruct* the mouth of the lacteals, so as the chyle may have a free passage into the blood. *Arbuthnot on Diet.*

DEO'BSTRUENT. *n. s.* [*deobstruens*, Latin.] A medicine that has the power to resolve viscidities, or to open by any means the animal passages.

All sopes are attenuating and *deobstruent*, resolving viscid substances. *Arbuthnot on Aliments.*

DE'ODAND. *n. s.* [*deo dandum*, Latin.] A thing given or forfeited to God for the pacifying his wrath, in case of any misfortune, by which any Christian comes to a violent end, without the fault of any reasonable creature; as, if a horse should strike his keeper, and so kill him; if a man, in driving a cart, and endeavouring to rectify something about it, should fall so as the cart-wheels, by running over him, should press him to death; if one should be felling a tree, and giving warning to company by, when the tree were near falling, to look to themselves, and any of them should nevertheless be slain by the fall of the tree; in these cases the horse, the cart-wheel, cart and horses, and the tree, are to be given to God; that is, sold and distributed to the poor, for an expiation of this dreadful event, though occasioned by unreasonable, senseless, and dead creatures: and though this be given to God, yet is it forfeited to the king by law, as executor in this case, to see the price of these distributed to the poor. *Cowel.*

To DEO'PPILATE. *v. a.* [*de* and *oppilo*, Latin.] To deobstruct; to clear a passage; to free from obstructions.

DEOPPILA'TION. *n. s.* [from *deoppilate.*] The act of clearing obstructions; the removal of whatever obstructs the vital passages.

Though the grosser parts be excluded again, yet are the dissoluble parts extracted, whereby it becomes effectual in *deoppilations.* *Brown's Vulgar Errours, b.* ii. *c.* 21.

DEO'PPILATIVE. *adj.* [from *deoppilate.*] Deobstruent.

A physician prescribed him a *deoppilative* and purgative apozem. *Harvey on Consumption.*

DEOSCULA'TION. *n. s.* [*deosculatio*, Latin.] The act of kissing.

We have an enumeration of the several acts of worship required to be performed to images, viz. processions, genuflections, thurifications and *deosculations.* *Stillingfleet.*

To DEPA'INT. *v. a.* [*depeint*, French.]

1. To picture; to describe by colours; to paint; to shew by a painted resemblance.

He did unwilling worship to the saint,
That on his sheild *depainted* he did see. *Fairy Queen, b.* ii.

2. To describe.

Such ladies fair would I *depaint*
In roundelay, or sonnet quaint. *Gay's Pastorals.*

To DEPA'RT. *v. n.* [*depart*, French.]

1. To go away from a place.

When the people *departed* away, Susanna went into her garden. *Susan.* vii.

He said unto him, go in peace; so he *departed* from him a little way. 2 *Kings* v. 19.

They *departed* quickly from the sepulchre, with fear and great joy, and did run to bring his disciples word. *Mat.* xxviii.

He, which hath no stomach to this fight,
Let him *depart*; his passport shall be made. *Shak. Henry* V.

Barbarossa stayed his course, and returned to Castronovum, whence, better appeased with presents, he *departed* out of that bay. *Knolles's History of the Turks.*

And could'st thou leave me, cruel, thus alone;
Not one kind kiss from a *departing* son!
No look, no last adieu! *Dryden's Æneis.*

2. To desist from a practice.

He cleaved unto the sins of Jeroboam, he *departed* not therefrom. 2 *Kings* iii. 3.

3. To be lost; to perish.

The good *departed* away, and the evil abode still. 2 *Esd.* iii.

4. To desert; to revolt; to fall away; to apostatise.

In transgressing and lying against the Lord, and *departing* away from our God. *Is.* lix. 13.

5. To desist from a resolution or opinion.

His majesty prevailed not with any of them to *depart* from the most unreasonable of all their demands. *Clarendon, b.* viii.

6. To dye; to decease; to leave the world.

As her soul was in *departing*; for she died. *Gen.* iii. 5. 18.

Lord, now lettest thou thy servant *depart* in peace, according to thy word. *Lu.* xxix.

As you wish Christian peace to souls *departed*,
Stand these poor people's friend. *Shakespeare's Henry* VIII.

To DEPA'RT. *v. a.* To quit; to leave; to retire from.

You have had dispatch in private by the consul;
You are will'd by him this evening
To *depart* Rome. *Ben. Johnson's Catiline.*

To DEPA'RT. *v. a.* [*partir*, French; *partior*, Latin.] To divide; to separate.

DEPA'RT. *n. s.* [*depart*, French.]

1. The act of going away.

I had in charge, at my *depart* from France,
To marry princess Marg'ret. *Shakespeare's Henry* VI. *p.* ii.

2. Death.

When your brave father breath'd his latest gasp,
Tidings, as swiftly as the post could run,
Were brought me of your loss and his *depart.* *Shak. H.* VI.

3. [With chymists.] An operation so named, because the particles of silver are *departed* or divided from gold, or other metal, when they were before melted together in the same mass, and could not be separated any other way. *Dict.*

DEPA'RTER. *n. s.* [from *depart.*] One that refines metals by separation.

DEPA'RTMENT. *n. s.* [*departement*, French.] Separate allotment; province or business assigned to a particular person.

The Roman fleets, during their command at sea, had their several stations and *departments:* the most considerable was the Alexandrian fleet, and the second was the African. *Arbuthnot.*

DEPA'RTURE. *n. s.* [from *depart.*]

1. A going away.

For thee, fellow,
Who needs must know of her *departure*, and
Do'st seem so ignorant, we'll force it from thee
By a sharp torture. *Shakespeare's Cymbeline.*
What besides
Of sorrow, and dejection, and despair,
Our frailty can sustain, thy tidings bring,
Departure from this happy place. *Milton's Paradise Lost, b.* xi.

2. Death; decease; the act of leaving the present state of existence.

Happy was their good prince in his timely *departure*, which barred him from the knowledge of his son's miseries. *Sidney.*

They were seen not only all the while our Saviour was upon earth, but survived after his *departure* out of this world. *Addison on the Christian Religion.*

3. A forsaking; an abandoning.

The fear of the Lord, and *departure* from evil, are phrases of like importance. *Tillotson, Sermon* 1.

DEPA'SCENT. *adj.* [*depascens*, Latin.] Feeding greedily.

To DEPA'STURE. *v. a.* [from *depascor*, Latin.] To eat up; to consume by feeding upon it.

They keep their cattle, and live themselves in bodies pasturing upon the mountains, and removing still to fresh land, as they have *depastured* the former. *Spenser's Ireland.*

To DEPAU'PERATE. *v. a.* [*depaupero*, Lat.] To make poor; to impoverish; to consume.

Liming does not *depauperate*; the ground will last long, and bear large grain. *Mortimer's Husbandry.*

Great evacuations, which carry off the nutritious humours, *depauperate* the blood. *Arbuthnot on Aliments.*

DEPE'CTIBLE. *adj.* [from *depecto*, Latin.] Tough; clammy; tenacious.

It may be also, that some bodies have a kind of lentor, and are of a more *depectible* nature than oil; as we see it evident in coloration; for a small quantity of saffron will tinct more than a very great quantity of brasil or wine. *Bacon's Nat. H.*

To Depe'inct. *v. a.* [*depeindre*, French.] To depaint; to paint; to describe in colours. A word of *Spenser*.

The red rose medlied with the white y fere,
In either cheek *depeincten* lively here. *Spenser's Pastorals.*

To DEPE'ND. *v. n.* [*dependeo*, Latin.]

1. To hang from.

From the frozen beard
Long isicles *depend*, and crackling sounds are heard. *Dryden.*
From gilded roofs *depending* lamps display
Nocturnal beams, that emulate the day. *Dryd. Virg. Æn.*
There is a chain let down from Jove,
So strong, that from the lower end,
They say, all human things *depend*. *Swift.*
The direful monster was afar descry'd
Two bleeding babes *depending* at her side. *Pope's Statius.*

2. To be in a state of servitude or expectation; to live subject to the will of others; to retain to others.

We work by wit, and not by witchcraft;
And wit *depends* on dilatory time. *Shakespeare's Othello.*

Never be without money, nor *depend* upon the curtesy of others, which may fail at a pinch. *Bacon's Advice to Villiers.*

3. To be in suspense; to be yet undetermined.

By no means be you persuaded to interpose yourself in any cause *depending*, or like to be *depending* in any court of justice. *Bacon's Advice to Villiers.*

The judge corrupt, the long *depending* cause,
And doubtful issue of misconstru'd laws. *Prior.*

4. *To* Depe'nd *upon.* To rely on; to trust to; to rest upon with confidence; to be certain of.

He resolved no more to *depend upon* the one, or to provoke the other. *Clarendon.*

But if you're rough, and use him like a dog,
Depend upon it—he'll remain incog. *Addison's Drum. Prol.*

I am a stranger to your characters, further than as common fame reports them, which is not to be *depended upon*. *Swift.*

5. To be in a state of dependance; to be at the discretion of others.

Be then desir'd
Of fifty to disquantity your train;
And the remainders, that shall still *depend*,
To be such men as may besort your age. *Shakes. K. Lear.*

6. To rest upon any thing as its cause.

The peace and happiness of a society *depend* on the justice and fidelity, the temperance and charity of its members. *Rogers.*

Depe'ndance. }
Depe'ndancy. } *n. s.* [from *depend.*]

1. The state of hanging down from a supporter.

2. Something hanging upon another.

On a neighb'ring tree descending light,
Like a large cluster of black grapes they show,
And make a large *dependance* from the bough. *Dryd. Virgil.*

3. Concatination; connexion; relation of one thing to another.

In all sorts of reasoning, the connexion and *dependance* of ideas should be followed, 'till the mind is brought to the source on which it bottoms. *Locke.*

4. State of being at the disposal or under the sovereignty of another.

Every moment we feel our *dependance* upon God, and find that we can neither be happy without him, nor think ourselves so. *Tillotson, Serm.* 1.

5. The things or persons of which any man has the dominion or disposal.

Never was there a prince bereaved of his *dependancies* by his council, except where there hath been either an over-greatness in one counsellor, or an over-strict combination in divers. *Bacon, Essay* 21.

The second natural division of power, is of such men who have acquired large possessions, and consequently *dependancies*; or descend from ancestors, who have left them great inheritances. *Swift on the Dissentions in Athens and Rome.*

6. Reliance; trust; confidence.

Their *dependencies* on him were drowned in this conceit. *Hooker, b.* i. *s.* 4.

They slept in peace by night,
Secure of bread, as of returning light;
And with such firm *dependance* on the day,
That need grew pamper'd, and forgot to pray. *Dryden.*

7. Accident; that of which the existence presupposes the existence of something else.

Modes I call such complex ideas, which, however compounded, contain not in them the supposition of subsisting by themselves, but are considered as *dependencies* on, or affections of substances; such are the ideas signified by the words triangle, gratitude, murder. *Locke.*

Depe'ndant. *adj.* [from *depend.*]

1. In the power of another.

On God, as the most high, all inferior causes in the world are *dependant*. *Hooker, b.* v. *s.* 23.

Depe'ndant. *n. s.* [from *depend.*] One who lives in subjection, or at the discretion of another; a retainer.

A great abatement of kindness appears as well in the general *dependants*, as in the duke himself also, and your daughter. *Shakespeare's King Lear.*

For a six-clerk a person recommended a *dependant* upon him, who paid six thousand pounds ready money. *Clarendon.*

His *dependants* shall quickly become his proselytes. *South.*

Depe'ndence. }
Depe'ndency. } *n. s.* [from *depend*, Latin. This word, with many others of the same termination, are indifferently written with *ance* or *ence*, *ancy* or *ency*, as the authors intended to derive them from the Latin or French.]

1. A thing or person at the disposal or discretion of another.

We invade the rights of our neighbours, not upon account of covetousness, but of dominion, that we may create *dependencies*. *Collier on Pride.*

2. State of being subordinate, or subject in some degree to the discretion of another; the contrary to sovereignty.

Let me report to him
Your sweet *dependency*, and you shall find
A conqu'ror that will pray in aid for kindness,
Where he for grace is kneel'd to. *Shak. Ant. and Cleopatra.*

At their setting out they must have their commission, or letters patents from the king, that so they may acknowledge their *dependency* upon the crown of England. *Bacon to Villiers.*

3. That which is not principal; that which is subordinate.

We speak of the sublunary worlds, this earth, and its *dependencies*, which rose out of a chaos about six thousand years ago. *Burnet's Theory of the Earth.*

4. Concatination; connexion; rise of consequents from premises.

Her madness hath the oddest frame of sense;
Such a *dependency* of thing on thing,
As e'er I heard in madness. *Shakesp. Measure for Measure.*

5. Relation of any thing to another, as of an effect to its cause.

I took pleasure to trace out the cause of effects, and the *dependence* of one thing upon another in the visible creation. *Burnet's Theory of the Earth.*

6. Trust; reliance; confidence.

The expectation of the performance of our desire, is that we call *dependence* upon him for help and assistance. *Stillingfleet.*

Depe'ndent. *adj.* [*dependens*, Latin. This, as many other words of like termination, are written with *ent* or *ant*, as they are supposed to flow from the Latin or French.] Hanging down.

None may wear this furr but princes; and there is a certain number of ranks allowed to dukes, marquisses, and earls, which they must not exceed in lining their caps therewith. In the time of Charles the Great, and long since, the whole furrs in the tails were *dependent*; but now that fashion is left, and the spots only worn, without the tails. *Peacham on Blazoning.*

Depe'ndent. *n. s.* [from *dependens*, Latin.] One subordinate; one at the discretion or disposal of another.

We are indigent, defenceless beings; the creatures of his power, and the *dependents* of his providence. *Rogers's Sermons.*

Depe'nder. *n. s.* [from *depend.*] A dependant; one that reposes on the kindness or power of another.

What shalt thou expect,
To be *depender* on a thing that leans? *Shakespeare's Cymbeline.*

Deperdi'tion. *n. s.* [from *deperditus*, Latin.] Loss; destruction.

It may be unjust to place all efficacy of gold in the non-omission of weights, or *deperdition* of any ponderous particles. *Brown.*

Dephlegma'tion. *n. s.* [from *dephlegm.*] An operation which takes away from the phlegm any spirituous fluid by repeated distillation, 'till it is at length left all behind. *Quincy.*

In divers cases it is not enough to separate the aqueous parts by *dephlegmation*; for some liquors contain also an unsuspected quantity of small corpuscles, of somewhat an earthy nature, which, being associated with the saline ones, do clog and blunt them, and thereby weaken their activity. *Boyle.*

To DEPHLE'GM. }
To DEPHLE'GMATE. } *v. a.* [*dephlegmo*, low Latin.] To clear from phlegm, or aqueous insipid matter.

We have sometimes taken spirit of salt, and carefully *dephlegmed* it. *Boyle.*

Dephle'gmedness. *n. s.* [from *dephlegm.*] The quality of being freed from phlegm or aqueous matter.

The proportion betwixt the coralline solution and the spirit of wine, depends so much upon the strength of the former liquor, and the *dephlegmedness* of the latter, that it is scarce possible to determine generally and exactly what quantity of each ought to be taken. *Boyle.*

To Depi'ct. *v. a.* [*depingo depictum*, Latin.]

1. To paint; to portray; to represent in colours.

The cowards of Lacedemon *depicted* upon their shields the most terrible beasts they could imagine. *Taylor's Worthy Comm.*

2. To describe; to represent an action to the mind.

When the distractions of a tumult are sensibly *depicted*, every object and every occurrence are so presented to your view, that while you read, you seem indeed to see them. *Felton.*

Depi'latory. *n. s.* [*de* and *pilus*, Latin.] An application used to take away hair.

De'pilous. *adj.* [*de* and *pilus*, Latin.] Without hair.

This

This animal is a kind of lizard, or quadruped, corticated and *depilous*; that is, without wool, furr, or hair. *Brown.*

DEPLANTA'TION. *n. s.* [*deplanto*, Latin.] The act of taking plants up from the bed. *Dict.*

DEPLE'TION. *n. s.* [*depleo depletus*, Lat.] The act of emptying.

Abstinence and a slender diet attenuates, because *depletion* of the vessels gives room to the fluid to expand itself. *Arbuthn.*

DEPLO'RABLE. *adj.* [from *deploro*, Latin.]

1. Lamentable; that which demands or causes lamentation; dismal; sad; calamitous; miserable; hopeless.

This was the *deplorable* condition to which the king was reduced. *Clarendon, b.* viii.

The bill of all weapons gives the most ghastly and *deplorable* wounds. *Temple.*

It will be considered in how *deplorable* a state learning lies in that kingdom. *Swift's Vindication of Isaac Bickerstaff.*

2. It is sometimes, in a more lax and jocular sense, used for contemptible; despicable: as, *deplorable* nonsense; *deplorable* stupidity.

DEPLO'RABLENESS. *n. s.* [from *deplorable.*] The state of being deplorable; misery; hopelesness. *Dict.*

DEPLO'RABLY. *adv.* [from *deplorable.*] Lamentably; miserably; hopelesly.

Notwithstanding all their talk of reason and philosophy, God knows, they are *deplorably* strangers to them. *South.*

DEPLO'RATE. *adj.* [*deploratus*, Lat.] Lamentable; hopeless.

The case is then most *deplorate* when reward goes over to the wrong side, and when interest shall be made the text and the measure. *L'Estrange, Fab.* 30.

DEPLORA'TION. *n. s.* [from *deplore.*] The act of deploring, or of lamenting.

To DEPLO'RE. *v. a.* [*deploro*, Latin.] To lament; to bewail; to wail; to mourn; to bemoan; to express sorrow.

But chaste Diana, who his death *deplor'd*,
With Æsculapian herbs his life restor'd. *Dryden's Æn.*

DEPLO'RER. *n. s.* [from *deplore.*] A lamenter; a mourner; one that laments.

DEPLUMA'TION. *n. s.* [*deplumatio*, Latin.]

1. A pluming, or plucking off the feathers.

2. [In surgery.] A swelling of the eyelids, accompanied with the fall of the hairs from the eye-brows. *Phillips.*

To DEPLU'ME. *v. a.* [*de* and *pluma*, Latin.] To strip of its feathers.

To DEPO'NE. *v. a.* [*depono*, Latin.]

1. To lay down as a pledge or security.

2. To risque upon the success of an adventure.

On this I would *depone*
As much, as any cause I've known. *Hudibras.*

DEPO'NENT. *n. s.* [from *depono*, Latin.]

1. One that deposes his testimony in a court of justice; an evidence; a witness.

2. [In grammar.] Such verbs as have no active voice are called *deponents*, and generally signify action only; as *fateor*, I confess. *Clark's Latin Grammar.*

To DEPO'PULATE. *v. a.* [*depopulor*, Latin.] To unpeople; to lay waste; to destroy inhabited countries.

Where is this viper,
That would *depopulate* the city, and
Be every man himself? *Shakespeare's Coriolanus.*

He turned his arms upon unarmed and unprovided people, to spoil only and *depopulate*, contrary to the laws both of war and peace. *Bacon's Henry* VII.

A land exhausted to the last remains,
Depopulated towns, and driven plains. *Dryden's Æn.*
Grim death, in different shapes,
Depopulates the nations, thousands fall
His victims. *Phillips.*

DEPOPULA'TION. *n. s.* [from *depopulate.*] The act of unpeopling; havock; waste; destruction of mankind.

How did'st thou grieve then, Adam! to behold
The end of all thy off-spring, end so sad,
Depopulation! Thee another flood,
Of tears and sorrow a flood, thee also drown'd,
And sunk thee as thy sons. *Milton's Paradise Lost, b.* xi.
Remote thou hear'st the dire effect of war,
Depopulation. *Phillips.*

DEPOPULA'TOR. *n. s.* [from *depopulate.*] A dispeopler; a destroyer of mankind; a waster of inhabited countries.

To DEPO'RT. *v. a.* [*deporter*, French.] To carry; to demean; to behave: it is used only with the reciprocal pronoun.

Let an ambassador *deport* himself in the most graceful manner before a prince. *Pope.*

DEPO'RT. *n. s.* [from the verb.] Demeanour; grace of attitude; behaviour; deportment.

She Delia's self
In gait surpass'd, and goddess-like *deport*. *Milt. Parad. Lost.*
Of middle age one rising, eminent
In wise *deport*, spake much of right and wrong. *Milton.*

DEPORTA'TION. *n. s.* [*deportatio*, Latin.] Transportation; exile into a remote part of the dominion, with prohibition to change the place of residence.

2. Exile in general.

An abjuration, which is a *deportation* for ever into a foreign land, was anciently with us a civil death. *Ayliffe's Parergon.*

DEPO'RTMENT. *n. s.* [*deportement*, French.]

1. Conduct; management; manner of acting.

I will but sweep the way with a few notes, touching the duke's own *deportment* in that island. *Wotton.*

2. Demeanour; behaviour.

The coldness of his temper, and the gravity of his *deportment*, carried him safe through many difficulties, and he lived and died in a great station. *Swift.*

To DEPO'SE. *v. a.* [*depono*, Latin.]

1. To lay down; to lodge; to let fall.

Its shores are neither advanced one jot further into the sea, nor its surface raised by additional mud *deposed* upon it by the yearly inundations of the Nile. *Woodward's Nat. History.*

2. To degrade from a throne or high station.

First, of the king: what shall of him become?
—The duke yet lives that Henry shall *depose*. *Shak. H.* VI.
May your sick fame still languish 'till it die;
Then, as the greatest curse that I can give,
Unpity'd, be *depos'd*, and after live. *Dryden's Aurengzebe.*

Deposed consuls, and captive princes, might have preceded him. *Tatler,* N°. 53.

3. To take away; to divest; to strip off.

You may my glory and my state *depose*,
But not my griefs; still am I king of those. *Shak. Rich.* III.

4. To give testimony; to attest.

'Twas he that made you to *depose*;
Your oath, my lord, is vain and frivolous. *Shak. Hen.* VI.

It was usual for him that dwelt in Southwark, or Tothill-street, to *depose* the yearly rent or valuation of lands lying in the North, or other remote part of the realm. *Bacon.*

5. To examine any one on his oath. Not now in use.

According to our law,
Depose him in the justice of his cause. *Shakes. Richard* III.

To DEPO'SE. *v. n.* To bear witness.

Love straight stood up and *deposed*, a lie could not come from the mouth of Zelmane. *Sidney, b.* ii.

DEPO'SITARY. *n. s.* [*depositarius*, Latin.] One with whom any thing is lodged in trust.

I gave you all.
—And in good time you gave it.
—Made you my guardians, my *depositaries*;
But kept a reservation to be follow'd
With such a number. *Shakespeare's King Lear.*

To DEPO'SITE. *v. a.* [*depositum*, Latin.]

1. To lay up; to lodge in any place.

The eagle got leave here to *deposite* her eggs. *L'Estrange.*

Dryden wants a poor square foot of stone, to shew where the ashes of one of the greatest poets on earth are *deposited*. *Garth.*

When vessels were open, and the insects had free access to the aliment within them, Redi diligently observed, that no other species were produced, but of such as he saw go in and feed, and *deposite* their eggs there, which they would readily do in all putrefaction. *Bentley's Sermons.*

2. To lay up as a pledge, or security.

3. To place at interest.

God commands us to return as to him, to the poor, his gifts, out of mere duty and thankfulness; not to *deposite* them with him, in hopes of meriting by them. *Sprat.*

4. To lay aside.

The difficulty will be to persuade the *depositing* of those lusts, which have, by I know not what fascination, so endeared themselves. *Decay of Piety.*

DEPO'SITE. *n. s.* [*depositum*, Latin.]

1. Any thing committed to the trust and care of another.

2. A pledge; a pawn; a thing given as a security.

3. The state of a thing pawned or pledged.

They had since Marseilles, and fairly left it: they had the other day the Valtoline, and now have put it in *deposite*. *Bacon.*

DEPOSI'TION. *n. s.* [from *depositio*, Latin.]

1. The act of giving publick testimony.

A witness is obliged to swear, otherwise his *deposition* is not valid. *Ayliffe's Parergon.*

2. The act of degrading a prince from sovereignty.

3. [In canon law.] Deposition properly signifies a solemn depriving of a man of his clerical orders. *Ayliffe's Parergon.*

DEPO'SITORY. *n. s.* [from *deposite.*] The place where any thing is lodged. *Depositary* is properly used of persons, and *depository* of places; but in the following example they are confounded.

The Jews themselves are the *depositories* of all the prophecies which tend to their own confusion. *Addison.*

DEPRAVA'TION. *n. s.* [*depravatio*, Latin.]

1. The act of making any thing bad; the act of corrupting; corruption.

The three forms of government have their several perfections, and are subject to their several *depravations*: however, few states are ruined by defect in their institution, but generally by corruption of manners. *Swift.*

2. The

2. The ſtate of being made bad; degeneracy; depravity.

We have a catalogue of the blackeſt ſins that human nature, in its higheſt *depravation*, is capable of committing. *South.*

3. Defamation; cenſure: a ſenſe not now in uſe.

Stubborn criticks are apt, without a theme
For *depravation*, to ſquare all the ſex. *Shakeſ. Troil. and Creſſ.*

To DEPRA'VE. *v. a.* [*depravo*, Latin.] To vitiate; to corrupt; to contaminate.

We admire the providence of God in the continuance of ſcripture, notwithſtanding the endeavours of Infidels to aboliſh, and the fraudulence of hereticks always to *deprave* the ſame. *Hooker, b.* v. *ſ.* 22.

Who lives that's not *depraved*, or *depraves*? *Shakeſ. Timon.*

But from me what can proceed,
But all corrupt; both mind and will *deprav'd*. *Milt. P. Loſt.*

A taſte which plenty does *deprave*,
Loaths lawful good, and lawleſs ill does crave. *Dryden.*

DEPRA'VEDNESS. *n. ſ.* [from *deprave*.] Corruption; taint; contamination; vitiated ſtate.

What ſins do you mean? Our original *depravedneſs*, and proneneſs of our eternal part to all evil. *Hammond's Pr. Catech.*

DEPRA'VEMENT. *n. ſ.* [from *deprave*.] A vitiated ſtate; corruption.

He maketh men believe, that apparitions are either deceptions of ſight, or melancholy *depravements* of fancy. *Brown.*

DEPRA'VER. *n. ſ.* [from *deprave*.] A corrupter; he that cauſes depravity.

DEPRA'VITY. *n. ſ.* [from *deprave*.] Corruption; a vitiated ſtate.

To DE'PRECATE. *v. n.* [*deprecor*, Latin.]

1. To pray earneſtly. *Dict.*
2. To requeſt; to petition. *Dict.*
3. To aſk pardon for. *Dict.*

To DE'PRECATE. *v. a.*

1. To implore mercy of.

At length he ſets
Thoſe darts, whoſe points make gods adore
His might, and *deprecate* his pow'r. *Prior.*

2. To avert; to remove; to turn away.
3. To beg off; to pray deliverance from.

In *deprecating* of evil, we make an humble acknowledgment of guilt, and of God's juſtice in chaſtiſing, as well as clemency, in ſparing the guilty. *Grew's Coſmol. Sac. b.* iii. *c.* 6.

Poverty indeed, in all its degrees, men are eaſily perſuaded to *deprecate* from themſelves. *Rogers, Sermon* ii.

The judgments which we would *deprecate*, are not removed. *Smalridge.*

The Italian entered them in his prayer: amongſt the three evils he petitioned to be delivered from, he might have *deprecated* greater evils. *Baker's Reflections on Learning.*

DEPRECA'TION. *n. ſ.* [*deprecatio*, Latin.]

1. Intreaty; petitioning.
2. An excuſing; a begging pardon for.
3. Prayer againſt evil.

I, with leave of ſpeech implor'd,
And humble *deprecation*, thus reply'd. *Milton's Parad. Loſt.*

Sternutation they generally conceived to be a good ſign, or a bad one; and ſo, upon this motion, they commonly uſed a gratulation for the one, and a *deprecation* for the other. *Brown.*

DEPRECA'TIVE. } *adj.* [from *deprecate*.] That ſerves to de-
DEPRECA'TORY. } precate; excuſive; apologizing.

Biſhop Fox underſtanding that the Scottiſh king was ſtill diſcontent, being troubled that the occaſion of breaking of the truce ſhould grow from his men, ſent many humble and *deprecatory* letters to the Scottiſh king to appeaſe him. *Bacon.*

DEPRECA'TOR. *n. ſ.* [*deprecator*, Latin.]

1. One that ſues for another; an interceſſor; a ſolicitor. *Dict.*
2. An excuſer.

To DEPRE'CIATE. *v. a.* [*depretiare*, Latin.]

1. To bring a thing down to a lower price.
2. To undervalue.

They preſumed upon that mercy, which, in all their converſations, they endeavour to *depreciate* and miſrepreſent. *Add.*

As there are none more ambitious of fame, than thoſe who are coiners in poetry, it is very natural for ſuch as have not ſucceeded in it to *depreciate* the works of thoſe who have. *Spect.*

To DE'PREDATE. *v. a.* [*deprædari*, Latin.]

1. To rob; to pillage.
2. To ſpoil; to devour.

It maketh the ſubſtance of the body more ſolid and compact, and ſo leſs apt to be conſumed and *depredated* by the ſpirits. *Bacon's Natural Hiſtory*, N°. 299.

DEPREDA'TION. *n. ſ.* [*deprædatio*, Latin.]

1. A robbing; a ſpoiling.

Commiſſioners were appointed to determine all matters of piracy and *depredations* between the ſubjects of both kingdoms. *Hayward.*

The land had never been before ſo free from robberies and *depredations* as through his reign. *Wotton.*

2. Voracity; waſte.

The ſpeedy *depredation* of air upon watry moiſture, and verſion of the ſame into air, appeareth in nothing more viſible than in the ſudden diſcharge or vaniſhing of a little cloud of breath, or vapour from glaſs, or the blade of a ſword, or any ſuch poliſhed body. *Bacon's Natural Hiſtory*, N°. 91.

DEPREDA'TOR. *n. ſ.* [*deprædator*, Lat.] A robber; a devourer.

It is reported, that the ſhrub called our Lady's Seal, which is a kind of briony, and coleworts, ſet near together, one or both will die: the cauſe is, for that they be both great *depredators* of the earth, and one of them ſtarveth the other. *Bacon.*

We have three that collect the experiments, which are in all books; theſe we call *depredators*. *Bacon's New Atlantis.*

To DEPREHE'ND. *v. a.* [*deprehendo*, Latin.]

1. To catch one; to take unawares; to take in the fact.

That wretched creature, being *deprehended* in that impiety, was held in ward. *Hooker, b.* iii. *ſ.* 11.

Who can believe men upon their own authority, that are once *deprehended* in ſo groſs and impious an impoſture. *More.*

2. To diſcover; to find out a thing; to come to the knowledge or underſtanding of.

The motions of the minute parts of bodies, which do ſo great effects, have not been obſerved at all, becauſe they are inviſible, and incur not to the eye; but yet they are to be *deprehended* by experience. *Bacon's Natural Hiſtory*, N°. 98.

DEPREHE'NSIBLE. *adj.* [from *deprehend*.]

1. That may be caught.
2. That may be apprehended, conceived, or underſtood. *Dict.*

DEPREHE'NSIBLENESS. *n. ſ.*

1. Capableneſs of being caught.
2. Intelligibleneſs; eaſineſs to be underſtood.

DEPREHE'NSION. *n. ſ.* [*deprehenſio*, Latin.]

1. A catching or taking unawares.
2. A diſcovery.

To DEPRE'SS. *v. a.* [from *depreſſus*, of *deprimo*, Latin.]

1. To preſs or thruſt down.
2. To let fall; to let down.

The ſame thing I have tried by letting a globe reſt, and raiſing or *depreſſing* the eye, or otherwiſe moving it to make the angle of a juſt magnitude. *Newton's Opt.*

3. To humble; to deject; to ſink.

Others *depreſs* their own minds, deſpond at the firſt difficulty, and conclude that the making any progreſs in knowledge is above their capacities. *Locke.*

If we conſider how often it breaks the gloom, which is apt to *depreſs* the mind, with tranſient unexpected gleams of joy, one would take care not to grow too wiſe for ſo great a pleaſure of life. *Addiſon's Spectator*, N°. 249.

Paſſion can *depreſs* or raiſe
The heavenly, as the human mind. *Prior.*

DEPRE'SSION. *n. ſ.* [*depreſſio*, Latin.]

1. The act of preſſing down.
2. The ſinking or falling in of a ſurface.

The beams of light are ſuch ſubtile bodies, that, in reſpect of them, even ſurfaces that are ſenſibly ſmooth, are not exactly ſo: they have their own degree of roughneſs, conſiſting of little protuberances and *depreſſions*; and conſequently ſuch inequalities may ſuffice to give bodies different colours, as we ſee in marble that appears white or black, or red or blue, even when moſt carefully poliſhed. *Boyle on Colours.*

If the bone be much depreſſed, and the fiſſure conſiderably large, it is then at your choice, whether you will enlarge that fiſſure, or continue it for the evacuation of the matter, and forbear the uſe of the trapan; not doubting but a ſmall *depreſſion* of the bone will either riſe, or caſt off, by the benefit of nature. *Wiſeman's Surgery.*

3. The act of humbling; abaſement.

Depreſſion of the nobility may make a king more abſolute, but leſs ſafe. *Bacon's Ornam. Ration.* 28.

DEPRE'SSION *of an Equation* [in algebra], is the bringing it into lower and more ſimple terms by diviſion. *Dict.*

DEPRE'SSION *of a Star* [with aſtronomers], is the diſtance of a ſtar from the horizon below, and is meaſured by the arch of the vertical circle or azimuth, paſſing through the ſtar, intercepted between the ſtar and the horizon. *Dict.*

DEPRE'SSOR. *n. ſ.* [*depreſſor*, Latin.]

1. He that keeps or preſſes down.
2. An oppreſſor.

DEPRE'SSOR. [In anatomy.] A term given to ſeveral muſcles of the body, whoſe action is to depreſs the parts to which they adhere.

DE'PRIMENT. *adj.* [from *deprimens*, of *deprimo*, Latin.] An epithet applied to one of the ſtraight muſcles that move the globe or ball of the eye, its uſe being to pull it downwards. *Phillips.*

All I ſhall farther take notice of, ſhall be only the exquiſite equilibration of all oppoſite and antagoniſt muſcles, affected partly by the natural poſture of the body and the eye, which is the caſe of the attollent and *depriment* muſcles. *Derham.*

DEPRIVA'TION. *n. ſ.* [from *de* and *privatio*, Latin.]

1. The act of depriving, or taking away from.

Fools whoſe end is deſtruction, and eternal *deprivation* of being. *Bentley.*

DEPRIVA'TION [in law], is when a clergyman, as a bishop, parson, vicar or prebend, is deprived, or deposed from his preferment, for any matter in fact or law. *Phillips.*

To DEPRI'VE. *v. a.* [from *de* and *privo*, Latin.]

1. To bereave one of a thing; to take it away from him.

God hath *deprived* her of wisdom, neither hath he imparted to her understanding. *Job* xxxix. 17.

He lamented the loss of an excellent servant, and the horrid manner in which he had been *deprived* of him. *Clarendon.*

Now wretched Oedipus, *depriv'd* of sight,
Led a long death in everlasting night. *Pope's Statius.*

2. To hinder; to debar from.

From his face I shall be hid, *depriv'd*
His blessed count'nance. *Milton's Paradise Lost*, *b.* xi.

The ghosts rejected, are th' unhappy crew
Depriv'd of sepulchres, and fun'ral due. *Dryden's Æn.* vi.

3. To release; to free from.

Most happy he,
Whose least delight sufficeth to *deprive*
Remembrance of all pains which him opprest. *Spenser.*

4. To put out of an office.

A minister, *deprived* for inconformity, said, that if they *deprived* him it should cost an hundred mens lives. *Bacon.*

DEPTH. *n. s.* [from *deep*, of *diep*, Dutch.]

1. Deepness; the measure of any thing from the surface downwards.

As for men, although they had buildings in many places higher than the *depth* of the water, yet that inundation had a long continuance. *Bacon's New Atlantis.*

We have large and deep caves of several *depths*: the deepest are sunk six hundred fathoms. *Bacon.*

The left to that unhappy region tends,
Which to the *depth* of Tartarus descends. *Dryden's Æn.*

For though, in nature, *depth* and height
Are equally held infinite,
In poetry the height we know
'Tis only infinite below. *Swift.*

2. Deep place; not a shoal.

The false tides skim o'er the cover'd land,
And seamen with dissembled *depths* betray. *Dryd. Ann. Mir.*

3. The abyss; a gulph of infinite profundity.

When he prepared the heavens I was there, when he set a compass upon the face of the *depth*. *Prov.* viii. 27.

4. The middle or height of a season.

And in the *depth* of winter, in the night,
You plow the raging seas to coasts unknown. *Denham.*

The earl of Newcastle, in the *depth* of Winter, rescued the city of York from the rebels. *Clarendon.*

5. Abstruseness; obscurity.

There are greater *depths* and obscurities in an elaborate and well written piece of nonsense, than in the most abstruse tract of school divinity. *Addison's Whig Examiner.*

DEPTH *of a Squadron or Batallion*, is the number of men in the file. *Milit. Dict.*

To DE'PTHEN. *v. a.* [*diepen*, Dutch.] To deepen, or make deeper. *Dict.*

To DEPU'CELATE. *v. a.* [*depuceler*, French.] To deflower; to bereave of virginity. *Dict.*

DEPU'LSION. *n. s.* [*depulsion*, Latin.] A beating or thrusting away.

DEPU'LSORY. *adj.* [from *depulsus*, Latin.] Putting away; averting. *Dict.*

To DE'PURATE. *v. a.* [*depurer*, French, from *depurgo*, Lat.] To purify; to cleanse; to free any thing from its impurities.

Chemistry enabling us to *depurate* bodies, and in some measure to analize them, and take asunder their heterogeneous parts, in many chemical experiments we may better than in others, know what manner of bodies we employ; art having made them more simple, or uncompounded, than nature alone is wont to present them to us. *Boyle.*

DE'PURATE. *adj.* [from the verb.]

1. Cleansed; freed from dregs and impurities.

2. Pure; not contaminated.

Neither can any boast a knowledge *depurate* from the defilement of a contrary, within this atmosphere of flesh. *Glanv.*

DEPURA'TION. *n. s.* [*depuratio*, Latin.]

1. The act of separating the pure from the impure part of any thing.

Brimstone is a mineral body, of fat and inflammable parts; and this is either used crude, and called *sulphur vive*, or is of a sadder colour, and, after *depuration*, such as we have in magdeleons, or rolls of a lighter yellow. *Brown's Vulgar Errours.*

What hath been hitherto discoursed, inclines us to look upon the ventilation and *depuration* of the blood as one of the principal and constant uses of respiration. *Boyle's Spring of the Air.*

2. The cleansing of a wound from its filth.

To DEPU'RE. *v. a.* [*depurer*, French.]

1. To cleanse; to free from impurities.

2. To purge; to free from some noxious quality.

It produced plants of such imperfection and harmful quality, as the waters of the general flood could not so wash out or *depure*, but that the same defection hath had continuance in the very generation and nature of mankind. *Raleigh.*

DEPUTA'TION. *n. s.* [*deputation*, French.]

1. The act of deputing, or sending away with a special commission.

2. Vicegerency; the possession of any commission given.

Cut me off the heads
Of all the fav'rites that the absent king
In *deputation* left behind him here,
When he was personal in the Irish war. *Shakesp. Henry* IV.

He looks not below the moon, but hath designed the regiment of sublunary affairs unto sublunary *deputations*. *Brown.*

The authority of conscience stands founded upon its vicegerency and *deputation* under God. *South's Sermons.*

To DEPU'TE. *v. a.* [*deputer*, French.] To send with a special commission; to impower one to transact instead of another.

And Absalom said unto him, See thy matters are good and right, but there is no man *deputed* of the king to hear. 2 *Sa.*

A bishop, by *deputing* a priest or chaplain to administer the sacraments, may correct and remove him for his demerits. *Ayliffe's Parergon.*

And Linus thus, *deputed* by the rest,
The heroes welcome, and their thanks express'd. *Roscomm.*

DE'PUTY. *n. s.* [*député*, Fr. from *deputatus*, Latin.] A lieutenant; a viceroy; one that is appointed by a special commission to govern and act instead of another.

He exerciseth dominion over them as the vicegerent and *deputy* of Almighty God. *Hale's Origin of Mankind.*

He was vouched his immediate *deputy* upon earth, and viceroy of the creation, and lord lieutenant of the world. *South.*

2. Any one that transacts business for another.

Presbyters, absent through infirmity from their churches, might be said to preach by those *deputies*, who, in their stead, did but read homilies. *Hooker, b.* v. *s.* 21.

A man hath a body, and that body is confined to a place; but where friendship is, all offices of life are, as it were, granted to him and his *deputy*; for he may exercise them by his friend. *Bacon, Essay* 28.

3. [In law.] One that exercises any office or other thing in another man's right, whose forfeiture or misdemeanour shall cause the officer or person for whom he acts to lose his office. *Phillips.*

To DEQUA'NTITATE. *v. a.* [from *de* and *quantitas*, Latin.] To diminish the quantity of.

This we affirm of pure gold; for that which is current, and passeth in stamp amongst us, by reason of its allay, which is a proportion of silver or copper mixed therewith, is actually *dequantitated* by fire, and possibly by frequent extinction. *Brown's Vulgar Errours, b.* ii. *c.* 2.

DER. A term used in the beginning of names of places. It is generally to be derived from ðeoꞃ, a wild beast, unless the place stands upon a river; for then it may rather be fetched from the British *dur*, i. e. water. *Gibson's Camden.*

To DERA'CINATE. *v. a.* [*deraciner*, French.]

1. To pluck or tear up by the roots.

Her fallow leas,
The darnel, hemlock, and rank fumitory
Doth root upon; while that the cutter rusts
That should *deracinate* such savagery. *Shakesp. Henry* V.

2. To abolish; to destroy; to extirpate.

To DERA'IGN. } *v. a.* [*disrationare*, or *dirationare*, Latin.]
To DERA'IN. }

1. To prove; to justify.

When the parson of any church is disturbed to demand tythes in the next parish by a writ of *indicavit*, the patron shall have a writ to demand the advowson of the tythes being in demand; and when it is *deraigned*, then shall the plea pass in the court christian, as far forth as it is *deraigned* in the king's court. *Blount.*

2. To disorder; to turn out of course. *Dict.*

DERA'IGNMENT. } *n. s.* [from *deraign*.]
DERA'INMENT. }

1. The act of deraigning or proving.

2. A disordering or turning out of course.

3. A discharge of profession; a departure out of religion.

In some places the substantive *dereignment* is used in the very literal signification with the French *disrayer*, or *desranger*; that is, turning out of course, displacing, or setting out of order; as *deraignment* or departure out of religion, and *dereignment* or discharge of their profession, which is spoken of those religious men who forsook their orders and professions. *Blount.*

DERA'Y. *n. s.* [from *desrayer*, French, to turn out of the right way.]

1. Tumult; disorder; noise.

2. Merriment; jollity; solemnity. *Douglass.*

To DERE. *v. a.* [ðeꞃian, Saxon.] To hurt. Obsolete.

So from immortal race he does proceed,
That mortal hands may not withstand his might;
Dred for his *derring* doe, and bloody deed;
For all in blood and spoil is his delight. *Fairy Queen, b.* ii.

DERELI'CTION.

Derelі'ction. *n. s.* [*derelictio*, Latin.] An utter forsaking or leaving; an abandoning.

There is no other thing to be looked for, but the effects of God's most just displeasure; the withdrawing of grace, *dereliction* in this world, and in the world to come confusion. *Hooker.*

De'relicts. *n. s.* pl. [In law.] Such goods as are wilfully thrown away, or relinquished by the owner. *Dict.*

To **DERI'DE.** *v. a.* [*derideo*, Latin.]

1. To laugh at; to mock; to turn to ridicule; to scorn.

And before whose presence to offend with any the least unseemliness, we would be surely as loth as they who most reprehend or *deride* what we do. *Hooker, b. v. s.* 29.

What shall be the portion of those who have *derided* God's word, and made a mock of every thing that is sacred and religious? *Tillotson, Serm.* ii.

These sons, ye gods, who with flagitious pride
Insult my darkness, and my groans *deride*. *Pope's Statius.*

Deri'der. *n. s.* [from the verb.]

1. A mocker; a scoffer.

Upon the wilful violation of oaths, execrable blasphemies, and like contempts offered by *deriders* of religion, fearful tokens of divine revenge have been known to follow. *Hooker.*

2. A droll; a buffoon.

Deri'sion. *n. s.* [*derisio*, Latin.]

1. The act of deriding or laughing at.

2. Contempt; scorn; a laughing-stock.

I am in *derision* daily; every one mocketh me. *Jer.* xx. 7.

Thou makest us a reproach to our neighbours, a scorn and a *derision* to them that are round about us. *Ps.* xliv. 13.

Ensnar'd, assaulted, overcome, led bound,
Thy foes *derision*, captive, poor and blind,
Into a dungeon thrust. *Milton's Agonistes, l.* 364.

Are we grieved with the scorn and *derision* of the prophane? Thus was the blessed Jesus despised and rejected of men. *Rogers.*

Vanity is the natural weakness of an ambitious man, which exposes him to the secret scorn and *derision* of those he converses with. *Addison's Spectator*, N°. 255.

Deri'sive. *adj.* [from *deride.*] Mocking; scoffing.

O'er all the dome they quaff, they feast;
Derisive taunts were spread from guest to guest,
And each in jovial mood his mate addrest. *Pope's Odyssey.*

Deri'sory. *adj.* [*derisorius*, Latin.] Mocking; ridiculing.

Deri'vable. *adj.* [from *derive.*] Attainable by right of descent or derivation.

God has declared this the eternal rule and standard of all honour *derivable* upon me, that those who honour him shall be honoured by him. *South's Sermons.*

Deriva'tion. *n. s.* [*derivatio*, Latin.]

1. A draining of water; a turning of its course; letting out.

When it began to swell, it would every way discharge itself by any descents or declivities of the ground; and these issues and *derivations* being once made, and supplied with new waters pushing them forwards, would continue their course 'till they arrived at the sea, just as other rivers do. *Burnet.*

2. [In grammar.] The tracing of a word from its original.

Your lordship here seems to dislike my taking notice, that the *derivation* of the word substance favours the idea we have of it; and your lordship tells me, that very little weight is to be laid on it, on a bare grammatical etymology. *Locke.*

3. The tracing of any thing from its source.

As touching traditional communication, and tradition of those truths that I call connatural and engraven, I do not doubt but many of those truths have had the help of that *derivation*. *Hale's Origin of Mankind.*

4. [In medicine.] The drawing of a humour from one part of the body to another.

Derivation differs from revulsion only in the measure of the distance, and the force of the medicines used: if we draw it to some very remote, or, it may be, contrary part, we call that revulsion; if only to some neighbouring place, and by gentle means, we call it *derivation*. *Wiseman on Tumours.*

Deri'vative. *adj.* [*derivativus*, Latin.] Derived or taken from another.

As it is a *derivative* perfection, so it is a distinct kind of perfection from that which is in God. *Hale's Origin of Mank.*

Deri'vative. *n. s.* [from the adjective.] The thing or word derived or taken from another.

For honour,
'Tis a *derivative* from me to mine,
And only that I stand for. *Shakespeare's Winter's Tale.*

The word honestus originally and strictly signifies no more than creditable, and is but a *derivative* from honour, which signifies credit or honour. *South's Sermons.*

Deri'vatively. *adv.* [from *derivative.*] In a derivative manner.

To **DERI'VE.** *v. a.* [*deriver*, French, from *derivo*, Latin.]

1. To turn the course of any thing; letting out; communicating.

Company lessens the shame of vice by sharing it, and abates the torrent of a common odium by *deriving* it into many channels. *South's Sermons.*

2. To deduce from its original.

They endeavour to *derive* the varieties of colours from the various proportion of the direct progress or motion of these globules to their circumvolution, or motion about their own centre. *Boyle on Colours.*

This property of it seems rather to have been *derived* from the Pretorian soldiers, who insolently assumed the disposing of the empire. *Decay of Piety.*

Men *derive* their ideas of duration from their reflection on the train of ideas they observe to succeed one another in their own understandings. *Locke.*

From these two causes of the laxity and rigidity of the fibres, the methodists, an ancient set of physicians, *derived* all diseases of human bodies with a great deal of reason; for the fluids *derive* their qualities from the solids. *Arbuthnot.*

3. To communicate to another, as from the origin and source.

Christ having Adam's nature as we have, but incorrupt, *deriveth* not nature, but incorruption, and that immediately from his own person, unto all that belong unto him. *Hooker.*

The censors of these wretches, who, I am sure, could *derive* no sanctity to them from their own persons; yet upon this account, that they had been consecrated by the offering incense in them, were, by God's special command, sequestered from all common use. *South's Sermons.*

4. To communicate to by descent of blood.

Besides the readiness of parts, an excellent disposition of mind is *derived* to your lordship from the parents of two generations, to whom I have the honour to be known. *Felton.*

5. To spread; to diffuse gradually from one place to another.

The streams of the publick justice were *derived* into every part of the kingdom. *Davies on Ireland.*

6. [In grammar.] To trace a word from its origin.

To **De'rive.** *v. n.*

1. To come from; to owe its origin to.

He that resists the pow'r of Ptolomy,
Resists the pow'r of heav'n; for pow'r from heav'n
Derives, and monarchs rule by gods appointed. *Prior.*

2. To descend from.

I am, my lord, as well *deriv'd* as he,
As well possest. *Shakespeare's Midsummer Night's Dream.*

Deri'ver. *n. s.* [from *derive.*]

1. One that draws or fetches from the original.

Such a one makes a man not only a partaker of other mens sins, but also a *deriver* of the whole intire guilt of them to himself. *South's Sermons.*

Dern. *adj.* [ꝺeaꞃn, Saxon.]

1. Sad; solitary.

2. Barbarous; cruel. Obsolete.

Dernie'r. *adj.* Last. It is a mere French word, and used only in the following phrase.

In the Imperial chamber, the term for the prosecution of an appeal is not circumscribed by the term of one or two years, as the law elsewhere requires in the Empire, this being the *dernier* resort and supreme court of judicature. *Ayliffe's Parerg.*

To **De'rogate.** *v. a.* [*derogo*, Latin.]

1. To do an act contrary to a preceding law or custom, so as to diminish its former value.

By several contrary customs and stiles used here, many of those civil and canon laws are controuled and *derogated*. *Hale.*

2. To lessen the worth of any person or thing; to disparage.

To **De'rogate.** *v. n.* To degenerate; to do a thing contrary to one's calling or dignity.

We should be injurious to virtue itself, if we did *derogate* from them whom their industry hath made great. *Hooker.*

De'rogate. *adj.* [from the verb.] Damaged; lessened in value.

Into her womb convey sterility;
Dry up in her the organs of increase,
And from her *derogate* body never spring
A babe to honour her! *Shakespeare's King Lear.*

Deroga'tion. *n. s.* [*derogatio*, Latin.]

1. The act of breaking and making void a former law or contract.

It was indeed but a wooing ambassage, with good respects to entertain the king in good affection; but nothing was done or handled to the *derogation* of the king's late treaty with the Italians. *Bacon's Henry* VII.

That which enjoins the deed is certainly God's law; and it is also certain, that the scripture, which allows of the will, is neither the *derogation* nor relaxation of that law. *South's Serm.*

2. A disparaging; lessening or taking away the worth of any person or thing. Sometimes with *to*, properly with *from*.

Which, though never so necessary, they could not easily now admit, without some fear of *derogation* from their credit; and therefore that which once they had done, they became for ever after resolute to maintain. *Hooker, Preface.*

So surely he is a very brave man, neither is that any thing which I speak to his *derogation*; for in that I said he is a mingled people, it is no dispraise. *Spenser on Ireland.*

The wisest princes need not think it any diminution to their greatness, or *derogation* to their sufficiency, to rely upon counsel. *Bacon, Essay* 21.

I say

I ſay not this in *derogation* to Virgil, neither do I contradict any thing which I have formerly ſaid in his juſt praiſe. *Dryden.*

I believe there are none of theſe patriots who will think it a *derogation* from their merit to have it ſaid, that they received many lights and advantages from their intimacy with my lord Somers. *Addiſon's Freeholder*, N° 39.

DERO'GATIVE. *adj.* [*derogativus*, Latin.] Derogating; leſſening the value of.

That ſpirits are corporeal ſeems to me a conceit *derogative* to himſelf, and ſuch as he ſhould rather labour to overthrow; yet thereby he eſtabliſheth the doctrine of luſtrations, amulets and charms, as we have declared before. *Brown's Vulgar Err.*

DERO'GATORILY. *adv.* [from *derogatory*.] In a detracting manner. *Dict.*

DERO'GATORINESS. *n. ſ.* [from *derogatory*.] The act of derogating. *Dict.*

DERO'GATORY. *adj.* [*derogatorius*, Latin.] That leſſens the value of.

They live and die in their abſurdities, paſſing their days in perverted apprehenſions and conceptions of the world, *derogatory* unto God and the wiſdom of the creation. *Brown.*

Theſe deputed beings, as they are commonly underſtood, are *derogatory* from the wiſdom and power of the Author of Nature, who doubtleſs can govern this machine he could create, by more direct and eaſy methods than employing theſe ſubſervient divinities. *Cheyne's Phil. Prin.*

DE'RVIS. *n. ſ.* [*dervis*, French.] A Turkiſh prieſt.

Even there, where Chriſt vouchſaf'd to teach,
Their *derviſes* dare an impoſtor preach. *Sandys.*

The *dervis* at firſt made ſome ſcruple of violating his promiſe to the dying brachman; but told him, at laſt, that he could conceal nothing from ſo excellent a prince. *Spectator.*

DE'SCANT. *n. ſ.* [*diſcanto*, Italian.]

1. A ſong or tune compoſed in parts.

Nay, now you are too flat,
And mar the concord with too harſh a *deſcant*. *Shakeſpeare.*
The wakeful nightingale
All night long her amorous *deſcant* ſung. *Milton's Par. Loſt.*

2. A diſcourſe; a diſputation; a diſquiſition branched out into ſeveral diviſions or heads. It is commonly uſed as a word of cenſure, or contempt.

Look you get a prayer-book in your hand,
And ſtand between two churchmen, good my lord;
For on that ground I'll build a holy *deſcant*. *Shak. Rich.* III.

Such kindneſs would ſupplant our unkind reportings, and ſevere *deſcants* upon our brethren. *Government of the Tongue.*

To DE'SCANT. *v. n.* [from the noun.]

1. To ſing in parts.

2. To diſcourſe at large; to make ſpeeches: in a ſenſe of cenſure or contempt.

Why I, in this weak piping time of peace,
Have no delight to paſs away the time;
Unleſs to ſpy my ſhadow in the ſun,
And *deſcant* on mine own deformity. *Shakeſ. Richard* III.

Com'ſt thou for this, vain boaſter, to ſurvey me,
To *deſcant* on my ſtrength, and give thy verdict? *Milton.*

A virtuous man ſhould be pleaſed to find people *deſcanting* upon his actions, becauſe, when they are thoroughly canvaſſed and examined, they turn to his honour. *Addiſon's Freeholder.*

To DESCE'ND. *v. a.* [*deſcendo*, Latin.]

1. To come from a higher place to a lower; to fall; to ſink.

The rain *deſcended*, and the floods came, and the winds blew, and beat upon that houſe; and it fell not, for it was founded upon a rock. *Matt.* vii. 25.

The brook that *deſcended* out of the mount. *Deutr.* ix. 21.

He cleft his head with one *deſcending* blow. *Dryden.*

Foul with ſtains
Of guſhing torrents and *deſcending* rains. *Addiſon's Cato.*

O goddeſs! who, *deſcending* from the ſkies,
Vouchſaf'd thy preſence to my wond'ring eyes. *Pope's Odyſſ.*

2. To come down in a popular ſenſe, implying only an arrival at one place from another.

He ſhall *deſcend* into battle, and periſh. 1 *Sa.* xxvi. 10.

3. To come ſuddenly or violently; to fall upon as an enemy.

For the pious ſire preſerve the ſon;
His wiſh'd return with happy pow'r befriend,
And on the ſuitors let thy wrath *deſcend*. *Pope's Odyſſey, b.* iv.

4. To make an invaſion.

The goddeſs gives th' alarm; and ſoon is known
The Grecian fleet, *deſcending* on the town. *Dryden.*
A foreign ſon upon the ſhore *deſcends*,
Whoſe martial fame from pole to pole extends. *Dryden.*

5. To proceed from an original; to be extracted from.

Deſpair *deſcends* from a mean original; the offspring of fear, lazineſs, and impatience. *Collier againſt Deſpair.*

Will is younger brother to a baronet, and *deſcended* of the ancient family of the Wimbles. *Addiſon's Spectator*, N°. 108.

6. To fall in order of inheritance to a ſucceſſor.

Should we allow that all the property, all the eſtate of the father, ought to *deſcend* to the eldeſt ſon; yet the father's natural dominion, the paternal power, cannot *deſcend* unto him by inheritance. *Locke.*

The inheritance of both rule over men and property, in things ſprung from the ſame original, and were to *deſcend* by the ſame rules. *Locke.*

Our author provides for the *deſcending* and conveyance down of Adam's monarchical power to poſterity, by the inheritance of his heir, ſucceeding to his father's authority. *Locke.*

7. To extend a diſcourſe from general to particular conſiderations.

Congregations diſcerned the ſmall accord that was among themſelves, when they *deſcended* to particulars. *Decay of Piety.*

To DESCE'ND. *v. a.* To walk downward upon any place.

He ended, and they both *deſcend* the hill;
Deſcended Adam to the bow'r, where Eve
Lay ſleeping. *Milton's Paradiſe Loſt.*

In all our journey through the Alps, as well when we climbed as when we *deſcended* them, we had ſtill a river running along with the road. *Addiſon on Italy.*

In the midſt of this plain ſtands a high hill, ſo very ſteep, that there would be no mounting or *deſcending* it, were not it made up of a looſe crumbled earth. *Addiſon on Italy.*

DESCE'NDANT. *n. ſ.* [*deſcendant*, Fr. *deſcendens*, Latin.] The offspring of an anceſtor; he that is in the line of generation at whatever diſtance.

The *deſcendants* of Neptune were planted there. *Bacon.*

O, true *deſcendant* of a patriot line,
Vouchſafe this picture of thy ſoul to ſee. *Dryden.*

He revealed his own will, and their duty, in a more ample manner than it had been declared to any of my *deſcendants* before them. *Atterbury's Sermons.*

DESCE'NDENT. *adj.* [*deſcendens*, Latin. It ſeems to be eſtabliſhed that the ſubſtantive ſhould derive the termination from the French, and the adjective from the Latin.]

1. Falling; ſinking; coming down; deſcending.

There is a regreſs of the ſap in plants from above downwards; and this *deſcendent* juice is that which principally nouriſhes both fruit and plant. *Ray on the Creation.*

2. Proceeding from another as an original or anceſtor.

More than mortal grace
Speaks thee *deſcendent* of æthereal race. *Pope's Odyſſey, b.* iv.

DESCE'NDIBLE. *adj.* [from *deſcend*.]

1. Such as may be deſcended; ſuch as may admit of a paſſage downwards.

2. Tranſmiſſible by inheritance.

According to the cuſtoms of other countries thoſe honorary fees and infeudations were *deſcendible* to the eldeſt, and not to all the males. *Hale's Common Law of England.*

DESCE'NSION. *n. ſ.* [*deſcenſio*, Latin.]

1. The act of falling or ſinking; deſcent.

2. A declenſion; a degradation.

From a god to a bull! a heavy *deſcenſion*:
It was Jove's caſe. From a prince to a 'prentice? a low transformation: that ſhall be mine. *Shakeſpeare's Henry* IV.

3. [In aſtronomy.] Right *deſcenſion* is the arch of the equator, which deſcends with the ſign or ſtar below the horizon of a direct ſphere.

Oblique *deſcenſion* is the arch of the equator, which deſcends with the ſign below the horizon of an oblique ſphere. *Ozenam.*

DESCE'NSIONAL. *adj.* [from *deſcenſion*.] Relating to deſcent.

DESCE'NT. *n. ſ.* [*deſcenſus*, Latin; *deſcente*, French.]

1. The act of paſſing from a higher place.

Why do fragments, from a mountain rent,
Tend to the earth with ſuch a ſwift *deſcent*? *Blackmore.*

2. Progreſs downwards.

Obſerving ſuch gradual and gentle *deſcents* downwards, in thoſe parts of the creation that are beneath men, the rule of analogy may make it probable, that it is ſo alſo in things above. *Locke.*

3. Obliquity; inclination.

The heads and ſources of rivers flow upon a *deſcent*, or an inclining plane, without which they could not flow at all. *Woodward's Natural Hiſtory, p.* iii.

4. Loweſt place.

From th' extremeſt upward of thy head,
To the *deſcent* and duſt below thy feet,
A moſt toad-ſpotted traitor. *Shakeſpeare's King Lear.*

5. Invaſion; hoſtile entrance into a kingdom: in alluſion to the height of ſhips.

At the firſt *deſcent* on ſhore, he was not immured with a wooden veſſel, but he did countenance the landing in his long-boat. *Wotton.*

The duke was general himſelf, and made that unfortunate *deſcent* upon the Iſle of Ree, which was attended with a miſerable retreat, in which the flower of the army was loſt. *Claren.*

Ariſe, true judges, in your own defence,
Controul thoſe foplings, and declare for ſenſe;
For ſhould the fools prevail, they ſtop not there,
But make their next *deſcent* upon the fair. *Dryden.*

6. Tranſmiſſion of any thing by ſucceſſion and inheritance.

If the agreement and conſent of men firſt gave a ſceptre into any one's hand, that alſo muſt direct its *deſcent* and conveyance. *Locke.*

7. The

7. The state of proceeding from an original or progenitor.

All of them, even without such a particular claim, had great reason to glory in their common *descent* from Abraham, Isaac and Jacob, to whom the promise of the blessed seed was severally made. *Atterbury's Sermons.*

8. Birth; extraction; process of lineage.

I give my voice on Richard's side,
To bar my master's heirs in true *descent!*
God knows, I will not do it. *Shakesp. Richard* III.

Turnus, for high *descent* and graceful mien,
Was first, and favour'd by the Latian queen. *Dryden's Æn.*

9. Offspring; inheritors; those proceeding in the line of generation.

The care of our *descent* perplexes us most,
Which must be born to certain woe. *Milton's Paradise Lost.*

From him
His whole *descent*, who thus shall Canaan win. *Milt. P. L.*

10. A single step in the scale of genealogy; a generation.

No man living is a thousand *descents* removed from Adam himself. *Hooker, b.* iii. *s.* 1.

Then all the sons of these five brethren reign'd
By due success, and all their nephews late,
Even thrice eleven *descents* the crown retain'd,
'Till aged Heli by due heritage it gain'd. *Fairy Queen, b.* ii.

11. A rank in the scale or order of being.

How have I then, with whom to hold converse,
Save with the creatures which I made, and those
To me inferior; infinite *descents*
Beneath what other creatures are to thee. *Milton's P. Lost.*

To DESCRI'BE. *v. a.* [*describo*, Latin.]

1. To mark out any thing by the mention of its properties.

I pray thee, overname them; and as thou nam'st them, I will *describe* them; and according to my description, level at my affection. *Shakespeare's Merchant of Venice.*

He that writes well in verse will often send his thoughts in search, through all the treasure of words that express any one idea in the same language, that so he may comport with the measures, or the rhyme of the verse which he writes, or with his own most beautiful and vivid sentiments of the thing he *describes*. *Watts's Improvement of the Mind.*

2. To delineate; to mark out; to trace: as a torch waved about the head *describes* a circle.

3. To distribute into proper heads or divisions.

Men passed through the land, and *described* it by cities into seven parts in a book. *Jos.* xviii. 9.

4. To define in a lax manner by the promiscuous mention of qualities general and peculiar. See DESCRIPTION.

DESCRI'BER. *n. s.* [from *describe.*] He that describes.

From a plantation and colony of theirs, an island near Spain was by the Greek *describers* named Erythra. *Brown.*

DESCRI'ER. *n. s.* [from the verb.] A discoverer; a detecter.

May think his labour vainly gone,
The glad *descrier* shall not miss
To taste the nectar of a kiss. *Crashaw.*

DESCRI'PTION. *n. s.* [*descriptio*, Latin.]

1. The act of describing or making out any person or thing by perceptible properties.

2. The sentence or passage in which any thing is described.

A poet must refuse all tedious and unnecessary *descriptions*: a robe which is too heavy, is less an ornament than a burthen. *Dryden's Dufresnoy, Preface.*

Sometimes misguided by the tuneful throng,
I look for streams immortaliz'd in song,
That lost in silence and oblivion lie,
Dumb are their fountains, and their channels dry,
That run for ever by the muse's skill,
And in the smooth *description* murmur still. *Addison.*

3. A lax definition.

This sort of definition, which is made up of a mere collection of the most remarkable parts or properties, is called an imperfect definition, or a *description*; whereas the definition is called perfect when it is composed of the essential difference, added to general nature or genus. *Watts's Logick.*

4. The qualities expressed in a description.

I'll pay six thousand, and deface the bond,
Before a friend of this *description*
Shall lose a hair. *Shakespeare's Merchant of Venice.*

To DESCRY'. *v. a.* [*descrier*, French.]

1. To give notice of any thing suddenly discovered; as, the scout *descried* the enemy, that he gave notice of their approach. This sense is now obsolete, but gave occasion to those which are now in use.

2. To spy out; to examine at a distance.

And the house of Joseph sent to *descry* Bethel. *Judg.* i. 23.

Edmund, I think, is gone to *descry*
Th' strength o' th' enemy. *Shakespeare's King Lear.*

3. To detect; to find out any thing concealed.

Of the king they got a sight after dinner in a gallery, and of the queen mother at her own table; in neither place *descryed*, no, not by Cadinet, who had been lately ambassador in England. *Wotton.*

4. To discover; to perceive by the eye; to see any thing distant or absent.

Thus dight, into the court he took his way;
Both through the guard, which never him *descry'd*,
And through the watchmen, who him never spy'd.
Hubbard's Tale.

The spirit of deep prophecy she hath;
What's past and what's to come she can *descry*. *Shak. H.* VI.

That planet would, unto our eyes, *descrying* only that part whereon the light falls, appear to be horned, as the moon seems. *Raleigh's History of the World, b.* i. *c.* 7.

And now their way to earth they had *descry'd*,
To Paradise first tending. *Milton's Paradise Lost, b.* x.

Although the motion of light be not *descried*, no argument can be made from thence to prove that light is not a body. *Digby on Bodies.*

A tow'r so high, it seem'd to reach the sky,
Stood on the roof, from whence we could *descry*
All Ilium. *Denham.*

Once more at least look back, said I;
Thyself in that large glass *descry*. *Prior.*

DESCRY'. *n. s.* [from the verb.] Discovery; thing discovered.

How near's the other army?
—Near, and on speedy foot, the main *descry*
Stands on the hourly thought. *Shakespeare's King Lear.*

To DE'SECRATE. *v. a.* [*desacro*, Lat.] To divert from the purpose to which any thing is consecrated.

The founders of monastries imprecated evil on those who should *desecrate* their donations. *Salmon's Survey.*

DESECRA'TION. *n. s.* [from *desecrate.*] The abolition of consecration.

DE'SERT. *n. s.* [*desertum*, Latin.] A wilderness; solitude; waste country; uninhabited place.

Be alive again,
And dare me to the *desert* with thy sword.
Of trembling I inhibit; then protest me
The baby of a girl. *Shakespeare's Macbeth.*

He, looking round on every side, beheld
A pathless *desert*, dusk with horrid shades. *Paradise Reg.*

DE'SERT. *adj.* [*desertus*, Latin.] Wild; waste; solitary; uninhabited; uncultivated; untilled.

I have words
That would be howl'd out in the *desert* air,
Where hearing should not catch them. *Shakesp. Macbeth.*

He found him in a *desert* land, and in the waste howling wilderness. *Deutr.* xxxii. 10.

The promises and bargains between two men in a *desert* island are binding to them, though they are perfectly in a state of nature, in reference to one another. *Locke.*

To DESE'RT. *v. a.* [*deserter*, French; *desero*, Latin.]

1. To forsake; to fall away from; to quit meanly or treacherously.

I do not remember one man, who heartily wished the passing of that bill, that ever *deserted* them 'till the kingdom was in a flame. *Dryden's Æn. Dedicat.*

2. To leave; to abandon.

What is it that holds and keeps them in fixed stations and intervals, against an incessant and inherent tendency to *desert* them? *Bentley's Sermons.*

3. To quit the army, or regiment, in which one is enlisted.

DESE'RT. *n. s.* [properly *dessert*: the word is originally French.] The last course; the fruit or sweetmeats with which a feast is concluded. See DESSERT.

DESE'RT. *n. s.* [from *desert.*]

1. Qualities or conduct considered with respect to rewards or punishments; degree of merit or demerit.

Being of necessity a thing common, it is, through the manifold persuasions, dispositions, and occasions of men, with equal *desert* both of praise and dispraise, shunned by some, by others desired. *Hooker, b.* v. *s.* 46.

The base o' th' mount
Is rank'd with all *deserts*, all kind of natures,
That labour on the bosom of this sphere
To propagate their states. *Shakespeare's Timon.*

Use every man after his *desert*, and who shall 'scape whipping? *Shakespeare's Hamlet.*

2. Proportional merit; claim to reward.

More to move you,
Take my *deserts* to his, and join them both. *Shakes. Timon.*

All *desert* imports an equality between the good conferred and the good deserved, or made due. *South's Sermons.*

3. Excellence; right to reward; virtue.

DESE'RTER. *n. s.* [from *desert.*]

1. He that has forsaken his cause or his post.

The members of both houses, who at first withdrew, were counted *deserters*, and outed of their places in parliament. *King Charles.*

Streight to their ancient calls, recall'd from air,
The reconcil'd *deserters* will repair. *Dryden's Virg. Georg.*

Hosts of *deserters*, who your honour sold,
And basely broke your faith for bribes of gold. *Dryd. Æn.*

2. He that leaves the army in which he is enlisted.

They are the ſame *deſerters*, whether they ſtay in our own camp, or run over to the enemies. *Decay of Piety.*

A *deſerter*, who came out of the citadel, ſays the garriſon is brought to the utmoſt neceſſity. *Tatler*, N°. 59.

3. He that forſakes another; an abandoner.

The fair ſex, if they had the *deſerter* in their power, would certainly have ſhewn him more mercy than the Bacchanals did Orpheus. *Dryden's Æn. Dedicat.*

Thou, falſe guardian of a charge too good,
Thou mean *deſerter* of thy brother's blood. *Pope.*

DESE'RTION. *n. ſ.* [from *deſert.*]

1. The act of forſaking or abandoning a cauſe or poſt.

Every compliance that we are perſuaded to by one, is a contradiction to the commands of the other; and our adherence to one, will neceſſarily involve us in a *deſertion* of the other. *Rogers, Serm* v.

3. [In theology.] Spiritual deſpondency; a ſenſe of the dereliction of God; an opinion that grace is withdrawn.

Chriſt hears and ſympathizes with the ſpiritual agonies of a ſoul under *deſertion*, or the preſſures of ſome ſtinging affliction. *South's Sermons.*

DESE'RTLESS. *adj.* [from *deſert.*] Without merit; without claim to favour or reward.

She ſaid ſhe lov'd;
Lov'd me *deſertleſs*, who, with ſhame, confeſt
Another flame had ſeiz'd upon my breaſt. *Dryd. Tyr. Love.*

To DESE'RVE. *v. a.* [*deſervir*, French.]

1. To be worthy of either good or ill.

Thoſe they honoured, as having power to work or ceaſe, as men *deſerved* of them. *Hooker, b.* i.

Some of us love you well; and ev'n thoſe ſome
Envy your great *deſervings*, and good name. *Shak. Hen.* IV.

All friends ſhall taſte
The wages of their virtue, and all foes
The cup of their *deſervings*. *Shakeſpeare's King Lear.*

What he *deſerves* of you and me I know. *Shak. H.* VIII.

Yet well, if here would end
The miſery: I *deſerv'd* it, and would bear
My own deſervings. *Milton's Paradiſe Loſt, b.* x. *l.* 727.

Courts are the places where beſt manners flouriſh,
Where the *deſerving* ought to riſe. *Otway's Orphan.*

A mother cannot give him death; though he
Deſerves it, he *deſerves* it not from me. *Dryden's Ovid.*

Since my Orazia's death I have not ſeen
A beauty ſo *deſerving* to be queen,

He had been a perſon of great *deſervings* from the republick, was an admirable ſpeaker, and very popular. *Swift.*

2. To be worthy of reward.

According to the rule of natural juſtice one man may merit and *deſerve* of another. *South's Sermons.*

DESE'RVEDLY. *adv.* [from *deſerve.*] Worthily; according to deſert, whether of good or evil.

For him I was not ſent, nor yet to free
That people victor once, now vile and baſe,
Deſervedly made vaſſal. *Milton's Paradiſe Regain'd, b.* iv.

A man *deſervedly* cuts himſelf off from the affections of that community which he endeavours to ſubvert. *Addiſ. Freeholder.*

DESE'RVER. *n. ſ.* [from *deſerve.*] A man who merits rewards. It is uſed, I think, only in a good ſenſe.

Their love is never link'd to the *deſerver*,
'Till his deſerts are paſs'd. *Shakeſp. Ant. and Cleopatra.*

Heavy, with ſome high minds, is an overweight of obligation; or otherwiſe great *deſervers* do perchance grow intolerable preſumers. *Wotton.*

Emulation will never be wanting amongſt poets, when particular rewards and prizes are propoſed to the beſt *deſervers*. *Dryden's Dufreſnoy, Preface.*

DESI'CCANTS. *n. ſ.* [from *deſiccate.*] Applications that dry up the flow of ſores; driers.

This, in the beginning, may be prevented by *deſiccants*, and waſted. *Wiſeman's Surgery.*

To DE'SICCATE. *v. a.* [*deſicco*, Latin.] To dry up; to exhale moiſture.

In bodies *deſiccated* by heat or age, when the native ſpirit goeth forth, and the moiſture with it, the air with time getteth into the pores. *Bacon's Natural Hiſtory*, N°. 842.

Where there is moiſture enough, or ſuperfluous, there wine helpeth to digeſt and *deſiccate* the moiſture. *Bacon's Nat. Hiſt.*

Seminal ferments were elevated from the ſea, or ſome *deſiccated* places thereof, by the heat of the ſun. *Hale.*

DESICCA'TION. *n. ſ.* [from *deſiccate.*] The act of making dry; the ſtate of being dried.

If the ſpirits iſſue out of the body, there followeth *deſiccation*, induration, and conſumption; as in brick, evaporation of bodies liquid, &c. *Bacon's Natural Hiſtory*, N°. 329.

DESI'CCATIVE. *adj.* [from *deſiccate.*] That which has the power of drying.

To DESI'DERATE. *v. a.* [*deſidero*, Lat.] To want; to miſs; to deſire in abſence. A word ſcarcely uſed.

Eclipſes are of wonderful aſſiſtance toward the ſolution of this ſo deſirable and ſo much *deſiderated* problem. *Cheyne.*

DESI'DIOSE. *adj.* [*deſidioſus*, Latin.] Idle; lazy; heavy. *Dict.*

To DESI'GN. *v. a.* [*deſigno*, Latin; *deſſiner*, French.]

1. To purpoſe; to intend any thing.

2. To form or order with a particular purpoſe: with *for*.

The acts of religious worſhip were purpoſely *deſigned for* the acknowledgment of a being, whom the moſt excellent creatures are bound to adore as well as we. *Stillingfleet.*

You are not for obſcurity *deſign'd*,
But, like the ſun, muſt cheer all human kind. *Dryden.*

3. To devote intentionally; with *to.*

One of thoſe places was *deſigned* by the old man *to* his ſon. *Clarendon.*

He was born to the inheritance of a ſplendid fortune; he was *deſigned to* the ſtudy of the law. *Dryden.*

4. To plan; to project; to form in idea.

We are to obſerve whether it be well drawn, or, as more elegant artizans term it, well *deſigned*; then, whether it be well coloured, which be the two general heads. *Wotton.*

Thus while they ſpeed their pace, the prince *deſigns*
The new elected ſeat, and draws the lines. *Dryden's Æn.*

5. To mark out.

'Tis not enough to make a man a ſubject, to convince him that there is regal power in the world; but there muſt be ways of *deſigning* and knowing the perſon to whom this regal power of right belongs. *Locke.*

DESI'GN. *n. ſ.* [from the verb.]

1. An intention; a purpoſe.

2. A ſcheme; a plan of action.

Is he a prudent man, as to his temporal eſtate, that lays *deſigns* only for a day, without any proſpect to the remaining part of his life? *Tillotſon, Sermon* i.

3. A ſcheme formed to the detriment of another.

A ſedate ſettled *deſign* upon another man's life, put him in a ſtate of war with him againſt whom he has declared ſuch an intention. *Locke.*

4. The idea which an artiſt endeavours to execute or expreſs.

I doubt not but in the *deſigns* of ſeveral Greek medals one may often ſee the hand of an Apelles or Protogenes. *Addiſon.*

Thy hand ſtrikes out ſome new *deſign*,
Where life awakes and dawns at every line. *Pope's Epiſtles.*

DESI'GNABLE. *adj.* [*deſigno*, Latin.] Diſtinguiſhable; capable to be particularly marked out.

The power of all natural agents is limited: the mover muſt be confined to obſerve theſe proportions, and cannot paſs over all theſe infinite *deſignable* degrees in an inſtant. *Digby.*

DESIGNA'TION. *n. ſ.* [*deſignatio*, Latin.]

1. The act of pointing or marking out by ſome particular token.

This is a plain *deſignation* of the duke of Marlborough: one kind of ſtuff uſed to fatten land is called marle, and every body knows that borough is a name for a town. *Swift.*

2. Appointment; direction.

William the Conqueror forbore to uſe that claim in the beginning, but mixed it with a titulary pretence, grounded upon the will and *deſignation* of Edward the Confeſſor. *Bacon.*

3. Import; intention.

Finite and infinite ſeem to be looked upon by the mind as the modes of quantity, and to be attributed primarily in their firſt *deſignation* only to thoſe things which have parts, and are capable of increaſe or diminution. *Locke.*

DESI'GNEDLY. *adv.* [from *deſign.*] Purpoſely; intentionally; by deſign or purpoſe; not ignorantly; not inadvertently; not fortuitouſly.

The next thing is ſometimes *deſignedly* to put them in pain; but care muſt be taken that this be done when the child is in good humour. *Locke.*

Uſes made things; that is to ſay, ſome things were made *deſignedly*, and on purpoſe, for ſuch an uſe as they ſerve to. *Ray on the Creation.*

DESI'GNER. *n. ſ.* [from *deſign.*]

1. A plotter; a contriver; one that lays ſchemes.

It has therefore always been both the rule and practice for ſuch *deſigners* to ſuborn the publick intereſt, to countenance and cover their private. *Decay of Piety.*

2. One that forms the idea of any thing in painting or ſculpture.

There is a great affinity between deſigning and poetry; for the Latin poets, and the *deſigners* of the Roman medals, lived very near one another, and were bred up to the ſame reliſh for wit and fancy. *Addiſon.*

DESI'GNING. *participial adj.* [from *deſign.*] Inſidious; treacherous; deceitful; fraudulently artful.

'Twould ſhew me poor, indebted, and compell'd,
Deſigning, mercenary; and I know
You would not wiſh to think I could be bought. *Southern.*

DESI'GNLESS. *adj.* [from *deſign.*] Without intention; without deſign; unknowing; inadvertent.

DESI'GNLESSLY. *adv.* [from *deſignleſs.*] Without intention; ignorantly; inadvertently.

In this great concert of his whole creation, the *deſignleſly* conſpiring voices are as differing as the conditions of the reſpective ſingers. *Boyle's Seraphick Love.*

DESI'GNMENT. *n. ſ.* [from *deſign.*]

1. A ſcheme of hoſtility.

News, lords, our wars are done:
The deſperate tempeſt hath ſo bang'd the Turks,
That their *deſignment* halts. *Shakeſpeare's Othello.*

2. A plot; a malicious intention.

She received advice both of the king's deſperate eſtate, and of the duke's *deſignments* againſt her. *Hayward.*

3. The idea, or ſketch of a work.

The ſcenes which repreſent cities and countries are not really ſuch, but only painted on boards and canvaſs; but ſhall that excuſe the ill painture or *deſignment* of them? *Dryden.*

When abſent, yet we conquer'd in his right;
For though that ſome mean artiſt's ſkill were ſhown
In mingling colours, or in placing light,
Yet ſtill the fair *deſignment* was his own. *Dryden.*

DESI'RABLE. *adj.* [from *deſire.*]

1. Pleaſing; delightful.

She then let drop ſome expreſſions about an agate ſnuff-box; I immediately took the hint, and bought one, being unwilling to omit any thing that might make me *deſirable* in her eyes. *Addiſon's Guardian*, N°. 97.

Our own ſex, our kindred, our houſes, and our very names, ſeem to have ſomething good and *deſirable* in them. *Watts.*

2. That which is to be wiſhed with earneſtneſs.

Adjudged caſes, collected by men of great ſagacity, will improve his mind, toward acquiring this *deſirable* amplitude and extent of thought. *Watts's Improvement of the Mind.*

He cannot but confeſs, that it is a thing the moſt *deſirable* to man, and moſt agreeable to the goodneſs of God, that he ſhould ſend forth his light and his truth by a ſpecial revelation of his will. *Rogers, Sermon* iii.

DESI'RE. *n. ſ.* [*deſir*, Fr. *deſeo*, Ital. *deſiderium*, Lat.] Wiſh; eagerneſs to obtain or enjoy.

Drink provokes, and unprovokes; it provokes the *deſire*, but it takes away the performance. *Shakeſpeare's Macbeth.*

Deſire's the vaſt extent of human mind;
It mounts above, and leaves poor hope behind. *Dryden.*

Deſire is the uneaſineſs a man finds in himſelf upon the abſence of any thing, whoſe preſent enjoyment carries the idea of delight with it. *Locke.*

It is in a man's power only to obſerve what the ideas are that take their turns in his underſtanding, or elſe to direct the ſort, and call in ſuch as he hath a *deſire* or uſe of. *Locke.*

To DESI'RE. *v. a.* [*deſirer*, French; *deſiderare*, Latin.]

1. To wiſh; to long for; to covet.

Thou ſhalt not *deſire* the ſilver or gold. *Deutr.* vii. 25.

2. To expreſs wiſhes; to appear to long.

Jove beheld it with a *deſiring* look. *Dryden.*

3. To aſk; to intreat.

Sir, I intreat you home with me to dinner.
—I humbly do *deſire* your grace of pardon;
I muſt away this night. *Shakeſp. Merchant of Venice.*

But ſince you take ſuch int'reſt in our woe,
And Troy's diſaſt'rous end *deſire* to know,
I will reſtrain my tears, and briefly tell
What in our laſt fatal night befell. *Dryden's Æn. b.* ii.

DESI'RER. *n. ſ.* [from *deſire.*] One that is eager of any thing; a wiſher.

I will counterfeit the bewitchment of ſome popular man, and give it bountifully to the *deſirers*. *Shakeſp. Coriolanus.*

DESI'ROUS. *adj.* [from *deſire.*] Full of deſire; eager; longing after; wiſhing for.

The ſame piety which maketh them that are in authority *deſirous* to pleaſe and reſemble God by juſtice, inflameth every way men of action with zeal to do good. *Hooker, b.* v. *ſ.* 1.

Be not *deſirous* of his dainties; for they are deceitful meat. *Prov.* xxiii. 3.

Men are drowſy and *deſirous* to ſleep before the fit of an ague, and yawn and ſtretch. *Bacon's Nat. Hiſtory*, N°. 296.

Adam the while,
Waiting *deſirous* her return, had wove
Of choiceſt flow'rs a garland. *Milton's Paradiſe Loſt, b.* ix.

Conjugal affection,
Prevailing over fear and timorous doubt,
Hath led me on, *deſirous* to behold
Once more thy face. *Milton's Agoniſtes.*

DESI'ROUSNESS. *n. ſ.* [from *deſirous.*] Fulneſs of deſire; eagerneſs. *Dict.*

DESI'ROUSLY. *adv.* [from *deſirous.*] Eagerly; with deſire; with ardent wiſhes. *Dict.*

To DESI'ST. *v. n.* [*deſiſto*, Latin.] To ceaſe from any thing; to ſtop.

Deſiſt, thou art diſcern'd,
And toil'ſt in vain; nor me in vain moleſt. *Milt. Pa. Loſt.*

There are many who will not quit a project, though they find it pernicious or abſurd; but will readily *deſiſt* from it, when they are convinced it is impracticable. *Addiſ. Freeholder.*

DESI'STANCE. *n. ſ.* [from *deſiſt.*] The act of deſiſting; ceſſation.

Men uſually give freelieſt where they have not given before; and make it both the motive and excuſe of their *deſiſtance* from giving any more, that they have given already. *Boyle.*

DESI'TIVE. *adj.* [*deſitus*, Latin.] Ending; concluded.

Inceptive and *deſitive* propoſitions are of this ſort: the fogs vaniſh as the ſun riſes, but the fogs have not yet begun to vaniſh; therefore the ſun is not yet riſen. *Watts's Logick, p.* iii.

DESK. *n. ſ.* [*diſch*, a table, Dutch.] An inclining table for the uſe of writers or readers, made commonly with a box or repoſitory under it.

Tell her in the *deſk*,
That's cover'd o'er with Turkiſh tapeſtry,
There is a purſe of ducats. *Shakeſp. Comedy of Errours.*

He is drawn leaning on a *deſk*, with his bible before him. *Walton's Angler.*

I have alſo been obliged to leave unfiniſhed in my *deſk* the heads of two eſſays. *Pope.*

Not the *deſk* with ſilver nails,
Nor bureau of expence,
Nor ſtandiſh well japann'd, avails
To writing of good ſenſe. *Swift.*

DE'SOLATE. *adj.* [*deſolatus*, Latin.]

1. Without inhabitants; uninhabited.

Let us ſeek ſome *deſolate* ſhade, and there
Weep our ſad boſoms empty. *Shakeſpeare's Macbeth.*

This hero appears at firſt in a *deſolate* iſland, ſitting upon the ſide of the ſea. *Broome on Epic Poetry.*

2. Deprived of inhabitants; laid waſte.

This city ſhall be *deſolate*, without an inhabitant. *Jer.* xxvi.

3. Solitary; without ſociety.

To DE'SOLATE. *v. a.* [*deſolo*, Latin.] To deprive of inhabitants; to lay waſte.

The iſland of Atlantis was not ſwallowed by an earthquake, but was *deſolated* by a particular deluge; for earthquakes are ſeldom in thoſe parts: but, on the other ſide, they have ſuch pouring rivers, as the rivers of Aſia, Africa, and Europe are but brooks to them. *Bacon, Eſſay* 59.

Thick around
Thunders the ſport of thoſe, who with the gun
And dog, impatient bounding at the ſhot,
Worſe than the ſeaſon, *deſolate* the fields. *Thomſon's Winter.*

DE'SOLATELY. *adv.* [from *deſolate.*] In a deſolate manner.

DESOLA'TION. *n. ſ.* [from *deſolate.*] Deſtruction of inhabitants; ravage.

What with your praiſes of the country, what with your diſcourſe of the lamentable *deſolation* thereof made by thoſe Scots, you have filled me with a great compaſſion of their calamities. *Spenſer's State of Ireland.*

Without her follows to myſelf and thee,
Herſelf, the land, and many a Chriſtian ſoul,
Death, *deſolation*, ruin, and decay. *Shakeſp. Richard* III.

To complete
The ſcene of *deſolation* ſtretch'd around,
The grim guards ſtand. *Thomſon's Summer, l.* 1075.

2. Gloomineſs; ſadneſs; melancholy.

That dwelling place is unnatural to mankind; and then the terribleneſs of the continual motion, the *deſolation* of the far being from comfort, the eye and the ear having ugly images before it, doth ſtill vex the mind, even when it is beſt armed againſt it. *Sidney, b.* ii.

Then your hoſe ſhall be ungartered, and every thing about you demonſtrate a careleſs *deſolation*. *Shakeſ. As you like it.*

My *deſolation* does begin to make
A better life. *Shakeſpeare's Anthony and Cleopatra.*

3. A place waſted and forſaken.

How is Babylon become a *deſolation* among the nations! *Jer.* l. 23.

DESPA'IR. *n. ſ.* [*deſeſpoir*, French.]

1. Hopeleſneſs; deſpondence; loſs of hope.

You had either never attempted this change, ſet on with hope, or never diſcovered it, ſtopt with *deſpair*. *Sidney, b.* ii.

We are troubled on every ſide, yet not diſtreſſed; we are perplexed, but not in *deſpair*. 2 *Cor.* iv. 8.

Weary'd, forſaken, and purſu'd at laſt,
All ſafety in *deſpair* of ſafety plac'd,
Courage he thence reſumes, reſolv'd to bear
All their aſſaults, ſince 'tis in vain to fear. *Denham.*

Equal their flame, unequal was their care;
One lov'd with hope, one languiſh'd with *deſpair*. *Dryden.*

Deſpair is the thought of the unattainableneſs of any good, which works differently in mens minds, ſometimes producing uneaſineſs or pain, ſometimes reſt and indolency. *Locke.*

2. That which cauſes deſpair; that of which there is no hope.

Strangely viſited people,
All ſwol'n and ulc'rous, pitiful to the eye;
The mere *deſpair* of ſurgery, he cures;
Hanging a golden ſtamp about their necks,
Put on with holy prayers. *Shakeſpeare's Macbeth.*

3. [In theology.] Loſs of confidence in the mercy of God.

Are not all or moſt evangelical virtues and graces in danger of extremes? As there is, God knows, too often a defect on the one ſide, ſo there may be an exceſs on the other: may not hope in God, or godly ſorrow, be perverted into preſumption or *deſpair*? *Sprat's Sermons.*

To

To Despa'ir. *v. n.* [*despero*, Latin.] To be without hope; to despond.

Though thou drewest a sword at thy friend, yet *despair* not; for there may be a turning. *Ecclus.* xxii. 21.

We commend the wit of the Chinese, who *despair* of making of gold, but are mad upon making of silver. *Bacon.*

Never *despair* of God's blessings here, or of his reward hereafter; but go on as you have begun. *Wake's Preparation.*

Despa'irer. *n. s.* [from *despair.*] One without hope.

He cheers the fearful, and commends the bold,
And makes *despairers* hope for good success. *Dryden.*

Despa'irful. *adj.* [*despair* and *full.*] Hopeless. Obsolete.

That sweet but sour *despairful* care *Sidney, b.* i.

Despa'iringly. *adv.* [from *despairing.*] In a manner betokening hopelessness or despondency.

He speaks severely and *despairingly* of our society. *Boyle.*

To DESPA'TCH. *v. a.* [*depescher*, French.]

1. To send away hastily.

Doctor Theodore Coleby, a sober and intelligent man, I *despatched* immediately to Utrecht, to bring me some of the moxa, and learn the exact method of using it, from the man that sold it. *Temple.*

The good Æneas, whose paternal care
Iulus' absence could no longer bear,
Despatch'd Achates to the ships in haste,
To give a glad relation of the past. *Dryden's Virg. Æn.*

2. To send out of the world; to put to death.

Edmund, I think, is gone,
In pity of his misery, to *despatch*
His nighted life. *Shakespeare's King Lear.*

And the company shall stone them with stones, and *despatch* them with their swords. *Ezek.* xxiii. 47.

In combating, but two of you will fall;
And we resolve we will *despatch* you all. *Dryden.*

Despatch me quickly, I may death forgive;
I shall grow tender else, and wish to live. *Dryd. Ind. Emp.*

3. To perform a business quickly; as, I *despatched* my affairs, and ran hither.

Therefore commanded he his chariot-man to drive without ceasing, and to *despatch* the journey, the judgment of God now following him. 2 *Mac.* ix. 4.

No sooner is one action *despatched*, which, by such a determination as the will, we are set upon, but another uneasiness is ready to set us on work. *Locke.*

4. To conclude an affair with another.

What, are the brothers parted?
—They have *despatch'd* with Pompey; he is gone. *Shakesp.*

Despa'tch. *n. s.* [from the verb.]

1. Hasty execution; speedy performance.

Affected *despatch* is one of the most dangerous things to business that can be. *Bacon.*

You'd see, could you her inward motions watch,
Feigning delay, she wishes for *despatch*;
Then to a woman's meaning would you look,
Then read her backward. *Granville.*

The *despatch* of a good office is very often as beneficial to the solicitor as the good office itself. *Addison's Spectator.*

2. Conduct; management. Obsolete.

You shall put
This night's great business into my *despatch*,
Which shall, to all our nights and days to come,
Give solely sovereign sway and masterdom. *Shakesp. Macbeth.*

3. Express; hasty messenger or message; as, *despatches* were sent away.

Despa'tchful. *adj* [from *despatch.*] Bent on haste; intent on speedy execution of business.

So saying, with *dispatchful* looks, in haste
She turns, on hospitable thoughts intent. *Milt. Parad. Lost.*

Let one *dispatchful* bid some swain to lead
A well fed bullock from the grassy mead. *Pope's Odyssey, b.* iii.

DE'SPERATE. *adj.* [*desperatus*, Latin.]

1. Without hope.

Since his exile she hath despis'd me most;
Forsworn my company, and rail'd at me,
That I am *desperate* of obtaining her. *Shakespeare.*

2. Without care of safety; rash; precipitant; fearless of danger.

Can you think, my lords,
That any Englishman dare give me counsel,
Or be a known friend 'gainst his highness' pleasure,
Though he be grown so *desperate* to be honest,
And live a subject. *Shakespeare's Henry* VIII.

He who goes on without any care or thought of reforming, such an one we vulgarly call a *desperate* person, and that sure is a most damning sin. *Hammond's Pract. Catech.*

3. Irretrievable; unsurmountable; irrecoverable.

These debts may be well called *desperate* ones; for a mad man owes them. *Shakespeare's Timon.*

In a part of Asia the sick, when their case comes to be thought *desperate*, are carried out and laid on the earth, before they are dead, and left there. *Locke.*

I am a man of *desperate* fortunes, that is, a man whose friends are dead; for I never aimed at any other fortune than in friends. *Pope to Swift.*

4. Mad; hot-brained; furious.

Were it not the part of a *desperate* physician to wish his friend dead, rather than to apply the best endeavours of his skill for his recovery? *Spenser's State of Ireland.*

5. It is sometimes used in a sense nearly ludicrous, and only marks any bad quality predominating in a high degree.

Concluding all mere *desp'rate* sots and fools,
That durst depart from Aristotle's rules. *Pope's Ess. on Crit.*

De'sperately. *adv.* [from *desperate.*]

1. Furiously; madly; without attention to safety or danger.

Your eldest daughters have foredone themselves,
And *desp'rately* are dead. *Shakes. King Lear.*

There might be somewhat in it, that he would not have done, or desired undone, when he broke forth as *desperately* as before he had done uncivilly. *Brown's Vulgar Errours, b.* i.

2. In a great degree; violently: this sense is ludicrous.

She fell *desperately* in love with him, and took a voyage into Sicily in pursuit of him, he having withdrawn thither on purpose to avoid her. *Addison's Spectator*, N°. 223.

De'sperateness. *n. s.* [from *desperate*] Madness; fury; precipitance.

The going on not only in terrours and amazement of conscience, but also boldly, hopingly, confidently, in wilful habits of sin, is called a *desperateness* also; and the more bold thus, the more desperate. *Hammond's Pract. Catech.*

Despera'tion. *n. s.* [from *desperate.*] Hopelesness; despair; despondency.

Desperation
Is all the policy, strength, and defence,
That Rome can make against them. *Shakes. Coriolanus.*

As long as we are guilty of any past sin, and have no promise of remission, whatever our future care be, this *desperation* of success chills all our industry, and we sin on, because we have sinned. *Hammond on Fundamentals.*

DE'SPICABLE. *adj.* [*despicabilis*, Latin.] Contemptible; vile; mean; sordid; worthless. It is applied equally to persons or things.

Our case were miserable, if that wherewith we most endeavour to please God, were in his sight so vile and *despicable* as mens disdainful speech would make it. *Hooker, b.* v. *s.* 23.

Their heads as low
Bow'd down in battle, sunk before the spears
Of *despicable* foes. *Milton's Paradise Lost, b.* i. 437.

All th' earth he gave thee to possess and rule,
No *despicable* gift! *Milton's Paradise Lost, b.* xi. *l.* 340.

All the quiet that could be expected from such a reign, must be the result of absolute power on the one hand, and a *despicable* slavery on the other. *Addison.*

When men of rank and figure pass away their lives in criminal pursuits and practices, they render themselves more vile and *despicable* than any innocent man can be, whatever low station his fortune and birth have placed him in. *Addison.*

Despi'cableness. *n. s.* [from *despicable.*] Meanness; vileness; worthlesness.

We consider the great disproportion between the infinity of the reward and the *despicableness* of our service. *Decay of Piety.*

De'spicably. *adv.* [from *despicable.*] Meanly; sordidly; vilely.

Here wanton Naples crowns the happy shore,
Nor vainly rich, nor *despicably* poor;
The town in soft solemnities delights,
And gentle poets to her arms invites. *Addison on Italy.*

Despi'sable. *adj.* [from *despise*] Contemptible; despicable; regarded with contempt. A word scarcely used but in low conversation.

I am extremely obliged to you for taking notice of a poor old distressed courtier, commonly the most *despisable* thing in the world. *Arbuthnot to Pope.*

To DESPI'SE. *v. a.* [*despiser*, old French, *Skinner*; *despicio*, Latin.]

1. To scorn; to contemn; to slight; to disrespect.

For, lo, I will make thee small among the Heathen, and *despised* among men. *Jer.* xlix. 15.

My sons their old unhappy sire *despise*,
Spoil'd of his kingdom, and depriv'd of eyes. *Pope's Statius.*

2. In *Shakespeare* it seems once to signify *abhor*, as from the Italian *despettare*.

Let not your ears *despise* my tongue for ever,
Which shall possess them with the heaviest sound
That ever yet they heard. *Shakespeare's Macbeth.*

Despi'ser. *n. s.* [from *despise.*] Contemner; scorner.

Art thou thus bolden'd, man, by thy distress?
Or else a rude *despiser* of good manners,
That in civility thou seem'st so empty? *Shak. As you like it.*

Wisdom is commonly, at long running, justified even of her *despisers*. *Government of the Tongue, s.* 7.

Thus the atheists, libertines, and *despisers* of religion, usually pass under the name of free-thinkers. *Swift.*

DESPI'TE. *n. s.* [*spijt*, Dutch; *dépit*, French.]

1. Malice; anger; malignity; maliciousness; spleen; hatred.

Thou wretch! *despite* o'erwhelm thee! *Shak. Coriolanus.*

With men these considerations are usually the causes of *despite*, disdain, or aversion from others; but with God they pass for reasons of our greater tenderness towards others. *Sprat.*

2. Defiance.

The life, thou gav'st me first, was lost and done;
'Till with thy warlike sword, *despite* of fate,
To my determin'd time thou gav'st new date. *Shak. H.* VI.

My life thou shalt command, but not my shame;
The one my duty owes; but my fair name,
Despite of death, that lives upon my grave,
To dark dishonour's use thou shalt not have. *Shak. Rich.* II.

Know I will serve the fair in thy *despite*. *Dryd. Fab.*

I have not quitted yet a victor's right;
I'll make you happy in your own *despite*. *Dryd. Aurengzebe.*

Say, would the tender creature, in *despite*
Of heat by day, and chilling dews by night,
Its life maintain? *Blackmore's Creation.*

Thou, with rebel insolence, did'st dare
To own and to protect that hoary ruffian;
And in *despite*, ev'n of thy father's justice,
To stir the factious rabble up to arms. *Row's Amb. S. Moth.*

3. Act of malice; act of opposition.

His punishment, eternal misery,
It would be all his solace and revenge,
As a *despite* done against the most High,
Thee once to gain companion of his woe. *Milt. Par. Lost.*

To DESPI'TE. *v. a.* [from the noun.] To vex; to affront; to give uneasiness to.

Saturn, with his wife Rhea, fled by night, setting the town on fire, to *despite* Bacchus. *Raleigh's History.*

DESPI'TEFUL. *adj.* [*despite* and *full.*] Malicious; full of spleen; full of hate; malignant; mischievous: used both of persons and things.

His taken labours bid him me forgive;
I, his *despiteful* Juno, sent him forth
From courtly friends with camping foes to live,
Where death and danger dog the heels of worth. *Shakes.*

Preserve us from the hands of our *despiteful* and deadly enemies. *King Charles.*

Mean while the heinous and *despiteful* act
Of Satan, done in Paradise, was known
In heav'n. *Milton's Paradise Lost, b.* x. *l.* 1.

DESPI'TEFULLY. *adv.* [from *despiteful.*] Maliciously; malignantly.

It requires us to pray for them that *despitefully* use us and persecute us. *Matthew* v. 44.

DESPI'TEFULNESS. *n. s.* [from *despiteful.*] Malice; hate; malignity.

Let us examine him with *despitefulness* and torture, that we know his meekness, and prove his patience. *Wisd.* ii. 19.

DESPI'TEOUS. *adj.* [from *despite.*] Malicious; furious. A word now out of use.

The knight of the red-cross, when him he spy'd
Spurring so hot with rage *despiteous*,
'Gan fairly couch his spear. *Fairy Queen, b.* i. *c.* 2.

To DESPO'IL. *v. a.* [*despolio*, Latin.]

1. To rob; to deprive. With *of*.

Despoil'd of warlike arms, and knowen shield. *Spenser.*

You are nobly born,
Despoiled of your honour in your life. *Shakes. Henry* VI.

He waits with hellish rancour imminent,
To intercept thy way, or send thee back
Despoil'd of innocence, *of* faith, *of* bliss. *Milt. Par. Lost.*

He, pale as death, *despoil'd of* his array,
Into the queen's apartment takes his way. *Dryden.*

Ev'n now thy aid,
Eugene, with regiments unequal prest,
Awaits: this day of all his honours gain'd
Despoils him, if thy succour opportune
Defends not the sad hour. *Phillips.*

DESPOLIA'TION. *n. s.* [from *despolio*, Latin.] The act of despoiling or stripping.

To DESPO'ND. *v. a.* [*despondeo*, Latin.]

1. To despair; to lose hope; to become hopeless or desperate.

It is every man's duty to labour in his calling, and not to *despond* for any miscarriages or disappointments that were not in his own power to prevent. *L'Estrange, Fab.* 110.

There is no surer remedy for superstitious and *desponding* weakness, than first to govern ourselves by the best improvement of that reason which providence has given us for a guide; and then, when we have done our own parts, to commit all chearfully, for the rest, to the good pleasure of heaven with trust and resignation. *L'Estrange.*

Besides, to change their pasture 'tis in vain,
Or trust to physick: physick is their bane:
The learned leaches in despair depart,
And shake their heads, *desponding* of their art. *Dryd. Virgil.*

Others depress their own minds, *despond* at the first difficulty; and conclude that making any progress in knowledge, farther than serves their ordinary business, is above their capacities. *Locke.*

2. [In theology.] To lose hope of the divine mercy.

He considers what is the natural tendency of such a virtue, or such a vice: he is well apprized that the representation of some of these things may convince the understanding, some may terrify the conscience, some may allure the slothful, and some encourage the *desponding* mind. *Watts's Improvement.*

DESPO'NDENCY. *n. s.* [from *despondent.*] Despair; hopelesness; desperation.

DESPO'NDENT. *adj.* [*despondens*, Latin.] Despairing; hopeless; without hope

Congregated thrushes, linnets, sit
On the dead tree, a dull *despondent* flock. *Thomson's Autumn.*

It is well known, both from ancient and modern experience, that the very boldest atheists, out of their debauches and company, when they chance to be surprised with solitude or sickness, are the most suspicious, timorous, and *despondent* wretches in the world. *Bentley's Sermons.*

To DESPO'NSATE. *v. a* [*desponso*, Latin.] To betroth; to affiance; to unite by reciprocal promises of marriage.

DESPONSA'TION. *n. s.* [from *desponsate.*] The betrothing persons to each other.

DE'SPOT. *n. s.* [δεσπότης] An absolute prince; one that governs with unlimited authority. This word is not in use, except as applied to some Dacian prince; as, the *despot* of Servia.

DESPO'TICAL. } *adj.* [from *despot.*] Absolute in power; unli-
DESPO'TICK. } mited in authority; arbitrary; unaccountable.

God's universal law
Gave to the man *despotick* power
Over his female in due awe,
Nor from that right to part an hour,
Smile she or lowre. *Milton's Agonistes.*

In all its directions of the inferior faculties, reason conveyed its suggestions with clearness, and enjoined them with power: it had the passions in perfect subjection; though its command over them was but persuasive and political, yet it had the force of coactive and *despotical*. *South's Sermons.*

We may see in a neighbouring government the ill consequences of having a *despotick* prince, in a state that is most of it composed of rocks and mountains; for notwithstanding there is vast extent of lands, and many of them better than those of the Swiss and Grisons, the common people among the latter are in a much better situation. *Addison on Italy.*

Patriots were forced to give way to the madness of the people, who, stirred up with the harangues of their orators, were now wholly bent upon single and *despotick* slavery. *Swift.*

DESPO'TICALNESS. *n. s.* [from *despotical.*] Absolute authority.

DE'SPOTISM. *n. s.* [*despotisme*, French, from *despot.*] Absolute power.

To DESPU'MATE. *v. n.* [*despumo*, Latin.] To throw off parts in foam; to froth; to work.

DESPUMA'TION. *n. s.* [from *despumate.*] The act of throwing off excrementitious parts in scum or foam.

DESQUAMA'TION. *n. s.* [from *squama*, Latin.] The act of scaling foul bones.

DESSE'RT. *n. s.* [*desserte*, French.] The last course at an entertainment; the fruit or sweetmeats set on the table after the meat.

To give thee all thy due, thou hast the art
To make a supper with a fine *dessert*. *Dryden's Persius.*

At your *dessert* bright pewter comes too late,
When your first course was well serv'd up in plate. *King.*

To DE'STINATE. *v. a.* [*destino*, Latin.] To design for any particular end or purpose.

Birds are *destinated* to fly among the branches of trees and bushes. *Ray on the Creation.*

DESTINA'TION. *n. s* [from *destinate.*] The purpose for which any thing is appointed; the ultimate design.

The passages through which spirits are conveyed to the members, being almost infinite, and each of them drawn through so many meanders, wherein other spirits are a journeying, it is wonderful that they should perform their regular *destinations* without losing their way. *Glanv. Sceps.*

There is a great variety of apprehensions and fancies of men, in the *destination* and application of things to several ends and uses. *Hale's Orign of Mankind.*

To DE'STINE. *v. a.* [*destino*, Latin.]

1. To doom; to appoint unalterably to any state or condition.

Wherefore cease we then?
Say they who counsel war: we are decreed,
Reserv'd, and *destin'd* to eternal woe:
Whatever doing, what can we suffer more? *Milt. Pa. Lost.*

All altars flame; before each altar lies,
Drench'd in his gore, the *destin'd* sacrifice. *Dryden's Æneis.*

2. To appoint to any use or purpose.

Too thin blood strays into the immediately subordinate vessels, which are *destined* to carry humours secreted from the blood. *Arbuthnot on Aliments.*

3. To devote; to doom to punishment or misery.

May heav'n around this *destin'd* head
The choicest of its curses shed. *Prior.*

4. To fix unalterably.

The infernal judge's dreadful pow'r,
From the dark urn shall throw thy *destin'd* hour. *Prior.*

DE'STINY. *n. s.* [*destinée*, French.]

1. The power that spins the life, and determines the fate of living beings.

Thou art neither like thy sire or dam;
But like a foul mis-shapen stigmatick,
Mark'd by the *destinies* to be avoided. *Shakes. Henry* VI.

2. Fate; invincible necessity.

He said, dear daughter, rightly may I rue
The fall of famous children born of me;
But who can turn the stream of *destiny*,
Or break the chain of strong necessity,
Which fast is ty'd to Jove's eternal seat? *Fairy Queen, b.* i.

How can hearts, not free, be try'd whether they serve
Willing or no, who will but what they must
By *destiny*, and can no other chuse? *Milton's Paradise Lost.*

Had thy great *destiny* but given thee skill
To know, as well as pow'r to act her will. *Denham.*

Chance, or forceful *destiny*,
Which forms in causes first whate'er shall be. *Dryden's Fab.*

3. Doom; condition in future time.

At the pit of Acheron
Meet me i' th' morning: thither he
Will come to know his *destiny*. *Shakespeare's Macbeth.*

DE'STITUTE. *adj.* [*destitutus*, Latin.]

1. Forsaken; abandoned.

To forsake the true God of heaven, is to fall into all such evils upon the face of the earth, as men, either *destitute* of grace divine, may commit, or unprotected from above, may endure. *Hooker, b.* v. *f.* 1.

He will regard the prayer of the *destitute*, and not despise their prayer. *Psal.* cii. 17.

2. In want of.

Living turfs upon his body lay;
This done, securely take the destin'd way
To find the regions *destitute* of day. *Dryden's Æn. b.* vi.

Nothing can be a greater instance of the love that mankind has for liberty, than such a savage mountain covered with people, and the Campania of Rome, which lies in the same country, *destitute* of inhabitants. *Addison's Remarks on Italy.*

DESTITU'TION. *n. s.* [from *destitute.*] Want; the state in which something is wanted.

That *destitution* in food and cloathing is such an impediment, as, 'till it be removed, suffereth not the mind of man to admit any other care. *Hooker, b.* i. *f.* 10.

They which want furtherance unto knowledge, are not left in so great *destitution*, that justly any man should think the ordinary means of eternal life taken from them. *Hooker, b.* v.

The order of paying the debts of contract or restitution is set down by the civil laws of a kingdom: in *destitution* or want of such rules, we are to observe the necessity of the creditor, the time of the delay, and the special obligations of friendship. *Taylor's Rule of living holy.*

To DESTRO'Y. *v. a.* [*destruo*, Latin; *destruire*, French.]

1. To overturn a city; to raze a building; to ruin.

The lord will *destroy* this city. *Gen.* xix. 14.

2. To lay waste; to make desolate.

Solyman sent a great part of his army out of the main unto the island, which burnt and *destroyed* the country villages. *Knolles's History of the Turks.*

3. To kill.

A people, great and many, and tall as the Anakims; but the Lord *destroyed* them before them, and they succeeded them, and dwelt in their stead. *Deutr.* ii. 21.

'Tis safer to be that which we *destroy*,
Than by destruction dwell in doubtful joy. *Shakes. Macbeth.*

The wise providence hath placed a certain antipathy between some animals and many insects, whereby they delight in their destruction, though they use them not as food; as the peacock *destroys* snakes and adders; the weasel, mice and rats; spiders, flies; and some sorts of flies *destroy* spiders. *Hale.*

4. To put an end to; to bring to nought.

Do we not see that slothful, intemperate and incontinent persons *destroy* their bodies with diseases, their reputations with disgrace, and their faculties with want? *Bentley.*

There will be as many sovereigns as fathers: the mother too hath her title, which *destroys* the sovereignty of one supreme monarch. *Locke.*

DESTRO'YER. *n. s.* [from *destroy.*] The person that destroys or lays waste; a murderer.

In all the translations it is said, that Assur both founded it and ruined it: it may be understood, that Assur the founder was the son of Shem, and Assur the *destroyer* was an Assyrian. *Raleigh's History of the World.*

For glory done
Of triumph, to be styl'd great conquerors,
Patrons of mankind, gods, and sons of gods!
Destroyers rightlier call'd, and slayers of men. *Milt. P. Lost.*

Yet, guiltless too, this bright *destroyer* lives;
At random wounds, nor knows the wound she gives. *Pope.*

DESTRU'CTIBLE. *adj.* [from *destruo*, Latin.] Liable to destruction.

DESTRUCTIBI'LITY. *n. s.* [from *destructible.*] Liableness to destruction.

DESTRU'CTION. *n. s.* [*destructio*, Latin.]

1. The act of destroying; waste.

2. Murder; massacre.

'Tis safer to be that which we destroy,
Than by *destruction* dwell in doubtful joy. *Shakes. Macbeth.*

If that your moody discontented souls
Do through the clouds behold this present hour,
Even for revenge mock my *destruction*. *Shakes. Richard* III.

When that which we immortal thought,
We saw so near *destruction* brought,
We felt what you did then endure,
And tremble yet, as not secure. *Waller.*

3. The state of being destroyed; ruin.

4. The cause of destruction; a destroyer; a depopulator: as a consuming plague.

The *destruction* that wasteth at noon-day. *Ps.* xci. 6.

5. [In theology.] Eternal death.

Broad is the way that leadeth to *destruction*. *Matth.* vii. 13.

DESTRU'CTIVE. *adj.* [*destructivus*, low Latin.]

1. That which destroys; wasteful; causing ruin and devastation; that which brings to destruction.

In ports and roads remote,
Destructive fires among whole fleets we send. *Dryden.*

One may think, by the name duration, that the continuation of existence, with a kind of resistance to any *destructive* force, is the continuation of solidity. *Locke.*

2. With *of.*

He will put an end to so absurd a practice, which makes our most refined diversions *destructive of* all politeness. *Addis.*

Both are defects equally *destructive of* true religion. *Rogers.*

3. With *to.*

In a firm building, even the cavities ought not to be filled with rubbish which is of a perishable kind, *destructive to* the strength. *Dryden's Æn. Dedicat.*

Excess of cold, as well as heat, pains us; because it is equally *destructive to* that temper which is necessary to the preservation of life. *Locke.*

DESTRU'CTIVELY. *adv.* [from *destructive.*] Ruinously; mischievously; with power to destroy.

What remains to him that ponders this epidemick folly, but to breathe out Moses's wish? O that men were not so *destructively* foolish. *Decay of Piety.*

DESTRU'CTIVENESS. *n. s.* [from *destructive.*] The quality of destroying or ruining.

The vice of professors exceeds the *destructiveness* of the most hostile assaults, as intestine treachery is more ruinous than foreign violence. *Decay of Piety.*

DESTRU'CTOR. *n. s.* [from *destroy.*] Destroyer; consumer.

Helmont wittily calls the fire the *destructor* and the artificial death of things. *Boyle.*

DESUDA'TION. *n. s.* [*desudatio*, Latin.] A profuse and inordinate sweating, from what cause soever.

DESU'ETUDE. *n. s.* [*desuetudo*, Latin.] Cessation to be accustomed; discontinuance of practice or habit.

By the irruption of numerous armies of barbarous people, those countries were quickly fallen off, with barbarism and *desuetude*, from their former civility and knowledge. *Hale.*

We see in all things how *desuetude* does contract and narrow our faculties, so that we can apprehend only those things wherein we are conversant. *Government of the Tongue.*

DESU'LTORY. } *adj.* [*desultorius*, Lat.] Roving from thing
DESULTO'RIOUS. } to thing; unsettled; immethodical; unconstant.

'Tis not for a *desultory* thought to attone for a lewd course of life, nor for any thing but the superinducing of a virtuous habit upon a vitious one, to qualify an effectual conversion. *L'Estrange.*

Let but the least trifle cross his way, and his *desultorious* fancy presently takes the scent, leaves the unfinished and half-mangled notion, and skips away in pursuit of the new game. *Norris.*

Take my *desultory* thoughts in their native order, as they rise in my mind, without being reduced to rules, and marshalled according to art. *Felton on the Classicks.*

To DESU'ME. *v. a.* [*desumo*, Latin.] To take from any thing; to borrow.

This pebble doth suppose, as pre-existent to it, the more simple matter out of which it is *desumed*, the heat and influence of the sun, and the due preparation of the matter. *Hale.*

They have left us relations suitable to those of Ælian and Pliny, whence they *desumed* their narrations. *Brown's Vul. Err.*

Laws, if convenient and useful, are never the worse, though they be *desumed* and taken from the laws of other countries. *Hale's Law of England.*

To DETA'CH. *v. a.* [*detacher*, French.]

1. To separate; to disengage; to part from something.

The heat takes along with it a sort of vegetative and terrestrial matter, which it *detaches* from the uppermost stratum. *Woodward's Natural History, p.* iii.

The several parts of it are *detached* one from the other, and yet join again one cannot tell how. *Pope.*

2. To send out part of a greater body of men on an expedition.

If ten men are in war with forty, and the latter *detach* only an equal number to the engagement, what benefit do they receive from their superiority? *Addison on the State of the War.*

DETA'CHMENT. *n. s.* [from *detach.*] A body of troops sent out from the main army.

The Czar dispatched instructions to send out *detachments* of his cavalry, to prevent the king of Sweden's joining his army. *Tatler*, N°. 55.

Besides materials, which are brute and blind,
Did not this work require a knowing mind?
Who for the task should fit *detachments* chuse
From all the atoms. *Blackmore's Creation.*

To DETA'IL. *v. a.* [*detailler*, French.] To relate particularly; to particularise; to display minutely and distinctly.

They will perceive the ground of the mistakes of these philosophers, and be able to answer their arguments, without my being obliged to *detail* them. *Cheyne's Phil. Princ.*

DETA'IL. *n. s.* [*detail*, French.] A minute and particular account.

I chuse, rather than trouble the reader with a *detail* here, to defer them to their proper place. *Woodward's Natural History.*

I was unable to treat this part of my subject more in *detail*, without becoming dry and tedious. *Pope.*

To DETA'IN. *v. a.* [*detineo*, Latin.]

1. To keep that which belongs to another.

Detain not the wages of the hireling; for every degree of detention of it, beyond the time, is injustice and uncharitableness. *Taylor's Rule of living holy.*

2. To withold; to keep back.

These doings sting him
So venomously, that burning shame *detains* him
From his Cordelia. *Shakespeare's King Lear.*

He has described the passion of Calypso, and the indecent advances she made to *detain* him from his country. *Broom.*

3. To restrain from departure.

Let us *detain* thee until we shall have made ready a kid. *Judg.* xiii. 15.

Had Orpheus sung it in the nether sphere,
So much the hymn had pleas'd the tyrant's ear,
The wife had been *detain'd* to keep her husband there. *Dry.*

4. To hold in custody.

DETA'INDER. *n. s.* [from *detain.*] The name of a writ for holding one in custody.

DETA'INER. *n. s.* [from *detain.*] He that holds back any one's right; he that detains any thing.

By proportion to these rules, we may judge of the obligation that lies upon all sorts of injurious persons; the sacrilegious, the *detainers* of tithes, and cheaters of mens inheritances. *Taylor's Rule of living holy.*

To DETE'CT. *v. a.* [*detectus*, Latin.] To discover; to find out any crime or artifice.

There's no true lover in the forest, else sighing every minute and groaning every hour, would *detect* the lazy foot of time as well as a clock. *Shakespeare's As you like it.*

Though should I hold my peace, yet thou
Would'st easily *detect* what I conceal. *Milton's Paradise Lost.*

DETE'CTER. *n. s.* [from *detect.*] A discoverer; one that finds out what another desires to hide.

Oh heavens! that this treason were not; or not I the *detecter*. *Shakespeare's King Lear.*

Hypocrisy has a secret hatred of its *detecter*; that which will bring it to a test which it cannot pass. *Decay of Piety.*

DETE'CTION. *n. s.* [from *detect.*]

1. Discovery of guilt or fraud, or any other fault.

Should I come to her with any *detection* in my hand, I could drive her then from the ward of her purity. *Shakespeare.*

That is a sign of the true evangelical zeal, and note for the *detection* of its contrary: it should abound more in the mild and good-natured affection, than in the vehement and wrathful passions. *Sprat's Sermons.*

Detection of the incoherence of loose discourses was wholly owing to the syllogistical form. *Locke.*

2. Discovery of any thing hidden.

Not only the sea, but rivers and rains also, are instrumental to the *detection* of amber, and other fossils, by washing away the earth and dirt that before covered and concealed them. *Woodward's Natural History.*

DETE'NTION. *n. s.* [from *detain.*]

1. The act of keeping what belongs to another.

How goes the world, that I am thus encountred
With clam'rous claims of debt, of broken bonds,
And the *detention* of long since due debts,
Against my honour? *Shakespeare's Timon.*

2. Confinement; restraint.

This worketh by *detention* of the spirits, and constipation of the tangible parts. *Bacon's Natural History*, N°. 341.

To DETE'R. *v. a.* [*deterreo*, Latin.] To discourage from any thing; to fright from any thing.

I never yet the tragick strain assay'd,
Deterr'd by thy inimitable maid. *Waller.*

Many and potent enemies tempt and *deter* us from our duty, yet our case is not hard, so long as we have a greater strength on our side. *Tillotson, Serm.* 6.

Beauty or unbecomingness are of more force to draw or *deter* imitation, than any discourses which can be made to them. *Locke.*

The ladies may not be *deterred* from corresponding with me by this method. *Addison's Guardian*, N°. 114.

My own face *deters* me from my glass;
And Kneller only shews what Celia was. *Prior.*

DETE'RMENT. *n. s.* [from *deter.*] Cause of discouragement; that by which one is deterred.

This will not be thought a discouragement unto spirits, which endeavour to advantage nature by art; nor will the ill success of some be made a sufficient *determent* unto others. *Brown's Vulgar Errours, b.* vi. *c.* 8.

These are not all the *determents* that opposed my obeying you. *Boyle.*

To DETE'RGE. *v. a.* [*detergo*, Latin.] To cleanse a sore; to purge any part from feculence or obstructions.

Consider the part and habit of body, and add or diminish your simples as you design to *deterge* or incarn. *Wiseman.*

Sea salt preserves bodies, through which it passeth, from corruption, and it *detergeth* the vessels, and keeps the fluids from putrefaction. *Arbuthnot on Aliments.*

DETE'RGENT. *adj.* [from *deterge.*] That which cleanses.

The food ought to be nourishing and *detergent*. *Arbuthnot.*

DETERIORA'TION. *n. s.* [from *deterior*, Latin.] The act of making any thing worse; the state of growing worse.

DETE'RMINABLE. *adj.* [from *determine.*] That which may be certainly decided.

Whether all plants have seeds were more easily *determinable*, if we could conclude concerning harts-tongue, ferne, and some others. *Brown's Vulgar Errours, b.* ii. *c.* 7.

About this matter, which seems so easily *determinable* by sense, accurate and sober men widely disagree. *Boyle.*

To DETE'RMINATE. *v. a.* [*determiner*, French.] To limit; to fix; to determine; to terminate.

The fly-slow hours shall not *determinate*
The dateless limit of thy dear exile. *Shakes. Richard* II.

DETE'RMINATE. *adj.* [*determinatus*, Latin.]

1. Limited; determined.

Demonstrations in numbers, if they are not more evident and exact than in extension, yet they are more general in their use, and *determinate* in their application. *Locke.*

To make all the planets move about the sun in circular orbs, there must be given to each, by a *determinate* impulse, those present particular degrees of velocity which they now have, in proportion to their distances from the sun, and to the quantity of the solar matter. *Bentley's Sermons.*

2. Established; settled by rule; positive.

Scriptures are read before the time of divine service, and, without either choice or stint, appointed by any *determinate* order. *Hooker, b.* v. *s.* 19.

3. Decisive; conclusive.

I' th' progress of this business,
E're a *determinate* resolution, he,
I mean the bishop, did require a respite. *Shak Henry* VIII.

4. Fixed; resolute.

Like men disused in a long peace, more *determinate* to do, than skilful how to do. *Sidney.*

5. Resolved.

My *determinate* voyage is mere extravagancy. *Shakespeare.*

DETE'RMINATELY. *adv.* [from *determinate.*]

1. Resolutely; with fixed resolve.

The queen obeyed the king's commandment, full of raging agonies, and *determinately* bent, that she would seek all loving means to win Zelmane. *Sidney.*

Think thus with yourselves, that you have not the making of things true or false; but that the truth and existence of things is already fixed and settled, and that the principles of religion are already either *determinately* true or false, before you think of them. *Tillotson, Serm.* 1.

DETERMINA'TION. *n. s.* [from *determinate.*]

1. Absolute direction to a certain end.

When we voluntarily waste much of our lives, that remissness can by no means consist with a constant *determination* of will or desire to the greatest apparent good. *Locke.*

2. The result of deliberation; conclusion formed; resolution taken.

They have acquainted me with their *determination*, which is indeed to go home, and to trouble you with no more suit. *Shakespeare's Merchant of Venice.*

The proper acts of the intellect are intellection, deliberation, and *determination* or decision. *Hale's Origin of Mankind.*

It

It is much disputed by divines, concerning the power of man's will to good and evil in the state of innocence; and, upon very nice and dangerous precipices, stand their *determinations* on either side. *South's Sermons.*

Consult thy judgment, affections and inclinations, and make thy *determination* upon every particular; and be always as suspicious of thyself as possible. *Calamy's Sermons.*

3 Judicial decision.

He confined the knowledge of governing to justice and lenity, and to the speedy *determination* of civil and criminal causes. *Gulliver's Travels.*

DETE'RMINATIVE. *adj.* [from *determinate.*]

1. That which uncontrolably directs to a certain end

That individual action which is justly punished as sinful in us, cannot proceed from the special influence and *determinative* power of a just cause. *Bramh. against Hobbs.*

2. That which makes a limitation.

If the term added to make up the complex subject does not necessarily or constantly belong to it, then it is *determinative*, and limits the subject to a particular part of its extension; as, every pious man shall be happy. *Watts's Logick.*

DETERMINA'TOR. *n. s.* [from *determinate*] One who determines.

Hereunto they have recourse as unto the oracles of life, unto the great *determinator* of virginity, conceptions, fertility, and the inscrutable infirmities of the whole body. *Brown.*

To DETE'RMINE. *v. a.* [*determiner*, Fr. *determino*, Latin.]

1. To fix; to settle.

It is concluded he shall be protector.
—It is *determin'd*, not concluded yet;
But so it must be, if the king miscarry. *Shakes. Richard* III.

More particularly to *determine* the proper season for grammar, I do not see how it can be made a study, but as an introduction to rhetorick. *Locke.*

2. To conclude; to fix ultimately.

Probability, in the nature of it, supposes that a thing may, or may not be so, for any thing that yet appears, or is certainly *determined* on the other side. *South's Sermons.*

Milton's subject was still greater than either of the former: it does not *determine* the fate of single persons or nations, but of a whole species. *Addison's Spectator*, N°. 267.

Destruction hangs on every word we speak,
On every thought, 'till the concluding stroke
Determines all, and closes our design. *Addison's Cato.*

3. To bound; to confine.

The knowledge of men hitherto hath been *determined* by the view or sight; so that whatsoever is invisible, either in respect of the fineness of the body itself, or the smallness of the parts, or of the subtilty of the motion, is little enquired. *Bacon's Natural History*, N°. 98.

No sooner have they climbed that hill, which thus *determines* their view at a distance, but a new prospect is opened. *Atterbury's Sermons.*

4. To adjust; to limit.

The principium individuationis is existence itself, which *determines* a being of any sort to a particular time and place, incommunicable to two beings of the same kind. *Locke.*

He that has settled in his mind *determined* ideas, with names affixed to them, will be able to discern their differences one from another, which is really distinguishing. *Locke.*

5. To direct to any certain point.

6. To influence the choice.

You have the captives,
Who were the opposites of this day's strife:
We do require them of you, so to use them
As we shall find their merits and our safety
May equally *determine*. *Shakespeare's King Lear.*

A man may suspend the act of his choice from being *determined* for or against the thing proposed, 'till he has examined it. *Locke.*

As soon as the studious man's hunger and thirst makes him uneasy, he, whose will was never *determined* to any pursuit of good cheer, is, by the uneasiness of hunger and thirst, presently *determined* to eating and drinking. *Locke.*

7. To resolve.

Jonathan knew that it was *determined* of his father to slay David. 1 *Sa.* xx. 33.

8. To decide.

I do not ask whether bodies so exist, that the motion of one cannot be without the motion of another: to *determine* this either way, is to beg the question for or against a vacuum. *Locke.*

9. To put an end to; to destroy.

Now where is he, that will not stay so long
'Till sickness hath *determin'd* me? *Shakespeare's Henry* IV.

To DETE'RMINE. *v. n.*

1. To conclude; to form a final conclusion.

Eve! now expect great tidings, which perhaps
Of us will soon *determine*, or impose
New laws to be observ'd. *Milton's Paradise Lost, b.* xi.

It is indifferent to the matter in hand which way the learned shall *determine* of it. *Locke.*

2. To end; to come to an end.

They were apprehended, and after conviction the danger *determined* by their deaths. *Hayward.*

All pleasure springing from a gratified passion, as most of the pleasure of sin does, must needs *determine* with that passion. *South's Sermons.*

3. To come to a decision.

She soon shall know of us,
How honourably and how kindly we
Determine for her. *Shakes. Ant. and Cleopatra.*

4. To end consequentially.

Revolutions of state, many times, make way for new institutions and forms; and often *determine* in either setting up some tyranny at home, or bringing in some conquest from abroad. *Temple.*

5. To resolve concerning any thing.

Now, noble peers, the cause why we are met
Is to *determine* of the coronation. *Shakesp. Richard* III.

DETERRA'TION. *n. s.* [*de* and *terra*, Latin; *deterrer*, French.] Discovery of any thing by removal of the earth that hides it; the act of unburying.

This concerns the raising of new mountains, *deterrations* or the devolution of earth down upon the valleys, from the hills and higher grounds. *Woodward's Natural History.*

DETE'RSION. *n. s.* [from *detergo*, Latin.] The act of cleansing a sore.

I endeavoured *detersion*; but the matter could not be discharged. *Wiseman's Surgery.*

DETE'RSIVE. *adj.* [from *deterge.*] Having the power to cleanse.

DETE'RSIVE. *n. s.* An application that has the power of cleansing wounds.

We frequently see simple ulcers afflicted with sharp humours, which corrode them, and render them painful sordid ulcers, if not timely relieved by *detersives* and lenients. *Wiseman.*

To DETE'ST. *v. a.* [*detestor*, Latin.] To hate; to abhor; to abominate.

Nigh thereto the ever-damned beast
Durst not approach; for he was deadly made,
And all that life preserved did *detest*. *Fairy Queen, b.* i. *c.* 12.

Glory grows guilty of *detested* crimes,
When for fame's sake, for praise, an outward part,
We bend to that the working of the heart. *Shakespeare.*

Since Cleopatra died,
I've liv'd in such dishonour, that the gods
Detest my baseness. *Shakespeare's Ant. and Cleopatra.*

There is that naturally in the heart of man which abhors sin as sin, and consequently would make him *detest* it both in himself and others too. *South's Sermons.*

Who dares think one thing, and another tell,
My heart *detests* him as the gates of hell. *Pope.*

DETE'STABLE. *adj.* [from *detest.*] Hateful; abhorred; abominable; odious.

Beguil'd, divorc'd, wrong'd, spighted, slain!
Most *detestable* death. *Shakesp. Romeo and Juliet.*

He desired him, and the residue of the Scottish nobility, to consider that both armies consisted of Christians, to whom nothing is more *detestable* than effusion of human blood. *Hayw.*

DETE'STABLY. *adv.* [from *detestable.*] Hatefully; abominably; odiously.

It stands here stigmatized by the apostle as a temper of mind, rendering man so *detestably* bad, that the great enemy of mankind, the devil himself, neither can nor desires to make them worse. *South's Sermons.*

DETESTA'TION. *n. s.* [from *detest.*]

1. Hatred; abhorrence; abomination.

Then only did misfortune make her see what she had done, especially finding in us rather *detestation* than pity. *Sidney, b.* ii.

2. It is sometimes used with *for*; but *of* seems more proper.

The *detestation* you can express
For vice in all its glitt'ring dress. *Swift.*

Our love of God will inspire us with a *detestation for* sin, as what is of all things most contrary to his divine nature. *Swift.*

DETE'STER. *n. s.* [from *detest.*] One that hates or abhors.

To DETHRO'NE. *v. a.* [*desthroner*, Fr. *de* and *thronus*, Latin.] To divest of regality; to throw down from the throne; to deprive of regal dignity.

DETI'NUE. *n. s.* [*detenue*, French.] A writ that lies against him, who, having goods or chattels delivered him to keep, refuses to deliver them again. *Cowel.*

DETONA'TION. *n. s.* [*detono*, Latin.] Somewhat more forcible than the ordinary crackling of salts in calcination; as in the going off of the pulvis or aurum fulminans, or the like. It is also used for that noise which happens upon the mixture of fluids that ferment with violence; as oil of turpentine with oil of vitriol, resembling the explosion of gunpowder. *Quincy.*

A new coal is not to be cast on the nitre, 'till the *detonation* occasioned by the former be either quite or almost altogether ended; unless it chance that the puffing matter do blow the coal too soon out of the crucible. *Boyle on Saltpetre.*

To DE'TONIZE. *v. a.* [from *detono*, Latin.] To calcine with detonation. A chemical term.

Nineteen parts in twenty of *detonized* nitre is deſtroyed in eighteen days. *Arbuthnot on Air.*

To DETO'RT. *v. a.* [*detortus*, of *detorqueo*, Latin.] To wreſt from the original import, meaning, or deſign.

They have aſſumed what amounts to an infallibility in the private ſpirit, and have *detorted* texts of ſcripture to the ſedition, diſturbance, and deſtruction of the civil government. *Dryden's Preface to Rel. Laici.*

To DETRA'CT. *v. a.* [*detractum*, Latin; *detracter*, French.] To derogate; to take away by envy and calumny, or otherwiſe, any thing from the reputation of another.

Thoſe were aſſiſtants in private, but not truſted to manage the affairs in publick; for that would *detract* from the honour of the principal ambaſſador. *Bacon's Advice to Villiers.*

No envy can *detract* from this: it will ſhine in hiſtory, and, like ſwans, grow whiter the longer it endures. *Dryden.*

DETRA'CTER. *n. ſ.* [from *detract.*] One that takes away another's reputation; one that impairs the honour of another injuriouſly.

I am right glad to be thus ſatisfied by you, in that I have often heard it queſtioned, and yet was never able till now to choke the mouth of ſuch *detracters* with the certain knowledge of their ſlanderous untruths. *Spenſer on Ireland.*

Whether we are ſo intirely ſure of their loyalty upon the preſent foot of government as you may imagine, their *detracters* make a queſtion. *Swift.*

Away the fair *detracters* went,
And gave by turns their cenſures vent. *Swift.*

DETRA'CTION. *n. ſ.* [*detractio*, Latin; *detraction*, French.]

Detraction, in the native importance of the word, ſignifies the withdrawing or taking off from a thing; and, as it is applied to the reputation, it denotes the impairing or leſſening a man in point of fame, rendering him leſs valued and eſteemed by others, which is the final aim of *detraction*, though purſued by various means. *Ayliffe.*

Even now
I put myſelf to thy direction, and
Unſpeak mine own *detraction*; here abjure
The taints and blames I laid upon myſelf,
For ſtrangers to my nature. *Shakeſpeare's Macbeth.*

Fame, that her high birth to raiſe,
Seem'd erſt ſo laviſh and profuſe,
We may juſtly now accuſe
Of *detraction* from her praiſe. *Milton.*

If *detraction* could invite us, diſcretion ſurely would contain us from any derogatory intention. *Brown.*

To put a ſtop to the inſults and *detractions* of vain men, I reſolved to enter a little farther into the examination. *Woodward's Natural Hiſtory.*

To conſider an author farther, as the ſubject of obloquy and *detraction*, we may obſerve with what pleaſure a work is received by the invidious part of mankind, in which a writer falls ſhort of himſelf. *Addiſon's Freeholder*, Nº. 40.

DETRA'CTORY. *adj.* [from *detract.*] Defamatory by denial of deſert; derogatory. Sometimes with *to*, properly *from.*

This is not only derogatory unto the wiſdom of God, who hath propoſed the world unto our knowledge, and thereby the notion of himſelf, but alſo *detractory* unto the intellect and ſenſe of man, expreſſedly diſpoſed for that inquiſition. *Brown.*

In mentioning the joys of heaven, I uſe the expreſſions I find leſs *detractory* from a theme above our praiſes. *Boyle.*

The *detractory* lye takes from a great man the reputation that juſtly belongs to him. *Arbuthnot's Hiſtory of J. Bull.*

DETRA'CTRESS. *n. ſ.* [from *detract.*] A cenſorious woman.

If any ſhall detract from a lady's character, unleſs ſhe be abſent, the ſaid *detractreſs* ſhall be forthwith ordered to the loweſt place of the room. *Addiſon's Freeholder*, Nº. 23.

DE'TRIMENT. *n. ſ.* [*detrimentum*, Latin.] Loſs; damage; miſchief; diminution; harm.

Difficult it muſt needs have been for one Chriſtian church to aboliſh that which all had received and held for the ſpace of many ages, and that without any *detriment* unto religion. *Hooker, b.* iv. *ſ.* 14.

I can repair
That *detriment*, if ſuch it be, to loſe
Self-loſt. *Milton's Paradiſe Loſt, b.* vii. *l.* 152.

If your joint pow'r prevail, th' affairs of hell
No *detriment* need fear: go, and be ſtrong. *Milton's P. Loſt.*

There often falls out ſo many things to be done on the ſudden, that ſome of them muſt of neceſſity be neglected for that whole year, which is the greateſt *detriment* to this whole myſtery. *Evelyn's Kalendar.*

Let a family burn but a candle a night leſs than the uſual number, and they may take in the Spectator without *detriment* to their private affairs. *Addiſon's Spectator*, Nº. 486.

DETRIME'NTAL. *adj.* [from *detriment.*] Miſchievous; harmful; cauſing loſs.

Among all honorary rewards, which are neither dangerous nor *detrimental* to the donor, I remember none ſo remarkable as the titles which are beſtowed by the emperor of China: theſe are never given to any ſubject 'till the ſubject is dead. *Addiſon's Guardian*, Nº. 96.

Obſtinacy in prejudices, which are *detrimental* to our country, ought not to be miſtaken for virtuous reſolution and firmneſs of mind. *Addiſon's Freeholder*, Nº. 25.

DETRI'TION. *n. ſ.* [*detero, detritus*, Latin.] The act of wearing away. *Dict.*

To DETRU'DE. *v. a.* [*detrudo*, Latin.] To thruſt down; To force into a lower place.

Such as are *detruded* down to hell,
Either, for ſhame, they ſtill themſelves retire;
Or, ty'd in chains, they in cloſe priſon dwell. *Davies.*

Philoſophers are of opinion, that the ſouls of men may, for their miſcarriages, be *detruded* into the bodies of beaſts. *Locke.*

At thy command the vernal ſun awakes
The torpid ſap, *detruded* to the root
By wintry winds. *Thomſon's Spring.*

To DETRU'NCATE. *v. a.* [*detrunco*, Latin.] To lop; to cut; to ſhorten by deprivation of parts.

DETRUNCA'TION. *n. ſ.* [from *detruncate.*] The act of lopping or cutting.

DETRU'SION. *n. ſ.* [from *detruſio*, Latin.] The act of thruſting or forcing down.

From this *detruſion* of the waters towards the ſide, the parts towards the pole muſt be much increaſed. *Keil againſt Burnet.*

DETURBA'TION. *n. ſ.* [*deturbo*, Latin.] The act of throwing down; degradation. *Dict.*

DEVASTA'TION. *n. ſ.* [*devaſto*, Latin.] Waſte; havock; deſolation; deſtruction.

By *devaſtation* the rough warrior gains,
And farmers fatten moſt when famine reigns. *Garth.*

That flood which overflowed Attica in the days of Ogyges, and that which drowned Theſſaly in Deucalion's Time, made cruel havock and *devaſtation* among them. *Woodward.*

DEUCE. *n. ſ.* [*deux*, French.] 1. Two: A word uſed in games.

You are a gentleman and a gameſter; then, I am ſure, you know how much the groſs ſum of *deuce* ace amounts to. *Shak.*

2. The devil. See DEUSE.

To DEVE'LOP. *v. a.* [*developer*, French.] To diſengage from ſomething that enfolds and conceals; to diſentangle; to clear from its covering.

Take him to *develop*, if you can,
And hew the block off, and get out the man. *Dunciad.*

DEVE'RGENCE. *n. ſ.* [*devergentiâ*, Latin.] Declivity; declination. *Dict.*

To DEVE'ST. *v. a.* [*deveſter*, French; *de* and *veſtis*, Latin.]

1. To ſtrip; to deprive of cloaths.

Then of his arms Androgeus he *deveſts*,
His ſword, his ſhield he takes, and plumed creſts. *Denham.*

2. To ſtrip; to take away any thing good.

What are thoſe breaches of the law of nature and nations, which do forfeit and *deveſt* all right and title in a nation to government? *Bacon.*

3. To free from any thing bad.

Come on, thou little inmate of this breaſt,
Which for thy ſake from paſſions I *deveſt.* *Prior.*

DEVE'X. *adj.* [*devexus*, Latin.] Bending down; declivous; incurvated downwards.

DEVE'XITY. *n. ſ.* [from *devex.*] Incurvation downwards; declivity.

To DE'VIATE. *v. n.* [*de via decedere*, Latin.]

1. To wander from the right or common way.

The reſt to ſome faint meaning make pretence,
But Shadwell never *deviates* into ſenſe. *Dryden.*

Thus Pegaſus, a nearer way to take,
May boldly *deviate* from the common track. *Pope.*

What makes all phyſical and moral ill?
There nature *deviates*, and here wanders will. *Pope's Eſſays.*

Beſides places which may *deviate* from the ſenſe of the author, it would be kind to obſerve any deficiencies in the diction. *Pope.*

2. To go aſtray; to err; to ſin; to offend.

DEVIA'TION. *n. ſ.* [from *deviate.*]

1. The act of quitting the right way; error; wandering.

Theſe bodies perſevere in their motions, and conſtantly move round in the ſame tracts, without making the leaſt *deviation.* *Cheyne's Phil. Princ.*

2. Variation from eſtabliſhed rule.

Having once ſurveyed the true and proper natural alphabet, we may eaſily diſcover the *deviations* from it in the character thereof, in all the alphabets in uſe, either by defect of ſingle characters, of letters, or by confuſion of them. *Holder.*

3. Offence; obliquity of conduct.

Worthy perſons, if inadvertently drawn into a *deviation*, will endeavour inſtantly to recover their loſt ground, that they may not bring error into habit. *Clariſſa.*

DEVI'CE. *n. ſ.* [*deviſe*, French; *diviſa*, Italian.]

1. A contrivance; a ſtratagem.

This is our *device*,
That Falſtaff at that oak ſhall meet with us. *Shakeſpeare.*

He intended it as a politick *device* to leſſen their intereſt, and keep them low in the world. *Atterbury's Sermons.*

2. A deſign; a ſcheme formed; project; ſpeculation.

Touching the exchange of laws in practice with laws in *device*,

device, which they say are better for the ſtate of the church, if they might take place: the farther we examine them, the greater cauſe we find to conclude, although we continue the ſame we are, the harm is not great. *Hooker, Dedicat.*

His *device* is againſt Babylon, to deſtroy it. *Jer.* li. 11.

There are many *devices* in a man's heart; nevertheleſs, the counſel of the Lord ſhall ſtand. *Prov.* xix. 21.

3. The emblem on a ſhield; the enſign armorial of a nation or family.

Then change we ſhields, and their *devices* bear;
Let fraud ſupply the want of force in war. *Dryden's Æn.*

Hibernia's harp, *device* of her command,
And parent of her mirth, ſhall there be ſeen. *Prior.*

They intend to let the world ſee what party they are of, by figures and deſigns upon theſe fans; as the knights-errant uſed to diſtinguiſh themſelves by *devices* on their ſhields. *Addiſ.*

4. Invention; genius.

He's gentle; never ſchooled, and yet learned; full of noble *device*, of all ſorts enchantingly beloved. *Shak. As you like it.*

DE'VIL. *n. ſ.* [ꝺioꝼul, Saxon; *diabolus*, Latin. It is more properly written *divel.*]

1. A fallen angel; the tempter and ſpiritual enemy of mankind.

Are you a man?
——Ay, and a bold one, that dare look on that
Which might appal the *devil.* *Shakeſpeare's Macbeth.*

2. A wicked man or woman.

See thyſelf, *devil:*
Proper deformity ſeems not in the fiend
So horrid as in woman. *Shakeſpeare's King Lear.*

3. A ludicrous term for miſchief.

A war of profit mitigates the evil;
But to be tax'd, and beaten, is the *devil.* *Granville.*

4. A kind of expletive, expreſſing wonder or vexation.

The things, we know, are neither rich nor rare;
But wonder how the *devil* they got there! *Pope, Epiſt.* ii.

5. A kind of ludicrous negative in an adverbial ſenſe.

The devil was well, the *devil* a monk was he. *A Proverb.*

DE'VILISH. *adj.* [from *devil.*]

1. Partaking of the qualities of the devil; diabolical; miſchievous; malicious; deſtructive.

Gynecia took a farther conceit of it, miſtruſting greatly Cecropia, becauſe ſhe had heard much of the *deviliſh* wickedneſs of her heart. *Sidney, b.* i.

For grief thereof, and *deviliſh* deſpight,
From his infernal furnaces forth he threw
Huge flames, that dimmed all the heaven's light,
Enroll'd in duſkiſh ſmoak and brimſtone blue. *Fairy Queen.*

In hollow cube
He trains his *deviliſh* engin'ry, impal'd
On ev'ry ſide with ſhadowy ſquadrons deep. *Milton's P. Loſt.*

2. Having communication with the devil.

The dutcheſs, by his ſubornation,
Upon my life began her *deviliſh* practices. *Shakeſ. Henry* VI.

3. An epithet of abhorrence or contempt.

A *deviliſh* knave! beſides the knave is handſome, young, and blyth: all thoſe requiſites are in him that delight. *Shakeſp.*

DE'VILISHLY. *adv.* [from *deviliſh.*] In a manner ſuiting the devil; diabolically.

Thoſe trumpeters threatened them with continual alarms of damnation, if they did not venture life, fortune, and all, in that which wickedly and *deviliſhly* thoſe impoſtors called the cauſe of God. *South's Sermons.*

DE'VILKIN. *n. ſ.* [from *devil.*] A little devil. *Clariſſa.*

DE'VIOUS. *adj.* [*devius*, Latin.]

1. Out of the common track.

Creuſa kept behind: by choice we ſtray
Through ev'ry dark and ev'ry *devious* way. *Dryden's Æn.*

In this minute *devious* ſubject I have been neceſſitated to explain myſelf in more words, than to ſome few may ſeem needful. *Holder's Elements of Speech.*

2. Wandering; roving; rambling.

Every muſe,
And every blooming pleaſure, wait without
To bleſs the wildly *devious* morning walk. *Thomſ. Summer.*

3. Erring; going aſtray from rectitude.

One *devious* ſtep, at firſt ſetting out, frequently leads a perſon into a wilderneſs of doubt and error. *Clariſſa.*

To DEVI'SE. *v. a.* [*deviſer*, French, as of *deviſare*, to look about. *Skinner.*]

1. To contrive; to form by art; to invent; to excogitate; to ſtrike out by thought.

Whether they, at their firſt coming into the land, or afterwards, by trading with other nations which had letters, learned them of them, or *deviſed* them among themſelves, is very doubtful. *Spenſer's State of Ireland.*

He could by his ſkill draw after him the weight of five thouſand buſhels of grain, and *deviſe* thoſe rare engines which ſhot ſmall ſtones at hand, but great ones afar off. *Peacham.*

Ye ſons of art, one curious piece *deviſe*,
From whoſe conſtructure motion ſhall ariſe. *Blackmore.*

2. To plan; to ſcheme.

Behold I frame evil againſt you, and *deviſe* a device againſt you. *Jer.* xiii. 11.

To DEVI'SE. *v. n.* To conſider; to contrive; to lay plans; to form ſchemes.

Her merry fit ſhe freſhly 'gan to rear,
And did of joy and jollity *deviſe*,
Herſelf to cheriſh and her gueſt to chear. *Fairy Queen, b.* ii.

But ſith now ſafe ye ſeiſed have the ſhore,
And well arrived are, high God be bleſt,
Let us *deviſe* of eaſe and everlaſting reſt. *Fairy Queen, b.* i.

Since we are ſo far entered, let us, I pray you, a little *deviſe* of thoſe evils by which that country is held in this wretched caſe, that it cannot, as you ſay, be recured. *Spenſer's Ireland.*

Deviſe but how you'll uſe him when he comes, and let us two *deviſe* to bring him thither. *Shak. Mer. Wives of Windſor.*

DEVI'SE. *n. ſ.* [*deviſe*, a will, old French.]

1. The act of giving or bequeathing by will.

This word is properly attributed, in our common law, to him that bequeaths his goods by his laſt will or teſtament in writing; and the reaſon is, becauſe thoſe that now appertain only to the deviſour, by this act are diſtributed into many parts. *Cowel.*

The alienation is made by *deviſe* in a laſt will only, and the third part of theſe profits is there demandable, by ſpecial proviſion thereof made in the ſtatute. *Bacon's Off. of Alienation.*

2. Contrivance. See DEVICE.

God hath omitted nothing needful to his purpoſe, nor left his intention to be accompliſhed by our *deviſes.* *Hooker.*

To DEVI'SE. *v. a.* [from the noun.] To grant by will. A law term.

DEVI'SER. *n. ſ.* [from *deviſe.*] A contriver; an inventer.

Being divided from truth in themſelves, they are yet farther removed by advenient deception; for true it is, if I ſay they are daily mocked into error by *deviſers.* *Brown's Vulg. Errours.*

The authors of uſeful inventions, the *deviſers* of wholſome laws, as were the philoſophers of ancient times, were honoured as the fathers and prophets of their country. *Grew's Coſmol.*

DE'VITABLE. *adj.* [*devitabilis*, Lat.] Poſſible to be avoided; avoidable. *Dict.*

DEVITA'TION. *n. ſ.* [*devitatio*, Latin.] The act of eſcaping or avoiding. *Dict.*

DEVO'ID. *adj.* [*vuide*, French.]

1. Empty; vacant; void.

When I awoke, and found her place *devoid*,
And nought but preſſed graſs where ſhe had lyen,
I ſorrow'd all ſo much as earſt I joy'd. *Fairy Queen, b.* i.

2. Without any thing, whether good or evil; free from; in want of.

He flung it from him, and *devoid* of dread,
Upon him lightly leaped without heed. *Fairy Queen, b.* ii.

That the ſoul and angels are *devoid* of quantity and dimenſion, hath the ſuffrage of the moſt; and that they have nothing to do with proper locality, is generally opinioned. *Glanv.*

The motion of this chariot will ſtill be eaſier as it aſcends higher, 'till at length it ſhall become utterly *devoid* of gravity, when the leaſt ſtrength will be able to beſtow upon it a ſwift motion. *Wilkins's Math. Magic.*

His warlike mind, his ſoul *devoid* of fear,
His high deſigning thoughts were figur'd there,
As when, by magick, ghoſts are made appear. *Dryden.*

We Tyrians are not ſo *devoid* of ſenſe,
Nor ſo remote from Phœbus' influence. *Dryden's Virg. Æn.*

DEVO'IR. *n. ſ.* [*devoir*, French.]

1. Service. A ſenſe now not uſed.

To reſtore again the kingdom of the Mamalukes, he offered him their utmoſt *devoir* and ſervice. *Knolles's Hiſtory.*

2. Act of civility or obſequiouſneſs.

Aukward and ſupple, each *devoir* to pay,
She flatters her good lady twice a day. *Pope.*

To DEVO'LVE. *v. a.* [*devolvo*, Latin.]

1. To roll down.

The matter which *devolves* from the hills down upon the lower grounds, does not conſiderably raiſe and augment them. *Woodward's Natural Hiſtory.*

Through ſplendid kingdoms he *devolves* his maze,
Now wanders wild through ſolitary tracts
Of life-deſerted ſand. *Thomſon's Summer, l.* 805.

2. To move from one hand to another.

Becauſe they found too much confuſion in ſuch a multitude of ſtateſmen, they *devolved* their whole authority into the hands of the council of ſixty. *Addiſon's Remarks on Italy.*

The whole power, at home and abroad, was *devolved* upon that family. *Swift.*

To DEVO'LVE. *v. n.* To fall in ſucceſſion into new hands.

Suppoſing people, by wanting ſpiritual bleſſings, did loſe all their right to temporal, yet that forfeiture muſt *devolve* only to the ſupreme Lord. *Decay of Piety.*

DEVOLU'TION. *n. ſ.* [*devolutio*, Latin.]

1. The act of rolling down.

What concerns the raiſing of new mountains, deterrations, or the *devolution* of earth down upon the valleys from the hills

hills and high grounds, will fall more properly under our conſideration on another occaſion. *Woodward's Natural Hiſtory.*

2. Removal from hand to hand.

The juriſdiction exerciſed in thoſe courts is derived from the crown of England, and the laſt *devolution* is to the king by way of appeal. *Hale's Common Law of England.*

DEVORA'TION. *n. ſ.* [from *devoro*, Latin.] The act of devouring. *Dict.*

To DEVO'TE. *v. a.* [*devoveo devotus*, Latin.]

1. To dedicate; to conſecrate; to appropriate.

No *devoted* thing that a man ſhall *devote* unto the Lord, of all that he hath, both of man and beaſt, and of the field of his poſſeſſion, ſhall be ſold or redeemed. *Lev.* xxvii. 21.

What black magician conjures up this fiend,
To ſtop *devoted* charitable deeds? *Shakeſp. Richard* III.

While we do admire
This virtue, and this moral diſcipline,
Let's be no ſtoicks, nor no ſtocks, I pray;
Or ſo *devote* to Ariſtotle's checks,
As Ovid be an outcaſt quite abjur'd. *Sh. Tam. of the Shrew.*

They, impious, dar'd to prey
On herds *devoted* to the god of day. *Pope's Odyſſey, b.* i.

If perſons of this make ſhould ever *devote* themſelves to ſcience, they ſhould be well aſſured of a ſolid and ſtrong conſtitution of body. *Watts's Improvement of the Mind.*

2. To addict; to give up to ill.

Aliens were *devoted* to their rapine and deſpight. *Dec. of Piety.*

Having once debauched their ſenſes with the pleaſures of other nations, they *devoted* themſelves unto all wickedneſs. *Grew's Coſm. Sac. b.* iii. *c.* 3.

Ah why, Penelope, this cauſeleſs fear,
To render ſleep's ſoft bleſſings inſincere?
Alike *devote* to ſorrow's dire extreme,
The day reflection, and the midnight dream. *Pope's Odyſſey.*

3. To curſe; to execrate; to doom to deſtruction.

Yet not for thy advice, or threats, I fly
Thoſe wicked tents *devoted*; leſt the wrath
Impendent, raging into ſudden flame,
Diſtinguiſh not. *Milton's Paradiſe Loſt, b.* v. *l.* 890.

To deſtruction ſacred, and *devote*,
He with his whole poſterity muſt die. *Milton's Parad. Loſt.*

Goddeſs of maids, and conſcious of our hearts,
So keep me from the vengeance of thy darts,
Which Niobe's *devoted* iſſue felt,
When, hiſſing through the ſkies, the feather'd deaths were dealt. *Dryden's Fables.*

Let her, like me, of ev'ry joy forlorn,
Devote the hour when ſuch a wretch was born:
Like me to deſerts and to darkneſs run. *Rowe's Jane Shore.*

DEVO'TEDNESS. *n. ſ.* [from *devote*.] The ſtate of being devoted or dedicated.

Whatever may fall from my pen to her diſadvantage, relates to her but as ſhe was, or may again be, an obſtacle to your *devotedneſs* to ſeraphick love. *Boyle's Seraphick Love.*

The owning of our obligation unto virtue, may be ſtiled natural religion; that is to ſay, a *devotedneſs* unto God, our liege Lord, ſo as to act in all things according to his will. *Grew's Coſmol. Sac. b.* iii. *c.* 5.

DEVOTE'E. *n. ſ.* [*devot*, French.] One erroneouſly or ſuperſtitiouſly religious; a bigot.

DEVO'TION. *n. ſ.* [*devotion*, French; *devotio*, Latin.]

1. The ſtate of being conſecrated or dedicated.

2. Piety; acts of religion.

Mean time her warlike brother on the ſeas
His waving ſtreamers to the winds diſplays,
And vows for his return, with vain *devotion*, pays. *Dryd.*

3. An act of external worſhip.

Religious minds are inflamed with the love of publick *devotion*. *Hooker.*

For as I paſſed by and beheld your *devotion*, I found an altar with this inſcription, To the unknown God. *Acts* xvii. 23.

In vain doth man the name of juſt expect,
If his *devotions* he to God neglect. *Denham.*

4. Prayer; expreſſion of devotion.

An aged holy man,
That day and night ſaid his *devotion*,
No other worldly buſineſs did apply. *Fairy Queen, b.* i.

Your *devotion* has its opportunity: we muſt pray always, but chiefly at certain times. *Sprat's Sermons.*

5. The ſtate of the mind under a ſtrong ſenſe of dependance upon God.

Grateful to acknowledge whence his good
Deſcends, thither with heart, and voice, and eyes
Directed in *devotion*, to adore
And worſhip God ſupreme, who made him chief
Of all his works. *Milton's Paradiſe Loſt, b.* vii. *l.* 514.

From the full choir, when loud Hoſanna's riſe,
And ſwell the pomp of dreadful ſacrifice;
Amid' that ſcene, if ſome relenting eye
Glance on the ſtone where our cold reliques lie,
Devotion's ſelf ſhall ſteal a thought from heav'n,
One human tear ſhall drop, and be forgiv'n. *Pope.*

Devotion may be conſidered either as an exerciſe of publick or private prayers at ſet times and occaſions, or as a temper of the mind, a ſtate and diſpoſition of the heart, which is rightly affected with ſuch exerciſes. *Law on Chriſt's Perfection.*

6. An act of reverence, reſpect, or ceremony.

Whither away ſo faſt?
—No farther than the Tower; and, as I gueſs,
Upon the like *devotion* as yourſelves,
To gratulate the gentle princes there. *Shakeſ. Richard* III.

7. Strong affection; ardent love; ſuch as makes the lover the ſole property of the perſon loved.

Be oppoſite, all planets of good luck,
To my proceeding, if, with pure heart's love,
Immaculate *devotion*, holy thoughts,
I tender not thy beauteous princely daughter. *Shak. R.* III.

He had a particular reverence for the perſon of the king; and the more extraordinary *devotion* for that of the prince, as he had had the honour to be truſted with his education. *Clar.*

8. Diſpoſal; power; ſtate of dependance on any one.

Arundel-caſtle would keep that rich corner of the country at his majeſty's *devotion*. *Clarendon, b.* viii.

DEVO'TIONAL. *adj.* [from *devotion*.] Pertaining to devotion; annexed to worſhip; religious.

Nor are the ſobereſt of them ſo apt for that *devotional* compliance and juncture of hearts, which I deſire to bear in holy offices, to be performed with me. *King Charles.*

The favourable opinion and good word of men comes often times at a very eaſy rate, by a few demure looks, with ſome *devotional* poſtures and grimaces. *South's Sermons.*

DEVO'TIONALIST. *n. ſ.* [from *devotion*.] A man zealous without knowledge; ſuperſtitiouſly devout.

To DEVOU'R. *v. a.* [*devoro*, Latin.]

1. To eat up ravenouſly, as a wild beaſt or animal of prey.

We will ſay ſome evil beaſt hath *devoured* him. *Gen.* xxxvii.

We've willing dames enough: there cannot be
That vulture in you to *devour* ſo many
As will to greatneſs dedicate themſelves,
Finding it ſo inclin'd. *Shakeſpeare's Macbeth.*

So looks the pent up lion o'er the wretch
That trembles under his *devouring* paws. *Shakeſ. Henry* VI.

2. To deſtroy or conſume with rapidity and violence.

A fire *devoureth* before them, and behind them a flame burneth. *Joel* ii. 3.

How dire a tempeſt from Mycenæ pour'd,
Our plains, our temples, and our town *devour'd*;
It was the waſte of war. *Dryden's Æn. b.* viii.

Notwithſtanding that Socrates lived in the time of this *devouring* peſtilence at Athens, he never caught the leaſt infection. *Addiſon's Spectator,* N°. 195.

3. To ſwallow up; to annihilate.

He ſeemed in ſwiftneſs to *devour* the way. *Shakeſpeare.*

Such a pleaſure as grows freſher upon enjoyment; and though continually fed upon, yet is never *devoured*. *South.*

Death ſtalks behind thee, and each flying hour
Does ſome looſe remnant of thy life *devour*. *Dryden.*

DEVOU'RER. *n. ſ.* [from *devour*.] A conſumer; he that devours; he that preys upon.

Rome is but a wilderneſs of tygers:
Tygers muſt prey, and Rome affords no prey
But me and mine: how happy art thou then,
From theſe *devourers* to be baniſhed? *Shak. Tit. Andronicus.*

Since thoſe leviathans are withdrawn, the leſſer *devourers* ſupply their place: fraud ſucceeds to violence. *Decay of Piety.*

Store the pond with carp and tench, which do the beſt together of any fiſh, all other fiſh being *devourers* of their ſpawn. *Mortimer's Husbandry.*

DEVO'UT. *adj.* [*devotus*, Latin.]

1. Pious; religious; devoted to holy duties.

We muſt be conſtant and *devout* in the worſhip of our God, and ready in all acts of benevolence to our neighbour. *Rogers, Sermon* 13.

2. Filled with pious thoughts.

For this, with ſoul *devout*, he thank'd the god;
And, of ſucceſs ſecure, return'd to his abode. *Dryd. Fables.*

3. Expreſſive of devotion or piety.

Anon dry ground appears, and from his ark
The ancient ſire deſcends, with all his train:
Then with uplifted hands, and eyes *devout*,
Grateful to heav'n. *Milton's Paradiſe Loſt, b.* xi. *l.* 863.

DEVO'UTLY. *adv.* [from *devout*.] Piouſly; with ardent devotion; religiouſly.

Her grace roſe, and with modeſt paces
Came to the altar, where ſhe kneel'd; and, ſaint-like,
Caſt her fair eyes to heav'n, and pray'd *devoutly*. *Sh. H.* VIII.

One of the wiſe men of the ſociety of Solomon's houſe, having a while attentively and *devoutly* viewed and contemplated this pillar and croſs, fell down upon his face. *Bacon.*

Her twilights were more clear than our mid-day,
She dreamt *devoutlier* than moſt uſe to pray;
Who being here fill'd with grace, yet ſtrove to be
Both where more grace and more capacity
At once is given. *Donne.*

Think, O my ſoul, *devoutly* think,
How, with affrighted eyes,
Thou ſaw'ſt the wide extended deep
In all its horrors riſe! *Addiſon's Spectator*, N°. 490.

To ſecond cauſes we ſeem to truſt, without expreſſing, ſo *devoutly* as we ought to do, our dependance on the firſt. *Atterb.*

DEUSE. *n.ſ.* [more properly than *deuce*, *Junius*, from *Duſius*, the name of a certain ſpecies of evil ſpirits.] The devil: a ludicrous word.

'Twas the prettieſt prologue, as he wrote it;
Well, the *deuce* take me if I ha'n't forgot it. *Congreve.*

DEUTERO'GAMY. *n.ſ.* [δεύτερος and γάμος.] A ſecond marriage. *Dict.*

DEUTERONO'MY. *n.ſ.* [δεύτερος νόμος.] The ſecond book of the law; being the book of Moſes.

DEUTERO'SCOPY. *n.ſ.* [δεύτερος and σκοπέω.] The ſecond intention; the meaning beyond the literal ſenſe.

Not attaining the *deuteroſcopy*, or ſecond intention of the words, they are fain to omit their conſequences, coherences, figures, or tropologies. *Brown's Vulgar Errours.*

DEW. *n.ſ.* [ꝺeaƿ, Saxon; *daaw*, Dutch.] The moiſture upon the ground.

Fogs, particularly thoſe which we frequently obſerve after ſun-ſetting, even in our hotteſt months, are nothing but a vapour, conſiſting of water, and of ſuch mineral matter as it meets with in its paſſage, and could well bring up along with it; which vapour was ſent up in greater quantity all the foregoing day, than now in the evening: but the ſun then being above the horizon, taking it at the ſurface of the earth, and rapidly mounting it up into the atmoſphere, it was not diſcernible, as now it is; becauſe the ſun being now gone off, the vapour ſtagnates at and near the earth, and ſaturates the air 'till it is ſo thick as to be eaſily viſible therein: and when at length the heat there is ſomewhat further ſpent, which is uſually about the middle of the night, it falls down again in a *dew*, alighting upon herbs and other vegetables, which it cheriſhes, cools and refreſhes, after the ſcorching heat of the foregoing day. *Woodward's Natural Hiſtory.*

Never yet one hour in bed
Did I enjoy the golden *dew* of ſleep,
But with his tim'rous dreams was ſtill awak'd. *Shak. R.* III.

That churchman bears a bounteous mind, indeed;
A hand as fruitful as the land that feeds us;
His *dew* falls ev'ry where. *Shakeſpeare's Henry* VIII.

She looks as clear
As morning roſes newly waſh'd with *dew*. *Shakeſpeare.*

Dews and rain are but the returns of moiſt vapours condenſed. *Bacon's Natural Hiſtory*, N°. 81.

Now ſliding ſtreams the thirſty plants renew,
And feed their fibres with reviving *dew*. *Pope.*

To DEW. *v. a.* [from the noun.] To wet as with dew; to moiſten; to bedew.

A trickling ſtream of balm moſt ſovereign,
And dainty dear, which on the ground ſtill fell,
And overflowed all the fertile plain,
As it had *dewed* been with timely rain. *Fairy Queen*, *b.* i.

Be we the med'cine of the ſickly weal,
And with him pour we in our country's purge,
Each drop of us.
——Or ſo much as it needs
To *dew* the ſovereign flower, and drown the weeds. *Shakeſ.*

Give me thy hand,
That I may *dew* it with my mournful tears. *Shakeſ. H.* VI.

He ceas'd; diſcerning Adam with ſuch joy
Surcharg'd, as had, like grief, been *dew'd* in tears,
Without the vent of words, which theſe he breath'd.
Milton's Paradiſe Loſt, *b.* xii. *l.* 373.

Palemon above the reſt appears,
In ſable garments, *dew'd* with guſhing tears. *Dryd. Fables.*

2. It is not uſed properly of an action of terrour.

In Gallick blood again
He *dews* his reeking ſword, and ſtrows the ground
With headleſs ranks. *Phillips.*

DE'WBERRY. *n.ſ.* [from *dew* and *berry*.]

Dewberries, as they ſtand here among the more delicate fruits, muſt be underſtood to mean raſberries, which are alſo of the bramble kind. *Hanmer.*

Feed him with apricocks and *dewberries*,
With purple grapes, green figs, and mulberries. *Shakeſpeare.*

DEWBESPRE'NT. *part.* [*dew* and *beſprent*.] Sprinkled with dew.

This evening late, by then the chewing flocks
Had ta'en their ſupper on the favoury herb
Of knot-graſs *dewbeſprent*, and were in fold,
I ſat me down to watch upon a bank
With ivy canopied, and interwove
With flaunting honey-ſuckle. *Milton.*

DEW-BURNING. *adj.* [from *dew* and *burning*.] The meaning of this compound is doubtful. Perhaps it alludes to the ſparkling of dew.

He, now to prove his late renewed might,
High-brandiſhing his bright *dew-burning* blade,
Upon his creſted ſcalp ſo ſore did ſmite,
That to the ſcull a yawning wound it made. *Fairy Queen.*

DE'WDROP. *n.ſ.* [*dew* and *drop*.] A drop of dew which ſparkles at ſun-riſe.

I muſt go ſeek ſome *dewdrops* here,
And hang a pearl in every cowſlip's ear. *Shakeſpeare.*

An hoſt
Innumerable! as the ſtars of night,
Or ſtars of morning, *dewdrops*, which the ſun
Impearls! on every leaf, and ev'ry flow'r. *Milton's Pa. Loſt.*

Reſt, ſweet as *dewdrops* on their flow'ry lawns,
When the ſky opens, and the morning dawns! *Tickell.*

DE'WLAP. *n.ſ.* [from *lapping* or *licking* the *dew*.]

1. The fleſh that hangs down from the throat of oxen.

Large rowles of fat about his ſhoulders flung,
And from his neck the double *dewlap* hung. *Addiſ. Ov. Met.*

2. It is uſed in *Shakeſpeare* for a lip flaccid with age, in contempt.

And ſometimes lurk I in a goſſip's bowl,
In very likeneſs of a roaſted crab;
And when ſhe drinks againſt her lips I bob,
And on the wither'd *dewlap* pour the ale. *Shakeſpeare.*

DE'WLAPT. *adj.* [from *dewlap*.] Furniſhed with dewlaps.

Who would believe, that there were mountaineers
Dewlapt like bulls, whoſe throats had hanging at 'em
Wallets of fleſh. *Shakeſpeare's Tempeſt.*

The *dewlapt* bull now chafes along the plain,
While burning love ferments in ev'ry vein. *Gay.*

DE'WWORM. *n.ſ.* [from *dew* and *worm*.] A worm found in dew.

For the trout, the *dew-worm*, which ſome call the lob-worm, and the brandliny, are the chief. *Walton's Angler.*

DE'WY. *adj.* [from *dew*.]

1. Reſembling dew; partaking of dew.

From the earth a *dewy* miſt
Went up, and water'd all the ground, and each
Plant of the field. *Milton's Paradiſe Loſt*, *b.* vii. *l.* 331.

Where two adverſe winds,
Sublim'd from *dewy* vapours in mid ſky,
Engage with horrid ſhock, the ruffled brine
Roars ſtormy. *Phillips.*

2. Moiſt with dew; roſcid.

The joyous day 'gan early to appear,
And fair Aurora from her *dewy* bed
Of aged Tithone, 'gan herſelf to rear,
With roſy cheeks, for ſhame as bluſhing red. *Fairy Queen.*

The bee with honied thigh,
That at her flow'ry work doth ſing,
And the waters murmuring,
With ſuch conſort as they keep,
Entice the *dewy* feather'd ſleep. *Milton.*

His *dewy* locks diſtill'd
Ambroſia. *Milton's Paradiſe Loſt*, *b.* v. *l.* 56.

His own Prænifte ſends a choſen band,
With thoſe who plough Saturnia's Gabine land;
Beſides the ſuccour which cold Ancien yields,
The rocks of Hernicus and *dewy* fields. *Dryden's Æn. b.* viii.

DE'XTER. *adj.* [Latin.] The right; not the left. A term uſed in heraldry.

My mother's blood
Runs on the *dexter* cheek, and this ſiniſter
Bounds in my ſire's. *Shakeſpeare's Troilus and Creſſida.*

DEXTE'RITY. *n.ſ.* [*dexteritas*, Latin.]

1. Readineſs of limbs; activity; readineſs to attain ſkill; ſkill; expertneſs.

2. Readineſs of contrivance; quickneſs of expedient; ſkill of management.

His wiſdom, by often evading from perils, was turned rather into a *dexterity* to deliver himſelf from dangers, when they preſſed him, than into a providence to prevent and remove them afar off. *Bacon's Henry* VII.

They attempted to be knaves, but wanted art and *dexterity*. *South's Sermons.*

The ſame Proteſtants may, by their *dexterity*, make themſelves the national religion, and diſpoſe the church-revenues among their paſtors. *Swift.*

DE'XTEROUS. *adj.* [*dexter*, Latin.]

1. Expert at any manual employment; active; ready; as, a *dexterous* workman.

2. Expert in management; ſubtle; full of expedients.

They confine themſelves, and are *dexterous* managers enough of the wares and products of that corner, with which they content themſelves. *Locke.*

DEXTE'ROUSLY. *adv.* [from *dexterous*.] Expertly; ſkilfully; artfully.

The magiſtrate ſometimes cannot do his own office *dexterouſly*, but by acting the miniſter. *South's Sermons.*

But then my ſtudy was to cog the dice,
And *dexterouſly* to throw the lucky ſice. *Dryden.*

De'xtral. *adj.* [*dexter*, Latin.] The right; not the left.

As for any tunicles or skins, which should hinder the liver from enabling the *dextral* parts, we must not conceive it diffuseth its virtue by meer irradiation, but by its veins and proper vessels. *Brown's Vulgar Errours, b.* iv. *c.* 5.

Dextra'lity. *n. s.* [from *dextral.*] The state of being on the right, not the left, side.

If there were a determinate prepotency in the right, and such as ariseth from a constant root in nature, we might expect the same in other animals, whose parts are also differenced by *dextrality*. *Brown's Vulgar Errours, b.* iv. *c.* 5.

Diabe'tes. *n. s.* [διαβήτης.] A morbid copiousness of urine; a fatal colliquation by the urinary passages.

An increase of that secretion may accompany the general colliquations; as in fluxes, hectick sweats and coughs, *diabetes*, and other consumptions. *Derham's Physico-Theology.*

Diabo'lical. } *adj.* [from *diabolus*, Latin.] Devilish; par-
Diabo'lick. } taking of the qualities of the devil; impious; atrocious; nefarious; pertaining to the devil.

This, in other beasts observ'd,
Doubt might beget of *diabolick* pow'r,
Active within, beyond the sense of brute. *Milt. Par. Lost.*

Does not the ambitious, the envious, and the revengeful man know very well, that the thirst of blood, and affectation of dominion by violence and oppression, is a most *diabolical* outrage upon the laws of God and Nature, and upon the common well-being of mankind? *L'Estrange.*

The practice of lying is a *diabolical* exercise, and they that use it are the devil's children. *Ray on the Creation.*

Damned spirits must needs be all envy, despair, and rage; and have so much of a *diabolical* nature in them, as to wish all men to share their misery. *Atterbury's Sermons.*

DIACO'DIUM. *n. s.* [Latin.] The syrup of poppies.

Diaco'ustics. *n. s.* [διακουστικά.] The doctrine of sounds.

DI'ADEM. *n. s.* [*diadema*, Latin.]

1. A tiara; an ensign of royalty bound about the head of Eastern monarchs.

The sacred *diadem* in pieces rent,
And purple robe gored with many a wound. *Fairy Queen.*

A lift the cobler's temples ties,
To keep the hair out of their eyes;
From whence 'tis plain the *diadem*,
That princes wear, derives from them. *Swift.*

2. The mark of royalty worn on the head; the crown.

A crown,
Golden in shew, is but a wreath of thorns;
Brings dangers, troubles, cares, and sleepless nights,
To him who wears the regal *diadem*. *Milton's Par. Lost.*

Why should he ravish then that *diadem*
From your grey temples, which the hand of time
Must shortly plant on his. *Denham's Sophy.*

Faction, that once made *diadems* her prey,
And stopt our prince in his triumphant way,
Fled like a mist before this radiant day. *Roscommon.*

Diade'med. *adj.* [from *diadem.*] Adorned with a diadem; crowned.

Not so, when *diadem'd* with rays divine,
Touch'd with the flame that breaks from virtue's shrine,
Her priestless muse forbids the good to dye,
And opes the temple of eternity. *Pope.*

Di'adrom. *n. s.* [διαδρομέω.] The time in which any motion is performed; the time in which a pendulum performs its vibration.

A gry is one tenth of a line, a line one tenth of one inch, an inch one tenth of a philosophical foot, a philosophical foot one third of a pendulum; whose *diadroms*, in the latitude of forty-five degrees, are each equal to one second of time, or a sixtieth of a minute. *Locke.*

Diæ'resis. *n. s.* [διαίρεσις.] The separation or disjunction of syllables; as *aër*.

Diagno'stick. *n. s.* [διαγινώσκω.] A symptom by which a disease is distinguished from others.

I shall lay down some indisputable marks of this vice, that whenever we see the tokens, we may conclude the plague is in the house:—let us hear your *diagnosticks*. *Collier on Pride.*

One of our physicians proved disappointed of his prognosticks, or rather *diagnosticks*. *Harvey on Consumptions.*

DIA'GONAL. *adj.* [διαγώνιος.] Reaching from one angle to another, so as to divide a parallelogram into equal parts.

The monstrosity of the badger is ill-contrived, and with some disadvantage; the shortness being fixed unto the legs of one side, that might have been more properly placed upon the *diagonal* movers. *Brown's Vulgar Errours, b.* iii. *c.* 5.

This, and all like sorts of stone that are composed of granules, will cut and rive in any direction, as well in a perpendicular, or in a *diagonal*, as horizontally and parallel to the side of the strata. *Woodward on Fossils.*

Dia'gonal. *n. s.* [from the adjective.] A line drawn from angle to angle, and dividing a square into equal parts.

When a man has in his mind the idea of two lines, viz. the side and *diagonal* of a square, whereof the *diagonal* is an inch long, he may have the idea also of the division of that line into a certain number of equal parts. *Locke.*

Dia'gonally. *adv.* [from *diagonal.*] In a diagonal direction.

The right and left are not defined by philosophers according to common acceptation, that is, respectively from one man unto another, or any constant site in each, as though that should be the right in one, which, upon confront or facing, stands athwart or *diagonally* unto the other; but were distinguished, according unto their activity and predominant locomotion, on the either side. *Brown's Vulgar Errours, b.* iv.

Di'agram. *n. s.* [διάγραμμα.] A delineation of geometrical figures; a mathematical scheme.

Many a fair precept in poetry is like a seeming demonstration in the mathematicks; very specious in the *diagram*, but failing in the mechanick operation. *Dryden.*

Why do not these persons make a *diagram* of these cogitative lines and angles, and demonstrate their properties of perception and appetite, as plainly as we know the other properties of triangles and circles? *Bentley's Sermons.*

Diagry'diates. *n. s.* [from *diagrydium*, Lat.] Strong purgatives made with diagrydium.

All cholerick humours ought to be evacuated by *diagrydiates*, mixed with tartar, or some acid, or rhubarb powder. *Floyer.*

DI'AL. *n. s.* [*diale*, *Skinner.*] A plate marked with lines, where a hand or shadow shews the hour.

O, gentlemen, the time of life is short:
To spend that shortness basely were too long,
Though life did ride upon a *dial*'s point,
Still ending at th' arrival of an hour. *Shakesp. Henry* IV.

If the motion be very slow, we perceive it not: we have no sense of the accretive motion of plants or animals; and the sly shadow steals away upon the *dial*, and the quickest eye can discover no more but that it is gone. *Glanv. Sceps. c.* 11.

Dial-plate. *n. s.* [*dial* and *plate.*] That on which hours or lines are marked.

He tells us that the two friends, being each of them possessed of one of these needles, made a kind of *dial-plate*, inscribing it with the four and twenty letters, in the same manner as the hours of the day are marked upon the ordinary *dial-plate*. *Addison's Spectator*, N°. 241.

DIALE'CT. *n. s.* [διάλεκτος.]

1. The subdivision of a language; as the Attic, Doric, Ionic, Æolic dialects.

2. Stile; manner of expression.

When themselves do practise that whereof they write, they change their *dialect*; and those words they shun, as if there were in them some secret sting. *Hooker, b.* v. *s.* 22.

3. Language; speech.

In her youth
There is a prone and speechless *dialect*,
Such as moves men. *Shakesp. Measure for Measure.*

If the conferring of a kindness did not bind the person, upon whom it was conferred, to the returns of gratitude, why, in the universal *dialect* of the world, are kindnesses still called obligations? *South's Sermons.*

Diale'ctical. *adj.* [from *dialectick.*] Logical; argumentative.

Those *dialectical* subtleties that the schoolmen too often employ about physiological mysteries, are wont much more to declare the wit of him that uses them, than increase the knowledge of sober lovers of truth. *Boyle.*

DIALE'CTICK. *n. s.* [διαλεκτική.] Logick; the act of reasoning.

Dia'lling. *n. s.* [from *dial.*] The sciaterick science; the knowledge of shadow; the act of constructing dials on which the shadow may shew the hour.

Dia'list. *n. s.* [from *dial.*] A constructer of dials.

Scientifick *dialists*, by the geometrick considerations of lines, have found out rules to mark out the irregular motion of the shadow in all latitudes, and on all planes. *Moxon.*

Dia'logist. *n. s.* [from *dialogue.*] A speaker in a dialogue or conference; a writer of dialogues.

DI'ALOGUE. *n. s.* [διάλογος.] A conference; a conversation between two or more, either real or feigned.

Will you hear the *dialogue* that the two learned men have compiled in praise of the owl and cuckow? *Shakespeare.*

Oh, the impudence of this wicked sex! Lascivious *dialogues* are innocent with you. *Dryden's Spanish Fryar.*

In easy *dialogues* is Fletcher's praise;
He mov'd the mind, but had not pow'r to raise. *Dryden.*

To Di'alogue. *v. a.* [from the noun.] To discourse with another; to confer.

Do'st *dialogue* with thy shadow? *Shakespeare's Timon.*

Dialy'sis. *n. s.* [διάλυσις.] The figure in rhetorick by which syllables or words are divided.

DIA'METER. *n. s.* [διὰ and μέτρον.] The line, which passing through the center of a circle, or other curvilinear figure, divides it into equal parts.

The space between the earth and the moon, according to Ptolemy and Alfraganus, is seventeen times the *diameter* of the earth, which makes, in a gross account, about one hundred and twenty thousand miles. *Raleigh's History of the World.*

The bay of Naples is the most delightful one that I ever saw: it lies in almost a round figure of about thirty miles in the *diameter*. *Addison's Remarks on Italy.*

DIA'METRAL. *adj.* [from *diameter.*] Describing the diameter; relating to the diameter.

DIA'METRALLY. *adv.* [from *diametral.*] According to the direction of a diameter.

Christian piety is, beyond all other things, *diametrally* opposed to profaneness and impiety of actions. *Hammond.*

DIAME'TRICAL. *adj.* [from *diameter.*]

1. Describing a diameter.
2. Observing the direction of a diameter.

The sin of calumny is set in a most *diametrical* opposition to the evangelical precept of loving our neighbours as ourselves. *Government of the Tongue, s.* v.

DIAME'TRICALLY. *adv.* [from *diametrical.*] In a diametrical direction.

He persuaded the king to consent to what was *diametrically* against his conscience and his honour, and, in truth, his security. *Clarendon, b.* viii.

When it is thus intercepted in its passage, the vapour, which cannot penetrate the stratum *diametrically*, glides along the lower surface of it, permeating the horizontal interval, which is betwixt the said dense stratum and that which lies underneath it. *Woodward.*

DIAMOND. *n. s.* [*diamant*, French; *adamas*, Latin.]

The *diamond*, the most valuable and hardest of all the gems, is, when pure, perfectly clear and pellucid as the purest water; and is eminently distinguished from all other substances by its vivid splendour, and the brightness of its reflexions. It is extremely various in shape and size, being found in the greatest quantity very small, and the larger ones extremely seldom met with. The largest ever known is that in the possession of the great Mogul, which weighs two hundred and seventy-nine carats, and is computed to be worth seven hundred and seventy-nine thousand two hundred and forty-four pounds. The diamond bears the force of the strongest fires, except the concentrated solar rays, without hurt; and even that infinitely fiercest of all fires does it no injury, unless directed to its weaker parts. It bears a glass-house fire for many days, and, if taken carefully out, and suffered to cool by degrees, is found as bright and beautiful as before; but if taken hastily out, it will sometimes crack, and even split into two or three pieces. The places where we have *diamonds* are the East Indies and the Brasils; and though they are usually found clear and colourless, yet they are sometimes slightly tinged with the colours of the other gems, by the mixture of some metalline particles. *Hill on Fossils.*

This *diamond* was my mother's: take it, heart;
But keep it 'till you woo another wife. *Shakesp. Cymbeline.*

Give me the ring of mine you had at dinner;
Or, for the *diamond*, the chain you promised. *Shakespeare.*

I see how thine eye would emulate the *diamond*: thou hast the right arched bent of the brow. *Shak. Mer. Wives of Windf.*

The *diamond* is preferable and vastly superior to all others in lustre and beauty; as also in hardness, which renders it more durable and lasting, and therefore much more valuable, than any other stone. *Woodward's Mett. Foss.*

The *diamond* is by mighty monarchs worn,
Fair as the star that ushers in the morn. *Blackm. Creation.*

The lively *diamond* drinks thy purest rays,
Collected light, compact. *Thomson's Summer, l.* 140.

DI'APASE. *n. s.* [διὰ πασῶν.] A chord including all tones. The old word for *diapason*. See DIAPASON.

And 'twixt them both a quadrant was the base,
Proportion'd equally by seven and nine;
Nine was the circle set in heaven's place,
All which compacted made a good *diapase*. *Fairy Queen.*

The sweet numbers and melodious measures,
With which I wont the winged words to tie,
And make a tuneful *diapase* of pleasures,
Now being let to run at liberty. *Spenser.*

DIAPA'SON. *n. s.* [διαπασῶν.]

Diapason denotes a chord which includes all tones: it is the same with that we call an eighth, or an octave; because there are but seven tones or notes, and then the eighth is the same again with the first. *Harris.*

It discovereth the true coincidence of sounds into *diapasons*, which is the return of the same sound. *Bacon's Nat. History.*

Harsh din
Broke the fair musick that all creatures made
To their great Lord, whose love their motion sway'd
In perfect *diapason*, whilst they stood
In first obedience, and their state of good. *Milton.*

Many a sweet rise, many as sweet a fall,
A full-mouth *diapason* swallows all. *Crashaw.*

From harmony, from heav'nly harmony,
This universal frame began:
From harmony to harmony
Through all the compass of the notes it ran,
The *diapason* closing full in man. *Dryden.*

DI'APER. *n. s.* [*diapre*, French, of uncertain etymology.]

1. Linen cloth woven in flowers, and other figures.

Not any damsel, which her vaunteth most
In skilful knitting of soft silken twine;
Nor any weaver, which his work doth boast
In *diaper*, in damask, or in lyne,
Might in their diverse cunning ever dare
With this so curious net-work to compare. *Spenser.*

2. A napkin; a towel.

Let one attend him with a silver bason
Full of rose-water, and bestrew'd with flowers;
Another bear the ewer, a third a *diaper*. *Shakespeare.*

To DI'APER. *v. a.* [from the noun.]

1. To variegate; to diversify; to flower.

For fear the stones her tender foot should wrong,
The ground he strew'd with flowers all along,
And *diaper'd* like the discoloured mead. *Spenser.*

Flora useth to cloath our grand-dame earth with a new livery, *diapered* with various flowers, and chequered with delightful objects. *Howel's Vocal Forrest.*

2. To draw flowers upon cloaths.

If you *diaper* upon folds, let your work be broken, and taken, as it were, by the half; for reason tells you, that your fold must cover somewhat unseen. *Peacham on Drawing.*

DIAPHANE'ITY. *n. s.* [from διαφανία.] Transparency; pellucidness; power of transmitting light.

Because the outward coat of the eye ought to be pellucid, to transmit the light, which, if the eyes should always stand open, would be apt to grow dry and shrink, and lose their *diaphaneity*; therefore are the eyelids so contrived as often to wink, that so they may, as it were, glaze and varnish them over with the moisture they contain. *Ray on the Creation.*

DIAPHA'NICK. *adj.* [διὰ and φαινῶ.] Transparent; pellucid; having the power to transmit light.

Air is an element superior, and lighter than water, through whose vast, open, subtile, *diaphanick*, or transparent body, the light, afterwards created, easily transpired. *Raleigh's History of the World.*

DIA'PHANOUS. *adj.* [διὰ and φαίνω.] Transparent; clear; translucent; pellucid; capable to transmit light.

Aristotle calleth light a quality inherent, or clearing to a *diaphanous* body. *Raleigh's History of the World.*

When he had taken off the insect, he found in the leaf very little and *diaphanous* eggs, exactly like to those which yet remained in the tubes of the fly's womb. *Ray on the Creation.*

DIAPHORE'TICK. *adj.* [διαφορητικὸς.] Sudorifick; promoting a diaphoresis or perspiration; causing sweat.

Diaphoreticks, or promoters of perspiration, help the organs of digestion, because the attenuation of the aliment make it perspirable. *Arbuthnot on Aliments.*

A *diaphoretick* medicine, or a sudorifick, is something that will provoke sweating. *Watts.*

DI'APHRAGM. *n. s.* [διάφραγμα.]

1. The midriff which divides the upper cavity of the body from the lower.
2. Any division or partition which divides a hollow body.

It consists of a fasciculus of bodies, round, about one sixth of an inch in diameter, hollow, and parted into numerous cells by means of *diaphragms*, thick set throughout the whole length of the body. *Woodward on Fossils.*

DIARRHOE'A. *n. s.* [διάῤῥοια.] A flux of the belly, whereby a person frequently goes to stool, and is cured either by purging off the cause, or restringing the bowels. *Quincy.*

During his *diarrhœa* I healed up the fontanels. *Wiseman.*

DIARRHOE'TICK. *adj.* [from *diarrhœa.*] Promoting the flux of the belly; solutive; purgative.

Millet is *diarrhœtick*, cleansing, and useful in diseases of the kidneys. *Arbuthnot on Aliments.*

DI'ARY. *n. s.* [*diarium*, Latin.] An account of the transactions, accidents, and observations of every day; a journal.

In sea-voyages, where there is nothing to be seen but sky and sea, men make *diaries*; but in land-travel, wherein so much is to be observed, they omit it. *Bacon, Essay* 19.

I go on in my intended *diary*. *Tatler*, N°. 60.

DIA'STOLE. *n. s.* [διαςολὴ.]

1. A figure in rhetorick, by which a short syllable is made long.
2. The dilation of the heart.

The systole seems to resemble the forcible bending of a spring, and the *diastole* its flying out again to its natural state. *Ray on the Creation.*

DIA'STYLE. [διὰ and ςύλος, a pillar.] A sort of edifice where the pillars stand at such a distance from one another, that three diameters of their thickness are allowed for intercolumniation. *Harris.*

DIATE'SSERON. *n. s.* [of διὰ and τέσσερα, four.] An interval in musick, composed of one greater tone, one lesser, and one greater semi-tone; its proportion being as four to three. It is called, in musical composition, a perfect fourth. *Harris.*

DIATO'NICK. [of διατόνος.] The ordinary sort of musick which proceeds by different tones, either in ascending or descending.

descending. It contains only the two greater and lesser tones, and the greater semi-tone. *Harris.*

DIAZE'NTICK *Tone.* [of δια and ζεύγνυμι.] In the ancient Greek musick, disjoined two fourths, one on each side of it; and which being joined to either, made a fifth. This is, in our musick, from A to B.

They allowed to this *diazentick* tone, which is our La, Mi, the proportion of nine to eight, as being the unalterable difference of the fifth and four h. *Harris.*

DI'BBLE. *n. s.* [from *dipsel*, Dutch, a sharp point, *Skinner*; from *dabble*, *Junius.*] A small spade; a pointed instrument with which the gardeners make holes for planting.

DICA'CITY. *n. s.* [*dicacitas*, Lat.] Pertness; sauciness. *Dict.*

DI'BSTONE. *n. s.* A little stone which children throw at another stone.

I have seen little girls exercise whole hours together, and take abundance of pains to be expert at *dibstones*, as they call it. *Locke.*

DICE. *n. s.* The plural of *die.* See DIE.

It is above a hundred to one against any particular throw, that you do not cast any given set of faces with four cubical *dice*; because there are so many several combinations of the six faces of four dice: now, after you have cast all the trials but one, it is still as much odds at the last remaining time, as it was at the first. *Bentley's Sermons.*

To DICE. *v. n.* [from the noun.] To game with dice.

I was as virtuously given as a gentleman need to be; virtuous enough; swore little; *diced* not above seven times a week; went to a bawdy-house not above once in a quarter of an hour. *Shakespeare's Henry IV. p. i.*

DICE-BOX. *n s.* [*dice* and *box.*] The box from which the dice are thrown.

What would you say, should you see the sparkler shaking her elbow for a whole night together, and thumping the table with a *dice-box?* *Addison's Guardian*, N°. 120.

DI'CER. *n. s.* [from *dice.*] A player at dice; a gamester.

They make marriage vows
As false as *dicers* oaths. *Shakespeare's Hamlet.*

DICH. *adj.* This word seems corrupted from *dit* for *do it.*

Rich men sin, and I eat root:
Much good *dich* thy good heart, Apemantus. *Shakes. Timon.*

DICHO'TOMY. *n. s.* [διχοτομία.] Distribution of ideas by pairs.

Some persons have disturbed the order of nature, and abused their readers by an affectation of *dichotomies*, trichotomies, sevens, twelves, &c. Let the nature of the subject, considered together with the design which you have in view, always determine the number of parts into which you divide it. *Watts.*

DI'CKENS. A kind of adverbial exclamation, importing, as it seems, much the same with the *devil*; but I know not whence derived.

Where had you this pretty weathercock?
—I cannot tell what the *dickens* his name is my husband had him of. *Shakesp. Merry Wives of Windsor.*

What a *dickens* does he mean by a trivial sum?
But han't you found it, sir? *Congreve's Old Batchelor.*

DI'CHER *of Leather.* *n. s.* [*dicra*, low Latin.] Ten hides. *Dict.*

To DI'CTATE. *v. a.* [*dicto*, Latin.] To deliver to another with authority; to declare with confidence.

The spoils of elephants the roofs inlay,
And studded amber darts a golden ray;
Such, and not nobler, in the realms above,
My wonder *dictates* is the dome of Jove. *Pope's Odyssey.*

Whatsoever is *dictated* to us by God himself, or by men who are divinely inspired, must be believed with full assurance. *Watts's Logick.*

DI'CTATE. *n. s.* [*dictatum*, Latin.] Rule or maxim delivered with authority; prescription; prescript.

Others cast about for new discoveries, and to seek in their own thoughts for those right helps of art which will scarce be found, I fear, by those who servilely confine themselves to the *dictates* of others. *Locke.*

I credit what the Grecian *dictates* say,
And Samian sounds o'er Scota's hills convey. *Prior.*

Then let this *dictate* of my love prevail;
Instant, to foreign realms prepare to sail,
To learn your father's fortunes. *Pope's Odyssey, b. i.*

DICTA'TION. *n. s.* [from *dictate.*] The act or practice of dictating or prescribing. *Dict.*

DICTA'TOR. *n. s.* [Latin.]

1. A magistrate of Rome made in times of exigence and distress, and invested with absolute authority.

Kind *dictators* made, when they came home,
Their vanquish'd foes free citizens of Rome. *Waller.*
Julius with honour tam'd Rome's foreign foes:
But patriots fell, ere the *dictator* rose. *Prior.*

2. One invested with absolute authority.

Unanimous they all commit the care,
And management of this main enterprize,
To him their great *dictator.* *Milton's Paradise Regain'd, b. i.*

3. One whose credit or authority enables him to direct the conduct or opinion of others.

Nor is it a small power it gives one man over another, to have the authority to be the *dictator* of principles, and teacher of unquestionable truths. *Locke.*

That riches, honours, and outward splendour, should set up persons for *dictators* to all the rest of mankind, is a most shameful invasion of the right of our understanding. *Watts.*

DICTATO'RIAL. *adj.* [from *dictator.*] Authoritative; confident; dogmatical; overbearing.

A young academick often dwells upon a journal, or an observator that treats of trade and politicks in a *dictatorial* style, and is lavish in the praise of the author. *Watts.*

DICTA'TORSHIP. *n. s.* [from *dictator.*]

1. The office of dictator.

This is the solemnest title they can confer under the princedom, being indeed a kind of *dictatorship.* *Wotton.*

2. Authority; insolent confidence.

This is that perpetual *dictatorship* which is exercised by Lucretius, though often in the wrong. *Dryden.*

DICTA'TURE. *n. s.* [*dictatura*, Latin.] The office of a dictator; dictatorship. *Dict.*

DI'CTION. *n. s.* [*diction*, French; *dictio*, Latin.] Stile; language; expression.

There appears in every part of his *diction*, or expression, a kind of noble and bold purity. *Dryden.*

DI'CTIONARY. *n. s.* [*dictionarium*, Latin.] A book containing the words of any language in alphabetical order, with explanations of their meaning; a lexicon; a vocabulary; a word-book.

Some have delivered the polity of spirits, and left an account that they stand in awe of charms, spells, and conjurations; that they are afraid of letters and characters, notes and dashes, which, set together, do signify nothing; and not only in the *dictionary* of man, but in the subtler vocabulary of satan. *Brown's Vulgar Errours, b. i. c. 10.*

Is it such a horrible fault to translate simulacra images? I see what a good thing it is to have a good catholick *dictionary.* *Still.*

An army, or a parliament, is a collection of men; a *dictionary*, or nomenclature, is a collection of words. *Watts.*

DID. of *do.* [ꝺiꝺ, Saxon.]

1. The preterite of do.

Thou can'st not say I *did* it. *Shakespeare.*
What *did* that greatness in a woman's mind?
Ill lodg'd and weak to act what it design'd. *Dryd. Aurengz.*

2. The sign of the preter-imperfect tense, or perfect.

When *did* his pen on learning fix a brand,
Or rail at arts he *did* not understand. *Dryden.*

3. It is sometimes used emphatically; as, I *did* really love him.

DIDA'CTICAL. } *adj.* [διδακτικός.] Preceptive; giving precepts:
DIDA'CTICK. } as a *didactick* poem is a poem that gives rules for some art; as the Georgicks.

The means used to this purpose are partly *didactical*, and partly protreptical, demonstrating the truth of the gospel; and then urging the professors of those truths to be stedfast in the faith, and to beware of infidelity. *Ward on Infidelity.*

DI'DAPPER. *n. s.* [from *dip.*] A bird that dives into the water.

DIDA'SCALICK. *adj.* [διδασκαλικός.] Preceptive; didactick; giving precepts in some art.

I found it necessary to form some story, and give a kind of body to the poem: under what species it may be comprehended, whether *didascalick* or heroick, I leave to the judgment of the criticks. *Prior.*

To DI'DDER. *v. a.* [*diddern*, Teut. *zittern*, Germ.] To quake with cold; to shiver. A provincial word. *Skinner.*

DIDST. The second person of the preter tense of *do.* See DID.

Oh last and best of Scots! who *didst* maintain
Thy country's freedom from a foreign reign. *Dryden.*

To DIE. *v. a.* [ꝺeaȝ, Saxon, a colour.] To tinge; to colour; to stain.

So much of death her thoughts
Had entertain'd, as *dy'd* her cheeks with pale. *Milt. P. L.*
All white, a virgin saint she sought the skies;
For marriage, though it sullies not, it *dies.* *Dryden.*

DIE. *n. s.* [from the verb.] Colour; tincture; stain; hue acquired.

It will help me nothing
To plead mine innocence; for that *die* is on me,
Which makes my whit'st part black. *Shakesp. Henry VIII.*

We have dainty works of feathers of wonderful lustre, excellent *dies*, and many. *Bacon's New Atlantis.*

Darkness we see emerges into light,
And shining suns descend to sable night:
Ev'n heav'n itself receives another *die*,
When weary'd animals in slumbers lie
Of midnight ease; another, when the gray
Of morn preludes the splendor of the day. *Dryden's Fables.*

It is very surprising to see the images of the mind stamped upon the aspect; to see the cheeks take the *die* of the passions, and appear in all the colours and complexions of thought. *Collier of the Aspect.*

First this
She sends on earth; then that of deeper *die*
Steals soft behind. *Thompson's Summer, l. 1685.*

To

To Die. *v. n.* [ꝺeaꝺian, Saxon.]

1. To lose life; to expire; to pass into another state of existence.

Thou do'st kill me with thy unkind falshood; and it grieves me not to *die*, but it grieves me that thou art the murtherer. *Sidney.*

Nor did the third his conquests long survive,
Dying ere scarce he had begun to live. *Addis. Ovid. Metam.*
Oh let me live my own, and *die* so too!
To live and *die* is all I have to do? *Pope's Epistles.*

2. To perish by violence or disease.

The dira only served to confirm him in his first opinion, that it was his destiny to *die* in the ensuing combat. *Dryden.*

Talk not of life or ransom, he replies,
Patroclus dead, whoever meets me, *dies:*
In vain a single Trojan sues for grace;
But least the sons of Priam's hateful race:
Die then, my friend! what boots it to deplore!
The great, the good Patroclus is no more!
He, far thy better, was foredoom'd to *die*;
And thou, dost thou, bewail mortality. *Pope's Hom. Iliad.*

3. It has *by* before an instrument of death.

4. *Of* before a disease.

They often come into the world clear, and with the appearance of sound bodies; which, notwithstanding, have been infected with disease, and have *died* of it, or at least have been very infirm. *Wiseman's Surgery.*

5. *For* commonly before a privative, and *of* before a positive cause.

At first she startles, then she stands amaz'd;
At last with terror she from thence doth fly,
And loaths the wat'ry glass wherein she gaz'd,
And shuns it still, although *for* thirst she *die*. *Davies.*
He in the loaden vineyard *dies for* thirst. *Addison.*

Hipparchus being passionately fond of his own wife, who was enamoured of Bathyllus, leaped and *died of* his fall. *Addis.*

6. To be punished with death.

If I *die* for it, as no less is threatened me, the king my old master must be relieved. *Shakesp. King Lear.*

What is the love of our neighbour?
—The valuing him as the image of God, one for whom Christ *died*. *Hammond's Pract. Catech.*

7. To be lost; to perish; to come to nothing.

How now, my lord, why do you keep alone?
Of sorriest fancies your companion making,
Using those thoughts which should indeed have *died*
With them they think on. *Shakesp. Macbeth.*

If any sovereignty, on account of his property, had been vested in Adam, which in truth there was not, it would have *died* with him. *Locke.*

Whatever pleasure any man may take in spreading whispers, he will find greater satisfaction by letting the secret *die* within his own breast. *Spectator*, N°. 595.

8. To sink; to faint.

His heart *died* within him, and he became as a stone. 1 *Sa.*

9. [In theology.] To perish everlastingly.

So long as God shall live, so long shall the damned *die*. *Hakewell on Providence.*

10. To languish with pleasure or tenderness.

To sounds of heav'nly harps she *dies* away,
And melts in visions of eternal day. *Pope's Eloi. to Abelard.*

11. To vanish.

This battle fares like to the morning's war,
When *dying* clouds contend with growing light. *Sh. H.* VI.

The smaller stains and blemishes may *die* away and disappear, amidst the brightness that surrounds them; but a blot of a deeper nature casts a shade on all the other beauties, and darkens the whole character. *Addison's Spectator*, N°. 256.

12. [In the stile of lovers.] To languish with affection.

The young men acknowledged in love-letters, that they *died* for Rebecca. *Tatler*, N°. 110.

13. To wither as a vegetable.

Except a corn of wheat fall into the ground, and *die*, it abideth alone; but if it *die*, it bringeth forth much fruit. *John* xii. 25.

14. To grow vapid, as liquor.

Die. *n. s.* pl. *dice.* [*dé*, French; *dis*, Welsh.]

1. A small cube, marked on its faces with numbers from one to six, which gamesters throw in play.

Keep a gamester from the *dice*, and a good student from his book, and it is wonderful. *Shakesp. Merry Wives of Windsor.*

I have set my life upon a cast,
And I will stand the hazard of the *die*. *Shakes. Richard* III.

He knows which way the lot and the *die* shall fall, as perfectly as if they were already cast. *South's Sermons.*

2. Hazard; chance;

Eftsoons his cruel hand Sir Guyon staid,
Temp'ring the passion with advisement slow,
And must'ring might on enemy dismay'd;
For th' equal *die* of war he well did know. *Fairy Queen.*
So both to battle fierce arranged are;
In which his harder fortune was to fall
Under my spear: such is the *die* of war. *Fairy Queen, b.* i.
Thine is the adventure, thine the victory:
Well has thy fortune turn'd the *die* for thee. *Dryden's Fables.*

3. Any cubick body.

Die. *n. s.* plur. *dies.* The stamp used in coinage.

There have been such variety of *dies* made use of by Wood in stamping his money, that it makes the discovery of counterfeits more difficult. *Swift.*

Di'er. *n. s.* [from *die.*] One who follows the trade of dying; one who dies cloaths.

The fleece, that has been by the *dier* stain'd,
Never again its native whiteness gain'd. *Waller.*

There were some of very low rank and professions, who acquired great estates: coblers, *diers*, and shoemakers gave publick shows to the people. *Arbuthnot on Coins.*

DI'ET. *n. s.* [*diœta*, low Latin; διαιτα.]

1. Food; provisions for the mouth; victuals.

They cared for no other delicacy of fare, or curiosity of *diet*, than to maintain life. *Raleigh's History of the World.*

Time may come, when men
With angels may participate; and find
No inconvenient *diet*, nor too light fare. *Milt. Par. Lost.*

No part of *diet*, in any season, is so healthful, so natural, and so agreeable to the stomach, as good and well-ripened fruits. *Temple.*

Milk appears to be a proper *diet* for human bodies, where acrimony is to be purged or avoided; but not so proper where the canals are obstructed, it being void of all saline quality. *Arbuthnot on Aliments.*

2. Food regulated by the rules of medicine, for the prevention or cure of any disease.

I commend rather some *diet* for certain seasons, than frequent use of physick; for those *diets* alter the body more, and trouble it less. *Bacon, Essay* 31.

I restrained myself to so regular a *diet*, as to eat flesh but once a day, and little at a time, without salt or vinegar. *Temp.*

To Di'et. *v. a.* [from the noun.]

1. To feed by the rules of medicine.

She *diets* him with fasting every day,
The swelling of his wounds to mitigate,
And made him pray both early and eke late. *Fairy Queen.*

Shew a while like fearful war,
To *diet* rank minds sick of happiness,
And purge th' obstructions, which begin to stop
Our very veins of life. *Shakespeare's Henry* IV. *p.* ii.

He was not taken well; he had not din'd:
The veins unfill'd, our blood is cold; and then
We powt upon the morning, are unapt
To give or to forgive; but when we've stuff'd
These pipes, and these conveyances of blood,
With wine and feeding, we have suppler souls
Than in our priestlike fasts; therefore I'll watch him
'Till he be *dieted* to my request. *Shakesp. Coriolanus.*

I will attend my husband, be his nurse,
Diet his sickness; for it is my office. *Shakesp. Com. of Err.*

Henceforth my early care
Shall 'tend thee, and the fertile burden ease
'Till *dieted* by thee, I grow mature
In knowledge as the gods, who all things know. *Milt. P. L.*

We have lived upon expedients, of which no country had less occasion: we have *dieted* a healthy body into a consumption, by plying it with physick instead of food. *Swift.*

2. To give food to.

I'm partly led to *diet* my revenge,
For that I do suspect the lusty Moor
Hath leapt into my seat. *Shakespeare's Othello.*

3. To board; to supply with diet.

To Di'et. *v. n.*

1. To eat by rules of physick.

2. To eat; to feed.

I join with thee calm peace and quiet;
Spare fast, that oft with gods doth *diet*. *Milton.*

Diet-drink. *n. s.* [*diet* and *drink.*] Medicated liquors; drink brewed with medicinal ingredients.

The observation will do that better than the lady's *diet-drinks*, or apothecary's medicines. *Locke.*

Di'et. *n. s.* [from *dies*, an appointed day, *Skinner:* from *diet*, an old German word signifying a multitude, *Junius.*] An assembly of princes or estates.

An emperour in title without territory, who can ordain nothing of importance but by a *diet*, or assembly of the estates of many free princes, ecclesiastical and temporal. *Raleigh.*

Di'etary. *adj.* [from *diet.*] Pertaining to the rules of diet. *Dict.*

Di'eter. *n. s.* [from *diet.*] One who prescribes rules for eating; one who prepares food by medicinal rules.

He sauc'd our broth as Juno had been sick,
And he her *dieter*. *Shakespeare's Cymbeline.*

Diete'tical. } *n. s.* [διαιτητική.] Relating to diet; belonging
Diete'tick. } to the medicinal cautions about the use of food.

He

He received no other counsel than to refrain from cold drink, which was but a *dietetical* caution, and such as, without a journey to Æsculapius, culinary prescription might have been afforded. *Brown's Vulgar Errours, b.* i.

This book was received by the publick with the respect that was due to the importance of its contents: it became the subject of conversation, and produced even sects in the *dietetick* philosophy. *Arbuthnot on Aliments, Pref.*

To DI'FFER. *v. n.* [*differo*, Latin.]

1. To be distinguished from; to have properties and qualities not the same with those of another person or thing.

If the pipe be a little wet on the inside, it will make a *differing* sound from the same pipe dry. *Bacon's Natural History.*

Thy prejudices, Syphax, wont discern
What virtues grow from ignorance and choice,
Nor how the hero *differs* from the brute. *Addison's Cato.*

The several parts of the same animal *differ* in their qualities. *Arbuthnot on Aliments.*

2. To contend; to be at variance.

A man that is of judgment and understanding shall sometimes hear ignorant men *differ*, and know well within himself that those which so *differ* mean one thing, and yet they themselves never agree. *Bacon's Essays.*

There are certain measures to be kept, which may leave a tendency rather to gain than to irritate those who *differ* with you in their sentiments. *Addison's Freeholder*, N°. 19.

Here uncontroll'd you may in judgment sit;
We'll never *differ* with a crowded pit. *Rowe.*

Others *differ* with me about the truth and reality of these speculations. *Cheyne's Phil. Princ.*

3. To be of a contrary opinion.

In things purely speculative, as these are, and no ingredients of our faith, it is free to *differ* from one another in our opinions and sentiments. *Burnet's Theory of the Earth.*

DI'FFERENCE. *n. s.* [*differentia*, Latin.]

1. State of being distinct from something; contrariety to identity.

Where the faith of the holy church is one, a *difference* between customs of the church doth no harm. *Hooker, b.* iv.

2. The quality by which one differs from another.

This nobility, or *difference* from the vulgar, was not in the beginning given to the succession of blood, but to the succession of virtue. *Raleigh's History of the World.*

Thus born alike, from virtue first began
The *diff'rence* that distinguish'd man from man:
He claim'd no title from descent of blood,
But that which made him noble, made him good. *Dryden.*

Though it be useful to discern every variety that is to be found in nature, yet it is not convenient to consider every *difference* that is in things, and divide them into distinct classes, under every such *difference*. *Locke.*

3. The disproportion between one thing and another caused by the qualities of each.

You shall see great *difference* betwixt our Bohemia and your Sicilia. *Shakespeare's Winter's Tale.*

Oh the strange *difference* of man and man!
To thee a woman's services are due;
My fool usurps my body. *Shakespeare's King Lear.*

Here might be seen a great *difference* between men practised to fight, and men accustomed only to spoil. *Hayward.*

4. Dispute; debate; quarrel; controversy.

What was the *difference*?
——It was a contention in publick. *Shakes. Cymbeline.*

He is weary of his life that hath a *difference* with any of them, and will walk abroad after daylight. *Sandys.*

5. Distinction.

Our constitution, under a good administration, does not only make a *difference* between the guilty and the innocent, but, even among the guilty, between such as are more or less criminal. *Addison's Freeholder*, N°. 31.

Nothing could have fallen out more unluckily than that there should be such *differences* among them, about that which they pretend to be the only means of ending *differences*. *Tillots.*

6. Point in question; ground of controversy.

Are you acquainted with the *difference*,
That holds this present question in the court? *Shakespeare.*

7. A logical distinction.

Some are never without a *difference*, and commonly, by amusing men with a subtilty, blanch the matter. *Bacon's Essays.*

8. Evidences of distinction; differential marks.

Henry had the title of sovereign, yet did not put those things in execution which are the true marks and *differences* of sovereignty. *Davies.*

To DI'FFERENCE. *v. a.* [from the noun.] To cause a difference; to make one thing not the same as another.

Most are apt to seek all the differences of letters in those articulating motions; whereas several combinations of letters are framed by the very same motions of those organs, which are commonly observed, and are *differenced* by other concurrent causes. *Holder's Elements of Speech.*

Grass *differenceth* a civil and well cultivated region from a barren and desolate wilderness. *Ray on the Creation.*

We see nothing that *differences* the courage of Mnestheus from that of Sergesthus. *Pope's Essay on Homer.*

DI'FFERENT. *adj.* [from *differ.*]

1. Distinct; not the same.

Happiness consists in things which produce pleasure, and, in the absence of those, which cause any pain: now these, to *different* men, are very *different* things. *Locke.*

There are covered galleries that lead from the palace to five *different* churches. *Addison on Italy.*

2. Of many contrary qualities.

The Britons change
Sweet native home for unaccustom'd air,
And other climes, where *diff'rent* food and soil
Portend distempers. *Phillips.*

3. Unlike; dissimilar.

Neither the shape of faces, nor the age, nor the colour, ought to be alike in all figures, any more than the hair; because men are as *different* from each other, as the regions in which they are born are *different*. *Dryden's Dufresnoy.*

DIFFERE'NTIAL *Method*, is applied to the doctrine of innnitesimals, or infinitely small quantities, called the arithmetick of fluxions; about the invention of which there has been a contest between Leibnitz and Sir Isaac Newton. It consists in descending from whole quantities to their infinitely small differences, and comparing together these infinitely small differences, of what kind soever they be: and from thence it takes the name of the *differential* calculus, or analysis of infinitesimals. *Harris.*

DI'FFERENTLY. *adv.* [from *different.*] In a different manner.

He may consider how *differently* he is affected by the same thought, which presents itself in a great writer, from what he is when he finds it delivered by a person of an ordinary genius. *Addison's Spectator*, N°. 409

DI'FFERINGLY. *adv.* [from *differing.*] In a different manner.

Such protuberant and concave parts of a surface may remit the light so *differingly*, as to vary a colour. *Boyle.*

DI'FFICIL. *adj.* [*difficilis*, Latin.]

1. Difficult; hard; not easy; not obvious. Little used.

That that should give motion to an unwieldy bulk, which itself hath neither bull nor motion, is of as *difficil* apprehension as any mystery in nature. *Glanv. Sceps. c.* 4.

Latin was not more *difficil*,
Than to a blackbird 'tis to whistle. *Hudibras.*

2. Scrupulous; hard to be persuaded.

The cardinal finding the pope *difficil* in granting the dispensation, doth use it as a principal argument, concerning the king's merit towards that see, that he had touched none of those deniers which had been levied by popes in England. *Bac.*

DI'FFICILNESS. *n. s.* [from *difficil.*] Difficulty to be persuaded; incompliance; impracticability.

There be that in their nature do not affect the good of others: the lighter sort of malignity turneth but to a crossness, or frowardness, or aptness to oppose, or *difficilness*, or the like; but the deeper sort, to envy and mere mischief. *Bacon's Essays.*

DIFFICULT. *adj.* [*difficilis*, Latin.]

1. Hard; not easy; not facil.

It is *difficult* in the eyes of this people. *Zachar.*

2. Troublesome; vexatious.

3. Hard to please; peevish; morose.

DI'FFICULTLY. *adv.* [from *difficult*] Hardly; with difficulty.

A man who has always indulged himself in the full enjoyment of his station, will *difficultly* be persuaded to think any methods unjust that offer to continue it. *Rogers's Sermons.*

DI'FFICULTY. *n. s.* [from *difficult*; *difficulte*, French.]

1. Hardness; contrariety to easiness or facility.

The religion which, by this covenant, we engage ourselves to observe, is a work of labour and *difficulty*; a service that requires our greatest care and attention to the discharge of it. *Rogers, Serm.* 13.

2. That which is hard to accomplish; that which is not easy.

They mistake *difficulties* for impossibilities: a pernicious mistake certainly; and the more pernicious, for that men are seldom convinced of it, 'till their convictions do them no good. *South's Sermons.*

3. Distress; opposition.

Thus, by degrees, he rose to Jove's imperial seat:
Thus *difficulties* prove a soul legitimately great. *Dryden.*

4. Perplexity in affairs; uneasiness of circumstances.

They lie at present under some *difficulties*, by reason of the emperor's displeasure, who has forbidden the importation of their manufactures. *Addison on Italy.*

5. Objection; cavil.

Men should consider, that raising *difficulties* concerning the mysteries in religion, cannot make them more wise, learned, or virtuous. *Swift.*

To DIFFI'DE. *v. n.* [*diffido*, Latin.] To distrust; to have no confidence in.

With hope and fear
The woman did the new solution hear:
The man *diffides* in his own augury,
And doubts the gods. *Dryden.*

DI'FFIDENCE. *n. s.* [from *diffide.*] Distrust, want of confidence; timidity.

No man almost thought himself secure, and men durst scarce commune or talk one with another; but there was a general *diffidence* every where. *Bacon's Henry* VII.

You have brought scandal
To Israel, *diffidence* of God, and doubt
In feeble hearts, propense enough before
To waver. *Milton's Agonistes.*

If the evidence of its being, or that this is its true sense, be only on probable proofs, our assent can reach no higher than an assurance or *diffidence*, arising from the more or less apparent probability of the proofs. *Locke.*

Be silent always, when you doubt your sense;
And speak, though sure, with seeming *diffidence.* *Pope.*

Whatsoever atheists think on, or whatsoever they look on, all do administer some reasons for suspicion and *diffidence*, least possibly they may be in the wrong; and then it is a fearful thing to fall into the hands of the living God. *Bentley's Serm.*

DI'FFIDENT. *adj.* [from *diffide.*] Not confident; not certain; distrustful.

I am not so confident of my own sufficiency as not willingly to admit the counsel of others; but yet I am not so *diffident* of myself, as brutishly to submit to any man's dictates. *K.Charles.*

Be not *diffident*
Of wisdom; she deserts thee not, if thou
Dismiss not her, when most thou need'st her nigh. *Milton.*

I was really so *diffident* of it, as to let it lie by me these two years, just as you now see it. *Pope.*

Pliny speaks of the Seres, the same people with the Chinese, as being very shy and *diffident* in their manner of dealing. *Arbuthnot.*

Distress makes the humble heart *diffident.* *Clarissa.*

To DIFFI'ND. *v a.* [*diffindo*, Latin.] To cleave in two; to split. *Dict.*

DIFFI'SION. *n. s.* [*diffissio*, Latin.] The act of cleaving or splitting. *Dict.*

DIFFLA'TION. *n. s.* [*difflare*, Latin.] The act of scattering with a blast of wind. *Dict.*

DI'FFLUENCE. } *n. s.* [from *diffluo*, Latin.] The quality of
DI'FFLUENCY. } falling away on all sides; the effect of fluidity; the contrary to consistency.

Ice is water congealed by the frigidity of the air, whereby it acquireth no new form; but rather a consistence or determination of its *diffluency*, and omitteth not its essence, but condition of fluidity. *Brown's Vulgar Errours, b.* ii. *c.* 1.

DI'FFLUENT. *adj.* [*diffluens*, Latin.] Flowing every way; not consistent; not fixed.

DI'FFORM. *adj.* [from *forma*, Latin.] Contrary to uniform; having parts of different structure; dissimilar; unlike; irregular; as a *difform* flower, one of which the leaves are unlike each other.

The unequal refractions of *difform* rays proceed not from any contingent irregularities; such as are veins, an uneven polish, or fortuitous position of the pores of glass. *Newton.*

DIFFO'RMITY. *n. s.* [from *difform.*] Diversity of form; irregularity; dissimilitude.

While they murmur against the present disposure of things, they rest not in their established natures; but desire in them a *difformity* from the primitive rule, and the idea of that mind, that formed all things best. *Brown's Vulgar Errours, b.* i. *c.* 11.

DIFFRA'NCHISEMENT. *n. s.* [*franchise*, French.] The act of taking away the privileges of a city.

To DIFFU'SE. *v. a.* [*diffusus*, Latin.]

1. To pour out upon a plane, so that the liquor may run every way.

When these waters began to rise at first, long before they could swell to the height of the mountains, they would *diffuse* themselves every way. *Burnet's Theory of the Earth.*

2. To spread; to scatter; to disperse.

Wisdom had ordain'd
Good out of evil to create; instead
Of spirits malign, a better race to bring
Into their vacant room, and thence *diffuse*
His good to worlds, and ages, infinite. *Milton's Par. Lost.*

No sect wants its apostles to propagate and *diffuse* it. *Decay of Piety.*

A chief renown'd in war,
Whose race shall bear aloft the Latian name,
And through the conquer'd world *diffuse* our fame. *Dryden.*

His eyes *diffus'd* a venerable grace,
And charity itself was in his face. *Dryden's Good Parson.*

DIFFU'SE. *adj.* [*diffusus*, Latin.]

1. Scattered; widely spread.
2. Copious; not concise.

DIFFU'SED. *participial adj.* [from *diffuse*] This word seems to have signified, in *Shakespeare's* time, the same as wild, uncouth, irregular.

Let them from forth a sawpit rush at once,
With some *diffused* song. *Shakes. Merry Wives of Windsor.*

He grows like savages,
To swearing and stern looks, *diffus'd* attire,
And every thing that seems unnatural. *Shakesp. Henry* V.

DIFFU'SEDLY. *adv.* [from *diffused.*] Widely; dispersedly; in manner of that which is spread every way.

DIFFU'SEDNESS. *n. s.* [from *diffused.*] The state of being diffused; dispersion.

DIFFU'SELY. *adv.* [from *diffuse.*]

1. Widely; extensively.
2. Copiously; not concisely.

DIFFU'SION. *n. s.* [from *diffuse.*]

1. Dispersion; the state of being scattered every way.

Whereas all bodies act either by the communication of their natures, or by the impressions and signatures of their motions, the *diffusion* of species visible seemeth to participate more of the former operation, and the species audible of the latter. *Bacon's Natural History*, N°. 269.

A sheet of very well sleeked marbled paper did not cast distinct colours upon the wall, nor throw its light with an equal *diffusion*; but threw its beams, unstained and bright, to this and that part of the wall. *Boyle on Colours.*

2. Copiousness; exuberance of stile.

DIFFU'SIVE. *adj.* [from *diffuse.*]

1. Having the quality of scattering any thing every way.

Diffusive of themselves, where-e'er they pass
They make that warmth in others they expect:
Their valour works like bodies on a glass,
And does its image on their men project. *Dryd. Ann. Mir.*

2. Scattered; dispersed; having the quality of suffering diffusion.

No man is of so general and *diffusive* a lust, as to prosecute his amours all the world over. *South's Sermons.*

The stars, no longer overlaid with weight,
Exert their heads from underneath the mass,
And upward shoot, and kindle as they pass,
And with *diffusive* light adorn their heav'nly place. *Dryden.*

Cherish'd with hope, and fed with joy it grows;
Its cheerful buds their opening bloom disclose,
And round the happy soil *diffusive* odour flows. *Prior.*

3. Extended; in full extension.

They are not agreed among themselves where infallibility is seated; whether in the pope alone, or a council alone, or in both together, or in the *diffusive* body of Christians. *Tillots.*

DIFFU'SIVELY. *adv.* [from *diffusive.*] Widely; extensively; every way.

DIFFU'SIVENESS. *n. s.* [from *diffusive.*]

1. Extension; dispersion; the power of diffusing; the state of being diffused.
2. Want of conciseness; large compass of expression.

The fault that I find with a modern legend, is its *diffusiveness*: you have sometimes the whole side of a medal overrun with it. *Addison on Ancient Medals.*

To DIG. *v. a.* preter. *dug*, or *digged*; part. pass. *dug*, or *digged.* [dic, Saxon, a ditch; *dyger*, Danish, to dig.]

1. To pierce with a spade.

Then said he unto me, Son of man, *dig* now in the wall; and when I had *digged* in the wall, I beheld a door. *Ezek.* viii. 8.

2. To form by digging.

Seek with heart and mouth to build up the walks of Jerusalem, which you have broken down; and to fill up the mines that you have *digged* by craft and subtlety, to overthrow the same. *Whitgift.*

He built towers in the desert, and *digged* many wells; for he had much cattle. 2 *Chro.* xxvi. 10.

3. To cultivate the ground by turning it with a spade.

The walls of your garden, without their furniture, look as ill as those of your house; so that you cannot *dig* up your garden too often. *Temple.*

Be first to *dig* the ground, be first to burn
The branches lopt. *Dryden's Virg. Georg.* ii.

4. To pierce with a sharp point.

A rav'nous vulture in his open'd side,
Her crooked beak and cruel talons try'd;
Still for the growing liver *digg'd* his breast,
The growing liver still supply'd the feast. *Dryden's Æn.*

5. To gain by digging.

It is *digged* out of even the highest mountains, and indeed all other parts of the earth contingently and indifferently; as the pyrites. *Woodward.*

Nor was the ground alone requir'd to bear
Her annual income to the crooked share;
But greedy mortals, rummaging her store,
Digg'd from her entrails first the precious ore. *Dryd Ovid.*

To DIG. *v. a.* To work with a spade; to work in making holes, or turning the ground.

They long for death, but it cometh not; and *dig* for it more than far hid treasures. *Job* iii. 21.

They have often *dug* into lands that are described in old authors, as the places where such particular statues or obelisks stood, and have seldom failed of success in their pursuits. *Addison's Travels.*

To DIG *up. v. a.* To throw up that which is covered with earth.

If

If I *digg'd up* thy forefather's graves,
And hung their rotten coffins up in chains,
It would not slake mine ire. *Shak. H.* VI.

DI'GERENT. *adj.* [*digerens*, Latin.] That which has the power of digesting, or causing digestion. *Dict.*

DIGE'ST. *n. s.* [*digesta*, Latin.] The pandect of the civil law, containing the opinions of the ancient lawyers.

I had a purpose to make a particular *digest*, or recompilement of the laws of mine own nation. *Bacon.*

Laws in the *digest* shew that the Romans applied themselves to trade. *Arbuthnot on Coins.*

To DIGE'ST. *v. a.* [*digero*, *digestum*, Latin.]

1. To distribute into various classes or repositories; to range or dispose methodically.

2. To concoct in the stomach, so as that the various particles of food may be applied to their proper use.

If little faults, proceeding on distemper,
Shall not be wink'd at, how shall we stretch our eye,
When capital crimes, chew'd, swallow'd, and *digested*,
Appear. *Shakespeare's Henry* V.

Each then has organs to *digest* his food;
One to beget, and one receive the brood. *Prior.*

3. To soften by heat, as in a boiler, or in a dunghil: a chemical term.

4. To range methodically in the mind; to apply knowledge by meditation to its proper use.

A few chosen friends, who sometimes deign
To bless my humble roof, with sense refin'd,
Learning *digested* well. *Thomson's Winter, l.* 550.

5. To reduce to any plan, scheme, or method.

Our play
Leaps o'er the vaunt and firstlings of those broils,
'Ginning i' th' middle: starting thence away,
To what may be *digested* in a play. *Shakes. Troil. and Cressid.*

6. To receive without loathing or repugnance; not to reject.

First, let us go to dinner.
—Nay, let me praise you while I have a stomach.
—No, pray thee, let it serve for table talk;
Then howsoe'er thou speak'st, 'mong other things
I shall *digest* it. *Shakespeare's Merchant of Venice.*

The pleasance of numbers, that rudeness and barbarism might the better taste and *digest* the lessons of civility. *Peacham.*

7. To receive and enjoy.

Cornwal and Albany,
With my two daughters dowers, *digest* the third. *Shakesp.*

8. [In chirurgery.] To dispose a wound; to generate pus in order to a cure.

To DIGE'ST. *v. n.* To generate matter as a wound, and tend to a cure.

DIGE'STER. *n. s.* [from *digest.*]

1. He that digests or concocts his food.

People that are bilious and fat, rather than lean, are great eaters and ill *digesters*. *Arbuthnot on Coins.*

2. A strong vessel or engine, contrived by M. Papin, wherein to boil, with a very strong heat, any bony substances, so as to reduce them into a fluid state. *Quincy.*

3. That which causes or strengthens the concoctive power.

Rice is of excellent use for all illnesses of the stomach, a great restorer of health, and a great *digester*. *Temple.*

DIGE'STIBLE. *adj.* [from *digest.*] That which is capable of being digested or concocted in the stomach.

Those medicines that purge by stool enter not into the mesentery veins; but are, at the first, not *digestible* by the stomach, and therefore move immediately downwards to the guts. *Bacon's Natural History*, N°. 43.

DIGE'STION. *n. s.* [from *digest.*]

1. The act of digesting or concocting food in the stomach.

Now good *digestion* wait on appetite,
And health on both. *Shakespeare's Macbeth.*

Digestion is a fermentation begun, because there are all the requisites of such a fermentation; heat, air, and motion: but it is not a complete fermentation, because that requires a greater time than the continuance of the aliment in the stomach: vegetable putrefaction resembles very much animal *digestion*. *Arbuthnot on Aliments.*

Quantity of food cannot be determined by measures and weights, or any general Lessian rules; but must vary with the vigour or decays of age or of health, and the use or disuse of air or of exercise, with the changes of appetite; and then, by what every man may find or suspect of the present strength or weakness of *digestion*. *Temple.*

Every morsel to a satisfied hunger, is only a new labour to a tired *digestion*. *South's Sermons.*

2. The preparation of matter by a chemical heat.

We conceive, indeed, that a perfect good concoction, or *digestion*, or maturation of some metals, will produce gold. *Bacon's Natural History*, N°. 327.

Did chymick chance the furnaces prepare,
Raise all the labour-houses of the air,
And lay crude vapours in *digestion* there. *Blackmore.*

3. Reduction to a plan; the act of methodising; the maturation of a scheme.

The *digestion* of the counsels in Sweden is made in senate, consisting of forty counsellors, who are generally the greatest men. *Temple.*

4. The act of disposing a wound to generate matter.

5. The disposition of a wound or sore to generate matter.

DIGE'STIVE. *adj.* [from *digest.*]

1. Having the power to cause digestion, or to strengthen the stomach.

A chilifactory menstruum, or a *digestive* preparation, drawn from species or individuals, whose stomachs peculiarly dissolve lapideous bodies. *Brown's Vulgar Errours, b.* ii. *c.* 5.

2. Capable by heat to soften and subdue.

The earth and sun were in that very same state; the one active, piercing, and *digestive* by its heat; the other passive, receptive, and stored with materials for such a production. *Hale's Origin of Mankind.*

3. Considerating; methodising.

To business, ripen'd by *digestive* thought,
This future rule is into method brought. *Dryden.*

DIGE'STIVE. *n. s.* [from *digest.*] An application which disposes a wound to generate matter.

I dressed it with *digestives*. *Wiseman of Abscesses.*

DI'GGER. *n. s.* [from *dig.*] One that opens the ground with a spade.

When we visited mines, we have been told by *diggers*, that even when the sky seemed clear, there would suddenly arise a steam so thick, that it would put out their candles. *Boyle.*

To DIGHT. *v. a.* [dihtan, to prepare, to regulate, Saxon.] To dress; to deck; to bedeck; to embellish; to adorn.

On his head his dreadful hat he *dight*,
Which maketh him invisible to sight. *Hubberd's Tale.*

Let my due feet never fail
To walk the studious cloisters pale,
And love the high embowed roof,
With antick pillar massy proof,
And storied windows richly *dight*,
Casting a dim religious light. *Milton.*

Just so the proud insulting lass
Array'd and *dighted* Hudibras. *Hudibras, p.* i. *cant.* 3.

DI'GIT. *n. s.* [*digitus*, Latin.]

1. The measure of length containing three fourths of an inch.

If the inverted tube of mercury be but twenty-five *digits* high, or somewhat more, the quicksilver will not fall, but remain suspended in the tube, because it cannot press the subjacent mercury with so great a force as doth the incumbent cylinder of the air, reaching thence to the top of the atmosphere. *Boyle's Spring of the Air.*

2. The twelfth part of the diameter of the sun or moon.

3. Any of the numbers expressed by single figures; any number to ten.

Not only the number seven and nine, from considerations abstruse, have been extolled by most, but all or most of other *digits* have been as mystically applauded. *Brown's Vulg. Errours.*

DI'GITATED. *adj.* [from *digitus*, Latin.] Branched out into divisions like fingers; as a *digitated* leaf is a leaf composed of many small leaves.

For animals multifidous, or such as are *digitated*, or have several divisions in their feet, there are but two that are uniparous; that is, men and elephants. *Brown's Vulgar Errours.*

DIGLADIA'TION. *n. s.* [*digladiatio*, Latin.] A combat with swords; any quarrel or contest.

Aristotle seems purposely to intend the cherishing of controversial *digladiations*, by his own affection of an intricate obscurity. *Glanv. Sceps. c.* 19.

DI'GNIFIED. *adj.* [from *dignify.*] Invested with some dignity: it is used chiefly of the clergy.

Abbots are stiled *dignified* clerks, as having some dignity in the church. *Ayliffe's Parergon.*

DIGNIFICA'TION. *n. s.* [from *dignify.*]

I grant that where a noble and ancient descent and merit meet in any man, it is a double *dignification* of that person. *Walton's Angler.*

To DI'GNIFY. *v. a.* [from *dignus* and *facio*, Latin.]

1. To advance; to prefer; to exalt. Used chiefly of the clergy.

2. To honour; to adorn; to give lustre.

Such a day,
So fought, so follow'd, and so fairly won,
Came not 'till now to *dignify* the times,
Since Cæsar's fortunes! *Shakespeare's Henry* IV.

Not that we think us worthy such a guest,
But your worth will *dignify* our feast. *Ben. Johnson's Epigr.*

No turbots *dignify* my boards;
But gudgeons, flounders, what my Thames affords. *Pope.*

DI'GNITARY. *n. s.* [from *dignus*, Latin.] A clergyman advanced to some dignity; to some rank above that of a parochial priest.

If there be any *dignitaries*, whose preferments are perhaps not liable to the accusation of superfluity, they may be persons of superior merit. *Swift.*

DI'GNITY. *n. s.* [*dignitas*, Latin.]

1. Rank of elevation.

Angels are not any where spoken so highly of as our Lord

and Saviour Jesus Christ, and are not in *dignity* equal to him. *Hooker, b.* ii. *s.* 6.

2. Grandeur of mien; elevation of aspect.

Some men have a native *dignity*, which will procure them more regard by a look, than others can obtain by the most imperious commands. *Clarissa.*

4. Advancement; preferment; high place.

Faster than spring-time show'rs comes thought on thought,
And not a thought but thinks on *dignity*. *Shakesf. Henry* VI.
For those of old,
And these late *dignities* heap'd up to them,
Shakespeare's Macbeth.

4. [Among ecclesiasticks.] By a *dignity* we understand that promotion or preferment to which any jurisdiction is annexed. *Ayliffe's Parergon.*

5. Maxims; general principles; κυρίαι δόξαι.

The sciences concluding from *dignities*, and principles known by themselves, receive not satisfaction from probable reasons, much less from bare and peremptory asseverations. *Brown's Vulgar Errours, b.* i. *c.* 7.

6. [In astrology.] The planet is in dignity when it is in any sign.

DIGNO'TION. *n. s.* [from *dignosco*, Lat.] Distinction; distinguishing mark.

That temperamental *dignotions*, and conjecture of prevalent humours, may be collected from spots in our nails, we are not averse to concede. *Brown's Vulgar Errours, b.* v. *c.* 21.

To DIGRE'SS. *v. n.* [*digressus*, Latin.]

1. To turn out of the road.

2. To depart from the main design of a discourse, or chief tenour of an argument.

In the pursuit of an argument there is hardly room to *digress* into a particular definition, as often as a man varies the signification of any term. *Locke.*

3. To wander; to expatiate.

It seemeth, to *digress* no farther, that the Tartarians, spreading so far, cannot be the Israelites. *Brerewood.*

4. To go out of the right way, or common track; to transgress; to deviate.

I am come to keep my word,
Though in some part am forced to *digress*,
Which at more leisure I will so excuse
As you shall well be satisfied. *Shak. Taming of the Shrew.*
Thy noble shape is but a form of wax,
Digressing from the valour of a man. *Shak. Romeo and Juliet.*

DIGRE'SSION. *n. s.* [*digressio*, Latin.]

1. A passage deviating from the main tenour or design of a discourse.

The good man thought so much of his late conceived commonwealth, that all other matters were but *digressions* to him. *Sidney, b.* i.

He, she knew, would intermix
Grateful *digressions*, and solve high dispute
With conjugal caresses. *Milton's Paradise Lost, b.* viii.
Here some *digression* I must make, t' accuse
Thee, my forgetful and ungrateful muse. *Denham.*

To content and fill the eye of the understanding, the best authors sprinkle their works with pleasing *digressions*, with which they recreate the minds of their readers. *Dryd. Dufresn.*

2. Deviation.

The *digression* of the sun is not equal; but near the equinoctial intersections, it is right and greater; near the solstices, more oblique and lesser. *Brown's Vulgar Errours, b.* vi. *c.* 4.

DIJUDICA'TION. *n. s.* [*dijudicatio*, Latin.] Judicial distinction.

DIKE *n. s.* [dic, Saxon; *dyk*, Erse.]

1. A channel to receive water.

The *dykes* are fill'd, and with a roaring sound
The rising rivers float the nether ground. *Dryd. Virg. Geo.*
The king of *dykes!* than whom no sluice of mud
With deeper sable blots the silver flood. *Pope's Dunciad.*

2. A mound to hinder inundations.

God, that breaks up the flood-gates of so great a deluge, and all the art and industry of man is not sufficient to raise up *dykes* and ramparts against it. *Cowley's Davideis.*

To DILA'CERATE. *v. a.* [*dilacero*, Latin.] To tear; to rend; to force in two.

The infant, at the accomplished period, struggling to come forth, *dilacerates* and breaks those parts which restrained him before. *Brown's Vulgar Errours, b.* iii. *c.* 6.

DILACERA'TION. *n. s.* [from *dilaceratio*, Latin.] The act of rending in two.

The greatest sensation of pain is by the obstruction of the small vessels, and *dilaceration* of the nervous fibres. *Arbuthnot on Diet.*

To DILA'NIATE. *v. a.* [*dilanio*, Latin.] To tear; to rend in pieces.

Rather than they would *dilaniate* the entrails of their own mother, and expose her thereby to be ravished, they met half way in a gallant kind. *Howel's Engl. Tears.*

To DILA'PIDATE. *v. a.* [*dilapido*, Latin.] To ruin; to throw down.

DILAPIDA'TION. *n. s.* [*dilapidatio*, Latin.] The incumbent's suffering the chancel, or any other edifices of his ecclesiastical living, to go to ruin or decay, by neglecting to repair the same: and it likewise extends to his committing, or suffering to be committed, any wilful waste in or upon the glebe-woods, or any other inheritance of the church. *Ayliffe's Parergon.*

'Tis the duty of all church-wardens to prevent the *dilapidations* of the chancel and mansion-house belonging to the rector or vicar. *Ayliffe's Parergon.*

DILATABI'LITY. *n. s.* [from *dilatable.*] The quality of admitting extension.

We take notice of the wonderful *dilatability* or extensiveness of the gullets of serpents: I have taken two adult mice out of the stomach of an adder, whose neck was not bigger than my little finger. *Ray on the Creation.*

By this continual contractibility and *dilatability*, by different degrees of heat, the air is kept in a constant motion. *Arbuthn.*

DILA'TABLE. *adj.* [from *dilate.*] Capable of extension.

The windpipe divides itself into a great number of branches called bronchia: these end in small air-bladders, *dilatable* and contractable, capable to be inflated by the admission of air, and to subside at the expulsion of it. *Arbuthnot on Aliment.*

DILATA'TION. *n. s.* [from *dilatatio*, Latin.]

1. The act of extending into greater space.

The motions of the tongue, by contraction and *dilatation*, are so easy and so subtle, that you can hardly conceive or distinguish them aright. *Holder.*

2. The state of being extended; the state in which the parts are at more distance from each other.

Joy causeth a cheerfulness and vigour in the eyes; singing, leaping, dancing, and sometimes tears: all these are the effects of the *dilatation*, and coming forth of the spirits into the outward parts, which maketh them more lively and stirring. *Bacon's Natural History.*

The image of the sun should be drawn out into an oblong form, either by a *dilatation* of every ray, or by any other casual inequality of the refractions. *Newton's Opt. Experim.*

To DILA'TE. *v. a.* [*dilato*, Latin.]

1. To extend; to spread out; to enlarge.

But ye thereby much greater glory gate,
Than had ye sorted with a prince's peer;
For now your light doth more itself *dilate*,
And in my darkness greater doth appear. *Spenser.*
Satan alarm'd,
Collecting all his might, *dilated* stood,
Like Teneriff, or Atlas, unremov'd. *Milton's Paradise Lost.*
Opener of mine eyes,
Dim erst; *dilated* spirits, ampler heart,
And growing up to godhead: which for thee
Chiefly I sought; without thee, can despise. *Milt. Pa. Lost.*
Through all the air his sounding strings *dilate*
Sorrow, like that which touch'd our hearts of late. *Waller.*
Diffus'd, it rises in a higher sphere;
Dilates its drops, and softens into air. *Prior.*
I mark the various fury of the winds;
These neither seasons guide, nor order binds:
They now *dilate*, and now contract their force;
Various their speed but endless is their course. *Prior.*

The second refraction would spread the rays one way as much as the first doth another, and so *dilate* the image in breadth as much as the first doth in length. *Newton's Opt.*

2. To relate at large; to tell diffusely and copiously.

But he would not endure that woful theam
For to *dilate* at large; but urged sore,
With piercing words, and pitiful implore,
Him hasty to arise. *Fairy Queen, b.* ii. *cant.* 5. *stan.* 37.
I observing,
Took once a pliant hour, and found good means
To draw from her a prayer of earnest heart,
That I would all my pilgrimage *dilate*,
Whereof by parcels she had something heard,
But not distinctively. *Shakespeare's Othello.*

To DILA'TE. *v. n.*

1. To widen; to grow wide.

His heart *dilates* and glories in his strength. *Addison.*

2. To speak largely and copiously.

It may be behoveful for princes, in matters of grace, to transact the same publickly, and by themselves; or their ministers to *dilate* upon it, and improve their lustre, by any addition or eloquence of speech. *Clarendon.*

DILA'TOR. *n. s.* [from *dilate.*] That which widens or extends.

The buccinatores, or blowers up of the cheeks, and the *dilators* of the nose, are too strong in cholerick people. *Arb.*

DI'LATORINESS. *n. s.* [from *dilatory.*] The quality of being dilatory; slowness; sluggishness.

DI'LATORY. *adj.* [*dilatoire*, French; *dilatorius*, Lat.] Tardy; slow; given to procrastination; addicted to delay; sluggish; loitering.

An inferior council, after former tedious suits in a higher court, would be but *dilatory*, and so to little purpose. *Hayward.*

What wound did ever heal but by degrees?

Thou

Thou know'ſt we work by wit, and not by witchcraft;
And wit depends on *dilatory* time. *Shakeſpeare's Othello.*
Theſe cardinals trifle with me: I abhor
This *dilatory* ſloth, and tricks of Rome. *Shak. Henry* VIII.
Dilatory fortune plays the jilt
With the brave, noble, honeſt, gallant man,
To throw herſelf away on fools and knaves *Otway's Orph.*

A *dilatory* temper commits innumerable cruelties without deſign *Addiſon's Spectator*, Nº. 469.

DILE'CTION. *n. ſ.* [*dilectio*, Latin.] The act of loving; kindneſs.

So free is Chriſt's *dilection*, that the grand condition of our felicity is our belief. *Boyle's Seraph. Love.*

DILE'MMA. *n. ſ.* [δίλημμα.]

1. An argument equally concluſive by contrary ſuppoſitions. A young rhetorician applied to an old ſophiſt to be taught the art of pleading, and bargained for a certain reward to be paid, when he ſhould gain a cauſe. The maſter ſued for his reward, and the ſcholar endeavoured to elude his claim by a *dilemma*: If I gain my cauſe, I ſhall withold your pay, becauſe the judge's award will be againſt you; if I loſe it, I may withhold it, becauſe I ſhall not yet have gained a cauſe. On the contrary, ſays the maſter, if you gain your cauſe, you muſt pay me, becauſe you are to pay me when you gain a cauſe; if you loſe it, you muſt pay me, becauſe the judges will award it.

A *dilemma*, that biſhop Morton the chancellor uſed, to raiſe benevolence, ſome called his fork, and ſome his crutch. *Bacon's Henry* VII.

Hope, whoſe weak being ruin'd is
Alike if it ſucceed, and if it miſs;
Whom good or ill does equally confound,
And both the horns of fate's *dilemma* wound. *Cowley.*

2. A difficult or doubtful choice; a vexatious alternative.

A ſtrong *dilemma* in a deſp'rate caſe!
To act with infamy, or quit the place. *Swift.*
A dire *dilemma*; either way I'm ſped;
If foes, they write, if friends, they read me dead. *Pope.*

DI'LIGENCE. *n. ſ.* [*diligentia*, Latin.] Induſtry; aſſiduity; conſtancy in buſineſs; continuance of endeavour; unintermitted application; the contrary to idleneſs.

Do thy *diligence* to come ſhortly unto me. 2 *Tim.* iv. 9.

Brethren, give *diligence* to make your calling and election ſure. 2 *Pet.* i. 10.

DI'LIGENT. *adj.* [*diligens*, Latin.]

1. Conſtant in application; perſevering in endeavour; aſſiduous; not idle; not negligent; not lazy.

Seeſt thou a man *diligent* in his buſineſs? he ſhall ſtand before kings. *Prov.* xxii. 29.

2. Conſtantly applied; proſecuted with activity and perſeverance; aſſiduous.

And the judges ſhall make *diligent* inquiſition. *Deutr* xix.

DI'LIGENTLY. *adv.* [from *diligent*.] With aſſiduity; with heed and perſeverance; not careleſly; not idly; not negligently.

If you inquire not attentively and *diligently*, you ſhall never be able to diſcern a number of mechanical motions. *Bacon.*

The ancients have *diligently* examined in what conſiſts the beauty of good poſtures. *Dryden's Dufreſnoy.*

DILL. *n. ſ.* [dile, Saxon.]

It hath a ſlender, fibroſe, annual root: the leaves are like thoſe of fennel; the ſeeds are oval, plain, ſtreaked, and bordered.

Dill is raiſed of ſeed, which is ripe in Auguſt. *Mortimer.*

DILU'CID. *adj.* [*dilucidus*, Latin.]

1. Clear; plain; not opaque.
2. Clear; plain; not obſcure.

To DILU'CIDATE. *v. a.* [from *dilucidare*, Latin.] To make clear or plain; to explain; to free from obſcurity.

I ſhall not traduce or extenuate, but explain and *dilucidate*, according to the cuſtom of the ancients. *Brown's Vu. Err. Pr.*

DILUCIDA'TION. *n. ſ.* [from *dilucidatio*.] The act of making clear; explanation; expoſition.

DI'LUENT. *adj.* [*diluens*, Latin.] Having the power to thin and attenuate other matter.

DI'LUENT. *n. ſ.* [from the adjective.] That which thins other matter.

There is no real *diluent* but water: every fluid is diluent, as it contains water in it. *Arbuthnot on Aliments.*

To DILU'TE. *v. a.* [*diluo*, Latin.]

1. To make thin; to attenuate by the admixture of other parts.

Drinking a large doſe of *diluted* tea, as ſhe was ordered by a phyſician, ſhe got to bed. *Locke.*

The aliment ought to be thin to *dilute*, demulcent to temper, or acid to ſubdue. *Arbuthnot on Aliments.*

2. To make weak.

If the red and blue colours were more *dilute* and weak, the diſtance of the images would be leſs than an inch; and if they were more intenſe and full, that diſtance would be greater. *Newton's Opt. Pro.* i. *Th.* I.

The chamber was dark, leſt theſe colours ſhould be *diluted* and weakened by the mixture of any adventitious light. *Newt.*

DILU'TER. *n. ſ.* [from *dilute*.] That which makes any thing elſe thin.

Water is the only *diluter*, and the beſt diſſolvent of moſt of the ingredients of our aliment. *Arbuthnot on Aliments.*

DILU'TION. *n. ſ.* [*dilutio*, Lat.] The act of making any thing thin or weak.

Oppoſite to *dilution* is coagulation, or thickening, which is performed by diſſipating the moſt liquid parts by heat, or by inſinuating ſome ſubſtances, which make the parts of the fluid cohere more ſtrongly. *Arbuthnot on Aliments.*

DILU'VIAN. *adj.* [from *diluvium*, Lat.] Relating to the deluge.

Suppoſe that this *diluvian* lake ſhould riſe to the mountain tops in one place, and not diffuſe itſelf equally into all countries about. *Burnet's Theory of the Earth.*

DIM. *adj.* dimme, Saxon; *dy*, Welſh; *dow*, Erſe.]

1. Not having a quick ſight; not ſeeing clearly.

For her true form, how can my ſpark diſcern,
Which, *dim* by nature, art did never clear? *Davies.*

2. Dull of apprehenſion.

The underſtanding is *dim*, and cannot by its natural light diſcover ſpiritual truths. *Rogers's Sermons.*

3. Not clearly ſeen; obſcure; imperfectly diſcovered.

We might be able to aim at ſome *dim* and ſeeming conception, how matter might begin to exiſt by the power of that eternal firſt Being. *Locke.*

Something, as *dim* to our internal view,
Is thus perhaps the cauſe of all we do. *Pope, Epiſt.* i.

4. Obſtructing the act of viſion; not luminous; ſomewhat dark.

Her face right wond'rous fair did ſeem to be,
That her broad beauty's beam great brightneſs threw
Through the *dim* ſhade, that all men might it ſee. *Fai. Qu.*

To DIM. *v. a.* [from the adjective.]

1. To cloud; to darken; to hinder from a full perception of light, and free exerciſe of viſion.

As where the Almighty's lightning brand does light,
It *dims* the dazed eyen, and daunts the ſenſes quite. *Fa. Qu.*

It hath been obſerved by the ancients, that much uſe of Venus doth *dim* the ſight; and yet eunuchs, which are unable to generate, are neverthelefs alſo *dim* ſighted. *Bacon's N. Hiſt.*

Every one declares againſt blindneſs, and yet who almoſt is not fond of that which *dims* his ſight? *Locke.*

For thee I *dim* theſe eyes, and ſtuff this head,
With all ſuch reading as was never read. *Pope's Dunciad.*

2. To make leſs bright; to obſcure.

A ſhip that through the ocean wide,
By conduct of ſome ſtar doth make her way,
When as a ſtorm hath *dimm'd* her truſty guide,
Out of her courſe doth wander far aſtray. *Spenſer.*
Siſter, have comfort: all of us have cauſe
To wail the *dimming* of our ſhining ſtar;
But none can help our harms by wailing them. *Shak. R.* III.
Thus while he ſpake, each paſſion *dimm'd* his face,
Thrice chang'd. *Milton's Paradiſe Loſt, b.* iv. *l.* 114.

DIME'NSION. *n. ſ.* [*dimenſio*, Latin.] Space contained in any thing; bulk; extent; capacity. It is ſeldom uſed but in the plural. The three dimenſions are length, breadth, and depth.

He try'd
The tomb, and found the ſtrait *dimenſions* wide. *Dryden.*

My gentleman was meaſuring my walls, and taking the *dimenſions* of the room. *Swift.*

DIME'NSIONLESS. *adj.* [from *dimenſion*.] Without any definite bulk.

In they paſs'd
Dimenſionleſs through heav'nly doors. *Milton's Paradiſe Loſt.*

DIME'NSIVE. *adj.* [*dimenſus*, Latin.] That which marks the boundaries or outlines.

All bodies have their meaſure, and their ſpace;
But who can draw the ſoul's *dimenſive* lines? *Davies.*

DIMICA'TION. *n. ſ.* [*dimicatio*, Latin.] A battle; the act of fighting; conteſt. *Dict.*

DIMIDIA'TION. *n. ſ.* [*dimidiatio*, Latin.] The act of halving; diviſion into two equal parts. *Dict.*

To DIMI'NISH. *v. a.* [*diminuo*, Latin.]

1. To make leſs by abſciſſion or deſtruction of any part: the oppoſite to increaſe.

That we call good which is apt to cauſe or increaſe pleaſure, or *diminiſh* pain in us. *Locke.*

2. To impair; to leſſen; to degrade.

Impiouſly they thought
Thee to *diminiſh*, and from thee withdraw
The number of thy worſhippers. *Milton's Paradiſe Loſt.*

4. To take any thing from that to which it belongs: the contrary to add.

Nothing was *diminiſhed* from the ſafety of the king by the impriſonment of the duke. *Hayward.*

Ye ſhall not add unto the word which I command you, neither ſhall you *diminiſh* aught from it. *Deut.* iv. 2.

To DIMI'NISH. *v. n.* To grow leſs; to be impaired.

What judgment I had increaſes rather than *diminiſhes*; and thoughts, ſuch as they are, come crowding in ſo faſt upon me, that my only difficulty is to chuſe or to reject. *Dryden.*

Crete's

Crete's ample fields *diminiſh* to our eye;
Before the Boreal blaſts the veſſels fly. *Pope's Odyſſey.*

DIMI'NISHINGLY. *adv.* [from *diminiſh.*] In a manner tending to vilify, or leſſen.

I never heard him cenſure, or ſo much as ſpeak *diminiſhingly* of any one that was abſent. *Locke.*

DIMINU'TION. *n. ſ.* [*diminutio*, Latin.]

1. The act of making leſs; oppoſed to augmentation.

The one is not capable of any *diminution* or augmentation at all by men; the other apt to admit both. *Hooker, b.* iii.

2. The ſtate of growing leſs; oppoſed to increaſe.

The gravitating power of the ſun is tranſmitted through the vaſt bodies of the planets without any *diminution*, ſo as to act upon all their parts, to their very centres, with the ſame force, and according to the ſame laws, as if the part upon which it acts were not ſurrounded with the body of the planet. *Newton's Opt.*

Finite and infinite ſeem to be looked upon as the modes of quantity, and to be attributed primarily to thoſe things which are capable of increaſe or *diminution*. *Locke.*

3. Diſcredit; loſs of dignity; degradation.

Gladly to thee
Heroick laurel'd Eugene yields the prime;
Nor thinks it *diminution* to be rank'd
In military honour next. *Phillips.*

They might raiſe the reputation of another, though they are a *diminution* to his. *Addiſon's Spectator*, Nº. 256.

4. Deprivation of dignity; injury of reputation.

Make me wiſe by thy truth, for my own ſoul's ſalvation, and I ſhall not regard the world's opinion or *diminution* of me. *King Charles.*

5. [In architecture.] The contraction of the diameter of a column, as it aſcends.

DIMI'NUTIVE. *adj.* [*diminutivus*, Latin.] Small; little; narrow; contracted.

The poor wren,
The moſt *diminutive* of birds, will fight,
Her young ones in her neſt, againſt the owl. *Shak. Macbeth.*

It is the intereſt of mankind, in order to the advance of knowledge, to be ſenſible they have yet attained it but in poor and *diminutive* meaſure. *Glanv. Scepſ. Preface.*

The light of man's underſtanding is but a ſhort, *diminutive*, contracted light, and looks not beyond the preſent. *South.*

If the ladies ſhould once take a liking to ſuch a *diminutive* race of lovers, we ſhould, in a little time, ſee mankind epitomized, and the whole ſpecies in miniature. *Addiſ. Guardian.*

They know how weak and aukward many of thoſe little *diminitive* diſcourſes are. *Watts's Improvement of the Mind.*

DIMI'NUTIVE. *n. ſ.* [from the adjective.]

1. A word formed to expreſs littleneſs; as *lapillus*, in Latin, a *little ſtone*; *maiſonette*, in French, a *little houſe*; *manniken*, in Engliſh, a *little man.*

He afterwards proving a dainty and effeminate youth, was commonly called, by the *diminutive* of his name, Peterkin or Perkin. *Bacon's Henry* VII.

Sim, while but Sim, in good repute did live;
Was then a knave, but in *diminutive*. *Cotton.*

2. A ſmall thing: a ſenſe not now in uſe.

Follow his chariot; monſter-like, be ſhewn
For poor'ſt *diminutives*, for doits! *Shakeſ. Ant. and Cleopatra.*

DIMI'NUTIVELY. *adv.* [from *diminutive.*] In a diminutive manner.

DIMI'NUTIVENESS. *n. ſ.* [from *diminutive.*] Smalneſs; littleneſs; pettyneſs; want of bulk; want of dignity.

DI'MISH. *adj.* [from *dim.*] Somewhat dim; ſomewhat obſcure.

'Tis true, but let it not be known,
My eyes are ſomewhat *dimiſh* grown;
For nature, always in the right,
To your decays adapts my ſight. *Swift.*

DI'MISSORY. *adj.* [*dimiſſorius*, Latin.] That by which a man is diſmiſſed to another juriſdicton.

A biſhop of another dioceſs ought neither to ordain or admit a clerk, with the conſent of his own proper biſhop, and without the letters *dimiſſory*. *Ayliffe's Parergon.*

DI'MITTY. *n. ſ.* A fine kind of fuſtian, or cloath of cotton.

I directed a trowze of fine dimitty. *Wiſeman's Surgery.*

DI'MLY. *adv.* [from *dim.*]

1. Not with a quick ſight; not with a clear perception.

Unſpeakable! who ſitt'ſt above theſe heav'ns,
To us inviſible, or *dimly* ſeen,
In theſe thy loweſt works. *Milton's Paradiſe Loſt, b.* v.

2. Not brightly; not luminouſly.

In the beginning of our pumping the air, the match appeared well lighted, though it had almoſt filled the receiver with its plentiful fumes; but by degrees it burnt more and more *dimly*. *Boyle's Spring of the Air.*

I ſaw th' angelick guards from earth aſcend,
Griev'd they muſt now no longer man attend;
The beams about their temples *dimly* ſhone;
One would have thought the crime had been their own. *Dry.*

DI'MNESS. *n. ſ.* [from *dim.*]

1. Dulneſs of ſight.

2. Want of apprehenſion; ſtupidity.

Anſwerable to this *dimneſs* of their perception was the whole ſyſtem and body of their religion. *Decay of Piety.*

DI'MPLE. *n. ſ.* [*dint*, a hole; *dintle*, a little hole; by a careleſs pronunciation *dimple*. *Skinner.*] The ſame cavity or depreſſion in the cheek or chin.

The *dimple* of the upper lip is the common meaſure of them all. *Grew's Coſm. Sac. b.* i. *c.* 5.

In her forehead's fair half-round,
Love ſits in open triumph crown'd;
He in the *dimple* of her chin,
In private ſtate, by friends is ſeen. *Prior.*

To DI'MPLE. *v. n.* [from the noun.] To ſink in ſmall cavities, or little inequalities.

The wild waves maſter'd him, and ſuck'd him in,
And ſmiling eddies *dimpled* on the main. *Dryd. Ann. Mirab.*
Eternal ſmiles his emptineſs betray,
As ſhallow ſtreams run *dimpling* all away. *Pope, Epiſtle* ii.

DI'MPLED. *adj.* [from *dimple.*] Set with dimples.

On each ſide her
Stood pretty *dimpled* boys like ſmiling Cupids. *Sh. Ant. and Cl.*

DI'MPLY. *adj.* [from *dimple.*] Full of dimples; ſinking in little inequalities.

As the ſmooth ſurface of the *dimply* flood,
The ſilver-ſlipper'd virgin lightly trod. *Wharton's Iſis.*

DIN. *n. ſ.* [dyn, a noiſe; dynan, to make a noiſe, Sax. *dyna*, to thunder, Iſlandick.] A loud noiſe; a violent and continued ſound.

And all the way he roared as he went,
That all the foreſt with aſtoniſhment
Thereof did tremble; and the beaſts therein
Fled faſt away from that ſo dreadful *din*. *Hubberd's Tale.*

O, 'twas a *din* to fright a monſter's ear;
To make an earthquake: ſure, it was the roar
Of a whole herd of lions. *Shakeſpeare's Tempeſt.*

While the cock with lively *din*
Scatters the rear of darkneſs thin,
And to the ſtack or the barn-door
Stoutly ſtruts, his dame before. *Milton.*

Now night over heav'n
Inducing darkneſs, grateful truce impos'd,
And ſilence, on the odious *din* of war. *Milton's Par. Loſt.*

How, while the troubled elements around,
Earth, water, air, the ſtunning *din* reſound,
Through ſtreams of ſmoak and adverſe fire he rides,
While ev'ry ſhot is levell'd at his ſides. *Smith.*

Some independent ideas, of no alliance to one another, are, by education, cuſtom, and the conſtant *din* of their party, ſo coupled in their minds, that they always appear there together. *Locke.*

To DIN. *v. a.* [from the noun.]

1. To ſtun with noiſe; to haraſs with clamour.

Rather live
To bait thee for his bread, and *din* your ears
With hungry cries. *Otway's Venice Preſerved.*

2. To impreſs with violent and continued noiſe.

What ſhall we do, if his majeſty puts out a proclamation commanding us to take Wood's half-pence? This hath been often *dinned* in my ears. *Swift.*

To DINE. *v. n.* [*diner*, French.] To eat the chief meal about the middle of the day.

Perhaps ſome merchant hath invited him,
And from the mart he's ſomewhere gone to dinner:
Good ſiſter, let us *dine*, and never fret. *Shakeſpeare.*

Myſelf, he, and my ſiſter,
To-day did *dine* together. *Shakeſp. Comedy of Errours.*

He would *dine* with him the next day. *Clarendon.*

Thus, of your heroes and brave boys,
With whom old Homer makes ſuch noiſe,
The greateſt actions I can find,
Are, that they did their work and *din'd*. *Prior.*

To DINE. *v. a.* To give a dinner to; to feed.

Boil this reſtoring root in gen'rous wine,
And ſet beſide the door the ſickly ſtock to *dine*. *Dryd Virg.*

DINE'TICAL. *adj.* [δινητικός.] Whirling round; vertiginous.

Some of late have concluded, from ſpots in the ſun, which appear and diſappear again, that, beſides the revolution it maketh with its orbs, it hath alſo a *dinetical* motion, and rolls upon its own poles. *Brown's Vulgar Errours, b.* vi. *c.* 6.

A ſpherical figure is moſt commodious for *dinetical* motion, or revolution upon its own axis. *Ray on the Creation.*

To DING. pret. *dung. v. a.* [*dringen*, Dutch.]

1. To daſh with violence.

2. To impreſs with force.

To DING. *v. n.* To bluſter; to bounce; to huff. A low word.

He huffs and *dings* at ſuch a rate, becauſe we will not ſpend the little we have left to get him the title and eſtate of lord Strut. *Arbuthnot's Hiſtory of John Bull.*

DING-DONG. *n. ſ.* A word by which the ſound of bells is imitated.

Let

Let us all ring fancy's knell;
Ding, dong bell. *Shakespeare's Merchant of Venice.*

DI'NGLE. *n. s.* [from ꝺen, or ꝺin, a hollow, Saxon.] A hollow between hills; a dale.

I know each lane, and every alley green,
Dingle or bushy dell of this wild wood;
And every bosky bourn from side to side,
My daily walks and ancient neighbourhood. *Milton.*

DINING-ROOM. *n. s.* [*dine* and *room.*] The principal apartment of the house; the room where entertainments are made.

He went out from the *dining-room* before he had fallen into errour by the intemperance of his meat, or the deluge of drink. *Taylor's Rule of living holy.*

DI'NNER. *n. s.* [*diner*, French.] The chief meal; the meal eaten about the middle of the day.

Let me not stay a jot for *dinner*:
Go, get it ready. *Shakespeare's King Lear.*

Before *dinner* and supper, as often as it is convenient, or can be had, let the publick prayers of the church, or some parts of them, be said publickly in the family. *Taylor.*

The jolly crew, unmindful of the past,
The quarry share, their plenteous *dinner* haste. *Dryd. Æn.*

DINNER-TIME. *n. s.* [*dinner* and *time.*] The time of dining.

At *dinner-time*,
I pray you, have in mind where we must meet. *Shakespeare.*

Then from the mint walks forth the man of rhyme,
Happy to catch me just at *dinner-time*. *Pope, Epistle* ii.

DINT. *n. s.* [ꝺynt, Saxon.]

1. A blow; a stroke.

Much daunted with that *dint*, her sense was daz'd;
Yet kindling rage, herself she gather'd round. *Fairy Queen.*

Neither vainly hope
To be invulnerable in these bright arms,
Though temper'd heav'nly; for that mortal *dint*,
Save he who reigns above, none can resist. *Milt. Par. Lost.*

2. The mark made by a blow; the cavity remaining after a violent pressure.

Now you weep; and, I perceive, you feel
The *dint* of pity. *Shakespeare's Julius Cæsar.*

He embrac'd her naked body o'er,
And, straining hard the statue, was afraid
His hands had made a *dint* and hurt the maid. *Dryden.*

3. Violence; force; power.

We are to wrest the whole Spanish monarchy out of the hands of the enemy; and, in order to it, to work our way into the heart of his country by *dint* of arms. *Addison.*

The dewlap'd bull now chafes along the plain,
While burning love ferments in ev'ry vein;
His well arm'd front against his rival aims,
And by the *dint* of war his mistress claims. *Gay.*

To DINT. *v. a.* [from the noun.] To mark with a cavity by a blow, or violent impression.

With greedy force each other doth assail,
And strike so fiercely, that they do impress
Deep *dinted* furrows in the batter'd mails:
The iron walls to ward their blows are weak and frail. *F. Q.*

Leave, leave, fair bride, your solitary bone,
No more shall you return to it alone;
It nurseth sadness; and your body's print,
Like to a grave, the yielding down doth *dint*. *Donne.*

Deep *dinted* wrinkles on her cheeks she draws;
Sunk are her eyes, and toothless are her jaws. *Dryd. Æn.*

DINUMERA'TION. *n. s.* [*dinumeratio*, Lat.] The act of numbering out singly.

DIOCE'SAN. *n. s.* [from *diocess.*] A bishop as he stands related to his own clergy or flock.

I have heard it has been advised by a *diocesan* to his inferior clergy, that they should read some of the most celebrated sermons printed by others, for the instruction of their congregation. *Tatler*, N°. 57.

DI'OCESS. *n. s.* [*diœcesis.* A Greek word compounded of διὰ and ὄμησις.] The circuit of every bishop's jurisdiction; for this realm has two divisions, one into shires or counties, in respect of temporal policy; another into *diocess*, in respect of jurisdiction ecclesiastical. *Cowel.*

None ought to be admitted by any bishop, but such as have dwelt and remained in his *diocess* a convenient time. *Whitgift.*

He should regard the bishop of Rome as the islanders of Jersey and Guernsey do him of Constance in Normandy; that is, nothing at all, since by that French bishop's refusal to swear unto our king, those isles were annexed to the *diocess* of Winchester. *Raleigh's Essays.*

St. Paul looks upon Titus as advanced to the dignity of a prince, ruler of the church, and intrusted with a large *diocess*, containing many particular cities, under the immediate government of their respective elders, and those deriving authority from his ordination. *South.*

DIO'PTRICAL. } *n. s.* [διόπτομαι.] Affording a medium for the
DIO'PTRICK. } sight; assisting the sight in the view of distant objects.

Being excellently well furnished with *dioptrical* gla... had not been able to see the sun spotted. *Bo...*

View the asperities of the moon through a *dioptrick* glass, and venture at the proportion of her hills by their shadows. *More's Antidote against Atheism.*

DIO'PTRICKS. *n. s.* A part of opticks, treating of the different refractions of the light passing through different mediums; as the air, water, glasses, &c. *Harris.*

DIORTHRO'SIS. *n. s* [διόρθρωσις, of διορθρόω, to make strait.] A chirurgical operation, by which crooked or distorted members are made even, and restored to their primitive and regular shape. *Harris.*

To DIP. *v. a.* particip. *dipped*, or *dipt.* [ꝺippan, Saxon; *doopen*, Dutch.]

1. To immerge; to put into any liquor.

The person to be baptized may be *dipped* in water; and such an immersion or dipping ought to be made thrice, according to the canon. *Ayliffe's Parergon.*

Old Corineus compass'd thrice the crew,
And *dipp'd* an olive-branch in holy dew,
Which thrice he sprinkl'd round, and thrice aloud
Invok'd the dead, and then dismiss'd the crowd. *Dryd. Æn.*

He turn'd a tyrant in his latter days,
And from the bright meridian where he stood,
Descending, *dipp'd* his hands in lovers blood. *Dryd. Fables.*

The kindred arts shall in their praise conspire;
One *dip* the pencil, and one string the lyre. *Pope's Epistles.*

Now on fancy's easy wing convey'd,
The king descended to th' Elysian shade;
There in a dusky vale, where Lethe rolls,
Old Bavius sits to *dip* poetick souls. *Pope's Dunciad, b.* iii.

So fishes rising from the main,
Can soar with moisten'd wings on high;
The moisture dry'd, they sink again,
And *dip* their wings again to fly. *Swift.*

2. To moisten; to wet.

And though not mortal, yet a cold shudd'ring dew
Dips me all o'er, as when the wrath of Jove
Speaks thunder. *Milton.*

3. To be engaged in any affair.

When men are once *dipt*, what with the encouragements of sense, custom, facility, and shame of departing from what they have given themselves up to, they go on 'till they are stifled. *L'Estrange, Fab.* 126.

In Richard's time, I doubt, he was a little *dipt* in the rebellion of the commons. *Dryden's Fables.*

4. To engage as a pledge; generally used for the first mortgage.

Be careful still of the main chance, my son;
Put out the principal in trusty hands,
Live on the use, and never *dip* thy lands. *Dryden's Pers.*

To DIP. *v. n.*

1. To sink; to immerge.

We have snakes in our cups, and in our dishes; and whoever *dips* too deep will find death in the pot. *L'Estrange's Fab.*

2. To enter; to pierce.

The vulture *dipping* in Prometheus' side,
His bloody beak with his torn liver dy'd. *Granville.*

3. To enter slightly into any thing.

When I think all the repetitions are struck out in a copy, I sometimes find more upon *dipping* in the first volume. *Pope.*

4. To drop by chance into any mass; to chuse by chance.

With what ill thoughts of Jove art thou possess't?
Wouldst thou prefer him to some man? Suppose
I *dipp'd* among the worst, and Staius chose? *Dryden's Pers.*

DIPCHI'CK. *n. s.* [from *dip* and *chick.*] The name of a bird.

Dipchick is so named of his diving and littleness. *Carew.*

DIPE'TALOUS. *adj.* [δὶς and πέταλον.] Having two flower-leaves.

DI'PPER. *n. s.* [from *dip.*] One that dips in the water.

DIPPING *Needle. n. s.* A device which shews a particular property of the magnetick needle, so that, besides its polarity or verticity, which is its direction of altitude, or height above the horizon, when duly poised about an horizontal axis, it will always point to a determined degree of altitude, or elevation above the horizon, in this or that place respectively. *Phil.*

DI'PHTHONG. *n. s.* [δίφθογγος.] A coalition of two vowels to form one sound; as *vain, leaf, Cæsar.*

We see how many disputes the simple and ambiguous nature of vowels created among grammarians, and how it has begot the mistake concerning *diphthongs*: all that are properly so are syllables, and not *diphthongs*, as is intended to be signified by that word. *Holder's Elements of Speech.*

Make a *diphthong* of the second *eta* and *iota*, instead of their being two syllables, and the objection is gone. *Notes on the Iliad.*

DI'PLOE. *n. s.* The inner plate or lamina of the skull.

DIPLO'MA. *n. s* [δίπλωμα.] A letter or writing conferring some privilege, so called because they used formerly to be written on waxed tables, and folded together.

DI'PSAS. *n. s.* [Latin, from διψάω, to thirst.] A serpent, whose bite produces the sensation of unquenchable thirst.

Scorpion, and asp, and amphisbœna dire,
Cerastes horn'd, hydrus, and elops drear,
And *dipsas*. *Milton's Par. Lost, b.* x. *l.* 526.

DI'PTOTE *n. s.* [δίπτωτα.] A noun consisting of two cases only. *Clark.*

DI'PTYCH. *n. s.* [*diptycha*, Latin.] A register of bishops and martyrs.

The commemoration of saints was made out of the *diptychs* of the church, as appears by multitudes of places in St. Austin. *Still.*

DIRE. *adj.* [*dirus*, Latin.] Dreadful; dismal; mournful; horrible; terrible; evil in a great degree.

Your eye in Scotland
Would create soldiers, and make women fight,
To doff their *dire* distresses. *Shakespeare's Macbeth.*

More by intemperance die
In meats, and drinks, which on the earth shall bring
Diseases *dire*; of which a monstrous crew
Before thee shall appear. *Milton's P. Lost, b.* xi. *l.* 474.

Hydras, and gorgons, and chimæras *dire* *Milton.*

Or what the cross, *dire*-looking planet smites,
Or hurtful worm with canker'd venom bites. *Milton.*

Dire was the tossing, deep the groans, despair
Tended the sick. *Milton.*

Discord! *dire* sister of the slaughtered pow'r,
Small at her birth, but rising ev'ry hour;
While scarce the skies her horrid head can bound,
She stalks on earth, and shakes the world around. *Pope's Il.*

DIRE'CT. *adj.* [*directus*, Latin.]

1. Strait, not crooked.

2. Not oblique.

The ships would move in one and the same surface; and consequently must needs encounter when they either advance towards one another in *direct* lines, or meet in the intersection of cross lines. *Bentley's Serm.*

3. [In astronomy.] Appearing to an eye on earth to move progressively through the zodiac, not retrograde.

Two geomantic figures were display'd,
Above his head, a warrior and a maid,
One when *direct*, and one when retrograde. *Dryd Fab.*

4. Not collateral, as the grandson succeeds his grandsire in a *direct* line.

5. Apparently tending to some end.

Such was as then the state of the king, as it was no time by *direct* means to seek her. And such was the state of his captivated will, as he would delay no time of seeking her. *Sid.*

He that does this, will be able to cast off all that is superfluous; he will see what is pertinent, what coherent, what is *direct* to, what slides by the question. *Locke.*

6. Open; not ambiguous.

There be, that are in nature faithful and sincere, and plain and *direct*; not crafty and involved. *Bacon's Essay,* 21.

7. Plain; express.

He no where, that I know, says it in *direct* words. *Locke.*

To DIRE'CT. *v. a.* [*dirigo*, *directum*, Latin.]

1. To aim in a strait line.

Two eagles from a mountain's height,
By Jove's command *direct* their rapid flight. *Pope's Od.*

2. To point against as a mark.

The spear flew hissing through the middle space,
And pierc'd his throat, *directed* at his face. *Dryd. Æn.*

3. To regulate; to adjust.

It is not in man that walketh to *direct* his steps. *Jer.* x. 23.

Wisdom is profitable to *direct*. *Ecclus* x. 10.

All that is in a man's power, is to mind what the ideas are that take their turns in his understanding; or else to *direct* and sort, and call in such as he desires. *Locke.*

4. To prescribe certain measure; to mark out a certain course.

He *directeth* it under the whole heavens, and his lightening unto the ends of the earth. *Job* xxxvii. 3.

5. To order; to command.

DIRE'CTER. *n. s.* [*director*, Latin.]

1. One that directs; one that prescribes.

2. An instrument that serves to guide any manual operation.

DIRE'CTION. *n. s.* [*directio*, Latin.]

1. Aim at a certain point.

The *direction* of good works to a good end, is the only principle that distinguishes charity. *Smalridge's Serm.*

2. Motion impressed by a certain impulse.

These mens opinions are not the product of judgment, or the consequence of reason; but the effects of chance and hazard, of a mind floating at all adventures, without choice, and without *direction*. *Locke.*

No particle of matter, nor any combination of particles, that is, no body can either move of itself, or of itself alter the *direction* of its motion. *Cheyney.*

3. Order; command; prescription.

From the counsel that St Jerome giveth Læta, of taking heed how she read the apocrypha; as also by the help of other learned mens judgments, delivered in like case, we may take *direction*. *Hooker b.* 5. *s.* 20.

Ev'n now
I put myself to thy *direction*. *Shakespeare's Macbeth.*

He needs not our mistrust, since he delivers
Our offices, and what we have to do,
To the *direction* just. *Shakespeare's Macbeth.*

The nobles of the people digged it by the *direction* of the law-giver. *Numb.* xxi. 18.

Mens passions and God's *direction* seldom agree. *K. Charles.*

All nature is but art unknown to thee,
All chance, *direction* which thou can'st not see. *Pope's Ess.*

General *directions* for scholastic disputers, is never to dispute upon mere trifles. *Watts's Improv. Mind, p.* 113.

DIRE'CTIVE. *n. s.* [from *direct*.]

1. Having the power of direction.

A law therefore generally taken, is a *directive* rule unto goodness of operation. *Hooker, b* 1. *s.* 7.

A power of command there is without all question, tho' there be some doubt in what faculty this command doth principally reside, whether in the will or the understanding. The true resolution is, that the *directive* command for counsel is in the understanding; and the applicative command, or empire, for putting in execution of what is directed, is in the will. *Bramh. against Hobbs.*

On the *directive* powers of the former, and the regularity of the latter, whereby it is capable of direction, depends the generation of all bodies. *Grew's Cosm. Sac. b.* ii. *c.* 1.

2. Informing; shewing the way.

Nor visited by one *directive* ray,
From cottage streaming, or from airy hall. *Thoms. Aut.*

DIRE'CTLY. *adj.* [from *direct*.]

1. In a strait line; rectilineally.

The more a body is nearer to the eyes, and the more *directly* it is opposed to them, the more it is enlightened; because the light languishes and lessens the farther it removes from its proper source. *Dryden's Dufresnoy.*

There was no other place assigned to any of this matter, than that whereinto its own gravity bore it, which was only *directly* downwards, whereby it obtained that place in the globe which was just underneath. *Woodward's N. Hist. p.* 4.

If the refracted ray be returned *directly* back to the point of incidence, it shall be refracted by the incident ray. *Newt. Opt.*

2. Immediately; apparently; without circumlocution; without any long train of consequence.

Infidels being clean without the church, deny *directly* and utterly reject the very principles of christianity, which hereticks embrace, and erroneously by misconstruction. *Hooker, b.* ii. *s.* 1.

No man hath hitherto been so impious, as plainly and *directly* to condemn prayer. *Hooker, b.* v. *s.* 2.

By asserting the scripture to be the canon of our faith, I have unavoidably created to myself enemies in the papists *directly*, because they have kept the scripture from us what they could, and have reserved to themselves a right of interpreting them. *Dryden's Pref. Rel. Laici.*

His work *directly* tends to raise sentiments of honour and virtue in his readers. *Addison's Freeholder.*

No reason can possibly be assigned, why it is best for the world that God Almighty hath such a power, which doth not *directly* prove that no mortal man should have the like *Swift on the Sent of a Ch. of Engl Man.*

DIRE'CTNESS. *n. s.* [from *direct*.] Straitness; tendency to any point; the nearest way.

They argued from celestial causes only, the constant vicinity of the sun, and the *directness* of his rays; never suspecting that the body of the earth had so great an efficiency in the changes of the air. *Bentley's Serm.*

DIRE'CTOR. *n. s.* [*director*, Latin.]

1. One that has authority over others; a superintendent; one that has the general management of a design or work.

Himself stood *director* over them, with nodding or stamping, shewing he did like or mislike those things he did not understand. *Sidney, b* i.

In all affairs thou sole *director*. *Swift's Miscel.*

What made *directors* cheat in south-sea year? *Pope's Ep.*

2. A rule; an ordinance.

Common forms were not design'd
Directors to a noble mind. *Swift's Miscel.*

3. An instructor; one who shews the proper methods of proceeding.

They are glad to use such as counsellors and *directors* in all their dealings which are of weight, as contracts, testaments. *Hooker's Pref.*

4. One who is consulted in cases of conscience.

I am her *director* and her guide in spiritual affairs. *Dryd. Sp. Fr.*

5. An instrument in surgery, by which the hand is guided in its operation.

The manner of opening with a knife, is by sliding it on a *director*, the groove of which prevents its being misguided. *Sharp's Surgery.*

DIRE'CTORY. *n. s.* [from *director*.] The book which the factious preachers published in the rebellion for the direction of their sect in acts of worship.

As to the ordinance concerning the *directory*, we cannot con-

consent to the taking away of the book of common prayer. *Oxford Reasons against the Cov.*

DI'REFUL. *adj.* [This word is frequent among the poets, but has been censured as not analogical; all other words compounded with *full* consisting of a substantive and *full*, as dreadful, or full of dread; joyful, or full of joy.] Dire; dreadful; dismal.

Point of spear it never piercen would,
Ne dint of *direful* sword, divide the substance could. *Fa. Qu.*
But yet at last, whereas the *direful* fiend,
She saw not stir, off shaking vain affright,
She nigher drew, and saw that joyous end;
Then God she pray'd, and thank'd her faithful knight. *Fa. Qu.*
Direful hap betide that hated wretch
That makes us wretched by the death of thee. *Sh. K. Rich.*

The voice of God himself speaks in the heart of men, whether they understand it or no; and by secret intimations gives the sinner a foretaste of that *direful* cup, which he is like to drink more deeply of hereafter. *South's Serm.*

I curs'd the *direful* author of my woes:
'Twas told again, and thence my ruin rose. *Dryden.*
The wrath of Peleus' son, the *direful* spring
Of all the Grecian woes, O goddess, sing. *Pope.*

DI'RENESS. *n. s.* [from *dire.*] Dismalness; horror; hideousness.

Direness, familiar to my slaught'rous thoughts,
Cannot once start me. *Shakesp. Macb.*

DIRE'PTION, *n. s.* [*direptio*, Lat.] the act of plundering.

DIRGE. [This is not a contraction of the Latin *dirige*, in the popish hymn *dirige gressus meos*, as some pretend; but from the Teutonick *dyrke*, *laudare*, to praise and extol. Whence it is possible their *dyrke*, and our *dirge*, was a laudatory song to commemorate and applaud the dead. *Verstegan. Bacon* apparently derives it from *dirige.*] A mournful ditty; a song of lamentation.

Th' imperial jointress of this warlike state,
Have we, as 'twere, with a defeated joy,
With mirth in funeral, and with *dirge* in marriage,
In equal scale weighing delight and dole,
Taken to wife. *Shakesp. Haml.*

Mean while the body of Richard, after many indignities and reproaches, the *dirigies* and obsequies of the common people towards tyrants, was obscurely buried. *Bacon's Hen.* VII.

You from above shall hear each day,
One *dirge* dispatch'd unto your clay,
These your own anthems shall become,
Your lasting epicedium. *Sandy's Paraph.*
All due measures of her mourning kept,
Did office at the *dirge*, and by infection wept. *Dryd. Sigis.*

DI'RIGENT. *adj.* [*dirigens*, Latin.]

The *dirigent* line in geometry is that along which the line describent is carried in the generation of any figure. *Harris.*

DIRK. *n. s.* [an Earse word.] A kind of dagger used in the Highlands of Scotland.

In vain thy hungry mountaineers
Come forth in all their warlike geers,
The shield, the pistol, *dirk*, and dagger,
In which they daily wont to swagger. *Tickell.*

To DIRKE, *v. a.* To spoil; to ruin. Obsolete.

Thy waste bigness but cumbers the ground,
And *dirkes* the beauties of my blossoms round. *Sp. Past.*

DIRT. *n. s.* [*dryt*, Dutch, *dirt*, Islandic.] Mud; filth; mire; any thing that sticks to the cloaths or body.

They gilding *dirt*, in noble verse
Rustick philosophy rehearse. *Denham.*

Numbers engage their lives and labours, to heap together a little *dirt*, that shall bury them in the end. *Wake's Pr.*

They all assured me that the sea rises as high as ever, tho' the great heaps of *dirt* it brings along with it are apt to choak up the shallows. *Addison.*

Mark by what wretched steps their glory grows;
From *dirt* and sea-weed as proud Venice rose:
In each how guilt and greatness equal ran,
And all that rais'd the hero sunk the man. *Pope's Ess.*
Is yellow *dirt* the passion of thy life?
Look but on Gripus, or on Gripus' wife. *Pope's Ess.*

2. Meanness; sordidness.

To DIRT. *v. a.* [from the noun.] To foul; to bemire; to make filthy; to bedawb; to soil; to pollute; to nasty.

Ill company is like a dog, who *dirts* those most whom he loves best. *Swift's Th. on var. Subj.*

DIRT-PIE. *n. s.* [*dirt* and *pie.*] Forms moulded by children of clay, in imitation of pastry.

Thou set'st thy heart upon that which has newly left off making of *dirt-pies*, and is but preparing itself for a greensickness. *Suckling.*

DI'RTILY. *adv.* [from *dirty.*]

1. Nastily; foully; filthily.
2. Meanly; sordidly; shamefully.

Such gold as that wherewithal
Almighty chimiques from each mineral
Are *dirtily* and desperately gull'd. *Donne.*

DI'RTINESS. *n. s.* [from *dirty.*]

1. Nastiness; filthiness; foulness.
2. Meanness; baseness; sordidness.

DI'RTY. *adj.* [from *dirt.*]

1. Foul; nasty; filthy.

Thy Dol and Helen of thy noble thoughts
Is in base durance, and contagious prison,
Haul'd thither by mechanic, *dirty* hands. *Sh. Hen.* IV.

2. Sullied; not elegant.

Pound an almond, and the clear white colour will be altered into a *dirty* one, and the sweet taste into an oily one. *Locke.*

3. Mean; base; despicable.

Such employments are the diseases of labour, and the rust of time, which it contracts not by lying still, but by *dirty* employment. *Taylor's Holy Living.*

Marriages would be made up upon more natural motives than meer *dirty* interests, and increase of riches without measure or end. *Temple's Miscellanies.*

They come at length to grow sots and epicures, mean in their discourses, and *dirty* in their practices. *South's Serm.*

To DI'RTY. *v. a.* [from the noun.]

1. To foul; to soil.

The Lords Strutts lived generously, and never used to *dirty* their fingers with pen, ink, and counters. *Arburth. Hist. Bull.*

2. To disgrace; to scandalize.

DI'RUPTION. *n. s.* [*diruptio*, Latin.]

1. The act of bursting, or breaking.
2. The state of bursting, or breaking.

DIS. An inseparable particle used in composition, implying commonly a privative or negative signification of the word to which it is joined; as to *arm*, to *disarm*; to join, to *disjoin.* It is borrowed from *des*, used by the French and Spaniards in the sense; as *desnouer*, to untie; *desterrar*, to banish; from the Latin *de*; as *struo*, to build; *destruo*, to destroy.

DISABI'LITY. *n. s.* [from *disable.*]

1. Want of power to do any thing; weakness; impotence.

Our consideration of creatures, and attention unto scriptures, are not in themselves things of like *disability* to breed or beget faith. *Hooker, b. v. s.* 22.

Many withdrew themselves out of pure faintness, and *disability* to attend the conclusion. *Raleigh's Hist. World.*

He that knows most of himself, knows least of his knowledge, and the exercised understanding is conscious of its *disability*. *Glanv. Sceps. c.* 27.

The ability of mankind does not lie in the impotency or *disabilities* of brutes. *Locke.*

2. Want of proper qualifications for any purpose; legal impediment.

A suit is commenced in a temporal court for an inheritance, and the defendant pleads in *disability*, that the plaintiff is a bastard. *Ayliffe's Parergon.*

It is true, indeed, that this disadvantage which the dissenters at present lie under, of a *disability* to receive church preferments, will be easily remedied by the repeal of the test. *Swift's Adv. Rep. Sacr. Test.*

To DISA'BLE. *v. a.* [*dis* and *able.*]

1. To deprive of natural force; to weaken; to crush.

The invasion of the Scots, and rebellion of the barons, did not only *disable* this king to be a conqueror, but deprived him both of his kingdom and life. *Davies's Ireland*

Nor so is overcome
Satan, whose fall from heav'n, a deadlier bruise
Disabled not to give thee thy death's wound. *Milt. P. Lost.*

A christian's life is a perpetual exercise a wrestling and warfare, for which sensual pleasure *disables* him, by yielding to that enemy with whom he must strive. *Taylor's Holy Living.*

2. To impair; to diminish.

'Tis not unknown to you Anthonio,
How much I have *disabled* mine estate,
By shewing something a more swelling port
Than my faint means would grant continuance. *Shakespeare.*

3. To make unactive.

I have known a great fleet *disabled* for two months, and thereby lose great occasions by an indisposition of the admiral. *Temple.*

4. To deprive of usefulness or efficacy.

Farewel, Monsieur Traveller; look you lisp, and wear strange suits; *disable* all the benefits of your own country. *Sh.*

Your days I will alarm, I'll haunt your nights,
And worse than age *disable* your delights. *Dryden's Aurenzebe.*

5. To exclude as wanting proper qualifications.

I will not *disable* any for proving a scholar, nor yet dissemble that I have seen many happily forced upon the course, to which by nature they seem much indisposed. *Wotton.*

To DISABU'SE. *v. a.* [*dis* and *abuse.*] To set free from a mistake; to disentangle from a fallacy; to set right; to undeceive.

The imposture and fallacy of our senses impose not only on common heads, but even more refined mercuries, who have the advantages of an improved reason to *disabuse* you. *Glanv.*

Those teeth fair Lyce must not show,
If she would bite her lovers: though
Like birds they stoop at seeming grapes,
Are *disabus'd*, when first she gapes. *Waller.*

If by ſimplicity you meant a general defect in thoſe that profeſs angling, I hope to *diſabuſe* you. *Waller's Angler.*

Chaos of thought and paſſion, all confus'd;
Still by himſelf abus'd, or *diſabus'd.* *Pope's Eſſ. on Man.*

DISACCOMMODA'TION. *n. ſ.* [*dis* and *accommodation.*] The ſtate of being unfit or unprepared.

Devaſtations have happened in ſome places more than in others, according to the accommodation or *diſaccommodation* of them to ſuch calamities. *Hale's Orig. of Mankind.*

To DISACCU'STOM. *v. a.* [*dis* and *accuſtom.*] To deſtroy the force of habit by diſuſe or contrary practice.

DISACQUA'INTANCE. *n. ſ.* [*dis* and *acquaintance.*] Diſuſe of familiarity.

Conſcience, by a long neglect of, and *diſacquaintance* with itſelf, contracts an inveterate ruſt or ſoil. *South.*

DISADVA'NTAGE. *n. ſ.* [*dis* and *advantage.*]

1. Loſs; injury to intereſt; as, he ſold to *diſadvantage.*
2. Diminution of any thing deſirable, as credit, fame, honour.

Our old Engliſh poet, Chaucer, in many things reſembled Ovid, and that with no *diſadvantage* on the ſide of the modern author. *Dryden's Fab. Pref.*

The moſt ſhining merit goes down to poſterity with *diſadvantage,* when it is not placed by writers in its proper light. *Addiſon's Freeholder.*

Thoſe parts already publiſhed give reaſon to think, that the Iliad will appear with no *diſadvantage* to that immortal poem. *Addiſon's Freeholder.*

Their teſtimony will not be of much weight to its *diſadvantage,* ſince they are liable to the common objection of condemning what they did not underſtand. *Swift.*

3. A ſtate not prepared for defence.

But all in vain; no fort can be ſo ſtrong,
Ne fleſhly breaſt can armed be ſo ſound,
But will at laſt be won with batt'ry long,
Or unawares at *diſadvantage* found. *Fairy Queen.*

To DISADVA'NTAGE. *v. a.* [from the noun.] To injure in intereſt of any kind.

All other violences are ſo far from advancing chriſtianity, that they extremely weaken and *diſadvantage* it. *Decay of Piety.*

DISADVA'NTAGEABLE. *adj.* [from *diſadvantage.*] Contrary to profit; producing loſs. A word not uſed.

In clearing of a man's eſtate, he may as well hurt himſelf in being too ſudden, as in letting it run on too long; for haſty ſelling is commonly as *diſadvantageable* as intereſt. *Bacon's Eſſ.*

DISADVANTA'GEOUS. *adj.* [from *diſadvantage.*] Contrary to intereſt; contrary to convenience; unfavourable.

A multitude of eyes will narrowly inſpect every part of him, conſider him nicely in all views, and not be a little pleaſed when they have taken him in the worſt and moſt *diſadvantageous* lights. *Add. Spect.* Nº. 256.

DISADVANTA'GEOUSLY. *adv.* [from *diſadvantageous.*] In a manner contrary to intereſt or profit; in a manner not favourable to any uſeful end.

An approving nod or ſmile ſerves to drive you on, and make you diſplay yourſelves more *diſadvantageouſly.* *Gov. Ton.*

DISADVANTA'GEOUSNESS. *n. ſ.* [from *diſadvantageous.*] Contrariety to profit; inconvenience; miſchief; loſs.

DISADVE'NTUROUS. *adj.* [*dis* and *adventurous.*] Unhappy; unproſperous.

Now he hath left you here,
To be the record of his rueful loſs,
And of my doleful *diſadventurous* death. *Fairy Queen, b.* i.

To DISAFFE'CT. *v. a.* [*diſ* and *affect.*] To fill with diſcontent; to diſcontent; to make leſs faithful or zealous.

They had attempted to *diſaffect* and diſcontent his majeſty's late army. *Clarendon.*

DISAFFE'CTED. *part. adj.* [from *diſaffect.*] Not diſpoſed to zeal or affection. Uſually applied to thoſe who are enemies to the government.

By denying civil worſhip to the emperor's ſtatues, which the cuſtom then was to give, they were proceeded againſt as *diſaffected* to the emperor. *Stilling. Def. of Diſ. on Ro. Idol.*

DISAFFE'CTEDLY. *adv.* [from *diſaffected.*] After a diſaffected manner.

DISAFFE'CTEDNESS. *n. ſ.* [from *diſaffected.*] The quality of being diſaffected.

DISAFFE'CTION. *n. ſ.* [from *diſaffect.*] Want of zeal for the government; want of ardour for the reigning prince.

In this age, every thing diſliked by thoſe who think with the majority, is called *diſaffection.* *Swift.*

DISAFFI'RMANCE. *n. ſ.* [*dis* and *affirm.*] Confutation; negation.

That kind of reaſoning which reduceth the oppoſite concluſion to ſomething that is apparently abſurd, is a demonſtration in *diſaffirmance* of any thing that is affirmed. *Hale's Or. of Man.*

To DISAFFO'REST. *v. a.* [*dis* and *foreſt*] To throw open to common purpoſes; to reduce from the privileges of a foreſt to the ſtate of common ground.

The commiſſioners of the treaſury moved the king to *diſafforeſt* ſome foreſts of his, explaining themſelves of ſuch foreſts as lay out of the way, not near any of the king's houſes. *Bacon.*

How happy's he, which hath due place aſſign'd
To his beaſts; and *diſafforeſted* his mind? *Donne.*

To DISAGR'EE. *v. n.* [*dis* and *agree.*]

1. To differ; not to be the ſame.

The mind clearly and infallibly perceives all diſtinct ideas to *diſagree*; that is, the one not to be the other. *Locke.*

2. To differ; not to be of the ſame opinion.

Why both the bands in worſhip *diſagree,*
And ſome adore the flow'r, and ſome the tree. *Dry. Fl.* and *L.*

3. To be in a ſtate of oppoſition: followed by *from* or *with,* before the oppoſite.

It containeth many improprieties, *diſagreeing* almoſt in all things *from* the true and proper deſcription. *Brown's V. Er.*

Strange it is, that they reject the plaineſt ſenſe of ſcripture, becauſe it ſeems to *diſagree with* what they call reaſon. *Atterbury's Sermons.*

DISAGREE'ABLE. *adj.* [from *diſagree.*]

1. Contrary; unſuitable.

Some demon, an enemy to the Greeks, had forced her to a conduct *diſagreeable* to her ſincerity. *Pope's Od. b.* iv. notes.

2. Unpleaſing; offenſive.

To make the ſenſe of eſteem or diſgrace ſink the deeper, and be of the more weight, either agreeable or *diſagreeable* things ſhould conſtantly accompany theſe different ſtates. *Locke.*

DISAGREE'ABLENESS. *n. ſ.* [from *diſagreeable.*]

1. Unſuitableneſs; contrariety.
2. Unpleaſantneſs; offenſiveneſs.

A father will hug and embrace his beloved ſon for all the dirt and foulneſs of his cloaths; the dearneſs of the perſon eaſily apologizing for the *diſagreeableneſs* of the habit. *South's S.*

DISAGREE'MENT. *n. ſ.* [from *diſagree.*]

1. Difference; diſſimilitude; diverſity; not identity.

Theſe carry ſuch plain and evident notes and characters, either of *diſagreement* or affinity with one another, that the ſeveral kinds of them are eaſily known and diſtinguiſhed. *Woodw. Nat. Hiſt.*

2. Difference of opinion; contrariety of ſentiments.

They ſeemed one to croſs another, as touching their ſeveral opinions about the neceſſity of ſacraments, whereas in truth their *diſagreement* is not great. *Hooker, b.* v. *ſ.* 57.

To DISALLO'W. *v a.* [*dis* and *allow.*]

1. To deny authority to any.

When, ſaid ſhe,
Were thoſe firſt councils *diſallow'd* by me?
Or where did I at ſure tradition ſtrike,
Provided ſtill it were apoſtolic. *Dryd. Hind. and Panth.*

2. To conſider as unlawful; not to permit an act.

Their uſual kind of diſputing ſheweth, that they do not *diſallow* only theſe Romiſh ceremonies which are unprofitable, but count all unprofitable which are Romiſh. *Hooker.*

3. To cenſure by ſome poſterior act.

It was known that the moſt eminent of thoſe who profeſſed his own principles, publickly *diſallowed* his proceedings. *Sw.*

4. Not to juſtify.

There is a ſecret, inward foreboding fear, that ſome evil or other will follow the doing of that which a man's own conſcience *diſallows* him in. *South's Serm.*

To DISALLOW. *v. n.* To refuſe permiſſion; not to grant; not to make lawful.

God doth in converts, being married, allow continuance with infidels, and yet *diſallow* that the faithful, when they are free, ſhould enter into bonds of wedlock with ſuch. *Hooker.*

DISALLO'WABLE. *adj.* [from *diſallow.*] Not allowable; not to be ſuffered.

DISALLO'WANCE. *n. ſ.* [from *diſallow.*] Prohibition.

God accepts of a thing ſuitable for him to receive, and for us to give, where he does not declare his refuſal and *diſallowance* of it. *South's Serm.*

To DIS'ANCHOR. *v. a.* [from *dis* and *anchor.*] to drive a ſhip from its anchor.

To DISANIMA'TE. *v: a.* [*dis* and *animate.*]

1. To deprive of life.
2. To diſcourage; to deject; to depreſs.

The preſence of a king engenders love amongſt his ſubjects, and his loyal friends, as it *diſanimates* his enemies. *Shakeſpeare's Henry* VI.

He was confounded and *diſanimated* at his preſence, and added, how can the ſervant of my lord talk with my lord? *Boyle's Seraph. Love.*

DISANIMA'TION. *n. ſ.* [from *diſanimate.*] Privation of life.

They cannot in reaſon retain that apprehenſion after death, as being affections which depend on life, and depart upon *diſanimation.* *Brown's Vulg. Er. b.* iii. *l.* 10.

To DISANNU'L. *v. a.* [*dis* and *annul.* This word is formed contrary to analogy by thoſe who not knowing the meaning of the word *annul,* intended to form a negative ſenſe by the needleſs uſe of the negative particle. It ought therefore to be rejected as ungrammatical and barbarous.] To annul; to deprive of authority; to vacate; to make null; to make void; to nullify.

The Jews ordinances for us to reſume, were to check our Lord himſelf, which hath *diſannulled* them. *Hooker, b.* iv. §. 11.

That gave him power of *diſannulling* of laws, and diſpoſing of mens fortunes and eſtates, and the like points of abſolute power, being in themſelves harſh and odious. *Bacon, Hen.* VII.

To be in both worlds full,
Is more than God was, who was hungry here:
Wouldſt thou his laws of faſting *diſannul?* *Herbert.*

Wilt thou my judgments *diſannul?* Defame
My equal rule, to clear thyſelf of blame? *Sandys.*

DISANNU'LMENT. *n. ſ.* [from *diſannul.*] The act of making void.

To DISAPPE'AR. *v. n.* [*diſparoitre*, French.] To be loſt to view; to vaniſh out of ſight; to fly; to go away.

She *diſappear'd*, and left me dark! I wak'd
To find her, or for ever to deplore. *Milton's Parad. Loſt.*

When the night and winter *diſappear*,
The purple morning, riſing with the year,
Salutes the Spring. *Dryden.*

The pictures drawn in our minds are laid in fading colours, and, if not ſometimes refreſhed, vaniſh and *diſappear.* *Locke.*

Criticks I ſaw, that other names deface,
And fix their own with labour in their place;
Their own, like others, ſoon their place reſign'd,
Or *diſappear'd*, and left the firſt behind. *Pope's Tem. of Fame.*

To DISAPPO'INT. *v. a.* [*dis* and *appoint.*]

1. To defeat of expectation; to balk; to hinder from ſomething expected.

The ſuperior Being can defeat all his deſigns, and *diſappoint* all his hopes. *Tillotſon, Sermon* i.

Whilſt the champion, with redoubled might,
Strikes home the jav'lin, his retiring foe
Shrinks from the wound, and *diſappoints* the blow. *Addiſon.*

There's nothing like ſurpriſing the rogues: how will they be *diſappointed*, when they hear that thou haſt prevented their revenge. *Arbuthnot's Hiſtory of John Bull.*

We are not only tortured by the reproaches which are offered us, but are *diſappointed* by the ſilence of men when it is unexpected, and humbled even by their praiſes. *Addiſ. Spectat.*

2. It has *of* before the thing loſt by diſappointment.

The Janizaries, *diſappointed* by the baſſas *of* the ſpoil of the merchants, eſpecially Chriſtians and Jews, received of the bounty of Solyman a great largeſs. *Knolles's Hiſt. of the Turks.*

DISAPPO'INTMENT. *n. ſ.* [from *diſappoint.*] Defeat of hopes; miſcarriage of expectations.

It is impoſſible for us to know what are calamities, and what are bleſſings: how many accidents have paſſed for misfortunes, which have turned to the welfare and proſperity of the perſons in whoſe lot they have fallen? How many *diſappointments* have, in their conſequences, ſaved a man from ruin? *Spectator.*

If we hope for things, of which we have not thoroughly conſidered the value, our *diſappointment* will be greater than our pleaſure in the fruition of them. *Addiſon's Spectator.*

DISAPPROB'ATION. *n. ſ.* [*dis* and *approbation.*] Cenſure; condemnation; expreſſion of diſlike.

Pope was obliged to publiſh his letters, to ſhew his *diſapprobation* of the publiſhing of others written in his youth. *Pope to Swift.*

To DISAPPRO'VE. *v. a.* [*diſapprover*, French.] To diſlike; to cenſure; to find fault with.

I reaſon'd much, alas! but more I lov'd;
Sent and recall'd, ordain'd and *diſapprov'd.* *Prior.*

Without good breeding, truth is *diſapprov'd*;
That only makes ſuperior ſenſe belov'd. *Pope's Eſſ. on Crit.*

A project for a treaty of barrier with the States was tranſmitted hither from Holland, and was *diſapproved* of by our court. *Swift.*

DI'SARD. *n. ſ.* [ꝺıſıṛ ꝺıſıᵹ, Saxon, a fool, *Skinner*; *diſeur*, French, *Junius.*] A prattler; a boaſting talker. This word is inſerted both by *Skinner* and *Junius*; but I do not remember it.

To DISA'RM. *v. a.* [*deſarmer*, French.]

1. To ſpoil or diveſt of arms; to deprive of arms.

I am ſtill the ſame,
By different ways ſtill moving to one fame;
And by *diſarming* you, I now do more
To ſave the town, than arming you before. *Dryd. In. Emp.*

2. It has *of* before the arms taken away.

They would be immediately *diſarmed* of their great magazine of artillery. *Locke.*

To DISARRA'Y. *v. a.* [*dis* and *array.*] To undreſs any one; to diveſt of cloaths.

So, as ſhe bad, the witch they *diſarray'd.* *Fairy Queen.*

Now night is come, now ſoon her *diſarray*,
And in her bed her lay. *Spenſer's Epithalamium.*

DISARRA'Y. *n. ſ.* [from the verb.]

1. Diſorder; confuſion; loſs of the regular order of battle.

He returned towards the river, to prevent ſuch danger as the *diſarray*, occaſioned by the narrowneſs of the bridge, might caſt upon them. *Hayward.*

Diſarray and ſhameful rout enſue,
And force is added to the fainting crew. *Dryden's Fables.*

2. Undreſs.

DISA'STER. *n. ſ.* [*deſaſtre*, French.]

1. The blaſt or ſtroke of an unfavourable planet.

Stars ſhone with trains of fire, dews of blood fall;
Diſaſters veil'd the ſun; and the moiſt ſtar,
Upon whoſe influence Neptune's empire ſtands,
Was ſick almoſt to doomſday with eclipſe. *Shakeſp. Hamlet.*

2. Misfortune; grief; miſhap; miſery; calamity.

This day black omens threat the brighteſt fair,
That e'er deſerv'd a watchful ſpirit's care,
Some dire *diſaſter*, or by force or ſlight;
But what, or where, the fates have wrapt in night. *Pope.*

To DISA'STER. *v. a.* [from the noun.]

1. To blaſt by the ſtroke of an unfavourable ſtar.

Ah, chaſte bed of mine, ſaid ſhe, which never heretofore couldſt accuſe me of one defiled thought, how canſt thou now receive that *diſaſtered* changling? *Sidney, b.* ii.

2. To afflict; to miſchief.

Theſe are the holes where eyes ſhould be, which pitifully *diſaſter* the cheeks. *Shakeſpeare's Anthony and Cleopatra.*

In his own fields, the ſwain
Diſaſter'd ſtands. *Thomſon's Winter, l.* 280.

DISA'STROUS. *adj.* [from *diſaſter.*]

1. Unlucky; not fortunate.

That day ſeemeth a moſt *diſaſtrous* day to the Scots, not only in regard of this overthrow, but for that upon the ſame day they were in like ſort defeated by the Engliſh at Flodden-field. *Hayward.*

2. Unhappy; calamitous; miſerable; ſtruck with affliction.

Then Juno, pitying her *diſaſtrous* fate,
Send Iris down, her pangs to mitigate. *Denham.*

Immediately after his return from this very expedition, ſuch *diſaſtrous* calamities befel his family, that he burnt two of his children himſelf. *South's Sermons.*

Fly the purſuit of my *diſaſtrous* love,
And from my unhappy neighbourhood remove. *Dryd. Auren.*

3. Gloomy; threatning misfortune.

The moon,
In dim eclipſe, *diſaſtrous* twilight ſheds
On half the nations. *Milton's Paradiſe Loſt, b.* i. *l.* 597.

DISA'STROUSLY. *adv.* [from *diſaſtrous.*] In a diſmal manner.

DISA'STROUSNESS. *n. ſ.* [from *diſaſtrous.*] Unluckineſs; unfortunateneſs. *Dict.*

To DISAVOU'CH. *v. a.* [*dis* and *avouch.*] To retract profeſſion; to diſown.

Thereupon they flatly *diſavouch*,
To yield him more obedience or ſupport. *Daniel's C. War.*

To DISAVO'W. *v. a.* [*dis* and *avow.*] To diſown; to deny knowledge of; to deny concurrence in any thing.

The heirs and poſterity of them which yielded the ſame, are, as they ſay, either ignorant thereof, or do wilfully deny, or ſtedfaſtly *diſavow* it. *Spenſer's State of Ireland.*

The Engliſh, that knew his noble ſpirit, did believe his name was therein abuſed, which he manifeſted to be true by *diſavowing* it openly afterwards. *Hayward.*

To deal in perſon is good, when a man's face breedeth regard, and generally when a man will reſerve to himſelf liberty either to *diſavow* or to expound. *Bacon, Eſſay* 48.

A man that acts below his rank, doth but *diſavow* fortune, and ſeemeth to be conſcious of his own want in worth, and doth but teach others to envy him. *Bacon, Eſſay* 9.

He only does his conqueſt *diſavow*,
And thinks too little what they found too much. *Dryden.*

We are reminded by the ceremony of taking an oath, that it is a part of that obedience which we learn from the goſpel, expreſly to *diſavow* all evaſions and mental reſervations whatſoever. *Addiſon's Freeholder.*

DISAVO'WAL. *n. ſ.* [from *diſavow.*] Denial.

An earneſt *diſavowal* of fear, often proceeds from fear. *Clariſſa.*

DISAVO'WMENT. *n. ſ.* [from *diſavow.*] Denial.

As touching the Tridentine hiſtory, his holineſs will not preſs you to any *diſavowment* thereof. *Wotton.*

To DISAU'THORISE. *v. a.* [*dis* and *authoriſe.*] To deprive of credit or authority.

The obtruſion of ſuch particular inſtances as theſe, are inſufficient to *diſauthoriſe* a note grounded upon the final intention of nature. *Wotton.*

To DISBA'ND. *v. a.* [*dis* and *band.*]

1. To diſmiſs from military ſervice; to break up an army; to diſmiſs ſoldiers from their colours.

They *disbanded* themſelves, and returned every man to his own dwelling. *Knolles's Hiſtory of the Turks.*

Pythagoras bids us in our ſtation ſtand,
'Till God, our general, ſhall us *disband.* *Denham.*

This if you do, to end all future ſtrife,
I am content to lead a private life;
Disband my army to ſecure the ſtate. *Dryden's Aurengzebe.*

Bid him *disband* his legions,
Reſtore the commonwealth to liberty. *Addiſon's Cato.*

2. To ſpread abroad; to ſcatter.

Some imagine that a quantity of water, ſufficient to make

ſuch

ſuch a deluge, was created upon that occaſion; and, when the buſineſs was done, all *diſbanded* again, and annihilated. *Woodw.*

To DISBA'ND. *v. n.* To retire from military ſervice; to ſeparate; to break up.

Our navy was upon the point of *diſbanding*, and many of our men come aſhore. *Bacon's War with Spain.*

The rang'd pow'rs
Diſband, and wand'ring, each his ſeveral way
Purſues. *Milton's Paradiſe Loſt, b.* ii. *l.* 525.

The common ſoldiers, and inferior officers, ſhould be fully paid upon their *diſbanding*. *Clarendon.*

Were it not for ſome ſmall remainders of piety and virtue, which are yet left ſcattered among mankind, human ſociety would in a ſhort ſpace *diſband* and run into confuſion, and the earth would grow wild and become a foreſt. *Tillotſon.*

To DISBA'RK. *v. a.* [*debarquer*, French.] To land from a ſhip; to put on ſhore.

Together ſail'd they, fraught with all the things
To ſervice done by land that might belong,
And, when occaſion ſerv'd, *diſbarked* them. *Fairfax, b.* i.

The ſhip we moor on theſe obſcure abodes;
Diſbark the ſheep, an offering to the gods. *Pope's Odyſſey.*

DISBELI'EF. *n. ſ.* [from *diſbelieve.*] Refuſal of credit; denial of belief.

Our belief or *diſbelief* of a thing does not alter the nature of the thing. *Tillotſon's Sermons.*

To DISBELI'EVE. *v. a.* [*dis* and *believe.*] Not to credit; not to hold true.

The thinking it impoſſible his ſins ſhould be forgiven, though he ſhould be truly penitent, is a ſin, but rather of infidelity than deſpair; it being the *diſbelieving* of an eternal truth of God's. *Hammond's Pract. Catech.*

Such, who profeſs to *diſbelieve* a future ſtate, are not always equally ſatisfied with their own reaſonings. *Atterbury.*

From a fondneſs to ſome vices, which the doctrine of futurity rendered uneaſy, they brought themſelves to doubt of religion; or, out of a vain affectation of ſeeing farther than other men, pretended to *diſbelieve* it. *Rogers, Sermon* 13.

DISBELI'EVER. *n. ſ.* [from *diſbelieve.*] One who refuſes belief; one who denies any poſition to be true.

An humble ſoul is frighted into any particular ſentiments, becauſe a man of great name pronounces hereſy upon the contrary ſentiments, and caſts the *diſbeliever* out of the church. *Watts's Logick.*

To DISBE'NCH. *v. a.* [*dis* and *bench.*] To drive from a ſeat.

Sir, I hope
My words *diſbench'd* you not?
——No, ſir; yet oft,
When blows have made me ſtay, I fled from words. *Shakeſ.*

To DISBRA'NCH. *v. a.* [*dis* and *branch.*] To ſeparate or break off, as a branch from a tree.

I fear your diſpoſition:
That nature which contemns its origine,
Cannot be border'd certain in itſelf:
She that herſelf will ſliver and *diſbranch*
From her maternal ſap, perforce muſt wither,
And come to deadly uſe. *Shakeſpeare's King Lear.*

But for ſuch as are newly planted, they need not be *diſbranched* 'till the ſap begins to ſtir, that ſo the wound may be healed without the ſcar, which our froſts do frequently leave. *Evelyn's Kalendar.*

To DISBU'D. *v. a.* [With gardeners.] To take away the branches or ſprigs newly put forth, that are ill placed. *Dict.*

To DISBU'RDEN. *v. a.* [*dis* and *burden.*]

1. To eaſe of a burden; to unload.

Better yet do I live, that though by my thoughts I be plunged
Into my life's bondage, I yet may *diſburden* a paſſion. *Sidney.*

The river, with ten branches or ſtreams, *diſburdens* himſelf within the Perſian ſea. *Peacham on Drawing.*

Diſburden'd heav'n rejoic'd. *Milton's Paradiſe Loſt, b.* vi.

2. To diſencumber, diſcharge, or clear.

They removed either by caſualty and tempeſt, or by intention and deſign, either out of lucre of gold, or for the *diſburdening* of the countries, ſurcharged with multitudes of inhabitants. *Hale's Origin of Mankind.*

We ſhall *diſburden* the piece of thoſe hard ſhadowings, which are always ungraceful. *Dryden's Dufreſnoy.*

3. To throw off a burden.

Lucia, *diſburden* all thy cares on me,
And let me ſhare thy moſt retired diſtreſs. *Addiſon's Cato.*

To DISBU'RDEN. *v. n.* To eaſe the mind.

To DISBU'RSE. *v. a.* [*debourſer*, French.] To ſpend or lay out money.

Money is now not *diſburſed* at once, as it might be; but drawn into a long length, by ſending over now twenty thouſand, and next half year ten thouſand pounds. *Spenſer.*

Nor would we deign him burial for his men,
'Till he *diſburs'd* at St. Colmeſkil Iſle,
Ten thouſand dollars to our general. *Shakeſpeare's Macbeth.*

As Alexander received great ſums, he was no leſs generous and liberal in *diſburſing* of them. *Arbuthnot on Coins.*

DISBU'RSEMENT. *n. ſ.* [*debourſement*, French.] A diſburſing or laying out.

It may be, Ireneus, that the queen's treaſure, in ſo great occaſions of *diſburſements*, is not always ſo ready, nor ſo plentiful, as it can ſpare ſo great a ſum together. *Spenſer's Ireland.*

DISBU'RSER. *n. ſ.* [from *diſburſe.*] One that diſburſes.

DISCA'LCEATED. *adj.* [*diſcalceatus*, Latin.] Stripped of ſhoes.

DISCALCEA'TION. *n. ſ.* [from *dicalceated.*] The act of pulling off the ſhoes.

The cuſtom of *diſcalceation*, or putting off their ſhoes at meals, is conceived to have been done, as by that means keeping their beds clean. *Brown's Vulgar Errours, b.* v. *c.* 6.

To DISCA'NDY. *v. n.* [from *dis* and *candy.*] To diſſolve; to melt. *Hanmer.*

The hearts,
That ſpaniel'd me at heels, to whom I gave
Their wiſhes, do *diſcandy*, melt their ſweets
On bloſſoming Cæſar. *Shakeſpeare's Ant. and Cleopatra.*

To DISCA'RD. *v. a.* [*dis* and *card.*]

1. To throw out of the hand ſuch cards as are uſeleſs.

2. To diſcharge or eject from ſervice or employment.

Theſe men being certainly jewels to a wiſe man, conſidering what wonders they were able to perform, yet were *diſcarded* by that unworthy prince, as not worthy the holding. *Sid.*

Their captains, if they liſt, *diſcard* whom they pleaſe, and ſend away ſuch as will perhaps willingly be rid of that dangerous and hard ſervice. *Spenſer's State of Ireland.*

Should we own that we have a very imperfect idea of ſubſtance, would it not be hard to charge us with *diſcarding* ſubſtance out of the world? *Locke.*

Juſtice *diſcards* party, friendſhip, kindred, and is always therefore repreſented as blind. *Addiſon's Guardian*, N°. 99.

They blame the favourites, and think it nothing extraordinary that the queen ſhould be at an end of her patience, and reſolve to *diſcard* them. *Swift.*

I do not conceive why a ſunk *diſcarded* party, who neither expect nor deſire more than a quiet life, ſhould be charged with endeavouring to introduce popery. *Swift.*

DISCA'RNATE. *adj.* [*dis* and *caro*, fleſh; *ſcarnato*, Ital.] Stripped of fleſh.

'Tis better to own a judgment, though but with a *curta ſuppellex* of coherent notions, than a memory, like a ſepulchre, furniſhed with a load of broken and *diſcarnate* bones. *Glanville's Sceps. c.* 17.

To DISCA'SE. *v. a.* [*dis* and *caſe.*] To ſtrip; to undreſs.

Fetch me the hat and rapier in my cell:
I will *diſcaſe* me, and myſelf preſent. *Shakeſp. Tempeſt.*

To DISCE'RN. *v. a.* [*diſcerno*, Latin.]

1. To deſcry; to ſee; to diſcover.

And behold among the ſimple ones, I *diſcerned* among the youths a young man void of underſtanding. *Prov.* vii. 7.

2. To judge; to have knowledge of.

What doth better become wiſdom than to *diſcern* what is worthy the loving? *Sidney, b.* ii.

Does any here know me? This is not Lear:
Does Lear walk thus, ſpeak thus? Where are his eyes?
Either his motion weakens, or his *diſcernings*
Are lethargied. *Shakeſpeare's King Lear.*

You ſhould be rul'd and led
By ſome diſcretion, that *diſcerns* your ſtate
Better than you yourſelf. *Shakeſpeare's King Lear.*

3. To diſtinguiſh.

To *diſcern* ſuch buds as are fit to produce bloſſoms, from ſuch as will diſplay themſelves but in leaves, is no difficult matter. *Boyle.*

4. To make the difference between.

They follow virtue for reward, to-day;
To-morrow vice, if ſhe give better pay:
We are ſo good, or bad, juſt at a price;
For nothing elſe *diſcerns* the virtue or vice. *Ben. Johnſon.*

To DISCE'RN. *v. n.* To make diſtinction.

Great part of the country was abandoned to the ſpoils of the ſoldiers, who not troubling themſelves to *diſcern* between a ſubject and a rebel, whilſt their liberty laſted, made indifferently profit of both. *Hayward.*

The cuſtom of arguing on any ſide, even againſt our perſuaſions, dims the underſtanding, and makes it by degrees loſe the faculty of *diſcerning* between truth and falſhood. *Locke.*

DISCE'RNER. *n. ſ.* [from *diſcern.*]

1. Diſcoverer; he that deſcries.

'Twas ſaid they ſaw but one; and no *diſcerner*
Durſt wag his tongue in cenſure. *Shakeſp. Henry* VIII.

2. Judge; one that has the power of diſtinguiſhing.

He was a great obſerver and *diſcerner* of mens natures and humours, and was very dextrous in compliance, where he found it uſeful. *Clarendon, b.* viii.

How unequal *diſcerners* of truth there are, and eaſily expoſed unto errour, will appear by their unqualified intellectuals. *Brown's Vulgar Errours, b.* i. *c.* 3.

DISCE'RNIBLE. *adj.* [from *diſcern.*] Diſcoverable; perceptible diſtinguiſhable; apparent.

It

Is is indeed a sin of so gross, so formidable a bulk, that there needs no help of opticks to render it *discernible*, and therefore I need not farther expatiate on it. *Gov. of the Tongue.*

All this is easily *discernible* by the ordinary discourses of the understanding. *South's Sermons.*

DISCE'RNIBLENESS. *n. s.* [from *discernible.*] Visibleness.

DISCE'RNIBLY. *adv.* [from *discernible.*] Perceptibly; apparently.

Consider what doctrines are infused *discernibly* among Christians, most apt to obstruct or interrupt the Christian life. *Ham.*

DISCE'RNING. *participial adj.* [from *discern.*] Judicious; knowing.

This hath been maintained not only by warm enthusiasts, but by cooler and more *discerning* heads. *Atterbury's Sermons.*

DISCE'RNINGLY. *adv.* [from *discerning.*] Judiciously; rationally; acutely.

These two errours Ovid has most *discerningly* avoided. *Garth.*

DISCE'RNMENT. *n. s.* [from *discern.*] Judgment; power of distinguishing.

A reader that wants *discernment*, loves and admires the characters and actions of men in a wrong place. *Freeholder.*

To DISCE'RP. *v. a.* [*discerpo*, Latin] To tear in pieces; to break; to destroy by separation of its parts. *Dict.*

DISCE'RPTIBLE. *adj.* [from *discerp.*] Frangible; separable; liable to be destroyed by the disunion of its parts.

What is most dense, and least porous, will be most coherent and least *discerptible.* *Glanville's Sceps.*

Matter is moveable, this immoveable; matter *discerptible*, this indiscerptible. *More's Div. Dialogues.*

DISCERPTIBI'LITY. *n. s.* [from *discerptible.*] Liableness to be destroyed by disunion of parts.

DISCE'RPTION. *n. s.* [from *discerp.*] The act of pulling to pieces, or destroying by disuniting the parts.

To DISCHA'RGE. *v. a.* [*descharger*, French.]

1. To disburden; to exonerate; to free from any load or inconvenience.

How rich in humble poverty is he,
Who leads a quiet country life;
Discharg'd of business, void of strife. *Dryden.*

When they have taken a degree, and are consequently grown a burden to their friends, who now think themselves fully *discharged*, they get into orders as soon as they can. *Swift.*

2. To unload; to disembark.

I will convey them by sea in floats, unto the place that thou shalt appoint me, and will cause them to be *discharged.* 1 *Ki.* v.

3. To throw off any thing collected or accumulated; to give vent to any thing; to let fly. It is used of any thing violent, or sudden.

Mounting his eyes,
He did *discharge* a horrible oath. *Shakespeare's Henry* VIII.

Infected minds,
To their deaf pillows will *discharge* their secrets. *Sh. Macb.*

Nor were those blust'ring brethren left at large,
On seas and shores their fury to *discharge.* *Dryden's Ovid.*

Soon may kind heav'n a sure relief provide;
Soon may your sire *discharge* the vengeance due,
And all your wrongs the proud oppressors rue. *Pope's Odyssey.*

Discharge thy shafts; this ready bosom rend. *Pope's Stat.*

4. To unload a gun.

A conceit runneth abroad, that there should be a white powder, which will *discharge* a piece without noise. *Bacon.*

The galleys also did oftentimes, out of their prows, *discharge* their great pieces against the city. *Knolles's History.*

We *discharged* a pistol, and had the sound returned upon us fifty-six times, though the air was foggy. *Addison on Italy.*

5. To clear a debt by payment.

Death of one person can be paid but once,
And that she has *discharged.* *Shakespeare's Ant. and Cleopatra.*

A grateful mind,
By owing, owes not, but still pays; at once
Indebted, and *discharg'd.* *Milton's Paradise Lost, b.* iv.

Now to the horrors of that uncouth place,
He passage begs with unregarded pray'r;
And wants two farthings to *discharge* his fare. *Dryd. Juven.*

When foreign trade imports more than our commodities will pay for, we contract debts beyond sea; and those are paid with money, when they will not take our goods to *discharge* them. *Locke.*

6. To send away a creditor by payment.

If he had
The present money to *discharge* the Jew,
He would not take it. *Shakesp. Merchant of Venice.*

7. To set free from obligation.

If one man's fault could *discharge* another man of his duty, there would be no place left for the common offices of society. *L'Estrange.*

8. To clear from an accusation or crime; to absolve.

They wanted not reasons to be *discharged* of all blame, who are confessed to have no great fault, even by their very word and testimony; in whose eyes no fault of ours hath ever hitherto been esteemed to be small. *Hooker, b.* v. *s.* 27.

They are imprudent enough to *discharge* themselves of this blunder, by laying the contradiction at Virgil's door. *Dryden.*

9. To perform; to execute.

Had I a hundred tongues, a wit so large,
As could their hundred offices *discharge.* *Dryden's Fables.*

10. To put away; to obliterate; to destroy.

It is done by little and little, and with many essays; but all this *dischargeth* not the wonder. *Bacon's Natural History.*

Trial would also be made in herbs poisonous and purgative, whose ill quality perhaps may be *discharged*, or attempered, by setting stronger poisons or purgatives by them. *Bac.*

11. To divest of any office or employment; to dismiss from service.

12. To dismiss; to release; to send away from any business or appointment.

Discharge your pow'rs unto their several counties. *Shakesp.*

When Cæsar would have *discharged* the senate, in regard of some ill presages, and especially a dream of Calphurnia, this man lifted him gently by the arm out of his chair, telling him, he hoped he would not dismiss the senate 'till his wife had dreamed a better dream. *Bacon, Essay* 28.

To DISCHA'RGE. *v. n.* To dismiss itself; to break up.

The cloud, if it were oily or fatty, would not *discharge.* *Bacon's Natural History.*

DISCHA'RGE. *n. s.* [from the verb.]

1. Vent; explosion; emission.

As the heat of all springs is owing to subterraneous fire, so wherever there are any extraordinary *discharges* of this fire, there also are the neighbouring springs hotter than ordinary. *Woodward.*

2. Matter vented.

The hæmorrhage being stopped, the next occurrence is a thin serous *discharge.* *Sharp's Surgery.*

3. Disruption; evanescence.

Mark the *discharge* of the little cloud upon glass or gems, or blades of swords, and you shall see it ever break up first in the skirts, and last in the middle. *Bacon's Natural History.*

4. Dismission from an office.

5. Release from an obligation or penalty.

He warns
Us, haply too secure of our *discharge*
From penalty, because from death releas'd
Some days. *Milton's Paradise Lost, b.* xi. *l.* 196.

6. Absolution from a crime.

The text expresses the sound estate of the conscience, not barely by its not accusing, but by its not condemning us; which word imports properly an acquittance or *discharge* of a man upon some precedent accusation, and a full trial and cognizance of his cause. *South's Sermons.*

7. Ransom; price of ransom.

O, all my hopes defeated
To free him hence! But death, who sets all free,
Hath paid his ransom now and full *discharge.* *Milt. Agonist.*

8. Performance; execution.

The obligations of hospitality and protection are so sacred, that nothing can absolve us from the *discharge* of those duties. *L'Estrange, Fable* 149.

9. An acquittance from a debt.

10. Exemption; privilege.

There is no *discharge* in that war, neither shall wickedness deliver those that are given to it. *Eccl.* viii. 8.

DISCHA'RGER. *n. s.* [from *discharge.*]

1. He that discharges in any manner.

2. He that fires a gun.

To abate the bombulation of gunpowder a way is promised by Porta, by borax and butter, which he says will make it so go off, as scarcely to be heard by the *discharger.* *Brown.*

DISCI'NCT. *adj.* [*discinctus*, Latin.] Ungirded; loosely dressed. *Dict.*

To DISCI'ND. *v. a.* [*discindo*, Latin.] To divide; to cut in pieces.

We found several concretions so soft, that we could easily *discind* them betwixt our fingers. *Boyle.*

DISCI'PLE. *n. s.* [*discipulus*, Latin.] A scholar; one that professes to receive instructions from another.

He rebuked *disciples*, who would call for fire from heaven upon whole cities, for the neglect of a few. *King Charles.*

The commemorating the death of Christ, is the professing ourselves the *disciples* of the crucified Saviour; and that engageth us to take up his cross and follow him. *Hammond.*

A young *disciple* should behave himself so well, as to gain the affection and the ear of his instructor. *Watts.*

To DISCI'PLE. *v. a.* [from the noun.] To punish; to discipline. This word is not in use.

She, bitter penance, with an iron whip,
Was wont him to *disciple* every day. *Spens. Fai. Queen.*

DISCI'PLESHIP. *n. s.* [from *disciple.*] The state or function of a disciple, or follower of a master.

That to which justification is promised, is certainly the giving up of the whole soul intirely unto Christ, undertaking *discipleship* upon Christ's terms. *Hammond's Pract. Catech.*

DISCIPLI'NABLE. *adj.* [*disciplinabilis*, Lat.] Capable of instruction; capable of improvement by discipline and learning.

DISCIPLI'NABLENESS. *n. s.* [from *disciplinable.*] Capacity of instruction; qualification for improvement by education and discipline.

We find in animals, especially some of them, as foxes, dogs, apes, horses, and elephants, not only perception, phantasy, and memory, common to most, if not all animals, but something of sagacity, providence, and *disciplinableness*. *Hale.*

DISCIPLINA'RIAN. *adj.* [from *discipline.*] Pertaining to discipline.

What eagerness in *disciplinarian* uncertainties, when the love of God and our neighbour, evangelical unquestionables, are neglected. *Glanv. Sceps. c.* 27.

DISCIPLINA'RIAN. *n. s.* [*disciplina*, Latin.]

1. One who rules or teaches with great strictness; one who allows no deviation from stated rules.

2. A follower of the presbyterian sect, so called from their perpetual clamour about discipline.

They draw those, that dissent, into dislike with the state, as puritans, or *disciplinarians*. *Sandersf. Pax. Eccl.*

DISCI'PLINARY. *adj.* [*disciplina*, Latin.] Pertaining to discipline; relating to a regular course of education.

These are the studies, wherein our noble and gentle youth ought to bestow their time in a *disciplinary* way. *Milton.*

DI'SCIPLINE. *n. s.* [*disciplina*, Latin.]

1. Education; instruction; the act of cultivating the mind; the act of forming the manners.

The cold of the northern parts is that which, without aid of *discipline*, doth make the bodies hardest, and the courage warmest. *Bacon, Essay* 59.

They who want that sense of *discipline*, hearing, are also by consequence deprived of speech. *Holder's Elements of Speech.*

It must be confessed, it is by the assistance of the eye and the ear especially, which are called the senses of *discipline*, that our minds are furnished with various parts of knowledge. *Watts.*

2. Rule of government; order; method of government.

They hold, that from the very apostles time 'till this present age, wherein yourselves imagine ye have found out a right pattern of sound *discipline*, there never was any time safe to be followed. *Hooker, Preface.*

As we are to believe for ever the articles of evangelical doctrine, so the precepts of *discipline* we are, in like sort, bound for ever to observe. *Hooker, b.* iii. *s.* 10.

While we do admire
This virtue and this moral *discipline*,
Let's be no stoicks. *Shakespeare.*

3. Military regulation.

This opens all your victories in Scotland,
Your *discipline* in war, wisdom in peace. *Shakesp. Rich.* III.

4. A state of subjection.

The most perfect among us, who have their passions in the best *discipline*, are yet obliged to be constantly on their guard. *Rogers, Sermon* 13.

5. Any thing taught; art; science.

Art may be said to overcome and advance nature in these mechanical *disciplines*, which, in this respect, are much to be preferred. *Wilkins's Math. Magick.*

6. Punishment; chastisement; correction.

A lively cobler kicked and spurred while his wife was carrying him, and had scarce passed a day without giving her the *discipline* of the strap. *Addison's Spectator*, N°. 499.

To DI'SCIPLINE. *v. a.* [from the noun.]

1. To educate; to instruct; to bring up.

We are wise enough to begin when they are very young, and *discipline* betimes those other creatures we would make useful and good for somewhat. *Locke.*

They were with care prepared and *disciplined* for confirmation, which they could not arrive at, 'till they were found upon examination to have made a sufficient progress in the knowledge of Christianity. *Addison on the Christian Religion.*

2. To regulate; to keep in order.

They look to us, as we should judge of an army of well *disciplined* soldiers at a distance. *Derham's Astro-Theology.*

3. To punish; to correct; to chastise.

4. To reform; to redress.

The law appear'd imperfect, and but giv'n
With purpose to resign them in full time
Up to a better covenant, *disciplin'd*
From shadowy types to truth, from flesh to spirit. *Milton.*

To DISCLA'IM. *v. a.* [*dis* and *claim.*] To disown; to deny any knowledge of; to retract any union with; to abrogate; to renounce.

You cowardly rascal! nature *disclaims* all share in thee: a taylor made thee. *Shakespeare's King Lear.*

He calls the gods to witness their offence;
Disclaims the war, asserts his innocence. *Dryden's Æn. b.* vii.

Let crooked steel invade
The lawless troops which discipline *disclaim*,
And their superfluous growth with rigour tame. *Dryd. Virg.*

We find our Lord, on all occasions, *disclaiming* all pretensions to a temporal kingdom. *Rogers, Sermon* 9.

Very few, among those who profess themselves Christians, *disclaim* all concern for their souls, disown the authority, or renounce the expectations of the gospel. *Rogers, Sermon* 13.

DISCLA'IMER. *n. s.* [from *disclaim.*]

1. One that disclaims, disowns, or renounces.

2. [In law.] A plea containing an express denial or refusal. *Cowel.*

To DISCLO'SE *v. a.* [*discludo*, Latin; *dis* and *close.*]

1. To uncover; to produce from a state of latitancy to open view.

In this deep quiet, from what source unknown,
Those seeds of fire their fatal birth *disclose*;
And first few scatt'ring sparks about were blown,
Big with the flames that to our ruin rose? *Dryd. Ann. Mir.*
Then earth and ocean various forms *disclose*. *Dryden.*

The shells being broken, struck off, and gone, the stone included in them is thereby *disclosed* and set at liberty. *Woodw.*

2. To hatch; to open.

It is reported by the ancients, that the ostrich layeth her eggs under sand, where the heat of the sun *discloseth* them. *Bac.*

3. To reveal; to tell; to impart what is secret.

There may be a reconciliation, except for upbraiding, or pride, or *disclosing* of secrets, or a treacherous wound; for from these things every friend will depart. *Ecclus.* xxii. 22.

If I *disclose* my passion,
Our friendship's at an end; if I conceal it,
The world will call me false. *Addison's Cato.*

DISCLO'SER. *n. s.* [from *disclose.*] One that reveals or discovers.

DISCLO'SURE. *n. s.* [from *disclose.*]

1. Discovery; production into view.

The producing of cold is a thing very worthy the inquisition, both for the use and *disclosure* of causes. *Bac. Nat. Hist.*

2. Act of revealing any thing secret.

After so happy a marriage between the king and her daughter, blessed with issue male, she was, upon a sudden mutability and *disclosure* of the king's mind, severely handled. *Bacon.*

DISCOLORA'TION. *n. s.* [from *discolour.*]

1. The act of changing the colour; the act of staining.

2. Change of colour; stain; die.

In a depravation of the humours from a sound state to what the physicians call by a general name of a cacochymy, spots and *discolorations* of the skin are signs of weak fibres. *Arbuth.*

To DISCO'LOUR. *v. a.* [*decoloro*, Latin.] To change from the natural hue; to stain.

Many a widow's husband groveling lies,
Coldly embracing the *discolour'd* earth. *Shakesp. K. John.*
Drink water, either pure, or but *discoloured* with malt. *Temp.*
Suspicious and fantastical surmise,
And jealousy with jaundice in her eyes,
Discolouring all she view'd. *Dryden.*

He who looks upon the soul through its outward actions, sees it through a deceitful medium, which is apt to *discolour* and pervert the object. *Addison's Spectator*, N°. 257.

Have a care lest some beloved notion, or some darling science, so prevail over your mind as to *discolour* all your ideas. *Watts.*

To DISCO'MFIT. *v. a.* [*desconfire*, Fr. *sconfiggere*, Ital. as if from *disconfigere*, Latin.] To defeat; to conquer; to vanquish; to overpower; to subdue; to beat; to overthrow.

Fight against that monstrous rebel, Cade,
Whom, since, I heard to be *discomfited*. *Shakesp. Hen.* VI.

Joshua *discomfited* Amelek and his people with the edge of the sword. *Exod.* xvii. 13.

He, fugitive, declin'd superior strength;
Discomfited, pursu'd, in the sad chace
Ten thousand ignominious fall. *Phillips.*

While many of my gallant countrymen are employed in pursuing rebels, half *discomfited* through the consciousness of their guilt, I shall labour to improve those victories to the good of my fellow subjects. *Addison's Freeholder*, N°. 16.

DISCO'MFIT. *n. s.* [from the verb.] Defeat; rout; overthrow.

Fly you must: incurable *discomfit*
Reigns in the hearts of all our present party. *Shakes. H.* VI.
Dagon must stoop, and shall ere long receive
Such a *discomfit*, as shall quite despoil him
Of all these boasted trophies. *Milton's Agonistes, l.* 468.

DISCO'MFITURE. *n. s.* [from *discomfit.*] Defeat; loss of battle; rout; ruin; overthrow.

Sad tidings bring I to you out of France,
Of loss, of slaughter, and *discomfiture*. *Shakes. Henry* VI.

Behold, every man's sword was against his fellow, and there was a very great *discomfiture*. 1 *Sa.* xiv. 20.

What a defeat and *discomfiture* is it to a man, when he comes to use this wealth, to find it all false metal? *Gov. Tongue.*

He sent his angels to fight for his people; and the *discomfiture* and slaughters of great hosts, is attributed to their assistance. *Atterbury's Sermons.*

DISCO'MFORT. *n. s.* [*dis* and *comfort.*] Uneasiness; sorrow; melancholy; gloom.

This himself did foresee, and therefore armed his church, to the end they might sustain it without *discomfort*. *Hooker.*

Discomfort guides my tongue,
And bids me speak of nothing but despair. *Shakes. Rich.* II.

In

In solitude there is not only *discomfort*, but weakness also. *Sou.*

To DISCO'MFORT. *v. a.* [from the noun.] To grieve; to sadden; to deject.

Her champion went away *discomforted* as much as discomfited. *Sidney.*

His funeral shall not be in our camp,
Lest it *discomfort* us. *Shakespeare's Julius Cæsar.*

DISCO'MFORTABLE. *n. s.* [from *discomfort.*]

1. One that is melancholy and refuses comfort.

Discomfortable cousin, know'st thou not,
That when the searching eye of heav'n is hid
Behind the globe, it lights the lower world. *Shakes. R. II.*

2. That causes sadness.

What! did that help poor Dorus, whose eyes could carry unto him no other news but *discomfortable?* *Sidney.*

To DISCOMME'ND. *v. a.* [*dis* and *commend.*] To blame; to censure; to mention with disapprobation.

Absolutely we cannot *discommend*, we cannot absolutely approve, either willingness to live, or forwardness to die. *Hooker.*

Now you will all be wits; and he, I pray,
And you, that *discommend* it, mend the play. *Denham.*

Neither do I *discommend* the lofty stile in tragedy, which is naturally pompous and magnificent. *Dryd. Span. Fry. Dedicat.*

DISCOMME'NDABLE. *adj.* [from *discommend.*] Blameable; censurable; deserving blame.

Pusillanimity is, according to Aristotle's morality, a vice very *discommendable.* *Ayliffe's Parergon.*

DISCOMME'NDABLENESS. *n. s.* [from *discommendable.*] Blameableness; liableness to censure. *Dict.*

DISCOMMENDA'TION. *n. s.* [from *discommend.*] Blame; reproach; censure.

Tully assigns three motions, whereby, without any *discommendation*, a man might be drawn to become an accuser of others. *Ayliffe's Parergon.*

DISCOMME'NDER. *n. s.* [from *discommend.*] One that discommends; a dispraiser.

To DISCOMMO'DE. *v. a.* [*dis* and *commode*, French.] To put to inconvenience; to molest; to incommode.

DISCOMMO'DIOUS. *adj.* [from *discommode.*] Inconvenient; troublesome; unpleasing.

So many thousand soldiers, unfit for any labour or other trade, must either seek service and employment abroad, which may be dangerous, or else employ themselves here at home, which may be *discommodious.* *Spenser's State of Ireland.*

DISCOMMO'DITY. *n. s.* [from *discommode.*] Inconvenience; disadvantage; hurt; mischief.

We speak now of usury, how the *discommodities* of it may be best avoided, and the commodities retained: or how in the balance of commodities and *discommodities*, the qualities of usury, are to be reconciled. *Bacon.*

It is better that a ship should be preserved with some *discommodity* to the sailors, than that, the sailors being in health, the ship should perish. *Hayward.*

To DISCOMPO'SE. *v. a.* [*decomposer*, French.]

1. To disorder; to unsettle.

The debate upon the self-denying ordinance had raised many jealousies, and *discomposed* the confidence that had formerly been between many of them. *Clarendon, b.* viii.

2. To ruffle; to disorder.

Now Betty from her master's bed had flown,
And softly stole to *discompose* her own. *Swift.*

3. To disturb the temper; to agitate by perturbation.

No more, dear mother: ill in death it shows,
Your peace of mind by rage to *discompose.* *Dryd. Tyr. Love.*

4. To offend; to fret; to vex.

Men, who possess all the advantages of life, are in a state where there are many accidents to disorder and *discompose*, but few to please them. *Swift.*

5. To displace; to discard.

Though he was a dark prince, and infinitely suspicious, he never put down or *discomposed* a counsellor, or near servant. *Bac.*

DISCOMPO'SURE. *n. s.* [from *discompose.*] Disorder; perturbation.

He threw himself upon his bed, lamenting with much passion, and with abundance of tears; and continued in this melancholick *discomposure* of mind many days. *Clarendon.*

To DISCONCE'RT. *v. a.* [*dis* and *concert.*]

1. To unsettle the mind; to discompose.

You need not provoke their spirits by outrages: a careless gesture, a word, or a look, is enough to *disconcert* them. *Collier.*

2. To break a scheme; to defeat a machination.

DISCONFO'RMITY. *n. s.* [*dis* and *conformity.*] Want of agreement; inconsistency.

Lies arise from errour and mistake, or malice and forgery; they consist in the disagreement and *disconformity* betwixt the speech and the conception of the mind, or the conceptions of the mind and the things themselves, or the speech and the things. *Hakewill on Providence.*

DISCONGRU'ITY. *n. s.* [*dis* and *congruity.*] Disagreement; inconsistency.

There is want of capacity in the thing, to sustain such a duration from the intrinsical *discongruity* of the one to the other. *Hale's Origin of Mankind.*

DISCO'NSOLATE. *adj.* [*dis* and *console.*] Without comfort; hopeless; sorrowful; melancholy.

See Cassius all *disconsolate*,
With Pindarus his bondman, on this hill. *Shak. Jul. Cæsar.*

If patiently thy bidding they obey,
Dismiss them not *disconsolate.* *Milton's Paradise Lost, b.* xi.

The ladies and the knights, no shelter nigh,
Were dropping wet, *disconsolate* and wan,
And through their thin array receiv'd the rain. *Dryden.*

The moon reflects the sunbeams to us, and so, by illuminating the air, takes away in some measure the *disconsolate* darkness of our winter-nights. *Ray on the Creation.*

DISCO'NSOLATELY. *adv.* [from *disconsolate.*] In a disconsolate manner; comfortlessly.

DISCO'NSOLATENESS. *n. s.* [from *disconsolate.*] The state of being disconsolate.

DISCONTE'NT. *n. s.* [*dis* and *content.*] Want of content; uneasiness at the present state.

I see your brows full of *discontent*,
Your hearts of sorrows, and your eyes of tears. *Shakespeare.*

Not that their pleasures caus'd her *discontent*
She sigh'd, not that they stay'd, but that she went. *Pope.*

DISCONTE'NT. *adj.* [*dis* and *content.*] Uneasy at the present state; dissatisfied.

They were of their own nature circumspect and slow, discountenanced and *discontent*, and those the earl singled as fittest for his purpose. *Hayward.*

To DISCO'NTENT. *v. a.* [from the noun.] To dissatisfy; to make uneasy at the present state.

I know a *discontented* gentleman,
Whose humble means match not his haughty spirit. *Shakes.*

The *discontented* now are only they
Whose crimes before did your just cause betray. *Dryden.*

DISCONTE'NTED. *participial adj.* [from *discontent.*] Uneasy; chearless; malevolent.

Let us know
What will tie up your *discontented* sword? *Shak. Ant. and Cl.*

These are, beyond comparison, the two greatest evils in this world, a diseased body and a *discontented* mind. *Tillotson.*

The goddess, with a *discontented* air,
Seems to reject him, though she grants his pray'r. *Pope.*

DISCONTE'NTEDNESS. *n. s.* [from *discontented.*] Uneasiness; want of ease; dissatisfaction.

A beautiful bust of Alexander the Great, casts up his face to heaven with a noble air of grief, or *discontentedness* in his looks. *Addison's Travels.*

DISCONTE'NTMENT. *n. s.* [from *discontent.*] The state of being discontented; uneasiness.

These are the voices that fill them with general *discontentment*, as though the bosom of that famous church, wherein they live, were more noisome than any dungeon. *Hooker.*

Certainly the politick and artificial nourishing and entertaining of hopes, and carrying men from hopes to hopes, is one of the best antidotes against the poison of *discontentments.* *Bacon, Essay* 16.

DISCONTI'NUANCE. *n. s.* [from *discontinue.*]

1. Want of cohesion of parts; want of union of one part with another; disruption.

The stillicides of water, if there be enough to follow, will draw themselves into a small thread, because they will not discontinue; but if there be no remedy, then they cast themselves into round drops, which is the figure that saveth the body most from *discontinuance.* *Bacon's Natural History.*

2. Cessation; intermission.

Let us consider, whether our approaches to him are sweet and refreshing, and if we are uneasy under any long *discontinuance* of our conversation with him. *Atterbury's Sermons.*

3. [In the common law.] An interruption or breaking off; as *discontinuance* of possession, or *discontinuance* of process. The effect of *discontinuance* of possession is, that a man may not enter upon his own land or tenement alienated, whatsoever his right be unto it, or by his own authority; but must seek to recover possession by law. The effect of *discontinuance* of plea is, that the instance may not be taken up again, but by a new writ to begin the suit afresh. *Cowel.*

DISCONTINUA'TION. *n. s.* [from *discontinue.*] Disruption of continuity; breach of union of parts; disruption; separation.

Upon any *discontinuation* of parts, made either by bubbles or by shaking the glass, the whole mercury falls. *Newt. Opt.*

To DISCONTI'NUE. *v. a.* [*discontinuer*, French.]

1. To lose the cohesion of parts; to suffer separation or disruption of substance.

All bodies, ductile and tensile, as metals that will be drawn into wires; wool and tow, that will be drawn into yarn, or thread, have in them the appetite of not *discontinuing* strong, which maketh them follow the force that pulleth them out; and yet so as not to *discontinue* or forsake their own body. *Bac.*

2. To lose an established or prescriptive custom.

Thyself shalt *discontinue* from thine heritage that I gave thee, and I will cause thee to serve thine enemies. *Jer.* xvii. 4.

To

To DISCONTI'NUE. *v. a.* To leave off; to cease any practice or habit.

Twenty puny lies I'll tell
That men shall swear I've *discontinued* school
Above a twelvemonth. *Shakespeare.*

Examine thy customs of diet, sleep, exercise, apparel, and the like, and try, in any thou shalt judge hurtful, to *discontinue* it by little and little; but so, as if thou find any inconvenience by the change, thou come back to it again. *Bacon's Essays.*

2. To break off; to interrupt.

There is that property, in all letters, of aptness to be conjoined in syllables and words, through the voluble motions of the organs from one stop or figure to another, that they modify and discriminate the voice, without appearing to *discontinue* it. *Holder's Elements of Speech.*

DISCONTINU'ITY. *n. s.* [*dis* and *continuity.*] Disunity of parts; want of cohesion.

That this *discontinuity* of parts is the principal cause of the opacity of bodies, will appear by considering that opaque substances become transparent by filling their pores with any substance of equal, or almost equal density with their parts. *Newton Opt.*

DISCONVE'NIENCE *n. s.* [*dis* and *convenience.*] Incongruity; disagreement; opposition of nature.

Fear ariseth many times out of natural antipathies of nature, but in these *disconveniences* of nature deliberation hath no place at all. *Bramhall's Answer to Hobbs.*

DI'SCORD. *n. s.* [*discordia*, Latin.]

1. Disagreement; opposition; mutual anger; reciprocal oppugnancy.

See what a scourge is laid upon your hate,
That heav'n finds means to kill your joys with love!
And I, for winking at your *discords* too,
Have lost a brace of kinsmen. *Shakesp. Rom. and Jul.*

Take but degree away, untune that string,
And hark what *discord* follows; each thing meets
In meer oppugnancy. *Shakesp. Troil. and Cress.*

He is a false witness that speaketh lies, and that soweth *discord* among brethren. *Prov.* vi. 19.

2. Difference, or contrariety of qualities.

Discord, like that of music's various parts,
Discord that makes the harmony of hearts;
Discord that only this dispute shall bring,
Who best shall love the duke and serve the king. *Dryd. Ep.*

All nature is but art unknown to thee;
All chance, direction which thou canst not see;
All *discord*, harmony not understood;
All partial evil, universal good. *Pope's Essay on Man.*

3. [In music.] Sounds not of themselves pleasing, but necessary to be mixed with others.

It is found alone that doth immediately and incorporeally affect most; this is most manifest in music, and concords and *discords* in music: for all sounds, whether they be sharp or flat, if they be sweet, have a roundness and equality; and if they be harsh, are unequal: for a *discord* itself is but a harshness of divers sounds meeting. *Bacon's N. Hist. Part* I. *p.* 400.

It is the lark that sings so out of tune,
Straining harsh *discords* and unpleasing sharps. *Shakesp.*

How doth music amaze us, when of *discords* she maketh the sweetest harmony? *Peacham.*

To DI'SCORD. *v. n.* [*discordo*, Latin.] To disagree; not to suit with.

Sounds do disturb and alter the one the other; sometimes the one drowning the other, and making it not heard; sometimes the one jarring and *discording* with the other, and making a confusion. *Bacon's Nat. Hist.* N°. 227.

DISCO'RDANCE } *n. s.* [from *discord.*] Disagreement; opposition; inconsistency.
DISCO'RDANCY. }

DISCO'RDANT. *adj.* [*discordans*, Latin.]

1. Inconsistent; at variance with itself.

Myrrha was joy'd the welcome news to hear,
But clogg'd with guilt, the joy was unsincere;
So various, so *discordant* is the mind,
That in our will a different will we find. *Dryden.*

2. Opposite; contrarious.

The *discordant* attraction of some wandering comets would certainly distract and disorder the harmony of the motions and revolutions of the planets, if they approached too near them. *Cheyne's Phil. Princip.*

3. Incongruous; not conformable.

Hither conscience is to be referred, if by a comparison of things done with the rule there be a consonancy, then follows the sentence of approbation; if *discordant* from it, the sentence of condemnation. *Hale's Origin of Mankind.*

DISCO'RDANTLY. *adv.* [from *discordant.*]

1. Inconsistently; in disagreement with itself.

2. In disagreement with another.

Two strings of a musical instrument being struck together, making two noises that arrive at the ear at the same time as to sense, yield a sound differing from either of them, and as it were compounded of both; insomuch, that if they be *discordantly* tuned, though each of them struck apart, would yield a pleasing sound; yet being struck together, they make a harsh and troublesome noise. *Boyle on Colours.*

3. Peevishly; in a contradictious manner.

To DISCO'VER. *v. a.* [*descouvrir*, French; *dis* and *cover.*]

1. To shew; to disclose; to bring to light.

Go draw aside the curtains, and *discover*
The several caskets to this noble prince. *Sh. Merch. of Ven.*

He *discovereth* deep things out of darkness, and bringeth out to light the shadow of death. *Job* xii. 22.

2. To make known.

We will pass over unto those men, and we will *discover* ourselves unto them. *Isa.* xiv. 8.

3. To find out; to espy.

He shall never by any alteration in me *discover* my knowledge of his mistake. *Pope's Letters.*

DISCO'VERABLE. *adj.* [from *discover.*]

1. That which may be found out.

That mineral matter which is so sparingly and dispersedly intermixed with the common and terrestrial matter, as not to be *discoverable* by human industry; or if *discoverable*, diffused and scattered amongst the crasser and more unprofitable matter, can never be separated. *Woodw. Nat. Hist.*

Revelation may assert two things to be joined, whose connection or agreement is not *discoverable* by reason. *Watts's Log.*

2. Apparent; exposed to view.

They were deceived by Satan, and that not in an invisible situation, but in an open and *discoverable* apparition, that is, in the form of a serpent. *Brown's Vulg. Err. b.* i. *c.* 6.

It is concluded by astronomers, that the atmosphere of the moon hath no clouds nor rains, but a perpetual and uniform serenity; because nothing *discoverable* in the lunar surface is ever covered and absconded by the interposition of any clouds or mists. *Bentley's Serm.*

DISCO'VERER. *n. s.* [from *discover.*]

1. One that finds any thing not known before; a finder out.

If more be found out, they will not recompence the *discoverer*'s pains, but will be fitter to be cast out. *Holder's El.*

Places receive appellations according to the language of the *discoverer*, from observations made upon the people. *Notes on Od.*

The Cape of Good Hope was doubled in those early times; and that the Portuguese were not the first *discoverers* of that navigation. *Arbuthnot on Coin.*

An old maiden gentlewoman is the greatest *discoverer* of judgments; she can tell you what sin it was that set such a man's house on fire. *Add. Spect.* N°. 483.

2. A scout; one who is put to descry the posture or number of an enemy; speculator.

Here stand, my lords, and send *discoverers* forth,
To know the numbers of our enemies. *Shakesp. Hen.* VI.

DISCO'VERY. *n. s.* [from *discover.*]

1. The act of finding any thing hidden.

Of all who since have us'd the open sea,
Than the bold English none more fame have won;
Beyond the year, and out of heaven's high way,
They make *discoveries* where they see no sun. *Dryd. A. M.*

2. The act of revealing or disclosing any secret.

What must I hold a candle to my shame?
They in themselves, good sooth, are too too light.
Why 'tis an office of *discovery*, love,
And I should be obscur'd. *Shakesp. Merch of Venice.*

Things that appeared amiable by the light of this world, appear of a different odious hue in the clear *discoveries* of the next. *South's Serm.*

It would be necessary to say something of the state to which the war hath reduced us; such a *discovery* ought to be made as late as possible. *Swift.*

To DISCOU'NSEL. *v. a.* [*dis* and *counsel.*] To dissuade; to give contrary advice.

But him that palmer from that vanity,
With temperate advice *discounselled*. *Spenser's Fa. Qu.*

DISCOU'NT. *n. s.* [*dis* and *count.*] The sum refunded in a bargain.

His whole intention was, to buy a certain quantity of copper money from Wood at a large *discount*, and sell them as well as he could. *Swift's Miscel.*

To DISCOU'NT. *v. a.* [from the noun.] To count back; to pay back again.

My father's, mother's, brother's death I pardon:
My prayers and penance shall *discount* for these,
And beg of heav'n to charge the bill on me. *Dryd Don Seb.*

The farmers spitefully combin'd,
Force him to take his tithes in kind;
And Parvisol *discounts* arrears,
By bills for taxes and repairs. *Swift's Miscel.*

To DISCOU'NTENANCE. *v. a.* [*dis* and *countenance.*]

1. To discourage by cold treatment.

Unwilling they were to *discountenance* any man who was willing to serve them. *Clarendon, b.* viii.

The truly upright judge will always countenance right, and *discountenance* wrong. *Atterbury's Serm.*

2. To

2. To abash; to put to shame.

Wisdom in discourse with her,
Loses *discountenanced*, and like folly shews. *Milt. Par. Lost.*
He came, and with him Eve, more loth, though first
To offend; *discountenanc'd* both, and discompos'd. *Milton.*
How would one look from his majestic brow,
Seated as on the top of virtue's hill,
Discount'nance her despis'd. *Milton.*

DISCOUNTENANCE. *n.s.* [*dis* and *countenance.*] Cold treatment; unfavourable aspect; unfriendly regard.

He thought a little *discountenance* upon those persons would suppress that spirit. *Clarendon.*

All accidental misfortunes, how inevitable soever, were still attended with very apparent *discountenance*. *Clarendon, b.* viii.

In expectation of the hour of judgment, he patiently bears all the difficulties of duty, and the *discountenance* he meets with from a wicked and prophane world. *Rogers's Serm.*

DISCOU'NTENANCER. *n.s.* [from *discountenance.*] One that discourages by cold treatment; one that depresses by unfriendly regard.

Rumours of scandal and murmurs against the king and his government, taxed him for a great taxer of his people and *discountenancer* of his nobility. *Bacon's Hen.* VII.

To DISCOURAGE. *v. a.* [*decourager*, Fr. *dis* and *courage.*]

1. To depress; to deprive of confidence; to deject; to dastardize.

I might neither encourage the rebels insolence, nor *discourage* the protestants loyalty and patience. *K. Charles.*

The apostle with great zeal *discourages* too unreasonable a presumption. *Roger's Serm.*

2. To deter; to fright from any attempt: with *from* before the thing.

Wherefore *discourage* ye the heart of the children of Israel *from* going over into the land? *Numb.* xxxii. 7.

3. It is irregularly used by *Temple*, with *to* before the following word.

You may keep your beauty and your health, unless you destroy them yourself, or *discourage* them to stay with you, by using them ill. *Temple's Miscell.*

DISCOU'RAGER. *n.s.* [from *discourage.*] One that impresses diffidence and terror.

Most men in years, as they are generally *discouragers* of youth, are like old trees, which being past bearing themselves, will suffer no young plants to flourish beneath them. *Pope.*

DISCOU'RAGEMENT. *n.s.* [from *discourage.*]

1. The act of deterring, or depressing hope.

2. Determent; that which deters from any thing.

Amongst other impediments of any inventions, it is none of the meanest *discouragements*, that they are so generally derided by common opinion. *Wilkins's Math. Magn.*

The books read at schools and colleges, are full of incitements to virtue, and *discouragements* from vice. *Swift.*

3. The cause of depression, or fear.

To things we would have them learn, the great and only *discouragement* is that they are called to them. *Locke.*

DISCOU'RSE. *n.s.* [*discours*, Fr. *discursus*, Latin.]

1. The act of the understanding, by which it passes from premises to consequences.

By reason of that original weakness in the instruments, without which the understanding part is not able in this world by *discourse* to work, the very conceit of painfulness is a bridle to stay us. *Hooker, b.* 1. *s.* 7.

Sure he that made us with such large *discourse*,
Looking before and after, gave us not
That capability and godlike reason
To rust in us unus'd. *Shakespeare.*

The third act of the mind is that which connects propositions, and deduceth conclusions from them: and this the schools call *discourse*; and we shall not miscall it, if we name it reason. *Glanv. Sceps. c.* 13.

2. Conversation; mutual intercourse of language; talk.

He waxeth wiser than himself, more by an hour's *discourse*, than by a day's meditation. *Bacon's Essays.*

In thy *discourse*, if thou desire to please,
All such is courteous, useful, new, or witty;
Usefulness come by labour, wit by ease,
Courtesy grows in court, news in the city. *Herbert.*
The vanquish'd party with the victors join'd,
Nor wanted sweet *discourse*, the banquet of the mind. *Dryd.*

3. Effusion of language; speech.

Topical and superficial arguments, of which there is store to be found on both sides, filling the head with variety of thoughts, and the mouth with copious *discourse*, serve only to amuse the understanding and entertain company. *Locke.*

4. A treatise; a dissertation either written or uttered.

The *discourse* here is about ideas, which, he says, are real things, and seen in God. *Locke.*

Plutarch, in his *discourse* upon garrulity, commends the fidelity of the companions of Ulysses. *Pope's Odyssey, Notes.*

To DISCOU'RSE. *v. n.* [from the noun.]

1. To converse; to talk; to relate.

How wert thou handled, being prisoner?
Discourse, I pr'ythee on this turret's top. *Shakesp. Hen.* IV.
Of various things *discoursing* as he pass'd,
Anchises hither bends. *Dryd.*

2. To treat upon in a solemn or set manner.

That the general maxims we are *discoursing* of are not known to children, ideots, and a great part of mankind, we have already sufficiently proved. *Locke.*

3. To reason; to pass from premises to consequences.

And yet the pow'rs of her *discoursing* thoughts,
From the collection is a diverse thing. *Davies.*
Brutes do want that quick *discoursing* pow'r. *Davies.*

To DISCOU'RSE. *v. a.* [from the noun.] To treat of.

Renowned duke, vouchsafe to take the pains
To go with us into the abbey here,
And let us there at large *discourse* all our fortunes. *Sh. Co. Err.*

DISCOU'RSER, *n. s.* [from *discourse.*]

1. A speaker; an haranguer.

The tract of every thing,
Would by a good *discourser* lose some life,
Which action's self was tongue to. *Shakespeare.*

2. A writer on any subject; a dissertator.

Philologers and critical *discoursers*, who look beyond the obvious exteriors of things, will not be angry at our narrower explorations. *Brown's Pref. to Vulgar Errours.*

But it seems to me, that such *discoursers* do reason upon short views, and a very moderate compass of thought. *Swift.*

DISCOU'RSIVE. *adj.* [from *discourse.*]

1. Passing by intermediate steps from premises to consequences.

The soul
Reason receives, and reason is her being,
Discoursive, or intuitive; discourse
Is oftest yours, the latter is most ours. *Milton's Par. Lost.*

2. Containing dialogue; interlocutory.

The epic is every where interlaced with dialogue or *discoursive* scenes. *Dryden on Dramatic Poesy.*

DISCOU'RTEOUS. *adj.* [*dis* and *courteous.*] Uncivil; uncomplaisant; defective in good manners.

He resolved to unhorse the first *discourteous* knight he should meet. *Motteux's Don Quixote.*

DISCOU'RTESY. *n. s.* [*dis* and *courtesy.*] Incivility; rudeness; act of disrespect.

As if chearfulness had been tediousness, and good entertainment had been turned to *discourtesy*, he would ever get himself alone. *Sidney.*

Be calm in arguing; for fierceness makes
Error a fault, and truth *discourtesy*. *Herbert.*

He made me many visits, maundering as if I had done him a *discourtesy*. *Wiseman's Surg.*

DISCOU'RTEOUSLY. *adv.* [from *discourteous.*] Uncivily; rudely.

DISCOU'S. [from *discus*, Latin.] Broad; flat; wide. Used by botanists to denote the middle, plain, and flat part of some flowers, such as the flos solis, &c. *Quincy.*

DISCRE'DIT. *n. s.* [*decrediter*, French.] Ignominy; reproach; lower degree of infamy; disgrace; imputation of a fault.

Had I been the finder out of this secret, it would not have relished among my other *discredits*. *Shakespeare's Winter's Tale.*

Idlers will ever live like rogues, and not fall to work, but be lazy, and then certify over their country to the *discredit* of a plantation. *Bacon.*

That they may quit their morals without any *discredit* to their intellectuals, they fly to several stale, trite, pitiful objections and cavils. *South.*

'Tis the duty of every christian to be concerned for the reputation or *discredit* his life may bring on his profession. *Rogers.*

Alas, the small *discredit* of a bribe,
Scarce hurts the lawyer, but undoes the scribe. *Pope.*

To DISCRE'DIT. *v a.* [*decrediter*, French.]

1. To deprive of credibility; to make not trusted.

He had fram'd to himself, by the instruction of his frailty, many deceiving promises of life, which I have *discredited* to him, and now is he resolved to die. *Shakes.*

2. To disgrace; to bring reproach upon; to shame; to make less reputable or honourable.

You had left unseen a wonderful piece of work, which not to have been blest withal, would have *discredited* you. *Shakes.*

He is commended that makes a saving voyage, and least *discredits* his travels, who returns the same man he went. *Wotton.*

He like a privileg'd spy, whom nothing can
Discredit, libels now 'gainst each great man. *Donne.*

Reflect how glorious it would be to appear in countenance of *discredited* duty, and by example of piety revive the declining spirit of religion. *Rogers.*

Without care our best actions will lose much of their influence, and our virtues will be often *discredited* with the appearance of evil. *Rogers's Serm.*

DISCRE'ET. *adj.* [*discret*, French.] Prudent; circumspect; cautious; sober; not rash; not precipitant; not careless; not hardily adventurous.

Honest, *discreet*, quiet, and godly learned men, will not be withdrawn by you. *Whitgifte.*

Less fearful than *discreet*,
You love the fundamental part of state,
More than you doubt the charge of 't. *Shakespeare's Coriol.*
To elder years to be *discreet* and grave,
Then to old age maturity she gave. *Denham.*

It is the *discreet* man, not the witty, nor the learned, nor the brave, who guides the conversation, and gives measures to society. *Addison's Spectator*, N°. 225.

2. Modest; not forward.

Dear youth, by fortune favour'd, but by Love
Alas! not favour'd less, be still as now
Discreet. *Thomson's Summer, l.* 1355.

DISCREE'TLY. *adv.* [from *discreet.*] Prudently; cautiously; circumspectly.

Poets lose half the praise they should have got,
Could it be known what they *discreetly* blot. *Waller.*

The labour of obedience, loyalty, and subjection, is no more but for a man honestly and *discreetly* to sit still. *South.*

Profit springs from husks *discreetly* d. *Philips.*

The dullest brain, if gently stirr'd,
Perhaps may waken to a humming bird;
The most recluse, *discreetly* open'd, find
Congenial object in the cockle kind. *Dunciad, b.* iv. *l.* 437.

DISCREE'TNESS. *n. s.* [from *discreet.*] The quality of being discreet; discretion.

DI'SCREPANCE. *n. s.* [*discrepantia*, Latin.] Difference; contrariety; disagreement.

DI'SCREPANT. *adj.* [*discrepans*, Latin.] Different; disagreeing; contrary.

DISCRE'TE. *adj.* [*discretus*, Latin.]

1. Distinct; disjoined; not continuous.

Discrete quantity, or different individuals, are measured by number, without any breaking continuity, that is, in things that have continuity, as continued quantity and motion. *Hale's Origin. of Mankind.*

2. Disjunctive; as, *I resign my life, but not my honour*, is a *discrete* proposition.

3. *Discrete* proportion is when the ratio between two pairs of numbers or quantities is the same; but there is not the same proportion between all the four: thus, 6 : 8 :: 3 : 4. *Harris.*

DISCRE'TION. *n. s.* [from *discretio*, Latin.]

1. Prudence; knowledge to govern or direct one's self; skill; wise management.

Nothing then was further thought upon for the manner of governing; but all permitted unto their wisdom and *discretion* which were to rule. *Hooker, b* i. *s.* 10.

A knife may be taken away from a child, without depriving them of the benefits thereof, which have years and *discretion* to use it. *Hooker, b.* iv. *s* 12.

It is not good that children should know any wickedness: old folks, you know, have *discretion*, as they say, and know the world. *Shakespeare's Merry Wives of Windsor.*

All this was order'd by the good *discretion*
Of the right reverend cardinal of York. *Shakesp. Hen.* VIII.

The pleasure of commanding our passions is to be preferred before any sensual pleasure; because it is the pleasure of wisdom and *discretion*. *Tillotson.*

But care in poetry must still be had,
It asks *discretion*, ev'n in running mad. *Pope's Ess. on Crit.*

There is no talent so useful towards rising in the world, or which puts men more out of the reach of fortune than *discretion*, a species of lower prudence. *Swift.*

2. Liberty of acting at pleasure; uncontrolled, and unconditional power; as, he surrenders at *discretion*; that is, without stipulation.

DISCRE'TIONARY. *adj.* [from *discretion.*] Left at large; unlimited; unrestrained.

A deacon may have a dispensation for entering into orders before he is twenty three years of age, and it is *discretionary* in the bishop to admit him to that order at what time he thinks fit. *Ayliff's Parergon.*

The major being a person of consummate experience, was invested with a *discretionary* power. *Tatler*, N° 61.

DISCRE'TIVE. *adj.* [*discretus*, Latin.]

1. [In logick.] *Discretive* propositions are such wherein various, and seemingly opposite judgements are made, whose variety or distinction is noted by the particles *but, tho', yet*, &c. as, *travellers may change their climate*, but *not their temper: Job was patient*, tho' *his grief was great.* *Watts's Logic.*

2. [In grammar.] *Discretive* conjunctions are such as imply opposition; as, *not a man* but *a beast.*

DISCRI'MINABLE. *adj.* [from *discriminate.*] Distinguishable by outward marks or tokens. *Dict.*

To DISCRI'MINATE. *v. a.* [*discrimino*, Latin.]

1. To mark with notes of difference; to distinguish by certain tokens from another.

Oysters and cockles and muscles, which move not, have no *discriminate* sex. *Bacon's Natural History*, N°. 875.

There are three sorts of it differing in fineness from each other, and *discriminated* by the natives by three peculiar names. *Boyle.*

The right hand is *discriminated* from the left by a natural, necessary, and never to be confounded distinction. *South.*

Although the features of his countenance be no reason of obedience, yet they may serve to *discriminate* him from any other person, whom she is not to obey. *Stillingfleet.*

There may be ways of *discriminating* the voice; as by acuteness and gravity, the several degrees of rising and falling from one tone or note to another. *Holder.*

2. To select or separate from others.

You owe little less for what you are not, than for what you are, to that *discriminating* mercy, to which alone you owe your exemption from miseries *Boyle.*

DISCRI'MINATENESS. *n. s.* [from *discriminate.*] Distinctness; marked difference. *Dict.*

DISCRIMINA'TION. *n. s.* [from *discriminatio*, Latin.]

1. The state of being distinguished from other persons or things.

There is a reverence left to be shewed them on the account of their *discrimination* from other places, and separation for sacred uses. *Stillingfleet's Def. of Disc. on Rom Id l.*

2. The act of distinguishing one from another; distinction; difference put.

A satire should expose nothing but what is corrigible, and make a due *discrimination* between those that are, and those who are not the proper objects of it. *Addison's Spectator.*

By that prudent *discrimination* made between the offenders of different degrees, he obliges those whom he has distinguished as objects of mercy. *Addison's Freeholder*, N°. 31.

3. The marks of distinction.

Take heed of abetting any factions, or applying any publick *discriminations* in matters of religion. *King Charles.*

Letters arise from the first original *discriminations* of voice, by way of articulation, whereby the ear is able to judge and observe the differences of vocal sounds. *Holder's El. of Speech.*

DISCRI'MINATIVE. *adj.* [from *discriminate.*]

1. That which makes the mark of distinction; characteristical.

The only standing test, and *discriminative* characteristick of any metal or mineral, must be sought for in the constituent matter of it. *Woodward.*

2. That which observes distinction.

Discriminative providence knew before the nature and course of all things. *More's Antidote again: Atheism.*

DISCRI'MINOUS. *adj.* [from *discrimen*, Latin.] Dangerous; hazardous.

Any kind of spitting of blood imports a very *discriminous* state, unless it happens upon the gaping of a vein opened by a plethory. *Harvey on Consumptions.*

DISCU'BITORY. *adj.* [*discubitorius*, Lat.] Fitted to the posture of leaning.

After bathing they retired to bed, and refreshed themselves with a repast; and so that custom, by degrees, changed their cubiculary beds into *discubitory* *Brown's Vulgar Errours, b.* v.

DISCU'MBENCY. *n. s.* [*discumbens*, Latin.] The act of leaning at meat, after the ancient manner.

The Greeks and Romans used the custom of *discumbency* at meals, which was upon their left side; for so their right hand was free and ready for all service. *Brown's Vulgar Errours.*

To DISCU'MBER. *v. a.* [*dis* and *cumber.*] To disengage from any troublesome weight or bulk.

His limbs *discumber'd* of the clinging vest,
He binds the sacred cincture round his breast. *Pope's Odyss.*

To DISCU'RE. *v. a.* [*decouvrir*, French.] To discover; to reveal. A word perhaps peculiar to *Spenser.*

I will, if please you it *discure*, assay
To ease you of that ill. *Fairy Queen.*

DISCU'RSIVE. *adj.* [*discursif*, French, from *discurro*, Latin.]

1. Moving here and there; roving.

Some noises help sleep; as the blowing of the wind, and the trickling of water: they move a gentle attention, and whatsoever moveth attention, without too much labour, stilleth the natural and *discursive* motion of the spirits. *Bacon's N. Hist.*

2. Proceeding by regular gradation from premises to consequences; argumentative. This is sometimes, perhaps not improperly, written *discoursive.*

There is a sanctity of soul and body, of more efficacy for the receiving of divine truths, than the greatest pretences to *discursive* demonstration. *More's Divine Dialogues.*

There hath been much dispute touching the knowledge of brutes, whether they have a kind of *discursive* faculty, which some call reason. *Hale's Origin of Mankind.*

DISCU'RSIVELY. *adv.* [from *discursive.*] By due gradation of argument.

We have a principle within, whereby we think, and we know we think; whereby we do *discursively*, and by way of ratiocination, deduce one thing from another. *Hale.*

DISCU'RSORY. *adj.* [*discursor*, Latin.] Argumental; rational.

DI'SCUS. *n. s.* [Latin.] A quoit; a heavy piece of iron thrown in the ancient sports.

From Elatreus' strong arm the *discus* flies,
And sings with unmatch'd force along the skies. *Pope's Odyss.*

To DISCU'SS. *v. a.* [*discutio, discussum*, Latin.]

1. To examine; to ventilate; to clear by disquisition.

We

We are to *discuss* only those general exceptions which have been taken. *Hooker, b. iv. s. 1.*

His usage was to commit the *discussing* of causes privately to certain persons learned in the laws. *Ayliffe's Parergon.*

This knotty point should you and I *discuss*,
Or tell a tale. *Pope.*

2. To disperse any humour or swelling.

DISCU'SSER. *n. s.* [from *discuss.*] He that discusses; an examiner.

DISCU'SSION. *n. s.* [from *discuss.*]

1. Disquisition; examination; ventilation of a question.

Truth cannot be found without some labour and intention of the mind, and the thoughts dwelling a considerable time upon the survey and *discussion* of each particular. *South.*

Various *discussions* tear our heated brain:
Opinions often turn; still doubts remain;
And who indulges thought, increases pain. *Prior.*

2. [In surgery.] *Discussion* or resolution is nothing else but breathing out the humours by insensible transpiration. *Wiseman.*

DISCU'SSIVE. *adj.* [from *discuss.*] Having the power to discuss or disperse any noxious matter.

DISCU'TIENT. *n. s.* [*discutiens*, Latin.] A medicine that has power to repel or drive back the matter or tumours in the blood, with tendency to separate. It sometimes means the same as carminative. *Quincy.*

The swellings arising from these require to be treated, in their beginning, with moderate repellents and *discutients*. *Wise.*

To DISDA'IN. *v. a.* [*dédaigner*, French.] To scorn; to consider as unworthy of one's character.

There is nothing so great, which I will fear to do for you; nor nothing so small, which I will *disdain* to do for you. *Sidn.*

They do *disdain* us much beyond our thoughts,
Which makes me sweat with wrath. *Shakesp. Coriolanus.*

What safe and nicely I might well delay
By rule of knighthood, I *disdain* and spurn. *Shakes. K. Lear.*

Tell him, Cato
Disdains a life which he has power to offer. *Addison's Cato.*

DISDA'IN. *n. s.* [*sdegno*, Ital.] Contempt; scorn; contemptuous anger; indignation.

Children being haughty, through *disdain* and want of nurture, do stain the nobility of their kindred. *Eccles.* xxii. 10.

But against you, ye Greeks, ye coward train,
Gods! how my soul is mov'd with just *disdain!* *Pope's Od.*

DISDA'INFUL. *adj.* [*disdain* and *full.*] Contemptuous; haughtily scornful; indignant.

There will come a time when three words, uttered with charity and meekness, shall receive a far more blessed reward than three thousand volumes, written with *disdainful* sharpness of wit. *Hooker, Preface.*

The queen is obstinate,
Stubborn to justice, apt t' accuse it,
Disdainful to be tried by't. *Shakespeare.*

Seek through this grove;
A sweet Athenian lady is in love
With a *disdainful* youth: anoint his eyes;
But do it when the next thing he espies
Shall be the lady. *Shakespeare's Midsummer Night's Dream.*

But those I can accuse, I can forgive:
By my *disdainful* silence let them live. *Dryden.*

The *disdainful* soul came rushing through the wound. *Dry.*

DISDA'INFULLY. *adv.* [from *disdainful.*] Contemptuously; with haughty scorn; with indignation.

Either greet him not,
Or else *disdainfully*, which shall shake him more
Than if not look'd on. *Shakespeare's Troil. and Cressida.*

It is not to insult and domineer, to look *disdainfully*, and revile imperiously, that procures esteem from any one. *South.*

DISDA'INFULNESS. *n. s.* [from *disdainful.*] Contempt; contemptuousness; haughty scorn.

Can I forget, when they in prison placing her,
With swelling heart, in spite and due *disdainfulness*,
She lay for dead, 'till I help'd with unlacing her. *Sidney.*

A proud *disdainfulness* of other good men in all honest matters. *Ascham's Schoolmaster.*

DISEA'SE. *n. s.* [*dis* and *ease.*] Distemper; malady; sickness; morbid state.

What's the *disease* he means?
——'Tis call'd the evil. *Shakespeare's Macbeth.*

It is idle to propose remedies before we are assured of the *disease*, or to be in pain 'till we are convinced of the danger. *Swift's Project for the Advancement of Religion.*

Then wasteful forth
Walks the dire power of pestilent *disease*. *Thoms. Summer.*

To DISEA'SE. *v. a.* [from the noun.]

1. To afflict with disease; to torment with sickness; to make morbid; to infect.

We are all *diseased*,
And with our surfeiting and wanton hours
Have brought ourselves into a burning fever,
And we must bleed for it. *Shakespeare's Henry IV. p. ii.*

Flatt'rers yet wear silk, drink wine, lie soft,
Hug their *diseas'd* perfumes, and have forgot
That ever Timon was. *Shakespeare's Timon.*

Let her alone, lady: as she is now, she will but *disease* our better mirth. *Shakespeare's Coriolanus.*

He was *diseased* in his feet. 1 *Kings* xv. 23.

2. To put to pain; to pain; to make uneasy.

Though great light be insufferable to our eyes, yet the highest degree of darkness does not at all *disease* them. *Locke.*

DISEA'SEDNESS. *n. s.* [from *diseased.*] Sickness; morbidness; the state of being diseased.

This is a restoration to some former state; not that state of indigency and *diseasedness*. *Burnet's Theory of the Earth.*

DISE'DGED. *adj.* [*dis* and *edge.*] Blunted; obtunded; dulled.

I grieve myself
To think, when thou shalt be *disedg'd* by her
Whom now thou tir'st on, how thy memory
Will then be pang'd by me. *Shakespeare's Cymbeline.*

To DISEMBA'RK. *v. a.* [*dis* and *embark.*] To carry to land.

I must unto the road, to *disembark*
Some necessaries. *Shakespeare's Two Gentlemen of Verona.*

To DISEMBA'RK. *v. n.* To land; to go on land.

There *disembarking* on the green sea-side,
We land our cattle, and the spoil divide. *Pope's Odyssey.*

To DISEMBI'TTER. *v. a.* [*dis* and *embitter.*] To sweeten; to free from bitterness; to clear from acrimony.

Encourage such innocent amusements as may *disembitter* the minds of men, and make them mutually rejoice in the same agreeable satisfactions. *Addison's Freeholder*, N°. 34.

DISEMBO'DIED. *adj.* [*dis* and *embodied.*] Divested of their bodies.

To DISEMBO'GUE. *v. a.* [*disemboucher*, old French. *Skinner.*] To pour out at the mouth of a river; to vent.

Rivers
In ample oceans *disembogu'd*, are lost. *Dryden's Ovid.*

Rolling down, the steep Timavus raves,
And through nine channels *disembogues* his waves. *Addison.*

To DISEMBO'GUE. *v. n.* To gain a vent; to flow.

By eminences placed up and down the globe, the rivers make innumberable turnings and windings and at last *disembogue* in several mouths into the sea. *Cheyne's Phil. Prin.*

DISEMBO'WELLED. *participial adj.* [*dis* and *embowel.*] Taken from out the bowels.

So her *disembowell'd* web,
Arachne in a hall or kitchen spreads,
Obvious to vagrant flies. *Phillips.*

To DISEMBRO'IL. *v. a.* [*debrouiller*, French.] To disentangle; to free from perplexity; to reduce from confusion.

Then earth from air, and seas from earth were driv'n,
And grosser air sunk from etherial heav'n;
Thus *disembroil'd*, they take their proper place. *Dryden.*

The system of his politicks is *disembroiled*, and cleared of all those incoherences and independent matters that are woven into this motly piece. *Addison's Whig Examiner.*

To DISENA'BLE. *v. a.* [*dis* and *enable.*] To deprive of power; to disable; to sink into weakness; to weaken.

Now age has overtaken me; and want, a more insufferable evil, through the change of the times, has wholly *disenabled* me. *Dryden's Juvenal, Dedication.*

To DISENCHA'NT. *v. a.* [*dis* and *enchant.*] To free from the force of an enchantment; to deliver from the power of charms or spells.

Alas! let your own brain *disenchant* you. *Sidney.*

Muse, stoop thy *disenchanted* wing to truth. *Denham.*

Haste to thy work; a noble stroke or two
Ends all the charms, and *disenchants* the grove. *Dryden.*

To DISENCU'MBER. *v. a.* [*dis* and *encumber.*]

1. To discharge from incumbrances; to free from clogs and impediments; to disburthen; to exonerate.

It will need the actual intention, the particular stress and application of the whole soul, to *disencumber* and set it free, to scour off its rust, and remove those hindrances which would otherwise clog and check the freedom of its operations. *Spratt.*

The *disencumber'd* soul
Flew off, and left behind the clouds and starry pole. *Dryd.*

Dreams look like the amusements of the soul, when she is *disencumbered* of her machine; her sports and recreations, when she has laid her charge asleep. *Spectator*, N°. 487.

2. To free from obstruction of any kind.

Dim night had *disencumber'd* heav'n. *Milton's Par. Lost.*

The church of St. Justina, designed by Palladio, is the most handsome, luminous, *disencumbered* building, in the inside, that I have ever seen; and is esteemed, by many artists, one of the finest works in Italy. *Addison's Remarks on Italy.*

DISENCU'MBRANCE. *n. s.* [from the verb.] Freedom from incumbrance.

There are many who make a figure below what their fortune or merit entitles them to, out of mere choice, and an elegant desire of ease and *disencumbrance*. *Spectator*, N°. 264.

To DISENGA'GE. *v. a.* [*dis* and *engage.*]

1. To separate from any thing with which it is in union.

Some others, being very light, would float up and down a good while, before they could wholly *disengage* themselves and descend. *Burnet's Theory of the Earth.*

2. To

2. To withdraw the affection; to wean; to abſtract the mind.

It is requiſite that we ſhould acquaint ourſelves with God, that we ſhould frequently *diſengage* our hearts from earthly purſuits. *Atterbury.*

The conſideration that ſhould *diſengage* our fondneſs from worldly things, is, that they are uncertain in their foundation, fading, tranſient, and corruptible in their nature. *Rogers.*

3. To diſentangle; to clear from impediments or difficulties.

From civil broils he did us *diſengage*;
Found nobler objects for our martial rage. *Waller.*

In the next paragraph I found my author pretty well *diſengaged* from quotations. *Atterbury.*

4. To free from any thing that powerfully ſeizes the attention.

When our mind's eyes are *diſengag'd* and free,
They clearer, farther, and diſtinctly ſee. *Denham.*

To DISENGA'GE. *v. n.* To ſet one's ſelf free from; to withdraw one's affections from.

Providence gives us notice, by ſenſible declenſions, that we may *diſengage* from the world by degrees. *Collier on Thought.*

DISENGA'GED. *participial adj.* [from *diſengage.*] Vacant; at leiſure; not fixed down to any particular object of attention.

DISENGA'GEDNESS. *n. ſ.* [from *diſengage.*] The quality of being diſengaged; vacuity of attention; freedom from any preſſing buſineſs.

DISENGA'GEMENT. *n. ſ.* [from *diſengage.*]
1. Releaſe from any engagement, or obligation.
2. Freedom of attention; vacancy.

To DISENTA'NGLE. *v. a.* [*dis* and *entangle.*]

1. To ſet free from impediments; to diſembroil; to clear from perplexity or difficulty.

'Till they could find ſome expedient to explicate and *diſentangle* themſelves out of this labyrinth, they made no advance towards ſupplying their armies. *Clarendon, b.* viii.

The welfare of their ſouls requires a better judgment than their own, either to guide them in their duty, or to *diſentangle* them from a temptation. *South.*

2. To unfold or looſe the parts of any thing interwoven with one another.

Though in concretions particles ſo entangle one another, that they cannot in a ſhort time clear themſelves, yet they do inceſſantly ſtrive to *diſentangle* themſelves, and get away. *Boyle.*

3. To diſengage; to ſeparate.

Neither can God himſelf be otherwiſe underſtood by us than as a mind free, and *diſentangled* from all corporeal mixtures. *Stillingfleet's Def. of Diſc. on Rom. Idol.*

To DISENTE'RRE. *v. a.* [*dis* and *enterrer*, French.] To unbury; to take out of the grave.

Though the blindneſs of ſome fanaticks have ſavaged on the bodies of the dead, and have been ſo injurious unto worms as to *diſenterre* the bodies of the deceaſed, yet had they therein no deſign upon the ſoul. *Brown's Vul. Errours, b.* vii. *c.* 19.

To DISENTHRA'L. *v. a.* [*dis* and *enthral.*] To ſet free; to reſtore to liberty; to reſcue from ſlavery.

But God my ſoul ſhall *diſenthral*;
For I upon his name will call. *Sandys.*

If religion were falſe, bad men would ſet the utmoſt force of their reaſon on work to diſcover that falſity, and thereby *diſenthral* themſelves. *South's Sermons.*

To DISENTHRO'NE. *v. a.* [*dis* and *enthrone.*] To depoſe from ſovereignty; to dethrone.

Either to *diſenthrone* the king of heav'n
We war, if war be beſt; or to regain
Our own right loſt. *Milton's Paradiſe Loſt, b.* ii. *l.* 229.

To DISENTRA'NCE. [*dis* and *entrance.*] To awaken from a trance, or deep ſleep.

Ralpho, by this time *diſentranc'd*,
Upon his bum himſelf advanc'd,
Though ſorely bruis'd. *Hudibras, p.* i. *cant.* 3.

To DISESPO'USE. *v. a.* [*dis* and *eſpouſe.*] To ſeparate after faith plighted.

Such was the rage
Of Turnus, for Lavinia *diſeſpous'd. Milton's Parad. Loſt.*

DISESTE'EM. *n. ſ.* [*dis* and *eſteem.*] Slight regard; a diſregard more moderate than contempt.

When any one, by miſcarriage, falls into *diſeſteem*, he will fall under neglect and contempt. *Locke.*

To DISESTE'EM. *v. a.* [from the noun.] To regard ſlightly; to conſider with a ſlight degree of contempt.

Should Mars ſee't,
That horrid hurrier of men, or ſhe that betters him,
Minerva, never ſo incens'd, they could not *diſeſteem. Chapm.*

But if this ſacred gift you *diſeſteem*,
Then cruel plagues ſhall fall on Priam's ſtate. *Denham.*

I would not be thought to *diſeſteem* or diſſuade the ſtudy of nature. *Locke.*

DISESTIMA'TION. *n. ſ.* [*dis* and *æſtimatio*, Lat.] Diſreſpect; diſeſteem. *Dict.*

DISFA'VOUR. *n. ſ.* [*dis* and *favour.*]

1. Diſcountenance; unpropitious regard; unfavourable aſpect; unfavourable circumſtance.

It was verily thought, that had it not been for four great *diſfavours* of that voyage, the enterprize had ſucceeded. *Bacon.*

2. A ſtate of ungraciouſneſs or unacceptableneſs; a ſtate in which one is not favoured.

While free from ſacrilege, he was at peace, as it were, with God and man; but after his ſacrilege, he was in *diſfavour* with both. *Spelman.*

3. Want of beauty. *Dict.*

To DISFA'VOUR. *v. a.* [from the noun.] To diſcountenance; to withold or withdraw kindneſs.

Might not thoſe of higher rank, and nearer acceſs to her majeſty, receive her own commands, and be countenanced or *diſfavoured* according as they obey? *Swift.*

DISFIGURA'TION. *n. ſ.* [from *diſfigure.*]
1. The act of diſfiguring.
2. The ſtate of being diſfigured.
3. Deformity.

To DISFI'GURE. *v. a* [*dis* and *figure.*] To change any thing to a worſe form; to deform; to mangle.

One
To whom you are but as a form in wax
By him imprinted, and within his power
To leave the figure, or *diſfigure* it. *Shakeſpeare.*

In this the antique and well-noted face
Of plain old form is much *diſfigured. Shakeſp. King John.*

Abject is their puniſhment,
Diſfiguring not God's likeneſs, but their own,
Or, if his likeneſs, by themſelves defac'd. *Milt. Par. Loſt.*

Uriel once warn'd, purſu'd him down
The way he went, and on the Aſſyrian mount
Saw him *diſfigur'd* more than could befall
Spirit of happy ſort. *Milton's Paradiſe Loſt, b.* iv. *l.* 127.

A noſe flatter, or a mouth wider, could have conſiſted, as well as the reſt of his figure, with ſuch a ſoul and ſuch parts as made him, *diſfigured* as he was, capable to be a dignitary in the church. *Locke.*

Nor would his ſlaughter'd army now have lain
On Africk's ſands, *diſfigur'd* with their wounds,
To gorge the wolves and vultures of Numidia. *Addiſ. Cato.*

His long abſence, and travels which had *diſfigured* him, made him altogether unknown. *Pope on Epick Poetry.*

DISFI'GUREMENT. *n. ſ.* [from *diſfigure.*] Defacement of beauty; change of a better form to a worſe.

The *diſfigurement* that travel or ſickneſs has beſtowed upon him, is not thought great by the lady of the iſle. *Suckling.*

And they, ſo perfect is their miſery,
Not once perceive their foul *diſfigurement. Milton's Comus.*

To DISFO'REST. *v. a.* [*dis* and *foreſt.*] To reduce land from the privileges of a foreſt to the ſtate of common land.

To DISFRA'NCHISE. *v. a.* [*dis* and *franchiſe.*] To deprive of privileges or immunities.

DISFRANCHI'SEMENT. *n. ſ.* [from *diſfranchiſe.*] The act of depriving of privileges. *Dict.*

To DISFU'RNISH. *v. a.* [*dis* and *furniſh.*] To deprive; to unfurniſh; to ſtrip.

My riches are theſe poor habiliments,
Of which if you ſhould here *diſfurniſh* me,
You take the ſum and ſubſtance that I have. *Shakeſpeare.*

He durſt not *diſfurniſh* that country either of ſo great a commander, or of the wonted garriſons. *Knolles's Hiſtory.*

To DISGA'RNISH. *v. a.* [*dis* and *garniſh.*]
1. To ſtrip of ornaments. *Dict.*
2. To take guns from a fortreſs.

To DISGLO'RIFY. *v. a.* [*dis* and *glorify.*] To deprive of glory; to treat with indignity.

So Dagon ſhall be magnify'd, and God,
Beſides whom is no god, compar'd with idols,
Diſglorify'd, blaſphem'd, and had in ſcorn. *Milt. Agoniſtes.*

To DISGO'RGE. *v. a.* [*degorger*, Fr. from *gorge*, the throat.]

1. To diſcharge by the mouth; to ſpew out; to vomit.

So, ſo, thou common dog, did'ſt thou *diſgorge*
Thy glutton boſom of the royal Richard?
And now thou wouldſt eat thy dead vomit up,
And howl'ſt to find it. *Shakeſpeare's Henry* IV. *p.* ii.

From the diſtant ſhore they loudly laugh'd,
To ſee his heaving breaſt *diſgorge* the briny draught. *Dryden.*

2. To pour out with violence.

All th' emboſſed ſores and headed evils,
That thou with licence of free foot haſt caught,
Would thou *diſgorge* into the general world. *Shakeſpeare.*

The deep drawing barks do there *diſgorge*
Their warlike fraughtage. *Shakeſ. Troilus and Creſſida, Prol.*

They move along the banks
Of four infernal rivers, that *diſgorge*
Into the burning lake their baleful ſtreams. *Milt. Par. Loſt.*

There are ſcarcely any countries much annoyed with earthquakes, that have not volcanoes, or fiery vents; and theſe are conſtantly all in flames, whenever any earthquake happens; they *diſgorging* that fire which, whilſt underneath, was the cauſe of the diſaſter. *Derham's Phyſico-Theology.*

DISGRA'CE. *n. s.* [*disgrace*, French.]

1. Shame; ignominy; dishonour.

Like a dull actor now,
I have forgot my part, and I am out
Even to a full *disgrace*. *Shakespeare's Coriolanus.*

Poetry, howsoever censured, is not fallen from the highest stage of honour to the lowest stair of *disgrace*. *Peacham.*

2. State of dishonour.

To such bondage he was for so many courses tied by her, whose *disgraces* to him were graced by her excellence. *Sidney.*

3. State of being out of favour.

To DISGRA'CE. *v. a.* [from the noun.]

1. To bring a reproach upon; to dishonour.

We may not so in any one special kind admire her, that we *disgrace* her in any other; but let all her ways be according unto their place and degree adored. *Hooker, b.* ii. *s.* 1.

Mens passions will carry them far in misrepresenting an opinion, which they have a mind to *disgrace*. *Burnet.*

2. To put out of favour: as, *the minister was* disgraced.

DISGRA'CEFUL. *adj.* [*disgrace* and *full.*] Shameful; ignominious; reproachful.

Masters must correct their servants with gentleness, prudence, and mercy; not with upbraiding and *disgraceful* language, but with such only as may express and reprove the fault, and amend the person. *Taylor's Rule of living holy.*

To retire behind their chariots was as little *disgraceful* then, as it is now to alight from one's horse in a battle. *Pope.*

DISGRA'CEFULLY. *adv.* [from *disgraceful.*] In disgrace; with indignity; ignominiously.

The senate have cast you forth
Disgracefully, to be the common tale
Of the whole city. *Ben. Johnson's Catiline.*

DISGRA'CEFULNESS. *n. s.* [from *disgraceful.*] Ignominy.

DISGRA'CER. *n. s.* [from *disgrace.*] One that exposes to shame; one that causes ignominy.

I have given good advice to those infamous *disgracers* of the sex and calling. *Swift.*

DISGRA'CIOUS. *adj.* [*dis* and *gracious.*] Unkind; unfavourable.

I do suspect I have done some offence,
That seems *disgracious* in the city's eye. *Shakes. Richard* III.

To DISGUI'SE. *v. a.* [*deguiser*, French; *dis* and *guise.*]

1. To conceal by an unusual dress.

How might we *disguise* him?
——Alas, I know not: there is no woman's gown big enough for him. *Shakespeare's Merry Wives of Windsor.*

Disguis'd he came; but those his children dear
Their parent soon discern'd, though in disguise. *Milt. P. L.*

2. To hide by a counterfeit appearance; to cloak by a false show; as, he *disguised* his anger.

3. To disfigure; to change the form.

They saw the faces, which too well they knew,
Though then *disguis'd* in death, and smear'd all o'er
With filth obscene, and dropping putrid gore. *Dryd. Æn.*

Ulysses wakes, not knowing the place where he was; because Minerva made all things appear in a *disguised* view. *Pope.*

4. To deform by liquor: a low term.

I have just left the right worshipful, and his myrmidons, about a sneaker of five gallons: the whole magistracy was pretty well *disguised* before I gave them the slip. *Spectator.*

DISGUI'SE. *n. s.* [from the verb.]

1. A dress contrived to conceal the person that wears it.

They generally act in a *disguise* themselves, and therefore mistake all outward show and appearances for hypocrisy in others. *Addison's Spectator*, N°. 170.

2. A false appearance; counterfeit show.

You see we've burnt our cheeks; and mine own tongue
Splits what it speaks: the wild *disguise* hath almost
Antickt us. *Shakespeare's Anthony and Cleopatra.*

A sudden thought then starting in his mind,
Since I in Arcite cannot Arcite find,
The world may search in vain with all their eyes,
But never penetrate through this *disguise*. *Dryden's Fables.*

Hence guilty joys, distastes, surmises,
False oaths, false tears, deceits, *disguises*. *Pope.*

DISGUI'SEMENT. *n. s.* [from *disguise.*] Dress of concealment.

Under that *disguisement* I should find opportunity to reveal myself to the owner of my heart. *Sidney.*

The marquis thought best to dismask his beard, and told him, that he was going covertly to take a secret view of the forwardness of his majesty's fleet, then in preparation: this did somewhat handsomely heal the *disguisement*. *Wotton.*

DISGUI'SER. *n. s.* [from *disguise.*]

1. One that puts on a disguise.

I hope he is grown more disengaged from his intentness on his own affairs, which is quite the reverse to you, unless you are a very dextrous *disguiser*. *Swift.*

2. One that conceals another by a disguise; one that disfigures.

Death's a great *disguiser*. *Shakesp. Measure for Measure.*

DISGU'ST. *n. s.* [*degout*, French.]

1. Aversion of the palate from any thing.

2. Ill-humour; malevolence; offence conceived.

The manner of doing is of more consequence than the thing done, and upon that depends the satisfaction or *disgust* wherewith it is received. *Locke.*

Thence dark *disgust* and hatred, winding wiles,
Coward deceit, and ruffian violence. *Thomson's Spring.*

To DISGU'ST. *v. a.* [*degouter*, French; *degusto*, Latin.]

1. To raise aversion in the stomach; to distaste.

2. To strike with dislike; to offend. It is variously constructed with *at* or *with.*

If a man were *disgusted* at marriage, he would never recommend it to his friend. *Atterbury.*

Those unenlarged souls are *disgusted* with the wonders which the microscope has discovered. *Watts's Impr. of the Mind.*

3. To produce aversion: with *from.*

What *disgusts* me *from* having to do with answer-jobbers is, that they have no conscience. *Swift.*

DISGU'STFUL. *adj.* [*disgust* and *full.*] Nauseous; that which causes aversion.

I have finished the most *disgustful* task that ever I undertook. *Swift.*

DISH. *n. s.* [ꝺırc, Saxon; *dysc*, Erse; *discus*, Latin.]

1. A broad wide vessel, in which solid food is served up at the table.

Of these he murders one; he boils the flesh,
And lays the mangled morsels in a *dish*. *Dryden.*

I saw among the ruins an old heathen altar, with this particularity in it, that it is hollowed like a *dish* at one end; but it was not this end on which the sacrifice was laid. *Addis.*

2. A deep hollow vessel for liquid food.

Who would rob a hermit of his weeds,
His few books, or his beads, or maple *dish*;
Or do his grey hairs any violence? *Milton.*

A ladle for our silver *dish*
Is what I want, is what I wish. *Prior.*

3. The meat served in a dish; any particular kind of food.

I have here a *dish* of doves, that I would bestow upon your worship. *Shakespeare's Merchant of Venice.*

Let's kill him boldly, but not wrathfully;
Let's carve him as a *dish* fit for the gods,
Not hew him as a carcass fit for hounds. *Shakes. Jul. Cæs.*

The contract you pretend with that base wretch,
One bred of alms and foster'd with cold *dishes*,
With scraps o' th' court; it is no contract, none. *Sh. Cymb.*

'Tis not the meat, but 'tis the appetite
Makes eating a delight;
And if I like one *dish*
More than another, that a pheasant is. *Suckling.*

The earth would have been deprived of a most excellent and wholsome fare, and very many delicious *dishes* that we have the use and benefit of. *Woodward.*

Many people would, with reason, prefer the griping of an hungry belly to those *dishes* which are a feast to others. *Locke.*

To DISH. *v. a.* [from the noun.] To serve in a dish; to send up to table.

For conspiracy,
I know not how it tastes, though it be *dish'd*
For me to try. *Shakespeare's Winter's Tale.*

DISH-CLOUT. *n. s.* [*dish* and *clout.*] The cloath with which the maids rub their dishes.

A *dish-clout* of Jaquenetta's, he wears next his heart for a favour. *Shakespeare's Love's Labour Lost.*

Send them up to their masters with a *dish-clout* pinned at their tails. *Swift's Directions to the Cook.*

DISH-WASHER. *n. s.* [*dish* and *washer.*] The name of a bird.

DISHABI'LLE. *adj.* [*deshabillé*, French.] Undressed; loosely or negligently dressed.

Queens are not to be too negligently dressed or *dishabille*. *Dryden's Dufresnoy.*

DISHABI'LLE. *n. s.* Undress; loose dress.

A woman, who would preserve a lover's respect to her person, will be careful of her appearance before him when in *dishabille*. *Clarissa.*

To DISHA'BIT. *v. a.* [This word I have found only in Shakespeare.] To throw out of place; to drive from their habitation.

But for our approach those sleeping stones,
By the compulsion of their ordinance,
By this time from their fixed beds of lime
Had been *dishabited*, and wide havock made. *Shakesp. K. Lear.*

DISHA'RMONY. *n. s.* [*dis* and *harmony.*] Contrary to harmony.

To DISHEA'RTEN. *v. a.* [*dis* and *hearten.*]

1. To discourage; to deject; to terrify; to depress.

To *dishearten* with fearful sentences, as tho' salvation could hardly be hoped for, is not in our understanding so consonant with christian charity. *Hooker, b.* v. *s.* 22.

Be not *disheartened* then, nor cloud those looks,
That wont to be more chearful and serene. *Milt. Par. Lost.*

Yet neither thus *dishearten'd* nor dismay'd,
The time prepar'd I waited. *Milton.*

It is a consideration that might *dishearten* those who are engaged against the common adversaries, that they promise themselves as much from the folly of enemies, as from the power of their friends. *Stillingfleet's Pref. to Def. Rom. Id.*

Men cannot ſay, that the greatneſs of an evil and danger is an encouragement to men to run upon it; and that the greatneſs of any good and happineſs ought in reaſon to *diſhearten* men from the purſuit of it. *Tillotſon, Serm.* i.

A true chriſtian fervour is more than the alliances of our potent friends, or even the fears of our *diſheartened* enemies. *Atterbury.*

DISHE'RISON. *n. ſ.* [*dis* and *heriſon.*] The act of debarring from inheritance.

To DISHE'RIT. *v. a.* [*dis* and *inherit.*] To cut off from hereditary ſucceſſion; to debar from an inheritance.

He tries to reſtore to their rightful heritage ſuch good old Engliſh words as have been long time out of uſe, almoſt *diſherited.* *Spencer's Paſt.*

How they were rank'd ſhall reſt untold by me,
With nameleſs nymphs that liv'd in ev'ry tree;
Nor how the Dryads and the woodland train,
Diſherited, ran howling o'er the plain. *Dryden's Fab.*

To DISHE'VEL. *v. a.* [*decheveler*, French.] To ſpread the hair diſorderly; to throw the hair of a woman negligently about her head. It is not often uſed but in the paſſive participle.

A gentle lady all alone,
With garments rent and hair *diſhevelled*,
Wringing her hands, and making piteous moan. *Sp. Fa. Qu.*

After followed great numbers of women weeping, with *diſhevelled* hair, ſcratching their faces and tearing themſelves after the manner of the country. *Knolles.*

A troop of Trojans mix'd with theſe appear,
And mourning matrons with *diſhevell'd* hair. *Dryd. Æneid.*

The flames involv'd in ſmoak
Of incence, from the ſacred altar broke,
Caught her *diſhevell'd* hair and rich attire. *Dryden's Æneid.*

You this morn beheld his ardent eyes,
Saw his arm lock'd in her *diſhevell'd* hair. *Smith's Ph. Hip.*

DI'SHING. *adj.* [from *diſh.*] Concave; a cant term among artificers.

For the form of the wheels, ſome make them more *diſhing*, as they call it, than others; that is, more concave, by ſetting off the ſpokes and fellies more outwards. *Mortimer's Huſband.*

DISHO'NEST. *adj.* [*dis* and *honeſt.*]

1. Void of probity; void of faith; faithleſs; wicked; fraudulent.

To-morrow will we be married—I do deſire it with all my heart; and I hope it is no *diſhoneſt* deſire, to deſire to be a woman of the world. *Shakeſpeare's As you like it.*

Juſtice then was neither blind to diſcern, nor lame to execute. It was not ſubject to be impoſed upon by a deluded fancy, nor yet to be bribed by a glozing appetite, for an utile or jucundum to turn the balance to a falſe or *diſhoneſt* ſentence. *South's Sermons.*

He lays it down as a principle, that right or wrong, honeſt and *diſhoneſt*, are defined only by laws and not by nature. *Locke.*

2. Diſgraced; diſhonoured.

Diſhoneſt with lopp'd arms the youth appears,
Spoil'd of his noſe, and ſhorten'd of his ears. *Dryden.*

3. Diſgraceful; ignominious. Theſe two ſenſes are ſcarcely Engliſh, being borrowed from the Latin idiom.

She ſaw her ſons with purple death expire,
Her ſacred domes involv'd in rolling fire,
A dreadful ſeries of inteſtine wars,
Inglorious triumphs and *diſhoneſt* ſcars. *Pope's Windſ. For.*

DISHO'NESTLY. *adv.* [from *diſhoneſt.*]

1. Without faith; without probity; faithleſly; wickedly.

I proteſt he had the chain of me,
Tho' moſt *diſhoneſtly* he doth deny it. *Shakeſp. Com. Err.*

2. Lewdly; wantonly; unchaſtely.

A wiſe daughter ſhall bring an inheritance to her huſband; but ſhe that liveth *diſhoneſtly* is her father's heavineſs. *Ecc.* xxii. 4.

DISHO'NESTY. *n. ſ.* [from *diſhoneſt.*]

1. Want of probity; faithleſsneſs; violation of truſt.

Their fortune depends upon their credit, and a ſtain of open public *diſhoneſty* muſt be to their diſadvantage. *Swift.*

2. Unchaſtity; incontinence; lewdneſs.

Mrs. Ford, the honeſt woman, the modeſt wife, the virtuous creature, that hath the jealous fool to her huſband! I ſuſpect without cauſe, miſtreſs, do I?—Heav'n be my witneſs you do, if you ſuſpect me in any *diſhoneſty.* *Shakeſpeare.*

DISHO'NOUR. *n. ſ.* [*dis* and *honour.*]

1. Reproach; diſgrace; ignominy.

Let not my jealouſies be your *diſhonours*,
But mine own ſafeties. *Shakeſpeare's Macbeth.*

He was pleaſed to own Lazarus even in the *diſhonours* of the grave, and vouchſafed him in that deſpicable condition the glorious title of his friend. *Boyle's Seraphick Love.*

Take him for your huſband and your lord,
'Tis no *diſhonour* to confer your grace
On one deſcended from a royal race. *Dryden's Fables.*

2. Reproach uttered; cenſure; report of infamy.

So good, that no tongue could ever
Pronounce *diſhonour* of her; by my life
She never knew harm-doing. *Shakeſpeare's Henry* VIII.

To DISHO'NOUR. *v. a.* [*dis* and *honour.*]

1. To diſgrace; to bring ſhame upon; to blaſt with infamy.

Make known,
It is no vicious blot, murther, or foulneſs,
No unchaſte action, or *diſhonour'd* ſtep,
That hath depriv'd me of your grace and favour. *Shakeſp.*

This no more *diſhonours* you at all,
Than to take in a town with gentle words,
Which elſe would put you to your fortune. *Shakeſp. Cor.*

A woman that honoureth her huſband, ſhall be judged wiſe of all; but ſhe that *diſhonoureth* him in her pride, ſhall be counted ungodly of all. *Eccl.* xxvi. 26.

We are not ſo much to ſtrain ourſelves to make thoſe virtues appear in us which really we have not, as to avoid thoſe imperfections which may *diſhonour* us. *Dryden's Dufreſnoy.*

2. To violate chaſtity.

3. To treat with indignity.

If I, celeſtial ſire! in ought
Have ſerv'd thy will, or gratify'd thy thought,
One glimpſe of glory to my iſſue give,
Grac'd for the little time he has to live:
Diſhonour'd by the king of men he ſtands;
His rightful prize is raviſh'd from his hands. *Dryd. Iliad.*

DISHO'NOURABLE. *adj.* [from *diſhonour.*]

1. Shameful, reproachful; ignominious.

He did *diſhonourable* find
Thoſe articles which did our ſtate decreaſe. *Dan. Civ. War.*

2. In a ſtate of neglect or diſeſteem.

He that is honoured in poverty, how much more in riches? and he that is *diſhonourable* in riches, how much more in poverty. *Ecclus,* x. 31.

DISHO'NOURER. *n. ſ.* [from *diſhonour.*]

1. One that treats another with indignity.

Preaching how meritorious with the gods
It would be, to enſnare an irreligious
Diſhonourer of Dagon. *Milton's Agon. l.* 857.

2. A violator of chaſtity.

To DISHO'RN. *v. a.* [*dis* and *horn.*] To ſtrip of horns.

We'll *diſhorn* the ſpirit,
And mock him home to Windſor. *Shakeſp. M. Wive Wind.*

DISHU'MOUR. *n. ſ.* [*dis* and *humour.*] Peeviſhneſs; ill humour; uneaſy ſtate of mind.

Speaking impatiently to ſervants, or any thing that betrays inattention or *diſhumour*, are alſo criminal. *Spectator,* Nº. 424.

DISIMPRO'VEMENT. *n. ſ.* [*dis* and *improvement.*] Reduction from a better to a worſe ſtate; the contrary to melioration; contrary to improvement.

The final iſſue of the matter would be, an utter neglect and *diſimprovement* of the earth. *Norris.*

I cannot ſee how this kingdom is at any height of improvement, while four parts in five of the plantations for thirty years paſt have been real *diſimprovements.* *Swift.*

To DISINCA'RCERATE. *n. ſ.* [*dis* and *incarcerate.*] To ſet at liberty; to free from priſon.

The arſenical bodies being now coagulated, and kindled into flaming atoms, require dry and warm, or ſubtilizing air, to melt and open the ſurface of the earth for to *diſincarcerate* the ſame venene bodies. *Harvey on the Plague.*

DISINCLINA'TION. *n. ſ.* [from *diſincline.*] Want of affection; ſlight; diſlike; ill will not heightened to averſion.

Diſappointment gave him a *diſinclination* to the fair ſex, for whom he does not expreſs all the reſpect poſſible. *Arb. and Pope.*

To DISINCLI'NE. *v. a.* [*dis* and *incline.*] To produce diſlike to; to make diſaffected; to alienate affection from.

They were careful to keep up the fears and apprehenſions in the people of dangers and deſigns, and to *diſincline* them from any reverence or affection to the queen, whom they begun every day more implacably to hate, and conſequently to diſoblige. *Clarendon.*

DISINGENU'ITY. *n. ſ.* [from *diſingenuous.*] Meanneſs of artifice; unfairneſs.

They contract a habit of ill-nature and *diſingenuity* neceſſary to their affairs, and the temper of thoſe upon whom they are to work. *Clarendon.*

DISINGE'NUOUS. *adj.* [*dis* and *ingenuous.*] Unfair; meanly artful; viciouſly ſubtle; ſly; cunning; illiberal; unbecoming a gentleman; crafty.

'Tis *diſingenuous* to accuſe our age
Of idleneſs, who all our pow'rs engage
In the ſame ſtudies, the ſame courſe to hold,
Nor think our reaſon for new arts too old. *Denham.*

It was a *diſingenuous* way of proceeding, to oppoſe a judgment of charity concerning their church, to a judgment of reaſon concerning the nature of actions. *Stillingfleet.*

There cannot be any thing ſo *diſingenuous* and miſbecoming any one who pretends to be a rational creature, as not to yield to plain reaſon and the conviction of clear arguments. *Locke.*

DISINGE'NUOUSLY. *adv.* [from *diſingenuous.*] In a diſingenuous manner.

DISINGE'NUOUSNESS. *n. ſ.* [from *diſingenuous.*] Mean ſubtilty; unfairneſs; low craft.

I might preſs them with the unreaſonableneſs, the *diſingenuouſneſs* of embracing a profeſſion to which their own hearts have an inward reluctance. *Government of the Tongue, ſ.* 3.

DISINHE'RISON. *n. f.* [*dis* and *inherit.*] The act of cutting off from any hereditary succession; the act of disinheriting.

If he stood upon his own title of the house of Lancaster, inherent in his person, he knew it was a title condemned by parliament, and generally prejudged in the common opinion of the realm, that it tended directly to the *disinherison* of the line of York. *Bacon's Henry* VII.

The chief minister of the revenue was obliged to prevent and even oppose such *disinherison*. *Clarendon.*

2. The state of being cut off from an hereditary right.

In respect of the effects and evil consequences, the adultery of the woman is worse, as bringing bastardy into a family, and *disinherisons* or great injuries to the lawful children. *Tayl.*

To DISINHE'RIT. *v. a.* [*dis* and *inherit.*] To cut off from an hereditary right; to deprive of an inheritance.

Is it then just with us to *disinherit*
The unborn nephews for the father's fault? *Davies.*

Unmuffle, ye faint stars, and thou fair moon,
Stoop thy pale visage through an amber cloud,
And *disinherit* chaos that reigns here
In double night of darkness, and of slander. *Milton.*

Posterity stands curs'd! fair patrimony,
That I must leave ye, sons! O were I able
To waste it all myself, and leave ye none;
So *disinherited*, how would ye bless
Me, now your curse! *Milton's Paradise Lost, b.* x. *l.* 521.

Of how fair a portion Adam *disinherited* his whole posterity by one single prevarication. *South's Sermons.*

To DISINTE'R. *v. a.* [from *dis* and *inter.*] To unbury; to take out of the grave.

The philosopher, the saint, or the hero, the wise, the good, or the great man, very often lie hid and concealed in a plebeian, which a proper education might have *disinterred*. *Addis. Spect.*

DISINTERE'SSED. *n. f.* [*dis* and *interesse*, French. It is written *disinterested* by those who derive it immediately from interest, and I think more properly.] Without regard to private advantage; not biassed by particular views; impartial.

Not that tradition's parts are useless here,
When general, old, *disinteress'd*, and clear. *Dryden.*

DISINTERE'SSMENT. *n. f.* [*dis* and *interessement*, French.] Disregard to private advantage; disinterest; disinterestedness. This word like *charges* in the same sentence, is merely gallick.

He has managed some of the charges of the kingdom with known ability, and laid them down with entire *disinteressment*. *Prior's Postscript.*

DISI'NTEREST. *n. f.* [*dis* and *interest.*]

1. What is contrary to one's wish or prosperity; that which any one is concerned to prevent.

They judge it the great *disinterest* to Rome. *Glanville.*

2. Indifference to profit; superiority to regards of private advantage.

DISI'NTERESTED. *adj.* [from *disinterest.*] Superior to regard of private advantage; not influenced by private profit.

My lord, as *disinterested* as you appear to the world, I am convinced, that no man is more in the power of prevailing favourite passion than yourself. *Swift.*

3. Without any concern in an affair; without fear or hope.

DISINTERE'STEDLY. *adv.* [from *disinterested.*] In a disinterested manner.

DISINTERE'STEDNESS. *n. f.* [from *disinterested.*] Contempt of private interest; neglect of personal profit.

These expressions of selfishness and *disinterestedness* have been used in a very loose and indeterminate manner. *Brown.*

To DISI'NTRICATE. *v. a.* [*dis* and *intricate.*] To disentangle. *Dict.*

To DISINVI'TE. *v. a.* [*dis* and *invite.*] To retract an invitation. *Dict.*

To DISJO'IN. *v. a.* [*dejoindre*, French; *dis* and *join.*] To separate; to part from each other; to disunite; to sunder.

Never shall my harp thy praise
Forget, nor from thy father's praise *disjoin*. *Milton's P. Lost.*

Lest different degree
Disjoin us, and I then too late renounce
Deity for thee, when fate will not permit. *Milton. P. Lost.*

Happier for me, that all our hours assign'd
Together we had liv'd: ev'n not in death *disjoin'd*. *Dryd.*

Never let us lay down our arms against France till we have utterly *disjoined* her from the Spanish monarchy. *Addison.*

To DISJO'INT. *v. a.* [*dis* and *joint.*]

1. To put out of joint.

Be all their ligaments at once unbound,
And their *disjointed* bones to powder ground. *Sandy's Paraph.*

Yet what could swords or poison, racks or flame,
But mangle and *disjoint* the brittle frame,
More fatal Henry's words; they murder Emma's fame. *Pr.*

2. To break at junctures; to separate at the part where there is a cement.

Mould'ring arches, and *disjointed* columns. *Irene.*

3. To break in pieces; to dilaniate.

Rotation must disperse in air,
All things which on the rapid orb appear;
And if no power that motion should controul,
It must *disjoint* and dissipate the whole. *Blackmore.*

Should a barbarous Indian, who had never seen a palace or a ship, view the separate and *disjointed* parts, he would be able to form but a very lame and dark idea of either of those excellent and useful inventions. *Watts's Improvm. of the Mind.*

4. To carve a fowl.

5. To make incoherent; to break the relation between the parts.

The constancy of your wit was not wont to bring forth such *disjointed* speeches. *Sidney, b.* ii.

But now her grief has wrought her into frenzy,
The images her troubled fancy forms
Are incoherent, wild; her words *disjointed*. *Smith.*

To DISJOI'NT. *v. n.* To fall in pieces.

Let both worlds *disjoint*, and all things suffer,
Ere we will eat our meal in fear. *Shakespeare's Macbeth.*

DISJOI'NT. *participle.* [from the verb.] Separated; divided.

Young Fortinbras,
Holding a weak supposal of our worth;
Thinks, by our late dear brother's death,
Our state to be *disjoint* and out of frame. *Shakesp. Hamlet.*

DISJUDICA'TION. *n. f.* [*dijudicatio*, Latin.] Judgment; determination; perhaps only mistaken for *dijudication.*

The disposition of the organ is of great importance in the *disjudications* we make of colours. *Boyle on Colours.*

DISJU'NCT. *adj.* [*disjunctus*, Latin.] Disjoined; separate.

DISJU'NCTION. *n. f.* [from *disjunctio*, Latin.] Disunion; separation; parting.

You may
Enjoy your mistress now, from whom, you see,
There's no *disjunction* to be made, but by
Your ruin. *Shakespeare's Winter's Tale.*

There is a great analogy between the body natural and politic, in which the ecclesiastical, or spiritual part, justly supplies the part of the soul; and the violent separation of this from the other, does as certainly infer death and dissolution, as the *disjunction* of the body and the soul in the natural. *South.*

DISJU'NCTIVE. *adj.* [*disjunctivus*, Latin.]

1. Incapable of union.

Such principles, whose atoms are of that *disjunctive* nature, as not to be united in a sufficient number to make a visible mass. *Grew's Cosm. Sac b.* i. *c.* 2.

2. That which marks separation or opposition; as *I love him*, or *fear him.*

There are such words as *disjunctive* conjunctions. *Watts.*

3. [In logick.] A disjunctive proposition is when the parts are opposed to one another by disjunctive particles; as, *It is either day or night: The weather is either shiny or rainy: Quantity is either length, breadth, or depth.* The truth of *disjunctives* depends on the necessary and immediate opposition of the parts, therefore only the last of these examples is true; but the two first are not strictly true, because twilight is a medium between day and night; and dry cloudy weather is a medium between shining and raining. *Watts's Logick.*

A *disjunctive* syllogysm is when the major proposition is *disjunctive*; as, *The earth moves in a circle, or an ellipsis*; but it does not move in a circle, therefore it moves in an ellipsis. *Watts's Logick.*

DISJU'NCTIVELY. *adv.* [from *disjunctive.*] Distinctly; separately.

What he observes of the numbers *disjunctively* and apart, reason suggests to be applicable to the whole body united. *Causes of the Decay of Piety.*

DISK. *n. f.* [*discus*, Latin.]

1. The face of the sun, or any other planet, as it appears to the eye.

The *disk* of Phæbus, when he climbs on high,
Appears at first but as a bloodshot eye. *Dryden.*

It is to be considered, that the rays, which are equally refrangible, do fall upon a circle answering to the sun's *disk*. *Newt.*

Mercury's *disk*
Can scarce be caught by philosophic eye,
Lost in the near effulgence. *Thomson's Summer.*

2. A broad piece of iron thrown in the antient sports; a quoit.

The crystal of the eye, which in a fish is a ball, in any land animal is a *disk* or bowl; being hereby fitted for the clearer sight of the object. *Grew's Cosm. Sac. b.* i. *c.* 5.

In areas vary'd with mosaic art,
Some whirl the *disk*, and some the jav'lin dart. *Pope's Od.*

DISKI'NDNESS. *n. f.* [*dis* and *kindness.*] Want of kindness; want of affection; want of benevolence.

2. Ill turn; injury; act of malignity; detriment.

This discourse is so far from doing any *diskindness* to the cause, that it does it a real service. *Woodward's Nat. Hist.*

DISLI'KE. *n. f.* [from the verb.]

1. Disinclination; absence of affection; the contrary to fondness.

He then them took, and tempering goodly well
Their contrary *dislikes* with loved means,
Did place them all in order, and compel
To keep themselves within their sundry reigns,
Together link'd with adamantine chains. *Spencer.*

Your *dislikes* to whom I would be pleasing,
Do cloud my joys with danger and with sorrow. *Shakesp.*

God's grace, that principle of his new birth, gives him continual *dislike* to sin. *Hammond's Pract. Catechism.*

Sorrow would have been as silent as thoughts, as severe as philosophy. It would have rested in inward senses, tacit *dislikes.* *South's Sermons.*

Our likings or *dislikes* are founded rather upon humour and fancy than upon reason. *L'Estrange.*

The jealous man is not angry if you *dislike* another; but if you find those faults which are in his own character, you discover not only your *dislike* of another, but of himself. *Addis.*

2. Discord; dissention; disagreement. This sense is not now in use.

This said Aletes, and a murmur rose
That shew'd *dislike* among the christian peers. *Fairfax.*

To DISLI'KE. *v. a.* [*dis* and *like.*] To disapprove; to regard without affection; to regard with ill-will or disgust.

What most he should *dislike*, seems pleasant to him;
What like, offensive. *Shakespeare's King Lear.*

Ye *dislike*, and so undo
The players, and disgrace the poet too. *Denh. Prol. Sophy.*

Whosoever *dislikes* the digressions, or grows weary of them, may throw them away. *Temple.*

DISLI'KEFUL. *adj.* [*dislike* and *full.*] Disaffected; malign.

I think it best, by an union of manners, and conformity of minds, to bring them to be one people, and to put away the *dislikeful* conceit of the one and the other. *Spenser's Ireland.*

To DISLI'KEN. *v. a.* [*dis* and *like.*] To make unlike.

Muffle your face,
Dismantle you; and, as you can, *disliken*
The truth of your own seeming. *Shakesp. Winter's Tale.*

DISLI'KENESS. *n. s.* [*dis* and *likeness.*] Dissimilitude; not resemblance; unlikeness.

That which is not designed to represent any thing but itself, can never be capable of a wrong representation, nor mislead us from the true apprehension of any thing by its *dislikeness* to it; and such, excepting those of substances, are all our own complex ideas. *Locke.*

DISLI'KER. *n. s.* [from *dislike.*] A disapprover; one that is not pleased.

There is a point, which whoever can touch, will never fail of pleasing a majority, so great that the *dislikers* will be forced to fall in with the herd. *Swift's Intell.*

To DISLI'MB. *v. a.* [*dis* and *limb.*] To dilaniate; to tear limb from limb. *Dict.*

To DISLI'MN. *v. a.* [*dis* and *limn.*] To unpaint; to strike out of a picture.

That which is now a horse, even with a thought
The rack *dislimns*, and makes it indistinct
As water is in water. *Shakespeare's Ant. and Cleop.*

To DI'SLOCATE. *v. a.* [*dis* and *locus*, Latin.]

1. To put out of the proper place.

The strata seemed to have been *dislocated*, borne from their original site, and distanced by some external power. *Woodw.*

After some time the strata were broken on all sides of the globe, that they were *dislocated*, and their situation varied, being elevated in some places, and depressed in others. *Woodw.*

2. To put out of joint; to disjoint.

Were't my fitness
To let these hands obey my boiling blood,
They're apt enough to *dislocate* and tear
Thy flesh and bones. *Shakespear's King Lear.*

DISLOCA'TION. *n. s.* [from *dislocate.*]

1. The act of shifting the places of things.

2. The state of being displaced.

The posture of rocks, often leaning or prostrate, shews that they had some *dislocation* from their natural site. *Burnet.*

3. A luxation; a violent pressure of a bone out of the socket; a joint put out.

It might go awry either within or without the upper, as often as it is forcibly pulled to it, and so cause a *dislocation*, or a strain. *Grew's Museum.*

To DISLO'DGE. *v. a.* [*dis* and *lodge.*]

1. To remove from a place.

The shell-fish which are resident in these places live and die there, and are never *dislodged* or removed by storms, nor cast upon the shores, which the littorales usually are. *Woodward.*

2. To remove from an habitation.

Those senses lost, behold a new defeat,
The soul *dislodging* from another seat. *Dryden's Juv.*

3. To drive an enemy from a station.

My sword can perfect what it has begun,
And from your walls *dislodge* that haughty son. *Dryd. Aur.*

4. To remove an army to other quarters.

The ladies have prevail'd,
The Volscians are *dislodg'd*, and Marcus gone. *Shakesp. Cor.*

To DISLO'DGE. *v. n.* To go away to another place.

Soon as midnight brought on the dusky hour,
Friendliest to sleep, and silence, he resolv'd
With all his legions to *dislodge*. *Milton's Par. Lost.*

DISLO'YAL. *adj.* [*desloyal*, French; *dis* and *loyal.*]

1. Not true to allegiance; faithless; false to a sovereign; disobedient.

Foul distrust, and breach
Disloyal on the part of man; revolt
And disobedience. *Milton's Paradise Lost, b.* ix. *l.* 7.

2. Dishonest; perfidious. Obsolete.

Such things, in a false *disloyal* knave,
Are tricks of custom; but, in a man that's just,
They're cold delations working from the heart,
That passion cannot rule. *Shakespeare's Othello.*

3. Not true to the marriage-bed.

The lady is *disloyal.*

——*Disloyal!* The word is too good to paint out her wickedness. *Shakespeare.*

Disloyal town!
Speak, did'st not thou
Forsake thy faith, and break the nuptial vow? *Dryden.*

4. False in love; not constant. The three latter senses are now obsolete.

DISLO'YALLY. *adv.* [from *disloyal.*] Not faithfully; treacherously; disobediently.

DISLO'YALTY. *n. s.* [from *disloyal.*]

1. Want of fidelity to the sovereign.

Let the truth of that religion I profess be represented to judgment, not in the disguises of levity, schism, heresy, novelty, and *disloyalty.* *King Charles.*

2. Want of fidelity in love. A sense now obsolete.

There shall appear such seeming truths of Hero's *disloyalty*, that jealousy shall be called assurance. *Sh. Much Ado about Noth.*

DI'SMAL. *adj.* [*dies malus*, Latin, an evil day.] Sorrowful; dire; horrid; melancholy; uncomfortable; unhappy; dark.

On the one hand set the most glittering temptations to discord, and on the other view the *dismal* effects of it. *Dec. of Piety.*

DI'SMALLY. *adv.* [from *dismal.*] Horribly; sorrowfully; uncomfortably.

DI'SMALNESS. *n. s.* [from *dismal.*] Horror; sorrow.

To DISMA'NTLE. *v. a.* [*dis* and *mantle.*]

1. To throw off a dress; to strip.

He that makes his prince despised and undervalued, and beats him out of his subjects hearts, may easily strip him of his other garrisons, having already dispossessed him of his strongest, by *dismantling* him of his honour, and seising his reputation. *South's Sermons.*

2. To loose; to unfold; to throw open.

This is most strange!
That she, who ev'n but now was your best object,
Dearest and best, should in this trice of time
Commit a thing so monstrous, to *dismantle*
So many folds of favour. *Shakespeare's King Lear.*

3. To strip a town of its outworks.

It is not sufficient to possess our own fort, without the *dismantling* and demolishing of our enemies. *Hakewill on Provid.*

4. To break down any thing external.

His eyeballs, rooted out, are thrown to ground;
His nose *dismantled*, in his mouth is found;
His jaws, cheeks, front, one undistinguish'd wound. *Dry.*

To DISMA'SK. *v. a.* [*dis* and *mask.*] To divest of a mask; to uncover from concealment.

Fair ladies mask'd, are roses in the bud;
Or angels veil'd in clouds: are roses blown,
Dismask'd, their damask sweet commixture shewn. *Shakesp.*

The marquis had no leisure to laugh, but thought best to *dismask* his beard; and so told him, that he was going covertly. *Wotton.*

To DISMA'Y. *v. a.* [*desmayar*, Spanish.] To terrify; to discourage; to affright; to depress; to deject.

Their mighty strokes their haberjeons *dismay'd*. *Fai. Qu.*

Enemies would not be so troublesome to the western coasts, nor that country itself would be so often *dismayed* with alarms as they have of late years been. *Raleigh's Essays.*

He will not fail thee; fear not, neither be *dismayed.* *Deutr.*

Nothing can make him remiss in the practice of his duty, no prospect of interest can allure him, no fear of danger *dismay* him. *Atterbury's Sermons.*

DISMA'Y. *n. s.* [*desmayo*, Spanish.] Fall of courage; terrour felt; desertion of mind; fear impressed.

All sat mute,
Pondering the danger with deep thoughts; and each
In others countenance read his own *dismay.* *Milt. Par. Lost.*

This then not minded in *dismay*, yet now
Assures me that the bitterness of death
Is past. *Milton's Paradise Lost, b.* xi. *l.* 156.

DISMA'YEDNESS. *n. s.* [from *dismay.*] Dejection of courage; dispiritedness.

The valiantest feels inward *dismayedness*, and yet the fearfullest is ashamed fully to shew it. *Sidney, b.* ii.

DI'SME. *n. s.* [French.] A tenth; the tenth part; tythe.

Since the first sword was drawn about this question,
Ev'ry tithe soul 'mongst many thousand *dismes*,
Hath been as dear as Helen. *Shakesp. Troilus and Cressida.*

The pope began to exercise his new rapines here in England, by a compliance with the said king Edward, in granting him two years *disme* from the clergy. *Ayliffe's Parergon.*

To DISMEʹMBER. *v. a.* [*dis* and *member.*] To divide member from member; to dilacerate; to cut in pieces.

I am with both, each army hath a hand;
And in their rage, I having hold of both,
They whirl asunder, and *dismember* me. *Shakesp. King John.*

O, that we then could come by Cæsar's spirit,
And not *dismember* Cæsar! But, alas!
Cæsar must bleed for it. *Shakespeare's Julius Cæsar.*

A state can never arrive to its period in a more deplorable crisis, than when some prince lies hovering, like a vulture, to devour, or *dismember* its dying carcass. *Swift.*

Fowls obscene *dismember'd* his remains,
And dogs had torn him on the naked plains. *Pope's Odyssey.*

Those who contemplate only the fragments or pieces of science, dispersed in short unconnected discourses, without relation to each other, can never survey an entire body of truth, but must always view it as deformed and *dismembered.* *Watts.*

To DISMIʹSS. *v. a.* [*dimissus*, Latin.]

1. To send away.

We commit thee thither,
Until his army be *dismiss'd* from him. *Shakesp. Henry IV.*

He *dismissed* the assembly. *Acts* xix. 41.

2. To give leave of departure.

If our young Iülus be no more,
Dismiss our navy from your friendly shore. *Dryd. Virg. Æn.*

3. To discard; to divest of an office.

DISMIʹSSION. *n. s.* [from *demissio*, Latin.]

1. Dispatch; act of sending away.

So pois'd, so gently she descends from high,
It seems a soft *dismission* from the sky. *Dryd. Hind and Pant.*

2. An honourable discharge from any office or place.

Not only thou degrad'st them, or remit'st
To life obscure, which were a fair *dismission*;
But throw'st them lower than thou didst exalt them high.
Milton's Agonistes, l. 687.

3 Deprivation; obligation to leave any post or place.

You must not stay here longer; your *dismission*
Is come from Cæsar. *Shakespeare's Anthony and Cleopatra.*

To DISMOʹRTGAGE. *v. a.* [*dis* and *mortgage.*] To redeem from mortgage.

He *dismortgaged* the crown demesnes, made an increase of munition, arms and treasure, and left behind a mass of gold. *Howel's Vocal Forrest.*

To DISMOʹUNT. *v. a.* [*demonter*, French.]

1. To throw off an horse.

From this flying steed unrein'd, as once
Bellerophon, though from a lower clime,
Dismounted, on th' Aleian field I fall. *Milton's Paradise Lost.*

2. To throw from any elevation or place of honour.

3. To throw cannon from its carriage.

The Turks artillery, planted against that tower, was, by the skilfulness of the Christian cannoneers, in short time *dismounted* with shot from the tower, and many of the gunners slain. *Knolles's History of the Turks.*

To DISMOʹUNT. *v. n.*

1. To alight from an horse.

When he came within sight of that prodigious army at Agincourt, he ordered all his cavalry to *dismount*, and implore upon their knees a blessing. *Addison's Freeholder*, N°. 49.

2. To descend from any elevation.

To DISNAʹTURALISE. *v. a.* [*dis* and *naturalise.*] To alienate; to make alien; to deprive of the privileges of birth.

DISNAʹTURED. *adj.* [*dis* and *nature.*] Unnatural; wanting natural tenderness; devoid of natural affection.

If she must teem,
Create her child of spleen, that it may live,
And be a thwart *disnatur'd* torment to her. *Shak. K. Lear.*

DISOBEʹDIENCE. *n. s.* [*dis* and *obedience.*]

1. Violation of lawful commands or prohibition; breach of duty due to superiours.

Th' offence is holy that she hath committed,
And this deceit loses the name of craft,
Of *disobedience*, or unduteous title. *Shak. M. W. of Windſ.*

Of man's first *disobedience*, and the fruit
Of that forbidden tree, sing heav'nly muse. *Milton.*

Murder, adultery, or *disobedience* to parents, have a general notion antecedently to laws. *Stillingfleet.*

This is not *disobedience*, but rebellion; 'tis disclaiming the sovereignty of Christ, and renouncing all allegiance to his authority. *Rogers, Sermon* 4.

2. Incompliance.

If planetary orbs the sun obey,
Why should the moon disown his sovereign sway;
Why in a whirling eddy of her own
Around the globe terrestrial should she run?
This *disobedience* of the moon will prove
The sun's bright orb does not the planets move. *Blackmore.*

DISOBEʹDIENT. *adj.* [*dis* and *obedient.*] Not observant of lawful authority; guilty of the breach of lawful commands or prohibition.

The man of God was *disobedient* unto the word of the Lord. 1 *Kings* xiii. 26.

To DISOBEʹY. *v. a.* [*dis* and *obey.*] To break commands or transgress prohibitions.

She absolutely bade him, and he durst not know how to *disobey.* *Sidney, b.* ii.

He's loth to *disobey* the god's command,
Nor willing to forsake this pleasant land. *Denham.*

DISOBLIGAʹTION. *n. s.* [*dis* and *obligation.*] Offence; cause of disgust.

If he receded from what he had promised, it would be such a *disobligation* to the prince that he would never forget it. *Clar.*

There can be no malice, and consequently no crime or *disobligation.* *L'Estrange.*

To DISOBLIʹGE. *v. a.* [*dis* and *oblige.*] To offend; to disgust; to give offence to. A term by which offence is tenderly expressed.

Ashley had been removed from that charge, and was thereby so much *disobliged* that he quitted the king's party. *Cla.*

Those, though in highest place, who slight and *disoblige* their friends, shall infallibly come to know the value of them, by having none, when they shall most need them. *South.*

Is is in the power of more particular persons in this kingdom, than in any other, to distress the government, when they are *disobliged.* *Addison's Freeholder*, N°. 48.

My plan has given offence to some gentlemen, whom it would not be very safe to *disoblige.* *Addison's Guardian*, N°. 108.

We love and esteem our clergy, and are apt to lay some weight upon their opinion, and would not willingly *disoblige* them. *Swift concerning the Sacramental Test.*

If a woman suffers her lover to see she is loth to *disoblige* him, let her beware of an encroacher. *Clarissa.*

DISOBLIʹGING. *participial adj.* [from *disoblige.*] Disgusting; unpleasing; offensive.

Peremptoriness can besit no form of understanding: it renders wise men *disobliging* and troublesome, and fools ridiculous and contemptible. *Government of the Tongue, s.* 11.

DISOBLIʹGINGLY. *adv.* [from *disobliging.*] In a disgusting or offensive manner; without attention to please.

DISOBLIʹGINGNESS. *n. s.* [from *disobliging.*] Offensiveness; readiness to disgust.

DISOʹRBED. *adj.* [*dis* and *orb.*] Thrown out of the proper orbit.

Fly like chidden Mercury from Jove,
Or like a star *disorb'd.* *Shakespeare's Troilus and Cressida.*

DISOʹRDER. *n. s.* [*dis* and *order*; *desordre*, French.]

1. Want of regular disposition; irregularity; confusion; immethodical distribution.

When I read an author of genius without method, I fancy myself in a wood that abounds with many noble objects, rising among one another in the greatest confusion and *disorder.* *Spectator*, N°. 476.

2. Tumult; disturbance; bustle.

A greater favour this *disorder* brought
Unto her servants, than your awful thought
Durst entertain, when thus compell'd they prest
The yielding marble of her snowy breast. *Waller.*

3. Neglect of rule; irregularity.

From vulgar bounds with brave *disorder* part,
And snatch a grace beyond the reach of art. *Pope's Essays.*

4. Breach of laws; violation of standing institution.

There reigned in all men blood, manslaughter, disquieting of good men, forgetfulness of good turns, and *disorder* in marriages. *Wisd.* xiv. 26.

5. Breach of that regularity in the animal œconomy which causes health; sickness; distemper. It is used commonly for a slight disease.

Pleasure and pain are only different constitutions of the mind, sometimes occasioned by *disorder* in the body, or sometimes by thoughts in the mind. *Locke.*

6. Discomposure of mind; turbulence of passions.

To DISOʹRDER. *v. a.* [*dis* and *order.*]

1. To throw into confusion; to confound; to put out of method; to disturb; to ruffle; to confuse.

Eve
Not so repuls'd, with tears that ceas'd not flowing,
And tresses all *disorder'd*, at his feet
Fell humble. *Milton's Paradise Lost, b.* x. *l.* 911.

Yon *disorder'd* heap of ruin lies,
Stones rent from stones, where clouds of dust arise. *Dryden.*

The incursions of the Goths, and other barbarous nations, *disordered* the affairs of the Roman empire. *Arbuthnot on Coins.*

2. To make sick; to disturb the body.

3. To discompose; to disturb the mind.

DISOʹRDERED. *adj.* [from *disorder.*] Disorderly; irregular; vicious; loose; unrestrained in behaviour; debauched.

Here do you keep a hundred knights and squires,
Men so *disorder'd*, so debauch'd and bold,
That this our court, infected with their manners,
Shews like a riotous inn. *Shakespeare's King Lear.*

DISOʹRDEREDNESS. *n. s.* [from *disordered.*] Irregularity; want of order; confusion.

By that *disorderedness* of the soldiers a great advantage was offered unto the enemy. *Knolles's History of the Turks.*

DISO'RDERLY. *adj.* [from *disorder.*]
1. Confused; immethodical; without proper distribution.
Those obsolete laws of Henry I. were but *disorderly*, confused, and general things; rather cases and shells of administration than institutions. *Hale.*
2. Irregular; tumultuous.
His thoughts, which are the pictures and results of passions, are generally such as naturally arise from those *disorderly* motions of our spirits. *Dryden.*
A *disorderly* multitude, contending with the body of the legislature, is like a man in a fit, under the conduct of one in the fulness of his health and strength. *Addison.*
3. Lawless; contrary to law; inordinate; contrary to the rules of life; vicious.
They thought it the extremest of evils to put themselves at the mercy of those hungry and *disorderly* people. *Bac. H.* VII.
He reproved them for their *disorderly* assemblies, against the peaceable people of the realms. *Hayward.*
DISO'RDERLY. *adv.* [from *disorder.*]
1. Without rule; without method; irregularly; confusedly.
Naked savages fighting *disorderly* with stones, by appointment of their commanders, may truly and absolutely be said to war. *Raleigh's Essays.*
2. Without law; inordinately.
We behaved not ourselves *disorderly* among you. 2 *Thess.* iii.
DISO'RDINATE. *adj.* [*dis* and *ordinate.*] Not living by the rules of virtue; inordinate.
These not *disordinate*, yet causeless suffer
The punishment of dissolute days. *Milton's Agonistes.*
DISO'RDINATELY. *adv.* [from *disordinate.*] Inordinately; viciously.
DISO'RIENTATED. *adj.* [*dis* and *orient.*] Turned from the East; turned from the right direction; thrown out of the proper place. *Harris.*
To DISO'WN. *v. a.* [*dis* and *own.*]
1. To deny; not to allow.
Then they, who brother's better claim *disown*,
Expel their parents, and usurp the throne. *Dryden's Æn.*
2. To abrogate; to renounce.
When an author has publickly *disowned* a spurious piece, they have disputed his name with him. *Swift.*
To DISPA'ND. *v. a.* [*dispando*, Latin.] To display; to spread abroad. *Dict.*
DISPA'NSION. *n. s.* [from *dispansus*, Lat.] The act of displaying; the act of spreading; diffusion; dilatation.
To DISPA'RAGE. *v. a.* [from *dispar*, Latin.]
1. To match unequally; to injure by union with something inferiour in excellence.
2. To injure by a comparison with something of less value.
3. To treat with contempt; to mock; to flout; to reproach.
Ahaz, his sottish conqueror he drew,
God's altar to *disparage* and displace,
For one of Syrian mode. *Milton's Paradise Lost.*
Thou durst not thus *disparage* glorious arms,
Which greatest hero's have in battle worn,
Their ornament and safety. *Milton's Agonistes, l.* 1130.
They will defy
That which they love most tenderly;
Quarrel with minc'd pies, and *disparage*
Their best and dearest friend, plum-porridge. *Hudibras*
4. To bring reproach upon; to be the cause of disgrace.
How shall frail pen, with fear *disparaged*,
Conceive such sovereign glory and great bountihed. *Fai. Qu.*
His religion sat easily, naturally, and gracefully upon him, without any of those forbidding appearances which sometimes *disparage* the actions of men sincerely pious. *Atterbury's Serm.*
5. To marry any one to another of inferiour condition.
DISPA'RAGEMENT. *n. s.* [from *disparage.*]
1. Injurious union or comparison with something of inferior excellence.
They take it for a *disparagement* to sort themselves with any other than the enemies of the publick peace. *L'Estrange.*
2. [In law.] Matching an heir in marriage under his or her degree, or against decency. *Cowel.*
You wrongfully do require Mopsa to so great a *disparagement*, as to wed her father's servant. *Sidney.*
She was much affectionate to her own kindred, even unto faction, which did stir great envy in the lords of the king's side, who counted her blood a *disparagement* to be mingled with the king's. *Bacon's Henry* VII.
3. Reproach; disgrace; indignity.
Gentle knight,
That doth against the dead his hand uprear,
His honour stains with rancour and despight,
And great *disparagement* makes to his former might. *Fa. Qu.*
In a commonwealth much *disparagement* is occasioned, when able spirits, attracted by a familiarity, are inflamed with faction. *Wotton.*
'Tis no *disparagement* to philosophy, that it cannot deify us. *Glanv. Apol.*
Reason is a weak, diminutive light, compared to revelation; but it ought to be no *disparagement* to a star that it is not a sun. *South's Sermons.*
Rely upon your beauty: 'twere a *disparagement* of that to talk of conditions, when you are certain of making your own terms. *Southern's Innocent Adultery.*
4. It has *to* before the person or thing disparaged.
Then *to* our age, when not to pleasure bent,
This seems an honour, not *disparagement*. *Denham.*
The play was never intended for the stage; nor, without *disparagement to* the author, could have succeeded. *Dryden.*
DISPA'RAGER. *n. s.* [from *disparage.*] One that disgraces; one that treats with indignity.
DISPARA'TES. *n. s.* [*disparata*, Latin.] Things so unlike that they cannot be compared with each other.
DISPA'RITY. *n. s.* [from *dispar*, Latin.]
1. Inequality; difference in degree either of rank or excellence.
Between Elihu and the rest of Job's familiars, the greatest *disparity* was but in years. *Hooker, b.* v. *s.* 47.
Among unequals, what society
Can sort, what harmony or true delight?
Which must be mutual, in proportion due,
Giv'n and receiv'd; but in *disparity*,
The one intense, the other still remiss,
Cannot well suit with either, but soon prove
Tedious alike. *Milton's Paradise Lost, b* viii. *l.* 386.
There was as great a *disparity* between the practical dictates of the understanding then and now, as there is between empire and advice, counsel and command. *South's Sermons.*
Men ought not to associate and join themselves together in the same office, under a *disparity* of condition or profession. *Ayliffe's Parergon.*
Some members must preside and direct, and others serve and obey; and a *disparity* between these, in the outward condition, is necessary to keep several orders in mutual dependance on each other. *Rogers's Sermons.*
2. Dissimilitude; unlikeness.
To DISPA'RK. *v. a.* [*dis* and *park.*]
1. To throw open a park.
You have fed upon my signiories,
Dispark'd my parks, and fell'd my forest woods. *Sh. R.* II.
2. To set at large without enclosure.
They were suppos'd
By narrow wits to be inclos'd,
'Till his free muse threw down the pale,
And did at once *dispark* them all. *Waller.*
To DISPA'RT. *v. a.* [*dis* and *part*; *departir*, French; *dispertior*, Latin.] To divide in two; to separate; to break; to burst; to rive.
The gate nor wood, nor of enduring brass,
But of more worthy substance framed was;
Doubly *disparted*, it did lock and close,
That when it locked, none might through it pass. *Fai. Qu.*
On either side
Disparted chaos overbuilt exclaim'd,
And with rebounding surge the bars assail'd,
That scorn'd his indignation. *Milton's Paradise Lost, b.* ix.
The rest to several places
Disparted, and between spun out the air. *Milt. Par. Lost.*
Disparted Britain mourn'd their doubtful sway,
And dreaded both, when neither would obey. *Prior.*
The pilgrim oft,
At dead of night, 'mid his orison, hears
Aghast, the voice of time *disparting* tow'rs. *Dier.*
DISPA'SSION. *n. s.* [*dis* and *passion.*] Freedom from mental perturbation; exemption from passion.
What is called by the Stoicks apathy, or *dispassion*, is called by the Scepticks indisturbance, by the Molenists quietism, by common men peace of conscience. *Temple.*
DISPA'SSIONATE. *adj.* [from *dis* and *passionate.*] Cool; calm; impartial; moderate; temperate.
Wise and *dispassionate* men thought he had been proceeded with very justly. *Clarendon.*
To DISPE'L. *v. a.* [*dispello*, Latin.] To drive by scattering; to dissipate.
If the night
Have gathered aught of evil, or conceal'd,
Disperse it, as now light *dispels* the dark. *Milton.*
When the spirit brings light into our minds, it *dispels* darkness: we see it, as we do that of the sun at noon, and need not the twilight of reason to shew it. *Locke.*
DISPE'NCE. *n. s.* [*despence*, Fr.] Expence; cost; charge.
It was a vault ybuilt for great *dispence*,
With many ranges rear'd along the wall,
And one great chimney, whose long funnel thence
The smoke forth threw. *Fairy Queen, b.* ii. *cant.* 9.
To DISPE'ND. *v. a.* [*dispendo*, Latin.] To spend; to consume; to expend.
Of their commodities they were now scarce able to *dispend* the third part. *Spenser's State of Ireland.*
DISPE'NSARY. *n. s.* [from *dispense.*] The place where medicines are dispensed.
To thee the lov'd *dispens'ry* I resign. *Garth.*
DISPENSA'TION. *n. s.* [from *dispensatio*, Latin.]
1. Distribution; the act of dealing out any thing.
This perpetual circulation is constantly promoted, by a *dispensation*

penſation of water promiſcuouſly and indifferently to all parts of the earth. *Woodward's Natural Hiſtory.*

2. The dealing of God with his creatures; method of providence; diſtribution of good and evil.

God delights in the miniſtries of his own choice, and the methods of grace, in the œconomy of heaven, and the *diſpenſations* of eternal happineſs. *Taylor's Worthy Communicant.*

Neither are God's methods or intentions different in his *diſpenſations* to each private man. *Rogers, Sermon* 16.

Do thou, my ſoul, the deſtin'd period wait,
When God ſhall ſolve the dark decrees of fate;
His now unequal *diſpenſations* clear,
And make all wiſe and beautiful appear. *Tickell.*

3. An exemption from ſome law; a permiſſion to do ſomething forbidden; an allowance to omit ſomething commanded.

A *diſpenſation* was obtained to enable Dr. Barrow to marry. *Ward.*

DISPENSA'TOR. *n. ſ.* [Latin.] One employed in dealing out any thing; a diſtributer.

As her majeſty hath made them *diſpenſators* of her favour towards her people, ſo it behoveth them to ſhew themſelves equal diſtributers of the ſame. *Bacon.*

DISPE'NSATORY. *n. ſ.* [from *diſpenſe*.] A book in which the compoſition of medicines is deſcribed and directed; in the Greek a *Pharmacopeia.*

The deſcription of the ointment is found in the chymical *diſpenſatory.* *Bacon's Natural Hiſtory*, N°. 98.

A whole *diſpenſatory* was little enough to meet with, and ſuffice to all their wants. *Hammond.*

Our materia medica is large enough; and to look into our *diſpenſatories*, one would think no diſeaſe incurable. *Baker.*

To DISPE'NSE. *v. a.* [*deſpenſer*, French.]

1. To deal out; to diſtribute.

Thoſe now, that were *diſpens'd*,
The burden of many ages, on me light
At once, by my foreknowledge. *Milton's Paradiſe Loſt.*

Thoſe to whom Chriſt has committed the *diſpenſing* of his goſpel. *Decay of Piety.*

At length the muſes ſtand reſtor'd again
While you *diſpenſe* the laws and guide the ſtate. *Dryden.*
To them but earth-born life they did *diſpenſe*,
To us, for mutual aid, celeſtial ſenſe. *Tate's Juvenal.*

2. To make up a medicine.

3. *To* DISPENSE *with.* To excuſe; to grant diſpenſation for; to allow.

To ſave a brother's life,
Nature *diſpenſes with* the deed. *Shak. Meaſure for Meaſure.*

How few kingdoms are there, wherein, by *diſpenſing with* oaths, abſolving ſubjects from allegiance, and curſing, or threatning to curſe, as long as their curſes were regarded, the popes have not wrought innumerable miſchiefs? *Raleigh's Eſſ.*

Rules of words may be *diſpenſed with.* *Watts's Logick.*

4. *To* DISPENSE *with.* To clear from; to ſet free from an obligation. This conſtruction ſeems ungrammatical.

I could not *diſpenſe with* myſelf from making a voyage to Caprea. *Addiſon's Remarks on Italy.*

5. *To* DISPENSE *with.* To obtain a diſpenſation from; to come to agreement with. This ſtructure is irregular, unleſs it be here ſuppoſed to mean, as it may, to diſcount; to pay an equivalent.

Haſt thou not ſworn allegiance unto me?
Canſt thou *diſpenſe* with heav'n for ſuch an oath? *Sh. H.VI.*

DISPE'NSE. *n. ſ.* [from the verb.] Diſpenſation; exemption.

Then reliques, beads,
Indulgences, *diſpenſes*, pardons, bulls,
The ſport of winds. *Milton's Paradiſe Loſt, b.* iii.

DISPE'NSER. *n. ſ.* [from *diſpenſe*.] One that diſpenſes; one that deals out any thing; a diſtributer.

The miniſters of that houſhold are the *diſpenſers* of that faith. *Spratt's Sermons.*

Thoſe who ſtand before earthly princes, who are the *diſpenſers* of their favours, and conveyers of their will to others, challenge high honours. *Atterbury's Sermons.*

To DISPE'OPLE. *v. a.* [*dis* and *people.*] To depopulate; to empty of people.

The Iriſh whom they baniſhed into the mountains, where they lived only upon white meats, ſeeing their lands ſo *diſpeopled* and weakened, came down into all the plains adjoining. *Spenſer's State of Ireland.*

Conflagrations, and great droughts, do not merely *diſpeople*, but deſtroy. *Bacon, Eſſay* 59.

His heart exalts him in the harm
Already done, to have *diſpeopled* heav'n. *Milton's Par. Loſt.*

Kings, furious and ſevere,
Who claim'd the ſkies, *diſpeopled* air and floods,
The lonely lords of empty wilds and woods. *Pope.*

DISPE'OPLER. *n. ſ.* [from *diſpeople.*] A depopulator; a waſter.

Nor drain I ponds, the golden carp to take;
Nor trowle for pikes, *diſpeoplers* of the lake. *Gay.*

To DISPE'RGE. *v. a.* [*diſpergo*, Latin.] To ſprinkle; to ſcatter. *Shakeſpeare.*

To DISPE'RSE. *v. a.* [*diſperſus*, Latin.]

1. To ſcatter; to drive to different parts.

And I ſcattered them among the heathen, and they were *diſperſed* through the countries. *Ezek.* xxxvi. 19.

2. To diſſipate.

Soldiers, *diſperſe* yourſelves. *Shakeſpeare's Henry* VI.

If the night
Have gather'd aught of evil, or conceal'd,
Diſperſe it, as now light diſpels the dark. *Milton.*

DISPE'RSEDLY. *adv.* [from *diſperſed.*] In a diſperſed manner; ſeparately.

The exquiſite wits of ſome few, peradventure, are able, *diſperſedly* here and there, to find now a word, and then a ſentence, which may be more probably ſuſpected than eaſily cleared of errour. *Hooker, b.* v. *ſ.* 23.

Thoſe minerals are either found in grains, *diſperſedly* intermixed with the corpuſcles of earth or ſand, or elſe amaſſed into balls or nodules. *Woodward.*

DISPE'RSEDNESS. *n. ſ.* [from *diſperſe.*] The ſtate of being diſperſed; diſperſion.

DISPE'RSENESS. *n. ſ.* [from *diſperſe.*] Thinneſs; ſcatteredneſs.

The torrid parts of Africk are by Piſo reſembled to a libbard's ſkin, the diſtance of whoſe ſpots repreſent the *diſperſeneſs* of habitations or towns in Africk. *Brerewood on Languages.*

DISPE'RSER. *n. ſ.* [from *diſperſe.*] A ſcatterer; a ſpreader.

Thoſe who are pleaſed with defamatory libels, ſo far as to approve the authors and *diſperſers* of them, are as guilty as if they had compoſed them. *Spectator*, N°. 451.

DISPE'RSION. *n. ſ.* [from *diſperſio*, Latin.]

1. The act of ſcattering or ſpreading.

2. The ſtate of being ſcattered.

Noah began from thence his *diſperſion.* *Raleigh's Hiſtory.*

After ſo many *diſperſions*, and ſo many diviſions, two or three of us may yet be gathered together, not to plot, but to divert ourſelves, and the world too if it pleaſes. *Pope.*

To DISPI'RIT. *v. a.* [*dis* and *ſpirit.*]

1. To diſcourage; to deject; to depreſs; to damp; to terrify; to intimidate; to fright; to ſtrike with fear.

Certain it is, that the poor man appeared ſo *diſpirited*, that he ſpoke but few words after he came upon the ſcaffold. *Clar.*

The providence of God ſtrikes not in with them, but daſhes, and even *diſpirits*, all their endeavours, and makes their deſigns heartleſs and ineffectual. *South's Sermons.*

Steady to my principles, and not *diſpirited* with my afflictions, I have overcome all difficulties. *Dryden's Æn. Dedicat.*

Amidſt all the honours that are paid him, he feels nothing in himſelf but a poor, weak, *diſpirited* mortal, yielding to the laws of corruption. *Rogers, Sermon* 5.

2. To exhauſt the ſpirits; to oppreſs the conſtitution of the body.

He has *diſpirited* himſelf by a debauch, and drank away his good humour. *Collier.*

DISPI'RITEDNESS. *n. ſ.* [from *diſpirit.*] Want of vigour; want of vivacity. *Dict.*

To DISPLA'CE. *v. a.* [*dis* and *place.*]

1. To put out of place; to place in another ſituation.

2. To put out of any ſtate, condition, office, truſt, or dignity.

To *diſplace* any who are in upon diſpleaſure, is by all means to be avoided, unleſs there be a manifeſt cauſe for it. *Bacon.*

Abdal, who commands
The city, is the prince's friend, and therefore
Muſt be *diſplac'd*, and thou ſhalt ſtrait ſucceed him. *Denh.*

A religion eſtabliſhed by God himſelf, ſhould not be *diſplaced* by any thing, under a demonſtration of that divine power that firſt introduced it. *South's Sermons.*

One then may be *diſplac'd*, and one may reign,
And want of merit render birthright vain. *Dryd. Aurengz.*

3. To diſorder.

You have *diſplac'd* the mirth, broke the good meeting,
With moſt admir'd diſorder. *Shakeſpeare's Macbeth.*

DISPLA'CENCY. *n. ſ.* [*diſplicentia*, Latin.]

1. Incivility; diſobligation.

2. Diſguſt; any thing unpleaſing.

The *diſplacencies* that he receives, by the conſequences of his exceſs, far outweigh all that is grateful in it. *Dec. of Piety.*

To DISPLA'NT. *v. a.* [*dis* and *plant.*]

1. To remove a plant.

2. To drive a people from the place in which they have fixed their reſidence.

All thoſe countries, which, lying near unto any mountains, or Iriſh deſarts, had been planted with Engliſh, were ſhortly *diſplanted* and loſt. *Spenſer's State of Ireland.*

Plantations are amongſt ancient, primitive, and heroical works: when the world was young, it begat more children; for I may juſtly account new plantations to be the children of former kingdoms: I like a plantation in a pure ſoil; that is, where people are not *diſplanted.* *Bacon's Eſſays.*

DISPLANTA'TION. *n. ſ.* [from *dis* and *plantation.*]

1. The removal of a plant.

2. The ejection of a people.

The Edenites were garriſoned to reſiſt the Aſſyrians, whoſe *diſplantation* Senacherib vaunted of. *Raleigh.*

To DISPLA'Y. *v. a.* [*deplier*, *deſployer*, French.]

1. To ſpread wide.

The

The northern wind his wings did broad *display*
At his command, and reared him up light. *Fairy Queen.*
Say, how this instrument of love began;
And in immortal strains *display* the fan. *Gay.*

2. To exhibit to the sight or mind.
You speak not like yourself, who ever yet
Have stood to charity, and *display'd* th' effects
Of disposition gentle. *Shakespeare's Henry* VIII.
Thou heav'n's alternate beauty can'st *display*,
The blush of morning, and the milky way. *Dryden.*
The works of nature, and the words of revelation, *display* truth to mankind in characters so visible, that those, who are not quite blind, may read. *Locke.*
The storm the dark Lycæan groves *display'd*,
And first to light expos'd the sacred shade. *Pope's Statius.*

3. To carve; to cut up.
He carves, *displays*, and cuts up to a wonder. *Spectator.*

4. To talk without restraint.
The other messenger,
Whose welcome I perceiv'd had poison'd mine,
Being the very fellow which of late
Display'd so saucily against your highness. *Shakesp. K. Lear.*

5. To set ostentatiously to view.
They are all couched in a pit, hard by Herne's oak, with obscured lights; which, at the very instant of Falstaff's and our meeting, they will at once *display* to the night. *Shakesp.*

DISPLA'Y. *n. s.* [from the verb.] An exhibition of any thing to view.
Our enobled understandings take the wings of the morning to visit the world above us, and have a glorious *display* of the highest form of created excellencies. *Glanv. Sceps. c.* 2.
We can with the greatest coldness behold the stupendous *displays* of omnipotence, and be in transports at the puny essays of human skill. *Spectator*, N°. 626.

DISPLE'ASANCE. *n. s.* [from *displease.*] Anger; discontent. Obsolete.
Cordell said, she lov'd him as behov'd;
Whose simple answer wanting colours fair
To paint it forth, him to *displeasance* mov'd. *Fairy Queen.*

DISPLEA'SANT. *adj.* [from *displease.*] Unpleasing; offensive; unpleasant.
What to one is a most grateful odour, to another is noxious and *displeasant*; and it were a misery to some to lie stretched on a bed of roses. *Glanv. Sceps. c.* 15.

To DISPLE'ASE. *v. a.* [*dis* and *please.*]
1. To offend; to make angry.
God was *displeased* with this thing. 1 *Chron.* xxi. 7.
Your extreme fondness was perhaps as *displeasing* to God before, as now your extreme affliction. *Temple.*
2. To disgust; to raise aversion.
Foul sights do rather *displease*, in that they excite the memory of foul things, than in the immediate objects; and therefore, in pictures, those foul sights do not much offend. *Bacon's Natural History*, N°. 275.
Sweet and stinking commonly serve our turn for these ideas, which, in effect, is little more than to call them pleasing or *displeasing*; though the smell of a rose and violet, both sweet, are certainly very distinct ideas. *Locke.*

DISPLE'ASINGNESS. *n. s.* [from *displeasing.*] Offensiveness; quality of offending.
It is a mistake to think that men cannot change the *displeasingness* or indifferency, that is in actions, into pleasure and desire, if they will do but what is in their power. *Locke.*

DISPLE'ASURE. *n. s.* [from *displease.*]
1. Uneasiness; pain received.
When good is proposed, its absence carries *displeasure* or pain with it. *Locke.*
2. Offence; pain given.
Now shall I be more blameless than the Philistines, though I do them a *displeasure.* *Judg.* xv. 3.
3. Anger; indignation.
True repentance may be wrought in the hearts of such as fear God, and yet incur his *displeasure*, the deserved effect whereof is eternal death. *Hooker, b.* v. *s.* 22.
He should beware that, by the fame of such a fact, he did not provoke Solyman's heavy *displeasure* against him. *Knolles.*
Undoubtedly he will relent, and turn
From his *displeasure.* *Milton's Paradise Lost, b.* x. *l.* 109.
Though the reciprocalness of the injury ought to allay the *displeasure* at it, yet men so much more consider what they suffer than what they do. *Decay of Piety.*
On me alone thy just *displeasure* lay;
But take thy judgments from this mourning land. *Dryden.*
Y' have shewn how much you my content design;
Yet, ah! would heaven's *displeasure* pass like mine. *Dryden.*
Nothing is in itself so pernicious to communities of learned men as the *displeasure* of their prince, which those may justly expect to feel who would make use of his favour to his own prejudice. *Addison's Freeholder*, N°. 33.
4. State of disgrace; state in which one does obtain discountenance; disfavour.
He went into Poland, being in *displeasure* with the pope for overmuch familiarity. *Peacham on Musick.*

To DISPLE'ASURE. *v. a.* [from the noun.] To displease; not to gain favour; not to win affection. A word not elegant, nor now in use.
When the way of pleasuring or *displeasuring* lieth by the favourite, it is impossible any other should be overgreat. *Bacon.*

To DISPLO'DE. *v. a.* [*displodo*, Latin.] To disperse with a loud noise; to vent with violence.
In view
Stood rank'd of seraphim another row,
In posture to *displode* their second fire
Of thunder. *Milton's Paradise Lost, b.* vi. *l.* 605.

DISPLO'SION. *n. s.* [from *displosus*, Lat.] The act of disploding; a sudden burst or dispersion with noise and violence.

DISPO'RT. *n. s.* [*dis* and *sport.*] Play; sport; pastime; diversion; amusement; merriment.
She list not hear, but her *disports* pursu'd;
And ever bade him stay, 'till time the tide renew'd. *Fai. Qu.*
His *disports* were ingenuous and manlike, whereby he always learned somewhat. *Hayward on Edward* VI.
She busied, heard the sound
Of rusling leaves; but minded not, as us'd
To such *disport* before her through the field. *Milt. P. Lost.*

To DISPO'RT. *v. a.* [from the noun.] To divert.
He often, but attended with weak guard,
Comes hunting this way to *disport* himself. *Shakesp. Hen.* VI.

To DISPO'RT. *v. n.* To play; to toy; to wanton.
Fresh gales and gentle airs
Whisper'd it to the woods, and from their wings
Flung rose, flung odours from the spicy shrub
Disporting! *Milton's Paradise Lost, b.* viii. *l.* 518.
Loose to the winds their airy garments flew;
The glitt'ring textures of the filmy dew,
Dipt in the richest tincture of the skies,
Where light *disports* in ever mingling dyes. *Pope.*

DISPO'SAL. *n. s.* [from *dispose.*]
1. The act of disposing or regulating any thing; regulation; dispensation; distribution.
Tax not divine *disposal*; wisest men
Have err'd, and by bad women been deluded. *Milt. Agon.*
2. The power of distribution; the right of bestowing.
I am called off from publick dissertations by a domestick affair of great importance, which is no less than the *disposal* of my sister Jenny for life. *Tatler*, N°. 75.
Are not the blessings both of this world and the next in his *disposal?* *Atterbury's Sermons.*
3. Government; management; conduct.
We shall get more true and clear knowledge by one rule, than by taking up principles, and thereby putting our minds into the *disposals* of others. *Locke.*

To DISPO'SE. *v. a.* [*disposer*, French; *dispono*, Latin.]
1. To employ to various purposes; to diffuse.
Thus whilst she did her various pow'r *dispose*,
The world was free from tyrants, wars, and woes. *Prior.*
2. To give; to place; to bestow.
Yet see, when noble benefits shall prove
Not well *dispos'd*, the mind grown once corrupt,
They turn to vicious forms, ten times more ugly
Than ever they were fair. *Shakespeare's Henry* VIII.
Of what you gathered, as most your own, you have *disposed* much in works of publick piety. *Spratt's Sermons.*
3. To turn to any particular end or consequence.
Endure, and conquer; Jove will soon *dispose*,
To future good, our past and present woes. *Dryden's Virgil.*
4. To adapt; to form for any purpose.
These, when the knights beheld, they 'gan *dispose*
Themselves to court, and each a damsel chose. *Fai. Queen.*
But if thee list unto the court to throng,
And there to haunt after the hoped prey,
Then must thou thee *dispose* another way. *Hulberd's Tale.*
5. To frame the mind; to give a proper propension; to incline.
Suspicions *dispose* kings to tyranny, husbands to jealousy, and wise men to irresolution and melancholy. *Bacon's Essays.*
The memory of what they had suffered, by being without it, easily *disposed* them to do this. *Clarendon, b.* viii.
He knew the seat of Paradise,
And, as he was *dispos'd*, could prove it
Below the moon, or else above it. *Hudibras, p.* i. *cant.* 1.
This *disposes* men to believe what it teaches, to follow what it advises. *Temple.*
A man might do this now, if he were maliciously *disposed*, and had a mind to bring matters to extremity. *Dryd. Spa. Fry.*
This may *dispose* me, perhaps, for the reception of truth; but helps me not to it. *Locke.*
Although the frequency of prayer and fasting may be of no efficacy to *dispose* God to be more gracious, yet it is of great use to *dispose* us to be more objects of his grace. *Smalridge.*
If mere moralists find themselves *disposed* to pride, lust, intemperance, or avarice, they do not think their morality concerned to check them. *Swift.*
6. To regulate; to adjust.

Wak'd

Wak'd by the cries, th' Athenian chief arose,
The knightly forms of combat to *dispose*. *Dryden's Fables.*

7. *To* DISPOSE *of.* To apply to any purpose; to transfer to any other person or use.

All men are naturally in a state of perfect freedom to order their actions, and *dispose of* their possessions and persons as they think fit, within the bounds of the law of nature. *Locke.*

Dispose of the meat with the butler, or any other crony. *Sw.*

8. *To* DISPOSE *of.* To put into the hands of another.

As she is mine, I may *dispose of* her;
Which shall be either to this gentleman,
Or to her death. *Shakespeare's Midsummer Night's Dream.*

I have *disposed of* her to a man of business, who will let her see, that to be well dressed in good humour, and chearful in her family, are the arts and sciences of female life. *Tatler.*

9. *To* DISPOSE *of.* To give away.

A rural judge *dispos'd of* beauty's prize. *Waller.*

10. *To* DISPOSE *of.* To employ to any end.

The lot is cast unto the lap; but the whole *disposing thereof* is of the Lord. *Prov.* xvi. 33.

They must receive instructions how to *dispose of* themselves when they come, which must be in the nature of laws unto them. *Bacon's Advice to Villiers.*

11. *To* DISPOSE *of.* To place in any condition.

For the remaining doubt,
What to resolve, and how *dispose of* me,
Be warn'd to cast that useless care aside. *Dryden's Fables.*

12. *To* DISPOSE *of.* To put away by any means.

They require more water than can be found, and more than can be *disposed of*, if it was found. *Burnet's Th. of Earth.*

To DISPO'SE. *v. n.* To bargain; to make terms. Obsolete.

When she saw you did suspect
She had *dispos'd* with Cæsar, and that your rage
Would not be purg'd, she sent word she was dead. *Shakesp.*

DISPO'SE. *n. s.* [from the verb.]

1. Power; management; disposal.

All that is mine I leave at thy *dispose*;
My goods, my lands, my reputation. *Shakespeare.*

It shall be my task
To render thee the Parthian at *dispose*. *Milton's Parad. Reg.*

Of all your goodness leaves to our *dispose*,
Our liberty's the only gift we chuse. *Dryden's Indian Emp.*

2. Distribution; act of government.

All is best, though oft we doubt
What th' unsearchable *dispose*
Of highest wisdom brings about,
And ever best found in the close. *Milton's Agonistes.*

3. Disposition; cast of behaviour. Obsolete.

He hath a person, and a smooth *dispose*,
To be suspected; fram'd to make women false. *Shak. Othello.*

4. Disposition; cast of mind; inclination. Obsolete.

He carries on the stream of his *dispose*
Without observance or respect of any,
In will peculiar. *Shakesp. Troil. and Cressid.*

DISPO'SER. *n. s.* [from *dispose.*]

1. Distributer; giver; bestower.

The magistrate is both the beggar and the *disposer* of what is got by begging. *Graunt's Bill of Mortality.*

2. Governor; regulator; director.

I think myself obliged, whatever my private apprehensions may be of the success, to do my duty, and leave events to their *disposer*. *Boyle.*

All the reason of mankind cannot suggest any solid ground of satisfaction, but in making that God our friend, who is the absolute *disposer* of all things. *South's Sermons.*

Would I had been *disposer* of thy stars,
Thou shouldst have had thy wish, and died in wars. *Dryd.*

3. One who gives to whom he pleases.

But brandish'd high, in an ill omen'd hour,
To thee, proud Gaul, behold thy justest fear,
The master sword, *disposer* of thy pow'r. *Prior.*

DISPO'SITION. *n. s.* [from *dispositio*, Latin.]

1. Order; method; distribution.

Touching musical harmony, whether by instrument or voice, it being of high and low, in due proportionable *disposition*, such notwithstanding is the force thereof, and so very pleasing effects it hath, in that very part of man, which is most divine, that some have been thereby induced to think, that the soul itself by nature is, or hath in it harmony. *Hooker.*

Under this head of invention is placed the *disposition* of the work, to put all things in a beautiful order and harmony, that the whole may be of a piece. *Dryden's Dufresnoy, Preface.*

I ask whether the connection of the extremes be not more clearly seen, in this simple and natural *disposition*, than in the perplexed repetitions and jumble of five or six syllogisms. *Locke.*

2. Natural fitness; quality.

Refrangibility of the rays of light is their *disposition* to be refracted, or turned out of their way, in passing out of one transparent body or medium into another. *Newton's Opt.*

3. Tendency to any act or state.

This argueth a great *disposition* to putrefaction in the soil and air. *Bacon's Natural History*, N°. 69.

Bleeding is to be used or omitted according to the symptoms which affect the brain: it relieves in any inflammatory *disposition* of the coat of the nerve. *Arbuthnot on Diet.*

4. Temper of mind.

I have suffered more for their sakes, more than the villanous inconstancy of man's *disposition* is able to bear. *Shakesp.*

Lesser had been
The thwartings of your *disposition*, if
You had not shew'd them how you were dispos'd,
'Ere they lack'd power to cross you. *Shakesp. Coriolanus.*

5. Affection of kindness or ill-will.

I take myself to be as well informed as most men in the *dispositions* of each people towards the other. *Swift.*

6. Predominant inclination.

As they pinch one another by the *disposition*, he cries out, no more. *Shakespeare's Anthony and Cleopatra.*

Disposition is when the power and ability of doing any thing is forward, and ready upon every occasion to break into action. *Locke.*

The love we bear to our friends is generally caused by our finding the same *disposition* in them which we feel in ourselves. *Pope.*

DISPO'SITIVE. *adj.* [from *dispose.*] That which implies disposal of any property; decretive.

The words of all judicial acts are written narratively, unless it be in sentences wherein *dispositive* and enacting terms are made use of. *Ayliffe's Parergon.*

DISPO'SITIVELY. *adv.* [from *dispositive.*]

1. In a dispositive manner.

2. Respecting individuals; distributively.

That axiom in philosophy, that the generation of one thing is the corruption of another, although it be substantially true, concerning the form and matter, is also *dispositively* verified in the efficient or producer. *Brown's Vulgar Errours*, *b.* iii.

DISPO'SITOR. *n. s.* [from *dispose.*] The lord of that sign in which the planet is, and by which therefore it is over-ruled.

To DISPOSSE'SS. *v. a.* [*dis* and *possess.*]

1. To put out of possession; to deprive; to disseize.

The blow from saddle forced him to fly;
Else might it needs down to his manly breast
Have cleft his head in twain, and life thence *dispossest*. *F. Q.*

Thou shalt hold the opinion of Pythagoras, ere I will allow of thy wits; and fear to kill a woodcock, lest thou *dispossess* the soul of thy grandame. *Shakespeare's Twelfth Night.*

Let us sit upon the ground, and tell
How some have been depos'd, some slain in war,
Some haunted by the ghosts they *dispossess'd*. *Shakesp. R.* II.

I will chuse
Mine heir from forth the beggars of the world,
And *dispossess* her all. *Shakespeare's Timon.*

In thee I hope; thy succours I invoke,
To win the crown whence I am *dispossess'd*;
For like renown awaiteth on the stroke,
To cast the haughty down, or raise th' oppress'd. *Fairfax.*

The children went to Gilead, and took it, and *dispossessed* the Amorite which was in it. *Numb.* xxxii. 39.

By their aid
This inaccessible high strength, the seat
Of deity supreme, us *dispossess'd*,
He trusted to have seiz'd. *Milton's Paradise Lost*, *b.* vii.

Restless Amata lay,
Fir'd with disdain for Turnus *dispossest*,
And the new nuptials of the Trojan guest. *Dryden's Æn.*

2. It is generally used with *of* before the thing taken away.

Charles resolved, with a puissant army, to pass over, and by arms to *dispossess* the pyrate *of* his new gotten kingdom in Tunis. *Knolles's History of the Turks.*

No pow'r shall *dispossess*
My thoughts of that expected happiness. *Denham.*

O, fairest of all creatures, last and best
Of what heav'n made, how art thou *dispossess'd*
Of all thy native glories! *Dryden's State of Innocence.*

Nothing can create more trouble to a man than to endeavour to *dispossess* him of this conceit. *Tillotson, Serm.* ii.

3. Formerly with *from.*

They arrogate dominion undeserv'd
Over their brethren, and quite *dispossess*
Concord and law of nature *from* the earth. *Milt. Par. Lost.*

It will be found a work of no small difficulty to *dispossess* and throw out a vice *from* that heart, where long possession begins to plead prescription. *South's Sermons.*

DISPO'SURE. *n. s.* [from *dispose.*]

1. Disposal; government; power; management.

In his *disposure* is the orb of earth,
The throne of kings, and all of human birth. *Sandys.*

They quietly surrendered both it and themselves to his *disposure*. *Sandys's Journey.*

Whilst they murmur against the present *disposure* of things, they do tacitly desire in them a difformity from the primitive rule, and the idea of that mind that formed all things best. *Brown's Vulgar Errours*, *b.* i. *c.* 11.

2. State; posture.

They remained in a kind of warlike *dispofure*, or perhaps little better. *Wotton.*

DISPRA'ISE. *n.f.* [*dis* and *praife.*] Blame; cenfure; difhonour.

If I can do it,
By aught that I can fpeak in his *difpraife*,
She fhall not long continue love to him. *Shakefpeare.*

To me reproach
Rather belongs, diftruft, and all *difpraife*. *Milt. Par. Loft.*

Nothing is here for tears, nothing to wail
Or knock the breafts; no weaknefs, no contempt,
Difpraife or blame. *Milton's Agoniftes, l.* 1723.

I need not raife
Trophies to thee from other mens *difpraife*. *Denham.*

Looks fright not men: the general has feen Moors
With as bad faces; no *difpraife* to Bertran's. *Dryd. Sp. Fry.*

If any writer fhall do this paper fo much honour as to infcribe the title of it to others, the whole praife or *difpraife* of fuch a performance will belong to fome other author. *Addifon.*

My faults will not be hid, and it is no *difpraife* to me that they will not: the cleannefs of one's mind is never better proved than in difcovering its own faults. *Pope.*

To DISPRA'ISE. *v. a.* [from the noun.] To blame; to cenfure; to condemn.

In praifing Anthony, I have *difprais'd* Cæfar. *Shakefp.*

No abufe, Ned, in the world; honeft Ned, none: I *difpraifed* him before the wicked, that the wicked might not fall in love with him; in which doing, I have done the part of a careful friend. *Shakefpeare's Henry* IV. *p.* ii.

The criticks, while they like my wares, may *difpraife* my writing. *Spectator*, N°. 288.

DISPRA'ISER. *n. f.* [from *difpraife.*] A cenfurer; one who blames. *Dict.*

DISPRA'ISIBLE. *adj.* [from *difpraife.*] Unworthy of commendation. *Dict.*

DISPRA'ISINGLY. *adv.* [from *difpraife.*] With blame; with cenfure.

Michael Caffio!
That came a wooing with you; many a time,
When I have fpoke of you *difpraifingly*,
Hath ta'en your part. *Shakefpeare's Othello.*

To DISPRE'AD. *v. a.* [*dis* and *fpread.*] To fpread different ways. In this word, and a few others, *dis* has the fame force as in Latin compofition, and means, different ways; in different directions.

As morning fun her beams *difpreaden* clear,
And in her face fair truth and mercy doth appear. *Fa. Qu.*

Over him, art ftriving to compare
With nature, did an arbour green *difpread*,
Framed of wanton ivy, flowing fair,
Through which the fragrant eglantine did fpread
His pricking arms, entrail'd with rofes red. *Fairy Queen.*

Above, below, around, with art *difpread*,
The fure inclofure folds the genial bed. *Pope's Odyffey.*

DISPRO'FIT. *n. f.* [*dis* and *profit.*] Lofs; damage; detriment. *Dict.*

DISPRO'OF. *n. f.* [*dis* and *proof.*] Confutation; conviction of errour or falfhood.

His remark contains the grounds of his doctrine, and offers at fomewhat towards the *difproof* of mine. *Atterbury.*

I need not offer any thing farther in fupport of one, or in *difproof* of the other. *Rogers, Serm.* 14.

To DISPRO'PERTY. *v. a.* [*dis* and *property.*] To difpoffefs of any property. *Dict.*

DISPROPO'RTION. *n. f.* [*dis* and *proportion.*] Unfuitablenefs in quantity of one thing, or one part of the fame thing, to another; want of fymmetry.

Not to affect many propofed matches
Of her own clime, complexion, and degree,
Whereto we fee in all things nature tends:
Foh! one may fmell, in fuch, a will moft rank,
Foul *difproportion*, thoughts unnatural. *Shakefpeare's Othello.*

Reafoning, I oft admire
How nature, wife and frugal, could commit
Such *difproportions*; with fuperfluous hand
So many nobler bodies to create,
Greater, fo many fold to this one ufe. *Milton's Par. Loft.*

Perhaps from greatnefs, ftate, and pride,
Thus furprifed, fhe may fall:
Sleep does *difproportion* hide,
And, death refembling, equals all. *Waller.*

For their ftrength,
The *difproportion* is fo great, we cannot but
Expect a fatal confequence. *Denham's Sophy.*

What, did the liquid to th' affembly call,
To give their aid to form the pond'rous ball?
Firft, tell us, why did any come? next why
In fuch a *difproportion* to the dry? *Blackmore's Creation.*

That we are defigned for a more exalted happinefs, than can be derived from the things of this life, we may infer from their vaft *difproportion* to the defires and capacities of our foul. *Rogers, Serm.* 5.

To DISPROPO'RTION. *v. a.* [from the noun.] To mifmatch; to join things unfuitable in quantity.

There fits deformity to mock my body,
To fhape my legs of an unequal fize,
To *difproportion* me in every part. *Shak. Henry* VI. *p.* iii.

Diftance and mens fears have fo enlarged the truth, and fo *difproportioned* every thing, that we have made the little troop of difcontents a gallant army, and already meafure by the evening fhadow. *Suckling.*

Mufick craveth your acquaintance: many are of fuch *difproportioned* fpirits, that they avoid her company. *Peacham.*

We on earth, with undifcording voice,
May rightly anfwer that melodious noife;
As once we did, 'till *difproportion'd* fin
Jarr'd againft nature's chime. *Milton.*

DISPROPO'RTIONABLE. *adj.* [from *difproportion.*] Unfuitable in quantity; not duly regulated in regard to fomething elfe.

Doubts and fears are the fharpeft paffions: through thefe falfe opticks all that you fee is like the evening fhadows, *difproportionable* to the truth, and ftrangely longer than the true fubftance. *Suckling.*

Had the obliquity been greater, the earth had not been able to endure the *difproportionable* differences of feafon. *Brown.*

We are apt to fet too great a value on temporal bleffings, and have too low and *difproportionable* efteem of fpiritual. *Smal.*

There is no wine of fo ftrong a body as to bear fuch a *difproportionable* quantity of water as fixty parts. *Pope's Od. Notes.*

DISPROPO'RTIONABLENESS. *n. f.* [from *difproportionable.*] Unfuitablenefs to fomething elfe.

DISPROPO'RTIONABLY. *adv.* [from *difproportion.*] Unfuitably; not fymmetrically.

DISPROPO'RTIONAL. *n. f.* [from *difproportion.*] Difproportionable; unfymmetrical; unfuitable in quantity to fomething elfe.

DISPROPO'RTIONALLY. *adv.* [from *difproportional.*] Unfuitably with refpect to quantity or value.

DISPROPO'RTIONATE. *adj.* [from *difproportion.*] Unfymmetrical; unfuitable to fomething elfe either in bulk or value.

None of our members are crooked or diftorted, or *difproportionate* to the reft, either in excefs or defect. *Ray.*

It is plain that men have agreed to a *difproportionate* and unequal poffeffion of the earth. *Locke.*

DISPROPO'RTIONATELY. *adv.* [from *difproportionate.*] Unfuitably; unfymmetrically.

DISPROPO'RTIONATENESS. *n. f.* [from *difproportionate.*] Unfuitablenefs in bulk or value.

To DISPRO'VE. *v. a.* [*dis* and *prove.*]

1. To confute an affertion; to convict of errour or falfhood.

This expofition they plainly *difprove*, and fhew by manifeft reafon, that of David the words of David could not poffibly be meant. *Hooker.*

This Weftmoreland maintains,
And Warwick fhall *difprove* it. *Shakefp. Henry* VI. *p.* iii.

Arcite with difdain,
In haughty language, thus reply'd again:
Forfworn thyfelf; the traytor's odious name
I firft return, and then *difprove* thy claim. *Dryden's Fables.*

It is eafier to affirm than to *difprove*. *Holder's Elements.*

That falfe fuppofition I advanced in order to *difprove* it, and by that means to prove the truth of my doctrine. *Atterbury's Sermons, Pref.*

We fee the fame affertions produced again, without notice of what hath been faid to *difprove* them. *Swift.*

2. To convict a practice of errour.

They behold thofe things *difproved*, difannulled, and rejected, which ufe had made in a manner natural. *Hooker, b.* iv.

If God did not forbid all indifferent ceremonies, then our conformity with the church of Rome in fome fuch is not hitherto as yet *difproved*, although papifts were unto us as heathens were unto Ifrael. *Hooker, b.* iv. *f.* 6.

DISPRO'VER. *n. f.* [from *difprove.*]

1. One that difproves or confutes.
2. One that blames; a cenfurer, if the following paffage be not ill printed for *difapprover*.

The fingle example that our annals have yielded of two extremes, within fo fhort time, by moft of the fame commenders and *difprovers*, would require no flight memorial. *Wotton.*

DISPU'NISHABLE. *adj.* [*dis* and *punifhable.*] Without penal reftraint.

No leafes of any part of the faid lands fhall ever be made, other than leafes for years not exceeding thirty-one, in poffeffion, and not in reverfion or remainder, and not *difpunifhable* of wafte. *Swift's laft Will.*

To DISPU'RSE. *v. a.* [*dis* and *purfe.*] To pay; to difburfe. It is not certain that the following paffage fhould not be written *difburfe*.

Many a pound of my own proper ftore,
Becaufe I would not tax the needy commons,
Have I *difpurfed* to the garrifons,
And never afk'd for reftitution. *Shakefpeare's Henry* VI.

DISPU'TABLE. *adj.* [from *dispute.*]

1. Liable to contest; controvertible; that for which something may be alleged on opposite sides.

If they are not in themselves *disputable*, why are they so much disputed? *South.*

2. Lawful to be contested.

Until any point is determined to be a law, it remains *disputable* by every subject. *Swift.*

DI'SPUTANT. *n. s.* [from *dispute*; *disputans*, Latin.] A controvertist; an arguer; a reasoner.

Our *disputants* put me in mind of the skuttle-fish, that when he is unable to extricate himself, blackens all the water about him 'till he becomes invisible. *Spectator*, N°. 476.

DI'SPUTANT. *adj.* Disputing; engaged in controversy.

Thou there wast found
Among the gravest rabbies, *disputant*
On points and questions fitting Moses chair. *Milt. Pa. Reg.*

DISPUTA'TION. *n. s.* [from *disputatio*, Latin.]

1. The skill of controversy; argumentation.

Consider what the learning of *disputation* is, and how they are employed for the advantage of themselves or others, whose business is only the vain ostentation of sounds. *Locke.*

2. Controversy; argumental contest.

Well do I find, by the wise knitting together of your answer, that any *disputation* I can use is as much too weak as I unworthy. *Sidney, b.* ii.

'Till some admirable or unusual accident happens, as it hath in some, to work the beginning of a better alteration in the mind, *disputation* about the knowledge of God commonly prevaileth little. *Hooker, b.* v.

DISPUTA'TIOUS. *adj.* [from *dispute.*] Inclined to dispute; cavilling.

A man must be of a very *disputatious* temper, that enters into state-controversies with any of the fair sex. *Add. Freehold.*

DISPU'TATIVE. *adj.* [from *dispute.*] Disposed to debate; argumentative.

Perhaps this practice might not so easily be perverted as to raise a cavilling, *disputative*, and sceptical temper in the minds of youth. *Watts's Improvement of the Mind.*

To DISPU'TE. *v. n.* [*disputo*, Latin.] To contend by argument; to altercate; to debate; to argue; to controvert.

If attempts of the pen have often proved unfit, those of the sword are more so, and fighting is a worse expedient than *disputing*. *Decay of Piety.*

The atheist can pretend no obligation of conscience, why he should *dispute* against religion. *Tillotson, Serm.* ii.

Did not Paul and Barnabas *dispute* with vehemence about a very little point of conveniency? *Atterbury.*

To DISPU'TE. *v. a.*

1. To contend for, whether by words or action.

Things were *disputed* before they came to be determined: men afterwards were not to *dispute* any longer, but to obey. *Hooker.*

So *dispute* the prize,
As if you fought before Cydaria's eyes. *Dryd. Ind. Emperor.*

One says the kingdom is his own: a Saxon drinks the quart, and swears he'll *dispute* that with him. *Tatler*, N°. 75.

2. To oppose; to question.

~~Now I am sent, and am not to *dispute*~~
My prince's orders, but to execute. *Dryden's Ind. Emperor.*

3. To discuss; to think on: a sense not in use.

Dispute it like a man.
——I shall do so:
But I must also feel it as a man. *Shakespeare's Macbeth.*

DISPU'TE. *n. s.* [from the verb.] Contest; controversy; argumental contention.

The question being about a fact, it is begging it, to bring as a proof an hypothesis which is the very thing in *dispute*. *Loc.*

The earth is now placed so conveniently, that plants thrive and flourish in it, and animals live: this is matter of fact, and beyond all *dispute*. *Bentley's Sermons.*

DISPU'TELESS. *adj.* [from *dispute.*] Undisputed; uncontrovertible. *Dict.*

DISPU'TER. *n. s.* [from *dispute.*] A controvertist; one given to argument and opposition.

Both were vehement *disputers* against the heathen idolatry. *Stillingfleet's Def. of Disc. on Rom. Idol.*

Those conclusions have generally obtained, and have been acknowledged even by *disputers* themselves, 'till with labour they had stifled their convictions. *Rogers's Sermons.*

DISQUALIFICA'TION. *n. s.* [from *disqualify.*] That which disqualifies; that which makes unfit.

It is recorded as a sufficient *disqualification* of a wife, that, speaking of her husband, she said, God forgive him. *Spectator.*

To DISQUA'LIFY. *v. a.* [*dis* and *qualify.*]

1. To make unfit; to disable by some natural or legal impediment.

Such persons as shall confer benefices on unworthy and *disqualified* persons, after a notice or correction given, shall for that turn be deprived of the power of presenting unto such benefices. *Ayliffe's Parergon.*

I know no employment for which piety *disqualifies*. *Swift.*

My common illness utterly *disqualifies* me for all conversation; I mean my deafness. *Swift.*

2. To deprive a right or claim by some positive restriction; to disable; to except from any grant.

The church of England is the only body of Christians which *disqualifies* those, who are employed to preach its doctrine, from sharing in the civil power, farther than as senators. *Swift on the Sacramental Test.*

To DISQUA'NTITY. *v. a.* [*dis* and *quantity.*] To lessen; to diminish.

Be entreated of fifty to *disquantity* your train;
And the remainders that shall still depend,
To be such men as may besort your age. *Shakes. K. Lear.*

DISQUI'ET. *n. s.* [*dis* and *quiet.*] Uneasiness; restlessness; want of tranquillity; vexation; disturbance; anxiety.

He that, upon a true principle, lives without any *disquiet* of thought, may be said to be happy. *L'Estrange's Fables.*

If we give way to our passions, we do but gratify ourselves for the present, in order to our future *disquiet*. *Tillotson.*

I had rather live in Ireland than under the frequent *disquiets* of hearing you are out of order. *Swift.*

DISQUI'ET. *adj.* Unquiet; uneasy; restless.

I pray you, husband, be not so *disquiet*;
The meat was well, if you were so content. *Shakespeare.*

To DISQUI'ET. *v. a.* [from the noun.] To disturb; to make uneasy; to harrass; to vex; to fret; to deprive of tranquillity.

The proud Roman him *disquieted*,
A warlike Cæsar, tempted with the name
Of this sweet island. *Fairy Queen, b.* ii. *cant.* 10. *stan.* 47.

Why art thou so vexed, O my soul? And why art thou so *disquieted* within me? *Psalm* i.

By anger and impatience the mind is *disquieted*, and is not able easily to compose itself to prayer. *Duppa.*

Thou, happy creature, art secure
From all the torments we endure;
Despair, ambition, jealousy,
Lost friends, nor love *disquiets* thee. *Roscommon.*

DISQUI'ETER. *n. s.* [from *disquiet.*] A disturber; a harrasser.

DISQUI'ETLY. *adv.* [from *disquiet.*] Without rest; anxiously; uneasily; without calmness.

We have seen the best of our machinations, hollowness, treachery, and all ruinous disorders, follow us *disquietly* to our graves. *Shakespeare's King Lear.*

He rested *disquietly* that night; but in the morning I found him calm. *Wiseman's Surgery.*

DISQUI'ETNESS. *n. s.* [from *disquiet.*] Uneasiness; restlessness; anxiety; disturbance.

All otherwise, said he, I riches rede,
And deem them root of all *disquietness*. *Fairy Queen, b.* ii.

Arius won to himself, both followers and great defenders; whereupon much *disquietness* ensued. *Hooker, b.* v. *s.* 49.

DISQUI'ETUDE. *n. s.* [from *disquiet.*] Uneasiness; anxiety; disturbance; want of tranquillity.

Little happiness attends a great character, and to a multitude of *disquietudes* the desire of it subjects an ambitious mind. *Addison's Spectator*, N°. 256.

'Tis the best preservative from all those temporal fears and *disquietudes*, which corrupt the enjoyment, and embitter the lives of men. *Rogers, Sermon* 1.

DISQUISI'TION. *n. s.* [*disquisitio*, Latin.] Examination; disputative enquiry.

God hath reserved many things to his own resolution, whose determinations we cannot hope from flesh; but with reverence must suspend unto that great day, whose justice shall either condemn our curiosity, or resolve our *disquisitions*. *Brown.*

'Tis indeed the proper place for this *disquisition* concerning the antediluvian earth, and it could not well have been brought in before. *Woodward's Natural History.*

The royal society had a good effect, as it turned many of the greatest geniuses of that age to the *disquisitions* of natural knowledge. *Addison's Spectator*, N°. 267.

The nature of animal diet may be discovered by taste, and other sensible qualities, and some general rules, without particular *disquisition* upon every kind. *Arbuthnot.*

To DISRA'NK. *v. a.* [*dis* and *rank.*] To degrade from his rank. *Dict.*

DISREGA'RD. *n. s.* [*dis* and *regard.*] Slight notice; neglect; contempt.

To DISREGA'RD. *v. a.* [from the noun.] To slight; to neglect; to contemn.

Since we are to do good to the poor, to strangers, to enemies, those whom nature is too apt to make us despise, *disregard*, or hate, then undoubtedly we are to do good to all. *Spratt's Sermons.*

Those fasts which God hath *disregarded* hitherto, he may regard for the time to come. *Smalridge's Sermons.*

Studious of good, man *disregarded* fame,
And useful knowledge was his eldest aim. *Blackmore.*

DISREGA'RDFUL.

DISREGA'RDFUL. *adj.* [*disregard* and *full.*] Negligent; contemptuous.

DISREGA'RDFULLY. *adj.* [from *disregardful.*] Negligently; contemptuously.

DISRE'LISH. *n. s.* [*dis* and *relish.*]

1. Bad taste; nauseousness.

Oft they assay'd,
Hunger and thirst constraining; drugg'd as oft
With hatefullest *disrelish*, writh'd their jaws,
With soot and cinders fill'd. *Milton's Paradise Lost, b.* x.

2. Dislike of the palate; squeamishness.

Bread or tobacco may be neglected, where they are shewn not to be useful to health, because of an indifferency or *disrelish* to them. *Locke.*

To DISRE'LISH. *v. a.* [from the noun.]

1. To make nauseous; to infect with an unpleasant taste.

Fruits of taste to please
True appetite, and not *disrelish* thirst
Of nectarous draughts between, from milky stream. *Milt.*

The same anxiety and solicitude that embittered the pursuit, *disrelishes* the fruition itself. *Rogers, Sermon* 19.

2. To want a taste of; to dislike.

The world is become too busy for me: every body is so concerned for the publick, that all private enjoyments are lost, or *disrelished.* *Pope.*

DISREPUTA'TION. *n. s.* [*dis* and *reputation.*]

1. Disgrace; dishonour.

I will tell you what was the course in the happy days of queen Elizabeth, whom it is no *disreputation* to follow. *Bacon.*

2. Loss of reputation; ignominy.

The king fearing lest that the bad success might discourage his people, and bring *disreputation* to himself, forbad any report to be made. *Hayward.*

Gluttony is not of so great *disreputation* amongst men as drunkenness. *Taylor's Rule of living holy.*

DISREPU'TE. *n. s.* [*dis* and *repute.*] Ill character; dishonour; want of reputation.

How studiously did they cast a slur upon the king's person, and bring his governing abilities under a *disrepute.* *South.*

DISRESPE'CT. *n. s.* [*dis* and *respect.*] Incivility; want of reverence; irreverence; an act approaching to rudeness.

Any *disrespect* to acts of state, or to the persons of statesmen, was in no time more penal. *Clarendon.*

Aristotle writ a methodical discourse concerning these arts, chusing a certain benefit before the hazard that might accrue from the vain *disrespects* of ignorant persons. *Wilkins.*

What is more usual to warriours than impatience of bearing the least affront or *disrespect?* *Pope.*

DISRESPE'CTFUL. *adj.* [*disrespect* and *full.*] Irreverent; uncivil.

DISRESPE'CTFULLY. *adv.* [from *disrespectful*] Irreverently; uncivilly.

We cannot believe our posterity will think so *disrespectfully* of their great grandmothers, as that they made themselves monstrous to appear amiable. *Addison's Spectator*, Nº. 127.

To DISRO'BE. *v. a.* [*dis* and *robe.*] To undress; to uncover; to strip.

Thus when they had the witch *disrobed* quite,
And all her filthy feature open shown,
They let her go at will, and wander ways unknown. *F. Qu.*

Kill the villain strait,
Disrobe him of the matchless monument,
Thy father's triumph o'er the savages. *Shakes. King John.*

These two great peers were *disrobed* of their glory, the one by judgment, the other by violence. *Wotton.*

Who will be prevailed with to *disrobe* himself at once of all his old opinions, and pretences to knowledge and learning, and turn himself out stark naked in quest afresh of new notions. *Locke.*

DISRU'PTION. *n. s.* [*diruptio*, Latin.] The act of breaking asunder; a breach; rent; dilaceration.

This secures them from *disruption*, which they would be in danger of, upon a sudden stretch or contortion. *Ray.*

The agent which effected this *disruption*, and dislocation of the strata, was seated within the earth. *Woodward's Nat. Hist.*

If raging winds invade the atmosphere,
Their force its curious texture cannot tear,
Nor make *disruption* in the threads of air. *Blackmore.*

DISSA'TISFACTION. *n. s.* [*dis* and *satisfaction.*] The state of being dissatisfied; discontent; want of something to compleat the wish.

He that changes his condition, out of impatience and *dissatisfaction*, when he has tried a new one, wishes for his old again. *L'Estrange.*

The ambitious man has little happiness, but is subject to much uneasiness and *dissatisfaction.* *Addison's Spectator.*

In vain we try to remedy the defects of our acquisition, by varying the object: the same *dissatisfaction* pursues us through the circle of created goods. *Rogers, Sermon* 5.

DISSA'TISFACTORINESS. *n. s.* [from *dissatisfactory.*] Inability to give content.

DISSATISFA'CTORY. *adj* [from *dissatisfy.*] That which is unable to give content.

To DISSA'TISFY. *v. a.* [*dis* and *satisfy.*]

1. To discontent; to displease.

The advantages of life will not hold out to the length of desire; and, since they are not big enough to satisfy, they should not be big enough to *dissatisfy.* *Collier.*

2. To fail to please; to want something requisite.

I still retain some of my notions, after your lordship's having appeared *dissatisfied* with them. *Locke.*

To DISSE'CT. *v. a.* [*disseco*, Latin.]

1. To cut in pieces. It is used chiefly of anatomical enquiries, made by separation of the parts of animal bodies.

No mask, no trick, no favour, no reserve;
Dissect your mind, examine every nerve. *Roscommon.*
Following life in creatures we *dissect*,
We lose it in the moment we detect. *Pope.*

2. To divide and examine minutely.

This paragraph, that has not one ingenuous word throughout, I have *dissected* for a sample. *Atterbury.*

DISSE'CTION. *n. s.* [*dissectio*, Lat.] The act of separating the parts of animal bodies; anatomy.

She cut her up; but, upon the *dissection*, found her just like other hens. *L'Estrange.*

I shall enter upon the *dissection* of a coquet's heart, and communicate particularities observed in that curious piece of anatomy. *Addison's Spectator.*

Such strict enquiries into nature, so true and so perfect a *dissection* of human kind, is the work of extraordinary diligence. *Granville.*

To DISSE'IZE. *v. a.* [*dissaiser*, French.] To dispossess; to deprive.

He so *disseized* of his griping gross,
The knight his thrillant spear again assay'd,
In his brass-plated body to emboss. *Fairy Queen, b.* i.

If a prince should give a man, besides his ancient patrimony, which his family had been *disseized* of, an additional estate, never before in the possession of his ancestors, he could not be said to re-establish lineal succession. *Locke.*

DISSE'ISIN. *n. s.* [from *dissaisir*, French] An unlawful dispossessing a man of his land, tenement, or other immoveable or incorporeal right. *Cowel.*

DISSE'IZOR. *n. s.* [from *disseize.*] He that dispossesses another.

To DISSE'MBLE. *v. a.* [*dissimulo*, Latin; *semblance*, *dissemblance*, and probably *dissembler*, in old French.]

1. To hide under false appearance; to conceal; to pretend that not to be which really is.

Your son Lucentio
Doth love my daughter, and she loveth him,
Or both *dissemble* deeply their affections. *Shakespeare.*

She answered, that her soul was God's; and touching her faith, as she could not change, so she would not *dissemble* it. *Hayward.*

2. To pretend that to be which is not. This is not the true signification.

In vain, on the *dissembl'd* mother's tongue,
Had cunning art and sly persuasion hung;
And real care in vain, and native love
In the true parent's panting breast had strove. *Prior.*

To DISSE'MBLE. *v. n.* To play the hypocrite.

Ye *dissembled* in your hearts when ye sent me unto the Lord your God, saying, pray for us. *Jer.* xlii. 20.

I would *dissemble* with my nature, where
My fortunes, and my friends, at stake, requir'd
I should do so in honour. *Shakespeare's Coriolanus.*

I am curtail'd of this fair proportion,
Cheated of feature by *dissembling* nature,
Deform'd, unfinish'd. *Shakesp. Richard* III.

Thy function too will varnish o'er our arts,
And sanctify *dissembling.* *Rowe's Ambitious Stepmother.*

DISSE'MBLER. *n. s.* [from *dissemble.*] An hypocrite; a man who conceals his true disposition.

Thou dost wrong me, thou *dissembler*, thou. *Shakesp.*

The French king, in the business of peace, was the greater *dissembler* of the two. *Bacon's Henry* VII.

Such an one, whose virtue forbiddeth him to be base and a *dissembler*, shall evermore hang under the wheel. *Raleigh.*

The queen, with rage inflam'd,
Thus greets him, Thou *dissembler*, wouldst thou fly
Out of my arms by stealth. *Denham.*

Men will trust no farther than they judge a person for sincerity fit to be trusted: a discovered *dissembler* can atchieve nothing great and considerable. *South's Sermons.*

DISSE'MBLINGLY. *adv.* [from *dissemble.*] With dissimulation; hypocritically.

They might all have been either *dissemblingly* spoken, or falsly reported of the equity of the barbarous king. *Knolles.*

To DISSE'MINATE. *v a.* [*dissemino*, Latin.] To scatter as seed; to sow; to spread every way.

Ill uses are made of it many times in stirring up seditions, rebellions, in *disseminating* of heresies, and infusing of prejudices. *Hammond's Fundamentals.*

There

There is a nearly uniform and conſtant fire or heat *diſſeminated* throughout the body of the earth. *Woodward's N. Hiſt.*

The Jews are indeed *diſſeminated* through all the trading parts of the world. *Addiſon's Spectator*, N°. 425.

By firmneſs of mind, and freedom of ſpeech, the goſpel was *diſſeminated* at firſt, and muſt ſtill be maintained. *Atterb.*

DISSE'MINATION. *n. ſ.* [*diſſeminatio*, Lat.] The act of ſcattering like ſeed; the act of ſowing or ſpreading.

Though now at the greateſt diſtance from the beginning of errour, yet we are almoſt loſt in its *diſſemination*, whoſe ways are boundleſs, and confeſs no circumſcription. *Brown.*

DISSEMINA'TOR. *n. ſ.* [*diſſeminator*, Lat.] He that ſcatters; a ſcatterer; a ſower; a ſpreader.

Men, vehemently thirſting after a name in the world, hope to acquire it by being the *diſſeminators* of novel doctrines. *Decay of Piety.*

DISS'ENSION. *n. ſ.* [*diſſenſio*, Latin.] Diſagreement; ſtrife; diſcord; contention; difference; quarrel; breach of union.

Friend now, faſt ſworn,
Whoſe hours, whoſe bed, whoſe meal, whoſe exerciſe,
Are ſtill together; who twine, as 'twere, in love,
Unſeparable, ſhall within this hour,
On a *diſſenſion* of a doit, break out
To bittereſt enmity. *Shakeſpeare's Coriolanus.*

Now join your hands, and with your hands your hearts,
That no *diſſenſion* hinder government. *Shakeſp. Henry VI.*

He appeaſed the *diſſenſion* then ariſing about religion. *Knolles.*

Grown
In wealth and multitude, factious they grow;
But firſt among the prieſts *diſſenſion* ſprings. *Milt. Pa. Loſt.*

Debates, *diſſenſions*, uproars are thy joy;
Provok'd without offence, and practis'd to deſtroy. *Dryden.*

DISSE'NSIOUS. *adj.* [from *diſſenſion.*] Diſpoſed to diſcord; quarrelſome; factious; contentious.

Either in religion they have a *diſſenſious* head, or in the commonwealth a factious head. *Aſcham's Schoolmaſter.*

Who are they that complain unto the king
That I am ſtern? They love his grace but lightly,
That fill his ears with ſuch *diſſenſious* rumours. *Shak. R. III.*

You *diſſenſious* rogues,
That rubbing the poor itch of your opinion,
Make yourſelves ſcabs? *Shakeſpeare's Coriolanus.*

To DISSE'NT. *v. n.* [*diſſentio*, Latin.]

1. To diſagree in opinion; to think in a contrary manner.

Let me not be any occaſion to defraud the publick of what is beſt, by any moroſe or perverſe *diſſentings.* *King Charles.*

What cruelty, in the moſt barbarous rites of heathens, has not been matched by the inhumanity of *diſſenting* chriſtians? *Decay of Piety.*

There are many opinions in which multitudes of men *diſſent* from us, who are as good and wiſe as ourſelves. *Addiſon.*

2. To differ; to be of a contrary nature.

We ſee a general agreement in the ſecret opinion of men, that every man ought to embrace the religion which is true, and to ſhun, as hurtful, whatſoever *diſſenteth* from it, but that moſt which doth fartheſt *diſſent.* *Hooker, b.* v. *ſ.* 1.

DISSE'NT. *n. ſ.* [from the verb.] Diſagreement; difference of opinion; declaration of difference of opinion.

In propoſitions, where though the proofs in view are of moſt moment, yet there are grounds to ſuſpect that there is proof as conſiderable to be produced on the contrary ſide, there ſuſpence or *diſſent* are voluntary actions. *Locke.*

What could be the reaſon of this general *diſſent* from the notion of the reſurrection, ſeeing that almoſt all of them did believe the immortality of the ſoul? *Bentley's Sermons.*

DISSENTA'NEOUS. *adj.* [from *diſſent.*] Diſagreeable; inconſiſtent; contrary.

DISSE'NTER. *n ſ.* [from *diſſent.*]

1. One that diſagrees, or declares his diſagreement from an opinion.

They will admit of matter of fact, and agree with *diſſenters* in that; but differ only in aſſigning of reaſons. *Locke.*

2. One who, for whatever reaſons, refuſes the communion of the Engliſh church.

DISSERTA'TION. *n. ſ.* [*diſſertatio*, Latin.] A diſcourſe; a diſquiſition; a treatiſe.

Plutarch, in his *diſſertation* upon the poets, quotes an inſtance of Homer's judgment in cloſing a ludicrous ſcene with decency and inſtruction. *Pope's Odyſſey, Notes.*

To DISSE'RVE. *v. a.* [*dis* and *ſerve.*] To do injury to; to miſchief; to damage; to hurt; to harm.

Having never done the king the leaſt ſervice, he took the firſt opportunity to *diſſerve* him, and engaged againſt him from the beginning of the rebellion. *Clarendon.*

Deſires of things of this world, by their tendency, promote or *diſſerve* our intereſts in another. *Rogers, Sermon* 2.

DISSE'RVICE. *n. ſ.* [*dis* and *ſervice.*] Injury; miſchief; ill turn.

We ſhall rather perform good offices unto truth, than any *diſſervice* unto relaters who have well deſerved. *Brown.*

Great ſickneſſes make a ſenſible alteration, but ſmaller indiſpoſitions do a proportionable *diſſervice.* *Collier on Hu. Reaſon.*

DISSE'RVICEABLE. *adj.* [from *diſſervice.*] Injurious; miſchievous; hurtful.

DISSE'RVICEABLENESS. *n. ſ.* [from *diſſerviceable.*] Injury; harm; hurt; miſchief; damage.

All action being for ſome end, and not the end itſelf, its aptneſs to be commanded or forbidden muſt be founded upon its ſerviceableneſs or *diſſerviceableneſs* to ſome end. *Norris.*

To DISSE'TTLE. *v. a.* [*dis* and *ſettle.*] To unſettle; to unfix.

To DISSE'VER. *v. a.* [*dis* and *ſever.* In this word the particle *dis* makes no change in the ſignification, and therefore the word, though ſupported by great authorities, ought to be ejected from our language.] To part in two; to break; to divide; to ſunder; to ſeparate; to diſunite.

Shortly had the ſtorm ſo *diſſevered* the company, which the day before had tarried together, that moſt of them never met again, but were ſwallowed up. *Sidney, b.* ii.

The *diſſevering* of fleets hath been the overthrow of many actions. *Raleigh's Eſſays.*

All downright rains *diſſever* the violence of outrageous winds, and level the mountainous billows. *Raleigh.*

Diſſever your united ſtrengths,
And part your mingled colours once again. *Shak. K. John.*

The meeting points the ſacred hair *diſſever*
From the fair head, for ever and for ever. *Pope.*

DISSI'DENCE. *n. ſ.* [*diſſideo*, Latin.] Diſcord; diſagreement. *Dict.*

DISSI'LIENCE. *n. ſ.* [*diſſilio*, Latin.] The act of ſtarting aſunder.

DISSI'LIENT. *adj.* [*diſſiliens*, Latin.] Starting aſunder; burſting in two.

DISSILI'TION. *n. ſ.* [*diſſilio*, Latin.] The act of burſting in two; the act of ſtarting different ways.

The air having much room to receive motion, the *diſſilition* of that air was great. *Boyle's Spring of the Air.*

DISSI'MILAR. *adj.* [*dis* and *ſimilar.*] Unlike; heterogeneous.

Simple oil is reduced into *diſſimilar* parts, and yields a ſweet oil, very differing from ſallet-oil. *Boyle.*

The light whoſe rays are all alike refrangible I call ſimple, homogeneal, and ſimilar; and that whoſe rays are ſome more refrangible than others, I call compound, heterogeneal, and *diſſimilar.* *Newton's Opt.*

If the fluid be ſuppoſed to conſiſt of heterogeneous particles, we cannot conceive how thoſe *diſſimilar* parts can have a like ſituation. *Bentley's Sermons.*

DISSIMILA'RITY. *n. ſ.* [from *diſſimilar.*] Unlikeneſs; diſſimilitude.

If the principle of reunion has not its energy in this life, whenever the attractions of ſenſe ceaſe, the acquired principles of *diſſimilarity* muſt repel theſe beings from their centre; ſo that the principle of reunion, being ſet free by death, muſt drive theſe beings towards God their centre, and the principle of *diſſimilarity* forcing him to repel them with infinite violence from him, muſt make them infinitely miſerable. *Cheyne.*

DISSIMI'LITUDE. *n. ſ.* [*diſſimilitudo*, Lat.] Unlikeneſs; want of reſemblance.

Thereupon grew marvellous *diſſimilitudes*, and by reaſon thereof jealouſies, heartburnings, jars and diſcords. *Hooker.*

We doubt whether the Lord, in different circumſtances, did frame his people unto any utter *diſſimilitude*, either with Egyptians, or any other nation. *Hooker, b.* iv. *ſ.* 6.

The *diſſimilitude* between the Divinity and images, ſhews that images are not a ſuitable means whereby to worſhip God. *Stillingfleet's Def. of Diſc. on Rom. Idolatry.*

As humane ſociety is founded in the ſimilitude of ſome things, ſo it is promoted by ſome certain *diſſimilitudes.* *Grew.*

Women are curious obſervers of the likeneſs of children to parents, that they may, upon finding *diſſimilitude*, have the pleaſure of hinting unchaſtity. *Pope's Odyſſey, Notes.*

DISSIMULA'TION. *n. ſ.* [*diſſimulatio*, Latin.] The act of diſſembling; hypocriſy; fallacious appearance; falſe pretenſions.

Diſſimulation is but a faint kind of policy; for it aſketh a ſtrong wit, and a ſtrong heart, to know when to tell truth, and to do it. *Bacon, Eſſay* 6.

He added not; and Satan, bowing low
His grey *diſſimulation*, diſappear'd
Into thin air diffus'd. *Milton's Paradiſe Regain'd, b.* i.

Diſſimulation may be taken for a bare concealment of one's mind, in which ſenſe we commonly ſay, that it is prudence to diſſemble injuries. *South's Sermons.*

DISSIPA'BLE. *adj.* [from *diſſipate.*] Eaſily ſcattered; liable to diſperſion.

The heat of thoſe plants is very *diſſipable*, which under the earth is contained and held in; but when it cometh to the air it exhaleth. *Bacon's Natural Hiſtory.*

The parts of plants are very tender, as conſiſting of corpuſcles which are extremely ſmall and light, and therefore the more eaſily *diſſipable.* *Woodward's Natural Hiſtory.*

To DI'SSIPATE. *v. a.* [*diſſipatus*, Latin.]

1. To ſcatter every way; to diſperſe.

The heat at length grows ſo great, that it again *diſſipates* and

and bears off those very corpuscles which before it brought. *Woodward's Natural History.*

The circling mountains eddy in,
From the bare wild, the *dissipated* storm. *Thomson's Autumn.*

2. To scatter the attention.

This slavery to his passions produced a life irregular and *dissipated*. *Savage's Life.*

3. To spend a fortune.

The wherry that contains
Of *dissipated* wealth the poor remains. *London.*

DISSIPA'TION. *n. s.* [*dissipatio*, Latin.]

1. The act of dispersion.

The effects of heat are most advanced when it worketh upon a body without loss or *dissipation* of the matter. *Bacon.*

Abraham was contemporary with Paleg, in whose time the famous *dissipation* of mankind and distinction of languages happened. *Hale's Origin of Mankind.*

Where the earth contains nitre within it, if that heat which is continually steaming out of the earth be preserved, its *dissipation* prevented, and the cold kept off by some building, this alone is ordinarily sufficient to raise up the nitre. *Woodward.*

2. The state of being dispersed.

Now
Foul *dissipation* follow'd, and forc'd rout. *Milt. Par. Lost.*

3. Scattered attention.

I have begun two or three letters to you by snatches, and been prevented from finishing them by a thousand avocations and *dissipations*. *Swift.*

To DISSO'CIATE. *v. a.* [*dissocio*, Latin.] To separate; to disunite; to part.

In the *dissociating* action, even of the gentlest fire, upon a concrete, there does perhaps vanish, though undiscernedly, some active and fugitive particles, whose presence was requisite to contain the concrete under such a determinate form. *Boyle.*

DISSO'LVABLE. *adj.* [from *dissolve.*] Capable of dissolution; liable to be melted.

Such things as are not *dissolvable* by the moisture of the tongue, act not upon the taste. *Newton's Opt.*

DISSO'LUBLE. *adj.* [*dissolubilis*, Latin.] Capable of separation of one part from another by heat or moisture.

Nodules, reposed in those cliffs amongst the earth, being hard and not so *dissoluble*, and likewise more bulky, are left behind. *Woodward's Natural History.*

DISSOLUBI'LITY. *n. s.* [from *dissoluble.*] Liableness to suffer a disunion of parts by heat or moisture; capacity of being dissolved.

Bodies seem to have an intrinsick principle of alteration, or corruption, from the *dissolubility* of their parts, and the coadlition of several particles endued with contrary and destructive qualities each to other. *Hale's Origin of Mankind.*

To DISSO'LVE. *v. a.* [*dissolvo*, Latin.]

1. To destroy the form of any thing by disuniting the parts with heat or moisture; to melt; to liquefy.

The whole terrestrial globe was taken all to pieces, and *dissolved* at the deluge. *Woodward's Nat. Hist. Preface.*

2. To break; to disunite in any manner.

Seeing then that all these things shall be *dissolved*, what manner of persons ought ye to be. *2 Pet.* iii. 11.

3. To loose; to break the ties of any thing.

Witness these ancient empires of the earth,
In height of all their flowing wealth *dissolv'd*. *Milt. P. Lost.*
The commons live, by no divisions rent;
But the great monarch's death *dissolves* the government. *Dry.*

4. To separate persons united.

She and I long since contracted,
Are now so sure that nothing can *dissolve* us. *Shakespeare.*

5. To break up assemblies.

By the king's authority alone, and by his writs, parliaments are assembled; and by him alone they are prorogued and *dissolved*, but each house may adjourn itself. *Bacon to Villiers.*

6. To solve; to clear.

And I have heard of thee, that thou can'st make interpretations and *dissolve* doubts. *Dan.* v. 16.

7. To break an enchantment.

Highly it concerns his glory now
To frustrate and *dissolve* the magick spells. *Milton's Agonist.*

8. To be relaxed by pleasure.

Angels *dissolv'd* in hallelujahs lye. *Dryden.*

To DISSO'LVE. *v. n.*

1. To be melted; to be liquefied.

As wax *dissolves*, as ice begins to run
And trickle into drops before the sun,
So melts the youth, and languishes away. *Addis. Ovid. Met.*

2. To sink away; to fall to nothing.

If there be more, more woful, hold it in;
For I am almost ready to *dissolve*,
Hearing of this *Shakespeare's King Lear.*

3. To melt away in pleasures.

DISSO'LVENT. *adj.* [from *dissolve.*] Having the power of dissolving or melting.

In man and viviparous quadrupeds, the food, moistened with the spittle, is first chewed, then swallowed into the stomach, where, being mingled with *dissolvent* juices, it is concocted, macerated, and reduced into a chyle. *Ray.*

DISSO'LVENT. *n. s.* [from the adjective.] Having the power of disuniting the parts of any thing.

Spittle is a great *dissolvent*, and there is a great quantity of it in the stomach, being swallowed constantly. *Arbuthnot.*

DISSO'LVER. *n. s.* [from *dissolve.*] That which has the power of dissolving.

Fire, and the more subtle *dissolver*, putrefaction, by dividing the particles of substances, turn them black. *Arbuthnot.*

Hot mineral waters are the best *dissolvers* of phlegm. *Arbut.*

DISSO'LVIBLE. *adj.* [from *dissolve.* It is commonly written *dissolvable*, but less properly.] Liable to perish by dissolution.

Man, that is even upon the intrinsick constitution of his nature *dissolvible*, must, by being in an eternal duration, continue immortal. *Hale's Origin of Mankind.*

DI'SSOLUTE. *adj.* [*dissolutus*, Latin.] Loose; wanton; unrestrained; dissolved in pleasures; luxurious; debauched.

A giant huge and tall,
Who him disarmed, *dissolute*, dismay'd,
Unawares surpriz'd. *Fairy Queen, b.* i. *cant.* 7.

Such stand in narrow lanes,
And beat our watch and rob our passengers;
While he, young, wanton, and effeminate boy,
Takes on the point of honour, to support
So *dissolute* a crew. *Shakespeare's Richard* II.

A man of little gravity, or abstinence in pleasures; yea, sometimes almost *dissolute*. *Hayward.*

They cool'd in zeal,
Thenceforth shall practise how to live secure,
Worldly, or *dissolute*, on what their lords
Shall leave them to enjoy. *Milton's Paradise Lost, b.* xi.

The true spirit of religion banishes indeed all levity of behaviour, all vicious and *dissolute* mirth; but, in exchange, fills the mind with a perpetual serenity. *Addison's Spectator.*

The beauty of religion the most *dissolute* are forced to acknowledge. *Rogers's Sermons.*

DI'SSOLUTELY. *adv.* [from *dissolute.*] Loosely; in debauchery; without restraint.

Whereas men have lived *dissolutely* and unrighteously, thou hast tormented them with their own abominations. *Wisd.* xii.

DI'SSOLUTENESS. *n. s.* [from *dissolute.*] Looseness; laxity of manners; debauchery.

If we look into the common management, we shall have reason to wonder, in the great *dissoluteness* of manners which the world complains of, that there are any footsteps at all left of virtue. *Locke.*

DISSOLU'TION. *n. s.* [*dissolutio*, Latin.]

1. The act of liquefying by heat or moisture.

2. The state of being liquefied.

3. The state of melting away; liquefaction.

I am as subject to heat as butter; a man of continual *dissolution* and thaw. *Shakesp. Merry Wives of Windsor.*

4. Destruction of any thing by the separation of its parts.

The elements were at perfect union in his body; and their contrary qualities served not for the *dissolution* of the compound, but the variety of the composure. *South's Sermons.*

5. The substance formed by dissolving any body.

Weigh iron and aqua-fortis severally; then dissolve the iron in the aqua-fortis, and weigh the *dissolution*. *Bacon.*

6. Death; the resolution of the body into its constituent elements.

The life of man is always either increasing towards ripeness and perfection, or declining and decreasing towards rottenness and *dissolution*. *Raleigh's History of the World.*

We expected
Immediate *dissolution*, which we thought
Was meant by death that day. *Milton's Paradise Lost, b.* x.

7. Destruction.

He determined to make a present *dissolution* of the world. *Hooker, b.* i. *s.* 3.

He thence shall come,
When this world's *dissolution* shall be ripe. *Milt. Par. Lost.*

Would they have mankind lay aside all care of provisions by agriculture or commerce, because possibly the *dissolution* of the world may happen the next moment? *Bentley's Sermons.*

8. Breach or ruin of any thing compacted or united.

Is a man confident of wealth and power? Why let him read of those strange unexpected *dissolutions* of the great monarchies and governments of the world. *South's Sermons.*

9. The act of breaking up an assembly.

10. Looseness of manners; laxity; remissness; dissipation.

Fame makes the mind loose and gayish, scatters the spirits, and leaves a kind of *dissolution* upon all the faculties. *South.*

An universal *dissolution* of manners began to prevail, and a professed disregard to all fixed principles. *Atterbury's Sermons.*

DI'SSONANCE. *n. s.* [*dissonans*, Latin; *dissonance*, French.] A mixture of harsh, unpleasing, unharmonious sounds; unsuitableness of one sound to another.

Still govern thou my song,
But drive far off the barbarous *dissonance*
Of Bacchus, and his revellers. *Milton's Paradise Lost, b.* vii.

The

The wonted roar was up amidſt the woods,
And fill'd the air with barbarous *diſſonance*,
At which I ceas'd, and liſten'd them a while. *Milton.*

The Latin tongue is a dead language, and none can decide with confidence on the harmony or *diſſonance* of the numbers of theſe times. *Garth's Pref. to Ovid.*

DI'SSONANT. *adj.* [*diſſonans*, Latin.]

1. Harſh; unharmonious

Dire were the ſtrain and *diſſonant*, to ſing
The cruel raptures of the ſavage kind. *Thomſon's Spring.*

2. Incongruous; diſagreeing

What can be more *diſſonant* from reaſon and nature, than that a man, naturally inclined to clemency, ſhould ſhew himſelf unkind and inhuman. *Hakewell on Providence.*

When conſcience reports any thing *diſſonant* to truth, it obliges no more than the falſhood reported by it. *South.*

To DISSU'ADE. *v. a.* [*diſſuadeo*, Latin.]

1. To dehort; to divert by reaſon or importunity from any thing.

We ſubmit to Cæſar, promiſing
To pay our wonted tribute, from the which
We were *diſſuaded* by our wicked queen. *Shakeſ. Cymbeline.*

2. To repreſent any thing as unfit or dangerous.

This would be worſe;
War therefore, open or conceal'd, alike
My voice *diſſuades*. *Milton's Paradiſe Loſt, b.* ii.

Not diffident of thee, do I *diſſuade*
Thy abſence from my ſight. *Milton's Paradiſe Loſt, b.* ix.

I'd fain deny this wiſh, which thou haſt made;
Or, what I can't deny, would fain *diſſuade* *Addiſon's Ovid.*

DISSU'ADER. *n. ſ.* [from *diſſuade*.] He that diſſuades.

DISSU'ASION. *n. ſ.* [*diſſuaſio*, Lat.] Urgency of reaſon or importunity againſt any thing; dehortation.

Endeavour to preſerve yourſelf from relapſe by ſuch *diſſuaſions* from love, as its votaries call invectives againſt it. *Boyle.*

DISSU'ASIVE. *adj.* [from *diſſuade*.] Dehortatory; tending to divert or deter from any purpoſe.

DISSU'ASIVE. *n. ſ.* Dehortation; argument or importunity employed to turn the mind off from any purpoſe or purſuit.

The meanneſs, or the ſin, will ſcarce be *diſſuaſives* to thoſe who have reconciled themſelves to both. *Govern. of the Tongue.*

To DISSU'NDER. *v. a.* [*dis* and *ſunder*. This is a barbarous word. See DISSEVER.] To ſunder; to ſeparate.

But when her draught the ſea and earth *diſſunder'd*,
The troubl'd bottoms turn'd up, and ſhe thunder'd. *Chapm.*

DISSY'LLABLE. *n. ſ.* [δισσύλλαβος.] A word of two ſyllables.

No man is tied, in modern poetry, to obſerve any farther rule in the feet of his verſe, but that they be *diſſyllables*; whether ſpondee, trochee, or iambique, it matters not. *Dryden.*

DI'STAFF. *n. ſ.* [dıſtæꝼ, Saxon.]

1. The ſtaff from which the flax is drawn in ſpinning.

In ſum, proud Boreas never ruled fleet,
Who Neptune's web on danger's *diſtaff* ſpins,
With greater power than ſhe did make them wend
Each way, as ſhe that ages praiſe did bend. *Sidney.*

Weave thou to end this web which I begin;
I will the *diſtaff* hold, come thou and ſpin. *Fairfax, b.* iv.

Ran Coll our dog, and Talbot with the band,
And Malkin with her *diſtaff* in her hand. *Dryden.*

2. It is uſed as an emblem of the female ſex.

In my civil government ſome ſay the croſier, ſome ſay the *diſtaff* was too buſy. *Howel's England's Tears.*

See my royal maſter murder'd,
His crown uſurp'd, a *diſtaff* in the throne. *Dryden.*

DISTAFF-THISTLE. *n. ſ.* A ſpecies of thiſtle. See THISTLE.

To DISTA'IN. *v. a.* [*dis* and *ſtain*.]

1. To ſtain; to tinge with an adventitious colour.

Nor ceas'd his arrows, 'till the ſhady plain
Sev'n mighty bodies with their blood *diſtain*. *Dryd. Virg.*

Place on their heads that crown *diſtain'd* with gore,
Which thoſe dire hands from my ſlain father tore. *Pope.*

2. To blot; to ſully with infamy.

He underſtood,
That lady whom I had to me aſſign'd,
Had both *diſtain'd* her honourable blood,
And eke the faith which ſhe to me did bind. *Fairy Queen.*

The worthineſs of praiſe *diſtains* his worth,
If he that's prais'd, himſelf bring the praiſe forth. *Shakeſp.*

DI'STANCE. *n. ſ.* [*diſtance*, French; *diſtantia*, Latin.]

1. *Diſtance* is ſpace conſidered barely in length between any two beings, without conſidering any thing elſe between them. *Locke.*

It is very cheap, notwithſtanding the great *diſtance* between the vineyards and the towns that ſell the wine. *Addiſ. on Italy.*

As he lived but a few miles *diſtance* from her father's houſe, he had frequent opportunities of ſeeing her. *Addiſon.*

2. Remoteneſs in place.

Cæſar is ſtill diſpoſed to give us terms,
And waits at *diſtance* 'till he hears from Cato. *Addiſ. Cato.*

Theſe dwell at ſuch convenient *diſtance*,
That each may give his friend aſſiſtance. *Prior.*

3. The ſpace kept between two antagoniſts in fencing.

We come to ſee fight; to ſee thy paſs, thy ſtock, thy reverſe, thy *diſtance*. *Shakeſpeare's Merry Wives of Windſor.*

4. Contrariety; oppoſition.

Banquo was your enemy,
So is he mine; and in ſuch bloody *diſtance*,
That every minute of his being thruſts
Againſt my near'ſt of life. *Shakeſpeare's Macbeth.*

5. A ſpace marked on the courſe where horſes run.

This was the horſe that ran the whole field out of *diſtance*, and won the race. *L'Eſtrange.*

6. Space of time.

You muſt do it by *diſtance* of time. 2 *Eſdr.* v. 47.

I help my preface by a preſcript, to tell that there is ten years *diſtance* between one and the other. *Prior.*

7. Remoteneſs in time either paſt or future.

We have as much aſſurance of theſe things, as things future and at a *diſtance* are capable of. *Tillotſon's Sermons.*

To judge right of bleſſings prayed for, and yet at a *diſtance*, we muſt be able to know things future. *Smalridge's Sermons.*

8. Ideal disjunction; mental ſeparation.

The qualities that affect our ſenſes are, in the things themſelves, ſo united and blended, that there is no ſeparation, no *diſtance* between them. *Locke.*

9. Reſpect; diſtant behaviour.

I hope your modeſty
Will know, what *diſtance* to the crown is due. *Dryden.*

'Tis by reſpect and *diſtance* that authority is upheld. *Atterb.*

If a man makes me keep my *diſtance*, the comfort is, he keeps his at the ſame time. *Swift.*

10. Retraction of kindneſs; reſerve; alienation.

On the part of heav'n,
Now alienated! *diſtance* and diſtaſte,
Anger, and juſt rebuke, and judgment giv'n. *Milt. P. Loſt.*

To DI'STANCE. *v. a.* [from the noun.]

1. To place remotely; to throw off from the view.

That which gives a relievo to a bowl is the quick light, or white which appears to be on the ſide neareſt to us, and the black by conſequence *diſtances* the object. *Dryd. Dufreſnoy.*

2. To leave behind at a race the length of a diſtance; to conquer in a race with great ſuperiority.

Each daring lover, with advent'rous pace,
Purſu'd his wiſhes in the dang'rous race;
Like the ſwift hind the bounding damſel flies,
Strains to the goal, the *diſtanc'd* lover dies. *Gay's Fan.*

DI'STANT. *adj.* [*diſtans*, Latin.]

1. Remote in place; not near.

The wond'rous rock the Parian marble ſhone,
And ſeem'd to *diſtant* ſight of ſolid ſtone. *Pope.*

Narrowneſs of mind ſhould be cured by reading hiſtories of paſt ages, and of nations and countries *diſtant* from our own. *Watts's Improvement of the Mind.*

The ſenſes will diſcover things near us with ſufficient exactneſs, and things *diſtant* alſo, ſo far as they relate to our neceſſary uſe. *Watts's Logick.*

2. Remote in time either paſt or future.

3. Remote to a certain degree; as, ten years, ten miles *diſtant*.

4. Reſerved; ſhy.

5. Not primary; not obvious.

It was one of the firſt diſtinctions of a well bred man to expreſs every thing obſcene in modeſt terms and *diſtant* phraſes, while the clown clothed thoſe ideas in plain homely terms that are the moſt obvious and natural. *Addiſon's Spectator.*

DISTA'STE. *n. ſ.* [*dis* and *taſte*.]

1. Averſion of the palate; diſreliſh; diſguſt.

He gives the reaſon of the *diſtaſte* of ſatiety, and of the pleaſure in novelty in meats and drinks. *Bacon's Nat. Hiſtory.*

2. Diſlike; uneaſineſs.

Proſperity is not without many fears and *diſtaſtes*, and adverſity is not without comforts and hopes. *Bacon's Eſſays.*

3. Anger; alienation of affection.

Julius Cæſar was by acclamation termed king, to try how the people would take it: the people ſhewed great murmur and *diſtaſte* at it. *Bacon, Apophth.* 221.

The king having taſted of the envy of the people, for his impriſonment of Edward Plantagenet, was doubtful to heap up any more *diſtaſtes* of that kind by the impriſonment of De la Pole alſo. *Bacon's Henry* VII.

On the part of heaven,
Now alienated, diſtance, and *diſtaſte*,
And juſt rebuke. *Milton's Parad. Loſt.*

With ſtern *diſtaſte* avow'd,
To their own diſtricts drive the ſuitor crowd. *Pope's Odyſſ.*

To DISTA'STE. *v. a.* [from the noun.]

1. To fill the mouth with nauſeouſneſs, or diſreliſh.

Dang'rous conceits are in their nature poiſons,
Which at firſt are ſcarce found to *diſtaſte*;
But with a little act upon the blood,
Burn like the mines of ſulphur. *Shakeſpeare's Othello.*

2. To diſlike; to loath.

I'd have it come to queſtion;
If he *diſtaſte* it, let him to my ſiſter. *Shakeſp. King Lear.*

3. To offend; to disgust.
He thought it no policy to *distaste* the English or Irish by a course of reformation, but sought to please them. *Davies.*
4. To vex; to exasperate; to sour.
The whistling of the winds is better musick to contented minds, than the opera to the spleenful, ambitious, diseased, *distasted*, and distracted souls. *Pope.*

DISTA'STEFUL. *adj.* [*distaste* and *full.*]
1. Nauseous to the palate; disgusting.
What to one palate is sweet and delicious, to another is odious and *distasteful.* *Glanv. Sceps. c.* 15.
2. Offensive; unpleasing.
The visitation, though somewhat *distasteful* to the Irish lords, was sweet and welcome to the common people. *Davies.*
None but a fool *distasteful* truth will tell;
So it be new and please, 'tis full as well. *Dryd. Tyran. Love.*
Distasteful humours, and whatever else may render the conversation of men grievous and uneasy to one another, are forbidden in the New Testament. *Tillotson, Sermon* 5.
3. Malignant; malevolent.
After *distasteful* looks,
With certain half-caps, and cold moving nods,
They froze me into silence. *Shakespeare's Timon.*
The ground that begot this assertion, might be the *distasteful* averseness of the Christian from the Jew. *Brown's Vul. Err.*

DISTE'MPER. *n. s.* [*dis* and *temper.*]
1. A disproportionate mixture of parts; want of a due temper of ingredients.
2. A disease; a malady; the peccant predominance of some humour; properly a slight illness; indisposition.
They heighten *distempers* to diseases. *Suckling.*
It argues sickness and *distemper* in the mind, as well as in the body, when a man is continually turning and tossing. *South.*
3. Want of due temperature.
It was a reasonable conjecture, that those countries which were situated directly under the tropick, were of a *distemper* uninhabitable. *Raleigh's History of the World.*
4. Bad constitution of the mind; predominance of any passion or appetite.
If little faults, proceeding on *distemper*,
Shall not be wink'd at, how shall we stretch our eye
At capital crimes? *Shakespeare's Henry* V.
5. Want of due ballance between contraries.
The true temper of empire is a thing rare, and hard to keep; for both temper and *distemper* consist of contraries. *Bac.*
6. Ill humour of mind; depravity of inclination.
I was not forgetful of those sparks, which some mens *distempers* formerly studied to kindle in parliament. *King Charles.*
7. Tumultuous disorder.
Still as you rise, the state exalted too,
Finds no *distemper* while 'tis chang'd by you. *Waller.*
8. Disorder; uneasiness.
There is a sickness,
Which puts some of us in *distemper*; but
I cannot name the disease, and it is caught
Of you that yet are well. *Shakespeare's Winter's Tale.*

To DISTE'MPER. *v. a.* [*dis* and *temper.*]
1. To disease.
Young son, it argues a *distemper'd* head,
So soon to bid good-morrow to thy bed. *Shak. Ro. and Jul.*
2. To disorder.
In madness,
Being full of supper and *distemp'ring* draughts,
Upon malicious bravery, do'st thou come
To start my guilt. *Shakespeare's Othello.*
He *distempered* himself one night with long and hard study. *Boyle's History of Fluids.*
3. To disturb; to fill with perturbation; to ruffle.
Thou see'st me much *distemper'd* in my mind;
Pull'd back, and then push'd forward to be kind. *Dryden.*
4. To destroy temper or moderation.
Distemper'd zeal, sedition, canker'd hate,
No more shall vex the church and tear the state. *Dryden.*
They will have admirers among posterity, and be equally celebrated by those whose minds will not be *distempered* by interest, passion, or partiality. *Addison's Freeholder.*
5. To make disaffected, or malignant.
Once more to-day well met, *distemper'd* lords;
The king by me requests your presence strait. *Sh. K. John.*

DISTE'MPERATE. *adj.* [*dis* and *temperate.*] Immoderate.
Aquinas objecteth the *distemperate* heat, which he supposeth to be in all places directly under the sun. *Raleigh's History.*

DISTE'MPERATURE. *n. s.* [from *distemperate.*]
1. Intemperateness; excess of heat or cold, or other qualities.
Through this *distemperature* we see
The seasons alter; hoary headed frosts
Fall in the fresh lap of the crimson rose. *Shakespeare.*
They profited little against him, but were themselves consumed by the discommodities of the country, and the *distemperature* of the air. *Abbot's Description of the World.*
2. Violent tumultuousness; outrageousness.
3. Perturbation of the mind.
Thy earliness doth me assure
Thou art uprouz'd by some *distemperature.* *Shakespeare.*
4. Confusion; commixture of extremes; loss of regularity.
At your birth
Our grandam earth, with this *distemperature*,
In passion shook. *Shakespeare's Henry* IV. *p.* i.
Tell how the world fell into this disease,
And how so great *distemperature* did grow. *Daniel's C. War.*

To DISTE'ND. *v. a.* [*distendo*, Latin.] To stretch out in breadth.
Thus all day long the full *distended* clouds
Indulge their genial stores, and well shower'd earth
Is deep enrich'd with vegetable life. *Thomson's Spring.*

DISTE'NT. *n. s.* [from *distend.*] The space through which any thing is spread; breadth.
Those arches are the gracefullest, which, keeping precisely the same height, shall yet be distended one fourteenth part longer; which addition of *distent* will confer much to their beauty, and detract but little from their strength. *Wotton.*

DISTE'NTION. *n. s.* [*distentio*, Latin.]
1. The act of stretching in breadth.
Wind and *distention* of the bowels are signs of a bad digestion in the intestines; for in dead animals, when there is no digestion at all, the *distention* is in the greatest extremity. *Arb.*
2. Breadth; space occupied by the thing distended.
3. The act of separating one part from another; divarication.
Our leggs do labour more in elevation than in *distention.* *Wotton's Architecture.*

To DISTHRONI'ZE. *v. a.* [*dis* and *throne.*] To dethrone; to depose from sovereignty.
By his death he it recovered;
But Peridure and Vigent him *disthronized.* *Fairy Queen.*

DI'STICH. *n. s.* [*distichon*, Latin.] A couplet; a couple of lines; an epigram consisting only of two verses.
The French compare anagrams, by themselves, to gems; but when they are cast into a *distich*, or epigram, to gems enchased in enamelled gold. *Camden's Remains.*
The bard, whose *distich* all commend,
In power, a servant; out of power, a friend. *Pope.*

To DISTI'L. *v. n.* [*distillo*, Latin.]
1. To drop; to fall by drops.
In vain kind seasons swell'd the teeming grain;
Soft show'rs *distill'd*, and suns grew warm in vain. *Pope.*
Crystal drops from min'ral roofs *distil.* *Pope.*
2. To flow gently and silently.
The Euphrates *distilleth* out of the mountains of Armenia, and falleth into the gulph of Persia. *Raleigh's History.*
3. To use a still; to practise the act of distillation.
Have I not been
Thy pupil long? Hast thou not learn'd me how
To make perfumes, *distil*, preserve? *Shakesp. Cymbeline.*

To DISTI'L. *v. a.*
1. To let fall in drops; to drop any thing down.
They pour down rain, according to the vapour thereof, which the clouds do drop and *distil* upon man abundantly. *Job.*
The dew, which on the tender grass
The evening had *distill'd*,
To pure rose-water turned was,
The shades with sweets that fill'd. *Drayton's Q. of Cynthia.*
From his fair head
Perfumes *distil* their sweets. *Prior.*
The roof is vaulted, and *distils* fresh water from every part of it, which fell upon us as fast as the first droppings of a shower. *Addison's Remarks on Italy.*
2. To force by fire through the vessels of distillation; to exalt, separate, or purify by fire.
Upon the corner of the moon
There hangs a vap'rous drop, profound;
I'll catch it ere it come to ground;
And that, *distill'd* by magick slights,
Shall raise artificial sprights. *Shakespeare's Macbeth.*
3. To draw by distillation; to extract by the force of fire.
The liquid, *distilled* from benzoin, is subject to frequent vicissitudes of fluidity and firmness. *Boyle.*

DISTILLA'TION. *n. s.* [*distillatio*, Latin.]
1. The act of dropping, or falling in drops.
2. The act of pouring out in drops.
3. That which falls in drops.
4. The act of distilling by fire.
Water by frequent *distillations* changes into fixed earth. *Newton's Opt.*
The serum of the blood, by a strong *distillation*, affords a spirit, or volatile alkaline salt, and two kinds of oil, and an earth. *Arbuthnot on Aliments.*
5. The substance drawn by the still.
I suffered the pangs of an egregious death, to be stopt in like a strong *distillation*, with cloaths. *Sh. Mer. Wi. of Winds.*

DISTI'LLATORY. *adj.* [from *distil.*] Belonging to distillation; used in distillation.

Besides those grosser elements of bodies, salt, sulphur and mercury, ingredients of a more subtile nature, extremely little, and not visible, may escape at the junctures of the *distillatory* vessels. *Boyle's Scept. Chym.*

DISTI'LLER. *n. s.* [from *distil.*]

1. One who practises the trade of distilling.

I sent for spirit of salt to a very eminent *distiller* of it. *Boyle.*

2. One who makes and sells pernicious and inflammatory spirits.

DISTI'LMENT. *n. s.* [from *distil.*] That which is drawn by distillation. A word formerly used, but now obsolete.

Upon my secure hour thy uncle stole,
And in the porches of mine ears did pour
The leperous *distilment*. *Shakespeare's Hamlet.*

DISTI'NCT. *adj* [*distinctus*, Latin.]

1. Different; not the same in number or in kind.

Bellarmin saith, it is idolatry to give the same worship to an image which is due to God: Vasquez saith, it is idolatry to give *distinct* worship: therefore, if a man would avoid idolatry, he must give none at all. *Stillingfleet.*

Fatherhood and property are *distinct* titles, and began presently, upon Adam's death, to be in *distinct* persons. *Locke.*

2. Different; apart; not conjunct.

The intention was, that the two armies, which marched out together, should afterwards be *distinct*. *Clarendon.*

Men have immortal spirits, capable of a pleasure and happiness *distinct* from that of our bodies. *Tillotson's Sermons.*

3. Clear; unconfused.

Heav'n is high,
High and remote, to see from thence *distinct*
Each thing on earth. *Milton's Paradise Lost, b.* ix.

4. Spotted; variegated.

Tempestuous fell
His arrows from the four-fold-visag'd four,
Distinct with eyes; and from the living wheels
Distinct alike with multitude of eyes. *Milton's Parad. Lost.*

5. Marked out; specified.

Dominion hold
Over all living things that move on th' earth,
Wherever thus created; for no place
Is yet *distinct* by name. *Milton's Paradise Lost, b.* vii.

DISTI'NCTION. *n. s.* [*distinctio*, Latin.]

1. Note of difference.

2. Honourable note of superiority.

3. That by which one differs from another.

This faculty of perception puts the *distinction* betwixt the animal kingdom and the inferior parts of matter. *Locke.*

4. Difference regarded; preference or neglect in comparison with something else.

Maids, women, wives, without *distinction* fall;
The sweeping deluge, love, comes on, and covers all. *Dryd.*

5. Separation of complex notions.

This fierce abridgment
Hath to it circumstantial branches, which
Distinction should be rich in. *Shakespeare's Cymbeline.*

6. Division into different parts.

The *distinction* of it into acts was not known unto them; or, if it were, it is yet so darkly delivered to us, that we cannot make it out. *Dryden on Dramatick Poesy.*

7. Notation of difference between things seemingly the same.

The mixture of those things by speech, which by nature are divided, is the mother of all error: to take away therefore that error, which confusion breedeth, *distinction* is requisite. *Hooker, b.* iii. *s.* 3.

Lawfulness cannot be handled without limitations and *distinctions*. *Bacon's Holy War.*

This will puzzle all your logick
And *distinctions* to answer it. *Denham's Sophy.*

From this *distinction* of real and apparent good, some distinguish happiness into two sorts, real and imaginary. *Norris.*

7. Discernment; judgment.

DISTI'NCTIVE. *adj.* [from *distinct.*]

1. That which marks distinction or difference.

For from the natal hour, *distinctive* names,
One common right the great and lowly claims. *Pope's Ody.*

2. Having the power to distinguish and discern; judicious.

Credulous and vulgar auditors readily believe it, and the more judicious and *distinctive* heads do not reject it. *Brown.*

DISTI'NCTIVELY. *adv.* [from *distinctive*] In right order; not confusedly.

I did all my pilgrimage dilate,
Whereof by parcels she had something heard,
But not *distinctively*. *Shakespeare's Othello.*

DISTI'NCTLY. *adv.* [from *distinct.*]

1. Not confusedly; without the confusion of one part with another.

To make an eccho that will report three, or four, or five words *distinctly*, it is requisite that the body percussing be a good distance off. *Bacon's Natural History,* N°. 248.

On its sides it was bounded pretty *distinctly*, but on its ends very confusedly and indistinctly. *Newton's Opt.*

2. Plainly; clearly.

The object I could first *distinctly* view,
Was tall streight trees, which on the waters flew. *Dryden.*

After the light of the sun was a little worn off my eyes, I could see all the parts of it *distinctly*, by a glimmering reflection that played upon them from the surface of the water. *Addison.*

DISTI'NCTNESS. *n. s.* [from *distinct.*]

1. Nice observation of the difference between different things.

The membranes and humours of the eye are perfectly pellucid, and void of colour, for the clearness, and for the *distinctness* of vision. *Ray on the Creation.*

2. Such separation of things as makes them easy to be separately observed.

To DISTI'NGUISH. *v. a.* [*distinguo*, Latin.]

1. To note the diversity of things.

Rightly to *distinguish*, is, by conceit of the mind, to sever things different in nature, and to discern wherein they differ. *Hooker, b.* iii. *s.* 3.

2. To separate from others by some mark of honour or preference.

They *distinguish* my poems from those of other men, and have made me their peculiar care. *Dryden's Fables, Dedicat.*

Let us revolve that roll with strictest eye,
Where, safe from time, *distinguish'd* actions lie. *Prior.*

3. To divide by proper notes of diversity.

Moses *distinguishes* the causes of the flood into those that belong to the heavens, and those that belong to the earth, the rains, and the abyss. *Burnet's Theory of the Earth.*

4. To know one from another by any mark or note of difference.

So long
As he could make me, with this eye or ear,
Distinguish him from others, he did keep
The deck. *Shakespeare's Cymbeline.*

We have not yet been seen in any house,
Nor can we be *distinguish'd* by our faces,
For man or master. *Shakesp. Taming of the Shrew.*

By our reason we are enabled to *distinguish* good from evil, as well as truth from falshood. *Watts's Logick.*

5. To discern critically; to judge.

Sweet, the untainted virtue of your years
Hath not yet div'd into the world's deceit;
Nor more can you *distinguish* of a man,
Than of his outward shew! *Shakespeare's Richard III.*

6. To constitute difference; to specificate; to make different from another.

St. Paul's Epistles contain nothing but points of christian instruction, amongst which he seldom fails to enlarge on the great and *distinguishing* doctrines of our holy religion. *Locke.*

7. To make known or eminent.

To DISTI'NGUISH. *v. n.* To make distinction; to find or shew the difference.

He would warily *distinguish* between the profit of the merchant and the gain of the kingdom. *Child's Disc. on Trade.*

The readers must learn by all means to *distinguish* between proverbs and those polite speeches which beautify conversation. *Swift.*

DISTI'NGUISHABLE. *adj.* [from *distinguish*]

1. Capable of being distinguished; capable of being known or made known by notes of diversity.

By the intervention of a liquor, it puts on the form of a fluid body; when, being dissolved in aqueous juices, it is by the eye *distinguishable* from the solvent body, and appears as fluid as it is. *Boyle.*

Impenitent, they left a race behind
Like to themselves, *distinguishable* scarce
From Gentiles, but by circumcision vain. *Milt. Parad Reg.*

The acting of the soul, as it relates to perception and decision, to choice and pursuit, or aversion, is *distinguishable* to us. *Hale's Origin of Mankind.*

I shall distribute duty into its principal and eminent parts, *distinguishable* as they relate to God, our neighbour, and ourselves. *Government of the Tongue, s.* 2.

A simple idea, being in itself uncompounded, contains nothing but one uniform appearance, or conception in the mind, and is not *distinguishable* into different ideas. *Locke.*

2. Worthy of note; worthy of regard.

I would endeavour that my betters should seek me by the merit of something *distinguishable*, instead of my seeking them. *Swift.*

DISTI'NGUISHED. *participial adj.* [from *distinguish.*] Eminent; transcendent; extraordinary.

For sins committed, with many aggravations of guilt, the furnace of wrath will be seven times hotter, and burn with a *distinguished* fury. *Rogers, Serm.* 3.

Never on man did heav'nly favour shine
With rays so strong, *distinguish'd*, and divine. *Pope's Odyss.*

DISTI'NGUISHER. *n. s.* [from *distinguish.*]

1. A judicious observer; one that accurately discerns one thing from another.

If writers be just to the memory of Charles II. they cannot deny

deny him to have been an exact knower of mankind, and a perfect *distinguisher* of their talents. *Dryd. Dedic. to K. Arthur.*

2. He that separates one thing from another by proper marks of diversity.

Let us admire the wisdom of God in this *distinguisher* of times, and visible deity, the sun. *Brown's Vulgar Errours.*

DISTI'NGUISHINGLY. *adv.* [from *distinguishing.*] With distinction; with some mark of eminent preference.

Some call me a Tory, because the heads of that party have been *distinguishingly* favourable to me. *Pope.*

DISTI'NGUISHMENT. *n. s.* [from *distinguish.*] Distinction; observation of difference.

To make corrections upon the searchers reports, I considered whether any credit at all were to be given to their *distinguishments.* *Graunt's Bills of Mortality.*

To DISTO'RT. *v. a.* [*distortus*, Latin.]

1. To writhe; to twist; to deform by irregular motions.

Now mortal pangs *distort* his lovely form. *Smith.*

2. To put out of the true direction or posture.

Wrath and malice, envy and revenge, do darken and *distort* the understandings of men. *Tillotson.*

3. To wrest from the true meaning.

Something must be *distorted*, beside the intent of the divine inditer. *Peacham on Poetry.*

DISTO'RTION. *n. s.* [*distortio*, Lat.] Irregular motion by which the face is writhed, or the parts disordered.

By his *distortions* he reveals his pains;
He by his tears, and by his sighs complains. *Prior.*

In England we see people lulled asleep with solid and elaborate discourses of piety, who would be warmed and transported out of themselves by the bellowings and *distortions* of enthusiasm. *Addison's Spectator*, N°. 407.

To DISTRA'CT. *v. a. part. pass. destracted*; anciently *destraught.* [*distractus*, Latin.]

1. To pull different ways at once.

2. To separate; to divide.

By sea, by sea.
—Most worthy sir, you therein throw away
The absolute soldiership you have by land;
Distract your army, which doth most consist
Of war-mark'd footmen. *Shakes. Anthony and Cleopatra.*

3. To turn from a single direction towards various points.

If he cannot wholly avoid the eye of the observer, he hopes to *distract* it by a multiplicity of the object. *South's Sermons.*

4. To fill the mind with contrary considerations; to perplex; to confound; to harrass.

While I suffer thy terrors I am *distracted.* *Ps.* lxxxviii. 15.

Come, cousin, can'st thou quake, and change thy colour,
Murther thy breath in middle of a word,
And then again begin, and stop again,
As if thou wert *distraught* and mad with terror? *Sh. R.* III.

It would burst forth; but I recover breath,
And sense *distract*, to know well what I utter. *Milt. Agonist.*

He possesses a quiet and cheerful mind, not afflicted with violent passions, or *distracted* with immoderate cares. *Ray.*

If our sense of hearing were a thousand times quicker than it is, how would a perpetual noise *distract* us? We should, in the quietest retirement, be less able to sleep or meditate than in the middle of a sea-fight. *Locke.*

5. To make mad.

Wherefore throng you hither?
——To fetch my poor *distracted* husband hence:
Let us come in, that we may bind him fast,
And bear him home for his recovery. *Shakes. Com. of Err.*

Better I were *distract*,
So should my thoughts be sever'd from my griefs,
And woes, by wrong imagination, lose
The knowledge of themselves. *Shakespeare's King Lear.*

She was unable, in strength of mind, to bear the grief of his decease, and fell *distracted* of her wits. *Bacon's Hen.* VII.

You shall find a *distracted* man fancy himself a king, and with a right inference require suitable attendance, respect, and obedience. *Locke.*

DISTRA'CTEDLY. *adv.* [from *distract.*] Madly; frantickly.

Methought her eyes had crost her tongue;
For she did speak in starts *distractedly.* *Shak. Twelfth Night.*

DISTRA'CTEDNESS. *n. s.* [from *distract.*] The state of being distracted; madness.

DISTRA'CTION. *n. s.* [*distractio*, Latin.]

1. Tendency to different parts; separation.

While he was yet in Rome,
His power went out in such *distractions* as
Beguil'd all spies. *Shakespeare's Anthony and Cleopatra.*

2. Confusion; state in which the attention is called different ways.

Never was known a night of such *distraction*;
Noise so confus'd and dreadful; jostling crowds,
That run, and knew not whither. *Dryden's Spanish Fryar.*

What may we not hope from him in a time of quiet and tranquillity, since, during the late *distractions*, he has done so much for the advantage of our trade? *Addison's Freeholder.*

3. Perturbation of mind; violence of some painful passion.

The *distraction* of the children, who saw both their parents expiring together, would have melted the hardest heart. *Tatler.*

4. Madness; franticknefs; loss of the wits.

Madam, this is a meer *distraction*:
You turn the good we offer into envy. *Shakesp. H.* VIII.

So to mad Pentheus double Thebes appears,
And furies howl in his distemper'd ears:
Orestes so, with like *distraction* tost,
Is made to fly his mother's angry ghost. *Waller.*

Commiserate all those who labour under a settled *distraction*, and who are shut out from all the pleasures and advantages of human commerce. *Atterbury's Sermons.*

5. Disturbance; tumult; difference of sentiments.

The two armies lay quiet near each other, without improving the confusion and *distraction* which the king's forces were too much inclined to. *Clarendon, b.* viii.

To DISTRA'IN. *v. a.* [from *distringo*, Latin.] To seize; to lay hold on as an indemnification for a debt.

Here's Beauford, that regards not God nor king,
Hath here *distrain'd* the Tower to his use. *Shakesp. Hen.* VI.

To DISTRA'IN. *v. n.* To make seizure.

The earl answered, I will not lend money to my superiour, upon whom I cannot *distrain* for the debt. *Camden's Remains.*

Blood his rent to have regain'd,
Upon the British diadem *distrain'd.* *Marvel.*

DISTRA'INER. *n. s.* [from *distrain.*] He that seizes.

DISTRA'INT. *n. s.* [from *distrain.*] Seizure. *Dict.*

DISTRA'UGHT. *part. adj.* [from *distract.*] Distracted.

He had been a good military man in his days, but was then *distraught* of his wits. *Camden's Remains.*

DISTRE'SS. *n. s.* [*destresse*, French.]

1. The act of making a legal seizure.

2. A compulsion in real actions, by which a man is assured to appear in court, or to pay a debt or duty which he refused. *Cow.*

When any one was indebted to another, he would first demand his debt; and, if he were not paid, he would straight go and take a *distress* of his goods and cattle, where he could find them, to the value, which he would keep 'till he were satisfied. *Spenser's State of Ireland.*

Quoth she, some say the soul's secure
Against *distress* and forfeiture. *Hudibras, p.* iii. *cant.* 1.

3. The thing seized by law.

4. Calamity; misery; misfortune.

There can I sit alone, unseen of any,
And to the nightingale's complaining notes
Tune my *distresses*, and record my woes. *Shakespeare.*

There shall be signs in the sun, and in the moon, and in the stars; and upon earth *distress* of nations, with perplexity, the sea and the waves roaring. *Luke* xxi. 25.

People in affliction or *distress* cannot be hated by generous minds. *Clarissa.*

To DISTRE'SS. *v. a.* [from the noun.]

1. To prosecute by law to a seizure.

2. To harrass; to make miserable; to crush with calamity.

Distress not the Moabites, neither contend with them in battle. *Deutr.* ii. 9.

I am *distressed* for thee, my brother Jonathan. 2 *Sa.* i. 26.

DISTRE'SSFUL. *adj.* [*distress* and *full.*] Miserable; full of trouble; full of misery.

He, with a body fill'd and vacant mind,
Gets him to rest, cramm'd with *distressful* bread. *Sh. H.* V.

I often did beguile her of her tears,
When I did speak of some *distressful* stroke
That my youth suffered. *Shakespeare's Othello.*

The ewes still folded, with distended thighs,
Unmilk'd, lay bleating in *distressful* cries. *Pope's Odyssey.*

Distressful and desolating events, which have attended the mistakes of politicians, should be present in their minds. *Watts.*

To DISTRI'BUTE. *v. a.* [*distribuo*, Lat.] To divide amongst more than two; to deal out.

The king sent over a great store of gentlemen and warlike people, amongst whom he *distributed* the land. *Spenser.*

The spoil got on the Antiates
Was not *distributed.* *Shakespeare's Coriolanus.*

She did *distribute* her goods to all them that were nearest of kindred. *Judith* xvi. 24.

DISTRI'BUTER. *n. s.* [from *distribute.*] One who deals out any thing; a bestower.

There were judges and *distributers* of justice appointed for the several parts of his dominions. *Addison on Italy.*

Of that peculiar matter out of which the bodies of vegetables, and consequently of animals, are formed, water is the common vehicle and *distributer* to the parts of those bodies. *Woodward's Natural History.*

DISTRIBU'TION. *n. s.* [*distributio*, Latin.]

1. The act of distributing or dealing out to others.

Of great riches there is no real use, except it be in the *distribution.* *Bacon's Essays.*

Providence has made an equal *distribution* of natural gifts, whereof each creature severally has a share. *L'Estrange.*

Every man in a great station would imitate the queen in the *distribution* of offices in his disposal. *Swift.*

2. Act

2. Act of giving in charity.

Let us govern our charitable *distributions* by this pattern of nature, and maintain a mutual circulation of benefits and returns. *Atterbury's Sermons.*

3. [In logick.] As an integral whole is distinguished into its several parts by division; so the word *distribution* is most properly used, when we distinguish an universal whole into its several kinds of species. *Watts's Logick.*

DISTRI'BUTIVE. *adj.* [from *distribute.*]

1. That which is employed in assigning to others their portions; as, *distributive* justice, that which allots to each his sentence or claim.

If justice will take all, and nothing give,
Justice methinks is not *distributive*. *Dryden's Conq. of Gran.*

Observe the *distributive* justice of the authors, which is constantly applied to the punishment of virtue, and the reward of vice, directly opposite to the rules of their best criticks. *Sw.*

2. That which assigns the various species of a general term.

DISTRI'BUTIVELY. *adv.* [from *distributive.*]

1. By distribution.

2. Singly; particularly.

Although we cannot be free from all sin collectively, in such sort that no part thereof shall be found inherent in us; yet, *distributively* at the least, all great and grievous actual offences, as they offer themselves one by one, both may, and ought to be, by all means avoided. *Hooker, b. v. s.* 48.

3. In a manner that expresses singly all the particulars included in a general term; not collectively.

An universal term is sometimes taken collectively for all its particular ideas united together, and sometimes *distributively*, meaning each of them single and alone. *Watts's Logick.*

DI'STRICT. *n. s.* [*districtus*, Latin.]

1. The circuit or territory within which a man may be thus compelled to appearance. *Cowel.*

2. Circuit of authority; province.

His governors of towns and provinces, who formed themselves upon the example of their grand monarque, practised all the arts of despotick government in their respective *districts.* *Addison.*

With stern distaste avow'd,
To their own *districts* drive the suitor crowd. *Pope's Odyss.*

3. Region; country; territory.

Those *districts* which between the tropicks lie,
The scorching beams, directly darted, fry. *Blackmore.*

To DISTRU'ST. *v. a.* [*dis* and *trust.*] To regard with diffidence; to diffide in; not to trust.

He sheweth himself unto such as do not *distrust* him. *Wisd.*

DISTRU'ST. *n. s.* [from the verb.]

1. Discredit; loss of credit; loss of confidence.

To me reproach
Rather belongs, *distrust*, and all dispraise. *Milt. Par. Lost.*

2. Suspicion; want of faith; want of confidence in another.

You doubt not me; nor have I spent my blood,
To have my faith no better understood:
Your soul's above the baseness of *distrust*;
Nothing but love could make you so unjust. *Dryd. Aureng.*

DISTRU'STFUL. *adj.* [*distrust* and *full.*]

1. Apt to distrust; suspicious.

Generals often harbour *distrustful* thoughts in their breasts. *Boyle's Seraphick Love.*

2. Not confident; diffident.

The great corrupters of discourse have not been so *distrustful* of themselves. *Government of the Tongue.*

3. Diffident of himself; modest; timorous.

Distrustful sense with modest caution speaks;
It still looks home, and short excursions makes;
But rattling nonsense in full vollies breaks. *Pope.*

DISTRU'STFULLY. *adv.* [from *distrustful.*] In a distrustful manner.

DISTRU'STFULNESS. *n. s.* [from *distrustful.*] The state of being distrustful; want of confidence.

To DISTU'RB. *v. a.* [*disturbo*, low Latin.]

1. To perplex; to disquiet; to deprive of tranquillity.

He that has his own troubles, and the happiness of his neighbours to *disturb* him, has work enough. *Collier on Envy.*

His youth with wants and hardships must engage;
Plots and rebellions must *disturb* his age. *Prior.*

2. To confound; to put into irregular motions.

3. To interrupt; to hinder.

4. To turn off from any direction: with *from*. This is not usual.

It oft-times may succeed, so as perhaps
Shall grieve him, if I fail not; and *disturb*
His inmost counsels *from* their destin'd aim. *Milt. Par. Lost.*

DISTU'RBANCE. *n. s.* [from *disturb.*]

1. Perplexity; interruption of tranquillity.

The denomination of money concerns trade, and the alteration of that necessarily brings *disturbance* to it. *Locke.*

2. Confusion; disorder.

They can survey a variety of complicated ideas without fatigue or *disturbance*. *Watts's Improvement of the Mind.*

3. Tumult; violation of peace.

This mischief had not then befall'n,
And more that shall befal: innumerable
Disturbances on earth through female snares. *Milt. Pa. Lost.*

DISTU'RBER. *n. s.* [from *disturb.*]

1. A violater of peace; he that causes tumults and publick disorders.

He stands in the sight both of God and men most justly blameable, as a needless *disturber* of the peace of God's church, and an author of dissension. *Hooker, b iv s.* 12.

Men that make an insult upon society, ought to be humbled as *disturbers* of the publick tranquillity. *Addis. Freeholder.*

Ye great *disturbers*, who in endless noise,
In blood and horror, seek unnatural joys;
For what is all this bustle, but to shun
Those thoughts with which you dare not be alone. *Granv.*

2. He that injures tranquillity; he that causes perturbation of mind.

Two deep enemies,
Foes to my rest, and my sweet sleep's *disturbers*,
Are they that I would have thee deal upon. *Shakesp. R.* III.

To DISTU'RN. *v. a.* [*dis* and *turn.*] To turn off; to turn aside.

He glad was to *disturn* that furious stream
Of war on us, that else had swallow'd them. *Daniel.*

DISVALUA'TION. *n. s.* [*dis* and *valuation.*] Disgrace; diminution of reputation.

What can be more to the *disvaluation* of the power of the Spaniard, than that eleven thousand English should, within two months, have marched into the heart of his countries? *Bacon's War with Spain.*

To DISVA'LUE. *v. a.* [*dis* and *value.*] To undervalue; to set a low price upon.

Her reputation was *disvalu'd*
In levity. *Shakespeare's Measure for Measure.*

The very same pride which prompts a man to vaunt and overvalue what he is, does as forcibly incline him to contemn and *disvalue* what he has. *Government of the Tongue.*

To DISVE'LOP. *v. a.* [*developer*, French.] To uncover. *Dict.*

DISU'NION. *n. s.* [*dis* and *union.*]

1. Separation; disjunction.

Rest is most opposite to motion, the immediate cause of *disunion*. *Glanv. Sceps. c* 7.

Disunion of the corporeal principles, and the vital, causeth death. *Grew's Cosmol. Sac.*

Let not peace be made before the *disunion* of France and Spain. *Addison's State of the War.*

The strength of it will join itself to France, and grow the closer to it by its *disunion* from the rest. *Addison on the War.*

2. Breach of concord.

To DISUNI'TE. *v. a.* [*dis* and *unite.*]

1. To separate; to divide.

The beast they then divide, and *disunite*
The ribs and limbs. *Pope's Odyssey.*

2. To part friends or allies.

To DISUNI'TE. *v. n.* [*dis* and *unite.*] To fall asunder; to become separate.

While every particular member of the publick provides solely for itself, the several joints of the body politick do separate and *disunite*, and so become unable to support the whole. *South's Sermons.*

DISU'NITY. *n. s.* [*dis* and *unity.*] A state of actual separation.

Disunity is the natural property of matter, which of itself is nothing else but an infinite congeries of physical monads. *More's Divine Dialogues.*

DISU'SAGE. *n. s.* [*dis* and *usage.*] The gradual cessation of use or custom.

They cut off presently such things as might be extinguished without danger, leaving the rest to be abolished by *disusage* through tract of time. *Hooker, b. iv. s.* 14.

DISU'SE. *n. s.* [*dis* and *use.*]

1. Cessation of use; dessuetude; want of practice.

The *disuse* of the tongue is the only effectual remedy against these. *Addison's Guardian,* N°. 121.

2. Cessation of custom.

That obligation upon the lands did not prescribe, or come into *disuse*, but by fifty consecutive years. *Arbuthnot.*

To DISU'SE. *v. a.* [*dis* and *use.*]

1. To cease to make use of.

'Tis law, though custom now diverts the course;
As nature's institute is yet in force,
Uncancell'd, though *disus'd*. *Dryden's Fables.*

Priam, in arms *disus'd*, invests his limbs decay'd. *Dryden.*

2. To disaccustom.

He shall his troops for fighting fields prepare,
Disus'd to toils and triumphs of the war. *Dryden's Æn.*

To DISVO'UCH. *v. a.* [*dis* and *vouch.*] To destroy the credit of; to contradict.

Every letter he hath writ hath *disvouched* another. *Shakesp.*

DISWI'TTED. *adj.* [*dis* and *wit.*] Deprived of the wits; mad; distracted. A word not in use.

She ran away alone;
Which when they heard, there was not one

But

But hasted after to be gone,
As she had been *diswitted*. *Drayton's Nymphid.*

DIT. *n. s.* [*dicht*, Dutch.] A ditty; a poem; a tune Obsolete.
No bird but did her shrill notes sweetly sing;
No song but did contain a lovely *dit*. *Fairy Queen, b.* ii.

DITCH. *n. s.* [dic, Saxon; *diik*, Erse.]
1. A trench cut in the ground usually between fields.
Some asked for manors, others for acres that lay convenient for them; that he would pull down his fences, and level his *ditches*. *Arbuthnot's History of John Bull.*
Sudden the *ditches* swell, the meadows swim. *Thomson.*
2. Any long narrow receptacle of water: used sometimes of a small river in contempt.
In the great plagues there were seen, in divers *ditches* and low grounds about London, many toads that had tails three inches long. *Bacon.*
3. The moat with which a town is surrounded.
The *ditches*, such as they were, were altogether dry, and easy to be passed over. *Knolles's History of the Turks.*
4. Ditch is used, in composition, of any thing worthless, or thrown away into ditches.
Poor Tom, when the foul fiend rages, eats cowdung for sallets, swallows the old rat, and the *ditch*-dog. *Shakespeare.*

To DITCH. *v. a.* [from the noun.] To make a ditch.
I have employed my time, besides *ditching*, in finishing my travels. *Swift.*

DITCH-DELIVERED. *adj.* [*ditch* and *deliver*.] Brought forth in a ditch.
Finger of birth-strangled babe,
Ditch-deliver'd by a drab. *Shakespeare's Macbeth.*

DI'TCHER. *n. s.* [from *ditch*.] One who digs ditches.
You merit new employments daily,
Our thatcher, *ditcher*, gard'ner, baily. *Swift.*

DITHYRA'MBICK. *n. s.* [*dithyrambus*, Latin.]
1. A song in honour of Bacchus; in which anciently, and now among the Italians, the distraction of ebriety is imitated.
2. Any poem written with wildness and enthusiasm.
Pindar does new words and figures roll
Down his impetuous *dithyrambick* tide. *Cowley.*

DITTA'NDER. *n. s.* The same with pepperwort, which see.

DI'TTANY. *n. s.* [*dictamnus*, Latin.]
Dittany hath been renowned for many ages, upon the account of its sovereign qualities in medicines. It is generally brought over dry from the Levant. *Millar.*
Virgil reports of *dittany*, that the wild goats eat it when they are shot with darts. *More's Antidote against Atheism.*

DI'TTIED. *adj.* [from *ditty*.] Sung; adapted to musick.
He, with his soft pipe, and smooth *dittied* song,
Well knows to still the wild winds when they roar. *Milton.*

DI'TTY. *n. s.* [*dicht*, Dutch.] A poem to be sung; a song.
Although we lay altogether aside the consideration of *ditty* or matter, the very harmony of sounds being framed in due sort, and carried from the ear to the spiritual faculties of our souls, is, by a native puissance and efficacy, greatly available to bring to a perfect temper whatsoever is there troubled. *Hook.*
Being young, I fram'd to the harp
Many an English *ditty*, lovely well,
And gave the tongue a helpful ornament. *Shakesp. Hen.* IV.
Strike the melodious harp, shrill timbrels ring,
And to the warbling lute soft *ditties* sing. *Sandys.*
His annual wound in Lebanon, allur'd
The Syrian damsels to lament his fate,
In am'rous *ditties*, all a Summer's day. *Milt. Paradise Lost.*
Mean while the rural *ditties* were not mute,
Temper'd to th' oaten flute;
Rough satyrs danc'd. *Milton.*
They will be sighing and singing under thy inexorable windows lamentable *dittie*, and call thee cruel. *Dryden.*

DIVA'N. *n. s.* [An Arabick or Turkish word.]
1. The council of the Oriental princes.
2. Any council assembled: used commonly in a sense of dislike.
Forth rush'd in haste the great consulting peers,
Rais'd from the dark *divan*, and with like joy
Congratulant approach'd him. *Milton's Paradise Lost, b.* x.
Swift to the queen the herald Medon ran,
Who heard the consult of the dire *divan*. *Pope's Odyssey.*

To DIVA'RICATE. *v. n.* [*divaricatus*, Latin.] To be parted into two; to become bifid.
The partitions are strained across; and as they tend towards the crust, they gradually lessen: one of them also *divaricates* into two, and another into several small ones. *Woodward.*

To DIVA'RICATE. *v. a.* To divide into two.
A slender pipe is produced forward towards the throat, whereinto it is at last inserted, and is there *divaricated*, after the same manner as the spermatick vessels. *Grew's Cosm. Sac.*

DIVARICA'TION. *n. s.* [*divaricatio*, Latin.]
1. Partition into two.
Dogs, running before their masters, will stop at a *divarication* of the way, 'till they see which hand their masters will take. *Ray on the Creation.*
2. Division of opinions.
To take away all doubt, or any probable *divarication*, the curse is plainly specified. *Brown's Vulgar Errours, b* vi. *c.* 11.

To DIVE. *v. n.* [dippan, Saxon.]
1. To sink voluntarily under water.
I am not yet informed, whether when a diver *diveth*, having his eyes open, and swimeth upon his back he sees things in the air greater or less. *Bacon's Natural History*, N°. 76.
Around our pole the spiry dragon glides,
And, like a winding stream, the Bears divides,
The less and greater; who, by fate's decree,
Abhor to *dive* beneath the Southern sea. *Dryd Virg. Georg.*
That the air in the blood-vessels of live bodies has a communication with the outward air, I think, seems plain, from the experiments of human creatures being able to bear air of much greater density in *diving*, and of much less upon the tops of mountains, provided the changes be made gradually. *Arb.*
2. To go under water in search of any thing.
Crocodiles defend those pearls which lie in the lakes: the poor Indians are eaten up by them, when they *dive* for the pearl. *Raleigh's History of the World.*
The knave deserves it, when he tempts the main,
Where folly fights for kings, or *dives* for gain. *Pope's Essays.*
3. To go deep into any question; doctrine; or science.
The wits that *div'd* most deep, and soar'd most high,
Seeking man's powers, have found his weakness such. *Davies.*
He performs all this out of his own fund, without *diving* into the arts and sciences for a supply. *Dryden.*
Whensoever we would proceed beyond those simple ideas, and *dive* farther into the nature of things, we fall presently into darkness and obscurity. *Locke.*
You swim a-top, and on the surface strive;
But to the depths of nature never *dive*. *Blackmore.*
You should have *div'd* into my inmost thoughts. *Phillips.*
4. To immerge into any business or condition.
Sweet prince, th' untainted virtue of your years
Hath not yet *div'd* into the world's deceit,
Nor can you distinguish. *Shakesp. Rich.* III.
5. To depart from observation.
Dive thoughts down to my soul, here Clarence comes.
Shakespeare's Richard III.

To DIVE. *v. a.* To explore by diving.
Then Brutus, Rome's first martyr I must name,
The Curtii bravely *div'd* the gulph of fame. *Denham.*

DI'VER. *n. s.* [from *dive*.]
1. One that sinks voluntarily under water.
If perseverance gain the *diver*'s prize,
Not everlasting Blackmore this denies. *Pope's Dunciad.*
2. One that goes under water in search of treasure.
It is evident, from the relation of *divers* and fishers for pearls, that there are many kinds of shell-fish which lie perpetually concealed in the deep, skreened from our sight. *Woodw.*
3. He that enters deep into knowledge or study.
He would have him, as I conceive it, to be no superficial and floating artificer; but a *diver* into causes, and into the mysteries of proportion. *Wotton's Architecture.*

To DIVE'RGE. *v. n.* [*divergo*, Latin.] To tend various ways from one point.
Homogeneal rays, which flow from several points of any object, and fall perpendicularly on any reflecting surface, shall afterwards *diverge* from so many points. *Newton's Opt.*

DIVE'RGENT. *adj.* [from *divergens*, Lat.] Tending to various parts from one point.

DI'VERS. *adj.* [*diversus*, Latin.] Several; sundry; more than one. It is now grown out of use.
We have *divers* examples in the primitive church of such as, by fear, being compelled to sacrifice to strange gods, after repented, and kept still the office of preaching the gospel. *Whitgift.*
The teeth breed when the child is a year and a half old: then they cast them, and new ones come about seven years; but *divers* have backward teeth come at twenty, some at thirty and forty. *Bacon's Natural History*, N°. 755.
Divers letters were shot into the city with arrows, wherein Solyman's councils were revealed. *Knolles's Hist. of the Turks.*
Divers friends thought it strange, that a white dry body should acquire a rich colour, upon the affusion of spring-water. *Boyle on Colours.*

DI'VERSE. *adj.* [*diversus*, Latin.]
1. Different from another.
Four great beasts came up from the sea, *diverse* one from another. *Dan.* vii. 3.
2. Different from itself; various; multiform; diffused.
Eloquence is a great and *diverse* thing, nor did she yet ever favour any man so much as to be wholly his. *Ben. Johnson.*
3. In different directions. It is little used but in the last sense.
To seize his papers, Curl, was next thy care;
His papers light, fly *diverse* tost in air. *Pope's Dunciad, b.* ii.

DIVERSIFICA'TION. *n. s.* [from *diversify*.]
1. The act of changing forms or qualities.
If you consider how variously several things may be compounded, you will not wonder that such fruitful principles, or manners

manners of *diversification*, should generate differing colours. *Boyle on Colours.*

2. Variation; variegation.
3. Variety of forms; multiformity.
4. Change; alteration.

This which is here called a change of will, is not a change of his will, but a change in the object, which seems to make a *diversification* of the will, but indeed is the same will diversified. *Hale's Origin of Mankind.*

To DIVE'RSIFY. *v. a.* [*diversifier*, French.]

1. To make different from another; to distinguish.

There may be many species of spirits, as much separated and *diversified* one from another as the species of sensible things are distinguished one from another. *Locke.*

Male souls are *diversified* with so many characters, that the world has not variety of materials sufficient to furnish out their different inclinations. *Addison's Spectator*, N°. 211.

It was easier for Homer to find proper sentiments for Grecian generals, than for Milton to *diversify* his infernal council with proper characters. *Addison's Spectator.*

2. To make different from itself; to vary; to variegate.

The country being *diversified* between hills and dales, woods and plains, one place more clear, another more darksome, it is a pleasant picture. *Sidney.*

There is, in the producing of some species, a composition of matter, which may be much *diversified*. *Bacon's Nat. Hist.*

DIVE'RSION. *n. s.* [from *divert.*]

1. The act of turning any thing off from its course.

Cutting off the tops, and pulling off the buds, work retention of the sap for a time, and *diversion* of it to the sprouts that were not forward. *Bacon's Natural History.*

2. The cause by which any thing is turned from its proper course or tendency.

Fortunes, honour, friends,
Are mere *diversions* from love's proper object,
Which only is itself. *Denham's Sophy.*

3. Sport; something that unbends the mind by turning it off from care. *Diversion* seems to be something lighter than *amusement*, and less forcible than *pleasure*.

You for those ends whole days in council sit,
And the *diversions* of your youth forget. *Waller.*

In the book of games and *diversions* the reader's mind may be supposed to be relaxed. *Addison's Spectator.*

Such productions of wit and humour as expose vice and folly, furnish useful *diversions* to readers. *Addison's Freeholder.*

4. [In war.] The act or purpose of drawing the enemy off from some design, by threatening or attacking a distant part.

DIVE'RSITY. *n. s.* [*diversité*, Fr. from *diversitas*, Latin.]

1. Difference; dissimilitude; unlikeness.

Then is there in this *diversity* no contrariety. *Hooker, b.* v.

They cannot be divided, but they will prove opposite; and not resting in a bare *diversity*, quickly rise into a contrariety. *South's Sermons.*

2. Variety.

The *diversity* of ceremonies in this kind ought not to cause dissension in churches. *Hooker, b.* iv. *s.* 13.

The most common *diversity* of human constitutions arises from the solid parts, as to their different degrees of strength and tension. *Arbuthnot on Aliments.*

3. Distinct being; not identity.

Society cannot subsist without a *diversity* of stations; and if God should grant every one a middle station, he would defeat the very scheme of happiness proposed in it. *Rogers.*

Considering any thing as existing, at any determined time and place, we compare it with itself existing at another time, and thereon form the ideas of identity and *diversity*. *Locke.*

4. Variegation.

A waving glow his bloomy beds display,
Blushing in bright *diversities* of day. *Pope, Epistle* 4.

DI'VERSLY. *adv.* [from *diverse.*]

1. In different ways; differently; variously.

Our common necessities, and the lack we all have as well of ghostly, as of earthly favours, is in each kind easily known; but the gifts of God are so *diversly* bestowed, that it seldom appeareth what all receive: what all stand in need of seldom lieth hid. *Hooker, b.* v. *s.* 43.

Both of them do *diversly* work, as they have their medium *diversly* disposed. *Bacon's Natural History*, N°. 264.

Whether the king did permit it to save his purse, or to communicate the envy of a business, displeasing to his people, was *diversly* interpreted. *Bacon.*

Leicester bewrayed a desire to plant him in the queen's favour, which was *diversly* interpreted by such as thought that great artizan of courts to do nothing by chance, nor much by affection. *Wotton.*

The universal matter, which Moses comprehendeth under the names of heaven and earth, is by divers *diversly* understood. *Raleigh's History of the World.*

William's arm
Could nought avail, however fam'd in war;
Nor armies leagu'd, that *diversly* assay'd
To curb his power. *Phillips.*

2. In different directions; to different points.

On life's vast ocean *diversly* we sail;
Reason the card, but passion is the gale. *Pope's Ess. on Man.*

To DIVE'RT. *v. a.* [*diverto*, Latin.]

1. To turn off from any direction or course.

I rather will subject me to the malice
Of a *diverted* blood and bloody brother. *Shakespeare.*

He finds no reason to have his rent abated, because a greater part of it is *diverted* from his landlord. *Locke.*

They *diverted* raillery from improper objects, and gave a new turn to ridicule. *Addison's Freeholder*, N°. 45.

Nothing more is requisite for producing all the variety of colours and degrees of refrangibility, than that the rays of light be bodies of different sizes; the least of which may make violet the weakest and darkest of the colours, and be more easily *diverted* by refracting surfaces from the right course; and the rest, as they are bigger and bigger, make the stronger and more lucid colours, blue, green, yellow, and red, and be more and more difficultly *diverted*. *Newton's Opt.*

2. To draw forces to a different part.

The kings of England would have had an absolute conquest of Ireland, if their whole power had been employed; but still there arose sundry occasions, which divided and *diverted* their power some other way. *Davies on Ireland.*

3. To withdraw the mind.

Alas, how simple, to these cates compar'd,
Was that crude apple that *diverted* Eve! *Milton's Pa. Reg.*

They avoid pleasure, lest they should have their affections tainted by any sensuality, and *diverted* from the love of him who is to be the only comfort. *Addison on Italy.*

Maro's muse, not wholly bent
On what is gainful, sometimes she *diverts*
From solid counsel. *Phillips.*

4. To please; to exhilerate. See DIVERSION.

An ingenious gentleman did *divert* or instruct the kingdom by his papers. *Swift.*

5. To subvert; to destroy, in *Shakespeare.*

Frights, changes, horrours,
Divert and crack, rend and deracinate
The unity and married calm of states. *Shak. Troil. and Cress.*

DIVE'RTER. *n. s.* [from the verb.] Any thing that diverts or alleviates.

Angling was, after tedious study, a rest to his mind, a cheerer of his spirits, and a *diverter* of sadness. *Walton's Angl.*

To DIVERTI'SE. *v. a.* [*divertiser*, French; *diverto*, Latin.] To please; to exhilerate; to divert. A word now little used.

Let orators instruct, let them *divertise*, and let them move us, this is what is properly meant by the word *salt*. *Dryden.*

DIVE'RTISEMENT. *n. s.* [*divertissement*, French.] Diversion; delight; pleasure. A word now not much in use.

How fond soever men are of bad *divertisement*, it will prove mirth which ends in heaviness. *Government of the Tongue.*

DIVE'RTIVE. *adj.* [from *divert.*] Recreative; amusive; exhilerating.

I would not exclude the common accidents of life, nor even things of a pleasant and *divertive* nature, so they are innocent, from conversation. *Rogers's Sermons.*

To DIVE'ST. *v. a.* [*devestir*, French. The English word is therefore more properly written *devest*. See DEVEST.] To strip; to make naked.

Then of his arms Androgeus he *divests*;
His sword, his shield he takes, and plumed crests. *Denham.*

Let us *divest* the gay phantom of temporal happiness, of all that false lustre and ornament in which the pride, the passions, and the folly of men have dressed it up. *Rogers's Serm.*

DIVE'STURE. *n. s.* [from *divest.*] The act of putting off.

The *divesture* of mortality dispenses them from those laborious and avocating duties which are here requisite to be performed. *Boyle's Seraphick Love.*

DI'VIDABLE. *adj.* [from *divide.*] Separate; different; parted. A word not used.

How could communities maintain
Peaceful commerce from *dividable* shores? *Shakespeare.*

DIVI'DANT. *adj.* [from *divide.*] Different; separate. A word not in use.

Twinn'd brothers of one womb,
Whose procreation, residence, and birth
Scarce is *dividant*, touch with several fortunes. *Shak. Timon.*

To DIVI'DE. *v. a.* [*divido*, Latin.]

1. To part one whole into different pieces.

Divide the living child in two, and give half to the one, and half to the other. *1 Kings* iii. 25.

Let old Timotheus yield the prize,
Or both *divide* the crown;
He rais'd a mortal to the skies,
She drew an angel down. *Dryden's St. Cecilia.*

They were *divided* into little, independent societies, speaking different languages. *Locke.*

2. To separate; to keep apart; to stand as a partition between.

Let there be firmament in the midſt of the waters, and let it *divide* the waters from the waters. *Gen.* i.

You muſt go
Where ſeas, and winds, and deſarts will *divide* you. *Dryd.*

3. To diſunite by diſcord.

There ſhall five in one houſe be *divided.* *Luke* xii.

4. To deal out; to give in ſhares.

Then in the midſt a tearing groan did break
The name of Anthony: it was *divided*
Between her heart and lips. *Shakeſ. Anthony and Cleopatra.*

Divide the prey into two parts, between them that took the war upon them, who went out to battle, and between all the congregation. *Num* xxxi. 27.

Cham and Japhet were heads and princes over their families, and had a right to *divide* the earth by families. *Locke.*

To Divi'de. *v. n.* To part; to ſunder; to break friendſhip.

Love cools, friendſhip falls off,
Brothers *divide.* *Shakeſpeare's King Lear.*

Di'vidend. *n. ſ.* [from *divide.*] A ſhare; the part allotted in diviſion.

Each perſon ſhould adapt to himſelf his peculiar ſhare, like other *dividends.* *Decay of Piety.*

If on ſuch petty merits you confer
So vaſt a prize, let each his portion ſhare:
Make a juſt *dividend*; and, if not all,
The greater part to Diomede will fall. *Dryden's Fables.*

Dividend is the number given to be parted or divided. *Cocker's Arithmetick.*

Divi'der. *n. ſ.* [from *divide.*]

1. That which parts any thing into pieces.

According as the body moved, the *divider* did more and more enter into the divided body; ſo it joined itſelf to ſome new parts of the medium, or divided body, and did in like manner forſake others. *Digby on the Soul.*

2. A diſtributer; he who deals out to each his ſhare.

Who made me a judge or *divider* over you? *Lu.* xii. 14.

3. A diſuniter; the perſon or cauſe that breaks concord.

Money, the great *divider* of the world, hath, by a ſtrange revolution, been the great uniter of a divided people. *Swift.*

4. A particular kind of compaſſes.

Divi'dual. *adj.* [*dividuus*, Latin.] Divided; ſhared or participated in common with others.

She ſhines,
Revolv'd on heav'n's great axle, and her reign
With thouſand leſſer lights *dividual* holds,
With thouſand thouſand ſtars! *Milton's Paradiſe Loſt, b.* vii.

Divina'tion. *n. ſ.* [*divinatio*, Latin.]

Divination is a prediction or foretelling of future things, which are of a ſecret and hidden nature, and cannot be known by any human means. *Ayliffe's Parergon.*

Certain tokens they noted in birds, or in the entrails of beaſts, or by other the like frivolous *divinations.* *Hooker.*

Surely there is no enchantment againſt Jacob, neither is there any *divination* againſt Iſrael. *Num.* xxiii. 23.

Tell thou thy earl his *divination* lies,
And I will take it as a ſweet diſgrace. *Shakeſp. Henry* IV.

His count'nance did imprint an awe;
And naturally all ſouls to his did bow,
As wands of *divination* downward draw,
And point to beds where ſov'reign gold doth grow. *Dryden.*

The excellency of the ſoul is ſeen by its power of divining in dreams: that ſeveral ſuch *divinations* have been made, none can queſtion who believes the holy writings. *Addiſon's Spectat.*

DIVI'NE. *adj.* [*divinus*, Latin.]

1. Partaking of the nature of God.

Her line
Was hero-make, half human, half *divine.* *Dryden.*

2. Proceeding from God; not natural; not human.

The benefit of nature's light is not thought excluded as unneceſſary, becauſe the neceſſity of a *divine* light is magnified. *Hooker.*

Inſtructed, you'd explore
Divine contrivance, and a God adore. *Blackmore's Creation.*

3. Excellent in a ſupreme degree.

The *divineſt* and richeſt mind,
Both by art's purchaſe and by nature's dower,
That ever was from heav'n to earth confin'd. *Davies.*

4. Preſageful; divining; preſcient.

Yet oft his heart, *divine* of ſomething ill,
Miſgave him; he the fault'ring meaſure felt. *Milt. Pa. Loſt.*

Divi'ne. *n. ſ.*

1. A miniſter of the goſpel; a prieſt; a clergyman.

Claudio muſt die to-morrow: let him be furniſhed with *divines*, and have all charitable preparation. *Sh. Meaſ. for Meaſ.*

Give Martius leave to proceed in his diſcourſe; for he ſpoke like a *divine* in armour. *Bacon's Holy War.*

A *divine* has nothing to ſay to the wiſeſt congregation, which he may not expreſs in a manner to be underſtood by the meaneſt among them. *Swift.*

2. A man ſkilled in divinity; a theologian.

Th' eternal cauſe in their immortal lines
Was taught, and poets were the firſt *divines.* *Denham.*

To Divi'ne. *v. a.* [*divino*, Latin.]

1. To foretell; to foreknow; to preſage.

Why do'ſt thou ſay king Richard is depos'd?
Dar'ſt thou, thou little better thing than earth,
Divine his downfall? *Shakeſpeare.*

To Divi'ne. *v. n.*

1. To utter prognoſtication.

Then is Cæſar and he knit together.——If I were to *divine* of this unity, I would not propheſy ſo. *Shakeſ.*

The prophets thereof *divine* for money. *Mic.* iii. 11.

2. To feel preſages.

If ſecret powers
Suggeſt but truth to my *divining* thoughts,
This pretty lad will prove our country's bliſs. *Shak. H.* VI.

3. To conjecture; to gueſs.

The beſt of commentators can but gueſs at his meaning; none can be certain he has *divined* rightly. *Dryd. Juv. Dedic.*

He took it with a bow, and ſoon *divin'd*
The ſeeming toy was not for nought deſign'd. *Dryd. Fables.*

In change of torment would be eaſe,
Could you *divine* what lovers bear;
Even you, Prometheus, would confeſs
There is no virtue like deſpair. *Granville.*

Divi'nely. *adv.* [from *divine.*]

1. By the agency or influence of God.

Faith, as we uſe the word, called commonly divine faith, has to do with no propoſitions but thoſe which are ſuppoſed to be *divinely* inſpired. *Locke.*

This topick was very fitly and *divinely* made uſe of by our apoſtle, in his conference with philoſophers, and the inquiſitive people of Athens. *Bentley's Sermons.*

2. Excellently in the ſupreme degree.

The Grecians moſt *divinely* have given to the active perfection of men, a name expreſſing both beauty and goodneſs. *Hooker.*

She fair, *divinely* fair! fit love for gods. *Milt. Par. Loſt.*

Exalted Socrates! *divinely* brave!
Injur'd he fell, and dying he forgave;
Too noble for revenge. *Creech's Juvenal, Sat.* 13.

3. In a manner noting a deity.

His golden horns appear'd,
That on the forehead ſhone *divinely* bright,
And o'er the banks diffus'd a yellow light. *Addiſon's Italy.*

Divi'neness. *n. ſ.* [from *divine.*]

1. Divinity; participation of the divine nature.

Is it then impoſſible to diſtinguiſh the *divineneſs* of this book from that which is humane? *Grew's Coſmol. Sac.*

2. Excellence in the ſupreme degree.

By Jupiter, an angel! or, if not,
An earthly paragon: behold *divineneſs*
No elder than a boy. *Shakeſpeare's Cymbeline.*

Divi'ner. *n. ſ.* [from *To divine.*]

1. One that profeſſes divination, or the art of revealing occult things by ſupernatural means.

This drudge of the devil, this *diviner*, laid claim to me, called me Dronio, and ſwore I was aſſured to her; told me what privy marks I had about me. *Shak. Comedy of Errours.*

Expelled his oracles, and common temples of deluſion, the devil runs into corners, exerciſing meaner trumperies, and acting his deceits in witches, magicians, *diviners*, and ſuch inferior ſeducers. *Brown's Vulgar Errours, b.* vii. *c.* 12.

2. Conjecturer; gueſſer.

If he himſelf be conſcious of nothing he then thought on, he muſt be a notable *diviner* of thoughts that can aſſure him that he was thinking. *Locke.*

Divi'neress. *n. ſ.* [from *diviner.*] A propheteſs; a woman profeſſing divination.

The mad *divinereſs* had plainly writ,
A time ſhould come, but many ages yet,
In which ſiniſter deſtinies ordain,
A dame ſhould drown with all her feather'd train. *Dryden.*

Divi'nity. *n. ſ.* [*divinité*, French, from *divinitas*, Latin.]

1. Participation of the nature and excellence of God; deity; godhead.

As with new wine intoxicated both,
They ſwim in mirth, and fancy that they feel
Divinity within them breeding wings,
Wherewith to ſcorn the earth. *Milton's Paradiſe Loſt, b.* ix.

When he attributes *divinity* to other things than God, it is only a *divinity* by way of participation. *Stillingfleet.*

2. God; the Deity; the Supreme Being; the Cauſe of cauſes.

3. Falſe god.

Vain idols, deities that ne'er before
In Iſrael's lands had fix'd their dire abodes,
Beaſtly *divinities*, and groves of Gods. *Prior.*

4. Celeſtial being.

God doubtleſs can govern this machine he could create, by more direct and eaſy methods than employing theſe ſubſervient *divinities.* *Cheyne's Phil. Princ.*

5. The ſcience of divine things; theology.

Hear him but reaſon in *divinity*,

And, all admiring with an inward wish,
You would desire the king were made a prelate. *Sh. H.* VI.
Trust not my age,
My reverence, calling, nor *divinity*,
If this sweet lady lie not guiltless here
Under some biting errour. *Shak. Much Ado about Nothing.*

Among hard words I number those which are peculiar to *divinity*, as it is a science. *Swift.*

6. Something supernatural.

They say there is *divinity* in odd numbers, either in nativity, chance, or death. *Shakesp. Merry Wives of Windsor.*

DIVI'SIBLE. *adj.* [*divisibilis*, Latin.] Capable of being divided into parts; discerptible; separable.

When we frame in our minds any notion of matter, we conceive nothing else but extension and bulk, which is impenetrable, or *divisible* and passive. *Bentley's Sermons.*

DIVISIBI'LITY. *n. s.* [*divisibilité*, French.] The quality of admitting division or separation of parts.

The most palpable absurdities will press the asserters of infinite *divisibility*. *Glanv. Sceps. c.* 7.

This will easily appear to any one, who will let his thoughts loose in the vast expansion of space, or *divisibility* of matter. *Locke.*

DIVI'SIBLENESS. *n. s.* [from *divisible.*] Divisibility.

Naturalists disagree about the origin of motion, and the indefinite *divisibleness* of matter. *Boyle.*

DIVI'SION. *n. s.* [*divisio*, Latin.]

1. The act of dividing any thing into parts.

Thou madest the spirit of the firmament, and commanded it to part asunder, and to make a *division* betwixt the waters. 2 *Esdr.* vi. 41.

2. The state of being divided.
3. That by which any thing is kept apart; partition.
4. The part which is separated from the rest by dividing.

If we look into communities and *divisions* of men, we observe that the discreet man, not the witty, guides the conversation. *Addison's Spectator*, N°. 225.

5. Disunion; discord; difference.

There was a *division* among the people, because of him. *Jo.* vii. 43.

As to our *divisions* with the Romanists, were our differences the product of heat, they would, like small clefts in the ground, want but a cool season to cement them. *Dec. of Piety.*

6. Parts into which a discourse is distributed.

In the *divisions* I have made, I have endeavoured, the best I could, to govern myself by the diversity of matter. *Locke.*

Express the heads of your *divisions* in as few and clear words as you can, otherwise I never can be able to retain them. *Swift.*

7. Space between the notes of musick, or parts of a musical composure; just time.

Thy tongue
Makes Welsh as sweet as ditties highly penn'd,
Sung by a fair queen, in a Summer's bower,
With ravishing *division* to her lute. *Shakespeare's Henry* IV.

Our tongue will run *divisions* in a tune, not missing a note, even when our thoughts are totally engaged elsewhere. *Glanv.*

8. Distinction.

I will put a *division* between my people and thy people. *Ex.*

9. [In arithmetick.] The separation or parting of any number or quantity given, into any parts assigned. *Cocker's Arithmetick.*

10. Subdivision; distinction of the general into species.

The king-becoming graces,
I have no relish of them; but abound
In the *division* of each several crime,
Acting it many ways. *Shakespeare's Macbeth.*

DIVI'SOR. *n. s.* [*divisor*, Latin.] The number given, by which the dividend is divided; the number which sheweth how many parts the dividend is to be divided into.

DIVO'RCE. *n. s.* [*divorce*, Fr. from *divortium*, Latin.] The legal separation of husband and wife.

Divorce is a lawful separation of husband and wife, made before a competent judge, on due cognizance had of the cause, and sufficient proof made thereof. *Ayliffe's Parergon.*

To restore the king,
He counsels a *divorce*, a loss of her,
That like a jewel has hung twenty years
About his neck, yet never lost her lustre. *Shak. Hen.* VIII.

He had in his eye the *divorce* which had passed betwixt the emperor and Scribonia. *Dryden's Dedicat. to the Æn.*

2. Separation; disunion.

Such motions may occasion a farther alienation of mind, and *divorce* of affections in her, from my religion. *K. Charles.*

These things, to be a bastard, and to be born out of lawful wedlock, are convertible the one with the other; and 'tis hard to make *divorce* between those things that are so near in nature to each other, as being convertible terms. *Ayliffe's Par.*

3. The sentence by which a marriage is dissolved.
4. The cause of any penal separation.

Go with me, like good angels, to my end;
And as the long *divorce* of steel falls on me,
Make of your prayers one sweet sacrifice,
And lift my soul to heav'n. *Shakespeare's Henry* VIII.

To DIVO'RCE *v. a.* [from the noun.]

1. To separate a husband or wife from the other.
2. To force asunder; to separate by violence.

Were it consonant unto reason to *divorce* these two sentences, the former of which doth shew how the latter is restrained, and not marking the former, to conclude by the latter of them? *Hooker, b.* ii. *s.* 5.

The continent and the island were continued together, within mens remembrance, by a draw-bridge; but is now *divorced* by the downfallen cliffs. *Carew's Survey of Cornwal.*

So seem'd her youthful soul not eas'ly forc'd,
Or from so fair, so sweet a seat *divorc'd*. *Waller.*

3. To separate from another.

If thou wer't not glad,
I would *divorce* me from thy mother's tomb,
Sepulch'ring an adultress. *Shakespeare's King Lear.*

If so be it were possible, that all other ornaments of mind might be had in their full perfection, nevertheless the mind, that should possess them *divorced* from piety, could be but a spectacle of commiseration. *Hooker.*

4. To take away.

I dare not make myself so guilty,
To give up willingly that noble title
Your master wed me to: nothing but death
Shall e'er *divorce* my dignities. *Shakespeare's Henry* VIII.

DIVO'RCEMENT. *n. s.* [from *divorce.*] Divorce; separation of marriage.

Write her a bill of *divorcement*, and give it in her hand, and send her out of his house. *Deutr.* xxiv. 1.

DIVO'RCER. *n. s.* [from *divorce.*] The person or cause which produces divorce or separation.

Death is the violent estranger of acquaintance, the eternal *divorcer* of marriage. *Drummond's Cypr. Grove.*

DIURE'TICK. *adj.* [διουρητικὸς.] Having the power to provoke urine.

Diureticks are decoctions, emulsions, and oils of emollient vegetables, that relax the *urinary* passages: such as relax ought to be tried before such as force and stimulate. Those emollients ought to be taken in open air, to hinder them from perspiring, and on empty stomachs. *Arbuthnot.*

DIU'RNAL. *adj.* [*diurnus*, Latin.]

1. Relating to the day.

We observe in a day, which is a short year, the greatest heat about two in the afternoon, when the sun is past the meridian, which is the *diurnal* solstice, and the same is evident from the thermometer. *Brown's Vulgar Errours, b.* iv.

Think, ere this *diurnal* star
Leave cold the night, how we his gather'd beams
Reflected, may with matter sere foment. *Milt. Par. Lost.*

2. Constituting the day.

Why does he order the *diurnal* hours
To leave earth's other part, and rise in our's? *Prior.*

3. Performed in a day; daily; quotidian.

The prime orb,
Incredible how swift, had thither rowl'd
Diurnal. *Milton's Paradise Lost, b.* iv. *l.* 594.

The *diurnal* and annual revolution of the sun have been, from the beginning of nature, constant, regular, and universally observable by all mankind. *Locke.*

DIU'RNAL. *n. s.* [*diurnal*, French.] A journal; a day-book.

DIU'RNALLY. *adv.* [from *diurnal.*] Daily; every day.

As we make the enquiries, we shall *diurnally* communicate them to the publick. *Tatler*, N°. 56.

DIUTU'RNITY. *n. s.* [*diuturnitas*, Latin.] Length of duration.

Such a coming, as it might be said, that that generation should not pass 'till it was fulfilled, they needed not suppose of such *diuturnity*. *Brown's Vulgar Errours, b.* vii. *c.* 10.

To DIVU'LGE. *v. a.* [*divulgo*, Latin.]

1. To publish; to make publick; to reveal to the world.

Men are better contented to have their commendations suppressed than the contrary much *divulged*. *Hooker, Dedicat.*

I will pluck the veil of modesty from the so seeming mistress Page, and *divulge* Page himself for a secure and wilful Acteon. *Shakespeare's Merry Wives of Windsor.*

These answers in the silent night receiv'd,
The king himself *divulg'd*, the land believ'd. *Dryden's Æn.*

You are deprived of the right over your own sentiments, of the privilege of every human creature, to *divulge* or conceal them. *Pope.*

The cabinets of the sick, and the closets of the dead, have been ransacked to publish our private letters, and *divulge* to all mankind the most secret sentiments of friendship. *Pope.*

2. To proclaim.

This is true glory and renown, when God
Looking on th' earth, with approbation, marks
The just man, and *divulges* him through heav'n
To all his angels, who with true applause
Recount his praises. *Milton's Paradise Lost, b.* iii.

DIVU'LGER. *n. s.* [from *divulge.*] A publisher; one that exposes to publick view.

I think not any thing in my letters could tend ſo much to my reproach, as the odious divulging of them did to the infamy of the *divulgers*. *King Charles.*

DIVU'LSION. *n. ſ.* [*divulſio*, Latin.] The act of plucking awry.

Ariſtotle, in his Ethicks, takes up the conceit of the beaver, and the *divulſion* of his teſticles. *Brown's Vulgar Errours, b.* i.

To DI'ZEN. *v. a.* [This word ſeems corrupted from *dight.*] To dreſs; to deck; to rig out. A low word.

Your ladyſhip lifts up the ſaſh to be ſeen;
For ſure I had *dizen'd* you out like a queen. *Swift.*

DI'ZZARD. *n. ſ.* [from *dizzy.*] A blockhead; a fool. *Dict.*

DI'ZZINESS. *n. ſ.* [from *dizzy.*] Giddineſs; whirl in the head.

Fixed ſerioufneſs heats the brain in ſome to diſtraction, and cauſeth an aching and *dizzineſs* in ſounder heads. *Glanv.*

DI'ZZY. *adj.* [dysi, dysiʒ, Saxon.]

1. Giddy; vertiginous; having in the head the ſenſation of turning round.

All on a ſudden miſerable pain
Surpriz'd thee, dim thine eyes, and *dizzy* ſwam
In darkneſs. *Milton's Paradiſe Loſt, b.* ii. *l.* 753.

2. Cauſing giddineſs.

How fearful
And *dizzy* 'tis to caſt one's eyes ſo low!
The crows and choughs that wing the midway air,
Shew ſcarce ſo groſs as beetles. *Shakeſp. King Lear.*

3. Giddy; thoughtleſs.

What followers, what retinue can'ſt thou gain?
Or at thy heels the *dizzy* multitude,
Longer than thou can'ſt feed them on thy coſt? *Milton.*

To DI'ZZY. *v. a.* [from the adjective.] To whirl round; to make giddy.

Not the dreadful ſpout,
Which ſhipmen do the hurricano call,
Shall *dizzy* with more clamour Neptune's ear
In his deſcent, than ſhall my prompted ſword
Falling on Diomede. *Shakeſp. Troilus and Creſſida.*

To DO. *v. a.* preter. *did*; part. paſſ. *done.* [don, Sax. *doen*, Dut.]

1. To practiſe or act any thing good or bad.

Thou haſt *done* evil above all that were before thee. 1 *Kings.*
Flee evil, and *do* good. *Pſalms.*

2. To perform; to atchieve.

They help, who hurt ſo ſmall;
And he hath nothing *done*, that *doth* not all. *Daniel's C. War.*
Learn to live well, that thou may'ſt die ſo too;
To live and die is all we have to *do*. *Denham.*

What is the reaſon a man's arm won't ſmile and frown, and *do* all the intellectual poſtures of the countenance? *Collier.*

3. To execute; to diſcharge.

May one, that is a herald and a prince,
Do a fair meſſage to his kingly ears? *Shak. Troil. and Creſſ.*
Pindarus is come
To *do* you ſalutation from his maſter. *Shakeſp. Jul. Cæſar.*

4. To cauſe.

A fatal plague which many *did* to dye. *Spenſer.*
Nought can quench mine inly flaming ſide,
Nor ſea of liquor cold, nor lake of mire,
Nothing but death can *do* me to reſpire. *Fairy Queen, b.* ii.

5. To tranſact.

The thing was not *done* in a corner. *Acts* xxvi. 26.

6. To produce any effect to another.

If he did not care whether he had their love or no, he waved indifferently 'twixt *doing* them neither good nor harm. *Shakeſpeare's Coriolanus.*

Thou haſt, Sebaſtian, *done* good feature ſhame. *Shakeſp.*
If there be any good thing to be done,
That may to thee *do* eaſe, and grace to me,
Speak to me. *Shakeſpeare's Hamlet.*
'Tis true, I did ſo; nor was it in vain:
She *did* me right, and ſatisfy'd my vengeance. *Rowe.*

You *do* her too much honour: ſhe hath neither ſenſe nor taſte, if ſhe dares to refuſe you. *Swift.*

7. To have recourſe to; to practiſe as the laſt effort, commonly in the form of a paſſionate interrogation.

What will ye *do* in the end thereof? *Jer.* v. 81.

8. To perform for the benefit of another.

I know what God will *do* for me. *Sa.* xxii. 3.

Acts of mercy *done* to the poor, ſhall then be accepted, and rewarded, as *done* to our Saviour himſelf. *Atterb. Sermons.*

9. To exert; to put forth.

Do thy diligence, to come ſhortly unto me. 2 *Tim.* iv. 9.

10. To manage by way of intercourſe or dealing; to have buſineſs; to deal.

No man, who hath to *do* with the king, will think himſelf ſafe, unleſs you be his good angel, and guide him. *Bacon.*

I have been deterred by an indiſpoſition from having much to *do* with ſteams of ſo dangerous a nature. *Boyle.*

What had I to *do* with kings and courts?
My humble lot had caſt me far beneath them. *Rowe.*

11. To gain a point; to effect by influence.

It is much, that a jeſt with a ſad brow will *do* with a fellow that never had the ache in his ſhoulders. *Shakeſp. Henry* IV.

His queen, notwithſtanding ſhe had preſented him with divers children, and with a crown alſo, though he would not acknowledge it, could *do* nothing with him. *Bacon's H.* VII.

12. To make any thing what it is not.

Off with the crown, and with the crown his head;
And whilſt we breathe take him to *do* him dead. *Sh. H.* VI.

13. To finiſh; to end.

As for this mercy,
Which he intends for Lear and for Cordelia,
The battle *done*, and they within our power,
Shall never ſee his pardon. *Shakeſpeare's King Lear.*

Go on to the reading of ſome part of the New Teſtament, not careleſly, or in haſte, as if you had a mind to have *done*, but attentively, as to be able to give ſome account of what you have read. *Duppa.*

Gigantick hinds, as ſoon as work was *done*,
To their huge pots of boiling pulſe would run. *Dryden.*

14. To conclude; to ſettle.

When all is *done*, there is no man can ſerve his own intereſt better than by ſerving God. *Tillotſon's Sermons.*

15. To put.

Why, Warwick, who ſhould *do* the duke to death? *Shak.*
The lord Aubrey Vere,
Was *done* to death? *Shakeſpeare's Henry* VI. *p.* iii.

16. This phraſe, *what to* DO *with*, ſignifies how to beſtow; what uſe to make of; what courſe to take; how to employ; which way to get rid of.

Men are many times brought to that extremity, that if it were not for God, they would not know *what to do with* themſelves, or how to enjoy themſelves for one hour. *Tillotſon.*

To DO. *v. n.*

1. To act or behave in any manner well or ill.

Unto this day they *do* after the former manners: they fear not the Lord, neither *do* they after the law and commandment which the Lord commanded the children of Jacob. 2 *Kings.*

As every prince ſhould govern as he would deſire to be governed, ſo every ſubject ought to obey as he would deſire to be obeyed, according to the maxim of *doing* as we would be *done* by. *Temple.*

2. To make an end; to conclude.

You may ramble a whole day, and every moment diſcover ſomething new; but when you have *done*, you will have but a confuſed notion of the place. *Spectator*, Nº. 47.

3. To ceaſe to be concerned with; to ceaſe to care about; to deſiſt from notice or practice.

No men would make uſe of diſunited parties to deſtroy one body, unleſs they were ſure to maſter them when they had *done* with them. *Stillingfleet's Def. of Diſc. on Rom. Idol.*

I have *done with* Chaucer, when I have anſwered ſome objections. *Dryden's Fables, Pref.*

We have not yet *done with* aſſenting to propoſitions at firſt hearing, and underſtanding their terms. *Locke.*

Having *done with* ſuch amuſements, we give up what we cannot diſown. *Pope.*

4. To fare; to be with regard to ſickneſs or health.

Good woman, how *do'ſt* thou?
——The better that it pleaſes your good worſhip to aſk. *Shak.*

5. To ſucceed; to fulfil a purpoſe.

Come, 'tis no matter; we ſhall *do* without him. *Addiſon.*

You would *do* well to prefer a bill againſt all kings and parliaments ſince the conqueſt; and, if that won't *do*, challenge the crown. *Collier on Duelling.*

6. *To* Do is uſed for any verb to ſave the repetition of the word; as, *I ſhall come, but if I* do *not, go away*; that is, *if I* come not.

Thus painters Cupid paint, thus poets *do*
A naked god, blind, young, with arrows two. *Sidney.*

If any thing in the world deſerve our ſerious ſtudy and conſideration, thoſe principles of religion *do*. *Tillotſon's Sermons.*

Take all things which relax the veins; for what *does* ſo, prevents too vigorous a motion through the arteries. *Arbuthn.*

7. Do is a word of vehement command, or earneſt requeſt; as, *help me*, do; *make haſte*, do.

If thou haſt loſt thy land, *do* not alſo loſe thy conſtancy; and if thou muſt die a little ſooner, yet *do* not die impatiently. *Taylor's Rule of living holy.*

I am enſnared;
Heaven's birdlime wraps me round, and glues my wings:
—Looſe me.—I will free thee.
—*Do*, and I'll be thy ſlave. *Dryden's King Arthur.*

8. *To* Do is put before verbs ſometimes expletively; as, *I* do *love*, or, *I love*; *I* did *love*, or, *I loved.*

The Turks *do* acknowledge God the father, creator of heaven and earth, being the firſt perſon in the Trinity, though they deny the reſt. *Bacon's Holy War.*

This juſt reproach their virtue *does* excite;
They ſtand, they join, they thicken to the fight. *Dryd. Æn.*
Expletives their feeble aid *do* join. *Pope.*

9. Sometimes emphatically; as, *I* do *hate him, but will not wrong him.*

Perdition catch my ſoul
But I *do* love thee; and when I love thee not,
Chaos is come again. *Shakeſpeare's Othello.*

10. Sometimes

10. Sometimes by way of oppofition; as, *I did love him, but fcorn him now.*

To Doat. *v. n.* See *To* Dote.

DO'CIBLE. *adj.* [*docilis*, Latin.] Tractable; docile; eafy to be taught.

The Afinine feaft of fow-thiftles and brambles is commonly fet before them, as all the food and entertainment of their tendereft and moft *docible* age. *Milton.*

Do'cibleness. *n. f.* [from *docible.*] Teachablenefs; docility; readinefs to learn.

I might enlarge in commendation of the noble hound, as alfo of the *docibleneſs* of dogs in general. *Walton's Angler.*

DO'CILE. *adj.* [*docilis*, Latin.]

1. Teachable; eafily inftructed; tractable.

Dogs foon grow accuftomed to whatever they are taught, and, being *docile* and tractable, are very ufeful. *Ellis's Voyage.*

2. With *to* before the thing taught.

Soon *docile to* the fecret acts of ill,
With fmiles I could betray, with temper kill. *Prior.*

Doci'lity. *n. f.* [*docilité*, French, from *docilitas*, Lat.] Aptnefs to be taught; readinefs to learn.

All the perfection they allowed his underftanding was aptnefs and *docility*, and all that they attributed to his will was a poffibility to be virtuous. *South's Sermons.*

What is more admirable than the fitnefs of every creature for ufe? The *docility* of an elephant, and the infitiency of a camel for travelling in defarts? *Grew's Cofm. Sac.*

Dock. *n. f.* [ðocca, Saxon.]

The cup of the flower confifts of fix leaves, three large, and red; the other three leffer, and green: in the middle of the cup are placed fix ftamina. The three outer fmall leaves of the cup fall away, when ripe; but the three inner large leaves join together, and form a triangular covering, in the middle of which are contained three fhining cornered feeds. The fpecies are feventeen, ten of which grow wild, feveral of them being ufed in medicine; and the fort called the oriental burdock, is faid to be the true rhubarb. *Millar.*

Nothing teems
But hateful *docks*, rough thiftles, keckfies, burs,
Lofing both beauty and utility. *Shakefpeare's Henry V.*

My love for gentle Dermot fafter grows
Than yon tall *dock* that rifes to thy nofe:
Cut down the *dock*, 'twill fprout again; but know
Love rooted out, again will never grow. *Swift.*

DOCK. *n. f.* The ftump of the tail, which remains after docking.

The tail of a great rhinoceros is not well defcribed by Bontius. The *dock* is about half an inch thick, and two inches broad, like an apothecary's fpatula. *Grew's Mufæum.*

Dock. *n. f.* [As fome imagine of δοχεῖον.] A place where water is let in or out at pleafure, where fhips are built or laid up.

There are *docks* for their gallies and men of war, moft of them full; as well as work-houfes for all land and naval preparations. *Addifon on Italy.*

To Dock. *v. a.* [from *dock*, a tail.]

1. To cut off a tail.

2. To cut any thing fhort.

One or two ftood conftant centry, who *docked* all favours handed down; and fpread a huge invifible net between the prince and fubject, through which nothing of value could pafs. *Swift's Examiner*, N°. 19.

3. To cut off a reckoning; to cut off an entail.

4. To lay the fhip in a dock

Do'cket. *n. f.* A direction tied upon goods; a fummary of a larger writing. *Dict.*

DO'CTOR. *n. f.* [*doctor*, Latin.]

1. One that has taken the higheft degree in the faculties of divinity, law, or phyfick. In fome univerfities they have doctors of mufick. In its original import it means a man fo well verfed in his faculty, as to be qualified to teach it.

No woman had it, but a civil *doctor*,
Who did refufe three thoufand ducats of me,
And begg'd the ring. *Shakefpeare's Merchant of Venice.*

Then ftood there up one in the council, a pharifee, named Gamaliel, a *doctor* of laws. *Acts* v. 34.

2. A man fkilled in any profeffion.

Then fubtle *doctors* fcriptures made their pride,
Cafuifts, like cocks, ftruck out each other's eyes. *Denham.*

Each profelyte would vote his *doctor* beft,
With abfolute exclufion to the reft. *Dryd Hind and Panth.*

3. A phyfician; one who undertakes the cure of difeafes.

By med'cine life may be prolong'd, yet death
Will feize the *doctor* too. *Shakefpeare's Cymbeline.*

How does your patient, *doctor?*
—Not fo fick, my lord,
As fhe is troubl'd with thick coming fancies. *Shakefp. Macb.*

Children will not take thofe medicines from the *doctor's* hand, which they will from a nurfe or mother. *Gov. of Tongue.*

To 'pothecaries let the learn'd prefcribe,
That men may die without a double bribe:
Let them, but under their fuperiors, kill,
When *doctors* firft have fign'd the bloody bill. *Dryden.*

He that can cure by recreation, and make pleafure the vehicle of health, is a *doctor* at it in good earneft. *Collier.*

In truth, nine parts in ten of thofe who recovered, owed their lives to the ftrength of nature and a good conftitution, while fuch a one happened to be the *doctor.* *Swift.*

4. Any able or learned man.

The fimpleft perfon, that can but apprehend and fpeak fenfe, is as much judge of it as the greateft *doctor* in the fchool. *Digby of Bodies.*

To Do'ctor. *v. a.* [from the noun.] To phyfick; to cure; to treat with medicines. A low word.

Do'ctoral. *adj.* [*doctoralis*, Latin.] Relating to the degree of a doctor.

Do'ctorally. *adv.* [from *doctoral.*] In manner of a doctor.

The phyficians reforted to him to touch his pulfe, and confider of his difeafe *doctorally* at their departure. *Hakewill.*

Do'ctorship. *n. f.* [from *doctor.*] The rank of a doctor.

From a fcholar he became a fellow, and then the prefident of the college, after he had received all the graces and degrees, the proctorfhip and the *doctorfhip*, that could be obtained there. *Clarendon.*

Doctri'nal. *adj.* [*doctrina*, Latin.]

1. Containing doctrine, or fomething formally taught.

The verfe naturally affords us the *doctrinal* propofition, which fhall be our fubject. *South's Sermons.*

Not fuch as affent to every word in Scripture, can be faid in *doctrinals* to deny Chrift. *South's Sermons.*

2. Pertaining to the act or means of teaching.

To this end the word of God no otherwife ferveth, than only in the nature of a *doctrinal* inftrument. *Hooker, b.* v.

What fpecial property or quality is that, which, being no where found but in fermons, maketh them effectual to fave fouls, and leaveth all other *doctrinal* means befides deftitute of vital efficacy. *Hooker, b.* v. *f.* 22.

Doctri'nally. *adv.* [from *doctrine.*] In the form of doctrine; pofitively; as neceffary to be held.

Scripture accommodates itfelf to common opinions, and employs the ufual forms of fpeech, without delivering any thing *doctrinally* concerning thefe points. *Ray on the Creation.*

Do'ctrine. *n. f.* [*doctrina*, Latin.]

1. The principles or pofitions of any fect or mafter; that which is taught.

To make new articles of faith and *doctrine*, no man thinketh it lawful: new laws of government, what church or commonwealth is there which maketh not either at one time or other? *Hooker, b.* iii. *f.* 10.

Ye are the fons of clergy, who bring all their *doctrines* fairly to the light, and invite men with freedom to examine them. *Atterbury's Sermons.*

That great principle in natural philofophy is the *doctrine* of gravitation, or mutual tendency of all bodies toward each other. *Watts's Improvement of the Mind.*

2. The act of teaching.

He faid unto them in his *doctrine.* *Mark* iv. 2.

Do'cument. *n. f.* [*documentum*, Latin.]

1. Precept; inftruction; direction.

It is a moft neceffary inftruction and *document* for them, that as her majefty made them difpenfators of her favour, fo it behoveth them to fhew themfelves equal diftributers. *Bacon.*

Learners fhould not be too much crouded with a heap or multitude of *documents* or ideas at one time. *Watts.*

2. Precept in an ill fenfe; a precept infolently authoritative, magifterially dogmatical, folemnly trifling.

Gentle infinuations pierce, as oil is the moft penetrating of all liquors; but in magifterial *documents* men think themfelves attacked, and ftand upon their guard. *Govern. of Tongue.*

It is not unneceffary to digeft the *documents* of cracking authors into feveral claffes. *Harr. on Confumptions.*

DO'DDER. *n. f.* [*touteren*, to fhoot up, Dutch. *Skinner.*]

Dodder is a fingular plant: when it firft fhoots from the feed it has little roots, which pierce the earth near the roots of other plants; but the capillaments of which it is formed, foon after clinging about thefe plants, the roots wither away. From this time it propagates itfelf along the ftalks of the plant, entangling itfelf about them in a very complicated manner. It has no leaves, but confifts of fuch capillaments or ftalks, as are brownifh with a caft of red, which run to great lengths. They have at certain diftances tubercles, which fix them faft down to the plant, and by means of which they abforb the juices deftined for its nourifhment. The flowers ftand in a kind of little round clufters on the ftalks, are fmall, of a whitifh or pale redifh colour, of the bell-fafhioned kind, and deeply divided into four or five fegments at the edge; The flower is fucceeded by a roundifh fruit with three or four ridges, that give it a trigonal or tetragonal form: this has only one cavity. The feeds are numerous: thefe fall upon the ground, and produce young plants. *Hill.*

Do'ddered. *adj.* [from *dodder.*] Overgrown with dodder, covered with fupercrefcent plants.

Near the hearth a lawrel grew,
Dodder'd with age, whofe boughs encompafs round
The houfhold gods, and fhade the holy ground. *Dryd. Æn.*

The peasants were enjoin'd
Sere-wood, and firs, and *dodder'd* oaks to find. *Dryd. Fables.*

DODE'CAGON. *n. s.* [δώδεκα and γωνία] A figure of twelve sides.

DODECATEMO'RION. *n. s.* [δωδεκατημόριον.] The twelfth part.
'Tis *dodecatemorion* thus describ'd:
Thrice ten degrees, which every sign contains,
Let twelve exhaust, that not one part remains;
It follows streight, that every twelfth confines
Two whole, and one half portion of the signs. *Creech.*

To DODGE. *v. n.* [probably corrupted from *dog*; to shift and play sly tricks like a dog.]

1. To use craft; to deal with tergiversation; to play mean tricks; to use low shifts.

If in good offices and due retributions we may not be pinching and niggardly, it argues an earthly and ignoble mind, where we have apparently wronged, to higgle and *dodge* in the amends. *Hale's Contemplation.*

The consideration should make men grow weary of *dodging* and shewing tricks with God. *South.*

2. To shift place as another approaches.
For he had, any time this ten years full,
Dodg'd with him betwixt Cambridge and the Bull. *Milton.*

3. To play fast and loose; to raise expectations and disappoint them.

You know my passion for Martha, and what a dance she has led me: she *dodged* with me above thirty years. *Addison.*

The chaffering with dissenters, and *dodging* about this or t'other ceremony, is but like opening a few wickets, and leaving them a-jar, by which no more than one can get in at a time. *Swift.*

DO'DKIN. *n. s.* [*duytken*, Dutch.] A doitkin or little doit; a contemptuous name for a low coin.

I would not buy them for a *dodkin*. *Lily's Gram. construed.*

DO'DMAN. *n. s.* The name of a fish.

Those that cast their shell are the lobster, the crab, the crawfish, the hodmandod or *dodman*, and the tortoise. *Bacon.*

DOE. *n. s.* [ða, Saxon; *daa*, Danish] A she-deer; the female of a buck.
Then but forbear your food a little while,
While, like a *doe*, I go to find my fawn,
And give it food. *Shakespeare's As you like it.*
Bucks have horns, *does* none. *Bacon's Natural History.*
The fearful *doe*
And flying stag amid'st the greyhounds go. *Dryden's Virgil.*

DOE. *n. s.* [from *To do.*] A feat; what one has to do; what one can perform.
No sooner he does peep into
The world, but he has done his *doe*. *Hudibras, p.* ii. *cant.* 3.

DO'ER. *n. s.* [from *To do.*] One that does any thing good or bad.
So foul a thing, O! thou Injustice art,
That tort'rest both the *doer* and distrest. *Daniel's Civ. War.*

It may be indeed a publick crime, or a national mischief; yet it is but a private act, and the *doer* of it may chance to pay his head for his presumption. *South's Sermons.*

2. Actor; agent.

Sith thus far we have proceeded in opening the things that have been done, let not the principal *doers* themselves be forgotten. *Hooker.*

3. Performer.

Then have they most commonly one, who judgeth the prize to the best *doer*, of which they are no less glad than great princes are of triumphs. *Sidney.*

4. An active, or busy, or valiant person.
Fear not, my lord, we will not stand to prate;
Talkers are no good *doers*: be assur'd,
We go to use our hands, and not our tongues. *Shak. R.* III.

They are great speakers, but small *doers*; greater in shew than in deed. *Knolles's History of the Turks.*

5. One that habitually performs or practises.

Be *doers* of the word, and not hearers only. *Comm. Prayer.*

In this we shew ourselves weak, and unapt to be *doers* of his will, in that we take upon us to be controllers of his wisdom. *Hooker, b.* ii. *s.* 6.

DOES. The third person from *do* for *doth*.

Though lending to foreigners, upon use, doth not at all alter the balance of trade between those countries, yet it *does* alter the exchange between those countries. *Locke.*

To DOFF. *v. a.* [from *do off.*]

1. To put off dress.
You have deceiv'd our trust,
And made us *doff* our easy robes of peace,
To crush our old limbs in ungentle steel. *Shakesp. Hen.* IV.
Doff those links. *Milton's Agonistes.*
Nature, in awe to him,
Had *doff'd* her gaudy trim,
With her great master so to sympathize. *Milton.*
That judge is hot, and *doffs* his gown; while this
O'er night was bowsy:
So many rubs appear, the time is gone
For hearing, and the tedious suit goes on. *Dryd. Juv. Sat.*
Alcides *doffs* the lion's tawny hide. *Rowe.*

2. To strip.
Why art thou troubled, Herod? What vain fear
Thy blood-revolving breast doth move?
Heaven's king, who *doffs* himself our flesh to wear,
Comes not to rule in wrath, but serve in love. *Crashaw.*

3. To put away; to get rid of.
Your eye in Scotland
Would create soldiers, and make women fight,
To *doff* their dire distresses. *Shakespeare's Macbeth.*

4. To shift off; to delay; to refer to another time.

Every day thou *doff'st* me with some device, Iago; and rather keep'st from me all conveniency, than supplieft me with the least advantage of hope. *Shakespeare's Othello.*

Away, I will not have to do with you.——
—Can'st thou so *doff* me? *Shakes. Much Ado about Nothing.*

5. This word is in all its senses obsolete, and scarcely used except by rusticks.

DOG. *n. s.* [*dogghe*, Dutch.]

1. A domestick animal remarkably various in his species; comprising the mastiff, the spaniel, the buldog, the greyhound, the hound, the terrier, the cur, with many others. The larger sort are used as a guard; the less for sports.
Such smiling rogues as these sooth every passion!
Renege, affirm, and turn their halcyon beaks
With ev'ry gale and vary of their masters,
As knowing nought, like *dogs*, but following. *Shak. K. Lear.*

Why should we not think a watch and pistol as distinct species one from another, as a horse and a *dog*. *Locke.*
The clamour roars of men and boys, and *dogs*,
Ere the soft fearful people, to the flood
Commit their woolly sides. *Thomson's Spring, l.* 375.

2. A constellation called Sirius, or Canicula, rising and setting with the sun during the canicular days, or dog days.

Among the southern constellations two there are who bear the name of the *dog*; the one in sixteen degrees latitude, containing on the left thigh a star of the first magnitude, usually called Procyon, or Anticanus. *Brown's Vulgar Errours, b.* iv.
It parts the twins and crab, the *dog* divides,
And Argo's keel that broke the frothy tides. *Creech.*

3. A reproachful name for a man.
I never heard a passion so confus'd,
So strange, outrageous, and so variable,
As the *dog* Jew did utter in the streets. *Shak. Mer. of Venice.*
Beware of *dogs*, beware of evil workers. *Phil.* iii. 2.

4. *To give or send to the* DOGS; to throw away. *To go to the* DOGS; to be ruined, destroyed, or devoured.
Had whole Colepeper's wealth been hops and hogs,
Could he himself have sent it to the *dogs*? *Pope's Epistles.*

5. It is used as the term for the male of several species; as, the *dog* fox, the *dog* otter.

If ever I thank any man, I'll thank you; but that they call compliments is like the encounter of two *dog* apes. *Shakesp.*

6. *Dog* is a particle added to any thing to mark meanness, or degeneracy, or worthlessness; as *dog* rose.

T DOG. *v. a.* [from the noun.] To hunt as a dog, insidiously and indefatigably.
I have *dogg'd* him like his murtherer. *Shakes. Twelfth Night.*
His taken labours bid him me forgive;
I, his despiteful Juno, sent him forth
From courtly friends, with camping foes to live,
Where death and danger *dog* the heels of worth. *Shakesp.*
Sorrow *dogging* sin,
Afflictions sorted. *Herbert.*

These spiritual joys are *dogged* by no such sad sequels as are the products of those titillations, that reach no higher than fancy and the senses. *Glanv. Sceps. Pref.*

I have been pursued, *dogged*, and way-laid through several nations, and even now scarce think myself secure. *Pope.*
Hate *dogs* their rise, and insult mocks their fall.
Vanity of Human Wishes.

DOG-TEETH. *n. s.* [*dog* and *teeth.*] The teeth in the human head next to the grinders; the eye-teeth.

The best instruments for dividing of herbs are incisor teeth; for cracking of hard substances, as bones and nuts, grinders, or mill-teeth; for dividing of flesh, sharp-pointed or *dog-teeth*. *Arbuthnot on Aliments.*

DOG-TRICK. *n. s.* [*dog* and *trick.*] An ill turn; surly or brutal treatment.

Learn better manners, or I shall serve you a *dog-trick*: come, down upon all four immediately; I'll make you know your rider. *Dryden's Don Sebastian.*

DO'GBANE. *n. s.* [*dog* and *bane.*]

The leaves are produced opposite by pairs upon the branches: the flower consists of one leaf, cut into several segments: from its flower-cup arises the pointal, fixed like a nail in the back-part of the flower. *Miller.*

DOGBERRY-TREE. See CORNELIAN-CHERRY.

DO'GBOLT. *n. s.* [*dog* and *bolt.*] Of this word I know not the meaning, unless it be, that when meal or flower is sifted or bolted to a certain degree, the coarser part is called *dogbolt*, or flower for *dogs*.

His only solace was, that now
His *dogbolt* fortune was so low,
That either it must quickly end,
Or turn about again, and mend. *Hudibras, p.* i. *cant.* 3.

DO'GBRIAR. *n. s.* [*dog* and *briar.*] The briar that bears the hip; the cynosbaton.

DOGCHEAP. *adj.* [*dog* and *cheap.*] Cheap as dogs meat; cheap as the offal bought for dogs.

Good store of harlots, say you, and *dogcheap?* *Dryden.*

DO'GDAYS. *n. s.* [*dog* and *days.*] The days in which the dogstar rises and sets with the sun, vulgarly reputed unwholesome.

Nor was it more in his power to be without promotion, and titles, and wealth, than for a healthy man to sit in the sun, in the brightest *dogdays,* and remain without warmth. *Clarendon.*

DO'GDRAW. *n. s.* [*dog* and *draw.*] A manifest deprehension of an offender against venison in the forest, when he is found drawing after a deer by the scent of a hound which he leads in his hand. *Cowel.*

DOGE. *n. s.* [*doge,* Italian] The title of the chief magistrate of Venice and Genoa.

Doria has a statue at the entrance of the *doge's* palace, with the title of deliverer of the commonwealth. *Addison.*

DO'GFISH. *n. s.* [from *dog* and *fish.*] Another name for a shark.

It is part of the jaw of a shark, or *dogfish.* *Woodward.*

DO'GFLY. *n. s.* [*dog* and *fly.*] A voracious biting fly.

Thump-buckler Mars began,
And at Minerva with a lance of brass he headlong ran;
These vile words ushering his blows, Thou *dogfly,* what's the cause
Thou mak'st gods fight thus? *Chapman's Iliad, b.* xxi.

DO'GGED. *adj.* [from *dog.*] Sullen; sour; morose; ill-humoured; gloomy.

Your uncle must not know but you are dead:
I'll fill these *dogged* spies with false reports. *Shakesp. K. John.*

Dogged York, that reaches at the moon,
Whose over-weening arm I have pluck'd back,
By false accuse doth level at my life. *Shakesp. Henry* VI.

Few miles on horseback had they jogged,
But fortune unto them turn'd *dogged.* *Hudibras, p.* i. *cant.* 1.

DO'GGEDLY. *adj.* [from *dogged.*] Sullenly; gloomily; sourly; morosely.

DO'GGEDNESS. *n. s.* [from *dogged.*] Gloom of mind; sullenness; moroseness.

DO'GGER. *n. s.* [from *dog,* for its meanness. *Skinner.*] A small ship with one mast.

DO'GGEREL. *adj.* [from *dog.*] Loosed from the measures of regular poetry; vile; despicable; mean.

Then hasten Og and Doeg to rehearse,
Two fools that crutch their feeble sense on verse;
Who by my muse, to all succeeding times,
Shall live in spite of their own *dogg'rel* rhymes. *Dryden.*

Your wit burlesque may one step higher climb,
And in his sphere may judge all *dogg'rel* rhyme. *Dryden.*

It is a dispute among the criticks, whether burlesque poetry runs best in heroick verse, like that of the Dispensary; or in *doggerel,* like that of Hudibras. *Addison's Spectator,* N°. 249.

DO'GGEREL. *n. s.* Mean, despicable, worthless verses.

The hand and head were never lost of those
Who dealt in *dogg'rel,* or who pin'd in prose. *Dryd. Juv.*

The vilest *dogg'rel* Grub-street sends,
Will pass for your's with foes and friends. *Swift.*

DO'GGISH. *adj.* [from *dog.*] Currish; brutal.

DOGHE'ARTED. *adj.* [*dog* and *heart.*] Cruel; pitiless; malicious.

His unkindness,
That stript her from his benediction, turn'd her
To foreign casualties, gave her dear rights
To his *doghearted* daughters. *Shakespeare's King Lear.*

DO'GHOLE. *n. s.* [*dog* and *hole.*] A vile hole; a mean habitation.

France is a *doghole,* and it no more merits the tread of a man's foot: to the wars. *Shakesp. All's well that ends well.*

But, could you be content to bid adieu
To the dear playhouse, and the players too,
Sweet country seats are purchas'd ev'ry where,
With lands and gardens, at less price than here;
You hire a darksom *doghole* by the year. *Dryden's Juv.*

Load some vain church with old theatrick state,
Turn arcs of triumph to a garden gate;
Reverse your ornaments, and hang them all
On some patch'd *doghole,* ek'd with ends of wall. *Pope.*

DOGKE'NNEL. *n. s.* [*dog* and *kennel.*] A little hut or house for dogs.

A certain nobleman, beginning with a *dogkennel,* never lived to finish the palace he had contrived. *Dryden.*

I am desired to recommend a *dogkennel* to any that shall want a pack. *Tatler,* N°. 62.

DO'GLOUSE. *n. s.* [*dog* and *louse.*] An insect that harbours on dogs.

DO'GMA. *n. s.* [Latin.] Established principle; settled notion.

Our poet was a stoick philosopher, and all his moral sentences are drawn from the *dogmas* of that sect. *Dryden.*

Dogma is that determination which consists in, and has a relation to, some casuistical point of doctrine, or some doctrinal part of the Christian faith. *Ayliffe's Parergon.*

DOGMA'TICAL. } *adj.* [from *dogma.*] Authoritative; magisterial; positive; in the manner of a philosopher laying down the first principles of a sect.
DOGMA'TICK. }

The dim and bounded intellect of man seldom prosperously adventures to be *dogmatical* about things that approach to infinite, whether in vastness or littleness. *Boyle.*

I laid by my natural diffidence and scepticism for a while, to take up that *dogmatical* way, which is so much his character. *Dryden.*

Learning gives us a discovery of our ignorance, and keeps us from being peremptory and *dogmatical* in our determinations. *Collier on Pride.*

Criticks write in a positive *dogmatick* way, without either language, genius, or imagination. *Spectator.*

One of these authors is indeed so grave, sententious, *dogmatical* a rogue, that there is no enduring him. *Swift.*

DOGMA'TICALLY. *adv.* [from *dogmatical.*] Magisterially; positively.

I shall not presume to interpose *dogmatically* in a controversy, which I look never to see decided. *South's Sermons.*

DOGMA'TICALNESS. *n. s.* [from *dogmatical.*] The quality of being dogmatical; magisterialness; mock authority.

DO'GMATIST. *n. s.* [*dogmatiste,* Fr.] A magisterial teacher; a positive asserter; a bold advancer of principles.

I could describe the poverty of our intellectual acquisitions, and the vanity of bold opinion, which the *dogmatists* themselves demonstrate in all the controversies they are engaged in. *Glanville's Sceps.*

A *dogmatist* in religion is not a great way off from a bigot, and is in high danger of growing up to be a bloody persecutor. *Watts's Improvement of the Mind.*

To DO'GMATIZE. *v. n.* [from *dogma.*] To assert positively; to advance without distrust; to teach magisterially.

These, with the pride of *dogmatizing* schools,
Impos'd on nature arbitrary rules;
Forc'd her their vain inventions to obey,
And move as learned frenzy trac'd the way. *Blackmore.*

DOGMATI'ZER. *n. s.* [from *dogmatize.*] An asserter; a magisterial teacher; a bold advancer of opinions.

Such opinions, being not entered into the confessions of our church, are not properly chargeable either on Papists or Protestants, but on particular *dogmatizers* of both parties. *Hamm.*

DO'GROSE. *n. s.* [*dog* and *rose.*] The flower of the hip.

Of the rough or hairy excrescence, those on the briar, or *dogrose,* are a good instance. *Derham's Physico-Theology.*

DO'GSLEEP. *n. s.* [*dog* and *sleep.*] Pretended sleep.

Juvenal indeed mentions a drowsy husband, who raised an estate by snoring; but then he is represented to have slept what the common people call *dogsleep.* *Addison's Spectator.*

DO'GSMEAT. *n. s.* [*dog* and *meat.*] Refuse; vile stuff; offal like the flesh sold to feed dogs.

His reverence bought of me the flower of all the market; these are but *dogsmeat* to 'em. *Dryden.*

DO'GSTAR. *n. s.* [*dog* and *star*; *canicula,* Lat.] The star which gives the name to the dogdays.

All shun the raging *dogstar's* sultry heat,
And from the half-unpeopled town retreat. *Addison.*

DO'GSTOOTH. *n. s.* [from *dog* and *tooth.*] A plant.

It hath a fleshy root, shaped like a dog's tooth: the leaves are broad, and spread upon the ground: the flower is naked, and produced single upon each stalk, each consisting of six leaves, shaped like a lily, and hanging downward. The pointal of the flower becomes a roundish fruit, containing oblong seeds: they produce their flowers early in March, for which they are valued. *Miller.*

DO'GTROT. *n. s.* [*dog* and *trot.*] A gentle trot like that of a dog.

This said, they both advanc'd, and rode
A *dogtrot* through the bawling crowd. *Hudibras, p.* ii.

DO'GWEARY. *adj.* [*dog* and *weary.*] Tired as a dog; excessively weary.

Oh, master, master, I have watch'd so long,
That I'm *dogweary.* *Shakesp. Taming of the Shrew.*

DO'GWOOD. See CORNELIAN-CHERRY, of which it is a species.

DO'ILY. *n. s.* A species of woollen stuff, so called, I suppose, from the name of the first maker.

We should be as weary of one set of acquaintance, though never so good, as we are of one suit, though never so fine: a fool, and a *doily* stuff, would now and then find days of grace, and be worn for variety. *Congreve's Way of the World.*

DO'INGS. *n. s.* [from *To do.* This word has hardly any singular.]

1. Things

1. Things done; events; transactions.

I have but kill'd a fly.
——But! how if that fly had a father and mother?
How would he hang his slender gilded wings,
And buz lamented *doings* in the air? *Shakesp. Tit. Andron.*

2. Feats; actions: good or bad.

The next degree was to mark all Zelmane's *doings*, speeches and fashions, and to take them unto herself, as a pattern of worthy proceeding. *Sidney, b.* ii.

If I'm traduc'd by tongues which neither know
My faculties nor person, yet will be
The chronicles of my *doing*; let me say
'Tis but the fate of place, and the rough brake
That virtue must go through. *Shakespeare's Henry* VIII.

At length a reverend sire among them came,
And of their *doings* great dislike declar'd,
And testify'd against their ways. *Milton's Paradise Lost.*

3. Behaviour; conduct.

Never the earth on his round shoulders bare,
A maid train'd up from high or low degree,
That in her *doings* better could compare
Mirth with respect, few words with curtesy. *Sidney.*

4. Conduct; dispensation.

After such miraculous *doings*, we are not yet in a condition of bringing France to our terms. *Swift.*

Dangerous it were for the feeble brains of man to wade far into the *doings* of the Most High. *Hooker, b.* i. *s.* 1.

5. Stir; bustle; tumult.

Shall there be then, in the mean while, no *doings?* *Hooker.*

6. Festivity; merriment.

7. This word is now only used in a ludicrous sense, or in low mean language.

DOIT. *n. s.* [*duyt*, Dutch; *doyght*, Erse.] A small piece of money.

When they will not give a *doit* to relieve a lame beggar, they will lay out ten to see a dead Indian. *Shakesp. Tempest.*

In Anna's wars a soldier, poor and old,
Had dearly earn'd a little purse of gold;
Tir'd with a tedious march, one luckless night
He slept, poor dog! and lost it to a *doit*. *Pope.*

DOLE. *n. s.* [from *deal*; ðælan, Saxon.]

1. The act of distribution or dealing.

The personal fruition in any man cannot reach to feel great riches: there is a custody of them, or a power of *dole* and donative of them, or a fame of them, but no solid use to the owner. *Bacon, Essay* 35.

At her general *dole*
Each receives his ancient soul. *Cleveland.*

2. Any thing dealt out or distributed.

Now, my masters, happy man be his *dole* say I; every man to his business. *Shakespeare's Henry* IV. *p.* i.

Let us, that are unhurt and whole,
Fall on, and happy man be's *dole*. *Hudibras, p.* i. *cant.* 3.

3. Provisions or money distributed in charity.

They had such firm dependance on the day,
That Need grew pamper'd, and forgot to pray;
So sure the *dole*, so ready at their call,
They stood prepar'd to see the manna fall. *Dryden.*

Clients of old were feasted; now a poor
Divided *dole* is dealt at th' outward door,
Which by the hungry rout is soon dispatch'd. *Dryd. Juven.*

4. Blows dealt out.

It was your presurmise,
That in the *dole* of blows your son might drop. *Sh. H.* IV.

What if his eye-sight, for to Israel's God
Nothing is hard, by miracle restor'd,
He now be dealing *dole* among his foes,
And over heaps of slaughter'd walk his way? *Milt. Agonist.*

5. [from *dolor.*] Grief; sorrow; misery.

Yonder they lie; the poor old man, their father, making such pitiful *dole* over them, that all beholders take his part with weeping. *Shakespeare's As you like it.*

Our sometime sister, now our queen,
Have we, as 'twere, with a defeated joy,
With mirth in funeral, and with dirge in marriage,
In equal scale weighing delight and *dole*,
Taken to wife. *Shakespeare's Hamlet.*

They might hope to change
Torment with ease, and soonest recompense
Dole with delight. *Milton's Paradise Lost, b.* iv. *l.* 892.

To DOLE. *v. a.* [from the noun] To deal; to distribute. *Dict.*

DOLE. *n. s.* Void space left in tillage. *Dict.*

DO'LEFUL. *adj.* [*dole* and *full.*]

1. Sorrowful; dismal; expressing grief.

She earnestly intreated to know the cause thereof, that either she might comfort, or accompany her *doleful* humour. *Sidney.*

For none but you, or who of you it learns,
Can rightfully aread so *doleful* lay. *Spens. Tears of the Muses.*

With screwed face, and *doleful* whine, they only ply with senseless harangues of conscience against carnal ordinances. *South's Sermons.*

Just then the hero cast a *doleful* cry,
And in those absent flames began to fry:
The blind contagion rag'd within his veins. *Dryd. Fables.*

2. Melancholy; afflicted; feeling grief.

How oft my *doleful* sire cry'd to me, tarry, son,
When first he spyed my love! *Sidney, b.* i.

3. Dismal; impressing sorrow.

It watereth the heart, to the end it may fructify; maketh the virtuous, in trouble, full of magnanimity and courage; serveth as a most approved remedy against all *doleful* and heavy accidents, which befall men in this present life. *Hooker, b.* v.

From those flames
No light, but rather darkness visible,
Serv'd only to discover sights of woe,
Regions of sorrow! *doleful* shades! where peace
And rest can never dwell! *Milton's Paradise Lost, b.* i.

Happy the mortal man! who now at last
Has through this *doleful* vale of mis'ry past;
Who to his destin'd stage has carry'd on
The tedious load, and laid his burden down. *Prior.*

DO'LEFULLY. *adv.* [from *doleful.*] In a doleful manner; sorrowfully; dismally; querulously.

DO'LEFULNESS. *n. s.* [from *doleful.*]

1. Sorrow; melancholy.

2. Querulousness.

3. Dismalness.

DO'LESOME. *adj.* [from *dole.*] Melancholy; gloomy; dismal; sorrowful; doleful.

Hell-ward bending o'er the beach descry
The *dolesome* passage to th' infernal sky. *Pope's Odyssey, b.* ii.

DO'LESOMELY. *adv.* [from *dolesome.*] In a dolesome manner.

DO'LESOMENESS. *n. s.* [from *dolesome.*] Gloom; melancholy; dismalness.

DOLL. *n. s.*

1. A contraction of Dorothy.

2. A little girl's puppet or baby.

DO'LLAR. *n. s.* [*daler*, Dutch.] A Dutch and German coin of different value, from about two shillings and sixpence to four and sixpence.

He disburs'd, at St. Colmeskill isle,
Ten thousand *dollars* for our gen'ral use. *Shakesp. Macbeth.*

DOLORI'FICK. *adj.* [*dolorificus*, Latin.] That which causes grief or pain.

The pain then by degrees returned, which I could attribute to nothing but the dissipating that vapour which obstructed the nerves, and giving the *dolorifick* motion free passage again. *Ray on the Creation.*

This, by the softness and rarity of the fluid, is insensible, and not *dolorifick*. *Arbuthnot on Air.*

DO'LOROUS. *adj.* [from *dolor*, Latin.]

1. Sorrowful; doleful; dismal; gloomy.

We are taught by his example, that the presence of *dolorous* and dreadful objects, even in minds most perfect, may, as clouds, overcast all seasonable joy. *Hooker, b.* v. *s.* 48.

You take me in too *dolorous* a sense:
I spake t'you for your comfort. *Shak. Anth. and Cleopatra.*

Through many a dark and dreary vale
They pass'd, and many a region *dolorous*,
O'er many a frozen, many a fiery alp,
Rocks, caves, lakes, fens, bogs, dens, and shades of death.
Milton's Paradise Lost, b. ii. *l.* 618.

Talk not of ruling in this *dol'rous* gloom,
Nor think vain words, he cry'd, can ease my doom. *Pope.*

2. Painful.

Their dispatch is quick, and less *dolorous* than the paw of the bear, or teeth of the lion. *More's Antidote against Atheism.*

DO'LOUR. *n. s.* [*dolor*, Latin.]

1. Grief; sorrow.

I've words too few to take my leave of you,
When the tongue's office should be prodigal,
To breathe th' abundant *dolour* of the heart. *Shakes. R.* II.

2. Lamentation; complaint.

3. Pain; pang.

A mind fixed and bent upon somewhat that is good, doth avert the *dolours* of death. *Bacon, Essay* 2.

DO'LPHIN. *n. s.* [*delphin*, Latin; though the dolphin is supposed to be not the same fish.] The name of a fish.

His delights
Were *dolphin* like; they shew'd his back above
The element they liv'd in. *Shakes. Anth. and Cleopatra.*

You may draw boys riding upon goats, eagles, and *dolphins*. *Peacham on Drawing.*

DOLT. *n. s.* [*dol*, Teutonick.] A heavy stupid fellow; a blockhead; a thickscul; a loggerhead.

Let *dolts* in haste some altar fair erect
To those high powers, which idlely sit above. *Sidney, b.* ii.

Thou hast not half that power to do me harm,
As I have to be hurt: oh, gull! oh, *dolt!*
As ignorant as dirt! *Shakespeare's Othello.*

Like men condemn'd to thunder-bolts,
Who, ere the blow, become mere *dolts*;

And

They neither have the hearts to ſtay,
Nor wit enough to run away. *Hudibras, p.* iii. *cant.* 2.
Wood's adult'rate copper,
Which, as he ſcatter'd, we, like *dolts*,
Miſtook at firſt for thunder-bolts. *Swift.*

DO'LTISH. *adj.* [from *dolt.*] Stupid; mean; dull; blockiſh.
Dametas, the moſt arrant *doltiſh* clown, that ever was without the privilege of a bauble. *Sidney.*

DO'MABLE. *adj.* [*domabilis*, Latin.] Tameable. *Dict.*

DOMA'IN. *n. ſ.* [*domaine*, French, from *dominium*, Latin.]
1. Dominion; empire.
Rome's great emperor, whoſe wide *domain*
Had ample territory, wealth and pow'r. *Milt. Parad. Reg.*
Ocean trembles for his green *domain.* *Thomſon.*
2. Poſſeſſion; eſtate.
A Latian field, with fruitful plains,
And a large portion of the king's *domains.* *Dryden's Æn.*

DOME. *n. ſ.* [*dome*, French, from *domus*, Latin.]
1. A building; a houſe; a fabrick.
Beſt be he call'd among good men,
Who to his God this column rais'd:
Though lightning ſtrike the *dome* again,
The man who built it ſhall be prais'd. *Prior.*
Stranger! whoe'er thou art, ſecurely reſt,
Affianc'd in my faith, a friendly gueſt:
Approach the *dome*, the ſocial banquet ſhare,
And then the purpoſe of thy ſoul declare. *Pope's Odyſſey.*
2. A hemiſpherical arch; a cupola.

DOME'STICAL. } DOME'STICK. } *adj.* [*domeſticus*, Latin.]
1. Belonging to the houſe; not relating to things publick.
The neceſſities of man had at the firſt no other helps and ſupplies than *domeſtical*; ſuch as that which the prophet implyeth, ſaying, can a mother forget her child? *Hooker.*
The practical knowledge of the *domeſtick* duties is the principal glory of a woman. *Clariſſa.*
2. Private; done at home; not open.
In this their *domeſtical* celebration of the Paſſover, they divided ſupper into two courſes. *Hooker, b.* iii.
Beholding thus, O, happy as a queen!
We cry; but ſhift the gaudy, flattering ſcene,
View her at home in her *domeſtick* light,
For thither ſhe muſt come, at leaſt at night. *Granville.*
3. Inhabiting the houſe; not wild.
The faithful prudent huſband is an honeſt, tractable, and *domeſtick* animal. *Addiſon's Spectator*, Nº. 128.
4. Not foreign; inteſtine.
Domeſtical evils, for that we think we can maſter them at all times, are often permitted to run on forward, 'till it be too late to recall them. *Hooker, Dedication.*
Equality of two *domeſtick* pow'rs
Breeds ſcrupulous faction. *Shakeſpeare's Anth. and Cleopatra.*
Combine together 'gainſt the enemy;
For theſe *domeſtick* and particular broils
Are not the queſtion here. *Shakeſpeare's King Lear.*
Next to the ſin of thoſe who began that rebellion, theirs muſt needs be who hindered the ſpeedy ſuppreſſing of it, by *domeſtick* diſſentions. *King Charles.*
Such they were, who might preſume t' have done
Much for the king and honour of the ſtate;
Having the chiefeſt actions undergone,
Both foreign and *domeſtical* of late. *Daniel's Civil War.*

To DOME'STICATE. *v. a.* [from *domeſtick.*] To make domeſtick; to withdraw from the publick. *Clariſſa.*

DOME'STICK. *n. ſ.* One kept in the ſame houſe.
A ſervant dwells remote from all knowledge of his lord's purpoſes: he lives as a kind of foreigner under the ſame roof; a *domeſtick*, and yet a ſtranger too. *South's Sermons.*

To DO'MIFY. *v. a.* [*domifico*, Latin.] To tame. *Dict.*

DO'MINANT. *adj.* [*dominant*, French; *dominans*, Latin.] Predominant; preſiding; aſcendant.

To DO'MINATE. *v. a.* [*dominatus*, Lat.] To predominate; to prevail over the reſt.
I thus conclude my theme,
The *dominating* humour makes the dream. *Dryden.*

DOMINA'TION. *n. ſ.* [*dominatio*, Latin.]
1. Power; dominion.
Thou and thine uſurp
The *domination*, royalties, and rights
Of this oppreſſed boy. *Shakeſpeare's King John.*
2. Tyranny; inſolent authority.
Maximinus traded with the Goths in the product of his own eſtate in Thracia, the place of his nativity, whither he retired, to withdraw from the unjuſt *domination* of Opilius Macrinus. *Arbuthnot on Coins.*
3. One highly exalted in power: uſed of angelick beings.
He heav'n of heav'ns, and all the pow'rs therein,
By thee created; and by thee threw down
Th' aſpiring *dominations.* *Milton's Paradiſe Loſt, b.* iii.
Hear all ye angels, progeny of light,
Thrones, *dominations*, princedoms, virtues, pow'rs. *Milton.*

DO'MINATIVE. *adj.* [from *dominate.*] Imperious; inſolent. *Dict.*

DOMINA'TOR. *n. ſ.* [Latin.] The preſiding or predominant power or influence.
Jupiter and Mars are *dominators* for this North-weſt part of the world, which maketh the people impatient of ſervitude, lovers of liberty, martial and courageous. *Camden's Remains.*

To DOMINE'ER. *v. n.* [*dominor*, Latin.] To rule with inſolence; to ſwell; to bluſter; to act without control.
Go to the feaſt, revel and *domineer*,
Carowſe full meaſure. *Shakeſp. Taming of the Shrew.*
The voice of conſcience now is low and weak, chaſtiſing the paſſions, as old Eli did his luſtful *domineering* ſons. *South.*
Both would their little ends ſecure;
He ſighs for freedom, ſhe for pow'r:
His wiſhes tend abroad to roam,
And her's to *domineer* at home. *Prior.*

DOMI'NICAL. *adj.* [*dominicalis*, Latin.] That which notes the Lord's day, or Sunday.
The cycle of the moon ſerves to ſhew the epacts, and that of the ſun the *dominical* letter, throughout all their variations. *Holder on Time.*

DOMI'NION. *n. ſ.* [*dominium*, Latin.]
1. Sovereign authority; unlimited power.
They on the earth
Dominion exerciſe, and in the air,
Chiefly on man. *Milton's Par. Loſt.*
He gave us only over beaſt, fiſh, fowl,
Dominion abſolute; that right we hold
By his donation: but man over man
He made not lord. *Milton.*
Bleſt uſe of pow'r, O virtuous pride in kings!
And like his bounty, whence *dominion* ſprings. *Tickell.*
2. Power; right of poſſeſſion or uſe, without being accountable.
He could not have private *dominion* over that, which was under the private *dominion* of another. *Locke.*
3. Territory; region; ſubject; diſtrict.
The donations of biſhopricks were a flower of the crown, which the kings of England did ever retain in all their *dominions*, when the pope's uſurped authority was at the higheſt. *Davies on Ireland.*
4. Predominance; aſcendant.
Objects placed foremoſt ought to be more finiſhed than thoſe caſt behind, and to have *dominion* over things confuſed and tranſient. *Dryden's Dufreſnoy.*
5. An order of angels.
By him were all things created, viſible and inviſible, whether they be thrones or *dominions*, or principalities or powers. *Col.* i. 16.

DON. *n. ſ.* [*dominus*, Latin.] The Spaniſh title for a gentleman; as, *don* Quixote.

To DON. *v. a.* [*To do on.*] To put on; to inveſt one with.
The purple morning left her crimſon bed,
And *don'd* her robes of pure vermilion hue. *Fairfax, b.* iii.
Her helm the virgin *don'd.* *Fairfax, b.* i. *ſtan.* 48.
What! ſhould I *don* this robe, and trouble you? *Shakeſp.*

DO'NARY. *n. ſ.* [*donarium*, Latin.] A thing given to ſacred uſes.

DONA'TION. *n. ſ.* [*donatio*, Latin.]
1. The act of giving any thing; the act of beſtowing.
He gave us only over beaſt, fiſh, fowl
Dominion abſolute; that right we hold
By his *donation.* *Milton's Paradiſe Loſt, b.* xii.
After *donation* there is an abſolute change and alienation made of the property of the thing given, and that as to the uſe of it too; which being ſo alienated, a man has no more to do with it than with a thing bought with another's money. *South's Sermons.*
2. The grant by which any thing is given or conferred.
Howſoever the letter of that *donation* may be unregarded by men, yet the ſenſe thereof is ſo imprinted in their hearts, as if every one laid claim for himſelf unto that which was conferred upon all. *Raleigh's Eſſays.*
The kingdoms of the world to thee were giv'n,
Permitted rather, and by thee uſurp'd,
Other *donation* none thou can'ſt produce. *Milt. Par. Reg.*

DO'NATIVE. *n. ſ.* [*donatif*, French, from *donatus*, Latin.]
1. A gift; a largeſs; a preſent; a dole of money diſtributed.
The Roman emperor's cuſtom was, at certain ſolemn times, to beſtow on his ſoldiers a *donative*; which *donative* they received, wearing garlands upon their heads. *Hooker.*
They were entertained with publick ſhows and *donatives*, to make them more eaſily digeſt their loſt liberty. *Dryden.*
2. [In law.] A benefice merely given and collated by the patron to a man, without either preſentation to the ordinary, or inſtitution by the ordinary, or induction by his orders. *Cowel.*
Never did ſteeple carry double truer;
His is the *donative*, and mine the cure. *Cleveland.*

DONE. *part. paſſ.* of the verb. To do.
Another like fair tree eke grew thereby,
Whereof who ſo did eat, eftſoons did know
Both good and evil: O mournful memory!
That tree, through one man's fault, hath *done* us all to dye.
Fairy Queen, b. i. *cant.* 11. *ſtanz.* 47.

DONE. *a kind of interjection.* The word by which a wager is concluded; when a wager is offered, he that accepts it says *done.*

Done: the wager? *Shakespeare's Tempest.*

One thing, sweet-heart, I will ask;
Take me for a new-fashion'd mask.
—*Done*: but my bargain shall be this,
I'll throw my mask off when I kiss. *Cleveland.*

'Twas *done* and *done*, and the fox, by consent, was to be the judge. *L'Estrange, Fab.* 133.

DO'NJON. *n. s.* [now corrupted to *dungeon*, from *domnionum*, low Latin, according to *Menage.*] The highest and strongest tower of the castle, in which prisoners were kept; as in *Chaucer.*

The grete toure, that was so thicke and strong,
Which of the castle was the chief *dongeon*,
Wherein the knightes were in prison,
Was evin joynant to the garden-wall,
Ther as this Emely had her playeing. *Chaucer.*

DO'NOR. *n. s.* [from *dono*, Latin.] A giver; a bestower; one who gives any thing.

Litters thick besiege the *donor*'s gate,
And begging lords and teeming ladies wait
The promis'd dole. *Dryden's Juvenal, Sat.* i.

It is a mighty check to beneficent tempers to consider how often good designs are frustrated by an ill execution of them, and perverted to purposes, which, could the *donors* themselves have foreseen, they would have been very loth to promote. *Atterbury's Sermons.*

DO'ODLE. *n. s.* [a cant word, perhaps corrupted from *do little*, *Faineant.*] A trifler; an idler.

To DOOM. *v. a.* [ꝺeman, Saxon.]

1. To judge.

Him through malice fall'n,
Father of mercy and grace! thou did'st not *doom*
So strictly, but much more to pity incline. *Milt. Par. Lost.*

2. To condemn to any punishment; to sentence.

He may be *doom'd* to chains, to shame, to death,
While proud Hippolitus shall mount his throne. *Smith.*

Justly th' impartial fates conspire,
Dooming that son to be the sire
Of such another son. *Granville.*

3. To pronounce condemnation upon any.

Minos, the strict inquisitor, appears,
And lives and crimes, with his assessors, hears;
Round in his urn the blended balls he rolls,
Absolves the just, and *dooms* the guilty souls. *Dryden's Æn.*

4. To command judicially or authoritatively.

Have I a tongue to *doom* my brother's death?
And shall that tongue give pardon to a slave? *Shakespeare.*

5. To destine; to command by uncontrolable authority.

Fate and the gods, by their supreme command,
Have *doom'd* our ships to seek the Latian land. *Dryd. Æn.*

I have no will but what your eyes ordain;
Destin'd to love, as they are *doom'd* to reign. *Granville.*

DOOM. *n. s.* [ꝺom, Saxon; *doem*, Dutch.]

1. Judicial sentence; judgment.

He's fled, my lord, and all his pow'rs do yield;
And humbly thus, with halters on their necks,
Expect your highness' *doom* of life or death. *Shakesp. H.* VI.

To Satan, first in sin, his *doom* apply'd,
Though in mysterious terms, judg'd as then best. *Milton.*

And now, without redemption, all mankind
Must have been lost, adjudg'd to death and hell
By *doom* severe. *Milton's Paradise Lost, b.* iii. *l.* 224.

In the great day, wherein the secrets of all hearts shall be laid open, no one shall be made to answer for what he knows nothing of; but shall receive his *doom*, his conscience accusing or excusing him. *Locke.*

2. The great and final judgment.

Search Windsor-castle, elves within and out:
Strew good luck, Ouphes, on every sacred room,
That it may stand 'till the perpetual *doom.* *Shakespeare.*

3. Condemnation.

Revoke thy *doom*,
Or whilst I can vent clamour from my throat,
I'll tell thee thou do'st evil. *Shakespeare's King Lear.*

4. Determination declared.

If friend or foe, let him be gently used.
—Revoke that *doom* of mercy; for 'tis Clifford. *Sh. H.* VI.

5. The state to which one is destined.

By day the web and loom,
And homely houshold-task, shall be her *doom.* *Dryd. Iliad.*

6. Ruin; destruction.

From the same foes, at last, both felt their *doom*,
And the same age saw learning fall, and Rome. *Pope.*

DO'OMSDAY. *n. s.* [*doom* and *day.*] The day of final and universal judgment; the last, the great day.

Men, wives, and children stare, cry out, and run,
As it were *doomsday.* *Shakespeare's Julius Cæsar.*

They may serve for any theme, and never be out of date until *doomsday.* *Brown's Vulgar Errours, b.* i. *c.* 6.

Our souls, not yet prepar'd for upper light,
'Till *doomsday* wander in the shades of night:
This only holiday of all the year,
We privileg'd in sunshine may appear. *Dryden.*

2. The day of sentence or condemnation.

All-souls day is my body's *doomsday.* *Shakespeare's R.* III.

DOOMSDAY-BOOK. *n. s.* [*doomsday* and *book.*] A book made by order of William the Conqueror, in which the estates of the kingdom were registered

The Danes also brought in a reckoning of money by *ores*, *per oras*, which is mentioned in *doomsday-book.* *Camden.*

DOOR. *n. s.* [ꝺoꞃ, ꝺuꞃe, Saxon; *dorris*, Erse.]

1. The gate of a house; that which opens to yield entrance. *Door* is used of houses and *gates* of cities, or publick buildings, except in the licence of poetry.

All the castle quaked from the ground,
And every *door* of free-will open flew. *Fairy Queen, b.* i.

In the side a *door*
Contriv'd; and of provisions laid in large,
For man and beast. *Milton's Paradise Lost, b.* xi.

To the same end men sev'ral paths may tread,
As many *doors* into one temple lead. *Denham.*

For without rules there can be no art, any more than there can be a house without a *door* to conduct you in. *Dryd. Dufres.*

2. In familiar language, a house.

Lay one piece of flesh or fish in the open air, and another of the same kind and bigness within *doors.* *Bacon's Nat. Hist.*

Let him doubt whether his cloaths be warm, and so go naked; whether his house be firm, and live without *doors.* *Decay of Piety.*

Martin's office is now the second *door* in the street, where he will see Parnel. *Arbuth.*

Lambs, though they are bred within *doors*, and never saw the actions of their own species, push at those who approach them with their foreheads. *Addison's Spectator*, N°. 121.

The sultan entered again the peasant's house, and turned the owner out of *doors.* *Addison's Guardian*, N°. 99.

3. Entrance; portal.

The tender blades of grass appear,
And buds, that yet the blast of Eurus fear,
Stand at the *door* of life, and doubt to clothe the year. *Dry.*

4. Passage; avenue; means of approach.

The indispensable necessity of sincere obedience, shuts the *door* against all temptations to carnal security. *Hammond.*

5. *Out of* DOOR, *or* DOORS. No more to be found; quite gone; fairly sent away.

Should he, who was thy lord, command thee now,
With a harsh voice and supercilious brow,
To servile duties, thou would'st fear no more;
The gallows and the whip are *out of door.* *Dryden's Pers.*

His imaginary title of fatherhood is *out of doors*, and Cain is no prince over his brother. *Locke.*

6. *At the* DOOR *of any one.* Imputable; chargeable upon him.

In any of which parts, if I have failed, the fault lies wholly *at my door.* *Dryden's Dufresnoy, Preface.*

7. *Next* DOOR *to.* Approaching to; near to; bordering upon.

A seditious word leads to a broil, and a riot unpunished is but *next door* to a tumult. *L'Estrange.*

DO'ORCASE. *n. s.* [*door* and *case.*] The frame in which the door is inclosed.

The making of frames for *doorcases*, is the framing of two pieces of wood athwart two other pieces. *Mox. Mech. Exer.*

DO'ORKEEPER. *n. s.* [*door* and *keeper.*] Porter; one that keeps the entrance of a house.

He that hath given the following assistances to thee, desires to be even a *doorkeeper* in God's house, and to be a servant to the meanest of God's servants. *Taylor's Preface.*

DO'QUET. *n. s.* A paper containing a warrant.

Before the institution of this form and office, no writ of covenant for the levying any final concord in chief, no *doquet* for licence to alien, nor warrant for pardon of alienation made, could be purchased and gotten, without an oath called an affidavit. *Bacon's Office of Alienation.*

DO'RMANT. *adj.* [*dormant*, French.]

1. Sleeping.

He a dragon! if he be, 'tis a very peaceful one: I can insure his anger is *dormant*; or should he seem to rouse, 'tis well lashing him, and he will sleep like a top. *Cong. Old Batchelor.*

2. In a sleeping posture.

If a lion were the coat of Judah, yet were it not a lion rampant, but rather couchant and *dormant.* *Brown's Vulg. Err.*

With this radius he is said to strike and kill his prey, for which he lies, as it were, *dormant*, 'till it swims within his reach. *Grew's Musæum.*

3. Private; not publick.

There were other *dormant* musters of soldiers throughout all parts of the realm, that were put in readiness, but not drawn together. *Bacon's War with Spain.*

4. Concealed; not divulged.

It would be prudent to reserve these privileges *dormant*, never to be produced but upon great occasions. *Swift.*

5. Leaning; not perpendicular.

Old *dormant* windows muſt confeſs
Her beams: their glimmering ſpectacles,
Struck with the ſplendor of her face,
Do th' office of a burning-glaſs. *Cleveland.*

DO'RMITORY. *n. ſ.* [*dormitorium*, Latin.]

1. A place to ſleep in: uſed commonly for a room with many beds.

Rooms that have thorough lights are left for entertainment, and thoſe that have windows on one ſide for *dormitories. Mort.*

Naked mourns the *dormitory* wall,
And Jones and Boyle's united labours fall. *Pope's Dunciad.*

2. A burial place.

The places where dead bodies are buried, are in Latin called *cœmiteria*, and in Engliſh *dormitories.* *Ayliffe's Parergon.*

DO'RMOUSE. *n. ſ.* [*dormio*, to ſleep, and *mouſe.*] A ſmall animal which paſſes a large part of the Winter in ſleep.

Come, we all ſleep, and are mere *dormice* flies,
A little leſs than dead: more dulneſs hangs
On us than on the moon. *Ben. Johnſon's Catiline.*

After they have lain a little while they grow as drowſy as *dormice*, unleſs they are rouſed. *Collier on Thought.*

DORN. *n. ſ.* [from *dorn*, German, a thorn.] The name of a fiſh; perhaps the ſame as the thornback.

The coaſt is ſtored both with ſhellfiſh, as ſcallops and ſheathfiſh, and flat, as turbets, *dorns*, and holybut. *Carew.*

DO'RNICK. *n. ſ.* [of *Deornick* in *Flanders*, where firſt made.] A ſpecies of linen cloath uſed in Scotland for the table.

To DORR. *v. a.* [*tor*, ſtupid, Teutonick.] To deafen or ſtupify with noiſe. This word I find only in *Skinner.*

DORR. *n. ſ.* [ſo named probably from the noiſe which he makes.] A kind of flying inſect, remarkable for flying with a loud noiſe.

The *dorr*, or hedge-chafer's chief marks are theſe: his head is ſmall, like that of the common beetle: this and his eyes black: his ſhoulder-piece, and the middle of his belly, alſo black; but juſt under the wing-ſhells ſpotted with white. His wing-ſhells, legs, and the end of his tail, which is long and flat-pointed, of a light cheſnut: his breaſt, eſpecially, covered with a downy hair. *Grew's Muſæum.*

DO'RSEL. } *n. ſ.* [from *dorſum*, the back.] A pannier; a baſket
DO'RSER. } or bag, one of which hangs on either ſide a beaſt of burthen, for the reception of things of ſmall bulk.

DORSI'FEROUS. } *n. ſ.* [*dorſum* and *fero*, or *pario*, Latin.]
DORSI'PAROUS. } Having the property of bearing or bringing forth on the back. It is uſed of plants that have the ſeeds on the back of their leaves, as fern; and may be properly uſed of the American frog, which brings forth young from her back.

DO'RTURE. *n. ſ.* [contracted from *dormiture*; *dormitura*, Lat. *dortoir*, French.] A dormitory; a place to ſleep in.

He led us to a gallery like a *dorture*, where he ſhewed us along the one ſide, for the other was but wall and window, ſeventeen cells, very neat, having partitions of cedar-wood. *Bacon's New Atlantis.*

DOSE. *n. ſ.* [δόσις.]

1. So much of any medicine as is taken at one time. *Quincy.*

The too vig'rous *doſe* too fiercely wrought,
And added fury to the ſtrength it brought. *Dryden's Virgil.*

In a vehement pain of the head he preſcribed the juice of the thapſia in warm water, without mentioning the *doſe.* *Arbuthnot.*

2. As much of any thing as falls to a man's lot.

No ſooner does he peep into
The world, but he has done his doe;
Married his punctual *doſe* of wives,
Is cuckolded, and breaks, or thrives. *Hudibras, p.* ii.

3. It is often uſed of the utmoſt quantity of ſtrong liquor that a man can ſwallow. He has his *doſe*, that is, he can carry off no more.

To DOSE. *v. a.*

1. To proportion a medicine properly to the patient or diſeaſe.

Plants ſeldom uſed in medicine, being eſteemed poiſonous, if corrected, and exactly *doſed*, may prove powerful medicines. *Derham's Phyſico-Theology.*

2. To give phyſick to any man in a ludicrous ſenſe.

DO'SSIL. *n. ſ.* [corrupted from *dorſel*, ſomething laid upon the part.] A pledget; a nodule or lump of lint, to be laid on a ſore.

Her complaints put me upon dreſſing with ſuch medicaments as baſilicon, with præcipitate, upon a *doſſil.* *Wiſeman.*

DOST. [the ſecond perſon of *do.*]

Why then *doſt* treat me with rebukes, inſtead
Of kind condoling cares, and friendly ſorrow? *Addiſ. Cato.*

DOT. *n. ſ.* [This is derived by *Skinner* from *dotter*, German, *the white of an egg*, and interpreted by him a grume of pus. It has now no ſuch ſignification, and ſeems rather corrupted from *jot*, a point.] A ſmall point or ſpot made to mark any place in a writing.

To DOT. *v. n.* [from the noun.] To make dots, or ſpots.

DO'TAGE. *n. ſ.* [from *dote.*]

1. Loſs of underſtanding; imbecillity of mind; deliriouſneſs.

The ſoul in all hath one intelligence;
Though too much moiſture in an infant's brain,
And too much drineſs in an old man's ſenſe,
Cannot the prints of outward things retain:
Then doth the ſoul want work, and idle ſit,
And this we childiſhneſs and *dotage* call. *Davies.*

I hold, that perfect joy makes all our parts
As joyful as our hearts:
Our ſenſes tell us, if we pleaſe not them,
Our love is but a *dotage*, or a dream. *Suckling.*

2. Exceſſive fondneſs.

If on your head my fury does not turn,
Thank that fond *dotage* which ſo much you ſcorn. *Dryden.*

DO'TAL. *adj.* [*dotalis*, Latin.] Relating to the portion of a woman; conſtituting her portion; compriſed in her portion.

Shall I, of one poor *dotal* town poſſeſt,
My people thin, my wretched country waſte?
An exil'd prince, and on a ſhaking throne,
Or riſk my patron's ſubjects, or my own? *Garth's Ovid.*

DO'TARD. *n. ſ.* [from *dote.*] A man whoſe age has impaired his intellects; a man in his ſecond childhood; called in ſome provinces a *twichild.*

Dotard, ſaid he, let be thy deep adviſe,
Seems that through many years thy wits thee fail,
And that weak old hath left thee nothing wiſe,
Elſe never ſhould thy judgement be ſo frail. *Fairy Queen.*

The ſickly *dotard* wants a wife,
To draw off his laſt dregs of life. *Prior.*

DOTA'TION. *n. ſ.* [*dotatio*, Latin.] The act of giving a dowry or portion. *Dict.*

To DOTE. *v. n.* [*doten*, Dutch; *radoter*, French.]

1. To have the intellect impaired by age or paſſion; to be delirious.

Unleſs the fear of death make me *dote*,
I ſee my ſon. *Shakeſp. Com. of Err.*

A ſword is upon the liars, and they ſhall *dote*: a ſword is upon her mighty men, and they ſhall be diſmayed. *Jer.* l. 36.

Time has made you *dote*, and vainly tell
Of arms imagin'd, in your lonely cell:
Go, be the temple and the gods your care;
Permit to men the thought of peace and war. *Dryd. Æn.*

When an old woman begins to *dote*, and grow chargeable to a pariſh, ſhe is turned into a witch, and fills the country with extravagant fancies. *Addiſon's Spectator*, N°. 117.

2. To be in love to extremity.

He was ſtriken with great affection towards me, which ſince is grown to ſuch a *doting* love, that, 'till I was fain to get this place, ſometimes to retire in freely: I was even choked with his tediouſneſs. *Sidney.*

I have long loved her, and beſtowed much on her, followed her with a *doting* obſervance. *Shak. M. Wives of Windſ.*

To DOTE *upon.* To regard with exceſſive fondneſs; to love to exceſs.

All their prayers and love
Were ſet on Hereford, whom they *doted* on,
And bleſs'd, and grac'd. *Shakeſpeare's Henry* IV.

Forgive me, that I do not dream on thee,
Becauſe thou ſeeſt me *dote* upon my love. *Shakeſpeare.*

All the beauties of the court beſides,
Are mad in love, and *dote* upon your perſon. *Denham.*

Mark thoſe who *dote* on arbitrary power,
And you ſhall find 'em either hot-brain'd youth,
Or needy bankrupts. *Dryden.*

Would you ſo *dote* upon your firſt deſire,
As not to entertain a nobler fire? *Dryden's Indian Emperor.*

We *dote* upon this preſent world, and the enjoyments of it; and 'tis not without pain and fear, and reluctancy, that we are torn from them, as if our hopes lay all within the compaſs of this life. *Burnet.*

O death, all eloquent! you only prove
What duſt we *dote* on, when 'tis man we love. *Pope.*

DO'TER. *n. ſ.* [from *dote.*]

1. One whoſe underſtanding is impaired by years; a dotard.

What ſhould a bald fellow do with a comb, a dumb *doter* with a pipe, or a blind man with a looking-glaſs? *Burton.*

2. A man fondly, weakly, and exceſſively in love.

If in black my lady's brow be deckt,
It mourns that painting and uſurping hair
Should raviſh *doters* with a falſe aſpect;
And therefore is ſhe born to make black fair. *Shakeſpeare.*

Our *doters* upon red and white are inceſſantly perplexed, by the incertainty both of the continuance of their miſtreſs's kindneſs, and of the laſting of her beauty. *Boyle.*

DO'TINGLY. *adv.* [from *doting.*] Fondly; by exceſſive fondneſs.

That he, to wedlock *dotingly* betray'd,
Should hope in this lewd town to find a maid! *Dryd. Juv.*

DO'TTARD. *n. ſ.* This word ſeems to ſignify a tree kept low by cutting.

For great trees, we ſee almoſt all overgrown trees in church-yards, or near ancient buildings, and the like, are pollards and *dottards*, and not trees at their full height. *Bacon's Nat. Hiſt.*

DO'TTEREL. *n. ſ.* [from *dote.*] The name of a bird that mimicks geſtures.

We fee how ready apes and monkeys are to imitate all motions of man; and in catching of *dotterels*, we fee how the foolifh bird playeth the ape in geftures. *Bacon's Nat. Hift.*

DO'UBLE. *adj.* [*double*, French; *duplex*, Latin; *duple*, Erfe.]

1. Two of a fort; one correfponding to the other; in pairs.

All things are *double* one againft another, and he hath made nothing imperfect. *Ecclus.* xlii. 24.

2. Twice as much; containing the fame quantity repeated.

Great honours are great burthens; but, on whom
They are caft with envy, he doth bear two loads:
His cares muft ftill be *double* to his joys,
In any dignity. *Ben. Johnfon's Catiline.*

I am not fo old in proportion to them as I formerly was, which I can prove by arithmetick; for then I was *double* their age, which now I am not. *Swift.*

This fum of forty thoufand pounds is almoft *double* to what is fufficient. *Swift's Draper's Letters.*

3. Having one added to another; having more than one in the fame order or parallel.

It is a curiofity alfo to make flowers *double*, which is effected by often removing them into new earth; as, on the contrary part, *double* flowers by neglecting, and not removing, prove fingle. *Bacon's Natural Hiftory*, N°. 513.

I met a reverend, fat, old gouty fryar,
With a paunch fwoln fo high, his *double* chin
Might reft upon't. *Dryden's Spanifh Fryar.*

4. Twofold; of two kinds.

Thus curfed fteel, and more accurfed gold,
Gave mifchief birth, and made that mifchief bold;
And *double* death did wretched man invade,
By fteel affaulted, and by gold betray'd. *Dryden's Ovid.*
No ftar appears to lend his friendly light;
Darknefs and tempeft make a *double* night. *Dryden.*

5. Two in number.

And if one power did not both fee and hear,
Our fights and founds would always *double* be. *Davies.*

6. Having twice the effect or influence; having the power of two.

The magnifico is much belov'd,
And hath in his effect a voice potential,
As *double* as the duke's. *Shakefpeare's Othello.*

7. Deceitful; acting two parts, one openly, the other in fecret.

I' th' prefence
He would fay untruths, and be ever *double*
Both in his words and meaning. *Shakefpeare's Henry* VIII.

Fifty thoufand could keep rank, that were not of *double* heart. 1 *Chron.* xii. 33.

DOUBLE-PLEA. *n. f.* [*duplex placitum*, Latin.] Is that in which the defendant alleges for himfelf two feveral matters, in bar of the action, whereof either is fufficient to effect his defire in debarring the plaintiff. *Cowel.*

DOUBLE-QUARREL, is a complaint made by any clerk or other to the archbifhop of the province, againft an inferiour ordinary, for delaying juftice in fome caufe ecclefiaftical. The effect is, that the archbifhop directs his letters, under the authentical feal, to all clerks of his province, commanding them to admonifh the faid ordinary within nine days to do the juftice required, or otherwife to cite him to appear before him or his official: and laftly to intimate to the faid ordinary, that if he neither performs the thing enjoined, nor appears at the day affigned, he himfelf will proceed to perform the juftice required. And this feems to be termed a *double quarrel*, becaufe it is moft commonly made againft both the judge, and him at whofe petition juftice is delayed. *Cowel.*

DOUBLE is much ufed in compofition, generally for *doubly*, two ways; as *double edged*, having an edge on each fide; or for twice the number or quantity, as *double died*, twice died.

DOUBLE-BITING. *adj.* [*double* and *bite.*] Biting or cutting on either fide.

But moft their looks on the black monarch bend,
His rifing mufcles and his brawn commend;
His *double-biting* ax, and beamy fpear,
Each afking a gigantick force to rear. *Dryden's Fables.*

DOUBLE-BUTTONED. *adj.* [*double* and *buttoned.*] Having two rows of buttons.

Others you'll fee, when all the town's afloat,
Wrapt in th' embraces of a kerfey coat,
Or *double-button'd* frieze. *Gay's Trivia.*

DOUBLE-DEALER. *n. f.* [*double* and *dealer.*] A deceitful, fubtle, infidious fellow; one who acts two parts at the fame time; one who fays one thing and thinks another.

Double-dealers may pafs mufter for a while; but all parties wafh their hands of them in the conclufion. *L'Eftrange.*

DOUBLE-DEALING. *n. f.* [*double* and *dealing.*] Artifice; diffimulation; low or wicked cunning.

Thou fhalt not be the worfe for me; there's gold.
—But that it would be *double-dealing*, fir, I would you could make it another. *Shakefpeare's Twelfth Night.*

Our poets have joined together fuch qualities as are by nature moft compatible; valour with anger, meeknefs with piety, and prudence with diffimulation: this laft union was neceffary for the goodnefs of Ulyffes; for without that, his diffimulation might have degenerated into wickednefs and *double-dealing*. *Pope's View of Epic Poetry.*

To DOUBLE-DIE. *v. a.* [*double* and *die.*] To die twice over.

Yes, I'll to the royal bed,
Where firft the myfteries of our love were acted,
And *double-die* it with imperial crimfon. *Dry. and Lee's Oed.*

DOUBLE-FOUNTED. *adj.* [*double* and *fount.*] Having two fources.

Here the *double-founted* ftream
Jordan, true limit eaftward. *Milton's Paradife Loft*, *b.* xii.

DOUBLE-HANDED. *adj.* [*double* and *hand.*] Having two hands.

All things being *double-handed*, and having the appearances both of truth and falfhood, where our affections have engaged us, we attend only to the former. *Glanv. Scepf. c.* 15.

DOUBLE-HEADED. *adj.* [*double* and *head.*] Having the flowers growing one to another.

The double rich fcarlet nonfuch is a large *double-headed* flower, of the richeft fcarlet colour. *Mortimer's Husbandry.*

To DOUBLE-LOCK. *v. a.* [*double* and *lock.*] To fhoot the lock twice; to faften with double fecurity.

He immediately *double-locked* his door, and fat down carefully to reading and comparing both his orders. *Tatler*, N°. 60.

DOUBLE-MINDED. *adj.* [from *double* and *mind.*] Deceitful; infidious.

A *double-minded* man is unftable in all his ways. *James* i. 8.

DOUBLE-SHINING. *adj.* [*double* and *fhine.*] Shining with double luftre.

He was
Among the reft that there did take delight,
To fee the fports of *double-fhining* day. *Sidney.*

DOUBLE-TONGUED. *adj.* [*double* and *tongue.*] Deceitful; giving contrary accounts of the fame thing.

The deacons muft be grave, not *double-tongued*, not given to much wine, not greedy of filthy lucre. 1 *Tim.* iii. 8.

For much fhe fear'd the Tyrians, *double-tongu'd*,
And knew the town to Juno's care belong'd. *Dryd. Virgil.*

To DO'UBLE. *v. a.* [from the adjective.]

1. To enlarge any quantity by addition of the fame quantity.

Rumour doth *double* voice, and echo
The numbers of the fear'd. *Shakefpeare's Henry* IV.
Pay him fix thoufand, and deface the bond;
Double fix thoufand, and then treble that. *Shakefpeare.*
Our foe's too proud the weaker to affail,
Or *doubles*, his difhonour if he fail. *Dryd. State of Innocence.*

This power of repeating or *doubling* any idea we have of any diftance, and adding it to the former, as often as we will, without being ever able to come to any ftop or ftint, let us enlarge it as much as we will, is that which gives us the idea of immenfity. *Locke.*

This was only the value of the filver: there was befides a tenth part of that number of talents of gold, which, if gold was reckoned in a decuple proportion, will juft *double* the fum. *Arbuthnot on Coins.*

2. To contain twice the quantity.

Thus reinforc'd againft the adverfe fleet,
Still *doubling* our's, brave Rupert leads the way. *Dryden.*

3. To repeat; to add.

He faw proud Arcite and fierce Palemon
In mortal battle, *doubling* blow on blow;
Like lightning flam'd their faulchions to and fro. *Dryden.*

4. To add one to another in the fame order or parallel.

Thou fhalt *double* the curtain in the tabernacle. *Ex.* xxvi. 9.

5. To fold.

He bought her fermons, pfalms, and graces,
And *doubled* down the ufeful places. *Prior.*

6. To pafs round a headland.

Prefently departing again, and failing along the coaft, he *doubled* the promontory of Carthage, yet famous for the ruins of that proud city. *Knolles's Hiftory of the Turks.*

Now we have the cape of Good Hope in fight, the tradewind is our own, if we can but *double* it. *Dryden.*

To DO'UBLE. *v. n.*

1. To increafe to twice the quantity.

'Tis obferved in particular nations, that within the fpace of three hundred years, notwithftanding all cafualties, the number of men *double*. *Burnet's Theory of the Earth.*

2. To enlarge the ftake to twice the fum in play.

Throw Ægypt's by, and offer in the ftead,
Offer—the crown on Berenice's head:
I am refolv'd to *double* 'till I win. *Dryden's Tyran. Love.*

3. To turn back, or wind in running.

Under the line the fun croffeth the line, and maketh two Summers and two Winters; but in the fkirts of the torrid zone it *doubleth* and goeth back again, and fo maketh one long Summer. *Bacon's Natural Hiftory*, N°. 398.

So keen thy hunters, and thy fcent fo ftrong,
Thy turns and *doublings* cannot fave thee long. *Swift.*

4. To play tricks; to ufe fleights.

Who knows which way fhe points?
Doubling and turning like an hunted hare!
Find out the meaning of her mind who can. *Dryd. Sp. Fry.*

Do'UBLE. *n. s.*

1. Twice the quantity or number.

In all the four great years of mortality abovementioned, I do not find that any week the plague increased to the *double* of the precedent week above five times. *Graunt's Mortality.*

2. Strong beer; beer of twice the common strength.

Here's a pot of good *double*, neighbour: drink, and fear not your man. *Shakespeare's Henry* VI.

3. A trick; a shift; an artifice.

Do'UBLENESS. *n. s.* [from *double.*] The state of being double.

If you think well to carry this as you may, the *doubleness* of the benefit defends the deceit from reproof. *Sh. Meas. for Meas.*

Do'UBLER. *n. s.* [from *double.*] He that doubles any thing.

Do'UBLET. *n. s.* [from *double.*]

1. The inner garment of a man; the waistcoat: so called from being double for warmth.

What a pretty thing a man is, when he goes in his *doublet* and hose, and leaves off his wit. *Sh. Much Ado about Nothing.*

His *doublet* was of sturdy buff,
And though not sword yet cudgel proof. *Hudibras, p.* i.

It is common enough to see a countryman in the *doublet* and breeches of his great grandfather. *Addison's Italy.*

They do but mimick ancient wits at best,
As apes our gransires, in their *doublets* drest. *Pope's Criticism.*

2. Two; a pair.

Those *doublets* on the sides of his tail seem to add strength to the muscles which move the tail-fins. *Grew's Musæum.*

DOUBLO'N. *n. s.* [French.] A Spanish coin containing the value of two pistoles.

Do'UBLY. *adv.* [from *double.*] In twice the quantity; to twice the degree.

Young Hollis, on a muse by Mars begot,
Born, Cæsar like, to write and act great deeds,
Impatient to revenge his fatal shot,
His right hand *doubly* to his left succeeds. *Dryd. Ann. Mirab.*

Haply at night he does with horror shun
A widow'd daughter, or a dying son:
His neighbour's offspring he to-morrow sees,
And *doubly* feels his want in their increase. *Prior.*

To DOUBT. *v. n.* [*doubter*, French; *dubito*, Latin.]

1. To question; to be in uncertainty.

Even in matters divine, concerning some things, we may lawfully *doubt* and suspend our judgment, inclining neither to one side or other; as, namely, touching the time of the fall both of man and angels. *Hooker, b.* ii. *s.* 7.

Let no man, while he lives here in the world, *doubt* whether there is any hell or no, and thereupon live so, as if absolutely there were none. *South's Sermons.*

I *doubt* not to make it appear to be a monstrous folly to deride these things. *Tillotson's Sermons.*

Can we conclude upon Luther's instability, because in a single notion, no way fundamental, an enemy writes that he had some *doubtings?* *Atterbury.*

2. To question any event, fearing the worst.

Doubting things go ill, often hurt more
Than to be sure they do. *Shakespeare's Cymbeline.*

3. Sometimes with *of* in both the foregoing senses.

Solyman said he had hitherto made war against divers nations, and always had the victory, whereof he *doubted* not now also. *Knolles's History of the Turks.*

Have I not manag'd my contrivance well,
To try your love, and make you *doubt of* mine? *Dryden.*

4. To fear; to be apprehensive.

I *doubt* there's deep resentment in his mind,
For the late slight his honour suffer'd there. *Otway's Orph.*

If there were no fault in the title, I *doubt* there are too many in the body of the work. *Baker on Learning.*

This is enough for a project, without any name; I *doubt* more than will be reduced into practice. *Swift.*

5. To suspect; to have suspicion.

The king did all his courage bend
Against those four which now before him were,
Doubting not who behind him doth attend. *Daniel's C. War.*

6. To hesitate; to be in suspense.

At first the tender blades of grass appear,
And buds that yet the blast of Eurus fear,
Stand at the door of life, and *doubt* to clothe the year. *Dry.*

To DOUBT. *v. a.*

1. To hold questionable; to think uncertain.

He from the terror of this arm so late
Doubted his empire. *Milton's Paradise Lost, b.* i. *l.* 113.

To teach vain wits a science little known,
T' admire superior sense, and *doubt* their own. *Pope.*

2. To fear; to suspect.

He did ordain the interdicts and prohibitions which we have to making entrance of strangers, which at that time was frequent, doubting novelties and commixture of manners. *Bacon.*

3. To distrust.

You that will be less fearful than discreet,
That love the fundamental part of state,
More than you *doubt* the change of it, prefer
A noble life before a long. *Shakespeare's Coriolanus.*

DOUBT. *n. s.* [from the verb.]

1. Uncertainty of mind; suspense; undetermined state of opinion.

Could any difficulty have been proposed, the resolution would have been as early as the proposal; it could not have had time to settle into *doubt.* *South's Sermons.*

Those who have examined it, are thereby got past *doubt* in all the doctrines they profess. *Locke.*

2. Question; point unsettled.

Hippocrates commends the flesh of the wild sow above the tame, and no *doubt* but the animal is more or less healthy according to the air it lives in. *Arbuthnot on Aliments.*

'Tis past a *doubt*,
All Bedlam or Parnassus is let out. *Pope.*

3. Scruple; perplexity; irresolution.

Our *doubts* are traytors,
And make us lose, by fearing to attempt,
The good we oft might win. *Shak. Measure for Measure.*

4. Uncertainty of condition.

And thy life shall hang in *doubt* before thee; and thou shalt fear day and night, and shalt have no assurance of thy life. *Deutr.* xxviii. 66.

5. Suspicion; apprehension of ill.

I desire to be present with you now, and to change my voice; for I stand in *doubt* of you. *Gal.* iv. 20.

6. Difficulty objected.

To every *doubt* your answer is the same,
It so fell out, and so by chance it came. *Blackmore's Creation.*

Do'UBTER. *n. s.* [from *doubt.*] One who entertains scruples; one who hangs in uncertainty.

Do'UBTFUL. *adj.* [*doubt* and *full.*]

1. Dubious; not settled in opinion.

Methinks I should know you, and know this man;
Yet I am *doubtful.* *Shakespeare's King Lear.*

2. Ambiguous; not clear in its meaning.

3. That about which there is doubt; that which is not yet determined or decided; obscure; questionable; uncertain.

In handling the right of a war, I am not willing to intermix matter *doubtful* with that which is out of doubt; for as in capital causes, wherein but one man's life is in question, the evidence ought to be clear; so much more in a judgment upon a war, which is capital to thousands. *Bacon.*

In *doubtful* cases, reason still determines for the safer side; especially if the case be not only *doubtful*, but also highly concerning, and the venture be a soul, and an eternity. *South.*

Themetes first, 'tis *doubtful* whether hir'd,
Or so the Trojan destiny requir'd,
Mov'd, that the ramparts might be broken down,
To lodge the monster fabrick in the town. *Dryden's Æn*

4. Not secure; not without suspicion.

Our manner is always to cast a *doubtful* and a more suspicious eye towards that, over which we know we have least power. *Hooker, Dedication.*

5. Not confident; not without fear.

With *doubtful* feet and wavering resolution
I come, still dreading thy displeasure, Samson. *Milt. Agonist.*

Do'UBTFULLY. *adv.* [from *doubtful.*]

1. Dubiously; irresolutely.

2. Ambiguously; with uncertainty of meaning.

Knowing how *doubtfully* all allegories may be construed, and this book of mine being a continual allegory, I have thought good to discover the general intention. *Spenser.*

Nor did the goddess *doubtfully* declare
Her alter'd mind, and alienated care. *Dryden.*

Do'UBTFULNESS. *n. s.* [from *doubtful.*]

1. Dubiousness; suspense; instability of opinion.

Though *doubtfulness* or uncertainty seems to be a medium between certain truth and certain falshood in our minds, yet there is no such medium in things themselves. *Watts's Logick.*

2. Ambiguity; uncertainty of meaning.

In arguing, the opponent uses as comprehensive and equivocal terms as he can, to involve his adversary in the *doubtfulness* of his expressions: this is expected, and therefore the answerer, on his side, makes it his play to distinguish as much as he can. *Locke.*

Most of his philosophy is, in broken sentences, delivered with much *doubtfulness.* *Baker's Reflections on Learning.*

Do'UBTINGLY. *adv.* [from *doubt.*] In a doubting manner; dubiously.

Whatsoever a man imagineth *doubtingly*, or with fear, must needs do hurt, if imagination have any power at all; for a man representeth that oftner that he feareth, than the contrary. *Bacon's Natural History*, N°. 945.

Do'UBTLESS. *adj.* [from *doubt.*] Without fear; without apprehension of danger.

Pretty child, sleep *doubtless* and secure,
That Hubert, for the wealth of all the world,
Will not offend them. *Shakespeare's King John.*

I am *doubtless*; I can purge
Myself of many I am charg'd withal. *Shakesp. Henry* IV.

Do'UBTLESS. *adv.* Without doubt; without question; unquestionably.

Doubtless he would have made a noble knight. *Sh. H.* VI.

All their desires, deserts, or expectations the Conqueror had no other means to satisfy, but by the estates of such as had appeared open enemies to him, and *doubtless* many innocent persons suffered in this kind. *Hale's Com. Law of England.*

Doubtless many men are finally lost, who yet have no mens sins to answer for, but their own. *South's Sermons.*

These mountains have been *doubtless* much higher than they are at present: the rains have washed away of the soil, that has left the veins of stones shooting out of them. *Woodward.*

Doubtless, oh guest! great laud and praise were mine,
If, after social rites and gifts bestow'd,
I stain'd my hospitable hearth with blood. *Pope's Odyssey.*

DOUCE'T. *n. s.* [*doucet*, French.] A custard. This word I find only in *Skinner*.

DO'UCKER. *n. s.* [from *To douck*, corrupted from *To duck.*] A bird that dips in the water.

The colymbi, or *douckers*, or loons, are admirably conformed for diving, covered with thick plumage, and their feathers so slippery, that water cannot moisten them. *Ray.*

DOVE. *n. s.* [*duvo*, old Teutonick; *taub*, *daub*, German.]

1. A wild pigeon.

So shews a snowy *dove* trooping with crows,
As yonder lady o'er her fellows shows. *Sh. Rom. and Juliet.*

Say, will the falcon, stooping from above,
Smit with her varying plumage, spare the *dove?* *Pope.*

Not half so swift the trembling *doves* can fly,
When the fierce eagle cleaves the liquid sky;
Not half so swiftly the fierce eagle moves,
When through the skies he drives the trembling *doves*. *Pope.*

2. A pigeon.

I have here a dish of *doves*, that I will bestow upon your worship. *Shakespeare's Merchant of Venice.*

DO'VECOT. *n. s.* [*dove* and *cot.*] A small building in which pigeons are bred and kept.

Like an eagle in a *dovecot*, I
Flutter'd your Volscians in Corioli;
Alone I did it. *Shakespeare's Coriolanus.*

DO'VEHOUSE. *n. s.* [*dove* and *house.*] A house for pigeons.

The hawk sets up for protector, and makes havock in the *dovehouse*. *L'Estrange, Fab.* 20.

But still the *dovehouse* obstinately stood. *Dryden.*

DO'VETAIL. *n. s.* [*dove* and *tail.*] A form of joining two bodies together, where that which is inserted has the form of a wedge reversed, and therefore cannot fall out.

DOUGH. *n. s.* [dah, Saxon; *deegh*, Dutch.]

1. The paste of bread, or pies, yet unbaked.

When the gods moulded up the paste of man,
Some of their *dough* was left upon their hands,
For want of souls, and so they made Egyptians. *Dryden.*

You that from pliant paste would fabricks raise,
Expecting thence to gain immortal praise,
Your knuckles try, and let your sinews know
Their pow'r to kneed, and give the form to *dough*. *King.*

2. *My cake is* DOUGH. My affair has miscarried; my undertaking has never come to maturity.

My cake is dough, but I'll in among the rest;
Out of hope of all, but my share of the feast. *Shakespeare.*

DOUGHBA'KED. *adj.* [*dough* and *baked.*] Unfinished; not hardened to perfection; soft.

For when, through tasteless flat humility,
In *doughbak'd* men some harmlessness we see,
'Tis but his phlegm that's virtuous, and not he. *Donne.*

DO'UGHTY. *adj.* [dohtig, Saxon; *deught*, virtue, Dutch.]

1. Brave; noble; illustrious; eminent. Used of men and things.

Such restless passion did all night torment
The flatt'ning courage of that fairy knight,
Devising how that *doughty* tournament,
With greatest honour, he atchieven might. *Fairy Queen.*

2. It is now seldom used but ironically, or in burlesque.

If this *doughty* historian hath any honour or conscience left, he ought to beg pardon. *Stillingfleet's Def. of Disc. on Rom Idol.*

She smil'd to see the *doughty* hero slain;
But, at her smile, the beau reviv'd again. *Pope.*

DO'UGHY. *adj.* [from *dough.*] Unsound; soft; unhardened.

Your son was misled with a snipt taffata fellow there, whose villanous saffron would have made all the unbaked and *doughy* youth of a nation in his colour. *Shakespeare.*

To DOUSE. *v. a.* [δούσω; but probably it is a cant word formed from the sound.] To put over head suddenly in the water.

To DOUSE. *v. n.* To fall suddenly into the water.

It is no jesting, trivial matter,
To swing i' th' air, or *douse* in water. *Hudibras, p.* ii.

DO'WAGER. *n. s.* [*douairiere*, French.]

1. A widow with a jointure.

She lingers my desires,
Like to a stepdame or a *dowager*,
Long wintering on a young man's revenue. *Shakespeare.*

Widows have a greater interest in property than either maids or wives; so that it is as unnatural for a *dowager* as a freeholder to be an enemy to our constitution. *Addis. Freehold.*

2. The title given to ladies who survive their husbands.

Catharine no more
Shall be call'd queen; but princess *dowager*,
And widow to prince Arthur. *Shakespeare's Henry* VIII.

DO'WDY. *n. s.* An aukward, ill-dressed, inelegant woman.

Laura, to his lady, was but a kitchen wench; Dido, a *dowdy*; Cleopatra, a gipsy; Helen and Hero, slidings and harlots. *Shakespeare's Romeo and Juliet.*

The bedlam train of lovers use
T' inhance the value, and the faults excuse;
And therefore 'tis no wonder if we see
They doat on *dowdies* and deformity. *Dryden.*

No houswifry the *dowdy* creature knew;
To sum up all, her tongue confess'd the shrew. *Gay's Past.*

DO'WER. }
DO'WERY. } *n. s.* [*douaire*, French.]

1. That which the wife bringeth to her husband in marriage.

His wife brought in *dow'r* Cilicia's crown,
And in herself a greater *dow'r* alone. *Dryden.*

His only daughter in a stranger's pow'r;
For very want, he could not pay a *dow'r*. *Pope's Epistles.*

2. That which the widow possesses.

His patrimonial territories of Flanders were partly in *dower* to his mother-in-law, and partly not serviceable, in respect of the late rebellions. *Bacon's Henry* VII.

3. The gifts of a husband for a wife.

Ask me never so much *dowery* and gift, and I will give according as ye shall say unto me; but give me the damsel to wife. *Gen.* xxxiv. 12.

4. Endowment; gift.

What spreading virtue, what a sparkling fire;
How great, how plentiful, how rich a *dow'r*,
Do'st thou within this dying flesh inspire! *Davies.*

DO'WERED. *adj.* [from *dower.*] Portioned; supplied with a portion.

Will you with those infirmities she owes,
Unfriended, new-adopted to our hate,
Dower'd with our curse, and stranger'd with our oath,
Take her, or leave her. *Shakespeare's King Lear.*

DO'WERLESS. *adj.* [from *dower.*] Without a fortune; unportioned.

Thy *dow'rless* daughter, king, thrown to my chance,
Is queen of us, and ours, and our fair France. *Sh. K. Lear.*

DO'WLAS. *n. s.* A coarse kind of linen.

Dowlas, filthy *dowlas*; I have given them away to bakers wives, and they have made boulters of them. *Shak. Hen.* IV.

DOWN. *n. s.* [*duun*, Danish.]

1. Soft feathers.

Virtue is the roughest way;
But proves at night a bed of *down*. *Wotton.*

Leave, leave, fair bride! your solitary bed,
No more shall you return to it alone;
It nurseth sadness; and your body's print,
Like to a grave, the yielding *down* doth dint. *Donne.*

Lie tumbling on our *down*, courting the blessing
Of a short minute's slumber. *Denham's Sophy.*

A tender weakly constitution is very much owing to the use of *down* beds. *Locke.*

2. Any thing that sooths or mollifies.

Thou bosom softness! *down* of all my cares!
I could recline my thoughts upon this breast
To a forgetfulness of all my griefs,
And yet be happy. *Southern's Oroonoko.*

3. Soft wool, or tender hair.

Scarce had the *down* to shade his cheeks begun;
One was their care, and their delight was one. *Dryden.*

I am not chang'd, I love my husband still;
But live him as he was when youthful grace,
And the first *down* began to shade his face. *Dryd. Aurengz.*

On thy chin the springing beard began
To spread a doubtful *down*, and promise man. *Prior.*

4. The soft fibres of plants which wing the seeds.

Any light thing that moveth, when we find no wind, sheweth a wind at hand; as when feathers, or *down* of thistles, fly to and fro in the air. *Bacon's Natural History*, N°. 822.

Like scatter'd *down* by howling Eurus blown,
By rapid whirlwinds from his mansion thrown. *Sandys.*

DOWN. *n. s.* [dun, Saxon; *dune*, Erse, a hill; but it is used now as if derived from the adverb.] A large open plain, or valley.

On the *downs* we see, near Wilton fair,
A hast'ned hare from greedy greyhound go. *Sidney.*

Lord of much riches, which the use renowns;
Seven thousand broad-tail'd sheep graz'd on his *downs*. *Sandys.*

Not all the fleecy wealth
That doth enrich those *downs* is worth a thought,
To this my errand, and the care it brought. *Milton.*

How Will-a-wisp misleads night-faring clowns
O'er hills, and sinking bogs, and pathless *downs*. *Gay.*

To compass this, his building is a town,
His pond an ocean, his parterre a *down*. *Pope, Epistle* iv.

2. A rising ground. This sense is very rare.

Hills afford pleaſant proſpects; as they muſt needs acknowledge who have been on the *downs* of Suſſex. *Ray on the Creat.*

DOWN. *prep.* [adune, Saxon.]

1. Along a deſcent; from a higher place to a lower.

Let go thy hold when a great wheel runs *down* hill, leſt it break thy neck with following it; but the great one that goes upward, let him draw after. *Shakeſpeare's King Lear.*

A man falling *down* a precipice, though in motion, is not at liberty, becauſe he cannot ſtop that motion if he would. *Loc.*

2. Towards the mouth of a river.

Mahomet put his chief ſubſtance into certain boats, to be conveyed *down* the river, as purpoſing to fly. *Knolles.*

DOWN. *adv.*

1. On the ground; from the height at which any thing was to a lower ſituation.

Whom they hit, none on their feet might ſtand,
Though ſtanding elſe as rocks; but *down* they fell
By thouſands. *Milton's Paradiſe Loſt, b.* vi. *l.* 593.

Down ſinks the giant with a thund'ring ſound,
His pond'rous limbs oppreſs the trembling ground;
Blood, brains, and foam, guſh from the gaping wound. *Dr.*

2. Tending towards the ground.

3. Out of ſight; below the horizon.

How goes the night, boy?
—The moon is *down*; I have not heard the clock,
And ſhe goes *down* at twelve. *Shakeſpeare's Macbeth.*

4. To a total maceration.

What remains of the ſubject, after the decoction, is continued to be boiled *down*, with the addition of freſh water, to a ſapid fat. *Arbuthnot on Aliments.*

5. Into diſgrace; into declining reputation.

He ſnar'd our dividend o' th' crown,
We had ſo painfully preach'd *down*;
And forc'd us, though againſt the grain,
T' have calls to teach it up again. *Hudibras, p.* iii. *cant.* 2.

It has been ſtill preached up, but acted *down*; and dealt with, as the eagle in the fable did with the oyſter, carrying it up on high, that, by letting it fall, he might daſh it in pieces. *South's Sermons.*

There is not a more melancholy object in the learned world, than a man who has written himſelf *down*. *Addiſon.*

6. [Anſwering to *up*.] Here and there.

Let them wander up and *down* for meat, and grudge if they be not ſatisfied. *Pſ.* lix. 15.

DOWN. *interj.*

1. An exhortation to deſtruction or demolition.

Go, ſome pull down the Savoy; others to the Inns of Courts: *down* with them all. *Shakeſpeare's Henry* VI. *p.* ii.

If there be ten, ſhrink not; but *down* with them. *Shakeſp.*

But now they cry, *down* with the palace, fire it,
Pull out th' uſurping queen. *Dryden's Spaniſh Fryar.*

2. A contemptuous threat.

Down, down to hell, and ſay I ſent thee thither. *Shakeſp.*

DOWN. [*To go.*] To be digeſted; to be received.

If he be hungry more than wanton, bread alone will *down*; and if he be not hungry, 'tis not fit he ſhould eat. *Locke.*

I know not how abſurd this may ſeem to the maſters of demonſtration; and probably it will hardly *down* with any body, at firſt hearing. *Locke.*

To DOWN. *v. a.* [from the particle.] To knock; to ſubdue; to ſuppreſs; to conquer.

The hidden beauties ſeem'd in wait to lie,
To *down* proud hearts, that would not willing die. *Sidney.*

DO'WNCAST. *adj.* [*down* and *caſt.*] Bent down; directed to the ground.

Wanton languiſhing borrowed of her eyes the *downcaſt* look of modeſty. *Sidney, b.* ii.

My wily nurſe by long experience found,
And firſt diſcover'd to my ſoul its wound,
'Tis love, ſaid ſhe; and then my *downcaſt* eyes,
And guilty dumbneſs, witneſs'd my ſurprize. *Dryden.*

Thy *downcaſt* looks, and thy diſorder'd thoughts,
Tell me my fate: I aſk not the ſucceſs
My cauſe has found. *Addiſon's Cato.*

DO'WNFAL. *n. ſ.* [*down* and *fall.*]

1. Ruin; calamity; fall from rank or ſtate.

Why do'ſt thou ſay king Richard is depos'd?
Dar'ſt thou, thou little better thing than earth,
Divine his *downfal?* *Shakeſpeare's Richard* II.

We have ſeen ſome, by the ways by which they had deſigned to riſe uncontrollably, to have directly procured their utter *downfal*. *South's Sermons.*

2. A ſudden fall, or body of things falling.

Each *downfal* of a flood the mountains pour
From their rich bowels, rolls a ſilver ſtream. *Dryd. Ind. Em.*

3. Deſtruction of fabricks.

Not more aghaſt the matrons of renown,
When tyrant Nero burn'd th' imperial town,
Shriek'd for the *downfal* in a doleful cry,
For which their guiltleſs lords were doom'd to die. *Dryden.*

DO'WNFALLEN. *participial adj.* [*down* and *fall.*] Ruined; fallen.

The land is now divorced by the *downfallen* ſteep cliffs on the farther ſide. *Carew's Survey of Cornwall.*

DO'WNGYRED. *adj.* [*down* and *gyred.*] Let down in circular wrinkles.

Lord Hamlet, with his ſtockings looſe,
Ungarter'd, and *downgyred* to his ancles. *Shakeſp. Hamlet.*

DO'WNHIL. *n. ſ.* [*down* and *hill.*] Declivity; deſcent.

Heavy the third, and ſtiff, he ſinks apace;
And though 'tis *downhil* all, but creeps along the race. *Dryd.*

DO'WNHIL. *adj.* Declivous; deſcending.

DO'WNLOOKED. *adj.* [*down* and *look.*] Having a dejected countenance; gloomy; ſullen; melancholy.

Jealouſy ſuffus'd, with jaundice in her eyes,
Diſcolouring all ſhe view'd, in tawney dreſs'd;
Downlook'd, and with a cuckow on her fiſt. *Dryd. Fables.*

DO'WNLYING. *adj.* [*down* and *lie.*] About to be in travail of childbirth.

DO'WNRIGHT. *adv.* [*down* and *right.*]

1. Strait or right down; down perpendicularly.

A giant's ſlain in fight,
Or mow'd o'erthwart, or cleft *downright*. *Hudibras, p.* i.

2. In plain terms; without ceremony.

Elves away;
We ſhall chide *downright*, if I longer ſtay. *Shakeſpeare.*

3. Completely; without ſtopping ſhort.

This paper put Mrs. Bull in ſuch a paſſion, that ſhe fell *downright* into a fit. *Arbuthnot's Hiſtory of John Bull.*

DO'WNRIGHT. *adj.*

1. Plain; open; apparent; undiſguiſed.

An admonition from a dead author, or a caveat from an impartial pen, will prevail more than a *downright* advice, which may be miſtaken as ſpoken magiſterially. *Bacon.*

It is *downright* madneſs to ſtrike where we have no power to hurt. *L'Eſtrange, Fab.* 44.

Religion ſeems not in danger from *downright* atheiſm, ſince rational men muſt reject that for want of proof. *Rogers's Serm.*

The merchant's wife, who abounds in plenty, is not to have *downright* money; but the mercenary part of her mind is engaged with a preſent of plate. *Spectator,* N°. 266.

2. Directly tending to the point; plain; artleſs.

I would rather have a plain *downright* wiſdom, than a fooliſh and affected eloquence. *Ben. Johnſon's Diſcoveries.*

3. Unceremonious; honeſtly ſurly.

When it came to the count to ſpeak, old fact ſo ſtared him in the face, after his plain *downright* way, that the count was ſtruck dumb. *Addiſon's Count Tariff.*

4. Plain; without palliation.

The idolatry was direct and *downright* in the people, whoſe credulity is illimitable. *Brown's Vulgar Errours, b.* i. *c.* 4.

DO'WNSITTING. *n. ſ.* [*down* and *ſit.*] Reſt; repoſe; the act of ſitting down, or going to reſt.

Thou knoweſt my *downſitting* and mine upriſing; thou underſtandeſt my thoughts afar off. *Pſ.* cxxxix. 2.

DO'WNWARD. } *adv.* [dunepeard, Saxon.]
DO'WNWARDS. }

1. Towards the center.

As you lift up the glaſſes the drop will aſcend ſlower and ſlower, and at length reſt, being carried *downward* by its weight, as much as upwards by the attraction. *Newton's Opt.*

2. From a higher ſituation to a lower.

Look *downward* on that globe, whoſe hither ſides,
With light from hence, ſhines. *Milton's Paradiſe Loſt, b.* iii.

Hills are ornamental to the earth, affording pleaſant proſpects to them that look *downwards* from them upon the ſubjacent countries. *Ray on the Creation.*

What would this man? Now upward will he ſoar,
And little leſs than angel, would be more:
Now looking *downwards*, juſt as griev'd, appears
To want the ſtrength of bulls, the fur of bears. *Pope.*

3. In a courſe of ſucceſſive or lineal deſcent.

A ring the count does wear,
That *downward* hath ſucceeded in his houſe,
From ſon to ſon, ſome four or five deſcents. *Shakeſpeare.*

DO'WNWARD. *adj.*

1. Moving on a declivity; tending towards the center; tending to the ground.

With *downward* force,
That drove the ſand along, he took his way,
And roll'd his yellow billows to the ſea. *Dryden's Æn.*

2. Declivous; bending.

When Aurora leaves our northern ſphere,
She lights the *downward* heaven, and riſes there. *Dryd. Virg.*

3. Depreſſed; dejected.

At the loweſt of my *downward* thoughts, I pulled up my heart to remember, that nothing is atchieved before it be thoroughly attempted, and that lying ſtill doth never go forward. *Sidney.*

DO'WNY. *adj.* [from *down.*]

1. Covered with down or nap.

By his gates of breath
There lies a *downy* feather, which ſtirs not:

Did he ſuſpire, that light and weightleſs down
Perforce muſt move. *Shakeſpeare's Henry* IV. *p.* ii.

There be plants that have prickles, yet have *downy* or velvet rind upon their leaves; as ſtock-gillyflowers and coltsfoot; which down or nap conſiſteth of a ſubtile ſpirit, in a ſoft ſubſtance. *Bacon's Natural Hiſtory*, Nº. 560.

In her hand ſhe held
A bough of faireſt fruit, that *downy* ſmil'd,
New-gather'd, and ambroſial ſmell diffus'd. *Milt. Par. Loſt.*

2. Made of down or ſoft feathers.

A ſide breeze from weſtward waits their ſails to fill,
And reſts in thoſe high beds his *downy* wings. *Dryden.*

Belinda ſtill her *downy* pillow preſt,
Her guardian ſylph prolong'd the balmy reſt. *Pope.*

3. Soft; tender; ſoothing.

Banquo! Donalbain! Malcolm! awake!
Shake off this *downy* ſleep, death's counterfeit,
And look on death itſelf. *Shakeſpeare's Macbeth.*

The night's companion kindly cheating them
Of all their cares, tam'd the rebellious eye
Of ſorrow with a ſoft and *downy* hand,
Sealing all breaſts in a lethean band. *Craſhaw.*

DO'WRE. } *n. ſ.* [*douaire*, French. It ought to be written
DO'WRY. } *dower.*]

1. A portion given with a wife.

I could marry this wench for this *dowre.* *Sidney.*

And aſk no other *dowry* but ſuch another jeſt. *Shakeſpeare.*

The king muſt die, that I may make you great,
And give a crown in *dowry* with my love. *Dryd. Span. Fry.*

Tethys all her waves in *dowry* gives. *Dryden's Virgil.*

2. A reward paid for a wife.

Thine own hand
An hundred of the faithleſs foe ſhall ſlay,
And for a *dowre* a hundred foreſkins pay. *Cowley's Davideis.*

3. A gift; a fortune given.

DOXO'LOGY. *n. ſ.* [δόξα and λόγος.] A form of giving glory to God.

David breaks forth into theſe triumphant praiſes and *doxologies* expreſſed in the text; Bleſſed be the Lord God of Iſrael, who has kept me this day from ſhedding blood, and from avenging myſelf with my own hand. *South's Sermons.*

Little did Athanaſius imagine, that ever it would have been received in the Chriſtian church, to conclude their books with a *doxology* to God and the bleſſed virgin. *Stillingfleet.*

DO'XY. *n. ſ.* A whore; a looſe wench.

When daffadils begin to pure,
With heigh! the *doxy* over the dale: *Shakeſ. Winter's Tale.*

To DOZE. *v. n.* [ꝺꞃæꞅ, Saxon; *daes*, Dutch.] To ſlumber; to live in a ſtate of drouſineſs; to be half aſleep.

There was no ſleeping under his roof: if he happened to *doze* a little, the jolly cobler waked him. *L'Eſtrange.*

It has happened to young men of the greateſt wit to waſte their ſpirits with anxiety and pain, ſo far as to *doze* upon their work with too much eagerneſs of doing well. *Dryd. Dufreſn.*

How to the banks, where bards departed *doze*,
They led him ſoft; how all the bards aroſe. *Pope's Dunciad.*

Chiefleſs armies *doz'd* out the campaign,
And navies yawn'd for orders on the main. *Pope's Dunciad.*

To DOZE. *v. a.* To ſtupify; to dull.

He was now much decayed in his parts, and with immoderate drinking *dozed* in his underſtanding. *Clarendon, b.* viii.

Two ſatyrs, on the ground,
Stretch'd at his eaſe, their ſire, Silenus, found
Doz'd with his fumes, and heavy with his load. *Dryden.*

DO'ZEN. *n. ſ.* [*douzaine*, French.] The number of twelve.

We cannot lodge and board a *dozen* or fourteen gentlewomen, but it will be thought we keep a bawdyhouſe ſtraight. *Shakeſpeare's Henry* V.

That they bear ſuch huge leaves, or delicate fruit, I could never find; yet I have travelled a *dozen* miles together under them. *Raleigh's Hiſtory of the World.*

By putting twelve units together, we have the complex idea of a *dozen*. *Locke.*

The number of diſſenters was ſomething under a *dozen* with them. *Swift concerning the Sacramental Teſt.*

DO'ZINESS. *n. ſ.* [from *dozy.*] Sleepineſs; drouſineſs.

A man, by a violent fit of the gout in his limbs, finds a *dozineſs* in his head, or a want of appetite. *Locke.*

DO'ZY. *adv.* [from *doze.*] Sleepy; drouſy; ſluggiſh.

The yawning youth, ſcarce half awake, eſſays
His lazy limbs and *dozy* head to raiſe. *Dryden's Perſ. Sat.*

DRAB. *n. ſ.* [ꝺꞃabbe, Saxon, lees.] A whore; a ſtrumpet.

That I, the ſon of a dear father murder'd,
Muſt, like a whore, unpack my heart with words,
And fall a curſing, like a very *drab!* *Shakeſp. Hamlet.*

If your worſhip will take order for the *drabs* and the knaves, you need not to fear the bawds. *Shakeſpeare.*

Babe,
Ditch-deliver'd by a *drab.* *Shakeſpeare's Macbeth.*

Curs'd be the wretch ſo venal, and ſo vain,
Paltry and proud as *drabs* in Drury-lane. *Pope.*

DRACHM. *n. ſ.* [*drachma*, Latin.]

1. An old Roman coin.

See here theſe movers, that do prize their honours
At a crack'd *drachm.* *Shakeſpeare's Macbeth.*

2. The eighth part of an ounce.

DRACUNCULUS. *n. ſ.* [Latin.] A worm bred in the hot countries, which grows to many yards length between the ſkin and fleſh.

DRAD. *adj.* [for *dread*, or the preterit of *To dread*] Terrible; formidable; dreaded.

Th' utmoſt ſand-breach they ſhortly fetch,
Whilſt the *drad* danger does behind remain. *Fairy Queen.*

DRAFF. *n. ſ.* [ꝺꞃoꝼ, dirty, Saxon; *draf*, Dutch, the ſediment of ale.] Any thing thrown away; ſweepings; refuſe; lees; dregs.

You would think I had a hundred and fifty tattered prodigals lately come from ſwinekeeping, from eating *draff* and huſks. *Shakeſpeare's Henry* IV. *p.* i.

'Twere ſimple fury, ſtill thyſelf to waſte
On ſuch as have no taſte;
To offer them a ſurfeit of pure bread
Whoſe appetite is dead!
No, give them grains their fill;
Huſks, *draff*, to drink and ſwill. *Ben. Johnſon.*

I call'd, and drew them thither,
My hell-hounds to lick up the *draff* and filth,
Which man's polluting ſin with taint had ſhed
On what was pure. *Milton's Paradiſe Loſt, b.* x. *l.* 630.

Here rather let me drudge, and earn my bread,
'Till vermin, or the *draff* of ſervile food,
Conſume me. *Milton's Agoniſtes.*

As Muley-Zeydan were not worth their care,
And younger brothers but the *draff* of nature. *Dryden.*

DRA'FFY. *adj.* [from *draff.*] Worthleſs; dreggy.

DRAFT. *adj.* [corrupt for *draught.*]

Ulyſſes and old Neſtor yoke you like *draft* oxen, and make you plough up the wair. *Shakeſp. Troilus and Creſſida.*

To DRAG. *v. a.* [ꝺꞃaȝan, Saxon.]

1. To pull along the ground by main force; to draw heavily along.

Such his aſpect, when, foil'd with bloody duſt,
Dragg'd by the cords which thro' his feet were thruſt. *Denh.*

2. To draw any thing burthenſome; any thing from which one cannot diſengage one's ſelf.

'Tis long ſince I, for my celeſtial wife,
Loath'd by the gods, have *dragg'd* a ling'ring life. *Dryden.*

Can I, who lov'd ſo well,
To part with all my bliſs to ſave my lover?
Oh! can I *drag* a wretched life without him? *Smith.*

While I have any ability to hold a commerce with you, I will never be ſilent; and this chancing to be a day that I can hold a pen, I will *drag* it as long as I am able. *Swift.*

3. To draw contemptuouſly along, as a thing unworthy to be carried.

They ſhall ſurprize
The ſerpent, prince of air, and *drag* in chains
Through all his realm, and there confounded leave. *Milton.*

To fall, that's juſtice;
But then, to *drag* him after! For to die,
And yet in death to conquer, is my wiſh. *Dryd. Cleomenes.*

He triumphs in St. Auſtin's opinion; and is not only content to *drag* me at his chariot-wheels, but he makes a ſhew of me. *Stillingfleet's Def. of Diſc. on Rom. Idol.*

4. To pull about with violence and ignominy.

The conſtable was no ſooner eſpied but he was reproached with diſdainful words, beaten and *dragged* in ſo barbarous a manner, that he hardly eſcaped with his life. *Clarendon.*

5. To pull roughly and forcibly.

In my fatal cauſe your ſword was drawn;
The weight of my misfortunes *dragg'd* you down. *Dryden.*

To DRAG. *v. n.* To hang ſo low as to trail or grate upon the ground.

From hence are heard the groans of ghoſts, the pains
Of ſounding laſhes, and of *dragging* chains. *Dryden's Æn.*

A door is ſaid to *drag*, when, by its ill hanging on its hinges, the bottom edge of the door rides in its ſweep upon the floor. *Moxon's Mech. Exer.*

DRAG. *n. ſ.* [from the verb.]

1. A net drawn along the bottom of the water.

Caſting nets were ſpread in ſhallow brooks,
Drags in the deep, and baits were hung on hooks. *Dryden.*

The creatures are but inſtruments in God's hand: the returning our acknowledgments to them is juſt the ſame abſurdity with theirs who burnt incenſe to the *drag*, and ſacrificed to the net. *Rogers's Sermons.*

2. An inſtrument with hooks to catch hold of things under water.

You may in the morning find it near to ſome fixed place, and then take it up with a *drag* hook, or otherwiſe. *Walton.*

3. A kind of car drawn by the hand.

The *drag* is made ſomewhat like a low car: it is uſed for

the

the carriage of timber, and then is drawn by the handle by two or more men. *Moxon's Mech. Exer.*

DRA'GNET. *n. s.* [*drag* and *net.*] A net which is drawn along the bottom of the water.

Dragnets were made to fish within the deep,
And castingnets did rivers bottoms sweep. *May's Virgil.*

Some fishermen, that had been out a whole day with a *dragnet*, and caught nothing, had a draught towards the evening, that came home very heavy, which put them in hope of a sturgeon at last. *L'Estrange, Fable* 112.

One of our late great poets is sunk in his reputation, because he could never forgive any conceit which came in his way, but swept, like a *dragnet*, great and small. *Dryden.*

Whatsoever old time, with his huge *dragnet*, has conveyed down to us along the stream of ages, whether it be shells or shellfish, jewels or pebbles, sticks or straws, seaweeds or mud, these are the ancients, these are the fathers. *Watts's Improvem.*

To DRA'GGLE. *v. a.* [from *drag.*] To make dirty by dragging on the ground.

You'll see a *draggled* damsel, here and there,
From Billingsgate her fishy traffick bear. *Gay's Trivia.*

He wore the same gown five years, without *draggling* or tearing *Swift.*

To DRA'GGLE. *v. n.* To grow dirty by being drawn along the ground.

His *draggling* tail hung in the dirt,
Which on his rider he would flirt. *Hudibras, p.* i. *cant.* 1.

DRA'GON. *n s.* [*draco*, Latin; *dragon*, French.]

1. A kind of winged serpent, perhaps imaginary, much celebrated in the romances of the middle age.

I go alone,
Like to a lonely *dragon*, that his fen
Makes fear'd and talk'd of more than seen. *Shak. Coriolan.*

Swift, swift, you *dragons* of the night! that dawning
May bear the raven's eye. *Shakespeare's Cymbeline.*

And you, ye *dragons!* of the scaly race,
Whom glittering gold and shining armours grace;
In other nations harmless are you found,
Their guardian genii and protectors own'd. *Rowe.*

On spiry volumes there a *dragon* rides;
Here, from our strict embrace, a stream he glides. *Pope.*

2. A fierce violent man or woman.

3. A constellation near the North pole.

DRA'GON. *n. s.* [*dracunculus*, Latin.] A plant.

The leaves are like those of arum, but divided into many parts: the stalk is spotted; but, in other respects, it agrees with the arum. *Miller.*

DRAGONET. *n. s.* [from *dragon.*] A little dragon.

Or in his womb might lurk some hidden nest
Of many *dragonets*, his fruitful seed. *Fairy Queen, b.* i.

DRA'GONFLY. *n. s.* [*dragon* and *fly.*] A fierce stinging fly.

The body of the cantharides is bright coloured; and it may be, that the delicate coloured *dragonflies* may have likewise some corrosive quality. *Bacon's Natural History*, N°. 729.

DRA'GONISH. *adj.* [from *dragon.*] Having the form of a dragon; dragonlike.

Sometime we see a cloud that's *dragonish*;
A vapour sometime like a bear or lion. *Shak. Ant. and Cleop.*

DRA'GONLIKE. *adj.* [*dragon* and *like.*] Furious; fiery.

He fights *dragonlike*, and does atchieve as soon
As draw his sword. *Shakespeare's Coriolanus.*

DRA'GONSBLOOD. *n. s.* [*dragon* and *blood.*] So called from a false opinion of the dragon's combat with the elephant.

Dragonsblood is a resin, so oddly named as to seem to have been imagined an animal production. It is moderately heavy, friable, and dusky red; but of a bright scarlet, when powdered: it has little smell, and is of a resinous and astringent taste. One sort is very compact: another sort less compact, and less pure, is called common *dragonsblood.* A third sort is tough and viscous, and of a blood colour; and in keeping it grows hard, like the first sort. Four vegetables afford *dragonsblood:* one is a tall tree in the Canaries: the *sanguis draconis* exsudates from the cracks of the bark in the great heats. Another grows to six or eight feet high in the island of Java, where the resin is extracted from the fruit, about the size of a hazelnut, by boiling. A third is a tall tree in New Spain, and a true *sanguis draconis* flows from the trunk. The fourth grows in Java, and has a red bark: its trunk and large branches yield a resinous juice, which seems to be our finest sort of *dragonsblood.* *Hill's Materia Medica.*

Take *dragonsblood*, beat it in a mortar, and put it in a cloth with *aqua vitæ*, and strain them together. *Peacham.*

DRA'GONSHEAD. *n. s.* A plant.

It hath a labiated flower, consisting of one leaf; whose upper lip, which is crested, and its under lip, which is divided into three segments, end in chaps or jaws, and have the representation of a dragon's head. *Miller.*

DRA'GONTREE. *n. s.* See PALMTREE, of which it is a species.

This tree is common in the Madeira and Canary islands, where they grow to a considerable size; and from it is supposed that the dragonsblood is obtained. *Miller.*

DRAGO'ON. *n. s.* [from *dragen*, German, to carry.] A kind of soldier that serves indifferently either on foot or horseback.

Two regiments of *dragoons* suffered much in the late action. *Tatler*, N°. 55.

To DRAGO'ON. *v. a.* [from the noun.] To persecute by abandoning a place to the rage of soldiers.

In politicks I hear you're stanch,
Directly bent against the French;
Deny to have your free-born foe
Dragoon'd into a wooden shoe. *Prior.*

To DRAIN. *v. a.* [*trainer*, French.]

1. To draw off gradually.

Salt water, *drained* through twenty vessels of earth, hath become fresh. *Bacon's Natural History*, N°. 2.

The fountains *drain* the water from the ground adjacent, and leave but sufficient moisture to breed moss. *Bacon.*

In times of dearth it *drained* much coin of the kingdom, to furnish us with corn from foreign parts. *Bacon to Villiers.*

Whilst a foreign war devoured our strength, and *drained* our treasures, luxury and expences increased at home. *Atterb.*

The last emperor *drained* the wealth of those countries into his own coffers, without increasing his troops against France. *Swift.*

2. To empty by drawing gradually away what it contains.

Sinking waters, the firm land to *drain*,
Fill'd the capacious deep, and form'd the main. *Roscommon.*

The royal babes a tawny wolf shall *drain.* *Dryden.*

While cruel Nero only *drains*
The mortal Spaniard's ebbing veins,
By study worn, and slack with age,
How dull, how thoughtless is his rage? *Prior.*

Had the world lasted from all eternity, these comets must have been *drained* of all their fluids. *Cheyne's Phil. Prin.*

3. To make quite dry.

When wine is to be bottled, wash your bottles, but do not *drain* them. *Swift's Directions to the Butler.*

DRAIN. *n. s.* [from the verb.] The channel through which liquids are gradually drawn; a watercourse; a sink.

If your *drains* be deep, that you fear cattle falling into them, fling in stones and brickbats, and cover them with wood, flags, and turf. *Mortimer's Husbandry.*

Why should I tell of ponds and *drains*,
What carps we met with for our pains? *Swift.*

DRAKE. *n. s.* [of uncertain etymology.]

1. The male of the duck.

The duck should hide her eggs from the *drake*, who will suck them if he finds them. *Mortimer's Husbandry.*

2. [from *draco*, dragon, French.] A small piece of artillery.

Two or three shots, made at them by a couple of *drakes*, made them stagger. *Clarendon, b.* viii.

DRAM. *n. s.* [from *drachm*, *drachma*, Latin.]

1. In weight the eighth part of an ounce.

The trial being made betwixt lead and lead, weighing severally seven *drams* in the air, the balance in the water weigheth only four *drams* and forty-one grains, and abateth of the weight in the air two *drams* and nineteen grains: the balance kept the same depth in the water as abovesaid. *Bacon.*

2. A small quantity, in a kind of proverbial sense.

One loving hour
For many years of sorrow can dispense;
A *dram* of sweet is worth a pound of sour. *Fairy Queen.*

No *dram* of judgment with thy force is join'd;
Thy body is of profit, and my mind. *Dryden's Fables.*

3. Such a quantity of distilled spirits as is usually drank at once.

I could do this, and that with no rash potion,
But with a ling'ring *dram*, that should not work
Maliciously like poison. *Shakespeare's Winter's Tale.*

Every *dram* of brandy, every pot of ale that you drink, raiseth your character. *Swift.*

4. Spirits; distilled liquors.

A second see, by meeker manners known,
And modest as the maid that sips alone;
From the strong fate of *drams* if thou get free,
Another Durfy, Ward! shall sing in thee. *Pope's Dunciad.*

To DRAM. *v. n.* [from the noun.] In low language, to drink drams; to drink distilled spirits.

DRA'MA. *n. s.* [δρᾶμα.] A poem accommodated to action; a poem in which the action is not related, but represented; and in which therefore such rules are to be observed as make the representation probable.

Many rules of imitating nature Aristotle drew from Homer, which he fitted to the *drama*; furnishing himself also with observations from the theatre, when it flourished under Eschylus, Euripides, and Sophocles. *Dryden's Æn. Dedicat.*

DRAMA'TICAL. } *adj.* [from *drama.*] Represented by action;
DRAMA'TICK. } not narrative.

I hope to make it appear, that in the great *dramatick* poem of nature, is a necessity of introducing a God. *Bentley.*

DRAMA'TICALLY. *adv.* [from *dramatick.*] Representatively; by representation.

Ignorance and errors are ſeverally reprehended, partly *dramatically*, partly ſimply. *Dryden's Juvenal, Dedicat.*

Dra'matist. *n. ſ.* [from *drama.*] The author of dramatick compoſitions.

The whole theatre reſounds with the praiſes of the great *dramatiſt*, and the wonderful art and order of the compoſition. *Burnet's Theory of the Earth.*

Drank. [the preterite of *drink.*]

To DRAPE. *v. n.* [*drap*, French; *drapus*, low Latin.]

1. To make cloth.

It was a rare thing to ſet prices by ſtatute; and this act did not preſcribe prices, but ſtinted them not to exceed a rate, that the clothier might *drape* accordingly as he might afford. *Bacon's Henry* VII.

2. To jeer, or ſatyrize. [*drapper*, French.] It is uſed in this ſenſe by the innovator *Temple*, whom nobody has imitated.

Dra'per. *n. ſ.* [from *drape.*] One who ſells cloth.

If a piece of cloth in a *draper*'s ſhop be variouſly folded, it will appear of differing colours. *Boyle on Colours.*

The *draper* and mercer may meaſure her as they pleaſe. *Howel's England's Tears.*

Dra'pery. *n. ſ.* [*drapperie*, French.]

1. Clothwork; the trade of making cloth.

He made ſtatutes for the maintenance of *drapery*, and the keeping of wools within the realm. *Bacon's Henry* VII.

The reverend clergy ſhould ſet us an example, by contenting themſelves with wearing gowns, and other habiliments, of Iriſh *drapery*. *Swift.*

2. Cloth; ſtuffs of wool.

The bulls and frogs had ſerved the lord Strut with *drapery* ware for many years. *Arbuthnot's Hiſtory of John Bull.*

3. The dreſs of a picture, or ſtatue.

Poets are allowed the ſame liberty in their deſcriptions and compariſons, as painters in their *draperies* and ornaments. *Pri.*

Dra'pet. *n. ſ.* [from *drape.*] Cloth; coverlet.

> Thence ſhe them brought into a ſtately hall,
> Wherein were many tables fair diſpred,
> And ready dight with *drapets* feaſtival,
> Againſt the viands ſhould be miniſtred. *Fairy Queen, b.* ii.

Dra'stick. *adj.* [δραστικὸς.] Powerful; vigorous; efficacious.

It is uſed of a medicine that works with ſpeed; as jalap, ſcammony, and the ſtronger purges. *Quincy.*

Drave. [the preterite of *drive.*]

> He *drave* them beyond Amon's flood,
> And their ſad bounds mark'd deep in their own blood. *Cowl.*
> The foe ruſh'd furious as he pants for breath,
> And through his navel *drave* the pointed death. *Pope's Iliad.*

Draugh. *n. ſ.* [corruptly written for *draff.*] Refuſe; ſwill. See **Draff.**

> We do not act, that often jeſt and laugh:
> 'Tis old, but true, ſtill ſwine eat all the *draugh*. *Shakeſp.*

Draught. *n. ſ.* [from *draw.*]

1. The act of drinking.

> Fill high the goblets with a ſparkling flood,
> And with deep *draughts* invoke our common god. *Dryden.*

They flung up one of their hogſheads, and I drank it off at a *draught*, which I might well do; for it did not hold half a pint. *Gulliver's Travels.*

2. A quantity of liquor drank at once.

He had once continued about nine days without drink; and he might have continued longer, if, by diſtempering himſelf one night with hard ſtudy, he had not had ſome inclination to take a ſmall *draught*. *Boyle.*

I have cured ſome very deſperate coughs by a *draught* every morning of ſpring-water, with a handful of ſage boiled in it. *Temple.*

Every *draught*, to him that has quenched his thirſt, is but a further quenching of nature; a proviſion for rheum and diſeaſes. *South's Sermons.*

> Long *draughts* of ſleep his monſtrous limbs enſlave;
> He reels, and, falling, fills the ſpacious cave. *Dryden's Æn.*

3. Liquor drank for pleaſure.

> Were it a *draught* for Juno when ſhe banquets,
> I would not taſte thy treaſonous offer. *Milton.*
> Number'd ills, that lie unſeen
> In the pernicious *draught*: the word obſcene,
> Or harſh, which, once elanc'd, muſt ever fly
> Irrevocable; the too prompt reply. *Prior.*
> Delicious wines th' attending herald brought;
> The gold gave luſtre to the purple *draught*. *Pope's Odyſſey.*

4. The act of drawing or pulling carriages.

A general cuſtom of uſing oxen for all ſorts of *draught*, would be perhaps the greateſt improvement. *Temple.*

The moſt occaſion that farmers have, is for *draught* horſes. *Mortimer's Husbandry.*

5. The quality of being drawn.

The Hertfordſhire wheel-plough is the beſt and ſtrongeſt for moſt uſes, and of the eaſieſt *draught*. *Mortimer's Husband.*

6. Repreſentation by picture.

> Her pencil drew whate'er her ſoul deſign'd,
> And oft the happy *draught* ſurpaſs'd the image in her mind. *Dryden.*

7. Delineation; ſketch.

A good inclination is but the firſt rude *draught* of virtue; but the finiſhing ſtrokes are from the will. *South's Sermons.*

I have, in a ſhort *draught*, given a view of our original ideas, from whence all the reſt are derived. *Locke.*

8. A picture drawn.

Whereas in other creatures we have but the trace of his footſteps, in man we have the *draught* of his hand: in him were united all the ſcattered perfections of the creature. *South.*

9. The act of ſweeping with a net.

Upon the *draught* of a pond not one fiſh was left, but two pikes grown to an exceſſive bigneſs. *Hale's Origin of Mankind.*

10. The quantity of fiſhes taken by once drawing the net.

He laid down his pipe, and caſt his net, which brought him a very great *draught*. *L'Eſtrange, Fable* 109.

11. The act of ſhooting with the bow.

Geffrey of Boullion, the glorious general, at one *draught* of his bow, ſhooting againſt David's tower in Jeruſalem, broached three feetleſs birds called allerions. *Camden's Rem.*

12. Diverſion in war; the act of diſturbing the main deſign; perhaps ſudden attack.

I conceive the manner of your handling of the ſervice, by drawing ſudden *draughts* upon the enemy, when he looketh not for you; and to watch advantages upon him, as he doth upon you. *Spenſer's Ireland.*

13. Forces drawn off from the main army; a detachment.

Such a *draught* of forces would leſſen the number of thoſe, that might otherwiſe be employed. *Addiſon.*

14. A ſink; a drain.

Whatſoever entereth in at the mouth goeth into the belly, and is caſt out into the *draught*. *Mat.* xv. 17.

15. The depth which a veſſel draws, or ſinks into the water.

> With roomy decks, her guns of mighty ſtrength,
> Deep in her *draught*, and warlike in her length. *Dryden.*

With a ſmall veſſel one may keep within a mile of the ſhore, go amongſt rocks, and paſs over ſhoals, where a veſſel of any *draught* would ſtrike. *Ellis's Voyage.*

16. [In the plural, *draughts.*] A kind of play reſembling cheſs.

Draughthouse. *n. ſ.* [*draught* and *houſe.*] A houſe in which filth is depoſited.

And they brake down the image of Baal, and brake down the houſe of Baal, and made it a *draughthouſe*. 2 *Kings* x. 27.

To DRAW. *v. a.* pret. *drew*; part. paſſ. *drawn.* [ꝺꞃaᵹan, Saxon.]

1. To pull along; not to carry.

Then ſhall all Iſrael bring ropes to that city, and we will *draw* it into the river. 2 *Sa.* xvii. 13.

2. To pull forcibly; to pluck.

He could not *draw* the dagger out of his belly. *Judg.* ii. 22.

The arrow is now *drawn* to the head. *Atterbury.*

3. To bring by violence; to drag.

Do not rich men oppreſs you, and *draw* you before the judgment-ſeats? *Ja.* ii. 6.

4. To raiſe out of a deep place.

They *drew* up Jeremiah with cords, and took him up out of the dungeon. *Jer.* xxxviii. 13.

Draw the water for the ſiege. *Nath.* iii. 14.

5. To ſuck.

He hath *drawn* thee dry. *Eccluſ.* xiii. 7.

There was no war, no dearth, no ſtop of trade or commerce; it was only the crown which had ſucked too hard, and now being full, upon the head of a young king, was like to *draw* leſs. *Bacon's Henry* VII.

Sucking and *drawing* the breaſt diſchargeth the milk as faſt as it can be generated. *Wiſeman on Tumours.*

6. To attract; to call towards itſelf.

We ſee that ſalt, laid to a cut finger, healeth it; ſo as it ſeemeth ſalt *draweth* blood, as well as blood *draweth* ſalt. *Bacon.*

Majeſty in an eclipſe, like the ſun, *draws* eyes, that would not have looked towards it, if it had ſhined out. *Suckling.*

He affected a habit different from that of the times, ſuch as men had only beheld in pictures, which *drew* the eyes of moſt, and the reverence of many towards him. *Clarendon.*

> All eyes you *draw*, and with the eyes the heart;
> Of your own pomp yourſelf the greateſt part. *Dryden.*

7. To inhale.

> Thus I call'd, and ſtray'd I know not whither,
> From where I firſt *drew* air, and firſt beheld
> This happy light. *Milton's Paradiſe Loſt, b.* viii. *l.* 284.
> While near the Lucrine lake, conſum'd to death,
> I *draw* the ſultry air, and gaſp for breath,
> You taſte the cooling breeze. *Addiſon's Remarks on Italy.*
> Why *drew* Marſeille's good biſhop purer breath,
> When nature ſicken'd, and each gale was death? *Pope.*

8. To take from any thing containing.

They *drew* out the ſtaves of the ark. 2 *Chron.* v. 9.

9. To take from a caſk.

> The wine of life is *drawn*, and the mere lees
> Are left this vault to brag of. *Shakeſpeare's Macbeth.*

10. To pull a ſword from the ſheath.

> We will our youth lead on to higher fields,
> And *draw* no ſwords but what are ſanctify'd. *Shakeſ. H.* IV.

I will *draw* my ſword; my hand ſhall deſtroy them. *Ex.* xv.

He proceeded ſo far in his inſolence as to *draw* out his ſword, with an intent to kill him. *Dryden's Conq. of Granada.*

In all your wars good fortune blew before you,
'Till in my fatal cauſe your ſword was *drawn*;
The weight of my misfortunes dragg'd you down. *Dryden.*

11. To let out any liquid.

Some blood *drawn* on me would beget opinion
Of my more fierce endeavour. *Shakeſpeare's King Lear.*

I opened the tumour by the point of a lancet, without *drawing* one drop of blood. *Wiſeman's Surgery.*

12. To take bread out of the oven.

The joyner puts boards into ovens after the batch is *drawn.* *Mortimer's Husbandry.*

13. To uncloſe or ſlide back curtains.

Go, *draw* aſide the curtains, and diſcover
The ſev'ral caſkets to this noble prince. *Shak. Merch. of Ven.*

Alarm'd, and with preſaging heart he came,
And *drew* the curtains, and expos'd the dame
To lothſome light. *Dryden's Sigiſm. and Guiſcar.*

Shouts, cries, and groans firſt pierce my ears, and then
A flaſh of lightning *draws* the guilty ſcene,
And ſhows new arms, and wounds, and dying men. *Dryden.*

14. To cloſe or ſpread curtains.

Philoclea earneſtly again intreated Pamela to open her grief, who, *drawing* the curtain, that the candle might not complain of her bluſhing, was ready to ſpeak. *Sidney, b.* ii.

15. To extract.

Spirits, by diſtillations, may be *drawn* out of vegetable juices, which ſhall flame and fume of themſelves. *Cheyne.*

16. To procure as an agent cauſe.

When he finds the hardſhip of ſlavery outweigh the value of life, 'tis in his power, by reſiſting his maſter, to *draw* on himſelf death. *Locke.*

17. To produce or bring as an efficient cauſe.

Have they invented tones to win
The women, and make them *draw* in
The men, as Indians with a female
Tame elephant inveigle the male? *Hudibras, p.* i. *cant.* 2.

Religion will requite all the honour we can do it, by the bleſſings it will *draw* down upon us. *Tillotſon.*

Our voluntary actions are the precedent cauſes of good and evil, which they *draw* after them, and bring upon us. *Locke.*

What would a man value acres of excellent land, ready cultivated, and well ſtocked too with cattle, where he had no hopes of commerce with other parts of the world to *draw* money to him, by the ſale of the product of the iſland. *Locke.*

Thoſe elucidations have given riſe or increaſe to his doubts, and *drawn* obſcurity upon places of ſcripture. *Locke.*

His ſword ne'er fell but on the guilty head;
Oppreſſion, tyranny, and pow'r uſurp'd,
Draw all the vengeance of his arm upon 'em. *Addiſ. Cato.*

18. To convey ſecretly.

The liers in wait *draw* themſelves along. *Judg.* xx. 37.

In proceſs of time, and as their people increaſed, they *drew* themſelves more weſterly towards the Red ſea. *Raleigh's Hiſtory of the World.*

19. To protract; to lengthen.

Do you note
How much her grace is alter'd on the ſudden?
How long her face is *drawn*? how pale ſhe looks,
And of an earthly cold? Obſerve her eyes! *Shak. H.* VIII.

If we ſhall meet again with more delight,
Then *draw* my life in length; let me ſuſtain,
In hopes of his embrace, the worſt of pain. *Dryden's Æn.*

In ſome similes men *draw* their compariſons into minute particulars of no importance. *Felton on the Claſſicks.*

20. To utter lingeringly.

The brand amid' the flaming fuel thrown,
Or *drew*, or ſeem'd to *draw*, a dying groan. *Dryd. Fables.*

21. To repreſent by picture; or in fancy.

I do arm myſelf
To welcome the condition of the time;
Which cannot look more hideouſly on me,
Than I have *drawn* it in my fantaſy. *Shakeſp. Henry* IV.

With his other hand, thus o'er his brow,
He falls to ſuch peruſal of my face,
As he would *draw* it. *Shakeſpeare's Hamlet.*

Draw the whole world expecting who ſhould reign,
After this combat, o'er the conquer'd main. *Waller.*

From the ſoft aſſaults of love
Poets and painters never are ſecure:
Can I, untouch'd, the fair one's paſſions move,
Or thou *draw* beauty, and not feel its pow'r? *Prior.*

22. To form a repreſentation.

The emperor one day took up a pencil which fell from the hand of Titian, who was then *drawing* his picture; and upon the compliment which Titian made him on that occaſion, he ſaid, Titian deſerves to be ſerved by Cæſar. *Dryden's Dufreſ.*

23. To derive; to have from ſome original cauſe or donor.

Shall freeborn men, in humble awe,
Submit to ſervile ſhame;
Who from conſent and cuſtom *draw*
The ſame right to be rul'd by law,
Which kings pretend to reign? *Dryden.*

Several wits entered into commerce with the Egyptians, and from them *drew* the rudiments of ſciences. *Temple.*

24. To deduce as from poſtulates

From the events and revolutions of theſe governments are *drawn* the uſual inſtruction of princes and ſtateſmen. *Temple.*

25. To imply; to produce as a conſequential inference.

What ſhews the force of the inference but a view of all the intermediate ideas that *draw* in the concluſion, or propoſition inferred. *Locke.*

26. To allure; to entice.

I'll raiſe ſuch artificial ſprights,
As, by the ſtrength of their illuſion,
Shall *draw* him on to his confuſion. *Shakeſpeare's Macbeth.*

We have *drawn* them from the city. *Joſ.* viii. 6.

Draw me not away with the wicked. *Pſ.* xxviii. 3.

Having the art, by empty promiſes and threats, to *draw* others to his purpoſe. *Hayward.*

The Spaniards, that were in the town, had ſo good memories of their loſſes in their former ſallies, as the confidence of an army, which came for their deliverance, could not *draw* them forth again. *Bacon's War with Spain.*

27. To lead as a motive.

Your way is ſhorter;
My purpoſes do *draw* me much about. *Sh. Ant. and Cleop.*

Æneas wond'ring ſtood, then aſk'd the cauſe
Which to the ſtream the crowding people *draws.* *Dryden.*

28. To perſuade to follow.

The poet
Did feign that Orpheus *drew* trees, ſtones, and floods;
Since nought ſo ſtockiſh, hard, and full of rage,
But muſick, for the time, doth change his nature. *Shakeſp.*

29. To induce; to perſuade.

The Engliſh lords, to ſtrengthen their parties, did ally themſelves with the Iriſh, and *drew* them in to dwell among them, and gave their children to be foſtered by them. *Davies.*

Their beauty or unbecomingneſs are of more force to *draw* or deter their imitation than diſcourſes. *Locke.*

30. To win; to gain: a metaphor from cards.

This ſeems a fair deſerving, and muſt *draw* me
That which my father loſes. *Shakeſpeare's King Lear.*

31. To receive; to take up.

For thy three thouſand ducats here is ſix.
—If every ducat in ſix thouſand ducats
Were in ſix parts, and every part a ducat,
I would not *draw* them, I would have my bond. *Shakeſp.*

32. To extort; to force.

So ſad an object, and ſo well expreſs'd,
Drew ſighs and groans from the griev'd hero's breaſt. *Dryd.*

Can you e'er forget
The fond embraces, and repeated bleſſings,
Which you *drew* from him in your laſt farewel? *Add. Cato.*

33. To wreſt; to diſtort.

I wiſh that both you and others would ceaſe from *drawing* the Scriptures to your fantaſies and affections. *Whitgifte.*

34. To compoſe; to form in writing.

In the mean time I will *draw* a bill of properties, ſuch as our play wants. *Shakeſp. Midſummer Night's Dream.*

Clerk, *draw* a deed of gift. *Shakeſ. Merch. of Venice.*

The report is not unartfully *drawn*, in the ſpirit of a pleader, who can find the moſt plauſible topicks. *Swift.*

Shall Ward *draw* contracts with a ſtateſman's ſkill? *Pope.*

35. To withdraw from judicial notice.

Go, waſh thy face, and *draw* thy action: come, thou muſt not be in this humour with me. *Shakeſpeare.*

36. To eviſcerate; to embowel.

In private *draw* your poultry, clean your tripe,
And from your eels their ſlimy ſubſtance wipe. *King's Cook.*

37. *To* Draw *in.* To apply to any purpoſe by diſtortion or violence.

A diſpute, where every little ſtraw is laid hold on, and every thing that can but be *drawn in* any way, to give colour to the argument, is advanced with oſtentation. *Locke.*

38. *To* Draw *in.* To contract; to pull back.

Now, ſporting muſe, *draw in* the flowing reins;
Leave the clear ſtreams awhile for ſunny plains. *Gay.*

39. *To* Draw *in.* To inveigle; to intice.

It was the proſtitute faith of faithleſs miſcreants that *drew* them *in*, and deceived them. *South's Sermons.*

40. *To* Draw *off.* To extract by diſtillation.

Authors, who have thus *drawn off* the ſpirits of their thoughts, ſhould lie ſtill for ſome time, 'till their minds have gathered freſh ſtrength, and by reading, reflection, and converſation, laid in a new ſtock of elegancies, ſentiments, and images of nature. *Addiſon's Freeholder*, Nº. 40.

41. To drain out by a vent.

Stop your veſſel, and have a little vent-hole ſtopped with a ſpill, which never allow to be pulled out 'till you *draw off* a great quantity. *Mortimer's Huſbandry.*

42. *To* Draw *off.* To withdraw; to abſtract.

It *draws* mens minds *off* from the bitterness of party. *Add.*

43. *To* DRAW *on*. To occasion; to invite.

Under colour of war, which either his negligence *draws on*, or his practices procured, he levied a subsidy. *Hayward.*

44. *To* DRAW *on*. To cause; to bring by degrees.

The examination of the subtile matter would *draw on* the consideration of the nice controversies that perplex philosophers. *Boyle on Fluids.*

45. *To* DRAW *over*. To raise in a still.

I took rectified oil of vitriol, and by degrees mixed with it essential oil of wormwood, *drawn over* with water in a limbeck. *Boyle on Colours.*

46. *To* DRAW *over*. To persuade to revolt; to induce to change a party.

Some might be brought into his interests by money, others *drawn over* by fear. *Addison on the State of the War.*

One of differing sentiments would have *drawn* Luther *over* to his party. *Atterbury.*

47. *To* DRAW *out*. To protract; to lengthen.

He must not only die the death,
But thy unkindness shall his death *draw out*
To ling'ring sufferance. *Shakesp. Measure for Measure.*

Virgil has *drawn out* the rules of tillage and planting into two books, which Hesiod has dispatched in half a one. *Addis.*

48. *To* DRAW *out*. To extract; to pump out by insinuation.

Philoclea found her, and, to *draw out* more, said she, I have often wondered how such excellencies could be. *Sidney.*

49. *To* DRAW *out*. To call to action; to detach for service; to range.

Draw out a file, pick man by man,
Such who dare die, and dear will sell their death. *Dryden.*

Th' Arcadian king
And Trojan youth the same oblations bring:
Next of his men, and ships, he makes review,
Draws out the best and ablest of the crew. *Dryden's Æn.*

50. To range in battle.

Let him desire his superior officer, that the next time he is *drawn out* the challenger may be posted near him. *Collier.*

51. *To* DRAW *up*. To form in order of battle.

The lord Bernard, with the king's troops, seeing there was no enemy left on that side, *drew up* in a large field opposite to the bridge. *Clarendon, b.* viii.

So Muley-Zeydan found us
Drawn up in battle to receive the charge. *Dryd. Don Sebast.*

52. *To* DRAW *up*. To form in writing; to contrive.

To make a sketch, or a more perfect model of a picture, is, in the language of poets, to *draw up* the scenary of a play. *Dry.*

A paper might be *drawn up*, and signed by two or three hundred principal gentlemen. *Swift.*

To DRAW. *v. n.*

1. To perform the office of a beast of draught.

An heifer which hath not been wrought with, and which hath not *drawn* in the yoke. *Deutr.* xxi. 3.

Think every bearded fellow, that's but yok'd,
May *draw* with you. *Shakespeare's Othello.*

2. To act as a weight.

They should keep a watch upon the particular bias in their minds, that it may not *draw* too much. *Addison's Spectator.*

3. To contract; to shrink.

I have not yet found certainly, that the water itself, by mixture of ashes, or dust, will shrink or *draw* into less room. *Bacon's Natural History,* N°. 34.

4. To advance; to move; to make progression.

Draw ye near hither all the chief of the people. 1 *Sa.* xiv.

He ended; and th' archangel soon *drew* nigh,
Not in his shape celestial, but as man
Clad to meet man. *Milton's Paradise Lost, b.* xi. *l.* 238.

Ambitious meteors! how willing they are to set themselves upon the wing, taking every occasion of *drawing* upward to the sun. *Dryden's Don Sebastian.*

Now nearer to the Stygian lake they *draw*,
Whom from the shore the surly boatman saw,
Observ'd their passage through the shady wood,
And mark'd their near approaches to the flood. *Dryden.*

And now I faint with grief; my fate *draws* nigh:
In all the pride of blooming youth I die. *Addison's Ovid.*

5. To draw a sword.

For his sake
Did I expose myself, pure; for his love
Drew to defend him, when he was beset. *Sh. Twelfth Night.*

6. To practise the act of delineation.

So much insight into perspective, and skill in *drawing*, as will enable him to represent tolerably on paper any thing he sees, should be got. *Locke.*

7. To take a card out of the pack; to take a lot.

He has *drawn* a black, and smiles. *Dryden.*

8. To make a sore run by attraction.

9. To retire; to retreat a little.

They returned to the camp where the king was, and the Scots *drew* a little back to a more convenient post for their residence. *Clarendon, b.* ii.

10. *To* DRAW *off*. To retire; to retreat.

When the engagement proves unlucky, the way is to *draw off* by degrees, and not to come to an open rupture. *Collier.*

11. *To* DRAW *on*. To advance; to approach.

The fatal day *draws on*, when I must fall. *Dryden.*

12. *To* DRAW *up*. To form troops into regular order.

DRAW. *n. s.* [from the verb.]

1. The act of drawing.

2. The lot or chance drawn.

DRAWBACK. *n. s.* [*draw* and *back.*] Money paid back for ready payment, or any other reason.

In poundage and *drawbacks* I lose half my rent;
Whatever they give me, I must be content. *Swift.*

DRA'WBRIDGE. *n. s.* [*draw* and *bridge.*] A bridge made to be lifted up, to hinder or admit communication at pleasure.

Half the buildings were raised on the continent, and the other half on an island, continued together by a *drawbridge.* *Carew's Survey of Cornwal.*

DRA'WER. *n. s.* [from *draw.*]

1. One employed in procuring water from the well.

From the hewer of thy wood unto the *drawer* of thy water. *Deutr.* xxix. 11.

2. One whose business is to draw liquors from the cask.

To drive away the time 'till Falstaff comes, I pray thee do thou stand in some bye room, while I question my puny *drawer* to what end he gave me the sugar. *Shakesp. Henry* IV.

Let the *drawers* be ready with wine and fresh glasses;
Let the waiters have eyes, though their tongues must be ty'd. *Ben. Johnson's Tavern Academy.*

A man of fire is a general enemy to all waiters, and makes the *drawers* abroad, and his footmen at home, know he is not to be provoked. *Tatler,* N°. 61.

3. That which has the power of attraction.

Love is a flame, and therefore we say beauty is attractive, because physicians observe that fire is a great *drawer.* *Swift.*

4. A box in a case, out of which it is drawn at pleasure.

There may be other and different intelligent beings, of whose faculties he has as little knowledge, or apprehension, as a worm, shut up in one *drawer* of a cabinet, hath of the senses or understanding of a man. *Locke.*

We will suppose the China dishes taken off, and a *drawer* of medals supplying their room. *Addison on Medals.*

5. [In the plural.] The lower part of a man's dress.

The Maltese harden the bodies of their children, and reconcile them to the heat, by making them go stark naked, without shirt or *drawers,* 'till they are ten years old. *Locke.*

DRA'WING. *n. s.* [from *draw.*] Delineation; representation.

They random *drawings* from your sheets shall take,
And of one beauty many blunders make. *Pope's Epistles.*

DRA'WINGROOM. *n. s.* [*draw* and *room.*]

1. The room in which company assembles at court.

What you heard of the words spoken of you in the *drawing-room* was not true: the sayings of princes are generally as ill related as the sayings of wits. *Pope.*

2. The company assembled there.

DRAWN. [participle from *draw.*]

An army was *drawn* together of near six thousand horse. *Cla.*

So lofty was the pile a Parthian bow,
With vigour *drawn,* must put the shaft below. *Dryd. Fab.*

1. Equal; where each party takes his own stake.

If we make a *drawn* game of it, or procure but moderate advantages, every British heart must tremble. *Addison.*

2. With a sword drawn.

What, art thou *drawn* among those heartless hinds? *Shak.*

3. Open; put aside, or unclosed.

A curtain *drawn,* presented to our view
A town besieg'd. *Dryden's Tyran. Love.*

4. Eviscerated.

There's no more faith in thee than in a stoned prune; no more truth in thee than in a *drawn* fox. *Shakesp.*

5. Induced as from some motive.

The Irish will better be *drawn* to the English, than the English to the Irish government. *Spenser on Ireland.*

As this friendship was *drawn* together by fear on both sides, so it was not like to be more durable than was the fear. *Hayw.*

DRA'WWELL. *n. s.* [*draw* and *well.*] A deep well; a well out of which water is drawn by a long cord.

The first conceit, tending to a watch, was a *drawwell:* the people of old were wont only to let down a pitcher with a handcord, for as much water as they could easily pull up. *Grew.*

To DRAWL. *v. n.* [from *draw.*] To utter any thing in a slow driveling way.

Then mount the clerks, and in one lazy tone
Through the long heavy page *drawl* on. *Pope's Dunciad.*

DRAY. } *n. s.* [ꝺpæᵹ, Saxon.] The car on which beer
DRA'YCART. } is carried.

Let him be brought into the field of election upon his *draycart,* and I will meet him there in a triumphant chariot. *Addis.*

When *drays* bound high, then never cross behind,
Where bubbling yest is blown by gusts of wind. *Gay's Triv.*

DRA'YHORSE. *n. s.* [*dray* and *horse.*] A horse which draws a dray.

This truth is illustrated by a discourse on the nature of the elephant and the *drayhorse.* *Tatler,* N°. 60.

DRA'YMAN. *n. ſ.* [*dray* and *man.*] One that attends a dray or cart.

A brace of *draymen* bid God ſpeed him well,
And had the tribute of his ſupple knee. *Shakeſpeare.*

Have not coblers, *draymen*, and mechanicks governed as well as preached? Nay, have not they by preaching come to govern? *South's Sermons.*

DRA'YPLOUGH. *n. ſ.* [*dray* and *plough.*] A plough of a particular kind.

The *drayplough* is the beſt plough in Winter for miry clays. *Mortimer's Husbandry.*

DRA'ZEL. *n. ſ.* [perhaps corrupted from *droſſel*, the ſcum or droſs of human nature; or from *droſleſſe*, French, a whore.] A low, mean, worthleſs wretch.

As the devil uſes witches,
To be their cully for a ſpace,
That, when the time's expir'd, the *drazels*
For ever may become his vaſſals. *Hudibras, p.* iii. *cant.* i.

DREAD. *n. ſ.* [ꝺɲaꝺ, Saxon.]

1. Fear; terrour; affright.

Think'ſt thou that duty ſhall have *dread* to ſpeak,
When pow'r to flatt'ry bows? To plainneſs honour
Is bound, when majeſty to folly falls. *Shakeſp. King Lear.*

But was ever any wicked man free from the ſtings of a guilty conſcience, from the ſecret *dread* of divine diſpleaſure, and of the vengeance of another world? *Tillotſon, Serm.* 4.

If our fears can be awakened with the *dread* of evil, he has armed his laws with the terrour of eternal miſery. *Rogers.*

2. Habitual fear; awe.

The fear of you, and the *dread* of you, ſhall be upon every beaſt of the earth. *Gen.* ix. 2.

3. The perſon or thing feared; the cauſe of fear.

To thee, of all our good the ſacred ſpring;
To thee, our deareſt *dread*; to thee, our ſofter king. *Prior.*

DREAD. *adj.* [ꝺɲæꝺ, Saxon.]

1. Terrible; frightful.

That e'er this tongue of mine,
That laid the ſentence of *dread* baniſhment
On yond' proud man, ſhould take it off again
With words of ſooth! *Shakeſpeare's Richard* II.

It cannot be, but thou haſt murther'd him:
So ſhould a murtherer look, ſo *dread*, ſo grim. *Shakeſpeare.*

To be expos'd againſt the warring winds?
To ſtand againſt the deep *dread* bolted thunder. *Shakeſp.*

Amaze
Be ſure, and terrour, ſeiz'd the rebel hoſt,
When, coming towards them, ſo *dread* they ſaw
The bottom of the mountains upward turn'd. *Milt. P. Loſt.*

2. Awful; venerable in the higheſt degree.

Thou, attended glorioully from heav'n,
Shalt in the ſky appear, and from thee ſend
The ſummoning archangels to proclaim
Thy *dread* tribunal. *Milton's Paradiſe Loſt, b.* iii. *l.* 323.

From this deſcent
Celeſtial virtues riſing, will appear
More glorious and more *dread* than from no fall. *Milton.*

3. This ſeems to be the meaning of that controverted phraſe *dread majeſty*. Some of the old acts of parliament are ſaid in the preface to be *metuendiſſimi regis*, our *dread* ſovereign's.

To DREAD. *v. a.* [from the noun.] To fear in an exceſſive degree.

You may deſpiſe that which terrifies others, and which yet all, even thoſe who moſt *dread* it, muſt in a little time encounter. *Wake.*

To DREAD. *v. n.* To be in fear.

Dread not, neither be afraid of them. *Deut.* i. 8.

DRE'ADER. *n. ſ.* [from *dread.*] One that lives in fear.

I have ſuſpended much of my pity towards the great *dreaders* of popery. *Swift.*

DRE'ADFUL. *n. ſ.* [*dread* and *full.*] Terrible; frightful; formidable.

Thy love, ſtill arm'd with fate,
Is *dreadful* as thy hate. *Granville.*

DRE'ADFULNESS. *n. ſ.* [from *dreadful.*] Terribleneſs; frightfulneſs.

It may juſtly ſerve for matter of extreme terrour to the wicked, whether they regard the *dreadfulneſs* of the day in which they ſhall be tried, or the quality of the judge by whom they are to be tried. *Hakewill on Providence.*

DRE'ADFULLY. *adv.* [from *dreadful.*] Terribly; frightfully.

Not ſharp revenge, nor hell itſelf can find
A fiercer torment than a guilty mind,
Which day and night doth *dreadfully* accuſe,
Condemns the wretch, and ſtill the charge renews. *Dryden.*

DRE'ADLESNESS. *n. ſ.* [from *dreadleſs.*] Fearleſneſs; intrepidity; undauntedneſs.

Zelmane, to whom danger then was a cauſe of *dreadleſneſs*, all the compoſition of her elements being nothing but fiery, with ſwiftneſs of deſire croſſed him. *Sidney.*

DRE'ADLESS. *adj.* [from *dread.*] Fearleſs; unaffrighted; intrepid; unſhaken; undaunted; free from terrour.

Dreadleſs, ſaid he, that ſhall I ſoon declare;
It was complain'd, that thou had'ſt done great tort
Unto an aged woman. *Fairy Queen, b.* ii. *cant.* 5. *ſtan.* 27.

All night the *dreadleſs* angel, unpurſu'd,
Through heav'n's wide champaign held his way. *Milton.*

DREAM. *n. ſ.* [*droom*, Dutch. This word is derived by *Meric Caſaubon*, with more ingenuity than truth, from δρᾶμα τοῦ βίου, *the comedy of life*; dreams being, as plays are, a repreſentation of ſomething which does not really happen. This conceit *Junius* has enlarged by quoting an epigram.

Σκηνὴ πᾶς ὁ βίος καὶ παίγνιον ἢ μάθε παίζειν,
Τὴν σπουδὴν μεταθεὶς, ἢ φέρε τὰς ὀδύνας. *Anthol.*

1. A phantaſm of ſleep; the thoughts of a ſleeping man.

We eat our meat in fear, and ſleep
In the affliction of thoſe terrible *dreams*
That ſhake us nightly. *Shakeſpeare's Macbeth.*

In *dreams* they fearful precipices tread;
Or, ſhipwreck'd, labour to ſome diſtant ſhore. *Dryden.*

Glorious *dreams* ſtand ready to reſtore
The pleaſing ſhapes of all you ſaw before. *Dryden.*

2. An idle fancy; a wild conceit; a groundleſs ſuſpicion.

Let him keep
A hundred knights; yes, that on ev'ry *dream*,
Each buz, each fancy, each complaint, diſlike,
He may enguard his dotage. *Shakeſpeare's King Lear.*

To DREAM. *v. n.* preter. *dreamed*, or *dreamt.* [from the noun.]

1. To have the repreſentation of ſomething in ſleep.

Dreaming is the having of ideas, whilſt the outward ſenſes are ſtopped, ſo that they receive not outward objects with their uſual quickneſs, in the mind; not ſuggeſted by any external objects, or known occaſion, nor under the rule or conduct of the underſtanding. *Locke.*

I have long *dream'd* of ſuch a kind of man,
But, being awake, I do deſpiſe my dream. *Shakeſ. H.* IV.

I have nightly ſince
Dreamt of encounters 'twixt thyſelf and me:
We have been down together in my ſleep,
Unbuckling helms, fiſting each other's throat,
And wak'd half dead with nothing. *Shakeſp. Coriolanus.*

I *dreamed* that I was conveyed into a wide and boundleſs plain. *Tatler*, N°. 81.

2. To think; to imagine.

Theſe boys know little they are ſons to th' king,
Nor Cymbeline *dreams* that they are alive. *Shak. Cymbeline.*

He never *dreamed* of the deluge, nor thought that firſt orb more than a tranſient cruſt. *Burnet's Theory of the Earth.*

He little *dream'd* how nigh he was to care,
'Till treach'rous fortune caught him in the ſnare. *Dryden.*

3. To think idly.

They *dream* on in a conſtant courſe of reading, but not digeſting. *Locke.*

I began to *dream* of nothing leſs than the immortality of my work. *Smith.*

3. To be ſluggiſh; to idle.

Why does Anthony *dream* out his hours,
And tempts not fortune for a noble day? *Dryd. All for Love.*

To DREAM. *v. a.* To ſee in a dream.

The Macedon, by Jove's decree,
Was taught to *dream* an herb for Ptolomey. *Dryden.*

At length in ſleep their bodies they compoſe,
And *dreamt* the future fight, and early roſe. *Dryden's Fab.*

DRE'AMER. *n. ſ.* [from *dream.*]

1. One who has dreams; one who has fancies in his ſleep.

The viſion ſaid, and vaniſh'd from his ſight;
The *dreamer* waken'd in a mortal fright. *Dryden.*

If our *dreamer* pleaſes to try whether the glowing heat of a glaſs furnace be barely a wandering imagination in a drowſy man's fancy, by putting his head into it, he may perhaps be wakened into a certainty. *Locke.*

2. An idle fanciful man; a viſionary.

Sometime he angers me,
With telling of the moldwarp, and the ant,
Of *dreamer* Merlin, and his prophecies. *Shakeſ. Henry* IV.

3. A mope; a man loſt in wild imagination; a *reveur.*

The man of ſenſe his meat devours,
But only ſmells the peel and flow'rs;
And he muſt be an idle *dreamer*,
Who leaves the pie, and gnaws the ſtreamer. *Prior.*

4. A ſluggard; an idler.

DRE'AMLESS. *adj.* [from *dream.*] Without dreams.

The ſavages of mount Atlas, in Barbary, were reported to be both nameleſs and *dreamleſs.* *Camden's Remains.*

DREAR. *adj.* [ꝺɲeoɲᵹ, Saxon, dreary.] Mournful; diſmal; ſorrowful.

In urns and altars round,
A *drear* and dying ſound
Affrights the flamens at their ſervice quaint. *Milton.*

DRE'ARIHEAD. *n. ſ.* [from *dreary.*] Horrour; diſmalneſs: a word now no longer in uſe.

That ſhortly from the ſhape of womanhed,
Such as ſhe was when Pallas ſhe attempted,

She grew to hideous ſhape of *drearihead*,
Pined with grief of folly late repented. *Spenſer.*

DRE'ARIMENT. *n. ſ.* [from *dreary.*]

1. Sorrow; diſmalneſs; melancholy.

I teach the woods and waters to lament
Your doleful *dreariment.* *Spenſer's Epithalamium.*

2. Horrour; dread; terrour. This word is now obſolete.

Almighty Jove, in wrathful mood,
To wreak the guilt of mortal ſins is bent;
Hurls forth his thundering dart with deadly food,
Inroll'd in flames and ſmould'ring *dreariment.* *Fairy Queen.*

DRE'ARY. *adj.* [ꝺꞃeoꞃıᵹ, Saxon.]

1. Sorrowful; diſtreſsful.

The meſſenger of death, the ghaſtly owl,
With *dreary* ſhrieks did alſo yell;
And hungry wolves continually did howl
At her abhorred face, ſo horrid and ſo foul. *Fairy Queen.*

2. Gloomy; diſmal; horrid.

Obſcure they went through *dreary* ſhades, that led
Along the vaſt dominions of the dead. *Dryden, Æn.* 6.

Towns, foreſts, herds and men promiſcuous drown'd,
With one great death deform the *dreary* ground. *Prior.*

DREDGE. *n. ſ.* [*To dretch*, in *Chaucer*, is to delay; perhaps a net ſo often ſtopped may be called from this.] A kind of net.

For oyſters, beſides gathering by hand, at a great ebb, they have a peculiar *dredge*; which is a thick ſtrong net, faſtened to three ſpills of iron, and drawn at the boat's ſtern, gathering whatſoever it meeteth lying in the bottom of the water. *Carew.*

To DREDGE. *v. a.* [from the noun.] To gather with a dredge.

The oyſters *dredged* in the Lyne, find a welcome acceptance. *Carew.*

DREDGER. *n. ſ.* [from *dredge.*] One who fiſhes with a dredge.

DRE'GGINESS. *n. ſ.* [from *dreggy.*] Fulneſs of dregs or lees; foulneſs; muddineſs; feculence.

DRE'GGISH. *adj.* [from *dregs.*] Foul with lees; feculent.

To give a ſtrong taſte to this *dreggiſh* liquor, they fling in an incredible deal of broom or hops, whereby ſmall beer is rendered equal in miſchief to ſtrong. *Harvey on Conſumptions.*

DRE'GGY. *adj.* [from *dregs.*] Containing dregs; conſiſting of dregs; muddy; feculent.

Theſe num'rous veins, ſuch is the curious frame,
Receive the pure inſinuating ſtream;
But no corrupt or *dreggy* parts admit,
To form the blood, or feed the limbs unfit. *Blackm. Creat.*

Ripe grapes, being moderately preſſed, their juice may, without much *dreggy* matter, be ſqueezed out. *Boyle.*

DREGS. *n. ſ.* [ꝺꞃeꞅꞇen, Saxon; *dreggian*, Iſlandick.]

1. The ſediment of liquors; the lees; the grounds; the feculence.

Fain would we make him author of the wine,
If for the *dregs* we could ſome other blame. *Davies.*

They often tread deſtruction's horrid path,
And drink the *dregs* of the revenger's wrath. *Sandys.*

We from the *dregs* of life think to receive,
What the firſt ſprightly running could not give. *Dryden.*

Such run on poets in a raging vein,
Ev'n to the *dregs* and ſqueezings of the brain. *Pope.*

2. Any thing by which purity is corrupted.

The king by this journey purged a little the *dregs* and leaven of the northern people, that were before in no good affections towards him. *Bacon.*

3. Droſs; ſweepings; refuſe.

Heav'n's favourite thou, for better fate's deſign'd,
Than we the *dregs* and rubbiſh of mankind. *Dryden's Juv.*

What diffidence we muſt be under, whether God will regard our ſacrifice, when we have nothing to offer him but the *dregs* and refuſe of life, the days of loathing and ſatiety, and the years in which we have no pleaſure. *Rogers's Sermons.*

To DREIN. *v. n.* [See DRAIN.] To empty.

I am ſure I can fiſh it out of her: ſhe is the ſluice of her lady's ſecrets: 'tis but ſetting her mill agoing, and I can *drein* her of them all. *Congreve's Old Batchelor.*

'Tis *drein'd* and empty'd of its poiſon now;
A cordial draught. *Southern.*

To DRENCH. *v. a.* [ꝺꞃencan, Saxon.]

1. To waſh; to ſoak; to ſteep.

In ſwiniſh ſleep
Their *drenched* natures lie, as in a death. *Shakeſp. Macbeth.*

Our garments being as they were *drenched* in the ſea, hold notwithſtanding their freſhneſs and gloſſes, being rather new-dy'd than ſtain'd with ſalt water. *Shakeſpeare's Tempeſt.*

To-day deep thoughts learn with me to *drench*
In mirth, that after no repenting draws. *Milton's Sam.*

Now dam the ditches, and the floods reſtrain;
Their moiſture has already *drench'd* the plain. *Dryd. Virgil.*

2. To ſaturate with drink or moiſture: in an ill ſenſe.

Too oft, alas! has mutual hatred *drench'd*
Our ſwords in native blood. *Phillips.*

3. To phyſick by violence.

If any of your cattle are infected, ſpeedily let both ſick and well blood, and *drench* them. *Mortimer's Huſbandry.*

DRENCH. *n. ſ.* [from the verb.]

1. A draught; a ſwill: by way of abhorrence or contempt.

Let ſuch bethink them, if the ſleepy *drench*
Of that forgetful lake benumb not ſtill,
That in our proper motion we aſcend. *Milton's Par. Loſt.*

2. Phyſick for a brute.

A *drench* is a potion or drink prepared for a ſick horſe, and compoſed of ſeveral drugs in a liquid form. *Farrier's Dict.*

Harry, ſays ſhe, how many haſt thou kill'd to-day? Give my roan horſe a *drench*, ſays he; and anſwers, fourteen, an hour after. *Shakeſpeare's Henry IV. p.* i.

A *drench* of wine has with ſucceſs been us'd,
And through a horn the gen'rous juice infus'd. *Dryden.*

3. Phyſick that muſt be given by violence.

Their counſels are more like a *drench*, that muſt be poured down, than a draught which might be leiſurely drank, if I liked it. *King Charles.*

4. A channel of water.

DRE'NCHER. *n. ſ.* [from *drench.*]

1. One that dips or ſteeps any thing.

2. One that gives phyſick by force. *Dict.*

DRENT. *participle.* Probably corrupted from *drenched*, to make a proverbial rhyme, *brent* or *burnt.*

What flames, quoth he, when I the preſent ſee,
In danger rather to be *drent* than brent? *Fairy Queen, b.* ii.

To DRESS. *v. a.* [*dreſſer*, French.]

1. To clothe; to inveſt with cloaths.

The firſt requeſt
He made, was, like his brothers to be *dreſs'd*;
And, as his birth requir'd, above the reſt. *Dryden.*

2. To clothe pompouſly or elegantly.

Look upon pleaſures not upon that ſide that is next the ſun, or where they look beauteouſly; that is, as they come towards you to be enjoyed; for then they paint and ſmile, and *dreſs* themſelves up in tinſel and glaſs gems and counterfeit imagery. *Taylour.*

Few admir'd the native red and white,
'Till poets *dreſs'd* them up to charm the ſight. *Dryd. Epiſtles.*

Lollia Paulina wore, in jewels only, when *dreſſed* out, about the value of three hundred twenty-two thouſand nine hundred and ſixteen pounds thirteen ſhillings and four pence. *Arbuthnot on Coins.*

3. To adorn; to deck; to embelliſh; to furniſh.

Where was a fine room in the middle of the houſe, handſomely *dreſſed* up, for the commiſſioners to ſit in. *Clarendon.*

Skill is uſed in *dreſſing* up power with all the ſplendour abſoluteneſs can add to it. *Locke.*

The mind loſes its natural reliſh of real truth, and is reconciled inſenſibly to any thing that can be *dreſſed* up, into any feint appearance of it. *Locke.*

4. To cover a wound with medicaments.

In time of my ſickneſs another chirurgeon *dreſſed* her. *Wiſem.*

5. To curry; to rub.

Our infirmities are ſo many, that we are forced to *dreſs* and tend horſes and aſſes, that they may help our needs. *Taylor.*

Three hundred horſes, in high ſtables fed,
Stood ready, ſhining all, and ſmoothly *dreſs'd.* *Dryd. Æn.*

6. To rectify; to adjuſt.

Adam! well may we labour ſtill to *dreſs*
This garden; ſtill to tend plant, herb, and flow'r,

7. To prepare for any purpoſe.

In Orkney they *dreſs* their leather with roots of tormentil, inſtead of bark. *Mortimer's Huſbandry.*

8. To trim; to fit any thing for ready uſe.

When he *dreſſeth* the lamps he ſhall burn incenſe. *Ex.* xxx.

When you *dreſs* your young hops, cut away roots or ſprigs. *Mortimer's Huſbandry.*

9. To prepare victuals for the table.

Thus the voluptuous youth, bred up to *dreſs*
For his fat grandſire ſome delicious meſs,
In feeding high his tutor will ſurpaſs,
An heir apparent of the gourmand race. *Dryden.*

DRESS. *n. ſ.* [from the verb.]

1. Cloaths; garment; habit.

Dreſſes laughed at in our forefathers wardrobes or pictures, when, by the circulation of time and vanity, they are brought about, we think becoming. *Government of the Tongue.*

A robe obſcene was o'er his ſhoulders thrown,
A *dreſs* by fates and furies worn alone. *Pope's Statius.*

2. Splendid cloaths; habit of ceremony.

Full *dreſs* creates dignity, augments conſciouſneſs, and keeps at diſtance an encroacher. *Clariſſa.*

3. The ſkill of adjuſting dreſs.

The men of pleaſure, *dreſs*, and gallantry. *Pope.*

DRE'SSER. *n. ſ.* [from *dreſs.*]

1. One employed in putting on the cloaths and adorning the perſon of another.

She hurries all her hand-maids to the taſk;
Her head alone will twenty *dreſſers* aſk. *Dryden's Juvenal.*

2. One employed in regulating, trimming, or adjusting any thing.

Said he unto the *dresser* of his vineyard, Behold, these three years I come seeking fruit on this fig-tree, and find none. *Luke.*

3. The bench in a kitchen on which meat is drest or prepared for the table.

'Tis burnt, and so is all the meat:
What dogs are these? Where is the rascal cook?
How durst you, villains, bring it from the *dresser*,
And serve it thus to me that love it not? *Shakespeare.*

A mapple *dresser* in her hall she had,
On which full many a slender meal she made. *Dryden.*

When you take down dishes, tip a dozen upon the *dresser*. *Swift's Directions to the Cook.*

DRE'SSING. *n. s.* [from *dress.*] The application made to a sore.

The second day after we took off the *dressings*, and found an eschar made by the catheretick. *Wiseman on Tumours.*

DRE'SSINGROOM. *n. s.* [*dress* and *room.*] The room in which clothes are put on.

Latin books might be found every day in his *dressingroom*, if it were carefully searched. *Swift.*

DREST. *part.* [from *dress.*]

In flow'ry wreaths the royal virgin *drest*
His bending horns, and kindly clapt his breast. *Addis. Ovid.*

To DRIB. *v. a.* [contracted from *dribble.*] To crop; to cut off; to defalcate. A cant word.

Merchants gains come short of half the mart;
For he who drives their bargains, *dribs* a part. *Dryd. Juv.*

To DRI'BBLE. *v. n.* [This word seems to have come from *drop* by successive alterations, such as are usual in living languages. *Drop*, *drip*, *dripple*, *dribble*, from thence *drivel* and *driveler*. *Drip* may indeed be the original word, from the Danish *drypp.*]

1. To fall in drops.

Semilunar processes on the surface, owe their form to the *dribbling* of water that passed over it. *Woodward on Fossils.*

A *dribbling*, difficulty, and a momentary suppression of urine, may be caused by the stone's shutting up the orifice of the bladder. *Arbuthnot on Aliments.*

2. To fall weakly and slowly.

Believe not that the *dribbling* dart of love
Can pierce a compleat bosom. *Shak. Measure for Measure.*

3. To slaver as a child or ideot.

To DRI'BBLE. *v. a.* To throw down in drops.

Let the cook follow with a ladle full of soup, and *dribble* it all the way up stairs. *Swift's Rules to Servants.*

DRI'BLET. *n. s.* [from *dribble.*] A small sum; odd money in a sum.

Twelve long years of exile born,
Twice twelve we number'd since his blest return:
So strictly wert thou just to pay,
Even to the *dribblet* of a day. *Dryden.*

DRI'ER. *n. s.* [from *dry.*] That which has the quality of absorbing moisture; a desiccative.

There is a tale, that boiling of daisy roots in milk, which it is certain are great *driers*, will make dogs little. *Bacon.*

DRIFT. *n. s.* [from *drive.*]

1. Force impellent; impulse; overbearing influence.

A man being under the *drift* of any passion, will still follow the impulse of it, 'till something interpose, and, by a stronger impulse, turn him another way. *South's Sermons.*

2. Violence; course.

The mighty trunk, half rent with rugged rift,
Doth roll adown the rocks, and fall with fearful *drift*. *F. Q.*

3. Any thing driven at random.

Some log, perhaps, upon the waters swam,
An useless *drift*, which rudely cut within,
And hollow'd, first a floating trough became,
And cross some riv'let passage did begin. *Dryd. Ann. Mirab.*

4. Any thing driven or born along in a body.

The ready racers stand,
Swift as on wings of wind up-borne they fly,
And *drifts* of rising dust involve the sky. *Pope's Odyssey.*

5. A storm; a shower.

Our thunder from the South
Shall rain their *drift* of bullets on this town. *Shak. K. John.*

6. A heap or stratum of any matter thrown together by the wind; as, a *snowdrift*, a deep body of snow.

7. Tendency, or aim of action.

The particular *drift* of every act, proceeding eternally from God, we are not able to discern; and therefore cannot always give the proper and certain reason of his works. *Hook.*

Their *drift* 'comes known, and they discover'd are;
For some, of many, will be false of course. *Daniel's C. War.*

8. Scope of a discourse.

The main *drift* of his book being to prove, that what is true is impossible to be false, he opposes nobody. *Tillot. Pref.*

The *drift* of the pamphlet is to stir up our compassion towards the rebels. *Addison.*

This by the stile, the manner, and the *drift*,
'Twas thought could be the work of none but Swift. *Swift.*

To DRIFT. *v. a.* [from the noun.]

1. To drive; to urge along.

Snow no larger than so many grains of sand, *drifted* with the wind in clouds from every plain. *Ellis's Voyage.*

2. Thrown together on heaps.

He wanders on
From hill to dale, still more and more astray,
Impatient flouncing through the *drifted* heaps. *Thomson.*

To DRILL. *v. a.* [*drillen*, Dutch; þirlian, Saxon, from þurgh, through.]

1. To pierce any thing with a drill.

The drill-plate is only a piece of flat iron, fixed upon a flat board, which iron hath an hole punched a little way into it, to set the blunt end of the shank of the drill in, when you *drill* a hole. *Moxon's Mech. Exer.*

2. To perforate; to bore; to pierce.

My body through and through he *drill'd*,
And Whacum by my side lay kill'd. *Hudibras, p.* ii. *can.* 3.

Tell, what could *drill* and perforate the poles,
And to th' attractive rays adapt their holes? *Blackm. Creat.*

3. To make a hole.

When a hole is *drilled* in a piece of metal, they hold the drill-bone in their right hand; but when they turn small work they hold the drill-bone in their left hand. *Moxon's Mech. Ex.*

4. To delay; to put off: in low phrase.

She has bubbled him out of his youth; she *drilled* him on to five and fifty, and she will drop him in his old age. *Addison.*

5. To draw from step to step. A low phrase.

When by such insinuations they have once got within him, and are able to *drill* him on from one lewdness to another, by the same arts they corrupt and squeeze him. *South's Sermons.*

6. To drain; to draw slowly. This sense wants better authority.

Drill'd through the sandy stratum every way,
The waters with the sandy stratum rise. *Thomson's Autumn.*

7. To range troops. An old cant word.

The foe appear'd drawn up and *drill'd*,
Ready to charge them in the field. *Hudibras, p.* i. *cant.* 3.

DRILL. *n. s.* [from the verb.]

1. An instrument with which holes are bored. It is pressed hard against the thing bored, and turned round with a bow and string.

The way of tempering steel to make gravers, *drills*, and mechanical instruments, we have taught artificers. *Boyle.*

Drills are used for the making such holes as punches will not conveniently serve for; as a piece of work that hath already its shape, and must have an hole or more made in it. *Moxon's Mech. Exer.*

2. An ape; a baboon.

Shall the difference of hair be a mark of a different internal specifick constitution between a changeling and a *drill*, when they agree in shape and want of reason? *Locke.*

3. A small dribbling brook. This I have found no where else, and suspect it should be *rill.*

Springs through the pleasant meadows pour their *drills*,
Which snake-like glide between the bordering hills. *Sandys.*

To DRINK. *v. n.* preter. *drank*, or *drunk*; part. pass. *drunk*, or *drunken*. [drincan, Saxon.]

1. To swallow liquors; to quench thirst.

Here, between the armies,
Let's *drink* together friendly, and embrace. *Shak. Henry* IV.

She said *drink*, and I will give thy camels drink also; so I *drank*, and she made the camels *drink* also. *Gen.* xxiv. 46.

He *drank* of the wine. *Gen.* ix. 21.

When delight is the only end, and rests in itself, and dwells there long, then eating and *drinking* is not a serving of God, but an inordinate action. *Taylor's Rule of living holy.*

2. To feast; to be entertained with liquors.

We came to fight you.——For my part, I am sorry it is turned to a *drinking*. *Shakespeare's Anthony and Cleopatra.*

3. To drink to excess; to be an habitual drunkard. A colloquial phrase.

4. *To* DRINK *to.* To salute in drinking; to invite to drink by drinking first.

I take your princely word for those redresses.
—I gave it you, and will maintain my word;
And thereupon I *drink* unto your grace. *Shakesp. Henay* IV.

5. *To* DRINK *to.* To wish well to in the act of taking the cup.

Give me some wine; fill full:
I *drink* to th' general joy of the whole table,
And to our dear friend Banquo, whom we miss. *Sh. Macb.*

I'll *drink* to master Bardolph, and to all the cavaleroes about London. *Shakespeare's Henry* IV. *p.* ii.

To DRINK. *v. a.*

1. To swallow: applied to liquids.

He had eaten no bread, nor *drunk* any water three days and three nights. 1 *Sa.* xxx. 12.

We have *drunken* our water for money. *Sam.* v. 4.

One man gives another a cup of poison, a thing as terrible as death; but at the same time he tells him that it is a cordial, and so he *drinks* it off, and dies. *South's Sermons.*

Alexander,

Alexander, after he had *drank* up a cup of fourteen pints, was going to take another. *Arbuthnot on Coins.*

2. To suck up; to absorb.

The body being reduced nearer unto the earth, and emptied, becometh more porous, and greedily *drinketh* in water. *Brown's Vulgar Errours, b.* ii. *c.* 5.

Set rows of rosemary with flow'ring stem,
And let the purple vi'lets *drink* the stream. *Dryden's Virgil.*

Brush not thy sweeping skirt too near the wall;
Thy heedless sleeve will *drink* the colour'd oil. *Gay's Trivia.*

3. To take in by any inlet; to hear; to see.

My ears have yet not *drunk* a hundred words
Of that tongue's uttering, yet I know the sound. *Shakesp.*

Thither write, my queen,
And with mine eyes I'll *drink* the words you send,
Though ink be made of gall. *Shakespeare's Cymbeline.*

Phemius! let acts of gods, and hero's old,
What ancient bards in hall and bow'r have told,
Attemper'd to the lyre, your voice employ;
Such the pleas'd ear will *drink* with silent joy. *Pope's Odyssey.*

I *drink* delicious poison from thy eye. *Pope.*

4. To act upon by drinking.

Come, we have a hot venison pasty to dinner: come, gentlemen, I hope we shall *drink* down all unkindness. *Shakesp.*

In the compass of some years he will drown his health and his strength in his belly; and, after all his *drunken* trophies, at length *drink* down himself too. *South's Sermons.*

5. To make drunk.

Benhadad was *drinking* himself *drunk* in the pavilions. *1 Kings* xx. 16.

DRINK. *n. s.* [from the verb.]

1. Liquor to be swallowed, opposed to meat.

When God made choice to rear
His mighty champion, strong above compare,
Whose *drink* was only from the liquid brook! *Milt. Agonist.*

2. Liquor of any particular kind.

We will give you rare and sleepy *drinks*. *Sh. Winter's Tale.*

The juices of fruits are either watry or oily: I reckon among the watry all the fruits out of which *drink* is expressed, as the grape, the apple, and the pear. *Bacon's Natural History.*

O madness, to think use of strongest wines,
And strongest *drinks*, our chief support of health! *Milton.*

These, when th' allotted orb of time's compleat,
Are more commended than the labour'd *drink*. *Phillips.*

Amongst *drinks*, austere wines are apt to occasion foul eruptions. *Arbuthnot on Aliments.*

DRI'NKMONEY. *n. s.* [*drink* and *money*.] Money given to buy liquor.

Peg's servants were always asking for *drinkmoney*. *Arbuthnot.*

DRI'NKABLE. *adj.* [from *drink*.] Potable; such as may be drank.

DRI'NKER. *n. s.* [from *drink*.] One that drinks to excess; a drunkard.

It were good for those that have moist brains, and are great *drinkers*, to take fume of lignum, aloes, rosemary, and frankincense, about the full of the moon. *Bacon's Natural History.*

The *drinker* and debauched person is the object of scorn and contempt. *South.*

The urine of hard *drinkers* afford a liquor extremely fetid, but no inflammable spirit: what is inflammable stays in the blood, and affects the brain. Great *drinkers* commonly die apoplectick. *Arbuthnot on Aliments.*

To DRIP. *v. n.* [*drippen*, Dutch.]

1. To fall in drops.

2. To have drops falling from it.

The soil, with fatt'ning moisture fill'd,
Is cloath'd with grass, and fruitful to be till'd;
Such as in fruitful vales we view from high,
Which *dripping* rocks, not rowling streams supply. *Dryden.*

The finest sparks, and cleanest beaux,
Drip from the shoulders to the toes. *Prior.*

To DRIP. *v. a.*

1. To let fall in drops.

Her flood of tears
Seem like the lofty barn of some rich swain,
Which from the thatch *drips* fast a shower of rain. *Swift.*

2. To drop fat in roasting.

Let what was put into his belly, and what he *drips*, be his sauce. *Walton's Angler.*

His offer'd entrails shall his crime reproach,
And *drip* their fatness from the hazle broach. *Dryd. Virgil.*

DRIP. *n. s.* [from the verb.] That which falls in drops.

Water may be procured for necessary occasions from the heavens, by preserving the *drips* of the houses. *Mortimer.*

DRI'PPING. *n. s.* [from *drip*.] The fat which housewives gather from roast meat.

Shews all her secrets of housekeeping;
For candles how she trucks her *dripping*. *Swift.*

DRI'PPINGPAN. *n. s.* [*drip* and *pan*.] The pan in which the fat of roast meat is caught.

When the cook turns her back, throw smoaking coals into the *drippingpan*. *Swift.*

DRI'PPLE. *adj.* [from *drip*.] This word is used somewhere by *Fairfax* for weak, or rare; *dripple shot*.

To DRIVE. *v. a.* preterite *drove*, anciently *drave*; part. pass. *driven*, or *drove*. [*dreiban*, Gothick; ðɲıfan, Saxon; *dryven*, Dutch.]

1. To produce motion in any thing by violence.

2. To force along by impetuous pressure.

On helmets, helmets throng,
Shield press'd on shield, and man *drove* man along. *Pope.*

3. To expel by force from any place.

Driven from his native land to foreign grounds,
He with a gen'rous rage resents his wounds. *Dryden's Virg.*

His ignominious flight the victors boast,
Beaux banish beaux, and swordknots swordknots *drive*. *Pope.*

4. To send by force to any place.

Time *drives* the flocks from field to fold,
When rivers rage and rocks grow cold. *Sh. M. W. of Win.*

Fate has *driven* 'em all
Into the net. *Dryden's Don Sebastian.*

5. To force or urge in any direction.

He stood and measured the earth: he beheld, and *drove* asunder the nations. *Heb.* iii. 6.

6. To impel to greater speed.

7. To guide and regulate a carriage.

He took off their chariot wheels, that they *drove* them heavily. *Ex.* xiv. 25.

8. To convey animals; to make animals march along under guidance.

There find a herd of heifers, wand'ring o'er
The neighb'ring hill, and *drive* 'em to the shore. *Addison.*

9. To clear any place by forcing away what is in it.

We come not with design of wasteful prey,
To *drive* the country, force the swains away. *Dryden's Virg.*

10. To force; to compel.

He *driven* to dismount, threatned, if I did not the like, to do as much for my horse as fortune had done for his. *Sidney.*

They did not think that tyranny was thoroughly extinguished, 'till they had *driven* one of their consuls to depart the city, against whom they found not in the world what to object, saving only that his name was Tarquin. *Hooker, b.* iv.

He was *driven* by the necessities of times, more than led by his own disposition to rigour. *King Charles.*

11. To distress; to straiten.

This kind of speech is in the manner of desperate men far *driven*. *Spenser's State of Ireland.*

12. To urge by violence, not kindness.

He taught the gospel rather than the law,
And forc'd himself to *drive*; but lov'd to draw. *Dryden.*

13. To impel by influence of passion.

I *drave* my suitor from his mad humour of love to a living humour of madness. *Shakespeare's As you like it.*

Discontents *drave* men into slidings. *King Charles.*

Lord Cottington, being master of temper, and of the most profound dissimulation, knew too well how to lead him into a mistake, and then *drive* him into choler. *Clarendon.*

It is better to marry than to burn, says St. Paul; where we may see what *drives* men into a conjugal life: a little burning pushes us more powerfully than greater pleasures in prospect. *Locke.*

14. To urge; to press to a conclusion.

The experiment of wood that shineth in the dark, we have diligently *driven* and pursued; the rather for that, of all things that give light here below, it is the most durable, and hath least apparent motion. *Bacon's Natural History*, N°. 352.

We have thus the proper notions of the four elements, and both them and their qualities, *driven* up and resolved into their most simple principles. *Digby on Bodies.*

To *drive* the argument farther, let us inquire into the obvious designs of this divine architect. *Cheyne's Phil. Princ.*

The design of these orators was to *drive* some particular point, either the condemnation or acquittal. *Swift.*

15. To carry on.

As a farmer cannot husband his ground so well, if he sit at a great rent; so the merchant cannot *drive* his trade so well, if he sit at great usury. *Bacon, Essay* 42.

The bees have common cities of their own,
And common sons, beneath one law they live,
And with one common stock their traffick *drive*. *Dryden.*

Your Pasimond a lawless bargain *drove*,
The parent could not sell the daughter's love. *Dryden.*

The trade of life cannot be *driven* without partners. *Collier.*

16. To purify by motion.

The one's in the plot, let him be never so innocent; and the other is as white as the *driven* snow, let him be never so criminal. *L'Estrange.*

17. *To* DRIVE *out*. To expel.

Tumults and their exciters *drave* myself and many of both houses *out* of their places. *King Charles.*

As soon as they heard the name of Roscetes, they forthwith *drave out* their governour, and received the Turks into the town. *Knolles's History of the Turks.*

To

To Drive. *v. n.*

1. To go as impelled by any external agent.

The needle endeavours to conform unto the meridian; but being distracted, *driveth* that way where the greater and powerfuller part of the earth is placed. *Brown's Vulgar Errours, b.* ii.

Love, fixt to one, still safe at anchor rides,
And dares the fury of the winds and tides;
But losing once that hold, to the wide ocean born,
It *drives* away at will, to every wave a scorn. *Dryden.*

Nor with the rising storm would vainly strive;
But left the helm, and let the vessel *drive*. *Dryden's Æn.*

2. To rush with violence.

Fierce Boreas *drove* against his flying sails,
And rent the sheets. *Dryden's Æn.*

Near as he draws, thick harbingers of smoke,
With gloomy pillars, cover all the place;
Whose little intervals of night are broke,
By sparks that *drive* against his sacred face. *Dryd. Ann. Mir.*

Then with so swift an ebb the flood *drove* backward,
It slipt from underneath the scaly herd. *Dryd. All for Love.*

The bees *drive* out upon each other's backs,
T' imboss their hives in clusters. *Dryden's Don Sebastian.*

While thus he stood,
Perithous' dart *drove* on, and nail'd him to the wood. *Dryd.*

As a ship, which winds and waves assail,
Now with the current *drives*, now with the gale;
She feels a double force, by turns obeys
The imperious tempest, and th' impetuous seas. *Dryden.*

The wolves scampered away, however, as hard as they could *drive*. *L'Estrange.*

Thick as autumnal leaves, or *driving* sand,
The moving squadrons blacken all the strand. *Pope's Iliad.*

3. To pass in a carriage.

There is a litter ready; lay him in't,
And *drive* tow'rd Dover. *Shakespeare's King Lear.*

Thy flaming chariot wheels, that shook
Heav'n's everlasting frame, while o'er the necks
Thou *drov'st* of warring angels disarray'd. *Milt. Par. Lost.*

4. To tend to; to consider as the scope and ultimate design.

Our first apprehensions are instructed in authors, which *drive* at these as the highest elegancies which are but the frigidities of wit. *Brown's Vulgar Errours, b.* i. *c.* 9.

We cannot widely mistake his discourse, when we have found out the point he *drives* at. *Locke.*

They look no further before them than the next line; whence it will inevitably follow, that they can *drive* to no certain point, but ramble from one subject to another. *Dryd.*

We have done our work, and are come within view of the end that we have been *driving* at. *Addison on the War.*

5. To aim; to strike at with fury.

Four rogues in buckram let *drive* at me. *Shakes. Hen.* IV.

At Auxur's shield he *drove*, and at the blow
Both shield and arm to ground together go. *Dryden's Æn.*

To DRI'VEL. *v. n.* [from *drip*, *dripple*, *dribble*, drivel.]

1. To slaver; to let the spittle fall in drops, like a child, an ideot, or a dotard.

I met with this Chremes, a *driveling* old fellow, lean, shaking both of head and hands, already half earth, and yet then most greedy of earth. *Sidney, b.* ii.

No man could spit from him, but would be forced to *drivel* like some paralytick, or a fool. *Grew's Cosm.*

2. To be weak or foolish; to dote.

This *driveling* love is like a great natural, that runs lolling up and down to hide his bauble. *Shakesp. Rom. and Juliet.*

I hate to see a brave bold fellow sotted,
Made sour and senseless, turn'd to whey by love;
A *driveling* hero, fit for a romance. *Dryden's Spanish Fryar.*

Dri'vel. *n. s.* [from the verb.]

1. Slaver; moisture shed from the mouth.

Besides th' eternal *drivel*, that supplies
The dropping beard, from nostrils, mouth and eyes. *Dryden.*

2. A fool; an ideot; a driveller. This sense is now out of use.

What fool am I, to mingle that *drivel's* speeches among my noble thoughts. *Sidney, b.* ii.

Millions of years this old *drivel* Cupid lives,
While still more wretch, more wicked he doth prove. *Sidney.*

Dri'veller. *n. s.* [from *drivel.*] A fool; an ideot; a slaverer.

I have heard the arrantest *drivellers* commended for their shrewdness, even by men of tolerable judgment. *Swift.*

Dri'ven. Participle of *drive.*

They were *driven* forth from among men. *Job* xxx. 5.

Dri'ver. *n. s.* [from *drive.*]

1. The person or instrument who gives any motion by violence.

2. One who drives beasts.

He from the many-peopl'd city flies;
Contemns their labours, and the *driver's* cries. *Sandys.*

The *driver* runs up to him immediately, and beats him almost to death. *L'Estrange's Fables.*

The multitude or common rout, like a drove of sheep, or an herd of men, may be managed by any noise or cry which their *driver* shall accustom them to. *South's Sermons.*

3. One who drives a carriage.

Not the fierce *driver* with more fury lends
The sounding lash, and, ere the stroke descends,
Low to the wheels his pliant body bends. *Dryd. Virg. Æn.*

To DRI'ZZLE. *v. a.* [*driselen*, German, to shed dew.] To shed in small slow drops; as Winter rains.

When the sun sets the air doth *drizzle* dew. *Shakespeare.*

Though now this face of mine be hid
In sap-consuming Winter's *drizzled* snow,
And all the conduits of my blood froze up,
Yet hath my night of life some memory. *Shakespeare.*

To Dri'zzle. *v. n.* To fall in short slow drops.

And *drizzling* drops that often do redound,
The firmest flint doth in continuance wear. *Spenser.*

Her heart did melt in great compassion,
And *drizzling* tears did shed for pure affection. *Fairy Queen.*

This day will pour down,
If I conjecture ought, no *drizzling* show'r,
But rattling storm of arrows barb'd with fire. *Milton.*

The neighbouring mountains, by reason of their height, are more exposed to the dews and *drizzling* rains than any of the adjacent parts. *Addison's Remarks on Italy.*

Drizzly. *adj.* [from *drizzle.*] Sheding small rain.

This during Winter's *drizzly* reign be done,
'Till the new ram receives th' exalted sun. *Dryden's Virgil.*

DROIL. *n. s.* [by *Junius* understood a contraction of *drivel.*] A drone; a sluggard.

To Droil. *v. n.* To work sluggishly and slowly; to plod.

Let such vile vassals, born to base vocation,
Drudge in the world, and for their living *droil*,
Which have no wit to live withouten toyle. *Spenser.*

We see in all things how desuetude does contract and narrow our faculties, so that we can apprehend only those things in which we are conversant: the *droiling* peasant scarce thinks there is any world beyond his own village, or the neighbouring markets. *Government of the Tongue.*

DROLL. *n. s.* [*droler*, French.]

1. One whose business is to raise mirth by petty tricks; a jester; a buffoon; a jackpudding.

As he was running home in all haste, a *droll* takes him up by the way. *L'Estrange.*

Why, how now, Andrew! cries his brother *droll*;
To-day's conceit, methinks, is something dull. *Prior.*

Democritus, dear *droll*, revisit earth,
And with our follies glut thy heighten'd mirth. *Prior.*

2. A farce; something exhibited to raise mirth.

Some as justly fame extols,
For lofty lines in Smithfield *drolls*. *Swift.*

To Droll. *v. n.* [*drôle*, French.] To jest; to play the buffoon.

Such august designs as inspire your inquiries used to be decided by *drolling* fantasticks, that have only wit enough to make others and themselves ridiculous. *Glanv. Sceps. Pref.*

Men that will not be reasoned into their senses, may yet be laughed or *drolled* into them. *L'Estrange.*

Let virtuosoes insult and despise on, yet they never shall be able to *droll* away nature. *South's Sermons.*

Dro'llery. *n. s.* [from *droll.*] Idle jokes; buffoonery.

They hang between heaven and hell, borrow the Christians faith, and the atheists *drollery* upon it. *Governm. of the Tongue.*

Dro'medary. *n. s.* [*dromedare*, Italian.]

A sort of camel so called from its swiftness, because it is said to travel a hundred miles a day, and some affirm one hundred and fifty. *Dromedaries* are smaller than common camels, slenderer, and more nimble, and are of two kinds: one larger, with two small bunches, covered with hair, on its back; the other lesser, with one hairy eminence, and more frequently called camel: both are capable of great fatigue, and very serviceable in the western parts of Asia, where they abound. Their hair is soft and shorn: they have no fangs and foreteeth, nor horn upon their feet, which are only covered with a fleshy skin; and they are about seven feet and a half high, from the ground to the top of their heads. They drink much at a time, and are said to disturb the water with their feet. They keep the water long in their stomachs, which, as some report, travellers in necessity will open for the sake of the water contained in them. The stomach of this animal is composed of four ventricles; and in the second are several mouths, which open a passage into twenty cavities, which serve for conservatories of water. See Camel. *Calmet.*

Straw for the horses and *dromedaries* brought they unto the place. *1 Kings* iv. 28.

DRONE. *n. s.* [ꝺꞃoen, Saxon.]

1. The bee which makes no honey, and is therefore driven out by the rest.

The sad-ey'd justice, with his surly hum,
Delivering o'er to executors pale
The lazy yawning *drone*. *Shakespeare's Henry* V.

Luxurious kings are to their people lost;
They live, like *drones*, upon the publick cost. *Dryd. Auren.*

All, with united force, combine to drive
The lazy *drones* from the laborious hive. *Dryden's Virgil.*

2. A sluggard; an idler.

He sleeps by day
More than the wild cat: *drones* hive not with me,
Therefore I part with him. *Shakespeare's Merch. of Venice.*
Sit idle on the houshold hearth
A burd'nous *drone*, to visitants a gaze. *Milton's Agonistes.*

It is my misfortune to be married to a *drone*, who lives upon what I get, without bringing any thing into the common stock. *Addison's Spectator*, N°. 211.

3. The hum, or instrument of humming.

To DRONE. *v. n.* [from the noun.] To live in idleness; to dream.

What have I lost by my forefathers fault?
Why, was not I the twentieth by descent
From a long restive race of *droning* kings? *Dryd. Span. Fry.*

DRO'NISH. *adj.* [from *drone.*] Idle; sluggish; dreaming; lazy; indolent; unactive.

The *dronish* monks, the scorn and shame of manhood,
Rouse and prepare once more to take possession,
To nestle in their ancient hives again. *Rowe's Jane Gray.*

To DROOP. *v. n.* [*droef*, sorrow, Dutch.]

1. To languish with sorrow.

Conceiving the dishonour of his mother,
He straight declin'd, *droop'd*, took it deeply;
Fasten'd, and fix'd the shame on't in himself. *Shakespeare.*
I *droop*, with struggling spent;
My thoughts are on my sorrows bent. *Sandys.*

2. To faint; to grow weak; to be despirited.

I find my zenith doth depend upon
A most auspicious star; whose influence
If now I court not, but omit, my fortunes
Will ever after *droop*. *Shakespeare's Tempest.*
Good things of day begin to *droop* and drowse,
While night's black agents to their prey do rowze. *Sh. Macb.*
When, by impulse from heav'n, Tyrtæus sung,
In *drooping* soldiers a new courage sprung. *Roscommon.*
Can flow'rs but *droop* in absence of the sun,
Which wak'd their sweets? and mine, alas! is gone. *Dryd.*
Time seems not now beneath his years to stoop,
Nor do his wings with sickly feathers *droop*. *Dryden.*
When factious rage to cruel exile drove
The queen of beauty and the court of love,
The muses *droop'd* with their forsaken arts. *Dryden.*
I'll animate the soldiers *drooping* courage,
With love of freedom and contempt of life. *Addis. Cato.*

I saw him ten days before he died, and observed he began very much to *droop* and languish. *Swift.*

3. To sink; to lean downwards.

I never from thy side henceforth must stray,
Where'er our day's work lies; though now enjoin'd
Laborious, 'till day *droop*. *Milton's Paradise Lost, b.* xi.
His head, though gay
Carnation, purple, azure, or speck'd with gold,
Hung *drooping*, unsustain'd. *Milton's Paradise Lost, b.* ix.
On her heav'd bosom hung her *drooping* head,
Which, with a sigh, she rais'd; and this she said. *Pope.*

DROP. *n. s.* [ꝺꞃoppa, Saxon.]

1. A globule of moisture; as much liquor as falls at once when there is not a continual stream.

Meet we the med'cine of our country's weal,
And with him pour we in our country's purge,
Each *drop* of us. *Shakespeare's Macbeth.*

Whereas Aristotle tells us, that if a *drop* of wine be put into ten thousand measures of water, the wine being overpowered by so vast a quantity of water, will be turned into it: he speaks, to my apprehension, very improbably. *Boyle.*

Admiring, in the gloomy shade,
Those little *drops* of light. *Waller.*
Had I but known that Sancho was his father,
I would have pour'd a deluge of my blood
To save one *drop* of his. *Dryden's Spanish Fryar.*

2. Diamond hanging in the ear.

The *drops* to thee, Brillante, we consign;
And, Momentilla, let the watch be thine. *Pope.*

DROP SERENE. *n. s.* [*gutta serena*, Latin.] A disease of the eye, proceeding from an inspissation of the humour.

So thick a *drop serene* hath quench'd their orbs,
Or dim suffusion veil'd! *Milton's Paradise Lost, b.* iii.

To DROP. *v. a.* [ꝺꞃoppan, Saxon.]

1. To pour in drops or single globules.

His heavens shall *drop* down dew. *Deut.* xxxiii. 28.

2. To let fall.

Others o'er chimney tops and turrets row,
And *drop* their anchors on the meads below. *Dryden.*
One only hag remain'd:
Against a wither'd oak she lean'd her weight,
Propp'd on her trusty staff, not half upright,
And *dropp'd* an aukward court'sy to the knight. *Dryden.*
St. John himself will scarce forbear
To bite his pen and *drop* a tear;
The rest will give a shrug, and cry,
I'm sorry, but we all must die! *Swift.*

3. To let go; to dismiss from the hand, or the possession.

Though I could
With barefac'd power sweep him from my sight,
And bid my will avouch it; yet I must not,
For certain friends that are both his and mine,
Whose loves I may not *drop*. *Shakespeare's Macbeth.*

Those who have assumed visible shapes for a season, can hardly be reckoned among this order of compounded beings; because they *drop* their bodies, and divest themselves of those visible shapes. *Watts's Logick.*

4. To utter slightly or casually.

Drop not thy word against the house of Isaac. *Amos* vii. 16.

5. To insert indirectly, or by way of digression.

St. Paul's epistles contain nothing but points of Christian instruction, amongst which he seldom fails to *drop* in the great and distinguishing doctrines of our holy religion. *Locke.*

6. To intermit; to cease.

Where the act is unmanly or immoral, we ought to *drop* our hopes, or rather never entertain them. *Collier on Despair.*

After having given this judgment in its favour, they suddenly *dropt* the pursuit. *Sharp's Surgery.*

7. To quit a master.

I have beat the hoof 'till I have worn out these shoes in your service, and not one penny left me to buy more; so that you must even excuse me, if I *drop* you here. *L'Estrange.*

8. To let go a dependant, or companion, without farther association.

She drilled him on to five and fifty, and will *drop* him in his old age, if she can find her account in another. *Addison.*

They have no sooner fetched themselves up to the fashion of the polite world, but the town has *dropped* them. *Addison.*

9. To suffer to vanish, or come to nothing.

Thus was the fame of our Saviour perpetuated by such records as would preserve the traditionary account of him to after-ages, and rectify it, if, by passing through several generations, it might *drop* any part that was material. *Addison.*

Opinions, like fashions, always descend from those of quality to the middle sort, and thence to the vulgar, where they are *dropped* and vanish. *Swift.*

10. To bedrop; to speckle; to variegate with spots. *Variis stellatus corpora guttis.*

Or, sporting with quick glance,
Shew to the sun their wav'd coats, *dropp'd* with gold. *Milt.*

To DROP. *v. n.*

1. To fall in drops, or single globules.

The quality of mercy is not strain'd;
It *droppeth*, as the gentle rain from heaven,
Upon the place beneath. *Shakesp. Merchant of Venice.*

2. To let drops fall; to discharge itself in drops.

The heavens *dropped* at the presence of God. *Ps.* lxvii. 8.
While cumber'd with my *dropping* cloaths I lay,
The cruel nation, covetous of prey,
Stain'd with my blood th' unhospitable coast. *Dryden's Æn.*
Beneath a rock he sigh'd alone,
And cold Lycæus wept from every *dropping* stone. *Dryden.*

3. To fall; to come from a higher place.

Philosophers conjecture that you *dropped* from the moon, or one of the stars. *Gulliver's Travels.*

In every revolution, approaching nearer and nearer to the sun, this comet must at last *drop* into the sun's body. *Cheyne.*

4. To fall spontaneously.

So may'st thou live, 'till, like ripe fruit, thou *drop*
Into thy mother's lap; or be with ease
Gather'd, not harshly pluck'd. *Milton's Paradise Lost, b.* xi.

5. To fall in death; to die suddenly.

It was your presurmise,
That in the dole of blows your son might *drop*. *Shakesp.*

6. To die.

Nothing, says Seneca, so soon reconciles us to the thoughts of our own death, as the prospect of one friend after another *dropping* round us. *Digby to Pope.*

7. To sink into silence; to vanish; to come to nothing: a familiar phrase.

Virgil's friends thought fit to let *drop* this incident of Helen. *Addison's Travels.*

I heard of threats, occasioned by my verses: I sent to acquaint them where I was to be found, and so it *dropped*. *Pope.*

8. To come unexpectedly.

He could never make any figure in company, but by giving disturbance at his entry; and therefore takes care to *drop* in when he thinks you are just seated. *Spectator*, N°. 448.

DRO'PPING. *n. s.* [from *drop.*]

1. That which falls in drops.

Thrifty wench scrapes kitchen-stuff,
And barreling the *droppings* and the snuff
Of wasting candles. *Donne.*

2. That which drops when the continuous stream ceases.

Strain out the last dull *droppings* of your sense,
And rhyme with all the rage of impotence. *Pope's Criticism.*

DRO'PLET. *n. s.* A little drop.

Thou abhorr'dst in us our human griefs,

Scorn'd

Scorn'd our brine's flow, and those our droplets, which
From niggard nature fall. *Shakespeare's Timon.*

Dro'pstone. *n. s.* [*drop* and *stone.*] Spar formed into the shape of drops. *Woodward's Foss.*

Dro'pwort. *n. s.* [*drop* and *wort.*] A plant of various species.

Dro'psical. *adj.* [from *dropsy.*] Diseased with a dropsy; hydropical; tending to a dropsy.

The diet of nephritick and *dropsical* persons ought to be such as is opposite to, and subdueth the alkalescent nature of the salts in the serum of the blood. *Arbuthnot on Aliments.*

Dro'psied. *adj.* [from *dropsy.*] Diseased with a dropsy.

Where great addition swells, and virtue none,
It is a *dropsied* honour: good alone
Is good. *Shakespeare's All's well that ends well.*

DRO'PSY. *n. s.* [*hydrops*, Latin; whence anciently *hydropisy*, thence *dropisy*, *dropsy.*] A collection of water in the body, from too lax a tone of the solids, whereby digestion is weakened, and all the parts stuffed. *Quincy.*

An anasarca, a species of *dropsy*, is an extravasation of water lodged in the cells of the membrana adiposa. *Sharp.*

DROSS. *n. s.* [ꝺꞃoꞅ, Saxon.]

1. The recrement or despumation of metals.

Some scumm'd the *dross* that from the metal came,
Some stirr'd the molton ore with ladles great,
And every one did swink, and every one did sweat. *Fai. Qu.*

Should the mixture of a little *dross* constrain the church to deprive herself of so much gold, rather than learn how, by art and judgment, to make separation of the one from the other? *Hooker, b. v. s. 20.*

2. Rust; incrustation upon metal.

An emperor, hid under a crust of *dross*, after cleansing, has appeared with all his titles fresh and beautiful. *Addis. on Medals.*

3. Refuse; leavings; sweepings; any thing remaining after the removal of the better part; dreggs; feculence; corruption.

Fair proud, now tell me, why should fair be proud,
Sith all world's glory is but *dross* unclean;
And in the shade of death itself shall shroud,
However now thereof ye little ween? *Spenser, Sonnet 2.*

That most divine light only shineth on those minds, which are purged from all worldly *dross* and human uncleanness. *Ral.*

All treasures and all gain esteem as *dross*,
And dignities and pow'rs all but the highest. *Milt. Pa. Lost.*

Such precepts exceedingly dispose us to piety and religion, by purifying our souls from the *dross* and filth of sensual delights. *Tillotson, Sermon 5.*

Dro'ssiness. *n. s.* [from *drossy.*] Foulness; feculence; rust.

The furnace of affliction refines us from earthly *drossiness*, and softens us for the impression of God's stamp. *Boyle.*

Dro'ssy. *adj.* [from *dross.*]

1. Full of scorious or recrementitious parts; full of dross.

So doth the fire the *drossy* gold refine. *Davies.*

For, by the fire, they emit not only many *drossy* and scorious parts, but whatsoever they had received either from earth or loadstone. *Brown's Vulgar Errours, b. ii. c. 4.*

2. Worthless; foul; feculent.

Your intention hold,
As fire these *drossy* rhymes to purify,
Or as elixir to change them into gold. *Donne.*

Dro'tchel. *n. s.* [corrupted perhaps from *dretchel. To dretch*, in *Chaucer*, is to *idle*, to *delay. Droch*, in *Frisick*, is *delay.*] An idle wench; a sluggard. In Scottish it is still used.

Drove. *n. s.* [from *drive.*]

1. A body or number of cattle: generally used of oxen or black cattle.

They brought to their stations many *droves* of cattle; and within a few days were brought out of the country two thousand muttons. *Hayward.*

A Spaniard is unacquainted with our northern *droves. Brown.*

2. A number of sheep driven.

A *drove* of sheep, or an herd of oxen, may be managed by any noise or cry which the drivers shall accustom them to. *South's Sermons.*

3. Any collection of animals.

The sounds and seas, with all their finny *drove*,
Now to the moon in wavering morrice move. *Milton.*

4. A crowd; a tumult.

But if to fame alone thou do'st pretend,
The miser will his empty palace lend,
Set wide with doors, adorn'd with plated brass,
Where *droves*, as at a city-gate, may pass. *Dryden's Juven.*

Dro'ven. *part.* from *drive.*

This is fought indeed;
Had we so done at first, we had *droven* them home
With clouts about their heads. *Shak. Anth. and Cleopatra.*

Dro'ver. *n. s.* [from *drove.*] One that fats oxen for sale, and drives them to market.

The prince hath got your hero.
——I wish him joy of her.
—Why, that's spoken like an honest *drover*; so they sell bullocks. *Shakespeare's Much Ado about Nothing.*

The *drover* who his fellow *drover* meets,
In narrow passages of winding streets. *Dryden's Juvenal.*

DROUGHT. *n. s.* [ꝺꞃuᵹoðe, Saxon; *drowth*, Scottish.]

1. Dry weather; want of rain.

O earth! I will befriend thee more with rain
Than youthful April shall with all his showers:
In Summer's *drought* I'll drop upon thee still. *Sh. Tit. Andr.*

Great *droughts* in Summer, lasting 'till the end of August, some gentle showers upon them, and then some dry weather, portend a pestilent Summer the year following. *Bacon.*

To south the Persian bay,
And inaccessible th' Arabian *drought. Milton's Parad. Reg.*

As torrents in the *drowth* of Summer fail,
So perisht man from death shall never rise. *Sandys.*

They were so learned in natural philosophy, that they foretold earthquakes and storms, great *droughts*, and great plagues. *Temple.*

In a *drought* the thirsty creatures cry,
And gape upon the gather'd clouds for rain. *Dryden.*

Upon a shower, after a *drought*, earthworms and landsnails innumerable come out of their lurking places. *Ray.*

2. Thirst; want of drink.

His carcase, pin'd with hunger and with *drought. Milton.*

One whose *drought*
Yet scarce allay'd, still eyes the current stream,
Whose liquid murmur heard, new thirst excites. *Milt. P. L.*

Drou'ghtiness. *n. s.* [from *droughty.*] The state of wanting rain.

Drou'ghty. *adj.* [from *drought.*]

1. Wanting rain; sultry.

That a camel, so patient of long thirst, should be bred in such *droughty* and parched countries, where it is of such eminent use for travelling over those dry and sandy desarts, where no water is to be had, must be acknowledged an act of providence and design. *Ray on the Creation.*

2. Thirsty; dry with thirst.

If the former years
Exhibit no supplies, alas! thou must
With tasteless water wash thy *droughty* throat. *Phillips.*

To Drown. *v. a.* [from *drunden*, below, German, *Skinner*, from ꝺꞃuncnian, Saxon, *Mr. Lye.*]

1. To suffocate in water.

They would soon *drown* those that refused to swim down the popular stream. *King Charles.*

When of God's image only eight he found
Snatch'd from the wat'ry grave, and sav'd from nations *drown'd.* *Prior.*

2. To overwhelm in water.

Or so much as it needs
To dew the sovereign flower, and *drown* the weeds. *Shakes.*

Galleys might be *drowned* in the harbour with the great ordnance, before they could be rigged. *Knolles's History.*

3. To overflow; to bury in an inundation; to deluge.

Betwixt the prince and parliament we stand,
The barriers of the state on either hand:
May neither overflow, for then they *drown* the land. *Dry.*

4. To immerge; to lose in any thing.

Most men being in sensual pleasures *drown'd*,
It seems their souls but in their senses are. *Davies.*

5. To lose in something that overpowers or covers.

Who cometh next will not follow that course, however good, which his predecessors held, for doubt to have his doings *drowned* in another man's praise. *Spenser on Ireland.*

To think that the brightness of the sun's body above doth *drown* our discerning of the lesser lights, is a popular errour. *Wotton's Architecture.*

My private voice is *drown'd* amid' the senate. *Add. Cato.*

Some aged man, who lives this act to see,
And who in former times remember'd me,
May say, the son, in fortitude and fame,
Outgoes the mark, and *drowns* his father's name. *Dryden.*

To Drown. *v. n.* To be suffocated in the waters.

There be, that keep them out of fire, and yet was never burned; that beware of water, and yet was never nigh *drowning.* *Ascham's Schoolmaster.*

Methought what pain it was to *drown!*
What dreadful noise of waters in my ears!
What sights of ugly death within mine eyes! *Shakes. R. III.*

To DROWSE. *v. a.* [*droosen*, Dutch.] To make heavy with sleep.

There gentle sleep
First found me, and with soft oppression seiz'd
My *drowsed* senses uncontroll'd. *Milton's Paradise Lost.*

To Drowse. *v. n.*

1. To slumber; to grow heavy with sleep.

All their shape
Spangled with eyes, more numerous than those
Of Argus; and more wakeful than to *drowse*,
Charm'd with Arcadian pipe, the pastoral reed
Of Hermes, or his opiate rod. *Milton's Paradise Lost, b. xi.*

2. To look heavy; not cheerful.

They rather *drows'd*, and hung their eyelids down,
Slept in his face, and render'd such aspect
As cloudy men use to their adversaries. *Shakesp. Henry VI.*

DRO'WSILY. *adv.* [from *drowsy.*]
1. Sleepily; heavily; with an inclination to sleep.
The air swarms thick with wand'ring deities,
Which *drowsily* like humming beetles rise. *Dryd. Ind. Emp.*
2. Sluggishly; idly; slothfully; lazily.
We do hastily satisfy our understanding with the first things, and, thereby satiated, slothfully and *drowsily* sit down. *Raleigh's History of the World.*

DRO'WSINESS. *n. s.* [from *drowsy.*]
1. Sleepiness; heaviness with sleep; disposition to sleep.
What a strange *drowsiness* possesses them? *Shakesp. Tempest.*
In deep of night, when *drowsiness*
Hath lock'd up mortal sense, then listen I
To the celestial syren's harmony. *Paradise Regained.*
What succour can I hope the muse will send,
Whose *drowsiness* hath wrong'd the muse's friend? *Crashaw.*
He passes his whole life in a dozed condition, between sleeping and waking, with a kind of *drowsiness* and confusion upon his senses. *South's Sermons.*
He that from his childhood has made rising betimes familiar to him, will not waste the best part of his life in *drowsiness* and lying a-bed. *Locke.*
A sensation of *drowsiness*, oppression, heaviness, and lassitude, are signs of a plentiful meal, especially in young people. *Arbuthnot on Aliments.*
2. Idleness; indolence; inactivity.
It falleth out well, to shake off your *drowsiness*; for it seemed to be the trumpet of a war. *Bacon's Holy War.*

DRO'WSIHED. *n. s.* Sleepiness; inclination to sleep.
The royal virgin shook off *drowsyhed*;
And rising forth out of her baser boure,
Look'd for her knight. *Fairy Queen, b.* i. *cant.* 2. *stan.* 7.

DRO'WSY. *adj.* [from *drowse.*]
1. Sleepy; heavy with sleep; lethargick.
Drowsy am I, and yet can rarely sleep. *Sidney.*
Men *drowsy*, and desirous to sleep, or before the fit of an ague, do use to yawn and stretch. *Bacon's Natural History.*
The flowers, call'd out of their beds,
Start and raise up their *drowsy* heads. *Cleaveland.*
Drunken at last, and *drowsy* they depart,
Each to his house. *Dryden.*
2. Heavy; lulling; causing sleep.
Sir Guyon, mindful of his vows yplight,
Up rose from *drowsy* couch. *Fairy Queen, b.* ii. *cant.* 3.
While thus she rested, on her arm reclin'd,
The hoary willows waving with the wind,
And feather'd quires that warbled in the shade,
And purling streams that through the meadow stray'd,
In *drowsy* murmurs lull'd the gentle maid. *Addison.*
3. Stupid; dull.
Those inadvertencies, a body would think, even our author, with all his *drowsy* reasoning, could never have been capable of. *Atterbury.*

To DRUB. *v. a.* [*druber*, to kill, Danish.] To thresh; to beat; to bang; to thump; to thwack; to cudgel. A word of contempt.
He that is valiant, and dares fight,
Though *drubb'd*, can lose no honour by't. *Hudibras, p.* i.
The little thief had been soundly *drubbed* with a good honest cudgel. *L'Estrange.*
Though the bread be not mine, yet, if it had been less than weight, I should have been *drubbed.* *Locke.*

DRUB. *n. s.* [from the verb.] A thump; a knock; a blow.
The blows and *drubs* I have receiv'd,
Have bruis'd my body, and bereav'd
My limbs of strength. *Hudibras, p.* i. *cant.* 3.
By setting such an unfortunate mark on their followers, they have exposed them to innumerable *drubs* and contusions. *Addison's Freeholder*, N°. 50.

To DRUDGE. *v. n.* [ðreccan, to vex, Saxon; *draghen*, to carry, Dutch.] To labour in mean offices; to toil without honour or dignity; to work hard; to slave.
And to crack'd fiddle, and hoarse tabour,
In merriment, did *drudge* and labour. *Hudibras, p.* i.
The poor sleep little: we must learn to watch
Our labours late, and early every morning,
Mid'st Winter frosts; then clad and fed with sparing,
Rise to our toils, and *drudge* away the day. *Otway.*
Advantages obtained by industry directed by philosophy, can never be expected from *drudging* ignorance. *Glanv. Sceps.*
Soon he came to court,
Proffering for hire his service at the gate,
To *drudge*, draw water, and to run or wait. *Dryd. Fables.*
I made no such bargain with you, to live always *drudging.* *Dryden's Dedicat. Æn.*
What is an age, in dull renown *drudg'd* o'er!
One little single hour of love is more. *Granville.*

DRUDGE. *n. s.* [from the verb.] One employed in mean labour; a slave; one doomed to servile occupation.
To conclude, this *drudge* of the devil, this diviner, laid claim to me. *Shakespeare's Comedy of Errours.*
He sits above, and laughs the while
At thee, ordain'd his *drudge*, to execute
Whate'er his wrath shall bid. *Milton's Paradise Lost, b.* ii.
Art thou our slave,
Our captive, at the publick mill our *drudge*,
And dar'st thou, at our sending and command,
Dispute thy coming. *Milton's Agonistes, l.* 392.
He is content to be their *drudge*,
And on their errands gladly trudge. *Hudibras, p.* iii. *cant.* 1.
The hard master makes men serve him for nought, who rewards his *drudges* and slaves with nothing but shame and sorrow, and misery. *Tillotson, Sermon* 4.

DRU'DGER. *n. s.* [from *drudge.*]
1. A mean labourer.
2. The drudging-box; the box out of which flower is thrown on roast meat. *Dict.*

DRU'DGERY. *n. s.* [from *drudge.*] Mean labour; ignoble toil; dishonourable work; servile occupation.
My old dame will be undone for one to do her husbandry, and her *drudgery.* *Shakespeare's Henry* IV. *p.* ii.
Were there not instruments for *drudgery* as well as offices of *drudgery?* Were there not people to receive orders as well as others to give and authorize them? *L'Estrange.*
You do not know the heavy grievances,
The toils, the labours, weary *drudgeries*,
Which they impose. *Southern's Oroonoko.*
To thee that *drudgery* of pow'r I give;
Cares be thy lot: reign thou, and let me live. *Dryd. Auren.*
Paradise was a place of bliss, as well as immortality, without *drudgery*, and without sorrow. *Locke.*
Even *drudgery* himself,
As at the car he sweats, or dusty hews
The palace-stone, looks gay. *Thomson's Summer, l.* 1445.
It is now handled by every dirty wench, and condemned to do her *drudgery.* *Swift's Meditations on a Broomstick.*

DRU'DGINGBOX. *n. s.* [*drudging* and *box.*] The box out of which flower is sprinkled upon roast meat.
But if it lies too long, the crackling's pall'd,
Not by the *drudgingbox* to be recall'd. *King's Cookery.*

DRU'DGINGLY. *adv.* [from *drudging.*] Laboriously; toilsomely.
He does now all the meanest and triflingest things himself *drudgingly*, without making use of any inferiour or subordinate minister. *Ray on the Creation.*

DRUG. *n. s.* [*drogue*, French.]
1. An ingredient used in physick; a medicinal simple.
Mortal *drugs* I have; but Mantua's law
Is death to any he that utters them. *Shak. Rom. and Juliet.*
A fleet descry'd
Hangs in the clouds, by equinoctial winds
Close sailing from Bengala, or the isles
Of Ternate and Tidore, whence merchants bring
Their spicy *drugs.* *Milton's Paradise Lost, b.* ii. *l.* 640.
And yet no doubts the poor man's draught control;
He dreads no poison in his homely bowl:
Then fear the deadly *drug*, when gems divine
Enchase the cup, and sparkle in the wine. *Dryden's Juven.*
Judicious physick's noble art to gain,
He *drugs* and plants explor'd, alas, in vain! *Smith.*
Bright Helen mix'd a mirth-inspiring bowl,
Temper'd with *drugs* of sov'reign use, t' assuage
The boiling bosom of tumultuous rage. *Pope's Odyssey, b.* iv.
In the names of *drugs* and plants, the mistake in a word may endanger life. *Baker's Reflections on Learning.*
2. Any thing without worth or value; any thing of which no purchaser can be found.
Each noble vice
Shall bear a price,
And virtue shall a *drug* become:
An empty name
Was all her fame,
But now she shall be dumb. *Dryden's Albion.*
3. A drudge.
He from his first swath proceeded
Through sweet degrees that this brief world affords,
To such as may the passive *drugs* of it freely command. *Shak.*

To DRUG. *v. a.* [from the noun.]
1. To season with medicinal ingredients.
The surfeited grooms
Do mock their charge with snores. I've *drugg'd* their possets,
That death and nature do contend about them. *Shak. Macb.*
2. To tincture with something offensive.
Oft they assay'd,
Hunger and thirst constraining: *drugg'd* as oft
With hatefulest disrelish, writh'd their jaws,
With soot and cinders fill'd. *Milton's Paradise Lost, b.* x.

DRU'GGET. *n. s.* A slight kind of woollen stuff.
In *druggets* drest, of thirteen pence a yard,
See Philip's son amid'st his Persian guard. *Swift.*

DRU'GGIST. *n. s.* [from *drug.*] One who sells physical drugs.
Common nitre we bought at the *druggist's.* *Boyle.*

DRU'GSTER. *n. s.* [from *drug.*] One who sells physical simples.

Common

Common oil of turpentine I bought at the *drugsters*. *Boyle.*

They set the clergy below their apothecaries, the physician of the soul below the *drugsters* of the body. *Atterbury.*

DRU'ID. *n. s.* [*deri*, oaks, and *hud*, incantation; which may be as ancient as the Grecian δρῦς. *Perron*; *darrach*, oak, Erse.]

The priests and philosophers of the antient Britons.

DRUM. *n. s.* [*tromme*, Danish; *drumme*, Erse.]

1. An instrument of military musick, consisting of vellum strained over a broad hoop on each side, and beaten with sticks.

Let's march without the noise of threat'ning *drums*. *Shak.*

In *drums* the closeness round about, that preserveth the sound from dispersing, maketh the noise come forth at the drum-hole, far more loud and strong than if you should strike upon the like skin extended in the open air. *Bacon's Nat. Hist.*

Tears trickling down their breasts bedew the ground,
And *drums* and trumpets mix their mournful sound. *Dryden.*
Now no more the *drum*
Provokes to arms, or trumpet's clangor shrill
Affrights the wives, and chills the virgin's blood. *Phillips.*

2. The tympanum of the ear, or the membrane which perceives the vibration of the air.

To DRUM. *v. n.*

1. To beat a drum; to beat a tune on a drum.

2. To beat with a pulsatory motion.

Now, heart,
Be ribb'd with iron for this one attempt;
Set ope thy sluices, send the vigorous blood
Through every active limb for my relief;
Then take thy rest within the quiet cell;
For thou shalt drum no more. *Dryden's Don Sebastian.*

To DRU'MBLE. *v. n.* To drone; to be sluggish. *Hanmer.*

Take up these cloaths here quickly: where's the cowlstaff? Look, how you *drumble*: carry them to the landress in Datchet mead. *Shakespeare's Merry Wives of Windsor.*

DRU'MFISH. *n. s.* The name of a fish.

The under jaw of the *drumfish* from Virginia. *Woodward.*

DRU'MMAJOR. *n. s.* [*drum* and *major.*] The chief drummer of a regiment.

Such company may chance to spoil the swearing;
And the *drummajor*'s oaths, of bulk unruly,
May dwindle to a feeble. *Cleaveland.*

DRU'MMAKER. *n. s.* [*drum* and *maker.*] He who deals in drums.

The *drummaker* uses it, and the cabinetmaker. *Mortimer.*

DRU'MMER. *n. s.* [from *drum.*] He whose office it is to beat the drum.

Drummer, strike up, and let us march away. *Shak. H.* IV.
Here rows of *drummers* stand in martial file,
And with their vellum-thunder shake the pile. *Gay's Trivia.*

DRU'MSTICK. *n. s.* [*drum* and *stick.*] The stick with which a drum is beaten.

DRUNK. *adj.* [from *drink.*]

1. Intoxicated with strong liquour; inebriated.

This was the morn when issuing on the guard,
Drawn up in rank and file, they stood prepar'd
Of seeming arms to make a short assay;
Then hasten to be *drunk*, the business of the day. *Dryden.*

We generally conclude that man *drunk*, who takes pains to be thought sober. *Spectator*, N°. 577.

2. Drenched or saturated with moisture.

I will make mine arrows *drunk* with blood. *Deut.* xxix. 6.

DRU'NKARD. *n. s.* [from *drunk.*] One given to excessive use of strong liquors; one addicted to habitual ebriety.

Some blood drawn on me would beget opinion
Of my more fierce endeavour. I've seen *drunkards*
Do more than this in sport. *Shakespeare's King Lear.*
My bowels cannot hide her woes,
But, like a *drunkard*, I must vomit them. *Shakesp. Tit. And.*

God will not take the *drunkard*'s excuse, that he has so long accustomed himself to intemperate drinking, that now he cannot leave it off. *South's Sermons.*

DRU'NKEN. *adj.* [from *drink.*]

1. Intoxicated with liquor; inebriated.

O monstrous beast! how like a swine he lies!
Sirs, I will practise on this *drunken* man. *Shakespeare.*

Drunken men imagine every thing turneth round: they imagine also, that things come upon them; they see not well things afar off; those things that they see near hand, they see out of their place; and sometimes they see things double. *Bac.*

2. Given to habitual ebriety.

3. Saturated with moisture.

Then let the earth be *drunken* with our blood. *Sh. H.* VI.

4. Done in a state of inebriation.

When your carters, or your waiting vassals,
Have done a *drunken* slaughter, and defac'd
The precious image of our dear Redeemer,
You strait are on your knees for pardon, pardon. *Sh. R.* III.
We should for honour take
The *drunken* quarrels of a rake. *Swift.*

DRU'NKENLY. *adj.* [from *drunken.*] In a drunken manner.

My blood already, like the pelican,
Hast thou tapt out, and *drunkenly* carows'd. *Shak. Rich.* II.

DRU'NKENNESS. *n. s.* [from *drunken.*]

1. Intoxication with strong liquour.

Every going off from our natural and common temper, and our usual severity of behaviour, is a degree of *drunkenness*. *Taylor's Rule of holy living.*

2. Habitual ebriety.

The Lacedemonians trained up their children to hate *drunkenness*, by bringing a drunken man into their company. *Watts's Improvement of the Mind*, p. i. c. 17.

3. Intoxication, or inebriation of any kind; disorder of the faculties.

Passion is the *drunkenness* of the mind, and therefore in its present workings not controllable by reason. *Spenser.*

DRY. *adj.* [ꝺꞃıᵹ, Saxon.]

1. Arid; without wet; without moisture; not wet; not moist.

If the pipe be a little wet on the inside, it will make a differing sound from the same pipe *dry*. *Bacon's Natural History.*

When God said,
Be gather'd now, ye waters under heav'n,
Into one place, and let *dry* land appear! *Milton's Par. Lost.*
Of turbid elements the sport;
From clear to cloudy tost, from hot to cold,
And *dry* to moist. *Thomson.*

2. Without rain.

A *dry* March and a *dry* May portend a wholsome Summer, if there be a showering April between. *Bacon's Nat. History.*

The weather, we agreed, was too *dry* for the season. *Addis.*

3. Not succulent; not juicy.

I will drain him *dry* as hay;
Sleep shall neither night nor day
Hang upon his penthouse lid:
He shall live a man forbid. *Shakespeare's Macbeth.*

4. Without tears.

Dry mourning will decays more deadly bring,
As a North wind burns a too forward Spring:
Give sorrow vent, and let the sluices go. *Dryden's Aurengz.*

5. Thirsty; a-thirst.

So *dry* he was for sway. *Shakespeare's Tempest.*
Void of a bulky charger near their lips,
With which, in often interrupted sleep,
Their frying blood compels to irrigate
Their *dry* furr'd tongues. *Phillips.*

6. Jejune; barren; plain; unembellished; without pathos.

As we should take care that our stile in writing be neither *dry* nor empty, we should look again it be not winding or wanton with far-fetched descriptions: either is a vice. *B. Johns.*

It remaineth to treat concerning ornaments within, or without the fabrick, a piece not so *dry* as the meer contemplation of proportions; and therefore, I hope, therein somewhat to refresh both the reader and myself. *Wotton's Architecture.*

That the fire burns by heat, is an empty *dry* return to the question, and leaves us still ignorant. *Glanv. Sceps.* c. 20.

It is a *dry* fable, with little or nothing in it. *L'Estrange.*

Authority and friendship work upon some, *dry* and sober reason works upon others. *L'Estrange.*

To clear up this theory, I was willing to lay aside *dry* subtilties with which the schools are filled. *Burnet's Theory.*

These epistles will become less *dry*, and more susceptible of ornament. *Pope.*

7. Hard; severe. [*Drien* anciently *to endure*, *dree*, Scottish.]

I rather hop'd I should no more
Hear from you o' th' gallanting score;
For hard *dry* bastings used to prove
The readiest remedies of love;
Next a *dry* diet. *Hudibras*, p. ii. *cant.* 1.

To DRY. *v. a.*

1. To free from moisture; to arefy; to exsiccate.

The meat was well, if you were so contented.
—I tell thee, Kate, 'twas burnt, and *dry'd* away,
And I expresly am forbid to touch it. *Shakespeare.*

Heat *drieth* bodies that do easily expire; as parchment, leaves, roots, and clay; and so doth time or age arefy, as in the same bodies. *Bacon's Natural History*, N°. 294.

Herbs and flowers, if they be *dried* in the shade, or *dried* in the hot sun a small time, keep best. *Bacon's Nat. History.*

The running streams are deep:
See, they have caught the father of the flock,
Who *drys* his fleece upon the neighbouring rock. *Dryden.*

2. To exhale moisture.

'Twas grief no more, or grief and rage were one,
Within her soul: at last 'twas rage alone;
Which burning upwards in succession, *dries*
The tears that stood considering in her eyes. *Dryd. Fables.*

The water of the sea, which formerly covered it, was in time exhaled and *dried* up by the sun. *Woodward's Nat. Hist.*

3. To wipe away moisture.

Then with her vest the wound she wipes and *dries*. *Denh.*
See, at your blest returning,
Rage disappears;
The widow'd isle in mourning,
Dries up her tears. *Dryden's Albion.*

4. To scorch with thirst.

Their honourable men are famished, and their multitude *dried* up with thirst. *Is.* v. 13.

5. To drain; to exhaust.

Rash Elpenor, in an evil hour,
Dry'd an immeasurable bowl, and thought
T' exhale his surfeit by irriguous sleep
Imprudent: him, death's iron sleep opprest. *Phillips.*

To DRY. *v. n.* To grow dry; to lose moisture; to be drained of its moisture.

DRY'ER. *n. s.* [from *dry.*] That which has the quality of absorbing moisture.

The ill effects of drinking are relieved by this plant, which is a great *dryer* and opener, especially by perspiration. *Temple.*

DRY'EYED. *adj.* [*dry* and *eye.*] Without tears; without weeping.

Sight so deform, what heart of rock could long
Dryey'd behold? Adam could not, but wept. *Milt. P. Lost.*

DRY'LY. *adv.* [from *dry.*]

1. Without moisture.
2. Coldly; frigidly; without affection.

The archduke, conscious to himself how *dryly* the king had been used by his council, did strive to recover the king's affection. *Bacon's Henry* VII.

Would'st thou to honour and preferments climb,
Be bold in mischief, dare some mighty crime,
Which dungeons, death, or banishment deserves;
For virtue is but *dryly* prais'd, and starves. *Dryden's Juven.*

3. Jejunely; barrenly; without ornament or embellishment.

Some *dryly* plain, without invention's aid,
Write dull receipts how poems may be made. *Pope.*

DRY'NESS. *n. s.* [from *dry.*]

1. Want of moisture; siccity.

The Africans are conceived to be peculiarly scorched and torrified by the sun, by *dryness* from the soil, from want and defect of water. *Brown's Vulgar Errours, b.* vi. *c.* 10.

Such was the discord which did first disperse
Form, order, beauty, through the universe;
While *dryness* moisture, coldness heat resists,
All that we have, and that we are, subsists. *Denham.*

The marrow supplies an oil for the inunction of the bones and ligaments in the articulations, and particularly of the ligaments, preserving them from *dryness* and rigidity, and keeping them supple and flexible. *Ray on the Creation.*

The difference of muscular flesh depends upon the hardness, tenderness, moisture, or *dryness* of the fibres. *Arbuthnot.*

Is the sea ever likely to be evaporated by the sun, or to be emptied with buckets? Why then must we fancy this impossible *driness*, and then, upon that fictitious account, calumniate nature? *Bentley's Sermons.*

2. Want of succulence.

If he fill'd
His vacancy with his voluptuousness,
Full surfeits, and the *dryness* of his bones,
Call on him for't. *Shakespeare's Anthony and Cleopatra.*

3. Want of embellishment; want of pathos; jejuneness; barrenness.

Their new flowers and sweetness do not as much corrupt, as the others *dryness* and squalor, if they chuse not carefully. *Ben. Johnson's Discoveries.*

Be faithful where the author excels, and paraphrase where penury of fancy or *dryness* of expression ask it. *Garth.*

4. Want of sensibility in devotion; want of ardour; aridity.

It may be, that by this *dryness* of spirit God intends to make us the more fervent and resigned in our direct and solemn devotions, by the perceiving of our wants and weakness. *Taylor's Worthy Communicant.*

DRY'NURSE. *n. s.* [*dry* and *nurse.*]

1. A woman who brings up and feeds a child without the breast.
2. One who takes care of another: with some contempt of the person taken care of.

Mistress Quickly is in the manner of his nurse, or his *drynurse*, or his cook, or his laundry, his washer, and his wringer. *Shakespeare's Merry Wives of Windsor.*

To DRY'NURSE. *v. a.* [from the noun.] To feed without the breast.

As Romulus a wolf did rear,
So he was *drynurs'd* by a bear. *Hudibras, p.* i. *cant.* 2.

DRY'SHOD. *adj.* [*dry* and *shod.*] Without wet feet; without treading above the shoes in the water.

He had embarked us in such disadvantage, as we could not return *dryshod.* *Sidney, b.* ii.

Dryshod to pass, she parts the floods in tway;
And eke huge mountains from their native seat
She would command, themselves to bear away. *Fairy Queen.*

Has honour's fountain then suck'd back the stream?
He has; and hooting boys may *dryshod* pass,
And gather pebbles from the naked ford. *Dryd. Don Sebast.*

DU'AL. *adj.* [*dualis*, Latin.] Expressing the number two.

Modern languages have only one variation, and so the Latin; but the Greek and Hebrew have one to signify two, and another to signify more than two: under one variation the noun is said to be of the *dual* number, and under the other of the plural. *Clarke's Latin Grammar.*

To DUB. *v. a.* [ꝺubban ꝫo ꞃıꝺeꞃe, Saxon; *addubba till riddara*, Islandick, to dub a knight. *Addubba*, in its primary sense, signifies to *strike*, knights being made by a blow with the sword.]

1. To make a man a knight.

Knight, knight, good mother! Basilisco like.
What! I am *dubb'd*; I have it on my shoulder. *Shakespeare.*

The robes which the kings then allowed to each knight, when he was *dubbed*, of green or burnet, as they spake in that age, appeareth upon record. *Camden's Remains.*

The king stood up under his cloth of state, took the sword from the lord protector, and *dubbed* the lord mayor of London knight. *Hayward on Edward* VI.

2. To confer any kind of dignity, or new character.

The jealous o'erworn widow and herself,
Since that our brother *dubb'd* them gentlewomen,
Are mighty gossips in this monarchy. *Shakesp. Richard* III.

He
Gave thee no instance why thou should'st do treason,
Unless to *dub* thee with the name of traitor. *Shakesp. H.* V.

Women commence by Cupid's dart,
As a king hunting *dubs* a hart. *Cleaveland.*

A plain gentleman, of an ancient family, is of better quality than a new knight, though the reason of his *dubbing* was meritorious. *Collier on Pride.*

O, poet! thou had'st been discreeter,
Hanging the monarch's hat so high,
If thou had'st *dubb'd* thy star a meteor,
That did but blaze, and rove, and die. *Prior.*

These demoniacks let me *dub*
With the name of legion club. *Swift.*

A man of wealth is *dubb'd* a man of worth;
Venus shall give him form, and Anstis birth. *Pope's Horace.*

DUB. *n. s.* [from the verb.] A blow; a knock.

As skilful coopers hoop their tubs
With Lydian and with Phrygian *dubs.* *Hudibras, p.* ii.

DUBIO'SITY. *n. s.* [from *dubious.*] A thing doubtful. A word not used.

Men often swallow falsities for truths, *dubiosities* for certainties, fesibilities for possibilities, and things impossible for possible. *Brown's Vulgar Errours, b.* i. *c.* 4.

DU'BIOUS. *n. s.* [*dubius*, Latin.]

1. Doubtful; not settled in an opinion.
2. Uncertain; that of which the truth is not fully known.

No quick reply to *dubious* questions make. *Denham.*

We also call it a *dubious* or doubtful proposition, when there are no arguments on either side. *Watts's Logick.*

3. Not plain; not clear.

Satan with less toil, and now with ease,
Wafts on the calmer wave by *dubious* light. *Milt. Pa. Lost.*

DU'BIOUSLY. *adv.* [from *dubious.*] Uncertainly; without any determination.

Authors write often *dubiously*, even in matters wherein is expected a strict definitive truth. *Brown's Vulgar Errours, b.* i.

Almanackmakers are so wise to wander in generals, and talk *dubiously*, and leave to the reader the business of interpreting. *Swift's Predictions for the Year* 1708.

DU'BIOUSNESS. *n. s.* [from *dubious.*] Uncertainty; doubtfulness.

DU'BITABLE. *adj.* [*dubito*, Latin.] Doubtful; uncertain; what may be doubted.

DUBITA'TION. *n. s.* [*dubitatio*, Latin.] The act of doubting; doubt.

Many of the ancients denied the antipodes; but the experience of our enlarged navigation can now assert them beyond all *dubitation.* *Brown's Vulgar Errours, b.* i. *c.* 7.

Dubitation may be called a negative perception; that is, when I perceive that what I see, is not what I would see. *Grew.*

DU'CAL. *adj.* [from *duke.*] Pertaining to a duke; as, a *ducal* coronet.

DU'CAT. *n. s.* [from *duke.*] A coin struck by dukes: in silver valued at about four shillings and six pence; in gold at nine shillings and six pence.

I cannot instantly raise up the gross
Of full three thousand *ducats.* *Shakesp. Merchant of Venice.*

There was one that died in debt: it was reported, where his creditors were, that he was dead: one said, he hath carried five hundred *ducats* of mine into the other world. *Bacon.*

DUCK. *n. s.* [*ducken*, to dip, Dutch.]

1. A water fowl, both wild and tame.

The *ducks* that heard the proclamation cry'd,
And fear'd a persecution might betide,
Full twenty mile from town their voyage take,
Obscure in rushes of the liquid lake. *Dryden's Nun's Priest.*

Grubs if you find your land subject to, turn *ducks* into it. *Mortimer's Husbandry.*

2. A word of endearment, or fondness.

Will you buy any tape, or lace for your cap,
My dainty *duck*, my dear-a? *Shakespeare's Winter's Tale.*

3. A declination of the head: fo called from the frequent action of a duck in the water.

Back, fhepherds, back; enough your play,
'Till next funfhine holyday:
Here be without *duck* or nod,
Other trippings to be trod,
Of lighter toes, and fuch court guife
As Mercury did firft devife. *Milton.*

4. A ftone thrown obliquely on the waters fo as to ftrike it and rebound.

Neither crofs and pile, nor *ducks* and drakes, are quite fo ancient as handy-dandy. *Arbuthn. and Pope's Mart. Scriblerus.*

To DUCK. *v. n.* [from the noun.]

1. To dive under water as a duck.

The varlet faw, when to the flood he came,
How without ftop or ftay he fiercely leapt;
And deep himfelf be *ducked* in the fame,
That in the lake his lofty creft was fteept. *Fairy Queen.*

Let the labouring bark climb hills of feas
Olympus high, and *duck* again as low
As hell's from heav'n. *Shakefpeare's Othello.*

Thou art wickedly devout;
In Tiber *ducking* thrice, by break of day. *Dryden's Perf.*

2. To drop down the head, as a duck.

As fome raw youth in country bred,
When at a fkirmifh firft he hears
The bullets whiftling round his ears,
Will *duck* his head afide, will ftart,
And feel a trembling at his heart. *Swift.*

3. To bow low; to cringe. In Scottifh *duyk*, or *juyk*, to make obeifance, is ftill ufed.

I cannot flatter and look fair,
Smile in mens faces, fmooth, deceive, and cog,
Duck with French nods and apifh courtefy. *Shakefp. R.* III.

The learned pate
Ducks to the golden fool. *Shakefpeare's Timon.*

DU'CKER. *n. f.* [from *duck.*]

1. A diver.
2. A cringer. *Dict.*

To DUCK. *v. a.* To put under water.

DU'CKINGSTOOL. *n. f.* [*duck* and *ftool.*] A chair in which fcolds are tied, and put under water.

She in the *duckingftool* fhould take her feat,
Dreft like herfelf in a great chair of ftate. *Dorfet.*

Reclaim the obftinately opprobrious and virulent women, and make the *duckingftool* more ufeful. *Addifon's Freeholder.*

DU'CKLEGGED. *adj.* [*duck* and *leg.*] Short legged.

Ducklegg'd, fhort waifted, fuch a dwarf fhe is,
That fhe muft rife on tiptoes for a kifs. *Dryden's Juv. Sat.*

DU'CKLING. *n. f.* [from *duck.*] A young duck; the brood of the duck.

Ducklings, though hatched and led by a hen, if fhe brings them to the brink of a river or pond, prefently leave her, and in they go. *Ray on the Creation.*

Ev'ry morn
Amid' the *ducklings* let her fcatter corn. *Gay's Paftorals.*

DU'CKMEAT. *n. f.* [*duck* and *meat.*] A common plant growing in ftanding waters.

DUCKCO'Y. *n. f.* [See *To* DUCKOY.] Any means of enticing and enfnaring.

Seducers have found it the moft compendious way to their defigns to lead captive filly women, and make them the *duckcoys* to their whole family. *Decay of Piety.*

To DUCKO'Y. *v. a.* [miftaken for *decoy*: the decoy being commonly practifed upon *ducks*, produced the errour.] To entice to a fnare.

This fifh hath a flender membranous ftring, which he projects and draws in at pleafure, as a ferpent doth his tongue: with this he *duckoys* little fifhes, and then preys upon them. *Grew's Mufæum.*

DU'CKSFOOT. *n. f.* Black fnakeroot, or Mayapple.

The cup of the flower confifts of one leaf: the flowers are hexapetalous; the footftalk of the flower comes out from the ftalk of the leaf: the fruit is fhaped like an urn, and contains many roundifh fimbriated feeds. *Miller.*

DU'CKWEED. *n. f.* [*duck* and *weed.*] The fame with duckmeat.

That we call *duckweed* hath a leaf no bigger than a thymeleaf, but of a frefher green; and putteth forth a little ftring into the water, far from the bottom. *Bacon's Natural Hiftory.*

DUCT. *n. f.* [*ductus*, Latin.]

1. Guidance; direction.

This doctrine, by faftening all our actions, by a fatal decree at the foot of God's chair, leaves nothing to us but only to obey our fate, to follow the *duct* of the ftars, or neceffity of thofe irony chains which we are born under. *Hammond.*

2. A paffage through which any thing is conducted.

A *duct* from each of thofe cells ran into the root of the tongue, where both joined together, and paffed forward in one common *duct* to the tip of it. *Addifon's Spectator*, N°. 275.

It was obferved, that the chyle in the thoracick *duct* retained the original tafte of the aliment. *Arbuthnot on Aliments.*

DU'CTILE. *adj.* [*ductilis*, Latin.]

1. Flexible; pliable.

Thick woods and gloomy night
Conceal the happy plant from human light:
One bough it bears; but, wond'rous to behold,
The *ductile* rind and leaves of radiant gold. *Dryden's Æn.*

2. Eafy to be drawn out into length, or expanded.

All bodies, *ductile* and tenfile, as metals, that will be drawn into wires; wool and tow, that will be drawn into yarn or thread, have in them the appetite of not difcontinuing ftrong. *Bacon's Natural Hiftory.*

Gold, as it is the pureft, fo it is the fofteft and moft *ductile* of all metals. *Dryden's Fables, Dedicat.*

3. Tractable; obfequious; complying; yielding.

He generous thoughts inftills
Of true nobility; forms their *ductile* minds
To human virtues. *Phillips.*

Their defigning leaders cannot defire a more *ductile* and eafy people to work upon. *Addifon's Freeholder*, N°. 7.

DU'CTILENESS. *n. f.* [from *ductile.*] Flexibility; ductility.

I, when I value gold, may think upon
The *ductilenefs*, the application;
The wholfomnefs, the ingenuity,
From ruft, from foil, from fire ever free. *Donne.*

DUCTI'LITY. *n. f.* [from *ductile.*]

1. Quality of fuffering extenfion; flexibility.

Yellow colour and *ductility* are properties of gold: they belong to all gold, but not only to gold; for faffron is alfo yellow, and lead is ductile. *Watts's Logick.*

2. Obfequioufnefs; compliance.

DU'DGEON. *n. f.* [*dolch*, German.]

1. A fmall dagger.

I fee thee ftill;
And, on the blade of thy *dudgeon*, gouts of blood. *Shakefp.*

I was a ferviceable *dudgeon*,
Either for fighting or for drudging. *Hudibras, p.* i. *cant.* i.

2. Malice; fullennefs; malignity; ill will.

Civil *dudgeon* firft grew high,
And men fell out they knew not why. *Hudibras, p.* i. *c.* i.

The cuckow took this a little in *dudgeon*. *L'Eftrange.*

DUE. *adj.* The participle paffive of *owe.* [*dû*, French.]

1. Owed; that which any one has a right to demand in confequence of a compact, or for any other reafon.

There is *due* from the judge to the advocate fome commendation and gracing, where caufes are well handled and fair pleaded. *Bacon, Effay* 57.

There is likewife *due* to the publick a civil reprehenfion of advocates, where there appeareth cunning, grofs neglect, or flight information. *Bacon, Effay* 57.

Mirth and chearfulnefs are but the *due* reward of innocency of life. *More's Divine Dialogues.*

A prefent bleffing upon our fafts is neither originally *due* from God's juftice, nor becomes *due* to us from his veracity. *Smalridge's Sermons.*

There is a refpect *due* to mankind, which fhould incline ever the wifeft of men to follow innocent cuftoms. *Watts.*

2. Proper; fit; appropriate.

Opportunity may be taken to excite, in perfons attending on thofe folemnities, a *due* fenfe of the vanity of earthly fatisfactions. *Atterbury.*

3. Exact; without deviation.

You might fee him come towards me beating the ground in fo *due* time, as no dancer can obferve better meafure. *Sidn.*

And Eve within, *due* at her hour, prepar'd
For dinner favoury fruits. *Milton's Paradife Loft, b.* v.

DUE. *adv.* [from the adjective.] Exactly; directly; duly.

Like the Pontick fea,
Whofe icy current, and compulfive courfe,
Ne'er feels retiring ebb, but keeps *due* on
To the Propontick and the Hellefpont. *Shakefp. Othello.*

DUE. *n. f.* [from the adjective.]

1. That which belongs to one; that which may be juftly claimed.

My *due* from thee is this imperial crown,
Which, as immediate from thy place and blood,
Derives itfelf to me. *Shakefpeare.*

The fon of Duncan,
From whom this tyrant holds the *due* of birth,
Lives in the Englifh court. *Shakefpeare's Macbeth.*

Thou better know'ft
The offices of nature, bond of childhood,
Effects of courtefy, *dues* of gratitude:
Thy half o' th' kingdom thou haft not forgot,
Wherein I thee endow'd. *Shakefpeare's King Lear.*

I defire of you a conduct over land.
—My lord, you are appointed for that purpofe;
The *due* of honour in no point omit. *Shakefp. Cymbeline.*

I take this garland, not as given by you,
But as my merit, and my beauty's *due*. *Dryd. Ind. Emperor.*

No popular affembly ever knew, or propofed, or declared what fhare of power was their *due*. *Swift.*

2. Right; juft title.

The

The key of this infernal pit by *due*,
And by command of heav'n's all-powerful king,
I keep. *Milton's Paradise Lost, b.* ii. *l.* 850.

3. Whatever custom or law requires to be done.

Befriend
Us thy vow'd priests, 'till outmost end
Of all thy *dues* be done, and none left out. *Milt. Par. Reg.*
They pay the dead his annual *dues*. *Dryden.*

4. Custom; tribute.

In respect of the exorbitant *dues* that are paid at most other ports, this deservedly retains the name of free. *Addison.*

To DUE. *v. a.* [from the noun.] To pay as due.

This is the latest glory of their praise,
That I thy enemy *due* thee withal. *Shakespeare's Henry* VI.

DU'EL. *n. s.* [*duellum*, Latin.] A combat between two; a single fight.

In many armies, if the matter should be tried by *duel* between two champions, the victory should go on the one side; and yet if it be tried by the gross, go on the other side. *Bacon.*

To whom thus Michael: dream not of your fight
As of a *duel*, or the local wounds
Of head or heel. *Milton's Paradise Lost, b.* xii. *l.* 387.
'Twas I that wrong'd you; you my life have sought:
No *duel* ever was more justly fought. *Waller.*

To DU'EL. *v. n.* [from the noun.] To fight a single combat.

The challenging and fighting with a man, a certain positive mode of action, by particular ideas distinguished from all others, is called *duelling*. *Locke.*

To DU'EL. *v. a.* To attack or fight with singly.

Who single
Duell'd their armies, rank'd in proud array,
Himself an army, now unequal match
To save himself against a coward arm'd,
At one spear's length. *Milton's Agonistes, l.* 344.

DU'ELLER. *n. s.* [from *duel*.] A single combatant.

They perhaps begin as single *duellers*, but then they soon get their troops about them. *Decay of Piety.*

DU'ELLIST. *n. s.* [from *duel*.]

1. A single combatant.

If the king ends the differences, the case will fall out no worse than when two *duellists* enter the field, where the worsted party hath his sword again, without further hurt. *Suckling.*

Henceforth let poets, ere allow'd to write,
Be search'd like *duellists* before they fight. *Dryden.*

2. One who professes to live by rules of honour.

His bought arms Mung not lik'd; for his first day
Of bearing them in field, he threw 'em away;
And hath no honour lost, our *duellists* say. *Ben. Johnson.*

DUE'LLO. *n. s.* [Italian.] The duel; the rule of duelling.

The gentleman will, for his honour's sake, have one bout with you: he cannot by the *duello* avoid it. *Sh. Twelfth Night.*

DUE'NNA. *n. s.* [Spanish.] An old woman kept to guard a younger.

I felt the ardour of my passion increase as the season advanced, 'till in the month of July I could no longer contain: I bribed her *duenna*, was admitted to the bath, saw her undressed, and the wonder displayed. *Arbuthnot and Pope.*

DUG. *n. s.* [*deggia*, to give suck, Islandick.]

1. A pap; a nipple; a teat: spoken of beasts, or in malice or contempt of human beings.

Of her there bred
A thousand young ones, which she daily fed,
Sucking upon her poisonous *dugs*; each one
Of sundry shape, yet all ill favoured. *Fairy Queen, b.* i.

They are first fed and nourished with the milk of a strange *dug*. *Raleigh's History of the World.*

Then shines the goat, whose brutish *dugs* supply'd
The infant Jove, and nurst his growing pride. *Creech.*

2. It seems to have been used formerly of the breast without reproach.

It was a faithless squire that was the source
Of all my sorrow, and of these sad tears;
With whom, from tender *dug* of common nourse,
At once I was up brought. *Fairy Queen, b.* ii. *cant.* 4.
As mild and gentle as the cradle-babe,
Dying with mother's *dug* between its lips. *Shakes. Hen.* VI.

DUG. *preterit.* and *part. pass.* of *dig.*

They had often found medals, and pipes of lead, as they *dug* among the rubbish. *Addison's Remarks on Italy.*

DUKE. *n. s.* [*duc*, French; *dux*, Latin.] One of the highest order of nobility in England; in rank a nobleman next to the royal family.

The *duke* of Cornwal, and Regan his dutchess, will be here with him this night. *Shakespeare's King Lear.*

Aurmarle, Surrey, and Exeter must lose
The names of *dukes*, their titles, dignities,
And whatsoever profits thereby rise. *Daniel's C. War.*

DU'KEDOM. *n. s.* [from *duke*.]

1. The seigniory or possessions of a duke.

Her brother found a wife,
Where he himself was lost; Prospero his *dukedom*
In a poor isle. *Shakespeare's Tempest.*

The cardinal never resigned his purple for the prospect of giving an heir to the *dukedom* of Tuscany. *Addison.*

2. The title or quality of a duke.

DU'LBRAINED. *adj.* [*dull* and *brain*.] Stupid; doltish; foolish.

This arm of mine hath chastised
The petty rebel, *dulbrain'd* Buckingham. *Shakes. Rich.* III.

DU'LCET. *adj.* [*dulcis*, Latin.]

1. Sweet to the taste; luscious.

From sweet kernels press'd,
She tempers *dulcet* creams; nor these to hold
Wants she fit vessels pure. *Milton's Paradise Lost, b.* v.

2. Sweet to the ear; harmonious; melodious.

I sat upon a promontory,
And heard a mermaid, on a dolphin's back,
Uttering such *dulcet* and harmonious breath,
That the rude sea grew civil at her song. *Shakespeare.*
A fabrick huge
Rose like an exhalation, with the sound
Of *dulcet* symphonies, and voices sweet. *Milt. Parad. Lost.*

DULCIFICA'TION. *n. s.* [from *dulcify*.] The act of sweetning; the act of freeing from acidity, saltness, or acrimony.

In colcothar the exactest calcination, followed by an exquisite *dulcification*, does not reduce the remaining body into elementary earth; for after the salt or vitriol, if the calcination have been too faint, is drawn out of the colcothar, the residue is not earth, but a mixt body, rich in medical virtues. *Boyle's Scept. Chym.*

To DU'LCIFY. *v. a.* [*dulcifier*, French.] To sweeten; to set free from acidity, saltness, or acrimony of any kind.

A decoction of wild gourd, or colocynthis, though somewhat qualified, will not from every hand be *dulcified* into aliment, by an addition of flower or meal. *Brown's Vulgar Err.*

I dressed him with a pledgit, dipt in a *dulcified* tincture of vitriol. *Wiseman's Surgery.*

Spirit of wine *dulcifies* spirit of salt; nitre, or vitriol have other bad effects. *Arbuthnot on Aliments.*

DU'LCIMER. *n. s.* [*dolcimello*, *Skinner*.] A musical instrument played by striking the brass wires with little sticks.

Ye hear the sound of the cornet, flute, harp, sackbut, psaltery, *dulcimer*, and all kinds of musick. *Dan.* iii. 5.

To DU'LCORATE. *v. a.* [from *dulcis*, Latin.] To sweeten; to make less acrimonious.

The ancients, for the *dulcorating* of fruit, do commend swine's dung above all other dung. *Bacon's Natural History.*

Turbith mineral, as it is sold in the shops, is a rough medicine; but being somewhat *dulcorated*, first procureth vomiting, and then salivation. *Wiseman's Surgery.*

DULCORA'TION. *n. s.* [from *dulcorate*.] The act of sweetening.

Malt gathereth a sweetness to the taste, which appeareth in the wort: the *dulcoration* of things is worthy to be tried to the full; for that *dulcoration* importeth a degree to nourishment: and the making of things inalimental to become alimental, may be an experiment of great profit for making new victuals. *Bacon's Natural History*, N°. 649.

DU'LHEAD. *n. s.* [*dull* and *head*.] A blockhead; a wretch foolish and stupid; a dolt.

This people be fools and *dulheads* to all goodness; but subtle, cunning, and bold in any mischief. *Ascham's Schoolm.*

DU'LIA. *n. s.* [δουλεια.] An inferiour kind of adoration.

Paleotus saith, that the same worship which is given to the prototype may be given to the image; but with the different degrees of latria and *dulia*. *Stillingfleet.*

DULL. *adj.* [*dwl*, Welsh; ꝺole, Saxon; *dol*, mad, Dutch.]

1. Stupid; doltish; blockish; unapprehensive; indocile; slow of understanding.

Such is their evil hap to play upon *dull* spirited men. *Hooker.*

He that hath learned no wit by nature, nor art, may complain of gross breeding, or comes of a very *dull* kindred. *Shak.*

Sometimes this perception, in some kind of bodies, is far more subtile than the sense; so that the sense is but a *dull* thing in comparison of it. *Bacon's Natural History.*

Every man, even the *dullest*, is thinking more than the most eloquent can teach him how to utter. *Dryden.*

2. Blunt; obtuse.

Meeting with time, Slack thing, said I,
Thy scythe is *dull*; whet it, for shame. *Herbert.*

3. Unready; aukward.

Gynecia a great while stood still, with a kind of *dull* amazement looking stedfastly upon her. *Sidney.*

O help thou my weak wit, and sharpen my *dull* tongue.
Fairy Queen, b. i. *stanz.* 2.

Memory is so necessary to all conditions of life, that we are not to fear it should grow *dull* for want of exercise, if exercise would make it stronger. *Locke.*

4. Hebetated; not quick.

This people's heart is waxed gross, and their ears are *dull* of hearing. *Math.* xiii. 15.

5. Sad; melancholy.

6. Sluggish; heavy; slow of motion.

Thenceforth the waters waxed *dull* and slow,
And all that drunk thereof did faint and feeble grow. *F. Q.*

7. Gross;

7. Grofs; cloggy; vile.

She excels each mortal thing
Upon the *dull* earth dwelling. *Shak. Two Gent. of Verona.*

8. Not exhilarating; not delightful; as, *to make dictionaries is* dull *work.*

9. Not bright; as, *the mirror is* dull, *the fire is* dull.

I'll not be made a foft and *dull* ey'd fool,
To fhake the head, relent, and figh, and yield
To Chriftian interceffors. *Shakefpeare's Merch. of Venice.*

10. Drowfy; fleepy.

To Dull. *v a.* [from the adjective.]

1. To ftupify; to infatuate

Nothing hath more *dulled* the wits, or taken away the will of children from learning, than care in making of Latin. *Afch.*

Thofe drugs fhe has
Will ftupify and *dull* the fenfe awhile. *Shakefp. Cymbeline.*

2. To blunt; to obtund.

This entrance of the battle did whet the courage of the Spaniards, though it *dulled* their fwords. *Bacon.*

3. To fadden; to make melancholy.

4. To hebetate; to weaken.

Now forc'd to overflow with brackifh tears,
The troublous noife did *dull* their dainty ears. *Spenfer.*

5. To damp; to clog.

Prayers were fhort, as if darts thrown out with a fudden quicknefs, left that vigilant and erect attention of mind, which in prayer is very neceffary, fhould be wafted or *dulled* through continuance. *Hooker, b.* v. *f.* 33.

In bodies, union ftrengtheneth and cherifheth any natural action; and, on the other fide, weakeneth and *dulleth* any violent impreffion, and even fo is it of minds. *Bacon's Effays.*

6. To make weary, or flow of motion.

7. To fully brightnefs.

The breath *dulls* the mirrour. *Bacon.*

Du'llard. *n.f.* [from *dull.*] A blockhead; a dolt; a ftupid fellow; a dunce.

What, mak'ft thou me a *dullard* in this act?
Wilt thou not fpeak to me? *Shakefpeare's Cymbeline.*

Thou muft make a *dullard* of the world,
If they not thought the profits of my death
Were very pregnant and potential fpurs
To make thee feek it. *Shakefpeare's King Lear.*

Du'lly. *adv.* [from *dull*]

1. Stupidly; doltifhly.

It is not fufficient to imitate nature in every circumftance *dully*, literally, and meanly; but it becomes a painter to take what is moft beautiful. *Dryden's Dufrefnoy.*

2. Slowly; fluggifhly.

The air, if it be moift, doth in a degree quench the flame, and howfoever maketh it burn more *dully*. *Bacon's Nat. Hift.*

3. Not vigoroufly; not gaily; not brightly; not keenly.

Du'lness. *n. f.* [from *dull.*]

1. Stupidity; weaknefs of intellect; indocility; flownefs of apprehenfion.

Nor is the *dulnefs* of the fcholar to extinguifh, but rather to inflame the charity of the teacher. *South's Sermons.*

Shadwel alone my perfect image bears,
Mature in *dulnefs* from his tender years. *Dryden.*

2. Want of quick perception.

Nature, by a continual ufe of any thing, groweth to a fatiety and *dulnefs*, either of appetite or working. *Bacon's Nat. Hift.*

3. Drowfinefs; inclination to fleep.

Here ceafe more queftions;
Thou art inclin'd to fleep. 'Tis a good *dulnefs*,
And give it way. *Shakefpeare's Tempeft.*

4. Sluggifhnefs of motion.

5. Dimnefs; want of luftre.

6. Bluntnefs; want of edge.

Du'ly. *adv.* [from *due.*]

1. Properly; fitly; in the due manner.

Ever fince they firmly have retained,
And *duly* well obferved his beheaft. *Spenfer.*

I do not know
What kind of my obedience I fhould tender,
More than my all, which is nothing; nor my prayers
Are not words *duly* hallow'd, nor my wifhes
More worth than vanities; yet prayers and wifhes
Are all I can return. *Shakefpeare's Henry* VIII.

In the body, when the principal parts, as the heart and liver, do their offices, and all the inferiour fmaller veffels act orderly and *duly*, there arifes a fweet enjoyment upon the whole, which we call health. *South's Sermons.*

If attention be *duly* engaged to thofe reflections, they cannot fail of influence. *Rogers, Sermon* 3.

2. Regularly; exactly.

Seldom at church, 'twas fuch a bufy life;
But *duly* fent his family and wife. *Pope, Epiftle* 3.

DUMB. *adj.* [דום he was filent; *dumbs*, Gothick; dumbe, Saxon; *dum*, Danifh; *dom*, Dutch, dull.]

1. Mute; incapable of fpeech.

It hath pleafed himfelf fometime to unloofe the very tongues even of *dumb* creatures, and to teach them to plead in their own defence, left the cruelty of man fhould perfift to afflict them. *Hooker, b.* v. *f.* 8.

They fpake not a word;
But like *dumb* ftatues, or unbreathing ftones,
Star'd each on other. *Shakefpeare's Richard* III.

Some pofitive terms fignify a negative idea: blind implies a privation of fight, *dumb* a denial of fpeech. *Watts's Logick.*

2. Deprived of fpeech.

They fung no more, or only fung his fame;
Struck *dumb*, they all admir'd the godlike man. *Dryden.*

3. Mute; not ufing words.

He is a proper man's picture; but, alas! who can converfe with a *dumb* fhow? *Shakefpeare's Merchant of Venice.*

His gentle *dumb* expreffion turn'd at length
The eye of Eve to mark his play. *Milton's Paradife Loft.*

Her humble geftures made the refidue plain,
Dumb eloquence perfuading more than fpeech. *Rofcommon.*

For he who covets gain in fuch excefs,
Does by *dumb* figns himfelf as much exprefs,
As if in words at length he fhow'd his mind. *Dryden's Juv.*

Nothing is more common than for lovers to complain, relent, languifh, defpair, and die in *dumb* fhow. *Addif. Spect.*

4. Silent; refufing to fpeak.

The good old feer withftood
Th' intended treafon, and was *dumb* to blood;
'Till tir'd with endlefs clamours, and purfuit
Of Ithacus, he ftood no longer mute. *Dryden's Æn.*

Du'mbly. *adv.* [from *dumb.*] Mutely; filently; without words.

Du'mbness. *n.f.* [from *dumb.*]

1. Incapacity to fpeak.

2. Omiffion of fpeech; mutenefs.

There was fpeech in their *dumbnefs*, language in their very gefture: they looked as they had heard of a world ranfomed, or one deftroyed. *Shakefpeare's Winter's Tale.*

To th' *dumbnefs* of the gefture
One might interpret. *Shakefpeare's Timon of Athens.*

3. Refufal to fpeak; filence.

'Tis love, faid fhe; and then my downcaft eyes,
And guilty *dumbnefs*, witnefs'd my furprize. *Dryden.*

To Du'mbfound. *v. a.* [from *dumb.*] To confufe; to ftrike dumb. A low phrafe.

They had like to have *dumbfounded* the juftice; but his clerk came in to his affiftance. *Spectator*, N°. 616.

DUMP. *n.f.* [from *dom*, ftupid, Dutch.]

1. Sorrow; melancholy; fadnefs.

Sing no more ditties, fing no mo
Of *dumps* fo dull and heavy;
The frauds of men were ever fo,
Since Summer firft was leafy. *Sh. Much Ado about Nothing.*

Vifit by night your lady's chamber window
With fome fweet confort: to their inftruments
Tune a deploring *dump*; the night's dead filence
Will well become fuch fweet complaining grievance. *Shak.*

Funerals with ftately pomp
March flowly on, in folemn *dump*. *Hudibras, p.* i. *cant.* 1.

The fquire who fought on bloody ftumps,
By future bards bewail'd in doleful *dumps*. *Gay's Paftorals.*

2. Abfence of mind; reverie.

This fhame *dumps* caufe to well-bred people, when it carries them away from the company. *Locke.*

Du'mpish. *adj.* [from *dump.*] Sad; melancholy; forrowful.

New year, forth looking out of Janus' gate,
Doth feem to promife hope of new delight;
And bidding th' old adieu, his paffed date
Bids all old thoughts to die in *dumpifh* fpight. *Spenfer.*

The life which I live at this age is not a dead, *dumpifh*, and four life; but chearful, lively, and pleafant. *Herbert.*

Du'mpling. *n. f.* [from *dump*, heavinefs.] A fort of pudding.

You prate too long, like a book-learn'd fot,
'Till pudding and *dumpling* burn to pot. *Dryden.*

Dun. *adj.* [dun, Saxon.]

1. A colour partaking of brown and black.

By mixing fuch powders we are not to expect a ftrong and full white, fuch as is that of paper; but fome dufky obfcure one, fuch as might arife from a mixture of light and darknefs, or from white and black, that is, a grey, or *dun*, or ruffet brown. *Newton's Opt.*

2. Dark; gloomy.

Come, thick night!
And pall thee in the *dunneft* fmoke of hell,
That my keen knife fee not the wound it makes;
Nor heav'n peep through the blanket of the dark,
To cry hold! hold! *Shakefpeare's Macbeth.*

He then furvey'd
Hell, and the gulph between, and Satan there
Coafting the wall of heav'n on this fide,
In the *dun* air fublime. *Milton's Paradife Loft, b.* iii. *l.* 69.

To DUN. *v. a.* [dunan, Saxon, to clamour.] To claim a debt with vehemence and importunity.

Borrow of thy back, and borrow of thy belly: they'll never afk thee again. I fhall be *dunning* thee every day. *Bacon.*

I remember

I remember what ſhe won:
And hath ſhe ſent ſo ſoon to *dun?* *Swift.*
When thou *dun'ſt* their parents, ſeldom they,
Without a ſuit before the tribune, pay. *Dryden's Juvenal.*

DUN. *n. ſ.* [from the verb.] A clamorous, importunate, troubleſome creditor.

Thus, while my joyleſs minutes tedious flow,
With looks demure, and ſilent pace, a *dun*,
Horrible monſter! hated by gods and men,
To my aerial citadel aſcends. *Phillips.*

It grieves my heart to be pulled by the ſleeve by ſome raſcally *dun*, Sir, remember my bill. *Arbuthn. Hiſtory of J. Bull.*

DUNCE. *n. ſ.* [A word of uncertain etymology; perhaps from *dum*, the Dutch ſtupid.] A dullard; a dolt; a thickſkul; a ſtupid indocile animal.

Dunce at the beſt; in ſtreets but ſcarce allow'd,
To tickle, on thy ſtraw, the ſtupid crowd. *Dryden's Virgil.*

Was Epiphanius ſo great a *dunce* to imagine a thing, indifferent in itſelf, ſhould be directly oppoſite to the law of God? *Stillingfleet.*

I never knew this town without *dunces* of figure, who had credit enough to give riſe to ſome new word. *Swift.*

DUNG. *n. ſ.* [dinȝ, Saxon.] The excrement of animals uſed to fatten ground.

For *dung*, all excrements are the refuſe and putrifactions of nouriſhment. *Bacon's Natural Hiſtory*, N°. 696.

I judge the likelieſt way to be the perforation of the body of the tree in ſeveral places, one above the other; and the filling of the holes with *dung*, mingled with the medicine; and the watering of thoſe lumps of *dung*, with ſquirts of an infuſion of the medicine in dunged water, once in three or four days. *Bacon's Natural Hiſtory*, N°. 500.

For when from herbs the pure part muſt be won,
From groſs by 'ſtilling, this is better done
By deſpis'd *dung* than by the fire or ſun. *Donne.*

He ſoon would learn to think like me,
And bleſs his raviſh'd eyes to ſee
Such order from confuſion ſprung,
Such gaudy tulips rais'd from *dung*. *Swift.*

To DUNG. *v. a.* [from the noun.] To fatten with dung.

It was received of old, that *dunging* of grounds, when the Weſt wind bloweth, and in the decreaſe of the moon, doth greatly help. *Bacon's Natural Hiſtory*, N°. 667.

There, as his dream foretold, a cart he found,
That carry'd compoſt forth to *dung* the ground. *Dryden.*

DU'NGEON. *n. ſ.* [from *donjon*, the tower in which priſoners were kept, whence all priſons eminently ſtrong were in time called *dungeons*.] A cloſe priſon: generally ſpoke of a priſon dark or ſubterraneous.

Then up he took the ſlumbered ſenſeleſs corſe,
And e're he could out of his ſwoon awake,
Him to his caſtle brought with haſty force,
And in a *dungeon* deep him threw without remorſe. *Fa. Qu.*

We know not that the king of heav'n hath doom'd
This place our *dungeon*; not our ſafe retreat
Beyond his potent arm. *Milton's Paradiſe Loſt, b.* ii.

Now from the North
Of Norumbeque, and the Samoed ſhore,
Burſting their brazen *dungeon*, arm'd with ice,
And ſnow, and hail, come ſtormy guſt, and flaw. *Milton.*

By imagination a man in a *dungeon* is capable of entertaining himſelf with ſcenes and landſkapes, more beautiful than any that can be found in the whole compaſs of nature. *Addiſ.*

DU'NGFORK. *n. ſ.* [*dung* and *fork.*] A fork to toſs out dung from ſtables.

Dungforks and paddles are common every where. *Mortimer.*

DU'NGHIL. *n. ſ.* [*dung* and *hill.*]

1. An heap or accumulation of dung.

I, his brother, gain nothing under him but growth; for the which his animals on his *dunghils* are as much bound to him as I. *Shakeſpeare's As you like it.*

Turn out that eyeleſs villain; throw this ſlave
Upon the *dunghil.* *Shakeſpeare's King Lear.*

Two cocks fought a duel for the maſtery of a *dunghil. L'Eſt.*

Never enter into a league of friendſhip with an ingrateful perſon; that is, plant not thy friendſhip upon a *dunghil:* it is too noble a plant for ſo baſe a ſoil. *South's Sermons.*

The *dunghil* having raiſed a huge muſhroom of ſhort duration, is now ſpread to enrich other mens land. *Swift.*

2. Any mean or vile abode.

Perhaps a thouſand other worlds, that lie
Remote from us, and latent in the ſky,
Are lighten'd by his beams, and kindly nurſt,
Of which our earthly *dunghil* is the worſt. *Dryden.*

3. Any ſituation of meanneſs.

The poor he raiſeth from the duſt,
Even from the *dunghil* lifts the juſt. *Sandys.*

4. A term of reproach for a man meanly born.

Out, *dunghil!* dar'ſt thou brave a nobleman? *Shakeſp.*

DU'NGHIL. *adj.* Sprung from the dunghil; mean; low; baſe; vile; worthleſs.

His *dunghil* thoughts, which do themſelves enure
To dirty droſs, no higher dare aſpire. *Spenſer on Love.*

DU'NGY. *adj.* [from *dung.*] Full of dung; mean; vile; baſe; low; odious; worthleſs.

If it be ſo,
We need no grave to bury honeſty;
There's not a grain of it, the face to ſweeten
Of the whole *dungy* earth. *Shakeſpeare's Winter's Tale.*

DU'NGYARD. *n. ſ.* [*dung* and *yard.*] The place of the dunghil.

Any manner of vegetables caſt into the *dungyard. Mortimer.*

DU'NNER. *n. ſ.* [from *dun.*] One employed in ſoliciting petty debts.

They are ever talking of new ſilks, and ſerve the owners in getting them cuſtomers, as their common *dunners* do in making them pay. *Spectator*, N°. 454.

DUO'DECUPLE. *adj.* [*duo* and *decuplus*, Latin.] Conſiſting of twelves.

Griſepſius, a learned Polander, endeavours to eſtabliſh the *duodecuple* proportion among the Jews, by comparing ſome paſſages of Scripture together. *Arbuthnot on Coins.*

DUPE. *n. ſ.* [*dupe*, French, from *duppe*, a fooliſh bird eaſily caught.] A credulous man; a man eaſily tricked.

An uſurping populace is its own *dupe*, a mere underworker, and a purchaſer in truſt for ſome ſingle tyrant. *Swift.*

Firſt ſlave to words, then vaſſal to a name,
Then *dupe* to party; child and man the ſame. *Dunciad.*

To DUPE. *v. a.* [from the noun.] To trick; to cheat.

The throne a bigot keep, a genius quit;
Faithleſs through piety, and *dup'd* through wit. *Pope's Epiſt.*

DU'PLE. *adj.* [*duplus*, Latin.] Double; one repeated.

To DU'PLICATE. *v. a.* [*duplico*, Latin.]

1. To double; to enlarge by the repetition of the firſt number or quantity.

And ſome alterations in the brain *duplicate* that which is but a ſingle object to our undiſtempered ſentiments. *Glanv.*

2. To fold together.

DU'PLICATE. *adj.* [from the verb.]

Duplicate proportion is the proportion of ſquares. Thus, in a rank of geometrical proportions, the firſt term to the third is ſaid to be in a *duplicate* ratio of the firſt to the ſecond, or as its ſquare is to the ſquare of the ſecond: ſo in 2, 4, 8, 16, the ratio of 2 to 8 is a duplicate of that of 2 to 4; or as the ſquare of 2 to the ſquare of 4. *Phillips. Harris. Bailey.*

It has been found, that the attraction is almoſt reciprocally in a *duplicate* proportion of the diſtance of the middle of the drop from the concourſe of the glaſſes, *viz.* reciprocally in a ſimple proportion, by reaſon of the ſpreading of the drop, and its touching each glaſs in a larger ſurface; and again reciprocally in a ſimple proportion, by reaſon of the attractions growing ſtronger within the ſame quantity of attracting ſurface. *Newton's Opt.*

DU'PLICATE. *n. ſ.* Another correſpondent to the firſt; a ſecond thing of the ſame kind, as a tranſcript of a paper.

Nothing is more needful for perfecting the natural hiſtory of bodies than the ſubjecting them to the fire; to which end I have reſerved *duplicates* of the moſt conſiderable. *Woodward.*

DUPLICA'TION. *n. ſ.* [from *duplicate.*]

1. The act of doubling.

What great pains hath been taken concerning the quadrature of a circle, and the *duplication* of a cube, and ſome other mathematical problems. *Hale's Origin of Mankind.*

2. The act of folding together.

3. A fold; a doubling.

The peritonæum is a ſtrong membrane, every where double; in the *duplications* of which all the viſcera of the abdomen are hid. *Wiſeman's Surgery.*

DU'PLICATURE. *n. ſ.* [from *duplicate.*] A fold; any thing doubled.

Vaſt bags are requiſite to contain the water which iſſues from the lymphеducts, either dilacerated or obſtructed, and exonerating themſelves into the foldings, or between the *duplicatures* of the membranes. *Ray on the Creation.*

DUPLI'CITY. *n. ſ.* [*duplicis*, Latin.]

1. Doubleneſs; the number of two.

This *duplicity* was ill contrived to place one head at both extremes, and had been more tolerable to have ſet three or four at one. *Brown's Vulgar Errours, b.* iii. *c.* 14.

Do not affect *duplicities* nor triplicities, nor any certain number of parts in your diviſion of things. *Watts's Logick.*

2. Deceit; doubleneſs of heart, or of tongue.

DURABI'LITY. *n. ſ.* [*durabilis*, Latin.] The power of laſting; continuance; endurance.

Stones though in dignity of nature inferior unto plants, yet exceed them in firmneſs of ſtrength, or *durability* of being. *Hooker, b.* i. *ſ.* 6.

Our times upon the earth have neither certainty nor *durability.* *Raleigh's Hiſtory of the World.*

DU'RABLE. *adj.* [*durabilis*, Latin.]

1. Laſting; having the quality of long continuance.

The bones of his body we may compare to the hard rocks and ſtones, and therefore ſtrong and *durable. Raleigh's Hiſtory.*

With pins of adamant,
And chains, they made all fast; too fast they made,
And *durable!* *Milton's Paradise Lost, b. x. l.* 320.

The glories of her majesty's reign ought to be recorded in words more *durable* than brass, and such as our posterity may read a thousand years hence. *Swift.*

2. Having successive existence.

When on a day,
For time, though in eternity, apply'd
To motion, measures all things *durable*
By present, past, and future, on such day
As heav'n's great year brings forth. *Milton's Paradise Lost.*

DU'RABLENESS. *n. s.* [from *durable.*] Power of lasting; continuance.

The different consistence and *durableness* of the strata whereof they consist, are more or less. *Woodward's Nat. Hist.*

A bad poet, if he cannot become immortal by the goodness of his verse, may by the *durableness* of the metal that supports it. *Addison on ancient Medals.*

DU'RABLY. *adv.* [from *durable.*] In a lasting manner.

There indeed he found his fame flourishing, his monuments engraved in marble, and yet more *durably* in mens memories. *Sidney.*

DU'RANCE. *n. s.* [from *duresse*, law French.]

1. Imprisonment; the custody or power of a jaylor; a prison.

Thy Dol, and Helen of thy noble thoughts,
Is in base *durance* and contagious prison;
Haul'd thither by mechanick dirty hands. *Shakesp. Hen.* IV.

A poor, innocent, forlorn stranger, languishing in *durance*, upon the false accusations of a lying, insolent, whorish woman. *South's Sermons.*

There's neither iron bar nor gate,
Portcullis, chain, nor bolt, nor grate;
And yet men *durance* there abide,
In dungeons scarce three inches wide. *Hudibras, p.* i. *cant.* 2.

Notwithstanding the warning and example before me, I commit myself to lasting *durance*. *Congreve's Old Batchelor.*

2. Endurance; continuance; duration.

Sick nature at that instant trembled round,
And mother earth sigh'd as she felt the wound:
Of how short *durance* was this new made state!
How far more mighty than heaven's love, hell's hate! *Dryd.*

DURA'TION. *n. s.* [*duratio*, Latin.]

1. A sort of distance or length, the idea whereof we get, not from the permanent parts of space, but from the fleeting and perpetually perishing parts of succession. *Locke.*

2. Power of continuance.

Duration is a circumstance so essential to happiness, that if we conceived it possible for the joys of heaven itself to pass from us in an instant, we should find ourselves not much concerned for the attainment of them. *Rogers's Sermons.*

3. Length of continuance.

Aristotle, by greatness of action, does not only mean it should be great in its nature, but also in its *duration*, that it should have a due length in it. *Addison's Spectator*, N°. 267.

To DURE. *v. n.* [*duro*, Latin.] To last; to continue; to endure.

The delights and pleasures of the world are most pleasing while they *dure*. *Raleigh's History of the World.*

DU'REFUL. *adj.* [from *endure* and *full.*] Lasting; of long continuance; durable.

The *dureful* oak, whose sap is not yet dry'd,
Is long e'er it conceive the kindling fire;
But when it once doth burn, it doth divide
Great heat, and makes his flames to heaven aspire. *Spenser.*

DU'RELESS. *adj.* [from *dure.*] Without continuance; fading; transitory; short.

Yet were that aptitude natural, more inclinable to follow and embrace the false and *dureless* pleasures of this stage-play world, than to become the shadow of God. *Raleigh's History.*

DU'RESSE. *n. s.* [French, hardship, severity.]

1. Imprisonment; constraint; confinement.

2. [In law.] A plea used by way of exception, by him who being cast into prison at a man's suit, or otherwise by threats, beating, &c. hardly used, seals any bond to him during his restraint. This the law holds as invalid, and supposes to be constrained. *Cowel.*

DU'RING. *prep.* [This word is rather a participle from *dure*; as, *during life*, *durante vita*, life *continuing*; *during my pleasure*, my pleasure continuing the same.] For the time of the continuance of; while any thing lasts.

If *during* his childhood he be constantly and rigorously kept from drinking cold liquor whilst he is hot, forbearance grows into a habit. *Locke.*

DU'RITY. *n. s.* [*dureté*, French; *durus*, Latin.] Hardness; firmness.

Ancients did burn fragments of marble, which in time became marble again, at least of indissoluble *durity*, as appeareth in the standing theatres. *Wotton's Architecture.*

Irradiancy or sparkling, found in many gems, is not discoverable in this; for it cometh short of their compactness and *durity*. *Brown's Vulgar Errours, b.* ii. *c.* 1.

DURST. The preterite of *dare*.

The Christians *durst* have no images of the Deity, because they would rather die than defile themselves with such an impiety. *Stillingfleet's Def. of Disc. on Rom. Idol.*

DUSK. *adj.* [*duyster*, Dutch.]

1. Tending to darkness. See DUSKY.

2. Tending to blackness; dark coloured.

The hills to their supply,
Vapour, and exhalation *dusk*, and moist,
Sent up amain. *Milton's Paradise Lost, b.* x. *l.* 741.

DUSK. *n. s.* [from the adjective.]

1. Tendency to darkness; incipient obscurity.

I will wait on you in the *dusk* of the evening, with my show upon my back. *Spectator*, N°. 271.

2. Darkness of colour; tendency to blackness.

Some sprinkled freckles on his face were seen,
Whose *dusk* set off the whiteness of the skin. *Dryden's Fab.*

To DUSK. *v. a.* [from the noun.] To make duskish. *Dict.*

To DUSK. *v. n.* To grow dark; to begin to lose light or brightness; to have lustre diminished. *Dict.*

DU'SKILY. *adv.* [from *dusky.*] With a tendency to darkness or blackness.

DU'SKISH. *adj.* [from *dusk.*]

1. Inclining to darkness; tending to obscurity.

From his infernal furnace forth he threw
Huge flames, that dimmed all the heaven's light,
Enroll'd in *duskish* smoak, and brimstone blue. *Fai. Queen.*

2. Tending to blackness; dark coloured.

Sight is not contented with sudden departments from one extreme to another; therefore rather a *duskish* tincture than an absolute black. *Wotton's Architecture.*

DU'SKISHLY. *adv.* [from *duskish.*] Cloudily; darkly.

The sawdust burned fair, 'till part of the candle consumed: the dust gathering about the snast, made the snast to burn *duskishly*. *Bacon's Natural History*, N°. 365.

DU'SKY. *adj.* [from *dusk*; *duyster*, Dutch.]

1. Tending to darkness; obscure; not luminous.

Here lies the *dusky* torch of Mortimer,
Chok'd with ambition of the meaner sort. *Shakesp. H.* VI.

There fierce winds o'er *dusky* valleys blow,
Whose every puff bears empty shades away. *Dryd. Ind. Em.*

Through the plains of one continual day,
Six shining months pursue their even way;
And six succeeding urge their *dusky* flight,
Obscur'd with vapours and o'erwhelm'd in night. *Prior.*

2. Tending to blackness; dark coloured; not clear; not bright.

They did plot
The means that *dusky* Dis my daughter got. *Shak. Tempest.*

It is not green, but of a *dusky* brown colour. *Bacon.*

When Jove in *dusky* clouds involves the skies,
And the faint crescent shoots by fits before their eyes. *Dryd.*

The surface is of a *dusky* yellow colour. *Woodward.*

By mixing such powders we are not to expect a strong and full white, such as is that of paper; but some *dusky* obscure one, such as might arise from a mixture of light and darkness, or from white and black; that is, a grey or dun, or russet brown. *Newton's Opt.*

3. Gloomy; sad; intellectually clouded.

While he continues in life, this *dusky* scene of horrour, this melancholy prospect of final perdition, will frequently occur to his fancy. *Bentley's Sermons.*

Umbriel, a *dusky*, melancholy sprite,
As ever sully'd the fair face of light,
Down to the central earth, his proper scene,
Repairs to search the gloomy cave of spleen. *Pope.*

DUST. *n. s.* [duꞅt, Saxon; *duist*, Erse.]

1. Earth or other matter reduced to small particles.

The *dust*
Should have ascended to the roof of heav'n,
Rais'd by your populous troops. *Shakesp. Anth. and Cleopat.*

Dust helpeth the fruitfulness of trees, insomuch as they cast *dust* upon them: that powdering, when a shower cometh, maketh a soiling to the tree, being earth and water finely laid on. *Bacon's Natural History*, N°. 666.

2. The grave; the state of dissolution.

The scepter, learning, physick must
All follow this, and come to *dust.* *Shakespeare's Cymbeline.*

Thou
Out of the ground wast taken, know thy birth;
For dust thou art, and shalt to *dust* return.
Milton's Paradise Lost.

3. A mean and dejected state.

God raiseth up the poor out of the *dust*, to set them among princes. 1 *Sam.* ii. 8.

To DUST. *v. a.* [from the noun.] To free from dust; to sprinkle with dust.

DU'STMAN. *n. s.* [*dust* and *man.*] One whose employment is to carry away the dust.

The *dustman*'s cart offends thy cloaths and eyes,
When through the street a cloud of ashes flies. *Gay.*

DU'STY. *adj.* [from *dust.*]

1. Filled with dust; clouded with dust.

Arms and the *dusty* field I less admire,
And soften strangely in some new desire. *Dryden.*

2. Covered or scattered with dust.

Even drudgery himself,
As at the car he sweats, or *dusty* hews
The palace stone, looks gay. *Thomson's Summer, l.* 1445.

DU'TCHESS. *n. s.* [*duchesse*, French.]

1. The lady of a duke.

The duke of Cornwal, and Regan his *dutchess*, will be here. *Shakespeare's King Lear.*

The duke was to command the army, and the *dutchess*, by the favour she possessed, to be near her majesty. *Swift.*

The gen'rous god, who wit and gold refines,
And ripens spirits as he ripens minds,
Kept dross for *dutchesses*, the world shall know it,
To you gave sense, good humour, and a poet. *Pope's Epist.*

2. A lady who has the sovereignty of a dukedom.

DU'TCHY. *n. s.* [*duché*, French.] A territory which gives title to a duke, or has a duke for its sovereign.

France might have swallowed up his whole *dutchy*. *Swift.*

Different states border on it; the kingdom of France, the *dutchy* of Savoy, and the canton of Bern. *Addison on Italy.*

DU'TCHYCOURT. *n. s.* A court wherein all matters appertaining to the dutchy of Lancaster are decided by the decree of the chancellor of that court. *Cowel.*

DU'TEOUS. *adj.* [from *duty.*]

1. Obedient; obsequious; respectful to those who have natural or legal authority.

Great Aurengzebe did *duteous* care express,
And durst not push too far his great success. *Dryd. Aureng.*

A female softness, with a manly mind;
A *duteous* daughter, and a sister kind;
In sickness patient, and in death resign'd. *Dryden.*

Who taught the bee with winds and rains to strive,
To bring her burden to the certain hive;
And through the liquid fields again to pass
Duteous, and hark'ning to the sounding brass? *Prior.*

2. Obsequious; obedient to good or bad purposes.

I know thee well; a serviceable villain!
As *duteous* to the vices of thy mistress,
As madness would desire. *Shakespeare's King Lear.*

Every beast, more *duteous* at her call,
Than at Circean call the herd disguis'd. *Milt. Parad. Lost.*

3. Enjoined by duty; enforced by the relation of one to another.

With mine own tongue deny my sacred right,
With mine own breath release all *duteous* ties. *Shakes. R.* II.

DU'TIFUL. *adj.* [*duty* and *full.*]

1. Obedient; submissive to natural or legal superiours; reverent.

She died in an extreme old age, without pain, under the care of the most *dutiful* son that I have ever known or heard of. *Swift to Pope.*

2. Expressive of respect; giving token of reverence; respectful; reverential.

There would she kiss the ground, and thank the trees, bless the air, and do *dutiful* reverence to every thing she thought did accompany her at their first meeting. *Sidney, b.* ii.

DU'TIFULLY. *adv.* [from *dutiful.*]

1. Obediently; submissively.

2. Reverently; respectfully.

His daughter Philoclea he found at that time *dutifully* watching by her mother, and Miso curiously watching her. *Sidney.*

He with joyful, nimble wing,
Flew *dutifully* back again,
And made an humble chaplet for the king. *Swift.*

DU'TIFULNESS. *n. s.* [from *dutiful.*]

1. Obedience; submission to just authority.

Piety, or *dutifulness* to parents, was a most popular virtue among the Romans. *Dryden's Æn.*

2. Reverence; respect.

It is a strange kind of civility, and an evil *dutifulness* in friends and relatives, to suffer him to perish without reproof or medicine, rather than to seem unmannerly to a great sinner. *Taylor's Rule of living holy.*

DU'TY. *n. s* [from *due.*]

1. That to which a man is by any natural or legal obligation bound.

When ye shall have done all those things which are commanded, you say we are unprofitable servants: we have done that which was our *duty* to do. *Lu* xvii. 10.

Good my lord,
You have begot me, bred me, lov'd me: I
Return those *duties* back, as are right fit;
Obey you, love you, and most honour you. *Shak. K. Lear.*

The pain children feel from any necessity of nature, it is the *duty* of parents to relieve. *Locke.*

2. Acts or forbearances required by religion or morality.

All our *duty* is set down in our prayers, because in all our *duty* we beg the Divine Assistance; and remember that you are bound to do all those *duties*, for the doing of which you have prayed for the Divine Assistance. *Taylor's Devotion.*

3. Obedience or submission due to parents, governors, or superiours; loyalty; piety to parents.

Thinkest thou that *duty* shall have dread to speak,
When pow'r to flatt'ry bows? To plainness honour
Is bound, when majesty to folly falls. *Shakesp. King Lear.*

God's party will appear small, and the king's not greater; it being not probable, that those should have sense of *duty* to him that had none to God. *Decay of Piety.*

4. Act of reverence or respect.

They both attone;
Did *duty* to their lady as became. *Fairy Queen, b.* ii.

5. The business of a soldier on guard.

The regiment did *duty* there punctually. *Clarendon, b.* viii.

Otho bribed his guards at a high rate; for as often as Galba supped with him, he used to give every soldier upon *duty* an aureus. *Arbuthnot on Coins.*

6. The business of war; service.

The night came and severed them, all parties being tired with the *duty* of the day. *Clarendon, b.* viii.

See how the madmen bleed! Behold the gains
With which their master, love, rewards their pains!
For sev'n long years, on *duty* ev'ry day,
Lo! their obedience, and their monarch's pay! *Dryden.*

7. Tax; impost; custom; toll.

All the wines that come down from Tuscany make their way through several *duties* and taxes, before they reach the port. *Addison's Travels.*

Such shekels as they now shew, were the old ones in which *duty* was to be paid by their law. *Arbuthnot on Coins.*

DWARF. *n. s.* [ꝺpeopᵹ, Sax. *dwerg*, Dutch; *dwerg*, Scottish.]

1. A man below the common size of men.

Get you gone, you *dwarf!*
You minimus, of hind'ring knot-grass made. *Shakespeare.*
Such *dwarfs* were some kind of apes. *Brown's Vulg. Err.*

They but now who seem'd
In bigness to surpass earth's giant sons,
Now less than smallest *dwarfs* in narrow room
Throng numberless. *Milton's Paradise Lost, b.* i. *l.* 779.

2. Any animal or plant below its natural bulk.

It is a delicate plantation of trees, all well-grown, fair, and smooth: one *dwarf* was knotty and crooked, and the rest had it in derision. *L'Estrange.*

Saw off the head of the stock in a smooth place; and for *dwarf* trees, graft them within four fingers of the ground. *Mortimer's Art of Husbandry.*

3. An attendant on a lady or knight in romances.

The champion stout,
Eftstoones dismounted from his courser brave,
And to the *dwarf* a-while his needless spear he gave. *F. Qu.*

4. It is used often by botanists in composition; as, *dwarf* elder, *dwarf* honeysuckle.

To DWARF. *v. a.* [from the noun.] To hinder from growing to the natural bulk; to lessen; to make little.

It is reported that a good strong canvas, spread over a tree grafted low, soon after it putteth forth, will *dwarf* it, and make it spread. *Bacon's Natural History*, N°. 534.

The whole sex is in a manner *dwarfed*, and shrunk into a race of beauties, that seems almost another species. *Addison.*

DWA'RFISH. *adj.* [from *dwarf.*] Below the natural bulk; low; small; little; petty; despicable.

Their *dwarfish* pages were
As cherubins, all gilt. *Shakespeare's Henry* VIII.

And are you grown so high in his esteem,
Because I am so *dwarfish* and so low? *Shakespeare.*

This unheard sawciness, and boyish troops,
The king doth smile at; and is well prepar'd
To whip this *dwarfish* war, these pigmy arms,
From out the circle of his territories. *Shakesp. King John.*

A thicket close beside the grove there stood,
With briars and brambles choak'd, and *dwarfish* wood. *Dry.*

We should have lost oaks and cedars, and the other tall and lofty sons of the forest, and have found nothing but *dwarfish* shrubs, and creeping moss, and despicable mushrooms. *Bentley's Sermons.*

DWA'RFISHLY. *adj.* [from *dwarfish.*] Like a dwarf.

DWA'RFISHNESS. *n. s.* [from *dwarfish.*] Minuteness of stature; littleness.

'Tis no wonder that science hath not outgrown the *dwarfishness* of its pristine stature, and that the intellectual world is such a microcosm. *Glanv. Sceps. c.* 17.

To DWAULE. *v. a.* [ꝺpelian, Sax. to wander; *dwaelen*, Dut.] To be delirious: a provincial word mentioned by *Junius.*

To DWELL. *v. n.* preterite *dwelt*, or *dwelled.* [*duala*, old Teutonick, is *stay, delay*; *duelia*, Islandick, to stay, to stand still.]

1. To inhabit; to live in a place; to reside; to have an habitation.

If thy brother that *dwelleth* by thee be waxen poor, and be sold unto thee, thou shalt not compel him to serve as a bond-servant. *Lev.* xxv. 39.

He

He ſhall *dwell* alone, without the camp ſhall his habitation be. *Lev.* xiii. 46.

John Haywood and Sir Thomas More, in the pariſh wherein I was born, *dwelt* and had poſſeſſions. *Peacham on Poetry.*

Why are you vex'd, lady? Why do you frown?
Here *dwell* no frowns, nor anger; from theſe gates
Sorrow flies far. *Milton.*

2. To live in any form of habitation.

Abraham ſojourned in the land of Promiſe as in a ſtrange country, *dwelling* in tabernacles. *Heb.* xi. 9.

3. To be in any ſtate or condition.

'Tis ſafer to be that which we deſtroy,
Than by deſtruction *dwell* in doubtful joy. *Shakeſ. Macbeth.*

4. To be ſuſpended with attention.

Th' attentive queen
Dwelt on his accents, and her gloomy eyes
Sparkled with gentler fires. *Smith's Phæd. and Hippolitus.*

5. To fix the mind upon; to hang upon with fondneſs.

Such was that face, on which I *dwelt* with joy,
Ere Greece aſſembled, ſtemm'd the tides to Troy;
But parting then for that deteſted ſhore,
Our eyes, unhappy! never greeted more. *Pope's Odyſſey.*

6. To continue long ſpeaking.

He preach'd the joys of heav'n and pains of hell,
And warn'd the ſinner with becoming zeal;
But on eternal mercy lov'd to *dwell.* *Dryd. Good Parſon.*

We have *dwelt* pretty long on the conſiderations of ſpace and duration. *Locke.*

Thoſe who defend our negotiators, *dwell* upon their zeal and patience. *Swift.*

To Dwell. *v. a.* To inhabit.

I ſaw and heard; for we ſometimes
Who *dwell* this wild, conſtrain'd by want, come forth
To town or village nigh. *Milton's Paradiſe Regained*, *b.* i.

Dwe'ller. *n. ſ.* [from *dwell.*] An inhabitant; one that lives in any place.

The houſes being kept up, did of neceſſity enforce a *dweller*; and the proportion of land for occupation being kept up, did of neceſſity enforce that *dweller* not to be beggar or cottager, but a man of ſome ſubſtance. *Bacon's Henry* VII.

Their cries ſoon waken all the *dwellers* near;
Now murmuring noiſes riſe in every ſtreet. *Dryden.*

Dwe'lling. *n. ſ.* [from *dwell.*]

1. Habitation; place of reſidence; abode.

His *dwelling* is low in a valley green,
Under the foot of Rauran moſſy hore. *Fairy Queen, b.* i.

Hazor ſhall be a *dwelling* for dragons, and a deſolation for ever. *Jer.* xlix. 33.

If he have ſeveral *dwellings*, let him ſort them ſo, that what he wanteth in the one he may find in the other. *Bacon.*

God will deign
To viſit oft the *dwellings* of juſt men,
Delighted. *Milton's Paradiſe Loſt*, *b.* vii. *l.* 570.

So it ſeems
To thee who haſt thy *dwelling* here on earth. *Milt. P. Loſt.*

All *dwellings* elſe
Flood overwhelm'd, and them with all their pomp
Deep under water roll'd; ſea cover'd ſea,
Sea without ſhore! *Milton's Paradiſe Loſt*, *b.* xi. *l.* 747.

The living few, and frequent funerals then,
Proclaim'd thy wrath on this forſaken place;
And now thoſe few, who are return'd again,
Thy ſearching judgments to their *dwellings* trace. *Dryden.*

The force of fire aſcended firſt on high,
And took its *dwelling* in the vaulted ſky. *Dryden's Ovid.*

2. State of life; mode of living.

My *dwelling* ſhall be with the beaſts of the field. *Dan.* iv. 25.

Dwe'llinghouse. *n. ſ.* [from *dwell* and *houſe.*] The houſe at which one lives.

A perſon ought always to be cited at the place of his *dwellinghouſe*, which he has in reſpect of his habitation and uſual reſidence; and not at the houſe which he has in reſpect of his eſtate, or the place of his birth. *Ayliffe's Parergon.*

Dwe'llingplace. *n. ſ.* [*dwell* and *place.*] The place of reſidence.

People do often change their *dwellingplaces*, and ſome muſt die, whilſt other ſome do grow up into ſtrength. *Spenſer.*

To Dwi'ndle. *v. n.* [ꝺpinan, Saxon.]

1. To ſhrink; to loſe bulk; to grow little.

Proper names, when familiarized in Engliſh, *dwindle* to monoſyllables; whereas in modern languages they receive a ſofter turn, by the addition of a new ſyllable. *Addiſon's Spect.*

Our drooping days are *dwindled* down to nought;
Their period finiſh'd e'er 'tis well begun. *Thomſon's Spring.*

2. To degenerate; to ſink.

'Tis now *dwindled* down to light frothy ſtuff. *Norris.*

If there have been ſuch a gradual diminution of the generative faculty of the earth, that it hath *dwindled* from nobler animals to puny mice and inſects, why was there not the like decay in the production of vegetables? *Bentley's Sermons.*

He found the expected council was *dwindling* into a conventicle, a packed aſſembly of Italian biſhops, not a free convention of fathers. *Atterbury.*

Religious ſocieties, though begun with excellent intentions, are ſaid to have *dwindled* into factious clubs. *Swift.*

3. To wear away; to loſe health; to grow feeble.

Weary ſev'nnights nine times nine,
Shall he *dwindle*, peak, and pine. *Shakeſpeare's Macbeth.*

How often do we ſee, that ſome ſmall part of the foot being injured by a wrench or a blow, the whole leg or thigh thereby loſes its ſtrength and nouriſhment, and *dwindles* away. *Locke.*

Phyſicians, with their milky cheer,
The love ſick maid and *dwindling* beau repair. *Gay's Triv.*

4. To fall away; to be diminiſhed; to moulder off.

Of all the forces under Greenvil, there were only five hundred foot and three hundred horſe left with him for the blocking up Plymouth; the reſt were *dwindled* away. *Clarendon.*

Dye. See Die.

Dy'ing. The participle of *die.*

1. Expiring; giving up the ghoſt.

2. Tinging; giving a new colour.

Dy'nasty. *n. ſ.* [δυναςεία.] Government; ſovereignty.

Some account him fabulous, becauſe he carries up the Egyptian *dynaſties* before the flood, yea, and long before the creation. *Hale's Origin of Mankind.*

Greece was then divided into ſeveral *dynaſties*, which our author has enumerated under their reſpective princes. *Notes on Pope's Iliad.*

Dy'scrasy. *n. ſ.* [δυσκρασία.] An unequal mixture of elements in the blood or nervous juice; a diſtemperature, when ſome humour or quality abounds in the body. *Dict.*

In this pituitous *dyſcraſy* of blood, we muſt vomit off the pituita, and purge upon intermiſſions. *Floyer on the Humours.*

Dyse'ntery. *n. ſ.* [*dyſenterie*, French, from δυσεντερία.] A looſeneſs wherein very ill humours flow off by ſtool, and are alſo ſometimes attended with blood. *Dict.*

From an unuſual inconſtancy of the weather, and perpetual changes of the wind from Eaſt to Weſt, proceed epidemical *dyſenteries.* *Arbuthnot on Air.*

Dyspe'psy. *n. ſ.* [δυσπεψία.] A difficulty of digeſtion, or bad fermentation in the ſtomach or guts. *Dict.*

Dy'sphony. *n. ſ.* [δυσφωνία.] A difficulty in ſpeaking, occaſioned by an ill diſpoſition of the organs. *Dict.*

Dyspno'ea. *n. ſ.* [δύσπνοια.] A difficulty of breathing; ſtraitneſs of breath.

Dy'sury. *n. ſ.* [δυσουρία.] A difficulty in making urine.

It doth end in a dyſentery, pains of the hæmorrhoids, inflammations of any of the lower parts, diabetes, a continual piſſing, or a hot *dyſury*, difficulty of making water. *Harvey.*

E.

E, Has two ſounds; long, as *ſcêne*, and ſhort, as *men*. *E* is the moſt frequent vowel in the Engliſh language; for it not only is uſed like the reſt in the beginning or end of words, but has the peculiar quality of lengthening the foregoing vowel, as *căn*, *cāne*; *măn*, *māne*; *găp*, *gāpe*; *glăd*, *glāde*; *brĕd*, *brēde*; *chĭn*, *chīne*; *whĭp*, *wīpe*; *thĭn*, *thīne*; *nŏd*, *nōde*; *tŭn*, *tūne*; *plŭm*, *plūme*. Yet it ſometimes occurs final, where yet the foregoing vowel is not lengthened; as *gŏne*, *knowlĕdge*, *ĕdge*, *gĭve*. Anciently almoſt every word ended with *e*; as for *can*, *canne*; for *year*, *yeare*; for *great*, *greate*; for *need*, *neede*; for *flock*, *flocke*. It is probable that this *e* final had at firſt a ſoft ſound, like the female *e* of the French; and that afterwards it was in poetry either mute or vocal, as the verſe required, 'till at laſt it became univerſally ſilent.

Ea has the ſound of *e* long: the *e* is commonly lengthened rather by the immediate addition of *a* than by the appoſition of *e* to the end of the word; as *mĕn*, *mēan*; *ſĕll*, *ſēal*; *mĕt*, *mēat*; *nĕt*, *nēat*.

EACH. *pron.* [elc, Saxon; *elch*, Dutch; *ilk*, Scottiſh.]

1. Either of two.

Though your orbs of diff'rent greatneſs be,
Yet both are for *each* other's uſe diſpos'd;
His to incloſe, and your's to be inclos'd. *Dryden.*

2. Every one of any number. This ſenſe is rare, except in poetry.

Th' invention all admir'd, and *each* how he
To be th' inventer miſs'd. *Milton, b.* vi.

Let *each*
His adamantine coat gird well, and *each*
Fit well his helm. *Milton, b.* vi.

By hunger, that *each* other creature tames,
Thou art not to be harm'd, therefore not mov'd;
Thy temperance invincible beſides. *Milton's Paradiſe Reg.*

Wiſe Plato ſaid, the world with men was ſtor'd,
That ſuccour *each* to other might afford. *Denham.*

To EACH the correſpondent word is *other*, whether it be uſed of two, or of a greater number.

'Tis ſaid they eat *each* other. *Shakeſpeare's Macbeth.*

Let *each* eſteem *other* better than themſelves. *Phil.* ii. 3.

Lovelieſt of women! heaven is in thy ſoul;
Beauty and virtue ſhine for ever round thee,
Bright'ning *each other!* Thou art all divine! *Addiſ. Cato.*

EAD. [*æd*, *ed.*] in the compound, and *eadig* in the ſimple names, denotes happineſs, or bleſſedneſs. Thus *Eadward* is a happy preſerver; *Eadulph*, happy aſſiſtance; *Eadgar*, happy power; *Eadwin*, happy conqueror; which *Macarius Eupolemus*, *Fauſta*, *Fortunatus*, *Felicianus*, &c. do in ſome meaſure reſemble. *Ead* may alſo in ſome caſes be derived from the Saxon *eath*, which ſignifies eaſy, gentle, mild. *Gib. Camden.*

EA'GER. *adj.* [eaȝoɲ, Saxon; *aigre*, French.]

1. Struck with deſire; ardently wiſhing; keenly deſirous; vehement in deſire; hotly longing.

Of action *eager*, and intent of thought,
The chiefs your honourable danger ſought. *Dryden's Ovid.*

Eager to read the reſt, Achates came. *Dryden's Æn.*

With joy th' ambitious youth his mother heard,
And *eager* for the journey ſoon prepar'd;
He longs the world beneath him to ſurvey,
To guide the chariot, and to give the day. *Dryden.*

Love inflam'd, and *eager* on his bliſs,
Smother'd her words. *Addiſon's Ovid's Metam. b.* ii.

2. It is uſed ſometimes with *of*, ſometimes with *on* or *after* before the thing ſought.

3. Hot of diſpoſition; vehement; ardent; impetuous.

Apt as well to quicken the ſpirits as to allay that which is too *eager*. *Hooker, b* v. *ſ.* 38.

Nor do the *eager* clamours of diſputants yield more relief to eclipſed truth, than did the ſounding braſs of old to the labouring moon. *Glanv. Scepſ. c.* 19.

This is not a general character of women, but a reproof of ſome *eager* ſpirited gipſies. *L'Eſtrange.*

Imperfect zeal is hot and *eager*, without knowledge. *Spratt.*

Palemon replies,
Eager his tone, and ardent were his eyes. *Dryden.*

A man, charged with a crime of which he thinks himſelf innocent, is apt to be too *eager in* his own defence. *Dryden.*

4. Quick; buſy; eaſily put in action.

His Numidian genius
Is well diſpos'd to miſchief, were he prompt
And *eager on* it; but he muſt be ſpurr'd. *Addiſon's Cato.*

5. Sharp; ſower; acid.

With a ſudden vigour it doth poſſet
And curd, like *eager* droppings into milk,
The thin and wholſome blood. *Shakeſpeare's Hamlet.*

6. Keen; ſevere; biting.

The air bites ſhrewdly; it is very cold.
—It is a nipping and an *eager* air. *Shakeſpeare's Hamlet.*

The reſiſtance of bone to cold is greater than of fleſh; for that the fleſh ſhrinketh, but the bone reſiſteth, whereby the cold becometh more *eager*. *Bacon's Natural Hiſtory*, N°. 688.

7. Brittle; inflexible; not ductile. A cant word of artificers.

Gold will be ſometimes ſo *eager*, as artiſts call it, that it will as little endure the hammer as glaſs itſelf. *Locke.*

EA'GERLY. *adv.* [from *eager.*]

1. With great ardour of deſire; with impetuoſity of inclination.

To the holy war how faſt and *eagerly* did men go, when the prieſt perſuaded them that whoſoever died in that expedition was a martyr? *South's Sermons.*

How *eagerly* he flew, when Europe's fate
Did for the ſeed of future actions wait. *Stepney.*

2. Ardently; hotly.

Brutus gave the word too early,
Who having ſome advantage on Octavius,
Took it too *eagerly*; his ſoldiers fell to ſpoil,
Whilſt we by Anthony were all inclos'd. *Shak. Jul. Cæſar.*

3. Keenly; ſharply.

Abundance of rain froze ſo *eagerly* as it fell, that it ſeemed the depth of Winter had of a ſudden been come in. *Knolles.*

EA'GERNESS. *n. ſ.* [from *eager.*]

1. Keenneſs of deſire; ardour of inclination.

She knew her diſtance, and did angle for me,
Madding my *eagerneſs* with her reſtraint. *Shakeſpeare.*

Have you not ſeen, when whiſtled from the fiſt,
Some falcon ſtoop'd at what her eye deſign'd,
And, with her *eagerneſs*, the quarry miſs'd. *Dryden.*

The *eagerneſs* and ſtrong bent of the mind after knowledge, if not warily regulated, is often an hindrance to it. *Locke.*

Detraction and obloquy are received with as much *eagerneſs* as wit and humour. *Addiſon's Freeholder.*

Juba lives to catch
That dear embrace, and to return it too,
With mutual warmth and *eagerneſs* of love. *Addiſon's Cato.*

His continued application to publick affairs diverts him from thoſe pleaſures, which are purſued with *eagerneſs* by princes who have not the publick ſo much at heart. *Addiſon.*

The things of this world, with whatever *eagerneſs* they engage our purſuit, leave us ſtill empty and unſatisfied with their fruition. *Rogers's Sermons.*

2. Impetuoſity; vehemence; violence.

It finds them in the *eagerneſs* and height of their devotion; they are ſpeechleſs for the time that it continues, and proſtrate and dead when it departs. *Dryden.*

I'll kill thee with ſuch *eagerneſs* of haſte,
As fiends, let looſe, would lay all nature waſte. *Dryd. Aur.*

EA'GLE. *n. ſ.* [*aigle*, French; *aquila*, Latin; *ealler*, Erſe.]

1. A bird of prey, which, as it is reported, renews its age when it grows old. But ſome think that this recovery of youth happens no otherwiſe in the eagle than in other birds, by caſting their feathers every year in the moulting ſeaſon, and having others in their room. It is alſo ſaid not to drink at all, like other birds with ſharp claws. It is given out, that when an eagle ſees its young ſo well grown as to venture upon flying, it hovers over their neſt, flutters with its wings, and excites them to imitate it, and take their flight; and when it ſees them weary, or fearful, it takes and carries them upon its back. Eagles are ſaid to be extremely ſharp-ſighted, and, when they take flight, ſpring perpendicularly upward, with their eyes ſteadily fixed upon the ſun, mounting 'till, by their diſtance, they diſappear. *Calmet.*

Diſmay'd not this
Our captains Macbeth and Banquo?
——Yes,
As ſparrows *eagles*, or the hare the lion. *Shakeſp. Macbeth.*

Draw forth the monſters of th' abyſs profound,
Or fetch th' aerial *eagle* to the ground. *Pope's Eſſ. on Man.*

2. The ſtandard of the ancient *Romans*.

Arts ſtill follow'd where Rome's *eagles* flew. *Pope.*

EAGLE-EYED. *adj.* [from *eagle* and *eye.*]

1. Sharp-ſighted as an eagle.

As he was rarely quick and perſpicacious, ſo was he inwardly *eagle-eyed*, and perfectly verſed in the humours of his ſubjects. *Howel's Vocal Forreſt.*

Ev'ry one is *eagle-ey'd* to ſee
Another's faults and his deformity. *Dryden's Perſ. Sat.* 4.

EA'GLESPEED. *n. ſ.* [*eagle* and *ſpeed.*] Swiftneſs like that of an eagle.

Abrupt, with *eagleſpeed* ſhe cut the ſky,
Inſtant inviſible to mortal eye. *Pope's Odyſſey, b.* i.

EA'GLESTONE. *n. ſ.* A ſtone ſaid to be found at the entrance of the holes in which the eagles make their neſts, and affirmed to have a particular virtue in defending the eagle's neſt from thunder. The ſtones of this kind which are moſt valued are flat and blackiſh, and ſound, if ſhaken near the ear; a leſſer ſtone being contained in the greater. *Calmet.*

The *eagleſtone* contains, in a cavity within it, a ſmall looſe ſtone, which rattles when it is ſhaken; and every foſſil, with a nucleus in it, has obtained the name. The ſort of analogy that was ſuppoſed to be between a ſtone, thus containing another within it, or, as the fanciful writers expreſs it, pregnant with another, and a woman big with child, led people to imagine that it muſt have great virtues and effects in accelerating or retarding delivery; ſo that, if tied to the arm of a woman with child, it prevents abortion; and if to the leg, it promotes delivery. It is pretended, that the eagles ſeek for theſe ſtones to lay in their neſts, and that they cannot hatch their young without. On ſuch idle and imaginary virtues was raiſed all the credit which this famous foſſil poſſeſſed for many ages. *Hill's Materia Medica.*

If you ſtop the holes of a hawk's bell it will make no ring, but a flat noiſe or rattle; and ſo doth the ætites, or *eagleſtone*, which hath a little ſtone within it. *Bacon's Nat. Hiſtory.*

EA'GLET. *n. ſ.* [from *eagle.*] A young eagle.

This treaſon of his ſons did the king expreſs in an emblem, wherein was an eagle with three *eaglets* tyring on her breaſt, and the fourth pecking at one of her eyes. *Davies.*

EA'GRE. *n. ſ.* [*æger*, in Runick, is the *ocean*; *eggia*, in Iſlandick, is *to agitate, to incite.*] A tide ſwelling above another tide, obſervable in the river Severn.

For as an *eagre* rides in triumph o'er the tide,
The tyrant paſſions, hope and fear,
Did in extremes appear,
And flaſh'd upon the ſoul with equal force. *Dryden.*

EA'LDERMAN. *n. ſ.* [ealdorman, Saxon.] The name of a Saxon magiſtrate; alderman.

EAME. *n. ſ.* [eam, Saxon; *eom*, Dutch.] Uncle: a word ſtill uſed in the wilder parts of Staffordſhire.

Daughter, ſays ſhe, fly, fly; behold, thy dame
Foreſhows the treaſon of thy wretched *eame!* *Fairfax.*

EAR. *n. ſ.* [eare, Saxon; *oor*, Dutch.]

1. The whole organ of audition or hearing.

What fire is in my *ears!* Can this be true?
Stand I condemn'd? *Shakeſp. Much Ado about Nothing.*

His *ears* are open unto their cry. *Pſ.* xxxiv. 15.

Valſalva diſcovered ſome paſſages into the region of the *ear* drum; of mighty uſe, among others, to make diſcharges of bruiſes. *Derham's Phyſico-Theology.*

2. That part of the ear that ſtands prominent.

You have heard of the news abroad: I mean, the whiſper'd ones; for they are yet but *ear* kiſſing arguments. *Sh. K. Lear.*

His maſter ſhall bore his *ear* through with an awl. *Ex.*

3. Power of judging of harmony; the ſenſe of hearing.

4. The head; or the perſon: in familiar language.

Their warlike force was ſore weakened, the city beaten down about their *ears*, and moſt of them wounded. *Knolles.*

Better paſs over an affront from one ſcoundrel, than draw the whole herd about a man's *ears*. *L'Eſtrange.*

Be not alarmed, as if all religion was falling about our *ears*. *Burnet's Theory.*

5. The higheſt part of a man; the top.

A cavalier was up to the *ears* in love with a very fine lady. *L'Eſtrange.*

6. The privilege of being readily and kindly heard; favour.

Ariſtippus was earneſt ſuitor to Dionyſius for ſome grant, who would give no *ear* to his ſuit: Ariſtippus fell at his feet, and then Dionyſius granted it. *Bacon's Apophthegms.*

They being told there was ſmall hope of eaſe,
Were willing at the firſt to give an *ear*
To any thing that ſounded liberty. *Ben. Johnſon's Catiline.*

If on a pillory, or near a throne,
He gain his prince's *ear*, or loſe his own. *Pope's Epiſtles.*

7. Diſpoſition to like or diſlike what is heard; judgment; opinion; taſte.

He laid his ſenſe cloſer, and in fewer words, according to the ſtyle and *ear* of thoſe times. *Denham.*

8. Any prominences from a larger body, raiſed for the ſake of holding it.

There are ſome veſſels, which, if you offer to lift by the belly or bottom, you cannot ſtir them; but are ſoon removed, if you take them by the *ears*. *Taylor's Rule of living holy.*

A quilted night-cap with one *ear*. *Congr. Way of the World.*

A pot without an *ear*. *Swift.*

9. The ſpike of corn; that part which contains the ſeeds.

He delivereth to each of them a jewel, made in the figure of an *ear* of wheat, which they ever after wear. *Bacon.*

The leaves on trees not more,
Nor bearded *ears* in fields, nor ſands upon the ſhore. *Dryd.*

From ſeveral grains he had eighty ſtalks, with very large *ears* full of large corn. *Mortimer's Huſbandry.*

10. *To fall together by the* EARS. To fight; to ſcuffle; to quarrel. [In Dutch *oorlogen.*] A familiar phraſe.

Poor naked men belaboured one another with ſhagged ſticks, or dully *fell together by the ears* at fiſty-cuffs. *More.*

Fools go together by the *ears*, to have knaves run away with the ſtakes. *L'Eſtrange, Fab.* 5.

All Aſia now was by the *ears*,
And gods beat up for voluntiers. *Prior.*

11. *To ſet by the* EARS. To make ſtrife; to quarrel: in low language.

A mean raſcal *ſets others together by the ears* without fighting himſelf. *L'Eſtrange, Fab.* 67.

She uſed to carry tales from one to another, 'till ſhe had ſet the neighbourhood together *by the ears*. *Arbuthnot.*

It is uſual to *ſet* theſe poor animals *by the ears*. *Addiſ. Freeh.*

EA'RLESS. *adj.* [from *ear.*] Without any ears.

Earleſs on high ſtood unabaſh'd Defoe,
And Tuthin flagrant from the ſcourge below. *Pope's Dunc.*

EA'RRING. *n. ſ.* [*ear* and *ring.*] Jewels ſet in a ring and worn at the ears; ornament of a woman's ear.

With gold and ſilver they increaſe his ſtore,
And gave the precious *earrings* which they wore. *Sandys.*

A lady beſtowed *earrings* upon a favourite lamprey. *Arbuth.*

EA'RSHOT. *n. ſ.* Reach of the ear; ſpace within which words may be heard.

Gomez, ſtand you out of *earſhot*.—I have ſomething to ſay to your wife in private. *Dryden's Spaniſh Fryar.*

EA'RWAX. *n. ſ.* [*ear* and *wax.*] The cerumen or exudation which ſmears the inſide of the ear.

The ear being to ſtand open, becauſe there was ſome danger that inſects might creep in thereat; therefore hath nature loricated or plaiſtered over the ſides of the hole with *earwax*, to entangle any inſects that ſhould attempt to creep in there. *Ray on the Creation.*

EA'RWIG. *n. ſ.* [eare and wigga, *a grub*, Saxon.] A ſheath-winged inſect, imagined to creep into the ear.

Himſelf he on an *earwig* ſet;
Yet ſcarce he on his back could get,
So oft and high he did curvet. *Drayton's Nymphid.*

Earwigs and ſnails ſeldom infect timber. *Mortimer's Huſb.*

Doll never flies to cut her lace,
Or throw cold water in her face,
Becauſe ſhe heard a ſudden drum,
Or found an *earwig* in a plum. *Swift.*

2. By way of reproach, a whiſperer; a prying informer.

EA'RWITNESS. *n. ſ.* [*ear* and *witneſs.*] One who atteſts, or can atteſt any thing as heard by himſelf.

All preſent were made *earwitneſſes*, even of each particular branch of a common indictment. *Hooker, b.* v. *ſ.* 36.

The hiſtories of mankind, written by eye or *earwitneſſes*, are built upon this principle. *Watts's Logick.*

To EAR. *v. a.* [*aro*, Latin.] To plow; to till.

He that *ears* my land ſpares my team, and gives me leave to enjoy the crop. *Shakeſpeare's All's well that ends well.*

Menecrates and Menas, famous pirates,
Make the ſea ſerve them, which they *ear* and wound
With keels of every kind. *Shakeſp. Ant. and Cleopatra.*

Then we bring forth weeds,
When our quick mind lies ſtill; and our ill, told us,
Is as our *earing*. *Shakeſpeare's Anthony and Cleopatra.*

A rough valley, which is neither *eared* nor ſown. *Deutr.*

Five years, in the which there ſhall neither be *earing* nor harveſt. *Gen.* xlv. 6.

The field of love, with plow of virtue *ear'd*. *Fairfax.*

To EAR. *v. n.* [from *ear.*] To ſhoot into ears.

EA'RED. *adj.* [from *ear.*]

1. Having ears, or organs of hearing.

2. Having ears, or ripe corn.

The covert of the thrice *ear'd* field
Saw ſtately Ceres to her paſſion yield. *Pope's Odyſſey, b.* iv.

EARL. *n. ſ.* [eorl, Saxon; *eoryl*, Erſe.] A title of nobility, anciently the higheſt of this nation, now the third.

Thanes and kinſmen,

Henceforth

Henceforth be *earls*, the first that ever Scotland
For such an honour nam'd. *Shakespeare's Macbeth.*

EARL-MARSHAL. *n. s.* [*earl* and *marshal.*] He that has chief care of military solemnities.

The marching troops through Athens take their way;
The great *earl-marshal* orders their array. *Dryden.*

EA'RLDOM. *n. s.* [from *earl.*] The seigniory of an earl; the title and dignity of an earl.

The duke of Clarence having married the heir of the earl of Ulster, and by her having all the *earldom* of Ulster, carefully went about the redressing evils. *Spenser's State of Ireland.*

When I am king, claim thou of me
The *earldom* of Hereford. *Shakespeare's Richard* III.

EA'RLINESS. *n. s.* [from *early.*] Quickness of any action with respect to something else: as *earliness* in the morning, the act of rising soon with respect to the sun; *earliness* of growth, the act of growing up soon in comparison with other things of the same kind.

The next morning we, having striven with the sun's *earliness*, were beyond the prospect of the highest turrets. *Sidney.*

The goodness of the crop is great gain, if the goodness answer the *earliness* of coming up. *Bacon's Natural History.*

EA'RLY. *adj.* [æɲ, Saxon, before] Soon with respect to something else: as, in the morning, with respect to the sun; in time, with respect to creation; in the season, in comparison with other products.

I am a tainted wether of the flock,
Meetest for death: the weakest kind of fruit
Drops *earliest* to the ground, and so let me. *Shakespeare.*

It is a curiosity to have several fruits upon one tree; and the more when some of them come *early*, and some come late, so that you may have upon the same tree ripe fruits all Summer. *Bacon's Natural History*, N°. 501.

God made all the world, that he might be worshipped in some parts of the world; and therefore, in the first and most *early* times of the church, what care did he manifest to have such places erected to his honour? *South's Sermons.*

And yet my numbers please the rural throng,
Rough satyrs dance, and Pan approves the song;
The nymphs, forsaking ev'ry cave and spring,
Their *early* fruit and milk-white turtles bring. *Pope.*

Sickness is *early* old age: it teaches us a diffidence in our earthly state, and inspires us with the thoughts of a future. *Pope.*

Oh soul of honour!
Oh *early* heroe! *Smith's Phædra and Hippolitus.*

EA'RLY. *adv.* [from the adjective.] Soon; betimes.

Early before the morn with crimson ray
The windows of bright heav'n opened had. *Fairy Queen.*

None in more languages can show
Those arts, which you so *early* know. *Waller.*

The princess makes her issue like herself, by instilling *early* into their minds religion, virtue and honour. *Addison's Freehol.*

To EARN. *v. a.* [eaɲnian, Saxon.]

1. To gain as the reward or wages of labour, or any performance.

Those that have joined with their honour great perils, are less subject to envy; for men think that they *earn* their honours hardly. *Bacon's Essays.*

Winning cheap the high repute,
Which he through hazard huge must *earn. Milt. Par. Lost.*

I to the evil turn
My obvious breast; arming to overcome
By suffering, and *earn* rest from labour won. *Milt. Pa. Lost.*

Men may discern
From what consummate virtue I have chose
This perfect man, by merit call'd my son,
To *earn* salvation for the sons of men. *Paradise Regained.*

Since they all beg, it were better for the state to keep them, even although they *earned* nothing. *Graunt's Bills of Mortality.*

This is the great expence of the poor, that takes up almost all their *earnings.* *Locke.*

The poems gained the plagiary wealth, while the author hardly *earned* his bread by repeating them. *Pope's Ess. on Homer.*

After toiling twenty days,
To *earn* a stock of pence and praise,
Thy labour's grown the critick's prey. *Swift.*

2. To gain; to obtain.

I can't say whore;
It does abhor me, now I speak the word:
To do the act, that might th' addition *earn*,
Not the world's mass of vanity could make me. *Sh. Othello.*

EA'RNEST. *adj.* [eoɲneꞅꞇ, Saxon.]

1. Ardent in any affection; warm; zealous; importunate.

He which prayeth in due sort, is thereby made the more attentive to hear; and he which heareth, the more *earnest* to pray for the time which we bestow, as well in the one as the other. *Hooker, b.* v. *s.* 34.

2. Intent; fixed; eager.

On that prospect strange
Their *earnest* eyes they fix'd; imagining,
For one forbidden tree, a multitude
Now ris'n, to work them further woe or shame. *Mi't. P. L.*

They are never more *earnest* to disturb us, than when they see us most *earnest* in this duty. *Duppa.*

EA'RNEST. *n. s.* [from the adjective.]

1. Seriousness; a serious event not a jest; reality not a feigned appearance.

Take heed that this jest do not one day turn to *earnest. Sid.*

I told you Klaius was the hapless wight,
Who *earnest* found what they accounted play. *Sidney.*

Therewith she laugh'd, and did her *earnest* end in jest. *F. Q.*

That high All-seer, which I dallied with,
Hath turn'd my feigned prayer on my head,
And given in *earnest* what I begg'd in jest. *Shak. Rich.* III.

Nor can I think that God, Creator wise!
Though threat'ning, will in *earnest* so destroy
Us, his prime creatures. *Milton's Paradise Lost, b.* ix.

But the main business and *earnest* of the world is money, dominion, and power. *L'Estrange, Fab.* 5.

We shall die in *earnest*, and it will not become us to live in jest. *Government of the Tongue, s.* 7.

Sempronius, you have acted like yourself;
One would have thought you had been half in *earnest. Add.*

2. [*ernitz penge*, Danish; *arres*, French.] Pledge; handsel; first fruits; token of something of the same kind in futurity.

The apostles term it the handsel or *earnest* of that which is to come. *Hooker, b.* v. *s.* 5.

Which leader shall the doubtful vict'ry bless,
And give an *earnest* of the war's success. *Waller.*

It may be looked upon as a pledge and *earnest* of quiet and tranquillity. *Smalridge's Sermons.*

The mercies received, great as they are, were *earnests* and pledges of greater. *Atterbury.*

3. The money which is given in token that a bargain is ratified.

You have conspir'd against our person,
Join'd with an enemy proclaim'd, and from his coffers
Receiv'd the golden *earnest* of our death. *Shakes. Henry* V.

Pay back the *earnest* penny received from Satan, and fling away his sin. *Decay of Piety.*

EA'RNESTLY. *adv.* [from *earnest.*]

1. Warmly; affectionately; zealously; importunately; intensely.

When *earnestly* they seek
Such proof, conclude they then begun to fail. *Milt. P. L.*

Shame is a banishment of him from the good opinion of the world, which every man most *earnestly* desires. *South.*

Earnestly invoke the goodness and power of an all merciful and almighty God. *Smalridge's Sermons.*

2. Eagerly; desirously.

Why so *earnestly* seek you to put up that letter? *Sh. K. Lear.*

EA'RNESTNESS. *n. s.* [from *earnest.*]

1. Eagerness; warmth; vehemence; impetuosity.

Often with a solemn *earnestness*,
More than, indeed, belong'd to such a trifle,
He begg'd of me to steal it. *Shakespeare's Othello.*

Audacity and confidence doth in business so great effects, as a man may doubt, that besides the very daring and *earnestness*, and persisting and importunity, there should be some secret binding, and stooping of other mens spirits to such persons. *Bacon's Natural History*, N°. 943.

Marcus is overwarm; his fond complaints
Have so much *earnestness* and passion in them,
I hear him with a secret kind of horror,
And tremble at his vehemence of temper. *Addison's Cato.*

2. Solemnity; zeal.

There never was a charge maintained with such a shew of gravity and *earnestness*, which had a slighter foundation to support it. *Atterbury's Sermons, Preface.*

3. Solicitude; care; intenseness.

With overstraining, and *earnestness* of finishing their pieces, they often did them more harm than good. *Dryden's Dufresn.*

EARSH. *n. s.* [from *ear*, to plow.] A plowed field.

Fires oft are good on barren *earshes* made,
With crackling flames to burn the stubble blade. *May's Virg.*

EARTH. *n. s.* [eoɲð, Saxon.]

1. The element distinct from air, fire, or water; soil; terrene matter.

The smiling god is seen; while water, *earth*,
And air attest his bounty. *Thomson's Spring, l.* 855.

2. The terraqueous globe; the world.

Nought so vile that on the *earth* doth live,
But to the *earth* some special good doth give. *Shakespeare.*

This solid globe we live upon is called the *earth*, though it contains in it a great variety of bodies, several whereof are not properly earth; which word, taken in a more limited sense, signifies such parts of this globe as are capable, being exposed to the air, to give rooting and nourishment to plants, so that they may stand and grow in it. *Locke.*

3. Different modification of terrene matter. In this sense it has a plural.

The five genera of *earths* are, 1. Boles. 2. Clays. 3. Marls. 4. Ochres. 5. Tripelas. *Hill's Mat. Medica.*

Earths

Earths are opake, insipid, and, when dried, friable, or consisting of parts easy to separate, and soluble in water; not disposed to burn, flame, or take fire. *Woodward's Met. Foss.*

4. This world opposed to other scenes of existence.

What are these,
So wither'd, and so wild in their attire,
That look not like th' inhabitants o' th' *earth*,
And yet are on't? *Shakesp. King Lear.*

They can judge as fitly of his worth,
As I can of those mysteries which heav'n
Will not have *earth* to know. *Shakespeare's Coriolanus.*

5. The inhabitants of the earth.

The whole *earth* was of one language. *Gen.* xi. 1.

6. Turning up the ground in tillage. [from *ear*, to plow.]

Such land as ye break up for barley to sow,
Two *earths*, at the least, ere ye sow it bestow. *Tuss. Husb.*

To EARTH. *v. a.* [from the noun.]

1. To hide in earth.

The fox is *earthed*; but I shall send my two terriers in after him. *Dryden's Spanish Fryar.*

2. To cover with earth.

Earth up with fresh mould the roots of those auricula's which the frost may have uncovered. *Evelyn's Kalendar.*

To EARTH. *v. n.* To retire under ground.

Hence foxes *earth'd*, and wolves abhorr'd the day,
And hungry churles ensnar'd the nightly prey. *Tickell.*

EA'RTHBOARD. *n. s.* [*earth* and *board.*] The board of the plow that shakes off the earth.

The plow reckoned the most proper for stiff black clays, is one that is long, large, and broad, with a deep head and a square *earthboard*, so as to turn up a great furrow. *Mortimer.*

EA'RTHBORN. *adj.* [*earth* and *born.*]

1. Born of the earth; terrigenous; meanly born.

The wounds I make but sow new enemies;
Which from their blood, like *earthborn* brethren rise. *Dryd.*

The God for ever great, for ever king,
Who slew the *earthborn* race, and measures right
To heav'n's great habitants? *Prior.*

2. Meanly born.

Earthborn Lycon shall ascend the throne. *Smith.*

EA'RTHBOUND. *adj.* [*earth* and *bound.*] Fastened by the pressure of the earth.

That will never be:
Who can impress the forest, bid the tree
Unfix his *earthbound* root? *Shakespeare's Macbeth.*

EA'RTHEN. *adj.* [from *earth.*] Made of earth; made of clay.

About his shelves
Green *earthen* pots, bladders, and musty seeds
Were thinly scatter'd. *Shakespeare.*

As a rustick was digging the ground by Padua, he found an urn, or *earthen* pot, in which there was another urn, and in this lesser a lamp clearly burning. *Wilkins's Math. Magic.*

The most brittle water-carriage was used among the Egyptians, who, as Strabo saith, would sail sometimes in the boats made of *earthen* ware. *Arbuthnot on Coins.*

EA'RTHFLAX. *n. s.* [*earth* and *flax.*] A kind of fibrous fossil.

Of English tile, the coarser sort is called plaister, or parget; the finer, *earthflax*, or salamander's hair. *Woodward.*

EA'RTHINESS. *n. s.* The quality of containing earth; grossness.

EA'RTHLING. *n. s.* [from *earth.*] An inhabitant of the earth; a mortal; a poor frail creature.

To *earthlings*, the footstool of God, that stage which he raised for a small time, seemeth magnificent. *Drummond.*

EA'RTHLY. *adj.* [from *earth.*]

1. Not heavenly; vile; mean; sordid.

But I remember now
I'm in this *earthly* world, where to do harm
Is often laudable; to do good, sometime
Accounted dangerous folly. *Shakespeare's Macbeth.*

When faith and love, which parted from thee never,
Had ripen'd thy just soul to dwell with God,
Meekly thou didst resign this *earthly* load
Of death, call'd life. *Milton.*

2. Belonging only to our present state; not spiritual.

Our common necessities, and the lack which we all have as well of ghostly as of *earthly* favours, is in each kind easily known. *Hooker.*

You have scarce time
To steal from spiritual leisure a brief span,
To keep your *earthly* audit. *Shakespeare's Henry* VIII.

It must be our solemn business and endeavour, at fit seasons, to turn the stream of our thoughts from *earthly* towards divine objects. *Atterbury's Sermons.*

3. Corporeal; not mental.

Great grace that old man to him given had,
For God he often saw, from heaven hight,
All were his *earthly* eyen both blunt and bad. *Fairy Queen.*

Sudden he view'd, in spite of all her art,
An *earthly* lover lurking at her heart. *Pope's Ra. of the Lock.*

4. Any thing in the world; a female hyperbole.

Oh! if to dance all night, and dress all day,
Charm'd the small-pox, or chas'd old age away,
Who would not scorn what housewife's cares produce?
Or who would learn one *earthly* thing of use? *Pope.*

EA'RTHNUT. *n. s.* [*earth* and *nut.*] A pignut; a root in shape and size like a nut.

It is an umbelliferous plant, with a rose-shaped flower, consisting of many leaves orbicularly placed, which turns to a fruit composed of small oblong smooth leaves, gibbous on one side, and plain on the other. It has a fleshy tuberose root. It is very common in shady woods and pastures, rising early in Spring, and flowering in May: in July the seeds are ripe, and soon after the leaves decay. Some dig up the roots, and eat them raw: they are very much like chestnuts, and not an unpleasant morsel; but boiled they are a very delicious food, eaten with butter and pepper, and are esteemed very nourishing. *Miller.*

Where there are *earthnuts* in several patches, though the roots lie deep in the ground, and the stalks be dead, the swine will by their scent root only where they grow. *Ray.*

EA'RTHQUAKE. *n. s.* [*earth* and *quake.*] Tremor or convulsion of the earth.

This subterranean heat or fire being in any part of the earth stopt, by some accidental glut or obstruction in the passages through which it used to ascend, and being preternaturally assembled in greater quantity into one place, causes a great rarefaction and intumescence of the water of the abyss, putting it into very great commotions; and making the like effort upon the earth, expanded upon the face of the abyss, occasions that agitation and concussion which we call an *earthquake.* *Woodward's Natural History.*

These tumults were like an *earthquake*, shaking the very foundations of all, than which nothing in the world hath more of horrour. *King Charles.*

Was it his youth, his valour, or success,
These might perhaps be found in other men:
'Twas that respect, that awful homage paid me;
That fearful love which trembled in his eyes,
And with a silent *earthquake* shook his soul. *Dryd. Sp. Fryar.*

The country, by reason of its vast caverns and subterraneous fires, has been miserably torn by *earthquakes*, so that the whole face of it is quite changed. *Addison's Remarks on Italy.*

EA'RTHSHAKING. *adj.* [*earth* and *shake.*] Having power to shake the earth, or to raise earthquakes.

By the *earthshaking* Neptune's mace,
And Tethys grave majestick pace. *Milton.*

Now scarce withdrawn the fierce *earthshaking* pow'r,
Jove's daughter Pallas watch'd the fav'ring hour;
Back to their caves she bad the winds to fly,
And hush'd the blust'ring brethren of the sky. *Pope.*

EA'RTHWORM. *n. s.* [*earth* and *worm.*]

1. A worm bred under ground.

Worms are found in snow commonly, like *earthworms*, and therefore it is not unlike that it may likewise put forth plants. *Bacon's Natural History,* N°. 569.

Upon a shower, after a drought, *earthworms* and landsnails innumerable come out of their lurking places. *Ray.*

2. A mean sordid wretch.

Thy vain contempt, dull *earthworm*, cease;
I won't for refuge fly. *Norris.*

EA'RTHY. *adj.* [from *earth.*]

1. Consisting of earth.

Long may'st thou live in Richard's seat to sit,
And soon lie Richard in an *earthy* pit! *Shakesp. Richard* II.

These lamps are inflamed by the admission of new air, when the sepulchres are opened, as we see in fat *earthy* vapours of divers sorts. *Wilkins's Math. Magic.*

All water, especially that of rain, is more or less stored with matter, light in comparison of the common mineral *earthy* matter. *Woodward's Natural History.*

2. Composed or partaking of earth; terrene.

To survey his dead and *earthy* image,
What were it but to make my sorrow greater. *Shak. H.* VI

Him lord pronounc'd, he, O indignity!
Subjected to his service angel-wings,
And flaming ministers to watch and tend
Their *earthy* charge. *Milton's Paradise Lost, b.* ix. *l.* 157.

3. Inhabiting the earth; terrestrial.

Those *earthy* spirits black and envious are;
I'll call up other gods of form more fair. *Dryd. Ind. Emper.*

4. Relating to earth.

Mine is the shipwreck, in a watry sign;
And in an *earthy*, the dark dungeon thine. *Dryden.*

5. Not mental; gross; not refined.

Teach me, dear creature, how to think and speak;
Lay open to my *earthy* gross conceit,
Smother'd in errors, feeble, shallow, weak,
The folded meaning of your words deceit. *Shakespeare.*

Nor is my flame

So *earthy*, as to need the dull material force
Of eyes, or lips, or cheeks. *Denham's Sophy.*

EASE. *n. s.* [*aise*, French.]

1. Quiet; rest; undisturbed tranquillity; no solicitude.

We should not find her half so brave and bold
To lead it to the wars, and to the seas;
To make it suffer watchings, hunger, cold,
When it might feed with plenty, rest with *ease*. *Davies.*

The priest on skins of off'rings takes his *ease*,
And nightly visions in his slumber sees. *Dryden's Æn.*

Lucan, content with praise, may lie at *ease*
In costly grotts and marble palaces. *Dryden's Juv. Sat.* 7.

Men of parts and penetration were not idly to dispute at their *ease*, but were to act according to the result of their debates. *Locke.*

No body is under an obligation to know every thing: knowledge and science in general is the business only of those who are at *ease* and leisure. *Locke.*

2. Freedom from pain; a neutral state between pain and pleasure.

That which we call *ease* is only an indolency, or a freedom from pain. *L'Estrange.*

Is it a small crime to wound himself by anguish of heart, to deprive himself of all the pleasures, or *eases*, or enjoyments of life? *Temple.*

3. Rest after labour; intermission of labour.

Give yourselves *ease* from the fatigue of waiting. *Swift.*

4. Facility; not difficulty.

The willing metal will obey thy hand,
Following with *ease*, if favour'd by thy fate,
Thou art foredoom'd to view the Stygian state;
If not, no labour can the tree constrain,
And strength of stubborn arms and steel are vain. *Dryden.*

5. Unconstraint; freedom from harshness, formality, forced behaviour, or conceits.

True *ease* in writing comes from art, not chance;
As those move easiest who have learn'd to dance. *Pope's Ess.*

To EASE. *v. a.* [from the noun.]

1. To free from pain.

Help and *ease* children the best you can; but by no means bemoan them. *Locke.*

2. To relieve; to assuage; to mitigate; to alleviate.

Thy father made our yoke grievous, now therefore *ease* thou somewhat the grievous servitude. 2 *Chro.* x. 4.

Complain, queen Margaret, and tell thy grief;
It shall be *eas'd*, if France can yield relief. *Shakesp. H.* VI.

As if with sports my sufferings I could *ease*. *Dryden.*

Though he speaks of such medicines as procure sleep, and *ease* pain, he doth not determine their doses. *Arbuthnot on Coins.*

Will he for sacrifice our sorrows *ease*?
And can our tears reverse his firm decrees? *Prior.*

3. To relieve from labour.

If ere night the gath'ring clouds we fear,
A song will help the beating storm to bear;
And that thou may'st not be too late abroad,
Sing, and I'll *ease* thy shoulders of thy load. *Dryden's Past.*

4. To set free from any thing that offends.

I will *ease* me of mine adversaries. *Is.* i. 24.

No body feels pain that he wishes not to be *eased* of, with a desire equal to that pain, and inseparable from it. *Locke.*

EA'SEFUL. *adj.* [*ease* and *full*.] Quiet; peaceable; fit for rest.

I spy a black, suspicious, threat'ning cloud,
That will encounter with our glorious sun,
Ere he attain his *easeful* western bed. *Shakesp. Henry* VI.

EA'SEMENT. *n. s.* [from *ease*.]

1. Assistance; support; relief from expences.

He has the advantage of a free lodging, and some other *easements*. *Swift.*

2. [In law.] A service that one neighbour has of another by charter or prescription, without profit; as a way through his ground, a sink, or such like. *Cowel.*

EA'SILY. *adv.* [from *easy*.]

1. Without difficulty.

Those move swiftly, and at great distance; but they require a medium well disposed, and their transmission is *easily* stopped. *Bacon's Natural History*, N°. 647.

She ask'd the reason of his woe;
She ask'd, but with an air and mien,
That made it *easily* foreseen
She fear'd too much to know. *Prior.*

3. Without pain; without disturbance; in tranquillity.

Is it not to bid defiance to all mankind to condemn their universal opinions and designs, if, instead of passing your life as well and *easily*, you resolve to pass it as ill and as miserable as you can? *Temple.*

3. Readily; without reluctance.

I can *easily* resign to others the praise of your illustrious family. *Dryden's Dedic. to State of Innocence.*

Not soon provok'd, she *easily* forgives;
And much she suffers, as she much believes. *Prior.*

EA'SINESS. *n. s.* [from *easy*.]

1. Freedom from difficulty.

Believe me, friends, loud tumults are not laid
With half the *easiness* that they are rais'd. *Ben. Johns. Catil.*

Easiness and difficulty are relative terms, and relate to some power; and a thing may be difficult to a weak man, which yet may be easy to the same person, when assisted with a greater strength. *Tillotson, Sermon* 6.

The seeming *easiness* of Pindarick verse has made it spread; but it has not been considered. *Dryden.*

You left a conquest more than half atchiev'd,
And for whose *easiness* I almost griev'd. *Dryden.*

This plea appears under a colour of friendship to religion, and to invite men to it by the *easiness* of the terms it offers. *Rogers, Sermon* 15.

2. Flexibility; compliance; readiness; not opposition; not reluctance.

His yielding unto them in one thing might happily put them in hope, that time would breed the like *easiness* of condescending further unto them. *Hooker, Pref.*

Since the custom of *easiness* to alter and change laws is so evil, no doubt but to bear a tolerable sore is better than to venture on a dangerous remedy. *Hooker, b.* iv. *s.* 14.

Give to him, and he shall but laugh at your *easiness*; save his life, but, when you have done, look to your own. *South.*

The safest way to secure honesty, is to lay the foundations of it early in liberality, and an *easiness* to part with to others whatever they have or like themselves. *Locke.*

3. Freedom from constraint; not effort; not formality.

Abstruse and mystick thoughts you must express
With painful care, but seeming *easiness*;
For truth shines brightest through the plainest dress. *Rosc.*

4. Rest; tranquillity.

I think the reason I have assigned hath a great interest in that rest and *easiness* we enjoy when asleep. *Ray on the Creation.*

EAST. *n. s.* [eaꞅt, Saxon; *heos*, Erse.]

1. The quarter where the sun rises.

They counting forwards towards the *East*, did allow 180 degrees to the Portugals eastward. *Abbot.*

2. The regions in the eastern parts of the world.

I would not be the villain that thou thinkest,
For the whole space that's in the tyrant's grasp,
And the rich *East* to boot. *Shakespeare's Macbeth.*

EA'STER. *n. s.* [eaꞅꞇꞃe, Saxon; *oster*, Dutch.] The day on which the Christian church commemorates our Saviour's resurrection.

Did'st thou not fall out with a taylor for wearing his new doublet before *Easter*? *Shakespeare's Romeo and Juliet.*

Victor's unbrother-like heat towards the Eastern churches, in the controversy about *Easter*, fomented that difference into a schism. *Decay of Piety.*

EA'STERLY. *adj.* [from *East*.]

1. Coming from the parts towards the East.

When the *easterly* winds or breezes are kept off by some high mountains from the vallies, whereby the air, wanting motion, doth become exceeding unhealthful. *Raleigh.*

2. Lying towards the East.

These give us a view of the most *easterly*, southerly, and westerly parts of England. *Graunt's Bills of Mortality.*

3. Looking towards the East.

Water he chuses clear, light, without taste or smell, drawn not from snow, but from springs with an *easterly* exposition. *Arbuthnot on Aliments.*

EA'STERN. *adj.* [from *East*.]

1. Dwelling or found in the East; oriental.

Eastern tyrants from the light of heaven
Seclude their bosom-slaves. *Thomson's Spring.*

2. Lying or being towards the East.

The *eastern* end of the isle rises up in precipices. *Addison.*

3. Going towards the East.

A ship at sea has no certain method in either her *eastern* or western voyages, or even in her less distant sailing from the coasts, to know her longitude, or how much she is gone *eastward* or westward, as can easily be known in any clear day or night how much she is gone northward or southward. *Addison.*

4. Looking towards the East.

EA'STWARD. *adv.* [*East* and *toward*.] Towards the East.

The moon, which performs its motion swifter than the sun, gets *eastward* out of his rays, and appears when the sun is set. *Brown's Vulgar Errours, b.* iv. *c.* 13.

What shall we do, or where direct our flight?
Eastward, as far as I could cast my sight,
From op'ning heav'ns, I saw descending light. *Dryden.*

EA'SY. *adj.* [from *ease*.]

1. Not difficult.

The service of God, in the solemn assembly of saints, is a work, though *easy*, yet withal very weighty, and of great respect. *Hooker, b.* v. *s.* 31.

There is a slave, whose *easy*-borrow'd pride
Dwells in the fickle grace of her he follows. *Shak. K. Lear.*

How much it is in every one's power to make resolutions

to himself, such as he may keep, is *easy* for every one to try. *Locke.*

The whole island was probably cut into several *easy* ascents, and planted with variety of palaces. *Addison on Italy.*

2. Quiet; at rest; not harrassed; not disturbed; without anxiety.

Those that are *easy* in their conditions, or their minds, refuse often to enter upon publick charges and employment. *Temple.*

Keep their thoughts *easy* and free, the only temper wherein the mind is capable of receiving new informations. *Locke.*

A marriage of love is pleasant, a marriage of interest *easy*, and a marriage where both meet happy. *Addison's Spectator.*

When men are *easy* in their circumstances, they are naturally enemies to innovations. *Addison's Freeholder*, N°. 42.

A man should direct all his studies and endeavours at making himself *easy* now, and happy hereafter. *Addison's Spectator.*

We plainly feel whether at this instant we are *easy* or uneasy, happy or miserable. *Smalridge's Sermons.*

3. Complying; unresisting; credulous.

Baited with reasons not unplausible,
Win me into the *easy* hearted man,
And hug him into snares. *Milton.*

With such deceits he gain'd their *easy* hearts,
Too prone to credit his perfidious arts. *Dryden's Æn.*

The kindest father I have ever found him,
Easy and good, and bounteous to my wishes. *Addison's Cato.*

4. Free from pain.

Another part, in squadrons and gross bands,
On bold adventure to discover wide
That dismal world, if any clime perhaps
Might yield them *easier* habitation. *Milton's Paradise Lost.*

Pleasure has been the bus'ness of my life,
And every change of fortune *easy* to me,
Because I still was *easy* to myself. *Dryden's Don Sebastian.*

5. Ready; not unwilling.

Pity and he are one;
So merciful a king did never live,
Loth to revenge, and *easy* to forgive. *Dryden's Span. Fryar.*

6. Without want of more.

They should be allowed each of them such a rent as would make them *easy*. *Swift's Arg. against abolishing Christianity.*

7. Without constraint; without formality.

Those move *easiest* that have learn'd to dance. *Pope.*

Praise the *easy* vigour of a line,
Where Denham's strength, and Waller's sweetness join. *Po.*

To EAT. *v. a.* preterite *ate*, or *eat*; part. *eat*, or *eaten*. [etan, Sax. *itan*, Gothick; *eich*, Erse.]

1. To devour with the mouth.

Locusts shall *eat* the residue of that which is escaped from the hail, and shall *eat* every tree which groweth. *Ex.* x. 5.

Other states cannot be accused for not staying for the first blow, or for not accepting Polyphemus's courtesy, to be the last that shall be *eaten* up. *Bacon's War with Spain.*

Even wormwood, *eat* with bread, will not bite, because it is mixed with a great quantity of spittle. *Arbuthnot on Aliments.*

2. To consume; to corrode.

Thou best of gold art worst of gold;
Other less fine in carrat is more precious,
Preserving life in med'cine potable:
But thou, most fine, most honour'd, most renown'd,
Hast *eat* thy bearer up. *Shakespeare's Henry* IV. *p.* ii.

They entail a secret curse upon their estates, which does either insensibly waste and consume it, or *eat* out the heart and comfort of it. *Tillotson, Sermon* 4.

There arises a necessity of keeping the surface even, either by pressure or *eating* medicines, that the eminence of the flesh may not resist the fibres of the skin in their tendency to cover the wound. *Sharp's Surgery.*

3. To swallow back; to retreat. This is only used of a man's word.

They cannot hold, but burst out those words, which afterwards they are forced to *eat*. *Hakewill on Providence.*

Credit were not to be lost
B' a brave knight errant of the post,
That *eats*, perfidiously, his word,
And swears his ears through a two inch board. *Hudibras.*

To EAT. *v. n.*

1. To go to meals; to take meals; to feed.

He did *eat* continually at the king's table. 2 *Sa.* ix. 13.

And when the scribes and pharisees saw him *eat* with publicans and sinners, they said unto his disciples, how is it that he *eateth* with publicans and sinners? *Mat.* ii. 16.

2. To take food.

He that will not *eat* 'till he has a demonstration that it will nourish him, he that will not stir 'till he infallibly knows the business he goes about will succeed, will have little else to do but sit still and perish. *Locke.*

3. To be maintained in food.

The righteous *eateth* to the satisfying of his soul, but the belly of the wicked shall want. *Prov.* xiii. 25.

Thou art past the tyrant's stroke;
Care no more to cloath and *eat*. *Shakespeare's Cymbeline.*

4. To make way by corrosion.

The plague of sin has even altered his nature, and *eaten* into his very essentials. *South's Sermons.*

A prince's court *eats* too much into the income of a poor state. *Addison's Italy.*

EA'TABLE. *n. s.* [from *eat.*] Any thing that may be eaten.

If you all sorts of persons would engage,
Suit well your *eatables* to ev'ry age. *King's Art of Cookery.*

EA'TER. *n. s.* [from *eat.*]

1. One that eats any thing.

The Caribees and the Cannibals, almost all, are *eaters* of man's flesh. *Abbot's Description of the World.*

A knave, a rascal, an *eater* of broken meats. *Sh. K. Lear.*

If the taste of this fruit maketh the *eaters* like gods, why remainest thou a beast? *Brown's Vulgar Errours, b.* i. *c.* 1.

As if the lotus grew only here, the virtue of whose fruit is to cause in the *eaters* an oblivion of all other soils. *Howel.*

2. A corrosive.

EATH. *adj.* [eað, Saxon.] Easy; not difficult. An old word.

Where ease abounds, it's *eath* to do amiss. *Fairy Queen.*

What works not beauty, man's relenting mind
Is *eath* to move with plaints and shews of woe. *Fairfax, b.* iv.

The way was strait and *eath*. *Fairfax.*

EATH. *adv.* [from the adjective] Easily. An old word.

Who hath the world not try'd,
From the right way full *eath* may wander wide. *Hubb. Tale.*

EA'TINGHOUSE. *n. s.* [*eat* and *house.*] A house where provisions are sold ready dressed.

An hungry traveller stept into an *eatinghouse* for his dinner. *L'Estrange.*

EAVES. *n. s.* [epese, Saxon.] The edges of the roof which overhang the house.

Every night he comes
With musick of all sorts, and songs compos'd
To her unworthiness: it nothing steads us
To chide him from our *eaves*; for he persists,
As if his life lay on't. *Shakespeare's All's well that ends well.*

His tears run down his beard, like Winter drops
From *eaves* of reeds. *Shakespeare's Tempest.*

If in the beginning of Winter the drops of the *eaves* of houses come more slowly down than they use, it portendeth a hard and frosty Winter. *Bacon*, N°. 811.

Usher'd with a shower still,
When the gust hath blown his fill,
Ending on the rusling leaves,
With minute drops from off the *eaves*. *Milton.*

The icicles hang down from the *eaves* of houses. *Woodward.*

To EA'VESDROP. *v. a.* [*eaves* and *drop.*] To catch what comes from the eaves; in common phrase, to listen under windows.

EA'VESDROPPER. *n. s.* [*eaves* and *drop.*] A listener under windows.

Under our tents I'll play the *eavesdropper*,
To hear if any mean to shrink from me. *Shakesp. Rich.* III.

EBB. *n. s.* [ebba, epplob, Saxon; *ebbe*, Dutch.]

1. The reflux of the tide towards the sea.

The clear sun on his wide wat'ry glass
Gaz'd hot, and of the fresh wave largely drew,
As after thirst; which made their flowing shrink
From standing lake to tripping *ebb*, that stole
With soft foot tow'rds the deep. *Milton's Paradise Lost.*

Hither the seas at stated times resort,
And shove the loaden vessels into port;
Then with a gentle *ebb* retire again,
And render back their cargo to the main. *Addison on Italy.*

2. Decline; decay; waste.

You have finished all the war, and brought all things to that low *ebb* which you speak of. *Spenser on Ireland.*

This tide of man's life, after it once turneth and declineth, ever runneth with a perpetual *ebb* and falling stream, but never floweth again. *Raleigh's History of the World.*

Thus all the treasure of our flowing years,
Our *ebb* of life for ever takes away. *Roscommon.*

The greatest age for poetry was that of Augustus Cæsar, yet painting was then at its lowest *ebb*, and perhaps sculpture was also declining. *Dryden's Dufresnoy, Preface.*

Near my apartment let him pris'ner be,
That I his hourly *ebbs* of life may see. *Dryden's Aurengzebe.*

What is it he aspires to?
Is it not this? To shed the slow remains,
His last poor *ebb* of blood in your defence? *Addison's Cato.*

To EBB. *v. n.* [from the noun.]

1. To flow back towards the sea.

Though my tide of blood
Hath proudly flow'd in vanity 'till now,
Now it doth turn and *ebb* back to the sea. *Shakesp. Hen.* IV.

From thence the tide of fortune left their shore,
And *ebb'd* much faster than it flow'd before. *Dryden's Æn.*

2. To decline; to decay; to waste.

Well, I am ſtanding water:
——I'll teach you how to flow.
——Do ſo: to *ebb*
Hereditary ſloth inſtructs me. *Shakeſpeare's Tempeſt.*
But oh he *ebbs!* the ſmiling waves decay!
For ever, lovely ſtream, for ever ſtay! *Halifax.*

E'BEN. } *n. ſ.* [*ebenus*, Latin.] A hard, heavy, black, valu-
EB'ON. } able wood, which admits a fine gloſs.
E'BONY. }

If the wood be very hard, as *ebony*, or lignum vitæ, they are to turn: they uſe not the ſame tools they do for ſoft woods. *Moxon's Mech. Exerciſes.*

Oft by the winds extinct the ſignal lies,
Or ſmother'd in the glimmering ſocket dies,
Ere night has half roll'd round her *ebon* throne. *Gay's Triv.*

EBRI'ETY. *n. ſ.* [*ebrietas*, Latin.] Drunkenneſs; intoxication by ſtrong liquors.

Bitter almonds, as an antidote againſt *ebriety*, hath commonly failed. *Brown's Vulgar Errours, b.* ii. *c.* 6.

EBRI'LLADE. n. ſ. [French.] A check of the bridle which a horſeman gives a horſe, by a jerk of one rein, when he refuſes to turn.

EBRIO'SITY. *n. ſ.* [*ebrioſitas*, Latin.] Habitual drunkenneſs.

That religion which excuſeth Noah in ſurpriſal, will neither acquit *ebrioſity* nor ebriety in their intended perverſion. *Brown.*

EB'ULLITION. *n. ſ.* [*ebullio*, Latin.]

1. The act of boiling up with heat.
2. Any inteſtine motion.
3. That ſtruggling or effervеſcence which ariſes from the mingling together any alkalizate and acid liquor; and hence any inteſtine violent motion of the parts of a fluid, occaſioned by the ſtruggling of particles of different properties, is ſo called. *Quincy.*

The diſſolution of gold and ſilver diſagree; ſo that in their mixture there is great *ebullition*, darkneſs, and, in the end, a precipitation of a black powder. *Bacon.*

Iron, in aqua fortis, will fall into *ebullition* with noiſe and emication; as alſo a craſſe and fumid exhalation, cauſed from the combat of the ſulphur of iron with the acid and nitrous ſpirits of aqua fortis. *Brown's Vulgar Errours, b.* ii.

When aqua fortis, or ſpirit of vitriol, poured upon filings of iron, diſſolves the filings with a great heat and *ebullition*, is not the heat and *ebullition* effected by a violent motion of the parts; and does not their motion argue, that the acid parts of the liquor ruſh towards the parts of the metal with violence, and run forcibly into its pores, 'till they get between its outmoſt particles and the main maſs of the metal. *Newton.*

A violent cold, as well as heat, may be produced by this *ebullition*; for if ſal ammoniack, or any pure volatile alkali, diſſolved in water, be mixed with an acid, an *ebullition*, with a greater degree of cold, will enſue. *Arbuthnot on Aliments.*

ECCE'NTRICAL. } *adj.* [*eccentricus*, Latin.]
ECCE'NTRICK. }

1. Deviating from the center.
2. Not having the ſame center with another circle: ſuch circles were ſuppoſed by the Ptolemaick philoſophy.

Thither his courſe he bends
Through the calm firmament; but up or down,
By centrick or *eccentrick*, hard to tell. *Milton's Parad. Loſt.*
They build, unbuild, contrive,
To ſave appearances: they gird the ſphere
With centrick, and *eccentrick*, ſcribbl'd o'er,
Cycle, and epicycle, orb in orb. *Milton's Paradiſe Loſt.*

Whence is it that planets move all one and the ſame way in orbs concentrick, while comets move all manner of ways in orbs very *eccentrick?* *Newton's Opt.*

3. Not terminating in the point; not directed by the ſame principle.

Whatſoever affairs paſs ſuch a man's hands, he crooketh them to his own ends; which muſt needs be often *eccentrick* to the ends of his maſter. *Bacon's Eſſays.*

4. Irregular; anamalous; deviating from ſtated and conſtant methods.

This motion, like others of the times, ſeems *eccentrick* and irregular. *King Charles.*

A character of an *eccentrick* virtue, is the more exact image of human life, becauſe it is not wholly exempted from its frailties. *Dryden's Dedicat. to the Conqueſt of Granada.*

Then from whate'er we can to ſenſe produce,
Common and plain, or wond'rous and abſtruſe,
From nature's conſtant or *eccentrick* laws,
The thoughtful ſoul this gen'ral inference draws,
That an effect muſt preſuppoſe a cauſe. *Prior.*

ECCENTRI'CITY. *n. ſ.* [from *eccentrick*.]

1. Deviation from a center.
2. The ſtate of having a different center from another circle.

In regard of *eccentricity*, and the epicycle wherein it moveth, the motion of the moon is unequal. *Brown's Vulgar Errours.*

By reaſon of the ſun's *eccentricity* to the earth, and obliquity to the equator, he appears to us to move unequally. *Holder.*

3. Excurſion from the proper orb.

The duke at his return from his *eccentricity*, for ſo I account favourites abroad, met no good news of the Cadiz attempt. *Wotton.*

4. *Eccentricity* of the earth is the diſtance between the focus and the center of the earth's elliptick orbit. *Harris.*

ECCHY'MOSIS. *n. ſ.* [ἐκχύμωσις] Livid ſpots or blotches in the ſkin, made by extravaſated blood. *Quincy.*

Ecchymoſis may be defined an extravaſation of the blood in or under the ſkin, the ſkin remaining whole. *Wiſeman's Surg.*

Laxations are accompanied with tumour and *ecchymoſis*. *Wiſ.*

ECCLESIA'STICAL. } *adj.* [*eccleſiaſticus*, Latin.]
ECCLESIA'STICK. }

1. Relating to the church; not civil.

Is diſcipline an *eccleſiaſtical* matter or civil? If an *eccleſiaſtical*, it muſt of neceſſity belong to the duty of the miniſter. *Hooker, Preface.*

Clergymen, otherwiſe little fond of obſcure terms, yet in their ſermons are liberal of thoſe which they find in *eccleſiaſtical* writers. *Swift.*

A church of England man has a true veneration for the ſcheme eſtabliſhed among us of *eccleſiaſtick* government. *Swift.*

ECCLESIA'STICK. *n. ſ.* [from the adjective.] A perſon dedicated to the miniſtries of religion.

The ambition of the *eccleſiaſticks* deſtroyed the purity of the church. *Burnet's Theory of the Earth.*

ECCOPRO'TICKS. *n. ſ.* [ἐκ and κόπρος.] Such medicines as gently purge the belly, ſo as to bring away no more than the natural excrements lodged in the inteſtines.

The body ought to be maintained in its daily excretions by ſuch means as are *eccoprotick*. *Harvey on the Plague.*

ECHINA'TE. } *adj.* [from *echinus*, Latin.] Briſtled like an
ECHINA'TED. } hedgehog; ſet with prickles.

An *echinated* pyrites in ſhape approaches the *echinated* cryſtalline balls. *Woodward on Foſſils.*

E'CHINUS. n. ſ. [Latin.]

1. A hedgehog.
2. A ſhellfiſh ſet with prickles.
3. [With botaniſts.] The prickly head, cover of the ſeed, or top of any plant.
4. [In architecture.] A member or ornament, taking its name from the roughneſs of the carving, reſembling the prickly rind of a cheſnut, and not unlike the thorny coat of a hedgehog.

This ornament is uſed by modern architects in cornices of the Ionick, Corinthian, and Compoſite orders; and generally ſet next to the abacus, being carved with anchors, darts, and ovals or eggs. *Harris.*

E'CHO. *n. ſ.* [ἠχώ.]

1. Echo was ſuppoſed to have been once a nymph, who pined into a ſound for love of Narciſſus.

The pleaſant myrtle may teach th' unfortunate *Echo*
In theſe woods to reſound the renowned name of a goddeſs. *Sidney, b.* i.

2. The return or repercuſſion of any ſound.

Babbling *echo* mocks the hounds,
Replying ſhrilly to the well-tun'd horns,
As if a double hunt were heard at once. *Shak. Titus Andron.*

The ſound, filling great ſpaces in arched lines, cannot be guided; therefore there hath not been any means to make artificial *echoes*. *Bacon's Natural Hiſtory,* N°. 242.

To you I mourn, nor to the deaf I ſing;
The woods ſhall anſwer, and the *echo* ring. *Pope's Summer.*
'Tis not enough no harſhneſs gives offence;
The ſound muſt ſeem an *echo* to the ſenſe. *Pope's Eſſ. Crit.*

3. The ſound returned.

Wilt thou hunt?
Thy hounds ſhall make the welkin anſwer them,
And fetch ſhrill *echoes* from their hollow earth. *Shakeſpeare.*
O woods, O fountains, hillocks, dales and bow'rs!
With other *echo* late I taught your ſhades
To anſwer, and reſound far other ſong! *Milt. Parad. Loſt.*

To E'CHO. *v. n.*

1. To reſound; to give the repercuſſion of a voice.

At the parting
All the church *echo'd*. *Shakeſpeare's Taming of the Shrew.*
Through rocks and caves the name of Delia ſounds;
Delia each cave and *echoing* rock rebounds. *Pope's Autumn.*

2. To be ſounded back.

Hark, how the ſound diſturbs imperious Rome!
Shakes her proud hills, and rolls from dome to dome!
Her miter'd princes hear the *echoing* noiſe,
And, Albion, dread thy wrath and awful voice. *Blackmore.*

To E'CHO. *v. a.* To ſend back a voice; to return what has been uttered.

Our modern ſeparatiſts do but *echo* the ſame note. *Decay of Piety.*

With peals of ſhouts the Tyrians praiſe the ſong;
Thoſe peals are *echo'd* by the Trojan throng. *Dryden's Æn.*
One great death deforms the dreary ground;
The *echo'd* woes from diſtant rocks reſound. *Prior.*

ECLAIRCI'SSEMENT. *n. ſ.* [French.] Explanation; the act of clearing up an affair by verbal expoſtulation.

ECLAT. *n. ſ.* [French.] Splendour; ſhow; luſtre.

Nothing more contributes to the variety, ſurprize, and *eclat* of Homer's battles, than that artificial manner of gaging his heroes by each other. *Pope's Eſſay on Homer.*

ECLE'CTICK. *adj.* [ἐκλεκτικος.] Selecting; chuſing at will.

Cicero gives an account of the opinions of philoſophers; but was of the *eclectick* ſect, and choſe out of each ſuch poſitions as came neareſt truth. *Watts's Improvement of the Mind.*

ECLE'GMA. *n. ſ.* [ἐκ and λείχειν.] A form of medicine made by the incorporation of oils with ſyrups, and which is to be taken upon a liquorice ſtick. *Quincy.*

ECLI'PSE. *n. ſ.* [ἔκλειψις.]

1. An obſcuration of the luminaries of heaven; the ſun is eclipſed by the intervention of the moon; the moon by the interpoſition of the earth. The word originally ſignifies *departure* from the place, to which *Milton* alludes.

Slips of yew,
Sliver'd in the moon's *eclipſe.* *Shakeſpeare's Macbeth.*

Planets, planet-ſtruck, real *eclipſe*
Then ſuffer'd. *Milton's Paradiſe Loſt, b.* x. *l.* 413.

So though the ſun victorious be,
And from a dark *eclipſe* ſet free,
The influence, which we fondly fear,
Afflicts our thoughts the following year. *Waller.*

An *eclipſe* of the moon is when the atmoſphere of the earth, being between the ſun and the moon, hinders the light of the ſun from falling upon and being reflected by the moon: if the light of the ſun is kept off from the whole body of the moon, it is a total *eclipſe*; if from a part only, it is a partial one. *Locke.*

2. Darkneſs; obſcuration.

All the poſterity of our firſt parents ſuffered a perpetual *eclipſe* of ſpiritual life. *Raleigh's Hiſtory of the World.*

Experience we have of the vanity of human glory, in our ſcatterings and *eclipſes.* *King Charles.*

To ECLI'PSE. *v. a.* [from the noun.]

1. To darken a luminary.

Let the *eclipſed* moon her throne reſign. *Sandys.*

Now if the earth were flat, the dark'ned moon
Would ſeem to all *eclipſ'd* as well as one. *Creech's Manilius.*

2. To extinguiſh; to put out.

Then here I take my leave of thee, fair ſon,
Born to *eclipſe* thy life this afternoon. *Shakeſp. Henry* VI.

3. To cloud; to obſcure.

They had ſeen tokens of more than common greatneſs, howſoever now *eclipſed* with fortune. *Sidney.*

Praiſe him to his father:
Let the prince's glory
Seem to *eclipſe*, and caſt a cloud on his. *Denham's Sophy.*

Let other muſes write his proſp'rous fate,
Of conquer'd nations tell, and kings reſtor'd;
But mine ſhall ſing of his *eclipſ'd* eſtate,
Which, like the ſun's, more wonders does afford. *Dryden.*

He deſcended from his father, and *eclipſed* the glory of his divine majeſty with a veil of fleſh. *Calamy's Sermons.*

4. To diſgrace.

She told the king, that her huſband was *eclipſed* in Ireland by the no-countenance his majeſty had ſhewed towards him. *Clarendon, b.* viii.

Another now hath to himſelf engroſs'd
All pow'r, and us *eclipſ'd.* *Milton's Paradiſe Loſt, b.* v.

ECLI'PTICK. *n. ſ.* [ἐκλειπτικὸς.] A great circle of the ſphere, ſuppoſed to be drawn through the middle of the Zodiack, and making an angle with the Equinoctial, in the points of Aries and Libra, of 23°. 30'. which is the ſun's greateſt declination. This is by ſome called *via ſolis*, or the way of the ſun, becauſe the ſun, in his annual motion, never deviates from this line It is this line which is drawn on the globe, and not the Zodiack. But in the new aſtronomy the *Ecliptick* is that path among the fixed ſtars, which the earth appears to deſcribe to an eye placed in the ſun, as in its annual motion it runs round the ſun from Weſt to Eaſt. If you ſuppoſe this circle to be divided into twelve equal parts, they will be the twelve ſigns, each of which is denoted or diſtinguiſhed by ſome aſteriſm or conſtellation. *Harris.*

All ſtars, that have their diſtance from the *Ecliptick* northwards not more than twenty-three degrees and a half, may, in progreſſion of time, have declination ſouthward, and move beyond the Equator. *Brown's Vulgar Errours, b.* iv. *c.* 13.

The terraqueous globe had the ſame ſite and poſition, in reſpect of the ſun, that it now hath: its axis was not parallel to that of the *Ecliptick*, but inclined in like manner as it is at preſent. *Woodward's Natural Hiſtory*, N°. 6.

The earth's rotation makes the night and day;
The ſun revolving through th' *Ecliptick* way,
Effects the various ſeaſons of the year. *Blackm. on the Creat.*

You muſt conceive an imaginary plane, which paſſing through the center of the ſun, and the earth, extends itſelf on all ſides as far as the firmament: this plane is called the *Ecliptick*, and in this the center of the earth is perpetually carried, without any deviation. *Bentley's Sermons.*

EC'LOGUE. *n. ſ.* [ἐκλογὴ.] A paſtoral poem ſo called, becauſe *Virgil* called his paſtorals eclogues.

What exclaiming praiſes Baſilius gave this *eclogue* any man may gueſs, that knows love is better than ſpectacles to make every thing ſeem great. *Sidney.*

It is not ſufficient that the ſentences be brief, the whole *eclogue* ſhould be ſo too. *Pope.*

ECO'NOMY. *n. ſ.* [οἰκονομία. This word is often written, from its derivation, *œconomy*; but *œ* being no diphthong in Engliſh, it is placed here with the authorities for different orthography.]

1. The management of a family; the government of a houſhold.

By St. Paul's *economy* the heir differs nothing from a ſervant, while he is in his minority; ſo a ſervant ſhould differ nothing from a child in the ſubſtantial part. *Taylor's Rule of living holy.*

2. Frugality; diſcretion of expence; laudable parſimony.

Particular ſums are not laid out to the greateſt advantage in his *economy*; but are ſometimes ſuffered to run waſte, while he is only careful of the main. *Dryden's State of Innocence, Preface.*

I have no other notion of *economy*, than that it is the parent of liberty and eaſe. *Swift to Lord Bolingbroke.*

3. Diſpoſition of things; regulation.

All the divine and infinitely wiſe ways of *economy* that God could uſe towards a rational creature, oblige mankind to that courſe of living which is moſt agreeable to our nature. *Hamm.*

4. The diſpoſition or arrangement of any work.

In the Greek poets, as alſo in Plautus, we ſhall ſee the *economy* and diſpoſition of poems better obſerved than in Terence. *Ben. Johnſon's Diſcoveries.*

If this *economy* muſt be obſerved in the minuteſt parts of an epick poem, what ſoul, though ſent into the world with great advantages of nature, cultivated with the liberal arts and ſciences, can be ſufficient to inform the body of ſo great a work? *Dryden's Dedication to the Æn.*

5. Syſtem of motions; diſtribution of every thing active or paſſive to its proper place.

Theſe the ſtrainers aid,
That, by a conſtant ſeparation made,
They may a due *economy* maintain,
Exclude the noxious parts, the good retain. *Blackm. Creat.*

ECO'NOMICK. } *adj.* [from *economy.*]
ECO'NOMICAL. }

1. Pertaining to the regulation of an houſhold.

Her quick'ning power in ev'ry living part,
Doth as a nurſe, or as a mother ſerve;
And doth employ her *economick* art,
And buſy care, her houſhold to preſerve. *Davies.*

In *economical* affairs, having propoſed the government of a family, we conſider the proper means to effect it. *Watts.*

2. Frugal.

Some are ſo plainly *economical*, as even to deſire that the ſeat be well watered, and well fuelled. *Wotton's Architect.*

ECPHRA'CTICKS. *n. ſ.* [ἐκ and φράττω.] Such medicines as render tough humours more thin, ſo as to promote their diſcharge. *Quincy.*

Procure the blood a free courſe, ventilation, and tranſpiration, by ſuitable purges and *ecphractick* medicines. *Harvey.*

E'CSTASY. *n. ſ.* [ἔκστασις.]

1. Any paſſion by which the thoughts are abſorbed, and in which the mind is for a time loſt.

Follow them ſwiftly,
And hinder them from what this *ecſtaſy*
May now provoke them to. *Shakeſpeare's Tempeſt.*

'T may be
No longer joy there, but an *ecſtaſy.* *Suckling.*

Whether what we call *ecſtaſy* be not dreaming with our eyes open, I leave to be examined. *Locke.*

2. Exceſſive joy; rapture.

O, love, be moderate! Allay thy *ecſtaſy!* *Shakeſpeare.*

The religious pleaſure of a well diſpoſed mind moves gently, and therefore conſtantly: it does not affect by rapture and *ecſtaſy*; but is like the pleaſure of health, ſtill and ſober. *South's Sermons.*

Each delighted, and delighting, gives
The pleaſing *ecſtaſy* which each receives. *Prior.*

A pleaſure, which no language can expreſs;
An *ecſtaſy*, that mothers only feel,
Plays round my heart. *Phillips's Diſtreſt Mother.*

3. Enthuſiaſm; exceſſive elevation of the mind.

He lov'd me well, and oft would beg me ſing;
Which when I did, he on the tender graſs
Would ſit, and hearken even to *ecſtaſy.* *Milton.*

4. Exceſſive grief or anxiety. This is not now uſed.

Sighs and groans, and ſhrieks that rend the air,
Are made, not mark'd; where violent ſorrow ſeems
A modern *ecſtaſy.* *Shakeſpeare's Macbeth.*

Better be with the dead,
Than on the torture of the mind to lie
In reſtleſs *ecſtaſy.* *Shakeſpeare's Macbeth.*

5. Madneſs; diſtraction. This ſenſe is not now in uſe.

Now ſee that noble and moſt ſovereign reaſon,

Like ſweet bells jangled out of tune, and harſh,
That unmatch'd form, and feature of blown youth,
Blaſted with *ecſtaſy*. *Shakeſpeare's Hamlet.*

E'CSTASIED. *adj.* [from *ecſtaſy*] Raviſhed; filled with enthuſiaſm.

These are as common to the inanimate things as to the moſt *ecſtaſied* ſoul upon earth. *Norris.*

ECSTA'TICAL. } *adj.* [ἐκςατικός.]
ECSTA'TICK. }

1. Raviſhed; rapturous; elevated to ecſtaſy.

There doth my ſoul in holy viſion ſit,
In penſive trance, and anguiſh, and *ecſtatick* fit. *Milton.*

When one of them, after an *ecſtatical* manner, fell down before an angel, he was ſeverely rebuked, and bidden to worſhip God. *Stillingfleet's Def. of Diſc. on Rom. Idol.*

In trance *ecſtatick* may thy pangs be drown'd;
Bright clouds deſcend, and angels watch thee round. *Pope.*

2. In the higheſt degree of joy.

To gain Peſcennius one employs his ſchemes;
One graſps a Cecrops in *ecſtatick* dreams. *Pope.*

3. Tending to external objects. This ſenſe is, I think, only to be found once, though agreeable enough to the derivation.

I find in me a great deal of *ecſtatical* love, which continually carries me out to good without myſelf. *Norris.*

E'CTYPE. *n. ſ.* [ἔκτυπος.] A copy.

The complex ideas of ſubſtances are *ectypes*, copies, but not perfect ones, not adequate. *Locke.*

E'CURIE. *n. ſ.* [French; *equus*, Latin.] A place covered for the lodging or houſing of horſes.

EDA'CIOUS *adj.* [*edax*, Latin.] Eating; voracious; devouring; predatory; ravenous; rapacious; greedy.

EDA'CITY. *n. ſ.* [*edacitas*, Latin.] Voracity; ravenouſneſs; greedineſs; rapacity.

The wolf is a beaſt of great *edacity* and digeſtion: it may be the parts of him comfort the bowels. *Bacon's Nat. Hiſtory.*

To E'DDER. *v. a.* [probably from *edge.*] To bind or interweave a fence.

To add ſtrength to the hedge, *edder* it; which is, bind the top of the ſtakes with ſome ſmall long poles on each ſide. *Mortimer's Huſbandry.*

E'DDER. *n. ſ.* [from the verb.] Such fencewood as is commonly put upon the top of fences, and binds or interweaves each other.

In lopping and felling, ſave *edder* and ſtake,
Thine hedges, as needeth, to mend or to make. *Tuſſer.*

E'DDY. *n. ſ.* [eð, *backward, again*, and ea, *water*, Saxon.]

1. The water that by ſome repercuſſion, or oppoſite wind, runs contrary to the main ſtream.

My praiſes are as a bulruſh upon a ſtream: if they ſink not, 'tis becauſe they are born up by the ſtrength of the current, which ſupports their lightneſs; but they are carried round again, and return on the *eddy* where they firſt began. *Dryden.*

2. Whirlpool; circular motion.

The wild waves maſter'd him, and ſuck'd him in,
And ſmiling *eddies* dimpled on the main. *Dryd. Ann. Mirab.*

So, where our wide Numidian waſtes extend,
Sudden th' impetuous hurricanes deſcend,
Wheel through the air, in circling *eddies* play,
Tear up the ſands, and ſweep whole plains away. *Add. Cato.*

E'DDY. *adj.* Whirling; moving circularly.

And chaff with *eddy* winds is whirl'd around,
And dancing leaves are lifted from the ground. *Dryd. Virgil.*

EDEMATO'SE. *adj.* [οἴδημα.] Swelling; full of humours. See ŒDEMATOUS.

A feroſity obſtructing the glands may be watery, *edematoſe*, and ſchirrous, according to the viſcoſity of the humour. *Arb.*

EDE'NTATED. *adj.* [*edentatus*, Latin.] Deprived of teeth. *Dict.*

EDGE *n. ſ.* [ecȝe, Saxon.]

1. The thin or cutting part of a blade.

Seize upon Fife; give to the *edge* o' th' ſword
His wife, his babes. *Shakeſpeare's Macbeth.*

He that will a good *edge* win,
Muſt forge thick, and grind thin. *Proverb.*

The *edge* of war, like an ill ſheathed knife,
No more ſhall cut his maſter. *Shakeſpeare's Henry* IV. *p.* i.

'Tis ſlander,
Whoſe *edge* is ſharper than the ſword. *Shakeſp. Cymbeline.*

If the iron be blunt, and he do not whet the *edge*, then muſt he put to more ſtrength. *Eccl.* x. 10.

2. A narrow part riſing from a broader.

Some harrow their ground over, and then plow it upon an *edge*. *Mortimer's Huſbandry.*

3. Brink; margin; extremity.

The rays which paſs very near to the *edges* of any body, are bent a little by the action of the body. *Newton's Opt.*

We have, for many years, walked upon the *edge* of a precipice, while nothing but the ſlender thread of human life has held us from ſinking into endleſs miſery. *Rogers's Sermons.*

Yes, the laſt pen for freedom let me draw,
When truth ſtands trembling on the *edge* of law. *Pope.*

4. Sharpneſs; proper diſpoſition for action or operation; intenſeneſs of deſire.

Give him a further *edge*,
And drive his purpoſe into theſe delights. *Shakeſp. Hamlet.*

But when long time the wretches thoughts refin'd,
When want had ſet an *edge* upon their mind,
Then various cares their working thoughts employ'd,
And that which each invented, all enjoy'd. *Creech's Manil.*

Silence and ſolitude ſet an *edge* upon the genius, and cauſe a greater application. *Dryden's Dufreſnoy.*

5. Keenneſs; acrimony of temper.

Abate the *edge* of traitors, gracious Lord!
That would reduce theſe bloody days again. *Shak. Rich.* III.

6. *To ſet teeth on* EDGE. To cauſe a tingling pain in the teeth.

A harſh grating tune *ſetteth the teeth on edge*. *Bacon.*

To EDGE. *v. a.* [from the noun.]

1. To ſharpen; to enable to cut.

There ſat ſhe rolling her alluring eyes,
To *edge* her champion's ſword, and urge my ruin. *Dryden.*

2. To furniſh with an edge.

I fell'd along a man of bearded face,
His limbs all cover'd with a ſhining caſe;
So wond'rous hard, and ſo ſecure of wound,
It made my ſword, though *edg'd* with flint, rebound. *Dryd.*

3. To border with any thing; to fringe.

Their long deſcending train,
With rubies *edg'd*, and ſaphires, ſwept the plain. *Dryden.*

I rid over hanging hills, whoſe tops were *edged* with groves, and whoſe feet were watered with winding rivers. *Pope.*

4. To exaſperate; to embitter.

By ſuch reaſonings the ſimple were blinded, and the malicious *edged*. *Hayward.*

He was indigent and low in money, which perhaps might have a little *edged* his deſperation. *Wotton's Life of D. of Bucks.*

5. To put forward beyond a line.

Edging by degrees their chairs forwards, they were in a little time got up cloſe to one another. *Locke.*

To EDGE. *v. n.* [perhaps from eð, backward, Saxon.] To move forward againſt any power; going cloſe upon a wind, as if upon its ſkirts or border, and ſo ſailing ſlow.

I muſt *edge* upon a point of wind,
And make ſlow way. *Dryden's Cleomenes.*

E'DGED. *participial adj.* [from *edge.*] Sharp; not blunt.

We find that ſubtile or *edged* quantities do prevail over blunt ones. *Digby on Bodies.*

E'DGING. *n. ſ.* [from *edge.*]

1. What is added to any thing by way of ornament.

The garland which I wove for you to wear,
And border'd with a roſy *edging* round. *Dryden.*

A woman branches out into a long diſſertation upon the *edging* of a petticoat. *Addiſon's Spectator*, N°. 247.

2. A narrow lace.

E'DGELESS. *adj.* [from *edge.*] Blunt; obtuſe; unable to cut.

To-morrow in the battle think on me,
And fall thy *edgeleſs* ſword; deſpair and die. *Shakeſ. R.* III.

They are only *edgeleſs* weapons it hath to encounter. *Decay of Piety.*

E'DGETOOL. *n. ſ.* [*edge* and *tool.*] A tool made ſharp to cut.

There muſt be no playing with things ſacred, nor jeſting with *edgetools*. *L'Eſtrange.*

Nurſes from their children keep *edgetools*. *Dorſet.*

I ſhall exerciſe upon ſteel, and its ſeveral ſorts; and what ſort is fitteſt for *edgetools*, which for ſprings. *Moxon's Mech. Ex.*

E'DGEWISE. *adv.* [*edge* and *wiſe.*] With the edge put into any particular direction.

Should the flat ſide be objected to the ſtream, it would be ſoon turned *edgewiſe* by the force of it. *Ray on the Creation.*

E'DIBLE. *adj.* [from *edo*, Latin.] Fit to be eaten; fit for food.

Some fleſh is not *edible*; as horſes and dogs. *Bacon.*

Wheat and barley, and the like, are made either *edible* or potable by man's art and induſtry. *More againſt Atheiſm.*

Some of the fungus kind, gathered for *edible* muſhrooms, have produced a difficulty of breathing. *Arbuthnot on Aliments.*

The *edible* creation decks the board. *Prior.*

E'DICT. *n. ſ.* [*edictum*, Latin.] A proclamation of command or prohibition; a law promulgated.

When an abſolute monarch commandeth his ſubjects that which ſeemeth good in his own diſcretion, hath not his *edict* the force of a law. *Hooker, b.* i. *ſ.* 10.

The great king of kings,
Hath in the table of his law commanded
That thou ſhalt do no murder; will you then
Spurn at his *edict*, and fulfil a man's? *Shakeſp. Richard* III.

Severe decrees may keep our tongues in awe,
But to our thoughts what *edict* can give law? *Dryd. Aureng.*

The miniſters are always preaching, and the governours putting out *edicts*, againſt gaming and fine cloaths. *Addiſon.*

EDIFICA'TION. *n. ſ.* [*ædificatio*, Latin.]

1. The act of building up man in the faith; improvement in holineſs.

Our bleſſed Saviour told us, that we muſt account for every idle word, not meaning that every word which is not deſigned to *edification*, or is leſs prudent, ſhall be reckoned for a ſin. *Taylor's Rule of living holy.*

2. Improvement;

2. Improvement; instruction.

Out of these magazines I shall supply the town with what may tend to their *edification*. *Addison's Guardian*, N°. 114.

E'DIFICE. *n. s.* [*ædificium*, Latin.] A fabrick; a building; a structure.

My love was like a fair house built on another man's ground; so that I have lost my *edifice* by mistaking the place where I erected it. *Shakesp. Merry Wives of Windsor.*

He built
So spacious, and his line stretch'd out so far,
That man may know he dwells not in his own;
An *edifice* too large for him to fill. *Milton's Paradise Lost.*

The *edifice*, where all were met to see him,
Upon their heads and on his own he pull'd. *Milton's Agon.*

As Tuscan pillars owe their original to this country, the architects always give them a place in *edifices* raised in Tuscany *Addison's Remarks on Italy.*

He must be an idiot that cannot discern more strokes of workmanship in the structure of an animal than in the most elegant *edifice*. *Bentley's Sermons.*

EDIFI'ER. *n. s.* [from *edify*.] One that improves or instructs another.

To EDIFY'. *v. a.* [*edifico*, Latin.]

1. To build.

Men have *edify'd*
A lofty temple, and perfum'd an altar to thy name. *Chapm.*

2. To instruct; to improve.

He who speaketh no more than *edifieth*, is undeservedly reprehended for much speaking. *Hooker, b.* v. *s.* 32.

Men are *edified*, when either their understanding is taught somewhat whereof, in such actions, it behoveth all men to consider, or when their hearts are moved with any affection suitable thereunto. *Hooker, b.* iv. *s.* 1.

Life is no life, without the blessing of a friendly and an *edifying* conversation. *L'Estrange.*

He gave, he taught; and *edify'd* the more,
Because he shew'd, by proof, 'twas easy to be poor. *Dryd.*

3. To teach; to persuade.

You shall hardly *edify* me, that those nations might not, by the law of nature, have been subdued by any nation that had only policy and moral virtue. *Bacon's holy War.*

E'DILE. *n. s.* [*ædilis*, Latin.] The title of a magistrate in old Rome, whose office seems in some particulars to have resembled that of our justices of peace.

The *edile*, ho! let him be apprehended. *Shak. Coriolanus.*

EDI'TION. *n. s.* [*editio*, Latin.]

1. Publication of any thing, particularly of a book.

These are of the second *edition*. *Shak. Mer. Wiv. of Winds.*

This English *edition* is not so properly a translation, as a new composition upon the same ground. *Burnet.*

2. Republication; generally with some revisal or correcting.

The business of our redemption is to rub over the defaced copy of the creation, to reprint God's image upon the soul, and to set forth nature in a second and a fairer *edition*. *South.*

I cannot go so far as he who published the last *edition* of him. *Dryden's Fables, Preface.*

The Code, composed hastily, was forced to undergo an emendation, and to come forth in a second *edition*. *Baker.*

E'DITOR. *n. s.* [*editor*, Latin.] Publisher; he that revises or prepares any work for publication.

When a different reading gives us a different sense, or a new elegance in an author, the *editor* does very well in taking notice of it. *Addison's Spectator*, N°. 450.

This nonsense got into all the editions by a mistake of the stage *editors*. *Pope's Notes on Shakesp. Henry* V.

To E'DUCATE. *v. a.* [*educo*, Latin.] To breed; to bring up; to instruct youth.

Their young succession all their cares employ;
They breed, they brood, instruct and *educate*,
And make provision for the future state. *Dryd. Virg. Georg.*

Education is worse, in proportion to the grandeur of the parents: if the whole world were under one monarch, the heir of that monarch would be the worst *educated* mortal since the creation. *Swift on Modern Education.*

EDUCA'TION. *n. s.* [from *educate*.] Formation of manners in youth; the manner of breeding youth; nurture.

Education and instruction are the means, the one by use, the other by precept, to make our natural faculty of reason both the better and the sooner to judge rightly between truth and error, good and evil. *Hooker, b.* i. *s.* 6.

All nations have agreed in the necessity of a strict *education*, which consisted in the observance of moral duties. *Swift.*

To EDU'CE. *v. a.* [*educo*, Latin.] To bring out; to extract; to produce from a state of occultation.

All that can be made of the power of matter, is a receptive capacity; and we may as well affirm, that the world was *educed* out of the power of space, and give that as a reason of its original: in this language, to grow rich, were to *educe* money out of the power of the pocket. *Glanv. Sceps.*

This matter must have lain eternally confined to its beds of earth, were there not this agent to *educe* it thence. *Woodward's Natural History, p.* iii.

Th' eternal art *educes* good from ill,
Grafts on this passion our best principle. *Pope's Ess. on Man.*

EDU'CTION. *n. s.* [from *educe*.] The act of bringing any thing into view.

To EDU'LCORATE. *v. n.* [from *dulcis*, Latin.] To sweeten.

EDULCORA'TION. *n. s.* [from *edulcorate*.] The act of sweetening.

To EEK. *v. a.* [eacan, ecan, ican, Sax. *eak*, Scott. *eck*, Erse.]

1. To make bigger by the addition of another piece.

2. To supply any deficiency. See EKE.

Hence endless penance for our fault I pay;
But that redoubled crime, with vengeance new,
Thou biddest me to *eke*. *Fairy Queen, b.* i. *c.* 5. *s.* 42.

EEL. *n. s.* [æl, Saxon; *aal*, German.] A serpentine slimy fish, that lurks in mud.

Is the adder better than the *eel*,
Because his painted skin contents the eye? *Shakespeare.*

The Cockney put the *eels* i' th' pasty alive. *Shak. K. Lear.*

E'EN. *adv.* Contracted from *even*. See EVEN.

Says the satyr, if you have a trick of blowing hot and cold out of the same mouth, I have *e'en* done with ye. *L'Estrange.*

EFF. *n. s.* See EFT.

E'FFABLE. *adj.* [*effabilis*, Latin.] Expressive; utterable. *Dict.*

To EFFA'CE. *v. a* [*effacer*, French.]

1. To destroy any form painted, or carved.

2. To make no more legible or visible; to blot out; to strike out.

Characters drawn on dust, the first breath of wind *effaces*. *Locke.*

It was ordered, that his name should be *effaced* out of all publick registers. *Addison's Remarks on Italy.*

Time, I said, may happily *efface*
That cruel image of the king's disgrace. *Prior.*

Otway fail'd to polish or refine,
And fluent Shakespeare scarce *effac'd* a line. *Pope.*

3. To destroy; to wear away.

Nor our admission shall your realm disgrace,
Nor length of time our gratitude *efface*. *Dryden's Æn.*

EFFE'CT. *n. s.* [*effectus*, Latin.]

1. That which is produced by an operating cause.

You may see by her example, in herself wise, and of others beloved, that neither folly is the cause of vehement love, nor reproach the *effect*. *Sidney, b.* ii.

Effect is the substance produced, or simple idea introduced into any subject, by the exerting of power? *Locke.*

We see the pernicious *effects* of luxury in the antient Romans, who immediately found themselves poor as soon as this vice got footing among them. *Addison on Italy.*

2. Consequence; event.

No man, in *effect*, doth accompany with others, but he learneth, ere he is aware, some gesture, or voice, or fashion. *Bacon's Natural History*, N°. 236.

To say of a celebrated piece that there are faults in it, is, in *effect*, to say that the author of it is a man. *Addis. Guard.*

3. Purpose; intention; general intent.

They spake to her to that *effect*. *2 Chro.* xxxiv. 22.

4. Consequence intended; success; advantage.

Christ is become of no *effect* unto you. *Gal.* v. 4.

He should depart only with a title, the *effect* whereof he should not be possessed of, before he had very well deserved it. *Clarendon, b.* viii.

The custom or institution has hitherto proved without *effect*, and has neither extinguished the practice of such crimes, nor lessened the numbers of such criminals. *Temple.*

5. Completion; perfection.

Semblant art shall carve the fair *effect*,
And full atchievement of thy great designs. *Prior.*

6. Reality; not mere appearance.

In shew, a marvellous indifferently composed senate ecclesiastical was to govern, but in *effect* one only man should, as the spirit and soul of the residue, do all in all. *Hooker.*

State and wealth, the business and the crowd,
Seems at this distance but a darker cloud;
And is to him, who rightly things esteems,
No other in *effect* than what it seems. *Denham.*

7. [In the plural.] Goods; moveables.

What form of prayer
Can serve my turn? Forgive me my foul murther!
That cannot be, since I am still possest
Of those *effects* for which I did the murther,
My crown, mine own ambition, and my queen. *Shakesp.*

The emperor knew that they could not convey away many of their *effects*. *Addison's Spectator*, N°. 499.

To EFFE'CT. *v. a.* [*efficio*, Latin.]

1. To bring to pass; to attempt with success; to atchieve; to accomplish as an agent.

Being consul, I not doubt t' *effect*
All that you wish. *Ben. Johns. Catil.*

2. To produce as a cause.

The change made of that syrup into a purple colour, was *effected* by the vinegar. *Boyle on Colours.*

EFFE'CTIBLE.

EFFE'CTIBLE. *adj.* [from *effect.*] Performable; practicable; feasible.

That a pot full of ashes will still contain as much water as it would without them, is not *effectible* upon the strictest experiment. *Brown's Vulgar Errours, b.* ii. *c.* 3.

EFFE'CTIVE. *adj.* [from *effect.*]

1. Having the power to produce effects.

They are not *effective* of any thing, nor leave no work behind them. *Bacon.*

If any mystery, rite, or sacrament be *effective* of any spiritual blessings, then this much more, as having the prerogative and principality above every thing else. *Taylor.*

There is nothing in words and stiles but suitableness, that makes them acceptable and *effective.* *Glanv. Sceps. Preface.*

2. Operative; active.

Nor do they speak properly who say that time consumeth all things; for time is not *effective*, nor are bodies destroyed by it. *Brown's Vulgar Errours, b.* iv. *c.* 12.

3. Producing effects; efficient.

Whosoever is an *effective* real cause of doing his neighbour wrong is criminal, by what instrument soever he does it. *Taylor.*

4. Having the power of operation; useful, as *effective* men in an army.

EFFE'CTIVELY. *adv.* [from *effective*] Powerfully; with real operation.

This *effectively* resists the devil, and suffers us to receive no hurt from him. *Taylor's Rule of living holy.*

EFFE'CTLESS. *adj.* [from *effect.*] Without effect; impotent; useless; unmeaning.

I'll chop off my hands;
In bootless prayer have they been held up,
And they have serv'd me to *effectless* use. *Shak. Tit. Andron.*

EFFE'CTOR. *n. s.* [*effector*, Latin.]

1. He that produces any effect.

2. Maker; Creator.

We commemorate the creation, and pay worship to that infinite Being who was the *effector* of it. *Derham's Phy. Theol.*

EFFE'CTUAL. *adj* [*effectuél*, French]

1. Productive of effects; powerful to a degree adequate to the occasion; operative; efficacious.

The reading of Scripture is *effectual*, as well to lay even the first foundation, as to add degrees of farther perfection, in the fear of God. *Hooker, b.* v. *s.* 22.

The communication of thy faith may become *effectual*, by the acknowledging of every good thing. *Philem.* 6.

2. Veracious; expressive of facts. A sense not in use.

Reprove my allegation, if you can;
Or else conclude my words *effectual.* *Shakesp. Henry* VI.

EFFE'CTUALLY. *adv.* [from *effectual*] In a manner productive of the consequence intended; efficaciously.

Sometimes the sight of the altar, and decent preparations for devotion, may compose and recover the wandering mind more *effectually* than a sermon. *South's Sermons.*

This is a subject of that vast latitude, that the strength of one man will scarcely be sufficient *effectually* to carry it on. *Woodward's Natural History.*

To EFFE'CTUATE. *v. a.* [*effectuer*, French.] To bring to pass; to fulfil.

He found means to acquaint himself with a nobleman, to whom discovering what he was, he found him a fit instrument to *effectuate* his desire. *Sidney, b.* ii.

EFFE'MINACY. *n. s.* [from *effeminate*]

1. Admission of the qualities of a woman; softness; unmanly delicacy; mean submission.

But foul *effeminacy* held me yok'd
Her bond-slave: O indignity, O blot
To honour and religion! *Milton's Agonistes, l.* 410.

2. Lasciviousness; loose pleasure.

So long as idleness is quite shut out from our lives, all the sins of wantonness, softness, and *effeminacy* are prevented. *Tayl.*

EFFE'MINATE. *adj.* [*effeminatus*, Latin.]

1. Having the qualities of a woman; womanish; soft to an unmanly degree; voluptuous; tender; luxurious.

After the slaughter of so many peers,
Shall we at last conclude *effeminate* peace? *Shak. Henry* VI.

The king, by his voluptuous life and mean marriage, became *effeminate*, and less sensible of honour. *Bacon's Hen.* VII.

From man's *effeminate* slackness it begins,
Who should better hold his place. *Milton.*
The more *effeminate* and soft his life,
The more his fame to struggle to the field. *Dryd. Don Seb.*

2. Womanlike; soft without reproach: a sense not in use.

As well we know your tenderness of heart,
And gentle, kind, *effeminate* remorse. *Shakespeare's R.* III.

To EFFE'MINATE. *v. a.* [*effemino*, Latin.] To make womanish; to weaken; to emasculate; to unman.

When one is sure it will not corrupt or *effeminate* childrens minds, and make them fond of trifles, I think all things should be contrived to their satisfaction. *Locke.*

To EFFE'MINATE. *v. n.* To grow womanish; to soften; to melt into weakness.

In a slothful peace both courage will *effeminate* and manners corrupt. *Pope.*

EFFE'MINATION. *n. s.* [from *effeminate.*] The state of one grown womanish; the state of one emasculated or unmanned.

Vices it figured; not only feneration, or usury, from its fecundity and superfetation, but from this mixture of sexes, degenerate *effemination.* *Brown's Vulgar Errours, b.* iii *c.* 17.

To EFFE'RVESCE. *v. n.* [*effervesco*, Latin.] To generate heat by intestine motion.

The compound spirit of nitre, put to oil of cloves, will *effervesce* even to a flame *Mead on Poisons.*

EFFE'RVESCENCE. *n. s.* [from *efferveo*, Latin.] The act of growing hot; production of heat by intestine motion.

In the chymical sense, *effervescence* signifies an intestine motion, produced by mixing two bodies together that lay at rest before; attended sometimes with a hissing noise, frothing, and ebullition. *Arbuthnot on Aliments.*

Take chalk, ignite it in a crucible, and then powder it: put it into strong spirit of nitre, 'till it becomes sweetish, and makes no *effervescence* upon the injection of the chalk. *Grew.*

Hot springs do not owe their heat to any colluctation or *effervescence* of the minerals in them, but to subterranean heat or fire. *Woodward's Natural History, p.* iii.

EFFE'TE. *adj.* [*effætus*, Latin.]

1. Barren; disabled from generation.

It is probable that females have in them the seeds of all the young they will afterwards bring forth, which, all spent and exhausted, the animal becomes barren and *effete.* *Ray.*

In most countries the earth would be so parched and *effete* by the drought, that it would afford but one harvest. *Bentley.*

2. Worn out with age.

All that can be allowed him now, is to refresh his decrepit, *effete* sensuality with the history of his former life. *South.*

EFFICA'CIOUS. *adj.* [*efficax*, Latin.] Productive of effects; powerful to produce the consequence intended.

A glowing drop with hollow'd steel
He takes, and by one *efficacious* breath
Dilates to cube or square. *Phillips.*

EFFICA'CIOUSLY. *adv* [from *efficacious.*] Effectually; in such a manner as to produce the consequence desired.

If we find that any other body strikes *efficaciously* enough upon it, we cannot doubt but it will move that way which the striking body impels it. *Digby on Bodies.*

E'FFICACY. *n s.* [from *efficax*, Latin.] Power to produce effects; production of the consequence intended.

Whatsoever is spoken concerning the *efficacy* or necessity of God's word, the same they tie and restrain only unto sermons. *Hooker, b.* v. *s.* 21.

Whether if they had tasted the tree of life before that of good and evil, they had suffered the curse of mortality; or whether the *efficacy* of the one had not overpowered the penalty of the other, we leave it unto God. *Brown's Vulg. Err.*

Efficacy is a power of speech which represents a thing, by presenting to our minds the lively ideas or forms of things. *Peacham on Drawing.*

The apostle tells us of the success and *efficacy* of the Gospel upon the minds of men; and, for this reason, he calls it the power of God unto salvation. *Tillotson's Sermons.*

The arguments drawn from the goodness of God have a prevailing *efficacy* to induce men to repent. *Rogers, Sermon* 16.

EFFI'CIENCE. } *n. s.* [from *efficio*, Latin.] The act of producing effects; agency.
EFFI'CIENCY. }

The manner of this divine *efficiency* being far above us, we are no more able to conceive by our reason, than creatures unreasonable by their sense are able to apprehend after what manner we dispose and order the course of our affairs. *Hooker, b.* i.

That they are carried by the manuduction of a rule, is evident; but what that regulating *efficiency* should be, is not easily determined. *Glanv. Sceps. c.* iv.

Sinning against conscience has no special productive *efficiency* of this particular sort of sinning, more than of any other. *South's Sermons.*

A pious will is the means to enlighten the understanding in the truth of Christianity, upon the account of a natural *efficiency*: a will so disposed, will engage the mind in a severe search. *South's Sermons.*

Gravity does not proceed from the *efficiency* of any contingent and unstable agents; but stands on a basis more firm, being entirely owing to the direct concourse of the power of the Author of nature. *Woodward's Natural History.*

EFFI'CIENT. *n s.* [*efficius*, Latin.]

1. The cause which makes effects to be what they are.

God, which moveth meer natural agents as an *efficient* only, doth otherwise move intellectual creatures, and especially his holy angels. *Hooker, b.* i. *s.* 3.

2. He that makes; the effector.

Observations of the order of nature are of use to carry the mind up to the admiration of the great *efficient* of the world. *Hale's Origin of Mankind.*

EFFI'CIENT. *adj.* Causing effects; that which makes the effect to be what it is.

Your

Your answering in the final cause, makes me believe you are at a loss for the *efficient*. *Collier on Thought.*

To EFFI'GIATE. *v. a.* [*effigio*, Latin.] To form in semblance; to image.

EFFIGIA'TION. *n. s.* [from *effigiate*.] The act of imaging; or forming the resemblance of things or persons. *Dict.*

EFFI'GIES. } *n. s.* [*effigies*, Latin.] Resemblance; image in
EFFI'GY. } painting or sculpture; representation; idea.

We behold the species of eloquence in our minds, the *effigies* or actual image of which we seek in the organs of our hearing. *Dryden's Dufresnoy, Preface.*

EFFLORE'SCENCE. } *n. s.* [*effloresco*, Latin.]
EFFLORE'SCENCY. }

1. Production of flowers.

Where there is less heat, there the spirit of the plant is digested, and severed ftom the grosser juice in *efflorescence*. *Bac.*

2. Excrescencies in the form of flowers.

Two white sparry incrustations, with *efflorescencies* in form of shrubs, formed by the trickling of water. *Woodward.*

3. [In physick.] The breaking out of some humours in the skin; as in the measles, and the like. *Quincy.*

A wart beginneth in the cutis, and seemeth to be an *efflorescence* of the serum of the blood. *Wiseman's Surgery.*

EFFLORE'SCENT. *adj.* [*effloresco*, Lat.] Shooting out in form of flowers.

Yellowish *efflorescent* sparry incrustations on stone. *Woodw.*

EFFLU'ENCE. *n. s.* [*effluo*, Latin.] That which issues from some other principle.

Bright *effluence* of bright essence increate. *Milt. P. Lost.*
From the bright *effluence* of his deed
They borrow that reflected light,
With which the lasting lamp they feed,
Whose beams dispel the damps of envious night. *Prior.*

EFFLU'VIA. } *n. s.* [from *effluo*, Latin.] Those small particles
EFFLU'VIUM. } which are continually flying off from bodies; the subtilty and fineness of which appears from their being able, a long time together, to produce very sensible effects, without any sensible diminution of the body from whence they arise. *Quincy.*

If the earth were an electrick body, and the air but the *effluvium* thereof, we might perhaps believe that from attraction, and by effluxion, bodies tended to the earth. *Brown's Vulgar Errours, b.* ii. *c.* 2.

Neither the earth's diurnal revolution upon its axis, nor any magnetick *effluvia* of the earth, nor the air, or atmosphere which environs the earth, can produce gravity. *Woodward.*

If these *effluvia*, which do upward tend,
Because less heavy than the air, ascend;
Why do they ever from their height retreat,
And why return to seek their central seat? *Blackm. Creat.*

E'FFLUX. *n. s.* [*effluxus*, Latin.]

1. The act of flowing out.

Through the daily and copious *efflux* of matter through the orifice of a deep ulcer in his thigh, he was reduced to a skeleton. *Harvey on Consumptions.*

2. Effusion.

The first *efflux* of mens piety, after receiving of the faith, was the selling and consecrating their possessions. *Hammond.*

3. That which flows from something else; emanation.

Prime chearer, light!
Of all material beings, first and best!
Efflux divine! *Thomson's Summer, l.* 80.

To EFFLU'X. *v. n.* [*effluo*, Latin.] To run out; to flow away.

Five thousand and some odd centuries of years are *effluxed* since the creation. *Boyle's Seraphick Love.*

EFFLU'XION. *n. s.* [*effluxum*, Latin.]

1. The act of flowing out.

By *effluxion* and attraction bodies tend towards the earth. *Brown.*

2. That which flows out; effluvium; emanation.

There are some light *effluxions* from spirit to spirit, when men are one with another; as from body to body. *Bacon.*

To EFFO'RCE. *v. a.* [*efforcer*, French.]

1. To force; to break through by violence.

In all that room was nothing to be seen,
But huge great iron chests and coffers strong,
All barr'd with double bonds, that ne'er could ween
Them to *efforce* by violence or wrong. *Fairy Queen, b.* ii.

2. To force; to ravish; to violate by force.

Then 'gan her beauty shine as brightest sky,
And burnt his beastly heart t' *efforce* her chastity. *Fa. Qu.*

To EFFO'RM. *n. s.* [*efformo*, Latin.] To make in any certain manner; to shape; to fashion.

Merciful and gracious, thou gavest us being, raising us from nothing, and *efforming* us after thy own image. *Taylor.*

EFFORMA'TION. *n. s.* [from *efform*.] The act of fashioning or giving form to.

They pretend to solve phænomena, and to give an account of the production and *efformation* of the universe. *Ray.*

Nature begins to set upon her work of *efformation*. *More.*

EFFO'RT. *n. s.* [*effort*, French.] Struggle; laborious endeavour.

If, after having gained victories, we had made the same *efforts* as if we had lost them, France could not have withstood us. *Addison on the State of the War.*

Though the same sun, with all diffusive rays,
Blush in the rose, and in the diamond blaze,
We prize the stronger *effort* of his pow'r,
And always set the gem above the flow'r. *Pope, Epist.* 1.

EFFO'SSION. *n. s.* [*effossumo*, Latin.] The act of digging up from the ground; deterration.

He set apart annual sums for the recovery of manuscripts, the *effossion* of coins, and the procuring of mummies. *Arbuthn.*

EFFRA'IABLE. *adj.* [*effroyable*, French.] Dreadful; frightful; terrible. A word not used.

Pestilential symptoms declare nothing a proportionate efficient of their *effraiable* nature, but arsenical fumes. *Harvey.*

E'FFRONTERY. *n. s.* [*effronterie*, Fr.] Impudence; shamelessness; contempt of reproach.

They could hardly contain themselves within one unworthy act, who had *effrontery* enough to commit or countenance it. *King Charles.*

Others with ignorance and insufficiency have self-admiration and *effrontery* to set up themselves. *Watts's Improv.*

A bold man's *effrontery*, in company with women, must be owing to his low opinion of them, and his high one of himself. *Clarissa.*

EFFU'LGENCE. *n. s.* [*effulgeo*, Latin.] Lustre; brightness; clarity; splendor.

On thee
Impress'd, th' *effulgence* of his glory abides. *Milt. Pa. Lost.*
Thy lustre, blest *effulgence*, can dispel
The clouds of error, and the gloom of hell. *Blackmore.*

EFFU'LGENT. *adj.* [*effulgens*, Latin.] Shining; bright; luminous.

How soon th' *effulgent* emanations fly
Through the blue gulph of interposing sky! *Blackmore.*
The downward sun
Looks out *effulgent*, from amid' the flash
Of broken clouds. *Thomson's Spring, l.* 185.

EFFU'MABILITY. *n. s.* [*fumus*, Latin.] The quality of flying away, or vapouring in fumes.

They seem to define mercury by volatility, or, if I may coin such a word, *effumability*. *Boyle's Scept. Chym.*

To EFFU'SE. *v. a.* [*effusus*, Latin.] To pour out; to spill; to shed.

He fell, and, deadly pale,
Groan'd out his soul, with gushing blood *effus'd*. *Milton.*
At last emerging from his nostrils wide,
And gushing mouth, *effus'd* the briny tide. *Pope's Odyssey.*

EFFU'SE. *n. s.* [from the verb.] Waste; effusion.

The air hath got into my deadly wounds,
And much *effuse* of blood doth make me faint. *Shak. H. VI.*

EFFU'SION. *n. s.* [*effusio*, Latin.]

1. The act of pouring out.

My heart hath melted at a lady's tears,
Being an ordinary inundation;
But this *effusion* of such manly drops,
This show'r, blown up by tempest of the soul,
Startles mine eyes, and makes me more amaz'd. *Shakesp.*

Our blessed Lord commanded the representation of his death, and sacrifice on the cross, should be made by breaking bread and *effusion* of wine. *Taylor's Worthy Communicant.*

If the flood-gates of heaven were any thing distinct from the forty days rain, their *effusion*, 'tis likely, was at this same time when the abyss was broken open. *Burnet's The. of Earth.*

2. Waste; the act of spilling or shedding.

When there was but as yet one only family in the world, no means of instruction, human or divine, could prevent *effusion* of blood. *Hooker, b.* i. *s.* 10.

Stop *effusion* of our Christian blood,
And 'stablish quietness. *Shakesp. Henry* VI.

Yet shall she be restor'd, since publick good
For private int'rest ought not be withstood,
To save th' *effusion* of my people's blood. *Dryd. Homer.*

3. The act of pouring out words.

Endless and senseless *effusions* of indigested prayers, often times disgrace, in most unsufferable manner, the worthiest part of Christian duty towards God. *Hooker, b.* v. *s.* 26.

4. Bounteous donation.

Such great force the gospel of Christ had then upon mens souls, melting them into that liberal *effusion* of all that they had. *Hammond on Fundamentals.*

5. The thing poured out.

Purge me with the blood of my redeemer, and I shall be clean; wash me with that precious *effusion*, and I shall be whiter than snow. *King Charles.*

EFFU'SIVE. *adj.* [from *effuse*.] Pouring out; dispersing.

The North-east spends its rage; and now shut up
Within its iron caves, th' *effusive* South
Warms the wide air. *Thomson's Spring, l.* 145.

EFT. *n.ſ.* [eꝼeꞇa, Saxon.] A newt; an evet; a ſmall kind of lizard that lives generally in the water.

Peacocks are beneficial to the places where they are kept, by clearing of them from ſnakes, adders and *efts*, upon which they will live. *Mortimer's Husbandry.*

The crocodile of Egypt is the lizard of Italy, and the *eft* in our country. *Nichols.*

EFT. *adv.* [eꝼꞇ, Saxon.] Soon; quickly; ſpeedily; ſhortly.

Eft through the thick they heard one rudely ruſh,
With noiſe whereof he from his lofty ſteed
Down fell to ground, and crept into a buſh,
To hide his coward head from dying dread. *Fairy Queen.*

Quite conſumed with flame,
The idol is of that eternal maid;
For ſo at leaſt I have preſerv'd the ſame,
With hands profane, from being *eft* betray'd. *Fairfax, b.* ii.

E'FTSOONS. *adv.* eꝼꞇ and ꞅoon.] Soon afterwards; in a ſhort time; again. An obſolete word.

He in their ſtead *eftſoons* placed Engliſhmen, who poſſeſſed all their lands. *Spenſer's State of Ireland.*

Eftſoons the nymphs, which now had flowers their fill,
Run all in haſte to ſee that ſilver brood. *Spenſer's Epithalam.*

The Germans deadly hated the Turks, whereof it was to be thought that new wars would *eftſoons* enſue. *Knolles's Hiſtory.*

Eftſoons, O ſweetheart kind, my love repay,
And all the year ſhall then be holiday. *Gay's Paſtorals.*

E. G. [*exempli gratia.*] For the ſake of an inſtance or example.

E'GER. *n ſ.* [See EAGER.] An impetuous and irregular flood or tide.

From the peculiar diſpoſition of the earth at the bottom, wherein quick excitations are made, may ariſe thoſe *egers* and flows in ſome eſtuaries and rivers; as is obſervable about Trent and Humber in England. *Brown's Vulgar Errours.*

To EGE'ST. *v. a* [*egero*, Latin.] To throw out food at the natural vents.

Divers creatures ſleep all the Winter; as the bear, the hedgehog, the bat, and the bee: theſe all wax fat when they ſleep, and *egeſt* not. *Bacon's Natural Hiſtory.* Nº. 899.

EGE'STION. *n.ſ.* [*egeſtus*, Latin.] The act of throwing out the digeſted food at the natural vents.

The animal ſoul or ſpirits manage as well their ſpontaneous actions as the natural or involuntary exertions of digeſtion, *egeſtion*, and circulation. *Hale's Origin of Mankind.*

EGG. *n.ſ.* [œᵹ, Saxon; *ough*, Erſe.]

1. That which is laid by feathered animals, from which their young is produced.

An *egg* was found, having lain many years at the bottom of a moat, where the earth had ſomewhat overgrown it; and this *egg* was come to the hardneſs of a ſtone, and the colours of the white and yolk perfect. *Bacon's Natural Hiſt.*

Eggs are perhaps the higheſt, moſt nouriſhing, and exalted of all animal food, and moſt indigeſtible. *Arbuthnot on Diet.*

2. The ſpawn or ſperm of other creatures.

Therefore think him as the ſerpent's *egg*,
Which, hatch'd, would, as his kind, grow miſchievous. *Sh.*

Ev'ry inſect of each different kind,
In its own *egg*, chear'd by the ſolar rays,
Organs involv'd and latent life diſplays. *Blackmore's Creation.*

3. Any thing faſhioned in the ſhape of an egg.

There was taken a great glaſs-bubble with a long neck, ſuch as chemiſts are wont to call a philoſophical *egg*. *Boyle.*

To EGG. *v. a.* [*eggia*, to incite, Iſlandick; eᵹᵹian, Saxon.] To incite; to inſtigate; to provoke to action.

Study becomes pleaſant to him who is purſuing his genius, and whoſe ardour of inclination *eggs* him forward, and carrieth him through every obſtacle. *Derham's Phyſico-Theology.*

E'GLANTINE. *n. ſ.* [*eſglantier*, French.] A ſpecies of roſe. See ROSE.

O'er canopied with luſcious woodbine,
With ſweet muſk roſes, and with *eglantine*. *Shakeſpeare.*

The leaf of *eglantine*, not to ſlander,
Outſweeten'd not thy breath. *Shakeſpeare's Cymbeline.*

Sycamores with *eglantine* were ſpread,
A hedge about the ſides, a covering over head. *Dryden.*

E'GOTISM. *n. ſ.* [from *ego*, Latin.] The fault committed in writing by the frequent repetition of the word *ego*, or *I*; too frequent mention of a man's ſelf, in writing or converſation.

The moſt violent *egotiſm* which I have met with, in the courſe of my reading, is that of cardinal Wolſey's; *ego & rex meus*, I and my king. *Spectator*, Nº. 562.

E'GOTIST. *n. ſ.* [from *ego.*] One that is always repeating the word *ego*, *I*; a talker of himſelf.

A tribe of *egotiſts*, for whom I have always had a mortal averſion, are the authors of memoirs, who are never mentioned in any works but their own. *Spectator*, Nº. 562.

To E'GOTIZE. *v. n.* [from *ego.*] To talk much of one's ſelf.

EGRE'GIOUS. *adj.* [*egregius*, Latin.]

1. Eminent; remarkable; extraordinary.

He might be able to adorn this preſent age, and furniſh hiſtory with the records of *egregious* exploits, both of art and valour. *More's Antidote againſt Atheiſm.*

One to empire born;
Egregious prince! whoſe manly childhood ſhew'd
His mingled parents, and portended joy
Unſpeakable. *Phillips.*

2. Eminently bad; remarkably vicious. This is the uſual ſenſe.

We may be bold to conclude, that theſe laſt times, for inſolence, pride and *egregious* contempt of all good order, are the worſt. *Hooker, Preface.*

Ah me, moſt credulous fool!
Egregious murtherer! *Shakeſpeare's Cymbeline.*

And hence th' *egregious* wizzard ſhall foredoom
The fate of Louis, and the fall of Rome. *Pope.*

EGRE'GIOUSLY. *adv.* [from *egregious.*] Eminently; ſhamefully.

Make the more thank me, love me, and reward me,
For making him *egregiouſly* an aſs,
And practiſing upon his peace and quiet,
Even to madneſs. *Shakeſpeare's Othello.*

He diſcovered that, beſides the extravagance of every article, he had been *egregiouſly* cheated. *Arbuthnot's John Bull.*

E'GRESS. *n. ſ.* [*egreſſus*, Latin.] The act of going out of any place; departure.

And gates of burning adamant,
Barr'd over us, prohibit all *egreſs*. *Milton's Paradiſe Loſt, b.* ii.

This water would have been locked up within the earth, and its *egreſs* utterly debarred, had the ſtrata of ſtone and marble remained continuous. *Woodward's Natural Hiſtory.*

EGRE'SSION. *n. ſ.* [*egreſſio*, Latin.] The act of going out.

The vaſt number of troops is expreſſed in the ſwarms; their tumultuous manner of iſſuing out of their ſhips, and the perpetual *egreſſion*, which ſeemed without end, are imaged in the bees pouring out. *Notes on the Iliads.*

E'GRET. *n. ſ.* A fowl of the heron kind, with red legs. *Bailey.*

E'GRIOT. *n. ſ.* [*aigret*, French; perhaps from *aigre*, ſour.] A ſpecies of cherry.

The cœur-cherry, which inclineth more to white, is ſweeter than the red; but the *egriot* is more ſour. *Bacon.*

To EJA'CULATE. *v. a.* [*ejaculor*, Latin.] To throw; to ſhoot; to dart out.

Being rooted ſo little way in the ſkin, nothing near ſo deeply as the quills of fowls, they are the more eaſy *ejaculated*. *Grew's Muſæum.*

The mighty magnet from the center darts
This ſtrong, though ſubtile force, through all the parts:
Its active rays, *ejaculated* thence,
Irradiate all the wide circumference. *Blackmore's Creation.*

EJA'CULATION. *n. ſ.* [from *ejaculate.*]

1. A ſhort prayer darted out occaſionally, without ſolemn retirement.

In your dreſſing let there be *ejaculations* fitted to the ſeveral actions of dreſſing; as at waſhing your hands, pray God to cleanſe your ſoul from ſin. *Taylor's Guide to Devotion.*

2. The act of darting or throwing out.

There ſeemeth to be acknowledged, in the act of envy, an *ejaculation* or irradiation of the eye. *Bacon's Eſſays.*

There is to be obſerved, in thoſe diſſolutions which will not eaſily incorporate, what the effects are; as the ebullition, the precipitation to the bottom, the *ejaculation* towards the top, the ſuſpenſion in the midſt, and the like. *Bacon.*

EJA'CULATORY. *adj.* [from *ejaculate*] Suddenly darted out; uttered in ſhort ſentences; ſudden; haſty.

The continuance of this poſture might incline to eaſe and drowſineſs: they uſed it rather upon ſome ſhort *ejaculatory* prayers, than in their larger devotions. *Duppa's Devotion.*

We are not to value ourſelves upon the merit of *ejaculatory* repentances, that take us by fits and ſtarts. *L'Eſtrange.*

To EJE'CT. *v. a.* [*ejicio ejectum*, Latin.]

1. To throw out; to caſt forth; to void.

Infernal lightning ſallies from his throat!
Ejected ſparks upon the billows float! *Sandys.*

The heart, as ſaid, from its contracted cave,
On the left ſide *ejects* the bounding wave. *Blackm. Creation.*

Tears may ſpoil the eyes, but not waſh away the affliction; ſighs may exhauſt the man, but not *eject* the burthen. *South.*

2. To throw out or expel from an office or poſſeſſion.

It was the force of conqueſt; force with force
Is well *ejected*, when the conquer'd can. *Milton's Agoniſtes.*

The French king was again *ejected* when our king ſubmitted to the church. *Dryden's Preface to Rel. Laici.*

3. To expel; to drive away; to diſmiſs with hatred.

We are peremptory to diſpatch
This viperous traitor; to *eject* him hence,
Were but our danger; and to keep him here,
Our certain death; therefore it is decreed
He dies to-night. *Shakeſpeare's Coriolanus.*

4. To caſt away; to reject.

To have *ejected* whatſoever the church doth make account of, be it never ſo harmleſs in itſelf, and of never ſo ancient continuance, without any other crime to charge it with, than only that it hath been the hap thereof to be uſed by the church of Rome, and not to be commanded in the word of God, could not have been defended. *Hooker.*

Will any man say, that if the words whoring and drinking were by parliament *ejected* out of the English tongue, we should all awake next morning chaste and temperate? *Swift.*

EJE'CTION. *n. s.* [*ejectio*, Latin.]

1. The act of casting out; expulsion.

These stories are founded on the *ejection* of the fallen angels from heaven. *Notes on the Odyssey.*

2. [In physick.] The discharge of any thing by vomit, stool, or any other emunctory. *Quincy.*

EJE'CTMENT. *n. s.* [from *eject.*] A legal writ by which any inhabitant of a house, or tenant of an estate, is commanded to depart.

EIGH. *interj.* An expression of sudden delight.

EIGHT. *adj.* [eahta, Saxon; *ahta*, Gothick; *acht*, Scottish.] Twice four. A word of number.

This island contains *eight* score and *eight* miles in circuit. *Sandys's Journey.*

EIGHTH. *adj.* [from *eight.*] Next in order to the seventh; the ordinal of eight.

Another yet?—A seventh! I'll see no more;
And yet the *eighth* appears! *Shakespeare's Macbeth.*

In the *eighth* month should be the reign of Saturn. *Bacon.*

I stay reluctant seven continu'd years,
And water her ambrosial couch with tears;
The *eighth*, she voluntary moves to part,
Or urg'd by Jove, or her own changeful heart. *Pope's Odyss.*

EI'GHTEEN. *adj.* [*eight* and *ten.*] Twice nine.

He can't take two from twenty, for his heart,
And leave *eighteen*. *Shakespeare's Cymbeline.*

If men naturally lived but twenty years, we should be satisfied if they died about *eighteen*; and yet *eighteen* years now are as long as *eighteen* years would be then. *Taylor.*

EI'GHTEENTH *adj.* [from *eighteen.*] The next in order to the seventeenth; twice nine.

In the *eighteenth* year of Jeroboam reigned Abijam. 1 *Kings.*

EI'GHTFOLD. *adj.* [*eight* and *fold.*] Eight times the number or quantity.

EI'GHTHLY. *adv.* [from *eighth.*] In the eighth place.

Eighthly, living creatures have voluntary motion, which plants have not. *Bacon's Natural History*, Nº. 607.

EI'GHTIETH. *adj.* [from *eighty.*] The next in order to the seventyninth; eighth tenth.

Some balances are so exact as to be sensibly turned with the *eightieth* part of a grain. *Wilkins's Math. Magic.*

EI'GHTSCORE. *adj.* [*eight* and *score.*] Eight times twenty; an hundred and sixty.

What! keep a week away? Seven days and nights?
Eightscore eight hours? And lovers absent hours,
More tedious than the dial *eightscore* times?
Oh weary reckoning. *Shakespeare's Othello.*

EI'GHTY. *adj.* [*eight* and *ten.*] Eight times ten; fourscore.

Eighty odd years of sorrow have I seen,
And each hour's joy wreck'd with a week of teen. *Shakesp.*

Among all other climactericks three are most remarkable; that is, seven times seven, or fortynine; nine times nine, or *eighty* one; and seven times nine, or the year sixtythree, which is conceived to carry with it the most considerable fatality. *Brown's Vulgar Errours, b.* iv. *c.* 12.

EI'GNE. *adj.* [*aisne*, Fr.] [In law.] Denotes the eldest or first born. Here it signifies unalienable, as being entailed.

Many assurances do also pass to godly and charitable uses alone; and it happeneth not seldom, that, to avoid the yearly oath, for averment of the continuance of some estate for life, which is *eigne*, and not subject to forfeiture for the alienation that cometh after it, the party will offer to sue a pardon uncompelled before the time; in all which, some mitigation of the uttermost value may well and worthily be offered. *Bacon.*

EI'SEL. *n. s.* [eopil, Saxon.] Vinegar; verjuice; any acid.

Woo't drink up *eisel*, eat a crocodile?
I'll do't. *Shakespeare's Hamlet.*

EI'THER. *pron.* [æᵹðeꞃ, Saxon; *auther*, Scottish.]

1. Which soever of the two; whether one or the other.

Lepidus flatters both,
Of both is flatter'd; but he neither loves,
Nor *either* cares for him. *Shakesp. Anthony and Cleopatra.*

So like in arms these champions were,
As they had been a very pair;
So that a man would almost swear,
That *either* had been *either*. *Drayton's Nymp.*

Goring made a fast friendship with Digby, *either* of them believing he could deceive the other. *Clarendon, b.* viii.

I do not ask whether bodies do so exist, that the motion of one body cannot really be without the motion of another: to determine this *either* way, is to beg the question for or against a vacuum. *Locke.*

2. Each; both.

In the process of natural beings, there seem some to be creatures placed, as it were, in the confines of several provinces, and participating something of *either*. *Hale.*

Sev'n times the sun has *either* tropick view'd,
The Winter banish'd, and the Spring renew'd. *Dryd. Virg.*

EI'THER. *adv.* [from the noun.] A distributive adverb, answered by *or*; either the one *or*.

We never heard of any ship that had been seen to arrive upon any shore of Europe; no nor of *either* the East *or* West Indies. *Bacon's New Atlantis.*

What perils shall we find,
If *either* place, *or* time, *or* other course,
Cause us to alter th' order now assign'd? *Daniel's C. War.*

Either your brethren have miserably deceived us, *or* power confers virtue. *Swift to Pope.*

EJULA'TION. *n. s.* [*ejulatio*, Latin.] Outcry; lamentation; moan; wailing.

Instead of hymns and praises, he breaks out into *ejulations* and effeminate wailings. *Government of the Tongue.*

With dismal groans
And *ejulation*, in the pangs of death,
Some call for aid neglected; some, o'erturn'd
In the fierce shock, lie gasping. *Phillips.*

EKE. *adv.* [eac, Saxon; *ook*, Dutch.] Also; likewise; beside; moreover.

If any strength we have, it is to ill;
But all the good is God's, both power and *eke* will. *Fa. Qu.*

Now if 'tis chiefly in the heart
That courage does itself exert,
'Twill be prodigious hard to prove,
That this is *eke* the throne of love. *Prior.*

To EKE. *v. a.* [eacan, Saxon.]

1. To increase.

I dempt there much to have *eked* my store,
But such *eking* hath made my heart sore. *Spenser's Pastorals.*

The little strength that I have, I would it were with you.
——And mine to *eke* out her's. *Shakesp. As you like it.*

2. To supply; to fill up deficiencies.

Still be kind,
And *eke* out our performance with your mind. *Shak. H. V.*

Your ornaments hung all,
On some patch'd doghole *ek'd* with ends of wall. *Pope.*

3. To protract; to lengthen.

I speak too long; but 'tis to piece the time,
To *eke* it, and to draw it out in length,
To stay you from election. *Shakesp. Merchant of Venice.*

4. To spin out by useless additions. [In this sense it seems borrowed from the use of our old poets, who put *eke* into their lines, when they wanted a syllable.]

Eusden *ekes* out Blackmore's endless line. *Pope's Dunciad.*

To ELA'BORATE. *v. a.* [*elaboro*, Latin.]

1. To produce with labour.

They in full joy *elaborate* a sigh. *Young.*

2. To heighten and improve by successive endeavours or operations.

The sap is diversified, and still more and more *elaborated* and exalted, as it circulates through the vessels of the plant. *Arbuthnot on Aliments.*

ELA'BORATE. *adj.* [*elaboratus*, Latin.] Finished with great diligence; performed with great labour.

Formalities of extraordinary zeal and piety are never more studied and *elaborate* than when politicians most agitate desperate designs. *King Charles.*

At least, on her bestow'd
Too much of ornament, of outward shew
Elaborate; of inward, less exact. *Milton's Paradise Lost.*

Man is thy theme, his virtue or his rage
Drawn to the life in each *elab'rate* page. *Waller.*

Consider the difference between *elaborate* discourses upon important occasions, delivered to parliaments, and a plain sermon intended for the lower people. *Swift.*

ELA'BORATELY. *adv.* [from *elaborate.*] Laboriously; diligently; with great study or labour.

Politick conceptions so *elaborately* formed and wrought, and grown at length ripe for delivery, do yet prove abortive *South.*

Some coloured powders, which painters use, may have their colours a little changed, by being very *elaborately* and finely ground. *Newton's Opt.*

I will venture once to incur the censure of some persons, for being *elaborately* trifling. *Bentley's Sermons.*

It is there *elaborately* shewn, that patents are good. *Swift.*

ELABORA'TION. *n. s.* [from *elaborate.*] Improvement by successive operations.

To what purpose is there such an apparatus of vessels for the *elaboration* of the sperm and eggs; such a tedious process of generation and nutrition? This is but an idle pomp. *Ray.*

To ELA'NCE. *v. a.* [*elancer*, French.] To throw out; to dart; to cast as a dart.

While thy unerring hand *elanc'd*
Another, and another dart, the people
Joyfully repeated Io! *Prior.*

Harsh words, that, once *elanc'd*, must ever fly
Irrevocable. *Prior.*

To ELA'PSE. *v. n.* [*elapsus*, Latin.] To pass away; to glide away; to run out without notice.

There is a docible season, a learning time in youth, which, suffered to *elapse*, and no foundation laid, seldom returns. *Clariss.*

ELA'STICAL. } *adj.* [from ἐλάω.] Having the power of re-
ELA'STICK. } turning to the form from which it is distorted or withheld; springy; having the power of a spring.

By what *elastick* engines did she rear
The starry roof, and roll the orbs in air. *Blackm. Creation.*

If the body is compact, and bends or yields inward to pression, without any sliding of its parts, it is hard and *elastick*, returning to its figure with a force rising from the mutual attraction of its parts. *Newton's Opt.*

The most common diversities of human constitutions arise from the solids, as to their different degrees of strength and tension; in some being too lax and weak, in others too *elastick* and strong. *Arbuthnot on Aliments.*

A fermentation must be excited in some assignable place, which may expand itself by its *elastical* power, and break through, where it meets with the weakest resistance. *Bentley.*

ELASTI'CITY. *n. s.* [from *elastick.*] Force in bodies, by which they endeavour to restore themselves to the posture from whence they were displaced by any external force. *Quincy.*

A lute string will bear a hundred weight without rupture; but, at the same time, cannot exert its *elasticity*: take away fifty, and immediately it raiseth the weight. *Arbuthn. on Alim.*

Me emptiness and dulness could inspire,
And were my *elasticity* and fire. *Pope's Dunciad, b.* i.

ELA'TE. *adj.* [*elatus*, Latin.] Flushed with success; elevated with prosperity; lofty; haughty.

Oh, thoughtless mortals! ever blind to fate!
Too soon dejected, and too soon *elate*! *Pope's Ra. of Lock.*
I, of mind *elate*, and scorning fear,
Thus with new taunts insult the monster's ear. *Pope's Odyss.*

To EL'ATE. *v. a.* [from the noun.]

1. To elevate with success; to puff up with prosperity.
2. To exult; to heighten. An unusual sense.

Or truth, divinely breaking on his mind,
Elates his being, and unfolds his power. *Thomson's Autumn.*

ELATE'RIUM. n. s. [Latin.] An inspissated juice, in fragments of flat and thin cakes, seldom thicker than a shilling. It is light, of a friable texture; a pale, dead, whitish colour, and an acrid and pungent taste. It is procured from the fruit of the wild cucumber; the seeds of which swim in a large quantity of an acrid and almost caustick liquor. It is a very violent and rough purge. *Hill.*

ELA'TION. *n. s.* [from *elate.*] Haughtiness proceeding from success; pride of prosperity.

God began to punish this vain *elation* of mind, by withdrawing his favours. *Atterbury's Sermons.*

E'LBOW. *n. s.* [elboʒa, Saxon.]

1. The next joint or curvature of the arm below the shoulder.

In some fair evening, on your *elbow* laid,
You dream of triumphs in the rural shade. *Pope.*

2. Any flexure, or angle.

Fruit-trees, or vines, set upon a wall between *elbows* or buttresses of stone, ripen more than upon a plain wall. *Bacon.*

3. *To be at the* ELBOW. To be near; to be at hand.

Here stand behind this bulk. Straight will he come:
Wear thy good rapier bare, and put it home:
Quick, quick; fear nothing, I'll *be at thy elbow. Shak. Othel.*

ELBOWCHA'IR. *n. s.* [*elbow* and *chair.*] A chair with arms to support the elbows.

Swans and *elbowchairs*, in the opera of Dioclesian, have danced upon the English stage with good success. *Gay.*

E'LBOWROOM. *n. s.* [*elbow* and *room.*] Room to stretch out the elbows on each side; perfect freedom from confinement.

Now my soul hath *elbowroom*;
It would not out at windows nor at doors. *Shakespeare.*

The natives are not so many, but that there may be *elbowroom* enough for them, and for the adventives also. *Bacon.*

A politican must put himself into a state of liberty, so to provide *elbowroom* for his conscience to have its full play in. *South's Sermons.*

To E'LBOW. *v. a.* [from the noun.]

1. To push with the elbow.

One *elbows* him, one justles in the shole. *Dryden's Juven.*

2. To push; to drive to distance; to encroach upon.

It thrusts and stretches out,
And *elbows* all the kingdoms round about. *Dryden.*
If fortune takes not off this boy betimes,
He'll make mad work, and *elbow* all his neighbours. *Dryden.*

To E'LBOW. *v. n.* To jut out in angles. *Dict.*

ELD. *n. s.* [ealԁ, Saxon; *eld*, Scottish.]

1. Old age; decrepitude.

Her heart with joy unwonted inly swel'd,
As feeling wond'rous comfort in her weaker *eld. Fa. Queen:*

2. Old people; persons worn out with years.

Thy blazed youth
Becomes assuaged, and doth beg the alms
Of palsied *eld.* *Shakespeare's Measure for Measure.*
He thought it touch'd his deity full near,
If likewise he some fair one wedded not,
Thereby to wipe away th' infamous blot
Of long uncoupled bed and childless *eld.* *Milton.*

E'LDER. *adj.* The comparative of *eld*, now corrupted to *old.* ealԁ, ealԁoꞃ, Saxon.] Surpassing another in years; survivor; having the privileges of primogeniture.

They bring the comparison of younger daughters conforming themselves in attire to the example of their *elder* sisters. *Hooker, b.* iv. *s.* 13.

Let still the woman take
An *elder* than herself; so wears she to him,
So sways she level in her husband's heart. *Sh. Twelfth Night.*
How I firmly am resolv'd, you know;
That is, not to bestow my youngest daughter,
Before I have a husband for the *elder. Sh. Tam. of the Shrew.*

The *elder* of his children comes to acquire a degree of authority among the younger, by the same means the father did among them. *Temple.*

Fame's high temple stands;
Stupendous pile! not rear'd by mortal hands!
Whate'er proud Rome, or artful Greece beheld,
Or *elder* Babylon, its frame excell'd. *Pope's Temp. of Fame.*

E'LDERS. *n. s.* [from *elder.*]

1. Persons whose age gives them a claim to credit and reverence.

Rebuke not an *elder*, but intreat him as a father, and the younger men as brethren. 1 *Tim.* v. 1.

Our *elders* say,
The barren, touched in this holy chase,
Shake off their steril curse. *Shakespeare's Julius Cæsar:*

Among the Lacedæmonians, the chief magistrates, as they were, so they are called, *elder* men. *Raleigh's H. of the World.*

The blushing youth their virtuous awe disclose,
And from their seats the reverend *elders* rose. *Sandys.*

2. Ancestors.

Says the goose, if it will be no better, e'en carry your head as your *elders* have done before ye. *L'Estrange.*

I lose my patience, and I own it too,
Where works are censur'd, not as bad, but new;
While, if our *elders* break all reason's laws,
Those fools demand not pardon, but applause. *Pope.*

3. Those who are older than others.

At the board, and in private, it very well becometh children's innocency to pray, and their *elders* to say amen. *Hooker.*

4. [Among the Jews.] Rulers of the people.
5. [In the New Testament.] Ecclesiasticks.
6. [Among presbyterians.] Laymen introduced into the kirk-polity in sessions, presbyteries, synods and assemblies.

Flea-bitten synod, an assembly brew'd
Of clerks and *elders* ana; like the rude
Chaos of presbytry, where laymen ride
With the tame woolpack clergy by their side. *Cleaveland.*

E'LDER. *n. s.* [ellaꞃa, Saxon.] The name of a tree.

The branches are full of pith, having but little wood: the flowers are monopetalous, divided into several segments, and expand in form of a rose: these are, for the most part, collected into an umbel, and are succeeded by soft succulent berries, having three seeds in each. It may be easily propagated from cuttings or seeds; but the former, being the most expeditious method, is generally practised. The season for planting their cuttings is any time from September to March, thrusting them six or eight inches into the ground. Dwarf elder is near London propagated for medicinal use. *Miller.*

Look for thy reward
Amongst the nettles at the *elder* tree,
Which overshades the mouth of that same pit. *Sh. Tit. And.*
Then seek the bank where flowering *elders* crowd. *Thom.*

E'LDERLY. *adj.* [from *elder.*] No longer young; bordering upon old age

I have a race of orderly *elderly* people of both sexes at command, who can bawl when I am deaf, and tread softly when I am giddy. *Swift to Pope.*

E'LDERSHIP. *n. s.* [from *elder.*]

1. Seniority; primogeniture.

That all should Alibech adore, 'tis true;
But some respect is to my birthright due:
My claim to her by *eldership* I prove. *Dryden's Ind. Emp.*
Nor were the *eldership*
Of Artaxerxes worth our least of fears,
If Memnon's interest did not prop his cause. *Rowe.*

2. Presbytery; ecclesiastical senate; kirk-session.

Here were the seeds sown of that controversy which sprang up between Beza and Erastus, about the matter of excommunications; whether there ought to be in all churches an *eldership*, having power to excommunicate, and a part of that *eldership* to be of necessity certain chosen out from amongst the laity for that purpose. *Hooker, Preface.*

E'LDEST. *adj.* The superlative of *eld*, now changed to *old.* [ealԁ, ealԁoꞃ, ealԁyꞅꞇe, Saxon.]

1. The oldest; the child that has the right of primogeniture.

We will establish our estate upon
Our *eldest* Malcolm, whom we name hereafter
The prince of Cumberland. *Shakespeare's Macbeth.*
The mother's and her *eldest* daughter's grace,
It seems, had brib'd him to prolong their space. *Dryden.*

2. The

2. The person that has lived most years.

Eldest parents signifies either the oldest men and women that have had children, or those who have longest had issue. *Locke.*

ELECAMPA'NE. *n. s.* [*helenium*, Latin.] A plant, named also starwort.

It hath a radiated flower, whose florets are hermaphrodite; but the semi-florets are female: both these are yellow. The ovaries rest on a naked placenta, crowned with down: all these parts are included in a scaly cup. To these notes may be added, the leaves growing alternately on the stalks, and the flowers on the top of the branches. Botanists enumerate thirty species of this plant. The first is the true elecampane, used in medicines: it grows wild in most fields and meadows, and is cultivated in gardens, to furnish the shops with roots, which is the only part of the plant in use. *Miller.*

The Germans have a method of candying *elecampane* root like ginger, to which they prefer it, and call it German spice. *Hill's Mat. Med.*

To ELE'CT. *v. a.* [*electus*, Latin.]

1. To choose for any office or use; to take in preference to others.

Henry his son is chosen king, though young;
And Lewis of France, *elected* first, beguil'd. *Dan. C. War.*

This prince, in gratitude to the people, by whose consent he was chosen, elected a hundred senators out of the commoners. *Swift on the Dissensions in Athens and Rome.*

2. [in theology.] To select as an object of eternal mercy.

Some I have chosen of peculiar grace,
Elect above the rest: so is my will. *Milton's Paradise Lost.*

ELE'CT. *adj.* [from the verb.]

1. Chosen; taken by preference from among others.

You have here, lady,
And of your choice, these reverend fathers,
Of singular integrity and learning;
Yea, the *elect* of the land, who are assembl'd
To plead your cause. *Shakespeare's Henry* VIII.

2. Chosen to an office, not yet in possession.

The bishop *elect* takes the oaths of supremacy, canonical obedience, and against simony; and then the dean of the arches reads and subscribes the sentences. *Ayliffe's Parergon.*

3. [In theology.] Chosen as an object of eternal mercy.

A vitious liver, believing that Christ died for none but the *elect*, shall have attempts made upon him to reform and amend his life. *Hammond.*

ELE'CTION. *n. s.* [*electio*, Latin.]

1. The act of chusing; the act of selecting one or more from a greater number for any use or office; choice.

If the *election* of the minister should be committed to every several parish, do you think that they would chuse the meetest. *Whitgift.*

I was sorry to hear with what partiality, and popular heat, *elections* were carried in many places. *King Charles.*

Him, not thy *election*,
But natural necessity, begot. *Milton's Paradise Lost, b.* x.

As charity is, nothing can more increase the lustre and beauty than a prudent *election* of objects, and a fit application of it to them. *Spratt's Sermons.*

2. The power of choice.

For what is man without a moving mind,
Which hath a judging wit, and chusing will!
Now, if God's pow'r should her *election* bind,
Her motions then would cease, and stand all still. *Davies.*

3. Voluntary preference.

He calls upon the sinners to turn themselves and live; he tells us, that he has set before us life and death, and referred it to our own *election* which we will chuse. *Rogers's Sermons.*

4. [In theology.] The predetermination of God by which any were selected for eternal life.

The conceit about absolute *election* to eternal life, some enthusiasts entertaining, have been made remiss in the practice of virtue. *Atterbury's Sermons.*

5. The ceremony of a publick choice.

Since the late dissolution of the club, many persons put up for the next *election*. *Addison's Spectator*, N°. 550.

ELE'CTIVE. *adj.* [from *elect.*] Exerting the power of choice; regulated or bestowed by election or choice.

I will say positively and resolutely, that it is impossible an *elective* monarchy should be so free and absolute as an hereditary. *Bacon.*

To talk of compelling a man to be good, is a contradiction; for where there is force, there can be no choice: whereas all moral goodness consisteth in the *elective* act of the understanding will. *Grew's Cosmol. Sac. b.* iii. *c* 2.

The last change of their government, from *elective* to hereditary, has made it seem hitherto of less force, and unfitter for action abroad. *Temple.*

ELE'CTIVELY. *adv.* [from *elect.*] By choice; with preference of one to another.

How or why that should have such an influence upon the spirits, as to drive them into those muscles *electively*, I am not subtile enough to discern. *Ray on the Creation.*

They work not *electively*, or upon proposing to themselves an end of their operations. *Grew's Cosm. Sac.*

ELE'CTOR. *n. s.* [from *elect.*]

1. He that has a vote in the choice of any officer.

From the new world her silver and her gold
Came, like a tempest, to confound the old;
Feeding with these the brib'd *electors'* hopes,
Alone she gave us emperors and popes. *Waller.*

2. A prince who has a voice in the choice of the German emperour.

ELE'CTORAL. *adj.* [from *elector.*] Having the dignity of an elector.

ELE'CTORATE. *n. s.* [from *elector.*] The territory of an elector.

He has a great and powerful king for his son-in-law; and can himself command, when he pleases, the whole strength of an *electorate* in the empire. *Addison's Freeholder*, N°. 24.

ELE'CTRE. *n. s.* [*electrum*, Latin.]

1. Amber; which, having the quality when warmed by friction of attracting bodies, gave to one species of attraction the name of *electricity*, and to the bodies that so attract the epithet *electrick*.

2. A mixed metal.

Change silver plate or vessel into the compound stuff, being a kind of silver *electre*, and turn the rest into coin. *Bacon.*

ELE'CTRICAL. } *adj.* [from *electrum.* See ELECTRE.]
ELE'CTRICK. }

1. Attractive without magnetism; attractive by a peculiar property, supposed once to belong chiefly to amber.

By *electrick* bodies do I conceive not such only as take up light bodies, in which number the ancients only placed jett and amber; but such as, conveniently placed, attract all bodies palpable. *Brown's Vulgar Errours, b.* ii. *c.* 4.

An *electrick* body can by friction emit an exhalation so subtile, and yet so potent, as by its emission to cause no sensible diminution of the weight of the *electrick* body, and to be expanded through a sphere, whose diameter is above two feet, and yet to be able to carry up lead, copper, or leaf-gold, at the distance of above a foot from the *electrick* body. *Newton.*

2. Produced by an electrick body.

If that attraction were not rather *electrical* than magnetical, it was wonderous what Helmont delivereth concerning a glass, wherein the magistery of loadstone was prepared, which retained an attractive quality. *Brown's Vulgar Errours.*

If a piece of white paper, or a white cloath, or the end of one's finger, be held at about a quarter of an inch from the glass, the *electrick* vapour, excited by friction, will, by dashing against the white paper, cloth, or finger, be put into such an agitation as to emit light. *Newton's Opt.*

ELECTRI'CITY. *n. s.* [from *electrick.* See ELECTRE.] A property in some bodies, whereby, when rubbed so as to grow warm, they draw little bits of paper, or such like substances, to them. *Quincy.*

Such was the account given a few years ago of electricity; but the industry of the present age, first excited by the experiments of *Gray*, has discovered in electricity a multitude of philosophical wonders. Bodies electrified by a sphere of glass, turned nimbly round, not only emit flame, but may be fitted with such a quantity of the electrical vapour, as, if discharged at once upon a human body, would endanger life. The force of this vapour has hitherto appeared instantaneous, persons at both ends of a long chain seeming to be struck at once. The philosophers are now endeavouring to intercept the strokes of lightning.

ELE'CTUARY. *n. s.* [*electarium*, *Collin's Aurel.* which is now written *electuary.*] A form of medicine made of conserves, and powders, in the consistence of honey. The form is attended with considerable inconveniencies; for *electuaries*, generally made up with honey, or syrup, when the consistence is too thin, are apt to ferment; and when too thick, to candy. By both which the ingredients will either be entirely altered in their nature, or impaired in their virtues. *Quincy.*

We meet with divers *electuaries*, which have no ingredient, except sugar, common to any two of them. *Boyle's Sc. Chym.*

ELEEMO'SYNARY. *adj.* [ἐλεημοσύνη.]

1. Living upon alms; depending upon charity.

It is little better than an absurdity, that the cause should be an *eleemosynary* for its subsistence to its effects, as a nature posteriour to and dependent on itself. *Glanv. Sceps. c.* 18.

2. Given in charity.

ELEGA'NCE. } *n. s.* [*elegantia*, Latin.] Beauty of art; ra-
ELEGA'NCY. } ther soothing than striking; beauty without grandeur.

St. Augustine, out of a kind of *elegancy* in writing, makes some difference. *Raleigh's History of the World.*

These questions have more propriety, and *elegancy*, understood of the old world. *Burnet.*

My compositions in gardening are altogether Pindarick, and run into the beautiful wildness of nature, without the nicer *elegancies* of art. *Spectator*, N°. 477.

ELE'GANT. *adj.* [*elegans*, Latin.]

1. Pleasing with minuter beauties.

Trifles themselves are *elegant* in him. *Pope.*
There may'st thou find some *elegant* retreat. *London.*
2. Nice; not coarse; not gross.
Polite with candour, *elegant* with ease. *Pope.*

E'LEGANTLY. *adv.* [from *elegant.*]
1. In such a manner as to please without elevation.
2. Neatly; nicely; with minute beauty.
Whoever would write *elegantly*, must have regard to the different turn and juncture of every period: there must be proper distances and pauses. *Pope's Odyssey, Notes.*

ELEGI'ACK. *adj.* [*elegiacus*, Latin.]
1. Used in elegies.
2. Pertaining to elegies.
3. Mournful; sorrowful.
Let *elegiack* lay the woe relate,
Soft as the breath of distant flutes. *Gay's Trivia.*

E'LEGY. *n. s.* [*elegus*, Latin.]
1. A mournful song.
He hangs odes upon hawthorns, and *elegies* upon brambles; all forsooth deifying the name of Rosalind. *Shak. As you like it.*
2. A funeral song.
So on meanders banks, when death is nigh,
The mournful swan sings her own *elegy*. *Dryden.*
3. A short poem without points or turns.

E'LEMENT. *n. s.* [*elementum*, Latin.]
1. The first or constituent principle of any thing.
If nature should intermit her course, those principal and mother *elements* of the world, whereof all things in this lower world are made, should lose the qualities which now they have. *Hooker, b.* i. *s.* 3.
A man may rationally retain doubts concerning the number of those ingredients of bodies, which some call *elements*, and others principles. *Boyle's Phys. Consider.*
Simple substances are either spirits, which have no manner of composition, or the first principles of bodies, usually called *elements*, of which other bodies are compounded. *Watts.*
2. The four elements, usually so called, are earth, fire, air, water, of which our world is composed.
The king is but a man: the violet smells to him as it doth to me; and the *element* shews to him as it doth to me. *Shakes.*
My dearest sister, fare thee well;
The *elements* be kind to thee, and make
Thy spirits all of comfort. *Shakes. Anth. and Cleopatra.*
The king,
Contending with the fretful *elements*,
Bids the wind blow the earth into the sea,
Or swell the curled waters. *Shakespeare's King Lear.*
The heavens and the earth will pass away, and the *elements* melt with fervent heat. *Peter.*
Here be four of you were able to make a good world; for you are as differing as the four *elements*. *Bacon's Hol. War.*
He from his flaming ship his children sent,
To perish in a milder *element*. *Waller.*
3. The proper habitation or sphere of any thing: as water of fish.
We are simple men; we do not know she works by charms, by spells, and such dawbry as is beyond our *element*. *Shakesp.*
Our torments may, in length of time,
Became our *elements*. *Milton's Paradise Lost, b.* ii *l.* 275.
They shew that they are out of their *element*, and that logick is none of their talent. *Baker's Reflections on Learning.*
4. An ingredient; a constituent part.
Who set the body and the limbs
Of this great sport together, as you guess?
——One sure that promises no *element*
In such a business. *Shakespeare's Henry* VIII.
5. The letters of any language.
6. The lowest or first rudiments of literature or science.
With religion it fareth as with other sciences; the first delivery of the *elements* thereof must, for like consideration, be framed according to the weak and slender capacity of young beginners. *Hooker, b.* v. *s.* 18.
Every parish should keep a petty schoolmaster, which should bring up children in the first *elements* of letters. *Spenser on Irel.*
We, when we were children, were in bondage under the *elements* of the world. *Gal.* iv. 3.
There is nothing more pernicious to a youth, in the *elements* of painting, than an ignorant master. *Dryden's Dufresn.*

To E'LEMENT. *v. a.* [from the noun.]
1. To compound of elements.
Whether any one such body be met with, in those said to be *elemented* bodies, I now question. *Boyle's Scept. Chym.*
2. To constitute; to make as a first principle.
Dull sublunary lover's love,
Whose soul is sense, cannot admit
Of absence, 'cause it doth remove
The thing which *elemented* it. *Donne.*

ELEME'NTAL. *adj.* [from *element.*]
1. Produced by some of the four elements.
If dusky spots are vary'd on his brow,
And streak'd with red, a troubl'd colour show;
That sullen mixture shall at once declare
Winds, rain and storms, and *elemental* war. *Dryden's Virg.*
Soft yielding minds to water glide away,
And sip, with nymphs, their *elemental* tea. *Pope.*
2. Arising from first principles.
Leeches are by some accounted poison not properly, that is, by temperamental contrariety, occult form, or so much as *elemental* repugnancy; but inwardly taken, they fasten upon the veins, and occasion an effusion of blood. *Brown's Vu. Err.*

ELEMENTA'RITY. *n. s.* [from *elementary.*] Containing the rudiments or first principles; simplicity of nature; absence of composition; being uncompounded.
A very large class of creatures in the earth, far above the condition of *elementarity*. *Brown's Vulgar Errours, b.* ii. *c.* 1.

ELEME'NTARY. *adj.* [from *elementary.*] Uncompounded; having only one principle or constituent part.
All rain water contains in it a copious sediment of terrestrial matter, and is not a simple *elementary* water. *Ray on the Creat.*
The *elementary* salts of animals are not the same as they appear by distillation. *Arbuthnot on Aliments.*

ELE'MI. *n. s.*
This drug is improperly called gum *elemi*, being a resin. The genuine *elemi* is brought from Æthiopia in flattish masses, or in cylinders, of a yellowish colour. Its smell is acrid and resinous. It is very rare in Europe, and supposed to be produced by a tree of the olive kind. The spurious or American *elemi*, almost the only kind known, is of a whitish colour, with a greater or less tinge of a greenish or yellowish. It is of an agreeable smell, and of an acrid and bitterish taste. It proceeds from a tall tree, which the Brasilians wound at night, and in the morning collect the resin that has run out. *Hill's Materia Medica.*

ELE'NCH. *n. s.* [*elenchus*, Latin.] An argument; a sophism.
The first delusion Satan put upon Eve, and his whole tentation might be the same *elench* continued, as when he said, Ye shall not die; that was, in his equivocation, you shall not incur present death. *Brown's Vulgar Errours, b.* i. *c.* 4.
Discover the fallacies of our common adversary, that old sophister, who puts the most abusive *elenchs* on us. *De. of Piety.*

ELE'OTS. *n. s.* Some name the apples in request in the cyder countries so; not known by that name in several parts of England. *Mortimer's Art of Husbandry.*

E'LEPHANT. *n. s.* [*elephas*, Latin.] The largest of all quadrupeds, of whose sagacity, faithfulness, prudence, and even understanding, many surprising relations are given. This animal is not carnivorous, but feeds on hay, herbs, and all sorts of pulse; and it is said to be extremely long lifed. It is naturally very gentle; but when enraged, no creature is more terrible. He is supplied with a trunk, or long hollow cartilage, like a large trumpet, which hangs between his teeth, and serves him for hands: by one blow with his trunk he will kill a camel or a horse, and will raise a prodigious weight with it. His teeth are the ivory so well known in Europe, some of which have been seen as large as a man's thigh, and a fathom in length. Wild elephants are taken with the help of a female ready for the male: she is confined to a narrow place, round which pits are dug; and these being covered with a little earth scattered over hurdles, the male elephants easily fall into the snare. In copulation the female receives the male lying upon her back; and such is his pudicity, that he never covers the female so long as any one appears in sight. *Calmet.*
He loves to hear,
That unicorns may be betray'd with trees,
And bears with glasses, *elephants* with holes. *Sh. Jul. Cæs.*
The *elephant* hath joints, but not for courtesy;
His legs are for necessity, not flexure. *Sh. Troil. and Cressida.*
2. Ivory; the teeth of elephants.
High o'er the gate, in *elephant* and gold,
The crowd shall Cæsar's Indian war behold. *Dryden's Virg.*

ELEPHANTI'ASIS. *n. s.* [*elephantiasis*, Latin.] A species of leprosy, so called from covering the skin with incrustations like those on the hide of an elephant.

ELEPHA'NTINE. *adj.* [*elephantinus*, Latin.] Pertaining to the elephant.

To E'LEVATE. *v. a.* [*elevo*, Latin.]
1. To raise up aloft.
This subterranean heat or fire, which *elevates* the water out of the abyss. *Woodward.*
2. To exalt; to dignify.
3. To raise the mind with great conceptions.
Others apart sat on a hill retired,
In thoughts more *elevate*, and reason'd high
Of providence, foreknowledge, will and fate. *Milt. P. L.*
In all that great extent, wherein the mind wanders, in those remote speculations it may seem to be *elevated* with, it stirs not beyond sense or reflection. *Locke.*
Now rising fortune *elevates* his mind,
He shines unclouded, and adorns mankind. *Savage.*
4. To elate the mind with vicious pride.

5. To

5. To leſſen by detraction. This ſenſe, though legitimately deduced from the Latin, is not now in uſe.

When the judgments of learned men are alledged againſt you, what do they but either *elevate* their credit, or oppoſe unto them the judgments of others as learned? *Hooker, b* ii.

E'LEVATE. *part. adj.* [from *elevated.*] Exalted; raiſed aloft.

On each ſide an imperial city ſtood,
With tow'rs and temples proudly *elevate*
On ſeven ſmall hills. *Milton's Paradiſe Regain'd, b.* ii.

ELEVA'TION. *n. ſ.* [*elevatio*, Latin.]

1. The act of raiſing aloft.

The diſruption of the ſtrata, the *elevation* of ſome, and depreſſion of others, did not fall out by chance, but were directed by a diſcerning principle. *Woodward's Nat. Hiſtory.*

2. Exaltation; dignity.

Angels, in their ſeveral degrees of *elevation* above us, may be endowed with more comprehenſive faculties. *Locke.*

3. Exaltation of the mind by noble conceptions.

We are therefore to love him with all poſſible application and *elevation* of ſpirit, with all the heart, ſoul and mind. *Norris.*

4. Attention to objects above us.

All which different *elevations* of ſpirit unto God, are contained in the name of prayer. *Hooker, b.* v. *ſ.* 48.

5. The height of any heavenly body with reſpect to the horizon.

Some latitudes have no canicular days, as thoſe which have more than ſeventy-three degrees of northern *elevation*, as Nova Zembla. *Brown's Vulgar Errours, b.* iv. *c.* 12.

ELEVA'TOR. *n. ſ.* [from *elevate.*] A raiſer or lifter up, applied to ſome chirurgical inſtruments put to ſuch uſes. *Quincy.*

ELE'VEN. *adj.* [ænblepen, Saxon.] Ten and one; one more than ten.

Had I a dozen ſons, each in my love alike, and none leſs dear than thine and my good Marcius, I had rather *eleven* die nobly for their country, than one voluptuouſly ſurfeit out of action. *Shakeſpeare's Coriolanus.*

ELE'VENTH. *adj.* [from *eleven.*] The next in order to the tenth.

In the *eleventh* chapter he returns to ſpeak of the building of Babel. *Raleigh's Hiſtory of the World.*

ELF. *n. ſ.* plural *elves.* [*eilf*, Welſh. *Baxter's* Gloſſ.]

1. A wandering ſpirit, ſuppoſed to be ſeen in wild unfrequented places.

Through this houſe give glimmering light,
By the dead and drowſie fire;
Every *elf*, and fairy ſprite,
Hop as light as bird from briar. *Shak. Midſ. Night's Dream.*

The king of *elfs* and little fairy queen
Gambol'd on heaths, and danc'd on ev'ry green. *Dryden.*

If e'er one viſion touch'd thy infant thought,
Of all the nurſe and all the prieſt have taught;
Of airy *elves* by moon-light ſhadow ſeen,
The ſilver token, and the circled green. *Pope's R. of the L.*

2. A devil.

That we may angels ſeem, we paint them *elves*;
And are but ſatires to ſet up ourſelves. *Dryden's Eſſ. on Sat.*

However it was civil, an angel or *elf*;
For he ne'er could have fill'd it ſo well of himſelf. *Swift.*

To ELF. *v. a.* [from the noun.] To entangle hair in ſo intricate a manner, that it is not to be unravelled. This the vulgar have ſuppoſed to be the work of fairies in the night; and all hair ſo matted together, hath had the name of *elf-locks.* *Hanmer.*

My face I'll grime with filth,
Blanket my loins, *elf* all my hair in knots. *Shakeſ. K. Lear.*

E'LFLOCK. *n. ſ.* [*elf* and *lock.*] Knots of hair twiſted by elves.

This is that very Mab,
That plats the manes of horſes in the night,
And cakes the *elflocks* in foul ſluttiſh hairs,
Which, once untangl'd, much misfortune bodes. *Shakeſp.*

To ELI'CITE. *v. a.* [*elicio*, Latin.] To ſtrike out; to fetch out by labour or art.

Although the ſame truths may be *elicited*, and explicated by the contemplation of animals, yet they are more clearly evidenced in the contemplation of man. *Hale's Origin of Mank.*

He *elicits* thoſe acts out of the meer lapſed ſtate of human nature. *Cheyne's Phil. Princ.*

ELI'CIT. *adj.* [*elicitus*, Latin.] Brought into act; brought from poſſibility to real exiſtence.

It is the virtue of humility and obedience, and not the formal *elicit* act of meekneſs; meekneſs being ordinarily annexed to theſe virtues. *Hammond's Pract. Catech.*

The ſchools diſpute whether, in morals, the external action ſuperadds any thing of good or evil to the internal *elicit* act of the will. *South's Sermons.*

ELICITA'TION. *n. ſ.* [from *elicio*, Latin.]

That *elicitation* which the ſchools intend, is a deducing of the power of the will into act: that drawing which they mention, is merely from the appetibility of the object. *Bramh.*

To ELI'DE. *v. a.* [*elido*, Latin.] To cut in pieces.

We are to cut off that whereunto they, from whom theſe objections proceed, fly for defence, when the force and ſtrength of the argument is *elided.* *Hooker, b.* iv. *ſ.* 4.

E'LIGIBILITY. *n. ſ.* [from *eligible.*] Worthineſs to be choſen.

The buſineſs of the will is not to judge concerning the nature of things, but to chuſe them in conſequence of the report made by the underſtanding, as to their *eligibility* or goodneſs. *Fiddes's Sermons.*

E'LIGIBLE. *adj.* [*eligibilis*, Latin] Fit to be choſen; worthy of choice; preferable.

A Britiſh miniſtry ought to be ſatisfied, if, allowing to every particular man that his private ſcheme is wiſeſt, they can perſuade him that next to his own plan, that of the government is the moſt *eligible.* *Addiſon's Freeholder*, N°. 48.

Did they really think, that going on with the war was more *eligible* for their country than the leaſt abatement of thoſe conditions? *Swift.*

That the moſt plain, ſhort, and lawful way to any good end, is more *eligible* than one directly contrary in ſome or all of theſe qualities. *Swift.*

Certainty, in a deep diſtreſs, is more *eligible* than ſuſpenſe. *Clariſſa.*

E'LIGIBLENESS. *n. ſ.* [from *eligible.*] Worthineſs to be choſen; preferableneſs.

ELIMINA'TION. *n. ſ.* [*elimino*, Latin.] The act of baniſhing, the act of turning out of doors; rejection. *Dict.*

ELI'SION. *n. ſ.* [*eliſio*, Latin.]

1. The act of cutting off: as, *th' attempt*, there is an eliſion of a ſyllable.

You will obſerve the abbreviations and *eliſions*, by which conſonants of moſt obdurate ſounds are joined together, without any ſoftening vowel to intervene. *Swift.*

2. Diviſion; ſeparation of parts.

The cauſe given of ſound, that it would be an *eliſion* of the air, whereby, if they mean any thing, they mean a cutting or dividing, or elſe an attenuating of the air, is but a term of ignorance. *Bacon's Natural Hiſtory*, N°. 124.

ELIXA'TION. *n. ſ.* [*elixus*, Latin.] The act of boiling or ſtewing any thing.

Even to ourſelves, and more perfect animals, water performs no ſubſtantial nutrition; ſerving for refrigeration, dilution of ſolid aliment, and its *elixation* in the ſtomach. *Brown.*

ELI'XIR. *n. ſ.* [Arabick.]

1. A medicine made by ſtrong infuſion, where the ingredients are almoſt diſſolved in the menſtruum, and give it a thicker conſiſtence than a tincture. *Quincy.*

For when no healing art prevail'd,
When cordials and *elixirs* fail'd,
On your pale cheek he dropp'd the ſhow'r,
Reviv'd you like a dying flow'r. *Waller.*

2. The liquor, or whatever it be, with which chymiſts hope to tranſmute metals to gold.

No chymiſt yet the *elixir* got,
But glorifies his pregnant pot,
If by the way to him befal
Some odoriferous thing, or medicinal. *Donne.*

3. The extract or quinteſſence of any thing.

In the ſoul, when the ſupreme faculties move regularly, the inferior paſſions and affections following, there ariſes a ſerenity infinitely beyond the higheſt quinteſſence and *elixir* of worldly delight. *South's Sermons.*

4. Any cordial; or invigorating ſubſtance.

What wonder then, if fields and regions here
Breathe forth *elixir* pure! *Milton's Paradiſe Loſt, b.* iii.

ELK. *n. ſ.* [ælc, Saxon]

The *elk* is a large and ſtately animal of the ſtag kind. The neck is ſhort and ſlender; the ears nine inches in length, and four in breath. The colour of its coat in Winter is greyiſh, in Summer it is paler; generally three inches in length, and equalling horſehair in thickneſs. The upper lip of the *elk* is large. The articulations of its legs are cloſe, and the ligaments hard, ſo that its joints are leſs pliable than thoſe of other animals. The horns of the male *elk* are ſhort and thick near the head, where it by degrees expands into a great breadth, with ſeveral prominences in its edges. Elks live in herds, and are very timorous. The hoof of the left hinder foot only, has been famous for the cure of epilepſies; but it is probable, that the hoof of any other animal will do as well. *Hill's Mat. Med.*

And, ſcarce his head
Rais'd o'er the heapy wreath, the branching *elk*
Lies ſlumb'ring ſullen in the white abyſs. *Thomſon's Winter.*

ELL. *n. ſ.* [eln, Saxon.]

1. A meaſure containing forty-five inches, or a yard and a quarter.

They are ſaid to make yearly forty thouſand pieces of linnen cloath, reckoning two hundred *ells* to the piece. *Addiſon.*

2. It is taken proverbially for a long meaſure.

Acquit thee bravely, play the man;
Look not on pleaſures as they come, but go:
Defer not the laſt virtue; life's poor ſpan
Make not an *ell* by trifling in thy woe. *Herbert.*

ELLI'PSIS.

ELLI'PSIS. *n. s.* [ἔλλειψις.]

1. A figure of rhetorick, by which something is left out necessary to be supplied by the hearer.

The words are delivered by way of *ellipsis*, *Rom.* iv. 18. *Hamm.*

2. [In geometry.] An oval figure, being generated from the section of a cone, by a plane cutting both sides of the cone, but not parallel to the base, which produces a circle, and meeting with the base when produced. *Harris.*

On the cylinder inclined, describe an *ellipsis* parallel to the horizon. *Wilkins's Dædalus.*

The planets could not possibly acquire such revolutions in circular orbs, or in *ellipses* very little eccentrick. *Bentley.*

ELLI'PTICAL. } *adj.* [from *ellipsis.*] Having the form of an
ELLI'PTICK. } ellipsis; oval.

Since the planets move in *elliptick* orbits, in one of whose foci the sun is, and by a radius from the sun describe equal areas in equal times, which no other law of a circulating fluid, but the harmonical circulation, can account for; we must find out a law for the paracentrical motion, that may make the orbits *elliptick*. *Cheyne's Phil. Prin.*

In animals, that gather food from the ground, the pupil is oval or *elliptical*; the greatest diameter going transversely from side to side. *Cheyne's Phil. Prin.*

ELM. *n. s.* [*ulmus*, Latin; elm, Saxon.]

1. The name of a tree. The flower consists of one leaf, striped like a bell, having many stamina in the center: from the bottom arises the pointal, which becomes a membranaceous or leafy fruit, almost heart-shaped; in the middle of which is placed a pear-shaped seed-vessel, containing one seed of the same shape. The species are, the common rough-leaved elm; the witch hazel, or broad-leaved elm, by some called the British elm; the smooth-leaved or witch elm. It is generally believed neither of them were originally natives of this country; but they have propagated themselves by seeds and suckers in such plenty as hardly to be rooted out, where they have had long possession; especially in hedgerows, where there is harbour for their roots, which will send forth various twigs. They are very proper to place in hedgerows upon the borders of fields, where they will thrive better than when planted in a wood or close plantation, and their shade will not be very injurious to whatever grows under them. They are also proper to plant at a distance from a garden, or building, to break the violence of winds; for they may be trained up in form of an hedge, keeping them cut every year, to the height of forty or fifty feet: but they should not be planted too near a garden where fruit-trees or other plants are placed, because the roots of the elm run superficially near the top of the ground, and will intermix with the roots of other trees, and deprive them of nourishment. *Miller.*

The rural seat,
Whose lofty *elms* and venerable oaks
Invite the rook, who high amid' the boughs,
In early Spring, his airy city builds. *Thomson's Spring.*

2. It was used to support vines, to which the poets allude.

Thou art an *elm*, my husband; I a vine,
Whose weakness married to thy stronger state,
Makes me with thy strength to communicate. *Shakespeare.*

ELOCU'TION. *n. s.* [*elocutio*, Latin.]

1. The power of fluent speech.

A travelled doctor of physick, of bold, and of able *elocution.* *Wotton.*

2. Eloquence; flow of language.

Whose taste, too long forborne, at first essay
Gave *elocution* to the mute, and taught
The tongue not made for speech to speak thy praise. *Milton.*

As I have endeavoured to adorn it with noble thoughts, so much more to express those thoughts with *elocution*. *Dryden.*

3. The power of expression or diction.

The third happiness of this poet's imagination is *elocution*, or the art of cloathing or adorning that thought so found, and varied, in apt, significant, and sounding words. *Dryden.*

E'LOGY. *n. s.* [*eloge*, French.] Praise; panegyrick.

Buckingham lay under millions of maledictions, which at the prince's arrival did vanish into praises and *elogies*. *Wotton.*

If I durst say all I know of the *elogies* received from abroad concerning him, I should offend the modesty of our author. *Boyle.*

Some excellent persons, above my approbation or *elogy*, have considered this subject. *Holder's Elements of Speech.*

To ELO'IGNE. *v. a.* [*eloigner*, French.] To put at a distance; to remove one far from another. Now disused.

From worldly cares himself he did *eloin*,
And greatly shunned many exercise. *Fairy Queen*, *b.* i. *c.* 4.

I'll tell thee now, dear love! what thou shalt do
To anger destiny, as she doth us;
How I shall stay, though she *eloigne* me thus,
And how posterity shall know it too. *Donne.*

To ELO'NGATE. *v. a.* [from *longus*, Latin.] To lengthen; to draw out; to protract; to stretch.

To ELO'NGATE. *v. n.* To go off to a distance from any thing.

About Cape Frio in Brasilia, the South point of the compass varyeth twelve degrees unto the West; but *elongating* from the coast of Brasilia, towards the shore of Africa, it varyeth eastward. *Brown's Vulgar Errours*, *b.* ii. *c.* 2.

ELONGA'TION. *n. s.* [from *elongate.*]

1. The act of stretching or lengthening itself.

To this motion of *elongation* of the fibres, is owing the union or conglutination of the parts of the body, when they are separated by a wound. *Arbuthnot on Aliments.*

2. The state of being stretched.

3. [In medicine.] An imperfect luxation, when the ligament of any joint is so extended or relaxed as to lengthen the limb, but yet not let the bone go quite out of its place. *Quincy.*

Elongations are the effect of an humour soaking upon a ligament, thereby making it liable to be stretched, and to be thrust quite out upon every little force. *Wiseman's Surgery.*

4. Distance; space at which one thing is distant from another.

The distant points in the celestial expanse appear to the eye in so small a degree of *elongation* from another, as bears no proportion to what is real. *Glanv. Sceps. c.* 11.

5. Departure; removal.

Nor then had it been placed in a middle point, but that of descent, or *elongation*. *Brown's Vulgar Errours*, *b.* vi. *c.* 2.

To ELO'PE. *v. a.* [*loopen*, to run, Dutch.] To run away; to break loose; to escape from law or restraint.

It is necessary to treat women as members of the body politick, since great numbers of them have *eloped* from their allegiance. *Addison's Freeholder*, Nº. 32.

What from the dame can Paris hope?
She may as well from him *elope*. *Prior.*

The fool whose wife *elopes* some thrice a quarter,
For matrimonial solace dies a martyr. *Pope's Ep. of Horace.*

ELO'PEMENT. *n. s.* [from *elope.*] Departure from just restraint; rejection of lawful power.

An *elopement* is the voluntary departure of a wife from her husband to live with an adulterer, and with whom she lives in breach of the matrimonial vow. *Ayliffe's Parergon.*

The negligent husband, trusting to the efficacy of this principle, was undone by his wife's *elopement* from him. *Arbuthnot.*

ELOPS. *n. s.* [ἔλοψ.] A fish; reckoned however by *Milton* among the serpents.

Scorpion and asp, and amphisbena dire,
Cerastes horn'd, hydrus, and *elops* drear,
And dipsas. *Milton's Paradise Lost*, *b.* x. *l.* 525.

ELOQUE'NCE. *n. s.* [*eloquentia*, Latin.]

1. The power of speaking with fluency and elegance; oratory.

Action is *eloquence*, and the eyes of th' ignorant
More learned than the ears. *Shakesp. Coriolanus.*

2. Elegant language uttered with fluency.

Say she be mute, and will not speak a word;
Then I'll commend her volubility,
And say she uttereth piercing *eloquence*. *Shakespeare.*

Fit words attended on his weighty sense,
And mild persuasion flow'd in *eloquence*. *Pope's Odyssey*, *b.* vii.

E'LOQUENT. *adj.* [*eloquens*, Latin.] Having the power of oratory; having the power of fluent and elegant speech.

The Lord of hosts doth take away the captain of fifty, and the honourable man, and the counsellor, and the cunning artificer, and the *eloquent* orator. *Is.* iii. 3.

O death! all *eloquent*, you only prove
What dust we dote on, when 'tis man we love. *Pope.*

ELSE. *pronoun.* [elleꞅ, Saxon.] Other; one besides: it is applied both to persons and things.

To stand stained with travel, and sweating with desire to see him; thinking of nothing *else*, putting all affairs *else* in oblivion, as if there were nothing *else* to be done but to see him. *Shakesp. Henry* IV. *p.* ii.

Should he or any *else* search, he will find evidence of the Divine Wisdom. *Hale's Origin of Mankind.*

He says, 'twas then with him, as now with you;
He did it when he had nothing *else* to do. *Denham.*

ELSE. *adv.* Otherwise.

Dare not, on thy life,
Touch ought of mine beside, by lot my due,
But stand aloof, and think profane to view:
This faulchion, *else*, not hitherto withstood,
These hostile fields shall fatten with thy blood. *Dryden.*

What ways are there whereby we should be assured, but either by an internal impression of the notion of a God upon our minds, or *else* by such external and visible effects as our reason tells us must be attributed to some cause. *Tillotson's Serm.*

2. Beside; except that mentioned.

Pleasures which no where *else* were to be found,
And all Elysium in a spot of ground. *Dryden.*

E'LSEWHERE. *adv.* [*else* and *where.*]

1. In any other place.

There are here divers trees, which are not to be found *elsewhere*. *Abbot's Description of the World.*

As he proved that Pison was not Ganges, or Gehon, Nilus; so where to find them *elsewhere* he knew not. *Raleigh's Hist.*

For, if we chance to fix our thoughts *elsewhere*,
Though our eyes open be, we cannot see. *Davies.*

Henceforth oracles are ceas'd,
And thou no more with pomp and sacrifice
Shalt be enquir'd at Delphos, or *elsewhere*. *Paradise Reg.*

Although seasoned bodies may and do live near as long in London as *elsewhere*, yet new-comers and children do not. *Graunt's Bills of Mortality.*

2. In other places; in some other place.

They which *elsewhere* complain, that disgrace and injury is offered to the meanest minister, when the magistrate appointeth him what to wear, think the gravest prelates no competent judges to appoint where it is fit for the minister to stand. *Hooker, b.* v. *s.* 29.

Let us no more contend, nor blame
Each other, blam'd enough *elsewhere*. *Milton's Paradise Lost.*

Bestow, base man, thy idle threats *elsewhere*;
My mother's daughter knows not how to fear. *Dryden.*

If it contradict what he says *elsewhere*, it is no new or strange thing. *Tillotson, Preface.*

To Elu'cidate. *v. a.* [*elucido*, Latin.] To explain; to clear; to make plain.

To *elucidate* a little the matter, let us consider it. *Boyle.*

Elucida'tion. *n. s.* [from *elucidate.*] Explanation; exposition.

We shall, in order to the *elucidation* of this matter, subjoin the following experiment. *Boyle.*

Elucida'tor. *n. s.* [from *elucidate.*] Explainer; expositor; commentator.

Obscurity is brought over them by the course of ignorance and age, and yet more by their pedantical *elucidators*. *Abbot.*

To ELU'DE. *v. a.* [*eludo*, Latin.]

1. To escape by stratagem; to avoid any mischief or danger by artifice.

Several pernicious vices, notorious among us, escape or *elude* the punishment of any law yet invented. *Swift.*

He who looks no higher for the motives of his conduct than the resentments of human justice, whenever he can presume himself cunning enough to *elude*, rich enough to bribe, or strong enough to resist it, will be under no restraint. *Rogers.*

2. To mock by an unexpected escape.

Me gentle Delia beckons from the plain,
Then, hid in shades, *eludes* her eager swain;
But feigns a laugh to see me search around,
And by that laugh the willing fair is found. *Pope's Spring.*

Elu'dible. *adj.* [from *elude.*] Possible to be defeated.

There is not any common place more insisted on than the happiness of trials by juries; yet if this blessed part of our law be *eludible* by power and artifice, we shall have little reason to boast. *Swift.*

Elves. The plural of *elf.* See Elf.

Ye sylphs and sylphids to your chief give ear;
Fays, fairies, genii, *elves* and demons hear. *Pope.*

Elvelo'ck. *n. s.* [from *elves* and *lock.*] Knots in the hair superstitiously supposed to be tangled by the fairies.

From the like might proceed the fears of polling *elvelocks*, or complicated hairs of the head. *Brown's Vulgar Errours, b.* v.

E'lvish. *adj.* [from *elves*, the plural of *elf*: it had been written more properly *elfish.*] Relating to elves, or wandering spirits.

Thou *elvish* markt, abortive, rioting hog!
The slave of nature, and the son of hell! *Shakesp. R.* III.

No muse hath been so bold,
Or of the latter, or the old,
Those *elvish* secrets to unfold,
Which lie from others reading. *Drayton.*

Elu'mbated. *adj.* [*elumbis*, Lat.] Weakened in the loins. *Dict.*

Elu'sion. *n. s.* [*elusio*, Latin.] An escape from enquiry or examination; a fraud; an artifice.

An appendix, relating to the transmutation of metals, detects the impostures and *elusions* of those who have pretended to it. *Woodward's Natural History.*

Elu'sive. *adj.* [from *elude.*] Practising elusion; using arts to escape.

Elusive of the bridal day, she gives
Fond hopes to all, and all with hopes deceives. *Pope's Odyss.*

Elu'sory. *adj.* [from *elude.*] Tending to elude; tending to deceive; fraudulent; deceitful; fallacious.

It may be feared they are but Parthian flights, ambuscade retreats, and *elusory* tergiversation. *Brown's Vulgar Errours.*

To Elu'te. *v. a.* [*eluo*, Latin.] To wash off.

The more oily any spirit is, the more pernicious; because it is harder to be *eluted* by the blood. *Arbuthnot on Aliments.*

To Elu'triate. *v. a.* [*elutrio*, Latin.] To decant; or strain out.

The pressure of the air upon the lungs is much less than it has been computed by some; but still it is something, and the alteration of one tenth of its force upon the lungs must produce some difference in *elutriating* the blood as it passes through the lungs. *Arbuthnot on Air.*

Ely'sian. *adj.* [*elysius*, Latin.] Pertaining to Elysium; pleasant; deliciously soft and soothing; exceedingly delightful.

The river of life, through midst of heaven,
Rolls o'er *elysian* flowers her amber stream. *Milton.*

Ely'sium. *n. s.* [Latin.] The place assigned by the heathens to happy souls; any place exquisitely pleasant.

To have thee with thy lips to stop my mouth,
So should'st thou either turn my flying soul,
Or I should breathe it so into thy body,
And then it liv'd in sweet *Elysium*. *Shakespeare's Henry* VI.

'Em. A contraction of them.

For he could coin and counterfeit
New words with little or no wit;
And when with hasty noise he spoke *'em*,
The ignorant for current took *'em*. *Hudibras.*

To EMA'CIATE. *v. a.* [*emacio*, Latin.] To waste; to deprive of flesh.

All dying of the consumption, die *emaciated* and lean. *Graunt's Bills of Mortality.*

To Ema'ciate. *v. n.* To lose flesh; to pine; to grow lean.

He *emaciated* and pined away in the too anxious enquiry of the sea's reciprocation, although not drowned therein. *Brown.*

Emacia'tion. *n. s.* [*emaciatus*, Latin.]

1. The act of making lean.
2. The state of one grown lean.

Searchers cannot tell whether this *emaciation* or leanness were from a phthisis, or from an hectick fever. *Graunt.*

Emacula'tion. *n. s.* [*emaculo*, Latin.] The act of freeing any thing from spots or foulness. *Dict.*

E'manant. *adj.* [*emanans*, Latin.] Issuing from something else.

The first act of the divine nature, relating to the world and his administration thereof, is an *emanant* act: the most wise counsel and purpose of Almighty God terminate in those two great transient or *emanant* acts or works, the work of creation and providence. *Hale's Origin of Mankind.*

Emana'tion. *n. s.* [*emanatio*, Latin.]

1. The act of issuing or proceeding from any other substance.

Aristotle said, that it streamed by connatural result and *emanation* from God, the infinite and eternal Mind, as the light issues from the sun. *South's Sermons.*

2. That which issues from another substance; an effluence; effluvium.

The experience of those profitable and excellent *emanations* from God, may be, and commonly are, the first motive of our love. *Taylor.*

Another way of attraction is delivered by a tenuous *emanation*, or continued effluvium, which, after some distance, retracteth unto itself; as in syrups, oils, and viscosities, which, spun, at length retire into their former dimensions. *Brown.*

Such were the features of her heav'nly face;
Her limbs were form'd with such harmonious grace;
So faultless was the frame, as if the whole
Had been an *emanation* of the soul. *Dryden.*

The letters, every judge will see, were by no means efforts of the genius, but *emanations* of the heart. *Pope.*

Each *emanation* of his fires
That beams on earth, each virtue he inspires;
Each art he prompts, each charm he can create;
Whate'er he gives, are giv'n for you to hate. *Pope's Dunciad.*

Ema'native. *adj.* [from *emano*, Latin.] Issuing from another. *Dict.*

To EMA'NCIPATE. *v. a.* [*emancipo*, Latin.] To set free from servitude; to restore to liberty.

Having received the probable inducements of truth, we become *emancipated* from testimonial engagements. *Brown.*

By the twelve tables, only those were called unto the intestate succession of their parents that were in the parents power, excluding all *emancipated* children. *Ayliffe's Parergon.*

They soon *emancipated* themselves from that dependance. *Arbuthnot on Coins.*

Emancipa'tion. *n. s.* [from *emancipate.*] The act of setting free; deliverance from slavery.

Obstinacy in opinions holds the dogmatist in the chains of error, without hope of *emancipation*. *Glanv. Sceps. c.* 27.

To Ema'rginate. *v. a.* [*margo*, Latin.] To take away the margin or edge of any thing. *Dict.*

To Ema'sculate. *v. a.* [*emasculo*, Latin.]

1. To castrate; to deprive of virility.

When it is found how many ews, suppose twenty, one ram will serve, we may geld nineteen, or thereabouts; for if you *emasculate* but ten, you shall, by promiscuous copulation, hinder the increase. *Graunt's Bills of Mortality.*

2. To effeminate; to weaken; to vitiate by unmanly softness.

From wars and from affairs of state abstain;
Women *emasculate* a monarch's reign. *Dryden's Aurengzebe.*

Dangerous principles not only impose upon our understandings, but *emasculate* our spirits, and spoil our temper. *Collier on Pride.*

Ema'sculation. *n. s.* [from *emasculate.*]

1. Castration.
2. Effeminacy; womanish qualities; unmanly softness.

To Emba'le. *v. a.* [*emballer*, French.]

1. To make up into a bundle.
2. To bind up; to inclose.

Below her ham her weed did somewhat train,
And her straight legs most bravely were *embal'd*
In golden buskins of costly cordwain. *Fairy Queen, b.* ii.

I would not be a queen
For all the world.
——In faith, for little England
You'd venture an *embaling*. *Shakespeare's Henry* VIII.

To EMBA'LM. *v. a.* [*embaumer*, French; *embalsamar*, Span.] To impregnate a body with aromaticks, that it may resist putrefaction.

Embalm me,
Then lay me forth; although unqueen'd, yet like
A queen, and daughter to a king, inter me. *Shak. H.* VIII.

I would shew future times
What you were, and teach them t' urge towards such:
Verse *embalms* virtue, and tombs or thrones of rhymes,
Preserve frail transitory fame as much
As spice doth bodies from corrupt air's touch. *Donne.*

Muse! at that name thy sacred sorrows shed;
Those tears eternal, that *embalm* the dead. *Pope.*

EMBA'LMER. *n. s.* [from *embalm.*] One that practises the art of embalming and preserving bodies.

The Romans were not so good *embalmers* as the Egyptians, so the body was utterly consumed. *Bacon's Natural History.*

To EMBA'R. *v. a.* [from *bar.*]
1. To shut; to enclose.

Themselves for fear into his jaws to fall,
He forc'd to castle strong to take their flight;
Where fast *embar'd* in mighty brazen wall,
He has them now four years besieg'd to make them thrall.
Fairy Queen, b. i. *cant.* 7. *stanz.* 44.

In form of airy members fair *embar'd*,
His spirits pure were subject to our sight. *Fairfax, b.* i.

2. To stop; to hinder by prohibition; to block up.

Translating the mart, which commonly followed the English cloth, unto Calis, he *embared* all further trade for the future. *Bacon's Henry* VII.

If this commerce 'twixt heav'n and earth were not
Embar'd, and all this traffick quite forgot,
She, for whose loss we have lamented thus,
Would work more fully and pow'rfully on us. *Donne.*

EMBA'RCATION. *n. s.* [from *embark.*]
1. The act of putting on shipboard.

The French gentlemen were very solicitous for the *embarcation* of the army, and for the departure of the fleet. *Clarendon.*

2. The act of going on shipboard.

EMBA'RGO. *n. s.* [*embargar*, Spanish.] A prohibition to pass; in commerce, a stop put to trade.

He knew that the subjects of Flanders drew so great commodity from the trade of England, as by *embargo* they would soon wax weary of Perkin. *Bacon's Henry* VII.

After an *embargo* of our trading ships in the river of Bourdeaux, and other points of sovereign affront, there did succeed the action of Rheez. *Wotton.*

I was not much concerned, in my own particular, for the *embargo* which was laid upon it. *Dryden's Preface to Cleomenes.*

To EMBA'RK. *v. a.* [*embarquer*, French.]
1. To put on shipboard.

Of mankind, so numerous late,
All left, in one small bottom swam *embark'd*. *Milt. P. Lost.*

The king had likewise provided a good fleet, and had caused a body of three thousand foot to be *embarked* on those ships. *Clarendon, b.* ii.

Straight to the ships Eneas took his way,
Embark'd his men, and skim'd along the sea. *Dryden's Æn.*

2. To engage another in any affair.

To EMBA'RK. *v. n.*
1. To go on shipboard.

I should with speed *embark*,
And with their embassy return to Greece. *A. Phillips.*

2. To engage in any affair.

To EMBA'RRASS. *v. a.* [*embarasser*, French.] To perplex; to distress; to entangle.

I saw my friend a little *embarrassed*, and turned away. *Spect.*

EMBA'RRASSMENT. *n. s.* [from *embarrass.*] Perplexity; entanglement.

Let your method be plain, that your hearers may run through it without *embarrassment*, and take a clear view of the whole. *Watts's Logick.*

To EMBA'SE. *v. a.* [from *base.*]
1. To vitiate; to depauperate; to lower; to deprave; to impair.

Grains are annual, so that the virtue of the seed is not worn out; whereas in a tree it is *embased* by the ground. *Bac.*

I have no service or ignoble end in my present labour, which may, on either side, restrain or *embase* the freedom of my poor judgment. *Wotton.*

I will rather chuse to wear a crown of thorns, than to exchange that of gold for one of lead, whose *embased* flexibleness shall be forced to bend. *King Charles.*

A pleasure high, rational, and angelical; a pleasure *embased* with no appendant sting; but such a one as being honey in the mouth, never turns to gall or gravel in the belly. *South.*

2. To degrade; to vilify.

Joy of my life, full oft for loving you
I bless my lot, that was so lucky plac'd;
But then the more your own mishap I rue,
That are so much by so mean love *embas'd*. *Spenser's Sonn.*

EMBA'SSADOR. *n. s.* [See AMBASSADOUR.] One sent on a publick message.

Mighty Jove's *embassador* appear'd
With the same message. *Denham.*

Myself, my king's *embassador*, will go. *Dryd. Ind. Emp.*

EMBA'SSADRESS. *n. s.* A woman sent on a publick message.

With fear the modest matron lifts her eyes,
And to the bright *embassadress* replies. *Garth's Ovid.*

E'MBASSAGE. } *n. s.* [It may be observed, that though our
E'MBASSY. } authors write almost indiscriminately *embassador* or *ambassador*, *embassage* or *ambassage*; yet there is scarcely an example of *ambassy*, all concurring to write *embassy*.]

1. A publick message; a message concerning business between princes or states.

Fresh *embassy* and suits,
Nor from the state nor private friends, hereafter,
Will I lend ear to. *Shakesp. Coriolanus.*

When he was at Newcastle he sent a solemn *embassage* unto James III. king of Scotland, to treat and conclude a peace with him. *Bacon's Henry* VII.

The peace polluted thus, a chosen band
He first commissions to the Latian land,
In threat'ning *embassy*. *Dryden's Æn.*

2. Any solemn message.

He sends the angels on *embassies* with his decrees. *Taylor.*

3. An errand in an ironical sense.

A bird was made fly with such art to carry a written *embassage* among the ladies, that one might say, if a live bird, how taught? If dead, how made? *Sidney, b.* ii.

Nimble mischance, that art so light of foot,
Doth not thy *embassage* belong to me?
And am I last that know it. *Shakespeare's Richard* II.

To EMBA'TTLE. *v. a.* [from *battle.*] To range in order or array of battle.

The English are *embattled*;
To horse! you gallant princes, strait to horse! *Shakespeare.*

I could drive her then from the ward of her purity, her reputation, her marriage-vow, and a thousand other her defences, which now are too strongly *embattled* against me.
Shakespeare's Merry Wives of Windsor.

On their *embattl'd* ranks the waves return,
And overwhelm the war! *Milton's Paradise Lost, b.* xii.

Embattl'd nations strive in vain
The hero's glory to restrain:
Streams arm'd with rocks, and mountains red with fire,
In vain against his force conspire. *Prior.*

To EMBA'Y. *v. a.* [from *baigner*, to bathe, French.]
1. To bathe; to wet; to wash.

In her lap a little babe did play;
His cruel sport;
For in her streaming blood he did *embay*
His little hands, and tender joints embrew. *Fairy Queen.*

Every sense the humour sweet *embay'd*,
And, slumb'ring soft, my heart did steal away. *Fai. Queen.*

2. [From *bay.*] To inclose in a bay; to land-lock.

If that the Turkish fleet
Be not inshelter'd and *embay'd*, they're drown'd. *Shakesp.*

To EMBE'LLISH. *v. a.* [*embellir*, French.] To adorn; to beautify; to grace with ornaments; to decorate.

How much more beauteous had the fountain been,
Embellish'd with her first created green;
Where crystal streams through living turf had run,
Contented with an urn of native stone. *Dryden's Juvenal.*

The names of the figures that *embellished* the discourses of those who understood the art of speaking, are not the art and skill of speaking well. *Locke.*

That which was once the most beautiful spot of Italy, covered with palaces, *embellished* by emperors, and celebrated by poets, has now nothing to shew but ruins. *Addison on Italy.*

EMBE'LLISHMENT. *n. s.* [from *embellish.*] Ornament; adventitious beauty; decoration; adscititious grace; any thing that confers the power of pleasing.

Cultivate the wild licentious savage
With wisdom, discipline, and liberal arts,
The *embellishments* of life. *Addison's Cato.*

Apparitions, visions, and intercourses of all kinds between the dead and the living, are the frequent and familiar *embellishments* of those pious romances, the legends of the Romish church. *Atterbury's Sermons.*

E'MBERING. *n. s.* The ember days. A word used by old authors, now obsolete.

For causes good so many ways,
Keep *emb'rings* well, and fasting days,

What

What law commands we ought to obey,
For Friday, Saturn, and Wednesday. *Tuss. Hus. for June.*

E'MBERS. *n. s.* without a singular. [æmyrıa, Saxon, ashes; *einmyria*, Islandick, hot ashes or cinders.] Hot cinders; ashes not yet extinguished.

Take hot *embers*, and put them about a bottle filled with new beer, almost to the very neck: let the bottle be well stopped, lest it fly out; and continue it, renewing the *embers* every day for the space of ten days. *Bacon's Natural History.*

Or if the air will not permit,
Some still removed place will fit,
While glowing *embers* through the room
Teach light to counterfeit a gloom. *Milton.*

While thus heav'n's highest counsels, by the low
Footsteps of their effects, he trac'd too well,
He tost his troubled eyes, *embers* that glow
Now with new rage, and wax too hot for hell. *Crashaw.*

He said, and rose, as holy zeal inspires;
He rakes hot *embers*, and renews the fires. *Dryden's Virgil.*

E'MBERWEEK. *n. s.* [The original of this word has been much controverted: some derive it from *embers* or ashes strewed by penitents on their heads; but *Nelson* decides in favour of *Mareschal*, who derives it from *ymbren* or *embren*, a *course* or *circumvolution.*] A week in which an ember day falls.

The ember days at the four seasons are the Wednesday, Friday, and Saturday after the first Sunday in Lent, the feast of Pentecost, September 14, December 13. *Comm. Prayer.*

Stated times appointed for fasting are Lent, and the four seasons of the year called *emberweeks.* *Ayliffe's Parergon.*

To EMBE'ZZLE. *v. a.* [This word seems corrupted by an ignorant pronunciation from *imbecil.*]

1. To appropriate by breach of trust; to turn what is intrusted in his hands to his own use.

He had *embezzled* the king's treasure, and extorted money by way of loan from all men. *Hayward.*

2. To waste; to swallow up in riot.

When thou hast *embezzl'd* all thy store,
Where's all thy father left? *Dryden's Pers. Sat.* vi.

EMBE'ZZLEMENT. *n. s.* [from *embezzle.*]

1. The act of appropriating to himself that which is received in trust for another.

2. The thing appropriated.

To EMBLA'ZE. *v. a.* [*blasonner*, French.]

1. To adorn with glittering embellishments.

Th' unsought diamonds
Would so *emblaze* the forehead of the deep,
And so bestud with stars, that they below
Would grow inur'd to light. *Milton.*

No weeping orphan saw his father's stores
Our shrines irradiate, or *emblaze* the floors. *Pope.*

2. To blason; to paint with ensigns armorial.

Nor shall this blood be wiped from thy point,
But thou shalt wear it as a herald's coat,
T' *emblaze* the honour which thy master got. *Shak. H.* VI.

He from the glittering staff unfurl'd
Th' imperial ensign, streaming to the wind,
With gems and golden lustre rich *emblaz'd*,
Seraphick arms and trophies. *Milton's Paradise Lost, b.* i.

To EMBLA'ZON. *v. a.* [*blasonner*, French.]

1. To adorn with figures of heraldry; to grace with ensigns armorial.

2. To deck in glaring colours; to set out pompously to shew.

We find Augustus, for some petty conquest, *emblazoned* by the poets to the highest pitch. *Hakewill on Providence.*

E'MBLEM. *n. s.* [ἔμβλημα.]

1. Inlay; enamel; any thing inserted into the body of another.

2. An occult representation; an allusive picture; a typical designation.

She had all the royal makings of a queen,
The rod, and bird of peace, and all such *emblems*,
Laid nobly on her. *Shakespeare's Henry* VIII.

If you draw your beast in an *emblem*, shew a landscape of the country natural to the beast. *Peacham on Drawing.*

Gentle Thames,
Thy mighty master's *emblem*, in whose face
Sate meekness, heighten'd with majestick grace. *Denham.*

He is indeed a proper *emblem* of knowledge and action, being all head and paws. *Addison's Guardian*, N°. 114.

To E'MBLEM. *v. a.* [from the noun.] To represent in an occult or allusive manner.

The primitive fight of elements doth fitly *emblem* that of opinions. *Glanv. Sceps. c.* 27.

EMBLEMA'TICAL. } *adj.* [from *emblem.*]
EMBLEMA'TICK. }

1. Comprising an emblem; allusive; occultly representative.

In the well fram'd models,
With *emblematick* skill and mystick order,
Thou shew'dst where tow'rs on battlements should rise,
Where gates should open, or where walls should compass. *Prior.*

The poets contribute to the explication of reverses purely *emblematical*, or when the persons are allegorical. *Addison.*

2. Dealing in emblems; using emblems.

By tongue and pudding to our friends explain
What does your *emblematick* worship mean. *Prior.*

EMBLEMA'TICALLY. *adv.* [from *emblematical*] In the manner of emblems; allusively; with occult representation.

Others have spoken *emblematically* and hieroglyphically, as to the Egyptians; and the phœnix was the hieroglyphick of the sun. *Brown's Vulgar Errours, b.* iii. *c.* 10.

He took a great stone, and put it up under the oak, *emblematically* joining the two great elements of masonry. *Swift.*

EMBLE'MATIST. *n. s.* [from *emblem.*] Writers or inventers of emblems.

These fables are still maintained by symbolical writers, *emblematists*, and heralds. *Brown's Vulgar Errours, b.* i. *c.* 9.

E'MBOLISM. *n. s.* [ἐμβολισμός.]

1. Intercalation; insertion of days or years to produce regularity and equation of time.

The civil constitutions of the year were after different manners in several nations; some using the sun's year, but in divers fashions; and some following the moon, finding out *embolisms* or equations, even to the addition of whole months, to make all as even as they could. *Holder on Time.*

2. The time inserted; intercalatory time.

E'MBOLUS. *n. s.* [ἔμβολος.] Any thing inserted and acting in another, as the sucker in a pump.

Our members make a sort of an hydraulick engine, in which a chemical liquor, resembling blood, is driven through elastick channels by the force of an *embolus*, like the heart. *Arbuthnot and Pope's Mart. Scriblerus.*

To EMBO'SS. *v. a.* [from *bosse*, a protuberance, French.]

1. To form with protuberances; to cover with something rising into lumps or bunches.

Timon hath made his everlasting mansion
Upon the beached verge of the salt flood;
Which once a day, with his *embossed* froth,
The turbulent surge shall cover. *Shakespeare's Timon.*

Thou art a bile,
A plague sore, or *embossed* carbuncle,
In my corrupted blood. *Shakespeare's King Lear.*

Botches and blains must all his flesh *emboss*,
And all his people. *Milton's Paradise Lost, b.* xii.

All croud in heaps, as at a night-alarm
The bees drive out upon each others backs,
T' *emboss* their hives in clusters. *Dryden's Don Sebastian.*

2. To engrave with relief, or rising work.

Then o'er the lofty gate his art *emboss'd*
Androgeo's death, and off'rings to his ghost. *Dryden's Virg.*

3. [from *emboister*, French, to inclose in a box.] To inclose; to include; to cover.

And in the way, as she did weep and wail,
A knight her met, in mighty arms *emboss'd*. *Fairy Queen.*

4. [*emboscare*, Italian.] To inclose in a thicket.

Like that self-begotten bird
In th' Arabian woods *embost*. *Milton's Agonistes.*

5. To hunt hard.

When a deer is hard run, and foams at the mouth, he is said to be *embost*: a dog also, when he is strained with hard running, especially upon hard ground, will have his knees swelled, and then he is said to be *embost*, from *bosse*, French, a tumour. *Hanmer.*

Oh, he is more mad
Than Telamon for his shield; the boar of Thessaly
Was never so *embost*. *Shakespeare's Ant. and Cleopatra.*

We have almost *embost* him: you shall see his fall to-night. *Shakespeare's All's well that ends well.*

EMBO'SSMENT. *n. s.* [from *emboss.*]

1. Any thing standing out from the rest; jut; eminence.

I wish also, in the very middle, a fair mount, with three ascents and alleys, enough for four to walk a-breast; which I would have to be perfect circles, without any bulwarks or *embossments.* *Bacon's Essays, Civ. and Moral.*

2. Relief; rising work.

They are at a loss about the word pendentis; some fancy it expresses only the great *embossment* of the figure, others believe it hung off the helmet in alto relievo. *Addison on Italy.*

To EMBO'TTLE. *v. a.* [*bouteille*, French.] To include in bottles; to bottle.

Stirom, firmest fruit
Embottled, long as Priamean Troy
Withstood the Greeks, endures. *Phillips.*

To EMBO'WEL. *v. a.* [from *bowel*] To eviscerate; to deprive of the entrails; to exenterate.

The schools,
Embowelled of their doctrine, have left off
The danger to itself. *Shakespeare's All's well that ends well.*

Embowell'd will I see thee by and by;
'Till then, in blood, by noble Percy lye. *Shak. Henry* IV.

The roar
Embowel'd with outrageous noise the air,
And all her entrails tore. *Milton's Paradise Lost, b.* vi.

Fossils and minerals that th' *embowel'd* earth
Displays. *Phillips.*

To

To EMBRA'CE. *v. a.* [*embraſſer*, French.]

1. To hold fondly in the arms; to ſqueeze in kindneſs.

Embrace again, my ſons! be foes no more;
Nor ſtain your country with her children's gore. *Dryden.*

2. To ſeize ardently or eagerly; to lay hold on; to welcome; to accept willingly any thing offered.

I take it, your own buſineſs calls on you,
And you *embrace* th' occaſion to depart. *Shakeſpeare.*

At firſt, her mother earth ſhe holdeth dear,
And doth *embrace* the world, and worldly things. *Davies.*

They who are repreſented by the wiſe virgins, *embraced* the profeſſion of the Chriſtian religion, as the fooliſh virgins alſo had done. *Tillotſon's Sermons.*

3. To comprehend; to take in; to encompaſs; to encircle.

4. To compriſe; to incloſe; to contain.

Low at his feet a ſpacious plain is plac'd,
Between the mountain and the ſtream *embrac'd.* *Denham.*

5. To admit; to receive.

Fenton, heav'n give thee joy!
What cannot be eſchew'd, muſt be *embraced.* *Shakeſpeare.*

If a man can be fully aſſured of any thing, without having examined, what is there that he may not *embrace* for truth? *Locke.*

6. To find; to take.

Fleance, his ſon,
Whoſe abſence is no leſs material to me
Than is his father's, muſt *embrace* the fate
Of that dark hour. *Shakeſpeare's Macbeth.*

7. To ſqueeze in a hoſtile manner.

To EMBRA'CE. *v. n.* To join in an embrace.

Let me *embrace* with old Vincentio;
And wander we to ſee thy honeſt ſon,
Who will of thy arrival be full joyous. *Shakeſpeare.*

EMBRA'CE. *n. ſ.* [from the verb.]

1. Claſp; fond preſſure in the arms; hug.

Thames, the moſt lov'd of all the ocean's ſons
By his old ſire, to his *embraces* runs. *Denham.*

2. An hoſtile ſqueeze; cruſh.

EMBRA'CEMENT. *n. ſ.* [from *embrace.*]

1. Claſp in the arms; hug; embrace.

Thus death becomes a rival to us all,
And hopes with foul *embracements* her to get,
In whoſe decay virtue's fair ſhrine muſt fall. *Sidney.*

There cheriſhing one another with dear, though chaſte *embracements*, with ſweet, though cold kiſſes, it might ſeem that love was come to play him there without darts. *Sidney, b.* ii.

2. Comprehenſion.

Nor can her wide *embracements* filled be. *Davies.*

3. State of being contained; incloſure.

The parts in man's body eaſily reparable, as ſpirits, blood, and fleſh, die in the *embracement* of the parts hardly reparable, as bones, nerves, and membranes. *Bacon's Natural Hiſtory.*

4. Conjugal endearment.

I would freelier rejoice in that abſence, wherein he won honour, than in the *embracements* of his bed, where he would ſhew moſt love. *Shakeſpeare's Coriolanus.*

EMBRA'CER. *n. ſ.* [from *embrace.*] The perſon embracing.

Yet are they the greateſt *embracers* of pleaſure of any other upon earth; and they eſteem of pearls as pebbles, ſo they may ſatisfy their guſt, in point of pleaſure or revenge. *Howel.*

EMBRA'SURE. *n. ſ.* [*embraſure*, French.] An aperture in the wall, through which the cannon is pointed; battlement.

To EMBRA'VE. *v. a.* [from *brave.*] To decorate; to embelliſh; to deck; to grace; to adorn.

So, both agree their bodies to engrave;
The great earth's womb they open to the ſky,
And, with ſad cypreſs, ſeemly it *embrave. Fairy Queen, b.* ii.

To E'MBROCATE. *v. a.* [ἐμβρέχω.] To rub any part diſeaſed with medicinal liquors.

I returned her a glaſs with oil of roſes and vinegar, to *embrocate* her arm. *Wiſeman on Inflammations.*

EMBROCA'TION. *n. ſ.* [from *embrocate.*]

1. The act of rubbing any part diſeaſed with medicinal liquors or ſpirits.

2. The lotion with which any diſeaſed part is waſhed or embrocated.

We endeavoured to eaſe by diſcutient and emollient cataplaſms, and *embrocations* of various ſorts. *Wiſeman's Surgery.*

To EMBRO'IDER. *v. a.* [*broder*, French.] To border with ornaments; to decorate with figured work; to diverſify with needlework; to adorn a ground with raiſed figures.

Embroider'd ſo with flowers it had ſtood,
That it became a garden of a wood. *Waller.*

Let no virgin be allowed to receive her lover, but in a ſuit of her own *embroidering.* *Spectator*, N°. 606.

Embroider'd purple clothes the golden beds;
This ſlave the floor, and that the table ſpreads. *Pope.*

EMBRO'IDERER. *n. ſ.* [from *embroider.*] One that adorns cloaths with needlework.

Blue ſilk and purple, the work of the *embroiderer.* *Eccluſ.*

EMBRO'IDERY. *n. ſ.* [from *embroider.*]

1. Figures raiſed upon a ground; variegated needlework.

Write,
In emrald tuffs, flow'rs purfled, blue and white,
Like ſaphire, pearl, in rich *embroidery*,
Buckled below fair knighthood's bending knee. *Shakeſpeare.*

Laces and *embroideries* are more coſtly than either warm or comely. *Bacon's Advice to Villiers.*

Next theſe a youthful train their vows expreſs'd,
With feathers crown'd, with gay *embroidery* dreſs'd. *Pope.*

2. Variegation; diverſity of colours

If the natural *embroidery* of the meadows were helpt and improved by art, a man might make a pretty landſkip of his own poſſeſſions *Spectator*, N°. 414.

To EMBRO'IL. *v. a.* [*brouiller*, French.] To diſturb; to confuſe; to diſtract; to throw into commotion; to involve in troubles by diſſenſion and diſcord.

I had no paſſion, deſign, or preparation to *embroil* my kingdom in a civil war. *King Charles.*

Rumour next, and chance,
And tumult and confuſion, all *embroil'd*,
And diſcord with a thouſand various mouths. *Milt. P. Loſt.*

When ſhe found her venom ſpread ſo far,
The royal houſe *embroil'd* in civil war,
Rais'd on her duſky wings ſhe cleaves the ſkies. *Dryden.*

2. In the following paſſage the word ſeems improperly uſed for *broil* or *burn.*

That knowledge, for which we boldly attempt to rifle God's cabinet, ſhould, like the coal from the altar, ſerve only to *embroil* and conſume the ſacrilegious invaders. *Dec. of Piety.*

To EMBRO'THEL. *v. a.* [*brothel*, *brodel.*] To incloſe in a brothel.

Men, which chuſe
Law practice for mere gain, boldly repute,
Worſe than *embrothel'd* ſtrumpets proſtitute. *Donne.*

E'MBRYO.
E'MBRYON. } *n. ſ.* [ἔμβρυον.]

1. The offspring yet unfiniſhed in the womb.

The bringing forth of living creatures may be accelerated, if the *embryo* ripeneth and perfecteth ſooner. *Bacon's Na. Hiſt.*

An excluſion before conformation, before the birth can bear the name of the parent, or be ſo much as properly called an *embryon.* *Brown's Vulgar Errours, b.* iii. *c.* 6.

The earth was form'd, but in the womb a yet
Of waters, *embryon* immature involv'd
Appear'd not. *Milton's Paradiſe Loſt, b.* vii. *l.* 277.

In that dark womb are the ſigns and rudiments of an *embryo* world. *Burnet's Theory of the Earth.*

When the crude *embryo* careful nature breeds,
See how ſhe works, and how her work proceeds. *Blackmore.*

While the promis'd fruit
Lies yet a little *embryo*, unperceiv'd
Within its crimſon folds. *Thomſon's Spring, l.* 100.

2. The ſtate of any thing yet not fit for production; yet unfiniſhed.

The company little ſuſpected what a noble work I had then in *embryo.* *Swift.*

EME. *n. ſ.* [eame, Saxon.] Unkle. Now obſolete.

Whilſt they were young, Caſſibelan their *eme*,
Was by the people choſen in their ſtead;
Who on him took the royal diadem,
And goodly well it long time governed. *Fairy Queen, b.* ii.

EME'NDABLE. *adj.* [*emendo*, Latin.] Capable of emendation; corrigible.

EMENDA'TION. *n. ſ.* [*emendo*, Latin.]

1. Correction; alteration of any thing from worſe to better.

The eſſence and the relation of every thing in being, is fitted, beyond any *emendation*, for its action and uſe; and ſhews it to proceed from a mind of the higheſt underſtanding. *Grew.*

2. An alteration made in the text by verbal criticiſm.

EMENDA'TOR. *n. ſ.* [*emendo*, Latin.] A corrector; an improver; an alterer for the better.

E'MERALD. *n. ſ.* [*emeraude*, French; *ſmaragdus*, Latin.] A green precious ſtone.

The emerald is evidently the ſame with the antient ſmaragdus; and, in its moſt perfect ſtate, is perhaps the moſt beautiful of all the gems: it is found from the ſixteenth of an inch in diameter, to the ſize of a walnut. The rough emerald is uſually of a very bright and naturally poliſhed ſurface, and is ever of a pure and beautiful green, without the admixture of any other colour. It is of all the various ſhades of green, from the deepeſt to the paleſt, and doubtleſs is found at times wholly colourleſs; but then it is eſteemed, by our jewellers, a white ſaphire. The oriental emerald is of the hardneſs of the ſaphire and ruby, and is ſecond only to the diamond in luſtre and brightneſs: they are only found in the kingdom of Cambay. The American, called by our jewellers oriental emeralds, are found in Peru, of the hardneſs of the garnet: the European are ſomewhat ſofter, but harder than cryſtal, and found in Sileſia. The coloured cryſtals, ſold as occidental emeralds, are from the mines of Germany. *Hill on Foſſ.*

Do you not ſee the graſs how in colour they excel the *emerald?* *Sidney.*

The *emerald* is a bright graſs green: it is found in fiſſures of rocks, along with copper ores. *Woodward's Foſſils.*

Nor

Nor deeper verdure dies the robe of Spring,
When first she gives it to the southern gale,
Than the green *emerald* shows. *Thomson's Summer*, *l.* 150.

To EME'RGE. *v. n.* [*emergo*, Latin.]

1. To rise out of any thing in which it is covered.

They *emerged*, to the upper part of the spirit of wine, as much of them as lay immersed in the spirit. *Boyle.*

The mountains *emerged*, and became dry land again, when the waters, after their violent agitation was abated, retired into the lower places. *Burnet's Theory of the Earth.*

Thetis, not unmindful of her son,
Emerging from the deep, to beg her boon,
Pursu'd their track. *Dryden's Homer.*

2. To issue; to proceed.

If the prism was turned about its axis that way, which made the rays *emerge* more obliquely out of the second refracting surface of the prism, the image soon became an inch or two longer or more. *Newton's Opt.*

3. To rise; to mount from a state of depression or obscurity; to rise into view.

Darkness, we see, *emerges* into light;
And shining suns descend to sable night. *Dryden's Fables.*

When, from dewy shade *emerging* bright,
Aurora streaks the sky with orient light,
Let each deplore his dead. *Pope's Odyssey, b.* iv. *l.* 470.

Then from antient gloom *emerg'd*
A rising world. *Thomson's Summer*, *l.* 995.

EME'RGENCE. } *n. s.* [from *emerge.*]
EME'RGENCY. }

1. The act of rising out of any fluid by which it is covered.

We have read of a tyrant, who tried to prevent the *emergence* of murdered bodies. *Brown's Vulgar Errours, b.* iv. *c.* 1.

2. The act of rising into view.

The *emergency* of colours, upon coalition of the particles of such bodies, as were neither of them of the colour of that mixture whereof they are ingredients, is very well worth our attentive observation. *Boyle on Colours.*

The white colour of all refracted light, at its very first *emergence*, where it appears as white as before its incidence, is compounded of various colours. *Newton's Opt.*

3. Any sudden occasion; unexpected casualty.

Most of our rarities have been found out by casual *emergency*, and have been the works of time and chance rather than of philosophy. *Glanv. Sceps. c.* 21.

4. Pressing necessity. A sense not proper.

In any case of *emergency*, he would employ the whole wealth of his empire, which he had thus amassed together in his subterraneous exchequer. *Addison's Freeholder.*

EME'RGENT. *adj.* [from *emerge.*]

1. Rising out of that which overwhelms or obscures it.

Love made my *emergent* fortune once more look
Above the main, which now shall hit the stars. *Ben. Johns.*

The man that is once hated, both his good and his evil deeds oppress him; he is not easily *emergent*. *Ben. Johnson.*

2. Rising into view, or notice.

Immediately the mountains huge appear
Emergent, and their broad bare backs unheave
Into the clouds, their tops ascend the sky. *Milt. Par. Lost.*

3. Proceeding or issuing from any thing.

The stoicks held a fatality, and a fixed unalterable course of events; but then they held also, that they fell out by a necessity *emergent* from and inherent in the things themselves, which God himself could not alter. *South's Sermons.*

4. Sudden; unexpectedly casual.

All the lords declared, that, upon any *emergent* occasion, they would mount their servants upon their horses. *Clarendon.*

E'MERODS. } *n. s.* [corrupted by ignorant pronunciation from
E'MEROIDS. } *hemorrhoids*, αἱμοῤῥοΐδες.] Painful swellings of the hemorrhoidal veins; piles.

He destroyed them, and smote them with *emerods.* 1 *Sa.* v.

EME'RSION. *n. s.* [from *emerge.*] The time when a star, having been obscured by its too near approach to the sun, appears again.

The time was in the heliacal *emersion*, when it becomes at greatest distance from the sun. *Brown's Vulgar Errours, b.* iv.

E'MERY. *n. s.* [*smyris*, Latin; *esmeril*, French.]

Emery is an iron ore, considerably rich. It is usually of a dusky brownish red on the surface; but, when broken, of a fine bright iron grey, but not without some tinge of redness, and is spangled all over with shining specks. It is also sometimes very red, and then contains veins of gold. It is found in the island of Guernsey, in Tuscany, and many parts of Germany. It has a near relation to the magnet. Emery has been recommended by the ancients as an abstergent, but it must be used with great caution. It is prepared by grinding in mills; and the lapidaries cut the ordinary gems on their wheels by sprinkling the wetted powder over them; but it will not cut diamonds. It is useful in cleaning and polishing steel. *Hill's Mat. Med.*

EME'TICAL. } *adj.* [ἐμέω.] Having the quality of provoking
EME'TICK. } vomits.

Various are the temperaments and operations of herbs; some purgative, some *emetick*, and some sudorifick. *Hale.*

EME'TICALLY. *adv.* [from *emetical.*] In such a manner as to provoke to vomit.

It has been complained of, that preparations of silver have produced violent vomits; whereas we have not observed duly refined silver to work *emetically*, even in women and girls. *Boyle.*

EMICA'TION. *n. s.* [*emicatio*, Latin.] Sparkling; flying off in small particles, as sprightly liquors.

Iron, in aqua fortis, will fall into ebullition with noise and *emication*, as also a crass and fumid exhalation. *Brown.*

EMI'CTION. *n. s.* [from *emictum*, Latin.] Urine; what is voided by the urinary passages.

Gravel and stone grind away the flesh, and effuse the blood apparent in a sanguine *emiction. Harvey on Consumptions.*

To E'MIGRATE. *v. n.* [*emigro*, Latin.] To remove from one place to another.

EMIGRA'TION. *n. s.* [from *emigrate.*] Change of habitation; removal from one place to another.

We find the originals of many kingdoms either by victories, or by *emigrations*, or intestine commotions. *Hale.*

E'MINENCE. } *n. s.* [*eminentia*, Latin.]
E'MINENCY. }

1. Loftiness; height.

2. Summit; highest part.

Mountains abound with different vegetables, every vertex or *eminency* affording new kinds. *Ray on the Creation.*

3. A part rising above the rest.

They must be smooth, almost imperceptible to the touch, and without either *eminence* or cavities. *Dryden's Dufresnoy.*

4. A place where one is exposed to general notice.

A satyr or libel on one of the common stamp, never meets with that reception as what is aimed at a person whose merit places him upon an *eminence*, and gives him a more conspicuous figure. *Addison's Spectator*, N°. 256.

5. Exaltation; conspicuousness; state of being exposed to view; reputation; celebrity; fame; preferment; greatness.

You've too a woman's heart, which ever yet
Affected *eminence*, wealth, sovereignty. *Shakes. Henry* VIII.

Alterations are attributed to the powerfullest under princes, where the *eminency* of one obscureth the rest. *Wotton.*

He deserv'd no such return
From me, whom he created what I was,
In that bright *eminence*; and with his good
Upbraided none. *Milton's Paradise Lost, b.* iv. *l.* 44.

Where men cannot arrive to any *eminency* of estate, yet religion makes a compensation, by teaching content. *Tillotson.*

These two were men of *eminency*, of learning as well as piety. *Stillingfleet's Def. of Disc. on Rom. Idol.*

6. Supreme degree.

Whatever pure thou in the body enjoy'st,
And pure thou wert created, we enjoy
In *eminence*. *Milton's Paradise Lost, b.* viii. *l.* 624.

7. Notice; distinction.

Let your remembrance still apply to Banquo;
Present him *eminence* both with eye and tongue. *Shak. Macb.*

8. A title given to cardinals.

E'MINENT. *adj.* [*eminens*, Latin.]

1. High; lofty.

Thou hast built unto thee an *eminent* place. *Ezek.* xvi. 24.

2. Dignified; exalted.

Rome for your sake shall push her conquests on,
And bring new titles home from nations won,
To dignify so *eminent* a son. *Dryden's Juv. Sat.* 8.

3. Conspicuous; remarkable.

Satan, in gesture proudly *eminent*,
Stood like a tow'r. *Milton.*

She is *eminent* for a sincere piety in the practice of religion. *Addison's Freeholder*, N°. 21.

E'MINENTLY. *adv.* [from *eminent.*]

1. Conspicuously; in a manner that attracts observation.

Thy love, which else
So *eminently* never had been known. *Milton's Parad. Lost.*

Lady, that in the prime of earliest youth,
Wisely has shun'd the broad way and the green,
And with those few art *eminently* seen,
That labour up the hill of heav'nly truth. *Milton.*

Such as thou hast solemnly elected,
With gifts and graces *eminently* adorn'd,
To some great work. *Milton's Agonistes*, *l.* 678.

2. In a high degree.

All men are equal in their judgment of what is *eminently* best. *Dryden.*

That simplicity, without which no human performance can arrive to perfection, is no where more *eminently* useful than in this. *Swift.*

E'MISSARY. *n. s.* [*emissarius*, Latin.]

1. One sent out on private messages; a spy; a secret agent.

Clifford, now become the state informer, was an *emissary* and spy of the king's, and he fled over into Flanders with his consent and privity. *Bacon's Henry* VII.

You shall neither eat nor sleep,
No, nor forth your window peep,

With your *emissary* eye,
To fetch in the forms go by. *Ben. Johnson's Underwoods.*

The Jesuits send over *emissaries*, with instructions to personate themselves members of the several sects amongst us. *Swift.*

2. One that emits or sends out. A technical sense.

Wherever there are *emissaries*, there are absorbent vessels in the skin; and, by the absorbent vessels, mercury will pass into the blood. *Arbuthnot on Aliments.*

EMI'SSION. *n. s.* [*emissio*, Latin.] The act of sending out; vent.

Tickling causeth laughter: the cause may be the *emission* of the spirits, and so of the breath by a flight from titillation. *Bac.*

Though it might restrain their dispersion, it could not their populosity, which necessarily requireth transmigration and *emission* of colonies. *Brown's Vulgar Errours, b.* i. *c.* 6.

Affection, in the state of innocence, was happily pitched upon its right object; it flamed up in direct fervours of devotion to God, and in collateral *emissions* of charity to its neighbour. *South's Sermons.*

Cover them with glasses; but upon all warm and benign *emissions* of the sun, and sweet showers, give them air. *Evelyn.*

To EMI'T. *v. a.* [*emitto*, Latin.]

1. To send forth; to let go; to give vent to.

These baths continually *emit* a manifest and very sensible heat; nay, some of them have been observed, at some times, to send forth an actual and visible flame. *Woodward's N. Hist.*

The soil, being fruitful and rich, *emits* steams, consisting of volatile and active parts. *Arbuthnot on Air.*

2. To let fly; to dart.

Pay sacred rev'rence to Apollo's song,
Lest, wrathful, the far-shooting god *emit*
His fatal arrows. *Prior.*

3. To issue out juridically.

That a citation be valid, it ought to be decreed and *emitted* by the judge's authority, and at the instance of the party. *Ayliffe's Parergon.*

EMME'NAGOGUES. *n. s.* [ἔμμηνα and ἄγω.] Medicines that promote the courses; and these do this, either by giving a greater force to the blood in its circulation, whereby its momentum against the vessels is increased; or by making it thinner, whereby it will more easily pass through any outlets. *Quin.*

Emmenagogues are such as produce a plethora, or fulness of the vessels, consequently such as strengthen the organs of digestion, so as to make good blood. *Arbuthnot on Diet.*

E'MMET. *n. s.* [æmette, Saxon.] An ant; a pismire.

When cedars to the ground fall down by the weight of an *emmet*,
Or when a rich ruby's just price be the worth of a walnut. *Sidney, b.* i.

To EMME'W. *v. a.* [from *mew*.] To mew or coop up.

This outward sainted deputy,
Whose settled visage and delib'rate word,
Nips youth i' th' head, and follies doth *emmew*,
As faulcon doth the fowl, is yet a devil. *Sh. Meas. for Meas.*

To EMMO'VE. *v. a.* [*emmouvoir*, French.] To excite; to rouse; to put into emotion.

One day, when him high courage did *emmove*,
He pricked forth. *Fairy Queen, b.* ii *c.* 1. *stan.* 50.

EMO'LLIENT. *adj.* [*emolliens*, Latin.] Softening; suppling.

Barley is *emollient*, moistening, and expectorating. *Arbuthn.*

Diureticks are decoctions, emulsions, and oils of *emollient* vegetables, so far as they relax the urinary passages: such as relax ought to be tried before such as stimulate. *Arbuthnot.*

EMO'LLIENTS. *n. s.* Such things as sheath and soften the asperities of the humours, and relax and supple the solids at the same time. *Quincy.*

Emollients ought to be taken in open air, to hinder them from perspiring, and on empty stomachs. *Arbuthnot.*

EMOLLI'TION. *n. s.* [*emollitio*, Latin.] The act of softening.

Lassitude is remedied by bathing, or anointing with oil and warm water: the cause is, for that all lassitude is a kind of contusion and compression of the parts, and bathing and anointing give a relaxation or *emollition*. *Bacon.*

Powerful menstruums are made for its *emollition*, whereby it may receive the tincture of minerals. *Brown's Vulgar Err.*

EMO'LUMENT. *n. s.* [*emolumentum*, Latin.] Profit; advantage.

Let them consult how politick they were, for a temporal *emolument* to throw away eternity. *South's Sermons.*

Nothing gives greater satisfaction than the sense of having dispatched a great deal of business to publick *emolument*. *Tatler.*

EMO'NGST. *prep.* [so written by *Spenser*.] Among.

The merry birds of every sort,
Chaunted aloud their chearful harmony;
And made *emongst* themselves a sweet consort,
That quick'ned the dull sp'rit with musical comfort. *F. Qu.*

EMO'TION. *n. s.* [*emotion*, French.] Disturbance of mind; vehemence of passion, or pleasing or painful.

I will appeal to any man, who has read this poet, whether he finds not the natural *emotion* of the same passion in himself, which the poet describes in his feigned persons? *Dryden.*

Those rocks and oaks that such *emotion* felt,
Were rural maids whom Orpheus taught to melt. *Granv.*

To EMPA'LE. *v. a.* [*empaler*, French.]

1. To fence with a pale.

How happy's he, which hath due place assign'd
T' his beasts, and disaforested his mind?
Empal'd himself to keep them out, not in;
Can sow, and dares trust corn, where they have been. *Donn.*

2. To fortify.

All that dwell near enemies *empale* villages, to save themselves from surprize. *Raleigh's Essays.*

The English *empaled* themselves with their pikes, and therewith bare off their enemies. *Hayward.*

3. To inclose; shut in.

Keep yourselves in breath,
And when I have the bloody Hector found,
Empale him with your weapons round about. *Shakespeare.*

They have *empal'd* within a zodiack
The free-born sun, and keep twelve signs awake
To watch his steps; the Goat and Crab controul
And fright him back. *Donne.*

Thank my charms,
I now *empale* her in my arms. *Cleaveland.*

Impenetrable, *empal'd* with circling fire,
Yet unconsum'd. *Milton's Paradise Lost, b.* ii. *l.* 647.

4. To put to death by spitting on a stake fixed upright.

Who can bear this, resolve to be *empal'd*?
His skin flead off, and roasted yet alive? *Southern's Oroonok.*

Let them each be broken on the rack;
Then, with what life remains, *empal'd*, and left
To writhe at leisure round the bloody stake. *Addis. Cato.*

Nay, I don't believe they will be contented with hanging; they talk of *empaling*, or breaking on the wheel. *Arbuthnot.*

EMPA'NNEL. *n. s.* [from *panne*, French.] The writing or entering the names of a jury into a parchment schedule, or roll of paper, by the sheriff, which he has summoned to appear for the performance of such publick service as juries are employed in. *Cowel.*

Who can expect any more upright verdicts from such packed, such corrupt juries? Why may we not be allowed to make exceptions against this so incompetent *empannel*? *Decay of Christian Piety.*

To EMPA'NNEL. *v. a.* [from the noun.] To summon to serve on a jury. A law term.

I shall not need to *empannel* a jury either of moralists or divines, every man's own breast sufficiently instructing him. *Government of the Tongue, s.* 8.

EMPA'RLANCE. *n. s.* [from *parler*, French.] It signifieth, in common law, a desire or petition in court of a day to pause what is best to do; and it is sometimes used for the conference of a jury in the cause committed to them. *Cowel.*

EMPA'SM. *n. s.* [ἐμπάσσω.] A powder to correct the bad scent of the body.

To EMPA'SSION. *v. a.* [from *passion*.] To move with passion; to affect strongly; to throw off from equanimity.

Unto my eyes strange shows presented were,
Picturing that which I in mind embrac'd,
That yet those sights *empassion* me full near. *Spenser.*

So, standing, moving, or to height upgrown,
The tempter, all *empassion'd*, thus began. *Milt. Par. Lost.*

To EMPE'OPLE. *v. a.* [from *people*.] To form into a people or community.

He wonder'd much, and 'gan enquire
What stately building durst so high extend
Her lofty towers unto the starry sphere,
And what unknown nation there *empeopled* were. *F. Queen.*

E'MPERESS. *n. s.* [from *emperour*, now written *empress*.]

1. A woman invested with imperial power.

Long, long, may you on earth our *emperess* reign,
E're you in heaven a glorious angel stand. *Davies.*

2. The queen of an emperour.

Lavinia will I make my *emperess*,
Rome's royal mistress, mistress of my heart. *Sh. Tit. Andr.*

E'MPEROUR. *n. s.* [*empereur*, French; *imperator*, Latin.] A monarch of title and dignity superiour to a king: as, the *emperour* of Germany.

Charles the *emperour*,
Under pretence to see the queen his aunt,
Makes visitation. *Shakespeare's Henry* VIII.

E'MPERY. *n. s.* [*empire*, French; *imperium*, Latin.] Empire; sovereign command. A word out of use.

A lady
So fair, and fasten'd to an *empery*,
Would make the great'st king double. *Shakesp. Cymbeline.*

Take on you the charge
And kingly government of this your land;
Not as protector, steward, substitute,
But as successively from blood to blood,
Your right of birth, your *empery*, your own. *Shak. R.* III.

E'MPHASIS. *n. s.* [ἔμφασις.] A remarkable stress laid upon a word or sentence; particular force impressed by stile or pronunciation.

Oh,

Oh, that brave Cæsar!
—Be choak'd with such another *emphasis. Sh. Ant. and Cleop.*

Emphasis must so much regards the time as a certain grandeur, whereby some letter, syllable, word, or sentence is rendered more remarkable than the rest, by a more vigorous pronunciation, and a longer stay upon it. *Holder's Elem. of Speech.*

These questions have force and *emphasis*, if they be understood of the antediluvian earth. *Burnet's Theory of the Earth.*

EMPHA'TICAL. } adj. [ἐμφαίνω.]
EMPHA'TICK. }

1. Forcible; strong; striking.

Where he endeavours to dissuade from carnivorous appetites, how *emphatical* is his reasoning! *Garth's Pref. to Ovid.*

In proper and *emphatick* terms thou didst paint the blazing comet's fiery tail. *Arbuthnot's History of John Bull.*

2. Striking the sight.

It is commonly granted, that *emphatical* colours are light itself, modified by refractions. *Boyle on Colours.*

3. Appearing; seeming not real.

EMPHA'TICALLY. *adv.* [from *emphatical.*]

1. Strongly; forcibly; in a striking manner.

How *emphatically* and divinely does every word proclaim the truth that I have been speaking of! *South's Sermons.*

2. According to appearance.

What is delivered of the incurvity of dolphins, must be taken *emphatically*, not really, but in appearance, when they leap above water, and suddenly shoot down again. *Brown.*

EMPHYSE'MATOUS. *adj.* [from ἐμφύσημα.] Bloated; puffed up; swollen.

The signs of a gangrene are these: the inflammation loses its redness, and becomes duskish and livid; the tenseness of the skin goes off, and feels to the touch flabby or *emphysematous*; and vesications, filled with ichor of different colours, spread all over it. *Sharp's Surgery.*

To EMPIE'RCE. *v. a.* [from *pierce.*] To pierce into; to enter into by violent appulse.

The weapon bright,
Taking advantage of his open jaw,
Ran through his mouth with so importune might,
That deep *empierc'd* his darksome hollow maw. *Fai. Queen.*

EMPI'GHT. *part.* [*To pight*, or *pitch.* See PITCH.] Set; pitched; put in a posture.

But he was wary, and ere it *empight*
In the meant mark, advanc'd his shield atween. *Fai. Queen.*

E'MPIRE. *n. s.* [*empire*, French; *imperium*, Latin.]

1. Imperial power; supreme dominion; sovereign command.

Assert, ye fair ones, who in judgment sit,
Your ancient *empire* over love and wit. *Rowe.*

2. The region over which dominion is extended.

A nation extended over vast tracts of land, and numbers of people, arrives in time at the ancient name of kingdom, or modern of *empire.* *Temple.*

Sextus Pompeius
Hath given the dare to Cæsar, and commands
The *empire* of the sea. *Shakesp. Ant. and Cleopatra.*

3. Command over any thing.

E'MPIRIC. *n. s.* [ἐμπειρικός.] A trier or experimenter; such persons as have no true education in, or knowledge of physical practice, but venture upon hearsay and observation only. *Quincy.*

The name of Hippocrates was more effectual to persuade such men as Galen, than to move a silly *empirick.* *Hooker.*

That every plant might receive a name, according unto the diseases it cureth, was the wish of Paracelsus; a way more likely to multiply *empiricks* than herbalists. *Brown.*

Such an aversion and contempt for all manner of innovators, as physicians are apt to have for *empiricks*, or lawyers for pettifoggers. *Swift.*

EMPI'RICAL. } adj. [from the noun.]
E'MPIRICK. }

1. Versed in experiments.

By fire
Of sooty coal, the *empirick* alchymist
Can turn, or holds it possible to turn,
Metals of drossiest ore to perfect gold. *Milton's Parad. Lost.*

2. Known only by experience; practised only by rote, without rational grounds.

The most sovereign prescription in Galen is but *empirick* to this preservative. *Shakespeare's Coriolanus.*

In extremes, bold counsels are the best;
Like *empirick* remedies, they last are try'd,
And by th' event condemn'd or justify'd. *Dryden's Aurengz.*

EMPI'RICALLY. *adv.* [from *empirical.*]

1. Experimentally; according to experience.

We shall *empirically* and sensibly deduct the causes of blackness from originals, by which we generally observe things denigrated. *Brown's Vulgar Errours, b.* vi. *c.* 12.

2. Without rational grounds; charlatanically; in the manner of quacks.

EMPI'RICISM. *n. s.* [from *empirick.*] Dependence on experience without knowledge or art; quackery.

EMPLA'STER. *n. s.* [ἔμπλαστρον. This word is now always pronounced, and generally written *plaster.*] An application to a sore of an oleaginous or viscous substance, spread upon cloth. See PLASTER.

All *emplasters*, applied to the breasts, ought to have a hole for the nipples. *Wiseman's Surgery.*

To EMPLA'STER. *v. a.* [from the noun.] To cover with a plaster.

They must be cut out to the quick, and the sores *emplastered* with tar. *Mortimer's Art of Husbandry.*

EMPLA'STICK. *adj.* [ἐμπλαστικός.] Viscous; glutinous: fit to be applied as a plaster.

Resin, by its *emplastick* quality, mixed with oil of roses, perfects the concoction. *Wiseman's Surgery.*

Emplastick applications are not sufficient to defend a wound from the air. *Arbuthnot on Air.*

To EMPLE'AD. *v. a.* [from *plead.*] To indict; to prefer a charge against; to accuse.

To terrify and torture them to their minds, and wind their necks more surely under their arm, their tyrannous masters did often *emplead* arrest, cast them into prison, and thereby consume them to worse than nothing. *Hayward.*

Antiquity thought thunder the immediate voice of Jupiter, and *empleaded* them of impiety that referred it to natural causalties. *Glanv. Sceps. c.* 14.

Since none the living villains dare *emplead*,
Arraign them in the persons of the dead. *Dryden's Juvenal.*

To EMPLO'Y. *v. a.* [*emploier*, French.]

1. To busy; to keep at work; to exercise.

For thrice, at least, in compass of the year,
Thy vineyard must *employ* the sturdy steer
To turn the glebe. *Dryden's Virgil's Georg. b.* ii. *l.* 551.

Their principal learning was applied to the course of the stars, and the rest was *employed* in displaying the brave exploits of their princes. *Temple.*

Our reason is often puzzled, because of the imperfection of the ideas it is *employed* about. *Locke.*

The proper business of the understanding is not that which men always *employ* it to. *Locke.*

Labour in the beginning gave a right of property, whereever any one was pleased to *employ* it upon what was common. *Locke.*

The cat became a blushing maid;
And, on the happy change, the boy
Employ'd his wonder and his joy. *Prior.*

This is a day in which the thoughts of our countrymen ought to be *employed* on serious subjects. *Addison's Freeholder.*

2. To use as an instrument.

The cleanly cheese-press she could never turn,
Her aukward fist did ne'er *employ* the churn. *Gay's Pastorals.*

3. To use as means.

The money was *employed* to the making of gallies. 2 *Mac.*

Peace is not freed from labour, but from noise;
And war more force, but not more pains *employs.* *Dryden.*

4. To use as materials.

The labour of those who felled and framed the timber *employed* about the plough, must be charged on labour. *Locke.*

5. To commission; to intrust with the management of any affairs.

Jonathan and Jahaziah were *employed* about this matter. *Ezra*, x. 15.

Jesus Christ is furnished with superior powers to the angels, because he is *employed* in superiour works, and appointed to be the sovereign Lord of all the visible and invisible worlds. *Watts.*

6. To fill up with business.

To study nature will thy time *employ*;
Knowledge and innocence are perfect joy. *Dryden.*

7. To pass or spend in business.

Why, whilst we struggle in this vale beneath,
With want and sorrow, with disease and death,
Do they more bless'd perpetual life *employ*
In songs of pleasure, and in scenes of joy? *Prior.*

EMPLO'Y. *n. s.* [from the verb.]

1. Business; object of industry.

Present to grasp, and future still to find,
The whole *employ* of body and of mind. *Pope's Ess. on Man.*

2. Publick office.

Lest animosities should obstruct the course of justice, if one of their own number had the distribution of it, they have always a foreigner for this *employ.* *Addison's Remarks on Italy.*

The honours and the burdens of great posts and *employs* were joined together. *Atterbury's Sermons.*

EMPLO'YABLE. *adj.* [from *employ.*] Capable to be used; proper for use.

The objections made against the doctrine of the chymists, seem *employable* against this hypothesis. *Boyle's Scept. Chym.*

EMPLO'YER. *n. s.* [from *employ.*] One that uses or causes to be used.

That man drives a great trade, and is owner or *employer* of much shipping, and continues and increases in trade and shipping. *Child's Discourses on Trade.*

EMPLO'YMENT.

Emplo'yment. *n. s.* [from *employ.*]
1. Business; object of industry; object of labour.
2. Business; the state of being employed.
3. Office; post of business.

If any station, any *employment* upon earth be honourable, their's was. *Atterbury's Sermons.*

Leaders on each side, instead of intending the publick weal, have their hearts wholly set upon ways and means to get or to keep *employments*. *Swift.*

4. Business intrusted.

Call not your stocks for me; I serve the king,
On whose *employment* I was sent to you. *Shakesp. K. Lear.*

To Empo'ison. *v. a.* [*empoisonner*, French.]
1. To destroy by poison; to destroy by venomous food or drugs; to poison.

Leaving no means unattempted of destroying his son, among others employing that wicked servant of his, who undertook to *empoison* him. *Sidney, b.* ii.

Mushrooms cause the incubus, or the mare in the stomach, and therefore the surfeit of them may suffocate and *empoison*. *Bacon's Natural History*, N°. 546.

2. To taint with poison; to envenom. This is the more usual sense.

Empo'isoner. *n. s.* [*empoisonneur*, French.] One who destroys another by poison

He is vehemently suspected to have been the *empoisoner* of his wife, thereby to make vacant his bed. *Bacon's Henry* VII.

Empo'isonment. *n. s.* [*empoisonnement*, French.] The practise of destroying by poison.

It were dangerous for secret *empoisonments*. *Bacon's N. Hist.*

Empore'tick. *adj.* [ἐμποϱητικος.] That which is used at markets, or in merchandize.

Empo'rium. *n. s.* [ἐμπόϱιον.] A place of merchandise; a mart; a town of trade; a commercial city.

And while this fam'd *emporium* we prepare,
The British ocean shall such triumphs boast,
That those who now disdain our trade to share,
Shall rob like pyrates on our wealthy coast. *Dryden.*

I take the prosperous estate of this great *emporium* to be owing to those instances of charity. *Atterbury's Sermons.*

To EMPO'VERISH. *v. a.* [*pauvre*, French.]
1. To make poor; to depauperate; to reduce to indigence.

Since they might talk better as they lay together, they *empoverished* their cloaths to enrich their bed, which, for that night, might well scorn the shrine of Venus. *Sidney, b.* ii.

Your's sounds aloud, and tells us you excel
No less in courage than in singing well;
While, unconcern'd, you let your country know,
They have *empoverish'd* themselves, not you. *Waller.*

For sense of honour, if it *empoverisheth* a man, it is, in his esteem, neither honour nor sense. *South's Sermons.*

Fresh roses bring
To strow my bed, 'till the *empoverish'd* Spring
Confess her want. *Prior.*

2. To lessen fertility.

Empo'verisher. *n. s.* [from *empoverish.*]
1. One that makes others poor.
2. That which impairs fertility.

They destroy the weeds, and fit the land for after-crops, being an improver, and not an *empoverisher* of land. *Mortimer.*

Empo'verishment. *n. s.* [from *empoverish.*] Diminution; cause of poverty; waste.

Being paid as it is, now some, and then some, it is no great burden unto her, nor any great *empoverishment* to her coffers. *Spenser's State of Ireland.*

All appeals for justice, or appellations for favour or preferment to another country, are so many grievous *empoverishments*. *Swift's View of Ireland.*

To Empo'wer. *v. a.* [from *power.*]
1. To authorise; to commission; to give power or authority to any purpose.

You are *empowered*, when you please, to give the final decision of wit. *Dryden's Juv. Dedication.*

The government shall be *empowered* to grant commissions to all Protestants whatsoever. *Swift on the Sacram. Test.*

2. To give natural force; to enable.

Does not the same power that enables them to heal, *empower* them to destroy? *Baker's Reflexions on Learning.*

E'mpress. *n. s.* [contracted from *emperess*, which is retained by *Johnson.*]
1. The queen of an emperour.

Let your nimble feet
Tread subtile circles, that may always meet
In point to him; and figures, to express
The grace of him, and his great *emperess*. *Ben. Johnson.*

2. A female invested with imperial dignity; a female sovereign.

Empress of this fair world, resplendent Eve! *Milton.*
Yet, London, *empress* of the northern clime,
By an high fate thou greatly didst expire. *Dryden.*
Wisdom, thou say'st, from heav'n receiv'd her birth;
Her beams transmitted to the subject earth:
Yet this great *empress* of the human soul,
Does only with imagin'd power controul,
If restless passion, by rebellious sway,
Compels the weak usurper to obey. *Prior.*

Empri'se. *n. s.* [*emprise*, French.] Attempt of danger; undertaking of hazard; enterprise.

Noble minds, of yore, allied were
In brave pursuit of chivalrous *emprise*. *Fairy Queen, b.* i.
A double conquest must you make,
If you atchieve renown by this *emprise*. *Fairfax, b.* ii.
Fierce faces threat'ning wars;
Giants of mighty bone, and bold *emprise*. *Milt. Par. Lost.*
Thus, 'till the sun had travell'd half the skies,
Ambush'd we lie, and wait the bold *emprise*. *Pope's Odyssey.*

E'mptier. *n. s.* [from *empty.*] One that empties; one that makes any place void by taking away what it contained.

The *emptiers* have emptied them out, and marred their vineyards. *Nah.* ii. 2.

E'mptiness. *n. s.* [from *empty.*]
1. Absence of plenitude; inanity.

Where cities stood,
Well fenc'd, and numerous, desolation reigns,
And *emptiness*; dismay'd, unfed, unhous'd,
The widow and the orphan stroll. *Phillips.*

2. The state of being empty.

His coffers sound
With hollow poverty and *emptiness*. *Shakesp. Henry* IV.

3. A void space; vacuity; *vacuum.*

Nor could another in your room have been,
Except an *emptiness* had come between. *Dryden.*

The ordinary air in which we live and respire, is of so thin a composition, that sixteen thousand one hundred and forty-nine parts of its dimensions are mere *emptiness* and nothing; and the remaining one only, material and real substance. *Bentley's Sermons.*

4. Want of substance or solidity.

'Tis this which causes the graces and the loves to take up their habitations in the hardest marble, and to subsist in the *emptiness* of light and shadow. *Dryden's Dufresnoy, Pref.*

5. Unsatisfactoriness; inability to fill up the desires.

O frail estate of human things,
Now to our cost your *emptiness* we know. *Dryden.*

Form the judgment about the worth or *emptiness* of things here, according as they are or are not of use, in relation to what is to come after. *Atterbury's Sermons.*

6. Vacuity of head; want of knowledge.

Eternal smiles his *emptiness* betray,
As shallow streams run dimpling all the way. *Pope's Epist.*

E'mption. *n. s.* [*emptio*, Latin.] The act of purchasing; a purchase.

There is a dispute among the lawyers, whether Glaucus his exchanging his golden armour with the brazen one of Tydides, was *emption* or commutation. *Arbuthnot on Coins.*

E'MPTY. *adj.* [æmtiᵹ, Saxon.]
1. Void; having nothing in it; not full.

I did never know so full a voice issue from so *empty* a heart; but the saying is true, the *empty* vessel makes the greatest sound. *Shakespeare's Henry* V.

The pit was *empty*, there was no water in it. *Gen.* xxxvii.

If you have two vessels to fill, and you empty one to fill the other, you gain nothing by that; there still remains one vessel *empty*. *Burnet's Theory of the Earth.*

2. Devoid; unfurnished.

Art thou thus boldened, man, by thy distress?
Or else a rude despiser of good manners,
That in civility thou seem'st so *empty*? *Shak. As you like it.*

Mr. Boyle has shewed, that air may be rarified above ten thousand times in vessels of glass; and the heavens are much *emptier* of air than any vacuum we can make below. *Newton.*

3. Unsatisfactory; unable to fill the mind or desires.
4. Without any thing to carry; unburthened; unfreighted.

He alleges that the satyrs carried platters full of fruit in their hands; but if they had been *empty* handed, had they been ever the larger satyrs? *Dryden's Juvenal, Dedication.*

Yet all the little that I got, I spent;
And still return'd as *empty* as I went. *Dryden's Virg. Past.*

5. Vacant of head; ignorant; unskilful; unfurnished with materials for thought.

How comes it that so many worthy and wise men depend upon so many unworthy and *empty* headed fools! *Raleigh.*

His answer is a handsome way of exposing an *empty*, trifling, pretending pedant; the wit lively, the satyr courtly and severe. *Felton on the Classicks.*

6. Without substance; without solidity; vain.

The god of sleep there hides his heavy head,
And *empty* dreams on ev'ry leaf are spread. *Dryden's Æn.*

To E'mpty. *v. a.* [from the adjective.] To evacuate; to exhaust; to deprive of that which was contained in it.

Boundless intemperance,
In nature is a tyranny: it hath been
Th' untimely *emptying* of the happy throne,
And fall of many kings. *Shakespeare's Macbeth.*

The

The emptiers have *emptied* them out, and marred their vine-branches. *Nah.* ii. 2.

Sheep are often blind by fulneſs of blood: cut their tails, and *empty* them of their blood. *Mortimer's Husbandry.*

The Euxine ſea is conveniently ſituated for trade, by the communication it has both with Aſia and Europe, and the great navigable rivers that *empty* themſelves into it. *Arbuthnot.*

To EMPU'RPLE. *v. a.* [from *purple.*] To make of a purple colour; to diſcolour with purple.

Now in looſe garlands, thick thrown off, the bright
Pavement, that like a ſea of jaſper ſhone,
Empurpled with celeſtial roſes ſmil'd. *Milton's Paradiſe Loſt.*
The deep,
Empurpl'd ran, with guſhing gore diſtain'd. *Phillips.*

To EMPU'ZZLE. *v. a.* [from *puzzle.*] To perplex; to put to a ſtand.

It hath *empuzzled* the enquiries of others to apprehend, and enforced them unto ſtrange conceptions to make out. *Brown.*

EMPYE'MA. *n. ſ.* [ἐμπύημα.] A collection of purulent matter in any part whatſoever; generally uſed to ſignify that in the cavity of the breaſt only, and which ſometimes happens upon the opening of abſceſſes, or ulcerations of the lungs, or membranes incloſing the breaſt. *Quincy.*

An *empyema*, or a collection of purulent matter in the breaſt, if not ſuddenly cured, doth undoubtedly impel the patient into a phthiſical conſumption. *Harvey on Conſumptions.*

There is likewiſe a conſumption from an *empyema*, after an inflammation of the lungs; which may be known from a weight upon the diaphragm, oppreſſion of the lungs, a difficulty of breathing, and inability to lie on one ſide, which is that which is found. *Arbuthnot on Diet.*

EMPY'REAL. *adj.* [ἔμπυρ☉.] Formed of the element of fire; refined beyond aerial; pertaining to the higheſt and pureſt region of heaven. [*Tickell* accents it on the penult.]

Now went forth the morn,
Such as in higheſt heav'n, array'd in gold
Empyreal. *Milton's Paradiſe Loſt, b.* vi. *l.* 13.
Go, ſoar with Plato to th' *empyreal* ſphere,
To the firſt good, firſt perfect, and firſt fair. *Pope.*
But *empyreal* forms, howe'er in fight
Gaſh'd and diſmember'd, eaſily unite. *Tickell.*

EMPYRE'AN. *n. ſ.* [ἔμπυρος.] The higheſt heaven where the pure element of fire is ſuppoſed to ſubſiſt.

Almighty Father from above,
From the pure *empyrean*, where he ſits
High thron'd above all height, bent down his eye. *Milton.*
Under his burning wheel
The ſtedfaſt *empyrean* ſhook throughout,
All but the throne itſelf of God. *Milton's Paradiſe Loſt.*
The *empyrean* rung
With hallelujahs. *Milton's Paradiſe Loſt, b.* vii. *l.* 633.

E'MPYREUM. } *n. ſ.* [ἐμπύρευμα.] The burning to of any mat-
EMPYRE'UMA. } ter in boiling or diſtillation, which gives a particular offenſive ſmell. *Quincy.*

It is ſo far from admitting an *empyreum*, that it burns clear away without leaving any cinders, or aduſt about it. *Harvey.*

The hopes of an elixir inſenſibly evaporate, and vaniſh to air, or leave in the recipient a foul *empyreuma.* *Dec. of Piety.*

EMPYREUMA'TICAL. *adj.* [from *empyreuma.*] Having the ſmell or taſte of burnt ſubſtances.

Many *empyreumatical* oils, diſtilled by ſtrong fires in retorts, may be brought to emulate eſſential oils drawn in limbicks. *Boyle's Hiſtory of Firmneſs.*

EMPYRO'SIS. *n. ſ.* [ἐμπυρόω.] Conflagration; general fire.

The former opinion that held theſe cataclyſms and *empyroſes* univerſal, was ſuch as held that it put a total conſummation unto things in this lower world, eſpecially that of conflagration. *Hale's Origin of Mankind.*

To E'MULATE. *v. a.* [*æmulor*, Latin.]

1. To rival; to propoſe as one to be equalled or excelled.
2. To imitate with hope of equality, or ſuperiour excellence.

I would have
Him *emulate* you: 'tis no ſhame to follow
The better precedent. *Ben. Johnſon's Catiline.*
Thoſe fair ideas to my aid I'll call,
And *emulate* my great original. *Dryden's Aurengzebe.*
What though no weeping loves thy aſhes grace,
Nor poliſh'd marble *emulate* thy face. *Pope.*

3. To be equal to; to riſe to equality with

I ſee how thy eye would *emulate* the diamond. *Shakeſp.*
We ſee no new-built palaces aſpire,
No kitchens *emulate* the veſtal fire. *Pope's Sat. of Donne.*

4. To imitate; to copy; to reſemble.

It is likewiſe attended with a delirium, fury, and an involuntary laughter, the convulſion *emulating* this motion. *Arbuth.*

EMULA'TION. *n. ſ.* [*æmulatio*, Latin.]

1. Rivalry; deſire of ſuperiority.

Mine *emulation*
Hath not that honour in't it had; for where
I thought to cruſh him in an equal force,
True ſword to ſword, I'll pitch at him ſome way,
Or wrath or craft may get him. *Shakeſpeare's Coriolanus.*

There was neither envy nor *emulation* amongſt them. 1 *Mac.*

Ariſtotle allows that ſome *emulation* may be good, and may be found in ſome good men; yet envy he utterly condemns, as wicked in itſelf, and only to be found in wicked minds. *Sprat.*

The apoſtle exhorts the Corinthians to an holy and general *emulation* of the charity of the Macedonians, in contributing freely to the relief of the poor ſaints at Jeruſalem. *South.*

A noble *emulation* heats your breaſt,
And your own fame now robs you of your reſt:
Good actions ſtill muſt be maintain'd with good,
As bodies nouriſh'd with reſembling food. *Dryden.*

2. Envy; deſire of depreſſing another; conteſt; contention; diſcord.

What madneſs rules in brainſick men!
When for ſo ſlight and frivolous a cauſe,
Such factious *emulations* ſhall ariſe. *Shakeſpeare's Henry* VI.

E'MULATIVE. *adj.* [from *emulate.*] Inclined to emulation; rivalling; diſpoſed to competition.

EMULA'TOR. *n. ſ.* [from *emulate.*] A rival; a competitor.

In ſuperiours it quencheth jealouſy, and layeth their competitors and *emulators* aſleep. *Bacon's Eſſays.*

To EMU'LGE. *v. a.* [*emulgeo*, Latin.] To milk out.

EMU'LGENT. *adj.* [*emulgens*, Latin.]

1. Milking or draining out.
2. *Emulgent* veſſels [in anatomy] are the two large arteries and veins which ariſe, the former from the deſcending trunk of the aorta, or great artery; the latter from the vena cava. They are both inſerted into the kidneys; the emulgent arteries carrying blood with the ſerum to them, and the emulgent veins bringing it back again, after the ſerum has been ſeparated therefrom by the kidneys. *Harris.*

Its deſcent doth furniſh the left *emulgent* with one vein, and the firſt vein of the loins on the right ſide with another. *Brown.*

Through the *emulgent* branches the blood is brought to the kidneys, and is there freed of its ſerum. *Cheyne's Phil. Princ.*

E'MULOUS. *adj.* [*æmulus*, Latin.]

1. Rivalling; engaged in competition.

What the Gaul or Moor could not effect,
Nor *emulous* Carthage, with their length of ſpite,
Shall be the work of one. *Ben. Johnſon's Catiline.*

She is in perpetual diffidence, or actual enmity with her, but always *emulous* and ſuſpectful of her. *Howel's Vocal Forreſt.*

2. Deſirous of ſuperiority; deſirous to riſe above another; deſirous of any excellence poſſeſſed by another. With *of* before the object of emulation.

By ſtrength
They meaſure all, *of* other excellence
Not *emulous*, nor care who them excels. *Milton's Par. Loſt.*
By fair rewards our noble youth we raiſe
To *emulous* merit, and to thirſt of praiſe. *Prior.*
Good Howard, *emulous of* the Grecian art. *Prior.*

3. Factious; contentious.

Whoſe glorious deeds, but in theſe fields of late,
Made *emulous* miſſions 'mongſt the gods themſelves,
And drave great Mars to faction. *Shakeſp. Troilus and Creſſ.*

E'MULOUSLY. *adv.* [from *emulous.*] With deſire of excelling or outgoing another.

So tempt they him, and *emulouſly* vie
To bribe a voice, that empires would not buy. *Granville.*

EMU'LSION. *n. ſ.* [*emulſio*, Latin.] A form of medicine, by bruiſing oily ſeeds and kernels, and drawing out their ſubſtances with ſome liquor, that thereby becomes milky. *Quincy.*

The aliment is diſſolved by an operation reſembling that of making an *emulſion*; in which operation the oily parts of nuts and ſeeds, being gently ground in a marble mortar, and gradually mixed with ſome watery liquor, are diſſolved into a ſweet, thick, turbid, milky liquor, reſembling the chyle in an animal body. *Arbuthnot on Aliments.*

EMU'NCTORIES. *n. ſ.* [*emunctorium*, Latin.] Thoſe parts of the body where any thing excrementitious is ſeparated and collected, to be in readineſs for ejectment. *Quincy.*

Superfluous matter deflows from the body unto their proper *emunctories.* *Brown's Vulgar Errours, b.* iii. *c.* 4.

There are receptacles in the body of man, and *emunctories* to drain them of ſuperfluous choler. *More againſt Atheiſm.*

Diſcourſing of the lungs, I ſhew that they are the grand *emunctory* of the body; that the main end of reſpiration is continually to diſcharge and expel an excrementitious fluid out of the maſs of blood. *Woodward's Natural Hiſtory.*

The regimen in quinſies, which proceed from an obſtruction of the glands, muſt be to uſe ſuch warm liquors as relax thoſe glands, ſuch as, by ſtimulating, open the *emunctories* to ſecern the humour. *Arbuthnot on Diet.*

EN. An inſeparable particle borrowed by us from the French, and by the French formed from the Latin *in.* Many words are uncertainly written with *en* or *in.*

To ENA'BLE. *v. a.* [from *able.*] To make able; to confer power; to give ſtrength or ability.

If thou would'ſt vouchſafe to overſpread
Me with the ſhadow of thy gentle wing,
I ſhould *enabled* be thy acts to ſing. *Spenſer's Hymn on Love.*

His great friendship with God might *enable* him, and his compassion might incline him. *Atterbury's Sermons.*

He points out to him the way of life, strengthens his weakness, restores his lapses, and *enables* him to walk and persevere in it. *Rogers, Sermon* 14.

To ENA'CT. *v. a.* [from *act.*]

1. To act; to perform; to effect.

In true ballancing of justice, it is flat wrong to punish the thought or purpose of any before it be *enacted*. *Spenser's State of Ireland.*

Three hours the fight continued,
Where valiant Talbot, above human thought,
Enacted wonders with his sword and lance. *Shak. Hen.* VI.

2. To establish; to decree.

It is *enacted* in the laws of Venice,
If it be proved against an alien,
He seeks the life of any citizen,
The party, 'gainst the which he doth contrive,
Shall seize on half his goods. *Shakes. Merchant of Venice.*

The senate were authors of all counsels in the state; and what was by them consulted and agreed, was proposed to the people, by whom it was *enacted* or commanded. *Temple.*

3. To represent by action.

I did *enact* Hector. *Shakespeare.*

ENA'CT. *n s.* [from the verb.] Purpose; determination.

ENA'CTOR. *n. s.* [from *enact.*]

1. One that forms decrees, or establishes laws.

The great Author of our nature, and *enactor* of this law of good and evil, is highly dishonoured. *Atterbury.*

2. One who practises or performs any thing.

The violence of either grief or joy,
Their own *enactors* with themselves destroy. *Shak. Hamlet.*

ENA'LLAGE. *n. s.* [from the Greek ἐναλλαγή.] A figure in grammar, whereby there is a change either of a pronoun, as when a possessive is put for a relative, or when one mood or tense of a verb is put for another. *Harris.*

To ENA'MBUSH. *v. a.* [from *ambush.*] To hide in ambush; to hide with hostile intention.

They went within a vale, close to a flood, whose stream
Us'd to give all their cattle drink, they there *enambush'd* them. *Chapman's Iliads, b.* i.

To ENA'MEL. *v. a.* [from *amel.* See AMEL.]

1. To inlay; to variegate with colours.

Must I, alas!
Frame and *enamel* plate, and drink in glass? *Donne.*

See Pan with flocks, with fruits Pomona crown'd;
Here blushing Flora paints th' *enamell'd* ground. *Pope.*

I bequeath to the earl of Orrery the *enamelled* silver plates, to distinguish bottles of wine by. *Swift's last Will.*

2. To lay upon another body so as to vary it.

Higher than that wall, a circling row
Of goodliest trees, loaden with fairest fruit,
Blossoms, and fruits at once of golden hue,
Appear'd with gay *enamel'd* colours mix'd. *Milton's Pa. Lost.*

To ENA'MEL. *v. n.* To practise the use of enamel.

Though it were foolish to colour or *enamel* upon the glasses of telescopes, yet to gild the tubes of them may render them more acceptable to the users, without lessening the clearness of the object. *Boyle.*

ENA'MEL. *n. s.* [from the verb.]

1. Any thing enamelled, or variegated with colours inlaid.

Down from her eyes welled the pearles round,
Upon the bright *enamel* of her face;
Such honey drops on springing flowers are found,
When Phœbus holds the crimson morn in chace. *Fairfax.*

There are various sorts of coloured glasses, pastes, *enamels*, and factitious gems. *Woodward on Fossils.*

2. The substance inlaid in other things.

ENA'MELLER. *n. s.* [from *enamel.*] One that practises the art of enamelling.

To ENA'MOUR. *v. a.* [*amour*, French.] To inflame with love; to make fond. With *of* before the thing or person loved.

Affliction is *enamour'd of* thy parts,
And thou art wedded to calamity. *Shakes. Rom. and Juliet.*

My Oberon! What visions have I seen!
I thought I was *enamour'd of* an ass. *Shakespeare.*

You are very near my brother in his love: he is *enamoured* on Hero. *Shakespeare's Much Ado about Nothing.*

Or should she, confident,
As sitting queen ador'd on beauty's throne,
Descend with all her winning charms begirt,
T' *enamour*, as the zone of Venus once
Brought that effect on Jove, so fables tell. *Milt. Par. Lost.*

He, on his side,
Leaning half-rais'd, with looks of cordial love
Hung over her *enamour'd*. *Milton's Paradise Lost, b.* 5.

Your uncle cardinal
Is not so far *enamour'd of* a cloyster,
But he will thank you for the crown. *Dryd Don Sebastian.*

'Tis hard to discern whether is in the greatest errour, he who is *enamoured of* all he does, or he whom nothing of his own can please. *Dryden's Dufresnoy.*

ENARRA'TION. *n. s.* [*enarro*, Latin.] Explanation; narrative. *Dict.*

ENARTHRO'SIS. *n. s.* [ἐν and ἄρθρον] The insertion of one bone into another to form a joint.

Enarthrosis is where a good round head enters into a cavity, whether it be cotyla, or profound cavity, as that of os coxæ, receiving the head of the os femoris; or glene, which is more shallow, as in the scapula, where it receives the humerus. *Wiseman's Surgery.*

ENATA'TION. *n. s.* [*enato*, Latin.] The act of swimming out; escape by swimming. *Dict.*

ENA'UNTER. *adv.* An obsolete word explained by *Spenser* himself to mean lest that.

Anger would not let him speak to the tree,
Enaunter his rage might cooled be,
But to the root bent his sturdy stroke *Spenser's Pastorals.*

To ENCA'GE. *v. a.* [from *cage.*] To shut up as in a cage; to coop up; to confine.

He suffer'd his kinsman March,
Who is, if every owner were right plac'd,
Indeed, his king, to be *encag'd* in Wales,
There without ransom to lie forfeited. *Shakesp. Henry* IV.

Like Bajazet *encag'd*, the shepherds scoff,
Or like slack-sinew'd Sampson, his hair off,
Languish our ships. *Donne.*

To ENCA'MP. *v. n.* [from *camp.*] To pitch tents; to sit down for a time in a march.

He *encamped* at the mount of God. *Exod.* xiii. 5.

The French knew how to make war with the English, by not putting things to the hazard of a battle, but wearing them by long sieges of towns, and strong fortified *encampings*. *Bacon.*

To ENCA'MP. *v. a.* To form an army into a regular camp; to order to encamp.

ENCA'MPMENT. *n. s.* [from *encamp.*]

1. The act of encamping, or pitching tents.

2. A camp; tents pitched in order.

Their enemies served to improve them in their *encampments*, weapons, or something else. *Grew's Cosmol. Sac. b.* iii.

When a gen'ral bids the martial train
Spread their *encampment* o'er the spacious plain,
Thick rising tents a canvas city build. *Gay's Trivia.*

To ENCA'VE. *v. a.* [from *cave.*] To hide as in a cave.

Do but *encave* yourself,
And mark the fleers, the gibes, and notable scorns,
That dwell in ev'ry region of his face;
For I will make him tell the tale anew. *Shakesp. Othello.*

ENCEINTE. n. s. [French.] Inclosure; ground inclosed with a fortification. A military term not yet naturalised.

To ENCHA'FE. *v. a.* [*eschauffer*, French.] To enrage; to irritate; to provoke.

The wind shak'd surge, with high and monstrous main,
Seems to cast water on the burning bear,
And quench the guards of th' ever-fired pole:
I never did like molestation view
On the *enchafed* flood. *Shakespeare's Othello.*

To ENCHA'IN. *v. a.* [*enchainer*, French.] To fasten with a chain; to hold in chains; to bind; to hold in bondage.

What should I do! while here I was *enchain'd*,
No glimpse of godlike liberty remain'd. *Dryden's Virgil.*

To ENCHA'NT. *v. a.* [*enchanter*, French.]

1. To give efficacy to any thing by songs of sorcery.

And now about the cauldron sing,
Like elves and fairies in a ring,
Enchanting all that you put in. *Shakespeare's Macbeth.*

These powerful drops thrice on the threshold pour,
And bathe with this *enchanted* juice her door;
That door where no admittance now is found,
But where my soul is ever hov'ring round. *Granville.*

2. To subdue by charms or spells.

Arcadia was the charmed circle, where all his spirits for ever should be *enchanted*. *Sidney, b.* ii.

One whom the musick of his own vain tongue
Doth ravish, like *enchanting* harmony. *Sh. Love's Lab. Lost.*

John thinks them all *enchanted*: he enquires if Nick had not given them some intoxicating potion. *Arbuthnot's J. Bull.*

3. To delight in a high degree.

Too dear I priz'd a fair *enchanting* face;
Beauty unchaste is beauty in disgrace. *Pope's Odyssey, b.* viii.

ENCHA'NTER. *n. s.* [*enchanteur*, French.] A magician; a sorcerer; one who has spirits or demons at his command; one who has the power of charms and spells.

Such phasms, such apparitions, are excellencies which men applaud in themselves, conjured up by the magick of a strong imagination, and only seen within that circle in which the *enchanter* stands. *Decay of Piety.*

Gladio, by valour and stratagem, put to death tyrants, *enchanters*, monsters, and knights. *Spectator*, N°. 597.

Ardan, that black *enchanter*, whose dire arts
Enslav'd our knights, and broke our virgin hearts. *Granv.*

ENCHA'NTINGLY. *adv.* [from *enchant.*] With the force of enchantment.

enchantment. It is improperly used in a passive sense in the following passage.

He's gentle; never school'd, and yet learned; full of noble device; of all sorts *enchantingly* belov'd. *Shakes. As you like it.*

ENCHA'NTMENT. *n. s.* [*enchantement*, French.]

1. Magical charms; spells; incantation; sorcery.

The Turks thought that horrible tempest was brought upon them by the charms and *enchantments* of the Persian magicians. *Knolles's History of the Turks.*

2. Irresistible influence; overpowering delight.

Warmth of fancy will carry the loudest and most universal applause, which holds the heart of a reader under the strongest *enchantment*. *Pope's Preface to the Iliad.*

ENCHA'NTRESS. *n. s.* [*enchanteresse*, French.]

1. A sorceress; a woman versed in magical arts.

Fell banning hag! *Enchantress*, hold thy tongue. *Shakes.*

I have it by certain tradition, that it was given to the first who wore it by an *enchantress*. *Tatler*, N°. 52.

2. A woman whose beauty or excellencies give irresistible influence.

From this *enchantress* all these ills are come;
You are not safe 'till you pronounce her doom. *Dryden.*
Oft with th' *enchantress* of his soul he talks,
Sometimes in crowds distress'd. *Thomson's Spring*, *l.* 1050.

To ENCHA'SE. *v. a.* [*enchasser*, French.]

1. To infix; to enclose in any other body so as to be held fast, but not concealed.

Like polish'd iv'ry, beauteous to behold;
Or Parian marble, when *enchas'd* in gold. *Dryden's Virgil.*

Words, which, in their natural situation, shine like jewels *enchased* in gold, look, when transposed into notes, as if set in lead. *Felton on the Classicks.*

2. To adorn by being fixed upon it.

What see'st thou there? King Henry's diadem,
Enchas'd with all the honours of the world! *Shak. Henry* VI.
They houses burn, and houshold gods deface,
To drink in bowls which glitt'ring gems *enchase*. *Dryden.*

ENCHE'ASON. *n. s.* [*encheson*, old law French.] Cause; occasion. *Skinner. Cowel. Bailey.*

Certes, said he, well mote I should to tell
The fond *encheason* that me hither led. *Fairy Queen*, *b.* ii.

To ENCI'RCLE. *v. a.* [from *circle.*] To surround; to environ; to inclose in a ring or circle; to enring.

That stranger-guest the Paphian realm obeys,
A realm defended with *encircling* seas. *Pope's Odyssey*, *b.* i.
Beneath a sculptur'd arch he sits inthron'd;
The peers *encircling*, form an awful round. *Pope's Odyssey.*

ENCI'RCLET. *n. s.* [from *circle.*] A circle; a ring.

In whose *encirclets* if ye gaze,
Your eyes may tread a lover's maze. *Sidney*, *b.* ii.

ENCLI'TICKS. *n. s.* [ἐγκλίτικα.] Particles which throw back the accent upon the foregoing syllable.

To ENCLO'SE. *v. a.* [*enclos*, French.]

1. To part from things or grounds common by a fence.

The protector caused a proclamation to be set forth against enclosures, commanding that they who had *enclosed* lands, accustomed to lie open, should lay them open again. *Hayward.*

As much land as a man tills, and can use the product of, so much he by his labour *encloses* from the common. *Locke.*

For *enclosing* of land, the usual way is with a bank set with quick. *Mortimer's Husbandry.*

2. To environ; to encircle; to surround; to encompass; to shut in between other things; to include.

The fourth row a beryl, and an onyx, and a jasper: they shall be set in gold in their *enclosings*. *Ex.* xxviii. 20.

The peer now spreads the glitt'ring forfex wide,
T' *enclose* the lock; now joins it, to divide. *Pope.*

ENCLO'SER. *n. s.* [from *enclose.*]

1. One that encloses, or separates common fields in several distinct properties.

If God had laid all common, certainly
Man would have been th' *encloser*; but since now
God hath impal'd us, on the contrary,
Man breaks the fence. *Herbert.*

2. Any thing in which another is enclosed.

ENCLO'SURE. *n. s.* [from *enclose.*]

1. The act of enclosing or environing any thing.

The membranes are for the comprehension or *enclosure* of all these together. *Wilkins's Math. Magick.*

2. The separation of common grounds into distinct possessions.

Enclosures began to be frequent, whereby arable land was turned into pasture. *Bacon's Henry* VII.

Touching *enclosures*, I am not ignorant what a profitable purchase is made thereby, because a company of lands inclosed are thereby improved in worth two or three parts at the least. *Hayward.*

3. The appropriation of things common.

Let no man appropriate what God hath made common; that is against justice and charity, and by miraculous accidents God hath declared his displeasure against such *enclosure*. *Taylor.*

4. State of being shut up in any place; encompassed, or environed.

This expresses particularly the *enclosure* of the waters within the earth. *Burnet's Theory of the Earth.*

For the young, during its *enclosure* in the womb, there are formed membranes inveloping it, called secundines. *Ray.*

5. The space enclosed; the space comprehended within certain limits.

And all, that else this world's *enclosure* base
Hath great or glorious in mortal eye,
Adorns the person of her majesty. *Fairy Queen*, *b.* ii. *can.* 2.

They are to live all in a body, and generally within the same *enclosure*; to marry among themselves, and to eat no meats that are not prepared their own way. *Addison's Spectator*

6. Several; ground enclosed; ground separated from the common.

'Tis not the common, but the *enclosure* must make him rich. *South's Sermons.*

ENCO'MIAST. *n. s.* [ἐγκωμιαστὴς.] A panegyrist; a proclaimer praise; a praiser.

The Jesuits are the great *encomiasts* of the Chinese. *Locke.*

ENCOMIA'STICAL. } *adj.* [ἐγκωμιάστικος.] Panegyrical; laudatory; containing praise; bestowing praise.
ENCOMIA'STICK. }

ENCO'MIUM. *n. s.* [ἐγκώμιον.] Panegyrick; praise; elogy.

How eagerly do some men propagate every little *encomium* their parasites make of them. *Government of the Tongue*, *s.* 9.

A vile *encomium* doubly ridicules;
There's nothing blackens like the ink of fools. *Pope.*

To ENCO'MPASS. *v. a* [from *compass.*]

1. To enclose; to encircle.

Look how my ring *encompasseth* thy finger;
Ev'n so thy breast encloseth my poor heart. *Shak. Rich.* III.

Two strong ligaments *encompass* the whole head of the femur. *Wiseman's Surgery.*

Poetick fields *encompass* me around,
And still I seem to tread on classick ground. *Addison.*

2. To shut in; to surround; to environ.

He, having scarce six thousand in his troop,
By three and twenty thousand of the French
Was round *encompassed*, and set upon. *Shakesp. Henry* VI.

3. To go round any place: as, *Drake* encompassed *the world.*

ENCO'MPASSMENT. *n. s.* [from *encompass.*] Circumlocution; remote tendency of talk.

Finding
By this *encompassment* and drift of question,
That they do know my son, come you more near. *Shakes.*

ENCO'RE. *adv.* [French.] Again; once more. A word used at publick shows when a singer, or fiddler, or buffoon is desired by the audience to do the same thing again.

To the same notes thy sons shall hum or snore,
And all thy yawning daughters cry *encore*. *Dunciad*, *b.* iv.

ENCO'UNTER. *n. s.* [*encontre*, French.]

1. Duel; single fight; conflict.

Thou hast beat me out
Twelve several times, and I have nightly since
Dreamt of *encounters* 'twixt thyself and me. *Shakespeare.*
Let's leave this keen *encounter* of our wits,
And fall something into a slower method. *Shakes. Rich.* III.
Pallas th' *encounter* seeks; but e're he throws,
To Tuscan Tiber thus address'd his vows:
O sacred stream, direct my flying dart,
And give to pass the proud Halesus' heart. *Dryden's Æn.*

2. Battle; fight in which enemies rush against each other.

Two black clouds
With heav'n's artillery fraught, come rattling on
Over the Caspian; then stand front to front,
Hov'ring a space, 'till winds the signal blow
To join their dark *encounter* in mid air. *Milt. Parad. Lost.*

3. Eager and warm conversation, either of love or anger.

The peaking cornuto comes to me in the instant of our *encounter*, after we had spoke the prologue of our comedy. *Shak.*

4. Accidental congress; sudden meeting.

Propitious Pallas, to secure her care,
Around him spread a veil of thicken'd air,
To shun th' *encounter* of the vulgar crowd. *Pope's Odyssey.*

5. Accosting.

But in what habit will you go along?
—Not like a woman; for I would prevent the loose *encounters* of lascivious men. *Shakespeare's Two Gentlemen of Verona.*

Three parts of Brutus
Is ours already; and the man entire,
Upon the next *encounter*, yields him ours. *Shakes. Jul. Cæs.*

6. Casual incident; occasion. This sense is scarcely English.

An equality is not sufficient for the unity of character: 'tis further necessary, that the same spirit appear in all sort of *encounters*. *Pope's View of Epick Poetry.*

To ENCO'UNTER. *v. a.* [from the noun.]

1. To meet face to face.

If I must die,
I will *encounter* darkness as a bride,
And hug it in mine arms. *Shakes. Measure for Measure.*

The fashion of the world is to avoid cost, and you *encounter* it. *Shakespeare's Much Ado about Nothing.*

Those

Thou ſtronger may'ſt endure the flood of light;
And, while in ſhades I chear my fainting ſight,
Encounter the deſcending excellence. *Dryd. State of Innocence.*

2. To meet in a hoſtile manner; to ruſh againſt in conflict.
Putting themſelves in order of battle, they *encountered* their enemies. *Knolles's Hiſtory of the Turks.*

3. To meet with reciprocal kindneſs.
See, they *encounter* thee with their hearts thanks;
Both ſides are even. *Shakeſpeare's Macbeth.*

4. To attack; to meet in the front.
Which way ſoever we turn ourſelves, we are *encountered* with clear evidences and ſenſible demonſtrations of a Deity. *Tillotſon, Sermon* 1.

5. To oppoſe; to oppugn.
Jurors are not bound to believe two witneſſes, if the probability of the fact does reaſonably *encounter* them. *Hale.*

6. To meet by accident.
I am moſt fortunate thus to *encounter* you:
You have ended my buſineſs, and I will merrily
Accompany you home. *Shakeſpeare's Coriolanus.*

To ENCO'UNTER. *v. n.*

1. To ruſh together in a hoſtile manner; to conflict.
And let belief and life *encounter* ſo,
As doth the fury of two deſperate men,
Which, in the very meeting, fall and die. *Shakeſ. K. John.*
Five times, Marcius,
Have I fought with thee; ſo often haſt thou beat me:
And wouldſt do ſo, I think, ſhould we *encounter*
As often as we eat. *Shakeſpeare's Coriolanus.*

2. To engage; to fight.
Our wars
Will turn into a peaceful comick ſport,
When ladies crave to be *encounter'd* with. *Shakeſp. H.* VI.
Both the wings of his fleet had begun to *encounter* with the Chriſtians. *Knolles's Hiſtory of the Turks.*
Thoſe who have the moſt dread of death, muſt in a little time be content to *encounter* with it, whether they will or no. *Wake's Preparation for Death.*

3. To meet face to face.

4. To come together by chance.

ENCO'UNTERER. *n. ſ.* [from *encounter.*]

1. Opponent; antagoniſt; enemy.
The lion will not kick with his feet, but he will ſtrike ſuch a ſtroke with his tail, that he will break the back of his *encounterer* with it. *More's Antidote againſt Atheiſm.*
The doctrines of the reformation have kept the field againſt all *encounterers*, and does he think they may be foiled by two or three remarks? *Atterbury's Pref. to Anſ. on Conſid. on Luther.*

2. One that loves to accoſt others. An old term.
Oh, theſe *encounterers!* ſo gilt of tongue,
They give a coaſting welcome ere it comes;
And wide unclaſp the tables of their thoughts
To every ticklish reader. *Shakeſp. Troilus and Creſſida.*

To ENCO'URAGE. *v. a.* [*encourager*, French.]

1. To animate; to incite to any thing.
They *encourage* themſelves in an evil matter. *Pſ.* lxiv. 5.

2. To give courage to; to ſupport the ſpirits; to inſpirit; to embolden.
I would neither *encourage* the rebels, nor diſcourage the proteſtants loyalty. *King Charles.*

3. To raiſe confidence; to make confident.
I doubt not but there are ways to be found, to aſſiſt our reaſon in this moſt uſeful part; and this the judicious Hooker *encourages* me to ſay. *Locke.*

ENCO'URAGEMENT. *n. ſ.* [from *encourage.*]

1. Incitement to any action or practice; incentive.
Such ſtrength of heart
Thy conduct and example gives; nor ſmall
Encouragement, Godolphin, wiſe and juſt. *Phillips.*

2. Favour; countenance; ſupport.
For when he dies, farewel all honour, bounty,
All generous *encouragement* of arts. *Otway's Orphan.*
The reproach of immorality will lie heavieſt againſt an eſtabliſhed religion, becauſe thoſe who have no religion will profeſs themſelves of that which has the *encouragement* of the law. *Rogers, Sermon* 9.

ENCO'URAGER. *n. ſ.* [from *encourage.*] One that ſupplies incitements to any thing; a favourer.
Live then, thou great *encourager* of arts,
Live ever in our thankful hearts. *Dryden.*
As the pope is himſelf a maſter of polite learning, and a great *encourager* of arts; ſo at Rome any of thoſe arts immediately thrives, under the encouragement of the prince. *Addiſon's Remarks on Italy.*

To ENCRO'ACH. *v. n.* [*accrocher*, from *croc*, a hook, Fr.]

1. To make invaſions upon the right of another; to put a hook into another man's poſſeſſions to draw them away.
Thoſe Iriſh captains of countries have *encroached* upon the queen's freeholders and tenants. *Spenſer on Ireland.*

2. To advance gradually and by ſtealth upon that to which one has no right.
The ſuperſtition that riſeth voluntarily, and by degrees mingleth itſelf with the rites, even of every divine ſervice, done to the only true God, muſt be conſidered of as a creeping and *encroaching* evil. *Hooker, b.* v. *ſ.* 3.
This hour is mine; if for the next I care, I grow too wide,
And do *encroach* upon death's ſide. *Herbert.*
They fabled how the ſerpent, whom they call'd
Ophion, with Eurynome, the wide
Encroaching Eve perhaps, had firſt the rule
Of high Olympus. *Milton's Paradiſe Loſt, b.* x. *l.* 582.
Th' *encroaching* ill you early ſhould oppoſe;
Flatter'd, 'tis worſe, and by indulgence grows. *Dryden.*
Next, fenc'd with hedges and deep ditches round,
Exclude th' *encroaching* cattle from thy ground. *Dryden.*
Tiſiphone, let looſe from under ground,
Before her drives diſeaſes and affright;
And every moment riſes to the fight,
Aſpiring to the ſkies, *encroaching* on the light. *Dryden.*

ENCRO'ACHER. *n. ſ.* [from *encroach.*]

1. One who ſeizes the poſſeſſion of another by gradual and ſilent means.
The bold *encroachers* on the deep,
Gain by degrees huge tracts of land,
'Till Neptune, with one gen'ral ſweep,
Turns all again to barren ſtrand. *Swift.*

2. One who makes ſlow and gradual advances beyond his rights.
Full dreſs creates dignity, augments conſciouſneſs, and keeps at diſtance an *encroacher*. *Clariſſa.*

ENCRO'ACHMENT. *n. ſ.* [from *encroach.*]

1. An unlawful gathering in upon another man. For example: if two mens grounds lying together, the one preſſes too far upon the other; or if a tenant owe two ſhillings rent-ſervice to the lord, and the lord takes three: ſo the Spencers encroached to themſelves royal power and authority. *Cowel.*
But this uſurper his *encroachment* proud
Stays not on man: to God his tow'r intends
Siege, and defiance. *Milton's Paradiſe Loſt, b.* xii. *l.* 72.
As a man had a right to all he could employ his labour upon, ſo he had no temptation to labour for more than he could make uſe of: this left no room for controverſy about the title, nor for *encroachment* on the right of others. *Locke.*
If it be a man's known principle to depart from his right, ill men will make unjuſt *encroachments* upon him. *Atterbury.*
The people, ſince the death of Solon, had already made great *encroachments*. *Swift on the Diſſent. in Athens and Rome.*

2. Advance into the territories or rights of another.
It gave the ancient Romans an opportunity of making ſo many *encroachments* on the ſea, and of laying the foundations of their palaces within the very borders of it. *Addiſon on Italy.*

To ENCU'MBER. *v. a.* [*encombrer*, French.]

1. To clog; to load; to impede.
We have, by this many years experience, found that exceeding great good, not *encumbered* with any notable inconvenience. *Hooker, b.* v. *ſ.* 20.
Encumber'd with his veſt, without defence. *Dryden.*

2. To entangle; to embarraſs; to obſtruct.
The verbal copier is *encumbered* with ſo many difficulties at once, that he can never diſentangle himſelf. *Dryden.*
The god awak'd,
And thrice in vain he ſhook his wing,
Encumber'd in the ſilken ſtring. *Prior.*

3. To load with debts: as, *his eſtate is* encumbered *with mortgages.*

ENCU'MBRANCE. *n. ſ.* [from *encumber.*]

1. Clog; load; impediment.
Philoſophers agreed in deſpiſing riches, at beſt, conſidering them as unneceſſary *encumbrances* of life. *Temple.*
Dead limbs are an *encumbrance* to the body, inſtead of being of uſe to it. *Addiſon's Freeholder,* Nº. 13.

2. Excreſcence; uſeleſs addition.
Strip from the branching Alps their piny load,
The huge *encumbrance* of horrifick woods. *Thomſ. Autumn.*

3. Burthen upon an eſtate.
In reſpect of the *encumbrances* of a living, conſider whether it be ſufficient for his family, and to maintain hoſpitality. *Ayl.*

ENCY'CLICAL. *adj.* [ἐγκυκλικός] Circular; ſent round through a large region.
This council was not received in patriarchal ſees, which is evident from Photius's *encyclical* epiſtle to the patriarch of Alexandria. *Stillingfleet's Def. of Diſc. on Rom. Idol.*

ENCYCLOPE'DIA. / ENCYCLOPE'DY } *n. ſ.* [ἐγκυκλοπαιδεία.] The circle of ſciences; the round of learning.
Every ſcience borrows from all the reſt, and we cannot attain any ſingle one without the *encyclopædy. Glanv. Scepſ. c.* 25.
This art may juſtly claim a place in the *encyclopædia*, eſpecially ſuch as ſerves for a model of education for an able politician. *Arbuthnot's Hiſtory of John Bull.*

ENCY'STED. *adj.* [κύστις.] Encloſed in a veſicle or bag.
Encyſted tumours borrow their names from a cyſt or bag in which they are contained, and are farther diſtinguiſhed by the nature of their contents. *Sharp's Surgery.*

END.

END. *n. ſ.* [enԁ, Saxon.]

1. The extremity of any thing materially extended.

Jonathan put forth the *end* of the rod that was in his hand, and dipt it in a honeycomb. 1 *Sam.* xiv. 27.

The extremity and bounds of all bodies we have no difficulty to arrive at; but, when the mind is there, it finds nothing to hinder its progreſs into this endleſs expanſion: of that it can neither find, nor conceive any *end.* *Locke.*

2. The laſt particle of any aſſignable duration.

If the world's age and death be argu'd well
By the ſun's fall, which now tow'rds earth doth bend,
Then we might fear that virtue, ſince ſhe fell
So low as woman, ſhould be near her *end.* *Donne.*

3. The concluſion or ceſſation of any action.

Jacob had made an *end* of commanding his ſons. *Gen.* xlix.

Yet vainly moſt their age in ſtudy ſpend;
No *end* of writing books, and to no end. *Denham.*

The cauſes and deſigns of an action are the beginning: the effects of theſe cauſes, and the difficulties that are met with in the execution of theſe deſigns, are the middle; and the unravelling and reſolution of theſe difficulties, are the *end.* *Pope's View of Epic Poem.*

4. The concluſion or laſt part of any thing; as, the *end* of a chapter; the *end* of a diſcourſe.

5. Ultimate ſtate; final doom.

6. The point beyond which no progreſſion can be made.

They reel to and fro, and ſtagger like a drunken man, and are at their wits *end.* *Pſ.* cvii. 27.

7. Final determination; concluſion of debate or deliberation.

My guilt be on my head, and there's an *end!* *Shakeſp.*

8. Death; fate; deceaſe.

I determine to write the life and the *end,* the nature and the fortunes of George Villiers. *Wotton.*

The ſoul receives intelligence,
By her near genius, of the body's *end,*
And ſo imparts a ſadneſs to the ſenſe. *Daniel's Civil War.*

'Tis the great buſineſs of life to fit ourſelves for our *end,* and no man can live well that has not death in his eye. *L'Eſtr.*

Remember Milo's *end,*
Wedg'd in that timber which he ſtrove to rend. *Roſcommon.*

My God, my father, and my friend,
Do not forſake me in my *end.* *Roſcommon.*

Unblam'd through life, lamented in thy *end.* *Pope.*

9. Abolition; total loſs.

There would be an *end* of all civil government, if the aſſignment of civil power were by ſuch inſtitution. *Locke.*

10. Cauſe of death; deſtroyer.

Take heed you dally not before your king,
Leſt he that is the ſupreme king of kings,
Confound your hidden falſhood, and award
Either of you to be the other's *end.* *Shakeſp. Richard* III.

11. Conſequence; event.

O, that a man might know
The *end* of this day's buſineſs ere it come!
But it ſufficeth that the day will end. *Shakeſp. Jul. Cæſar.*

The *end* of theſe things is death. *Rom.* vi. 21.

12. Fragment; broken piece.

Thus I cloathe my naked villany
With old odd *ends,* ſtol'n forth of Holy Writ,
And ſeem a ſaint. *Shakeſpeare's Richard* III.

13. Purpoſe; intention

There was a purpoſe to reduce the monarchy to a republick, which was far from the *end* and purpoſe of that nation. *Claren.*

I have lov'd!
What can thy *ends,* malicious beauty, be?
Can he who kill'd thy brother, live for thee? *Dryd. Ind. Emp.*

Heav'n, as its inſtrument, my courage ſends;
Heav'n ne'er ſent thoſe who fight for private *ends.* *Dryden.*

Others are apt to attribute them to ſome falſe *end* or intention. *Addiſon's Spectator,* N°. 255.

14. Thing intended; final deſign.

Wiſdom may have framed one and the ſame thing to ſerve commodiouſly for divers *ends,* and of thoſe *ends* any one may be ſufficient cauſe for continuance, though the reſt have ceaſed. *Hooker, b.* v. *ſ.* 42.

All thoſe things which are done by him, have ſome *end* for which they are done; and the *end* for which they are done, is a reaſon of his will to do them. *Hooker, b.* i. *ſ.* 2.

Her only *end* is never-ending bliſs;
Which is, the eternal face of God to ſee,
Who laſt of ends, and firſt of cauſes is;
And to do this, ſhe muſt eternal be. *Davies.*

The *end* of the commandment is charity. 1 *Tim.* i. 5.

Two things I ſhall propound to you, as *ends;* ſince the wiſe men of this world have made them theirs. *Suckling.*

Such conditions did fully comply with all thoſe *ends,* for which the parliament had firſt taken up arms. *Clarendon.*

Hear and mark
To what *end* I have brought thee hither, and ſhewn
All this fair ſight. *Milton's Paradiſe Regained, b.* iii.

Life, with my Indamora, I would chuſe;
But, loſing her, the *end* of living loſe. *Dryden's Aurengz.*

For when ſucceſs a lover's toil attends,
Few aſk if fraud or force attain'd his *ends.* *Pope.*

The *end* of our faſt is to pleaſe God, and make him propitious. *Smalridge's Sermons.*

15. *An* END. [Probably corrupted from *on end.*] Upright; erect: as, his hair ſtands *an end.*

16. *An* END has a ſignification in low language not eaſily explained; as, *moſt an end, commonly:* perhaps it is properly *on end,* at the concluſion; or corrupted from ſome old word not eaſily recoverable.

Stay'ſt thou to vex me here?
Slave, that, ſtill *an end,* turns me to ſhame. *Shakeſpeare.*

To END. *v. a.* [from the noun.]

1. To terminate; to conclude; to finiſh.

That but this blow
Might be the be-all, and the *end*-all. *Shakeſp. Macbeth.*

He would in one battle *end* quarrel with them, either win or loſe the empire. *Knolles's Hiſtory of the Turks.*

That expenſive war under which we have ſo long groaned, is not yet *ended.* *Smalridge's Sermons.*

2. To deſtroy; to put to death.

The lord of Stafford dear to-day hath bought
Thy likeneſs; for inſtead of thee, king Harry,
This ſword hath *ended* him. *Shakeſpeare's Henry* IV.

To END. *v. n.*

1. To come to an end; to be finiſhed.

Yet happy were my death, mine *ending* bleſt,
If this I could obtain, that, breaſt to breaſt,
Thy boſom might receive my yielded ſpright. *Fairfax, b.* ii.

Then eaſe your weary Trojans will attend,
And the long labours of your voyage *end.* *Dryden's Æn.*

2. To terminate; to conclude; to ceaſe; to fail.

Our laughing, if it be loud and high, commonly *ends* in a deep ſigh; and all the inſtances of pleaſure have a ſting in the tail. *Taylor's Rule of living holy.*

His ſovereignty, built upon either of theſe titles, could not have deſcended to his heir, but muſt have *ended* with him. *Loc.*

To ENDA'MAGE. *v. a.* [from *damage.*] To miſchief; to prejudice; to harm.

Nor ought he car'd whom he *endamaged*
By tortous wrong, or whom bereav'd of right. *Fa. Queen.*

And it cometh ſometime to paſs, that a thing unneceſſary in itſelf, touching the whole direct purpoſe, doth notwithſtanding appear convenient to be ſtill held, even without uſe, leſt, by reaſon of that coherence which it hath with ſomewhat moſt neceſſary, the removal of the one ſhould *endamage* the other. *Hooker, b.* v. *ſ.* 42.

Where your good word cannot advantage him,
Your ſlander never can *endamage* him. *Shakeſpeare.*

Gather our ſoldiers, ſcatter'd and diſperſt,
And lay new platforms to *endamage* them. *Shak. Hen.* VI.

The trial hath *endamag'd* thee no way;
Rather more honour left, and more eſteem. *Milton.*

When an erroneous opinion is publiſhed, the publick is *endamaged,* and therefore it becomes puniſhable by the magiſtrate. *South's Sermons.*

A great alteration doth ſeldom any wiſe *endamage* or diſorder the globe. *Woodward's Natural Hiſtory.*

To ENDA'NGER. *v. a.* [from *danger.*]

1. To put into hazard; to bring into peril.

Every one deſires his own preſervation and happineſs, and therefore hath a natural dread of every thing that can deſtroy his being, or *endanger* his happineſs. *Tillotſon, Sermon* 4.

He rais'd the reſt,
To force the foes from the Lavinian ſhore,
And Italy's *endanger'd* peace reſtore. *Dryden's Æn. b.* vii.

My kingdom claims your birth; my late defence,
Of our *endanger'd* fleet, may claim your confidence. *Dryden.*

Volatile ſalts never exiſt in an animal body; the heat required to make them volatile, *endangers* the animal. *Arbuthnot on Aliments.*

The intereſt *endangered* is no leſs than our title to heaven. *Rogers, Sermon* 4.

2. To incur the danger of; to hazard.

He that turneth the humours back, and maketh the wound bleed inwards, *endangereth* malign ulcers. *Bacon's Eſſays.*

To ENDE'AR. *v. a.* [from *dear.*] To make dear; to make beloved.

All thoſe inſtances of charity which uſually *endear* each other, ſweetneſs of converſation, frequent admonition, all ſignifications of love muſt be expreſſed towards children. *Tayl.*

And in the mixture of all theſe appears
Variety, which all the reſt *endears.* *Denham.*

The only thing that can *endear* religion to your practice, will be to raiſe your affections above this world. *Wake.*

ENDE'ARMENT. *n. ſ.* [from *endear.*]

1. The cauſe of love; means by which any thing is endeared.

Her firſt *endearments,* twining round the ſoul. *Thomſon.*

2. The ſtate of being endeared; the ſtate of being loved.

Is not the ſeparate property of a thing the great cauſe of its *endearment* amongſt all mankind? *South's Sermons.*

When a man shall have done all that he can to make one his friend, and emptied his purse to create *endearment* between them, he may, in the end, be forced to write vanity and frustration. *South's Sermons.*

ENDE'AVOUR. *n. s.* [*devoir*, French; *endevoir.*] Labour directed to some certain end; effort to obtain or avoid.

My studied purposes went
Beyond all man's *endeavours*. *Shakespeare's Henry* VIII.

Heav'n doth divide
The state of man in divers functions,
Setting *endeavour* in continual motion. *Shakesp. Henry* V.

Here their appointment we may best discover,
And look on their *endeavour*. *Shakesp. Ant. and Cleopatra.*

I take imitation of an author, in their sense, to be an *endeavour* of a later poet to write like one, who has written before him on the same subject. *Dryden.*

The bold and sufficient pursue their game with more passion, *endeavour*, and application, and therefore often succeed. *Temple.*

She could not make the least *endeavour* towards the producing of any thing that hath vital and organical parts. *Ray.*

Such an assurance as will quicken mens *endeavours* for the obtaining of a lesser good, ought to animate men more powerfully in the pursuit of that which is infinitely greater. *Tillots.*

This is the hinge on which turns the liberty of intellectual beings, in their constant *endeavours* after, and steady prosecution of true felicity. *Locke.*

To ENDEA'VOUR. *v. n.* [from the noun.] To labour to a certain purpose; to work for a certain end.

I could wish that more of our country-clergy would *endeavour* after a handsome elocution. *Addison's Spectator*, Nº. 106.

Of old, those met rewards who could excel;
And those were prais'd, who but *endeavour'd* well. *Pope.*

To ENDEA'VOUR. *v. a.* To attempt; to try.

To pray'r, repentance, and obedience due,
Though but *endeavour'd* with sincere intent,
Mine ear shall not be slow, mine ear not shut. *Milt. P. L.*

ENDEA'VOURER. *n. s.* [from *endeavour.*] One who labours to a certain end.

He appears an humble *endeavourer*, and speaks honestly to no purpose. *Rymer's Tragedies of the last Age.*

ENDECA'GON. *n. s.* [ἑνδέκαγον.] A plain figure of eleven sides and angles.

ENDE'MIAL. } ENDE'MICAL. } ENDE'MICK. } *adj.* [ἔνδημος.] Peculiar to a country; used of any disease that affects several people together in the same country, proceeding from some cause peculiar to the country where it reigns: such as the scurvy to the northern climes. *Quincy.*

We may bring a consumption under the notion of a pandemick, or *endemick*, or rather a vernacular disease, to England. *Harvey on Consumptions.*

Solenander, from the frequency of the plants springing up in any region, could gather what *endemial* diseases the inhabitants were subject to. *Ray on the Creation.*

An *endemial* disease is what is common to the people of the country. *Arbuthnot on Air.*

What demonstrates the plague to be *endemial* to Egypt, is its invasion and going off at certain seasons. *Arbuthn. on Air.*

To ENDE'NIZE. *v. a.* [from *denizen.*] To make free; to enfranchise.

It hath been beautified and enriched out of other good tongues, partly by enfranchising and *endenizing* strange words. *Camden's Remains.*

To ENDI'CT. } To ENDI'TE. } *v. a.* [*enditer*, French; *dictum*, Latin.]

1. To charge any man by a written accusation before a court of justice: as, *he was* endited *for felony.*

2. To draw up; to compose; to write.

Your battles they hereafter shall *indite*,
And draw the image of our Mars in fight. *Waller.*

How shall Filbert unto me *indite*,
When neither I can read, nor he can write. *Gay.*

Hear how learn'd Greece her useful rules *indites*,
When to repress, and when indulge our flights! *Pope.*

ENDI'CTMENT. } ENDI'TEMENT. } *n. s.* [from *endite.*] A bill or declaration made in form of law, for the benefit of the commonwealth; or an accusation for some offence exhibited unto jurours, and by their verdict found and presented to be true, before an officer can have power to punish the same offence. *Cowel.*

'Tis necessary that the species of the crime be described in the libel or articles, which our English lawyers call an *indictment* or information. *Ayliffe's Parergon.*

We never draw any *indictment* at all against them, but think commendably even of them. *Hooker.*

The hand-writing against him may be cancelled in the court of heaven, and yet the *indictment* run on in the court of conscience. *South's Sermons.*

Attend the court, and thou shalt briefly find
In that one place the manners of mankind;
Hear the *endictments*, then return again,
Call thyself wretch, and, if thou dar'st, complain. *Dryden.*

E'NDIVE. *n. s.* [*endive*, French; *intybum*, Latin.]

Endive, or succory, is of several sorts; as the white, the green, and the curled, which are only propagated by seed, that is longish, of a white-grey colour, flat at one end, and roundish at the other. It grows upon the stocks or stems of the preceding year's growth. *Mortimer's Husbandry.*

E'NDLESS. *adj.* [from *end.*]

1. Without end; without conclusion or termination.

Nothing was more *endless* than the common method of comparing eminent writers by an opposition of particular passages in them. *Pope's Preface to the Iliad.*

2. Infinite in longitudinal extent.

As it is pleasant to the eye to have an *endless* prospect, so it is some pleasure to a finite understanding to view unlimited excellencies. *Tillotson.*

3. Infinite in duration; perpetual.

None of the heathens, how curious soever in searching out all kinds of outward ceremonies, could ever once endeavour to resemble herein the church's care for the *endless* good of her children. *Hooker, b.* v. *s.* 18.

But after labours long, and sad delay,
Brings them to joyous rest, and *endless* bliss. *Fairy Queen.*

All our glory extinct, and happy state,
Here swallow'd up in *endless* misery! *Milton's Paradise Lost.*

4. Incessant; continual.

All the priests and friars in my realm,
Shall in procession sing her *endless* praise. *Shakesp. Hen.* VI.

Each pleasing Blount shall *endless* smiles bestow,
And soft Belinda's blush for ever glow. *Pope.*

E'NDLESSLY. *adv.* [from *endless.*]

1. Incessantly; perpetually.

Though his promise has made a sure entail of grace to all those who humbly seek, yet it no where engages that it shall importunately and *endlessly* renew its assaults on those who have often repulsed it. *Decay of Piety.*

2. Without termination of length.

E'NDLESSNESS. *n. s.* [from *endless.*]

1. Perpetuity; endless duration.

2. The quality of being round without an end.

The Tropick circles have,
Yea, and those small ones, which the poles engrave,
All the same roundness, evenness, and all
The *endlessness* of the Equinoctial. *Donne.*

E'NDLONG. *adv.* [*end* and *long.*] In a strait line.

Then spurring at full speed, ran *endlong* on,
Where Theseus sat on his imperial throne. *Dryden.*

E'NDMOST. *adj.* [*end* and *most.*] Remotest; furthest; at the farther end. *Dict.*

To ENDO'RSE. *v. a.* [*endosser*, French; *dorsum*, Latin.]

1. To register on the back of a writing; to superscribe.

A French gentleman speaking with an English of the law salique, the English said that was meant of the women themselves, not of males claiming by women. The French gentleman said, where do you find that gloss? The English answered, look on the backside of the record of the law salique, and there you shall find it *endorsed*. *Bacon's Apophth.*

Upon credential letters was *endorsed* this superscription, To the king who hath the sun for his helmet. *Howel's Vocal Forr.*

All the letters I can find of your's I have fastened in a folio cover, and the rest in bundles *endorsed*. *Swift to Pope.*

2. To cover on the back

Chariots, or elephants *endors'd* with tow'rs
Of archers. *Milton's Paradise Regain'd, b.* iii. *l.* 329.

ENDO'RSEMENT. *n s.* [from *endorse.*]

1. Superscription; writing on the back.

2. Ratification.

Th' *endorsement* of supreme delight,
Writ by a friend, and with his blood. *Herbert.*

To ENDO'W. *v. a.* [*indotare*, Latin; *endouairer*, French.]

1. To enrich with a portion.

He shall surely *endow* her to be his wife. *Exod.* xxii. 16.

2. To supply with any external goods.

An alms-house I intend to *endow* very handsomely for a dozen superannuated husbandmen. *Addison's Spectator.*

3. To enrich with any excellence.

I at first with two fair gifts
Created him *endow'd*; with happiness
And immortality; that fondly lost,
This other serv'd but to eternize woe. *Milt. Parad. Lost.*

Among those who are the most richly *endowed* by nature, and accomplished by their own industry, how few are there whose vertues are not obscured? *Addison's Spectator*, Nº. 255.

God did never command us to believe, nor his ministers to preach any doctrine contrary to the reason he hath pleased to *endow* us with. *Swift.*

4. To be the fortune of any one.

I do not think
So fair an outward, and such stuff within,
Endows a man but him. *Shakespeare's Cymbeline.*

ENDO'WMENT. *n. s.* [from *endow.*]

1. Wealth bestowed to any person or use.

2. The bestowing or assuring a dower; the setting forth or severing

ſevering a ſufficient portion for a vicar toward his perpetual maintenance, when the benefice is appropriated. *Cowel.*

A chapel will I build, with large *endowment.* *Dryden.*

3. Gifts of nature.

By a deſire of fame, great *endowments* are not ſuffered to lie idle and uſeleſs to the publick. *Addiſon's Spectator*, Nº. 255.

If providence ſhews itſelf even in the blemiſhes of theſe creatures, how much more does it diſcover itſelf in their ſeveral *endowments*, according to the condition in which they are poſted. *Addiſon's Spectator*, Nº. 121.

To ENDU'E. *v. a.* [*induo*, Latin.]

1. To ſupply with mental excellencies; to inveſt with intellectual powers.

Endue them with thy holy ſpirit. *Common Prayer.*

Wiſdom was Adam's inſtructor in Paradiſe: wiſdom *endued* the fathers, who lived before the law, with the knowledge of holy things. *Hooker*, *b.* ii. *ſ.* 7.

Theſe baniſh'd men that I have kept withal,
Are men *endu'd* with worthy qualities. *Shakeſpeare.*

With what eaſe,
Endu'd with royal virtues as thou art,
Appearing and beginning noble deeds,
Might'ſt thou expel this monſter from his throne. *Milton.*

Whatſoever other knowledge a man may be *endued* withal, he is but an ignorant perſon who doth not know God, the author of his being. *Tillotſon's Sermons.*

Every Chriſtian is *endued* with a power, whereby he is enabled to reſiſt and conquer temptations. *Tillotſon, Sermon* 6.

2. In the following paſſage it ſeems incorrectly printed for *endow*.

Leah ſaid, God hath *endued* me with a good dowry. *Gen.*

ENDU'RANCE. *n. ſ.* [from *endure.*]

1. Continuance; laſtingneſs.

Some of them are of very great antiquity and continuance, others more late and of leſs *endurance*. *Spenſer's State of Ireland.*

2. Patience; the act of ſupporting; ſufferance.

Great things of ſmall
One can create; and in what place ſoe'er
Thrive under evil, and work eaſe out of pain,
Through labour and *endurance*. *Milton's Paradiſe Loſt, b.* ii.

Their fortitude was moſt admirable in their patience and *endurance* of all evils, of pain, and of death. *Temple.*

3. Delay; procraſtination. Obſolete.

I ſhould have ta'en ſome pains to bring together
Yourſelf and your accuſers, and have heard you,
Without *endurance* further. *Shakeſpeare's Henry* VIII.

To ENDU'RE. *v. a.* [*endurer*, French; *durare*, Latin.] To bear; to undergo; to ſuſtain; to ſupport.

By thine own tongue thou art condemn'd, and muſt
Endure our law. *Shakeſpeare's Cymbeline.*

The hardneſs of bodies is cauſed chiefly by the jejuneneſs of the ſpirits, and their imparity with the tangible parts, which make them not only hard, but fragile, and leſs *enduring* of preſſure. *Bacon's Natural Hiſtory*, Nº. 844.

So dear I love him, that with him all deaths
I could *endure*; without him, live no life. *Milt. Par. Loſt.*

The gout haunts uſually the eaſy and the rich, the nice and the lazy, who grow to *endure* much, becauſe they can *endure* little. *Temple.*

I wiſh to die, yet dare not death *endure*. *Dryd. Aurengz.*

Both were of ſhining ſteel, and wrought ſo pure,
As might the ſtrokes of two ſuch arms *endure*. *Dryden.*

To ENDU'RE. *v. n.*

1. To laſt; to remain; to continue.

Labour not for the meat which periſheth, but for that meat which *endureth* unto everlaſting life. *John* vi. 27.

Doth the crown *endure* to every generation? *Prov.* xxvii.

By being able to repeat meaſures of time, or ideas of ſtated length of duration in our minds, we can imagine duration, where nothing does really *endure* or exiſt. *Locke.*

A charm, that ſhall to age *endure*
The mind benevolent and pure. *Anon.*

2. To brook; to bear; to admit.

For how can I *endure* to ſee the evil that ſhall come unto my people? Or how can I *endure* to ſee the deſtruction of my kindred? *Eſth.* viii. 6.

Our great Engliſh lords could not *endure* that any kings ſhould reign in Ireland but themſelves; nay, they could hardly *endure* that the crown of England ſhould have any power over them. *Davies on Ireland.*

ENDU'RER. *n. ſ.* [from *endure.*]

1. One that can bear or endure; ſuſtainer; ſufferer.

They are very valiant and hardy; for the moſt part great *endurers* of cold, labour, hunger, and all hardineſs. *Spenſer.*

2. Continuer; laſter.

E'NDWISE. *adv.* [*end* and *wiſe.*] Erectly; uprightly; on end.

A rude and unpoliſhed America, peopled with ſlothful and naked Indians, living in pitiful huts and cabbins, made of poles ſet *endwiſe*. *Ray on the Creation.*

To E'NECATE. *v. a.* [*eneco*, Latin.] To kill; to deſtroy.

Some plagues partake of ſuch a pernicious degree of malignity, that, in the manner of a moſt preſentaneous poiſon, they *enecate* in two or three hours, ſuddenly corrupting or extinguiſhing the vital ſpirits. *Harvey on the Plague.*

E'NEMY. *n. ſ.* [*ennemi*, French; *inimicus*, Latin.]

1. A publick foe.

All theſe ſtatutes ſpeak of Engliſh rebels and Iriſh *enemies*, as if the Iriſh had never been in condition of ſubjects, but always out of the protection of the law. *Davies on Ireland.*

The *enemy* thinks of raiſing threeſcore thouſand men for the next Summer. *Addiſon on the State of the War.*

2. A private opponent; an antagoniſt.

3. Any one who regards another with malevolence; not a friend.

Kent, in diſguiſe,
Follow'd his *enemy* king, and did him ſervice
Improper for a ſlave. *Shakeſpeare's King Lear.*

4. One that diſlikes.

He that deſignedly uſes ambiguities, ought to be looked on as an *enemy* to truth and knowledge. *Locke.*

Bold is the critick, who dares prove
Theſe heroes were no friends to love;
And bolder he who dares aver,
That they were *enemies* to war. *Prior.*

5. [In theology.] The fiend; the devil.

Defend us from the danger of the *enemy*. *Common Prayer.*

ENERGE'TICK. *adj.* [ἐνεργητικος.]

1. Forcible; active; vigorous; powerful in effect; efficacious.

2. Operative; active; working; not at reſt.

If then we will conceive of God truly, and, as far as we can, adequately, we muſt look upon him not only as an eternal Being, but alſo as a Being eternally *energetick*. *Grew.*

E'NERGY. *n. ſ.* [ἐνέργεια.]

1. Power not exerted in action.

They are not effective of any thing, nor leave no work behind them, but are *energies* merely; for their working upon mirrours, and places of echo, doth not alter any thing in thoſe bodies. *Bacon.*

2. Force; vigour; efficacy; influence.

Whether with particles of heav'nly fire
The God of nature did his ſoul inſpire;
Or earth, but new divided from the ſky,
And pliant ſtill, retain'd th' ethereal *energy*. *Dryden.*

God thinketh with operation infinitely perfect, with an omnipotent as well as an eternal *energy*. *Grew's Coſmol. Sac.*

Beg the bleſſed Jeſus to give an *energy* to your imperfect prayers, by his moſt powerful interceſſion. *Smalridge's Serm.*

What but God!
Inſpiring God! who, boundleſs ſpirit all,
And unremitting *energy*, pervades,
Adjuſts, ſuſtains, and agitates the whole. *Thomſon's Spring.*

3. Faculty; operation.

Matter, though divided into the ſubtileſt parts, moved ſwiftly, is ſenſeleſs and ſtupid, and makes no approach to vital *energy*. *Ray on the Creation.*

How can concuſſion of atoms beget ſelf-conſciouſneſs, and other powers and *energies* that we feel in our minds? *Bentley.*

4. Strength of expreſſion; force of ſignification; ſpirit; life

Who did ever, in French authors, ſee
The comprehenſive Engliſh *energy*. *Roſcommon.*

Swift and ready, and familiar communication is made by ſpeech; and, when animated by elocution, it acquires a greater life and *energy*, raviſhing and captivating the hearers. *Holder.*

Many words deſerve to be thrown out of our language, and not a few antiquated to be reſtored, on account of their *energy* and ſound. *Swift.*

To ENE'RVATE. *v. a.* [*enervo*, Latin.] To weaken; to deprive of force; to emaſculate.

Great empires, while they ſtand, do *enervate* and deſtroy the forces of the natives which they have ſubdued, reſting upon their own protecting forces. *Bacon, Eſſay* 59.

Sheepiſh ſoftneſs often *enervates* thoſe who are bred like fondlings at home. *Locke.*

On each *enervate* ſtring they taught the note,
To pant, or tremble through an eunuch's throat. *Pope.*

Footmen exerciſe themſelves, whilſt their *enervated* lords are ſoftly lolling in their chariots. *Arbuthn. and Pope's M. Scrib.*

ENERVA'TION. *n. ſ.* [from *enerve.*]

1. The act of weakening; emaſculation.

2. The ſtate of being weakened; effeminacy.

To ENE'RVE. *v. a.* [*enervo*, Latin.] To weaken; to break the force of; to cruſh.

We ſhall be able perfectly to ſolve and *enerve* their force. *Digby on Bodies.*

Such object hath the pow'r to ſoft'n and tame
Severeſt temper, ſmooth the rugged'ſt brow,
Enerve, and with voluptuous hope diſſolve. *Milt. Par. Reg.*

To ENFA'MISH. *v. a.* [from *famiſh.*] To ſtarve; to famiſh; to kill with hunger. *Dict.*

To ENFE'EBLE. *v. a.* [from *feeble.*] To weaken; to enervate; to deprive of ſtrength.

I've belied a lady,
The princess of this country; and the air on't
Revengingly *enfeebles* me *Shakespeare's Cymbeline.*

My people are with sickness much *enfeebled. Shak. H.* V.

Much hath hell debas'd, and pain
Enfeebl'd me, to what I was in heav'n! *Milt. Parad. Lost.*

Some there are that employ their time in affairs infinitely below the dignity of their persons; and being called by God, or the republick, to bear great burdens, do *enfeeble* their understandings, and disable their persons, by sordid and brutish business. *Taylor's Rule of living holy.*

Sure, nature form'd me of her softest mould,
Enfeebled all my soul with tender passions,
And sunk me even below my own weak sex. *Addis. Cato.*

To ENFE'OFF. *v. a.* [*feoffamentum*, low Latin.] To invest with any dignities or possessions. A law term.

If the eldest son *enfeoff* the second, reserving homage, and that homage paid, and then the second son dies without issue, it will descend to the eldest as heir, and the seignory is extinct. *Hale's Common Law of England.*

ENFE'OFFMENT. *n. s.* [from *enfeoff.*]

1. The act of enfeoffing.
2. The instrument or deed by which one is invested with possessions.

To ENFE'TTER. *v. a.* [from *fetter.*] To bind in fetters; to enchain.

His soul is so *enfetter'd* to her love,
That she may make, unmake, do what she list. *Sh. Othello.*

ENFILA'DE. n. s. [Fr.] A strait passage; any thing through which a right line may be drawn.

To ENFILA'DE. *v. a.* [from the noun.] To pierce in a right line.

The avenues, being cut through the wood in right lines, were *enfiladed* by the Spanish canon. *Expedition to Carthagena.*

To ENFI'RE. *v. a.* [from *fire.*] To fire; to set on fire; to kindle.

So hard those heavenly beauties be *enfir'd*,
As things divine, least passions do impress. *Spenser.*

To ENFO'RCE. *v. a.* [*enforcir*, French.]

1. To give strength to; to strengthen; to invigorate.
2. To make or gain by force.

The idle stroke, *enforcing* furious way,
Missing the mark of his misaimed sight,
Did fall to ground. *Fairy Queen, b.* i. *cant.* 8. *stan.* 8.

3. To put in act by violence.

Sker away as swift as stones
Enforced from the old Assyrian slings. *Shakesp. Henry* V.

4. To instigate; to provoke; to urge on; to animate.

Fear gave her wings, and rage *enforc'd* my flight
Through woods and plains. *Fairy Queen, b.* ii. *cant.* 4.

If you knew to whom you shew this honour,
I know you would be prouder of the work,
Than customary bounty can *enforce* you. *Sh. Merch of Ven.*

5. To urge with energy.

Let them assemble;
And, on a safer judgment, all revoke
Your ignorant election; *enforce* his pride,
And his old hate to you. *Shakespeare's Coriolanus.*

He prevailed with him, by *enforcing* the ill consequence of his refusal to take the office, which would be interpreted to his dislike of the court. *Clarendon.*

To avoid all appearance of disaffection, I have taken care to *enforce* loyalty by an invincible argument. *Swift.*

6. To compel; to constrain.

For competence of life I will allow you,
That lack of means *enforce* you not to evil. *Shak. H.* IV.

A just disdain conceived by that queen, that so wicked a rebel should prevail against her, did move and almost *enforce* her to send over that mighty army. *Davies on Ireland.*

7. To press with a charge. Little used.

In this point charge him home, that he affects
Tyrannick pow'r: if he evade us there,
Enforce him with his envy to the people;
And that the spoil got on the Antiates
Was ne'er distributed. *Shakespeare's Coriolanus.*

To ENFO'RCE. *v. n.* To prove; to evince; to shew beyond contradiction.

Which laws in such case we must obey, unless there be reason shewed, which may necessarily *enforce* that the law of reason, or of God, doth enjoin the contrary. *Hooker, b.* i.

ENFO'RCE. *n. s.* [from *force.*] Power; strength.

He now defies thee thrice to single fight,
As a petty enterprise of small *enforce*. *Milton's Agonistes.*

ENFO'RCEDLY. *adv.* [from *enforce.*] By violence; not voluntarily; not spontaneously; not by choice.

If thou didst put this sow'r cold habit on,
To castigate thy pride, 'twere well; but thou
Do'st it *enforcedly*: thoud'st courtier be,
Wert thou not beggar. *Shakespeare's Timon.*

ENFO'RCEMENT. *n s.* [from *enforce.*]

1. An act of violence; compulsion; force offered.

Confess 'twas her's, and by what rough *enforcement*
You got it from her. *Shakesp. All's well that ends well.*

He that contendeth against these *enforcements*, may easily master or resist them. *Raleigh's History of the World.*

2. Sanction; that which gives force to a law.

The rewards and punishments of another life, which the Almighty has established as the *enforcements* of his law, are of weight enough to determine the choice. *Locke.*

3. Motive of conviction; urgent evidence.

The personal descent of God himself, and his assumption of our flesh to his divinity, was an *enforcement* beyond all the methods of wisdom that were ever made use of in the world. *Hammond on Fundamentals.*

4. Pressing exigence.

More than I have said,
The leisure and *enforcement* of the time
Forbids to dwell on. *Shakespeare's Richard* III.

ENFO'RCER. *n. s.* [from *enforce.*] Compeller; one who effects by violence.

When a man tumbles a cylinder or roller down an hill, 'tis certain that the man is the violent *enforcer* of the first motion of it. *Hammond's Fundamentals.*

ENFO'ULDRED. *adj.* [from *foudre*, French.] Mixed with lightning.

Heart cannot think what outrage and what cries,
With foul *enfouldred* smoak and flashing fire,
The hell-bred beast threw forth unto the skies. *Fairy Queen.*

To ENFRA'NCHISE *v. a.* [from *franchise.*]

1. To admit to the privileges of a freeman.

The English colonies, and some septs of the Irishry, *enfranchised* by special charters, were admitted to the benefit of the laws. *Davies on Ireland.*

Romulus was the natural parent of all those people that were the first inhabitants of Rome, or of those that were after incorporated and *enfranchised* into that name, city, or government. *Hale's Origin of Mankind.*

2. To set free from slavery.

Men, forbearing wine, come from drinking healths to a draught at a meal; and, lastly, to discontinue altogether: but if a man have the fortitude and resolution to *enfranchise* himself at once, that is the best. *Bacon's Essays.*

If they won a battle, prisoners became slaves, and continued so in their generations, unless *enfranchised* by their masters. *Temple.*

3. To free or release from custody.

The gentleman, I told your ladyship,
Had come along with me, but that his mistress
Did hold his eyes lockt in her crystal looks.
—Belike, that now she hath *enfranchis'd* them,
Upon some other pawn for fealty. *Shakespeare.*

4. To denisen; to endenisen.

These words have been *enfranchised* amongst us. *Watts.*

ENFRA'NCHISEMENT. *n. s.* [from *enfranchise.*]

1. Investiture of the privileges of a denisen.

The incorporating a man into any society, or body politick. For example, he that is by charter made denizen of England, is said to be enfranchised; and so is he that is made a citizen of London, or other city, or burgess of any town corporate, because he is made partaker of those liberties that appertain to the corporation. *Cowel.*

His coming hither hath no farther scope,
Than for his lineal royalties, and to beg
Enfranchisement immediate on his knees. *Shakesp. Rich.* II.

2. Release from prison or from slavery.

Never did captive with a freer heart
Cast off his chains of bondage, and embrace
His golden uncontroul'd *enfranchisement*. *Shakes. Richard* II.

ENFRO'ZEN. *particip.* [from *frozen.*] Congealed with cold.

Yet to augment the anguish of my smart,
Thou hast *enfrozen* her disdainful breast,
That no one drop of pity there doth rest. *Spenser on Love.*

To ENGA'GE. *v. a.* [*engager*, French.]

1. To make liable for a debt to a creditor.

I have *engag'd* myself to a dear friend,
Engag'd my friend to his meer enemy,
To feed my means. *Shakesp. Merchant of Venice.*

2. To impawn; to stake.

They most perfidiously condemn
Those that *engag'd* their lives for them. *Hudibras, p.* ii.

3. To enlist; to bring into a party.

All wicked men are of a party against religion: some lust or interest *engageth* them against it. *Tillotson's Sermons.*

4. To embark in an affair; to enter in an undertaking.

So far had we *engaged* ourselves, unfortunate souls, that we listed not to complain, since our complaints could not but carry the greatest accusation to ourselves. *Sidney, b.* ii.

Before I *engage* myself in giving any answer to this objection of inconsumptible lights, I would see the effect certainly averred. *Digby on Bodies.*

5. To unite; to attach; to make adherent.

This humanity and good-nature *engages* every body to him, so that when he is pleasant upon any of them, all his family are in good humour. *Addison's Spectator,* N°. 106.

2

6. To

6. To induce; to win by pleasing means; to gain.

To ev'ry duty he cou'd minds *engage*,
Provoke their courage, and command their rage. *Waller.*
His beauty these, and those his blooming age,
The rest his house and his own fame *engage*. *Dryden's Æn.*
So shall I court thy dearest truth,
When beauty ceases to *engage*;
So thinking on thy charming youth,
I'll love it o'er again in age. *Prior.*

7. To bind by any appointment or contract.

We have been firm to our allies, without declining any expence to which we had *engaged* ourselves, and we have even exceeded our engagement. *Atterbury's Sermons.*

8. To seize by the attention.

9. To employ; to hold in business.

For I shall sing of battles, blood and rage,
Which princes and their people did *engage*. *Dryden.*

10. To encounter; to fight.

The rebel knave, who dares his prince *engage*,
Proves the just victim of his royal rage. *Pope.*

To ENGA'GE. *v. n.*

1. To conflict; to fight.

Upon advertisement of the Scots army, the earl of Holland was sent with a body to meet and *engage* with it. *Clarendon.*

2. To embark in any business; to enlist in any party.

'Tis not, indeed, my talent to *engage*
In lofty trifles, or to swell my page
With wind and noise. *Dryden's Pers. Sat.* 5.

ENGA'GEMENT. *n. s.* [from *engage*; *engagement*, French.]

1. The act of engaging, impawning, or making liable to a debt.

2. Obligation by contract.

We have, in expence of blood, exceeded our *engagements*. *Atterbury's Sermons.*

3. Adherence to a party or cause; partiality.

This practice may be obvious to any who impartially, and without *engagement*, is at the pains to examine. *Swift.*

4. Employment of the attention.

Play, either by our too constant or too long *engagement* in it, becomes like an employment or profession. *Rogers's Serm.*

5. Fight; conflict; battle.

Our army, led by valiant Torrismond,
Is now in hot *engagement* with the Moors. *Dryden.*
Encourag'd by despair, or obstinate
To fall like men in arms, some dare renew
Feeble *engagement*, meeting glorious fate
On the firm land. *Phillips.*

6. Obligation; motive.

This is the greatest *engagement* not to forfeit an opportunity. *Hammond's Fundamentals.*

To ENGA'OL. *v. a.* [from *gaol.*] To imprison; to confine.

Within my mouth you have *engaol'd* my tongue,
Doubly portcullis'd with my teeth and lips. *Shakes. R.* II.

To ENGA'RRISON. *v. a.* [from *garrison.*] To protect by a garrison.

Neptune with a flying guard doth *engarrison* her strongly. *Howel's Vocal Forrest.*

To ENGE'NDER. *v. a.* [*engendrer*, French.]

1. To beget between different sexes.

This bastard love is *engendered* betwixt lust and idleness. *Sid.*

2. To produce; to form.

Oh nature! thou, who of the self-same mettle,
Whereof thy proud child, arrogant man, is pufft,
Engender'st the black toad and adder blue. *Shakesp. Timon.*
Again, if souls do other souls beget,
'Tis by themselves, or by the body's pow'r:
If by themselves, what doth their working let,
But they might souls *engender* ev'ry hour? *Davies.*

3. To excite; to cause; to produce.

Say, can you fast? Your stomachs are too young,
And abstinence *engenders* maladies. *Shakes. Love's Lab. Lost.*
The presence of a king *engenders* love
Amongst his subjects and his loyal friends. *Shakes. Henry* VI.
That *engenders* thunder in his breast,
And makes him roar these accusations forth. *Shakes. H.* VI.

It unloads the mind, *engenders* thoughts, and animates virtue. *Addison's Spectator*, N°. 93.

4. To bring forth.

Vice *engenders* shame, and folly broods o'er grief. *Prior.*

To ENGE'NDER. *v. n.* To be caused; to be produced.

Thick clouds are spread, and storms *engender* there. *Dryd.*

E'NGINE. *n. s.* [*engin*, French; *ingegno*, Italian.]

1. Any mechanical complication, in which various movements and parts concur to one effect.

2. A military machine.

This is our *engine*, towers that overthrows;
Our spear that hurts, our sword that wounds our foes. *Fairf.*

3. Any instrument.

The sword, the arrow, the gun, with many terrible *engines* of death, will be well employed. *Raleigh's Essays.*

He takes the scissars, and extends
The little *engine* on his fingers ends. *Pope's Rape of the Lock.*

4. Any instrument to throw water upon burning houses.

Some cut the pipes, and some the *engines* play;
And some, more bold, mount ladders to the fire. *Dryden.*

5. Any means used to bring to pass, or to effect. Usually in an ill sense.

Prayer must be divine and heavenly, which the devil with all his *engines* so violently opposeth. *Duppa's Rules for Devotion.*

6. An agent for another. In contempt.

They had th' especial *engines* been, to rear
His fortunes up into the state they were.

ENGINE'ER. *n. s.* [*engingnier*, French.] One who manages engines; one who directs the artillery of an army.

For 'tis the sport to have the *engineer*
Hoist with his own petard. *Shakespeare's Hamlet.*
Him thus enrag'd,
Descrying from afar, some *engineer*,
Dext'rous to guide th' unerring charge, design'd
By one nice shot to terminate the war. *Phillips.*

An author, who points his satire at a great man, is like the *engineer* who signalized himself by this ungenerous practice. *Addison's Freeholder*, N°. 19.

E'NGINERY. *n. s.* [from *engine.*]

1. The act of managing artillery.

They may descend in mathematicks to fortification, architecture, *enginery*, or navigation. *Milton on Education.*

2. Engines of war; artillery.

We saw the foe
Approaching, gross and huge, in hollow cube
Training his dev'lish *enginery*. *Milton.*

To ENGI'RD. *v. a.* [from *gird.*] To encircle; to surround; to environ; to encompass.

My heart is drown'd with grief,
My body round *engirt* with misery;
For what's more miserable than discontent? *Shak. Hen.* VI.
That gold must round *engirt* these brows of mine. *Shakes.*

E'NGLE. *n. s.* [derived from the French *engluer*, to catch with birdlime.] A gull; a put; a bubble. *Hanmer.*

I spied
An ancient *engle* going down the hill,
Will serve our turn. *Shakesp. Taming of the Shrew.*

An alteration of *Theobald's* for *angel.*

E'NGLISH. *adj.* [englyꞅ, Saxon.] Belonging to England; thence English is the language of England.

He hath neither Latin, French, nor Italian; and you may come into the court, and swear that I have a poor pennyworth in the *English*. *Shakespeare's Merchant of Venice.*

Of *English* talc, the coarser sort is called plaister, or parget; the finer, spoad. *Woodward.*

To E'NGLISH. *v. a.* [from the noun.] To translate into English.

We find not a word in the text can properly be rendered anise, which is what the Latins call anethum, and properly *Englished* dill. *Brown's Vulgar Errours, b.* vii. *c.* 7.

To ENGLU'T. *v. a.* [*engloutir*, French.]

1. To swallow up.

Neither my place, nor ought I heard of business,
Hath rais'd me from my bed; nor doth the general
Take hold on me: for my particular grief
Engluts and swallows other sorrows. *Shakespeare's Othello.*
Certainly, thou art so near the gulf,
Thou needs must be *englutted*. *Shakespeare's Henry* V.
How many prodigal bits have slaves and peasants
This night *englutted*! *Shakespeare's Timon.*

2. To glut; to pamper.

Whose grieved minds, which choler did *englut*,
Against themselves turning their wrathful spight. *Fai. Qu.*

Being once *englutted* with vanity, he will straightway loath all learning. *Ascham's Schoolmaster.*

To ENGO'RE. *v. a.* [from *gore.*] To pierce; to prick.

As savage bull, whom two fierce mastiffs bait,
When rancour doth with rage him once *engore*,
Forgets with wary ward them to await,
But with his dreadful horns them drives afore. *Fairy Queen.*

To ENGO'RGE. *v. a.* [from *gorge*, French, a throat.] To swallow; to devour; to gorge.

Then fraught with rancour and *engorged* ire,
He cast at once him to avenge for all. *Fairy Queen, b.* i.
That is the gulf of greediness, they say,
That deep *engorgeth* all this world is prey. *Spenser's Fa. Qu.*

To ENGO'RGE. *v. n.* To devour; to feed with eagerness and voracity; to riot.

Greedily she *engorg'd* without restraint,
And knew not eating death! *Milton's Paradise Lost, b.* ix.

To ENGRA'IL. *v. a.* [from *grele*, French, hail.] To batter; to bruise as with hail. A word now used only in heraldry, for, to indent in curve lines.

Æacides then shews
A long lance, and a caldron, new, *engrail'd* with twenty hues. *Chapman's Iliads.*

Polwheel beareth a saultier *engrailed*. *Carew's Survey.*

To ENGRA'IN. *v. a.* [from *grain.*] To die deep; to die in grain.

Sees

Sees thou how fresh my flowers being spread,
Dyed in lilie white and crimson red,
With leaves *engrain'd* in lusty green. *Spenser's Pastorals.*

To Engra'pple. *v. n.* [from *grapple.*] To close with; to contend with hold on each other.

There shall young Hotspur, with a fury led,
Engrapple with thy son, as fierce as he. *Daniel's Civ. War.*

To Engra'sp. *v. a.* [from *grasp.*] To seize; to hold fast in the hand; to gripe.

Now 'gan Pyrrocles wax as wood as he,
And him affronted with impatient might;
And both together fierce *engrasped* he,
Whiles Guyon standing by, their uncouth strife does see.
Fairy Queen, b. ii. *cant.* 5. *stan.* 20.

To Engra've. *v. a.* preter. *engraved*; part. pass. *engraved* or *engraven.* [*engraver*, French.]

1. To picture by incisions in any matter.

Her ivory forehead, full of bounty brave,
Like a broad table, did itself dispread,
For love his lofty triumphs to *engrave*,
And write the battles of his great godhead. *Fairy Queen.*

O'er all, the heav'n's refulgent image shines;
On either gate were six *engraven* signs. *Addison's Ovid's Met.*

Names fresh *engrav'd* appear'd of wits renown'd;
I look'd again, nor could their trace be found. *Pope.*

2. To mark wood or stone.

Engrave the two stones with the names. *Ex.* xxviii. 11.

3. To impress deeply; to imprint.

It will scarce seem possible, that God should *engrave* principles, in men's minds, in words of uncertain signification. *Locke.*

Our Saviour makes this return, fit to be *engraven* in the hearts of all promoters of charity. *Atterbury's Sermons.*

Sounds which address the ear, are lost and die
In one short hour; but that which strikes the eye,
Lives long upon the mind: the faithful sight
Engraves the knowledge with a beam of light. *Watts.*

4. [from *grave.*] To bury; to inhume; to inter.

The son had charge of them now being dead,
In seemly sort their corses to *engrave*,
And deck with dainty flowers their bridal bed. *Fai. Queen.*

Engra'ver. *n. s.* [from *engrave*] A cutter in stone or other matter.

Images are not made in the brain itself, as the pencil of a painter or *engraver* makes the images in the table or metal, but are imprinted in a wonderful method in the very soul itself. *Hale's Origin of Mankind.*

To Engri'eve. *v. a.* [from *grieve.*] To pain; to vex; to afflict; to disconsolate.

The gnawing anguish, and sharp jealousy,
Which his sad speech infixed in my breast,
Rankled so sore, and fester'd inwardly,
That my *engrieved* mind could find no rest. *Fairy Queen.*

Aches, and hurts, and corns, do *engrieve* either towards rain, or towards frost. *Bacon's Natural History*, N°. 828.

To Engro'ss. *v. a.* [*grossir*, French.]

1. To thicken; to make thick.

But more happy he than wise,
Of that sea's nature did him not avise;
The waves thereof so slow and sluggish were,
Engross'd with mud, which did them foul agriese,
That every weighty thing they did upbear. *Fairy Queen.*

2. To encrease in bulk.

Though pillars, by channeling, be seemingly *engrossed* to our sight, yet they are truly weakened in themselves. *Wotten.*

3. To fatten; to plump up.

Not sleeping, to *engross* his idle body;
But praying, to enrich his watchful soul. *Shakes. Rich.* III.

4. To seize in the gross; to seize the whole of any thing.

If thou *engrossest* all the griefs as thine,
Thou robb'st me of a moiety. *Shak. All's well that ends well.*

Those two great things that so *engross* the desires and designs of both the nobler and ignobler sort of mankind, are to be found in religion; namely, wisdom and pleasure. *South's Serm.*

A dog, a parrot, or an ape,
Or some worse brute in human shape,
Engross the fancies of the fair. *Swift.*

5. To purchase the whole of any commodity for the sake of selling at a high price.

6. To copy in a large hand.

Here is th' indictment of the good lord Hastings,
Which in a set hand fairly is *engross'd*. *Shakes. Rich.* III.

A clerk, foredoom'd his father's soul to cross,
Who pens a stanza when he should *engross*. *Pope's Epistles.*

Engro'sser. *n. s.* [from *engross.*] He that purchases large quantities of any commodity, in order to sell it at a high price.

A new sort of *engrossers*, or forestallers, having the feeding and supplying this numerous body of workmen in the woollen manufactures, out of their warehouses, set the price upon the poor landholder. *Locke.*

Engro'ssment. *n. s.* [from *engross.*] Appropriation of things in the gross; exorbitant acquisition.

Our thighs are packt with wax, our mouths with honey:
We bring it to the hive; and, like the bees,
Are murder'd for our pains! This bitter taste
Yield his *engrossments* to the dying father. *Shakes. Henry* IV.

Those held their immoderate *engrossments* of power and favour by no other tenure than presumption. *Swift.*

To Engua'rd. *v. a.* [from *guard.*] To protect; to defend; to surround as guards.

A hundred knights! yes, that on ev'ry dream
He may *enguard* his dotage with their pow'rs,
And hold our lives at mercy. *Shakespeare's King Lear.*

To Enha'nce. *v. a.* [*hausser*, *enhausser*, French.]

1. To lift up; to raise on high. A sense now obsolete.

Both of them high at once their hands *enhanc'd*,
And both at once their huge blows down did sway. *Fa. Qu.*

2. To raise; to advance; to heighten in price.

The desire of money is every where the same; its vent varies very little, but as its greater scarcity *enhances* its price, and increases the scramble. *Locke.*

3. To raise in esteem.

What is it but the experience of want that *enhances* the value of plenty. *L'Estrange.*

The remembrance of the difficulties we now undergo, will contribute to *enhance* our pleasure. *Atterbury's Sermons.*

4. To aggravate; to increase from bad to worse.

To believe or pretend that whatever our hearts incite is the will of God within us, is the principle of villainy that hath acted in the children of disobedience, *enhanced* and improved with circumstances of greater impudence than the most abominable heathens were guilty of. *Hammond.*

The relation which those children bore to the priesthood, contributed to *enhance* their guilt, and increase their punishment. *Atterbury's Sermons.*

Enha'ncement. *n s.* [from *enhance.*]

1. Encrease; augmentation of value.

Their yearly rents are not improved, the landlords making no less gain by fines than by *enhancement* of rents. *Bacon.*

2. Aggravation; encrease of ill.

Jocular slanders have, from the slightness of the temptation, an *enhancement* of guilt. *Government of the Tongue, s.* 5.

ENI'GMA. *n. s.* [*ænigma*, Latin; αἴνιγμα.] A riddle; an obscure question; a position expressed in remote and ambiguous terms.

The dark *enigma* will allow
A meaning; which, if well I understand,
From sacrilege will free the god's command. *Dryden.*

A custom was amongst the ancients of proposing an *enigma* at festivals, and adjudging a reward to him that solved it. *Pope.*

Enigma'tical. *adj.* [from *enigma.*]

1. Obscure; ambiguously or darkly expressed.

Your answer, sir, is *enigmatical.* *Sh. Much Ado about Noth.*

Enigmatical deliveries comprehend useful verities; but being mistaken by liberal expositors at first, they have been misunderstood by most since. *Brown's Vulgar Erronrs.*

2. Cloudy; obscurely conceived or apprehended.

Faith here is the assent to those things which come to us by hearing, and are so believed by adherence, or dark *enigmatical* knowledge, but hereafter are seen or known demonstratively. *Hammond's Practical Catechism.*

Enigma'tically. *adv.* [from *enigma.*] In a sense different from that which the words in their familiar acceptation imply.

Homer speaks *enigmatically*, and intends that these monsters are merely the creation of poetry. *Notes on the Odyssey.*

Eni'gmatist. *n. s.* [from *enigma.*] One who deals in obscure and ambiguous matters; maker of riddles.

That I may deal more ingenuously with my reader than the abovementioned *enigmatist* has done, I shall present him with a key to my riddle; which, upon application, he will find exactly fitted to all the words of it. *Addison's Whig Exam.*

To ENJO'IN. *v. a.* [*enjoindre*, French.] To direct; to order; to prescribe. It is more authoritative than *direct*, and less imperious than *command.*

To satisfy the good old man,
I would bend under any heavy weight
That he'll *enjoin* me to. *Shakes. Much Ado about Nothing.*

Monks and philosophers, and such as do continually *enjoin* themselves. *Bacon's Natural History*, N°. 292.

It endeavours to secure every man's interest, by *enjoining* that truth and fidelity be inviolably preserved. *Tillots. Sermons.*

Enjo'iner. *n. s.* [from *enjoin.*] One who gives injunctions. *Dict.*

Enjo'inment. *n. s.* [from *enjoin.*] Direction; command.

Critical trial should be made by publick *enjoinment*, whereby determination might be settled beyond debate. *Brown's V. Err.*

To ENJO'Y. *v. a.* [*jouir*, *enjouir*, French]

1. To feel or perceive with pleasure; to have a pleasing sense of; to be delighted with.

I could *enjoy* the pangs of death,
And smile in agony. *Addison's Cato.*

2. To

2. To obtain poſſeſſion or fruition of.

Edward the ſaint, in whom it pleaſed God, righteous and juſt, to let England ſee what a bleſſing ſin and iniquity would not ſuffer it to *enjoy*. *Hooker, b.* iv. *ſ.* 14.

He, who to *enjoy*
Plato's elyſium, leap'd into the ſea,
Cleombrotus. *Milton's Paradiſe Loſt, b.* iii. *l.* 471.

5. To pleaſe; to gladden; to exhilarate; to glad; to delight. This ſenſe is uſual with the reciprocal pronoun, and is derived from *enjouir*.

Creatures are made to *enjoy* themſelves, as well as to ſerve us. *More's Antidote againſt Atheiſm.*

When a man ſhall, with a ſober, ſedate, diabolical rancour, look upon and *enjoy* himſelf in the ſight of his neighbour's ſin and ſhame, can he plead the inſtigation of any appetite in nature? *South's Sermons.*

To ENJO'Y. *v. n.* To live in happineſs.

Then I ſhall be no more!
And Adam, wedded to another Eve,
Shall live with her *enjoying*, I extinct. *Milton's Parad. Loſt.*

ENJO'YER. *n. ſ.* [from *enjoy.*] One that has fruition or poſſeſſion. *Dict.*

ENJO'YMENT. *n. ſ.* [from *enjoy.*] Pleaſure; happineſs; fruition.

His hopes and expectations are bigger than his *enjoyments*. *Tillotſon, Sermon* 1.

To ENKI'NDLE. *v. a.* [from *kindle.*]

1. To ſet on fire; to inflame; to put in a flame.

Edmund, *enkindle* all the ſparks of nature
To quit this horrid act. *Shakeſp. King Lear.*

2. To rouſe paſſions; to ſet the ſoul into a flame.

Your hand
Gave ſign for me to leave you: ſo I did,
Fearing to ſtrengthen that impatience,
Which ſeem'd too much *enkindled*. *Shak. Jul. Cæſar.*

3. To incite to any act or hope.

Do you not hope your children ſhall be kings?
When thoſe that gave the thane of Cawder to me,
Promis'd no leſs to them?
——That, truſted home,
Might yet *enkindle* you unto the crown. *Shakeſp. Macbeth.*

To ENLA'RGE. *v. a.* [*elargir*, French.]

1. To make greater in quantity or appearance.

The wall, in luſtre and effect like glaſs,
Which o'er each object caſting various dyes,
Enlarges ſome, and others multiplies. *Pope's Temp. of Fame.*

2. To encreaſe any thing in magnitude; to extend.

Where there is ſomething both laſting and ſcarce, and ſo valuable to be hoarded up, there men will not be apt to *enlarge* their poſſeſſions of land. *Locke.*

3. To encreaſe by repreſentation; to magnify; to exaggerate.

4. To dilate; to expand.

O ye Corinthians, our mouth is open unto you, our heart is *enlarged*. 2 *Cor.* vi. 11.

5. To ſet free from limitation.

Though ſhe appear honeſt to me, yet at other places ſhe *enlargeth* her mirth ſo far, that there is ſhrewd conſtruction made of her. *Shakeſpeare's Merry Wives of Windſor.*

6. To extend to more purpoſes or uſes.

It hath grown from no other root than only a deſire to *enlarge* the neceſſary uſe of the word of God, which deſire hath begotten an errour, *enlarging* it farther than ſoundneſs of truth will bear. *Hooker, b.* ii. *ſ.* 1.

7. To amplify; to aggrandiſe.

This is that ſcience which would truly *enlarge* mens minds, were it ſtudied. *Locke.*

Could the mind, as in number, come to ſo ſmall a part of extenſion or duration as excluded diviſibility, that would be the indiviſible unit, or idea; by repetition of which it would make its more *enlarged* ideas of extenſion and duration. *Locke.*

8. To releaſe from confinement.

Enlarge the man committed yeſterday,
That rail'd againſt our perſon. *Shakeſpeare's Henry* V.

9. To diffuſe in eloquence.

They *enlarged* themſelves upon this ſubject with all the invidious inſinuations they could deviſe. *Clarendon, b.* viii.

To ENLA'RGE. *v. n.* To expatiate; to ſpeak in many words.

They appointed the chancellor of the Exchequer to *enlarge* upon any of thoſe particulars. *Clarendon, b.* viii.

This is a theme ſo unpleaſant, I delight not to *enlarge* on it; rather wiſh the memory of it were extinct. *Decay of Piety.*

ENLA'RGEMENT. *n. ſ.* [from *enlarge.*]

1. Encreaſe; augmentation; farther extenſion.

The king afterwards enlarged the conſtant obedience of the city with *enlargement* both of liberties and of revenues. *Hayw.*

The ocean, which ſo long our hopes confin'd,
Could give no limits to his vaſter mind:
Our bounds *enlargement* was his lateſt toil,
Nor hath he left us pris'ners to our iſle. *Waller.*

There never were any iſlands, or other conſiderable parcels of land, amaſſed or heaped up; nor any *enlargement*, or addition of earth, made to the continent by the mud that is carried down into the ſea by rivers. *Woodward's Nat. Hiſt.*

The commons in Rome generally purſued the *enlargement* of their power by more ſet quarrels of one entire aſſembly againſt another. *Swift on the Diſſent. in Athens and Rome.*

The Greek tongue received many *enlargements* between the time of Homer and that of Plutarch. *Swift.*

2. Releaſe from confinement or ſervitude.

Lieutenant,
At our *enlargement* what are thy due fees? *Shak. Henry* VI.

If thou holdeſt thy peace at the time, then ſhall there *enlargement* and deliverance ariſe to the Jews from another place. *Eſther* iv. 14.

3. Magnifying repreſentation.

And all who told it, added ſomething new;
And all who heard it, made *enlargements* too. *Pope.*

4. Expatiating ſpeech; copious diſcourſe.

He concluded with an *enlargement* upon the vices and corruptions which were got into the army. *Clarendon, b.* viii.

ENLA'RGER. *n. ſ.* [from *enlarge.*] Amplifier; one that encreaſes or dilates any thing.

We ſhall not contentiouſly rejoin, but confer what is in us unto his name and honour, ready to be ſwallowed in any worthy *enlarger*. *Brown's Vulgar Errours.*

To ENLI'GHT. *v. a.* [from *light.*] To illuminate; to ſupply with light; to enlighten.

Wit from the firſt has ſhone on ages paſt,
Enlights the preſent, and ſhall warm the laſt. *Pope.*

To ENLI'GHTEN. *v. a.* [from *light.*]

1. To illuminate; to ſupply with light.

As one ſun ſhineth to the whole world, ſo there is no faith but this one publiſhed, the brightneſs whereof muſt *enlighten* all that come to the knowledge of the truth. *Hooker, b.* v. *ſ.* 46.

2. To inſtruct; to furniſh with encreaſe of knowledge.

This doctrine is ſo agreeable to reaſon, that we meet with it in the writings of the *enlightened* heathens. *Spectator.*

'Tis he who *enlightens* our underſtanding, corrects our wills, and enables us to ſubdue our affections to the law of God. *Rog.*

3. To cheer; to exhilarate; to gladden.

4. To ſupply with ſight; to quicken in the faculty of viſion.

Love never fails to maſter what he finds;
The fool *enlightens*, and the wiſe he blinds. *Dryden.*

ENLI'GHTENER. *n. ſ.* [from *enlighten.*]

1. Illuminator; one that gives light.

O, ſent from heav'n,
Enlight'ner of my darkneſs! gracious things
Thou haſt reveal'd. *Milton's Paradiſe Loſt, b.* xii. *l.* 271.

2. Inſtructor.

To ENLI'NK. *v. a.* [from *link.*] To chain to; to bind.

What is it then to me, if impious war,
Array'd in flames like to the prince of fiends,
Do with his ſmirch'd complexion all fell feats,
Enlinkt to waſte and deſolation. *Shakeſp. Henry* V.

To ENLI'VEN. *v. a.* [from *life, live.*]

1. To make quick; to make alive; to animate.

2. To make vigorous or active.

In a glaſs-houſe the workmen often fling in a ſmall quantity of freſh coals, which ſeems to diſturb the fire, but very much *enlivens* it. *Swift's Thoughts on various Subjects.*

3. To make ſprightly or vivacious.

4. To make gay or cheerful in appearance.

ENLI'VENER. *n. ſ.* [from *enliven.*] That which animates; that which puts in motion; that which invigorates.

But fire, th' *enlivener* of the general frame,
Is one, its operation ſtill the ſame:
Its principle is in itſelf; while ours
Works, as confederates war, with mingled pow'rs. *Dryden.*

To ENLU'MINE. *v. a.* [*enluminer*, French.] To illumine; to illuminate; to enlighten. See ILLUMINE.

For having yet, in his deducted ſpright,
Some ſparks remaining of that heav'nly fire,
He is *enlumin'd* with that goodly light,
Unto like goodly ſemblance to aſpire. *Spenſ. Hymn on Love.*

E'NMITY. *n. ſ.* [from *enemy*; as if *enemity, inamity.*]

1. Unfriendly diſpoſition; malevolence; averſion.

Their being forced to their books, in an age at *enmity* with all reſtraint, has been the reaſon why many have hated books. *Locke.*

2. Contrariety of intereſts or inclinations; mutual malignity.

They ſhall within this hour,
On a diſſenſion of a doit, break out
In bittereſt *enmity*. *Shakeſpeare's Coriolanus.*

Between thee and the woman I will put
Enmity; and between thine and her ſeed:
Her ſeed ſhall bruiſe thy head, thou bruiſe his heel. *Milton.*

How far theſe controverſies, and appearing *enmities* of thoſe glorious creatures, may be carried, is not my buſineſs to ſhew or determine. *Dryden's Juven. Dedication.*

3. State of oppoſition.

Know ye not that the friendſhip of the world is *enmity* with God? *Jam.* iv. 4.

You muſt firmly be convinced, that every ſin you commit

ſets

ſets you at *enmity* with heaven, and will, if not forſaken, render you incapable of it. *Wake's Preparation for Death.*

4. Malice; miſchievous attempts.

I abjure all roofs, and chuſe
To wage againſt the *enmity* o' th' air. *Shakeſ. King Lear.*

He who performs his duty in a ſtation of great power, muſt needs incur the utter *enmity* of many, and the high diſpleaſure of more. *Atterbury's Sermons.*

To ENMA'RBLE. *v. a.* [from *marble.*] To turn to marble; to harden.

Their dying to delay,
Thou do'ſt *enmarble* the proud heart of her,
Whoſe love before their life they do prefer. *Spenſer.*

To ENME'SH. *v. a.* [from *meſh.*] To net; to intangle; to intrap.

So will I turn her virtue into pitch;
And out of her own goodneſs make the net
That ſhall *enmeſh* them all. *Shakeſpeare's Othello.*

ENNE'AGON. *n. ſ.* [ἐννέα and γωνία.] A figure of nine angles.

ENNEA'TICAL. *adj.* [ἐννέα.] *Enneatical days,* are every ninth day of a ſickneſs; and *enneatical years,* every ninth year of one's life.

To ENNO'BLE. *v. a.* [*ennoblir,* French.]

1. To raiſe from commonalty to nobility.

Many fair promotions
Are given daily to *ennoble* thoſe,
That ſcarce ſome two days ſince were worth a noble. *Shak.*

2. To dignify; to aggrandiſe; to exalt; to raiſe.

God raiſed up the ſpirit of this great perſon, and *ennobled* his courage and conduct with the entire overthrow of this mighty hoſt. *South's Sermons.*

What can *ennoble* ſots, or ſlaves, or cowards!
Alas! not all the blood of all the Howards. *Pope's Eſſays.*

3. To elevate; to magnify.

None ſo lovely, ſweet and fair,
Or do more *ennoble* love. *Waller.*
Ennobled, yet unchang'd, if nature ſhine. *Anon.*

4. To make famous or illuſtrious.

The breath of Scotland the Spaniards could not endure; neither durſt they as invaders land in Ireland, but only *ennobled* ſome of the coaſts thereof with ſhipwrecks. *Bacon.*

ENNO'BLEMENT. *n. ſ.* [from *ennoble.*]

1. The act of raiſing to the rank of nobility.

He added during parliament, to his former creations, the *ennoblement* or advancement in nobility of a few others. *Bacon.*

2. Exaltation; elevation; dignity.

The eternal wiſdom enriched us with all *ennoblements,* ſuitable to the meaſures of an unſtraitned goodneſs. *Glanv. Scepſ.*

ENODA'TION. *n. ſ.* [*enodatio,* Latin.]

1. The act of untying a knot.

2. Solution of a difficulty. *Dict.*

ENO'RMITY. *n. ſ.* [from *enormous.*]

1. Deviation from rule; irregularity.

2. Deviation from right; depravity; corruption.

We ſhall ſpeak of the particular abuſes and *enormities* of the government. *Spenſer's State of Ireland.*

That the mean, which this law provideth, will be always ſufficient to bridle or reſtrain *enormity,* no man can warrant. *Hooker, b.* iii. *ſ.* 10.

There are many little *enormities* in the world, which our preachers would be very glad to ſee removed; but at the ſame time dare not meddle with them, for fear of betraying the dignity of the pulpit. *Addiſon's Guardian,* Nº. 116.

3. Atrocious crimes; flagitious villanies; crimes exceeding the common meaſure.

It is not a bare ſpeculation that kings may run into *enormities;* the practice may be proved by examples. *Swift.*

ENO'RMOUS. *adj.* [*enormis,* Latin.]

1. Irregular; out of rule; not regulated by any ſtated meaſures; excurſive beyond the limits of a regular figure.

Nature here
Wanton'd, as in her prime; and plaid at will
Her virgin fancies, pouring forth more ſweets,
Wild above rule, or art, *enormous* bliſs! *Milton's Par. Loſt.*

The *enormous* part of the light in the circumference of every lucid point, ought to be leſs diſcernible in ſhorter teleſcopes than in longer, becauſe the ſhorter tranſmit leſs light to the eye. *Newton's Opt.*

2. Diſordered; confuſed.

I ſhall find time
From this *enormous* ſtate, and ſeek to give
Loſſes their remedies. *Shakeſpeare's King Lear.*

3. Wicked beyond the common meaſure.

4. Exceeding in bulk the common meaſures: always uſed with ſome degree of diſlike, or horror, or wonder.

A giant-ſhepherd here his flock maintains,
Far from the reſt, and ſolitary reigns,
A form *enormous!* far unlike the race
Of human birth, in ſtature, or in face. *Pope's Odyſſey.*

ENO'RMOUSLY. *adv.* [from *enormous.*] Beyond meaſure.

One who could ever eſpouſe a notion ſo *enormouſly* abſurd and ſenſeleſs, as that the world was framed by chance. *Woodw.*

ENO'RMOUSNESS. *n. ſ.* [from *enormous.*] Immeaſurable wickedneſs.

When thoſe who have no opportunity to examine our faith, ſee the *enormouſneſs* of our works, what ſhould hinder them from meaſuring the maſter by the diſciples? *Dec. of Piety.*

ENO'UGH. *adj.* [genoh, Saxon; *ganah,* Gothick; *genoeg,* Dut. It is not eaſy to determine whether this word be an adjective or adverb; perhaps, when it is joined with a ſubſtantive, it is an adjective, of which *enow* is the plural. In other ſituations it ſeems an adverb; except that after the verb to *have,* or to *be,* either expreſſed or underſtood, it may be accounted a ſubſtantive. It is pronounced as if it were written *enuf.*] In a ſufficient meaſure; ſo as may ſatisfy; ſo as may ſuffice.

Why wou'dſt thou go, with one conſent they cry,
When thou hadſt gold *enough,* and Emily. *Dryden.*

When there was not room *enough* for their herds, they by conſent ſeparated, and enlarged their paſture. *Locke.*

ENO'UGH. *n. ſ.*

1. Something ſufficient in greatneſs or excellence.

'Tis *enough* for me to have endeavoured the union of my country, whilſt I continued in publick employments. *Temple.*

The indolency and enjoyment we have, ſufficing for our preſent happineſs, we deſire not to venture the change, being content, and that is *enough.* *Locke.*

Enough for me that to the liſt'ning ſwains,
Firſt in thoſe fields I ſung the ſilvan ſtrains. *Pope.*

I will not quarrel with the preſent age: it has done *enough* for me, in making and keeping you two my friends. *Pope.*

2. Something equal to a man's powers or faculties.

He could not have been without ſome great defects and main errours in his nature, cuſtoms, and proceedings, which he had *enough* to do to ſave and help, with a thouſand little induſtries and watches. *Bacon's Henry* VII.

ENO'UGH. *adv.*

1. In a ſufficient degree; in a degree that gives ſatisfaction.

2. It notes a ſlight augmentation of the poſitive degree: as, *I am ready* enough *to quarrel;* that is, I am rather quarrelſome than peaceable.

I am apt *enough* to think, that this ſame binarium of a ſtronger and a weaker, like unto maſculine and feminine, doth hold in all living bodies. *Bacon.*

It is ſometimes pleaſant *enough* to conſider the different notions which different perſons have of the ſame thing. *Addiſon.*

They are now in priſon at Florence; and, as it is ſaid, treated hardly *enough.* *Addiſon on Italy.*

3. Sometimes it notes diminution; as, the ſong is well *enough;* that is, not quite well, though not much amiſs.

4. An exclamation noting fulneſs or ſatiety.

Macbeth, beware Macduff!
Beware the thane of Fife! Diſmiſs me.—*Enough.* *Shakeſp.*
Henceforth I'll bear
Affliction, 'till it do cry out itſelf,
Enough, enough, and die. *Shakeſpeare's King Lear.*

ENO'W. The plural of *enough.* In a ſufficient number.

The earth hath ſince born *enow* bleeding witneſſes, that it was no want of true courage. *Sidney, b.* ii.

The walls of the church there are *enow* contented to build, and to underſet it with goodly pillars: the marbles are poliſhed, the roofs ſhine with gold, the altar hath precious ſtones to adorn it, and of Chriſt's miniſters no choice at all. *Hooker, b.* v. *ſ.* 15.

As if
Man had not ſelfiſh foes *enow* beſides,
That, day and night, for his deſtruction wait. *Milt. P. Loſt.*
My conquering brother will have ſlaves *enow,*
To pay his cruel vows for victory. *Dryden's Don Sebaſtian.*

There are at Rome *enow* modern works of architecture to employ any reaſonable man. *Addiſon on ancient Medals.*

EN PASSANT. *adv.* [French.] By the way.

To ENRA'GE. *v. a.* [*enrager,* French.] To irritate; to provoke; to make furious; to exaſperate.

The juſtice of their quarrel ſhould not ſo much encourage as *enrage* them, being to revenge the diſhonour done to their king, and to chaſtiſe the deceitful dealings of their enemies. *Hayward.*

Enrag'd at this, upon the bawd I flew;
And that which moſt *enrag'd* me was, 'twas true. *Walſh.*

To ENRA'NGE. *v. a.* [from *range.*] To place regularly; to put into order.

In their jaw
Three ranks of iron teeth *enranged* were. *Fairy Queen, b.* i.
As fair Diana, in freſh Summer's day,
Beholds her nymphs *enrang'd* in ſhady wood. *Fai. Queen.*

To ENRA'NK. *v. a.* [from *rank.*] To place in orderly ranks.

No leiſure had he to *enrank* his men. *Shakeſp. Hen.* VI.

To ENRA'PT. *v. a.* [from *rapt.*]

1. To throw into an extaſy; to tranſport with enthuſiaſm.

I myſelf
Am, like a prophet, ſuddenly *enrapt*
To tell thee, that this day is ominous. *Shak. Ant. and Cleop.*

2. In the following quotation it ſeems erroneouſly written for *enwrapt,* involved; wrapt up.

Nor

Nor hath he been so *enrapt* in those studies as to neglect the polite arts of painting, architecture, musick, and poetry. *Arbuthnot and Pope's Mart. Scriblerus.*

To ENRA'PTURE. *v. a.* [from *rapture.*] To transport with pleasure; to delight highly.

To ENRA'VISH. *v. a.* [from *ravish.*] To throw into extasy; to transport with delight.

What wonder,
Frail men, whose eyes seek heavenly things to see,
At sight thereof so much *enravish'd* be? *Spenser.*

ENRA'VISHMENT. *n. s.* [from *enravish.*] Extasy of delight.

They contract a kind of splendor from the seemingly obscuring vail, which adds to the *enravishments* of her transported admirers. *Glanv. Sceps.*

To ENRI'CH. *v. a.* [*enricher*, French.]

1. To make wealthy; to make opulent.

The king will *enrich* him with great riches, and will give him his daughter. 1 *Sa.* xvii. 25.

Henry is able to *enrich* his queen,
And not to seek a queen to make him rich. *Shak. Henry* VI.

The city, which thou seest, no other deem
Than great and glorious Rome, queen of the earth,
So far renown'd, and with the spoils *enrich'd*
Of nations. *Milton's Paradise Regain'd, b.* iv. *l.* 446.

Those are so unhappy as to rob others, without *enriching* themselves. *Denham.*

2. To fertilise; to make fruitful.

See the sweet brooks in silver mazes creep,
Enrich the meadows, and supply the deep. *Blackm. Creation.*

3. To store; to supply with augmentation of any thing desireable.

There is not any one among them that could ever *enrich* his own understanding with any certain truth, or ever edify others therein. *Raleigh's History of the World.*

ENRI'CHMENT. *n. s.* [from *enrich.*]

1. Augmentation of wealth.

2. Amplification; improvement by addition.

I have procured a translation of that book into the general language, not without great and ample additions, and *enrichment* thereof. *Bacon's Holy War.*

It is a vast hindrance to the *enrichment* of our understandings, if we spend too much of our time and pains among infinites and unsearchables. *Watts's Logick.*

To ENRI'DGE. *v. a.* [from *ridge.*] To form with longitudinal protuberances or ridges.

He had a thousand noses,
Horns walk'd and wav'd like the *enridged* sea:
It was some fiend. *Shakespeare's King Lear.*

To ENRI'NG. *v. a.* [from *ring.*] To bind round; to encircle.

Ivy so
Enrings the barky fingers of the elm. *Shakespeare.*

To ENRI'PEN. *v. a.* [from *ripe.*] To ripen; to mature; to bring to perfection.

The Summer, how it *enripen'd* the year;
And Autumn, what our golden harvests were. *Donne.*

To ENRO'BE. *v. a.* [from *robe.*] To dress; to cloath; to habit; to invest.

Her mother hath intended,
That, quaint in green, she shall be loose *enrob'd*,
With ribbands pendant, flaring 'bout her head. *Shakespeare.*

To ENRO'LL. *v. a.* [*enroller*, French.]

1. To insert in a roll or register.

There be *enrolled* amongst the king's forces about thirty thousand men of the Jews. 1 *Mac.* x. 36.

We find ourselves *enrolled* in this heavenly family as servants, and as sons. *Spratt's Sermons.*

The champions, all of high degree,
Who knighthood lov'd, and deeds of chivalry,
Throng'd to the lists, and envy'd to behold
The names of others, not their own, *enroll'd.* *Dryden.*

Mentes, an ever-honour'd name of old,
High in Ulysses' social list *enroll'd* *Pope's Odyssey, b.* i.

Heroes and heroines of old,
By honour only were *enroll'd*
Among their brethren of the skies;
To which, though late, shall Stella rise. *Swift.*

2. To record; to leave in writing.

He swore consent to your succession;
His oath *enrolled* in the parliament. *Shakespeare's Henry* VI.

Laws, which none shall find
Left them *enroll'd*; or what the spirit within
Shall on the heart engrave. *Milton's Paradise Lost, b.* xii.

3. To involve; to inwrap.

From his infernal furnace forth he threw
Huge flames, that dimmed all the heaven's light,
Enroll'd in duskish smoak and brimstone blue. *Fairy Queen.*

ENRO'LLER. *n. s.* [from *enrol.*] He that enrols; he that registers.

ENRO'LMENT. *n. s.* [from *enrol.*] Register; writing in which any thing is recorded; record.

The king himself caused to be enrolled, and testified by a notary publick; and delivered the *enrolments*, with his own hands, to the bishop of Salisbury. *Davies on Ireland.*

To ENRO'OT. *v. a.* [from *root.*] To fix by the root; to implant deep.

Full well he knows
He cannot so precisely weed this land,
As his misdoubts present occasion:
His foes are so *enrooted* with his friends,
That, plucking to unfix an enemy,
He doth unfasten so and shake a friend. *Shakesp. Henry* IV.

To ENRO'UND. *v. a.* [from *round.*] To environ; to surround; to encircle; to inclose.

Upon his royal face there is no note
How dread an army hath *enrounded* him. *Shakesp. Henry* V.

ENS. *n. s.* [Latin.]

1. Any being or existence.

2. [In chymistry.] Some things that are pretended to contain all the qualities or virtues of the ingredients they are drawn from in a little room.

ENSA'MPLE. *n. s.* [*essempio*, Italian.] Example; pattern; subject of imitation. This orthography is now justly disused.

Such life should be the honour of your light;
Such death, the sad *ensample* of your might. *Spenser's Sonnets.*

Ye have us for an *ensample.* *Phil.* iii. 17.

Such persons as would be willing to make use of our *ensample* to do the same thing, where there is not the same necessity, may do it upon their own score, and not be able to vouch our practice for their excuse. *Sanderson's Judgment.*

To ENSA'MPLE. *v. a.* [from the noun.] To exemplify; to shew by example; to give as a copy.

I have followed all the ancient poets historical: first, Homer, who, in the person of Agamemnon, *ensampled* a good governor and a virtuous man. *Spenser.*

To ENSA'NGUINE. *v. a.* [*sanguis*, Latin; *ensanglanter*, Fr.] To smear with gore; to suffuse with blood.

With cruel tournament the squadrons join,
Where cattle pastur'd late; now scatter'd lies,
With carcasses and arms, th' *ensanguin'd* field
Deserted. *Milton's Paradise Lost, b.* xi. *l.* 654.

To ENSCHE'DULE. *v. a.* [from *schedule.*] To insert in a schedule or writing.

You must buy that peace
With full accord to all our just demands,
Enschedul'd here. *Shak. Hen.* V.

To ENSCO'NCE. *v. a.* [from *sconce.*] To cover as with a fort; to secure. *Hanmer.*

I myself sometimes, hiding mine honour in my necessity, am fain to shuffle, to hedge, and to lurch; and yet your rogue will *ensconce* your rags, your cat-a-mountain looks, your red lettice phrases, your bold bearing oaths under the shelter of your honour. *Shakesp. Merry Wives of Windsor.*

She shall not see me: I will *ensconce* me behind the arras. *Shakespeare's Merry Wives of Windsor.*

We make trifles of terrours, *ensconcing* ourselves in seeming knowledge. *Shakespeare's All's well that ends well.*

A fort of error to *ensconce*
Absurdity and ignorance. *Hudibras, p.* iii. *cant.* 3.

This he courageously invaded,
And having enter'd, barricado'd,
Ensconc'd himself as formidable
As could be underneath a table. *Hudibras, p.* iii. *cant.* 1.

To ENSE'AM. *v. a.* [from *seam.*] To sow up; to inclose by a seam or juncture of needlework.

A name engraved in the revestiary of the temple, watched by two brazen dogs, one stole away, and *enseamed* it in his thigh. *Camden's Remains.*

To ENSE'AR. *v. a.* [from *sear.*] To cauterise; to stanch or stop with fire.

Ensear thy fertile and conceptious womb;
Let it no more bring out t' ingrateful man. *Shakesp. Timon.*

To ENSHI'ELD. *v. a.* [from *shield.*] To shield; to cover; to protect.

These black masks
Proclaim an *enshield* beauty, ten times louder
Than beauty could display. *Shak. Measure for Measure.*

To ENSHRI'NE. *v. a.* [from *shrine.*] To inclose in a chest or cabinet; to preserve and secure as a thing sacred.

He seems
A phœnix, gaz'd by all, as that sole bird,
When to *enshrine* his reliques in the sun's
Bright temple, to Egyptian Thebes he flies. *Milt. Pa. Lost.*

The sots combine
With pious care a monkey to *enshrine.* *Tate's Juv. Sat.*

Fair fortune next, with looks serene and kind,
Receives 'em, in her ancient fane *enshrin'd.* *Addison.*

E'NSIFORM. *adj.* [*ensiformis*, Latin.] Having the shape of a sword, as the xiphoeides or *ensiform* cartilage.

E'NSIGN. *n. s.* [*enseigne*, French.]

1. The flag or standard of a regiment.

Hang up your *ensigns*, let your drums be still;
For here we entertain a solemn peace. *Shakespeare's H.* VI.

The Turks still pressing on, got up to the top of the walls with eight *ensigns*, from whence they had repulsed the defendants. *Knolles's History of the Turks.*

Men taking occasion from the qualities, wherein they observe often several individuals to agree, range them into sorts, in order to their naming, for the convenience of comprehensive signs; under which individuals, according to their conformity to this or that abstract idea, come to be ranked as under *ensigns*. *Locke.*

2. Any signal to assemble.

He will lift up an *ensign* to the nations from far. *Is.* v.

3. Badge; or mark of distinction, rank or office.

Princes that fly, their sceptres left behind,
Contempt or pity, where they travel, find;
The *ensigns* of our pow'r about we bear,
And ev'ry land pays tribute to the fair. *Waller.*

The marks or *ensigns* of virtues contribute not a little, by their nobleness, to the ornament of the figures; such, for example, as are the decorations belonging to the liberal arts, to war or sacrifices. *Dryden's Dufresnoy.*

4. The officer of foot who carries the flag. [Formerly written *ancient.*]

E'NSIGNBEARER. *n. s.* [*ensign* and *bear.*] He that carries the flag; the ensign.

If it be true that the giants ever made war against heaven, he had been a fit *ensignbearer* for that company. *Sidney, b.* ii.

To ENSLA'VE. *v. a.* [from *slave.*]

1. To reduce to servitude; to deprive of liberty.

The conquer'd also, and *enslav'd* by war,
Shall, with their freedom lost, their virtue lose. *Milt. P. L.*

2. To make over to another as his slave or bondman.

I to do this! I, whom you once thought brave,
To sell my country, and my king *enslave*. *Dryd. Ind. Emp.*
Long draughts of sleep his monstrous limbs *enslave*;
He reels, and falling fills the spacious cave. *Dryden's Æn.*

He is certainly the most subjected, the most *enslaved*, who is so in his understanding. *Locke.*

While the balance of power is equally held, the ambition of private men gives neither danger nor fear, nor can possibly *enslave* their country. *Swift.*

No man can make another man to be his slave, unless he hath first *enslaved* himself to life and death, to pleasure or pain, to hope or fear: command those passions, and you are freer than the Parthian king. *Taylor's Rule of living holy.*

The more virtuously any man lives, and the less he is *enslaved* to any lust, the more ready he is to entertain the principles of religion. *Tillotson, Sermon* 1.

A man, not having the power of his own life, cannot by compact, or his own consent, *enslave* himself to any one, nor put himself under the absolute arbitrary power of another, to take away life when he pleases. *Locke.*

ENSLA'VEMENT. *n. s.* [from *enslave.*] The state of servitude; slavery; abject subjection.

The children of Israel, according to their method of sinning, after mercies, and thereupon returning to a fresh *enslavement* to their enemies, had now passed seven years in cruel subjection. *South's Sermons.*

ENSLA'VER. *n. s.* [from *enslave.*] He that reduces others to a state of servitude.

What indignation in her mind,
Against *enslavers* of mankind! *Swift.*

To ENSU'E. *v. a.* [*ensuiver*, French.] To follow; to pursue.

Flee evil, and do good; seek peace, and *ensue* it. *Com. Pray.*

But now these Epicures begin to smile,
And say, my doctrine is more safe than true;
And that I fondly do myself beguile,
While these receiv'd opinions I *ensue*. *Davies.*

To ENSU'E. *v. n.*

1. To follow as a consequence to premises.

Let this be granted, and it shall hereupon plainly *ensue*, that the light of Scripture once shining in the world, all other light of nature is therewith in such sort drowned, that now we need it not. *Hooker, b.* ii. *s.* 4.

2. To succeed in a train of events, or course of time.

The man was noble;
But with his last attempt he wip'd it out,
Destroy'd his country, and his name remains
To the *ensuing* age abhorr'd. *Shakespeare's Coriolanus.*

Bishops are placed by collation of the king, without any precedent election or confirmation *ensuing*. *Hayward.*

Of worse deeds worse sufferings must *ensue*. *Milt. P. L.*

With mortal heat each other shall pursue;
What wars, what wounds, what slaughter shall *ensue*! *Dryd.*

Impute not then those ills which may *ensue*
To me, but those who with incessant hate
Pursue my life. *Rowe's Ambitious Stepmother.*

Then grave Clarissa graceful wav'd her fan;
Silence *ensu'd*, and thus the nymph began. *Pope.*

ENSU'RANCE. *n. s.* [from *ensure.*]

1. Exemption from hazard, obtained by the payment of a certain sum.

2. The sum paid for security.

ENSU'RANCER. *n. s.* [from *ensurance.*] He who undertakes to exempt from hazard.

The vain *ensurancers* of life,
And they who most perform'd, and promis'd less,
Ev'n Short and Hobbes, forsook th' unequal strife. *Dryden.*

To ENSU'RE. *v. a.* [from *sure*, *assurer*, French.]

1. To ascertain; to make certain; to secure.

It is easy to entail debts on succeeding ages, but how to *ensure* peace for any term of years is difficult enough. *Swift.*

2. To exempt any thing from hazard by paying a certain sum, on condition of being reimbursed for miscarriage.

3. To promise reimbursement of any miscarriage for a certain reward stipulated.

A mendicant contracted with a country fellow for a quantity of corn, to *ensure* his sheep for that year. *L'Estrange.*

ENSU'RER. *n. s.* [from *ensure.*] One who makes contracts of ensurance; one who for a certain sum exempts any thing from hazard.

ENTA'BLATURE. } *n. s.* [from *table.*] [In architecture.] Signifies the architrave, frise, and cornice of a pillar; being in effect the extremity of the flooring, which is either supported by pillars, or by a wall, if there be no columns. *Harris.*
ENTA'BLEMENT. }

ENTA'IL. *n. s.* [*feudum talliatum*, from the French *entaillé*, cut, from *tailler*, to cut.]

1. The estate entailed or settled, with regard to the rule of its descent.

2. The rule of descent settled for any estate.

3. Engraver's work; inlay. Obsolete.

Well it appeared to have been of old
A work of rich *entail*, and curious mold,
Woven with anticks and wild imagery. *Fairy Queen, b.* ii.

To ENTA'IL. *v. a.* [*tailler*, to cut; *entailler*, French.]

1. To settle the descent of any estate so that it cannot be by any subsequent possessor bequeathed at pleasure.

I here *entail*
The crown to thee and to thine heirs for ever. *Shak. H.* VI.

Had Richard unconstrain'd resign'd the throne,
A king can give no more than is his own:
The title stood *entail'd*, had Richard had a son. *Dryden.*

2. To fix unalienably upon any person or thing.

None ever had a privilege of infallibility *entailed* to all he said. *Digby on Bodies.*

The intemperate and unjust transmit their bodily infirmities and diseases to their children, and *entail* a secret curse upon their estates. *Tillotson, Sermon* 4.

3. To cut. Obsolete.

The mortal steel dispiteously *entail'd*,
Deep in their flesh, quite through the iron walls,
That a large purple stream adown their giambeux falls. *F. Q.*

To ENTA'ME. *v. a.* [from *tame.*] To tame; to subjugate; to subdue.

'Tis not your inky brows, your black silk hair,
Your bugle eyeballs, and your cheek of cream,
That can *entame* my spirits to your worship. *Shakespeare.*

To ENTA'NGLE. *v. a.* [A word of uncertain etymology.]

1. To inwrap or ensnare with something not easily extricable, as a net; or something adhesive, as briars.

2. To lose in multiplied involutions; as in a labyrinth.

3. To twist, or confuse in such a manner as that a separation cannot easily be made; to make an *entangled* knot.

4. To involve in difficulties; to embarrass; to perplex.

He knew not how to wrestle with desperate contingencies, and so abhorred to be *entangled* in such. *Clarendon.*

5. To puzzle; to bewilder.

The duke, being questioned, neither held silence as he might, nor constantly denied it, but *entangled* himself in his doubtful tale. *Hayward.*

I suppose a great part of the difficulties that perplex mens thoughts, and *entangle* their understandings, would be easily resolved. *Locke.*

6. To ensnare by captious questions or artful talk.

The Pharisees took counsel how they might *entangle* him in his talk. *Mat.* xxii. 15.

7. To distract with variety of cares.

No man that warreth *entangleth* himself with the affairs of this life. 2 *Tim.* ii. 4.

8. To multiply the intricacies or difficulties of a work.

Now all labour,
Marrs what it does, yea very force *entangles*
Itself with strength. *Shakespeare's Anth. and Cleopatra.*

ENTA'NGLEMENT. *n. s.* [from *entangle.*]

1. Involution of any thing intricate or adhesive.

The highest and most improved spirits are frequently caught in the *entanglements* of a tenacious imagination. *Glanv. Sceps.*

2. Perplexity; puzzle.

There will be no greater *entanglements*, touching the notion of God and his providence. *More's Divine Dialogues.*

It is to fence against the *entanglements* of equivocal words, and the art of sophistry, that distinctions have been multiplied. *Locke.*

ENTA'NGLER. *n. s.* [from *entangle.*] One that entangles.

To E'NTER. *v. a.* [*entrer*, French.]

1. To go or come into any place.

A king of repute and learning *entered* the lists against him. *Atterbury.*

2. To initiate in a business, method, or society.

The eldest being thus *entered*, and then made the fashion, it would be impossible to hinder them. *Locke.*

3. To introduce or admit into any counsel.

So your opinion is, Aufidius,
That they of Rome are *enter'd* in our counsels,
And know how we proceed. *Shakespeare's Coriolanus.*

4. To set down in a writing.

Mr. Phang, have you *enter'd* the action?
—It is *enter'd*. *Shakespeare's Henry IV. p. ii.*

Agues and fevers are *entered* promiscuously, yet in the few bills they have been distinguished. *Graunt's Bills of Mortality.*

To E'NTER. *v. n.*

1. To come in; to go in.

Be not slothful to go and to *enter* to possess the land. *Judg.*

Other creature here,
Beast, bird, insect, or worm, durst *enter* none. *Milton.*

2. To penetrate mentally; to make intellectual entrance.

He is particularly pleased with Livy for his manner of telling a story, and with Sallust for his *entering* into internal principles of action. *Addison's Spectator*, N°. 409.

They were not capable of *entering* into the numerous concurring springs of action. *Watts's Improvement of the Mind.*

3. To engage in.

The French king hath often *entered* on several expensive projects, on purpose to dissipate wealth. *Addison on the War.*

Gentlemen did not care to *enter* upon business 'till after their morning draught. *Tatler*, N°. 86.

4. To be initiated in.

As soon as they once *entered* into a taste of pleasure, politeness, and magnificence, they fell into a thousand violences, conspiracies and divisions. *Addison on Italy.*

ENTERDE'AL. *n. s.* [*entre* and *deal.*] Reciprocal transactions.

For he is practis'd well in policy,
And thereto doth his courting most apply;
To learn the *enterdeal* of princes strange,
To mark th' intent of counsels, and the change
Of states. *Hubberd's Tale.*

E'NTERING. *n. s.* [from *enter.*] Entrance; passage into a place.

It is laid waste, so that there is no house, no *entering* in. *Is.*

To ENTERLA'CE. *v. a.* [*entrelasser*, French.] To intermix; to interweave.

This lady walked outright, 'till she might see her enter into a fine close arbor: it was of trees, whose branches so lovingly *enterlaced* one another, that it could resist the strongest violence of the sight. *Sidney.*

ENTERO'CELE. *n. s.* [*enterocele*, Latin.] A rupture from the bowels pressing through or dilating the peritonæum, so as to fall down into the groin. The remedy in such cases, is chiefly by trusses and bolsters. *Quincy.*

If the intestine only is fallen, it becomes an *enterocele*; if the omentum or epiploon, epipocele; and if both, enteroepiplocele. *Sharp's Surgery.*

ENTERO'LOGY. *n. s.* [ἔντερον and λόγος.] The anatomical account of the bowels and internal parts.

ENTERO'MPHALOS. *n. s.* [ἔντερον and ὀμφαλος.] An umbilical or navel rupture.

ENTERPA'RLANCE. *n. s.* [*entre* and *parler*, French.] Parley; mutual talk; conference.

During the *enterparlance* the Scots discharged against the English without harm, but not without breach of the laws of the field. *Hayward.*

ENTERPLE'ADER. *n. s.* [*entre* and *plead.*] The discussing of a point incidentally falling out, before the principal cause can take end. For example: two several persons, being found heirs to land by two several officers in one county, the king is brought in doubt whether livery ought to be made; and therefore, before livery be made to either, they must enterplead; that is, try between themselves who is the right heir. *Cowel.*

E'NTERPRISE. *n. s.* [*entreprise*, French.] An undertaking of hazard; an arduous attempt.

Now is the time to execute mine *enterprises* to the destruction of the enemies. *Judith* ii. 5.

Whet on Warwick to this *enterprise*. *Shakesp. Henry* VI.

The day approach'd, when fortune should decide
Th' important *enterprise*, and give the bride. *Dryden.*

To E'NTERPRISE. *v. a.* [from the noun.]

1. To undertake; to attempt; to essay.

Nor shall I to the work thou *enterprisest*
Be wanting, but afford thee equal aid. *Milton's Parad. Lost.*

Princes were only chiefs of those assemblies, by whose consultations and authority the great actions were resolved and *enterprised*. *Temple.*

An epick poem, or the heroick action of some great commander, *enterprised* for the common good and honour of the Christian cause, and executed happily, may be as well written now as it was of old by the heathens. *Dryden's Juv. Dedicat.*

Haste then, and lose no time:
The business must be *enterpris'd* this night;
We must surprise the court in its delight. *Dryden.*

2. To receive; to entertain. Obsolete.

In goodly garments, that her well became,
Fair marching forth in honourable wise,
Him at the threshold met, and well did *enterprise*. *Fa. Qu.*

E'NTERPRISER. *n. s.* [from *enterprise.*] A man of enterprise; one who undertakes great things; one who engages himself in important and dangerous designs.

They commonly proved great *enterprisers* with happy success. *Hayward on Edward* VI.

To ENTERTA'IN. *v. a.* [*entretenir*, French.]

1. To converse with; to talk with.

His head was so well stored a magazine, that nothing could be proposed which he was not readily furnished to *entertain* any one in. *Locke.*

2. To treat at the table.

You shall find an apartment fitted up for you, and shall be every day *entertained* with beef or mutton of my own feeding. *Addison's Spectator*, N°. 549.

3. To receive hospitably.

Be not forgetful to *entertain* strangers; for thereby some have *entertained* angels unawares. *Heb.* iii. 2.

Heav'n, set ope thy everlasting gates,
To *entertain* my vows of thanks and praise. *Shak. Hen.* VI.

4. To keep in one's service.

How many men would you require to the furnishing of this which you take in hand? And how long space would you have them *entertained*? *Spenser's Ireland.*

You, sir, I *entertain* for one of my hundred; only, I do not like the fashion of your garments. *Shakesp. King Lear.*

I'll weep and sigh,
And, leaving so his service, follow you,
So please you *entertain* me. *Shakespeare's Cymbeline.*

5. To reserve in the mind.

This is the severest purpose God can *entertain* towards us. *Decay of Piety.*

6. To please; to amuse; to divert.

David *entertained* himself with the meditations of God's law, not his hidden decrees or counsels. *Decay of Piety.*

The history of the Royal Society shews how well philosophy becometh a narration: the progress of knowledge is as *entertaining* as that of arms. *Felton on the Classicks.*

They were capable of *entertaining* themselves on a thousand different subjects, without running into the common topicks. *Addison on Ancient Medals.*

In gardens, art can only reduce the beauties of nature to a figure which the common eye may better take in, and is therefore more *entertained* with. *Pope's Pref. to the Iliads.*

7. To admit with satisfaction.

Reason can never permit the mind to *entertain* probability, in opposition to knowledge and certainty. *Locke.*

ENTERTA'INER. *n. s.* [from *entertain.*]

1. He that keeps others in his service.

He was, in his nature and constitution of mind, not very apprehensive or forecasting of future events afar off, but an *entertainer* of fortune by the day. *Bacon's Henry* VII.

2. He that treats others at his table.

He shews both to the guests and to the *entertainer* their great mistake. *Smalridge's Sermons.*

It is little the sign of a wise or good man to suffer temperance to be transgressed, in order to purchase the repute of a generous *entertainer*. *Atterbury's Sermons.*

3. He that pleases, diverts, or amuses.

ENTERTA'INMENT. *n. s.* [from *entertain.*]

1. Conversation.

2. Treatment at the table; convivial provision.

Arrived there, the little house they fill,
Ne look for *entertainment* where none was;
Rest is their feast, and all things at their will;
The noblest mind the best contentment has. *Fairy Queen.*

With British bounty in his ship he feasts
Th' Hesperian princes, his amazed guests,
To find that watry wilderness exceed
The *entertainment* of their great Madrid. *Waller.*

3. Hospitable reception.

4. Reception; admission.

It is not easy to imagine how it should at first gain *entertainment*, but much more difficult to conceive how it should be universally propagated. *Tillotson, Sermon* 1.

5. The state of being in pay as soldiers or servants.

Have you an army ready, say you?
——A most royal one. The centurions and their charges distinctly billeted, already in the *entertainment*, and to be on foot at an hour's warning. *Shakespeare's Coriolanus.*

6. Payment of soldiers or servants. Now obsolete.

The *entertainment* of the general, upon his first arrival, was but six shillings and eight pence. *Davies on Ireland.*

The captains did covenant with the king to serve him with certain numbers of men, for certain wages and *entertainments*. *Davies on Ireland.*

7. Amusement;

7. Amusement; diversion.

Because he that knoweth least is fittest to ask questions, it is more reason, for the *entertainment* of the time, that he ask me questions than that I ask you. *Bacon's New Atlantis.*

Passions ought to be our servants, and not our masters; to give us some agitation for *entertainment*, but never to throw reason out of its seat. *Temple.*

8. Dramatick performance; the lower comedy.

A great number of dramatick *entertainments* are not comedies, but five act farces. *Gay's Pref. to What d'ye Call it.*

ENTERTI'SSUED. *adj.* [*entre* and *tissue.*] Enterwoven or intermixed with various colours or substances.

The sword, the mace, the crown imperial,
The *entertissued* robe of gold and pearl. *Shakesp. Henry* V.

To ENTHRO'NE. *v. a.* [from *throne.*]

1. To place on a regal seat.

Mercy is above this scepter'd sway;
It is *enthroned* in the hearts of kings;
It is an attribute to God himself. *Shak. Merchant of Venice.*

On a tribunal silver'd,
Cleopatra and himself, in chairs of gold,
Were publickly *enthron'd*. *Shakespeare's Ant. and Cleopatra.*

Beneath a sculptur'd arch he sits *enthron'd*,
The peers, encircling, form an awful round. *Pope's Odyssey.*

2. To invest with sovereign authority.

This pope was no sooner elected and *enthroned*, but that he began to exercise his new rapines. *Ayliffe's Parergon.*

ENTHU'SIASM. *n. s.* [ἐνθουσιασμὸς.]

1. A vain belief of private revelation; a vain confidence of divine favour or communication.

Enthusiasm is founded neither on reason nor divine revelation, but rises from the conceits of a warmed or overweening brain. *Locke.*

2. Heat of imagination; violence of passion; confidence of opinion.

3. Elevation of fancy; exaltation of ideas.

Imaging is, in itself, the very height and life of poetry, which, by a kind of *enthusiasm*, or extraordinary emotion of soul, makes it seem to us that we behold those things which the poet paints. *Dryden's Juv. Preface.*

ENTHU'SIAST. *n. s.* [ἐνθουσιάω.]

1. One who vainly imagines a private revelation; one who has a vain confidence of his intercourse with God.

Let an *enthusiast* be principled that he or his teacher is inspired, and acted by an immediate communication of the Divine Spirit, and you in vain bring the evidence of clear reasons against his doctrine. *Locke.*

2. One of a hot imagination, or violent passions.

Chapman seems to have been of an arrogant turn, and an *enthusiast* in poetry. *Pope's Pref. to the Iliads.*

3. One of elevated fancy, or exalted ideas.

At last divine Cecilia came,
Inventress of the vocal frame;
The sweet *enthusiast*, from her sacred store,
Enlarg'd the former narrow bounds,
And added length to solemn sounds,
With nature's mother-wit, and arts unknown before. *Dryd.*

ENTHUSIA'STICAL. } *adj.* [ἐνθουσιαστικὸς.]
ENTHUSIA'STICK. }

1. Persuaded of some communication with the Deity.

He pretended not to any seraphick *enthusiastical* raptures, or inimitable unaccountable transports of devotion. *Calamy.*

2. Vehemently hot in any cause.

3. Elevated in fancy; exalted in ideas.

It commonly happens in an *enthusiastick* or prophetick style, that, by reason of the eagerness of the fancy, it doth not always follow the even thread of discourse. *Burnet.*

At last, sublim'd
To rapture and *enthusiastick* heat,
We feel the present Deity. *Thomson's Spring, l.* 895.

E'NTHYMEME. *n. s.* [ἐνθύμημα.] An argument consisting only of an antecedent and consequential proposition; a syllogism where the major proposition is suppressed, and only the minor and consequence produced in words.

Playing much upon the simple or lustrative argumentation, to induce their *enthymemes* unto the people, they take up popular conceits. *Brown's Vulgar Errours, b.* i. *c.* 9.

What is an *enthymeme*, quoth Cornelius. Why, an *enthymeme*, replied Crambe, is when the major is indeed married to the minor, but the marriage kept secret. *Arb. and Pope's M. S.*

To ENTI'CE. *v. a.* [of uncertain etymology.] To allure; to attract; to draw by blandishments or hopes to something sinful or destructive.

The readiest way to entangle the mind with false doctrine, is first to *entice* the will to wanton living. *Ascham's Schoolmaster.*

If a man *entice* a maid that is not betrothed, he shall surely endow her to be his wife. *Ex.* xxii. 16.

So sang the syrens, with enchanting sound,
Enticing all to listen, and be drown'd. *Granville.*

ENTI'CEMENT. *n. s.* [from *entice.*]

1. The act or practice of alluring to ill.

Suppose we that the sacred word of God can at their hands receive due honour, by whose *enticement* the holy ordinances of the church endure every where open contempt? *Hooker.*

And here to every thirsty wanderer,
By sly *enticement* gives his baneful cup,
With many murmurs mixt. *Milton.*

2. The means by which one is allured to ill; blandishment; allurement.

In all these instances we must separate intreaty and *enticements* from deceit or violence. *Taylor's Rule of living holy.*

ENTI'CER. *n. s.* [from *entice*] One that allures to ill.

ENTICI'NGLY. *adv.* [from *entice.*] Charmingly; in a winning manner.

She strikes a lute well, and sings most *enticingly*. *Addis. Spect.*

E'NTIERTY. *n. s.* [*entierte*, French.] The whole; not barely a part.

Sometime the attorney thrusteth into the writ the uttermost quantity; or else setteth down an *entierty*, where but a moiety was to be passed. *Bacon's Off. of Alienation.*

ENTI'RE. *adj.* [*entier*, French; *integer*, Latin.]

1. Whole; undivided.

It is not safe to divide, but to extol the *entire*, still in general. *Bacon's Collection of Good and Evil.*

2. Unbroken; complete in its parts.

An antique model of the famous Laocoon is the more remarkable, as it is *entire* in those parts where the statue is maimed. *Addison on Italy.*

Water and earth, composed of old worn particles and fragments of particles, would not be of the same nature and texture now with water and earth composed of *entire* particles in the beginning. *Newton's Opt.*

3. Full; complete; comprising all requisites in itself.

The church of Rome hath rightly also considered that publick prayer is a duty *entire* in itself, a duty requisite to be performed much oftener than sermons can possibly be made. *Hook.*

Love's not love,
When it is mingled with regards that stand
Aloof from th' *entire* point. *Shakesp. King Lear.*

An action is *entire* when it is complete in all its parts; or, as Aristotle describes it, when it consists of a beginning, a middle, and an end. *Spectator,* N°. 267.

4. Sincere; hearty.

He run a course more *entire* with the king of Arragon, but more laboured and officious with the king of Castile. *Bacon.*

5. Firm; sure; solid; fixed.

Entire and sure the monarch's rule must prove,
Who founds her greatness on her subjects love. *Prior.*

6. Unmingled; unallayed.

Wrath shall be no more
Thenceforth, but in thy presence joy *entire*. *Milt. P. Lost.*

7. Honest; firmly adherent; faithful.

No man had ever a heart more *entire* to the king, the church, or his country; but he never studied the easiest ways those ends. *Clarendon.*

They had many persons, of whose *entire* affections they were well assured. *Clarendon, b.* viii.

8. In full strength; with vigour unabated; with power unbroken.

Then back to fight again, new breathed and *entire*. *F. Q.*

ENTI'RELY. *adv.* [from *entire.*]

1. In the whole; without division.

Euphrates, running, sinketh partly into the lakes of Chaldea, and falls not *entirely* into the Persian sea. *Raleigh's History.*

2. Completely; fully.

Here finish'd he, and all that he had made
View'd, and beheld! all was *entirely* good. *Milt. Par. Lost.*

Chyle may be said to be a vegetable juice in the stomach and intestines; and, poured upon blood, it seems like oil: as it passeth into the lacteals it grows still more animal, and when it has circulated often with the blood, it is *entirely* so. *Arbuth.*

General consent *entirely* altered the whole frame of their government. *Swift.*

3. With firm adherence; faithfully.

Which when his pensive lady saw from far,
Great woe and sorrow did her soul assay,
As weening that the sad end of the war,
And 'gan to highest God *entirely* pray. *Fairy Queen, b.* i.

ENTI'RENESS. *n. s.* [from *entire.*]

1. Totality; compleatness; fulness.

In an arch where each single stone, which, if severed from the rest, would be perhaps defenceless, is sufficiently secured by the solidity and *entireness* of the whole fabrick, of which it is a part. *Boyle.*

2. Honesty; integrity.

To ENTI'TLE. *v. a.* [*entituler*, French.]

1. To grace or dignify with a title or honourable appellation.

2. To give a title or discriminative appellation; as, to *entitle* a book.

Besides the Scripture, the books which they call ecclesiastical were thought not unworthy some time to be brought into publick audience, and with that name they *entitled* the books which we term apocryphal. *Hooker, b.* v. *s.* 20.

Next favourable thou,
Who highly thus to *entitle* me vouchsaf'st,
Far other name deserving! *Milton's Paradise Lost, b.* x.

3. To superscribe or prefix as a title.

How ready zeal for party is to *entitle* christianity to their designs, and to charge atheism on those who will not submit. *Locke.*

4. To give a claim to any thing.

But we, descended from your sacred line,
Entitled to your heav'n, and rites divine,
Are banish'd earth. *Dryden's Virg. Æn.*

He discovers the martyr and confessor without the trial of flames and tortures, and will hereafter *entitle* many to the reward of actions which they had never the opportunity of performing. *Addison's Spectator*, N°. 257.

He *entitled* himself to the continuance of the divine protection and goodness, by humiliation and prayer. *Atterbury.*

Thus hardly even is the penitent sinner saved; thus difficult is that duty, by which alone he can be reconciled to his Creator, and *entitled* to the mercies of the gospel. *Rogers.*

5. To grant any thing as claimed by a title.

This is to *entitle* God's care how and to what we please. *Loc.*

E'NTITY. *n. s.* [*entitas*, low Latin.]

1. Something which really is; a real being.

Dear hope! earth's dowry and heaven's debt,
The *entity* of things that are not yet:
Subt'lest, but surest being. *Crashaw.*

Fortune is no real *entity*, nor physical essence, but a mere relative signification. *Bentley's Sermons.*

God's decrees of salvation and damnation both Romish and Reformed affix to mens particular *entity*, absolutely considered, without any respect to demeanours. *Hammond's Fundamentals.*

Here *entity* and quiddity
The souls of defunct bodies fly. *Hudibras.*

2. A particular species of being.

All eruptions of air, though small and slight, give an *entity* of sound, which we call crackling, puffing, and spitting; as in bay salt and bay leaves, cast into the fire. *Bacon's Nat. Hist.*

To ENTO'IL. *v. a.* [from *toil.*] To ensnare; to intangle; to bring into toils or nets.

He cut off their land forces from their ships, and *entoiled* both their navy and their camp with a greater power than their's, both by sea and land. *Bacon's New Atlantis.*

To ENTO'MB. *v. a.* [from *tomb.*] To put into a tomb; to bury.

These processions were first begun for the interring of holy martyrs, and the visiting of those places where they were *entombed. Hooker, b.* v. *s.* 41.

The cry went once for thee,
And yet it may again,
If thou would'st not *entomb* thyself alive,
And case thy reputation in a tent. *Shakesp. Troil. and Cress.*

They, within the beast's vast womb,
The choice and flow'r of all their troops *entomb. Denham.*

E'NTRAILS. *n. s.* without a singular. [*entrailles*, Fr. ἔντερα.]

1. The intestines; the bowels; the inward parts; the guts.

What, hath thy firy heart so parch'd thine *entrails*,
That not a tear can fall? *Shak. H.* VI.

As for the *entrails*, they are all without bones; save that a bone is sometimes found in the heart of a stag, and it may be in some other creature. *Bacon's Natural History*, N°. 749.

The earth hath lost
Most of her ribs, as *entrails*; being now
Wounded no less for marble than for gold. *Ben. Johns. Catil.*

I tear that harden'd heart from out her breast,
Which with her *entrails* makes my hungry hounds a feast. *Dr.*

2. The internal parts; recess; caverns.

A precious ring that lightens all the hole,
And shews the ragged *entrails* of this pit. *Shakes. Tit. Andr.*

He had brought to light but little of that treasure, that lay so long hid in the dark *entrails* of America. *Locke.*

To ENTRA'IL. *v. a.* To mingle; to interweave; to diversify.

Over him, art striving to compare
With nature, did an arbor green dispred,
Framed of wanton ivy, flow'ring fair,
Through which the fragrant eglantine did spread,
His pricking arms *entrail'd* with roses red. *Fairy Queen.*

A little wicker basket,
Made of fine twigs, *entrailed* curiously,
In which they gather'd flowers. *Spenser's Prothal.*

E'NTRANCE. *n. s.* [*entrant*, French.]

1. The power of entering into a place.

Whence are you, sir? Has the porter his eyes in his head, that he gives *entrance* to such companions? Pray, get you out. *Shakespeare's Coriolanus.*

Where diligence opens the door of the understanding, and impartially keeps it, truth is sure to find both an *entrance* and a welcome too. *South's Sermons.*

2. The act of entering.

The reason, that I gather, he is mad,
Is a mad tale he told to-day at dinner,
Of his own door being shut against his *entrance. Shakespeare.*

Better far, I guess,
That we do make our *entrance* several ways. *Shak. Hen.* VI.

All the world's a stage,
And all the men and women meerly players;
They have their exits and their *entrances. Shak. As you like it.*

3. The passage by which a place is entered; avenue.

He charged them to keep the passages of the hilly country; for by them there was an *entrance* into Judea. *Judith* iv. 7.

Palladio did conclude, that the principal *entrance* was never to be regulated by any certain dimensions, but by the dignity of the master. *Wotton's Architecture.*

Many are the ways that lead
To his grim cave, all dismal! yet to sense
More terrible at th' *entrance* than within. *Milt. Parad. Lost.*

Let this, and every other anxious thought,
At th' *entrance* of my threshold be forgot. *Dryden's Juven.*

4. Initiation; commencement.

This is that which, at first *entrance*, balks and cools them they want their liberty. *Locke.*

5. Intellectual ingress; knowledge.

He that travelleth into a country before he hath some *entrance* into the language, goeth to school, and not to travel. *Bacon's Essays.*

6. The act of taking possession of an office or dignity.

From the first *entrance* of this king to his reign, never was king either more loving, or better beloved. *Hayw. Edw.* VI.

7. The beginning of any thing.

St. Augustine, in the *entrance* of one of his sermons, makes a kind of apology. *Hakewill on Providence.*

The earl of Holland we have had occasion to mention before in the first *entrance* upon this discourse. *Clarendon.*

To ENTRA'NCE. *v. n.* [from *trance*; *transe*, French, from *transeo*, Latin, to pass over; to pass for a time from one region to another.]

1. To put into a trance; to withdraw the soul wholly to other regions, while the body appears to lye in dead sleep.

2. To put into an extasy; to make insensible of present objects.

With delight I was all the while *entranced*, and carried so far from myself, as that I am right sorry that you ended so soon. *Spenser's Ireland.*

Adam, now enforc'd to close his eyes,
Sunk down, and all his spirits became *entranc'd. Milton.*

And I so ravish'd with her heav'nly note,
I stood *entranc'd*, and had no room for thought;
But all o'erpower'd with ecstasy of bliss,
Was in a pleasing dream of paradise. *Dryden.*

To ENTRA'P. *v. a.* [from *trap.*]

1. To ensnare; to catch in a trap or snare.

Take heed, mine eyes, how ye do stare
Henceforth too rashly on that guileful net;
In which, if ever eyes *entrapped* are,
Out of her bands ye by no means shall get. *Spenser.*

2. To involve unexpectedly in difficulties or distresses; to entangle.

Misfortune waits advantage to *entrap*
The man most wary, in her whelming lap. *Fairy Queen.*

The fraud of England, not the force of France,
Hath now *entrapt* the noble minded Talbot. *Shak. Hen.* VI.

He fought to *entrap* me by intelligence. *Shakes. Hen.* IV.

3. To take advantage of.

An injurious person lies in wait to *entrap* thee in thy words. *Ecclus.* viii. 11.

To ENTRE'AT. *v. a.* [*traiter*, French.]

1. To petition; to solicite; to importune.

Isaac *entreated* the Lord for his wife. *Gen.* xxv. 21.

2. To prevail upon by solicitation.

I have a wife, whom, I protect, I love;
I would she were in heaven, so she could
Entreat some pow'r to change this currish Jew. *Shakespeare.*

The Lord was *entreated* of him, and Rebecah his wife conceived. *Gen.* xxv. 21.

It were a fruitless attempt to appease a power, whom no prayers could *entreat*, no repentance reconcile. *Rogers's Serm.*

3. To treat or use well or ill.

Whereas thy servant worketh truly, *entreat* him not evil. *Ecclus.* vii. 20.

Must you, sir John, protect my lady here?
Entreat her not the worse in that I pray
You use her well. *Shakespeare's Henry* VI. *p.* ii.

Well I *entreated* her, who well deserv'd:
I call'd her often; for she always serv'd:
Use made her person easy to my sight,
And ease insensibly produc'd delight. *Prior.*

4. To entertain; to amuse.

My lord, I must *entreat* the time alone.
—God shield I should disturb devotion. *Sh. Rom. and Juliet.*

5. To entertain; to receive.

The garden of Proserpina this hight,
And in the midst thereof a silver seat,
With a thick arbour goodly overdight,
In which she often us'd, from open heat,
Herself to shroud, and pleasures to *entreat. Fairy Queen.*

5 8 E To

To ENTRE'AT. *v. n.*

1. To offer a treaty or compact.

Alexander was the first that *entreated* peace with them. *1 Mac.* xvi. 47.

2. To treat; to discourse.

The most admirable mystery of nature is the turning of iron, touched with the loadstone, toward the North pole, of which I shall have farther occasion to *entreat*. *Hakewill.*

3. To make a petition.

They charged me, on pain of perpetual displeasure, neither to speak of him, *entreat* for him, or any way sustain him. *Shak.*

The Janizaries *entreated* for them, as valiant men. *Knolles.*

ENTRE'ATANCE. *n. s.* [from *entreat.*] Petition; entreaty; solicitation.

These two *entreatance* made they might be heard,
Nor was their just petition long deny'd. *Fairfax, b.* ii.

ENTRE'ATY. *n. s.* [from *entreat.*] Petition; prayer; solicitation; supplication; request.

If my weak orator
Can from his mother win the duke of York,
Anon expect him here; but if she be
Obdurate to *entreaties*, God forbid
We should infringe the holy privilege
Of sanctuary. *Shakespeare's Richard* III.

ENTREMETS. n. s. [French.] Small plates set between the main dishes.

Chards of beet are plants of white beet transplanted, producing great tops, which, in the midst, have a large white main shoot, which is the true chard used in pottages and *entremets*. *Mortimer's Art of Husbandry.*

E'NTRY. *n. s.* [from *enter*; *entree*, French.]

1. The passage by which any one enters a house.

Some there are that know the resorts and falls of business, that cannot sink into the main of it; like a house that hath convenient stairs and *entries*, but never a fair room. *Bacon's Essays.*

A strait long *entry* to the temple led,
Blind with high walls, and horror over head. *Dryden.*

Is all this hurry made
On this account, because thou art afraid
A dirty hall or *entry* should offend
The curious eyes of thy invited friend? *Dryden's Juven.*

We proceeded through the *entry*, and were necessarily kept in order by the situation. *Tatler*, N°. 86.

2. The act of entrance; ingress.

Bathing and anointing give a relaxation or emollition; and the mixture of oil and water is better than either of them alone, because water entereth better into the pores, and oil after *entry* softeneth better. *Bacon's Natural History*. N°. 730.

I took horse to the lake of Constance, which lies at two leagues distance from it, and is formed by the *entry* of the Rhine. *Addison on Italy.*

By the *entry* of the chyle and air into the blood, by the lacteals, the animal may again revive. *Arbuthnot on Aliments.*

3. The act of taking possession of any estate.

4. The act of registering or setting down in writing.

A notary made an *entry* of this act. *Bacon's New Atlantis.*

5. The act of entering publickly into any city.

The day being come, he made his *entry*: he was a man of middle stature and age, and comely. *Bacon.*

To ENU'BILATE. *v. a.* [*e* and *nubile*, Latin.] To clear from clouds. *Dict.*

To ENU'CLEATE. *v. a.* [*enucleo*, Latin.] To solve; to clear; to disentangle. *Dict.*

To ENVE'LOP. *v. a.* [*enveloper*, French.]

1. To inwrap; to cover; to invest with some integument.

2. To cover; to hide; to surround.

The best and wholesom'st spirits of the night *envelop* you, good provost. *Shakespeare's Measure for Measure.*

A cloud of smoke *envelops* either host,
And all at once the combatants are lost:
Darkling they join adverse, and shock unseen,
Coursers with coursers justing, men with men. *Dryden.*

It is but to approach nearer, and that mist that *enveloped* them will remove. *Locke.*

Nocturnal shades
This world *envelop*, and th' inclement air
Persuades men to repel benumming frosts. *Phillips.*

3. To line; to cover on the inside.

His iron coat, all over grown with rust,
Was underneath *enveloped* with gold,
Darkned with filthy dust. *Fairy Queen.*

ENVELO'PE. *n. s.* [French.] A wrapper; an outward case; an integument; a cover.

Send these to paper-sparing Pope;
And, when he sits to write,
No letter with an *envelope*
Could give him more delight. *Swift.*

To ENVE'NOM. *v. a.* [from *venom.*]

1. To tinge with poison; to poison; to impregnate with venom. It is never used of the person to whom poison is given, but of the draught, meat, or instrument by which it is conveyed.

The treacherous instrument is in thy hand,
Unbated and *envenom'd*. *Shakespeare.*

Alcides, from Oechalia, crown'd
With conquest, felt th' *envenom'd* robe, and tore,
Through pain, up by the roots Thessalian pines. *Milton.*

Nor with *envenom'd* tongue to blast the fame
Of harmless men. *Phillips.*

2. To make odious.

Oh, what a world is this, when what is comely
Envenoms him that bears it! *Shakesp. As you like it.*

3. To enrage.

With her full force she threw the pois'nous dart,
And fix'd it deep within Amata's heart;
That thus *envenom'd* she might kindle rage,
And sacrifice to strife her house and husband's age. *Dryden.*

E'NVIABLE. *adj.* [from *envy.*] Deserving envy; such as may excite envy.

They, in an *enviable* mediocrity of fortune, do happily possess themselves. *Carew's Survey of Cornwall.*

E'NVIER. *n. s.* [from *envy.*] One that envies another; a maligner; one that desires the downfall of another.

Men had need beware how they be too perfect in compliments; for that *enviers* will give them that attribute, to the disadvantage of their virtues. *Bacon's Essays, Civ. and Mor.*

They ween'd
That self-same day, by fight or by surprize,
To win the mount of God, and on his throne
To set the *envier* of his state, the proud
Aspirer; but their thoughts prov'd fond and vain. *Milton.*

All preferments in church and state were given by him, all his kindred and friends promoted, and all his enemies and *enviers* discountenanced. *Clarendon.*

E'NVIOUS *adj.* [from *envy.*] Infected with envy; pained by the excellence or happiness of another.

A man of the most *envious* disposition that ever infected the air with his breath, whose eyes could not look right upon any happy man, nor ears bear the burden of any man's praise. *Sidn.*

Still in thy right hand carry gentle peace,
To silence *envious* tongues. *Shakespeare's Henry* VIII.

Be not thou *envious* against evil men. *Prov.* xxiv. 19.

Neither be thou *envious* at the wicked. *Prov.* xxiv. 19.

Sure you mistake the precept, or the tree;
Heav'n cannot *envious* of his blessings be. *Dryden.*

E'NVIOUSLY. *adj.* [from *envious.*] With envy; with malignity; with ill will.

Damned spirits, being fallen from heaven, endeavour *enviously* to obstruct the ways that may lead us thither. *Duppa.*

How *enviously* the ladies look,
When they surprise me at my book!
And sure as they're alive at night,
As soon as gone, will shew their spight. *Swift.*

To ENVI'RON. *v. a.* [*environner*, French.]

1. To surround; to encompass; to encircle.

I stand as one upon a rock,
Environ'd with a wilderness of sea. *Shakes. Tit. Andronicus.*

The country near unto the city of Sultania is on every side *environed* with huge mountains. *Knolles's History.*

The manifold streams of goodly navigable rivers, as so many chains, *environed* the same site and temple. *Bacon.*

On a plain, within the *environing* rocks, stood the city. *Sandys's Journey.*

A wand'ring
Compact of unctuous vapour, which the night
Condenses, and the cold *environs* round. *Milt. Parad. Lost.*

Thought following thought, and step by step led on,
He enter'd now the bordering desart wild,
And with dark shades and rocks *environ'd* round,
His holy meditation thus pursu'd. *Milton's Par. Regain'd.*

God hath scattered several degrees of pleasure and pain in all the things that *environ* and affect us, and blended them together in almost all that our thoughts. *Locke.*

2. To involve; to envelope.

May never glorious sun reflect his beams
Upon the country where you make abode!
But darkness and the gloomy shade of death
Environ you, 'till mischief and despair
Drive you to break your necks. *Shakespeare's Henry* VI.

Since she must go, and I must mourn, come, night,
Environ me with darkness whilst I write. *Donne.*

3. To surround in a hostile manner; to besiege; to hem in.

Methought a legion of foul fiends
Environ'd me, and howled in mine ears
Such hideous cries, that with the very thought
I trembling wak'd. *Shakespeare's Richard* III.

In thy danger,
If ever danger do *environ* thee,
Commend thy grievance to my holy prayer. *Shakespeare.*

I did but prompt the age to quit their clogs,
By the known rules of ancient liberty,
When straight a barbarous noise *environs* me. *Milton.*

4. To inclose; to invest.

The

The soldier, that man of iron,
Whom ribs of horrour all *environ*. *Cleaveland.*

ENVI'RONS. *n. s.* [*environs*, French.] The neighbourhood or neighbouring places round about the country.

To ENU'MERATE. *v. a.* [*enumero*, Latin.] To reckon up singly; to count over distinctly; to number.

You must not only acknowledge to God that you are a sinner, but must particularly *enumerate* the kinds of sin whereof you know yourself guilty. *Wake's Preparation for Death.*

Besides *enumerating* the gross defect of duty to the queen, I shew how all things were managed wrong. *Swift.*

ENUMERA'TION. *n. s.* [*enumeratio*, Latin.] The act of numbering or counting over; number told out.

Whosoever reads St. Paul's *enumeration* of duties incumbent upon it, must conclude, that well nigh the business of Christianity is laid on charity. *Sprat's Sermons.*

The chemists make spirit, salt, sulphur, water, and earth their five elements, though they are not all agreed in this *enumeration* of elements. *Watts's Logick.*

To ENU'NCIATE. *v. a.* [*enuncio*, Latin.] To declare; to proclaim; to relate; to express.

ENUNCIA'TION. *n. s.* [*enunciatio*, Latin.]

1. Declaration; publick attestation; open proclamation.

This preaching is to strangers and infants in Christ, to produce faith; but this sacramental *enunciation* is the declaration and confession of it by men in Christ, declaring it to be done, and owned, and accepted, and prevailing. *Taylor.*

2. Intelligence; information.

It remembers and retains such things as were never at all in the sense; as the conceptions, *enunciations*, and actions of the intellect and will. *Hale's Origin of Mankind.*

ENU'NCIATIVE. *adj.* [from *enunciate.*] Declarative; expressive.

This presumption only proceeds in respect of the dispositive words, and not in regard of the *enunciative* terms thereof. *Ayl.*

ENU'NCIATIVELY. *adv.* [from *enunciative.*] Declaratively.

E'NVOY. *n. s.* [*envoye*, French.]

1. A publick minister sent from one power to another.

Now the Lycian lots conspire
With Phœbus; now Jove's *envoy* through the air
Brings dismal tydings. *Denham.*

Perseus sent *envoys* to Carthage, to kindle their hatred against the Romans. *Arbuthnot on Coins.*

2. A publick messenger, in dignity below an ambassador.

3. A messenger.

The watchful sentinels at ev'ry gate,
At ev'ry passage to the senses wait;
Still travel to and fro' the nervous way,
And their impressions to the brain convey;
Where their report the vital *envoys* make,
And with new orders are commanded back. *Blackm. Creat.*

To E'NVY. *v. a.* [*envier*, French; *invidere*, Latin.]

1. To hate another for excellence, happiness, or success.

Envy thou not the oppressor, and chuse none of his ways. *Prov.* iii. 31.

A woman does not *envy* a man for fighting courage, nor a man a woman for her beauty. *Collier of Envy.*

2. To grieve at any qualities of excellence in another.

I have seen the sight,
When I have *envied* thy behaviour. *Shakesp. Ant. and Cleop.*

You cannot *envy* your neighbour's wisdom, if he gives you good counsel; nor his riches, if he supplies you in your wants; nor his greatness, if he employs it to your protection. *Swift.*

3. To grudge; to impart unwillingly; to withold maliciously.

Johnson, who, by studying Horace, had been acquainted with the rules, seemed to *envy* others that knowledge. *Dryden.*

To E'NVY. *v. n.* To feel envy; to feel pain at the sight of excellence or felicity.

In seeking tales and informations
Against this man, whose honesty the devil
And his disciples only *envy* at,
Ye blew the fire that burns ye. *Shakespeare's Henry* VIII.

He that loves God is not displeased at accidents which God chuses, nor *envies* at those gifts he bestows *Taylor.*

Who would *envy* at the prosperity of the wicked, and the success of persecutors? *Taylor's Rule of living holy.*

E'NVY. *n. s.* [from the verb.]

1. Pain felt and malignity conceived at the sight of excellence or happiness.

Envy is a repining at the prosperity or good of another, or anger and displeasure at any good of another which we want, or any advantage another hath above us. *Ray on the Creation.*

All the conspirators, save only he,
Did that they did in *envy* of great Cæsar. *Shak. Jul. Cæsar.*

Many suffered death merely in *envy* to their virtues and superiour genius. *Swift.*

Envy, to which th' ignoble mind's a slave,
Is emulation in the learn'd or brave. *Pope's Essay on Man.*

2. Rivalry; competition.

You may see the parliament of women, the little *envies* of them to one another. *Dryden on Dramatick Poesy.*

3. Malice; malignity.

Madam, this is a meer distraction;
You turn the good we offer into *envy*. *Shakesp. Henry* VIII.

4. Publick odium; ill repute.

Edward Plantagenet should be, in the most publick and notorious manner, shewed unto the people; to discharge the king of the *envy* of that opinion and bruit, how he had been put to death privily. *Bacon's Henry* VII.

To ENWHE'EL. *v. a.* [from *wheel.*] To encompass; to encircle. A word probably peculiar to *Shakespeare.*

Hail to thee, lady! and the grace of heav'n,
Before, behind thee, and on ev'ry hand
Enwheel thee round. *Shakespeare's Othello.*

To ENWO'MB. *v. a.* [from *womb.*]

1. To make pregnant.

Me then he left *enwombed* of this child,
This luckless child, whom thus ye see with blood. *Fa. Qu.*

I'm your mother;
And put you in the catalogue of those
That were *enwombed* mine. *Shak. All's well that ends well.*

2. To bury; to hide as in a womb.

Or as the Africk niger stream *enwombs*
Itself into the earth, and after comes,
Having first made a natural bridge to pass,
For many leagus, far greater than it was;
May't not be said, that her grave shall restore
Her greater, purer, finer than before. *Donne.*

EO'LIPILE. *n. s.* [from *Æolus* and *pila.*] A hollow ball of metal with a long pipe; which ball, filled with water, and exposed to the fire, sends out, as the water heats, at intervals, blasts of cold wind through the pipe.

Considering the structure of that globe, the exterior crust, and the waters lying round under it, both exposed to the sun, we may fitly compare it to an *eolipile*, or an hollow sphere with water in it, which the heat of the fire rarefies, and turns into vapours and wind. *Burnet's Theory of the Earth.*

EPA'CT. *n. s.* [ἐπακτη.] A number, whereby we note the excess of the common solar year above the lunar, and thereby may find out the age of the moon every year. For the solar year consisting of 365 days, the lunar but of 354, the lunations every year get eleven days before the solar year; and thereby, in 19 years, the moon completes 20 times 12 lunations, or gets up one whole solar year; and having finished that circuit, begins again with the sun, and so from 19 to 19 years. For the first year afterwards the moon will go before the sun but 11 days; the second year 22 days; the third 33 days: but 30 being an entire lunation, cast that away, and the remainder 3 shall be that year's epact; and so on, adding yearly 11 days. To find the epact, having the prime or golden number given, you have this rule:

Divide by three; for each one left add ten;
Thirty reject: the prime makes *epact* then. *Harris.*

As the cycle of the moon seems to shew the *epacts*, and that of the sun the dominical letter, throughout all their variations; so this Dionysian period serves to shew these two cycles both together, and how they proceed or vary all along, 'till at last they accomplish their period, and both together take their beginning again, after every 532d year. *Holder on Time.*

EPA'ULMENT. *n. s.* [French, from *epaule*, a shoulder.] In fortification, a sidework made either of earth thrown up, of bags of earth, gabions, or of fascines and earth; of which latter are made the epaulments of the places of arms for the cavalry behind the trenches. It sometimes denotes a semibastion and a square orillion, or mass of earth faced and lined with a wall, designed to cover the cannon of a cazemate. *Harr.*

EPE'NTHESIS. *n. s.* [ἐπένθεσις.] [In grammar.] The addition of a vowel or consonant in the middle of a word *Harris.*

E'PHA. *n. s.* [Hebrew.] A measure among the Jews, containing fifteen solid inches.

The *epha* and the bath shall be of one measure; that the bath may contain the tenth part of an homer, and the *epha* the tenth part of an homer. *Ezek.* xlv. 11

EPHE'MERA. *n. s.* [ἐφήμερα.]

1. A fever that terminates in one day.

2. An insect that lives only one day.

EPHE'MERAL. } *n. s.* [ἐφημέριος.] Diurnal; beginning and end-
EPHE'MERICK. } ing in a day.

This was no more than a meer bubble or blast, and like an *ephemeral* fit of applause. *Wotton.*

EPHE'MERIS. *n. s.* [ἐφημερίς.]

1. A journal; an account of daily transactions.

2. An account of the daily motions and situations of the planets.

When casting up his eyes against the light,
Both month, and day, and hour he measur'd right;
And told more truly than the *ephemeris*;
For art may err, but nature cannot miss *Dryd. Nun's Tale.*

EPHE'MERIST. *n. s.* [from *ephemeris*] One who consults the planets; one who studies or practises astrology.

The night immediately before, he was discoursing of and slighting the art of those foolish astrologers, and genethiacal *ephemerists*, that use to pry into the horoscope of nativities. *Howel's Vocal Forrest.*

EPHEMERON-

EPHEMERON-WORM. *n. ſ.* [from ἐφήμερον and *worm.*] A ſort of worm that lives but a day.

Swammerdam obſerves of the *ephemeron-worms*, that their food is clay, and that they make their cells of the ſame. *Derh.*

E'PHOD. *n. ſ.* [.אפוד] A ſort of ornament worn by the Hebrew prieſts That worn by the high prieſt was richly compoſed of gold, blue, purple, crimſon, and twiſted cotton; and upon the part which came over his two ſhoulders, were two large precious ſtones, upon which were engraven the names of the twelve tribes of Iſrael, upon each ſtone ſix names Where the ephod croſſed the high prieſt's breaſt, was a ſquare ornament, called the breaſt-plate; in which twelve precious ſtones were ſet, with the names of the twelve tribes of Iſrael engraved on them, one on each ſtone. The ephods worn by the other prieſts were only of plain linen. *Calmet.*

He made the *ephod* of gold, blue, and purple, and ſcarlet, and fine twined linen. *Ex.* xxxix. 2.

Array'd in *ephods*; nor ſo few
As are thoſe pearls of morning dew,
Which hang on herbs and flowers. *Sandys's Paraphr.*

E'PIC. *adj.* [*epicus*, Latin; ἔπος] Narrative; compriſing narrations, not acted, but rehearſed. It is uſually ſuppoſed to be heroick, or to contain one great action atchieved by a hero.

Holmes, whoſe name ſhall live in *epic* ſong,
While muſic numbers, or while verſe has feet. *Dryden.*

The *epic* poem is more for the manners, and the tragedy for the paſſions. *Dryden.*

From morality they formed that kind of poem and fable which we call *epic*. *Pope's View of Epic Poems.*

EPICE'DIUM. *n. ſ.* [ἐπικήδιος] An elegy; a poem upon a funeral.

You from above ſhall hear each day
One dirge diſpatch'd unto your clay;
Theſe, your own anthems, ſhall become
Your laſting *epicedium*. *Sandys's Paraphraſe.*

E'PICURE. *n. ſ.* [*epicureus*, Latin.] A follower of Epicurus; a man given wholly to luxury.

Then fly falſe thanes,
And mingle with the Engliſh *epicures*. *Shakeſp. Macbeth.*

The *epicure* buckles to ſtudy, when ſhame, or the deſire to recommend himſelf to his miſtreſs, ſhall make him uneaſy in the want of any ſort of knowledge. *Locke.*

EPICURE'AN. *n. ſ.* [*epicureus*, Latin.] One who holds the phyſiological principles of Epicurus.

The Platoniſts have their ſoul of the world, and the *Epicureans* their ſoul of the world, and the *Epicureans* their endeavour towards motion in their atoms when at reſt. *Locke.*

EPICU'REAN. *adj.* Luxurious; contributing to luxury.

Tie up the libertine in a field of feaſts,
Keep his brain fuming; *epicurean* cooks,
Sharpen with cloyleſs ſauce his appetite. *Shak. Ant. and Cleop.*

What a damn'd *epicurean* raſcal is this! *Shakeſpeare.*

EPICU'RISM. *n. ſ.* [from *epicure.*] Luxury; ſenſual enjoyment; groſs pleaſure.

Here you do keep a hundred knights and ſquires;
Men ſo diſorder'd, ſo debauch'd and bold,
That this our court, infected with their manners,
Shews like a riotous inn; *epicuriſm* and luſt
Make it a tavern or a brothel. *Shakeſpeare's King Lear.*

There is not half ſo much *epicuriſm* in any of their moſt ſtudied luxuries, as a bleeding fame at their mercy. *Government of the Tongue, ſ.* 6.

Some good men have ventured to call munificence, the greateſt ſenſuality, a piece of *epicuriſm*. *Calamy's Sermons.*

EPICY'CLE. *n. ſ.* [ἐπὶ and κύκλος.] A little circle whoſe center is in the circumference of a greater; or a ſmall orb, which, being fixed in the deferent of a planet, is carried along with its motion; and yet, with its own peculiar motion, carries the body of the planet faſtened to it round about its proper center. *Harris.*

In regard of the *epicycle*, or leſſer orb, wherein it moveth, the motion of the moon is various and unequal. *Brown.*

Gird the ſphere
With centric and eccentric, ſcribbl'd o'er;
Cycle and *epicycle*, orb in orb. *Milton's Paradiſe Loſt, b.* viii.

EPICY'CLOID. *n. ſ.* [ἐπικυκλοειδής.] A curve generated by the revolution of the periphery of a circle along the convex or concave part of another circle. *Harris.*

EPIDE'MICAL. }
EPIDE'MICK. } *n. ſ.* [ἐπὶ and δῆμος.]

1. That which falls at once upon great numbers of people, as a plague.

It was conceived not to be an *epidemick* diſeaſe, but to proceed from a malignity in the conſtitution of the air, gathered by the prediſpoſitions of ſeaſons. *Bacon's Henry* VII.

As the proportion of acute and *epidemical* diſeaſes ſhews the aptneſs of the air to ſudden and vehement impreſſions, ſo the chronical diſeaſes ſhew the ordinary temper of the place. *Graunt's Bills of Mortality.*

2. Generally prevailing; affecting great numbers.

The more *epidemical* and prevailing this evil is, the more honourable are thoſe who ſhine as exceptions. *South's Sermons.*

He ought to have been buſied in loſing his money, or in other amuſements equally laudable and *epidemick* among perſons of honour. *Swift.*

3. General; univerſal.

They're citizens o' th' world, they're all in all;
Scotland's a nation *epidemical*. *Cleaveland.*

EPIDE'RMIS. *n. ſ.* [ἐπιδερμίς.] The ſcarf-ſkin of a man's body.

EPIGRA'M. *n. ſ.* [*epigramma*, Latin.] A ſhort poem terminating in a point.

A college of witcrackers cannot flout me out of my humour: doſt thou think I care for a ſatire or an *epigram*? *Shak.*

What can be more witty than the *epigram* of Moore upon the name of Nicolaus, an ignorant phyſician, that had been the death of thouſands? *Peacham of Poetry.*

I writ
An *epigram* that boaſts more truth than wit. *Gay.*

EPIGRAMMA'TICAL. }
EPIGRAMMA'TICK. } *adj.* [*epigrammaticus*, Latin.]

1. Dealing in epigrams; writing epigrams.

Our good *epigrammatical* poet, old Godfrey of Wincheſter, thinketh no ominous foreſpeaking to lie in names. *Camden.*

2. Suitable to epigrams; belonging to epigrams.

He is every where above conceits of *epigrammatick* wit and groſs hyperboles: he maintains majeſty in the midſt of plainneſs; he ſhines, but glares not; and is ſtately, without ambition. *Addiſon.*

He has none of thoſe little points and puerilities that are ſo often to be met with in Ovid; none of the *epigrammatick* turns of Lucan; none of thoſe ſwelling ſentiments which are ſo frequent in Statius and Claudian; none of thoſe mixt embelliſhments of Taſſo. *Addiſon's Spectator*, Nº. 279.

EPIGRA'MMATIST. *n. ſ.* [from *epigram.*] One who writes or deals in epigrams.

A jeſt upon a poor wit, at firſt might have had an *epigrammatiſt* for its father, and been afterwards gravely underſtood by ſome painful collector. *Pope.*

Such a cuſtomer the *epigrammatiſt* Martial meets withal, one who, after he had walked through the faireſt ſtreet twice or thrice, cheapening jewels, plate, rich hangings, came away with a wooden diſh. *Peacham on Blazoning.*

EPI'GRAPHE. *n. ſ.* [ἐπιγραφὴ.] An inſcription on a ſtatue. *Dict.*

E'PILEPSY. *n. ſ.* [ἐπίληψις.] An convulſion, or convulſive motion of the whole body, or of ſome of its parts, with a loſs of ſenſe. A convulſive motion happens when the blood, or nervous fluid, runs into any parts with ſo great violence, that the mind cannot reſtrain them from attraction. *Quincy.*

My lord is fell into an *epilepſy*:
This is the ſecond fit. *Shak. Othello.*

Melancholy diſtempers are deduced from ſpirits drawn from that cacochymia; the phrenitis from cholerick ſpirits, and the *epilepſy* from fumes. *Floyer on the Humours.*

EPILE'PTICK. *adj.* [from *epilepſy.*] Convulſed; diſeaſed with an epilepſy.

A plague upon your *epileptick* viſage!
Smile you my ſpeeches, as I were a fool? *Shakeſ. K. Lear.*

Epilepticks ought to breathe a pure air, unaffected with any ſteams, even ſuch as are very fragrant. *Arbuthnot on Diet.*

E'PILOGUE. *n. ſ.* [*epilogus*, Latin.] The poem or ſpeech at the end of a play.

If it be true that good wine needs no buſh, 'tis true that a good play needs no *epilogue*; yet to good wine they do uſe good buſhes, and good plays prove the better by the help of good *epilogues*. *Shakeſpeare's As you like it.*

Are you mad, you dog;
I am to riſe and ſpeak the *epilogue*. *Dryden's Tyran. Love.*

EPINY'CTIS. *n. ſ.* [ἐπινυκτίς.] A ſore at the corner of the eye.

The *epinyctis* is of the bigneſs of a lupin, of a duſky red, and ſometimes of a livid and pale colour, with great inflammation and pain: it diſchargeth firſt a ſanies of bloody matter. *Wiſeman's Surgery.*

EPI'PHANY. *n. ſ.* [ἐπιφανεία.] A church feſtival, celebrated on the twelth day after Chriſtmas, in commemoration of our Saviour's being manifeſted to the world, by the appearance of a miraculous blazing ſtar, which conducted the magi to the place where he was. *Dict.*

EPIPHONE'MA. *n. ſ.* [ἐπιφώνημα.] An exclamation; a concluſive ſentence not cloſely connected with the words forgoing.

I know a gentleman, who made it a rule in reading to ſkip over all ſentences where he ſpied a note of admiration at the end. I believe, if thoſe preachers who abound in *epiphomenas* would but look about them, they would find one part of their congregation out of countenance, and the other aſleep, except perhaps an old female beggar or two in the iſles; who, if they be ſincere, may probably groan at the ſound. *Swift.*

EPI'PHORA. *n. ſ.* [ἐπίφορα.] An inflammation of any part, but more eſpecially a defluxion of humours on the eyes. *Harris.*

Epiphyllospe'rmous. *adj.* [from ἐπὶ, φύλλον and σπέρμα.] Is applied to plants that bear their ſeed on the back part of their leaves, being the ſame with capillaries. *Harris.*

Epi'physis. *n. ſ.* [ἐπίφυσις.] Accretion; the part added by accretion; one bone growing to another by ſimple contiguity, without any proper articulation *Quincy.*

The *epiphyſis* of the os femoris is a diſtinct bone from it in a child, whereas in a man they do entirely unite. *Wiſeman.*

Epi'ploce. *n. ſ.* [ἐπιπλοκή.] A figure of rhetorick, by which one aggravation, or ſtriking circumſtance, is added in due gradation to another; as, *he not only ſpared his enemies, but continued them in employment; not only continued, but advanced them.*

Epi'scopacy. *n. ſ.* [*epiſcopatus*, Latin.] The government of biſhops; the government of the church eſtabliſhed by the apoſtles.

They durſt not conteſt with the aſſembly in juriſdiction; ſo that there was little more than the name of *epiſcopacy* preſerved. *Clarendon.*

Prelacy itſelf cannot be proved by preſcription, ſince *epiſcopacy* is not preſcribed by any time whatſoever. *Ayliffe's Par.*

Epi'scopal. *adj.* [from *epiſcopus*, Latin.]

1. Belonging to a biſhop.

The apoſtle commands Titus not only to be a pattern of good works himſelf, but to uſe his *epiſcopal* authority in exhorting every rank and order of men. *Rogers's Sermons.*

2. Veſted in a biſhop.

The plot of diſcipline ſought to erect a popular authority of elders, and to take away *epiſcopal* juriſdiction. *Hooker.*

Epi'scopate. *n. ſ.* [*epiſcopatus*, Latin.] A biſhoprick; the office and dignity of a biſhop.

E'PISODE. *n. ſ.* [ἐπισωδη.] An incidental narrative, or digreſſion in a poem, ſeparable from the main ſubject, yet riſing naturally from it.

The poem, which we have now under our conſideration, hath no other *epiſodes* than ſuch as naturally ariſe from the ſubject. *Addiſon's Spectator.*

Episo'dical. } *adj.* [from *epiſode.*] Contained in an epiſode;
Episo'dick. } pertaining to an epiſode

Epiſodical ornaments, ſuch as deſcriptions and narrations, were delivered to us from the obſervations of Ariſtotle. *Dryd.*

I diſcover the difference between the *epiſodick* and principal action, as well as the nature of epiſodes. *Notes on the Odyſſey.*

Epispa'stick. *n. ſ.* [ἐπὶ and σπάω.]

1. Drawing.

2. Bliſtering. This is now the more frequent, though leſs proper ſenſe.

The matter ought to be ſolicited, by all poſſible methods, to the lower parts, by fomentations, bathing, *epiſpaſticks*, and bliſtering. *Arbuthnot on Diet.*

EPI'STLE. *n. ſ.* [ἐπιςολή.] A letter. This word is ſeldom uſed but in poetry, or on occaſions of dignity and ſolemnity.

When looſe *epiſtles* violate chaſte eyes,
She half conſents, who ſilently denies. *Dryden.*

Epi'stolary. *adj.* [from *epiſtle.*]

1. Relating to letters; ſuitable to letters.

2. Tranſacted by letters.

I ſhall carry on an *epiſtolary* correſpondence between the two heads. *Addiſon's Guardian*, Nº. 114.

Epi'stler. *n. ſ.* [from *epiſtle.*] A ſcribbler of letters.

E'pitaph. *n. ſ.* [ἐπιτάφιο.] An inſcription upon a tomb.

Live ſtill, and write mine *epitaph.* *Shakeſpeare.*

Some thy lov'd duſt in Parian ſtones enſhrine,
Others immortal *epitaphs* deſign;
With wit, and ſtrength, that only yields to thine *Smith.*

Epithala'mium. *n. ſ.* [ἐπὶ θάλαμος.] A nuptial ſong; a compliment upon marriage.

I preſume to invite you to theſe ſacred nuptials: the *epithalamium* ſung by a crowned muſe. *Sandys's Paraphraſe.*

The forty-fifth pſalm is an *epithalamium* to Chriſt and the church, or to the lamb and his ſpouſe. *Burnet.*

E'pithem. *n. ſ.* [ἐπίθημα.] A liquid medicament externally applied.

Epithems, or cordial applications, are juſtly applied unto the left breaſt. *Brown's Vulgar Errours, b.* iv. *c.* 1.

Cordials and *epithems* are alſo neceſſary, to reſiſt the putrefaction and ſtrengthen the vitals. *Wiſeman's Surgery.*

E'pithet. *n. ſ.* [ἐπίθετον.]

1. An adjective denoting any quality good or bad: as, the *verdant* grove, the *craggy* mountain's *lofty* head.

I affirm with phlegm, leaving the *epithets* of falſe, ſcandalous and villainous to the author. *Swift.*

2. It is uſed by ſome writers improperly for *title, name.*

The *epithet* of ſhades belonged more properly to the darkneſs than the refreſhment. *Decay of Piety.*

3. It is uſed improperly for *phraſe, expreſſion.*

For which of my good parts did you firſt ſuffer love for me? —Suffer love! a good *epithet:* I do ſuffer love indeed; for I love thee againſt my will. *Shakeſpeare.*

EPI'TOME. *n. ſ.* [ἐπιτομή.] Abridgment; abbreviature; compendious abſtract; compendium.

This is a poor *epitome* of your's,
Which, by th' interpretation of full time,
May ſhew like all yourſelf. *Shakeſpeare's Coriolanus.*

Epitomes are helpful to the memory, and of good private uſe; but ſet forth for publick monuments, accuſe the induſtrious writers of delivering much impertinency. *Wotton.*

I think it would be well, if there were a ſhort and plain *epitome* made, containing the chief and moſt material heads. *Locke on Education.*

Such abſtracts and *epitomes* may be reviewed in their proper places. *Watts's Improvement of the Mind.*

To Epi'tomise. *v. a.* [from *epitome.*]

1. To abſtract; to contract into a narrow ſpace.

Who did the whole world's ſoul contract, and drove
Into the glaſſes of your eyes·
So made ſuch mirrours and ſuch ſpies,
That they did all to you *epitomiſe.* *Donne.*

2. Leſs properly, to diminiſh; to curtail.

We have *epitomiſed* many particular words, to the detriment of our tongue. *Addiſon's Spectator*, Nº 135.

Epi'tomiser. } *n. ſ.* [from *epitomiſe.*] An abridger; an ab-
Epi'tomist. } ſtracter; a writer of epitomes.

E'poch. } *n. ſ.* [ἐποχή.] The time at which a new compu-
E'pocha. } tation is begun; the time from which dates are numbered.

Moſes diſtinctly ſets down this account, computing by certain intervals, memorable æras and *epochas*, or terms of time. *Brown's Vulgar Errours, b.* vi. *c.* 1.

Theſe are the practices of the world, ſince the year ſixty; the grand *epoch* of falſhood, as well as debauchery. *South.*

Some lazy ages, loſt in ſleep and eaſe,
No action leave to buſy chronicles;
Such whoſe ſupine felicity but makes
In ſtory chaſms, in *epochas* miſtakes. *Dryden.*

Their ſeveral *epochas* or beginnings, as from the creation of the world, from the flood, from the firſt olympiad, from the building of Rome, or from any remarkable paſſage or accident, give us a pleaſant proſpect into the hiſtories of antiquity and of former ages. *Holder on Time.*

Time is always reckoned from ſome known parts of this ſenſible world, and from ſome certain *epochs* marked out to us by the motions obſerveable in it. *Locke.*

Time, by neceſſity compel'd, ſhall go
Through ſcenes of war, and *epochas* of woe. *Prior.*

Epo'de. *n. ſ.* [ἐπῳδός.] The ſtanza following the ſtrophe and antiſtrophe.

Epope'e. *n. ſ.* [ἐποποιία.] An epick or heroick poem.

Tragedy borrows from the *epopee*, and that which borrows is of leſs dignity, becauſe it has not of its own. *Dryd. Virgil.*

Epula'tion. *n. ſ.* [*epulatio*, Latin.] Banquet; feaſt.

Contented with bread and water, when he would dine with Jove, and pretended to *epulation*, he deſired no other addition than a piece of cheeſe. *Brown's Vulgar Errours, b.* vii. *c.* 17.

Epulo'tick. *n. ſ.* [ἐπουλωτικός.] A cicatriſing medicament.

The ulcer, incarned with common ſarcoticks, and the ulcerations about it, were cured by ointment of tuty, and ſuch like *epuloticks.* *Wiſeman of Inflammation.*

Equabi'lity. *n. ſ.* [from *equable.*] Equality to itſelf; evenneſs; uniformity.

For the celeſtial bodies, the *equability* and conſtancy of their motions argue them ordained by Wiſdom. *Ray.*

The *equability* of the temperature of the air rendered the Aſiaticks lazy. *Arbuthnot on Air.*

E'QUABLE. *adj.* [*æquabilis*, Latin.] Equal to itſelf; even; uniform in reſpect to form, motion, or temperature.

He would have the vaſt body of a planet to be as elegant and round as a factitious globe repreſents it; to be every where ſmooth and *equable*, and as plain as elyſian fields. *Bentley.*

Nothing abates acrimony of the blood more than an *equable* motion of it, neither too ſwift nor too ſlow; for too quick a motion produceth an alkaline, and too ſlow an acid acrimony. *Arbuthnot on Diet.*

E'quably. *adv.* [from *equable.*] Uniformly; in the ſame tenour; evenly; equally to itſelf.

If bodies move *equably* in concentrick circles, and the ſquares of their periodical times be as the cubes of their diſtances from the common center, their centripetal forces will be reciprocally as the ſquares of the diſtances. *Cheyne.*

E'qual. *adj.* [*æqualis*, Latin.]

1. Like another in bulk, excellence, or any other quality that admits compariſon; neither greater nor leſs; neither worſe nor better.

If thou be among great men, make not thyſelf *equal* with them. *Ecclus.* xxxii. 9.

Equal lot
May join us; *equal* joy, as *equal* love. *Milton's Par. Loſt.*

Although there were no man in the world to take notice of it, every triangle would contain three angles *equal* to two right angles. *Hale's Origin of Mankind.*

2. Adequate to any purpoſe.

The Scots truſted not their own numbers, as *equal* to fight with the Engliſh. *Clarendon, b.* viii.

3. Even; uniform.

He laughs at all the vulgar cares and fears,
At their vain triumphs, and their vainer tears;
An *equal* temper in his mind he found,
When fortune flatter'd him, and when she frown'd. *Dryden.*

Think not of me: perhaps my *equal* mind
May learn to bear the fate the gods allot me. *Smith.*

4. In just proportion.

It is not permitted me to make my commendations *equal* to your merit. *Dryden's Fab. Dedication.*

5. Impartial; neutral.

Each to his proper fortune stand or fall;
Equal and unconcern'd I look on all:
Rutilians, Trojans, are the same to me,
And both shall draw the lots their fates decree. *Dryd. Æn.*

6. Indifferent.

They who are not disposed to receive them, may let them alone, or reject them; it is *equal* to me. *Cheyne's Phil. Prin.*

7. Equitable; advantageous alike to both parties.

He submitted himself, and sware to all *equal* conditions. *2 Mac.* xiii. 23.

8. Upon the same terms.

They made the married, orphans, widows, yea and the aged also, *equal* in spoils with themselves. *2 Mac.* viii. 30.

E'QUAL. *n. s.* [from the adjective.]

1. One not inferiour or superiour to another.

He is enamoured on Hero: I pray you, dissuade him from her; she is no *equal* for his birth. *Sh. Much Ado about Nothing.*

He would make them all *equals* to the citizens of Rome. *2 Mac.* ix. 15.

Those who were once his *equals*, envy and defame him, because they now see him their superiour; and those who were once his superiours, because they look upon him as their *equal*. *Addison's Spectator*, N°. 256.

To my dear *equal*, in my native land,
My plighted vow I gave: I his receiv'd:
Each swore with truth; with pleasure each believ'd:
The mutual contract was to heav'n convey'd. *Prior.*

2. One of the same age.

I profited in the Jews religion above many my *equals* in mine own nation. *Gal.* i. 14.

To E'QUAL. *v. a.* [from the noun.]

1. To make one thing or person equal to another.
2. To rise to the same state with another person.

I know no body so like to *equal* him, even at the age he wrote most of them, as yourself. *Trumbull to Pope.*

3. To be equal to.

One whose all not *equals* Edward's moiety. *Shakespeare.*

4. To recompense fully.

Then sought Sicheus through the shady grove,
Who answer'd all her cares, and *equal'd* all her love. *Dryd.*

Nor you, great queen, these offices repent,
Which he will *equal*, and perhaps augment. *Dryden's Virg.*

To E'QUALISE. *v. a.* [from *equal.*]

1. To make even.

To *equalise* accounts we will allow three hundred years, and so long a time as we can manifest from the Scripture. *Bro.*

2. To be equal to: a sense not used.

That would make the moved body, remaining what it is, in regard of its bigness, to *equalise* and fit a thing bigger than it is. *Digby on Bodies.*

Ye lofty beeches, tell this matchless dame,
That if together ye fed all one flame,
It could not *equalise* the hundredth part
Of what her eyes have kindled in my heart. *Waller.*

EQUA'LITY. *n. s.* [from *equal.*]

1. Likeness with regard to any quantities compared.

Equality of two domestick powers,
Breeds scrupulous faction: the hated, grown to strength,
Are newly grown to love. *Shakesp. Anthony and Cleopatra.*

2. The same degree of dignity.

One shall rise,
Of proud ambition; who, not content
With fair *equality*, fraternal state,
Will arrogate dominion undeserv'd,
Over his brethren. *Milton's Paradise Lost*, *b.* xii. *l.* 26.

According to this *equality* wherein God hath placed all mankind, with relation to himself, in all the relations between man and man there is a mutual dependance. *Swift.*

3. Evenness; uniformity; constant tenour; equability.

Measure out the lives of men, and periodically define the alterations of their tempers, conceive a regularity in mutations, with an *equality* in constitutions, and forget that variety which physicians therein discover. *Brown's Vulgar Errours.*

E'QUALLY. *adv.* [from *equal.*]

1. In the same degree with another person or thing; alike.

To reconcile mens vices to their fears is the aim of all the various schemes and projects of sin, and is *equally* intended by atheism and immorality. *Rogers, Sermon* 15.

They are *equally* impatient of their condition, *equally* tempted with the wages of unrighteousness, as if they were indeed poor. *Rogers, Sermon* 2.

2. Evenly; equably; uniformly.

If the motion of the sun were as unequal as of a ship, sometimes slow, and at others swift; or, if being constantly *equally* swift, it yet was not circular, and produced not the same appearances, it would not help us to measure time more than the motion of a comet does. *Locke.*

3. Impartially.

We shall use them,
As we shall find their merits and our safety
May *equally* determine. *Shakespeare's King Lear.*

EQU'ANGULAR. *adj.* [from *equus* and *angulus*, Latin.] Consisting of equal angles.

EQUANI'MITY. *n. s.* [*æquanimitas*, Latin.] Evenness of mind neither elated nor depressed.

EQUA'NIMOUS. *adj.* [*æquanimis*, Latin.] Even; not dejected; not elated.

EQUA'TION. *n. s.* [*æquare*, Latin.] The investigation of a mean proportion collected from the extremities of excess and defect, to be applied to the whole.

We are to find out the extremities on both sides, and from and between them the middle daily motions of the sun along the Ecliptick; and to frame tables of *equation* of natural days, to be applied to the mean motion by addition or substraction, as the case shall require. *Holder on Time.*

By an argument taken from the *equations* of the times of the eclipses of Jupiter's satellites, it seems that light is propagated in time, spending in its passage from the sun to us about seven minutes of time. *Newton's Opt.*

EQUATION. [In algebra.] Is an expression of the same quantity in two dissimilar terms, but of equal value; as 3 *s.* = 36 *d.* *Dict.*

EQUATION. [In astronomy.] The difference between the time marked out by the sun's apparent motion, and the time that is measured by its real or middle motion; according to which clocks and watches ought to be adjusted. *Dict.*

EQUA'TOR. *n. s.* [*æquator*, Latin.] On the earth, or equinoctial in the heavens, is a great circle, whose poles are the poles of the world. It divides the globe into two equal parts, the northern and southern hemispheres. It passes through the east and west points of the horizon; and at the meridian is raised as much above the horizon as is the complement of the latitude of the place. Whenever the sun comes to this circle, it makes equal days and nights all round the globe, because he then rises due east and sets due west, which he doth at no other time of the year. *Harris.*

By reason of the convexity of the earth, the eye of man, under the *equator*, cannot discover both the poles; neither would the eye, under the poles, discover the sun in the *equator*. *Brown's Vulgar Errours, b.* vi. *c.* 5.

On the other side the *equator* there is much land still remaining undiscovered. *Ray on the Creation.*

Rocks rich in gems, and mountains big with mines,
That on the high *equator* ridgy rise,
Whence many a bursting stream auriferous plays. *Thomson.*

EQUATO'RIAL. *adj.* [from *equator.*] Pertaining to the equator; taken at the equator.

The planets have spheroidical figures, and obliquities of their *equatorial* to their ecliptick planes. *Cheyne.*

EQUE'STRIAN. *adj.* [*equestris*, Latin.]

1. Appearing on horseback.

An *equestrian* lady appeared upon the plains. *Spectator.*

2. Skilled in horsemanship.
3. Belonging to the second rank in *Rome.*

EQUE'RRY. *n. s.* [*ecurie*, Dutch.] Master of the horse.

EQUICRU'RAL. } *adj.* [*æquus* and *crus*, Latin.]
EQUICRU'RE. }

1. Having the legs of an equal length.
2. Having the legs of an equal length, and longer than the base; isosceles.

An *equicrure* triangle goes upon a certain proportion of length and breadth. *Digby on the Soul.*

We begin with Saturn, and successively draw lines from angle to angle, until seven *equicrural* triangles be described. *Brown's Vulgar Errours, b.* v. *c.* 22.

EQUIDI'STANT. *adj.* [*æquus* and *distans*, Latin.] At the same distance.

The fixt stars are not all placed in the same concave spherical superficies, and *equidistant* from us, as they seem to be. *Ray on the Creation.*

EQUIDI'STANTLY. *adv.* [from *equidistant.*] At the same distance.

The liver, though seated on the right side, yet by the subclavian division *equidistantly* communicates unto either arm. *Brown's Vulgar Errours, b.* iv. *c.* 4.

EQUIFO'RMITY. *n. s.* [*æquus* and *forma*, Latin.] Uniform equality.

No diversity or difference, but a simplicity of parts and *equiformity* of motion. *Brown's Vulgar Errours, b.* iv. *c.* 5.

EQUILA'TERAL. *adj.* [*æquus* and *latus*, Latin.] Having all sides equal.

Circles or squares, or triangles *equilateral*, which are all figures of equal lines, can differ but in greater or lesser. *Bacon.*

Trifling futility appears in their twelve signs of the zodiack

diack and their aspects: why no more aspects than diametrically opposite, and such as make *equilateral* figures? *Bentley.*

To EQUILI'BRATE. *v. a.* [from *equilibrium.*] To balance equally; to keep even with equal weight on each side.

If the point of the knife, drawn over the loadstone, have in this affriction been drawn from the equator of the loadstone towards the pole, it will attract one of the extremes of an *equilibrated* magnetick needle. *Boyle's Experiments.*

The bodies of fishes are *equilibrated* with the water in which they swim. *Arbuthnot on Air.*

EQUILIBRA'TION. *n. s.* [from *equilibrate.*] Equipoise; the act of keeping the balance even.

The accession of bodies upon, or secession thereof from the earth's surface, perturb not the *equilibration* of either hemisphere. *Brown's Vulgar Errours, b.* i. *c.* 2.

In so great a variety of motions, as running, leaping, and dancing, nature's laws of *equilibration* are always observed. *Derham's Physico-Theology.*

EQUILI'BRIUM. *n. s.* [Latin.]

1. Equipoise; equality of weight.

2. Equality of evidence, motives, or powers of any kind.

Things are not left to an *equilibrium*, to hover under an indifference whether they shall come to pass, or not come to pass. *South's Sermons.*

It is in *equilibrio*
If deities descend or no;
Then let th' affirmative prevail,
As requisite to form my tale. *Prior.*

Health consists in the *equilibrium* between those two powers, when the fluids move so equally that they don't press upon the solids with a greater force than they can bear. *Arbuth. on Alim.*

EQUINE'CESSARY. *adj.* [*æquus* and *necessarius*, Latin.] Needful in the same degree.

For both to give blows and to carry,
In fights, are *equinecessary*. *Hudibras, p.* i. *cant.* 3.

EQUINO'CTIAL. *n. s.* [*æquus* and *nox*, Latin.] The line that encompasses the world at an equal distance from either pole, to which circle when the sun comes, he makes equal days and nights all over the globe.

EQUINO'CTIAL. *adj.* [from *equinox.*]

1. Pertaining to the equinox.

Thrice th' *equinoctial* line
He circled; four times cross'd the car of night
From pole to pole, traversing each colure. *Milton's Pa. Lost.*
Some say the sun
Was bid turn reins from th' *equinoctial* road,
Like distant breadth. *Milton's Paradise Lost, b.* x.

2. Happening about the time of the equinoxes.

3. Being near the equinoctial line; having the properties of things near the equator.

In vain they covet shades, and Thracia's gales,
Pining with *equinoctial* heat. *Phillips.*

EQUINO'CTIALLY. *adv.* [from *equinoctial.*] In the direction of the equinoctial.

They may be refrigerated inclanaterly, or somewhat *equinoctially*; that is, towards the eastern and western points. *Brown.*

E'QUINOX. *n. s.* [*æquus* and *nox*, Latin.]

1. Equinoxes are the precise times in which the sun enters into the first point of Aries and Libra; for then, moving exactly under the equinoctial, he makes our days and nights equal. This he doth twice a year, about the 21st of *March* and 23d of *September*, which therefore are called the vernal and autumnal equinoxes. *Harris.*

It ariseth not unto Biarmia, and heliacally about the autumnal *equinox*. *Brown's Vulgar Errours, b.* iv. *c.* 13.

The time when this kid was taken out of the womb was about the vernal *equinox*. *Ray on the Creation.*

'Twas now the month in which the world began,
If March beheld the first created man;
And since the vernal *equinox*, the sun
In Aries twelve degrees or more had run. *Dryden.*

2. Equality; even measure. Improper.

Do but see his vice;
'Tis to his virtues a just *equinox*,
The one as long as th' other. *Shakespeare's Othello.*

3. Equinoctial wind: a poetical use.

The passage yet was good; the wind, 'tis true,
Was somewhat high, but that was nothing new,
No more than usual *equinoxes* blew. *Dryden.*

EQUINU'MERANT. *adj.* [*æquus* and *numerus*, Latin.] Having the same number; consisting of the same number.

This talent of gold, though not *equinumerant*, nor yet equiponderant, as to any other; yet was equivalent to some correspondent talent in brass. *Arbuthnot on Coins.*

To EQUIP. *v. a.* [*equipper*, French.]

1. To furnish for a horseman or cavalier.

2. To furnish; to accoutre; to dress out.

The country are led astray in following the town; and *equipped* in a ridiculous habit, when they fancy themselves in the height of the mode. *Addison's Spectator*, N°. 129.

E'QUIPAGE. *n. s.* [*equipage*, French.]

1. Furniture for a horseman.

2. Carriage of state; vehicle.

Winged spirits, and chariots wing'd,
From th' armory of God; where stand of old
Myriads, between two brazen mountains lodg'd
Against a solemn day, harness'd at hand,
Celestial *equipage*! *Milton's Paradise Lost, b.* vii. *l.* 203.

3. Attendance; retinue.

Think what an *equipage* thou hast in air,
And view with scorn two pages and a chair. *Pope.*

4. Accoutrements; furniture.

Soon as thy dreadful trump begins to sound,
The god of war, with his fierce *equipage*,
Thou do'st awake, sleep never he so sound. *Fairy Queen.*
I will not lend thee a penny.—
I will retort the sum in *equipage*.
Shakespeare's Merry Wives of Windsor.

E'QUIPAGED. *adj.* [from *equipage.*] Accoutred; attended; with fine habits; with splendid retinue.

She forth issued with a goodly train
Of squires and ladies, *equipaged* well,
And entertained them right fairly, as befell. *Fairy Queen.*

EQUIPE'NDENCY. *n. s.* [*æquus* and *pendeo*, Latin.] The act of hanging in equipoise; not determined either way.

Doubtless the will of man, in the state of innocence, had an entire freedom, a perfect *equipendency* and indifference to either part of the contradiction, to stand or not to stand. *South.*

EQUI'PMENT. *n. s.* [from *equip.*]

1. The act of equipping or accoutering.

2. Accoutrement; equipage.

E'QUIPOISE. *n. s.* [*æquus*, Latin, and *poids*, French.] Equality of weight; equilibration; equality of force.

In the temperate zone of our life there are few bodies at such an *equipoise* of humours; but that the prevalency of some one indisposeth the spirits. *Glanv. Sceps. c.* 14.

EQUIPO'LLENCE. *n. s.* [*æquus* and *pollentia*, Latin.] Equality of force or power.

EQUIPO'LLENT. *adj.* [*æquipollens*, Lat.] Having equal power or force; equivalent.

Votary resolution is made *equipollent* to custom, even in matter of blood. *Bacon's Essays, Civil and Moral.*

EQUIPO'NDERANCE. } *n. s.* [*æquus* and *pondus*, Latin.] Equa-
EQUIPO'NDERANCY. } lity of weight; equipoise. *Dict.*

EQUIPO'NDERANT. *adj.* [*æquus* and *ponderans*, Latin.] Being of the same weight.

Their lungs may serve to render their bodies *equiponderant* to the water. *Ray on the Creation.*

A column of air, of any given diameter, is *equiponderant* to a column of quicksilver of between twenty-nine and thirty inches height. *Locke.*

To EQUIPO'NDERATE. *v. n.* [*æquus* and *pondero*, Latin.] To weigh equal to any thing.

The heaviness of any weight doth increase proportionably to its distance from the center: thus one pound A at D, will *equiponderate* unto two pounds at B, if the distance AD is double unto AB. *Wilkins's Mathem. Magick.*

EQUIPO'NDIOUS. *adj.* [*æquus* and *pondus*, Lat.] Equilibrated; equal on either part.

The Scepticks affected an indifferent *equipondious* neutrality, as the only means to their ataraxia. *Glanv. Sceps. c.* 27.

E'QUITABLE. *adj.* [*equitable*, French.]

1. Just; due to justice.

It seems but *equitable* to give the artists leave to name them as they please. *Boyle's Scept. Chym.*

2. Loving justice; candid; impartial.

E'QUITABLY. *adv.* [from *equitable.*] Justly; impartially.

E'QUITY. *n. s.* [*equite*, French; *æquitas*, Latin.]

1. Justice; right; honesty.

Foul subornation is predominant,
And *equity* exil'd your highness' land. *Shakesp. Henry* VI.

Christianity secures both the private interests of men and the publick peace, enforcing all justice and *equity*. *Tillotson.*

2. Impartiality.

Liking their own somewhat better than other mens, even because they are their own, they must in *equity* allow us to be like unto them in this affection. *Hooker, b.* iv. *s.* 13.

3. [In law.] The rules of decision observed by the court of Chancery.

EQUI'VALENCE. } *n. s.* [*æquus* and *valeo*, Latin.] Equality of
EQUI'VALENCY. } power or worth.

Must the servant of God be assured that which he nightly prays for shall be granted? Yes, either formally or by way of *equivalence*, either that or something better. *Hamm. Pract. Cat.*

That there is any *equivalence* or parity of worth betwixt the good we do to our brother, and the good we hope for from God, all good Protestants do deny. *Smalridge.*

Civil causes are equivalent unto criminal causes, and of as great importance; but that this *equivalency* only respects the careful and diligent admission of proofs. *Ayliffe's Parergon.*

To EQUI'VALENCE. *v. a.* [from the noun.] To equiponderate; to be equal to.

Whether the transgression of Eve seducing did not exceed Adam seduced, or whether the resistibility of his reason did

not

not *equivalence* the facility of her ſeduction, we ſhall refer to ſchoolmen. *Brown's Vulgar Errours, b.* i. *c.* i.

EQUI'VALENT. *adj.* [*æquus* and *valens*, Latin.]

1. Equal in value.

Things
Well nigh *equivalent*, and neighb'ring value,
By lot are parted; but the value, high heav'n, thy ſhare,
In equal balance laid with earth and hell,
Flings up the adverſe ſcale, and ſhuns proportion. *Prior.*

2. Equal in value, or in any excellence.

No fair to thine
Equivalent, or ſecond! which compell'd
Me thus, though importune perhaps, to come
And gaze, and worſhip thee. *Milton's Paradiſe Loſt, b.* ix.

3. Equal in force or power.

The dread of Iſrael's foes, who, with a ſtrength
Equivalent to angels, walk'd their ſtreets,
None offering fight. *Milton's Agoniſtes, l.* 342.

4. Of the ſame cogency or weight.

The conſideration of publick utility is, by very good advice, judged at the leaſt *equivalent* with the eaſier kind of neceſſity. *Hooker, b.* v. *ſ.* 9.

5. Of the ſame import or meaning.

The uſe of the word miniſter is brought down to the literal ſignification of it, a ſervant; for now to ſerve and to miniſter, ſervile and miniſterial, are terms *equivalent*. *South's Sermons.*

EQUI'VALENT. *n. ſ.* A thing of the ſame weight, dignity, or value.

The ſlave without a ranſom ſhall be ſent;
It reſts for you to make th' *equivalent*. *Dryden's Homer.*

Fancy a regular obedience to one law will be a full *equivalent* for their breach of another. *Rogers, Sermon* 13.

EQUI'VOCAL. *adj.* [*æquivocus*, Latin.]

1. Of doubtful ſignification; meaning different things; ſtanding for different notions.

Theſe ſentences to ſugar, or to gall,
Being ſtrong on both ſides, are *equivocal*. *Shakeſp. Othello.*

Words of different ſignifications, taken in general, are of an *equivocal* ſenſe; but being conſidered with all their particular circumſtances, they have their ſenſe reſtrained. *Stillingfleet.*

The greater number of thoſe who held this were miſguided by *equivocal* terms. *Swift.*

2. Uncertain; doubtful; happening different ways.

Equivocal generation is the production of plants without ſeed, or of inſects or animals without parents in the natural way of coition between male and female; which is now believed never to happen, but that all bodies are univocally produced. *Harr.*

My affirmation is, that there is no ſuch thing as *equivocal* or ſpontaneous generation; but that all animals are generated by animal parents of the ſame ſpecies with themſelves. *Ray.*

Thoſe half-learn'd witlings, num'rous in our iſle
As half-form'd inſects on the banks of Nile;
Unfiniſh'd things, one knows not what to call,
Their generation's ſo *equivocal*. *Pope's Eſſay on Criticiſm.*

EQUI'VOCAL. *n. ſ.* Ambiguity; word of doubtful meaning.

Shall two or three wretched *equivocals* have the force to corrupt us. *Dennis.*

EQUI'VOCALLY. *adv.* [from *equivocal*.]

1. Ambiguouſly; in a doubtful or double ſenſe.

Words abſtracted from their proper ſenſe and ſignification, loſe the nature of words, and are only *equivocally* ſo called. *South.*

2. By uncertain or irregular birth; by equivocal generation; by generation out of the ſtated order.

No inſect or animal did ever proceed *equivocally* from putrefaction, unleſs in miraculous caſes; as in Egypt by the Divine judgments. *Bentley's Sermons.*

EQUI'VOCALNESS. *n. ſ.* [from *equivocal*.] Ambiguity; double meaning.

Diſtinguiſh the *equivocalneſs* or latitude of the word, and then point out that determinate part which is the ground of my demonſtration. *Norris.*

To EQUI'VOCATE. *v. n.* [*æquivocatio*, Latin.] To uſe words of double meaning; to uſe ambiguous expreſſions; to mean one thing and expreſs another.

Not only Jeſuits can *equivocate*. *Dryden's Hind and Panth.*

My ſoul diſdain'd a promiſe;
But yet your falſe *equivocating* tongue,
Your looks, your eyes, your ev'ry motion promis'd:
But you are ripe in frauds, and learn'd in falſhoods. *Smith.*

EQUIVOCA'TION. *n. ſ.* [*æquivocatio*, Latin.] Ambiguity of ſpeech; double meaning.

Reproof is eaſily miſapplied, and, through *equivocation*, wreſted. *Hooker, b.* ii. *ſ.* 8.

I pull in reſolution, and begin
To doubt the *equivocation* of the fiend,
That lies like truth. *Shakeſpeare's Macbeth.*

EQUIVOCA'TOR. *n. ſ.* [from *equivocate*.] One who uſes ambiguous language; one who uſes mental reſervation.

Here's an *equivocator*, that could ſwear in both the ſcales againſt either ſcale; who committed treaſon, yet could not equivocate to heaven. *Shakeſpeare's Macbeth.*

ER, a ſyllable in the middle of names or places, comes by contraction from the Saxon *wara*, dwellers. *Gibſon's Camden.*

E'RA. *n. ſ.* [*æra*, Latin.] The account of time from any particular date or epoch.

From the bleſſings they beſtow
Our times are dated, and our *eras* move:
They govern, and enlighten all below,
As thou do'ſt all above. *Prior.*

ERADIA'TION. *n. ſ.* [*e* and *radius*, Latin.] Emiſſion of radiance.

God gives me a heart humbly to converſe with him, from whom alone are all the *eradiations* of true majeſty. *K. Charles.*

To ERA'DICATE. *v. a.* [*eradico*, Latin.]

1. To pull up by the root.

He ſuffereth the poiſon of Nubia to be gathered, and Aconite to be *eradicated*, yet this not to be moved. *Brown's Vulg. Err.*

2. To completely deſtroy; to end; to cut off.

If a gouty perſon can bring himſelf entirely to a milk diet, he may ſo change the whole juices of his body as to *eradicate* the diſtemper. *Arbuthnot on Diet.*

If vice cannot wholly be *eradicated*, it ought at leaſt to be confined to particular objects. *Swift's Examiner, N°.* 27.

ERADICA'TION. *n. ſ.* [from *eradicate*.]

1. The act of tearing up by the root; deſtruction; exciſion.
2. The ſtate of being torn up by the roots.

They affirm the roots of mandrakes give a ſhriek upon *eradication*, which is falſe below confutation. *Brown's Vulg. Err.*

ERA'DICATIVE. *adj.* [from *eradicate*.] That which cures radically; that which drives quite away.

To ERA'SE. *v. a.* [*raſer*, French.] To deſtroy; to exſcind; to expunge; to rub out.

The heads of birds, for the moſt part, are given *eraſed*; that is, plucked off. *Peacham on Blazoning.*

ERA'SEMENT. *n. ſ.* [from *eraſe*.]

1. Deſtruction; devaſtation.
2. Expunction; abolition.

ERE. *adv.* [ær, Saxon; *air*, Gothick; *eer*, Dutch. This word is ſometimes vitiouſly written *e'er*, as if from *ever*. It is likewiſe written *or* before *ever*, or and ær in Saxon being indiſcriminately written. Mr. *Lye*.]

1. Before; ſooner than.

Ere he would have hang'd a man for the getting a hundred baſtards, he would have paid for the nurſing a thouſand. *Shak.*

The lions brake all their bones in pieces *or ever* they came to the bottom of the den. *Daniel.*

Juſt trial, *ere* I merit
My exaltation without change or end. *Milt. Par. Regain'd.*

The mountain trees in diſtant proſpect pleaſe,
Ere yet the pine deſcended to the ſeas;
Ere ſails were ſpread new oceans to explore. *Dryden's Ovid.*

Our fruitful Nile
Flow'd *ere* the wonted ſeaſon. *Dryden's All for Love.*

The birds ſhall ceaſe to tune their ev'ning ſong,
The winds to breathe, the waving woods to move,
And ſtreams to murmur, *ere* I ceaſe to love. *Pope's Autumn.*

ERELO'NG. *adv.* [from *ere* and *long*.] Before a long time had elapſed. *Nec longum tempus.*

The wild horſe having enmity with the ſtag, came to a man to deſire aid, who mounted upon his back, and, following the ſtag, *erelong* ſlew him. *Spenſer on Ireland.*

The anger already began to paint revenge in many colours, *erelong* he had not only gotten pity but pardon. *Sidney.*

Nothing is laſting that is feigned: it will have another face than it had *erelong*. *Ben. Johnſon's Diſcoveries.*

They ſwim in joy,
Erelong to ſwim at large, and laugh, for which
The world *erelong* a world of tears muſt weep. *Milt. P. Loſt.*

I ſaw two ſtock-doves billing, and *erelong*
Will take the neſt. *Dryden's Virgil, Paſt.* 3.

It pleaſes me to think, that I who know ſo ſmall a portion of the works of the Creator, and with ſlow and painful ſteps creep up and down on the ſurface of this globe, ſhall *erelong* ſhoot away with the ſwiftneſs of imagination, and trace the ſprings of nature's operations. *Spectator, N°.* 635.

ERENO'W. *adv.* [from *ere* and *now*.] Before this time.

Ah, gentle ſoldiers, ſome ſhort time allow;
My father has repented him *erenow*. *Dryd. Conq. of Granad.*

Had the world eternally been, ſcience had been brought to perfection long *erenow*. *Cheyne's Phil. Prin.*

EREWHI'LE. } *adv.* [from *ere* and *while*.] Some time ago;
EREWHI'LES. } before a little while.

I am as fair now as I was *erewhile*:
Since night you lov'd me, yet ſince night you left me. *Shak.*

We ſit down to our meals, ſuſpect not the intruſion of armed uninvited gueſts, who *erewhiles*, we know, were wont to ſurpriſe us. *Decay of Piety.*

To ERE'CT. *v. a.* [*erectus*, Latin.]

1. To raiſe in a ſtrait line; to place perpendicularly to the horizon.
2. *To* ERECT *a Perpendicular*. To croſs one line by another at right angles.

3. To

3. To raise; to build.

Happier walls expect,
Which, wand'ring long, at last thou shalt *erect*. *Dryd. Virg.*

There are many monuments *erected* to benefactors to the republick. *Addison's Remarks on Italy.*

4. To establish anew; to settle.

Great difference there is between their proceedings, who *erect* a new commonwealth which is to have neither regiment nor religion the same that was, and theirs who only reform a decayed estate. *Hooker, b.* v. *s.* 17.

He suffers seventy-two distinct nations to be *erected* out of the first monarchy, under distinct governours. *Raleigh.*

5. To elevate; to exalt.

I, who am a party, am not to *erect* myself into a judge. *Dryden's Fables, Preface.*

I am far from pretending infallibility: that would be to *erect* myself into an apostle. *Locke on St. Paul's Epistles.*

6. To raise consequences from premises.

Men being too hasty to *erect* to themselves general notions and ill-grounded theories, find themselves deceived in their stock of knowledge. *Locke.*

Malebranche *erects* this proposition, of seeing all things in God, upon their ruin. *Locke.*

7. To animate; not to depress; to encourage.

Why should not hope
As much *erect* our thoughts, as fear deject them. *Denham.*

To Ere'ct. *v. n.* To rise upright.

The trefoil against rain swelleth in the stalk, and so standeth more upright; for by wet stalks do *erect*, and leaves bow down. *Bacon's Natural History*, Nº. 827.

Ere'ct. *adj.* [*erectus*, Latin.]

1. Upright; not leaning; not prone.

Birds, far from proneness, are almost *erect*; advancing the head and breast in progression, only prone in volitation. *Brown.*

Basil tells us, that the serpent went *erect* like man. *Brown.*

2. Directed upwards.

Vain were vows,
And plaints, and suppliant hands, to heav'n *erect*. *Phillips.*

3. Bold; confident; unshaken.

Let no vain fear thy gen'rous ardour tame;
But stand *erect*, and sound as loud as fame. *Granville.*

4. Vigorous; not depressed.

That vigilant and *erect* attention of mind, which in prayer is very necessary, is wasted or dulled. *Hooker, b.* v. *s.* 35.

Ere'ction. *n. s.* [from *erect.*]

1. The act of raising, or state of being raised upward.

We are to consider only the *erection* of the hills above the ordinary land. *Brerewood on Languages.*

2. The act of building or raising edifices.

The first thing which moveth them thus to cast up their poison, are certain solemnities usual at the first *erection* of churches. *Hooker, b.* v. *s.* 12.

Pillars were set up above one thousand four hundred and twenty-six years before the flood, counting Seth to be an hundred years old at the *erection* of them. *Raleigh's History.*

3. Establishment; settlement.

It must needs have a peculiar influence upon the *erection*, countinuance, and dissolution of every society. *South's Serm.*

4. Elevation; exaltation of sentiments.

Her peerless height my mind to high *erection* draws up. *Sidn.*

Ere'ctness. *n. s.* [from *erect.*] Uprightness of posture or form.

We take *erectness* strictly as Galen defined it: they only, sayeth he, have an erect figure, whose spine and thighbone are carried on right lines. *Brown's Vulgar Errours, b.* iv. *c.* 1.

E'REMITE. *n. s.* [*eremita*, Latin; ἐρημῖτης.] One who lives in a wilderness; one who lives in solitude; an hermit; a solitary.

Antonius the *eremite* findeth a fifth commodity not inferior to any of these four. *Raleigh's History of the World.*

And many more too long,
Embryoes and idiots, *eremites* and friars,
White, black, and grey, with all their trumpery. *Milton.*

Eremi'tical. *adj.* [from *eremite.*] Religiously solitary; leading the life of an hermit.

They have multitudes of religious orders, *eremitical* and cenobitical. *Stillingfleet.*

Erepta'tion. *n. s.* [*erepto*, Latin.] A creeping forth. *Bail.*

Ere'ption. *n. s.* [*ereptio*, Latin.] A snatching or taking away by force. *Bail.*

E'rgot. *n. s.* A sort of stub, like a piece of soft horn, about the bigness of a chesnut, which is placed behind and below the pastern joint, and is commonly hid under the tuft of the fetlock. *Farrier's Dict.*

Eri'ngo. *n. s.* Sea-holly, a plant.

Eri'stical. *adj.* [ἔρις.] Controversial; relating to dispute; containing controversies.

Erke. *n. s.* [eaɼᵹ, Saxon.] Idle; lazy; slothful. An old word.

For men therein should hem delite;
And of that dede be not *erke*,
But oft sithes haunt that werke. *Chaucer.*

E'rmelin. *n. s.* [*diminutive*, of *ermin*; *armelin*, French.] An ermine. See Ermine.

Silver skins,
Passing the hate spot *ermelins*. *Sidney, b.* ii.

E'RMINE. *n. s.* [*hermine*, French, from *armenius*, Latin.] An animal that is found in cold countries, and which very nearly resembles a weasle in shape; having a white pile, and the tip of the tail black, and furnishing a choice and valuable fur. The fellmongers and furriers put upon it little bits of Lombardy lambskin, which is noted for its shining black colour, the better to set off the whiteness of the ermine. *Trevoux.*

Ermine is the fur of a little beast, about the bigness of a weasel, called Mus Armenius; for they are found in Armenia. *Peacham on Blazoning.*

A lady's honour must be touch'd;
Which, nice as *ermines*, will not bear a soil. *Dryden.*
Fair *ermines*, spotless as the snows they press. *Thomson.*

E'rmined. *adj.* [from *ermine.*] Cloathed with ermine.

Arcadia's countess, here in *ermin'd* pride,
Is there Pastora by a fountain side. *Pope's Epistles.*

E'rne. } Do immediately flow from the Saxon eɲn, eaɲn, a
E'ron. } cottage, or place of retirement. *Gibson's Camden.*

To ERO'DE. *v. a.* [*erodo*, Latin.] To canker, or eat away; to corrode.

It hath been anciently received, that the sea-hare hath antipathy with the lungs, if it cometh near the body, and *erodeth* them. *Bacon's Natural History*, Nº. 983.

The blood, being too sharp or thin, *erodes* the vessel. *Wise.*

Eroga'tion. *n. s.* [*erogatio*, Latin.] The act of giving or bestowing; distribution.

Ero'sion. *n. s.* [*erosio*, Latin.]

1. The act of eating away.

2. The state of being eaten away; canker; corrosion.

As sea-salt is a sharp solid body, when taken in too great quantities, in a constant diet of salt meat, it breaks the vessels, produceth *erosions* of the solid parts, and all the symptoms of the sea-scurvy. *Arbuthnot on Aliments.*

To ERR. *v. n.* [*erro*, Latin.]

1. To wander; to ramble.

A storm of strokes, well meant, with fury flies,
And *errs* about their temples, ears, and eyes. *Dryden's Virg.*
The rains arise, and fires their warmth dispense;
And fix'd and *erring* stars dispose their influence. *Dryd. Virg.*

2. To miss the right way; to stray.

We have *erred* and strayed like lost sheep. *Common Prayer.*

3. To deviate from any purpose.

But *errs* not nature from this gracious end,
From burning suns when livid deaths descend. *Pope's Essays.*

4. To commit errours; to mistake.

It is a judgment maim'd and most imperfect,
That will confess perfection so could *err*,
Against all rules of nature. *Shakespeare's Othello.*

Do they not *err* that devise evil? *Prov.* xiv. 22.

Possibly the man may *err* in his judgment of circumstances, and therefore let him fear; but because it is not certain he is mistaken, let him not despair. *Taylor's Rule of living holy.*

Nor has it only been the heat of *erring* persons that has been thus mischievous, but sometimes men of right judgments have too much contributed to the breach. *Decay of Piety.*

The muses' friend, unto himself severe,
With silent pity looks on all that *err*. *Waller.*

He who from the reflected image of the sun in water would conclude of light and heat, could not *err* more grosly. *Cheyne.*

E'rrand. *n. s.* [æɲenꝺ, Saxon; *arend*, Danish.] A message; something to be told or done by a messenger; a mandate; a commission. It is generally used now only in familiar language.

Servants being commanded to go, shall stand still, 'till they have their *errand* warranted unto them. *Hooker, b.* ii. *s.* 8.

But hast thou done thy *errand* to Baptista?
—I told him that your father was in Venice. *Shakespeare.*

A quean! have I not forbid her my house? She comes of *errands*, does she? *Shakespeare's Merry Wives of Windsor.*

When he came, behold the captains of the host were sitting, and he said, I have an *errand* to thee, O captain. 2 *Kings* ix. 5.

From them I go
This uncouth *errand* sole. *Milton's Paradise Lost, b.* ii.

His eyes,
That run through all the heav'ns, or down to th' earth,
Bear his swift *errands*, over moist and dry,
O'er sea and land. *Milton's Paradise Lost, b.* iii. *l.* 652.

Well thou do'st to hide from common sight
Thy close intrigues, too bad to bear the light;
Nor doubt I, but the silver-footed dame,
Tripping from sea, on such an *errand* came. *Dryd. Homer.*

E'rrable. *adj.* [from *err.*] Liable to err; liable to mistake.

E'rrableness. *n. s.* [from *errable.*] Liableness to error; liableness to mistake.

We may infer, from the *errableness* of our nature, the reasonableness of compassion to the seduced. *Decay of Piety.*

Erra'nt. *adj.* [*errans*, Latin; *errant*, French.]

1. Wandering; roving; rambling. Particularly applied to an

an order of knights much celebrated in romances, who roved about the world in search of adventures.

There are just seven planets, or *errant* stars, in the lower orbs of heaven; but it is now demonstrable unto sense, that there are many more. *Brown's Vulgar Errours, b.* iv. *c.* 12.

Chief of domestick knights and *errant*,
Either for chattel or for warrant. *Hudibras.*

2. Vile; abandoned; completely bad. See ARRANT.

Any way, so thou wilt do it, good impertinence:
Thy company, if I slept not very well
A-nights, would make me an *errant* fool with questions.
Johnson's Catiline.

E'RRANTRY. *n. s.* [from *errant*]

1. An errant state; the condition of a wanderer.

After a short space of *errantry* upon the seas, he got safe back to Dunkirk. *Addison's Freeholder*, N°. 36.

2. The employment of a knight errant.

ERRA'TA. *n. s.* [Latin.] The faults of the printer inserted in the beginning or end of the book.

If he meet with faults, besides those that the *errata* take notice of, he will consider the weakness of the author's eyes. *Boyle.*

ERRA'TICK. *adj.* [*erraticus*, Latin.]

1. Wandering; uncertain; keeping no certain order; holding no established course.

The earth, and each *erratick* world,
Around the sun their proper center whirl'd,
Compose but one extended vast machine. *Blackm. Creation.*
Through the vast waves the dreadful wonders move,
Hence nam'd *erratick*. *Pope's Odyssey, b.* xii. *l.* 75.

2. Irregular; changeable.

They are incommoded with a slimy mattery cough, stink of breath, and an *erratick* fever. *Harvey on Consumptions.*

ERRA'TICALLY. *adv.* [from *erratical* or *erratick.*] Without rule; without any established method or order.

They come not forth in generations *erratical*, or different from each other; but in specifical and regular shapes.
Brown's Vulgar Errours, b. ii. *c.* 6.

E'RRHINE. *n. s.* [ἔῤῥινα.] Snuffed up the nose; occasioning sneezing.

We see sage or betony bruised, sneezing powder, and other powders or liquors, which the physicians call *errhines*, put into the nose to draw phlegm and water from the head.
Bacon's Natural History, N°. 38.

ERRO'NEOUS. *adj.* [from *erro*, Latin.]

1. Wandering; unsettled.

They roam
Erroneous and disconsolate, themselves
Accusing, and their chiefs improvident
Of military chance. *Phillips.*

This circle, by being placed here, stopped much of the *erroneous* light, which otherwise would have disturbed the vision. *Newton's Opt.*

Unblam'd abundance crown'd the royal board,
What time this done rever'd her prudent lord;
Who now, so heav'n decrees, is doom'd to mourn,
Bitter constraint! *erroneous* and forlorn. *Pope's Odyssey, b.* i.

2. Irregular; wandering from the right road.

If the vessels, instead of breaking, yield, it subjects the person to all the inconveniencies of *erroneous* circulation; that is, when the blood strays into the vessels destined to carry serum or lymph. *Arbuthnot on Aliments.*

3. Mistaking; misled by errour.

Thou art far from destroying the innocent with the guilty, and the *erroneous* with the malicious. *King Charles.*

There is the *erroneous* as well as the rightly informed conscience. *South's Sermons.*

4. Mistaken; not conformable to truth.

Their whole counsel is in this point utterly condemned, as having either proceeded from the blindness of those times, or from negligence, or from desire of honour and glory, or from an *erroneous* opinion that such things might be for a while.
Hooker, b. iv. *s.* 14.

A wonderful *erroneous* observation that walketh about, is commonly received, contrary to all the true account of time and experience. *Bacon's War with Spain.*

The phænomena of light have been hitherto explained by supposing that they arise from new modifications of the rays, which is an *erroneous* supposition. *Newton's Opt.*

ERRO'NEOUSLY. *adv.* [from *erroneous.*] By mistake; not rightly.

The minds of men are *erroneously* persuaded, that it is the will of God to have those things done which they fancy. *Hook.*

I could not discover the lenity and favour of this sentence; but conceived it, perhaps *erroneously*, rather to be rigorous than gentle. *Gulliver's Travels.*

ERRO'NEOUSNESS. *n. s.* [from *erroneous.*] Physical falsehood; inconformity to truth.

The phænomena may be explained by his hypothesis, whereof he demonstrates the truth, together with the *erroneousness* of ours. *Boyle's Spring of the Air.*

E'RROUR. *n. s.* [*error*, Latin.]

1. Mistake; involuntary deviation from truth.

Errour is a mistake of our judgment giving assent to that which is not true. *Locke.*

Oh, hateful *errour*, melancholy's child!
Why do'st thou shew to the apt thoughts of men,
The things that are not? *Shakespeare's Jul. Cæsar.*

2. A blunder; an act or assertion in which a mistake is committed.

In religion,
What damned *errour*, but some sober brow
Will bless it. *Shakespeare's Merchant of Venice.*
He look'd like nature's *errour*, as the mind
And body were not of a piece design'd,
But made for two, and by mistake in one were join'd. *Dryd.*

3. Roving excursion; irregular course.

What brought you living to the Stygian state?
Driv'n by the winds and *errours* of the sea,
Or did you heav'n's superiour doom obey? *Dryden's Æn.*

4. [In theology.] Sin.

Blood he offered for himself, and for the *errours* of the people. *Heb.* ix. 7.

5. [In law, more especially in our common law.] An errour in pleading, or in the process; and the writ, which is brought for remedy of this oversight, is called a writ of errour, which lies to redress false judgment given in any court of record. *Cowel.*

ERST. *adv.* [*erst*, German; ærest, Saxon.]

1. First.

Sir knight, if knight thou be,
Abandon this forestalled place at *erst*,
For fear of further harm, I counsel thee. *Spens. Fai. Queen.*

2. At first; in the beginning.

Fame that her high worth to raise,
Seem'd *erst* so lavish and profuse,
We may justly now accuse
Of detraction from her praise. *Milton.*

3. Once; when time was.

He taught us *erst* the heifer's tail to view. *Gay.*
The future few or more, howe'er they be,
Were destin'd *erst*, nor can by fate's decree
Be now cut off. *Prior.*

4. Formerly; long ago.

5. Before; till then; till now.

As signal now in low dejected state,
As *erst* in highest, behold him. *Milton's Agonistes, l.* 338.
Opener mine eyes,
Dim *erst*; dilated spirits, ampler heart. *Milton's Par. Lost.*

The Rhodians, who *erst* thought themselves at great quiet, were now overtaken with a sudden and unexpected mischief.
Knolles's History of the Turks.

ERUBE'SCENCE. } *n. s.* [*erubescentia*, Latin.] The act of growing red; redness.
ERUBE'SCENCY. }

ERUBESCENT. *adj.* [*erubescens*, Latin.] Reddish; somewhat red; inclining to redness.

To ERU'CT. *v. a.* [*eructo*, Latin.] To belch; to break wind from the stomach.

ERUCTA'TION. *n. s.* [from *eruct.*]

1. The act of belching.

2. Belch; the matter vented from the stomach.

The signs of the functions of the stomach being depraved, are *eructations*, either with the taste of the aliment, acid, inodorous, or fetid. *Arbuthnot.*

3. Any sudden burst of wind or matter.

Thermæ, are hot springs, or fiery *eructations*; such as burst forth of the earth during earthquakes. *Woodward's Nat. Hist.*

ERUDI'TION. *n. s.* [*eruditio*, Latin.] Learning; knowledge obtained by study and instruction.

Fam'd be thy tutor, and thy parts of nature;
Thrice fam'd beyond all *erudition*. *Shakespeare.*

The earl was of good *erudition*, having been placed at study in Cambridge very young. *Wotton.*

To your experience in state affairs you have also joined no vulgar *erudition*, which all your modesty is not able to conceal; for to understand critically the delicacies of Horace, is a height to which few of our noblemen have arrived. *Dryden.*

Some gentlemen, abounding in their university *erudition*, are apt to fill their sermons with philosophical terms and notions, metaphysical. *Swift.*

ERU'GINOUS. *adj.* [*æruginosus*, Latin.] Partaking of the substance and nature of copper.

Agues depend upon a corrupt incinerated melancholy, or upon an adust stibial or *eruginous* sulphur. *Harvey on Consumpt.*

Copperas is a rough and acrimonious kind of salt, drawn out of ferreous and *eruginous* earths, partaking chiefly of iron and copper; the blue of copper, the green of iron. *Browne.*

ERU'PTION. *n. s.* [*eruptio*, Latin.]

1. The act of breaking or bursting forth from any confinement.

In part of Media there are *eruptions* of flames out of plains. *Bacon's Natural History*, N°. 361.

Finding themselves pent in by the exterior earth, they pressed with violence against that arch, to make it yield and give

give way to their dilatation and *eruption*. *Burnet's Theory.*

2. Burst; emission.

Upon a signal given the *eruption* began; fire and smoak, mixed with several unusual prodigies and figures, made their appearance. *Addison's Guardian*, N°. 103.

3. Sudden excursion of an hostile kind.

Thither, if but to pry, shall be perhaps
Our first *eruption*, thither or elsewhere;
For this infernal pit shall never hold
Celestial spirits in bondage. *Milton's Paradise Lost*, *b.* i.
Such command we had,
To see that none thence issu'd forth a spy,
Or enemy, while God was in his work;
Lest he, incens'd at such *eruption* bold,
Destruction with creation might have mix'd. *Milt. P. Lost.*

4. Violent exclamation.

It did not run out in voice or indecent *eruptions*, but filled the soul, as God does the universe, silently and without noise. *South's Sermons.*

5. Efflorescence; pistules.

Diseased nature oftentimes breaks forth
In strange *eruptions*. *Shakespeare's Henry* IV. *p.* i.

An *eruption* of humours, in any part, is not cured merely by outward applications, but by alterative medicines. *Government of the Tongue*, *s.* 6.

Unripe fruits are apt to occasion foul *eruptions* on the skin. *Arbuthnot on Aliments.*

ERU'PTIVE. *adj.* [*eruptus*, Latin.] Bursting forth.

'Tis listening fear, and dumb amazement all,
When to the startled eye the sudden glance
Appears far south *eruptive* through the cloud. *Thomson.*

ERYSI'PELAS. *n. s.* [ἐρυσίπελας.]

An *erysipelas* is generated by a hot serum in the blood, and affects the superficies of the skin with a shining pale red, or citron colour, without pulsation or circumscribed tumour, spreading from one place to another. *Wiseman's Surgery.*

ESCALA'DE. *n. s.* [French.] The act of scaling the walls of a fortification.

In Geneva one meets with the ladders, petard, and other utensils, which were made use of in their famous *escalade*. *Add.*

E'SCALOP. *n. s.* A shellfish, whose shell is regularly indented.

The shells of those cockles, *escalops*, and periwinkles, which have greater gravity, were enclosed in the strata of stone. *Woodward's Natural History.*

To ESCA'PE. *v. a.* [*echaper*, French.]

1. To obtain exemption from; to obtain security from; to fly; to avoid.

Since we cannot *escape* the pursuit of passions, and perplexity of thoughts, there is no way left but to endeavour all we can either to subdue or divert them. *Temple.*

Had David died sooner, how much trouble had he *escaped*, which by living he endured in the rebellion of his son. *Wake.*

2. To pass unobserved.

Men are blinded with ignorance and errour: many things may *escape* them, and in many things they may be deceived. *Hooker*, *b.* ii. *s.* 7.

'Tis still the same, although their airy shape
All but a quick poetick sight *escape*. *Denham.*

The reader finds out those beauties of propriety in thought and writing, which *escaped* him in the tumult and hurry of representing. *Dryden's Don Sebastian*, *Pref.*

To ESCA'PE. *v. n.* To fly; to get out of danger.

Benhadad, the king of Syria, *escaped* on horse. *Chronicles.*

They *escaped* all safe to land. *Acts* xxvii. 44.

The sinner shall not *escape* with his spoil, and the patience of the godly shall not be frustrated. *Ecclus.* xvi. 13.

Escape for thy life; look not behind thee, neither stay thou in all the plain: *escape* to the mountain, lest thou be consumed. *Gen.* xix. 17.

Whoso pleaseth God shall *escape* from her, but the sinner shall be taken by her. *Eccl.* vii. 26.

There is no woman's gown big enough for him; otherwise he might put on a hat, a muffler, and a kerchief, and so *escape*. *Shakes. Merry Wives of Windsor.*

To convince us that there was no way to *escape* by climbing up to the mountains, he assures us that the highest were all covered. *Woodward's Natural History.*

Laws are not executed, men of virtue are disgraced, and murderers *escape*. *Watts's Logick.*

ESCA'PE. *n. s.* [from the verb.]

1. Flight; the act of getting out of danger.

I would hasten my *escape* from the windy storm and tempest. *Ps.* lv. 7.

He enjoyed neither his *escape* nor his honour long; for he was hewn in pieces. *Hayward.*

Men of virtue have had extraordinary *escapes* out of such dangers as have enclosed them, and which have seemed inevitable. *Addison's Guardian*, N°. 117.

2. Excursion; sally.

We made an *escape*, not so much to seek our own,
As to be instruments of your safety. *Denham's Sophy.*

3. [In law.] Violent or privy evasion out of some lawful restraint. For example, if the sheriff, upon a capias directed unto him, takes a person, and endeavours to carry him to gaol, and he in the way, either by violence or by flight, breaks from him, this is called an escape. *Cowel.*

4. Excuse; subterfuge; evasion.

St. Paul himself did not despise to remember whatsoever he found agreeable to the word of God among the heathen, that he might take from them all *escape* by way of ignorance. *Ral.*

5. Sally; flight; irregularity.

Thousand '*scapes* of wit,
Make thee the father of their idle dreams,
And rack thee in their fancies. *Shakesp. Meas. for Measure.*
Loose '*scapes* of love. *Milton.*

6. Oversight; mistake.

In transcribing there would be less care taken, as the language was less understood, and so the *escapes* less subject to observation. *Brerewood on Languages.*

ESCA'RGATOIRE. *n. s.* [French.] A nursery of snails.

At the Capuchins I saw *escargatoires*, which I took the more notice of, because I do not remember to have met with any thing of the same kind in other countries. It is a square place boarded in, and filled with a vast quantity of large snails that are esteemed excellent food, when they are well dressed. *Add.*

ESCHALO'T. *n. s.* [French.] Pronounced *shallot*.

Eschalots are now from France become an English plant, being increased and managed after the same manner as garlick; only they are to be set earlier, because they spring sooner, and taken up as soon as the leaves begin to wither, lest either they rot there, or the Winter kills them. They give a fine relish to most sauces, and the breath of those that eat them is not offensive to others. *Mortimer's Husbandry.*

E'SCHAR. *n. s.* [ἐσχάρα.] A hard crust or scar made by hot applications.

When issues are made, or bones exposed, the *eschar* should be cut out immediately. *Sharp's Surgery.*

ESCHA'ROTICK. *adj.* [from *eschar*.] Caustick; having the power to sear or burn the flesh.

An eschar was made by the catharetick, which we thrust off, and continued the use of *escharoticks*. *Wiseman's Surgery.*

Escaraticks applied of ash-ashes, or blistering plaister. *Floyer.*

ESCHE'AT. *n. s.* [from the French *eschevir*.] Any lands, or other profits, that fall to a lord within his manor by forfeiture, or the death of his tenant, dying without heir general or especial. *Escheat* is also used sometimes for the place in which the king, or other lord, has escheats of his tenants. Thirdly, escheat is used for a writ, which lies where the tenant, having estate of fee-simple in any lands or tenements holden of a superiour lord, dies seised, without heir general or especial; for, in this case, the lord brings this writ against him that possesses the lands after the death of his tenant, and shall thereby recover them. *Cowel.*

If the king's ordinary courts of justice do not extend to protect the people, if he have no certain revenue or *escheats*, I cannot justly say that such a country is wholly conquered. *Davies on Ireland.*

To ESCHE'AT. *v. a.* [from the noun.] To fall to the lord of the manor by forfeiture, or for want of heirs.

In the last general wars there, I knew many good freeholders executed by martial law, whose lands were thereby saved to their heirs, which should have otherwise *escheated* to her majesty. *Spenser on Ireland.*

He would forbear to alienate any of the forfeited *escheated* lands in Ireland, which should accrue to the crown by reason of this rebellion. *Clarendon.*

ESCHE'ATOR. *n. s.* [from *escheat*.] An officer that observes the escheats of the king in the county whereof he is escheator, and certifies them into the Exchequer. *Cowel.*

At a Bartholomew fair at London an *escheator* of the city arrested a clothier, and seised his goods. *Camden's Remains.*

To ESCHE'W. *v. a.* [*eschevir*, old French.] To fly; to avoid; to shun; to decline. A word almost obsolete.

She was like a young fawn, who, coming in the wind of the hunters, doth not know whether it be a thing or no to be *eschewed*. *Sidney*, *b.* ii.

So let us, which this change of weather view,
Change eke our minds, and former lives amend;
The old year's sins forepast let us *eschew*,
And fly the faults with which we did offend. *Spenser.*

He who obeys, destruction shall *eschew*;
A wise man knows both when and what to do. *Sandys.*

Of virtue and vice the obligations are such, that men are universally to practise the one and *eschew* the other. *Atterbury's Sermons*, *Preface.*

ESCHU'TCHEON. *n. s.* The shield of the family; the picture of the ensigns armorial.

Eschutcheon is a French word, from the Latin *scutum*, leather; and hence cometh our English word buckler, lere in the old Saxon signifying leather, and buck or bock a buck or stag; of whose skins, quilted close together with horn or hard wood, the ancient Britons made their shields. *Peacham.*

We

There be now, for martial encouragement, some degrees and orders of chivalry, and some remembrance perhaps upon the *eschutcheon*. *Bacon's Essays.*

We will pass over the *eschutcheons* of the tribes of Israel, as they are usually described in the maps of Canaan. *Brown.*

ESCO'RT. *n. s.* [*escort*, French.] Convoy; guard from place to place.

To ESCO'RT. *v. a.* [*escorter*, French.] To convoy; to guard from place to place.

ESCO'T. *n. s.* [French.] A tax paid in boroughs and corporations towards the support of the community, which is called scot and lot.

To ESCO'T. *v. a.* [from the noun.] To pay a man's reckoning; to support.

What, are they children? Who maintains them? How are they *escoted*? *Shakespeare's Hamlet.*

ESCO'UT. *n. s.* [*escouter*, French.] Listeners or spies; persons sent for intelligence.

They were well entrenched, having good *escout* abroad, and sure watch within. *Hayward.*

ESCRI'TOIR. *n. s.* [French.] A box with all the implements necessary for writing.

ESCU'AGE. *n. s.* [from *escu*, French, a shield.]

Escuage, that is service of the shield, is either uncertain or certain. *Escuage* uncertain is likewise twofold: first, where the tenant by his tenure is bound to follow his lord, going in person to the king's wars against his enemies, either himself, or to send a sufficient man in his place, at his cost, so many days as were agreed upon between the lord and his first tenant at the granting of the fee; and the days of such service seem to have been rated by the quantity of the land so holden: as, if it extend to a whole knight's fee, then the tenant was bound thus to follow his lord forty days. A knight's fee was so much land as, in those days, was accounted a sufficient living for a a knight; and that was six hundred and eighty acres as some think, or eight hundred as others, or 15 *l. per Annum.* Sir Thomas Smith saith that *census equestris* is 40 *l.* revenue in free lands. If the law extend but to half a knight's fee, then the tenant is bound to follow his lord, as above is said, but twenty days. The other kind of this *escuage* uncertain is called castleward, where the tenant by his land is bound, either by himself or by some other, to defend a castle as often as it shall come to his course. *Escuage* certain is where the tenant is set at a certain sum of money, to be paid in lieu of such uncertain services: as that a man yearly pay for a knight's fee twenty shillings; for half his fee, ten shillings, or some like rate. *Cowel.*

E'SCULENT. *adj.* [*esculentus*, Latin.] Good for food; eatable.

I knew a man that would fast five days; but the same man used to have continually a great wisp of herbs that he smelled on, and some *esculent* herbs of strong scent, as garlick. *Bacon.*

E'SCULENT. *n. s.* Something fit for food.

This cutting off the leaves in plants, where the root is the *esculent*, as radish and parsnips, it will make the root the greater, and so it will do to the heads of onions; and where the fruit is the *esculent*, by strengthening the root, it will make the fruit also the greater. *Bacon's Natural History*, N°. 474.

ESPA'LIER. *n. s.* Trees planted and cut so as to join.

Plant your fairest tulips in places of shelter, and under *espaliers*. *Evelyn's Kalendar.*

Behold Villario's ten years toil complete,
His arbours darken, his *espaliers* meet. *Pope, Epistle* iv.

ESPA'RCET. *n. s.* A kind of saint-foin, and by some judged to be the same. *Mortimer's Husbandry.*

ESPE'CIAL. *adj.* [*specialis*, Latin.] Principal; chief.

They had th' *especial* engines been, to rear
His fortunes up. *Daniel's Civil War.*

ESPE'CIALLY. *adv.* [from *especial.*] Principally; chiefly; particularly; in an uncommon degree above any other.

I somewhat marvel, that they *especially* should think it absurd to oppose church government, a plain matter of action, unto matter of faith, who know that themselves divide the gospel into doctrine and discipline. *Hooker, b.* iii. *s.* 3.

Would you proceed *especially* against Caius Marcius? *Shak.*

This delight they take in doing of mischief, whereby I mean spoiling of any thing to no purpose; but more *especially* the pleasure they take to put any thing to pain that is capable of it, I cannot persuade myself to be any other than a foreign and introduced disposition. *Locke.*

Providence hath planted in all men a natural desire and curiosity of knowing things to come; and such things *especially* as concern our particular happiness, or the general fate of mankind. *Burnet's Theory of the Earth.*

ESPE'RANCE. *n. s.* [French.] Hope.

To be worst,
The lowest, most dejected things of fortune,
Stands still in *esperance*, lives not in fear. *Shakesp. K. Lear.*
Yet there is a credence in my heart,
An *esperance* so obstinately strong,
That doth invert th' attest of eyes and ears. *Shakespeare.*

ESPI'AL. *n. s.* [French, from *espier.*] A spy; a scout; one sent to bring intelligence.

Those four garrisons, issuing forth at such convenient times as they shall have intelligence, or *espial* upon the enemy, will drive him from one side to another. *Spenser on Ireland.*

As he march'd along,
By your *espials* were discovered
Two mightier troops. *Shakesp.*
'*Spials* have informed me,
The English in the suburbs close entrench'd,
Went through a secret grate. *Shakesp. Hen.* VI.

She had some secret *espials* to look abroad for graceful youths, to make Plantagenets. *Bac. H.* VII.

ESPLANADE. *n. s.* [French.] In fortification, the same with the glacis of the counterscarpe originally; but now it is taken for the empty space between the glacis of a citadel and the first houses of the town. *Harris.*

ESPO'USALS. *n. s.* without a singul. [*sponsalia*, Latin; *espous*, French.] The act of contracting or affiancing a man and woman to each other; the act or ceremony of betrothing.

ESPO'USAL. *adj.* Used in the act of espousing or betrothing.

The ambassador put his leg, stript naked to the knee, between the *espousal* sheets; that the ceremony might amount to a consummation. *Bacon's Henry* VII.

To ESPO'USE. *v. a.* [*espouser*, French.]

1. To contract or betroth to another.

Deliver me my wife Michal, which I *espoused* to me. 2 *Sa.*

He had received him as a suppliant, protected him as a person fled for refuge, and *espoused* him with his kinswoman. *Bac.*

2. To marry; to wed.

Lavinia will I make my emperess,
And in the sacred Pantheon her *espouse*. *Shakesp. Tit. Andr.*
Here, in close recess,
With flow'rs, garlands, and sweet smelling herbs,
Espoused Eve deck'd first her nuptial bed. *Milton's Par. Lost.*
They soon *espous'd*; for they with ease were join'd,
Who were before contracted in the mind. *Dryden.*
If her sire approves,
Let him *espouse* her to the peer she loves. *Pope's Odyssey, b.* ii.

3. To adopt; to take to himself.

In gratitude unto the duke of Bretagne, for his former favours, he *espoused* that quarrel, and declared himself in aid of the duke. *Bacon's Henry* VII.

4. To maintain; to defend.

Their gods did not only interest themselves in the event of wars, but also *espoused* the several parties in a visible corporeal descent. *Dryden's Juvenal, Dedication.*

The city, army, court, *espouse* my cause. *Dryd. Sp. Fry.*

Men *espouse* the well-endowed opinions in fashion, and then seek arguments either to make good their beauty, or varnish over their deformity. *Locke.*

The righteousness of the best cause may be over balanced by the iniquities of those that *espouse* it. *Smalridge's Sermons.*

The cause of religion and goodness, which is the cause of God, is ours by descent, and we are doubly bound to *espouse* it. *Atterbury's Sermons.*

To E'SPY. *v. a.* [*espier*, French.]

1. To see a thing at a distance.

2. To discover a thing intended to be hid.

He who before he was *espied* was afraid, after being perceived was ashamed, now being hardly rubbed upon, left both fear and shame, and was moved to anger. *Sidney.*

Few there are of so weak capacity but publick evils they easily *espy*; fewer so patient as not to complain, when the grievous inconveniencies thereof doth work sensible smart. *Hook.*

3. To see unexpectedly.

And as one of them opened his sack, he *espied* his money. *Gen.* xl. 27.

4. To discover as a spy.

Moses sent me to *espy* out the land, and I brought him word again. *Jos.* xiv. 7.

To ESPY'. *v. n.* To watch; to look about.

Stand by the way and *espy*; ask him that fleeth what is done. *Jer.* xlvii. 19.

ESQU'IRE. *n. s.* [*escuer*, French.] See SQUIRE.

1. The armour-bearer or attendant on a knight.

2. A title of dignity, and next in degree below a knight. Those to whom this title is now of right due, are all the younger sons of noblemen, and their heirs male for ever; the four esquires of the king's body; the eldest sons of all baronets; so also of all knights of the Bath, and knights batchelors, and their heirs male in the right line; those that serve the king in any worshipful calling, as the serjeant chirurgeon, serjeant of the ewry, master cook, &c. such as are created esquires by the king with a collar of S. S. of silver, as the heralds and serjeants at arms. The chief of some ancient families are likewise esquires by prescription; those that bear any superior office in the commonwealth, as high sheriff of any county, who retains the title of esquire during his life, in respect of the great trust he has had of the *posse comitatus*. He who is a justice of the peace has it during the time he is in commission, and no longer, if not otherwise qualified to bear it. Utter barristers, in the acts of parliament for poll-money, were ranked among esquires. *Blount.*

What are our English dead?
—Sir Richard Ketley, Davy Gam *esquire*. *Shakesf. Hen.* V.

To ESSA'Y. *v. a.* [*essayer*, French.]

1. To attempt; to try; to endeavour.

While I this unexampled task *essay*,
Pass awful gulphs, and beat my painful way,
Celestial dove, divine assistance bring. *Blackmore's Creation.*
No conquest she, but o'er herself desir'd;
No arts *essay'd*, but not to be admir'd. *Pope, Epistle* 5.

2. To make experiment of.

3. To try the value and purity of metals.

The standard in our mint being now settled, the rules and methods of *essaying* suited to it should remain unvariable. *Locke.*

E'SSAY. *n. s.* [from the verb. The accent is used on either syllable.]

1. Attempt; endeavour.

Fruitless our hopes, though pious our *essays*;
Your's to preserve a friend, and mine to praise. *Smith.*

2. A loose sally of the mind; an irregular indigested piece; not a regular and orderly composition.

My *essays*, of all my other works, have been most current. *Bac.*

Yet modestly he does his work survey,
And calls his finish'd poem an *essay*. *Poem to Roscommon.*

3. A trial; an experiment.

He wrote this but as an *essay*, or taste of my virtue. *Shak.*

Repetitions wear us into a liking of what possibly, in the first *essay*, displeased us. *Locke.*

4. First taste of any thing; first experiment.

Translating the first of Homer's Iliads, I intended as an *essay* to the whole work. *Dryden's Fables, Preface.*

E'SSENCE. *n. s.* [*essentia*, Latin.]

1. Essence is but the very nature of any being, whether it be actually existing or no: a rose in Winter has an *essence*; in Summer it has existence also. *Watts's Logick.*

One thinks the soul is air; another, fire;
Another, blood diffus'd about the Heart;
Another saith, the elements conspire,
And to her *essence* each doth give a part. *Davies.*

I could wish the nature of a spirit were more unknown to me than it is, that I might believe its existence, without meddling at all with its *essence*. *More's Divine Dialogues.*

He wrote the nature of things upon their names: he could view *essences* in themselves, and read forms without the comment of their respective properties. *South's Sermons.*

2. Formal existence; that which makes any thing to be what it is.

The visible church of Jesus is one in outward profession of those things, which supernaturally appertain to the very *essence* of Christianity, and are necessarily required in every particular Christian man. *Hooker, b.* iii. *s.* 1.

3. Existence; the quality of being.

In such cogitations have I stood, with such a darkness and heaviness of mind, that I might have been persuaded to have resigned my very *essence*. *Sidney.*

4. Being; existent person.

As far as gods, and heav'nly *essences*
Can perish. *Milton's Paradise Lost, b.* i. *l.* 138.

5. Species of existent being.

Here be four of you, as differing as the four elements; and yet you are friends: as for Eupolis, because he is temperate, and without passion, he may be the fifth *essence*. *Bacon.*

6. Constituent substance.

For spirits, when they please,
Can either sex assume, or both; so soft
And uncompounded is their *essence* pure;
Not ty'd or manacled with joint or limb. *Milton's Pa. Lost.*

7. The cause of existence. This sense is not proper.

She is my *essence*; and I leave to be,
If I be not by her fair influence
Foster'd, illumin'd, cherish'd, kept alive. *Shakespeare.*

8. [In medicine.] The chief properties or virtues of any simple, or composition collected in a narrow compass.

9. Perfume; odour; scent.

Our humble province is to 'tend the fair;
To save the powder from too rude a gale,
Nor let th' imprison'd *essences* exhale. *Pope's Rape of the Lock.*

To E'SSENCE. *v. a.* [from *essence*.] To perfume; to scent.

The husband rails, from morning to night, at *essenced* fops and tawdry courtiers. *Addison's Spectator*, N°. 128.

ESSE'NTIAL. *adj.* [*essentialis*, Latin.]

1. Necessary to the constitution or existence of any thing.

The discipline of our church, although it be not an *essential* part of our religion, should not be rashly altered, as the very substance of our religion will be interested in it. *Bacon.*

From that original of doing good, that is *essential* to the infinite being of our Creator, we have an excellent copy transcribed. *Spratt's Sermon.*

This power cannot be innate and *essential* to matter; and if it be not *essential*, it is consequently most manifest it could never supervene to it, unless impressed and infused into it by an immaterial and divine power. *Bentley's Sermons.*

A great minister puts you a case, and asks your opinion; but conceals an *essential* circumstance, upon which the whole weight of the matter turns. *Swift.*

And if each system in gradation roll,
Alike *essential* to th' amazing whole,
The least confusion but in one, not all
That system only, but the whole must fall. *Pope.*

2. Important in the highest degree; principal.

Judgment's more *essential* to a general,
Than courage. *Denham's Sophy.*

3. Pure; highly rectified; subtilly elaborated; extracted so as to contain all the virtues of its elemental parts contracted into a narrow compass.

The juice of the seed is an *essential* oil or balm, designed by nature to preserve the seed from corruption. *Arbuthnot.*

ESSE'NTIAL. *n. s.*

1. Existence; being.

His utmost ire to the height enrag'd,
Will either quite consume us, or reduce
To nothing this *essential*. *Milton's Paradise Lost, b.* ii.

2. Nature; first or constituent principles.

The plague of sin has even altered his nature, and eaten into his very *essentials*. *South's Sermons.*

3. The chief point; that which is in any respect of great importance.

ESSE'NTIALLY. *adv.* [*essentialiter*, Latin.] By the constitution of nature.

He that loves himself,
Hath not *essentially*, but by circumstance,
The name of valour. *Shakespeare's Henry* VI. *p.* ii.

Body and spirit are *essentially* divided, though not locally distant. *Glanville.*

All sin *essentially* is, and must be, mortal. *South's Sermons.*

Knowledge is that which, next to virtue, truly and *essentially* raises one man above another. *Addison's Guardian.*

ESSO'INE. *n. s.* [of the French *essonie*, or *exonnie*.]

1. He that has his presence forborn or excused upon any just cause; as sickness.

2. Allegment of an excuse for him that is summoned, or sought for, to appear and answer to an action real, or to perform suit to a court-baron, upon just cause of absence. *Cowel.*

3. Excuse; exemption.

From every work he challenged *essoin*,
For contemplation sake; yet otherwise
His life he led in lawless riotise. *Fairy Queen, b.* i. *c.* 4.

To ESTA'BLISH. *v. a.* [*etablir*, French.]

1. To settle firmly; to fix unalterably.

He may *establish* thee to-day for a people unto himself. *Deut.*

Upon the throne of David, and upon his kingdom, to order it, and to *establish* it with judgment and with justice. *Is.* ix.

I will *establish* my covenant with him for an everlasting covenant, *Gen.* xvii. 19.

The Normans never obtained this kingdom by such a right of conquest, as did or might alter the *established* laws of the kingdom. *Hale's Common Law of England.*

2. To settle in any privilege or possession; to confirm.

Soon after the rebellion broke out, the Presbyterian sect was *established* in all its forms by an ordinance of the lords and commons. *Swift.*

3. To make firm; to ratify.

Every vow, and every binding oath to afflict the soul, her husband may *establish* it, or her husband may make it void. *Num.*

4. To fix or settle in an opinion.

So were the churches *established* in the faith. *Acts* xvi. 5.

5. To form or model.

He appointed in what manner his family should be *established*. *Clarendon, b.* viii.

6. To found; to build firmly; to fix immoveably. A sense not in use.

For he hath founded it upon the seas, and *established* it upon the floods. *Ps.* xxiv. 12.

7. To make a settlement of any inheritance. A sense not in use.

We will *establish* our estate upon
Our eldest Malcolm, whom we name hereafter
The prince of Cumberland. *Shakespeare's Macbeth.*

ESTA'BLISHMENT. *n. s.* [from *establish*; *etablissement*, French.]

1. Settlement; fixed state.

All happy peace, and goodly government,
Is settled there in sure *establishment*. *Fairy Queen, b.* ii. *c.* 11.

2. Confirmation of something already done; ratification.

He had not the act penned by way of recognition of right; as, on the other side, he avoided to have it by new law; but chose rather a kind of middle way, by way of *establishment*. *Bacon's Henry* VII.

3. Settled regulation; form; model of a government or family.

Now come unto that general reformation, and bring in that *establishment* by which all men should be contained in duty. *Spenser's State of Ireland.*

4. Foundation; fundamental principle; settled law.

The sacred order to which you belong, and even the *establishment* on which it subsists, have often been struck at; but in vain. *Atterbury's Sermons.*

5. Allowance;

5. Allowance; income; salary.

His excellency, who had the sole disposal of the emperor's revenue, might easily provide against that evil, by gradually lessening your *establishment*. *Gulliver's Travels.*

Esta'te. *n. s.* [*estat*, French.]

1. The general interest; the business of the government; the publick. In this sense it is now commonly written *state.*

Many times the things adduced to judgment may be *meum & tuum*, when the reason and consequence thereof may reach to point of *estate*: I call matters of *estate* not only the parts of sovereignty, but whatsoever introduceth any great alteration, or dangerous precedent, or concerneth manifestly any great portion of people. *Bacon's Essays.*

2. Condition of life, with regard to prosperity or adversity.

Thanks to giddy chance,
She cast us headlong from our high *estate*. *Dryden.*

3. Condition; circumstances in general.

Truth and certainty are not at all secured by innate principles; but men are in the same uncertain, floating *estate* with as without them. *Locke.*

4. Fortune; possession: generally meant of possessions in land, or realities.

She accused us to the king, as though we went about to overthrow him in his own *estate*. *Sidney, b.* ii.

Go, miser! go; for lucre sell thy soul;
Truck wares for wares, and trudge from pole to pole,
That men may say, when thou art dead and gone,
See what a vast *estate* he left his son! *Dryden's Pers. Sat.*

5. Rank; quality.

Who hath not heard of the greatness of your *estate*? Who seeth not that your *estate* is much excelled with that sweet uniting of all beauties. *Sidney, b.* ii.

6. A person of high rank. This sense is disused.

She is a dutchess, a great *estate*. *Latimer.*

Herod, on his birthday, made a supper to his lords, high captains, and chief *estates* of Galilee. *Mar.* vi. 21.

To Esta'te. *v. a.* [from the noun.] To settle as a fortune.

Why hath thy queen
Summon'd me hither?
—A contract of true love to celebrate,
And some donation freely to *estate*
On the bless'd lovers. *Shakespeare's Tempest.*

To ESTE'EM. *v. a.* [*estimer*, French; *æstimo*, Latin.]

1. To set a value whether high or low upon any thing.

The worth of all men by their end *esteem*,
And then due praise, or due reproach them yield. *Fa. Queen.*

I preferred her before sceptres and thrones, and *esteemed* riches nothing in comparison of her. *Wisd.* vii. 8.

2. To compare; to estimate by proportion.

Besides, those single forms she doth *esteem*,
And in her balance doth their values try. *Davies.*

3. To prize; to rate high; to regard with reverence.

Who would not be loved more, though he were *esteemed* less? *Dryden.*

4. To hold in opinion; to think; to imagine.

One man *esteemeth* one day above another: another *esteemeth* every day alike. *Rom.* xiv. 5.

Este'em. *n. s.* [from the verb.] High value; reverential regard.

Who can see,
Without *esteem* for virtuous poverty,
Severe Fabritius, or can cease t' admire
The ploughman consul in his coarse attire. *Dryden's Æn.*

Both those poets lived in much *esteem* with good and holy men in orders. *Dryden's Fables, Preface.*

I am not uneasy that many, whom I never had any *esteem* for, are likely to enjoy this world after me. *Pope.*

Este'emer. *n. s.* [from *esteem.*] One that highly values; one that sets an high rate upon any thing.

This might instruct the proudest *esteemer* of his own parts, how useful it is to talk and consult with others. *Locke.*

E'STIMABLE. *adj.* [French.]

1. Valuable; worth a large price.

A pound of man's flesh, taken from a man,
Is not so *estimable* or profitable
As flesh of muttons, beefs, or goats. *Shak. Mer. of Venice.*

2. Worthy of esteem; worthy of some degree of honour and respect.

A lady said of her two companions, that one was more amiable, the other more *estimable*.

You lost one who gave hopes of being, in time, every thing that was *estimable* and good. *Temple.*

E'stimableness. *n. s.* [from *estimable.*] The quality of deserving regard.

To E'STIMATE. *v. a.* [*æstimo*, Latin.]

1. To rate; to adjust the value of; to judge of any thing by its proportion to something else.

When a man shall sanctify his house to the Lord, then the priest shall *estimate* it whether it be good or bad: as the priest shall *estimate* it, so shall it stand. *Lev.* xxvii. 14.

It is by the weight of silver, and not the name of the piece, that men *estimate* commodities and exchange them. *Locke.*

2. To calculate; to compute.

E'stimate. *n. s.* [from the verb.]

1. Computation; calculation.

Upon a moderate *estimate* and calculation of the quantity of water now actually contained in the abyss, I found that this alone was full enough to cover the whole globe to the height assigned by Moses. *Woodward.*

2. Value.

I'd love
My country's good, with a respect more tender,
More holy and profound than mine own life,
My dear wife's *estimate*, her womb's increase,
The treasure of my loins. *Shakespeare's Coriolanus.*

3. Valuation; assignment of proportional value; comparative judgment.

The only way to come to a true *estimate* upon the odds betwixt a publick and a private life, is to try both. *L'Estrange.*

Outward actions can never give a just *estimate* of us, since there are many perfections of a man which are not capable of appearing in actions. *Addison's Spectator,* N°. 257.

Estima'tion. *n. s.* [from *estimate.*]

1. The act of adjusting proportional value.

If a man shall sanctify unto the Lord some part of a field, the *estimation* shall be according to the seed, and homer of barley. *Levit.*

2. Calculation; computation.

3. Opinion; judgment.

In our own *estimation* we account such particulars more worthy than those that are already tried and known. *Bacon.*

4. Esteem; regard; honour.

Crimes there were laid to his charge many, the least whereof being just, had bereaved him of *estimation* and credit with men. *Hooker, b.* v. *s.* 42.

Of your brace of unprizeable *estimations*, the one is but frail, and the other casual. *Shakespeare's Cymbeline.*

I know the gentleman
To be of worth and worthy *estimation*,
And not without desert so well reputed. *Shakespeare.*

I shall have *estimation* among the multitude, and honour with the elders. *Wisd.* viii. 10.

A plain reason of the publick honours due to the magistrate is, that he may be in due *estimation* and reverence. *Atterbury.*

E'stimative. *adj.* [from *estimate.*] Having the power of comparing and adjusting the preference.

We find in animals an *estimative* or judicial faculty, an appetition or aversation, and loco-motive faculty answering the will. *Hale's Origin of Mankind.*

Estima'tor. *n. s.* [from *estimate.*] A setter of rates; a computist.

E'stival. *adj.* [*æstivus*, Latin.]

1. Pertaining to the Summer.

2. Continuing for the Summer.

Estiva'tion. *n. s.* [*æstivatio*, Latin.] The act of passing the Summer.

A grotto is a place of shade, or *estivation*. *Bacon's Essays.*

Estra'de. *n. s.* [French; *stratum*, Latin.] An even or level space. *Dict.*

To ESTRA'NGE. *v. a.* [*estranger*, French.]

1. To keep at a distance; to withdraw.

Had we not only cut off their corruptions, but also *estranged* ourselves from them in things indifferent, who seeth not how greatly prejudicial this might have been to so good a cause? *Hooker, b.* iv. *s.* 7.

They know it is our custom of simple reading, not for conversion of infidels *estranged* from the house of God, but for instruction of men baptized, bred, and brought up in the bosom of the church. *Hooker, b.* v. *s.* 22.

See, she weeps;
Thinks me unkind, or false, and knows not why
I thus *estrange* my person from her bed. *Dryden.*

2. To alienate; to divert from its original use or possessor.

They have *estranged* this place, and have burnt incense in it to other gods. *Jer.* xix. 4.

3. To alienate from affection; to turn from kindness to malevolence or indifference.

How comes it now, my husband, oh, how comes it,
That thou art thus *estranged* from thyself?
Thyself I call it, being strange to me. *Shakes. Com. of Err.*

Adam, *estrang'd* in look, and alter'd style,
Speech intermitted, thus to Eve renew'd. *Milton's Par. Lost.*

I came to grieve a father's heart *estrang'd*;
But little thought to find a mistress chang'd. *Dryd. Aurengz.*

I do not know, to this hour, what it is that has *estranged* him from me. *Pope.*

4. To withdraw or withold.

We must endeavour to *estrange* our belief from every thing which is not clearly and distinctly evidenced to our faculties. *Glanv. Sceps. c.* 14.

Estra'ngement. *n. s.* [from *estrange.*] Alienation; distance; removal; voluntary abstraction.

Desires, by a long *estrangement* from better things, come at length perfectly to loath, and fly off from them. *South.*

ESTRAPA'DE. *n s.* [French.] The defence of a horse that will

will not obey, who, to get rid of his rider, rises mightily before; and while his forehand is yet in the air, yerks furiously with his hind legs. *Farrier's Dict.*

ESTRE'ATE. *n. s.* [*extractum*, Latin.] The true copy of an original writing: for example, of amerciaments or penalties, set down in the rolls of a court, to be levied by the bailiff, or other officer, of every man for his offence. A law term. *Cowel.*

ESTRE'PEMENT. *n. s.* [of the French word *estrepier.*] Spoil made by the tenant for term of life upon any lands or woods, to the prejudice of him in the reversion. *Cowel.*

E'STRICH. *n. s.* [commonly written *ostrich.*] The largest of birds.

To be furious,
Is to be frighted out of fear; and, in that mood,
The dove will peck the *estridge*. *Shak. Anth. and Cleopatra.*
The peacock, not at thy command, assumes
His glorious train; nor *estrich* her rare plumes. *Sandys.*

E'STUARY. *n. s.* [*æstuarium*, Latin.] An arm of the sea; the mouth of a lake or river in which the tide reciprocates; a frith.

To E'STUATE. *v. a.* [*æstuo*, Latin.] To swell and fall reciprocally; to boil; to be in a state of violent commotion. *Dict.*

ESTUA'TION. *n. s.* [from *æstuo*, Latin.] The state of boiling; reciprocation of rise and fall; agitation; commotion.

Rivers and lakes, that want fermenting parts at the bottom, are not excited unto *estuations*; therefore some seas flow higher than others. *Brown's Vulgar Errours, b.* vii. *c.* 13.

The motion of the will is accompanied with a sensible commotion of the spirits, and an *estuation* of the blood. *Norris.*

E'STURE. *n. s.* [*æstus*, Latin.] Violence; commotion.

The seas retain
Not only their outrageous *esture* there,
But supernatural mischief they expire. *Chapman's Odyssey.*

E'SURIENT. *adj.* [*esuriens*, Latin.] Hungry; voracious. *Dict.*

E'SURINE. *adj.* [*esurio*, Latin.] Corroding; eating.

Over much piercing is the air of Hampstead, in which sort of air there is always something *esurine* and acid. *Wiseman.*

ETC. A contraction of the two Latin words *et cætera*, which signifies *and so on*; *and the rest*; *and others of the like kind.*

To ETCH. *v. a.* [*etizen*, German.]

1. A way used in making of prints, by drawing with a proper needle upon a copper-plate, covered over with a ground of wax, &c. and well blacked with the smoke of a link, in order to take off the figure of the drawing or print; which having its backside tinctured with white lead, will, by running over the strucken out lines with a stift, impress the exact figure on the black or red ground; which figure is afterwards with needles drawn deeper quite through the ground, and all the shadows and hatchings put in; and then a wax border being made all round the plate, there is poured on a sufficient quantity of well tempered *aqua fortis*, which, insinuating into the strokes made by the needles, usually eats, in about half an hour, into the figure of the print or drawing on the copper plate. *Harris.*

2. To scetch; to draw; to delineate [unless this word be mistaken by *Locke* for *eke.*]

There are many empty terms to be found in some learned writers, to which they had recourse to *etch* out their systems. *Locke.*

3. [This word is evidently mistaken by *Ray* for *edge.*] To move forwards towards one side.

When we lie long awake in the night, we are not able to rest one quarter of an hour without shifting of sides, or at least *etching* this way and that way, more or less. *Ray.*

ETCH. *n. s.* A country word, of which I know not the meaning.

When they sow their *etch* crops, they sprinkle a pound or two of clover on an acre. *Mortimer's Husbandry.*

Where you find dunging of land makes it rank, lay dung upon the *etch*, and sow it with barley. *Mortimer's Husbandry.*

ETE'RNAL. *adj.* [*æternus*, Latin.]

1. Without beginning or end.

The *eternal* God is thy refuge. *Deut.* xxxiii. 27.

2. Without beginning.

It is a question quite different from our having an idea of eternity, to know whether there were any real being, whose duration has been *eternal.* *Locke.*

3. Without end; endless; immortal.

Thou know'st that Banquo and his Fleance lives.
—But in them nature's copy's not *eternal.* *Shakes. Macbeth.*

4. Perpetual; constant; unintermitting.

Burnt off'rings morn and ev'ning shall be thine,
And fires *eternal* in thy temple shine. *Dryd. Knight's Tale.*

5. Unchangeable.

Hobbes believed the *eternal* truths which he opposed. *Dryd.*

ETE'RNAL. *n. s.* [*eternel*, French.] One of the appellations of the Godhead.

That law whereby the *eternal* himself doth work. *Hooker.*

The *eternal*, to prevent such horrid fray,
Hung out of heav'n his golden scales. *Milton.*

ETE'RNALIST. *n. s.* [*æternus*, Latin.] One that holds the past existence of the world infinite.

I would ask the *eternalists* what mark is there that they could expect or desire of the novelty of a world, that is not found in this? Or what mark is there of eternity that is found in this? *Burnet's Theory of the Earth.*

To ETE'RNALISE. *v. a.* [from *eternal.*] To make eternal. *Dict.*

ETE'RNALLY. *adv.* [from *eternal.*]

1. Without beginning or end.

2. Unchangeably; invariably.

That which is morally good, or evil, at any time, or in any case, must be also *eternally* and unchangeably so, with relation to that time and to that case. *South's Sermons.*

3. Perpetually; without intermission.

Bear me, some god, to Baja's gentle seats,
Or cover me in Umbria's green retreats,
Where western gales *eternally* reside,
And all the seasons lavish all their pride. *Addison.*

ETE'RNE. *adj.* [*æternus*, Latin.] Eternal; perpetual; endless.

The Cyclops hammers fall
On Mars his armour, forg'd for proof *eterne. Shak. Hamlet.*

ETE'RNITY. *n. s.* [*æternitas*, Latin.]

1. Duration without beginning or end.

In this ground his precious root
Still lives, which, when weak time shall be pour'd out
Into *eternity*, and circular joys
Dancing an endless round, again shall rise. *Crashaw.*

Thy immortal rhyme
Makes this one short point of time,
To fill up half the orb of round *eternity.* *Cowley.*

By repeating the idea of any length of duration which we have in our minds, with all the endless addition of number, we come by the idea of *eternity.* *Locke.*

2. Duration without end.

Beyond is all abyss,
Eternity, whose end no eye can reach! *Milt. Parad. Lost.*
Eternity, thou pleasing, dreadful thought!
Through what variety of untried being,
Through what new scenes and changes must we pass. *Add.*

To ETE'RNIZE. *v. a.* [*æterno*, Latin.]

1. To make endless; to perpetuate.

I with two fair gifts
Created him endow'd; with happiness,
And immortality: that fondly lost,
This other serv'd but to *eternize* woe. *Milton's Parad. Lost.*

2. To make for ever famous; to immortalize.

Mankind by all means seeking to *eternize* himself, so much the more as he is near his end, doth it by speeches and writings. *Sidney.*

And well beseems all knights of noble name,
That covet in th' immortal book of fame
To be *eternized*, that same to haunt. *Fairy Queen, b.* i.
I might relate of thousands, and their names
Eternize here on earth; but those elect
Angels, contented with their fame in heav'n,
Seek not the praise of men. *Milton's Paradise Lost, b.* vi.

The four great monarchies have been celebrated by the writings of many famous men, who have *eternized* their fame, and thereby their own. *Temple.*

Both of them are set on fire by the great actions of heroes, and both endeavour to *eternize* them. *Dryden's Dufresnoy.*

Hence came its name, in that the grateful Jove
Hath *eterniz'd* the glory of his love. *Creech's Manilius.*

E'THER. *n. s.* [*æther*, Latin; αἰθήρ.]

1. An element more fine and subtle than air; air refined or sublimed.

If any one should suppose that *ether*, like our air, may contain particles which endeavour to recede from one another; for I do not know what this *ether* is; and that its particles are exceedingly smaller than those of air, or even than those of light, the exceeding smallness of its particles may contribute to the greatness of the force, by which those particles may recede from one another. *Newton's Opt.*

The parts of other bodies are held together by the eternal pressure of the *ether*, and can have no other conceivable cause of their cohesion and union. *Locke.*

2. The matter of the highest regions above.

There fields of light and liquid *ether* flow,
Purg'd from the pond'rous dregs of earth below. *Dryden.*

ETHE'REAL. *adj.* [from *ether.*]

1. Formed of ether.

Man feels me, when I press th' *ethereal* plains. *Dryden.*

2. Celestial; heavenly.

Go, heav'nly guest, *ethereal* messenger,
Sent from whose sov'reign goodness I adore. *Milton.*
Thrones and imperial pow'rs, offspring of heav'n,
Ethereal virtues! *Milton's Paradise Lost, b.* ii. *l.* 311.

Such as these, being in good part freed from the entanglements of sense and body, are employed, like the spirits above, in contemplating the Divine Wisdom in the works of nature; a kind of anticipation of the *ethereal* happiness and employment. *Glanv. Apol.*

Vaſt chain of being, which from God began,
Natures *ethereal*, human; angel, man. *Pope.*

ETHE'REOUS. *adj.* [from *ether*] Formed of ether; heavenly.
Behold the bright ſurface
Of this *ethereous* mould, whereon we ſtand. *Milt. Pa. Loſt.*

E'THICAL. *adj.* [ἠθικός.] Moral; treating on morality.

E'THICALLY. *adv.* [from *ethical.*] According to the doctrines of morality.

My ſubject leads me not to diſcourſe *ethically*, but chriſtianly of the faults of the tongue. *Government of the Tongue.*

E'THICK. *adj.* [ἠθικός.] Moral; delivering precepts of morality. Whence *Pope* entitled part of his works *Ethick* Epiſtles.

E'THICKS. *n. ſ.* without the ſingular. [ἠθική.] The doctrine of morality; a ſyſtem of morality.

For of all moral virtues, ſhe was all
That *ethicks* ſpeak of virtues cardinal. *Donne.*

I will never ſet politicks againſt *ethicks*; eſpecially for that true *ethicks* are but as a handmaid to divinity and religion. *Bacon's War with Spain.*

Perſius profeſſes the ſtoick philoſophy; the moſt noble, generous, and beneficial amongſt all the ſects who have given rules of *ethicks*. *Dryden's Juvenal, Dedicat.*

If the atheiſts would live up to the *ethicks* of Epicurus himſelf, they would make few or no proſelytes from the Chriſtian religion. *Bentley's Sermons.*

E'THNICK. *adj.* [ἐθνικός.] Heathen; Pagan; not Jewiſh; not Chriſtian.

Such contumely as the *ethnick* world durſt not offer him, is the peculiar inſolence of degenerated Chriſtians. *Gov. of Tongue.*

I ſhall begin with the agreement of profane, whether Jewiſh or *ethnick*, with the Sacred Writings. *Grew's Coſm. Sac.*

E'THNICKS. *n. ſ.* Heathens; not Jews; not Chriſtians.

This firſt Jupiter of the *ethnicks* was then the ſame Cain, the ſon of Adam. *Raleigh's Hiſtory of the World.*

ETHOLO'GICAL. *adj.* [ἦθος and λόγος.] Treating of morality.

ETIO'LOGY. *n. ſ.* [αἰτιολογία.] An account of the cauſes of any thing, generally of a diſtemper.

I have not particulars enough to enable me to enter into the *etiology* of this diſtemper. *Arbuthnot on Air.*

ETYMOLO'GICAL. *adj.* [from *etymology.*] Relating to etymology; relating to the derivation of words.

Excuſe this conceit, this *etymological* obſervation. *Locke.*

ETYMO'LOGIST. *n. ſ.* [from *etymology.*] One who ſearches out the original of words; one who ſhows the derivation of words from their original.

ETYMO'LOGY. *n. ſ.* [*etymologia*, Lat. [ἔτυμος and λόγος.]

1. The deſcent or derivation of a word from its original; the deduction of formations from the radical word; the analyſis of compound words into primitives.

Conſumption is generally taken for any univerſal diminution and colliquation of the body, which acception its *etymology* implies. *Harvey on Conſumptions.*

When words are reſtrained, by common uſage, to a particular ſenſe, to run up to *etymology*, and conſtrue them by dictionary, is wretchedly ridiculous. *Collier's View of the Stage.*

Pelvis is uſed by comick writers for a looking-glaſs, by which means the *etymology* of the word is viſible, and pelvidera will ſignify a lady who looks in her glaſs. *Addiſon's Spectator.*

If the meaning of a word could be learned by its derivation or *etymology*, yet the original derivation of words is oftentimes very dark. *Watts's Logick.*

2. The part of grammar which delivers the inflections of nouns and verbs.

E'TYMON. *n. ſ.* [ἔτυμον.] Origin; primitive word.

Blue hath its *etymon* from the High Dutch blaw; from whence they call himmel-blue, that which we call ſky-colour or heaven's blue. *Peacham on Drawing.*

To EVA'CATE. *v. a.* [*vaco*, Latin.] To empty out; to throw out.

Dry air opens the ſurface of the earth to diſincarcerate venene bodies, or to *evacate* them. *Harvey on the Plague.*

To EVA'CUATE. *v. a.* [*evacuo*, Latin.]

1. To make empty; to clear.

There is no good way of prevention but by *evacuating* clean, and emptying the church. *Hooker, b.* iv. *ſ.* 10.

We tried how far the air would manifeſt its gravity in ſo thin a medium, as we could make in our receiver, by *evacuating* it. *Boyle's Spring of the Air.*

2. To throw out as noxious, or offenſive.

3. To void by any of the excretory paſſages.

Boerhaave gives an inſtance of a patient, who, by a long uſe of whey and water, and garden fruits, *evacuated* a great quantity of black matter, and recovered his ſenſes. *Arbuthnot.*

4. To make void; to evacate; to nullify; to annul.

The defect, though it would not *evacuate* a marriage, after cohabitation and actual conſummation; yet it was enough to make void a contract. *Bacon's Henry* VII.

If the prophecies recorded of the Meſſiah are not fulfilled in Jeſus of Nazareth, it is impoſſible to know when a prophecy is fulfilled, and when not, in any thing or perſon whatſoever, which would utterly *evacuate* the uſe of them. *South.*

5. To quit; to withdraw from out of a place.

As this neutrality was never obſerved by the emperor, ſo he never effectually *evacuated* Catalonia. *Swift.*

EVA'CUANT. *n. ſ.* [*evacuans*, Latin.] Medicine that procures evacuation by any paſſage.

EVACUA'TION. *n. ſ.* [from *evacuate.*]

1. Such emiſſions as leave a vacancy; diſcharge.

Conſider the vaſt *evacuations* of men that England hath had, by aſſiſtances lent to foreign kingdoms. *Hale's Orig. of Mank.*

2. Abolition; nullification.

Popery hath not been able to re-eſtabliſh itſelf in any place, after proviſion made againſt it by utter *evacuation* of all Romiſh ceremonies. *Hooker, b.* iv. *ſ.* 9.

2. The practice of emptying the body by phyſick.

The uſual practice of phyſick among us, turns in a manner wholly upon *evacuation*, either by bleeding, vomit, or ſome purgation. *Temple.*

3. Diſcharges of the body by any vent natural or artificial.

To EVA'DE. *v. a.* [*evado*, Latin.]

1. To elude; to eſcape by artifice or ſtratagem.

In this point charge him home, that he affects
Tyrannick power: if he *evade* us there,
Inforce him with his envy to the people. *Shakeſ. Coriolanus.*

Or, if thou covet death, as utmoſt end
Of miſery, ſo thinking to *evade*
The penalty pronounc'd, doubt not but God
Hath wiſelier arm'd his vengeful ire, than ſo
To be foreſtall'd. *Milton's Paradiſe Loſt, b.* x. *l.* 1021.

He might *evade* the accompliſhment of theſe afflictions he now gradually endureth. *Brown's Vulgar Errours, b.* i.

2. To avoid; to decline by ſubterfuge.

Our queſtion thou *evad'ſt*; how did'ſt thou dare
To break hell bounds? *Dryden's State of Innocence.*

3. To eſcape or elude by ſophiſtry.

My argument evidently overthrows all that he brings to *evade* the teſtimonies of the fathers. *Stillingfleet.*

4. To eſcape as imperceptible, or unconquerable, as too great or too ſubtle to be ſeized or ſubdued.

We have ſeen how a contingent event baffles man's knowledge, and *evades* his power. *South's Sermons.*

To EVA'DE. *v. n.*

1. To eſcape; to ſlip away.

His wiſdom, by often *evading* from perils, was turned rather into a dexterity to deliver himſelf from dangers, than into a providence to prevent. *Bacon's Henry* VII.

2. To practiſe ſophiſtry or evaſions.

Unarm'd they might
Have eaſily, as ſpirits, *evaded* ſwift
By quick contraction, or remove. *Milton's Paradiſe Loſt.*

The miniſters of God are not to *evade* or take refuge in any of theſe two forementioned ways. *South's Sermons.*

EVAGA'TION. *n. ſ.* [*evagor*, Latin.] The act of wandering; excurſion; ramble; deviation.

Theſe long chains of lofty mountains, which run through whole continents eaſt and weſt, ſerve to ſtop the *evagation* of the vapours to the north and ſouth in hot countries. *Ray.*

EVANE'SCENT. *adj.* [*evaneſcens*, Latin.] Vaniſhing; imperceptible; leſſening beyond the perception of the ſenſes.

As the canal is wire-drawn, it grows ſtill ſmaller and ſlenderer, ſo as that the *evaneſcent* ſolid and fluid will ſcarce differ. *Arbuthnot on Aliments.*

The difference between right and wrong, on ſome petty caſes, is almoſt *evaneſcent*. *Wollaſton.*

The downy orchard, and the melting pulp
Of mellow fruit, the nameleſs nations feed
Of *evaneſcent* inſects. *Thomſon's Spring, l.* 300.

EVANGE'LICAL. *adj.* [*evangelique*, French; *evangelicus*, Latin.]

1. Agreeable to goſpel; conſonant to the Chriſtian law revealed in the holy goſpel.

This diſtinction between moral goodneſs and *evangelical* perfection, ought to have been obſerved. *Atterbury's Sermons.*

God will indeed judge the world in righteouſneſs; but 'tis by an *evangelical*, not a legal righteouſneſs, and by the intervention of the man Chriſt Jeſus, who is the Saviour as well as the judge of the world. *Atterbury's Sermons.*

2. Contained in the goſpel.

Thoſe *evangelical* hymns they allow not to ſtand in our liturgy. *Hooker, b.* v. *ſ.* 35.

EVANGE'LISM. *n. ſ.* [from *evangely.*] The promulgation of the bleſſed goſpel.

Thus was this land ſaved from infidelity, through the apoſtolical and miraculous *evangeliſm*. *Bacon's New Atlantis.*

EVA'NGELIST. *n. ſ.* [εὐαγγελιστής.]

1. A writer of the hiſtory of our Lord Jeſus.

Each of theſe early writers aſcribe to the four *evangeliſts* by name their reſpective hiſtories. *Addiſon's Chriſt. Religion.*

2. A promulgator of the Chriſtian laws.

Thoſe to whom he firſt entruſted the promulgating of the goſpel, had inſtructions; and it were fit our new *evangeliſts* ſhould ſhow their authority. *Decay of Piety.*

To EVANGE'LIZE. *v. a.* [*evangelizo*, Latin; εὐαγγελίζω.] To inſtruct in the goſpel, or law of Jeſus.

The ſpirit
Pour'd firſt on his apoſtles, whom he ſends
T' *evangelize* the nations; then on all
Baptiz'd, ſhall them with wond'rous gifts endue. *Milton.*

EVA'NGELY. *n. ſ.* [ἐυαγγέλιον, that is, good tidings.] Good tidings; the meſſage of pardon and ſalvation; the holy goſpel; the goſpel of *Jeſus.*

Good Lucius,
That firſt received Chriſtianity,
The ſacred pledge of Chriſt's *evangely.* *Fairy Queen, b.* ii.

EVA'NID. *adj.* [*evanidus,* Latin.] Faint; weak; evaneſcent.

Where there is heat and ſtrength enough in the plant to make the leaves odorate, there the ſmell of the flower is rather *evanid* and weaker than that of the leaves. *Bacon's Nat. Hiſt.*

The decoctions of ſimples, which bear the viſible colours of bodies decocted, are dead and *evanid,* without the commixtion of allum, argol, and the like. *Brown's Vulgar Errours.*

I put as great difference between our new lights and ancient truths, as between the ſun and an *evanid* meteor. *Glanv. Scepſ.*

To EVA'NISH. *v. a.* [*evaneſco,* Latin.] To vaniſh; to eſcape from notice or perception.

EVA'PORABLE. *adj.* [from *evaporate.*] Eaſily diſſipated in fumes or vapours.

Such cordial powders as are aromatick, their virtue lies in parts that are of themſelves volatile, and eaſily *evaporable.* *Grew's Muſæum.*

To EVA'PORATE. *v. n.* [*evaporo,* Latin.] To fly away in vapours or fumes; to waſte inſenſibly as a volatile ſpirit.

Poeſy is of ſo ſubtile a ſpirit, that in the pouring out of one language into another it will all *evaporate.* *Denham.*

Our works unhappily *evaporated* into words; we ſhould have talked leſs, and done more. *Decay of Piety.*

Being weary with attending the ſo ſlow conſumption of the liquor, we ſet it in a digeſting furnace to *evaporate* more nimbly. *Boyle on Saltpetre.*

This vapour falling upon joints which have not heat enough to diſpel it, cannot be cured otherwiſe than by burning, by which it *evaporates.* *Temple.*

The enemy takes a ſurer way to conſume us, by letting our courage *evaporate* againſt ſtones and rubbiſh. *Swift.*

To EVA'PORATE. *v. a.*

1. To drive away in fumes; to diſperſe in vapours.

If we compute that prodigious maſs of water daily thrown into the ſea from all the rivers, we ſhould then know how much is perpetually *evaporated,* and caſt again upon the continents to ſupply thoſe innumerable ſtreams. *Bentley's Sermons.*

Convents abroad are ſo many retreats for the ſpeculative, the melancholy, the proud, the ſilent, the politick, and the moroſe, to ſpend themſelves, and *evaporate* the noxious particles. *Swift's Argument againſt aboliſhing Chriſtianity.*

We perceive clearly, that fire will warm or burn us, and will *evaporate* water. *Watts's Logick.*

2. To give vent to; to let out in ebullition or ſallies.

My lord of Eſſex *evaporated* his thoughts in a ſonnet to be ſung before the queen. *Wotton.*

EVAPORA'TION. *n. ſ.* [from *evaporate.*]

1. The act of flying away in fumes or vapours; vent; diſcharge.

They are but the fruits of aduſted choler, and the *evaporations* of a vindicative ſpirit. *Howel's Vocal Forreſt.*

Evaporations are at ſome times greater, according to the greater heat of the ſun; ſo wherever they alight again in rain, 'tis ſuperior in quantity to the rain of colder ſeaſons. *Woodw.*

2. The act of attenuating matter, ſo as to make it fume away.

Thoſe waters, by rarifaction and *evaporation,* aſcended. *Raleigh's Hiſtory of the World.*

3. [In pharmacy.] An operation by which liquids are ſpent or driven away in ſteams, ſo as to leave ſome part ſtronger, or of a higher conſiſtence than before. *Quincy.*

EVA'SION. *n. ſ.* [*evaſum,* Latin.] Excuſe; ſubterfuge; ſophiſtry; artifice; artful means of eluding or eſcaping.

We are too well acquainted with thoſe anſwers;
But his *evaſion,* wing'd thus ſwift with ſcorn,
Cannot outfly our apprehenſions. *Shak. Troilus and Creſſida.*

Him, after all diſputes,
Forc'd I abſolve: all my *evaſions* vain,
And reaſonings, though through mazes, lead me ſtill
But to my own conviction. *Milton's Paradiſe Loſt, b.* x.

In vain thou ſtriv'ſt to cover ſhame with ſhame;
For by *evaſions* thy crime uncover'ſt more. *Milton's Agoniſtes.*

EVA'SIVE. *adj.* [from *evade.*]

1. Practiſing evaſion; eluſive.

Thus he, though conſcious of th' etherial gueſt,
Anſwer'd *evaſive* of the ſly requeſt. *Pope's Odyſſey, b.* i.

2. Containing an evaſion; ſophiſtical; diſhoneſtly artful.

EVA'SIVELY. *adv.* [from *evaſive.*] By evaſion; eluſively; ſophiſtically.

EU'CHARIST. *n. ſ.* [ἐυχαριςία.] The act of giving thanks; the ſacramental act in which the death of our Redeemer is commemorated with a thankful remembrance; the ſacrament of the Lord's ſupper.

Himſelf did better like of common bread to be uſed in the *euchariſt.* *Hooker, Preface.*

Some receive the ſacrament as a means to procure great graces and bleſſings, others as an *euchariſt* and an office of thankſgiving for what they have received. *Taylor.*

EUCHARI'STICAL. *adj.* [from *euchariſt.*]

1. Containing acts of thankſgiving.

The latter part was *euchariſtical,* which began at the breaking and bleſſing of the bread. *Brown's Vulgar Errours, b.* v.

It would not be amiſs to put it into the *euchariſtical* part of our daily devotions: we praiſe thee, O God, for our limbs and ſenſes. *Ray on the Creation.*

2. Relating to the ſacrament of the ſupper of the Lord.

EUCHO'LOGY. *n. ſ.* [ἐυχολόγιον.] A formulary of prayers.

EUCRASY. *n. ſ.* [ἐυκρασία.] An agreeable well proportioned mixture of qualities, whereby a body is ſaid to be in a good ſtate of health. *Quincy.*

EVE. }
E'VEN. } *n. ſ.* [æpen, Saxon; *avend,* or *avond,* Dutch.]

1. The cloſe of the day; the latter part of the day; the interval between bright light and darkneſs.

They like ſo many Alexanders,
Have in theſe parts from morn 'till *even* fought,
And ſheath'd their ſwords for lack of argument. *Sh. H.* V.

Such ſights as youthful poets dream
On Summer *eves* by haunted ſtream. *Milton.*

O, nightingale, that on yon bloomy ſpray
Warbleſt at *eve,* when all the woods are ſtill. *Milton.*

When the ſun's orb both *even* and morn is bright,
Then let no fear of ſtorms thy mind affright. *May's Virgil.*

Th' unerring ſun by certain ſigns declares,
What the late *ev'n,* or early morn prepares. *Dryd. Virgil.*

Winter, oft at *eve,* reſumes the breeze,
Chills the pale morn. *Thomſon's Spring, l.* 20.

2. The vigil or faſt to be obſerved before an holiday. In this ſenſe only *eve* is uſed, not *even.*

Let the immediate preceding day be kept as the *eve* to this great feaſt. *Duppa's Rule to Devotion.*

E'VEN. *adj.* [eꝼen, Saxon; *even,* Dutch; *æquus,* Latin.]

1. Level; not rugged; not unequal.

To ſee a beggar's brat in riches flow,
Adds not a wrinkle to my *even* brow. *Dryden's Perſ. Sat.* 6.

The preſent face of Rome is much more *even* and level than it was formerly. *Addiſon's Remarks on Italy.*

The ſuperficies of ſuch plates are not *even,* but have many cavities and ſwellings, which, how ſhallow ſoever, do a little vary the thickneſs of the plate. *Newton's Opt.*

2. Uniform; equal to itſelf; ſmooth as oppoſed to rough.

Lay the rough paths of peeviſh nature *ev'n,*
And open in each heart a little heav'n. *Prior.*

3. Level with; parallel to.

That the net may be *even* to the midſt of the altar. *Ex.*
And ſhall lay thee *even* with the ground. *Luk.* xix. 44.

4. Without inclination any way; not leaning to any ſide.

He was
A noble ſervant to them; but he could not
Carry his honours *even.* *Shakeſpeare's Coriolanus.*

5. Without any part higher or lower than the other.

When Alexander demanded of one what was the fitteſt ſeat of his empire, he laid a dry hide before him, and deſired him to ſet his foot on one ſide thereof; which being done, all the other parts of the hide did riſe up; but when he did ſet his foot in the middle, all the other parts lay flat and *even.* *Davies.*

Upheld by me, yet once more he ſhall ſtand
On *even* ground againſt his mortal foe. *Milton's Par. Loſt.*

6. Equal on both ſides: as, the account is *even.*

Even reckoning makes laſting friends; and the way to make reckonings *even,* I am ſure, is to make them often. *South.*

7. Without any thing owed, either good or ill; out of debt.

We reckon with your ſeveral loves,
And make us *even* with you;
Henceforth be earls. *Shakeſpeare's Macbeth.*

I will be *even* with thee, doubt it not. *Shak. Ant. and Cleop.*

I do confeſs
The blind lad's pow'r, whilſt he inhabits there;
But I'll be *ev'n* with him nevertheleſs. *Suckling.*

In taking revenge, a man is but *even* with his enemy; but in paſſing it over, he is ſuperior. *Bacon's Eſſays.*

The publick is always *even* with an author who has not a juſt deference for them: the contempt is reciprocal. *Addiſon.*

The true reaſon of their flying to this ſtrange doctrine was to be *even* with the magiſtrate, who, they found, was againſt them; and they reſolved, therefore, at any rate to be againſt him. *Atterbury's Sermons.*

8. Calm; not ſubject to elevation or depreſſion.

Deſires compos'd, affections ever *ev'n,*
Tears that delight, and ſighs that waft to heav'n. *Pope.*

9. Capable to be divided into equal parts; not odd.

Let him tell me whether the number of the ſtars be *even* or odd. *Taylor's Rule of living holy.*

What verity there is in that numeral conceit, in the lateral diviſion

division of man by *even* and odd, ascribing the odd unto the right side, and *even* unto the left. *Brown's Vulgar Errours.*

To E'VEN. *v. a.* [from the noun.]

1. To make even.

2. To make out of debt; to put in a state in which either good or ill is fully repaid.

Nothing can, or shall content my soul,
'Till I am *evened* with him, wife for wife. *Shakesp. Othello.*

3. To level; to make level.

This temple Xerxes *evened* with the soil, which Alexander is said to have repaired. *Raleigh's History of the World.*

Beat, roll, and mow carpet-walks and cammomile; for now the ground is supple, and it will *even* all inequalities. *Evelyn.*

To E'VEN. *v. n.* To be equal to. Now disused.

A like strange observation taketh place here as at Stonehenge, that a redoubled numbering never *eveneth* with the first. *Carew's Survey of Cornwal.*

E'VEN. *adv.* [often contracted to *ev'n.*]

1. A word of strong assertion; verily.

Even so did those Gauls possess the coasts. *Spenser's Ireland.*

Thou wast a soldier
Even to Cato's wish; not fierce, and terrible
Only in strokes. *Shakspeare's Macbeth.*

Dang'rous rocks,
Which, touching but my gentle vessel's side,
Would scatter all the spices on the stream,
Enrobe the roaring waters with my silks;
And, in a word, yea *even* now worth this,
And now worth nothing. *Shakesp. Merchant of Venice.*

It is not much that the good man ventures; and after this life, if there be no God, is as well as the bad; but if there be a God, is infinitely better, *even* as much as unspeakable and eternal happiness is better than extreme and endless misery. *Tillotson's Sermons.*

2. Notwithstanding; though it was so that.

All I can say for those passages is, that I knew they were bad enough to please, *even* when I wrote them. *Dryden.*

3. Likewise; not only so, but also.

The motions of all the lights of heaven might afford measures of time, if we could number them; but most of those motions are not evident, and the great lights are sufficient, and serve also to measure *even* the motions of those others. *Holder.*

He might *even* as well have employed his time, as some princes have done, in the frivolous and low delights of catching moles. *Atterbury.*

Here all their rage, and *ev'n* their murmurs cease,
And sacred silence reigns, and universal peace. *Pope.*

4. So much as.

Books give the same turn to our thoughts that company does to our conversation, without loading our memories, or making us *even* sensible of the change. *Swift.*

5. A word of exaggeration in which a secret comparison is implied: as, *even* the great, that is, *the great like the mean.*

Nor death itself can wholly wash your stains,
But long contracted filth *ev'n* in the soul remains. *Dryden.*

I have made several discoveries which appear new, *even* to those who are versed in critical learning. *Addison's Spectator.*

6. A term of concession.

Since you refined the notion, and corrected the malignity, I shall *e'en* let it pass. *Collier of Friendship.*

EVENHA'NDED. *adj.* [*even* and *hand.*] Impartial; equitable.

Evenhanded justice
Returns th' ingredients of our poison'd chalice
To our own lips. *Shakespeare's Macbeth.*

E'VENING. *n. s.* [æfen, Saxon; *avend*, Dutch.] The close of the day; the beginning of night.

I shall fall
Like a bright exhalation in the *evening*,
And no man see me more. *Shakesp. Henry VIII.*

The devil is now more laborious than ever, the long day of mankind drawing fast towards an *evening*, and the world's tragedy and time near at an end. *Raleigh's Hist. of the World.*

Mean time the sun descended from the skies,
And the bright *evening* star began to rise. *Dryden's Æn.*

It was a sacred rule among the Pythagoreans, that they should every *evening* thrice run over the actions and affairs of the day. *Watts's Improvement of the Mind, p.* i.

E'VENLY. *adj.* [from *even.*]

1. Equally; uniformly; in an equipoise.

In an infinite chaos nothing could be formed; no particles could convene by mutual attraction; for every one there must have infinite matter around it, and therefore must rest for ever, being *evenly* balanced between infinite attractions. *Bentley.*

2. Levelly; without asperities.

The first shall be a palish clearness, *evenly* and smoothly spread; not overthin and washy, but of a pretty solid consistence. *Wotton.*

3. Without inclination to either side; in a posture parallel to the horizon; horizontally.

The upper face of the sea is known to be level by nature, and *evenly* distant from the center, and waxes deeper and deeper the farther one saileth from the shore. *Brerewood.*

4. Impartially; without favour or enmity.

You serve a great and gracious master, and there is a most hopeful young prince: it behoves you to carry yourself wisely and *evenly* between them both. *Bacon's Advice to Villiers.*

E'VENNESS. *n. s.* [from *even.*]

1. State of being even.

2. Uniformity; regularity.

The ether most readily yieldeth to the revolutions of the celestial bodies, and the making them with that *evenness* and celerity is requisite in them all. *Grew's Cosm log. Sa. r. b.* i.

3. Equality of surface; levelness.

4. Freedom from inclination to either side.

A crooked stick is not straitned, unless it be bent as far on the clear contrary side, that so it may settle itself at the length in a middle estate of *evenness* between both. *Hooker, b.* iv. *s.* 8.

5. Impartiality; equal respect.

6. Calmness; freedom from perturbation.

Though he appeared to relish these blessings as much as any man, yet he bore the loss of them, when it happened, with great composure and *evenness* of mind. *Atterbury's Sermons.*

E'VENSONG. *n. s.* [*even* and *song.*]

1. The form of worship used in the evening.

Thee, 'chantress of the woods among,
I woo to hear thy *evensong.* *Milton.*

If a man were but of a day's life, it is well if he lasts 'till *evensong*, and then says his compline an hour before the time. *Taylor's Rule of living holy.*

2. The evening; the close of the day.

He tun'd his notes both *evensong* and morn. *Dryden.*

EVENTI'DE. *n. s.* [*even* and *tide.*] The time of evening.

A swarm of gnats at *eventide*,
Out of the fens of Allan do arise,
Their murmuring small trumpets sounding wide. *Fa. Queen.*

Isaac went out to meditate at the *eventide.* *Gen.* xxiv. 63.

EVE'NT. *n. s.* [*eventus*, Latin.]

1. An incident; any thing that happens, good or bad.

There is one *event* to the righteous, and to the wicked. *Eccl.*

Oh heavy times, begetting such *events!* *Shak. Hen.* VI.

2. The consequence of an action; the conclusion; the upshot.

Two spears from Meleager's hand were sent,
With equal force, but various in th' *event*;
The first was fixt in earth, the second stood
On the boar's bristled back, and deeply drank his blood. *Dry.*

To EVE'NTERATE. *v. a.* [*eventero*, Latin.] To rip up; to open by ripping the belly.

In a bear, which the hunters *eventerated*, or opened, I beheld the young ones with all their parts distinct. *Brown.*

EVE'NTFUL. *adj.* [*event* and *full.*] Full of incidents; full of changes of fortune.

Last scene of all,
That ends this strange *eventful* history,
Is second childishness. *Shakespeare's As you like it.*

To EVE'NTILATE. *v. n.* [*eventilo*, Latin.]

1. To winnow; to sift out.

2. To examine; to discuss. *Dict.*

EVE'NTUAL. *adj.* [from *event.*] Happening in consequence of any thing; consequential.

EVE'NTUALLY. *adv.* [from *eventual.*] In the event; in the last result; in the consequence.

Hermione has but intentionally, not *eventually*, disobliged you; and hath made your flame a better return, by restoring you your own heart, than she could have done by exchanging her's for it. *Boyle's Seraphick Love.*

E'VER. *adv.* [æfre, Saxon.]

1. At any time.

Men know by this time, if *ever* they will know, whether it be good or evil which hath been so long retained. *Hooker.*

If thou hast that, which I have greater reason to believe now than *ever*, I mean valour, this might shew it. *Sh. Othello.*

You serve a master who is as free from the envy of friends, as *ever* any king was. *Bacon's Advice to Villiers.*

So few translations deserve praise, that I scarce *ever* saw any which deserved pardon. *Denham.*

The most sensual man that *ever* was in the world, never felt so delicious a pleasure as a clear conscience. *Tillotson's Sermons.*

By repeating any such idea of any length of time, as of a minute, a year, or an age, as often as we will in our own thoughts, and adding them to one another, without *ever* coming to the end of such addition, we come by the idea of eternity. *Locke.*

2. At all times; always; without end.

God hath had *ever*, and *ever* shall have, some church visible upon the earth. *Hooker, b.* iii. *s.* 1.

I see things may serve long, but not serve *ever.* *Shakesp.*

Riches endless is as poor as Winter,
To him that *ever* fears he shall be poor. *Shakesp. Othello.*

Blinded greatness, *ever* in turmoil,
Still seeking happy life, makes life a toil. *Daniel's Civ. War.*

There under ebon shades, and low-brow'd rocks,
In dark cimmerian desart *ever* dwell. *Milton.*

The inclinations of the people must *ever* have a great influence. *Temple.*

He

He shall *ever* love, and always be
The subject of my scorn and cruelty. *Dryden's Ind. Emp.*

Mankind is *ever* the same, and nothing lost out of nature, though every thing is altered. *Dryden's Fables, Pref.*

Ever since that time Lisander has been at the house. *Tatler.*

Immortal Vida! on whose honour'd brow
The poet's bays and critick's ivy grow,
Cremona now shall *ever* boast thy name,
As next in place to Mantua, next in fame. *Pope's Essays.*

3. For ever; eternally; to perpetuity.

Men are like a company of poor insects, whereof some are bees, delighted with flowers and their sweetness; others beetles, delighted with other kinds of viands; which, having enjoyed for a season, they cease to be, and exist no more for *ever*. *Loc.*

We'll to the temple: there you'll find your son;
And there be crown'd, or give him up for *ever*. *A. Phillips.*

4. It is sometimes reduplicated.

For ever, and for *ever*, farewel, Cassius. *Shakespeare.*

I know a lord who values no lease, though for a thousand years, nor any estate that is not for *ever* and *ever*. *Temple.*

The meeting points the fatal lock dissever
From the fair head, for *ever* and for *ever*. *Pope.*

5. At one time, as, *ever* and anon: that is, at one time and another; now and then.

So long as Guyon with her communed,
Unto the ground she cast her modest eye;
And *ever* and anon, with rosy red,
The bashful blood her snowy cheeks did dye. *Fairy Queen.*

The fat ones would be *ever* and anon making sport with the lean, and calling them starvelings. *L'Estrange.*

He lay stretch'd along,
And *ever* and anon a silent tear
Stole down and trickled from his hoary beard. *Dryden.*

6. In any degree.

Let no man fear that harmful creature *ever* the less, because he sees the apostle safe from that poison. *Hall.*

For a mine undiscovered, neither the owner of the ground or any body else are *ever* the richer. *Collier on Pride.*

It suffices to the unity of any idea, that it be considered as one representation or picture, though made up of *ever* so many particulars. *Locke.*

There must be somewhere such a rank as man;
And all the question, wrangle *e'er* so long,
Is only this, if God has plac'd him wrong. *Pope's Essays.*

7. A word of enforcement, or aggravation. *As soon as* ever *he had done it*; that is, immediately after he had done it. In this sense it is scarcely used but in familiar language.

That *ever* this fellow should have fewer words than a parrot, and yet the son of a woman. *Shakespeare's Henry* IV. *p.* I.

They brake all their bones in pieces, or *ever* they came at the bottom of the den. *Dan.* iv. 24.

That purse in your hand, as a twin brother, is as like him as *ever* he can look. *Dryden's Spanish Fryar.*

As soon as *e'er* the bird is dead,
Opening again, he lays his claim
To half the profit, half the fame. *Prior.*

The title of duke had been sunk in the family *ever* since the attainder of the great duke of Suffolk. *Addison on Italy.*

8. Ever a. Any: [as *every*, that is, everich or ever each is each one, all.] This word is still retained in the Scottish dialect.

I am old, I am old.
—I love thee better than I love *e'er a* scurvy young boy of them all *Shakespeare's Henry* IV. *p.* ii.

9. It is often contracted into *e'er*.

10. It is much used in composition in the sense of always: as, *evergreen*, green throughout the year; *everduring*, enduring without end. It is added almost arbitrarily to neutral participles and adjectives, and will be sufficiently explained by the following instances.

Everbu'bbling. *adj.* [*ever* and *bubbling*] Boiling up with perpetual murmurs.

Panting murmurs, still'd out of her breast,
That *everbubbling* spring. *Crashaw.*

Everbu'rning. *adj.* [*ever* and *burning.*] Unextinguished.

His tail was stretched out in wond'rous length,
That to the house of heavenly gods it raught;
And with extorted power and borrow'd strength,
The *everburning* lamps from thence it brought. *Fai. Queen.*

Torture without end
Still urges, and a fiery deluge, fed
With *everburning* sulphur unconsum'd! *Milton's Par. Lost.*

Everdu'ring. *adj.* [*ever* and *during.*] Eternal; enduring without end.

Our souls, piercing through the impurity of flesh, behold the highest heavens, and thence bring knowledge to contemplate the *everduring* glory and termless joy. *Raleigh.*

Heav'n open'd wide
Her *everduring* gates, harmonious sound!
On golden hinges moving. *Milton's Paradise Lost, b.* vii.

Evergre'en *adj.* [*ever* and *green*] Verdant throughout the year.

There will I build him
A monument, and plant it round with shade
Of laurel, *evergreen*, and branching palm. *Milton's Agonist.*

The juice, when in greater plenty than can be exhaled by the sun, renders the plant *evergreen*. *Arbuthnot on Aliments.*

E'vergreen. *n. s.* A plant that retains its verdure through all the seasons.

Some of the hardiest *evergreens* may be transplanted, especially if the weather be moist and temperate. *Evelyn's Kalend.*

I find you are against filling an English garden with *evergreens*. *Addison's Spectator*, N°. 477.

Everho'noured. *adj.* [*ever* and *honoured.*] Always held in honour or esteem.

Mentes, an *everhonour'd* name, of old
High in Ulysses' social list enroll'd. *Pope's Odyssey, b.* i.

Everla'sting. *adj.* [*ever* and *lasting.*]

1. Lasting or enduring without end; perpetual; immortal; eternal.

Whether we shall meet again, I know not;
Therefore our *everlasting* farewel take:
For ever, and for ever, farewel, Cassius. *Shak. Jul. Cæsar.*

The *everlasting* life, both of body and soul, in that future state, whether in bliss or woe, hath been added. *Hammond.*

And what a trifle is a moment's breath,
Laid in the scale with *everlasting* death! *Denham.*

2. It is used of past as well as future eternity, though not so properly.

Everla'sting. *n. s.* Eternity; eternal duration whether past or future.

From *everlasting* to *everlasting* thou art God. *Ps.* xc. 2.

We are in God through the knowledge which is had of us, and the love which is born towards us, from *everlasting*. *Hooker.*

Everla'stingly. *adv.* [from *everlasting.*] Eternally; without end.

I'll hate him *everlastingly*,
That bids me be of comfort any more. *Shakes. Rich.* II.

Many have made themselves *everlastingly* ridiculous. *Swift.*

Everla'stingness. *n. s.* [from *everlasting.*] Eternity; perpetuity; an indefinite duration.

Nothing could make me sooner to confess,
That this world had an *everlastingness*,
Than to consider that a year is run
Since both this lower world's, and the sun's sun,
The lustre and the vigour of this all,
Did set. *Donne.*

Everli'ving. *adj.* [*ever* and *living.*] Living without end; immortal; eternal; incessant.

Is not from hence the way, that leadeth right
To that most glorious house, that glist'reth bright
With burning stars and *everliving* fires. *Fairy Queen, b.* i.

In that he is man, he received life from the Father, as from the fountain of that *everliving* Deity. *Hooker, b.* v. *s.* 56.

God's justice in the one, and his goodness in the other, is exercised for evermore, as the *everliving* subjects of his reward and punishment. *Raleigh's History of the World.*

The instinct of brutes and insects can be the effect of nothing else than the wisdom and skill of a powerful *everliving* Agent. *Newton's Opt.*

Evermo're. *adv.* [*ever* and *more.*] Always; eternally. *More* seems an expletive accidentally added, unless it signified originally *from this time*: as, *evermore, always henceforward*; but this sense has not been strictly preserved.

It govern'd was, and guided *evermore*,
Through wisdom of a matron grave and hoare. *Fa. Queen.*

Sparks by nature *evermore* aspire,
Which makes them now to such a highness flee. *Davies.*

Religion prefers those pleasures which flow from the presence of God for *evermore*, infinitely before the transitory pleasures of this world. *Tillotson, Sermon* i.

Evero'pen. *adv.* [*ever* and *open.*] Never closed; not at any time shut.

God is the great eye of the world, always watching over our actions, and has an *everopen* ear to hear all our words. *Taylor's Rule of living holy.*

Everple'asing. *adj.* [*ever* and *pleasing.*] Delighting at all times; never ceasing to give pleasure.

The *everpleasing* Pamela was content to urge a little farther for me. *Sidney.*

Forsaking Scheria's *everpleasing* shore,
The winds to Marathon the virgin bore. *Pope's Odyssey.*

To Eve'rse. *v. a.* [*eversus*, Latin.] To overthrow; to subvert; to destroy.

The foundation of this principle is totally *eversed* by the ingenious commentator upon immaterial beings. *Glanv. Sceps.*

To Eve'rt. *v. a.* [*everto*, Latin.] To destroy; to overthrow.

A process is valid, if the jurisdiction of the judge is not yet *everted* and overthrown. *Ayliffe's Parergon.*

Everwa'tchful. *adj.* [*ever* and *watchful*] Always vigilant.

Plac'd at the helm he sat, and mark'd the skies,
Nor clos'd in sleep his *everwatchful* eyes. *Pope's Odyssey, b.* iv.

E'very. *adj.* [in old language *everich*, that is, ever each; æfeꝛ ealc, Saxon.]

1. Each one of all. *Every* has therefore no plural signification.

He

He propoſeth unto God their neceſſities, and they their own requeſts for relief in *every* of them. *Hooker, b.* v. *ſ.* 39.

All the congregation are holy, *every* one of them. *Num.* xvi.

The king made this ordonance, that *every* twelve years there ſhould be ſet forth two ſhips. *Bacon's New Atlantis.*

The virtue and force of *every* of theſe three is ſhrewdly allayed. *Hammond's Fundamentals.*

Ariſtotle has long ſince obſerved, how unreaſonable it is to expect the ſame kind of proof for *every* thing, which we have for ſome things. *Tillotſon's Sermons.*

Every one, that has any idea of a foot, finds that he can repeat that idea, and, joining it to the former, make the idea of two feet. *Locke.*

From pole to pole the thunder roars aloud,
And broken lightnings flaſh from *ev'ry* cloud. *Pope's Statius.*

2. EVERY-WHERE. In all places; in each place.

The ſubſtance of the body of Chriſt was not *every-where* ſeen, nor did it *every-where* ſuffer death; *every-where* it could not be entombed: it is not *every-where* now, being exalted into heaven. *Hooker, b.* v. *ſ.* 55.

If I ſend my ſon abroad, how is it poſſible to keep him from vice, which is *every-where* ſo in faſhion? *Locke.*

'Tis no-where to be found, or *every-where.* *Pope.*

E'VERYOUNG. *adj.* [*ever* and *young*] Not ſubject to old age, or decay; undecaying.

Joys *everyoung,* unmix'd with pain or fear,
Fill the wide circle of th' eternal year. *Pope's Odyſſey, b.* iv.

E'VESDROPPER. *n.ſ.* [*eves* and *dropper.*] Some mean fellow that ſkulks about a houſe in the night.

What makes you liſtening there? Get farther off; I preach not to thee, thou wicked *eveſdropper.* *Dryden's Spaniſh Fryar.*

Do but think how decent a habit you have on, and how becoming your function it is to be diſguiſed like a ſlave, and an *eveſdropper,* under the women's windows. *Dryd. Don Sebaſt.*

To EVE'STIGATE. *v. a.* [*eveſtigo,* Lat.] To ſearch out. *Dict.*

EUGH. *n.ſ.* [This word is ſo written by moſt writers; but ſince the original ıp, Saxon, or Welſh *ywen,* more favours the eaſier orthography of *yew,* I have referred it thither.] A tree.

At the firſt ſtretch of both his hands he drew,
And almoſt join'd the horns of the tough *eugh.* *Dryd. Æn.*

To EVI'CT. *v. a.* [*evinco,* Latin.]

1. To diſpoſſeſs of by a judicial courſe.

The law of England would ſpeedily *evict* them out of their poſſeſſion, and therefore they held it the beſt policy to caſt off the yoke of Engliſh law. *Davies on Ireland.*

2. To take away by a ſentence of law.

His lands were *evicted* from him. *K. James's Declaration.*

3. To prove; to evince. Little uſed.

This nervous fluid has never been diſcovered in live animals by the ſenſes, however aſſiſted; nor its neceſſity *evicted* by any cogent experiment. *Cheyne's Phil. Princ.*

EVI'CTION. *n.ſ.* [from *evict.*]

1. Diſpoſſeſſion or deprivation by a definitive ſentence of a court of judicature.

If any of the parties be laid aſleep, under pretence of arbitrement, and the other party doth cautiouſly get the ſtart at common law, yet the pretorian court will ſet back all things, and no reſpect had to *eviction* or diſpoſſeſſion. *Bacon.*

2. Proof; evidence; certain teſtimony.

A plurality of voices carries the queſtion, in all our debates, but rather as an expedient for peace than an *eviction* of the right. *L'Eſtrange's Fables.*

E'VIDENCE. *n.ſ.* [French.]

1. The ſtate of being evident; clearneſs; indubitable certainty; notoriety.

2. Teſtimony; proof.

I had delivered the *evidence* of the purchaſe unto Baruch. *Jer.* xxxii. 16.

Unreaſonable it is to expect the ſame kind of proof and *evidence* for every thing, which we have for ſome things. *Tillot.*

Cato major, who had borne all the great offices, has left us an *evidence,* under his own hand, how much he was verſed in country affairs. *Locke.*

They bear *evidence* to a hiſtory in defence of Chriſtianity, the truth of which hiſtory was their motive to embrace Chriſtianity. *Addiſon on the Chriſtian Religion.*

3. Witneſs; one that gives evidence. In this ſenſe it is ſometimes plural; as, *the* evidence *were ſworn:* but ſometimes regularly augmented, as *evidences.*

To ſwear he ſaw three inches through a door,
As Aſiatick *evidences* ſwore. *Dryden's Juvenal, Sat.* vii.

There are books extant, which they muſt needs allow of as proper *evidence;* even the mighty volumes of viſible nature, and the everlaſting tables of right reaſon. *Bentley.*

To E'VIDENCE. *v. a.* [from the noun.]

1. To prove; to evince.

If they be principles evident of themſelves, they need nothing to *evidence* them. *Tillotſon's Sermons, Preface.*

Theſe things the Chriſtian religion require, as might be *evidenced* from texts. *Tillotſon, Sermon* v.

2. To ſhew; to make diſcovery of.

Thou on earth had'ſt proſper'd, which thy looks
Now alſo *evidence.* *Milton's Paradiſe Loſt, b.* x. *l.* 361.

E'VIDENT. *adj.* [French.] Plain; apparent; notorious.

It is *evident,* in the general frame of nature, that things moſt manifeſt unto ſenſe have proved obſcure unto the underſtanding. *Brown's Vulgar Errours, b.* vi. *c.* 10.

In this ſtate they are incapable of making conqueſts upon their neighbours, which is *evident* to all that know their conſtitutions. *Temple.*

Children minded not what was ſaid, when it was *evident* to them that no attention was ſufficient. *Locke.*

E'VIDENTLY. *adv.* [from *evident.*] Apparently; certainly; undeniably.

Laying their eggs, they *evidently* prove
The genial pow'r and full effects of love. *Prior.*

The printing private letters is the worſt ſort of betraying converſation, as it has *evidently* the moſt extenſive ill conſequences. *Pope.*

E'VIL. *adj.* [ẏpel, Saxon; *euvel,* Dutch.]

1. Having bad qualities of any kind; not good.

He hath brought up an *evil* name upon a virgin of Iſrael. *Deut* xxii. 19.

An *evil* diſeaſe cleaveth faſt unto him; and now that he lieth, he ſhall riſe up no more. *Pſ.* xli. 8.

The good fig's very good, and the *evil* very *evil,* that cannot be eaten they are ſo *evil.* *Jeremiah* xxiv. 3.

That hour he cured many of *evil* ſpirits. *Luke* vii. 21.

2. Wicked; bad; corrupt.

Is thine eye *evil,* becauſe I am good? *Matt.* xx. 15.

The imagination of man's heart is *evil* from his youth. *Gen.*

3. Unhappy; miſerable; calamitous.

And the officers did ſee that they were in *evil* caſe. *Ex.* v.

All the days of the afflicted are *evil.* *Prov.* xv. 15.

4. Miſchievous; deſtructive; ravenous.

It is my ſon's coat; an *evil* beaſt hath devoured him. *Gen.*

E'VIL. *n.ſ.* [generally contracted to *ill.*]

1. Wickedneſs; a crime.

Not in the legions
Of horrid hell can come a devil more damn'd
In *evils* to top Macbeth. *Shakeſpeare's Macbeth.*

2. Injury; miſchief.

Whoſo rewardeth *evil* for good, *evil* ſhall not depart from his houſe. *Prov.* xvii. 13.

Let thine enemies, and they that ſeek *evil* to my Lord, be as Nabal. 1 *Sa.* xxv. 26.

3. Malignity; corruption.

The heart of the ſons of men is full of *evil.* *Eccleſ.* ix. 3.

4. Misfortune; calamity.

Shall we receive good at the hand of God, and ſhall we not receive *evil.* *Job* ii. 10.

A prudent man foreſeeth the *evil,* and hideth himſelf. *Prov.*

If we will ſtand boggling at imaginary *evils,* let us never blame a horſe for ſtarting at a ſhadow. *L'Eſtrange.*

Evil is what is apt to produce or increaſe any pain, or diminiſh any pleaſure in us; or elſe to procure us any *evil,* or deprive us of any good. *Locke.*

5. Malady; diſeaſe: as, the *king's evil.*

At his touch,
Such ſanctity hath heaven given his hand,
They preſently amend.
——What's the diſeaſe he means?
——'Tis call'd the *evil.* *Shakeſpeare's Macbeth.*

E'VIL. *adv.* [commonly contracted to *ill.*]

1. Not well in whatever reſpect.

Ah, froward Clarence, *evil* it beſeems thee,
To flatter Henry, and forſake thy brother! *Shak. Hen.* VI.

2. Not well; not virtuouſly; not innocently.

If I have ſpoken *evil,* bear witneſs of the *evil;* but if well, why ſmiteſt thou me. *John* xviii. 22.

3. Not well; not happily; not fortunately.

It went *evil* with his houſe. *Deut.* vii. 23.

4. Injuriouſly; not kindly.

The Egyptians *evil* entreated us, and afflicted us. *Deut.* xxvi.

5. It is often uſed in compoſition to give a bad meaning to a word; but in this, as in all other caſes, it is in the modern dialect generally contracted to *ill.*

EVILAFFE'CTED. *adj.* [*evil* and *affected.*] Not kind; not diſpoſed to kindneſs.

The unbelieving Jews ſtirred up the Gentiles, and made their minds *evilaffected* againſt the brethren. *Acts* xiv. 2.

EVILDO'ER. *n.ſ.* [*evil* and *doer.*] Malefactor; one that commits crimes.

Whereas they ſpeak evil againſt you as *evildoers,* they may by your good works glorify God. 1 *Pet.* ii. 12.

EVILFA'VOURED. *adj.* [*evil* and *favour.*] Illcountenanced; having no good aſpect.

Machiavel well noteth, though in an *evilfavoured* inſtance, there is no truſting to the force of nature, nor the bravery of words, except it be corroborate by cuſtom. *Bacon's Eſſays.*

EVILFA'VOUREDNESS. *n.ſ.* [from *evilfavoured.*] Deformity.

Thou ſhalt not ſacrifice unto the Lord any bullock, or ſheep, wherein is blemiſh or any *evilfavouredneſs*. *Deutr.* xvii.

E'VILLY. *adv.* [from *evil.*] Not well.

This act, ſo *evilly* born, ſhall cool the hearts
Of all his people, and freeze up their zeal. *Shak. K. John.*

EVILMI'NDED. *adj.* [*evil* and *mind.*] Malicious; miſchievous; malignant; wicked; inſidious.

But moſt ſhe fear'd, that travelling ſo late,
Some *evilminded* beaſts might lie in wait,
And, without witneſs, wreak their hidden hate. *Dryden.*

E'VILNESS. *n. ſ.* [from *evil.*] Contrariety to goodneſs; badneſs of whatever kind.

The moral goodneſs and congruity, or *evilneſs*, unfitneſs, and unſeaſonableneſs of moral or natural actions, falls not within the verge of a brutal faculty. *Hale's Orig of Mankind.*

EVILSPE'AKING. *n. ſ.* [*evil* and *ſpeaking.*] Slander; defamation; calumny; cenſoriouſneſs.

Wherefore laying aſide all malice and all guile, and hypocriſies and envies, and all *evilſpeakings*. 1 *Pet.* ii. 1.

EVILWI'SHING. *adj.* [*evil* and *wiſh.*] Wiſhing evil to; having no good will.

They having heard of this ſudden going out with ſo ſmall a company, in a country full of *evilwiſhing* minds towards him, followed him. *Sidney, b.* ii.

EVILWO'RKER. *n. ſ.* [*evil* and *work.*] One who does ill.

Beware of dogs, beware of *evilworkers.* *Phil.* iii. 3.

To EVI'NCE. *v. a.* [*evinco*, Latin.] To prove; to ſhow; to manifeſt; to make evident.

Doubt not but that ſin
Will reign among them, as of thee begot;
And therefore was law given them, to *evince*
Their natural pravity. *Milton's Paradiſe Loſt, b.* xii.

That religion, teaching a future ſtate of ſouls, is a probability; and that its contrary cannot, with equal probability, be proved, we have *evinced.* *South's Sermons.*

The greater the abſurdities are, the more ſtrongly do they *evince* the falſity of that ſuppoſition from whence they flow. *Atterbury's Sermons, Preface.*

EVI'NCIBLE. *adj.* [from *evince.*] Capable of proof; demonſtrable.

Implanted inſtincts in brutes are in themſelves highly reaſonable and uſeful to their ends, and *evincible* by true reaſon to be ſuch. *Hale's Origin of Mankind.*

EVI'NCIBLY. *adv.* [from *evincible.*] In ſuch a manner as to force conviction.

To E'VIRATE. *v. a.* [*eviratus*, Latin.] To deprive of manhood; to emaſculate. *Dict.*

To EVI'SCERATE. *v. a.* [*eviſcero*, Latin.] To embowel; to draw; to deprive of the entrails; to ſearch within the entrails.

E'VITABLE. *adj.* [*evitabilis*, Latin.] Avoidable; that may be eſcaped or ſhunned.

Of divers things evil, all being not *evitable*, we take one; which one, ſaving only in caſe of ſo great urgency, were not otherwiſe to be taken. *Hooker, b.* i. *ſ.* 8.

To E'VITATE. *v. a.* [*evito*, Latin.] To avoid; to ſhun; to eſcape.

Therein ſhe doth *evitate* and ſhun
A thouſand irreligious curſed hours,
Which forced marriage would have brought upon her *Shak.*

EVITA'TION. *n. ſ.* [from *evitate.*] The act of avoiding. *Dict.*

EVITE'RNAL. *adj.* [*æviternus*, Latin.] Eternal in a limited ſenſe; of duration not infinitely but indefinitely long.

EVITE'RNITY. *n. ſ.* [*æviternitas*, low Lat.] Duration not infinitely, but indefinitely long.

EU'LOGY. *n. ſ.* [εὖ and λόγ☉.] Praiſe; encomium; panegyrick.

Many brave young minds have oftentimes, through hearing the praiſes and famous *eulogies* of worthy men, been ſtirred up to affect the like commendations. *Spenſer on Ireland.*

EU'NUCH. *n. ſ.* [εὐνοῦχ☉.] One that is caſtrated or emaſculated.

He hath gelded the commonwealth, and made it an *eunuch.* *Shakeſpeare's Henry* VI. *p.* ii.

It hath been obſerved by the ancients, that much of Venus doth dim the ſight; and yet *eunuchs*, which are unable to generate, are neverthelefs alſo dimſighted. *Bacon's Nat. Hiſtory.*

So charm'd you were, you ceas'd awhile to doat
On nonſenſe gargl'd in an *eunuch*'s throat. *Fenton.*

To EU'NUCHATE. *v. a.* To make an eunuch.

It were an impoſſible act to *eunuchate* or caſtrate themſelves. *Brown's Vulgar Errours, b.* viii. *c.* 4.

EVOCA'TION. *n. ſ* [*evocatio*, Latin.] The act of calling out.

Inſtead of a deſcent into hell, it ſeems rather a conjuring up or an *evocation* of the dead from hell. *Notes to Pope's Odyſſey.*

EVOLA'TION. *n. ſ.* [*evolo*, Latin.] The act of flying away.

To EVO'LVE. *v. a.* [*evolvo*, Latin.] To unfold; to diſentangle.

The animal ſoul ſooner expands and *evolves* itſelf to its full orb and extent than the human ſoul. *Hale's Orig. of Mank.*

This little active principle, as the body increaſeth and dilateth, *evolveth*, diffuſeth, and expandeth, if not his ſubſtantial exiſtence, yet his energy. *Hale's Origin of Mankind.*

To EVO'LVE. *v. n.* To open itſelf; to diſcloſe itſelf.

Ambroſial odours
Does round the air *evolving* ſcents diffuſe;
The holy ground is wet with heav'nly dews. *Prior.*

EVO'LVENT. *n. ſ.* [*evolvens*, Latin.] *Harris.*

EVOLU'TION. *n. ſ.* [*evolutus*, Latin.]

1. The act of unrolling or unfolding.

2. The ſeries of things unrolled or unfolded.

The whole *evolution* of ages, from everlaſting to everlaſting, is ſo collectedly and preſentifickly repreſented to God at once, as if all things which ever were, are, or ſhall be, were at this very inſtant, and ſo always, really preſent and exiſtent before him. *More's Divine Dialogues.*

3. [In geometry.] The equable evolution of the periphery of a circle, or any other curve, is ſuch a gradual approach of the circumference to rectitude, as that all its parts do meet together, and equally evolve or unbend; ſo that the ſame line becomes ſucceſſively a leſs arch of a reciprocally greater circle, 'till at laſt they turn into a ſtrait line. In the Philoſ. Tranſactions, N°. 260. you have a new quadratrix to the circle, found by this means. *Harris.*

4. [In tacticks.] The motion made by a body of men in changing their poſture, or form of drawing up, either to make good the ground they are upon, or to poſſeſs themſelves of another; that ſo they may attack the enemy, or receive his onſet more advantageouſly. And theſe evolutions are doubling of ranks or files, countermarches, and wheelings. *Harris.*

This ſpontaneous coagulation of the little ſaline bodies was preceded by almoſt innumerable *evolutions*, which were ſo various, that the little bodies came to obvert to each other thoſe parts by which they might be beſt faſtened together. *Boyle.*

5. EVOLUTION *of Powers* [in algebra]. Extracting of roots from any given power, being the reverſe of involution. *Harr.*

EVOMI'TION. *n. ſ.* [*evomo*, Latin.] The act of vomiting out. *Dict.*

EUPHO'NICAL. *adj.* [from *euphony.*] Sounding agreeably. *Dict.*

EU'PHONY. *n. ſ.* [εὐφωνία.] An agreeable ſound; the contrary to harſhneſs.

EUPHO'RBIUM. *n. ſ.*

1. A plant.

It hath flowers and fruit like the ſpurge, and is alſo full of an hot ſharp milky juice. The plants are angular, and ſhaped ſomewhat like the cereus or torch-thiſtle. It is commonly beſet with ſpines, and for the moſt part hath no leaves. *Miller.*

2. A gum reſin, brought to us always in drops or grains, of a bright yellow, between a ſtraw and a gold colour, and a ſmooth gloſſy ſurface. It has no great ſmell, but its taſte is violently acrid and nauſeous. It is produced in the remoter parts of Africa, whence it is ſent to Sallee, and thence tranſported into Europe. The plant is alſo common on the coaſt of Malabar; but the Africans only know the ſecret of collecting the gum. It is uſed medicinally in ſinapiſms. *Hill.*

EU'PHRASY. *n. ſ.* [*euphraſia*, Latin.] The herb eyebright; a plant ſuppoſed to clear the ſight.

Then purg'd with *euphraſy*, and rue,
The viſual nerve; for he had much to ſee;
And from the well of life three drops inſtill'd. *Milt. P. Loſt.*

EURO'CLYDON. *n. ſ.* [εὐροκλύδων.] A wind which blows between the Eaſt and North, and is very dangerous in the Mediterranean. It is of the nature of a whirlwind, which falls ſuddenly on ſhips, makes them tack about, and ſometimes cauſes them to founder, as Pliny obſerves. *Calmet.*

There aroſe againſt it a tempeſtuous wind called *euroclydon.* *Acts* xxvii. 14.

EUROPE'AN. *adj.* [*europæus*, Latin.] Belonging to Europe.

Mean while the Spaniards in America,
Near to the line the ſun approaching ſaw,
And hop'd their *European* coaſts to find
Clear'd from our ſhips by the autumnal wind. *Waller.*

What was the waſte of war, what fierce alarms
Shook Aſia's crown with *European* arms! *Dryden's Æn.*

He alone defy'd
The *European* thrones combin'd, and ſtill
Had ſet at nought their machinations vain. *Phillips.*

EU'RUS. *n. ſ.* [Latin.] The Eaſt wind.

Eurus, as all other winds, muſt be drawn with blown cheeks, wings upon his ſhoulders, and his body the colour of the tawny moon. *Peacham.*

E'URYTHMY. *n. ſ.* [εὐρυθμ☉.] Harmony; regular and ſymmetrical meaſure.

EUTHAN'ASIA. / EUTHA'NASY. } *n. ſ.* [εὐθανασία.] An eaſy death.

A recovery, in my caſe, and at my age, is impoſſible: the kindeſt wiſh of my friends is *euthanaſia.* *Arbuthnot.*

EVU'LSION. *n. ſ.* [*evulſio*, Latin.] The act of plucking out.

From a ſtrict enquiry we cannot maintain the *evulſion*, or biting off any parts. *Brown's Vulgar Errours, b.* iii. *c.* 2.

EVULGA'TION. *n. ſ.* [*evulgo*, Latin.] The act of divulging; publication. *Dict.*

Ewe. *n. s.* [eope, Saxon.] The she-sheep; the female to the ram.

Abraham set seven *ewe* lambs by themselves. *Gen.* xxi. 28.

Rams have more wreathed horns than *ewes*. *Bac. N. Hist.*

Haste the sacrifice;
Sev'n bullocks yet unyok'd, for Phœbus chuse;
And for Diana seven unspotted *ewes*. *Dryden's Æn. b.* viii.

E'WER. *n. s.* [from *eau*, perhaps anciently *eu*, water.] A vessel in which water is brought for washing the hands.

I dreamt of a silver bason and *ewer* to-night. *Shakes. Timon.*

Let one attend him with a silver bason
Full of rosewater, and bestrew'd with flowers;
Another bear the *ewer*; a third a diaper;
And say, wil't please your lordship cool your hands? *Shak.*

The golden *ewer* a maid obsequious brings,
Replenish'd from the cool, translucent springs;
With copious water the bright vase supplies
A silver laver, of capacious size:
They wash. *Pope's Odyssey, b.* i. *l.* 179.

E'wry. *n. s.* [from *ewer*.] An office in the king's houshold, where they take care of the linen for the king's table, lay the cloth, and serve up water in silver *ewers* after dinner. *Dict.*

Ex. A Latin preposition often prefixed to compounded words; sometimes meaning *out*, as *exhaust*, to draw *out*; sometimes only enforcing the meaning, and sometimes producing little alteration.

To EXACE'RBATE. *v. a.* [*exacerbo*, Latin.] To imbitter; to exasperate; to heighten any malignant quality.

Exacerba'tion. *n. s.* [from *exacerbate*.]

1. Encrease of malignity; augmented force or severity.

2. Height of a disease; paroxysm.

The patient may strive, by little and little, to overcome the symptom in *exacerbation*; and so, by time, turn suffering into nature. *Bacon's Natural History*, N°. 61.

Watchfulness and delirium, and *exacerbation*, every other day. *Arbuthnot on Diet.*

Exacerva'tion. *n. s.* [*acervus*, Latin.] The act of heaping up. *Dict.*

EXA'CT. *adj.* [*exactus*, Latin.]

1. Nice; without failure; without deviation from rule.

All this, *exact* to rule, were brought about,
Were but in a combat in the lists left out. *Pope's Ess. on Crit.*

2. Methodical; not negligently performed.

What if you and I enquire how money matters stand between us?—With all my heart, I love *exact* dealing; and let Hocus audit. *Arbuthnot's John Bull.*

3. Accurate; not negligent.

Many gentlemen turn out of the seats of their ancestors, to make way for such new masters as have been more *exact* in their accounts than themselves. *Spectator*, N°. 174.

4. Honest; strict; punctual.

In my doings I was *exact*. *Ecclus.* li. 19.

To Exa'ct. *v. a.* [*exigo*, *exactus*, Latin.]

1. To require authoritatively.

Thou now *exact'st* the penalty,
Which is a pound of this poor merchant's flesh. *Shakesp.*

Of a foreigner thou mayest *exact* it again; but that which is thine with thy brother, thine hand shall release. *Deut.* xv. 3.

Exact of servants to be faithful and diligent. *Taylor.*

From us his foes pronounc'd glory he *exacts*. *Milton.*

The hand of fate is over us, and heaven
Exacts severity from all our thoughts. *Addison's Cato.*

2. To demand of right.

Years of service past,
From grateful souls *exact* reward at last. *Dryd. Knight's Tale.*

Where they design a recompence for benefits received, they are less solicitous to make it when it is *exacted*. *Smalridge.*

3. To summon; to enjoin.

Let us descend now therefore from this top
Of speculation; for the hour precise
Exacts our parting hence. *Milton's Paradise Lost, b.* xii.

Duty,
And justice to my father's soul, *exact*
This cruel piety. *Denham's Sophy.*

To Exa'ct. *v. n.* To practise extortion.

The enemy shall not *exact* upon him. *Ps.* lxxx. 22.

Exa'cter. *n. s.* [from *exact*.]

1. Extortioner; one who claims more than his due, or claims his due with outrage and severity.

The poller and *exacter* of fees justifies the common resemblance of the courts of justice to the bush, whereunto while the sheep flies for defence in weather, he is sure to lose part of the fleece. *Bacon's Essays, Civ. and Mor.*

I will also make thy officers peace, and thine *exacters* righteousness. *Is.* lx. 17.

2. He that demands by authority.

Light and lewd persons, especially that the *exacter* of the oath did neither use exhortation, nor examining of them for taking thereof, were easily suborned to make an affidavit for money. *Bacon's Office of Alienation.*

3. One who is severe in his injunctions or his demands.

No men are prone to be greater tyrants, and more rigorous *exacters* upon others, than such whose pride was formerly least disposed to the obedience of lawful constitutions. *K. Charles.*

The grateful person being still the most severe *exacter* of himself, not only confesses, but proclaims his debts. *South.*

There is no way to deal with this man of reason, this rigid *exacter* of strict demonstration for things which are not capable of it. *Tillotson.*

Exa'ction. *n. s.* [from *exact*.]

1. The act of making an authoritative demand, or levying by force.

If he should break his day, what should I gain
By the *exaction* of the forfeiture? *Shak. Merch. of Venice.*

2. Extortion; unjust demand.

They vent reproaches
Most bitterly on you, for putter-on
Of these *exactions*. *Shakespeare's Henry* VIII.

Remove violence and spoil, and execute judgment and justice; take away your *exactions* from my people. *Ez.* xlv. 9.

As the first earl did first raise the greatness of that house, by Irish *exactions* and oppressions; so Girald the last earl did at last ruin and reduce it to nothing, by using the like extortions. *Davies's State of Ireland.*

3. A toll; a tribute severely levied.

They have not made bridges over the rivers for the convenience of their subjects as well as strangers, who pay an unreasonable *exaction* at every ferry upon the least using of the waters. *Addison's Remarks on Italy.*

Exa'ctly. *adv.* [from *exact*.] Accurately; nicely; thoroughly.

Both of 'em knew mankind *exactly* well; for both of 'em began that study in themselves. *Dryden's Don Sebastian.*

The religion they profess is such, that the more *exactly* it is sifted by pure unbiassed reason, the more reasonable still it will be found. *Atterbury's Sermons.*

Exa'ctness. *n. s.* [from *exact*.]

1. Accuracy; nicety; strict conformity to rule or symmetry.

The experiments were all made with the utmost *exactness* and circumspection. *Woodward on Fossils.*

In wit, as nature, what affects our hearts
Is not th' *exactness* of peculiar parts;
'Tis not a lip, or eye, we beauty call,
But the joint force and full result of all. *Pope's Ess. on Crit.*

The balance must be held by a third hand, who is to deal power with the utmost *exactness* into the several scales. *Swift.*

2. Regularity of conduct; strictness of manners; care not to deviate.

I preferred not the outward peace of my kingdoms with men, before that inward *exactness* of conscience before God. *King Charles.*

They think that their *exactness* in one duty will attone for their neglect of another. *Rogers.*

To EXA'GGERATE. *v. a.* [*exaggero*, Latin.] To heighten by representation; to enlarge by hyperbolical expressions.

He had *exaggerated*, as pathetically as he could, the sense the people generally had, even despair of ever seeing an end of the calamities. *Clarendon, b.* viii.

A friend *exaggerates* a man's virtues, an enemy inflames his crimes. *Addison's Spectator*, N°. 399.

Exaggera'tion. *n. s.* [from *exaggerate*.]

1. The act of heaping together; an heap; an accumulation.

Some towns, that were anciently havens and ports, are now, by *exaggeration* of sand between those towns and the sea, converted into firm land. *Hale's Origin of Mankind.*

2. Hyperbolical amplification.

Exaggerations of the prodigious condescensions in the prince to pass good laws, would have an odd sound at Westminster. *Swift.*

To Exa'gitate. *v. a.* [*exagito*, Latin.]

1. To shake; to put in motion.

The warm air of the bed *exagitates* the blood. *Arbuthnot.*

2. To reproach; to pursue with invectives. This sense is now disused, being purely Latin.

This their defect and imperfection I had rather lament in such case than *exagitate*. *Hooker, b.* iii.

Exagita'tion. *n. s.* [from *exagitate*.] The act of shaking, or agitating. *Dict.*

To EXA'LT. *v. a.* [*exalter*, French; *altus*, Latin; *exalto*, low Latin.]

1. To raise on high.

And thou, Capernaum, which art *exalted* unto heaven, shalt be brought down to hell. *Mat.* xi. 23.

2. To elevate to power, wealth, or dignity.

Exalt him that is low, and abase him that is high. *Ezek.*

As yet *exaltest* thou thyself against my people, that thou wilt not let them go? *Ex.* ix. 17.

How long shall mine enemy be *exalted* over me? *Ps.* xiii. 2.

3. To elevate to joy or confidence.

The covenanters who understood the court, and their own want of strength, were very reasonably *exalted* with this success. *Clarendon, b.* iii.

How much soever the king's friends were dejected upon the passing those two acts, it is certain, they who thought they got

whatsoever

whatsoever he lost were mightily *exalted*, and thought themselves now superior to any opposition. *Dryden's Æn. Dedicat.*

4. To praise; to extol; to magnify.

O magnify the Lord with me, and let us *exalt* his name together. *Ps.* xxxiv. 3.

5. To raise up in opposition: a scriptural phrase.

Against whom hast thou *exalted* thy voice, and lift up thine eyes on high? *2 Kings* xix. 22.

6. To intend; to enforce.

Now Mars, she said, let fame *exalt* her voice;
Nor let thy conquests only be her choice. *Prior.*

7. To heighten; to improve; to refine by fire, as in chemistry.

The wild animals have more exercise, have their juices more elaborated and *exalted*; but, for the same reason, the fibres are harder, especially when old. *Arbuthnot on Aliments.*

With chymick art *exalts* the min'ral pow'rs,
And draws the aromatick souls of flow'rs. *Pope.*

They meditate what will be the effect of their composition, and whether the virtues of the one will *exalt* or diminish the force of the other, or correct any of its nocent qualities. *Watts.*

8. To elevate in diction or sentiment.

But hear, oh hear, in what *exalted* strains,
Sicilian muses, through these happy plains,
Proclaim Saturnian times, our own Apollo reigns. *Rosc.*

EXALTA'TION. *n. s.* [from *exalt.*]

1. The act of raising on high.

2. Elevation to power, or dignity.

She put off the garments of widowhood, for the *exaltation* of those that were oppressed. *Judith* xvi. 8.

The former was an humiliation of Deity, the latter an humiliation of manhood; for which cause there followed, upon the latter, an *exaltation* of that which was humbled; for with power he created the world, but restored it by obedience. *Hooker, b.* v. *s.* 54.

3. Most elevated state; state of greatness or dignity.

I wonder'd at my flight and change
To this high *exaltation*. *Milton's Paradise Lost, b.* v. *l.* 90.

In God all perfections, in their highest degree and *exaltation*, meet together. *Tillotson, Sermon* i.

You are as much esteemed, and as much beloved, perhaps more dreaded, than ever you were in your highest *exaltation*. *Swift.*

4. [In pharmacy.] Raising a medicine to a higher degree of virtue, or an increase of the most remarkable property of any body. *Quincy.*

5. Dignity of a planet in which its powers are increased.

Astrologers tell us, that the sun receives his *exaltation* in the sign Aries. *Dryden.*

EXA'MEN. *n. s.* [Latin.] Examination; disquisition; enquiry.

This considered together with a strict account, and critical *examen* of reason, will also distract the witty determinations of astrology. *Brown's Vulgar Errours, b.* iv. *c.* 12.

EXA'MINATE. *n. s.* [*examinatus*, Latin.] The person examined.

In an examination where a freed servant, who having power with Claudius, very saucily had almost all the words, asked in scorn one of the *examinates*, who was likewise a freed servant of Scribonianus; I pray, sir, if Scribonianus had been emperor, what would you have done? He answered, I would have stood behind his chair and held my peace. *Bacon.*

EXAMINA'TION. *n. s.* [*examinatio*, Latin.] The act of examining by questions, or experiment; accurate disquisition.

I have brought him forth, that, after *examination* had, I might have somewhat to write. *Acts* xxv. 26.

Different men leaving out or putting in several simple ideas, according to their various *examination*, skill, or observation of the subject, have different essences. *Locke.*

EXAMINA'TOR. *n. s.* [Latin.] An examiner; an enquirer.

An inference, not of power to persuade a serious *examinator*. *Brown's Vulgar Errours, b.* vi. *c.* 6.

To EXA'MINE. *v. a.* [*examino*, Latin.]

1. To try a person accused or suspected by interrogatories.

Let them *examine* themselves whether they repent them truly. *Ch. Cat.*

If we this day be *examined* of the good deed done to the impotent man. *Acts* iv. 9.

We ought, before it be too late, to *examine* our souls, and provide for futurity. *Wake's Preparation for Death.*

2. To interrogate a witness.

Command his accusers to come unto thee, by *examining* of whom thyself mayest take knowledge of all these things. *Acts.*

3. To try the truth or falshood of any proposition.

4. To try by experiment, or observation; narrowly sift; scan.

To write what may securely stand the test
Of being well read over thrice at least,
Compare each phrase, *examine* ev'ry line,
Weigh ev'ry word, and every thought refine.

5. To make enquiry into; to search into; to scrutinise.

When I began to *examine* the extent and certainty of our knowledge, I found it had a near connexion with words. *Locke.*

EXA'MINER. *n. s.* [from *examine.*]

1. One who interrogates a criminal or evidence.

A crafty clerk, commissioner, or *examiner*, will make a witness speak what he truly never meant. *Hale's Law of Engl.*

2. One who searches or tries any thing; one who scrutinises.

So much diligence is not altogether necessary, but it will promote the success of the experiments, and by a very scrupulous *examiner* of things deserves to be applied. *Newt. Opt.*

EXA'MPLARY. *adj.* [from *example.*] Serving for example or pattern; proposed to imitation.

We are not of opinion that nature, in working, hath before her certain *examplary* draughts or patterns, which subsisting in the bosom of the Highest, and being thence discovered, she fixeth her eye upon them. *Hooker, b.* i. *s.* 3.

EXA'MPLE. *n. s.* [*exemple*, French; *exemplum*, Latin.]

1. Copy or pattern; that which is proposed to be resembled or imitated.

The *example* and pattern of those his creatures he beheld in all eternity. *Raleigh's History of the World.*

2. Precedent; former instance of the like.

So hot a speed, with such advice dispos'd,
Such temp'rate order in so fierce a course,
Doth want *example*. *Shakespeare's King John.*

3. Precedent of good.

Let us shew an *example* to our brethren. *Judith* viii. 24.

Taught this by his *example*, whom I now
Acknowledge my Redeemer ever blest! *Milt. Parad. Lost.*

4. A person fit to be proposed as a pattern.

Be thou an *example* of the believers. *1 Tim.* iv. 12.

5. One punished for the admonition of others.

Sodom and Gomorrah, giving themselves over to fornication, are set forth for an *example*, suffering the vengeance of eternal fire. *Jude* vii.

6. Influence which disposes to imitation.

When virtue is present, men take *example* at it; and when it is gone, they desire it. *Wisd.* iv. 2.

Example is a motive of a very prevailing force on the actions of men. *Rogers, Sermon* 4.

7. Instance; illustration of a general position by some particular specification.

Can we, for *example*, give the praise of valour to a man, who, seeing his gods prophaned, should want the courage to defend them? *Dryden's Virg. Æn. Dedication.*

8. Instance in which a rule is illustrated by an application.

My reason is sufficiently convinced both of the truth and usefulness of his precepts: it is to pretend that I have, at least in some places, made *examples* to his rules. *Dryden.*

To EXA'MPLE. *v. a.* [from the noun.] To examplify; to give an instance of.

The proof whereof I saw sufficiently *exampled* in these late wars of Munster. *Spenser's State of Ireland.*

EXA'NGUIOUS. *adj.* [*exanguis*, Latin.] Having no blood; formed with animal juices, not sanguineous.

Hereby they confound the generation of perfect animals with imperfect, sanguineous with *exanguious*. *Brown.*

The insects, if we take in the *exanguious*, both terrestial and aquatick, may for number vie even with plants. *Ray.*

EXA'NIMATE. *adj.* [*exanimatus*, Latin.]

1. Lifeless; dead.

2. Spiritless; depressed.

The grey morn
Lifts her pale lustre on the paler wretch,
Exanimate by love. *Thomson's Spring, l.* 1045.

EXANIMA'TION. *n. s.* [from *exanimate.*] Deprivation of life. *Dict.*

EXA'NIMOUS. *adj.* [*exanimis*, Latin.] Lifeless; dead; killed.

EXANTHE'MATA. *n. s.* [ἐξανθήματα.] Efflorescencies; eruptions; breaking out; pustules.

EXANTHE'MATOUS. *adj.* [from *exanthemata.*] Pustulous; efflorescent; eruptive.

To EXANTLA'TE. *n. s.* [*exantlo*, Latin.]

1. To draw out.

2. To exhaust; to waste away.

By time those seeds are wearied or *exantlated*, or unable to act their parts any longer. *Boyle's Scept. Chym.*

EXANTLA'TION. *n. s.* [from *exantlate.*] The act of drawing out; exhaustion.

EXARA'TION. *n. s.* [*exaro*, Lat.] The manual act of writing; the manner of manual writing. *Dict.*

EXARTICULA'TION. *n. s.* [*ex* and *articulus*, Latin.] The dislocation of a joint. *Dict.*

To EXA'SPERATE. *v. a.* [*exaspero*, Latin.]

1. To provoke; to enrage; to irritate; to anger; to make furious.

To take the widow,
Exasperates, makes mad her sister Goneril. *Shak. K. Lear.*

The people of Italy, who run into news and politicks, have something to *exasperate* them against the king of France. *Addison's Remarks on Italy.*

2. To heighten a difference; to aggravate; to embitter.

Matters grew more *exasperate* between the two kings of England

England and France, for the auxiliary forces of French and English were much blooded one against another. *Bacon.*

When our ambition is unable to attain its end, it is not only wearied, but *exasperated* too at the vanity of its labours. *Parnel to Pope.*

3. To exacerbate; to heighten malignity.

The plaister alone would pen the humour already contained in the part, and so *exasperate* it *Bacon's Natural History.*

EXASPERA'TER. *n. s.* [from *exasperate.*] He that exasperates, or provokes; a provoker.

EXASPERA'TION. *n. s.* [from *exasperate.*]

1. Aggravation; malignant representation.

My going to demand justice upon the five members, my enemies loaded with all the obloquies and *exasperations* they could. *King Charles.*

2. Provocation; irritation; incitement to rage.

Their ill usage and *exasperations* of him, and his zeal for maintaining his argument, dispofed him to take liberty. *Woodw.*

To EXAU'CTORATE. *v. a.* [*exauctoro*, Latin.]

1. To dismiss from service.

2. To deprive of a benefice.

Arch hereticks, in the primitive days of Christianity, were by the church treated with no other punishment than excommunication, and by *exauctorating* and depriving them of their degrees therein. *Ayliffe's Parergon.*

EXAUTORA'TION. *n. s.* [from *exauctorate.*]

1. Dismission from service.

2. Deprivation; degradation.

Deposition, degradation, or *exauctoration*, is nothing else but the removing of a person from some dignity or order in the church, and the depriving him of his ecclesiastical preferments. *Ayliffe's Parergon.*

EXCANDE'SCENCE. } EXCANDE'SCENCY. } *n. s.* [*excandesco*, Latin.]

1. Heat; the state of growing hot.

2. Anger; the state of growing angry.

EXCANTA'TION. *n. s.* [*excanto*, Latin.] Disenchantment by a counter-charm.

To EXCA'RNATE. *v. a.* [*ex* and *carnes*, Latin.] To clear from flesh.

The spleen is most curiously *excarnated*, and the vessels filled with wax, whereby its fibres and vessels are very well seen. *Grew's Musæum.*

EXCARNIFICA'TION. *n. s.* [*excarnifico*, Latin.] The act of taking away the flesh.

To E'XCAVATE. *v. a.* [*excavo*, Latin.] To hollow; to cut into hollows.

The cups, gilt with a golden border about the brim, were of that wonderful smalness, that Faber put a thousand of them into an *excavated* pepper-corn. *Ray on the Creation.*

Though nitrous tempests, and clandestine death,
Fill'd the deep caves, and num'rous vaults beneath,
Which form'd with art, and wrought with endless toil,
Ran through the faithless *excavated* soil,
See the unweary'd Briton delves his way,
And to the caverns lets in war and day. *Blackm. Creation.*

Flat thecæ, some like hats, some like buttons, *excavated* in the middle. *Derham's Physico-Theology.*

EXCAVA'TION. *n. s.* [from *excavate.*]

1. The act of cutting into hollows.

2. The hollow formed; the cavity.

While our eye measures the eminent and the hollowed parts of pillars, the total object appeareth the bigger; and so, as much as those *excavations* do substract, is supplied by a fallacy of the sight. *Wotton's Architecture.*

To EXCE'ED. *v. a.* [*excedo*, Latin.]

1. To go beyond; to outgo.

Nor did any of the crusts much *exceed* half an inch in thickness. *Woodward on Fossils.*

2. To excel; to surpass.

Solomon *exceeded* all the kings of the earth. *1 Kings* x. 23.

To EXCE'ED. *v. n.*

1. To go too far; to pass the bounds of fitness.

In your prayers, and places of religion, use reverent postures and great attention, remembering that we speak to God, in our reverence to whom we cannot possibly *exceed*. *Taylor.*

2. To go beyond any limits.

Forty stripes he may give him, and not *exceed*. *Deutr.* xxv.

3. To bear the greater proportion.

Justice must punish the rebellious deed;
Yet punish so, as pity shall *exceed*. *Dryd. State of Innocence.*

EXCE'EDING. *participial adj.* [from *exceed.*] Great in quantity, extent, or duration.

He saith, that cities were built an *exceeding* space of time before the great flood. *Raleigh's History of the World.*

EXCE'EDING. *adv.* [This word is not analogical, but has been long admitted and established.] In a very great degree; eminently.

The country is supposed to be *exceeding* rich. *Abbot.*

The Genoese were *exceeding* powerful by sea, and had many places in the East, and contended often with the Venetians for superiority. *Raleigh.*

Talk no more so *exceeding* proudly; let not arrogance come out of your mouth. *1 Sa.* ii. 3.

The action of the Iliad and that of the Æneid were in themselves *exceeding* short; but are beautifully extended and diversified by the invention of episodes, and the machinery of the gods. *Addison's Spectator*, N°. 267.

The serum of the blood affords, by distillation, an *exceeding* limpid water, neither acid nor alkaline. *Arbuthn. on Alim.*

EXCE'EDINGLY. *adv.* [from *exceeding.*] To a great degree; greatly; very much.

They cried out the more *exceedingly*, crucify him. *Mar.* xv.

Isaac trembled *exceedingly*. *Gen.* xxvii. 33.

The earl of Surrey, lieutenant of Ireland, was much feared of the king's enemies, and *exceedingly* beloved of the king's subjects. *Davies on Ireland.*

Precious stones look *exceedingly* well, when they are set in those places which we would make to come out of the picture. *Dryden's Dufresnoy.*

Is not this medium *exceedingly* more rare and subtile than the air, and *exceedingly* more elastick and active? *Newt. Opt.*

To EXCE'L. *v. a.* [*excello*, Latin.] To outgo in good qualities; to surpass.

Venus her myrtle, Phœbus has his bays;
Tea both *excels*, which you vouchsafe to praise. *Waller.*

How heroes rise, how patriots set,
Thy father's bloom and death may tell;
Excelling others, these were great;
Thou, greater still, must these *excel*. *Prior.*

To EXCE'L. *v. n.* To have good qualities in a great degree; to be eminent; to be excellent.

Then to Silvia let us sing,
That Silvia is *excelling*. *Shakesp. Two Gent. of Verona.*

Reuben, unstable as water, thou shalt not *excel*. *Gen.* xlix.

It is not only in order of nature for him to govern, that is, the more intelligent; but there is no less required, courage to protect, and, above all, honesty and probity to abstain from injury: so fitness to govern is a perplexed business. Some men, some nations, *excel* in the one ability, some in the other. *Bacon's Holy War.*

Company are to be avoided that are good for nothing; those to be sought and frequented that *excel* in some quality or other. *Temple.*

He match'd their beauties where they most *excel*;
Of love sung better, and of arms as well. *Dryden.*

Let those teach others, who themselves *excel*;
And censure freely, who have written well. *Pope.*

EXCELLE'NCE. } EXCELLE'NCY. } *n. s.* [*excellence*, French; *excellentia*, Latin.]

1. The state of abounding in any good quality.

2. Dignity; high rank in existence.

Is it not wonderful, that base desires should so extinguish in men the sense of their own *excellency*, as to make them willing that their souls should be like to the souls of beasts, mortal and corruptible with their bodies? *Hooker, b.* v. *s.* 2.

I know not why a fiend may not deceive a creature of more *excellency* than himself, but yet a creature. *Dryden's Juv. Dedic.*

3. The state of excelling in any thing.

I have, amongst men of parts and business, seldom heard any one commended for having an *excellency* in musick. *Locke.*

4. That in which one excels.

The criticisms have been made rather to discover beauties and *excellencies* than their faults and imperfections. *Addis. Spect.*

5. Purity; goodness.

She loves him with that *excellence*,
That angels love good men with. *Shakespeare's Henry* VIII.

6. A title of honour. It is now usually applied to generals of an army, ambassadors, and governors.

They humbly sue unto your *excellence*,
To have a goodly peace concluded of. *Shakesp. Henry* VI.

E'XCELLENT. *adj.* [*excellens*, Latin.]

1. Of great virtue; of great worth; of great dignity.

Arts and sciences are *excellent*, in order to certain ends. *Tayl.*

2. Eminent in any good quality.

He is *excellent* in power and in judgment. *Job* xxxvii. 23.

E'XCELLENTLY. *adv.* [from *excellent.*]

1. Well; in a high degree.

He determines that man was erect, because he was made with hands, as he *excellently* declareth. *Brown's Vulg. Errours.*

That was *excellently* observed, says I, when I read a passage in an author, where his opinion agrees with mine. *Swift.*

2. To an eminent degree.

Comedy is both *excellently* instructive and extremely pleasant; satyr lashes vice into reformation; and humour represents folly, so as to render it ridiculous. *Dryd. St. of Inn. Pref.*

To EXCE'PT. *v. a.* [*excipio*, Latin.]

1. To leave out, and specify as left out of a general precept, or position.

But when he saith, all things are put under him, it is manifest, that he is *excepted* which did put all things under him. *1 Cor.* xv. 27.

Adam, behold
Th' effects, which thy original crime hath wrought

In

In some to spring from thee, who never touch'd
Th' *excepted* tree. *Milton's Paradise Lost*, *b.* xi. *l.* 426.

To EXCE'PT. *v. n.* To object; to make objections.

A succession which our author could not *except* against. *Locke.*

EXCE'PT. *preposit.* [from the verb. This word, long taken as a preposition or conjunction, is originally the participle passive of the verb; which, like most others, had for its participle two terminations, *except* or *excepted*. *All* except *one*, is *all*, *one* excepted. *Except* may be, according to the *Teutonick* idiom, the imperative mood: *all*, except *one*; that is, all but one, which you must except.]

1. Exclusively of; without inclusion of.

Richard *except*, those, whom we fight against,
Had rather have us win than him they follow. *Shak. R.* III.
God and his son *except*,
Nought valued he nor fear'd. *Milton.*

2. Unless.

It is necessary to know our duty, because 'tis necessary for us to do it; and it is impossible to do it, *except* we know it. *Till.*

EXCE'PTING. *preposit.* [from *except*. See EXCEPT.] Without inclusion of; with exception of. An improper word.

What, since the pretor did my fetters loose,
May I not live without controul and awe,
Excepting still the letter of the law. *Dryden's Pers. Sat.* 5.

People come into the world in Turkey the same way they do here; and yet, *excepting* the royal family, they get but little by it. *Collier on Duelling.*

EXCE'PTION. *n. s.* [from *except*; *exceptio*, Latin.]

1. Exclusion from the things comprehended in a precept, or position; exclusion of any person from a general law.

When God renewed this charter of man's sovereignty over the creatures to Noah and his family, we find no *exception* at all; but that Cham stood as fully invested with this right as any of his brethren. *South's Sermons.*

2. It should have *from* before the rule or law to which the exception refers; but it is sometimes inaccurately used with *to*.

Let the money be raised on land, with an *exception* to some of the more barren parts, that might be tax-free. *Addison.*

Pleads, in *exception to* all gen'ral rules,
Your taste of follies with our scorn of fools. *Pope's Epistles.*

3. Thing excepted or specified in exception.

Every act of parliament was not previous to what it enacted; unless those two, by which the earl of Strafford and sir John Fenwick lost their heads may pass for *exceptions*. *Swift.*

Who first taught souls enslav'd, and realms undone,
Th' enormous faith of many made for one;
That proud *exception to* all nature's laws,
T' invert the world and counterwork its cause. *Pope's Essays.*

4. Objection; cavil. With *against* or *to*.

Your assertion hath drawn us to make search whether these be just *exceptions against* the customs of our church, when ye plead that they are the same which the church of Rome hath, or that they are not the same which some other reformed churches have devised. *Hooker, Preface.*

He may have *exceptions* peremptory *against* the jurors, of which he then shall shew cause. *Spenser.*

Revelations will soon be discerned to be extremely conducible to reforming men's lives, such as will answer all objections and *exceptions* of flesh and blood *against* it. *Hammond.*

I will answer what *exceptions* they can have *against* our account, and confute all the reasons and explications they can give of their own. *Bentley's Sermons.*

5. Peevish dislike; offence taken.

I fear'd to shew my father Julia's letter,
Lest he should take *exceptions* to my love. *Shakespeare.*
He first took *exception* at this badge,
Pronouncing, that the paleness of this flow'r
Bewray'd the faintness of my master's heart. *Shak. Hen.* VI.

Rodorigo, thou hast taken against me an *exception*; but I protest I have dealt most directly in thy affair. *Sh. Othello.*

He gave sir James Tirrel great thanks; but took *exception* to the place of their burial, being too base for them that were king's children. *Bacon's Henry* VII.

EXCE'PTIONABLE. *adj.* [from *exception*.] Liable to objection.

The only piece of pleasantry is where the evil spirits rally the angels upon the success of their artillery: this passage I look upon to be the most *exceptionable* in the whole poem. *Add.*

EXCE'PTIOUS. *adj.* [from *except*.] Peevish; froward; full of objections; quarrelsome.

They are so supercilious, sharp, troublesome, fierce, and *exceptious*, that they are not only short of the true character of friendship, but become the very sores and burdens of society. *South's Sermons.*

EXCE'PTIVE. *adj.* [from *except*.] Including an exception.

Exceptive propositions will make complex syllogisms, as none but physicians came to the consultation: the nurse is no physician, therefore the nurse came not to the consultation. *Watts's Logick.*

EXCE'PTLESS. *adj.* [from *except*.] Omitting or neglecting all exception; general; universal.

Forgive my gen'ral and *exceptless* rashness,
Perpetual sober gods! I do proclaim
One honest man. *Shakespeare's Timon.*

EXCE'PTOR. *n. s.* [from *except*.] Objecter; one that makes exceptions.

The *exceptor* makes a reflection upon the impropriety of those expressions. *Burnet's Theory of the Earth.*

To EXCE'RN. *v. a.* [*excerno*, Latin.] To strain out; to separate or emit by strainers; to send out by excretion.

That which is dead, or corrupted, or *excerned*, hath antipathy with the same thing when it is alive and sound, and with those parts which do *excern*. *Bacon's Natural History.*

Exercise first sendeth nourishment into the parts; and secondly, helpeth to *excern* by sweat, and so maketh the parts assimilate. *Bacon's Natural History*, N°. 299.

An unguent or pap prepared, with an open vessel to *excern* it into. *Ray on the Creation.*

EXCE'RPTION. *n. s.* [*excerptio*, Latin.]

1. The act of gleaning; selecting.

2. The thing gleaned or selected.

Times have consumed his works, saving some few *excerptions*. *Raleigh.*

EXCE'SS. *n. s.* [*excessus*, Latin.]

1. More than enough; superfluity.

Amongst the heaps of these *excesses* and superfluities, there is espied the want of a principal part of duty. *Hooker, b.* v. *s.* 43.

Goodness answers to the theological virtue charity, and admits no *excess* but error: the desire of power in *excess* caused the angels to fall; the desire of knowledge in *excess* caused man to fall; but in charity there is no *excess*, neither can angel or man come in danger by it. *Bacon's Essays.*

Members are crooked or distorted, or disproportionate to the rest, either in *excess* or defect. *Ray on the Creation.*

2. Exuberance; act of exceeding; comparative exuberance.

Let the superfluous and lust dieted man,
That braves your ordinance, feel your power quickly;
So distribution shall undo *excess*,
And each man have enough. *Shakespeare's King Lear.*

The several rays in that white light retain their colorifick qualities, by which those of any sort, whenever they become more copious than the rest, do by their *excess* and predominance cause their proper colour to appear. *Newton's Opt.*

3. Intemperance; unreasonable indulgence in meat and drink.

It was *excess* of wine that set him on,
And on his more advice we pardon him. *Shakesp. Hen.* V.

There will be need first of temperance in diet; for the body, once heavy with *excess* and surfeits, hangs plummets on the nobler parts. *Duppa's Rules for Devotion.*

4. Violence of passion.

5. Transgression of due limits.

A popular sway, by forcing kings to give
More than was fit for subjects to receive,
Ran to the same extremes; and one *excess*
Made both, by striving to be greater, less. *Denham.*

Hospitality sometimes degenerates into profuseness: even parsimony itself, which sits but ill upon a publick figure, is yet the more pardonable *excess* of the two. *Atterbury's Sermons.*

EXCE'SSIVE. *adj.* [*excessif*, French; from *excess*.]

1. Beyond the common proportion of quantity or bulk.

If panicum be laid below and about the bottom of a root, it will cause the root to grow to an *excessive* bigness. *Bacon.*

2. Vehement beyond measure in kindness or dislike.

Be not *excessive* toward any. *Ecclus.* xxxiii 29.

The people whose property it is, by *excessive* favour, to bring great men to misery, and then to be *excessive* in pity, departed away grieved and afraid. *Hayward.*

EXCE'SSIVELY. *adv.* [from *excessive*.] Exceedingly; eminently; in a great degree.

A man must be *excessively* stupid, as well as uncharitable, who believes there is no virtue but on his own side. *Addison.*

To EXCHA'NGE. *v. a.* [*exchanger*, French; *excambiare*, low Latin.]

1. To give or quit one thing for the sake of gaining another.

They shall not sell of it, neither *exchange* nor alienate the first fruits. *Ezek.* xlviii. 14.

Exchange his sheep for shells, or wool for a sparkling pebble, or a diamond. *Locke.*

Take delight in the good things of this world, so as to remember that we are to part with them, and to *exchange* them for more excellent and durable enjoyments. *Atterbury's Serm.*

2. To give and take reciprocally.

Exchange forgiveness with me, noble Hamlet;
Mine and my father's blood, be not upon thee,
Nor thine on me. *Shakespeare's Hamlet.*

Words having naturally no signification, the idea must be learned by those who would *exchange* thoughts, and hold intelligible discourse with others. *Locke.*

Here then *exchange* we mutually forgiveness,
So may the guilt of all my broken vows,
My perjuries to thee, be all forgotten. *Rowe's Jane Shore.*

3. It has *with* before the person with whom the exchange is made, and *for* before the thing taken in exchange.

The king called in the old money, and erected exchanges where the weight of old money was *exchanged for* new. *Camd.*

Being acquainted with the laws and fashions of his own country, he has something to *exchange* with those abroad. *Locke.*

Excha'nge. *n. s.* [from the verb.]

1. The act of giving and receiving reciprocally.

And thus they parted with *exchange* of harms;
Much blood the monsters lost, and they their arms. *Waller.*

They lend their corn, they make *exchanges*; they are always ready to serve one another. *Addison.*

2. Traffick by permutation.

The world is maintained by intercourse; and the whole course of nature is a great *exchange*, in which one good turn is, and ought to be, the stated price of another. *South's Serm.*

3. The form or act of transferring, properly by bills or notes.

I have bills for money by *exchange*
From Florence, and must here deliver them. *Shakespeare.*

4. The balance of the money of different nations.

He was skilful in the *exchange* beyond seas, and in all the circumstances and practices thereof. *Hayward on Edward VI.*

5. The thing given in return for something received.

Thou art arm'd, Glo'ster; let the trumpet sound:
If none appear to prove upon thy person
Thy heinous, manifest, and many treasons,
There is my pledge: I'll prove it on thy heart.
—There's my *exchange*; what in the world he is
That names me traitor, villain-like he lies. *Shak. K. Lear.*

Spend all I have, only give me so much time in *exchange* of it. *Shakesp. Merry Wives of Windsor.*

It made not the silver coined go for more than its value in all things to be bought; but just so much as the denomination was raised, just so much less of commodity had the buyer in *exchange* for it. *Locke.*

If blood you seek, I will my own resign:
O spare her life, and in *exchange* take mine. *Dryd. Ind. Emp.*

6. The thing received in return for something given.

The respect and love which was paid you by all, who had the happiness to know you, was a wise *exchange* for the honours of the court. *Dryden.*

7. The place where the merchants meet to negociate their affairs; place of sale.

He that uses the same words sometimes in one, and sometimes in another signification, ought to pass, in the schools, for as fair a man, as he does, in the market and *exchange*, who sells several things under the same name. *Locke.*

No thing, no place is strange,
While his fair bosom is the world's *exchange*. *Denham.*

Excha'nger. *n. s.* [from *exchange.*] One who practises exchange.

Whilst bullion may be had for a small price more than the weight of our current cash, these *exchangers* generally chuse rather to buy bullion than run the risk of melting down our coin, which is criminal by the law. *Locke.*

Exche'at. *n. s.* See Escheat.

The sons of day he favoureth, I see,
And by my ruins thinks to make them great:
To make one great by others loss, is bad *excheat*. *Fai. Qu.*

Exche'ator. *n. s.* See Escheator.

These earls and dukes appointed their special officers; as sheriff, admiral, receiver, havener, customer, butler, searcher, comptroller, gager, *excheator*, feodary, auditor, and clerk of the market. *Carew's Survey of Cornwal.*

Exche'quer. *n. s.* [*eschequeir*, Norman French; *scaccharium*, low Latin, from *schatz*, a treasure, German.] The court to which are brought all the revenues belonging to the crown. It consists of two parts; whereof one dealeth specially in the hearing and deciding of all causes appertaining to the king's coffers: the other is called the receipt of the exchequer, which is properly employed in the receiving and paying of money. It is also a court of record, wherein all causes touching the revenues of the crown are handled. *Harris.*

I will be cheater to them both, and they shall be *exchequers* to me: they shall be my East and West Indies. *Shakespeare.*

Your treasures
Are quite exhausted, the *exchequer*'s empty. *Denham's Sophy.*

Clipped money will pass whilst the king's bankers and at last the *exchequer* takes it. *Locke.*

EXCI'SE. *n. s.* [*accijs*, Dutch; *excisum*, Latin.] A hateful tax levied upon commodities, and adjudged not by the common judges of property, but wretches hired by those to whom excise is paid.

The people should pay a ratable tax for their sheep, and an *excise* for every thing which they should eat. *Hayward.*

Ambitious now to take *excise*
Of a more fragrant paradise. *Cleaveland.*

Excise,
With hundred rows of teeth, the shark exceeds,
And on all trades like Cassawar she feeds. *Marvel.*

Can hire large houses, and oppress the poor,
By farm'd *excise*. *Dryden's Juvenal, Sat.* 3.

To Exci'se. *v. a.* [from the noun.] To levy excise upon a person or thing.

In South-sea days, not happier when surmis'd
The lord of thousands, than if now *excis'd*. *Pope's Horace.*

Exci'seman. *n. s.* [*excise* and *man.*] An officer who inspects commodities, and rates their excise.

Exci'sion. *n. s.* [*excisio*, Latin.] Extirpation; destruction; ruin; the act of cutting off; the state of being cut off.

Pride is one of the fatallest instruments of *excision*. *Decay of Piety.*

Such conquerors are the instruments of vengeance on those nations that have filled up the measure of iniquities, and are grown ripe for *excision*. *Atterbury's Sermons.*

Excita'tion. *n. s.* [from *excito*, to *excite*, Latin.]

1. The act of exciting, or putting into motion.

All putrefactions come from the ambient body, either by ingress of the ambient body into the body putrefied, or by *excitation* and solicitation of the body putrefied by the body ambient. *Bacon's Natural History*, N°. 836.

2. The act of rousing or awakening.

The original of sensible and spiritual ideas may be owing to sensation and reflection, the recollection and fresh *excitation* of them to other occasions. *Watts's Logick.*

To EXCI'TE. *v. a.* [*excito*, Latin.]

1. To rouse; to animate; to stir up; to encourage.

The Lacedemonians were more *excited* to desire of honour with the excellent verses of the poet Tirtæus, than with all the exhortations of their captains, or authority of their rulers and magistrates. *Spenser's State of Ireland.*

That kind of poesy which *excites* to virtue the greatest men, is of greatest use to human kind. *Dryden.*

2. To put into motion; to awaken; to raise.

Exci'tement. *n. s.* [from *excite.*] The motive by which one is stirred up, animated, or put in action.

How stand I then,
That have a father kill'd, a mother stain'd,
Excitements of my reason and my blood,
And let all sleep? *Shakespeare's Tempest.*

Exci'ter. *n. s.* [from *excite.*]

1. One that stirs up others, or puts them in motion.

They never punished the delinquency of the tumults and their *exciters*. *King Charles.*

2. The cause by which any thing is raised or put in motion.

Hope is the grand *exciter* of industry. *Decay of Piety.*

To EXCLA'IM. *v. n.* [*exclamo*, Latin.]

1. To cry out with vehemence; to make an outcry; to cry out querulously and outrageously.

This ring,
Which, when you part from, lose, or give away,
Let it presage the ruin of your love,
And be my 'vantage to *exclaim* on you. *Sh. Merch. of Venice.*

Those who *exclaim* against all foreign tyranny, do, to this intestine usurper, make an entire dedition of themselves. *Decay of Piety.*

The most insupportable of tyrants *exclaim* against the exercise of arbitrary power. *L'Estrange.*

2. To declare with loud vociferation.

Is Cade the son of Henry the fifth,
That thus you do *exclaim* you'll go with him? *Shak. H.VI.*

Excla'im. *n. s.* [from the verb.] Clamour; outcry. Now disused.

Alas, the part I had in Glo'ster's blood
Doth more solicit me than your *exclaims*,
To stir against the butchers of his life. *Shakes. Richard* II.

Exclama'tion. *n. s.* [*exclamatio*, Latin.]

1. Vehement outcry; clamour; outrageous vociferation.

The ears of the people are continually beaten with *exclamations* against abuses in the church. *Hooker, Dedication.*

Either be patient, and intreat me fair,
Or with the clamorous report of war
Thus will I drown your *exclamations*. *Shakesp. Richard* III.

2. An emphatical utterance; a pathetical sentence.

O Musidorus! Musidorus! but what serve *exclamations*, where there are no ears to receive the sound? *Sidney, b.* ii.

3. A note by which a pathetical sentence is marked thus!

Excla'mer. *n. s.* [from *exclaim.*] One that makes vehement outcries; one that speaks with great heat and passion.

I must tell this *exclaimer*, that, if that were his real aim, his manner of proceeding is very strange and unaccountable. *Atterbury's Sermons, Preface.*

Excla'matory. *adj.* [from *exclaim.*]

1. Practising exclamation.

2. Containing exclamation.

To EXCLU'DE. *v. a.* [*excludo*, Latin.]

1. To shut out; to hinder from entrance or admission.

Fenc'd with hedges and deep ditches round,
Exclude th' incroaching cattle from thy ground. *Dryd. Virg.*

Sure I am, unless I win in arms,
To stand *excluded* from Emilia's charms. *Dryd Knight's Tale.*

Bodies do each singly possess its proper portion, according to the extent of its solid parts, and thereby *exclude* all other bodies from that space. *Locke.*

Though these three sorts of substances do not *exclude* one another out of the same place, yet we cannot conceive but that they must necessarily each of them *exclude* any of the same kind out of the same place. *Locke.*

If the church be so unhappily contrived as to *exclude* from its communion such persons likeliest to have great abilities, it should be altered. *Swift.*

2. To debar; to hinder from participation; to prohibit.

Justice, that sits and frowns where publick laws
Exclude soft mercy from a private cause,
In your tribunal most herself does please;
There only smiles, because she lives at ease. *Dryden.*

This is Dutch partnership, to share in all our beneficial bargains, and *exclude* us wholly from theirs. *Swift.*

3. To except in any position.

4. Not to comprehend in any grant or privilege.

They separate from all apparent hope of life and salvation, thousands whom the goodness of Almighty God doth not *exclude*. *Hooker, b.* v. *s.* 22.

EXCLU'SION. *n. s.* [from *exclude*.]

1. The act of shutting out or denying admission.

In bodies that need detention of spirits, the *exclusion* of the air doth good; but in bodies that need emission of spirits, it doth hurt. *Bacon's Natural History*, N°. 343.

2. Rejection; not reception in any manner.

If he is for an entire *exclusion* of fear, which is supposed to have some influence in every law, he opposes himself to every government. *Addison's Freeholder*, N°. 31.

3. The act of debarring from any privilege, or participation.

4. Exception.

There was a question also asked at the table, whether the French king would agree to have the disposing of the marriage of Bretagne, with an exception and *exclusion* that he should not marry her himself. *Bacon's Henry* VII.

5. The dismission of the young from the egg or womb.

How were it possible the womb should contain the child, nay sometimes twins, 'till they come to their due perfection and maturity for *exclusion*? *Ray on the Creation.*

EXCLU'SIVE. *adj.* [from *exclude*.]

1. Having the power of excluding or denying admission.

They obstacle find none
Of membrane, joint, or limb, *exclusive* bars:
Easier than air with air, if spirits embrace,
Total they mix. *Milton's Paradise Lost, b.* viii. *l.* 625.

2. Debarring from participation.

In Scripture there is no such thing as an heir that was, by right of nature, to inherit all, *exclusive* of his brethren. *Locke.*

3. Not taking into an account or number; opposed to inclusive.

I know not whether he reckons the dross *exclusive* or inclusive with his three hundred and sixty tons of copper. *Swift.*

4. Excepting.

EXCLU'SIVELY. *adv.* [from *exclusive*.]

1. Without admission of another to participation.

It is not so easy to discern, among the many differing substances that may be obtained from the same portion of matter, which ought to be esteemed, *exclusively* to all the rest, its inexistent elementary ingredients; much less what primogeneal and simple bodies, convened together, compose it. *Boyle.*

Ulysses addresses himself to the queen chiefly or primarily, but not *exclusively* of the king. *Notes to Pope's Odyssey.*

2. Without comprehension in an account or number.

The first part lasts from the date of the citation to the joining of issue, *exclusively*: the second continues to a conclusion in the cause, inclusively. *Ayliffe's Parergon.*

To EXCO'CT. *v. a.* [*excoctus*, Latin.] To boil up; to make by boiling.

Salt and sugar, *excocted* by heat, are dissolved by cold and moisture. *Bacon's Natural History*, N°. 843.

To EXCO'GITATE. *v. a.* [*excogito*, Latin.] To invent; to strike out by thinking.

If the wit of man had been to contrive this organ for himself, what could he have possibly *excogitated* more accurate? *More's Antidote against Atheism.*

The tradition of the origination of mankind seems to be universal; but the particular methods of that origination, *excogitated* by the heathen, were particular. *Hale's Orig. of Mank.*

We shall find them to be little else than *excogitated* and invented models, not much arising from the true image of the things themselves. *Hale's Origin of Mankind.*

To EXCO'MMUNICATE. *v. a.* [*excommunico*, low Latin.] To eject from the communion of the visible church by an ecclesiastical censure; to interdict from the participation of holy mysteries.

Thou shalt stand curst and *excommunicate*;
And blessed shall he be, that doth revolt
From his allegiance to an heretick. *Shakesp. King John.*

What if they shall *excommunicate* me, hath the doctrine of meekness any salve for me then? *Hammond's Pract. Catech.*

The office is performed by the parish-priest at interment, but not unto persons *excommunicated.* *Ayliffe's Parergon.*

EXCOMMUNICA'TION. *n. s.* [from *excommunicate*.] An ecclesiastical interdict; exclusion from the fellowship of the church.

As for *excommunication*, it neither shutteth out from the mystical, nor clean from the visible church; but only from fellowship with the visible in holy duties. *Hooker, b.* iii. *s.* 1.

To EXCO'RIATE. *v. a.* To flay; to strip off the skin.

An hypersarcosis arises upon the *excoriated* eyelid, and turneth it outward. *Wiseman's Surgery.*

A looseness proves often a fatal symptom in fevers; for it weakens, *excoriates*, and inflames the bowels. *Arbuthnot.*

EXCORIA'TION. *n. s.* [from *excoriate*.]

1. Loss of skin; privation of skin; the act of flaying.

The pituite secerned in the nose, mouth, and intestines, is not an excrementitious, but a laudable humour, necessary for defending those parts from *excoriations*. *Arbuthn. on Aliments.*

2. Plunder; spoil; the act of stripping of possessions.

It hath marvellously enhanced the revenues of the crown to many millions more than it was, though with a pitiful *excoriation* of the poorer sort. *Howel's Vocal Forrest.*

EXCORTICA'TION. *n. s.* [from *cortex* and *ex*, Latin.] Pulling the bark off any thing. *Quincy.*

To E'XCREATE. *v. a.* [*excreo*, Latin.] To eject at the mouth by hawking, or forcing matter from the throat.

E'XCREMENT. *n. s.* [*excrementum*, Latin.] That which is thrown out as useless, noxious, or corrupted from the natural passages of the body.

We see that those *excrements*, that are of the first digestion, smell the worst; as the *excrements* from the belly. *Bacon.*

It fares with politick bodies as with the physical; each would convert all into their own proper substance, and cast forth as *excrement* what will not so be changed. *Raleigh's Essays.*

Their sordid avarice rakes
In *excrements*, and hires the very jakes. *Dryden's Juv. Sat.* 3.

Farce, in itself, is of a nasty scent;
But the gain smells not of the *excrement*. *Dryden.*

You may find, by dissection, not only their stomachs full of meat, but their intestines full of *excrement*. *Bentley's Sermons.*

The *excrements* of horses are nothing but hay, and, as such, combustible. *Arbuthnot on Aliments.*

EXCREME'NTAL. *adj.* [from *excrement*.] That which is voided as excrement.

God hath given virtues to springs, fountains, earth, plants, and the *excremental* parts of the basest living creatures. *Raleigh.*

EXCREMENTI'TIOUS. *adj.* [from *excrement*.] Containing excrements; consisting of matter excreted from the body; offensive or useless to the body.

The *excrementitious* moisture of living creatures passeth in birds through a fairer and more delicate strainer than in beasts. *Bacon's Natural History*, N°. 5.

Toil of the mind destroys health, by attracting the spirits from their task of concoction to the brain; whither they carry along with them clouds of vapours and *excrementitious* humours. *Harvey on Consumptions.*

The lungs are the grand emunctory of the body; and the main end of respiration is continually to discharge and expel an *excrementitious* fluid out of the mass of blood. *Woodward.*

An animal fluid no ways *excrementitious*, mild, elaborated, and nutritious. *Arbuthnot on Aliments.*

EXCRE'SCENCE. } *n. s.* [*excresco*, Latin.] Somewhat growing
EXCRE'SCENCY. } out of another without use, and contrary to the common order of production; preternatural production.

All beyond this is monstrous, 'tis out of nature, 'tis an *excrescence*, and not a living part of poetry. *Dryden.*

We have little more than the *excrescencies* of the Spanish monarchy. *Addison on the State of the War.*

They are the *excrescences* of our souls; which, like our hair and beards, look horrid or becoming, as we cut or let them grow. *Tatler*, N°. 54.

Tumours and *excrescences* of plants, out of which generally issues a fly or a worm, are at first made by such insects which wound the tender buds. *Bentley.*

EXCRE'SCENT. *adj.* [*excrescens*, Latin.] That which grows out of another with preternatural superfluity.

Expunge the whole, or lop the *excrescent* parts
Of all, our vices have created arts:
Then see how little the remaining sum,
Which serv'd the past, and must the times to come. *Pope.*

EXCRE'TION. *n. s.* [*excretio*, Latin.] Separation of animal substance; ejecting somewhat quite out of the body, as of no further use, which is called excrement. *Quincy.*

The symptoms of the *excretion* of the bile vitiated, are a yellowish skin, white hard fæces, loss of appetite, and lixivial urine. *Arbuthnot on Aliments.*

EXCRE'TIVE. *adj.* [*excretus*, Latin.] Having the power of separating and ejecting excrements.

A diminution of the body happens by some fault in the *excretive* faculty, excerning or evacuating more than necessary. *Harvey on Consumptions.*

E'XCRETORY. *adj.* [from *excretion*.] Having the quality of separating and ejecting superfluous parts.

Excretories of the body are nothing but slender slips of the arteries, deriving an appropriated juice from the blood. *Cheyne.*

EXCRU'CIABLE. *adj.* [from *excruciate*.] Liable to torment. *Dict.*

To EXCRU'CIATE. *v. a.* [*excrucio*, Latin.] To torture; to torment.

And here my heart, long time *excruciate*,
Amongst the leaves I rested all that night. *Chapm. Odyssey.*

Leave them, as long as they keep their hardnefs and impenitent hearts, to thofe gnawing and *excruciating* fears, thofe whips of the Divine Nemefis, that frequently fcourge even atheifts themfelves. *Bentley's Sermons.*

EXCUBA'TION. *n. f.* [*excubatio*, Latin.] The act of watching all night. *Dict.*

To EXCU'LPATE. *v. a.* [*ex* and *culpo*, Latin.] To clear from the imputation of a fault.

A good child will not feek to *exculpate* herfelf at the expence of the moft revered characters. *Clariffa.*

EXCU'RSION. *n. f.* [*excurfion*, French; *excurro*, Latin.]

1. The act of deviating from the ftated or fettled path; a ramble.

The mufe whofe early voice you taught to fing,
Prefcrib'd her heights, and prun'd her tender wing;
Her guide now loft, no more attempts to rife,
But in low numbers fhort *excurfions* tries. *Pope's Effays.*

2. An expedition into fome diftant part.

The mind extends its thoughts often even beyond the utmoft expanfion of matter, and makes *excurfions* into that incomprehenfible *Locke.*

3. Progreffion beyond fixed limits.

The caufes of thofe great *excurfions* of the feafons into the extremes of cold and heat, are very obfcure. *Arbuthn. on Air.*

4. Digreffion; ramble from a fubject.

Expect not that I fhould beg pardon for this *excurfion*, 'till I think it a digreffion, to infift on the bleffednefs of Chrift in heaven. *Boyle's Seraphick Love.*

I am too weary to allow myfelf any *excurfion* from the main defign. *Atterbury.*

EXCU'RSIVE. *adj.* [from *excurro*, Latin.] Rambling; wandering; deviating.

But why fo far *excurfive*? when at hand
Along thefe blufhing borders, bright with dew,
Fair-handed Spring unbofoms every grace? *Thomf. Spring.*

EXCU'SABLE. *adj.* [from *excufe.*] Pardonable; that for which fome excufe or apology may be admitted.

Though he were already ftept into the winter of his age, he found himfelf warm in thofe defires, which were in his fon far more *excufable.* *Sidney, b.* ii.

Learned men are *excufable* in particulars, whereupon our falvation dependeth not. *Raleigh's Hiftory of the World.*

Not only that;
That were *excufable*, that and thoufands more
Of femblable import. *Shakefpeare's Anthony and Cleopatra.*

For his intermeddling with arms he is the more *excufable*, becaufe many others of his coat are not only martial directors, but commanders. *Howel's Vocal Forreft.*

Before the Gofpel, impenitency was much more *excufable*, becaufe men were ignorant. *Tillotfon, Sermon* 5.

EXCU'SABLENESS. *n. f.* [from *excufable.*] Pardonablenefs; capability to be excufed.

It may fatisfy others of the *excufablenefs* of my diffatisfaction, to perufe the enfuing relation. *Boyle's Phyfiol. Confiderat.*

EXCUSA'TION. *n. f.* [from *excufe.*] Excufe; plea; apology.

Prefaces, *excufations*, and other fpeeches of reference to the perfon, though they feem to proceed of modefty, they are bravery. *Bacon's Effays.*

And goodnefs to be admired, that it refuted not his argument in the punifhment of his *excufation.* *Brown's Vul. Err.*

EXCU'SATORY. *adj.* [from *excufe.*] Pleading excufe; apologetical; making apology.

To EXCU'SE. *v. a.* [*excufo*, Latin.]

1. To extenuate by apology.

Bad men *excufe* their faults, good men will leave them;
He acts the third crime that defends the firft. *B. Johnf. Catil.*

2. To difengage from an obligation; remit attendance.

I have bought a piece of ground, and I muft needs go and fee it: I pray thee, have me *excufed.* *Luke* xiv. 19.

Laud attended throughout that whole journey, which he was not obliged to do, and no doubt would have been *excufed* from it. *Clarendon.*

3. To remit; not to exact.

4. To weaken or mollify obligation to any thing; to obtain remiffion.

Nor could the real danger of leaving their dwellings to go up to the temple, *excufe* their journey. *South's Sermons.*

5. To pardon by allowing an apology.

O thou, whoe'er thou art, *excufe* the force
Thefe men have us'd; and O befriend our courfe. *Addifon.*
Excufe fome courtly ftrains;
No whiter page than Addifon's remains. *Pope.*

6. To throw off imputation by a feigned apology.

Think you that we *excufe* ourfelves unto you? 2 *Cor.* xii.

EXCU'SE. *n. f.* [from the verb. The laft fyllable of the verb is founded as if written *excuze*, that of the noun with the natural found.]

1. Plea offered in extenuation; apology.

I was fet upon by fome of your fervants, whom becaufe I have in my juft defence evil entreated, I came to make my *excufe* to you. *Sidney.*

Be gone, I will not hear thy vain *excufe*;
But, as thou lov'ft thy life, make fpeed from hence. *Shakef.*

As good fuccefs admits no examination, fo the contrary allows of no *excufe*, how reafonable or juft foever. *Raleigh.*

We find out fome *excufe* or other for deferring good refolutions, 'till our intended retreat is cut off by death. *Addifon.*

2. The act of excufing or apologifing.

Heav'n put it in thy mind to take it hence,
That thou might'ft win the more thy father's love,
Pleading fo wifely in *excufe* of it. *Shakefpeare's Henry* IV.

3. Caufe for which one is excufed.

Let no vain hope your eafy mind feduce;
For rich ill poets are without *excufe.* *Rofcommon.*
Nothing but love this patience could produce;
And I allow your rage that kind *excufe.* *Dryden's Aurengzebe.*

EXCU'SELESS. *adj.* [from *excufe.*] That for which no excufe or apology can be given.

The voluntary enflaving myfelf is *excufelefs.* *Decay of Piety.*

EXCU'SER. *n. f.* [from *excufe.*]

1. One who pleads for another.

In vain would his *excufers* endeavour to palliate his enormities, by imputing them to madnefs. *Swift.*

2. One who forgives another.

To EXCU'SS. *v. a.* [*excuffus*, Lat.] To feize and detain by law.

The perfon of a man ought not, by the civil law, to be taken for a debt, unlefs his goods and eftate has been firft *excuffed.* *Ayliffe's Parergon.*

EXCU'SSION. *n. f.* [*excuffio*, Latin.] Seizure by law.

If upon an *excuffion* there are not goods to fatisfy the judgment, his body may be attached. *Ayliffe's Parergon.*

EXE'CRABLE. *adj.* [*execrabilis*, Latin.] Hateful; deteftable; accurfed; abominable.

For us to change that which he hath eftablifhed, they hold it *execrable* pride and prefumption. *Hooker, b.* iii. *f.* 10.

Of the vifible church of Jefus Chrift thofe may be, in refpect of their outward profeffion; who, in regard of their inward difpofition, are moft worthily both hateful in the fight of God himfelf, and in the eyes of the founder parts of the vifible church moft *execrable.* *Hooker, b.* iii. *f.* 1.

Give fentence on this *execrable* wretch,
That hath been breeder of thefe dire events. *Shak. Tit. And.*
When *execrable* Troy in afhes lay,
Through fires, and fwords, and feas, they forc'd their way.
Dryden's Æn. b. vii. *l.* 408.

EXE'CRABLY. *adv.* [from *execrable.*] Curfedly; abominably.

'Tis fuftian all, 'tis *execrably* bad;
But if they will be fools, muft you be mad? *Dryden'. Perf.*

To E'XECRATE. *v. a.* [*execror*, Latin.] To curfe; to imprecate ill upon; to abominate.

Extinction of fome tyranny, by the indignation of a people, makes way for fome form contrary to that which they lately *execrated* and detefted. *Temple.*

EXECRA'TION. *n. f.* [from *execrate.*] Curfe; imprecation of evil.

Mifchance and forrow go along with you,
And threefold vengeance tend upon your fteps!
—Ceafe, gentle queen, thefe *execrations.* *Shakef. Hen.* VI.
For this we may thank Adam! but his thanks
Shall be the *execration.* *Milton's Paradife Loft, b.* x.

The Indians, at naming the devil, did fpit on the ground in token of *execration.* *Stillingfleet's Def. of Difc. on Rom. Idol.*

To EXE'CT. *v. a.* [*execo*, Latin.] To cut out; to cut away.

Were it not for the effufion of blood which would follow an exection, the liver might not only be *exected*, but its office fupplied by the fpleen and other parts. *Harvey on Confumptions.*

EXE'CTION. *n. f.* [from *exect.*] The act of cutting out. See EXECT.

To E'XECUTE. *v. a.* [*exequor*, Latin.]

1. To perform; to practife.

Againft all the gods of Egypt I will *execute* judgment. *Ex.*

He cafts into the balance the promife of a reward to fuch as fhould *execute*, and of punifhment to fuch as fhould neglect their commiffion. *South's Sermons.*

2. To put in act; to do what is planned or determined.

Men may not devife laws, but are bound for ever to ufe and *execute* thofe which God hath delivered. *Hooker, b.* iii. *f.* 7.

The government here is fo regularly difpofed, that it almoft *executes* itfelf. *Swift.*

Abfalom pronounced fentence of death againft his brother, and had it *executed* too. *Locke.*

3. To put to death according to form of juftice; to punifh capitally.

Sir William Bremingham was *executed* for treafon. *Davies.*

Fitzofborn was *executed* under him, or difcarded into foreign fervice for a pretty fhadow of exilement. *Spenfer.*

O Tyburn, cou'dft thou reafon and difpute,
Cou'dft thou but judge as well as *execute*,
How often wou'dft thou change the felon's doom,
And trufs fome ftern chief juftice in his room. *Dryden.*

4. To put to death; to kill.

The treacherous Faftolfe wounds my peace,
Whom with my bare fifts I would *execute*,
If I now had him. *Shakefpeare's Henry* VI. *p.* i.

EXECU'TION. *n. s.* [from *execute.*]

1. Performance; practice.

When things are come to the *execution*, there is no secrecy comparable to celerity. *Bacon's Essays.*

I wish no better
Than have him hold that purpose, and to put it
In *execution*. *Shakespeare's Coriolanus.*

I like thy counsel; and how well I like it,
The *execution* of it shall make known. *Shakespeare.*

The excellency of the subject contributed much to the happiness of the *execution*. *Dryden.*

2. The last act of the law in civil causes, by which possession is given of body or goods.

Sir Richard was committed to the Fleet in *execution* for the whole six thousand pounds. *Clarendon, b.* viii.

3. Capital punishment; death inflicted by forms of law.

Good rest.
—As wretches have o'er night,
That wait for *execution* in the morn. *Shak. Two Gent. of Ver.*

I have seen,
When, after *execution*, judgment hath
Repented o'er his doom. *Shakes. Measure for Measure.*

Laws support those crimes they checkt before,
And *executions* now affright no more. *Creech's Manilius.*

4. Destruction; slaughter.

Brave Macbeth, with his brandish'd steel,
Which smok'd with bloody *execution*, carv'd out his passage. *Shakespeare's Macbeth.*

The *execution* had been too cruel, and far exceeding the bounds of ordinary hostility. *Hayward.*

When the tongue is the weapon, a man may strike where he cannot reach, and a word shall do *execution* both further and deeper than the mightiest blow. *South's Sermons.*

Ships of such height and strength, that his vessels could do no *execution* upon them. *Arbuthnot on Coins.*

EXECU'TIONER. *n. s.* [from *execution.*]

1. He that puts in act, or executes.

Is not the causer of the timeless deaths,
As blameful as the *executioner*? *Shakesp. Richard* III.

It is a singular comfort to the *executioners* of this office, when they consider that they cannot be guilty of oppression. *Bacon's Office of Alienation.*

The heart of every man was in the hand of God, and he could have made them *executioners* of his wrath upon one another. *Woodward's Natural History.*

In this case every man hath a right to punish the offender, and be the *executioner* of the law of nature. *Locke.*

2. He that inflicts capital punishment; he that puts to death according to the sentence of the law.

He, born to the greatest expectation, and of the greatest blood, submitted himself to be servant to the *executioner* that should put to death Musidorus. *Sidney, b.* ii.

The deluge was not sent only as an *executioner* to mankind, but its prime errand was to reform the earth. *Woodward.*

3. He that kills; he that murthers.

I would not be thy *executioner*:
I fly thee, for I would not injure thee;
Thou tell'st me, there is murder in mine eyes. *Shakespeare.*

4. The instrument by which any thing is performed.

All along
The walls, abominable ornaments!
Are tools of wrath, anvils of torments hung,
Fell *executioners* of foul intents. *Crashaw.*

EXE'CUTIVE. *adj.* [from *execute.*]

1. Having the quality of executing or performing.

They are the nimblest, agil, strongest instruments, fittest to be *executive* of the commands of the souls. *Hale.*

2. Active; not deliberative; not legislative; having the power to put in act the laws.

The Roman emperors were possessed of the whole legislative as well as *executive* power. *Addison's Freeholder*, N°. 51.

Hobbes confounds the *executive* with the legislative power, though all well instituted states have ever placed them in different hands. *Swift.*

E'XECUTER. *n. s.* [from *execute.*]

1. He that performs or executes any thing.

My sweet mistress
Weeps when she sees me work, and says such baseness
Had ne'er like *executer*. *Shakespeare's Tempest.*

Sophocles and Euripides, in their most beautiful pieces, are impartial *executers* of poetick justice. *Dennis.*

2. He that is intrusted to perform the will of a testator. In this sense the accent is on the second syllable.

Let's chuse *executers*, and talk of wills;
And yet not so; for what can we bequeath? *Shak. R.* II.

3. An executioner; one who puts others to death. Disused.

The sad-ey'd justice, with his surly hum,
Delivers o'er to *executers* pale
The lazy yawning drone. *Shakespeare's Henry* V.

EXE'CUTERSHIP. *n. s.* [from *executer.*] The office of him that is appointed to perform the will of the defunct.

For fishing for testaments and *executorships* it is worse, by how much men submit themselves to mean persons, than in service. *Bacon's Essays, Civil and Moral.*

EXE'CUTRIX. *n. s.* [from *execute.*] A woman intrusted to perform the will of the testator.

He did, after the death of the earl, buy of his *executrix* the remnant of the term. *Bacon's Office of Alienation.*

EXEGE'SIS. *n. s.* [ἐξήγησις.] An explanation.

EXEGE'TICAL. *adj.* [ἐξηγητικὸς.] Explanatory; expository.

I have here and there interspersed some critical and some *exegetical* notes, fit for learners to know, and not unfit for some teachers to read. *Walker's Pref. to Ex. of the Lat. Synt.*

EXE'MPLAR. *n. s.* [*exemplar*, Latin.] A pattern; an example to be imitated.

The idea and *exemplar* of the world was first in God. *Raleigh.*

They began at a known body, a barleycorn, the weight whereof is therefore called a grain; which ariseth, being multiplied to scruples, drachms, ounces, and pounds, and then those weights, as they happen to take them, are fixed by authority, and *exemplars* of them publickly kept. *Holder.*

If he intends to murder his prince, as Cromwel did, he must persuade him that he resolves nothing but his safety; as the same grand *exemplar* of hypocrisy did before. *South.*

Best poet! fit *exemplar* for the tribe
Of Phœbus. *Phillips.*

EXE'MPLARILY. *adv.* [from *exemplary.*]

1. In such a manner as deserves imitation.

She is *exemplarily* loyal in a high exact obedience. *Howel.*

2. In such a manner as may warn others.

If he had shut the commons house to have been quiet, whilst their champions were *exemplarily* punished, their jurisdiction would probably in a short time have been brought within the due limits. *Clarendon.*

EXE'MPLARINESS. *n. s.* [from *exemplary.*] State of standing as a pattern to be copied.

In Scripture we find several titles given to Christ, which import his *exemplariness* as of a prince and a captain, a master and a guide. *Tillotson's Sermons.*

EXE'MPLARY. *adj.* [from *exemplar.*]

1. Such as may deserve to be proposed to imitation, whether persons or things.

The archbishops and bishops have the government of the church: be not you the mean to prefer any to those places, but only for their learning, gravity, and worth: their lives and doctrine ought to be *exemplary*. *Bacon's Advice to Villiers.*

If all these were *exemplary* in the conduct of their lives, religion would receive a mighty encouragement. *Swift.*

2. Such as may give warning to others.

Had the tumults been repressed by *exemplary* justice, I had obtained all that I designed. *King Charles.*

3. Such as may attract notice and imitation.

Awaking therefore, as who long had dream'd,
Much of my women and their gods asham'd,
From this abyss of *exemplary* vice
Resolv'd, as time might aid my thought, to rise. *Prior.*

When any duty is fallen under a general disuse and neglect, in such a case the most visible and *exemplary* performance is required. *Rogers, Sermon* 18.

EXEMPLIFICA'TION. *n. s.* [from *exemplify.*] A copy; a transcript.

An ambassador of Scotland demanded an *exemplification* of the articles of peace. *Hayward.*

A love of vice as such, a delighting in sin for its own sake, is an imitation, or rather an *exemplification* of the malice of the devil. *South's Sermons.*

To EXE'MPLIFY. *v. a.* [from *exemplar.*]

1. To illustrate by example.

This might be *exemplified* even by heaps of rites and customs, now superstitious in the greatest part of the Christian world. *Hooker, b.* v. *s.* 3.

Our author has *exemplified* his precepts in the very precepts themselves. *Spectator*, N°. 253.

A satire may be *exemplified* by pictures, characters, and *examples*. *Pope to Swift.*

2. To transcribe; to copy.

To EXE'MPT. *v. a.* [*exemptus*, Latin.] To privilege; to grant immunity from.

Things done well,
And with a care, *exempt* themselves from fear:
Things done without example, in their issue
Are to be fear'd. *Shakespeare's Henry* VIII.

The religious were not *exempted*, but fought among the other soldiers. *Knolles's History of the Turks.*

The emperors *exempted* them from all taxes, to which they subjected merchants without exception. *Arbuthnot on Coins.*

EXE'MPT. *adj.* [from the verb.]

1. Free by privilege.

Be it my wrong you are from me *exempt*;
But wrong not that wrong with a mere contempt. *Shakesp.*

An abbot cannot, without the advice of his convent, subject a monastery to any, from whose jurisdiction such monastery was *exempted*. *Ayliffe's Parergon.*

2. Not subject; not liable to.

Do not once hope, that thou canst tempt
A spirit so resolved to tread
Upon thy throat, and live *exempt*
From all the nets that thou canst spread. *Ben. Johnson.*

No man, not even the most wealthy and powerful among the sons of men, is *exempt* from the chances of human life. *Atterbury's Sermons.*

The god constrains the Greek to roam,
A hopeless exile from his native home,
From death alone *exempt*. *Pope's Odyssey, b.* i. *l.* 96.

3. Clear; not included.

His dreadful imprecation hear;
'Tis laid on all, not any one *exempt*. *Lee's Oedipus.*

4. Cut off from. Disused.

Was not thy father for treason 'headed?
And by his treason stand'st not thou attainted,
Corrupted, and *exempt* from ancient gentry? *Shak. Hen.* VI.

Exe'mption. *n. s.* [from *exempt.*] Immunity; privilege; freedom from imposts or burdensome employments.

The like *exemption* hath the writ to enquire of a man's death, which also must be granted freely. *Bacon's Off. of Alien.*

The Roman laws gave particular *exemptions* to such as built ships, or traded in corn. *Arbuthnot on Coins.*

Exempti'tious. *adj.* [from *exemptus*, Latin.] Separable; that which may be taken from another.

If motion were loose or *exemptitious* from matter, I could be convinced that it had extension of its own. *More.*

To Exe'nterate. *v. a.* [*exentero*, Latin.] To embowel; to deprive of the entrails.

A toad contains not those urinary parts which are found in other animals to avoid that serous excretion, which may appear unto any that *exenterates* or dissects them. *Brown.*

Exentera'tion. *n. s.* [*exenteratio*, Lat.] The act of taking out the bowels; embowelling.

Belonius not only affirms that chamelions feed on flies, caterpillars, beetles, and other insects; but upon *exenteration* he found these animals in their bellies. *Brown's Vulg. Errours.*

Exe'quial. *adj.* [from *exequiæ*, Latin.] Funeral; relating to funerals. *Dict.*

Exe'quies. *n. s.* without a singular. [*exequiæ*, Lat.] Funeral rites; the ceremony of burial; the procession of burial. For this word *obsequies* is often used, but not so properly.

Let's not forget
The noble duke of Bedford late deceas'd,
But see his *exequies* fulfill'd in Roan. *Shakespeare's Hen.* VI.

The tragical end of the two brothers, whose *exequies* the next successor had leisure to perform. *Dryden's Dedic. to Æn.*

Exe'rcent. *adj.* [*exercens*, Latin.] Practising; following any calling or vocation.

The judge may oblige every *exercent* advocate to give his patronage and assistance unto a litigant in distress for want of an advocate. *Ayliffe's Parergon.*

E'XERCISE. *n. s.* [*exercitium*, Latin.]

1. Labour of the body; labour considered as conducive to the cure or prevention of diseases.

Men ought to beware that they use not *exercise* and a spare diet both; but if much *exercise*, a plentiful diet; if sparing diet, little *exercise*. *Bacon's Natural History*, N°. 298.

The wise for cure on *exercise* depend;
God never made his work for man to mend. *Dryden.*

He is exact in prescribing the *exercises* of his patients, ordering some of them to walk eighty stadia in a day, which is about nine English miles. *Arbuthnot on Coins.*

The purest *exercise* of health,
The kind refresher of the Summer heats. *Thomson's Summer.*

2. Something done for amusement.

As a watchful king, he would not neglect his safety, thinking nevertheless to perform all things rather as an *exercise* than as a labour. *Bacon's Henry* VII.

3. Habitual action by which the body is formed to gracefulness, air, and agility.

He was strong of body, and so much the stronger as he, by a well disciplined *exercise*, taught it both to do and to suffer. *Sidney, b.* ii.

The French apply themselves more universally to their *exercises* than any nation: one seldom sees a young gentleman that does not fence, dance, and ride. *Addison.*

4. Preparatory practice in order to skill: as, the *exercise* of soldiers.

5. Use; actual application of any thing.

The sceptre of spiritual regimen over us in this present world, is at the length to be yielded up into the hands of the Father which gave it; that is, the use and *exercise* thereof shall cease, there being no longer on earth any militant church to govern. *Hooker, b.* v. *s.* 54.

6. Practice; outward performance.

The same prince refused even those of the church of England, who followed their master to St. Germain's, the publick *exercise* of their religion. *Addison on Italy.*

7. Employment.

The learning of the situation and boundaries of kingdoms, being only an *exercise* of the eyes and memory, a child with pleasure will learn them. *Locke.*

Children, by the *exercise* of their senses about objects that affect them in the womb, receive some few ideas before they are born. *Locke.*

Exercise is very alluring and entertaining to the understanding, while its reasoning powers are employed without labour. *Watts.*

8. Task; that which one is appointed to perform.

Patience is more oft the *exercise*
Of saints, the trial of their fortitude
Making them each his own deliverer,
And victor over all
That tyranny or fortune can inflict. *Milton's Agonistes.*

9. Act of divine worship whether publick or private.

Good sir John,
I'm in your debt for your last *exercise*;
Come the next Sabbath, and I will content you. *Shakesp.*

To E'xercise. *n. a.* [*exerceo*, Latin.]

1. To employ; to engage in employment.

This faculty of the mind, when it is *exercised* immediately about things, is called judgment. *Locke.*

2. To train by use to any act.

The Roman tongue was the study of their youth: it was their own language they were instructed and *exercised* in. *Locke.*

3. To make skilful or dexterous by practice; to habituate.

Strong meat belongeth to them who, by reason of use, have their senses *exercised* to discern both good and evil. *Hebr.*

Reason, by its own penetration, where it is strong and *exercised*, usually sees quicker and clearer without syllogism. *Locke.*

And now the goddess, *exercis'd* in ill,
Who watch'd an hour to work her impious will,
Ascends the roof. *Dryden's Æn. b.* vii. *l.* 713.

4. To busy; to keep busy.

He will *exercise* himself with pleasure, and without weariness, in that godlike employment of doing good which is assigned him. *Atterbury's Sermons.*

5. To task; to keep employed as a penal injunction.

Sore travel hath God given to the sons of man, to be *exercised* therewith. *Eccl.* i. 13.

Where pain of unextinguishable fire
Must *exercise* us, without hope of end. *Milton's Par. Lost.*

6. To practise; to perform.

A man's body is confined to a place; but where friendship is, all offices are granted to him and his deputy: for he may *exercise* them by his friend. *Bacon's Essays.*

Age's chief arts, and arms, are to grow wise;
Virtue to know, and, known, to *exercise*. *Denham.*

7. To exert; to put in use.

The princes of the Gentiles *exercise* dominion over them, and they that are great *exercise* authority upon them. *Mat.* xx.

Their consciences oblige them to submit to that dominion which their governours had a right to *exercise* over them. *Locke.*

8. To practise or use in order to habitual skill.

Mean while I'll draw up my Numidian troop
Within the square, to *exercise* their arms. *Addison's Cato.*

To E'xercise. *v. n.* To use exercise; to labour for health or for amusement.

The Lacedemonians were remarkable for the use of this sport, and Alexander the Great frequently *exercised* at it. *Notes to the Odyssey.*

E'xerciser. *n. s.* [from *exercise.*] He that directs or uses exercise. *Dict.*

Exercita'tion. *n. s.* [*exercitatio*, Latin.]

1. Exercise.

It were some extenuation of the curse, if *in sudore vultus tui* were confinable unto corporal *exercitations*. *Brown's Vulg. Err.*

2. Practice; use.

By frequent *exercitations* we form them within us. *Felton.*

To EXE'RT. *v. a.* [*exero*, Latin.]

1. To use with an effort; to use with ardour and vehemence.

When the service of Britain requires your courage and conduct, you may *exert* them both. *Dryden's Fables, Dedicat.*

Whate'er I am, each faculty,
The utmost power of my *exerted* soul,
Preserves a being only for your service. *Rowe.*

2. To put forth; to perform.

When the will has *exerted* an act of command upon any faculty of the soul, or member of the body, it has done all that the whole man, as a moral agent, can do for the actual exercise or employment of such a faculty or member. *South.*

3. To enforce; to push to an effort. With the reciprocal pronoun.

Strong virtue, like strong nature, struggles still;
Exerts itself, and then throws off the ill. *Dryd. Aurengzebe.*

Exe'rtion. *n. s.* [from *exert.*] The act of exerting; effort.

Exe'sion. *n. s.* [*exesus*, Latin.] The act of eating through.

Theophrastus denieth the *exesion* or forcing of vipers through the belly of the dam. *Brown's Vulgar Errours, b.* iii.

Exestua'tion. *n. s.* [*exæstuo*, Latin.] The state of boiling; tumultuous heat; effervescence; ebullition.

Saltpetre

Saltpetre is in operation a cold body: phyficians and chymifts give it in fevers, to allay the inward *exeftuations* of the blood and humours. *Boyle.*

To EXFO'LIATE. *v. n.* [*ex* and *folium*, Latin.] To fhell off; feparate, as a corrupt bone from the found part. A term of chirurgery.

Our work went on fuccefsfully, the bone *exfoliating* from the edges. *Wifeman's Surgery.*

EXFOLIA'TION. *n. f.* [from *exfoliate.*] The procefs by which the corrupted part of the bone feparates from the found.

If the bone be dreffed, the flefh will foon arife in that cut of the bone, and make *exfoliation* of what is neceffary, and incarn it. *Wifeman's Surgery.*

EXFO'LIATIVE. *adj.* [from *exfoliate.*] That which has the power of procuring exfoliation.

Drefs the bone with the milder *exfoliatives*, 'till the burnt bone is caft off. *Wifeman's Surgery.*

EXHA'LABLE. *adj.* [from *exhale.*] That which may be evaporated or exhaled.

The fire may refolve fome of the more fpirituous and *exhalable* parts, whereof diftillation has fhewn me that alabafter is not deftitute, into vapours. *Boyle.*

EXHALA'TION. *n. f.* [*exhalatio*, Latin.]

1. The act of exhaling or fending out in vapours; emiffion.
2. The ftate of evaporating or flying out in vapours; evaporation.
3. That which rifes in vapours, and fometimes takes the form of meteors.

No nat'ral *exhalation* in the fky,
No 'fcape of nature, no diftemper'd day,
But they will pluck away its nat'ral caufe,
And call them meteors, prodigies, and figns,
Abortives, and prefages, tongues of heav'n
Plainly denouncing vengeance upon John. *Shak. King John.*

While moving in fo high a fphere, and with fo vigorous a luftre, he muft needs, as the fun, raife many envious *exhalations*; which, condenfed by a popular odium, are capable to caft a cloud upon the brighteft merit and integrity. *K. Charles.*

Anon, out of the earth, a fabrick huge
Rofe like an *exhalation*, with the found
Of dulcet fymphonies and voices fweet. *Milton's Par. Loft.*

It is no wonder if the earth be often fhaken, there being quantities of *exhalations* within thofe mines, or cavernous paffages, that are capable of rarefaction and inflammation. *Burn.*

The growing tow'rs like *exhalations* rife,
And the huge columns heave into the fkies. *Pope.*

To EXHA'LE. *v. a.* [*exhalo*, Latin.]

1. To fend or draw out in vapours or fumes.

Yon light is not daylight, I know it well:
It is fome meteor that the fun *exhales*,
To be to thee this night a torch-bearer. *Sh. Rom. and Jul.*

I flattered myfelf with hopes that the vapour had been *exhaled.* *Temple.*

Fear freezes minds; but love, like heat,
Exhales the foul fublime to feek her native feat. *Dryden.*

2. To draw out.

See, dead Henry's wounds
Open their congeal'd mouths, and bleed afrefh!
Blufh, blufh, thou lump of foul deformity;
For 'tis thy prefence that *exhales* this blood
From cold and empty veins, where no blood dwells. *Shakef.*

EXHA'LEMENT. *n. f.* [from *exhale.*] Matter exhaled; vapour.

Nor will polifhed amber, although it fend forth a grofs and corporal *exhalement*, be found a long time defective upon the exacteft fcales. *Brown's Vulgar Errours, b.* ii. *c.* 5.

To EXHA'UST. *v. a.*

1. To drain; to diminifh; to deprive by draining.

Single men be many times more charitable, becaufe their means are lefs *exhaufted.* *Bacon's Effays.*

Spermatick matter of a vitious fort abounds in the blood, *exhaufts* it of its beft fpirits, and derives the flower of it to the feminal veffels. *Wifeman's Surgery.*

2. To draw out totally; to draw 'till nothing is left.

Though the knowledge they have left us be worth our ftudy, yet they *exhaufted* not all its treafures: they left a great deal for the induftry and fagacity of after-ages. *Locke.*

The nurfling grove
Seems fair awhile, cherifh'd with fofter earth;
But when the alien compoft is *exhauft*,
Its native poverty again prevails. *Phillips.*

EXHA'USTION. *n. f.* [from *exhauft.*] The act of drawing or draining.

EXHA'USTLESS. *adj.* [from *exhauft.*] Not to be emptied; not to be all drawn off; inexhauftible.

Of heat and light, what everduring ftores
Brought from the fun's *exhauftlefs* golden fhores,
Through gulphs immenfe of intervening air,
Enrich the earth, and every lofs repair. *Blackm. Creation.*

To EXHI'BIT. *v. a.* [*exhibeo*, Latin.]

1. To offer to view or ufe; to offer or propofe in a formal or publick manner.

If any claim redrefs of injuftice, they fhould *exhibit* their petitions in the ftreet. *Shakefp. Meafure for Meafure.*

He fuffered his attorney-general to *exhibit* a charge of high treafon againft the earl. *Clarendon.*

2. To fhow; to difplay.

One of an unfortunate conftitution is perpetually *exhibiting* a miferable example of the weaknefs of mind and body. *Pope.*

EXHI'BITER. *n. f.* [from *exhibit.*] He that offers any thing, as a petition or charge, in a publick manner.

He feems indifferent,
Or rather fwaying more upon our part,
Than cherifhing th' *exhibiters* againft us. *Shakefp. Henry* V.

EXHIBI'TION. *n. f.* [from *exhibit.*]

1. The act of exhibiting; difplay; fetting forth.

What are all mechanick works, but the fenfible *exhibition* of mathematick demonftrations? *Grew's Cofmol. Sac. b.* ii.

2. Allowance; falary; penfion.

I crave fit difpofition for my wife,
Due preference of place and *exhibition*,
As levels with her breeding. *Shakefpeare's Othello.*

What maintenance he from his friends receives,
Like *exhibition* thou fhalt have from me. *Shakefpeare.*

All was affigned to the army and garrifons there, and fhe received only a penfion or *exhibition* out of his coffers. *Bacon.*

He is now neglected, and driven to live in exile upon a fmall *exhibition.* *Swift.*

EXHI'BITIVE. *adj.* [from *exhibit.*] Reprefentative; difplaying.

Truths muft have an eternal exiftence in fome underftanding; or rather, they are the fame with that underftanding itfelf, confidered as varioufly *exhibitive* or reprefentative, according to the various modes of inimitability or participation. *Norris.*

EXHI'LARATE. *v. a.* [*exhilaro*, Latin.] To make cheerful; to cheer; to fill with mirth; to enliven; to glad; to gladden.

The coming into a fair garden, the coming into a fair room richly furnifhed, a beautiful perfon, and the like, do delight and *exhilarate* the fpirits much. *Bacon's Natural Hiftory.*

The force of that fallacious fruit,
That with *exhilarating* vapours bland
About their fpirits, had play'd, and inmoft pow'rs
Made err, was now exhal'd. *Milton's Paradife Loft, b.* ix.

Continual tide
Flows from th' *exhilarating* fount. *Phillips.*

Let them thank
Boon nature, that thus annually fupplies
Their vaults, and with her former liquid gifts
Exhilarates their languid minds, within
The golden mean confin'd. *Phillips.*

EXHILARA'TION. *n. f.* [from *exhilarate.*]

1. The act of giving gaiety.
2. The ftate of being enlivened.

And therefore *exhilaration* hath fome affinity with joy, though it be a much lighter motion. *Bacon's Natural Hiftory.*

To EXHO'RT. *v. a.* [*exhortor*, Latin.] To incite by words to any good action.

We befeech you, and *exhort* you by the Lord Jefus, that as ye have received of us, how you ought to walk, fo ye would abound. *1 Thef.* iv. 1.

My duty is to *exhort* you to confider the dignity of that holy myftery. *Common Prayer.*

EXHORTA'TION. *n. f.* [from *exhort.*]

1. The act of exhorting; incitement to good.

If we will not encourage publick beneficence, 'till we are fecure that no ftorm fhall overturn what we help to build, there is no room for *exhortations* to charity. *Atterbury.*

2. The form of words by which one is exhorted.

I'll end my *exhortation* after dinner. *Shakefpeare.*

EXHORTA'TORY. *adj.* [from *exhort.*] Tending to exhort.

EXHO'RTER. *n. f.* [from *exhort.*] One who exhorts or encourages by words.

To EXI'CCATE. *v. a.* [*exficco*, Latin.] To dry; to dry up. *Dict.*

EXICCA'TION. *n. f.* [from *exiccate.*] Arefaction; act of drying up; ftate of being dried up.

What is more eafily refuted than that old vulgar affertion of an univerfal drought and *exiccation* of the earth? As if the fun could evaporate the leaft drop of its moifture, fo that it fhould never defcend again, but be attracted and elevated quite out of the atmofphere. *Bentley's Sermons.*

EXI'CCATIVE. *adj.* [from *exiccate.*] Drying in quality; having the power of drying.

E'XIGENCE. } *n. f.* [This word is probably only a corruption
E'XIGENCY. } of *exigents*, vitiated by an unfkilful pronounciation.]

1. Demand; want; need.

As men, we are at our own choice, both for time and place and form, according to the *exigence* of our own occafions in private. *Hooker, b.* v. *f.* 24.

You have heard what the prefent condition and *exigencies* of thefe feveral charities are. *Atterbury's Sermons.*

While our fortunes exceed not the meafure of real convenience,

nience, and are adapted to the *exigencies* of our station, we perceive the hand of providence in our gradual and successive supplies. *Rogers, Sermon* 2.

2. Pressing necessity; distress; sudden occasion.

This dissimulation in war may be called stratagem and conduct; in other *exigencies* address and dexterity. *Notes on the Ody.*

Now in such *exigencies* not to need,
Upon my word you must be rich indeed!
A noble superfluity it craves,
Not for yourself, but for your fools and knaves. *Pope.*

E'XIGENT. *n. s.* [*exigens*, Latin.]

1. Pressing business; occasion that requires immediate help.

In such an *exigent* I see not how they could have staid to deliberate about any other regiment than that which already was devised to their hands. *Hooker, Preface.*

The council met, your guards to find you sent,
And know your pleasure in this *exigent*. *Waller.*

2. [A law term.] A writ sued when the defendant is not to be found, being part of the process leading to an outlawry. *Shakespeare* uses it for any extremity. *Hanmer.*

3. End.

These eyes, like lamps whose wasting oil is spent,
Wax dim, as drawing to their *exigent*. *Shakes. Henry* VI.

EXIGU'ITY. *n. s.* [*exiguitas*, Latin.] Smallness; diminutiveness; slenderness.

The *exiguity* and shape of the extant particles is now supposed. *Boyle on Colours.*

EXIGU'OUS. *adj.* [*exiguus*, Latin.] Small; diminutive; little.

Their subtile parts and *exiguous* dose are consumed and evaporated in less than two hours time. *Harvey.*

E'XILE. *n. s.* [*exilium*, Latin. It seems anciently to have had the accent indifferently on either syllable: now it is uniformly on the first.]

1. Banishment; state of being banished from one's country.

Our state of bodies would bewray what life
We've led since thy *exile*. *Shakespeare's Coriolanus.*
Welcome is *exile*, welcome were my death. *Shak. H.VI.*
Let them pronounce the steep Tarpeian death,
Vagabond *exile*, slaying, pent to linger
But with a grain of day, I would not buy
Their mercy at the price of one fair word. *Shak. Coriolanus.*

2. The person banished.

O must the wretched *exiles* ever mourn,
Nor after length of rowling years return? *Dryden's Virg.*
Ulysses, sole of all the victor train,
An *exile* from his dear paternal coast,
Deplor'd his absent queen, and empire lost. *Pope's Odyssey.*

EXI'LE. *adj.* [*exilis*, Latin.] Small; slender; not full; not powerful. Not in use, except in philosophical writings.

It were also good to enquire what other means may be to draw forth the *exile* heat which is in the air; for that may be a secret of great power to produce cold weather. *Bacon.*

In a virginal, when the lid is down, it maketh a more *exile* sound than when the lid is open. *Bacon's Natural History.*

To E'XILE. *v. a.* [from the noun. This had formerly the accent on the last syllable, now generally on the first, though *Dryden* has used both.] To banish; to drive from a country; to transport.

Call home our *exil'd* friends abroad,
That fled the snares of watchful tyranny. *Shakes. Macbeth.*
Foul subornation is predominant,
And equity *exil'd* your highness' land. *Shakesp. Henry* VI.
For that offence,
Immediately we do *exile* him hence. *Shak. Rom. and Juliet.*

They fettered with the bonds of a long night, lay there *exiled* from the eternal providence. *Wisd.* xvii. 2.

His brutal manners from his breast *exil'd*,
His mien he fashion'd, and his tongue he fil'd. *Dryden.*
Arms and the man I sing, who forc'd by fate,
And haughty Juno's unrelenting hate,
Expel'd and *exil'd*. *Dryden's Virgil's Æn.*

EXI'LEMENT. *n. s.* [from *exile.*] Banishment.

Fitzosborn was discarded into foreign service for a pretty shadow of *exilement*. *Wotton.*

EXILI'TION. *n. s.* [*exilitio*, Latin.] The act of springing or rushing out suddenly.

From saltpetre proceedeth the force and report; for sulphur and small-coal, mixt, will not take fire with noise or *exilition*; and powder, which is made of impure and greasy petre, hath but a weak emission, and gives but a faint report. *Brown.*

EXI'LITY. *n. s.* [*exilis*, Latin.] Slenderness; smalness; diminution.

Certain flies, called ephemera, live but a day: the cause is the *exility* of the spirit, or perhaps the absence of the sun. *Bac.*

For *exility* of the voice, or other sounds, it is certain that the voice doth pass through solid and hard bodies, if they be not too thick; and through water, which is likewise a very close body, and such an one as letteth not in air. *Bacon.*

A body, by being subtilized, can lose nothing of its corporeity; neither can it hereby gain any thing but *exility*; for all degrees of subtility are essentially the same thing. *Grew.*

EXI'MIOUS. *adj.* [*eximius*, Latin.] Famous; eminent; conspicuous; excellent. *Dict.*

EXINANI'TION. *n. s.* [*exinanitio*, Latin.] Privation; loss.

He is not more impotent in his glory than he was in his *exinanition*. *Decay of Piety.*

To EXI'ST. *v. n.* [*existo*, Latin.] To be; to have a being.

It is as easy to conceive that an infinite Almighty Power might produce a thing out of nothing, and make that to *exist de novo*, which did not *exist* before; as to conceive the world to have had no beginning, but to have *existed* from eternity. *South's Sermons.*

It seems reasonable to enquire, how such a multitude comes to make but one idea, since that combination does not always *exist* together in nature. *Locke.*

One year is past; a different scene!
No farther mention of the dean:
Who now, alas, no more is mist
Than if he never did *exist*. *Swift.*

EXI'STENCE. } *n. s.* [*existentia*, low Latin.] State of being;
EXI'STENCY. } actual possession of being.

Nor is only the *existency* of this animal considerable, but many things delivered thereof. *Brown's Vulgar Errours, b.* iii.

It is impossible any being can be eternal with successive eternal physical changes, or variety of states or manner of *existency*, naturally and necessarily concomitant unto it. *Hale.*

The soul, secur'd in her *existence*, smiles
At the drawn dagger, and defies its point. *Addison's Cato.*

When a being is considered as possible, it is said to have an essence or nature: such were all things before the creation. When it is considered as actual, then it is said to have *existence* also. *Watts's Logick.*

EXI'STENT. *adj.* [from *exist.*] In being; in possession of being or of existence.

Whatsoever sign the sun possessed, whose recess or vicinity defineth the quarters of the year, those seasons were actually *existent*. *Brown's Vulgar Errours, b.* vi. *c.* 2.

The eyes and minds are fastened on objects which have no real being, as if they were truly *existent*. *Dryden.*

EXISTIMA'TION. *n. s.* [*existimatio*, Latin.]

1. Opinion.

2. Esteem.

E'XIT. *n. s.* [*exit*, Latin.]

1. The term set in the margin of plays to mark the time at which the player goes off the stage.

2. Recess; departure; act of quitting the stage; act of quitting the theatre of life.

All the world's a stage,
And all the men and women meerly players:
They have their *exits* and their entrances,
And one man in his time plays many parts. *Shakespeare.*

A regard for fame becomes a man more towards the *exit* than at his entrance into life. *Swift.*

Many of your old comrades live a short life, and make a figure at their *exit*. *Swift.*

3. Passage out of any place.

In such a pervious substance as the brain, they might find an easy either entrance or *exit*, almost every where. *Glanville.*

4. Way by which there is a passage out.

The fire makes its way, forcing the water forth through its ordinary *exits*, wells, and the outlets of rivers. *Woodw.*

EXI'TAL. } *adj.* [*exitialis*, Latin.] Destructive; fatal;
EXI'TIOUS. } mortal.

Most *exitial* fevers, although not concomitated with the tokens, exanthemata, anthraces, or carbuncles, are to be censured pestilential. *Harvey on the Plague.*

E'XODUS. } *n. s.* [ἔξοδος.] Departure; journey from a place:
E'XODY. } the second book of *Moses* is so called, because it describes the journey of the Israelites from Egypt.

In all probability their years continued to be three hundred and sixty-five days, ever since the time of the Jewish *exody* at least. *Hale's Origin of Mankind.*

EXOLE'TE. *adj.* [*exoletus*, Lat.] Obsolete; out of use. *Dict.*

To EXO'LVE. *v. a.* [*exolvo*, Latin.] To loose; to pay. *Dict.*

EXO'MPHALOS. *n. s.* [ἐξ and ὀμφαλός.] A navel rupture.

To EXO'NERATE. *v. a.* [*exonero*, Latin.] To unload; to disburthen; to free from any heavy charge.

The glands being a congeries of vessels curled, circumgyrated, and complicated, give the blood time to separate through the capillary vessels into the secretory ones, which afterwards all *exonerate* themselves into one common ductus. *Ray.*

EXONERA'TION. *n. s.* [from *exonerate.*] The act of disburthening, or discharging.

The body is adapted unto eating, drinking, nutrition, and other ways of repletion and *exoneration*. *Grew.*

EXO'PTABLE. *adj.* [*exoptabilis*, Lat.] Desireable; to be sought with eagerness or desire.

E'XORABLE. *adj.* [*exorabilis*, Latin.] To be moved by intreaty.

EXO'RBITANCE. } *n. s.* [from *exorbitance.*]
EXO'RBITANCY. }

1. The act of going out of the track prescribed.

2. Enormity;

I see some degree of this fault cleave to those, who have eminently corrected all other *exorbitancies* of the tongue. *Government of the Tongue, s.* 4.

2. Enormity; gross deviation from rule or right.

The reverence of my presence may be a curb to your *exorbitancies*. *Dryden's Spanish Fryar.*

The people were grossly imposed on, to commit such *exorbitancies* as could not end but in the dissolution of the government. *Swift on the Dissentions in Athens and Rome.*

3. Boundless depravity.

They riot still,
Unbounded in *exorbitance* of ill. *Garth's Dispensary.*

Exo'rbitant. *adj.* [*ex* and *orbito*, Latin.]

1. Going out of the prescribed track; deviating from the course appointed or rule established.

What signifies the fiction of the tortoise riding upon the wings of the wind, but to prescribe bounds and measures to our *exorbitant* passions? *L'Estrange.*

These phenomena are not peculiar to the earthquakes which have happened in our times, but have been observed in all ages, and particularly those *exorbitant* commotions of the waters of the globe. *Woodward's Natural History.*

2. Anomalous; not comprehended in a settled rule or method.

The Jews, who had laws so particularly determining in all affairs what to do, were notwithstanding continually inured with causes *exorbitant*, and such as their laws had not provided for. *Hooker, b.* iii. *s.* 11.

3. Enormous; beyond due proportion; excessive.

Their subjects would live in great plenty, were not the impositions so very *exorbitant*; for the courts are too splendid for the territories. *Addison's Remarks on Italy.*

So endless and *exorbitant* are the desires of men, that they will grasp at all, and can form no scheme of perfect happiness with less. *Swift on the Dissentions in Athens and Rome.*

To Exo'rbitate. *v. n.* [*ex* and *orbito*, Latin.] To deviate; to go out of the track or road prescribed.

The planets sometimes would have approached the sun as near as the orb of Mercury, and sometimes have *exorbitated* beyond the distance of Saturn. *Bentley's Sermons.*

To E'XORCISE. *v. a.* [ἐξορκίζω.]

1. To adjure by some holy name.

2. To drive away spirits by certain forms of adjuration.

3. To purify from the influence of malignant spirits by religious ceremonies.

And fry'rs, that through the wealthy regions run,
Resort to farmers rich, and bless their halls,
And *exorcise* the beds, and cross the walls. *Dryden.*

E'xorciser. *n. s.* [from *exorcise.*] One who practises to drive away evil spirits.

E'xorcism. *n. s.* [ἐξορκισμός.] The form of adjuration, or religious ceremony by which evil and malignant spirits are driven away.

Will his lordship behold and hear our *exorcisms?* *Shakesp.*

Symptoms supernatural, must be only curable by supernatural means; namely, by devout prayers or *exorcisms. Harvey.*

E'xorcist. *n. s.* [ἐξορκιστής.]

1. One who by adjurations, prayers, or religious acts, drives away malignant spirits.

Then certain of the vagabond Jews, *exorcists*, took upon them to call over them which had evil spirits. *Acts* xix. 13.

2. An enchanter; a conjurer. Improperly.

Soul of Rome!
Thou, like an *exorcist*, hast conjur'd up
My mortified spirit. *Shakespeare's Julius Cæsar.*

Is there no *exorcist*
Beguiles the truer office of mine eyes?
Is't real that I see? *Shakespeare's All's well that ends well.*

EXO'RDIUM. n. s. [Latin.] A formal preface; the proemial part of a composition.

Nor will I thee detain
With poets fictions, nor oppress thine ear
With circumstance, and long *exordiums* here. *May's Virgil.*

I have been distasted at this way of writing, by reason of long prefaces and *exordiums*. *Addison on ancient Medals.*

Exorna'tion. *n. s.* [*exornatio*, Latin.] Ornament; decoration; embellishment.

It seemeth that all those curious *exornations* should rather cease. *Hooker, b.* v. *s.* 15.

Hyperbolical *exornations* and elegancies many much affect. *Hale's Origin of Mankind.*

Exo'ssated. *adj.* [*exossatus*, Latin.] Deprived of bones. *Dict.*

Exosto'sis. *n. s.* [ἐκ and ὀστέον.] Any protuberance of a bone that is not natural, as often happens in venereal cases. *Quincy.*

Exo'sseous. *adj* [*ex* and *ossa*, Latin.] Wanting bones; boneless; formed without bones.

Thus we daily observe in the heads of fishes, as also in snails and soft *exosseous* animals, nature near the head hath placed a flat white stone, or testaceous concretion. *Brown.*

Exo'tick. *adj.* [ἐξωτικός.] Foreign; not produced in our own country; not domestick.

Some learned men treat of the nature of letters as of some remote *exotick* thing, whereof we had no knowledge but by fabulous relations. *Holder's Elements of Speech.*

Continue fresh hot-beds to entertain such *exotick* plants as arrive not to their perfection without them. *Evelyn's Kalendar.*

Exo'tick. *n. s.* A foreign plant.

Claudian was seated on the other summit, which was barren, and produced, on some spots, plants that are unknown to Italy, and such as the gardeners call *exoticks*. *Addison's Guard.*

To EXPA'ND. *v. a.* [*expando*, Latin.]

1. To spread; to lay open as a net or sheet.

2. To dilate; to spread out every way; to diffuse.

An animal growing, *expands* its fibres in the air as a fluid. *Arbuthnot on Air.*

Along the stream of time thy name
Expanded flies, and gathers all its fame. *Pope's Ess. on Man.*

Expa'nse. *n. s.* [*expansum*, Latin.] A body widely extended without inequalities.

A murmuring sound
Of waters issu'd from a cave, and spread
Into a liquid plain; then stood unmov'd,
Pure as th' *expanse* of heav'n. *Milton's Paradise Lost, b.* iv.

Bright as th' ethereal glows the green *expanse*. *Savage.*

On the smooth *expanse* of crystal lakes,
The sinking stone at first a circle makes;
The trembling surface, by the motion stirr'd,
Spreads in a second circle, then a third;
Wide, and more wide, the floating rings advance,
Fill all the watry plain, and to the margin dance. *Pope.*

Expansibi'lity. *n. s.* [from *expansible.*] Capacity of extension; possibility to be expanded or spread into a wider surface.

Together with the rotundity common to the atoms of all fluids, there is some difference in bulk, by which the atoms in one fluid are distinguished from those of another; else all fluids would be alike in weight, *expansibility*, and all other qualities. *Grew's Cosmolog. Sacr. b.* i. *c.* 3.

Expa'nsible. *adj.* [from *expansus*, Latin.] Capable to be extended; capable to be spread into a wider surface.

Bodies are not *expansible* in proportion to their weight, or to the quantity of matter to be expanded. *Grew's Cosmol.*

Expa'nsion. *n. s.* [from *expand.*]

1. The state of being expanded into a wider surface or greater space.

'Tis demonstrated that the condensation and *expansion* of any portion of the air is always proportional to the weight and pressure incumbent upon it. *Bentley's Sermons.*

2. The act of spreading out.

The easy *expansion* of the wing of a bird, and the lightness, strength, and shape of the feathers, are all fitted for her better flight. *Grew's Cosmolog. Sac. b.* i. *c.* 5.

3. Extent; space to which any thing is extended.

The capacious mind of man takes its flight farther than the stars, and cannot be confined by the limits of the world: it extends its thoughts often even beyond the utmost *expansion* of matter, and makes excursions into that incomprehensible inane. *Locke.*

4. Pure space, as distinct from extension in solid matter.

Distance or space, in its simple abstract conception, I call *expansion*, to distinguish it from extension, which expresses this distance only as it is in the solid parts of matter. *Locke.*

It would for ever take an useless flight,
Lost in *expansion*, void and infinite. *Blackmore's Creation.*

Expa'nsive. *adj.* [from *expand.*] Having the power to spread into a wider surface, or greater space.

The elastick or *expansive* faculty of the air, whereby it dilates itself when compressed, hath been made use of in the common weather-glasses. *Ray on the Creation.*

Then no more
Th' *expansive* atmosphere is cramp'd with cold. *Thomson.*

To Expa'tiate. *v. n.* [*expatior*, Latin.]

1. To range at large; to rove without any prescribed limits.

Religion contracts the circle of our pleasures, but leaves it wide enough for her votaries to *expatiate* in. *Addison's Spectat.*

He looks in heav'n with more than mortal eyes,
Bids his free soul *expatiate* in the skies;
Amidst her kindred stars familiar roam,
Survey the region, and confess her home. *Pope.*

Expatiate free o'er all this scene of man;
A mighty maze! but not without a plan. *Pope's Ess. on Man.*

With wonder seiz'd, we view the pleasing ground,
And walk delighted, and *expatiate* round. *Pope's Odyssey.*

2. To enlarge upon in language.

They had a custom of offering the tongues to Mercury, because they believed him the giver of eloquence: Dacier *expatiates* upon this custom. *Notes on Pope's Odyssey, b.* iii.

3. To let loose; to allow to range. This sense is very improper.

Make choice of a subject, which, being of itself capable of all that colours and the elegance of design can possibly give, shall afterwards afford art an ample field of matter wherein to *expatiate* itself. *Dryden's Dufresnoy.*

To EXPE'CT. *v. a.* [*expecto*, Latin.]

1. To have a previous apprehension of either good or evil.

2. To wait for; to attend the coming.

While, *expecting* there the queen, he rais'd
His wond'ring eyes, and round the temple gaz'd. *Dryden.*

To EXPE'CT. *v. n.* To wait; to stay.

Elihu had *expected* 'till Job had spoken. *Job.*

EXPE'CTABLE. *adj.* [from *expect.*] To be expected; to be hoped or feared.

Occult and spiritual operations are not *expectable* from ice; for being but water congealed, it can never make good such qualities. *Brown's Vulgar Errours.*

EXPE'CTANCE. } *n. s.* [from *expect.*]
EXPE'CTANCY. }

1. The act or state of expecting; expectation.

Every moment is *expectancy*
Of more arrivance. *Shakespeare's Othello.*

Satyrs leave your petulance,
Or else rail upon the moon,
Your *expectance* is too soon;
For before the second cock
Crow, the gates will not unlock. *Ben. Johns. Fairy Prince.*

This blessed *expectance* must be now my theme. *Boyle.*

But fy, my wand'ring muse, how thou do'st stay!
Expectance calls thee now another way. *Milton.*

2. Something expected.

There is *expectance* here from both the sides,
What further you will do. *Shakes. Troilus and Cressida.*

3. Hope; that of which the expectation is accompanied with pleasure.

Oh, what a noble mind is here o'erthrown!
The *expectancy* and rose of the fair state. *Shakesp. Hamlet.*

EXPE'CTANT. *adj.* [French.] Waiting in expectation.

Her majesty has offered concessions, in order to remove scruples raised in the mind of the *expectant* heir. *Swift.*

EXPE'CTANT. *n. s.* [from *expect.*] One who waits in expectation of any thing; one held in dependance by his hopes.

They, vain *expectants* of the bridal hour,
My stores in riotous expence devour. *Pope's Odyssey, b.* i.

This treatise was agreeable to the sentiments of the whole nation, except of those gentlemen who had employments, or were *expectants.* *Swift to Pope.*

EXPECTA'TION. *n. s.* [*exspectatio*, Latin.]

1. The act of expecting.

The trees
Should have borne men, and *expectation* fainted,
Longing for what it had not. *Shak. Anth. and Cleopatra.*

The rest,
That are within the note of *expectation*,
Already are i' th' court. *Shakespeare's Macbeth.*

2. The state of expecting either with hope or fear.

Live in a constant and serious *expectation* of that day, when we must appear before the Judge of heaven and earth. *Rogers.*

3. Prospect of any thing good to come.

My soul, wait thou only upon God; for my *expectation* is from him. *Ps.* lxii. 5.

4. The object of happy expectation; the Messiah expected.

Now clear I understand,
What oft my steadiest thoughts have search'd in vain,
Why our great *expectation* should be call'd
The seed of woman. *Milton's Paradise Lost, b.* xii.

5. A state in which something excellent is expected from us

How fit it will be for you, born so great a prince, and of so rare not only *expectation* but proof, to divert your thoughts from the way of goodness. *Sidney.*

You first came home
From travel with such hopes as made you look'd on,
By all men's eyes, a youth of *expectation*;
Pleas'd with your growing virtue, I receiv'd you. *Otway.*

EXPE'CTER. *n. s.* [from *expect.*]

1. One who has hopes of something.

These are not great *expecters* under your administration, according to the period of governors here. *Swift.*

2. One who waits for another.

Signify this loving interview
To the *expecters* of our Trojan part. *Shak. Troil. and Cress.*

To EXPE'CTORATE. *v. a.* [*ex* and *pectus*, Latin.] To eject from the breast.

Excrementitious humours are *expectorated* by a cough after a cold or an asthma. *Harvey on Consumptions.*

Morbifick matter is either attenuated so as to be returned into the channels, or *expectorated* by coughing. *Arbuthnot.*

EXPE'CTORATION. *n. s.* [from *expectorate.*]

1. The act of discharging from the breast.

2. That discharge which is made by coughing, as bringing up phlegm, or any thing that obstructs the vessels of the lungs, and strengthens the breath. *Quincy.*

With water, vinegar, and honey, in pleurisies and inflammations of the lungs, he mixeth spices, for promoting *expectoration.* *Arbuthnot on Aliments.*

EXPE'CTORATIVE. *adj.* [from *expectorate.*] Having the quality of promoting expectoration.

Syrups and other *expectoratives*, in coughs, must necessarily occasion a greater cough. *Harvey on Consumptions.*

EXPE'DIENCE. } *n. s.* [from *expedient.*]
EXPE'DIENCY. }

1. Fitness; propriety; suitableness to an end.

Solemn dedications of things set apart for Divine Worship, could never have been universally practised, had not right reason dictated the high *expediency* and great use of such practices. *South's Sermons.*

2. It is used in *Shakespeare* for expedition; adventure; or attempt.

Let me hear
What yesternight our council did decree,
In forwarding this dear *expedience.* *Shakespeare's Henry* IV.

3. It is also used by *Shakespeare* for expedition; haste; dispatch.

I shall break
The cause of our *expedience* to the queen,
And get her leave to part. *Shakesp. Anth. and Cleopatra.*

Eight tall ships, three thousand men of war,
Are making hither with all due *expedience.* *Shak. Richard* II.

EXPE'DIENT. *adj.* [*expedit*, Latin.]

1. Proper; fit; convenient; suitable.

All things are not *expedient*: in things indifferent there is a choice; they are not always equally *expedient.* *Hooker, b.* ii.

When men live as if there were no God, it becomes *expedient* for them that there should be none; and then they endeavour to persuade themselves so. *Tillotson's Sermons.*

2. In *Shakespeare*, quick; expeditious.

The adverse winds,
Whose leisure I have staid, have given him time
To land his legions all as soon as I:
His marches are *expedient* to this town. *Shakes. King John.*

EXPE'DIENT. *n. s.* [from the adjective.]

1. That which helps forward; as means to an end.

God, who delights not to grieve the children of men, does not project for our sorrow, but our innocence; and would never have invited us to the one, but as an *expedient* to the other. *Decay of Piety.*

2. A shift; means to an end which are contrived in an exigence.

Th' *expedient* pleas'd, where neither lost his right;
Mars had the day, and Venus had the night. *Dryden.*

He flies to a new *expedient* to solve the matter, and supposes an earth of a make and frame like that of Des Cartes. *Woodw.*

EXPE'DIENTLY. *adv.* [from *expedient.*]

1. Fitly; suitably; conveniently.

2. Hastily; quickly.

Let my officers of such a nature
Make an extent upon his house and lands:
Do this *expediently*, and turn him going. *Shak. As you like it.*

To E'XPEDITE. *v. a.* [*expedio*, Latin.]

1. To facilitate; to free from impediment.

By sin and death a broad way now is pav'd,
To *expedite* your glorious march. *Milton's Paradise Lost.*

2. To hasten; to quicken.

An inquisition would still be a further improvement, and would *expedite* the conversion of the Papists. *Swift.*

3. To dispatch; to issue from a publick office.

Though such charters be *expedited* of course, and as of right, yet they are varied by discretion. *Bacon's New Atlantis.*

E'XPEDITE. *adj.* [*expeditus*, Latin.]

1. Quick; hasty; soon performed.

Wholesome advice, and *expedite* execution in freeing the state of those monsters. *Sandys.*

2. Easy; disencumbered; clear from impediments.

Nature can teach the church but in part; neither so fully as is requisite for man's salvation, nor so easily as to make the way plain and *expedite* enough, that many may come to the knowledge of it, and so be saved, and therefore the Scripture has been given. *Hooker, b.* iii. *s.* 3.

3. Nimble; active; agile.

The more any man's soul is cleansed from sensual lusts, the more nimble and *expedite* it will be in its operations. *Tillot.*

4. It seems to be used by *Bacon* for *light armed* in the Roman signification.

He sent the lord chamberlain with *expedite* forces to speed to Exeter, to the rescue of the town. *Bacon's Henry* VII.

E'XPEDITELY. *adv.* [from *expedite.*] With quickness, readiness, haste.

Nature hath left his ears naked, that he may turn them more *expeditely* for the reception of sounds from every quarter. *Grew's Musæum.*

EXPEDI'TION. *n. s.* [from *expedite.*]

1. Haste; speed; activity.

Prayers, whereunto devout minds have added a piercing kind of brevity, thereby the better to express that quick and speedy *expedition* wherewith ardent affections, the very wings of prayer, are delighted to present our suits in heaven. *Hooker.*

Ev'n with the speediest *expedition*
I will dispatch him to the emperor's court. *Shakespeare.*

2. A march or voyage with martial intentions.

Young Octavius, and Mark Antony,
Come down upon us with a mighty power,
Bending their *expedition* tow'rd Philippi. *Shak. Jul. Cæsar.*

2

To

To EXPE'L. *v. a.* [*expello*, Latin.]

1. To drive out; to force away.

The Lord your God shall *expel* them from before you, and drive them from out of your sight. *Jos.* xxiii. 5.

I may know the let why gentle peace
Should not *expel* these inconveniencies. *Shakes. Henry* V.

Suppose a mighty rock to fall there, it would *expel* the waters out of their places with such violence as to fling them among the clouds. *Burnet's Theory of the Earth.*

2. To eject; to throw out.

Whatsoever cannot be digested by the stomach, is either put up by vomit, or put down to the guts, and other parts of the body are moved to *expel* by consent. *Bacon's Nat. History.*

3. To banish; to drive from the place of residence.

Arms and the man I sing, who forc'd by fate,
And haughty Juno's unrelenting hate,
Expel'd and exil'd left the Trojan shore. *Dryden's Virg. Æn.*

EXPE'LLER. *n. s.* [from *expel.*] One that expels or drives away.

To EXPE'ND. *v. a.* [*expendo*, Latin.] To lay out; to spend.

If my death might make this island happy,
I would *expend* it with all willingness. *Shakesp. Henry* VI.

The king of England wasted the French king's country, and thereby caused him to *expend* such sums of money as exceeded the debt. *Hayward.*

The publick burthens, though they may be a good reason for our not *expending* so much in charity, yet will not justify us in giving nothing. *Atterbury's Sermons.*

EXPE'NSE. *n. s.* [*expensum*, Latin.] Cost; charges; money expended.

Hence comes that wild and vast *expense*,
That hath enforc'd Rome's virtue thence,
Which simple poverty first made. *Ben. Johnson's Catiline.*

A feast prepar'd with riotous *expense*,
Much cost, more care, and most magnificence. *Dryden.*

I can see no reason by which we were obliged to make those prodigious *expenses*. *Swift.*

EXPE'NSEFUL. *adj.* [*expense* and *full.*] Costly; chargeable; expensive.

No part of structure is either more *expenceful* than windows or more ruinous, as being exposed to all violence of weather. *Wotton's Architecture.*

EXPE'NSELESS. *adj.* [from *expense.*] Without cost.

A physician may save any army by this frugal and *expenseless* means only. *Milton on Education.*

What health promotes, and gives unenvy'd peace,
Is all *expenseless*, and procur'd with ease. *Blackm. Creation.*

EXPE'NSIVE. *adj.* [from *expense.*]

1. Given to expense; extravagant; luxurious.

Frugal and industrious men are friendly to the established government, as the idle and *expensive* are dangerous. *Temple.*

2. Costly; requiring expense: as, *expensive* dress; an *expensive* journey.

3. Liberal; generous; distributive.

This requires an active, *expensive*, indefatigable goodness, such as our apostle calls a work and labour of love. *Spratt.*

EXPE'NSIVELY. *adv.* [from *expensive.*] With great expense; at great charge.

I never knew him live so great and *expensively* as he hath done since his return from exile. *Swift.*

EXPE'NSIVENESS. *n. s.* [from *expensive.*]

1. Addiction to expense; extravagance.

2. Costliness.

Their highways, for their extent, solidity, or *expensiveness*, are some of the greatest monuments of the grandeur of the Roman empire. *Arbuthnot on Coins.*

EXPE'RIENCE. *n. s.* [*experientia*, Latin.]

1. Practice; frequent trial.

Hereof *experience* hath informed reason, and time hath made those things apparent which were hidden. *Raleigh.*

2. Knowledge gained by trial and practice.

Boys immature in knowledge,
Pawn their *experience* to their present pleasure,
And so rebel to judgment. *Shakes. Ant. and Cleopatra.*

But if you'll prosper, mark what I advise,
Whom age and long *experience* render wise. *Pope.*

To EXPE'RIENCE. *v. a.* [from the noun.]

1. To try; to practise.

2. To know by practice.

EXPE'RIENCED. *participial adj.* [from *experience.*]

1. Made skilful by experience.

We must perfect, as much as we can, our ideas of the distinct species; or learn them from such as are used to that sort of things, and are *experienced* in them. *Locke.*

2. Wise by long practice.

To him *experienc'd* Nestor thus rejoin'd,
O friend! what sorrows do'st thou bring to mind! *Pope.*

EXPE'RIENCER. *n. s.* One who makes trials; a practiser of experiments.

A curious *experiencer* did affirm, that the likeness of any object, if strongly enlightned, will appear to another, in the eye of him that looks strongly and steadily upon it, 'till he be dazzled by it; even after he shall have turned his eyes from it. *Digby on Bodies.*

EXPE'RIMENT. *n. s.* [*experimentum*, Latin.] Trial of any thing; something done in order to discover an uncertain or unknown effect.

That which sheweth them to be wise, is the gathering of principles out of their own particular *experiments*; and the framing of our particular *experiments*, according to the rule of their principles, shall make us such as they are. *Hooker, b.* v.

It is good also not to try *experiments* in states, except the necessity be urgent, or the utility evident. *Bacon.*

Adam! by sad *experiment* I know,
How little weight with thee my words can find,
Found so erroneous. *Milton's Paradise Lost, b.* x.

'Till his fall it was ignorant of nothing but of sin; or, at least, it rested in the notion without the smart of the *experiment*. *South's Sermons.*

When we are searching out the nature or properties of any being by various methods of trial, this sort of observation is called *experiment*. *Watts's Improvement of the Mind.*

To EXPE'RIMENT. *v. a.* [from the noun.] To try; to search out by trial.

Francisco Redi *experimented* that no putrified flesh will of itself, if all insects be carefully kept from it, produce any. *Ray.*

EXPERIME'NTAL. *adj.* [from *experiment.*]

1. Pertaining to experiment.

2. Built upon experiment; formed by observation.

Call me a fool;
Trust not my reading, nor my observations,
Which with *experimental* seal do warrant
The tenor of my book. *Shak. Much Ado about Nothing.*

The *experimental* testimony of Gillius is most considerable of any, who beheld the course thereof. *Brown's Vulgar Err.*

3. Known by experiment or trial.

We have no other evidence of universal impenetrability, besides a large experience, without an *experimental* exception. *Newton's Opt.*

These are so far from being subservient to atheists in their audacious attempts, that they rather afford an *experimental* confirmation of the universal deluge. *Bentley's Sermons.*

EXPERIME'NTALLY. *adv.* [from *experimental.*] By experience; by trial; by experiment; by observation.

The miscarriage being sometimes universal, has made us impart what we have *experimentally* learned by our own observations. *Evelyn's Kalendar.*

While the man is under the scourge of affliction, he is willing to abjure those sins which he now *experimentally* finds attended with such bitter consequences. *Rogers's Sermons.*

EXPE'RIMENTER. *n. s.* [from *experiment.*] One who makes experiment.

Galileus and Marsenius, two exact *experimenters*, do think they find this verity by their experiences; but surely this is impossible to be done. *Digby on Bodies.*

EXPE'RT. *adj.* [*expertus*, Latin.]

1. Skilful; addressful; intelligent in business.

Now we will take some order in the town,
Placing therein some *expert* officers. *Shakes. Henry* VI.

Again fair Alma sits confest,
On Florimel's *experter* breast;
When she the rising sigh constrains,
And by concealing speaks her pains. *Prior.*

2. Ready; dexterous.

The meanest sculptor in th' Æmilian square,
Can imitate in brass the nails and hair;
Expert in trifles, and a cunning fool,
Able t' express the parts, but not dispose the whole. *Dryden.*

They have not the good luck to be perfectly knowing in the forms of syllogism, or *expert* in mode and figure. *Locke.*

3. Skilful by practice or experience. This sense is rare.

Expert men can execute, and judge of particulars, one by one; but the general counsels, and the plots and marshalling of affairs, come best from those that are learned. *Bacon.*

4. It is used by *Pope* with *of* before the object of skill, generally with *in*.

Thy offspring bloom,
Expert of arms, and prudent in debate,
The gifts of heav'n to guard thy hoary state. *Pope's Odyssey.*

EXPE'RTLY. *adv.* [from *expert.*] In a skilful, ready and dexterous manner.

EXPE'RTNESS. *n. s.* [from *expert.*] Skill; readiness; dexterity.

What his reputation, what his valour, honesty, and *expertness* in war. *Shak. All's well that ends well.*

This army, for the *expertness* and valour of the soldiers, was thought sufficient to have met the greatest army of the Turks. *Knolles's History of the Turks.*

E'XPIABLE. *adj.* [from *expiate.*] Capable to be expiated, or attoned.

To E'XPIATE. *v. a.* [*expio*, Latin.]

1. To annul the guilt of a crime by subsequent acts of piety; to attone for.

Strong and able petty felons, in true penitence, implore permission

permission to *expiate* their crimes by their assiduous labours in so innocent and so hopeful a work. *Bacon's Phys. Remarks.*

The odium which some men's rigour or remissness had contracted upon my government, I resolved to *expiate* by regulations. *King Charles.*

For the cure of this disease an humble, serious, hearty repentance is the only physick; not to *expiate* the guilt of it, but to qualify us to partake of the benefit of Christ's attonement. *Ray on the Creation.*

2. To avert the threats of prodigies.

EXPIA'TION. *n. s.* [from *expiate.*]

1. The act of expiating or attoning for any crime.

2. The means by which we attone for crimes; attonement.

Law can discover sin, but not remove,
Save by those shadowy *expiations* weak,
The blood of bulls and goats. *Milton's Paradise Lost, b.* xii.

The former part of this poem is but a due *expiation* for my not serving my king and country in it. *Dryden.*

Let a man's innocence be what it will, let his virtues rise to the highest pitch of perfection, there will be still in him so many secret sins, so many human frailties, so many offences of ignorance, passion and prejudice, so many unguarded words and thoughts, that without the advantage of such an *expiation* and attonement, as Christianity has revealed to us, it is impossible he should be saved. *Addison's Spectator*, N°. 50.

3. Practices by which the threats of ominous prodigies were averted.

Upon the birth of such monsters the Grecians and Romans did use divers sorts of *expiations*, and to go about their principal cities with many solemn ceremonies and sacrifices. *Hayw.*

E'XPIATORY. *adj.* [from *expiate.*] Having the power of expiation or attonement.

His voluntary death for others prevailed with God, and had the force of an *expiatory* sacrifice. *Hooker, b.* v. *s.* 56.

EXPILA'TION. *n. s.* [*expilatio*, Latin.] Robbery; the act of committing waste upon land to the loss of the heir.

EXPIRA'TION. *n. s.* [from *expire.*]

1. That act of respiration which thrusts the air out of the lungs, and contracts the cavity of the breast. *Quincy.*

In all *expiration* the motion is outwards, and therefore rather driveth away the voice than draweth it. *Bacon's Nat. History.*

Of an inflammation of the diaphragm, the symptoms are a violent fever, and a most exquisite pain increases upon inspiration; by which it is distinguished from a pleurisy, in which the greatest pain is in *expiration.* *Arbuthnot on Diet.*

2. The last emission of breath; death.

We have heard him breathe the groan of *expiration. Rambler.*

3. Evaporation; act of fuming out.

4. Vapour; matter expired.

Words of this sort resemble the wind in fury and impetuousness, in transientness and sudden *expiration. Decay of Piety.*

Close air is warmer than open air, as the cause of cold is an *expiration* from the earth, which in open places is stronger. *Bacon's Natural History*, N°. 866.

5. The cessation of any thing to which life is figuratively ascribed.

To satisfy ourselves of its *expiration* we darkened the room, and in vain endeavoured to discover any spark of fire. *Boyle.*

6. The conclusion of any limited time.

If 'till the *expiration* of your month,
You will return and sojourn with my sister,
Dismissing half your train, come there to me. *Shak. K. Lear.*

This he did in a fortnight after the *expiration* of the treaty of Uxbridge. *Clarendon, b.* viii.

To EXPI'RE. *v. a.* [*expiro*, Latin.]

1. To breathe out.

To save his body from the scorching fire,
Which he from hellish entrails did *expire.* *Fairy Queen.*

Anatomy exhibits the lungs in a continual motion of inspiring and *expiring* air. *Harvey on Consumptions.*

This chaff'd the boar; his nostrils flames *expire*,
And his red eyeballs roll with living fire. *Dryden's Ovid.*

2. To exhale; to send out in exhalations.

The fluid which is thus secreted, and *expired* forth along with the air, goes off in insensible parcels. *Woodward.*

3. To close; to conclude; to bring to an end.

When as time flying with wings swift,
Expired had the term that these two javels
Should render up a reck'ning of their travels. *Hubb. Tale.*

To EXPI'RE. *v. n.*

1. To make an emission of the breath.

If the inspiring and *expiring* organ of any animal be stopt, it suddenly dies. *Walton's Angler.*

2. To die; to breathe the last.

For when the fair in all their pride *expire*,
To their first elements the souls retire. *Pope.*

3. To perish; to fall; to be destroyed.

All thy praise is vain,
Save what this verse, which never shall *expire*,
Shall to thee purchase. *Spenser.*

The dead man's knell,
Is there scarce ask'd, for whom; and good mens lives
Expire before the flowers in their caps,
Dying or ere they sicken. *Shakespeare's Macbeth.*

4. To fly out with a blast.

The distance judg'd for shot of every size,
The linstocks touch, the pond'rous ball *expires*;
The vig'rous seaman every porthole plies,
And adds his heart to every gun he fires. *Dryden.*

5. To conclude; to terminate; to come to an end.

A month before
This bond *expires*, I do expect return
Of thrice three times the value of this bond. *Shakespeare.*

To EXPLA'IN. *v. a.* [*explano*, Latin.] To expound; to illustrate; to clear by notes or commentaries.

Such is the original design, however we may *explain* it away. *Ayliffe's Parergon.*

You will have variety of commentators to *explain* the difficult passages to you. *Gay.*

Some *explain'd* the meaning quite away. *Pope.*

EXPLA'INABLE. *adj.* [from *explain.*] Capable of being explained or interpreted.

It is symbolically *explainable*, and implieth purification and cleanness. *Brown's Vulgar Errours, b.* v. *c.* 21.

EXPLA'INER. *n. s.* [from *explain.*] Expositor; interpreter; commentator.

EXPLANA'TION. *n. s.* [from *explain.*]

1. The act of explaining or interpreting.

2. The sense given by an explainer or interpreter.

Before this *explanation* be condemned, and the bill found upon it, some lawyers should fully inform the jury. *Swift.*

EXPLA'NATORY. *adj.* [from *explain.*] Containing explanation.

Had the printer given me notice, I would have printed the names, and writ *explanatory* notes. *Swift.*

E'XPLETIVE. *n. s.* [*expletivum*, Latin.] Something used only to take up room; something of which the use is only to prevent a vacancy.

These are not only useful *expletives* to matter, but great ornaments of style. *Swift.*

Oft the ear the open vowels tire,
While *expletives* their feeble aid do join. *Pope's Ess. on Critic.*

Another nicety is in relation to *expletives*, whether words or syllables, which are made use of purely to supply a vacancy: *do*, before verbs plural, is absolutely such; and future refiners may explode *did* and *does.* *Pope.*

E'XPLICABLE. *adj.* [from *explicate.*] Explainable; possible to be explained.

Many difficulties, scarce *explicable* with any certainty, occur in the fabrick of human nature. *Hale's Origin of Mankind.*

Great variety there is in compound bodies, and little many of them seem to be *explicable.* *Boyle.*

To E'XPLICATE. *v. a.* [*explico*, Latin.]

1. To unfold; to expand.

They *explicate* the leaves, and ripen food
For the silk labourers of the mulberry wood. *Blackmore.*

2. To explain; to clear; to interpret.

They do not understand that part of Christian philosophy which *explicates* the secret nature of this divine sacrament. *Taylor's Worthy Communicant.*

Although the truths may be elicited and *explicated* by the contemplation of animals, yet they are more clearly evidenced in the contemplation of man. *Hale's Origin of Mankind.*

The last verse of his last satyr is not yet sufficiently *explicated.* *Dryden's Juvenal, Dedicat.*

EXPLICA'TION. *n. s.* [from *explicate.*]

1. The act of opening; unfolding or expanding.

2. The act of explaining; interpretation; explanation.

The church preacheth, first publishing, by way of testimony, the truth which from them she hath received, written in the sacred volumes of Scripture; secondly, by way of *explication*, discovering the mysteries which lie hid therein. *Hooker.*

Many things are needful for *explication*, and many for application unto particular occasions. *Hooker, b.* i.

Allowances are made in the *explication* of our Saviour's parables, which hold only as to the main scope. *Atterbury.*

3. The sense given by an explainer; interpretation.

'Tis the substance of this theory I mainly depend upon: many single *explications* and particularities may be rectified upon farther thoughts. *Burnet's Theory of the Earth, Preface.*

E'XPLICATIVE. *adj.* [from *explicate.*] Having a tendency to explain.

If the term which is added to the subject of a complex proposition be either essential or any way necessary to it, then it is called *explicative*; for it only explains the subject, as every mortal man is a son of Adam. *Watts's Logick.*

EXPLICA'TOR. *n. s.* [from *explicate.*] Expounder; interpreter; explainer.

EXPLI'CIT. *adj.* [*explicitus*, Latin.] Unfolded; plain; clear; not obscure; not merely implied.

We must lay aside that lazy and fallacious method of censuring by the lump, and bring things close to *explicit* proof and evidence. *Burnet's Theory of the Earth, Preface.*

These speculations, when most refined, serve only to shew

how

how impossible it is for us to have a clear and *explicit* notion of that which is infinite. *South's Sermons.*

EXPLI'CITLY. *adv.* [from *explicit.*] Plainly; directly; not merely by inference or implication.

This querulous humour carries an implicit repugnance to God's disposals; but where it is indulged, it usually is its own expositor, and *explicitly* avows it. *Government of the Tongue.*

To EXPLO'DE. *v. a.* [*explodo*, Latin.]

1. To drive out disgracefully with some noise of contempt; to treat with open contempt; to treat not only with neglect, but open disdain or scorn.

Him old and young
Exploded, and had seiz'd with violent hands,
Had not a cloud descending snatch'd him thence
Unseen amid' the throng. *Milton's Paradise Lost, b.* xi.

Thus was th' applause they meant,
Turn'd to *exploding* hiss, triumph to shame,
Cast on themselves from their own mouths. *Milt. Par. Lost.*

Old age *explodes* all but morality. *Roscommon.*

There is pretended, that a magnetical globe or terrella, being placed upon its poles, would have a constant rotation; but this is commonly *exploded*, as being against all experience. *Wilkins's Dædalus.*

Shall that man pass for a proficient in Christ's school, who would have been *exploded* in the school of Zeno or Epictetus. *South's Sermons.*

Provided that no word, which a society shall give a sanction to, be afterwards antiquated and *exploded*, they may receive whatever new ones they shall find occasion for. *Swift's Letter to the Lord High Treasurer.*

2. To drive out with noise and violence.

But late the kindled powder did *explode*
The massy ball, and the brass tube unload. *Blackmore.*

EXPLO'DER. *n. s.* [from *explode.*] An hisser; one who drives out any person or thing with open contempt.

EXPLO'IT. *n. s.* [*expletum*, Latin, *res expleta.*] A design accomplished; an atchievement; a successful attempt.

Know'st thou not any whom corrupting gold
Would tempt into a close *exploit* of death? *Shak. Rich.* III.

Flight cannot stain the honour you have won;
But mine it will, that no *exploit* have done. *Shak. Hen.* VI.

How shall I relate
To human sense th' invisible *exploits*
Of warring spirits? *Milton's Paradise Lost, b.* v.

He breaks fierce Hannibal's insulting heats;
Of which *exploit* thus our friend Ennius treats. *Denham.*

Will you thus dishonour
Your past *exploits*, and sully all your wars? *Addison's Cato.*

To EXPLO'IT. *v. a.* [from the noun.] To perform; to atchieve.

He *exploited* great matters in his own person in Gallia, and by his son in Spain. *Camden's Remains.*

To EXPLO'RATE. *v. a.* [*exploro*, Latin.] To search out; to try by searching.

Snails exclude their horns, and therewith *explorate* their way. *Brown's Vulgar Errours, b.* iii. *c.* 20.

EXPLORA'TION. *n. s.* [from *explorate.*] Search; examination.

For exact *exploration* they should be suspended where the air is quiet, that, clear of impediments, they may the more freely convert upon their natural verticity. *Brown's Vulgar Errours.*

Use may be made of the like way of *exploration* in that enquiry which puzzles so many modern naturalists. *Boyle.*

EXPLORA'TOR. *n. s.* [from *explorate.*] One who searches; a searcher; an examiner.

EXPLO'RATORY. *adj.* [from *explorate.*] Searching; examining.

To EXPLO'RE. *v. a.* [*exploro*, Latin.] To try; to search into; to examine by trial.

Abdiel that fight endur'd not, where he stood
Among the mightiest, bent on highest deeds,
And thus his own undaunted heart *explores*. *Milt. Par. Lost.*

Divers opinions I have been inclined to question, not only as a naturalist, but as a chymist, whether they be agreeable to true grounds of philosophy, or the *exploring* experiments of the fire. *Boyle.*

But Capys, and the rest of sounder mind,
The fatal present to the flames design'd,
Or to the wat'ry deep; at least to bore
The hollow sides, and hidden frauds *explore*. *Dryden's Æn.*

The mighty Stagyrite first left the shore,
Spread all his sails, and durst the deeps *explore*;
He steer'd securely, and discover'd far,
Led by the light of the Mœonian star. *Pope's Ess. on Crit.*

EXPLO'REMENT. *n. s.* [from *explore.*] Search; trial.

The frustrated search of Porta, upon the *explorement* of many, could scarce find one. *Brown's Vulgar Errours, b.* iii.

EXPLO'SION. *n. s.* [from *explode.*] The act of driving out any thing with noise and violence.

Those parts which abound with strata of stone, or marble, making the strongest opposition, are the most furiously shattered; an event observable not only in this, but all other *explosions* whatever. *Woodward's Natural History.*

In gunpowder the charcoal and sulphur easily take fire, and set fire to the nitre; and the spirit of the nitre being thereby rarified into vapour, rushes out with *explosion*, after the manner that the vapour of water rushesout of an æolipile: the sulphur also, being volatile, is converted into vapour, and augments the *explosion*. *Newton's Opt.*

With *explosion* vast,
The thunder raises his tremendous voice. *Thomson.*

EXPLO'SIVE. *adj.* [from *explode.*] Driving out with noise and violence.

These minerals constitute in the earth a kind of natural gunpowder, which takes fire; and by the assistance of its *explosive* power, renders the shock greater. *Woodward's N. Hist.*

EXPO'NENT. *n. s.* [from *expono*, Latin.]

Exponent of the ratio, or proportion between any two numbers or quantities, is the exponent arising when the antecedent is divided by the consequent: thus six is the exponent of the ratio which thirty hath to five. Also a rank of numbers in arithmetical progression, beginning from 0, and placed over a rank of numbers in geometrical progression, are called indices or exponents: and in this is founded the reason and demonstration of logarithms; for addition and subtraction of these exponents answers to multiplication and division in the geometrical numbers. *Harris.*

EXPONE'NTIAL. *adj.* [from *exponent.*]

Exponential curves are such as partake both of the nature of algebraick and transcendental ones. They partake of the former, because they consist of a finite number of terms, though those terms themselves are indeterminate; and they are in some measure transcendental, because they cannot be algebraically constructed. *Harris.*

To EXPO'RT. *v. a.* [*exporto*, Latin.] To carry out of a country, generally in the way of traffick.

Glorious followers taint business for want of secrecy, and *export* honour from a man, and make him a return in envy. *Bacon's Essays, Civil and Moral.*

Edward III. by his encouragement of trade, turned the scale so much in favour of English merchandize, that, by a balance of trade taken in his time, the *exported* commodities amounted to two hundred ninety-four thousand pounds, and the imported but to thirty-eight thousand. *Addison's Freeholder.*

Great ships brought from the Indies precious wood, and *exported* pearls and robes. *Arbuthnot on Coins.*

E'XPORT. *n. s.* [from the verb.] Commodity carried out in traffick.

EXPORTA'TION. *n. s.* [from *export.*] The act or practice of carrying out commodities into other countries.

The cause of a kingdom's thriving is fruitfulness of soil to produce necessaries, not only sufficient for the inhabitants, but for *exportation* into other countries. *Swift.*

EXPO'RTER. *n. s.* [from *export.*] He that carries out commodities, in opposition to the *importer*, who brings them in.

Money which is weight, according to its denomination by the standard of the mint, will be that which will be melted down, or carried away in coin by the *exporter*, whether the pieces of each species be by the law bigger or less. *Locke.*

To EXPO'SE. *v. a.* [*expono*, *expositum*, Lat. *exposer*, French.]

1. To lay open; to make liable to.

Take physick, pomp;
Expose thyself to feel what wretches feel,
That thou may'st shake the superflux to them,
And shew heav'n just. *Shakespeare's King Lear.*

Who here
Will envy whom the highest place *exposes*
Foremost to stand against the Thunderer's aim? *Milt. P. L.*

To pass the riper period of his age,
Acting his part upon a crowded stage,
To lasting toils *expos'd*, and endless cares,
To open dangers, and to secret snares. *Prior.*

2. To put in the power of any thing.

But still he held his purpose to depart;
For as he lov'd her equal to his life,
He would not to the seas *expose* his wife. *Dryden.*

3. To lay open; to make bare; to put in a state of being acted upon.

Then joyous birds frequent the lonely grove,
And beasts, by nature strong, renew their love;
Then fields the blades of bury'd corn disclose,
And while the balmy western spirit blows,
Earth to the breath her bosom dares *expose*. *Dryden's Virgil.*

4. To lay open to censure or ridicule; to show in such a state as brings contempt.

Like Horace, you only *expose* the follies of men, without arraigning their vices. *Dryden's Juv. Dedication.*

Tully has justly *exposed* a precept, that a man should live with his friend in such a manner, that if he became his enemy, it should not be in his power to hurt him. *Addison's Spect.*

A fool might once himself alone *expose*;
Now one in verse makes many more in prose. *Pope.*

Your fame and your property suffer alike, you are at once *exposed* and plundered. *Pope.*

5. To lay open to examination.

Those

Those who seek truth only, freely *expose* their principles to the test, and are pleased to have them examined. *Locke.*

6. To put in danger.

The *exposing* himself notoriously did sometimes change the fortune of the day, when his troops begun to give ground. *Clarendon, b.* viii.

7. To cast out to chance.

A father, unnaturally careless of his child, gives him to another man; and he again *exposes* him: a third man finding him, breeds up and provides for him as his own. *Locke.*

Helpless and naked on a woman's knees,
To be *expos'd* or rear'd as she may please,
Feel her neglect, and pine from her disease. *Prior.*

8. To censure; to treat with dispraise. A colloquial abuse of the word.

A little wit is equally capable of *exposing* a beauty, and of aggravating a fault. *Addison's Spectator,* N°. 29.

EXPOSI'TION. *n. s.* [from *expose.*]

1. The situation in which any thing is placed with respect to the sun or air.

Water he chuses clear, light, without taste or smell; drawn not from snow, but from springs with an easterly *exposition.* *Arbuthnot on Aliments.*

The diversity of *exposition* of the several kitchens in this city, whereby some receive the rays of the sun sooner, and others later, will occasion great irregularity as to the time of dining. *Arbuthnot.*

2. Explanation; interpretation; [from *expound, expono,* Latin.]

My lord of York, it better shew'd with you,
When that your flock, assembled by the bell,
Encircled you, to hear with reverence
Your *exposition* on the holy text. *Shakespeare's Henry* IV.

You are a worthy judge;
You know the law: your *exposition*
Hath been most sound. *Shakespeare's Merch. of Venice.*

I have sometimes very boldly made such *expositions* of my authors, as no commentator will forgive me. *Dryden.*

EXPO'SITOR. *n. s.* [*expositor,* Latin.] Explainer; expounder; interpreter.

A mirth-moving jest,
Which his fair tongue, conceit's *expositor,*
Delivers in such apt and gracious words,
That aged ears play truant at his tales. *Shakespeare.*

In the picture of Abraham's sacrificing his son, Isaac is described as a little boy, which is not consentaneous unto the authority of *expositors.* *Brown's Vulgar Errours, b.* v. *c.* 8.

The sinner's conscience is the best *expositor* of the mind of God, under any judgment or affliction. *South's Sermons.*

Commentators and scholiasts, those copious *expositors* of places, pour out a vain overflow of learning on passages plain and easy. *Locke.*

To EXPO'STULATE. *v. n.* [*expostulo,* Latin.] To canvass with another; to altercate; to debate without open rupture.

More bitterly could I *expostulate,*
Save that for reverence of some alive
I give a sparing limit to my tongue. *Shakes. Richard* III.

The emperor's ambassador did *expostulate* with the king, that he had broken his league with the emperor. *Hayward.*

It is madness for friendless and unarmed innocence to *expostulate* with invincible power. *L'Estrange.*

Durst I *expostulate* with providence, I then might ask. *Cotton.*

The bishop will *expostulate,* and the tenant will have regard to the reasonableness of the demand, rather than engage in a suit. *Swift.*

EXPOSTULA'TION. *n. s.* [from *expostulate.*]

1. Debate; altercation; discussion of an affair in private without rupture.

Expostulations end well between lovers, but ill between friends. *Spect.*

2. Charge; accusation.

This makes her bleeding patients to accuse
High heav'n, and these *expostulations* use;
Could nature then no private woman grace,
Whom we might dare to love, with such a face? *Waller.*

Expostulation is a private accusation of one friend touching another, supposed not to have dealt singly or considerately in the course of good friendship. *Ayliffe's Parergon.*

EXPOSTULA'TOR. *n. s.* [from *expostulate.*] One that debates with another without open rupture.

EXPO'STULATORY. *adj.* [from *expostulate.*] Containing expostulation.

This fable is a kind of an *expostulatory* debate between bounty and ingratitude. *L'Estrange.*

EXPO'SURE. *n. s.* [from *expose.*]

1. The act of exposing or setting out to observation.

2. The state of being open to observation.

When we have our naked frailties hid,
That suffer in *exposure,* let us meet. *Shakes. Macbeth.*

3. The state of being exposed, or being liable to any thing.

Determine on some course,
More than a wild *exposure* to each chance
That starts i' th' way before thee. *Shakes. Coriolanus.*

4. The state of being in danger.

Ajax sets Thersites
To match us in comparisons with dirt;
To weaken and discredit our *exposure,*
How hard soever rounded in with danger. *Shakespeare.*

5. Exposition; the situation in which the sun or air is received.

The cold now advancing, set such plants as will not endure the house, in pots two or three inches lower than the surface of some bed, under a southern *exposure.* *Evelyn.*

To EXPO'UND. *v. a.* [*expono,* Lat.]

1. To explain; to clear; to interpret; to shew the meaning of.

We cannot better interpret the meaning of those words than pope Leo himself *expounded* them, whose speech concerning our Lord's ascension may serve instead of a marginal gloss. *Hooker, b.* v. *s.* 45.

This by Calphurnia's dream is signified.
—And this way you have well *expounded* it. *Shak. Ju. Cæs.*

He *expounded* unto them in all the Scriptures the things concerning himself. *Lu.* xxiv. 27.

Those right holy fathers, as in matters of faith they did not make truth, but religiously *expounded* it; so in matters of ecclesiastical government, they did not create provinces for themselves, but ordered the countries which they then had. *Raleigh's Essays.*

2. To examine; to lay open: a Latinism.

He *expounded* both his pockets,
And found a watch with rings and lockets. *Hudibras.*

EXPO'UNDER. *n. s.* [from *expound.*] Explainer; interpreter.

This they did partly as faithful witnesses, making a mere relation of what God himself had revealed unto them; and partly as careful *expounders,* teachers, and persuaders thereof. *Hooker.*

The best he was,
And faithfullest *expounder* of the laws. *Dryden's Juv. Sat.* 4.

To EXPRE'SS. *v. a.* [*exprimo, expressus,* Latin.]

1. To copy; to resemble; to represent.

So kids and whelps their sires and dams *express,*
And so the great I measur'd by the less. *Dryden's Virgil.*

Adorn a dream, *expressing* human form,
The shape of him who suffer'd in the storm;
And send it fleeting to the Thracian court,
The wreck of wretched Ceyx to report. *Dryden.*

2. To represent by any of the imitative arts: as poetry, sculpture, painting.

Each skilful artist shall *express* thy form
In animated gold. *Smith's Phædra and Hippolitus.*

3. To represent in words; to exhibit by language; to utter; to declare.

Less than half we find *exprest,*
Envy bid conceal the rest. *Milton.*

Though they have learned those sounds, yet there are no determined ideas laid up in their minds, which are to be *expressed* to others by them. *Locke.*

In moral ideas we have no sensible marks that resemble them, whereby we can set them down: we have nothing but words to *express* them by. *Locke.*

True wit is nature to advantage drest,
What oft was thought, but ne'er so well *exprest.* *Pope.*

Others for language all their care *express,*
And value books, as women men, for dress. *Pope.*

To shed tears, among the ancients, when they should *express* their gratitude to the gods with joy, was esteemed a prophanation. *Notes to Pope's Odyssey.*

4. To show or make known in any manner.

No longer shall thy bodice aptly lace,
That air and shape of harmony *express,*
Fine by degrees, and delicately less. *Prior.*

5. To utter; to declare, with the reciprocal pronoun.

Mr. Philips did *express* himself with much indignation against me one evening. *Pope.*

6. To denote; to designate.

Moses and Aaron took these men *expressed* by their names. *Numb.* i. 17.

7. To squeeze out; to force out by compression.

Among the watry juices of fruit are all the fruits out of which drink is *expressed;* as the grape, and the apple. *Bacon.*

8. To extort by violence: a Latinism.

Halters and racks cannot *express* from thee
More than thy deeds: 'tis only judgment waits thee. *Ben. Johnson's Catiline.*

EXPRE'SS. *adj.* [from the verb.]

1. Copied; resembling; exactly like.

Of his presence many a sign
Still following thee, still compassing thee round
With goodness and paternal love; his face
Express, and of his steps the track divine. *Milton's P. Lost.*

2. Plain; apparent; in direct terms.

There hath been some doubt whether containing in Scripture do import *express* setting down in plain terms; or else comprehending in such sort, that by reason we may from thence conclude all things which are necessary. *Hooker, b.* i.

There is not any positive law of men, whether general or particular, received by formal *express* consent, as in councils; or by secret approbation; but the same may be taken away, if occasion serves. *Hooker, b.* iv. *s.* 14.

All the gazers on the skies,
Read not in fair heaven's story
Expresser truth, or truer glory,
Than they might in her bright eyes. *Ben. Johns. Epigr.*

3. Clear; not dubious.

I love to feel myself of an *express* and settled judgment and affection, in things of the greatest moment. *More's Div. Dial.*

As to the testimonies of the fathers, let them be never so *express* against all sorts of prayers and invocations, they hold only of such a sort of prayer. *Stillingfleet.*

Where reason or scripture is *express* for any opinion, or action, we may receive it as of divine authority. *Locke.*

4. On purpose; for a particular end.

They who are not induced to believe and live as they ought, by those discoveries which God hath made in Scripture, would stand out against any evidence whatsoever; even that of a messenger sent *express* from the other world. *Atterbury's Serm.*

Expre'ss. *n. s.* [from the adjective.]

1. A messenger sent on purpose.

The king sent an *express* immediately to the marquis, with all the particular informati ns. *Clarendon, b.* viii.

As if *expresses* from al parts had come,
With fresh alarms threat ning the fate of Rome. *Dryd. Juv.*

Upon the first moment I was discovered sleeping on the ground, after my landing, the emperor had early notice of it by an *express*. *Gulliver's Travels.*

2. A message sent.

I am content my heart should be discovered to the world, without any of those popular captations which some men use in their speeches and *expresses*. *King Charles.*

3. A declaration in plain terms. Not usual.

They do not only contradict the general design and particular *expresses* of the gospel, but trespass against all logick and common sense. *Norris.*

Expre'ssible. *adj.* [from *express.*]

1. That may be uttered or declared.

They had not only a memory and tradition of it in general, but even of several particular accidents of it likewise, which they handed downwards to the succeeding ages, with notes of the greatest terror *expressible*. *Woodward's Natural History.*

2. That may be drawn by squeezing or expression.

Expre'ssion. *n. s.* [from *express.*]

1. The act or power of representing any thing.

There is nothing comparable to the variety of instructive *expressions* by speech, wherewith a man alone is endowed, as with an instrument suitable to the excellency of his soul, for the communication of his thoughts. *Holder's Elem. of Speech.*

2. The form or cast of language in which any thoughts are uttered.

But ill *expression* sometimes gives allay
To noble thoughts, whose flame shall ne'er decay. *Buckingh.*

The poet, to reconcile Helen to his reader, brings her in as a penitent, condemning her own infidelity in very strong *expressions*. *Notes on the Odyssey.*

3. A phrase; a mode of speech.

4. The act of squeezing or forcing out any thing by a press.

Those juices that are so fleshy, as they cannot make drink by *expression*, yet may make drink by mixture of water. *Bacon.*

The juices of the leaves are obtained by *expression*: from this juice proceeds the taste. *Arbuthnot on Aliments.*

Expre'ssive. *adj.* [from *express.*] Having the power of utterance or representation. With *of* before the thing expressed.

Each verse so swells *expressive of* her woes,
And ev'ry tear in lines so mournful flows,
We, spite of fame, her fate revers'd believe,
O'erlook her crimes, and think she ought to live. *Tickell.*

And four fair queens, whose hands sustain a flow'r,
Th' *expressive* emblem of their softer pow'r. *Pope.*

A visible and exemplary obedience to God's laws is the most *expressive* acknowledgment of the majesty and sovereignty of God, and disposes others to glorify him by the same observances. *Rogers, Sermon* 18.

Expre'ssively. *adv.* [from *expressive.*] In a clear and representative way.

Expre'ssiveness. *n. s.* [from *expressive.*] The power of expression, or representation by words.

The murrain at the end has all the *expressiveness* that words can give: it was here that the poet strained hard to outdo Lucretius. *Addison.*

Expre'ssly. *adv.* [from *express.*] In direct terms; plainly; clearly; not by implication; not generally.

It doth not follow, that of necessity we shall sin, unless we *expressly* extend this in every particular. *Hooker, b.* ii. *s.* 2.

Articles of belief, and things which all men must of necessity do, to the end they may be saved, are either *expressly* set down in Scripture, or else plainly thereby to be gathered. *Hooker, b.* iii. *s.* 10.

Who dare cross 'em,
Bearing the king's will from his mouth *expressly*? *Shakes.*

The beginning of the worship of images in these western parts, was by the folly and superstition of the people, *expressly* against the will of their own bishop. *Stillingfleet.*

This account I *expressly* give of them, when I enter on the argument. *Atterbury's Sermons.*

All the duties that the best political laws enjoin, as conducive to the quiet and order of social life, are *expressly* commanded by our religion. *Rogers, Sermon* 17.

Expre'ssure. *n. s.* [from *express.* Now disused.]

1. Expression; utterance.

There is a mystery in the soul of state,
Which hath an operation more divine,
Than breath or pen can give *expressure* to. *Sh. Troil. and Cr.*

2. The form; the likeness represented.

I will drop some obscure epistles of love, wherein, by the colour of his beard, the manner of his gait, the *expressure* of his eye, forehead, and complexion, he shall find himself personated. *Shakes. Twelfth Night.*

3. The mark; the impression.

And nightly, meadow fairies, look you sing,
Like to the garter-compass in a ring:
Th' *expressure* that it bears, green let it be,
More fertile fresh than all the field to see. *Shakespeare.*

To EXPROBRA'TE. *v. a.* [*exprobro,* Latin.] To charge upon with reproach; to impute openly with blame; to upbraid.

To *exprobrate* their stupidity, he induces the providence of storks: now, if the bird had been unknown, the illustration had been obscure, and the exprobration not so proper. *Brown.*

Exprobra'tion. *n. s.* [from *exprobrate.*] Scornful charge; reproachful accusation; act of upbraiding.

The only goodness we glory in, is to find out somewhat whereby we may judge others to be ungodly: each other's fault we observe as matter of *exprobration*, and not of grief. *Hooker's Sermons, Preface.*

The Parthians, with *exprobration* of Crassus's thirst after money, poured molten gold into his mouth after he was dead. *Abbot's Description of the World.*

It will be a denial with scorn, with a taunting *exprobration*; and to be miserable without commiseration, is the height of misery. *South's Sermons.*

No need such boasts, or *exprobrations* false
Of cowardice: the military mound
The British files transcend in evil hour
For their proud foes. *Philips.*

To Expro'priate. *v. a.* [*ex* and *proprius,* Latin.] To make no longer our own; to hold no longer as a property. Not in use.

When you have resigned, or rather consigned, your *expropriated* will to God, and thereby entrusted him to will for you, all his dispensations towards you are, in effect, the acts of your own will. *Boyle's Seraphick Love.*

To EXPU'GN. *v. a.* [*expugno,* Latin.] To conquer; to take by assault.

Expugna'tion. *n. s.* [from *expugn.*] Conquest; the act of taking by assault.

The *expugnation* of Vienna he could never accomplish. *Sand.*

To EXPU'LSE. *v. a.* [*expulsus,* Latin.] To drive out; to expel; to force away.

For ever should they be *expuls'd* from France,
And not have title of an earldom there. *Shak. Henry* VI.

Suppose a nation where the custom were, that after full age the sons should *expulse* their fathers and mothers out of possessions, and put them to their pensions. *Bacon's holy War.*

Although inwardly received, it may be very diuretick, and *expulse* the stone in the kidneys; yet how it should resolve or break that in the bladder, will require a farther dispute. *Brown.*

Dictys relates, that Peleus was *expulsed* from his kingdom by Acastus. *Notes on the Odyssey.*

Expu'lsion. *n. s.* [from *expulse.*]

1. The act of expelling or driving out.

A wooer,
More hateful than the foul *expulsion* is
Of thy dear husband. *Shakes. Cymbeline.*

Sole victor from th' *expulsion* of his foes,
Messiah his triumphal chariot turn'd. *Milton's Paradise Lost.*

Others think it possible so to contrive several pieces of steel and a load-stone, that, by their continual attraction and *expulsion* of one another, they may cause a perpetual revolution of a wheel. *Wilkins's Dædalus.*

Coffee-coloured urine proceeds from a mixture of a small quantity of blood with the urine; but often prognosticates a resolution of the obstructing matter, and the *expulsion* of gravel or a stone. *Arbuthnot on Diet.*

2. The state of being driven out.

To what end had the angel been set to keep the entrance into Paradise, after Adam's *expulsion*, if the universe had been Paradise? For then must Adam have been chased also out of the world. *Raleigh's History of the World.*

This magnificent temple was not finished 'till after the *expulsion* of Tarquin. *Stillingfleet.*

Expu'lsive. *adj.* [from *expulse.*] Having the power of expulsion.

If the member be dependent, by raising of it up, and placing it equal with or higher than the rest of the body, the influx

influx may be restrained, and the part strengthened by *expulsive* bandages. *Wiseman's Surgery.*

EXPU'NCTION. *n. s.* [from *expunge.*] Abolition; the act of expunging, blotting, or effacing.

To EXPU'NGE. *v. a.* [*expungo*, Latin.]

1. To blot out; to rub out.

The difference of the denarius and drachm having been done in the manuscript, it was needless to *expunge* it. *Arbuthn.*

Neither do they remember the many alterations, additions, and *expungings* made by great authors in those treatises which they prepare for the publick. *Swift.*

2. To efface; to annihilate.

Wilt thou not to a broken heart dispense
Thy balm of mercy, and *expunge* th' offence? *Sandys.*

Deduct what is but vanity, or dress,
Or learning's luxury, or idleness,
Or tricks to shew the stretch of human brain
Mere curious pleasure, or ingenious pain;
Expunge the whole, or lop th' excrescent parts
Of all, our vices have created arts:
Then see how little the remaining sum,
Which serv'd the past, and must the times to come! *Pope.*

EXPURGA'TION. *n. s.* [*expurgatio*, Latin.]

1. The act of purging or cleansing.

All the intestines, but especially the great ones, kidneys and ureters, serve for *expurgation.* *Wiseman's Surgery.*

2. Purification from bad mixture, as of errour or falshood.

Wise men know, that arts and learning want *expurgation*; and if the course of truth be permitted to itself, it cannot escape many errours. *Brown's Preface to Vulgar Errours.*

EXPU'RGATORY. *adj.* [*expurgatorius*, Latin.] Employed in purging away what is noxious: as, the *expurgatory* index of the Romanists directs the abolition or expunction of passages admitted by any authors contrary to popery.

There wants *expurgatory* animadversions, whereby we might strike out great numbers of hidden qualities; and having once a conceded list, we might with more safety attempt their reasons. *Brown's Vulgar Errours, b.* ii. *c.* 7.

E'XQUISITE. *adj.* [*exquisitus*, Latin.]

1. Farsought; excellent; consummate; complete.

His absolute exactness they imitate by tending unto that which is most *exquisite* in every particular. *Hooker, b.* i. *s.* 5.

Why should the state be troubled with this needless charge of keeping and maintaining so great a navy in such *exquisite* perfection and readiness? *Raleigh's Essays.*

Adam and Eve, before the fall, were a different species; and none but a poet of the most unbounded invention, and the most *exquisite* judgment, could have fitted their conversation and behaviour to their state of innocence. *Addison.*

The pleasures of sense are probably relished by beasts in a more *exquisite* degree than they are by men; for they taste them sincere and pure, without being distracted in the pursuit, or disquieted in the use of them. *Atterbury's Sermons.*

2. Consummately bad.

With *exquisite* malice they have mixed the gall and vinegar of falsity and contempt. *King Charles.*

EXQU'ISITELY. *adv.* [from *exquisite.*] Perfectly; completely: in either a good or ill sense.

We see more *exquisitely* with one eye shut than with both open; for that the spirits visual unite themselves, and become stronger. *Bacon's Natural History*, N°. 86.

A collection of rare manuscripts, *exquisitely* written in Arabick, and sought in the most remote parts by Epenius, the most excellent linguist. *Wotton.*

The soldier then, in Grecian arts unskill'd,
Returning rich with plunder from the field,
If cups of silver or of gold he brought,
With jewels set, and *exquisitely* wrought,
To glorious trappings strait the plate he turn'd,
And with the glitt'ring spoil his horse adorn'd. *Dryden.*

The poetry of opera's is generally as *exquisitely* ill as the musick is good. *Addison's Remarks on Italy.*

EXQU'ISITENESS. *n. s.* [from *exquisite.*] Nicety; perfection.

We suppose the superficies of the two glasses should be so exactly flat and smooth, that no air at all can come between them; and experience has informed us, that it is extremely difficult to procure from our ordinary tradesmen either glasses or marbles so much as approaching such an *exquisiteness.* *Boyle.*

E'XSCRIPT. *n. s.* [*exscriptum*, Latin.] A copy; a writing copied from another.

EXSI'CCANT. *adj.* [from *exsiccate.*] Drying; having the power to dry up.

Some are moderately moist, and require to be treated with medicines of the like nature, such as fleshy parts; others dry in themselves, yet require *exsiccants*, as bones. *Wiseman.*

To EXSI'CCATE. *v. a.* [*exsicco*, Latin.] To dry.

If in a dissolution of steel a separation of parts be made by precipitation, or exhalation, the *exsiccated* powder ascends not unto the loadstone. *Brown's Vulgar Errours, b.* ii. *c.* 3.

Great heats and droughts *exsiccate* and waste the moisture and vegetative nature of the earth. *Mortimer's Husbandry.*

EXSICCA'TION. *n. s.* [from *exsiccate.*] The act of drying.

That which is concreted by *exsiccation*, or expression of humidity, will be resolved by humectation; as earth, dirt, and clay. *Brown's Vulgar Errours, b.* ii. *c.* 1.

EXSI'CCATIVE. *adj.* [from *exsiccate.*] Having the power of drying.

EXSPUI'TION. *n. s.* [*exspuo*, Latin.] A discharge of saliva by spitting. *Quincy.*

EXSU'CTION. *n. s.* [*exugo*, Latin.] The act of sucking out, or draining out, without immediate contact of the power sucking with the thing sucked.

If you open the valve, and force up the sucker, after this first *exsuction* you will drive out almost a whole cylinder full of air. *Boyle.*

EXSUDA'TION. *n. s.* [from *exudo*, Latin.] A sweating out; an extillation; an emission.

They seemed to be made by an *exsudation*, or extillation of some petrifying juices out of the rocky earth. *Derham.*

To EXSU'FFOLATE. *v. a.* [a word peculiar to *Shakespeare.*] To whisper; to buzz in the ear, [from the Italian verb *suffolar.* *Hanmer.*

Exchange me for a goat,
When I shall turn the business of my soul
To such *exsuffolate* and blown surmises. *Shakesp. Othello.*

EXSUFFLA'TION. *n. s.* [*ex* and *sufflo*, Latin.] A blast working underneath.

Of volatility the utmost degree is when it will fly away without returning: the next is when it will fly up, but with ease return: the next is when it will fly upwards over the helm, by a kind of *exsufflation*, without vapouring. *Bacon.*

To EXSU'SCITATE. *v. a.* [*exsuscito*, Latin.] To rouse up; to stir up. *Dict.*

E'XTANCY. *n. s.* [from *extant.*] Parts rising up above the rest; in opposition to those depressed.

The order of the little *extancies*, and consequently that of the little depressions in point of situation, will be altered likewise. *Boyle on Colours.*

E'XTANT. *adj.* [*extans*, Latin.]

1. Standing out to view; standing above the rest.

That part of the teeth which is *extant* above the gums is naked, and not invested with that sensible membrane called periosteum, wherewith the other bones are covered. *Ray.*

2. Publick; not suppressed.

The first of the continued weekly bills of mortality, *extant* at the parish clerks hall, begins the twenty-ninth of December 1603. *Graunt's Bills of Mortality.*

EXTA'TICAL. } *adj.* [ἐκςατικὸς. See ECSTACY.]
EXTA'TICK. }

1. Tending to something external.

I find in me a great deal of *extatical* love, which continually carries me to good without myself. *Boyle.*

2. Rapturous.

In trance *extatick* may thy pangs be drown'd;
Bright clouds descend, and angels watch thee round. *Pope.*

EXTE'MPORAL. *adj.* [*extemporalis*, Latin.]

1. Uttered without premeditation; quick; ready; sudden.

Alcidimus the sophister hath many arguments to prove, that voluntary and *extemporal* far excelleth premeditated speech. *Hooker, b* v. *s.* 22.

A man of pleasant and popular conversation, of good *extemporal* judgment and discourse, for the satisfying of publick ministers. *Wotton's Life of the Duke of Buckingham.*

2. Speaking without premeditation.

Many foolish things fall from wise men, if they speak in haste, or be *extemporal.* *Ben. Johnson's Discoveries.*

EXTE'MPORALLY. *adv.* [from *extemporal.*] Quickly; without premeditation.

The quick comedians
Extemporally will stage us, and present
Our Alexandrian revels. *Shakes. Anthony and Cleopatra.*

EXTEMPORA'NEOUS. *adj.* [*extemporaneus*, Latin.] Without premeditation; sudden.

EXTE'MPORARY. *adj.* [*extemporareus*, Latin.] Uttered or performed without premeditation; sudden; quick.

This custom was begun by our ancestors out of an ambition of shewing their *extemporary* ability of speaking upon any subject. *More's Divine Dialogues.*

That men should confer at very distant removes by an *extemporary* intercourse, is another reputed impossibility. *Glanv.*

They write in so diminutive a manner, with such frequent interlineations, that they are hardly able to go on without perpetual hesitations, or *extemporary* expletives. *Swift.*

EXTE'MPORE. *adv.* [*extempore*, Latin.]

1. Without premeditation; suddenly; readily; without any previous care or preparation.

You may do it *extempore*; for it is nothing but roaring. *Sh.*

Nothing great ought to be ventured upon without preparation; but, above all, how sottish is it to engage *extempore*, where the concern is eternity? *South's Sermons.*

Hast thou no mark at which to bend thy bow?
Or, like a boy, pursu'st the carrion-crow
With pellets and with stones from tree to tree,
A fruitless toil, and liv'st *extempore*? *Dryden's Pers. Sat.* 3.

2. It is sometimes used as an adjective, but very improperly.

I have known a woman branch out into a long *extempore* dissertation upon a petticoat. *Addison's Spectator*, No. 247.

Exte'mporiness. *n. s.* [from *extempore.*] The faculty of speaking or acting without premeditation.

To Exte'mporize. *v. n.* [from *extempore.*] To speak extempore, or without premeditation.

The *extemporizing* faculty is never more out of its element than in the pulpit; though, even here, it is much more excusable in a sermon than in a prayer. *South's Sermons.*

To EXTE'ND. *v. a.* [*extendo*, Latin.]

1. To stretch out towards any part.

See the figure of his lifeless friend,
And his old sire, his helpless hand *extend*. *Dryden's Virgil.*
Should'ring god's altar a vile image stands,
Belies his features, nay *extends* his hands. *Pope.*

2. To spread abroad; to diffuse; to expand.

He much magnifies the capacity of his understanding, who persuades himself that he can *extend* his thoughts farther than God exists, or imagine any expansion where he is not. *Locke.*

3. To widen to a large comprehension.

Few *extend* their thoughts towards universal knowledge *Locke.*

4. To stretch into assignable dimensions; to make local; to magnify so as to fill some assignable space.

The mind, say they, while you sustain
To hold her station in the brain;
You grant, at least she is *extended*,
Ergo, the whole dispute is ended. *Prior.*

5. To enlarge; to continue.

To Helen's bed the gods alone assign
Hermione, t' *extend* the regal line. *Pope's Odyssey, b.* iv.

6. To encrease in force or duration.

If much you note him,
You shall offend him, and *extend* his passion:
Feed and regard him not. *Shakespeare's Macbeth.*

7. To enlarge the comprehension of any position.

Seeing it is not set down how far the bounds of his speech concerning dissimilitude reach, who can assure us that it *extendeth* farther than to those things only wherein the nations were idolatrous. *Hooker, b.* iv. *s.* 6.

8. To impart; to communicate.

Let there be none to *extend* mercy unto him. *Ps.* civ. 12.

9. To seize by a course of law.

The law, that settles all you do,
And marries where you did but woo;
And if it judge upon your side,
Will soon *extend* her for your bride;
And put her person, goods or lands,
Or which you like best, int' your hands. *Hudibras, p.* iii.

Exte'nder. *n. s.* [from *extend.*] The person or instrument by which any thing is extended.

The extension made, the *extenders* are to be loosened gently. *Wiseman's Surgery.*

Exte'ndible. *adj.* [from *extend.*] Capable of extension; capable to be made wider or longer.

Tubes, recently made of fluids, are easily lengthened; such as have often suffered force, grow rigid, and hardly *extendible*. *Arbuthnot on Aliments.*

Exte'ndlessness. *n. s.* [from *extend.*] Unlimited extension. In this sense it is once found; but, I think, with little propriety.

Certain *moleculæ seminales* must keep the world from an infinitude, and *extendlessness* of excursions every moment into new figures and animals. *Hale's Origin of Mankind.*

Extensibili'ty. *n. s.* [from *extensible.*] The quality of being extensible.

In what manner they are mixed, so as to give a fibre *extensibility*, who can say? *Grew's Cosmol. Sac. b.* ii. *c.* 5.

Exte'nsible. *adj.* [*extensio*, Latin.]

1. Capable of being stretched into length or breadth.

The malleus being fixed to an *extensible* membrane, follows the traction of the muscle, and is drawn inward. *Holder.*

2. Capable of being extended to a larger comprehension.

That love is blind, is *extensible* beyond the object of poetry. *Glanv. Sceps. c.* 15.

Exte'nsibleness. *n. s.* [from *extensible.*] Capacity of being extended.

Exte'nsion. *n. s.* [from *extensio*, Latin.]

1. The act of extending.

2. The state of being extended.

The hiccough cometh of fulness of meat, especially in children, which causeth an *extension* of the stomach. *Bacon.*

All rest satisfied at the postures of moderation, and none endure the extremity of flexure or *extension*. *Brown's Vul. Err.*

This foundation of the earth upon the waters, or *extension* of it above the waters, doth agree to the antediluvian earth. *Burnet's Theory of the Earth.*

By this idea of solidity is the *extension* of body distinguished from the *extension* of space: the *extension* of body being nothing but the cohesion or continuity of solid, separable, moveable parts; and the *extension* of space, the continuity of unsolid, inseparable, and immoveable parts. *Locke.*

Exte'nsive. *adj.* [*extensivus*, Latin.] Wide; large.

I would not be understood to recommend to all a pursuit of those sciences, to those *extensive* lengths to which the moderns have advanced them. *Watts's Improvement of the Mind.*

Exte'nsively. *adv.* [from *extensive.*] Widely; largely.

'Tis impossible for any to pass a right judgment concerning them, without entering into most of these circumstances, and surveying them *extensively*, and comparing and balancing them all aright. *Watts's Improvement of the Mind.*

Exte'nsiveness. *n. s.* [from *extensive.*]

1. Largeness; diffusiveness; wideness.

As we have reason to admire the excellency of this contrivance, so have we to applaud the *extensiveness* of the benefit. *Government of the Tongue, s.* 1.

An *extensiveness* of understanding and a large memory are of service. *Watts's Logick.*

2. Possibility to be extended.

We take notice of the wonderful dilatability or *extensiveness* of the throats and gullets of serpents: I myself have taken two entire adult mice out of the stomach of an adder, whose neck was not bigger than my little finger. *Ray on the Creation.*

Exte'nsor. *n. s.* [Latin.] The muscle by which any limb is extended.

Extensors are muscles so called, which serve to extend any part. *Quincy.*

Complaisant and civil people had the flexors of the head very strong; but in the proud and insolent there was a great overbalance of strength in the *extensors* of the neck and the muscles of the back. *Arbuthnot and Pope's Mart. Scriblerus.*

Exte'nt. *participle.* from *extend.* Extended.

Both his hands most filthy feculent,
Above the water were on high *extent*,
And fain'd to wash themselves incessantly. *Spens. Fai. Queen.*

Exte'nt. *n. s.* [*extentus*, Latin.]

1. Space or degree to which any thing is extended.

If I mean to reign
David's true heir, and his full sceptre sway
To just *extent* over all Israel's sons. *Milton's Paradise Lost.*

2. Communication; distribution.

An emperour of Rome
Troubled, confronted thus, and for th' *extent*
Of equal justice us'd with such contempt. *Shak. Tit. Andron.*

3. Execution; seizure.

Let my officers
Make an *extent* upon his house and land,
And turn him going. *Shakespeare's As you like it.*

To EXTE'NUATE. *v. a.* [*extenuo*, Latin.]

1. To lessen; to make small or slender in bulk.

His body behind his head becomes broad, from whence it is again *extenuated* all the way to the tail. *Grew's Musæum.*

2. To lessen; to diminish in any quality.

To persist
In doing wrong, *extenuates* not wrong,
But makes it much more heavy. *Shak. Troilus and Cressida.*
But fortune there *extenuates* the crime;
What's vice in me, is only mirth in him. *Dryden's Juvenal.*

3. To lessen; to degrade; to diminish in honour.

Righteous are thy decrees on all thy works;
Who can *extenuate* thee? *Milton's Paradise Lost, b.* x.

4. To lessen in representation; to palliate. Opposite to *aggravate*.

When you shall these unlucky deeds relate,
Speak of me, as I am: nothing *extenuate*,
Nor set down aught in malice. *Shakes. Othello.*

Upon his examination he denied little of that wherewith he was charged, nor endeavoured much to excuse or *extenuate* his fault; so that, not very wisely thinking to make his offence less by confession, he made it enough for condemnation. *Bac.*

Yet hear me, Sampson, not that I endeavour
To lessen or *extenuate* my offence. *Milton's Agonistes.*

5. To make lean.

Extenua'tion. *n. s.* [from *extenuate.*]

1. The act of representing things less ill than they are; contrary to aggravation; palliation.

2. Mitigation; alleviation of punishment.

When sin is to be judged, the kindest enquiry is what deeds of charity we can allege in *extenuation* of our punishment. *Att.*

3. A loss of plumpness, or a general decay in the muscular flesh of the whole body. *Quincy.*

EXTE'RIOR. *adj.* [*exterior*, Latin.] Outward; external; not intrinsick.

And what is faith, love, virtue unessay'd
Alone, without *exterior* help sustain'd? *Milton's Par. Lost.*

Seraphick and common lovers behold *exterior* beauties as children and astronomers consider Galileo's optick glasses. *Boyle.*

Father, blacker, and merrier, are words which, together with the thing they denominate, imply also something else separate and *exterior* to the existence of that thing. *Locke.*

Exte'riorly. *adv.* [from *exterior.*] Outwardly; externally; not intrinsically.

You have slander'd nature in my form;
Which, howsoever rude *exteriorly*,

Is yet the cover of a fairer mind,
Than to be butcher of an innocent child. *Shakes. K. John.*

To EXTE'RMINATE. *v. a.* [*extermino*, Latin.] To root out; to tear up; to drive away; to abolish; to destroy.

Unlucky vices, on which the *exterminating* lot happened to fall. *Decay of Piety.*

Alexander left Grecian colonies in the Indies; but they were *exterminated* by Sandrocothus. *Arbuthnot on Coins.*

This discovery alone is sufficient, if the vices of men did not captivate their reason, to explode and *exterminate* rank atheism out of the world. *Bentley's Sermons.*

EXTERMINA'TION. *n. s.* [from *exterminate.*] Destruction; excision.

The question is, how far an holy war is to be pursued, whether to displanting and *extermination* of people. *Bacon.*

EXTERMINA'TOR. *n. s.* [*exterminator*, Latin.] The person or instrument by which any thing is destroyed.

To EXTE'RMINE. *v. a.* [*extermino*, Latin.] To exterminate; to destroy.

If you do sorrow at my grief in love,
By giving love, your sorrow and my grief
Were both *extermin'd*. *Shakes. As you like it.*

EXTE'RN. *adj.* [*externus*, Latin.]

1. External; outward; visible.

When my outward action doth demonstrate
The native act and figure of my heart
In compliment *extern*, 'tis not long after
But I will wear my heart upon my sleeve,
For daws to peck at. *Shakespeare's Othello.*

2. Without itself; not inherent; not intrinsick; not depending on itself.

When two bodies are pressed one against another, the rare body not being so able to resist division as the dense, and being not permitted to retire back, by reason of the *extern* violence impelling it, the parts of the rare body must be severed. *Digby.*

EXTE'RNAL. *adj.* [*externus*, Latin.]

1. Outward; not proceeding from itself; operating or acting from without; opposite to internal.

We come to be assured that there is such a being, either by an internal impression of the notion of a God upon our minds, or else by such *external* and visible effects as our reason tells us must be attributed to some cause, and which we cannot attribute to any other but such as we conceive God to be. *Tillotson.*

These shells being thus exposed loose upon the surface of the earth to the injuries of weather, to be trod upon by horses and other cattle, and to many other *external* accidents, are, in tract of time, worn, fretted, and broken to pieces. *Woodward's Natural History.*

2. Having the outward appearance; having to the view or outward perception any particular nature.

Adam was then no less glorious in his *externals*: he had a beautiful body as well as an immortal soul. *South's Sermons.*

He that commits only the *external* act of idolatry is as guilty as he that commits the *external* act of theft. *Stillingfleet.*

EXTE'RNALLY. *adv.* [from *external.*] Outwardly.

The exterior ministry, *externally* and alone, hath in it nothing excellent, as being destitute of the sanctity that God requires, and it is common to wicked men and good. *Taylor.*

To EXTI'L. *v. n.* [*ex* and *stillo*, Lat.] To drop or distil from.

EXTILLA'TION. *n. s.* [from *ex* and *stillo*, Latin.] The act of falling in drops.

They seemed made by an exsudation or *extillation* of putrifying juices out of the rocky earth. *Derham's Phys. Theology.*

To EXTI'MULATE. *v. a.* [*extimulo*, Latin.] To prick; to incite by stimulation.

Choler is one excretion whereby nature excludeth another, which, descending unto the bowels, *extimulates* and excites them unto expulsion. *Brown's Vulgar Errours, b.* iii. *c.* 2.

EXTIMULA'TION. *n. s.* [from *extimulatio*, Latin.] Pungency; power of exciting motion or sensation.

The native spirits admit great diversity; as hot, cold, active, dull, *&c.* whence proceed most of the virtues of bodies; but the air intermixed is without virtues, and maketh things insipid, and without any *extimulation*. *Bacon's Natural History.*

EXTI'NCT. *adj.* [*extinctus*, Latin.]

1. Extinguished; quenched; put out.

Their purple vengeance bath'd in gore retires,
Her weapons blunted, and *extinct* her fires. *Pope.*

2. At a stop; without progressive succession.

The royal family is all *extinct*,
And she who reigns bestows her crown on me. *Dryden.*

The nobility are never likely to be *extinct*, because the greatest part of their titles descend to heirs general. *Swift.*

3. Abolished; out of force.

A censure inflicted *a jure* continues, though such law be *extinct*, or the lawgiver removed from his office. *Ayliffe.*

EXTI'NCTION. *n. s.* [*extinctio*, Latin.]

1. The act of quenching or extinguishing.

Red-hot needles or wires, extinguished in quicksilver, do yet acquire a verticity according to the laws of position and *extinction*. *Brown's Vulgar Errours, b.* ii. *c.* 2.

2. The state of being quenched.

The parts are consumed through *extinction* of their native heat, and dissipation of their radical moisture. *Harvey.*

3. Destruction; excision.

The *extinction* of nations, and the desolation of kingdoms, were but the effects of this destructive evil. *Rogers's Sermons.*

4. Suppression.

They lie in dead oblivion, losing half
The fleeting moments of too short a life,
Total *extinction* of th' enlighten'd soul. *Thomson's Summer.*

To EXTI'NGUISH. *v. a.* [*extinguo*, Latin.]

1. To put out; to quench.

The soft god of pleasure that warm'd our desires,
Has broken his bow, and *extinguish'd* his fires. *Dryden.*
Then rose the seed of chaos and of night,
To blot out order, and *extinguish* light. *Dunciad, b.* iv.

2. To suppress; to destroy.

They *extinguish* the love of the people to the young king, by remembring some imperfections of his father. *Hayward.*

My fame of chastity, by which the skies
I reacht before, by thee *extinguish'd* dies. *Denham.*

3. To cloud; to obscure.

Bethink thee on her virtues that surmount,
Her nat'ral graces that *extinguish* art. *Shakesp. Henry* VI.

EXTI'NGUISHABLE. *adj.* [from *extinguish.*] That may be quenched, suppressed, or destroyed.

EXTI'NGUISHER. *n. s.* [from *extinguish.*] A hollow cone put upon a candle to quench it.

If it should ever offer to flame out again, I would use the conicum as an *extinguisher* to smother it. *More's Div. Dialog.*

Of it a broad *extinguisher* he makes,
And hoods the flames that to their quarry strove. *Dryden.*

'Tis better to cover the vital flame with an *extinguisher* of honour, than let it consume 'till it burns blue, and lies agonizing within the socket. *Collier on the Value of Life.*

EXTI'NGUISHMENT. *n. s.* [from *extinguish.*]

1. Extinction; suppression; act of quenching; destruction.

When death's form appears, she feareth not
An utter quenching, or *extinguishment*;
She would be glad to meet with such a lot,
That so she might all future ill prevent. *Davies.*

He moved him to a war upon Flanders, for the better *extinguishment* of the civil wars of France. *Bacon.*

The immediate cause of death is the resolution or *extinguishment* of the spirits. *Bacon's Natural History,* N°. 400.

2. Abolition; nullification.

Divine laws of Christian church polity may not be altered by *extinguishment*. *Hooker, b.* iii.

3. Termination of a family or succession.

His heart easily conceived treason against the crown, wherein he perished himself, and made a final *extinguishment* of his house and honour. *Davies on Ireland.*

To EXTI'RP. *v. a.* [*extirpo*, Latin.] To eradicate; to root out.

Which to *extirp* he laid him privily
Down in a darksome lowly place far in. *Fairy Queen, b.* i.
Nor shall that nation boast it so with us,
But be *extirped* from our provinces. *Shakespeare's Henry* VI.

To EXTI'RPATE. *v. a.* [*extirpo*, Latin.] To root out; to eradicate; to exscind; to destroy.

The rebels were grown so strong, that they made account speedily to *extirpate* the British nation in that kingdom. *Dryd.*

We in vain endeavour with noise, and weapons of law, to drive the wolf from our own to another's door: the breed ought to be *extirpated* out of the island. *Locke.*

It is not the business of virtue to *extirpate* the affections, but to regulate them. *Addison's Spectator,* N°. 494.

EXTIRPA'TION. *n. s.* [from *extirpate.*] The act of rooting out; eradication; excision; destruction.

It is said that popery, for want of utter *extirpation*, hath in some places taken root and flourished again. *Hooker, b.* iv.

Religion requires the *extirpation* of all those passions and vices which render men unsociable and troublesome to one another. *Tillotson, Sermon* 3.

EXTIRPA'TOR. *n. s.* [from *extirpate.*] One who roots out; a destroyer.

EXTISPI'CIOUS. *adj.* [*extispicium*, Latin.] Augurial; relating to the inspection of entrails in order to prognostication.

Thus hath he deluded many nations unto his augurial and *extispicious* inventions, from casual and uncontrived contingences, divining events succeeding. *Brown's Vulgar Errours.*

To EXTO'L. *v. a.* [*extollo*, Latin.] To praise; to magnify; to laud; to celebrate.

When a rich man speaketh, every man holdeth his tongue; and look, what he saith they *extol* it to the clouds. *Ecclus.* xiii.

For which both heav'n and earth shall high *extol*
Thy praises, with th' innumerable sound
Of hymns, and sacred songs, wherewith thy throne
Encompass'd shall resound thee ever bless'd. *Milt. Par. Lost.*
Let Araby *extol* her happy coast,
Her cinnamon and sweet amomum boast. *Dryden's Ovid.*

EXTO'LLER. *n. s.* [from *extol.*] A praiser; a magnifier; one that praises to the skies.

EXTO'RSIVE. *adj.* [from *extort.*] Having the quality of drawing by violent means.

EXTO'RSIVELY.

EXTO'RSIVELY. *adv.* [from *extorsive.*] In an extorsive manner; by violence.

To EXTO'RT. *v. a.* [*extorqueo, extortus*, Latin.]

1. To draw by force; to force away; to wrest; to wring from one.

'Till the injurious Roman did *extort*
This tribute from us, we were free. *Shakesf. Cymbeline.*
Newness
Of Cloten's death may drive us to a render,
Where we have liv'd; and so *extort* from us
That which we've done. *Shakesf. Cymbeline.*
That glory never shall his wrath or might
Extort from me, to bow and sue for grace
With suppliant knee, and deify his pow'r. *Milt. Par. Lost.*
I remember well the impious oath,
Hardly *extorted* from my trembling youth. *Rowe.*

My earnest desires, not any doubts of your goodness, but my real concern for your welfare, *extort* this from me. *Wake.*

2. To gain by violence or oppression.

His tail was stretch'd out in wond'rous length,
That to the house of heav'nly gods it raught,
And with *extorted* power and borrow'd strength,
The ever-burning lamps from thence it brought. *Spenser.*
Are my chests fill'd up with *extorted* gold? *Shakesf. H.* VI.

To EXTO'RT. *v. n.* To practise oppression and violence. Now disused.

To whom they never gave any penny of entertainment, but let them feed upon the countries, and *extort* upon all men where they come. *Spenser on Ireland.*

Before they did *extort* and oppress the people only by colour of a lewd custom, they did afterwards use the same extortions by warrant. *Davies on Ireland.*

EXTO'RTER. *n. s.* [from *extort.*] One who practises oppression or extortion.

Edric the *extorter* was deprived by king Cnute of the government of Mercia. *Camden's Remains.*

EXTO'RTION. *n. s.* [from *extort.*]

1. The act or practice of gaining by violence and rapacity.

That goodness
Of gleaning all the land's wealth into one,
Into your own hands, cardinal, by *extortion*. *Shak. H.* VIII.

Oppression and *extortion* did maintain the greatness, and oppression and *extortion* did extinguish the greatness of that house. *Davies on Ireland.*

2. Force by which any thing is unjustly taken away.

Because the lords had power to impose this charge, the freeholders were glad to give a great part of their lands to hold the rest free from that *extortion*. *Davies on Ireland.*

A succeeding king's just recovery of rights from unjust usurpations and *extortions*, shall never be prejudiced by any act of mine. *King Charles.*

EXTO'RTIONER. *n. s.* [from *extortion.*] One who practises extortion; one who grows rich by violence and rapacity.

There will be always tyrants, murderers, thieves, adulterers, *extortioners*, church-robbers, traitors, and other of the same rabblement. *Camden's Remains.*

The covetous *extortioner* is involved in the same sentence. *Decay of Piety.*

To EXTRA'CT. *v. a.* [*extraho, extractum*, Latin.]

1. To draw out of something.

The drawing one metal or mineral out of another, we call *extracting*. *Bacon's Physical Remarks.*

Out of the ashes of all plants they *extract* a salt which they use in medicines. *Bacon's Natural History*, N°. 645.

If the metallick or mineral matter is discoverable, it is so diffused and scattered amongst the crasser and more unprofitable matter, that it would never be possible to separate and *extract* it. *Woodward's Natural History.*

2. To draw by chemical operation.

They
Whom sunny Borney bears, are stor'd with streams
Egregious, rum and rice's spirit *extract*. *Phillips.*

3. To take from something of which the thing taken was a part.

I now see
Bone of my bone, flesh of my flesh, myself
Before me: woman is her name, of man
Extracted. *Milton's Paradise Lost, b.* viii. *l.* 497.

4. To draw out of any containing body or cavity.

These waters were *extracted*, and laid upon the surface of the ground. *Burnet's Theory of the Earth.*

5. To select and abstract from a larger treatise.

To see how this case is represented, I have *extracted* out of that pamphlet a few notorious falshoods. *Swift.*

E'XTRACT. *n. s.* [from the verb.]

1. The substance extracted; the chief parts drawn from any thing.

In tinctures, if the superfluous spirit of wine be distilled off, it leaves at the bottom that thicker substance, which chymists call the *extract* of the vegetables. *Boyle's Scept. Chym.*

To dip our tongues in gall, to have nothing in our mouth but the *extract* and exhalation of our inward bitterness, is no great sensuality. *Government of the Tongue, s.* 10.

2. The chief heads drawn from a book; an abstract; an epitome.

I will present a few *extracts* out of authors. *Camden's Rem.*

Some books may be read by *extracts* made of them by others, but only in the less important arguments, and the meaner books; else distilled books are like common distilled waters, flashy things. *Bacon's Essays, Civil and Moral.*

Spend some hours every day in reading, and making *extracts*, if your memory be weak. *Swift.*

EXTRA'CT. *partic. adj.* See the verb.

EXTRA'CTION. *n. s.* [*extractio*, Latin.]

1. The act of drawing one part out of a compound; the act of drawing out the principal substance by chemical operation.

Although the charge of *extraction* should exceed the worth, at least it will discover nature and possibility. *Bacon.*

They have fallen upon the distillations of waters, *extractions* of oils, and such like experiments unknown to the ancients. *Hakewill on Providence.*

It would not defray the charge and labour of the *extraction*, and must needs be all irretrievably lost. *Woodward's Nat. Hist.*

2. Derivation from an original; lineage; descent.

One whose *extraction*'s from an ancient line,
Gives hope again that well-born men may shine;
The meanest in your nature mild and good,
The noble rest secured in your blood. *Waller.*

A family of an ancient *extraction*, transported with the conqueror out of Normandy. *Clarendon.*

EXTRA'CTOR. *n. s.* [Latin.] The person or instrument by which any thing is extracted.

EXTRADI'CTIONARY. *adj.* [*extra* and *dictio*, Latin.] Not consisting in words but realities.

Of these *extradictionary* and real fallacies, Aristotle and logicians make six; but we observe men are commonly deceived by four thereof. *Brown's Vulgar Errours, b.* i. *c.* 4.

EXTRAJUDI'CIAL. *adj.* [*extra* and *judicium*, Latin.] Out of the regular course of legal procedure.

A declaratory or *extrajudicial* absolution is conferred in *foro pœnitentiali.* *Ayliffe's Parergon.*

EXTRAJUDI'CIALLY. *adv.* [from *extrajudicial.*] In a manner different from the ordinary course of legal procedure.

The confirmation of an election, though done by a previous citation of all persons concerned, may be said to be done *extrajudicially*, when opposition ensues thereupon. *Ayliffe.*

EXTRAMI'SSION. *n. s.* [*extra* and *mitto*, Latin.] The act of emitting outwards; opposite to intromission.

Aristotle, Alhazen, and others, hold that sight is by reception, and not by *extramission*; by receiving the rays of the object unto the eye, and not by sending any out. *Brown.*

EXTRAMUNDA'NE. *adj.* [*extra* and *mundus*, Latin.] Beyond the verge of the material world.

'Tis a philosophy that gives the exactest topography of the *extramundane* spaces. *Glanv. Sceps. c.* 18.

EXTRA'NEOUS. *adj.* [*extraneus*, Latin.] Not belonging to any thing; foreign; of different substance; not intrinsick.

Relation is not contained in the real existence of things, but something *extraneous* and superinduced. *Locke.*

When the mind refers any of its ideas to any thing *extraneous* to them, they are then called true or false. *Locke.*

Gold, when equally pure, and freed from *extraneous* matter, is absolutely alike in colour, consistence, specifick gravity, and all other respects. *Woodward on Fossils.*

EXTRAO'RDINARILY. *adv.* [from *extraordinary.*]

1. In a manner out of the common method and order.

In the affairs which were not determinable one way or other by the Scripture, himself gave an *extraordinarily* direction and counsel, as oft as they sought it at his hands. *Hooker.*

In government it is good to use men of one rank equally; for to countenance some *extraordinarily*, is to make them insolent, and the rest discontent. *Bacon's Essays, Civ. and Moral.*

2. Uncommonly; particularly; eminently; remarkably.

He quotes me right; and I hope all his quotations, wherein he is so *extraordinarily* copious and elaborate, are so. *Howel.*

The temple of Solomon was a type, and therefore was so *extraordinarily* magnificent; otherwise perhaps a cheaper structure might have been as serviceable. *Wilkins's Math. Magick.*

EXTRAO'RDINARINESS. *n. s.* [from *extraordinary.*] Uncommonness; eminence; remarkableness.

I chuse some few, which either for the *extraordinariness* of their guilt, or the frequency of their practice, are the most eminent. *Government of the Tongue, s.* 4.

EXTRAO'RDINARY. *adj.* [*extraordinarius*, Lat. This word and its derivatives are generally pronounced *extrordinary*, whereby the *a* is liquified into the *o.*]

1. Different from common order and method; not ordinary.

Evils must be judged inevitable, if there be no apparent ordinary way to avoid them; because where council and advice bear rule of God's *extraordinary* power, without *extraordinary* warrant, we cannot presume. *Hooker, b.* v. *s.* 9.

At that time Spain had no other wars, save those which were grown into an ordinary: now they have coupled therewith the *extraordinary* of the Voltaline and the Palatinate. *Bacon's War with Spain.*

Let us see what *extraordinary* armies have been transmitted thither, and what ordinary forces have been maintained there. *Davies's State of Ireland.*

2. Different from the common course of law.

If they proceeded in a martial or any other *extraordinary* way,

way, without any form of law, his majesty should declare his justice and affection to an old faithful servant. *Clarendon.*

3. Eminent; remarkable; more than common.

The house was built of fair and strong stone, not affecting so much any *extraordinary* kind of fineness, as an honourable representing of a firm stateliness. *Sidney.*

The Indians worshipped rivers, fountains, rocks, or great stones, &c. and all things which seemed to have something *extraordinary* in them. *Stillingfleet's Def. of Disc. on Rom. Idol.*

EXTRAO'RDINARY. *adv.* [This word seems only a colloquial barbarism, used for the ease of pronunciation.] Extraordinarily.

I ran over their cabinet of medals, but don't remember to have met with any things in it that are *extraordinary* rare. *Add.*

EXTRAPARO'CHIAL. *adj.* [*extra* and *parochia*, Latin.] Not comprehended within any parish.

EXTRAPROVI'NCIAL. *adj.* [*extra* and *provincia*, Latin.] Not within the same province; not within the jurisdiction of the same archbishop.

An *extraprovincial* citation is not valid, *ultra duas diætas*, above two day's journey; nor is a citation valid that contains many conditions manifestly inconvenient. *Ayliffe's Parergon.*

EXTRARE'GULAR. *adj.* [*extra* and *regula*, Latin.] Not comprehended within a rule.

His providence is *extraregular*, and produces strange things beyond common rules; and he led Israel through a sea, and made a rock pour forth water. *Taylor's Rule of living holy.*

EXTRA'VAGANCE. }
EXTRA'VAGANCY. } *n. s.* [*extravagans*, Latin.]

1. Excursion or sally beyond prescribed limits.

I have troubled you too far with this *extravagance*: I shall make no delay to recall myself into the road again, having been taught by you those several particulars. *Hammond.*

2. Irregularity; wildness.

3. Outrage; violence; outrageous vehemence.

How many, by the wild fury and *extravagancy* of their own passions, have put their bodies into a combustion, and by stirring up their rage against others, have armed that fierce humour against themselves. *Tillotson, Sermon 4.*

4. Unnatural tumour; bombast.

I remember some verses of my own, Maximin and Almanzor, which cry vengeance upon me for their *extravagance*. *Dryden's Spanish Fryar, Dedication.*

5. Waste; vain and superfluous expence.

She used to come home in her cups, and break the china and the looking-glasses; and was of such an irregular temper, and so entirely given up to her passion, that you might argue as well with the North-wind as with her ladyship; so expensive, that the income of three dukes was not enough to supply her *extravagance*. *Arbuthnot.*

EXTRA'VAGANT. *adj.* [*extravagans*, Latin.]

1. Wandering out of his bounds. This is the primogeneal sense, but not now in use.

At his warning
The *extravagant* and erring spirit hies
To his confine. *Shakespeare's Hamlet.*

2. Roving beyond just limits or prescribed methods.

I dare not ask for what you would not grant:
But wishes, madam, are *extravagant*;
They are not bounded with things possible;
I may wish more than I presume to tell. *Dryden's Aurengz.*

3. Not comprehended in any thing.

Twenty constitutions of pope John XXII. are called the *extravagants*; for that they being written in no order or method, *vagantu extra corpus collectionum canonum*. *Ayliffe's Parer.*

4. Irregular; wild.

For a dance they seem'd
Somewhat *extravagant*, and wild. *Milton's Paradise Lost.*

There appears something nobly wild and *extravagant* in great natural geniuses, infinitely more beautiful than turn and polishing. *Addison's Spectator, N°. 160.*

New ideas employed my fancy all night, and composed a wild *extravagant* dream. *Addison's Spectator.*

5. Wasteful; prodigal; vainly expensive.

An *extravagant* man, who has nothing else to recommend him but a false generosity, is often more beloved than a person of a much more finished character, who is defective in this particular. *Addison's Spectator, N°. 243.*

EXTRA'VAGANT. *n. s.* One who is confined in no general rule or definition.

We pity or laugh at those fatuous *extravagants*. *Glanville.*

There are certain *extravagants* among people of all sizes and professions; and there must be no drawing of general rules from particular exceptions. *L'Estrange.*

EXTRA'VAGANTLY. *adv.* [from *extravagant*.]

1. In an extravagant manner; wildly.

Her passion was *extravagantly* new;
But mine is much the madder of the two. *Dryden.*

2. In an unreasonable degree.

Some are found to praise our author, and others as rashly and *extravagantly* contradict his admirers. *Pope's Ess. on Homer.*

3. Expensively; luxuriously; wastefully.

EXTRAVAGA'NTNESS. *n. s.* [from *extravagant*.] Excess; excursion beyond limits.

To EXTRA'VAGATE. *v. n.* [*extra* and *vagor*, Latin.] To wander out of limits. *Dict.*

EXTRA'VASATED. *adj.* [*extra* and *vasa*, Latin.] Forced out of the properly containing vessels.

The viscous matter, which lies like leather upon the *extravasated* blood of pleuretick people, may be dissolved by a due degree of heat. *Arbuthnot on Aliments.*

EXTRAVASA'TION. *n. s.* [from *extravasated*.] The act of forcing, or state of being forced out of the proper containing vessels.

Aliment, too viscous, obstructing the glands, and by its acrimony corroding the small vessels of the lungs, after a rupture and *extravasation* of blood, easily produces an ulcer. *Arb.*

EXTRAVE'NATE. *adj.* [*extra* and *vena*, Latin.] Let out of the veins.

That there is a magnetick way of curing wounds, by anointing the weapon; and that the wound is affected in like manner as is the *extravenate* blood by the sympathetick medicine, as to matter of fact, is with circumstances of good evidence asserted. *Glanv. Sceps. c. 24.*

EXTRAVE'RSION. *n. s.* [*extra* and *versio*, Latin.] The act of throwing out; the state of being thrown out.

Nor does there intervene heat to afford them any colour to pretend that there is made an *extraversion* of the sulphur, or of any of the two other supposed principles. *Boyle.*

EXTRA'UGHT. *part.* [This is an obsolete participle from *extract*; as *distraught* from *distract*.] Extracted.

Sham'st thou not, knowing whence thou art *extraught*,
To let thy tongue detect thy baseborn heart? *Shak. H. VI.*

EXTRE'ME. *adj.* [*extremus*, Latin. This word is sometimes corrupted by the superlative termination, of which it is by no means capable, as it has in itself the superlative signification.]

1. Greatest; of the highest degree.

He that will take away *extreme* heat by setting the body in extremity of cold, shall undoubtedly remove the disease; but together with it the diseased too. *Hooker, b. iv. s. 8.*

The Lord shall smite thee with a fever, an inflammation, and an *extreme* burning. *Deutr. xxviii. 22.*

They thought it the *extremest* of evils to put themselves at the mercy of those hungry and disorderly people. *Bacon.*

2. Utmost.

The hairy fool
Stood on th' *extremest* verge of the swift brook,
Augmenting it with tears. *Shakes. As you like it.*
Miseno's cape and Bauli last he view'd,
That on the sea's *extremest* borders stood. *Addison on Italy.*

3. Last; that beyond which there is nothing.

Farewel, ungrateful and unkind! I go,
Condemn'd by thee, to those sad shades below:
I go th' *extremest* remedy to prove,
To drink oblivion, and to drench my love. *Dryden.*

4. Pressing in the utmost degree.

Cases of necessity being sometime but urgent, sometime *extreme*, the consideration of publick utility is urged equivalent to the easier kind of necessity. *Hooker, b. v. s. 9.*

EXTRE'ME. *n. s.* [from the adjective.]

1. Utmost point; highest degree of any thing.

Thither by harpy-footed furies hal'd,
At certain revolutions, all the damn'd
Are brought; and feel by turns the bitter change
Of fierce *extremes*, *extremes* by change more fierce;
From beds of raging fire to starve in ice
Their soft ethereal warmth, and there to pine
Immoveable, infix'd, and frozen round
Periods of time; thence hurried back to fire. *Milt. Pa. Lost.*
Avoid *extremes*, and shun the faults of such
Who still are pleas'd too little, or too much. *Pope.*

They cannot bear that human nature, which they know to be imperfect, should be praised in an *extreme*, without opposition. *Pope's Essay on Homer.*

2. Points at the greatest distance from each other; extremity.

The true Protestant religion is seated in the golden mean; the enemies unto her are the *extremes* on either hand. *Bacon.*

The syllogistical form only shews, that if the intermediate idea agrees with those it is on both sides immediately applied to, then those two remote ones, or, as they are called, *extremes*, do certainly agree. *Locke.*

EXTRE'MELY. *adv.* [from *extreme*.]

1. In the utmost degree.

She might hear, not far from her, an *extremely* doleful voice; but so suppressed with a kind of whispering note, that he could not conceive the words distinctly. *Sidney.*

2. Very much; greatly: in familiar language.

Whoever sees a scoundrel in a gown reeling home at midnight, is apt to be *extremely* comforted in his own vices. *Swift.*

EXTRE'MITY. *n. s.* [*extremitas*, Latin.]

1. The utmost point; the highest degree.

He that will take away extreme heat by setting the body in *extremity* of cold, shall undoubtedly remove the disease; but together with it the diseased too. *Hooker, b. iv. s. 8.*

Should

Should any one be cruel and uncharitable to that *extremity*, yet this would not prove that propriety gave any authority. *Locke.*

2. The utmost parts; the parts most remote from the middle.

It is commonly set forth green or yellow: in its proper colour it is inclining to white, excepting the *extremities* or tops of the wing-feathers, which are black. *Brown.*

The *extremities* of the joints must be seldom hidden, and the *extremities* or end of the feet never. *Dryden's Dufresnoy.*

The extremity of pain often creates a coldness in the *extremities*; but such a sensation is very consistent with an inflammatory distemper. *Arbuthnot on Diet.*

3. The points in the utmost degree of opposition, or at the utmost distance from each other.

He's a man of that strange composition,
Made up of all the worst *extremities*
Of youth and age. *Denham's Sophy.*

4. Remotest parts; parts at the greatest distance.

They sent fleets out of the Red Sea to the *extremities* of Æthiopia, and imported quantities of precious goods. *Arbuth.*

5. Violence of passion.

With equal measure she did moderate
The strong *extremities* of their outrage. *Spenser's Fa. Queen.*

If I shew no colour for my *extremity*, let me be your table-sport. *Shakespeare.*

6. The utmost violence, rigour, or distress.

Why should not the same laws take good effect on that people, being prepared by the sword, and brought under by *extremity*? *Spenser on Ireland.*

Their hearts she guesseth,
And yields her to *extremity* of time. *Fairy Queen, b.* i.

He promised, if they should be besieged, to do all he could to relieve them, before they should be reduced to *extremity*. *Clarendon, b.* viii.

It should be never so exposed to the *extremity* of war as to fall into those barbarous hands. *Clarendon.*

I wish peace, and any terms prefer
Before the last *extremities* of war. *Dryden's Ind. Emperor.*

To EXTRICATE. *v. a.* [*extrico*, Latin.] To disembarrass; to set free any one in a state of perplexity; to disentangle.

We run into great difficulties about free created agents, which reason cannot well *extricate* itself out of. *Locke.*

These are great reliefs to nature, as they give her an opportunity of *extricating* herself from her oppressions, and recovering the several tones and springs of her distended vessels. *Addison's Spectator*, Nº. 195.

EXTRICA'TION. *n. s.* [from *extricate.*] The act of disentangling; disentanglement.

Crude salt has a taste not properly acid, but such as predominates in brine; and it does not appear, that this acid spirit did as such pre-exist in the salt whence it was obtained, so that we may suppose it to have been made rather by transmutation than *extrication*. *Boyle.*

EXTRI'NSICAL. *adj.* [*extrinsecus*, Latin.] External; outward; not intimately belonging; not intrinsick. It is commonly written so, but analogy requires *extrinsecal*.

A body cannot move, unless it be moved by some *extrinsical* agent: we may easily frame a conceit, how absurd it is to think that a body, by a quality in it, can work upon itself. *Digby on Bodies.*

Neither is the atom by any *extrinsical* impulse diverted from its natural course. *Ray on the Creation.*

Outward objects, that are *extrinsical* to the mind; and its own operations, proceeding from powers intrinsical, and proper to itself, which, when reflected on by itself, become also objects of its contemplation, are the original of all knowledge. *Locke.*

EXTRI'NSICALLY. *adv.* [from *extrinsical.*] From without.

If to suppose the soul a distinct substance from the body, and *extrinsically* advenient, be an error, almost all the world hath been mistaken. *Glanville.*

EXTRI'NSICK. *adj.* [*extrinsecus*, Latin.] Outward; external.

When they cannot shake the main fort, they must try if they can possess themselves of the outworks, raise some prejudice against his carriage and his most *extrinsick* adherents. *Government of the Tongue, s.* 7.

Extrinsick modes are such as arise from something that is not in the subject or substance itself; but it is a manner of being which some substances attain, by reason of something that is external or foreign to the subject; as, this globe lies within two yards of the wall; this man is beloved or hated. *Watts's Logick.*

To EXTRU'CT. *v. a.* [*extruo*, *extructum*, Latin.] To build; to raise; to form into a structure.

EXTRU'CTOR. *n. s.* [from *extruct.*] A builder; a fabricator; a contriver.

To EXTRU'DE. *v. a.* [*extrudo*, Latin.] To thrust off; to drive off; to push out with violence.

If in any part of the continent they found the shells, they concluded that the sea had been *extruded* and driven off by the mud. *Woodward's Natural History.*

EXTRU'SION. *n. s.* [*extrusus*, Latin.] The act of thrusting or driving out.

They suppose the channel of the sea to have been formed, and mountains and caverns, by a violent depression of some parts of the earth, and an *extrusion* and elevation of others. *Burnet's Theory of the Earth.*

EXTU'BERANCE. *n. s.* [*ex* and *tuber*, Latin.] Knobs, or parts protuberant; parts that rise from the rest of the body.

The gouge takes off the irregularities or *extuberances* that lie farthest from the axis of the work. *Moxon's Mech. Exer.*

EXU'BERANCE. *n. s.* [*exuberatio*, Latin.] Overgrowth; superfluous shoots; useless abundance; luxuriance.

Men esteem the overflowing of gall the *exuberance* of zeal, and all the promises of the faithful combatant they confidently appropriate. *Decay of Piety.*

Though he expatiates on the same thoughts in different words, yet in his similes that *exuberance* is avoided. *Garth.*

EXU'BERANT. *adj.* [*exuberans*, Latin.]

1. Growing with superfluous shoots; overabundant; superfluously plenteous; luxuriant.

Another Flora there of bolder hues,
And richer sweets, beyond our gardens pride,
Plays o'er the fields, and showers with sudden hand
Exuberant spring. *Thomson's Spring, l.* 685.

His similes have been thought too *exuberant*, and full of circumstances. *Pope's Preface to the Iliad.*

2. Abounding in the utmost degree.

We might there discern such immense power, such unsearchable wisdom, and such *exuberant* goodness, as may justly ravish us to an amazement, rather than a bare admiration. *Boyle's Seraphick Love.*

A part of that *exuberant* devotion, with which the whole assembly raised and animated one another, catches a reader at the greatest distance of time. *Addison's Freeholder*, Nº. 49.

EXU'BERANTLY. *adv.* [from *exuberant.*] Abundantly; to a superfluous degree.

A considerable quantity of the vegetable matter lay at the surface of the antediluvian earth, and rendered it *exuberantly* fruitful. *Woodward's Natural History.*

To EXU'BERATE. *v. n.* [*exubero*, Latin.] To abound in the highest degree.

All the loveliness imparted to the creature is lent it, to give us enlarged conceptions of that vast confluence and immensity that *exuberates* in God. *Boyle's Seraph. Love.*

EXU'CCOUS. *adj.* [*exsuccus*, Latin.] Without juice; dry.

This is to be effected not only in the plant yet growing, but in that which is brought *exuccous* and dry unto us. *Brown.*

EXU'DATION. *n. s.* [from *exudo*, Latin.]

1. The act of emitting in sweat; the act of emitting moisture through the pores.

The tumour sometimes arises by a general *exudation* out of the cutis. *Wiseman's Surgery.*

2. The matter issuing out by sweat from any body.

The gum of trees, which we see shining and clear, is but a fine passage or straining of the juice of the tree through the wood and bark; and in like manner Cornish diamonds, and rock rubies, which are yet more resplendent than gums, are the fine *exudations* of stone. *Bacon's Natural History.*

If it hath more dew at noon than in the morning, then it seemeth to be an *exudation* of the herb itself. *Bacon.*

Cuckowspittle, or woodsere, that spumous frothy dew, or *exudation*, or both, is found especially about the joints of lavender and rosemary. *Brown's Vulgar Errours, b.* v. *c.* 3.

To EXU'DATE. } *v. n.* [*exudo*, Latin.] To sweat out; to issue
To EXU'DE. } out by sweat.

Some perforations in the part itself, through which the humour included doth *exudate*, may be observed in such as are fresh. *Brown's Vulg. Err.*

The juices of the flowers are, first, the expressed juice; secondly, a volatile oil, wherein the smell of the plant presides; thirdly, honey, *exuding* from all flowers, the bitter not excepted. *Arbuthnot on Aliments.*

To EXU'LCERATE. *v. a.* [*exulcero*, Latin.]

1. To make sore with an ulcer; to affect with a running or eating sore.

Cantharides, applied to any part of the body, touch the bladder and *exulcerate* it, if they stay on long. *Bac. Nat. Hist.*

That the saliva hath a virtue of macerating bodies, appears by the effects in taking away warts, sometimes *exulcerating* the jaws, and rotting the teeth. *Ray on the Creation.*

The stagnating serum turning acrimonious, *exulcerates* and putrifies the bowels, producing most dismal symptoms. *Arbuthnot on Diet.*

2. To afflict; to corrode; to enrage.

Thoughts, my tormentors, arm'd with deadly stings,
Mangle my apprehensive tenderest parts,
Exasperate, *exulcerate*, and raise
Dire inflammation, which no cooling herb
Or medicinal liquor can asswage. *Milton's Agonistes, l.* 623.

EXULCERA'TION. *n. s.* [from *exulcerate.*]

1. The beginning erosion, which wears away the substance and forms an ulcer. *Quincy.*

2. Exacerbation;

2. Exacerbation; corroſion.

This *exulceration* of mind made him apt to take all occaſions of contradiction. *Hooker, b.* ii. *ſ.* 5.

Exu'lceratory. *adj.* [from *exulcerate*] Having a tendency to cauſe ulcers.

To EXU'LT. *v. n.* [*exulto*, Latin] To rejoice above meaſure; to triumph; to be in high exaltation of gladneſs.

The whole world did ſeem to *exult* that it had occaſion of pouring out gifts to ſo bleſſed a purpoſe. *Hooker, b.* v. *ſ.* 13.

Who might be your mother,
That you inſult, *exult*, and rail, at once
Over the wretched. *Shakeſpeare's As you like it.*

Exu'ltance. *n. ſ.* [from *exult.*] Tranſport; joy; triumph; gladneſs; exultation.

We have great cauſe of *exultance* and joy, God's ſervice being the moſt perfect freedom. *Government of the Tongue.*

Exulta'tion. *n. ſ.* [*exultatio*, Latin.] Joy; triumph; rapturous delight.

Good effects may grow in each of the people towards other, in them all towards their paſtor, and in their paſtor towards every of them; between whom there daily and interchangeably paſs, in the hearing of God himſelf, and in the preſence of his holy angels, ſo many heavenly acclamations, *exultations*, provocations, petitions. *Hooker, b.* v. *ſ.* 39.

Devotion inſpires men with ſentiments of religious gratitude, and ſwells their hearts with inward tranſports of joy and *exultation*. *Addiſon's Freeholder*, N°. 49.

To EXU'NDATE. *v. n.* [*exundo*, Lat.] To overflow. *Dict.*

Exunda'tion. *n. ſ.* [from *exundate.*] Overflow; abundance.

It is more worthy the Deity to attribute the creation of the world to the *exundation* and overflowing of his tranſcendent and infinite goodneſs. *Ray on the Creation.*

Exu'perable. *adv.* [*exuperabilis*, Latin.] Conquerable; ſuperable; vincible.

Exu'perance. *n. ſ.* [*exuperantia*, Lat.] Overbalance; greater proportion.

Rome hath leſs variation than London; for on the Weſt ſide of Rome are ſeated France, Spain and Germany, which take off the *exuperance*, and balance the vigour of the Eaſtern parts. *Brown's Vulgar Errours, b.* ii. *c.* 2.

To Exu'scitate. *v. a.* [*exſuſcito*, Latin.] To ſtir up; to rouſe.

Exu'stion. *n. ſ.* [*exuſtio*, Latin.] The act of burning up; conſumption by fire.

EXU'VIÆ. n. ſ. [Latin.] Caſt ſkins; caſt ſhells; whatever is thrown off, or ſhed by animals.

The fiſhes upon this ſtone have taken up ſo little room in the ſtone, that they appear to be only the ſkins or *exuviæ*, rather than entire bodies of fiſhes. *Woodward on Fiſhes.*

Ey. Ea. Ee. } May either come from ıᵹ, an iſland, by melting the Saxon ᵹ into ẏ, which is uſually done; or from the Saxon ea, which ſignifies a water, river, &c. or, laſtly, from ıeaᵹ, a field, by the ſame kind of melting. *Gibſon.*

Ey'as. *n. ſ.* [*niais*, French.] A young hawk juſt taken from the neſt, not able to prey for itſelf. *Hanmer.*

There is, ſir, an aiery of children, little *eyaſes*, that cry out. *Shakeſpeare's Hamlet.*

Ey'asmusket. *n. ſ.* A young unfledged male hawk of the muſket kind. *Hanmer.*

Here comes little Robin.—How now, my *eyaſmuſket*; what news with you? *Shakeſp. Merry Wives of Windſor.*

EYE. *n. ſ.* obſolete plural *eyne*, now *eyes.* [*auga*, Gothick; eaᵹ, Saxon; *oog*, Dutch; *ee*, Scottiſh, plur. *eene.*]

1. The organ of viſion; the medium of the ſenſe of ſight.

Good ſir John, as you have one *eye* upon my follies, turn another into the regiſter of your own, that I may paſs with a reproof off the eaſier. *Shakeſ. Merry Wives of Windſor.*

My face is but a moon, and clouded too.
—Bleſſed are clouds to do as ſuch clouds do:
Vouchſafe, bright moon, and theſe thy ſtars to ſhine,
Thoſe clouds remov'd, upon our watry *eyne.* *Shakeſpeare.*

Nor doth the *eye* itſelf,
That moſt pure ſpirit of ſenſe, behold itſelf,
Not going from itſelf; but *eyes* oppos'd,
Salute each other with each other's form. *Sh. Troil. and Creſſ.*

He kept him as the apple of his *eye*. *Deutr.* xxxii. 10.

As long looking againſt the ſun or fire hurteth the *eye* by dilatation; ſo curious printing in ſmall volumes, and reading of ſmall letters, do hurt the *eye* by contraction. *Bacon.*

His awful preſence did the crowd ſurprize,
Nor durſt the raſh ſpectator meet his *eyes*;
Eyes that confeſs'd him born for kingly ſway,
So fierce, they flaſh'd intolerable day. *Dryd. Knight's Tale.*

But ſure the *eye* of time beholds no name
So bleſt as thine in all the rolls of fame. *Pope's Odyſſey.*

2. Sight; ocular knowledge.

Who hath bewitched you, that you ſhould not obey the truth, before whoſe *eyes* Jeſus Chriſt hath been evidently ſet forth? *Gal.* iii. 1.

3. Look; countenance.

I'll ſay yon grey is not the morning's *eye*,
'Tis but the pale reflex of Cynthia's brow. *Sh. Rom. and Jul.*

4. Front; face.

To juſtify this worthy nobleman,
Her ſhall you hear diſproved to your *eyes*. *Shakeſpeare's Meaſure for Meaſure.*

5. A poſture of direct oppoſition, where one thing is in the ſame line with another.

Now paſs'd, on either ſide they nimbly tack,
Both ſtrive to intercept and guide the wind;
And in its *eye* more cloſely they come back,
To finiſh all the deaths they left behind. *Dryd. Ann. Mirab.*

6. Aſpect; regard.

Having an *eye* to a number of rites and orders in the church of England, as marrying with a ring, &c. ſundry church-offices, dignities and callings, for which they found no commandment in the holy Scripture, they thought by the one only ſtroke of an axiom to have cut them off. *Hooker, b.* iii. *ſ.* 4.

As in Scripture a number of laws, particular and poſitive, being in force, may not by any law of man be violated; we are, in making laws, to have thereunto an eſpecial *eye. Hooker.*

The man that is tender among you, and very delicate, his *eyes* ſhall be evil towards his brother. *Deutr.* xxviii. 54.

He that hath a bountiful *eye* ſhall be bleſſed. *Prov.* xxii. 9.

None ſhould be put into either of thoſe commiſſions, with an *eye* of favour to their perſons, to give them countenance or reputation in the places where they live. *Bacon to Villiers.*

Winds and hurricanes at land, tempeſts and ſtorms at ſea, have always been looked upon with as evil an *eye* as earthquakes. *Woodward's Natural Hiſtory.*

In this diſpoſal of my ſiſter, I have had an *eye* to her being a wit, and provided that the bridegroom be a man of ſound judgment. *Tatler*, N°. 75.

Bookſellers mention with reſpect the authors they have printed, and conſequently have an *eye* to their own advantage. *Addiſon's Spectator*, N°. 92.

7. Notice; attention; obſervation.

Not ſatisfied with our oath, he appointed a band of horſemen to have an *eye* that we ſhould not go beyond appointed limits. *Sidney, b.* ii.

Lawmakers muſt have an *eye* to the place where, and to the men amongſt whom. *Hooker, b.* i. *ſ.* 10.

His majeſty hath caſt his *eyes* upon you, as finding you to be ſuch as you ſhould be, or hoping to make you to be ſuch as he would have you to be. *Bacon.*

If the Engliſh had driven the Iriſh into the plains and open countries, where they might have an *eye* and obſervation upon them, the Iriſh had been eaſily kept in order. *Davies on Irel.*

Spenſer has followed both Virgil and Theocritus in the charms which he employs for curing Britomartis of her love; but he had alſo our poet's Ceiris in his *eye*. *Dryden's Æn.*

Miſdoubt my conſtancy, and do not try;
But ſtay and ever keep me in your *eye*. *Dryd. Ind. Emperor.*

After this jealouſy he kept a ſtrict *eye* upon him. *L'Eſtrange.*

This method of teaching children by a repeated practice, under the *eye* and direction of the tutor, 'till they have got the habit of doing well, has many advantages. *Locke.*

Theſe are intrinſick difficulties ariſing from the text itſelf, as the uncertainty ſometimes who are the perſons he ſpeaks to, or the opinions or practices which he has in his *eye*. *Locke.*

Several performances have been juſtly applauded for their wit, which have been written with an *eye* to this predominant humour of the town. *Addiſon's Freeholder*, N°. 35.

We were the moſt obedient creatures in the world, conſtant to our duty, and kept a ſteddy *eye* on the end for which we were ſent hither. *Spectator*, N°. 577.

8. Opinion formed by obſervation.

She told her huſband, ſhe deſigned to be beautiful in no body's *eye* but his. *Sidney.*

It hath, in their *eye*, no great affinity with the form of the church of Rome. *Hooker, b.* v. *ſ.* 27.

Like one of two contending in a prize,
That thinks he hath done well in people's *eyes. Shakeſpeare.*

I was as far from meditating a war as I was, in the *eye* of the world, from having any preparations for one. *K. Charles.*

Though he in all the people's *eyes* ſeem'd great,
Yet greater he appear'd in his retreat. *Denham.*

9. Sight; view; the place in which any thing may be ſeen.

There ſhall he practiſe tilts and tournaments,
Hear ſweet diſcourſe, converſe with noblemen;
And be, in *eye* of every exerciſe,
Worthy his youth and nobleneſs of birth. *Shakeſpeare.*

10. Any thing formed like an eye.

Or ſee colours like the *eye* of a peacock's feather, by preſſing our eyes on either corner, whilſt we look the other way. *Newton's Opt.*

11. Any ſmall perforation.

This Ajax has not ſo much wit as will ſtop the *eye* of Helen's needle. *Shakeſp. Troilus and Creſſida.*

Does not our Saviour himſelf ſpeak of the intolerable difficulty which they cauſe in men's paſſage to heaven? Do not they make the narrow way much narrower, and contract the

gate

gate which leads to life to the ſtreightneſs of a needle's *eye?* *South's Sermons.*

12. A ſmall catch into which a hook goes.

Thoſe parts, if they cohere to one another but by reſt only, may be much more eaſily diſſociated, and put into motion by any external body, than they could be, if they were by little hooks and *eyes*, or other kind of faſtenings entangled in one another. *Boyle.*

13. Bud of a plant.

Prune and cut off all your vine-ſhoots to the very root, ſave one or two of the ſtouteſt, to be left with three or four *eyes* of young wood. *Evelyn's Kalendar.*

14. A ſmall ſhade of colour.

The ground indeed is tawny.
—With an *eye* of green in't. *Shakeſ. Tempeſt.*

Red with an *eye* of blue, makes a purple. *Boyle on Colours.*

15. Power of perception.

The *eyes* of your underſtanding being enlightened. *Eph.* i.

A gift doth blind the *eyes* of the wiſe. *Deutr.* xvi. 19.

To E'YE. *v. a.* [from the noun.] To watch; to keep in view; to obſerve.

When they are laid in garriſon, they may better hide their defaults than when they are in camp, where they are continually *eyed* and noted of all men. *Spenſer on Ireland.*

Full many a lady
I've *ey'd* with beſt regard. *Shakeſpeare's Tempeſt.*

The kitchen Malkin pins
Her richeſt lockram 'bout her reeky neck,
Clamb'ring the walls to *eye* him. *Shakeſ. Coriolanus.*

Bid the cheek be ready with a bluſh,
Modeſt as morning, when ſhe coldly *eyes*
The youthful Phœbus. *Shakeſ. Troilus and Creſſida.*

Bold deed thou haſt preſum'd, advent'rous Eve,
And peril great provok'd, who thus hath dar'd,
Had it been only coveting to *eye*
That ſacred fruit. *Milton's Paradiſe Loſt, b.* ix. *l.* 923.

Such a ſtory as the baſiliſk is that of the wolf, concerning priority of viſion, that a man becomes hoarſe and dumb, if the wolf have the advantage firſt to *eye* him. *Brown's Vulg. Err.*

It was needful for her perpetually to *eye* her purſuing enemy. *More's Antidote againſt Atheiſm.*

Then gave it to his faithful ſquire,
With leſſons how t'obſerve and *eye* her. *Hudibras, p.* iii.

Eye nature's walks, ſhoot folly as it flies,
And catch the manners living as they riſe. *Pope's Eſſ. on Man.*

Have a box when eunuchs ſing,
And foremoſt in the circle *eye* a king. *Pope's Epiſt. of Hor.*

To EYE. *v. n.* To appear; to ſhow; to bear an appearance.

Forgive me,
Since my becomings kill me when they do not
Eye well to you. *Shakeſ. Anthony and Cleopatra.*

EY'EBALL. *n. ſ.* [*eye* and *ball.*] The apple of the eye; the pupil.

Oh, were mine *eyeballs* into bullets turn'd,
That I in rage might ſhoot them at your faces! *Shak. H.*VI.

Be ſubject to no ſight but mine: inviſible
To every *eyeball* elſe. *Shakeſpeare's Tempeſt.*

I feel my hair grow ſtiff, my *eyeballs* rowl;
This is the only form could ſhake my ſoul. *Dryd. Ind. Emp.*

Not when a gilt buffet's reflected pride
Turns you from ſound philoſophy aſide,
Not when from plate to plate your *eyeballs* roll,
And the brain dances to the mantling bowl. *Pope's Horace.*

EYEBRI'GHT. *n. ſ.* [*euphraſia*, Latin.] It hath an anomalous perſonated flower of one leaf, divided into two lips; the upper one upright, parted into ſeveral diviſions; and the lower one divided into three parts, each of which is again divided into two: out of the flowercup riſes the pointal, which afterwards turns to a fruit, or oblong huſk, divided into two parts, and replete with ſmall ſeeds. *Miller.*

EY'EBROW. *n. ſ.* [*eye* and *brow.*] The hairy arch over the eye.

The lover,
Sighing like a furnace, with a woful ballad
Made to his miſtreſs *eyebrow*. *Shakeſp. As you like it.*

On the ſeventh day he ſhall ſhave all his hair off his head, his beard, and his *eyebrows*. *Lev.* xiv. 9.

Above ſtand the *eyebrows*, to keep any thing from running down upon them; as drops of ſweat from the forehead, or duſt. *Ray on the Creation.*

The balls of his broad eyes roll'd in his head,
And glar'd betwixt a yellow and a red;
He look'd a lion with a gloomy ſtare,
And o'er his *eyebrows* hung his matted hair. *Dryden.*

EY'EDROP. *n. ſ.* [*eye* and *drop.*] Tear.

That tyranny which never quaft but blood,
Would by beholding him have waſh'd his knife
With gentle *eyedrops*. *Shakeſpeare's Henry* IV. *p.* ii.

EY'EGLANCE. *n. ſ.* [*eye* and *glance.*] Quick notice of the eye.

His countenance was bold, and baſhed not
For Guyon's looks; but ſcornful *eyeglance* at him ſhot. *F. Q.*

EY'EGLASS. *n. ſ.* [*eye* and *glaſs.*] Spectacles; glaſs to aſſiſt the ſight.

Ha' not you ſeen, Camillo?
But that's paſt doubt you have; or your *eyeglaſs*
Is thicker than a cuckold's horn. *Shakeſ. Winter's Tale.*

By comparing it with a good perſpective of four foot in length, made with a concave *eyeglaſs*, I could read at a greater diſtance with my own inſtrument than with the glaſs. *Newton.*

EY'ELESS. *adj.* [from *eye.*] Without eyes; ſightleſs; deprived of ſight.

A proclaim'd prize! moſt happy!
That *eyeleſs* head of thine was firſt fram'd fleſh
To raiſe my fortunes. *Shakeſp. King Lear.*

Promiſe was, that I
Should Iſrael from Philiſtian yoke deliver:
Aſk for this great deliverer now, and find him
Eyeleſs in Gaza, at the mill with ſlaves:
Himſelf is bound under Philiſtian yoke. *Milton's Agoniſtes.*

Pentheus durſt deride
The cheated people, and the *eyeleſs* guide.
Addiſon's Ovid's Metamorph.

Eyeleſs he grop'd about with vengeful haſte,
And juſtled promontories as he paſs'd. *Garth's Ovid.*

Meonides,
Poor *eyeleſs* pilgrim. *Phillips.*

Cyclop, if any pitying thy diſgrace,
Aſk who disfigur'd thus that *eyeleſs* face. *Pope's Odyſſey.*

EY'ELET. *n. ſ.* [*œillet*, French, a little eye.] A hole through which light may enter; any ſmall perforation for a lace to go through.

Slitting the back and fingers of a glove, I made *eyelet* holes to draw it cloſe. *Wiſeman's Surgery.*

EY'ELID. *n. ſ.* [*eye* and *lid.*] The membrane that ſhuts over the eye.

Therewith her dim *eyelids* ſhe up 'gan rear,
On which the dreary death did ſit, as ſad
As lump of lead, and made dark clouds appear. *Fai. Queen.*

Mark when ſhe ſmiles with amiable chear,
And tell me whereto can ye liken it!
When on each *eyelid* ſweetly do appear
An hundred graces as in ſhade to ſit. *Spenſer's Sonnets.*

On my *eyelids* is the ſhadow of death. *Job* xvi. 16.

Fetch me that flower; the herb I ſhew'd thee once;
The juice of it, on ſleeping *eyelids* laid,
Will make or man or woman madly doat
Upon the next live creature that it ſees. *Shakeſpeare.*

The Turks have a black powder, made of a mineral called alcohol, which with a fine long pencil they lay under their *eyelids*, which doth colour black, whereby the white of the eye is ſet off more white. *Bacon's Natural Hiſtory.*

At length, the crackling noiſe and dreadful blaze
Call'd up ſome waking lover to the ſight;
And long it was ere he the reſt could raiſe,
Whoſe heavy *eyelids* yet were full of night. *Dryden.*

EYESE'RVANT. *n. ſ.* [*eye* and *ſervant.*] A ſervant that works only while watched.

EYESE'RVICE. *n. ſ.* [*eye* and *ſervice.*] Service performed only under inſpection.

Servants, obey in all things your maſter; not with *eyeſervice*, as men pleaſers, but in ſingleneſs of heart. *Col.* iii.

EY'ESHOT. *n. ſ.* [*eye* and *ſhot.*] Sight; glance; view.

I muſt carry off my prize as others do; and not think of ſharing the booty before I am free from danger, and out of *eyeſhot* from the other windows. *Dryden's Don Sebaſtian.*

I have preſerved many a young man from her *eyeſhot* by this means. *Spectator*, Nº. 284.

EY'ESIGHT. *n. ſ.* [*eye* and *ſight.*] Sight of the eye.

The Lord hath recompenſed me according to my cleanneſs in his *eyeſight*. 2 *Sam.* xxii. 22.

I have an ill-divining ſoul:
Methinks I ſee thee, now thou art below,
As one dead in the bottom of a tomb;
Either my *eyeſight* fails, or thou look'ſt pale. *Shakeſpeare.*

I love you, ſir,
Dearer than *eyeſight*, ſpace and liberty,
Beyond what can be valued, rich or rare. *Shakeſ. K. Lear.*

Though ſight be loſt,
Life yet hath many ſolaces, enjoy'd
Where other ſenſes want not their delights,
At home in leiſure and domeſtick eaſe,
Exempt from many a care and chance, to which
Eyeſight expoſes daily men abroad. *Milton's Agoniſtes.*

Joſephus ſets this down from his own *eyeſight*, being himſelf a chief captain at the ſiege of Jopata, where theſe events happened. *Wilkins's Math. Magic.*

He blinds the wiſe, gives *eyeſight* to the blind,
And molds and ſtamps anew the lover's mind. *Dryden.*

EY'ESORE. *n. ſ.* [*eye* and *ſore.*] Something offenſive to the ſight.

Hath the church of Chriſt, from the firſt beginning, by a ſecret univerſal inſtinct of God's good ſpirit, always tied itſelf to to end neither ſermon, nor almoſt any ſpeech of moment, which hath concerned matters of God, without ſome ſpecial words of honour and glory to the Trinity which we all adore; and is the like concluſion of pſalms become now, at length, an *eyeſore*, or a galling to the ears that hear it? *Hooker*, *b*. v.

Fy, doff this habit; ſhame to your eſtate,
And *eyeſore* to our ſolemn feſtival. *Shak. Tam. of the Shrew.*

As ſoon as the two lords came thither they covered, to the trouble of the other; but having preſently to ſpeak, they were quickly freed from that *eyeſore*. *Clarendon*, *b*. viii.

Mordecai was an *eyeſore* to Haman. *L'Eſtrange*, *Fable* 38.

He's the beſt piece of man's fleſh in the market; not an *eyeſore* in his whole body. *Dryden's Don Sebaſtian.*

EYESPO'TTED. *adj*. [*eye* and *ſpot*.] Marked with ſpots like eyes.

Nor Juno's bird, in her *eyeſpotted* train,
So many goodly colours doth contain. *Spenſer.*

EYESTRI'NG. *n. ſ.* [*eye* and *ſtring*.] The ſtring of the eye; the tendon by which the eye is moved.

I would have broke mine *eyeſtrings*; crackt them, but
To look upon him. *Shakeſpeare's Cymbeline.*

To know whether the ſheep are ſound or not, ſee that their gums be red, the briſket-ſkin red, and the *eyeſtrings* ruddy. *Mortimer's Huſbandry.*

EY'ETOOTH. *n. ſ.* [*eye* and *tooth*.] The tooth on the upper jaw next on each ſide to the grinders; the fang.

The next one on each ſide ſtronger and deeper rooted, and more pointed, called canini, in Engliſh *eyeteeth*, to tear the more tough ſort of aliments. *Ray on the Creation.*

EY'EWINK. *n. ſ.* [*eye* and *wink*.] A wink, as a hint or token.

They would have won any woman's heart; and, I warrant you, they could never get an *eyewink* of her. *Shakeſpeare.*

EYEWI'TNESS. *n. ſ.* [*eye* and *witneſs*.] An ocular evidence; one who gives teſtimony to facts ſeen with his own eyes.

We made known unto you the power and coming of our Lord Jeſus Chriſt, and were *eyewitneſſes* of his majeſty. 2 *Pet.*

To meet him all his ſaints, who ſilent ſtood
Eyewitneſſes of his almighty acts,
With jubilee advanc'd. *Milton's Paradiſe Loſt*, *b*. vi.

Give us, if thou can'ſt,
Eyewitneſs of what firſt or laſt was done,
Relation more particular and diſtinct. *Milton's Agoniſtes.*

The curious, by laying together circumſtances, atteſtations, and characters of thoſe who are concerned in them, either receive or reject what at firſt but *eyewitneſſes* could abſolutely believe or diſbelieve. *Addiſon on the Chriſtian Religion.*

EYRE. *n. ſ.* [*eyre*, French; *iter*, Latin.] The court of juſtices itinerants; and juſtices in *eyre* are thoſe only, which *Bracton* in many places calls *juſticiarios itinerantes*. The *eyre* alſo of the foreſt is nothing but the juſtice-ſeat, otherwiſe called; which is, or ſhould by ancient cuſtom, be held every three years by the juſtices of the foreſt, journeying up and down to that purpoſe. *Cowel.*

EY'RY. *n. ſ.* [from *ey*, an egg.] The place where birds of prey build their neſts and hatch

But I was born ſo high,
Our *eyrie* buildeth in the cedars top,
And dallies with the wind, and ſcorns the ſun. *Shak. R.* III.

The eagle, and the ſtork,
On cliffs and cedar-tops their *eyries* build. *Milt. Par. Loſt.*

Some haggard hawk, who had her *eyry* nigh,
Well pounc'd to faſten, and well wing'd to fly. *Dryden.*

F.

F.

F, A consonant generally reckoned by authors, and admitted by *Scaliger*, among the semi-vowels, and according to that opinion distinguished in the enumeration of the alphabet by a name beginning with a vowel, yet has so far the nature of a mute, that it is easily pronounced before a liquid in the same syllable. It has in English an invariable sound, formed by compression of the whole lips and a forcible breath. Its kindred letter is V, which, in the Islandick alphabet, is only distinguished from it by a point in the body of the letter.

FABA'CEOUS. *adj.* [*fabaceus*, Latin.] Having the nature of a bean. *Dict.*

FA'BLE. *n. s.* [*fable*, French; *fabula*, Latin.]

1. A feigned story intended to enforce some moral precept.
   Jotham's *fable* of the bees is the oldest extant, and as beautiful as any made since. *Addison's Spectator.*
2. A fiction in general.
   Triptolemus, so sung the nine,
   Strew'd plenty from his cart divine;
   But, spite of all those *fable* makers,
   He never sow'd on Almaign acres. *Dryden.*
3. A vitious or foolish fiction.
   But refuse profane and old wives *fables.* 1 *Tim.* iv. 7.
4. The series or contexture of events which constitute a poem epick or dramatick.
   The moral is the first business of the poet: this being formed, he contrives such a design or *fable* as may be most suitable to the moral. *Dryden's Dufresnoy.*
   The first thing to be considered in an epick poem is the *fable*, which is perfect or imperfect, according as the action, which it relates, is more or less so. *Addison's Spectator.*
5. A lye. This sense is merely familiar.

To FA'BLE. *v. n.* [from the noun.]

1. To feign; to write not truth but fiction.
   That Saturn's sons receiv'd the three-fold reign
   Of heav'n, of ocean, and deep hell beneath,
   Old poets mention, *fabling.* *Prior.*
   Vain now the tales which *fabling* poets tell,
   That wav'ring conquest still desires to rove!
   In Marlbro's camp the goddess knows to dwell. *Prior.*
2. To tell falshoods; to lye.
   He *fables* not: I hear the enemy. *Shakesp. Henry* VI.

To FA'BLE. *v. a.* To feign; to tell of falsety.
   We mean to win,
   Or turn this heav'n itself into the hell
   Thou *fablest.* *Milton's Paradise Lost, b.* vi. *l.* 292.
   Ladies of th' Hesperides, that seem'd
   Fairer than feign'd of old, or *fabl'd* since
   Of fairy damsels met in forest wide,
   By knights. *Milton's Parad. Lost.*

FA'BLED. *adj.* [from *fable.*] Celebrated in fables.
   Hail, *fabled* grotto! hail, Elysian soil!
   Thou fairest spot of fair Britannia's isle! *Tickell.*

FA'BLER. *n. s.* [from *fable.*] A dealer in fiction; a writer of feigned stories.

To FA'BRICATE. *v. a.* [*fabricor*, Latin.]

1. To build; to construct.
2. To forge; to devise falsely. This sense is retained among the Scottish lawyers; for when they suspect a paper to be forged, they say it is *fabricate.*

FABRICA'TION. *n. s.* [from *fabricate.*] The act of building; construction.
   This *fabrication* of the human body is the immediate work of a vital principle, that formeth the first rudiments of the human nature. *Hale's Origin of Mankind.*

FA'BRICK. *n. s.* [*fabrica*, Latin.]

1. A building; an edifice.
   There must be an exquisite care to place the columns, set in several stories, most precisely one over another, that so the solid may answer to the solid, and the vacuities to the vacuities, as well for beauty as strength of the *fabrick.* *Wotton.*
2. Any system or compages of matter; any body formed by the conjunction of dissimilar parts.
   Still will ye think it strange,
   That all the parts of this great *fabrick* change;
   Quit their old station and primeval frame. *Prior.*

To FA'BRICK. *v. a.* [from the noun.] To build; to form; to construct.
   Shew what laws of life
   The cheese inhabitants observe, and how
   Fabrick their mansions. *Phillips.*

FA'BULIST. *n. s.* [*fabuliste*, French.] A writer of fables.
   Quitting Esop and the *fabulists*, he copies from Boccace. *Croxal.*
   Our bard's a *fabulist*, and deals in fiction. *Garrick.*

FABULO'SITY. *n. s.* [*fabulositas*, Latin.] Lyingness; fulness of stories; fabulous invention.
   In their *fabulosity* they would report, that they had observations for twenty thousand years. *Abbot's Description of the World.*

FA'BULOUS. *adj.* [*fabulosus*, Latin.] Feigned; full of fables, or invented tales.
   A person terrified with the imagination of spectres, is more reasonable than one who thinks the appearance of spirits *fabulous* and groundless. *Addison's Spectator*, N°. 110.

FA'BULOUSLY. *adv.* [from *fabulous.*] In fiction; in a fabulous manner.
   There are many things *fabulously* delivered, and are not to be accepted as truths. *Brown's Vulgar Errours, b.* vi. *c.* 8.

FACE. *n. s.* [*face*, French, from *facies*, Latin.]

1. The visage.
   The children of Israel saw the *face* of Moses, that the skin of Moses's *face* shone. *Exod.* xxxiv. 35.
   A man shall see *faces*, which, if you examine them part by part, you shall never find good; but take them together, are not uncomely. *Bacon, Essay* 44.
   From beauty still to beauty ranging,
   In ev'ry *face* I found a dart. *Addison's Spectator.*
2. Countenance; cast of the features; look; air of the face.
   Seiz'd and ty'd down to judge, how wretched I!
   Who can't be silent, and who will not lye:
   To laugh, were want of goodness and of grace;
   And to be grave, exceeds all pow'r of *face.* *Pope's Epistles.*
3. The surface of any thing.
   A mist watered the whole *face* of the ground. *Gen.* ii. 6.
4. The front or forepart of any thing.
   The breadth of the *face* of the house, towards the East, was an hundred cubits. *Ezek.* xli. 14.
4. State of affairs.
   He look'd, and saw the *face* of things quite chang'd,
   The brazen throat of war had ceas'd to roar;
   All now was turn'd to jollity and game,
   To luxury and riot, feast and dance. *Milton's Par. Lost.*
   This would produce a new *face* of things in Europe. *Addis.*
5. Appearance; resemblance.
   Keep still your former *face*, and mix again
   With these lost spirits; run all their mazes with 'em;
   For such are treasons. *Ben. Johnson.*
   At the first shock, with blood and powder stain'd,
   Nor heav'n, nor sea, their former *face* retain'd;
   Fury and art produce effects so strange,
   They trouble nature, and her visage change. *Waller.*
   His dialogue has so much the *face* of probability, that some have mistaken it for a real conference. *Baker.*
6. Presence; sight.
   Ye shall give her unto Eleazar, and one shall slay her before his *face.* *Numb.* xix. 3.
   Jove cannot fear; then tell me to my *face*,
   That I of all the gods am least in grace. *Dryden's Iliad.*
7. Confidence; boldness.
   Thinking, by this *face*,
   To fasten in our thoughts that they have courage;
   But 'tis not so. *Shakespeare's Julius Cæsar.*
   How many things are there which a man cannot, with any *face* or comliness, say or do himself? A man can scarce allege his own merits with modesty, much less extol them: a man cannot sometimes brook to supplicate or beg. *Bacon, Essay* 28.
   You'll find the thing will not be done
   With ignorance and *face* alone. *Hudibras, p.* ii.
   You, says the judge to the wolf, have the *face* to challenge that

that which you never lost; and you, says he to the fox, have the confidence to deny that which you have certainly stolen. *L'Estrange, Fable* 415.

This is the man that has the *face* to charge others with false citations. *Tillotson, Preface.*

8. Distortion of the face.

Shame itself!
Why do you make such *faces*? *Shakespeare's Macbeth.*

FACE *to* FACE. [An adverbial expression.]

1. When both parties are present.

It is not the manner of the Romans to deliver any man to die, before that he which is accused have his accusers *face to face.* *Acts* xxv. 16.

2. Nakedly; without the interposition of other bodies.

Now we see through a glass darkly; but then *face to face.* 1 *Cor.* xiii. 12.

To FACE. *v. n.* [from the noun.]

1. To carry a false appearance; to play the hypocrite.

Thou needs must learn to laugh, to lye,
To *face*, to forge, to scoff, to company. *Hubberd's Tale.*

2. To turn the face; to come in front.

Face about, man; you a soldier, and afraid of the enemy! *Dryden's Spanish Fryar.*

Then thrice the mounted squadrons ride around
The fire, and Arcite's name they thrice resound;
Hail and farewel they shouted thrice amain,
Thrice *facing* to the left, and thence they turn'd again. *Dry.*

To FACE. *v. a.*

1. To meet in front; to oppose with confidence and firmness.

I'll *face*
This tempest, and deserve the name of king. *Dryden.*

We get intelligence of the force of the enemy, and cast about for a sufficient number of troops to *face* the enemy in the field of battle. *Addison on the War.*

They are as loth to see the fires kindled in Smithfield as his lordship; and, at least, as ready to *face* them under a popish perseeution. *Swift.*

2. To oppose with impudence.

We trapann'd the state, and *fac'd* it down
With plots and projects of our own. *Hudibras, p.* iii. *c.* 2.
Because he walk'd against his will,
He *fac'd* men down that he stood still. *Prior.*

3. To stand opposite to.

On one side is the head of the emperor Trajan; the reverse has on it the circus Maximus, and a view of the side of the Palatine mountain that *faces* it. *Addison on Italy.*

The temple is described to be square, and the four fronts with open gates, *facing* the different quarters of the world. *Pope's Temple of Fame.*

4. To cover with an additional superficies; to invest with a covering.

The whole fortification of Soleurre is *faced* with marble. *Addison's Remarks on Italy.*

Where your old bank is hollow, *face* it with the first spit of earth that you dig out of the ditch. *Mortimer's Husbandry.*

FA'CELESS. *adj.* [from *face.*] Without a face. *Bailey.*

FACEPAI'NTER. *n. s.* [*face* and *painter.*] A drawer of portraits; a painter who draws from the life.

FACEPAI'NTING. *n. s.* [*face* and *painting.*] The art of drawing portraits.

Georgione, the cotemporary of Titian, excelled in portraits or *facepainting.* *Dryden's Dufresnoy.*

FA'CET. *n. s.* [*facette*, French.] A small surface; a superficies cut into several angles.

Honour that is gained and broken upon another, hath the quickest reflection, like diamonds cut with *facets.* *Bacon.*

FACE'TIOUS. *adj.* [*facetieux*, French; *facetiæ*, Lat.] Gay; cheerful; lively; merry; witty. It is used both of persons and sentiments.

Socrates, informed of some derogating speeches used of him behind his back, made this *facetious* reply, Let him beat me too when I am absent. *Government of the Tongue, s.* 6.

FACE'TIOUSLY. *adv.* [from *facetious.*] Gayly; cheerfully; wittily; merrily.

FACE'TIOUSNESS. *n. s.* [from *facetious.*] Cheerful wit; mirth; gaiety.

FA'CILE. *adj.* [*facile*, French; *facilis*, Latin.]

1. Easy; not difficult; performable or attainable with little labour.

Then also those poets, which are now counted most hard, will be both *facile* and pleasant. *Milton on Education.*

To confine the imagination is as *facile* a performance as the Goteham's design of hedging in the cuckoo. *Glanv. Sceps.*

By dividing it into parts so distinct, the order in which they shall find each disposed, will render the work *facile* and delightful. *Evelyn's Kalendar.*

This may at first seem perplexed with many difficulties, yet many things may be suggested to make it more *facile* and commodious. *Wilkins's Math. Magic.*

2. Easily surmountable; easily conquerable.

The *facile* gates of hell too slightly barr'd. *Milt. P. Lost.*

3. Easy of access or converse; not haughty; not supercilious not austere.

I meant she should be courteous, *facile*, sweet,
Hating that solemn vice of greatness, pride;
I meant each softest virtue there should meet,
Fit in that softer bosom to reside. *Ben. Johnson's Epigrams.*
Raphael now, to Adam's doubt propos'd,
Benevolent and *facile*, thus reply'd. *Milton's Paradise Lost.*

4. Pliant; flexible; easily persuaded to good or bad; ductile to a fault.

Too *facile* then, thou did'st not much gainsay;
Nay did'st permit, approve, and fair dismiss. *Milt. P. Lost.*
Since Adam and his *facile* consort Eve
Lost Paradise, deceiv'd by me. *Milton's Paradise Regain'd.*

Some men are of that *facile* temper, that they are wrought upon by every object they converse with, whom any affectionate discourse, or serious sermon, or any notable accident, shall put into a fit of religion, which yet usually lasts no longer than till somewhat else comes in their way. *Calamy.*

To FACI'LITATE. *v. a.* [*faciliter*, French.] To make easy; to free from difficulty; to clear from impediments.

Choice of the likeliest and best prepared metal for the version will *facilitate* the work. *Bacon's Natural History.*

They renewed their assault two or three days together, and planted cannon to *facilitate* their passage, which did little hurt; but they still lost many men in the attempt. *Clarendon, b.* viii.

Though perspective cannot be called a certain rule, or a finishing of the picture, yet it is a great succour and relief to art, and *facilitates* the means of execution. *Dryden's Dufresn.*

What produceth a due quantity of animal spirits, necessarily *facilitates* the animal and natural motions. *Arbuthnot on Diet.*

A war on the side of Italy would cause a great diversion of the French forces, and *facilitate* the progress of our arms in Spain. *Swift.*

FACI'LITY. *n. s.* [*facilitè*, French; *facilitas*, Latin.]

1. Easiness to be performed; freedom from difficulty.

Yet reason saith, reason should have ability
To hold these worldly things in such proportion,
As let them come or go with even *facility.* *Sidney, b.* ii.

Piety could not be diverted from this to a more commodious business by any motives of profit or *facility.* *Raleigh.*

A war upon the Turks is more worthy than upon any other Gentiles, both in point of religion and in point of honour; though *facility* and hope of success might invite some other choice. *Bacon's holy War.*

2. Readiness in performing; dexterity.

They who have studied have not only learned many excellent things, but also have acquired a great *facility* of profiting themselves by reading good authors. *Dryden's Dufresnoy.*

The *facility* which we get of doing things, by a custom of doing, makes them often pass in us without our notice. *Locke.*

3. Vitious ductility; easiness to be persuaded to good or bad; to ready compliance.

Facility is worse than bribery; for bribes come now and then: but if importunity or idle respects lead a man, he shall never be without. *Bacon, Essay* 11.

'Tis a great error to take *facility* for good-nature; tenderness, without discretion, is no better than a more pardonable folly. *L'Estrange, Fable* 30.

4. Easiness of access; complaisance; condescension; affability.

He opens and yields himself to the man of business with difficulty and reluctancy; but offers himself to the visits of a friend with *facility*, and all the meeting readiness of appetite and desire. *South's Sermons.*

FACINE'RIOUS. *adj.* [corrupted by *Shakespeare* from *facinorous*; *facinus, facinoris*, Latin.] Wicked; facinorous.

'Tis strange, 'tis very strange, that is the brief and the tedious of it; and he's of a most *facinerious* spirit that will not acknowledge it. *Shakes. All's well that ends well.*

FA'CING. *n. s.* [from *To face.*] An ornamental covering; that which is put on the outside of any thing by way of decoration.

These offices and dignities were but the *facings* and fringes of his greatness. *Wotton.*

FACI'NOROUS. *adj.* [*facinora*, Latin.] Wicked; atrocious; detestably bad.

FACI'NOROUSNESS. *n. s.* [from *facinorous*] Wickedness in a high degree.

FACT. *n. s.* [*factum*, Latin]

1. A thing done; an effect produced; something not barely supposed or suspected, but really done.

In matter of *fact* there is some credit to be given to the testimony of man; but not in matter of opinion and judgment: we see the contrary both acknowledged and universally practised also throughout the world. *Hooker, b.* ii. *s.* 7.

As men are not to mistake the causes of these operations, so much less are they to mistake the *fact* or effect, and rashly to take that for done which is not done. *Bacon's Nat. History.*

Matter of *fact* breaks out and blazes with too great an evidence to be denied. *South's Sermons.*

2. Reality; not supposition; not speculation.

Those

Those effects which are wrought by the percussion of the sense, and by things in *fact*, are produced likewise in some degree by the imagination: therefore if a man see another eat sour or acid things, which set the teeth on edge, that object tainteth the imagination. *Bacon's Natural History*, N°. 795.

If this were true in *fact*, I do not see any colour for such a conclusion. *Addison on the State of the War.*

Manifold sins, though in speculation they may be separable from war, in reality and *fact* never fail to attend it. *Smalridge.*

3. Action; deed.

Unhappy man! to break the pious laws
Of nature, pleading in his children's cause:
Howe'er the doubtful *fact* is understood,
'Tis love of honour and his country's good;
The consul, not the father, sheds the blood. *Dryden.*

FA'CTION. *n. s.* [*faction*, French; *factio*, Latin.]

1. A party in a state.

The queen is valued thirty thousand strong;
If she hath time to breathe, be well assur'd
Her *faction* will be full as strong as ours. *Shakes. Henry* VI.

He has been known to commit outrages,
And cherish *factions*. *Shakespeare's Timon.*

Their hatred went so far, that by one of Simon's *faction* murders were committed. 2 *Mac.* iv. 9.

By the weight of reason I should counterpoise the overbalancings of any *factions*. *King Charles.*

2. Tumult; discord; dissension.

They remained at Newbery in great *faction* among themselves. *Clarendon.*

FA'CTIONARY. *n. s.* [*factionaire*, French.] One of a faction; a party man. A word not in use.

Pr'ythee, fellow, remember my name is Menenius; always *factionary* of the party of your general. *Shakes. Coriolanus.*

FA'CTIOUS. *adj.* [*factieux*, French.]

1. Given to faction; loud and violent in a party; publickly dissensious; addicted to form parties and raise publick disturbances.

He is a traitor; let him to the Tower,
And crop away that *factious* pate of his. *Shakes. Hen.* VI.

Be *factious* for redress of all these griefs. *Shak. Jul. Cæsar.*

2. Proceeding from publick dissensions; tending to publick discord.

Grey-headed men and grave, with warriors mix'd,
Assemble; and harangues are heard; but soon
In *factious* opposition. *Milton's Paradise Lost, b.* xi. *l.* 664.

Factious tumults overbore the freedom and honour of the two houses. *King Charles.*

Why these *factious* quarrels, controversies, and battles amongst themselves, when they were all united in the same design? *Dryden's Juvenal, Dedication.*

FA'CTIOUSLY. *adv.* [from *factious.*] In a manner criminally dissensious or tumultuous.

I intended not only to oblige my friends, but mine enemies also; exceeding even the desires of those that were *factiously* discontented. *King Charles.*

FA'CTIOUSNESS. *n. s.* [from *factious.*] Inclination to publick dissension; violent clamourousness for a party.

FACTI'TIOUS. *adj.* [*factitius*, Latin.] Made by art, in opposition to what is made by nature.

In the making and distilling of soap, by one degree of fire the salt, the water, and the oil or grease, whereof that *factitious* concrete is made up, being boiled up together, are easily brought to incorporate. *Boyle.*

Hardness wherein some stones exceed all other bodies, and among them the adamant all other stones, being exalted to that degree that art in vain endeavours to counterfeit it; the *factitious* stones of chymists, in imitation, being easily detected by an ordinary lapidist. *Ray on the Creation.*

FA'CTOR. *n. s.* [*facteur*, French; *factor*, Latin.]

1. An agent for another; one who transacts business for another. Commonly a substitute in mercantile affairs.

Take on you the charge
And kingly government of this your land;
Not as protector, steward, substitute,
Or lowly *factor* for another's gain. *Shakes. Richard* III.

Percy is but my *factor*, good my lord,
T' engross up glorious deeds on my behalf. *Shak. Hen.* IV.

You all three,
The senators alone of this great world,
Chief *factors* for the gods. *Shakes. Anthony and Cleopatra.*

We agreed that I should send up an English *factor*, that whatsoever the island could yield should be delivered at a reasonable rate. *Raleigh's Apology.*

It was conceived that the Scots had good intelligence, having some *factors* doubtless at this mart, albeit they did not openly trade. *Hayward.*

Vile arts and restless endeavours are used by some sly and venomous *factors* for the old republican cause. *South's Sermons.*

All the reason that I could ever hear alleged, by the chief *factors* for a general intromission of all sorts, sects and persuasions, into our communion, is, that those who separate from us are stiff and obstinate, and will not submit to the rules and orders of our church, and that therefore they ought to be taken away. *South's Sermons.*

Forc'd into exile from his rightful throne,
He made all countries where he came his own;
And viewing monarchs secret arts of sway,
A royal *factor* for their kingdoms lay. *Dryden.*

2. [In arithmetick.] The multiplicator and multiplicand. *Harris.*

FA'CTORY. *n. s.* [from *factor.*]

1. A house or district inhabited by traders in a distant country.

2. The traders embodied in one place.

FACTO'TUM. *n. s.* [*fac totum*, Latin. It is used likewise in burlesque French.] A servant employed alike in all kinds of business: as *Scrub* in the *Stratagem.*

FA'CTURE. *n. s.* [French.] The act or manner of making any thing.

FA'CULTY. *n. s.* [*faculté*, French; *facultas*, Latin.]

1. The power of doing any thing; ability whether corporal or intellectual.

There is no kind of *faculty* or power in man, or any creature, which can rightly perform the functions allotted to it without perpetual aid and concurrence of that supreme cause of all things. *Hooker, b.* i. *s.* 8.

Orators may grieve; for in their sides,
Rather than heads, their *faculty* abides. *Denham.*

Reason in man supplies the defect of other *faculties* wherein we are inferior to beasts, and what we cannot compass by force we bring about by stratagem. *L'Estrange.*

2. Powers of the mind, imagination, reason, memory.

For well I understand in the prime end
Of nature, her the inferior; in the mind
And inward *faculties*, which most *excel. Milt. Parad. Lost.*

In the ordinary way of speaking, the understanding and will are two *faculties* of the mind. *Locke.*

Neither did our Saviour think it necessary to explain to us the nature of God, because it would be impossible, without bestowing on us other *faculties* than we possess at present. *Swift.*

3. [In physick.] A power or ability to perform any action natural, vital, and animal: by the first they understand that by which the body is nourished and augmented, or another like it generated: the vital faculty is that by which life is preserved, and the ordinary functions of the body performed; and the animal faculty is what conducts the operations of the mind. *Quincy.*

4. A knack; habitual excellence; dexterity.

He had none of those *faculties*, which the other had, of reconciling men to him. *Clarendon, b.* viii.

A sober man would have wondered how our author found out monarchical absolute power in that text, had he not had an exceeding good *faculty* to find it himself where he could not shew it others. *Locke.*

He had an excellent *faculty* in preaching, if he were not too refined. *Swift.*

5. Quality; disposition or habit of good or ill.

I'm traduc'd by tongues which neither know
My *faculties* nor person, yet will be
The chronicles of my doing. *Shakespeare's Henry* VIII.

6. Power; authority.

This Duncan
Hath born his *faculties* so meek, hath been
So clear in his great office, that his virtues
Will plead like angels. *Shakespeare's Macbeth.*

7. Privilege; right to do any thing.

Law hath set down to what persons, in what causes, with what circumstances, almost every *faculty* or favour shall be granted. *Hooker, b.* v.

8. Faculty, in an university, denotes the masters and professors of the several sciences: as, a meeting of the *faculty* or *faculties.*

FACU'ND. *adj.* [*facundus*, Latin.] Eloquent. *Dict.*

To FA'DDLE. *v. n.* [corrupted from *To fiddle*, or toy with the fingers.] To trifle; to toy; to play.

To FADE. *v. n.* [*fade*, French, insipid, languid.]

1. To tend from greater to less vigour; to grow weak; to languish.

2. To tend from a brighter to a weaker colour.

The greenness of a leaf ought to pass for apparent, because soon *fading* into a yellow, it scarce lasts at all, in comparison of the greenness of an emerald. *Boyle on Colours.*

The spots in this stone are of the same colour throughout, even to the very edges; there being an immediate transition from white to black, and the colours not *fading* or declining gradually. *Woodward on Fossils.*

3. To wither: as a vegetable.

Ye shall be as an oak whose leaf *fadeth*, and as a garden that hath no water. *If.* i. 30.

4. To die away gradually; to vanish; to be worn out.

Where either through the temper of the body, or some other default, the memory is very weak, ideas in the mind quickly *fade*. *Locke.*

The stars shall *fade* away, the sun himself
Grow dim with age, and nature sink in years. *Addis. Cato.*

5. To

5. To be naturally not durable; to be transient; easily to lose vigour or beauty.

The glorious beauty on the head of the fat valley shall be a *fading* flower. *Is.* xxviii. 4.

The pictures drawn in our minds are laid in *fading* colours, and, if not sometimes refreshed, vanish and disappear. *Locke.*

Narcissus' change, to the vain virgin shows
Who trusts to beauty, trusts the *fading* rose. *Gay's Fan.*

To FADE. *v. a.* To wear away; to reduce to languor; to deprive of freshness or vigour; to wither.

This is a man old, wrinkled, *faded*, withered;
And not a maiden, as thou say'st he is. *Shakespeare.*

His palms, though under weights they did not stand,
Still thriv'd; no Winter could his laurels *fade*. *Dryden.*

Restless anxiety, forlorn despair,
And all the *faded* family of care. *Garth's Dispens.*

To FADGE. *v. n.* [ȝeꝼeȝan, Saxon; *fugen*, German.]

1. To suit; to fit; to have one part consistent with another.

How will this *fadge*? my master loves her dearly,
And I, poor monster, fond as much on him;
And she, mistaken, seems to dote on me. *Shakespeare.*

2. To agree; not to quarrel; to live in amity.

When they thriv'd they never *fadg'd*,
But only by the ears engag'd;
Like dogs that snarl about a bone,
And play together when they've none. *Hudibras, p.* iii.

3. To succeed; to hit.

The fox had a fetch; and when he saw it would not *fadge*, away goes he presently. *L'Estrange's Fables.*

4. This is a mean word not now used, unless perhaps in ludicrous and low compositions.

FÆCES. *n. s.* [Latin.] Excrements; but often used to express the ingredients and settlings after distillation and infusion. *Quincy.*

To FAG. *v. a.* [*fatigo*, Latin.] To grow weary; to faint with weariness.

Creighton witheld his force 'till the Italian begun to *fag*, and then brought him to the ground. *Mackenzie's Lives.*

FAGE'ND. *n. s.* [from *fag* and *end.*]

1. The end of a web of cloath, generally made of coarser materials.

2. The refuse or meaner part of any thing.

In the world's *fagend*
A nation lies. *Fanshaw.*

When they are the worst of their way, and fixt in the *fagend* of business, they are apt to look not kindly upon those who go before them. *Collier of Envy.*

FA'GOT. *n. s.* [*fagod*, Welsh and Armorick; *fagot*, French.]

1. A bundle of sticks bound together for the fire.

About the pile of *fagots*, sticks and hay,
The bellows raised the newly kindled flame. *Fairfax, b.* ii.

Spare for no *fagots*, let there be enow;
Place pitchy barrels on the fatal stake. *Shakes. Henry* VI.

Mitres or *fagots* have been the rewards of different persons, according as they pronounced these consecrated syllables or not. *Watts's Improvement of the Mind.*

2. A bundle of sticks for any purpose.

The black prince filled a ditch with *fagots* as successfully as the generals of our times do it with fascines. *Addis. Spectator.*

3. A soldier numbered in the muster-roll, but not really existing.

To FA'GOT. *v. a.* [from the noun] To tie up; to bundle together.

He was too warm on picking work to dwell,
But *fagoted* his notions as they fell,
And if they rhym'd and rattled, all was well. *Dryden.*

To FAIL. *v. n.* [*failler*, French; *faeln*, Welsh. *Pezron.*]

1. To be deficient; to cease from former plenty; to fall short; not to be equal to demand or use.

The waters *fail* from the sea, and the flood decayeth and drieth up. *Job* xiv. 11.

Where the credit and money *fail*, barter alone must do. *Locke.*

2. To be extinct; to cease to be produced.

Help, Lord, for the godly man ceaseth; for the faithful *fail* from among the children of men. *Ps.* xii. 1.

Let there not *fail* from the house of Joab one that hath an issue. 2 *Sa.* iii. 29.

3. To cease; to perish; to be lost.

For Titan, by the mighty loss dismay'd,
Among the heavens th' immortal fact display'd,
Lest the remembrance of his grief should *fail*. *Addison.*

4. To die; to lose life.

Had the king in his last sickness *fail'd*,
Their heads should have gone off. *Shakes. Henry* VIII.

Both he that helpeth shall fall, and he that is holpen shall fall down, and they all shall *fail* together. *Is.* xxxi. 3.

5. To sink; to be torn down; to languish through resistance.

Neither will I be always wroth; for the spirit should *fail* before me. *Is.* lvii. 16.

6. To decay; to decline; to languish.

Mine eyes *fail*. *Ps.* cxix. 82.

I perceive
Thy mortal sight to *fail*: objects divine
Must needs impair and weary human sense. *Milt. Par. Lost.*

7. To miss; not to produce its effect.

Consider of deformity not as a sign which is deceiveable, but as a cause which seldom *faileth* of the effect. *Bacon's Essays.*

This jest was first of th' other house's making,
And, five times try'd, has never *fail'd* of taking. *Dryden.*

A persuasion that we shall overcome any difficulties, that we meet with in the sciences, seldom *fails* to carry us through them. *Locke.*

He does not remember whether every grain came up or not; but he thinks that very few *failed*. *Mortimer's Husband.*

8. To miss; not to succeed in a design.

I am enjoin'd, by oath, if I *fail*
Of the right casket, never in my life
To woo a maid in way of marriage. *Shak. Merch. of Venice.*

In difficulties of state, the true reason of *failing* proceeds from failings in the administration. *L'Estrange.*

Men who have been busied in the pursuit of the philosopher's stone, have *failed* in their design. *Addison's Guardian.*

9. To be deficient in duty.

Endeavour to fulfill God's commands, to repent as often as you *fail* of it, and to hope for pardon and acceptance of him. *Wake's Preparation for Death.*

To FAIL. *v. a.*

1. To desert; not to continue to assist or supply.

The ship was now left alone, as proud lords be when fortune *fails* them. *Sidney, b.* ii.

So hast thou oft with guile thine honour blent;
But little may such guile thee now avail,
If wonted force and fortune do not much me *fail*. *Fai. Qu.*

There shall be signs in the sun, the moon, and the stars, mens hearts *failing* them for fear. *Lu.* xxi. 26.

Her heart *failed* her, and she would fain have compounded for her life. *L'Estrange.*

He presumes upon his parts that they will not *fail* him at time of need, and so thinks it superfluous labour to make any provision beforehand. *Locke.*

2. Not to assist; to neglect; to omit to help.

Since nature *fails* us in no needful thing,
Why want I means my inward self to see? *Davies.*

3. To omit; not to perform.

The inventive god who never *fails* his part,
Inspires the wit, when once he warms the heart. *Dryden.*

4. To be wanting to.

There shall not *fail* thee a man on the throne. 1 *Kings* ii. 4.

FAIL. *n. s.* [from the verb.]

1. Miscarriage; miss; unsuccessfulness.

2. Omission; non-performance.

Mark and perform it, seest thou? for the *fail*
Of any point in't shall not only be
Death to thyself, but to thy lewd-tongu'd wife. *Shakespeare.*

He will without *fail* drive out from before you the Canaanites. *Jos.* iii. 10.

3. Deficience; want.

4. Death; extinction.

How grounded he his title to the crown
Upon our *fail*? *Shakespeare's Henry* VIII.

FAI'LING. *n. s.* [from *fail.*] Deficiency; imperfection; faults not atrocious; lapse.

Besides what *failings* may be in the matter, even in the expressions there must often be great obscurities. *Digby.*

To *failings* mild, but zealous for desert;
The clearest head, and the sincerest heart. *Pope.*

Even good men have many temptations to subdue, many conflicts with those enemies which war against the soul, and many *failings* and lapses to lament and recover. *Rogers.*

FA'ILURE. *n. s.* [from *fail.*]

1. Deficience; cessation.

There must have been an universal *failure* and want of springs and rivers all the Summer season. *Woodward's N. Hist.*

2. Omission; non-performance; slip.

He that, being subject to an apoplexy, used still to carry his remedy about him; but upon a time shifting his cloaths, and not taking that with him, chanced upon that very day to be surprised with a fit: he owed his death to a mere accident, to a little inadvertency and *failure* of memory. *South's Sermons.*

3. A lapse; a slight fault.

FAIN. *adj.* [ꝼeaȝn, Saxon.]

1. Glad; merry; chearful; fond. It is still retained in Scotland in this sense.

And in her hand she held a mirrour bright,
Wherein her face she often viewed *fain*. *Fairy Queen.*

My lips will be *fain* when I sing unto thee, and so will my soul whom thou hast delivered. *Psalm* lxxi.

2. Forced; obliged; compelled. [This signification seems to have arisen from the mistake of the original signification in some ambiguous expressions; as, *I was* fain *to do this*, would equally

equally suit with the rest of the sentence, whether it was understood to mean *I was compelled*, or *I was glad to do it for fear of worse*. Thus the primary meaning seems to have been early lost.]

Every weight to shroud it did constrain,
And this fair couple eke to shroud themselves were *fain*.
Fairy Queen, *b.* i. *cant.* 1. *stan.* 6.

Whosoever will hear, he shall find God; whosoever will study to know, shall be also *fain* to believe. *Hooker*, *b.* v.

I was *fain* to forswear it; they would else have married me to the rotten medlar. *Shakes. Measure for Measure.*

When Hildebrand had accursed Henry IV. there were none so hardy as to defend their lord; wherefore he was *fain* to humble himself before Hildebrand. *Raleigh's Essays.*

The learned Castalio was *fain* to make trenchers at Basle, to keep himself from starving. *Locke.*

FAIN. *adv.* [from the adjective.] Gladly; very desirously; according to earnest wishes.

Now I would give a thousand furlongs of sea for an acre of barren ground: I would *fain* die a dry death. *Shakespeare.*

Why would'st thou urge me to confess a flame
I long have stifled, and would *fain* conceal. *Addison's Cato.*

Fain wou'd I Raphael's godlike art rehearse,
And show th' immortal labours in my verse. *Addison.*

The plebeians would *fain* have a law enacted to lay all mens rights and privileges upon the same level. *Swift.*

To FAIN. *v. n.* [from the noun.] To wish; to desire fondly.

Fairer than fairest, in his *faining* eye,
Whose sole aspect he counts felicity. *Spenser on Love.*

To FAINT. *v. n.* [*faner*, French.]

1. To decay; to wear or waste away quickly.

Those figures in the gilded clouds, while we gaze upon them, *faint* before the eye, and decay into confusion. *Pope.*

2. To lose the animal functions; to sink motionless and senseless.

Their young children were out of heart, and their women and young men *fainted* for thirst, and fell down in the streets. *Judith* vii. 22.

We are ready to *faint* with fasting. 1 *Mac.* iii. 17.

Upon hearing the honour intended her, she *fainted* away, and fell down as dead. *Guardian*, N°. 167.

3. To grow feeble.

They will stand in their order, and never *faint* in their watches. *Ecclus.* xliii. 10.

The imagination cannot be always alike constant and strong, and if the success follow not speedily it will *faint* and lose strength. *Bacon's Natural History*, N°. 953.

4. To sink into dejection.

Lest they *faint*
At the sad sentence rigorously urg'd,
All terror hide. *Milton's Paradise Lost*, *b.* xi. *l.* 108.

To FAINT. *v. a.* To deject; to depress; to enfeeble. A word little in use.

It *faints* me
To think what follows. *Shakespeare's Henry* VIII.

FAINT. *adj.* [*fane*, French.]

1. Languid; weak; feeble.

In the more intemperate climates the spirits, either exhaled by heat or comprest by cold, are rendered *faint* and sluggish. *Temple.*

2. Not bright; not vivid; not striking.

The blue compared with these is a *faint* and dark colour, and the indigo and violet are much darker and *fainter*. *Newt.*

The length of the image I measured from the *faintest* and utmost red at one end, to the *faintest* and utmost blue at the other end, excepting only a little penumbra. *Newton's Opt.*

From her naked limbs of glowing white,
In folds loose floating, fell the *fainter* lawn. *Thomson.*

3. Not loud; not piercing.

The pump after this being employed from time to time, the sound grew *fainter* and *fainter*. *Boyle.*

4. Feeble of body.

Two neighbouring shepherds, *faint* with thirst, stood at the common boundary of their grounds. *Rambler.*

5. Cowardly; timorous; not vigorous; not ardent.

Faint heart never won fair lady. *Proverb in Camden's Rem.*

Our *faint* Egyptians pray for Antony;
But in their servile hearts they own Octavius. *Dryden.*

6. Dejected; depressed.

Consider him that endureth such contradiction against himself, lest ye be wearied and *faint* in your minds. *Hebr.* xii. 3.

7. Not vigorous; not active.

The defects which hindered the conquest, were the *faint* prosecution of the war, and the looseness of the civil government. *Davies on Ireland.*

FAINTHEA'RTED. *adj.* [*faint* and *heart.*] Cowardly; timorous; dejected; easily depressed.

Fear not, neither be *fainthearted* for the two tails of these smoaking firebrands. *Is.* vii. 4.

They should resolve the next day as victorious conquerors to take the city, or else there as *fainthearted* cowards to end their days. *Knolles's History of the Turks.*

Now the late *fainthearted* rout,
O'erthrown and scatter'd round about,
Chac'd by the horrour of their fear,
From bloody fray of knight and bear,
Took heart again and fac'd about,
As if they meant to stand it out. *Hudibras*, *p.* i. *cant.* 3.

Villain, stand off! base, groveling, worthless wretches,
Mongrils in faction; poor *fainthearted* traitors. *Addis. Cato.*

FAINTHEA'RTEDLY. *adv.* [from *fainthearted.*] Timorously; in a cowardly manner.

FAINTHEA'RTEDNESS. *n. s.* [from *fainthearted.*] Cowardice; timorousness; want of courage.

FA'INTING. *n. s.* [from *faint.*] Deliquium; temporary loss of animal motion.

These *faintings* her physicians suspect to proceed from contusions. *Wiseman's Surgery.*

FA'INTISHNESS. *n. s.* [from *faint.*] Weakness in a slight degree; incipient debility.

A certain degree of heat lengthens and relaxes the fibres; whence proceeds the sensation of *faintishness* and debility in a hot day. *Arbuthnot on Air.*

FA'INTLING. *adj.* [from *faint.*] Timorous; feebleminded. A burlesque or low word.

There's no having patience, thou art such a *faintling* silly creature. *Arbuthnot's History of John Bull.*

FA'INTLY. *adv.* [from *faint.*]

1. Feebly; languidly.

Love's like a torch, which, if secur'd from blasts,
Will *faintly* burn; but then it longer lasts:
Expos'd to storms of jealousy and doubt,
The blaze grows greater, but 'tis sooner out. *Walsh.*

2. Not in bright colours.

Nature affords at least a glimm'ring light;
The lines, tho' touch'd but *faintly*, are drawn right. *Pope.*

3. Without force of representation.

I have told you what I have seen and heard but *faintly*; nothing like the image and horrour of it. *Shakes. King Lear.*

An obscure and confused idea represents the object so *faintly*, that it doth not appear plain to the mind. *Watts.*

4. Without strength of body.

With his loll'd tongue he *faintly* licks his prey,
His warm breath blows her flix up as she lies. *Dryden.*

5. Not vigorously; not actively.

Though still the famish'd English, like pale ghosts,
Faintly besiege us one hour in a month. *Shakes. Henry* VI.

6. Timorously; with dejection; without spirit.

Loth was the ape, though praised, to adventure;
Yet *faintly* 'gan into his work to enter. *Hubberd's Tale.*

He *faintly* now declines the fatal strife;
So much his love was dearer than his life. *Denham.*

FA'INTNESS. *n. s.* [from *faint.*]

1. Languour; feebleness; want of strength.

If the prince of the lights of heaven, which now as a giant doth run his unwearied courses, should through a languishing *faintness* begin to stand. *Hooker*, *b.* i. *s.* 3.

This proceeded not from any violence of pain, but from a general languishing and *faintness* of spirits, which made him think nothing worth the trouble of one careful thought. *Temp.*

2. Inactivity; want of vigour.

This evil proceeds rather of the unsoundness of the counsels laid for the reformation, or of *faintness* in following and effecting the same, than of any such fatal course appointed of God. *Spenser's State of Ireland.*

3. Timorousness; dejection.

The paleness of this flow'r
Bewray'd the *faintness* of my master's heart. *Shak. Hen.* VI.

FA'INTY. *adj.* [from *faint.*] Weak; feeble; languid; debilitated; enfeebled.

When Winter frosts constrain the field with cold,
The *fainty* root can take no steady hold. *Dryd. Virg. Georg.*

The ladies gasp'd, and scarcely could respire;
The breath they drew, no longer air, but fire:
The *fainty* knights were scorch'd, and knew not where
To run for shelter; for no shade was near. *Dryden.*

FAIR. *adj.* [fæger, Saxon; *faur*, Danish.]

1. Beautiful; elegant of feature; handsome. *Fair* seems in the common acceptation to be restrained, when applied to women, to the beauty of the face.

Thou art a *fair* woman to look upon. *Gen.* xii. 11.

My decay'd *fair*,
A sunny look of his will soon repair. *Shak. Comed. of Err.*

2. Not black; not brown; white in the complexion.

I never yet saw man,
But she would spell him backward; if *fair* fac'd,
She'd swear the gentleman should be her sister;
If black, why, nature, drawing of an antick,
Made a foul blot. *Shak. Much Ado about Nothing.*

Let us look upon men in several climates: the Ethiopians are black, flat-nosed, and crisp-haired: the Moors tawny; the Northern people large, and *fair* complexioned. *Hale.*

3. Pleasing to the eye; beautiful in general.

Carry him gently to my *fairest* chamber,
And hang it round with all my wanton pictures. *Shakespeare.*

Thus was he *fair* in his greatness, and in the length of his branches. *Ezek.* xxxi. 7.

4. Clear; pure.

A standard of a damask-rose, with the root on, was set in a chamber where no fire was, upright in an earthen pan, full of *fair* water, half a foot under the water. *Bacon's Nat. Hist.*

Even *fair* water, falling upon white paper or linnen, will immediately alter the colour of them, and make it sadder than that of the unwetted parts. *Boyle on Colours.*

5. Not cloudy; not foul; not tempestuous.

Fair is foul, and foul is *fair*;
Hover through the fog and filthy air. *Shakespeare's Macbeth.*

Fair weather cometh out of the earth. *Job* xxxvii. 22.

About three of the clock in the afternoon the weather was very *fair* and very warm. *Clarendon, b.* viii.

6. Favourable; prosperous: as, a *fair* wind.

In vain you tell your parting lover,
You wish *fair* winds may waft him over. *Prior.*

7. Likely to succeed.

Yourself, renowned prince, stood as *fair*
As any comer I have look'd on yet,
For my affection. *Shakespeare's Merchant of Venice.*

The Caliphs obtained a mighty empire, which was in a *fair* way to have enlarged, until they fell out. *Raleigh's Essays.*

O pity and shame! that they who to live well
Enter'd so *fair*, should turn aside to tread
Paths indirect, or in the midway faint. *Milt. Paradise Lost.*

8. Equal; just.

The king did so much desire a peace, that no man need advise him to it, or could divert him from it, if *fair* and honourable conditions of peace were offered to him. *Clarendon.*

9. Not effected by any insidious or unlawful methods; not foul.

After all these conquests he passed the rest of his age in his own native country, and died a *fair* and natural death. *Temple.*

10. Not practising any fraudulent or insidious arts: as, a *fair* rival, a *fair* disputant.

Virtuous and vicious ev'ry man must be,
Few in th' extreme, but all in the degree;
The rogue and fool by fits is *fair* and wise,
And ev'n the best, by fits, what they despise. *Pope.*

11. Open; direct.

For still, methought, she sung not far away;
At last I found her on a laurel-spray:
Close by my side she sat, and *fair* in sight,
Full in a line, against her opposite. *Dryden.*

12. Gentle; mild; not compulsory.

All the lords came in, and, being by *fair* means wrought thereunto, acknowledged king Henry. *Spenser on Ireland.*

For to reduce her by main force,
Is now in vain; by *fair* means, worse. *Hudibras, p.* iii.

13. Mild; not severe.

Not only do'st degrade them, or remit
To life obscur'd, which were a *fair* dismission;
But throw'st them lower than thou did'st exalt them high.
Milton's Agonistes.

14. Pleasing; civil.

Good sir, why do you start, and seem to fear
Things that do sound so *fair*? *Shakespeare's Macbeth.*

When *fair* words and good counsel will not prevail upon us, we must be frighted into our duty. *L'Estrange.*

15. Equitable; not injurious.

His doom is *fair*,
That dust I am, and shall to dust return. *Milt. Parad. Lost.*

16. Commodious; easy.

Hereby, upon the edge of yonder coppice,
A stand where you may make the *fairest* shoot. *Shakespeare.*

FAIR. *adv.* [from the adjective.]

1. Gently; decently; without violence.

He who *fair* and softly goes steadily forward, in a course that points right, will sooner be at his journey's end than he that runs after every one, though he gallop. *Locke.*

2. Civilly; complaisantly.

Well, you must now speak sir John Falstaff *fair*. *Shakesp.*

One of the company spoke him *fair*, and would have stopt his mouth with a crust. *L'Estrange, Fable* 21.

In this plain fable you th' effect may see
Of negligence, and fond credulity;
And learn besides of flatt'rers to beware,
Then most pernicious when they speak too *fair*. *Dryden.*

His promise Palamon accepts; but pray'd
To keep it better than the first he made:
Thus *fair* they parted 'till the morrow's dawn;
For each had laid his plighted faith to pawn. *Dryden.*

Kalib ascend, my *fair* spoke servant rise,
And sooth my heart with pleasing prophecies. *Dryd. In. Emp.*

This promised *fair* at first. *Addison on Italy.*

3. Happily; successfully.

O, princely Buckingham, I'll kiss thy hand,
In sign of league and amity with thee:
Now *fair* befal thee and thy noble house!
Thy garments are not spotted with our blood. *Shak. R.* III

4. On good terms.

There are other nice, though inferior cases, in which a man must guard, if he intends to keep *fair* with the world, and turn the penny. *Collier of Popularity.*

FAIR. *n. s.*

1. A beauty; elliptically a fair woman.

Of sleep forsaken, to relieve his care,
He sought the conversation of the *fair*. *Dryden's Fables.*

Gentlemen who do not design to marry, yet pay their devoirs to one particular *fair*. *Spectator*, N°. 288.

2. Honesty; just dealing.

I am not much for that present; we'll settle it between ourselves: *fair* and square, Nic, keeps friends together. *Arbuthnot.*

FAIR. *n. s.* [*foire*, French; *feriæ*, or *forum*, Latin.] An annual or stated meeting of buyers and sellers; a time of traffick more frequented than a market. The privilege of holding fairs in England is granted by the king.

With silver, iron, tin and lead they traded in thy *fairs*. *Ezek.* xxvii. 12.

His corn, his cattle, were his only care,
And his supreme delight a country *fair*. *Dryden.*

The ancient Nundinæ, or *fairs* of Rome, were kept every ninth day: afterwards the same privileges were granted to the country markets, which were at first under the power of the consuls. *Arbuthnot on Coins.*

FA'IRING. *n. s.* [from *fair*.] A present given at a fair.

Sweetheart, we shall be rich ere we depart,
If *fairings* come thus plentifully in. *Shakesp. Love's Lab. Lost.*

What pretty things they are, we wonder at!
Like children that esteem every trifle,
And prefer a *fairing* before their fathers:
What difference is between us and them?
That we are dearer fools, cockscombs at
A higher rate. *Ben. Johnson's Discoveries.*

Now he goes on, and sings of fairs and shows;
For still new fairs before his eyes arose:
How pedlars stalls with glitt'ring toys are laid,
The various *fairings* of the country maid. *Gay's Pastorals.*

FA'IRLY. *adv.* [from *fair*.]

1. Beautifully: as, a city *fairly* situated.

2. Commodiously; conveniently; suitably to any purpose or design.

Waiting 'till willing winds their sails supply'd,
Within a trading town they long abide,
Full *fairly* situate on a haven's side. *Dryden.*

3. Honestly; justly; without shift; without fraud.

To the first advantages we may *fairly* lay claim; I wish we had as good a title to the latter. *Atterbury's Sermons.*

It is a church of England man's opinion, that the freedom of a nation consists in an absolute unlimited legislative power, wherein the whole body of the people are *fairly* represented, and in an executive duly limited. *Swift.*

4. Ingenuously; plainly; openly.

The stage how loosely does Astrea tread,
Who *fairly* puts all characters to bed. *Pope's Epist. of Hor.*

5. Candidly; without sinistrous interpretations.

As I interpret *fairly* your design,
So look not with severer eyes on mine. *Dryden's Aurengz.*

6. Without violence to right reason.

Where I have enlarged them, I desire the false criticks would not always think that those thoughts are wholly mine; but that either they are secretly in the poet, or may be *fairly* deduced from him. *Dryden.*

This nutritious juice being a subtile liquor, scarce obtainable by a human body, the serum of the blood is *fairly* substituted in its place. *Arbuthnot on Aliments.*

7. Without blots.

Here is th' indictment of the good lord Hastings,
Which in a set hand *fairly* is engross'd. *Shakes. Rich.* III.

8. Completely; without any deficience.

All this they *fairly* overcame, by reason of the continual presence of their king. *Spenser's State of Ireland.*

Let them say, 'tis grossly done; so it be *fairly* done, no matter. *Shakespeare's Merry Wives of Windsor.*

Our love is not so great, Hortensio, but we may blow our nails together, and fast it *fairly* out. *Shak. Tam. of the Shrew.*

FA'IRNESS. *n. s.* [from *fair*.]

1. Beauty; elegance of form.

That which made her *fairness* much the fairer, was that it was but a fair embassador of a most fair mind, full of wit, and a wit which delighted more to judge itself than to show itself. *Sidney.*

2. Honesty; candour; ingenuity.

There may be somewhat of wisdom, but little of goodness or *fairness* in this conduct. *Atterbury's Sermons, Preface.*

FA'IRSPOKEN. *adj.* [from *fair* and *speak*.] Bland and civil in language and address.

Arius, a priest in the church of Alexandria, a subtlewitted

 and

and a marvellous *fairſpoken* man, but diſcontented that we ſhould be placed before him in honour, whoſe ſuperior he thought himſelf in deſert, becauſe through envy and ſtomach prone unto contradiction. *Hooker, b.* v. *ſ.* 42.

FAI'RY. *n. ſ.* [ꝼeɲhꝺ, Saxon; *fee*, French.]

Ab ἔρα, terra, fit & ϝέρα Macedonum dialecto; unde ἔνεροι ἔνϝεροι, & Romanis inferi, qui Scoto-Saxonibus dicuntur *feries*, noſtratiq; vulgo corruptius *fairies*, καταχόνιοι δαίμονες, ſive dii manes. *Baxter's Gloſſary.*

1. A kind of fabled beings ſuppoſed to appear in a diminutive human form, and to dance in the meadows, and reward cleanlineſs in houſes; an elf; a fay.

Nan Page, my daughter, and my little ſon,
And three or four more of their growth, we'll dreſs
Like urchins, ouphes, and *fairies*, green and white,
With rounds of waxen tapers on their heads,
And rattles in their hands. *Shakeſ. Merry Wives of Windſor.*

Then let them all encircle him about,
And *fairy* like too pinch the unclean knight;
And aſk him, why, that hour of *fairy* revel,
In their ſo ſacred paths he dares to tread
In ſhape prophane. *Shakeſp. Merry Wives of Windſor.*

By the idea any one has of *fairies*, or centaurs, he cannot know that things, anſwering thoſe ideas, exiſt. *Locke.*

Fays, *fairies*, genii, elves, and demons hear. *Pope.*

2. Enchantreſs. *Warburton.*

To this great *fairy* I'll commend thy acts,
Make her thanks bleſs thee. *Shakeſ. Anth. and Cleopatra.*

FA'IRY. *adj.*

1. Given by fairies.

Be ſecret and diſcrete; theſe *fairy* favours
Are loſt when not conceal'd. *Dryden's Spaniſh Fryar.*

Such borrowed wealth, like *fairy* money, though it were gold in the hand from which he received it, will be but leaves and duſt when it comes to uſe. *Locke.*

2. Belonging to fairies.

This is the *fairy* land: oh, ſpight of ſpights,
We talk with goblings, owls, and elviſh ſprights. *Shakeſp.*

FA'IRYSTONE. *n. ſ.* [*fairy* and *ſtone.*] It is found in gravel-pits, being of an hemiſpherical figure; hath five double lines ariſing from the centre of its baſis, which meet in the pole. *Brown's Vulgar Errours.*

FAITH. *n. ſ.* [*foi*, French; *fede*, Italian; *fides*, Latin.]

1. Belief of the revealed truths of religion.

The name of *faith* being properly and ſtrictly taken, it muſt needs have reference unto ſome uttered word, as the object of belief. *Hooker, b.* ii. *ſ.* 4.

Faith, if it have not works, is dead. *Jam.* ii. 17.

Viſion in the next life is the perfecting of that *faith* in this life, or that *faith* here is turned into viſion there, as hope into enjoying. *Hammond's Pract. Catech.*

Then *faith* ſhall fail, and holy hope ſhall die;
One loſt in certainty, and one in joy. *Prior.*

2. The ſyſtem of revealed truths held by the Chriſtian church; the *credenda*.

Felix heard Paul concerning the *faith*. *Acts* xxiv. 24.

This is the catholick *faith*. *Common Prayer.*

3. Truſt in God.

Faith is an entire dependence upon the truth, the power, the juſtice, and the mercy of God; which dependence will certainly incline us to obey him in all things. *Swift.*

4. Tenet held.

Which to believe of her,
Muſt be a *faith*, that reaſon, without miracle,
Should never plant in me. *Shakeſpeare's King Lear.*

5. Truſt in the honeſty or veracity of another.

6. Fidelity; unſhaken adherence.

Her failing, while her *faith* to me remains,
I ſhould conceal, and not expoſe to blame
By my complaint. *Milton's Paradiſe Loſt, b.* x. *l.* 129.

7. Honour; ſocial confidence.

For you alone
I broke my *faith* with injur'd Palamon. *Dryd. Knight's Tale.*

8. Sincerity; honeſty; veracity.

Sir, in good *faith*, in meer verity. *Shakeſ. King Lear.*

They are a very froward generation, children in whom is no *faith*. *Deutr.* xxxii. 20.

9. Promiſe given.

I have been forſworn,
In breaking *faith* with Julia whom I lov'd. *Shakeſpeare.*

FAI'THBREACH. *n. ſ.* [*faith* and *breach.*] Breach of fidelity; diſloyalty; perfidy.

Now minutely revolts upbraid his *faithbreach*;
Thoſe he commands, move only in command,
Nothing in love. *Shakeſpeare's Macbeth.*

FAI'THED. *adj.* [from *faith.*] Honeſt; ſincere. A word not in uſe.

Thou baſtard! would the repoſal
Of any truſt, virtue, or worth in thee,
Make thy words *faith'd?* *Shakeſpeare's King Lear.*

FA'ITHFUL. *adj.* [*faith* and *full.*]

1. Firm in adherence to the truth of religion.

To the ſaints which are at Epheſus, and the *faithful* in Chriſt Jeſus. *Eph.* i. 1.

Be thou *faithful* unto death, and I will give thee a crown of life. *Rev.* ii. 10.

2. Of true fidelity; loyal; true to the allegiance or duty profeſſed.

I have this day receiv'd a traitor's judgment,
And by that name muſt die; yet, heav'n bear witneſs,
And, if I have a conſcience, let it ſink me,
Ev'n as the axe falls, if I be not *faithful*. *Shak. Hen.* VIII.

So ſpake the ſeraph Abdiel, *faithful* found;
Among the faithleſs, *faithful* only he. *Milton's Parad. Loſt.*

3. Honeſt; upright; without fraud.

My ſervant Moſes is *faithful* in all mine houſe. *Numb.* xii.

4. Obſervant of compact or promiſe; true to his contract; ſincere; veracious.

Well I know him;
Of eaſy temper, naturally good,
And *faithful* to his word. *Dryden's Don Sebaſtian.*

FAI'THFULLY. *adv.* [from *faithful.*]

1. With firm belief in religion.

2. With full confidence in God.

3. With ſtrict adherence to duty and allegiance.

His noble grace would have ſome pity
Upon my wretched women, that ſo long
Have follow'd both my fortunes *faithfully*. *Shakeſ. H.* VIII.

4. Without failure of performance; honeſtly; exactly.

If on my wounded breaſt thou drop a tear,
Think for whoſe ſake my breaſt that wound did bear;
And *faithfully* my laſt deſires fulfil,
As I perform my cruel father's will. *Dryden's Ovid.*

5. Sincerely; with ſtrong promiſes.

For his own part, he did *faithfully* promiſe to be ſtill in the king's power. *Bacon's H.* VII.

6. Honeſtly; without fraud, trick, or ambiguity.

They ſuppoſe the nature of things to be truly and *faithfully* ſignified by their names, and thereupon believe as they hear, and practiſe as they believe. *South's Sermons.*

7. In *Shakeſpeare*, according to Mr. *Warburton*, fervently, perhaps rather confidently; ſteadily.

If his occaſions were not virtuous,
I ſhould not urge it half ſo *faithfully*. *Shakeſp. Timon.*

FA'ITHFULNESS. *n. ſ.* [from *faithful.*]

1. Honeſty; veracity.

For there is no *faithfulneſs* in your mouth; your inward part is very wickedneſs. *Pſ.* lix.

The band that knits together and ſupports all compacts, is truth and *faithfulneſs*. *South's Sermons.*

2. Adherence to duty; loyalty.

The ſame zeal and *faithfulneſs* continues in your blood, which animated one of your noble anceſtors to ſacrifice his life in the quarrel of his ſovereign. *Dryden.*

FA'ITHLESS. *adj.* [from *faith.*]

1. Without belief in the revealed truths of religion; unconverted.

Whatſoever our hearts be to God and to his truth, believe we, or be we as yet *faithleſs*, for our converſion or confirmation, the force of natural reaſon is great. *Hooker, b.* iii. *ſ.* 8.

Never dare misfortune croſs her foot,
Unleſs ſhe doth it under this excuſe,
That ſhe is iſſue to a *faithleſs* Jew. *Shakeſ. Merch. of Venice.*

2. Perfidious; diſloyal; not true to duty, profeſſion, promiſe, or allegiance.

Both
Fell by our ſervants, by thoſe men we lov'd moſt;
A moſt unnatural and *faithleſs* ſervice. *Shakeſp. Hen.* VIII.

So ſpake the ſeraph Abdiel, faithful found;
Among the *faithleſs*, faithful only he. *Milton's Parad. Loſt.*

FA'ITHLESSNESS. *n. ſ.* [from *faithleſs.*]

1. Treachery; perfidy.

2. Unbelief as to revealed religion.

FA'ITOUR. *n. ſ.* [*faitard*, French.] A ſcoundrel; a raſcal; a mean fellow; a poltron. An old word now obſolete.

To Philemon, falſe *faitour*, Philemon,
I caſt to pay, that I ſo dearly bought. *Fairy Queen, b.* ii.

Into new woes unweeting I was caſt,
By this falſe *faitour*. *Fairy Queen, b.* i. *cant.* 4. *ſtan.* 47.

FAKE. *n. ſ.* [Among ſeamen.] A coil of rope. *Harris.*

FALCA'DE. *n. ſ.* [from *falx, falcis*, Latin.]

A horſe is ſaid to make *falcades*, when he throws himſelf upon his haunches two or three times, as in very quick curvets, which is done in forming a ſtop, and half a ſtop; therefore a *falcade* is that action of the haunches and of the legs, which bend very low, when you make a ſtop and half a ſtop. *Farrier's Dict.*

FA'LCATED. *adj.* [*falcatus*, Latin.] Hooked; bent like a reaping hook or ſcythe.

The enlightened part of the moon appears in the form of a ſickle, or reaping hook, which is while ſhe is moving from the conjunction to the oppoſition, or from the new moon to the full; but from full to a new again, the enlightened part appears gibbous, and the dark *falcated*. *Harris.*

FALCA'TION. *n. ſ.* [*falcis*, Latin.] Crookedneſs; form like that of a reaper's hook.

The locuſts have antennæ, or long horns before, with a long *falcation* or forcipated tail behind. *Brown's Vulgar Err.*

FA'LCHION. *n. ſ.* [*enſis falcatus*; in French *fauchon*.] A ſhort crooked ſword; a cymeter.

I've ſeen the day, with my good biting *falchion*,
I would have made them ſkip: I am old now. *Sh. K. Lear.*

Old *falchions* are new temper'd in the fires;
The ſounding trumpet ev'ry ſoul inſpires. *Dryden's Æn.*

What ſighs and tears
Hath Eugene cauſed! how many widows curſe
His cleaving *falchion!* *Phillips.*

FA'LCON. *n. ſ.* [*faulcon*, French; *falconne*, Italian; *falco*, Latin. *Credo, a roſtro falcato* ſive *adunco*, from the falcated or crooked bill.]

1. A hawk trained for ſport.

As Venus' bird, the white, ſwift, lovely dove,
O! happy dove that art compar'd to her,
Doth on her wings her utmoſt ſwiftneſs prove,
Finding the gripe of *falcon* fierce not far. *Sidney.*

Air ſtops not the high ſoaring of my noble generous *falcon*. *Walton's Angler.*

Apulian farms, for the rich ſoil admir'd,
And thy large fields where *falcons* may be tir'd. *Dryd. Juv.*

Say, will the *falcon*, ſtooping from above,
Smit with her varying plumage, ſpare the dove? *Pope.*

2. A ſort of cannon, whoſe diameter at the bore is five inches and a quarter, weight ſeven hundred and fifty pounds, length ſeven foot, load two pounds and a quarter, ſhot two inches and a half diameter, and two pounds and a half weight. *Harris.*

FA'LCONER. *n. ſ.* [*faulconnier*, French.] One who breeds and trains hawks; one who follows the ſport of fowling with hawks.

Hiſt! Romeo, hiſt! O for a *falc'ner's* voice,
To lure this taſſel gentle back again. *Shak. Rom. and Jul.*

The univerſal remedy was ſwallowing of pebbleſtones, in imitation of *falconers* curing hawks. *Temple.*

I have learnt of a *falconer* never to feed up a hawk, when I would have him fly. *Dryden's Don Sebaſtian.*

A *falc'ner* Henry is, when Emma hawks;
With her of tarſels and of lures he talks. *Prior.*

FA'LCONET. *n. ſ.* [*falconette*, French.] A ſort of ordnance, whoſe diameter at the bore is four inches and a quarter, weight four hundred pounds, length ſix foot, load one pound and a quarter, ſhot ſomething more than two inches diameter, and one pound and a quarter weight. *Harris.*

Mahomet ſent janizaries and nimble footmen, with certain *falconets* and other ſmall pieces, to take the ſtreights. *Knolles.*

FA'LDAGE. *n. ſ.* [*faldagium*, barbarous Latin.] A privilege which anciently ſeveral lords reſerved to themſelves of ſetting up folds for ſheep, in any fields within their manors, the better to manure them; and this not only with their own, but their tenants ſheep, which they called *ſecta faldæ*. This *faldage* in ſome places they call a foldcourſe, or freefold; and in ſome old charters 'tis called foldſoca, that is, *libertas foldæ*, or *faldagii*. *Harris.*

FA'LDFEE. *n. ſ.* [*fald* and *fee*.] A compoſition paid anciently by tenants for the privilege of faldage. *Dict.*

FA'LDING. *n. ſ.* A kind of coarſe cloth. *Dict.*

FA'LDSTOOL. *n. ſ.* [*fald* or *fold* and *ſtool*.] A kind of ſtool placed at the ſouth-ſide of the altar, at which the kings of England kneel at their coronation.

To FALL. *v. n.* pret. *I fell*; compound pret. *I have fallen*, or *faln*. [ꝼeallan, Saxon; *fallen*, German.]

1. To drop from a higher place.

Thou ſhalt make a battlement for thy roof, that thou bring not blood upon thine houſe, if any man *fall* from thence. *Deut.*

I was walking in the open fields 'till the night inſenſibly *fell* upon me. *Spectator*, N°. 565.

I ſhall *fall*
Like a bright exhalation in the evening,
And no man ſee me more. *Shakeſpeare's Henry* VIII.

2. To drop from an erect to a prone poſture.

Saul *fell* all along on the earth. 1 *Sa.* xxviii. 20.

Where he bowed, there he *fell* down dead. *Judg.* v. 27.

That is a ſtep,
On which I muſt *fall* down, or elſe o'erleap;
For in my way it lies. *Shakeſpeare's Macbeth.*

3. To drop; to be held no longer.

His chains *fell* off from his hands. *Acts* xii. 7.

4. To move down any deſcent.

All liquid bodies are diffuſive; for their parts being in motion, have no connexion one with another, but glide and *fall* off any way, as gravity and the air preſſeth them. *Burnet.*

5. To drop ripe from the tree.

As the leaf *falleth* off from the vine, and as a *falling* fig from the fig-tree. *Iſ.* xxxiv. 4.

6. To paſs at the outlet: as a river.

Cæſar therefore gave orders to build his gallies on the Loir, and the rivers that *fall* into it. *Arbuthnot on Coins.*

7. To be determined to ſome particular direction.

Birds and fowls that reſt one foot to eaſe the other, naturally lay their heads under their wings, that the center of gravity may *fall* upon the foot they ſtand on. *Cheyne's Phil. Princ.*

8. To apoſtatiſe; to depart from faith or goodneſs.

Labour to enter into that reſt, leſt any man *fall* after the ſame example of unbelief. *Heb.* iv. 11.

They brought ſcandal
To Iſrael, diffidence of God, and doubt
In feeble hearts, propenſe enough before
To waver or *fall* off, and join with idols. *Milton's Agoniſt.*

Whether ſome ſpirit on holy purpoſe bent,
Or ſome *fall'n* angel from below broke looſe,
Who comes with envious eyes, and curſt intent,
To view this world and its created Lord. *Dryden.*

9. To die by violence.

God and good angels fight on Richmond's ſide,
And Richard *fall* in height of all his pride. *Shak. Rich.* III.

If one ſhould be a prey, how much the better
To *fall* before the lion than the wolf! *Shakeſpeare.*

What other oath,
Than honeſty to honeſty engag'd?
That this ſhall be, or we will *fall* for it. *Shak. Jul. Cæſar.*

A thouſand ſhall *fall* at thy ſide, and ten thouſand at thy right hand; but it ſhall not come nigh thee. *Pſ.* xci. 7.

Ye ſhall chaſe your enemies, and they ſhall *fall* before you by the ſword. *Lev.* xxvi. 7.

They not obeying,
Incurr'd, what could they leſs? the penalty;
And manifold in ſin, deſerv'd to *fall*. *Milton's Parad. Loſt.*

Almon *falls*, old Tyrrheus' eldeſt care,
Pierc'd with an arrow from the diſtant war. *Dryden's Æn.*

10. To come to a ſudden end.

The greatneſs of theſe Iriſh lords ſuddenly *fell* and vaniſhed, when their oppreſſions and extortions were taken away. *Davies.*

He firſt the fate of Cæſar did foretell,
And pity'd Rome, when Rome in Cæſar *fell*;
In iron clouds conceal'd the publick light,
And impious mortals fear'd eternal night. *Dryd. Virg. Geor.*

11. To be degraded from an high ſtation; to ſink into meanneſs or diſgrace; to be plunged into ſudden miſery.

They ſhall *fall* among them that *fall*; at the time that I viſit them they ſhall be caſt down. *Jer.* vi. 15.

What can be their buſineſs
With a poor weak woman *fall'n* from favour! *Shak. H.* VIII.

12. To decline from power or empire; to be overthrown.

What men could do,
Is done already: heaven and earth will witneſs,
If Rome muſt *fall*, that we are innocent. *Addiſon's Cato.*

13. To enter into any ſtate worſe than the former.

He *fell* at difference with Ludovico Sfortia, who carried the keys which brought him in, and ſhut him out. *Bacon's H.* VII.

Some of the ableſt painters taking precepts in too literal a ſenſe, have *fallen* thereby into great inconveniencies. *Dryden's Dufreſnoy.*

14. To come into any ſtate of weakneſs, terrour, or miſery.

Theſe, by obtruding the beginning of a change for the entire work of new life, will *fall* under the former guilt. *Hamm.*

One would wonder how ſo many learned men could *fall* into ſo great an abſurdity, as to believe this river could preſerve itſelf unmixt with the lake. *Addiſon on Italy.*

The beſt men generally *fall* under the ſevereſt preſſures. *Wake's Preparation for Death.*

15. To decreaſe; to be diminiſhed.

From the pound weight, as Pliny tells us, the as *fell* to two ounces in the firſt Punick war: when Hannibal invaded Italy, to one ounce; then, by the Papirian law, to half an ounce. *Arbuthnot on Coins.*

16. To ebb; to grow ſhallow.

17. To decreaſe in value; to bear leſs price.

When the price of corn *falleth*, men generally break no more ground than will ſupply their own turn. *Carew.*

But now her price is *fall'n*. *Shakeſpeare's King Lear.*

His rents will *fall*, and his income every day leſſen, 'till induſtry and frugality, joined to a well ordered trade, ſhall reſtore to the kingdom the riches it had formerly. *Locke.*

18. To ſink; not to amount to the full.

The greatneſs of an eſtate, in bulk and territory, doth *fall* under meaſure; and the greatneſs of finances and revenue doth *fall* under computation. *Bacon, Eſſay* 30.

19. To be rejected; to become null.

This book muſt ſtand or *fall* with thee; not by any opinion I have of it, but thy own. *Locke.*

20. To decline from violence to calmneſs, from intenſeneſs to remiſſion.

He was ſtirr'd,
And ſomething ſpoke in choler, ill and haſty;
But he *fell* to himſelf again, and ſweetly
In all the reſt ſhew'd a moſt noble patience. *Shakeſ. H.* VIII.

At length her fury *fell*, her foaming ceas'd;
And ebbing in her ſoul, the god decreas'd. *Dryden's Æn.*

21. To enter into any new ſtate of the body or mind.

In sweet musick is such art,
Killing care and grief of heart,
Fall asleep, or hearing die. *Shakesf. Henry* VIII.

Solyman, chafed with the loss of his gallies and best soldiers, and with the double injury done unto him by the Venetians, *fell* into such a rage that he cursed Barbarossa. *Knolles.*

When about twenty, upon the falseness of a lover, she *fell* distracted. *Temple.*

A spark like thee, of the man-killing trade,
Fell sick; and thus to his physician said:
Methinks I am not right in ev'ry part,
I feel a kind of trembling at my heart;
My pulse unequal, and my breath is strong;
Besides a filthy furr upon my tongue. *Dryden's Pers. Sat.*

And have you known none in health who have pitied you; and behold, they are gone before you, even since you *fell* into this distemper? *Wake's Preparation for Death.*

He died calmly, and with all the easiness of a man *falling* asleep. *Atterbury.*

Portius himself oft *falls* in tears before me,
As if he mourn'd his rival's ill success. *Addison's Cato.*

For as his own bright image he survey'd,
He *fell* in love with the fantastick shade. *Addis. Ovid. Met.*

I *fell* in love with the character of Pomponius Atticus: I longed to imitate him. *Blount to Pope.*

22. To sink into an air of discontent or dejection.

If thou persuade thyself that they shall not be taken, let not thy countenance *fall*: I have spoken it, and none of my words shall be in vain. *Judith* vi. 9.

If you have any other request to make, hide it not; for ye shall find we will not make your countenance to *fall* by the answer ye shall receive. *Bacon's New Atlantis.*

Syphax, I joy to meet thee thus alone;
I have observ'd of late thy looks are *fallen*,
O'ercast with gloomy cares and discontent. *Addison's Cato.*

23. To sink below something in comparison.

Fame of thy beauty and thy youth,
Among the rest, me hither brought:
Finding this fame *fall* short of truth,
Made me stay longer than I thought. *Waller.*

24. To happen; to befall.

For such things as do *fall* scarce once in many ages, it did suffice to take such order as was requisite when they *fell*. *Hook.*

Oft it *falls* out, that while one thinks too much of his doing, he leaves to do the effect of this thinking. *Sidney, b.* i.

A long advertent and deliberate connexing of consequents, which *falls* not in the common road of ordinary men. *Hale.*

Since this fortune *falls* to you,
Be content and seek no new. *Shakesf. Merchant of Venice.*

If the worst *fall* that ever *fell*, I hope, I shall make shift to go without him. *Shakespeare's Merchant of Venice.*

O, how feeble is man's power,
That if good fortune *fall*,
Cannot add another hour,
Nor a lost hour recall! *Donne.*

Since both cannot possess what both pursue,
I'm griev'd, my friend, the chance should *fall* on you. *Dry.*

I had more leisure, and disposition, than have since *fallen* to my share. *Swift.*

25. To come by chance; to light on.

I have two boys
Seek Percy and thyself about the field;
But seeing thou *fall'st* on me so luckily,
I will assay thee. *Shakespeare's Henry* IV. *p.* i.

The Romans *fell* upon this model by chance, but the Spartans by thought and design. *Swift.*

26. To come in a stated method.

The odd hours at the end of the solar year, are not indeed fully six, but are deficient 10′ 44″; which deficiency, in 134 years, collected, amounts to a whole day: and hence may be seen the reason why the vernal equinox, which at the time of the Nicene council *fell* upon the 21st of March, *falls* now about ten days sooner. *Holder on Time.*

It does not *fall* within my subject to lay down the rules of odes. *Felton on the Classicks.*

27. To come unexpectedly.

I am *fallen* upon the mention of mercuries. *Boyle.*

It happened this evening that we *fell* into a very pleasing walk, at a distance from his house. *Addison's Spectator.*

28. To begin any thing with ardour and vehemence.

The king understanding of their adventure, suddenly *falls* to take pride in making much of them with infinite praises. *Sidney, b.* ii.

Each of us *fell* in praise of our country mistresses. *Shakesp.*

And the mixt multitude *fell* a lusting. *Num.* ii. 4.

It is better to sound a person afar off, than to *fall* upon the point at first; except you mean to surprize him by some short question. *Bacon, Essay* 48.

When a horse is hungry, and comes to a good pasture, he *falls* to his food immediately. *Hale's Origin of Mankind.*

They *fell* to blows, insomuch that the Argonauts slew the most part of the Deliones, with their king Cyzicus. *L'Estr.*

29. To handle or treat directly.

We must immediately *fall* into our subject, and treat every part of it in a lively manner. *Addison's Spectator,* N°. 124.

30. To come vindictively: as a punishment.

There *fell* wrath for it against Israel. 2 *Chron.* xv. 9.

31. To come by any mischance to any new possessor.

The stout bishop could not well brook that his province should *fall* into their hands. *Knolles's History of the Turks.*

32. To drop or pass by carelesness or imprudence.

Ulysses let no partial favours *fall*,
The people's parent, he protected all. *Pope's Odyssey, b.* iv.

Some expressions *fell* from him, not very favourable to the people of Ireland. *Swift.*

33. To come forcibly and irresistibly.

Fear *fell* on them all. *Acts* xix. 17.

A kind refreshing sleep is *fallen* upon him:
I saw him stretcht at ease, his fancy lost
In pleasing dreams. *Addison's Cato.*

34. To become the property of any one by lot, chance, inheritance, or otherwise.

All the lands, which will *fall* to her majesty thereabouts, are large enough to contain them. *Spenser on Ireland.*

If you do chance to hear of that blind traitor,
Preferment *falls* on him that cuts him off. *Shakesf. K. Lear.*

Then 'tis most like
The sovereignty will *fall* upon Macbeth. *Shakesf. Macbeth.*

After the flood, arts to Chaldea *fell*;
The father of the faithful there did dwell,
Who both their parent and instructor was. *Denham.*

You shall see a great estate *fall* to you, which you would have lost the relish of, had you known yourself born to it. *Addison's Spectator,* N°. 123.

If to her share some female errours *fall*,
Look on her face, and you'll forget them all. *Pope.*

In their spiritual and temporal courts the labour *falls* to their vicars-general, secretaries, proctors, apparitors and seneschals. *Swift's Considerations on two Bills.*

35. To languish; to grow faint.

Their hopes or fears for the common cause rose or *fell* with your lordship's interest. *Addison's Remarks on Italy.*

36. To be born; to be yeaned.

Lambs must have care taken of them at their first *falling*, else, while they are weak, the crows and magpies will be apt to pick out their eyes. *Mortimer's Husbandry.*

37. *To* Fall *away.* To grow lean.

Watery vegetables are proper, and fish rather than flesh: in a Lent diet people commonly *fall away*. *Arbuthnot on Diet.*

38. *To* Fall *away.* To revolt; to change allegiance.

The fugitives *fell away* to the king of Babylon. 2 *Kings* xxv.

39. *To* Fall *away.* To apostatise; to sink into wickedness.

These for a while believe, and in time of temptation *fall away.* *Luke* viii. 13.

Say not thou it is through the Lord that I *fell away*; for thou oughtest not to do the things that he hateth. *Ecclus.* xv.

The old giants *fell away* in the strength of their foolishness. *Ecclus.* xvi.

40. *To* Fall *away.* To perish; to be lost.

Still propagate; for still they *fall away*;
'Tis prudence to prevent th' entire decay. *Dryd. Virg. Geo.*

How can it enter into the thoughts of man, that the soul, which is capable of such immense perfections, and of receiving new improvement to all eternity, shall *fall away* into nothing, almost as soon as it is created? *Addison's Spectator,* N°. 111.

41. *To* Fall *away.* To decline gradually; to fade; to languish.

In a curious brede of needlework one colour *falls away* by such just degrees, and another rises so insensibly, that we see the variety, without being able to distinguish the total vanishing of the one from the first appearance of the other. *Addison.*

42. *To* Fall *back.* To fail of a promise or purpose.

We have often *fallen back* from our resolutions. *Taylor.*

43. *To* Fall *back.* To recede; to give away.

44. *To* Fall *down.* [*down* is sometimes added to *fall*, though it adds little to the signification.] To prostrate himself in adoration.

All kings shall *fall down* before him; all nations shall serve him. *Ps.* lxxii. 11.

Shall I *fall down* to the stock of a tree? *Is.* xliv. 19.

45. *To* Fall *down.* To sink; not to stand.

As she was speaking, she *fell down* for faintness. *Esth.* xv.

Down fell the beauteous youth; the yawning wound
Gush'd out a purple stream, and stain'd the ground. *Dryden.*

46. *To* Fall *down.* To bend as a suppliant.

They shall *fall down* unto thee; they shall make supplication unto thee. *Is.* xlv. 14.

47. *To* Fall *from.* To revolt; to depart from adherence.

Clarence
Is very likely now to *fall from* him. *Shakespeare's Henry* VI.

The emperor being much solicited by the Scots not to be a help to ruin their kingdom, *fell* by degrees *from* the king of England. *Hayward.*

48. *To* Fall *in*. To concur; to coincide.

Objections *fall in* here, and are the cleareſt and moſt convincing arguments of the truth. *Woodward's Nat. Hiſtory.*

His reaſonings in this chapter ſeem to *fall in* with each other; yet, upon a cloſer examination, we ſhall find them propoſed with great variety and diſtinction. *Atterbury.*

Any ſingle paper that *falls in* with the popular taſte, and pleaſes more than ordinary, brings one in a great return of letters. *Addiſon's Spectator*, N°. 482.

When the war was begun, there ſoon *fell in* other incidents at home, which made the continuance of it neceſſary. *Swift.*

49. To comply; to yield to.

Our fine young ladies readily *fall in* with the direction of the graver ſort. *Spectator*, N°. 536.

It is a double misfortune to a nation, which is thus given to change, when they have a ſovereign that is prone to *fall in* with all the turns and veerings of the people. *Addiſon's Freeh.*

You will find it difficult to perſuade learned men to *fall in* with your projects. *Addiſon on ancient Medals.*

That prince applied himſelf firſt to the church of England; and, upon their refuſal to *fall in* with his meaſures, made the like advances to the diſſenters. *Swift.*

50. *To* Fall *off*. To ſeparate; to be broken.

Love cools, friendſhip *falls off*, brothers divide; in cities, mutinies; in countries, diſcord. *Shakeſ. King Lear.*

51. *To* Fall *off*. To periſh; to die away.

Languages need recruits to ſupply the place of thoſe words that are continually *falling off* through diſuſe. *Felton.*

52. *To* Fall *off*. To apoſtatiſe; to revolt; to forſake.

Oh, Hamlet, what a *falling off* was there! *Shak. Haml.*

Revolted Mortimer?
—He never did *fall off*, my ſovereign liege,
But by the chance of war. *Shakeſpeare's Henry* IV. *p.* i.

They, accuſtomed to afford at other times either ſilence or ſhort aſſent to what he did purpoſe, did then *fall off* and forſake him. *Hayward.*

What cauſe
Mov'd our grand parents, in that happy ſtate,
Favour'd of heav'n ſo highly, to *fall off*
From their Creator, and tranſgreſs his will? *Milt. P. Loſt.*

As for thoſe captive tribes, themſelves
Who wrought their own captivity, *fell off*
From God to worſhip calves. *Milton's Paradiſe Loſt.*

Were I always grave, one half of my readers would *fall off* from me. *Addiſon's Spectator*, N°. 179.

53. *To* Fall *on*. To begin eagerly to do any thing.

Some coarſe cold ſallad is before thee ſet;
Bread with the bran perhaps, and broken meat;
Fall on, and try thy appetite to eat. *Dryden's Perſ. Sat.*

54. *To* Fall *on*. To make an aſſault; to begin the attack.

They *fell on*, I made good my place: at length they came to th' broomſtaff with me; I defied 'em ſtill. *Shak. Hen.* VIII.

Fall on, *fall on*, and hear him not;
But ſpare his perſon for his father's ſake. *Dryd. Span. Fryar.*

Draw all; and when I give the word *fall on*. *Oedipus.*

He pretends, amongſt the reſt, to quarrel with me, to have *fallen* foul *on* prieſthood. *Dryden's Fables, Pref.*

55. *To* Fall *over*. To revolt; to deſert from one ſide to the other.

And do'ſt thou now *fall over* to my foes?
Thou wear a lion's hide! doff it, for ſhame,
And hang a calve's ſkin on thoſe recreant limbs. *Sh. K. John.*

56. *To* Fall *out*. To quarrel; to jar; to grow contentious.

Little needed thoſe proofs to one who would have *fallen out* with herſelf, rather than make any conjectures to Zelmane's ſpeeches. *Sidney, b.* ii.

How *fell* you *out*, ſay that?
—No contraries hold more antipathy,
Than I and ſuch a knave. *Shakeſpeare's King Lear.*

Meeting her of late behind the wood,
Seeking ſweet favours for this hateful fool,
I did upbraid her, and *fall out* with her. *Shakeſpeare.*

The cedar, by the inſtigation of the loyaliſts, *fell out* with the homebians, who had elected him to be their king. *Howel.*

A ſoul exaſperated in ills, *falls out*
With every thing, its friend, itſelf. *Addiſon's Cato.*

It has been my misfortune to live among quarrelſome neighbours: there is but one thing can make us *fall out*, and that is the inheritance of lord Strut's eſtate. *Arbuthnot's John Bull.*

57. *To* Fall *out*. To happen; to befall.

Who think you is my Dorus *fallen out* to be? *Sidney.*

Now, for the moſt part, it ſo *falleth out*, touching things which generally are received, that although in themſelves they be moſt certain, yet, becauſe men preſume them granted of all, we are hardlieſt able to bring proof of their certainty. *Hooker.*

It ſo *fell out*, that certain players
We o'er-rode on the way; of thoſe we told him. *Shakeſp.*

Yet ſo it may *fall out*, becauſe their end
Is hate, not help to me. *Milton's Agoniſtes.*

There *fell out* a bloody quarrel betwixt the frogs and the mice. *L'Eſtrange, Fable* 41.

If it ſo *fall out* that thou art miſerable for ever, thou haſt no reaſon to be ſurpriſed, as if ſome unexpected thing had happened. *Tillotſon, Sermon* 5.

58. *To* Fall *to*. To begin eagerly to eat.

The men were faſhion'd in a larger mould,
The women fit for labour, big and bold;
Gigantick hinds, as ſoon as work was done,
To their huge pots of boiling pulſe would run;
Fall to, with eager joy, on homely food. *Dryden's Juven.*

59. *To* Fall *to*. To apply himſelf to.

They would needs *fall to* the practice of thoſe virtues which they before learned. *Sidney, b.* ii.

I know thee not, old man; *fall to* thy prayers:
How ill white hairs become a fool and jeſter! *Shak. H.* IV.

Having been brought up an idle horſeboy, he will never after *fall to* labour; but is only made fit for the halter. *Spenſer.*

They *fell to* raiſing money under pretence of the relief of Ireland. *Clarendon.*

My lady *falls to* play: ſo bad her chance,
He muſt repair it. *Pope's Epiſt.*

60. *To* Fall *under*. To be ſubject to; to become the object of.

We know the effects of heat will be ſuch as will ſcarce *fall under* the conceit of man, if the force of it be altogether kept in. *Bacon's Natural Hiſtory*, N°. 99.

Thoſe things which are wholly in the choice of another, *fall under* our deliberation. *Taylor's Rule of living holy.*

The idea of the painter and the ſculptor is undoubtedly that perfect and excellent example of the mind, by imitation of which imagined form all things are repreſented, which *fall under* human ſight. *Dryden's Dufreſnoy.*

61. *To* Fall *under*. To be ranged with; to be reckoned with.

No rules that relate to paſtoral can affect the Georgicks, which *fall under* that claſs of poetry which conſiſts in giving plain inſtructions to the reader. *Addiſon on the Georgicks.*

62. *To* Fall *upon*. To attack; to invade; to aſſault.

Auria *falling upon* theſe gallies, had with them a cruel and deadly fight. *Knolles.*

An infection in a town firſt *falls upon* children, weak conſtitutions, or thoſe that are ſubject to other diſeaſes; but, ſpreading further, ſeizes upon the moſt healthy. *Temple.*

Man *falls upon* every thing that comes in his way; not a berry or a muſhrome can eſcape him. *Addiſon's Spectator.*

To get rid of fools and ſcoundrels was one part of my deſign in *falling upon* theſe authors. *Pope to Swift.*

63. *To* Fall *upon*. To attempt.

I do not intend to *fall upon* nice philoſophical diſquiſitions about the nature of time. *Holder on Time.*

64. *To* Fall *upon*. To ruſh againſt.

At the ſame time that the ſtorm bears upon the whole ſpecies, we are *falling* foul *upon* one another. *Addiſon's Spectator.*

This is one of thoſe general words of which it is very difficult to aſcertain or detail the full ſignification. It retains in moſt of its ſenſes ſome part of its primitive meaning, and implies either literally or figuratively deſcent, violence, or ſuddenneſs. In many of its ſenſes it is oppoſed to *riſe*; but in others has no counterpart, or correlative.

To Fall. *v. a.*

1. To drop; to let fall.

To-morrow in the battle think on me,
And *fall* thy edgeleſs ſword, deſpair and die. *Shak. Rich.* III.

If that the earth could teem with woman's tears,
Each drop, ſhe *falls*, would prove a crocodile. *Shak. Othello.*

Draw together;
And when I rear my hand, do you the like,
To *fall* it on Gonzalo. *Shakeſpeare's Tempeſt.*

I am willing to *fall* this argument: 'tis free for every man to write or not to write in verſe, as he thinks it is or is not his talent, or as he imagines the audience will receive it. *Dryd.*

2. To ſink; to depreſs.

If a man would endeavour to raiſe or *fall* his voice ſtill by half notes, like the ſtops of a lute, or by whole notes alone without halfs, as far as an eight, he will not be able to frame his voice unto it. *Bacon's Natural Hiſtory.*

3. To diminiſh in value; to let ſink in price.

Upon leſſening intereſt to four *per cent.* you *fall* the price of your native commodities, or leſſen your trade, or elſe prevent not the high uſe. *Locke.*

4. To yean; to bring forth.

They then conceiving, did in yeaning time
Fall party-colour'd lambs, and thoſe were Jacob's. *Shakeſp.*

Fall. *n. ſ.* [from the verb.]

1. The act of dropping from on high.

High o'er their heads a mould'ring rock is plac'd,
That promiſes a *fall*, and ſhakes at ev'ry blaſt. *Dryd. Æn.*

2. The act of tumbling from an erect poſture.

I ſaw him run after a gilded butterfly; and when he caught it, he let it go again, and after it again; and over and over he comes, and up again, and caught it again; or whether his *fall* enraged him, or how it was, he did ſo ſet his teeth, and did tear it. *Shakeſpeare's Coriolanus.*

3. The violence suffered in dropping from on high.

My son coming into his marriage-chamber, happened to have a *fall*, and died. 2 *Esdr.* x. 48.

Spirit of wine, mingled with common water, if the first *fall* be broken, by means of a sop, or otherwise, stayeth above; and if once mingled, it severeth not again, as oil doth. *Bacon's Phys. Rem.*

A fever or *fall* may take away my reason. *Locke.*

Some were hurt with the *falls* they got by leaping upon the ground. *Gulliver's Travels.*

4. Death; overthrow; destruction incurred.

Wail his *fall*,
Whom I myself struck down. *Shakes. Macbeth.*

Our fathers were given to the sword, and for a spoil, and had a great *fall* before our enemies. *Judith* viii. 9.

I will begin to pray for myself and for them; for I see the *falls* of us that dwell in the land. 2 *Esdr.* viii. 17.

5. Ruin; dissolution.

Paul's, the late theme of such a muse, whose flight
Has bravely reach'd and soar'd above thy height;
Now shalt thou stand though sword, or time, or fire,
Or zeal more fierce than they, thy *fall* conspire. *Denham.*

6. Downfal; loss of greatness; declension from eminence; degradation; state of being deposed from a high station; plunge from happiness or greatness into misery or meanness.

Her memory served as an accuser of her change, and her own handwriting was there to bear testimony against her *fall*. *Sidney, b.* ii.

Perhaps thou talk'st of me, and do'st enquire
Of my restraint; why here I live alone;
And pitiest this my miserable *fall*. *Daniel's Civil War.*

He, careless now of int'rest, fame, or fate,
Perhaps forgets that Oxford e'er was great;
Or deeming meanest what we greatest call,
Beholds thee glorious only in thy *fall*. *Pope to Parnel.*

7. Declension of greatness, power, or dominion.

'Till the empire came to be settled in Charles the Great, the *fall* of the Romans huge dominion concurring with other universal evils, caused those times to be days of much affliction and trouble throughout the world. *Hooker, b.* v. *f.* 41.

8. Diminution; decrease of price.

That the improvement of Ireland is the principal cause why our lands in purchase rise not, as naturally they should, with the *fall* of our interest, appears evidently from the effect the *fall* of interest hath had upon houses in London. *Child.*

9. Declination or diminution of sound; cadence; close of musick.

That strain again; it had a dying *fall*:
O, it came o'er my ear, like the sweet South
That breathes upon a bank of violets,
Stealing and giving odours. *Shakesp. Twelfth Night.*

How sweetly did they float upon the wings
Of silence, through the empty-vaulted night,
At ev'ry *fall* smoothing the raven down
Of darkness 'till it smil'd! *Milton.*

10. Declivity; steep descent.

Waters when beat upon the shore, or straitned, as the *falls* of bridges, or dashed against themselves by winds, give a roaring noise. *Bacon's Natural History,* N°. 115.

11. Cataract; cascade; rush of water down a steep place.

There will we sit upon the rocks,
And see the shepherds feed their flocks
By shallow rivers, to whose *falls*
Melodious birds sing madrigals. *Shakespeare.*

A whistling wind, or a melodious noise of birds among the spreading branches, or a pleasing *fall* of water running violently, these things made them to swoon for fear. *Wisd.* xvii.

Down through the crannies of the living walls
The crystal streams descend in murm'ring *falls*. *Dryd. Virg.*

The swain, in barren deserts, with surprize
Sees lilies spring, and sudden verdure rise;
And starts, amidst the thirsty wilds, to hear
New *falls* of water murm'ring in his ear. *Pope's Messiah.*

Now under hanging mountains,
Beside the *falls* of fountains,
He makes his moan;
And calls her ghost,
For ever, ever, ever lost! *Pope's St. Cecilia.*

12. The outlet of a current into any other water.

Before the *fall* of the Po into the gulph, it receives into its channel the most considerable rivers of Piedmont, Milan, and the rest of Lombardy. *Addison's Remarks on Italy.*

13. Autumn; the fall of the leaf; the time when the leaves drop from the trees.

What crowds of patients the town-doctor kills,
Or how last *fall* he rais'd the weekly bills. *Dryden's Juven.*

14. Any thing that falls in great quantities.

Upon a great *fall* of rain the current carried away a huge heap of apples. *L'Estrange.*

15. The act of felling or cutting down: as, *the* fall *of timber.*

FALLA'CIOUS. *adj.* [*fallax*, Latin; *fallacieux*, French.]

1. Producing mistake; sophistical. It is never used of men, but of writings, propositions, or things.

They believed and assented to things neither evident nor certain, nor yet so much as probable, but actually false and *fallacious*; such as were the absurd doctrines and stories of their rabbies. *South's Sermons.*

2. Deceitful; mocking expectation.

Soon as the force of that *fallacious* fruit,
That with exhilerating vapour bland
About their spirits had play'd, and inmost pow'rs
Made err, was now exhal'd. *Milton's Paradise Lost, b.* ix.

False philosophy inspires
Fallacious hope. *Milton.*

FALLA'CIOUSLY. *adv.* [from *fallacious*.] Sophistically; with purpose to deceive; with unsound reasoning.

We shall so far encourage contradiction, as to promise not to oppose any pen that shall *fallaciously* refute us. *Brown.*

We have seen how *fallaciously* the author has stated the cause, by supposing that nothing but unlimited mercy, or unlimited punishment, are the methods that can be made use of. *Addis.*

FALLA'CIOUSNESS. *n. s.* [from *fallacious*.] Tendency to deceive; inconclusiveness.

FA'LLACY. *n. s.* [*fallacia*, Latin; *fallace*, French.] Sophism; logical artifice; deceit; deceitful argument; delusory mode of ratiocination.

Most princes make themselves another thing from the people by a *fallacy* of argument, thinking themselves most kings when the subject is most basely subjected. *Sidney, b.* ii.

Until I know this sure uncertainty,
I'll entertain the favour'd *fallacy*. *Shak. Comedy of Errours.*

It were a mere *fallacy*, and mistaking to ascribe that to the force of imagination upon another body, which is but the force of imagination upon the proper body. *Bacon's Na. Hist.*

All men, who can see an inch before them, may easily detect gross *fallacies*. *Dryden.*

FALLIBI'LITY. *n. s.* [from *fallible*.] Liableness to be deceived; uncertainty; possibility of errour.

There is a great deal of *fallibility* in the testimony of men; yet there are some things we may be almost as certain of as that the sun shines, or that five twenties make an hundred. *Watts's Logick.*

FA'LLIBLE. *adj.* [*fallo*, Latin.] Liable to errour; such as may be deceived.

Do not falsify your resolution with hopes that are *fallible*: to-morrow you must die. *Shakesp. Measure for Measure.*

He that creates to himself thousands of little hopes, uncertain in the promise, *fallible* in the event, and depending upon a thousand circumstances, shall often fail in his expectations. *Taylor's Rule of living holy.*

Our intellectual or rational powers need some assistance, because they are so frail and *fallible* in the present state. *Watts.*

FA'LLING. *n. s.* [from *fall*.] Indentings opposed to prominence.

It shows the nose and eyebrows, with the several prominencies and *fallings* in of the features, much more distinctly than any other kind of figure. *Addison on ancient Medals.*

FA'LLINGSICKNESS. *n. s.* [*fall* and *sickness*.] The epilepsy; a disease in which the patient is without any warning deprived at once of his senses, and falls down.

Did Cæsar swoon?—He fell down in the market-place, and foam'd at mouth, and was speechless.—He hath the *falling-sickness*. *Shakespeare's Julius Cæsar.*

The dogfisher is good against the *fallingsickness*. *Walton.*

FA'LLOW. *adj.* [ꝼalepe, Saxon.]

1. Pale red, or pale yellow.

How does your *fallow* greyhound, sir?
I heard say, he was out-run at Cotsale. *Shakespeare.*

The king, who was excessively affected to hunting, had a great desire to make a great park for red as well as *fallow* deer between Richmond and Hampton-court. *Clarendon.*

2. Unsowed; left to rest after the years of tillage. [Supposed to be so called from the colour of naked ground.]

The ridges of the *fallow* field lay traversed, so as the English must cross them in presenting the charge. *Hayward.*

3. Plowed, but not sowed; plowed as prepared for a second aration.

Her predecessors, in their course of government, did but sometimes cast up the ground; and so leaving it *fallow*, it became quickly overgrown with weeds. *Howel's Vocal Forrest.*

4. Unplowed; uncultivated.

Her *fallow* lees
The darnel, hemlock, and rank fumitory,
Doth root upon. *Shakespeare's Henry* V.

5. Unoccupied; neglected.

Shall saints in civil bloodshed wallow
Of saints, and let the cause lie *fallow*. *Hudibras, p.* i. *c.* 2.

FA'LLOW. *n. s.* [from the adjective.]

1. Ground plowed in order to be plowed again.

The plowing of *fallows* is a very great benefit to land. *Mortimer's Husbandry.*

They are the best ploughs to plow up Summer *fallow* with. *Mortimer's Husbandry.*

2. Ground

2. Ground lying at rest.

Within an ancient forest's ample verge,
There stands a lonely but a healthful dwelling,
Built for convenience, and the use of life;
Around it *fallows*, meads, and pastures fair,
A little garden, and a limpid brook,
By nature's own contrivance seems dispos'd. *Row's J. Shore.*

To FA'LLOW. *v. n.* To plow in order to a second plowing.

Begin to plow up fallows: this first *fallowing* ought to be very shallow. *Mortimer's Husbandry.*

But the ground ought to be well plowed and *fallowed* the Summer before. *Mortimer.*

FA'LLOWNESS. *n. s.* [from *fallow.*] Barrenness; an exemption from bearing fruit.

Like one, who, in her third widowhood, doth profess
Herself a nun, ty'd to retiredness,
S' affects my muse now a chaste *fallowness*. *Donne.*

FALSE. *adj.* [*falsus*, Latin; *faux*, *fausse*, French.]

1. Not morally true; expressing that which is not thought.

Innocence shall make
False accusation blush, and tyranny
Tremble at patience. *Shakespeare's Winter's Tale.*

There are *false* witnesses among men. *L'Estrange.*

2. Not physically true; conceiving that which does not exist.

For how can that be *false*, which ev'ry tongue
Of ev'ry mortal man affirms for true?
Which truth hath in all ages been so strong,
As, loadstone like, all hearts it ever drew. *Davies.*

A farce is that in poetry which grotesque is in a picture: the persons and action of a farce are all unnatural, and the manners *false*; that is, inconsisting with the characters of mankind. *Dryden's Dufresnoy.*

3. Suppositious; succedaneous.

Take a vessel, and make a *false* bottom of coarse canvass: fill it with earth above the canvass. *Bacon's Nat. History.*

4. Deceiving expectation.

The heart of man looks fair to the eye; but when we come to lay any weight upon't, the ground is *false* under us. *L'Estrange, Fable* 54.

5. Not agreeable to rule, or propriety.

Now, fy upon my *false* French; by mine honour, in true English, I love thee, Kate. *Shakespeare's Henry* V.

6. Not honest; not just.

What thou would'st highly,
That thou would'st holily; would'st not play *false*,
And yet would'st wrongly win. *Shakespeare's Macbeth.*

The true prince may, for recreation sake, prove a *false* thief; for the poor abuses of the times want countenance. *Shakespeare's Henry* IV. *p.* i.

Men are spunges, which, to pour out, receive;
Who know *false* play, rather than lose, deceive. *Donne.*

7. Treacherous; perfidious; traiterous; deceitful; hollow.

I grant him bloody,
Luxurious, avaricious, *false*, deceitful,
Sudden, malicious, smacking of ev'ry sin
That has a name. *Shakespeare's Macbeth.*

False of heart, light of ear, bloody of hand. *Shakespeare.*

A man to whom he had committed the trust of his person, in making him his chamberlain; this man, no ways disgraced, no ways discontent, no ways put in fear, turns *false* unto him. *Bacon's Henry* VII.

So hast thou cheated Theseus with a wile,
Against thy vow, returning to beguile
Under a borrow'd name; as *false* to me,
So *false* thou art to him who set thee free. *Dryden.*

The ladies will make a numerous party against him, for being *false* to love in forsaking Dido. *Dryd. Virg. Æn. Ded.*

8. Counterfeit; hypocritical; not real.

False tears true pity moves: the king commands
To loose his fetters. *Dryden's Æn. b.* ii.

9. In all these senses *true* is the word opposed.

To FALSE. *v. a.* [from the noun.]

1. To violate by failure of veracity.

Is't not enough that to this lady mild,
Thou *falsed* hast thy faith with perjury. *Fairy Queen, b.* i.

2. To deceive.

Fair seemly pleasance each to other makes,
With goodly purposes there as they sit;
And in his *falsed* fancy he, her takes
To be the fairest wight that lived yet. *Fairy Queen, b.* i.

3. To defeat; to balk; to shift; to evade, as fencers commonly do.

But, Guyon, in the heat of all his strife,
Was wary wise, and closely did await
Advantage, whilst his foe did rage most rife;
Sometimes athwart, sometimes he strook him strait,
And *falsed* oft his blows t' illude him with such bait. *F. Qu.*

4. This word is now out of use.

FALSEHEA'RTED. *adj.* [*false* and *heart.*]

1. Treacherous; perfidious; deceitful; hollow.

The traitorous or treacherous, who have misled others, are severely punished; and the neutrals and *falsehearted* friends and followers, who have started aside like a broken bow, he noted. *Bacon's Advice to Villiers.*

FA'LSEHOOD. *n. s.* [from *false.*]

1. Want of truth; want of veracity.

All deception in the course of life is, indeed, nothing else but a lie reduced to practice, and *falsehood* passing from words to things. *South's Sermons.*

2. Want of honesty; treachery; deceitfulness; perfidy.

3. A lie; a false assertion.

FA'LSELY. *adv.* [from *false.*]

1. Contrarily to truth; not truly.

Simeon and Levi spake not only *falsely* but insidiously, nay hypocritically, abusing proselytes and religion. *Gov. of Tongue.*

Already were the Belgians on our coast,
Whose fleet more mighty every day became
By late success, which they did *falsely* boast,
And now by first appearing seem'd to claim. *Dryd. Ann. Mir.*

Tell him, I did in vain his brother move,
And yet he *falsely* said he was in love;
Falsely; for had he truly lov'd, at least
He would have giv'n one day to my request. *Dryd. Aureng.*

Such as are treated ill, and upbraided *falsely*, find out an intimate friend that will hear their complaints, and endeavour to sooth their secret resentments. *Addison's Spectator.*

2. Erroneously; by mistake.

He knows that to be inconvenient which we *falsely* think convenient for us. *Smalridge's Sermons.*

3. Perfidiously; treacherously; deceitfully.

FA'LSENESS. *n. s.* [from *false.*]

1. Contrariety to truth.

2. Want of veracity; violation of promise.

Suppose the reverse of virtue were solemnly enacted, and the practice of fraud and rapine, and perjury and *falseness* to a man's word, and all vice were established by a law, would that which we now call vice gain the reputation of virtue, and that which we now call virtue grow odious to human nature? *Tillotson, Sermon* 3.

3. Duplicity; deceit; double dealing.

Piety is opposed to hypocrisy and insincerity, and all *falseness* or foulness of intentions, especially to personated devotion. *Hammond's Fundamentals.*

4. Treachery; perfidy; traitorousness.

King Richard might create a perfect guess,
That great Northumberland, then *false* to him,
Would of that seed grow to a greater *falseness*. *Shak. H.* IV.

The prince is in no danger of being betrayed by the *falseness*, or cheated by the avarice of such a servant. *Rogers.*

FA'LSER. *n. s.* [from *false.*] A deceiver; an hypocrite. Now obsolete.

Such end had the kid; for he would weaned be
Of craft coloured with simplicity;
And such end, pardie, does all them remain,
That of such *falsers* friendship been fain. *Spenser's Pastorals.*

FALSIFIA'BLE. *adv.* [from *falsify.*] Liable to be counterfeited or corrupted.

FALSIFICA'TION. *n. s.* [*falsification*, French, from *falsify.*]

1. The act of counterfeiting any thing so as to make it appear what it is not.

Concerning the word of God, whether it be by misconstruction of the sense, or by *falsification* of the words, wittingly to endeavour that any thing may seem divine which is not, is very plainly to abuse, and even to falsify Divine evidence, which injury, offered but unto men, is most worthily counted heinous. *Hooker, b.* iii. *s.* 5.

To counterfeit the dead image of a king in his coin is an high offence; but to counterfeit the living image of a king in his person, exceedeth all *falsifications*; except it should be that of a Mahomet, that counterfeits divine honour. *Bacon.*

2. Confutation.

The poet invents this fiction to prevent posterity from searching after this isle, and to preserve his story from detection of *falsification*. *Notes on the Odyssey.*

FA'LSIFIER. *n. s.* [from *falsify.*]

1. One that counterfeits; one that makes any thing to seem what it is not.

It happens in theories built on too obvious or too few experiments, what happens to *falsifiers* of coin; for counterfeit money will endure some one proof, others another, but none of them all proofs. *Boyle.*

2. A liar; one that contrives falshoods.

Boasters are naturally *falsifiers*, and the people, of all others, that put their shams the worst together. *L'Estrange's Fables.*

To FA'LSIFY. *v. a.* [*falsifier*, French.]

1. To counterfeit; to forge; to produce something for that which in reality it is not.

We cannot excuse that church, which either through corrupt translations of Scripture, delivereth, instead of divine speeches, any thing repugnant unto that which God speaketh; or, through *falsified* additions, proposeth that to the people of God as Scripture which is in truth no Scripture. *Hooker, b.* v. *s.* 19.

The Irish bards use to forge and *falsify* every thing as they list, to please or displease any man. *Spenser on Ireland.*

2. To

2. To confute; to prove false.

Our Saviour's prophecy stands good in the destruction of the temple, and the dissolution of the Jewish œconomy, when Jews and Pagans united all their endeavours, under Julian the apostate, to baffle and *falsify* the prediction. *Addison.*

3. To violate; to break by falsehood.

It shall be thy work, thy shameful work, which is in thy power to shun, to make him live to see thy faith *falsified*, and his bed defiled. *Sidney, b. ii.*

He suddenly *falsified* his faith, and villainously slew Selymes the king, as he was bathing himself, mistrusting nothing less than the falsehood of the pyrate. *Knolles's History of the Turks.*

This superadds treachery to all the other pestilent ingredients of the crime; 'tis the *falsifying* the most important trust. *Decay of Piety.*

4. To pierce; to run through.

His crest is rash'd away, his ample shield
Is *falsify'd*, and round with jav'lins fill'd. *Dryden's Æn.*

Of this word Mr. *Dryden* writes thus. My friends quarrelled at the word *falsified*, as an innovation in our language. The fact is confessed; for I remember not to have read it in any English author; though perhaps it may be found in *Spenser*'s Fairy Queen. But suppose it be not there: why am I forbidden to borrow from the Italian, a polished language, the word which is wanting in my native tongue? Horace has given us a rule for coining words, *si græco fonte cadant*, especially when other words are joined with them which explain the sense. I use the word *falsify*, in this place, to mean that the shield of Turnus was not of proof against the spears and javelins of the Trojans, which had pierced it through and through in many places. The words which accompany this new one, makes my meaning plain:

Ma si l' Usbergo d' Ambi era perfetto,
Che mai poter falsarlo *in nessum canto.* Ariosto, cant. xxvi.

Falsar cannot otherwise be turned than by *falsified*; for his shield was *falsed*, is not English. I might indeed have contented myself with saying his shield was pierced, and bored, and stuck with javelins. *Dryden.*

Dryden, with all this effort, was not able to naturalise the new signification, which I have never seen copied, except once by some obscure nameless writer, and which indeed deserves not to be received.

To FA'LSIFY. *v. n.* To tell lies; to violate truth.

This point have we gained, that it is absolutely and universally unlawful to lie and *falsify*. *South's Sermons.*

FA'LSITY. *n. s.* [*falsitas*, Latin.]

1. Falsehood; contrariety to truth.

Neither are they able to break through those errours, wherein they are so determinately settled, that they pay unto *falsity* the whole sum of whatsoever love is owing unto God's truth. *Hooker, b. v. s.* 49.

Can you on him such *falsities* obtrude?
And as a mortal the most wise delude? *Sandys's Paraphrase.*

Probability does not properly make any alteration, either in the truth or *falsity* of things; but only imports a different degree of their clearness or appearance to the understanding. *South's Sermons.*

2. A lye; an errour; a false assertion or position.

That Danubius ariseth from the Pyrenean hills, that the earth is higher towards the North, are opinions truly charged on Aristotle by the restorer of Epicurus, and all easily confutable *falsities*. *Glanv. Sceps. c.* 20.

To FA'LTER. *v. n.* [*faltar*, to be wanting, Spanish; *vaulttur*, a stammerer, Islandick, which is probably a word from the same radical.]

1. To hesitate in the utterance of words.

With *faltering* tongue, and trembling ev'ry vein,
Tell on, quoth she. *Fairy Queen, b.* i.

The pale assistants on each other star'd,
With gaping mouths for issuing words prepar'd;
The still-born sounds upon the palate hung,
And dy'd imperfect on the *falt'ring* tongue. *Dryden.*

He changes, gods! and *falters* at the question:
His fears, his words, his looks declare him guilty. *Smith.*

2. To fail in any act of the body.

This earth shall have a feeling; and these stones
Prove armed soldiers, ere her native king
Shall *fa'ter* under foul rebellious arms. *Shakesp. Richard* II.

3. To fail in any act of the understanding.

How far ideots are concerned in the want or weakness of any or all faculties, an exact observation of their several ways of *faltering* would discover. *Locke.*

To FA'LTER. *v a.* To sift; to cleanse. This word seems to be merely rustick or provincial.

Barley for malt must be bold, dry, sweet, and clean *faltered* from foulness, seeds and oats. *Mortimer's Husbandry.*

FA'LTERINGLY. *adv.* [from *falter.*] With hesitation; with difficulty; with feebleness.

To FA'MBLE. *v. a.* [*famler*, Danish.] To hesitate in the speech. This word I find only in *Skinner*.

FAME. *n. s.* [*fama*, Latin; φαμα, Dorick.]

1. Celebrity; renown.

The house to be builded for the Lord must be exceeding magnifical, of *fame* and of glory throughout all countries. *1 Chro.* xxii. 5.

The desire of *fame* will not suffer endowments to lie useless. *Addison's Spectator.*

What is this *fame*, for which we thoughts employ,
The owner's wife, which other men enjoy? *Pope.*

2. Report; rumour.

We have heard the *fame* of him, and all that he did in Egypt. *Jos.* ix. 9.

I shall shew what are true *fames*. *Bacon.*

FA'MED. *adj.* [from *fame.*] Renowned; celebrated; much talked of.

He is *fam'd* for mildness, peace and prayer. *Shak. H.* VI.

He purposes to seek the Clarian god,
Avoiding Delphos, his more *fam'd* abode,
Since Phlegyan robbers made unsafe the road. *Dryden.*

Aristides was an Athenian philosopher, *famed* for his learning and wisdom; but converted to Christianity. *Addison.*

FA'MELESS. *adj.* [from *fame.*] Without fame; without renown.

Then let me, *fameless*, love the fields and woods,
The fruitful water'd vales and running floods. *May's Virgil.*

FAMILIAR. *adj.* [*familiaris*, Latin.]

1. Domestick; relating to a family.

They range *familiar* to the dome. *Pope.*

2. Affable; not formal; easy in conversation.

Be thou *familiar*, but by no means vulgar. *Shak. Hamlet.*

Be not too *familiar* with Poins; for he misuses thy favours so much, that he swears thou art to marry his sister Nell. *Shak.*

3. Unceremonious; free, as among persons long acquainted.

Kalandar streight thought he saw his niece Parthenia, and was about in such *familiar* sort to have spoken unto her; but she, in grave and honourable manner, gave him to understand that he was mistaken. *Sidney.*

4. Well known; brought into knowledge by frequent practice or custom.

I see not how the Scripture could be possibly made *familiar* unto all, unless far more should be read in the people's hearing than by a sermon can be opened. *Hooker, b. v. s.* 22.

Let us chuse such limbs of noble counsel,
That the great body of our state may go
In equal rank with the best govern'd nation;
That war, or peace, or both at once, may be
As things acquainted and *familiar* to us. *Shakes. Henry* IV.

Our sweet
Recess, and only consolation left
Familiar to our eyes! *Milton's Paradise Lost, b.* xi.

One idea which is *familiar* to the mind, connected with others which are new and strange, will bring those new ideas into easy remembrance. *Watts's Improvement of the Mind.*

5. Well acquainted with; accustomed; habituated by custom.

Or chang'd at length, and to the place conform'd
In temper and in nature, will receive
Familiar the fierce heat, and void of pain. *Milton's P. Lost.*

The senses at first let in particular ideas; and the mind, by degrees, growing *familiar* with some of them, they are lodged in the memory, and names got to them. *Locke.*

He was amazed how so impotent and groveling an insect as I could entertain such inhuman ideas, and in so *familiar* a manner, as to appear wholly unmoved at all the scenes of blood and desolation. *Gulliver's Travels.*

Patient permit the sadly-pleasing strain;
Familiar now with grief, your tears refrain. *Pope's Odyssey.*

6. Common; frequent.

To a wrong hypothesis, may be reduced the errors that may be occasioned by a true hypothesis, but not rightly understood: there is nothing more *familiar* than this. *Locke.*

7. Easy; unconstrained.

He unreins
His muse, and sports in loose *familiar* strains. *Addison.*

8. Too nearly acquainted.

A poor man found a priest *familiar* with his wife, and because he spake it abroad, and could not prove it, the priest sued him for defamation. *Camden.*

FA'MILIAR. *n. s.*

1. An intimate; one long acquainted.

The king is a noble gentleman, and my *familiar*. *Shakesp.*

When he finds himself avoided and neglected by his *familiars*, this affects him. *Rogers, Sermon* 10.

2. A demon supposed to attend at call.

Love is a *familiar*; there is no evil angel but love. *Shakesp.*

FAMILIA'RITY. *n. s.* [*familiarité*, French, from *familiar.*]

1. Easiness of conversation; omission of ceremony; affability.

2. Acquaintance; habitude.

We contract at last such an intimacy and *familiarity* with them, as makes it difficult and irksome for us to call off our minds. *Atterbury's Sermons.*

3. Easy intercourse.

They say any mortals may enjoy the most intimate *familiarities* with these gentle spirits. *Pope.*

To

To FAMILIARI'ZE. *v. a.* [*familiariser*, French.]

1. To make familiar; to make easy by habitude.
2. To bring down from a state of distant superiority.

The genius smiled upon me with a look of compassion and affability that *familiarized* him to my imagination, and at once dispelled all fear and apprehensions. *Addison's Spectator.*

FA'MILIARLY. *adv.* [from *familiar.*]

1. Unceremoniously; with freedom like that of long acquaintance.

Because that I *familiarly* sometimes
Do use you for my fool, and chat with you,
Your sawciness will jest upon my love. *Shak. Comed. of Err.*

He talks as *familiarly* of John of Gaunt as if he had been sworn brother to him; and I'll be sworn he never saw him but once in the Tiltyard, and then he broke his head. *Sh.*

The governour came to us, and, after salutations, said *familiarly*, that he was come to visit us, and called for a chair and sat him down. *Bacon's New Atlantis.*

2. Commonly; frequently; with the unconcernedness or easiness of long habitude or acquaintance.

Lesser mists and fogs than those which covered Greece with so long darkness, do *familiarly* present our senses with as great alterations in the sun and moon. *Raleigh's Hist. of the World.*

3. Easily; without solemnity; without formality.

Horace still charms with graceful negligence,
And without method talks us into sense;
Will, like a friend, *familiarly* convey
The truest notions in the easiest way. *Pope's Ess. on Critic.*

FAMI'LLE. *en famille*, French. In a family way; domestically.

Deluded mortals, whom the great
Chuse for companions *tete à tete*;
Who at their dinners, *en famille*,
Get leave to sit whene'er you will. *Swift.*

FA'MILY. *n. s.* [*familia*, Latin; *famille*, French.]

1. Those who live in the same house; household.

The night made little impression on myself; but I cannot answer for my whole *family*; for my wife prevailed on me to take somewhat. *Swift.*

2. Those that descend from one common progenitor; a race; a tribe; a generation.
3. A class; a tribe; a species.

There be two great *families* of things, sulphureous and mercurial, inflammable and not inflammable, mature and crude, oily and watry. *Bacon's Natural History*, N°. 354.

FA'MINE. *n. s.* [*famine*, French; *fames*, Latin.] Scarcity of food; dearth; distress for want of victuals.

Our castle's strength
Will laugh a siege to scorn: here let them lie,
'Till *famine* and the ague eat them up. *Shakesp. Macbeth.*

Famines have not been of late observed, partly because of the industry of mankind, partly by those supplies that come by sea to countries in want, but principally by the goodness of God. *Hale's Origin of Mankind.*

This city never felt a siege before,
But from the lake receiv'd its daily store;
Which now shut up, and millions crowded here,
Famine will soon in multitudes appear. *Dryd. Indian Emp.*

To FA'MISH. *v. a.* [from *fames*, Latin; *famis*, old French.]

1. To kill with hunger; to starve; to destroy by want of food.

What, did he marry me to *famish* me? *Shakespeare.*

The pains of *famish'd* Tantalus he'll feel,
And Sisyphus, that labours up the hill
The rowling rock in vain; and curst Ixion's wheel. *Dryd.*

2. To kill by deprivation or denial of any thing necessary to life.

Thin air
Above the clouds will pine his entrails gross,
And *famish* him of breath, if not of bread. *Milt. P. Lost.*

To FA'MISH. *v. n.* To die of hunger.

You are all resolved rather to die than to *famish. Sh. Coriol.*

FA'MISHMENT. *n. s.* [from *famish.*] The pain of hunger; want of food.

Apicius, thou did'st on thy gut bestow
Full ninety millions; yet, when this was spent,
Ten millions still remain'd to thee; which thou,
Fearing to suffer thirst and *famishment*,
In poison'd potion drank'st. *Hakewill on Providence.*

FAMO'SITY. *n. s.* [from *famous.*] Renown; celebrity. *Dict.*

FA'MOUS. *adj.* [*fameux*, French; *famosus*, Latin.]

1. Renowned; celebrated; much talked of and praised.

Henry the fifth, too *famous* to live long;
England ne'er lost a king of so much worth. *Shak. Hen.* VI.

There rose up before Moses two hundred and fifty princes of the assembly, *famous* in the congregation, men of renown. *Num.* xvi. 2.

She became *famous* among women; for they had executed judgment upon her. *Ezek.* xxiii. 10.

Pyreius was only *famous* for counterfeiting all base things; as earthen pitchers, a scullery, rogues together by the ears, and swine tumbling in the mire; whereupon he was firnamed Rupographus. *Peacham on Drawing.*

I shall be nam'd among the *famousest*
Of women, sung at solemn festivals. *Milton's Agonistes.*

Many, besides myself, have heard our *famous* Waller own, that he derived the harmony of his numbers from the Godfrey of Bulloign, which was turned into English by Mr. Fairfax. *Dryden's Fables, Dedication.*

2. It has sometimes a middle signification, and imports fame whether for good or ill.

Menecrates and Menas, *famous* pyrates,
Make the sea serve them. *Shakesp. Anthony and Cleopatra.*

FA'MOUSLY. *adv.* [from *famous.*] With great renown; with great celebration.

Then this land was *famously* enriched
With politick grave counsel; then the king
Had virtuous uncles to protect his grace. *Shakesp. Rich.* III.

They looked on the particulars as things *famously* spoken of, and believed, and worthy to be recorded and read. *Grew's Cos.*

FA'MOUSNESS. *n. s.* [from *famous.*] Celebrity; great fame.

FAN. *n. s.* [*vannus*, Latin.]

1. An instrument used by ladies to move the air and cool themselves.

With scarfs, and *fans*, and double change of brav'ry,
With amber bracelets, beads, with all this knav'ry. *Shakesp.*

Flavia, the least and slightest toy
Can with resistless art employ:
In other hands the *fan* would prove
An engine of small force in love;
But she, with such an air and mien,
Not to be told or safely seen,
Directs its wanton motions so,
That it wounds more than Cupid's bow;
Gives coolness to the matchless dame,
To every other breast a flame. *Atterbury.*

The modest *fan* was lifted up no more,
And virgins smil'd at what they blush'd before. *Pope.*

2. Any thing spread out like a woman's fan into a triangle with a broad base.

As a peacock and crane were in company, the peacock spread his tail, and challenged the other to shew him such a *fan* of feathers. *L'Estrange.*

3. The instrument by which the chaff is blown away when corn is winnowed. [*Van*, French.]

Flaile, strawfork, and rake with a *fan* that is strong. *Tuss.*

Asses shall eat clean provender, winnowed with the shovel and with the *fan*. *Is.* xxx. 24.

In the wind and tempest of fortune's frown,
Distinction, with a broad and powerful *fan*,
Puffing at all, winnows the light away. *Shak. Troil. and Cr.*

For the cleansing of corn is commonly used either a wicker-fan, or a *fan* with sails. *Mortimer's Husbandry.*

4. Any thing by which the air is moved; wings.

The pris'ner with a spring from prison broke;
Then stretch'd his feather'd *fans* with all his might,
And to the neighb'ring maple wing'd his flight. *Dryden.*

5. An instrument to raise the fire.

Nature worketh in us all a love to our own counsels: the contradiction of others is a *fan* to inflame that love. *Hooker.*

To FAN. *v. a.*

1. To cool or recreate with a fan.

She was *fanned* into slumbers by her slaves. *Spectator.*

2. To ventilate; to affect by air put in motion.

Let every feeble humour shake your hearts;
Your enemies, with nodding of their plumes,
Fan you into despair. *Shakespeare's Coriolanus.*

The Norweyan banners flout the sky,
And *fan* our people cold. *Shakespeare's Macbeth.*

The air
Floats as they pass, *fann'd* with unnumber'd plumes:
From branch to branch the smaller birds with song
Solac'd the woods, and spread their painted wings,
'Till ev'n. *Milton's Paradise Lost*, *b.* vii. *l.* 432.

The *fanning* wind upon her bosom blows;
To meet the *fanning* wind the bosom rose:
The *fanning* wind and purling streams continue her repose. *Dryden's Cymon and Iphigenia.*

Calm as the breath which *fans* our eastern groves,
And bright, as when thy eyes first lighted up our loves. *Dryd.*

And now his shorter breath, with sultry air,
Pants on her neck, and *fans* her parting hair. *Pope.*

3. To separate, as by winnowing.

I have collected some few, therein *fanning* the old, not omitting any. *Bacon's Apophthegms.*

Not so the wicked; but as chaff, which, *fann'd*,
The wind drives, so the wicked shall not stand
In judgment. *Milton.*

FANA'TICISM. *n. s.* [from *fanatick.*] Enthusiasm; religious frenzy.

A church whose doctrines are derived from the clear fountains of the Scriptures, whose polity and discipline are formed upon the most uncorrupted models of antiquity, which has stood unshaken by the most furious assaults of popery on the one hand, and *fanaticism* on the other; has triumphed over all

all the arguments of its enemies, and has nothing now to contend with but their slanders and calumnies. *Rogers's Sermons.*

FANA'TICK. *adj.* [*fanaticus*, Latin; *fanatique*, Fr.] Enthusiastick; struck with a superstitious frenzy.

After these appear'd
A crew, who, under names of old renown,
Osiris, Isis, Orus, and their train,
With monst'rous shapes and sorceries abus'd
Fanatick Egypt, and her priests, to seek
Their wand'ring gods disguis'd in brutish forms. *Milt. P. L.*

FANA'TICK. *n. s.* [from the adjective.] An enthusiast; a man mad with wild notions of religion.

The double armature of St. Peter is a more destructive engine than the tumultary weapon snatcht up by a *fanatick*. *Decay of Piety.*

FA'NCIFUL *adj.* [*fancy* and *full*.]

1. Imaginative; rather guided by imagination than reason.

Some *fanciful* men have expected nothing but confusion and ruin from those very means, whereby both that and this is most effectually prevented. *Woodward's Natural History.*

2. Directed by the imagination, not the reason; full of wild images.

What treasures did he bury in his sumptuous buildings? and how foolish and *fanciful* were they? *Hayward.*

It would show as much singularity to deny this, as it does a *fanciful* facility to affirm it. *Garth's Preface to Ovid.*

FA'NCIFULLY. *adv.* [from *fanciful.*] According to the wildness of imagination.

FA'NCIFULNESS. *n. s.* [from *fanciful.*] Addiction to the pleasures of imagination; habit of following fancy rather than reason.

Albertus Magnus, with somewhat too much curiosity, was somewhat transported with too much *fancifulness* towards the influences of the heavenly motions, and astrological calculations. *Hale's Origin of Mankind.*

FA'NCY. *n. s.* [contracted from *phantasy*, *phantasia*, Latin; φαντασία.]

1. Imagination; the power by which the mind forms to itself images and representations of things, persons, or scenes of being.

Shakespeare, *fancy*'s sweetest child! *Milton.*

In the soul
Are many lesser faculties, that serve
Reason as chief: among these *fancy* next
Her office holds; of all external things,
Which the five watchful senses represent,
She forms imaginations, airy shapes,
Which reason joining, or disjoining, frames
All what we affirm, or what deny, and call
Our knowledge, or opinion. *Milton's Paradise Lost, b.* v.

Though no evidence affects the *fancy* so strongly as that of sense, yet there is other evidence, which gives as full satisfaction and as clear a conviction to our reason. *Atterbury.*

Love is by *fancy* led about,
From hope to fear, from joy to doubt:
Whom we now a goddess call,
Divinity grac'd in every feature,
Strait's a deform'd, a perjur'd creature;
Love and hate are *fancy* all. *Granville.*

2. An opinion bred rather by the imagination than the reason.

Mens private *fancies* must give place to the higher judgment of that church which is in authority over them. *Hooker.*

A person of a full and ample fortune, who was not disturbed by any *fancies* in religion. *Clarendon, b.* viii.

I have always had a *fancy*, that learning might be made a play and recreation to children. *Locke.*

3. Taste; idea; conception of things.

The little chapel called the Salutation is very neat, and built with a pretty *fancy*. *Addison on Italy.*

4. Image; conception; thought.

How now, my lord, why do you keep alone?
Of sorriest *fancies* your companions making,
Using those thoughts which should indeed have died
With them they think on? *Shakespeare's Macbeth.*

5. Inclination; liking; fondness.

Tell me where is *fancy* bred,
Or in the heart, or in the head?
How begot, how nourished?
It is engender'd in the eyes,
With gazing fed, and *fancy* dies
In the cradle where it lies. *Shakes. Merchant of Venice.*

His *fancy* lay extremely to travelling. *L'Estrange.*

For you, fair Hermia, look you arm yourself,
To fit your *fancies* to your father's will;
Or else the law of Athens yields you up
To death, or to a vow of single life. *Shakespeare.*

A resemblance in humour or opinion, a *fancy* for the same business or diversion, is oftentimes a ground of affection. *Collier of Friendship.*

6. Caprice; humour; whim.

True worth shall gain me, that it may be said
Desert, not *fancy*, once a woman led. *Dryden's Ind. Emp.*

The sultan of Egypt kept a good correspondence with the Jacobites towards the head of the Nile, for fear they should take a *fancy* to turn the course of that river. *Arbuthnot.*

7. Frolick; idle scheme; vagary.

One that was just entring upon a long journey, took up a *fancy* of putting a trick upon Mercury. *L'Estrange.*

8. Something that pleases or entertains.

The altering of the scent, colour, or taste of fruit, by infusing, mixing, or cutting into the bark or root of the tree, herb, or flower, any coloured, aromatical, or medicinal substance, are but *fancies*: the cause is, for that those things have passed their period, and nourish not. *Bacon's Nat. History.*

London-pride is a pretty *fancy*, and does well for borders. *Mortimer's Husbandry.*

To FA'NCY. *v. n.* [from the noun.] To imagine; to believe without being able to prove.

All are not always bound to hate and punish the true enemies of religion, much less any whom they may *fancy* to be so: all are always obliged to love its true friends, and to pray for its very enemies. *Spratt's Sermons.*

If our search has reached no farther than simile and metaphor, we rather *fancy* than know, and are not yet penetrated into the inside and reality of the thing; but content ourselves with what our imaginations furnish us with. *Locke.*

To FA'NCY. *v. a.*

1. To portray in the mind; to image to himself; to imagine.

But he whose noble genius is allow'd,
Who with stretch'd pinions soars above the crowd;
Who mighty thought can clothe with manly dress,
He whom I *fancy*, but can ne'er express. *Dryd. Juven. Sat.*

2. To like; to be pleased with.

Ninus both admiring her judgment and valour, together with her person and external beauty, *fancied* her so strongly, as, neglecting all princely respects, he took her from her husband. *Raleigh's History of the World.*

It is a little hard that the queen cannot demolish this town in whatever manner she pleaseth to *fancy*. *Swift.*

FANCYMO'NGER. *n. s.* [from *fancy*.] One who deals in tricks of imagination.

There is a man haunts the forest, that abuses our young plants with carving Rosalind on their barks; hangs odes upon hawthorns, and elegies on brambles; all, forsooth, deifying the name of Rosalind. If I could meet that *fancymonger*, I would give him some good counsel; for he seems to have the quotidian of love upon him. *Shakesp. As you like it.*

FA'NCYSICK. *adj.* [*fancy* and *sick*.] One whose imagination is unsound; one whose distemper is in his own mind.

'Tis not necessity, but opinion, that makes men miserable; and when we come once to be *fancysick*, there's no cure for it. *L'Estrange.*

FANE. *n. s.* [*fane*, French; *fanum*, Latin.] A temple; a place consecrated to religion.

Nor *fane*, nor capitol,
The prayers of priests, nor times of sacrifice,
Embarments all of fury, shall lift up
Their rotten privilege. *Shakesp. Coriolanus.*

Old Calibe, who kept the sacred *fane*
Of Juno, now she seem'd. *Dryden's Æn. b.* vii. *l.* 589.

Yet some to *fanes* repair'd, and humble rites
Perform'd to Thor and Woden, fabled gods,
Who with their vot'ries in one ruin shar'd. *Phillips.*

A sacred *fane* in Egypt's fruitful lands,
Hewn from the Theban mountain's rocky womb. *Tickell.*

The fields are ravish'd from th' industrious swains,
From men their cities, and from gods their *fanes*. *Pope.*

FA'NFARON. *n. s.* [French, from the Spanish. Originally in Arabick it signifies one who promises what he cannot perform. *Menage.*]

1. A bully; a hector.

2. A blusterer; a boaster of more than he can perform.

There are *fanfarons* in the trials of wit too, as well as in feats of arms; and none so forward to engage in argument or discourse as those that are least able to go through with it. *L'Est.*

Virgil makes Æneas a bold avower of his own virtues, which, in the civility of our poets, is the character of a *fanfaron* or hector. *Dryden on Dramatick Poesy.*

FANFARONA'DE. *n. s.* [from *fanfaron*, French.] A bluster; a tumour of fictitious dignity.

The bishop copied this proceeding from the *fanfaronade* of monsieur Boufflei.s, when the earl of Portland and that general had an interview. *Swift.*

To FANG. *v. a.* [fangan, Saxon; *vangen*, Dutch.] To seize; to gripe; to clutch.

Destruction *fang* mankind! *Shakespeare's Timon.*

FANG. *n. s.* [from the verb.]

1. The long tusks of a boar or other animal; any thing like 'em.

Here feel we but the penalty of Adam,
The season's difference; as the icy *fang*
And churlish chiding of the Winter's wind;
Which, when it bites and blows upon my body,
Ev'n 'till I shrink with cold, I smile and say
This is no flattery. *Shakespeare's As you like it.*

Some

Some creatures have overlong or outgrowing teeth, which we call *fangs*, or tusks; as boars, pikes, salmons, and dogs, though less. *Bacon's Natural History*, No. 752.

Prepar'd to fly,
The fatal *fang* drove deep within his thigh,
And cut the nerves: the nerves no more sustain
The bulk; the bulk, unprop'd, falls headlong on the plain. *Dryden's Ovid, b.* viii.

Then charge him close, provoke him to the rage
Of *fangs* and claws, and, stooping from your horse,
Rivet the panting savage to the ground. *Addison's Cato.*

2. The nails; the talons.
3. Any shoot or other thing by which hold is taken.

The protuberant *fangs* of the yuca are to be treated like the tuberoses. *Evelyn's Kalendar.*

FA'NGED. *adj.* [from *fang*.] Furnished with fangs or long teeth; furnished with any instruments of destruction, which can be exercised in imitation of fangs.

My two schoolfellows,
Whom I will trust as I will adders *fang'd*,
They bear the mandate. *Shakespeare's Hamlet.*

Not Scythians, nor fierce Dacians, onward rush
With half the speed, nor half so swift retreat:
In chariots, *fang'd* with scythes, they scour the field,
Drive through our wedg'd battalions with a whirl,
And strew a dreadful harvest on the plain. *Phillips's Briton.*

FA'NGLE. *n. s.* [from fengan, Saxon, to attempt. *Skinner.*] Silly attempt; trifling scheme. It is never used, or rarely, but in contempt with the epithet *new*; as, *new fangles*, *new fangleness*.

FA'NGLED. *adj.* [from *fangle*.] This word seems to signify gaudy; ridiculously shewy; vainly decorated. This is still retained in Scotland: as, he's new *fangled*, or whimsical, and very fond of novelty.

Quick wits be in desire new *fangled*, and in purpose unconstant. *Ascham.*

A book! oh, rare one!
Be not, as in this *fangled* world, a garment
Nobler than that it covers. *Shakespeare's Cymbeline.*

FA'NGLESS. *adj.* [from *fang*.] Toothless; without teeth.

The king hath wasted all his rods
On late offenders, that he now doth lack
The very instruments of chastisement;
So that his pow'r, like to a *fangless* lion,
May offer, but not hold. *Shakespeare's Henry* IV. *p.* ii.

FA'NGOT. *n. s.* [ ] A quantity of wares: as raw silk, &c. containing from one or two hundred weight three quarters. *Dict.*

FA'NNEL. *n. s.* [*fanon*, French.] A sort of ornament like a scarf, worn about the left arm of a mass-priest when he officiates. *Dict.*

FA'NNER. *n. s.* [from *fan*.] One that plays a fan.

I will send unto Babylon *fanners* that shall fan her. *Jerem.*

FA'NTASIED. *adj.* [from *fantasy*.] Filled with fancies or wild imaginations.

As I travell'd hither through the land,
I found the people strangely *fantasied*. *Shakes. King John.*

FANTA'SM. *n. s.* [See PHANTASM.]

FANTA'STICAL. } FANTA'STICK. } *adj.* [*fantastique*, Fr. from *fantasy*.]

1. Irrational; bred only in the imagination.

The delight that a man takes from another's sin, can be nothing else but a *fantastical*, preternatural complacency, arising from that which he really has no feeling of. *South.*

2. Subsisting only in the fancy; imaginary.

Present feats
Are less than horrible imaginings:
My thought, whose murther yet is but *fantastical*,
Shakes so my single state of man, that function
Is smother'd in surmise; and nothing is,
But what is not. *Shakespeare's Macbeth.*

Men are so possessed with their own fancies, that they take them for oracles; and are arrived to some extraordinary revelations of truth, when indeed they do but dream dreams, and amuse themselves with the *fantastick* ideas of a busy imagination. *Decay of Piety.*

3. Unreal; apparent only; having the nature of phantoms which only assume visible forms occasionally.

Are ye *fantastical*, or that indeed
Which outwardly ye shew? *Shakespeare's Macbeth.*

4. Capricious; humourous; unsteady; irregular.

Nor happiness can I, nor misery feel,
From any turn of her *fantastick* wheel. *Prior.*

5. Whimsical; fanciful; indulgent to one's own imagination.

They put such words in the mouths of one of these *fantastical* mind-infected people, that children and musicians call lovers. *Sidney.*

I'll knit it up in silken strings,
With twenty odd conceited true love knots:
To be *fantastick*, may become a youth
Of greater time than I. *Shakes. Two Gentlemen of Verona.*

Duumvir is provided with an imperious, expensive and *fantastick* mistress; to whom he retires from the conversation of a discreet and affectionate wife. *Tatler.*

We are apt to think your medallists a little *fantastical* in the different prices they set upon their coins, without any regard to the metal of which they are composed. *Addison.*

FANTA'STICALLY. *adj.* [from *fantastical*.]

1. By the power of imagination.
2. Capriciously; humourously; unsteadily.

England is so idly king'd,
Her sceptre so *fantastically* borne,
By a vain, giddy, shallow, humourous youth,
That fear attends her not. *Shakespeare's Henry* V.

3. Whimsically; in compliance with mere imagination.

One cannot so much as *fantastically* chuse, even or odd, he thinks not why. *Grew's Cosmol. b.* ii. *c.* 4.

FANTA'STICALNESS. } FANTA'STICKNESS. } *n. s.* [from *fantastical*.]

1. Humourousness; mere compliance with fancy.
2. Whimsicalness; unreasonableness.

I dare not assume to myself to have put him out of conceit with it, by having convinced him of the *fantasticalness* of it. *Tillotson, Preface.*

3. Caprice; unsteadiness.

FA'NTASY. *n. s.* [*fantasie*, Fr. *phantasia*, Latin; Φαντασία.]

1. Fancy; imagination; the power of imagining. See FANCY.

How now, Horatio? you tremble and look pale!
Is not this something more than *fantasy*? *Shakes. Hamlet.*

I talk of dreams,
Which are the children of an idle brain,
Begot of nothing but vain *fantasy*;
Which is as thin of substance as the air,
And more unconstant than the wind. *Shak. Rom. and Juliet.*

He is superstitious grown of late,
Quite from the main opinion he held once
Of *fantasy*, of dreams, and ceremonies. *Shak. Jul. Cæsar.*

Go you, and where you find a maid,
That ere she sleep hath thrice her prayers said,
Rein up the organs of her *fantasy*,
Sleep she as sound as careless infancy. *Shakespeare.*

These spirits of sense, in *fantasy*'s high court,
Judge of the forms of objects, ill or well;
And so they send a good or ill report
Down to the heart, where all affections dwell. *Davies.*

By the power of *fantasy* we see colours in a dream, or a mad man sees things before him which are not there. *Newton.*

2. Idea; image of the mind.

And with the sug'ry sweet thereof allure,
Chaste ladies ears to *fantasies* impure. *Hubberd's Tale.*

3. Humour; inclination.

I would wish that both you and others would cease from drawing the Scriptures to your *fantasies* and affections. *Whitg.*

FA'NTOM. *n. s.* [See PHANTOM.]

FAP. *adj.* Fuddled; drunk. It seems to have been a cant word in the time of *Shakespeare*.

The gentleman had drunk himself out of his five senses; and being *fap*, sir, was, as they say, cashiered. *Shakespeare.*

FAR. *adv.* [feon, Saxon; *fatt*, Erse.]

1. To great extent in length.

Pay sacred rev'rence to Apollo's song,
Lest wrathful the *far*-shooting god emit
His fatal arrows. *Prior.*

2. To a great extent every way. This less proper.

Vast and great
Is what I love: the *far* extended ocean
To a little riv'let I prefer. *Prior.*

With costly cates she stain'd her frugal board;
Then with ill-gotten gold she bought a lord:
Corruption, discord, luxury combin'd,
Down sunk the *far* fam'd mistress of mankind. *Arbuthnot.*

From the same lineage stern Æetes came,
The *far* fam'd brother of th' enchantress dame. *Pope.*

3. To a great distance progressively.

Be factious for redress of all these griefs,
And I will set this foot of mine as *far*
As who goes farthest. *Shakespeare's Julius Cæsar.*

Is it *far* you ride?
—As *far*, my lord, as will fill up the time
'Twixt this and supper. *Shakespeare's Macbeth.*

Far from that hated face the Trojans fly;
All but the fool who sought his destiny. *Dryden's Æn.*

4. Remotely: at a great distance.

He meant to travel into *far* countries, until his friends affection either ceased or prevailed. *Sidney.*

In a kingdom rightly ordered, after a law is once published, it presently takes effect *far* and wide; all states framing themselves thereunto. *Hooker, b.* i. *s.* 3.

And after that long strayed here and there,
Through every field and forrest *far* and near. *Hubb. Tale.*

Far be it from me to justify the cruelties which were at first used towards them, which had their reward soon after. *Bacon's Holy War.*

He sent light horsemen into Mesopotamia with a guide, because

cause the country was unto him best known; following not *far* after himself with all his army. *Knolles's Hist. of the Turks.*

And yet the lights which in my tower do shine,
Mine eyes, which view all objects nigh and *far*,
Look not into this little world of mine. *Davies.*

God hath bid dwell *far* off all anxious cares,
And not molest us; unless we ourselves
Seek them with wand'ring thoughts, and notions vain. *Milt.*

I have been hunting up and down, *far* and near, since your unhappy indisposition, to find out a remedy. *L'Estrange.*

The nations *far* and near contend in choice,
And send the flow'r of war by publick voice. *Dryden.*

The painted lizard and the birds of prey,
Foes of the frugal kind, be *far* away. *Dryden's Virg. Geor.*

But from the reading of my book and me,
Be *far*, ye foes of virtuous poetry!
Who fortune's fault upon the poor can throw,
Point at the tatter'd coat and ragged shoe. *Dryden's Pers.*

Far off you view'd them with a longing eye
Upon the topmost branch. *Dryden.*

These words are so *far* from establishing any dominion, that we find the quite contrary. *Locke.*

'Till on the Po his blasted corps was hurl'd,
Far from his country, in the western world. *Addison's Ovid.*

5. To a distance.

As *far* as the East is from the West, so *far* hath he removed our transgressions from him. *Ps.* ciii. 12.

Neither did those that were sent, and travelled *far* off, undertake so difficult enterprizes without a conductor. *Raleigh.*

But all in vain! which when he saw, he ceas'd
Contending, and remov'd his tents *far* off. *Milt. Par. Lost.*

I had always a curiosity to look back into the sources of things, and view in my mind, so *far* as I was able, the beginning and progress of a rising world. *Burn. Th. of the World.*

A lion's hide around his loins he wore;
The well-poiz'd javelin to the field he bore,
Inur'd to blood; the *far* destroying dart,
And the best weapon, an undaunted heart. *Addison's Ovid.*

6. In a great part.

When they were by Jebus the day was *far* spent. *Judg.*

7. In a great proportion; by many degrees.

Who can find a virtuous woman? for her price is *far* above rubies. *Prov.* xxxi. 10.

Such a communication passeth *far* better through the water than air. *Bacon's Natural History*, N°. 134.

Those countries have *far* greater rivers, and *far* higher mountains to pour down waters, than any part of the old world. *Bacon's New Atlantis.*

The face of war,
In ancient times, doth differ *far*
From what our fiery battles are. *Waller.*

Of negatives we have *far* the least certainty, and they are usually hardest, and many times impossible to be proved. *Tillot.*

Latin is a more succinct language than either the Italian, Spanish, French, or even than the English, which, by reason of its monosyllables, is *far* the most compendious of them. *Dryden.*

Besides, he's lovely *far* above the rest,
With you immortal, and with beauty blest. *Pope.*

Ah! hope not yet to breathe thy native air;
Far other journey first demands thy care. *Pope's Odyssey.*

8. To a great height; magnificently. This is perhaps only in *Shakespeare.*

I do not think
So fair an outward, and such stuff within,
Endows a man but him.
——You speak him *far*.
——I don't extend him, sir. *Shakespeare's Cymbeline.*

9. To a certain point; to a certain degree.

The substance of the service of God, so *far* forth as it hath in it any thing more than the law of reason doth teach, may not be invented of men, as it is amongst the heathen; but must be received from God himself. *Hooker, b.* i.

Answer them
How *far* forth you do like their articles. *Shakes. Henry* IV.

Not to resolve, is to resolve; and many times it breeds as many necessities, and engageth as *far* in some other sort, as to resolve. *Bacon.*

Of this I need not many words to declare how *far* it is from being so much as any part of repentance. *Hammond.*

My discourse is so *far* from being equivalent to the position he mentions, that it is a perfect contradiction to it. *Tillotson.*

The custom of these tongues sometimes so *far* influences the expressions, that in these epistles one may observe the force of the Hebrew conjugations. *Locke on St. Paul's Epistles.*

10. It is used often in composition: as *farshooting*, *farseeing*.

FAR-FE'TCH. *n. s.* [*far* and *fetch.*] A deep stratagem. A ludicrous word.

But Jesuits have deeper reaches,
In all their politick *farfetches*;
And from their Coptick priest, Kircherus,
Found out this mystick way to jeer us. *Hudibras, p.* iii.

FAR-FE'TCHED. *adj.* [*far* and *fetch.*]

1. Brought from places remote.

Of these things others quickly will dispose,
Whose pains have earn'd the *farfetch'd* spoil *Milt. Pa. Lost.*

By his command we boldly cross'd the line,
And bravely fought where southern stars arise:
We trac'd the *farfetch'd* gold unto the mine,
And that which brib'd our fathers made our prize. *Dryden.*

2. Studiously sought; elaborately strained; not easily or naturally introduced.

York, with all his *farfetch'd* policy. *Shakes. Henry* VI.

For *farfetch'd* rhymes make puzzled angels strain,
And in low prose dull Lucifer complain. *Smith.*

Under this head we may rank those words, which signify different ideas, by a sort of an unaccountable *farfetched* analogy, or distant resemblance, that fancy has introduced between one thing and another; as when we say, the meat is green when it is half roasted. *Watts's Logick.*

FAR-PIE'RCING. *adj.* [*far* and *pierce.*] Striking, or penetrating a great way.

Atlas, her sire, to whose *farpiercing* eye
The wonders of the deep expanded lie;
Th' eternal columns which on earth he rears,
End in the starry vault, and prop the spheres. *Pope's Odyss.*

FAR-SHOO'TING. *adj.* [*far* and *shoot.*] Shooting to a great distance.

Then loud he call'd Æneas thrice by name;
The loud repeated voice to glad Æneas came;
Great Jove, he said, and the *farshooting* god,
Inspire thy mind to make thy challenge good. *Dryd. Æn.*

FAR. *adj.*

1. Distant; remote.

But we must beg our bread in climes unknown,
Beneath the scorching or the freezing zone;
And some to *far* Oaxis shall be sold,
Or try the Lybian heat, or Scythian cold. *Dryden's Virgil.*

2. It was formerly used not only as an adverb but an adjective, with *off*.

These things seem small and undistinguishable,
Like *far* off mountains turned into clouds. *Shakespeare.*

If we may behold in any creature any one spark of that eternal fire, or any *far off* dawning of God's glorious brightness, the same in the beauty, motion, and virtue of this light may be perceived. *Raleigh's History of the World.*

3. *From* FAR. In this sense is used elliptically for a *far* or remote place.

The Lord shall bring a nation against thee *from far*, from the end of the earth. *Deutr.* xxvii. 49.

4. Remoter of the two; in horsemanship, the right side of the horse, which the rider turns from him when he mounts.

No true Egyptian ever knew in horses
The *far* side from the near. *Dryden's Cleomenes.*

FAR. *n. s.* [contracted from *farrow.*] The offspring of a sow; young pigs.

Sows, ready to farrow this time of the year,
Are for to be made of and counted full dear;
For now is the loss of the *far* of the sow
More great than the loss of two calves of the cow. *Tuss.*

To FARCE. *v. a.* [*farcio*, Latin; *farcir*, French.]

1. To stuff; to fill with mingled ingredients.

Wrestling is a pastime which either the Cornishmen derived from Corineus, their first pretended founder, or at least it ministred some stuff to the *farcing* of that fable. *Carew.*

2. To extend; to swell out.

'Tis not the balm, the sceptre and the ball,
The sword, the mace, the crown imperial,
The entertissu'd robe of gold and pearl,
The *farced* title running 'fore the king. *Shakes. Henry* V.

FARCE *n. s.* [from the verb; or from *farcer*, French, to mock.] A dramatick representation written without regularity, and stuffed with wild and ludicrous conceits.

There is yet a lower sort of poetry and painting, which is out of nature; for a *farce* is that in poetry which grotesque is in a picture: the persons and actions of a *farce* are all unnatural, and the manners false; that is, inconsistent with the characters of mankind: grotesque painting is the just resemblance of this. *Dryden's Dufresnoy.*

What should be great, you turn to *farce*. *Prior.*

They object against it as a *farce*, because the irregularity of the plot should answer to the extravagance of the characters, which they say this piece wants, and therefore is no *farce*. *Gay.*

FA'RCICAL. *adj.* [from *farce.*] Belonging to a farce; appropriated to a farce.

They deny the characters to be *farcical*, because they are actually in nature. *Gay's Preface to the What d'ye Call it.*

FA'RCY. *n. s.* [*farcina*, Italian; *farcin*, French.] The leprosy of horses. It is probably curable by antimony.

FA'RDEL *n. s.* [*fardello*, Italian; *fardeau*, Fr.] A bundle; a little pack.

Let us to the king: there is that in this *fardel* will make him scratch his beard. *Shakespeare's Winter's Tale.*

Who would *fardels* bear,
To groan and ſweat under a weary life? *Shakeſp. Hamlet.*

To FARE. *v. n.* [ꝼaɲan, Saxon; *varen*, Dutch.]

1. To go; to paſs; to travel.

At laſt, reſolving forward ſtill to *fare*,
Until the bluſt'ring ſtorm is overblown. *Fairy Queen, b.* i.

His ſpirits pure were ſubject to our ſight,
Like to a man in ſhew and ſhape he *fared*. *Fairfax.*

So on he *fares*, and to the border comes
Of Eden. *Milton's Paradiſe Loſt, b.* iv. *l.* 131.

Sadly they *far'd* along the ſea-beat ſhore;
Still heav'd their hearts. *Pope.*

2. To be in any ſtate good or bad.

So bids thee well to *fare* thy nether friend. *Fairy Queen.*

A ſtubborn heart ſhall *fare* evil at the laſt. *Ecclus.* iii. 26.

Well *fare* the hand, which to our humble ſight
Preſents that beauty, which the dazzling light
Of royal ſplendor. *Waller.*

So in this throng bright Sachariſſa *far'd*,
Oppreſs'd by thoſe who ſtrove to be her guard:
As ſhips, though never ſo obſequious, fall
Foul in a tempeſt on their admiral. *Waller.*

So *fares* the ſtag among th' enraged hounds;
Repels their force, and wounds returns for wounds. *Denh.*

But as a barque, that in foul weather,
Toſs'd by two adverſe winds together,
Is bruis'd and beaten to and fro,
And knows not which to turn him to;
So *far'd* the knight between two foes,
And knew not which of them t' oppoſe. *Hudibras, p.* i.

If you do as I do, you may *fare* as I *fare*. *L'Eſtrange.*

Thus *fares* the queen, and thus her fury blows
Amid'ſt the crowd. *Dryden's Æn.*

Engliſh miniſters never *fare* ſo well as in a time of war with a foreign power, which diverts the private feuds and animoſities of the nation, and turns their efforts upon the common enemy. *Addiſon's Freeholder*, N°. 49.

Some give out there is no danger at all; others are comforted that it will be a common calamity, and they ſhall *fare* no worſe than their neighbours. *Swift.*

3. To proceed in any train of conſequences good or bad.

Thus it *fareth* when too much deſire of contradiction cauſeth our ſpeeches rather to paſs by number than to ſtay for weight. *Hooker, b.* ii. *ſ.* 5.

So *fares* it when with truth falſehood contends. *Milton.*

4. To happen to any one well or ill. With *it* preceding in an imperſonal form.

When the hand finds itſelf well warmed and covered, let it refuſe the trouble of feeding the mouth, or guarding the head, 'till the body be ſtarved or killed, and then we ſhall ſee how it will *fare* with the hand. *South's Sermons.*

5. To feed; to eat; to be entertained with food.

The rich man *fared* ſumptuouſly every day. *Luke.*

Feaſt your ears with the muſick awhile, if they will *fare* ſo harſhly as on the trumpet's ſound. *Shakeſpeare's Timon.*

Men think they have *fared* hardly, if, in times of extremity, they have deſcended ſo low as dogs; but Galen delivereth, that, young, fat, and gelded, they were the food of many nations. *Brown's Vulgar Errours, b.* iii. *c.* 25.

Fare. *n. ſ.* [from the verb.]

1. Price of paſſage in a vehicle by land or by water. Uſed only of that which is paid for the perſon, not the goods.

He found a ſhip going to Tarſiſh; ſo he paid the *fare* thereof, and went down into it to go with them unto Tarſiſh. *Jon.*

He paſſage begs with unregarded pray'r,
And wants two farthings to diſcharge his *fare*. *Dryd. Juv.*

2. Food prepared for the table; proviſions.

But come, ſo well refreſh'd, now let us play,
As meet is, after ſuch delicious *fare*. *Milton's Paradiſe Loſt.*

But when the weſtern winds with vital pow'r
Call forth the tender graſs and budding flow'r,
Then, at the laſt, produce in open air
Both flocks, and ſend them to their Summer's *fare*. *Dryden.*

This is what nature's want may well ſuffice;
He that would more is covetous, not wiſe:
But ſince among mankind ſo few there are,
Who will conform to philoſophick *fare*,
This much I will indulge thee for thy eaſe,
And mingle ſomething of our times to pleaſe. *Dryd. Juv.*

Upon his riſing up he ordered the peaſant to ſet before him whatever food he had in his houſe: the peaſant brought out a great deal of coarſe *fare*, of which the emperor eat very heartily. *Addiſon's Guardian*, N°. 99.

Farewe'll. *adv.* [This word is originally the imperative of the verb *fare well*, or *fare* you *well*; *ſis felix, abi in bonam rem*; or *bene ſit tibi*; but in time uſe familiariſed it to an adverb, and it is uſed both by thoſe who go and thoſe who are left.]

1. The parting compliment; adieu.

But *farewell*, king; ſith thus thou wilt appear,
Freedom lives hence, and baniſhment is here. *Shak. K. Lear.*

Farewell, maſter Silence: I will not uſe many words with you; *fare* you *well*, gentlemen, both. *Shakeſp. Henry* IV.

Whether we ſhall meet again, I know not,
Therefore our everlaſting farewell take;
For ever, and for ever, *farewell*, Caſſius. *Shak. Jul. Cæſar.*

Be not amazed, call all your ſenſes to you; defend your reputation, or bid *farewell* to your good life for ever. *Shakeſp.*

An iron ſlumber ſhuts my ſwimming eyes;
And now *farewell*, involv'd in ſhades of night,
For ever I am raviſh'd from thy ſight. *Dryden's Virg. Geo.*

Farewell, ſays he; the parting ſound ſcarce fell
From his faint lips, but ſhe replied *farewell*. *Dryden.*

O queen, *farewell!* be ſtill poſſeſt
Of dear remembrance, bleſſing ſtill and bleſt! *Pope's Odyſſ.*

2. It is ſometimes uſed only as an expreſſion of ſeparation without kindneſs.

Farewell the year which threaten'd ſo
The faireſt light the world can ſhow. *Waller.*

Treading the path to nobler ends,
A long *farewell* to love I gave;
Reſolv'd my country and my friends
All that remain'd of me ſhould have. *Waller.*

Farewe'll. *n. ſ.*

1. Leave; act of departure.

See how the morning opes her golden gates,
And takes her *farewell* of the glorious ſun. *Shakeſ. Hen.* VI.

If chance the radiant ſun, with *farewell* ſweet,
Extend his ev'ning beam, the fields revive,
The birds their notes renew, and bleating herds
Atteſt their joy, that hill and valley ring. *Milt. Par. Loſt.*

As in this grove I took my laſt *farewell*,
As on this very ſpot of earth I fell. *Dryden.*

Before I take my *farewell* of this ſubject, I ſhall adviſe the author for the future to ſpeak his meaning more plainly. *Addiſ.*

2. It is ſometimes uſed as an adjective; leave-taking.

Several ingenious writers, who have taken their leave of the publick in *farewell* papers, will not give over ſo, but intend to appear again; though perhaps under another form, and with a different title. *Spectator*, N°. 445.

Farina'ceous. *adj.* [from *farina*, Latin.] Mealy; taſting like meal or flower of corn.

The propereſt food of the vegetable kingdom for mankind, is taken from the *farinaceous* or mealy ſeeds of ſome culmiferous plants; as oats, barley, wheat, rice, rye, maize, panick, and millet. *Arbuthnot on Aliments.*

FARM. *n. ſ.* [*ferme*, French; ꝼeoɲm, proviſion, Saxon.]

1. Ground let to a tenant; ground cultivated by another man upon condition of paying part of the profit to the owner or landlord.

Touching their particular complaint for reducing lands and *farms* to their ancient rents, it could not be done without a parliament. *Hayward.*

2. The ſtate of lands let out to the culture of tenants.

The lords of land in Ireland do not uſe to ſet out their land in *farm*, for term of years, to their tenants; but only from year to year, and ſome during pleaſure. *Spenſer on Ireland.*

To Farm. *v. a.* [from the noun.]

1. To let out to tenants at a certain rent.

We are enforc'd to *farm* our royal realm,
The revenue whereof ſhall furniſh us
For our affairs in hand. *Shakeſpeare's Richard* II.

2. To take at a certain rate.

They received of the bankers ſcant twenty ſhillings for thirty, which the earl of Cornwall *farmed* of the king. *Camden's Rem.*

3. To cultivate land.

Fa'rmer. *n. ſ.* [*fermier*, French; or from *farm.*]

1. One who cultivates hired ground.

Thou haſt ſeen a *farmer's* dog bark at a beggar, and the creature run from the cur: there thou might'ſt behold the great image of authority; a dog's obey'd in office. *Shakeſp.*

2. One who cultivates ground, whether his own or another's.

Nothing is of greater prejudice to the *farmer* than the ſtocking of his land with cattle that are larger than it will bear. *Mortimer's Huſbandry.*

Fa'rmost. *n. ſ.* [ſuperlative of *far.*] Moſt diſtant; remoteſt.

A ſpacious cave, within its *farmoſt* part,
Was hew'd and faſhion'd by laborious art,
Through the hill's hollow ſides. *Dryden's Æn. b.* vi.

Fa'rness. *n. ſ.* [from *far.*] Diſtance; remoteneſs.

Their nearneſs on all quarters to the enemy, and their *farneſs* from timely ſuccour by their friends, have forced the commanders to call forth the uttermoſt number of able hands to fight. *Carew's Survey of Cornwall.*

Farra'ginous. *adj.* [from *farrago*, Latin.] Formed of different materials.

Being a confuſion of knaves and fools, and a *farraginous* concurrence of all conditions, tempers, ſexes and ages, it is but natural if their determinations be monſtrous, and many ways inconſiſtent with truth. *Brown's Vulgar Errours.*

FARRA'GO. *n. ſ.* [Latin.] A maſs formed confuſedly of ſeveral ingredients; a medley.

FA'RRIER. *n. s.* [*ferrier*, French; *ferrarius*, Latin.]

1. A shoer of horses.

But the utmost exactness in these particulars belong to *farriers*, saddlers, smiths, and other tradesmen. *Digby.*

2. One who professes the medicine of horses.

If you are a piece of a *farrier*, as every good groom ought to be, get sack, brandy, or strong-beer to rub your horses. *Swift's Directions to the Groom.*

To FA'RRIER. *v. n.* [from the noun.] To practise physick or chirurgery on horses.

Though there are many pretenders to the art of *farriering* and cowleeching, yet many of them are very ignorant. *Mort.*

FA'RROW. *n. s.* [fearh, Saxon.] A little pig.

Pour in sow's blood that hath litter'd
Her nine *farrow*. *Shakespeare's Macbeth.*

To FA'RROW. *v. a.* To bring pigs. It is used only of swine.

Sows ready to *farrow* this time of the year,
Are for to be made of. *Tuss. Husb.*

The swine, although multiparous, yet being bisulcous, and only cloven-hoofed, is *farrowed* with open eyes, as other bisulcous animals. *Brown.*

Ev'n her, who did her numerous offspring boast,
As fair and fruitful as the sow that carry'd
The thirty pigs, at one large litter *farrow'd*. *Dryd. Juven.*

FART. *n. s.* [fert, Saxon.] Wind from behind.

Love is the *fart*
Of every heart;
It pains a man when 'tis kept close;
And others doth offend, when 'tis let loose. *Suckling.*

To FART. *v. a.* [from the noun.] To break wind behind.

As when we a gun discharge,
Although the bore be ne'er so large,
Before the flame from muzzle burst,
Just at the breech it flashes first;
So from my lord his passion broke,
He *farted* first, and then he spoke. *Swift.*

FA'RTHER. *adv.* [This word is now generally considered as the comparative degree of *far*; but by no analogy can *far* make *farther* or *farthest*: it is therefore probable, that the ancient orthography was nearer the true, and that we ought to write *further* and *furthest*, from *forth*, *forther*, *forthest*, forðor, furðer, Saxon; the *o* and *u*, by resemblance of sound, being first confounded in speech, and afterwards in books.] At a greater distance; to a greater distance; more remotely; beyond; moreover.

To make a perfect judgment of good pictures, when compared with one another, besides rules, there is *farther* required a long conversation with the best pieces. *Dryden's Dufresnoy.*

They contented themselves with the opinions, fashions and things of their country, without looking any *farther*. *Locke.*

FA'RTHER. *adj.* [supposed from *far*, more, probably from *forth*.]

1. More remote.

Let me add a *farther* truth, that without those ties of gratitude, I have a most particular inclination to honour you. *Dryden's Juven. Dedication.*

2. Longer; tending to greater distance.

Before our *farther* way the fates allow,
Here must we fix on high the golden bough. *Dryden's Æn.*

FA'RTHERANCE. *n. s.* [more properly *furtherance*, from *further*.] Encouragement; promotion.

That was the foundation of the learning I have, and of all the *fartherance* that I have obtained. *Ascham's Schoolmaster.*

FARTHERMO'RE. *adv.* [more properly *furthermore*.] Besides; over and above; likewise.

Farthermore the leaves, body and boughs of this tree, by so much exceed all other plants, as the greatest men of power and worldly ability surpass the meanest. *Raleigh's History.*

To FA'RTHER. *v. a.* [more proper *To further*.] To promote; to facilitate; to advance.

If he had *farthered* or hindered the taking of the town, *Dryden's Dedicat. to the Æn.*

FA'RTHEST. *adv.* [more properly *furthest*. See FARTHER.]

1. At the greatest distance.
2. To the greatest distance.

FA'RTHEST. *adj.* Most distant; remotest.

Yet it must be withal considered, that the greatest part of the world are they which be *farthest* from perfection. *Hooker.*

FA'RTHING. *n. s.* [feorðling, Saxon, from feower, four, that is, the fourth part of a penny.]

1. The fourth of a penny; the smallest English coin.

A *farthing* is the least denomination or fraction of money used in England. *Cocker's Arithmetick.*

Else all those things we toil so hard in,
Would not avail one single *farthing*. *Prior.*

2. Copper money.

The parish find, 'tis true; but our church-wardens
Feed on the silver, and give us the *farthings*. *Gay.*

You are not obliged to take money not of gold or silver; not the halfpence or *farthings* of England. *Swift.*

3. It is used sometimes in a sense hyperbolical: as, it is not worth a *farthing*; or proverbial.

His son builds on, and never is content,
'Till the last *farthing* is in structure spent *Dryden's Juven.*

FA'RTHINGALE. *n. s.* [This word has much exercised the etymology of *Skinner*, who at last seems to determine that it is derived from *vertu garde*: if he had considered what *vert* signifies in Dutch, he might have found out the true sense.] A hoop; circles of whalebone used to spread the petticoat to a wide circumference.

With silken coats, and caps, and golden rings,
With ruffs, and cuffs, and *farthingales*, and things. *Shakesp.*

Tell me,
What compass will you wear your *farthingale?* *Shakesp.*

Arthur wore in hall
Round table, like a *farthingal*. *Hudibras, p.* i. *cant.* 1.

Some will have it that it portends the downfal of the French king; and observe, that the *farthingale* appeared in England a little before the ruin of the Spanish monarchy. *Addison.*

She seems a medley of all ages,
With a huge *farthingale* to swell her fustian stuff,
A new commode, a topknot, and a ruff. *Swift.*

FA'RTHINGSWORTH. *n. s.* [*farthing* and *worth*.] As much as is sold for a farthing.

They are thy customers; I hardly ever sell them a *farthingsworth* of any thing. *Arbuthnot's History of John Bull.*

FA'SCES. *n. s.* [Latin.] Rods anciently carried before the consuls as a mark of their authority.

The duke beheld, like Scipio, with disdain,
That Carthage, which he ruin'd, rise once more;
And shook aloft the *fasces* of the main,
To fright those slaves with what they felt before. *Dryden.*

FA'SCIA. *n. s.* [Latin.] A fillet; a bandage.

FA'SCIATED. *adj.* [from *fascia*.] Bound with fillets; tied with a bandage. *Dict.*

FASCIA'TION. *n. s.* [from *fascia*.] Bandage; the act or manner of binding diseased parts.

Three especial sorts of *fasciation*, or rowling, have the worthies of our profession commended to posterity. *Wiseman.*

To FA'SCINATE. *v. a.* [*fascino*, Latin.] To bewitch; to enchant; to influence in some wicked and secret manner.

There be none of the affections which have been noted to *fascinate* or bewitch, but love and envy. *Bacon, Essay* 9.

Such a *fascinating* sin this is, as allows men no liberty of consideration. *Decay of Piety.*

FASCINA'TION. *n. s.* [from *fascinate*.] The power or act of bewitching; enchantment; unseen inexplicable influence.

He had such a crafty and bewitching fashion, both to move pity and to induce belief, as was like a kind of *fascination* and enchantment to those that saw him or heard him. *Bacon.*

The Turks hang old rags, or such like ugly things, upon their fairest horses, and other goodly creatures, to secure them against *fascination*. *Waller.*

There is a certain bewitchery or *fascination* in words, which makes them operate with a force beyond what we can naturally give an account of. *South's Sermons.*

FA'SCINE. *n. s.* [French.] A faggot. Military cant.

The black prince passed many a river without the help of pontoons, and filled a ditch with faggots as successfully as the generals of our times do with *fascines*. *Addison's Spectator.*

FA'SCINOUS. *adj.* [*fascinum*, Latin.] Caused or acting by witchcraft, or enchantment.

I shall not discuss the possibility of *fascinous* diseases, farther than refer to experiment. *Harvey on Consumptions.*

FA'SHION. *n. s.* [*façon*, French; *facies*, Latin.]

1. Form; make; state of any thing with regard to its outward appearance.

They pretend themselves grieved at our solemnities in erecting churches, at their form and *fashion*, at the stateliness of them and costliness, and at the opinion which we have of them. *Hooker, b.* v. *s.* 17.

The *fashion* of his countenance was altered. *Luke* ix. 29.

Stand these poor people's friend.
—I will,
Or let me lose the *fashion* of a man. *Shakes. Henry* VIII.

2. The make or cut of cloaths.

I'll be at charges for a looking-glass,
And entertain a score or two of taylors,
To study *fashions* to adorn my body. *Shakes. Richard* III.

You, sir, I entertain for one of my hundred; only, I do not like the *fashion* of your garments. *Shakesp. King Lear.*

3. Manner; sort; way.

For that I love your daughter
In such a righteous *fashion* as I do,
Perforce against all checks, rebukes, and manners,
I must advance. *Shakespeare's Merry Wives of Windsor.*

Pluck Casca by the sleeve,
And he will, after his sour *fashion*, tell you
What hath proceeded. *Shakespeare's Julius Cæsar.*

The commissioners either pulled down or defaced all images in churches; and that in such unseasonable and unseasoned *fashion*, as if it had been done in hostility against them. *Hayw.*

4. Custom operating upon dress, or any domestick ornaments.

Here's

Here's the note
How much your chain weighs to the utmoſt carat,
The fineneſs of the gold, the chargeful *faſhion*. *Shakeſpeare.*

5. Cuſtom; general practice.

Zelmane again, with great admiration, begun to ſpeak of him; aſking whether it were the *faſhion* or no, in Arcadia, that ſhepherds ſhould perform ſuch valorous enterprizes. *Sidn.*

Though the truth of this hath been univerſally acknowledged, yet becauſe the *faſhion* of the age is to call every thing into queſtion, it will be requiſite to ſatisfy mens reaſon about it. *Tillotſon, Sermon* 3.

Why truly, wife, it was not eaſily reconciled to the common method; but then it was the *faſhion* to do ſuch things. *Arbuthnot's Hiſtory of John Bull.*

6. Manner imitated from another; way eſtabliſhed by precedent.

Sorrow ſo royally in you appears,
That I will deeply put the *faſhion* on,
And wear it in my heart. *Shakeſpeare.*

7. General approbation; mode.

A young gentleman accommodates himſelf to the innocent diverſions in *faſhion*. *Locke.*

His panegyricks were beſtowed only on ſuch perſons as he had familiarly known, and only at ſuch times as others ceaſe to praiſe, when out of power, or out of *faſhion*. *Pope.*

8. Rank; condition above the vulgar. It is uſed in a ſenſe below that of quality.

It is ſtrange that men of *faſhion*, and gentlemen, ſhould ſo groſly belie their own knowledge. *Raleigh.*

9. Any thing worn.

Now, by this maiden bloſſom in my hand,
I ſcorn thee, and thy *faſhion*, peeviſh boy. *Shak. Hen.* VI.

10. The farcy; a diſtemper in horſes; the horſes leproſy. A barbarous word.

His horſe is poſſeſt with the glanders, infected with the *faſhions*, and full of windgalls. *Shak. Taming of the Shrew.*

To FA'SHION. *v. a.* [*façonner*, French, from the noun.]

1. To form; to mould; to figure.

He loves me well, and I have giv'n him reaſons;
Send him but hither, and I'll *faſhion* him. *Shak. Jul. Cæſar.*

Did not he that made me in the womb, make him? And did not one *faſhion* us in the womb? *Job* xxxi. 15.

The graves of the rebellious generations were already *faſhioned* in the clouds, which ſoon after ſhould ſwallow up all living creatures. *Raleigh's Hiſtory of the World.*

The rib he form'd, and *faſhion'd* with his hands:
Under his forming hands a creature grew,
Man like, but different ſex. *Milton's Paradiſe Loſt, b.* viii.

Inability will every one find in himſelf, who ſhall go about to *faſhion* in his underſtanding any ſimple idea, not received by his ſenſes from external objects, or by reflection from the operations of his mind about them. *Locke.*

How could this noble fabrick be deſign'd,
And *faſhion'd*, by a maker brute and blind?
Could it of art ſuch miracles invent?
And raiſe a beauteous world of ſuch extent? *Blackm. Creat.*

A different toil another forge employs,
Here the loud hammer *faſhions* female toys;
Each trinket that adorns the modern dame,
Firſt to theſe little artiſts ow'd its frame. *Gay's Fan.*

2. To fit; to adapt; to accommodate.

Laws ought to be *faſhioned* unto the manners and conditions of the people to whom they are meant, and not to be impoſed upon them according to the ſimple rule of right. *Spenſer.*

Ne do, I doubt, but that ye well can *faſhion*
Yourſelves thereto, according to occaſion. *Hubb. Tale.*

Nature, as it grows again tow'rds earth,
Is *faſhion'd* for the journey, dull and heavy. *Shakeſ. Timon.*

This cardinal,
Though from an humble ſtock undoubtedly,
Was *faſhion'd* to much honour from his cradle. *Sh. H.* VIII.

3. To caſt into external appearance.

It better fits my blood to be diſdained of all, than to *faſhion* a carriage to rob love from any. *Sh. Much Ado about Nothing.*

4. To make according to the rule preſcribed by cuſtom.

The value of the labour employed about one parcel of ſilver more than another, makes a difference in their price; and thus *faſhioned* plate ſells for more than its weight. *Locke.*

FA'SHIONABLE. *adj.* [from *faſhion.*]

1. Approved by cuſtom; eſtabliſhed by cuſtom; modiſh.

The eminence of your condition, and the gallantry of your principles, will invite gentlemen to the uſeful and ennobling ſtudy of nature, and make philoſophy *faſhionable*. *Glan.*

Examine how the *faſhionable* practice of the world can be reconciled to this important doctrine of our religion. *Rogers.*

'Tis prevailing example that hath now made it *faſhionable*. *Bentley.*

2. Made according to the mode.

Rich, *faſhionable* robes her perſon deck;
Pendants her ears, and pearls adorn her neck. *Dryd. Ovid.*

3. Obſervant of the mode.

Time is like a *faſhionable* hoſt,
That ſlightly ſhakes his parting gueſt by th' hand;
But with his arms outſtretch'd, as he would fly,
Graſps in the comer: welcome ever ſmiles,
And farewell goes out ſighing. *Shakeſ. Troilus and Creſſida.*

4. Having rank above the vulgar, and below nobility.

FA'SHIONABLENESS. *n. ſ.* [from *faſhionable.*] Modiſh elegance; ſuch appearance as is according to the preſent cuſtom.

Why ſhould they not continue to value themſelves for this outſide *faſhionableneſs* of the taylor or tirewoman's making, when their parents have ſo early inſtructed them to do ſo? *Locke.*

FA'SHIONABLY. *adv.* [from *faſhionable.*] In a manner conformable to cuſtom; with modiſh elegance.

He muſt at length die dully of old age at home, when here he might ſo *faſhionably* and genteelly have been duelled or fluxed into another world. *South's Sermons.*

FA'SHIONIST. *n. ſ.* [from *faſhion.*] A follower of the mode; a fop; a coxcomb. *Dict.*

To FAST. *v. n.* [*faſtan*, Gothick; fæſtan, Saxon.]

1. To abſtain from food.

Our love is not ſo great, Hortenſio,
But we may blow our nails together,
And *faſt* it fairly out. *Shak. Taming of the Shrew.*

I had rather *faſt* from all four days than drink ſo much in one. *Shakſpeare's Anthony and Cleopatra.*

We have ſome meats, and breads, and drinks, which taken by men enable them to *faſt* long after. *Bacon's New Atlantis.*

2. To mortify the body by religious abſtinence.

When thou *faſteſt*, anoint thy head and waſh thy face, that thou appear not unto men to *faſt*. *Mat.* vi.

Laſt night the very god ſhew'd me a viſion:
I *faſt*, and pray'd for their intelligence. *Shakeſ. Cymbeline.*

FAST. *n. ſ.* [from the verb.]

1. Abſtinence from food.

A thouſand men have broke their *faſts* to-day,
That ne'er ſhall dine, unleſs thou yield the crown. *Shakeſ.*

Where will this end? Four times ten days I've paſs'd,
Wand'ring this woody maze, and human food
Nor taſted, nor had appetite; that *faſt*
To virtue I impute not, or count part
Of what I ſuffer here. *Milton's Paradiſe Loſt, b.* ii.

Happy and innocent were the ages of our fore-fathers, who broke their *faſts* with herbs and roots; and when they were permitted fleſh, eat it only dreſſed with hunger and fire. *Taylor.*

She's gone unkindly, and refus'd to caſt
One glance to feed me for ſo long a *faſt*. *Dryd. Tyran. Love.*

2. Religious mortification by abſtinence; religious humiliation.

We humble ourſelves before God this day, not merely by the outward ſolemnities of a *faſt*, but by afflicting our ſouls as well as bodies for our ſins. *Atterbury's Sermons.*

Nor pray'rs nor *faſts* its ſtubborn pulſe reſtrain;
Nor tears, for ages, taught to flow in vain. *Pope.*

FAST. *adj.* [fæſt, Saxon.]

1. Firm; immoveable.

He by his ſtrength ſetteth *faſt* mountains. *Pſ.* lxv. 6.

Laſt, the ſire and his three ſons,
With their four wives; and God made *faſt* the door. *Milt.*

Be ſure to find,
What I foretold thee, many a hard aſſay
Of dangers and adverſities, and pains,
Ere thou of Iſrael's ſceptre get *faſt* hold. *Milt. Par. Reg.*

2. Strong; impregnable.

England, by report of the chronicles, was infeſted with robbers and outlaws; which, lurking in woods and *faſt* places, uſed often to break forth to rob and ſpoil. *Spenſer on Ireland.*

3. Fixed.

Lodronius, with the breaking in and force of the horſemen, was driven into a marſh; where, after that he, being ſore wounded, and almoſt *faſt* in the deep mud, had done the uttermoſt of that his laſt endeavour, he yielded himſelf. *Knolles.*

A man in a boat, who tugs at a rope that's *faſt* to a ſhip, looks as if he reſolved to draw the ſhip to him. *Temple.*

4. Deep; ſound.

I have ſeen her riſe from her bed, take paper, fold it, ſeal it, and again return to bed; yet all this while in a moſt *faſt* ſleep. *Shakeſpeare's Macbeth.*

5. Firm in adherence.

Quick wits be in deſire new-fangled; in purpoſe, unconſtant; light to promiſe any thing, ready to forget every thing, both benefit and injury; and thereby neither *faſt* to friend, nor fearful to foe. *Aſcham's Schoolmaſter.*

6. [from *ffeſt*, Welſh, quick] Speedy; quick; ſwift.

This work goeth *faſt* on, and proſpereth in their hands. *Ezra* v. viii.

Skill comes ſo ſlow, and life ſo *faſt* doth fly,
We learn ſo little, and forget ſo much. *Davies.*

The prince groweth up *faſt* to be a man, and is of a ſweet and excellent diſpoſition: it would be a ſtain upon you if you ſhould miſlead, or ſuffer him to be miſled. *Bacon to Villiers.*

7. FAST *and looſe.* Uncertain; variable; inconſtant; deceitful.

A rope of fair pearl, which now hiding, now hidden by the hair, did, as it were, play at *fast and loose* each with other, giving and receiving richness. *Sidney.*

If she perceived by his outward chear,
That any would his love by talk bewray,
Sometimes she heard him, sometimes stopt her ear,
And play'd *fast and loose* the live-long day. *Fairfax, b.* v.

The folly and wickedness of men, that think to play *fast and loose* with God Almighty! *L'Estrange.*

If they cohered, yet by the next conflict with other atoms they might be separated again; and so on in an eternal vicissitude of *fast and loose*, without ever consociating into the huge condense bodies of planets. *Bentley's Sermons.*

FAST. *adv.*

1. Firmly; immoveably.

Bind the boy, which you shall find with me,
Fast to the chair. *Shakespeare's King John.*

This love of theirs myself have often seen,
Haply when they have judg'd me *fast* asleep. *Shakespeare.*

2. Closely; nearly.

Barbarossa left fourteen galleys in the lake; but the tacklings, sails, oars, and ordnance he had laid up in the castle *fast* by. *Knolles's History of the Turks.*

Siloa's brook, that flow'd
Fast by the oracle of God. *Milton's Paradise Lost, b.* i.

Let purling streams be in her fancy seen,
And flow'ry meads, and vales of chearful green;
And in the midst of deathless groves
Soft sighing wishes lie,
And smiling hopes *fast* by,
And just beyond 'em ever-laughing loves. *Dryd. Tyr. Love.*

Fast by the throne obsequious fame resides,
And wealth incessant rolls her golden tides. *Pope's Odyssey.*

Well known to me the palace you inquire;
For *fast* beside it dwells my honour'd fire. *Pope's Odyssey.*

Here o'er the martyr-king the marble weeps,
And *fast* beside him once-fear'd Edward sleeps. *Pope.*

3. Swiftly; nimbly.

I would give a thousand pound I could run as *fast* as thou can'st. *Shakespeare's Henry* IV. *p.* 1.

There streams a spring of blood so *fast*,
From those deep wounds, as all embru'd the face. *Daniel.*

The heaviest muse the swiftest course has gone,
As clocks run *fastest* when most lead is on. *Pope.*

You are to look upon me as one going *fast* out of the world. *Swift to Pope.*

4. Frequently.

Being tried only with a promise, he gave full credit to that promise, and still gave evidence of his fidelity as *fast* as occasions were offered. *Hammond's Pract. Catech.*

To FA'STEN. *v. a.* [from *fast.*]

1. To make fast; to make firm; to fix immoveably.

A mantle coming under her right arm, and covering most of that side, had no *fastening* on the left side. *Sidney.*

Moses reared up the tabernacle, and *fastened* his sockets. *Ex.*

By chance a ship was *fasten'd* to the shore,
Which from old Clusium king Osinius bore. *Dryden's Æn.*

2. To hold together; to cement; to link.

She had all magnetick force alone,
To draw and *fasten* sundred parts in one. *Donne.*

In the sea-coast of India there is no iron, which flies not like a bird unto those mountains, and therefore their ships are *fastened* with wood. *Brown's Vulgar Errours, b.* ii. *c.* 8.

3. To affix; to conjoin.

The words Whig and Tory have been pressed to the service of many successions of parties, with very different ideas *fastened* to them. *Swift's Examiner*, N°. 43.

4. To stamp; to impress.

Thinking, by this face,
To *fasten* in our thoughts that they have courage;
But 'tis not so. *Shakespeare's Julius Cæsar.*

5. To settle; to confirm.

Their oppressors have changed the scene, and combated the opinions in their true shape, upon which they could not so well *fasten* their disguise. *Decay of Piety.*

6. To lay on with strength.

Could he *fasten* a blow, or make a thrust, when not suffered to approach? *Dryden's Æn. Dedication.*

To FA'STEN. *v. n.* To fix himself.

This paucity of blood may be observed in other sorts of lizards, in frogs, and other fishes; and therefore an horseleech will hardly *fasten* upon a fish. *Brown's Vulgar Errours.*

He *fasten'd* on my neck; and bellow'd out,
As he'd burst heaven. *Shakespeare's King Lear.*

The wrong judgment that misleads us, and makes the will often *fasten* on the worse side, lies in misreporting upon comparisons. *Locke.*

FA'STENER. *n. s.* [from *fasten.*] One that makes fast or firm.

FA'STER. *n. s.* [from *fast.*] He who abstains from food. *Ainf.*

FA'STHANDED. *adj.* [*fast* and *hand.*] Avaricious; closehanded; closefisted; covetous.

The king being *fasthanded*, and loth to part with a second dowry, prevailed with the prince to be contracted with the princess Catharine. *Bacon's Henry* VII.

FASTIDIO'SITY. *n. s.* [from *fastidious.*] Disdainfulness; contemptuousness. *Swift.*

FASTI'DIOUS. *adj.* [*fastidiosus*, Latin; *fastidieux*, *fastidieuse*, French.] Disdainful; squeamish; delicate to a vice; insolently nice.

Reasons plainly delivered, and always after one manner, especially with fine and *fastidious* minds, enter but heavily and dully. *Bacon's Collection of Good and Evil.*

Let their *fastidious* vain
Commission of the brain,
Run on and rage, sweat, censure, and condemn,
They were not made for thee, less thou for them. *B. Johns.*

A squeamish *fastidious* niceness, in meats and drinks, must be cured by starving. *L'Estrange.*

All hopes, raised upon the promises or supposed kindnesses of the *fastidious* and fallacious great ones of the world, shall fail. *South's Sermons.*

FASTI'DIOUSLY. *adv.* [from *fastidious.*] Disdainfully; contemptuously; squeamishly.

Their sole talent is pride and scorn: they look *fastidiously*, and speak disdainfully, on any one who want them; concluding, if a man shall fall short of their garniture at the knees and elbows, he is much inferior to them in the furniture of his head. *Government of the Tongue, s.* 7.

FASTIGI'ATED. *adv.* [*fastigiatus*, Latin.] Roofed; narrowed up to the top. *Dict.*

FA'STINGDAY. *n. s* [*fast* and *day.*] Day of mortification by religious abstinence.

Do not call it a *fastingday*, unless also it be a day of extraordinary devotion and of alms. *Taylor's Guide to Devotion.*

FA'STNESS. *n. s.* [from *fast.*]

1. Firmness; firm adherence.

Such as had given the king any distaste, did content by their forwardness to shew it was but their *fastness* to the former government, and that those affections ended with the time. *Bacon's History of Great Britain.*

2. Strength; security.

All the places are cleared, and places of *fastness* laid open, which are the proper walls and castles of the Irish, as they were of the British in the times of Agricola. *Davies on Ireland.*

The foes had left the *fastness* of their place,
Prevail'd in fight, and had his men in chace. *Dryden's Æn.*

3. A strong place; a place not easily forced.

If his adversary be not well aware of him, he entrenches himself in a new *fastness*, and holds out the siege with a new artillery. *Watts's Improvement of the Mind.*

4. Closeness; conciseness; not diffusion.

Bring his stile from all loose grossness to such firm *fastness* in Latin, as in Demosthenes. *Ascham's Schoolmaster.*

FA'STUOUS. *adj.* [*fastuosus*, Latin; *fastueux-se*, Fr.] Proud; haughty. *Dict.*

FAT. *adj.* [fæt, Saxon.]

1. Fullfed; plump; fleshy; the contrary to lean.

When gods have hot backs, what shall poor men do? For me, I am here a Windsor stag, and the *fattest*, I think, i' th' forest. *Shakespeare's Merry Wives of Windsor.*

Let our wives
Appoint a meeting with this old *fat* fellow. *Shakespeare.*

'Tis a fine thing to be *fat* and smooth. *L'Estrange.*

Spare diet and labour will keep constitutions, where this disposition is the strongest, from being *fat*: you may see in an army forty thousand foot-soldiers without a *fat* man; and I dare affirm, that by plenty and rest twenty of the forty shall grow *fat*. *Arbuthnot on Aliments.*

2. Coarse; gross; dull. [*fat*, French.]

O souls! in whom no heav'nly fire is found,
Fat minds, and ever-grov'ling on the ground. *Dryd. Pers.*

3. Wealthy; rich.

Some are allured to law, not on the contemplation of equity, but on the promising and pleasing thoughts of litigious terms, *fat* contentions, and flowing fees. *Milton.*

A *fat* benefice is that which so abounds with an estate and revenues, that a man may expend a great deal in delicacies of eating and drinking. *Ayliffe's Parergon.*

FAT. *n. s.* An oily and sulphureous part of the blood, deposited in the cells of the membrana adiposa, from the innumerable little vessels which are spread amongst them. The fat is to be found immediately under the skin, in all the parts of the body, except in the forehead, eyelids, lips, upper part of the ear, yard, and scrotum. In some the vesicles of the membrana adiposa are so full, that the fat is an inch or more thick; and in others they are almost flat, containing little or no fat. There are two sorts of fat; one yellow, soft, and lax, which is easily melted, called pinguedo; another firm, white, brittle, and which is not so easily melted, called sebum, suet, or tallow. Some reckon the marrow of the bones for a third sort of fat. *Quincy.*

In this ointment the strangest and hardest ingredients to come by, are the moss upon the skull of a dead man unburied,

 and

and the *fats* of a boar and a bear, killed in the act of generation. *Bacon's Natural History*, N°. 998.

This membrane separates an oily liquor called *fat*: when the fibres are lax, and the aliment too redundant, great part of it is converted into this oily liquor. *Arbuthnot on Aliments.*

FAT. *n. s.* [fæt, Saxon; *vatte*, Dutch. This is generally written *vat*.] A vessel in which any thing is put to ferment or be soaked.

The *fats* shall overflow with wine and oil. *Joel* ii. 24.

A white stone used for flagging floors, for cisterns, and tanners *fats*. *Woodward on Fossils.*

To FAT. *v. a.* [from the noun.] To make fat; to fatten; to make plump and fleshy with abundant food.

Oh how this villany
Doth *fat* me with the very thoughts of it! *Shak. Tit. Andr.*

Ere this
I should have *fatted* all the region kites
With this slave's offal. *Shakespeare's Hamlet.*

They *fat* such enemies as they take in the wars, that they may devour them. *Abbot's Description of the World.*

The Caribbees were wont to geld their children, on purpose to *fat* and eat them. *Locke.*

Cattle *fatted* by good pasturage, after violent motion, sometimes die suddenly. *Arbuthnot on Diet.*

To FAT. *v. n.* To grow fat; to grow full fleshed.

Clarence, he is well repaid;
He is frank'd up to *fatting* for his pains. *Shakes. Rich.* III.

The one labours in his duty with a good conscience; the other, like a beast, but *fatting* up for the slaughter. *L'Estrange.*

An old ox *fats* as well, and is as good, as a young one. *Mortimer's Husbandry.*

FA'TAL. *adj.* [*fatalis*, Latin; *fatal*, French.]

1. Deadly; mortal; destructive; causing destruction.

O *fatal* maid! thy marriage is endow'd
With Phrygian, Latian, and Rutilian blood. *Dryden's Æn.*

A palsy in the brain is most dangerous; when it seizeth the heart, or organs of breathing, *fatal*. *Arbuthnot on Diet.*

2. Proceeding by destiny; inevitable; necessary.

Others delude their trouble by a graver way of reasoning, that these things are *fatal* and necessary, it being in vain to be troubled at that which we cannot help. *Tillotson's Sermons.*

3. Appointed by destiny.

It was *fatal* to the king to fight for his money; and though he avoided to fight with enemies abroad, yet he was still enforced to fight for it with rebels at home. *Bacon's Henry* VII.

Fatal course
Had circled his full orb. *Milton's Paradise Lost, b.* v.

It was
Still *fatal* to stout Hudibras,
In all his feats of arms, when least
He dreamt of it, to prosper best. *Hudibras, p.* i. *cant.* 3.

Behold the destin'd place of your abodes;
For thus Anchises prophecy'd of old,
And this our *fatal* place of rest foretold. *Dryden's Æn. b.* vii.

O race divine!
For beauty still is *fatal* to the line. *Dryden.*

FA'TALIST. *n. s.* [from *fate*.] One who maintains that all things happen by invincible necessity.

Will the obstinate *fatalists* find sufficient apology. *Watts.*

FATA'LITY. *n. s.* [*fatalité*, French, from *fatal*.]

1. Predestination; predetermined order or series of things and events; preordination of inevitable causes acting invincibly in perpetual succession.

The stoicks held a *fatality*, and a fixed unalterable course of events; but then they held also, that they fell out by a necessity emergent from and inherent in the things themselves, which God himself could not alter. *South's Sermons.*

2. Decree of fate.

By a strange *fatality* men suffer their dissenting to be drawn into the stream of the present vogue. *King Charles.*

All the father's precaution could not secure the son from the *fatality* of dying by a lion. *L'Estrange's Fables.*

3. Tendency to danger; tendency to some great or hazardous event.

Seven times seven, or forty-nine, nine times nine, or eighty-one, and seven times nine, or the years sixty-three, is conceived to carry with it the most considerable *fatality*. *Bro.*

FA'TALLY. *adv.* [from *fatal*.]

1. Mortally; destructively; even to death.

The stream is so transparent, pure and clear,
That had the self-enamour'd youth gaz'd here,
So *fatally* deceiv'd he had not been,
While he the bottom, not his face had seen. *Denham.*

'Tis the procession of a funeral vow,
Which cruel laws to Indian wives allow,
When *fatally* their virtue they approve;
Chearful in flames, and martyrs of their love. *Dryd. Auren.*

2. By the decree of fate; by inevitable and invincible determination.

To say that the world was made casually by the concurrence of atoms, is to affirm that the atoms composed the world mechanically and *fatally*; only they were not sensible of it. *Bentley's Sermons.*

FA'TALNESS. *n. s.* [from *fatal*.] Invincible necessity.

FATE. *n. s.* [*fatum*, Latin.]

1. Destiny; an eternal series of successive causes.

Necessity or chance
Approach not me; and what I will is *fate*. *Milton.*

There is a necessity in *fate*
Why still the brave bold man is fortunate. *Dryden.*

You must obey me soon or late;
Why will you vainly struggle with your *fate*! *Dryden.*

When empire in its childhood first appears,
A watchful *fate* o'ersees its rising years. *Dryden.*

Random chance, or wilful *fate*,
Guides the shaft from Cupid's bow. *A. Phillips.*

2. Event predetermined.

Tell me what *fates* attend the duke of Suffolk?
By water shall he die, and take his end. *Shakespeare.*

3. [De]ath; destruction.

Viewing a neighbouring hill, whose top of late
A chapel crown'd, 'till in the common *fate*
Th' adjoining abbey fell. *Denham.*

Looking, he feeds alone his famish'd eyes;
Feeds ling'ring death, but looking not he dies;
Yet still he chose the longest way to *fate*,
Wasting at once his life and his estate. *Dryden.*

Courage uncertain dangers may abate;
But who can bear th' approach of certain *fate*! *Dryden.*

The whizzing arrow sings,
And bears thy *fate*, Antinous, on its wings. *Pope.*

4. Cause of death.

With full force his deadly bow he bent,
And feather'd *fates* among the mules and sumpters sent. *Dry.*

FA'TED. *adj.* [from *fate*.]

1. Decreed by fate.

She fled her father's rage, and with a train
Driv'n by the southern blasts was *fated* here to reign. *Dryd.*

2. Determined in any manner by fate.

Bright Vulcanian arms,
Fated from force of steel by Stygian charms,
Suspended, shone on high. *Dryden's Æn.*

3. Endued with any quality by fate.

Her aukward love indeed was oddly *fated*;
She and her Polly were too near related. *Prior.*

4. Invested with the power of fatal determination. Peculiar to *Shakespeare.*

Thy *fated* sky
Gives us free scope. *Shakespeare.*

FA'THER. *n. s.* [fæðeꞃ, Saxon; *aaher*, Erse. This word is found likewise in the Persian language.]

1. He by whom the son or daughter is begotten.

Father is a notion superinduced to the substance, or man, and refers only to an act of that thing called man, whereby he contributed to the generation of one of his own kind. *Locke.*

Son of Bensalem, thy *father* saith it; the man by whom thou hast breath and life speaketh the word. *Bacon.*

He shall forget
Father and mother, and to his wife adhere. *Milt. Pa. Lost.*

2. The first ancestor.

It was said
It should not stand in thy posterity;
But that myself should be the root and *father*
Of many kings. *Shakespeare's Macbeth.*

Abraham is the *father* of us all. *Rom.* iv. 16.

3. The appellation of an old man.

A poor blind man was accounted cunning in prognosticating weather: Epsom, a lawyer, said in scorn, Tell me, *father*, when doth the sun change? The old man answered, when such a wicked lawyer as you goeth to heaven. *Camden.*

4. The title of any man reverend for age, learning, and piety.

You shall find one well accompanied
With reverend *fathers* and well learned bishops. *Sh. R.* III.

5. One who has given original to any thing good or bad.

Jubal was the *father* of all such as handle the harp and organ. *Gen.* iv. 21.

6. The ecclesiastical writers of the first centuries.

Men may talk of the *fathers*, and magnify the *fathers*, and seem to make the authority of the *fathers* next to infallible; and yet none expose them more to contempt than they which give such answers as these. *Stillingfleet.*

7. One who acts with paternal care and tenderness.

I was a *father* to the poor. *Job* xxix. 16.

He hath made me a *father* to Pharaoh, and lord of all his house. *Gen.* xlv. 8.

8. The title of a popish confessor, particularly of a Jesuit.

Formal in apparel,
In gait and countenance surely like a *father*. *Shakespeare.*

There was in this place a *father* of a convent, who was very much renowned for his piety and exemplary life; and as it is usual, under any great affliction, to apply themselves to the most eminent confessors, our beautiful votary took the opportunity of confessing herself to this celebrated *father*. *Add.*

9. The title of a senator of old Rome.

From hence the race of Alban *fathers* come,
And the long glories of majestick Rome. *Dryden's Virgil.*

10.

10. The appellation of the first person of the adorable Trinity.
The eternal son of God esteemed it his meat and drink to do the will of his *Father*, and for his obedience alone obtained the greatest glory. *Taylor's Rule of living holy.*
11. The compellation of God as Creator.
We have one *Father*, even God. *John* viii. 41.
Almighty and most merciful *Father*. *Common Prayer.*

FA'THER-IN-LAW. *n. s.* [from *father.*] The father of one's husband or wife.
I must make my *father-in-law* a visit with a great train and equipage. *Addison's Spectator*, N°. 547.

To FA'THER. *v. a.*
1. To take; to adopt as a son or daughter.
Ay, good youth,
And rather *father* thee than master thee. *Shakes. Cymbeline.*
2. To supply with a father.
I am no stronger than my sex,
Being so *father'd* and so husbanded. *Shakes. Julius Cæsar.*
How light and portable my pain seems now,
When that which makes me bend makes the king bow;
He childed as I *father'd*. *Shakespeare's King Lear.*
3. To adopt a composition.
Men of wit,
Often *father'd* what he writ. *Swift.*
4. To ascribe to any one as his offspring, or production.
And lest we seem to *father* any thing upon them more than is their own, let them read. *Hooker, b.* iv. *s.* 4.
My name was made use of by several persons, one of which was pleased to *father* on me a new set of productions. *Swift.*
Magical relations comprehend effects derived and *fathered* upon hidden qualities, whereof, from received grounds of art, no reasons are derived. *Brown's Vulgar Errours, b.* ii. *c.* 3.

FA'THERHOOD. *n. s.* [from *father.*] The character of a father; the authority of a father.
Who can abide, that against their own doctors, both of the middle and latest age, six whole books should by their *fatherhoods* of Trent be under pain of a curse, imperiously obtruded upon God and his church. *Hall.*
We might have had an entire notion of this *fatherhood*, or fatherly authority. *Locke.*

FA'THERLESS. *adj.* [from *father.*] Without a father; destitute of a father.
Ye shall not afflict any widow, or *fatherless* child. *Ex.* xxii.
Our *fatherless* distress was left unmoan'd;
Your widow dolours likewise be unwept. *Shakes. R.* III.
The *fatherless* had no friend. *Sandys.*
He caught his death the last county-sessions, where he would go to see justice done to a poor widow woman and her *fatherless* children. *Addison's Spectator*, N°. 517.

FA'THERLINESS. *n. s.* [from *father.*] The tenderness of a father; parental kindness.

FA'THERLY. *adj.* [from *father.*] Paternal; like a father; tender; protecting; careful.
Let me but move one question to your daughter,
And, by that *fatherly* and kindly power
That you have in her, bid her answer truly. *Shakespeare.*
The part which describes the fire, I owe to the piety and *fatherly* affection of our monarch to his suffering subjects. *Dry.*

FA'THERLY. *adv.* In the manner of a father.
Thus Adam, *fatherly* displeas'd:
O execrable son! so to aspire
Above his brethren! *Milton.*

FA'THOM. *n. s.* [fæðm, Saxon.]
1. A measure of length containing six foot, or two yards; the space to which a man can extend both arms.
The extent of this *fathom*, or distance between the extremity of the fingers of either hand upon expansion, is equal unto the space between the sole of the foot and the crown. *Brown's Vulgar Errours, b.* iv. *c.* 5.
The arms spread cross in a streight line, and measured from the end of the long finger on one hand to that of the other, made a measure equal to the stature, and is named a *fathom*. *Holder on Time.*
2. It is the usual measure applied to the depth of the sea, when the line for sounding is called the *fathom-line*.
Dive into the bottom of the deep,
Where *fathom-line* could never touch the ground. *Sh. H.* IV.
3. Reach; penetration; depth of contrivance; compass of thought.
Another of his *fathom* they have none
To lead their business. *Shakespeare's Othello.*

To FA'THOM. *v. a.* [from the noun.]
1. To encompass with the arms extended or encircling.
2. To reach; to master.
Leave, leave to *fathom* such high points as these;
Nor be ambitious, ere the time, to please. *Dryden's Pers.*
3. To sound; to try with respect to the depth.
'Tis too strong for weak heads to try the heights and *fathom* the depths of his flights. *Felton on the Classicks.*
Our depths who *fathoms*? *Pope.*
4. To penetrate into; to find the bottom or utmost extent: as, *I cannot* fathom *his design.*

FA'THOMLESS. *adj.* [from *fathom.*]
1. That of which no bottom can be found.
2. That of which the circumference cannot be embraced.
Will you with counters sum
The vast proportion of his infinite;
And buckle in a waste most *fathomless*,
With spans and inches so diminutive
As fears and reasons? *Shakespeare's Troilus and Cressida.*

FATI'DICAL. *adj.* [*fatidicus*, Latin; *fatidique*, French.] Prophetick; having the power to foretell future events.
The oak, of all other trees only *fatidical*, told them what a fearful unfortunate business this would prove. *Howel.*

FATI'FEROUS. *adj.* [*fatifer*, Latin.] Deadly; mortal; destructive. *Dict.*

FA'TIGABLE. *adj.* [*fatigo*, Lat.] Easily wearied; susceptible of weariness.

To FA'TIGATE. *v. a.* [*fatigo*, Latin.] To weary; to fatigue; to tire; to exhaust with labour; to oppress with lassitude.
By and by the din of war 'gan to pierce
His ready sense, when straight his doubled spirit
Requicken'd what in flesh was *fatigate*,
And to the battle came he. *Shakespeare's Coriolanus.*

FATI'GUE. *n. s.* [*fatigue*, French; *fatigo*, Latin.]
1. Weariness; lassitude.
2. The cause of weariness; labour; toil.
The great Scipio sought honours in his youth, and endured the *fatigues* with which he purchased them. *Dryden.*

To FA'TIGUE. *v. a.* [*fatigue*, French; *fatigo*, Latin.] To tire; to weary; to harrass with toil; to exhaust with labour.
The man who struggles in the fight,
Fatigues left arm as well as right. *Prior.*

FATKI'DNEYED. *adj.* [*fat* and *kidney.*] Fat: by way of reproach or contempt.
Peace, ye *fatkidneyed* rascal; what a brawling do'st thou keep! *Shakespeare's Henry* IV.

FA'TLING. *n. s.* [from *fat.*] A young animal fed fat for the slaughter.
The calf and the young lion, and the *fatling* shall lie down together, and a little child shall lead them. *Is.* xi. 6.

FA'TNER. *n. s.* [from *fat.*] That which gives fatness.
The wind was west, on which that philosopher bestowed the encomium of *fatner* of the earth. *Arbuthn. Mart. Scribl.*

FA'TNESS. *n. s.* [from *fat.*]
1. The quality of being fat, plump, or full-fed.
2. Fat; grease; fulness of flesh.
And by his side rode loathsome gluttony,
Deformed creature, on a filthy swine;
His belly was upblown with luxury,
And eke with *fatness* swollen were his eyen. *Fai. Queen, b.* i.
3. Unctuous or greasy matter.
Earth and water, mingled by the help of the sun, gather a nitrous *fatness*. *Bacon's Natural History*, N°. 355.
4. Oleaginousness; sliminess.
By reason of the *fatness* and heaviness of the ground, Egypt did not produce metals, wood, pitch, and some fruits. *Arbuth.*
5. Fertility; fruitfulness.
God give thee of the dew of heaven, and the *fatness* of the earth, and plenty of corn and wine. *Gen.* xxvii. 28.
6. That which causes fertility.
When around
The clouds drop *fatness*, in the middle sky
The dew suspended staid, and left unmoist
The execrable glebe. *Phillips.*
Vapours and clouds feed the plants of the earth with the balm of dews and the *fatness* of showers. *Bentley's Sermons.*

To FA'TTEN. *v. a.* [from *fat.*]
1. To feed up; to make fleshy; to plump with fat.
Frequent blood-letting, in small quantities, often increaseth the force of the organs of digestion, and *fatteneth* and increaseth the distemper. *Arbuthnot on Diet.*
2. To make fruitful.
Town of stuff to *fatten* land. *Lib. Londiniensis.*
Dare not, on thy life,
Touch aught of mine;
This falchion else, not hitherto withstood,
These hostile fields shall *fatten* with thy blood. *Dryden.*
3. To feed grosly; to increase.
Obscene Orontes
Conveys his wealth to Tyber's hungry shores,
And *fattens* Italy with foreign whores. *Dryden's Juvenal.*

To FA'TTEN. *v. n.* [from *fat.*] To grow fat; to be pampered; to grow fleshy.
All agree to spoil the publick good,
And villains *fatten* with the brave man's labour. *Otway.*
Apollo check'd my pride, and bad me feed
My *fatt'ning* flocks, nor dare beyond the reed. *Dryden.*
Yet then this little spot of earth well till'd,
A num'rous family with plenty fill'd,
The good old man and thrifty housewife spent
Their days in peace, and *fatten'd* with content;
Enjoy'd the dregs of life, and liv'd to see
A long-descending healthful progeny. *Dryden's Juvenal.*

Tygers and wolves shall in the ocean breed,
The whale and dolphin *fatten* on the mead,
And every element exchange its kind,
When thriving honesty in courts we find. *Granville.*

FA'TUOUS. *adj.* [*fatuus*, Latin.]

1. Stupid; foolish; feeble of mind.

We pity or laugh at those *fatuous* extravagants, while yet ourselves have a considerable dose of what makes them so. *Glan.*

2. Impotent; without force; illusory; alluding to an *ignis fatuus*.

And when that flame finds combustible earth,
Thence *fatuous* fires and meteors take their birth. *Denham.*

FATU'ITY. *n. s.* [*fatuité*, French; from *fatuus*.] Foolishness; weakness of mind; some degree of frenzy.

It had argued a very short sight of things, and extreme *fatuity* of mind in me, to bind my own hands at their request. *King Charles.*

These symptoms were so high in some as to produce a sort of *fatuity* or madness. *Arbuthnot on Air.*

FA'TWITTED. *adj.* [*fat* and *wit.*] Heavy; dull; stupid.

Thou art so *fatwitted* with drinking old sack, and unbottoning thee after supper, and sleeping upon benches in the afternoon, that thou hast forgotten. *Shakesp. Henry* IV.

FA'TTY. *adj.* [from *fat.*] Unctuous; oleaginous; greasy; partaking of the nature of fat.

The like cloud, if oily or *fatty*, will not discharge; not because it sticketh faster, but because air preyeth upon water, and flame and fire upon oil. *Bacon's Natural History.*

The gourd
And thirsty cucumber, when they perceive
Th' approaching olive, with resentment fly
Her *fatty* fibres, and with tendrils creep
Diverse, detesting contact. *Phillips.*

The common symptoms of the muriatick scurvy are, a saline taste in the spittle, and a lixivial urine, sometimes with a *fatty* substance like a thin skin a-top. *Arbuthnot on Aliments.*

FA'UCET. *n. s.* [*fausset*, French; *fauces*, Latin.] The pipe inserted into a vessel to give vent to the liquor, and stopped up by a peg or spigot. It is sometimes improperly written *fosset*.

You were out a good wholesome forenoon in hearing a cause between an orange-wife and a *fosset*-seller, and adjourned a controversy of three-pence to a second audience. *Shakesp.*

If you are sent down to draw drink, and find it will not run, blow strongly into the *faucet*, and it will immediately pour into your mouth. *Swift's Direct. to the Butler.*

FA'UCHION. *n. s.* [See FALCHION.] A crooked sword.

But good Æneas order'd on the shore
A stately tomb, whose top a trumpet bore;
A soldier's *fauchion*, and a seaman's oar. *Dryden's Æn.*

FA'UFEL. *n. s.* [French.] The fruit of a species of the palm-tree. See PALM.

FAVI'LLOUS. *adj.* [*favilla*, Latin.] Consisting of ashes.

As to foretelling of strangers, from the fungous particles about the wicks of the candle, it only signifieth a moist air about them, hindering the avolation of light and the *favillous* particles. *Brown's Vulgar Errours, b.* v. *c.* 22.

FA'ULCON. } See { FALCON.
FA'ULCONRY. } See { FALCONRY.

FAULT. *n. s.* [*faut, faute*, Fr. *faltar*, to be deficient, Spanish. The *l* is sometimes sounded, and sometimes mute. In conversation it is generally suppressed.]

1. Offence; slight crime; somewhat liable to censure or objection.

The prophet chuseth rather to charge them with the *fault* of making a law unto themselves, than the crime of transgressing a law which God had made. *Hooker, b.* iii. *s.* 6.

He finds no *fault* with their opinion about the true God, but only that it was not clear and distinct enough. *Stillingfleet.*

He that but conceives a crime in thought,
Contracts the danger of an actual *fault*:
Then what must he expect that still proceeds
To commit sin, and work up thoughts to deeds. *Dryden.*

If you like not my poem, the *fault* may possibly be in my writing; but more probably 'tis in your morals, which cannot bear the truth of it. *Dryden.*

They wholly mistake the nature of criticism, who think its business is principally to find *fault*. *Dryden.*

To be desirous of a good name, and careful to do every thing, that we innocently may, to obtain it, is so far from being a *fault*, even in private persons, that it is their great and indispensible duty. *Atterbury's Sermons.*

Before his sacred name flies ev'ry *fault*,
And each exalted stanza teems with thought. *Pope.*

Which of our thrum-cap'd ancestors found *fault*,
For want of sugar-tongs or spoons for salt? *King.*

Being void of all friendship and enmity, they never complain, nor find *fault* with the times. *Swift.*

2. Defect; want; absence.

I could tell to thee, as to one it pleases me, for *fault* of a better, to call my friend, I could be sad, and sad indeed too. *Shakespeare's Henry* IV. *p.* ii.

There is no straw given unto thy servants, and they say unto us, make brick; and behold, thy servants are beaten; but the *fault* is in thine own people. *Ex.* v. 16.

3. Puzzle; difficulty: as, the enquirer is at a *fault*.

To FAULT. *v. n.* [from the noun.] To be wrong; to fail.

Which moved him rather in eclogues than otherwise to write, minding to furnish our tongue in this kind wherein it *faulteth*. *Spenser.*

To FAULT. *v. a.* To charge with a fault; to accuse.

For that I will not *fault* thee,
But for humbleness exalt thee. *Old Song.*

FA'ULTER. *n. s.* [from *fault.*] An offender; one who commits a fault.

Then she, behold the *faulter* here in sight;
This hand committed that supposed offence. *Fairfax, b.* ii.

FA'ULTFINDER. *n. s.* [*fault* and *find.*] A censurer; an objector.

FA'ULTILY. *adv.* [from *faulty.*] Not rightly; improperly; defectively; erroneously.

FA'ULTINESS. *n. s.* [from *faulty.*]

1. Badness; vitiousness; evil disposition.

When her judgment was to be practised in knowing *faultiness* by his first tokens, she was like a young fawn, who coming in the wind of the hunters, doth not know whether it be a thing or no to be eschewed. *Sidney, b.* ii.

2. Delinquency; actual offences.

The inhabitants will not take it in evil part, that the *faultiness* of their people heretofore is by us so far forth laid open. *Hooker, Preface.*

FA'ULTLESS. *adj.* [from *fault.*] Without fault; perfect; completely excellent.

Where for our sins he *faultless* suffered pain,
There where he died, and where he liv'd again. *Fairfax.*

Who durst thy *faultless* figure thus deface? *Dryden's Æn.*

Whoever thinks a *faultless* piece to see,
Thinks what ne'er was, nor is, nor e'er shall be. *Pope.*

FA'ULTY. *adj.* [*fautif*, French, from *fault.*]

1. Guilty of a fault; blameable; criminal; not innocent.

The king doth speak as one which is *faulty*. 2 *Sa.* xiv. 13.

Can thus
Th' image of God in man, created once
So goodly and erect, though *faulty* since!
To such unsightly sufferings be debas'd! *Milton's Par. Lost.*

2. Wrong; erroneous.

The form of polity by them set down for perpetuity, is three ways *faulty*; *faulty* in omitting some things which in Scripture are of that nature, as, namely, the difference that ought to be of pastors, when they grow to any great multitude; *faulty* in requiring doctors, deacons, and widows, as things of perpetual necessity by the law of God, which in truth are nothing less; *faulty* also in urging some things by Scripture mutable, as their lay-elders. *Hooker, b.* iii.

3. Defective; bad in any respect; not fit for the use intended.

By accident of a *faulty* helmet that Parker had on, he was stricken into the mouth at the first course, so that he died presently. *Bacon's Henry* VII.

To FA'VOUR. *v. a.* [*faveo*, Latin.]

1. To support; to regard with kindness; to be propitious to; to countenance.

Of all the race of silver-winged flies
Was none more favourable, nor more fair,
Whilst heaven did *favour* his felicities,
Than Clarion, the eldest son and heir
Of Muscarol. *Spenser.*

The self-same gods that arm'd the queen of Troy,
May *favour* Tamora the queen of Goths. *Shak. Tit. Andr.*

Men *favour* wonders. *Bacon's Natural History*, N°. 495.

Fortune so *favoured* him, that the town at his first coming surrendered unto him. *Knolles's History of the Turks.*

The good Æneas am I call'd; a name,
While fortune *favour'd*, not unknown to fame. *Dryden.*

Oh happy youth! and *favour'd* of the skies,
Distinguish'd care of guardian deities. *Pope's Odyssey, b.* iii.

2. To assist with advantages or conveniences.

No one place about it is weaker than another, to *favour* an enemy in his approaches. *Addison's Whig Examiner.*

3. To resemble in feature.

The porter owned that the gentleman *favoured* his master. *Spectator.*

4. To conduce to; to contribute.

FA'VOUR. *n. s.* [*favor*, Latin; *faveur*, French.]

1. Countenance; kindness; kind regard; propitious aspect.

It pleas'd your majesty to turn your looks
Of *favour* from myself, and all our house. *Shakesp. H.* IV.

The child Samuel was in *favour* both with the Lord and also with men. 1 *Sa.* ii. 26.

The race is not to the swift, nor yet *favour* to men of skill. *Eccl.* ix. 11.

His

His dreadful navy, and his lovely mind,
Gave him the fear and *favour* of mankind. *Waller.*

This *favour*, had it been employed on a more deserving subject, had been an effect of justice in your nature; but, as placed on me, is only charity. *Dryden's Aurengzebe, Preface.*

At play, among strangers, we are apt to find our hopes and wishes engaged on a sudden in *favour* of one side more than another. *Swift.*

2. Support; defence; vindication.

The pleasures which these Scriptures ascribe to religion, are of a kind very different from those in *favour* of which they are here alleged. *Rogers, Sermon* 15.

3. Kindness granted.

All *favours* and punishments passed by him, all offices and places of importance were distributed to his favourites. *Sidney.*

O, my royal master!
The gods, in *favour* to you, made her cruel. *A. Phillips.*

4. Lenity; mildness; mitigation of punishment.

I could not discover the lenity and *favour* of this sentence; but conceived it rather to be rigorous than gentle. *Gulliv. Trav.*

5. Leave; good will; pardon.

Worthy Macbeth, we stay upon your leisure.
—Give me your *favour*; my dull brain was wrought
With things forgot. *Shakespeare's Macbeth.*

Yet e're we enter into open act,
With *favour*, 'twere no loss if 't might be inquir'd
What the condition of these arms would be. *B. Johns. Cat.*

They got not the land by their own sword; but thy right hand and thine arm, and the light of thy countenance, because thou hast a *favour* unto them. *Ps.* xliv. 3.

Come down, said Reynard, let us treat of peace:
A peace, with all my soul, said Chanticleer;
But, with your *favour*, I will treat it here. *Dryden.*

6. Object of favour; person or thing favoured.

All these his wond'rous works, but chiefly man,
His chief delight and *favour*; him, for whom
All these his works so wond'rous he ordain'd. *Milt. P. L.*

7. Something given by a lady to be worn.

And every one his lovesuit will advance
Unto his several mistress, which they'll know
By *favours* several which they did bestow. *Shakespeare.*

It is received that it helpeth to continue love, if one wear the hair of the party beloved; and perhaps a glove, or other like *favour*, may as well do it. *Bacon's Natural History.*

A blue ribband tied round the sword-arm, I conceive to be the remains of that custom of wearing a mistress's *favour* on such occasions of old. *Spectator*, N°. 436.

8. Any thing worn openly as a token.

Here, Fluellen, wear thou this *favour* for me, and stick it in thy cap: when Alanson and myself were down together, I pluck'd this glove from his helm. *Shakesp. Henry* V.

9. Feature; countenance.

That is only suitable in laying a foul complexion upon a filthy *favour*, setting forth both in sluttishness. *Sidney.*

Young though thou art, thine eye
Hath staid upon some *favour* that it loves. *Shakespeare.*

Disseat thy *favour* with an usurped beard. *Shakes. Othello.*

There's no goodness in thy face: if Antony
Be free and healthful, why so tart a *favour*
To trumpet such good tidings. *Shakes. Ant. and Cleopatra.*

Yet well I remember
The *favours* of these men: were they not mine?
Did they not sometime cry, all hail! to me? *Shakes. R.* II.

A youth of fine *favour* and shape. *Bacon's Henry* VII.

By their virtuous behaviour they compensate hardness of their *favour*, and by the pulchritude of their souls, make up what is wanting in the beauty of their bodies. *South.*

FA'VOURABLE. *adj.* [*favorable*, French; *favorabilis*, Latin.]

1. Kind; propitious; affectionate.

Famous Plantagenet! most gracious prince,
Lend *favourable* ear to our requests. *Shakes. Richard* III.

2. Palliative; tender; averse from censure.

None can have the *favourable* thought,
That to obey a tyrant's will they fought. *Dryden's Juvenal.*

3. Conducive to; contributing to; propitious.

People are multiplied in a country by the temper of the climate, *favourable* to generation, to health, and long life. *Temple.*

4. Accommodate; convenient.

Many good officers were willing to stay there, as a place very *favourable* for the making levies of men. *Clarendon.*

5. Beautiful; well favoured; well featured. Obsolete.

Of all the race of silver-winged flies
Which do possess the empire of the air,
Betwixt the centred earth and azure skies
Was none more *favourable*, nor more fair,
Than Clarion, the eldest son and heir
Of Muscarol. *Spenser.*

FA'VOURABLENESS. *n. s.* [from *favourable.*] Kindness; benignity.

FA'VOURABLY. *adv.* [from *favourable.*] Kindly; with favour; with tenderness; with kind regard.

Touching actions of common life, there is not any defence more *favourably* heard than theirs who allege sincerely for themselves, that they did as necessity constrained them. *Hook.*

She goeth about seeking such as are worthy of her, and sheweth herself *favourably* unto them in the ways. *Wisd.* vi.

The violent will condemn the character of Absalom, as either too *favourably* or too hardly drawn. *Dryden.*

We are naturally inclined to think *favourably* of those we love *Rogers's Sermons.*

FA'VOURED. *participial adj.* [from *favour.*]

1. Regarded with kindness.

Oft with some *favour'd* traveller they stray,
And shine before him all the desert way. *Pope's Odyssey.*

2. [From *favour*, the noun.] Featured. Always conjoined with *well* or *ill*.

Of her there bred
A thousand young ones, which she daily fed;
Sucking upon her poisonous dugs, each one
Of sundry shape, yet all *ill-favoured.* *Fairy Queen, b.* i.

FA'VOUREDLY. *adv* [from *favoured*] Always joined with *well* or *ill*, in a fair or foul way.

FA'VOURER. *n. s.* [from *favour*.] One who favours; one who regards with kindness or tenderness; a wellwisher; a friend.

If we should upbraid them with irreligious, as they do us with superstitious *favourers*, the answer which herein they would make us, let them apply unto themselves *Hooker, b.* iv.

Do I not know you for a *favourer*
Of this new sect? ye are not sound. *Shak. Henry* VIII.

Being now a *favourer* to the Briton. *Shakes. Cymbeline.*

Conjure their friends they had, labour for more,
Solicit all reputed *favourers.* *Daniel's Civil War.*

All the *favourers* of magick were the most profest and bitter enemies to the Christian religion. *Addis. on the Christ. Rel.*

FA'VOURITE. *n. s.* [*favori*, *favorite*, French; *favorita*, Ital.]

1. A person or thing beloved; one regarded with favour; any thing in which pleasure is taken; that which is regarded with particular approbation or affection.

Every particular master in criticism has his *favourite* passages in an author. *Addison's Spectator*, N°. 202.

So fathers speak, persuasive speech and mild!
Their sage experience to the *fav'rite* child. *Pope's Odyssey.*

2. One chosen as a companion by his superiour; a mean wretch whose whole business is by any means to please.

All favours and punishments passed by him, all offices and places of importance were distributed to his *favourites. Sidney.*

I was a Thessalian gentleman, who, by mischance, having killed a *favourite* of the prince of that country, was pursued so cruelly, that in no place but by favour or corruption they would obtain my destruction. *Sidney, b.* i.

The great man down, you mark, his *fav'rite* flies;
The poor advanc'd, makes friends of enemies. *Shak. Haml.*

Bid her steal into the plashed bower,
Where honeysuckles, ripen'd by the sun,
Forbid the sun to enter; like to *favourites*,
Made proud by princes, that advance their pride
Against that power that bred it. *Shakespeare.*

Nothing is more vigilant, nothing more jealous than a *favourite*, especially towards the waining time, and suspect of satiety. *Wotton.*

This man was very capable of being a great *favourite* to a great king. *Clarendon.*

What *fav'rites* gain, and what the nation owes,
Fly the forgetful world. *Pope.*

FA'VOURLESS. *adj.* [from *favour.*]

1. Unfavoured; not regarded with kindness; without patronage; without countenance.

2. Unfavouring; unpropitious.

Of that goddess I have sought the sight,
Yet no where can her find; such happiness
Heaven doth me envy, and fortune *favourless. Fairy Queen.*

FA'USEN. *n. s.* A sort of large eel.

He left the waves to wash;
The wave sprung entrails, about which *fausens* and other fish
Did shole. *Chapman's Iliads, b.* xxi.

FA'USSEBRAYE. *n. s.* A small mount of earth, four fathom wide, erected on the level round the foot of the rampart, made use of to fire upon the enemy, when he is so far advanced that you cannot force him back; and also to receive the ruins which the cannons make in the body of the place. *Harris.*

FA'UTOR. *n. s.* [Latin; *fauteur*, French.] Favourer; countenancer; supporter.

I am neither author or *fautor* of any sect: I will have no man addict himself to me; but, if I have any thing right, defend it as truth's, not mine. *Ben. Johnson.*

The new mountain in the Lucrine lake, which is alleged, by the *fautors* of this opinion, as an instance in behalf of it, was not raised thus. *Woodward.*

FA'UTRESS. *n. s.* [*fautrix*, Latin; *fautrice*, Fr.] A woman that favours, or shows countenance.

It made him pray, and prove
Minerva's aid his *fautress* still. *Chapman's Iliads.*

He comes from banishment to the *fautress* of liberty, from the barbarous to the polite. *Garth's Dedicat. to Ovid.*

FAWN. *n. ſ.* [*faon*, French, from *fan*, in old French a child, probably from *infans*, Latin.] A young deer.

Looking my love, I go from place to place,
Like a young *fawn* that late hath loſt the hind;
And ſeek each where, where laſt I ſaw her face,
Whoſe image yet I carry freſh in mind. *Spenſer's Sonnets.*

The buck is called the firſt year a *fawn*, the ſecond year a pricket. *Shakeſpeare's Love's Labour Loſt.*

The colt hath about four years of growth; and ſo the *fawn*, and ſo the calf. *Bacon's Natural Hiſtory*, N. 759.

Who for thy table feeds the wanton *fawn*,
For him as kindly ſpreads the flow'ry lawn. *Pope.*

To FAWN. *v. n.* [of uncertain original. Perhaps a contraction of the French *fanfan*, a term of fondneſs for children.

1. To court by friſking before one: as a dog.

The dog ſtraight *fawned* upon his maſter for old knowledge. *Sidney.*

Holding Corioli in the name of Rome,
Even like a *fawning* greyhound. *Shakeſpeare's Coriolanus.*

2. To court by any means. Uſed by animals.

Inſtead thereof he kiſs'd her weary feet,
And lick'd her lily hands with *fawning* tongue,
As he her wrong'd innocence did weet. *Fairy Queen, b.* i.

Is it not ſtrange that a rational man ſhould worſhip an ox? that he ſhould *fawn* upon his dog? bow himſelf before a cat? and adore leeks and garlick? *South's Sermons.*

3. To court ſervilely.

My love, forbear to *fawn* upon their frowns;
What danger or what ſorrow can befal thee,
So long as Edward is thy conſtant friend? *Shak. Henry* VI.

And thou, ſly hypocrite, who now would'ſt be
Patron of liberty, who more than thou
Once *fawn'd*, and cring'd, and ſervilely ador'd
Heav'n's awful monarch? *Milton's Paradiſe Loſt, b.* iv.

Whom Ancus follows, with a *fawning* air;
But vain within, and proudly popular. *Dryden's Æn. b.* vi.

Dext'rous the craving *fawning* crowd to quit,
And pleas'd to 'ſcape from flattery to wit. *Pope.*

4. To bring forth a fawn.

FA'WNER. *n. ſ.* [from *fawn.*] One that fawns; one that pays ſervile courtſhip.

By ſoftneſs of behaviour we have arrived at the appellation of *fawners.* *Spectator*, Nº. 304.

FA'WNINGLY. *adv.* [from *fawn.*] In a cringing ſervile way.

FA'XED. *adj.* [from ꝼæx, Saxon, hair.] Hairy. Now obſolete.

They could call a comet a *faxed* ſtar, which is all one with ſtella crinita, or cometa. *Camden's Remains.*

FAY. *n. ſ.* [*feé*, French.]

1. A fairy; an elf.

And the yellow-ſkirted *fays*
Fly after the night-ſteeds, leaving their moon-lov'd maze. *Milton.*

Ye ſylphs and ſylphids, to your chief give ear;
Fays, fairies, genii, elves and demons hear! *Pope.*

2. [from *foi*, French.] Faith. Wholly obſolete.

They plainly to ſpeak of ſhepherds moſt what,
Bad is the beſt, this Engliſh is flat;
Their ill 'haviour garres men miſſay,
Both of their doctrine and their *fay*. *Spenſer's Paſtorals.*

FE'ABERRY. *n. ſ.* A gooſeberry. *Dict.*

To FEAGUE. *v. a.* [*Gower* uſes *To feige*, free to cenſure; *fegen*, German, to ſweep; *fyken*, Dutch, to ſtrike.] To whip; to chaſtiſe; to beat. In Scottiſh *feake*, to flutter; to be idly or officiouſly buſy.

FE'ALTY. *n. ſ.* [*feaulté*, French.] Duty due to a ſuperior lord; fidelity to a maſter; loyalty.

I am in parliament pledge for his truth,
And laſting *fealty* to the new-made king. *Shak. Rich.* III.

Let my ſovereign
Command my eldeſt ſon, nay all my ſons,
As pledges of my *fealty* and love. *Shakeſ. Henry* IV. *p.* ii.

Man diſobeying,
Diſloyal, breaks his *fealty*, and ſins
Againſt the high ſupremacy of heav'n. *Milton's Par. Loſt.*

Each bird and beaſt behold
After their kinds: I bring them to receive
From thee their names, and pay thee *fealty*
With low ſubjection. *Milton's Paradiſe Loſt, b.* viii.

Whether his firſt deſign be to withdraw
Our *fealty* from God, or to diſturb
Conjugal love. *Milton's Paradiſe Loſt, b.* ix.

FEAR. *n. ſ.* [ꝼeaꞃan, Sax. to fear; *vaer*, Dut. *feakle*, Erſe.]

1. Dread; horrour; painful apprehenſion of danger.

Fear is an uneaſineſs of the mind, upon the thought of future evil likely to befal us. *Locke.*

Trembling *fear* ſtill to and fro did fly,
And found no place where ſafe ſhe ſhrowd him might. *F. Q.*

For *fear* was upon them, becauſe of the people of thoſe countries. *Ezra* iii. 3.

What then remains? Are we depriv'd of will?
Muſt we not wiſh, for *fear* of wiſhing ill? *Dryden's Juv.*

Fear, in general, is that paſſion of our nature whereby we are excited to provide for our ſecurity upon the approach of evil. *Rogers, Sermon* 1.

2. Awe; dejection of mind at the preſence of any perſon or thing.

And the *fear* of you, and the dread of you, ſhall be upon every beaſt. *Gen.* ix. 2.

3. Anxiety; ſolicitude.

The greateſt and principal *fear* was for the holy temple. 2 *Mac.* xv. 18.

4. That which cauſes fear.

Antony, ſtay not by his ſide:
Thy demon, that's the ſpirit that keeps thee, is
Noble, courageous, high, unmatchable,
Where Cæſar's is not; but near him, thy angel
Becomes a *fear*, as being o'erpower'd. *Shak. Ant. and Cleop.*

5. The object of fear.

Except the God of Abraham and the *fear* of Iſaac had been with me. *Gen.* xxxi. 42.

6. Something hung up to ſcare deer by its colour or noiſe.

He who fleeth from the noiſe of the *fear* ſhall fall into the pit, and he that cometh up out of the midſt of the pit ſhall be taken in the ſnare. *Iſ.* xxiv. 18.

FEAR. *n. ſ.* [ꝼoeꞃa, Saxon.] A companion. Obſolete.

But fair Chariſſa to a lovely *fear*
Was linked, and by him had many pledges dear. *Fairy Qu.*

To FEAR. *v. a.* [ꝼeaꞃan, Saxon.]

1. To dread; to conſider with apprehenſions of terrour; to be afraid of.

Now, for my life, Hortenſio *fears* his widow.
—Then never truſt me if I be afraid.
---You are very ſenſible, yet you miſs my ſenſe;
I mean Hortenſio is afraid of you. *Shak. Tam. of the Shrew.*

To *fear* the foe, ſince fear oppreſſeth ſtrength,
Gives, in your weakneſs, ſtrength unto your foe. *Sh. R.* II.

There ſhall riſe up a kingdom, and it ſhall be *feared* above all the kingdoms before it. 2 *Eſdr.* xii. 13.

When I view the beauties of thy face,
I *fear* not death, nor dangers, nor diſgrace. *Dryden.*

2. To fright; to terrify; to make afraid.

The inhabitants, being *feared* with the Spaniards landing and burning, fled from their dwellings. *Carew.*

If he be taken, he ſhall never more
Be *fear'd* of doing harm: make your own purpoſe
How in my ſtrength you pleaſe. *Shakeſ. King Lear.*

We muſt not make a ſcarecrow of the law,
Setting it up to *fear* the birds of prey. *Sh. Meaſ. for Meaſ.*

Some, ſitting on the hatches, would ſeem there,
With hideous gazing, to *fear* away fear. *Donne.*

To FEAR. *v. n.*

1. To live in horrour; to be afraid.

Well you may *fear* too far.
---Safer than truſt too far:
Let me ſtill take away the harms I fear,
Not fear ſtill to be harm'd. *Shakeſpeare's King Lear.*

2. To be anxious.

If any ſuch be here, if any *fear*
Leſs for his perſon than an ill report;
If any think brave death outweighs bad life. *Shak. Coriolan.*

Then let the greedy merchant *fear*
For his ill-gotten gain;
And pray to gods that will not hear,
While the debating winds and billows bear
His wealth into the main. *Dryden's Horace.*

See, pious king, with diff'rent ſtrife,
Thy ſtruggling Albion's boſom torn:
So much ſhe *fears* for William's life,
That Mary's fate ſhe dare not mourn. *Prior.*

FE'ARFUL. *adj.* [*fear* and *full.*]

1. Timorous; timid; eaſily made afraid.

He's gentle, and not *fearful.* *Shakeſpeare's Tempeſt.*

2. Afraid. It has *of* before the object of fear.

The Iriſh are more *fearful* to offend the law than the Engliſh. *Davies on Ireland.*

I have made my heroine *fearful of* death, which neither Caſſandra nor Cleopatra would have been. *Dryd. Auren. Pref.*

3. Awful; to be reverenced.

Who is like thee, glorious in holineſs, *fearful* in praiſes. *Ex.* xv. 11.

4. Terrible; dreadful; frightful; impreſſing fear.

Neither faſt to friend, nor *fearful* to foe. *Aſcham's Schoolm.*

Againſt ſuch monſters God maintained his own, by *fearful* execution of extraordinary judgment upon them. *Hooker.*

What God did command touching Canaan, concerneth not us any otherwiſe than only as a *fearful* pattern of his juſt diſpleaſure. *Hooker, b.* v. *ſ.* 17.

All torment, trouble, wonder, and amazement
Inhabits here: ſome heav'nly power guide us
Out of this *fearful* country. *Shakeſpeare's Tempeſt.*

It is a *fearful* thing to fall into the hands of the living God. *Hebr.* x. 31.

Lay down by thoſe pleaſures the *fearful* and dangerous thunders

thunders and lightnings, the horrible and frequent earthquakes, and then there will be found no comparison. *Raleigh.*

This is the natural fruit of sin, and the present revenge which it takes upon sinners, besides that *fearful* punishment which shall be inflicted on them in another life. *Tillotson.*

FE'ARFULLY. *adv.* [from *fearful*]

1. Timorously; in fear.

In such a night
Did Thisbe *fearfully* o'ertrip the dew,
And saw the lion's shadow. *Shakesp. Merchant of Venice.*

2. Terribly; dreadfully.

There is a cliff, whose high and bending head
Looks *fearfully* on the confined deep. *Shakes. King Lear.*

FE'ARFULNESS. *n. s.* [from *fearful.*]

1. Timorousness; habitual timidity.

2. State of being afraid; awe; dread.

Is it credible that the acknowledgment of our own unworthiness, our professed *fearfulness* to ask any thing, otherwise than only for his sake to whom God can deny nothing, that this should be noted for a popish errour. *Hooker, b.* v.

A third thing that makes a government justly despised, is *fearfulness* of and mean compliances with bold popular offenders. *South's Sermons.*

FE'ARLESLY. *adv.* [from *fearless.*] Without terrour.

'Tis matter of the greatest astonishment to observe the stupid, yet common boldness of men, who so *fearlesly* expose themselves to this most formidable of perils. *Decay of Piety.*

FE'ARLESNESS. *n. s.* [from *fearless.*] Exemption from fear; intrepidity.

He gave instances of an invincible courage, and *fearlessness* in danger. *Clarendon, b.* viii.

FE'ARLESS. *adj.* [from *fear.*] Free from fear; intrepid; courageous; bold.

From the ground she *fearless* doth arise,
And walked forth without suspect of crime. *Fairy Queen.*
The flaming seraph, *fearless*, though alone
Encompass'd round with foes, thus answer'd bold. *Milton.*

A nation, whose distinguishing character it is to be more *fearless* of death and danger than any other. *Temple.*

FE'ASIBILITY. *n. s.* [from *feasible.*] A thing practicable.

Men often swallow falsities for truths, dubiosities for certainties, possibilities for *feasibilities*, and things impossible for possibilities themselves. *Brown's Vulgar Errours, b.* i. *c.* 5.

FE'ASIBLE. *adj.* [*faisible*, French.] Practicable; such as may be effected; such as may be done.

We conclude many things impossibilities, which yet are easy *feasibles*. *Glanville's Sceps. c.* 14.

Things are *feasible* in themselves; else the eternal wisdom of God would never have advised, and much less have commanded them. *South's Sermons.*

FE'ASIBLY. *adv.* [from *feasible.*] Practicably.

FEAST. *n. s.* [*feste*, French; *festum*, Latin.]

1. An entertainment of the table; a sumptuous treat of great numbers.

Here's our chief guest.
----If he had been forgotten,
It had been as a gap in our great *feast*. *Shakes. Macbeth.*

On Pharaoh's birthday he made a *feast* unto all his servants. *Gen.* xl. 20.

The lady of the leaf ordain'd a *feast*,
And made the lady of the flow'r her guest;
When lo! a bow'r ascended on the plain,
With sudden seats ordain'd, and large for either train. *Dry.*

2. An anniversary day of rejoicing either on a civil or religious occasion. Opposed to a fast.

This day is call'd the *feast* of Crispian. *Shakes. Hen.* V.

3. Something delicious to the palate.

Many people would, with reason, prefer the griping of an hungry belly to those dishes which are a *feast* to others. *Locke.*

To FEAST. *v. n.* [from the noun.] To eat sumptuously; to eat together on a day of joy.

Richard and Northumberland, great friends,
Did *feast* together. *Shakespeare's Henry* IV. *p.* ii.
The parish finds, indeed; but our church-wardens
Feast on the silver, and give us the farthings. *Gay.*

To FEAST. *v. a.*

1. To entertain sumptuously; to entertain magnificently.

He was entertained and *feasted* by the king with great shew of favour. *Hayward.*

2. To delight; to pamper.

All these are our's, all nature's excellence,
Whose taste or smell can bless the *feasted* sense. *Dryden.*

FE'ASTER. *n. s.* [from *feast.*]

1. One that fares deliciously.

Those *feasters* could speak of great and many excellencies in manna. *Taylor's Worthy Communicant.*

2. One that entertains magnificently.

FE'ASTFUL. *adj.* [*feast* and *full.*]

1. Festive; joyful.

The virgins also shall on *feastful* days
Visit his tomb with flowers, only bewailing
His lot unfortunate in nuptial choice,
From whence captivity and loss of eyes. *Milton's Agonistes.*

Therefore be sure
Thou, when the bridegroom with his *feastful* friends
Passes to bliss at the mid-hour of night,
Hast gain'd thy entrance, virgin wise and pure. *Milton.*

2. Luxurious; riotous.

The suitor train
Who crowd his palace, and with lawless pow'r
His herds and flocks in *feastful* rites devour. *Pope's Odyssey.*

FE'ASTRITE. *n. s.* [*feast* and *rite.*] Custom observed in entertainments.

His hospitable gate,
Unbarr'd to all, invites a num'rous train
Of daily guests; whose board with plenty crown'd,
Revives the *feastrites* old. *Phillips.*

FEAT. *n. s* [*fait*, French.]

1. Act; deed; action; exploit.

Pyrocles is his name, renowned far
For his bold *feats*, and hardy confidence;
Full oft approved in many a cruel war. *Fairy Queen, b.* ii.
Tarquin's self he met,
And struck him on his knee: in that day's *feats*,
When he might act the woman in the scene,
He prov'd th' best man i' th' field. *Shakesp. Coriolanus.*

Our soldiers are men of strong heads for action, and perform such *feats* as they are not able to express. *Addis. Spectat.*

2. A trick; a festive or ludicrous performance.

The joints are more supple to all *feats* of activity and motion in youth than afterwards. *Bacon's Essays.*

FEAT. *adj.* [*fait*, *bien fait*, French; *homo factus ad unguem.*]

1. Ready; skilful; ingenious.

Never master had
A page so kind, so duteous, diligent;
So tender over his occasions, true,
So *feat*, so nurse-like. *Shakespeare's Cymbeline.*

2. It is now only used in irony and contempt.

That *feat* man at controversy. *Stillingfleet.*

3. Nice; neat.

Look how well my garments sit upon me,
Much *feater* than before. *Shakespeare's Tempest.*

FE'ATEOUS. *adj.* [from *feat.*] Neat; dexterous Obsolete.

FE'ATEOUSLY. *adv.* [from *feateous.*] Neatly; dexterously.

And with fine fingers cropt full *feateously*
The tender stalks on high. *Spenser.*

FE'ATHER. *n. s.* [ꝼeðeꞃ, Saxon; *feder*, German.]

1. The plume of birds.

Look, as I blow this *feather* from my face. *Shak. H.* VI.
The brave eagle does with sorrow see
The forest wasted, and that lofty tree,
Which holds her nest, about to be o'erthrown,
Before the *feathers* of her young are grown;
She will not leave them, nor she cannot stay,
But bears them boldly on her wings away. *Waller.*

When a man in the dark presses either corner of his eye with his finger, and turns his eye away from his finger, he will see a circle of colours like those in the *feathers* of a peacock's tail. *Newton's Opt.*

I am bright as an angel, and light as a *feather*. *Swift.*

2. Kind; nature; species: from the proverbial expression, *birds of a* feather; that is, of a species.

The proud insulting queen,
With Clifford and the haught Northumberland,
And of their *feather* many more proud birds,
Have wrought the easy-melting king, like wax. *Sh H.* VI.
I am not of that *feather* to shake off
My friend, when he most needs me. *Shakesp. Timon.*

3. An ornament; an empty title.

4. [Upon a horse.] A sort of natural frizzling of hair, which, in some places, rises above the lying hair, and there makes a figure resembling the tip of an ear of corn. *Farrier's Dict.*

To FE'ATHER *v a.* [from the noun]

1. To dress in feathers.

2. To fit with feathers.

3. To tread as a cock.

Dame Partlet was the sovereign of his heart;
Ardent in love, outrageous in his play,
He *feather'd* her a hundred times a day. *Dryden.*

4. To enrich; to adorn; to exalt.

They stuck not to say, that the king cared not to plume his nobility and people, to *feather* himself. *Bacon's Henry* VII.

5. *To* FEATHER *one's Nest.* Alluding to birds which collect feathers, among other materials, for making their nests; to get riches together.

FE'ATHERBED. *n. s.* [*feather* and *bed.*] A bed stuffed with feathers; a soft bed.

The husband cock looks out, and strait is sped,
And meets his wife, which brings her *featherbed*. *Donne.*

FE'ATHERDRIVER. *n. s.* [*feather* and *drive.*] One who cleanses feathers by whisking them about.

A *featherdriver* had the residue of his lungs filled with the fine dust or down of feathers. *Derham's Physico-Theology.*

FE'ATHERED. *adj.* [from *feather.*]

1. Cloathed

3. Cloathed with feathers.

I saw young Harry with his beaver on,
His cuisses on his thighs, gallantly arm'd,
Rise from the ground like *feather'd* Mercury. *Shak. H. IV.*

So when the new-born phœnix first is seen,
Her *feather'd* subjects all adore their queen. *Dryden.*

Dark'ning the sky, they hover o'er, and shroud
The wanton sailors with a *feather'd* cloud. *Prior.*

Then ships of uncouth form shall stem the tide,
And *feather'd* people crowd my wealthy side. *Pope.*

Vultures, harpies, ravens, cormorants, and, among many other *feathered* creatures, several little winged boys perch upon the middle arches. *Addison's Spectator*, Nº. 159.

2. Fitted with feathers; carrying feathers

An eagle had the ill hap to be struck with an arrow, *feather'd* from her own wing. *L'Estrange's Fables.*

Not the bow they bend, nor boast the skill
To give the *feather'd* arrow wings to kill. *Pope's Odyssey.*

FE'ATHEREDGE. *n. s.*

Boards or planks that have one edge thinner than another, are called *featheredge* stuff. *Moxon's Mech. Exer.*

FE'ATHEREDGED. *adj.* [*feather* and *edge.*] Belonging to a feather edge.

The cover must be made of *featheredged* boards, in the nature of several doors with hinges fixed thereon. *Mortimer.*

FE'ATHERFEW. *n. s.* A plant both single and double: it is increased by seeds or slips, and also by dividing the roots: it flowereth most part of the Summer. *Mortimer's Husbandry.*

FE'ATHERLESS *adj.* [from *feather.*] Without feathers.

This so high grown ivy was like that *featherless* bird, which went about to beg plumes of other birds to cover his nakedness. *Howel's Vocal Forrest.*

FE'ATHERSELLER. *n. s.* [*feather* and *seller.*] One who sells feathers for beds.

FE'ATHERY. *adj.* [from *feather.*] Cloathed with feathers.

Or whistle from the lodge, or village cock
Count the night-watches to his *feathery* dames. *Milton.*

FE'ATLY. *adv.* [from *feat.*] Neatly; nimbly; dexterously.

Foot it *featly* here and there,
And sweet sprites the burthen bear. *Shakesp. Tempest.*

The moon was up, and shot a gleamy light;
He saw a quire of ladies in a round,
That *featly* footing seem'd to skim the ground. *Dryden.*

There haply by the ruddy damsel seen,
Or shepherd-boy, they *featly* foot the green. *Tickell.*

FE'ATNESS. *n. s.* [from *feat.*] Neatness; nicety; dexterity.

FE'ATURE. *n. s.* [*faiture*, old French.]

1. The cast or make of the face.

Report the *feature* of Octavia, her years. *Shakespeare.*

2. Any lineament or single part of the face.

Though ye be the fairest of God's creatures,
Yet think that death shall spoil your goodly *features. Spenser.*

We may compare the face of a great man with the character, and try if we can find out in his looks and *features* the haughty, cruel, or unmerciful temper that discovers itself in the history. *Addison on ancient Medals.*

Though various *features* did the sisters grace,
A sister's likeness was in every face. *Addison's Ovid's Met.*

To FE'ATURE. *v. a.* To resemble in countenance; to favour.

He liv'd in court most prais'd, most lov'd,
A sample to the young'st; to th' more mature,
A glass that *featur'd* them. *Shakespeare's Cymbeline.*

To FEAZE. *v. a.* [See FAXED, perhaps from ꝼax, Saxon, hair.]

1. To untwist the end of a rope, and reduce it again to its first stamina.

2. To beat; to whip with rods. *Ainsw.*

To FEBRI'CITATE. *v. n.* [*febricitor*, Latin.] To be in a fever. *Dict.*

FEBRI'CULOSE. *adj.* [*febriculosus*, Latin.] Troubled with a fever. *Dict.*

FEBRIFU'GE. *n. s.* [*febris* and *fugo*, Latin; *febrifuge*, Fr.] Any medicine serviceable in a fever. *Quincy.*

Bitters, like choler, are the best sanguifiers, and also the best *febrifuges*. *Floyer on the Humours.*

FEBRIFU'GE. *adj.* Having the power to cure fevers.

Febrifuge draughts had a most surprising good effect. *Arbuth.*

FE'BRILE. *adj.* [*febrilis*, Latin; *febrile*, Fr.] Constituting a fever; proceeding from a fever.

The spirits, embroiled with the malignity in the blood, and turgid and tumified by the *febrile* fermentation, are by phlebotomy relieved. *Harvey on Consumptions.*

FE'BRUARY. *n. s.* [*februarius*, Latin.] The name of the second month in the year.

You have such a *February* face,
So full of frost, of storm, and cloudiness? *Shakespeare.*

FE'CES. *n. s.* [*fæces*, Latin; *feces*, French.]

1. Dregs; lees; sediment; subsidence.

Hence the surface of the ground with mud
And slime besmear'd, the *feces* of the flood,
Receiv'd the rays of heav'n; and sucking in
The seeds of heat, new creatures did begin. *Dryden.*

2. Excrement.

The symptoms of such a constitution are a sour smell in their *feces*. *Arbuthnot on Aliments.*

FE'CULENCE. } FE'CULENCY. } *n. s.* [*fæculentia*, Latin.]

1. Muddiness; quality of abounding with lees or sediment.

2. Lees; feces; sediment; dregs.

Pour upon it some very strong lee, to facilitate the separation of its *feculencies*. *Boyle.*

Whether the wilding's fibres are contriv'd
To draw th' earth's purest spirit, and resist
Its *feculence*, which in more porous stocks
Of cyder plants finds passage free. *Phillips.*

FE'CULENT. *adj.* [*fæculentus*, Lat. *feculent*, French.] Foul; dreggy; excrementitious.

But both his hands, most filthy *feculent*,
Above the water were on high extent,
And fain'd to wash themselves incessantly,
Yet nothing cleaner were for such intent. *Fairy Queen.*

We may affirm them to be to the body as the light of a candle to the gross and *feculent* snuff, which as it is not pent up in it, so neither doth it partake of its stench and impurity. *Glanv. Apology.*

FECU'ND. *adj.* [*fœcundus*, Latin; *fecond*, Fr.] Fruitful; prolifick.

The more sickly the years are, the less *fecund* or fruitful of children also they be. *Graunt's Bills of Mortality.*

FECUNDA'TION. *n. s.* [*fœcundo*, Latin.] The act of making fruitful or prolifick.

She requested these plants as a medicine of *fecundation*, or to make her fruitful. *Brown's Vulgar Errours, b.* vii. *c.* 7.

To FECU'NDIFY. *v. a.* To make fruitful; to make prolifick. *Dict.*

FECU'NDITY. *n. s.* [from *fecund*; *fecondité*, French.]

1. Fruitfulness; quality of producing or bringing forth in great abundance.

I appeal to the animal and vegetable productions of the earth, the vast numbers whereof notoriously testify the extreme luxuriance and *fecundity* of it. *Woodward's Nat. Hist.*

2. Power of producing or bringing forth.

Some of the ancients mention some seeds that retain their *fecundity* forty years; and I have found, from a friend, that melon-seeds, after thirty years, are best for raising of melons. *Ray on the Creation.*

He could never create so ample a world, but he could have made a bigger; the *fecundity* of his creative power never growing barren, nor being exhausted. *Bentley's Sermons.*

FED. Preterite and participle pass. of *To feed.*

For on the grassy verdure as he lay,
And breath'd the freshness of the early day,
Devouring dogs the helpless infant tore,
Fed on his trembling limbs, and lapp'd the gore. *Pope.*

FE'DARY. *n. s.* [*fœdus*, Latin, or from *feudum.*] This word, peculiar to *Shakespeare*, may signify either a confederate; a partner; or a dependant.

Damn'd paper!
Black as the ink that's on thee, senseless bauble!
Art thou a *fedary* for this act, and lookest
So virgin-like without? *Shakespeare's Cymbeline.*

FE'DERAL. *adj.* [from *fœdus*, Latin.] Relating to a league or contract.

It is a *federal* rite betwixt God and us, as eating and drinking, both among the Jews and Heathens, was wont to be. *Hammond's Fundamentals.*

The Romans compelled them, contrary to all *federal* right and justice, both to part with Sardinia, their lawful territory, and also to pay them for the future a double tribute. *Grew.*

FE'DERARY. *n. s.* [from *fœdus*, Latin.] A confederate; an accomplice.

She's a traitor, and Camillo is
A *federary* with her. *Shakespeare.*

FE'DERATE. *adj.* [*fœderatus*, Latin.] Leagued; joined in confederacy.

FEE. *n. s.* [ꝼeoh, Saxon; *fee*, Danish, cattle; *feudum*, low Latin; *feu*, Scottish.]

1. [In law.] All lands and tenements that are held by any acknowledgment of superiority to a higher lord. All lands and tenements, wherein a man hath a perpetual estate to him and his heirs, &c. are divided into *allodium* and *feudum*: *allodium* is every man's own land, which he possesses merely in his own right, without acknowledgment of any service, or payment of any rent to any other. *Feudum*, or fee, is that which we hold by the benefit of another, and in name whereof we owe services, or pay rent, or both, to a superior lord. And all our land in England, the crown-land, which is in the king's own hands, in right of his crown, excepted, is in the nature of feudum: for though a man have land by descent from his ancestors, or bought it for his money; yet is the land of such a nature, that it cannot come to any, either by descent or purchase, but with the burthen that was laid upon him who had novel fee, or first of all received it as a benefit from his lord, to him and to all such to whom it might descend, or be

be any way conveyed from him. So that no man in England has *directum dominium*, that is, the very property or demesne in any land, but the prince in right of his crown: for though he that has fee has *jus perpetuum & utile dominium*, yet he owes a duty for it, and therefore it is not simply his own. Fee is divided into two sorts; fee-absolute, otherwise called fee-simple, and fee-conditional, otherwise termed fee-tail: fee-simple is that whereof we are seized in those general words, To us and our heirs for ever: fee-tail is that whereof we are seised to us and our heirs, with limitation; that is, the heirs of our body, &c. And fee-tail is either general or special: general is where land is given to a man, and the heirs of his body: fee-tail special is that where a man and his wife are seised of land to them and the heirs of their two bodies. *Cowel.*

Now like a lawyer, when he land would let,
Or sell *fee*-simples in his master's name. *Hubberd's Tale.*

Here's the lord of the soil come to seize me for a stray, for entering his *fee*-simple without leave. *Shakespeare's Henry* VI.

2. Property; peculiar.

What concern they?
The general cause; or is it a *fee*-grief,
Due to some single breast? *Shakespeare's Macbeth.*

3. Reward; gratification; recompense.

These be the ways by which, without reward,
Livings in courts be gotten, though full hard;
For nothing there is done without a *fee*. *Hubberd's Tale.*

Not helping, death's my *fee*;
But if I help, what do you promise me? *Shakespeare.*

4. Payments occasionally claimed by persons in office.

Now that God and friends
Have turn'd my captive state to liberty,
At our enlargement what are thy due *fees*? *Shak. Hen.* VI.

5. Reward paid to physicians or lawyers.

He does not reject the person's pretensions, who does not know how to explain them; or refuse doing a good office for a man, because he cannot pay the *fee* of it. *Addison's Spectat.*

6. Portion; pittance; share. Obsolete.

In pruning and trimming all manner of trees,
Reserve to each cattle their property *fees*. *Tuss. Husbandry.*

FE'EFARM. *n. s.* [*fee* and *farm.*] Tenure by which lands are held from a superiour lord.

John surrendered his kingdoms to the pope, and took them back again, to hold in *feefarm*; which brought him into such hatred, as all his lifetime after he was possest with fear. *Davies.*

To FEE. *v. a.* [from the noun.]

1. To reward; to pay.

No man *fees* the sun, no man purchases the light, nor errs if he walks by it. *South's Sermons.*

Watch the disease in time; for when within
The dropsy rages and extends the skin,
In vain for hellebore the patient cries,
And *fees* the doctor; but too late is wise. *Dryden's Pers.*

2. To bribe.

I have long loved her, and ingrossed opportunities to meet her; *feed* every slight occasion, that could but niggardly give me sight of her. *Shakesp. Merry Wives of Windsor.*

3. To keep in hire.

There's not a thane of them but in his house
I have a servant *fee'd*. *Shakespeare's Macbeth.*

FE'EBLE. *adj.* [*foible*, French.] Weak; debilitated; sickly; infirm; without strength of body or mind.

The men carried all the *feeble* upon asses to Jericho. 2 *Chron.*

Command th' assistance of a faithful friend,
But *feeble* are the succours I can send. *Dryden's Æn.*

How I have lov'd, excuse my falt'ring tongue;
My spirits *feeble*, and my pains are strong. *Dryden.*

We carry the image of God in us, a rational and immortal soul; and though we be now miserable and *feeble*, yet we aspire after eternal happiness, and finally expect a great exaltation of all our natural powers. *Bentley's Sermons.*

A crutch that helps the weak along,
Supports the *feeble*, but retards the strong. *Smith.*

To FE'EBLE. *v. a.* [from the noun.] To weaken; to enfeeble; to deprive of strength or power. Not in use.

Or as a castle reared high and round,
By subtile engines and malicious slight
Is undermined from the lowest ground,
And her foundation forc'd and *feebled* quite. *Fairy Queen.*

Shall that victorious hand be *feebled* here,
That in your chambers gave you chastisement? *Sh. K. John.*

FEEBLEMI'NDED. *adj.* [*feeble* and *mind.*] Weak of mind; defective in resolution and constancy.

Warn them that are unruly, comfort the *feebleminded*, support the weak, be patient toward all men. 1 *Thess.* v. 14.

FE'EBLENESS. *n. s.* [from *feeble.*] Weakness; imbecility; infirmity; want of strength.

A better head Rome's glorious body fits,
Than his that shakes for age and *feebleness*. *Shak. Tit Andr.*

Some in their latter years, through the *feebleness* of their limbs, have been forced to study upon their knees. *South.*

FE'EBLY. *adv.* [from *feeble.*] Weakly; without strength.

Like mine, thy gentle numbers *feebly* creep;
Thy tragick muse gives smiles, thy comick sleep. *Dryden.*

To FEED. *v. a.* [*fodan*, Gothick; ꝼeðan, ꝼoeðan, Saxon.]

1. To supply with food.

Her heart and bowels through her back he drew,
And *fed* the hounds that help'd him to pursue. *Dryden.*

Boerhaave *fed* a sparrow with bread four days, in which time it eat more than its own weight. *Arbuthnot on Diet.*

2. To supply; to furnish.

A constant smoke arises from the warm springs that *feed* the many baths with which this island is stocked. *Addison.*

The breadth of the bottom of the hopper must be half the length of a barleycorn, and near as long as the rollers, that it may not *feed* them too fast. *Mortimer's Husbandry.*

3. To graze; to consume by cattle.

Once in three years *feed* your mowing lands, if you cannot get manure constantly to keep them in heart. *Mortimer.*

The frost will spoil the grass; for which reason take care to *feed* it close before Winter. *Mortimer's Husbandry.*

4. To nourish; to cherish.

How oft from pomp and state did I remove,
To *feed* despair, and cherish hopeless love? *Prior.*

5. To keep in hope or expectation.

Barbarossa learned the strength of the emperor, craftily *feeding* him with the hope of liberty. *Knolles's Hist. of the Turks.*

6. To delight; to entertain; to keep from satiety.

The alteration of scenes, so it be without noise, *feeds* and relieves the eye, before it be full of the same object. *Bacon.*

To FEED. *v. n.*

1. To take food. Chiefly applied to animals food.

To *feed* were best at home;
From thence the sawce to meat is ceremony;
Meeting were bare without it. *Shakespeare's Macbeth.*

2. To prey; to live by eating.

I am not covetous of gold;
Nor care I, who doth *feed* upon my cost. *Shakes. Hen.* V.

You cry against the noble senate, who,
Under the gods, keep you in awe, which else
Would *feed* on one another. *Shakesp. Coriolanus.*

Galen speaketh of the curing of the scirrhus of the liver by milk of a cow, that *feedeth* upon certain herbs. *Bacon.*

Some birds *feed* upon the berries of this vegetable. *Brown.*

He *feeds* on fruits, which, of their own accord,
The willing grounds and laden trees afford. *Dryden's Virg.*

The Brachmans were all of the same race, lived in fields and woods, and *fed* only upon rice, milk, or herbs. *Temple.*

All *feed* on one vain patron, and enjoy
Th' extensive blessing of his luxury. *Pope's Essay on Man.*

3. To pasture; to place cattle to feed.

If a man shall cause a field to be eaten, and shall put in his beast, and shall *feed* in another man's field, he shall make restitution. *Ex.* xxii. 5.

4. To grow fat or plump.

FEED. *n. s.* [from the verb.]

1. Food; that which is eaten.

A fearful deer then looks most about when he comes to the best *feed*, with a shruging kind of tremor through all her principal parts. *Sidney, b.* ii.

An old worked ox fats as well as a young one: their *feed* is much cheaper, because they eat no oats. *Mortimer's Husb.*

2. Pasture.

Besides his cote, his flocks and bounds of *feed*
Are now on sale. *Shakespeare's As you like it.*

FE'EDER. *n. s.* [from *feed.*]

1. One that gives food.

The beast obeys his keeper, and looks up,
Not to his master's but his *feeder*'s hand. *Denham.*

2. An exciter; an encourager.

When thou do'st hear I am as I have been,
Approach me, and thou shalt be as thou was't,
The tutor and the *feeder* of my riots. *Shakes. Henry* IV.

3. One that eats.

With eager feeding, food doth choak the *feeder*. *Shakes.*

We meet in Aristotle with one kind of thrush, called the missel-thrush, or *feeder* upon misseltoe. *Brown's Vulgar Err.*

4. One that eats nicely; one that lives luxuriously.

But that our feasts
In every mess have folly, and the *feeders*
Jest with it as a custom, I should blush
To see you so attired. *Shakespeare's Winter's Tale.*

But such fine *feeders* are no guests for me;
Riot agrees not with frugality:
Then, that unfashionable man am I,
With me they'd starve for want of ivory. *Dryden's Juven.*

To FEEL. pret. *felt*; part. pass. *felt. v. n.* [ꝼelan, Saxon.]

1. To have perception of things by the touch.

The sense of *feeling* can give us a notion of extension, shape, and all other ideas that enter at the eye, except colours. *Addison's Spectator*, Nº. 411.

2. To search by feeling. See FEELER.

3. To have a quick sensibility of good or evil, right or wrong.

Man, who *feels* for all mankind. *Pope.*

4. To appear to the touch.
The difference of these tumours will be distinguished by the feel: one *feels* flaccid and rumpled; the other more even, flatulent and springy. *Sharp's Surgery.*

To FEEL. *v. a.*

1. To perceive by the touch.
Suffer me that I may *feel* the pillars. *Judg.* xxvi. 26.

2. To try; to sound.
He hath writ this to *feel* my affection to your honour. *Shak.*

3. To have sense of pain or pleasure.
Nor did they not perceive the evil plight
In which they were, or the fierce pains not *feel*? *Milton.*
But why should those be thought to 'scape, who *feel*
Those rods of scorpions and those whips of steel? *Creech's Juvenal.*
The well sung woes shall sooth my pensive ghost;
He best can paint them who can *feel* them most. *Pope.*
Not youthful kings in battle seiz'd alive,
E'er *felt* such grief, such terrour, and despair. *Pope.*

4. To be affected by.
Would I had never trod this English earth,
Or *felt* the flatteries that grow upon it. *Shakes. Hen.* VIII.

5. To know; to be acquainted with.
His overthrow heap'd happiness upon him;
For then, and not 'till then, he *felt* himself,
And found the blessedness of being little. *Shakes. Hen.* VIII.

FEEL. *n. s.* [from the verb.] The sense of feeling; the touch.
The difference of these tumours will be distinguished by the *feel*: one feels flaccid and rumpled, the other more even, flatulent, and springy. *Sharp's Surgery.*

FE'ELER. *n. s.* [from *feel.*]

1. One that feels.
This hand, whose touch,
Whose ev'ry touch would force the *feeler's* soul
To th' oath of loyalty. *Shakespeare's Cymbeline.*

2. The horns or antennæ of insects.
Insects clean their eyes with their forelegs as well as antennæ; and as they are perpetually feeling and searching before them with their *feelers* or antennæ, I am apt to think that besides wiping and cleaning the eyes, the uses here named may be admitted. *Derham's Physico-Theology.*

FEE'LING. *participial adj.* [from *feel.*]

1. Expressive of great sensibility.
O wretched state of man in self-division!
O well thou say'st a *feeling* declaration
Thy tongue hath made of Cupid's deep incision. *Sidney.*
Thy wailing words do much my spirits move,
They uttered are in such a *feeling* fashion. *Sidney, b.* ii.
Write 'till your ink be dry, and with your tears
Moist it again; and frame some *feeling* line,
That may discover such integrity. *Sh. Two Gent. of Verona.*

2. Sensibly felt. This sense is not sufficiently analogical.
A most poor man made tame to fortune's blows,
Who, by the art of known and *feeling* sorrows,
Am pregnant to good pity. *Shakespeare's King Lear.*
I had a *feeling* sense
Of all your royal favours; but this last
Strikes through my heart. *Southerne.*

FE'ELING. *n. s.* [from *feel.*]

1. The sense of touch.
Why was the sight
To such a tender ball as th' eye confin'd?
So obvious and so easy to be quench'd,
And not, as *feeling*, through all parts diffus'd,
That she might look at will through ev'ry pore. *Milton.*

2. Sensibility; tenderness.
The apprehension of the good,
Gives but the greater *feeling* to the worse. *Shakes. Rich.* II.
Their king, out of a princely *feeling*, was sparing and compassionate towards his subjects. *Bacon's Henry* VII.

3. Perception.
Great persons had need to borrow other men's opinions to think themselves happy; for if they judge by their own *feeling*, they cannot find it. *Bacon's Essays.*
As we learn what belongs to the body by the evidence of sense, so we learn what belongs to the soul by an inward consciousness, which may be called a sort of internal *feeling*. *Watts.*

FEE'LINGLY. *adv.* [from *feeling.*]

1. With expression of great sensibility.
The princess might judge that he meant himself, who spake so *feelingly*. *Sidney.*
He would not have talked so *feelingly* of Codrus's bed, if there had been room for a bedfellow in it. *Pope.*

2. So as to be sensibly felt.
Here feel we but the penalty of Adam,
The season's difference; as the icy phang,
And churlish chiding of the Winter's wind,
Which when it bites and blows upon my body,
Ev'n 'till I shrink with cold, I smile and say,
This is no flattery: these are counsellors,
That *feelingly* persuade me what I am. *Shakesp. As you like it.*

He *feelingly* knew, and had trial of the late good, and of the new purchased evil. *Raleigh's History of the World.*

FEET. *n. s.* The plural of *foot.*
His brother's image to his mind appears,
Inflames his heart with rage, and wings his *feet* with fears. *Pope's Statius.*

FEE'TLESS. *adj.* [from *feet.*] Without feet.
Geoffroy of Boulloin broched three *feetless* birds, called Allerions, upon his arrow. *Camden.*

To FEIGN. *v. a.* [*feindre*, French; *fingo*, Latin.]

1. To invent.
And these three voices differ; all the things done, the doing and the doer; the thing *feigned*, the feigning and the feigner; so the poem, the poesy and the poet. *Ben. Johnson's Discover.*
No such things are done as thou sayest, but thou *feignest* them out of thine own heart. *Neh.* vi. 8.

2. To make a show of.
Both his hands, most filthy feculent,
Above the water were on high extent,
And *feigned* to wash themselves incessantly. *Spens. Fairy Qu.*

3. To make a shew of; to do upon some false pretence.
Me gentle Delia beckons from the plain,
Then, hid in shades, eludes her eager swain;
But *feigns* a laugh to see me search around. *Pope.*

4. To dissemble; to conceal. Now obsolete.
Each trembling leaf and whistling wind they hear,
As ghastly bug their hair on end does rear;
Yet both do strive their fearfulness to *feign*. *Fairy Queen.*

To FEIGN. *v. n.* To relate falsely; to image from the invention.
Therefore the poet
Did *feign* that Orpheus drew trees, stones, and floods;
Since nought so stockish, hard and full of rage,
But musick for the time doth change his nature. *Shakesp.*

FE'IGNEDLY. *adv.* [from *feign.*] In fiction; not truly.
Such is found to have been falsely and *feignedly* in some of the heathens. *Bacon, Essay* 28.

FE'IGNER. *n. s.* [from *feign.*] Inventer; contriver of a fiction.
And these three voices differ; all the things done, the doing and the doer; the thing feigned, the feigning and the *feigner*; so the poem, the poesy and the poet. *Ben. Johnson.*

FEINT. *participial adj.* [from *feign*, for *feigned*; or *feint*, Fr.]
The mind by degrees loses its natural relish of real, solid truth, and is reconciled insensibly to any thing that can be but dressed up into any *feint* appearance of it. *Locke.*

FEINT. *n. s.* [*feint*, French.]

1. A false appearance; an offer of something not intended to be.
Courtly's letter is but a *feint* to get off. *Spectator*, Nº. 286.

2. A mock assault; an appearance of aiming at one part when another is intended to be struck.
But, in the breast encamp'd, prepares
For well-bred *feints* and future wars. *Prior.*

FE'LANDERS. *n. s.* Worms in hawks. *Ainsworth.*

FE'LDFARE. *n. s.* See FIELDFARE.

To FELI'CITATE. *v. a.* [*feliciter*, French; *felicita*, Latin.]

1. To make happy.
I profess
Myself an enemy to all other joys;
And find I am alone *felicitate*
In your dear highness' love. *Shakespeare's King Lear.*
What a glorious entertainment and pleasure would fill and *felicitate* his spirit, if he could grasp all in a single survey. *Watts.*

2. To congratulate.
They might proceed unto forms of speeches, *felicitating* the good, or deprecating the evil to follow. *Brown's Vulgar Err.*

FELICITA'TION. *n. s.* [French, from *felicitate.*] Congratulation. *Dict.*

FELI'CITOUS. *adj.* [*felix*, Latin.] Happy. *Dict.*

FELI'CITOUSLY. *adv.* [from *felicitous.*] Happily. *Dict.*

FELI'CITY. *n. s.* [*felicitas*, Latin; *felicité*, Fr.] Happiness; prosperity; blissfulness; blessedness.
The joyous day, dear Lord, with joy begin,
And grant that we, for whom thou didest die,
Being with thy dear blood clean wash'd from sin,
May live for ever in *felicity*. *Spenser, Sonnet* 68.
Others in virtue plac'd *felicity*;
But virtue join'd with riches and long life,
In corporal pleasure he, and careless ease. *Milt. Par. Reg.*
So the *felicities* of her wonderful reign may be complete. *Atterbury's Sermons.*
How great, how glorious a *felicity*, how adequate to the desires of a reasonable nature, is revealed to our hopes in the gospel! *Rogers, Sermon* iii.

FE'LINE. *adj.* [*felinus*, Latin.] Like a cat; pertaining to a cat.
Even as in the beaver; from which he differs principally in his teeth, which are canine, and in his tail, which is *feline*, or a long taper. *Grew's Musæum.*

FELL. *adj.* [felle, Saxon.]

1. Cruel; barbarous; inhuman.

It

It seemed fury, discord, madness *fell*,
Flew from his lap when he unfolds the same. *Fairfax, b.* ii.
So *fellest* foes,
Whose passions and whose plots have broke their sleep,
To take the one the other, by some chance,
Some trick not worth an egg, shall grow dear friends. *Shak.*
That instant was I turn'd into a hart,
And my desires, like *fell* and cruel hounds,
E'er since pursue me. *Shakespeare's Twelfth Night.*

2. Savage; ravenous; bloody.
I know thee, love! wild as the raging main,
More *fell* than tygers on the Lybian plain. *Pope's Autumn.*
Scorning all the taming arts of man,
The keen hyena, *fellest* of the *fell*. *Thomson's Spring.*

FELL. *n. s.* [fell, Saxon.] The skin; the hide.
Wipe thine eye;
The goujers shall devour them, flesh and *fell*,
Ere they shall make us weep. *Shakespeare's King Lear.*
The time has been my senses would have cool'd
To hear a night-shriek; and my *fell* of hair
Would at a dismal treatise rouze and stir. *Shakes. Macbeth.*

To FELL. *v. a.* [*fellen*, German.]

1. To knock down; to bring to the ground.
Villain, stand, or I'll *fell* thee down. *Shakesp. Henry* V.
Up and down he traverses his ground;
Now wards a *felling* blow, now strikes again. *Daniel.*

Taking the small end of his musket in his hand, he struck him on the head with the stock, and *felled* him. *Raleigh.*

His fall, for the present, struck an earthquake into all minds; nor could the vulgar be induced to believe he was *felled*. *Howel's Vocal Forrest.*

On their whole host I flew
Unarm'd, and with a trivial weapon *fell'd*
Their choicest youth: they only liv'd who fled. *Milt. Agon.*
Whom with such force he struck he *fell'd* him down,
And cleft the circle of his golden crown. *Dryden.*
I *fell'd* along a man of bearded face,
His limbs all cover'd with a shining case. *Dryd. Ind. Emp.*

2. To hew down; to cut down.
Then would he seem a farmer that would sell
Bargains of woods, which he did lately *fell*. *Hubb. Tale.*
Proud Arcite and fierce Palamon,
In mortal battle, doubling blow on blow;
Like lightning flam'd their fauchions to and fro,
And shot a dreadful gleam; so strong they struck,
There seem'd less force requir'd to *fell* an oak. *Dryden.*

FELL. The preterite of *To fall.*
None on their feet might stand,
Though standing else as rocks; but down they *fell*
By thousands, angel on archangel roll'd. *Milton.*

FE'LLER. *n. s.* [from *fell.*] One that hews down.
Since thou art laid down, no *feller* is come up against us. *Is.* xiv. 8.

FELLI'FLUOUS. *adj.* [*fel* and *fluo*, Latin.] Flowing with gall. *Dict.*

FE'LLMONGER. *n. s.* [from *fell.*] A dealer in hides.

FE'LLNESS. *n. s.* [from *fell.*] Cruelty; savageness; fury; rage.
When his brother saw the red blood trail
Adown so fast, and all his armour steep,
For very *felness* loud he 'gan to weep. *Fairy Queen, b.* ii.

FE'LLOE. *n. s.* [*felge*, Danish.] The circumference of a wheel; the outward part. It is often written *fally* or *felly*.
Out, out, thou strumpet fortune! all you gods,
In general synod, take away her power;
Break all the spokes and *fellies* from her wheel,
And bowl the round nave down the hill of heav'n. *Shakesp.*
Their axle-trees, naves, *felloes*, and spokes were all molten. 1 *Kings* vii. 33.

FE'LLOW. *n. s.* [*quasi*, to follow, *Minshew*; from fe, faith, and lag, bound, Saxon, *Junius*; *fallow*, Scottish.]

1. A companion; one with whom we consort.
In youth I had twelve *fellows* like unto myself, but not one of them came to a good end. *Ascham's Schoolmaster.*

To be your *fellow*,
You may deny me; but I'll be your servant,
Whether you will or no. *Shakespeare's Tempest.*
Have we not plighted each our holy oath,
That one should be the common good of both;
One soul should both inspire, and neither prove
His *fellow*'s hindrance in pursuit of love? *Dryden.*

2. An associate; one united in the same affair.
Each on his *fellow* for assistance calls;
At length the fatal fabrick mounts the walls. *Dryden's Virg.*

3. One of the same kind.
Let partial spirits still aloud complain,
Think themselves injur'd that they cannot reign;
And own no liberty, but where they may
Without controul upon their *fellows* prey. *Waller.*

A shepherd had one favourite dog: he fed him with his own hand, and took more care of him than of any of his *fellows*. *L'Estrange's Fables.*

4. Equal; peer.
Chieftain of the rest
I chose him here: the earth shall him allow;
His *fellows* late, shall be his subjects now. *Fairfax, b.* i.

So you are to be hereafter *fellows*, and no longer servants. *Sidney.*

5. One thing suited to another; one of a pair.
When virtue is lodged in a body, that seems to have been prepared for the reception of vice: the soul and the body do not seem to be *fellows*. *Addison's Spectator*, N°. 86.

6. One like another: as, this knave hath not his *fellow*.

7. A familiar appellation used sometimes with fondness; sometimes with esteem; but generally with some degree of contempt.
This is Othello's ancient, as I take it.
—The same indeed; a very valiant *fellow*. *Shakes. Othello.*

An officer was in danger to have lost his place, but his wife made his peace; whereupon a pleasant *fellow* said, that he had been crushed, but that he saved himself upon his horns. *Bacon, Apophthegm* 4.

Full fifteen thousand lusty *fellows*
With fire and sword the fort maintain;
Each was a Hercules, you tell us,
Yet out they march'd like common men. *Prior.*

8. A word of contempt: the foolish mortal; the mean wretch; the sorry rascal.
Those great *fellows* scornfully receiving them, as foolish birds fallen into their net, it pleased the eternal justice to make them suffer death by their hands. *Sidney, b.* ii.

Cassio hath here been set on in the dark
By Rodorigo, and *fellows* that are 'scap'd:
He's almost slain, and Rodorigo dead. *Shakesp. Othello.*

I have great comfort from this *fellow*: methinks he hath no drowning mark about him; his complexion is perfect gallows. *Shakespeare's Tempest.*

Opinion, that did help me to the crown,
Had still kept loyal to possession;
And left me in reputeless banishment,
A *fellow* of no mark nor likelihood. *Shakesp. Henry* IV.
How oft the sight of means, to do ill deeds,
Makes deeds ill done? for had'st not thou been by,
A *fellow* by the hand of nature mark'd,
Quoted, and sign'd to do a deed of shame,
This murder had not come into my mind. *Shakes. K. John.*
The Moor's abus'd by some most villainous knave,
Some base notorious knave, some scurvy *fellow*. *Shak. Othell.*

The *fellow* had taken more fish than he could spend while they were sweet. *L'Estrange.*

As next of kin, Achilles' arms I claim;
This *fellow* would ingraft a foreign name
Upon our stock, and the Sisyphian seed
By fraud and theft asserts his father's breed. *Dryden.*

You will wonder how such an ordinary *fellow*, as this Mr. Wood, could have got his majesty's broad seal. *Swift.*

You'll find, if once the monarch acts the monk,
Or, cobler like, the parson will be drunk,
Worth makes the man, and want of it the *fellow*;
The rest is all but leather and prunella. *Pope's Ess. on Man.*

9. Sometimes it implies a mixture of pity with contempt.
The provost commanded his men to hang him up on the nearest tree: then the *fellow* cried out that he was not the miller, but the miller's man. *Hayward.*

10. A member of a college that shares its revenues.

To FE'LLOW. *v. a.* To suit with; to pair with; to match.
Fellow is often used in composition to mark community of nature, station, or employment.
Imagination,
With what's unreal, thou co-active art,
And *fellow'st* nothing. *Shakespeare's Winter's Tale.*

FELLOW-CO'MMONER. *n. s.*

1. One who has the same right of common.
He cannot appropriate, he cannot inclose, without the consent of all his *fellowcommoners*, all mankind. *Locke.*

2. A commoner at Cambridge of the higher order, who dines with the fellows.

FELLOW-CREA'TURE. *n. s.* One that has the same creator.
Reason is the glory of human nature, and one of the chief eminencies whereby we are raised above our *fellowcreatures* the brutes in this lower world. *Watts's Logick, Introduction.*

FELLO'W-HEIR. *n. s.* Coheir; partner of the same inheritance.
The Gentiles should be *fellowheirs*. *Eph.* iii. 6.

FELLOW-HE'LPER. *n. s.* Coadjutor; one who concurs in the same business.
We ought to receive such, that we might be *fellowhelpers* to the truth. 3 *Jo.* viii.

FELLOW-LA'BOURER. *n. s.* One who labours in the same design.
My *fellowlabourers* have likewise commissioned me to perform in their behalf this office of dedication. *Dryd. Juv. Ded.*

FELLOW-SE'RVANT. *n. s.* One that has the same master.

Nor leſs think we in heav'n of thee on earth,
Than of our *fellowſervant*; and inquire
Gladly into the ways of God with man. *Milt. Parad. Loſt.*
Fair *fellowſervant!* may your gentle ear
Prove more propitious to my ſlighted care
Than the bright dame's we ſerve. *Waller.*

Their fathers and yours were *fellowſervants* to the ſame heavenly maſter while they lived; nor is that relation diſſolved by their death, but ought ſtill to operate among their ſurviving children. *Atterbury's Sermons.*

FELLOW-SO'LDIER. *n. ſ.* One who fights under the ſame commander. An endearing appellation uſed by officers to their men.

Come, *fellowſoldier*, make thou proclamation. *Shakeſp.*

Epaphroditus, my brother and companion in labour, and *fellowſoldier*. *Phil.* ii. 25.

FELLOW-STU'DENT. *n. ſ.* One who ſtudies in company with another.

I pr'ythee, do not mock me, *fellowſtudent*;
I think it was to ſee my mother's wedding. *Shakeſ. Hamlet.*

If you have no *fellowſtudent* at hand, tell it over with your acquaintance. *Watts's Logick.*

FELLOW-SU'BJECT. *n. ſ.* One who lives under the ſame government.

The bleeding condition of their *fellowſubjects* was a feather in the balance with their private ends. *Swift.*

FELLOW-SU'FFERER. *n. ſ.* One who ſhares in the ſame evils; one who partakes the ſame ſufferings with another.

How happy was it for thoſe poor creatures, that your grace was made their *fellowſufferer?* And how glorious for you, that you choſe to want rather than not relieve the wants of others? *Dryden's Fables, Dedication.*

We in ſome meaſure ſhare the neceſſities of the poor at the ſame time that we relieve them, and make ourſelves not only their patrons but *fellowſufferers*. *Addiſon's Spectator.*

FELLOW-WRITER. *n. ſ.* One who writes at the ſame time, or on the ſame ſubject.

Since they cannot raiſe themſelves to the reputation of their *fellow-writers*, they muſt ſink it to their own pitch, if they would keep themſelves upon a level with them. *Addiſ. Spectat.*

FELLOWFE'ELING. *n. ſ.* [*fellow* and *feeling.*]

1. Sympathy.

It is a high degree of inhumanity not to have a *fellowfeeling* of the misfortune of my brother. *L'Eſtrange.*

2. Combination; joint intereſt.

Even your milkwoman and your nurſerymaid have a *fellowfeeling*. *Arbuthnot's Hiſtory of John Bull.*

FE'LLOWLIKE. } *adj.* [*fellow* and *like.*] Like a companion;
FE'LLOWLY. } on equal terms; companionable.

All which good parts he graceth with a good *fellowlike*, kind, and reſpectful carriage. *Carew's Survey of Cornwal.*

One ſeed for another, to make an exchange,
With *fellowly* neighbourhood ſeemeth not ſtrange. *Tuſſer.*

FE'LLOWSHIP. *n. ſ.* [from *fellow.*]

1. Companionſhip; conſort; ſociety.

This boy cannot tell what he would have,
But kneels and holds up hands for *fellowſhip*. *Shak. Coriolan.*
From bliſsful bow'rs
Of amarantine ſhade, fountain, or ſpring,
By the waters of life, where'er they ſat
In *fellowſhips* of joy, the ſons of light
Haſted. *Milton's Paradiſe Loſt, b.* xi. *l.* 80.

There is no man but God puts excellent things into his poſſeſſion, to be uſed for the common good; for men are made for ſociety and mutual *fellowſhip*. *Calamy's Sermons.*

God having deſigned man for a ſociable creature, made him not only with an inclination and under the neceſſity to have *fellowſhip* with thoſe of his own kind, but furniſhed him alſo with language, which was to be the great inſtrument and cementer of ſociety. *Locke.*

2. Aſſociation; confederacy; combination.

We would not die in that man's company,
That fears his *fellowſhip* to die with us. *Shakeſp. Henry* V.

Thoſe laws do bind men abſolutely, even as they are men, although they have never any ſettled *fellowſhip*, never any ſolemn agreement amongſt themſelves what to do, or not to do. *Hooker, b* i. *ſ.* 10.

Moſt of the other Chriſtian princes were drawn into the *fellowſhip* of that war. *Knolles's Hiſtory of the Turks.*

3. Equality.

4. Partnerſhip; joint intereſt.

Nearer acquainted, now I feel by proof
That *fellowſhip* in pain divides not ſmart,
Nor lightens aught each man's peculiar load. *Parad. Reg.*
O love! thou ſternly do'ſt thy pow'r maintain,
And wilt not bear a rival in thy reign;
Tyrants and thou all *fellowſhip* diſdain. *Dryden.*

5. Company; ſtate of being together.

The great contention of the ſea and ſkies
Parted our *fellowſhip*. But hark, a ſail! *Shakeſp. Othello.*

6. Frequency of intercourſe; ſocial pleaſure.

In a great town friends are ſcattered, ſo that there is not that *fellowſhip* which is in leſs neighbourhoods. *Bacon's Eſſays.*

7. Fitneſs and fondneſs for feſtal entertainments, with *good* prefixed.

He had by his exceſſive *good fellowſhip*, which was grateful to all the company, made himſelf popular with all the officers of the army. *Clarendon, b.* viii.

8. An eſtabliſhment in the college with ſhare in its revenue.

Coruſodes having, by the moſt extreme parſimony, ſaved thirty-four pounds out of a beggarly *fellowſhip*, went up to London. *Swift.*

9. [In arithmetick.] That rule of plural proportion whereby we balance accompts, depending between divers perſons, having put together a general ſtock, ſo that they may every man have his proportional gain, or ſuſtain his proportional part of loſs. *Cocker's Arithmetick.*

10. A rule in arithmetick, by which two or more independent operations of the rule of three may divide any given number into unequal parts, proportional to certain other numbers. It is ſo called, becauſe the more common and uſeful application thereof is in the diviſion of gains, loſſes, or other things, among partners in company. *Malcolm.*

FE'LLY. *adv.* [from *fell.*] Cruelly; inhumanly; ſavagely; barbarouſly.

Fair ye be ſure, but cruel and unkind;
As is a tyger, that with greedineſs
Hunts after blood, when he by chance doth find
A feeble beaſt, doth *felly* him oppreſs. *Spenſer's Sonnets.*

FELO-DE-SE. *n. ſ.* [In law.] He that committeth felony by murdering himſelf.

FE'LON. *n. ſ.* [*felon*, French; *felo*, low Latin; ꝼel, Saxon.]

1. One who has committed a capital crime.

I apprehend thee for a *felon* here. *Shak. Romeo and Juliet.*
And often have you brought the wily fox,
Chas'd even amid' the folds; and made to bleed,
Like *felons*, where they did the murd'rous deed. *Dryden.*

2. A whitlow; a tumour formed between the bone and its inveſting membrane, very painful.

The malign paronychia is that which is commonly called a *felon*. *Wiſeman's Surgery.*

FE'LON. *adj.* Cruel; traitorous; inhuman.

Ay me! what thing on earth, that all things breeds,
Might be the cauſe of ſo impatient plight!
What fury, or what fiend with *felon* deeds,
Hath ſtirred up ſo miſchievous deſpight! *Spenſer.*
Then bids prepare th' hoſpitable treat,
Vain ſhews of love to veil his *felon* hate. *Pope's Odyſſey.*

FE'LONIOUS. *adj.* [from *felon.*] Wicked; traitorous; villanous; malignant; perfidious; deſtructive.

This man conceived the duke's death; but what was the motive of that *felonious* conception is in the clouds. *Wotton.*

O thieviſh night!
Why ſhould'ſt thou, but for ſome *felonious* end,
In thy dark lanthorn thus cloſe up the ſtars
That nature hung in heav'n, and fill'd the lamps
With everlaſting oil, to give due light
To the miſled and lonely traveller? *Milton.*
In thy *felonious* heart though venom lies,
It does but touch thy Iriſh pen and dies. *Dryden.*

FELO'NIOUSLY. *adj.* [from *felonious.*] In a felonious way.

FE'LONOUS. *adj.* [from *felon.*] Wicked; felonious.

I am like for deſperate dole to die,
Through *felonous* force of mine enemy. *Spenſer's Paſtorals.*

FE'LONY. *n. ſ.* [*felonie*, Fr. *felonia*, low Latin, from *felon.*] A crime denounced capital by the law; an enormous crime.

I will make it *felony* to drink ſmall beer. *Shakeſ. Henry* VI.

FELT. The preterite of FEEL, which ſee.

FELT. *n. ſ.* [ꝼeltz, Saxon.]

1. Cloath made of wool united without weaving.

It were a delicate ſtratagem to ſhoe
A troop of horſe with *felt*. *Shakeſpeare's King Lear.*

2. A hide or skin.

To know whether ſheep are ſound or not, ſee that the *felt* be looſe. *Mortimer's Huſbandry.*

To FELT. *v. a.* [from the noun.] To unite without weaving.

The ſame wool one man *felts* into a hat, another weaves it into cloath, another into kerſey. *Hale's Origin of Mankind.*

To FE'LTRE. *v. a.* [from *felt.*] To clot together like felt.

His *feltred* locks, that on his boſom fell,
On rugged mountains briers and thorns reſemble. *Fairfax.*

FELU'CCA. *n. ſ.* [*feleu*, Fr. *feluken*, Arab.] A ſmall open boat with ſix oars. *Dict.*

FE'MALE. *n. ſ.* [*femelle*, French; *femella*, Latin.] A ſhe; one of the ſex which brings young.

God created man in his own image, male and *female* created he them. *Gen.* i. 27.

Man, more divine,
Lord of the wide world, and wide wat'ry ſeas,
Indu'd with intellectual ſenſe and ſoul,
Are maſters to their *females*, and their lords. *Shakeſpeare.*

FE'MALE. *adj.*

1. Not maſculine; belonging to a ſhe.

If by a *female* hand he had foreſeen
He was to die, his wiſh had rather been
The lance and double ax of the fair warrior queen. *Dryd.*

2. Female *Rhymes.* Double rhymes so called, because in French, from which the term is taken, they end in *e* weak or feminine. These rhymes are female:

Th' excess of heat is but a fable;
We know the torrid zone is now found habitable. *Cowley.*

The *female rhymes* are in use with the Italian in every line, with the Spaniard promiscuously, and with the French alternately, as appears from the Alarique, the Pucelle, or any of their later poems. *Dryden's Preface to Ann. Mirab.*

Feme *Covert. n. s.* [French.] A married woman; who is also said to be under covert baron. *Blount.*

Feme *Sole. n. s.* [French.] A single woman; an unmarried woman.

Femina'lity. *n. s.* [from *fœmina*, Latin.] Female nature.

If in the minority of natural vigour the parts of *feminality* take place, upon the increase or growth thereof the masculine appears. *Brown's Vulgar Errours, b.* iii. *c.* 17.

Fe'minine *adj.* [*fœmininus*, Latin.]

1. Of the sex that brings young; female.

Thus we chastise the god of wine
With water that is *feminine*,
Until the cooler nymph abate
His wrath, and so concorporate. *Cleaveland.*

2. Soft; tender; delicate.

Her heav'nly form
Angelick, but more soft and *feminine. Milton's Parad. Lost.*

3. Effeminate; emasculated.

Ninias was no man of war at all, but altogether *feminine* and subjected to ease and delicacy. *Raleigh's Hist. of the World.*

Fe'minine. *n. s.* A she; one of the sex that brings young; a female.

O! why did God create at last
This novelty on earth, this fair defect
Of nature? And not fill the world at once
With men, as angels, without *feminine? Milt. Par. Lost.*

Fe'moral. *adj.* [*femoralis*, Latin.] Belonging to the thigh.

The largest crooked needle should be used in taking up the *femoral* arteries in amputation. *Sharp's Surgery.*

FEN. *n. s.* [fenn, Saxon; *venne*, Dutch.] A marsh; low flat and moist ground; a moor; a bog.

Mexico is a city that stands in the midst of a great marsh or *fen. Abbot's Description of the World.*

I go alone,
Like to a lonely dragon, that his *fen*
Makes fear'd and talk'd of more than seen. *Shakesp. Coriolan.*

Yon common cry of curs, whose breath I hate,
As reek o' th' rotten *fens. Shakespeare's Coriolanus.*

The surface is of black *fen* earth. *Woodward on Fossils.*

He to Portina's wat'ry marshes went;
A long canal the muddy *fen* divides,
And with a clear unsully'd current glides. *Addison.*

Fe'nberry. *n. s.* [*fen* and *berry.*] A kind of blackberry. *Skinner.*

Fence. *n. s.* [from *defence.*]

1. Guard; security; outwork; defence.

That proved not *fence* enough to the reputation of their oppressors. *Decay of Piety.*

There's no *fence* against inundations, earthquakes, or hurricanes. *L'Estrange, Fable* 167.

To put them out of their parents view, at a great distance, is to expose them to the greatest dangers of their whole life, when they have the least *fence* and guard against them. *Locke.*

Let us bear this awful corps to Cæsar,
And lay it in his sight, that it may stand
A *fence* betwixt us and the victor's wrath. *Addison's Cato.*

2. Inclosure; mound; hedge.

In vain did nature's wise command
Divide the waters from the land,
If daring ships, and men prophane,
Invade th' inviolable main;
Th' eternal *fences* overleap,
And pass at will the boundless deep. *Dryden's Horace.*

Shall I mention make
Of the vast mound that binds the Lucrine lake?
Or the disdainful sea, that, shut from thence,
Roars round the structure, and invades the *fence? Dryden.*

Employ their wiles and unavailing care,
To pass the *fences* and surprise the fair. *Pope.*

3. The art of fencing; defence.

I bruised my skin th' other day, with playing at sword and dagger with a master of *fence. Shakes. Merry Wives of Winds.*

4. Skill in defence.

I'll prove it on his body, if he dare,
Despite his nice *fence* and his active practice. *Shakespeare.*

To Fence. *v. a.*

1. To inclose; to secure by an inclosure or hedge.

Th' inhabitants each pasture and each plain
Destroyed have, each field to waste is lade;
In *fenced* towers bestowed is their grain,
Before thou cam'st this kingdom to invade. *Fairfax, b.* ii.

He hath *fenced* up my way that I cannot pass, and set darkness in my paths. *Job* xix. 8.

Thou hast cloathed me with skin and flesh, and hast *fenced* me with bones and sinews. *Job* x. 11.

He went about to make a bridge to a strong city, which was *fenced* about with walls. 2 *Mac.* xii. 13.

See that the churchyard be *fenced* in with a decent rail, or other inclosure. *Ayliffe's Parergon.*

2. To guard.

So much of adders wisdom I have learnt,
To *fence* my ear against thy sorceries. *Milton's Agonistes.*

With love to friend, th' impatient lover went,
Fenc'd from the thorns, and trod the deep descent. *Dryden.*

To Fence. *v. n.*

1. To practise the arts of manual defence; to practise the use of weapons.

He having got some iron, should have it beaten into swords, and put into his servants hands to *fence* with, and bang one another. *Locke.*

2. To guard against; to act on the defensive.

Vice is the more stubborn as well as the more dangerous evil, and therefore in the first place to be *fenced* against. *Locke.*

3. To fight according to art.

If a throstle sing, he falls strait a capering:
He will *fence* with his own shadow. *Shak. Merch. of Venice.*

A beauteous heifer in the wood is bred;
The stooping warriors, aiming head to head,
Engage their clashing horns; with dreadful sound
The forest rattles, and the rocks rebound;
They *fence* and push, and, pushing, loudly roar,
Their dewlaps and their sides are bath'd in gore. *Dryden.*

A man that cannot *fence* will keep out of bullies and gamesters company. *Locke.*

These, being polemical arts, could no more be learned alone than *fencing* or cudgelplaying. *Arbuth. and Pope's Ma. Sc.*

Fe'nceless. *adj.* [from *fence.*] Without inclosure; open.

Each motion of the heart rises to fury,
And love in their weak bosoms is a rage
As terrible as hate, and as destructive:
So the wind roars o'er the wide *fenceless* ocean,
And heaves the billows of the boiling deep,
Alike from North, from South, from East, from West.
Rowe's Jane Shore.

Fe'ncer. *n. s.* [from *fence.*] One who teaches or practises the use of weapons, or science of defence.

Calmness is great advantage: he that lets
Another chafe, may warm him at his fire,
Mark all his wand'rings, and enjoy his frets;
As cunning *fencers* suffer heat to tire. *Herbert.*

A nimble *fencer* will put in a thrust so quick, that the foil will be in your bosom when you thought it a yard off. *Digby.*

Fe'ncible. *adj.* [from *fence.*] Capable of defence. *Addison.*

Fe'ncingmaster. *n. s.* [*fence* and *master.*] One who teaches the use of weapons.

Fe'ncingschool. *n. s.* [*fence* and *school.*] A place in which the use of weapons is taught.

If a man be to prepare his son for duels, I had rather mine should be a good wrestler than an ordinary fencer, which is the most a gentleman can attain to, unless he will be constantly in the *fencingschool*, and every day exercising. *Locke.*

To Fend. *v. a.* [from *defend.*] To keep off; to shut out.

Spread with straw the bedding of thy fold,
With fern beneath, to *fend* the bitter cold. *Dryden's Virgil.*

To Fend. *v. n.* To dispute; to shift off a charge.

The dexterous management of terms, and being able to *fend* and prove with them, passes for a great part of learning; but it is learning distinct from knowledge. *Locke.*

Fe'nder. *n. s.* [from *fend.*]

1. An iron plate laid before the fire to hinder coals that fall from rolling forward to the floor.

2. Any thing laid or hung at the side of a ship to keep off violence.

Fenera'tion. *n. s.* [*fœneratio*, Latin.] Usury; the gain of interest; the practice of increasing money by lending.

The hare figured not only pusilanimity and timidity from its temper, but *feneration* and usury from its fecundity and superfetation. *Brown's Vulgar Errours, b* iii. *c.* 17.

Fe'nugreek. *n. s.* [*fœnum Græcum*, Latin.] A plant.

It hath a papilionaceous flower, out of whose empalement rises the pointal, which afterwards becomes a pod, somewhat plain, shaped like a horn, and full of seeds, for the most part rhomboid or kidney-shaped. *Miller.*

Fe'nnel. *n. s.* [*fœniculum*, Latin.] A plant of strong scent.

It is an umbelliferous plant, whose leaves are divided into capillaceous jags: the petals of the flower are intire, and placed orbicularly, expanding in form of a rose: each flower is succeeded by two oblong thick gibbous seeds, chaucled on one side, and plain on the other. *Miller.*

A sav'ry odour blown, more pleas'd my sense
Than smell of sweetest *fennel*, or the teats
Of ewe, or goat, dropping with milk at ev'n. *Milton.*

Fe'nnelflower. *n. s.* A plant.

Fe'nnelgiant. *n. s.* A plant.

It hath a large succulent milky root: the stalks are spongy, and filled with pith: the flowers consist of many leaves, expanded in form of a rose, growing in an umbel: each flower is succeeded by two large oval-shaped flat seeds, which are very thin, and turn black when ripe: the leaves are like those of fennel. *Miller.*

FE'NNY. *adj.* [from *fen.*]

1. Marshy; boggy; moorish.

Driving in of piles is used for stone or brick houses, and that only where the ground proves *fenny* or moorish. *Moxon.*

The hungry crocodile, and hissing snake,
Lurk in the troubl'd stream and *fenny* brake. *Prior.*

2. Inhabiting the marsh.

Fillet of a *fenny* snake,
In the caudron boil and bake. *Shakespeare's Macbeth.*

FE'NNYSTONES. *n. s.* A plant.

FE'NSUCKED. *adj.* [*fen* and *suck.*] Sucked out of marshes.

Infect her beauty,
You *fensuck'd* fogs, drawn by the pow'rful sun. *Sh. K. Lear.*

FE'OD. *n. s.* [*feodum*, low Latin.] Fee; tenure. *Dict.*

FE'ODAL. *adj.* [*feodal*, French, from *feod.*] Held from another.

FE'ODARY. *n. s.* [from *feodum*, Latin.] One who holds his estate under the tenure of suit and service to a superiour lord. *Hanmer.*

To FEOFF. *v. a.* [*fief*, *fieffer*, French; *feoffare*, low Latin.] To put in possession; to invest with right.

FEOFFEE. *n. s.* [*feoffatus*, Latin; *fieffé*, French.] One put in possession.

The late earl of Desmond, before his breaking forth into rebellion, conveyed secretly all his lands to *feoffees* in trust, in hope to have cut off her majesty from the escheat of his lands. *Spenser's State of Ireland.*

FE'OFFER. *n. s.* [*feoffator*, low Latin.] One who gives possession of any thing. See FEOFFMENT.

FE'OFFMENT. *n. s.* [*feoffamentum*, Latin.] The act of granting possession.

Any gift or grant of any honours, castles, lands, or other immoveable things, to another in fee-simple, that is, to him and his heirs for ever, by the delivery of seisin of the thing given: when it is in writing, it is called a deed of *feoffment*; and in every *feoffment* the giver is called the feoffor, *feoffator*, and he that receiveth by virtue thereof the feoffee, *feoffatus*. The proper difference between a feoffor and a donor is, that the feoffor gives in fee-simple, the donor in fee-tail. *Cowel.*

The act of parliament cut off and frustrated all such conveyances as had, by the space of twelve years before his rebellion, been made; within the compass whereof the fraudulent *feoffment* of others, his accomplices and fellow-traytors, were contained. *Spenser's State of Ireland.*

FERA'CITY. *n. s.* [*feracitas*, Lat.] Fruitfulness; fertility. *Dict.*

FE'RAL. *adj.* [*feralis*, Latin.] Funereal; mournful; deadly. *Dict.*

FERIA'TION. *n. s.* [*feriatio*, Lat.] The act of keeping holiday; cessation from work.

As though there were any *feriation* in nature, this season is commonly termed the physicians vacation. *Brown's Vulg. Err.*

FE'RINE. *adj.* [*ferinus*, Latin.] Wild; savage.

The only difficulty that remains is touching those *ferine*, noxious, and untameable beasts; as lions, tygers, wolves and bears. *Hale's Origin of Mankind.*

FERI'NENESS. *n. s.* [from *ferine.*] Barbarity; savageness; wildness.

A ferine and necessitous kind of life, a conversation with those that were fallen into a barbarous habit of life, would assimilate the next generation to barbarism and *ferineness*. *Hale.*

FE'RITY. *n. s.* [*feritas*, Latin.] Barbarity; cruelty; wildness; savageness.

He reduced him from the most abject and stupid *ferity* to his senses, and to sober reason. *Woodward's Natural History.*

To FERME'NT. *v. a.* [*fermento*, Latin; *fermenter*, French.] To exalt or rarify by intestine motion of parts.

Ye vig'rous swains! while youth *ferments* your blood,
And purer spirits swell the sprightly flood,
Now range the hills, the thickest woods beset,
Wind the shrill horn, or spread the waving net. *Pope.*

To FERME'NT. *v. n.* To have the parts put into intestine motion.

FE'RMENT. *n. s.* [*ferment*, French; *fermentum*, Latin.]

1. That which causes intestine motion.

The semen puts females into a fever, upon impregnation; and all animal humours which poison, are putrefying *ferments*. *Floyer on the Humours.*

Subdue and cool the *ferment* of desire. *Rogers's Sermons.*

2. The intestine motion; tumult.

FERME'NTABLE. *adj.* [from *ferment.*] Capable of fermentation.

FERME'NTAL. *adj.* [from *ferment.*] Having the power to cause fermentation

Cucumbers, being waterish, fill the veins with crude and windy serosities, that contain little salt or spirit, and debilitate the vital acidity and *fermental* faculty of the stomach. *Brown.*

FERMENTA'TION. *n. s.* [*fermentatio*, Latin.] A slow motion of the intestine particles of a mixt body, arising usually from the operation of some active acid matter, which rarifies, exalts, and subtilizes the soft and sulphureous particles: as when leaven or yest rarifies, lightens, and ferments bread or wort, &c. And this motion differs much from that usually called ebullition or effervescence, which is a violent boiling and struggling between an acid and an alkali, when mixed together. *Harris.*

The juice of grapes, after *fermentation*, will yield a *spiritus ardens*. *Boyle.*

A man, by tumbling his thoughts, and forming them into expressions, gives them a new kind of *fermentation*; which works them into a finer body, and makes them much clearer than they were before. *Collier of Friendship.*

The sap, in fluent dance,
And lively *fermentation*, mounting, spreads
All this innumerous colour'd scene of things. *Thomson.*

FERME'NTATIVE. *adj.* [from *ferment.*] Causing fermentation; having the power to cause fermentation.

Aromatical spirits destroy by their *fermentative* heat. *Arbuth.*

FERN. *n. s.* [ꝼeaꝛn, Saxon.] A plant.

The male *fern* is common on the stumps of trees in woods, and on the banks of ditches: the leaves are formed of a number of small pinnules, dentated on the edges, and set close by one another on slender ribs. On the back of these pinnules are produced the seeds, small and extremely numerous. Decoctions of the root and diet drinks have been used in chronick disorders and obstructions. The country people esteem it a sovereign remedy for the rickets in children. *Hill.*

Black was the forest, thick with beech it stood,
Horrid with *fern*, and intricate with thorn;
Few paths of human feet or tracks of beasts were worn. *Dryden's Æneid.*

There are great varieties of *fern* in different parts of the world; but they are seldom cultivated in gardens. *Miller.*

FE'RNY. *adj.* [from *fern.*] Overgrown with fern.

The herd suffic'd, did late repair
To *ferny* heaths, and to their forest-lare. *Dryden.*

FERO'CIOUS. *adj.* [*ferox*, Latin; *feroce*, French.]

1. Savage; fierce.

2. Ravenous; rapacious.

The hare, that becometh a prey unto man, unto beasts and fowls of the air, is fruitful even unto superfetation; but the lion and *ferocious* animal hath young ones but seldom, and but one at a time. *Brown's Vulgar Errours, b.* iii. *c.* 16.

Smedley rose in majesty of mud;
Shaking the horrors of his ample brows,
And each *ferocious* feature grim with ooze. *Pope's Dunciad, b.* ii.

FERO'CITY. *n. s.* [*ferocitas*, Lat. *ferocité*, Fr. from *ferocious.*] Savageness; wildness; fierceness.

An uncommon *ferocity* in my countenance, with the remarkable flatness of my nose, and extent of my mouth, have procured me the name of lion. *Addison's Guardian.*

Untaught, uncultivated, as they were
Inhospitable, full of *ferocity*. *Phillips's Briton.*

FE'RREOUS. *adj.* [*ferreus*, Latin.] Irony; of iron.

In the body of glass there is no *ferreous* or magnetical nature. *Brown's Vulgar Errours, b.* ii. *c.* 3.

FE'RRET. *n. s.* [*fured*, Welsh; *furet*, French; *ferret*, Dutch; *viverra*, Lat.]

1. A kind of rat with red eyes and a long snout, used to catch rabbits.

With what an eager earnestness she looked, having threatning not only in her *ferret* eyes, but while she spoke her nose seemed to threaten her chin. *Sidney, b.* ii.

Cicero
Looks with such *ferret* and such firy eyes,
As we have seen him. *Shakespeare's Julius Cæsar.*

Coneys are destroyed or taken either by *ferrets* or pursenets. *Mortimer's Husbandry.*

2. A kind of narrow ribband.

To FE'RRET. *v. a.* [from the noun.] To drive out of lurking places, as the ferret drives the coney.

The archbishop had *ferreted* him out of all his holds. *Heylin.*

FE'RRETER. *n. s.* [from *ferret.*] One that hunts another in his privacies.

FE'RRIAGE. *n. s.* [from *ferry.*] The fare paid at a ferry.

FERRU'GINOUS. *adj.* [*ferrugineux*, Fr. *ferrugineus*, Latin.] Partaking of the particles and qualities of iron.

They are cold, hot, purgative, diuretick, *ferrugineous*, saline, petrefying and bituminous. *Ray on the Creation.*

FE'RRULE. *n. s.* [from *ferrum*, iron, Latin.] An iron ring put round any thing to keep it from cracking.

The fingers ends are strengthened with nails, as we fortify the ends of our staves or forks with iron hoops or *ferrules*. *Ray.*

To FE'RRY. *v. a.* [ꝼaꝛan, to pass, Saxon; *fahr*, German, a passage. *Skinner* imagines that this whole family of words may be deduced from the Latin *veho*. I do not love Latin originals; but if such must be sought, may not these words be more naturally derived from *ferri*, to be carried?] To carry over in a boat.

Cymocles heard and ſaw,
He loudly call'd to ſuch as were aboard,
The little bark unto the ſhore to draw,
And him to *ferry* over that deep ford. *Fairy Queen, b.* ii.

To FE'RRY. *v. n.* To paſs over water in a veſſel of carriage.

Thence hurried back to fire,
They *ferry* over this Lethæan ſound
Both to and fro, their ſorrow to augment. *Milt. Par. Loſt.*

FE'RRY. *n. ſ.* [from the verb.]

1. A veſſel of carriage; a veſſel in which goods or paſſengers are carried over water.

By this time was the worthy Guyon brought
Unto the other ſide of that wide ſtrand,
Where ſhe was rowing, and for paſſage ſought:
Him needed not long call, ſhe ſoon to hand
Her *ferry* brought. *Fairy Queen, b.* ii. *cant.* 6.

There went a *ferryboat* to carry over the king's houſhold. 2 *Sa.* xix. 18.

Bring them with imagin'd ſpeed
Unto the Traject, to the common *ferry*
Which trades to Venice. *Shakeſ. Merchant of Venice.*

I went down to the river Brent in the ordinary *ferry. Addiſ.*

2. The paſſage over which the ferryboat paſſes.

FE'RRYMAN. *n. ſ.* [*ferry* and *man.*] One who keeps a ferry; one who for hire tranſports goods and paſſengers over the water.

I paſt, methought, the melancholy flood,
With that grim *ferryman*, which poets write of,
Unto the kingdom of perpetual night. *Shakeſ. Richard* III.

The common *ferryman* of Egypt, that wafted over the dead bodies from Memphis, was made by the Greeks the *ferryman* of hell, and ſolemn ſtories raiſed after him. *Brown.*

The griſly *ferryman* of hell deny'd
Æneas entrance, 'till he knew his guide. *Roſcommon.*

FERTH, or *forth.* Common terminations are the ſame as in Engliſh an army; coming from the Saxon word ꝼyꞃð. *Gibſon.*

FE'RTILE. *adj.* [*fertile*, French; *fertilis*, Latin.]

1. Fruitful; abundant; plenteous.

I had hope of France,
As firmly as I hope for *fertile* England. *Shakeſ. Henry* VI.

I have had a large, a fair, and a pleaſant field; ſo *fertile*, that it has given me two harveſts in a Summer. *Dryden.*

I aſk whether in the uncultivated waſte of America, left to nature, without any improvement, a thouſand acres yield the needy inhabitants as many conveniencies of life as ten acres of equally *fertile* land do in Devonſhire? *Locke.*

View the wide earth adorn'd with hills and woods,
Rich in her herds, and *fertile* by her floods. *Blackm. Creat.*

2. With *of* before the thing produced.

The earth is *fertile of* all kind of grain. *Camden's Remains.*

This happy country is extremely *fertile*, as of thoſe above, ſo likewiſe of its productions under ground. *Woodward.*

FE'RTILENESS. *n. ſ.* [from *fertile.*] Fruitfulneſs; fecundity.

To FERTI'LITATE. *v. a.* [from *fertile.*] To fecundate; to fertilize; to make fruitful or productive.

A cock will in one day *fertilitate* the whole racemation or cluſter of eggs, which are not excluded in many weeks after. *Brown's Vulgar Errours, b.* iii.

FERTI'LITY. *n. ſ.* [*fertilitas*, Latin.] Fecundity; abundance; fruitfulneſs; plenteouſneſs.

I will go root away
The noiſom weeds, that without profit ſuck
The ſoil's *fertility* from wholeſome flowers. *Shak. Rich.* II.

Paradiſe itſelf exceeded in beauty and *fertility*; and theſe places had but a reſemblance thereof. *Raleigh's Hiſtory.*

To inundations Egypt, through which the Nile flows, and the Indies owe their extraordinary *fertility*, and thoſe mighty crops they produce after theſe waters are withdrawn. *Woodw.*

To FE'RTILIZE. *v. a.* [*fertiliſer*, French.] To make fruitful; to make plenteous; to make productive; to fecundate.

Rain-water carries along with it a ſort of terreſtrial matter that *fertilizes* the land, as being proper for the formation of vegetables. *Woodward's Natural Hiſtory.*

FE'RTILY. *adv.* [from *fertile.*] Fruitfully; plenteouſly; plentifully; abundantly.

FE'RVENCY. *n. ſ.* [*fervens*, Latin.]

1. Heat of mind; ardour; eagerneſs.

Your diver
Did hang a ſaltfiſh on his hook, which he
With *fervency* drew up. *Shakeſpeare's Ant. and Cleopatra.*

2. Pious ardour; flame of devotion; zeal.

We have on all ſides loſt much of our firſt *fervency* towards God. *Hooker, Dedication.*

There muſt be zeal and *fervency* in him which propoſeth for the reſt thoſe ſuits and ſupplications, which they by their joyful acclamations muſt ratify. *Hooker, b.* v. *ſ.* 25.

When you pray, let it be with attention, with *fervency*, and with perſeverance. *Wake's Preparation for Death.*

FE'RVENT. *adj.* [*fervens*, Latin; *fervent*, French.]

1. Hot; boiling.

From the phlegmatick humour, the proper allay of *fervent* blood, will flow a future quietude and ſerenitude. *Wotton.*

2. Hot in temper; vehement.

They that are more *fervent* to diſpute, be not always the moſt able to determine. *Hooker, b.* iv. *ſ.* 14.

3. Ardent in piety; warm in zeal; flaming with devotion.

This man being *fervent* in the ſpirit, taught diligently the things of the Lord. *Acts* xviii. 25.

So ſpake the *fervent* angel; but his zeal
None ſeconded, as out of ſeaſon judg'd,
Or ſingular and raſh. *Milton's Paradiſe Loſt, b.* v.

Let all enquiries into the myſterious points of theology be carried on with *fervent* petitions to God, that he would diſpoſe their minds to direct all their ſkill to the promotion of a good life. *South's Sermons.*

FE'RVENTLY. *adv.* [from *fervent.*]

1. Eagerly; vehemently.

They all that charge did *fervently* apply,
With greedy malice and importune toil. *Fairy Queen, b.* ii.

2. With pious ardour; with holy zeal.

Epaphras ſaluteth you, labouring *fervently* for you in prayers. *Col.* iv. 12.

He cares not how or what he ſuffers, ſo he ſuffer well, and be the friend of Chriſt; nor where nor when he ſuffers, ſo he may do it frequently, *fervently*, and acceptably. *Taylor.*

FE'RVID. *adj.* [*fervidus*, Latin.]

1. Hot; burning; boiling.
2. Vehement; eager; zealous.

FERVI'DITY. *n. ſ.* [from *fervid.*]

1. Heat.
2. Zeal; paſſion; ardour. *Dict.*

FE'RVIDNESS. *n. ſ.* [from *fervid.*] Ardour of mind; zeal; paſſion.

As to the healing of Malchus's ear, in the act of the meek lamb of God, it was a kind of injury done to him by the *fervidneſs* of St. Peter, who knew not yet what ſpirit he was of. *Bentley's Sermons.*

FE'RULA. *n. ſ.* [*ferule*, Fr. from *ferula*, giant fennel, Lat.] An inſtrument of correction with which young ſcholars are beaten on the hand: ſo named becauſe anciently the ſtalks of fennel were uſed for this purpoſe.

Theſe differ as much as the rod and *ferula. Shaw's Gramm.*

To FE'RULE. *v. a.* To chaſtiſe with the ferula.

FE'RVOUR. *n. ſ.* [*fervor*, Latin; *ferveur*, French.]

1. Heat; warmth.

Were it an undeniable truth that an effectual *fervour* proceeded from this ſtar, yet would not the ſame determine the opinion. *Brown's Vulgar Errours, b.* iv.

Like bright Aurora, whoſe refulgent ray
Foretells the *fervour* of enſuing day,
And warns the ſhepherd with his flocks retreat
To leafy ſhadows, from the threatned heat. *Waller.*

Theſe ſilver drops, like morning dew,
Foretell the *fervour* of the day;
So from one cloud ſoft ſhow'rs we view,
And blaſting lightnings burſt away. *Pope.*

2. Heat of mind; zeal; ardour of devotion.

Odious it muſt needs have been to aboliſh that which all had held for the ſpace of many ages, without reaſon ſo great as might in the eyes of impartial men appear ſufficient to clear them from all blame of raſh proceedings, if in *fervour* of zeal they had removed ſuch things. *Hooker, b.* iv. *ſ.* 14.

Haply deſpair hath ſeiz'd her;
Or, wing'd with *fervour* of her love, ſhe's flown
To her deſir'd Poſthumus. *Shakeſpeare's Cymbeline.*

There will be at Loretto, in a few ages more, jewels of the greateſt value in Europe, if the devotion of its princes continues in its preſent *fervour. Addiſon's Remarks on Italy.*

FESCUE. *n. ſ.* [*veeſe*, Dutch; *feſtu*, French.] A ſmall wire by which thoſe who teach to read point out the letters.

Teach him an alphabet upon his fingers, making the points of his fingers of his left hand both on the inſide to ſignify ſome letter, when any of them is pointed at by the forefinger of the right hand, or by any kind of *feſcue. Holder.*

Teach them how manly paſſions ought to move;
For ſuch as cannot think, can never love;
And ſince they needs will judge the poet's art,
Point 'em with *feſcues* to each ſhining part. *Dryden.*

FE'SELS. *n. ſ.* A kind of baſe grain.

Diſdain not *feſels* or poor vech to ſow,
Or care to make Egyptian lentils thrive. *May's Virg. Georg.*

FESSE. *n. ſ.* [In heraldry.]

The *feſſe* is ſo called of the Latin word *faſcia*, a band or girdle, poſſeſſing the third part of the eſcutcheon over the middle: if there be above one, you muſt call them bars; if with the field there be odd pieces, as ſeven or nine, then you muſt name the field, and ſay ſo many bars; if even, as ſix, eight, or ten, you muſt ſay barwiſe, or barry of ſix, eight, or ten, as the king of Hungary bears argent and gules barry of eight. *Peacham on Blazoning.*

To FE'STER. *v. n.* [*feſſe*, in Bavarian, a ſwelling corrupted, *Junius.*] To rankle; to corrupt; to grow virulent.

I might, even in my lady's preſence, diſcover the ſore which had deeply *feſtered* within me. *Sidney, b.* ii.

How should our *festered* sores be cured? *Hooker, b.* i.

Inward corruption and infected sin,
Not purg'd, not heal'd, behind remained still,
And *festering* sore did rankle yet within. *Fairy Queen, b.* i.

I have some wounds upon me, and they smart
To hear themselves remember'd.
—Well might they *fester* 'gainst ingratitude,
And tent themselves with death. *Shakespeare's Coriolanus.*

Mind that their souls
May make a peaceful and a sweet retire
From off these fields, where, wretches, their poor bodies
Must lie and *fester*. *Shakespeare's Henry* V.

There was imagination, that between a knight whom the duke had taken into some good degree of favour, and Felton, there had been ancient quarrels not yet well healed, which might perhaps be *festering* in his breast, and by a certain inflammation produce this effect. *Wotton.*

Passion, anger, and unkindness may give a wound that shall bleed and smart; but it is treachery only that makes it *fester*. *South's Sermons.*

FE'STINATE. *adj* [*festinatus*, Latin.] Hasty; hurried. A word not in use.

Advise the duke, where you are going, to a most *festinate* preparation: we are bound to the like. *Shakes. King Lear.*

FE'STINATELY. *adv.* [from *festinate.*] Hastily; speedily, with speed. Not in use.

Take this key; give enlargement to the swain, and bring him *festinately* hither. *Shakesp. Love's Labour Lost.*

FESTINA'TION. *n. s.* [*festinatio*, Latin.] Haste; hurry.

FE'STIVAL. *adj.* [*festivus*, Latin.] Pertaining to feasts; joyous.

He appeared at great tables, and *festival* entertainments, that he might manifest his divine charity to men. *Atterbury.*

FE'STIVAL. *n. s.* Time of feast; anniversary-day of civil or religious joy.

So tedious is this day,
As is the night before some *festival*,
To an impatient child that hath new robes,
And may not wear them. *Shakes. Romeo and Juliet.*

Th' invited sisters with their graces blest
Their *festivals*. *Sandys.*

The morning trumpets *festival* proclaim'd
Through each high street. *Milton's Agonistes.*

Follow, ye nymphs and shepherds all,
Come celebrate this *festival*,
And merrily sing, and sport, and play;
For 'tis Oriana's nuptial day. *Granville.*

By sacrifice of the tongues they purged away whatever they had spoken amiss during the *festival*. *Notes on the Odyssey.*

The *festival* of our Lord's resurrection we have celebrated, and may now consider the chief consequence of his resurrection, a judgment to come. *Atterbury's Sermons.*

FE'STIVE. *adj.* [*festivus*, Latin.] Joyous; gay; befiting a feast.

The glad circle round them yield their souls
To *festive* mirth and wit that knows no gall. *Thomson.*

FESTI'VITY. *n. s.* [*festivitas*, Latin, from *festive.*]

1. Festival; time of rejoicing.

The daughter of Jephtha came to be worshipped as a deity, and had an annual *festivity* observed unto her honour. *Brown.*

There happening a great and solemn *festivity*, such as the sheep-shearings used to be, David condescends to beg of a rich man some small repast. *South.*

2. Gaiety; joyfulness; temper or behaviour befitting a feast.

To those persons there is no better instrument to cause the remembrance, and to endear the affection to the article, than the recommending it by *festivity* and joy of a holyday. *Taylor.*

FE'STOON. *n. s.* [*feston*, French.] In architecture, an ornament of carved work in the form of a wreath or garland of flowers, or leaves twisted together, thickest at the middle, and suspended by the two extremes, whence it hangs down perpendicularly. *Harris.*

FE'STUCINE. *adj.* [*festuca*, Latin.] Straw-colour between green and yellow.

Therein may be discovered a little insect of a *festucine* or pale green, resembling a locust or grasshopper. *Brown.*

FESTU'COUS. *adj.* [*festuca*, Latin.] Formed of straw.

We speak of straws, or *festucous* divisions, lightly drawn over with oil. *Brown's Vulgar Errours.*

To FET. *v. a.* To fetch; to go and bring.

Get home with thy fewel, made ready to *fet*,
The sooner the easier carriage to get. *Tuss. Husbandry.*

He in a chair was set,
Tossing and turning them withouten end;
But for he was unable them to *fet*,
A little boy did on him still attend. *Fairy Queen, b.* ii.

And they *fet* forth Urijah out of Egypt to Jehoiakim, who slew him with the sword. *Jer.* xxvi. 23.

FET. *n. s.* [I suppose from *fait*, French, a part or portion.] A piece.

The bottom clear,
Now laid with many a *fet*
Of seed-pearl, ere she bath'd her there
Was known as black as jet. *Drayton.*

To FETCH. *v. a.* preter. *fetched*; anciently *fet*, unless it rather came from *To fet*. [feccan, fettan, Saxon.]

1. To go and bring.

They have devis'd a mean
How he her chamber-window will ascend,
And with a corded ladder *fetch* her down. *Shakespeare.*

We will take men to *fetch* victuals for the people. *Judg.* xx.

Go to the flock, and *fetch* me from thence two kid goats. *Gen.* xxvii. 9.

The seat of empire, where the Irish come,
And the unwilling Scotch, to *fetch* their doom. *Waller.*

Draw forth the monsters of th' abyss profound,
Or *fetch* th' aerial eagle to the ground. *Pope's Ess. on Man.*

2. To derive; to draw.

On, you noblest English,
Whose blood is *fetcht* from fathers of war-proof. *Sh. H.* V.

3. To strike at a distance.

The conditions of weapons, and their improvements, are the *fetching* afar off; for that outruns the danger, as it is seen in ordnance and muskets. *Bacon's Essays.*

4. To bring to any state by some powerful operation.

In smells we see their great and sudden effect in *fetching* men again, when they swoon. *Bacon's Natural History.*

At Rome any of those arts immediately thrives, under the encouragement of the prince, as may be *fetched* up to its perfection in ten or a dozen years, which is the work of an age or two in other countries. *Addison on Italy.*

5. To draw within any confinement or prohibition.

General terms may sufficiently convey to the people what our intentions are, and yet not *fetch* us within the compass of the ordinance. *Sanderson.*

6. To produce by some kind of force.

These ways, if there were any secret excellence among them, would *fetch* it out, and give it fair opportunities to advance itself by. *Milton on Education.*

An human soul without education is like marble in the quarry, which shews none of its beauties 'till the skill of the polisher *fetches* out the colours. *Addison's Spectator.*

7. To perform any excursion.

I'll *fetch* a turn about the garden, pitying
The pangs of barr'd affections; though the king
Hath charg'd you should not speak together. *Shak. Cymbel.*

When evening grey doth rise, I *fetch* my round
Over the mount, and all this hollow ground. *Milton.*

To come to that place they must *fetch* a compass three miles on the right hand through a forest. *Knolles's History.*

8. To perform with suddenness or violence.

Note a wild and wanton herd,
Or race of youthful and unhandled colts,
Fetching mad bounds, bellowing and neighing loud. *Shakes.*

The fox *fetched* a hundred and a hundred leaps at a delicious cluster of grapes. *L'Estrange.*

Talk to her of an unfortunate young lady that lost her beauty by the small-pox, she *fetches* a deep sigh. *Addison.*

9. To reach; to arrive at; to come to.

Mean time flew our ships, and streight we *fetcht*
The syrens isle; a spleenless wind so stretcht
Her wings to waft us, and so urg'd our keel. *Chapman.*

It needs not thy belief,
If earth, industrious of herself, *fetch* day
Travelling East; and with her part averse
From the sun's beam, meet night; her other part
Still luminous by his ray. *Milton's Paradise Lost, b.* viii.

The hare laid himself down, and took a nap; for, says he, I can *fetch* up the tortoise when I please. *L'Estrange.*

10. To obtain as its price.

During such a state, silver in the coin will never *fetch* as much as the silver in bullion. *Locke.*

To FETCH. *v. n.* To move with a quick return.

Like a shifted wind unto a sail,
It makes the course of thoughts to *fetch* about. *Shakespeare.*

FETCH. *n. s.* [from the verb.] A stratagem by which any thing is indirectly performed; by which one thing seems intended and another is done; a trick; an artifice.

An envious neighbour is easy to find,
His cumbersome *fetches* are seldom behind:
His *fetch* is to flatter, to get what he can;
His purpose once gotten, a pin for thee than. *Tuss. Husband.*

It is a *fetch* of wit;
You laying these slight sullies on my son,
As 'twere a thing a little soil'd i' th' working. *Shak. Hamlet.*

But Sidrophel, as full of tricks
As rota men of politicks,
Streight cast about to over-reach
Th' unwary conqu'ror with a *fetch*. *Hudibras, p.* ii.

With this *fetch* he laughs at the trick he hath plaid me. *Still.*

The fox had a *fetch* in't. *L'Estrange, Fab.* 42.

From these instances and *fetches*
Thou mak'st of horses, clocks and watches,

Quoth

3

Quoth Mat, thou seem'st to mean
That Alma is a mere machine. *Prior.*

FE'TCHER. *n. s.* [from *fetch.*] One that fetches any thing.

FE'TID. *adj.* [*fœtidus*, Latin; *fetide*, Fr.] Stinking; rancid; having a smell strong and offensive.

Most putrefactions are of an odious smell; for they smell either *fetid* or mouldy. *Bacon's Natural History.*

In the most severe orders of the church of Rome, those who practise abstinence, feel after it *fetid* hot eructations. *Arbuth.*

Plague, fiercest child of Nemesis divine,
Descends from Ethiopia's poison'd woods,
From stifled Cairo's filth and *fetid* fields. *Thomson's Summer.*

FE'TIDNESS. *n. s.* [from *fetid.*] The quality of stinking.

FE'TLOCK. *n. s.* [*feet* and *lock.*] A tuft of hair as big as the hair of the mane that grows behind the pastern-joint of many horses: horses of a low size have scarce any such tuft. *Farrier's Dict.*

Their wounded steeds
Fret *fetlock* deep in gore, and with wild rage
Yerk out their armed heels at their dead masters. *Sh. H. V.*

White were the *fetlocks* of his feet before,
And on his front a snowy star he bore. *Dryd. Virg. Æn.*

FE'TOR. *n. s.* [*fœtor*, Latin.] A stink; a stench; a strong and offensive smell.

The *fetor* may discover itself by sweat and humour. *Brown.*

When the symptoms are attended with a *fetor* of any kind, such a disease will be cured by acescent substances, and none better than whey. *Arbuthnot on Diet.*

FE'TTER. *n. s.* It is commonly used in the plural *fetters.* [from *feet*; feꞇꞇeꞃe, Saxon.] Chains for the feet; chains by which walking is hindered.

Doctrine unto fools is as *fetters* on the feet, and like manacles on the right hand. *Eccluf.* xxi. 19.

Drawing after me the chains and *fetters* whereunto I have been thirteen years tied, I have by other mens errours failed. *Raleigh's Apology.*

Passion's too fierce to be in *fetters* bound,
And nature flies him like enchanted ground. *Dryden.*

The wretch in double *fetters* bound,
Your potent mercy may release. *Prior.*

I thought her pride
Had broke your *fetters*, and assur'd your freedom. *A. Phill.*

To FE'TTER. *v. a.* [from the noun.] To bind; to enchain; to shackle; to tie.

Neither her great worthiness nor his own suffering for her, could *fetter* his fickleness. *Sidney.*

My conscience! thou art *fetter'd*
More than my shanks and wrists. *Shakes. Cymbeline.*

Fetter strong madness in a silken thread;
Charm ach with air, and agony with words. *Shakespeare.*

Doth a master chide his servant because he doth not come, yet knows that the servant is chained and *fettered*, so as he cannot move? *Bramhall against Hobbes.*

A chain which man to *fetter* man has made;
By artifice impos'd, by fear obey'd. *Prior.*

To FE'TTLE. *v. n.* [A cant word from *feel*] To do trifling business; to ply the hands without labour.

When your master is most busy in company, come in and pretend to *fettle* about the room; and if he chides, say you thought he rung the bell. *Swift's Direct. to the Footman.*

FE'TUS. *n. s.* [*fœtus*, Latin.] Any animal in embrio; any thing yet in the womb; any thing unborn.

Nor are we at leisure to examine that paradox of Hippocrates, which some learned physicians have of late revived, that the *fetus* respires in the womb. *Boyle.*

FEUD. *n. s.* [ꝼæhð, enmity, Saxon.] Quarrel; contention; opposition; war.

Though men would find such mortal *feuds*
In sharing of their publick goods. *Hudibras, p.* iii. *cant.* I.

In former ages it was a constant policy of France to raise and cherish intestine *feuds* and discords in the isle of Great Britain. *Addison's Freeholder.*

Scythia mourns
Our guilty wars, and earth's remotest regions
Lie half unpeopled by the *feuds* of Rome. *Addison's Cato.*

FE'UDAL. *adj.* [*feudalis*, low Latin.] Pertaining to fees, feus, or tenures by which lands are held of a superiour lord.

FE'UDAL. *n. s.* A dependance; something held by tenure; a fee; a feu.

Wales, that was not always the *feudal* territory of England, having been governed by a prince of their own, had laws utterly strange to the laws of England. *Hale.*

FEU'DATORY. *n. s.* [from *feudal.*] One who holds not in chief, but by some conditional tenure from a superiour.

The duke of Parma was reasonably well tempted to be true to that enterprize, by no less promise than to be made a *feudatary*, or beneficiary king of England, under the seignory in chief of the pope, and the protection of the king of Spain. *Bacon's War with Spain.*

FE'VER. *n. s.* [*fievre*, French; *febris*, Latin.] A disease in which the body is violently heated, and the pulse quickened, or in which heat and cold prevail by turns. It is sometimes continual, sometimes intermittent.

Think'st thou the firy *fever* will go out
With titles blown from adulation?
Will it give place to flexure and low bending? *Shak. H. V.*

Duncan is in his grave;
After life's fitful *fever* he sleeps well. *Shakesp. Macbeth.*

Should not a ling'ring *fever* be remov'd,
Because it long has rag'd within my blood? *Dryden.*

He had never dreamed in his life, 'till he had the *fever* he was then newly recovered of. *Locke.*

To FE'VER. *v. a.* [from the noun.] To put into a fever.

The white hand of a lady *fever* thee!
Shake to look on't. *Shakespeare's Ant. and Cleopatra.*

FE'VERET. *n. s.* [from *fever.*] A slight fever; febricula.

A light *feveret*, or an old quartan ague, is not a sufficient excuse for non-appearance. *Ayliffe's Parergon.*

FE'VERFEW. *n. s.* [*febris* and *fugo*, Latin.]

It has a fibrose root: the leaves are conjugated, and divided into many segments: the cup of the flower is squamose and hemispherical: the flowers grow in an umbel upon the top of the stalks, and the rays of the flower are generally white. The species are nine; but the first, called common feverfew, is the sort used in medicine, and is found wild in many parts of England; but is, however, cultivated in medicinal gardens. *Miller.*

FE'VERISH. *adj.* [from *fever.*]

1. Troubled with a fever.

To other climates beasts and birds retire,
And *feverish* nature burns in her own fire. *Creech.*

When an animal that gives suck turns *feverish*, that is, its juices more alkaline, the milk turns from its native genuine whiteness to yellow. *Arbuthnot on Aliments.*

2. Tending to a fever.

A *feverish* disorder disabled me. *Swift to Pope.*

3. Uncertain; inconstant; now hot, now cold.

We toss and turn about our *feverish* will,
When all our ease must come by lying still;
For all the happiness mankind can gain,
Is not in pleasure, but in rest from pain. *Dryd. Ind. Emp.*

4. Hot; burning.

And now four days the sun had seen our woes,
Four nights the moon beheld th' incessant fire;
It seem'd as if the stars more sickly rose,
And farther from the *feverish* North retire. *Dryd. Ann. Mir.*

FE'VERISHNESS. *n. s.* [from *feverish.*] A slight disorder of the feverish kind.

FE'VEROUS. *adj.* [*fievreux-se*, French, from *fever.*]

1. Troubled with a fever or ague.

Thou mad'st thine enemies shake, as if the world
Were *feverous*, and did tremble. *Shakespeare's Coriolanus.*

2. Having the nature of a fever.

All *fev'rous* kinds,
Convulsions, epilepsies, fierce catarrhs. *Milton's Par. Lost.*

3. Having a tendency to produce fevers.

It hath been noted by the ancients, that southern winds, blowing much, without rain, do cause a *feverous* disposition of the year; but with rain, not. *Bacon's Natural History.*

FE'VERY. *adj.* [from *fever.*] Diseased with a fever.

O Rome, thy head
Is drown'd in sleep, and all thy body *fev'ry. B. Johns. Catil.*

FE'UILLAGE. *n. s.* [French.] A bunch or row of leaves.

I have done Homer's head; and I inclose the outline, that you may determine whether you would have it so large, or reduced to make room for *feuillage* or laurel round the oval. *Jervas to Pope.*

FE'UILLEMORT. *n. s.* [French.] The colour of a faded leaf, corrupted commonly to *philemot.*

FE'UTERER. *n. s.* A dogkeeper: perhaps the cleaner of the kennel.

FEW. *adj.* [ꝼeo, ꝼeopa, Saxon; *fua*, Danish.]

1. Not many; not in a great number.

We are left but *few* of many. *Jer.*

So much the thirst of honour fires the blood;
So many would be great, so *few* be good;
For who would virtue for herself regard,
Or wed without the portion of reward? *Dryd. Juvenal.*

On Winter seas we *fewer* storms behold,
Than foul diseases that infect the fold. *Dryden's Virg. Geor.*

Men have *fewer* or more simple ideas from without, according as the objects they converse with afford greater or less variety. *Locke.*

The *fewer* still you name, you wound the more;
Bond is but one, but Harpax is a score. *Pope's Hor. Imitat.*

Party is the madness of many, for the gain of a *few. Swift.*

The imagination of a poet is a thing so nice and delicate, that it is no easy matter to find out images capable of giving pleasure to one of the *few*, who, in any age, have come up to that character. *Berkley to Pope.*

2. Sometimes elliptically; not many words.

To answer both allegations at once, the very substance of that they contain is in *few* but this. *Hooker, b.* v. *s.* 22.

 So

So having said, he thus to Eve in *few:*
Say, woman, what is this which thou hast done? *Milton.*
Thus Jupiter in *few* unfolds the charge. *Dryden's Æn.*
The firm resolve I here in *few* disclose. *Pope's Odyssey.*

FE'WEL. *n. s.* [*feu*, French.] Combustible matter; materials for keeping fire: as firewood, coal.

If a spark of error have thus far prevailed, falling even where the wood was green, and farthest off from any inclination unto furious attempts, must not the peril thereof be greater in men, whose minds are as dry *fewel*, apt beforehand unto tumults, seditions and broils? *Hooker, Dedication.*

Others may give the *fewel* or the fire;
But they the breath, that makes the flame, inspire. *Denham.*

A known quantity of *fewel*, all kindled at once, will cause water to boil, which being lighted gradually will never be able to do it. *Bentley's Sermons.*

To FE'WEL. *v. a.* [from the noun.] To feed with fewel.

Never, alas! the dreadful name,
That *fewels* the infernal flame. *Cowley.*

FE'WNESS. *n. s.* [from *few.*]

1. Paucity; smalness of number.

These, by reason of their *fewness*, I could not distinguish from the numbers of the rest with whom they are embodied. *Dryden's Preface to the Hind and Panther.*

2. Paucity of words; brevity; conciseness.

Fewness and truth, 'tis thus. *Shakes. Meas. for Measure.*

To FEY. *v. a.* [*veghen*, Dutch.] To cleanse a ditch of mud.

Such muddy deep ditches and pits in the field,
That all a dry Summer no water will yield,
By *feying* and casting that mud upon heaps,
Commodities many the husbandman reaps. *Tuss. Husband.*

FIB. *n. s.* [A cant word among children.] A lye; a falsehood.

Destroy his *fib* or sophistry; in vain,
The creature's at his dirty work again. *Pope's Epistles.*
I so often lie,
Scarce Harvey's self has told more *fibs* than I. *Pope.*

To FIB. *v. n.* [from the noun.] To lie; to tell lyes; to speak falsely.

If you have any particular mark, whereby one may know when you *fib*, and when you speak truth, you had best tell it me. *Arbuthnot's History of John Bull.*

FI'BBER. *n. s.* [from *fib.*] A teller of fibs.

FI'BRE. *n. s.* [*fibre*, Fr. *fibra*, Latin.] A small thread or string; the first constituent parts of bodies.

Now sliding streams the thirsty plants renew,
And feed their *fibres* with reviving dew. *Pope.*

2. A *fibre*, in physick, is an animal thread, of which there are different kinds: some are soft, flexible, and a little elastick; and these are either hollow, like small pipes, or spongious and full of little cells, as the nervous and fleshy *fibres:* others are more solid, flexible, and with a strong elasticity or spring, as the membranous and cartilaginous *fibres:* and a third sort are hard and flexible, as the *fibres* of the bones. Now of all those some are very sensible, and others destitute of all sense: some so very small as not to be easily perceived; and others, on the contrary, so big as to be plainly seen; and most of them, when examined with a microscope, appear to be composed of still smaller *fibres:* these *fibres* first constitute the substance of the bones, cartilages, ligaments, membranes, nerves, veins, arteries and muscles. And again, by the various texture and different combination of some or all of those parts, the more compound organs are framed; such as the lungs, stomach, liver, legs and arms, the sum of all which make up the body. *Quincy.*

My heart sinks in me while I hear him speak,
And every slacken'd *fibre* drops its hold,
Like nature letting down the springs of life:
The name of father awes me still. *Dryd. Spanish Fryar.*

FI'BRIL. *n. s.* [*fibrille*, French.] A small fibre or string.

The muscles consist of a number of fibres, and each fibre of an incredible number of little *fibrils* bound together, and divided into little cells. *Cheyne's Phil. Princ.*

FI'BROUS. *adj.* [*fibreux*, French, from *fibre.*] Composed of fibres or stamina.

The difference between bodies *fibrous* and bodies viscous is plain; for all wool and tow, and cotton and silk, have a greediness of moisture. *Bacon's Natural History.*

I saw Petræus' arms employ'd around
A well-grown oak, to root it from the ground;
This way and that he wrench'd the *fibrous* bands,
The trunk was like a sapling in his hands. *Dryden.*

The *fibrous* and solid parts of plants pass unaltered through the intestines. *Arbuthnot on Aliments.*

FI'BULA. *n. s.* [Latin.] The outer and lesser bone of the leg, much smaller than the tibia: it lies on the outside of the leg; and its upper end, which is not so high as the knee, receives the lateral knob of the upper end of the tibia into a small sinus, which it has in its inner side. Its lower end is received into the small sinus of the tibia, and then it extends into a large process, which forms the outer ankle. *Quincy.*

FI'CKLE. *adj.* [ficol, Saxon.]

1. Changeable; unconstant; irresolute; wavering; unsteady; mutable; changeful; without steady adherence.

Remember where we are,
In France amongst a *fickle* wavering nation. *Shak. Hen.* VI.
A slave, whose easy borrow'd pride
Dwells in the *fickle* grace of her he follows. *Shak. K. Lear.*
Or likest hovering dreams,
The *fickle* pensioners of Morpheus' train. *Milton.*
They know how *fickle* common lovers are;
Their oaths and vows are cautiously believ'd;
For few there are but have been once deceiv'd. *Dryden.*
We in vain the *fickle* sex pursue,
Who change the constant lover for the new. *Prior.*

2. Not fixed; subject to vicissitude.

He would be loth
Us to abolish; lest the adversary
Triumph, and say, *fickle* their state, whom God
Most favours! *Milton's Paradise Lost, b.* ix.

FI'CKLENESS. *n. s.* [from *fickle.*] Inconstancy; uncertainty; unsteadiness.

Neither her great worthiness, nor his own suffering for her, could fetter his *fickleness*; but, before his marriage-day, he had taken to wife that Baccha of whom she complained. *Sidney.*

Beware of fraud, beware of *fickleness*,
In choice and change of thy dear loved dame. *Fairy Queen.*
I am a soldier, and unapt to weep,
Or to exclaim on fortune's *fickleness*. *Shakes. Henry* VI.

Instability of temper ought to be checked, when it disposes men to wander from one scheme of government to another, since such a *fickleness* cannot but be attended with fatal consequences. *Addison's Freeholder*, N°. 25.

Whether out of *fickleness* or design I can't tell, I found that what she liked one day she disliked another. *Addison.*

FI'CKLY. *adv.* [from *fickle.*] Without certainty or stability.

Do not now,
Like a young wasteful heir, mortgage the hopes
Of godlike majesty on bankrupt terms,
To raise a present pow'r that's *fickly* held
By the frail tenure of the people's will. *Southern.*

FI'CO. *n. s.* [Italian.] An act of contempt done with the fingers, expressing a *fig for you.*

Having once recovered his fortress, he then gives the *fico* to all that his adversaries can by siege, force, or famine attempt against him. *Carew's Survey of Cornwal.*

FI'CTILE. *adj.* [*fictilis*, Latin.] Moulded into form; manufactured by the potter.

The cause of fragility is an impotency to be extended; and therefore stone is more fragil than metal, and so *fictile* earth is more fragil than crude earth. *Bacon's Nat. History.*

FI'CTION. *n. s.* [*fictio*, Latin; *fiction*, French.]

1. The act of feigning or inventing.

If the presence of God in the image, by a mere *fiction* of the mind, be a sufficient ground to worship that image, is not God's real presence in every creature a far better ground to worship it? *Stillingfleet.*

Fiction is of the essence of poetry, as well as of painting: there is a resemblance in one of human bodies, things, and actions, which are not real; and in the other of a true story by a *fiction.* *Dryden's Dufresnoy.*

2. The thing feigned or invented.

If through mine ears pierce any consolations,
By wise discourse, sweet tunes, or poets *fictions*;
If ought I cease these hideous exclamations,
While that my soul, she, she lives in affliction. *Sidney.*

So also was the *fiction* of those golden apples kept by a dragon, taken from the serpent, which tempted Evah. *Raleigh.*

3. A falsehood; a lye.

FI'CTIOUS. *adj.* [*fictus*, Latin.] Fictitious; imaginary; invented. A word coined by *Prior.*

With fancy'd rules and arbitrary laws
Matter and motion man restrains,
And study'd lines and *fictious* circles draws. *Prior.*

FICTI'TIOUS. *adj.* [*fictitius*, Latin.]

1. Counterfeit; false; not genuine.

Draw him strictly so,
That all who view the piece may know
He needs no trappings of *fictitious* fame. *Dryden.*

2. Feigned; imaginary.

The human persons are as *fictitious* as the airy ones; and Belinda resembles you in nothing but in beauty. *Pope.*

3. Not real; not true.

Milton, sensible of this defect in the subject of his poem, brought into it two characters of a shadowy and *fictitious* nature, in the persons of sin and death, by which means he has interwoven in his fable a very beautiful allegory. *Addis. Spect.*

FICTI'TIOUSLY. *adv.* [from *fictitious.*] Falsely; counterfeitly.

These pieces are *fictitiously* set down, and have no copy in nature. *Brown's Vulgar Errours, b.* v. *c.* 20.

FID. *n. s.* [*fitta*, Italian.] A pointed iron with which seamen untwist their cords. *Skinner.*

FI'DDLE. *n. s.* [fiðele, Saxon; *vedel*, Dutch; *fidel*, German; *fidicula*, Latin; *fidil*, Erse.]

1. A stringed instrument of musick; a violin.

In

In trials of musical skill the judges did not crown the *fiddle*, but the performer. *Stillingfleet.*

The adventure of the bear and *fiddle*
Is sung; but breaks off in the middle. *Hudibras.*

She tried the *fiddle* all over, by drawing the bow over every part of the strings; but could not, for her heart, find whereabout the tune lay. *Addison's Guardian*, N°. 98.

To Fi'ddle. *v. n.* [from the noun.]

1. To play upon a fiddle.

Themistocles being desired at a feast to touch a lute, he said he could not *fiddle*, but he could make a small town a great city. *Bacon's Essays.*

Others import yet nobler arts from France,
Teach kings to *fiddle*, and make senates dance. *Pope.*

2. To trifle; to shift the hands often, and do nothing, like a fellow that plays upon a fiddle.

A cunning fellow observed, that old Lewis had stole away part of the map, and saw him *fiddling* and turning the map, trying to join the two pieces together. *Arbuth. H. of J. Bull.*

Good cooks cannot abide what they justly call *fiddling* work, where abundance of time is spent, and little done. *Swift.*

Fi'ddlefaddle. *n. s.* [A cant word.] Trifles.

She said that their grandfather had a horse shot at Edgehill, and their uncle was at the siege of Buda; with abundance of *fiddlefaddle* of the same nature. *Spectator*, N°. 299.

Fi'ddlefaddle. *adj.* Trifling; giving trouble, or making a bustle about nothing.

She was a troublesome *fiddlefaddle* old woman, and so ceremonious that there was no bearing of her. *Arbuthn. J. Bull.*

Fi'ddler. *n. s.* [from *fiddle.*] A musician; one that plays upon the fiddle.

Let no sawcy *fiddler* presume to intrude,
Unless he is sent for to vary our bliss. *Ben. Johnson.*

Nero put the *fiddlers* to death, for being more skilful in the trade than he was. *Taylor's Rule of living holy.*

These will appear such chits in story,
'Twill turn all politicks to jests,
To be repeated like John Dory,
When *fiddlers* sing at feasts. *Dryden.*

When miss delights in her spinnet,
A *fiddler* may a fortune get. *Swift.*

Fi'ddlestick. *n. s.* [*fiddle* and *stick.*] The bow and hair which a fiddler draws over the strings of a fiddle.

His grisly beard was long and thick,
With which he strung his *fiddlestick*. *Hudibras, p.* i.

Fi'ddlestring. *n. s.* [*fiddle* and *string.*] The string of a fiddle; that which makes the noise.

A *fiddlestring*, moistened with water, will sink a note in a little time, and consequently must be relaxed or lengthened one sixteenth. *Arbuthnot on Air.*

Fide'lity. *n. s.* [*fidelitas*, Latin; *fidelité*, French.]

1. Honesty; veracity.

The church, by her publick reading of the book of God, preached only as a witness; now the principal thing required in a witness is a *fidelity*. *Hooker, b.* v. *s.* 19.

2. Faithful adherence.

They mistake credulity for *fidelity*. *Clarke.*

To Fidge. } *v. n.* [A cant word.] To move nimbly and
To Fi'dget. } irregularly. It implies in Scotland agitation.

Tim, thou'rt the Punch to stir up trouble in;
You wriggle, *fidge*, and make a rout,
Put all your brother puppets out;
Run on in a perpetual round,
To teaze, perplex, disturb, confound. *Swift.*

Fidu'cial. *adj.* [*fiducia*, Latin.] Confident; undoubting.

Faith is cordial, and such as God will accept of, when it affords *fiducial* reliance on the promises, and obediential submission to the commands. *Hammond's Pract. Catech.*

Fidu'ciary. *n. s.* [*fiduciarius*, Latin.]

1. One who holds any thing in trust.

2. One who depends on faith without works.

The second obstructive is that of the *fiduciary*, that faith is the only instrument of his justification; and excludes good works from contributing any thing toward it. *Hammond.*

Fidu'ciary. *adj.*

1. Confident; steady; undoubting; untouched with doubt.

That faith, which is required of us, is then perfect, when it produces in us a *fiduciary* assent to whatever the Gospel has revealed. *Wake's Preparation for Death.*

2. Not to be doubted.

Elaiana can rely no where upon mere love and *fiduciary* obedience, unless at her own home, where she is exemplarily loyal to herself in a high exact obedience. *Howel's Voc. Forest.*

FIEF. *n. s.* [*fief*, French.] A fee; a manor; a possession held by some tenure of a superiour.

To the next realm she stretch'd her sway,
For painture near adjoining lay,
A plenteous province and alluring prey;
A chamber of dependencies was fram'd,
And the whole *fief*, in right of poetry, she claim'd. *Dryd.*

As they were honoured by great privileges, so their lands were in the nature of *fiefs*, for which the possessors were obliged to do personal service at sea. *Arbuthnot on Coins.*

Field. *n. s.* [feld, Saxon; *feld*, German; *veld*, Dutch.]

1. Ground not inhabited; not built on.

Live with me, and be my love,
And we will all the pleasure prove,
That hills and vallies, dale and *field*,
And all the craggy mountains yield. *Raleigh.*

By the civil law the corpse of persons deceased were buried out of the city in the *fields*. *Ayliffe's Parergon.*

2. Ground not enclosed.

Field lands are not exempted from mildews, nor yet from smut, where it is more than in inclosed lands. *Mortim. Husb.*

3. Cultivated tract of ground.

Or great Osiris, who first taught the swain
In Pharian *fields* to sow the golden grain. *Pope's Statius.*

4. The open country: opposed to quarters.

Since his majesty went into the *field*,
I have seen her rise from her bed. *Shakespeare's Macbeth.*

5. The ground of battle.

What though the *field* be lost,
All is not lost. *Milton's Paradise Lost, b.* i.

When a man is in the *field*, a moderate skill in fencing rather exposes him to the sword of his enemy than secures him from it. *Locke.*

6. A battle; a campaign; the action of an army while it keeps the field.

You maintain several factions;
And whilst a *field* should be dispatch'd and fought,
You are disputing of your generals. *Shakesp. Henry* VI.

7. A wide expanse.

The god a clearer space for heav'n design'd;
Where *fields* of light and liquid ether flow,
Purg'd from the pond'rous dregs of earth below. *Dryden.*

Ask of yonder argent *fields* above,
Why Jove's satellites are less than Jove. *Pope's Ess. on Man.*

8. Space; compass; extent.

The ill-natured man gives himself a large *field* to expatiate in: he exposes failings in human nature. *Addison's Spectator.*

I should enter upon a *field* too wide, and too much beaten, if I should display all the advantages of peace. *Smalridge.*

Who can this *field* of miracles survey,
And not with Galen all in rapture say,
Behold a God, adore him and obey. *Blackmore's Creation.*

9. The ground or blank space on which figures are drawn.

Let the *field* or ground of the picture be clean, light, and well united with colour. *Dryden's Dufresnoy.*

10. [In heraldry.] The surface of a shield.

Fi'elded. *adj.* [from *field.*] Being in field of battle.

Now, Mars, I pr'ythee, make us quick in work;
That we with smoking swords may march from hence,
To help our *fielded* friends. *Shakespeare's Coriolanus.*

Field-basil. *n. s.* [*field* and *basil.*] A plant with a labiated flower, consisting of one leaf, whose upper lip is upright, roundish, and generally split in two; but the beard, or under lip, is divided into three segments: these flowers are disposed in whorles round the stalks, and are succeeded by oblong seeds. *Miller.*

Fi'eldbed. *n. s.* [*field* and *bed.*] A bed contrived to be set up easily in the field.

Romeo, good-night; I'll to my trucklebed,
This *fieldbed* is too cold for me to sleep. *Shak. Rom. and Jul.*

Fi'eldfare. *n. s.* [feld and faran, to wander in the fields.] A bird.

Winter birds, as woodcocks and *fieldfares*, if they come early out of the northern countries, with us shew cold Winters. *Bacon's Natural History*, N°. 816.

Fi'eldmarshal. *n. s.* [*field* and *marshal.*] Commander of an army in the field.

Fi'eldmouse. *n. s.* [*field* and *mouse.*] A mouse that burrows in banks, and makes her house with various apartments.

The *fieldmouse* builds her garner under ground. *Dryden.*

Fieldmice are apt to gnaw their roots, and kill them in hard Winters. *Mortimer's Husbandry.*

Fi'eldofficer. *n. s.* [*field* and *officer.*] An officer whose command in the field extends to a whole regiment: as the colonel, lieutenant-colonel, and major.

Fi'eldpiece. *adj.* [*field* and *piece.*] Small cannon used in battles, but not in sieges.

The bassa planting his *fieldpieces* upon the hills on the North-side, did from thence grievously annoy the defendants. *Knolles's History of the Turks.*

Fiend. *n. s.* [feond, fiond, Saxon, a foe.]

1. An enemy; the great enemy of mankind; satan; the devil.

Tom is followed by the foul *fiend*. *Shakespeare's K. Lear.*

2. Any infernal being.

What now, had I a body again, I could,
Coming from hell; what *fiends* would wish should be,
And Hannibal could not have wish'd to see. *B. Johns. Cat.*

The hell-hounds, as ungorg'd with flesh and blood,
Pursue their prey, and seek their wonted food;
The *fiend* remounts his courser. *Dryden's Theo. and Hon.*

O woman! woman! when to ill thy mind
Is bent, all hell contains no fouler *fiend*. *Pope's Odyssey.*

FIERCE. *adj.* [*fier*, French; *ferox*, Latin.]

1. Savage; ravenous; easily enraged.

Thou huntest me as a *fierce* lion. *Job.*

2. Vehement in rage; eager of mischief.

Destruction enters in the treacherous wood,
And vengeful slaughter, *fierce* for human blood. *Pope.*
Tyrants *fierce*, that unrelenting die. *Pope.*
With that the god, whose earthquakes rock the ground,
Fierce to Phœacia crost the vast profound. *Pope's Odyssey.*

3. Violent; outrageous.

Cursed be their anger, for it was *fierce*; and their wrath, for it was cruel. *Gen.* xlix. 7.

4. Passionate; angry; furious.

This *fierce* abridgment
Hath to it circumstantial branches, which
Distinction should be rich in. *Shakespeare's Cymbeline.*

A man brings his mind to be positive and *fierce* for positions whose evidence he has never examined. *Locke.*

5. Strong; forcible.

The ships, though so great, are driven of *fierce* winds; yet are they turned about with a very small helm. *Ja.* iii. 2.

FI'ERCELY. *adv.* [from *fierce*.] Violently; furiously.

Battle join'd, and both sides *fiercely* fought. *Shak. H.* VI.

The defendants, *fiercely* assailed by their enemies before, and beaten with the great ordnance behind, were grievously distressed. *Knolles's History of the Turks.*

The air, if very cold, irritateth the flame, and maketh it burn more *fiercely*, as fire scorcheth in frosty weather, and so furthereth the consumption. *Bacon's Natural History.*

FI'ERCENESS. *n. s.* [from *fierce*.]

1. Ferocity; savageness.

The same defect of heat which gives a *fierceness* to our natures, may contribute to that roughness of our language. *Swift's Letter to the Lord High Treasurer.*

2. Eagerness for blood; fury.

Suddenly there came out of a wood a monstrous lion, with a she-bear not far from him, of little less *fierceness*. *Sidney.*

3. Quickness to attack; keenness in anger and resentment.

The Greeks are strong, and skilful to their strength,
Fierce to their skill, and to their *fierceness* valiant. *Shakes.*

4. Violence; outrageous passion.

His pride and brutal *fierceness* I abhor;
But scorn your mean suspicions of me more. *Dryd. Aureng.*

FIERIFA'CIAS. [In law.] A judicial writ, that lies at all times within the year and day, for him that has recovered in an action of debt or damages, to the sheriff, to command him to levy the debt, or the damages of his goods, against whom the recovery was had. *Cowel.*

FI'ERINESS. *n. s.* [from *fiery*.]

1. Hot qualities; heat; acrimony.

The ashes, by their heat, their *fieriness*, and their dryness, belong to the element of earth. *Boyle.*

2. Heat of temper; intellectual ardour.

The Italians, notwithstanding their natural *fieriness* of temper, affect always to appear sober and sedate. *Addison.*

FI'ERY. *adj.* [from *fire*.]

1. Consisting of fire.

Scarcely had Phœbus in the gloomy East
Yet harnessed his *fiery* footed team,
Ne rear'd above the earth his flaming crest,
When the last deadly smoak aloft did steam. *Fairy Queen.*
I know, thou'dst rather
Follow thine enemy in a *fiery* gulph
Than flatter him in a bower. *Shakespeare's Coriolanus.*

2. Hot like fire.

Hath thy *fiery* heart so parcht thy entrails,
That not a tear can fall for Rutland's death? *Shak. H.* VI.

3. Vehement; ardent; active.

Then *fiery* expedition be my wing,
Jove's Mercury, and herald for a king. *Shakes. Rich.* III.
I drew this gallant head of war,
And cull'd these *fiery* spirits from the world,
To outlook conquest, and to win renown
Ev'n in the jaws of danger and of death. *Shakes. K. John.*

4. Passionate; outrageous; easily provoked.

You know the *fiery* quality of the duke;
How unremoveable, and fixt he is
In his own course. *Shakespeare's King Lear.*

5. Unrestrained; fierce.

Then, as I said, the duke, great Bolingbroke,
Mounted upon a hot and *fiery* steed,
Which his aspiring rider seem'd to know,
With slow but stately pace kept on his course. *Shak. R.* II.
Through Elis and the Grecian towns he flew;
Th' audacious wretch four *fiery* coursers drew. *Dryden.*

6. Heated by fire.

The sword which is made *fiery* doth not only cut, by reason of the sharpness which simply it hath, but also burn by means of that heat which it hath from fire. *Hooker, b.* v. 54.

See! from the brake the whirring pheasant springs,
And mounts exulting on triumphant wings:
Short is his joy; he feels the *fiery* wound,
Flutters in blood, and panting beats the ground. *Pope.*

FIFE. *n. s.* [*fifre*, French.] A pipe blown to the drum; military wind-musick.

Farewell the plumed troops, and the big war
That make ambition virtue! oh farewell!
Farewell the neighing steed and the shrill trump,
The spirit-stirring drum, th' ear-piercing *fife*. *Shak. Othello.*
Thus the gay victim, with fresh garlands crown'd,
Pleas'd with the sacred *fife's* enlivening sound,
Through gazing crowds in solemn state proceeds. *Phillips.*

FI'FTEEN. *adj.* [fyftyne, Saxon.] Five and ten.

I have dreamed and slept above some *fifteen* years and more. *Shakespeare's Taming of the Shrew.*

FI'FTEENTH. *adj.* [fifteoða, Sax.] The ordinal of fifteen; the fifth after the tenth.

A *fifteenth* part of silver incorporate with gold, will not be recovered by any water of separation, except you put a greater quanty of silver to draw up the less. *Bacon's Natural History.*

London sends but four burgesses to parliament, although it bear the *fifteenth* part of the charge of the whole nation in all publick taxes and levies. *Graunt's Bills of Mortality.*

FIFTH. *adj.* [fifta, Saxon.]

1. The ordinal of five; the next to the fourth.

With smiling aspect you serenely move,
In your *fifth* orb, and rule the realm of love. *Dryden.*
Just as I wish'd, the lots were cast on four,
Myself the *fifth*. *Pope's Odyssey, b.* ix.

2. All the ordinals are taken elliptically for the part which they express: a *fifth*, a *fifth* part; a *third*, a *third* part.

The publick shall have lost four *fifths* of its annual income for ever. *Swift.*

FI'FTHLY. *adv.* [from *fifth*.] In the fifth place.

Fifthly, living creatures have a more exact figure than plants. *Bacon's Natural History*, N°. 607.

FI'FTIETH. *adj.* [fifteogoþa, Saxon.] The ordinal of fifty.

If this medium be rarer within the sun's body than at its surface, and rarer there than at the hundred part of an inch from its body, and rarer there than at the *fiftieth* part of an inch from its body, and rarer there than at the orb of Saturn, I see no reason why the increase of density should stop any where. *Newton's Opt.*

FI'FTY. *adj.* [fiftig, Saxon.] Five tens.

A wither'd hermit, five score Winters worn,
Might shake off *fifty* looking in her eye. *Shakespeare.*

Judas ordained captains over thousands, hundreds, *fifties*, and tens. 1 *Mac.* iii. 55.

The breadth of the ark shall be *fifty* cubits. *Gen.* vi. 15.

In the Hebrew there is a particle consisting but of one letter, of which there are reckoned up above *fifty* several significations. *Locke.*

FIG. *n. s.* [*ficus*, Latin; *figo*, Spanish; *figue*, French.]

1. A tree that bears figs.

The characters are: the flowers, which are always inclosed in the middle of the fruit, consist of the leaf, and are male and female in the same fruit: the male flowers are situated towards the crown of the fruit; and the female, growing near the stalk, are succeeded by small hard seeds: the intire fruit is, for the most part, turbinated and globular, or of an oval shape, is fleshy, and of a sweet taste. *Miller.*

Full on its crown a *fig's* green branches rise,
And shoot a leafy forest to the skies. *Pope's Odyssey, b.* xii.
Or lead me through the maze,
Embowering endless of the Indian *fig*. *Thomson's Summer.*

2. A luscious soft fruit: the fruit of the figtree.

It maketh *figs* better, if a figtree, when it beginneth to put forth leaves, have his top cut off. *Bacon's Nat. History.*

Figs are great subduers of acrimony. *Arbuthnot on Diet.*

To FIG. *v. a.* [See FICO.]

1. To insult with fico's or contemptuous motions of the fingers.

When Pistol lies, do this, and *fig* me like
The bragging Spaniard. *Shakespeare's Henry* IV.

2. To put something useless into one's head. Low cant.

Away to the sow she goes, and *figs* her in the crown with another story. *L'Estrange.*

FI'GAPPLE. *n. s.* A fruit.

A *figapple* hath no core or kernel, in these resembling a *fig*, and differing from other apples. *Mortimer's Husbandry.*

FI'GMARIGOLD. *n. s.* A plant. It is succulent, and has the appearance of houseleek: the leaves grow opposite by pairs. *Mill.*

To FIGHT. *v. n.* preter. *fought*; part. pass. *fought*. [feohtan, Saxon.]

1. To contend in battle; to war; to make war; to battle; to contend in arms. It is used both of armies and single combatants.

King Henry, be thy title right or wrong,
Lord Clifford vows to *fight* in thy defence. *Shak. Hen.* VI.
Fierce fiery warriors *fight* upon the clouds
In ranks and squadrons, and right form of war. *Shakesp.*

The common question is, if we must now surrender Spain, what

what have we been *fighting* for all this while? The answer is ready: we have been *fighting* for the ruin of the publick interest, and the advancement of a private. *Swift.*

For her confederate nations *fought*, and kings were slain,
Troy was o'erthrown, and a whole empire fell. *Phillips.*

2. To combat; to duel; to contend in single fight.

One shall undertake to *fight* against another. 2 *Esdr.* xiii.

The poor wren,
The most diminutive of birds, will *fight*,
The young ones in her nest, against the owl. *Shakesp. Macb.*

3. To act as a soldier in any case.

Richard, that robb'd the lion of his heart,
And *fought* the holy wars in Palestine,
By this brave duke came early to his grave. *Shak. K. John.*

Greatly unfortunate, he *fights* the cause
Of honour, virtue, liberty and Rome. *Addison's Cato.*

4. It has *with* before the person opposed.

5. To contend.

The hot and cold, the dry and humid *fight*. *Sandys.*

To FIGHT. *v. a.* To war against; to combat against.

Himself alone, an equal match he boasts,
To *fight* the Phrygian and the Ausonian hosts. *Dryd. Æn.*

FIGHT. *n. s.* [from the verb.]

1. Battle.

2. Combat; duel.

Herilus in single *fight* I slew,
Whom with three lives Feronia did endue;
And thrice I sent him to the Stygian shore,
'Till the last ebbing soul return'd no more. *Dryden's Æn.*

3. Something to screen the combatants in ships.

FI'GHTER. *n. s.* [from *fight.*] Warriour; duellist.

I will return again into the house, and desire some conduct of the lady: I am no *fighter*. *Shakespeare's Twelfth Night.*

O, 'tis the coldest youth upon a charge,
The most deliberate *fighter!* *Dryden's All for Love.*

FI'GHTING. *participial adj.* [from *fight.*]

1. Qualified for war; fit for battle.

An host of *fighting* men went out to war by bands. 2 *Chro.*

2. Occupied by war; being the scene of war.

In *fighting* fields, as far the spear I throw
As flies the arrow from the well-drawn bow. *Pope's Odyss.*

FI'GMENT. *n. s.* [*figmentum*, Latin.] An invention; a fiction; the idea feigned.

Upon the like grounds was raised the *figment* of Briareus, who, dwelling in a city called Hecatonchiria, the fancies of those times assigned him an hundred hands. *Brown's Vulg. Err.*

The most frightful passages, probably so strange as to be hardly credible; it carried rather an appearance of *figment* and invention, in those that handed down the memory of it, than of truth and reality. *Woodward's Natural History.*

FI'GPECKER. *n. s.* [*fig* and *peck.*] A bird.

FI'GULATE. *adj.* [from *figulus*, Latin.] Made of potters clay.

FI'GURABLE. *adj.* [from *figuro*, Latin.] Capable of being brought to certain form, and retained in it. Thus lead is *figurable*, but not water.

The differences of impressible and not impressible, *figurable* and not *figurable*, scissible and not scissible, are plebeian notions. *Bacon's Natural History.*

FIGURABI'LITY. *n. s.* [from *figurable.*] The quality of being capable of a certain and stable form.

FI'GURAL. *adj.* [from *figure.*]

1. Represented by delineation.

Incongruities have been committed by geographers in the *figural* resemblances of several regions. *Brown's Vulg. Err.*

2. FIGURAL *Numbers.* Such numbers as do or may represent some geometrical figure, in relation to which they are always considered, and are either lineary, superficial, or solid. *Harris.*

FI'GURATE. *adj.* [*figuratus*, Latin.]

1. Of a certain and determinate form.

Plants are all *figurate* and determinate, which inanimate bodies are not; for look how far the spirit is able to spread and continue itself, so far goeth the shape or figure, and then is determined. *Bacon.*

2. Resembling any thing of a determinate form: as, *figurate* stones retaining the forms of shells in which they were formed by the deluge.

3. FI'GURATE *Counterpoint.* [In musick.] That wherein there is a mixture of discords along with the concords. *Harris.*

5. FIGURATE *Descant.* [In musick.] That wherein discords are concerned, as well, though not so much, as concords; and may well be termed the ornament or rhetorical part of musick, in regard that in this are introduced all the varieties of points, figures, syncopes, diversities of measures, and whatever else is capable of adorning the composition. *Harris.*

FIGURA'TION. *n. s.* [*figuratus*, Latin.]

1. Determination to a certain form.

Neither doth the wind, as far as it carrieth a voice, with motion thereof confound any of the delicate and articulate *figurations* of the air in variety of words. *Bacon's Nat. Hist.*

2. The act of giving a certain form.

If motion be in a certain order, there followeth vivification and *figuration* in living creatures perfect. *Bacon's Nat. Hist.*

FI'GURATIVE. *adj.* [*figuratif-ve*, Fr. from *figura*, Latin.]

1. Representing something else; typical; representative.

This, they will say, was *figurative*, and served by God's appointment but for a time, to shadow out the true everlasting glory of a more divine sanctity; whereinto Christ being long since entered, it seemeth that all these curious exornations should rather cease. *Hooker, b.* v. *s.* 15.

2. Changed by rhetorical figures from the primitive meaning; not literal.

How often have we been railed at for understanding words in a *figurative* sense, which cannot be literally understood without overthrowing the plainest evidence of sense and reason. *Stillingfleet's Def. of Disc. on Rom. Idol.*

This is a *figurative* expression, where the words are used in a different sense from what they signify in their first ordinary intention. *Rogers, Sermon* 14.

3. Full of figures; full of rhetorical exornations; full of changes from the original sense.

Sublime subjects ought to be adorned with the sublimest and with the most *figurative* expressions. *Dryden's Juvenal, Pref.*

FI'GURATIVELY. *adj.* [from *figurative.*] By a figure; in a sense different from that which words originally imply; not literally.

The custom of the apostle is *figuratively* to transfer to himself, in the first person, what belongs to others. *Hammond.*

The words are different, but the sense is still the same; for therein are *figuratively* intended Uziah and Ezechias. *Brown.*

Satyr is a kind of poetry in which human vices are reprehended, partly dramatically, partly simply; but, for the most part, *figuratively* and occultly. *Dryden's Juvenal, Dedicat.*

FI'GURE. *n. s.* [*figura*, Latin.]

1. The form of any thing as terminated by the outline.

Flowers have all exquisite *figures*, and the flower numbers are chiefly five and four; as in primroses, briar-roses, single muskroses, single pinks and gilliflowers, &c. which have five leaves; lilies, flower-de-luces, borage, buglass, &c. which have four leaves. *Bacon's Natural History.*

Men find green clay that is soft as long as it is in the water, so that one may print on it all kind of *figures*, and give it what shape one pleases. *Boyle.*

Figures are properly modifications of bodies; for pure space is not any where terminated, nor can be: whether there be or be not body in it, it is uniformly continued. *Locke.*

2. Shape; form; semblance.

He hath borne himself beyond the promise of his age, doing in the *figure* of a lamb the feats of a lion. *Shakespeare.*

3. Person; external form; appearance graceful or inelegant, mean or grand.

The blue German shall the Tigris drink,
E'er I, forsaking gratitude and truth,
Forget the *figure* of that godlike youth. *Dryden's Virgil.*

I was charmed with the gracefulness of his *figure* and delivery, as well as with his discourses. *Addison's Spectator.*

A good *figure*, or person, in man or woman, gives credit at first sight to the choice of either. *Clarissa.*

4. Distinguished appearance; eminence; remarkable character.

While fortune favour'd, while his arms support
The cause, and rul'd the counsels of the court,
I made some *figure* there; nor was my name
Obscure, nor I without my share of fame. *Dryden's Æn.*

The speech, I believe, was not so much designed by the knight to inform the court, as to give him a *figure* in my eye, and keep up his credit in the country. *Addison's Spectator.*

Not a woman shall be unexplained that makes a *figure* either as a maid, a wife, or a widow. *Addison's Guardian.*

Whether or no they have done well to set you up for making another kind of *figure*, time will witness. *Addison.*

Many princes made very ill *figures* upon the throne, who before were the favourites of the people. *Addison's Freeholder.*

5. A statue; an image; something formed in resemblance of somewhat else.

The several statues, which seemed at a distance to be made of the whitest marble, were nothing else but so many *figures* in snow. *Addison's Freeholder.*

6. Representations in painting; persons exhibited in colours.

In the principal *figures* of a picture the painter is to employ the sinews of his art; for in them consists the principal beauty of his work. *Dryden's Dufresnoy.*

My favourite books and pictures sell;
Kindly throw in a little *figure*,
And set the price upon the bigger. *Prior.*

7. Arrangement; disposition; modification.

The *figure* of a syllogism is the proper disposition of the middle term with the parts of the question. *Watts's Logick.*

8. A character denoting a number.

Hearts, tongues, *figures*, scribes, bards, poets cannot
Think, speak, cast, write, sing, number
His love to Anthony. *Shakespeare's Ant. and Cleopatra.*

He that seeketh to be eminent amongst able men, hath a great

great task; but that is ever good for the publick: but he that plots to be the only *figure* among cyphers, is the decay of a whole age. *Bacon's Essays.*

As in accounts cyphers and *figures* pass for real sums, so in human affairs words pass for things themselves. *South's Serm.*

9. The horoscope; the diagram of the aspects of the astrological houses.

We do not know what's brought to pass under the profession of fortunetelling: she works by charms, by spells, by the *figure*, and dawbry beyond our element. *Shakespeare.*

He set a *figure* to discover
If you were fled to Rye or Dover. *Hudibras, p.* iii. *cant.* I.

Figure flingers and star-gazers pretend to foretell the fortunes of kingdoms, and have no foresight in what concerns themselves. *L'Estrange, Fable* 94.

10. [In theology.] Type representative.

Who was the *figure* of him that is to come. *Romans.*

11. [In rhetorick.] Any mode of speaking in which words are detorted from their literal and primitive sense. In strict acceptation, the change of a word is a *trope*, and any affection of a sentence a *figure*; but they are generally confounded by the exactest writers.

Silken terms precise,
Three pil'd hyperboles, spruce affectation,
Figures pedantical, these Summer flies
Have blown me full of maggot ostentation. *Shakespeare.*

Here is a strange *figure* invented against the plain and natural sense of the words; for by praying to bestow, must be understood only praying to pray. *Stillingfleet.*

They have been taught rhetorick, but yet never taught to express themselves in the language they are always to use; as if the names of the *figures* that embellished the discourse of those, who understood the art of speaking, were the very art and skill of speaking well. *Locke.*

12. [In grammar.] Any deviation from the rules of analogy or syntax.

To FI'GURE. *v. a.* [*figuro*, Latin.]

1. To form into any determinate shape.

Trees and herbs, in the growing forth of their boughs and branches, are not *figured*, and keep no order. *Bacon.*

Accept this goblet, rough with *figur'd* gold. *Dryd. Virgil.*

2. To show by a corporeal resemblance: as in picture or statuary.

Arachne *figur'd* how Jove did abuse
Europa like a bull, and on his back
Her through the sea did bear; so lively seen,
That it true sea, and true bull ye would ween. *Spenser.*

Now marks the course of rolling orbs on high,
O'er *figur'd* worlds now travels with his eye. *Pope.*

3. To cover or adorn with figures.

I'll give my jewels for a set of beads,
My gorgeous palace for a hermitage,
My gay apparel for an almsman's gown,
My *figur'd* goblets for a dish of wood. *Shakes. Richard* II.

4. To diversify; to variegate with adventitious forms or matter.

But this effusion of such manly drops,
Startle mine eyes, and makes me more amaz'd
Than had I seen the vaulty top of heav'n
Figur'd quite o'er with burning meteors. *Shakesp. K. John.*

5. To represent by a typical or figurative resemblance.

When sacraments are said to be visible signs of invisible grace, we thereby conceive how grace is indeed the very end for which these heavenly mysteries were instituted; and the matter whereof they consist is such as signifieth, *figureth*, and representeth their end. *Hooker, b.* v.

There is a history in all mens lives,
Figuring the nature of the times deceased. *Shakes. Hen.* IV.

Marriage rings are not of this stuff:
Oh! why should ought less precious or less tough
Figure our loves? *Donne.*

The emperor appears as a rising sun, and holds a globe in his hand to *figure* out the earth that is enlightened and actuated by his beams. *Addison on ancient Medals.*

6. To image in the mind.

None that feels sensibly the decays of age, and his life wearing off, can *figure* to himself those imaginary charms in riches and praise, that men are apt to do in the warmth of their blood. *Temple.*

If love, alas! be pain, the pain I bear
No thought can *figure*, and no tongue declare. *Prior.*

7. To prefigure; to foreshow.

Three glorious suns, each one a perfect sun,
In this the heaven *figures* some event. *Shakes. Henry* VI.

8. To form figuratively; to use in a sense not literal.

Figured and metaphorical expressions do well to illustrate more abstruse and unfamiliar ideas, which the mind is not yet thoroughly accustomed to. *Locke.*

FIGURE-FLINGER. *n. s.* [*figure* and *fling.*] A pretender to astrology and prediction.

Quacks, *figure-flingers*, pettifoggers, and republican plotters cannot well live without it. *Collier of Confidence.*

FI'GWORT. *n. s.* [*fig* and *wort.*] A plant

It hath an anomalous flower, consisting of one leaf, gaping at both sides, and generally globular, cut as it were into two lips, under the upper one of which are two small leaves. *Mill.*

FILA'CEOUS. *adj.* [from *filum*, Lat.] Consisting of threads; composed of threads.

They make cables of the bark of lime-trees: it is the stalk that maketh the *filaceous* matter commonly, and sometimes the down that groweth above. *Bacon's Natural History.*

FI'LACER. *n. s.* [*filazarius*, low Lat. *filum.*] An officer in the Common Pleas, so called because he files those writs whereon he makes process. There are fourteen of them in their several divisions and counties: they make out all original process, as well real as personal and mixt. *Harris.*

FI'LAMENT. *n. s.* [*filament*, Fr. *filamenta*, Latin.] A slender thread; a body slender and long like a thread.

The effluvium passing out in a smaller thread, and more enlightened *filament*, it stirreth not the bodies interposed. *Bro.*

The lungs of consumptives have been consumed, nothing remaining but the ambient membrane, and a number of withered veins and *filaments*. *Harvey on Consumptions.*

The ever-rolling orb's impulsive ray
On the next threads and *filaments* does bear,
Which form the springy texture of the air
And those still strike the next, 'till to the sight
The quick vibration propagates the light. *Blackm. Creation*

The dung of horses is nothing but the *filaments* of the hay, and as such combustible. *Arbuthnot on Aliments.*

FI'LBERT. *n. s.* [This is derived by *Junius* and *Skinner* from the long beards or husks, as corrupted from *full beard*, or *full of beard*. It probably had its name, like many other fruits, from some one that introduced or cultivated it; and is therefore corrupted from *Filbert* or *Filibert*, the name of him who brought it hither.] A fine hazel nut with a thin shell.

In August comes fruit of all sorts; as plumbs, pears, apricots, barberries, *filberts*, muskmelons, monkshoods of all colours. *Bacon, Essay* 47.

Thou hast a brain, such as it is indeed!
On what else should thy worm of fancy feed?
Yet in a *filbert* I have often known
Maggots survive, when all the kernel's gone. *Dorset.*

There is also another kind, called the *filbert* of Constantinople; the leaves and fruit of which are bigger than either of the former: the best are those of a thin shell. *Mortimer.*

To FILCH. *v. a.* [A word of uncertain etymology. The French word *filer*, from which some derive it, is of very late production, and therefore cannot be its original.] To steal; to take by theft; to pilfer; to pillage; to rob; to take by robbery. It is usually spoken of petty thefts.

He shall find his wealth wonderfully enlarged by keeping his cattle in inclosures, where they shall always have safe being, that none are continually *filched* and stolen. *Spenser.*

The champion robbeth by night,
And prowleth and *filcheth* by daie. *Tusser's Husbandry.*

Who steals my purse, steals trash; 'tis something, nothing;
'Twas mine, 'tis his, and has been slave to thousands;
But he that *filches* from me my good name,
Robs me of that which not enriches him,
And makes me poor indeed. *Shakespeare's Othello.*

His thefts were too open; his *filching* was like an unskilful singer, he kept no time. *Shakes. Merry Wives of Windsor.*

He could discern cities like hives of bees, wherein every bee did nought else but sting; some like hornets, some like *filching* wasps, others as drones. *Burton on Melancholy.*

What made thee venture to betray,
And *filch* the lady's heart away. *Hudibras, p.* iii. *cant.* I.

The pismire was formerly a husbandman, that secretly *filched* away his neighbour's goods. *L'Estrange's Fables.*

Fain would they *filch* that little food away,
While unrestrain'd those happy gluttons prey. *Dryden.*

So speeds the wily fox, alarm'd by fear,
Who lately *filch'd* the turkey's callow care. *Gay's Trivia.*

FI'LCHER. *n. s.* [from *filch.*] A thief; a petty robber.

FILE. *n. s.* [*file*, French; *filum*, a thread, Latin.]

1. A thread.

But let me resume the *file* of my relation, which this object of books, best agreeable to my course of life, hath a little interrupted. *Wotton.*

2. A line on which papers are strung to keep them in order.

All records, wherein there was any memory of the king's attainder, should be cancelled and taken off the *file*. *Bacon.*

The petitions being thus prepared, do you continually set apart an hour in a day to peruse those, and then rank them into several *files*, according to the subject matters. *Bacon.*

Th' apothecary-train is wholly blind;
From *files* a random recipe they take,
And many deaths of one prescription make. *Dryden.*

3. A catalogue; roll; series.

Our present musters grow upon the *file*
To five and twenty thousand men of choice. *Shakes. H.* IV.

The valu'd *file*
Distinguishes the swift, the slow, the subtle. *Shak. Macb.*

4. A

4. A line of soldiers ranged one behind another.

Those goodly eyes,
That o'er the *files* and musters of the war
Have glow'd like plated Mars, now bend, now turn
Upon a tawny front. *Shakespeare's Ant. and Cleopatra.*
So saying, on he led his radiant *files*,
Dazzling the moon. *Milton's Paradise Lost, b.* iv.

5. [feol, Saxon; *vijle*, Dutch.] An instrument to rub down prominences.

The rough or coarse-toothed *file*, if it be large, is called a rubber, and is to take off the unevenness of your work which the hammer made in the forging: the bastard-toothed *file* is to take out of your work the deep cuts, or file-strokes, the rough *file* made: the fine-toothed *file* is to take out the cuts, or file-strokes, the bastard *file* made; and the smooth *file* is to take out those cuts, or file-strokes, that the fine *file* made. *Moxon.*

Yet they had a *file* for the mattocks and for the coulters. 1 *Sa.* xiii. 21.

The smiths and armourers on palfreys ride,
Files in their hands and hammers at their side,
And nails for loosen'd spears, and thongs for shields provide. *Dryden's Knight's Tale.*

Filecu'tter. *s. n.* [*file* and *cutter*.] A maker of files.

Gad-steel is a tough sort of steel: *filecutters* use it to make their chissels, with which they cut their files. *Moxon.*

To File. *v. a.* [from *filum*, a thread.]

1. To string upon a thread or wire. Whence to *file a bile* is to offer it in its order to the notice of the judge.

From the day his first bill was *filed* he began to collect reports. *Arbuthnot and Pope's Mart. Scrib.*

2. [from feolan, Saxon.] To cut with a file.

They which would *file away* most from the largeness of that offer, do in more sparing terms acknowledge little less. *Hooker, b.* v. *s.* 27.

His humour is lofty, his discourse peremptory, his tongue *filed*, and his eye ambitious. *Shakesp. Love's Labour Lost.*

Let men be careful how they attempt to cure a blemish by *filing* or cutting off the head of such an overgrown tooth. *Ray.*

3. [from fylan.] To foul; to sully; to pollute. This sense is retained in Scotland.

For Banquo's issue have I *fil'd* my mind,
For them the gracious Duncan have I murder'd. *Shakesp.*
His weeds, divinely fashioned,
All *fil'd* and mangl'd. *Chapman's Iliads, b.* xviii.

To File. *v. n.* [from the noun.] To march in a file, not abreast, but one behind another.

All ran down without order or ceremony, 'till we drew up in good order, and *filed* off. *Tatler,* N°. 86.

Did all the grosser atoms at the cell
Of chance *file* off to form the pond'rous ball,
And undetermin'd into order fall? *Blackmore's Creation.*

Fi'lemot. *n. s.* [corrupted from *feueille morte*, a dead leaf, French.] A brown or yellow-brown colour.

The colours you ought to wish for are blue or *filemot*, turned up with red. *Swift's Direct. to the Footman.*

Fi'ler. *n. s.* [from *file*.] One who files; one who uses the file in cutting metals.

FILIAL. *adj.* [*filial-le*, French; *filius*, Latin.]

1. Pertaining to a son; befitting a son.

My mischievous proceeding may be the glory of his *filial* piety, the only reward now left for so great a merit. *Sidney.*

From imposition of strict laws, to free
Acceptance of large grace; from servile fear
To *filial*; works of law, to works of faith. *Milt. Pa. Lost.*
He griev'd, he wept, the sight an image brought
Of his own *filial* love; a sadly pleasing thought. *Dryden.*

2. Bearing the character or relation of a son.

And thus the *filial* godhead answ'ring spoke. *Milt. P. L.*
Where the old myrtle her good influence sheds,
Sprigs of like leaf erect their *filial* heads;
And when the parent rose decays and dies,
With a resembling face the daughter buds arise. *Prior.*

Filia'tion. *n. s.* [from *filius*, Latin.] The relation of a son to a father; correlative to paternity.

The relation of paternity and *filiation*, between the first and second person, and the relation between the sacred persons of the Trinity, and the denomination thereof, must needs be eternal, because the terms of relation between whom that relation ariseth were eternal. *Hale's Origin of Mankind.*

Fi'lings. *n. s.* [without a singular; from *file*.] Fragments rubbed off by the action of the file.

The *filings* of iron infused in vinegar, will, with a decoction of galls, make good ink, without any copperose at all. *Brown's Vulgar Errours, b.* vi. *c.* 12.

The chippings and *filings* of those jewels are of more value than the whole mass of ordinary authors. *Felton on the Class.*

To FILL. *v. n.* [fyllan, Saxon.]

1. To store 'till no more can be admitted.

Fill thine horn with oil. 1 *Sa.* xvi. 1.

Fill the waterpots with water, and they *filled* them up to the brim. *Jo.* ii. 7.

The earth is *filled* with violence through them. *Gen.* vi. 13.

2. To store abundantly.

Be fruitful and multiply, and *fill* the waters in the seas. *Gen.*

3. To satisfy; to content.

Nothing but the supreme and absolute Infinite can adequately *fill* and super-abundantly satisfy the infinite desires of intelligent beings. *Cheyne's Phil. Princ.*

4. To glut; to surfeit.

Thou art going to lord Timon's feast.
—Ay, to see meat *fill* knaves, and wine heat fools. *Shakes.*

5. *To* Fill *out.* To pour out liquor for drink.

6. *To* Fill *out.* To extend by something contained.

I only speak of him
Whom pomp and greatness sits so loose about,
That he wants majesty to *fill* them out. *Dryden.*

7. *To* Fill *up.* [*Up* is often used without much addition to the force of the verb.] To make full.

Hope leads from goal to goal,
And opens still, and opens on his soul;
'Till lengthen'd on to faith, and unconfin'd,
It pours the bliss that *fills up* all the mind. *Pope's Ess. on Man.*

8. *To* Fill *up.* To supply.

When the several trades and professions are supplied, you will find most of those that are proper for war absolutely necessary for *filling up* the laborious part of life, and carrying on the underwork of the nation. *Addison on the War.*

9. *To* Fill *up.* To occupy by bulk.

There would not be altogether so much water required for the land as for the sea, to raise them to an equal height; because mountains and hills would *fill up* part of that space upon the land, and so make less water requisite. *Burnet.*

10. *To* Fill *up.* To engage; to employ.

Is it far you ride?
—As far, my lord, as will *fill up* the time
'Twixt this and supper. *Shakespeare's Macbeth.*

To Fill. *v. n.*

1. To give to drink.

In the cup which she hath filled, *fill* to her double. *Rev.* xviii.
We *fill* to th' general joy of the whole table,
And to our dear friend Banquo, whom we miss. *Shak. Mac.*

2. To grow full.

3. To glut; to satiate.

Things that are sweet and fat are more *filling*, and do swim and hang more about the mouth of the stomach, and go not down so speedily. *Bacon's Natural History.*

4. *To* Fill *up.* To grow full.

Neither the Palus Meotis nor the Euxine, nor any other seas, *fill up*, or by degrees grow shallower. *Woodward.*

The first stage of healing, or the discharge of matter, is by surgeons called digestion; the second, or the *filling up* with flesh, incarnation; and the last, or skining over, cicatrization. *Sharp's Surgery.*

Fill. *n. s.* [from the verb.]

1. As much as may produce complete satisfaction.

Her neck and breasts were ever open bare,
That aye thereof her babes might suck their *fill*. *Fairy Qu.*
But thus inflam'd bespoke the captain,
Who scorneth peace shall have his *fill* of war. *Fairfax, b.* ii.

When ye were thirsty, did I not cleave the rock, and waters flowed out to your *fill*? 2 *Esd.* i. 20.

Mean while enjoy
Your *fill*, what happiness this happy state
Can comprehend, incapable of more. *Milton's Par. Lost.*
Amid' the tree now got, where plenty hung
Tempting so nigh, to pluck and eat my *fill*
I spar'd not. *Milton's Paradise Lost, b.* ix.
Which made me gently first remove your fears,
That so you might have room to entertain
Your *fill* of joy. *Denham's Sophy.*

Your barbarity, which I have heard so long exclaimed against in town and country, may have its *fill* of destruction. *Pope.*

2. [More properly *thill*.] The place between the shafts of a carriage.

This mule being put in the *fill* of a cart, run away with the cart and timber. *Mortimer's Husbandry.*

Fi'ller. *n. s.* [from *fill*.]

1. Any thing that fills up room without use.

'Tis a meer *filler*, to stop a vacancy in the hexameter, and connect the preface to the work of Virgil. *Dryd. Æn. Dedic.*

A mixture of tender gentle thoughts and suitable expressions, of forced and inextricable conceits, and of needless *fillers* up to the rest. *Pope.*

2. One whose employment is to fill vessels of carriage.

They commonly have three, four, five or six hewers or diggers to four *fillers*, being proportioned so as to keep the *fillers* always at work. *Mortimer's Husbandry.*

FI'LLET. *n. s.* [*filet*, French; *filum*, Latin.]

1. A band tied round the head or other part.

His baleful breath inspiring, as he glides,
Now like a chain around her neck he rides;

Now

Now like a *fillet* to her head repairs,
And with his circling volumes folds her hairs. *Dryd. Æn.*
She ſcorn'd the praiſe of beauty, and the care;
A belt her waiſt, a *fillet* binds her hair. *Pope's Windſ. For.*

2. The fleſhy part of the thigh: applied commonly to veal.
The youth approach'd the fire, and as it burn'd,
On five ſharp broachers rank'd, the roaſt they turn'd:
Theſe morſels ſtay'd their ſtomachs; then the reſt
They cut in legs and *fillets* for the feaſt. *Dryden's Iliad.*

3. Meat rolled together, and tied round.
Fillet of a fenny ſnake,
In the cauldron boil and bake. *Shakeſpeare's Macbeth.*
The mixture thus, by chymick art
United cloſe in every part,
In *fillets* roll'd, or cut in pieces,
Appear'd like one continu'd ſpecies. *Swift.*

4. [In architecture.] A little member which appears in the ornaments and mouldings, and is otherwiſe called liſtel. *Harris.*

To FI'LLET. *v. a.* [from the noun.]
1. To bind with a bandage or fillet.
2. To adorn with an aſtragal.
He made hooks for the pillars, and overlaid their chapiters and *filletted* them. *Ex.* xxxviii. 28.

To FI'LLIP. *v. a.* [A word, ſays *Skinner*, formed from the ſound. This reſemblance I am not able to diſcover, and therefore am inclined to imagine it corrupted from *fill up*, by ſome combination of ideas which cannot be recovered.] To ſtrike with the nail of the finger by a ſudden ſpring or motion.
If I do, *fillip* me with a three-man beetle. *Shak. Hen.* IV.
Then let the pebbles on the hungry beach
Fillip the ſtars: then let the mutinous winds
Strike the proud cedars 'gainſt the fiery ſun. *Shakeſ. Coriol.*
We ſee, that if you *fillip* a luteſtring, it ſheweth double or treble. *Bacon's Natural Hiſtory*, N°. 183.

FI'LLIP. *n. ſ.* [from the verb.] A jerk of the finger let go from the thumb.

FI'LLY. *n. ſ.* [*filoy*, Welſh; *fille*, French.]
1. A young horſe or mare.
Geld *fillies*, but tits, yer a nine days of age,
They die elſe of gelding, or gelders do rage:
Young *fillies* ſo likely of bulk and of bone,
Keep ſuch to be breeders, let gelding alone. *Tuſſ. Husband.*
A well-wayed horſe will convey thee to thy journey's end, when an unbacked *filly* may give thee a fall. *Suckling.*
2. A young mare, oppoſed to a colt or young horſe.
I jeſt to Oberon, and make him ſmile,
When I a fat and bean-fed horſe beguile,
Neighing in likeneſs of a *filly* foal. *Shakeſpeare.*
I am joined in wedlock, for my ſins, to one of thoſe *fillies* who are deſcribed in the old poet. *Addiſon's Spectator.*

FILM. *n. ſ.* [ꝼylmeꞅa, Saxon.] A thin pellicle or ſkin.
While the ſilver needle did work upon the ſight of his eye, to remove the *film* of the cataract, he never ſaw any thing more clear or perfect than that white needle. *Bacon's N. Hiſt.*
Michael from Adam's eyes the *film* remov'd,
Which that falſe fruit that promis'd clearer ſight
Had bred. *Milton's Paradiſe Loſt, b.* ii. *l.* 412.
A ſtone is held up by the *films* of the bladder, and ſo kept from grating or offending it. *Graunt's Bills of Mortality.*
There is not one infidel ſo ridiculous as to pretend to ſolve the phænomena of ſight, fancy, or cogitation, by thoſe fleeting ſuperficial *films* of bodies. *Bentley's Sermons.*
He from thick *films* ſhall purge the viſual ray,
And on the ſightleſs eyeballs pour the day. *Pope's Meſſiah.*

To FILM. *v. a.* [from the noun.] To cover with a pellicle or thin ſkin.
It will but ſkin and *film* the ulcerous place,
Whilſt rank corruption, mining all within,
Infects unſeen. *Shakeſpeare's Hamlet.*

FI'LMY. *adj.* [from *film.*] Compoſed of thin membranes or pellicles.
So the falſe ſpider, when her nets are ſpread,
Deep ambuſh'd in her ſilent den does lie;
And feels, far off, the trembling of her thread,
Whoſe *filmy* cord ſhould bind the ſtruggling fly. *Dryden.*
They with fruitleſs toil
Flap *filmy* pinions oft, to extricate
Their feet in liquid ſhackles bound, 'till death
Bereave them of their worthleſs ſouls; ſuch doom
Waits luxury, and lawleſs love of gain. *Phillips.*
Looſe to the winds their airy garments flew,
Thin glitt'ring textures of the *filmy* dew;
Dipt in the richeſt tincture of the ſkies,
Where light diſports in ever-mingling dyes. *Pope.*

To FI'LTER. *v. a.* [*filtro*, low Latin; *per filum trahere.*]
1. To defecate by drawing off liquor by depending threads.
2. To ſtrain; to percolate.
Dilute this liquor with fair water, *filtre* it through a paper, and ſo evaporate it. *Grew's Muſæum.*

FI'LTER. *n. ſ.* [*filtrum*, Latin.]
1. A twiſt of thread, of which one end is dipped in the liquor to be defecated, and the other hangs below the bottom of the veſſel, ſo that the liquor drips from it. See NEW DISPENSATORY.
2. A ſtrainer; a ſearce.
That the water, paſſing through the veins of the earth, ſhould be rendered freſh and potable, which it cannot be by any percolations we can make, but the ſaline particles will paſs through a tenfold *filter*. *Ray on the Creation.*

FILTH. *n. ſ.* [ꝼılð, Saxon.]
1. Dirt; naſtineſs; any thing that ſoils or fouls.
When we in our viciouſneſs grow hard,
The wiſe gods ſeal our eyes;
In our own *filth* drop our clear judgments. *Shakeſpeare.*
Wiſdom and goodneſs to the vile ſeem vile;
Filths ſavour but themſelves. *Shakeſpeare's King Lear.*
Neither may you truſt waters that taſte ſweet; for they are commonly found in riſing grounds of great cities, which muſt needs take in a great deal of *filth*. *Bacon's Natural Hiſtory.*
How perfect then is man? From head to foot
Defil'd with *filth*, and rotten at the root. *Sandys.*
Though perhaps among the rout
He wildly flings his *filth* about;
He ſtill has gratitude and ſap'ence,
To ſpare the folks that give him ha'pence. *Swift.*
2. Corruption; groſſneſs; pollution.
Such do likewiſe exceedingly diſpoſe us to piety and religion, by purifying our ſouls from the droſs and *filth* of ſenſual delights. *Tillotſon's Sermons.*

FI'LTHILY. *adv.* [from *filthy.*] Naſtily; foully; groſsly.
It ſtuck *filthily* in the camel's ſtomach that bulls, bears, and the like, ſhould be armed, and that a creature of his ſize ſhould be left defenceleſs. *L'Eſtrange, Fable* 78.

FI'LTHINESS. *n. ſ.* [from *filthy.*]
1. Naſtineſs; foulneſs; dirtineſs.
Men of virtue ſuppreſſed it, leſt their ſhining ſhould diſcover the others *filthineſs*. *Sidney, b.* ii.
2. Corruption; pollution.
They held this land, and with their *filthineſs*
Polluted this ſame gentle ſoil long time,
That their own mother loath'd their beaſtlineſs,
And 'gan abhor her brood's unkindly crime,
All were they born of her own native ſlime. *Fairy Queen.*
They never duly improved the utmoſt of ſuch a power, but gave themſelves up to all the *filthineſs* and licentiouſneſs of life imaginable. *South's Sermons.*

FI'LTHY. *adj.* [from *filth.*]
1. Naſty; foul; dirty.
Fair is foul, and foul is fair;
Hover through the fog and *filthy* air. *Shakeſp. Macbeth.*
2. Groſs; polluted.
As all ſtories are not proper ſubjects for an epick poem or a tragedy, ſo neither are they for a noble picture: the ſubjects both of the one and of the other, ought to have nothing of immoral, low, or *filthy* in them. *Dryden's Dufreſnoy.*

To FI'LTRATE. *v. a.* [from *filter.*] To ſtrain; to percolate; to filter.
The extract obtained by the former operation, burnt to aſhes, and thoſe aſhes boiled in water and *filtrated*, yield a fiery ſalt. *Arbuthnot on Aliments.*

FI'LTRATION. *n. ſ.* [from *filtrate.*] A method by which liquors are procured fine and clear. The filtration in uſe is ſtraining a liquor through paper, which, by the ſmallneſs of its pores, admits only the finer parts through, and keeps the reſt behind. *Quincy.*
We took then common nitre, and having, by the uſual way of ſolution, *filtration*, and coagulation, reduced it into cryſtals, we put four ounces of this purified nitre into a ſtrong new crucible. *Boyle.*

FI'MBLE *Hemp. n. ſ.*
The ſeaſon of pulling of it is firſt about Lambas, when good part of it will be ripe; that is, the light Summer hemp, that bears no ſeed, which is called *fimble hemp. Mortim. Husb.*
Good flax and good hemp, for to have of her own,
In May a good houſewife will ſee it be ſown;
And afterwards trim it, to ſerve at a need,
The *fimble* to ſpin, and the carle for her ſeed. *Tuſſ. Husb.*

FIN. *n. ſ.* [ꝼın, Saxon; *vin*, Dutch.] The wing of a fiſh; the limb by which he balances his body, and moves in the water.
He that depends
Upon your favours, ſwims with *fins* of lead,
And hews down oaks with ruſhes. *Shakeſpeare's Othello.*
Their *fins* conſiſt of a number of griſtly bones, long and ſlender, like pins and needles. *More's Antid. againſt Atheiſm.*
Thus at half-ebb a rowling ſea
Returns, and wins upon the ſhore;
The watry herd, affrighted at the roar,
Reſt on their *fins* awhile, and ſtay,
Then backward take their wond'ring way. *Dryden.*
Still at his oar th' induſtrious Libys plies;
But as he plies, each buſy arm ſhrinks in,
And by degrees is faſhion'd to a *fin*. *Addiſ. Ovid's Metam.*

FIN-FOO'TED. *adj.* [*fin* and *foot*] Palmipedous; having feet with membranes between the toes.

It is described like fissipedes, or birds which have their feet or claws divided; whereas it is palmipedous or *fin-footed*, like swans and geese, according to the method of nature in latirostrous or flat-billed birds; which being generally swimmers, the organ is wisely contrived unto the action, and they are framed with fins or oars upon their feet. *Brown's Vulg. Err.*

FI'NABLE. *adj.* [from *fine.*] That admits a fine.

This is the order for writs of covenant that be *finable*. *Bac.*

He sent letters to the council, wherein he acknowledged himself favoured in bringing his cause *finable*. *Hayward.*

FI'NAL. *adj.* [*final*, French; *finalis*, Latin.]

1. Ultimate; last.

And over them triumphant death his dart
Shook; but delay'd to strike, though oft invok'd
With vows, as their chief good, and *final* hope. *Milt. P. L.*

2. Conclusive; decisive.

There be many examples where sea-fights have been *final* to the war. *Bacon, Essay* 30.

Henry spent his reign in establishing himself, and had neither leisure nor opportunity to undertake the *final* conquest of Ireland. *Davies on Ireland.*

3. Mortal; destructive.

At last resolv'd to work his *final* smart,
He lifted up his hand, but back again did start. *Fai. Queen.*

4. Respecting the end or motive.

Some things in such sort are allowed, that they be also required as necessary unto salvation, by way of direct, immediate, and proper necessity *final*; so that, without performance of them, they cannot by ordinary course be saved, nor by any means be excluded from life, observing them. *Hooker, b.* ii.

By its gravity fire raises the water in pumps, siphons, and other engines; and performs all those feats which former philosophers, through ignorance of the efficient cause, attributed to a *final*, namely, nature's abhorrence of a vacuity. *Ray.*

Your answering in the *final* cause, makes me believe you are at a loss for the efficient. *Collier on Thought.*

FI'NALLY. *adv.* [from *final.*]

1. Ultimately; lastly; in conclusion.

Sight bereav'd
May chance to number thee with those
Whom patience *finally* must crown. *Milton's Agonistes.*

2. Completely; without recovery.

Their houses were many times in danger of ruin; yet was there not any house of noble English in Ireland utterly destroyed, or *finally* rooted out by the hand of justice, but the house of Desmond only. *Davies on Ireland.*

Doubtlesly many men are *finally* lost, who yet have no mens sins to answer for but their own. *South's Sermons.*

FI'NANCE. *n. s.* [French.] Revenue; income; profit. It is seldom used in the singular.

This sort of *finance* hath been increased by this new device. *Bacon's Off. of Alienation.*

The residue of these ordinary *finances* be casual or uncertain; as be the escheats and forfeitures. *Bacon.*

His pretence for making war upon his neighbours was their pyracies, though he practised the same trade when he was straitened in his *finances* at the siege of Byzantium. *Arbuthnot.*

FI'NANCIER. n. s. [French.] One who collects or farms the publick revenue.

FI'NARY. *n. s.* [from *To fine.*] In the iron works, the second forge at the iron mills. *Dict.*

FINCH. *n. s.* [ꝼinc, Saxon.] A small bird of which we have three kinds, the goldfinch, chaffinch, and bulfinch.

To FIND. *v. a.* [ꝼinꝺan, Saxon; *vinden*, Dutch.]

1. To obtain by searching or seeking.

Ask, and it shall be given you; seek, and ye shall *find*. *Matt.* vii. 7.

Whereas thou hast searched all my stuff, what hast thou *found* of all thy houshold stuff? *Gen.* xxxi. 37.

A bird that flies about,
And beats itself against the cage,
Finding at last no passage out,
It sits and sings. *Cowley.*

2. To obtain something lost.

When he hath *found* his sheep, he layeth it on his shoulders rejoicing. *Luke* xv. 5.

In my school days, when I had lost one shaft,
I shot his fellow of the self-same flight
The self-same way, with more advised watch,
To *find* the other forth; by vent'ring both,
I oft *found* both. *Shakespeare's Merchant of Venice.*

3. To meet with; to fall upon.

There watchful at the gate they *find*
Suspicion with her eyes behind. *Dodsley's Miscell.*
In woods and forests thou art *found*. *Cowley.*
The bad must miss, the good unsought shall *find*. *Pope.*

4. To know by experience.

How oft will he
Of thy chang'd faith complain!
And his fortunes *find* to be
So airy and so vain! *Cowley.*

The torrid zone is now *found* habitable. *Cowley.*

5. To discover by study.

Physicians
With sharpen'd sight some remedies may *find*. *Dryden.*
Thy maid! ah, *find* some nobler theme,
Whereon thy doubts to place. *Cowley.*

6. To discover what is hidden.

A curse on him who *found* the oar. *Cowley.*

7. To hit on by chance; to perceive by accident.

They build on sands, which if unmov'd they *find*,
'Tis but because there was no wind. *Cowley.*

8. To gain by any mental endeavour.

If we for happiness could leisure *find*,
And wand'ring time into a method bind,
We should not then the great mens favour need. *Cowley.*
We oft review, each *finding* like a friend
Something to blame, and something to commend. *Pope.*

9. To remark; to observe.

Beauty or wit in all I *find*. *Cowley.*

10. To detect; to deprehend; to catch.

When first *found* in a lie, talk to him of it as a strange monstrous matter, and so shame him out of it. *Locke.*

11. To reach; to attain.

They are glad when they can *find* the grave. *Job* iii. 22.
He did the utmost bounds of knowledge *find*,
Yet found them not so large as was his mind. *Cowley.*

12. To meet.

A clear conscience and heroick mind,
In ills their business and their glory *find*. *Cowley.*

13. To settle; to fix any thing in one's own opinion.

Some men
The marks of old and catholick would *find*. *Cowley.*

14. To determine by judicial verdict.

His peers, upon this evidence,
Have *found* him guilty of high treason. *Shakesp. Hen.* VIII.

15. To supply; to furnish: as, he *finds* me in money and in victuals.

16. [In law.] To approve: as, to *find* a bill.

17. *To* FIND *himself*. To be; to fare with regard to ease or pain, health or sickness.

Pray, sir, how d'ye *find yourself*? says the doctor. *L'Estr.*

18. *To* FIND *out*. To unriddle; to solve.

The *finding out* of parables is a wearisome labour of the mind. *Ecclus.* xiii. 26.

19. *To* FIND *out*. To discover something hidden.

Can'st thou by searching *find out* God? Can'st thou *find out* the Almighty unto perfection? *Job* ii. 7.

There are agents in nature able to make the particles of bodies stick together by very strong attractions, and it is the business of experimental philosophy to *find* them *out*. *Newton.*

What hinders then, but that thou *find* her *out*,
And hurry her away by manly force? *Addison's Cato.*

20. *To* FIND *out*. To obtain the knowledge of.

The principal part of painting is to *find out* and thoroughly to understand what nature has made most beautiful. *Dryden.*

21. *To* FIND *out*. To invent; to excogitate.

A man of Tyre, skilful to work in gold, and to *find out* every device which shall be put to him. *2 Chron.* ii. 14.

22. The particle *out* is added often without any other use than that it adds some force or emphasis to the verb.

While she proudly march'd about,
Greater conquests to *find out*,
She beat out Susan by the by. *Cowley.*

It is agreeable to compare the face of a great man with the character, and to try if we can *find out* in his looks and features either the haughty, cruel, or merciful temper. *Addison.*

He was afraid of being insulted with Greek; for which reason he desired a friend to *find* him *out* a clergyman rather of plain sense than much learning. *Addison's Spectator.*

FI'NDER. *n. s.* [from *find.*]

1. One that meets or falls upon any thing.

We will bring the device to the bar, and crown thee for a *finder* of mad men. *Shakespeare's Twelfth Night.*

2. One that picks up any thing lost.

Some lewd squeaking cryer,
Well pleas'd with one lean thread-bare groat for hire,
May like a devil roar through every street,
And gall the *finder*'s conscience, if they meet. *Donne.*
O yes! if any happy eye
This roving wanton shall descry,
Let the *finder* surely know
Mine is the wag; 'tis I that owe
The winged wand'rer. *Crashaw.*

FINDFA'ULT. *n. s.* [*find* and *fault.*] A censurer; a caviller.

We are the makers of manners, Kate; and the liberty that follows our places, stops the mouth of all *findfaults*. *Shakesp.*

FI'NDY. *adj.* [ꝼynꝺiᵹ, Saxon.] Plump; weighty; firm; solid. Thus the proverb,

A cold May and a windy,
Makes the barn fat and *findy*.

means that it stores the barn with plump and firm grain. *Jun.*

FINE. *adj.* [*finne*, French; *fijn*, Dutch and Erse, perhaps from *finitus*, completed, Latin.]

1. Not coarse.

Not any skill'd in loops of fingering *fine*,
With this so curious net-work might compare. *Spenser.*

He was arrayed in purple and *fine* linen. *Luke.*

2. Refined; pure; free from dross.

Two vessels of *fine* copper, precious as gold. *Ezra* viii. 27.

3. Subtle; thin; tenuous: as, the *fine* spirits evaporate.

4. Refined; subtilely excogitated.

In substance he promised himself money, honour, friends, and peace in the end; but those things were too *fine* to be fortunate, and succeed in all parts. *Bacon.*

Whether the scheme has not been pursued so far as to draw it into practice, or whether it be too *fine* to be capable of it, I will not determine. *Temple.*

5. Keen; thin; smoothly sharp.

Great affairs are commonly too rough and stubborn to be wrought upon by the *finer* edges or points of wit. *Bacon.*

6. Clear; pellucid; transparent: as, the wine is *fine*.

7. Nice; exquisite; delicate.

Are they not senseless then, that think the soul
Nought but a *fine* perfection of the sense. *Davies.*

The irons of planes are set *fine* or rank: they are set *fine*, when they stand so shallow below the sole of the plane, that in working they take off a thin shaving. *Moxon's Mech. Exer.*

8. Artful; dexterous.

The wisdom of all these latter times, in princes affairs, is rather *fine* deliveries, and shiftings of dangers and mischiefs, than solid and grounded courses to keep them aloof. *Bacon.*

9. Fraudulent; sly; knavishly subtle.

Through his *fine* handling, and his cleanly play,
He all those royal signs had stol'n away. *Hubberd's Tale.*

10. Elegant; with elevation.

To call the trumpet by the name ofthe metal was*fine*. *Dry.*

11. Applied to person, it means beautiful with dignity.

12. Accomplished; elegant of manners.

He was not only the *finest* gentleman of his time, but one of the *finest* scholars. *Felton on the Classicks.*

13. Showy; splendid.

It is with a *fine* genius as with a *fine* fashion; all those are displeased at it who are not able to follow it. *Pope.*

The satirical part of mankind will needs believe, that it is not impossible to be very *fine* and very filthy. *Swift.*

14. [Ironically.] Something that will serve the purpose; something worth contemptuous notice.

That same knave, Ford, her husband, hath the *finest* mad devil of jealousy in him, master Brook, that ever governed frenzy. *Shakespeare's Merry Wives of Windsor.*

They taught us, indeed, to cloath, to dwell in houses,
To feast, to sleep on down, to be profuse:
A *fine* exchange for liberty. *Phillips's Briton.*

FINE. *n. s.* [*ffin*, Cimbr.]

1. A mulct; a pecuniary punishment.

The killing of an Irishman was not punished by our law, as manslaughter, which is felony and capital; but by a *fine* or pecuniary punishment, called an ericke. *Davies on Ireland.*

2. Penalty.

Ev'n this ill night your breathing shall expire,
Paying the *fine* of rated treachery. *Shakesp. King John.*

3. Forfeit; money paid for any exemption or liberty.

The spirit of wantonness is sure scared out of him: if the devil have him not in fee-simple, with *fine* and recovery, he will never, I think, in the way of waste, attempt us again. *Shakespeare's Merry Wives of Windsor.*

Beside *fines* set upon plays, games, balls and feasting, they have many customs which contribute to their simplicity. *Addis.*

How vain that second life in others breath,
Th' estate which wits inherit after death!
Ease, health, and life for this they must resign,
Unsure the tenure, but how vast the *fine*! *Pope.*

4. [From *finis*, Latin; *fin*, *enfin*, French.] The end; conclusion. It is seldom used but adverbially, *in fine*.

In fine, whatsoever he was, he was nothing but what it pleased Zelmane, the powers of his spirit depending of her. *Sid.*

His resolution, *in fine*, is, that in the church a number of things are strictly observed, whereof no law of scripture maketh mention one way or other. *Hooker, b.* ii. *s.* 5.

Still the *fine*'s the crown;
Whate'er the course, the end is the renown. *Shakespeare.*

Your daughter, ere she seems as won,
Desires this ring; appoints him an encounter;
In fine, delivers me to fill the time,
Herself most chastly absent. *Shak. All's well that ends well.*

The blessings of fortune are the lowest: the next are the bodily advantages of strength and health; but the superlative blessings, *in fine*, are those of the mind. *L'Estrange.*

In fine, he wears no limbs about him sound,
With sores and sicknesses beleaguer'd round. *Dryden's Juv.*

In fine, let there be a perfect relation betwixt the parts and the whole, that they may be entirely of a piece. *Dryden.*

To FINE. *v. a.* [from *fine*, the adjective.]

1. To refine; to purify.

The *fining* pot is for silver, and the furnace for gold. *Prov.*

There is a vein for the silver, and a place for gold, where they *fine* it. *Job* xxviii. 1.

2. To embellish; to decorate. Now not in use.

Hugh Capet also, who usurp'd the crown,
To *fine* his title with some shews of truth,
Convey'd himself as heir to th' lady Lingare. *Shakes. H. V.*

3. To make less coarse.

It *fines* the grass, but makes it short, though thick. *Mortim.*

4. To make transparent.

It is good also for fuel, not to omit the shavings of it for the *fining* of wine. *Mortimer's Husbandry.*

5. [From the substantive.] To punish with pecuniary penalty.

To *fine* men one third of their fortune, without any crime committed, seems very hard. *Locke.*

To FINE. *v. n.* To pay a fine.

What poet ever *fin'd* for sheriff? or who
By rhymes and verse did ever lord mayor grow? *Oldham.*

To FINEDRA'W. *v. a.* [*fine* and *draw*.] To sow up a rent with so much nicety that it is not perceived.

FINEDRA'WER. *n. s.* [from *finedraw*.] One whose business is to sow up rents.

FINEFI'NGERED. *adj.* [*fine* and *finger*.] Nice; artful; exquisite.

The most *finefinger'd* workman on the ground,
Arachne, by his means was vanquished. *Spenser.*

FI'NELY. *adv.* [from *fine*.]

1. Beautifully; elegantly; more than justly.

Plutarch says very *finely*, that a man should not allow himself to hate even his enemies; because, says he, if you indulge this passion on some occasions, it will rise of itself in others. *Addison's Spectator*, N°. 125.

The walls are painted, and represent the labours of Hercules: many of them look very *finely*, though a great part of the work has been cracked. *Addison on Italy.*

2. Keenly; sharply; with a thin edge or point.

Get you black lead, sharpened *finely*, and put it into quills. *Peacham on Drawing.*

3. Not coarsely; not meanly; gaily.

He was alone, save that he had two persons of honour, on either hand one, *finely* attired in white. *Bacon's New Atlantis.*

4. In small parts; subtilly; not grossly.

Saltpetre was but grossly beaten; for it should not be *finely* powdered. *Boyle.*

5. [Ironically.] Wretchedly; in such a manner as to deserve contemptuous notice.

Let laws be made to obey, and not to be obeyed, and you will find that kingdom *finely* governed in a short time. *South.*

For him she loves:
She nam'd not me; that may be Torrismond,
Whom she has thrice in private seen this day:
Then I am *finely* caught in my own snare. *Dryd. Sp. Fryar.*

FI'NENESS. *n. s.* [from *fine*.]

1. Elegance; beauty; delicacy.

Every thing was full of a choice *fineness*, that, if it wanted any thing in majesty, it supplied with increase in pleasure; and if at the first it struck not admiration, it ravished with delight. *Sidney.*

The softness of her sex, and the *fineness* of her genius, conspire to give her a very distinguishing character. *Prior.*

2. Show; splendour; gaiety of appearance.

The *fineness* of cloaths destroys the ease: it often helps men to pain, but can never rid them of any: the body may languish under the most splendid cover. *Decay of Piety.*

3. Subtility; artfulness; ingenuity.

Those, with the *fineness* of their souls,
By reason guide his execution. *Shakesp. Troil. and Cressida.*

4. Purity; freedom from dross or base mixtures.

Our works are, indeed, nought else
But the protractive tryals of great Jove,
To find persistive constancy in men;
The *fineness* of which metal is not found
In fortune's love. *Shakespeare's Troilus and Cressida.*

I am doubtful whether men have sufficiently refined metals; as whether iron, brass, and tin be refined to the height: but when they come to such a *fineness* as serveth the ordinary use, they try no farther. *Bacon's Natural History.*

The ancients were careful to coin their money in due weight and *fineness*, only in times of exigence they have diminished both the weight and *fineness*. *Arbuthnot on Coins.*

FI'NERY. *n. s.* [from *fine*.] Show; splendour of appearance; gaiety of colours.

Dress up your houses and your images,
And put on all the city's *finery*,
To consecrate this day a festival. *Southern.*

The capacities of a lady are sometimes apt to fall short in cultivating cleanliness and *finery* together. *Swift.*

Don't chuse your place of study by the *finery* of the prospects, or the most various scenes of sensible things. *Watts.*

FINE'SSE. *n. ſ.* [French.] Artifice; ſtratagem: an unneceſſary word which is creeping into the language.

A circumſtance not much to be ſtood upon, in caſe it were not upon ſome *fineſs.* *Hayward.*

Fi'ner. *n. ſ.* [from *fine.*] One who purifies metals.

Take away the droſs from the ſilver, and there ſhall come forth a veſſel for the *finer.* *Prov.* xxv. 4.

FI'NGER. *n. ſ.* [ꝼinᵹeꞃ, Saxon, from *fangen,* to hold.]

1. The flexible member of the hand by which men catch and hold.

The *fingers* and thumb in each hand conſiſt of fifteen bones, there being three to each *finger:* they are a little convex and round towards the back of the hand, but hollow and plain towards the palm, except the laſt, where the nails are. The order of their diſpoſitions is called firſt, ſecond, and third phalanx: the firſt is longer than the ſecond, and the ſecond longer than the third. The upper extremity of the firſt bone on each *finger* has a little ſinus, which receives the round head of the bones of the metacarpus. The upper extremity of the ſecond and third bones of each *finger* hath two ſmall ſinuſes, parted by a ſmall protuberance; and the lower extremity of the firſt and ſecond bones of each *finger* has two protuberances, divided by a ſmall ſinus: the two protuberances are received into the two ſinuſes of the upper extremity of the ſecond and third bones; and the ſmall ſinus receives the little protuberance of the ſame end of the ſame bones. The firſt bone of the thumb is like the bones of the metacarpus, and it is joined to the wriſt and ſecond of the thumb, as they are to the wriſt and firſt of the *fingers.* The ſecond bone of the thumb is like the firſt bones of the *fingers,* and it is joined to the firſt and third, as they are to the bones of the metacarpus and ſecond of the *fingers.* The *fingers* are moved ſideways only upon their firſt joint. Beſides theſe there are ſome ſmall bones, called *oſſa ſeſamoidea,* becauſe they reſemble ſeſamum grains: they are reckoned about twelve in each hand: they are placed at the joint of the fingers, under the tendons of the flexors, to which they ſerve as pullies. *Quincy.*

You ſeem to underſtand me,
By each at once her choppy *finger* laying
Upon her ſkinny lips. *Shakeſpeare's Macbeth.*

Diogenes, who is never ſaid,
For aught that ever I could read,
To whine, put *finger* i' th' eye and ſob,
Becauſe h' had ne'er another tub. *Hudibras.*

The hand is divided into four *fingers* bending forward, and one oppoſite to them bending backwards, and of greater ſtrength than any of them ſingly, which we call the thumb, to join with them ſeverally or united; whereby it is fitted to lay hold of objects of any ſize or quantity. *Ray on the Creat.*

A hand of a vaſt extenſion, and a prodigious number of *fingers* playing upon all the organ pipes of the world, and making every one ſound a particular note. *Keil againſt Burnet.*

Poor Peg ſewed, ſpun, and knit for a livelihood, 'till her *finger* ends were ſore. *Arbuthnot's Hiſt. of John Bull.*

2. A ſmall meaſure of extenſion.

Go now, go truſt the wind's uncertain breath,
Remov'd four *fingers* from approaching death;
Or ſeven at moſt, when thickeſt is the board. *Dryd. Juv.*

One of theſe bows with a little arrow did pierce through a piece of ſteel three *fingers* thick. *Wilkins's Math. Mag.*

3. The hand; the inſtrument of work; manufacture; art.

Fool, that forgets her ſtubborn look
This ſoftneſs from thy *finger* took. *Waller.*

To Fi'nger. *v. a.* [from the noun.]

1. To touch lightly; to toy with.

Go, get you gone, and let the papers lie;
You would be *fingering* them to anger me. *Shakeſpeare.*

One that is covetous is not ſo highly pleaſed with the meer ſight and *fingering* of money, as with the thoughts of his being conſidered as a wealthy man. *Grew's Coſmol. Sac.*

2. To touch unſeaſonably or thieviſhly.

His ambition would needs be *fingering* the ſcepter, and hoiſting him into his father's throne. *South's Sermons.*

3. To touch an inſtrument of muſick.

She hath broke the lute;
I did but tell her ſhe miſtook her frets,
And bow'd her hand to teach her *fingering.* *Shakeſpeare.*

4. To perform any work exquiſitely with the fingers.

Not any ſkill'd in loops of *fingering* fine,
With this ſo curious net-work might compare. *Spenſer.*

Fi'nglefangle. *n. ſ.* [from *fangle.*] A trifle: a burleſque word.

We agree in nothing but to wrangle,
About the ſlighteſt *fiᵹlefangle.* *Hudibras, p.* iii. *cau.* 3.

Fi'nical. *adj.* [from *fine.*] Nice; foppiſh; pretending to ſuperfluous elegance.

A whorſon, glaſſgazing, ſuperſerviceable, *finical* rogue. *Shakeſpeare's King Lear.*

I cannot hear a *finical* fop romancing, how the king took him aſide at ſuch a time; what the queen ſaid to him at another. *L'Eſtrange, Fable* 34.

Fi'nically. *adv.* [from *finical.*] Foppiſhly.

Fi'nicalness. *n. ſ.* [from *finical.*] Superfluous nicety; foppery.

To FI'NISH. *v. a.* [*finir,* French; *finio,* Latin.]

1. To bring to the end purpoſed; to complete.

For which of you, intending to build a tower, ſitteth not down firſt and counteth the coſt, whether he have ſufficient to *finiſh* it? *Luke* xiv. 28.

As he had begun, ſo he would alſo *finiſh* in you the ſame grace. 2 *Cor.* viii. 6.

A poet uſes epiſodes; but epiſodes, taken ſeparately, *finiſh* nothing. *Notes on the Odyſſey.*

2. To perfect; to poliſh to the excellency intended.

Though here you all perfection ſhould not find,
Yet is it all th' Eternal Will deſign'd;
It is a *finiſh'd* work, and perfect in his kind. *Blackmore.*

I would make what bears your name as *finiſhed* as my laſt work ought to be; that is, more *finiſhed* than the reſt. *Pope.*

3. To end; to put an end to.

Fi'nisher. *n. ſ.* [from *finiſh.*]

1. Performer; accompliſher.

He that of greateſt works is *finiſher,*
Oft does them by the weakeſt miniſter. *Shakeſpeare.*

2. One that puts an end; ender.

This was the plain condition of thoſe times; the whole world againſt Athanaſius, and Athanaſius againſt it: half an hundred of years ſpent in doubtful trials which of the two, in the end, would prevail; the ſide which had all, or elſe that part which had no friend but God and death, the one a defender of his innocency, the other a *finiſher* of all his troubles. *Hooker, b.* v. *ſ.* 42.

3. One that completes or perfects.

The author and *finiſher* of our faith. *Hebrews.*

O prophet of glad tidings! *finiſher*
Of utmoſt hope! *Milton's Paradiſe Loſt, b.* xii.

FI'NITE. *adj.* [*finitus,* Latin.] Limited; bounded; terminated.

Servius conceives no more thereby than a *finite* number for indefinite. *Brown's Vulgar Errours, b.* iv. *c.* 12.

Finite of any magnitude holds not any proportion to infinite. *Locke.*

That ſuppoſed infinite duration will, by the very ſuppoſition, be limited at two extremes, though never ſo remote aſunder, and conſequently muſt needs be *finite.* *Bentley's Serm.*

Fi'niteless. *adj.* [from *finite.*] Without bounds; unlimited.

It is ridiculous unto reaſon, and *finiteleſs* as their deſires. *Brown's Vulgar Errours.*

Fi'nitely. *adv.* [from *finite.*] Within certain limits; to a certain degree.

They are creatures ſtill, and that ſets them at an infinite diſtance from God; whereas all their excellencies can make them but *finitely* diſtant from us. *Stillingfleet.*

Fi'niteness. *n. ſ.* [from *finite.*] Limitation; confinement within certain boundaries.

I ought now to unbay the current of my paſſion, and love without other boundary than what is ſet by the *finiteneſs* of my natural powers. *Norris.*

Fi'nitude. *n. ſ.* [from *finite.*] Limitation; confinement within certain boundaries.

Finitude, applied to natural or created things, imports the proportions of the ſeveral degrees of affections, or properties of theſe things to one another; infinitude, the unboundedneſs of theſe degrees of affections, or properties. *Cheyne.*

Fi'nless. *adj.* [from *fin.*] Without fins.

He angers me
With telling of the moldwarp and the ant,
And of a dragon and a *finleſs* fiſh. *Shakeſp. Henry* IV.

Fi'nlike. *adj.* [*fin* and *like.*] Formed in imitation of fins.

In ſhipping ſuch as this, the Iriſh kern
And untaught Indian, on the ſtream did glide;
Ere ſharp-keel'd boats to ſtem the flood did learn,
Or *finlike* oars did ſpread from either ſide. *Dryd. Ann. Mir.*

Fi'nned. *adj.* [from *fin.*] Having broad edges ſpread out on either ſide.

They plow up the turf with a broad *finned* plough. *Mor*

Fi'nny. *adj.* [from *fin.*] Furniſhed with fins; forme the element of water.

High o'er the main in wat'ry pomp he rides,
His azure car and *finny* courſers guides;
Proteus his name. *Dryden's Virg. Georg.*

New herds of beaſts he ſends the plains to ſhare;
New colonies of birds to people air;
And to their oozy beds the *finny* fiſh repair. *Dryd. Ovid.*

While black with ſtorms the ruffled ocean rolls,
And from the fiſher's art defends her *finny* ſhoals. *Black*

With hairy ſpringes we the birds betray;
Slight lines of hair ſurprize the *finny* prey. *Pope.*

Fi'ntoed. *adj.* [*fin* and *toe.*] Palmipedous; having a membrane between the toes.

Such creatures as are whole footed, or *fintoed,* viz. ſome birds and quadrupeds, are naturally directed to go into the water and ſwim there. *Ray on the Crea*

FI'NOCHIO. *n. s.* See FENNEL, of which plant it is a species.

FI'PPLE. *n. s.* [from *fibula*, Latin.] A stopper.

You must know, that in recorders, which go with a gentle breath, the concave of the pipe, were it not for the *fipple* that straitneth the air, much more than the simple concave, would yield no sound. *Bacon's Natural History.*

FIR. *n. s.* [*fyrr*, Welsh; ꝼuꞃh, Saxon; *fyr*, Danish.] The tree of which deal-boards are made.

It is ever green: the leaves are single, and for the most part produced on every side of the branches: the male flowers, or catkins, are placed at remote distances from the fruit on the same tree. The seeds are propagated on cones, which are squamose. See PINE-TREE. *Miller.*

He covered the floor of the house with planks of *fir*. 1 *Kings.*

The 'spiring *fir* and stately box adorn. *Pope.*

FIRE. *n. s.* [ꝼẏꞃ, Saxon; *fewr*, German.]

1. The igneous element.
2. Any thing burning.

A little *fire* is quickly trodden out,
Which, being suffer'd, rivers cannot quench. *Shakes. H. VI.*

Where two raging *fires* meet together,
They do consume the thing that feeds their fury. *Shakesp.*

So contraries on Etna's top conspire;
Here hoary frosts, and by them breaks out *fire*. *Cowley.*

3. A conflagration of towns or countries.

There is another liberality to the citizens, who had suffered damage by a great *fire*. *Arbuthnot on Coins.*

Though safe thou think'st thy treasure lies,
Conceal'd in chests from human eyes,
A *fire* may come, and it may be
Bury'd, my friend, as far from thee. *Granville.*

4. Flame; light; lustre.

Stars, hide your *fires*!
Let not night see my black and deep desires! *Shakes. Macb.*

5. Torture by burning.

Did Shadrach's zeal my glowing breast inspire,
To weary tortures, and rejoice in *fire*? *Prior.*

6. The punishment of the damned.

Who among us shall dwell with the devouring *fire*? Who among us shall dwell with everlasting burnings? *Isa.* xxxiii.

7. Any thing provoking; any thing that inflames the passions.

What *fire* is in my ears? Can this be true?
Stand I condemn'd for pride and scorn so much? *Shakesp.*

8. Ardour of temper; violence of passion.

He had *fire* in his temper, and a German bluntness; and, upon provocations, might strain a phrase. *Atterbury.*

9. Liveliness of imagination; vigour of fancy; intellectual activity; force of expression; spirit of sentiment.

Nor can the snow that age does shed
Upon thy rev'rend head,
Quench or allay the noble *fire* within,
But all that youth can be thou art. *Cowley.*

They have no notion of life and *fire* in fancy and in words, and any thing that is just in grammar and in measure is good oratory and poetry to them. *Felton on the Classicks.*

He brings
The reasoner's weapons and the poet's *fire*. *Blackmore.*

Exact Racin, and Corneille's noble *fire*,
Taught us that France had something to admire. *Pope.*

The bold Longinus all the nine inspire,
And warm the critick with a poet's *fire*. *Pope.*

Oh may some spark of your celestial *fire*,
The last, the meanest of your sons inspire. *Pope.*

10. The passion of love.

Love various hearts does variously inspire,
It stirs in gentle bosoms gentle *fire*,
Like that of incense on the altar laid;
But raging flames tempestuous souls invade;
A *fire* which every windy passion blows,
With pride it mounts, and with revenge it glows. *Dryden.*

The *fire* of love in youthful blood,
Like what is kindled in brush-wood,
But for a moment burns. *Shadwell.*

The god of love retires;
Dim are his torches, and extinct his *fires*. *Pope.*

New charms shall still increase desire,
And time's swift wing shall fan the *fire*. *Moore's Fables.*

11. Eruptions or imposthumations: as, St. Anthony's *fire*.
12. *To set* FIRE *on*, or *set on* FIRE. To kindle; to inflame.

Hermosilla courageously set upon the horsemen, and set *fire* also upon the stables where the Turks horses stood. *Knolles.*

He that set a *fire* on a plane-tree to spite his neighbour, and the plane-tree set on his neighbour's house, is bound to pay all the loss, because it did all rise from his own ill intention. *Taylor's Rule of living holy.*

FI'REARMS. *n. s.* [*fire* and *arms*.] Arms which owe their efficacy to fire; guns.

Nor had they ammunition to supply their few *firearms*: horses they had, and officers they had, which made all their shew. *Clarendon, b.* ii.

Before the use of *firearms* there was infinitely more scope for personal valour than in the modern battles. *Pope.*

FI'REBALL. *s. n.* [*fire* and *ball*.] Grenado; ball filled with combustibles, and bursting where it is thrown.

Judge of those insolent boasts of conscience; which, like so many *fireballs*, or mouth grenadoes, are thrown at our church. *South's Sermons.*

The same great man hath sworn to make us swallow his coin in *fireballs*. *Swift.*

FI'REBRUSH. *n. s.* [*fire* and *brush*.] The brush which hangs by the fire to sweep the hearth.

When you are ordered to stir up the fire, clean away the ashes from betwixt the bars with the *firebrush*. *Swift.*

FI'REDRAKE. *n. s.* [*fire* and *drake*.] A fiery serpent: I suppose the prester.

By the hissing of the snake,
The rustling of the *firedrake*,
I charge thee thou this place forsake,
Nor of queen Mab be prattling. *Drayton's Nymphia.*

FI'RENEW. *adj.* [*fire* and *new*.] New from the forge; new from the melting-house.

Armado is a most illustrious wight,
A man of *firenew* words, fashion's own knight. *Shakesp.*

Some excellent jests, *firenew* from the mint. *Shakespeare.*

Upon the wedding-day I put myself, according to custom, in another suit *firenew*, with silver buttons to it. *Addis. Guard.*

FI'REPAN. *n. s.* [*fire* and *pan*.] Vessel of metal to carry fire.

His *firepans*, and all the vessels thereof, thou shalt make of brass. *Ex.* xxvii. 3.

Pour of it upon a *firepan* well heated, as they do rosewater and vinegar. *Bacon's Natural History.*

FI'RER. *n. s.* [from *fire*.] An incendiary.

Others burned Moussel, and the rest marched as a guard for defence of these *firers*. *Carew's Survey of Cornwall.*

FI'RESIDE. *n. s.* [*fire* and *side*.] The hearth; the chimney; the focus.

My judgment is, that they ought all to be despised, and ought to serve but for Winter talk by the *fireside*. *Bacon.*

By his *fireside* he starts the hare,
And turns her in his wicker chair:
His feet, however lame, you find,
Have got the better of his mind. *Prior.*

What art thou asking of them, after all? Only to sit quietly at thy own *fireside*. *Arbuthnot's Hist. of John Bull.*

FI'RESTICK. *n. s.* [*fire* and *stick*.] A lighted stick or brand.

Children, when they play with *firesticks*, move and whirle them round so fast, that the motion will cozen their eyes, and represent an intire circle of fire to them. *Digby on Bodies.*

FI'REWORK. *n. s.* [*fire* and *work*.] Shows of fire; pyrotechnical performances.

The king would have me present the princess with some delightful ostentation, or pageant, or antick, or *firework*. *Shak.*

We represent also ordnance, and new mixtures of gunpowder, wildfires burning in water and unquenchable; and also *fireworks* of all variety. *Bacon's New Atlantis.*

The ancients were imperfect in the doctrine of meteors, by their ignorance of gunpowder and *fireworks*. *Brown.*

In *fireworks* give him leave to vent his spite;
Those are the only serpents he can write. *Dryden.*

Our companion proposed a subject for a *firework*, which he thought would be very amusing. *Addison's Guardian.*

Their *fireworks* are made up in paper. *Tatler*, N°. 88.

To FIRE. *v. a.* [from the noun.]

1. To set on fire; to kindle.

They spoiled many parts of the city, and *fired* the houses of those whom they esteemed not to be their friends; but the rage of the fire was at first hindered, and then appeased by the fall of a sudden shower of rain. *Hayward.*

The breathless body, thus bewail'd, they lay,
And *fire* the pile. *Dryden.*

A second Paris, diff'ring but in name,
Shall *fire* his country with a second flame. *Dryden's Æn.*

2. To inflame the passions; to animate.

Yet, if desire of fame, and thirst of pow'r,
A beauteous princess, with a crown in dow'r,
So *fire* your mind, in arms assert your right. *Dryden.*

3. To drive by fire.

He that parts us, shall bring a brand from heav'n
And *fire* us hence. *Shakespeare's King Lear.*

To FIRE. *v. n.*

1. To take fire; to be kindled.
2. To be inflamed with passion.
3. To discharge any firearms.

FIREBRA'ND. *n. s.* [*fire* and *brand*.]

1. A piece of wood kindled.

I have eased my father-in-law of a *firebrand*, to set my own house in a flame. *L'Estrange.*

2. An incendiary; one who inflames factions; one who causes mischief.

Troy must not be, nor goodly Ilion stand;
Our *firebrand* brother, Paris, burns us all. *Shakespeare.*

He sent Surrey with a competent power against the rebels, who fought with the principal band of them, and defeated them, and took alive John Chamber, their *firebrand*. *Bacon.*

FI'RECROSS. *n. s.* [*fire* and *cross.*] A token in Scotland for the nation to take arms: the ends thereof burnt black, and in some parts smeared with blood. It is carried like lightning from one place to another. Upon refusal to send it forward, or to rise, the last person who has it shoots the other dead.

He sent his heralds through all parts of the realm, and commanded the *firecross* to be carried; namely, two firebrands set in fashion of a cross, and pitched upon the point of a spear. *Haywood.*

FI'RELOCK. *n. s.* [*fire* and *lock.*] A soldier's gun; a gun discharged by striking steel with flint.

Prime all your *firelocks*, fasten well the stake. *Gay.*

FI'REMAN. *n. s.* [*fire* and *man.*]

1. One who is employed to extinguish burning houses.

The *fireman* sweats beneath his crooked arms;
A leathern casque his vent'rous head defends,
Boldly he climbs where thickest smoke ascends. *Gay.*

2. A man of violent passions.

I had last night the fate to drink a bottle with two of these *firemen.* *Tatler*, Nº. 61.

FI'REPAN *n. s.* [*fire* and *pan.*]

1. A pan for holding fire.

2. [In a gun.] The receptacle for the priming powder.

FI'RESHIP. *n. s.* [*fire* and *ship.*] A ship filled with combustible matter to fire the vessels of the enemy.

Our men bravely quitted themselves of the *fireship*, by cutting the spritsail tackle. *Wiseman's Surgery.*

FI'RESHOVEL. *n. s.* [*fire* and *shovel.*] The instrument with which the hot coals are thrown up in kitchens.

Nim and Bardolph are sworn brothers in filching; and in Calais they stole a *fireshovel.* *Shakespeare's Henry V.*

Culinary utensils and irons often feel the force of fire; as tongs, *fireshovels*, prongs, and irons. *Brown's Vulgar Errours.*

The neighbours are coming out with forks and *fireshovels*, and spits, and other domestick weapons. *Dryd. Span. Fryar.*

FI'RESTONE. *n. s.* [*fire* and *stone.*]

The *firestone*, or pyrites, is a compound metallick fossil, composed of vitriol, sulphur, and an unmetallick earth, but in very different proportions in the several masses. The most common sort, which is used in medicine, is a greenish shapeless kind found in our clay-pits, out of which the green vitriol or copperas is procured. It has its name of pyrites, or *firestone*, from its giving fire on being struck against a steel much more freely than a flint will do; and all the sparks burn a longer time, and grow larger as they fall, the inflammable matter struck from off the stone burning itself out before the spark becomes extinguished. *Hill's Mat. Med.*

Firestone is a kind of stone called also Rygate stone, from the place whence it is chiefly brought, being very good for firehearths, ovens, and stoves. *Builder's Dict.*

Firestone, if broke small, and laid on cold lands, must be of advantage. *Mortimer's Husbandry.*

FI'REWOOD. *n. s.* [*fire* and *wood.*] Wood to burn; fewel.

FI'RING. *n. s.* [from *fire.*] Fewel.

They burn the cakes, *firing* being there scarce. *Mortimer.*

To FIRK. *v. a.* [from *ferio*, Latin.] To whip; to beat; to correct; to chastise.

Besides, it is not only foppish,
But vile, idolatrous and popish,
For one man out of his own skin
To *firk* and whip another's sin. *Hudibras, p. ii. can. 2.*

FI'RKIN. *n. s.* [from feoper, Saxon, the fourth part of a vessel.]

1. A vessel containing nine gallons.

Strutt's servants get such a haunt about that shop, that it will cost us many a *firkin* of strong beer to bring them back again. *Arbuthnot's History of John Bull.*

2. A small vessel.

You heard of that wonder of the lightning and thunder,
Which made the lye so much the louder;
Now list to another, that miracle's brother,
Which was done with a *firkin* of powder. *Denham.*

FIRM. *adj.* [*firmus*, Latin.]

1. Strong; not easily pierced or shaken; hard, opposed to soft.

The flakes of his flesh are joined together: they are *firm* in themselves, and they cannot be moved. *Job* xli. 23.

Love's artillery then checks
The breastworks of the *firmest* sex. *Cleaveland.*

There is nothing to be left void in a *firm* building; even the cavities ought to be filled with rubbish. *Dryden.*

That body, whose parts are most *firm* in themselves, and are by their peculiar shapes capable of the greatest contacts, is the most *firm*; and that which has parts very small, and capable of the least contact, will be most soft. *Woodward.*

2. Constant; steady; resolute; fixed; unshaken.

We hold *firm* to the works of God, and to the sense which is God's lamp. *Bacon's Natural History.*

He straight obeys;
And *firm* believes. *Milt. Paradise Lost.*

The great encouragement is the assurance of a future reward, the *firm* persuasion whereof is enough to raise us above any thing in this world. *Tillotson, Sermon* 6.

The man that's resolute and just,
Firm to his principles and trust,
Nor hopes nor fears can blind. *Walsh.*

To FIRM. *v. a.* [*firmo*, Latin.]

1. To settle; to confirm; to establish; to fix.

He declared the death of the emperor; which after they had seen to be true, they by another secret and speedy messenger advertised Solyman again thereof, *firming* those letters with all their hands and seals. *Knolles's History of the Turks.*

'Tis ratify'd above by every god,
And Jove has *firm'd* it with an awful nod. *Dryd. Albion.*

The pow'rs, said he,
To you, and your's, and mine, propitious be,
And *firm* our purpose with their augury. *Dryden's Æn.*

Oh thou, who free'st me from my doubtful state,
Long lost and wilder'd in the maze of fate!
Be present still: oh goddess, in our aid
Proceed, and *firm* those omens thou hast made. *Pope's Stat.*

2. To fix without wandering.

He on his card and compass *firms* his eye,
The masters of his long experiment. *Fairy Queen, b.* ii.

FI'RMAMENT. *n. s.* [*firmamentum*, Latin.] The sky; the heavens.

Even to the heavens their shouting shrill
Doth reach, and all the *firmament* doth fill. *Spenser.*

I am constant as the northern star,
Of whose true, fixt, and resting quality,
There is no fellow in the *firmament.* *Shakesp. Jul. Cæsar.*

The Almighty, whose hieroglyphical characters are the unnumbered stars, sun and moon, written on these large volumes of the *firmament.* *Raleigh's History of the World.*

The *firmament* expanse of liquid, pure,
Transparent, elemental air, diffus'd
In circuit to the uttermost convex
Of this great round. *Milton's Paradise Lost, b.* vii.

The steeds climb up the first ascent with pain;
And when the middle *firmament* they gain,
If downward from the heavens my head I bow,
And see the earth and ocean hang below,
Ev'n I am seiz'd with horror. *Addison's Ovid's Metamorph.*

What an immensurable space is the *firmament*, wherein a great number of stars, lesser and lesser, and consequently farther and farther off, are seen with our naked eye, and many more discovered with our glasses! *Derham's Astro-Theology.*

FIRMAME'NTAL. *adj.* [from *firmament.*] Celestial; of the upper regions.

An hollow crystal pyramid he takes,
In *firmamental* waters dipt above. *Dryden's Ann. Mirab.*

FI'RMLY. *adv.* [from *firm.*]

1. Strongly; impenetrably; immoveably.

Thou shalt come of force,
Though thou art *firm'ier* fasten'd than a rock. *Milt. Agonist.*

How very hard particles, which touch only in a few points, can stick together so *firmly*, without something which causes them to be attracted towards one another, is difficult to conceive. *Newton's Opt.*

2. Steadily; constantly.

Himself to be the man the fates require;
I *firmly* judge, and what I judge desire. *Dryden's Æn. b.* vii.

The common people of Lucca are *firmly* persuaded, that one Lucquese can beat five Florentines. *Addison on Italy.*

FI'RMNESS. *n. s.* [from *firm.*]

1. Stability; hardness; compactness; solidity.

It would become by degrees of greater consistency and *firmness*, so as to resemble an habitable earth. *Burnet.*

2. Durability.

Both the easiness and *firmness* of union might be conjectured, for that both people are of the same language. *Hayw.*

3. Certainty; soundness.

In persons already possessed with notions of religion, the understanding cannot be brought to change them, but by great examination of the truth and *firmness* of the one, and the flaws and weakness of the other. *South's Sermons.*

4. Steadiness; constancy; resolution.

That thou should'st my *firmness* doubt
To God, or thee, because we have a foe
May tempt us, I expected not to hear. *Milt. Paradise Lost.*

Nor can th' Egyptian patriarch blame my muse,
Which for his *firmness* does his heat excuse. *Roscommon.*

This armed Job with *firmness* and fortitude. *Atterbury.*

FIRST. *adj.* [fynyт, Saxon.]

1. The ordinal of one; that which is in order before any other.

Thy air,
Thou other gold-bound brow, is like the *first.*
—A third is like the former. *Shakespeare's Macbeth.*

In the six hundreth and *first* year, in the *first* month, the *first* day of the month, the waters were dried up from off the earth. *Gen.* viii. 13.

Arms and the man I sing, the *first* who bore
His course to Latium from the Trojan shore. *Æn.*

2. Earliest in time.

The *first* covenant had also ordinances of divine service. *Heb.* ix. 1.

I find,

I find, quoth Mat, reproof is vain!
Who *first* offend, will *first* complain. *Prior.*

3. Highest in dignity.
Three presidents, of whom Daniel was *first*. *Dan.*
First with the dogs, and king among the squires. *Spect.*

4. Great; excellent.
My *first* son,
Where will you go? Take good Cominius
With thee. *Shakespeare's Coriolanus.*

FIRST. *adv.*

1. Before any thing else; earliest.
He, not unmindful of his usual art,
First in dissembled fire attempts to part;
Then roaring beasts and running streams he tries. *Dryden.*
Thy praise, and thine was then the publick voice,
First recommended Guiscard to my choice. *Dryden.*
Heav'n, sure, has kept this spot of earth uncurst,
To shew how all things were created *first*. *Prior.*

2. Before any other consideration.
First, metals are more durable than plants; secondly, they are more solid and hard; thirdly, they are wholly subterraneous; whereas plants are part above earth, and part under the earth. *Bacon's Natural History*, N°. 603.

3. It has often *at* before it, and means at the beginning.
At first the silent venom slid with ease,
And seiz'd her cooler senses by degrees. *Dryden's Æn.*
Excepting fish and insects, there are very few or no creatures that can provide for themselves *at first*, without the assistance of parents. *Bentley's Sermons.*

4. FIRST *or last*. At one hour or other.
But sure a general doom on man is past,
And all are fools and lovers *first or last*. *Dryden.*

FIRST-BEGOT. } *n. s.* [from *first* and *begot*.] The eldest
FIRST-BEGOTTEN. } of children.
His *first-begot*, we know; and sore have felt,
When his fierce thunder drove us to the deep. *Parad. Reg.*

FIRST-BORN. *n. s.* [*first* and *born*.] Eldest; the first by the order of nativity.
Last, with one midnight stroke, all the *first-born*
Of Egypt must lie dead. *Milton's Paradise Lost*, *b.* xii.
Hail, holy light, offspring of heav'n *first-born!* *Milton.*
The *first-born* has not a sole or peculiar right, by any law of God and nature; the younger children having an equal title with him. *Locke.*

FIRST-FRUITS. *n. s.* [*first* and *fruits*.]

1. What the season first produces or matures of any kind.
A sweaty reaper from his tillage brought
First-fruits, the green ear, and the yellow sheaf. *Milt. P. L.*
The blooming hopes of my then very young patron have been confirmed by most noble *first-fruits*, and his life is going on towards a plentiful harvest of all accumulated virtues. *Prior.*

2. The first profits of any thing.
Although the king loved to employ and advance bishops, because, having rich bishopricks, they carried their reward upon themselves; yet he did use to raise them by steps, that he might not lose the profit of the *first-fruits*, which by that course of gradation was multiplied. *Bacon's Henry* VII.

3. The earliest effect of any thing.
See, Father, what *first-fruits* on earth are sprung,
From thy implanted grace in man! *Milton's Parad. Lost.*

FI'RSTLING. *adj.* [from *first*.] That which is first produced or brought forth.
All the *firstling* males that come of thy herd, and of thy flock, thou shalt sanctify unto the Lord thy God. *Deutr.* xv.

FI'RSTLING. *n. s.* [from *first*.]

1. The first produce or offspring.
A shepherd next,
More meek, came with the *firstlings* of his flock,
Choicest and best. *Milton's Paradise Lost*, *b.* xi.
The tender *firstlings* of my woolly breed,
Shall on his holy altar often bleed. *Dryden's Virg. Past.*
The *firstlings* of the flock are doom'd to die;
Rich fragrant wines the cheering bowl supply. *Pope's Odyss.*

2. The thing first thought or done.
Our play
Leaps o'er the vaunt and *firstlings* of these broils,
'Ginning i' th' middle. *Shakes. Troil. and Cress. Prologue.*
The flighty purpose works o'erlook,
Unless the deed go with it: from this moment,
The very *firstlings* of my heart shall be
The *firstlings* of my hand. *Shakespeare's Macbeth.*

FI'SCAL. *n. s.* [from *fiscus*, a treasury, Latin.] Exchequer; revenue.
War, as it is entertained by diet, so can it not be long maintained by the ordinary *fiscal* and receipt. *Bacon.*

FISH. *n. s.* [ꝼırc, Saxon; *visch*, Dutch.] An animal that inhabits the water.
The beasts, the *fishes*, and the winged fowls,
Are their males subjects. *Shakes. Comedy of Errours.*
I fight when I cannot chuse, and I eat no *fish*. *Sh. K. Lear.*
And now the *fish* ignoble fates escape,
Since Venus ow'd her safety to their shape. *Creech.*
There are *fishes*, that have wings, that are not strangers to the airy region; and there are some birds that are inhabitants of the water, whose blood is cold as *fishes*; and their flesh is so like in taste, that the scrupulous are allowed them on fish-days. *Locke.*

To FISH. *v. n.*

1. To be employed in catching fishes.

2. To endeavour at any thing by artifice.
While others *fish*, with craft, for great opinion,
I, with great truth, catch meer simplicity. *Shakespeare.*

To FISH. *v. a.* To search water in quest of fish, or any thing else.
Some have *fished* the very jakes for papers left there by men of wit. *Swift.*
Oft, as he *fish'd* her nether realms for wit,
The goddess favour'd him, and favours yet. *Pope's Dunciad.*

FISH-HOOK. *n. s.* [*fish* and *hook*.] A hook baited, with which fish are caught.
A sharp point, bended upward and backward, like a *fish-hook*. *Grew's Musæum.*

FISH-POND. *n. s.* [*fish* and *pond*.] A small pool for fish.
Fish-ponds are no small improvement of watry boggy lands. *Mortimer's Husbandry.*
Fish-ponds were made where former forests grew,
And hills were levell'd to extend the view. *Prior.*
After what I have said of the great value the Romans put upon fishes, it will not appear incredible that C. Hirrius should sell his *fish-ponds* for quadragies H. S. 32,291 *l.* 13 *s.* 4 *d.* *Arbuthnot on Coins.*

FI'SHER. *n. s.* [from *fish*.] One who is employed in catching fish.
In our sight the three were taken up
By fishermen of Corinth, as we thought:
At length another had seiz'd on us,
And would have reft the *fishers* of their prey,
Had not they been very slow of sail. *Shakes. Comedy of Err.*
We know that town is but with *fishers* fraught,
Where Theseus govern'd and where Plato taught. *Sandys.*
Lest he should suspect it, draw it from him,
As *fishers* do the bait, to make him follow it. *Denham.*
A soldier now he with his coat appears;
A *fisher* now, his trembling angle bears;
Each shape he varies. *Pope.*

FI'SHERBOAT. *n. s.* [*fisher* and *boat*.] A boat employed in catching fish.

FI'SHERMAN. *n. s.* [*fisher* and *man*.] One whose employment and livelihood is to catch fish.
How fearful
And dizzy 'tis to cast one's eyes so low!
The *fishermen* that walk upon the beach
Appear like mice. *Shakespeare's King Lear.*
At length two monsters of unequal size,
Hard by the shore, a *fisherman* espies. *Waller.*
Do scales and fins bear price to this excess?
You might have bought the *fisherman* for less. *Dryd. Juven.*

FI'SHERTOWN. *n. s.* [*fisher* and *town*.] A town inhabited by fishermen.
Others of them, in that time, burned that *fishertown* Mousehole. *Carew's Survey of Cornwal.*
Lime in Dorsetshire, a little *fishertown*. *Clarendon*, *b.* vii.

FISHERS-COAT. *n. s.* [*fisher* and *coat*.] A coat worn by a fisher.
When Simon-Peter heard that it was the Lord, he girt his *fishers-coat* unto him, for he was naked, and did cast himself into the sea. *Jo.* xxi. 7.

FI'SHERY. *n. s.* [from *fisher*.] The business of catching fish.
We shall have plenty of mackerel this season: our *fishery* will not be disturbed by privateers. *Addison's Spectator.*

FI'SHFUL. *adj.* [from *fish*.] Abounding with fish; stored with fish.
Thus mean in state, and calm in sprite,
My *fishful* pond is my delight. *Carew's Survey of Cornwal.*
It is walled and guarded with the ocean, most commodious for traffick to all parts of the world, and watered with pleasant, *fishful* and navigable rivers. *Camden's Remains.*

To FI'SHIFY. *v. a.* [from *fish*.] To turn to fish: a cant word.
Here comes Romeo
—Without his roe, like a dried herring:
O flesh, flesh, how art thou *fishified!* *Shak. Rom. and Juliet.*

FI'SHING. *n. s.* [from *fish*.] Commodity of taking fish.
There also would be planted a good town, having both a good haven and a plentiful *fishing*. *Spenser on Ireland.*

FI'SHKETTLE. *n. s.* [*fish* and *kettle*.] A caldron made long for the fish to be boiled without bending.
It is probable that the way of embalming amongst the Egyptians was by boiling the body, in a long caldron like a *fish-kettle*, in some kind of liquid balsam. *Grew's Musæum.*

FI'SHMEAL.

FI'SHMEAL. *n. s.* [*fish* and *meal.*] Diet of fish; abstemious diet.

'Thin drink doth overcool their blood, and making many *fishmeals*, they fall into a kind of male greensickness. *Sharp.*

FI'SHMONGER. *n. s.* [from *fish.*] A dealer in fish; a seller of fish.

I fear to play the *fishmonger*; and yet so large a commodity may not pass in silence. *Carew's Survey of Cornwal.*

The surgeon left the *fishmonger* to determine the controversy between him and the pike. *L'Estrange.*

FI'SHY. *adj.* [from *fish.*]

1. Consisting of fish.

My absent mates
Roam the wild isle in search of rural cates,
Bait the barb'd steel, and from the *fishy* flood
Appease th' afflictive fierce desire of food. *Pope's Odyssey.*

2. Having the qualities of fish.

Few eyes have escaped the picture of mermaids, that is, according to Horace, a monster with a woman's head above, and *fishy* extremity below. *Brown's Vulgar Errours.*

FI'SSILE. *adj.* [*fissilis*, Latin.] Having the grain in a certain direction, so as to be cleft

This crystal is a pellucid *fissile* stone, clear as water or crystal of the rock, and without colour; enduring a red heat without losing its transparency, and in a very strong heat calcining without fusion. *Newton's Opt.*

FISSI'LITY. *n. s.* from *fissile.*[The quality of admitting to be cloven.

FI'SSURE. *n. s.* [*fissura*, Latin; *fissure*, French.] A cleft; a narrow chasm where a breach has been made.

The stone and other terrestrial matter was distinguished into strata or layers, as it is in England: those strata were divided by parallel *fissures*, that were inclosed in the stone. *Woodward's Natural History.*

I see
The gaping *fissures* to receive the rain. *Thomson's Autumn.*

To FI'SSURE. *v. a.* [from the noun.] To cleave; to make a fissure.

By a fall or blow the skull may be *fissured* or fractured. *Wise.*

FIST. *n. s.* [fyst, Saxon.] The hand clenched with the fingers doubled down, in order to give a blow, or keep hold.

She quick and proud, and who did Pas despise,
Up with her *fist*, and took him on the face;
Another time, quoth she, become more wise;
Thus Pas did kiss her hand with little grace. *Sidney.*

And being down, the villain sore did beat
And bruise with clownish *fists* his manly face. *Fairy Queen.*

Anger causeth paleness in some; in others trembling, swelling, foaming at the mouth, stamping, and bending the *fist.* *Bacon's Natural History*, N°. 716.

And the same hand into a *fist* may close,
Which instantly a palm expanded shows. *Denham.*

Tyrrheus, the foster-father of the beast,
Then clench'd a hatchet in his horny *fist.* *Dryden's Æn.*

To FIST. *v. a.*

1. To strike with the fist.

I saw him spurning and *fisting* her most unmercifully. *Dryd.*

2. To gripe with the fist.

We have been down together in my sleep,
Unbuckling helms, *fisting* each other's throat,
And wak'd half dead with nothing. *Shakes. Coriolanus.*

FI'STINUT. *n. s.* A pistachio nut.

FI'STICUFFS. *n. s.* [*fist* and *cuff.*] Battle with the fist; blows with the fist.

Naked men belabouring one another with snagged sticks, or dully falling together by the ears at *fisticuffs.* *More.*

She would seize upon John's commons; for which they were sure to go to *fisticuffs.* *Arbuthn. History of John Bull.*

My invention and judgment are perpetually at *fisticuffs*, 'till they have quite disabled each other. *Swift.*

FI'STULA. *n. s.* [Latin; *fistule*, French.]

1. A sinuous ulcer callous within; any sinuous ulcer.

That *fistula* which is recent is the easiest of cure: those of a long continuance are accompanied with ulcerations of the gland and caries in the bone. *Wiseman's Surgery.*

2. FISTULA *Lachrimalis.* A disorder of the canals leading from the eye to the nose, which obstructs the natural progress of the tears, and makes them trickle down the cheek; but this is only the first and mildest stage of the disease: in the next there is matter discharged with the tears from the *puncta lachrimalia*, and sometimes from an orifice broke through the skin between the nose and angle of the eye. The last and worst degree of it is when the matter of the eye, by its long continuance, has not only corroded the neighbouring soft parts, but also affected the subjacent bone. *Sharp's Surgery.*

FI'STULAR. *adj.* [from *fistula.*] Hollow like a pipe.

FI'STULOUS. *adj* [from *fistula*; *fistuleux*, French.] Having the nature of a fistula; callous or sinuous like a fistula.

How these sinuous ulcers become *fistulous*, I have shewn you. *Wiseman's Surgery.*

FIT. *n s.* [from *fight*, *Skinner*, every fit of a disease being a struggle of nature; from *viit*, in Flemish, frequent, *Junius.*]

1. A paroxysm or exacerbation of any intermittent distemper.

Small stones and gravel collect and become very large in the kidneys, in which case a *fit* of the stone in that part is the cure. *Sharp's Surgery.*

2. Any short return after intermission; interval.

Sometimes 'tis grateful to the rich to try
A short vicissitude, and *fit* of poverty. *Dryden's Horace.*

Men that are habitually wicked may now and then, by *fits* and starts, feel certain motions of repentance. *L'Estrange.*

By *fits* my swelling grief appears,
In rising sighs and falling tears. *Addison on Italy.*

Thus o'er the dying lamp th' unsteady flame
Hangs quivering on a point, leaps off by *fits*,
And falls again as loth to quit its hold. *Addison's Cato.*

Religion is not the business of some *fits* only and intervals of our life, to be taken up at certain days and hours, and laid aside for the rest of our time; but a system of precepts to be regarded in all our conduct. *Rogers's Sermons.*

All *fits* of pleasure we balanced by an equal degree of pain or languor: 'tis like spending this year part of the next year's revenue. *Swift.*

3. Any violent affection of mind or body.

The life did flit away out of her nest,
And all his senses were with deadly *fit* opprest. *Fairy Queen.*

An ambitious man subjects himself to others, and puts it in the power of every malicious tongue to throw him into a *fit* of melancholy. *Addison's Spectator.*

4. Disorder; distemperature.

For your husband,
He's noble, wise, judicious, and best knows
The *fits* o' th' season. *Shakespeare's Macbeth.*

5. It is used, without an epithet of discrimination, for the hysterical disorders of women, and the convulsions of children; and by the vulgar for the epilepsy.

Mrs. Bull was so much enraged, that she fell downright into a *fit.* *Arbuthnot's History of John Bull.*

FIT. *adj.* [*vitten*, Flemish, *Junius*]

1. Qualified; proper: with *for* before the noun, and *to* before the verb.

Mighty men of valour, *fit to* go out for war and battle. 1 *Chron.* vii. 11.

He lends him vain Goliah's sacred sword,
The *fittest* help just fortune could afford. *Cowley's Davideis.*

This fury *fit for* her intent she chose,
One who delights in wars and human woes. *Dryden's Æn.*

It is a wrong use of my understanding to make it the rule and measure of another man's; a use which it is neither *fit for*, nor capable of. *Locke.*

2. Convenient; meet; proper; right.

Since we have said it were good not to use men of ambitious natures, except it be upon necessity, it is *fit* we speak in what cases they are so. *Bacon, Essay* 37.

See how thou could'st judge of *fit* and meet. *Milt. P. L.*

It is *fit* for a man to know his own abilities and weaknesses, and not think himself obliged to imitate all that he thinks *fit* to praise. *Boyle.*

If our forefathers thought *fit* to be grave and serious, I hope their posterity may laugh without offence. *Addison.*

To FIT. *v. a.* [*vitten*, Flemish, *Junius.*]

1. To accommodate to any thing; to suit one thing to another.

The carpenter marketh it out with a line: he *fitteth* it with planes. *Is.* xliv. 13.

Would fate permit
To my desires I might my fortune *fit*,
Troy I would raise. *Denham.*

2. To accommodate a person with any thing: as, the taylor *fits* his customer.

A trussmaker *fitted* the child with a pair of boddice, stiffened on the lame side *Wiseman's Surgery.*

3. To be adapted to; to suit any thing.

She shall be our messenger to this paultry knight: trust me I thought on her; she'll *fit* it. *Shakespeare.*

As much of the stone as was contiguous to the marcasite, *fitted* the marcasite so close as if it had been formerly liquid. *Bo.*

4. *To* FIT *out.* To furnish; to equip; to supply with necessaries or decoration.

A play, which if you dare but twice *fit out*,
You'll all be slander'd, and be thought devout. *Dryden.*

The English fleet could not be paid and manned, and *fitted out*, unless we encouraged trade and navigation. *Addis. Freeh.*

5. *To* FIT *up.* To furnish; to make proper for the use or reception of any.

He has *fitted up* his farm. *Pope to Swift.*

To FIT. *v. n.* To be proper; to be fit.

Nor *fits* it to prolong the heavenly feast,
Timeless, indecent, but retire to rest. *Pope's Odyssey, b.* iii.

FITCH. *n. s.* [A colloquial corruption of *vetch.*] A small kind of wild pea.

Now is the season
For sowing of *fitches*, of beans, and of peason. *Tusser.*

FI'TCHAT. } *n. s.* [*fissau*, French; *fisse*, Dutch.] A stinking
FI'TCHEW. } little beast, that robs the henroost and warren. *Skinner*

Skinner calls him the ſtinking ferret; but he is much larger; at leaſt as ſome provinces diſtinguiſh them, in which the polecat is termed a fitchat, and the ſtinking ferret a ſtoat.

'Tis ſuch another fitchew! marry, a perfum'd one:
What do you mean by this haunting of me? *Shakeſpeare.*

The fitchat, the fulimart, and the like creatures, live upon the face and within the bowels of the earth. *Walton's Angler.*

FI'TFUL. *adj.* [fit and full.] Varied by paroxyſms; diſordered by change of maladies.

Duncan is in his grave;
After life's fitful fever he ſleeps well. *Shakeſp. Macbeth.*

FI'TLY. *adv.* [from fit.]

1. Properly; juſtly; reaſonably.

Mutinous parts
That envied his receit, even ſo moſt fitly
As you malign our ſenators. *Shakeſpeare's Coriolanus.*

Where a man cannot fitly play his own part, if he have not a friend, he may quit the ſtage. *Bacon, Eſſay 28.*

I cannot fitlier compare marriage than to a lottery; for, in both, he that ventures may ſucceed, and may miſs; and if he draw a prize, he hath a rich return of his venture: but in both lotteries there lie pretty ſtore of blanks for every prize. *Boyle.*

The whole of our duty may be expreſſed moſt fitly by departing from evil. *Tillotſon's Sermons.*

An animal, in order to be moveable, muſt be flexible; and therefore is fitly made of ſeparate and ſmall ſolid parts, replete with proper fluids. *Arbuthnot on Aliments.*

2. Commodiouſly; meetly.

To take a latitude,
Sun or ſtars are fitlieſt view'd
At their brighteſt; but to conclude
Of longitudes, what other way have we
But to mark when, and where the dark eclipſes be. *Donne.*

FI'TNESS. *n.ſ.* [from fit.]

1. Propriety; meetneſs; juſtneſs; reaſonableneſs.

In things the fitneſs whereof is not of itſelf apparent, nor eaſy to be made ſufficiently manifeſt unto all, yet the judgment of antiquity, concurring with that which is received, may induce them to think it not unfit. *Hooker, b. v. ſ. 7.*

The queen being abſent, 'tis a needful fitneſs
That we adjourn this court. *Shakeſpeare's Henry VIII.*

Wer't my fitneſs
To let theſe hands obey my boiling blood,
They're apt enough to diſlocate and tear
Thy fleſh and bones. *Shakeſpeare's King Lear.*

2. Convenience; commodity; the ſtate of being fit.

Nor time nor place
Did then cohere, and yet you would make both:
They've made themſelves, and that their fitneſs now
Does unmake you. *Shakeſpeare's Macbeth.*

FI'TMENT. *n.ſ.* [from fit.] Something adapted to a particular purpoſe.

Poor beſeeming: 'twas a fitment for
The purpoſe I then follow'd. *Shakeſpeare's Cymbeline.*

FI'TTER. *n.ſ.* [from fit.]

1. The perſon or thing that confers fitneſs for any thing.

Sowing the ſandy gravelly land in Devonſhire and Cornwal with French furze-ſeed, they reckon a great improver of their land, and a fitter of it for corn. *Mortimer's Husbandry.*

2. [from fetta, Italian: fetzen, German.] A ſmall piece: as, to cut into fitters. *Skinner.*

FITZ. *n.ſ.* [Norman, from fils, a ſon, Fr.] A ſon. Only uſed in law and genealogy: as Fitzherbert, the ſon of Herbert; Fitzthomas, the ſon of Thomas; Fitzroy, the ſon of the king. It is commonly uſed of illegitimate children.

FIVE. *adj.* [ꝼiꝼ, Saxon.] Four and one; half of ten.

And five of them were wiſe, and five were fooliſh. *Mat.*

No perſon, no incident, but muſt be of uſe to carry on the main deſign: all things elſe are like ſix fingers to the hand, when nature, which is ſuperfluous in nothing, can do her work with five. *Dryden's Dufreſnoy.*

Five herds, five bleating flocks, his paſtures fill'd;
His lands a hundred yoke of oxen till'd. *Dryden's Æn.*

Our Britiſh youth loſe their figure by that time they are five and twenty. *Addiſon's Guardian, Nº. 111.*

FIVELE'AVED *Graſs. n.ſ.* Cinquefoil; a ſpecies of clover.

FIVES. *n.ſ.*

1. A kind of play with a bowl.
2. A diſeaſe of horſes.

His horſe ſped with ſpavins rayed with the yellows, paſt cure of the fives, and ſtark ſpoiled with the ſtaggers. *Shakeſp.*

To FIX. *v. a.* [fixer, French; fixus, Latin.]

1. To make faſt, firm, or ſtable.

Hell heard the unſufferable noiſe, hell ſaw
Heav'n ruining from heav'n, and would have fled
Affrighted, but that fate had fix'd too deep
Her dark foundations, and too faſt had bound. *Milt. P. L.*

2. To ſettle; to eſtabliſh invariably.

Brighteſt ſeraph! tell
In which of all theſe orbs hath man
His fixed ſeat, or fixed ſeat hath none,
But all theſe ſhining orbs his choice to dwell! *Milt. P. L.*

One loves fixed laws, and the other arbitrary power. *Temple.*

When cuſtom hath fixed his eating to certain ſtated periods, his ſtomach will expect victuals at the uſual hour. *Locke.*

3. To direct without variation.

Why are thine eyes fixt to the ſullen earth,
Gazing at that which ſeems to dim thy ſight! *Shak. H. VI.*

Thus while the Trojan prince employs his eyes,
Fix'd on the walls with wonder and ſurprize. *Dryden's Æn.*

4. To deprive of volatility.

We pronounce concerning gold, that it is fixed. *Locke.*

5. To pierce; to transfix. A ſenſe purely Latin.

While from the raging ſword he vainly flies,
A bow of ſteel ſhall fix his trembling thighs. *Sandys.*

6. To withold from motion.

To FIX. *v. n.*

1. To ſettle the opinion; to determine the reſolution.

If we would be happy, we muſt fix upon ſome foundation that can never deceive us. *L'Eſtrange.*

He made himſelf their prey,
T' impoſe on their belief and Troy betray;
Fix'd on his aim, and obſtinately bent
To die undaunted, or to circumvent. *Dryden's Æn.*

Here hope began to dawn; reſolv'd to try,
She fix'd on this her utmoſt remedy,
Death was behind; but hard it was to die. *Dryden.*

In moſt bodies, not propagated by ſeed, it is the colour we muſt fix on, and are moſt led by. *Locke.*

2. To reſt; to ceaſe to wander.

Your kindneſs baniſhes your fear,
Reſolv'd to fix for ever here. *Waller.*

3. To loſe volatility, ſo as to be malleable.

In the midſt of molten lead, when it beginneth to congeal, make a little dent, and put quickſilver, wrapped in a piece of linen, in that hole, and the quickſilver will fix and run no more, and endure the hammer. *Bacon's Natural Hiſtory.*

FIXA'TION. *n.ſ.* [French.]

1. Stability; firmneſs; ſteadineſs.

Your fixation in matters of religion will not be more neceſſary for your ſoul's than your kingdom's peace. *King Charles.*

2. Reſidence in a certain place.

To light, created in the firſt day, God gave no proper place or fixation. *Raleigh's Hiſtory of the World.*

3. Confinement; forbearance of excurſion.

They are ſubject to errors from a narrowneſs of ſoul, a fixation and confinement of thought to a few objects. *Watts.*

4. Want of volatility; deſtruction of volatility.

Upon the compound body three things are chiefly to be obſerved; the colour, the fragility or pliantneſs, and the volatility or fixation, compared with the ſimple bodies. *Bacon.*

It is more difficult to make gold of other metals leſs ponderous and leſs materiate, than, via verſa, to make ſilver of lead or quickſilver, both which are more ponderous than ſilver; ſo that they need rather a degree of fixation than any condenſation. *Bacon's Natural Hiſtory.*

5. Reduction from fluidity to firmneſs.

Salt diſſolved, upon a fixation returns to its affected cubes. *Glanv. Scepſ. c. 7.*

FI'XEDLY. *adv.* [from fixed.] Certainly; firmly; in a manner ſettled and eſtabliſhed.

If we pretend that the diſtinction of ſpecies, or ſorts, is fixedly eſtabliſhed by the real and ſecret conſtitutions of things. *Locke.*

FI'XEDNESS. *n.ſ.* [from fixed.]

1. Stability; firmneſs.
2. Want or loſs of volatility.

Fixedneſs, or a power to remain in the fire unconſumed, is an idea that always accompanies our complex idea ſignified by the word gold. *Locke.*

3. Solidity; coherence of parts.

All matter is either fluid or ſolid, to comprehend all the middle degrees between extreme fixedneſs and coherency, and the moſt rapid inteſtine motion of the particles of bodies. *Bentley's Sermons.*

4. Steadineſs; ſettled opinion or reſolution.

A fixedneſs in religion will not give my conſcience leave to conſent to innovations. *King Charles.*

FIXI'DITY. *n.ſ.* [from fixed.] Coherence of parts, oppoſed to volatility. A word of *Boyle.*

Bodies mingled by the fire are differing as to fixidity and volatility, and yet are ſo combined by the firſt operation of the fire, that itſelf does ſcarce afterwards ſeparate them. *Boyle.*

FI'XITY. *n.ſ.* [fixité, French.] Coherence of parts, oppoſed to volatility.

And are not the ſun and fixed ſtars great earths vehemently hot, whoſe heat is conſerved by the greatneſs of the bodies, and the mutual action and reaction between them, and the light which they emit, and whoſe parts are kept from fuming away, not only by their fixity, but alſo by the vaſt weight and denſity of the atmoſpheres incumbent upon them? *Newt. Opt.*

FI'XURE. *n. s.* [from *fix.*]

1. Position.

The *fixure* of her eye hath motion in't,
As we were mock'd with art. *Shakesp. Winter's Tale.*

2. Stable pressure.

The firm *fixure* of thy foot would give an excellent motion to thy gait. *Shakes. Merry Wives of Windsor.*

3. Firmness; stable state.

Frights, changes, horrours;
Divert and crack, rend and deracinate
The unity and married calm of states
Quite from their *fixure.* *Shakespeare's Troil. and Cressida.*

FI'ZGIG. *n. s.* A kind of dart or harpoon with which seamen strike fish.

FLA'BBY. *adj.* [*flaccidus,* Latin.] Soft; not firm; easily shaking or yielding to the touch.

Paleness, a weak pulse, palpitations of the heart, *flabby* and black flesh, are symptoms of weak fibres. *Arbuthnot.*

Pulls out the rags contriv'd to prop
Her *flabby* dugs, and down they drop. *Swift.*

FLA'BILE. *adj.* [*flabilis,* Latin.] Blown about by the wind; subject to be blown. *Dict.*

FLA'CCID. *adj.* [*flaccidus,* Latin] Weak; limber; not stiff; lax; not tense.

The bowing and inclining the head is found in the great flower of the sun: the cause I take to be is, that the part against which the sun beateth waxeth more faint and *flaccid* in the stalk, and thereby less able to support the flower. *Bacon.*

They whose muscles are weak or *flaccid,* are unapt to pronounce the letter *r.* *Holder's Elements of Speech:*

The surgeon ought to vary the diet as he finds the fibres are too *flaccid* and produce funguses, or as they harden and produce callosities. *Arbuthnot on Diet.*

FLACCI'DITY. *n. s.* [from *flaccid.*] Laxity; limberness; want of tension; want of stiffness.

There is neither fluxion nor pain, but *flaccidity* joined with insensibility. *Wiseman's Surgery.*

To FLAG. *v. n.* [*flaggeren,* Dutch; ꝼleoᵹan, Saxon, to fly.]

1. To hang loose without stiffness or tension.

Beds of cotton wool hung up between two trees, not far from the ground; in the which, *flagging* down in the middle, men, wives and children lie together. *Abbot.*

The jades
That drag the tragick melancholy night,
Who with their drowsy, slow, and *flagging* wings
Clip dead men's graves. *Shakespeare's Henry* VI.

It keeps those slender aerial bodies separated and stretched out, which otherwise, by reason of their flexibleness and weight, would *flag* or curl. *Boyle's Spring of the Air.*

Like a fiery meteor sunk the sun,
The promise of a storm; the shifting gales
Forsake by fits, and fill the *flagging* sails. *Dryden.*

2. To grow spiritless or dejected.

My *flagging* soul flies under her own pitch,
Like fowl in air too damp, and lags along
As if she were a body in a body:
My senses too are dull and stupify'd,
Their edge rebated: sure some ill approaches. *Dryd. D. Seb.*

The pleasures of the town begin to *flag* and grow languid, giving way daily to cruel inroads from the spleen. *Swift.*

3. To grow feeble; to lose vigour.

Juice in language is somewhat less than blood; for if the words be but becoming and signifying, and the sense gentle, there is juice: but where that wanteth, the language is thin, *flagging,* poor, starved, scarce covering the bone, and shews like stones in a sack: some men, to avoid redundancy, run into that; and while they strive to hinder ill blood or juice, they lose their good. *Ben. Johnson's Discoveries:*

His stomach will expect victuals at the usual hour, and grow peevish if he passes it; either fretting itself into a troublesome excess, or *flagging* into a downright want of appetite. *Locke.*

There must be a noble train of actions to preserve his fame in life and motion; for, when it is once at a stand, it naturally *flags* and languishes. *Addison's Spectator,* Nº. 256.

If on sublimer wings of love and praise,
My love above the starry vault I raise,
Lur'd by some vain conceit of pride or lust,
I *flag,* I drop, and flutter in the dust. *Arbuthnot.*

He sees a spirit hath been raised against him, and he only watches 'till it begins to *flag:* he goes about watching when to devour us. *Swift.*

To FLAG. *v. a.*

1. To let fall; to suffer to droop.

Take heed, my dear, youth flies apace;
As well as Cupid, Time is blind:
Soon must those glories of thy face
The fate of vulgar beauty find:
The thousand loves, that arm thy potent eye,
Must drop their quivers, *flag* their wings, and die. *Prior.*

2. [From *flag,* a species of stone.] To lay with broad stone.

The sides and floor are all *flagged* with excellent marble. *Sandys.*

A white stone used for *flagging* floors. *Woodward on Fossils.*

FLAG. *n. s.* [from the verb.]

1. A water plant with a broad bladed leaf and yellow flower, so called from its motion in the wind.

She took an ark of bulrushes, and laid it in the *flags* by the river's brink *Ex.* ii 3.

Can bulrushes but by the river grow?
Can *flags* there flourish where no waters flow. *Sandys.*

There be divers fishes that cast their spawn on *flags* or stones. *Walton's Angler.*

Cut *flag* roots, and the roots of other weeds. *Mortimer.*

2. The colours or ensign of a ship or land forces, by which signals are made at sea, or regiments are distinguished in the field.

These *flags* of France that are advanced here,
Before the eye and prospect of your town,
Have hither march'd to your endamagement. *Shak. K. John.*

He hangs out as many *flags* as he descryeth vessels; square, if ships; if gallies, pendants. *Sandys's Travels.*

Let him be girt
With all the grisly legions that troop
Under the sooty *flag* of Acheron,
Harpies and hydras, or all the monstrous forms
'Twixt Africa and Inde, I'll find him out,
And force him to restore his purchase back,
Or drag him by the curls to a foul death. *Milton.*

The French and Spaniard, when your *flags* appear,
Forget their hatred, and consent to fear. *Waller.*

The interpretation of that article about the *flag* is a ground at pleasure for opening a war. *Temple.*

In either's *flag* the golden serpents bear,
Erecting crests alike, like volumes rear,
And mingle friendly hissings in the air. *Dryden's Aurengz.*

Then they, whose mothers, frantick with their fear,
In woods and wilds the *flags* of Bacchus bear,
And lead his dances with dishevell'd hair. *Dryden's Æn.*

3. A species of stone used for smooth pavements. [*flache,* old French]

Part of two *flags* striated, but deeper on one side than the other. *Woodward on Fossils.*

Flagstone will not split, as slate does, being found formed into *flags,* or thin plates, which are no other than so many strata. *Woodward's Met. Foss.*

FLAG-BROOM. *n. s.* [from *flag* and *broom.*] A broom for sweeping flags or pavements, commonly made of birch-twigs, or of the leaves of the dwarf palm, imported from Spain.

FLAG-OFFICER. *n. s.* [*flag* and *officer.*] A commander of a squadron.

Her grandfather was a *flag-officer.* *Addison's Spectator.*

FLAG-SHIP. *n. s.* [*flag* and *ship.*] The ship in which the commander of a fleet is.

FLAG-WORM. *n. s.* [*flag* and *worm.*] A grub bred in watry places among flags or sedge.

He will in the three hot months bite at a *flag-worm,* or a green gentle. *Walton's Angler.*

FLA'GELET. *n s.* [*flageolet,* French.] A small flute; a small instrument of wind musick.

Play us a lesson on your *flagelet.* *More's Divine Dialogues.*

FLAGELLA'TION. *n. s.* [from *flagello,* Latin.] The use of the scourge.

By Bridewell all descend,
As morning pray'r and *flagellation* end. *Garth's Dispens.*

FLA'GGINESS. *n. s.* [from *flaggy.*] Laxity; limberness; want of tension.

FLA'GGY. *adj.* [from *flag.*]

1. Weak; lax; limber; not stiff; not tense.

His *flaggy* wings, when forth he did display,
Were like two sails, in which the hollow wind
Is gather'd full, and worketh speedy way. *Fairy Queen, b.* i.

That basking in the sun thy bees may lye,
And resting there, their *flaggy* pinions dry. *Dryden's Virgil.*

2. Weak in taste; insipid.

Graft an apple-cion upon the stock of a colewort, and it will bear a great *flaggy* apple. *Bacon's Natural History.*

FLAGI'TIOUS. *adj.* [from *flagitius,* Latin.] Wicked; villainous; atrocious.

No villany or *flagitious* action was ever yet committed, but, upon a due enquiry into the causes of it, it will be found that a lye was first or last the principal engine to effect it. *South.*

There's no working upon a *flagitious* and perverse nature by kindness and discipline. *L'Estrange.*

First, those *flagitious* times,
Pregnant with unknown crimes,
Conspire to violate the nuptial bed. *Roscommon.*

Perjury is a crime of so *flagitious* a nature, we cannot be too careful in avoiding every approach towards it. *Addison.*

But if in noble minds some dregs remain,
Not yet purg'd off, of spleen and sour disdain,
Discharge that rage on more provoking crimes,
Nor fear a dearth in these *flagitious* times. *Pope.*

FLAGI'TIOUSNESS. *n. ſ.* [from *flagitious.*] Wickedneſs; villany.

FLA'GON. *n. ſ.* [*ffacced*, Welſh; flaxe, Saxon; *flaſke*, Daniſh; *flacon*, French; *fiaſco*, Italian; *flaſco*, Spaniſh.] A veſſel of drink with a narrow mouth.

A mad rogue! he pour'd a *flagon* of Rheniſh on my head once. *Shakeſpeare's Hamlet.*

More had ſent him by a ſuitor in Chancery two ſilver *flagons*. *Bacon's Apophth.*

Did they coin piſpots, bowls, and *flagons*
Int' officers of horſe and dragoons? *Hudibras, p.* i. *cant.* 2.

His truſty *flagon*, full of potent juice,
Was hanging by, worn thin with age and uſe. *Roſcommon.*

One *flagon* walks the round, that none ſhould think
They either change, or ſtint him of his drink. *Dryd. Juv.*

FLA'GRANCY. *n. ſ.* [*flagrantia*, Latin.] Burning; heat; fire.

Luſt cauſeth a *flagrancy* in the eyes, as the ſight and the touch are the things deſired, and therefore the ſpirits reſort to thoſe parts. *Bacon's Natural Hiſtory.*

FLA'GRANT. *adj.* [*flagrans*, Latin.]

1. Ardent; burning; eager.

A thing which filleth the mind with comfort and heavenly delight, ſtirreth up *flagrant* deſires and affections, correſpondent unto that which the words contain. *Hooker, b.* v. *ſ.* 39.

2. Glowing; fluſhed.

See Sapho, at her toilet's greaſy taſk,
And iſſuing *flagrant* to an evening maſk:
So morning inſects, that in muck begun,
Shine, buz, and fly-blow in the ſetting ſun. *Pope's Epiſtles.*

3. Red; imprinted red.

Their common loves, a lewd abandon'd pack,
The beadle's laſh ſtill *flagrant* on their back. *Prior.*

4. Notorious; flaming.

When fraud is great, it furniſhes weapons to defend itſelf; and at worſt, if the crimes be ſo *flagrant* that a man is laid aſide out of perfect ſhame, he retires loaded with the ſpoils of the nation. *Swift.*

With equal poize let ſteddy juſtice ſway,
And *flagrant* crimes with certain vengeance pay;
But, 'till the proofs are clear, the ſtroke delay. *Smith.*

FLAGRA'TION. *n. ſ.* [*flagro*, Latin.] Burning. *Dict.*

FLA'GSTAFF. *n. ſ.* [*flag* and *ſtaff.*] The ſtaff on which the flag is fixed.

The duke, leſs numerous, but in courage more,
On wings of all the winds to combat flies:
His murdering guns a loud defiance roar,
And bloody croſſes on his *flagſtaffs* riſe. *Dryd. Ann. Mirab.*

FLAIL. *n. ſ.* [*flagellum*, Latin; *flegel*, German.] The inſtrument with which grain is beaten out of the ear.

Our ſoldiers, like the night owl's lazy flight,
Or like a lazy threſher with a *flail*,
Fell gently down as if they ſtruck their friends. *Sh. H.* VI.

When in one night, ere glimpſe of morn,
His ſhadowy *flail* hath threſh'd the corn,
That ten day-labourers could not end,
Then lies him down the lubbar-fend. *Milton.*

In this pile ſhould reign a mighty prince,
Born for a ſcourge of wit, and *flail* of ſenſe. *Dryden.*

The dextrous handling of the *flail*, or the plough, and being good workmen with theſe tools, did not hinder Gideon's and Cincinnatus's ſkill in arms, nor make them leſs able in the arts of war and government. *Locke.*

The threſher, Duck, could o'er the queen prevail;
The proverb ſays, no fence againſt a *flail*. *Swift.*

FLAKE. *n. ſ.* [*floccus*, Latin.]

1. Any thing that appears looſely held together, like a flock of wool.

O crimſon circles, like red *flakes* in the element, when the weather is hotteſt. *Sidney, b.* ii.

And from his wide devouring oven ſent
A *flake* of fire, that fluſhing in his beard,
Him all amaz'd, and almoſt made affear'd. *Fairy Queen.*

The earth is ſometimes covered with ſnow two or three feet deep, made up only of little *flakes* or pieces of ice. *Burn.*

Small drops of a miſling rain, deſcending through a freezing air, do each of them ſhoot into one of thoſe figured icicles; which, being ruffled by the wind, in their fall are broken, and cluſtered together into ſmall parcels, which we call *flakes* of ſnow. *Grew's Coſmolog. Sacr. b.* i. *c.* 3.

Upon throwing in a ſtone the water boils for a conſiderable time, and at the ſame time are ſeen little *flakes* of ſcurf riſing up. *Addiſon on Italy.*

2. A ſtratum; layer; lamina.

The *flakes* of his tough fleſh ſo firmly bound,
As not to be divorced by a wound. *Sandys.*

A labourer in his left hand holding the head of the centerpin, and with his right drawing about the beam and teeth, which cut and tore away great *flakes* of the metal, 'till it received the perfect form the teeth would make. *Moxon.*

To FLAKE. *v. a.* [from the noun.] To form in flakes or bodies looſely connected.

From the bleak pole no winds inclement blow,
Mold the round hail, or *flake* the fleecy ſnow. *Pope's Odyſſ.*

FLA'KY. *adj.* [from *flake.*]

1. Looſely hanging together.

The ſilent hour ſteals on,
And *flaky* darkneſs breaks within the Eaſt. *Shakeſ. Rich.* III.

The trumpet roars, long *flaky* flames expire,
With ſparks that ſeem to ſet the world on fire. *Pope.*

Hence, when the ſnows in Winter ceaſe to weep,
And undiſſolv'd their *flaky* texture keep,
The banks with eaſe their humble ſtreams contain,
Which ſwell in Summer, and thoſe banks diſdain. *Blackm.*

2. Lying in layers or ſtrata; broken into laminæ.

FLAM. *n. ſ.* [A cant word of no certain etymology.] A falſehood; a lye; an illuſory pretext.

A *flam* more ſenſeleſs than the rog'ry
Of old aruſpicy and aug'ry. *Hudibras, p.* ii. *cant.* 3.

'Till theſe men can prove the things, ordered by our church, to be either intrinſically unlawful or indecent, all pretences or pleas of conſcience to the contrary are nothing but cant and cheat, *flam* and deluſion. *South's Sermons.*

What are moſt of the hiſtories of the world but lyes? Lyes immortalized and conſigned over as a perpetual abuſe and *flam* upon poſterity. *South's Sermons.*

FLAM. *n. ſ.* [from the French *flamme*, a flame.] A tranſient blaze; a ſudden exploſion of flame from fat or dripping: and ſo in Scotland transferred to any thing glozing and flaſhily illuſory.

To FLAM. *v. a.* [from the noun.] To deceive with a lye. Merely cant.

For ſo our ignorance was *flamm'd*,
To damn ourſelves t' avoid being damn'd. *Hudibras, p.* iii.

God is not to be *flammed* off with lyes, who knows exactly what thou can'ſt do, and what not. *South's Sermons.*

FLA'MBEAU. *n. ſ.* [French.] A lighted torch.

The king ſeiz'd a *flambeau* with zeal to deſtroy. *Dryden.*

As the attendants carried each of them a *flambeau* in their hands, the ſultan, after having ordered all the lights to be put out, gave the word to enter the houſe, find out the criminal, and put him to death. *Addiſon's Guardian.*

FLAME. *n. ſ.* [*flamma*, Latin; *flamme*, French.]

1. Light emitted from fire.

Is not *flame* a vapour, fume, or exhalation heated red hot, that is, ſo hot as to ſhine? For bodies do not flame without emitting a copious fume, and this fume burns in the *flame*. *Newton's Opt.*

What *flame*, what lightning e'er
So quick an active force did bear! *Cowley.*

2. Fire.

Jove, Prometheus' theft allow;
The *flames* he once ſtole from thee, grant him now. *Cowley.*

3. Ardour of temper or imagination; brightneſs of fancy; vigour of thought.

Of all our elder plays,
This and Philaſter have the loudeſt fame;
Great are their faults, and glorious is their *flame*:
In both our Engliſh genius is expreſt,
Lofty and bold, but negligently dreſt. *Waller.*

4. Ardour of inclination.

Smit with the love of kindred arts we came,
And met congeneal, mingling *flame* with *flame*. *Pope.*

5. Paſſion of love.

My heart's on *flame*, and does like fire
To her aſpire. *Cowley.*

Come arm'd in *flames*; for I would prove
All the extremities of love. *Cowley.*

No warning of th' approaching *flame*;
Swiftly like ſudden death it came:
I lov'd the moment I beheld. *Granville.*

To FLAME. *v. n.* [from the noun]

1. To ſhine as fire; to burn with emiſſion of light.

Can you think to blow out the intended fire your city is ready to *flame* in, with ſuch weak breath as this? *Shakeſp.*

He fell *flaming* through th' ethereal ſky
To bottomleſs perdition. *Milton.*

Hell all around
As one great furnace *flam'd*. *Milton.*

2. To ſhine like flame.

Behold it like an ample curtain ſpread,
Now ſtreak'd and glowing with the morning red;
Anon at noon in *flaming* yellow bright,
And chuſing ſable for the peaceful night. *Prior.*

3. To break out in violence of paſſion.

FLAMECO'LOURED. *adj.* [*flame* and *colour.*] Of a bright yellow colour.

'Tis ſtrong, and it does indifferent well in *flamecoloured* ſtockings. *Shakeſpeare's Twelfth Night.*

Auguſt ſhall bear the form of a young man of a fierce and cholerick aſpect, in a *flamecoloured* garment. *Peacham.*

FLA'MEN. *n. ſ.* [Latin.] A prieſt; one that officiates in ſolemn offices.

Then firſt the *flamen* taſted living food;
Next his grim idol ſmear'd with human blood. *Pope.*

FLAMMA'TION. *n. s.* [*flammatio*, Latin.] The act of setting on flame.

White or crystalline arsenick, being artificial, and sublimed with salt, will not endure *flammation*. *Brown's Vulgar Err.*

FLAMMABI'LITY. *n. s.* [*flamma*, Latin.] The quality of admitting to be set on fire.

In the sulphur of bodies torrified, that is, the oily, fat and unctuous parts, consist the principles of *flammability*. *Brown.*

FLA'MMEOUS. *adj.* [*flammeus*, Latin.] Consisting of flame; resembling flame.

This *flammeous* light is not over all the body. *Brown.*

FLAMMI'FEROUS. *adj.* [*flammifer*, Lat.] Bringing flame. *Dict.*

FLAMMI'VOMOUS. *adj.* [*flamma* and *vomo*, Latin.] Vomiting out flame. *Dict.*

FLA'MY. *adj.* [from *flame*.]

1. Inflamed; burning; flaming.

My thoughts imprison'd in my secret woes,
With *flamy* breaths do issue oft in sound. *Sidney, b.* ii.

2. Having the nature of flame.

The vital spirits of living creatures are a substance compounded of an airy and *flamy* matter; and though air and flame, being free, will not well mingle, yet bound in by a body they will. *Bacon's Natural History.*

FLANK. *n. s.* [*flanc*, French, according to *Menage*, from λαγὼν; more probably from *latus*, Latin.]

1. That part of the side of a quadruped near the hinder thigh.

The belly shall be eminent by shadowing the *flank*. *Peach.*

2. [In men.] The lateral part of the lower belly.

He said, and, pois'd in air, the jav'lin sent:
Through Paris shield the forceful weapon went,
His corslet pierces, and his garment rends,
And glancing downward near his *flank* descends. *Pope.*

3. The side of any army or fleet.

Great ordnance and small shot thundered and showered upon our men from the rampier in front, and from the gallies that lay at sea in *flank*. *Bacon's War with Spain.*

The other half of the battle, and the whole *flank* of the rear, was closed by the carriages. *Hayward.*

Gray was appointed to stand on the left side, in such sort as he might take the *flank* of the enemy. *Hayward.*

To right and left the front
Divided, and to either *flank* retir'd. *Milton's Paradise Lost.*

4. [In fortification.] That part of the bastion which reaches from the curtain to the face, and defends the opposite face, the flank and the curtain. *Harris.*

To FLANK. *v. a.*

1. To attack the side of a battalion or fleet.

2. To be posted so as to overlook or command any pass on the side; to be on the side.

With fates averse, against their king's command,
Arm'd on the right, and on the left they stand,
And *flank* the passage. *Dryden's Æn.*
By the rich scent we found our perfum'd prey,
Which, *flank'd* with rocks, did close in covert lay. *Dryden.*

FLA'NKER. *n. s.* [from *flank*.] A fortification jutting out so as to command the side of a body marching to the assault.

The Turks, discouraged with the loss of their fellows, and sore beaten by the Spaniards out of their *flankers*, were enforced to retire. *Knolles's History of the Turks.*

To FLA'NKER. *v. a.* [*flanquer*, French.] To defend by lateral fortifications.

FLA'NNEL. *n. s.* [*gwlanen*, Welch, from *gwlan*, wool, *Davies.*] A soft nappy stuff of wool.

I cannot answer the Welch *flannel*. *Shakespeare.*

FLAP. *n. s.* [lœppe, Saxon.]

1. Any thing that hangs broad and loose, fastened only by one side.

There is a peculiar provision for the windpipe, that is, a cartilaginous *flap* upon the opening of the larinx, which hath an open cavity for the admission of the air. *Brown's Vulg. Err.*

Some surgeons make a crucial incision, upon the supposition that the wound will more easily heal by turning down the *flaps*. *Sharp's Surgery.*

2. The motion of any thing broad and loose.

3. [A disease in horses.]

When a horse is said to have the *flaps*, you may perceive his lips to be swelled on both sides of his mouth; and that which is in the blisters is like the white of an egg: you must, to cure it, cut some slashes with a knife, and rub it once with salt, and it will cure. *Farrier's Dict.*

To FLAP. *v. a.* [from the noun.]

1. To beat with a flap, as flies are beaten.

A hare, hard put to it by an eagle, took sanctuary in a ditch with a beetle: the eagle *flapt* off the former, and devoured the other. *L'Estrange.*

Yet let me *flap* this bug with gilded wings,
This painted child of dirt, that stinks and stings. *Pope.*

2. To move with a flap or noise made by the stroke of any thing broad.

The dira *flapping* on the shield of Turnus, and fluttering about his head, disheartened him in the duel. *Dryden's Æn. Dedicat.*

With fruitless toil
Flap filmy pinions oft, to extricate
Their feet in liquid shackles bound. *Phillips.*

Three times, all in the dead of night,
A bell was heard to ring;
And shrieking at her window thrice
The raven *flapp'd* his wing. *Tickell.*

To FLAP. *v. n.*

1. To ply the wings with noise.

'Tis common for a duck to run *flapping* and fluttering away, as if maimed, to carry people from her young. *L'Estrange.*

2. To fall with flaps, or broad parts depending.

When suffocating mists obscure the morn,
Let thy worst wig, long us'd to storms, be worn;
This knows the powder'd footman, and with care
Beneath his *flapping* hat secures his hair. *Gay's Trivia.*

FLA'PDRAGON. *n. s.*

1. A play in which they catch raisins out of burning brandy, and, extinguishing them by closing the mouth, eat them.

2. The thing eaten at flapdragon.

He plays at quoits well, and eats conger and fennel, and drinks candles ends for *flapdragons*, and rides the wild mare with the boys. *Shakespeare's Henry* IV. *p.* ii.

To FLA'PDRAGON. *v. a.* [from the noun.] To swallow; to devour.

But to make an end of the ship, to see how the sea *flapdragoned* it. *Shakespeare's Winter's Tale.*

FLA'PEARED. *adj.* [*flap* and *ear*.] Having loose and broad ears.

A whoreson, beetleheaded, *flapeared* knave. *Shakespeare.*

To FLARE. *v. n.* [from *flederen*, to flutter, Dutch, *Skinner*; perhaps accidentally changed from *glare*.]

1. To flutter with a splendid show.

She shall be loose enrob'd,
With ribbands pendant *flaring* 'bout her head. *Shakespeare.*

2. To glitter with transient lustre.

Doctrine and life, colours and light, in one
When they combine and mingle, bring
A strong regard and awe; but speech alone
Doth vanish like a *flaring* thing,
And in the ear, not conscience, ring. *Herbert.*

3. To glitter offensively.

When the sun begins to fling
His *flaring* beams, me, goddess, bring
To arched walks of twilight groves. *Milton.*

4. To be in too much light.

I cannot stay
Flaring in sunshine all the day. *Prior.*

FLASH. *n. s.* [φλὸξ, *Minshew.*]

1. A sudden, quick, transitory blaze.

When the cross blue lightning seem'd to open
The breast of heav'n, I did present myself
Ev'n in the aim and very *flash* of it. *Shakesp. Jul. Cæsar.*

We see a *flash* of a piece is seen sooner than the noise is heard. *Bacon's Natural History,* N°. 210.

One with a *flash* begins, and ends in smoak;
The other out of smoak brings glorious light. *Roscommon.*

And as Ægeon, when with heaven he strove,
Defy'd the forky lightning from afar,
At fifty mouths his flaming breath expires,
And *flash* for *flash* returns, and fires for fires. *Dryd. Æn.*

2. Sudden burst of wit or merriment.

Where be your gibes now? your gambols? your songs? your *flashes* of merriment, that were wont to set the table in a roar? *Shakespeare's Hamlet.*

Wicked men prefer the light *flashes* of a wanton mirth, which for a while suspend reflection, and hide the sinner from himself, to such discourses as awaken conscience. *Rogers.*

3. A short transient state.

The Persians and Macedonians had it for a *flash*. *Bacon.*

4. A body of water driven by violence.

To FLASH. *v. n.*

1. To glitter with a quick and transient flame.

This salt powdered, and put into a crucible, was, by the injection of well kindled charcoal, made to *flash* divers times almost like melted nitre. *Boyle.*

2. To burst out into any kind of violence.

By day and night he wrongs me; ev'ry hour
He *flashes* into one gross crime or other,
That sets us all at odds. *Shakespeare's King Lear.*

3. To break out into wit, merriment, or bright thought.

They *flash* out sometimes into an irregular greatness of thought. *Felton on the Classicks.*

To FLASH. *v. a.* To strike up large bodies of water from the surface.

With his raging arms he rudely *flash'd*
The waves about, and all his armour swept,
That all the blood and filth away was wash'd. *Fairy Queen.*

If the sea-water be *flashed* with a stick or oar, the same casteth a shining colour, and the drops resemble sparkles of fire. *Carew's Survey of Cornwal.*

FLA'SHER.

FLA'SHER. *n. s.* [from *flash*.] A man of more appearance of wit than reality. *Dict.*

FLA'SHILY. *adv.* [from *flashy*.] With empty show; without real power of wit or solidity of thought.

FLA'SHY. *adj.* [from *flash*.]

1. Empty; not solid; showy without substance.

Flashy wits cannot fathom the whole extent of a large discourse. *Digby on the Soul, Dedicat.*

When they list, their lean and *flashy* songs
Grate on their scrannel pipes of wretched straw. *Milton.*

This mean conceit, this darling mystery,
Which thou think'st nothing, friend! thou shalt not buy;
Nor will I change for all the *fleshy* wit. *Dryden's Pers. Sat.*

2. [From *flaccidus*, *Skinner*.] Insipid; without force or spirit.

Distilled books are, like common distilled waters, *flashy* things. *Bacon, Essay 51.*

The tastes that most offend in fruits, herbs and roots, are bitter, harsh, sour, waterish or *flashy*. *Bacon's Nat. History.*

FLASK. *n. s.* [*flasque*, French.]

1. A bottle; a vessel.

Then for the Bourdeaux you may freely ask;
But the Champaigne is to each man his *flask*. *King.*

2. A powder-horn.

Powder in a skilless soldier's *flask*
Is set on fire. *Shakespeare.*

FLA'SKET. *n. s.* [from *flask*.] A vessel in which viands are served.

Another plac'd
The silver stands, with golden *flaskets* grac'd. *Pope's Odyss.*

FLAT. *adj.* [*plat*, French.]

1. Horizontally level without inclination.

Thou all-shaking thunder,
Strike *flat* the thick rotundity o' th' world. *Shak. K. Lear.*

The houses are *flat* roofed to walk upon, so that every bomb that fell on them would take effect. *Addison on Italy.*

2. Smooth; without protuberances.

In the dawning of the next day we might plainly discern it was a land *flat* to our sight, and full of boscage. *Bacon.*

3. Without elevation.

Cease t' admire, and beauty's plumes
Fall *flat*, and shrink into a trivial toy,
At every sudden slighting quite abasht. *Milton's Par. Lost.*

4. Level with the ground.

In them is plainest taught, and easiest learnt,
What makes a nation happy, and keeps it so,
What ruins kingdoms, and lays cities *flat*. *Milt. Par. Reg.*

That Christ-church stands above ground, and that the church of Westminster lies not *flat* upon it, is your lordship's commendation. *South.*

5. Lying horizontally prostrate; lying along.

The wood-born people fall before her *flat*,
And worship her as goddess of the wood. *Fairy Queen, b.* i.

That lamentable wound,
Which laid that wretched prince *flat* on the ground. *Daniel.*

6. [In painting.] Without relief; without prominence of the figures.

7. Tasteless; insipid; dead.

He, like a puling cuckold, would drink up
The lees and dregs of a *flat* tamed piece. *Sh. Troil. and Cres.*

Taste so divine! that what of sweet before
Hath touch'd my sense, *flat* seems to this and harsh. *Milton.*

The miry fields,
Rejoicing in rich mold, most ample fruit
Of beauteous form produce; pleasing to sight,
But to the tongue inelegant and *flat*. *Phillips.*

8. Dull; unanimated; frigid.

Short speeches fly abroad like darts, and are thought to be shot out of secret intentions; but as for large discourses, they are *flat* things, and not so much noted. *Bacon, Essay 16.*

Some short excursions of a broken vow
He made indeed, but *flat* insipid stuff. *Dryd. Don Sebastian.*

9. Depressed; spiritless; dejected.

My hopes all *flat*, nature within me seems
In all her functions weary of herself. *Milton's Agonistes.*

10. Unpleasing; tasteless.

How weary, stale, *flat* and unprofitable
Seem to me all the uses of this world! *Shakesp. Hamlet.*

To one firmly persuaded of the reality of heavenly happiness, and earnestly desirous of obtaining it, all earthly satisfactions must needs look little, and grow *flat* and unsavoury. *Atterbury's Sermons.*

11. Peremptory; absolute; downright.

His horse with *flat* tiring taught him, that discrete stays make speedy journeys. *Sidney.*

It is a *flat* wrong to punish the thought or purpose of any before it be enacted; for true justice punisheth nothing but the evil act or wicked word. *Spenser's State of Ireland.*

As it is in the nature of all men to love liberty, so they become *flat* libertines, and fall to all licentiousness. *Spenser.*

You start away,
And lend no ear unto my purposes;
Those prisoners you shall keep:
——I will, that's *flat*. *Shakespeare's Henry* IV. *p.* i.

Thus repuls'd, our final hope
Is *flat* despair: we must exasperate
Th' Almighty Victor to spend all his rage,
And that must end us. *Milton's Paradise Lost, b.* ii.

If thou sin in wine or wantonness,
Boast not thereof, nor make thy shame thy glory;
Frailty gets pardon by submissiveness:
But he that boasts, shuts that out of his story:
He makes *flat* war with God, and doth defy
With his meer clod of earth the spacious sky. *Herbert.*

You had broke and robb'd his house,
And stole his talismanique louse;
And all his new-found old inventions,
With *flat* felonious intentions. *Hudibras, p.* iii. *cant.* i.

12. Not shrill; not acute; not sharp in sound.

If you stop the holes of a hawk's bell it will make no ring, but a *flat* noise or rattle. *Bacon's Natural History.*

The upper end of the windpipe is endued with several cartilages and muscles to contract or dilate it, as we would have our voice *flat* or sharp. *Ray on the Creation.*

FLAT. *n. s.*

1. A level; an extended plane.

The strings of a lute, viol, or virginals, give a far greater sound, by reason of the knot, board and concave underneath, than if there were nothing but only the *flat* of a board to let in the upper air into the lower. *Bacon's Nat Hist.*

Because the air receiveth great tincture from the earth, expose flesh or fish, both upon a stake of wood some height above the earth, and upon the *flat* of the earth. *Bacon's Nat. Hist.*

It comes near an artificial miracle to make divers distinct eminences appear a *flat* by force of shadows, and yet the shadows themselves not to appear. *Wotton's Architecture.*

He has cut the side of the rock into a *flat* for a garden; and by laying on it the waste earth, that he has found in several of the neighbouring parts, furnished out a kind of luxury for a hermit. *Addison on Italy.*

2. Even ground; not mountainous.

Now pile your dust upon the quick and dead,
'Till of this *flat* a mountain you have made,
T' o'ertop old Pelion, or the skyish head
Of blue Olympus. *Shakespeare's Hamlet.*

The way is ready and not long,
Beyond a row of myrtles, on a *flat*,
Fast by a mountain. *Milton's Paradise Lost, b.* ix.

3. A smooth low ground exposed to inundations.

The ocean, overpeering of his list,
Eats not the *flats* with more impetuous haste,
Than young Laertes, in a riotous head,
O'erbears your officers. *Shakespeare's Hamlet.*

All the infections, that the sun sucks up
From bogs, fens, *flats*, on Prospero fall. *Shakesp. Tempest.*

Half my pow'rs this night,
Passing these *flats*, are taken by the tide;
These Lincoln washes have devoured them. *Shak. K. John.*

4. Shallow; strand; place in the sea where the water is not deep enough for ships.

I should not see the sandy hour-glass run,
But I should think of shallows and of *flats*. *Shakespeare.*

The difficulty is very great to bring them in or out through so many *flats* and sands, if wind and weather be not very favourable. *Raleigh's Essays.*

Having newly left these grammatick *flats* and shallows, where they stuck unreasonably, to learn a few words with lamentable constructions, we are now on the sudden turmoiled with their unballasted wits in fathomless and unquiet deeps of controversy. *Milton on Education.*

Full in the prince's passage hills of sand,
And dang'rous *flats*, in secret ambush lay,
Where the false tides skim o'er the cover'd land,
And seamen with dissembled depths betray. *Dryden.*

The sea could not be narrower than it is, without a great loss to the world; and must we now have an ocean of mere *flats* and shallows, to the utter ruin of navigation? *Bentley.*

5. The broad side of a blade.

A darted mandate came
From that great will which moves this mighty frame,
Bid me to thee, my royal charge, repair,
To guard thee from the dæmons of the air;
My flaming sword above 'em to display,
All keen and ground upon the edge of day,
The *flat* to sweep the visions from thy mind,
The edge to cut 'em through that stay behind. *Dryden.*

6. Depression of thought or language.

Milton's Paradise Lost is admirable; but am I therefore bound to maintain, that there are no *flats* amongst his elevations, when 'tis evident he creeps along sometimes for above an hundred lines together? *Dryden.*

7. A surface without relief, or prominences.

Are there then such ravishing charms in a dull unvaried *flat*, to make a sufficient compensation for the chief things of the ancient mountains, and for the precious things of the lasting hills. *Bentley's Sermons.*

To Flat. *v. a.* [from the noun.]

1. To level; to depress; to make broad and smooth.

The ancients say, if you take two twigs of several fruit-trees, and *flat* them on the sides, and bind them close, and set them in the ground, they will come up in one stock. *Bacon.*

With horrid shapes she does her sons expose,
Distends their swelling lips, and *flats* their nose. *Creech.*

2. To make vapid.

An orange, lemon and apple, wrapt in a linen cloth, being buried for a fortnight four foot deep within the earth, though in a moist place and rainy time, were become a little harder than they were; otherwise fresh in their colour, but their juice somewhat *flatted.* *Bacon's Natural History,* N°. 377.

To Flat. *v. n.*

1. To grow flat: opposed to swell.

I burnt it the second time, and observed the skin shrink, and the swelling to *flat* yet more than at first. *Temple.*

2. To obstruct; retard; hinder; to render unanimated or evanid.

Nor are constant forms of prayer more likely to *flat* and hinder the spirit of prayer and devotion, than unpremeditated and confused variety to distract and lose it. *K. Charles.*

Fla'tlong. *adv.* [*flat* and *long.*] With the flat downwards; not edgewise.

What a blow was there given?
—An it had not fallen *flatlong.* *Shakespeare's Tempest.*

Fla'tly. *adv.* [from *flat.*]

1. Horizontally; without inclination.
2. Without prominence or elevation.
3. Without spirit; dully; frigidly.
4. Peremptorily; downright.

He in these wars had *flatly* refused his aid. *Sidney, b.* ii.

Thereupon they *flatly* disavouch
To yield him more obedience, or support. *Daniel's Ci. War.*

Unjust, thou say'st,
Flatly unjust, to bind with laws the free. *Milt. Parad. Lost.*

Not any interpreters allow it to be spoken of such as *flatly* deny the being of God; but of them that believing his existence, do yet seclude him from directing the affairs of the world. *Bentley's Sermons.*

Fla'tness. *n. s.* [from *flat*]

1. Evenness; level extension.
2. Want of relief or prominence.

It appears so very plain and uniform, that one would think the coiner looked on the *flatness* of a figure, as one of the greatest beauties in sculpture. *Addison on ancient Medals.*

3. Deadness; insipidity; vapidness.

Deadness or *flatness* in cyder is often occasioned by the too free admission of air into the vessel. *Mortimer's Husbandry.*

4. Dejection of state.

The emperor of Russia was my father:
Oh, that he were alive, and here beholding
His daughter's trial! that he did but see
The *flatness* of my misery! *Shakespeare's Winter's Tale.*

5. Dejection of mind; want of life; want of spirit.
6. Dulness; insipidity; frigidity.

How fast does obscurity, *flatness,* and impertinency flow in upon our meditations? 'Tis a difficult task to talk to the purpose, and to put life and perspicuity into our discourses. *Collier.*

Some of Homer's translators have swelled into fustian, and others sunk into *flatness.* *Pope's Preface to Homer.*

7. The contrary to shrilness or acuteness of sound.

Take two saucers, and strike the edge of the one against the bottom of the other within a pail of water, and you shall find the sound groweth more flat, even while part of the saucer is above the water; but that *flatness* of sound is joined with a harshness. *Bacon's Natural History,* N°. 157.

To Fla'tten. *v. a.* [*flatir,* French, from *flat.*]

1. To make even or level, without prominence or elevation.
2. To beat down to the ground.

If they should lie in it, and beat it down, or *flatten* it, it will rise again. *Mortimer's Husbandry.*

3. To make vapid.
4. To deject; to depress; to dispirit.

To Fla'tten. *v. n.*

1. To grow even or level.
2. To grow dull and insipid.

Here joys that endure for ever, fresh and in vigour, are opposed to satisfactions that are attended with satiety and surfeits, and *flatten* in the very tasting. *L'Estrange, Fable* 161.

Fla'tter. *n. s.* [from *flat.*] The workman or instrument by which bodies are flattened.

To FLA'TTER. *v. a.* [*flater,* French.]

1. To sooth with praises; to please with blandishments; to gratify with servile obsequiousness; to gain by false compliments.

When I tell him he hates flatterers,
He says he does; being then most *flattered.* *Shak. Jul. Cæs.*

His nature is too noble for the world;
He would not *flatter* Neptune for his trident,
Or Jove for's power to thunder: his heart's his mouth;
What his breast forges, that his tongue must vent. *Shakesp.*

He that *flattereth* his neighbour, spreadeth a net for his feet. *Prov.* xxix. 5.

He *flattereth* himself in his own eyes, until his iniquity be found hateful. *Ps.* xxxvi. 2.

After this way of *flattering* their willing benefactors out of part, they contrived another of forcing their unwilling neighbours out of all their possessions. *Decay of Piety.*

Averse alike to *flatter* or offend. *Pope.*

They *flatter'd* ev'ry day, and some days eat. *Pope.*

I scorn to *flatter* you or any man. *Dr. Newton's Ded. to Milt.*

2. To praise falsely.

Flatter'd crimes of a licentious age,
Provoke our censure. *Young.*

3. To please; to sooth. This sense is purely Gallick.

A consort of voices supporting themselves by their different parts make a harmony, pleasingly fills the ears and *flatters* them. *Dryden's Dufresnoy.*

4. To raise false hopes.

He always vacant, always amiable,
Hopes thee, of *flatt'ring* gales
Unmindful. *Milton.*

Fla'tterer. *n. s.* [from *flatter.*] One who flatters; a fawner; a wheedler; one who endeavours to gain favour by pleasing falsities.

When I tell him he hates *flatterers,*
He says he does; being then most flattered. *Shak. Jul. Cæs.*

Some praises proceed merely of flattery; and if he be an ordinary *flatterer,* he will have certain common attributes, which may serve every man: if he be a cunning *flatterer,* he will follow the arch *flatterer,* which is a man's self. But if he be an impudent *flatterer,* look wherein a man is conscious to himself that he is most defective, and is most out of countenance in himself, that will the *flatterer* entitle him to perforce. *Bacon, Essay* 54.

If we from wealth to poverty descend,
Want gives to know the *flatt'rer* from the friend. *Dryden.*

After treating her like a goddess, the husband uses her like a woman: what is still worse, the most abject *flatterers* degenerate into the greatest tyrants. *Addison's Guardian,* N°. 113.

The publick should know this of your ladyship; yet whoever goes about to inform them, shall be censured for a *flatterer.* *Swift.*

Fla'ttery. *n. s.* [from *flatter*; *flaterie,* French] False praise; artful obsequiousness; adulation.

Minds, by nature great, are conscious of their greatness,
And hold it mean to borrow aught from *flattery.* *Rowe.*

Simple pride for *flatt'ry* makes demands. *Pope.*

See how they beg an alms of *flattery*!
They languish, O! support them with a lye. *Young.*

Fla'ttish. *adj.* [from *flat.*] Somewhat flat; approaching to flatness.

These are from three inches over to six or seven, and of a *flattish* shape. *Woodward on Fossils.*

Fla'tulency. *n. s.* [from *flatulent.*]

1. Windiness; fulness of wind; turgescence by wind confined.

Vegetable substances contain a great deal of air, which expands itself, producing all the disorders of *flatulency.* *Arbuthn.*

2. Emptiness; vanity; levity; airiness.

Whether most of them are not the genuine derivations of the hypothesis they claim to, may be determined by any that considers the natural *flatulency* of that airy scheme of notions. *Glanville.*

FLA'TULENT. *adj.* [*flatulentus, flatus,* Latin.]

1. Turgid with air; windy.

Pease are mild and demulcent; but being full of aerial particles, are *flatulent,* when dissolved by digestion. *Arbuthnot.*

Flatulent tumours are such as easily yield to the pressure of the finger; but readily return, by their elasticity, to a tumid state again: these are so light as scarce to be felt by the patient, and no otherwise incommodious than by their unsightliness or bulk. *Quincy.*

2. Empty; vain; big without substance or reality; puffy.

To talk of knowledge, from those few indistinct representations which are made to our grosser faculties, is a *flatulent* vanity. *Glanv. Sceps. c.* 23.

How many of these *flatulent* writers have sunk in their reputation, after seven or eight editions of their works. *Dryden.*

Flatuo'sity. *n. s.* [*flatuosité,* French, from *flatus,* Latin.] Windiness; fulness of air.

The cause is *flatuosity*; for wind stirred, moveth to expel; and all purgers have in them a raw spirit or wind, which is the principal cause of tension in the stomach and belly. *Bacon.*

Fla'tuous. *adj.* [from *flatus,* Latin.] Windy; full of wind.

Rhubarb in the stomach, in a small quantity, doth digest and overcome, being not *flatuous* nor loathsome; and so sendeth it to the mesentery veins, and, being opening, it helpeth down urine. *Bacon's Natural History,* N°. 44.

FLA'TUS. *n. s.* [Latin.] Wind gathered in any cavities of the body, caused by indigestion and a gross internal perspiration; which is therefore discussed by warm aromaticks. *Quinc.*

Fla'twise. *adj.* [*flat* and *wise*: so it should be written, not *flatways.*] With the flat downwards; not the edge.

Its posture in the earth was *flatwise,* and parallel to the site of the stratum in which it was reposited. *Woodward on Fossils.*

To FLAUNT. *v. n.*

1. To make a fluttering ſhow in apparel.

With ivy canopy'd, and interwove
With *flaunting* honeyſuckle. *Milton.*

Theſe courtiers of applauſe deny themſelves things convenient to *flaunt* it out, being frequently enough fain to immolate their own deſires to their vanity. *Boyle.*

Here, attir'd beyond our purſe, we go,
For uſeleſs ornament and *flaunting* ſhow:
We take on truſt, in purple robes to ſhine,
And poor, are yet ambitious to be fine. *Dryden's Juvenal.*

You ſot, you loiter about alehouſes, or *flaunt* about the ſtreets in your new-gilt chariot, never minding me nor your numerous family. *Arbuthnot's Hiſtory of John Bull.*

2. To be hung with ſomething looſe and flying. This ſeems not to be proper.

Fortune in men has ſome ſmall diff'rence made;
One *flaunts* in rags, one flutters in brocade. *Pope's Eſſays.*

FLAUNT. *n. ſ.* Any thing looſe and airy.

How would he look to ſee his work ſo noble,
Wildly bound up, what would he ſay! or how
Should I in theſe my borrow'd *flaunts* behold
The ſternneſs of his preſence! *Shakeſp. Winter's Tale.*

FLA'VOUR. *n. ſ.*

1. Power of pleaſing the taſte.

They have a certain *flavour*, at their firſt appearance, from ſeveral accidental circumſtances, which they may loſe, if not taken early. *Addiſon's Spectator*, N°. 488.

2. Sweetneſs to the ſmell; odour; fragrance.

Myrtle, orange, and the bluſhing roſe,
With bending heaps, ſo nigh their bloom diſcloſe,
Each ſeems to ſmell the *flavour* which the other blows. *Dry.*

FLA'VOUROUS. *adj.* [from *flavour.*]

1. Delightful to the palate.

Sweet grapes degen'rate there, and fruits declin'd
From their firſt *flav'rous* taſte, renounce their kind. *Dryden.*

2. Fragrant; odorous.

FLAW. *n. ſ.* [φλάω, to break; floh, Saxon, a fragment; *flauw*, Dutch, broken in mind.]

1. A crack or breach in any thing.

This heart ſhall break into a thouſand *flaws*,
Or ere I weep. *Shakeſpeare's King Lear.*

Wool, new-ſhorn, being laid caſually upon a veſſel of verjuice, after ſome time had drunk up a great part of the verjuice, though the veſſel were whole, without any *flaw*, and had not the bunghole open. *Bacon's Natural Hiſtory.*

We found it exceeding difficult to keep out the air from getting in at any imperceptible hole or *flaw*. *Boyle.*

A *flaw* is in thy ill-bak'd veſſel found;
'Tis hollow, and returns a jarring ſound. *Dryden's Perſ.*

As if great Atlas, from his height,
Should ſink beneath his heavenly weight;
And with a mighty *flaw* the flaming wall, as once it ſhall,
Should gape immenſe, and, ruſhing down, o'erwhelm this nether ball. *Dryden.*

Whether the nymph ſhall break Diana's law,
Or ſome frail China-jar receive a *flaw*. *Pope.*

He that would keep his houſe in repair, muſt attend every little breach or *flaw*, and ſupply it immediately, elſe time alone will bring all to ruin. *Swift.*

2. A fault; defect.

Yet certain though it be, it hath *flaws*; for that the ſcriveners and brokers do value unſound men to ſerve their own turn. *Bacon's Eſſays.*

Traditions were a proof alone,
Could we be certain ſuch they were, ſo known:
But ſince ſome *flaws* in long deſcents may be,
They make not truth, but probability. *Dryden.*

And laid her dowry out in law,
To null her jointure with a *flaw*. *Hudibras, p.* iii. *c.* 1.

Their judgment has found a *flaw* in what the generality of mankind admires. *Addiſon's Spectator.*

So many *flaws* had this vow in its firſt conception. *Atterb.*

3. A ſudden guſt; a violent blaſt. [from *flo*, Latin.]

Being incens'd, he's flint;
As humourous as Winter, and as ſudden
As *flaws* congealed in the ſpring of day. *Shakeſ. Hen.* IV.

Oh, that that earth, which kept the world in awe,
Should patch a wall, t' expel the Winter's *flaw*. *Shak. Ham.*

As a huge fiſh, laid
Near to the cold weed-gathering ſhore, is with a north *flaw*
Shoots back; ſo, ſent againſt the ground, [fraid,
Was foil'd Eurialus. *Chapman's Iliads.*

Burſting their brazen dungeon, arm'd with ice,
And ſnow, and hail, and ſtormy guſt, and *flaw*,
Boreas, and Cæcias, and Argeſtes loud,
And Thraſcias rend the woods, and ſeas upturn. *Milton.*

I heard the rack,
As earth and ſky would mingle; but myſelf
Was diſtant; and theſe *flaws*, though mortals fear them,
As dangerous to the pillar'd frame of heav'n,
Or to the earth's dark baſis underneath,
Are to the main inconſiderable. *Milton's Paradiſe Loſt.*

4. A tumult; a tempeſtuous uproar.

And this fell tempeſt ſhall not ceaſe to rage,
Until the golden circuit on my head
Do calm the fury of this madbrain'd *flaw*. *Shak. Hen.* VI.

The fort's revolted to the emperor,
The gates are open'd, the portcullis drawn,
And deluges of armies from the town
Came pouring in: I heard the mighty *flaw*;
When firſt it broke, the crowding enſigns ſaw
Which choak'd the paſſage. *Dryden's Aurengzebe.*

5. A ſudden commotion of mind.

Oh theſe *flaws* and ſtarts,
Impoſtors to true fear, would become
A woman's ſtory at a Winter's fire. *Shakeſpeare's Macbeth.*

To FLAW. *v. a.* [from the noun.]

1. To break; to crack; to damage with fiſſure.

But his *flaw'd* heart,
Alack, too weak the conflict to ſupport,
'Twixt two extremes of paſſion, joy and grief,
Burſt ſmilingly. *Shakeſpeare's King Lear.*

The cup was *flawed* with ſuch a multitude of little cracks, that it looks like a white, not like a cryſtalline cup. *Boyle.*

The brazen cauldrons with the froſts are *flaw'd*,
The garment ſtiff with ice, at hearths is thaw'd. *Dryden.*

2. To break; to violate. Out of uſe.

France hath *flaw'd* the league, and hath attach'd
Our merchants goods. *Shakeſpeare's Henry* VIII.

FLA'WLESS. *adj.* [from *flaw.*] Without cracks; without defects.

A ſtar of the firſt magnitude, which the more high, more vaſt, and more *flawleſs*, ſhines only bright enough to make itſelf conſpicuous. *Boyle on Colours.*

FLAWN. *n. ſ.* [flena, Saxon; *flan*, French; *vlaeye*, Dutch.] A ſort of cuſtard; a pie baked in a diſh. *Dict.*

To FLA'WTER. *v. a.* To ſcrape or pare a ſkin. *Ainſworth.*

FLA'WY. *adj.* [from *flaw.*] Full of flaws.

FLAX. *n. ſ.* [fleax, flex, Saxon; *vlas*, Dutch.]

1. The fibrous plant of which the fineſt thread is made.

The leaves, for the moſt part, grow alternately on branches: the cup of the flower conſiſts of one leaf, is tubulous, and divided into five parts at the top: the flower conſiſts of five leaves, which expand in form of a clove-gilliflower: the ovary, which riſes from the centre of the flowercup, becomes an almoſt globular fruit, which is generally pointed, and compoſed of many cells, in which are lodged many plain ſmooth ſeeds, which are blunt at one end, and generally ſharp at the other. The ſpecies are ſix. The firſt ſort is that which is cultivated for uſe in divers parts of Europe, and is reckoned an excellent commodity. It ſhould be cultivated. *Miller.*

2. The fibres of flax cleanſed and combed for the ſpinner.

I'll fetch ſome *flax*, and whites of eggs,
T' apply to's bleeding face. *Shakeſpeare's King Lear.*

Then on the rock a ſcanty meaſure place
Of vital *flax*, and turn'd the wheel apace,
And turning ſung. *Dryden's Ovid, b.* viii.

FLA'XCOMB. *n. ſ.* [*flax* and *comb.*] The inſtrument with which the fibres of flax are cleanſed from the brittle parts.

FLA'XDRESSER. *n. ſ.* [*flax* and *dreſs.*] He that prepares flax for the ſpinner.

FLA'XEN. *adj.* [from *flax.*]

1. Made of flax.

The matron, at her nightly taſk,
With penſive labour draws the *flaxen* thread. *Thomſ. Winter.*

The beſt materials for making ligatures are the *flaxen* thread that ſhoemakers uſe. *Sharp's Surgery.*

2. Fair, long and flowing, as if made of flax.

I bought a fine *flaxen* long wig, that coſt me thirty guineas. *Addiſon's Guardian*, N°. 97.

FLA'XWEED. *n. ſ.* A plant.

To FLAY. *v. a.* [*ad flaa*, Iſlandick; *flae*, Daniſh; *vlaen*, Dut.]

1. To ſtrip of the ſkin.

I muſt have ſuffered famine, been eaten with wild beaſts, or have fallen into the hands of the Spaniards, and been *flayed* alive. *Raleigh's Apology.*

While the old levitical hierarchy continued, it was part of the miniſterial office to *flay* the ſacrifices. *South.*

Then give command the ſacrifice to haſte;
Let the *flay'd* victims in the plains be caſt;
And ſacred vows, and myſtick ſong, apply'd
To griſly Pluto and his gloomy bride. *Pope's Odyſſey, b.* x.

2. To take off the ſkin or ſurface of any thing.

They *flay* their ſkin from off them, break their bones, and chop them in pieces. *Mac.* iii. 3.

Neither ſhould that odious cuſtom be allowed of cutting ſcraws, which is *flaying* off the green ſurface of the ground, to cover their cabins, or make up their ditches. *Swift.*

FLA'YER. *n. ſ.* [from *flay.*] He that ſtrips off the ſkin of any thing.

FLEA. *n. ſ.* [flea, Saxon; *vloye*, Dutch; *fleach*, Scottiſh.] A ſmall red inſect remarkable for its agility in leaping, which ſucks the blood of larger animals.

While wormwood hath ſeed, get a handful or twain,
To ſave againſt March to make *flea* to refrain:

Where chamber is sweeped, and wormwood is strown,
No *flea* for his life dare abide to be known. *Tuss. Husband.*

Fleas breed principally of straw or mats, where there hath been a little moisture. *Bacon's Natural History.*

A valiant *flea*, that dares eat his breakfast on the lip of a lion. *Shakespeare's Henry V.*

To FLEA. *v. a.* [from the noun.] To clean from fleas.

FLE'ABANE. *n. s.* [*flea* and *bane.*] A plant.

It hath undivided leaves, which, for the most part, are glutinous, and have a strong scent: the cup of the flower is for the most part scaly, and of a cylindrical form: the flower is composed of many florets, which are succeeded by seeds with a downy substance adhering to them. *Miller.*

FLE'ABITE. } *n. s.* [*flea* and *bite.*]
FLE'ABITING. }

1. Red marks caused by fleas.

The attendance of a cancer is commonly a breaking out all over the body, like a *fleabiting*. *Wiseman's Surgery.*

2. A small hurt or pain like that caused by the sting of a flea.

A gout, a cholick, a cutting off an arm or leg, or searing the flesh, are but *fleabites* to the pains of the soul. *Harvey.*

The same expence that breaks one man's back, is not a *fleabiting* to another. *L'Estrange, Fable* 229.

FLE'ABITTEN. *adj.* [*flea* and *bite.*]

1. Stung by fleas.
2. Mean; worthless.

Fleabitten synod, an assembly brew'd
Of clerks and elders ana, like the rude
Chaos of presbyt'ry, where laymen guide,
With the tame woolpack clergy by their side. *Cleaveland.*

FLE'AK. *v. a.* [from *floccus*, Latin. See FLAKE.] A small lock, thread, or twist.

The businesses of men depend upon these little long *fleaks* or threads of hemp and flax. *More's Antidote against Atheism.*

FLEAM. *n. s.* [corrupted from φλεβότομον, the instrument used in phlebotomy.] An instrument used to bleed cattle, which is placed on the vein, and then driven by a blow.

FLE'AWORT. *n. s.* [*flea* and *wort.*] A plant.

This plant agrees with plantain and buckshorn-plantain in every respect, excepting that this rises up with leafy stalks, and divides into many branches; whereas both the others produce their flowers upon naked pedicles. *Miller.*

To FLECK. *v. a.* [*fleck*, German, a spot; *Skinner*: perhaps it is derived from *fleak*, or *fleke*, an old word for a grate, hurdle, or any thing made of parts laid transverse, from the Islandick *flake.*] To spot; to streak; to stripe; to dapple; to variegate.

Let it not see the dawning *fleck* the skies,
Nor the grey morning from the ocean rise. *Sandys.*

Fleck'd in her face, and with disorder'd hair,
Her garments ruffled, and her bosom bare. *Dryden's Juven.*

Both *fleck'd* with white, the true Arcadian strain. *Dryden.*

To FLE'CKER. *v. a.* [from *fleck.*] To spot; to mark with strokes or touches of different colours; to mark with red whelkes.

The grey-ey'd morn smiles on the frowning night,
Check'ring the eastern clouds with streaks of light;
And darkness *flecker'd*, like a drunkard, reels
From forth day's path, and Titan's burning wheels. *Shakesp.*

FLED. The preterite and participle not properly of *fly*, to use the wings, but of *flee*, to run away.

The truth is *fled* far away, and leasing is hard at hand. 2 *Esdr.* xiv. 18.

In vain for life he to the altar *fled*;
Ambition and revenge have certain speed. *Prior.*

FLEDGE. *adj.* [*flederen*, to fly, Dutch.] Full-feathered; able to fly; qualified to leave the nest.

We did find
The shells of *fledge* souls left behind. *Herbert.*

His locks behind,
Illustrious on his shoulders, *fledge* with wings,
Lay waving round. *Milton's Paradise Lost, b.* iii.

To FLEDGE. *v. a.* [from the adjective.] To furnish with wings; to supply with feathers.

The birds were not as yet *fledged* enough to shift for themselves. *L'Estrange, Fable* 72.

The speedy growth of birds that are hatched in nests, and fed by the old ones 'till they be *fledged*, and come almost to full bigness in about a fortnight, seems to me an argument of providence. *Ray on the Creation.*

The sandals of celestial mould,
Fledg'd with ambrosial plumes, and rich with gold,
Surround her feet. *Pope's Odyssey, b.* i.

To FLEE. *v. n.* pret. *fled.* [This word is now almost universally written *fly*, though properly to *fly*, ꝼleoᵹan, is *to move with wings*, and *flee*, ꝼlean, *to run away*. They are now confounded.] To run from danger; to have recourse to shelter.

Behold, this city is near to *flee* unto. *Gen.* xix. 20.

Were men so dull they could not see
That Lyce painted; should they *flee*
Like simple birds into a net,
So grosly woven and ill set? *Waller.*

There are none of us fall into those circumstances of danger, want, or pain, that we can have hopes of relief but from God alone; none in all the world to *flee* to, but him. *Tillotson, Sermon* 1.

FLEECE. *n. s.* [ꝼlyꞅ, ꝼleꞅ, Saxon; *vleese*, Dutch] As much wool as is shorn from one sheep.

Giving account of the annual increase
Both of their lambs and of their woolly *fleece*. *Hubb. Tale.*

So many days my ewes have been with young,
So many months ere I shall sheer the *fleece*. *Shak. Hen.* VI.

I am shepherd to another man,
And do not sheer the *fleeces* that I graze. *Shak. As you like it.*

Her sunny locks
Hang on her temples like a golden *fleece*. *Shakespeare.*

Sailors have used every night to hang *fleeces* of wool on the sides of their ships, towards the water; and they have crushed fresh water out of them in the morning. *Bacon's Nat. History.*

The sheep will prove much to the advantage of the woollen manufacture, by the fineness of the *fleeces*. *Gulliver's Travels.*

To FLEECE. *v. a.* [from the noun.]

1. To clip the fleece off a sheep.
2. To strip; to pull; to plunder, as a sheep is robbed of his wool.

Courts of justice have a small pension, so that they are tempted to take bribes, and to *fleece* the people. *Addison.*

FLE'ECED. *adj.* [from *fleece*] Having fleeces of wool.

As when two rams, stirr'd with ambitious pride,
Fight for the rule of the rich *fleeced* flock,
Their horned fronts so fierce on either side
Do meet, that with the terror of the shock
Astonied both stand senseless as a block. *Fairy Queen, b.* i.

FLE'ECY. *adj.* [from *fleece.*] Woolly; covered with wool.

Not all the *fleecy* wealth
That doth enrich these downs, is worth a thought
To that my errand. *Milton.*

From eastern point
Of Libra, to the *fleecy* star, that bears
Andromeda far off Atlantic seas. *Milton's Paradise Lost.*

Let her glad valleys smile with wavy corn;
Let *fleecy* flocks her rising hills adorn. *Prior.*

The good shepherd tends his *fleecy* care,
Seeks freshest pasture, and the purest air;
Explores the lost, the wand'ring sheep directs. *Pope's Mess.*

To FLEER. *v. n.* [ꝼleaꞃdian, to trifle, Saxon; *fleardan*, Scottish. *Skinner* thinks it formed from *leer.*]

1. To mock; to gibe; to jest with insolence and contempt.

You speak to Casca, and to such a man
That is no *fleering* tell-tale. *Shakespeare's Julius Cæsar.*

Dares the slave
Come hither, cover'd with an antick face,
To *fleer* and scorn at our solemnity! *Shak. Rom. and Juliet.*

Do I, like the female tribe,
Think it well to *fleer* and gibe? *Swift.*

2. To leer; to grin with an air of civility.

How popular and courteous; how they grin and *fleer* upon every man they meet! *Burton on Melancholy.*

FLEER. *n. s.* [from the verb.]

1. Mockery expressed either in words or looks.

Encave yourself,
And mark the *fleers*, the gibes, and notable scorns,
That dwell in ev'ry region of his face. *Shakesp. Othello.*

2. A deceitful grin of civility.

If a man will but observe such persons exactly, he shall generally spy such false lines, and such a sly treacherous *fleer* upon their face, that he shall be sure to have a cast of their eye to warn him, before they give him a cast of their nature to betray him. *South's Sermons.*

FLE'ERER. *n. s.* [from *fleer.*] A mocker; a fawner. *Dict.*

FLEET. FLEOT. FLOT. Are all derived from the Saxon ꝼleoꞇ, which signifies a bay or gulph. *Gibson's Camden.*

FLEET. *n. s.* [ꝼlota, Saxon.] A company of ships; a navy.

Our pray'rs are heard; our master's *fleet* shall go
As far as winds can bear, or waters flow. *Prior.*

FLEET. *n. s.* [ꝼleoꞇ, Saxon, an estuary, or arm of the sea.] A creek; an inlet of water. A provincial word, from which the Fleet-prison and Fleet-street are named.

They have a very good way in Essex of draining of lands that have land-floods or *fleets* running through them, which make a kind of a small creek. *Mortimer's Husbandry.*

FLEET. *adj.* [*fliotur*, Islandick] Swift of pace; quick; nimble; active.

Upon that shore he spied Atin stand;
There by his master left, when late he far'd
In Phædria's *fleet* bark. *Fairy Queen.*

I take him for the better dog:
——Thou art a fool: if Echo were as *fleet*,
I would esteem him worth a dozen such. *Shakespeare.*

He had in his stables one of the *fleetest* horses in England. *Clar*

His fear was greater than his haste;

For fear, though *fleeter* than the wind,
Believes 'tis always left behind. *Hudibras, p.* iii. *cant.* 3.
So fierce they drove, their courſers were ſo *fleet*,
That the turf trembled underneath their feet. *Dryden.*
He told us, that the welkin would be clear
When ſwallows *fleet* ſoar high and ſport in air. *Gay.*
Ten thouſand thouſand *fleet* ideas
Croud faſt into the mind. *Thomſon's Autumn.*

2. [In the huſbandry of ſome provinces.] Light; ſuperficially fruitful.

Marl cope-ground is a cold, ſtiff, wet clay, unleſs where it is very *fleet* for paſture. *Mortimer.*

3. Skimming the ſurface.

Thoſe lands muſt be plowed *fleet*. *Mortimer's Huſbandry.*

To FLEET. *v. n.* [ꝼlotan, Saxon.]

1. To fly ſwiftly; to vaniſh.

How all the other paſſions *fleet* to air,
As doubtful thoughts, and raſh embrac'd deſpair! *Shakeſp.*
A wolf, who, hang'd for human ſlaughter,
Ev'n from the gallows did his fell ſoul *fleet*. *Shakeſpeare.*

2. To be in a tranſient ſtate; the ſame with *flit*.

Our underſtanding, to make a complete notion, muſt add ſomething elſe to this *fleeting* and unremarkable ſuperficies, that may bring it to our acquaintance. *Digby on Bodies.*

O *fleeting* joys
Of Paradiſe, dear-bought with laſting woes! *Milt. P. Loſt.*
While I liſten to thy voice,
Chloris! I feel my life decay:
That powerful noiſe
Calls my *fleeting* ſoul away. *Waller.*
As empty clouds by riſing winds are toſt,
Their *fleeting* forms ſcarce ſooner found than loſt. *Prior.*

To FLEET. *v. a.*

1. To ſkim the water.

Who ſwelling ſails in Caſpian ſea doth croſs,
And in frail wood an Adrian gulph doth *fleet*,
Doth not, I ween, ſo many evils meet. *Fairy Queen, b.* ii.

2. To live merrily, or paſs time away lightly.

Many young gentlemen flock to him every day, and *fleet* the time careleſly as they did in the golden age. *Shakeſpeare.*

3. [In the country.] To ſkim milk; to take off the cream: whence the word *fleeting* diſh.

FLEE'TINGDISH. *n. ſ.* [from *fleet* and *diſh.*] A ſkimming bowl.

FLE'ETLY. *adv.* [from *fleet.*] Swiftly; nimbly; with ſwift pace.

FLEE'TNESS. *n. ſ.* [from *fleet.*] Swiftneſs of courſe; nimbleneſs; celerity; velocity; ſpeed; quickneſs.

FLESH. *n. ſ.* [ꝼlæc, ꝼlæſc, Saxon; *vleeſch*, Dutch; *feol*, Erſe.]

1. The body diſtinguiſhed from the ſoul.

As if this *fleſh*, which walls about our life,
Were braſs impregnable. *Shakeſpeare's Richard* II.
A diſeaſe that's in my *fleſh*,
Which I muſt needs call mine. *Shakeſpeare's King Lear.*
And thou, my ſoul, which turn'ſt with curious eye
To view the beams of thine own form divine,
Know, that thou can'ſt know nothing perfectly,
While thou art clouded with this *fleſh* of mine. *Davies.*

2. The muſcles diſtinguiſhed from the ſkin, bones, tendons.

A ſpirit hath not *fleſh* and bones. *New Teſtament.*

3. Animal food diſtinguiſhed from vegetable.

Fleſh ſhould be forborne as long as he is in coats, or at leaſt 'till he is two or three years old. *Locke.*

Fleſh, without being qualified with acids, is too alkaleſcent a diet. *Arbuthnot on Aliments.*

Acidity in the infant may be cured by a *fleſh* diet in the nurſe. *Arbuthnot on Aliments.*

4. The body of beaſts or birds uſed in food, diſtinct from fiſhes.

There is another indictment upon thee, for ſuffering *fleſh* to be eaten in thy houſe, contrary to the law. *Shakeſp. H.* IV.

We mortify ourſelves with the diet of fiſh; and think we fare coarſely, if we abſtain from the *fleſh* of other animals. *Brown's Vulgar Errours.*

5. Animal nature.

The end of all *fleſh* is come before me. *Gen.* vi. 13.

6. Carnality; corporal appetites.

Name not religion; for thou lov'ſt the *fleſh*. *Shakeſ.*

Faſting ſerves to mortify the *fleſh*, and ſubdue the luſts thereof. *Smalridge's Sermons.*

7. A carnal ſtate; worldly diſpoſition.

They that are in the *fleſh* cannot pleaſe God. *Rom.* viii. 8.

The *fleſh* luſteth againſt the ſpirit, and the ſpirit againſt the *fleſh*. *Gal.* v. 16.

8. Near relation.

Let not our hand be upon him; for he is our *fleſh*. *Gen.*

When thou ſeeſt the naked, cover him; and hide not thyſelf from thine own *fleſh*. *Iſa.* lviii. 7.

9. The outward or literal ſenſe. The Orientals termed the immediate or literal ſignification of any precept or type *the fleſh*, and the remote or typical meaning *the ſpirit*. This is frequent in St *Paul*.

Ye judge after the *fleſh*. *John* viii. 15.

To FLESH. *v. a.*

1. To initiate: from the ſportſman's practiſe of feeding his hawks and dogs with the firſt game that they take, or training them to purſuit by giving them the *fleſh* of animals.

Good man boy, if you pleaſe; come, I'll *fleſh* ye. *Shakeſp.*

Every puny ſwordſman will think him a good tame quarry to enter and *fleſh* himſelf upon. *Government of the Tongue.*

2. To harden; to eſtabliſh in any practice, as dogs by often feeding on any thing.

Theſe princes finding them ſo *fleſhed* in cruelty, as not to be reclaimed, ſecretly undertook the matter alone. *Sidney, b.* ii.

The women ran all away, ſaving only one, who was ſo *fleſhed* in malice, that neither during nor after the fight ſhe gave any truce to her cruelty. *Sidney, b.* ii.

3. To glut; to ſatiate.

Harry from curb'd licence plucks
The muzzle of reſtraint; and the wild dog
Shall *fleſh* his tooth on every innocent. *Shakeſp. Henry* IV.

He hath perverted a young gentlewoman, and this night he *fleſhes* his will in the ſpoil of her honour. *Shakeſpeare.*

The kindred of him hath been *fleſh'd* upon us;
And he is bred out of that bloody ſtrain,
That hunted us in our familiar paths. *Shakeſ. Henry* V.
Full bravely haſt thou *fleſht*
Thy maiden ſword. *Shakeſpeare's Henry* IV.

FLE'SHBROATH. *n. ſ.* [*fleſh* and *broath.*] Broath made by decocting fleſh.

Her leg being emaciated, I adviſed bathing it with *fleſhbroath*, wherein had been decocted emollient herbs. *Wiſeman.*

FLE'SHCOLOUR. *n. ſ.* [*fleſh* and *colour.*] The colour of fleſh.

A complication of ideas together makes up the ſingle complex idea, which he calls man, whereof white or *fleſhcolour* in England is one. *Locke.*

A looſe earth of a pale *fleſhcolour*, that is, white with a bluſh of red, is found in ſmall fiſſures of a brown ſoft ſtone in the Skrees, a mountain in Cumberland. *Woodward on Foſſils.*

FLE'SHFLY. *n. ſ.* [*fleſh* and *fly.*] A fly that feeds upon fleſh, and depoſites her eggs in it.

I would no more endure
This wooden ſlavery, than I would ſuffer
The *fleſhfly* blow my mouth. *Shakeſpeare's Tempeſt.*

It is a wonderful thing in *fleſhflies*, that a fly-maggot, in five days ſpace after it is hatched, arrives at its full growth and perfect magnitude. *Ray on the Creation.*

FLE'SHHOOK. *n. ſ.* [*fleſh* and *hook.*] A hook to draw fleſh from the caldron.

All that the *fleſhhook* brought up the prieſt took. 1 *Sa.* ii. 12.

FLE'SHLESS. *adj.* [from *fleſh.*] Without fleſh.

FLE'SHLINESS. *n. ſ.* [from *fleſhly.*] Carnal paſſions or appetites.

When ſtrong paſſions or weak *fleſhlineſs*
Would from the right way ſeek to draw him wide,
He would, through temperance and ſtedfaſtneſs,
Teach him the weak to ſtrengthen, and the ſtrong ſuppreſs.
Fairy Queen, b. ii. *cant.* 4. *ſtan.* 2.

Corrupt manners in living, breed falſe judgment in doctrine: ſin and *fleſhlineſs* bring forth ſects and hereſies. *Aſcham.*

FLE'SHLY. *adj.* [from *fleſh.*]

1. Corporeal.

Nothing reſembles death ſo much as ſleep;
Yet then our minds themſelves from ſlumber keep,
When from their *fleſhly* bondage they are free. *Denham.*

2. Carnal; laſcivious.

From amid'ſt them roſe
Belial, the diſſoluteſt ſpirit that fell,
The ſenſualeſt; and, after Aſmodai,
The *fleſhlieſt* incubus. *Paradiſe Regained, b.* ii.

3. Animal; not vegetable.

'Tis then for nought that mother earth provides
The ſtores of all ſhe ſhows, and all ſhe hides,
If men with *fleſhly* morſels muſt be fed,
And chaw with bloody teeth the breathing bread. *Dryden.*

4. Human; not celeſtial; not ſpiritual.

Elſe, never could the force of *fleſhly* arm
Ne molten metal in his fleſh embrue. *Fairy Queen, b.* i.
What time th' eternal Lord in *fleſhly* ſhrine
Enwombed was, from wretched Adam's line,
To purge away the guilt of ſinful crime. *Fairy Queen.*
Much oſtentation, vain of *fleſhly* arm,
And of frail arms, much inſtrument of war
Before mine eyes thou'ſt ſet. *Milton's Par. Regained, b.* iii.

FLE'SHMEAT. *n. ſ.* [*fleſh* and *meat.*] Animal food; the fleſh of animals prepared for food.

The moſt convenient diet is that of *fleſhmeats*. *Floyer.*

In this prodigious plenty of cattle and dearth of human creatures, *fleſhmeat* is monſtrouſly dear. *Swift.*

FLE'SHMENT. *n. ſ.* [from *fleſh.*] Eagerneſs gained by a ſucceſsful initiation.

He got praiſes of the king,
For him attempting who was ſelf-ſubdued;
And in the *fleſhment* of this dread exploit,
Drew on me here again. *Shakeſpeare's King Lear.*

FLE'SHMONGER. *n. ſ.* [from *fleſh.*] One who deals in fleſh; a pimp.

Was the duke a *fleſhmonger*, a fool, and a coward, as you then reported him? *Shakeſpeare's Meaſure for Meaſure.*

FLE'SHPOT. *n. ſ.* [*fleſh* and *pot.*] A veſſel in which fleſh is cooked; thence plenty of fleſh.

If he takes away the *fleſhpots*, he can alſo alter the appetite. *Taylor's Rule for living holy.*

FLE'SHQUAKE. *n. ſ.* [*fleſh* and *quake.*] A tremor of the body: a word formed by *Johnſon* in imitation of earthquake.

They may, blood-ſhaken then,
Feel ſuch a *fleſhquake* to poſſeſs their powers,
As they ſhall cry like ours:
In ſound of peace or wars,
No harp e'er hit the ſtars. *Ben. Johnſon's New-Inn.*

FLE'SHY. *adj.* [from *fleſh.*]

1. Plump; full of fleſh; fat; muſculous.

All Ethiopes are *fleſhy* and plump, and have great lips; all which betoken moiſture retained, and not drawn out. *Bacon.*

We ſay it is a *fleſhy* ſtile when there is much periphraſes and circuit of words, and when with more than enough it grows fat and corpulent. *Ben. Johnſon's Diſcoveries.*

The ſole of his foot is flat and broad, being very *fleſhy*, and covered only with a thick ſkin; but very fit to travel in ſandy places. *Ray.*

2. Pulpous; plump: with regard to fruits.

Thoſe fruits that are ſo *fleſhy*, as they cannot make drink by expreſſion, yet may make drink by mixture of water. *Bacon.*

FLE'TCHER. *n. ſ.* [from *fleche*, an arrow, French.] A manufacturer of bows and arrows.

It is commended by our *fletchers* for bows, next unto yew. *Mortimer's Husbandry.*

FLET. *participle paſſive* of *To fleet.* Skimmed; deprived of the cream.

They teach them to drink *flet* milk, which they juſt warm. *Mortimer's Husbandry.*

FLEW. The preterite of *fly.*

The people *flew* upon the ſpoil. 1 *Sa.* xiv. 32.

O'er the world of waters Hermes *flew*,
'Till now the diſtant iſland roſe in view. *Pope's Odyſſey, b.* v.

FLEW. *n. ſ.* The large chaps of a deep-mouthed hound. *Hanm.*

FLEWED. *adj.* [from *flew.*] Chapped; mouthed.

My hounds are bred out of the Spartan kind,
So *flew'd*, ſo ſanded, and their heads are hung
With ears that ſweep away the morning dew. *Shakeſpeare.*

FLEXA'NIMOUS. *adj.* [*flexanimus*, Latin.] Having power to change the diſpoſition of the mind. *Dict.*

FLEXIBI'LITY. *n. ſ.* [*flexibilité*, French, from *flexible.*]

1. The quality of admitting to be bent; pliancy.

Do not the rays which differ in refrangibility differ alſo in *flexibility?* And are they not, by their different inflexions, ſeparated from one another, ſo as after ſeparation to make the colours? *Newton's Opt.*

Corpuſcles of the ſame ſet agree in every thing; but thoſe that are of diverſe kinds differ in ſpecifick gravity, in hardneſs, and in *flexibility*, as in bigneſs and figure. *Woodward.*

2. Eaſineſs to be perſuaded; ductility of mind; compliance; facility.

Adviſe me to reſolve rather to err by too much *flexibility* than too much perverſeneſs, by meekneſs than by ſelf-love. *Hammond's Pract. Catech.*

FLE'XIBLE. *adj.* [*flexibilis*, Latin; *flexible*, French.]

1. Poſſible to be bent; not brittle; eaſy to be bent; pliant; not ſtiff.

When ſplitting winds
Make *flexible* the knees of knotted oaks. *Sh. Troil. and Creſſ.*

Take a ſtock-gillyflower and tie it upon a ſtick, and put them both into a ſtoop glaſs full of quickſilver, ſo that the flower be covered: after four or five days you ſhall find the flower freſh, and the ſtalk harder and leſs *flexible* than it was. *Bacon's Natural Hiſtory*, N°. 796.

2. Not rigid; not inexorable; complying; obſequious.

Phocyon was a man of great ſeverity, and no ways *flexible* to the will of the people. *Bacon.*

3. Ductile; manageable.

Under whoſe care ſoever a child is put to be taught, during the tender and *flexible* years of his life, it ſhould be one who thinks Latin and language the leaſt part of education. *Locke.*

4. That may be accommodated to various forms and purpoſes.

This was a principle more *flexible* to their purpoſe. *Rogers.*

FLE'XIBLENESS. *n. ſ.* [from *flexible.*]

1. Poſſibility to be bent; not brittleneſs; eaſineſs to be bent; not ſtiffneſs; pliantneſs; pliancy.

I will rather chuſe to wear a crown of thorns, than to exchange that of gold for one of lead, whoſe embaſed *flexibleneſs* ſhall be forced to bend. *King Charles.*

Keep thoſe ſlender aerial bodies ſeparated and ſtretched out, which otherwiſe, by reaſon of their *flexibleneſs* and weight, would flag or curl. *Boyle's Spring of the Air.*

2. Facility; obſequiouſneſs; compliance.

3. Ductility; manageableneſs.

The *flexibleneſs* of the former part of a man's age, not yet grown up to be headſtrong, makes it more governable. *Locke.*

FLE'XILE. *adj.* [*flexilis*, Latin.] Pliant; eaſily bent; obſequious to any power or impulſe.

Every *flexile* wave
Obeys the blaſt, th' aerial tumult ſwells. *Thomſon's Summer.*

FLE'XION. *n. ſ.* [*flexio*, Latin.]

1. The act of bending.

2. A double; a bending; part bent; joint.

Of a ſinuous pipe that may have ſome four *flexions*, trial would be made. *Bacon's Natural Hiſtory*, N°. 222.

3. A turn towards any part or quarter.

Pity cauſeth ſometimes tears, and a *flexion* or caſt of the eye aſide. *Bacon's Natural Hiſtory*, N°. 71.

FLE'XOR. n. ſ. [Latin.] The general name of the muſcles which act in contracting the joints.

Flatterers, who have the *flexor* muſcles ſo ſtrong that they are always bowing and cringing, might in ſome meaſure be corrected by being tied down upon a tree by the back. *Arbuth.*

FLE'XUOUS. *adj.* [*flexuoſus*, Latin.]

1. Winding; full of turns and meanders; tortuous.

In regard of the ſoul, the numerous and crooked narrow cranies, and the reſtrained *flexuous* rivulets of corporeal things, are all contemptible. *Digby on the Soul.*

2. Bending; not ſtrait; variable; not ſteady.

The trembling of a candle diſcovers a wind, that otherwiſe we do not feel; and the *flexuous* burning of flames doth ſhew the air beginneth to be unquiet. *Bacon's Natural Hiſtory.*

FLE'XURE. *n. ſ.* [*flexura*, Latin.]

1. The form or direction in which any thing is bent.

Contrary is the *flexure* of the joints of our arms and legs to that of quadrupeds: our knees bend forward, whereas the ſame joint of their hind legs bends backward. *Ray.*

2. The act of bending.

The elephant hath joints, but none for courteſy;
His legs are for neceſſity, not *flexure*. *Shak. Troil. and Creſſ.*

3. The part bent; the joint.

His mighty ſtrength lies in his able loins,
And where the *flexure* of his navel joins. *Sandys.*

4. Obſequious or ſervile cringe.

Think'ſt thou the fiery fever will go out
With titles blown from adulation?
Will it give place to *flexure* and low bends? *Shak. Hen.* V.

To FLI'CKER. *v. a.* [*fligheren*, Dutch; flicceꞃian, Saxon.] To flutter; to play the wings; to have a fluttering motion.

Under th' allowance of your grand aſpect,
Whoſe influence, like the wreath of radiant fire,
On *flickering* Phœbus' front. *Shakeſpeare's King Lear.*

'Twas ebbing darkneſs, paſt the mid' of night,
And Phoſpher, on the confines of the light,
Promis'd the ſun, ere day began to ſpring;
The tuneful lark already ſtretch'd her wing,
And *flick'ring* on her neſt, made ſhort eſſays to ſing. *Dry.*

At all her ſtretch her little wings ſhe ſpread,
And with her feather'd arms embrac'd the dead;
Then *flickering* to his pallid lips, ſhe ſtrove
To print a kiſs, the laſt eſſay of love. *Dryden.*

FLI'ER. *n. ſ.* [from *fly.*]

1. One that runs away; a fugitive; a runaway.

Cam'ſt thou from where they made the ſtand?
——I did;
Though you, it ſeems, came from the *fliers*. *Shak. Cymbel.*

The gates are ope, now prove good ſeconds;
'Tis for the followers fortune widens them,
Not for the *fliers*. *Shakeſpeare's Coriolanus.*

Now the *fliers* from and forſakers of their places, carry the parliamentary power along with them. *King Charles.*

2. That part of a machine which, by being put into a more rapid motion than the other parts, equalizes and regulates the motion of the reſt; as in a jack.

The *flier*, tho't had leaden feet,
Turn'd ſo quick, you ſcarce could ſee't. *Swift.*

FLIGHT. *n. ſ.* [from *To fly.*]

1. The act of flying or running from danger.

And now, too late, he wiſhes for the fight,
That ſtrength he waſted in ignoble *flight*. *Denham.*

He thinks by *flight* his miſtreſs muſt be won,
And claims the prize becauſe he beſt did run. *Dryd. Ind. Em.*

As eager of the chace, the maid
Beyond the foreſt's verdant limits ſtray'd;
Pan ſaw and lov'd, and, burning with deſire,
Purſu'd her *flight*; her *flight* increas'd his fire. *Pope.*

2. Removal to another place.

The fury ſprang above the Stygian flood;
And on her wicker wings, ſublime through night,
She to the Latian palace took her *flight*. *Dryden's Æn.*

3. The act of uſing wings; volation.

For he ſo ſwift and nimble was of *flight*,
That from this lower tract he dar'd to fly
Up to the clouds, and thence with pinions light
To mount aloft unto the cryſtal ſky. *Spenſer's Muiopotmos.*

Winds that tempeſts brew,
When through Arabian groves they take their *flight*,
Made wanton with rich odours, loſe their ſpite. *Dryden.*

4. Removal from place to place by means of wings.
Ere the bat hath flown
His cloyster'd *flight*. *Shakespeare's Macbeth.*
The fowls shall take their *flight* away together. 2 *Esd.* v. 6.
Fowls, by Winter forc'd, forsake the floods,
And wing their hasty *flight* to happier lands. *Dryden's Æn.*
5. A flock of birds flying together.
Flights of angels wing thee to thy rest. *Shakesp. Hamlet.*
They take great pride in the feathers of birds; and this they took from their ancestors of the mountains, who were invited unto it by the infinite *flights* of birds that came up to the high grounds. *Bacon's New Atlantis.*
I can at will, doubt not,
Command a table in this wilderness;
And call swift *flights* of angels ministrant,
Array'd in glory, on my cup t' attend. *Milton's Par. Lost.*
6. The birds produced in the same season: as, the harvest *flight* of pigeons.
7. A volley; a shower; as much shot as is discharged at once.
At the first *flight* of arrows sent,
Full threescore Scots they slew. *Chevy Chase.*
Above an hundred arrows discharged on my left hand, pricked me like so many needles; and besides they shot another *flight* into the air, as we do bombs. *Gulliver's Travels.*
8. The space past by flying.
9. Heat of imagination; sally of the soul.
Old Pindar's *flights* by him are reacht,
When on that gale his wings are stretcht. *Denham.*
He shewed all the stretch of fancy at once; and if he has failed in some of his *flights*, it was but because he attempted every thing. *Pope's Preface to the Iliad.*
Strange graces still, and stranger *flights* she had;
Was just not ugly, and was just not mad. *Pope, Epistle* ii.
Trust me, dear! good humour can prevail,
When airs and *flights*, and screams and scolding fail. *Pope.*
10. Excursion on the wing.
If there were any certain height where the *flights* of ambition end, one might imagine that the interest of France were but to conserve its present greatness. *Temple.*
It is not only the utmost pitch of impiety, but the highest *flight* of folly, to deride these things. *Tillotson, Sermon* 2.
11. The power of flying.
In my school-days, when I had lost one shaft,
I shot his fellow of the self-same *flight*
The self-same way. *Shakespeare's Merchant of Venice.*

FLI'GHTY. *adj.* [from *flight.*]
1. Fleeting; swift.
Time, thou anticipat'st my dread exploits:
The *flighty* purpose never is o'ertook,
Unless the deed go with it. *Shakespeare's Macbeth.*
2. Wild; full of imagination.

FLI'MSY. *adj.* [Of this word I know not any original, and suspect it to have crept into our language from the cant of manufacturers.]
1. Weak; feeble; without strength of texture.
2. Mean; spiritless; without force.
Proud of a vast extent of *flimsy* lines. *Pope, Epistle* ii.

To FLINCH. *v. n.* [corrupted from *fling. Skinner.*]
1. To shrink from any suffering or undertaking; to withdraw from any pain or danger.
Every martyr could keep one eye steadily fixed upon immortality, and look death and danger out of countenance with the other; nor did they *flinch* from duty, for fear of martyrdom. *South's Sermons.*
A child, by a constant course of kindness, may be accustomed to bear very rough usage without *flinching* or complaining. *Locke.*
Oh ingratitude, that John Bull, whom I have honoured with my friendship, should *flinch* at last, and pretend that he can disburse no more money. *Arbuthnot's History of John Bull.*
2. In *Shakespeare* it signifies to fail.
If I break time, or *flinch* in property
Of what I spoke, unpitied let me die. *Shakespeare.*

FLI'NCHER. *n. s.* [from the verb.] He who shrinks or fails in any matter.

To FLING. preter. *flung*; part. *flung* or *flong*. *v. a.* [from *fligo*, Latin, *Skinner*: according to others from *flying*; so to fling is to *set flying.*]
1. To cast from the hand; to throw.
The matrons *flung* their gloves,
Ladies and maids their scarfs and handkerchiefs
Upon him. *Shakespeare's Coriolanus.*
'Tis fate that *flings* the dice; and as she *flings*,
Of kings makes peasants, and of peasants kings. *Dryden.*
2. To dart; to cast with violence.
How much unlike that Hector who return'd
Clad in Achilles' spoils; when he, among
A thousand ships, like Jove, his lightning *flung*. *Denham.*
3. To scatter.
Ev'ry beam new transient colours *flings*,
Colours that change whene'er they wave their wings. *Pope.*
4. To drive by violence.
A heap of rocks, falling, would expel the waters out of their places with such a violence as to *fling* them among the highest clouds. *Burnet's Theory of the Earth.*
5. To move forcibly.
The knight seeing his habitation reduced to so small compass, ordered all the apartments to be *flung* open. *Addis. Spect.*
6. To eject; to dismiss.
Cromwell, I charge thee *fling* away ambition;
By that sin fell the angels. *Shakespeare's Henry* VIII.
7. To cast reproach.
I know thy gen'rous temper:
Fling but the appearance of dishonour on it,
It strait takes fire. *Addison's Cato.*
8. To force into another condition, properly into a worse.
Squalid fortune, into baseness *flong*,
Doth scorn the pride of wonted ornaments. *Spenser.*
9. *To* FLING *down.* To demolish; to ruin.
These are so far from raising mountains, that they overturn and *fling down* some of those which were before standing. *Woodward's Natural History.*
10. *To* FLING *off.* To baffle in the chace; to defeat of a prey.
These men are too well acquainted with the chace to be *flung off* by any false steps or doubles. *Addison's Spectator.*

To FLING. *v. n.*
1. To flounce; to wince; to fly into violent and irregular motions.
The angry beast
Began to kick, and *fling*, and wince,
As if h' had been beside his sense. *Hudibras, p.* i. *cant.* 2.
Their consciences are galled by it, and this makes them wince and *fling* as if they had some mettle. *Tillotson's Sermons.*
2. *To* FLING *out.* To grow unruly or outrageous: from the act of any angry horse that throws out his legs.
Duncan's horses,
Turn'd wild in nature, broke their stalls, *flung out*,
Contending 'gainst obedience. *Shakespeare's Macbeth.*

FLING. *n. s.* [from the verb.]
1. A throw; a cast.
2. A gibe; a sneer; a contemptuous remark.
No little scribbler is of wit so bare,
But has his *fling* at the poor wedded pair. *Addison.*
I, who love to have a *fling*
Both at senate-house and king,
Thought no method more commodious
Than to show their vices odious. *Swift.*

FLI'NGER. *n. s.* [from the verb.]
1. He who throws.
2. He who jeers.

FLINT. *n. s.* [ꝼlınt, Saxon.]
1. A semi-pellucid stone, composed of crystal debased, of a blackish grey, of one similar and equal substance, free from veins, and naturally invested with a whitish crust. It is sometimes smooth and equal, more frequently rough: its size is various. It is well known to strike fire with steel. It is useful in glassmaking. *Hill on Fossils.*
Searching the window for a *flint*, I found
This paper. *Shakespeare's Julius Cæsar.*
Love melts the rigour which the rocks have bred;
A *flint* will break upon a featherbed. *Cleaveland.*
There is the same force and the same refreshing virtue in fire kindled by a spark from a *flint*, as if it were kindled by a beam from the sun. *South's Sermons.*
Take this, and lay your *flint* edg'd weapon by. *Dryden.*
I'll fetch quick fuel from the neighb'ring wood,
And strike the sparkling *flint*, and dress the food. *Prior.*
2. Any thing eminently or proverbially hard.
Your tears, a heart of *flint*
Might tender make. *Spenser.*
Throw my heart
Against the *flint* and hardness of my fault. *Sh. Ant. and Cleop.*

FLI'NTY. *adj.* [from *flint.*]
1. Made of flint; strong.
Tyrant custom
Hath made the *flinty* and steel couch of war
My thrice-driven bed of down. *Shakesp. Othello.*
A pointed *flinty* rock, all bare and black,
Grew gibbous from behind the mountain's back. *Dryden.*
2. Full of stones.
The gathering up of flints in *flinty* ground, and laying them on heaps, is no good husbandry. *Bacon's Natural History.*
3. Hard of heart; cruel; savage; inexorable.
I did him a desired office,
Dear almost as his life; which gratitude,
Through *flinty* Tartar's bosom, would peep forth,
And answer thanks. *Shakespeare's All's well that ends well.*

FLIPP. *n. s.* [A cant word.] A liquor much used in ships, made by mixing beer with spirits and sugar.
The tarpawlin and swabber is lolling at Madagascar, with some drunken sunburnt whore, over a can of *flip*. *Dennis.*

FLIPPA'NT. *adj.* [A word of no great authority, probably derived from *flip-flap.*]

1. Nimble; moveable. It is used only of the act of speech.

An excellent anatomist promised to dissect a woman's tongue, and examine whether there may not be in it certain juices, which render it so wonderfully voluble or *flippant*. *Addison.*

2. Pert; talkative.

Away with *flippant* epilogues. *Thomson.*

Fli'ppantly. *adv.* [from the adjective.] In a flowing prating way.

To FLIRT. *v. a.* [*Skinner* thinks it formed from the sound.]

1. To throw any thing with a quick elastick motion.

Dick the scavenger
Flirts from his cart the mud in Walpole's face. *Swift.*

2. To move with quickness.

Permit some happier man
To kiss your hand, or *flirt* your fan. *Dorset.*

To Flirt. *v. n.*

1. To jeer; to gibe at one.
2. To run about perpetually; to be unsteady and fluttering.

Flirt. *n. s.* [from the verb.]

1. A quick elastick motion.

In unfurling the fan are several little *flirts* and vibrations, as also gradual and deliberate openings. *Addison's Spectator.*

Before you pass th' imaginary sights
While the spread fan o'ershades your closing eyes,
Then give one *flirt*, and all the vision flies. *Pope.*

2. A sudden trick.

Have licence to play,
At the hedge a *flirt*,
For a sheet or a shirt. *Ben. Johnson's Gypsies.*

3. A pert young hussey.

Scurvy knave, I am none of his *flirt* gills; I am none of his skains mates. *Shakesp. Romeo and Juliet.*

Several young *flirts* about town had a design to cast us out of the fashionable world. *Addison's Guardian*, Nº. 109.

Flirta'tion. *n. s.* [from *flirt.*] A quick sprightly motion. A cant word among women.

A muslin flounce, made very full, would give a very agreeable *flirtation* air. *Pope.*

To Flit. *v. n.* [from *To fleet*; or from *flitter*, Danish, to remove.]

1. To fly away.

Likest it seemeth, in my simple wit,
Unto the fair sunshine in Summer's day,
That when a dreadful storm away is *flit*,
Through the broad world doth spread his goodly ray. *Spens.*
His grudging ghost did strive
With the frail flesh; at last it *flitted* is,
Whither the souls do die of men that live amiss. *Fairy Qu.*

2. To remove; to migrate. In Scotland it is still used for removing from one place to another at quarter-day, or the usual term.

So hardly he the *flitted* life does win,
Unto her native prison to return. *Fairy Queen, cant.* 7.

It became a received opinion, that the souls of men, departing this life, did *flit* out one body into some other. *Hooker.*

3. To flutter; to rove on the wing.

He made a glancing shot, and miss'd the dove;
Yet miss'd so narrow, that he cut the cord
Which fasten'd, by the foot, the *flitting* bird. *Dryd. Æn.*
Fear the just gods, and think of Scylla's fate!
Chang'd to a bird, and sent to *flit* in air. *Pope.*

4. To be flux or unstable.

Himself up high he lifted from the ground,
And with strong flight did forcibly divide
The yielding air, which nigh too feeble found
Her *flitting* parts, and element unsound. *Fairy Queen, b.* i.
He stopt at once the passage of his wind,
And the free soul to *flitting* air resign'd. *Dryden's Æn.*

Flit. *adj.* [from *fleet.*] Swift; nimble; quick.

And in his hand two darts exceeding *flit*,
And deadly sharp, he held; whose heads were dight,
In poison and in blood, of malice and despight. *Fairy Qu.*

Flitch. *n. s.* [flicce, Saxon; *flycke*, Danish; *fleche*, *floche*, French. *Skinner.*] The side of a hog salted and cured.

But heretofore 'twas thought a sumptuous feast,
On birthdays, festivals, or days of state,
A salt dry *flitch* of bacon to prepare;
If they had fresh meat, 'twas delicious fare. *Dryden's Juv.*
While he from out the chimney took
A *flitch* of bacon off the hook,
Cut out large slices to be fry'd. *Swift.*

He sometimes accompanies the present with a *flitch* of bacon. *Addison.*

Fli'ttermouse. *n. s.* The bat.

Fli'tting. *n. s.* [flit, Saxon, scandal.] An offence; a fault.

Thou tellest my *flittings*, put my tears into thy bottle. *Psalm* lvi.

Flix. *n. s.* [corrupted from *flax.*] Down; fur; soft hair.

With his loll'd tongue he faintly licks his prey;
His warm breath blows her *flix* up as she lies:
She trembling creeps upon the ground away,
And looks back to him with beseeching eyes. *Dryden.*

Fli'xwood. *n. s.* See Hedge-mustard.

To FLOAT. *v. n.* [*flotter*, French.]

1. To swim on the surface of the water.

When the sea was calm, all boats alike
Shew'd mastership in *floating*. *Shakespeare's Coriolanus.*
The ark no more now *floats*, but seems on ground,
Fast on the top of some high mountain fix'd. *Milt. P. L.*

That men, being drowned and sunk, do *float* the ninth day, when their gall breaketh, are popular affirmations. *Brown.*

Three blust'ring nights, born by the southern blast,
I *floated*; and discover'd land at last. *Dryden's Æn. b.* vi.
His rosy wreath was dropt not long before,
Born by the tide of wine, and *floating* on the floor. *Dryden.*
On frothy billows thousands *float* the stream,
In cumb'rous mail, with love of farther shore. *Phillips.*

Carp are very apt to *float* away with fresh water. *Mortimer.*

2. To move without labour in a fluid.

What divine monsters, O ye gods, were these
That *float* in air, and fly upon the seas! *Dryd. Ind. Emp.*
Swift they descend, with wing to wing conjoin'd,
Stretch their broad plumes, and *float* upon the wind. *Pope.*

3. To pass with a light irregular course.

Floating visions make not deep impressions enough to leave in the mind clear, distinct, lasting ideas. *Locke.*

To Float. *v. a.* To cover with water.

Proud Pactolus *floats* the fruitful lands,
And leaves a rich manure of golden sands. *Dryden's Æn.*

Venice looks, at a distance, like a great town half *floated* by a deluge. *Addison's Remarks on Italy.*

Now smoaks with show'rs the misty mountain-ground,
And *floated* fields lie undistinguish'd round. *Pope's Statius.*
The vast parterres a thousand hands shall make:
Lo! Cobham comes, and *floats* them with a lake. *Pope.*

Float. *n. s.* [from the verb.]

1. The act of flowing; the flux; the contrary to the ebb. A sense now out of use.

Our trust in the Almighty is, that with us contentions are now at their highest *float*. *Hooker, Preface.*

Of this kind is some disposition of bodies to rotation, particularly from East to West; of which kind we conceive the main *float* and refloat of the sea is, which is by consent of the universe, as part of the diurnal motion. *Bacon's Nat. History.*

2. Any body so contrived or formed as to swim upon the water.

They took it for a ship, and, as it came nearer, for a boat; but it proved a *float* of weeds and rushes. *L'Estrange's Fables.*

A passage for the weary people make;
With osier *floats* the standing water strow,
Of massy stones make bridges, if it flow. *Dryden's Virgil.*

3. The cork or quill by which the angler discovers the bite of a fish.

You will find this to be a very choice bait, sometimes casting a little of it into the place where your *float* swims. *Walton.*

4. A cant word for a level.

Banks are measured by the *float* or floor, which is eighteen foot square, and one deep. *Mortimer's Husbandry.*

Flo'aty. *adj.* Buoyant and swimming a-top.

The hindrance to stay well is the extreme length of a ship, especially if she be *floaty*, and want sharpness of way forwards. *Raleigh's Essays.*

FLOCK. *n. s.* [flocc, Saxon.]

1. A company; usually a company of birds or beasts.

She that hath a heart of that fine frame,
To pay this debt of love but to a brother,
How will she love when the rich golden shaft
Hath kill'd the *flock* of all affections else
That live in her. *Shakesp. Twelfth Night.*

2. A company of sheep, distinguished from *herds*, which are of oxen.

The cattle in the fields, and meadows green,
Those rare and solitary; these in *flocks*
Pasturing at once, and in broad herds upsprung. *Milton.*

France has a sheep by her, not only as a sacrifice, but to shew that the riches of the country consisted chiefly in *flocks* and pasturage. *Addison on ancient Medals.*

3. A body of men.

The heathen that had fled out of Judea came to Nicanor by *flocks.* 2 *Mac.* xiv. 14.

4. [From *floccus.*] A lock of wool.

A house well furnish'd shall be thine to keep;
And, for a *flock* bed, I can sheer my sheep. *Dryden.*

To Flock. *v. n.* [from the noun.] To gather in crowds or large numbers.

Many young gentlemen *flock* to him every day, and fleet the time carelesly. *Shakes. As you like it.*

Upon the return of the ambassadors, the poor of all sorts *flocked* together to the great master's house. *Knolles's History.*

Others ran *flocking* out of their houses to the general supplication. 2 *Mac.* iii. 18.

Stilpo, when the people *flocked* about him, and that one said, The people come wondering about you, as if it were to see

see some strange beast; no, saith he, it is to see a man which Diogenes sought with his lanthorn at noon-day. *Bacon.*

Seeing the spirits swelling the nerves cause the arm's motion, upon its resistance they *flock* from other parts of the body to overcome it. *Digby on Bodies.*

The wits of the town came thither;
'Twas strange to see how they *flock'd* together;
Each strongly confident of his own way,
Thought to gain the laurel that day. *Suckling.*

Friends daily *flock.* *Dryden's Æn.*

The Trojan youth about the captive *flock,*
To wonder, or to pity, or to mock. *Denham.*

People do not *flock* to courts so much for their majesties service, as for making their fortunes. *L'Estrange.*

To FLOG. *v. a.* [from *flagrum,* Latin.] To lash; to whip; to chastise.

The schoolmaster's joy is to *flog.* *Swift.*

FLONG. *particip. passive,* from *To fling,* used by *Spenser.* See FLING.

FLOOD. *n. s.* [flod, Saxon; *flot,* French.]

1. A body of water; the sea; a river.

What need the bridge much broader than the *flood?* *Shak.*

His dominion shall be also from the one sea to the other, and from the *flood* unto the world's end. *Psalm* lxxii. 8.

Or thence from Niger *flood* to Atlas mount,
The kingdoms of Almanzor, Fez, and Sus,
Morocco, and Algiers, and Tremisen. *Milton's Par. Lost.*

All dwellings else
Flood overwhelm'd, and them with all their pomp
Deep under water roll'd; sea cover'd sea,
Sea without shore. *Milton's Paradise Lost, b.* xi.

Arcadia's flow'ry plains and pleasing *floods.* *Dryden's Virg.*

2. A deluge; an inundation.

When went there by an age since the great *flood,*
But it was fam'd with more than with one man? *Shakesp.*

You see this confluence, this great *flood* of visiters. *Shak.*

By sudden *floods,* and fall of waters,
Buckingham's army is dispers'd and scatter'd. *Shak. R.* III.

3. Flow; flux; not ebb; not reflux; the swelling of a river by rain or inland flood.

We seek to know the moving of each sphere,
And the strange cause o' th' ebbs and *floods* of Nile. *Davies.*

4. Catamenia.

Those that have the good fortune of miscarrying, or being delivered, escape by means of their *floods* revelling the humours from their lungs. *Harvey on Consumptions.*

To FLOOD. *v. a.* [from the noun.] To deluge; to cover with waters.

Where meadows are *flooded* late in Spring, roll them with a large barley-roller. *Mortimer's Husbandry.*

FLO'ODGATE. *n. s.* [*flood* and *gate.*] Gate or shutter by which the watercourse is closed or opened at pleasure.

As if the opening of her mouth to Zelmane had opened some great *floodgate* of sorrow, whereof her heart could not abide the violent issue, she sunk to the ground. *Sidney.*

Yet there the steel staid not; but inly bate
Deep in his flesh, and opened wide a red *floodgate.* *Fai. Qu.*

His youth, and want of experience in maritime service, had somewhat been shrewdly touched, even before the sluices and *floodgates* of popular liberty were yet set open. *Wotton.*

The rain descended for forty days, the cataracts or *floodgates* of heaven being opened. *Burnet's Theory of the Earth.*

FLOOK. *n. s.* [*pflug,* a plow, German.] The broad part of the anchor which takes hold of the ground.

FLOOR. *n. s.* [flor, flore, Saxon.]

1. The pavement: a pavement is always of stone, the floor of wood or stone; the part on which one treads.

His stepmother, making all her gestures counterfeit affliction, lay almost groveling upon the *floor* of her chamber. *Sidn.*

He rent that iron door
With furious force, and indignation fell;
Where entered in, his foot could find no *floor,*
But all a deep descent as dark as hell. *Fairy Queen, b.* i,

Look how the *floor* of heav'n
Is thick inlay'd with patens of bright gold:
There's not the smallest orb which thou behold'st,
But in his motion like an angel sings,
Still quiring to the young ey'd cherubims. *Shakespeare.*

The ground lay strewed with pikes so thick as a *floor* is usually strewed with rushes. *Hayward.*

He winnoweth barley to-night in the threshing *floor.* *Ruth.*

2. A story; a flight of rooms.

He that building stays at one
Floor, or the second, hath erected none. *Johnson's Catiline.*

To FLOOR. *v. a.* [from the noun.] To cover the bottom with a floor.

Hewn stone and timber to *floor* the houses. 2 *Chro.* xxxiv.

FLO'ORING. *n. s.* [from *floor.*] Bottom; floor.

The *flooring* is a kind of red plaister made of brick, ground to powder, and afterwards worked into mortar. *Addison.*

To FLOP. *v. a.* [from *flap.*] To clap the wings with noise; to play with any noisy motion of a broad body.

A blackbird was frighted almost to death with a huge *flopping* kite that she saw over her head. *L'Estrange.*

FLO'RAL. *adj.* [*floralis,* Latin.] Relating to Flora, or to flowers.

Let one great day
To celebrated sports and *floral* play
Be set aside. *Prior.*

FLO'RENCE. *n. s.* [from the city *Florence.*] A kind of cloath. *Dict.*

FLO'REN. *n. s.* [so named, says *Camden,* because made by *Florentines.*] A gold coin of Edward III. in value six shillings.

FLO'RET. *n. s.* [*fleurette,* French.] A small imperfect flower.

FLO'RID. *adj.* [*floridus,* Latin.]

1. Productive of flowers; covered with flowers.

2. Bright in colour; flushed with red.

Our beauty is in colour inferiour to many flowers; and when it is most *florid* and gay, three fits of an ague can change it into yellowness and leanness. *Taylor's Rule of living holy.*

The qualities of blood in a healthy state are to be *florid,* when let out of the vessel, the red part congealing strongly and soon. *Arbuthnot on Aliments.*

3. Embellished; splendid; brilliant with decorations.

The *florid,* elevated, and figurative way is for the passions; for love and hatred, fear and anger, are begotten in the soul, by shewing their objects out of their true proportion. *Dryden.*

How did, pray, the *florid* youth offend,
Whose speech you took, and gave it to a friend? *Pope.*

FLORI'DITY. *n. s.* [from *florid.*] Freshness of colour.

There is a *floridity* in the face from the good digestion of the red part of the blood. *Floyer on the Humours.*

FLO'RIDNESS. *n. s.* [from *florid.*]

1. Freshness of colour.

2. Embellishment; ambitious elegance.

Though a philosopher need not delight readers with his *floridness,* yet he may take a care that he disgust them not by flatness. *Boyle.*

FLORI'FEROUS. *adj.* [*florifer,* Latin.] Productive of flowers.

FLO'RIN. *n. s.* [French.] A coin first made by the Florentines. That of Germany is in value 2 *s.* 4 *d.* that of Spain 4 *s.* 4 *d.* halfpenny; that of Palermo and Sicily 2 *s.* 6 *d.* that of Holland 2 *s.*

In the Imperial chamber the proctors have half a *florin* taxed and allowed them for every substantial recess. *Ayliffe.*

FLO'RIST. *n. s.* [*fleuriste,* French.] A cultivater of flowers.

Some botanists or *florists* at the least. *Dunciad, b.* iv.

And while they break
On the charm'd eye, th' exulting *florist* marks
With secret pride the wonders of his hand. *Thoms. Spring.*

FLO'RULENT. *adj.* [*floris,* Latin.] Flowery; blossoming.

FLO'SCULOUS. *adj.* [*flosculus,* Latin.] Composed of flowers; having the nature or form of flowers.

The outward part is a thick and carnous covering, and the second a dry and *flosculous* coat. *Brown's Vulgar Errours.*

To FLOTE. *v. a.* [See *To fleet.*] To skim.

Such cheeses, good Cisley, ye *floted* too nigh. *Tusser.*

FLO'TSON. *n. s.* [from *flote.*] Goods that swim without an owner on the sea.

FLO'TTEN. *part.* [from *flote.*] Skimmed. *Skinner.*

To FLOUNCE. *v. n.* [*plonsen,* Dutch, to plunge.]

1. To move with violence in the water or mire; to struggle or dash in the water.

With his broad fins and forky tail he laves
The rising surge, and *flounces* in the waves. *Addison's Ovid.*

2. To move with weight and tumult.

Six *flouncing* Flanders mares
Are e'en as good as any two of theirs. *Prior.*

3. To move with passionate agitation.

When I'm duller than a post,
Nor can the plainest word pronounce,
You neither fume, nor fret, nor *flounce.* *Swift.*

To FLOUNCE. *v. a.* To deck with flounces.

She was *flounced* and furbelowed from head to foot; every ribbon was crinkled, and every part of her garments in curl. *Addison's Spectator,* N°. 129.

They have got into the fashion of *flouncing* the petticoat so very deep, that it looks like an entire coat of lutestring. *Pope.*

FLOUNCE. *n. s.* [from the verb.] Any thing sewed to the garment, and hanging loose, so as to swell and shake.

Nay, oft in dreams invention we bestow,
To change a *flounce,* or add a furbelow. *Pope.*

A muslin *flounce,* made very full, would be very agreeable. *Pope.*

FLO'UNDER. *n. s.* [*flynder,* Danish; *fluke,* Scottish.] The name of a small flat fish.

Like the *flounder,* out of the frying-pan into the fire. *Camd.*

Flounders will both thrive and breed in any pond. *Mortimer.*

To FLO'UNDER. *v. n.* [from *flounce.*] To struggle with violent and irregular motions: as a horse in the mire.

Down goes at once the horseman and the horse;
That courser stumbles on the fallen steed,
And *flound'ring* throws the rider o'er his head. *Dryden.*

The

The more inform'd, the leſs he underſtood,
And deeper ſunk by *flound'ring* in the mud. *Dryden.*
He champs the bit, impatient of his loſs,
And ſtarts aſide, and *flounders* at the croſs. *Dryden.*
He plung'd for ſenſe, but found no bottom there;
Then writ and *flounder'd* on, in mere deſpair. *Pope's Dunc.*

To FLO'URISH. *v. n.* [*floreo, floreſco*, Latin.]

1. To be in vigour; not to fade.

The righteous ſhall *flouriſh* like the palm-tree. *Pſ.* xcii. 12.

Where e'er you tread, the bluſhing flow'rs ſhall riſe,
And all things *flouriſh* where you turn your eyes. *Pope.*

2. To be in a proſperous ſtate.

If I could find example
Of thouſands, that had ſtruck anointed kings,
And *flouriſh'd* after, I'd not do't: but ſince
Nor braſs, nor ſtone, nor parchment, bears not one,
Let villany itſelf forſwear't. *Shakeſp. Winter's Tale.*

Harry, that propheſied thou ſhould'ſt be king,
Doth comfort thee in ſleep; live thou and *flouriſh. Shakeſp.*

He was the patron of my manhood, when I *flouriſhed* in the opinion of the world, though with ſmall advantage to my fortune. *Dryden's Dedicat. to Lord Clifford.*

3. To uſe florid language; to ſpeak with ambitious copiouſneſs and elegance.

Whilſt Cicero acts the part of a rhetorician, he dilates and *flouriſhes*, and gives example inſtead of rule. *Baker.*

You ſhould not affect to *flouriſh* in a copious harangue and a diffuſive ſtyle in company. *Watts's Improvement of the Mind.*

They dilate ſometimes, and *flouriſh* long upon little incidents, and they ſkip over and but lightly touch the drier part of their theme. *Watts's Logick.*

4. To deſcribe various figures by interſecting lines; to play in wanton and irregular motions.

Impetuous ſpread
The ſtream and ſmoaking, *flouriſh'd* o'er his head. *Pope.*

5. To boaſt; to brag.

6. [In muſick.] To play ſome prelude.

To FLO'URISH. *v. a.*

1. To adorn with vegetable beauty.

With ſhadowy verdure *flouriſh'd* high,
A ſudden youth the groves enjoy. *Fenton.*

2. To adorn with figures of needle work.

3. To work with a needle into figures.

All that I ſhall ſay will be but like bottoms of thread cloſe wound up, which, with a good needle, perhaps may be *flouriſhed* into large works. *Bacon's War with Spain.*

4. To move any thing in quick circles or vibrations by way of ſhow or triumph.

And all the powers of hell in full applauſe
Flouriſh'd their ſnakes, and toſs'd their flaming brands. *Cra.*

Againſt the poſt their wicker ſhields they cruſh,
Flouriſh the ſword, and at the plaſtron puſh. *Dryden's Juv.*

5. To adorn with embelliſhments of language; to grace with eloquence oſtentatiouſly diffuſive.

We ſhould add the labours of Hercules, though *flouriſhed* with much fabulous matter; yet it doth notably ſet forth the conſent of all nations and ages in the approbation of the extirpating and debellating giants, monſters and tyrants. *Bacon.*

6. To adorn; to embelliſh; to grace.

To bring you thus together, 'tis no ſin,
Sith that the juſtice of your title to him
Doth *flouriſh* the deceit. *Shakeſ. Meaſure for Meaſure.*

FLO'URISH. *n. ſ.* [from the verb.]

1. Bravery; beauty.

I call'd thee then vain *flouriſh* of my fortune;
I call'd thee then poor ſhadow, painted queen,
The preſentation of but what I was. *Shakeſp. Richard* III.

The *flouriſh* of his ſober youth,
Was the pride of naked truth. *Craſhaw.*

2. An oſtentatious embelliſhment; ambitious copiouſneſs; farfetched elegance.

This is a *flouriſh*: there follow excellent parables. *Bacon.*

We can excuſe the duty of our knowledge, if we only beſtow the *flouriſh* of poetry thereon, or thoſe commendatory conceits which popularly ſet forth the eminence of this creature. *Brown's Vulgar Errours, b.* vi. *c.* 5.

The apprehenſion is ſo deeply rivetted into my mind, that ſuch rhetorical *flouriſhes* cannot at all looſen or bruſh it out. *More's Divine Dialogues.*

Villanies have not the ſame countenance, when there are great intereſts, plauſible colours, and *flouriſhes* of wit and rhetorick interpoſed between the ſight and the object. *L'Eſtr.*

The ſo much repeated ornament and *flouriſh* of their former ſpeeches was commonly the trueſt word they ſpoke, tho' leaſt believed by them. *South's Sermons.*

Studious to pleaſe the genius of the times,
With periods, points, and tropes he ſlurs his crimes;
He lards with *flouriſhes* his long harangue;
'Tis fine, ſay'ſt thou; what to be prais'd, and hang? *Dryd.*

3. Figures formed by lines curiouſly or wantonly drawn.

A child with delight looks upon emblems finely drawn and painted, and takes ſome pleaſure in beholding the neat characters and *flouriſhes* of a bible curiouſly printed. *Boyle.*

They were intended only for ludicrous ornaments of nature, like the *flouriſhes* about a great letter that ſignify nothing, but are made only to delight the eye. *More againſt Atheiſm.*

FLO'URISHER. *n. ſ.* [from *flouriſh.*] One that is in prime or in proſperity.

They count him of the green-hair'd eld, they may, or in his flow'r;
For not our greateſt *flouriſher* can equal him in pow'r. *Chapman's Iliads.*

To FLOUT. *v. a.* [*fluyten*, Dutch; *flouwe*, Friſick.] To mock; to inſult; to treat with mockery and contempt.

You muſt *flout* my inſufficiency. *Shakeſpeare.*

The Norweyan banners *flout* the ſky,
And fan our people cold. *Shakeſpeare's Macbeth.*

He mock'd us when he begg'd our voices;
Certainly he *flouted* us downright. *Shakeſp. Coriolanus.*

She railed at her, that ſhe ſhould be ſo immodeſt to write to one ſhe knew would *flout* her. *Shakeſpeare.*

Phillida *flouts* me. *Walton's Angler.*

To FLOUT. *v. n.* To practiſe mockery; to behave with contempt; to ſneer.

Though nature hath given us wit to *flout* at fortune, hath not fortune ſent in this fool to cut off this argument? *Shakeſ.*

With talents well endu'd
To be ſcurrilous and rude;
When you pertly raiſe your ſnout,
Fleer and gibe, and laugh and *flout.* *Swift.*

FLOUT. *n. ſ.* [from the verb.] A mock; an inſult; a word or act of contempt.

He would aſk of thoſe that had been at the other's table,
Tell truly, was there never a *flout* or dry blow given? *Bacon.*

She opened it, and read it out,
With many a ſmile and leering *flout.* *Hudibras, p.* iii.

Their doors are barr'd againſt a bitter *flout*;
Snarl, if you pleaſe; but you ſhall ſnarl without. *Dryden.*

How many *flouts* and jeers muſt I expoſe myſelf to by this repentance? How ſhall I anſwer ſuch an old acquaintance when he invites me to an intemperate cup? *Calamy's Serm.*

FLO'UTER. *n. ſ.* [from *flout.*] One who jeers.

To FLOW. *v. n.* [flopan, Saxon.]

1. To run or ſpread as water.

The god am I, whoſe yellow water *flows*
Around theſe fields, and fattens as it goes. *Dryden's Æn.*

Fields of light and liquid ether *flow*,
Purg'd from the pond'rous dregs of earth below. *Dryden.*

Endleſs tears *flow* down in ſtreams. *Swift.*

2. To run: oppoſed to ſtanding waters.

With oſier floats the ſtanding water ſtrow;
Of maſſy ſtones make bridges, if it *flow.* *Dryden.*

2. To riſe; not to ebb.

This river hath thrice *flow'd*, no ebb between. *Shakeſp.*

3. To melt.

Oh that thou wouldſt rent the heavens, that the mountains might *flow* down at thy preſence. *Iſ.* lxiv. 1.

4. To proceed; to iſſue.

I'll uſe that tongue I have: if wit *flow* from 't,
I ſhall do good. *Shakeſpeare's Winter's Tale.*

The knowledge drawn from experience is quite of another kind from that which *flows* from ſpeculation or diſcourſe. *South.*

5. To glide ſmoothly without aſperity: as, a *flowing* period.

This diſcourſe of Cyprian, and the flowers of rhetorick in it, ſhew him to have been of a great wit and *flowing* eloquence. *Hakewill on Providence.*

6. To write ſmoothly; to ſpeak volubly.

Virgil is ſweet and *flowing* in his hexameters. *Dryden.*

Did ſweeter ſounds adorn my *flowing* tongue
Than ever man pronounc'd, or angel ſung. *Prior.*

7. To abound; to be crowded.

The dry ſtreets *flow'd* with men. *Chapman.*

8. To be copious; to be full.

Then ſhall our names,
Be in their *flowing* cups freſhly remember'd. *Shak. Hen.* V.

There ev'ry eye with ſlumb'rous chains ſhe bound,
And daſh'd the *flowing* goblet to the ground. *Pope's Odyſſey.*

9. To hang looſe and waving.

He was cloathed in a *flowing* mantle of green ſilk, interwoven with flowers. *Spectator,* N°. 425.

To FLOW. *v. a.* To overflow; to deluge.

In a hot dry Summer watering would be a very great advantage to hops; but it is ſcarce practicable, unleſs you have a ſtream at hand to *flow* the ground. *Mortimer's Husbandry.*

FLOW. *n. ſ.* [from the verb.]

1. The riſe of water; not the ebb.

Some, from the diurnal and annual motion of the earth, endeavour to ſolve the *flows* and motions of theſe ſeas, illuſtrating the ſame by water in a bowl, that riſes or falls according to the motion of the veſſel. *Brown's Vulgar Errours.*

The ebb of tides, and their myſterious *flow*,
We as arts elements ſhall underſtand. *Dryden's Ann. Mirab.*

2. A ſudden plenty or abundance.

The noble power of ſuffering bravely is as far above that of of enterpriſing greatly, as an unblemiſhed conſcience and inflexible reſolution are above an accidental *flow* of ſpirits, or a ſudden tide of blood. *Pope.*

3. A ſtream of diction; volubility of tongue.

Teaching is not a *flow* of words, nor the draining of an hour-glaſs; but an effectual procuring that a man know ſomething which he knew not before, or to know it better. *South.*

FLO'WER. *n. ſ.* [*fleur*, French; *flos, flores*, Latin.]

1. The part of a plant which contains the ſeeds.

Such are reckoned perfect *flowers* which have petala, a ſtamen, apex and ſtylus; and whatever *flower* wants either of theſe is reckoned imperfect. Perfect *flowers* are divided into ſimple ones, which are not compoſed of other ſmaller ones, and which uſually have but one ſingle ſtyle; and compounded, which conſiſt of many floſculi, all making but one *flower*. Simple *flowers* are monopetalous, which have the body of the *flower* all of one intire leaf, though ſometimes cut or divided a little way into many ſeeming petala, or leaves; as in borage, bugloſs, &c. or polypetalous, which have diſtinct petala, and thoſe falling off ſingly, and not all together, as the ſeeming petala of monopetalous *flowers* always do: but thoſe are further divided into uniform and difform *flowers*: the former have their right and left hand parts, and the forward and backward parts all alike; but the difform have no ſuch regularity, as in the *flowers* of ſage, deadnettle, &c. A monopetalous difform *flower* is likewiſe further divided into, firſt, ſemi-fiſtular, whoſe upper part reſembles a pipe cut off obliquely, as in the ariloſtochia: 2d, labiate; and this either with one lip only, as in the acanthum and ſcordium, or with two lips, as in the far greater part of the labiate flowers: and here the upper lip is ſometimes turned upwards, and ſo turns the convex part downwards, as in the chamæciſſus, &c. but moſt commonly the upper lip is convex above, and turns the hollow part down to its fellow below, and ſo repreſents a kind of helmet or monkſhood; and from thence theſe are frequently called galeate, cucullate, and galericulate *flowers*; and in this form are the *flowers* of the lamium, and moſt verticillate plants. Sometimes alſo the lamium is intire, and ſometimes jagged or divided. 3d, Corniculate; that is, ſuch hollow *flowers* as have on their upper part a kind of ſpur, or little horn, as in the linaria, delphinum, &c. and the carniculum, or calcar, is always impervious at the tip or point. Compounded *flowers* are either, firſt, diſcous or diſcoidal; that is, whoſe floſculi are ſet together ſo cloſe, thick, and even, as to make the ſurface of the *flower* plain and flat, which therefore, becauſe of its round form, will be like a diſcus; which diſk is ſometimes radiated, when there is a row of petala ſtanding round in the diſk, like the points of a ſtar, as in the matricaria, chamæmelum, &c. and ſometimes naked, having no ſuch radiating leaves round the limb of its diſk, as in the tanacetum: 2d, planifolious, which is compoſed of plain flowers, ſet together in circular rows round the centre, and whoſe face is uſually indented, notched uneven and jagged, as the hieracia, &c. 3d, fiſtular, which is compounded of many long hollow little *flowers*, like pipes, all divided into large jags at the ends. Imperfect *flowers*, becauſe they want the petala, are called ſtamineous, apetalous, and capillaceous; and thoſe which hang pendulous by fine threads, like the juli, are by Tournefort called amentaceous, and we call them cats-tail. The term campaniformis is uſed for ſuch as are in the ſhape of a bell, and infundibuliformis for ſuch as are in the form of a funnel. *Miller.*

Good men's lives
Expire before the *flowers* in their caps,
Dying or ere they ſicken. *Shakeſpeare's Macbeth.*

With *flow'r* inwoven treſſes torn,
The nymphs in twilight ſhade of tangled thickets mourn. *Milton.*

Beauteous *flow'rs* why do we ſpread
Upon the monuments of the dead? *Cowley.*

Though the ſame ſun with all-diffuſive rays
Bluſh in the roſe and in the diamond blaze,
We praiſe the ſtronger effort of his power,
And always ſet the gem above the *flower*. *Pope.*

If the bloſſom of the plant be of moſt importance, we call it a *flower*; ſuch are daiſies, tulips, and carnations. *Watts.*

2. An ornament; an embelliſhment.

This diſcourſe of Cyprian, and the excellent *flowers* of rhetorick in it, ſhew him to have been a ſweet and powerful orator. *Hakewill on Providence.*

Truth needs no *flow'rs* of ſpeech. *Pope.*

3. The prime; the flouriſhing part.

Alas! young man, your days can ne'er be long:
In *flow'r* of age you periſh for a ſong. *Pope's Horace Impr.*

4. The edible part of corn; the meal.

The bread I would have in *flower*, ſo as it might be baked ſtill to ſerve their neceſſary want. *Spenſer on Ireland.*

I can make my audit up, that all
From me do back receive the *flow'r* of all,
And leave me but the bran. *Shakeſpeare's Coriolanus.*

The *flowers* of grains, mixed with water, will make a ſort of glue. *Arbuthnot on Aliments.*

But by thy care twelve urns of wine be fill'd,
Next theſe in worth, and firm thoſe urns be ſeal'd;
Be twice ten meaſures of the choiceſt *flour*
Prepar'd, ere yet deſcends the evening hour. *Pope's Odyſſey.*

5. The moſt excellent or valuable part of any thing; quinteſſence.

The choice and *flower* of all things profitable the Pſalms do more briefly contain, and more movingly expreſs, by reaſon of their poetical form. *Hooker.*

Thou haſt ſlain
The *flower* of Europe for his chivalry. *Shakeſp. Henry VI.*

The French monarchy is exhauſted of its braveſt ſubjects: the *flower* of the nation is conſumed in its wars. *Addiſon.*

6. That which is moſt diſtinguiſhed for any thing valuable.

He is not the *flower* of courteſy; but, I warrant him, as gentle as a lamb. *Shakeſp. Romeo and Juliet.*

FLO'WER *de Luce*. *n. ſ.* A bulbous iris.

It hath a lily flower of one leaf, ſhaped like that of the common iris: the pointal has three leaves, and the empalement turns to a fruit ſhaped like that of the common iris. Its root is bulbous. *Miller* ſpecifies thirty-four ſpecies of this plant; and among them the Perſian *flower de luce* is greatly eſteemed for the ſweetneſs and beauty of its variegated flowers, which are in perfection in February, or the beginning of March.

Crop'd are the *flower de luces* in your arms;
Of England's coat one half is cut away. *Shakeſ. Henry VI.*

The iris is the *flower de luce.* *Peacham.*

To FLO'WER. *v. n.* [*fleurir*, French, or from the noun.]

1. To be in flower; to be in bloſſom; to bloom; to put forth flowers.

So forth they marched in this goodly ſort,
To take the ſolace of the open air,
And in freſh *flowering* fields themſelves to ſport. *Fairy Qu.*

Sacred hill, whoſe head full high,
Is, as it were, for endleſs memory
Of that dear Lord, who oft thereon was found,
For ever with a *flow'ring* garland crown'd. *Fairy Queen.*

Then herbs of every leaf, that ſudden *flower'd*,
Op'ning their various colours. *Milton's Paradiſe Loſt, b.* vii.

Mark well the *flow'ring* almonds in the wood,
If od'rous blooms the bearing branches load. *Dryd. Georg.*

To leafleſs ſhrubs the *flow'ring* palms ſucceed,
And od'rous myrtle to the noiſome weed. *Pope's Meſſiah.*

2. To be in the prime; to flouriſh.

Whilome in youth, when *flower'd* my youthful ſpring,
Like ſwallow ſwift, I wandered here and there;
For heat of heedleſs luſt me did ſo ſting,
That I of doubted danger had no fear. *Spenſer's Paſtorals.*

This cauſe detain'd me all my *flow'ring* youth,
Within a loathſome dungeon there to pine. *Shak. Hen.* VI.

3. To froth; to ferment; to mantle, as new bottled beer.

Thoſe above water were the beſt, and that beer did *flower* a little; whereas that under water did not, though it were freſh. *Bacon's Natural Hiſtory,* Nº. 385.

An extreme clarification doth ſpread the ſpirits ſo ſmooth that they become dull, and the drink dead, which ought to have a little *flowering.* *Bacon's Natural Hiſtory.*

4. To come as cream from the ſurface.

If you can accept of theſe few obſervations, which have *flowered* off, and are, as it were, the burniſhing of many ſtudious and contemplative years, I here give you them to diſpoſe of. *Milton on Education.*

To FLO'WER. *v. a.* [from the noun.] To adorn with fictitious or imitated flowers.

FLO'WERAGE. *n. ſ.* [from *flower*.] Store of flowers. *Dict.*

FLO'WERET. *n. ſ.* [*fleuret*, French.] A flower; a ſmall flower.

Sometimes her head ſhe fondly would aguiſe
With gaudy garlands, or freſh *flow'rets* dight,
About her neck, or rings of ruſhes plight. *Fairy Queen.*

No more ſhall trenching war channel her fields,
Nor bruiſe her *flow'rets* with the armed hoofs
Of hoſtile pacer. *Shakeſpeare's Henry* IV.

That ſame dew, which ſometime on the buds
Was wont to ſwell, like round and orient pearls,
Stood now within the pretty *flow'ret's* eyes,
Like tears that did their own diſgrace bewail. *Shakeſpeare.*

So to the ſylvan lodge
They came, that like Pomona's arbour ſmil'd,
With *flow'rets* deck'd, and fragrant ſmells. *Milt. Par. Loſt.*

Then laughs the childiſh year with *flow'rets* crown'd,
And laviſhly perfumes the fields around;
But no ſubſtantial nouriſhment receives,
Infirm the ſtalks, unſolid are the leaves. *Dryden's Fables.*

FLO'WERGARDEN. *n. ſ.* [*flower* and *garden*.] A garden in which flowers are principally cultivated.

Obſerving that this manure produced flowers in the field, I made my gardener try thoſe ſhells in my *flowergarden*, and I never ſaw better carnations or flowers. *Mortimer's Husbandry.*

FLO'WERINESS. *n. ſ.* [from *flowery*.]

1. The ſtate of abounding in flowers.

2. Floridneſs of ſpeech.

FLO'WERINGBUSH. *n. ſ.* A plant.

The leaves are triangular and graſſy, the ſtalks naked, and the flowers diſpoſed in an umbella upon the top of the ſtalk, each conſiſting of ſix leaves: three of them are large, and three ſmall, which are expanded in form of a roſe. *Miller.*

FLO'WERY. *adj.* [from *flower.*] Full of flowers; adorned with flowers real or fictitious.

My mother Circe, with the ſyrens three,
Amid'ſt the *flow'ry* kirtl'd Naiades. *Milton.*

Day's harbinger
Comes dancing from the Eaſt, and leads with her
The *flow'ry* May, who from her green lap throws
The yellow cowſlip and the pale primroſe. *Milton.*

O'er his fair limbs a *flow'ry* veſt he threw. *Pope's Odyſſey.*

To her the ſhady grove, the *flow'ry* field,
The ſtreams and fountains, no delight could yield. *Pope.*

FLO'WINGLY. *adv.* [from *flow.*] With volubility; with abundance.

FLOWK. *n. ſ.* [*fluke*, Scott.] A flounder; the name of a fiſh.

Amongſt theſe the *flowk*, ſole, and plaice follow the tide up into the freſh waters. *Carew's Survey of Cornwal.*

FLO'WKWORT. *n ſ.* The name of a plant.

FLOWN. Participle of *fly*, or *flee*, they being confounded.

1. Gone away.

For thoſe,
Appointed to ſit there, had left their charge,
Flown to the upper world. *Milton's Paradiſe Loſt, b.* x.

Where, my deluded ſenſe! was reaſon *flown?*
Where the high majeſty of David's throne? *Prior.*

2. Puffed; inflated; elate.

And when night
Darkens the ſtreets, then wander forth the ſons
Of Beliah, *flown* with inſolence and wine. *Milton's P. L.*

FLU'CTUANT. *adj.* [*fluctuans*, Latin.] Wavering; uncertain.

To be longing for this thing to-day, and for that thing to-morrow; to change likings for loathings, and to ſtand wiſhing and hankering at a venture, how is it poſſible for any man to be at reſt in this *fluctuant* wandering humour and opinion? *L'Eſtrange.*

To FLU'CTUATE. *v. n.* [*fluctuo*, Latin.]

1. To roll to and again as water in agitation.

The *fluctuating* fields of liquid air,
With all the curious meteors hov'ring there,
And the wide regions of the land, proclaim
The Pow'r Divine, that rais'd the mighty frame. *Blackmore.*

2. To float backward and forward, as with the motion of water.

3. To move with uncertain and haſty motion.

The tempter
New part puts on; and, as to paſſion mov'd,
Fluctuates diſturb'd. *Milton's Paradiſe Loſt, b.* ix.

4. To be in an uncertain ſtate; to feel ſudden viciſſitudes.

As the greateſt part of my eſtate has been hitherto of an unſteady and volatile nature, either toſt upon ſeas, or *fluctuating* in funds, it is now fixed and ſettled in ſubſtantial acres and tenements. *Addiſon's Spectator*, N°. 549.

5. To be irreſolute; to be undetermined.

FLUCTUA'TION. *n. ſ.* [*fluctuatio*, Latin; *fluctuation*, French, from *fluctuate.*]

1. The alternate motion of the water.

Its *fluctuations* are but motions ſubſervient, which winds, ſtorms, ſhores, ſhelves, and every interjacency irregulates. *Brown's Vulgar Errours, b.* vii. *c.* 17.

They were cauſed by the impulſes and *fluctuation* of water in the bowels of the earth. *Woodward's Natural Hiſtory.*

2. Uncertainty; indetermination.

It will not hinder it from making a proſelyte of a perſon, that loves *fluctuation* of judgment little enough to be willing to be eaſed of it by any thing but errour. *Boyle.*

FLUE. *n. ſ.* [A word of which I know not the etymology, unleſs it be derived from *flew* of *fly.*]

1. A ſmall pipe or chimney to convey air, heat, or ſmoke.

2. Soft down or fur, ſuch as may fly in the wind.

FLUE'LLIN. *n. ſ.* The herb SPEEDWELL.

FLU'ENCY. *n. ſ.* [from *fluent.*]

1. The quality of flowing; ſmoothneſs; freedom from harſhneſs or aſperity.

Fluency of numbers, and moſt expreſſive figures for the poet, morals for the ſerious, and pleaſantries for admirers of points of wit. *Garth's Preface to Ovid.*

2. Readineſs; copiouſneſs; volubility.

Our publick liturgy muſt be caſhiered, the better to pleaſe thoſe men who gloried in their extemporary vein and *fluency.* *King Charles.*

Th' unthinking victors vainly boaſt their pow'rs;
Be their's the muſquet, while the tongue is our's:
We reaſon with ſuch *fluency* and fire,
The beaux we baffle, and the learned tire. *Tickell.*

The common *fluency* of ſpeech in many men, and moſt women, is owing to a ſcarcity of matter, and a ſcarcity of words; for whoever is a maſter of language, and hath a mind full of ideas, will be apt, in ſpeaking, to heſitate upon the choice of both. *Swift's Thoughts on various Subjects.*

3. Affluence; abundance. This ſenſe is obſolete.

Thoſe who grow old in *fluency* and eaſe,
Behold him toſt on ſeas. *Sandys's Paraphraſe on Job.*

God riches and renown to men imparts,
Even all they wiſh; and yet their narrow hearts
Cannot ſo great a *fluency* receive,
But their fruition to a ſtranger leave. *Sandys.*

FLU'ENT. *adj.* [*fluens*, Latin.]

1. Liquid.

It is not malleable; but yet is not *fluent*, but ſtupified. *Bac.*

2. Flowing; in motion; in flux.

Motion being a *fluent* thing, and one part of its duration being abſolutely independent upon another, it doth not follow that becauſe any thing moves this moment, it muſt neceſſarily continue to do ſo the next. *Ray on the Creation.*

3. Ready; copious; voluble.

Thoſe have ſome natural diſpoſitions, which have better grace in youth than in age, ſuch as is a *fluent* and luxurious ſpeech. *Bacon.*

I ſhall lay before you all that's within me,
And with moſt *fluent* utterance. *Denham's Sophy.*

FLU'ENT. *n. ſ.* Stream; running water.

Confiding in their hands, that ſed'lous ſtrive
To cut th' outrageous *fluent*; in this diſtreſs,
Ev'n in the ſight of death. *Phillips.*

FLU'ID. *adj.* [*fluidus*, Latin; *fluide*, French.] Having parts eaſily ſeparable; not ſolid.

Or ſerve they as a flow'ry verge to bind
The *fluid* ſkirts of that ſame wat'ry cloud,
Leſt it again diſſolve, and ſhow'r the earth? *Milt. P. Loſt.*

If particles ſlip eaſily, and are of a fit ſize to be agitated by heat, and the heat is big enough to keep them in agitation, the body is *fluid*; and if it be apt to ſtick to things, it is humid. *Newton's Opt.*

FLU'ID. *n. ſ.* [In phyſick.] Any animal juice: as the blood.

Conſider how luxury hath introduced new diſeaſes, and with them, not improbably, altered the whole courſe of the *fluids.* *Arbuthnot and Pope's Mart. Scriblerus.*

FLU'IDITY. *n. ſ.* [*fluidité*, Fr. from *fluid.*] The quality in bodies oppoſite to ſolidity; want of adherence between the parts.

Heat promotes *fluidity* very much, by diminiſhing the tenacity of bodies: it makes many bodies fluid, which are not fluid in cold, and increaſes the *fluidity* of tenacious liquids; as of oil, balſam and honey; and thereby decreaſes their reſiſtance. *Newton's Opt.*

A diſeaſe oppoſite to this ſpiſſitude is too great *fluidity.* *Arb.*

FLU'IDNESS. *n. ſ.* [from *fluid.*] That quality in bodies oppoſite to ſtability.

What if we ſhould ſay that *fluidneſs* and ſtability depends ſo much upon the texture of the parts, that, by the change of that texture, the ſame parts may be made to conſtitute either a fluid or a dry body, and that permanently too? *Boyle.*

FLU'MMERY. *n. ſ.* A kind of food made by coagulation of wheatflower or oatmeal.

Milk and *flummery* are very fit for children. *Locke.*

FLUNG. *participle* and *preterite* of *fling.* Thrown; caſt.

Several ſtatues the Romans themſelves *flung* into the river, when they would revenge themſelves. *Addiſon on Italy.*

FLU'OR. *n. ſ.* [Latin.]

1. A fluid ſtate.

The particles of fluids which do not cohere too ſtrongly, and are of ſuch a ſmallneſs as renders them moſt ſuſceptible of thoſe agitations which keep liquors in a *fluor*, are moſt eaſily ſeparated and rarified into vapours. *Newton's Opt.*

2. Catamenia.

FLU'RRY. *n. ſ.*

1. A guſt or ſtorm of wind; a haſty blaſt.

The boat was overſet by a ſudden *flurry* from the North. *Gulliver's Travels.*

2. Hurry; a violent commotion.

To FLUSH. *v. n.* [*fluyſen*, Dutch, to flow; *flus*, or *flux*, Fr.]

1. To flow with violence.

The pulſe of the heart he attributes to an ebullition and ſudden expanſion of the blood in the ventricles, after the manner of the milk, which, being heated to ſuch a degree, doth ſuddenly, and all at once, *fluſh* up and run over the veſſel. *Ray.*

It *fluſhes* violently out of the cock for about a quart, and then ſtops. *Mortimer's Huſbandry.*

2. To come in haſte.

If the place but affords
Any ſtore of lucky birds,
As I make 'em to *fluſh*,
Each owl out of his buſh. *Ben Johnſon's Owls.*

3. To glow in the ſkin; to produce a colour in the face by a ſudden afflux of blood.

Ere yet the ſalt of moſt unrighteous tears
Had left the *fluſhing* in her gauled eyes,
She married. *Shakeſpeare's Hamlet.*

Thus Eve with count'nance blithe her ſtory told,
But in her cheek diſtemper *fluſhing* glow'd. *Milt. Par. Loſt.*

What can be more ſignificant than the ſudden *fluſhing* and confuſion of a bluſh? *Collier of the Aſpect.*

What means that lovely fruit? What means, alas!
That blood, which *flushes* guilty in your face? *Dryden.*
At once, array'd
In all the colours of the *flushing* year,
The garden glows. *Thomson's Spring, l.* 95.
4. To shine. Obsolete.
A flake of fire, that *flushing* in his beard,
Him all amaz'd. *Spenser.*
To Flush. *v. a.*
1. To colour; to redden.
The glowing dames of Zama's royal court,
Have faces *flush'd* with more exalted charms. *Addis. Cato.*
Some court, or secret corner seek,
Nor *flush* with shame the passing virgin's cheek. *Gay's Triv.*
2. To elate; to elevate.
A prosperous people, *flushed* with great victories and successes, are rarely known to confine their joys within the bounds of moderation and innocence. *Atterbury's Sermons.*
Flush. *adj.*
1. Fresh; full of vigour.
He took my father grosly, full of bread,
With all his crimes broad blown, and *flush* as May;
And how his audit stands, who knows, save heav'n? *Shak.*
I love to wear cloths that are *flush*,
Not prefacing old rags with plush. *Cleaveland.*
2. Affluent; abounding. A cant word.
Lord Strut was not very *flush* in ready, either to go to law or clear old debts; neither could he find good bail. *Arbuthnot.*
Flush. *n. s.* Afflux; sudden impulse; violent flow.
Never had any man such a loss, cries a widower, in the *flush* of his extravagancies for a dead wife. *L'Estrange.*
The pulse of the arteries is not only caused by the pulsation of the heart, driving the blood through them in manner of a wave or *flush*, but by the coats of the arteries themselves. *Ray.*
Success may give him a present *flush* of joy; but when the short transport is over, the apprehension of losing succeeds to the care of acquiring. *Rogers's Sermons.*
2. Cards all of a sort.
To Flu'ster. *v. a.* [from *To flush.*] To make hot and rosy with drinking; to make half drunk.
Three lads of Cyprus, noble swelling spirits,
Have I to-night *fluster'd* with flowing cups,
And they watch too. *Shakespeare's Othello.*
FLUTE. *n. s.* [*fluste, flute*, French; *fluyte*, Dutch.]
1. A musical pipe; a pipe with stops for the fingers.
Th' oars were silver,
Which to the tune of *flutes* kept stroke. *Shak. Ant. and Cleo.*
The soft complaining *flute*
In dying notes discovers
The woes of hopeless lovers,
Whose dirge is whisper'd by the warbling lute. *Dryden.*
2. A channel or furrow in a pillar, like the concave of a flute split.
To Flute. *v. a.* To cut columns into hollows.
To FLU'TTER. *v. n.* [floteran, Saxon; *flotter*, French.]
1. To take short flights with great agitation of the wings.
As an eagle stirreth up her nest, *fluttereth* over her young, and spreadeth abroad her wings, so the Lord alone did lead him. *Deutr.* xxxii. 11.
When your hands untie these strings,
Think you've an angel by the wings;
One that gladly will be nigh,
To wait upon each morning-sigh;
To *flutter* in the balmy air
Of your well-perfumed pray'r. *Crashaw.*
They fed, and, *flutt'ring*, by degrees withdrew. *Dryden.*
2. To move about with great show and bustle without consequence.
Excess muddies the best wit, and only makes it *flutter* and froth high. *Grew.*
No rag, no scrap of all the beau or wit,
That once so *flutter'd*, and that once so writ. *Pope's Dunc.*
3. To be moved with quick vibrations or undulations.
Ye spirits! to your charge repair;
The *flutt'ring* fan be Zephyretta's care. *Pope.*
They the tall mast above the vessel rear,
Or teach the *flutt'ring* sail to float in air. *Pope's Odyssey.*
4. To be in agitation; to move irregularly; to be in a state of uncertainty.
The relation being brought him what a glorious victory was got, and with what difficulty, and how long she *fluttered* upon the wings of doubtful success, he was not surprised. *Howel's Vocal Forest.*
It is impossible that men should certainly discover the agreement or disagreement of ideas, whilst their thoughts *flutter* about, or stick only in sounds of doubtful signification. *Locke.*
Esteem we these, my friends! event and chance,
Produc'd by atoms from their *flutt'ring* dance! *Prior.*
Some never arrive at any deep, solid, or valuable knowledge, because they are perpetually *fluttering* over the surface of things. *Watts.*
His thoughts are very *fluttering* and wandering, and cannot be fixed attentively to a few ideas successively. *Watts.*
To Flutter. *v. a.*
1. To drive in disorder, like a flock of birds suddenly roused.

Like an eagle in a dovecoat, I
Flutter'd your Volscians in Corioli. *Shakes. Coriolanus.*
2. To hurry the mind.
3. To disorder the position of any thing.
Flu'tter. *n. s.* [from the verb.]
1. Vibration; undulation; quick and irregular motion.
An infinite variety of motions are to be made use of in the *flutter* of a fan: there is the angry *flutter*, the modest *flutter*, and the timorous *flutter*. *Addison's Spectator*, N°. 102.
2. Hurry; tumult; disorder of mind.
3. Confusion; irregular position.
Fluvia'tick. *adj.* [*fluviaticus*, Latin.] Belonging to rivers.
FLUX. *n. s.* [*fluxus*, Latin; *flux*, French.]
1. The act of flowing; passage.
The most simple and primary motion of fire is a *flux*, in a direct line from the centre of the fuel to its circumference. *Digby on Bodies.*
By the perpetual *flux* of the liquids, a great part of them is thrown out of the body. *Arbuthnot.*
2. The state of passing away and giving place to others.
The heat of the sun in animals whose parts are successive, and in a continual *flux*, can produce a deep and perfect gloss of blackness. *Brown's Vulgar Errours, b.* vi. *c.* 10.
What the stated rate of interest should be, in the constant change of affairs, and *flux* of money, is hard to determine. *Locke.*
In the constituent matter of one body, turning naturally to another like body, the stock or fund can never be exhausted, nor the *flux* and alteration sensible. *Woodward.*
Languages, like our bodies, are in a perpetual *flux*, and stand in need of recruits to supply the place of those words that are continually falling through disuse. *Felton on the Class.*
3. Any flow or issue of matter.
Quinces stop *fluxes* of blood. *Arbuthnot on Diet.*
4. Dysentery; disease in which the bowels are excoriated and bleed; bloody flux.
Eat eastern spice, secure
From burning *fluxes* and hot calenture. *Hallifax.*
5. Excrement; that which falls from bodies.
Civet is the very uncleanly *flux* of a cat. *Shakespeare.*
6. Concourse; confluence.
Left and abandon'd of his velvet friends;
'Tis right, quoth he; thus misery doth part
The *flux* of company. *Shakesp. As you like it.*
7. The state of being melted.
8. That which mingled with a body makes it melt.
Flux. *adj.* [*fluxus*, Latin.] Unconstant; not durable; maintained by a constant succession of parts.
To Flux. *v. a.*
1. To melt.
2. To salivate; to evacuate by spitting.
He might fashionably and genteelly have been duelled or *fluxed* into another world. *South.*
Flu'xility. *n. s.* [*fluxus*, Latin.] Easiness of separation of parts; possibility of liquefaction.
Experiments seem to teach, that the supposed aversation of nature to a vacuum is but accidental, or in consequence, partly of the weight and fluidity, or at least *flexility* of the bodies here below. *Boyle.*
Flu'xion. *n. s.* [*fluxio*, Latin.]
1. The act of flowing.
2. The matter that flows.
3. [In mathematicks.] The arithmetick or analysis of infinitely small variable quantities; or it is the method of finding an infinite small or infinitely small quantity, which, being taken an infinite number of times, becomes equal to a quantity given. *Harris.*
A penetration into the abstruse difficulties and depths of modern algebra and *fluxions*, are not worth the labour of those who design the learned professions as the business of life. *Watts.*
To FLY. pret. *flew* or *fled*; part. *fled* or *flown. v. n.* [fleogan, Saxon. To *fly* is properly *to use wings*, and gives *flew* and *flown*. To *flee* is to *escape*, or *go away*, flean, Saxon, and makes *fled*. They are now confounded.]
1. To move through the air with wings.
Ere the bat hath *flown*
His cloister'd flight. *Shakespeare's Macbeth.*
Fowl that may *fly* above the earth in the open firmament of heaven. *Gen.* i. 20.
These men's hastiness the warier sort of you do not commend: ye wish they had held themselves longer in, and not *flown* so dangerously abroad before the feathers of the cause had been grown. *Hooker.*
2. To pass through the air.
Man is born unto trouble, as the sparks *fly* upward. *Job* v.
3. To pass away.
Ev'n a romance, a tune, a rhime,
Help thee to pass the tedious time,
Which else would on thy hand remain;
Though *flown*, it ne'er looks back again. *Prior.*
4. To pass swiftly.
The scouts with *flying* speed
Return, and through the city spread the news. *Dryden.*
Earth rolls back beneath the *flying* steed. *Pope.*

5. To ſpring with violence; to fall on ſuddenly.

A ſervant that he bred, thrill'd with remorſe,
Oppos'd againſt the act, bending his ſword
To his great maſter; who, thereat enrag'd,
Flew on him, and amongſt them fell'd him dead. *Shakeſp.*

Though the dogs have never ſeen the dog killer, yet they will come forth, and bark and *fly* at him. *Bacon's Nat. Hiſt.*

No honour, no fortune, can keep a man from being miſerable, when an enraged conſcience ſhall *fly* at him, and take him by the throat. *South's Sermons.*

6. To move with rapidity.

Glad to catch this good occaſion,
Moſt thoroughly to be winnow'd, where my chaff
And corn ſhall *fly* aſunder. *Shakeſpeare's Henry* VIII.

A fair example to his maſter gave;
He baſſas heads, to ſave his own, made *fly*;
And now, the ſultan to preſerve, muſt die. *Waller.*

7. To burſt aſunder with a ſudden exploſion.

Behold, a frothy ſubſtance riſe;
Be cautious, or your bottle *flies*. *Swift.*

8. To break; to ſhiver.

9. [ꝼlean, Saxon; *fliehen*, German.] To run away; to attempt eſcape. [In this ſenſe the verb is properly to *flee*, when *fled* is formed; but the following examples ſhew that they are confounded.]

Which when the valiant elf perceiv'd, he leapt,
As lion fierce, upon the *flying* prey. *Spenſer.*

Macduff is *fled* to England. *Shakeſpeare's Macbeth.*

Ye ſhall flee, as ye *fled* from before the earthquake. *Zech.* xiv. 5.

Abiathar eſcaped, and *fled* after David. 1 *Sa.* xxii. 20.

What wonder if the kindly beams he ſhed,
Reviv'd the drooping arts again;
If ſcience rais'd her head,
And ſoft humanity, that from rebellion *fled*. *Dryden.*

He oft deſir'd to *fly* from Iſrael's throne,
And live in ſhades with her and love alone. *Prior.*

I'll *fly* from ſhepherds, flocks, and flow'ry plains;
From ſhepherds, flocks, and plains I may remove,
Forſake mankind, and all the world but love. *Pope.*

10. *To* FLY *in the face.* To inſult.

This would diſcourage any man from doing you good, when you will either neglect him, or *fly in his face*; and he muſt expect only danger to himſelf. *Swift's Drapier's Letters.*

11. To act in defiance.

Fly in nature's *face*:
—But how, if nature *fly in* my *face* firſt?
—Then nature's the aggreſſor. *Dryden's Spaniſh Fryar.*

12. *To* FLY *off.* To revolt.

Deny to ſpeak with me? They're ſick, they're weary,
They have travell'd all the night! mean fetches;
The images of revolt, and *flying off*. *Shakeſp. King Lear.*

The traytor Syphax
Flew off at once with his Numidian horſe. *Addiſon's Cato.*

13. *To* FLY *out.* To burſt into paſſion.

How eaſy is a noble ſpirit diſcern'd,
From harſh and ſulphurous matter that *flies out*
In contumelies, makes a noiſe, and ſtinks. *Ben Johnſ. Catil.*

Paſſion is apt to ruffle, and pride will *fly out* into contumely and neglect. *Collier of Friendſhip.*

14. *To* FLY *out.* To break out into licence.

You uſe me like a courſer ſpurr'd and rein'd:
If I *fly out*, my fierceneſs you command. *Dryden.*

Papiſts, when unoppoſed, *fly out* into all the pageantries of worſhip; but in times of war, when they are hard preſſed by arguments, lie cloſe intrenched behind the council of Trent. *Dryden's Medal, Dedicat.*

15. *To* FLY *out.* To ſtart violently from any direction.

All bodies, moved circularly, have a perpetual endeavour to recede from the centre, and every moment would *fly out* in right lines, if they were not reſtrained. *Bentley's Sermons.*

16. *To let* FLY. To diſcharge.

The noiſy culverin, o'ercharg'd, *lets fly*,
And burſts, unaiming, in the rended ſky. *Granville.*

17. To be light and unencumbered: as, a *flying* camp.

To FLY. *v. a.*

1. To ſhun; to avoid; to decline.

Love like a ſhadow flies, when ſubſtance love purſues;
Purſuing that which flies, and *flying* what purſues. *Shakeſp.*

O Jove, I think
Foundations *fly* the wretched; ſuch I mean,
Where they ſhould be relieved. *Shakeſpeare.*

If you *fly* phyſick in health altogether, it will be too ſtrange for your body when you ſhall need it. *Bacon's Eſſays.*

O whither ſhall I run, or which way *fly*
The ſight of this ſo horrid ſpectacle. *Milton's Agoniſtes.*

2. To refuſe aſſociation with.

Sleep *flies* the wretch; or when with cares oppreſt,
And his toſs'd limbs are weary'd into reſt,
Then dreams invade. *Dryden's Juvenal, Sat.* 13.

Nature *flies* him like enchanted ground. *Dryden.*

3. To quit by flight.

Dedalus, to *fly* the Cretan ſhore,
His heavy limbs on jointed pinions bore,
The firſt who ſail'd in air. *Dryden's Æn. b.* vi.

4. To attack by a bird of prey.

If a man can tame this monſter, and with her *fly* other ravening fowl, and kill them, it is ſomewhat worth. *Bacon.*

5. It is probable that *flew* was originally the preterite of *fly*, when it ſignified volation, and *fled* when it ſignified eſcape: *flown* ſhould be confined likewiſe to volation; but theſe diſtinctions are now confounded.

FLY. *n. ſ.* [ꝼleoᵹe, Saxon.]

1. A ſmall winged inſect of many ſpecies.

As *flies* to wanton boys, are we to th' gods;
They kill us for their ſport. *Shakeſpeare's King Lear.*

My country neighbours begin to think of being in general, before they come to think of the *fly* in their ſheep, or the tares in their corn. *Locke.*

To prevent the *fly*, ſome propoſe to ſow aſhes with the ſeed. *Mortimer's Huſbandry.*

To heedleſs *flies* the window proves
A conſtant death. *Thomſon's Summer.*

2. That part of a machine which, being put into a quick motion, regulates and equaliſes the motion of the reſt.

If we ſuppoſe a man tied in the place of the weight, it were eaſy, by a ſingle hair faſtened unto the *fly* or balance of the jack, to draw him up from the ground. *Wilkins.*

3. FLY, in a compaſs. That part which points how the wind blows.

To FLY'BLOW. *v. a.* [*fly* and *blow.*] To taint with flies; to fill with maggots.

I cannot diſcern any labyrinth, unleſs in the perplexity of his own thoughts; for I am unwilling to believe that he doth it with a deſign to play tricks, and to *flyblow* my words, to make others diſtaſte them. *Stillingfleet.*

Like a *flyblown* cake of tallow;
Or, on parchment, ink turn'd yellow. *Swift.*

So morning inſects, that in muck begun,
Shine, buz, and *flyblow* in the ſetting ſun. *Pope's Epiſtles.*

FLY'BOAT. *n. ſ.* [*fly* and *boat.*] A kind of veſſel nimble and light for ſailing.

FLYCA'TCHER. *n. ſ.* [*fly* and *catch.*] One that hunts flies.

There was more need of Brutus in Domitian's days, to redeem or mend, than of Horace, to laugh at a *flycatcher*. *Dry.*

The ſwallow was a *flycatcher* as well as the ſpider. *L'Eſtr.*

FLY'ER. *n. ſ.* [from *fly.*]

1. One that flies or runs away.

They hit one another with darts, as the others do with their hands, which they never throw counter, but at the back of the *flyer*. *Sandys's Journey.*

He grieves ſo many Britons ſhould be loſt;
Taking more pains, when he beheld them yield,
To ſave the *flyers* than to win the field. *Waller.*

2. One that uſes wings.

3. The fly of a jack.

4. [In architecture.] Stairs made of an oblong ſquare figure, whoſe fore and backſides are parallel to each other, and ſo are their ends: the ſecond of theſe *flyers* ſtands parallel behind the firſt, the third behind the ſecond, and ſo are ſaid to fly off from one another. *Moxon's Mech. Exer.*

To FLY'FISH. *v. n.* [*fly* and *fiſh.*] To angle with a hook baited with a fly.

I ſhall next give you ſome other directions for *flyfiſhing*. *Walton's Angler.*

FOAL. *n. ſ.* [ꝼola, Saxon.] The offspring of a mare, or other beaſt of burthen. The cuſtom now is to uſe *colt* for a young horſe, and *foal* for a young mare; but there was not originally any ſuch diſtinction.

Alſo flew his ſteed,
And with his winged heels did tread the wind,
As he had been a *foal* of Pegaſus's kind. *Fairy Queen, b.* i.

Twenty ſhe-aſſes and ten *foals*. *Gen.* xxxii. 15.

To FOAL. *v. a.* [from the noun.] To bring forth a foal.

Give my horſe to Timon: it *foals* me ſtraight
Ten able horſes. *Shakeſpeare's Timon.*

Such colts as are
Of generous race, ſtraight, when they firſt are *foal'd*,
Walk proudly. *May's Georgicks.*

About September take your mares into the houſe, where keep them 'till they *foal*. *Mortimer's Huſbandry.*

FO'ALBIT. } *n. ſ.* Plants.
FO'ALFOOT. }

FOAM. *n. ſ.* [ꝼam, Saxon.] The white ſubſtance which agitation or fermentation gathers on the top of liquors; froth; ſpume.

The *foam* upon the water. *Hoſ.* x. 7.

Whitening, down their moſſy tinctur'd ſtream
Deſcends the billowy *foam*. *Thomſon's Spring.*

To FOAM. *v. n.* [from the noun.]

1. To froth; to gather foam.

What a beard of the general's cut will do among *foaming* bottles and ale-waſh'd wits, is wonderful. *Shakeſp. Henry* V.

Cæſar fell down in the market-place, and *foam'd* at mouth, and was ſpeechleſs. *Shakeſpeare's Julius Cæſar.*

To Pallas high the *foaming* bowl he crown'd,
And sprinkl'd large libations on the ground. *Pope's Odyssey.*
Upon a *foaming* horse
There follow'd strait a man of royal port. *Rowe.*

2. To be in rage; to be violently agitated.
He *foameth*, and gnasheth with his teeth. *Mar.* ix. 18.

Fo'AMY. *adj.* [from *foam.*] Covered with foam; frothy.
More white than Neptune's *foamy* face,
When struggling rocks he would embrace. *Sidney, b.* ii.
Behold how high the *foamy* billows ride!
The winds and waves are on the juster side. *Dryden.*

FOB. *n. s.* [*fuppe, fupsacke*, German.] A small pocket.
Who pick'd a *fob* at holding forth,
And where a watch for half the worth
May be redeem'd. *Hudibras, p.* ii. *cant.* 3.
When were the dice with more profusion thrown?
The well-fill'd *fob*, not empty'd now alone. *Dryd. Juven.*
He put his hand into his *fob*, and presented me in his name with a tobacco-stopper. *Addison's Spectator.*
There were two pockets which we could not enter; these he called his *fobs*: they were two large slits cut into the top of his middle cover, but squeezed close by the pressure of his belly. *Gulliver's Travels.*
Orphans around his bed the lawyer sees,
And takes the plaintiff's and defendant's fees;
His fellow pick-purse, watching for a job,
Fancies his fingers in the cully's *fob*. *Swift.*

To FOB. *v. a.* [*fuppen*, German.]
1. To cheat; to trick; to defraud.
I think it is scurvy, and begin to find myself *fobb'd* in it. *Shakespeare's Othello.*
Shall there be a gallows standing in England when thou art king, and resolution thus *fobb'd* as it is with the rusty curb of old father antick the law. *Shakespeare's Henry* IV. *p.* i.
He goes pressing forward, 'till he was *fobbed* again with another story. *L'Estrange.*

2. *To* FOB *off.* To shift off; to put aside with an artifice; to delude by a trick.
You must not think
To *fob off* our disgraces with a tale. *Shakesp. Coriolanus.*
For they, poor knaves, were glad to cheat,
To get their wives and children meat;
But these will not be *fobb'd off* so,
They must have wealth and power too. *Hudibras, p.* i.
By a Ravenna vintner once betray'd,
So much for wine and water mix'd I paid;
But when I thought the purchas'd liquor mine,
The rascal *fobb'd* me *off* with only wine. *Addison.*
Being a great lover of country-sports, I absolutely determined not to be a minister of state, nor to be *fobb'd off* with a garter. *Addison's Freeholder,* N°. 3.

Fo'CAL. *adj.* [from *focus.*] Belonging to the focus. See FOCUS.
Schelhammer demandeth whether the convexity or concavity of the drum collects rays into a *focal* point, or scatters them. *Derham's Physico-Theology.*

Fo'CIL. *n. s.* [*focile*, French.] The greater or less bone between the knee and ankle, or elbow and wrist.
The fracture was of both the *focils* of the left leg. *Wisem.*

FOCILLA'TION. *n. s.* [*focillo*, Lat.] Comfort; support. *Dict.*

FO'CUS. *n. s.* [Latin.]
1. [In opticks.] The focus of a glass is the point of convergence or concourse, where the rays meet and cross the axis after their refraction by the glass. *Harris.*
The point from which rays diverge, or to which they converge, may be called their *focus.* *Newton's Opt.*
2. FOCUS *of a Parabola.* A point in the axis within the figure, and distant from the vertex by a fourth part of the parameter, or *latus rectum.* *Harris.*
3. FOCUS *of an Ellipsis.* A point towards each end of the longer axis; from whence two right lines being drawn to any point in the circumference, shall be together equal to that longer axis. *Harris.*
4. FOCUS *of the Hyperbola.* A point in the principal axis, within the opposite hyperbola's; from which if any two right lines are drawn, meeting in either of the opposite hyperbolas, the difference will be equal to the principal axis. *Dict.*

FO'DDER. *n. s.* [ꝼoꝺꝺne, ꝼoꝺꝺeꞃ, Saxon.] Dry food stored up for cattle against Winter.
Their cattle, starving for want of *fodder*, corrupted the air. *Knolles's History of the Turks.*
Being not to be raised without wintering, they will help to force men into improvement of land by a necessity of *fodder.* *Temple.*
Of grass and *fodder* thou defraud'st the dams,
And of their mothers dugs the starving lambs. *Dryd. Virgil.*

To FO'DDER. *v. a.* [from the noun.] To feed with dry food.
Natural earth is taken the first half spit from just under the turf of the best pasture ground, in a place that has been well *foddered* on. *Evelyn's Kalendar.*
From Winter keep,
Well *fodder'd* in the stalls, thy tender sheep. *Dryd. Virgil.*

A farm of fifty pound hath commonly three barns, with as many cowyards to *fodder* cattle in. *Mortimer's Husbandry.*
Straw will do well enough to *fodder* with. *Mortim. Hus b.*

Fo'DDERER. *n. s.* [from *fodder.*] He who fodders cattle.

FOE. *n. s.* [ꝼah, Saxon; *fae*, Scottish.]
1. An enemy in war.
Ere he had established his throne,
He fought great battles with his savage *fone*,
In which he them defeated ever more. *Fairy Queen, b.* ii.
Never but one more was either like
To meet so great a *foe.* *Milton.*
2. A persecutor; an enemy in common life.
God's benison go with you, and with those
That would make good of bad, and friends of *foes.* *Shakes.*
Forc'd by thy worth, thy *foe* in death become;
Thy friend has lodg'd thee in a costly tomb. *Dryden's Fab.*
Thy defects to know,
Make use of ev'ry friend, and ev'ry *foe.* *Pope.*
3. An opponent; an illwisher.
He that considers and enquires into the reason of things, is counted a *foe* to received doctrines. *Watts's Imp. of the Mind.*

Fo'EMAN. *n. s.* [from *foe* and *man.*] Enemy in war; antagonist. An obsolete word.
Here haunts that fiend, and does his daily spoil;
Therefore henceforth be at your keeping well,
And ever ready for your *foeman* fell. *Fairy Queen, b.* i.
What valiant *foemen*, like to Autumn's corn,
Have we mow'd down in top of all their pride? *Sh. H.* VI.

FO'ETUS. *n. s.* [Latin.] The child in the womb after it is perfectly formed: but before, it is called embryo. *Quincy.*
A *fœtus*, in the mother's womb, differs not much from the state of a vegetable. *Locke.*

FOG. *n. s.* [*fog*, Danish, a storm.] A thick mist; a moist dense vapour near the surface of the land or water.
Infect her beauty,
You fensuck'd *fogs*, drawn by the pow'rful sun,
To fall and blast her pride. *Shakespeare's King Lear.*
Lesser mists and *fogs* than those which covered Greece with so long darkness, present great alterations in the sun and moon. *Raleigh's History of the World.*
Fly, fly, prophane *fogs!* far hence fly away;
Taint not the pure streams of the springing day
With your dull influence: it is for you
To sit and scoule upon night's heavy brow. *Crashaw.*
Fogs we frequently observe after sun-setting, even in our hottest months. *Woodward's Natural History.*

FOG. *n. s.* [*fogagium*, low Latin. *Gramen in foresta regis locatur pro* fogagio. *Leges forest. Scoticæ.*] Aftergrass; grass which grows in Autumn after the hay is mown.

Fo'GGILY. *adv.* [from *foggy.*] Mistily; darkly; cloudily.

Fo'GGINESS. *n. s.* [from *foggy.*] The state of being dark or misty; cloudiness; mistiness.

Fo'GGY. *adj.* [from *fog.*]
1. Misty; cloudy; dank; full of moist vapours.
Alas! while we are wrapt in *foggy* mist
Of our self-love, so passions do deceive,
We think they hurt, when most they do assist. *Sidney, b.* ii.
And Phœbus flying so, most shameful sight,
His blushing face in *foggy* cloud implys,
And hides for shame. *Fairy Queen, b.* i. *cant.* 6.
Whence have they this mettle?
Is not their climate *foggy*, raw and dull? *Shakes. Henry* V.
Let not air be too gross, nor too penetrative; not subject to any *foggy* noisomeness, from fens or marshes near adjoining. *Wotton's Architecture.*
About Michaelmas, the weather fair, and by no means *foggy*, retire your rarest plants. *Evelyn's Kalendar.*
2. Cloudy in understanding; dull.

FOH. *interject.* [from ꝼah, Saxon, an enemy.] An interjection of abhorrence: as if one should at sight of any thing hated cry out *a foe!*
Not to affect many proposed matches
Of her own clime, complection and degree,
Whereto we see in all things nature tends,
Foh! one may smell in such a will most rank,
Foul disproportions, thoughts unnatural. *Shakes. Othello.*

FO'IBLE. *n. s.* [French.] A weak side; a blind side; a failing.
He knew the *foibles* of human nature. *Freind's Hist. of Phys.*
The witty men sometimes have sense enough to know their own *foible*, and therefore they craftily shun the attacks of argument. *Watts's Logick.*

To FOIL. *v. a.* [*affoler*, to wound, old French.] To put to the worst; to defeat, though without a complete victory.
Amazement seiz'd
The rebel thrones; but greater rage to see
Thus *foil'd* their mightiest. *Milton's Paradise Lost, b.* vi.
Leader of those armies bright,
Which but th' omnipotent none could have *foil'd!* *Milton.*
Yet these subject not: I to thee disclose
What inward thence I feel, not therefore *foil'd*:
Who meet with various objects, from the sense

Variouſly repreſenting; yet ſtill free,
Approve the beſt, and follow what I approve. *Milt. P. Loſt.*

Strange, that your fingers ſhould the pencil *foil*,
Without the help of colours or of oil! *Waller.*

He had been *foiled* in the cure, and had left it to nature. *Wiſeman's Surgery.*

In their conflicts with ſin they have been ſo often *foiled*, that they now deſpair of ever getting the day. *Calamy's Serm.*

Virtue, diſdain, deſpair, I oft have try'd;
And, *foil'd*, have with new arms my foe defy'd. *Dryden.*

But I, the conſort of the Thunderer,
Have wag'd a long and unſucceſsful war;
With various arts and arms in vain have toil'd,
And by a mortal man at length am *foil'd*. *Dryden's Æn.*

Foil. *n. ſ.* [from the verb.]

1. A defeat; a miſcarriage; an advantage gained without a complete conqueſt.

We of thy cunning had no diffidence;
One ſudden *foil* ſhall never breed diſtruſt. *Shakeſ. Hen.* VI.

Whoſoever overthroweth his mate in ſuch ſort, as that either his back, or the one ſhoulder, and contrary heel do touch the ground, ſhall be accounted to give the fall: if he be endangered, and make a narrow eſcape, it is called a *foil*. *Carew.*

So after many a *foil* the tempter proud,
Renewing freſh aſſaults, amidſt his pride,
Fell whence he ſtood to ſee his victor fall. *Milton's P. Loſt.*

When age ſhall level me to impotence,
And ſweating pleaſure leave me on the *foil*. *Southern.*

Death never won a ſtake with greater toil,
Nor e'er was fate ſo near a *foil*. *Dryden.*

2. [*Feuille*, French.] Leaf; gilding.

A ſtately palace, built of ſquared brick,
Which cunningly was without mortar laid,
Whoſe walls were high, but nothing ſtrong nor thick,
And golden *foil* all over them diſplay'd. *Fairy Queen, b.* i.

Fame is no plant that grows on mortal ſoil,
Nor in the gliſtering *foil*
Set off to th' world, nor in broad rumour lies. *Milton.*

3. Something of another colour near which jewels are ſet to raiſe their luſtre.

As ſhe a black ſilk cap on him begun
To ſet for *foil* of his milk-white to ſerve. *Sidney.*

Like bright metal on a ſullen ground,
My reformation glittering o'er my fault,
Shall ſhew more goodly, and attract more eyes,
Than that which hath no *foil* to ſet it off. *Shak. Hen.* IV.

The ſullen paſſage of thy weary ſteps
Eſteem a *foil*, wherein thou art to ſet
The precious jewel of thy home. *Shakeſpeare.*

'Tis the property of all true diamonds to unite the *foil* cloſely itſelf, and thereby better augment its luſtre: the *foil* is a mixture of maſtich and burnt ivory. *Grew's Muſæum.*

Hector has a *foil* to ſet him off: we are perpetually oppoſing the incontinence of Paris to the temperance of Hector. *Notes on the Odyſſey.*

4. [From *fouiller*, French.] A blunt ſword uſed in fencing.

He that plays the king ſhall be welcome; his majeſty ſhall have tribute of me: the adventurous knight ſhall uſe his *foil* and target. *Shak. Hamlet.*

Fo'iler. *n. ſ.* [from *foil.*] One who has gained advantage over another.

To **FOIN.** *v. n.* [*poindre*, Fr. *Skinner.*] To puſh in fencing.

He hew'd, and laſh'd, and *foin'd*, and thunder'd blows,
And every way did ſeek into his life;
Ne plate, ne mail, could ward ſo mighty throws,
But yielded paſſage to his cruel knife. *Fairy Queen, b.* ii.

He cares not what miſchief he doth, if his weapon be out: he will *foin* like any devil; he will ſpare neither man, woman, nor child. *Shakeſpeare's Henry* IV. *p.* i.

Then both, no moment loſt, at once advance
Againſt each other, arm'd with ſword and lance:
They laſh, they *foin*, they paſs, they ſtrive to bore
Their corſlets, and the thinneſt parts explore. *Dryden.*

Foin. *n. ſ.* [from the verb.] A thruſt; a puſh.

Fo'iningly. *adv.* [from *foin.*] In a puſhing manner.

Fo'ison. *n. ſ.* [ꝼoiſon, Saxon.] Plenty; abundance. A word now out of uſe.

Pay juſtly thy tithes, whatſoever thou be,
That God may in bleſſing ſend *foiſon* to thee. *Tuſſ. Huſb.*

Be wilful to kill, and unſkilful to ſtore,
And look for no *foiſon*, I tell thee before. *Tuſſer's Huſband.*

Nature ſhould bring forth,
Of its own kind, all *foiſon*, all abundance,
To feed my innocent people. *Shakeſpeare's Tempeſt.*

As thoſe that feed grow full, as bloſſoming time
That from the ſeedneſs the bare fallow brings
To teeming *foiſon*; ſo her plenteous womb
Expreſſeth his full tilth and huſbandry. *Shak. Meaſ. for Meaſ.*

To **Foist.** *v. a.* [*fauſſer*, French.] To inſert by forgery.

Leſt negligence or partiality might admit or *foiſt* in abuſes and corruption, an archdeacon was appointed to take account of their doings. *Carew's Survey of Cornwal.*

Forge law, and *foiſt* it into ſome by-place
Of ſome old rotten roll. *Dryden's Don Sebaſtian.*

Fo'istiness. *n. ſ.* [from *foiſty.*] Fuſtineſs; mouldineſs.

Dreſs muſtard, and lay it in cellar up ſweet,
Leſt *foiſtineſs* make it for table unmeet. *Tuſſ. Huſbandry.*

Fo'isty. *adj.* [See **Fusty.**] Mouldy; fuſty.

FOLD. *n. ſ.* [ꝼalæð, ꝼalð, Saxon.]

1. The ground in which ſheep are confined.

His eyes he open'd, and beheld a field
Part arable and tilth; whereon were ſheaves
New reap'd; the other part, ſheepwalks and *folds*. *Milton.*

In thy book record their groans,
Who were thy ſheep, and in their ancient *fold*
Slain. *Milton.*

2. The place where ſheep are houſed.

Time drives the flocks from field to *fold*,
When rivers rage and rocks grow cold;
And Philomel becometh dumb,
And all complain of cares to come. *Raleigh.*

3. The flock of ſheep.

And this you ſee I ſcarcely drag along,
Who yeaning on the rocks has left her young,
The hope and promiſe of my failing *fold*. *Dryden's Virgil.*

4. A limit; a boundary.

Secure from meeting, they're diſtinctly roll'd;
Nor leave their ſeats, and paſs the dreadful *fold*. *Creech.*

5. [From ꝼılð, Saxon.] A double; a complication; an involution; one part added to another; one part doubled upon another.

She in this trice of time
Commits a thing ſo monſtrous, to diſmantle
So many *folds* of favour! *Shakeſpeare's King Lear.*

The ancient Egyptian mummies were ſhrowded in a number of *folds* of linen, beſmeared with gums. *Bacon's N. Hiſt.*

Not with indented wave,
Prone on the ground, as ſince; but on his rear
Circular baſe of riſing *folds*, that tower'd
Fold above *fold*, a ſurging maze! *Milton's Paradiſe Loſt.*

Let the draperies be nobly ſpread upon the body, and let the *folds* be large: the parts ſhould be often traverſed by the flowing of the *folds*. *Dryden's Dufreſnoy.*

With fear and wonder ſeiz'd, the crowd beholds
The gloves of death, with ſeven diſtinguiſh'd *folds*
Of tough bull hides. *Dryden's Virg. Æn.*

The inward coat of a lion's ſtomach has ſtronger *folds* than a human, but in other things not much different. *Arbuthnot.*

6. From the foregoing ſignification is derived the uſe of *fold* in compoſition. *Fold* ſignifies the ſame quantity added: as, *two fold*, twice the quantity; *twenty fold*, twenty times repeated.

But other fell into good ground, and brought forth fruit; ſome an *hundred fold*, ſome *ſixty fold*, ſome *thirty fold*. *Matt.*

At laſt appear
Hell bounds, high reaching to the horrid roof,
And thrice *three fold* the gates: *three folds* were braſs,
Three iron, three of adamantine rock. *Milt. Parad. Loſt.*

Their martyr'd blood and aſhes ſow
O'er all th' Italian fields, where ſtill doth ſway
The triple tyrant; that from theſe may grow
A *hundred fold*. *Milton.*

To **Fold.** *v. a.* [from the noun.]

1. To ſhut ſheep in the fold.

The ſtar that bids the ſhepherd *fold*,
Now the top of heav'n doth hold. *Milton.*

We ſee that the *folding* of ſheep helps ground, as well by their warmth as by their compoſt. *Bacon's Natural Hiſtory.*

She in pens his flocks will *fold*,
And then produce her dairy ſtore,
With wine to drive away the cold,
And unbought dainties of the poor. *Dryden's Horace.*

2. [ꝼalðan, Saxon.] To double; to complicate.

As a veſture ſhalt thou *fold* them up. *Heb.* i. 12.

Yet a little ſleep, a little ſlumber, a little *folding* of the hands to ſleep. *Prov* vi. 10.

They be *folden* together as thorns. *Nah.* i. 10.

I have ſeen her riſe from her bed, unlock her cloſet, take forth paper, *fold* it, write upon't, read it, ſeal it, and again return to bed. *Shakeſpeare.*

Conſcious of its own impotence, it *folds* its arms in deſpair, and ſits curſing in a corner. *Collier of Envy.*

Both furl their ſails, and ſtrip them for the fight;
Their *folded* ſheets diſmiſs the uſeleſs air. *Dryd. Ann. Mir.*

3. To incloſe; to include; to ſhut.

We will deſcend and *fold* him in our arms. *Shak. Rich.* II.

Witneſs my ſon, now in the ſhade of death,
Whoſe bright outſhining beams thy cloudy wrath
Hath in eternal darkneſs *folded* up. *Shakeſp. Richard* III.

The fires i' th' loweſt hell *fold* in the people! *Shak. Coriol.*

To **Fold.** *v. n.* To cloſe over another of the ſame kind; to join with another of the ſame kind.

The two leaves of the one door were *folding*, and the two leaves of the other door were *folding*. 1 *Kings* vi. 34.

FOLIA'CEOUS.

FOLIA'CEOUS. *adj.* [*foliaceus*, from *folium*, Latin.] Conſiſting of laminæ or leaves.

A piece of another, conſiſting of an outer cruſt, of a ruddy talky ſpar, and a blue talky *foliaceous* ſpar. *Woodward on Foſſ.*

FO'LIAGE. *n. ſ.* [*folium*, Latin; *feuillage*, French.] Leaves; tufts of leaves; the apparel of leaves to a plant.

The great columns are finely engraven with fruits and *foliage*, that run twiſting about them from the very top to the bottom. *Addiſon on Italy.*

When ſwelling buds their od'rous *foliage* ſhed,
And gently harden into fruit, the wiſe
Spare not the little offſprings, if they grow
Redundant. *Phillips.*

To FO'LIATE. *v. a.* [*foliatus*, *folium*, Latin.] To beat into laminas or leaves.

Gold *foliated*, or any metal *foliated*, cleaveth. *Bacon.*

If gold be *foliated*, and held between your eyes and the light, the light looks of a greeniſh blue. *Newton's Opt.*

FOLIA'TION. *n. ſ.* [*foliatio*, *folium*, Latin.]

1. The act of beating into thin leaves.

2. Foliation is one of the parts of the flower of a plant, being the collection of thoſe fugacious coloured leaves called petala, which conſtitute the compaſs of the flower; and alſo ſometimes to ſecure and guard the fruit which ſucceeds the foliation, as in apples, pears, &c. and ſometimes ſtands within it, as in cherries, apricots, &c. for theſe, being of a tender and pulpous body, and coming forth in the colder parts of the Spring, would be often injured by the extremities of weather, if they were not thus protected and lodged up within their flowers. *Quincy.*

FO'LIATURE. *n. ſ.* [from *folium*, Latin.] The ſtate of being hammered into leaves. *Dict.*

FO'LIO. *n. ſ.* [*in folio*, Latin.] A large book, of which the pages are formed by a ſheet of paper once doubled.

Plumbinus and Plumeo made leſs progreſs in knowledge, though they had read over more *folio's*. *Watts's Improvement.*

FO'LIOMORT. *adj.* [*folium mortuum*, Latin.] A dark yellow; the colour of a leaf faded: vulgarly called *philomot*.

A flinty pebble was of a dark-green colour, and the exteriour cortex of a *foliomort* colour. *Woodward on Foſſils.*

FOLK. *n. ſ.* [folc, Saxon; *volk*, Dutch.]

1. People, in familiar language.

Never troubling him, either with aſking queſtions, or finding fault with his melancholy, but rather fitting to his dolor dolorous diſcourſes of their own and other *folks* misfortune. *Sidney.*

Dorilaus having married his ſiſter, had his marriage in ſhort time bleſt, for ſo are *folk* wont to ſay, how unhappy ſoever the children after grow, with a ſon. *Sidney.*

When with greateſt art he ſpoke,
You'd think he talk'd like other *folk*;
For all a rhetorician's rules
Teach nothing but to name his tools. *Hudibras, p.* i.

2. Nations; mankind.

Thou ſhalt judge the *folk* righteouſly, and govern the nations upon earth. *Pſalm* lvii. 4.

3. Any kind of people as diſcriminated from others.

The river thrice hath flow'd, no ebb between;
And the old *folk*, time's doting chronicles,
Say it did ſo a little time before. *Shakeſp.*

Anger is a kind of baſeneſs; as it appears well in the weakneſs of children, women, old *folks*, and ſick *folks*. *Bacon's Eſſ.*

4. It is now uſed only in familiar or burleſque language.

Old good man Dobſon of the green,
Remembers he the tree has ſeen,
And goes with *folks* to ſhew the ſight. *Swift.*
He walk'd, and wore a threadbare cloak;
He din'd and ſupp'd at charge of other *folk*. *Swift.*

FO'LKMOTE. *n. ſ.* [from *folk* and *mote*.]

Thoſe hills were appointed for two ſpecial uſes, and built by two ſeveral nations: the one is that which you call *folkmotes*, built by the Saxons, and ſignifies in the Saxon a meeting of folk. *Spenſer on Ireland.*

FO'LLICLE. *n. ſ.* [*folliculus*, Latin.]

1. A cavity in any body with ſtrong coats.

Although there be no eminent and circular *follicle*, no round bag or veſicle, which long containeth this humour; yet is there a manifeſt receptacle of choler from the liver into the guts. *Brown's Vulgar Errours, b.* iii. *c.* 2.

2. *Follicle* is a term in botany ſignifying the ſeed-veſſels, capſula ſeminalis, or caſe, which ſome fruits and ſeeds have over them; as that of the alkengi, pedicularis, &c. *Quincy.*

To FO'LLOW. *v. a.* [folgian, Saxon; *volgen*, Dutch.]

1. To go after; not before or ſide by ſide.

I had rather, forſooth, go before you like a man, than *follow* him like a dwarf. *Shakeſpeare's Merry Wives of Windſor.*

2. To purſue as an enemy.

Wherever guilt can fly, revenge can *follow*. *Irene.*

3. To attend as a dependant.

And the three eldeſt ſons of Jeſſe went and *followed* Saul to the battle. 1 *Sa.* xvii. 13.

Such ſmiling rogues as theſe ſooth every paſſion,
That in the nature of their lords rebels:
As knowing nought, like dogs, but *following*. *Shak. K. Lear.*
Let not the muſe then flatter lawleſs ſway,
Nor *follow* fortune where ſhe leads the way. *Pope.*

4. To purſue.

Not yielding over to old age his country delights, he was at that time *following* a merlin. *Sidney, b.* ii.

Some pious tears the pitying hero paid,
And *follow'd* with his eyes the fleeting ſhade. *Dryden's Æn.*
We *follow* fate, which does too faſt purſue. *Dryden.*

5. To ſucceed in order of time.

6. To be conſequential, as effects to cauſes.

7. To imitate; to copy.

Where Rome keepeth that which is ancienter and better, others, whom we much more affect, leaving it for newer, and changing it for worſe, we had rather *follow* the perfections of them whom we like not, than in defects reſemble them whom we love. *Hooker, b.* v. *ſ.* 28.

Ill patterns are ſure to be *followed* more than good rules. *Locke on Education.*

8. To obey; to obſerve.

If all who do not *follow* oral tradition as their only rule of faith are out of the church, then all who *follow* the council of Trent are no Chriſtians. *Tillotſon, Preface.*

Moſt men admire
Virtue, who *follow* not her lore. *Paradiſe Regain'd, b.* vii.

9. To confirm by new endeavours; to keep up indefatigably.

They bound themſelves to his laws and obedience; and in caſe it had been *followed* upon them, as it ſhould have been, they ſhould have been reduced to perpetual civility. *Spenſer.*

10. To attend to; to be buſied with.

He that undertaketh and *followeth* other mens buſineſs for gain, ſhall fall into ſuits. *Eccluſ.* xxix. 9.

To FO'LLOW. *v. n.*

1. To come after another.

Peter *followed* afar off. *Luke* xxii. 54.
The famine ſhall *follow* cloſe after you. *Jer.* xlii. 16.
Welcome all that lead or *follow*
To the oracle of Apollo. *Ben. Johnſon.*

2. To be poſteriour in time.

3. To be conſequential, as effect to cauſe.

If the neglect or abuſe of liberty to examine what would really and truly make for his happineſs miſleads him, the miſcarriages that *follow* on it muſt be imputed to his own election. *Locke.*

To tempt them to do what is neither for their own nor the good of thoſe under their care, great miſchiefs cannot but *follow*. *Locke.*

4. To be conſequential, as inference to premiſes.

Though there are or have been ſometimes dwarfs, and ſometimes giants in the world; yet it does not *follow* that there muſt be ſuch in every age, nor in every country. *Temple.*

This dangerous doctrine muſt neceſſarily *follow*, from making all political power to be nothing elſe but Adam's paternal power. *Locke.*

5. To continue endeavours.

Then ſhall we know, if we *follow* on to know the Lord. *Hoſ.*

FO'LLOWER. *n. ſ.* [from *follow*.]

1. One who comes after another; not before him, or ſide by ſide.

Little gallant, you were wont to be a *follower*; but now you are a leader: whether had you rather lead mine eyes, or eye your maſter's heels? *Shakeſpeare's Merry Wives of Windſor.*

No ſtop, no ſtay, but clouds of ſand ariſe,
Spurn'd and caſt backward on the *follower*'s eyes. *Dryden.*

2. A dependant.

3. An attendant.

No *follower*, but a friend. *Pope.*

4. An aſſociate; a companion.

How accompanied, can'ſt thou tell that?
—With Poins, and other his continual *followers*. *Sh. H.* IV.

5. One under the command of another.

I hold it no wiſdom to leave unto them too much command over their kindred, but rather withdraw their *followers* from them as much as may be, and gather them under the command of law. *Spenſer's State of Ireland.*

The underſtanding that ſhould be eyes to the blind faculty of the will, is blind itſelf; and ſo brings all the inconveniences that attend a blind *follower*, under the conduct of a blind guide. *South's Sermons.*

And forc'd Æneas, when his ſhips were loſt,
To leave his *followers* on a foreign coaſt. *Dryden's Æn.*

6. A ſcholar; an imitator; a copyer; one of the ſame ſort.

Be ye *followers* of me, even as I am of Chriſt. 1 *Cor.* xi. 1.

The true profeſſion of Chriſtianity inviolably engages all its *followers* to do good to all men. *Sprat's Sermons.*

Every one's idea of identity will not be the ſame that Pythagoras and thouſands of his *followers* have. *Locke.*

The ſtudious head or gen'rous mind,
Follow'r of God, or friend of human kind,
Poet or patriot, roſe but to reſtore
The faith and moral nature gave before. *Pope's Eſſays.*

FO'LLY. *n. s.* [*folie*, French.]

1. Want of understanding; weakness of intellect.

2. Criminal weakness; depravity of mind.

Think'st thou, that duty shall have dread to speak,
When pow'r to flattery bows? To plainness honour
Is bound, when majesty to *folly* falls. *Shakesp. King Lear.*

3. Act of negligence or passion unbecoming gravity or deep wisdom. In this sense it has a plural.

Love is blind, and lovers cannot see
The pretty *follies* that themselves commit;
For if they could, Cupid himself would blush
To see me thus transformed to a boy. *Shakespeare.*

Leave such to trifle with more grace and ease,
Whom folly pleases, or whose *follies* please. *Pope's Horace.*

To FOME'NT. *v. a.* [*fomentor*, Latin; *fomenter*, French.]

1. To cherish with heat.

Every kind that lives,
Fomented by his virtual power, and warm'd. *Milton's P. L.*

2. To bathe with warm lotions.

He *fomented* the head with opiates to procure sleep, and a solution of opium in water to *foment* the forehead. *Arbuthnot.*

3. To encourage; to support; to cherish.

They love their givings, and *foment* their deeds no less than parents do their children. *Wotton.*

Blame then thyself, as reason's law requires,
Since nature gave, and thou *foment'st* my fires. *Dryden.*

They are troubled with those ill humours, which they themselves infused and *fomented* in them. *Locke.*

FOMENTA'TION. *n. s.* [*fomentation*, Fr. from *foment.*]

1. A fomentation is partial bathing, called also stuping, which is applying hot flannels to any part, dipped in medicated decoctions, whereby the steams breathe into the parts, and discuss obstructed humours. *Quincy.*

Fomentation calleth forth the humour by vapours; but yet, in regard of the way made by the poultis, draweth gently the humours out: for it is a gentle *fomentation*, and hath withal a mixture of some stupefactive. *Bacon's Natural History.*

2. The lotion prepared to foment the parts.

The medicines were prepared by the physicians, and the lotions or *fomentations* by the nurses. *Arbuthnot on Coins.*

FOME'NTER. *n. s.* [from *foment.*] An encourager; a supporter

These fatal distempers, as they did much hurt to the body politick at home, being like humours stirred in the natural without evacuation, so did they produce disadvantageous effects abroad; and better had it been, that the raisers and *fomenters* of them had never sprung up in Druina. *Howel.*

FON. *n. s.* [Scott. A word now obsolete.] A fool; an ideot.

Sicker I hold him for a greater *fon*,
That loves the thing he cannot purchase. *Spenser's Past.*

FOND. *n. s.* [*fonn*, Scottish. A word of which I have found no satisfactory etymology. To *fonne* is in *Chaucer* to doat, to be foolish.]

1. Foolish; silly; indiscreet; imprudent; injudicious.

This we know that the Grecians or Gentiles did account foolishness; but that they ever did think it a *fond* or unlikely way to seek men's conversion by sermons, we have not heard. *Hooker, b. v. s. 22.*

He was beaten out of all love of learning by a *fond* schoolmaster. *Ascham.*

Tell these sad women,
'Tis *fond* to wail inevitable strokes,
As 'tis to laugh at them. *Shakespeare's Coriolanus.*

Grant I may never prove so *fond*
To trust man on his oath or bond. *Shakespeare's Timon.*

I am weaker than a woman's tear,
Tamer than sleep, *fonder* than ignorance. *Shakespeare.*

Fond thoughts may fall into some idle brain;
But one belief of all, is ever wise. *Davies.*

Thou see'st
How subtly to detain thee I devise,
Inviting thee to hear while I relate;
Fond! were it not in hope of thy reply. *Milt. Paradise Lost.*

So *fond* are mortal men,
Fall'n into wrath divine,
As their own ruin on themselves t' invite. *Milton's Agonistes.*

'Twas not revenge for griev'd Apollo's wrong
Those ass's ears on Midas' temples hung;
But *fond* repentance of his happy wish. *Waller.*

But reason with your *fond* religion fights;
For many gods are many infinites. *Dryden's Tyran. Love.*

This is *fond*, because it is the way to cheat thyself. *Tillotson.*

2. Trifling; valued by folly.

Not with *fond* shekles of the tested gold,
Or stones, whose rate are either rich or poor
As fancy values them. *Shakespeare's Meas. for Measure.*

3. Foolishly tender; injudiciously indulgent.

I'm a foolish *fond* wife. *Addison.*

Like Venus I'll shine,
Be *fond* and be fine. *Addison.*

4. Pleased in too great a degree; foolishly delighted.

Fame is in itself a real good, if we may believe Cicero, who was perhaps too *fond* of it *Dryden's Juvenal, Dedication.*

I, *fond* of my well-chosen seat,
My pictures, medals, books complete. *Prior.*

Some are so *fond* to know a great deal at once, and love to talk of things with freedom and boldness before they thoroughly understand them *Watts's Improvem. of the Mind.*

To FOND. } *v. a.* [from the noun.] To treat with great
To FO'NDLE. } indulgence; to caress; to cocker.

Howe'er unjust your jealousy appear,
It does my pity, not my anger move:
I'll *fond* it as the froward child of love. *Dryden's Aurengz.*

When amidst the fervour of the feast,
The Tyrian hugs, and *fonds* thee on her breast,
And with sweet kisses in her arms constrains,
Thou may'st infuse thy venom in her veins. *Dryden's Æn.*

They are allowed to kiss the child at meeting and parting; but a professor, who always stands by, will not suffer them to use any *fondling* expressions. *Gulliver's Travels.*

To FOND. *v. n.* To be fond of; to be in love; to doat on.

How will this fadge? My master loves her dearly;
And I, poor monster, *fond* as much on him;
And she, mistaken, seems to dote on me. *Shakespeare.*

FO'NDLER. *n. s.* [from *fond.*] One who fondles.

FO'NDLING. *n. s.* [from *fondle.*] A person or thing much fondled or caressed; something regarded with great affection.

Partiality in a parent is commonly unlucky; for *fondlings* are in danger to be made fools, and the children that are least cockered make the best and wisest men. *L'Estrange.*

The bent of our own minds may favour any opinion or action, that may shew it to be a *fondling* of our own. *Locke.*

Any body would have guessed miss to have been bred up under a cruel stepdame, and John to be the *fondling* of a tender mother. *Arbuthnot's History of John Bull.*

Bred a *fondling* and an heiress.
Dress'd like any lady may'ress;
Cocker'd by the servants round,
Was too good to touch the ground. *Swift.*

FO'NDLY. *adv.* [from *fond.*]

1. Foolishly; weakly; imprudently; injudiciously.

Most shallowly did you these arms commence,
Fondly brought here, and foolishly sent hence. *Shak. H. IV.*

Sorrow and grief of heart
Makes him speak *fondly*, like a frantick man. *Shakes. R. II.*

Ficinus *fondly* adviseth, for the prolongation of life, that a vein be opened in the arm of some wholesome young man, and the blood to be sucked. *Bacon's Natural History.*

The military mound
The British files transcend, in evil hour
For their proud foes, that *fondly* brav'd their fate. *Phillips.*

Some valuing those of their own side or mind,
Still make themselves the measure of mankind:
Fondly we think we merit honour then,
When we but praise ourselves in other men. *Pope's Criticism.*

Under those sacred leaves, secure
From common lightning of the skies,
He *fondly* thought he might endure
The flashes of Ardelia's eyes. *Swift.*

2. With great or extreme tenderness.

Ev'n before the fatal engine clos'd,
A wretched sylph too *fondly* interpos'd:
Fate urg'd the sheers, and cut the sylph in twain. *Pope.*

Fondly or severely kind. *Savage.*

FO'NDNESS. *n. s.* [from *fond.*]

1. Foolishness; weakness; want of sense; want of judgment.

Fondness it were for any, being free,
To covet fetters, though they golden be. *Spenser's Sonnets.*

2. Foolish tenderness.

My heart had still some foolish *fondness* for thee;
But hence! 'tis gone: I give it to the winds. *Addis. Cato.*

Hopeless mother!
Whose *fondness* could compare her mortal offspring
To those which fair Latona bore to Jove. *Prior.*

3. Tender passion.

Your jealousy perverts my meaning still;
My very hate is construed into *fondness*. *A. Phill. Dist. Moth.*

Corinna, with that youthful air,
Is thirty and a bit to spare:
Her *fondness* for a certain earl
Began when I was but a girl. *Swift.*

4. Unreasonable liking.

They err that either through indulgence to others, or *fondness* to any sin in themselves, substitute for repentance any thing that is less than a sincere resolution of new obedience, attended with faithful endeavour, and meet fruits of this change. *Hammond's Fundamentals.*

FONT. *n. s.* [*fons*, Latin; *fonte*, French.] A stone vessel in which the water for holy baptism is contained in the church.

The presenting of infants at the holy *font* is by their godfathers. *Hooker, b. ii. s. 7.*

I have

I have no name, no title;
No, not that name was given me at the *font*. *Shakes. R.* II.

FO'NTANEL. *n. s.* [*fontanelle*, French.] An issue; a discharge opened in the body.

A person plethorick, subject to hot defluxions, was advised to a *fontanel* in her arm. *Wiseman of Inflammation.*

FONTA'NGE. n. s. [from the name of the first wearer.] A knot of ribbonds on the top of the head-dress. Out of use.

These old fashioned *fontanges* rose an ell above the head: they were pointed like steeples, and had long loose pieces of crape, which were fringed, and hung down their backs. *Addis.*

FOOD. *n. s.* [fædan, Sax. *voeden*, Dut. to feed; *feed*, Scott.]

1. Victuals; provision for the mouth.

On my knees I beg,
That you'll vouchsafe me raiment, bed, and *food*. *Shakesp.*

Much *food* is in the tillage of the poor. *Prov.* xiii. 23.

Under whose lowly roof thou hast vouchsaf'd
To enter, and these earthly fruits to taste;
Food not of angels, yet accepted so,
As that more willingly thou could'st not seem
At heav'n's high feasts t' have fed. *Milton's Paradise Lost.*

They give us *food*, which may with nectar vie,
And wax that does the absent sun supply. *Waller.*

2. Any thing that nourishes.

Give me some musick: musick, moody *food*
Of us that trade in love. *Shakes. Antony and Cleopatra.*

O dear son Edgar,
The *food* of thy abused father's wrath,
Might I but live to see thee in my touch,
I'd say, I had eyes again. *Shakespeare's King Lear.*

FOO'DFUL. *adj.* [*food* and *full*.] Fruitful; full of food; plenteous.

There Tityus was to see, who took his birth
From heav'n, his nursing from the *foodful* earth. *Dryden.*

FOO'DY. *adj.* [from *food*.] Eatable; fit for food.

To vessels, wine she drew;
And into well sew'd sacks pour'd *foody* meal. *Chapman.*

FOOL. *n. s.* [*ffol*, Welsh; *fol*, Islandick; *fol*, French.]

1. One whom nature has denied reason; a natural; an idiot.

Do'st thou call me *fool*, boy?
—All thy other titles thou hast given away that thou wast born with. *Shakespeare's King Lear.*

The *fool* multitude, that chuse by show,
Not learning more than the fond eye doth teach,
Which pry not to the interior. *Shak. Merchant of Venice.*

It may be asked, whether the eldest son, being a *fool*, shall inherit paternal power before the younger, a wise man. *Locke.*

He thanks his stars he was not born a *fool*. *Pope.*

2. [In Scripture.] A wicked man.

The *fool* hath said in his heart there is no God. *Ps.* xiv. 1.

3. A term of indignity and reproach.

To be thought knowing, you must first put the *fool* upon all mankind. *Dryden's Juvenal, Preface.*

4. One who counterfeits folly; a buffoon; a jester.

Where's my knave, my *fool?* Go you, and call my *fool* hither. *Shakespeare's King Lear.*

I scorn, although their drudge, to be their *fool* or jester. *Milt.*

If this disguise sit not naturally on so grave a person, yet it may become him better than that *fool's* coat. *Denham.*

5. *To play the* FOOL. To play pranks like a hired jester; to jest; to make sport.

I returning where I left his armour, found another instead thereof, and armed myself therein to *play the fool*. *Sidney.*

6. *To play the* FOOL. To act like one void of common understanding.

Well, thus we *play the fools* with the time,
And the spirits of the wise sit in the clouds
And mock us. *Shakespeare's Henry* IV. *p.* ii.

Is it worth the name of freedom to be at liberty to *play the fool*, and draw shame and misery upon a man's self? *Locke.*

7. *To make a* FOOL. To disappoint; to defeat.

'Twere as good a deed as to drink when a man's a-hungry, to challenge him to the field, and then to break promise with him, and *make a fool* of him. *Shakes. Twelfth Night.*

To FOOL. *v. n.* [from the noun.] To trifle; to toy; to play; to idle; to sport.

I, in this kind of merry *fooling*, am nothing to you; so you may continue and laugh at nothing still. *Shakesp. Tempest.*

Fool not; for all may have,
If they dare try, a glorious life, a grave. *Herbert.*

If you have the luck to be court-fools, those that have either wit or honesty, you may *fool* withal, and spare not. *Denham.*

It must be an industrious youth that provides against age; and he that *fools* away the one, must either beg or starve in the other. *L'Estrange.*

He must be happy that knows the true measures of *fooling*. *L'Estrange, Fable* 74.

Is this a time for *fooling?* *Dryden's Spanish Fryar.*

To FOOL. *v. a.*

1. To treat with contempt; to disappoint; to frustrate; to defeat.

And shall it in more shame be further spoken,
That you are *fool'd*, discarded, and shook off? *Shak. H.IV.*

If it be you that stir these daughters hearts
Against their father, *fool* me not so much
To bear it tamely. *Shakespeare's King Lear.*

When I am read, thou feign'st a weak applause,
As if thou wert my friend, but lackest a cause:
This but thy judgment *fools*; the other way
Would both thy folly and thy spite betray. *Ben. Johnson.*

Him over-weaning
To over-reach; but with the serpent meeting,
Fool'd and beguil'd. *Milton's Paradise Lost, b.* x.

If men loved to be deceived and *fooled* about their spiritual estate, they cannot take a surer course than by taking their neighbour's word for that, which can be known only from their own heart. *South's Sermons.*

When I consider life, 'tis all a cheat;
For *fool'd* with hope, men favour the deceit.
I'm tir'd with waiting for this chemick gold,
Which *fools* us young, and beggars us when old. *Dryden.*

I would advise this blinded set of men not to give credit to those, by whom they have been so often *fooled* and imposed upon. *Addison's Freeholder*, N°. 7.

2. To infatuate.

It were an handsome plot,
But full of difficulties, and uncertain;
And he's so *fool'd* with downright honesty,
He'll ne'er believe it. *Denham's Sophy.*

A long and eternal adieu to all unlawful pleasures: I will no longer be *fooled* or imposed upon by them. *Calamy's Serm.*

A boor of Holland, whose cares of growing still richer and richer, perhaps *fool* him so far as to make him enjoy less in his riches than others in poverty. *Temple.*

3. To cheat: as, to *fool* one of his money.

FOO'LBORN. *adj.* [*fool* and *born*.] Foolish from the birth.

Reply not to me with a *foolborn* jest. *Shakes. Henry* IV.

FOO'LERY. *n. s.* [from *fool*.]

1. Habitual folly.

Foolery, sir, does walk about the orb like the sun; it shines every where: I would be sorry, sir, but the fool should be as oft with your master as with my mistress. *Shak. Twelfth Night.*

2. An act of folly; trifling practice.

It is mere *foolery* to multiply distinct particulars in treating of things, where the difference lies only in words. *Watts.*

3. Object of folly.

That Pythagoras, Plato, or Orpheus believed in any of these *fooleries*, it cannot be suspected. *Raleigh's History.*

We are transported with *fooleries*, which, if we understood, we should despise. *L'Estrange's Fables.*

FOOLHA'PPY. *adj.* [*fool* and *happy*.] Lucky without contrivance or judgment.

As when a ship, that flies fair under sail,
An hidden rock escaped unawares,
That lay in wait her wreck for to bewail;
The mariner, yet half amazed, stares
At perils past, and yet in doubt ne dares
To joy at his *foolhappy* oversight. *Fairy Queen, b.* i. *cant.* 6.

FOOLHA'RDINESS. *n. s.* [from *foolhardy*.] Mad rashness; courage without sense.

A false glozing parasite would call his *foolhardiness* valour, and then he may go on boldly, because blindly. *South's Serm.*

There is a difference betwixt daring and *foolhardiness:* Lucan and Statius often ventured them too far, our Virgil never. *Dryden's Dufresnoy.*

FOOLHA'RDISE. *n. s.* [*fool* and *hardiesse*, French.] Foolhardiness; adventurousness without judgment. Obsolete.

More huge in strength than wise in works he was,
And reason with *foolhardise* over-ran;
Stern melancholy did his courage pass,
And was, for terror more, all arm'd in shining brass. *F. Q.*

FOOLHA'RDY. *adj.* [*fool* and *hardy*.] Daring without judgment; madly adventurous; foolishly bold.

One mother, when as her *foolhardy* child
Did come too near, and with his talons play,
Half dead through fear, her little babe revil'd. *Fairy Queen.*

Some would be so *foolhardy* as to presume to be more of the cabinet-council of God Almighty than the angels. *Howel.*

If any yet be so *foolhardy*,
T' expose themselves to vain jeopardy;
If they come wounded off, and lame,
No honour's got by such a maim. *Hudibras, p.* i. *cant.* 1.

FOO'LTRAP. *n. s.* [*fool* and *trap*.] A snare to catch fools in: as a flytrap.

Betts, at the first, were *fooltraps*, where the wise
Like spiders lay in ambush for the flies. *Dryden.*

FOO'LISH. *adj.* [from *fool*.]

1. Void of understanding; weak of intellect.

Thou *foolish* woman, seest thou not our mourning? 2 *Esdr.*

He, of all the men that ever my *foolish* eyes looked upon, was the best deserving a fair lady. *Shakes. Merchant of Venice.*

2. Imprudent; indiscreet.

We are come off

Like

Like Romans; neither *fooliſh* in our ſtands,
Nor cowardly in retire. *Shakeſpeare's Coriolanus.*

3. Ridiculous; contemptible.

It is a *fooliſh* thing to make a long prologue, and to be ſhort in the ſtory itſelf. *2 Mac.* ii. 32.

Pray do not mock me;
I am a very *fooliſh* fond old man:
I fear I am not in my perfect mind. *Shakeſp. King Lear.*

What could the head perform alone,
If all their friendly aids were gone?
A *fooliſh* figure he muſt make;
Do nothing elſe but ſleep and ake. *Prior.*

4. [In Scripture.] Wicked; ſinful.

Foo'lishly. *adv.* [from *fooliſh.*] Weakly; without underſtanding. In Scripture, wickedly.

Although we boaſt our Winter ſun looks bright,
And *fooliſhly* are glad to ſee it at its height;
Yet ſo much ſooner comes the long and gloomy night. *Swift.*

Foo'lishness. *n. ſ.* [from *fooliſh.*]

1. Folly; want of underſtanding.

2. Fooliſh practice; actual deviation from the right.

Fooliſhneſs being properly a man's deviation from right reaſon, in point of practice, muſt needs conſiſt in his pitching upon ſuch an end as is unſuitable to his condition, or pitching upon means unſuitable to the compaſſing of his end. *South.*

Charm'd by their eyes, their manners I acquire,
And ſhape my *fooliſhneſs* to their deſire. *Prior.*

Foo'lsstones. *n. ſ.* A plant.

The characters are: it hath an anomalous flower, conſiſting of ſix diſſimilar leaves; the five uppermoſt of which are ſo diſpoſed as to imitate in ſome manner a helmet. *Miller.*

FOOT. *n. ſ.* plural *feet.* [ꝼoꞇ, Saxon; *voet*, Dutch; *fut*, Scottiſh.]

1. The part upon which we ſtand.

The queen that bore thee,
Oft'ner upon her knees than on her *feet*,
Died ev'ry day ſhe liv'd. *Shakeſpeare's Macbeth.*

His affection to the church was ſo notorious, that he never deſerted it 'till both it and he were over-run and trod under *foot.* *Clarendon.*

2. That by which any thing is ſupported in the nature of a foot.

3. The lower part; the baſe.

Yond' towers, whoſe wanton tops do buſs the clouds,
Muſt kiſs their own *feet.* *Shakeſ. Troilus and Creſſida.*

Fretting, by little and little, waſhes away and eats out both the tops and ſides and *feet* of mountains. *Hakewill on Provid.*

4. The end; the lower part.

What diſmal cries are thoſe?
—Nothing; a trifling ſum of miſery,
New added to the *foot* of thy account:
Thy wife is ſeiz'd by force, and born away. *Dryd. Cleomen.*

5. The act of walking.

Antiochus departed, weening in his pride to make the land navigable, and the ſea paſſable by *foot.* *2 Mac.* v. 21.

6. *On* Foot. Walking; without carriage.

Iſrael journeyed about ſix hundred thouſand *on foot.* *Ex.* xii.

7. A poſture of action.

The centurions and their charges diſtinctly billeted, already in the entertainment, and to be on *foot* at an hour's warning. *Shakeſpeare's Coriolanus.*

8. Infantry; footmen in arms. In this ſenſe it has no plural.

Luſias gathered threeſcore thouſand choice men of *foot*, and five thouſand horſemen. *1 Mac.* iv. 28.

Himſelf with all his *foot* entered the town, his horſe being quartered about it. *Clarendon, b.* viii.

Thrice horſe and *foot* about the fires are led,
And thrice with loud laments they wail the dead. *Dryden.*

9. State; character; condition.

See on what *foot* we ſtand; a ſcanty ſhore,
The ſea behind, our enemies before. *Dryden's Æn.*

In ſpecifying the word Ireland, it would ſeem to inſinuate that we are not upon the ſame *foot* with our fellow ſubjects in England. *Swift's Drapier's Letters.*

What colour of excuſe can be for the contempt with which we treat this part of our ſpecies, that we ſhould not put them upon the common *foot* of humanity, that we ſhould only ſet an inſignificant fine upon the man who murders them? *Addiſ.*

10. Scheme; plan; ſettlement.

There is no wellwiſher to his country without a little hope, that in time the kingdom may be on a better *foot.* *Swift.*

I aſk, whether upon the *foot* of our conſtitution, as it ſtood in the reign of the late king James, a king of England may be depoſed? *Swift.*

11. A ſtate of incipient exiſtence.

If ſuch a tradition were at any time ſet on *foot*, it is not eaſy to imagine how it ſhould at firſt gain entertainment; but much more difficult how it ſhould come to be univerſally propagated. *Tillotſon's Sermons.*

12. It ſeems to have been once proverbially uſed for the level, the ſquare, par.

Were it not for this eaſy borrowing upon intereſt, men's neceſſities would draw upon them a moſt ſudden undoing, in that they would be forced to ſell their means, be it lands or goods, far under *foot.* *Bacon's Eſſays.*

13. A certain number of ſyllables conſtituting a diſtinct part of a verſe.

Feet, in our Engliſh verſifying, without quantity and joints, be ſure ſigns that the verſe is either born deformed, unnatural, or lame. *Aſcham's Schoolmaſter.*

Did'ſt thou hear theſe verſes?
—O yes, I heard them all, and more too; for ſome o' them had in them more *feet* than the verſes would bear. *Shakeſpeare.*

14. Motion; action.

While other jeſts are ſomething rank on *foot*,
Her father hath commanded her to ſlip
Away with Slender to marry. *Shakeſ. Mer. Wives of Windſ.*

In the government of the world the number and variety of the ends on *foot*, with the ſecret nature of moſt things to which they relate, muſt make a diſtinct remark of their congruity, in ſome caſes very difficult, and in ſome unattainable. *Grew.*

15. A meaſure containing twelve inches.

When it ſignifies meaſure it has often, but vitiouſly, *foot* in the plural.

An orange, lemon, and apple, wrapt in a linnen cloth, being buried for a fortnight's ſpace four *foot* deep within the earth, came forth no ways mouldy or rotten. *Bacon.*

16. Step.

This man's ſon would, every *foot* and anon, be taking ſome of his companions into the orchard. *L'Eſtrange.*

To Foot. *v. n.* [from the noun.]

1. To dance; to tread wantonly; to trip.

Lonely the vale and full of horror ſtood,
Brown with the ſhade of a religious wood;
The moon was up, and ſhot a gleamy light;
He ſaw a quire of ladies in a round,
That featly *footing* ſeem'd to ſkim the ground. *Dryden.*

2. To walk; not ride; not fly.

By this the dreadful beaſt drew nigh to land,
Half flying, and half *footing* in his haſte. *Fairy Queen.*

Take heed, have open eye; for thieves do *foot* by night. *Sh.*

The man ſet the boy upon the aſs, and *footed* it himſelf. *L'Eſtrange.*

With them a man ſometimes cannot be a penitent, unleſs he alſo turns vagabond, and *foots* it to Jeruſalem; or wanders over this or that part of the world, to viſit the ſhrine of ſuch or ſuch a pretended ſaint. *South.*

If you are for a merry jaunt, I'll try, for once, who can *foot* it fartheſt. *Dryden's Spaniſh Fryar.*

To Foot. *v. a.*

1. To ſpurn; to kick.

You, that did void your rheum upon my beard, and *foot* me as you ſpurn a ſtranger cur over your threſhold. *Shakeſpeare.*

2. To ſettle; to begin to fix.

What confed'racy have you with the traitors
Late *footed* in the kingdom? *Shakeſpeare's King Lear.*

3. To tread.

Saint Withold *footed* thrice the wold:
He met the night-mare, and her name told;
Bid her alight, and her troth plight,
And aroynt thee, witch, aroynt thee right. *Shak. K. Lear.*

There haply by the ruddy damſel ſeen,
Or ſhepherd boy, they featly *foot* the green. *Tickell.*

Foo'tball. *n. ſ.* [*foot* and *ball.*] A ball commonly made of a blown bladder caſed with leather, driven by the foot.

Am I ſo round with you as you with me,
That like a *football* you do ſpurn me thus? *Shakeſpeare.*

Such a Winter-piece ſhould be beautified with all manner of works and exerciſes of Winter; as *footballs*, felling of wood, and ſliding upon the ice. *Peacham.*

As when a ſort of luſty ſhepherds try
Their force at *football*, care of victory
Makes them ſalute ſo rudely, breaſt to breaſt,
That their encounter ſeems too rough for jeſt. *Waller.*

One rolls along a *football* to his foes,
One with a broken truncheon deals his blows. *Dryden.*

He was ſenſible the common *football* was a very imperfect imitation of that exerciſe. *Arbuthnot and Pope's Mart. Scribl.*

Foo'tboy. *n. ſ.* [*foot* and *boy.*] A low menial; an attendant in livery.

Was it diſcretion, lords, to let this man,
This honeſt man, wait like a lowſy *footboy*
At chamber-door? *Shakeſpeare's Henry* VIII.

Though I had no body to aſſiſt but a *footboy*, yet I made ſhift to try a pretty number of things. *Boyle on Colours.*

Whenever he imagines advantage will redound to one of his *footboys* by oppreſſion of me, he never diſputes it. *Swift.*

Foo'tbridge. *n. ſ.* [*foot* and *bridge.*] A bridge on which paſſengers walk; a narrow bridge.

Palemon's ſhepherd, fearing the *footbridge* was not ſtrong enough, loaded it ſo long, 'till he broke that which would have born a bigger burden. *Sidney.*

Foo'tcloath. *n. ſ.* [*foot* and *cloath.*] A ſumpter cloath.

Three times to-day my *footcloath* horse did stumble,
And started when he look'd upon the Tower,
As loth to bear me to the slaughterhouse. *Shakes. Rich.* III.

FOO'TED. *adj.* [from *foot.*] Shaped in the foot.

Snouted and tailed like a boar, and *footed* like a goat. *Grew.*

FOO'TFIGHT. *n. s.* [*foot* and *fight.*] A fight made on foot, in opposition to that on horseback.

So began our *footfight* in such sort, that we were well entered to blood of both sides. *Sidney, b.* ii.

FOO'THOLD. *n. s.* [*foot* and *hold.*] Space to hold the foot; space on which one may tread surely.

So they all fell to work at the roots of the tree, and left it so little *foothold*, that the first blast of wind laid it flat upon the ground. *L'Estrange.*

He's never well 'till he's at the top: he has nothing above him to aspire to, nor any *foothold* left him to come down by. *L'Estrange, Fable* 6.

FOO'TING. *n. s.* [from *foot.*]

1. Ground for the foot.

I'll read you matter deep and dangerous;
As full of peril and advent'rous spirit
As to o'erwalk a current, roaring loud,
On the unsteadfast *footing* of a spear. *Shakesp. Henry* IV.

As Noah's pigeon, which return'd no more,
Did shew she *footing* found, for all the flood. *Davies.*

In ascents, every step gained is a *footing* and help to the next. *Holder's Elements of Speech.*

2. Foundation; basis; support; root.

Cloven stakes; and, wond'rous to behold,
Their sharpen'd ends in earth their *footing* place,
And the dry poles produce a living race. *Dryd. Virg. Georg.*

All those sublime thoughts take their rise and *footing* here: the mind stirs not one jot beyond those ideas which sense or reflection have offered. *Locke.*

The reasoning faculties of the soul would not know how to move, for want of a foundation and *footing* in most men, who cannot trace truth to its fountain and original. *Locke.*

3. Place.

Whether they unctuous exhalations are,
Fir'd by the sun, or seeming so alone;
Or each some more remote and slippery star,
Which loses *footing* when to mortals shewn. *Dryden.*

4. Tread; walk.

I would outnight you did no body come:
But hark, I hear the *footing* of a man. *Shak. Merch. of Ven.*

Break off, break off; I feel the different sound
Of some chaste *footing* near about this ground:
Run to your shrouds, within these brakes and trees;
Our number may affright. *Milton.*

5. Dance.

Make holyday: your ryestraw hats put on,
And these fresh nymphs encounter every one
In country *footing.* *Shakespeare's Tempest.*

6. Steps; road; track.

He grew strong among the Irish; and in his *footing* his son continuing, hath increased his said name. *Spenser on Ireland.*

Like running weeds, that have no certain root; or like *footings* up and down, impossible to be traced. *Bacon's H.* VII.

7. Entrance; beginning; establishment.

Ever since our nation had any *footing* in this land, the state of England did desire to perfect the conquest. *Davies.*

The defeat of colonel Bellasis gave them their first *footing* in Yorkshire. *Clarendon, b.* viii.

No useful arts have yet found *footing* here;
But all untaught and savage does appear. *Dryd. Ind. Emp.*

8. State; condition; settlement.

Gaul was on the same *footing* with Egypt, as to taxes. *Arb.*

FOO'TLICKER. *n. s.* [*foot* and *lick.*] A slave; an humble fawner; one who licks the foot.

Do that good mischief which may make this island
Thine own for ever; and I, thy Caliban,
For ay thy *footlicker.* *Shakespeare's Tempest.*

FOO'TMAN. *n. s.* [*foot* and *man.*]

1. A soldier that marches and fights on foot.

The numbers levied by her lieutenant did consist of *footmen* three millions, of horsemen one million. *Raleigh's History.*

2. A low menial servant in livery.

He was carried in a rich chariot, litterwise, with two horses at either end, and two *footmen* on each side. *Bacon.*

Like *footmen* running before coaches,
To tell the inn what lord approaches. *Prior.*

3. One who practises to walk or run.

FOO'TMANSHIP. *n. s.* [from *footman.*] The art or faculty of a runner.

The Irish archers espying this, suddenly broke up, and committed the safety of their lives to their nimble *footmanship.* *Hayward.*

Yet, says the fox, I have baffled more of them with my wiles and shifts than ever you did with your *footmanship. L'Est.*

FOO'TPACE. *n. s.* [*foot* and *pace.*]

1. Part of a pair of stairs, whereon, after four or five steps, you arrive to a broad place, where you make two or three paces before you ascend another step, thereby to ease the legs in ascending the rest of the stairs. *Moxon's Mech. Exercises.*

2. A pace no faster than a slow walk.

FOO'TPAD. *n. s.* [*foot* and *pad.*] A highwayman that robs on foot, not on horseback.

FOO'TPATH. *n. s.* [*foot* and *path.*] A narrow way which will not admit horses or carriages.

Know'st thou the way to Dover?
—Both stile and gate, horseway and *footpath. Shak. K. Lear.*

FOO'TPOST. *n. s.* [*foot* and *post.*] A post or messenger that travels on foot.

For carrying such letters, every thoroughfare weekly appointeth a *footpost*, whose dispatch is well near as speedy as the horses. *Carew's Survey of Cornwal.*

FOO'TSTALL. *n. s.* [*foot* and *stall.*] A woman's stirrup.

FOO'TSTEP. *n. s.* [*foot* and *step.*]

1. Trace; track; impression left by the foot.

Clear-sighted reason wisdom's judgment leads,
And sense, her vassal, in her *footsteps* treads. *Denham.*

A man shall never want crooked paths to walk in, if he thinks that he is in the right way, where ever he has the *footsteps* of others to follow. *Locke.*

2. Token; mark; notice given.

Let us turn our thoughts to the frame of our system, if there we may trace any visible *footsteps* of Divine Wisdom and Beneficence. *Bentley's Sermons.*

3. Example.

FOO'TSTOOL. *n. s.* [*foot* and *stool.*] Stool on which he that sits places his feet.

Thus have we swept suspicion from our seat,
And made our *footstool* of security. *Shakesp. Henry* VI.

They whose sacred office 'tis to bring
Kings to obey their God, and men their king,
By these mysterious links to fix and tye
Men to the *footstool* of the Deity. *Denham's Sophy.*

Let ecchoing anthems make his praises known
On earth, his *footstool*, as in heav'n his throne *Roscommon.*

By the phrase of worshipping his *footstool*, no more is meant than worshipping God at his *footstool.* *Stillingfleet.*

FOP. *n. s.* [A word probably made by chance, and therefore without etymology.] A simpleton; a coxcomb; a man of small understanding and much ostentation; a pretender; a man fond of show, dress, and flutter; an impertinent.

A whole tribe of *fops*,
Got 'tween asleep and wake. *Shakespeare's King Lear.*

When such a positive abandon'd *fop*,
Among his numerous absurdities,
Stumbles upon some tolerable line,
I fret to see them in such company. *Roscommon.*

The leopard's beauty, without the fox's wit, is no better than a *fop* in a gay coat. *L'Estrange.*

In a dull stream, which moving slow,
You hardly see the current flow;
When a small breeze obstructs the course,
It whirls about for want of force,
And in its narrow circle gathers
Nothing but chaff, and straws, and feathers:
The current of a female mind
Stops thus, and turns with ev'ry wind;
Thus whirling round, together draws
Fools, *fops*, and rakes, for chaff and straws. *Swift.*

FO'PDOODLE. *n. s.* [*fop* and *doodle.*] A fool; an insignificant wretch.

Where sturdy butchers broke your noddle,
And handled you like a *fopdoodle.* *Hudibras, p.* ii.

FO'PPERY. *n. s.* [from *fop.*]

1. Folly; impertinence.

Let not the sound of shallow *foppery* enter
My sober house. *Shakespeare's Merchant of Venice.*

I was three or four times in the thought they were not fairies; and yet the guiltiness of my mind, the sudden surprise of my powers, drove the grossness of the *foppery* into a received belief, in despight of the teeth of all rhime and reason, that they were fairies. *Shakesp. Merry Wives of Windsor.*

This is the excellent *foppery* of the world, that when we are sick in fortune, often the surfeits of our own behaviour, we make guilty of our disasters the sun, the moon and stars, as if we were villains on necessity. *Shakesp. King Lear.*

2. Affectation of show or importance; showy folly.

3. Foolery; vain or idle practice; idle affectation.

They thought the people were better let alone in their *fopperies*, than to be suffered to break loose from that subjection which your superstition kept them in. *Stillingfleet.*

But though we fetch from Italy and France
Our *fopperies* of tune, and mode of dance,
Our sturdy Britons scorn to borrow sense. *Granville.*

I wish I could say quaint *fopperies* were wholly absent from graver subjects. *Swift to the Lord High Treasurer.*

FO'PPISH. *adj* [from *fop.*]

1. Foolish; idle; vain.

Fools

Fools ne'er had leſs grace in a year;
For wiſe men are grown *foppiſh*,
And know not how their wits to wear,
Their manners are ſo apiſh. *Shakeſpeare's King Lear.*

2. Vain in ſhow; fooliſhly oſtentatious; vain of dreſs.

With him the preſent ſtill ſome virtues have;
The vain are ſprightly, and the ſtupid grave;
The ſlothful negligent, the *foppiſh* neat;
The lewd are airy, and the ſly diſcreet. *Garth's Diſpenſat.*

The Romans grew extremely expenſive and *foppiſh* in this article; ſo that the emperor Aurelian forbid men that variety of colours on their ſhoes, allowing it ſtill to women. *Arbuth.*

Fo'ppishly. *adv.* [from *foppiſh.*] Vainly; oſtentatiouſly.

Fo'ppishness. *n. ſ.* [from *foppiſh.*] Vanity; ſhowy or oſtentatious vanity.

Fo'ppling. *n. ſ.* [from *fop.*] A petty fop; an under-rate coxcomb.

Thy works in Chloe's toilet gain a part,
And, with his tailor, ſhare the *foppling's* heart *Tickell.*

FOR. *prep.* [ꝼoꞃ, Saxon; *voor*, Dutch.]

1. Becauſe of.

That which we *for* our unworthineſs are afraid to crave, our prayer is, that God *for* the worthineſs of his ſon would notwithſtanding vouchſafe to grant. *Hooker, b.* v. *ſ.* 47.

Edward and Richard,
With fiery eyes ſparkling *for* very wrath,
Are at our backs. *Shakeſpeare's Henry* VI. *p.* iii.

Speak, good Cominius;
Leave nothing out *for* length. *Shakeſp.*

For as much as the queſtion cannot be ſcanned, unleſs the time of Abraham's journey be conſidered of, I will ſearch into a tradition concerning his travels. *Raleigh's Hiſt. of the World.*

An aſtrologer ſaith, if it were not *for* two things that are conſtant, no individual would laſt one moment. *Bacon.*

For as much as it is a fundamental law in the Turkiſh empire, that they may, without any other provocation, make war upon Chriſtendom *for* the propagation of their laws; ſo the Chriſtians may at all times, as they think good, be upon the prevention. *Bacon's War with Spain.*

The governour, ſallying out, took great ſtore of victual and warlike proviſion, which the Turks had *for* haſte left behind them. *Knolles's Hiſtory of the Turks.*

Their offer he willingly accepted, knowing that he was not able to keep that place three days, *for* lack of victual. *Knolles.*

Quit, quit, *for* ſhame; this will not move,
This cannot take her:
If of herſelf ſhe will not love,
Nothing can make her. *Suckling.*

Care not *for* frowns or ſmiles. *Denham's Sophy, Prol.*

The hypocrite or carnal man hopes, and is the wickeder *for* hoping. *Hammond's Pract. Catech.*

Let no man, *for* his own poverty, become more oppreſſing in his bargains; but quietly recommend his eſtate to God, and leave the ſucceſs to him. *Taylor.*

Perſons who have loſt moſt of their grinders, having been compelled to uſe three or four only in chewing, wore them ſo low that the inward nerve lay bare, and they would no longer *for* pain make uſe of them. *Ray on the Creation.*

I but revenge my fate; diſdain'd, betray'd;
And ſuff'ring death *for* this ungrateful maid. *Dryden.*

Sole on the barren ſands, the ſuff'ring chief
Roar'd out *for* anguiſh, and indulg'd his grief. *Dryden.*

For his long abſence church and ſtate did groan,
Madneſs the pulpit, faction ſeiz'd the throne. *Dryden.*

Nor with a ſuperſtitious fear is aw'd
For what befalls at home, or what abroad. *Dryd. Virg. Geo.*

I, my own judge, condemn'd myſelf before;
For pity, aggravate my crime no more. *Dryden's Aurengz.*

Matrons of renown,
When tyrant Nero burnt th' imperial town,
Shriek'd *for* the downfal in a doleful cry,
For which their guiltleſs lords were doom'd to die. *Dryden.*

Children, diſcountenanced by their parents *for* any fault, find a refuge in the careſſes of fooliſh flatterers. *Locke.*

A ſound mind in a ſound body is a ſhort but full deſcription of a happy ſtate in this world: he that has theſe two has little more to wiſh for, and he that wants either of them will be but little the better *for* any thing elſe. *Locke.*

The middle of the gulph is remarkable *for* tempeſts. *Addiſ.*

My open'd thought to joyous proſpect raiſe,
And *for* thy mercy let me ſing thy praiſe. *Prior.*

Which beſt or worſt, you could not think;
And die you muſt, *for* want of drink. *Prior.*

It is a moſt infamous ſcandal upon the nation, to reproach them *for* treating foreigners with contempt. *Swift.*

We can only give them that liberty now *for* ſomething, which they have ſo many years exerciſed *for* nothing, of railing and ſcribbling againſt us. *Swift.*

Your ſermons would be leſs valuable, *for* want of time. *Swift.*

2. With reſpect to; with regard to.

Rather our ſtate's defective *for* requital,
Than we to ſtretch it out. *Shakeſpeare's Coriolanus.*

A paltry ring
That ſhe did give me, whoſe poeſy was,
For all the world, like cutlers poetry
Upon a knife; love me and leave me not. *Shakeſpeare.*

For all the world,
As thou art at this hour, was Richard then. *Shakeſ. H.* IV.

It was young counſel *for* the perſons, and violent counſel *for* the matters. *Bacon, Eſſay* 21.

Authority followeth old men, and favour and popularity youth; but *for* the moral part, perhaps, youth will have the pre-eminence, as age hath for the politick. *Bacon's Eſſays.*

Comets are rather gazed upon than wiſely obſerved in their effects; that is, what kind of comet *for* magnitude or colour, produceth what kind of effects. *Bacon, Eſſay* 54.

For me, if there be ſuch a thing as I. *Waller.*

He ſaith theſe honours conſiſted in preſerving their memories, and praiſing their virtues; but *for* any matter of worſhip towards them, he utterly denies it. *Stillingfleet.*

Our laws were *for* their matter foreign. *Hales.*

Now *for* the government, it is abſolute monarchy; there being no other laws in China but the king's command. *Temple.*

For me, no other happineſs I own,
Than to have born no iſſue to the throne. *Dryd. Tyr. Love.*

For me, my ſtormy voyage at an end,
I to the port of death ſecurely tend. *Dryden's Æn. b.* xii.

After death, we ſprights have juſt ſuch natures
We had, *for* all the world, when human creatures. *Dryden.*

Such little waſps, and yet ſo full of ſpite;
For bulk mere inſects, yet in miſchief ſtrong. *Tate's Juv.*

Hobbes has given us a correct explanation of the ſenſe in general; but *for* particulars and circumſtances, he continually lops them. *Pope's Preface to the Iliad.*

Lo, ſome are vellom, and the reſt as good,
For all his lordſhip knows, but they are wood. *Pope.*

3. In this ſenſe it has often *as* before it.

As for Maramaldus the general, they had no juſt cauſe to miſlike him, being an old captain of great experience. *Knolles.*

4. In the character of.

If a man can be fully aſſured of any thing *for* a truth, without having examined, what is there that he may not embrace *for* truth? *Locke.*

She thinks you favour'd:
But let her go, *for* an ungrateful woman. *A. Phillips.*

Say, is it fitting in this very field,
This field, where from my youth I've been a carter,
I, in this field, ſhould die *for* a deſerter? *Gay.*

5. With reſemblance of.

I hear *for* certain, and do ſpeak the truth,
The gentle York is up. *Shakeſpeare's Henry* IV. *p.* ii.

Now, now *for* ſure, deliverance is at hand,
The kingdom ſhall to Iſrael be reſtor'd. *Paradiſe Regain'd.*

The ſtartling ſteed was ſeiz'd with ſudden fright,
And, bounding, o'er the pommel caſt the knight:
Forward he flew, and pitching on his head,
He quiver'd with his feet, and lay *for* dead. *Dryden.*

6. Conſidered as; in the place of.

Our preſent lot appears
For happy, though but ill; *for* ill, not worſt,
If we procure not to ourſelves more woe. *Milton's Pa. Loſt.*

The council-table and ſtar-chamber held *for* honourable that which pleaſed, and *for* juſt that which profited. *Clarendon.*

Read all the prefaces of Dryden,
For thoſe our criticks much confide in;
Though meerly writ at firſt *for* filling,
To raiſe the volume's price a ſhilling. *Swift.*

7. In advantage of; for the ſake of.

An ant is a wiſe creature *for* itſelf; but it is a ſhrewd thing in an orchard. *Bacon, Eſſay* 24.

He refuſed not to die *for* thoſe that killed him, and ſhed his blood *for* ſome of thoſe that ſpilt it. *Boyle.*

Whether ſome hero's fate,
In words worth dying *for*, he celebrate. *Cowley.*

Shall I think the world was made *for* one,
And men are born *for* kings, as beaſts *for* men,
Not *for* protection, but to be devour'd? *Dryd. Span. Fryar.*

8. Conducive to; beneficial to.

It is *for* the general good of human ſociety, and conſequently of particular perſons, to be true and juſt; and it is *for* mens health to be temperate. *Tillotſon, Sermon* 1.

It can never be *for* the intereſt of a believer to do me a miſchief, becauſe he is ſure, upon the balance of accounts, to find himſelf a loſer by it. *Addiſon's Spectator,* Nº. 186.

9. With intention of going to a certain place.

We ſailed from Peru, where we had continued for the ſpace of one whole year, *for* China and Japan, taking with us victuals for twelve months. *Bacon's New Atlantis.*

As ſhe was brought *for* England, ſhe was caſt away near Harwich haven. *Hayward.*

We ſailed directly *for* Genoa, and had a fair wind. *Addiſon.*

10. In comparative reſpect.
For tuſks with Indian elephants he ſtrove,
And Jove's own thunder from his mouth he drove. *Dryden.*

11. In proportion to
As he could ſee clear, *for* thoſe times, through ſuperſtition; ſo he would be blinded, now and then, by human policy. *Bacon's Henry* VII
Your underſtandings are not bright enough *for* the exerciſe of the higheſt acts of reaſon. *Tillotſon, Sermon* 4.

12. With appropriation to.
Shadow will ſerve *for* Summer: prick him; for we have a number of ſhadows to fill up the muſter-book. *Shakeſ. H.* IV.

13. After O an expreſſion of deſire.
O for a muſe of fire, that would aſcend
The brighteſt heaven of invention! *Shak. H.* V. *Prologue.*

14. In account of; in ſolution of.
Thus much *for* the beginning and progreſs of the deluge. *Burnet's Theory of the Earth.*

15. Inducing to as a motive.
There is a natural, immutable, and eternal reaſon *for* that which we call virtue, and againſt that which we call vice. *Till.*

16. In expectation of.
He muſt be back again by one and twenty, to marry and propagate: the father cannot ſtay any longer *for* the portion, nor the mother *for* a new ſet of babies to play with. *Locke.*

17. Noting power or poſſibility.
For a holy perſon to be humble, *for* one whom all men eſteem a ſaint, to fear leſt himſelf become a devil, is as hard as *for* a prince to ſubmit himſelf to be guided by tutors. *Taylor.*

18. Noting dependence.
The colours of outward objects, brought into a darkened room, depend *for* their viſibility upon the dimneſs of the light they are beheld by. *Boyle on Colours.*

19. In prevention of; for fear of.
Corn being had down, any way ye allow,
Should wither as needeth *for* burning in mow. *Tuſſ. Huſb.*
And, *for* the time ſhall not ſeem tedious,
I'll tell thee what befel me on a day,
In this ſelf place. *Shakeſpeare's Henry* VI. *p.* iii.
There muſt be no alleys with hedges at the hither end, *for* letting your proſpect upon this fair hedge from the green; nor at the farther end, *for* letting your proſpect from the hedge through the arches upon the heath. *Bacon, Eſſay* 47.

20. In remedy of.
Sometimes hot, ſometimes cold things are good *for* the toothach. *Garretſon.*

21. In exchange for.
He made conſiderable progreſs in the ſtudy of the law, before he quitted that profeſſion *for* this of poetry. *Dryden.*

22. In the place of; inſtead of.
To make him copious is to alter his character; and to tranſlate him line *for* line, is impoſſible. *Dryden.*
We take a falling meteor *for* a ſtar. *Cowley.*

23. In ſupply of; to ſerve in the place of.
Moſt of our ingenious young men take up ſome cried-up Engliſh poet *for* their model, adore him, and imitate him, as they think, without knowing wherein he is defective. *Dryden.*

24. Through a certain duration.
Some pleaſe *for* once, ſome will *for* ever pleaſe. *Roſcom.*
Thoſe who ſleep without dreaming, can never be convinced that their thoughts are *for* four hours buſy, without their knowing it. *Locke.*
The adminiſtration of this bank is *for* life, and partly in the hands of the chief citizens. *Addiſon's Remarks on Italy.*
Since, hir'd *for* life, thy ſervile muſe muſt ſing
Succeſſive conqueſts, and a glorious king;
And bring him laurels, whatſoe'er they coſt. *Prior.*
The youth tranſported, aſks without delay
To guide the ſun's bright chariot *for* a day. *Garth's Ovid.*

25. In ſearch of; in queſt of.
Some of the philoſophers have run ſo far back *for* arguments of comfort againſt pain, as to doubt whether there were any ſuch thing; and yet, for all that, when any great evil has been upon them, they would cry out as loud as other men. *Tillotſon, Sermon* 5.

26. According to.
Chymiſts have not been able, *for* aught is vulgarly known, by fire alone to ſeparate true ſulphur from antimony. *Boyle.*

27. Noting a ſtate of fitneſs or readineſs.
Nay, if you be an undertaker, I am *for* you *Shakeſpeare.*
If he be brave, he's ready *for* the ſtroke. *Dryden.*

28. In hope of; for the ſake of; noting the final cauſe.
How quickly nature
Falls to revolt, when gold becomes her object!
For this the fooliſh, over-careful fathers,
Have broke their ſleeps with thought, their brains with care,
Their bones with induſtry: *for* this, engroſs'd
The canker'd heaps of ſtrong atchieved gold:
For this they have been thoughtful to inveſt
Their ſons with arts and martial exerciſes. *Shakeſ. H.* IV.
The kingdom of God was firſt rent by ill counſel; upon which counſel there are ſet, *for* our inſtruction, two marks. *Bacon.*
For he writes not *for* money, nor *for* praiſe,
Nor to be call'd a wit, nor to wear bays. *Denham.*
There we ſhall ſee, a ſight worthy dying *for*, that bleſſed Saviour, who ſo highly deſerves of us. *Boyle.*
He is not diſpoſed to be a fool, and to be miſerable *for* company. *Tillotſon, Sermon* 1.
Even death's become to me no dreadful name;
In fighting fields, where our acquaintance grew,
I ſaw him, and contemn'd him firſt *for* you *Dryd. Aureng.*
For this, 'tis needful to prevent her art,
And fire with love the proud Phœnician's heart *Dryd. Virg.*
Some pray *for* riches; riches they obtain;
But watch'd by robbers, *for* their wealth are ſlain. *Dryden.*
Let them, who truly would appear my friends,
Employ their ſwords like mine *for* noble ends. *Dryd Auren.*
Scholars are frugal of their words, and not willing to let any go *for* ornament, if they will not ſerve *for* uſe. *Felton.*

29. Of tendency to; towards.
It were more *for* his honour to raiſe his ſiege, than to ſpend ſo many good men in the winning of it by force. *Knolles.*
The kettle to the top was hoiſt;
But with the upſide down, to ſhow
Its inclination *for* below. *Swift.*

30. In favour of; on the part of; on the ſide of.
Ye ſuppoſe the laws *for* which ye ſtrive are found in Scripture; but thoſe not againſt which we ſtrive. *Hooker, Preface.*
It becomes me not to draw my pen in the defence of a bad cauſe, when I have ſo often drawn it *for* a good one. *Dryden.*
Jove was *for* Venus; but he fear'd his wife. *Dryden.*
He *for* the world was made, not us alone. *Cowley.*
They muſt be void of all zeal *for* God's honour, who do not with ſighs and tears intercede with him. *Smalridge's Serm.*
Ariſtotle is *for* poetical juſtice. *Dennis.*
They are all *for* rank and foul feeding. *Felton.*

31. Noting accommodation or adaptation.
Fortune, if there be ſuch a thing as ſhe,
Spies that I bear ſo well her tyranny,
That ſhe thinks nothing elſe ſo fit *for* me. *Donne.*
A few rules of logick are thought ſufficient, in this caſe, *for* thoſe who pretend to the higheſt improvement. *Locke.*
It is *for* wicked men to dread God; but a virtuous man may have undiſturbed thoughts, even of the juſtice of God. *Tillotſon, Sermon* 4.
His country has good havens, both *for* the Adriatick and Mediterranean. *Addiſon's Remarks on Italy.*
Perſia is commodiouſly ſituated *for* trade both by ſea and land. *Arbuthnot on Coins.*

32. With intention of.
And by that juſtice haſt remov'd the cauſe
Of thoſe rude tempeſts, which, *for* rapine ſent
Too oft, alas, involv'd the innocent. *Waller.*
Here huntſmen with delight may read
How to chuſe dogs *for* ſcent or ſpeed. *Waller.*
God hath made ſome things *for* as long a duration as they are capable of. *Tillotſon, Sermon* 1.
For this, from Trivia's temple and her wood,
Are courſers driv'n, who ſhed their maſters blood. *Dryden.*
Such examples ſhould be ſet before them, as patterns *for* their daily imitation. *Locke.*
The next queſtion uſually is, what is it *for?* *Locke.*
Achilles is *for* revenging himſelf upon Agamemnon, by means of Hector. *Pope's View of Epick Poem.*

33. Becoming; belonging to.
It were not *for* your quiet, nor your good,
Nor *for* my manhood, honeſty, and wiſdom,
To let you know my thoughts. *Shakeſpeare's Othello.*
Th' offers he doth make,
Were not *for* him to give, nor them to take. *Daniel.*
Jeſts *for* Dutchmen and Engliſh boys. *Cowley.*
Is it *for* you to ravage ſeas and land,
Unauthoriz'd by my ſupreme command! *Dryd. Virg. Æn.*
His fire already ſigns him *for* the ſkies,
And marks the ſeat amidſt the deities. *Dryden's Æn.*
It is a reaſonable account *for* any man to give, why he does not live as the greateſt part of the world do, that he has no mind to die as they do, and periſh with them. *Tillotſon.*

34. Notwithſtanding.
This, *for* any thing we know to the contrary, might be the ſelf-ſame form which Philojudæus expreſſeth *Hooker, b.* v.
God's deſertion ſhall, *for* ought he knows the next minute, ſupervene. *Decay of Piety.*
Probability ſuppoſes that a thing may, or may not be ſo, *for* any thing that yet is certainly determined on either ſide. *South's Sermons.*
For any thing that legally appears to the contrary, it may be a contrivance to fright us. *Swift's Drapier's Letters.*
If ſuch vaſt maſſes of matter had been ſituated nearer to the ſun, or to each other, as they might as eaſily have been, *for* any mechanical or fortuitous agent, they muſt neceſſarily have cauſed a conſiderable diſorder in the whole ſyſtem. *Bentley.*

35. For *all*. Notwithstanding.

Neither doubt you, because I wear a woman's apparel, I will be the more womanish; since I assure you, *for all* my apparel, there is nothing I desire more than fully to prove myself a man in this enterprize. *Sidney.*

For all the carefulness of the Christians the English bulwark was undermined by the enemy, and upon the fourth of September part thereof was blown up *Knolles's History.*

But as Noah's pigeon, which return'd no more,
Did shew she footing found *for all* the flood. *Davies.*

They resolute, *for all* this, do proceed
Unto that judgment. *Daniel.*

For all his exact plot, down was he cast from all his greatness, and forced to end his days in a mean condition. *South.*

If we apprehend the greatest things in the world of the emperor of China or Japan, we are well enough contented, *for all* that, to let them govern at home. *Stillingfleet.*

Though that very ingenious person has anticipated part of what I should say, yet you will, *for all* that, expect that I should give you a fuller account. *Boyle on Colours.*

She might have passed over all such petty businesses; but the raising of my rabble is not to be mumbled up in silence, *for all* her pertness. *Dryden's Don Sebastian.*

36. To the use of; to be used in.

The oak *for* nothing ill,
The osier good *for* twigs, the poplar *for* the mill. *Spenser.*

37. In consequence of.

For love they force through thickets of the wood,
They climb the steepy hills and stem the flood. *Dryden.*

38. In recompense of.

Now, *for* so many glorious actions done,
For peace at home, and *for* the publick wealth,
I mean to crown a bowl for Cæsar's health;
Besides, in gratitude *for* such high matters,
Know I have vow'd two hundred gladiators. *Dryden's Pers.*

First the wily wizard must be caught;
For unconstrain'd, he nothing tells *for* naught. *Dryd. Virg.*

39. In proportion to.

He is not very tall, yet *for* his years he's tall. *Shakespeare.*

Exalted Socrates! divinely brave!
Injur'd he fell, and dying he forgave;
Too noble *for* revenge. *Dryden's Juven. Sat.* 13.

40. By means of; by interposition of.

Moral consideration can no way move the sensible appetite, were it not *for* the will. *Hale's Origin of Mankind.*

Of some calamity we can have no relief but from God alone; and what would men do in such a case, if it were not *for* God? *Tillotson's Sermons.*

41. In regard of; in preservation of. I *cannot for my life*, is, I cannot if my life might be saved by it.

I bid the rascal knock upon your gate;
But could not get him *for* my heart. *Shakespeare.*

I cannot *for* my heart leave a room, before I have thoroughly examined the papers pasted upon the walls. *Addison's Spect.*

42. For *to*. In the language used two centuries ago, *for* was commonly used before *to* the sign of the infinitive mood, to note the final cause. As, I come *for to* see you, for I love to see you: in the same sense with the French *pour*. Thus it is used in the translation of the Bible. But this distinction was by the best writers sometimes forgotten; and *for*, by wrong use, appearing superfluous, is now always omitted.

Who shall let me now
On this vile body *for to* wreak my wrong? *Fairy Queen.*

A large posterity
Up to your happy palaces may mount,
Of blessed saints *for to* increase the count. *Spenser.*

These things may serve *for* to represent how just cause of fear this kingdom may have towards Spain. *Bacon.*

For. *conj.*

1. The word by which the reason is given of something advanced before.

Heav'n doth with us as we with torches deal,
Not light them for themselves; *for* if our virtues
Did not go forth of us, 'twere all alike
As if we had them not. *Shakesp. Measure for Measure.*

Old husbandmen I at Sabinum know,
Who for another year dig, plough, and sow;
For never any man was yet so old,
But hop'd his life one Winter more would hold. *Denham.*

Tell me what kind of thing is wit?
For the first matter loves variety less. *Cowley.*

Thus does he who, for fear of any thing in this world, ventures to displease God; *for* in so doing he runs away from men, and falls into the hands of the living hand. *Tillotson.*

2. Because; on this account that.

I doubt not but great troops would be ready to run; yet *for* that the worst men are most ready to remove, I would wish them chosen by discretion of wise men. *Spenser on Ireland.*

Jealous souls will not be answer'd so:
They are not ever jealous for a cause,
But jealous *for* they're jealous. *Shakespeare's Othello.*

Heaven defend your good souls, that you think
I will your serious and great business scant;
For she is with me. *Shakespeare's Othello.*

Nor swell'd his breast with uncouth pride,
That heav'n on him above his charge had laid;
But, *for* his great Creator would the same,
His will increas'd; so fire augmenteth flame. *Fairfax.*

Many excrescences of trees grow chiefly where the tree is dead or faded; *for* that the natural sap of the tree corrupteth into some preternatural substance. *Bacon's Natural History.*

3. For *as much*. In regard that; in consideration of.

For as much as in publick prayer we are not only to consider what is needful, in respect of God; but there is also in men that which we must regard: we somewhat incline to length, lest overquick dispatch should give occasion to deem, that the thing itself is but little accounted of. *Hooker, b.* v.

For as much as the thirst is intolerable, the patient may be indulged the free use of spaw water. *Arbuthnot on Diet.*

4. For *why*. Because; for this reason that.

Solyman had three hundred fieldpieces, that a camel might well carry one of them, being taken from the carriage; *for why*, Solyman purposing to draw the emperor unto battle, had brought no greater pieces of battery with him. *Knolles.*

To Fo'rage. *v. n.* [from *foris*, abroad, Latin.]

1. To wander far; to rove at a distance.

Forage, and run
To meet displeasure farther from the doors,
And grapple with him, ere he come so nigh. *Shak. K. John.*

2. To wander in search of spoil, generally of provisions.

As in a stormy night,
Wolves, urged by their raging appetite,
Forage for prey. *Denham.*

There was a brood of young larks in the corn, and the dam went abroad to *forage* for them. *L'Estrange's Fables.*

Nor dare they stray
When rain is promis'd, or a stormy day;
But near the city walls their wat'ring take,
Nor *forage* far, but short excursions make. *Dryden's Virgil.*

3. To ravage; to feed on spoil.

His most mighty father on a hill
Stood smiling, to behold his lion's whelp
Forage in blood of French nobility. *Shakesp. Henry* V.

To Fo'rage *v. a.* To plunder; to strip; to spoil.

They will both strengthen all the country round, and also be as continual holds for her majesty, if the people should revolt; for without such it is easy to *forage* and over-run the whole land. *Spenser on Ireland.*

FO'RAGE. *n. s.* [*fourage*, German and French, from *foris*, Latin.]

1. Search of provisions; the act of feeding abroad.

One way a band select from *forage* drives
A herd of beeves, fair oxen, and fair kine,
From a fat meadow ground; or fleecy flock,
Ewes, and their bleating lambs, over the plains
Their booty. *Milton's Paradise Lost, b.* xi.

2. Provisions sought abroad.

Some o'er the publick magazines preside,
And some are sent new *forage* to provide. *Dryden's Georg.*

3. Provisions in general.

Provided *forage*, our spent arms renew'd. *Dryd. Fables.*

Fora'minous. *adj.* [from *foramen*, Latin.] Full of holes; perforated in many places; porous.

Soft and *foraminous* bodies, in the first creation of the sound, will deaden it; but in the passage of the sound they will admit it better than harder bodies. *Bacon's Nat. History.*

To FORBE'AR. *v. n.* pret. *I forbore*, anciently *forbare*; part. *forborn.* [ꝼoꞃbæꞃan, Saxon. *For* has in composition the power of privation; as, *forbear*: or depravation; as *forswear*, and other powers not easily explained.]

1. To cease from any thing; to intermit.

The wolf, the lion, and the bear,
When they their prey in pieces tear,
To quarrel with themselves *forbear*. *Denham.*

2. To pause; to delay.

I pray you, tarry: pause a day or two,
Before you hazard; for in chusing wrong,
I lose your company; therefore *forbear* a while. *Shakesp.*

3. To omit voluntarily; not to do; to abstain.

He *forbare* to go forth. 1 *Sa.* xxiii. 13.

At this he started, and *forbore* to swear;
Not out of conscience of the sin, but fear. *Dryden's Juv.*

Who can *forbear* to admire and adore him who weighed the mountains in scales, and the hills in a balance. *Cheyne.*

4. To restrain any violence of temper; to be patient.

By long *forbearing* is a prince persuaded, and a soft tongue breaketh the bone. *Prov.* xxv. 15.

To Fo'rbear. *v. a.*

1. To decline; to omit voluntarily.

Forbear his presence, until time hath qualified the heat of his displeasure. *Shakespeare's King Lear.*

So angry bulls the combat do *forbear*,
When from the wood a lion does appear. *Waller.*

2. To abstain from; to shun to do.

If it passed only by the house of peers, it should be looked upon as invalid and void, and execution should be thereupon *forborn* or suspended. *Clarendon, b.* viii.

There is not any one action whatsoever which a man ought to do, or to *forbear*, but the Scripture will give him a clear precept or prohibition for it. *South's Sermons.*

3. To spare; to treat with clemency.

With all lowliness and meekness, with long suffering, *forbearing* one another in love. *Eph.* iv. 2.

4. To withold.

Forbear thee from meddling with God, who is with me, that he destroy thee not. 2 *Chro.* xxxv. 21.

FORBE'ARANCE. *n. s.* [from *forbear.*]

1. The care of avoiding or shunning any thing; negation of practice.

True nobleness would
Learn him *forbearance* from so foul a wrong. *Shakesp. R.* III.

This may convince us how vastly greater a pleasure is consequent upon the *forbearance* of sin, than can possibly accompany the commission of it. *South's Sermons.*

Liberty is the power a man has to do, or forbear doing, any particular action, according as its doing or *forbearance* has the actual preference in the mind. *Locke.*

2. Intermission of something.

3. Command of temper.

Have a continent *forbearance*, 'till the speed of his rage goes slower. *Shakespeare's King Lear.*

4. Lenity; delay of punishment; mildness.

Nor do I take notice of this instance of severity in our own country to justify such a proceeding, but only to display the mildness and *forbearance* made use of under the reign of his present majesty. *Addison's Freeholder*, N°. 52.

He applies to our gratitude by obligations of kindness and beneficence, of long suffering and *forbearance.* *Rogers.*

FORBE'ARER. *n. s.* [from *forbear.*] An intermitter; interceptor of any thing.

The West as a father all goodness doth bring,
The East a *forbearer*, no manner of thing. *Tuss. Husbandry.*

To FO'RBID. *v. a.* pret. *I forbade*; part. *forbidden* or *forbid.* [ꝼoꞃbeoðan, Saxon; *verbieden*, Dutch.]

1. To prohibit; to interdict any thing.

A witch, a quean, an old cozening quean; have I not *forbid* her my house? *Shakesp. Merry Wives of Windsor.*

By tasting of that fruit *forbid*,
Where they sought knowledge, they did error find. *Davies.*

The voice of reason, in all the dictates of natural morality, ought carefully to be attended to, by a strict observance of what it commands, but especially of what it *forbids.* *South.*

All hatred of persons, by very many Christian principles, we are most solemnly and indispensably *forbid.* *Spratt's Serm.*

The chaste and holy race
Are all *forbidden* this polluted place. *Dryden's Æn. b.* vi.

2. To command to forbear any thing.

She with so sweet a rigour *forbad* him, that he durst not rebel. *Sidney, b.* ii.

It is the shameful work of Hubert's hand,
The practice and the purpose of the king,
From whose obedience I *forbid* my soul. *Shakespeare.*

They have determined to consume all those things that God hath *forbidden* them to eat by his laws. *Judith* xi. 12.

3. To oppose; to hinder.

The moisture being *forbidden* to come up in the plant, stayeth longer in the root, and so dilateth it. *Bacon's Nat. History.*

The plaister alone would pen the humour, and so exasperate it as well as *forbid* new humour. *Bacon's Natural History.*

Thy throne is darkness in th' abyss of light,
A blaze of glory that *forbids* the sight!
O teach me to believe thee thus conceal'd,
And search no farther than thyself reveal'd. *Dryden.*

4. To accurse; to blast. Now obsolete. To *bid* is in old language to *pray*; to *forbid* therefore is to *curse.*

Sleep shall neither night nor day
Hang upon his penthouse lid;
He shall live a man *forbid.* *Shakespeare's Macbeth.*

To FO'RBID. *v. n.* To utter a prohibition.

Now the good gods *forbid*,
That our renowned Rome
Should now eat up her own! *Shakespeare's Coriolanus.*

FORBI'DDANCE. *n. s.* [from *forbid.*] Prohibition; edict against any thing.

How hast thou yielded to transgress
The strict *forbiddance!* how to violate
The sacred fruit forbidden! *Milton's Paradise Lost, b.* ix.

FO'RBIDDENLY. *adv.* [from *forbid.*] In an unlawful manner.

With all confidence he swears, as he had seen't,
That you have touch'd his queen *forbiddenly.* *Shakespeare.*

FO'RBIDDER. *n. s.* [from *forbid.*] One that prohibits; one that enacts a prohibition.

This was a bold accusation of God, making the fountain of good the contriver of evil, and the *forbidder* of the crime an abettor of the fact prohibited. *Brown's Vul. Err.*

Other care, perhaps,
May have diverted from continual watch
Our great *forbidder!* *Milton's Paradise Lost, b.* ix.

FO'RBIDDING. *participial adj.* [from *forbid.*] Raising abhorrence; repelling approach; causing aversion.

Tragedy was made *forbidding* and horrible. *A. Hill.*

FORCE. *n. s.* [*force*, French; *fortis*, Latin.]

1. Strength; vigour; might; active power.

He never could maintain his part but in the *force* of his will. *Shakesp. Much Ado about Nothing.*

A ship, which hath struck sail, doth run
By *force* of that *force* which before it won. *Donne.*

2. Violence.

Thus got the house of Lancaster the crown,
Which now they hold by *force*, and not by right. *Sh. H.* VI.

The shepherd Paris bore the Spartan bride
By *force* away, and then by *force* enjoy'd;
But I by free consent. *Dryden.*

3. Virtue; efficacy.

Manifest it is, that the very majesty and holiness of the place where God is worshipped, hath, in regard of us, great virtue, *force* and efficacy; for that it serveth as a sensible help to stir up devotion. *Hooker, b.* v. *s.* 16.

No definitions, no suppositions of any sect, are of *force* enough to destroy constant experience. *Locke.*

4. Validness; power of law.

A testament is of *force* after men are dead. *Heb.* ix. 17.

Not long in *force* this charter stood;
Wanting that seal, it must be seal'd in blood. *Denham.*

5. Armament; warlike preparation. Often *forces* in the plural.

O Thou! whose captain I account myself,
Look on my *forces* with a gracious eye. *Shakesp. Richard* III.

The secret of the power of Spain consisteth in a veteran army, compounded of miscellany *forces* of all nations. *Bacon.*

A greater *force* than that which here we find,
Ne'er press'd the ocean, nor employ'd the wind. *Waller.*

Those victorious *forces* of the rebels were not able to sustain your arms. *Dryden.*

6. Destiny; necessity; fatal compulsion.

To FORCE. *v. a.* [from the noun.]

1. To compel; to constrain.

Dangers are light, if they once seem light; and more dangers have deceived men than *forced* them. *Bacon.*

I have been *forced* to use the cant words of Whig and Tory. *Swift's Examiner.*

The actions and operations did *force* them upon dividing the single idea. *Pope's View of Epick Poem.*

2. To overpower by strength.

O that fortune
Had brought me to the field where thou art fam'd
To have wrought such wonders with an ass's jaw,
I should have *forc'd* thee soon with other arms. *Milton.*

With fates averse, the rout in arms resort,
To *force* their monarch and insult the court. *Dryden's Æn.*

3. To impel; to press.

Thou shalt not destroy the trees by *forcing* an ax against them. *Deutr.* 20. 19.

4. To draw or push by main strength.

Stooping, the spear descended on his chine,
Just where the bone distinguish'd either loin:
It stuck so fast, so deeply bury'd lay,
That scarce the victor *forc'd* the steel away. *Dryden's Æn.*

5. To enforce; to urge.

Three blust'ring nights, born by the southern blast,
I floated, and discover'd land at last:
High on a mounting wave my head I bore,
Forcing my strength, and gath'ring to the shore. *Dryd. Æn.*

6. To drive by violence or power.

This way of flattering their willing benefactors out of part, contrived another of *forcing* their unwilling neighbours out of all their possessions. *Decay of Piety.*

To free the ports, and ope the Punique land
To Trojan guests; lest, ignorant of fate,
The queen might *force* them from her town and state. *Dryd.*

7. To gain by violence or power.

My heart was your's; but, oh! you left it here
Abandon'd to those tyrants hope and fear:
If they *forc'd* from me one kind look or word,
Could you not that, nor that small part afford? *Dryden.*

8. To storm; to take or enter by violence.

Troy wall'd so high,
Atrides might as well have *forc'd* the sky. *Waller.*

Heav'n from all ages wisely did provide
This wealth, and for the bravest nation hide;
Who with four hundred foot, and forty horse,
Dare boldly go a new-found world to *force.* *Dryd. Ind. Emp.*

9. To ravish; to violate by force.

Force her.—I like it not. *Dryden.*

10. To constrain; to distort; not to obtain naturally or with ease.

Our general taste in England is for epigram, turns of wit, and *forced* conceits. *Addison's Spectator*, N°. 409.

11. To man; to strengthen by soldiers; to garrison.

Here

Here let them lye,
'Till famine and the ague eat them up:
Were they not *forc'd* with those that should be our's,
We might have met them dareful, beard to beard. *Shakesp.*

If you find that any great number of soldiers be newly sent into Oroonoque, and that the passages be already *forced*, then be well advised how you land. *Raleigh's Apology.*

11. *To* FORCE *out*. To extort.

The tricks used in convening synods might *force out* an expression from him, that did not carry all the respect due to those great names. *Atterbury.*

The heat of the dispute had *forced out* from him expressions that seemed to make his doctrine run higher than really it did. *Atterbury.*

To FORCE. *v. n.* To lay stress upon. This word I have only found in the following passage.

That morning that he was to join battle with Harold, his armorer put on his backpiece before, and his breastplate behind; the which being espied by some that stood by, was taken among them for an ill token, and therefore advised him not to fight that day; to whom the duke answered, I *force* not of such fooleries; but if I have any skill in soothsaying, as in sooth I have none, it doth prognosticate that I shall change copy from a duke to a king. *Camden's Remains.*

FO'RCEDLY. *adv.* [from *force.*] Violently; constrainedly; unnaturally.

This foundation of the earth upon the waters doth most aptly agree to that structure of the abyss and antediluvian earth; but very improperly and *forcedly* to the present form of the earth and the waters. *Burnet's Theory of the Earth.*

FO'RCEFUL. *adj.* [*force* and *full.*] Violent; strong; driven with great might; impetuous.

Why, what need we
Commune with you of this, but rather follow
Our *forceful* instigation? *Shakesp. Winter's Tale.*

Against the steed he threw
His *forceful* spear, which, hissing as it flew,
Pierc'd through the yielding planks. *Dryden's Æn.*

Were it by chance, or *forceful* destiny,
Which forms in causes first whate'er shall be,
Assisted by a friend, one moonless night,
This Palamon from prison took his flight. *Dryden.*

He pois'd in air, the jav'lin sent,
Through Paris' shield the *forceful* weapon went. *Pope.*

FO'RCEFULLY. *adv.* [from *forceful.*] Violently; impetuously.

FO'RCELESS. *adj.* [from *force.*] Without force; weak; feeble; impotent.

FO'RCEPS. *n. s.* [Latin.]

Forceps properly signifies a pair of tongs; but is used for an instrument in chirurgery, to extract any thing out of wounds, and the like occasions. *Quincy.*

FO'RCER. *n. s.* [from *force.*]

1. That which forces, drives, or constrains.
2. The embolus of a pump working by pulsion, in contradistinction to a sucker, which acts by attraction.

The usual means for the ascent of water is either by suckers or *forcers*. *Wilkins's Dædalus.*

FO'RCIBLE. *adj.* [from *force.*]

1. Strong; mighty: opposed to weak.

That punishment, which hath been sometimes *forcible* to bridle sin, may grow afterwards too weak and feeble. *Hooker.*

2. Violent; impetuous.
3. Efficacious; active; powerful.

Sweet smells are most *forcible* in dry substances, when broken; and so likewise in oranges, the ripping of their rind giveth out their smell more. *Bacon's Natural History.*

4. Prevalent; of great influence.

God hath assured us, that there is no inclination or temptation so *forcible* which our humble prayers and desires may not frustrate and break asunder. *Raleigh's Hist. of the World.*

Jersey, belov'd by all; for all must feel
The influence of a form and mind,
Where comely grace and constant virtue dwell,
Like mingl'd streams, more *forcible* when join'd:
Jersey shall at thy altars stand,
Shall there receive the azure band. *Prior.*

5. Done by force.

The abdication of king James, the advocates on that side look upon to have been *forcible* and unjust, and consequently void. *Swift.*

6. Valid; binding; obligatory.

FO'RCIBLENESS. *n. s.* [from *forcible.*] Force; violence.

FO'RCIBLY. *adv.* [from *forcible.*]

1. Strongly; powerfully.

The Gospel offers such considerations as are fit to work very *forcibly* upon two of the most swaying and governing passions in the mind, our hopes and our fears. *Tillotson.*

2. Impetuously.
3. By violence; by force.

He himself with greedy great desire
Into the castle enter'd *forcibly*. *Fairy Queen, b.* i. *cant.* 8.

The taking and carrying away of women *forcibly*, and against their will, except female wards and bondwomen, was made capital. *Bacon's Henry* VII.

This doctrine brings us down to the level of horse and mule, whose mouths are *forcibly* holden with bit and bridle. *Hamm.*

FO'RCIPATED. *adj.* [from *forceps.*] Formed like a pair of pincers to open and inclose.

The locusts have antennæ, or long horns before, with a long falcation or *forcipated* tail behind. *Brown's Vulgar Err.*

When they have seized their prey, they will so tenaciously hold it with their *forcipated* mouth, that they will not part therewith, even when taken out of the waters. *Derham.*

FORD. *n. s.* [ꝼoꞃꝺ, Saxon, from ꝼaꞃan, to pass.]

1. A shallow part of a river when it may be passed without swimming.

Her men the paths rode through made by her sword;
They pass the stream, when she had found the *ford*. *Fairfax.*

2. It sometimes signifies the stream, the current, without any consideration of passage or shallowness.

Medusa with Gorgonian terror guards
The *ford*, and of itself the water flies
All taste of living wight. *Milton's Paradise Lost, b.* ii.

Rise, wretched widow! rise; nor undeplor'd
Permit my ghost to pass the Stygian *ford*:
But rise, prepar'd in black to mourn thy perish'd lord. *Dry.*

To FORD. *v. a.* [from the noun.] To pass without swimming.

Adam's shin-bones must have contained a thousand fathom, and much more, if he had *forded* the ocean. *Raleigh's Hist.*

FO'RDABLE. *adj.* [from *ford.*] Passable without swimming.

Pliny placeth the Schenitæ upon the Euphrates, where the same beginneth to be *fordable*. *Raleigh's Hist. of the World.*

A countryman sounded a river up and down, to try where it was most *fordable*; and where the water ran too smooth, he found it deepest; and, on the contrary, shallowest where it made most noise. *L'Estrange.*

FORE. *adj.* [ꝼoꞃe, Saxon.] Anterior; that which comes first in a progressive motion.

Resistance in fluids arises from their greater pressing on the *fore* than hind part of the bodies moving in them. *Cheyne.*

FORE. *adv.*

1. Anteriorly; in the part which appears first to those that meet it.

Each of them will bear six demiculverins and four saikers, needing no other addition than a slight spar deck *fore* and aft, which is a slight deck throughout. *Raleigh's Essays.*

2. *Fore* is a word much used in composition to mark priority of time, of which some examples shall be given.

To FOREADVI'SE. *v. n.* [*fore* and *advise.*] To counsel early; to counsel before the time of action, or the event.

Thus to have said,
As you were *foreadvis'd*, had touch'd his spirit,
And tried his inclination. *Shakespeare's Coriolanus.*

To FOREAPPO'INT. [*fore* and *appoint.*] To order beforehand.

To FOREA'RM. *v. a.* [*fore* and *arm.*] To provide for attack or resistance before the time of need.

A man should fix and *forearm* his mind with this persuasion, that, during his passion, whatsoever is offered to his imagination tends only to deceive. *South's Sermons.*

He *forearms* his care
With rules to push his fortune, or to bear. *Dryden's Æn.*

To FOREBO'DE. *v. n.* [*fore* and *bode.*]

1. To prognosticate; to foretell.

An ancient augur, skill'd in future fate,
With these *foreboding* words restrains their hate. *Dryden.*

2. To foreknow; to be prescient of; to feel a secret sense of something future.

Fate makes you deaf, while I in vain implore:
My heart *forebodes* I ne'er shall see you more. *Dryd. In. Emp.*

My soul *foreboded* I should find the bow'r
Of some fell monster, fierce with barb'rous pow'r. *Pope.*

FOREBO'DER. *n. s.* [from *forebode.*]

1. A prognosticator; a soothsayer.

Your raven has a reputation in the world for a bird of omen, and a kind of small prophet: a crow that had observed the raven's manner and way of delivering his predictions, sets up for a *foreboder*. *L'Estrange's Fables.*

2. A foreknower.

FOREBY'. *prep.* [*fore* and *by.*] Near; hard by; fast by.

Not far away he hence doth won
Foreby a fountain, where I late him left. *Fairy Queen, b.* i.

To FORECA'ST. *v. a.* [*fore* and *cast.*]

1. To scheme; to plan before execution.

He shall *forecast* his devices against the strong holds. *Dan.* xi.

2. To adjust; to contrive.

The feast was serv'd; the time so well *forecast*,
That just when the dessert and fruits were plac'd,
The fiend's alarm began. *Dryden's Theod. and Honoria.*

3. To foresee; to provide against.

It is wisdom to consider the end of things before we embark, and to *forecast* consequences. *L'Estrange, Fable* 83.

To Foreca'st. *v. n.* To form schemes; to contrive beforehand.

And whatso heavens in their secret doom
Ordained have, how can frail fleshy wight
Forecast, but it must needs to issue come? *Spenser.*
When broad awake, she finds in troublous fit,
Forecasting how his foe he might annoy. *Fairy Queen, b.* i.

Fo'recast. *n. s.* [from the verb.] Contrivance beforehand; scheme; plan; antecedent policy.

Alas! that Warwick had no more *forecast*,
But while he thought to steal the single ten,
The king was slily finger'd from the deck! *Shak. Hen.* VI.

He makes this difference to arise from the *forecast* and predetermination of the gods. *Addison on ancient Medals.*

The last, scarce ripen'd into perfect man,
Saw helpless him from whom their life began:
Mem'ry and *forecast* just returns engage;
That pointed back to youth, this on to age. *Pope.*

Foreca'ster. *n. s.* [from *forecast.*] One who contrives beforehand.

Fo'recastle. *n. s.* [*fore* and *castle.*] In a ship, is that part where the foremast stands, and is divided from the rest of the floor by a bulk-head: that part of the *forecastle* which is aloft, and not in the hold, is called the prow. *Harris.*

The commodity of the new cook-room the merchants have found to be so great, as that, in all their ships, the cook-rooms are built in their *forecastles*, contrary to that which had been anciently used. *Raleigh's Essays.*

Forecho'sen. *partic.* [*fore* and *chosen.*] Pre-elected.

Foreci'ted. *part.* [*fore* and *cite.*] Quoted before, or above.

Greaves is of opinion, that the alteration mentioned in that *forecited* passage is continued. *Arbuthnot on Coins.*

To Foreclo'se. *v. a.* [*fore* and *close.*]

1. To shut up; to preclude; to prevent.

The embargo with Spain *foreclosed* this trade. *Carew.*

2. *To* Foreclose *a Mortgage*, is to cut off the power of redemption.

Fo'redeck. *n. s.* [*fore* and *deck.*] The anterior part of the ship.

I to the *foredeck* went, and thence did look
For rocky Scylla. *Chapman's Odyssey, b.* xii.

To Foredesi'gn. *v. a.* [*fore* and *design.*] To plan beforehand.

All the steps of the growth and vegetation both of animals and plants, have been foreseen and *foredesigned* by the wise Author of nature. *Cheyne's Phil. Princ.*

To Foredo'. *v. a.* [from *for* and *do*, not *fore.*]

1. To ruin; to destroy. A word obsolete. Opposed to making happy.

Beseeching him, if either salves or oils,
A *foredone* wight from door of death might raise,
He would at her request prolong her nephew's days. *Fa. Qu.*
That drew on men God's hatred and his wrath,
And many souls in dolours had *foredone*. *Fairy Queen, b.* i.
This doth betoken,
The corse they follow did with desperate hand
Foredo its own life. *Shakespeare's Hamlet.*
This is the night
That either makes me, or *foredoes* me quite. *Shakespeare.*

2. To overdo; to weary; to harrass.

Whilst the heavy plowman snoars,
All with weary task *foredone*. *Shakespeare.*

To Foredo'om. *v. a.* [*fore* and *doom.*] To predestinate; to determine beforehand.

Through various hazards and events we move
To Latium, and the realms *foredoom'd* by Jove. *Dryd. Æn.*
The willing metal will obey thy hand,
Following with ease: if favour'd by thy fate,
Thou art *foredoom'd* to view the Stygian state. *Dryden.*
Fate *foredoom'd*, and all things tend
By course of time to their appointed end. *Dryden.*
Here Britain's statesmen oft the fall *foredoom*
Of foreign tyrants, and of nymphs at home. *Pope.*

Foree'nd. *n. s.* [*fore* and *end.*] The anteriour part.

I have liv'd at honest freedom; paid
More pious debts to heaven than in all
The *fore-end* of my time. *Shakespeare's Cymbeline.*

In the *fore-end* of it, which was towards him, grew a small green branch of palm; and when the wise man had taken it into his boat, it opened of itself, and there were found in it a book and a letter. *Bacon's New Atlantis.*

Forefa'ther. *n. s.* [*fore* and *father.*] Ancestor; one who in any degree of ascending genealogy precedes another.

The custom of the people of God, and the decrees of our *forefathers*, are to be kept, touching those things whereof the Scripture hath neither one way or other given us charge. *Hook.*

If it be a generous desire in men to know from whence their own *forefathers* have come, it cannot be displeasing to understand the place of our first ancestor. *Raleigh's History.*

Conceit is still deriv'd
From some *forefather* grief; mine is not so. *Shak. Rich.* II.
Shall I not be distraught,
And madly play with my *forefathers* joints? *Sh. Ro. and Jul.*
Our great *forefathers*
Had left him nought to conquer but his country. *Addison.*

When a man sees the prodigious pains our *forefathers* have been at in these barbarous buildings, one cannot but fancy what miracles of architecture they would have left us, had they been instructed in the right way. *Addison on Italy.*

Blest peer! his great *forefathers* ev'ry grace
Reflecting, and reflected in his race. *Pope, Epist.* i.

To Forefe'nd. *v. a.* [*fore* and *defend.*]

1. To prohibit; to avert.

I would not kill thy unprepared spirit;
No, heav'ns *forefend!* I would not kill thy soul. *Shakesp.*
Perhaps a fever, which the gods *forefend*,
May bring your youth to some untimely end. *Dryden.*

2. To provide for; to secure.

Down with the nose,
Down with it flat: take the bridge quite away
Of him, that, his particular to *forefend*,
Smells from the gen'ral weal. *Shakes. Timon of Athens.*

Forefi'nger. *n. s.* [*fore* and *finger.*] The finger next to the thumb; the index.

An agate-stone
On the *forefinger* of an alderman. *Shak. Romeo and Juliet.*

Polymnia shall be drawn, as it were, acting her speech with her *forefinger*. *Peacham on Drawing.*

Some wear this on the middlefinger, as the ancient Gauls and Britons; and some upon the *forefinger*. *Brown's Vul. Err.*

Fo'refoot. *n. s.* plur. *forefeet.* [*fore* and *foot.*] The anterior foot of a quadruped: in contempt, a hand.

Give me thy fist, thy *forefoot* to me give. *Shak. Hen.* V.

He ran fiercely, and smote at Heliodorus with his *forefeet*. 2 *Mac.* iii. 25.

I continue my line from thence to the heel; then making the breast with the eminency thereof, bring out his near *forefoot*, which I finish. *Peacham on Drawing.*

To Forego'. *v. a.* [*for* and *go.*]

1. To quit; to give up; to resign.

Is it her nature, or is it her will,
To be so cruel to an humbled foe?
If nature, then she may it mend with skill;
If will, then she at will may will *forego*. *Spenser, Son.* 41.

Having all before absolutely in his power, it remaineth so still, he having already neither foregiven nor *foregone* any thing thereby unto them, but having received something from them. *Spenser's State of Ireland.*

He is a great adventurer, said he,
That hath his sword through hard assay *forgone*;
And now hath vowed, 'till he avenged be
Of that despite, never to wearen none. *Fairy Queen, b.* ii.

Special reason oftentimes causeth the will to prefer one good thing before another; to leave one for another's sake, to *forego* meaner for the attainment of higher degrees. *Hooker, b.* v.

Must I then leave you? Must I needs *forgo*
So good, so noble, and so true a master? *Shakes. H.* VIII.
Let us not *forgo*
That for a trifle which was bought with blood. *Shakespeare.*
How can I live without thee! how *forego*
Thy sweet converse, and love so dearly join'd,
To live again in these wild woods forlorn! *Milt. Pa. Lost.*

This argument might prevail with you to *forego* a little of your repose for the publick benefit. *Dryd. Juv. Dedic.*

What they have enjoyed with great pleasure at one time, has proved insipid or nauseous at another; and therefore they see nothing in it, for which they should *forego* a present enjoyment. *Locke.*

2. To go before; to be past. [from *fore* and *go.*]

By our remembrances of days *foregone*,
Such were our faults: O! then we thought them not. *Shak.*

It is to be understood of Cain, that many years *foregone*, and when his people were increased, he built the city of Enoch. *Raleigh's History of the World.*

Lest what has been said of the differences between true and apparent colours be interpreted in too unlimited a sense, reflect upon the two *foregoing* objections. *Boyle on Colours.*

This *foregoing* remark gives the reason why imitation pleases. *Dryden's Dufresnoy.*

I was seated in my elbow-chair, where I had indulged the *foregoing* speculations, with my lamp burning by me as usual. *Addison's Spectator*, N°. 463.

In the *foregoing* part of this work I promised further proofs. *Woodward's Natural History.*

3. To lose.

This is the very ecstasy of love,
Whose violent property *forgoes* itself,
And leads the will to desp'rate undertakings. *Shak. Hamlet.*

Fo'regoer. *n. s.* [from *forego.*] Ancestor; progenitor.

Honours best thrive,
When rather from our acts we them derive
Than our *foregoers*. *Shakespeare's All's well that ends well.*

Fo'reground.

FO'REGROUND. *n.s.* [*fore* and *ground.*] The part of the field or expanse of a picture which seems to lie before the figures.

All agree that white can subsist on the *foreground* of the picture: the question therefore is to know, if it can equally be placed upon that which is backward, the light being universal, and the figures supposed in an open field. *Dryden.*

FO'REHAND. *n.s.* [*fore* and *hand.*]

1. The part of a horse which is before the rider.

2. The chief part.

The great Achilles, whom opinion crowns
The sinew and the *forehand* of our host. *Shakespeare.*

FO'REHAND. *adj.* A thing done too soon.

You'll say she did embrace me as a husband,
And so extenuate the *forehand* sin. *Shakespeare.*

FOREHA'NDED. *n.s.* [from *fore* and *hand.*]

1. Early; timely.

If by thus doing you have not secured your time by an early and *forehanded* care, yet be sure, by a timely diligence, to redeem the time. *Taylor's Rule of living holy.*

2. Formed in the foreparts.

Bauble, do you call him? He's a substantial true-bred beast, bravely *forehanded:* mark but the cleanness of his shapes too. *Dryden's Don Sebastian.*

FO'REHEAD. *n.s.* [*fore* and *head.*]

1. That part of the face which reaches from the eyes upward to the hair.

The breast of Hecuba,
When she did suckle Hector, look'd not lovelier
Than Hector's *forehead*, when it spit forth blood
At Grecian swords contending. *Shakespeare's Coriolanus.*
Some angel copy'd, while I slept, each grace,
And molded ev'ry feature from my face:
Such majesty does from her *forehead* rise,
Her cheeks such blushes cast, such rays her eyes. *Dryden.*

2. Impudence; confidence; assurance; audaciousness; audacity.

A man of confidence presseth forward upon every appearance of advantage, and thinks nothing above his management or his merit: where his force is too feeble, he prevails by dint of impudence: these men of *forehead* are magnificent in promises, and infallible in their prescriptions. *Collier.*

I would fain know to what branch of the legislature they can have the *forehead* to apply. *Swift's Presbyterian Plea.*

FOREHO'LDING. *n.s.* [*fore* and *hold.*] Predictions; ominous accounts; superstitious prognostications.

How are superstitious men hagged out of their wits with the fancy of omens, *foreholdings*, and old wives tales! *L'Estr.*

FO'REIGN. *adj.* [*forain*, French; *forano*, Spanish, from *foris*, Latin.]

1. Not of this country; not domestick.

Your son, that with a fearful soul
Leads discontented steps in *foreign* soil,
This fair alliance quickly shall call home. *Shakesp. Rich.* III.
The learned correspondence you hold in *foreign* parts. *Milt.*

The positions are so far from being new, that they are commonly to be met with in both ancient and modern, domestick and *foreign* writers. *Atterbury's Serm. Pref.*

The parties and divisions amongst us may several ways bring destruction upon our country, at the same time that our united force would secure us against all the attempts of a *foreign* enemy. *Addison's Freeholder*, N°. 34.

2. Alien; remote; not allied; not belonging; without relation. It is often used with *to*; but more properly with *from.*

I must dissemble,
And speak a language *foreign to* my heart. *Addison's Cato.*

Fame is a good so wholly *foreign to* our natures, that we have no faculty in the soul adapted to it, nor any organ in the body to relish it, placed out of the possibility of fruition. *Addis.*

This design is not *foreign from* some people's thoughts. *Swift on the Sacramental Test.*

3. Excluded; not admitted; held at a distance.

They will not stick to say you envied him;
And fearing he would rise, he was so virtuous,
Kept him a *foreign* man still; which so griev'd him,
That he ran mad and died. *Shakespeare's Henry* VIII.

4. [In law.] A foreign plea, *plantum forinsecum*; as being a plea out of the proper court of justice.

5. Extraneous; adventitious in general.

There are who, fondly studious of increase,
Rich *foreign* mold in their ill-natur'd land
Induce. *Phillips.*

FO'REIGNER. *n.s.* [from *foreign.*] A man that comes from another country; not a native; a stranger.

Joy is such a *foreigner*,
So mere a stranger to my thoughts, I know
Not how to entertain him. *Denham's Sophy.*
To this false *foreigner* you give your throne,
And wrong a friend, a kinsman, and a son:
Resume your ancient care. *Dryd. Æn.*

Water is the only native of England made use of in punch; but the lemons, the brandy, the sugar, and the nutmegs, are all *foreigners.* *Addison's Freeholder.*

Nor could the majesty of the English crown appear in a greater lustre, either to *foreigners* or subjects. *Swift.*

FO'REIGNNESS. *n.s.* [from *foreign.*] Remoteness; want of relation to something.

Let not the *foreignness* of the subject hinder you from endeavouring to set me right. *Locke.*

To FOREIMA'GINE. *v.a.* [*fore* and *imagine.*] To conceive or fancy before proof.

We are within compass of a *foreimagined* possibility in that behalf. *Camden's Remains.*

To FOREJU'DGE. *v.a.* [*fore* and *judge.*] To judge beforehand; to be prepossessed.

To FOREKNO'W. *v.a.* [*fore* and *know.*] To have prescience of; to foresee.

We *foreknow* that the sun will rise and set, that all men born in the world shall die again; that after Winter the Spring shall come; after the Spring, Summer and harvest; yet is not our foreknowledge the cause of any of those. *Raleigh.*

He *foreknew* John should not suffer a violent death, but go into his grave in peace. *Brown's Vulgar Errours, b.* vii. *c.* 10.

Calchas the sacred seer, who had in view
Things present and the past, and things to come *foreknew.* *Dryden's Iliad.*
Who would the miseries of man *foreknow?*
Not knowing, we but share our part of woe. *Dryden.*

FOREKNO'WABLE. *adj.* [from *foreknow.*] Possible to be known before they happen.

It is certainly *foreknowable* what they will do in such and such circumstances. *More's Divine Dialogues.*

FOREKNO'WLEDGE. *n.s.* [*fore* and *knowledge.*] Prescience; knowledge of that which has not yet happened.

Our being in Christ by eternal *foreknowledge*, saveth us not without our actual and real adoption into the fellowship of his saints in this present world. *Hooker, b.* v. *s.* 56.

I told him you was asleep: he seems to have a *foreknowledge* of that too, and therefore chuses to speak with you. *Shakesp.*

If I foreknew,
Foreknowledge had no influence on their fault,
Which had no less prov'd certain unforeknown. *Milton.*

I hope the *foreknowledge* you had of my esteem for you, is the reason that you do not dislike my letters. *Pope.*

FO'RELAND. *n.s.* [*fore* and *land.*] A promontory; headland; high land jutting into the sea; a cape.

As when a ship, by skilful steersman wrought,
Nigh river's mouth, or *foreland*, where the wind
Veers oft, as oft so steers, and shifts her sails. *Milt. P. L.*

To FORELA'Y. *v.a.* [*fore* and *lay.*] To lay wait for; to intrap by ambush.

A serpent shoots his sting at unaware;
An ambush'd thief *forelays* a traveller:
The man lies murder'd, while the thief and snake,
One gains the thickets, and one thrids the brake. *Dryden.*

To FORELI'FT. *v.a.* [*fore* and *lift*] To raise aloft any anterior part.

So dreadfully he towards him did pass,
Forelifting up aloft his speckled breast;
And often bounding on the bruised grass,
As for great joy of his new comen guest. *Fairy Queen, b.* i.

FO'RELOCK. *n.s.* [*fore* and *lock.*] The hair that grows from the forepart of the head.

Tell her the joyous time will not be staid,
Unless she do him by the *forelock* take. *Spenser, Sonnet* 70.
Hyacinthine locks
Round from his parted *forelock* manly hung,
Clust'ring, but not beneath his shoulders broad. *Milton.*
Zeal and duty are not slow,
But on occasion's *forelock* watchful wait. *Milt. Parad. Reg.*

Time is painted with a lock before, and bald behind, signifying thereby that we must take time by the *forelock*; for, when it is once past, there is no recalling it. *Swift.*

FO'REMAN. *n.s.* [*fore* and *man.*] The first or chief person.

He is a very sensible man, shoots flying, and has been several times *foreman* of the petty jury. *Addison's Spectator.*

FOREME'NTIONED. *adj.* [*fore* and *mentioned.*] Mentioned or recited before. It is observeable that many participles are compounded with *fore*, whose verbs have no such composition.

Dacier, in the life of Aurelius, has not taken notice of the *forementioned* figure on the pillar. *Addison on Italy.*

FO'REMOST. *adj.* [from *fore.*]

1. First in place.

Our women in the *foremost* ranks appear;
March to the fight, and meet your mistress there. *Dryden.*
I stand astonish'd! what, the bold Sempronius,
That still broke *foremost* through the crowd of patriots,
As with a hurricane of zeal transported,
And virtuous ev'n to madness! *Addison's Cato.*

2. First in dignity.

All three were set among the *foremost* ranks of fame, for great minds to attempt, and great force to perform what they did attempt. *Sidney, b.* ii.

These ride *foremost* in the field,
As they the *foremost* rank of honour held. *Dryden.*

FO'RENAMED.

FORENA'MED. *adj.* [*fore* and *name.*] Nominated before.

And such are sure ones,
As Curius, and the *forenam'd* Lentulus. *Ben. Johns. Catil.*

FO'RENOON. *n. s.* [*fore* and *noon.*] The time of day reckoned from the middle point, between the dawn and the meridian, to the meridian: opposed to afternoon.

The manner was, that the *forenoon* they should run at tilt, the afternoon in a broad field in manner of a battle, 'till either the strangers or the country knights won the field. *Sidney.*

Curio, at the funeral of his father, built a temporary theatre, consisting of two parts turning on hinges, according to the position of the sun, for the conveniency of *forenoon's* and afternoon's diversion. *Arbuthnot on Coins.*

FORENO'TICE. *n. s.* [*fore* and *notice.*] Information of an event before it happens.

So strange a revolution never happens in poetry, but either heaven or earth gives some *forenotice* of it. *Rymer's Tragedies.*

FORE'NSICK. *adj.* [*forensis*, Latin.] Belonging to courts of judicature.

Person is a *forensick* term, appropriating actions and their merit; and so belongs only to intelligent agents, capable of a law, and happiness and misery. This personality extends itself beyond present existence to what is past, only by consciousness. *Locke.*

The forum was a publick place in Rome, where lawyers and orators made their speeches before the proper judges in matters of property, or in criminal cases: thence all sorts of disputations in courts of justice, where several persons make their distinct speeches, may come under the name of *forensick* disputes. *Watts's Improvement of the Mind.*

To FOREORDA'IN. *v. a.* [*fore* and *ordain.*] To predestinate; to predetermine; to preordain.

The church can discharge, in manner convenient, a work of so great importance; by *foreordaining* some short collect wherein briefly to mention thanks. *Hooker, b. v.*

FO'REPART. *n. s.* [*fore* and *part.*] The anteriour part.

Had it been so raised, it would deprive us of the sun's light all the *forepart* of the day. *Raleigh's Hist. of the World.*

The ribs have no cavity in them, and towards the *forepart* or breast are broad and thin, to bend and give way without danger of fracture. *Ray on the Creation.*

FOREPA'ST. *adj.* [*fore* and *past.*] Past before a certain time.

Now cease, ye damsels, your delights *forepast*;
Enough it is that all the day is your's. *Spenser's Epithalam.*

My *forepast* proofs, howe'er the matter fall,
Shall tax my fears of little vanity,
Having vainly fear'd too little. *Shakespeare.*

Such is the treaty which he negotiates with us, an offer and tender of a reconciliation, an act of oblivion, of all *forepast* sins, and of a new covenant. *Hammond on Fundamentals.*

FOREPOSSE'SSED. *adj.* [*fore* and *possess.*] Preoccupied; prepossessed; pre-engaged.

The testimony either of the ancient fathers, or of other classical divines, may be clearly and abundantly answered, to the satisfaction of any rational man, not extremely *forepossessed* with prejudice. *Sanderson's Judgment.*

FO'RERANK. *n. s.* [*fore* and *rank.*] First rank; front.

Yet leave our cousin Catharine here with us;
She is our capital demand, compris'd
Within the *forerank* of our articles. *Shakes. Henry V.*

FORERECI'TED. *adj.* [*fore* and *recite.*] Mentioned or enumerated before.

Bid him recount
The *forerecited* practices, whereof
We cannot feel too little, hear too much. *Shak. Hen. VIII.*

To FORERU'N. *v. a.* [*fore* and *run.*]

1. To come before as an earnest of something following; to introduce as an harbinger.

Against ill chances men are ever merry;
But heaviness *foreruns* the good event. *Shakes. Henry IV.*

The sun
Was set, and twilight from the East came on,
Forerunning night. *Milton's Paradise Lost, b. vii.*

She bids me hope: oh heav'ns, she pities me!
And pity still *foreruns* approaching love,
As lightning does the thunder. *Dryden's Spanish Fryar.*

2. To precede; to have the start of.

I heard it to be a maxim at Dublin to follow, if not *forerun*, all that is or will be practised in London. *Graunt.*

FORERU'NNER. *n. s.* [from *forerun.*]

1. An harbinger; a messenger sent before to give notice of the approach of those that follow.

The six strangers seek for you, madam, to take their leave; and there is a *forerunner* come from a seventh, the prince of Morocco. *Shakespeare's Merchant of Venice.*

A cock was sacrificed as the *forerunner* of day and the sun, thereby acknowledging the light of life to be derived from the divine bounty, the daughter of providence. *Stillingfleet.*

My elder brothers, my *forerunners* came,
Rough draughts of nature, ill design'd, and lame:
Blown off, like blossoms, never made to bear;
'Till I came finish'd, her last labour'd care. *Dryd. Aurengz.*

Already opera prepares the way,
The sure *forerunner* of her gentle sway. *Pope's Dunciad.*

2. A prognostick; a sign foreshowing any thing.

O Eve! some further change awaits us nigh,
Which heav'n, by these mute signs in nature, shews
Forerunners of his purpose. *Milton's Paradise Lost, b. xi.*

Loss of sight is the misery of life, and usually the *forerunner* of death. *South's Sermons.*

The keeping insensible perspiration up in due measure is the cause as well as sign of health, and the least deviation from that due quantity, the certain *forerunner* of a disease. *Arbuthn.*

To FORESA'Y. *v. a.* [*fore* and *say.*] To predict; to prophesy; to foretell.

Let ordinance
Come as the gods *foresay* it. *Shakespeare's Cymbeline.*

To FORESE'E. *v. a.* [*fore* and *see.*] To see beforehand; to see what has not yet happened; to have prescience; to foreknow.

With Cupid she *foresees* and goes god Vulcan's pace. *Sidney.*

The first of them could things to come *foresee*;
The next, could of things present best advise;
The third, things past could keep in memory. *Fairy Queen.*

If there be any thing *foreseen* that is not usual, be armed for it by any hearty though a short prayer, and an earnest resolution beforehand, and then watch when it comes. *Taylor.*

At his *foreseen* approach, already quake
The Caspian kingdoms and Meotian lake:
Their seers behold the tempest from afar,
And threat'ning oracles denounce the war. *Dryden's Æn.*

To FORESHA'ME. *v. a.* [*for* and *shame.*] To shame; to bring reproach upon.

Oh bill, *foreshaming*
Those rich-left heirs, that let their fathers lie
Without a monument. *Shakespeare's Cymbeline.*

To FO'RESHEW. *v. a.* [See FORESHOW.]

FO'RESHIP. *n. s.* [*fore* and *ship.*] The anteriour part of the ship.

The shipmen would have cast anchors out of the *foreship*. *Acts* xxvii. 30.

To FORESHO'RTEN. *v. a.* [*fore* and *shorten.*] To shorten figures for the sake of shewing those behind.

The greatest parts of the body ought to appear foremost; and he forbids the *foreshortenings*, because they make the parts appear little. *Dryden's Dufresnoy.*

To FORESHO'W. *v. a.* [*fore* and *show.*]

1. To discover before it happens; to predict; to prognosticate.

Christ had called him to be a witness of his death, and resurrection from the dead, according to that which the prophets and Moses had *foreshowed*. *Hooker, b. iii. s. 8.*

Next, like Aurora, Spenser rose,
Whose purple blush the day *foreshows*. *Denham.*

You chose to withdraw yourself from publick business, when the face of heaven grew troubled, and the frequent shifting of the wind *foreshowed* a storm. *Dryden.*

2. To represent before it comes.

What else is the law but the gospel *foreshowed*? What other the gospel than the law fulfilled? *Hooker, b. v.*

FO'RESIGHT. *n. s.* [*fore* and *sight.*]

1. Prescience; prognostication; foreknowledge. The accent anciently on the last syllable.

Let Eve, for I have drench'd her eyes,
Here sleep below; while thou to *foresight* wak'st;
As once thou slept'st, whilst she to life was form'd. *Milton.*

2. Provident care of futurity.

He had a sharp *foresight*, and working wit,
That never idle was, ne once could rest a whit. *Fai. Qu.*

In matters of arms he was both skilful and industrious, and as well in *foresight* as resolution present and great. *Hayward.*

Difficulties and temptations will more easily be born or avoided, if with prudent *foresight* we arm ourselves against them. *Rogers's Sermons.*

FORESI'GHTFUL. *adj.* [*forsight* and *full.*] Prescient; provident.

Death gave him no such pangs as the *foresightful* care he had of his silly successor. *Sidney, b. ii.*

To FORESI'GNIFY. *v. a.* [*fore* and *signify.*] To betoken beforehand; to foreshow; to typify.

Discoveries of Christ already present, whose future coming the Psalms did but *foresignify*. *Hooker, b. v.*

Yet as being past times noxious, where they light
On man, beast, plant, wasteful and turbulent,
They oft *foresignify*, and threaten ill. *Milton's Par. Reg.*

FO'RESKIN. *n. s.* [*fore* and *skin.*] The prepuce.

Their own hand
An hundred of the faithless foe shall slay,
And for a dow'r their hundred *foreskins* pay,
Be Michel thy reward. *Cowley's Davideis.*

FO'RESKIRT. *n. s.* [*fore* and *skirt.*] The pendulous or loose part of the coat before.

A thousand

A thousand pounds a year for pure respect!
No other obligation?
That promises more thousands: honour's train
Is longer than his *foreskirt*. *Shakespeare's Henry* VIII.

To FORESLA'CK. *v. a.* [*fore* and *slack*.] To neglect by idleness.

It is a great pity that so good an opportunity was omitted, and so happy an occasion *foreslacked*, that might have been the eternal good of the land. *Spenser's State of Ireland.*

To FORESLO'W. *v. a* [*fore* and *slow*.]

1. To delay; to hinder; to impede; to obstruct.

No stream, no wood, no mountain could *foreslow*
Their hasty pace. *Fairfax, b.* i.

Now the illustrious nymph return'd again,
Brings every grace triumphant in her train:
The wond'ring Nereids, though they rais'd no storm,
Foreslow'd her passage, to behold her form. *Dryden.*

2. To neglect; to omit.

When the rebels were on Blackheath, the king knowing well that it stood him upon, by how much the more he had hitherto protracted the time in not encountering them, by so much the sooner to dispatch with them, that it might appear to have been no coldness in *foreslowing*, but wisdom in chusing his time, resolved with speed to assail them. *Bacon's Hen.* VII.

Chremes, how many fishers do you know
That rule their boats and use their nets aright,
That neither wind, nor time, nor tide *foreslow?*
Some such have been: but, ah! by tempests spite
Their boats are lost; while we may sit and moan
That few were such, and now these few are none. *P. Fletch.*

To FORESLO'W. *v. n.* To be dilatory; to loiter.

This may plant courage in their quailing breasts,
For yet is hope of life and victory:
Foreslow no longer, make we hence amain. *Shak. Hen.* VI.

To FORESPE'AK. *v. n.* [*fore* and *speak*.]

1. To predict; to foresay; to foreshow; to foretell.

Old Godfrey of Winchester, thinketh no ominous *forespeaking* to lie in names. *Camden's Remains.*

2. To forbid.

Thou hast *forespoke* my being in these wars,
And say'st it is not fit. *Shakesp. Ant. and Cleopatra.*

FORESPE'NT. *adj.* [*fore* and *spent*.]

1. Wasted; tired; spent.

After him came spurring hard
A gentleman, almost *forespent* with speed. *Shak. Henry* IV.

2. Forepassed; past.

Is not enough thy evil life *forespent?* *Fairy Queen, b.* i.

You shall find his vanities *forespent*,
Were but the outside of the Roman Brutus,
Covering discretion with a coat of folly. *Shakesp. Hen.* V.

3. Bestowed before.

We must receive him
According to the honour of his sender;
And towards himself, his goodness *forespent* on us,
We must extend our notice. *Shakespeare.*

FORESPU'RRER. *n. s.* [*fore* and *spur*.] One that rides before.

A day in April never came so sweet,
To show how costly Summer was at hand,
As this *forespurrer* comes before his lord. *Shakespeare.*

FO'REST. *n. s.* [[*forest*, French; *foresta*, Italian.]

1. A wild uncultivated tract of ground, with wood.

By many tribulations we enter into the kingdom of heaven, because, in a *forest* of many wolves, sheep cannot chuse but feed in continual danger of life. *Hooker, b.* v. *s.* 48.

Macbeth shall never vanquish'd be, until
Great Birnam-wood to Dunsinane's high hill
Shall come against him.
——That will never be:
Who can impress the *forest*, bid the tree
Unfix his earth-bound root? *Shakespeare's Macbeth.*

There be airs which the physicians advise their patients to remove unto, which commonly are plain champaigns, but grasing, and not overgrown with heath; or else timber-shades, as in *forests*. *Bacon's Natural History,* N°. 936.

How the first *forest* rais'd its shady head. *Roscommon.*

2. [In law.] A certain territory of woody grounds and fruitful pastures, privileged for wild beasts, and fowls of forest, chase, and warren, to rest and abide in, in the safe protection of the king, for his pleasure; which territory of ground is bounded with irremoveable marks, and replenished with beasts of venery or chase, and with great coverts of vert for their succour and abode: for the preservation of which place, vert, and venison, there are certain particular laws. The manner of making forests is this: the king sends out his commission, under the broad seal of England, directed to certain discreet persons, for viewing, perambulating, and bounding the place that he has a mind to afforest: which returned into Chancery, proclamation is made throughout all the country where the ground lies, that none shall hunt or chase any wild beasts within that precinct, without the king's special licence; after which he appoints ordinances, laws, and officers for the preservation of the vert and venison; and this becomes a forest by matter of record. The properties of a forest are these: a forest, as it is strictly taken, cannot be in the hands of any but the king, who hath power to grant commission to a justice in eyre for the forest; the courts; the officers for preserving the vert and venison, as the justices of the forest, the warden or keeper, the verders, the foresters, agistors, regarders, bailiffs, and beadles. The chief property of a forest is the swainmote, which is no less incident to it than the court of pyepowders to a fair. *Cowel.*

To FORESTA'LL. *v. a.* [ꝼoꝛeꞅtallan, Saxon.]

1. To anticipate; to take up beforehand.

If thou be master-gunner, spend not all
That thou can'st speak at once; but husband it,
And give men turns of speech: do not *forestall*
By lavishness thine own and others wit,
As if thou mad'st thy will. *Herbert.*

What need a man *forestall* his date of grief,
And run to meet what he would most avoid. *Milton.*

2. To hinder by preoccupation or prevention.

And though good luck prolonged hath thy date,
Yet death then would the like mishap *forestall*. *Fairy Queen.*

What's in prayer, but this twofold force
To be *forestalled* e're we come to fall,
Or pardon'd being down. *Shakespeare's Hamlet.*

May
This night *forestall* him of the coming day. *Shak. Cymbeline.*

But for my tears,
I had *forestall'd* this dear and deep rebuke,
Ere you with grief had spoke. *Shakespeare's Henry* IV.

If thou covet death, as utmost end
Of misery, so thinking to evade
The penalty pronounc'd, doubt not but God
Hath wiselier arm'd his vengeful ire, than so
To be *forestall'd*. *Milton's Paradise Lost, b.* x.

I will not *forestall* your judgment of the rest. *Pope.*

3. To seize or gain possession of before another; to buy before another in order to raise the price.

He bold spake, Sir knight, if knight thou be,
Abandon this *forestalled* place at erst,
For fear of further harm, I counsel thee. *Fairy Queen.*

FORESTA'LLER. *n. s.* [from *forestall*.] One that anticipates the market; one that purchases before others to raise the price.

Commodities, good or bad, the workman must take at his master's rate, or sit still and starve; whilst, by this means, this new sort of ingrossors or *forestallers* having the feeding and supplying this numerous body of workmen, set the price upon the poor landholder. *Locke.*

FORESTBO'RN. *adj.* [*forest* and *born*.] Born in a wild.

This boy is *forestborn*,
And hath been tutor'd in the rudiments
Of desperate studies. *Shak. As you like it.*

FO'RESTER. *n. s.* [*forestier*, French, from *forest*.]

1. An officer of the forest.

Forester, my friend, where is the bush,
That we may stand and play the murtherer in?
—Here by, upon the edge of yonder copice. *Shakespeare.*

2. An inhabitant of the wild country.

FO'RESWAT. } *adj.* [from *fore* and *swat*, from *sweat*.] Spent
FO'RESWART. } with heat.

Miso and Mopsa, like a couple of *foreswat* melters, were getting the pure silver of their bodies out of the ore of their garments. *Sidney, b.* ii.

To FORETA'STE. *v. a.* [*fore* and *taste*.]

1. To have antepast of; to have prescience of.

2. To taste before another.

Perhaps the fact
Is not so heinous now, *foretasted* fruit,
Profan'd first by the serpent, by him first
Made common, and unhallow'd, ere our taste. *Milt. P. L.*

FO'RETASTE. *n. s.* Anticipation of.

A pleasure that a man may call as properly his own as his soul and his conscience, neither liable to accident, nor exposed to injury: it is the *foretaste* of heaven, and the earnest of eternity. *South's Sermons.*

To FORETE'LL. *v. a.* [*fore* and *tell*.]

1. To predict; to prophesy.

What art thou, whose heavy looks *foretell*
Some dreadful story hanging on thy tongue? *Shak. H.* VI.

I found
The new-created world, which fame in heaven
Long had *foretold*. *Milton's Paradise Lost, b.* x.

Mercia's king,
Warn'd in a dream, his murder did *fortell*,
From point to point, as after it befell. *Dryden.*

When great Ulysses fought the Phrygian shores,
Deeds then undone my faithful tongue *foretold*;
Heaven seal'd my words, and you those deeds behold. *Pope.*

2. To

2. To foretoken; to foreshow.

To Forete'll. *v. n.* To utter prophecy.

All the prophets from Samuel, and those that follow after, have likewise *foretold* of these days. *Acts* iii. 24.

Forete'ller. *n. s.* [from *foretell.*] Predicter; foreshower.

Others are proposed, not that the foretold events should be known; but that the accomplishment that expounds them may evince, that the *foreteller* of them was able to foresee thee. *Boyle on Colours.*

To Forethi'nk. *v. a.* [*fore* and *think.*] To anticipate in the mind; to have prescience of.

The soul of every man
Prophetically does *forethink* thy fall. *Shakes. Henry* IV.
I do pray to thee,
Thou virtuous Dauphin, alter not the doom
Forethought by heav'n. *Shakespeare's King John.*

Adam could not be ignorant of the punishments due to neglect and disobedience; and felt, by the proof thereof, in himself another terror than he had *forethought*, or could imagine. *Raleigh's History of the World.*

Friday, the fatal day! when next it came,
Her soul *forethought* the fiend would change his game. *Dryd.*

To Forethi'nk. *v. n.* To contrive beforehand.

With this you blot my name, and clear your own;
And what's my frenzy will be call'd my crime:
What then is thine? Thou cool deliberate villain!
Thou wise, *forethinking*, weighing politician! *Smith.*

Foretho'ught. *n. s.* [from *forethink.*]

1. Prescience; anticipation.

He that is undone, is equally undone, whether it be by spitefulness of *forethought*, or by the folly of oversight, or evil counsel. *L'Estrange.*

2. Provident care.

To Foreto'ken. *v. a.* [*fore* and *token.*] To foreshow; to prognosticate as a sign.

The king from Ireland hastes; but did no good;
Whilst strange prodigious signs *foretoken* blood. *Daniel.*

Foreto'ken. *n. s.* [from the verb.] Prevenient sign; prognostick.

It may prove some ominous *foretoken* of misfortune. *Sidney.*

They misliked nothing more in king Edward the Confessor, than that he was Frenchified; and accounted the desire of foreign language then to be a *foretoken* of bringing in of foreign powers, which indeed happened. *Camden's Remains.*

Foreto'oth. *n. s.* [*fore* and *tooth.*] The tooth in the anterior part of the mouth; the incisor.

The *foreteeth* should be formed broad, and with a thin sharp edge like chizzles. *Ray on the Creation.*

Fo'retop. *n. s.* [*fore* and *top.*] That part of a woman's headdress that is forward, or the top of a periwig.

So may your hats your *foretops* never press,
Untouch'd your ribbons, sacred be your dress. *Dryden.*

Forevou'ched. *part.* [*fore* and *vouch.*] Affirmed before; formerly told.

Sure her offence
Must be of such unnatural degree,
That monsters it; or your *forevouch'd* affection
Fall'n into taint. *Shakespeare's King Lear.*

Fo'reward. *n. s.* [*fore* and *ward.*] The van; the front.

They that marched in the *foreward* were all mighty men. *1 Mac.* ix. 11.

To Forewa'rn. *v. a.* [*fore* and *warn.*]

1. To admonish beforehand.

I will *forewarn* you whom you shall fear: fear him which, after he hath killed, hath power to cast into hell. *Lu.* xii. 5.

2. To inform previously of any future event.

Divine interpreter, by favour sent
Down from the empyrean, to *forewarn*
Us timely of what might else have been our loss
Unknown. *Milton's Paradise Lost, b.* vii.

3. To caution against any thing beforehand.

Well I will arm me, being thus *forewarn'd. Shak. H.*VI.
Thy pride,
And wand'ring vanity, when least was safe,
Rejected my *forewarning*, and disdain'd
Not to be trusted. *Milton's Paradise Lost, b.* x.

Tho' Phœbus had *forewarned* him of singing wars, yet the search of nature was free. *Dryd. Virg. Dedic. to Ld. Clifford.*

Young Chorœbus, who by love was led
To win renown and fair Cassandra's bed,
Had lately brought his troops to Priam's aid;
Forewarn'd in vain by the prophetick maid. *Dryden's Æn.*

To Forewa'ste. *v. a.* [*fore* and *waste.*] To desolate; to destroy. Out of use.

Vespasian, with great spoil and rage,
Forewasted all, until Gemissa gent
Persuaded him to cease. *Fairy Queen, b.* ii.
High time 'gan it wex for Una fair,
To think of those her captive parents dear,
And their *forewasted* kingdom to repair. *Fairy Queen, b.* i.

To Forewi'sh. *part.* [*fore* and *wish.*] To desire beforehand.

The wiser sort ceased not to do what in them lay, to procure that the good commonly *forewished* might in time come to effect. *Knolles's History of the Turks.*

Forewo'rn. *part.* [*fore* and *worn*, from *wear.*] Worn out; wasted by time or use.

Neither the light was enough to read the words, and the ink was already *foreworn*, and in many places blotted. *Sidney.*

FO'RFEIT. *n. s.* [*forfait*, French; *fforfed*, Welsh.]

1. Something lost by the commission of a crime; something paid for expiation of a crime; a fine; a mulct.

Thy slanders I forgive, and therewithal
Remit thy other *forfeits*. *Shak. Measure for Measure.*
Th' execution leave to high disposal,
And let another hand, not thine, exact
Thy penal *forfeit* from thyself. *Milton's Agonistes, l.* 506.
Thy life, Melantius! I am come to take,
Of which foul treason does a *forfeit* make. *Waller.*

2. A person obnoxious to punishment; one whose life is forfeited by his offence. Now obsolete.

Your brother is a *forfeit* of the law,
And you but waste your words. *Shak. Meas. for Measure.*

Claudio, whom here you have warrant to execute, is no greater *forfeit* to the law than Angelo, who hath sentenced him. *Shakespeare's Measure for Measure.*

To Fo'rfeit. *v. a.* [from the noun.] To lose by some breach of condition; to lose by some offence.

If then a man, on light conditions, gain
A great estate to him, and his, for ever;
If wilfully he *forfeit* it again,
Who doth bemoan his heir, or blame the giver? *Davies.*

Men displeased God, and consequently *forfeited* all right to happiness. *Boyle.*

A father cannot alien the power he has over his child: he may perhaps to some degrees *forfeit* it, but cannot transfer it. *Locke.*

Fo'rfeit. *participial adj.* [from the verb.] Liable to penal seizure; alienated by a crime; lost either as to the right or possession, by breach of conditions.

All the souls that are, were *forfeit* once;
And he that might the 'vantage best have took,
Found out the remedy. *Shakesp. Measure for Measure.*
Beg that thou may'st have leave to hang thyself;
And yet, thy wealth being *forfeit* to the state,
Thou hast not left the value of a cord. *Shakespeare.*
This now fenceless world,
Forfeit to death. *Milton's Paradise Lost, b.* x. *l.* 303.
Straight all his hopes exhal'd in empty smoke,
And his long toils were *forfeit* for a look. *Dryd. Virg. Geor.*
Methought with wond'rous ease he swallow'd down
His *forfeit* honour, to betray the town. *Dryd. Indian Emp.*
How the murd'rer paid his *forfeit* breath;
What lands so distant from that scene of death,
But trembling heard the fame! *Pope's Odyssey, b.* iii.

Fo'rfeitable. *adj.* [from *forfeit.*] Possessed on conditions, by the breach of which any thing may be lost.

Fo'rfeiture. *n. s.* [*forfaiture*, French, from *forfeit.*]

1. The act of forfeiting; the punishment discharged by loss of something possessed.

2. The thing forfeited; a mulct; a fine.

The court is as well a Chancery to save and debar *forfeitures*, as a court of common law to decide rights; and there would be work enough in Germany and Italy, if Imperial *forfeitures* should go for good titles. *Bacon's War with Spain.*

Ancient privileges and acts of grace indulged by former kings, must not, without high reason, be revoked by their successors; nor *forfeitures* be exacted violently, nor penal laws urged rigorously. *Taylor's Rule of living holy.*

He fairly abdicates his throne,
He has a *forfeiture* incurr'd. *Swift.*

To Forfe'nd. *v. a.* To prevent; to forbid. *Hanmer.*

Forga've. The preterite of *forgive.*

FORGE. *n. s.* [*forge*, French.]

1. The place where iron is beaten into form. In common language we use *forge* for large work, and *smithy* for small; but in books the distinction is not kept.

Now behold,
In the quick *forge* and working-house of thought,
How London doth pour out her citizens. *Shak. Henry* V.
In other part stood one, who at the *forge*
Labouring, two massy clods of iron and brass
Had melted. *Milton's Paradise Lost, b.* xi.
Th' o'er-labour'd Cyclop from his task retires,
Th' Æolian *forge* exhausted of its fires. *Pope's Statius.*

2. Any place where any thing is made or shaped.

From no other *forge* hath proceeded a strange conceit, that to serve God with any set form of common prayer is superstitious. *Hooker, b.* v. *s.* 26.

To Forge. *v. a.* [*forger*, old French.]

1. To form by the hammer; to beat into shape.

The queen of martials,

And

And Mars himself conducted them; both which being *forg'd* of gold,
Must needs have golden furniture. *Chapman's Iliad, b.* xviii.

Tyger with tyger, bear with bear you'll find
In leagues offensive and defensive join'd;
But lawless man the anvil dares profane,
And *forge* that steel by which a man is slain,
Which earth at first for plough-shares did afford,
Nor yet the smith had learn'd to form a sword. *Tate's Juv.*

2. To make by any means.

He was a kind of nothing, titleless,
'Till he had *forg'd* himself a name i' th' fire
Of burning Rome. *Shakespeare's Coriolanus.*

His heart's his mouth:
What his breast *forges*, that his tongue must vent. *Shakesp.*

Those few names that the schools *forged*, and put into the mouths of their scholars, could never yet get admittance into common use, or obtain the licence of publick approbation. *Locke.*

3. To counterfeit; to falsify.

Were I king,
I should cut off the nobles for their lands:
My more having would be as sauce
To make me hunger more, that I should *forge*
Quarrels unjust against the good and loyal,
Destroying them for wealth. *Shakespeare's Macbeth.*

FO'RGER. *n. s.* [from *forge.*]

1. One who makes or forms.
2. One who counterfeits any thing; a falsifier.

As in stealing, if there were no receivers there would be no thieves; so in slander, if there were fewer spreaders there would be fewer *forgers* of libels. *Government of the Tongue.*

No *forger* of lyes willingly and wittingly furnishes out the means of his own detection. *West on the Resurrection.*

FO'RGERY. *n. s.* [from *forge.*] The crime of falsification.

Has your king married the lady Gray?
And now, to sooth your *forgery* and his,
Sends me a paper to persuade me patience. *Shakes. Hen.* VI.

Nothing could have been easier than for the Jews, the enemies of Jesus Christ, to have disproved these facts, had they been false, to have shewn their falshood, and to have convicted them of *forgery*. *Stephens's Sermons.*

A *forgery*, in setting a false name to a writing, which may prejudice another's fortune, the law punishes with the loss of ears; but has inflicted no adequate penalty for doing the same thing in print, though books sold under a false name are so many *forgeries*. *Swift.*

2. Smith's work; fabrication; the act of the forge.

He ran on embattl'd armies clad in iron,
And weaponless himself,
Made arms ridiculous, useless the *forgery*
Of brazen shield and spear, the hammer'd cuirass,
Chalybean temper'd steel, and frock of mail
Adamantean proof. *Milton's Agonistes, l.* 129.

To FORGE'T. *v. a.* preter. *forgot*; part. *forgotten*, or *forgot*. [ꝼoɲᵹytan, Saxon; *vergeten*, Dutch.]

1. To lose memory of; to let go from the remembrance.

That is not *forgot*
Which ne'er I did remember; to my knowledge,
I never in my life did look on him. *Shakesp. Richard* II.

When I am *forgotten*, as I shall be,
And sleep in dull cold marble, where no mention
Of me must more be heard. *Shakes. Henry* VIII.

Oh, my oblivion is a very Anthony,
And I am all *forgotten*. *Shakes. Anthony and Cleopatra.*

Forget not thy friend in thy mind, and be not unmindful of him in thy riches. *Ecclus.* xxxvii. 6.

No sooner was our deliverance compleated, but we *forgot* our danger and our duty. *Atterbury's Sermons.*

Alive, ridiculous; and dead, *forgot*. *Pope.*

2. Not to attend; to neglect.

Can a woman *forget* her sucking child? Yea, they may *forget*; yet will I not *forget* thee. *Isa.* xlix. 5.

The mass of mean *forgotten* things. *Anon.*

FORGE'TFUL. *adj.* [from *forget.*]

1. Not retaining the memory of.
2. Causing oblivion; oblivious.

But when a thousand rolling years are past,
So long their punishments and penance last,
Whole droves of minds are by the driving god
Compell'd to drink the deep Lethean flood,
In large *forgetful* draughts to steep the cares
Of their past labours, and their irksome years. *Dryd. Æn.*

3. Inattentive; negligent; neglectful; careless.

Be not *forgetful* to entertain strangers. *Hebr.* xiii. 2.

The queen is comfortless, and we *forgetful*
In our long absence. *Shakespeare's Henry* VIII.

Have you not love enough to bear with me,
When that rash humour, which my mother gave me,
Makes me *forgetful*? *Shakespeare's Julius Cæsar.*

I, in fact, a real interest have,
Which to my own advantage I would save;
And, with the usual courtier's trick, intend
To serve myself, *forgetful* of my friend. *Prior.*

FORGE'TFULNESS. *n. s.* [from *forgetful.*]

1. Oblivion; cessation to remember; loss of memory.

O gentle sleep!
Nature's soft nurse, how have I frighted thee,
That thou no more wilt weigh my eyelids down,
And steep my senses in *forgetfulness*! *Shakesp. Henry* IV.

All birds and beasts lie hush'd; sleep steals away
The wild desires of men and toils of day;
And brings, descending through the silent air,
A sweet *forgetfulness* of human care. *Pope's Statius.*

2. Negligence; neglect; inattention.

The church of England is grievously charged with *forgetfulness* of her duty. *Hooker, b.* iv. *s.* 13.

FORGE'TTER. *n. s.* [from *forget.*]

1. One that forgets.
2. A careless person.

To FORGI'VE. *v. a.* [ꝼoɲᵹiꝼan, Saxon.]

1. To pardon a person; not to punish.

Then heaven *forgive* him too! *Shakespeare's Macbeth.*

I do beseech your grace for charity;
If ever any malice in your heart
Were hid against me, now *forgive* me frankly.
—Sir Thomas Lovell, I as free *forgive* you,
As I would be *forgiven*: I *forgive* all. *Shakes. Henry* VIII.

Slowly provok'd, she easily *forgives*. *Prior.*

2. To pardon a crime.

The people that dwell therein shall be *forgiven* their iniquity. *Is.* xxxiii. 24.

3. To remit; not to exact debt or penalty.

The lord of that servant was moved with compassion, loosed him, and *forgave* him the debt. *Mat.* xviii. 27.

FORGI'VENESS. *n. s.* [ꝼoɲᵹiꝼenneꝼꝼe, Saxon.]

1. The act of forgiving.

To the Lord our God belong mercies and *forgivenesses*. *Dan.*

2. Pardon of an offender.

Thou hast promised repentance and *forgiveness* to them that have sinned against thee. *Prayer of Manass.*

Exchange *forgiveness* with me, noble Hamlet;
Mine and my father's death come not on thee,
Nor thine on me. *Shakespeare's Hamlet.*

Forgiveness to the injur'd does belong;
But they ne'er pardon who commit the wrong. *Dryden.*

3. Pardon of an offence.

God has certainly promised *forgiveness* of sin to every one who repents. *South's Sermons.*

4. Tenderness; willingness to pardon.

Here are introduced more heroick principles of meekness, *forgiveness*, bounty and magnanimity, than all the learning of the heathens could invent. *Sprat's Sermons.*

Mercy above did hourly plead
For her resemblance here below;
And mild *forgiveness* intercede
To stop the coming blow. *Dryden.*

5. Remission of a fine or penalty.

FORGI'VER. *n. s.* [from *forgive.*] One who pardons.

FORGO'T. } *part. pass.* of *forget*. Not remembered.
FORGO'TTEN. }

This song shall not be *forgotten*. *Deutr.* xxxi. 21.

Great Strafford! worthy of that name, though all
Of thee could be *forgotten*, but thy fall. *Denham.*

The soft ideas of the cheerful note,
Lightly receiv'd, were easily *forgot*. *Prior.*

To FORHA'IL. *v. a.* [An old word. Probably for *forhaul*, from *for* and *haul.*] To harrass; tear; torment.

All this long tale
Nought easeth the care that doth me *forhail*. *Spenser's Past.*

FORK. *n. s.* [*furca*, Latin; *fforch*, Welsh; *fourche*, French.]

1. An instrument divided at the end into two or more points or prongs, used on many occasions.

At Midsummer down with the brembles and brakes,
And after abroad with thy *forks* and thy rakes. *Tuss. Husb.*

The vicar first, and after him the crew,
With *forks* and staves the felon to pursue,
Ran Coll our dog. *Dryden's Nun's Priest.*

I dine with *forks* that have but two prongs. *Swift.*

2. It is sometimes used for the point of an arrow.

The bow is bent and drawn: make from the shaft.
—Let it fall rather, though the *fork* invade
The region of my heart. *Shakespeare's King Lear.*

3. A point of a fork.

Several are amazed at the wisdom of the ancients that represented a thunderbolt with three *forks*, since nothing could have better explained its triple quality of piercing, burning, and melting. *Addison on ancient Medals.*

To FORK. *v. n.* [from the noun.] To shoot into blades, as corn does out of the ground.

The corn beginneth to *fork*. *Mortimer's Husbandry.*

Fo'rked. *adj.* [from *fork.*] Opening into two or more parts.

When he was naked he was, for all the world, like a *forked* radish, with a head fantastically carved upon it with a knife. *Shakespeare's Henry* IV. *p.* ii.

Sometimes we see a cloud that's dragonish,
A *forked* mountain, or blue promontory. *Shakespeare.*

Come, shall we go and kill us venison?
And yet it irks me the poor dappled fools
Should, in their own confines, with *forked* heads,
Have their round haunches goar'd. *Shakesp. As you like it.*

He would have spoke;
But hiss for hiss return'd, with *forked* tongue
To *forked* tongue. *Milton's Paradise Lost, b.* x.

Ye dragons, whose contagious breath
Peoples the dark retreats of death,
Change your fierce hissing into joyful song,
And praise your maker with your *forked* tongue. *Roscommon.*

Fo'rkedly. *adv.* [from *forked.*] In a forked form.

Fo'rkedness. *n. s.* [from *forked.*] The quality of opening into two parts.

Fo'rkhead *n. s.* [*fork* and *head.*] Point of an arrow.

It seizing, no way enter might;
But back rebounding, left the *forkhead* keen,
Eftsoons it fled away, and might no where be seen. *Fa. Qu.*

Fo'rky. *adj.* [from *fork*] Forked; furcated; opening into two parts.

The smiling infant in his hand shall take
The crested basilisk and speckled snake;
Pleas'd the green lustre of the scales survey,
And with their *forky* tongue and pointless sting shall play. *Pope's Messiah.*

Forlo're. [The preterite and participle of the Saxon ꝼoꞃleoꞃan, in Dutch *verloren.*] Deserted; forsook; forsaken.

Such as Diana by the sandy shore
Of swift Eurotas, or on Cynthus' green,
Where all the nymphs have her *forlore*. *Fairy Queen, b.* ii.

That wretched world he 'gan for to abhor,
And mortal life 'gan loath, as thing *forlore*. *Fairy Queen.*

Thus fell the trees, with noise the desarts roar;
The beasts their caves, the birds their nests *forelore*. *Fairf.*

FORLO'RN. *adj.* [ꝼoꞃloꞃen, from ꝼoꞃleoꞃan, Saxon; *verloren*, Dutch.]

1. Deserted; destitute; forsaken; wretched; helpless; solitary.

Make them seek for that they wont to scorn;
Of fortune and of hope at once *forlorn*. *Hubberd's Tale.*

Tell me, good Hobinol, what gars thee greet?
What! hath some wolf thy tender lambs ytorn?
Or is thy bagpipe broke, that sounds so sweet?
Or art thou of thy loved lass *forlorne*? *Spenser's Pastorals.*

In every place was heard the lamentation of women and children; every thing shewed the heaviness of the time, and seemed as altogether lost and *forlorn*. *Knolles's History.*

How can I live without thee! how forego
Thy sweet converse, and love so dearly join'd,
To live again in these wild woods *forlorn*! *Milt. Par. Lost.*

Their way
Lies through the perplex'd paths of this drear wood;
The nodding horrour of whose shady brows,
Threats the *forlorn* and wand'ring passenger. *Milton.*

My only strength and stay! *forlorn* of thee,
Whither shall I betake me, where subsist! *Milt. Par. Lost.*

Like a declining statesman, left *forlorn*
To his friends pity and pursuers scorn. *Denham.*

The good old man, *forlorn* of human aid,
For vengeance to his heav'nly patron pray'd. *Dryd. Iliad.*

Philomel laments *forlorn*. *Fenton.*

As some sad turtle his lost love deplores,
Thus, far from Delia, to the winds I mourn;
Alike unheard, unpity'd, and *forlorn*. *Pope's Autumn.*

2. Lost; desperate.

What is become of great Acrates' son?
Or where hath he hung up his mortal blade,
That hath so many haughty conquests won?
Is all his force *forlorn*, and all his glory done? *Fairy Queen.*

3. Small; despicable: in a ludicrous sense.

He was so *forlorn*, that his dimensions to any thick sight were invincible. *Shakespeare's Henry* IV. *p.* ii.

Forlo'rn. *n. s.* A lost, solitary, forsaken man.

Henry
Is of a king become a banish'd man,
And forc'd to live in Scotland a *forlorn*. *Shakesp. Henry* VI.

2. Forlorn *Hope.* The soldiers who are sent first to the attack, and are therefore doomed to perish.

Criticks in plume,
Who lolling on our foremost benches sit,
And still charge first, the true *forlorn* of wit. *Dryden.*

Forlo'rnness. *n. s.* [from *forlorn.*] Destitution; misery; solitude.

Men displeased God, and consequently forfeited all right to happiness; even whilst they compleated the *forlornness* of their condition by the lethargy of not being sensible of it. *Boyle.*

To Fo'rlye. *v. n.* [from *for* and *lye.*] To lye across.

Knit with a golden baldric, which *forlay*
Athwart her snowy breast, and did divide
Her dainty paps, which, like young fruit in May,
Now little 'gan to swell; and being ty'd,
Through her thin weed, their places only signify'd. *Fa. Qu.*

FORM. *n. s.* [*forma*, Latin; *forme*, French.]

1. The external appearance of any thing; representation; shape.

Nay, women are frail too.
——Ay, as the glasses where they view themselves,
Which are as easy broke as they make *forms*. *Shakespeare.*

It stood still; but I could not discern the *form* thereof. *Job.*

Gold will endure a vehement fire, without any change, and after it has been divided by corrosive liquors into invisible parts; yet may presently be precipitated, so as to appear again in its *form*. *Grew's Cosmol. Sac. b.* i.

Matter, as wise logicians say,
Cannot without a *form* subsist;
And *form*, say I as well as they,
Must fail, if matter brings no grist. *Swift.*

2. Being, as modified by a particular shape.

When noble benefits shall prove
Not well dispos'd, the mind grown once corrupt,
They turn to vicious *forms*, ten times more ugly
Than ever they were fair. *Shakespeare's Henry* VIII.

Here toils and death, and death's half-brother, sleep,
Forms terrible to view, their sentry keep;
With anxious pleasures of a guilty mind,
Deep frauds before, and open force behind. *Dryden's Æn.*

3. Particular model or modification.

He that will look into many parts of Asia and America, will find men reason there perhaps as acutely as himself, who yet never heard of a syllogism, nor can reduce any one argument to those *forms*. *Locke.*

It lengthens out every act of worship, and produces more lasting and permanent impressions in the mind, than those which accompany any transient *form* of words that are uttered in the ordinary method of religious worship. *Addison.*

4. Beauty; elegance of appearance.

He hath no *form* nor comeliness. *Isa.* liii. 2.

5. Regularity; method; order.

What he spoke, though it lack'd *form* a little,
Was not like madness. *Shakespeare's Hamlet.*

6. External appearance without the essential qualities; empty show.

Then those whom *form* of laws
Condemn'd to die, when traitors judg'd their cause. *Dryden.*

They were young heirs sent only for *form* from schools, where they were not suffered to stay three months in the year. *Swift's Essay on Modern Education.*

7. Ceremony; external rites.

Though well we may not pass upon his life,
Without the *form* of justice; yet our pow'r
Shall do a court'sy to our wrath, which men
May blame, but not controul. *Shakespeare's King Lear.*

A long table, and a square table, or seat about the walls, seem things of *form*, but are things of substance; for at a long table, a few at the upper end, in effect, sway all the business; but in the other form, there is more use of the counsellors opinions that sit lower. *Bacon, Essay* 21.

That the parliaments of Ireland might want no decent or honourable *form* used in England, he caused a particular act to pass that the lords of Ireland should appear in parliament robes. *Davies in Ireland.*

Their general used, in all dispatches made by himself, to observe all decency in their *forms*. *Clarendon, b.* viii.

How am I to interpret, sir, this visit?
Is it a compliment of *form*, or love? *A. Phill. Dist. Moth.*

8. Stated method; established practice.

He who affirmeth speech to be necessary amongst all men, throughout the world, doth not thereby import that all men must necessarily speak one kind of language; even so the necessity of polity and regimen in all churches may be held, without holding any one certain *form* to be necessary in them all. *Hooker, b.* iii. *s.* 2.

Nor are constant *forms* of prayer more likely to flat and hinder the spirit of prayer and devotion, than unpremeditated and confused variety to distract and lose it. *King Charles.*

Nor seek to know
Their process, or the *forms* of law below. *Dryden's Æn.*

9. A long seat.

If a chair be defined a seat for a single person, with a back belonging to it, then a stool is a seat for a single person without a back; and a *form* is a seat for several persons, without a back. *Watts's Logick.*

I was seen with her in the manorhouse, sitting with her upon the *form*, and taken following her into the park. *Shakesp.*

10. A class; a rank of students.

It will be necessary to see and examine those works which have

have given so great a reputation to the masters of the first *form*. *Dryden's Dufresnoy.*

11. The seat or bed of a hare.

Now for a clod-like hare in *form* they peer;
Now bolt and cudgel squirrels leap do move;
Now the ambitious lark, with mirrour clear,
They catch, while he, fool! to himself makes love. *Sidn.*
Have you observ'd a sitting hare,
List'ning, and fearful of the storm
Of horns and hounds, clap back her ear,
Afraid to keep or leave her *form*. *Prior.*

12. *Form* is the essential, specifical, or distinguishing modification of the matter of which any thing is composed, so as thereby to give it such a peculiar manner of existence. *Harris.*

In definitions, whether they be framed larger to augment, or stricter to abridge the number of sacraments, we find grace expresly mentioned as their true essential *form*, and elements as the matter whereunto that *form* doth adjoin itself. *Hooker.*

They inferred, if the world were a living creature, it had a soul and spirit, by which they did not intend God, for they did admit of a deity besides, but only the soul or essential *form* of the universe. *Bacon's Natural History.*

13. A formal cause; that which gives essence.

To FORM. *v. a.* [*formo*, Latin.]

1. To make out of materials.

God *formed* man of the dust of the ground. *Gen.* ii. 7.
She *form'd* the phantom of well-bodied air. *Pope.*

2. To model to a particular shape.

3. To modify; to scheme; to plan.

Lucretius taught him not to *form* his heroe, to give him piety or valour for his manners. *Dryden's Æn. Dedicat.*

4. To arrange; to combine in any particular manner: as, he *formed* his troops.

5. To adjust; to settle.

Our differences with the Romanists are thus *formed* into an interest, and become the design not of single persons, but of corporations and successions. *Decay of Piety.*

6. To contrive; to coin.

The defeat of the design is the routing of opinions *formed* for promoting it. *Decay of Piety.*

He dies too soon;
And fate, if possible, must be delay'd:
The thought that labours in my *forming* brain,
Yet crude and immature, demands more time. *Rowe.*

7. To model by education or institution.

Let him to this with easy pains be brought,
And seem to labour when he labours not:
Thus *form'd* for speed, he challenges the wind,
And leaves the Scythian arrow far behind. *Dryd. Virg. Geo.*

FO'RMAL. *adj.* [*formel*, French; *formalis*, Latin.]

1. Ceremonious; solemn; precise; exact to affectation:

The justice,
In fair round belly, with good capon lin'd,
With eyes severe, and beard of *formal* cut,
Full of wise saws and modern instances,
And so he plays his part. *Shakespeare's As you like it.*
Formal in apparel,
In gait and countenance surely like a father. *Shakespeare.*

Ceremonies especially be not to be omitted to strangers and *formal* natures; but the exalting them above the mean is not only tedious, but doth diminish the credit of him that speaks. *Bacon, Essay* 53.

2. Done according to established rules and methods; not irregular; not sudden; not extemporaneous.

There is not any positive law of men, whether it be general or particular, received by *formal* express consent, as in councils; or by secret approbation, as in customs it cometh to pass, but the same may be taken away, if occasion serve. *Hooker, b.* iv. *s.* 14.

As there are *formal* and written leagues, respective to certain enemies; so there is a natural and tacit confederation amongst all men against the common enemy of human society, so as there needs no intimation or denunciation of the war; but all these formalities the law of nature supplies, as in the case of pyrates. *Bacon's Holy War.*

3. Regular; methodical.

The *formal* stars do travel so,
As we their names and courses know;
And he that on their changes looks,
Would think them govern'd by our books. *Waller.*

4. External; having the appearance but not the essence.

Of *formal* duty, make no more thy boast;
Thou disobey'st where it concerns me most. *Dryd. Aureng.*

5. Depending upon establishment or custom.

Still in constraint your suffering sex remains,
Or bound in *formal* or in real chains. *Pope.*

6. Having the power of making any thing what it is; constituent; essential.

Of letters the material part is breath and voice: the *formal* is constituted by the motions and figure of the organs of speech affecting breath with a peculiar found, by which each letter is discriminated. *Holder's Elements of Speech.*

Bellarmine agrees in making the *formal* act of adoration to be subjection to a superior; but withal he makes the mere apprehension of excellency to include the *formal* reason of it: whereas mere excellency, without superiority, doth not require any subjection, but only estimation. *Stillingfleet.*

The very life and vital motion, and the *formal* essence and nature of man, is wholly owing to the power of God. *Bentl.*

7. Retaining its proper and essential characteristick.

Thou shou'dst come like a fury cover'd with snakes,
Not like a *formal* man. *Shakesp. Ant. and Cleopatra.*
I will not let him stir,
'Till I have us'd th' approved means I have;
With wholsome syrups, drugs, and holy prayers,
To make of him a *formal* man again. *Shakesp. Com. of Err.*

FO'RMALIST. *n. s.* [*formaliste*, French, from *form*.] One who practises external ceremony; one who prefers appearance to reality; one who seems what he is not.

It is a ridiculous thing, and fit for a satyr to persons of judgment, to see what shifts *formalists* have, and what prospectives to make superficies to seem a body that hath depth and bulk. *Bacon, Essay* 27.

A grave, stanch, skilfully managed face, set upon a grasping aspiring mind, having got many a sly *formalist* the reputation of a primitive and severe piety. *South's Sermons.*

FORMA'LITY. *n. s.* [*formalite*, French, from *form*.]

1. Ceremony; established mode of behaviour.

The attire, which the minister of God is by order to use at times of divine service, is but a matter of mere *formality*, yet such as for comeliness sake hath hitherto been judged not unnecessary. *Hooker, b.* v. *s.* 29.

Formalities of extraordinary zeal and piety are never more studied and elaborate than in desperate designs. *King Charles.*

Many a worthy man sacrifices his peace to *formalities* of compliment and good manners. *L'Estrange, Fable* 184.

Nor was his attendance on divine offices a matter of *formality* and custom, but of conscience. *Atterbury's Sermons.*

2. Solemn order, habit, or dress.

If men forswear the deeds and bonds they draw,
Though sign'd with all *formality* of law;
And though the signing and the seal proclaim
The barefac'd perjury, and fix the shame. *Dryden's Juven.*

The pretender would have infallibly landed in our northern parts, and found them all sat down in their *formalities*, as the Gauls did the Roman senators. *Swift.*

3. Essence; the quality by which any thing is what it is.

To fix on God the *formality* of faculties, or affections, is the imposture of our fancies, and contradictory to his divinity. *Glanv Sceps. c.* 13.

May not a man vow to A. and B. that he will give a hundred pound to an hospital? Here the vow is made both to God and to A. and B. But here A. and B. are only witnesses to the vow; but the *formality* of the vow lies in the promise made to God. *Stillingfleet's Def. of Disc. on Rom. Idol.*

To FO'RMALIZE. *v. a.* [*formaliser*, French, from *formal*.]

1. To model; to modify. A word not now in use.

The same spirit which anointed the blessed soul of our Saviour Christ, doth so *formalize*, unite, and actuate his whole race, as if both he and they were so many limbs compacted into one body. *Hooker, b.* v. *s.* 56.

2. To affect formality; to be fond of ceremony.

FO'RMALLY. *adv.* [from *formal*.]

1. According to established rules, methods, ceremonies or rites.

Formally, according to our law,
Depose him. *Shakespeare's Richard* II.

2. Ceremoniously; stifly; precisely.

To be stiff and *formally* reserved, as if the company did not deserve our familiarity, is a downright challenge of homage. *Collier on Pride.*

3. In open appearance; with visible and apparent show.

You and your followers do stand *formally* divided against the authorised guides of the church, and the rest of the people. *Hooker.*

4. Essentially; characteristically.

This power and dominion is not adequately and *formally* the image of God, but only a part of it. *South's Sermons.*

The Heathens and the Christians may agree in material acts of charity; but that which *formally* makes this a Christian grace, is the spring from which it flows. *Smalridge's Sermons.*

FORMA'TION. *n. s.* [*formation*, French, from *formo*, Latin.]

1. The act of forming or generating.

The matter discharged forth of vulcano's, and other spiracles, contributes to the *formation* of meteors. *Woodward's Nat. Hist.*

The solids are originally formed of a fluid, from a small point, as appears by the gradual *formation* of a fœtus. *Arbuth.*

Complicated ideas, growing up under observation, give not the same confusion, as if they were all offered to the mind at once, without your observing the original and *formation* of them. *Watts's Improvement of the Mind.*

2. The manner in which a thing is formed.

The chorion, a thick membrane obscuring the *formation*, the dam doth tear asunder. *Brown's Vulgar Errours.*

Fo'rmative. *adj.* [from *formo*, Latin.] Having the power of giving form; plaſtick.

As we have eſtabliſhed our aſſertion of the ſeminal production of all kinds of animals; ſo likewiſe we affirm, that the meaneſt plant cannot be raiſed without ſeed, by any *formative* power reſiding in the ſoil. *Bentley's Sermons.*

Fo'rmer. *n. ſ.* [from *form.*] He that forms; maker; contriver; planner.

The wonderful art and providence of the contriver and *former* of our bodies, appears in the multitude of intentions he muſt have in the formation of ſeveral parts for ſeveral uſes. *Ray on the Creation.*

Fo'rmer. *adj.* [from ꝼoꞃma, Saxon, firſt; whence *former*, and *formoſt* now commonly written *foremoſt*, as if derived from *before*. *Formoſt* is generally applied to place, rank, or degree, and *former* only to time; for when we ſay, the laſt rank of the proceſſion is like the *former*, we reſpect time rather than place, and mean that which we ſaw *before*, rather than that which had precedence in place.]

1. Before another in time.

Thy air,
Thou other gold-bound brow, is like the firſt:
—A third is like the *former*. *Shakeſpeare's Macbeth.*

2. Mentioned before another.

A bad author deſerves better uſage than a bad critick: a man may be the *former* merely through the misfortune of an ill judgment; but he cannot be the latter without both that and an ill temper. *Pope.*

3. Paſt: as, *this was the cuſtom in* former *times*.

Fo'rmerly. *adv.* [from *former.*] In times paſt.

The places mentioned were all of them *formerly* the cool retirements of the Romans, where they uſed to hide themſelves among the woods and mountains, during the exceſſive heats of their Summer. *Addiſon on Italy.*

As an animal degenerates by diſeaſes, the animal ſalts, *formerly* benign, approach towards an alkaline nature. *Arbuthnot.*

FO'RMIDABLE. *adj.* [*formidabilis*, Latin; *formidable*, Fr.] Terrible; dreadful; tremendous; terrifick; to be feared.

I ſwell my preface into a volume, and make it *formidable*, when you ſee ſo many pages behind. *Dryden's Æn. Dedicat.*

They ſeem'd to fear the *formidable* ſight,
And roll'd their billows on, to ſpeed his flight. *Dryden.*

Fo'rmidableness. *n. ſ.* [from *formidable.*]

1. The quality of exciting terror or dread.

2. The thing cauſing dread.

They rather chuſe to be ſhewed the *formidableneſs* of their danger, than, by a blind embracing it, to periſh in it. *Decay of Piety.*

Fo'rmidably. *adv.* [from *formidable.*] In a terrible manner.

Behold! e'en to remoter ſhores,
A conquering navy proudly ſpread;
The Britiſh cannon *formidably* roars. *Dryden.*

Fo'rmless. *adj.* [from *form.*] Shapeleſs; without regularity of form.

All form is *formleſs*, order orderleſs,
Save what is oppoſite to England's love. *Shakeſp. K. John.*

Fo'rmulary. *n. ſ.* [*formulaire*, French, from *formule.*] A book containing ſtated and preſcribed models or ſet forms.

FO'RMULE. *n. ſ.* [*formule*, French; *formula*, Latin.] A ſet or preſcribed model.

To FO'RNICATE. *v. a.* [from *fornix*, Latin.] To commit lewdneſs.

It is a new way to *fornicate* at a diſtance. *Brown's Vul. Err.*

Fornica'tion. *n. ſ.* [*fornication*, French; *fornicatio*, Latin.]

1. Concubinage or commerce with an unmarried woman.

Bleſs me! what a fry of *fornication* is at the door. *Shakeſ.*

The law ought to be ſtrict againſt *fornications* and adulteries; for, if there were univerſal liberty, the increaſe of mankind would be but like that of foxes at beſt. *Graunt.*

2. In Scripture, ſometimes idolatry.

Thou didſt truſt in thine own beauty, and playedſt the harlot, becauſe of thy renown, and pouredſt out thy *fornications*, on every one that paſſed by. *Ezek.* xvi. 15.

Fornica'tor. *n. ſ.* [*fornicateur*, French, from *fornix*, Latin.] One that has commerce with unmarried women.

A *fornicator* or adulterer ſteals the ſoul as well as diſhonours the body of his neighbour. *Taylor's Rule of living holy.*

Fornica'tress. *n. ſ.* [from *fornicator.*] A woman who without marriage cohabits with a man.

See you the *fornicatreſs* be remov'd;
Let her have needful but not ſlaviſh means. *Shakeſpeare.*

To FORSA'KE. *v. a.* preter. *forſook*; part. paſſ. *forſook*, or *forſaken*. [*verſaeken*, Dutch.]

1. To leave in reſentment, neglect, or diſlike.

'Twas now the time when firſt Saul God *forſook*,
God Saul; the room in's heart wild paſſions took. *Cowley.*

Oreſtes comes in time
To ſave your honour: Pyrrhus cools apace;
Prevent his falſhood, and *forſake* him firſt:
I know you hate him. *A. Phillips's Diſtreſt Mother.*

Daughter of Jove! whoſe arms in thunder wield
Th' avenging bolt, and ſhake the dreadful ſhield,
Forſook by thee, in vain I ſought thy aid. *Pope's Odyſſey.*

2. To leave; to go away from; to depart from.

Unwilling I *forſook* your friendly ſtate,
Commanded by the gods, and forc'd by fate. *Dryden's Æn.*

3. To deſert; to fail.

Truth, modeſty, and ſhame the world *forſook*;
Fraud, avarice, and force their places took. *Dryd. Ovid.*

When ev'n the flying ſails were ſeen no more,
Forſaken of all ſight ſhe left the ſhore. *Dryden.*

Their purple majeſty,
And all thoſe outward ſhows which we call greatneſs,
Languiſh and droop, ſeem empty and *forſaken*,
And draw the wond'ring gazers eyes no more. *Rowe.*

Forsa'ker. *n. ſ.* [from *forſake.*] Deſerter; one that forſakes.

Thou did'ſt deliver us into the hands of lawleſs enemies, moſt hateful *forſakers* of God. *Apocrypha.*

Forsoo'th. *adv.* [ꝼoꞃſoðe, Saxon.]

1. In truth; certainly; very well. It is uſed almoſt always in an ironical or contemptuous ſenſe.

Wherefore doth Lyſander
Deny your love, ſo rich within his ſoul,
And tender me, *forſooth*, affection? *Shakeſpeare.*

A fit man, *forſooth*, to govern a realm, who had ſo goodly government in his own eſtate. *Hayward.*

Unlearned perſons uſe ſuch letters as juſtly expreſs the power or ſound of their ſpeech; yet *forſooth*, we ſay, write not true Engliſh, or true French. *Holder's Elem. of Speech.*

In the Eaſt-Indies a widow, who has any regard to her character, throws herſelf into the flames of her huſband's funeral pile, to ſhew, *forſooth*, that ſhe is faithful to the memory of her deceaſed lord. *Addiſon's Freeholder.*

She would cry out murder, and diſturb the whole neighbourhood; and when John came running down the ſtairs to enquire what the matter was, nothing, *forſooth*, only her maid had ſtuck a pin wrong in her gown. *Arbuthn. Hiſt. of J. Bull.*

Some queſtion the genuineneſs of his books, becauſe, *forſooth*, they cannot diſcover in them that *flumen orationis* that Cicero ſpeaks of. *Baker's Reflections on Learning.*

2. It is ſuppoſed to have been once a word of honour in addreſs to women. It is probablethat an inferior, being called, ſhewed his attention by anſwering in the word yes, *forſooth*, which in time loſt its true meaning; and inſtead of a mere exclamatory interjection, was ſuppoſed a compellation. It appears in *Shakeſpeare* to have been uſed likewiſe to men.

Our old Engliſh word *forſooth* has been changed for the French madam. *Guardian.*

To FORSWE'AR. *v. a.* pret. *forſwore*; part. *forſworn*. [ꝼoꞃſƿæꞃian, Saxon.]

1. To renounce upon oath.

I firmly vow
Never to wooe her more; but do *forſwear* her,
As one unworthy all the former favours,
That I have fondly flatter'd her withal. *Shakeſpeare.*

2. To deny upon oath.

And that ſelf chain about his neck,
Which he *forſwore* moſt monſtrouſly to have. *Shakeſpeare.*

Obſerve the wretch who hath his faith forſook,
How clear his voice, and how aſſur'd his look!
Like innocence, and as ſerenely bold
As truth, how loudly he *forſwears* thy gold! *Dryd. Juven.*

3. With the reciprocal pronoun: as, *to forſwear himſelf*; to be perjured; to ſwear falſely.

To leave my Julia, ſhall I be *forſworn?*
To love fair Silvia, ſhall I be *forſworn?*
To wrong my friend, ſhall I be much *forſworn?*
And ev'n that power which gave me firſt my oath,
Provokes me to this threefold perjury. *Shakeſpeare.*

One ſays, he never ſhould endure the ſight
Of that *forſworn*, that wrongs both land and laws. *Daniel.*

I too have ſworn, ev'n at the altar ſworn,
Eternal love and endleſs faith to Theſeus;
And yet am falſe, *forſworn:* the hallow'd ſhrine,
That heard me ſwear, is witneſs to my falſhood. *Smith.*

To Forswe'ar. *v. n.* To ſwear falſely; to commit perjury.

Take heed; for he holds vengeance in his hand,
To hurl upon their heads that break his law.
—And that ſame vengeance doth hurl on thee,
For falſe *forſwearing*, and for murder too. *Shakeſ. Rich.* III.

Forswea'rer. *n. ſ.* [from *forſwear.*] One who is perjured.

FORT. *n. ſ.* [*fort*, French.] A fortified houſe; a caſtle.

They erected a *fort*, which they called the *fort de l'or*; and from thence they bolted like beaſts of the foreſt. *Bacon.*

Now to their *fort* they are about to ſend
For the loud engines which their iſle defend. *Waller.*

He that views a *fort* to take it,
Plants his artillery 'gainſt the weakeſt part. *Denham's Sophy.*

My fury does, like jealous *forts*, purſue
With death, ev'n ſtrangers who but come to view. *Dryden.*

Fo'rted. *adj.* [from *fort.*] Furniſhed or guarded by forts. Not uſed now.

Your deſert ſpeaks loud, and I ſhould wrong
To lock it in the wards of covert boſom,
When it deſerves with characters of braſs
A *forted* reſidence, 'gainſt the tooth of time
And raſure of oblivion. *Shakeſ. Meaſure for Meaſure.*

FORTH. *adv.* [ꝼoꞃð, Saxon; whence *further* and *furtheſt.*]

1. Forward; onward in time.

From that day *forth* I lov'd that face divine;
From that day *forth* I caſt in careful mind
To ſeek her out. *Fairy Queen, b.* i. *cant.* 9.

2. Forward in place or order.

Look at the ſecond admonition, and ſo *forth*, where they ſpeak in moſt unchriſtian manner. *Whitgifte.*

Mad Pandarus ſteps *forth*, with vengeance vow'd
For Bitias' death. *Dryden's Æn.*

3. Abroad; out of doors.

Uncle, I muſt come *forth.* *Shakeſpeare's Othello.*

I have no mind of feaſting *forth* to-night. *Shakeſpeare.*

Attend you here the door of our ſtern daughter?
Will ſhe not *forth?* *Shakeſpeare.*

When Winter paſt, and Summer ſcarce begun,
Invites them *forth* to labour in the ſun. *Dryden's Virg. Æn.*

4. Out away; beyond the boundary of any place.

They will privily relieve their friends that are *forth*; they will ſend the enemy ſecret advertiſements; and they will not alſo ſtick to draw the enemy privily upon them. *Spenſer.*

Even that ſunſhine brew'd a ſhow'r for him,
That waſh'd his father's fortunes *forth* of France. *Shakeſp.*

5. Out into publick ſtate; publick view.

You may ſet *forth* the ſame with farmhouſes. *Peacham.*

But when your troubled country call'd you *forth*,
Your flaming courage, and your matchleſs worth,
To fierce contention gave a proſp'rous end. *Waller.*

6. Throughly; from beginning to end.

You, couſin,
Whom it concerns to hear this matter *forth*,
Do with your injuries as ſeems you beſt. *Shakeſp.*

7. To a certain degree.

Hence we learn, how far *forth* we may expect juſtification and ſalvation from the ſufferings of Chriſt; no *further* than we are wrought on by his renewing grace. *Hammond.*

8. On to the end.

I repeated the Ave Maria: the inquiſitor bad me ſay *forth*; I ſaid I was taught no more. *Memoir in Strype.*

Forth. *prep.* Out of.

And here's a prophet, that I brought with me
From *forth* the ſtreets of Pomfret. *Shakeſpeare.*

Some *forth* their cabbins peep,
And trembling aſk what news, and do hear ſo
As jealous huſbands, what they would not know. *Donne.*

Forthco'ming. *adj.* [*forth* and *coming.*] Ready to appear; not abſconding; not loſt.

Carry this mad knave to jail: I charge you ſee that he be *forthcoming.* *Shakeſpeare's Taming of the Shrew.*

We'll ſee your trinkets here *forthcoming* all. *Shak. H.* VI.

Forthi'ssuing. *adj.* [*forth* and *iſſue.*] Coming out; coming forward from a covert.

Forthiſſuing thus, ſhe gave him firſt to wield
A weighty axe, with trueſt temper ſteel'd,
And double edg'd. *Pope's Odyſſey, b.* v.

Forthri'ght. *adv.* [*forth* and *right.*] Strait forward; without flexions.

He ever going ſo juſt with the horſe, either *forthright* or turning, that it ſeemed as he borrowed the horſe's body, ſo he lent the horſe his mind. *Sidney, b.* ii.

The river not running *forthright*, but almoſt continually winding, as if the lower ſtreams would return to their ſpring, or that the river had a delight to play with itſelf. *Sidney, b.* ii.

Arrived there, they paſſed in *forthright*;
For ſtill to all the gate ſtood open wide. *Fairy Queen, b.* i.

Here's a maze trod, indeed,
Through *forthrights* and meanders. *Shakeſpeare's Tempeſt.*

Thither *forthright* he rode to rouſe the prey,
That ſhaded by the fern in harbour lay,
And thence diſlodg'd. *Dryden's Knight's Tale.*

Forthwi'th. *adv.* [*forth* and *with.*] Immediately; without delay; at once; ſtrait.

Forthwith he runs, with feigned faithful haſte,
Unto his gueſt; who, after troublous ſights
And dreams, 'gan now tó take more ſound repaſt. *Fa. Qu.*

Few things are ſo reſtrained to any one end or purpoſe, that the ſame being extinct, they ſhould *forthwith* utterly become fruſtrate. *Hooker, b.* v. *ſ.* 42.

Neither did the martial men dally or proſecute the ſervice faintly, but did *forthwith* quench that fire. *Davies on Ireland.*

Forthwith began theſe fury-moving ſounds,
The notes of wrath, the muſick brought from hell,
The rattling drums. *Daniel's Civil War.*

The winged heralds, by command
Of ſov'reign pow'r, throughout the hoſt proclaim
A ſolemn council *forthwith* to be held
At Pandæmonium. *Milton's Paradiſe Loſt, b.* i.

In his paſſage thither one put into his hand a note of the whole conſpiracy, deſiring him to read it *forthwith*, and to remember the giver of it as long as he lived. *South's Sermons.*

Fo'rtieth. *adj.* [from *forty.*] The fourth tenth; next after the thirty-ninth.

What doth it avail
To be the *fortieth* man in an entail? *Donne.*

Burnet ſays, Scotland is not above a *fortieth* part in value to the reſt of Britain; and, with reſpect to the profit that England gains from hence, not the forty thouſandth part. *Swift.*

Fo'rtifiable. *adj.* [from *fortify.*] What may be fortified.

Fortifica'tion. *n. ſ.* [*fortification*, French, from *fortify.*]

1. The ſcience of military architecture.

Fortification is an art ſhewing how to fortify a place with ramparts, parapets, moats, and other bulwarks; to the end that a ſmall number of men within may be able to defend themſelves, for a conſiderable time, againſt the aſſaults of a numerous army without; ſo that the enemy, in attacking them, muſt of neceſſity ſuffer great loſs. It is either regular or irregular; and, with reſpect to time, may be diſtinguiſhed into durable and temporary. *Harris.*

The Phœacians, tho' an unwarlike nation, yet underſtood the art of *fortification.* *Notes on the Odyſſey.*

2. A place built for ſtrength.

Excellent devices were uſed to make even their ſports profitable; images, battles, and *fortifications* being then delivered to their memory, which, after ſtronger judgments, might diſpenſe ſome advantage. *Sidney, b.* ii.

Fo'rtifier. *n. ſ.* [from *fortify.*]

1. One who erects works for defence.

The *fortifier* of Pendennis made his advantage of the commodity afforded by the ground. *Carew's Survey of Cornwal.*

2. One who ſupports or ſecures; one who upholds.

He was led forth by many armed men, who often had been the *fortifiers* of wickedneſs, to the place of execution. *Sidney.*

To **FO'RTIFY.** *v. a.* [*fortifier*, French.]

1. To ſtrengthen againſt attacks by walls or works.

Great Dunſinane he ſtrongly *fortifies.* *Shakeſ. Macbeth.*

He *fortified* the city againſt beſieging. *Eccluſ.* l. 4.

2. To confirm; to encourage.

It greatly *fortified* her deſires, to ſee that her mother had the like deſires. *Sidney, b.* ii.

3. To fix; to eſtabliſh in reſolution.

But in-born worth that fortune can controul,
New-ſtrung and ſtiffer bent her ſofter ſoul:
The heroine aſſum'd the woman's place,
Confirm'd her mind, and *fortify'd* her face. *Dryden.*

A young man, before he leaves the ſhelter of his father's houſe, ſhould be *fortified* with reſolution to ſecure his virtues. *Locke.*

Fortila'ge. *n. ſ.* [from *fort.*] A little fort; a blockhouſe.

In all ſtraights and narrow paſſages there ſhould be ſome little *fortilage*, or wooden caſtle ſet, which ſhould keep and command the ſtraight. *Spenſer on Ireland.*

FO'RTIN. *n. ſ.* [French.] A little fort raiſed to defend a camp, particularly in a ſiege. *Hanmer.*

Thou haſt talk'd
Of paliſadoes, *fortins*, parapets. *Shakeſ. Henry* IV. *p.* i.

Fo'rtitude. *n. ſ.* [*fortitudo*, Latin.]

1. Courage; bravery; magnanimity; greatneſs of mind; power of acting or ſuffering well.

The king-becoming graces,
Devotion, patience, courage, *fortitude*,
I have no reliſh of them. *Shakeſpeare's Macbeth.*

The better *fortitude*
Of patience, and heroick martyrdom
Unſung. *Milton's Paradiſe Loſt, b.* ix.

Fortitude is the guard and ſupport of the other virtues; and without courage, a man will ſcarce keep ſteady to his duty, and fill up the character of a truly worthy man. *Locke.*

2. Strength; force. Not in uſe.

He wrongs his fame,
Deſpairing of his own arm's *fortitude*,
To join with witches and the help of hell! *Shakeſ. H.* VI.

Fo'rtlet. *n. ſ.* [from *fort.*] A little fort.

Fo'rtnight. *n. ſ.* [contracted from *fourteen nights*, ꝼeoꞃꞇyne niht, Saxon. It was the cuſtom of the ancient northern nations to count time by nights: thus we ſay, *this day ſevennight.* So *Tacitus, Non dierum numerum ut nos, ſed noctium computant.*] The ſpace of two weeks.

She would give her a leſſon for walking ſo late, that ſhould make her keep within doors for one *fortnight.* *Sidney, b.* ii.

Hanging in a deep well, ſomewhat above the water, for ſome *fortnights* ſpace, is an excellent means of making drink freſh and quick. *Bacon's Natural Hiſtory.*

About a *fortnight* before I had finiſhed it, his majeſty's declaration for liberty of conſcience came abroad. *Dryden.*

He often had it in his head, but never, with much apprehenſion, 'till about a *fortnight* before. *Swift.*

Fo'rtress. *n. ſ.* [*fortereſſe*, French.] A ſtrong hold; a fortified place; a caſtle of defence.

Breaking forth like a ſudden tempeſt, he over-ran all, breaking down all the holds and *fortreſſes*. *Spenſer on Ireland.*

The trump of death ſounds in their hearing ſhrill;
Their weapon, faith; their *fortreſs* was the grave. *Fairfax.*

God is our *fortreſs*, in whoſe conqu'ring name
Let us reſolve to ſcale their flinty bulwarks. *Shak. Hen.* VI.

There is no ſuch way to give defence to abſurd doctrines, as to guard them round about with legions of obſcure and undefined words; which yet makes theſe retreats more like the dens of robbers, or holes of foxes, than the *fortreſſes* of fair warriors. *Locke.*

FORTUITOUS. *adj.* [*fortuit*, French; *fortuitus*, Lat.] Accidental; caſual; happening by chance.

A wonder then it muſt be, that there ſhould be any man found ſo ſtupid as to perſuade himſelf that this moſt beautiful world could be produced by the *fortuitous* concourſe of atoms. *Ray on the Creation.*

If caſual concourſe did the world compoſe,
And things and acts *fortuitous* aroſe,
Then any thing might come from any thing;
For how from chance can conſtant order ſpring. *Blackmore.*

FORTU'ITOUSLY. *adv.* [from *fortuitous.*] Accidentally; caſually; by chance.

It is partly evaporated into air, and partly diluted into water, and *fortuitouſly* ſhared between all the elements. *Rogers.*

FORTU'ITOUSNESS. *n. ſ.* [from *fortuitous.*] Accident; chance; hit.

FO'RTUNATE. *adj.* [*fortunatus*, Latin.] Lucky; happy; ſucceſsful; not ſubject to miſcarriage. Uſed of perſons or actions.

I am moſt *fortunate* thus accidentally to encounter you: you have ended my buſineſs, and I will merrily accompany you home. *Shakeſpeare's Coriolanus.*

He ſigh'd; and could not but their fate deplore,
So wretched now, ſo *fortunate* before. *Dryd. Knight's Tale.*

No, there is a neceſſity in fate
Why ſtill the brave bold man is *fortunate*:
He keeps his object ever full in ſight,
And that aſſurance holds him firm and right:
True, 'tis a narrow path that leads to bliſs,
But right before there is no precipice;
Fear makes men look aſide, and ſo their footing miſs. *Dry.*

FO'RTUNATELY. *adv.* [from *fortunate.*] Happily; ſucceſsfully.

Bright Eliza rul'd Britannia's ſtate,
And boldly wiſe, and *fortunately* great. *Prior.*

FO'RTUNATENESS. *n. ſ.* [from *fortunate.*] Happineſs; good luck; ſucceſs.

O me, ſaid ſhe, whoſe greateſt *fortunateneſs* is more unfortunate than my ſiſter's greateſt unfortunateneſs. *Sidney, b.* ii.

FO'RTUNE. *n. ſ.* [*fortuna*, Latin; *fortune*, French.]

1. The power ſuppoſed to diſtribute the lots of life according to her own humour.

Fortune, that arrant whore,
Ne'er turns the key to th' poor. *Shakeſpeare's King Lear.*

Though *fortune's* malice overthrow my ſtate,
My mind exceeds the compaſs of her wheel. *Shakeſ. H.* VI.

2. The good or ill that befals man.

Rejoice, ſaid he, to-day;
In you the *fortune* of Great Britain lies:
Among ſo brave a people you are they
Whom heav'n has choſe to fight for ſuch a prize. *Dryden.*

The adequate meaning of chance, as diſtinguiſhed from *fortune*, in that the latter is underſtood to befal only rational agents, but chance to be among inanimate bodies. *Bentley.*

3. The chance of life; means of living.

His father dying, he was driven to London to ſeek his *fortune*. *Swift.*

4. Event; ſucceſs good or bad.

This terreſtrial globe has been ſurrounded by the *fortune* and boldneſs of many navigators. *Temple.*

No, he ſhall eat, and die with me, or live;
Our equal crimes ſhall equal *fortune* give. *Dryd. Innocence.*

5. Eſtate; poſſeſſions.

If thou do'ſt
As this inſtructs thee, thou do'ſt make thy way
To noble *fortunes*. *Shakeſpeare's King Lear.*

That eyeleſs head of thine was firſt fram'd fleſh
To raiſe my *fortunes*. *Shakeſpeare's King Lear.*

But tell me, Tityrus, what heav'nly power
Preſerv'd your *fortunes* in that fatal hour? *Dryd. Virg. Paſt.*

The fate which governs poets, thought it fit
He ſhould not raiſe his *fortunes* by his wit. *Dryden.*

He was younger ſon to a gentleman of a good birth, but ſmall *fortune*. *Swift.*

6. The portion of a man or woman: generally of a woman.

I am thought ſome heireſs rich in lands,
Fled to eſcape a cruel guardian's hands;
Which may produce a ſtory worth the telling,
Of the next ſparks that go a *fortune* ſtealing. *Prol. to Orphan.*

The *fortune* hunters have already caſt their eyes upon her, and take care to plant themſelves in her view. *Spectator.*

When miſs delights in her ſpinnet,
A fiddler may a *fortune* get. *Swift.*

7. Futurity; future events.

You who mens *fortunes* in their faces read,
To find out mine, look not, alas, on me:
But mark her face, and all the features heed;
For only there is writ my deſtiny. *Cowley's Miſtreſs.*

To FO'RTUNE. *v. n.* [from the noun.] To befall; to fall out; to happen; to come caſually to paſs.

It *fortuned*, as fair it then befell,
Behind his back, unweeting, where he ſtood,
Of ancient time there was a ſpringing well,
From which faſt trickled forth a ſilver flood. *Fairy Queen.*

It *fortuned* the ſame night that a Chriſtian, ſerving a Turk in the camp, ſecretly gave the watchmen warning that the Turks prepared the next day to give a general aſſault. *Knolles.*

I'll tell you as we paſs along,
That you will wonder what hath *fortuned*. *Shakeſpeare.*

Here *fortun'd* Curl to ſlide. *Pope's Dunciad.*

FO'RTUNED. *adj.* Supplied by fortune.

Not th' imperious ſhew
Of the full *fortun'd* Cæſar ever ſhall
Be brook'd with me. *Shakeſp. Ant. and Cleopatra.*

FO'RTUNEBOOK. *n. ſ.* [*fortune* and *book.*] A book conſulted to know fortune or future events.

Thou know'ſt a face, in whoſe each look
Beauty lays ope love's *fortunebook*;
On whoſe fair revolutions wait
The obſequious motions of love's fate. *Craſhaw.*

FORTUNEHU'NTER. *n. ſ.* [*fortune* and *hunt.*] A man whoſe employment is to enquire after women with great portions to enrich himſelf by marrying them.

We muſt, however, diſtinguiſh between *fortunehunters* and fortuneſtealers. *Spectator*, N°. 312.

To FO'RTUNETELL. *v. n.* [*fortune* and *tell.*]

1. To pretend to the power of revealing futurity.

We are ſimple men; we do not know what's brought to paſs under the profeſſion of *fortunetelling*. *Shakeſpeare.*

I'll conjure you, I'll *fortunetell* you. *Shakeſpeare.*

The gypſies were to divide the money got by ſtealing linnen, or by *fortunetelling*. *Walton's Angler.*

2. To reveal futurity.

Here, while his canting drone-pipe ſcan'd
The myſtick figures of her hand,
He tipples palmeſtry, and dines
On all her *fortunetelling* lines. *Cleaveland.*

FO'RTUNETELLER. *n. ſ.* [*fortune* and *teller.*] One who cheats common people by pretending to the knowledge of futurity.

They brought one Pinch, a hungry lean-fac'd villain,
A thread-bare juggler, and a *fortuneteller*. *Shakeſpeare.*

A Welchman being at a ſeſſions-houſe, and ſeeing the priſoners hold up hands at the bar, related to ſome of his acquaintance that the judges were good *fortunetellers*; for if they did but look upon their hand, they could certainly tell whether they ſhould live or die. *Bacon's Apophthegms.*

Haſt thou given credit to vain predictions of men, to dreams or *fortunetellers*, or gone about to know any ſecret things by lot? *Duppa's Rules for Devotion.*

There needs no more than impudence on one ſide, and a ſuperſtitious credulity on the other, to the ſetting up of a *fortuneteller*. *L'Eſtrange, Fable* 94.

Long ago a *fortuneteller*
Exactly ſaid what now befell her. *Swift.*

FO'RTY. *adj.* [feopeꞃꞇıᵹ, Saxon.] Four times ten.

On fair ground I could beat *forty* of them. *Shak. Coriol.*

He that upon levity quits his ſtation, in hopes to be better, 'tis *forty* to one loſes. *L'Eſtrange.*

FO'RUM. *n. ſ.* [Latin.] Any publick place.

The *forum* was a publick place in Rome, where lawyers and orators made their ſpeeches before the proper judge in matters of property, or in criminal caſes, to accuſe or excuſe, to complain or defend. *Watts's Improvement of the Mind.*

Cloſe to the bay great Neptune's fane adjoins,
And near a *forum* flank'd with marble ſhines,
Where the bold youth, the num'rous fleets to ſtore,
Shape the broad ſail, or ſmooth the taper oar. *Pope.*

To FORWA'NDER. *v. a.* [*for* and *wander.*] To wander wildly and wearily.

The better part now of the ling'ring day
They travelled had, when as they far eſpy'd
A weary wight *forwand'ring* by the way. *Fairy Queen, b.* i.

FO'RWARD. *adv.* [fopeapꝺ, Saxon.] Towards; to a part or place before; onward; progreſſively.

When fervent ſorrow ſlaked was,
She up aroſe, reſolving him to find
Alive or dead, and *forward* forth doth paſs. *Fairy Queen.*

From ſmaller things the mind of the hearers may go *forward* to the knowledge of greater, and climb up from the loweſt to the higheſt things. *Hooker, b.* v. *ſ.* 20.

He that is uſed to go *forward*, and findeth a ſtop, falleth of his own favour, and is not the thing he was. *Bacon's Eſſays.*

FO'RWARD. *adj.* [from the adverb.]

1. Warm; earnest.

They would that we should remember the poor, which I also was *forward* to do. *Gal.* ii. 10.

2. Ardent; eager; hot; violent.

You'll still be too *forward*. *Shakesp. Two Gent. of Verona.*

Unskill'd to dart the pointed spear,
Or lead the *forward* youth to noble war. *Prior.*

3. Ready; confident; presumptuous.

Old Butes' form he took, Anchises' squire,
Now left to rule Ascanius by his sire;
And thus salutes the boy, too *forward* for his years. *Dryd.*

4. Not reserved; not over modest.

'Tis a per'lous boy,
Bold, quick, ingenious, *forward*, capable;
He's all the mother's from the top to toe. *Shakes. Rich.* III.

5. Premature; early ripe.

Short Summer lightly has a *forward* Spring. *Sh. R.* III.

6. Quick; ready; hasty.

The mind makes not that benefit it should of the information it receives from civil or natural historians, in being too *forward* or two slow in making observations on the particular facts recorded in them. *Locke.*

Had they, who would persuade us that there are innate principles, considered separately the parts out of which these propositions are made, they would not perhaps have been so *forward* to believe they were innate. *Locke.*

7. Antecedent; anterior: opposed to posterior.

Let us take the instant by the *forward* top;
For we are old, and on our quick'st decrees
Th' inaudible and noiseless foot of time
Steals, ere we can effect them. *Shakespeare.*

8. Not behindhand; not inferiour.

My good Camillo,
She is as *forward* of her breeding, as
She is i' th' rear o' our birth. *Shakesp. Winter's Tale.*

To FO'RWARD. *v. a.* [from the adverb.]

1. To hasten; to quicken; to accelerate in growth or improvement.

As we house hot country plants, as lemons, to save them; so we may house our own country plants to *forward* them, and make them come in the cold seasons. *Bacon's Nat. Hist.*

Whenever I shine,
I *forward* the grass and I ripen the vine. *Swift.*

2. To patronise; to advance.

FO'RWARDER. *n. s.* [from *forward.*] He who promotes any thing.

FO'RWARDLY. *adv.* [from the adjective.] Eagerly; hastily; quickly.

The sudden and surprising turns we ourselves have felt, should not suffer us too *forwardly* to admit presumption. *Atter.*

FO'RWARDNESS. *n. s.* [from *forward.*]

1. Eagerness; ardour; readiness to act.

Absolutely we cannot discommend, we cannot absolutely approve either willingness to live, or *forwardness* to die. *Hook.*

Is it so strange a matter to find a good thing furthered by ill men of a sinister intent and purpose, whose *forwardness* is not therefore a bridle to such as favour the same cause with a better and sincere meaning. *Hooker, b.* iv. *s.* 9.

If the great ones were in *forwardness*, the people were in fury, entertaining this airy phantasm with incredible affection. *Bacon's Henry* VII.

2. Quickness; readiness.

He had such a dextrous proclivity, as his teachers were fain to restrain his *forwardness*; to the end that his brothers, who were under the same training, might hold pace with him. *Wotton.*

3. Earliness; early ripeness.

4. Confidence; assurance; want of modesty.

In France it is usual to bring their children into company, and to cherish in them, from their infancy, a kind of *forwardness* and assurance. *Addison on Italy.*

FO'RWARDS. *adv.* Straight before; progressively.

The Rhodian ship passed through the whole Roman fleet, backwards and *forwards* several times, carrying intelligence to Drepanum. *Arbuthnot on Coins.*

FOSSE. *n. s.* [*fossa*, Latin; *fos*, Welch] A ditch; a moat; an intrenchment thrown up by the spade.

FO'SSET. See FAUCET.

FO'SSEWAY. *n. s.* [*fosse* and *way.*] One of the great Roman inroads through England, so called from the ditches on each side.

FO'SSIL. *adj.* [*fossilis*, Latin; *fossile*, French.] That which is dug out of the earth.

The *fossil* shells are many of them of the same kinds with those that now appear upon the neighbouring shores; and the rest such as may be presumed to be at the bottom of the adjacent seas. *Woodward's Natural History.*

Fossil or rock salt, and sal gemm, differ not in nature from each other; nor from the common salt of salt springs, or that of the sea, when pure. *Woodward's Natural History.*

It is of a middle nature, between *fossil* and animal, being produced from animal excrements, intermixed with vegetable salts. *Arbuthnot on Aliments.*

FO'SSIL. *n. s.*

In this globe are many other bodies, which, because we discover them by digging into the bowels of the earth, are called by one common name *fossils*; under which are comprehended metals and minerals. *Locke.*

Many kinds of *fossils* are very oddly and elegantly shaped. *Bentley's Sermons.*

By the word *fossil*, used as a denomination of one of three general divisions of natural productions, we understand bodies formed usually within the earth, sometimes on its surface, and sometimes in waters; of a plain and simple structure, in which there is no visible difference of parts, no distinction of vessels and their contents, but every portion of which is similar to and perfect as the whole. *Hill's Mat. Med.*

To FO'STER. *v. a.* [fostrian, Saxon.]

1. To nurse; to feed; to support; to train up.

Thy threat'ning colours now wind up,
And tame the savage spirit of wild war;
That, like a lion *foster'd* up at hand,
It may lie gently at the foot of peace. *Shakesp. King John.*

Some say that ravens *foster* forlorn children. *Shakespeare.*

Our kingdom's earth should not be soil'd
With that dear blood, which it hath *fostered.* *Shakes. R.* II.

That base wretch,
Bred on alms, and *foster'd* with cold dishes,
With scraps o' th' court. *Shakespeare's Cymbeline.*

Fostering has always been a stronger alliance than blood. *Davies on Ireland.*

No more let Ireland brag her harmless nation
Fosters no venom, since that Scots plantation. *Cleaveland.*

The son of Mulciber,
Found in the fire, and *foster'd* in the plains,
A shepherd and a king at once he reigns. *Dryd. Æn. b.* vii.

2. To pamper; to encourage.

A prince of great courage and beauty, but *fostered* up in blood by his naughty father. *Sidney, b.* ii.

3. To cherish; to forward.

Ye *fostering* breezes, blow;
Ye softening dews, ye tender showers descend. *Thomson.*

FO'STERAGE. *n. s.* [from *foster.*] The charge of nursing; alterage.

Some one adjoining to this lake had the charge and *fosterage* of this child, who being, perchance, but some base and obscure creature, was cast from the top of her temple into the lake adjoining; and, as the poets have feigned, changed by Venus into a fish, all but her face. *Raleigh's History.*

FOSTERBRO'THER. *n. s.* [fostеr broðer, Saxon.] One bred at the same pap; one fed by the same nurse.

FOSTERCHI'LD. *n. s.* [fostеr cild, Saxon.] A child nursed by a woman not the mother, or bred by a man not the father.

The *fosterchildren* do love and are beloved of their fosterfathers. *Davies on Ireland.*

The goddess thus beguil'd,
With pleasant stories, her false *fosterchild.* *Addis. Ov. Met.*

FOSTERDA'M. *n. s.* [*foster* and *dam.*] A nurse; one that performs the office of a mother by giving food to a young child.

There, by the wolf, were laid the martial twins:
Intrepid on her swelling dugs they hung;
The *fosterdam* loll'd out her fawning tongue. *Dryden's Æn.*

FOSTEREA'RTH. *n. s.* [*foster* and *earth.*] Earth by which the plant is nourished, though it did not grow at first in it.

In vain, the nursling grove
Seems fair a while, cherish'd with *fosterearth*;
But when the alien compost is exhaust,
Its native poverty again prevails! *Phillips.*

FO'STERER. *n. s.* [from *foster.*] A nurse; one who gives food in the place of a parent.

In Ireland they put their children to *fosterers*; the rich men selling, the meaner sort buying the alterage of their children: in the opinion of the Irish fostering has always been a stronger alliance than blood; and the fosterchildren do love, and are beloved of their fosterfathers and their sept, more than of their own natural parents and kindred. *Davies on Ireland.*

FOSTERFA'THER. *n. s.* [fostеrfaðer, Saxon.] One who gives food in the place of the father.

In Ireland fosterchildren do love and are beloved of their *fosterfathers*, and their sept, more than of their own natural parents and kindred. *Davies on Ireland.*

The duke of Bretagne having been an host and a kind of parent or *fosterfather* to the king, in his tenderness of age and weakness of fortune, did look for aid this time from king Henry. *Bacon's Henry* VII.

Tyrrheus, the *fosterfather* of the beast,
Then clench'd a hatchet in his horny fist. *Dryden's Æn.*

FOSTERMO'THER. *n. s.* [*foster* and *mother.*] A nurse.

FOSTERNU'RSE. *n. s.* [*foster* and *nurse.*] This is an improper compound, because *foster* and *nurse* mean the same.] A nurse.

Our *fosternurse* of nature is repose,
The which he lacks. *Shakespeare's King Lear.*

FO'STERSON. *n. s.* [*foster* and *son.*] One fed and educated, though not the son by nature.

Mature in years, to ready honours move;
O of celestial seed! O *fosterson* of Jove! *Dryd. Virg. Past.*

FOUGA'DE. *n. s.* [French.] In the art of war, a sort of little mine in the manner of a well, scarce more than ten feet wide and twelve deep, dug under some work or fortification, and charged with barrels or sacks of gunpowder to blow it up, and covered over with earth. *Dict.*

FOUGHT. The preterite and participle of *fight.*

FO'UGHTEN. [The passive participle of *fight.* Rarely used.] Contested; disputed by arms.

On the *foughten* field
Michael and his angels, prevalent
Encamping, plac'd in guard their watches round
Cherubick waving fires. *Milton's Paradise Lost, b.* vi.

FOUL. *adj.* [*fuls,* Gothick; ful, Saxon.]

1. Not clean; filthy; dirty; miry. Through most of its significations it is opposed to *fair.*

My face is *foul* with weeping. *Job* xvi. 16.

It's monstrous labour when I wash my brain,
And it grows *fouler.* *Shakes. Ant. and Cleopatra.*

He that can travel in deep and *foul* ways, ought not to say that he cannot walk in fair. *Tillotson's Sermons.*

The stream is *foul* with stains
Of rushing torrents and descending rains. *Addison.*

2. Impure; polluted; full of filth.

With *foul* mouth,
And in the witness of his proper ear,
To call him villain. *Shakes. Measure for Measure.*

Kill thy physician, and the fee bestow
Upon the *foul* disease. *Shakespeare's King Lear.*

Intemperance and sensuality debase mens minds, clog their spirits, and make them gross, *foul,* listless and unactive. *Tillots.*

3. Wicked; detestable; abominable.

Jesus rebuked the *foul* spirit. *Mar.* ix. 25.

He hates *foul* leasings and vile flattery,
Two filthy blots in noble gentery. *Hubberd's Tale.*

This is the grossest and most irrational supposition, as well as the *foulest* atheism, that can be imagined. *Hale.*

Satire has always shone among the rest,
And is the boldest way, if not the best,
To tell men truly of their *foulest* faults,
To laugh at their vain deeds, and vainer thoughts. *Dryden.*

4. Not lawful; not according to the established rules.

By *foul* play were we heav'd thence,
But blessedly help'd hither. *Shakespeare's Tempest.*

5. Hateful; ugly; loathsome.

Th' other half did woman's shape retain,
Most loathsom, filthy, *foul,* and full of vile disdain. *F. Qu.*

Hast thou forgot
The *foul* witch Sycorax, who with age and envy
Was grown into a hoop? *Shakespeare's Tempest.*

Foul sights do rather displease, in that they excite the memory of *foul* things than in the immediate objects; and therefore, in pictures, those *foul* sights do not much offend. *Bacon.*

6. Disgraceful; shameful.

Too well I see and rue the dire event,
That with sad overthrow and *foul* defeat
Hath lost us heav'n. *Milton's Paradise Lost, b.* i.

Who first seduc'd them to that *foul* revolt? *Milt. P. Lost.*

Reason half extinct,
Or impotent, or else approving, sees
The *foul* disorder. *Thomson's Spring.*

7. Coarse; gross.

You will have no notion of delicacies, if you table with them: they are all for rank and *foul* feeding, and spoil the best provisions in cooking. *Felton on the Classicks.*

8. Full of gross humours, or bad matter; wanting purgation or mundification.

You perceive the body of our kingdom,
How *foul* it is; what rank diseases grow,
And with what danger near the heart of it. *Shakes. H.* IV.

9. Not bright; not serene.

Who's there besides *foul* weather?
One minded like the weather, most inquietly. *Sh. K. Lear.*

Be fair or *foul,* or rain or shine,
The joys I have profess'd, in spite of fate are mine. *Dryd.*

10. With rough force; with unseasonable violence.

So in this throng bright Sacharissa far'd,
Oppress'd by those who strove to be her guard:
As ships, though never so obsequious, fall
Foul in a tempest on their admiral. *Waller.*

In his sallies their men might fall *foul* of each other. *Clarend.*

The great art of the devil, and the principal deceit of the heart, is to keep fair with God himself, while men fall *foul* upon his laws. *South's Sermons.*

11. [Among seamen.] Entangled: as, a rope is *foul* of the anchor.

To FOUL. *v. a.* [fulan, Saxon.] To daub; to bemire; to make filthy; to dirty.

Sweep and cleanse your walks from autumnal leaves, lest the worms draw them into their holes, and *foul* your gardens. *Evelyn's Kalendar.*

While Traulus all his ordure scatters,
To *foul* the man he chiefly flatters. *Swift.*

She *fouls* a smock more in one hour than the kitchen-maid doth in a week. *Swift's Directions to Servants.*

FO'ULFACED. *adj.* [*foul* and *faced.*] Having an ugly or hateful visage.

If black scandal, or *foulfac'd* reproach,
Attend the sequel of your imposition,
Your mere enforcement shall acquittance me
From all the impure blots and stains thereof. *Shakes. R.* III.

FO'ULLY. *adv.* [from *foul.*] Filthily; nastily; odiously; hatefully; scandalously; disgracefully; shamefully.

We in the world's wide mouth
Live scandaliz'd, and *foully* spoken of. *Shakesp. Henry* IV.

The letter to the protector was gilded over with many smooth words; but the other two did fully and *foully* set forth his obstinacy, avarice and ambition. *Hayward.*

O brother, brother! Filbert still is true;
I *foully* wrong'd him: do, forgive me, do. *Gay.*

FOULMOU'THED. *adj.* [*foul* and *mouth.*] Scurrilous; habituated to the use of opprobrious terms and epithets.

My lord, he speaks most vilely of you, like a *foulmouth'd* man as he is, and said he would cudgel you. *Shak. H.* IV.

It was allowed by every body, that so *foulmouthed* a witness never appeared in any cause. *Addison.*

My reputation is too well established in the world to receive any hurt from such a *foulmouthed* scoundrel as he. *Arbuth.*

Now singing shrill, and scolding oft between,
Scolds answer *foulmouth'd* scolds; bad neighbourhood I ween. *Swift.*

FO'ULNESS. *n. s.* [from *foul.*]

1. The quality of being foul; filthiness; nastiness.

The ancients were wont to make garments that were not destroyed but purified by fire; and whereas the spots or *foulness* of other cloaths are washed out, in these they were usually burnt away. *Wilkins's Math. Magic.*

2. Pollution; impurity.

It is no vicious blot, murder, or *foulness,*
No unchaste action, or dishonour'd step,
That hath depriv'd me of your grace and favour. *Shakesp.*

There is not so chaste a nation as this, nor so free from all pollution or *foulness*: it is the virgin of the world. *Bacon.*

3. Hatefulness; atrociousness.

He by an affection sprung up from excessive beauty, should not delight in horrible *foulness.* *Sidney.*

Consul, you are too mild:
The *foulness* of some facts takes thence all mercy:
Report it to the senate. *Ben. Johnson's Catiline.*

It is the wickedness of a whole life, discharging all its filth and *foulness* into this one quality, as into a great sink or common shore. *South's Sermons.*

4. Ugliness; deformity.

He's fallen in love with your *foulness,* and she'll fall in love with my anger. *Shakespeare's As you like it.*

The fury laid aside
Her looks and limbs, and with new methods tried
The *foulness* of th' infernal form to hide. *Dryden's Æn.*

5. Dishonesty; want of candour.

Piety is opposed to hypocrisy and insincerity, and all falseness or *foulness* of intentions; especially to that personated devotion, under which any kind of impiety is wont to be disguised. *Hammond's Fundamentals.*

FOUND. The preterite and participle passive of *find.*

I am sought of them that asked not for me: I am *found* of them that sought me not. *Is.* lxv. 1.

To FOUND. *v. a.* [*fundare,* Latin; *fonder,* French.]

1. To lay the basis of any building.

It fell not; for it was *founded* upon a rock. *Math.* vii.

He hath *founded* it upon the seas, and established it upon the floods. *Ps.* xxiv. 2.

2. To build; to raise.

These tunes of reason are Amphion's lyre,
Wherewith he did the Theban city *found.* *Davies.*

They Gabian walls, and strong Fidenæ rear,
Nomentum, Bola with Pometia *found,*
And raise Colatian tow'rs on rocky ground. *Dryden's Æn.*

3. To establish; to erect.

This also shall they gain by their delay
In the wide wilderness; there they shall *found*
Their government, and their great senate chuse,
Through the twelve tribes, to rule by laws ordain'd. *Milt.*

He *founding* a library, gathered together the acts of the kings and prophets. *2 Mac.* ii. 13.

4. To give birth or original to: as, he *founded* an art; he *founded* a family.

5. To raise upon, as on a principle or ground.

Though some have made use of the opinion of some schoolmen,

ſchoolmen, that dominion is *founded* in grace; yet as that is but an opinion, ſo were it admitted as the moſt certain truth, it could never warrant any ſuch ſanguinary method. *Decay of Piety.*

A right to the uſe of the creatures is *founded* originally in the right a man has to ſubſiſt. *Locke.*

Power, *founded* on contract, can deſcend only to him who has right by that contract. *Locke.*

The reputation of the Iliad they *found* upon the ignorance of his times. *Pope's Preface to the Iliad.*

6. To fix firm.

Fleance is eſcap'd.
—Then comes my fit again: I had elſe been perfect,
Whole as the marble, *founded* as the rock. *Shakeſ. Macbeth.*

To Found. *v. a.* [*fundere*, Latin; *fondre*, French.] To form by melting and pouring into moulds; to caſt.

Founda'tion. *n. ſ.* [*fondation*, French.]

1. The baſis or lower parts of an edifice.

The ſtatelineſs of houſes, the goodlineſs of trees, when we behold them, delighteth the eye; but that *foundation* which beareth up the one, that root which miniſtreth unto the other nouriſhment and life, is in the boſom of the earth concealed. *Hooker, b.* i. *ſ.* 1.

That is the way to make the city flat,
To bring the roof to the *foundation*,
To bury all. *Shakeſpeare's Coriolanus.*

O Jove, I think,
Foundations fly the wretched; ſuch, I mean,
Where they ſhould be reliev'd. *Shakeſpeare's Coriolanus.*

I draw a line along the ſhore;
I lay the deep *foundations* of a wall,
And Enos, nam'd from me, the city call. *Dryden's Æn.*

2. The act of fixing the baſis.

Ne'er to theſe chambers where the mighty reſt,
Since their *foundation*, came a nobler gueſt. *Tickel.*

3. The principles or ground on which any notion is raiſed.

If we give way to our paſſions, we do but gratify ourſelves for the preſent, in order to our future diſquiet; but if we reſiſt and conquer them, we lay the *foundation* of perpetual peace in our minds. *Tillotſon, Sermon* 6.

That ſhe ſhould be ſubject to her huſband, the laws of mankind and cuſtoms of nations have ordered it ſo; and there is a *foundation* in nature for it. *Locke.*

4. Original; riſe.

Throughout the world, even from the firſt *foundation* thereof, all men have either been taken as lords or lawful kings in their own houſes. *Hooker, b.* i. *ſ.* 10.

5. A revenue ſettled and eſtabliſhed for any purpoſe, particularly charity.

He had an opportunity of going to ſchool on a *foundation*. *Swift.*

6. Eſtabliſhment; ſettlement.

Fo'under. *n. ſ.* [from *found*.]

1. A builder; one who raiſes an edifice; one who preſides at the erection of a city.

Of famous cities we the *founders* know;
But rivers, old as ſeas to which they go,
Are nature's bounty: 'tis of more renown
To make a river than to build a town. *Waller.*

Nor was Prœneſte's *founder* wanting there,
Whom fame reports the ſon of Mulciber;
Found in the fire, and foſter'd in the plains;
A ſhepherd and a king at once he reigns. *Dryden's Æn.*

2. One who eſtabliſhes a revenue for any purpoſe.

The wanting orphans ſaw with wat'ry eyes
Their *founders* charity in the duſt laid low. *Dryden.*

This hath been experimentally proved beyond contradiction, by the honourable *founder* of this lecture in his treatiſe of the air. *Bentley.*

3. One from whom any thing has its original or beginning.

And the rude notions of pedantick ſchools
Blaſpheme the ſacred *founder* of our rules. *Roſcommon.*

When Jove, who ſaw from high, with juſt diſdain,
The dead inſpir'd with vital breath again,
Struck to the center with his flaming dart
Th' unhappy *founder* of the godlike art. *Dryden's Æn.*

King James I. the *founder* of the Stuart race, had he not confined all his views to the peace of his own reign, his ſon had not been involved in ſuch fatal troubles. *Addiſ. Freehold.*

Nor can the ſkilful herald trace
The *founder* of thy ancient race. *Swift.*

4. [*Fondeur*, French.] A caſter; one who forms figures by caſting melted matter into moulds.

Founders add a little antimony to their bell-metal, to make it more ſonorous; and ſo pewterers to their pewter, to make it ſound more clear like ſilver. *Grew's Muſæum.*

To Fo'under. *v. a* [*fondre*, French.] To cauſe ſuch a ſoreneſs and tenderneſs in a horſe's foot, that he is unable to ſet it to the ground.

Phœbus' ſteeds are *founder'd*,
Or night kept chain'd below. *Shakeſpeare's Tempeſt.*

I have *foundered* nine ſcore and odd poſts; and here, travel-tainted as I am, have, in my pure and immaculate valour, taken Sir John Colevile of the Dale, a moſt furious knight: but what of that? he ſaw me and yielded. *Shakeſ. Henry* IV.

Thy ſtumbling *founder'd* jade can trot as high
As any other Pegaſus can fly;
So the dull eel moves nimbler in the mud,
Than all the ſwift-finn'd racers of the flood. *Dorſet.*

Brutes find out where their talents lie:
A bear will not attempt to fly;
A *founder'd* horſe will oft debate,
Before he tries a five-barr'd gate. *Swift.*

If you find a gentleman fond of your horſe, perſuade your maſter to ſell him, becauſe he is vicious, and *foundered* into the bargain. *Swift's Directions to the Groom.*

Men of diſcretion, whom people in power may with little ceremony load as heavy as they pleaſe, drive them through the hardeſt and deepeſt roads, without danger of *foundering* or breaking their backs, and will be ſure to find them neither reſty nor vicious. *Swift.*

To Fo'under. *v. n.* [from *fond*, French, the bottom.]

1. To ſink to the bottom.

New ſhips, built at thoſe rates, have been ready to *founder* in the ſeas with every extraordinary ſtorm. *Raleigh's Eſſays.*

2. To fail; to miſcarry.

In this point
All his tricks *founder*; and he brings his phyſick
After his patient's death. *Shakeſpeare's Henry* VIII.

Fo'undery. *n. ſ.* [*fonderi*, Fr. from *found*.] A place where figures are formed of melted metal; a caſtinghouſe.

Fo'undling. *n. ſ.* [from *found* of *find*.] A child expoſed to chance; a child found without any parent or owner.

We, like baſtards, are laid abroad, even as *foundlings*, to be trained up by grief and ſorrow. *Sidney.*

I paſs the *foundling* by, a race unknown,
At doors expos'd, whom matrons make their own,
And into noble families advance
A nameleſs iſſue; the blind work of chance. *Dryd. Juven.*

I ſhall mention a piece of charity which is practiſed by moſt of the nations about us: I mean a proviſion for *foundlings*, or for thoſe children who, for want of ſuch a proviſion, are expoſed to the barbarity of cruel and unnatural parents. *Addiſon.*

The goddeſs long had mark'd the child's diſtreſs,
And long had ſought his ſuff'rings to redreſs;
She prays the gods to take the *foundling*'s part,
To teach his hands ſome beneficial art
Practis'd in ſtreets. *Gay's Trivia.*

Fo'undress. *n. ſ.* [from *founder*.]

1. A woman that founds, builds, eſtabliſhes, or begins any thing.

2. A woman that eſtabliſhes any charitable revenue.

For of their order ſhe was patroneſs,
Albe Chariſſa was their chiefeſt *foundreſs*. *Fairy Queen, b.* i.

For zeal like her's, her ſervants were to ſhow;
She was the firſt, where need requir'd to go;
Herſelf the *foundreſs*, and attendant too. *Dryden.*

FOUNT.
FOUNTAIN. } *n. ſ.* [*fons*, Latin; *fontaine*, French.]

1. A well; a ſpring.

He ſet before him ſpread
A table of celeſtial food divine,
Ambroſial fruits, fetcht from the tree of life;
And from the *fount* of life ambroſial drink. *Milt. Par. Reg.*

2. A ſmall baſon of ſpringing water.

Proofs as clear as *founts* in July, when
We ſee each grain of gravel. *Shakeſpeare's Henry* VIII.

Can a man drink better from the *fountain* when it is finely paved with marble, than when it ſwells over the green turf? *Taylor's Rule of living holy.*

Narciſſus on the graſſy verdure lies;
But whilſt within the cryſtal *fount* he tries
To quench his heat, he feels new heat ariſe. *Addiſon.*

3. A jet; a ſpout of water.

Fountains I intend to be of two natures: the one that ſprinkleth or ſpouteth water; the other a fair receipt of water, without fiſh, or ſlime, or mud. *Bacon, Eſſay* 47.

4. The head or firſt ſpring of a river.

All actions of your grace are of a piece, as waters keep the tenor of their *fountains*: your compaſſion is general, and has the ſame effect as well on enemies as friends. *Dryden.*

5. Original; firſt principle; firſt cauſe.

Almighty God, the *fountain* of all goodneſs. *Comm. Prayer.*

You may reduce many thouſand bodies to theſe few general figures, as unto their principal heads and *fountains*. *Peacham.*

This one city may well be reckoned not only the ſeat of trade and commerce, not only the *fountain* of habits and faſhions, and good breeding, but of morally good or bad manners to all England. *Spratt's Sermons.*

Fo'untainless. *adj.* [from *fountain*.] Without a fountain; without a ſpring.

So large
The proſpect was, that here and there was room
For barren deſert *fountainleſs* and dry. *Milton's Parad. Reg*

FO'UNTFUL. *adj.* [*fount* and *full.*] Full of ſprings.

But when the *fountful* Ida's top they ſcal'd with utmoſt haſte,
All fell upon the high-hair'd oaks. *Chapman's Iliads.*

To FOUPE. *v. a.* To drive with ſudden impetuoſity. A word out of uſe.

We pronounce, by the confeſſion of ſtrangers, as ſmoothly and moderately as any of the northern nations, who *foupe* their words out of the throat with fat and full ſpirits. *Camden.*

FOUR. *adj.* [ꝼeopeꞃ, Saxon.] Twice two.

Juſt as I wiſh'd, the lots were caſt on *four*;
Myſelf the fifth. *Pope's Odyſſey, b.* ix.

FOURBE. n. ſ. [French.] A cheat; a tricking fellow. Not in uſe.

Jove's envoy, through the air,
Brings diſmal tydings; as if ſuch low care
Could reach their thoughts, or their repoſe diſturb!
Thou art a falſe impoſtor, and a *fourbe.* *Denham.*

FOURFO'LD. *adj.* [*four* and *fold.*] Four times told.

He ſhall reſtore the lamb *fourfold*, becauſe he had no pity. 2 *Sa.* xii. 6.

FOURFO'OTED. *adj.* [*four* and *foot.*] Quadruped; having twice two feet.

Augur Aſtylos, whoſe art in vain
From fight diſſuaded the *fourfooted* train,
Now beat the hoof with Neſſus on the plain. *Dryden.*

FOURSCO'RE. *adj.* [*four* and *ſcore.*]

1. Four times twenty; eighty.

When they were out of reach, they turned and croſſed the ocean to Spain, having loſt *fourſcore* of their ſhips, and the greater part of their men. *Bacon's War with Spain.*

The Chiots were firſt a free people, being a commonwealth, maintaining a navy of *fourſcore* ſhips. *Sandys.*

The Liturgy had, by the practice of near *fourſcore* years, obtained great veneration from all ſober Proteſtants. *Clarend.*

2. It is uſed elliptically for fourſcore years in numbering the age of man.

At ſeventeen years many their fortunes ſeek;
But at *fourſcore* it is too late a week. *Shak. As you like it.*

Some few might be of uſe in council upon great occaſions, 'till after threeſcore and ten; and the two late miniſters in Spain were ſo 'till *fourſcore.* *Temple.*

FOURSQUA'RE. *adj.* [*four* and *ſquare.*] Quadrangular; having four ſides and angles equal.

The temple of Bel was invironed with a wall carried *fourſquare*, of great height and beauty; and on each ſquare certain brazen gates curiouſly engraven. *Raleigh's Hiſtory.*

FOURTE'EN. *adj.* [ꝼeopeꞃꞇyn, Saxon.] Four and ten; twice ſeven.

She ſays I am not *fourteen* pence on the ſcore for ſheer ale. *Shakeſpeare's Taming of the Shrew.*

FOURTE'ENTH. *adj.* [from *fourteen.*] The ordinal of fourteen; the fourth after the tenth.

I have not found any that ſee the ninth day, few before the twelfth, and the eyes of ſome not open before the *fourteenth* day. *Brown's Vulgar Errours, b.* iii. *c.* 26.

FOURTH. *adj.* [from *four.*] The ordinal of four; the firſt after the third.

A third is like the former: filthy hags!
Why do you ſhew me this? A *fourth?* ſtart eye!
What! will the line ſtretch out to th' crack of doom? *Shak.*

FO'URTHLY. *adv.* [from *fourth.*] In the fourth place.

Fourthly, plants have their ſeed and ſeminal parts uppermoſt, and living creatures have them lowermoſt. *Bacon's Nat. Hiſt.*

FOURWHE'ELED. *adj.* [*four* and *wheel.*] Running upon twice two wheels.

Scarce twenty *fourwheel'd* cars, compact and ſtrong,
The maſſy load could bear, and roll along. *Pope's Odyſſey.*

FO'UTRA. *n. ſ.* [from *foutre*, French.] A fig; a ſcoff; an act of contempt.

A *foutra* for the world, and worldlings baſe. *Shak. H.* IV.

FOWL. *n. ſ.* [ꝼugel, ꝼuhl, Saxon; *vogel*, Dutch.] A winged animal; a bird. It is colloquially uſed of edible birds, but in books of all the feathered tribes.

The beaſts, the fiſhes, and the winged *fowls*,
Are their males ſubjects, and at their controuls. *Shakeſp.*

Lucullus entertained Pompey in a magnificent houſe: Pompey ſaid, this is a marvellous houſe for the Summer; but methinks very cold for Winter. Lucullus anſwered, do you not think me as wiſe as divers *fowls*, to change my habitation in the Winter ſeaſon. *Bacon's Apophthegms.*

This mighty breath
Inſtructs the *fowls* of heaven. *Thomſon's Spring.*

To FOWL. *v. n.* [from the noun.] To kill birds for food or game.

FO'WLER. *n. ſ.* [from *fowl.*] A ſportſman who purſues birds.

The *fowler*, warn'd
By thoſe good omens, with ſwift early ſteps
Treads the crimp earth, ranging through fields and glades,
Offenſive to the birds. *Phillips.*

With ſlaught'ring guns th' unweary'd *fowler* roves,
When froſts have whiten'd all the naked groves. *Pope.*

FO'WLINGPIECE. *n. ſ.* [*fowl* and *piece.*] A gun for birds.

'Tis neceſſary that the countryman be provided with a good *fowlingpiece*, to deſtroy and ſcare them away. *Mortimer.*

FOX. *n. ſ.* [ꝼox, Saxon; *vos*, *voſch*, Dutch.]

1. A wild animal of the canine kind, with ſharp ears and a buſhy tail, remarkable for his cunning, living in holes, and preying upon fowls or ſmall animals.

The *fox* barks not when he would ſteal the lamb. *Shakeſ.*

He that truſts to you,
Where he ſhould find you lions, finds you hares;
Where *foxes*, geeſe. *Shakeſpeare's Macbeth.*

Theſe retreats are more like the dens of robbers, or holes of *foxes*, than the fortreſſes of fair warriours. *Locke.*

2. By way of reproach, applied to a knave or cunning fellow.

FO'XCASE. *n. ſ.* [*fox* and *caſe.*] A fox's ſkin.

One had better be laughed at for taking a *foxcaſe* for a fox, than be deſtroyed by taking a live fox for a caſe. *L'Eſtrange.*

FO'XCHASE. *n. ſ.* [*fox* and *chaſe.*] The purſuit of the fox with hounds.

See the ſame man, in vigour, in the gout;
Alone, in company; in place or out;
Early at buſineſs, and at hazard late;
Mad at a *foxchaſe*, wiſe at a debate. *Pope, Epiſtle* i.

FO'XEVIL. *n. ſ.* [*fox* and *evil.*] A kind of diſeaſe in which the hair ſheds.

FO'XGLOVES. *n. ſ.* A plant.

The leaves are produced alternately on the branches: the cup of the flower conſiſts of one leaf, which is divided into ſix ample long ſegments: the flower conſiſts of one leaf, is tubuloſe and compreſſed, and a little reflexed at the brim: theſe flowers are diſpoſed in a long ſpike, and always grow upon one ſide of the ſtalk: the ovary of the flower becomes a roundiſh fruit, which ends in a point, and opens in the middle: it has two cells, in which many ſmall ſeeds are contained. *Miller.*

FOXHU'NTER. *n. ſ.* [*fox* and *hunter.*] A man whoſe chief ambition is to ſhew his bravery in hunting foxes. A term of reproach uſed of country gentlemen.

The *foxhunters* went their way, and then out ſteals the fox. *L'Eſtrange, Fable* 104.

John Wildfire, *foxhunter*, broke his neck over a ſix-bar gate. *Spectator*, N°. 561.

FO'XSHIP. *n. ſ.* [from *fox.*] The character or qualities of a fox; cunning; miſchievous art.

Had'ſt thou *foxſhip*
To baniſh him that ſtruck more blows for Rome,
Than thou haſt ſpoken words. *Shakeſpeare's Coriolanus.*

FO'XTRAP. *n. ſ.* [*fox* and *trap.*] A gin or ſnare to catch foxes.

Anſwer a queſtion, at what hour of the night to ſet a *foxtrap.* *Tatler*, N°. 56.

FOY. *n. ſ.* [*foi*, French.] Faith; allegiance. An obſolete word.

He Eaſterland ſubdued, and Denmark won,
And of them both did *foy* and tribute raiſe. *Fairy Queen.*

To FRACT. *v. a.* [*fractus*, Latin.] To break; to violate; to infringe. Found perhaps only in the following paſſage.

His days and times are paſt,
And my reliance on his *fracted* dates
Has ſmit my credit. *Shakeſpeare's Timon.*

FRA'CTION. *n. ſ.* [*fraction*, Fr. *fractio*, Latin.]

1. The act of breaking; the ſtate of being broken.

It hath been obſerved by ſeveral, that the ſurface of the earth hath been broke, and the parts of it diſlocated; but more particularly ſeveral parcels of nature retain ſtill the evident marks of *fraction* and ruin. *Burnet's Theory of the Earth.*

2. A broken part of an integral.

Neither the motion of the moon, whereby months are computed, nor the ſun, whereby years are accounted, conſiſteth of whole numbers, but admits of *fractions* and broken parts. *Brown's Vulgar Errours, b.* iv. *c.* 13.

Pliny put a round number near the truth, rather than a *fraction.* *Arbuthnot on Coins.*

FRA'CTIONAL. *adj.* [from *fraction.*] Belonging to a broken number.

We make a cypher the medium between increaſing and decreaſing numbers, commonly called abſolute or whole numbers, and negative or *fractional* numbers. *Cocker's Arithmetick.*

FRA'CTURE. *n. ſ.* [*fractura*, Latin.]

1. Breach; ſeparation of continuous parts.

That may do it without any great *fracture* of the more ſtable and fixed parts of nature, or the infringement of the laws thereof. *Hale's Origin of Mankind.*

2. The ſeparation of the continuity of a bone in living bodies.

But thou wilt ſin and grief deſtroy,
That ſo the broken bones may joy,
And tune together in a well-ſet ſong,
Full of his praiſes,
Who dead men raiſes;
Fractures well cur'd, make us more ſtrong. *Herbert.*

Fractures of the ſcull are dangerous, not in conſequence of the injury done to the cranium itſelf, but as the brain becomes affected. *Sharp's Surgery.*

To FRA'CTURE. *v. a.* [from the noun.] To break a bone.

The leg was dreſſed, and the *fractured* bones united together. *Wiſeman's Surgery.*

FRA'GILE. *adj.* [*fragile*, French; *fragilis*, Latin.]

1. Brittle; eaſily ſnapped or broken.

To eaſe them of their griefs,
Their pangs of love, and other incident throes,
That nature's *fragile* veſſel doth ſuſtain
In life's uncertain voyage. *Shakeſpeare's Timon.*

The ſtalk of ivy is tough, and not *fragile*. *Bacon's N. Hiſt.*

When ſubtle wits have ſpun their threads too fine,
'Tis weak and *fragile*, like Arachne's line. *Denham.*

A dry ſtick will be eaſily broken, when a green one will maintain a ſtrong reſiſtance; and yet in the moiſt ſubſtance there is leſs reſt than in what is drier and more *fragile*. *Glanv.*

2. Weak; uncertain; eaſily deſtroyed.

Much oſtentation, vain of fleſhly arms,
And *fragile* arms, much inſtrument of war,
Long in preparing, ſoon to nothing brought,
Before mine eyes thou'ſt ſet. *Milton's Paradiſe Regain'd.*

FRAGI'LITY. *n. ſ.* [from *fragile.*]

1. Brittleneſs; eaſineſs to be broken.

To make an induration with toughneſs, and leſs *fragility*, decoct bodies in water for two or three days. *Bacon's N. Hiſt.*

2. Weakneſs; uncertainty; eaſineſs to be deſtroyed.

Fearing the uncertainty of man's *fragility*, the common chance of war, the violence of fortune. *Knolles's Hiſtory.*

3. Frailty; liableneſs to fault.

All could not be right, in ſuch a ſtate, in this lower age of *fragility*. *Wotton.*

FRA'GMENT. *n. ſ.* [*fragmentum*, Latin.] A part broken from the whole; an imperfect piece.

He who late a ſceptre did command,
Now graſps a floating *fragment* in his hand. *Dryden.*

Cowley, in his unfiniſhed *fragment* of the Davideis, has ſhewn us this way to improvement. *Watts's Improvement.*

If a thinned or plated body, which, being of an even thickneſs, appears all over of one uniform colour, ſhould be ſlit into threads, or broken into *fragments* of the ſame thickneſs with the plate, I ſee no reaſon why every thread or *fragment* ſhould not keep its colour. *Newton's Opt.*

FRA'GMENTARY. *adj.* [from *fragment.*] Compoſed of fragments. A word not elegant, nor in uſe.

She, ſhe is gone; ſhe's gone: when thou know'ſt this,
What *fragmentary* rubbiſh this world is,
Thou know'ſt, and that it is not worth a thought;
He knows it too too much that thinks it nought. *Donne.*

FRA'GOR. *n. ſ.* [Latin.] A noiſe; a crack; a craſh.

Purſu'd by hideous *fragors*, as before
The flames deſcend, they in their breaches roar. *Sandys.*

FRA'GRANCE. } *n. ſ.* [*fragrantia*, Lat.] Sweetneſs of ſmell;
FRA'GRANCY. } pleaſing ſcent; grateful odour.

Eve ſeparate he ſpies,
Veil'd in a cloud of *fragrance*, where ſhe ſtood
Half-ſpy'd. *Milton's Paradiſe Loſt*, *b.* ix.

I am more pleaſed to ſurvey my rows of coleworts and cabbages ſpringing up in their full *fragrancy* and verdure, than to ſee the tender plants of foreign countries kept alive by artificial heats. *Addiſon's Spectator*, N°. 47.

Not lovelier ſeem'd Narciſſus to the eye;
Nor, when a flower, could boaſt more *fragrancy*. *Garth.*

Such was the wine; to quench whoſe fervent ſteam
Scarce twenty meaſures from the living ſtream
To cool one cup ſuffic'd: the goblet crown'd,
Breath'd aromatick *fragrancies* around. *Pope's Odyſſey*, *b.* ix.

FRA'GRANT. *adj.* [*fragrans*, Latin.] Odorous; ſweet of ſmell.

The nymph vouchſaf'd to place
Upon her head the various wreath:
The flow'rs, leſs blooming than her face;
Their ſcent, leſs *fragrant* than her breath. *Prior.*

FRA'GRANTLY. *adv.* [from *fragrant.*] With ſweet ſcent.

As the hops begin to change colour, and ſmell *fragrantly*, you may conclude them ripe. *Mortimer's Huſbandry.*

FRAIL. *n. ſ.*

1. A baſket made of ruſhes.

2. A ruſh for weaving baſkets.

FRAIL. *adj.* [*fragilis*, Latin.]

1. Weak; eaſily decaying; ſubject to caſualties; eaſily deſtroyed.

I know my body's of ſo *frail* a kind,
As force without, fevers within can kill. *Davies.*

When with care we have raiſed this imaginary treaſure of happineſs, we find, at laſt, that the materials of the ſtructure are *frail* and periſhing, and the foundation itſelf is laid in the ſand. *Rogers, Sermon* 5.

2. Weak of reſolution; liable to errour or ſeduction.

The truly virtuous do not eaſily credit evil that is told them of their neighbours; for if others may do amiſs, then may theſe alſo ſpeak amiſs: man is *frail*, and prone to evil, and therefore may ſoon fail in words. *Taylor's Guide to Devotion.*

FRA'ILNESS. *n. ſ.* [from *frail.*] Weakneſs; inſtability.

There is nothing among all the *frailneſſes* and uncertainties of this ſublunary world ſo tottering and unſtable as the virtue of a coward. *Norris.*

FRA'ILTY. *n. ſ.* [from *frail.*]

1. Weakneſs of reſolution; inſtability of mind; infirmity.

Though Page be a ſecure fool, and ſtands ſo firmly on his wife's *frailty*, yet I cannot put off my opinion ſo eaſily. *Shak.*

Nor ſhould'ſt thou have truſted that to woman's *frailty*:
Ere I to thee, thou to thyſelf waſt cruel. *Milton's Agoniſtes.*

God knows our *frailty*, pities our weakneſs, and requires of us no more than we are able to do. *Locke.*

2. Fault proceeding from weakneſs; ſins of infirmity.

Love did his reaſon blind,
And love's the nobleſt *frailty* of the mind. *Dryd. Ind. Emp.*

Kind wits will thoſe light faults excuſe;
Thoſe are the common *frailties* of the muſe. *Dryden.*

Death, only death, can break the laſting chain;
And here, ev'n then, ſhall my cold duſt remain;
Here all its *frailties*, all its flames reſign,
And wait, 'till 'tis no ſin to mix with thine. *Pope.*

FRA'ISCHEUR. *n. ſ.* [French.] Freſhneſs; coolneſs. A word fooliſhly innovated by *Dryden.*

Hither in Summer-ev'nings you repair,
To taſte the *fraiſcheur* of the purer air. *Dryden.*

FRAISE. *n. ſ.* [French, the caul of an animal.] A pancake with bacon in it.

To FRAME. *v. a.*

1. To form or fabricate by orderly conſtruction and union of various parts.

The double gates he findeth locked faſt;
The one fair *fram'd* of burniſh'd ivory,
The other all with ſilver overcaſt. *Spenſer.*

2. To fit one to another.

They rather cut down their timber to *frame* it, and to do other ſuch neceſſaries to their convenient uſe, than to fight. *Abbot's Deſcription of the World.*

Hew the timber, ſaw it out, *frame* it, and ſet it together. *Mortimer's Huſbandry.*

3. To make; to compoſe.

Then chuſing out few words moſt horrible,
Thereof did verſes *frame.* *Spenſer.*

Fight valiantly to-day;
And yet I do thee wrong to mind thee of it;
For thou art *fram'd* of the firm truth of valour. *Shakeſp.*

4. To regulate; to adjuſt.

Let us not deceive ourſelves by pretending to this excellent knowledge of Chriſt Jeſus our Lord, if we do not *frame* our lives according to it. *Tillotſon.*

5. To form to any rule or method by ſtudy or precept.

Thou art their ſoldier, and, being bred in broils,
Haſt not the ſoft way; but thou wilt *frame*
Thyſelf forſooth hereafter theirs. *Shakeſp. Coriolanus.*

I have been a truant to the law;
I never yet could *frame* my will to it,
And therefore *frame* the law unto my will. *Shakeſp. H.* VI.

6. To form and digeſt by thought.

The moſt abſtruſe ideas are only ſuch as the underſtanding *frames* to itſelf, by joining together ideas that it had either from objects of ſenſe, or from its own operations about them. *Locke.*

Full of that flame his tender ſcenes he warms,
And *frames* his goddeſs by your matchleſs charms. *Granv.*

Urge him with truth to *frame* his ſure replies;
And ſure he will; for wiſdom never lies. *Pope's Odyſſey.*

How many excellent reaſonings are *framed* in the mind of a man of wiſdom and ſtudy in a length of years? *Watts.*

7. To contrive; to plan.

Unpardonable the preſumption and inſolence in contriving and *framing* this letter was. *Clarendon*, *b.* viii.

8. To ſettle; to ſcheme out.

Though I cannot make true wars,
I'll *frame* convenient peace. *Shakeſpeare's Coriolanus.*

9. To invent; to fabricate, in a bad ſenſe: as, to *frame* a ſtory or lie.

Aſtronomers, to ſolve the phænomena, *framed* to their conceit eccentricks and epicycles. *Bacon.*

FRAME. *n. ſ.* [from the verb.]

1. A fabrick; any thing conſtructed of various parts or members.

If the *frame* of the heavenly arch ſhould diſſolve itſelf, if celeſtial ſpheres ſhould forget their wonted motions, and by irregular volubility turn themſelves any way, as it might happen. *Hooker*, *b.* i. *ſ.* 3.

Caſtles made of trees upon *frames* of timber, with turrets and arches, were anciently matters of magnificence. *Bacon.*

Theſe are thy glorious works, parent of good!
Almighty! thine this univerſal *frame.* *Milt. Parad. Loſt.*

Divine Cecilia came,
Inventreſs of the vocal *frame.* *Dryden.*

The gate was adamant; eternal *frame*,
Which, hew'd by Mars himſelf, from Indian quarries came,
The labour of a god; and all along
Tough iron plates were clench'd to make it ſtrong. *Dryd.*

We ſee this vaſt *frame* of the world, and an innumerable multitude of creatures in it; all which we, who believe a God, attribute to him as the author. *Tillotſon, Sermon* 1.

2. Any thing made ſo as to incloſe or admit ſomething elſe.

Put both the tube and the veſſel it leaned on into a convenient wooden *frame*, to keep them from miſchances. *Boyle.*

His picture ſcarcely would deſerve a *frame*. *Dryden's Juvenal.*

A globe of glaſs, about eight or ten inches in diameter, being put into a *frame* where it may be ſwiftly turned round its axis, will, in turning, ſhine, where it rubs againſt the palm of one's hand. *Newton's Opt.*

3. Order; regularity; adjuſted ſeries or diſpoſition.

A woman, that is like a German clock,
Still a repairing, ever out of *frame*,
And never going aright. *Shakeſpeare.*

Your ſteddy ſoul preſerves her *frame*;
In good and evil times the ſame. *Swift.*

4. Scheme; order.

Another party did reſolve to change the whole *frame* of the government in ſtate as well as church. *Clarendon.*

5. Contrivance; projection.

John the Baſtard,
Whoſe ſpirits toil in *frame* of villanies. *Shakeſpeare.*

6. Mechanical conſtruction.

7. Shape; form; proportion.

A bear's a ſavage beaſt,
Whelp'd without form, until the dam
Has lick'd it into ſhape and *frame*. *Hudibras.*

FRA'MER. *n. ſ.* [from *frame*; ꝼꞃemman, Saxon.] Maker; former; contriver; ſchemer.

The forger of his own fate, the *framer* of his fortune, ſhould be improper, if all his actions were predetermined. *Hammond's Fundamentals.*

There was want of accurateneſs in experiments in the firſt original *framer* of thoſe medals. *Arbuthnot on Coins.*

FRA'MPOLD. *n. ſ.* [This word is written by Dr. *Hacket frampul.* I know not its original.] Peeviſh; boiſterous; rugged; croſſgrained.

Her huſband! Alas, the ſweet woman leads an ill life with him: ſhe leads a very *frampold* life with him. *Shakeſpeare.*

The *frampul* man could not be pacified. *Hacket's Life of Williams.*

FRA'NCHISE. *n. ſ.* [*franchiſe*, French.]

1. Exemption from any onerous duty.

2. Privilege; immunity; right granted.

They granted them markets, and other *franchiſes*, and erected corporate towns among them. *Davies on Ireland.*

His gracious edict the ſame *franchiſe* yields
To all the wild increaſe of woods and fields. *Dryden.*

3. Diſtrict; extent of juriſdiction.

There are other privileges granted unto moſt of the corporations, that they ſhall not be travelled forth of their own *franchiſes*. *Spenſer's State of Ireland.*

To FRANCHI'SE. *v. a.* [from the noun.] To enfranchiſe; to make free; to keep free.

I loſe no honour
In ſeeking to augment it; but ſtill keep
My boſom *franchis'd*, and allegiance clear. *Shak. Macbeth.*

FRA'NGIBLE. *adj.* [*frango*, Latin.] Fragile; brittle; eaſily broken.

Though it ſeem the ſolideſt wood, if wrought before it be well ſeaſoned, it will ſhew itſelf very *frangible*. *Boyle.*

FRA'NION. *n. ſ.* [Of this word I know not the derivation.] A paramour; a boon companion.

Firſt, by her ſide did ſit the bold Sanſloy,
Fit mate for ſuch a mincing minion,
Who in her looſeneſs took exceeding joy,
Might not be found a franker *franion*. *Fairy Queen, b.* ii.

FRANK. *adj.* [*franc*, French.]

1. Liberal; generous; not niggardly.

The moiſter ſorts of trees yield little moſs, which is for the reaſon of the *frank* putting up of the ſap into the boughs. *Bacon's Natural Hiſtory.*

They were left deſtitute, either by narrow proviſion, or by their *frank* hearts and their open hands, and their charity towards others. *Spratt's Sermons.*

'Tis the ordinary practice of the world to be *frank* of civilities that coſt them nothing. *L'Eſtrange.*

2. Open; ingenuous; ſincere; not reſerved.

3. Without conditions; without payment.

Thou haſt it won; for it is of *frank* gift,
And he will care for all the reſt to ſhift. *Hubberd's Tale.*

4. Not reſtrained; licentious.

Might not be found a *franker* franion. *Spenſer.*

FRANK. *n. ſ.* [from the adjective.]

1. A place to feed hogs in; a ſty: ſo called from liberality of food.

Where ſups here? Doth the old boar feed in the old *frank*? *Shakeſpeare's Henry* IV.

2. A letter which pays no poſtage.

You'll have immediately, by ſeveral *franks*, my epiſtle to lord Cobham. *Pope to Swift.*

3. A French coin.

To FRANK. *v. a.* [from the noun.]

1. To ſhut up in a frank or ſty. *Hanmer.*

Tell Richmond this from me,
That in the ſty of this moſt bloody boar,
My ſon George Stanly is *frank'd* up in hold:
If I revolt, off goes young George's head. *Shak. Rich.* III.

2. To feed high; to fat; to cram. *Junius* and *Ainſworth.*

3. [From the adjective.] To exempt letters from poſtage.

My lord Orrery writes to you to-morrow; and you ſee I ſend this under his cover, or at leaſt *franked* by him. *Swift.*

Gazettes ſent gratis down, and *frank'd*,
For which thy patron's weekly thank'd. *Pope.*

FRANKALMOI'GNE. *n. ſ.* The ſame which we in Latin call *libera eleemoſyna*, or free alms in Engliſh; whence that tenure is commonly known among our Engliſh lawyers by the name of a tenure in *frank aumone*, or *frankalmoigne*, which, according to *Britton*, is a tenure by divine ſervice. *Ayliffe's Parerg.*

FRA'NKINCENSE. *n. ſ.* [*frank* and *incenſe*; ſo called perhaps from its liberal diſtribution of odour.]

Frankincenſe is a dry reſinous ſubſtance in pieces or drops, of a pale yellowiſh white colour; a ſtrong ſmell, but not diſagreeable, and a bitter, acrid, and reſinous taſte. It is very inflammable. The earlieſt hiſtories inform us, that *frankincenſe* was uſed among the ſacred rites and ſacrifices, as it ſtill continues to be in many different parts of the world. As well however as the world has at all times been acquainted with the drug itſelf, we are ſtill uncertain as to the place whence *frankincenſe* is brought, and much more ſo as to the tree which produces it. It is commended againſt diſorders in the head and breaſt, and againſt diarrhœas and dyſenteries. *Hill.*

Take unto thee ſweet ſpices, with pure *frankincenſe*. *Exod.*

I find in Dioſcorides record of *frankincenſe* gotten in India. *Brerewood on Languages.*

Black ebon only will in India grow,
And od'rous *frankincenſe* on the Sabœan bough. *Dryd. Virg.*

Cedar and *frankincenſe*, an od'rous pile,
Flam'd on the hearth, and wide perfum'd the iſle. *Pope.*

FRA'NKLIN. *n. ſ.* [from *frank*.] A ſteward; a bailiff of land. It ſignifies originally a little gentleman, and is not improperly Engliſhed a gentleman ſervant.

A ſpacious court they ſee,
Both plain and pleaſant to be walked in,
Where them does meet a *franklin* fair and free. *Fai. Queen.*

FRA'NKLY. *adv.* [from *frank*.]

1. Liberally; freely; kindly; readily.

Oh, were it but my life,
I'd throw it down for your deliverance,
As *frankly* as a pin. *Shakeſpeare's Meaſure for Meaſure.*

If ever any malice in your heart
Were hid againſt me, now forgive me *frankly*. *Sh. H.* VIII.

When they had nothing to pay, he *frankly* forgave them both. *Lu.* vii. 42.

By the toughneſs of the earth the ſap cannot get up to ſpread ſo *frankly* as it ſhould do. *Bacon's Natural Hiſtory.*

I value my garden more for being full of blackbirds than cherries, and very *frankly* give them fruit for their ſongs. *Spect.*

2. Without conſtraint; without reſerve.

The lords mounted their ſervants upon their own horſes; and they, with the voluntiers, who *frankly* liſted themſelves, amounted to a body of two hundred and fifty horſe. *Clarend.*

He entered very *frankly* into thoſe new deſigns, which were contrived at court. *Clarendon, b.* viii.

FRA'NKNESS. *n. ſ.* [from *frank*.]

1. Plainneſs of ſpeech; openneſs; ingenuouſneſs.

When the conde duke had ſome eclairciſſment with the duke, in which he made all the proteſtations of his ſincere affection, the other received his proteſtations with all contempt; and declared, with a very unneceſſary *frankneſs*, that he would have no friendſhip with him. *Clarendon.*

Tom made love to a woman of ſenſe, and always treated her as ſuch during the whole time of courtſhip: his natural temper and good breeding hindered him from doing any thing diſagreeable, as his ſincerity and *frankneſs* of behaviour made him converſe with her before marriage in the ſame manner he intended to do afterwards. *Addiſon's Guardian.*

2. Liberality; bounteouſneſs.

3. Freedom from reſerve.

Upon occaſion of the pictures preſent, he delivered with the *frankneſs* of a friend's tongue, as near as he could, word by word, what Kalander had told him touching the ſtrange ſtory. *Sidney.*

The ableſt men that ever were, have had all an openneſs and *frankneſs* of dealing, and a name of certainty and veracity. *Bacon, Eſſay* 6.

FRA'NKPLEDGE.

FRANKPLE'DGE. *n. s.* [*franciplegium*, Latin, of *franc*, i. e. *liber & pleige*, i. e. *fidei jussor.*] A pledge or surety for freemen. For the ancient custom of England, for the preservation of the publick peace, was that every freeborn man at fourteen years of age, religious persons, clerks, knights and their eldest sons excepted, should find security for his fidelity to the king, or else be kept in prison: whence it became customary for a certain number of neighbours to be bound for one another, to see each man of their pledge forthcoming at all times, or to answer the trangression of any one absenting himself. This was called *frankpledge*, and the circuit thereof was called *decenna*, because it commonly consisted of ten housholds; and every particular person, thus mutually bound, was called *decennier*. This custom was so strictly observed, that the sheriffs, in every county, did from time to time take the oaths of young ones as they grew to the age of fourteen years, and see that they combined in one dozen or other: whereupon this branch of the sheriff's authority was called *visus franciplegii*, view of frankpledge. *Cowel.*

FRA'NTICK. *adj.* [corrupted from *phrenetick*, *phreneticus*, Latin; φρενητικός.]

1. Mad; deprived of understanding by violent madness; outrageously and turbulently mad.

Far off, he wonders what makes them so glad;
Of Bacchus merry fruit they did invent,
Or Cebel's *frantick* rites have made them mad. *Fairy Queen.*

2. Transported by violence of passion; outrageous; turbulent.

Esteeming, in the *frantick* error of their minds, the greatest madness in the world to be wisdom, and the highest wisdom foolishness. *Hooker, b.* iii. *s.* 8.

The lover, *frantick*,
Sees Helen's beauty in a brow of Egypt. *Shakespeare.*

To such height their *frantick* passion grows,
That what both love, both hazard to destroy. *Dryden.*

She tears her hair, and, *frantick* in her griefs,
Calls out Lucia. *Addison's Cato.*

FRA'NTICKLY. *adv.* [from *frantick.*] Madly; outrageously.

Fie, fie, how *franticklyI* square my talk! *Shakespeare.*

FRA'NTICKNESS. *n. s.* [from *frantick.*] Madness; fury of passion.

FRATE'RNAL. *adj.* [*fraternel*, French; *fraternus*, Latin.] Brotherly; pertaining to brothers; becoming brothers.

One shall rise
Of proud ambitious heart; who, not content
With fair equality, *fraternal* state,
Will arrogate dominion undeserv'd,
Over his brethren. *Milton's Paradise Lost, b.* xii.

The admonitions, *fraternal* or paternal, of his fellow Christians, or of the governors of the church, then more publick reprehensions; and upon their unsuccessfulness, the censures of the church, until he reform and return. *Hammond's Fundam.*

Plead it to her,
With all the strength and heats of eloquence
Fraternal love and friendship can inspire. *Addison's Cato.*

FRATE'RNALLY. *adv.* [from *fraternal.*] In a brotherly manner.

FRATE'RNITY. *n. s.* [*fraternité*, French; *fraternitas*, Latin.]

1. The state or quality of a brother.

2. Body of men united; corporation; society; association; brotherhood.

'Tis a necessary rule in alliances, societies, and *fraternities*, and all manner of civil contracts, to have a strict regard to the humour of those we have to do withal. *L'Estrange's Fables.*

3. Men of the same class or character.

With what terms of respect knaves and sots will speak of their own *fraternity*. *South's Sermons.*

FRA'TRICIDE. *n. s.* [*fratricide*, French; *fratricidium*, Latin.] The murder of a brother.

FRAUD. *n. s.* [*fraus*, Latin; *fraude*, Fr.] Deceit; cheat; trick; artifice; subtility; stratagem.

None need the *frauds* of sly Ulysses fear. *Dryden's Æn.*

If success a lover's toil attends,
Who asks if force or *fraud* obtain'd his ends. *Pope.*

FRA'UDFUL. *adj.* [*fraud* and *full.*] Treacherous; artful; trickish; deceitful; subtle.

The welfare of us all
Hangs on the cutting short that *fraudful* man. *Shak. H. VI.*

He, full of *fraudful* arts,
This well-invented tale for truth imparts. *Dryden's Æn.*

FRA'UDFULLY. *adv.* [from *fraudful.*] Deceitfully; artfully; subtilly; treacherously; by stratagem.

FRA'UDULENCE. } *n. s.* [*fraudulentia*, Latin.] Deceitfulness;
FRA'UDULENCY. } trickishness; proneness to artifice.

We admire the providence of God in the continuance of Scripture, notwithstanding the endeavours of infidels to abolish, and the *fraudulence* of hereticks always to deprave the same. *Hooker, b.* v. *s.* 22.

FRA'UDULENT. *adj.* [*frauduleux*, Fr. *fraudulentus*, Latin.]

1. Full of artifice; trickish; subtle; deceitful.

He with serpent tongue
His *fraudulent* temptation thus began. *Milton.*

She mix'd the potion, *fraudulent* of soul;
The potion mantled in the golden bowl. *Pope's Odyssey.*

2. Performed by artifice; deceitful; treacherous.

Now thou hast aveng'd
Supplanted Adam,
And frustrated the conquest *fraudulent*. *Milt. Parad. Reg.*

FRA'UDULENTLY. *adv.* [from *fraudulent.*] By fraud; by deceit; by artifice; deceitfully.

He that by fact, word, or sign, either *fraudulently* or violently, does hurt to his neighbour, is bound to make restitution. *Taylor's Rule of living holy.*

FRAUGHT. *particip. pass.* [from *fraight*, now written *freight.*]

1. Laden; charged.

In the narrow seas that part
The French and English, there miscarried
A vessel of our country, richly *fraught*. *Shakespeare.*

With joy
And tidings *fraught*, to hell he now return'd. *Milt. P. Lost.*

And now approach'd their fleet from India, *fraught*
With all the riches of the rising sun,
And precious sand from southern climates brought. *Dryden.*

2. Filled; stored; thronged.

The Scripture is *fraught* even with laws of nature. *Hooker.*

By this sad Una, *fraught* with anguish sore,
Arriv'd, where they in earth their fruitless blood had spilt. *Fairy Queen, b.* i *cant.* 6.

I am so *fraught* with curious business, that I leave out ceremony. *Shakespeare's Winter's Tale.*

Whosoever hath his mind *fraught* with many thoughts, his wits and understanding do clarify and break up in the communicating and discoursing with another. *Bacon, Essay* 28.

Hell, their fit habitation, *fraught* with fire
Unquenchable, the house of woe and pain. *Milt Par. Lost.*

Abdallah and Balsora were so *fraught* with all kinds of knowledge, and possessed with so constant a passion for each other, that their solitude never lay heavy on them. *Guardian.*

FRAUGHT. *n. s.* [from the participle.] A freight; a cargo.

Yield up, oh love, thy crown and parted throne
To tyrannous hate! swell, bosom, with thy *fraught*;
For 'tis of aspicks tongues. *Shakespeare's Othello.*

The bark that all our blessings brought,
Charg'd with thyself and James, a doubly royal *fraught*. *Dry.*

To FRAUGHT. *v. a.* [for *freight*, by corruption.] To load; to crowd.

Hence from my sight:
If after this command thou *fraught* the court
With thy unworthiness, thou dy'st. *Shakesp. Cymbeline.*

FRA'UGHTAGE. *n. s.* [from *fraught.*] Lading; cargo. A bad word.

Our *fraughtage*, sir,
I have convey'd aboard. *Shakes. Comedy of Errours.*

FRAY. *n. s.* [*effrayer*, to fright, French.]

1. A broil; a battle; a fight.

Time tells, that on that ever blessed day,
When Christian swords with Persian blood were dy'd,
The furious prince Tancredie from that *fray*
His coward foes chased through forests wide. *Fairfax.*

I'll speak between the change of man and boy
With a reed voice, and turn two mincing steps
Into a manly stride; and speak of *frays*,
Like a fine bragging youth. *Shak. Merchant of Venice.*

After the bloody *fray* at Wakefield fought. *Shak. H.* VI.

He left them to the fates in bloody *fray*,
To toil and struggle through the well-fought day. *Pope.*

2. A duel; a combat.

Since, if we fall before th' appointed day,
Nature and death continue long their *fray*. *Denham.*

The boaster Paris oft desir'd the day
With Sparta's king to meet in single *fray*. *Pope's Iliad.*

To FRAY. *v. a.* [*effrayer*, French.] To fright; to terrify.

The panther, knowing that his spotted hide
Doth please all beasts, but that his looks them *fray*,
Within a bush his dreadful head doth hide,
To let them gaze, whilst he on them may prey. *Spenser.*

So diversely themselves in vain they *fray*,
Whilst some more bold to measure him stand nigh. *Fa. Qu.*

Fishes are thought to be *frayed* with the motion caused by noise upon the water. *Bacon's Natural History.*

These vulturs prey only on carcases, on such stupid minds as have not life and vigour enough to *fray* them away. *Government of the Tongue.*

2. [*frayer*, French.] To rub.

FREAK. *n. s.* [*frech*, German, saucy, petulant; ꝼꞃæc, Saxon, fugitive.]

1. A sudden and causeless change of place.

2. A sudden fancy; a humour; a whim; a capricious prank.

O! but I fear the fickle *freaks*, quoth she,
Of fortune, and the odds of arms in field. *Fairy Queen.*

When that *freak* has taken possession of a fantastical head, the distemper is incurable. *L'Estrange, Fable* 100.

She is so restless and peevish that she quarrels with all about her, and sometimes in a *freak* will instantly change her habitation. *Spectator,* N°. 427.

To vex me more, he took a *freak*
To slit my tongue, and make me speak. *Swift.*

To Freak. *v. a.* [A word, I suppose, Scotch, brought into England by *Thomson.*] To variegate; to checquer.

There furry nations harbour:
Sables of glossy black, and dark embrown'd,
Or beauteous, *freak'd* with many a mingled hue. *Thomson.*

Fre'akish. *adj.* [from *freak.*] Capricious; humoursome.

It may be a question, whether the wife or the woman was the more *freakish* of the two; for she was still the same uneasy fop. *L'Estrange, Fable* 173.

Fre'akishly. *adv.* [from *freakish.*] Capriciously; humoursomely.

Fre'akishness. *n. s.* [from *freakish.*] Capriciousness; humoursomness; whimsicalness.

To Fream. *v. n.* [*fremere*, Lat. *fremir*, French.] To growl or grunt as a boar. *Bailey.*

FRE'CKLE. *n. s.* [*flech*, a spot, German; whence *fleckle*, *freckle.*]

1. A spot raised in the skin by the sun.

Ruddy his lips, and fresh and fair his hue;
Some sprinkled *freckles* on his face were seen,
Whose dusk set off the whiteness of the skin. *Dryden.*

2. Any small spot or discoloration.

The cowslips tall her pensioners be;
In their gold coats spots you see:
Those be rubies fairy favours;
In those *freckles* live their savours. *Sh. Midsf. Night's Dream.*

The farewel frosts and easterly winds now spot your tulips; therefore cover such with mats, to prevent *freckles.* *Evelyn.*

Fre'ckled. *adj.* [from *freckle.*] Spotted; maculated; discoloured with small spots.

Sometimes we'll angle at the brook,
The *freckled* trout to take
With silken worms. *Drayton's Cynthia.*

The even mead, that erst brought sweetly forth
The *freckled* cowslip,
Wanting the scythe, all uncorrected, rank,
Conceives by idleness. *Shakespeare's Henry* V.

Now thy face charms ev'ry shepherd,
Spotted over like a leopard;
And, thy *freckled* neck display'd,
Envy breeds in ev'ry maid. *Swift.*

Fre'ckly. *adj.* [from *freckle.*] Full of freckles.

Fred. The same with peace; upon which our forefathers called their sanctuaries *fredstole*, *i. e.* the seats of peace. So *Frederic* is powerful, or wealthy in peace; *Winfred*, victorious peace; *Reinfred*, sincere peace. *Gibson's Camden.*

FREE. *adj.* [ꝼꞃeah, Saxon; *vry*, Dutch.]

1. At liberty; not a vassal; not enslaved; not a prisoner; not dependant.

Do faithful homage, and receive *free* honours,
All which we pine for now. *Shakespeare's Macbeth.*

A *free* nation is that which has never been conquered, or thereby entered into any conditions of subjection. *Temple.*

Free, what, and fetter'd with so many chains? *Dryden.*

How can we think any one *freer* than to have the power to do what he will? *Locke.*

This wretched body trembles at your pow'r:
Thus far could fortune; but she can no more:
Free to herself my potent mind remains,
Nor fears the victor's rage, nor feels his chains. *Prior.*

Set an unhappy pris'ner *free*,
Who ne'er intended harm to thee. *Prior.*

2. Uncompelled; unrestrained.

Their use of meats was not like unto our ceremonies, that being a matter of private action in common life, where every man was *free* to order that which himself did; but this is a publick constitution for the ordering of the church. *Hooker.*

It was *free*, and in my choice whether or no I should publish these discourses; yet the publication being once resolved, the dedication was not so indifferent. *South.*

3. Not bound by fate; not necessitated.

Freely they stood who stood, and fell who fell:
Not *free*, what proof could they have giv'n sincere
Of true allegiance, constant faith, or love,
Where only what they needs must do, appear'd;
Not what they would? *Milton's Paradise Lost, b.* iii.

4. Permitted; allowed.

Why, sir, I pray, are not the streets as *free*
For me as for you? *Shakesp. Taming of the Shrew.*

Defaming as impure what God declares
Pure; and commands to some, leaves *free* to all. *Milton.*

5. Licentious; unrestrained.

O conspiracy!
Sham'st thou to shew thy dang'rous brow by night,
When evils are most *free?* *Shak. Julius Cæsar.*

Physicians are too *free* upon the subject, in the conversation of their friends. *Temple.*

The criticks have been very *free* in their censures. *Felton.*

I know there are to whose presumptuous thoughts
Those *freer* beauties, ev'n in them, seem faults. *Pope.*

6. Open; ingenuous.

'Tis not to make me jealous;
To say my wife is fair, feeds well, loves company,
Is *free* of speech, sings, plays, and dances well,
Where virtue is, these make more virtuous. *Shak. Othello.*

Castalio, I have doubts within my heart;
Will you be *free* and candid to your friend? *Otway's Orph.*

7. Acquainted; conversing without reserve.

Being one day very *free* at a great feast, he suddenly broke forth into a great slaughter. *Hakewill on Providence.*

Free and familiar with misfortune grow,
Be us'd to sorrow, and inur'd to woe. *Prior.*

8. Liberal; not parsimonious.

Glo'ster too, a foe to citizens,
O'ercharging your *free* purses with large fines,
That seeks to overthrow religion. *Shakespeare's Henry* IV.

No statute in his favour says,
How *free* or frugal I shall pass my days;
I, who at sometimes spend as others spare. *Pope's Horace.*

Alexandrian verses, of twelve syllables, should never be allowed but when some remarkable beauty or propriety in them atones for the liberty: Mr. Dryden has been too *free* of these in his latter works. *Pope.*

9. Frank; not gained by importunity; not purchased.

We wanted words to express our thanks his noble *free* offers left us nothing to ask. *Bacon's New Atlantis.*

10. Clear from distress.

Who alone suffers, suffers most i' th' mind,
Leaving *free* things and happy shows behind. *Shak. K. Lear.*

11. Guiltless; innocent.

Make mad the guilty, and appall the *free*,
Confound the ign'rant. *Shakespeare's Hamlet.*

My hands are guilty, but my heart is *free.* *Dryden.*

12. Exempt.

These
Are such allow'd infirmities, that honesty
Is never *free* of. *Shakespeare's Winter's Tale.*

Who fears not to do ill, yet fears the name;
And *free* from conscience, is a slave to fame. *Denham.*

Let envy, then, those crimes within you see,
From which the happy never must be *free.* *Dryden.*

Their steeds around,
Free from the harness, graze the flow'ry ground. *Dryden.*

The will, *free* from the determination of such desires, is left to the pursuit of nearer satisfactions. *Locke.*

13. Invested with franchises; possessing any thing without vassalage; admitted to the privileges of any body.

He therefore makes all birds of every sect
Free of his farm, with promise to respect
Their several kinds alike, and equally protect. *Dryden.*

Friend!
What do'st thou make a-shipboard? To what end
Art thou of Bethlem's noble college *free?*
Stark-staring mad, that thou shou'dst tempt the sea? *Dryd.*

14. Without expence; by charity, as a *freeschool.*

To Free. *v. a.* [from the adjective.]

1. To set at liberty; to rescue from slavery or captivity; to manumit; to loose.

The child was prisoner to the womb, and is
By law and process of great nature thence
Freed and enfranchis'd; not a party to
The anger of the king, nor guilty of,
If any be, the trespass of the queen. *Shakes. Winter's Tale.*

He recovered the temple, *freed* the city, and upheld the laws which were going down. 2 *Mac.* ii. 22.

Can'st thou no other master understand,
Than him that *freed* thee by the pretor's wand? *Dryden.*

Should thy coward tongue
Spread its cold poison through the martial throng,
My jav'lin shall revenge so base a part,
And *free* the soul that quivers in thy heart. *Pope.*

2. To rid from; to clear from any thing ill.

It is no marvail, that he could think of no better way to be *freed* of these inconveniencies the passions of those meetings gave him, than to dissolve them. *Clarendon.*

Hercules
Freed Erymanthus from the foaming boar. *Dryden.*

Our land is from the rage of tygers *freed.* *Dryden's Virg.*

3. To clear from impediments or obstructions.

The chaste Sibylla shall your steps convey,
And blood of offer'd victims *free* the way. *Dryden.*

Fierce was the fight; but hast'ning to his prey,
By force the furious lover *freed* his way. *Dryden.*

4. To banish; to send away; to rid.

We may again
Give to our tables meat, sleep to our nights,
Free from our feasts and banquets bloody knives. *Shakespeare.*

5. To exempt.

For he that is dead is *freed* from sin. *Rom.* vi. 7.

6. To unlock; to open.

This master-key
Frees every lock, and leads us to his person. *Dryden.*

Freebo'oter. *n. s.* [*free* and *booty.*] A robber; a plunderer; a pillager.

The Kentishmen, perceiving that Perkin was not followed by any English of name, and that his forces consisted mostly of base people and *freebooters*, fitter to spoil a coast than to recover a kingdom, professed their loyalty to the king. *Bacon.*

The earl of Warwick had, as often as he met with any Irish frigates, or such *freebooters* as sailed under their commission, taken all the seamen who became prisoners to them of that nation, and bound them back to back, and thrown them overboard into the sea. *Clarendon, b.* viii.

Freeboo'ting. *n. s.* Robbery; plunder; the act of pillaging.

Under it he may cleanly convey any fit pillage, that cometh handsomely in his way; and when he goeth abroad in the night on *freebooting*, it is his best and surest friend. *Spenser.*

Fre'eborn. *n. s.* [*free* and *born*] Not a slave; inheriting liberty.

O baseness, to support a tyrant's throne,
And crush your *freeborn* brethren of the world! *Dryden.*

I shall speak my thoughts like a *freeborn* subject, such things perhaps as no Dutch commentator could, and I am sure no Frenchman durst. *Dryden's Æn. Dedication.*

Shall *freeborn* men, in humble awe,
Submit to servile shame;
Who from consent and custom draw
The same right to be rul'd by law,
Which kings pretend to reign? *Dryden.*

Freecha'ppel. *n. s.* [*free* and *chappel.*] Such chappels as are of the king's foundation, and by him exempted from the jurisdiction of the ordinary. The king may also license a subject to found such a chappel, and by his charter exempt it from the ordinary's visitation. *Cowel.*

Fre'ecost. *n. s.* [*free* and *cost.*] Without expence; free from charges.

We must not vouch any man for an exact master in the rules of our modern policy, but such a one as has brought himself so far to hate and despise the absurdity of being kind upon *freecost*, as not so much as to tell a friend what it is o'clock for nothing. *South's Sermons.*

Fre'edman. *n. s.* [*freed* and *man.*] A slave manumitted. *Libertus.*

The *freedman* jostles, and will be preferr'd;
First come, first serv'd, he cries. *Dryden's Juv. Sat.* I.

Fre'edom. *n. s.* [from *free.*]

1. Liberty; exemption from servitude; independence.

The laws themselves they do specially rage at, as most repugnant to their liberty and natural *freedom. Spenser on Ireland.*

O *freedom!* first delight of human kind!
Not that which bondmen from their masters find,
The privilege of doles; nor yet t' inscribe
Their names in this or t'other Roman tribe:
That false enfranchisement with ease is found;
Slaves are made citizens by turning round. *Dryden's Pers.*

2. Privileges; franchises; immunities.

By our holy Sabbath have I sworn
To have the due and forfeit of my bond:
If you deny it, let the danger light
Upon your charter, and your city's *freedom.* *Shakespeare.*

3. Power of enjoying franchises.

This prince first gave *freedom* to servants, so as to become citizens of equal privileges with the rest, which very much increased the power of the people. *Swift.*

4. Exemption from fate, necessity, or predetermination.

I else must change
Their nature, and revoke the high decree
Unchangeable, eternal, which ordain'd
Their *freedom*; they themselves ordain'd their fall. *Milton.*

In every sin, by how much the more free will is in its choice, by so much is the act the more sinful; and where there is nothing to importune, urge, or provoke the will to any act, there is so much an higher and perfecter degree of *freedom* about that act. *South's Sermons.*

5. Unrestraint.

I will that all the feasts and sabbaths shall be all days of immunity and *freedom* for the Jews in my realm. 1 *Mac.* x.

6. The state of being without any particular evil or inconvenience.

7. Ease or facility in doing or showing any thing.

Freefo'oted. *adj.* [*free* and *foot.*] Not restrained in the march.

We will fetters put upon this fear,
Which now goes too *freefooted.* *Shakespeare's Hamlet.*

Freehe'arted. *adj.* [*free* and *heart.*] Liberal; unrestrained.

Love must *freehearted* be, and voluntary;
And not inchanted, or by fate constrain'd. *Davies.*

Freeho'ld. *n. s.* [*free* and *hold.*] That land or tenement which a man holdeth in fee, fee-tail, or for term of life. *Freehold* in deed is the real possession of lands or tenements in fee, fee-tail, or for life. *Freehold* in law is the right that a man has to such land or tenements before his entry or seisure. *Freehold* is sometimes taken in opposition to villenage. Land, in the time of the Saxons, was called either bockland, that is, holden by book or writing, or foleland, that is, holden without writing. The former was held by far better conditions, and by the better sort of tenants, as noblemen and gentlemen, being such as we now call *freehold.* The latter was commonly in the possession of clowns, being that which we now call at the will of the lord. *Cowel.*

No alienation of lands holden in chief should be available, touching the *freehold* or inheritance thereof, but only where it were made by matter of record, to be found in some of her majesty's treasuries. *Bacon's Office of Alienation.*

There is an unspeakable pleasure in calling any thing one's own: a *freehold*, though it be but in ice and snow, will make the owner pleased in the possession, and stout in the defence of it. *Addison's Freeholder,* N°. 1.

My friends here are very few, and fixed to the *freehold*, from whence nothing but death will remove them. *Swift.*

I should be glad to possess a *freehold* that could not be taken from me by any law to which I did not give my own consent. *Swift to Lord Middleton.*

Freeho'lder. *n. s.* [from *freehold.*] One who has a freehold.

As extortion did banish the old English *freeholder*, who could not live but under the law; so the law did banish the Irish lord, who could not live but by extortion. *Davies.*

Free'ly. *adv.* [from *free.*]

1. At liberty; without vassalage; without slavery; without dependance.

2. Without restraint; lavishly.

If my son were my husband, I would *freelier* rejoice in that absence wherein he won honour, than in the embracements of his bed, where he would shew most love. *Shakesp. Coriolan.*

I pledge your grace; and if you knew what pains
I have bestow'd to breed this present peace,
You would drink *freely.* *Shakes. Henry* IV.

3. Without scruple; without reserve.

Let such teach others who themselves excel,
And censure *freely* who have written well. *Pope's Ess. on Crit.*

4. Without impediment.

To follow rather the Goths in rhyming than the Greeks in true versifying, were even to eat acorns with swine, when we may *freely* eat wheat-bread among men. *Ascham's Schoolmaster.*

The path to peace is virtue: what I show,
Thyself may *freely* on thyself bestow:
Fortune was never worshipp'd by the wise;
But, set aloft by fools, usurps the skies. *Dryden's Juv. Sat.*

5. Without necessity; without predetermination.

Freely they stood who stood, and fell who fell. *Milton.*

He leaves us to chuse with the liberty of reasonable beings: they who comply with his grace, comply with it *freely*; and they who reject it, do also *freely* reject it. *Rogers's Sermons.*

6. Frankly; liberally.

By nature all things have an equally common use: nature *freely* and indifferently opens the bosom of the universe to all mankind. *South's Sermons.*

7. Spontaneously; of its own accord.

Fre'eman. *n. s.* [*free* and *man.*]

1. One not a slave; not a vassal.

Had you rather Cæsar were living, and die all slaves, than that Cæsar were dead, to live all *freemen? Shakesp. Jul. Cæsar.*

If to break loose from the conduct of reason, and to want that restraint of examination and judgment which keeps us from chusing or doing the worse, be liberty, true liberty, mad men and fools are only the *freemen.* *Locke.*

2. One partaking of rights, privileges, or immunities.

He made us *freemen* of the continent,
Whom nature did like captives treat before. *Dryden.*

What this union was is expressed in the preceding verse, by their both having been made *freemen* on the same day. *Addison's Remarks on Italy.*

Freemi'nded. *adj.* [*free* and *mind.*] Unconstrained; without load of care.

To be *freeminded*, and cheerfully disposed at hours of meat, sleep, and exercise, is one of the best precepts of long lasting. *Bacon, Essay* 31.

Fre'eness. *n. s.* [from *free.*]

1. The state or quality of being free.

2. Openness; unreservedness; ingenuousness; candour.

The reader may pardon it, if he please, for the *freeness* of the confession. *Dryden.*

3. Generosity; liberality.

I hope it will never be said that the laity, who by the clergy are taught to be charitable, shall in their corporations exceed the clergy itself, and their sons, in *freeness* of giving. *Sprat.*

Freescho'ol. *n. s.* [*free* and *school.*] A school in which learning is given without pay.

To give a civil education to the youth of this land in the time

time to come, proviſion was made by another law, that there ſhould be one *freeſchool* at leaſt erected in every dioceſs. *Davies.*

Two clergymen ſtood candidates for a ſmall *freeſchool* in ——ſhire, where a gentleman of intereſt in the country, who happened to have a better underſtanding than his neighbours, procured the place for him who was the better ſcholar. *Swift.*

FREESPO'KEN. *adj.* [*free* and *ſpoken.*] Accuſtomed to ſpeak without reſerve.

Nerva one night ſupped privately with ſome ſix or ſeven; amongſt whom there was one that was a dangerous man, and began to take the like courſes as Marcellus and Regulus had done: the emperor fell into diſcourſe of the injuſtice and tyranny of the former time, and, by name, of the two accuſers; and ſaid, what ſhould we do with them, if we had them now? One of them that was at ſupper, and was a *free-ſpoken* ſenator, ſaid, Marry, they ſhould ſup with us. *Bacon.*

FRE'ESTONE. *n. ſ.* [*free* and *ſtone.*] Stone commonly uſed in building.

Freeſtone is ſo named from its being of ſuch a conſtitution as to be wrought and cut freely in any direction. *Woodward.*

I ſaw her hand: ſhe has a leathern hand, a *freeſtone*-coloured hand. *Shakeſpeare's As you like it.*

The ſtreets are generally paved with brick or *freeſtone*, and always kept very neat. *Addiſon on Italy.*

FREETHI'NKER. *n. ſ.* [*free* and *think.*] A libertine; a contemner of religion.

Atheiſt is an old-faſhion'd word: I'm a *freethinker*, child. *Addiſon's Drummer.*

Of what uſe is freedom of thought, if it will not produce freedom of action, which is the ſole end, how remote ſoever in appearance, of all objections againſt Chriſtianity? And therefore the *freethinkers* conſider it as an edifice, wherein all the parts have ſuch a mutual dependance on each other, that if you pull out one ſingle nail, the whole fabrick muſt fall to the ground. *Swift's Argument againſt aboliſhing Chriſtianity.*

FREEWI'LL. *n. ſ.* [*free* and *will.*]

1. The power of directing our own actions without conſtraint by neceſſity or fate.

We have a power to ſuſpend the proſecution of this or that deſire: this ſeems to me the ſource of all liberty; in this ſeems to conſiſt that which is improperly called *freewill.* *Locke.*

2. Voluntarineſs; ſpontaneity.

I make a decree, that all they of the people of Iſrael in my realm, which are minded of their own *freewill* to go up to Jeruſalem, go with thee. *Ezr.* vii. 13.

FREEWO'MAN. *n. ſ.* [*free* and *woman.*] A woman not enſlaved.

All her ornaments are taken away of a *freewoman*; ſhe is become a bondſlave. 1 *Mac.* ii. 11.

To FREEZE. *v. n.* preter. *froze.* [*vrieſen*, Dutch.]

1. To be congealed with cold.

The aqueous humour of the eye will not *freeze*, which is very admirable, ſeeing it hath the perſpicuity and fluidity of common water. *Ray on the Creation.*

The *freezing* of water, or the blowing of a plant, returning at equidiſtant periods in all parts of the earth, would as well ſerve men to reckon their years by as the motions of the ſun. *Locke.*

2. To be of that degree of cold by which water is congealed.

Orpheus with his lute made trees
And mountain tops, that *freeze*,
Bow themſelves when he did ſing. *Shakeſpeare's Henry* VIII.
Thou art all ice, thy kindneſs *freezes.* *Shakeſ. Rich.* III.
Heav'n *froze* above ſevere, the clouds congeal,
And thro' the cryſtal vault appear'd the ſtanding hail. *Dryd.*

To FREEZE. *v. a.* pret. *froze*; part. *frozen* or *froze.*

1. To congeal with cold.

2. To kill by cold.

When we both lay in the field,
Frozen almoſt to death, how did he lap me,
Ev'n in his garments! *Shakeſpeare's Richard* III.

My maſter and miſtreſs are almoſt *frozen* to death. *Shakeſp.*

3. To chill by the loſs of power or motion.

I have a faint cold fear thrills through my veins,
That almoſt *freezes* up the heat of life. *Sh. Rom. and Juliet.*
Death came on amain,
And exercis'd below his iron reign;
Then upward to the ſeat of life he goes;
Senſe fled before him, what he touch'd he *froze.* *Dryden.*

To FREIGHT. *v. a.* preter. *freighted*; part. *fraught*; which being now uſed as an adjective, *freighted* is adopted. [*fretter*, French.]

1. To load a ſhip or veſſel of carriage with goods for tranſportation.

The princes
Have to the port of Athens ſent their ſhips,
Fraught with the miniſters and inſtruments
Of cruel war. *Shak. Troilus and Creſſida, Prologue.*
Nor is, indeed, that man leſs mad than theſe,
Who *freights* a ſhip to venture on the ſeas;
With one frail interpoſing plank to ſave
From certain death, roll'd on by ev'ry wave. *Dryden's Juv.*
Freighted with iron, from my native land
I ſteer my voyage. *Pope's Odyſſey, b* i.

2. To load as the burthen; to be the thing with which a veſſel is freighted.

I would
Have ſunk the ſea within the earth, or ere
It ſhould the good ſhip ſo have ſwallow'd, and
The *freighting* ſouls within her. *Shakeſpeare's Tempeſt.*

FREIGHT. *n. ſ.*

1. Any thing with which a ſhip is loaded.

He clears the deck, receives the mighty *freight*;
The leaky veſſel groans beneath the weight. *Dryden's Æn.*

2. The money due for tranſportation of goods.

FRE'IGHTER. *n. ſ.* [*fretteur*, French.] He who freights a veſſel.

FREN. *n. ſ.* A worthleſs woman. An old word wholly forgotten.

But now from me his madding mind is ſtart,
And wooes the widow's daughter of the glen;
And now fair Roſalind hath bred his ſmart,
So now his friend is changed for a *fren.* *Spenſer's Paſt.*

FRENCH *Chalk. n. ſ.*

French chalk is an indurated clay, extremely denſe, of a ſmooth gloſſy ſurface, and ſoft and unctuous to the touch; of a greyiſh white colour, variegated with a duſky green. *Hill.*

French chalk is unctuous to the touch, as ſteatites is, but harder, and nearer approaching the conſiſtence of ſtone. *Wood.*

To FRE'NCHIFY. *v. a.* [from *French.*] To infect with the manner of France; to make a coxcomb.

They miſliked nothing more in king Edward the Confeſſor than that he was *Frenchified*; and accounted the deſire of foreign language then to be a foretoken of bringing in foreign powers, which indeed happened. *Camden's Remains.*

Has he familiarly diſlik'd
Your yellow ſtarch, or ſaid your doublet
Was not exactly *Frenchified.* *Shakeſpeare's As you like it.*

FRE'NETICK. *adj.* [*frenetique*, French; φρενιτικὸς; generally therefore written *phrenetick.*] Mad; diſtracted.

He himſelf impotent,
By means of his *frenetick* malady. *Daniel's Civil War.*

FRE'NZY. *n. ſ.* [φρενῖτις; *phrenitis*, Latin: whence *phrenetiſy*, *phrenetſy*, *phrenzy*, or *frenzy.*] Madneſs; diſtraction of mind; alienation of underſtanding; any violent paſſion approaching to madneſs.

That knave, Ford, hath the fineſt mad devil of jealouſy in him that ever governed *frenzy.* *Shakeſ. Mer. Wives of Windſ.*

True fortitude is ſeen in great exploits,
That juſtice warrants, and that wiſdom guides;
All elſe is touring *frenzy* and diſtraction. *Addiſon's Cato.*

Why ſuch a diſpoſition of the body induceth ſleep, another diſturbs all the operations of the ſoul, and occaſions a lethargy or *frenzy:* this knowledge exceeds our narrow faculties. *Bent.*

FRE'QUENCE. *n. ſ.* [*frequence*, Fr. *frequentia*, Latin.] Crowd; concourſe; aſſembly.

The *frequence* of degree,
From high to low throughout. *Shakeſpeare's Timon.*
He, in full *frequence* bright
Of angels, thus to Gabriel ſmiling ſpake. *Paradiſe Reg.*

FRE'QUENCY. *n. ſ.* [*frequentia*, Latin.]

1. Common occurrence; the condition of being often ſeen or done.

Should a miracle be indulged to one, others would think themſelves equally intitled to it; and if indulged to many, it would no longer have the effect of a miracle; its force and influence would be loſt by the *frequency* of it. *Atterb.*

2. Concourſe; full aſſembly.

Thou cam'ſt e're while into this ſenate: who
Of ſuch a *frequency*, ſo many friends
And kindred thou haſt here, ſaluted thee? *Ben. Johnſ. Catil.*

FRE'QUENT. *adj.* [*frequent*, French; *frequens*, Latin.]

1. Often done; often ſeen; often occurring.

An ancient and imperial city falls;
The ſtreets are fill'd with *frequent* funerals. *Dryden's Æn.*
Frequent herſes ſhall beſiege your gates. *Pope.*

2. Uſed often to practiſe any thing.

Every man thinks he may pretend to any employment, provided he has been loud and *frequent* in declaring himſelf hearty for the government. *Swift.*

3. Full of concourſe.

Frequent and full. *Milton.*

To FREQU'ENT. *v. a.* [*frequento*, Latin; *frequenter*, French.] To viſit often; to be much in any place; to reſort often to.

Latter day,
Finding in it fit ports for fiſhers trade,
'Gan more the ſame *frequent*, and further to invade. *F. Q.*

There were ſynagogues for men to reſort unto: our Saviour himſelf, and after him the apoſtles, *frequented* them. *Hooker, b.* v. *ſ.* 11.

This fellow here, this thy creature,
By night *frequents* my houſe. *Shakeſpeare's Timon.*

At

At that time this land was known and *frequented* by the ships and vessels. *Bacon.*

With tears
Wat'ring the ground, and with our sighs the air
Frequenting, sent from hearts contrite, in sign
Of sorrow unfeign'd, and humiliation meek. *Milt. P. L.*

To serve my friends, the senate I *frequent*;
And there what I before digested, vent. *Denham.*

That he *frequented* the court of Augustus, and was well received in it, is most undoubted. *Dryden's Ovid, Preface.*

FREQUE'NTABLE. *adj.* [from *frequent.*] Conversable; accessible. A word not now used, but not inelegant.

While youth lasted in him, the exercises of that age and his humour, not yet fully discovered, made him somewhat the more *frequentable* and less dangerous. *Sidney, b.* ii.

FREQUE'NTATIVE. *adj.* [*frequentatif*, French; *frequentativus*, Latin.] A grammatical term applied to verbs signifying the frequent repetition of an action.

FREQUE'NTER. *n. s.* [from *frequent.*] One who often resorts to any place.

Persons under bad imputations are no great *frequenters* of churches. *Swift.*

FRE'QUENTLY. *adv.* [*frequenter*, Latin.] Often; commonly; not rarely; not seldom; a considerable number of times; manifold times.

I could not, without much grief, observe how *frequently* both gentlemen and ladies are at a loss for questions and answers. *Swift's Introduction to Genteel Conversation.*

FRE'SCO. n. s. [Italian.]

1. Coolness; shade; duskiness, like that of the evening or morning.

Hellish sprites
Love more the *fresco* of the nights. *Prior.*

2. A picture not drawn in glaring light, but in dusk.

Here thy well-study'd marbles fix our eye;
A fading *fresco* here demands a sigh. *Pope.*

FRESH. *adj.* [ꝼꞃeꞅc, Saxon; *fraiche*, French.]

1. Cool; not vapid with heat.

I'll cull the farthest mead for thy repast;
The choicest herbs I to thy board will bring,
And draw thy water from the *freshest* spring. *Prior.*

2. Not salt

They keep themselves unmixt with the salt water; so that, a very great way within the sea, men may take up as *fresh* water as if they were near the land. *Abbot's Desc. of the World.*

3. New; not impaired by time.

This second source of men, while yet but few,
And while the dread of judgment past remain
Fresh in their minds, fearing the Deity,
With some regard to what's just and right,
Shall lead their lives. *Milton's Paradise Lost, b.* xii.

That love which first was set, will first decay;
Mine of a *fresher* date will longer stay. *Dryd. Indian Emp.*

4. In a state like that of recentness.

We will revive those times, and in our memories
Preserve and still keep *fresh*, like flowers in water. *Denham.*

With such a care
As roses from their stalks we tear,
When we would still preserve them new,
And *fresh* as on the bush they grew. *Waller.*

Thou sun, said I, fair light!
And thou enlighten'd earth, so *fresh* and gay! *Milt. P. L.*

5. Recent; newly come.

Amidst the spirits Palinurus press'd;
Yet *fresh* from life, a new admitted guest. *Dryden's Æn.*

Fresh from the fact, as in the present case,
The criminals are seiz'd upon the place;
Stiff in denial, as the law appoints,
On engines they distend their tortur'd joints. *Dryden.*

6. Repaired from any loss or diminution.

Nor lies she long; but, as her fates ordain,
Springs up to life, and *fresh* to second pain;
Is sav'd to-day, to-morrow to be slain. *Dryden.*

7. Florid; vigorous; chearful; unfaded; unimpaired.

This pope is decrepid, and the bell goeth for him: take order that when he is dead there be chosen a pope of *fresh* years, between fifty and threescore. *Bacon's holy War.*

Two swains,
Fresh as the morn, and as the season fair. *Pope.*

8. Healthy in countenance; ruddy.

Tell me,
Hast thou beheld a *fresher* gentlewoman,
Such war of white and red within her cheeks? *Shakespeare.*

It is no rare observation in England to see a *fresh* coloured lusty young man yoked to a consumptive female, and him soon after attending her to the grave. *Harvey on Consumptions.*

They represent to themselves a thousand poor, tall, innocent, *fresh* coloured young gentlemen. *Addison's Spectator.*

9. Brisk; strong; vigorous.

As a *fresh* gale of wind fills the sails of a ship. *Holder.*

10. Fasting: opposed to eating or drinking. A low word.

11. Sweet: opposed to stale or stinking.

FRESH. *n. s.* Water not salt.

He shall drink nought but brine; for I'll not shew him
Where the quick *freshes* are. *Shakespeare's Tempest.*

To FRE'SHEN. *v. a.* [from *fresh.*] To make fresh.

Prelusive drops let all their moisture flow
In large effusion o'er the *freshen'd* world. *Thomson's Spring.*

To FRE'SHEN. *v. n.* To grow fresh.

A *freshening* breeze the magick power supply'd,
While the wing'd vessel flew along the tide. *Pope's Odyssey.*

FRE'SHET. *n. s.* [from *fresh.*] A pool of fresh water.

All fish from sea or shore,
Freshet or purling brook, or shell or fin. *Milt. Parad. Lost.*

FRE'SHLY. *adv.* [from *fresh.*]

1. Coolly.

2. Newly; in the former state renewed.

The weeds of heresy being grown unto such ripeness as that was, do, even in the very cutting down, scatter oftentimes those seeds which for a while lie unseen and buried in the earth; but afterwards *freshly* spring up again, no less pernicious than at the first. *Hooker, b.* v. *s.* 42.

Then shall our names,
Familiar in their mouth as houshold words,
Be in their flowing cups *freshly* remember'd. *Shak. Hen.* V.

They are now *freshly* in difference with them. *Bacon.*

3. With a healthy look; ruddily.

Looks he as *freshly* as he did the day he wrestled? *Shakesp.*

FRE'SHNESS. *n. s.* [from *fresh.*]

1. Newness; vigour; spirit; the contrary to vapidness.

Most odours smell best broken or crushed; but flowers pressed or beaten, do lose the *freshness* and sweetness of their odour. *Bacon's Natural History.*

2. Freedom from diminution by time; not staleness.

For the constant *freshness* of it, it is such a pleasure as can never cloy or overwork the mind; for surely no man was ever weary of thinking that he had done well or virtuously. *South.*

3. Freedom from fatigue; newness of strength.

The Scots had the advantage both for number and *freshness* of men. *Hayward.*

4. Coolness.

There are some rooms in Italy and Spain for *freshness*, and gathering the winds and air in the heats of Summer; but they be but pennings of the winds, and enlarging them again, and making them reverberate in circles. *Bacon.*

Say, if she please, she hither may repair,
And breathe the *freshness* of the open air. *Dryden's Aureng.*

She laid her down to rest,
And to the winds expos'd her glowing breast,
To take the *freshness* of the morning air. *Addison on Italy.*

5. Ruddiness; colour of health.

The secret venom, circling in her veins,
Works through her skin, and bursts in bloating stains;
Her cheeks their *freshness* lose and wonted grace,
And an unusual paleness spreads her face. *Granville.*

6. Freedom from saltness.

FRESHWA'TER. [A compound word of *fresh* and *water*, used as an adjective.] Raw; unskilled; unacquainted. A low term borrowed from the sailors, who stigmatise those who come first to sea as *freshwater* men or novices.

The nobility, as *freshwater* soldiers which had never seen but some light skirmishes, in their vain bravery made light account of the Turks. *Knolles's History of the Turks.*

FRET. *n. s.* [Of this word the etymology is very doubtful: some derive it from ꝼꞃeꞇan, to eat; others from ꝼꞃeꞇpan, to adorn; some from φρίττω; *Skinner* more probably from *fremo*, or the French *fretiller*: perhaps it comes immediately from the Latin *fretum.*]

1. A frith, or strait of the sea, where the water by confinement is always rough.

Euripus generally signifieth any strait, *fret*, or channel of the sea, running between two shores. *Brown's Vulg. Errours.*

2. Any agitation of liquors by fermentation, confinement, or other cause.

The channel of this river is white with rocks, and the surface covered with froth and bubbles; for it runs along upon the *fret*, and is still breaking against the stones that oppose its passage. *Addison's Remarks on Italy.*

The blood in a fever, if well governed, like wine upon the *fret*, dischargeth itself of all heterogeneous mixtures. *Derham's Physico-Theology.*

3. That stop of the musical instrument which causes or regulates the vibrations of the string.

It requireth good winding of a string before it will make any note; and in the tops of lutes, &c. the higher they go, the less distance is between the *frets*. *Bacon's Nat. History.*

The harp
Had work, and rested not: the solemn pipe
And dulcimer, all organs of sweet stop,
All sounds on *fret* by string or golden wire,
Temper'd soft tunings, intermix'd with voice
Choral or unison. *Milton's Paradise Lost, b.* vii.

They are fitted to answer the most variable harmony: two or

or three pipes to all those of a church-organ, or to all the strings and *frets* of a lute. *Grew's Cosmolog. Sac. b* i.

4. Work rising in protuberances.

The *frets* of houses, and all equal figures, please; whereas unequal figures are but deformities. *Bacon's Natural History.*

We take delight in a prospect well laid out, and diversified with fields and meadows, woods and rivers, in the curious *fret* works of rocks and grottos. *Spectator*, Nº. 414.

5. Agitation of the mind; commotion of the temper; passion.

Calmness is great advantage: he that lets
Another chafe, may warm him at his fire,
Mark all his wand'rings, and enjoy his *frets*,
As cunning fencers suffer heat to tire. *Herbert.*

The incred'lous Pheac, having yet
Drank but one round, reply'd in sober *fret*. *Tate's Juven.*

You, too weak the slightest loss to bear,
Are on the *fret* of passion, boil and rage. *Creech's Juven.*

Yet then did Dennis rave in furious *fret*;
I never answer'd, I was not in debt. *Pope, Epistle* ii.

To Fret. *v. a.* [from the noun.]

1. To rub against any thing; to agitate violently.

You may as well forbid the mountain pines
To wag their high tops, and to make a noise
When they are *fretted* with the gusts of heav'n. *Shakespeare.*

2. To wear away by rubbing.

Drop them still upon one place,
'Till they have *fretted* us a pair of graves
Within the earth. *Shakespeare's Richard* II.

In the banks of rivers, with the washing of the water, there were divers times *fretted* out big pieces of gold. *Abbot.*

Before I ground the object metal on the pitch, I always ground the putty on it with the concave copper, 'till it had done making a noise; because, if the particles of the putty were not made to stick fast in the pitch, they would, by rolling up and down, grate and *fret* the object metal, and fill it full of little holes. *Newton's Opt.*

3. To hurt by attrition.

The better part with Mary and with Ruth
Chosen thou hast; and they that over-ween,
And at thy growing virtues *fret* their spleen,
No anger find in thee, but pity and ruth. *Milton.*

4. To corrode; to eat away.

It is *fret* inward, whether it be bare within or without. *Lev.* xiii. 55.

The painful husband, plowing up his ground,
Shall find all *fret* with rust, both pikes and shields,
And empty helms under his harrow found. *Hakewill.*

5. To form into raised work.

Nor did there want
Cornice or freeze, with bossy sculptures grav'n;
The roof was *fretted* gold. *Milton's Paradise Lost, b.* i.

6. To variegate; to diversify.

Yon grey lines,
That *fret* the clouds, are messengers of day. *Shak. Jul. Cæs.*

7. To make angry; to vex.

Antony
Is valiant and dejected; and, by starts,
His *fretted* fortunes give him hope and fear
Of what he has and has not. *Shakes. Ant. and Cleopatra.*

Because thou hast *fretted* me in all these things, behold I will recompense thy way upon thine head. *Ezek.* xvi. 43.

Such an expectation, cries one, will never come to pass: therefore I'll even give it up, and go and *fret* myself. *Collier.*

Injuries from friends *fret* and gall more, and the memory of them is not so easily obliterated. *Arbuthn. Hist. of John Bull.*

To Fret. *v. n.*

1. To be in commotion; to be agitated.

No benefits whatsoever shall ever alter or allay that diabolical rancour, that *frets* and ferments in some hellish breasts, but that upon all occasions it will foam out at its foul mouth in slander and invective. *South's Sermons.*

Th' adjoining brook, that purls along
The vocal grove, now *fretting* o'er a rock,
Now scarcely moving through a reedy pool. *Thoms. Summ.*

2. To be worn away; to be corroded.

Take a piece of glovers leather that is very thin, and put your gold therein, binding it close, and then hang it up: the sal armoniack will *fret* away, and the gold remain behind. *Peacham on Drawing.*

3. To make way by attrition.

These do but indeed scrape off the extuberances, or *fret* into the wood, and therefore they are very seldom used to soft wood. *Moxon's Mech. Exer.*

It inflamed and swelled very much; many wheals arose, and *fretted* one into another with great excoriation. *Wiseman.*

4. To be angry; to be peevish; to vex himself.

They trouble themselves with *fretting* at the ignorance of such as withstand them in their opinion. *Hooker, b.* v. *s.* 22.

We are in a *fretting* mind at the church of Rome, and with angry disposition enter into cogitation. *Hooker.*

Helpless, what may it boot
To *fret* for anger, or for grief to moan! *Fairy Queen.*

Their wounded steeds
Fret fetlock deep in gore, and with wild rage
Yerk out their armed heels at their dead masters *Sh. H.* V.

Be lion-mettled, proud, and take no care
Who chafes, who *frets*, or where conspirers are. *Sh. Macb.*

His heart *fretteth* against the Lord. *Prov.* xix. 3.

Hudibras *fretting*
Conquest should be so long a getting,
Drew up his force. *Hudibras, b.* i. *cant.* 2.

He swells with wrath, he makes outrageous moan,
He *frets*, he fumes, he stares, he stamps the ground. *Dryd.*

How should I *fret* to mangle ev'ry line,
In rev'rence to the sins of thirty-nine. *Pope.*

Fre'tful. *adj.* [from *fret.*] Angry; peevish; in a state of vexation.

Thy knotty and combined locks to part,
And each particular hair to stand on end,
Like quills upon the *fretful* porcupine. *Shakesp. Hamlet.*

Where's the king?
—Contending with the *fretful* elements;
Bids the wind blow the earth into the sea. *Shakes. K. Lear.*

They are extremely *fretful* and peevish, never well at rest; but always calling for this or that, or changing their posture of lying or sitting. *Harvey on Consumptions.*

Are you positive and *fretful*?
Heedless, ignorant, forgetful? *Swift.*

Fre'tfully. *adv.* [from *fretful.*] Peevishly.

Fre'tfulness. *n. s.* [from *fretful.*] Passion; peevishness.

Fre'tty. *adj.* [from *fret.*] Adorned with raised work.

Friabi'lity. *n. s.* [from *friable.*] Capacity of being reduced to powder.

Hardness, *friability*, and power to draw iron, are qualities to be found in a loadstone. *Locke.*

FRI'ABLE. *adj.* [*friable*, French; *friabilis*, Latin.] Easily crumbled; easily reduced to powder.

A spongy excrescence groweth upon the roots of the laser-tree, and sometimes on cedar, very white, light, and *friable*, which we call agarick. *Bacon's Natural History.*

The liver, of all the viscera, is the most *friable*, and easily crumbled or dissolved. *Arbuthnot on Diet.*

FRI'AR. *n. s.* [A corruption of *frere*, French.] A religious; a brother of some regular order.

Holy Franciscan *friar*! brother! ho! *Sh. Rom. and Jul.*

All the priests and *friars* in my realm,
Shall in procession sing her endless praise. *Shakesp. H.* VI.

He says he's but a *friar*, but he's big enough to be a pope. *Dryden's Spanish Fryar.*

Many jesuits and *friars* went about, in the disguise of Presbyterian and Independent ministers, to preach up rebellion. *Swift.*

A *friar* would needs shew his talent in Latin. *Swift.*

Fri'arlike. *adj.* [from *friar.*] Monastick; unskilled in the world.

Their *friarlike* general would the next day make one holy-day in the Christian calendars, in remembrance of thirty thousand Hungarian martyrs slain of the Turks. *Knolles's History.*

Fri'arly. *adv.* [*friar* and *like.*] Like a friar, or man untaught in life.

Seek not proud riches, but such as thou may'st get justly, use soberly, distribute cheerfully, and leave contentedly; yet have no abstract nor *friarly* contempt of them. *Bacon's Essays.*

Fri'arscowl. *n. s.* [*friar* and *cowl.*] A plant.

It agrees with the dragon and arum, from both which it differs only in having a flower resembling a cowl.

Fri'ary. *n. s.* [from *friar.*] A monastry or convent of friars.

Fri'ary. *adj.* Like a friar.

Francis Cornfield did scratch his elbow when he had sweetly invented to signify his name, St. Francis, with a *friary* cowl in a cornfield. *Camden's Remains.*

To FRI'BBLE. *v. n.* To trifle.

Though cheats, yet more intelligible
Than those that with the stars do *fribble*. *Hudibras, p.* ii.

Fri'bbler. *n. s.* [from the verb.] A trifler.

A *fribbler* is one who professes rapture for the woman, and dreads her consent. *Spectator*, Nº. 288.

FRICASSE'E. *n. s.* [French.] A dish made by cutting chickens or other small things in pieces, and dressing them with strong sauce.

Oh, how would Homer praise their dancing dogs,
Their stinking cheese, and *fricacy* of frogs!
He'd raise no fables, sing no flagrant lye,
Of boys with custard choak'd at Newberry. *King.*

Frica'tion *n. s.* [*fricatio*, Latin.] The act of rubbing one thing against another.

Gentle *frication* draweth forth the nourishment, by making the parts a little hungry, and heating them: this *frication* I wish to be done in the morning. *Bacon's Natural History.*

Resinous or unctuous bodies, and such as will flame, attract vigorously, and most thereof without *frication*, as good hard wax,

wax, which will convert the needle almost as actively as the loadstone. *Brown's Vulgar Errours, b.* ii. *c.* 4.

FRI'CTION. *n. s.* [*friction*, Fr. *frictio*, from *frico*, Latin.]

1. The act of rubbing two bodies together.

Do not all bodies which abound with terrestrial parts, and especially with sulphureous ones, emit light as often as those parts are sufficiently agitated, whether the agitation be made by heat, *friction*, percussion, putrefaction, or by any vital motion? *Newton's Opt.*

2. The resistance in machines caused by the motion of one body upon another.

3. Medical rubbing with the fleshbrush or cloaths.

Frictions make the parts more fleshy and full, as we see both in men and in the currying of horses; for that they draw a greater quantity of spirits to the parts. *Bacon.*

FRI'DAY. *n. s.* [ꝼꞃiᵹe dæᵹ, Saxon.] The sixth day of the week, so named of *Freya*, a Saxon deity.

An' she were not kin to me, she would be as fair on *Friday* as Helen is on Sunday. *Shakespeare's Troilus and Cressida.*

For Venus, like her day, will change her cheer,
And seldom shall we see a *Friday* clear. *Dryden.*

FRIEND. *n. s.* [*vriend*, Dutch; ꝼꞃeonԁ, Saxon. This word, with its derivatives, is pronounced *frend*, *frendly*: the *i* totally neglected.

1. One joined to another in mutual benevolence and intimacy: opposed to foe or enemy.

Friends of my soul, you twain
Rule in this realm, and the gor'd state sustain. *Shakesp.*

Some man is a *friend* for his own occasion, and will not abide in the day of thy trouble. *Ecclus.* vi. 8.

God's benison go with you, and with those
That would make good of bad, and *friends* of foes. *Shakes.*

Wonder not to see this soul extend
The bounds, and seek some other self, a *friend*. *Dryden.*

2. One without hostile intentions.

Who comes so fast in silence of the night?
—A *friend*.
—What *friend*? your name? *Shakesp. Merchant of Venice.*

3. One reconciled to another: this is put by the custom of the language somewhat irregularly in the plural number.

He's *friends* with Cæsar,
In state of health thou say'st, and thou say'st free. *Shakesp.*

My son came then into my mind; and yet my mind
Was then scarce *friends* with him. *Shak. King Lear.*

4. An attendant, or companion.

The king ordains their entrance, and ascends
His regal seat, surrounded by his *friends*. *Dryden's Æn.*

5. Favourer; one propitious.

Aurora riding upon Pegasus, sheweth her swiftness, and how she is a *friend* to poetry and all ingenious inventions. *Peacham.*

6. A familiar compellation.

Friend, how camest thou in hither? *Mat.* xxii. 12.

What supports me, do'st thou ask?
The conscience, *friend*, t'have lost mine eyes o'erply'd
In liberty's defence. *Milton.*

To FRIEND. *v. a.* [from the noun.] To favour; to befriend; to countenance; to support.

I know that we shall have him well to *friend*. *Shakesp.*

When vice makes mercy, mercy's so extended,
That, for the fault's love, is th' offender *friended*. *Shakesp.*

FRI'ENDLESS. *adj.* [from *friend*.]

1. Wanting friends; wanting support; without countenance; destitute; forlorn.

Alas! I am a woman, *friendless*, hopeless. *Shak. H.* VIII.

Woe to him that is alone, is verified upon none so much as upon the *friendless* person. *South's Sermons.*

To some new clime, or to thy native sky,
Oh *friendless* and forsaken virtue fly. *Dryden's Aurengzebe.*

To what new clime, what distant sky,
Forsaken, *friendless*, will ye fly?
Say, will ye bless the bleak Atlantick shore,
Or bid the furious Gaul be rude no more? *Pope.*

2. FRIENDLESS *Man*. The Saxon word for him whom we call an outlaw, because he was, upon his exclusion from the king's peace and protection, denied all help of friends.

FRI'ENDLINESS. *n. s.* [from *friendly*.]

1. A disposition to friendship.

Such a liking and *friendliness* as hath brought forth the effects. *Sidney.*

2. Exertion of benevolence.

Let all the intervals be employed in prayers, charity, *friendliness* and neighbourhood, and means of spiritual and corporal health. *Taylor's Rule of holy living.*

FRI'ENDLY. *adj.* [from *friend*.]

1. Having the temper and disposition of a friend; kind; favourable; benevolent.

They gave them thanks, desiring them to be *friendly* still unto them. 2 *Mac.* xii. 31.

Thou to mankind
Be good, and *friendly* still, and oft return! *Milton's P. Lost.*

How art thou
To me so *friendly* grown above the rest
Of brutal kind? *Milton's Paradise Lost, b.* ix.

Let the Nassau-star in rising majesty appear,
And guide the prosp'rous mariner
With everlasting beams of *friendly* light. *Prior.*

2. Disposed to union.

Like *friendly* colours found our hearts unite,
And each from each contract new strength and light. *Pope.*

3. Salutary; homogeneal.

Not that Nepentes, which the wife of Thone
In Egypt gave to Jove-born Helena,
Is of such power to stir up joy as this,
To life so *friendly*, or so cool to thirst. *Milton.*

FRI'ENDLY. *adv.* In the manner of friends; with appearance of kindness.

Here between the armies,
Let's drink together *friendly*, and embrace;
That all their eyes may bear those tokens home
Of our restored love and amity. *Shakesp. Henry* IV. *p.* ii.

FRIE'NDSHIP. *n. s.* [*vriendschap*, Dutch.]

1. The state of minds united by mutual benevolence.

There is little *friendship* in the world, and least of all between equals, which was wont to be magnified: that that is, is between superior and inferior, whose fortunes may comprehend the one the other. *Bacon, Essay* 49.

He lived rather in a fair intelligence than any *friendship* with the favourites. *Clarendon.*

My sons, let your unseemly discord cease,
If not in *friendship*, live at least in peace. *Dryd. Ind. Emp.*

2. Highest degree of intimacy.

His *friendships*, still to few confin'd,
Were always of the middling kind. *Swift.*

3. Favour; personal kindness.

Raw captains are usually sent only preferred by *friendship*, and not chosen by sufficiency. *Spenser on Ireland.*

4. Assistance; help.

Gracious, my lord, hard-by here is a hovel:
Some *friendship* will it lend you 'gainst the tempest;
Repose you there. *Shakespeare's King Lear.*

5. Conformity; affinity; correspondence; aptness to unite.

We know those colours which have a *friendship* with each other, and those which are incompatible, in mixing together those colours of which we would make trial. *Dryd. Dufresnoy.*

FRIEZE. *n. s.* [*drap de frieze*, French.] A coarse warm cloath, made perhaps first in *Friesland*.

If all the world
Should in a pet of temperance feed on pulse,
Drink the clear stream, and nothing wear but *frieze*,
The All-giver would be unthank'd. *Milton.*

The captive Germans, of gigantick size,
Are rank'd in order, and are clad in *frieze*. *Dryd. Pers.*

He could no more live without his *frieze* coat than without his skin. *Addison's Guardian*, N°. 102.

See how the double nation lies,
Like a rich coat with skirts of *frieze*;
As if a man, in making poesies,
Should bundle thistles up with roses. *Swift.*

FRIEZE. } *n. s.* [In architecture.] A large flat member which
FRIZE. } separates the architrave from the cornice; of which there are as many kinds as there are orders of columns. *Harr.*

No jutting *frieze*,
Buttrice, nor coigne of 'vantage, but this bird
Hath made his pendant-bed, and procreant cradle. *Shakes.*

Nor did there want
Cornice or *frieze* with bossy sculptures grav'n;
The roof was fretted gold. *Milton's Paradise Lost, b.* i.

Polydore designed admirably well, as to the practical part, having a particular genius for *friezes*. *Dryden's Dufresnoy.*

FRI'EZED. *adj.* [from *frieze*.] Shagged or napped with frieze.

FRI'EZELIKE. *adj.* [*frieze* and *like*.] Resembling a frieze.

I have seen the figure of Thalia, the comick muse, sometimes with an entire headpiece and a little *friezelike* tower, running round the edges of the face, and sometimes with a mask for the face only. *Addison's Remarks on Italy.*

FRI'GAT. *n. s.* [*frigate*, French; *fregata*, Italian.]

1. A small ship. Ships under fifty guns are generally termed *frigats*.

The treasure they fought for was, in their view, embezzled in certain *frigats*. *Raleigh's Apology.*

On high-rais'd decks the haughty Belgians ride,
Beneath whose shade our humble *frigats* go. *Dryden.*

2. Any small vessel on the water.

Behold the water work and play
About her little *frigat*, therein making way. *Fairy Queen.*

FRIGEFA'CTION. *n. s.* [*frigus* and *facio*, Latin.] The act of making cold.

To FRIGHT. *v. a.* [ꝼꞃyhꞇan, Saxon.] To terrify; to disturb with fear; to shock with fear; to daunt.

The herds
Were strongly clam'rous in the *frighted* fields. *Shak. H.* IV.

Nor exile or danger can *fright* a brave spirit,
With innocence guarded,
With virtue rewarded,
I make of my sufferings a merit. *Dryden's Albion.*

The

The mind *frights* itself with any thing reflected on in grofs, and at a diftance: things thus offered to the mind, carry the fhew of nothing but difficulty. *Locke.*

Whence glaring oft with many a broaden'd orb,
He *frights* the nations. *Thomfon's Autumn.*

FRIGHT. *n. f.* [from the verb.] A fudden terrour.

You, if your goodnefs does not plead my caufe,
May think I broke all hofpitable laws,
To bear you from your palace-yard by might,
And put your noble perfon in a *fright.* *Dryden.*

To FRI'GHTEN. *v. a.* To terrify; to fhock with dread.

The rugged bear's, or fpotted lynx's brood,
Frighten the valleys and infeft the wood. *Prior.*

FRI'GHTFUL. *adj.* [from *fright.*]

1. Terrible; dreadful; full of terrour.

Tetchy and wayward was thy infancy,
Thy fchooldays *frightful*, defp'rate, wild, and furious. *Shak.*
Without aid you durft not undertake
This *frightful* paffage o'er the Stygian lake. *Dryden's Æn.*

2. A cant word among women for any thing unpleafing.

FRI'GHTFULLY. *adv.* [from *frightful.*]

1. Dreadfully; horribly.

This will make a prodigious mafs of water, and looks *frightfully* to the imagination; 'tis huge and great. *Burnet.*

2. Difagreeably; not beautifully. A woman's word.

Then to her glafs; and Betty, pray,
Don't I look *frightfully* to-day? *Swift.*

FRI'GHTFULNESS. *n. f.* [from *frightful.*] The power of impreffing terrour.

FRI'GID. *adj.* [*frigidus*, Latin.]

1. Cold; without warmth. In this fenfe it is feldom ufed but in fcience.

In the torrid zone the heat would have been intolerable, and in the *frigid* zones the cold would have deftroyed both animals and vegetables. *Cheyne's Phil. Princ.*

2. Without warmth of affection.
3. Impotent; without warmth of body.
4. Dull; without fire of fancy.

If juftice Phillip's coftive head
Some *frigid* rhymes difburfes,
They fhall like Perfian tales be read,
And glad both babes and nurfes. *Swift.*

FRI'GIDITY. *n. f.* [*frigiditas*, Latin.]

1. Coldnefs; want of warmth.
2. Dulnefs; want of intellectual fire.

Driving at thefe as at the higheft elegancies, which are but the *frigidities* of wit. *Brown's Vulgar Errours, b.* i. *c.* 9.

Of the two extremes, one would fooner pardon phrenzy than *frigidity.* *Pope's Preface to the Iliad.*

3. Want of corporeal warmth.

The boiling blood of youth agitating the fluid air, hinders that ferenity which is neceffary to fo fevere an intentnefs; and the *frigidity* of decrepit age is as much its enemy, by reafon of its dulling moifture. *Glanv. Scepf. c.* 14.

4. Coldnefs of affection.

FRI'GIDLY. *adv.* [from *frigid.*] Coldly; dully; without affection.

FRI'GIDNESS. *n. f.* [from *frigid.*] Coldnefs; dulnefs; want of affection.

FRIGORI'FICK. *adj.* [*frigorificus*, *frigus* and *facio*, Lat.] Caufing cold. A word ufed in fcience.

Frigorifick atoms or particles mean thofe nitrous falts which float in the air in cold weather, and occafion freezing. *Quincy.*

To FRILL. *v. a.* [*frilleux*, French.] To quake or fhiver with cold. Ufed of a hawk; as, the hawk *frills.* *Dict.*

FRINGE. *n. f.* [*friggio*, Italian; *frange*, French.] Ornamental appendages added to drefs or furniture.

Thofe offices and dignities were but the facings or *fringes* of his greatnefs. *Wotton.*

The golden *fringe* ev'n fet the ground on flame,
And drew a precious trail. *Dryden's Flower and Leaf.*

The fhadows of all bodies, in this light, were bordered with three parallel *fringes*, or bands of coloured light, whereof that which was contiguous to the fhadow was broadeft and moft luminous; and that which was remoteft from it was narroweft, and fo faint as not eafily to be vifible. *Newton's Opt.*

To FRINGE. *v. a.* [from the noun.] To adorn with fringes; to decorate with ornamental appendages.

Either fide of the bank, *fringed* with moft beautiful trees, refifted the fun's darts. *Sidney, b.* ii.

Of filver wings he took a fhining pair,
Fringed with gold. *Fairfax, ftan.* 14.

Here, by the facred bramble ting'd,
My petticoat is doubly *fring'd.* *Swift.*

FRI'PPERER. *n. f.* [from *frippier*, French.] One who deals in old things vamped up.

FRI'PPERY. *n. f.* [*fripperie*, French; *fripperia*, Italian.]

1. The place where old cloaths are fold.

Oh, oh, monfter, we know what belongs to a *frippery.* *Shakefpeare's Tempeft.*

Lurana is a *frippery* of bankrupts, who fly thither from Druina to play their after-game. *Howel's Vocal Forreft.*

2. Old cloaths; caft dreffes; tattered rags.

Poor poet ape, that would be thought our chief,
Whofe works are e'en the *frippery* of wit;
From brocage is become fo bold a thief,
As we, the robb'd, leave rage, and pity it. *Ben. Johnfon.*
The fighting-place now feamens rage fupply,
And all the tackling is a *frippery.* *Donne.*

Ragfair is a place near the Tower of London, where old cloaths and *frippery* are fold. *Notes to Pope's Dunciad.*

To FRISK. *v. n.* [*frizzare*, Italian.]

1. To leap; to fkip.

Put water into a glafs, and wet your finger, and draw it round about the lip of the glafs, preffing it fomewhat hard; and after drawing it fome few times about, it will make the water *frifk* and fprinkle up in a fine dew. *Bacon's Nat. Hift.*

The fifh fell a *frifking* in the net. *L'Eftrange's Fables.*

Whether every one hath experimented this troublefome intrufion of fome *frifking* ideas, which thus importune the underftanding, and hinder it from being better employed, I know not. *Locke.*

2. To dance in frolick or gaiety.

We are as twinn'd lamb, that did *frifk* i' th' fun,
And bleat the one at the other: what we chang'd,
Was innocence for innocence; we knew not
The doctrine of ill-doing. *Shakefpeare's Winter's Tale.*
About them *frifking* play'd
All beafts of th' earth. *Milton's Paradife Loft, b* iv.

A wanton heifer *frifked* up and down in a meadow, at eafe and pleafure. *L'Eftrange.*

Watch the quick motions of the *frifking* tail,
Then ferve their fury with the rufhing male. *Dryd. Virgil.*
So Bacchus through the conquer'd Indies rode,
And beafts in gambols *frifk'd* before their honeft god. *Dryd.*
Oft to the mountains airy tops advanc'd,
The *frifking* fatyrs on the fummits danc'd. *Addifon.*
Thofe merry blades,
That *frifk* it under Pindus' fhades. *Prior.*

Peg faints at the found of an organ, and yet will dance and *frifk* at the noife of a bagpipe. *Arbuthn. Hift. of John Bull.*

Sly hunters thus, in Borneo's ifle,
To catch a monkey by a wile,
The mimick animal amufe;
They place before him gloves and fhoes;
Which when the brute puts aukward on,
All his agility is gone:
In vain to *frifk* or climb he tries;
The huntfmen feize the grinning prize. *Swift.*

FRISK. *n. f.* [from the verb.] A frolick; a fit of wanton gaiety.

FRI'SKER. *n. f.* [from *frifk.*] A wanton; one not conftant or fettled.

Now I will wear this, and now I will wear that;
Now I will wear I cannot tell what:
All new fafhions be pleafant to me:
Now I am a *frifker*, all men on me look;
What fhould I do but fet cock on the hoop? *Camden.*

FRI'SKINESS. *n. f.* [from *frifk.*] Gaiety; livelinefs. A low word.

FRI'SKY. *adj.* [*frifque*, French, from *frifk.*] Gay; airy. A low word.

FRIT. *n. f.* [Among chymifts.] Afhes or falt baked or fried together with fand. *Dict.*

FRITH. *n. f.* [*fretum*, Latin.]

1. A ftrait of the fea where the water being confined is rough.

What defp'rate madman then would venture o'er
The *frith*, or haul his cables from the fhore? *Dryd. Virg.*
Batavian fleets
Defraud us of the glittering finny fwarms
That heave our *friths*, and crowd upon our fhores. *Thomfon.*

2. A kind of net. I know not whether this fenfe be now retained.

The Wear is a *frith*, reaching through the Ofe, from the land to low water mark, and having in it a bunt or cod with an eye-hook; where the fifh entering, upon their coming back with the ebb, are ftopt from iffuing out again. *Carew.*

FRITI'LLARY. *n. f.* [*fritillaire*, French.] A plant.

The flower confifts of fix leaves, and is of the bell-fhaped lily flowers, pendulous, naked, and, for the moft part, chequered: the ftyle of the flower becomes an oblong fruit, divided into three cells, and filled with flat feeds, lying in a double row: the root confifts of two flefhy knobs, for the moft part femi-globular, betwixt which arifes the flower-ftalk. *Miller.*

FRI'TINANCY. *n. f.* [from *fritinnio*, Latin.] The fcream of an infect, as the cricket or cicada.

The note or *fritinancy* thereof is far more fhrill than that of the locuft, and its life fhort. *Brown's Vulgar Errours.*

FRI'TTER. *n. f.* [*friture*, French.]

1. A fmall piece cut to be fried.

Maids, *fritters* and pancakes ynow fee ye make;
Let Slut have one pancake for company fake. *Tuff. Hufb.*

2. A fragment; a fmall piece.

Sense and putter! have I lived to stand in the taunt of one that makes *fritters* of English! *Shak. Merry Wives of Windſ.*

If you strike a solid body that is brittle, as glass or sugar, it breaketh not only where the immediate force is, but breaketh all about into shivers and *fritters*; the motion, upon the pressure, searching all ways, and breaking where it findeth the body weakest. *Bacon's Natural History.*

The ancient errant knights
Won all their ladies hearts in fights;
And cut whole giants into *fritters*,
To put them into amorous twitters. *Hudibras, p.* iii.

3. A cheesecake; a wigg. *Ainsworth.*

To FRI'TTER. *v. a.* [from the noun.]

1. To cut meat into small pieces to be fried.

2. To break into small particles or fragments.

Joy to great chaos! let division reign!
My racks and tortures soon shall drive them hence,
Break all their nerves, and *fritter* all their sense. *Dunciad.*
How prologues into prefaces decay,
And these to notes are *fritter'd* quite away. *Pope's Dunciad.*

FRI'VOLOUS. *adj.* [*frivolus*, Latin; *frivole*, Fr.] Slight; trifling; of no moment.

It is *frivolous* to say we ought not to use bad ceremonies of the church of Rome, and presume all such bad as it pleaseth themselves to dislike. *Hooker, b.* iv. *s.* 4.

These seem very *frivolous* and fruitless; for, by the breach of them, little damage can come to the commonwealth. *Spenser.*

She tam'd the brinded lioness,
And spotted mountain pard; but set at nought
The *frivolous* bolt of Cupid. *Milton.*
Those things which now seem *frivolous* and slight,
Will be of serious consequence to you,
When they have made you once ridiculous. *Roscommon.*

All the impeachments in Greece and Rome seem to have agreed in a notion they had of being concerned, in point of honour, to condemn whatever person they impeached, however *frivolous* the articles, or however weak the surmises, whereon they were to proceed in their proofs. *Swift.*

I will not defend any mistake, and do not think myself obliged to answer every *frivolous* objection. *Arbuthnot.*

FRI'VOLOUSNESS. *n. s.* [from *frivolous.*] Want of importance; triflingness.

FRI'VOLOUSLY. *adv.* [from *frivolous.*] Triflingly; without weight.

To FRIZLE. *v. a.* [*friser*, Fr.] To curl in short curls like nap of frieze.

Th' humble shrub
And bush, with *frizl'd* hair implicit. *Milton's Parad. Lost.*

They *frizled* and curled their hair with hot irons. *Hakewill.*

I doff'd my shoe, and swear
Therein I spy'd this yellow *frizled* hair. *Gay's Pastorals.*

FRI'ZLER. *n. s.* [from *frizle.*] One that makes short curls.

FRO. *adv.* [of ꝼꞃa, Saxon.]

1. Backward; regressively. It is only used in opposition to the word *to*; *to* and *fro*, backward and forward.

The Carthaginians, in all the long Punick war, having spoiled all Spain, rooted out all that were affected to the Romans; and the Romans, having recovered that country, did cut off all that favoured the Carthaginians: so betwixt them both, to and *fro*, there was scarce a native Spaniard left. *Spens.*

As when a heap of gather'd thorns is cast,
Now to, now *fro*, before th' autumnal blast,
Together clung, it rolls around the field. *Pope's Odyssey.*

2. It is a contraction of *from*: not now used.

They turn round like grindlestones,
Which they dig out *fro'* the delves,
For their bairns bread, wives and selves. *Ben. Johnson.*

FROCK. *n. s.* [*froc*, French.]

1. A dress; a coat.

That monster, custom, is angel yet in this,
That to the use of actions fair and good,
He likewise gives a *frock* or livery,
That aptly is put on. *Shakespeare's Hamlet.*
Chalybean temper'd steel, and *frock* of mail
Adamantean proof. *Milton's Agonistes, l.* 129.

2. A kind of close coat for men.

I strip my body of my shepherd's *frock*. *Dryden.*

3. A kind of gown for children.

FROG. *n. s.* [ꝼꞃogga, Saxon.]

1. A small animal with four feet, living both by land and water, and placed by naturalists among mixed animals, as partaking of beast and fish. There is likewise a small green frog that perches on trees, said to be venomous.

Poor Tom, that eats the swimming *frog*, the toad, the todpole. *Shakespeare's King Lear.*

Auster is drawn with a pot or urn, pouring forth water, with which shall descend *frogs*. *Peacham on Drawing.*

2. The hollow part of the horse's hoof.

FRO'GBIT. *n. s.* [*frog* and *bit.*] An herb. *Ainsworth.*

FRO'GFISH. *n. s.* [*frog* and *fish.*] A kind of fish. *Ainsworth.*

FRO'GGRASS. *n. s.* [*frog* and *grass.*] A kind of herb.

FRO'GLETTUCE. *n. s.* [*frog* and *lettuce.*] A plant.

FROISE. *n. s.* [from the French *froisser*, as the pancake is crisped or crimpled in frying.] A kind of food made by frying bacon inclosed in a pancake.

FRO'LICK. *adj.* [*vrolijck*, Dutch.] Gay; full of levity; full of pranks.

We fairies, that do run
By the triple Hecate's team,
From the presence of the sun,
Following darkness like a dream,
Now are *frolick*. *Shakespeare's Midsum. Night's Dream.*
Whether, as some sages sing,
The *frolick* wind that breathes the Spring,
Zephyr with Aurora playing,
As he met her once a Maying;
There on beds of violets blue,
And fresh-blown roses wash'd in dew,
Fill'd her with thee a daughter fair,
So buxom, blithe, and debonnair. *Milton.*
Who ripe, and *frolick* of his full-grown age,
Roving the Celtick and Iberian fields,
At last betakes him to this ominous wood. *Milton.*
The gay, the *frolick*, and the loud. *Waller.*

FRO'LICK. *n. s.* [from the adjective.] A wild prank; a flight of whim and levity.

He would be at his *frolick* once again,
And his pretensions to divinity. *Roscommon.*

Alcibiades, having been formerly noted for the like *frolicks* and excursions, was immediately accused of this. *Swift.*

While rain depends, the pensive cat gives o'er
Her *frolicks*, and pursues her tail no more. *Swift.*

To FRO'LICK. *v. n.* [from the noun.] To play wild pranks; to play tricks of levity and gaiety.

Then to her new love let her go,
And deck her in golden array;
Be finest at ev'ry fine show,
And *frolick* it all the long day. *Rowe.*

FRO'LICKLY. *adv.* [from *frolick.*] Gaily; wildly.

FRO'LICKSOME. *adj.* [from *frolick.*] Full of wild gaiety.

FRO'LICKSOMENESS. *n. s.* [from *frolicksome.*] Wildness of gaiety; pranks.

FRO'LICKSOMELY. *adv.* [from *frolicksome.*] With wild gaiety.

FROM. *prep.* [ꝼꞃam, Saxon and Scottish.]

1. Away; noting privation.

Your slighting Zulema, this very hour
Will take ten thousand subjects *from* your power. *Dryden.*
In fetters one the barking porter ty'd,
And took him trembling *from* his sov'reign's side. *Dryden.*
Clarissa drew, with tempting grace,
A two-edg'd weapon *from* the shining case. *Pope.*

2. Noting reception.

What time would spare *from* steel receives its date. *Pope.*

3. Noting procession, descent, or birth.

Thus the hard and stubborn race of man
From animated rock and flint began. *Blackmore's Creation.*
The song began *from* Jove. *Dryden.*
Succeeding kings rise *from* the happy bed. *Irene.*

4. Noting transmission.

The messengers *from* our sister and the king. *Shakesp.*

5. Noting abstraction; vacation from.

I shall find time
From this enormous state, and seek to give
Losses their remedies. *Shakespeare's King Lear.*

6. With *to* following; noting succession.

These motions we must examine *from* first *to* last, to find out what was the form of the earth. *Burn. Theo of the Earth.*

He bid her *from* time *to* time be comforted. *Addis. Spectat.*

7. Out of; noting emission.

When the most high
Eternal Father, *from* his secret cloud
Amidst, in thunder utter'd thus his voice. *Milt. Par. Lost.*
Then pierc'd with pain, she shook her haughty head,
Sigh'd *from* her inward soul, and thus she said. *Dryd. Æn.*

8. Noting progress from premisses to inferences.

If an objection be not removed, the conclusion of experience *from* the time past to the time present will not be found and perfect. *Bacon's War with Spain.*

This is evident *from* that high and refined morality, which shined forth in some of the ancient heathens. *South's Sermons.*

9. Noting the place or person from whom a message is brought.

The king is coming, and I must speak with him *from* the bridge.——How now, Fluellen, cam'st thou *from* the bridge? *Shakespeare's Henry* V.

10. Out of: noting extraction.

From high Meonia's rocky shores I came,
Of poor descent; Acætes is my name. *Addis. Ovid. Met.*

11. Because of. Noting the reason or motive of an act or effect.

You are good, but *from* a nobler cause;
From your own knowledge, not *from* nature's laws. *Dryden.*

David celebrates the glory of God *from* the consideration of the greatness of his works. *Tillotson, Sermon* 4.

We sicken soon *from* her contagious care;
Grieve for her sorrows, groan for her despair. *Prior.*

Relaxations *from* plenitude is cured by ſpare diet, and *from* any cauſe by that which is contrary to it. *Arbuthnot on Alim.*

12. Out of. Noting the ground or cauſe of any thing.

They who believe that the praiſes which ariſe *from* valour are ſuperiour to thoſe which proceed *from* any other virtues, have not conſidered. *Dryden's Virg. Æn. Dedication.*

What entertainment can be raiſed *from* ſo pitiful a machine? We ſee the ſucceſs of the battle from the very beginning. *Dryd.*

'Tis true *from* force the ſtrongeſt titles ſpring. *Dryden.*

13. Not near to. Noting diſtance.

His regiment lies half a mile at leaſt
South *from* the mighty power of the king. *Shak. Rich.* III.

14. Noting ſeparation or receſſion.

To die by thee, were but to die in jeſt;
From thee to die, were torture more than death. *Sh. H.* VI.

By the ſacred radiance of the ſun,
The myſteries of Hecate, and the night;
By all the operations of the orbs,
From whom we do exiſt, and ceaſe to be,
Here I diſclaim all my paternal care. *Shakeſp. King Lear.*

Haſt thou beheld, when *from* the goal they ſtart,
The youthful charioteers, with heaving heart,
Ruſh to the race, and, panting, ſcarcely bear
Th' extremes of feveriſh hope and chilling fear. *Dryd. Virg.*

15. Noting exemption or deliverance.

From jealouſy's tormenting ſtrife,
For ever be thy boſom free. *Prior.*

16. At a diſtance. Noting abſence.

Our father he hath writ, ſo hath our ſiſter,
Of diff'rences, which I beſt thought it fit
To anſwer *from* our home. *Shakeſpeare's King Lear.*

17. Noting derivation.

I lay the deep foundations of a wall,
And Enos, nam'd *from* me, the city call. *Dryden's Æn.*

18. Since. Noting diſtance from the paſt.

The flood was not the cauſe of mountains, but there were mountains *from* the creation. *Raleigh's Hiſtory of the World.*

I had, *from* my childhood, a wart upon one of my fingers. *Bacon's Natural Hiſtory*, N°. 997.

The other had been trained up *from* his youth in the war of Flanders. *Clarendon, b.* viii.

The milk of tygers was his infant food,
Taught *from* his tender years the taſte of blood. *Dryden.*

Were there, *from* all eternity, no memorable actions done 'till about that time? *Tillotſon, Sermon* 1.

19. Contrary to.

Any thing ſo overdone is *from* the purpoſe of playing; whoſe end, both at the firſt and now, was and is to hold, as 'twere, the mirrour up to nature. *Shakeſpeare's Hamlet.*

Do not believe,
That *from* the ſenſe of all civility,
I thus would play and trifle with your reverence. *Shakeſp.*

Did you draw bonds to forfeit? Sign, to break?
Or muſt we read you quite *from* what we ſpeak,
And find the truth out the wrong way? *Donne.*

20. Noting removal.

Thrice *from the ground* ſhe leap'd. *Dryden's Æn. b.* ii.

21. *From* is very frequently joined by an ellipſis with adverbs: as, *from above*, *from* the parts *above*; *from below*, *from* the places *below*; of which ſome are here exemplified.

22. From *above*.

He, which gave them *from above* ſuch power, for miraculous confirmation of that which they taught, endued them alſo with wiſdom *from above*, to teach that which they ſo did confirm. *Hooker, b.* iii. *ſ.* 8.

No ſooner were his eyes in ſlumber bound,
When, *from above*, a more than mortal ſound
Invades his ears. *Dryden's Æn. b.* viii.

23. From *afar*.

Light demilances *from afar* they throw. *Dryden's Æn.*

24. From *beneath*.

With whirlwinds *from beneath* ſhe toſs'd the ſhip,
And bare expos'd the boſom of the deep. *Dryden's Virgil.*

An arm ariſes of the Stygian flood,
Which, breaking *from beneath* with bellowing ſound,
Whirls the black waves and rattling ſtones around. *Dryden.*

25. From *behind*.

See, to their baſe reſtor'd, earth, ſeas, and air,
And joyful ages *from behind*, in crowding ranks appear. *Dry.*

26. From *far*.

The train, proceeding on their way,
From far the town and lofty tow'rs ſurvey. *Dryden's Æn.*

27. From *high*.

Then heav'n's imperious queen ſhot down *from high*. *Dryd.*

28. From *thence*. Here *from* is ſuperfluous.

In the neceſſary differences which ariſe *from thence*, they rather break into ſeveral diviſions than join in any one publick intereſt; and *from hence* have always riſen the moſt dangerous factions, which have ruined the peace of nations. *Clarendon.*

29. From *whence*. *From* is here ſuperfluous.

While future realms his wand'ring thoughts delight,
His daily viſion, and his dream by night,
Forbidden Thebes appears before his eye,
From whence he ſees his abſent brother fly. *Pope's Statius.*

30. From *where*.

From where high Ithaca o'erlooks the floods,
Brown with o'er-arching ſhades and pendent woods,
Us to theſe ſhores our filial duty draws. *Pope's Odyſſey.*

31. From *without*.

When the plantation grows to ſtrength, then it is time to plant it with women as well as with men, that it may ſpread into generations, and not be pieced *from without*. *Bacon.*

If native power prevail not, ſhall I doubt
To ſeek for needful ſuccour *from without*. *Dryden's Æn.*

32. *From* is ſometimes followed by another prepoſition, with its proper caſe.

33. From *amidſt*.

Thou too ſhalt fall by time or barb'rous foes,
Whoſe circling walls the ſev'n fam'd hills encloſe;
And thou, whoſe rival tow'rs invade the ſkies,
And, *from amidſt* the waves, with equal glory riſe. *Addiſon.*

34. From *among*.

Here had new begun
My wand'ring, had not he, who was my guide
Up hither, *from among* the trees appear'd,
Preſence divine! *Milton's Paradiſe Loſt, b.* viii.

35. From *beneath*.

My worthy wife our arms miſlaid,
And *from beneath* my head my ſword convey'd. *Dryd. Æn.*

36. From *beyond*.

There followed him great multitudes of people from Galilee, and *from beyond* Jordan. *Mat.* iv. 25.

37. From *forth*.

Young Aretus, *from forth* his bridal bow'r,
Brought the full laver o'er their hands to pour,
And caniſters of conſecrated flour. *Pope's Odyſſey.*

38. From *off*.

The ſea being conſtrained to withdraw *from off* certain tracts of lands, which lay 'till then at the bottom of it. *Woodw.*

Knights, unhors'd, may riſe *from off* the plain,
And fight on foot, their honour to regain. *Dryden.*

39. From *out*.

The king with angry threatnings *from out* a window, where he was not aſhamed the world ſhould behold him a beholder, commanded his guard and the reſt of his ſoldiers to haſten their death. *Sidney, b.* ii.

And join thy voice unto the angel-quire,
From out his ſecret altar touch'd with hallow'd fire. *Milton.*

Now ſhake, *from out* thy fruitful breaſt, the ſeeds
Of envy, diſcord, and of cruel deeds. *Dryden's Æn. b.* vii.

Strong god of arms, whoſe iron ſceptre ſways
The freezing North and hyperborean ſeas,
Terror is thine; and wild amazement, flung
From out thy chariot, withers ev'n the ſtrong. *Dryden.*

40. From *out of*.

Whatſoever ſuch principle there is, it was at the firſt found out by diſcourſe, and drawn *from out of* the very bowels of heaven and earth. *Hooker, b.* i. *ſ.* 8.

41. From *under*.

He, though blind of ſight,
Deſpis'd, and thought extinguiſh'd quite,
With inward eyes illuminated,
His fiery virtue rous'd
From under aſhes into ſudden flame. *Milton's Agoniſtes.*

42. From *within*.

From within
The broken bowels, and the bloated ſkin,
A buzzing noiſe of bees his ears alarms. *Dryd. Virg. Geor.*

FRO'MWARD. *prep.* [ꝼꞃam and ꝼeaꞃð, Saxon.] Away from; the contrary to the word *towards*.

As chearfully going towards as Pyrocles went froward *fromward* his death. *Sidney.*

The common horizontal needle is continually varying towards Eaſt and Weſt; and ſo the dipping or inclining needle is varying up and down, towards or *fromwards* the zenith. *Cheyne's Phil. Princ.*

FRONDI'FEROUS. *adj.* [*frondifer*, Lat.] Bearing leaves. *Dict.*

FRONT. *n. ſ.* [*frons*, Latin; *front*, French.]

1. The face.

His *front* yet threatens, and his frowns command. *Prior.*

They ſtand not *front* to *front*, but each doth view
The other's tail, purſu'd as they purſue. *Creech's Manilius.*

The patriot virtues that diſtend thy thought,
Spread on thy *front*, and in thy boſom glow. *Thomſon.*

2. The face, in a ſenſe of cenſure or diſlike: as, a hardened *front*; a fierce *front*. This is the uſual ſenſe.

3. The face as oppoſed to an enemy.

His forward hand, inur'd to wounds, makes way
Upon the ſharpeſt *fronts* of the moſt fierce. *Daniel's C. W.*

4. The part or place oppoſed to the face.

The acceſs of the town was only by a neck of land: our men had ſhot that thundered upon them from the rampier in *front*, and from the gallies that lay at ſea in flank. *Bacon.*

5. The van of an army.

> 'Twixt hoſt and hoſt but narrow ſpace was left,
> A dreadful interval! and *front* to *front*
> Preſented, ſtood in terrible array. *Milton's Paradiſe Loſt.*

6. The forepart of any thing, as of a building.

Both theſe ſides are not only returns, but parts of the *front*; and uniform without, though ſeverally partitioned within, and are on both ſides of a great and ſtately tower, in the midſt of the *front*. *Bacon, Eſſay* 46.

Palladius adviſeth the *front* of his edifice ſhould ſo reſpect the South, that in its firſt angle it receive the riſing rays of the Winter ſun, and decline a little from the Winter ſetting thereof. *Brown's Vulgar Errours, b.* vi.

> The prince approach'd the door,
> Poſſeſs'd the porch, and on the *front* above
> He fix'd the fatal bough. *Dryden's Æn. b.* vi.

One ſees the *front* of a palace covered with painted pillars of different orders. *Addiſon's Remarks on Italy.*

7. The moſt conſpicuous part or particular.

To FRONT. *v. a.* [from the noun.]

1. To oppoſe directly, or face to face; to encounter.

You four ſhall *front* them in the narrow lane; we will walk lower: if they 'ſcape from your encounter, then they light on us. *Shakeſpeare's Henry* IV. *p.* i.

Can you, when you have puſh'd out of your gates the very defender of them, think to *front* his revenges with eaſy groans. *Shakeſpeare's Coriolanus.*

Some are either to be won to the ſtate in a faſt and true manner, or *fronted* with ſome other of the ſame party that may oppoſe them, and ſo divide the reputation. *Bacon's Eſſays.*

> I ſhall *front* thee, like ſome ſtaring ghoſt,
> With all my wrongs about me. *Dryden's Don Sebaſtian.*

2. To ſtand oppoſed or overagainſt any place or thing.

The ſquare will be one of the moſt beautiful in Italy when this ſtatue is erected, and a townhouſe built at one end to *front* the church that ſtands at the other. *Addiſon on Italy.*

To FRONT. *v. n.* To ſtand foremoſt.

> I *front* but in that file,
> Where others tell ſteps with me. *Shakeſpeare's Henry* VIII.

FRO'NTAL. *n. ſ.* [*frontale*, Lat. *frontal*, Fr.] Any external form of medicine to be applied to the forehead, generally compoſed amongſt the ancients of coolers and hypnoticks. *Quincy.*

We may apply intercipients upon the temples of maſtick: *frontales* may alſo be applied. *Wiſeman's Surgery.*

The torpedo, being alive, ſtupifies at a diſtance; but after death produceth no ſuch effect; which had they retained, they might have ſupplied opium, and ſerved as *frontals* in phrenſies. *Brown's Vulgar Errours, b.* iii.

FRO'NTATED. *adj.* [from *frons*, Latin.] In botany, the *frontated* leaf of a flower grows broader and broader, and at laſt perhaps terminates in a right line: uſed in oppoſition to cuſpated, which is, when the leaves of a flower end in a point. *Quincy.*

FRO'NTBOX. *n. ſ.* [*front* and *box*.] The box in the playhouſe from which there is a direct view to the ſtage.

> How vain are all theſe glories, all our pains,
> Unleſs good ſenſe preſerve what beauty gains!
> That men may ſay, when we the *frontbox* grace,
> Behold the firſt in virtue, as in face. *Pope's Ra. of the Lock.*

FRO'NTED. *adj.* [from *front*.] Formed with a front.

> Part *fronted* brigades form. *Milton.*

FRO'NTIER. *n. ſ.* [*frontiere*, French.] The marches; the limit; the utmoſt verge of any territory; the border: properly that which terminates not at the ſea, but fronts another country.

Draw all the inhabitants of thoſe borders away, or plant garriſons upon all thoſe *frontiers* about him. *Spenſer on Ireland.*

> I upon my *frontiers* here
> Keep reſidence,
> That little which is left ſo to defend. *Milton's Paradiſe Loſt.*

FRO'NTIER. *adj.* Bordering.

> A place there lies on Gallia's utmoſt bounds,
> Where riſing ſeas inſult the *frontier* grounds. *Addiſon.*

FRO'NTISPIECE. *n. ſ.* [*frontiſpicium, id quod in fronte conſpicitur*; *frontiſpice*, French.] That part of any building or other body that directly meets the eye.

> With *frontiſpiece* of diamond and gold
> Embelliſh'd, thick with ſparkling orient gems
> The portal ſhone. *Milton's Paradiſe Loſt, b.* iii.

Who is it has informed us that a rational ſoul can inhabit no tenement, unleſs it has juſt ſuch a ſort of *frontiſpice*? *Locke.*

The *frontiſpiece* of the townhouſe has pillars of a beautiful black marble, ſtreaked with white. *Addiſon on Italy.*

FRO'NTLESS. *adj.* [from *front*.] Without bluſhes; without ſhame; without diffidence.

> Thee, *frontleſs* man, we follow'd from afar,
> Thy inſtruments of death and tools of war. *Dryd. Iliad.*
> For vice, though *frontleſs* and of harden'd face,
> Is daunted at the ſight of awful grace. *Dryden.*
> Strike a bluſh through *frontleſs* flattery. *Pope.*

FRO'NTLET. *n. ſ.* [from *frons*, Latin; *frontcau*, French.] A bandage worn upon the forehead.

How now, daughter, what makes that *frontlet* on? You are too much of late i' th' frown. *Shakeſpeare's King Lear.*

They ſhall be as *frontlets* between thine eyes. *Deutr.* vi. 8.

To the forehead *frontlets* were applied, to reſtrain and intercept the influx. *Wiſeman's Surgery.*

FRONTROO'M. *n. ſ.* [*front* and *room*.] An apartment in the forepart of the houſe.

If your ſhop ſtands in an eminent ſtreet, the *frontrooms* are commonly more airy than the backrooms; and it will be inconvenient to make the *frontroom* ſhallow. *Moxon's Mech. Ex.*

FRORE. *adj.* [*bevroren*, Dutch, frozen.] Frozen. This word is not uſed ſince the time of *Milton*.

> The parching air
> Burns *frore*, and cold performs th' effect of fire. *Milt. P. L.*

FRORNE. *adj.* [*bevroren*, frozen, Dutch.] Frozen; congealed with cold. Obſolete.

> O, my heart-blood is well nigh *frorne* I feel,
> And my galage grown faſt to my heel. *Spenſer's Paſtorals.*

FROST. *n. ſ.* [ꝼꞃoꞅꞇ, Saxon.]

1. The laſt effect of cold; the power or act of congelation.

> This is the ſtate of man: to-day he puts forth
> The tender leaves of hopes, to-morrow bloſſoms,
> And bears his bluſhing honours thick upon him;
> The third day comes a *froſt*, a killing *froſt*,
> And when he thinks, good eaſy man, full ſurely
> His greatneſs is a ripening, nips his root,
> And then he falls. *Shakeſpeare's Henry* VIII.

When the *froſt* ſeizes upon wine, only the more wateriſh parts are congealed: there is a mighty ſpirit which can retreat into itſelf, and within its own compaſs lie ſecure from the freezing impreſſion. *South's Sermons.*

2. The appearance of plants and trees ſparkling with congelation of dew.

> Behold the groves that ſhine with ſilver *froſt*,
> Their beauty wither'd, and their verdure loſt. *Pope's Winter.*

FRO'STBITTEN. *adj.* [*froſt* and *bitten*.] Nipped or withered by the froſt.

The leaves, gathered ſomewhat before they are too much *froſtbitten*, make excellent matreſſes. *Mortimer.*

FRO'STED. *adj.* [from *froſt*.] Laid on in inequalities like thoſe of the hoar froſt upon plants.

> The rich brocaded ſilk unfold,
> Where riſing flow'rs grow ſtiff with *froſted* gold. *Gay.*

FRO'STILY. *adv.* [from *froſty*.]

1. With froſt; with exceſſive cold.
2. Without warmth of affection.

> Courtling, I rather thou ſhould'ſt utterly
> Diſpraiſe my work, than praiſe it *froſtily*. *Ben. Johnſon.*

FRO'STINESS. *n. ſ.* [from *froſty*.] Cold; freezing cold.

FRO'STNAIL. *n. ſ.* [*froſt* and *nail*.] A nail with a prominent head driven into the horſe's ſhoes, that it may pierce the ice.

The claws are ſtrait only to take hold, for better progreſſion; as a horſe that is ſhod with *froſtnails*. *Grew's Coſmol.*

FRO'STWORK. *n. ſ.* [*froſt* and *work*.] Work in which the ſubſtance is laid on with inequalities, like the dew congealed upon ſhrubs.

> By nature ſhap'd to various figures, thoſe
> The fruitful rain, and theſe the hail compoſe;
> The ſnowy fleece and curious *froſtwork* theſe,
> Produce the dew, and thoſe the gentle breeze. *Blackmore.*

FRO'STY. *adj.* [from *froſt*.]

1. Having the power of congelation; exceſſive cold.

> For all my blood in Rome's great quarrel ſhed,
> For all the *froſty* nights that I have watch'd,
> Be pitiful to my condemned ſons. *Shakeſp. Titus Andronicus.*

The air, if very cold, irritateth the flame, and maketh it burn more fiercely; as fire ſcorcheth in *froſty* weather. *Bacon.*

A gnat, half ſtarved with cold and hunger, went out one *froſty* morning to a bee-hive. *L'Eſtrange.*

2. Chill in affection; without warmth of kindneſs or courage.

What a *froſty* ſpirited rogue is this! *Shakeſp. Henry* IV.

3. Hoary; gray-haired; reſembling froſt.

> Where is loyalty?
> If it be baniſh'd from the *froſty* head,
> Where ſhall it find a harbour in the earth? *Shak. H.* VI.

FROTH. *n. ſ.* [*froe*, Daniſh and Scottiſh.]

1. Spume; foam; the bubbles cauſed in liquors by agitation.

> His hideous tail then hurled he about,
> And therewith all enwrapt the nimble thighs
> Of his *froth* foamy ſteed. *Fairy Queen, b.* i. *cant.* 11.

When wind expireth from under the ſea, as it cauſeth ſome reſounding of the water, ſo it cauſeth ſome light motions of bubbles, and white circles of *froth*. *Bacon's Nat. Hiſtory.*

> Surging waves againſt a ſolid rock,
> Though all to ſhivers daſh'd, th' aſſault renew;
> Vain batt'ry, and in *froth* or bubbles end. *Milton's Pa. Reg.*

The uſeleſs *froth* ſwims on the ſurface, but the pearl lies covered with a maſs of waters. *Glanv. Scepſ. c.* 9.

The scatter'd ocean flies;
Black sands, discolour'd *froth*, and mingled mud arise. *Dry.*

They were the *froth* my raging folly mov'd
When it boil'd up; I knew not then I lov'd,
Yet then lov'd most. *Dryden's Aurengzebe.*

If now the colours of natural bodies are to be mingled, let water, a little thickened with soap, be agitated to raise a *froth*; and after that *froth* has stood a little, there will appear, to one that shall view it intently, various colours every where in the surfaces of the several bubbles; but to one that shall go so far off that he cannot distinguish the colours from one another, the whole *froth* will grow white, with a perfect whiteness. *Newton's Opt.*

A painter, having finished the picture of a horse, excepting the loose *froth* about his mouth and his bridle; and after many unsuccessful essays, despairing to do that to his satisfaction, in a great rage threw a spunge at it, all besmeared with the colours, which fortunately hitting upon the right place, by one bold stroke of chance most exactly supplied the want of skill in the artist. *Bentley's Sermons.*

2. Any empty or senseless show of wit or eloquence.
3. Any thing not hard, solid, or substantial.

Who eateth his veal, pig and lamb being *froth*,
Shall twice in a week go to bed without broth. *Tuss. Husb.*

To FROTH. *v. n.* [from the noun.] To foam; to throw out spume; to generate spume.

He frets within, *froths* treason at his mouth,
And churns it through his teeth. *Dryden's Don Sebastian.*

FRO'THILY. *adv.* [from *frothy.*]
1. With foam; with spume.
2. In an empty trifling manner.

FRO'THY. *adj.* [from *froth.*]
1. Full of foam, froth, or spume.

The sap of trees is of differing natures; some watery and clear, as vines, beeches, pears; some thick, as apples; some gummy, as cherries; and some *frothy*, as elms. *Bacon.*

Behold a *frothy* substance rise;
Be cautious, or your bottle flies. *Swift.*

2. Soft; not solid; wasting.

Their bodies are so solid and hard as you need not fear that bathing should make them *frothy*. *Bacon's Natural History.*

3. Vain; empty; trifling.

What's a voluptuous dinner, and the *frothy* vanity of discourse that commonly attends these pompous entertainments? What is it but a mortification, to a man of sense and virtue? *L'Estrange, Fable 185.*

Though the principles of religion were never so clear and evident, yet they may be made ridiculous by vain and *frothy* men; as the gravest and wisest person in the world may be abused by being put in a fool's coat. *Tillotson, Sermon 1.*

FROUNCE. *n. s.* A word used by falconers for a distemper, in which white spittle gathers about the hawk's bill. *Skinner and Ainsworth.*

To FROUNCE. *v. a.* [from the noun.] To frizzle or curl the hair about the face. This word was at first probably used in contempt.

Some *frounce* their curled hair in courtly guise,
Some prank their ruffs, and others timely dight
Their gay attire. *Fairy Queen, b.* i. *cant.* 4.

Some warlike sign must be used; either a slovenly buskin, or an overstaring *frounced* head. *Ascham's Schoolmaster.*

Thus, night, oft see me in thy pale career,
'Till civil suited morn appear;
Not trick'd and *frounc'd* as she was wont,
With the Attick boy to hunt. *Milton.*

FRO'UZY. *adj.* [A cant word.] Dim; fœtid; musty.

Petticoats in *frouzy* heaps. *Swift.*

When first Diana leaves her bed,
Vapours and steams her looks disgrace;
A *frouzy* dirty-colour'd red
Sits on her cloudy wrinkled face. *Swift.*

FRO'WARD. *adj.* [ꝼꞃampeaꞃꝺ, Saxon.] Peevish; ungovernable; angry; perverse: the contrary to *toward.*

The *froward* pain of mine own heart made me so delight to punish him, whom I esteemed the chiefest let in the way. *Sidney.*

She's not *froward*, but modest as the dove:
She is not hot, but temperate as the morn. *Shakespeare.*

Whose ways are crooked, and they *froward* in their paths. *Prov.* ii. 15.

Time moveth so round, that a *froward* retention of custom is as turbulent a thing as innovation. *Bacon, Essay* 25.

'Tis with *froward* men, and *froward* factions too, as 'tis with *froward* children; they'll be sooner quieted by fear than by any sense of duty. *L'Estrange.*

They help or occasion sleep, as we find by the common use and experience of rocking *froward* children in cradles. *Temple.*

FRO'WARDLY. *adv.* [from *froward.*] Peevishly; perversely.

I hid me and was wroth, and he went *frowardly* in the way of his heart. *Is.* lvii. 17.

FRO'WARDNESS. *n. s.* [from *froward.*] Peevishness; perverseness.

How many *frowardnesses* of ours does he smother? how many indignities does he pass by? how many affronts does he put up at our hands? *South's Sermons.*

We'll mutually forget
The warmth of youth and *frowardness* of age. *Addis. Cato.*

FRO'WER. *n. s.* [I know not the etymology.] A cleaving tool.

A *frower* of iron for cleaving of lath,
With roll for a sawpit, good husbandry hath. *Tuss. Husb.*

To FROWN. *v. a.* [*frogner*, old French, to wrinkle. *Skinner.*] To express displeasure by contracting the face to wrinkles; to look stern.

Say, that she *frowns*; I'll say, she looks as clear
As morning roses newly wash'd with dew. *Shakespeare.*

They chuse their magistrate;
And such a one as he, who puts his shall,
His popular shall, against a graver bench
Than ever *frown'd*. *Shakespeare's Coriolanus.*

How now, daughter, what makes that frontlet on? You are too much of late i' th' frown.
——Thou wast a pretty fellow, when thou hadst no need to care for her *frowning*. *Shakespeare's King Lear.*

Heroes in animated marble *frown.* *Pope.*

The wood,
Whose shady horrors on a rising brow
Wav'd high, and *frown'd* upon the stream below. *Pope.*

FROWN. *n. s.* [from the verb.] A wrinkled look; a look of displeasure.

Patiently endure that *frown* of fortune, and by some notable exploit win again her favour. *Knolles's History of the Turks.*

In his half-clos'd eyes
Stern vengeance yet and hostile terror stand;
His front yet threatens, and his *frowns* command. *Prior.*

FRO'WNINGLY. *adv.* [from *frown.*] Sternly; with a look of displeasure.

What, look'd he *frowningly?*
—A count'nance more in sorrow than in anger. *Shak. Ham.*

FRO'WY. *adj.* Musty; mossy. This word is now not used; but instead of it *frouzy.*

But if they with thy gotes should yede,
They soon might be corrupted;
Or like not of the *frowy* fede,
Or with the weeds be glutted. *Spenser's Pastorals.*

FRO'ZEN. *part. pass.* of *freeze.*

Against whom was the fine *frozen* knight, *frozen* in despair; but his armour so naturally representing ice, and all his furniture so lively answering thereto, as yet did I never see any thing that pleased me better. *Sidney, b.* ii.

How dire a tempest from Mycenæ pour'd,
Our plains, our temples, and our town devour'd:
What was the waste of war, what fierce alarms
Shook Asia's crown with European arms;
Ev'n such have heard, if any such there be,
Whose earth is bounded by the *frozen* sea. *Dryden's Æn.*

Fierce Boreas, with his offspring, issues forth
T' invade the *frozen* waggon of the North. *Dryd. Ovid.*

A cheerful blaze arose, and by the fire
They warm'd their *frozen* feet, and dry'd their wet attire. *Dryden's Flower and Leaf.*

F. R. S. *Fellow* of the *Royal Society.*

Who this profess,
Shine in the dignity of *F. R. S.* *Pope.*

FRU'CTIFEROUS. *adj.* [*fructifer*, Latin.] Bearing fruit. *Ains.*

To FRU'CTIFY. *v. a.* [*fructifier*, French.] To make fruitful; to fertilise.

The legal levies the sovereign raises, are as vapours which the sun exhales, which fall down in sweet showers to *fructify* the earth. *Howel's Vocal Forest.*

Where e'er she looks, behold some sudden birth
Adorns the trees, and *fructifies* the earth. *Granville.*

To FRU'CTIFY. *v. n.* To bear fruit.

It watereth the heart, to the end it may *fructify*; maketh the virtuous, in trouble, full of magnanimity and courage; and serveth as a most approved remedy against all doleful and heavy accidents which befall men in this present life. *Hooker.*

Thus would there nothing *fructify*, either near or under them, the sun being horizontal to the poles. *Brown's Vu. Err.*

FRUCTIFICA'TION. *n. s.* [from *fructify.*] The act of causing or of bearing fruit; fecundation; fertility.

That the sap doth powerfully rise in the Spring, to put the plant in a capacity of *fructification*, he that hath beheld how many gallons of water may be drawn from a birch-tree, hath slender reason to doubt. *Brown's Vulgar Errours, b.* ii.

FRU'CTUOUS. *adj.* [*fructueux*, Fr. from *fructify.*] Fruitful; fertile; impregnating with fertility.

Here to the sight
Apples of price, and plenteous sheaves of corn
Oft interlac'd occur; and both imbibe
Fitting congenial juice, so rich the soil,
So much does *fructuous* moisture o'erabound! *Phillips.*

FRU'GAL. *adj.* [*frugalis*, Latin; *frugal*, Fr.] Thrifty; sparing; parsimonious; not prodigal; not profuse; not lavish.

If through mists he shoots his sullen beams,
Frugal of light, in loose and straggling streams,
Suspect a drisling day. *Dryden's Virgil's Georgicks.*

FRU'GALLY. *adv.* [from *frugal.*] Parsimoniously; sparingly; thriftily.

Mean time young Pasimond his marriage press'd,
And *frugally* resolv'd, the charge to shun,
To join his brother's bridal with his own. *Dryden.*

FRUGA'LITY. *n. s.* [*frugalité*, French; *frugalitas*, Latin.] Thrift; parsimony; good husbandry.

As for the general sort of men, *frugality* may be the cause of drinking water; for that is no small saving, to pay nothing for one's drink. *Bacon.*

Frugality and bounty too,
Those diff'ring virtues, meet in you. *Waller.*

In this *frugality* of your praises, some things I cannot omit. *Dryden's Fables, Dedication.*

The boundaries of virtues are indivisible lines: it is impossible to march up close to the frontiers of *frugality*, without entering the territories of parsimony. *Arbuthnot's John Bull.*

FRU'GIFEROUS. *adj.* [*frugifer*, Latin.] Bearing fruit. *Ainf.*

FRUIT. *n. s.* [*fructus*, Latin; *frwyth*, Welsh; *fruit*, French.]

1. The product of a tree or plant in which the seeds are contained.

The strawberry grows underneath the nettle,
And wholsome berries thrive and ripen best,
Neighbour'd by *fruit* of baser quality. *Shakesp. Henry V.*

2. That part of a plant which is taken for food.

By tasting of that *fruit* forbid,
Where they sought knowledge, they did error find. *Davies.*
See how the rising *fruits* the gardens crown,
Imbibe the sun, and make his light their own. *Blackmore.*

3. Production.

The *fruit* of the spirit is in all goodness and righteousness, and truth. *Ez.* v. 9.

4. The offspring of the womb; the young of any animal.

Can'st thou their reck'nings keep? the time compute,
When their swol'n bellies shall enlarge their *fruit*. *Sandys.*

5. Advantage gained by any enterprise or conduct.

What is become of all the king of Sweden's victories? Where are the *fruits* of them at this day? Or of what benefit will they be to posterity? *Swift.*

Another *fruit*, from considering things in themselves, will be, that each man will pursue his thoughts in that method which will be most agreeable to the nature of the thing, and to his apprehension of what it suggests to him. *Locke.*

6. The effect or consequence of any action.

She blushed when she considered the effect of granting; she was pale, when she remembered the *fruits* of denying. *Sidney.*

They shall eat of the *fruit* of their own way. *Prov.* i. 31.

If I live in the flesh, this is the *fruit* of my labour *Philip* i.

FRU'ITAGE. *n. s.* [*fruitage*, French.] Fruit collectively; various fruits.

In heav'n the trees
Of life ambrosial *fruitage* bear, and vines
Yield nectar. *Milton's Paradise Lost*, *b.* v.

Greedily they pluck'd
The *fruitage*, fair to sight, like that which grew
Near that bituminous lake where Sodom flam'd. *Milton.*

What is more ordinary with them than the taking in flowers and *fruitage* for the garnishing of their work? *More.*

FRU'ITBEARER. *n. s.* [*fruit* and *bearer.*] That which produces fruit.

Trees, especially *fruitbearers*, are often infected with the measles. *Mortimer's Husbandry.*

FRU'ITBEARING. *adj.* [*fruit* and *bear.*] Having the quality of producing fruit.

By this way graft trees of different kinds one on another, as *fruitbearing* trees on those that bear not. *Mort. Husbandry.*

FRU'ITERER. *n. s.* [*fruitier*, French.] One who trades in fruit.

I did fight with one Sampson Stockfish, a *fruiterer*, behind Gray's-inn. *Shakespeare's Henry* IV. *p.* ii.

Walnuts the *fruit'rer's* hand in Autumn stain;
Blue plumbs and juicy pears augment his gain. *Gay.*

FRU'ITERY. *n. s.* [*fruiterie*, French.]

1. Fruit collectively taken.

Oft, notwithstanding all thy care
To help thy plants, on the small *fruitery*
Exempt from ills, an oriental blast
Disastrous flies. *Phillips.*

2. A fruit-loft; a repository for fruit.

FRU'ITFUL. *adj.* [*fruit* and *full.*]

1. Fertile; abundantly productive; liberal of product.

If she continued cruel, he could no more sustain his life than the earth remain *fruitful* in the sun's continual absence. *Sidney*, *b.* ii.

2. Actually bearing fruit.

Adonis' gardens,
That one day bloom'd, and *fruitful* were the next. *Shakesp.*

3. Prolifick; childbearing; not barren.

Hear, nature, hear; dear goddess, hear a father!
Suspend thy purpose, if thou did'st intend
To make this creature *fruitful*:
Into her womb convey sterility. *Shakespeare's King Lear.*

I have copied nature, making the youths amorous and the damsels *fruitful*. *Gay's Preface to the What d'ye Call it.*

4. Plenteous; abounding in any thing.

While you, my lord, the rural shades admire,
And from Britannia's publick posts retire,
Me into foreign realms my fate conveys,
Through nations *fruitful* of immortal lays. *Addison.*

FRU'ITFULLY. *adv.* [from *fruitful.*]

1. In such a manner as to be prolifick.

How sacred seeds of sea, and air, and earth,
And purer fire through universal night,
And empty space, did *fruitfully* unite. *Roscommon.*

2. Plenteously; abundantly.

You have many opportunities to cut him off: if your will want not, time and place will be *fruitfully* offered. *Shakesp.*

FRU'ITFULNESS. *n. s.* [from *fruitful.*]

1. Fertility; fecundity; plentiful production.

Neither can we ascribe the same *fruitfulness* to any part of the earth, nor the same virtue to any plant thereon growing, that they had before the flood. *Raleigh's Hist. of the World.*

2. The quality of being prolifick.

The goddess, present at the match she made,
So bless'd the bed, such *fruitfulness* convey'd,
That ere ten moons had sharpen'd either horn,
To crown their bliss, a lovely boy was born. *Dryd. Ovid.*

3. Exuberant abundance

The remedy of *fruitfulness* is easy, but no labour will help the contrary: I will like and praise some things in a young writer, which yet, if he continues in, I cannot but justly hate him for. *Ben. Johnson's Discoveries.*

FRUITGRO'VES. *n. s.* [*fruit* and *groves.*] Shades, or close plantations of fruit trees.

The faithful slave,
Whom to my nuptial train Icarius gave,
To tend the *fruitgroves*? *Pope's Odyssey*, *b.* iv.

FRUI'TION. *n. s.* [*fruor*, Latin.] Enjoyment; possession; pleasure given by possession or use.

Man doth not seem to rest satisfied either with *fruition* of that wherewith his life is preserved, or with performance of such actions as advance him most deservedly in estimation. *Hooker*, *b.* i.

I am driv'n, by breath of her renown,
Either to seek shipwreck, or arrive
Where I may have *fruition* of her love. *Shakesp. Henry* VI.

God riches and renown to men imparts,
Ev'n all they wish; and yet their narrow hearts
Cannot so great a fluency receive,
But their *fruition* to a stranger leave. *Sandys's Paraphrase.*

Affliction generally disables a man from pursuing those vices in which the guilt of men consists: if the affliction be on his body, his appetites are weakened, and capacity of *fruition* destroyed. *Rogers's Sermons.*

Wit once, like beauty, without art or dress,
Naked and unadorn'd, could find success;
'Till by *fruition*, novelty destroy'd,
The nymph must find new charms to be enjoy'd. *Granv.*

FRU'ITIVE. *adj.* [from the noun.] Enjoying; possessing; having the power of enjoyment.

To whet our longings for *fruitive* or experimental knowledge, it is reserved among the prerogatives of being in heaven to know how happy we shall be, when there. *Boyle.*

FRU'ITLESS. *adj.* [from *fruit.*]

1. Barren of fruit; not bearing fruit.

The Spaniards of Mexico, for the first forty years, could not make our kind of wheat bear seed; but it grew up as high as the trees, and was *fruitless*. *Raleigh's History.*

2. Vain; productive of no advantage; idle; unprofitable.

O! let me not, quoth he, return again
Back to the world, whose joys so *fruitless* are;
But let me here for ay in peace remain,
Or straightway on that last long voyage fare. *Fairy Queen.*

Serpent! we might have spar'd our coming hither;
Fruitless to me, though fruit be here t' excess. *Milt. P. L.*

3. Without offspring.

Upon my head they plac'd a *fruitless* crown,
And put a barren scepter in my gripe;
No son of mine succeeding. *Shakespeare's Macbeth.*

FRU'ITLESSLY. *adv.* [from *fruitless.*] Vainly; idly; unprofitably.

After this fruit curiosity *fruitlessly* enquireth, and confidence blindly determineth. *Brown's Vulgar Errours*, *b.* vii.

Walking they talk'd, and *fruitlessly* divin'd
What friend the priestess by those words design'd. *Dryden.*

FRUIT-TIME. *n. s.* [*fruit* and *time.*] The Autumn; the time for gathering fruit.

FRU'IT-TREE *n. s.* [*fruit* and *tree.*] A tree of that kind whose principal value arises from the fruit produced by it.

Lady,

Lady, by yonder blessed moon I vow,
That tips with silver all these *fruittree* tops. *Shakespeare.*

They took strong cities, possessed houses full of all goods, wells digged, vineyards and oliveyards, and *fruittrees* in abundance. *Neh.* ix. 25.

All with a border of rich *fruittrees* crown'd,
Whose loaded branches hide the lofty mound. *Waller.*

FRUMENTA'CIOUS. *adj.* [from *frumentum*, Latin.] Made of grain. *Dict.*

FRUME'NTY. *n. s.* [*frumentum*, corn, Latin.] Food made of wheat boiled in milk.

To FRUMP. *v. a.* To mock; to browbeat. *Skinner. Ainsw.*

To FRUSH. *v. a.* [*froisser*, French.] To break, bruise, or crush. *Hanmer.*

I like thy armour well;
I'll *frush* it, and unlock the rivets all,
But I'll be master of it. *Shakespeare's Troilus and Cressida.*

FRUSH. *n. s.* [from the verb.] A sort of tender horn that grows in the middle of the sole, and at some distance from the toe: it divides into two branches, running towards the heel, in the form of a fork. *Farrier's Dict.*

FRUSTRA'NEOUS. *adj.* [*frustra*, Latin.] Vain; useless; unprofitable; without advantage.

Their attempts being so *frustraneous*, and the demonstrations to the contrary so perspicuous, it is a marvel that any man, virtuously and piously disposed, should be so partially and zealously affected in a cause that has neither truth nor any honest usefulness in it. *More's Divine Dialogues.*

He timely withdraws his *frustraneous* baffled kindnesses, and sees the folly of endeavouring to stroke a tyger into a lamb, or to court an Ethiopian out of his colour. *South's Sermons.*

To FRU'STRATE. *v. a.* [*frustror*, Latin; *frustrer*, Fr.]

1. To defeat; to disappoint; to balk.

It is an axiom of nature, that natural desire cannot utterly be *frustrate.* *Hooker, b.* i.

I survive,
To mock the expectations of the world;
To *frustrate* prophecies, and to raze out
Rotten opinion, which hath writ me down
After my seeming. *Shakespeare's Henry* IV. *p.* ii.

Stern look'd the fiend, as *frustrate* of his will;
Not half suffic'd, and greedy yet to kill. *Dryden.*

Not more almighty to resist our might,
Than wise to *frustrate* all our plots and wiles. *Milt. P. Lost.*

2. To make null; to nullify.

The act of parliament which gave all his lands to the queen, did cut off and *frustrate* all such conveyances. *Spenser.*

Now thou hast aveng'd
Supplanted Adam; and by vanquishing
Temptation, hast regain'd lost paradise,
And *frustrated* the conquest fraudulent. *Milton's Par. Reg.*

The peculiar strength of the motive may of itself perhaps contribute to *frustrate* the efficacy of it, rendering it liable to be suspected by him to whom it is addressed. *Atterbury's Serm.*

FRU'STRATE. *participial adj.* [from the verb.]

1. Vain; ineffectual; useless; unprofitable.

He is drown'd
Whom thus we stray to find, and the sea mocks
Our *frustrate* search on land. *Shakespeare's Tempest.*

The ruler of the province of Judea being by Julian busied in the re-edifying of this temple, flaming balls of fire issuing near the foundation, and oft consuming the workmen, made the enterprise *frustrate.* *Raleigh's History.*

All at once employ their thronging darts;
But out of order thrown, in air they join,
And multitude makes *frustrate* the design. *Dryden's Ovid.*

2. Null; void.

Few things are so restrained to any one end or purpose, that, the same being extinct, they should forthwith utterly become *frustrate.* *Hooker, b.* v. *s.* 42.

FRUSTRA'TION. *n. s.* [*frustratio*, Latin, from *frustrate.*] Disappointment; defeat.

In states notoriously irreligious, a secret and irresistible power countermands their deepest projects, splits their counsels, and smites their most refined policies with *frustration* and a curse. *South's Sermons.*

FRU'STRATIVE. *adj.* [from *frustrate.*] Fallacious; disappointing. *Ainsworth.*

FRU'STRATORY. *adj.* [from *frustrate.*] That which makes any procedure void; that which vacates any former process.

Bartolus restrains this to a *frustratory* appeal. *Ayliffe's Par.*

FRU'STUM. *n. s.* [Latin.] A piece cut off from a regular figure. A term of science.

FRY. *n. s.* [from *froe*, foam, Danish. *Skinner.*]

1. The swarm of little fishes just produced from the spawn.

They come to us, but us love draws;
He swallows us, and never chaws:
By him, as by chain'd shot, whole ranks do die;
He is the tyrant pike, and we the *fry.* *Donne.*

Forthwith the sounds and seas, each creek and bay,
With *fry* innumerable swarm, and shoals
Of fish, that with their fins and shining scales
Glide under the green wave in sculls, that oft
Bank the mid-sea. *Milton's Paradise Lost, b.* vii.

The angler had the hap to draw up a very little fish from among the *fry.* *L'Estrange.*

So close behind some promontory lie
The huge leviathans, t' attend their prey;
And give no chace, but swallow in the *fry*,
Which through their gaping jaws mistake the way. *Dryd.*

2. Any swarm of animals; or young people in contempt.

Out of the *fry* of these rakehell horseboys, growing up in knavery and villany, are their kern continually supplied and maintained. *Spenser on Ireland.*

Them before the *fry* of children young,
Their wanton sports and childish mirth did play,
And to the maidens sounding timbrels sung. *Fairy Queen.*

Draw me no constellations there,
Nor dog, nor goat, nor bull, nor bear;
Nor any of that monstrous *fry*
Of animals that stock the sky. *Oldham.*

The young *fry* must be held at a distance, and kept under the discipline of contempt. *Collier on Pride.*

FRY. *n. s.* A kind of sieve.

He dresseth the dust from malt, by running it through a fan or *fry.* *Mortimer's Husbandry.*

To FRY. *v. a.* [*frigo*, Lat. *ffrio*, Welsh; *frijck*, Erse.] To dress food by roasting it in a pan on the fire.

To FRY. *v. n.*

1. To be roasted in a pan on the fire.

2. To suffer the action of fire.

So when with crackling flames a cauldron *fries*,
The bubbling waters from the bottom rise;
Above the brims they force their fiery way,
Black vapours climb aloft, and cloud the day. *Dryd. Æn.*

3. To melt with heat.

Spices and gums about them melting *fry*,
And, phenix like, in that rich nest they die. *Waller.*

4. To be agitated like liquor in the pan on the fire.

Oil of sweet almonds, newly drawn with sugar, and a little spice, spread upon bread toasted, is an excellent nourisher; but then, to keep the oil from *frying* in the stomach, drink mild beer after it. *Bacon's Natural History.*

Where no ford he finds, no water *fries*,
Nor billows with unequal murmurs roar,
But smoothly slide along, and swell the shoar,
That course he steer'd. *Dryden's Æn.*

FRY. *n. s.* [from the verb.] A dish of things fried.

FRY'INGPAN. *n. s.* [*fry* and *pan.*] The vessel in which meat is roasted on the fire.

If I pass by sea, I may chance to fall from the *fryingpan* into the fire. *Howel's Vocal Forest.*

We understand by out of the *fryingpan* into the fire, that things go from bad to worse. *L'Estrange.*

A freeman of London has the privilege of disturbing a whole street, for an hour together, with the twanking of a brass kettle or a *fryingpan.* *Addison's Spectator.*

To FUB. *v. a.* To put off; to delay by false pretences; to cheat. It is generally written *fob.* See FOB.

A hundred mark is a long lone for a poor lone woman to bear; and I have borne, and borne, and borne, and have been *fubb'd* off and *fubb'd* off from this day to that day, that it is a shame to be thought on. *Shakespeare's Henry* IV. *p.* ii.

FUB. *n. s.* A plump chubby boy. *Ainsworth.*

FU'CATED. *adj.* [*fucatus*, Latin.]

1. Painted; disguised with paint.

2. Disguised by false show.

FU'CUS. *n. s.* [Latin.] Paint for the face.

Women chat
Of *fucus* this, and *fucus* that. *Ben. Johnson.*

Those who paint for debauchery should have the *fucus* pulled off, and the coarseness underneath discovered. *Collier.*

To FU'DDLE. *v. a.* [Of unknown etymology.] To make drunk.

Earnest brimming bowls
Leave every soul the table floating round,
And pavement faithless to the *fuddled* feet. *Thoms. Autumn*

To FU'DDLE. *v. n.* To drink to excess.

Men, we see, will be whoring and *fuddling* on still. *L'Estr.*

FUEL. *n. s.* [from *feu*, fire, French.] The matter or aliment of fire.

This shall be with burning and *fuel* of fire. *Is.* ix. 5.

This spark will prove a raging fire,
If wind and *fuel* be brought to feed it with. *Shak. H.* VI.

Mov'd by my charms, with them your love may cease;
And as the *fuel* sinks, the flame decrease. *Prior.*

To FU'EL. *v. a.* [from the noun.]

1. To feed fire with combustible matter.

And yet she cannot waste by this,
Nor long endure this torturing wrong;
For more corruption needful is,
To *fuel* such a fever long. *Donne.*

Never,

Never, alas! the dreadful name
That *fuels* the infernal flame *Cowley.*
The *fuel'd* chimney blazes wide. *Thomson's Autumn.*

2. To store with firing.

Some are plainly oeconomical, as that the seat be well watered, and well *fuelled.* *Wotton's Architecture.*

FUE'ILLEMORTE. [French.] Corruptly pronounced and written *philomot.*

Fueillemorte colour signifies the colour of withered leaves in Autumn. *Locke.*

FUGA'CIOUSNESS. *n. s.* [*fugax*, Latin.] Volatility; the quality of flying away.

FUGA'CITY. *n. s.* [*fugax*, Latin.]

1. Volatility; quality of flying away.

Spirits and salts, which, by their *fugacity*, colour, smell, taste, and divers experiments that I purposely made to examine them, were like the salt and spirit of urine and soot. *Boyle.*

2 Uncertainty; instability.

FUGH. *interj.* [perhaps from φεῦ.] An expression of abhorrence.

A very filthy fellow: how odiously he smells of his country garlick! *fugh*, how he stinks of Spain! *Dryd. Don Sebastian.*

FU'GITIVE. *adj.* [*fugitif*, French; *fugitivus*, Latin.]

1. Not tenable; not to be held or detained.

Our idea of infinity is a growing and *fugitive* idea, still in a boundless progression, that can stop no where. *Locke.*

Happiness, object of that waking dream,
Which we call life, mistaking: *fugitive* theme
Of my pursuing verse, ideal shade,
Notional good, by fancy only made. *Prior.*

2. Unsteady; unstable; not durable.

3. Volatile; apt to fly away.

The more tender and *fugitive* parts, the leaves, of many of the more sturdy vegetables, fall off for want of the supply from beneath: those only which are more tenacious, making a shift to subsist without such recruit. *Woodward's Nat. History.*

4. Flying; running from danger.

Whilst yet with Parthian blood thy sword is warm,
The *fugitive* Parthians follow. *Shakes. Ant. and Cleopatra.*

The Trojan chief
Thrice *fugitive* about Troy wall. *Milton.*

5. Flying from duty; falling off.

Can a *fugitive* daughter enjoy herself, while her parents are in tears? *Clarissa.*

6. Wandering; runnagate; vagabond.

It was the most malicious surmise that had been ever brewed, howsoever countenanced by a libellous pamphlet of a *fugitive* physician. *Wotton.*

FU'GITIVE. *n. s.* [from the adjective.]

1. One who runs from his station or duty.

Unmarried men are best friends, best masters, best servants, but not always best subjects; for they are light to run away, and almost all *fugitives* are of that condition. *Bacon, Essay* 8.

Back to thy punishment,
False *fugitive!* and to thy speed add wings,
Lest with a whip of scorpions I pursue
Thy ling'ring. *Milton's Paradise Lost, b.* ii.

We understand by some *fugitives* that he hath commanded
The generals to return with victory, or expect
A shameful death. *Denham's Sophy.*

2. One who takes shelter under another power from punishment.

There are also in this realm of England too many, which, being men of good inheritance, are fled beyond the seas, where they live under princes which are her majesty's professed enemies; and converse and are confederates with other traytors and *fugitives*, which are there abiding. *Spenser on Ireland.*

Your royal highness is too great and too just a monarch either to want or to receive the homage of rebellious *fugitives.* *Dryden.*

FU'GITIVENESS. *n. s.* [from *fugitive.*]

1. Volatility; fugacity.

That divers salts, emerging upon the analysis of many concretes, are very volatile, is plain from the *fugitiveness* of salt and of hartshorn ascending in distillation. *Boyle.*

2. Instability; uncertainty.

FUGUE. *n. s.* [French, from *fuga*, Latin.] In musick, some point consisting of four, five, six, or any other number of notes begun by some one single part, and then seconded by a third, fourth, fifth and sixth part, if the composition consists of so many; repeating the same, or such like notes, so that the several parts follow, or come in one after another in the same manner, the leading parts still flying before those that follow. *Harris.*

The reports and *fugues* have an agreement with the figures in rhetorick of repetition and traduction. *Bacon's Nat. Hist.*

The skilful organist plies his grave and fancied descant in lofty *fugues*; or through the whole symphony artful and unimaginable touches adorn and grace the well-studied chords of some choice composer. *Milton on Education.*

His volant touch
Instinct through all proportions, low and high,
Fled, and pursu'd transverse the resonant *fugue.* *Milt. P. L.*

Long has a race of heroes fill'd the stage,
That rant by note, and through the gamut rage;
In songs and airs express their martial fire,
Combat in trills, and in a *fugue* expire. *Addison.*

FU'LCIMENT. *n. s.* [*fulcimen*, *fulcimentum*, Latin.] That on which a body rests, which acts or is acted upon at each end, as a balance or a lever.

The power that equiponderates with any weight, must have the same proportion unto it as there is betwixt their several distances from the center or *fulciment.* *Wilkins.*

To FULFI'L. *v. a.* [*full* and *fill.*]

1. To fill till there is no room for more. This sense is now not used.

Six gates i' th' city, with massy staples,
And corresponsive and *fulfilling* bolts,
Sparre up the sons of Troy. *Shak. Troil. and Cressida, Prol.*

2. To answer any prophecy or promise by performance.

They knew him not, nor yet the voices of the prophets which are read every sabbath-day, they have *fulfilled* them in condemning him. *Acts* xiii. 27.

The fury bath'd them in each other's blood;
Then, having fix'd the fight, exulting flies,
And bears *fulfill'd* her promise to the skies. *Dryden's Æn.*

3. To answer any purpose or design.

Here nature seems *fulfill'd* in all her ends. *Milt. P. Lost.*

4. To answer any desire by compliance or gratification.

If on my wounded breast thou drop'st a tear,
Think for whose sake my breast that wound did bear;
And faithfully my last desires *fulfil*,
As I perform my cruel father's will. *Dryden's Ovid.*

5. To answer any law by obedience.

Love worketh no ill to his neighbour, therefore love is the *fulfilling* of the law. *Ro.* xiii. 10.

This I my glory account,
My exaltation, and my whole delight,
That thou in me well-pleas'd, declar'st thy will
Fulfill'd, which to *fulfil* is all my bliss. *Milton's Par. Lost.*

FULFRA'UGHT. *adj.* [*full* and *fraught.*] Fully stored.

Thy fall hath left a kind of blot
To mark the *fulfraught* man, the best endu'd,
With some suspicion. *Shakespeare's Henry* V.

FU'LGENCY. *n. s.* [*fulgens*, Latin.] Splendour; glitter. *Dict.*

FU'LGENT. *adj.* [*fulgens*, Latin.] Shining; dazzling; exquisitely bright.

As from a cloud, his *fulgent* head,
And shape star-bright, appear'd. *Milton's Paradise Lost.*

The illumination is not so bright and *fulgent* as to obscure or extinguish all perceptibility of reason. *More's Divine Dial.*

FU'LGID. *adj.* [*fulgidus*, Latin.] Shining; glittering; dazzling.

FULGI'DITY. *n. s.* [from *fulgid.*] Splendour; dazzling glitter. *Dict.*

FU'LGOUR. *n. s.* [*fulgor*, Latin.]

1. Splendour; dazzling brightness like that of lightning.

Glow-worms alive project a lustre in the dark; which *fulgour*, notwithstanding, ceaseth after death. *Brown.*

When I set my eyes on this side of things, there shines from them such an intellectual *fulgour*, that methinks the very glory of the Deity becomes visible through them. *More.*

FULGURA'TION. *n. s.* [*fulguratio*, Latin.] The act of lightening.

FU'LHAM. *n. s.* A cant word for false dice. *Hanmer.*

Let vultures gripe thy guts, for gourd and *Fulham's* hold,
And high and low beguile the rich and poor. *Shakespeare.*

FULI'GINOUS. *adj.* [*fuligineux-se*, Fr. *fuliginosus*, Lat.] Sooty smoky.

The leaf of burrage hath an excellent spirit to repress the *fuliginous* vapours of dusky melancholy, and so cure madness. *Bacon's Natural History.*

Whereas history should be the torch of truth, he makes her in divers places a *fuliginous* link of lies. *Howel.*

FU'LIMART. *n. s.* [This word, of which *Skinner* observes that he found it only in this passage, seems to mean the same with *fitchat.*] A kind of stinking ferret.

The fichat, the *fulimart*, and the ferret, live upon the face, and within the bowels of the earth. *Walton's Angler.*

FULL. *adj.* [ꝼulle, Saxon; *vol*, Dutch.]

1. Replete; without vacuity; without any space void.

Better is an handful with quietness than both the hands *full* with travel and vexation of spirit. *Eccl.* iv. 6.

2. Abounding in any quality good or bad.

With pretence from Strephon her to guard,
He met her full, but *full* of warefulness. *Sidney.*

You should tread a course
Pretty and *full* of view. *Shakespeare's Cymbeline.*

Followers, who make themselves as trumpets of the commendation of those they follow, are *full* of inconvenience; for they taint business through want of secresy, and they export honour from a man, and make him a return in envy. *Bacon, Essay* 49.

In that sweet season, as in bed I lay,

I turn'd

I turn'd my weary side, but still in vain,
Though *full* of youthful health and void of pain. *Dryden.*

He is *full* of wants which he cannot supply, and compassed about with infirmities which he cannot remove. *Tillotf. Serm.*

From yon bright heaven our author fetch'd his fire,
And paints the passions that your eyes inspire;
Full of that flame, his tender scenes he warms,
And frames his goddess by your matchless charms. *Granv.*

3. Stored with any thing; well supplied with any thing.

Full of days was he;
Two ages past, he liv'd the third to see. *Tickell.*

4. Plump; saginated; fat.

A gentleman of a *full* body having broken his skin by a fall, the wound inflamed. *Wiseman's Surgery.*

5. Saturated; sated.

I am *full* of the burnt offerings of rams. *Isa.* i. 11.

The alteration of scenes feeds and relieves the eye, before it be *full* of the same object. *Bacon.*

6. Crouded in the imagination or memory.

Every one is *full* of the miracles done by cold baths on decayed and weak constitutions. *Locke.*

7. That which fills or makes full; large; great in effect.

Water digesteth a *full* meal sooner than any other liquor. *Arbuthnot on Aliments.*

8. Complete; such as that nothing further is desired or wanted.

That day had seen the *full* accomplishment
Of all his travels. *Daniel's Civil War.*

Being tried at that time only with a promise, he gave *full* credit to that promise, and still gave evidence of his fidelity as fast as occasions were offered. *Hammond's Pract. Catechism.*

The resurrection of Jesus from the dead hath given the world *full* assurance of another life. *Tillotson, Sermon* 5.

9. Complete without abatement; at the utmost degree.

At the end of two *full* years Pharaoh dreamed. *Genesis.*

After hard riding plunge the horses into water, and allow them to drink as they please; but gallop them *full* speed, to warm the water in their bellies. *Swift's Direct. to the Groom.*

10 Containing the whole matter; expressing much.

Where my expressions are not so *full* as his, either our language or my art were defective; but where mine are *fuller* than his, they are but the impressions which the often reading of him hath left upon my thoughts. *Denham.*

Should a man go about with never so set study to describe such a natural form of the year before the deluge as that which is at present established, he could scarcely do it in so few words, so fit and proper, so *full* and express. *Woodward.*

11. Strong; not faint; not attenuated.

I did never know so *full* a voice issue from so empty a heart; but the saying is true, the empty vessel makes the greatest sound. *Shakespeare's Henry* V.

Barrels placed under the floor of a chamber, make all noises in the same more *full* and resounding. *Bacon's Nat. History.*

Dryden taught to join
The varying verse, the *full* resounding line. *Pope.*

12. Mature; perfect.

In the sultanry of the Mamalukes, slaves reigned over families of free men; and much like were the case, if you suppose a nation, where the custom were that after *full* age the sons should expulse their fathers and mothers out of their possessions. *Bacon's Holy War.*

13. [Applied to the moon.] Complete in its orb.

Towards the *full* moon, as he was coming home one morning, he felt his legs faulter. *Wiseman's Surgery.*

14. Noting the conclusion of any matter, or a full stop.

Therewith he ended, making a *full* point of a hearty sigh. *Sidney.*

15. Spread to view in all dimensions.

'Till about the end of the third century, I do not remember to have seen the head of a Roman emperor drawn with a *full* face: they always appear in profile. *Addison on Medals.*

FULL. *n.s.* [from the adjective.]

1. Complete measure; freedom from deficiency.

When we return,
We'll see those things effected to the *full*. *Shak. Henry* VI.

He liked the pomp and absolute authority of a general well, and preserved the dignity of it to the *full*. *Clarendon, b.* viii.

The picture of Ptolemy Philopater is given by the forementioned authors to the *full*. *Dryden's Preface to Cleomenes.*

Sicilian tortures and the brazen bull,
Are emblems, rather than express the *full*
Of what he feels. *Dryden's Pers. Sat.* iii.

If where the rules not far enough extend,
Some lucky licence answer to the *full*
Th' intent propos'd, that licence is a rule. *Pope's Criticism.*

2. The highest state or degree.

The swan's down feather,
That stands upon the swell at *full* of tide,
Neither way inclines. *Shakesp. Ant. and Cleopatra.*

3. The whole; the total.

The king hath won, and hath sent out
A speedy pow'r to encounter you, my lord:
This is the news at *full*. *Shakespeare's Henry* IV. *p.* ii.

But what at *full* I know, thou know'st no part;
I knowing all my peril, thou no art. *Shakespeare.*

4. The state of being full.

When I had fed them to the *full*. *Jer.* v. 7.

5. [Applied to the moon.] The time in which the moon makes a perfect orb.

Brains in rabbits, woodcocks, and calves, are fullest in the *full* of the moon. *Bacon's Natural History.*

FULL. *adv.*

1. Without abatement.

In the unity of place they are *full* as scrupulous; for many of their criticks limit to that very spot of ground where the play is supposed to begin. *Dryden's Dramatick Poesy.*

A modest blush he wears, not form'd by art;
Free from deceit his face, and *full* as free his heart. *Dryden.*

The most judicious writer is sometimes mistaken after all his care; but the hasty critick, who judges on a view, is *full* as liable to be deceived. *Dryden's Aurengz. Preface.*

Since you may
Suspect my courage, if I should not lay,
The pawn I proffer shall be *full* as good. *Dryd. Virg. Past.*

2. With the whole effect.

'Tis the pencil, thrown luckily *full* upon the horse's mouth to express the foam, which the painter, with all his skill, could not perform without it. *Dryden's Dufresnoy.*

From harmony, from heavenly harmony,
This universal frame began:
From harmony to harmony,
Through all the compass of the notes it ran,
The diapason closing *full* in man. *Dryden.*

3. Exactly.

Full in the centre of the sacred wood,
An arm ariseth of the Stygian flood. *Addison on Italy.*

Full nineteen sailors did the ship convey,
A shole of nineteen dolphins round her play. *Addis. Ovid.*

4. Directly.

He met her *full*, but full of warefulness. *Sidney.*

He then confronts the bull,
And on his ample forehead aiming *full*,
The deadly stroke descending pierc'd the skull. *Dryden.*

At length resolv'd, he throws with all his force
Full at the temples of the warrior horse. *Dryden's Æn.*

5. It is placed before adverbs and adjectives, to intend or strengthen their signification.

Why on your shield, so goodly scor'd,
Bear ye the picture of that lady's head?
Full lively is the semblant, though the substance dead. *F. Q.*

I was set at work
Among my maids; *full* little, God knows, looking
Either for such men or such business. *Shakes. Henry* VIII.

Full well ye reject the commandment. *Mar.* vii. 9.

Adam was all in tears, and to his guide
Lamenting turn'd *full* sad. *Milton's Paradise Lost, b.* xi.

You *full* little think that you must be the beginner of the discourse yourself. *More's Divine Dialogues.*

Full little thought of him the gentle knight. *Dryden.*

Full well the god his sister's envy knew,
And what her aims and what her arts pursue. *Dryden.*

There is a perquisite *full* as honest, by which you have the best part of a bottle of wine for yourself. *Swift.*

FULL is much used in composition to intimate any thing arrived at its highest state, or utmost degree.

FULL-BLO'WN. *adj.* [*full* and *blown.*]

1. Spread to the utmost extent, as a perfect blossom.

My glories are past danger; they're *full-blown*:
Things, that are blasted, are but in the bud. *Denh. Sophy.*

My *full-blown* youth already fades apace;
Of our short being 'tis the shortest space! *Dryden's Juven.*

2. Stretched by the wind to the utmost extent.

He who with bold Cratinus is inspir'd,
With zeal and equal indignation fir'd;
Who at enormous villany turns pale,
And steers against it with a *full-blown* sail. *Dryd. Pers. Sat.*

FULL-BO'TTOMED. *adj.* [*full* and *bottom.*] Having a large bottom.

I was obliged to sit at home in my morning-gown, having pawned a new suit of cloaths and a *full-bottomed* wig for a sum of money. *Guardian*, N°. 166.

FULL-EA'RED. [*full* and *ear.*] Having the heads full of grain.

As flames roll'd by the winds conspiring force,
O'er *full-ear'd* corn, or torrents raging course. *Denham.*

FULL-EY'ED. [*full* and *eye.*] Having large prominent eyes.

FULL-FE'D. [*full* and *fed.*] Sated; fat; saginated.

All as a partridge plump, *full-fed* and fair,
She form'd this image of well-bodied air. *Pope's Dunciad.*

FULL-LA'DEN. [*full* and *laden.*] Laden 'till there can be no more.

It were unfit that so excellent a reward as the Gospel promises should stoop down, like fruit upon a *full-laden* bough, to be plucked by every idle and wanton hand. *Tillotson's Serm.*

FULL-SPRE'AD. [*full* and *spread.*] Spread to the utmost extent.

How easy 'tis, when destiny proves kind,
With *full-spread* sails to run before the wind;
But those that 'gainst stiff gales laveering go,
Must be at once resolv'd and skilful too. *Dryden.*

FULL-SU'MMED. [*full* and *summed.*] Complete in all its parts.

The time was that the cedar stretched forth his imperial branches as far as the mountains of the moon, and that the king of birds nested within his leaves, thick feathered, and with *full-summed* wings fastening his talons East and West; but now the eagle is become half naked. *Howel's Voc. Forest.*

To FULL. *v. a.* [*fullo*, Latin.] To cleanse cloath from its oil or grease.

FU'LLAGE. *n. s.* [from *full.*] The money paid for fulling or cleansing cloath.

FU'LLER. *n. s.* [*fullo*, Latin.] One whose trade is to cleanse cloath.

The clothiers have put off
The spinsters, carders, *fullers*, weavers. *Shakesf. H. VIII.*

His raiment became shining, exceeding white as snow; so as no *fuller* on earth can whiten them. *Mar.* ix. 3.

FU'LLERS *Earth. n. s.*

Fullers earth is a marl of a close texture, extremely soft and unctuous to the touch: when dry it is of a greyish brown colour, in all degrees, from very pale to almost black, and generally has something of a greenish cast in it. The finest *fullers earth* is dug in our own island. *Hill's Mat. Medica.*

The *fullers earth* of England is very various, and it very much exceeds any yet discovered abroad in goodness; which is one great reason why the English surpass all other nations in the woollen manufacture. *Woodward on Fossils.*

FU'LLERY. *n. s.* [from *fuller.*] The place where the trade of a fuller is exercised.

FU'LLINGMILL. *n. s.* [*full* and *mill.*] A mill where the water raises hammers which beat the cloath 'till it be cleansed.

By large hammers, like those used for paper and *fulling-mills*, they beat their hemp. *Mortimer.*

FU'LLY. *adv.* [from *full.*]

1. Without vacuity.
2. Completely; without lack; without more to be desired.

There are many graces for which we may not cease hourly to sue, graces which are in bestowing always, but never come to be *fully* had in this present life; and therefore, when all things here have an end, endless thanks must have their beginning in a state which bringeth the full and final satisfaction of all such perpetual desires. *Hooker, b.* v. *s.* 43.

He *fully* possessed the entire revelation he had received from God, and had thoroughly digested it. *Locke.*

The goddess cry'd
It is enough, I'm *fully* satisfy'd. *Addison's Ovid's Metam.*

FU'LMINANT. *adj.* [*fulminant*, Fr. *fulminans*, Latin.] Thundering; making a noise like thunder.

To FU'LMINATE. *v. n.* [*fulmino*, Lat. *fulminer*, French.]

1. To thunder.
2. To make a loud noise or crack.

Whilst it was in fusion we cast into it a live coal, which presently kindled it, and made it boil and flash for a pretty while: after which we cast in another glowing coal, which made it *fulminate* afresh. *Boyle.*

In damps one is called the suffocating, and the other the *fulminating* damp. *Woodward's Natural History.*

3. To issue out ecclesiastical censures.

To FU'LMINATE. *v. a.* To throw out as an object of terrour.

As excommunication is not greatly regarded here in England, as now *fulminated*; so this constitution is out of use among us in a great measure. *Ayliffe's Parergon.*

FULMINA'TION. *n. s.* [*fulminatio*, Latin; *fulmination*, French, from *fulminate.*]

1. The act of thundering.
2. Denunciations of censure.

The *fulminations* from the vatican were turned into ridicule. *Ayliffe's Parergon.*

FU'LMINATORY. *adj.* [*fulmineus*, Latin; from *fulminate.*] Thundering; striking horror.

FU'LNESS. *n. s.* [from *full.*]

1. The state of being filled so as to have no part vacant.

Your heave-offering shall be reckoned the *fulness* of the wine-press. *Numb.* xviii. 27.

To the houses I wished nothing more than safety, *fulness*, and freedom. *King Charles.*

2. The state of abounding in any quality good or bad.
3. Completeness; such as leaves nothing to be desired.

Your enjoyments are so complete, I turn wishes into gratulations, and congratulating their *fulness* only wish their continuance. *South.*

4. Completeness from the coalition of many parts.

The king set forwards to London, receiving the acclamations and applauses of the people as he went; which indeed were true and unfeigned, as might well appear in the very demonstrations and *fulness* of the cry. *Bacon's Henry* VII.

5. Completeness; freedom from deficiency.

He is the half part of a blessed man,
Left to be finished by such as she;
And she a fair divided excellence,
Whose *fulness* of perfection lies in him. *Shakesf. K. John.*

6. Repletion; satiety.

I need not instance in the habitual intemperance of rich tables, nor the evil accidents and effects of *fulness*, pride and lust, wantonness and softness. *Taylor's Rule of living holy.*

7. Plenty; wealth.

To lapse in *fulness*
Is sorer than to lie for need; and falshood
Is worse in kings than beggars. *Shakespeare's Cymbeline.*

8. Struggling perturbation; swelling in the mind.

A principal fruit of friendship is the ease and discharge of the *fulness* of the heart, which passions of all kinds do cause and induce. *Bacon, Essay* 28.

9. Largeness; extent.

There wanted the *fulness* of a plot, and variety of characters to form it as it ought; and perhaps something might have been added to the beauty of the style. *Dryden.*

10. Force of sound, such as fills the ear; vigour.

This sort of pastoral derives almost its whole beauty from a natural ease of thought and smoothness of verse; whereas that of most other kinds consists in the strength and *fulness* of both. *Pope.*

FU'LSOME. *adj.* [from fulle, Saxon, foul.]

1. Nauseous; offensive.

The skilful shepherd peel'd me certain wands;
And in the doing of the deed of kind,
He stuck them up before the *fulsome* ewes. *Shakespeare.*

He that brings *fulsome* objects to my view,
With nauseous images my fancy fills,
And all goes down like oxymel of squills. *Roscommon.*

Now half the youth of Europe are in arms,
How *fulsome* must it be to stay behind,
And die of rank diseases here at home? *Otway's Orphan.*

2. Of a rank odious smell.

White satyrion is of a dainty smell, and bean-flowers: again, if the plant puts forth white flowers only, and those not thin or dry, they are commonly of rank and *fulsome* smell. *Bacon's Natural History*, N°. 507.

3. Tending to obscenity.

A certain epigram, which is ascribed to the emperor, is more *fulsome* than any passage I have met with in our poet. *Dryden.*

FU'LSOMELY. *adv.* [from *fulsome.*] Nauseously; rankly; obscenely.

FU'LSOMENESS. *n. s.* [from *fulsome.*]

1. Nauseousness.
2. Rank smell.
3. Obscenity.

No decency is considered, no *fulsomeness* is omitted, no venom is wanting, as far as dulness can supply it. *Dryden.*

FU'MADO. *n. s.* [*fumus*, Latin.] A smoked fish.

Fish that serve for the hotter countries, they used at first to fume, by hanging them up on long sticks one by one, drying them with the smoke of a soft and continual fire, from which they purchased the name of *fumadoes*. *Carew.*

FU'MAGE. *n. s.* [from *fumus*, Latin.] Hearthmoney. *Dict.*

FU'MATORY. *n. s.* [*fumaria*, Lat. *fumeterre*, Fr.] See FUMITORY.

It hath divided leaves resembling those of the umbelliferous plants: the flowers, which are collected into a spike, are of an anomalous figure, somewhat resembling a papilionaceous flower, consisting of two petals or leaves, open like two lips, the upper lip ending in a spur: the footstalk is joined to the middle part of the flower: the fruit is either of a long or a round figure, which is like a pod. *Miller.*

Her fallow leas
The darnel, hemlock, and rank *fumatory*,
Doth root upon. *Shakespeare's Henry* V.

To FU'MBLE. *v. n.* [*fommelen*, Dutch.]

1. To attempt any thing aukwardly or ungainly.

Our mechanick theists will have their atoms never once to have *fumbled* in these their motions, nor to have produced any inept system. *Cudworth.*

2. To puzzle; to strain in perplexity.

Am not I a friend to help you out? You would have been *fumbling* half an hour for this excuse. *Dryden's Spanish Fryar.*

3. To play childishly.

I saw him *fumble* with the sheets, and play with flowers, and smile upon his finger's end. *Shakespeare's Henry* V.

To FU'MBLE. *v. a.* To manage aukwardly.

As many farewels as be stars in heav'n,
With distinct breath and consign'd kisses to them,
He *fumbles* up all in one loose adieu. *Shakespeare.*

His greasy bald-pate choir
Came *fumbling* o'er the beads, in such an agony,
They told 'em false for fear. *Dryden's Spanish Fryar.*

FU'MBLER. *n. s.* [from *fumble.*] One who acts aukwardly.

FU'MBLINGLY. *adv.* [from *fumble.*] In an aukward manner.

FUME. *n. s.* [*fumée*, French; *fumus*, Latin.]

1. Smoke.

Thus fighting fires a while themſelves conſume;
But ſtreight, like Turks, forc'd on to win or die,
They firſt lay tender bridges of their *fume*,
And o'er the breach in unctuous vapours fly. *Dryden.*

2. Vapour; any volatile parts flying away.

Love is a ſmoke rais'd with the *fume* of ſighs;
Being purg'd, a fire ſparkling in lovers eyes *Shakeſpeare.*

It were good to try the taking of *fumes* by pipes, as they do in tobacco, of other things, to dry and comfort. *Bacon.*

In Winter, when the heat without is leſs, it becomes ſo far condenſed as to be viſible, flowing out of the mouth in form of a *fume*, or craſſer vapour; and may, by proper veſſels, ſet in a ſtrong freezing mixture, be collected in a conſiderable quantity. *Woodward's Natural Hiſtory.*

3. Exhalation from the ſtomach.

The *fumes* of drink diſcompoſe and ſtupify the brains of a man overcharged with it. *South's Sermons.*

Plung'd in ſloth we lie, and ſnore ſupine,
As fill'd with *fumes* of undigeſted wine. *Dryden's Perſ. Sat.*

Pow'r, like new wine, does your weak brain ſurprize,
And its mad *fumes* in hot diſcourſes riſe;
But time theſe yielding vapours will remove:
Mean while I'll taſte the ſober joys of love. *Dryden's Auren.*

4. Rage; heat of mind; paſſion.

The *fumes* of his paſſion do really intoxicate and confound his judging and diſcerning faculty. *South.*

5. Any thing unſubſtantial.

When Duncan is aſleep, his two chamberlains
Will I with wine and waſſel ſo convince,
That memory, the warder of the brain,
Shall be a *fume*. *Shakeſpeare's Macbeth.*

6. Idle conceit; vain imagination.

Plato's great year would have ſome effect, not in renewing the ſtate of like individuals; for that is the *fume* of thoſe, that conceive the celeſtial bodies have more accurate influences upon theſe things below, than indeed they have, but in groſs. *Bacon, Eſſay* 59.

To lay aſide all that may ſeem to have a ſhew of *fumes* and fancies, and to ſpeak ſolids, a war with Spain is a mighty work. *Bacon's War with Spain.*

To FUME. *v. n.* [*fumer*, French; *fumo*, Latin.]

1. To ſmoke.

Their pray'rs paſs'd
Dimenſionleſs through heav'nly doors; then clad
With incenſe, where the golden altar *fum'd*,
By their great interceſſor; came in ſight
Before the Father's throne. *Milton's Paradiſe Loſt, b.* xi.

From thence the *fuming* trail began to ſpread,
And lambent glories danc'd about her head. *Dryd. Æn.*

Strait hover round the fair her airy band;
Some, as ſhe ſipp'd, the *fuming* liquor fann'd. *Pope.*

2. To vapour; to yield exhalations.

Tie up the libertine in a field of feaſts,
Keep his brain *fuming*. *Shakeſpeare's Ant. and Cleopatra.*

Silenus lay,
Whoſe conſtant cups lay *fuming* to his brain,
And always boil in each extended vein. *Roſcommon.*

3. To paſs away in vapours.

We have
No anger in our eyes, no ſtorm, no lightning:
Our hate is ſpent and *fum'd* away in vapour,
Before our hands be at work. *Ben. Johnſon's Catiline.*

Their parts are kept from *fuming* away by their fixity, and alſo by the vaſt weight and denſity of the atmoſpheres incumbent upon them. *Cheyne's Phil. Princ.*

The firſt freſh dawn then wak'd the gladden'd race
Of uncorrupted man, nor bluſh'd to ſee
The ſluggard ſleep beneath its ſacred beam;
For their light ſlumbers gentle *fum'd* away. *Thomſon's Spring.*

4. To be in a rage.

When he knew his rival free'd and gone,
He ſwells with wrath; he makes outrageous moan:
He frets, he *fumes*, he ſtares, he ſtamps the ground,
The hollow tow'r with clamours rings around. *Dryden.*

To FUME. *v. a.*

1. To ſmoke; to dry in the ſmoke.

Thoſe that ſerve for hot countries they uſed at firſt to *fume*, by hanging them upon long ſticks one by one, and drying them with the ſmoke of a ſoft fire. *Carew.*

2. To perfume with odours in the fire.

She *fum'd* the temples with an od'rous flame,
And oft before the ſacred altars came,
To pray for him who was an empty name. *Dryden.*

The *fuming* of the holes with brimſtone, garlick, or other unſavory things, will drive moles out of the ground. *Mortim.*

3. To diſperſe in vapours.

The heat will *fume* away moſt of the ſcent. *Mortimer.*

FUMETTE. *n. ſ.* [French.] A word introduced by cooks, and the pupils of cooks, for the ſtink of meat.

A haunch of ven'ſon made her ſweat,
Unleſs it had the right *fumette*. *Swift.*

FU'MID. *adj.* [*fumidus*, Latin.] Smoky; vaporous.

A craſs and *fumid* exhalation is cauſed from the combat of the ſulphur and iron with the acid and nitrous ſpirits of *aquafortis*. *Brown's Vulgar Errours, b.* ii. *c.* 5.

FUMI'DITY. *n. ſ.* [from *fumid.*] Smokineſs; tendency to ſmoke. *Dict.*

To FU'MIGATE. *v. n.* [from *fumus*, Latin; *fumiger*, Fr.]

1. To ſmoke; to perfume by ſmoke or vapour.

Would'ſt thou preſerve thy famiſh'd family,
With fragrant thyme the city *fumigate*,
And break the waxen walls to ſave the ſtate. *Dryden's Virg.*

2. To medicate or heal by vapours.

FUMIGA'TION. *n. ſ.* [*fumigatio*, Latin; *fumigation*, French; from *fumigate*.]

1. Scents raiſed by fire.

Fumigations, often repeated, are very beneficial. *Arbuthnot.*

My *fumigation* is to Venus, juſt
The ſouls of roſes, and red coral's duſt:
And, laſt, to make my *fumigation* good,
'Tis mixt with ſparrows brains and pigeons blood. *Dryden.*

2. The application of medicines to the body in fumes.

FU'MINGLY. *adv.* [from *fume.*] Angrily; in a rage.

That which we move for our better learning and inſtruction ſake, turneth unto anger and choler in them: they grow altogether out of quietneſs with it; they anſwer *fumingly*, that they are aſhamed to defile their pens with making anſwer to ſuch idle queſtions. *Hooker, b.* v. *ſ.* 22.

FU'MITER. *n. ſ.* See FUMATORY.

Why, he was met even now,
As mad as the vext ſea; ſinging aloud,
Crown'd with rank *fumiter* and furrow-weeds. *Shakeſpeare.*

FU'MOUS. } *adj.* [*fumeux-ſe*, French; from *fume.*] Producing
FU'MY. } fumes.

From dice and wine the youth retir'd to reſt,
And puff'd the *fumy* god from out his breaſt:
Ev'n then he dreamt of drink and lucky play;
More lucky had it laſted 'till the day. *Dryden's Æn.*

FUN. *n. ſ.* [A low cant word.] Sport; high merriment; frolickſome delight.

Don't mind me, though, for all my *fun* and jokes,
You bards may find us bloods good-natur'd folks. *Moore.*

FU'NCTION. *n. ſ.* [*functio*, Latin.]

1. Diſcharge; performance.

There is hardly a greater difference between two things than there is between a repreſenting commoner in the *function* of his publick calling, and the ſame perſon in common life. *Swift.*

2. Employment; office.

The miniſtry is not now bound to any one tribe: now none is ſecluded from that *function* of any degree, ſtate, or calling. *Whitgifte.*

You have paid the heav'ns your *function*, and the priſoner the very debt of your calling. *Shakeſ. Meaſure for Meaſure.*

Nor was it any policy of ſtate, or obſtinacy of will, or partiality of affection either to the men or their *function*, which fixed me. *King Charles.*

This double *function* of the goddeſs gives a conſiderable light and beauty to the ode which Horace has addreſſed to her. *Addiſon's Remarks on Italy.*

Let not theſe indignities diſcourage us from aſſerting the juſt privileges and pre-eminence of our holy *function* and character. *Atterbury's Sermons.*

3. Single act of any office.

Without difference thoſe *functions* cannot, in orderly ſort, be executed. *Hooker.*

They have ſeveral offices and prayers againſt fire, tempeſts, and eſpecially for the dead, in which *functions* they uſe ſacerdotal garments. *Stillingfleet's Def. of Diſc. on Rom. Idol.*

4. Trade; occupation.

Follow your *function*; go, and batten on cold bits. *Shakeſp.*

5. Office of any particular part of the body.

The bodies of men, and other animals, are excellently well fitted for life and motion; and the ſeveral parts of them well adapted to their particular *functions*. *Bentley's Sermons.*

6. Power; faculty.

Tears in his eyes, diſtraction in his aſpect,
A broken voice, and his whole *function* ſuiting
With forms to his conceit. *Shakeſpeare's Hamlet.*

Nature ſeems
In all her *functions* weary of herſelf:
My race of glory run, and race of ſhame;
And I ſhall ſhortly be with them that reſt. *Milton.*

Whatever warms the heart, or fills the head,
As the mind opens, and its *functions* ſpread,
Imagination plies her dang'rous art,
And pours it all upon the peccant part. *Pope.*

Though every human conſtitution is morbid, yet are their diſeaſes conſiſtent with the common *functions* of life. *Arbuthn.*

FUND. *n. ſ.* [*fond*, French; *funda*, a bag, Latin.]

1. Stock; capital; that by which any expence is ſupported.

He touches the paſſions more delicately than Ovid, and performs all this out of his own *fund*, without diving into the arts and ſciences for a ſupply. *Dryden.*

Part

Part must be left, a *fund* when foes invade,
And part employ'd to roll the watry tide. *Dryden.*

In preaching, no men succeed better than those who trust entirely to the stock or *fund* of their own reason, advanced indeed, but not overlaid by commerce with books. *Swift.*

2. Stock or bank of money.

As my estate has been hitherto either tost upon seas, or fluctuating in *funds*, it is now fixed in substantial acres. *Add.*

FU'NDAMENT. *n. s.* [*fundamentum*, Latin.] The back part of the body.

FUNDAME'NTAL. *adj.* [*fundamentalis*, Lat. from *fundament.*] Serving for the foundation; that upon which the rest is built; essential; important; not merely accidental.

Until this can be agreed upon, one main and *fundamental* cause of the most grievous war is not like to be taken from the earth. *Raleigh's Essays.*

You that will be less fearful than discreet,
That love the *fundamental* part of state,
More than you doubt the charge of't. *Shakes. Coriolanus.*

Others, when they were brought to allow the throne vacant, thought the succession should go to the next heir, according to the *fundamental* laws of the kingdom, as if the last king were actually dead. *Swift's Examiner.*

Gain some general and *fundamental* truths, both in philosophy, in religion, and in human life. *Watts.*

Such we find they are, as can controul
The servile actions of our wav'ring soul,
Can fright, can alter, or can chain the will;
Their ills all built on life, that *fundamental* ill. *Prior.*

Yet some there were among the sounder few,
Of those who less presum'd, and better knew,
Who durst assert the juster ancient cause,
And here restor'd wit's *fundamental* laws. *Pope on Criticism.*

FUNDAME'NTAL. *n. s.* Leading proposition; important and essential part which is the groundwork of the rest.

We will propose the question, whether those who hold the *fundamentals* of faith may deny Christ damnably, in respect of those superstructures and consequences that arise from them. *South's Sermons.*

It is a very just reproach, that there should be so much violence and hatred in religious matters among men who agree in all *fundamentals*, and only differ in some ceremonies, or mere speculative points. *Swift.*

FUNDAME'NTALLY. *adv.* [from *fundamental.*] Essentially; originally.

As virtue is seated *fundamentally* in the intellect, so perspectively in the fancy; so that virtue is the force of reason, in the conduct of our actions and passions to a good end. *Grew.*

Religion is not only useful to civil society, but *fundamentally* necessary to its very birth and constitution. *Bentley.*

The unlimited power placed *fundamentally* in the body of a people, the legislators endeavour to deposite in such hands as would preserve the people. *Swift on the Diss. in Ath. and Rome.*

FU'NERAL. *n. s.* [*funus*, Latin; *funerailles*, French.]

1. The solemnization of a burial; the payment of the last honours to the dead; obsequies.

Here, under leave of Brutus, and the rest,
Come I to speak in Cæsar's *funeral.* *Shak. Julius Cæsar.*

All things that we ordained festival,
Turn from their office to black *funeral.* *Shakespeare.*

He that had cast out many unburied, had none to mourn for him, nor any solemn *funerals*, nor sepulchre with his fathers. *2 Mac.* v. 10.

No widow at his *funeral* shall weep. *Sandys.*

2. The pomp or procession with which the dead are carried.

The long *fun'rals* blacken all the way. *Pope.*

You are sometimes desirous to see a *funeral* pass by in the street. *Swift's Directions to the Chambermaid.*

3. Burial; interment.

May he find his *funeral*
I' th' sands, when he before his day shall fall. *Denham.*

FU'NERAL. *adj.* Used at the ceremony of interrring the dead.

Our instruments to melancholy bells,
Our wedding chear to a sad *funeral* feast. *Shak. R. and Jul.*

Let such honours
And *funeral* rites, as to his birth and virtues
Are due, be first perform'd. *Denham's Sophy.*

Thy hand o'er towns the *fun'ral* torch displays,
And forms a thousand ills ten thousand ways. *Dryden.*

FUNE'REAL. *adj.* [*funerea*, Latin.] Suiting a funeral; dark; dismal.

But if his soul hath wing'd the destin'd flight,
Inhabitant of deep disastrous night,
Homeward with pious speed repass the main,
To the pale shade *funereal* rites ordain. *Pope's Odyssey, b.* i.

FUNGO'SITY. *n. s.* [from *fungus.*] Unsolid excrescence. *Dict.*

FU'NGOUS. *adj.* [from *fungus.*] Excrescent; spongy; wanting firmness.

It is often employed to keep down the *fungous* lips that spread upon the bone; but it is much more painful than the escharotick medicines. *Sharp's Surgery.*

FU'NGUS. *n. s.* [Latin.] Strictly a mushroom: a word used to express such excrescences of flesh as grow out upon the lips of wounds, or any other excrescence from trees or plants not naturally belonging to them; as the agarick from the larch-tree, and auriculæ Judæ from elder. *Quincy.*

The surgeon ought to vary the diet as the fibres lengthen too much, are too fluid, and produce *funguses*, or as they harden and produce callosities. *Arbuthnot on Diet.*

FU'NICLE. *n. s.* [*funiculus*, Latin.] A small cord; a small ligature; a fibre.

FUNI'CULAR. *adj.* [*funiculaire*, Fr. from *funicle.*] Consisting of a small cord or fibre.

FUNK. *n. s.* A stink. A low word.

FU'NNEL. *n. s.* [*infundibulum*, Latin; whence *fundible, fundle, funnel.*]

1. An inverted hollow cone with a pipe descending from it, through which liquors are poured into vessels with narrow mouths; a tundish.

If you pour a glut of water upon a bottle, it receives little of it; but with a *funnel*, and by degrees, you shall fill many of them. *Ben. Johnson's Discoveries.*

Some the long *funnel*'s curious mouth extend,
Through which ingested meats with ease descend. *Blackm.*

The outward ear or auricula is made hollow, and contracted by degrees, to draw the sound inward, to take in as much as may be of it, as we use a *funnel* to pour liquor into any vessel. *Ray on the Creation.*

2. A pipe or passage of communication.

Towards the middle are two large *funnels*, bored through the roof of the grotto, to let in light or fresh air. *Addison.*

FUR. *n. s.* [*fourrure*, French.]

1. Skin with soft hair with which garments are lined for warmth, or covered for ornament.

December must be expressed with a horrid and fearful countenance; as also at his back a bundle of holly, holding in *fur* mittens the sign of Capricorn. *Peacham on Drawing.*

'Tis but dressing up a bird of prey in his cap and *furs* to make a judge of him. *L'Estrange.*

And lordly gout wrapt up in *fur*,
And wheezing asthma, loth to stir. *Swift.*

2. Soft hair of beasts found in cold countries, where nature provides coats suitable to the weather; hair in general.

This night, wherein the cubdrawn bear would couch,
The lion and the belly-pinched wolf
Keep their *fur* dry, unbonnetted he runs,
And bids what will take all. *Shakespeare's King Lear.*

Such animals as feed upon flesh qualify it, the one by swallowing the hair or *fur* of the beasts they prey upon, the other by devouring some part of the feathers of the birds they gorge themselves with. *Ray on the Creation.*

3. Any moisture exhaled to such a degree as that the remainder sticks on the part.

Methinks I am not right in ev'ry part;
I feel a kind of trembling at my heart:
My pulse unequal, and my breath is strong;
Besides a filthy *fur* upon my tongue. *Dryden's Pers. Sat.* 3.

To FUR. *v. a.* [from the noun.]

1. To line or cover with skins that have soft hair.

How mad a sight it was to see Dametas, like rich tissue *furred* with lambskins? *Sidney, b.* ii.

Through tatter'd cloaths small vices do appear;
Robes and *furr'd* gowns hide all. *Shakesp. King Lear.*

You are for dreams and slumbers, brother priest;
You *fur* your gloves with reasons. *Shakes. Troil. and Cress.*

To cover with soft matter.

To make lampblack, take a torch and hold it under the bottom of a latten bason; and, as it groweth to be *furred* and black within, strike it with a feather into some shell. *Peacham.*

The sisters, mourning for their brother's loss,
Their bodies hid in bark, and *furr'd* with moss. *Dryden.*

Their frying blood compels to irrigate
Their dry *furr'd* tongues. *Phillips.*

A dungeon wide and horrible; the walls
On all sides *furr'd* with mouldy damps, and hung
With clots of ropy gore. *Addison.*

FUR. *adv.* [It is now commonly written *far.*] At a distance.

The white lovely dove
Doth on her wings her utmost swiftness prove,
Finding the gripe of falcon fierce not *fur.* *Sidney.*

FUR-WROUGHT. *adj.* [*fur* and *wrought.*] Made of fur.

Silent along the mazy margin stray,
And with the *fur-wrought* fly delude the prey. *Gay's Past.*

FURA'CIOUS. *adj.* [*furax*, Latin.] Thievish; inclined to steal. *Dict.*

FURA'CITY. *n. s.* [from *furax*, Latin.] Disposition to theft; thievishness.

FU'RBELOW. *n. s.* [*fur* and *below.*] Fur sewed on the lower part of the garment; an ornament of dress.

Nay, oft in dreams invention we bestow
To change a flounce, or add a *furbelow.* *Pope.*

To

To FU'RBELOW. *v. a.* [from the noun.] To adorn with ornamental appendages of dress.

When arguments too fiercely glare,
You calm them with a milder air;
To break their points, you turn their force,
And *furbelow* the plain discourse. *Prior.*

She was flounced and *furbelowed* from head to foot; every ribbon was crinkled, and every part of her garments in curl. *Addison's Spectator*, N°. 129.

To FU'RBISH. *v. a.* [*fourbir*, French.] To burnish; to polish; to rub to brightness.

It may enter Mowbray's waxen coat,
And *furbish* new the name of John o' Gaunt. *Shak. R.* II.

Furbish the spears, and put on the brigandines. *Jer.* xlvi. 4.

Some others who *furbish* up and reprint his old errours, hold that the sufferings of the damned are not to be, in a strict sense, eternal; but that, after a certain period of time, there shall be a general gaol-delivery of the souls in prison, and that not for a farther execution, but a final release. *South's Serm.*

As after Numa's peaceful reign,
The martial Ancus did the sceptre wield;
Furbish'd the rusty sword again,
Resum'd the long-forgotten shield,
And led the Latins to the dusty field. *Dryden.*

Inferior ministers, for Mars repair
His broken axle-tree, and blunted war;
And send him forth again, with *furbish'd* arms. *Dryden.*

FU'RBISHER. *n. s.* [*fourbisseur*, French, from *furbish*.] One who polishes any thing.

FURCA'TION. *n. s.* [*furca*, Latin.] Forkiness; the state of shooting two ways like the blades of a fork.

When they grow old they grow less branched, and first do lose their brow-antlers, or lowest *furcations* next the head. *Brown's Vulgar Errours*, *b.* iii. *c.* 9.

FU'RFUR. *n. s.* [Latin.] Husk or chaff, scurff or dandriff, that grows upon the skin, with some likeness to bran. *Quincy.*

FURFURA'CEOUS. *adj.* [*furfuraceus*, Latin.] Husky; branny; scaly.

FU'RIOUS. *adj.* [*furieux*, French; *furiosus*, Latin.]

1. Mad; phrenetick.

No man did ever think the hurtful actions of *furious* men and innocents to be punishable. *Hooker*, *b.* i. *s.* 9.

2. Raging; violent; transported by passion beyond reason.

Who can be wise, amaz'd, temp'rate and *furious*,
Loyal and neutral in a moment? No man. *Shakesp. Macb.*

To be *furious*,
Is to be frighted out of fear; and, n that mood,
The dove will peck the estridge. *Shakesp. Ant. and Cleopat.*

FU'RIOUSLY. *adv.* [from *furious*.] Madly; violently; vehemently.

Which when his brother saw, fraught with great grief
And wrath, he to him leapt *furiously*. *Fairy Queen*, *b.* ii.

They observe countenance to attend the practice; and this carries them on *furiously* to that which of themselves they are inclined. *South's Sermons.*

She heard not half, so *furiously* she flies;
Fear gave her wings. *Dryden.*

FU'RIOUSNESS. *n. s.* [from *furious*.] Frenzy; madness; transport of passion.

To FURL. *v. a.* [*fresler*, French.] To draw up; to contract.

When fortune sends a stormy wind,
Then shew a brave and present mind;
And when with too indulgent gales
She swells too much, then *furl* thy sails. *Creech.*

FU'RLONG. *n. s.* [fuplang, Saxon.] A measure of length; the eighth part of a mile.

If a man stand in the middle of a field and speak aloud, he shall be heard a *furlong* in round, and that in articulate sounds. *Bacon's Natural History*, N°. 289.

Coming within a few *furlongs* of the temple, they passed through a very thick grove. *Addison's Freeholder.*

FU'RLOUGH. *n. s.* [*verloef*, Dutch.] A temporary dismission from military service; a licence given to a soldier to be absent.

Brutus and Cato might discharge their souls,
And give them *furlo's* for another world;
But we, like sentries, are oblig'd to stand
In starless nights, and wait th' appointed hour. *Dryden.*

FU'RMENTY. *n. s.* [More properly *frumenty*, or *frumety*, of *frumentum*, Latin.] Food made by boiling wheat in milk.

Remember, wife, therefore, though I do it not,
The seed-cake, the pasties, and *furmenty* pot. *Tuss. Husb.*

FU'RNACE. *n. s.* [*furnus*, Latin.] An inclosed fireplace.

Heat not a *furnace* for your foe so hot
That it may singe yourself. *Shakesp. Henry* VIII.

The fining pot is for silver and the *furnace* for gold. *Prov.*

We have also *furnaces* of great diversities, that keep great diversity of heats. *Bacon's New Atlantis.*

The kings of Spain have erected divers *furnaces* and forges, for the trying and fining of their gold. *Abbo..*

Whoso falleth not down and worshippeth, shall the same hour be cast into the midst of a burning fiery *furnace*. *Dan.*

A dungeon horrible, on all sides around,
As one great *furnace*, flam'd. *Milton's Paradise Lost*, *b.* i.

To FU'RNACE. *v. a.* [from the noun.] To throw out as sparks from a furnace. A bad word.

He *furnaces*
The thick sighs from him. *Shakespeare's Cymbeline.*

To FU'RNISH. *v. a.* [*fournir*, French.]

1. To supply with what is necessary.

She hath directed
How I shall take her from her father's house;
What gold and jewels she is *furnish'd* with. *Shakespeare.*

His training such,
That he may *furnish* and instruct great teachers,
And never seek for aid out of himself. *Shak. Henry* VIII.

Thou shalt *furnish* him liberally out of thy flock. *Deut.* xv.

Auria, having driven the Turks from Corone, both by sea and land, *furnished* the city with corn, wine, victual, and powder. *Knolles's History of the Turks.*

Come, thou stranger, and *furnish* a table, and feed me of that thou hast ready. *Ecclus.* xxix. 26.

I shall not need to heap up instances; every one's reading and conversation will sufficiently *furnish* him, if he wants to be better stored. *Locke.*

2. To give things for use.

These simple ideas, the materials of all our knowledge, are suggested and *furnished* to the mind only by these two ways, sensation and reflection. *Locke.*

It is not any action of the state, but a compact among private persons that hath *furnished* out these several remittances. *Addison's Remarks on Italy.*

3. To fit up; to fit with appendages.

Something deeper,
Whereof perchance these are but *furnishings*. *Shakespeare.*

Plato entertained some of his friends at dinner, and had in the chamber a bed or couch, neatly and costly *furnished*. Diogenes came in, and got up upon the bed, and trampled it, saying, I trample upon the pride of Plato. Plato mildly answered, But with greater pride, Diogenes. *Bacon's Apophth.*

We were led into another great room, *furnished* with old inscriptions. *Addison on Italy.*

4. To equip; to fit out for any undertaking.

Will your lordship lend me a thousand pounds to *furnish* me? *Shakespeare's Henry* IV. *p.* i.

Ideas, forms, and intellects,
Have *furnish'd* out three diff'rent sects. *Prior.*

Doubtless the man Jesus Christ is *furnished* with superior powers to all the angels in heaven, because he is employed in superior work. *Watts's Improvement of the Mind.*

5. To decorate; to adorn.

The wounded arm would *furnish* all their rooms,
And bleed for ever scarlet in the looms. *Halifax.*

FU'RNISHER. *n. s.* [*fournisseur*, French, from *furnish*.] One who supplies or fits out.

FU'RNITURE. *n. s.* [*fourniture*, Fr. from *furnish*.]

1. Moveables; goods put in a house for use or ornament.

No man can transport his large retinue, his sumptuous fare, and his rich *furniture* into another world. *South's Sermons.*

There are many noble palaces in Venice: their *furniture* is not commonly very rich, if we except the pictures from the hands of the best masters. *Addison.*

2. Appendages.

By a general conflagration mankind shall be destroyed, with the form and all the *furniture* of the earth. *Tillotson.*

3. Equipage; embellishments; decorations.

Young Clarion, with vauntful lustyhed,
After his guise did cast abroad to fare,
And thereto 'gan his *furnitures* prepare. *Spenser.*

The duke is coming: see, the barge be ready,
And fit it with such *furniture* as suits
The greatness of his person. *Shakespeare's Henry* VIII.

The ground must be of a mixt brown, and large enough, or the horse's *furniture* must be of very sensible colours. *Dryd.*

FU'RRIER. *n. s.* [from *fur*.] A dealer in furs.

FU'RROW. *n. s.* [funh, Saxon.]

1. A small trench made by the plow for the reception of seed.

Wheat must be sowed above *furrow* before Michaelmas. *Mortimer's Husbandry.*

Then ploughs for seed the fruitful *furrows* broke,
And oxen labour'd first beneath the yoke. *Dryden's Ovid.*

2. Any long trench or hollow: as a wrinkle.

My lord it is, though time has plow'd that face
With many *furrows* since I saw it first;
Yet I'm too well acquainted with the ground quite to forget it. *Dryd. and Lee's Oedipus.*

FU'RROW-WEED. *n. s.* [*furrow* and *weed*.] A weed that grows in furrowed land.

Crown'd with rank fumiter, and *furrow-weeds*. *Shakesp.*

To FU'RROW. *v. a.* [from the noun; fynian, Saxon.]

1. To cut in furrows.

While the plowman near at hand,
Whistles o'er the *furrow'd* land. *Milton.*

2. To divide in long hollows.

No briny tear has *furrow'd* her ſmooth cheek. *Suckling.*

The billows fall, while Neptune lays his mace
On the rough ſea, and ſmooths its *furrow'd* face. *Dryden.*

3. To make by cutting.

There go the ſhips that *furrow* out their way;
Yea, there of whales enormous ſights we ſee. *Wotton.*

FU'RRY. *adj.* [from *fur.*]

1. Covered with fur; dreſſed in fur.

From Volga's banks th' imperious Czar
Leads forth his *furry* troops to war. *Felton to Lord Gower.*

2. Conſiſting of fur.

Not arm'd with horns of arbitrary might,
Or claws to ſeize their *furry* ſpoils in fight. *Dryden.*

FU'RTHER. *adj.* [from *forth*, not from *far*, as is commonly imagined; *forth*, *further*, *furtheſt*, corrupted from *forther*, *fortheſt*, forðer, Saxon. *Forther* is uſed by Sir *Thomas More.* See FORTH and FARTHER, of which the examples are to be referred to this word.]

1. At a greater diſtance.

2. Beyond this.

What *further* need have we of witneſſes. *Mat.* xxvi. 65.

FU'RTHER. *adv.* [from *forth.*] To a greater diſtance.

And the angel of the Lord went *further*, and ſtood in a narrow place. *Numb.* xxii. 2.

To FU'RTHER. *v. a.* [from the adverb; forðrian, Saxon.] To put onward; to forward; to promote; to countenance; to aſſiſt; to help.

Things thus ſet in order, in quiet and reſt,
Shall *further* thy harveſt, and pleaſure thee beſt. *Tuſſ. Husb.*

Could their fond ſuperſtition have *furthered* ſo great attempts, without the mixture of a true perſuaſion concerning the irreſiſtible force of divine power. *Hooker, b.* v. *ſ.* 1.

Grant not, O Lord, the deſires of the wicked; *further* not his wicked device. *Pſ.* cxl. 8.

This binds thee then to *further* my deſign,
As I am bound by vow to *further* thine. *Dryden.*

FU'RTHERANCE. *n. ſ.* [from *further.*] Promotion; advancement; help.

The Gauls learned them firſt, and uſed them only for the *furtherance* of their trade and private buſineſs. *Spenſer.*

Our diligence muſt ſearch out all helps and *furtherances* of direction, which ſcriptures, councils, fathers, hiſtories, the laws and practices of all churches afford. *Hooker.*

For gain and work, and ſucceſs in his affairs, he ſeeketh *furtherance* of him that hath no manner of power. *Hooker.*

Cannot my body, nor blood-ſacrifice,
Intreat you to your wonted *furtherance?* *Shak. Henry* VI.

If men were minded to live righteouſly, to believe a God would be no hindrance or prejudice to any ſuch deſign, but very much for the advancement and *furtherance* of it. *Till.*

FU'RTHERER. *n. ſ.* [from *further.*] Promoter; advancer.

That earneſt favourer and *furtherer* of God's true religion, that faithful ſervitor to his prince and country. *Aſcham.*

FU'RTHERMORE. [*further* and *more.*] Moreover; beſides.

This ring I do accept moſt thankfully,
And ſo, I pray you, tell him: *furthermore*,
I pray you, ſhew my youth old Shylock's houſe. *Shakeſp.*

FU'RTIVE. *adj.* [*furtive*, Fr. *furtivus*, Latin.] Stolen; gotten by theft.

Or do they, as your ſchemes, I think, have ſhown,
Dart *furtive* beams and glory not their own,
All ſervants to that ſource of light, the ſun? *Prior.*

FU'RUNCLE. *n. ſ.* [*furoncle*, Fr. *furunculus*, Latin.] A bile; an angry puſtule.

A *furuncle* is in its beginning round, hard, and inflamed; and as it increaſeth, it riſeth up with an acute head, and ſometimes a puſtule; and then it is more inflamed and painful, when it arrives at its ſtate, which is about the eighth or ninth day. *Wiſeman's Surgery.*

FU'RY. *n. ſ.* [*furor*, Latin; *fureur*, French.]

1. Madneſs.

2. Rage; paſſion of anger; tumult of mind approaching to madneſs.

I do oppoſe my patience to his *fury*; and am arm'd
To ſuffer with a quietneſs of ſpirit
The very tyranny and rage of his. *Shakeſp. Mer. of Venice.*

He hath given me to know the natures of living creatures, and the *furies* of wild beaſts. *Wiſd.* vii. 20.

3. Enthuſiaſm; exaltation of fancy.

Taking up the lute, her wit began to be with a divine *fury* inſpired; and her voice would, in ſo beloved an occaſion, ſecond her wit. *Sidney, b.* ii.

A ſybil, that had number'd in the world
The ſun to courſe two hundred compaſſes,
In her prophetick *fury* ſew'd the work. *Shakeſp. Othello.*

Greater than human kind ſhe ſeem'd to look,
And with an accent more than mortal ſpoke;
Her ſtaring eyes with ſparkling *fury* roll,
When all the god came ruſhing on her ſoul. *Dryden's Æn.*

4. [From *furia*, Latin.] One of the deities of vengeance, and thence a ſtormy, turbulent, violent, raging woman.

The ſight of any of the houſe of York,
Is as a *fury* to torment my ſoul. *Shakeſp. Henry* VI. *p.* iii.

It was the moſt proper place for a *fury* to make her exit; and I believe every reader's imagination is pleaſed, when he ſees the angry goddeſs thus ſinking in a tempeſt, and plunging herſelf into hell, amidſt ſuch a ſcene of horror and confuſion. *Addiſon's Remarks on Italy.*

FURZE. *n. ſ.* [fyrr, Saxon.] Gorſe; goſs.

The whole plant is very thorny: the flowers, which are of the pea-bloom kind, are diſpoſed in ſhort thick ſpikes, which are ſucceeded by ſhort compreſſed pods, in each of which are contained three or four kidney-ſhaped ſeeds. The ſpecies are three, each of which grow wild on the heaths and upland-commons in England: the firſt is ſometimes uſed to make hedges, for which purpoſe it will do very well for a few years. *Miller.*

Carry out gravel to fill up a hole,
Both timber and *furzin*, the turf and the cole. *Tuſſ. Husb.*

For fewel, there groweth generally in all parts great ſtore of *furze*, of which the ſhrubby ſort is called tame, and the better grown French. *Carew's Survey of Cornwal.*

From hence uncertain ſeaſons we may know,
And when to reap the grain, and when to ſow,
Or when to fell the *furzes.* *Dryden's Virg. Georg.*

FU'RZY. *adj.* [from *furze.*] Overgrown with furze; full of gorſe.

Wide through the *furzy* field their route they take,
Their bleeding boſoms force the thorny brake. *Gay.*

FUSCA'TION. *n. ſ.* [*fuſcus*, Latin.] The act of darkening or obſcuring. *Dict.*

To FUSE. *v. a.* [*fundo*, *fuſum*, Latin.] To melt; to put into fuſion; to liquify by heat.

To FUSE. *v. n.* To be melted; to be capable of being liquified by heat.

FU'SEE. *n. ſ.* [*fuſeau*, French.]

1. The cone round which is wound the cord or chain of a clock or watch.

The reaſon of the motion of the balance is by the motion of the next wheel, and that by the motion of the next, and that by the motion of the *fuſee*, and that by the motion of the ſpring: the whole frame of the watch carries a reaſonableneſs in it, the paſſive impreſſion of the intellectual idea that was in the artiſt. *Hale's Origin of Mankind.*

2. A firelock [from *fuſil*, Fr.]; a ſmall neat muſquet. This is more properly written *fuſil.*

FUSEE of a bomb or granado ſhell, is that which makes the whole powder or compoſition in the ſhell take fire, to do the deſigned execution. 'Tis uſually a wooden pipe or tap filled with wildfire, or ſome ſuch matter; and is intended to burn no longer than is the time of the motion of the bomb from the mouth of the mortar to the place where it is to fall, which time Anderſon makes twenty-ſeven ſeconds. *Harris.*

FU'SEE. Track of a buck. *Ainſworth.*

FU'SIBLE. *adj.* [from *fuſe.*] Capable of being melted; capable of being made liquid by heat.

Colours afforded by metalline bodies, either colliquate with or otherwiſe penetrate into other bodies, eſpecially *fuſible* ones. *Boyle.*

FUSIBI'LITY. *n. ſ.* [from *fuſible.*] Capacity of being melted; quality of growing liquid by heat.

The ancients obſerving in that material a kind of metalical nature, or at leaſt a *fuſibility*, ſeem to have reſolved it into a nobler uſe. *Wotton's Architecture.*

The bodies of moſt uſe, that are ſought for out of the depths of the earth, are the metals, which are diſtinguiſhed from other bodies by their weight, *fuſibility*, and malleableneſs. *Locke.*

FU'SIL. *adj.* [*fuſile*, French; *fuſilis*, Latin.]

1. Capable of being melted; liquifiable by heat.

The liquid ore he drain'd
Into fit molds prepar'd; from which he form'd
Firſt his own tools: then, what might elſe be wrought
Fuſile, or grav'n in metal. *Milton's Paradiſe Loſt, b.* xi.

Some, leſs ſkilful, fancy theſe ſcapi that occur in moſt of the larger Gothick buildings of England are artificial; and will have it, that they are a kind of *fuſil* marble. *Woodward.*

2. Running by the force of heat.

Perpetual flames,
O'er ſand and aſhes, and the ſtubborn flint,
Prevailing, turn into a *fuſil* ſea. *Phillips.*

FU'SIL. *n. ſ.* [*fuſil*, French.]

1. A firelock; a ſmall neat muſquet.

2. [In heraldry, from *fuſus*, Latin.] Something like a ſpindle.

Fuſils muſt be made long, and ſmall in the middle, in the ancient coat of Mountague, argent three *fuſils* in feſſe gules. *Peacham on Blazoning.*

FU'SILIER. *n. ſ.* [from *fuſil.*] A ſoldier armed with a fuſil.

FU'SION. *n. ſ.* [*fuſio*, Latin; *fuſion*, French.]

1. The act of melting.

2. The ſtate of being melted, or of running with heat.

Metals in *fuſion* do not flame for want of a copious fume, except ſpelter, which fumes copiouſly, and thereby flames. *Newton's Opt.*

FUSS. *n. ſ.* [A low cant word.] A tumult; a buſtle.

End as it befits your ftation;
Come to ufe and application;
Nor with fenates keep a *fufs*:
I fubmit, and anfwer thus. *Swift.*

FUST. *n. f.* [*fufte*, French.]

1. The trunk or body of a column.

2. [From *fufté*, French.] A ftrong fmell, as that of a mouldy barrel.

To Fust. *v. n.* [from the noun.] To grow mouldy; to fmell ill.

FU'STIAN. *n. f.* [*futaine*, French, from *fufte*, a tree, becaufe cotton grows on trees.]

1. A kind of cloth made of linen and cotton, and perhaps now of cotton only.

Is fupper ready, the houfe trimm'd, the ferving-men in their new *fuftian* and their white ftockings? *Shakefpeare.*

2. A high fwelling kind of writing made up of heterogeneous parts, or of words and ideas ill affociated; bombaft.

Nor will you raife in me combuftion,
By dint of high heroick *fuftian*. *Hudibras, p.* ii. *cant.* 1.

What *fuftian* have I heard thefe gentlemen find out in Mr. Cowley's odes! In general, I will fay, that nothing can appear more beautiful to me than the ftrength of thofe images which they condemn. *Dryden.*

I am much deceived if this be not abominable *fuftian*; that is, thoughts and words ill forted, and without the leaft relation to each other. *Dryden's Spanifh Fryar, Dedication.*

Chance thoughts, when govern'd by the clofe,
Oft rife to *fuftian*, or defcend to profe. *Smith.*

Fu'stian. *adj.* [from the noun.]

1. Made of fuftian.

2. Swelling; unnaturally pompous; ridiculoufly tumid. Ufed of ftile.

When men argue, th' greateft part
O' th' conteft falls on terms of art,
Until the *fuftian* ftuff be fpent,
And then they fall to th' argument. *Hudibras, p.* i. *can.* 3.

Virgil, if he could have feen the firft verfes of the Sylvæ, would have thought Statius mad in his *fuftian* defcription of the ftatue on the brazen horfe. *Dryden's Dufrefnoy.*

Fu'stic. *n. f.* A fort of wood brought from the Weft-Indies, ufed in dying of cloath. *Dict.*

To Fu'stigate. *v. a.* [*fuftigo*, Latin.] To beat with a ftick; to cane. *Dict.*

Fustilarian. *n. f.* [from *fufty*.] A low fellow; a ftinkard; a fcoundrel. A word ufed by *Shakefpeare* only.

Away, you fcullion, you rampallian, you *fuftilarian*: I'll tickle your cataftrophe. *Shakefpeare's Henry* IV. *p.* ii.

Fu'stiness. *n. f.* [from *fufty*.] Mouldinefs; ftink.

Fu'sty. *adj.* [from *fuft*.] Ill fmelling; mouldy.

Hector fhall have a great catch, if he knock out either of your brains: he were as good crack a *fufty* nut with no kernel. *Shakefpeare's Troilus and Creffida.*

The *fufty* plebeians hate thine honours. *Shak. Coriolan.*

The large Achilles, at this *fufty* ftuff,
From his deep cheft laughs out a loud applaufe. *Shakefp.*

FU'TILE. *adj.* [*futile*, French; *futilis*, Latin.]

1. Talkative; loquacious.

One *futile* perfon, that maketh it his glory to tell, will do more hurt than many that know it their duty to conceal. *Bacon.*

2. Trifling; worthlefs; of no weight.

Futi'lity. *n. f.* [*futilité*, French, from *futile*.]

1. Talkativenefs; loquacity.

This fable does not ftrike fo much at the *futility* of women, as at the incontinent levity of a prying humour. *L'Eftrange.*

2. Triflingnefs; want of weight; want of folidity.

Trifling *futility* appears in their figns of the zodiack, and their mutual relations and afpects. *Bentley.*

Fu'ttocks. *n. f.* [corrupted from *foot hooks*. *Skinner.*] The lower timbers that hold the fhip together.

FU'TURE. *adj.* [*futurus*, Latin; *futur*, French.] That which will be hereafter; to come: as, the *future* ftate.

Glory they fung to the moft High! good will
To *future* men, and in their dwellings peace. *Milt. P. L.*

He fows the teeth at Pallas's command,
And flings the *future* people from his hand. *Addifon's Ovid.*

Fu'ture. *n. f.* [from the adjective.] Time to come; fomewhat to happen hereafter.

Thy letters have tranfported me beyond
This ign'rant prefent time; and I feel now
The *future* in the inftant. *Shakefpeare's Macbeth.*

The mind, once jaded by an attempt above its power, either is difabled for the *future*, or elfe checks at any vigorous undertaking ever after. *Locke.*

Fu'turely. *adv.* [from *future*.] In time to come.

This prefcience of God, as it is prefcience, is not the caufe of any thing *futurely* fucceeding; neither doth God's foreknowledge impofe any neceffity, or bind. *Raleigh.*

Futuri'tion. *n. f.* [from *future*.] The ftate of being to be; of being to come to pafs hereafter.

Is it imaginable, that the great means of the world's redemption fhould reft only in the number of poffibilities, and hang fo loofe in refpect of its *futurition*, as to leave the event in an equal poife, whether ever there fhould be fuch a thing or no? *South's Sermons.*

Fu'turity. *n. f.* [from *future*.]

1. Time to come; events to come.

Not my fervice paft, nor prefent forrows,
Nor purpos'd merit in *futurity*,
Can ranfom me. *Shakefpeare's Othello.*

All *futurities* are naked before that All-feeing Eye, the fight of which is no more hindred by diftance of time than the fight of an angel can be determined by diftance of place. *South.*

I will contrive fome way to make it known to *futurity*, that I had your lordfhip for my patron. *Swift.*

This, great Amphiarus, lay hid from thee,
Though fkill'd in fate and dark *futurity*. *Pope's Statius.*

2. The ftate of being to be; futurition.

It may be well reckoned among the bare poffibilities, which never commence into a *futurity*; it requiring fuch a free, fedate and intent mind, as, it may be, is no where found but among the platonical ideas. *Glanv. Scepf. c.* 10.

To FUZZ. *v. n.* [without etymology.] To fly out in fmall particles.

Fu'zzball. *n. f.* [*fuzz* and *ball*.] A kind of fungus, which, when preffed, burfts and fcatters duft in the eyes.

Fy. *interj.* [*fy*, French and Flemifh; φεῦ, Greek; *vah*, Lat.] A word of blame and difapprobation.

And *fy* on fortune, mine avowed foe,
Whofe wrathful wreaks themfelves do now allay. *Fa. Queen.*

Fy, my lord, *fy*! a foldier, and afraid? What need we fear who knows it, when none can call our power to account? *Shakefpeare's Macbeth.*

A bawd, fir, *fy* upon him! *Shakef. Meafure for Meafure.*

But *fy*, my wand'ring mufe, how thou do'ft ftray!
Expectance calls thee now another way. *Milton.*

Nay, *fy*, what mean you in this open place?
Unhand me, or, I fwear, I'll fcratch your face:
Let go, for fhame; you make me mad for fpite:
My mouth's my own; and if you kifs, I'll bite. *Dryden.*

Fy, madam, he cried, we muft be paft all thefe gaities. *Tatler*, N°. 54.

G.

G.

G Has two sounds, one from the Greek Γ, and the Latin, which is called that of the hard *G*, because it is formed by a pressure somewhat hard of the forepart of the tongue against the upper gum. This sound *G* retains before *a, o, u, l, r*; as, *gate, go, gull*. The other sound, called that of the soft *G*, resembles that of *J*, and is commonly, though not always, found before *e, i*; as, *gem, gibbet*. Before *n*, at the end of a word, *g* is commonly melted away; as in the French, from which these words are commonly derived: thus, for *benign, malign, condign*, we pronounce *benine, maline, condine*. It is often silent in the middle of words before *h*; as, *might*. The Saxon Ꞡ, ȝ, seems to have had generally the sound of *y* consonant; whence *gate* is by rusticks still pronounced *yate*.

GA'BARDINE. *n. s.* [*gavardina*, Italian.] A coarse frock; any mean dress.

My best way is to creep under his *gabardine*; there is no other shelter hereabout. *Shakespeare's Tempest.*

You call me misbeliever, cut-throat dog,
And spit upon my Jewish *gabardine*. *Shakes. Mer. of Venice.*

The knight did straight submit,
And laid his weapons at her feet:
Next he disrob'd his *gabardine*,
And with it did himself resign. *Hudibras, b.* i.

To GA'BBLE. *v. n.* [*gabbare*, Italian; *gabberen*, Dutch.]

1. To make an inarticulate noise.

When thou could'st not, savage,
Shew thine own meaning, but would'st *gabble* like
A thing most brutish, I endow'd thy purposes
With words that made them known. *Shakesp. Tempest.*

Flocks of fowl, that when the tempests roar,
With their hoarse *gabbling* seek the silent shoar. *Dryd. Æn.*

2. To prate loudly without meaning.

Have you no wit, manners, nor honesty, but to *gabble* like tinkers at this time of night? Do ye make an alehouse of my lady's house? *Shakespeare's Twelfth Night.*

Which made some think, when he did *gabble*,
Th' had heard three labourers of Babel. *Hudibras, p.* i.

Such a rout, and such a rabble,
Run to hear Jack Pudding *gabble*. *Swift.*

GA'BBLE. *n. s.* [from the verb.]

1. Inarticulate noise like that of brute animals.

Not to know what we speak one to another, so we seem to know, is to know straight our purpose: chough's language, *gabble* enough, and good enough. *Shak. All's well that ends well.*

2. Loud talk without meaning.

Forthwith a hideous *gabble* rises loud
Among the builders; each to other calls,
Not understood. *Milton's Paradise Lost, b.* xii.

GA'BBLER. *n. s.* [from *gabble.*] A prater; a chattering fellow.

GA'BEL. *n. s.* [*gabelle*, French; *gabello*, Italian; ȝaꝼel, Saxon, a tribute.] An excise; a tax.

The *gabels* of Naples are very high on oil, wine, and tobacco. *Addison's Remarks on Italy.*

GA'BION. *n. s.* [French.] A wicker basket which is filled with earth to make a fortification or intrenchment.

His battery was defended all along with *gabions*, and casks filled with sand. *Knolles's History of the Turks.*

GA'BLE. *n. s.* [*gaval*, Welsh; *gable*, French.] The sloping roof of a building.

Take care that all your brick-work be covered with the tiling, according to the new way of building, without *gable* ends, which are very heavy, and very apt to let the water into the brick-work. *Mortimer's Husbandry.*

GAD. *n. s.* [ȝaꝺ, Saxon; *gaddur*, Islandick, a club.]

1. A wedge or ingot of steel.

Flemish steel is brought down the Rhine to Dort, and other parts of Holland and Flanders, some in bars, and some in *gads*; and therefore called Flemish steel, and sometimes *gad* steel. *Moxon's Mech. Exer.*

2. It seems to be used by *Shakespeare* for a stile or graver, [from ȝaꝺ, Saxon, a goad.]

I will go get a leaf of brass,
And with a *gad* of steel will write these words. *Shakespeare.*

To GAD. *v. n.* [Derived by *Skinner* from *gadfly*; by *Junius* from *gadaw*, Welsh, to forsake.] To ramble about without any settled purpose; to rove loosely and idly.

How now, my headstrong, where have you been *gadding*?
—Where I have learnt me to repent. *Shakes. Rom. and Jul.*

Give the water no passage, neither a wicked woman liberty to *gad* abroad. *Ecclus.* xxv. 25.

The lesser devils arose with ghastly rore,
And thronged forth about the world to *gad*;
Each land they fill'd, river, stream and shore. *Fairfax, b.* iv.

Envy is a *gadding* passion, and walketh the streets, and doth not keep home. *Bacon, Essay* 9.

Gad not abroad at ev'ry quest and call
Of an untrained hope or passion;
To court each place or fortune that doth fall,
Is wantonness in contemplation. *Herbert.*

Thee, shepherd, thee the woods and desart caves,
With wild thyme and the *gadding* vine o'ergrown,
And all their echo's moan. *Milton.*

A fierce loud buzzing breeze; their stings draw blood,
And drive the cattle *gadding* through the wood. *Dryd. Virg.*

She wreaks her anger on her rival's head;
With furies frights her from her native home,
And drives her *gadding*, round the world to roam. *Dryden.*

Gull 'em with freedom,
And you shall see 'em toss their tails, and *gad*
As if the breeze had stung them. *Dryd. and Lee's Oedipus.*

There's an ox lost, and this coxcomb runs a *gadding* after wild fowl. *L'Estrange.*

No wonder their thoughts should be perpetually shifting from what disgusts them, and seek better entertainment in more pleasing objects, after which they will unavoidably be *gadding*. *Locke.*

GA'DDER. *n. s.* [from *gad.*] A rambler; one that runs much abroad without business.

A drunken woman, and a *gadder* abroad, causeth great anger, and she will not cover her own shame. *Ecclus.* xxvi. 8.

GA'DDINGLY. *adv.* [from *gad.*] In a rambling, roving manner.

GA'DFLY. *n. s.* [*gad* and *fly*; but by *Skinner*, who makes it the original of *gad*, *goadfly*. Supposed to be originally from *goad*, in Saxon ȝaꝺ, and *fly*.] A fly that when he stings the cattle makes them gad or run madly about; the breese.

The fly called the *gadfly* breedeth of somewhat that swimeth upon the top of the water, and is most about ponds. *Bac.*

Light fly his slumbers, if perchance a flight
Of angry *gadflies* fasten on the herd. *Thomson's Summer.*

GAFF. *n. s.* A harpoon or large hook. *Ainsworth.*

GA'FFER. *n. s.* [ȝeꝼeꞃe, companion, Saxon.] A word of respect now obsolete, or applied only in contempt to a mean person.

For *gaffer* Treadwell told us by the bye,
Excessive sorrow is exceeding dry. *Gay's Pastorals.*

GA'FFLES. *n. s.* [ȝaꝼelucaꞅ, spears, Saxon.]

1. Artificial spurs put upon cocks when they are set to fight.

2. A steel contrivance to bend cross-bows. *Ainsworth.*

To GAG. *v. n.* [from *gaghel*, Dutch, the palate, *Minshew.*] To stop the mouth with something that may allow to breathe, but hinder to speak.

He's out of his guard already: unless you laugh and minister occasion to him, he is *gagg'd*. *Shakesp. Twelfth Night.*

There foam'd rebellious logick, *gagg'd* and bound. *Pope.*

GAG. *n. s.* [from the verb.] Something put into the mouth to hinder speech or eating.

Some, when the kids their dams too deeply drain,
With *gags* and muzzles their soft mouths restrain. *Dryden.*

Your woman would have run up stairs before me; but I have secured her below with a *gag* in her chaps. *Dryden.*

GAGE. *n. s.* [*gage*, French.] A pledge; a pawn; a caution; any thing given in security.

Who, when the shamed shield of slain Sansfoy
He spy'd, with that same fairy champion's page,
He to him leapt; and that same envious *gage*,
Of victor's glory, from him snatcht away. *Fairy Queen.*

There I throw my *gage*
Disclaiming here the kindred of a king,
And lay aside my high blood's royalty. *Shakesp. Richard* II.

There is my *gage*, the manual seal of death,
That marks thee out for hell. *Shakesp. Richard* II.

They from their mothers breasts poor orphans rend,
Nor without *gages* to the needy lend. *Sandys's Paraphrase.*

I am made the cautionary pledge,
The *gage* and hostage of your keeping it. *Southern's Oroonok.*

But since it was decreed, auspicious king,
In Britain's right that thou should'st wed the main,
Heav'n, as a *gage*, would cast some previous thing,
And therefore doom'd that Lawson should be slain. *Dryden.*

In any truth, that gets not possession of our minds by self-evidence or demonstration, the arguments, that gain it assent, are the vouchers and *gage* of its probability. *Locke.*

To GAGE. *v. a.* [*gager*, French.]

1. To wager; to depone as a wager; to impawn; to give as a caution, pledge, or security.

Against the which, a moiety competent
Was *gaged* by our king. *Shakespeare's Hamlet.*

Drawing near the shore, he found the Turkish merchants making merry upon the main: unto these merchants he gave due salutations, *gaging* his faith for their safety, and they likewise to him. *Knolles's History of the Turks.*

2. To measure; to take the contents of any vessel of liquids particularly. More properly *gauge*. See GAUGE.

We shall see your bearing.
—Nay, but I bar to-night: you shall not *gage* me
By what we do to-night. *Shakesp. Merchant of Venice.*

To GA'GGLE. *v. n.* [*gagen*, *gagelen*, Dutch] To make noise like a goose.

Birds prune their feathers, geese *gaggle*, and crows seem to call upon rain; which is but the comfort they receive in the relenting of the air. *Bacon's Natural History*, N°. 823.

May fat geese *gaggle* with melodious voice,
And ne'er want gooseberries or apple-sauce. *King.*

GAI'ETY. See GAYETY.

GAILY. *adv.* [from *gay.*]

1. Airily; cheerfully.

2. Splendidly; pompously; with great show.

The ladies *gaily* dress'd, the Mall adorn
With curious dyes, and paint the sunny morn. *Gay's Trivia.*

Like some fair flow'r that early Spring supplies,
That *gaily* blooms, but ev'n in blooming dies. *Pope.*

GAIN. *n. s.* [*gain*, French.]

1. Profit; advantage.

But what things were *gain* to me, those I counted loss for Christ. *Phil.* iii. 7.

Besides the purpose it were now, to teach how victory should be used, or the *gains* thereof communicated to the general content. *Raleigh's Essays.*

It is in praise of men as in gettings and *gains*; for light *gains* make heavy purses; for light *gains* come thick, whereas great come but now and then. *Bacon, Essay* 53.

This must be made by some governor upon his own private account, who has a great stock that he is content to turn that way, and is invited by the *gains*. *Temple.*

2. Interest; lucrative views.

That sir, which serves for *gain*,
And follows but for form,
Will pack, when it begins to rain,
And leave thee in the storm. *Shakespeare's King Lear.*

3. Unlawful advantage.

Did I make a *gain* of you by any of them whom I sent unto you? 2 *Cor.* xii. 17.

4. Overplus in a comparative computation; any thing opposed to loss.

To GAIN. *v. a.* [*gagner*, French.]

1. To obtain as profit or advantage.

Thou hast taken usury and increase, and thou hast greedily *gained* of thy neighbours by extortions. *Ezek.* xxii. 12.

2. To have the overplus in comparative computation.

If you have two vessels to fill, and you empty one to fill the other, you *gain* nothing by that. *Burnet's Theory of the Earth.*

3. To obtain; to procure.

If such a tradition were endeavoured to be set on foot, it is not easy to imagine how it should at first *gain* entertainment; but much more difficult to conceive how ever it should come to be universally propagated. *Tillotson's Sermons.*

4. To obtain increase of any thing allotted.

I know that ye would *gain* the time, because ye see the king is gone from me. *Dan.* ii. 8.

5. To obtain whatever good or bad.

Ye should not have loosed from Crete, and have *gained* this harm and loss. *Acts* xxvii. 21.

6. To win.

They who were sent to the other pass, after a short resistance, *gained* it. *Clarendon, b.* viii.

Fat fees from the defended Umbrian draws,
And only *gains* the wealthy client's cause. *Dryd. Pers. Sat.*

O love! for Sylvia let me *gain* the prize,
And make my tongue victorious as her eyes. *Pope's Spring.*

7. To draw into any interest or party.

Come, with presents, laden from the port,
To gratify the queen and *gain* the court. *Dryd. Virg. Æn.*

If Pyrrhus must be wrought to pity,
No woman does it better than yourself:
If you *gain* him, I shall comply of course. *A. Phillips.*

8. To reach; to attain.

The West glimmers with some streaks of day:
Now spurs the lated traveller apace,
To *gain* the timely inn. *Shakespeare's Macbeth.*

Death was the post, which I almost did *gain*:
Shall I once more be tost into the main? *Waller.*

We came to the roots of the mountain, and had a very troublesome march to *gain* the top of it. *Addison on Italy.*

Thus sav'd from death, they *gain* the Phestan shores,
With shatter'd vessels and disabled oars. *Pope's Odyssey, b.* iii.

9. *To* GAIN *over.* To draw to another party or interest.

The court of Hanover should have endeavoured to *gain over* those who were represented as their enemies. *Swift.*

To GAIN. *v. n.*

1. To encroach; to come forward by degrees.

When watchful herons leave their wat'ry stand,
And mounting upward with erected flight,
Gain on the skies, and soar above the sight. *Dryd. Virg. Geo.*

On the land while here the ocean *gains*,
In other parts it leaves wide sandy plains. *Pope on Criticism.*

2. To get ground; to prevail against.

The English have not only *gained* upon the Venetians in the Levant, but have their cloth in Venice itself. *Addison.*

3. To obtain influence with.

My good behaviour had *gained* so far on the emperor, that I began to conceive hopes of liberty. *Gulliver's Travels.*

To GAIN. *v. n.* To grow rich; to have advantage; to be advanced in interest or happiness.

GAIN. *adj.* [An old word now out of use.] Handy; ready; dexterous.

GA'INER. *n. s.* [from *gain.*] One who receives profit or advantage.

The client, besides retaining a good conscience, is always a *gainer*, and by no means can be at any loss, as seeing, if the composition be overhard, he may relieve himself by recourse to his oath. *Bacon's Off. of Alienation.*

If what I get in empire
I lose in fame, I think myself no *gainer*. *Denham's Sophy.*

He that loses any thing, and gets wisdom by it, is a *gainer* by the loss. *L'Estrange, Fable* 59.

By extending a well regulated trade, we are as great *gainers* by the commodities of many other countries as those of our own nation. *Addison's Freeholder.*

GAI'NFUL. *adj.* [*gain* and *full.*]

1. Advantageous; profitable.

He will dazzle his eyes, and bait him in with the luscious proposal of some *gainful* purchase, some rich match, or advantageous project. *South.*

2. Lucrative; productive of money.

Nor knows he merchants *gainful* care. *Dryden's Horace.*

Maro's muse,
Thrice sacred muse! commodious precepts gives,
Instructive to the swains, not wholly bent
On what is *gainful*: sometimes she diverts
From solid counsels. *Phillips.*

GA'INFULLY. *adv.* [from *gainful.*] Profitably; advantageously.

GA'INFULNESS. *n. s.* [from *gainful.*] Profit; advantage.

GAI'NGIVING *n. s.* ['*gainst* and *give.*] The same as misgiving; a giving against: as gainsaying, which is still in use, is saying against, or contradicting. *Hanmer.*

It is but foolery; but it is such a kind of *gaingiving* as would, perhaps, trouble a woman. *Shakespeare's Hamlet.*

GA'INLESS. *adj.* [from *gain.*] Unprofitable; producing no advantage.

GAI'NLESSNESS. *n. s.* [from *gainless.*] Unprofitableness; want of advantage.

The parallel holds too in the *gainlessness* as well as laboriousness of the work: those wretched creatures, buried in earth and darkness, were never the richer for all the ore they digged; no more is the insatiable miser. *Decay of Piety.*

GA'INLY. *adv.* [from *gain.*] Handily; readily; dexterously.

To GA'INSAY. *v. a.* ['*gainst* and *say.*]

1. To contradict; to oppose; to controvert with; to dispute against.

Speeches which *gainsay* one another, must of necessity be applied both unto one and the same subject. *Hooker, b.* v.

Too facile then, thou didst not much *gainsay*;
Nay, didst permit, approve, and fair dismiss. *Milton's P. L.*

2. To deny any thing.

I never heard yet
That any of those bolder vices wanted
Less impudence to *gainsay* what they did,
Than to perform it first. *Shakespeare's Winter's Tale.*

GA'INSAYER. *n. s.* [from *gainsay.*] Opponent; adversary.

Such as may satisfy *gainsayers*, when suddenly, and besides expectation, they require the same at our hands. *Hooker, b.* v.

We are, for this cause, challenged as manifest *gainsayers* of Scripture, even in that which we read for Scripture unto the people. *Hooker, b.* v. *s.* 19.

It was full matter of conviction to all *gainsayers. Hammond.*

'GAINST. *prep.* [for *against.*] See AGAINST.

Tremble, ye nations! who, secure before,
Laugh'd at those arms, that *'gainst* ourselves we bore. *Dryd.*

To GA'INSTAND. *v. a.* [*'gainst* and *stand.*] To withstand; to oppose; to resist.

Love proved himself valiant, that durst with the sword of reverent duty *gainstand* the force of so many enraged desires. *Sidney, b.* ii.

GA'IRISH. *adj.* [ʒeaɲɲuan, to dress fine, Saxon.]

1. Gaudy; showy; splendid; fine.

I call'd thee then poor shadow, painted queen,
The presentation of but what I was;
A mother, only mock'd with two fair babes;
A dream of what thou wast, a *gairish* flag,
To be the aim of every dangerous shot. *Shakesp. Rich.* III.

There in close covert by some brook,
Where no profaner eye may look,
Hide me from day's *gairish* eye. *Milton.*

2. Extravagantly gay; flighty.

Fame and glory transports a man out of himself: it makes the mind loose and *gairish*, scatters the spirits, and leaves a kind of dissolution upon all the faculties. *South's Sermons.*

GA'IRISHNESS. *n. s.* [from *gairish.*]

1. Finery; flaunting gaudiness.

2. Flighty or extravagant joy.

Let your hope be without vanity, or *garishness* of spirit, but sober, grave and silent. *Taylor's Rule of living holy.*

GAIT. *n. s.* [*gat*, Dutch.]

1. A way: as, *gang your gait.*

Good youth, address thy *gait* unto her;
Be not denied access, stand at her door. *Shakespeare.*

2. March; walk.

Nought regarding, they kept on their *gait*,
And all her vain allurements did forsake. *Fairy Queen, b.* ii.

Thou art so lean and meagre waxen late,
That scarce thy legs uphold thy feeble *gait. Hubb. Tale.*

3. The manner and air of walking.

Great Juno comes; I know her by her *gait. Shakespeare.*

He had in his person, in his aspect, the appearance of a great man, which he preserved in his *gait* and motion. *Claren.*

A third, who, by his *gait*
And fierce demeanour, seems the prince of hell. *Milton.*

Leviathans
Wallowing, unwieldy, enormous in their *gait. Milton.*

I describ'd his way,
Bent all on speed, and mark'd his airy *gait. Milt. Pa. Lost.*

GALA'GE. *n. s.* A shepherd's clog.

My heart-blood is well nigh frorne, I feel;
And my *galage* grown fast to my heel. *Spenser's Pastorals.*

GALA'NGAL. *n. s.* [*galange*, French.] A medicinal root, of which there are two species. The lesser galangal is in pieces, about an inch or two long, of the thickness of a man's little finger; a brownish red colour, extremely hot and pungent. The larger galangal is in pieces, about two inches or more in length, and an inch in thickness: its colour is brown, with a faint cast of red in it: it has a disagreeable, but much less acrid and pungent taste than the smaller sort. They are both brought from the East-Indies; the small kind from China, and the larger from the island of Java, wherewith the people, while it is fresh, by way of spice, season their dishes. The small sort is used with us in medicine as a stomachick, and is an ingredient in almost all bitter infusions and mixtures. *Hill.*

GALA'XY. *n. s.* [γαλαξία; *galaxie*, Fr.] The milky way; a stream of light in the sky.

A broad and ample road, whose dust is gold,
And pavement stars, as stars to thee appear,
Seen in the *galaxy. Milton's Paradise Lost, b.* vii.

A brown, for which heaven would disband
The *galaxy*, and stars be tann'd. *Cleaveland.*

Men doubt, because they stand so thick i' th' sky,
If those be stars that paint the *galaxy. Cowley.*

We dare not undertake to shew what advantage is brought to us by those innumerable stars in the *galaxy. Bentley's Serm.*

GA'LBANUM. *n. s.*

We meet with *galbanum* sometimes in loose granules, called drops or tears, which is the purest, and sometimes in large masses. It is soft, like wax, and ductile between the fingers; of a yellowish or reddish colour: its smell is strong and disagreeable; its taste acrid, nauseous and bitterish. It is of a middle nature between a gum and a resin, being inflammable as a resin, and soluble in water as a gum, and will not dissolve in oil as pure resins do. It is the produce of an umbelliferous plant, whose stalks are about an inch thick, and five or six feet high: its leaves are like the common anise, of a strong smell, and acrid taste; but the flowers, and especially the seeds, much more so. The whole plant abounds with a viscous milky juice, which it yields when wounded, and which soon concretes into substance called *galbanum.* The plant is frequent in Persia, and in many parts of Africa. Its medicinal virtues are considerable in asthmas, coughs, and hysterick complaints. *Hill's Materia Medica.*

I yielded indeed a pleasant odour, like the best myrrh; as *galbanum. Ecclus.* xxiv. 15.

GALE. *n. s.* [*gahling*, hasty, sudden, German.] A wind not tempestuous, yet stronger than a breeze.

What happy *gale*
Blows you to Padua here, from old Verona? *Shakespeare.*

Winds
Of gentlest *gale* Arabian odours fann'd
From their soft wings, and Flora's earliest smells. *Milton.*

Fresh *gales* and gentle air. *Milton.*

Umbria's green retreats,
Where western *gales* eternally reside. *Addison.*

GA'LEAS. *n. s.* [*galeasse*, French.] A heavy low-built vessel, with both sails and oars. It carries three masts, but they cannot be lowered, as in a galley. It has thirty-two seats for rowers, and six or seven slaves to each. They carry three tire of guns at the head, and at the stern there are two tire of guns. *Dict.*

The Venetians pretend they could set out, in case of great necessity, thirty men of war, a hundred gallies, and ten *galeasses. Addison's Remarks on Italy.*

GA'LEATED. *adj.* [*galeatus*, Latin.]

1. Covered as with a helmet.

A *galeated* eschinus copped, and in shape somewhat more conick than any of the foregoing. *Woodward on Fossils.*

2. [In botany.] Such plants as bear a flower resembling an helmet, as the monkshood.

GALERI'CULATE. *adj.* [from *galerus*, Latin.] Covered as with a hat.

GA'LIOT. *n. s.* [*galiotte*, French.] A little galley or sort of brigantine, built very slight and fit for chase. It carries but one mast, and two or three pattereroes. It can both sail and row, and has sixteen or twenty seats for the rowers, with one man to each oar. *Dict.*

Barbarossa sent before him Dragut and Corsetus, two notable pyrates, with thirty *galiots*, who, landing their men, were valiantly encountered by Sarmentus, and forced again to their *galiots. Knolles's History of the Turks.*

GALL. *n. s.* [ʒeala, Saxon; *galle*, Dutch.]

1. The bile; an animal juice remarkable for its supposed bitterness.

Come to my woman's breast,
And take my milk for *gall*, you murth'ring ministers! *Shak.*

A honey tongue, a heart of *gall*,
Is fancy's spring, but sorrow's fall. *Shakespeare.*

It drew from my heart all love,
And added to the *gall. Shakespeare's King Lear.*

This position informs us of a vulgar errour, terming the *gall* bitter, as their proverb more peremptorily implies, It's as bitter as *gall*; whereas there's nothing gustable sweeter; and what is most unctuous must needs partake of a sweet favour. *Harvey on Consumptions.*

Gall is the greatest resolvent of curdled milk: Boerhaave has given at a time one drop of the *gall* of an eel with success. *Arbuthnot on Diet.*

2. The part which contains the bile.

The married couple, as a testimony of future concord, did cast the *gall* of the sacrifice behind the altar. *Brown's Vu. Err.*

3. Any thing extremely bitter.

Thither write, my queen,
And with mine eyes I'll drink the words you send,
Though ink be made of *gall. Shakespeare's Cymbeline.*

Poison be their drink!
Gall, worse than *gall*, the daintiest meat they taste! *Shakes.*

She still insults, and you must still adore;
Grant that the honey's much, the *gall* is more. *Dryd. Juv.*

4. Rancour; malignity.

They did great hurt unto his title, and have left a perpetual *gall* in the mind of the people. *Spenser's State of Ireland.*

5. A slight hurt by fretting off the skin. [From the verb.]

This is the fatalest wound of the tongue, carries least smart, but infinitely more of danger; and is as much superior to the former, as a gangrene is to a *gall* or scratch: this may be sore and vexing, but that stupifying and deadening. *Government of the Tongue, s.* 8.

6 Anger; bitterness of mind.

Suppose your hero were a lover,
Though he before had *gall* and rage;
He grows dispirited and low,
He hates the fight, and shuns the blow. *Prior.*

7. [From

7. [From *galla*.]

Galls or galnuts are a kind of preternatural and accidental tumours, produced on various trees; but those of the oak only are used in medicine. We have two kinds, the Oriental and the European *galls:* the Oriental are brought from Aleppo, of the bigness of a large nutmeg, with tubercles on their surface, of a very firm and solid texture, and a disagreeable, acerb, and astringent taste. The European *galls* are of the same size, with perfectly smooth surfaces: they are light, often spongy, and cavernous within, and always of a lax texture. They have a less austere taste, and are of much less value than the first sort, both in manufactures and medicine. The general history of galls is this: an insect of the fly kind, for the safety of her young, wounds the branches of the trees, and in the hole deposites her egg: the lacerated vessels of the tree discharging their contents, form a tumour or woody case about the hole, where the egg is thus defended from all injuries. This tumour also serves for the food of the tender maggot, produced from the egg of the fly, which, as soon as it is perfect, and in its winged state, gnaws its way out, as appears from the hole found in the gall; and where no hole is seen on its surface, the maggot, or its remains, are sure to be found within, on breaking it. It has been observed, that the oak does not produce galls in cold countries: but this observation should be confined to the medicinal galls; for all those excrescencies which we find on this tree in our own woods, and call oak-apples, oak-grapes, and oak-cones, are true and genuine galls, though less firm in their texture. The true reason of the hard ones not being produced with us, seems to be that we want the peculiar species of insect to which they owe their origin, which is a fly of the ichneumon kind, only found in hot countries. The species of fly that occasions, by its punctures, the soft galls of France and Italy, is different both from the Syrian one and from ours, though still of the ichneumon kind; and we find the several kinds, which occasion the different galls in our own kingdom, produce different kinds, and those of different degrees of hardness, on the same tree. Galls are used in making ink, and in dying and dressing leather, and many other manufactures. In medicine they are very astringent, and good under proper management. *Hill.*

Besides the acorns, the oak beareth *galls*, oak-apples, and oak-nuts. *Bacon's Natural History*, N°. 635.

Malpighi, in his treatise of *galls*, under which name he comprehends all preternatural and morbose excrescences, demonstrates that all such excrescences, where any insects are found, are excited by some venenose liquor, which, together with their eggs, such insects shed. *Ray on the Creation.*

The Aleppo *galls*, wherewith we make ink, are no other than cases of insects, which are bred in them. *Derham.*

To GALL. *v. a.* [*galer*, French.]

1. To hurt by fretting the skin.

I'll touch my point
With this contagion, that, if I *gall* him slightly,
It may be death. *Shakespeare's Hamlet.*

His yoke is easy, when by us embrac'd;
But loads and *galls*, if on our necks 'tis cast. *Denham.*

A carrier, when he would think of a remedy for his *galled* horse, begins with casting his eye upon all things. *Locke.*

On the monarch's speech Achilles broke,
And furious thus, and interrupting spoke,
Tyrant, I well deserv'd thy *galling* chain. *Pope's Iliad.*

2. To impair; to wear away.

He doth object, I am too great of birth;
And that my state being *gall'd* with my expence,
I seek to heal it only by his wealth. *Shakespeare.*

If it should fall down in a continual stream like a river, it would *gall* the ground, wash away plants by the roots, and overthrow houses. *Ray on the Creation.*

3. To teaze; to fret; to vex.

In honour of that action, and to *gall* their minds who did not so much commend it, he wrote his book. *Hooker*, *b.* ii.

What they seem contented with, even for that very cause we reject; and there is nothing but it pleaseth us the better, if we espy that it *galleth* them. *Hooker*, *b.* iv. *s.* 9.

When I shew justice,
I pity those I do not know;
Which a dismiss'd offence would after *gall.* *Shakespeare.*

Let it not *gall* your patience, good Iago,
That I extend my manners: 'tis my breeding,
That gives me this bold shew of courtesy. *Shakesp. Othello.*

All studies here I solemnly defy,
Save how to *gall* and pinch this Bolingbroke. *Shak H.* IV.

No man commits any sin but his conscience smites him, and his guilty mind is frequently *galled* with the remembrance of it. *Tillotson's Sermons.*

5. To harrass; to mischief.

The Helots had gotten new heart, and with divers sorts of shot from corners of streets and house-windows *galled* them. *Sidney.*

Light demilances from afar they throw,
Fasten'd with leathern thongs, to *gall* the foe. *Dryd. Æn.*

In our wars against the French of old, we used to *gall* them with our long bows, at a greater distance than they could shoot their arrows. *Addison on the State of the War.*

To GALL. *v. n.* To fret.

I have seen you glecking and *galling* at this gentleman twice or thrice. *Shakespeare's Henry* V.

GA'LLANT. *adj.* [*galant*, French, from *gala*, fine dress, Spanish.]

1. Gay; well dressed; showy; splendid; magnificent.

A place of broad rivers, wherein shall go no gally with oars, neither shall *gallant* ships pass thereby. *Is.* xxxiii. 21.

The gay, the wise, the *gallant*, and the grave,
Subdu'd alike, all but one passion have. *Waller.*

2. Brave; high spirited; daring; magnanimous.

Scorn, that any should kill his uncle, made him seek his revenge in manner *gallant* enough. *Sidney*, *b.* ii.

But, fare thee well, thou art a *gallant* youth. *Shakespeare.*

A *gallant* man, whose thoughts fly at the highest game, requires no further insight into them than to satisfy himself by what way they may be performed. *Digby on the Soul, Dedicat.*

3. Fine; noble; specious.

There are no tricks in plain and simple faith;
But hollow men, like horses hot at hand,
Make *gallant* shew and promise of their mettle. *Shakesp.*

He discoursed, how *gallant* and how brave a thing it would be for his highness to make a journey into Spain, and to fetch home his mistress. *Clarendon.*

4. Inclined to courtship.

When first the soul of love is sent abroad,
The gay troops begin
In *gallant* thought to plume their painted wings. *Thomson.*

GA'LLANT. *n. s.* [from the adjective.]

1. A gay, sprightly, airy, splendid man.

The new proclamation.
——What is't for?
—The reformation of our travell'd *gallants*,
That fill the court with quarrels, talk, and taylors. *Shakesp.*

The *gallants* and lusty youths of Naples came and offered themselves unto Vastius. *Knolles's History of the Turks.*

The *gallants*, to protect the lady's right,
Their fauchions brandish'd at the grisly spright. *Dryden.*

Gallants, look to't, you say there are no sprights;
But I'll come dance about your beds at nights. *Dryden.*

2. A whoremaster, who caresses women to debauch them.

One, worn to pieces with age, shews himself a young *gallant.* *Shakespeare's Merry Wives of Windsor.*

The next carried a handsome young fellow upon her back: she had left the good man at home, and brought away her *gallant.* *Addison's Spectator.*

3. A wooer; one who courts a woman for marriage. In the two latter senses it has commonly the accent on the last syllable.

GA'LLANTLY. *adv.* [from *gallant.*]

1. Gayly; splendidly.

2. Bravely; nobly; generously.

You have not dealt so *gallantly* with us as we did with you in a parallel case: last year a paper was brought here from England, which we ordered to be burnt by the common hangman. *Swift.*

GA'LLANTRY. *n. s.* [*galanterie*, French.]

1. Splendour of appearance; show; magnificence; glittering grandeur; ostentatious finery.

Make the sea shine with *gallantry*, and all
The English youth flock to their admiral. *Waller.*

2. Bravery; nobleness; generosity.

The eminence of your condition, and the *gallantry* of your principles, will invite gentlemen to the useful and enobling study of nature. *Glanv. Sceps. Preface.*

3. A number of gallants.

Hector, Deiphobus, and all the *gallantry* of Troy, I would have arm'd to-day. *Shakespeare's Troilus and Cressida.*

4. Courtship; refined address to women.

The martial Moors, in *gallantry* refin'd,
Invent new arts to make their charmers kind. *Granville.*

5. Vicious love; lewdness; debauchery.

It looks like a sort of compounding between virtue and vice, as if a woman were allowed to be vicious provided she be not a profligate; as if there were a certain point where *gallantry* ends, and infamy begins. *Swift.*

GA'LLEASS. *n. s.* [*galeas*, French.] A large galley; a vessel of war driven with oars.

My father hath no less
Than three great argosies, besides two *galleasses*,
And twelve tight gallies. *Shakesp. Taming of the Shrew.*

The number of vessels were one hundred and thirty, whereof *galleasses* and galleons seventy-two, goodly ships, like floating towers. *Bacon's War with Spain.*

GALLE'ON. *n. s.* [*galion*, French.] A large ship with four or sometimes five decks, now in use only among the Spaniards.

I assured them that I would stay for them at Trinidado, and that no force should drive me thence, except I were sunk or set on fire by the Spanish *galleons.* *Raleigh's Apology.*

The

The number of vessels were one hundred and thirty, whereof galleasses and *galleons* seventy-two, goodly ships, like floating towers or castles. *Bacon's War with Spain.*

GA'LLERY. *n. s.* [*galerie*, French, derived by *Du Cange* from *galeria*, low Latin, a fine room.]

1. A kind of walk along the floor of a house, into which the doors of the apartments open; in general, any building of which the length much exceeds the breadth.

In most part there had been framed by art such pleasant arbors, that, one answering another, they became a *gallery* aloft from tree to tree, almost round about, which below gave a perfect shadow. *Sidney, b.* i.

High lifted up were many lofty towers,
And goodly *galleries* fair overlaid. *Fairy Queen, b.* i.

Your *gallery*
Have we pass'd through, not without much content. *Shakesp.*

The row of return on the banquet side, let it be all stately *galleries*, in which *galleries* let there be three cupola's. *Bacon.*

A private *gallery* 'twixt th' apartments led,
Not to the foe yet known. *Denham.*

Nor is the shape of our cathedral proper for our preaching auditories, but rather the figure of an amphitheatre, with *galleries* gradually overlooking each other; for into this condition the parish-churches of London are driving apace, as appears by the many *galleries* every day built in them. *Graunt.*

There are covered *galleries* that lead from the palace to five different churches. *Addison on Italy.*

2. The seats in the playhouse above the pit, in which the meaner people sit.

While all its throats the *gallery* extends,
And all the thunder of the pit ascends. *Pope's Ep. of Horace.*

GA'LLETYLE. *n. s.* I suppose this word has the same import with gallipot.

Make a compound body of glass and *galletyle*; that is, to have the colour milky like a chalcedon, being a stuff between a porcellane and a glass. *Bacon's Phys. Rem.*

GA'LLEY. *n. s.* [*galea*, Italian; *galere*, French; derived, as some think, from *galea*, a helmet pictured anciently on the prow; as others from γαλεώτης, the swordfish; as others from *galleon*, expressing in Syriac men exposed to the sea. From *galley* come *galeass*, *galleon*, *galliot*.]

1. A vessel driven with oars, much in use in the Mediterranean, but found unable to endure the agitation of the main ocean.

Great Neptune grieved underneath the load
Of ships, hulks, *gallies*, barks and brigandines. *Fairfax.*

In the ages following, navigation did every where greatly decay, and especially far voyages; the rather by the use of *gallies*, and such vessels as could hardly brook the ocean. *Bacon's New Atlantis.*

Jason ranged the coasts of Asia the Less in an open boat, or kind of *galley*. *Raleigh's History of the World.*

On oozy ground his *gallies* moor;
Their heads are turn'd to sea, their sterns to shore. *Dryden.*

2. It is proverbially considered as a place of toilsome misery, because criminals are condemned to row in them.

The most voluptuous person, were he tied to follow his hawks and his hounds, his dice and his courtships every day, would find it the greatest torment that could befal him: he would fly to the mines and the *gallies* for his recreation, and to the spade and the mattock for a diversion from the misery of a continual uninterrupted pleasure. *South's Sermons.*

GA'LLEY-SLAVE. *n. s.* [*galley* and *slave.*] A man condemned for some crime to row in the gallies.

As if one chain were not sufficient to load poor man, but he must be clogged with innumerable chains: this is just such another freedom as the Turkish *galley-slaves* do enjoy. *Bramh.*

Hardened *galley-slaves* despise manumission. *Decay of Piety.*

The surges gently dash against the shore,
Flocks quit the plains, and *galley-slaves* their oar. *Garth.*

GA'LLIARD. *n. s.* [*gaillard*, French; imagined to be derived from the Gaulish *ard*, genius, and *gay*.]

1. A gay, brisk, lively man; a fine fellow.

Selden is a *galliard* by himself. *Cleaveland.*

2. An active, nimble, spritely dance. It is in both senses now obsolete.

I did think by the excellent constitution of thy leg, it was form'd under the star of a *galliard*. *Shakesp. Twelfth Night.*

There's nought in France
That can be with a nimble *galliard* won:
You cannot revel into dukedoms there. *Shakesp. Henry V.*

If there be any that would take up all the time, let him find means to take them off, and bring others on; as musicians use to do with those that dance too long *galliards*. *Bacon.*

The tripla's and changing of times have an agreement with the changes of motion; as when *galliard* time and measure time are in the medley of one dance. *Bacon's Natural History.*

GA'LLIARDISE. *n. s.* [French.] Merriment; exuberant gaiety.

At my nativity my ascendant was the watry sign of Scorpius: I was born in the planetary hour of Saturn, and I think I have a piece of that leaden planet in me: I am no way facetious, nor disposed for the mirth and *galliardise* of company. *Brown's Rel. Med.*

GA'LLICISM. *n. s.* [*gallicisme*, French, from *gallicus*, Latin.] A mode of speech peculiar to the French language: such as, he *figured* in controvery; he *held* this conduct; he *held* the same language that another had *held* before: with many other expressions to be found in the pages of *Bolinbroke*.

In English I would have *Gallicisms* avoided, that we may keep to our own language, and not follow the French mode in our speech. *Felton on the Classicks.*

GA'LLIGASKINS. *n. s.* [*Caligæ Gallo-Vasconum. Skinner.*] Large open hose.

My *galligaskins*, that have long withstood
The Winter's fury, and encroaching frosts,
By time subdu'd, what will not time subdue,
An horrid chasm disclose. *Phillips.*

GALLIMA'TIA. *n. s.* [*galimathias*, French.] Nonsense; talk without meaning.

GALLIMAU'FRY. *n. s.* [*galimafreé*, French.]

1. A hoch-poch, or hash of several sorts of broken meat; a medley. *Hanmer.*

They have made of our English tongue a *gallimaufry*, or hodge-podge of all other speeches. *Spenser.*

2. Any inconsistent or ridiculous medley.

They have a dance, which the wenches say is a *gallimaufry* of gambols, because they are not in't. *Shakesp. Winter's Tale.*

The painter who, under pretence of diverting the eyes, would fill his picture with such varieties as alter the truth of history, would make a ridiculous piece of painting, and a mere *gallimaufry* of his work. *Dryden's Dufresnoy.*

3. It is used by *Shakespeare* ludicrously of a woman.

Sir John affects thy wife.
—Why, sir, my wife is not young.
—He wooes both high and low, both rich and poor;
He loves thy *gallimaufry*, friend. *Shakespeare.*

GA'LLIOT. *n. s.* [*galiotte*, French.] A small swift galley.

Barbarossa departing out of Hellespontus with eighty gallies, and certain *galliots*, shaped his course towards Italy. *Knolles.*

GA'LLIPOT. *n. s.* [*gleye*, Dutch, shining earth. *Skinner.* The true derivation is from *gala*, Spanish, finery. *Gala*, or gallypot, is a fine painted pot.] A pot painted and glazed, commonly used for medicines.

Plato said his master Socrates was like the apothecary's *gallipots*, that had on the outsides apes, owls, and satyrs; but within, precious drugs. *Bacon, Apophth.* 227.

Here phials in nice discipline are set;
There *gallipots* are rang'd in alphabet. *Garth's Dispensatory.*

Alexandrinus thought it unsafe to trust the real secret of his phial and *gallipot* to any man. *Spectator*, N°. 426.

Thou that do'st Æsculapius deride,
And o'er his *gallipots* in triumph ride. *Fenton.*

GA'LLON. *n. s.* [*gelo*, low Latin.] A liquid measure of four quarts.

Beat them into powder, and boil them in a *gallon* of wine, in a vessel close stopped. *Wiseman's Surgery.*

GALLO'ON. *n. s.* [*galon*, French.] A kind of close lace, made of gold or silver, or of silk alone.

To GA'LLOP. *v. n.* [*galoper*, French. Derived by all the etymologists, after *Budæus*, from καλπάζειν; but perhaps it comes from *gaut*, all, and *loopen*, to run, Dutch; that is, to go on full speed.]

1. To move forward by leaps, so that all the feet are off the ground at once.

I did hear
The *galloping* of horse: who was't came by? *Shak. Macb.*

His steeds will be restrain'd,
But *gallop* lively down the western hill. *Donne.*

In such a shape grim Saturn did restrain
His heav'nly limbs, and flow'd with such a mane,
When half surpriz'd, and fearing to be seen,
The leacher *gallop'd* from his jealous queen. *Dryden's Virgil.*

2. To ride at the pace which is performed by leaps.

Seeing such streams of blood as threatned a drowning life, we *galloped* toward them to part them. *Sidney, b.* ii.

They 'gan espy
An armed knight towards them *gallop* fast,
That seem'd from some feared foe to fly. *Fairy Queen, b.* i.

He who fair and softly goes steadily forward, in a course that points right, will sooner be at his journey's end than he that runs after every one he meets, though he *gallop* all day full speed. *Locke.*

3. To move very fast.

The golden sun salutes the morn,
And, having gilt the ocean with his beams,
Gallops the zodiack in his glist'ring coach. *Shak. Tit. Andr.*

Whom doth time *gallop* withal?
—With a thief to the gallows. *Shakesp. As you like it.*

He that rides post through a country may, from the transient view, tell how in general the parts lie: such superficial ideas he may collect in *galloping* over it. *Locke.*

GA'LLOP. *n. s.* [from the verb.] The motion of a horse when he he runs at full speed; in which, making a kind of a leap forwards, he lifts both his forelegs very near at the same time; and while these are in the air, and just upon the point of touching the ground, he lifts both his hindlegs almost at once. *Farrier's Dict.*

GA'LLOPER. *n. s.* [from *gallop*.]

1. A horse that gallops.

Mules bred in cold countries are much better to ride than horses for their walk and trot; but they are commonly rough *gallopers*, though some of them are very fleet. *Mortim. Husb.*

2. A man that rides fast, or makes great haste.

GA'LLOWAY. *n. s.* A horse not more than fourteen hands high, much used in the North; probably as coming originally from Galloway, a shire in Scotland.

To GA'LLOW. *v. a.* [azælpan, to fright, Saxon.] To terrify; to fright.

The wrathful skies
Gallow the very wand'rers of the dark,
And make them keep their caves. *Shakespeare's King Lear.*

GA'LLOWGLASSES. *n. s.*

1. It is worn then likewise of footmen under their shirts of mail, the which footmen call *gallowglasses*: the which name doth discover them also to be ancient English; for *gallogla* signifies an English servitor or yeoman. And he being so armed in a long shirt of mail, down to the calf of his leg, with a long broad ax in his hand, was then *pedes gravis armaturæ*; and was instead of the footman that now weareth a corslet, before the corslet was used, or almost invented. *Spenser on Ireland.*

2. [*Hanmer*, otherwise than *Spenser*.] Soldiers among the wild Irish, who serve on horseback.

A puissant and mighty pow'r
Of *gallowglasses* and stout kernes,
Is marching hitherward in proud array. *Shakes. Henry* VI.

GA'LLOW. } *n. s.* [It is used by some in the singular; but by
GA'LLOWS. } more only in the plural, or sometimes has another plural *gallowses*. *Galga*, Gothick; zealza, Saxon; *galge*, Dutch; which some derive from *gabalus*, *furca*, Latin; others from גבה high; others from *gallu*, Welsh, power: but it is probably derived like *gallow*, to fright, from azælpan, the gallows being the great object of legal terrour.]

1. A beam laid over two posts, on which malefactors are hanged.

This monster sat like a hangman upon a pair of *gallows*: in his right hand he was painted holding a crown of laurel, in his left hand a purse of money. *Sidney, b.* ii.

I would we were all of one mind, and one mind good; O, there were desolation of gaolers and *gallowses*. *Shakesp. Cymbel.*

I prophesied, if a *gallows* were on land,
This fellow could not drown. *Shakespeare's Tempest.*

A little before dinner he took the major aside, and whispered him in the ear, that execution must that day be done in the town, and therefore required him that a pair of *gallows* should be erected. *Hayward.*

A production that naturally groweth under *gallowses*, and places of execution. *Brown's Vulgar Errours, b.* ii.

A poor fellow, going to the *gallows*, may be allowed to feel the smart of wasps while he is upon Tyburn road. *Swift.*

2. A wretch that deserves the gallows.

Cupid hath been five thousand years a boy.
—Ay, and a shrewd unhappy *gallows* too. *Shakespeare.*

GA'LLOWSFREE. *adj.* [*gallows* and *free*.] Exempt by destiny from being hanged.

Let him be *gallowfree* by my consent,
And nothing suffer, since he nothing meant. *Dryden.*

GA'LLOWTREE. *n. s.* [*gallows* and *tree*.] The tree of terrour; the tree of execution.

He hung their conquer'd arms, for more defame,
On *gallowtrees*, in honour of his dearest dame. *Fai. Queen.*
A Scot, when from the *gallowtree* got loose,
Drops into Styx, and turns a soland goose. *Cleaveland.*

GAMBA'DE. } *n. s.* [*gamba*, Italian, a leg.] Spatterdashes;
GAMBA'DO. } boots worn upon the legs above the shoe.

The pettifogger ambles to her in his *gambadoes* once a week. *Dennis's Letters.*

GA'MBLER. *n. s.* [A cant word, I suppose, for *game* or *gamester*.] A knave whose practice it is to invite the unwary to game and cheat them.

GA'MBOGE. *n. s.*

Gamboge is a concreted vegetable juice, partly of a gummy, partly of a resinous nature. It is heavy, of a bright yellow colour, and scarce any smell. It is brought from America, and from many parts of the East Indies, particularly from Cambaja, or Cambogia, whence it has its name. Gamboge was not known in Europe 'till 1603, and soon after got into use as a purgative medicine; but the roughness of its operation rendering it less esteemed as such, it got into use in painting, where it yet retains its credit. *Hill.*

To GA'MBOL. *v. n.* [*gambiller*, French.]

1. To dance; to skip; to frisk; to jump for joy; to play merry frolicks.

Bears, tigers, ounces, pards,
Gambol'd before them. *Milton's Paradise Lost, b.* iv.

The king of elfs, and little fairy queen,
Gambol'd on heaths, and danc'd on ev'ry green. *Dryden.*
The monsters of the flood
Gambol around him in the wat'ry way,
And heavy whales in aukward measures play. *Pope.*

2. To leap; to start.

'Tis not madness
That I have utter'd; bring me to the test,
And I the matter will record, which madness
Would *gambol* from. *Shakespeare's Hamlet.*

GA'MBOL. *n. s.* [from the verb.]

1. A skip; a hop; a leap for joy.

A gentleman had got a favourite spaniel, that would be still toying and leaping upon him, and playing a thousand pretty *gambols*. *L'Estrange's Fables.*

Bacchus through the conquer'd Indies rode,
And beasts in *gambols* frisk'd before their honest god. *Dryden.*

2. A frolick; a wild prank.

For who did ever play his *gambo's*,
With such insufferable rambles? *Hudibras, p.* iii. *cant.* 2.

GA'MBREL. *n. s.* [from *gamba*, *gambarella*, Italian.] The leg of a horse.

What can be more admirable than for the principles of the fibres of a tendon to be so mixed as to make it a soft body, and yet to have the strength of iron? as appears by the weight which the tendon, lying on a horse's *gambrel*, doth then command, when he rears up with a man upon his back. *Grew.*

GAME. *n. s.* [*gaman*, a jest, Islandick.]

1. Sport of any kind.

We have had pastimes here, and pleasing *game*. *Shakesp.*

2. Jest, opposed to earnest or seriousness.

Then on her head they set a garland green,
And crowned her 'twixt earnest and 'twixt *game*. *Fai. Qu.*

3. Insolent merriment; sportive insult.

Do they not seek occasion of new quarrels,
On my refusal, to distress me more;
Or make a *game* of my calamities. *Milton's Agonistes.*

4. A single match at play.

5. Advantage in play.

Mutual vouchers for our fame we stand,
And play the *game* into each other's hand. *Dryden.*

6. Scheme pursued; measures planned.

This seems to be the present *game* of that crown, and that they will begin no other 'till they see an end of this. *Temple.*

7. Field sports: as, the chase, falconry.

If about this hour he make his way,
Under the colour of his usual *game*,
He shall here find his friends with horse and men,
To set him free from his captivity. *Shakespeare's Henry* VI.

What arms to use, or nets to frame
Wild beasts to combat, or to tame,
With all the myst'ries of that *game*. *Waller.*

Some sportsmen, that were abroad upon *game*, spied a company of bustards and cranes. *L'Estrange.*

8. Animals pursued in the field; animals appropriated to legal sportsmen.

Hunting, and men, not beasts, shall be his *game*,
With war, and hostile snare, such as refuse
Subjection to his empire tyrannous. *Milton's Parad. Lost.*

There is such a variety of *game* springing up before me, that I am distracted in my choice, and know not which to follow. *Dryden's Fables, Preface.*

A bloodhound will follow the tract of the person he pursues, and all hounds the particular *game* they have in chace. *Arbuthnot on Aliments.*

Go, with thy Cynthia hurl the pointed spear
At the rough bear, or chace the flying deer;
I and my Chloe take a nobler aim,
At human hearts we fling, nor ever miss the *game*. *Prior.*
Proud Nimrod first the bloody chace began,
A mighty hunter, and his prey was man:
Our haughty Norman boasts that barb'rous name,
And makes his trembling slaves the royal *game*. *Pope.*

9. Solemn contests exhibited as spectacles to the people.

The *games* are done, and Cæsar is returning. *Shakespeare.*
Milo, when ent'ring the Olympick *game*,
With a huge ox upon his shoulders came. *Denham.*

To GAME. *v. n.* [zaman, Saxon.]

1. To play at any sport.

2. To play wantonly and extravagantly for money.

Gaming leaves no satisfaction behind it: it no way profits either body or mind. *Locke.*

GA'MECOCK. *n. s.* [*game* and *cock*.] Cocks bred to fight.

They managed the dispute as fiercely as two *gamecocks* in the pit. *Locke.*

GAME-EGG. *n. s.* [*game* and *egg*.] Eggs from which fighting cocks are bred.

Thus boys hatch *game-eggs* under birds of prey,
To make the fowl more furious for the fray. *Garth.*

GA'MEKEEPER. *n. s.* [*game* and *keep*.] A person who looks after game, and sees it is not destroyed.

GA'MESOME. *adj.* [from *game.*] Frolickſome; gay; ſportive; playful; ſportful.

Geron, though old, yet *gameſome*, kept one end with Coſma. *Sidney.*

I am not *gameſome*; I do lack ſome part
Of that quick ſpirit that is in Antony. *Shakeſ. Jul. Cæſar.*

The *gameſome* wind among her treſſes play,
And curleth up thoſe growing riches ſhort. *Fairfax, b.* iv.

Belial, in like *gameſome* mood. *Milton's Paradiſe Loſt.*

This *gameſome* humour of children ſhould rather be encouraged, to keep up their ſpirits and improve their ſtrength and health, than curbed or reſtrained. *Locke.*

GA'MESOMENESS. *n. ſ.* [from *gameſome.*] Sportiveneſs; merriment.

GA'MESOMELY. *adv.* [from *gameſome.*] Merrily.

GA'MESTER. *n. ſ.* [from *game.*]

1. One who is vitiouſly addicted to play.

Keep a *gameſter* from the dice, and a good ſtudent from his book, and it is wonderful. *Shak. Merry Wives of Windſor.*

A *gameſter*, the greater maſter he is in his art, the worſe man he is. *Bacon.*

Gameſters for whole patrimonies play;
The ſteward brings the deeds, which muſt convey
The whole eſtate. *Dryden's Juvenal, Sat.* I.

Could we look into the mind of a common *gameſter*, we ſhould ſee it full of nothing but trumps and mattadores: her ſlumbers are haunted with kings, queens and knaves. *Addiſon.*

All the ſuperfluous whims relate,
That fill a female *gameſter's* pate;
What agony of ſoul ſhe feels
To ſee a knave's inverted heels. *Swift.*

2. One who is engaged at play.

When lenity and cruelty play for kingdoms,
The gentler *gameſter* is the ſooneſt winner. *Shakeſ. Hen.* V.

A man may think, if he will, that two eyes ſee no more than one; or that a *gameſter* ſeeth always more than a looker-on: but, when all is done, the help of good counſel is that which ſetteth buſineſs ſtrait. *Bacon, Eſſay* 28.

3. A merry frolickſome perſon.

You're a merry *gameſter*,
My lord Sands. *Shakeſp. Henry* VIII.

4. A proſtitute.

She's impudent, my lord,
And was a common *gameſter* to the camp. *Shakeſpeare.*

GA'MMER. *n. ſ.* [Of uncertain etymology; perhaps from *grand mere*, and therefore uſed commonly to old women.] The compellation of a woman correſponding to gaffer.

GA'MMON. *n. ſ.* [*gambone*, Italian.]

1. The buttock of an hog ſalted and dried; the lower end of the flitch.

Aſk for what price thy venal tongue was ſold:
A ruſty *gammon* of ſome ſev'n years old. *Dryden's Juv. Sat.*

Gammons, that give a reliſh to the taſte,
And potted fowl, and fiſh, come in ſo faſt,
That ere the firſt is out, the ſecond ſtinks. *Dryden's Perſ.*

2. A kind of play with dice.

The quick dice,
In thunder leaping from the box, awake
The ſounding *gammon.* *Thomſon's Autumn.*

GA'MUT. *n. ſ.* [*gama*, Italian.] The ſcale of muſical notes.

Madam, before you touch the inſtrument,
To learn the order of my fingering,
I muſt begin with rudiments of art,
To teach you *gamut* in a briefer ſort. *Shakeſpeare.*

When by the *gamut* ſome muſicians make
A perfect ſong, others will undertake,
By the ſame *gamut* chang'd, to equal it:
Things ſimply good can never be unfit. *Donne.*

Long has a race of heroes fill'd the ſtage,
That rant by note, and through the *gamut* rage;
In ſongs and airs expreſs their martial fire,
Combat in trills, and in a feuge expire. *Addiſon.*

'GAN, for *began*, from *'gin* for *begin.*

The noble knight *'gan* feel
His vital force to faint. *Spenſer.*

To GANCH. *v. a.* [*ganciare*, from *gancio*, a hook, Italian; *ganche*, French.] To drop from a high place upon hooks by way of puniſhment: a practice in Turkey, to which *Smith* alludes in his *Pocockius.*

Cohors catenis qua pia ſtridulis
Gemunt onuſti, vel ſude trans ſinum
Luctantur actâ, pendulive
Sanguineis luctantur in unæs. *Muſæ Angl.*

GA'NDER. *n. ſ.* [ʒanꝺꝛa, Saxon.] The male of the gooſe.

As deep drinketh the gooſe as the *gander.* *Camden's Rem.*

One *gander* will ſerve five geeſe. *Mortimer's Huſbandry.*

To GANG. *v. n.* [*gangen*, Dutch; ʒanʒan, Saxon; *gang*, Scottiſh.] To go; to walk: an old word not now uſed, except ludicrouſly.

But let them *gang* alone,
As they have brewed, ſo let them bear blame. *Spenſer.*

Your flaunting beaus *gang* with their breaſts open. *Arbuthn.*

GANG. *n. ſ.* [from the verb.] A number herding together; a troop; a company; a tribe; a herd. It is ſeldom uſed but in contempt or abhorrence.

Oh, you panderly raſcals! there's a knot, a *gang*, a pack, a conſpiracy againſt me. *Shakeſ. Merry Wives of Windſor.*

As a *gang* of thieves were robbing a houſe, a maſtiff fell a barking. *L'Eſtrange, Fable* 21.

Admitted in among the *gang*,
He acts and talks as they befriend him. *Prior.*

GA'NGHON. [French] A kind of flower. *Ainſworth.*

GA'NGLION. *n. ſ.* [γαγγλίον.] A tumour in the tendinous and nervous parts, proceeding from a fall or ſtroke. It reſiſts, if ſtirred; if preſſed upon the ſide, is not diverted, nor can be turned round. *Harris.*

Boneſetters uſually repreſent every bone diſlocated, though poſſibly it be but a *ganglion*, or other crude tumour or preternatural protuberance of ſome part of a joint. *Wiſeman.*

GA'NGRENE. *n. ſ.* [*gangrene*, Fr. *gangræna*, Lat.] A mortification; a ſtoppage of circulation followed by putrefaction.

This experiment may be transferred unto the cure of *gangrenes*, either coming of themſelves, or induced by too much applying of opiates. *Bacon's Natural Hiſtory.*

She ſaves the lover, as we *gangrenes* ſtay,
By cutting hope, like a lopt limb, away. *Waller.*

A diſcolouring in the part was ſuppoſed an approach of a *gangrene.* *Wiſeman's Surgery.*

If the ſubſtance of the ſoul is feſtered with theſe paſſions, the *gangrene* is gone too far to be ever cured: the inflammation will rage to all eternity. *Addiſon's Spectator.*

To GA'NGRENE. *v. a.* [*gangrener*, French, from the noun.] To corrupt to mortification.

In cold countries, when men's noſes and ears are mortified, and, as it were, *gangrened* with cold, if they come to a fire they rot off preſently; for that the few ſpirits, that remain in thoſe parts, are ſuddenly drawn forth, and ſo putrefaction is made complete. *Bacon's Natural Hiſtory.*

Gangren'd members muſt be lop'd away,
Before the nobler parts are tainted to decay. *Dryden.*

To GA'NGRENE. *v. n.* To become mortified.

My griefs not only pain me
As a ling'ring diſeaſe;
But finding no redreſs, ferment and rage,
Nor leſs than wounds immedicable
Rankle and feſter, and *gangrene*
To black mortification. *Milton's Agoniſtes.*

As phlegmons are ſubject to mortification, ſo alſo in fat bodies they are apt to *gangrene* after opening, if that fat be not ſpeedily digeſted out. *Wiſeman's Surgery.*

GA'NGRENOUS. *adj.* [from *gangrene.*] Mortified; producing or betokening mortification.

The blood, turning acrimonious, corrodes the veſſels, producing hæmorrhages, puſtules red, lead-coloured, black and *gangrenous.* *Arbuthnot on Aliments.*

GA'NGWAY. *n. ſ.* In a ſhip, the ſeveral ways or paſſages from one part of it to the other. *Dict.*

GA'NGWEEK. *n. ſ.* [*gang* and *week.*] Rogation week, when proceſſions are made to luſtrate the bounds of pariſhes *Dict.*

GA'NTELOPE. } *n. ſ.* [*gantlet* is only corrupted from *gantelope*,
GA'NTLET. } *gant*, all, and *loopen*, to run, Dutch] A military puniſhment, in which the criminal running between the ranks receives a laſh from each man.

But would'ſt thou, friend, who haſt two legs alone,
Would'ſt thou to run the *ganlet* theſe expoſe,
To a whole company of hob-nail'd ſhoes? *Dryden's Juv.*

Young gentlemen are driven with a whip, to run the *gantlet* through the ſeveral claſſes. *Locke.*

GA'NZA. *n. ſ.* [*ganſa*, Spaniſh, a gooſe.] A kind of wild gooſe, by a flock of which a virtuoſo was fabled to be carried to the lunar world.

They are but idle dreams and fancies,
And ſavour ſtrongly of the *ganza's.* *Hudibras, p.* ii.

GAOL. *n. ſ.* [*geol*, Welſh; *geole*, French.] A priſon; a place of confinement. It is always pronounced and too often written *jail*, and ſometimes *goal.*

Then am I the priſoner, and his bed my *gaol.* *Sh. K. Lear.*

Have I been ever free, and muſt my houſe
Be my retentive enemy, my *gaol?* *Shakeſpeare's Timon.*

If we mean to thrive and do good, break open the *gaols*, and let out the priſoners. *Shakeſpeare's Henry* VI. *p.* ii.

GA'OLDELIVERY. *n. ſ.* [*gaol* and *deliver.*] The judicial proceſs, which by condemnation or acquittal of perſons confined evacuates the priſon.

Then doth th' aſpiring ſoul the body leave,
Which we call death; but were it known to all,
What life our ſouls do by this death receive,
Men would it birth or *gaoldelivery* call. *Davies.*

Theſe make a general *gaoldelivery* of ſouls, not for puniſhment. *South.*

GA'OLER. *n. ſ.* [from *gaol.*] Keeper of a priſon; he to whoſe care the priſoners are committed.

This is a gentle provoſt; ſeldom, when
The ſteeled *gaoler* is the friend of men. *Sh. Meaſ. for Meaſ.*
I know not how or why my ſurly *goaler*,
Hard as his irons, and inſolent as pow'r
When put in vulgar hands, Cleanthes,
Put off the brute. *Dryden's Cleomenes.*

From the polite part of mankind ſhe had been baniſhed and immured, 'till the death of her *gaoler* *Tatler*, Nº. 53.

GAP. *n. ſ.* [from *gape.*]

1. An opening in a broken fence.

Behold the deſpair,
By cuſtom and covetous pates,
By *gaps* and opening of gates. *Tuſſer's Huſbandry.*

With terrours and with furies to the bounds
And cryſtal wall of heav'n; which, opening wide,
Roll'd inward, and a ſpacious *gap* diſcloſ'd
Into the waſteful deep. *Milton's Paradiſe Loſt, b.* vi.

Buſhes are moſt laſting of any for dead hedges, or to mend *gaps.* *Mortimer's Huſbandry.*

I ſought for a man, ſays God, that ſhould make up the hedge, and ſtand in the *gap* before me, for the land that I ſhould not deſtroy it. *Rogers, Sermon* 18.

2. A breach.

The loſs of that ſtrong city concerned the Chriſtian commonweal: manifold and lamentable miſeries afterwards enſued by the opening of that *gap*, not unto the kingdom of Hungary only, but to all that ſide of Chriſtendom. *Knolles.*

3. Any paſſage.

He's made maſter
O' th' rolls and the king's ſecretary: further
Stands in the *gap*, and treads for more preferment. *Shakeſp.*

So ſtands the Thracian herdſman with his ſpear
Full in the *gap*, and hopes the hunted bear,
And hears him ruſtling in the wood. *Dryden.*

4. An avenue; an open way.

The former kings of England paſſed into them a great part of their prerogatives; which though then it was well intended, and perhaps well deſerved, yet now ſuch a *gap* of miſchief lies open thereby, that I could wiſh it were well ſtopt. *Spenſer.*

5. A hole; a deficiency.

If you violently proceed againſt him, miſtaking his purpoſe, it would make a great *gap* in your honour. *Shak. King Lear.*

Nor is it any botch or *gap* at all in the works of nature. *More's Antidote againſt Atheiſm.*

6. Any interſtice; a vacuity.

Each one demand, and anſwer to his part
Perform'd in this wide *gap* of time, ſince firſt
We were diſſever'd. *Shakeſpeare's Winter's Tale.*

That I might ſleep out this great *gap* of time my Antony is away. *Shakeſpeare's Ant. and Cleopatra.*

To make 'twixt words and lines huge *gaps*,
Wide as meridians in maps. *Hudibras, p.* ii. *cant.* 3.

One can revive a languiſhing converſation by a ſudden ſurpriſing ſentence; another is more dexterous in ſeconding; a third can fill the *gap* with laughing. *Swift's Genteel Converſat.*

7. An opening of the mouth in ſpeech during the pronunciation of two ſucceſſive vowels.

The hiatus, or *gap* between two words, is cauſed by two vowels opening on each other. *Pope.*

8. *To ſtop a* GAP, is to eſcape by ſome mean ſhift: alluding to hedges mended with dead buſhes, 'till the quickſets will grow.

His policy conſiſts in ſetting traps,
In finding ways and means, and *ſtopping gaps.* *Swift.*

GA'P-TOOTHED. *adj.* [*gap* and *tooth.*] Having interſtices between the teeth.

The reeve, miller, and cook, are diſtinguiſhed from each other as much as the mincing lady prioreſs and the broad-ſpeaking *gap-toothed* wife of Bath. *Dryden's Fables, Preface.*

To GAPE. *v. n.* [ȝeapan, Saxon.]

1. To open the mouth wide; to yawn.

Some men there are love not a *gaping* pig;
Some, that are mad, if they behold a cat. *Shakeſpeare.*

Gaping or yawning, and ſtretching, do paſs from man to man; for that that cauſeth *gaping* and ſtretching is when the ſpirits are a little heavy by any vapour. *Arbuthnot.*

She ſtretches, *gapes*, unglues her eyes,
And aſks if it be time to riſe. *Swift.*

2. To open the mouth for food, as a young bird.

As callow birds,
Whoſe mother's kill'd in ſeeking of the prey,
Cry in their neſt, and think her long away;
And at each leaf that ſtirs, each blaſt of wind,
Gape for the food which they muſt never find. *Dryden.*

As in a drought the thirſty creatures cry,
And *gape* upon the gather'd clouds for rain,
Then firſt the martlet meets it in the ſky,
And with wet wings joys all the feather'd train. *Dryden.*

3. To deſire earneſtly; to crave. With *for.*

To her grim death appears in all her ſhapes;
The hungry grave *for* her due tribute *gapes.* *Denham.*

To thy fortune be not thou a ſlave;
For what haſt thou to fear beyond the grave?
And thou, who *gap'ſt for* my eſtate, draw near;
For I would whiſper ſomewhat in thy ear. *Dryden's Perſ.*

4. With *after.*

What ſhall we ſay of thoſe who ſpend their days in *gaping after* court-favour and preferments? *L'Eſtrange.*

5. With *at.*

Many have *gaped at* the church revenues; but, before they could ſwallow them, have had their mouths ſtopped in the church-yard. *South's Sermons.*

6. To open in fiſſures or holes.

If it aſſume my noble father's perſon,
I'll ſpeak to it, though hell itſelf ſhould *gape*
And bid me hold my peace. *Shakeſpeare's Hamlet.*

May that ground *gape*, and ſwallow me alive,
Where I ſhall kneel to him that ſlew my father. *Sh. H.* VI.

The great horſe-muſſel, with the fine ſhell, doth *gape* and ſhut as the oyſters do. *Bacon's Natural Hiſtory.*

The reception of one is as different from the admiſſion of the other, as when the earth falls open under the inciſions of the plough, and when it *gapes* and greedily opens itſelf to drink in the dew of heaven, or the refreſhments of a ſhower. *South.*

The mouth of a little artery and nerve *gapes* into the cavity of theſe veſicles. *Cheyne's Phil. Princ.*

7. To open with a breach.

The planks, their pitchy coverings waſh'd away,
Now yield, and now a yawning breach diſplay:
The roaring waters, with a hoſtile tide,
Ruſh through the ruins of her *gaping* ſide. *Dryden.*

That all theſe actions can be performed by aliment, as well as medicines, is plain; by obſerving the effects of different ſubſtances upon the fluids and ſolids, when the veſſels are open and *gape* by a wound. *Arbuthnot.*

8. To open; to have an hiatus.

There is not, to the beſt of my remembrance, one vowel *gaping* on another for want of a cæſura in this whole poem. *Dryden's Æn. Dedication.*

9. To make a noiſe with open throat.

And, if my muſe can through paſt ages ſee,
That noiſy, nauſeous, *gaping* fool is he. *Roſcommon.*

10. To ſtare with hope or expectation.

Others will *gape* t' anticipate
The cabinet deſigns of fate;
Apply to wizards, to foreſee
What ſhall, and what ſhall never be. *Hudibras, p.* ii.

11. To ſtare with wonder.

Parts of different ſpecies jumbled together, according to the mad imagination of the dawber; and the end of all this to cauſe laughter: a very monſter in a Bartholomew fair, for the mob to *gape* at. *Dryden's Dufreſnoy.*

Where elevated o'er the *gaping* croud,
Claſp'd in the board the perjur'd head is bow'd,
Betimes retreat. *Gay's Trivia.*

12. To ſtare irreverently.

They have *gaped* upon me with their mouth. *Job* xvi. 10.

GA'PER. *n. ſ.* [from *gape.*]

1. One who opens his mouth.
2. One who ſtares fooliſhly.
3. One who longs or craves.

The golden ſhower of the diſſolved abbey-lands rained well near into every *gaper's* mouth. *Carew's Survey of Cornwal.*

GAR, in Saxon, ſignifies a weapon: ſo *Eadgar* is a happy weapon; *Ethelgar*, a noble weapon. *Gibſon's Camden.*

To GAR. *v. a.* [*giera*, Iſlandick.] To cauſe; to make. It is ſtill in uſe in Scotland.

Tell me, good Hobbinol, what *gars* thee greet?
What! hath ſome wolf thy tender lambs ytorn?
Or is thy bagpipe broke, that ſounds ſo ſweet?
Or art thou of thy loved loſs forlorne. *Spenſer's Paſtorals.*

GARB. *n. ſ.* [*garbe*, French.]

1. Dreſs; cloaths; habit.

Thus Belial, with words cloath'd in reaſon's *garb*,
Counſel'd ignoble eaſe, and peaceful ſloth.
Milton's Paradiſe Loſt.

He puts himſelf into the *garb* and habit of a profeſſor of phyſick, and ſets up. *L'Eſtrange, Fable* 37.

2. Faſhion of dreſs.

Horace's wit, and Virgil's ſtate,
He did not ſteal, but emulate;
And when he would like them appear,
Their *garb*, but not their cloaths, did wear. *Denham.*

3. Exteriour appearance.

This is ſome fellow,
Who, having been prais'd for bluntneſs, doth affect
A ſaucy roughneſs, and conſtrains the *garb*
Quite from his nature. *Shakeſpeare's King Lear.*

GA'RBAGE. *n. ſ.* [*garbear*, Spaniſh. This etymology is very doubtful.]

1. The bowels; the offal; that part of the inwards which is ſeparated and thrown away.

The cloyed will,
That ſatiate, yet unſatisfy'd deſire, that tub

Both fill'd and running, ravening firſt the lamb,
Longs after for the *garbage* *Shakeſpeare's Cymbeline.*
Luſt, though to a radiant angel link'd,
Will ſate itſelf in a celeſtial bed,
And prey on *garbage.* *Shakeſpeare's Hamlet.*
A flam more ſenſeleſs than the rog'ry
Of old Aruſpicy and aug'ry,
That out of *garbages* of cattle
Preſag'd th' events of truce or battle. *Hudibras, p.* ii.
Who, without averſion, ever look'd
On holy *garbage*, though by Homer cook'd? *Roſcommon.*

When you receive condign puniſhment, you run to your confeſſor, that parcel of guts and *garbage. Dryd. Span. Fryar.*

GA'RBEL. *n. ſ.* A plank next the keel of a ſhip. *Bailey.*

GA'RBIDGE. *n. ſ.* Corrupted for *garbage.*

All ſhavings of horns, hoofs of cattle, blood, and *garbidge* is good manure for land. *Mortimer's Husbandry.*

GA'RBISH. *n. ſ.* Corrupted from *garbage.*

In Newfoundland they improve their ground with the *garbiſh* of fiſh. *Mortimer's Husbandry.*

To GA'RBLE. *v. a.* [*garbellare*, Italian.] To ſift; to part; to ſeparate the good from the bad.

But you who fathers and traditions take,
And *garble* ſome, and ſome you quite forſake. *Dryden.*

Had our author ſet down this command without *garbling*, as God gave it, and joined mother to father, it had made directly againſt him. *Locke.*

The underſtanding works to collate, combine, and *garble* the images and ideas, the imagination and memory preſent to it. *Cheyne's Phil. Princ.*

GA'RBLER. *n. ſ.* [from *garble.*] He who ſeparates one part from another.

A farther ſecret in this clauſe may beſt be diſcovered by the projectors, or at leaſt the *garblers* of it. *Swift's Examiner.*

GA'RBOIL. *n. ſ.* [*garbouille*, French; *garbuglio*, Italian.] Diſorder; tumult; uproar. *Hanmer.*

Look here, and at thy ſovereign leiſure read
What *garboils* ſhe awak'd. *Shak. Ant. and Cleopatra.*

GARD. *n. ſ.* [*garde*, French] Wardſhip; care; cuſtody.

GA'RDEN. *n. ſ.* [*gardd*, Welſh; *jardin*, French; *giardino*, Italian.]

1. A piece of ground incloſed, and cultivated with extraordinary care, planted with herbs or fruits for food, or laid out for pleaſure.

Thy promiſes are like Adonis' *gardens*,
Which one day bloom'd and fruitful were the next. *Shakeſ.*
My lord of Ely, when I was laſt in Holbourn,
I ſaw good ſtrawberries in your *garden* there. *Shakeſ. R.* III.

In the royal ordering of *gardens*, there ought to be *gardens* for all the months in the year. *Bacon's Eſſays.*

In every *garden* ſhould be provided flowers, fruit, ſhade and water. *Temple.*

2. A place particularly fruitful or delightful.

I am arriv'd from fruitful Lombardy,
The pleaſant *garden* of great Italy. *Shak. Tam. of the Shrew.*

3. GARDEN is often uſed in compoſition for *hortenſis*, or belonging to a garden.

GARDEN-MOULD. *n. ſ.* Mould fit for a garden.

They delight moſt in rich black *garden-mould*, that is deep and light, and mixed rather with ſand than clay. *Mortimer.*

GARDEN-TILLAGE. *n. ſ.* Tillage uſed in cultivating gardens.

Peas and beans are what belong to *garden tillage* as well as that of the field. *Mortimer's Husbandry.*

GARDEN-WARE. *n. ſ.* The produce of gardens.

A clay bottom is a much more pernicious ſoil for trees and *garden-ware* than gravel. *Mortimer's Husbandry.*

To GA'RDEN. *v. n.* [from the noun.] To cultivate a garden; to lay out gardens.

At firſt, in Rome's poor age,
When both her kings and conſuls held the plough,
Or *garden'd* well. *Ben. Johnſon's Catiline.*

When ages grow to civility and elegancy, men come to build ſtately, ſooner than to *garden* finely; as if *gardening* were the greater perfection *Bacon, Eſſay* 47.

GA'RDENER. *n. ſ.* [from *garden.*] He that attends or cultivates gardens.

Our bodies are our gardens, to the which our wills are *gardeners*; ſo that, if we will plant nettles, or ſow lettuce, the power lies in our will. *Shakeſpeare's Othello.*

Gardeners tread down any looſe ground, after they have ſown onions or turnips. *Bacon's Natural Hiſtory.*

The *gardener* may lop religion as he pleaſe. *Howel.*

The life and felicity of an excellent *gardener* is preferable to all other diverſions. *Evelyn's Kalendar.*

Then let the learned *gard'ner* mark with care
The kinds of ſtocks, and what thoſe kinds will bear. *Dryd.*

GA'RDENING. *n. ſ.* [from *garden.*] The act of cultivating or planning gardens.

My compoſitions in *gardening* are after the Pindarick manner, and run into the beautiful wildneſs of nature, without affecting the nicer elegancies of art. *Spectator*, N°. 477.

GARE. *n. ſ.* Coarſe wool growing on the legs of ſheep. *Dict.*

GA'RGARISM. *n. ſ.* [γαργαρισμὸς; *gargariſme*, French.] A liquid form of medicine to waſh the mouth with. *Quincy.*

Apophlegmatiſms and *gargariſms* draw the rheum down by the palate. *Bacon's Natural Hiſtory.*

To GARGARI'ZE. *v. a.* [γαργαρίζω; *gargariſer*, French.] To waſh the mouth with medicated liquors.

Vinegar, put to the noſtrils, or *gargarized*, doth eaſe the hiccough; for that it is aſtringent, and inhibiteth the motion of the ſpirit. *Bacon's Natural Hiſtory.*

This being relaxed, may make a ſhaking of the larynx; as when we *gargarize.* *Holder's Elements of Speech.*

GA'RGET. *n. ſ.* A diſtemper in cattle.

The *garget* appears in the head, maw, or in the hinder parts. *Mortimer's Husbandry.*

To GA'RGLE. *v. a.* [*gargouiller*, French; *gargogliare*, Ital. *gurgel*, German, the throat.]

1. To waſh the throat with ſome liquor not ſuffered immediately to deſcend.

Gargle twice or thrice with ſharp oxycrate. *Harvey.*

The exciſion made, the bleeding will ſoon be ſtopt by *gargling* with oxycrate. *Wiſeman's Surgery.*

They comb, and then they order ev'ry hair;
Next *gargle* well their throats. *Dryden's Perſ. Sat.*

2. To warble; to play in the throat. An improper uſe.

Thoſe which only warble long,
And *gargle* in their throats a ſong. *Waller.*
So charm'd you were, you ceas'd a while to doat
On nonſenſe *gargl'd* in an eunuch's throat. *Fenton.*

GA'RGLE. *n. ſ.* [from the verb.] A liquor with which the throat is waſhed.

His throat was waſhed with one of the *gargles* ſet down in the method of cure. *Wiſeman's Surgery.*

GA'RGLION. *n. ſ.* An exſudation of nervous juice from a bruiſe, or the like, which indurates into a hard immoveable tumour. *Quincy.*

GA'RGOL. *n. ſ.* A diſtemper in hogs.

The ſigns of the *gargol* in hogs are, hanging down of the head, moiſt eyes, ſtaggering, and loſs of appetite. *Mortimer.*

GA'RLAND. *n. ſ.* [*garlande*, *guirland*, French.] A wreath of branches or flowers.

Strephon, with leavy twigs of laurel-tree,
A *garland* made, on temples for to wear;
For he then choſen was the dignity
Of village-lord that Whitſuntide to bear. *Sidney.*
With every minute you do change a mind,
And call him noble, that was now your hate,
Him vile, that was your *garland.* *Shakeſpeare.*
A reeling world will never ſtand upright,
'Till Richard wear the *garland* of the realm.
—How! wear the *garland!* do'ſt thou mean the crown?
—Ay, my good lord. *Shakeſpeare's Richard* III.
Then party-colour'd flow'rs of white and red
She wove, to make a *garland* for her head. *Dryden's Fables.*
Vanquiſh again; though ſhe be gone,
Whoſe *garland* crown'd the victor's hair,
And reign; though ſhe has left the throne,
Who made thy glory worth thy care. *Prior.*
Her gods and godlike heroes riſe to view,
And all her faded *garlands* bloom anew. *Pope.*

GA'RLICK. *n. ſ.* [ȝar, Saxon, a lance, and *leek*, the leek that ſhoots up in blades. *Skinner.*]

It has a bulbous root, conſiſting of many ſmall tubercles included in its coats: the leaves are plain: the flowers conſiſt of ſix leaves, formed into a corymbus on the top of the ſtalk; and are ſucceeded by ſubrotund fruit, divided into three cells, which contain roundiſh ſeeds. *Miller.*

Garlick is of an extremely ſtrong, and to moſt people a diſagreeable ſmell, and of an acrid and pungent taſte. It is an extremely active and penetrating medicine, as may be proved by applying plaiſters of *garlick* to the ſoles of the feet, which will in a very little time give a ſtrong ſmell to the breath. Iſſues will ſmell ſtrongly of *garlick* three or four hours after a perſon has eaten it; and given to fowls, it communicates its taſte ſtrongly to their fleſh, and in ſome degree to their eggs. Bruiſed, and laid on any tender part of the ſkin, it corrodes it, and raiſes bliſters. Some are very fond of it in food; and a little of it is not only agreeable this way, but aſſiſts digeſtion, and ſtrengthens the ſtomach. *Hill.*

Garlick has, of all our plants, the greateſt ſtrength, affords moſt nouriſhment, and ſupplies moſt ſpirits to thoſe who eat little fleſh. *Temple.*

'Tis mortal ſin an onion to devour;
Each clove of *garlick* is a ſacred pow'r:
Religious nations ſure, and bleſt abodes,
Where ev'ry orchard is o'er-run with gods. *Tate's Juven.*

GA'RLICK *Pear-tree. n. ſ.*

It hath an anomalous flower, conſiſting of four petals or leaves, which ſtand erect, the lower part being occupied by a number of chives: the pointal, which is fixed on a long footſtalk,

ſtalk, riſes from the centre of the empalement, and afterward becomes a globular fleſhy fruit; in the centre of which are included many ſeeds, which are ſhaped almoſt like kidneys. This tree is pretty common in Jamaica, and ſeveral other places in the warmer parts of America, where it uſually riſes to the height of thirty or forty feet, and ſpreads into many branches. When the flowers fall off the pointal, it becomes a round fruit about the ſize of a tennis-ball, which, when ripe, has a rough browniſh rind, and a mealy ſweet pulp, ſomewhat like ſome of the European pears; but has a ſtrong ſcent of garlick. *Miller.*

GARLICK *Wild. n. ſ.*

The characters are: it agrees in every reſpect with the garlick; but hath, for th e moſt part, a ſweet ſcent; and the flowers are produced in an umbel. *Miller.*

GARLICKEA'TER. *n. ſ.* [*garlick* and *eat.*] A mean fellow.

You've made good work,
You and your apron men, that ſtood ſo much
Upon the voice of occupation, and
The breath of *garlickeaters.* *Shakeſpeare's Coriolanus.*

GA'RMENT. *n. ſ.* [*guarniment*, old French.] Any thing by which the body is covered; cloaths; dreſs.

Hence, rotten thing, or I ſhall ſhake thy bones
Out of thy *garments.* *Shakeſp. Coriolanus.*
Haſt any of thy late maſter's *garments* in thy poſſeſſion? *Shakeſpeare's Cymbeline.*

Our leaf, once fallen, ſpringeth no more; neither doth the ſun or ſummer adorn us again with the *garments* of new leaves and flowers. *Raleigh's Hiſtory of the World.*

Three worthy perſons from his ſide it tore,
And dy'd his *garment* with their ſcatter'd gore. *Waller.*

The peacock, in all his pride, does not diſplay half the colours that appear in the *garments* of a Britiſh lady, when ſhe is dreſſed. *Addiſon's Spectator*, N°. 265.

GA'RNER. *n. ſ.* [*grenier*, French.] A place in which threſhed grain is ſtored up.

Earth's increaſe, and foyſon plenty,
Barns and *garners* never empty. *Shakeſpeare's Tempeſt.*
For ſundry foes the rural realm ſurround;
The fieldmouſe builds her *garner* under ground:
For gather'd grain the blind laborious mole,
In winding mazes, works her hidden hole. *Dryd. Vir. Geo.*

To GA'RNER. *v. a.* [from the noun.] To ſtore as in garners.

There, where I have *garner'd* up my heart,
Where either I muſt live, or bear no life. *Shakeſ. Othello.*

GA'RNET. *n. ſ.* [*garnato*, Italian; *granatus*, low Latin, from its reſemblance in colour to the grain of the pomegranate.]

The *garnet* is a gem of a middle degree of hardneſs, between the ſaphire and the common cryſtal. It is found of various ſizes. Its ſurfaces are not ſo ſmooth or polite as thoſe of a ruby, and its colour is ever of a ſtrong red, with a plain admixture of blueiſh: its degree of colour is very different, and it always wants much of the brightneſs of the ruby. *Hill.*

The *garnet* ſeems to be a ſpecies of the carbuncle of the ancients: the Bohemian is red, with a ſlight caſt of a flame-colour; and the Syrian is red, with a ſlight caſt of purple. *Woodward's Met. Foſſils.*

To GA'RNISH. *v. a.* [*garnir*, French.]

1. To decorate with ornamental appendages.

There were hills which *garniſhed* their proud heights with ſtately trees. *Sidney.*

All within with flowers was *garniſhed*,
That, when mild Zephyrus amongſt them blew,
Did breathe out bounteous ſmells, and painted colours ſhew. *Fairy Queen, b.* ii. *cant.* 5.

With taper light
To ſeek the beauteous eye of heav'n to *garniſh*,
Is waſteful and ridiculous exceſs. *Shakeſp. King John.*

Paradiſe was a terreſtrial garden, *garniſhed* with fruits, delighting both the eye and taſte. *Raleigh's Hiſtory of the World.*

All the ſtreets between the Bridge-foot and palace of Paul's, where the king then lay, were *garniſhed* with the citizens, ſtanding in their liveries. *Bacon's Henry* VII.

2. To embelliſh a diſh with ſomething laid round it.

With what expence and art, how richly dreſt!
Garniſh'd with 'ſparagus, himſelf a feaſt! *Dryd. Juven. Sat.*
No man lards ſalt pork with orange peel,
Or *garniſhes* his lamb with ſpitchcok'd eel. *King's Cookery.*

3. To fit with fetters.

GA'RNISH. *n. ſ.* [from the verb.]

1. Ornament; decoration; embelliſhment.

So are you, ſweet,
Ev'n in the lovely *garniſh* of a boy. *Shak. Merch. of Venice.*
Matter and figure they produce;
For *garniſh* this, and that for uſe;
They ſeek to feed and pleaſe their gueſts. *Prior.*

2. Things ſtrewed round a diſh.
3. [In gaols.] Fetters.
4. *Penſiuncula carceraria*; an acknowledgment in money when firſt a priſoner goes into a gaol. *Ainſworth.*

GA'RNISHMENT. *n. ſ.* [from *garniſh.*] Ornament; embelliſhment.

The church of Sancta Guiſtiniana in Padoua is a ſound piece of good art, where the materials being but ordinary ſtone, without any *garniſhment* of ſculpture, do raviſh the beholders. *Wotton's Architecture.*

GA'RNITURE. *n. ſ.* [from *garniſh.*] Furniture; ornament.

They conclude, if they fall ſhort in the *garniture* of their knees, that they are inferior in the furniture of their heads. *Government of the Tongue.*

Plain ſenſe, which pleas'd your ſires an age ago,
Is loſt, without the *garniture* of ſhow. *Granville.*

As nature has poured out her charms upon the female part of our ſpecies, ſo they are very aſſiduous in beſtowing upon themſelves the fineſt *garnitures* of art. *Addiſon's Spectator.*

GA'ROUS. *adj.* [from *garum.*] Reſembling pickle made of fiſh.

In a civet-cat a different and offenſive odour proceeds, partly from its food, that being eſpecially fiſh; whereof this humour may be a *garous* excretion, and olidous ſeparation. *Brown's Vulgar Errours, b.* iii. *c.* 4.

GA'RRAN. *n. ſ.* [Erſe. It imports the ſame as gelding. The word is ſtill retained in Scotland.] A ſmall horſe; a hobby. A Highland horſe which when brought into the North of England takes the name of *galloway.*

When he comes forth he will make their cows and *garrans* to walk, if he doth no other harm to their perſons. *Spenſer.*

Every man would be forced to provide Winter-fodder for his team, whereas common *garrans* ſhift upon graſs the year round; and this would force men to the encloſing of grounds, ſo that the race of *garrans* would decreaſe. *Temple.*

GA'RRET. *n. ſ.* [*garite*, the tower of a citadel, French.]

1. A room on the higheſt floor of the houſe.

The mob, commiſſion'd by the government,
Are ſeldom to an empty *garret* ſent. *Dryden's Juven. Sat.*

John Bull ſkipped from room to room; ran up ſtairs and down ſtairs, from the kitchen to the *garret.* *Arbuthn. J. Bull.*

On earth the god of wealth was made
Sole patron of the building trade;
Leaving the arts the ſpacious air,
With licence to build caſtles there:
And 'tis conceiv'd their old pretence,
To lodge in *garrets*, comes from thence. *Swift.*

2. Rotten wood.

The colour of the ſhining part of rotten wood, by daylight, is in ſome pieces white, and in ſome pieces inclining to red, which they call the white and red *garret.* *Bacon.*

GARRETE'ER. *n. ſ.* [from *garret.*] An inhabitant of a garret.

GA'RRISON. *n. ſ.* [*garniſon*, French.]

1. Soldiers placed in a fortified town or caſtle to defend it.

How oft he ſaid to me,
Thou art no ſoldier fit for Cupid's *garriſon.* *Sidney, b.* i.

2. Fortified place ſtored with ſoldiers.

Whom the old Roman wall ſo ill confin'd,
With a new chain of *garriſons* you bind. *Waller.*

3. The ſtate of being placed in a fortification for its defence.

Some of them that are laid in *garriſon* will do no great hurt to the enemies. *Spenſer on Ireland.*

To GA'RRISON. *v. a.* [from the verb.] To ſecure by fortreſſes.

Others thoſe forces join,
Which *garriſon* the conqueſts near the Rhine. *Dryd. Juven.*

GARRU'LITY. *n. ſ.* [*garrulitas*, Latin.]

1. Loquacity; incontinence of tongue; inability to keep a ſecret.

Let me here
Expiate, if poſſible, my crime,
Shameful *garrulity.* *Milton's Agoniſtes.*

2. The quality of talking too much; talkativeneſs.

Some vices of ſpeech muſt carefully be avoided: firſt of all, loquacity or *garrulity.* *Ray on the Creation.*

GA'RRULOUS. *adj.* [*garrulus*, Latin.] Prattling; talkative.

Old age looks out,
And *garrulous* recounts the feats of youth. *Thomſon.*

GA'RTER. *n. ſ.* [*gardus*, Welſh; *jartier*, French, from *gar*, Welſh, the binding of the knee.]

1. A ſtring or ribband by which the ſtocking is held upon the leg.

Let their heads be ſleekly comb'd, their blue coats bruſh'd, and their *garters* of an indifferent knit. *Sh. Tam. of the Shrew.*

When we reſt in our cloaths we looſen our *garters*, and other ligatures, to give the ſpirits free paſſage. *Ray.*

Handſome *garters* at your knees. *Swift.*

There lay three *garters*, half a pair of gloves,
And all the trophies of his former loves. *Pope.*

2. The mark of the order of the garter, the higheſt order of Engliſh knighthood.

Now by my george, my *garter.*
—The george, profan'd, hath loſt his holy honour;
The *garter*, blemiſh'd, pawn'd his knightly virtue. *Sh. R.* III.

You owe your Ormond nothing but a son,
To fill in future times his father's place,
And wear the *garter* of his mother's race. *Dryden.*

3. The principal king at arms.

To Ga'rter. *v. a.* [from the noun.] To bind with a garter.

He, being in love, could not see to *garter* his hose. *Shakesp.*

A person was wounded in the leg, below the *gartering* place. *Wiseman's Surgery.*

Garth. *n. s.* [as if *girth*, from *gird.*] The bulk of the body measured by the girdle.

Gas. *n. s.* [A word invented by the chymists.] It is used by Van Helmont, and seems designed to signify, in general, a spirit not capable of being coagulated: but he uses it loosely in many senses, and very unintelligibly and inconsistently. *Har.*

GASCONA'DE. *n. s.* [French, from *Gascon*, a nation eminent for boasting.] A boast; a bravado.

Was it a *gasconade* to please me, that you said your fortune was increased to one hundred a year since I left you? *Swift.*

To Gascona'de. *v. n.* [from the noun.] To boast; to brag; to bluster.

To GASH. *v. a* [from *hacher*, to cut, French. *Skinner.*] To cut deep so as to make a gaping wound; to cut with a blunt instrument so as to make the wound wide.

Where the Englishmen at arms had been defeated, many of their horses were found grievously *gashed* or gored to death. *Hayward.*

Wit is a keen instrument, and every one can cut and *gash* with it; but to carve a beautiful image requires great art. *Tillotson, Sermon 2.*

See me *gash'd* with knives,
Or sear'd with burning steel. *Rowe's Royal Convert.*

Streaming with blood, all over *gash'd* with wounds,
He reel'd, he groan'd, and at the altar fell. *A. Phillips.*

Gash. *n. s.* [from the verb.]

1. A deep and wide wound.

He glancing on his helmet, made a large
And open *gash* therein; were not his targe,
That broke the violence of his intent,
The weary soul from thence it would discharge. *Fai. Queen.*

A perilous *gash*, a very limb lopt off. *Shakesp. Henry IV.*

Hamilton drove Newton almost to the end of the lists; but Newton on a sudden gave him such a *gash* on the leg, that therewith he fell to the ground. *Hayward.*

But th' ethereal substance clos'd,
Not long divisible; and from the *gash*
A stream of nectarous humour issuing flow'd. *Milt. P. Lost.*

2. The mark of a wound. I know not if this be proper.

I was fond of back-sword and cudgel play, and I now bear in my body many a black and blue *gash* and scar. *Arbuthnot.*

Ga'skins. *n. s.* [from *Gascoigne.* See Galligaskins.] Wide hose; wide breeches. An old ludicrous word.

If one point break, the other will hold;
Or, if both break, your *gaskins* fall. *Shak. Twelfth Night.*

To Gasp. *v. n.* [from *gape*, *Skinner*; from *gispe*, Danish, to sob, *Junius.*]

1. To open the mouth wide to catch breath.

The sick for air before the portal *gasp.* *Dryd. Virg. Geo.*

They rais'd a feeble cry with trembling notes;
But the weak voice deceiv'd their *gasping* throats. *Dryden.*

The *gasping* head flies off; a purple flood
Flows from the trunk. *Dryden's Æn.*

The ladies *gasp'd*, and scarcely could respire;
The breath they drew no longer air, but fire. *Dryden.*

A scantling of wit lay *gasping* for life, and groaning beneath a heap of rubbish. *Dryden's Spanish Fryar.*

Pale and faint,
He *gasps* for breath; and, as his life flows from him,
Demands to see his friends. *Addison's Cato.*

2. To emit breath by opening the mouth convulsively.

I lay me down to *gasp* my latest breath;
The wolves will get a breakfast by my death. *Dryden.*

He staggers round, his eyeballs roll in death,
And with short sobs, he *gasps* away his breath. *Dryden's Æn.*

3. To long for. This sense is, I think, not proper, as nature never expresses desire by gasping.

The Castilian and his wife had the comfort to be under the same master, who, seeing how dearly they loved one another, and *gasped* after their liberty, demanded a most exorbitant price for their ransom. *Spectator,* N°. 198.

Gasp. *n. s.* [from the verb.]

1. The act of opening the mouth to catch breath.

2. The short catch of breath in the last agonies.

His fortunes all lie speechless, and his name
Is at last *gasp.* *Shakespeare's Cymbeline.*

Ah, Warwick, Montague hath breath'd his last;
And to the latest *gasp* cry'd out for Warwick. *Shak. H. VI.*

If in the dreadful hour of death,
If at the latest *gasp* of breath,
When the cold damp bedews your brow,
You hope for mercy, shew it now. *Addison's Rosamond.*

Life's business at one *gasp* be o'er. *Pope.*

To Gast. *v. a.* [from ᵹarꞇ, Saxon. See Aghast.] To make aghast; to fright; to shock; to terrify; to fear; to affray.

When he saw my best alarmed spirits,
Bold in the quarrel's right, rous'd to th' encounter,
Or whether *gasted* by the noise I made,
Full suddenly he fled. *Shakespeare's King Lear.*

Ga'strick. *adj.* [from γαςὴρ.] Belonging to the belly.

Gastro'raphy. *n. s* [γαςὴρ and ῥάπτω.] In strictness of etymology, signifies no more than sewing up any wound of the belly; yet in common acceptation it implies, that the wound of the belly is complicated with another of the intestine. *Sharp's Surgery.*

Gastro'tomy. *n. s.* [γαςὴρ and τέτομα.] The act of cutting open the belly.

Gat. The preterite of *get.*

Moses *gat* him up into the mount. *Ex.* xxiv. 18.

GATE. *n. s.* [ᵹeaꞇ, Saxon.]

1. The door of a city, a castle, palace, or large building.

Open the *gate* of mercy, gracious God!
My soul flies through these wounds to seek thee. *Shakesp.*

Gates of monarchs
Are arch'd so high, that giants may jet through,
And keep their impious turbands on, without
Good-morrow to the sun. *Shakespeare's Cymbeline.*

2. A frame of timber upon hinges to give a passage into inclosed grounds.

Know'st thou the way to Dover?
—— Both stile and *gate*, horseway and footpath. *Shakesp.*

3. An avenue; an opening.

Auria had done nothing but wisely and politickly, in setting the Venetians together by the ears with the Turks, and opening a *gate* for a long war. *Knolles's History of the Turks.*

Ga'tevein. *n. s.* The *vena portæ.*

Being a king that loved wealth, he could not endure to have trade sick, nor any obstruction to continue in the *gatevein* which disperseth that blood. *Bacon's Henry VII.*

Ga'teway. *n. s.* [*gate* and *way.*] A way through gates of inclosed grounds.

Gateways between inclosures are so miry, that they cannot cart between one field and another. *Mortimer's Husbandry.*

To GA'THER. *v. a.* [ᵹaꝺeꞃan, Saxon.]

1. To collect; to bring into one place; to get in harvest.

I *gathered* me silver and gold. *Ecclus.* ii. 8.

Gather stones—and they took stones and made an heap. *Gen.*

The seventh year we shall not sow, nor *gather* in our increase. *Lev.* xxv. 20.

2. To pick up; to glean; to pluck.

His opinions
Have satisfied the king for his divorce,
Gather'd from all the famous colleges. *Shak. Henry* VIII.

Cast up the highway, *gather* out the stones. *Is.* lxii. 10.

I will spend this preface upon those from whom I have *gathered* my knowledge; for I am but a gatherer. *Wotton.*

To pay the creditor, that lent him his rent, he must *gather* up money by degrees, as the sale of his commodities shall bring it in. *Locke.*

3. To crop.

What have I done?
To see my youth, my beauty, and my love
No sooner gain'd, but slighted and betray'd;
And like a rose just *gather'd* from the stalk,
But only smelt, and cheaply thrown aside,
To wither on the ground! *Dryden's Spanish Fryar.*

4. To assemble.

They have *gathered* themselves together against me. *Job.*

Come ye heathen, and *gather* yourselves together. *Joel* iii.

He led us through three fair streets; and all the way we went there were *gathered* some people on both sides, standing in a row. *Bacon's New Atlantis.*

5. To heap up; to accumulate.

He that by usury and unjust gain increaseth his substance, shall *gather* it for him that will pity the poor. *Prov.* xxviii. 8.

6. To select and take.

Save us, O Lord, and *gather* us from among the heathen, to give thanks unto thy holy name. *Ps.* cvi. 47.

7. To sweep together.

The kingdom of heaven is like unto a net that was cast into the sea, and *gathered* of every kind. *Mat.* xiii. 47.

8. To collect charitable contributions.

9. To bring into one body or interest.

I will *gather* others to him, besides those that are *gathered* unto him. *Is.* lvi. 8.

10. To draw together from a state of diffusion; to compress; to contract.

Immortal Tully shone,
The Roman rostra deck'd the consul's throne;
Gath'ring his flowing robe he seem'd to stand,
In act to speak, and graceful stretch'd his hand. *Pope.*

11. To gain.

He *gathers* ground upon her in the chace;
Now breathes upon her hair with nearer pace. *Dryden.*

12. To pucker needlework.

13. To collect logically; to know by inference.

That which, out of the law either of reason or of God, men probably *gathering* to be expedient, they make it law. *Hooker, b. i. ſ. 3.*

The reason that I *gather* he is mad,
Is a mad tale he told to-day at dinner,
Of his own door being ſhut againſt his entrance. *Shakeſp.*

After he had ſeen the viſion, we endeavoured to get into Macedonia, aſſuredly *gathering* that the Lord had called us. *Acts* xvi. 10.

Return'd
By night, and liſtening where the hapleſs pair
Sat in their ſad diſcourſe, and various plaint,
Thence *gather'd* his own doom. *Milton's Paradiſe Loſt, b.* x.

Madamoiſelle de Scudery, who is as old as Sibyl, is at this time tranſlating Chaucer into modern French: from which I *gather*, that he has formerly been tranſlated into the old Provençal. *Dryden's Fables, Preface.*

We may eaſily *gather* from this paſſage what notion the ancients had concerning a future ſtate. *Notes on the Odyſſey.*

14. *To* GATHER *Breath.* [A proverbial expreſſion.] To have reſpite from any calamity.

The luckleſs lucky maid
A long time with that ſavage people ſtaid,
To *gather breath*, in many miſeries. *Spenſer.*

To GA'THER. *v. n.*

1. To be condenſed; to thicken.

If ere night the *gath'ring* clouds we fear,
A ſong will help the beating ſtorm to bear. *Dryden's Paſt.*
When *gath'ring* clouds o'erſhadow all the ſkies,
And ſhoot quick lightnings, weigh, my boys! he cries. *Dry.*
When the rival winds their quarrel try,
South, Eaſt and Weſt, on airy courſers born,
The whirlwind *gathers*, and the woods are torn. *Dryden.*
Think on the ſtorm that *gathers* o'er your head,
And threatens every hour to burſt upon it. *Addiſon's Cato.*

2. To grow larger by the accretion of ſimilar matter.

Their ſnow-ball did not *gather* as it went; for the people came in to them. *Bacon's Henry* VIII.

3. To aſſemble.

There be three things that mine heart feareth; the ſlander of a city, the *gathering* together of an unruly multitude, and a falſe accuſation. *Eccluſ.* xxvi. 5.

4. To generate pus or matter.

Aſk one, who by repeated reſtraints hath ſubdued his natural rage, how he likes the change, and he will tell you 'tis no leſs happy than the eaſe of a broken impoſthume after the painful *gathering* and filling of it. *Decay of Piety.*

GA'THER. *n. ſ.* [from the verb.] Pucker; cloth drawn together in wrinkles.

Give laws for pantaloons,
The length of breeches, and the *gathers*,
Part cannons, perriwigs and feathers. *Hudibras, p.* i.

GA'THERER. *n. ſ.* [from *gather.*]

1. One that gathers; one that collects; a collector.

I will ſpend this preface about thoſe from whom I have gathered my knowledge; for I am but a *gatherer* and diſpoſer of other mens ſtuff. *Wotton's Preface to Elem. of Architecture.*

2. One that gets in a crop of any kind.

I was a herdman and a *gatherer* of ſycamore-fruit. *Amos* vii.

Nor in that land
Do poiſonous herbs deceive the *gatherer's* hand. *May's Virg.*

GA'THERING. *n. ſ.* [from *gather.*] Collection of charitable contributions.

Let every one lay by him in ſtore, that there be no *gatherings* when I come. 1 *Cor.* xvi. 2.

GA'TTEN-TREE. See CORNELIAN-CHERRY, of which it is a ſpecies.

GAUDE *n. ſ.* [The etymology of this word is uncertain: *Skinner* imagines it may come from *gaude*, French, a yellow flower, yellow being the moſt gaudy colour. *Junius*, according to his cuſtom, talks of ἀγαυός; and Mr. *Lye* finds *gaude*, in *Douglaſs*, to ſignify deceit or fraud, from *gwawdio*, Welſh, to cheat. It ſeems to me moſt eaſily deducible from *gaudium*, Latin, joy; the cauſe of joy; a token of joy: thence aptly applied to any thing that gives or expreſſes pleaſure. In Scotland this word is ſtill retained, both as a ſhowy bawble, and the perſon fooled. It is alſo retained in Scotland to denote a yellow flower.] An ornament; a fine thing; any thing worn as a ſign of joy.

He ſtole th' impreſſion of her fantaſy,
With bracelets of thy hair, rings, *gaudes*, conceits,
Knacks, trifles, noſegays, ſweetmeats. *Shakeſpeare.*
The ſun is in the heav'n, and the proud day,
Attended with the pleaſures of the world,
Is all too wanton, and too full of *gaudes*,
To give me audience. *Shakeſpeare's King Lear.*
My love to Hermia
Is melted as the ſnow; ſeems to me now
As the remembrance of an idle *gaude*,
Which in my childhood I did doat upon. *Shakeſpeare.*

Some bound for Guiney, golden ſand to find,
Bore all the *gaudes* the ſimple natives wear;
Some for the pride of Turkiſh courts deſign'd,
For folded turbants fineſt holland bear. *Dryd. Ann. Mirab.*

To GAUDE. *v. a.* [*gaudeo*, Latin.] To exult; to rejoice at any thing.

Go to a goſſip's feaſt, and *gaude* with me,
After ſo long grief ſuch nativity. *Shakeſpeare.*

GA'UDERY. *n. ſ.* [from *gaude.*] Finery; oſtentatious luxury of dreſs.

The triumph was not pageants and *gaudery*, but one of the wiſeſt and nobleſt inſtitutions that ever was. *Bacon's Eſſays.*

Age, which is but one remove from death, and ſhould have nothing about us but what looks like a decent preparation for it, ſcarce ever appears, of late, but in the high mode, the flaunting garb, and utmoſt *gaudery* of youth, with cloaths as ridiculouſly, and as much in the faſhion, as the perſon that wears them is uſually grown out of it. *South's Sermons.*

A plain ſuit, ſince we can make but one,
Is better than to be by tarniſh'd *gaud'ry* known. *Dryden.*

GA'UDILY. *adv.* [from *gaudy.*] Showily.

GAU'DINESS. *n. ſ.* [from *gaudy.*] Showineſs; tinſel appearance.

GA'UDY. *adj.* [from *gaude.*] Showy; ſplendid; pompous; oſtentatiouſly fine.

Coſtly thy habit as thy purſe can buy,
But not expreſt in fancy; rich, not *gaudy*;
For the apparel oft proclaims the man. *Shakeſp. Hamlet.*
Fancies fond with *gaudy* ſhapes poſſeſs,
As thick and numberleſs
As the gay motes that people the ſun-beams. *Milton.*

A man who walks directly to his journey's end, will arrive thither much ſooner than him who wanders aſide to gaze at every thing, or to gather every *gaudy* flower. *Watts.*

A goldfinch there I ſaw, with *gaudy* pride
Of painted plumes, that hopp'd from ſide to ſide. *Dryden.*
The Bavarian duke his brigades leads,
Gallant in arms, and *gaudy* to behold. *Phillips.*

GA'UDY. *n. ſ.* [*gaudium*, Latin.] A feaſt; a feſtival; a day of plenty.

He may ſurely be content with a faſt to-day, that is ſure of a *gaudy* to-morrow. *Cheyne.*

GAVE. The preterite of *give.*

Thou can'ſt not every day give me thy heart;
If thou can'ſt give it, then thou never *gav'ſt* it:
Lovers riddles are, that though thy heart depart,
It ſtays at home, and thou with loſing ſav'ſt it. *Donne.*

GA'VEL. *n. ſ.* A provincial word for ground.

Let it lie upon the ground or *gavel* eight or ten days. *Mort.*

GA'VELKIND. *n. ſ.* [In law.] A cuſtom whereby the lands of the father are equally divided at his death amongſt all his ſons, or the land of the brother equally divided among the brothers, if he have no iſſue of his own. This cuſtom is of force in divers places of England, but eſpecially in Kent. *Cowel.*

Among other Welſh cuſtoms he aboliſhed that of *gavelkind*, whereby the heirs female were utterly excluded, and the baſtards did inherit as well as the legitimate, which is the very Iriſh *gavelkind*. *Davies on Ireland.*

To GAUGE. *v. a.* [*gauge, jauge*, a meaſuring rod, French. It is pronounced *gage.*]

1. To meaſure with reſpect to the contents of a veſſel.

2. To meaſure with regard to any proportion.

The vanes nicely *gauged* on each ſide, broad on one ſide, and narrow on the other, both which miniſter to the progreſſive motion of the bird. *Derham's Phyſico-Theology.*

There is nothing more perfectly admirable in itſelf than that artful manner in Homer's battles of taking meaſure or *gaging* his heroes by each other, and thereby elevating the character of one perſon by the oppoſition of it to ſome other he is made to excel. *Pope's Eſſay on Homer's Battles.*

GAUGE. *n. ſ.* [from the verb.] A meaſure; a ſtandard.

This plate muſt be a *gage* to file your worm and groove to equal breadth by. *Moxon's Mech. Exer.*

If money were to be hired, as land is, or to be had from the owner himſelf, it might then be had at the market rate, which would be a conſtant *gauge* of your trade and wealth. *Loc.*

Timothy propoſed to his miſtreſs, that ſhe ſhould entertain no ſervant that was above four foot ſeven inches high; and for that purpoſe had prepared a *gage*, by which they were to be meaſured. *Arbuthnot's Hiſtory of John Bull.*

GAU'GER. *n. ſ.* [from *gauge.*] One whoſe buſineſs is to meaſure veſſels or quantities.

Thoſe earls and dukes have, from the beginning, been privileged with royal juriſdiction; and, to this end, appointed their ſpecial officers, as ſheriff, admiral, *gauger*, and eſcheator. *Carew's Survey of Cornwal.*

GAUNT. *adj.* [As if *gewant*, from ʒepanian, to leſſen, Saxon.] Thin; ſlender; lean; meagre.

Oh, how that name befits my compoſition!
Old *Gaunt*, indeed, and *gaunt* in being old:
Within me grief hath kept a tedious faſt;
And who abſtains from meat that is not *gaunt*?

For ſleeping England long time have I watch'd;
Watching breeds leanneſs, leanneſs is all *gaunt*:
The pleaſure that ſome fathers feed upon,
Is my ſtrict faſt; I mean my childrens looks;
And therein faſting, thou haſt made me *gaunt*:
Gaunt am I for the grave, *gaunt* as a grave,
Whoſe hollow womb inherits nought but bones. *Sh. R.* II.
Two maſtiffs, *gaunt* and grim, her flight purſu'd,
And oft their faſten'd fangs in blood embru'd. *Dryd. Fables.*

GA'UNTLY. *adv.* [from *gaunt*.] Leanly; ſlenderly; meagerly.

GA'UNTLET. *n. ſ.* [*gantelet*, French.] An iron glove uſed for defence, and thrown down in challenges. It is ſometimes in poetry uſed for the *ceſtus*, or boxing glove.

A ſcaly *gauntlet* now, with joints of ſteel,
Muſt glove this hand. *Shakeſp. Henry* IV. *p.* i.
Feel but the difference, ſoft and rough;
This a *gauntlet*, that a muff. *Cleaveland.*
Some ſhall in ſwiftneſs for the goal contend,
And others try the twanging bow to bend;
The ſtrong with iron *gauntlets* arm'd ſhall ſtand,
Oppos'd in combat, on the yellow ſand. *Dryd. Virg. Æn.*
Who naked wreſtled beſt, beſmear'd with oil;
Or who with *gaunlets* gave or took the foil. *Dryd. Fables.*
The funeral of ſome valiant knight
May give this thing its proper light:
View his two *gauntlets*; theſe declare
That both his hands were us'd to war. *Prior.*
So to repel the Vandals of the ſtage,
Our vet'ran bard reſumes his tragick rage;
He throws the *gauntlet* Otway us'd to wield,
And calls for Engliſhmen to judge the field. *Southern.*

GA'VOT. *n. ſ.* [*gavotte*, French.] A kind of dance.

The diſpoſition in a fiddle to play tunes in preludes, ſarabands, jigs and *gavots*, are real qualities in the inſtrument. *Arbuthnot and Pope's Mart. Scriblerus.*

GAUZE. *n. ſ.* A kind of thin tranſparent ſilk.

Silken cloaths were uſed by the ladies; and it ſeems they were thin, like *gauze*. *Arbuthnot on Coins.*
Brocadoes and damaſks, and tabbies and *gauzes*,
Are lately brought over. *Swift.*

GAWK. *n. ſ.* [ȝeac, Saxon.]
1. A cuckow.
2. A fooliſh fellow. In both ſenſes it is retained in Scotland.

GAWN. *n. ſ.* [corrupted for *gallon*.] A ſmall tub, or lading veſſel.

GA'WNTREE. *n. ſ.* [Scottiſh.] A wooden frame on which beer-caſks are ſet when tunned.

GAY. *adj.* [*gay*, French.]
1. Airy; chearful; merry; frolick.

Smooth flow the waves, the zephyrs gently play;
Belinda ſmil'd, and all the world was *gay*. *Pope.*
Ev'n rival wits did Voiture's fate deplore,
And the *gay* mourn'd, who never mourn'd before. *Pope.*

2. Fine; ſhowy.

A virgin that loves to go *gay*. *Bar.* vi. 9.

GAY. *n. ſ.* [from the adjective.] An ornament; an embelliſhment.

Moroſe and untractable ſpirits look upon precepts in emblem, as they do upon *gays* and pictures, the fooleries of ſo many old wives tales. *L'Eſtrange.*

GA'YETY. *n. ſ.* [*gayeté*, French, from *gay*.]
1. Chearfulneſs; airineſs; merriment.
2. Acts of juvenile pleaſure.

And from thoſe *gayeties* our youth requires
To exerciſe their minds, our age retires. *Denham.*

3. Finery; ſhow.

Our *gayety* and our gilt are all beſmirch'd,
With rainy marching in the painful field. *Shakeſp. H.* V.

GA'YLY. *adv.* Merrily; chearfully; ſhowily.

GA'YNESS. *n. ſ.* [from *gay*.] Gayety; finery. Not much in uſe.

To GAZE. *v. n.* [ἀγάζεσθαι, or rather ȝeyean, to ſee, Sax.] To look intently and earneſtly; to look with eagerneſs.

What ſee'ſt thou there? King Henry's diadem,
Inchas'd with all the honours of the world:
If ſo, *gaze* on. *Shakeſpeare's Henry* IV. *p.* ii.
From ſome ſhe caſt her modeſt eyes below;
At ſome her *gazing* glances roving flew. *Fairfax, b.* iv.
Gaze not on a maid, that thou fall not by thoſe things that are precious in her. *Eccluſ.* ix. 5.
A lover's eyes will *gaze* an eagle blind. *Shakeſpeare.*
Strait toward heav'n my wond'ring eyes I turn'd,
And *gaz'd* a while the ample ſky. *Milton's Paradiſe Loſt.*

GAZE. *n. ſ.* [from the verb.]
1. Intent regard; look of eagerneſs or wonder; fixed look.

Being light'ned with her beauty's beam,
And thereby fill'd with happy influence,
And lifted up above the worldis *gaze*,
To ſing with angels her immortal praiſe. *Spenſer.*
Do but note a wild and wanton herd,
If any air of muſick touch their ears,
You ſhall perceive them make a mutual ſtand,
Their ſavage eyes turn'd to a modeſt *gaze*,
By the ſweet power of muſick. *Shakeſp. Merch. of Venice.*
Not a month
'Fore your queen dy'd, ſhe was more worth ſuch *gazes*
Than what you look on now. *Shakeſpeare's Winter's Tale.*
With ſecret *gaze*,
Or open admiration, him behold,
On whom the great Creator hath beſtow'd
Worlds. *Milton's Paradiſe Loſt, b.* iii.
Pindar is a dark writer, wants connexion as to our underſtanding, ſoars out of ſight, and leaves his readers at a *gaze*. *Dryden's Preface to Ovid.*
After having ſtood at *gaze* before this gate, he diſcovered an inſcription. *Addiſon's Freeholder*, Nº. 27.

2. The object gazed on.

I muſt die
Betray'd, captiv'd, and both my eyes put out;
Made of my enemies the ſcorn and *gaze*;
To grind in brazen fetters, under taſk,
With my heav'n-gifted ſtrength. *Milton's Agoniſtes.*

GA'ZER. *n. ſ.* [from *gaze*.] He that gazes; one that looks intently with eagerneſs or admiration.

In her cheeks the vermil red did ſhew,
Like roſes in a bed of lilies ſhed;
The which ambroſial odours from them threw,
And *gazers* ſenſe with double pleaſure fed. *Fairy Queen.*
I'll ſlay more *gazers* than the baſiliſk. *Shakeſp. Hen.* VI.
Come, baſiliſk,
And kill the innocent *gazer* with thy ſight. *Shak. Hen.* VI.
Bright as the ſun, her eyes the *gazers* ſtrike;
And, like the ſun, they ſhine on all alike. *Pope.*
His learned ideas give him a tranſcendent delight; and yet, at the ſame time, diſcover the blemiſhes which the common *gazer* never obſerved. *Watts's Logick.*

GA'ZEFUL. *adj.* [*gaze* and *full*.] Looking intently.

The brightneſs of her beauty clear,
The raviſht hearts of *gazeful* men might rear
To admiration of that heavenly light. *Spenſer on Beauty.*

GA'ZEHOUND. *n. ſ.* [*gaze* and *hound*; *canis agaſæus*, *Skinner*.] A hound that purſues not by the ſcent, but by the eye.

See'ſt thou the *gazehound!* how with glance ſevere
From the cloſe herd he marks the deſtin'd deer! *Tickell.*

GAZETTE. *n. ſ.* [*gazetta* is a Venetian halfpenny, the price of a news paper, of which the firſt was publiſhed at Venice.] A paper of news; a paper of publick intelligence. It is accented indifferently on the firſt or laſt ſyllable.

And ſometimes when the loſs is ſmall,
And danger great, they challenge all;
Print new additions to their feats,
And emendations in *gazettes*. *Hudibras, p.* iii. *cant.* 3.
An Engliſh gentleman, without geography, cannot well underſtand a *gazette*. *Locke.*
One cannot hear a name mentioned in it that does not bring to mind a piece of a *gazette*. *Addiſon's Guardian.*
All, all but truth, falls dead-born from the preſs;
Like the laſt *gazette*, or the laſt addreſs. *Pope.*

GAZETTE'ER. *n. ſ.* [from *gazette*.]
1. A writer of news.
2. It was lately a term of the utmoſt infamy, being uſually applied to wretches who were hired to vindicate the court.

Satire is no more: I feel it die:
No *gazetteer* more innocent than I. *Pope.*

GA'ZINGSTOCK. *n. ſ.* [*gaze* and *ſtock*.] A perſon gazed at with ſcorn or abhorrence.

Theſe things are offences to us, by making us *gazingſtocks* to others, and objects of their ſcorn and deriſion. *Ray.*

GAZO'N. *n. ſ.* [French.] In fortification, pieces of freſh earth covered with graſs, cut in form of a wedge, about a foot long and half a foot thick, to line parapets and the traſverſes of galleries. *Harris.*

GEAR. *n. ſ.* [ȝẏꞃian, to cloath; ȝeaꞃpe, furniture, Saxon.]
1. Furniture; accoutrements; dreſs; habit; ornaments.

Array thyſelf in her moſt gorgeous *gear*. *Fairy Queen.*
When he found her bound, ſtript from her *gear*,
And vile tormenters ready ſaw in place,
He broke through. *Fairfax, b.* ii. *ſtan.* 27.
When once her eye
Hath met the virtue of this magick duſt,
I ſhall appear ſome harmleſs villager,
Whom thrift keeps up about his country *gear*. *Milton.*
I fancy every body obſerves me as I walk the ſtreet, and long to be in my old plain *gear* again. *Addiſon's Guardian.*
To ſee ſome radiant nymph appear
In all her glitt'ring birthday *gear*,
You think ſome goddeſs from the ſky
Deſcended, ready cut and dry. *Swift.*

2. The traces by which horſes or oxen draw.

Apollo's ſpite Pallas diſcern'd, and flew to Tydeus' ſon;
His ſcourge reacht, and his horſe made freſh; then took her angry run
At king Eumelus, brake his *gears*. *Chapman's Iliads.*

The frauds he learn'd in his fanatick years
Made him uneasy in his lawful *gears*. *Dryden.*

3. Stuff. *Hanmer.*

If fortune be a woman, she is a good wench for this *gear*. *Shakespeare's Merchant of Venice.*

4. [In *Scotland.*] Goods or riches: as, he has *gear* enough.

Ge'ason. *adj.* [A word which I find only in *Spenser.*] Wonderful.

It to Leeches seemed strange and *geason*. *Hubberd's Tale.*

Geat. *n. s.* [corrupted from *jett.*] The hole through which the metal runs into the mold. *Moxon's Mech. Exer.*

Geck. *n. s.* [geac, a cuckow; *geck*, German, a fool; *gawk*, Scottish.] A bubble easily imposed upon. *Hanmer.*

Why did you suffer Jachimo to taint his noble heart and brain with needless jealousy, and to become the *geek* and scorn o' th' other's villany? *Shakespeare's Cymbeline.*

Why have you suffer'd me to be imprison'd,
And made the most notorious *geek* and gull
That e'er invention plaid on? *Shakesp. Twelfth Night.*

To Geck. *v. a.* [from the noun.] To cheat; to trick.

Gee. A term used by waggoners to their horses when they would have them go faster.

Geese. The plural of *goose.*

Ge'lable. *adj.* [from *gelu*, Latin.] What may be congealed or concreted into a gelly.

Ge'latine. } *adj.* [*gelatus*, Latin.] Formed into a gelly;
Gela'tinous. } viscous; stiff and cohesive.

That pellucid *gelatinous* substance is an excrement cast off from the shoals of fish that inhabit the main. *Woodward.*

You shall always see their eggs laid carefully up in that spermatick *gelatine* matter, in which they are reposited. *Derh.*

To GELD. *v. a.* preter. *gelded* or *gelt*; part. pass. *gelded* or *gelt.* [*gelten*, German.]

1. To castrate; to deprive of the power of generation.

Geld bull-calf and ram lamb as soon as they fall. *Tusser.*

Lord Say hath *gelded* the commonwealth, and made it an eunuch. *Shakesp. Henry VI.*

2. To deprive of any essential part.

He bears his course, and runs me up
With like advantage on the other side,
Gelding th' oppos'd continent as much
As on the other side it takes from you. *Shakesp. Henry IV.*

3. To deprive of any thing immodest, or liable to objection.

They were diligent enough to make sure work, and to *geld* it so clearly in some places that they took away the very manhood of it. *Dryden's Preface to Cleomenes.*

Ge'lder. *n. s.* [from *geld.*] One that performs the act of castration.

Geld later with *gelders*, as many one do,
And look of a dozen to geld away two. *Tuss. Husbandry.*
No sow *gelder* did blow his horn
To geld a cat, but cry'd reform. *Hudibras, p. i. cant. 2.*

Ge'lder-rose. *n. s.* [I suppose brought from *Guelderland.*]

The leaves are like those of the maple-tree: the flowers consist of one leaf, which expands in a circular rose form, and is divided at the top into five parts: these are collected in form of an umbel, the largest of which grow on the outside, and are barren; but those in the middle are fruitful, producing red berries, in each of which is contained one flat heart-shaped seed.

The species are three. If the soil be moist, this plant affords a very agreeable prospect, both in the season when it is in flower, and also in the Autumn, when the fruit is ripe, which generally grows in large clusters, and is of a beautiful colour. *Miller.*

The *gelder-rose* is increased by suckers and cuttings. *Mort.*

Ge'lding. *n. s.* [from *geld.*] Any animal castrated, particularly an horse.

Though naturally there be more males of horses, bulls or rams than females; yet artificially, that is, by making *geldings*, oxen and weathers, there are fewer. *Graunt.*

The lord lieutenant may chuse out one of the best horses, and two of the best *geldings*; for which shall be paid one hundred pounds for the horse, and fifty pounds a-piece for the *geldings*. *Temple.*

GE'LID. *adj.* [*gelidus*, Latin.] Extremely cold.

From the deep ooze and *gelid* cavern rous'd,
They flounce. *Thomson's Spring.*

Geli'dity *n. s.* [from *gelid.*] Extreme cold. *Dict.*

Ge'lidness *n. s.* [from *gelid.*] Extreme cold. *Dict.*

Ge'lly. *n. s.* [*gelatus*, Latin.] Any viscous body; viscidity; glue; gluey substance.

My best blood turn
To an infected *gelly*. *Shakespeare's Winter's Tale.*
The tapers of the gods,
The sun and moon, became like waxen globes,
The shooting stars end all in purple *gellies*,
And chaos is at hand. *Dryden and Lee's Oedipus.*

The white of an egg will coagulate by a moderate heat, and the hardest of animal solids are resolvable again into *gellies*. *Arbuthnot on Aliments.*

Gelt. *n. s.* [from *geld.*] A castrated animal; gelding.

The spayed *gelts* they esteem the most profitable. *Mortimer.*

Gelt. *n. s.* [corrupted for the sake of rhyme from *gilt.*] Tinsel; gilt surface.

I won her with a girdle of *gelt*,
Emboss with bugle about the belt. *Spenser's Pastorals.*

Gelt. The participle passive of *geld.*

Let the others be *gelt* for oxen. *Mortimer's Husbandry.*

GEM. *n. s.* [*gemma*, Latin.]

1. A jewel; a precious stone of whatever kind.

Love his fancy drew;
And so to take the *gem* Urania sought. *Sidney.*
I saw his bleeding rings,
Their precious *gems* new lost, became his guide,
Led him, begg'd for him, sav'd him from despair. *Shakesp.*

It will seem a hard matter to shadow a *gem*, or well pointed diamond, that hath many sides, and to give the lustre where it ought. *Peacham on Drawing.*

Stones of small worth may lie unseen by day;
But night itself does the rich *gem* betray. *Cowley.*

The basis of all *gems* is, when pure, wholly diaphanous, and either crystal or an adamantine matter; but we find the diaphaneity of this matter changed, by means of a fine metallick matter. *Woodward.*

2. The first bud.

From the joints of thy prolifick stem
A swelling knot is raised, call'd a *gem*;
Whence, in short space, itself the cluster shows. *Denham.*
Embolden'd out they come,
And swell the *gems*, and burst the narrow room. *Dryden.*
The orchard loves to wave
With Winter winds, before the *gems* exert
Their feeble heads. *Phillips.*

To Gem. *v. a.* [*gemma*, Latin.] To adorn, as with jewels or buds.

To Gem. *v. n.* [*gemmo*, Latin.] To put forth the first buds.

Last rose, in dance, the stately trees, and spread
Their branches; hung with copious fruit; or *gemm'd*
Their blossoms. *Milton's Paradise Lost, b. vii.*

Geme'lliparous. *adj.* [*gemelli* and *pario*, Latin.] Bearing twins. *Dict.*

To GE'MINATE. *v. a.* [*gemino*, Latin.] To double. *Dict.*

Gemina'tion. *n. s.* [from *geminate.*] Repetition; reduplication.

Be not afraid of them that kill the body: fear him, which, after he hath killed, hath power to cast into hell; yea, I say unto you, a *gemination*, which the present controversy shews not to have been causeless, fear him. *Boyle.*

Ge'miny. *n. s.* [*gemini*, Latin.] Twins; a pair; a brace; a couple.

I have grated upon my good friends for three reprieves for you, and your couch-fellow, Nim; or else you had looked through the grate, like a *geminy* of baboons. *Shakespeare.*

A *geminy* of asses split, would make just four of you. *Congr.*

Ge'minous. *adj.* [*geminus*, Latin.] Double.

Christians have baptized these *geminous* births, and double connascencies, with several names, as conceiving in them a distinction of souls. *Brown's Vulgar Errours, b. iii.*

Ge'mmary. *adj.* [from *gem.*] Pertaining to gems or jewels.

The principle and *gemmary* affection is its translucency: as for irradiancy, which is found in many gems, it is not discoverable in this. *Brown's Vulgar Errours, b. i. c. 2.*

Ge'mmeous. *adj.* [*gemmeus*, Latin.]

1. Tending to gems.

Sometimes we find them in the *gemmeous* matter itself. *Woodw.*

2. Resembling gems.

Gemmo'sity. *n. s.* [from *gem.*] The quality of being a jewel. *Dict.*

Ge'mote *n. s.* The court of the hundred. Obsolete.

Ge'nder. *n. s.* [*genus*, Latin; *gendre*, French.]

1. A kind; a sort.

Our bodies are our gardens, to the which our wills are gardeners; so that if we will supply it with one *gender* of herbs, or distract it with many, the power and corrigible authority of this lies in our will. *Shakespeare's Othello.*

The other motive,
Why to a publick court I might not go,
Is the great love the general *gender* bear me. *Shak. Hamlet.*

2. A sex.

3. [In grammar.] A denomination given to nouns, from their being joined with an adjective in this or that termination. *Clark.*

Cubitus, sometimes cubitum in the neutral *gender*, signifies the lower part of the arm on which we lean. *Arbuthnot.*

Ulysses speaks of Nausicaa, yet immediately changes the words into the masculine *gender*. *Notes on the Odyssey.*

To Ge'nder. *v. a.* [*engendrer*, French.]

1. To beget.

2. To produce; to cause.

Foolish and unlearned questions avoid, knowing that they do *gender* strife. *2 Tim. ii. 23.*

To

To GE'NDER. *v. n.* To copulate; to breed.
A cistern for foul toads
To gender in. *Shakespeare's Othello.*
Thou shalt not let thy cattle *gender* with a diverse kind. *Lev.* xix. 19.

GENEALO'GICAL. *adj.* [from *genealogy.*] Pertaining to descents or families; pertaining to the history of the successions of houses.

GENEA'LOGIST. *n. s.* [γενεαλογέω; *genealogiste*, French.] He who traces descents.

GENEA'LOGY. *n. s.* [γενεὰ and λόγος.] History of the succession of families; enumeration of descent in order of succession; a pedigree.
The ancients ranged chaos into several regions; and in that order successively rising one from another, as if it was a pedigree or *genealogy*. *Burnet's Theory of the Earth.*

GE'NERABLE. *adj.* [from *genero*, Latin.] That may be produced or begotten.

GE'NERAL. *adj.* [*general*, French; *generalis*, Latin.]
1. Comprehending many species or individuals; not special; not particular.
To conclude from particulars to *generals* is a false way of arguing. *Notes to Pope's Odyssey.*
2. Lax in signification; not restrained to any special or particular import.
Where the author speaks more strictly and particularly on any theme, it will explain the more loose and *general* expressions. *Watts's Improvement of the Mind.*
3. Not restrained by narrow or distinctive limitations.
A *general* idea is an idea in the mind, considered there as separated from time and place, and so capable to represent any particular being that is conformable to it. *Locke.*
4. Relating to a whole class or body of men, or a whole kind of any being.
They, because some have been admitted without trial, make that fault *general* which is particular. *Whitgifte.*
5. Publick; comprising the whole.
Nor would we deign him burial of his men,
'Till he disburs'd, at Saint Colmeskill isle,
Ten thousand dollars to our *gen'ral* use. *Shakesp. Macbeth.*
Nor fail'd they to express how much they prais'd,
That for the *general* safety he despis'd
His own. *Milton's Paradise Lost, b.* ii.
6. Not directed to any single object.
If the same thing be peculiarly evil, that *general* aversion will be turned into a particular hatred against it. *Spratt.*
7. Extensive, though not universal.
8. Common; usual.
I've been bold,
For that I knew it the most *general* way. *Shakesp. Timon.*
9. *General* is appended to several offices: as, *Attorney General, Solicitor General, Vicar General.*

GE'NERAL. *n. s.*
1. The whole; the totality; the main, without insisting on particulars.
That which makes an action fit to be commanded or forbidden, can be nothing else, in *general*, but its tendency to promote or hinder the attainment of some end. *Norris.*
In particulars our knowledge begins, and so spreads itself by degrees to *generals*. *Locke.*
I have considered Milton's Paradise Lost in the fable, the characters, the sentiments, and the language; and have shewn that he excels, in *general*, under each of these heads. *Addison.*
2. The publick; the interest of the whole. Not in use.
Neither my place, nor aught I heard of business,
Hath raised me from my bed; nor doth the *general*
Take hold on me; for my particular grief
Ingluts and swallows other sorrows. *Shakespeare's Othello.*
3. The vulgar. Not in use.
The play, I remember, pleased not the million; 'twas caviare to the *general*: but it was, as I received it, and others, whose judgment in such matters cried in the top of mine, an excellent play. *Shakespeare's Hamlet.*
4. [*General*, Fr.] One that has the command over an army.
A *general* is one that hath power to command an army. *Locke.*
The *generals* on the enemy's side are inferior to several that once commanded the French armies. *Addison on the War.*
The war's whole art each private soldier knows,
And with a *gen'ral's* love of conquest glows. *Addison.*

GENERALI'SSIMO. *n. s.* [*generalissime*, French, from *general.*] The supreme commander. It is often rather a title of honour than office.
Commission of *generalissimo* was likewise given to the prince. *Clarendon, b.* viii.
Pompey had deserved the name of great; and Alexander, of the same cognomination, was *generalissimo* of Greece. *Brown.*

GENERA'LITY. *n. s.* [*generalité*, French, from *general.*]
1. The state of being general; the quality of including species or particulars.
Because the curiosity of man's wit doth with peril wade farther in the search of things than were convenient, the same is thereby restrained unto such *generalities* as, every where offering themselves, are apparent to men of the weakest conceit. *Hooker, b.* i. *s.* 6.
These certificates do only in the *generality* mention the parties contumacies and disobedience. *Ayliffe's Parergon.*
2. The main body; the bulk; the common mass.
There is a great necessity, though not apparent, as not extending to the *generality*, but resting upon private heads. *Raleigh's Essays.*
By his own principles he excludes from salvation the *generality* of his own church; that is, all that do not believe upon his grounds. *Tillotson, Sermon* 1.
The *generality* of the English have such a favourable opinion of treason, nothing can cure them. *Addison's Freeholder.*
They publish their ill-natured discoveries with a secret pride, and applaud themselves for the singularity of their judgment, which has found a flaw in what the *generality* of mankind admires. *Addison's Spectator.*
Such treatment has its effect among the *generality* of those whose hands it falls into. *Addison's Spectator.*
The wisest were distracted with doubts, while the *generality* wandered without any ruler. *Rogers, Sermon* 3.

GE'NERALLY. *adv.* [from *general.*]
1. In general; without specification or exception.
I am not a woman to be touch'd with so many giddy fancies as he hath *generally* taxed their whole sex withal. *Shakespeare.*
Generally we would not have those that read this work of Sylva Sylvarum, account it strange that we have set down particulars untried. *Bacon's Natural History.*
2. Extensively, though not universally.
3. Commonly; frequently.
4. In the main; without minute detail; in the whole taken together.
Generally speaking, they live very quietly. *Addis. Guardian.*
Generally speaking, they have been gaining ever since, though with frequent interruptions. *Swift.*

GE'NERALNESS. *n. s.* [from *general.*] Wide extent, though short of universality; frequency; commonness.
They had with a general consent, rather springing by the *generalness* of the cause than of any artificial practice, set themselves in arms. *Sidney.*

GE'NERALTY. *n. s.* [from *general.*] The whole; the totality.
The municipal laws of this kingdom are of a vast extent, and include in their *generalty* all those several laws which are allowed as the rule of justice and judicial proceedings. *Hale.*

GE'NERANT. *n. s.* [*generans*, Latin.] The begetting or productive power.
Some believe that the soul is made by God, some by angels, and some by the *generant*: whether it be immediately created or traduced hath been the great ball of contention to the later ages. *Glanv. Sceps. c.* 4.
In such pretended generations the *generant* or active principle is supposed to be the sun, which, being an inanimate body, cannot act otherwise than by his heat. *Ray on the Creat.*

To GE'NERATE. *v. a.* [*genero*, Latin.]
1. To beget; to propagate.
Those creatures which being wild *generate* seldom, being tame, *generate* often. *Bacon's Natural History.*
2. To cause; to produce.
God created the great whales, and each
Soul living, each that crept, which plenteously
The waters *generated* by their kinds. *Milton's Paradise Lost.*
Or find some other way to *generate*
Mankind. *Milton's Paradise Lost, b.* x. *l.* 894.
Sounds are *generated* where there is no air at all. *Bacon.*
Whatever *generates* a quantity of good chyle, must likewise *generate* milk. *Arbuthnot on Aliments.*

GENERA'TION. *n. s.* [*generation*, French, from *generate.*]
1. The act of begetting or producing.
Seals make excellent impressions; and so it may be thought of sounds in their first *generation*: but then the dilation of them, without any new sealing, shews they cannot be impressions *Bacon's Natural History.*
He longer will delay, to hear thee tell
His *generation*, and the rising birth
Of nature from the unapparent deep. *Milton's Paradise Lost.*
If we deduce the several races of mankind in the several parts of the world from *generation*, we must imagine the first numbers of them, who in any place agree upon any civil constitutions, to assemble as so many heads of families whom they represent. *Temple.*
2. A family; a race.
Y'are a dog.
——Thy mother's of my *generation*: what's she, if I be a dog? *Shakespeare's Timon of Athens.*
3. Progeny; offspring.
The barb'rous Scythian,
Or he that makes his *generation* messes,
To gorge his appetite, shall to my bosom
Be as well neighbour'd. *Shakespeare's King Lear.*

4. A ſingle ſucceſſion; one gradation in the ſcale of genealogical deſcent.

This *generation* ſhall not paſs 'till all theſe things be fulfilled. *Mat.* xxiv. 34.

In the fourth *generation* they ſhall come hither again. *Gen.*

A marvellous number were excited to the conqueſt of Paleſtine, which with ſingular virtue they performed, and held that kingdom ſome few *generations*. *Raleigh's Eſſays.*

5. An age.

By ſome of the ancients a *generation* was fixed at an hundred years; by others at an hundred and ten; by others at thirty-three, thirty, thirty-five, and twenty: but it is remarked, that the continuance of *generations* is ſo much longer as they come nearer to the more ancient times. *Calmet.*

Every where throughout all *generations* and ages of the Chriſtian world, no church ever perceived the word of God to be againſt it. *Hooker.*

GE'NERATIVE. *adj.* [*generatif*, French, from *genero*, Latin.]

1. Having the power of propagation.

He gave to all, that have life, a power *generative*, thereby to continue their ſpecies and kinds. *Raleigh's Hiſtory.*

In grains and kernels the greateſt part is but the nutriment of that *generative* particle, ſo diſproportionable unto it. *Brown.*

2. Prolifick; having the power of production; fruitful.

If there hath been ſuch a gradual diminution of the *generative* faculty upon the earth, why was there not the like decay in the production of vegetables? *Bentley's Sermons.*

GENERA'TOR. *n.ſ.* [from *genero*, Latin.] The power which begets, cauſes, or produces.

Imagination aſſimilates the idea of the *generator* into the reality in the thing engendered. *Brown's Vulgar Errours.*

GENE'RICAL. } *adj.* [*generique*, French, from *genus*, Latin.]
GENE'RICK. } That which comprehends the genus, or diſtinguiſhes from another genus, but does not diſtinguiſh the ſpecies.

The word conſumption being applicable to a proper, and improper to a true and baſtard conſumption, requires a *generical* deſcription quadrate to both. *Harvey on Conſumptions.*

Though wine differs from other liquids, in that it is the juice of a certain fruit; yet this is but a general or *generick* difference; for it does not diſtinguiſh wine from cyder or perry: the ſpecifick difference of wine, therefore, is its preſſure from the grape. *Watts's Logick.*

GENE'RICALLY. *adv.* [from *generick.*] With regard to the genus, though not the ſpecies.

Theſe have all the eſſential characters of ſea-ſhells, and ſhew that they are of the very ſame ſpecifick gravity with thoſe to which they are ſo *generically* allied. *Woodward.*

GENERO'SITY. *n.ſ.* [*generoſité*, French; *generoſitas*, Latin.] The quality of being generous; magnanimity; liberality.

Can he be better principled in the grounds of true virtue and *generoſity* than his young tutor is? *Locke on Education.*

It would not have been your *generoſity*, to have paſſed by ſuch a fault as this. *Locke.*

GE'NEROUS. *adj.* [*generoſus*, Latin; *genereux*, French.]

1. Not of mean birth; of good extraction.

2. Noble of mind; magnanimous; open of heart.

His *gen'rous* ſpouſe, Theano, heav'nly fair,
Nurs'd the young ſtranger. *Pope.*

3. Liberal; munificent.

4. Strong; vigorous.

Having in a digeſtive furnace drawn off the ardent ſpirit from ſome good ſack, the phlegm, even in this *generous* wine, was copious. *Boyle.*

GE'NEROUSLY. *adv.* [from *generous.*]

1. Not meanly with regard to birth.

2. Magnanimouſly; nobly.

When all the gods our ruin have foretold,
Yet *generouſly* he does his arms withold. *Dryd. Ind. Emp.*

3. Liberally; munificently.

GEN'EROUSNESS. *n.ſ.* [from *generous.*] The quality of being generous.

Is it poſſible to conceive that the overflowing *generouſneſs* of the Divine Nature would create immortal beings with mean or envious principles? *Collier on Kindneſs.*

GE'NESIS. *n.ſ.* [γένεσις; *geneſe*, French.] Generation; the firſt book of *Moſes*, which treats of the production of the world.

GE'NET. *n.ſ.* [French. The word originally ſignified a horſeman, and perhaps a gentleman or knight.] A ſmall ſized well proportioned Spaniſh horſe.

You'll have your nephews neigh to you; you'll have courſers for couſins, and *genets* for germanes. *Shak. Othello.*

It is no more likely that frogs ſhould be engendered in the clouds than Spaniſh *genets* be begotten by the wind. *Ray.*

He ſhews his ſtatue too, where, plac'd on high,
The *genet* underneath him ſeems to fly. *Dryd. Juven. Sat.*

GENETHLI'ACAL. *adj.* [γενεθλιακὸς.] Pertaining to nativities as calculated by aſtronomers; ſhewing the configurations of the ſtars at any birth.

The night immediately before he was ſlighting the art of thoſe fooliſh aſtrologers, and *genethliacal* ephemeriſts, that uſe to pry into the horoſcope of nativities. *Howel's Vocal Foreſt.*

GENETHLI'ACKS. *n.ſ.* [from γενέθλη.] The ſcience of calculating nativities, or predicting the future events of life from the ſtars predominant at the birth.

GENETHLIA'TICK. *n.ſ.* [γενέθλη.] He who calculates nativities.

The truth of aſtrological predictions is not to be referred to the conſtellations: the *genethliaticks* conjecture by the diſpoſition, temper, and complexion of the perſon. *Drummond.*

GENE'VA. *n.ſ.* [A corruption of *genevre*, French, a juniperberry.]

We uſed to keep a diſtilled ſpirituous water of juniper in the ſhops; but the making of it became the buſineſs of the diſtiller, who ſold it under the name of *geneva*. At preſent only a better kind is diſtilled from the juniper-berry: what is commonly ſold is made with no better an ingredient than oil of turpentine, put into the ſtill, with a little common ſalt, and the coarſeſt ſpirit they have, which is drawn off much below proof ſtrength, and is conſequently a liquor that one would wonder any people could accuſtom themſelves to drink with pleaſure. *Hill's Mat. Medica.*

GE'NIAL. *adj.* [*genialis*, Latin.]

1. That which contributes to propagation.

Higher of the *genial* bed by far,
And with myſterious reverence I deem. *Milt. Parad. Loſt.*

Creator Venus, *genial* pow'r of love,
The bliſs of men below and gods above! *Dryden's Fables.*

2. That gives chearfulneſs or ſupports life.

Nor th' other light of life continue long,
But yields to double darkneſs nigh at hand;
So much I feel my *genial* ſpirits droop. *Milton's Agoniſtes.*

3. Natural; native.

It chiefly proceedeth from natural incapacity, and *genial* indiſpoſition. *Brown's Vulgar Errours, b.* i.

GE'NIALLY. *adv.* [from *genial.*]

1. By genius; naturally.

Some men are *genially* diſpoſed to ſome opinions, and naturally as averſe to others. *Glanv. Scepſ. c.* 15.

2. Gayly; chearfully.

GENICULA'TED. *adj.* [*geniculatus*, Latin.] Knotted; jointed.

A piece of ſome *geniculated* plant, ſeeming to be part of a ſugar-cane. *Woodward on Foſſils.*

GENICULA'TION. *n.ſ.* [*geniculatio*, Latin.] Knottineſs; the quality in plants of having knots or joints.

GE'NIO. *n.ſ.* [*genio*, Italian; *genius*, Latin.] A man of a particular turn of mind.

Some *genio's* are not capable of pure affection; and a man is born with talents for it as much as for poetry, or any other ſcience. *Tatler*, N°. 53.

GE'NITALS. *n.ſ.* [*genitalis*, Lat.] Parts belonging to generation.

Ham is conceived to be Jupiter, who was the youngeſt ſon, who is ſaid to have cut off the *genitals* of his father. *Brown.*

GE'NITING. *n.ſ.* [A corruption of *Janeton*, French, ſignifying *Jane* or *Janet*, having been ſo called in honour of ſome lady of that name; and the Scottiſh dialect calls them *Janet* apples, which is the ſame with *Janeton*: otherwiſe ſuppoſed to be corrupted from *Juneting*.] An early apple gathered in June.

In July come early pears and plumbs in fruit, *genitings* and codlins. *Bacon, Eſſay* 47.

GE'NITIVE. *adj.* [*genitivus*, Latin.] In grammar, the name of a caſe, which, among other relations, ſignifies one begotten, as, the father *of a ſon*; or one begetting, as ſon *of a father*.

GE'NIUS. *n.ſ.* [Latin; *genie*, French.]

1. The protecting or ruling power of men, places, or things.

There is none but he
Whoſe being I do fear: and, under him,
My *genius* is rebuk'd; as it is ſaid
Antony's was by Cæſar. *Shakeſpeare's Macbeth.*

The *genius* and the mortal inſtruments
Are then in council; and the ſtate of man,
Like to a little kingdom, ſuffers then. *Shakeſ. Jul. Cæſar.*

And as I awake, ſweet muſick breathe,
Sent by ſome ſpirit to mortals good,
Or th' unſeen *genius* of the wood. *Milton.*

And the tame demon that ſhould guard my throne,
Shrinks at a *genius* greater than his own. *Dryden.*

To your glad *genius* ſacrifice this day;
Let common meats reſpectfully give way. *Dryden*

2. A man endowed with ſuperiour faculties.

There is no little writer of Pindarick who is not mentioned as a prodigious *genius*. *Addiſon.*

3. Mental power or faculties.

The ſtate and order does proclaim
The *genius* of that royal dame. *Waller.*

4. Diſpoſition of nature by which any one is qualified for ſome peculiar employment.

A happy *genius* is the gift of nature. *Dryden's Dufreſnoy.*

Your majeſty's ſagacity, and happy *genius* for natural hiſtory, is a better preparation for enquiries of this kind than all the dead learning of the ſchools. *Burnet's Theory, Preface.*

One ſcience only will one *genius* fit;
So vaſt is art, ſo narrow human wit. *Pope on Criticiſm.*

The Romans, though they had no great *genius* for trade, yet were not entirely neglectful of it. *Arbuthnot on Coins.*

5. Nature;

5. Nature; disposition.

Studious to please the *genius* of the times,
With periods, points and tropes he slurs his crimes. *Dryd.*

Another *genius* and disposition improper for philosophical contemplations is not so much from the narrowness of their spirit and understanding, as because they will not take time to extend them. *Burnet's Theory of the Earth, Preface.*

He tames the *genius* of the stubborn plain. *Pope.*

GENT. *adj.* [*gent*, old French.] Elegant; soft; gentle; polite. A word now disused.

Vespasian, with great spoil and rage,
Forewasted all: 'till Genuissa *gent*
Persuaded him to cease. *Fairy Queen, b.* ii. *cant.* 10.

She that was noble, wise, as fair and *gent*,
Cast how she might their harmless lives preserve. *Fairfax.*

GENTE'EL. *adj.* [*gentil*, French.]

1. Polite; elegant in behaviour; civil.

He had a *genteeler* manner of binding the chains of this kingdom than most of his predecessors. *Swift to Gay.*

Their poets have no notion of *genteel* comedy, and fall into the most filthy double meanings when they have a mind to make their audience merry. *Addison's Remarks on Italy.*

2. Graceful in mien.

GENTE'ELLY. *adv.* [from *genteel*.]

1. Elegantly; politely.

Those that would be *genteelly* learned, need not purchase it at the dear rate of being atheists. *Glanv. Sceps. Preface.*

After a long fatigue of eating and drinking, and babbling, he concludes the great work of dining *genteelly*. *South.*

2. Gracefully; handsomely.

GENTE'ELNESS. *n. s.* [from *genteel*.]

1. Elegance; gracefulness; politeness.

He had a genius full of *genteelness* and spirit, having nothing that was ungraceful in his postures and dresses. *Dryd. Dufresn.*

2. Qualities befitting a man of rank.

GE'NTIAN. *n. s.* [*gentiane*, French; *gentiana*, Latin.] Felwort or baldmony.

The leaves grow by pairs opposite to each other: the flower consists of one leaf, shaped like a cup, being cut into four, five, or more segments: it is succeeded by a membranous oval shaped fruit, ending in a sharp point, opening lengthwise into two parts, and containing many flat roundish seeds, bordered with a leafy rim. *Miller.*

The root of the *gentian* is large and long, of a tolerably firm texture, and remarkably tough: it has a faintish and somewhat disagreeable smell, and an extremely bitter taste. It is brought cheap from Germany. *Hill's Mat. Medica.*

If it be fistulous, and the orifice small, dilate it with *gentian* roots. *Wiseman's Surgery.*

GENTIANE'LLA. *n. s.* A kind of blue colour.

GE'NTILE. *n. s.* [*gentilis*, Latin.]

1. One of an uncovenanted nation; one who knows not the true God.

Tribulation and anguish upon every soul that doeth evil, of the Jew first, and also of the *gentile*. *Rom.* ii. 2.

Gentiles or infidels, in those actions, upon both the spiritual and temporal good, have been in one pursuit conjoined. *Bacon.*

2. A person of rank. Obsolete.

Fine Basil desireth it may be her lot
To grow, as a gilliflower, trim in a pot;
That ladies and *gentiles*, for whom ye do serve,
May help him as needeth, poor life to preserve. *Tusser.*

GENTILE'SSE. *n. s.* [French.] Complaisance; civility.

She with her wedding-cloaths undresses
Her complaisance and *gentilesses*. *Hudibras, p.* iii. *cant.* 1.

GE'NTILISM. *n. s.* [*gentilisme*, French, from *gentile*.] Heathenism; paganism.

If invocation of saints had been introduced in the apostolical times, it would have looked like the introducing of *gentilism* again. *Stillingfleet's Def. of Disc. on Rom. Idol.*

GENTILI'TIOUS. *adj.* [*gentilitius*, Latin.]

1. Endemial; peculiar to a nation.

That an unsavory odour is *gentilitious*, or national unto the Jews, reason or sense will not induce. *Brown's Vulgar Err.*

2. Hereditary; entailed on a family.

The common cause of this distemper is a particular and perhaps a *gentilitious* disposition of body. *Arbuthnot on Aliment.*

GENTI'LITY. *n. s.* [*gentilité*, French, from *gentil*, French; *gentilis*, Latin.]

1. Good extraction; dignity of birth.
2. Elegance of behaviour; gracefulness of mien; nicety of taste.
3. Gentry; the class of persons well born.

Gavelkind must needs, in the end, make a poor *gentility*. *Davies on Ireland.*

4. Paganism; heathenism.

When people began to espy the falshood of oracles, whereupon all *gentility* was built, their hearts were utterly averted from it. *Hooker, b.* v. *s.* 2.

GE'NTLE. *adj.* [*gentilis*, Latin.]

1. Well born; well descended; ancient, though not noble.

They entering and killing all of the *gentle* and rich faction, for honesty sake broke open all prisons. *Sidney.*

These are the studies wherein our noble and *gentle* youth ought to bestow their time. *Milton on Education.*

Of *gentle* blood, part shed in honour's cause,
Each parent sprung. *Pope.*

2. Soft; bland; mild; tame; meek; peaceable.

I am one of those *gentle* ones that will use the devil himself with curtesy. *Shakespeare's Twelfth Night.*

Her voice was ever soft,
Gentle and low; an excellent thing in woman. *Shakespeare.*

As *gentle*, and as jocund, as to jest,
Go I to fight. *Shakespeare's Richard* II.

A virtuous and a good man, reverend in conversation, and *gentle* in condition. 2 *Mac.* xv. 12.

The *gentlest* heart on earth is prov'd unkind. *Fairfax.*

Your change was wise; for, had she been deny'd,
A swift revenge had follow'd from her pride:
You from my *gentle* nature had no fears;
All my revenge is only in my tears. *Dryden's Ind. Emp.*

He had such a *gentle* method of reproving their faults, that they were not so much afraid as ashamed to repeat them. *Atter.*

3. Soothing; pacifick.

And though this sense first *gentle* musick found,
Her proper object is the speech of men. *Davies.*

GE'NTLE. *n. s.*

1. A gentleman; a man of birth. Now out of use.

Gentles, do not reprehend;
If you pardon, we will mend. *Shakespeare.*

Where is my lovely bride?
How does my father? *Gentles*, methinks you frown. *Shakes.*

2. A particular kind of worm.

He will in the three hot months bite at a flagworm, or at a green *gentle*. *Walton's Angler.*

To GE'NTLE. *v. a.* To make gentle; to raise from the vulgar. Obsolete.

He to-day that sheds his blood with me,
Shall be my brother; be he never so vile,
This day shall *gentle* his condition. *Shakespeare's Henry* V.

GE'NTLEFOLK. *n. s.* [*gentle* and *folk*.] Persons distinguished by their birth from the vulgar.

The queen's kindred are made *gentlefolk*. *Shakes. Rich.* III.

Gentlefolks will not care for the remainder of a bottle of wine; therefore always set a fresh one before them after dinner. *Swift's Directions to the Butler.*

GE'NTLEMAN. *n. s.* [*gentilhomme*, French; *gentilhuomo*, Ital. that is, *homo gentilis*, a man of ancestry. All other derivations seem to be whimsical.]

1. A man of birth; a man of extraction, though not noble.

A civil war was within the bowels of that state, between the *gentlemen* and the peasants. *Sidney.*

I freely told you, all the wealth I had
Ran in my veins; I was a *gentleman*. *Shak. Merch. of Venice.*

He hither came a private *gentleman*,
But young and brave, and of a family
Ancient and noble. *Otway's Orphan.*

You say a long descended race
Makes *gentlemen*, and that your high degree
Is much disparag'd to be match'd with me. *Dryden.*

2. A man raised above the vulgar by his character or post.

Inquire me out some mean-born *gentleman*,
Whom I will marry strait to Clarence' daughter. *Shakesp.*

3. A term of complaisance.

The same *gentlemen* who have fixed this piece of morality on the three naked sisters dancing hand in hand, would have found out as good a one had there been four of them sitting at a distance, and covered from head to foot. *Addison.*

4. The servant that waits about the person of a man of rank.

Sir Thomas More, the Sunday after he gave up his chancellorship, came to his wife's pew, and used the usual words of his *gentleman* usher, Madam, my lord is gone. *Camden.*

Let be call'd before us
That *gentleman* of Buckingham's in person. *Shak. H.* VIII.

5. It is used of any man however high.

The earl of Hereford was reputed then
In England the most valiant *gentleman*. *Shakes. Henry* IV.

The king is a noble *gentleman*, and my familiar. *Shakesp.*

GENTLEMANLI'KE. } *adj.* [*gentleman* and *like*.] Becoming a
GE'NTLEMANLY. } man of birth.

He holdeth himself a gentleman, and scorneth to work, which, he saith, is the life of a peasant or churl; but enureth himself to his weapon, and to the *gentlemanly* trade of stealing. *Spenser on Ireland.*

Pyramus is a sweet-fac'd man; a proper man as one shall see in a Summer's day; a most lovely *gentlemanlike* man. *Shak.*

You have train'd me up like a peasant, hiding from me all *gentlemanlike* qualities. *Shakespeare's As you like it.*

A gentleman uses the words of gallantry, and *gentlemanlike* very often in his petition. *Spectator*, N°. 629.

Two clergymen stood candidates for a freeschool, where a gentleman, who happened to have understanding, procured the place for him who was the better scholar and more *gentlemanly* person of the two. *Swift.*

GE'NTLENESS. *n. s.* [from *gentle*.]

1. Dignity

1. Dignity of birth; goodneſs of extraction.
2. Softneſs of manners; ſweetneſs of diſpoſition; meekneſs; tenderneſs.

My lord Sebaſtian,
The truth, you ſpeak, doth lack ſome *gentleneſs*. *Shakeſp.*

Still ſhe retains
Her maiden *gentleneſs*, and oft at eve
Viſits the herds. *Milton.*

The perpetual *gentleneſs* and inherent goodneſs of the Ormond family. *Dryden's Fables, Dedication.*

Changes are brought about ſilently and inſenſibly, with all imaginable benignity and *gentleneſs*. *Woodward's Nat. Hiſt.*

Maſters muſt correct their ſervants with *gentleneſs*, prudence, and mercy. *Rogers.*

Women ought not to think *gentleneſs* of heart deſpicable in a man. *Clariſſa.*

3. Kindneſs; benevolence. Obſolete.

The *gentleneſs* of all the gods go with thee. *Shakeſpeare.*

GE'NTLESHIP. *n. ſ.* [from *gentle.*] Carriage of a gentleman. Obſolete.

Some in France, which will needs be gentlemen, have more *gentleſhip* in their hat than in their head. *Aſcham's Schoolmaſter.*

GE'NTLEWOMAN. *n. ſ.* [*gentle* and *woman.* See GENTLEMAN.]

1. A woman of birth above the vulgar; a woman well deſcended.

The *gentlewomen* of Rome did not ſuffer their infants to be ſo long ſwathed as poorer people. *Abbot's Deſcr. of the World.*

Doth this ſir Protheus
Often reſort unto this *gentlewoman?* *Shakeſpeare.*

Gentlewomen may do themſelves much good by kneeling upon a cuſhion, and weeding. *Bacon's Natural Hiſtory.*

2. A woman who waits about the perſon of one of high rank.

The late queen's *gentlewoman*, a knight's daughter,
To be her miſtreſs' miſtreſs! *Shakeſp. Henry VIII.*

Her *gentlewomen*, like the nereids,
So many mermaids, tended her i' th' eyes,
And made their bends adorings. *Shakeſp. Ant. and Cleopat.*

3. A word of civility or irony.

Now, *gentlewoman*, you are confeſſing your enormities; I know it by that hypocritical down-caſt look. *Dryden.*

GE'NTLY. *adv.* [from *gentle.*]

1. Softly; meekly; tenderly; inoffenſively; kindly.

My miſtreſs *gently* chides the fault I made. *Dryden.*

The miſchiefs that come by inadvertency, or ignorance, are but very *gently* to be taken notice of. *Locke.*

2. Softly; without violence.

Fortune's blows,
When moſt ſtruck home, being *gently* warded, craves
A noble cunning. *Shakeſpeare's Coriolanus.*

In the ſame iſland a ſort of great bat, as men lie aſleep with their legs naked, will ſuck their blood at a wound ſo *gently* made as not to awake them. *Grew's Muſæum.*

GE'NTRY. *n. ſ.* [*gentlery, gentry,* from *gentle.*]

1. Birth; condition.

You are certainly a gentleman,
Clerk-like experienc'd, which no leſs adorns
Our *gentry* than our parents' noble name,
In whoſe ſucceſs we are gentle. *Shakeſp. Winter's Tale.*

2. Claſs of people above the vulgar; thoſe between the vulgar and the nobility.

They ſlaughtered many of the *gentry*, for whom no ſex or age could be accepted for excuſe. *Sidney.*

Let ſtates, that aim at greatneſs, take heed how their nobility and *gentry* multiply too faſt. *Bacon's Ornam. Ration.*

How chearfully the hawkers cry
A ſatire, and the *gentry* buy. *Swift.*

2. A term of civility real or ironical.

The many-colour'd *gentry* there above,
By turns are rul'd by tumult and by love. *Prior.*

3. Civility; complaiſance. Obſolete.

Shew us ſo much *gentry* and good-will,
As to extend your time with us a-while. *Shakeſp. Hamlet.*

GE'NUFLECTION. *n. ſ.* [*genuflexion*, French; *genu* and *flecto*, Latin.] The act of bending the knee; adoration expreſſed by bending the knee.

Here they make uſe of all the rites of adoration, *genuflections*, wax-candles, incenſe, oblations, prayers only excepted. *Stillingfleet's Defence of Diſc. on Rom. Idol.*

GE'NUINE. *adj.* [*genuinus*, Latin.] Not ſpurious; not counterfeit; real; natural; true.

Experiments were at one time tried with *genuine* materials, and at another time with ſophiſticated ones. *Boyle.*

The belief and remembrance, and love and fear of God, have ſo great influence to make men religious, that where any of theſe is, the reſt, together with the true and *genuine* effects of them, are ſuppoſed to be. *Tillotſon's Sermons.*

A ſudden darkneſs covers all;
True *genuine* night: night added to the groves:
The fogs are blown full in the face of heaven. *Dryd. Oedip.*

GENU'INELY. *adv.* [from *genuine.*] Without adulteration; without foreign admixtures; naturally.

There is another agent able to analize compound bodies leſs violently, more *genuinely*, and more univerſally than the fire. *Boyle.*

GENU'INENESS. *n. ſ.* [from *genuine.*] Freedom from any thing counterfeit; freedom from adulteration; purity; natural ſtate.

It is not eſſential to the *genuineneſs* of colours to be durable. *Boyle.*

GE'NUS. *n. ſ.* [Latin.] In ſcience, a claſs of being, comprehending under it many ſpecies: as *quadruped* is a *genus* comprehending under it almoſt all terreſtrial beaſts.

A general idea is called by the ſchools *genus*, and it is one common nature agreeing to ſeveral other common natures: ſo animal is a *genus*, becauſe it agrees to horſe, lion, whale, and butterfly. *Watts's Logick.*

If minerals are not convertible into another ſpecies, though of the ſame *genus*, much leſs can they be ſurmiſed reducible into a ſpecies of another *genus.* *Harvey on Conſumptions.*

GE'OCENTRICK. *adj.* [γῆ and κέντρον; *geocentrique*, French.] Applied to a planet or orb having the earth for its centre, or the ſame centre with the earth. *Harris.*

GE'ODÆSIA. *n. ſ.* [γεωδαισία; *geodeſie*, French.] That part of geometry which contains the doctrine or art of meaſuring ſurfaces, and finding the contents of all plane figures. *Harris.*

GE'ODÆTICAL. *adj.* [from *geodæſia.*] Relating to the art of meaſuring ſurfaces; comprehending or ſhowing the art of meaſuring land.

GE'OGRAPHER. *n. ſ.* [γῆ and γράφω; *geographe*, French.] One who deſcribes the earth according to the poſition of its different parts.

A greater part of the earth hath ever been peopled than hath been known or deſcribed by *geographers*. *Brown.*

The bay of Naples is called the Crater by the old *geographers*. *Addiſon.*

From ſea to ſea, from realm to realm I rove,
And grow a meer *geographer* by love. *Tickell.*

GEOGRA'PHICAL. *adj.* [*geographique*, French, from *geography.*] Relating to geography; belonging to geography.

GEOGRA'PHICALLY. *adv.* [from *geographical.*] In a geographical manner; according to the rules of geography.

Minerva lets Ulyſſes into the knowledge of his country: ſhe *geographically* deſcribes it to him. *Broome on the Odyſſey.*

GEO'GRAPHY. *n. ſ.* [γῆ and γράφω; *geographie*, Fr.] *Geography* in a ſtrict ſenſe, ſignifies the knowledge of the circles of the earthly globe, and the ſituation of the various parts of the earth. When it is taken in a little larger ſenſe, it includes the knowledge of the ſeas alſo; and in the largeſt ſenſe of all, it extends to the various cuſtoms, habits, and governments of nations. *Watts.*

Olympus is extolled by the Greeks as attaining unto heaven; but *geography* makes ſlight account hereof, when they diſcourſe of Andes or Teneriff. *Brown's Vulgar Errours, b.* vi.

According to ancient fables the Argonauts ſailed up the Danube, and from thence paſſed into the Adriatick, carrying their ſhips upon their ſhoulders: a mark of great ignorance in *geography*. *Arbuthnot on Coins.*

GEO'LOGY. *n. ſ.* [γῆ and λόγος] The doctrine of the earth; the knowledge of the ſtate and nature of the earth.

GE'OMANCER. *n. ſ.* [γῆ and μάντις.] A fortuneteller; a caſter of figures; a cheat who pretends to foretell futurity by other means than the aſtrologer.

Fortunetellers, jugglers, *geomancers*, and the incantatory impoſtors, though commonly men of inferior rank, daily delude the vulgar. *Brown's Vulgar Errours, b.* i.

GE'OMANCY. *n. ſ.* [γῆ and μαντία; *geomance*, French.] The act of caſting figures; the act of foretelling by figures what ſhall happen.

According to ſome perſons there are four kinds of divination; hydromancy, pyromancy, aeromancy, and *geomancy*. *Ayliffe's Parergon.*

GEOMA'NTICK. *adj.* [from *geomancy.*] Pertaining to the act of caſting figures.

Two *geomantick* figures were diſplay'd
Above his head, a warrior and a maid;
One when direct, and one when retrograde. *Dryden.*

GE'OMETER. *n. ſ.* [γεωμέτρης; *geometre*, French.] One ſkilled in geometry; a geometrician.

He became one of the chief *geometers* of his age. *Watts.*

GE'OMETRAL. *adj.* [*geometral*, French, from *geometry.*] Pertaining to geometry. *Dict.*

GE'OMETRICAL. / GE'OMETRICK. } *adj.* [γεωμετρικὸς; *geometrique*, French, from *geometry.*]

1. Pertaining to geometry.

A *geometrical* ſcheme is let in by the eyes, but the demonſtration is diſcerned by reaſon. *More's Antid against Atheiſm.*

This mathematical diſcipline, by the help of *geometrical* principles, doth teach to contrive ſeveral weights and powers unto motion or reſt. *Wilkins's Math. Magick.*

2. Preſcribed or laid down by geometry.

Muſt men take the meaſure of God juſt by the ſame *geometrical* proportions that he did, that gather'd the height and bigneſs of Hercules by his foot? *Stillingfleet*

Does

Does not this wise philosopher assert,
That the vast orb, which casts so fair his beams,
Is such, or not much bigger than he seems?
That the dimensions of his glorious face
Two *geometrick* feet do scarce surpass? *Blackmore's Creation.*

3. Disposed according to geometry.

Geometrick jasper seemeth of affinity with the *lapis sanguinalis* described by Boetius; but it is certainly one sort of *lapis cruciformis.* *Grew's Musæum.*

GEOME'TRICALLY. *adv.* [from *geometrical.*] According to the laws of geometry.

'Tis possible *geometrically* to contrive such an artificial motion as shall be of greater swiftness than the revolutions of the heavens. *Wilkins's Math. Magick.*

All the bones, muscles, and vessels of the body are contrived most *geometrically*, according to the strictest rules of mechanicks. *Ray on the Creation.*

GEOMETRI'CIAN. *n. s.* [γεωμέτρης.] One skilled in geometry; a geometer.

Although there be a certain truth therein, *geometricians* would not receive satisfaction without demonstration thereof. *Brown's Vulgar Errours, b.* i.

How easily does an expert *geometrician*, with one glance of his eye, take in a complicated diagram, made up of many lines and circles! *Watts's Improvement of the Mind.*

To GEO'METRIZE. *v. n.* [γεωμετρέω.] To act according to the laws of geometry.

We obtained good store of crystals, whose figures were differing enough, though prettily shaped, as if nature had at once affected variety in their figuration, and yet confined herself to *geometrize.* *Boyle.*

GEO'METRY. *n. s.* [γεωμετρία; *geometrie*, French.] Originally signifies the art of measuring the earth, or any distances or dimensions on or within it: but it is now used for the science of quantity, extension, or magnitude abstractedly considered, without any regard to matter.

Geometry very probably had its first rise in Egypt, where the Nile annually overflowing the country, and covering it with mud, obliged men to distinguish their lands one from another, by the consideration of their figure; and after which, 'tis probable, to be able also to measure the quantity of it, and to know how to plot it, and lay it out again in its just dimensions, figure and proportion: after which, it is likely, a farther contemplation of those draughts and figures helped them to discover many excellent and wonderful properties belonging to them; which speculations were continually improving, and are still to this day. *Geometry* is usually divided into speculative and practical; the former of which contemplates and treats of the properties of continued quantity abstractedly; and the latter applies these speculations and theorems to use and practice, and to the benefit and advantage of mankind. *Harris.*

In the muscles alone there seems to be more *geometry* than in all the artificial engines in the world. *Ray on the Creation.*

Him also for my censor I disdain,
Who thinks all science, as all virtue, vain;
Who counts *geometry* and numbers toys,
And with his foot the sacred dust destroys. *Dryd. Pers. Sat.*

GEOPO'NICAL. *adj.* [γῆ and πόνος; *geoponique*, French.] Relating to agriculture; relating to the cultivation of the ground.

Such expressions are frequent in authors *geoponical*, or such as have treated *de re rustica.* *Brown's Vulgar Errours, b.* vi.

GEOPO'NICKS. *n. s.* [γῆ and πόνος.] The science of cultivating the ground; the doctrine of agriculture.

GEORGE. *n. s.* [*Georgius*, Latin.]

1. A figure of St. George on horseback worn by the knights of the garter.

Look on my *George*, I am a gentleman;
Rate me at what thou wilt. *Shakespeare's Henry* VI. *p.* ii.

2. A brown loaf. Of this sense I know not the original.

Cubb'd in a cabbin, on a mattress laid,
On a brown *george*, with lousy swobbers, fed. *Dryd. Pers.*

GEO'RGICK. *n. s.* [γεωργικόν; *georgiques*, Fr.] Some part of the science of husbandry put into a pleasing dress, and set off with all the beauties and embellishments of poetry. *Addison.*

GEO'RGICK. *adj.* Relating to the doctrine of agriculture.

Here I peruse the Mantuan's *georgick* strains,
And learn the labours of Italian swains. *Gay's Rural Sports.*

GEO'TICK. *adj.* [from γῆ.] Belonging to the earth; terrestrial. *Dict.*

GE'RENT. *adj.* [*gerens*, Latin.] Carrying; bearing. *Dict.*

GE'RFALCON. *n. s.* A bird of prey, in size between a vulture and a hawk, and of the greatest strength next to the eagle. *Bailey.*

GE'RMAN. *n. s.* [*germain*, French; *germanus*, Lat.] Brother; one approaching to a brother in proximity of blood: thus the children of brothers or sisters are called cousins *german.*

They knew it was their cousin *german*, the famous Amphialus. *Sidney, b.* ii.

And to him said, go now, proud miscreant,
Thyself thy message do to *german* dear. *Fairy Queen, b.* i.
These *Germans* did subdue all Germany,
Of whom it hight; but in the end their sire,
With foul repulse, from France was forced to retire. *F. Q.*

Wert thou a bear, thou wouldst be kill'd by the horse; wert thou a horse, thou wouldst be seiz'd by the leopard; wert thou a leopard, thou wert *german* to the lion, and the spots of thy kindred were juries on thy life. *Shakesp. Timon.*

You'll have your nephews neigh to you; you'll have coursers for cousins, and genets for *germans.* *Shakesp. Othello.*

GE'RMAN. *adj.* [*germanus*, Latin.] Related.

Not he alone shall suffer what wit can make heavy, and vengeance bitter; but those that are *german* to him, though removed fifty times, shall come under the hangman. *Shakesp.*

GE'RMANDER. *n. s.* [*germandrée*, French.]

It has small thick leaves, which are laciniated somewhat like those of the oak: the flowers, which are produced at the wings of the leaves, are labiated: the stamina or threads supply the place of the crest, or upper lip: the beard or lower lip of the flower is divided into five parts: the middle segment, which is largest, is hollow like a spoon, and sometimes divided into two parts: the cup of the flower is fistulous. *Miller.*

GE'RME. *n. s.* [*germen*, Latin.] A sprout or shoot; that part which grows and spreads.

Whether it be not made out of the *germe*, or treadle of the egg, doth seem of lesser doubt. *Brown's Vulgar Errours.*

GE'RMIN. *n. s.* [*germen*, Latin.] A shooting or sprouting seed.

Though palaces and pyramids do slope
Their heads to their foundations; though the treasure
Of nature's *germins* tumble all together,
Even 'till destruction sicken; answer me
To what I ask you. *Shakespeare's Macbeth.*

Thou all-shaking thunder,
Strike flat the thick rotundity o' th' world;
Crack nature's mould, all *germins* spill at once
That make ungrateful man. *Shakespeare's King Lear.*

To GE'RMINATE. *v. n.* [*germino*, Latin.] To sprout; to shoot; to bud; to put forth.

This action is furthered by the chalcites, which hath within a spirit that will put forth and *germinate*, as we see in chymical trials. *Bacon's Natural History.*

The seeds of all kinds of vegetables being planted near the surface of the earth, in a convenient soil, amongst matter proper for the formation of vegetables, would *germinate*, grow up, and replenish the face of the earth. *Woodward's Na. Hist.*

GERMINA'TION. *n. s.* [*germination*, French, from *germinate.*] The act of sprouting or shooting; growth.

For acceleration of *germination*, we refer it over unto the place, where we shall handle the subject of plants generally. *Bacon's Natural History.*

The duke of Buckingham had another kind of *germination*; and surely, had he been a plant, he would have been reckoned among the *sponte nascentes.* *Wotton.*

There is but little similitude between a terreous humidity and plantal *germinations.* *Glanv. Sceps. c.* 25.

Suppose the earth should be carried to the great distance of Saturn; there the whole globe would be one frigid zone; there would be no life, no *germination.* *Bentley's Sermons.*

GE'RUND. *n. s.* [*gerundium*, Latin.] In the Latin grammar, a kind of verbal noun, which governs cases like a verb.

GEST. *n. s.* [*gestum*, Latin.]

1. A deed; an action; an atchievement.

Who fair them quites, as him beseemed best,
And goodly can discourse of many a noble *gest.* *Fai. Qu.*

2. Show; representation.

Gests should be interlarded after the Persian manner, by ages, young and old.

3. The roll or journal of the several days, and stages prefixed, in the progresses of our kings, many of them being still extant in the herald's office. [From *giste*, or *gite*, Fr.] *Hanmer.*

I'll give you my commission,
To let him there a month, behind the *gest*,
Prefix'd for's parting. *Shakespeare's Winter's Tale.*

He distinctly sets down the *gests* and progress thereof; and are conceits of eminent use, to solve magnetical phenomenas. *Brown's Vulgar Errours, b.* ii. *c.* 2.

GESTA'TION. *n. s.* [*gestatio*, Latin.] The act of bearing the young in the womb.

Aristotle affirmeth the birth of the infant, or time of its *gestation*, extendeth sometimes unto the eleventh month; but Hippocrates avers that it exceedeth not the tenth. *Brown.*

Why in viviparous animals, in the time of *gestation*, should the nourishment be carried to the embryo in the womb, which at other times goeth not that way? *Ray on the Creation.*

To GESTI'CULATE. *v. n.* [*gesticulor*, Latin; *gisticuler*, Fr.] To play antick tricks; to shew postures. *Dict.*

GESTICULA'TION. *n. s.* [*gesticulatio*, Latin; *gesticulation*, Fr. from *gesticulate.*] Antick tricks; various postures.

GE'STURE. *n. s.* [*gero*, *gestum*, Latin; *geste*, French.]

1. Action or posture expressive of sentiment.

Ah, my sister, if you had heard his words, or seen his *gestures*,

gestures, when he made me know what and to whom his love was, you would have matched in yourself, those two rarely matched together, pity and delight. *Sidney*, *b.* ii.

When we make profession of our faith, we stand; when we acknowledge our sins, or seek unto God for favour, we fall down; because the *gesture* of constancy becometh us best in the one, in the other the behaviour of humility. *Hooker*.

To the dumbness of the *gesture*
One might interpret. *Shakespeare's Timon of Athens*.

2. Movement of the body.

Grace was in all her steps, heav'n in her eye,
In ev'ry *gesture* dignity and love! *Milton's Paradise Lost*.

Every one will agree in this, that we ought either to lay aside all kinds of *gesture*, or at least to make use of such only as are graceful and expressive. *Addison's Spectator*, N°. 408.

To GE'STURE. *v. a.* [from the noun.] To accompany with action or posture.

Our attire disgraceth it; it is not orderly read, nor *gestured* as beseemeth. *Hooker*, *b.* v.

Undertaking so to *gesture* and muffle up himself in his hood, as the duke's manner was, that none should discern him. *Wotton's Life of the Duke of Buckingham*.

To GET. *v. a.* pret. *I got*, anciently *gat*; part. pass. *got*, or *gotten*. [ᵹetan, ᵹettan, Saxon.]

1. To procure; to obtain.

Thine be the cosset, well hast thou it *got*. *Spenser's Past*.

Of that which was our father's hath he *gotten* all this glory. *Gen.* xxxi. 1.

We *gat* our bread with the peril of our lives. *Sam.* v. 9.

The pains of hell *gat* hold upon me. *Ps.* cxvi. 3.

David *gat* him a name when he returned from smiting of the Syrians. 2 *Sa.* viii. 13.

Most of these things might be more exactly tried by the Torricellian experiments, if we could *get* tubes so accurately blown that the cavity were perfectly cylindrical. *Boyle*.

Such a conscience, as has not been wanting to itself, in endeavouring to *get* the utmost and clearest information about the will of God, that its power, advantages, and opportunities could afford it, is that great internal judge, whose absolution is a rational and sure ground of confidence. *South's Sermons*.

He insensibly *got* a facility, without perceiving how; and that is attributed wholly to nature, which was much more the effect of use and practice. *Locke*.

He who attempts to *get* another man into his absolute power, does thereby put himself into a state of war with him. *Locke*.

The man who lives upon alms, *gets* him his set of admirers, and delights in superiority. *Addison's Spectator*, N°. 219.

Sphinx was a monster that would eat
Whatever stranger she could *get*,
Unless his ready wit disclos'd,
The subtle riddle she propos'd. *Addison's Whig Examiner*.

This practice is to be used at first, in order to *get* a fixed habit of attention, and in some cases only. *Watts*.

The word *get* is variously used: we say to *get* money, to *get* in, to *get* off, to *get* ready, to *get* a stomach, and to *get* a cold. *Watts's Logick*.

2. To force; to seize.

Such losels and scatterlings cannot easily, by any constable, or other ordinary officer, be *gotten*, when they are challenged for any such fact. *Spenser on Ireland*.

The king seeing this, starting from where he sat,
Out from his trembling hand his weapon *gat*. *Daniel*.

All things, but one, you can restore;
The heart you *get* returns no more. *Waller*.

3. To win.

Henry the sixth hath lost
All that which Henry the fifth had *gotten*. *Shakes. Hen.* VI.

He *gat* his people great honour, and he made battles, protecting the host with his sword. 1 *Mac.* iii. 3.

To *get* the day of them of his own nation, would be a most unhappy day for him. 2 *Mac.* v. 6.

Auria held that course to have drawn the gallies within his great ships, who thundering amongst them with their great ordnance, might have opened a way unto his gallies to have *gotten* a victory. *Knolles's History of the Turks*.

4. To have possession of; to hold.

Then forcing thee, by fire he made thee bright;
Nay, thou hast *got* the face of man. *Herbert*.

5. To beget upon a female.

These boys are boys of ice; they'll none of her: sure they are bastards to the English, the French never *got* them. *Shak*.

Women with study'd arts they vex:
Ye gods destroy that impious sex;
And if there must be some t' invoke
Your pow'rs, and make your altars smoke,
Come down yourselves, and, in their place,
Get a more just and nobler race. *Waller*.

Children they *got* on their female captives. *Locke*.

If you'll take 'em as their fathers *got* 'em, so and well; if not, you must stay 'till they *get* a better generation. *Dryden*.

Has no man, but who has kill'd
A father, right to *get* a child? *Prior*.

Let ev'ry married man, that's grave and wise,
Take a tartuff of known ability,
Who shall so settle lasting reformation;
First *get* a son, then give him education. *Dorset*.

The god of day, descending from above,
Mixt with the day, and *got* the queen of love. *Granville*.

6. To gain as profit.

Though creditors will lose one fifth of their principal and use, and landlords one fifth of their income, yet the debtors and tenants will not *get* it. *Locke*.

7. To gain as superiority or advantage.

If they *get* ground and 'vantage of the king,
Then join you with them like a rib of steel. *Shakes. H.* IV.

8. To earn; to gain by labour.

Nature and necessity taught them to make certain vessels of a tree, which they *got* down, not with cutting, but with fire. *Abbot's Description of the World*.

Having no mines, nor any other way of *getting* or keeping of riches but by trade, so much of our trade as is lost, so much of our riches must necessarily go with it. *Locke*.

If it be so much pains to count the money I would spend, what labour did it cost my ancestors to *get* it? *Locke*.

9. To receive as a price or reward.

Any tax laid on foreign commodities in England raises their price, and makes the importer *get* more for them; but a tax laid on your homemade commodities lessens their price. *Locke*.

10. To learn.

Get by heart the more common and useful words out of some judicious vocabulary. *Watts*.

11. To procure to be.

I shall shew how we may *get* it thus informed, and afterwards preserve and keep it so. *South's Sermons*.

12. To put into any state.

Take no repulse, whatever she doth say;
For, *get* you gone, she doth not mean away. *Shakespeare*.

About a fortnight before your ewes bring forth their young, they may be pretty well kept, to *get* them a little into heart. *Mortimer's Husbandry*.

Helim, who was taken up in embalming the bodies, visited the place very frequently: his greatest perplexity was how to *get* the lovers out of it, the gates being watched. *Guardian*.

13. To prevail on; to induce.

Though the king could not *get* him to engage in a life of business, he made him however his chief companion. *Spectat*.

14. To draw; to hook.

With much communication will he tempt thee, and smiling upon thee *get* out thy secrets. *Ecclus.* xiii. 11.

By the marriage of his grandson Ferdinand he *got* into his family the kingdoms of Bohemia and Hungary. *Addison*.

After having *got* out of you every thing you can spare, I scorn to trespass. *Guardian*, N°. 167.

15. To betake; to remove.

Get you to bed on th' instant; I will be return'd forthwith. *Shakespeare's Othello*.

Arise, *get* thee out from this land. *Gen.* xxxi. 13.

Get thee out, and depart hence. *Luke* xiii. 31.

Lest they join also unto our enemies, and fight against us, and so *get* them up out of the land. *Ex.* i. 10.

Get ye up in peace unto your father. *Gen.* xliv. 17.

Thus perplexed, he with all speed *got* himself with his followers to the strong town of Mega, in hope to shrowd himself. *Knolles's History of the Turks*.

16. To remove by force or art.

By the good direction of Auria she was quickly *got* off the land again, and entered with the rest. *Knolles's History*.

The roving fumes of quicksilver, in evaporating, would oftentimes fasten upon the gold in such plenty, as would put him to much trouble to *get* them off from his rings. *Boyle*.

When mercury is *got* by the help of the fire out of a metal, or other mineral body, we may suppose this quicksilver to have been a perfect body of its own kind. *Boyle*.

They are offended to see them wilful, and would be glad to *get* out those weeds which their own hands have planted, and which now have taken too deep root to be easily extirpated. *Locke on Education*.

17. To put.

Get on thy boots; we'll ride all night. *Shakesp. Henry* IV.

18. *To* GET *off*. To sell or dispose of by some expedient.

Wood, to *get* his halfpence *off*, offered an hundred pounds in his coin for seventy in silver. *Swift*.

To GET. *v. n.*

1. To arrive at any state or posture by degrees with some kind of labour, effort, or difficulty.

Phalantus was entrapped, and saw round about him, but could not *get* out. *Sidney*.

You knew he walk'd o'er perils, on an edge
More likely to fall in than to *get* o'er. *Shakesp. Henry* IV.

Away, *get* thee down. *Ex.* xix. 24.

If

If it displeaſe thee, I will *get* me back again. *Num.* xxii.

The ſtranger ſhall *get* up above thee very high, and thou ſhalt come down very low. *Deuter.* xxviii. 43.

The fox bragged what a number of ſhifts and devices he had to *get* from the hounds, and the cat ſaid he had but one, which was to climb a tree. *Bacon.*

Thoſe that are very cold, and eſpecially in their feet, cannot *get* to ſleep. *Bacon's Natural Hiſtory.*

I utterly condemn the practice of the later times, that ſome who are pricked for ſheriffs, and were fit, ſhould *get* out of the bill. *Bacon's Advice to Villiers.*

Being entered unto the Mahometan religion, he *got* away unto the Chriſtians, and hardly eſcaped from the battle. *Knolles's Hiſtory of the Turks.*

He would be at their backs before they could *get* out of Armenia. *Knolles's Hiſtory of the Turks.*

She plays with his rage, and *gets* above his anger. *Denham.*

The latitant air had *got* away in bubbles. *Boyle.*

There are few bodies whoſe minute parts ſtick ſo cloſe together, but that it is poſſible to meet with ſome other body whoſe ſmall parts may *get* between, and ſo disjoin them. *Boyle.*

There was but an inſenſible diminution of the liquor upon the receſs of whatever it was that *got* through the cork. *Boyle.*

Although the univerſe, and every part thereof, are objects full of excellency, yet the multiplicity thereof is ſo various, that the underſtanding falls under a kind of deſpondency of *getting* through ſo great a taſk. *Hale's Origin of Mankind.*

If there ſhould be any leak at the bottom of the veſſel, yet very little water would *get* in, becauſe no air could *get* out. *Wilkins's Math. Magick.*

O heav'n, in what a lab'rinth am I led!
I could *get* out, but ſhe detains the thread! *Dryden.*

So have I ſeen ſome fearful hare maintain
A courſe, 'till tir'd before the dog ſhe lay;
Who, ſtretch'd behind her, pants upon the plain,
Paſt pow'r to kill, as ſhe to *get* away. *Dryden's Ann. Mirab.*

The more oily and light part of this maſs would *get* above the other, and ſwim upon it. *Burnet's Theory of the Earth.*

Having *got* through the foregoing paſſage, let us go on to his next argument. *Locke.*

The removing of the pains we feel is the *getting* out of miſery, and conſequently the firſt thing to be done, in order to happineſs, abſent good. *Locke.*

If, having *got* into the ſenſe of the epiſtles, we will but compare what he ſays, in the places where he treats of the ſame ſubject, we can hardly be miſtaken in his ſenſe. *Locke.*

I *got* up as faſt as poſſible, girt on my rapier, and ſnatched up my hat, when my landlady came up to me. *Tatler.*

Bucephalus would let nobody *get* upon him but Alexander the Great. *Addiſon on Italy.*

Impriſon'd fires, in the cloſe dungeons pent,
Roar to *get* looſe, and ſtruggle for a vent;
Eating their way, and undermining all,
'Till with a mighty burſt whole mountains fall. *Addiſon.*

When Alma now, in diff'rent ages,
Has finiſh'd her aſcending ſtages,
Into the head at length ſhe *gets*,
And there in publick grandeur ſits,
To judge of things. *Prior.*

I reſolved to break through all meaſures to *get* away. *Swift.*

Happy are they who meet with civil people that will comply with their ignorance, and help them to *get* out of it. *Locke.*

2. To fall; to come by accident.

Two or three men of the town are *got* among them. *Tatler.*

3. To find the way.

When an egg is made hard by boiling, ſince there is nothing that appears to *get* in at the ſhell, unleſs ſome colorifick atoms, and ſome little particles of the water it is boiled in, it is not eaſy to diſcover from whence elſe this change of conſiſtency proceeds than from a change made in the texture of the parts. *Boyle.*

He raves; his words are looſe
As heaps of ſand, and ſcattering wide from ſenſe:
You ſee he knows not me, his natural father;
But aiming to poſſeſs th' uſurping queen,
So high he's mounted in his airy hopes,
That now the wind is *got* into his head,
And turns his brains to frenzy. *Dryden's Spaniſh Fryar.*

A child runs to overtake and *get* up to the top of his ſhadow, which ſtill advances at the ſame rate that he does. *Locke.*

Should dreſſing, feaſting, and balls once *get* among the Cantons, their military roughneſs would be quickly loſt. *Addiſ.*

The fluids which ſurround bodies, upon the ſurface of the globe, *get* in between the ſurfaces of bodies when they are at any diſtance. *Cheyne's Phil. Princ.*

4. To move; to remove.

Get home with thy fewel made ready to ſet;
The ſooner, the eaſier carriage to get. *Tuſſer.*

Many of the gallies rode it out at ſea, where they were by ſhot out of the city enforced to *get* them farther off. *Knolles.*

Riſe up and *get* you forth from amongſt my people. *Ex.* xii.

5. To have recourſe to.

The Turks made great haſte through the midſt of the town ditch, to *get* up into the bulwark to help their fellows. *Knolles.*

Lying is ſo cheap a cover for any miſcarriage, and ſo much in faſhion, that a child can ſcarce be kept from *getting* into it. *Locke.*

6. To go; to repair.

They ran to their weapons, and furiouſly aſſailed the Turks, now fearing no ſuch matter, and were not as yet all *got* into the caſtle. *Knolles's Hiſtory of the Turks.*

A knot of ladies, *got* together by themſelves, is a very ſchool of impertinence. *Swift.*

7. To put one's ſelf in any ſtate.

To-morrow *get* you early on your way. *Judg.* xix. 9.

They might *get* over the river Avon at Stratford, and *get* between the king and Worceſter. *Clarendon.*

We can neither find ſource nor iſſue for ſuch an exceſſive maſs of waters, neither where to have them; nor, if we had them, how to *get* quit of them. *Burnet's Theory of the Earth.*

Without his aſſiſtance we can no more *get* quit of our affliction, than but by his permiſſion we ſhould have fallen into it. *Wake's Preparation for Death.*

There is a ſort of men who pretend to diveſt themſelves of partiality on both ſides, and to *get* above that imperfect idea of their ſubject which little writers fall into. *Pope on Homer.*

As the obtaining the love of valuable men is the happieſt end of this life, ſo the next felicity is to *get* rid of fools and ſcoundrels. *Pope to Swift.*

8. To become by any act what one was not before.

The laughing ſot, like all unthinking men,
Bathes and *gets* drunk; then bathes and drinks again. *Dryd.*

9. To be a gainer; to receive advantage.

Like jewels to advantage ſet,
Her beauty by the ſhade does *get*. *Waller.*

10. *To* GET *off*. To eſcape.

The gallies, by the benefit of the ſhores and ſhallows, *got off*. *Bacon's War with Spain.*

Whate'er thou do'ſt, deliver not thy ſword;
With that thou may'ſt *get off*, tho' odds oppoſe thee. *Dryd.*

11. *To* GET *over*. To conquer; to ſuppreſs; to paſs without being ſtopped in thinking or acting.

'Tis very pleaſant, on this occaſion, to hear the lady propoſe her doubts, and to ſee the pains he is at to *get over* them. *Addiſon's Spectator*, Nº. 475.

I cannot *get over* the prejudice of taking ſome little offence at the clergy, for perpetually reading their ſermons. *Swift.*

To remove this difficulty, the earl of Peterborough was diſpatched to Vienna, and *got over* ſome part of thoſe diſputes, to the ſatisfaction of the duke of Savoy. *Swift.*

12. *To* GET *up*. To riſe from repoſe.

Sheep will *get up* betimes in the morning to feed againſt rain. *Bacon's Natural Hiſtory.*

13. *To* GET *up*. To riſe from a ſeat.

Get you *up* from about the tabernacle of Koran, Dathan, and Aboriam. *Numb.* xvi.

GE'TTER. *n.ſ.* [from *get*.]

1. One who procures or obtains.
2. One who begets on a female.

Peace is a very apoplexy, lethargy, null'd, deaf, ſleepy, inſenſible; a *getter* of more baſtard-children than war's a deſtroyer of men. *Shakeſpeare's Coriolanus.*

GE'TTING. *n.ſ.* [from *get*.]

1. Act of getting; acquiſition.

Wiſdom is the principal thing, therefore get wiſdom; and with all thy *getting* get underſtanding. *Prov.* iv. 7.

2. Gain; profit.

Who hath a ſtate to repair may not deſpiſe ſmall things; and it is leſs diſhonourable to abridge a petty charge than to ſtoop to petty *gettings*. *Bacon, Eſſay* 29.

The meaner families, are obliged to return to the ſteward a ſmall monthly ſhare of their *gettings*, to be a portion for the child. *Gulliver's Travels.*

GE'WGAW. *n.ſ.* [ȝeȝap, Saxon; *joyau*, French.] A ſhowy trifle; a toy; a bauble; a ſplendid plaything.

That metal they exchanged for the meaneſt trifles and *gewgaws* which the others could bring. *Abbot's Deſcr. of the World.*

Prefer that which providence has pronounced to be the ſtaff of life, before a glittering *gewgaw* that has no other value than what vanity has ſet upon it. *L'Eſtrange, Fable* 1.

As children, when they throw one toy away,
Straight a more fooliſh *gewgaw* comes in play. *Dryden.*

A heavy *gewgaw*, call'd a crown, that ſpread
About his temples, drown'd his narrow head,
And would have cruſh'd it. *Dryden's Juvenal, Sat.* 10.

Some looſe the bands
Of ancient friendſhip, cancel nature's laws
For pageantry and tawdry *gewgaws*. *Phillips.*

The firſt images were fans, ſilks, ribbands, laces, and many other *gewgaws*, which lay ſo thick that the whole heart was nothing elſe but a toyſhop. *Addiſon's Guard.*

GE'WGAW. *adj.* Splendidly trifling; showy without value.
Let him that would learn the happiness of religion, see the poor *gewgaw* happiness of Feliciano. *Law's Serious Call.*

GHA'STFUL. *adj.* [ȝarꞇ and fulle, Saxon.] Dreary; dismal; melancholy; fit for walking spirits.

Here will I dwell apart,
In *ghastful* grave, 'till my last sleep
Do close mine eyes:
Help me, ye baneful birds, whose shrieking sound
Is sign of dreary death. *Spenser's Pastorals.*

GHA'STLINESS. *n. s.* [from *ghastly.*]
1. Horrour of countenance; resemblance of a ghost; paleness.

GHA'STLY. *adj.* [ȝarꞇ, or *ghost*, and *like.*]
1. Like a ghost; having horrour in the countenance; pale; dreadful; dismal.

Why looks your grace so heavily to-day?
—O, I have past a miserable night;
So full of ugly sights, of *ghastly* dreams,
So full of dismal terrour was the time. *Shakesp. Rich.* III.

Envy quickly discovered in court Solyman's changed countenance upon the great bassa, and began now to shew her *ghastly* face. *Knolles's History of the Turks.*

Death
Grinn'd horrible a *ghastly* smile, to hear
His famine should be fill'd. *Milton's Paradise Lost, b.* ii.

Those departed friends, whom at our last separation we saw disfigured by all the *ghastly* horrours of death, we shall then see assisting about the majestick throne of Christ, with their once vile bodies transfigured into the likeness of his glorious body, mingling their glad acclamations with the hallelujahs of thrones, principalities and powers. *Boyle.*

This poor man's desolate wife,
Expects some happy day;
This *ghastly* thing, the comfort of her life. *Flatman.*

He came, but with such alter'd looks,
So wild, so *ghastly*, as if some ghost had met him,
All pale and speechless. *Dryden's Spanish Fryar.*

I did not for these *ghastly* visions send;
Their sudden coming does some ill portend. *Dryd. Ind. Em.*

I who make the triumph of to-day,
May of to-morrow's pomp one part appear,
Ghastly with wounds, and lifeless on the bier! *Prior.*

2. Horrible; shocking; dreadful.

To be less than gods
Disdain'd; but meaner thoughts learn'd in their flight,
Mangled with *ghastly* wounds through plate and mail. *Milt.*

GHA'STNESS. *n. s.* [from ȝarꞇ, Saxon.] Ghastliness; horrour of look.

Look you pale, mistress?
Do you perceive the *ghastness* of the eye? *Shakesp. Othello.*

GHE'RKIN. *n. s.* [from *gurcke*, German, a cucumber.] A pickled cucumber. *Skinner.*

To GHESS. *v. n.* [See To GUESS. *Ghess* is by criticks considered as the true orthography, but *guess* has universally prevailed.] To conjecture.

GHOST. *n. s.* [ȝarꞇ, Saxon.]
1. The soul of man.

Vex not his *ghost*: O, let him pass! He hates him,
That would upon the rack of this rough world
Stretch him out longer. *Shakespeare's King Lear.*

Often did I strive
To yield the *ghost*; but still the envious flood
Kept in my soul. *Shak. R.* III.

Man, when once cut down, when his pale *ghost*
Fleets into air, is for ever lost. *Sandys's Paraphrase.*

2. A spirit appearing after death.

The mighty *ghosts* of our great Harrys rose,
And armed Edwards look'd with anxious eyes,
To see this fleet among unequal foes,
By which fate promis'd them their Charles should rise. *Dryd.*

3. *To give up the* GHOST. To die; to yield up the spirit into the hands of God.

Their shadows seem
A canopy most fatal, under which
Our army lies ready to *give up the ghost. Shakesp. Jul. Cæs.*

4. The third person in the adorable Trinity, called the Holy Ghost.

To GHOST. *v. n.* [from the noun.] To yield up the ghost; to die. Not in use.

Euryalus taking leave of Lucretia, precipitated her into such a love-fit, that within a few hours she *ghosted*; which course Euryalus was like to have steered, upon the news. *Sidney.*

To GHOST. *v. a.* To haunt with apparitions of departed men. Obsolete.

Julius Cæsar,
Who at Philippi the good Brutus *ghosted*,
There saw you labouring for him. *Shakes. Ant. and Cleopat.*

GHO'STLINESS. *n. s.* [from *ghostly.*] Spiritual tendency; quality of having reference chiefly to the soul.

GHO'STLY. *adj.* [from *ghost.*]
1. Spiritual; relating to the soul; not carnal; not secular.

Our common necessities, and the lack which we all have, as well of *ghostly* as of earthly favours, is in each kind so easily known, but the gifts of God, according to these degrees and times, which he in his secret wisdom seeth meet, are so diversly bestowed, that it seldom appeareth what all receive, what all stand in need of, it seldom lieth hid. *Hooker, b.* v.

The graces of the spirit are much more precious than worldly benefits, and our *ghostly* evils of greater importance than any harm which the body feeleth. *Hooker, b.* v. *s.* 35.

To deny me the *ghostly* comfort of my chaplains, seems a greater barbarity than is ever used by Christians. *King Charles.*

2. Having a character from religion; spiritual.

Hence will I to my *ghostly* friar's close cell,
His help to crave, and my dear hap to tell. *Sh. Ro. and Jul.*
The *ghostly* father now hath done his shrift. *Shakesp. H.* VI.

GIA'LALINA. n. s. [Italian.] Earth of a bright gold colour, found in the kingdom of Naples, very fine, and much valued by painters. *Woodward's Met. Foss.*

GIA'MBEUX. *n. s.* [*jambes*, French.] Legs, or armour for legs; greaves.

The mortal steel dispiteously entail'd,
Deep in their flesh, quite through the iron walls,
That a large purple stream adown their *giambeux* falls. *F. Q.*

GI'ANT. *n. s.* [*geant*, French; *gigas*, Latin.] A man of size above the ordinary rate of men; a man unnaturally large. It is observable, that the idea of a giant is always associated with pride, brutality, and wickedness.

Now does he feel his axle
Hang loose about him, like a *giant's* robe
Upon a dwarfish thief. *Shakespeare's Macbeth.*

Gates of monarchs
Are arch'd so high that *giants* may jet through,
And keep their impious turbands on, without
Good-morrow to the sun. *Shakespeare's Cymbeline.*

Woman's gentle brain
Could not drop forth such *giant* rude invention;
Such Ethiop words. *Shakesp. As you like it.*

Fierce faces threat'ning wars,
Giants of mighty bone, and bold emprise! *Milt. Pa. Lost.*

Those *giants*, those mighty men, and men of renown, far exceeded the proportion, nature, and strength of those *giants* remembered by Moses of his own time. *Raleigh's History.*

The *giant* brothers, in their camp, have found
I was not forc'd with ease to quit my ground. *Dryden's Æn.*

By weary steps and slow
The groping *giant* with a trunk of pine
Explor'd his way. *Addison.*

Neptune, by pray'r repentant, rarely won,
Afflicts the chief t' avenge his *giant* son,
Great Polypheme, of more than mortal might. *Pope.*

GI'ANTESS. *n. s.* [from *giant.*] A she-giant; a woman of unnatural bulk and height.

I had rather be a *giantess*, and lie under mount Pelion. *Shak.*

Were this subject to the cedar, she would be able to make head against that huge *giantess*. *Howel.*

GI'ANTLIKE. } *adj.* [from *giant* and *like.*] Gigantick; vast;
GI'ANTLY. } bulky.

Single courage, has often, without romance, overcome *giantly* difficulties. *Decay of Piety.*

Notwithstanding all their talk of reason and philosophy, which they are deplorably strangers to, and those unanswerable doubts and difficulties, which, over their cups, they pretend to have against Christianity; persuade but the covetous man not to deify his money, the proud man not to adore himself, and I dare undertake that all their *giantlike* objections against the Christian religion shall presently vanish and quit the field. *South's Sermons.*

GI'ANTSHIP. *n. s.* [from *giant.*] Quality or character of a giant.

His *giantship* is gone somewhat crest-fall'n,
Stalking with less unconscionable strides,
And lower looks. *Milton's Agonistes.*

GI'BBE. *n. s.* Any old worn-out animal. *Hanmer.*

For who that's but a queen, fair, sober, wise,
Would from a paddock, from a bat, a *gibbe*,
Such dear concernings hide? *Shakespeare's Hamlet.*

To GI'BBER. *v. n.* [from *jabber.*] To speak inarticulately.

The sheeted dead
Did squeak and *gibber* in the Roman streets. *Shakesp. Haml.*

GI'BBERISH. *n. s.* [Derived by *Skinner* from *gaber*, French, to cheat; by others conjectured to be formed by corruption from *jabber*. But as it was anciently written *gebrish*, it is probably derived from the chymical cant, and originally implied the jargon of *Geber* and his tribe.] Cant; the private language of rogues and gipsies; words without meaning.

Some, if they happen to hear an old word, albeit very natural and significant, cry out straitway, that we speak no English, but *gibberish*. *Spenser.*

Some of both sexes writing down a number of letters, just as it came into their heads; upon reading this *gibberish*, that which the men had wrote sounded like High Dutch, and the other by the women like Italian. *Swift.*

GI'BBET. *n.s.* [*gibet*, French.]

1. A gallows; the post on which malefactors are hanged, or on which their carcases are exposed.

When was there ever cursed atheist brought
Unto the *gibbet*, but he did adore
That blessed pow'r which he had set at nought? *Davies.*

You scandal to the stock of verse, a race
Able to bring the *gibbet* in disgrace. *Cleaveland.*

Haman suffered death himself upon the very *gibbet* that he had provided for another. *L'Estrange.*

Papers of universal approbation, lay such principles to the whole body of the Tories, as, if they were true, our next business should be to erect *gibbets* in every parish, and hang them out of the way. *Swift.*

2. Any traverse beams.

To GI'BBET. *v. n.* [from the noun.]

1. To hang or expose on a gibbet.

I'll *gibbet* up his name. *Oldham.*

2. To hang on any thing going traverse: as the beam of a gibbet.

He shall come off and on swifter than he that *gibbets* on the brewer's bucket. *Shakespeare's Henry* IV. *p.* ii.

GI'BBIER. *n.s.* [French.] Game; wild fowl.

These imposts are laid on all butcher's meat, while, at the same time, the fowl and *gibbier* are tax free. *Addison on Italy.*

GIBBO'SITY. *n.s.* [*gibbosité*, Fr. from *gibbous.*] Convexity; prominence; protuberance.

When two ships, sailing contrary ways, lose the sight one of another, what should take away the sight of ships from each other, but the *gibbosity* of the interjacent water? *Ray.*

GI'BBOUS. *adj.* [*gibbus*, Latin; *gibbeux*, Fr.]

1. Convex; protuberant; swelling into inequalities.

The bones will rise, and make a *gibbous* member. *Wiseman.*

A pointed flinty rock, all bare and black,
Grew *gibbous* from behind the mountain's back. *Dryden.*

The sea, by this access and recess, shuffling the empty shells, wears them away, reducing those that are concave and *gibbous* to a flat. *Woodward's Natural History.*

2. Crookbacked.

I shall demand how the camels of Bactria came to have two bunches in their back, whereas the camels of Arabia, in all relations, have but one? How oxen, in some countries, began and continue *gibbous*, or hunch-backed? *Brown.*

GI'BBOUSNESS. *n.s.* [from *gibbous.*] Convexity; prominence.

To make the convexity of the earth discernible, suppose a man lifted in the air, that he may have a spacious horizon; but then, because of the distance, the convexity and *gibbousness* would vanish away, and he would only see a great circular flat. *Bentley's Sermons.*

GI'BCAT. *n.s.* [*gib* and *cat.*] An old worn-out cat.

I am as melancholy as a *gibcat*, or a lugg'd bear. *Shakesp.*

To GIBE. *v. n.* [*gaber*, old French, to sneer, to ridicule.] To sneer; to join censoriousness with contempt.

They seem to imagine that we have erected of late a frame of some new religion, the furniture whereof we should not have borrowed from our enemies, lest they should afterwards laugh and *gibe* at our party. *Hooker*, *b.* iv. *s.* 9.

When he saw her toy, and *gibe*, and geer,
And pass the bounds of modest merry-make,
Her dalliance he despis'd. *Fairy Queen*, *b.* ii. *cant.* 6.

Why that's the way to choke a *gibing* spirit,
Whose influence is begot of that loose grace
Which shallow laughing hearers give to fools. *Shakespeare.*

Thus with talents well endu'd
To be scurrilous and rude,
When you pertly raise your snout,
Fleer and *gibe*, and laugh and flout. *Swift.*

To GIBE. *v. a.* To reproach by contemptuous hints; to flout; to scoff; to ridicule; to treat with scorn; to sneer; to taunt.

When rioting in Alexandria: you
Did pocket up my letters, and with taunts
Did *gibe* my missive out of audience. *Shakes. Ant. and Cleop.*

Draw the beasts as I describe them,
From their features, while I *gibe* them. *Swift.*

GIBE. *n.s.* [from the verb.] Sneer; hint of contempt by word or look; scoff; act or expression of scorn; taunt.

Mark the fleers, the *gibes*, and notable scorns
That dwell in ev'ry region of his face. *Shakesp. Othello.*

The rich have still a *gibe* in store,
And will be monstrous witty on the poor. *Dryden's Juven.*

If they would hate from the bottom of their hearts, their aversion would be too strong for little *gibes* every moment. *Spectator*, N°. 300.

But the dean, if this secret shou'd come to his ears,
Will never have done with his *gibes* and his jeers. *Swift.*

GI'BER. *n.s.* [from *gibe.*] A sneerer; one who turns others to ridicule by contemptuous hints; a scoffer; a taunter.

You are well understood to be a more perfect *giber* of the table, than a necessary bencher of the capitol. *Shakes. Cor.*

Come, Sempronia, leave him;
He is a *giber*, and our present business
Is of more serious consequence. *Ben. Johnson's Catiline.*

GI'BINGLY. *adv.* [from *gibe.*] Scornfully; contemptuously.

His present portance,
Gibingly and ungravely he did fashion
After th' inveterate hate he bears to you. *Shakes. Coriolanus.*

GI'BLETS. *n.s.* [According to *Minshew* from *gobbet*, *gobblet*: according to *Junius* more probably from *gibier*, game, Fr.] The parts of a goose which are cut off before it is roasted.

'Tis holyday; provide me better cheer:
'Tis holyday; and shall be round the year:
Shall I my houshold gods and genius cheat,
To make him rich who grudges me my meat?
That he may loll at ease; and pamper'd high,
When I am laid, may feed on *giblet* pie? *Dryden's Pers.*

GI'DDILY. *adv.* [from *giddy.*]

1. With the head seeming to turn round.

2. Inconstantly; unsteadily.

To roam
Giddily, and be every where but at home,
Such freedom doth a banishment become. *Donne.*

3. Carelesly; heedlesly; negligently.

The parts that fortune hath bestow'd upon her,
Tell her, I hold as *giddily* as fortune. *Shak. Twelfth Night.*

GI'DDINESS. *n.s.* [from *giddy.*]

1. The state of being giddy or vertiginous; the sensation which we have when every thing seems to turn round.

Megrims and *giddiness* are rather when we rise after long sitting, than while we sit. *Bacon's Natural History.*

2. Inconstancy; unsteadiness; mutability; changeableness.

There be that delight in *giddiness*, and count it a bondage to fix a belief. *Bacon, Essay* 1.

3. Quick rotation; inability to keep its place.

The indignation of heaven rolling and turning us, 'till at length such a *giddiness* seized upon government, that it fell into the very dregs of sectaries. *South's Sermons.*

4. Frolick; wantonness of life.

Thou, like a contrite penitent,
Charitably warn'd of thy sins, do'st repent
These vanities and *giddinesses*. *Donne.*

GI'DDY. *adj.* [ȝiðiȝ, Saxon. I know not whether this word may not come from *gad*, to wander, to be in motion, *gad*, *gid*, *giddy.*]

1. Vertiginous; having in the head a whirl, or sensation of circular motion, such as happens by disease or drunkenness.

Them rev'ling thus the Tentyrites invade,
By *giddy* heads and stagg'ring legs betray'd. *Tate's Juvenal.*

2. Rotatory; whirling; running round with celerity.

As Ixion fix'd, the wretch shall feel
The *giddy* motion of the whirling mill. *Pope.*

3. Inconstant; mutable; unsteady; changeful.

Our fancies are more *giddy* and unfirm,
More longing, wavering, sooner lost and won,
Than womens are. *Shakespeare's Twelfth Night.*

It may be gnats and flies have their imagination more mutable and *giddy*, as small birds likewise have. *Bacon's N. Hist.*

Thanks to *giddy* chance, which never bears
That mortal bliss should last for length of years,
She cast us headlong from our high estate,
And here in hope of thy return we wait. *Dryden's Fables.*

The *giddy* vulgar, as their fancies guide,
With noise say nothing, and in parts divide. *Dryden's Æn.*

You are as *giddy* and volatile as ever, the reverse of Pope, who hath always loved a domestick life. *Swift to Gay.*

4. That which causes giddiness.

The frequent errors of the pathless wood,
The *giddy* precipice, and the dang'rous flood. *Prior.*

The sylphs through mystick mazes guide their way,
Through all the *giddy* circle they pursue. *Pope.*

5. Heedless; thoughtless; uncautious; wild.

Too many *giddy* foolish hours are gone,
And in fantastick measures danc'd away. *Rowe's Ja. Shore.*

How inexcusable are those *giddy* creatures, who, in the same hour, leap from a parent's window to a husband's bed. *Clarissa.*

6. Tottering; unfixed.

As we pac'd along
Upon the *giddy* footing of the hatches,
Methought that Glo'ster stumbled. *Shakespeare's Rich.* III.

7. Intoxicated; elated to thoughtlesness; overcome by any overpowering inticement.

Art thou not *giddy* with the fashion too, that thou hast shifted out of thy tale into telling me of the fashion? *Shakesp.*

Like one of two contending in a prize,
That thinks he hath done well in people's eyes;
Hearing applause and universal shout,
Giddy in spirit, gazing still in doubt,
Whether those peals of praise be his or no. *Shakespeare.*

GI'DDYBRAINED. *adj.* [*giddy* and *brain.*] Careless; thoughtless.

Turn him out again, you unnecessary, useless, *giddybrain'd* ass! *Otway's Venice Preserved.*

GI'DDYHEADED. *adj.* [*giddy* and *head.*] Without thought or caution; without steadiness or constancy.

And sooner may a gulling weather spy,
By drawing forth heav'n's scheme descry
What fashion'd hats or ruffs, or suits, next year,
Our *giddyheaded* antick youth will wear. *Donne.*

That men are so misaffected, melancholy, *giddyheaded*, hear the testimony of Solomon. *Burton on Melancholy.*

GI'DDYPACED. *adj.* [*giddy* and *pace.*] Moving without regularity.

More than light airs, and recollected terms,
Of these most brisk and *giddypaced* times. *Shakespeare.*

GI'ER-EAGLE. *n. s.* [Sometimes it is written *jer-eagle.*] An eagle of a particular kind.

These fowls shall not be eaten, the swan and the pelican, and the *gier-eagle.* *Lev.* xi. 18.

GIFT. *n. s.* [from *give.*]

1. A thing given or bestowed; something conferred without price.

They presented unto him *gifts*, gold, and frankincense and myrrh. *Mat.* ii. 11.

Recall your *gift*, for I your pow'r confess;
But first take back my life, a *gift* that's less. *Dryd. Aureng.*

2. The act of giving.

No man has any antecedent right or claim to that which comes to him by free *gift.* *South's Sermons.*

3. Oblation; offering.

Many nations shall come with *gifts* in their hands, even *gifts* to the king of heaven: *Tob.* xiii. 11.

4. A bribe.

Thou shalt not wrest judgment, thou shalt not respect persons, neither take a *gift*; for a *gift* doth blind the eyes of the wise. *Deuter.* xvi. 19.

5. Power; faculty.

And if the boy have not a woman's *gift*,
To rain a shower of commanded tears,
An onion will do well for such a shift. *Shakespeare.*

He who has the *gift* of ridicule, finds fault with any thing that gives him an opportunity of exerting his beloved talent. *Addison's Spectator*, Nº. 291.

GI'FTED. *adj.* [from *gift.*]

1. Given; bestowed.

Made of my enemies the scorn and gaze,
To grind in brazen fetters, under task,
With my heav'n *gifted* strength. *Milton's Agonistes.*

2. Endowed with extraordinary powers. It is commonly used ironically.

Two of their *gifted* brotherhood, Hacket and Coppinger, got up into a pease-cart, and harangued the people to dispose them to an insurrection. *Dryd. Rel. Laici, Preface.*

There is no talent so pernicious as eloquence, to those who have it not under command: women, who are so liberally *gifted* by nature in this particular, ought to study the rules of female oratory. *Addison's Freeholder*, Nº. 23.

GIG. *n. s.* [Etymology uncertain.]

1. Any thing that is whirled round in play.]

Playthings, as tops, *gigs*, battledores, should be procured them. *Locke.*

2. [*Gigia*, Islandick.] A fiddle. Now out of use.

GI'GANTICK. *adj.* [*gigantes*, Latin.] Suitable to a giant; big; bulky; enormous; likewise wicked; atrocious.

Others from the wall defend
With dart and jav'lin, stones, and sulphurous fire;
On each hand slaughter and *gigantick* deeds! *Milt. Pa.Lost.*

I dread him not, nor all his giant-brood,
Though fame divulg'd him father of five sons,
All of *gigantick* size, Goliah chief. *Milton's Agonistes.*

The son of Hercules he justly seems,
By his broad shoulders and *gigantick* limbs. *Dryden's Æn.*

The Cyclopean race in arms arose;
A lawless nation of *gigantick* foes. *Pope's Odyssey*, *b.* vi.

To GI'GGLE. *v. n.* [*gichgelen*, Dutch.] To laugh idly; to titter; to grin with merry levity. It is retained in Scotland.

GI'GGLER. *n. s.* [from *giggle.*] A laugher; a titterer; one idly and foolishly merry.

A sad wise valour is the brave complexion,
That leads the van, and swallows up the cities:
The *giggler* is a milk-maid, whom infection,
Or the fir'd beacon, frighteth from his ditties. *Herbert.*

We shew our present, joking, *giggling* race;
True joy consists in gravity and grace. *Garrick's Epilogue.*

GI'GLET. *n. s.* [ȝeaȝl, Saxon; *geyl*, Dutch; *gillet*, Scottish, is still retained.] A wanton; a lascivious girl. Now out of use.

Young Talbot was not born
To be the pillage of a *giglet* wench. *Shakesp. Henry* VI.

The fam'd Cassibelan was once at point,
Oh *giglet* fortune! to master Cæsar's sword. *Shak. Cymbel.*

Away with those *giglets* too, and with the other confederate companion. *Shakespeare's Measure for Measure.*

GI'GOT. *n. s.* [French.] The hip joint.

To GILD. *v. a.* pret. *gilded*, or *gilt.* [ȝilđan, Saxon.]

1. To wash over with gold; to cover with foliated gold.

The room was large and wide,
As it some *gilt* or solemn temple were:
Many great golden pillars did uprear
The massy roof, and riches huge sustain. *Fairy Queen*, *b.* ii.

Gilded wood may worms infold. *Shak. Merch. of Venice.*

To *gild* refined gold, to paint the lily,
To throw a perfume on the violet. *Shakespeare's K. John.*

And the *gilded* car of day
His glowing axle doth allay
In the steep Atlantick stream. *Milton.*

Purchasing riches with our time and care,
We lose our freedom in a *gilded* snare. *Roscommon.*

When Britain, looking with a just disdain
Upon this *gilded* majesty of Spain,
And knowing well that empire must decline,
Whose chief support and sinews are of coin. *Waller.*

Her joy in *gilded* chariots, when alive;
And love of ombre after death survive. *Pope.*

2. To cover with any yellow matter.

Thou did'st drink
The stale of horses and the *gilded* puddle,
Which beasts would cough at. *Shakes. Ant. and Cleopatra.*

3. To adorn with lustre.

No more the rising sun shall *gild* the morn,
Nor ev'ning Cynthia fill her silver horn. *Pope's Messiah.*

4. To brighten; to illuminate.

The lightsome passion of joy was not that trivial, vanishing, superficial thing, that only *gilds* the apprehension and plays upon the surface of the soul. *South.*

5. To recommend by adventitious ornaments.

For my part, if a lie may do thee grace,
I'll *gild* it with the happiest terms I have. *Shakes. Hen.* IV.

Yet, oh! th' imperfect piece moves more delight;
'Tis *gilded* o'er with youth, to catch the sight. *Dryd. Auren.*

GI'LDER. *n. s.* [from *gild.*]

1. One who lays gold on the surface of any other body.

Gilders use to have a piece of gold in their mouth, to draw the spirits of the quicksilver. *Bacon's Natural History.*

We have here a *gilder*, with his anvil and hammer. *Notes on the Odyssey.*

2. A coin, from one shilling and sixpence, to two shillings. *Phil.*

I am bound
To Persia, and want *gilders* for my voyage. *Shakespeare.*

GI'LDING. *n. s.* [from *gild.*] Gold laid on any surface by way of ornament.

Silvering will sully and canker more than *gilding*, which, if it might be corrected with a little mixture of gold, there is profit. *Bacon's Phys. Rem.*

The church of the Annunciation, all but one corner of it, is covered with statues, *gilding*, and paint. *Addison on Italy.*

Could laureate Dryden Pimp and Fry'r engage,
And I not strip the *gilding* off a knave,
Unplac'd, unpension'd, no man's heir or slave? *Pope's Hor:*

GILL. *n. s.* [*agulla*, Spanish; *gula*, Latin.]

1. The apertures at each side of a fish's head.

The leviathan,
Stretch'd like a promontory, sleeps or swims,
And seems a moving land; and at his *gills*
Draws in, and at his trunk spouts out a sea. *Milt. P. Lost.*

Fishes perform their respiration under water by the *gills.* *Ray on the Creation.*

He hath, on the bottom of his sides, two *gill*-fins; not behind the *gills*, as in most fishes, but for a good part before them. *Walton.*

'Till they, of farther passage quite bereft,
Were in the mash with *gills* entangl'd left. *King's Fisherman.*

2. The flaps that hang below the beak of a fowl.

The turkeycock hath great and swelling *gills*, and the hen hath less. *Bacon's Natural History.*

3. The flesh under the chin.

In many there is no paleness at all; but, contrariwise, redness about the cheeks and *gills*, which is by the sending forth of spirits in an appetite to revenge. *Bacon's Natural History.*

Like the long bag of flesh hanging down from the *gills* of the people in Piedmont. *Swift.*

4. [*Gilla*, barbarous Latin.] A measure of liquids containing the fourth part of a pint.

Every bottle must be rinced with wine: some, out of mistaken thrift, will rince a dozen with the same: change the wine at every second bottle: a *gill* may be enough. *Swift.*

5. [From *gillian*, the old English way of writing *Julian*, or *Juliana.*] The appellation of a woman in ludicrous language.

I can, for I will,
Here at Burley o' th' Hill,
Give you all your fill,
Each Jack with his *Gill.* *Ben. Johnson's Gypsies.*

6. The

6. The name of a plant; ground-ivy.
7. Malt liquor medicated with ground-ivy.

GI'LLHOUSE. *n. ſ.* [*gill* and *houſe.*] A houſe where gill is ſold.

Thee ſhall each alehouſe, thee each *gillhouſe* mourn,
And anſw'ring ginſhops ſourer ſighs return. *Pope.*

GIL'LYFLOWER. *n. ſ.* [Either corrupted from *July flower*, or from *giroflée*, French.]

Gillyflowers, or rather *Julyflowers*, ſo called from the month they blow in, are of a very great variety; but they may be reduced to theſe ſorts; red and white, purple and white, ſcarlet and white, the various kinds of which are too many to enumerate. *Mortimer's Husbandry.*

In July come *gillyflowers* of all varieties. *Bacon, Eſſay* 47.

Fair is the *gillyflow'r* of gardens ſweet,
Fair is the marygold, for pottage meet. *Gay's Paſtorals.*

GILT. *n. ſ.* [from *gild.*] Golden ſhow; gold laid on the ſurface of any matter. Now obſolete.

Our gayneſs and our *gilt* are all beſmirch'd,
With rainy marching in the painful field. *Shakeſ. Hen.* V.

When thou waſt in thy *gilt*, and thy perfume, they mockt thee for too much curioſity: in thy rags thou know'ſt none, but art deſpis'd for the contrary. *Shakeſ. Timon of Athens.*

The double *gilt* of this opportunity you let time waſh off. *Shakeſpeare's Twelfth Night.*

GILT. The participle of GILD, which ſee.

Where the *gilt* chariot never mark'd its way. *Pope.*

GI'LTHEAD. *n. ſ.* [*gilt* and *head.*] A ſeafiſh. *Dict.*

GILT-TAIL. *n. ſ.* [*gilt* and *tail.*] A worm ſo called from his yellow tail.

GIM. *adj.* [An old word.] Neat; ſpruce; well dreſſed.

GI'MCRACK. *n. ſ.* [Suppoſed by *Skinner* to be ludicrouſly formed from *gin*, derived from *engine.*] A ſlight or trivial mechaniſm.

For though theſe *gimcracks* were away,
However, more reduc'd and plain,
The watch would ſtill a watch remain;
But if the horal orbit ceaſes,
The whole ſtands ſtill, or breaks to pieces. *Prior.*

What's the meaning of all theſe trangrams and *gimcracks?* What, in the name of wonder, are you going about, jumping over my maſter's hedges, and running your lines croſs his grounds? *Arbuthnot's Hiſt. of J. Bull.*

GI'MLET. *n. ſ.* [*gibelet*, *guimbelet*, French.] A borer with a ſcrew at its point.

The *gimlet* hath a worm at the end of its bit. *Moxon.*

GI'MMAL. *n. ſ.* [Suppoſed by *Skinner* and *Ainſworth* to be derived from *gimellus*, Latin, and to be uſed only of ſomething conſiſting of correſpondent parts, or double. It ſeems rather to be gradually corrupted from *geometry* or *geometrical.*] Some little quaint devices or pieces of machinery. *Hanmer.*

I think by ſome odd *gimmals* or device
Their arms are ſet like clocks, ſtill to ſtrike on,
Elſe they could not hold out ſo as they do. *Shakeſ. Hen.* VI.

GI'MMER. *n. ſ.* [See GIMMAL.] Movement; machinery.

The holding together of the parts of matter has ſo confounded me, that I have been prone to conclude with myſelf, that the *gimmers* of the world hold together not ſo much by geometry as ſome natural magick. *More's Divine Dialogues.*

GIMP. *n. ſ.* [See GIM. *Gimp*, in old Engliſh, is neat, ſpruce.] A kind of ſilk twiſt or lace.

GIN. *n. ſ.* [from *engine.*]

1. A trap; a ſnare.

As the day begins,
With twenty *gins* we will the ſmall birds take,
And paſtime make. *Sidney, b.* i.

Which two, through treaſon and deceitful *gin*,
Hath ſlain ſir Mordant. *Fairy Queen, b.* ii.

So ſtrives the woodcock with the *gin*;
So doth the cony ſtruggle in the net. *Shakeſp. Henry* VI.

Be it by *gins*, by ſnares, by ſubtilty. *Shakeſ. Hen.* VI.

If thoſe, who have but ſenſe, can ſhun
The engines that have them annoy'd;
Little for me had reaſon done,
If I could not thy *gins* avoid. *Ben. Johnſon's Foreſt.*

I know thy trains,
Though dearly to my coſt, thy *gins* and toils;
No more on me have pow'r, their force is null'd. *Milton.*

He made a planetary *gin*,
Which rats would run their own heads in,
And come on purpoſe to be taken,
Without th' expence of cheeſe and bacon. *Hudibras, p.* ii.

Keep from flaying ſcourge thy ſkin,
And ankle free from iron *gin*. *Hudibras, p.* i. *cant.* 2.

2. Any thing moved with ſcrews, as an engine of torture.

Typhæus' joints were ſtretched on a *gin*. *Fairy Queen.*

3. A pump worked by rotatory ſails.

A bituminous plate, alternately yellow and black, formed by water driveling on the outſide of the *gin* pump of Moſtyn coalpits. *Woodward on Foſſils.*

4. [Contracted from GENEVA, which ſee.] The ſpirit drawn by diſtillation from juniper berries.

This calls the church to deprecate our ſin,
And hurls the thunder of our laws on *gin*. *Pope, Dial.* 1.

Thee ſhall each alehouſe, thee each gillhouſe mourn,
And anſw'ring *gin* ſhops ſourer ſighs return. *Pope's Dunciad.*

GI'NGER. *n. ſ.* [*zinziber*, Latin; *gingero*, Italian.]

The flower conſiſts of five leaves, which are ſhaped ſomewhat like thoſe of the iris: theſe are produced in an head or club, each coming out of a ſeparate leafy ſcale. The ovary afterwards becomes a triangular fruit, having three cells which contain their ſeeds. *Miller.*

The root of *ginger* is of the tuberous kind, knotty, crooked and irregular; of a hot, acrid, and pungent taſte, though aromatick, and of a very agreeable ſmell. The Indians eat both the young ſhoots of the leaves and the roots themſelves, cut ſmall in their ſallads, and make an excellent ſweetmeat of them. *Ginger* is an excellent carminative and ſtomachick. *Hill's Mat. Medica.*

Or waſting *ginger* round the ſtreets to go,
And viſit alehouſe where ye firſt did grow. *Pope's Dunciad.*

GI'NGERBREAD. *n. ſ.* [*ginger* and *bread.*] A kind of farinaceous ſweetmeat made of dough, like that of bread or biſcuit, ſweetened with treacle, and flavoured with ginger and ſome other aromatick ſeeds. It is ſometimes gilt.

An' I had but one penny in the world, thou ſhould'ſt have it to buy *gingerbread.* *Shakeſpeare's Love's Labour Loſt.*

Her currans there and gooſeberries were ſpread,
With the enticing gold of *gingerbread.* *King's Cookery.*

'Tis a loſs you are not here, to partake of three weeks froſt, and eat *gingerbread* in a booth by a fire upon the Thames. *Swift.*

GI'NGERLY. *adv.* [I know not whence derived.] Cautiouſly; nicely.

What is't that you
Took up ſo *gingerly?* *Shakeſpeare's Two Gent. of Verona.*

GI'NGERNESS. *n. ſ.* Niceneſs; tenderneſs. *Dict.*

GI'NGIVAL. *adj.* [*gingiva*, Latin.] Belonging to the gums.

Whilſt the Italians ſtrive to cut a thread in their pronunciation between D and T, ſo to ſweeten it, they make the occluſe appulſe, eſpecially the *gingival*, ſofter than we do, giving a little of perviouſneſs. *Holder's Elements of Speech.*

To GIN'GLE. *v. n.*

1. To utter a ſharp clattering noiſe; to utter a ſharp noiſe in quick ſucceſſion.

The foot grows black that was with dirt embrown'd,
And in thy pocket *gingling* halfpence ſound. *Gay's Trivia.*

Once, we confeſs, beneath the patriot's cloak,
From the crack'd bag the dropping guinea ſpoke,
And *gingling* down the backſtairs, told the crew,
Old Cato is as great a rogue as you. *Pope's Epiſtles.*

2. To make an affected ſound in periods or cadence.

To GI'NGLE. *v. a.* To ſhake ſo that a ſharp ſhrill clattering noiſe ſhould be made.

Her infant grandame's whiſtle next it grew;
The bells ſhe *gingled*, and the whiſtle blew. *Pope.*

GI'NGLE. *n. ſ.* [from the verb.]

1. A ſhrill reſounding noiſe.
2. Affectation in the ſound of periods.

GI'NGLYMOID. *adj.* [γιγλυμος and εἶδος.] Reſembling a ginglymus; approaching to a ginglymus.

The malleus lies along, fixed to the tympanum, and on the other end is joined to the incus by a double or *ginglymoid* joint. *Holder's Elements of Speech.*

GI'NGLYMUS. *n. ſ.* [*ginglime*, French.] A mutual indenting of two bones into each other's cavity, of which the elbow is an inſtance. *Wiſeman.*

GI'NNET. *n. ſ.* [γιννος.] A nag; a mule; a degenerated breed. Hence, according to ſome, but, I believe, erroneouſly, a Spaniſh *gennet*, improperly written for *ginnet.*

GI'NSENG. *n. ſ.* [I ſuppoſe *Chineſe.*] A root brought lately into Europe. It never grows to any great ſize, and is of a browniſh colour on the outſide, and ſomewhat yellowiſh within; and ſo pure and fine, that it ſeems almoſt tranſparent. It is of a very agreeable and aromatick ſmell, though not very ſtrong. Its taſte is acrid and aromatick, and has ſomewhat bitter in it. We have it from China; and there is of it in the ſame latitudes in America. The Chineſe value this root ſo highly, that it ſells with them for three times its weight in ſilver. The Aſiaticks in general think the ginſeng almoſt an univerſal medicine. The virtues moſt generally believed to be in it are thoſe of a reſtorative, and a cordial. The European phyſicians eſteem it a good medicine in convulſions, vertigoes, and all nervous complaints; and recommend it as one of the beſt reſtoratives known. *Hill.*

To GIP. *v. a.* To take out the guts of herrings. *Bailey.*

GI'PSY. *n. ſ.* [Corrupted from *Egyptian*; for when they firſt appeared in Europe they declared, and perhaps truly, that they were driven from Egypt by the Turks. They are now mingled with all nations.]

1. A vagabond who pretends to foretell futurity, commonly by palmeſtry or phyſiognomy.

The butler, though he is ſure to loſe a knife, a fork, or a ſpoon every time his fortune is told him, ſhuts himſelf up in the

the pantry with an old *gipſy* for above half an hour. *Addiſon.*

A frantick *gipſey* now, the houſe he haunts,
And in wild phraſes ſpeaks diſſembled wants. *Prior.*

I, near yon ſtile, three ſallow *gypſies* met;
Upon my hand they caſt a poring look,
Bid me beware, and thrice their heads they ſhook. *Gay.*

In this ſtill labyrinth around her lie
Spells, philters, globes, and ſpheres of palmiſtry;
A ſigil in this hand the *gipſy* bears,
In th' other a prophetick ſieve and ſheers. *Garth's Diſpenſat.*

2. A reproachful name for a dark complexion.

Laura, to his lady, was but a kitchen-wench; Dido a dowdy; Cleopatra a *gipſy*; Helen and Hero hildings and harlots. *Shakeſpeare's Romeo and Juliet.*

3. A name of ſlight reproach to a woman.

The widow play'd the *gypſy*, and ſo did her confidant too, in pretending to believe her. *L'Eſtrange.*

A ſlave I am to Clara's eyes:
The *gipſy* knows her pow'r, and flies. *Prior.*

GIR'ASOLE. *n. ſ.* [*giraſol*, French.]

1. The herb turnſol.

2. The opal ſtone.

To GIRD. *v. a.* pret. *girded*, or *girt*. [ᵹẏꞃdan, Saxon.]

1. To bind round.

They ſprinkled earth upon their heads, and *girded* their loins with ſackcloth. 2 *Mac.* x. 25.

2. To put on ſo as to ſurround or bind.

Cords of the bigneſs of packthread were faſtened to bandages, which the workmen had *girt* round my neck. *Gulliver.*

3. To faſten by binding.

He *girt* his warlike harneſs about him. 1 *Mac.* iii. 3.

My bow and thunder, my almighty arms
Gird on, and ſword upon thy puiſſant thigh. *Milt. P. Loſt.*

No, let us riſe at once, *gird* on our ſwords,
And, at the head of our remaining troops,
Attack the foe. *Addiſon's Cato.*

The combatant too late the field declines,
When now the ſword is *girded* to his loins. *Prior.*

4. To inveſt.

Stoop then, and ſet your knee againſt my foot;
And in reguerdon of that duty done,
I *gird* thee with the valiant ſword of York. *Shakeſp. H.* VI.

The ſon appear'd,
Girt with omnipotence. *Milton's Paradiſe Loſt*, *b.* vii.

5. To dreſs; to habit; to clothe.

I *girded* thee about with fine linen, and I covered thee with ſilk. *Ezek.* xvi. 10.

Tyſiphone there keeps the ward,
Girt in her ſanguine gown, by night and day,
Obſervant of the ſouls that paſs the downward way. *Dryd.*

6. To cover round as a garment.

Theſe, with what ſkill they had, together ſow'd,
To *gird* their waiſt: vain covering, if to hide
Their guilt, and dreaded ſhame! *Milton's Paradiſe Loſt.*

7. To reproach; to gibe.

Being mov'd, he will not ſpare to *gird* the gods. *Shakeſ.*

8. To furniſh; to equip.

So to the coaſt of Jordan he directs
His eaſy ſteps, *girded* with ſnaky wiles. *Paradiſe Regain'd.*

9. To incloſe; to incircle.

That Nyſeian iſle,
Girt with the river Triton, where old Cham
Hid Amalthea, and her florid ſon
Young Bacchus, from his ſtepdame Rhea's eye. *Milt. P. L.*

To GIRD. *v. n.* To break a ſcornful jeſt; to gibe; to ſneer.

Men of all ſorts take a pride to *gird* at me: the brain of this fooliſh compounded clay, man, is not able to invent any thing that tends to laughter more than I invent, or is invented on me: I am not only witty in myſelf, but the cauſe that wit is in other men. *Shakeſpeare's Henry* IV. *p.* ii.

GIRD. *n. ſ.* [from the verb] A twitch; a pang: from the ſenſation cauſed by a bandage or girdle drawn hard ſuddenly. This word is now ſeldom uſed.

Sweet king! the biſhop hath a kindly *gird*:
For ſhame, my lord of Wincheſter, relent. *Shakeſ. H.* VI.

They give ſatisfaction to his mind, and his conſcience by this means is freed from many fearful *girds* and twinges which the atheiſt feels. *Tillotſon, Sermon* 2.

He has the glory of his conſcience, when he doth well, to ſet againſt the checks and *girds* of it when he doth amiſs. *Goodman's Winter Evening Con.*

GI'RDER. *n. ſ.* [from *gird.*] In architecture, the largeſt piece of timber in a floor. Its end is uſually faſtened into the ſummers, or breaſt ſummers, and the joiſts are framed in at one arm to the girders. *Harris.*

The *girders* are alſo to be of the ſame ſcantling the ſummers and ground-plates are of, though the back *girder* need not be ſo ſtrong as the front *girder*. *Moxon's Mech. Exer.*

Theſe mighty *girders* which the fabrick bind,
Theſe ribs robuſt and vaſt in order join'd. *Blackm. Creation.*

GI'RDLE. *n. ſ.* [ᵹẏꞃdel. Saxon.]

1. Any thing drawn round the waiſt, and tied or buckled.

There will I make thee beds of roſes,
With a thouſand fragrant poſies;
A cap of flowers, and a *girdle*,
Embroider'd all with leaves of myrtle. *Shakeſpeare.*

Many conceive there is ſomewhat amiſs, until they put on their *girdle*. *Brown's Vulgar Errours, b.* v. *c.* 21.

On him his mantle, *girdle*, ſword and bow,
On him his heart and ſoul he did beſtow. *Cowley.*

2. Encloſure; circumference.

Suppoſe within the *girdle* of theſe walls
Are now confin'd two mighty monarchies. *Shakeſ. Hen.* V.

3. The equator; the torrid zone.

Great breezes in great circles, ſuch as are under the *girdle* of the world, do refrigerate. *Bacon.*

To GI'RDLE. *v. a.* [from the noun.]

1. To gird; to bind as with a girdle.

Lay the gentle babes, *girdling* one another
Within their innocent alabaſter arms. *Shakeſ. Rich.* III.

2. To incloſe; to ſhut in; to environ.

Thoſe ſleeping ſtones,
That as a waiſt do *girdle* you about,
By this time from their fixed beds of lime
Had been diſhabited. *Shakeſpeare's King John.*

Let me look back upon thee, O thou wall,
That *girdleſt* in thoſe wolves! *Shakeſpeare's Timon.*

GI'RDLEBELT. *n. ſ.* [*girdle* and *belt.*] The belt that incircles the waiſt.

Nor did his eyes leſs longingly behold
The *girdlebelt*, with nails of burniſh'd gold. *Dryden's Æn.*

GI'RDLER. *n. ſ.* [from *girdle.*] A maker of girdles.

GIRE. *n. ſ.* [*gyrus*, Latin.] A circle deſcribed by any thing in motion. See GYRE.

GIRL. *n. ſ.* [About the etymology of this word there is much queſtion: *Meric Caſaubon*, as is his cuſtom, derives it from κόρη, of the ſame ſignification; *Minſhew* from *garrula*, Latin, a prattler, or *girella*, Italian, a weathercock; *Junius* thinks that it comes from *herlodes*, Welſh, from which, ſays he, *harlot* is very eaſily deduced. *Skinner* imagines that the Saxons, who uſed ceoꞃl for a man, might likewiſe have ceoꞃla for a woman, though no ſuch word is now found. Dr. *Hickes* derives it moſt probably from the Iſlandick *karlinna*, a woman.] A young woman, or female child.

In thoſe unfledg'd days was my wife a *girl*. *Shakeſpeare.*

And let it not diſpleaſe thee, good Bianca;
For I will love thee ne'er the leſs, my *girl*. *Shakeſpeare.*

A weather-beaten lover, but once known,
Is ſport for every *girl* to practiſe on. *Donne.*

Tragedy ſhould bluſh as much to ſtoop
To the low mimick follies of a farce,
As a grave matron would to dance with *girls*. *Roſcommon.*

A boy, like thee, would make a kingly line;
But oh, a *girl*, like her, muſt be divine! *Dryden.*

GI'RLISH. *adj.* [from *girl.*] Suiting a girl; youthful.

In her *girliſh* age ſhe kept ſheep on the moor. *Carew.*

GI'RLISHLY. *adv.* [from *girliſh.*] In a girliſh manner.

To GIRN. *v. n.* Seems to be a corruption of *grin*. It is ſtill uſed in Scotland, and is applied to a crabbed, captious, or peeviſh perſon.

GI'RROCK. *n. ſ.* A kind of fiſh. *Dict.*

GIRT. *part. paſſ.* [from *To gird.*]

To GIRT. *v. a.* [from *gird.*] To gird; to encompaſs; to encircle. Not proper.

In the dread ocean, undulating wide
Beneath the radiant line, that *girts* the globe,
The circling Typhon whirl'd from point to point. *Thomſon.*

GIRT. *n. ſ.* [from the verb.]

1. A band by which the ſaddle or burthen is fixed upon the horſe.

Here lies old Hobſon, death hath broke his *girt*;
And here, alas! hath laid him in the dirt. *Milton.*

2. A circular bandage.

The moſt common way of bandage is by that of the *girt*, which *girt* hath a bolſter in the middle, and the ends are tacked firmly together. *Wiſeman's Surgery.*

GIRTH. *n. ſ.* [from *gird.*]

1. The band by which the ſaddle is fixed upon the horſe.

Or the ſaddle turn'd round, or the *girths* brake;
For low on the ground, woe for his ſake,
The law is found. *Ben. Johnſon's Underwoods.*

Nor Pegaſus could bear the load,
Along the high celeſtial road;
The ſteed oppreſs'd, would break his *girth*,
To raiſe the lumber from the earth. *Swift.*

Mordanto gallops on alone;
The roads are with his foll'wers ſtrown;
This breaks a *girth*, and that a bone. *Swift.*

2. The compaſs meaſured by the girdle, or encloſing bandage.

He's a luſty jolly fellow that lives well, at leaſt three yards in the *girth*. *Addiſon's Freeholder.*

To GIRTH. *v. a.* To bind with a girth.

To GISE *Ground.* *v. a.* Is when the owner of it does not feed it with his own ſtock, but takes in other cattle to graze. *Bailey.*

Gi'sle. Among the English Saxons, signifies a pledge: thus, *Fredgisle* is a pledge of peace; *Gisiebert* an illustrious pledge, like the Greek *Homerus*. *Gibson's Camden.*

Gith. *n. s.* An herb called Guiney pepper.

To GIVE. *v. a.* preter. *gave*; part. pass. *given*. [ʒifan, Saxon.]

1. To bestow; to confer without any price or reward.

This opinion abated the fear of death in them which were so resolved, and *gave* them courage to all adventures. *Hooker.*

Give us of your oil, for our lamps are gone out. *Mat.* xxv.

Give us also sacrifices and burnt offerings, that we may sacrifice unto the Lord. *Ex.* x. 25.

I had a master that *gave* me all I could ask, but thought fit to take one thing from me again. *Temple.*

Constant at church and change; his gains were sure,
His *givings* rare, save farthings to the poor. *Pope's Epistles.*

2. To transmit from himself to another by hand, speech, or writing; to deliver; to impart; to communicate.

The woman whom thou *gavest* to be with me, she *gave* me of the tree, and I did eat. *Gen.* iii. 12.

They were eating and drinking, marrying and *giving* in marriage. *Mat.* xxiv. 38.

Those bills were printed not only every week, but also a general account of the whole year was *given* in upon the Thursday before Christmas. *Graunt's Bills of Mortality.*

We shall *give* an account of these phenomena. *Burnet.*

Aristotle advises not poets to put things evidently false and impossible into their poems, nor *gives* them licence to run out into wildness. *Broome's Notes on the Odyssey.*

3. To put into one's possession; to consign.

Nature *gives* us many children and friends, to take them away; but takes none away to *give* them us again. *Temple.*

Give me, says Archimedes, where to stand firm, and I will remove the earth. *Temple.*

If the agreement of men first *gave* a sceptre into any one's hands, or put a crown on his head, that almost must direct its conveyance. *Locke.*

4. To pay as price or reward, or in exchange.

All that a man hath will he *give* for his life. *Job* ii. 4.

If you did know to whom I *gave* the ring,
If you did know for whom I *gave* the ring,
And would conceive for what I *gave* the ring,
And how unwillingly I left the ring,
You would abate the strength of your displeasure. *Shakesp.*

He would *give* his nuts for a piece of metal, and exchange his sheep for shells, or wool for a sparkling pebble. *Locke.*

5. To yield; not to withold.

Philip, Alexander's father, gave sentence against a prisoner what time he was drowsy, and seemed to *give* small attention. The prisoner, after sentence was pronounced, said, I appeal: the king, somewhat stirred, said, To whom do you appeal? The prisoner answered, From Philip, when he *gave* no ear, to Philip, when he shall *give* ear. *Bacon's Apophthegms.*

Constantia accused herself for having so tamely *given* an ear to the proposal. *Addison's Spectator.*

6. To quit; to yield as due.

Give place, thou stranger, to an honourable man. *Eccluf.*

7. To confer; to impart.

I will bless her, and *give* thee a son also of her. *Gen.* xvii.

Nothing can *give* that to another which it hath not itself. *Bramh. against Hobbs.*

What beauties I lose in some places, I *give* to others which had them not originally. *Dryden's Fables, Preface.*

8. To expose.

All clad in skins of beasts the jav'lin bear;
Give to the wanton winds their flowing hair. *Dryd. Æn.*

9. To grant; to allow.

'Tis *given* me once again to behold my friend. *Rowe.*

He has not *given* Luther fairer play. *Atterbury.*

10. To yield; not to deny.

I *gave* his wife proposal way;
Nay, urg'd him to go on: the shallow fraud
Will ruin him. *Rowe's Ambitious Stepmother.*

11. To yield without resistance.

12. To permit; to commission.

Prepare
The due libation and the solemn pray'r;
Then *give* thy friend to shed the sacred wine. *Pope's Odyss.*

13. To enable; to allow.

God himself requireth the lifting up of pure hands in prayers; and hath *given* the world to understand, that the wicked, although they cry, shall not be heard. *Hooker.*

Give me to know
How this foul rout began, who set it on. *Shakes. Othello.*

So some weak shoot, which else would poorly rise,
Jove's tree adopts, and lifts into the skies;
Through the new pulpil fost'ring juices flow,
Thrust forth the gems, and *give* the flow'rs to blow. *Tickel.*

14. To pay.

The applause and approbation, most reverend for thy stretcht-out life, I *give* to both your speeches. *Shak. Troil. and Cressida.*

15. To utter; to vent; to pronounce.

So you must be the first that *gives* this sentence,
And he that suffers. *Shakesp. Measure for Measure.*

The Rhodians seeing their enemies turn their backs, *gave* a great shout in derision of them. *Knolles's Hist. of the Turks.*

Let the first honest discoverer *give* the word about, that Wood's halfpence have been offered, and caution the poor people not to receive them. *Swift.*

16. To exhibit; to express.

This instance *gives* the impossibility of an eternal existence in any thing essentially alterable or corruptible. *Hale.*

17. To exhibit as the product of a calculation.

The number of men being divided by the number of ships, *gives* four hundred and twenty-four men a-piece. *Arbuthnot.*

18. To do any act of which the consequence reaches others.

As we desire to *give* no offence ourselves, so neither shall we take any at the difference of judgment in others. *Burnet.*

19. To exhibit; to send forth as odours from any body.

In oranges the ripping of their rind *giveth* out their smell more. *Bacon.*

20. To addict; to apply.

The Helots, of the other side, shutting their gates, *gave* themselves to bury their dead, to cure their wounds, and rest their wearied bodies. *Sidney.*

After men began to grow to number, the first thing we read they *gave* themselves into, was the tilling of the earth and the feeding of cattle. *Hooker, b.* i.

Groves and hill-altars were dangerous, in regard of the secret access which people superstitiously *given* might have always thereunto with ease. *Hooker, b.* v. *s.* 17.

The duke is virtuous, mild, and too well *given*,
To dream on evil, or to work my downfal. *Shakesp. H.* VI.

Fear him not, Cæsar, he's not dangerous:
He is a noble Roman, and well *given*. *Shakes. Jul. Cæsar.*

His name is Falstaff: if that man should be lewdly *given*, he deceives me; for, Harry, I see virtue in his looks. *Shakesp.*

Huniades, the scourge of the Turks, was dead long before; so was also Mathias: after whom succeeded others, *given* all to pleasure and ease. *Knolles's History of the Turks.*

Though he was *given* to pleasure, yet he was likewise desirous of glory. *Bacon's Henry* VII.

He that *giveth* his mind to the law of the most High, will seek out the wisdom of all the ancients. *Ecclus.* xxxix. 1.

He is much *given* to contemplation, and the viewing of this theatre of the world. *More's Antidote against Atheism.*

They who *gave* themselves to warlike action and enterprises, went immediately to the palace of Odin. *Temple.*

Men are *given* to this licentious humour of scoffing at personal blemishes and defects. *L'Estrange.*

Besides, he is too much *given* to horseplay in his raillery; and comes to battle, like a dictator from the plough. *Dryden.*

I have some business of importance with her; but her husband is so horribly *given* to be jealous. *Dryd. Spanish Fryar.*

What can I refuse to a man so charitably *given*? *Dryden.*

21. To resign; to yield up.

Finding ourselves in the midst of the greatest wilderness of waters, without victual, we *gave* ourselves for lost men, and prepared for death. *Bacon's New Atlantis.*

Who say, I care not, those I *give* for lost;
And to instruct them, will not quit the cost. *Herbert.*

Virtue giv'n for lost,
Deprest and overthrown, as seem'd;
Like that self-begott'n bird
In the Arabian woods embost,
That no second knows, nor third,
And lay erewhile a holocaust,
From out her ashy womb now teem'd. *Milton's Agonistes.*

Since no deep within her gulph can hold
Immortal vigour, though oppress'd and fall'n,
I *give* not heaven for lost. *Milton's Paradise Lost, b.* ii.

For a man to *give* his name to Christianity in those days, was to list himself a martyr. *South.*

Ours *gives* himself for gone; you've watch'd your time,
He fights this day unarm'd, without his rhyme. *Dryden.*

The parents, after a long search for the body, *gave* him for drowned in one of the canals. *Addison's Spectator.*

As the hinder feet of the horse stuck to the mountain, while the body reared up in the air, the poet with great difficulty kept himself from sliding off his back, in so much that the people *gave* him for gone. *Addison's Guardian.*

22. To conclude; to suppose.

Whence came you here, O friend, and whither bound?
All *gave* you lost on far Cyclopean ground. *Garth's Ovid.*

23. *To* Give *away.* To alienate from one's self; to make over to another; to transfer.

The more he got, the more he shewed that he *gave away* to his new mistress, when he betrayed his promises to the former. *Sidney, b.* ii.

If you shall marry,
You *give away* this hand, and that is mine;
You *give away* heav'n's vows, and those are mine;
You *give away* myself, which is known mine. *Shakespeare.*

Honest company, I thank you all,
That have beheld me *give away* myself
To this most patient, sweet, and virtuous wife. *Shakespeare.*

I know not how they sold themselves; but thou, like a kind fellow, *gav'st* thyself *away* gratis, and I thank thee for thee. *Shakespeare's Henry IV. p. ii.*

Love *gives away* all things, that so he may advance the interest of the beloved person. *Taylor's Rule of living holy.*

But we who *give* our native rights *away*,
And our enslav'd posterity betray,
Are now reduc'd to beg an alms, and go
On holidays to see a puppet-show. *Dryden's Juvenal's Sat.*

Alas, said I, man was made in vain! How is he *given away* to misery and mortality! *Addison's Spectator, N°. 159.*

Theodosius arrived at a religious house in the city, where Constantia resided, and made himself one of the order, with a private vow never to inquire after Constantia, whom he looked upon as *given away* to his rival, upon the day on which their marriage was to have been solemnized. *Addison's Spectat.*

Whatsoever we employ in charitable uses, during our lives, is *given away* from ourselves: what we bequeath at our death, is *given* from others only, as our nearest relations. *Atterbury.*

24. *To* GIVE *back.* To return; to restore.

'Till their vices perhaps *give back* all those advantages which their victories procured. *Atterbury's Sermons.*

25. *To* GIVE *forth.* To publish; to tell.

Soon after it was *given forth*, and believed by many, that the king was dead. *Hayward.*

26. *To* GIVE *the hand.* To yield pre-eminence, as being subordinate or inferior.

Lessons being free from some inconveniences, whereunto sermons are more subject, they may in this respect no less take than in others they must *give the hand*, which betokeneth pre-eminence. *Hooker.*

27. *To* GIVE *over.* To leave; to quit; to cease.

Let novelty therefore in this *give over* endless contradictions, and let ancient customs prevail. *Hooker.*

It may be done rather than that be *given over.* *Hooker.*

Never *give* her *o'er*;
For scorn at first makes after love the more. *Shakespeare.*

If Desdemona will return me my jewels, I will *give over* my suit, and repent my unlawful solicitation. *Shakes. Othello.*

Abdemelech, as one weary of the world, *gave over* all, and betook himself to a solitary life, and became monk. *Knolles.*

All the soldiers, from the highest to the lowest, had solemnly sworn to defend the city, and not to *give* it *over* unto the last man. *Knolles's History of the Turks.*

Sleep hath forsook and *giv'n* me *o'er*
To death's benuming opium, as my only cure. *Milton.*

Those troops, which were levied, have *given over* the prosecution of the war. *Clarendon, b. viii.*

But worst of all to *give* her *over*,
'Till she's as desperate to recover. *Hudibras, p. iii. cant. 3.*

'Tis not amiss, e'er y' are *giv'n o'er*,
To try one desp'rate med'cine more;
And where your case can be no worse,
The desp'ratest is the wisest course. *Hudibras, p. ii.*

A woman had a hen that laid every day an egg: she fancied that upon a larger allowance this hen might lay twice a day; but the hen grew fat, and *gave* quite *over* laying. *L'Estrange.*

Many have *given over* their pursuits after fame, either from the disappointments they have met, or from their experience of the little pleasure which attends it. *Addison's Spectator.*

28. *To* GIVE *over.* To addict; to attach to.

Zelmane, govern and direct me; for I am wholly *given over* unto thee. *Sidney, b. ii.*

When the Babylonians had *given* themselves *over* to all manner of vice, it was time for the Lord, who had set up that empire, to pull it down. *Grew's Cosmol. b. iii. c. 3.*

I used one thing ill, or *gave* myself so much *over* to it as to neglect what I owed either to him or the rest of the world. *Temple's Miscellanies.*

29. *To* GIVE *over.* To conclude lost.

Since it is lawful to practise upon them that are forsaken and *given over*, I will adventure to prescribe to you. *Suckling.*

The abbess, finding that the physicians had *given* her *over*, told her that Theodosius was just gone before her, and had sent her his benediction. *Addison's Spectator, N°. 164.*

Her condition was now quite desperate, all regular physicians, and her nearest relations, having *given* her *over*. *Arbuth.*

Yet this false comfort never *gives* him *o'er*,
That, whilst he creeps, his vigorous thoughts can soar. *Pope.*

Not one foretells I shall recover;
But all agree to *give* me *over*. *Swift.*

30. *To* GIVE *over.* To abandon.

The duty of uniformity throughout all churches, in all manner of indifferent ceremonies, will be very hard, and therefore best to *give* it *over*. *Hooker, b. iv. s. 13.*

The cause, for which we fought and swore
So boldly, shall we now *give o'er?* *Hudibras, p. i. cant. 2.*

31. *To* GIVE *out.* To proclaim; to publish; to utter.

The fathers *give* it *out* for a rule, that whatsoever Christ is said in Scripture to have received, the same we ought to apply only to the manhood of Christ. *Hooker, b. v. s. 54.*

It is *given out*, that, sleeping in my orchard,
A serpent stung me. So the whole ear of Denmark
Is, by a forged process of my death,
Rankly abused. *Shakespeare's Hamlet.*

One that *gives out* himself prince Florizel,
Son of Polixenes, with his princess. *Shakes. Winter's Tale.*

It hath been *given out*, by an hypocritical thief, who was the first master of my ship, that I carried with me out of England twenty-two thousand of twenty-two shillings per piece. *Raleigh's Apology.*

He *gave out* general summons for the assembly of his council for the wars. *Knolles's History of the Turks.*

The night was distinguished by the orders which he *gave out* to his army, that they should forbear all insulting of their enemies. *Addison's Freeholder, N°. 49.*

32. *To* GIVE *out.* To show in false appearance.

His *givings out* were of an infinite distance
From his true meant design. *Shakesp. Meas. for Measure.*

She that, so young, could *give out* such a seeming,
To seal her father's eyes up close as oak. *Shakesp. Othello.*

33. *To* GIVE *up.* To resign; to quit; to yield.

The people, weary of the miseries of war, would *give* him *up*, if they saw him shrink. *Sidney, b. ii.*

He has betray'd your business, and *given up*
For certain drops of salt your city Rome. *Shak. Coriolanus.*

The sun, breaking out with his cheerful beams, revived many, before ready to *give up* the ghost for cold, and gave comfort to them all. *Knolles's History of the Turks.*

He found the lord Hopton in trouble for the loss of the regiment of foot at Alton, and with the unexpected assurance of the *giving up* of Arundel-castle. *Clarendon, b. viii.*

Let us *give* ourselves wholly *up* to Christ in heart and desire. *Taylor's Rule of living holy.*

Such an expectation will never come to pass; therefore I'll e'en *give it up*, and go and fret myself. *Collier against Despair.*

I can *give up* to the historians of your country the names of so many generals and heroes which crowd their annals. *Dryd.*

He declares himself to be now satisfied to the contrary, in which he has *given up* the cause. *Dryden.*

The leagues made between several states, disowning all claim to the land in the other's possession, have, by common consent, *given up* their pretences to their natural right. *Locke.*

If they *give* them *up* to their reasons, then they with them *give up* all truth and farther enquiry, and think there is no such thing as certainty. *Locke.*

We should see him *give up* again to the wild common of nature, whatever was more than would supply the conveniencies of life. *Locke.*

Juba's surrender, since his father's death,
Would *give up* Africk into Cæsar's hands,
And make him lord of half the burning zone. *Addis. Cato.*

Learn to be honest men, *give up* your leaders,
And pardon shall descend on all the rest. *Addison's Cato.*

A popish priest threatened to excommunicate a Northumberland squire, if he did not *give up* to him the church lands. *Addison's Freeholder.*

He saw the celestial deities acting in a confederacy against him, and immediately *gave up* a cause which was excluded from all possibility of success. *Addison's Freeholder.*

An old gentleman, who had been engaged in an argument with the emperor, upon his friend's telling him he wondered he would *give up* the question when he had the better, I am never ashamed, says he, to be confuted by one who is master of fifty legions. *Addison's Spectator, N°. 239.*

He may be brought to *give up* the clearest evidence. *Atterb.*

The constant health and longevity of men must be *given up* also, as a groundless conceit. *Bentley's Sermons.*

Have the physicians *giv'n up* all their hopes?
Cannot they add a few days to a monarch? *Rowe.*

These people were obliged to demand peace, and *give up* to the Romans all their possessions in Sicily. *Arbuthnot.*

Every one who will not ask for the conduct of God in the study of religion, has just reason to fear he shall be left of God, and *given up* a prey to a thousand prejudices, that he shall be consigned over to the follies of his own heart. *Watts.*

Give yourself *up* to some hours of leisure. *Watts.*

34. *To* GIVE *up.* To abandon.

If any be *given up* to believe lyes, some must be first *given up* to tell them. *Stillingfleet's Def. of Disc. on Rom. Idol.*

Our minds naturally *give* themselves *up* to every diversion which they are much accustomed to; and we always find that play, when followed with assiduity, engrosses the whole woman. *Addison's Guardian, N°. 120.*

Give up your fond paternal pride,
Nor argue on the weaker side. *Swift.*

A good poet no sooner communicates his works, but it is imagined he is a vain young creature *given up* to the ambition of fame. *Pope.*

I am

I am obliged at this time to *give up* my whole application to Homer. *Pope.*

Persons who, through misfortunes, chuse not to dress, should not, however, *give up* neatness. *Clarissa.*

35. *To* GIVE *up.* To deliver.

And Joab *gave up* the sum of the number of the people to the king. *2 Sa.* xxiv. 9.

His accounts were confused, and he could not then *give* them *up.* *Swift on the Dissent. in Athens and Rome.*

To GIVE. *v. n.*

1. To rush; to fall on; to give the assault. A phrase merely French, and not worthy of adoption.

Your orders come too late, the fight's begun;
The enemy *gives* on with fury led. *Dryd. Ind. Emp.*

Hannibal *gave upon* the Romans. *Hooke's Rom. Hist.*

2. To relent; to grow moist; to melt or soften; to thaw.

Some things are harder when they come from the fire, and afterwards *give* again, and grow soft; as the crust of bread, bisket, sweetmeats, and salt. *Bacon's Natural History.*

Only a sweet and virtuous soul,
Like season'd timber, never *gives*;
But though the whole world turn to coal,
Then chiefly lives. *Herbert.*

Unless it is kept in a hot house, it will so *give* again, that it will be little better than raw malt. *Mortimer.*

Before you carry your large cocks in, open them once, and spread them: hay is apt to *give* in the cock. *Mortimer.*

3. To move. A French phrase.

Up and down he traverses his ground,
Then nimbly shifts a thrust, then lends a wound;
Now back he *gives*, then rushes on amain. *Daniel's C. War.*

4. *To* GIVE *in.* To go back; to give way.

The charge was given with so well governed fury, that the left corner of the Scots battalion was enforced to *give in. Haywo.*

5. *To* GIVE *in to.* [A French phrase.] To adopt; to embrace.

This is a geography particular to the medallists: the poets, however, have sometimes *given in to* it, and furnish us with very good lights for the explication of it. *Addison on Medals.*

This consideration may induce a translator to *give in to* those general phrases, which have attained a veneration in our language from being used in the Old Testament. *Pope.*

The whole body of the people are either stupidly negligent, or else *giving in* with all their might *to* those very practices that are working their destruction. *Swift.*

6. *To* GIVE *off.* To cease; to forbear.

The punishment would be kept from being too much, if we *gave off* as soon as we perceived that it reached the mind. *Locke on Education.*

7. *To* GIVE *over.* To cease; to act no more.

If they will speak to the purpose, they must *give over*, and stand upon such particulars only as they can shew we have either added or abrogated, otherwise than we ought, in the matter of church polity. *Hooker, b.* iii.

Neither hath Christ, thro' union of both natures, incurred the damage of either; lest, by being born a man, we should think he hath *given over* to be God, or that because he continued God, therefore he cannot be man also. *Hooker, b.* v.

Give not *o'er* so: to him again; intreat him,
Kneel down before him, hang upon his gown;
You are too cold. *Shakespeare's Measure for Measure.*

The state of human actions is so variable, that to try things oft, and never to *give over*, doth wonders. *Bacon's Nat. Hist.*

Demetrius, king of Macedon, had a petition offered him divers times by an old woman, and still answered he had no leisure; whereupon the woman said aloud, Why then *give over* to be king. *Bacon's Apophthegms.*

So Satan, whom repulse upon repulse
Met ever, and to shameful silence brought,
Yet *gives* not *o'er*, though desperate of success. *Milton.*

Shall we kindle all this flame
Only to put it out again?
And must we now *give o'er*,
And only end where we begun?
In vain this mischief we have done,
If we can do no more. *Denham.*

It would be well for all authors, if they knew when to *give over*, and to desist from any farther pursuits after fame. *Addis.*

He coined again, and was forced to *give over* for the same reason. *Swift.*

8. *To* GIVE *out.* To publish; to proclaim.

Simon bewitched the people of Samaria, *giving out* that himself was some great one. *Acts* viii. 9.

Julius Cæsar laid asleep Pompey's preparations, by a fame that he cunningly *gave out* how Cæsar's own soldiers loved him not. *Bacon, Essay* 60.

Your ill-wishers will *give out* you are now going to quit your school. *Swift.*

9. *To* GIVE *out.* To cease; to yield.

We are the earth; and they,
Like moles within us, heave and cast about:
And 'till they foot and clutch their prey;
They never cool, much less *give out.* *Herbert.*

Madam, I always believ'd you so stout,
That for twenty denials you would not *give out.* *Swift.*

10. *To* GIVE *way.* To yield; not to resist; to make room for.

Private respects, with him, *gave way* to the common good. *Carew's Survey of Cornwal.*

Perpetual pushing and assurance put a difficulty out of countenance, and make a seeming impossibility *give way.* *Collier.*

Scarce had he spoken when the cloud *gave way*;
The mists flew upward, and dissolv'd in day. *Dryd. Æn.*

His golden helm *gives way* with stony blows,
Batter'd and flat, and beaten to his brows. *Dryden's Æn.*

GI'VER. *n. s.* [from *give.*] One that gives; donor; bestower; distributer; granter.

Well we may afford
Our *givers* their own gifts. *Milton's Paradise Lost, b.* v.

By thee how fairly is the *giver* now
Repaid? But gratitude in thee is lost
Long since. *Milton's Paradise Regain'd, b.* iv.

I have not liv'd since first I heard the news;
The gift the guilty *giver* doth accuse. *Dryden's Aurengzebe.*

Both gifts destructive to the *givers* prove;
Alike both lovers fall by those they love. *Pope.*

GI'ZZARD. *n. s.* [*gesier*, French; *gigeria*, Latin. It is sometimes called *gizzern.*]

1. The strong musculous stomach of a fowl.

Fowls have two ventricles, and pick up stones to convey them into their second ventricle, the *gizzerne.* *More.*

In birds there is no mastication in the mouth; but in such as are not carnivorous, it is immediately swallowed into the crop, a kind of antestomach, where it is moistened by some proper juice from the glandules distilling in there, and thence transferred into the *gizzard*, or musculous stomach. *Ray.*

Flutt'ring there they nestle near the throne,
And lodge in habitations not their own;
By their high crops and corny *gizzards* known. *Dryden.*

2. It is proverbially used for apprehension or conception of mind: as, he *frets his gizzard*, he harrasses his imagination.

But that which does them greatest harm,
Their spiritual *gizzards* are too warm;
Which puts the overheated sots
In fevers still. *Hudibras, p.* iii. *cant.* ii.

Satisfaction and restitution lie so cursedly hard upon the *gizzards* of our publicans, that the blood in their veins is not half so dear to them as the treasure they have in their coffers. *L'Estrange.*

GLA'BRITY. *n. s.* [from *glaber*, Latin.] Smoothness; baldness. *Dict.*

GLA'CIAL. *adj.* [*glacial*, French; *glacialis*, Latin.] Icy; made of ice; frozen.

To GLA'CIATE. *v. n.* [*glacies*, Latin; *glacer*, French.] To turn into ice.

GLACIA'TION. *n. s.* [from *glaciate.*] The act of turning into ice; ice formed.

Ice is plain upon the surface of water, but round in hail, which is also a *glaciation*, and figured in its guttulous descent from the air. *Brown's Vulgar Errours, b.* ii. *c.* 1.

GLA'CIS. *n. s.* [French.] In fortification, a sloping bank. It is more especially taken for that which rangeth from the parapet of the covered way to the level on the side of the field. *Harris.*

GLAD. *adj.* [ᵹlæd, Saxon; *glad*, Danish.]

1. Cheerful; gay; in a state of hilarity.

He will be *glad* in his heart. *Ex.* iv. 14.

They blessed the king, and went unto their tents joyful and *glad* of heart. *1 Kings* viii. 66.

2. Wearing a gay appearance; fertile; bright; showy.

The wilderness and the solitary place shall be *glad* for them, and the desert shall rejoice and blossom as the rose. *Is.* xxxv.

3. Pleased; elevated with joy. It has generally *of*, sometimes *at* or *with* before the cause of gladness: perhaps *of* is most proper, when the cause of joy is something gained or possessed; and *at* or *with*, when it is some accident befallen himself or another.

I am *glad* to see your worship. *Shakespeare's Henry* IV.

He hath an uncle in Messina will be very much *glad of* it. *Shakespeare's Much Ado about Nothing.*

He that is *glad at* calamities shall not be unpunished. *Prov.*

If he be my enemy, let him triumph; if he be my friend, he will be *glad of* my repentance. *Dryden's Fables, Pref.*

The gaping wound gush'd out a crimson flood;
The Trojan, *glad with* sight of hostile blood,
His fauchion drew. *Dryden's Æn.*

I would be *glad* to learn from those who pronounce that the human soul always thinks, how they know it. *Locke.*

4. Pleasing; exhilarating.

Her conversation
More *glad* to me than to a miser money is. *Sidney, b.* i.

5. Expressing gladness.

Hark! a *glad* voice the lonely desert cheers:
Prepare the way, a God, a God appears! *Pope's Messiah.*

To GLAD. *v. a.* [from the adjective.] To make glad; to cheer; to exhilarate.

He saw rich nectar-thaws release the rigour
Of th' icy North; from frost-bound Atlas' hands
His adamantine fetters fall: green vigour
Gladding the Scythian rocks, and Lybian sands. *Crashaw.*

It *glads* me
To see so many virtues thus united,
To restore justice and dethrone oppression. *Otway.*

Each drinks the juice that *glads* the heart of man. *Pope.*

If justice Philips' costive head
Some frigid rhymes disburses,
They shall like Persian tales be read,
And *glad* both babes and nurses. *Swift.*

To GLA'DDEN. *v. a.* [from *glad.*] To cheer; to delight; to make glad; to exhilarate.

Oh, he was all made up of love and charms!
Delight of every eye! When he appear'd,
A secret pleasure *gladden'd* all that saw him. *Addison's Cato.*

A kind of vital heat in the soul cheers and *gladdens* her, when she does not attend to it. *Addison's Spectator.*

GLA'DDER. *n. s.* [from *glad.*] One that makes glad; one that gladdens; one that exhilarates.

Thou *gladder* of the mount of Cytheron,
Have pity, goddess. *Dryden.*

GLADE. *n. s.* [from gloȝan, to be hot, or to shine; whence the Danish *glod*, and the obsolete English *gleed*, a red hot coal.] A lawn or opening in a wood. *Lucus.* It is taken for an avenue through a wood, whether open or shaded, and has therefore epithets of opposite meaning.

So flam'd his eyen with rage and rancorous ire;
But far within, as in a hollow *glade*,
Those glaring lamps were set, that made a dreadful shade.
Fairy Queen, b. i. *cant.* 11.

Lo where they spy'd, how in a gloomy *glade*
The lion sleeping lay in secret shade. *Hubberd's Tale.*

O might I here
In solitude live savage, in some *glade*
Obscur'd, where highest woods, impenetrable
To star or sun-light, spread their umbrage broad,
And brown as evening. *Milton's Paradise Lost, b.* ix.

When any, favour'd of high Jove,
Chances to pass through this adventurous *glade*,
Swift as a sparkle of a glancing star
I shoot from heav'n to give him safe convoy. *Milton.*

For noonday's heat are closer arbours made,
And for fresh ev'ning air the op'ner *glade*. *Dryd. Innocence.*

There, interspers'd in lawns and opening *glades*,
Thin trees arise that shun each other's shades. *Pope.*

By the heroes armed shades,
Glitt'ring through the gloomy *glades*;
By the youths that dy'd for love,
Wand'ring in the myrtle grove,
Restore, restore Eurydice to life!
Oh, take the husband, or restore the wife! *Pope's St. Cecil.*

GLA'DEN. } *n. s.* [from *gladius*, Latin, a sword.] Swordgrass: a
GLA'DER. } general name of plants that rise with a broad blade like sedge. *Junius.*

GLA'DFULNESS. *n. s.* [*glad* and *fulness.*] Joy; gladness.

And there him rests in riotous suffisance
Of all his *gladfulness*, and kingly joyance. *Spenser.*

GLADIA'TOR. *n s.* [Latin; *gladiateur*, Fr.] A swordplayer; a prizefighter.

Then whilst his foe each *gladiator* foils,
The atheist, looking on, enjoys the spoils. *Denham.*

Besides, in gratitude for such high matters,
Know I have vow'd two hundred *gladiators*. *Dryden's Pers.*

GLA'DLY. *adv.* [from *glad.*] Joyfully; with gayety; with merriment; with triumph; with exultation.

For his particular, I'll receive him *gladly*;
But not one follower. *Shakespeare's King Lear.*

You are going to set us right; and 'tis an advantage every body will *gladly* see you engross the glory of. *Blount to Pope.*

GLA'DNESS. *n. s.* [from *glad.*] Cheerfulness; joy; exultation.

By such degrees the spreading *gladness* grew
In every heart, which fear had froze before:
The standing streets with so much joy they view,
That with less grief the perish'd they deplore. *Dryden.*

GLA'DSOME. *adj.* [from *glad.*]

1. Pleased; gay; delighted.

The highest angels to and fro descend,
From highest heaven in *gladsome* company. *Fairy Queen.*

The *gladsome* ghosts in circling troops attend,
And with unweary'd eyes behold their friend:
Delight to hover near. *Dryden's Æn. b.* iv.

2. Causing joy; having an appearance of gayety.

Each morn they wak'd me with a sprightly lay;
Of opening heav'n they sung and *gladsome* day. *Prior.*

GLA'DSOMELY. *adv.* [from *gladsome.*] With gayety and delight.

GLA'DSOMNESS. *n. s.* [from *gladsome.*] Gayety; showiness; delight.

GLAIRE. *n. s.* [ȝlæꞃ, Saxon, amber; *glar*, Danish, glass; *glaire*, French; *glarea*, Latin.]

1. The white of an egg.

Take the *glaire* of eggs, and strain it as short as water.
Peacham on Drawing.

2. A kind of halbert. *Dict.*

To GLAIRE. *v. a.* [*glairer*, French; from the noun.] To smear with the white of an egg. This word is still used by the bookbinders.

GLANCE. *n. s.* [*glantz*, German, glitter.]

1. A sudden shoot of light or splendour.

His off'ring soon propitious fire from heav'n
Consum'd with nimble *glance*, and grateful steam:
The other's not; for his was not sincere. *Milt. Parad. Lost.*

2. A stroke or dart of the beam of sight.

The aspects which procure love are not gazings, but sudden *glances* and dartings of the eye. *Bacon's Nat. History.*

There are of those sort of beauties which last but for a moment; some particularity of a violent passion, some graceful action, a smile, a *glance* of an eye, a disdainful look, and a look of gravity. *Dryden's Dufresnoy.*

3. A snatch of sight; a quick view.

The ample mind takes a survey of several objects with one *glance*. *Watts's Improvement of the Mind.*

To GLANCE. *v. n.* [from the noun.]

1. To shoot a sudden ray of splendour.

He double blows about him fiercely laid,
That *glancing* fire out of the iron play'd,
As sparkles from the anvil use,
When heavy hammers on the wedge are sway'd. *Fai. Queen.*

When through the gloom the *glancing* lightnings fly,
Heavy the rattling thunders roll on high. *Rowe.*

2. To fly off in an oblique direction.

He has a little gall'd me, I confess;
But as the jest did *glance* away from me,
'Tis ten to one it maim'd you two outright. *Shakespeare.*

3. To strike in an oblique direction.

Pois'd in air, the jav'lin sent,
Through Paris' shield the forceful weapon went,
His corslet pierces, and his garment rends,
And *glancing* downwards near his flank descends. *Pope.*

4. To view with a quick cast of the eye; to play the eye.

O' th' sudden up they rise and dance,
Then sit again, and sigh and *glance*;
Then dance again, and kiss. *Suckling.*

Mighty dulness crown'd,
Shall take through Grub-street her triumphant round;
And her Parnassus *glancing* o'er at once,
Behold a hundred sons, and each a dunce. *Pope's Dunciad.*

The cooing dove
Flies thick in am'rous chace, and wanton rolls
The *glancing* eye, and turns the changeful scene. *Thomson.*

5. To censure by oblique hints.

How can'st thou thus, for shame, Titania,
Glance at my credit with Hippolita,
Knowing I know thy love to Theseus? *Shakespeare.*

Some men *glance* and dart at others, by justifying themselves by negatives; as to say, this I do not. *Bacon, Essay* 23.

I have never *glanced* upon the late designed procession of his holiness and his attendants, notwithstanding it might have afforded matter to many ludicrous speculations. *Addis. Spect.*

It was objected against him that he had written verses, wherein he *glanced* at a certain reverend doctor, famous for dulness. *Swift.*

To GLANCE. *v. a.* To move nimbly; to shoot obliquely.

Glancing an eye of pity on his losses,
Enough to press a royal merchant down. *Shak. Mer. of Ven.*

GLA'NCINGLY. *adv.* [from *glance.*] In an oblique broken manner; transiently.

Sir Richard Hawkins hath done something in this kind, but brokenly and *glancingly*, intending chiefly a discourse of his own voyage. *Hakewill on Providence.*

GLAND. *n. s.* [*glans*, Latin; *gland*, French.]

All the *glands* of a human body are reduced to two sorts, viz. conglobate and conglomerate. A conglobate *gland* is a little smooth body, wrapt up in a fine skin, by which it is separated from all the other parts, only admitting an artery and nerve to pass in, and giving way to a vein and excretory canal to come out: of this sort are the *glands* in the brain, the labial *glands*, and testes. A conglomerate *gland* is composed of many little conglobate *glands*, all tied together, and wrapt up in the common tunicle or membrane. *Quincy.*

I observed the abscess to have begun deep in the body of the *glands*. *Wiseman's Surgery.*

The *glands*, which o'er the body spread,
Fine complicated clues of nervous thread,
Involv'd and twisted with th' arterial duct,
The rapid motion of the blood obstruct. *Blackm. Creation.*

GLA'NDERS. *n. s.* [from *gland.*] In a horse, is the running of corrupt matter from the nose, which differs in colour according to the degree of the malignity, being white, yellow, green or black. *Farrier's Dict.*

His

His horse is possest with the *glanders*, and like to mose in the chine. *Shakespeare's Taming of the Shrew.*

GLANDI'FEROUS. *adj.* [*glans* and *fero*, Latin.] Bearing mast; bearing acorns, or fruit like acorns.

The beech is of two sorts, and numbered amongst the *glandiferous* trees. *Mortimer's Husbandry.*

GLA'NDULE. *n. s.* [*glandula*, Latin; *glandule*, Fr.] A small gland serving to the secretion of humours.

Nature hath provided several *glandules* to separate this juice from the blood, and no less than four pair of channels to convey it into the mouth, which are called *ductus salivales*. *Ray.*

GLANDULO'SITY. *n. s.* [from *glandulous*.] A collection of glands.

In the upper parts of worms are found certain white and oval *glandulosities*. *Brown's Vulgar Errours, b.* iii.

GLA'NDULOUS. *adj.* [*glandulosus*, Latin; *glanduleux*, Fr. from *glandule*.] Pertaining to the glands; subsisting in the glands; having the nature of glands.

There are no testicles, or parts official unto generation, but *glandulous* substances, that hold the nature of emunctories. *Brown's Vulgar Errours, b.* iii. *c.* 17.

Such constitutions must be subject to *glandulous* tumours and ruptures of the lymphatick, and all the diseases thereon dependant. *Arbuthnot on Aliments.*

To GLARE. *v. n.* [*glaeren*, Dutch.]

1. To shine so as to dazzle the eyes.

After great light, if you come suddenly into the dark, or, contrariwise, out of the dark into a *glaring* light, the eye is dazzled for a time, and the sight confused. *Bacon's Nat. Hist.*

His *glaring* eyes with anger's venom swell,
And like the brand of foul Alecto flame. *Fairfax, b.* ii.

He is every where above conceits of epigrammatick wit, and gross hyperboles: he maintains majesty in the midst of plainness; he shines, but *glares* not; and is stately without ambition. *Dryden.*

The court of Cacus stands reveal'd to sight;
The cavern *glares* with new admitted light. *Dryden's Æn.*

Alas, thy dazzled eye
Beholds this man in a false *glaring* light,
Which conquest and success have thrown upon him. *Addis.*

2. To look with fierce piercing eyes.

Avaunt, and quit my sight! let the earth hide thee!
Thou hast no speculation in those eyes,
Which thou do'st *glare* with. *Shakespeare's Macbeth.*

Look, how pale he *glares!*
His form and cause conjoin'd, preaching to stones,
Would make them capable. *Shakespeare's Hamlet.*

Now friends no more, nor walking hand in hand;
But when they met they made a surly stand,
And *glar'd*, like angry lions, as they pass'd,
And wish'd that ev'ry look might be their last. *Dryd. Fables.*

3. To shine ostentatiously, or with too much laboured lustre.

The most *glaring* and notorious passages are none of the finest, or most correct. *Felton on the Classicks.*

To GLARE. *v. a.* To shoot such splendour as the eye cannot bear.

One spirit in them rul'd, and every eye
Glar'd lightning, and shot forth pernicious fire
Among th' accurst, that wither'd all their strength. *Milton.*

GLARE. *n. s.* [from the verb.]

1. Overpowering lustre; splendour, such as dazzles the eye.

The frame of burnish'd steel that cast a *glare*
From far, and seem'd to thaw the freezing air. *Dryd. Fab.*

I have grieved to see a person of quality gliding by me in her chair at two o'clock in the morning, and looking like a spectre amidst a *glare* of flambeaux. *Addison's Guardian.*

Here in a grotto, shelter'd close from air,
And screen'd in shades from day's detested *glare*,
She sighs for ever. *Pope's Rock of the Lock.*

2. A fierce piercing look.

About them round,
A lion now he stalks with fiery *glare*. *Milt. Parad. Lost.*

GLA'REOUS. *adj.* [*glaireux*, Fr. *glareosus*, Latin, from *glaire*.] Consisting of viscous transparent matter, like the white of an egg.

GLA'RING. *adj.* Applied to any thing very shocking: as, a *glaring* crime.

GLASS. *n. s.* [ʒlæꞅ, Saxon; *glas*, Dutch, as *Pezon* imagines from *glâs*, British, green. In Erse it is called *klânn*, and this primarily signifies clean or clear, being so denominated from its transparency.

1. An artificial substance made by fusing fixed salts and flint or sand together, with a vehement fire.

The word *glass* cometh from the Belgick and High Dutch: *glass*, from the verb *glansen*, which signifies amongst them to shine; or perhaps from *glacies* in the Latin, which is ice, whose colour it resembles. *Peacham on Drawing.*

Glass is thought so compact and firm a body that it is indestructible by art or nature, and is also of so close a texture that the subtlest chymical spirits cannot pervade it. *Boyle.*

Show'rs of granadoes rain, by sudden burst
Disploding murd'rous bowels, fragments of steel
And stones, and *glass* and nitrous grain adust. *Phillips.*

2. A glass vessel of any kind.

I'll see no more;
And yet the eighth appears, who bears a *glass*
Which shews me many more. *Shakespeare's Macbeth.*

3. A looking-glass; a mirrour.

He was the mark and *glass*, copy and book,
That fashion'd others. *Shakespeare's Henry* IV. *p.* ii.

He spreads his subtile nets from sight,
With twinkling *glasses*, to betray
The larks that in the meshes light. *Dryden's Horace.*

4. *An Hour* GLASS. A glass used in measuring time by the flux of sand.

Were my wife's liver
Infected as her life, she would not live
The running of one *glass*. *Shakes. Winter's Tale.*

5. A cup of glass used to drink in.

To this last costly treaty,
That swallow'd so much treasure, and like a *glass*
Did break i' th' rinsing. *Shakespeare's Henry* VIII.

When thy heart
Dilates with fervent joys, and eager soul
Prompts to pursue the sparkling *glass*, be sure
'Tis time to shun it. *Phillips.*

6. The quantity of wine usually contained in a glass; a draught.

While a man thinks one *glass* more will not make him drunk, that one *glass* hath disabled him from well discerning his present condition. *Taylor's Rule of living holy.*

The first *glass* may pass for health, the second for good-humour, the third for our friends; but the fourth is for our enemies. *Temple.*

7. A perspective glass.

Like those who have surveyed the moon by *glasses*, I can only tell of a new and shining world above us; but not relate the riches and glories of the place. *Dryden.*

GLASS. *adj.* Vitreous; made of glass.

Get thee *glass* eyes;
And, like a scurvy politician, seem
To see the things thou do'st not. *Shakesp. King Lear.*

Glass bottles are more fit for this second fining than those of wood. *Mortimer's Husbandry.*

To GLASS. *v. a.*

1. To see as in a glass; to represent as in a glass or mirrour.

Methinks I am partaker of thy passion,
And in thy case do *glass* mine own debility. *Sidney, b.* ii.

2. To case in glass.

Methought all his senses were lockt in his eye,
As jewels in crystal for some prince to buy;
Who tend'ring their own worth, from whence they were *glasst*,
Did point out to buy them, along as you past. *Shakesp.*

3. To cover with glass; to glaze.

I have observed little grains of silver to lie hid in the small cavities, perhaps *glassed* over by a vitrifying heat, in crucibles wherein silver has been long kept in fusion. *Boyle.*

GLA'SSFURNACE. *n. s.* [*glass* and *furnace*.] A furnace in which glass is made by liquefaction.

If our dreamer pleases to try whether the glowing heat of a *glassfurnace* be barely a wandering imagination in a drowsy man's fancy, by putting his hand into it, he may perhaps be awakened into a certainty that it is something more than bare imagination. *Locke.*

GLA'SSGAZING. *adj.* [*glass* and *gazing*] Finical; often contemplating himself in a mirrour.

A whorson, *glassgazing*, superserviceable, finical rogue. *Shakespeare's King Lear.*

GLA'SSGRINDER. *n. s.* [*glass* and *grinder*.] One whose trade is to polish and grind glass.

The *glassgrinders* complain of the trouble they meet with. *Boyle.*

GLA'SSHOUSE. *n. s.* [*glass* and *house*.] A house where glass is manufactured.

I remember to have met with an old Roman Mosaic, composed of little pieces of clay half vitrified, and prepared at the *glasshouses*. *Addison's Remarks on Italy.*

GLA'SSMAN. *n. s.* [*glass* and *man*.] One who sells glass.

The profit of glasses consists only in a small present made by the *glassman*. *Swift.*

GLA'SSMETAL. *n. s.* [*glass* and *metal*.] Glass in fusion.

Let proof be made of the incorporating of copper or brass with *glassmetal*. *Bacon's Phys. Rem.*

GLA'SSWORK. *n. s.* [*glass* and *work*.] Manufactory of glass.

The crystalline Venice glass is a mixture, in equal portions, of stones brought from Pavia, and the ashes of a weed called kali, gathered in a desert between Alexandria and Rosetta; and is by the Egyptians used first for fuel, and then they crush the ashes into lumps like a stone, and so sell them to the Venetians for their *glassworks*. *Bacon's Natural History.*

GLA'SSWORT. *n. s.* [*salicornia*, or saltwort.]

It hath an apetalous flower, wanting the empalement; for the stamina, or chives, and the embryoes grow on the extreme part of the leaves: these embryoes afterward become pods or bladders, which for the most part contain one seed. The species are two. These plants grow on the sea-coasts in many parts of Europe, and upon the shores in several places of England which are washed every tide with the salt water. The inhabitants, near the sea-coast where these plants grow, cut them up toward the latter end of Summer, when they are fully grown; and, after having dried them in the sun, they burn them for their ashes, which are used in making of glass and soap. These herbs are by the country people called kelp, and are promiscuously gathered for use. From the ashes of these plants is extracted the salt called sal kali, or alkali, much used by the chymists. *Miller.*

For the fine glass we use the purest of the finest sand, and the ashes of chali or *glasswort*; and for the coarser or green sort, the ashes of brake or other plants. *Brown's Vulgar Errours.*

GLA'SSY. *adj.* [from *glass.*]

1. Made of glass; vitreous.

In the valley near mount Carmel in Judea there is a sand, which, of all others, hath most affinity with glass; insomuch as other minerals laid in it turn to a *glassy* substance. *Bacon.*

2. Resembling glass, as in smoothness or lustre, or brittleness.

Man! proud man!
Drest in a little brief authority,
Most ignorant of what he's most assur'd:
His *glassy* essence, like an angry ape,
Plays such fantastick tricks before high heav'n,
As makes the angels weep. *Shakesp. Meas. for Measure.*

There is a willow grows aslant a brook,
That shews his hoary leaves in the *glassy* stream. *Shak. Ham.*

The magnet attracteth the shining or *glassy* powder brought from the Indies, usually employed in writing-dust. *Brown.*

Whose womb produc'd the *glassy* ice? Who bred
The hoary frosts that fall on Winter's head? *Sandys.*

A hundred sweep,
With stretching oars, the *glassy* deep. *Dryden's Æn.*

GLA'STONBURY *Thorn. n. s.* A species of MEDLAR, whichsee.

This species of thorn produces some bunches of flowers in Winter, and flowers again in the Spring, and in no other respect differs from the common hawthorn. *Miller.*

GLAUCO'MA. *n. s.* [γλαύκωμα; *glaucome*, French.] A fault in the eye, which changes the crystalline humour into a greyish colour, without detriment of sight, and therein differs from what is commonly understood by suffusion. *Quincy.*

The *glaucoma* is no other disease than the cataract. *Sharp.*

GLAVE. *n. s.* [*glaive*, French; *glaif*, a hook, Welsh. *Glaive* is Erse for a broad sword.] A broad sword; a falchion.

Two hundred Greeks came next in fight well try'd,
Not surely arm'd in steel or iron strong,
But each a *glave* had pendant by his side. *Fairfax, b.* i.

When zeal, with aged clubs and *glaves*,
Gave chace to rockets and white staves. *Hudibras, p.* iii.

To GLAVER. *v. n.* [*glave*, Welsh, flattery; ᵹliꝑan, Saxon, to flatter. It is still retained in Scotland.] To flatter; to wheedle. A low word.

Kingdoms have their distempers, intermissions, and paroxysms, as well as natural bodies; and a *glavering* council is as dangerous on the one hand as a wheedling priest, or a flattering physician is on the other. *L'Estrange's Fables.*

To GLAZE. *v. a.* [*To glass*, only accidentally varied.]

1. To furnish with windows of glass.

Let there be two delicate cabinets daintily paved, richly hanged, and *glazed* with crystalline glass. *Bacon's Essays.*

2. To cover with glass, as potters do their earthen ware; [from the French *glâise*, *argilla.*]

3. To overlay with something shining and pellucid.

Sorrow's eye, *glaz'd* with blinding tears,
Divides one thing entire to many objects. *Shakesp. R.* II.

The reason of one man operates on that of another in all true oratory; wherein though with other ornaments he may *glaze* and brandish the weapons, yet is it found reason that carries the stroke home. *Grew's Cosm. Sac. b.* ii. *c.* 6.

White, with other strong colours, with which we paint that which we intend to *glaze*, are the life, the spirit, and the lustre of it. *Dryden's Dufresnoy.*

GLA'ZIER. *n. s.* [corrupted from *glasier*, or *glassier*, of *glass.*] One whose trade is to make glass windows. Other manufacturers of glass are otherwise named.

Into rabbets the several panes of glasswork are set, and fastened by the *glazier*. *Moxon's Mech. Exer.*

The dext'rous *glazier* strong returns the bound,
And gingling sashes on the penthouse sound. *Gay's Trivia.*

GLEAD. *n. s.* A buzzard hawk; a kite. It retains that name in Scotland.

GLEAM. *n. s.* [ᵹeleoma, Saxon.] Sudden shoot of light; lustre; brightness.

Then was the fair Dodonian tree far seen
Upon seven hills to spread his gladsome *gleam*;
And conquerors bedecked with his green,
Along the banks of the Ausonian stream. *Spenser.*

At last a *gleam*
Of dawning light turn'd thitherward in haste
His travell'd steps. *Milton's Paradise Lost, b.* iii.

As I bent down to look just opposite,
A shape within the wat'ry *gleam* appear'd,
Bending to look on me. *Milton's Paradise Lost, b.* iv.

Mine is a *gleam* of bliss, too hot to last;
Wat'ry it shines, and will be soon o'ercast. *Dryd. Aurengz.*

We ken them from afar; the setting sun
Plays on their shining arms and burnish'd helmets,
And covers all the field with *gleams* of fire. *Addison's Cato.*

In the clear azure *gleam* the flocks are seen,
And floating forests paint the waves with green. *Pope.*

Nought was seen, and nought was heard,
Around the dreary coast,
But dreadful *gleams*,
Fires that glow,
Shrieks of woe. *Pope's St. Cecilia.*

To GLEAM. *v. n.* [from the noun.]

1. To shine with sudden coruscation.

Observant of approaching day,
The meek-ey'd morn appears, mother of dews,
At first faint *gleaming* in the dappled East. *Thoms. Summer.*

Ye *gleamings* of departed peace
Shine out your last. *Thomson's Spring.*

2. To shine.

On each hand the gushing waters play,
And down the rough cascade white dashing fall,
Or *gleam* in lengthen'd vista's through the trees. *Thomson.*

GLE'AMY. *adj.* [from *gleam.*] Flashing; darting sudden coruscations of light.

In brazen arms, that cast a *gleamy* ray,
Swift through the town the warriour bends his way. *Pope.*

To GLEAN. *v. a.* [*glaner*, French, as *Skinner* thinks, from *granum.*]

1. To gather what the gatherers of the harvest leave behind.

She came and *gleaned* in the field after the reapers. *Ruth* ii.

Cheap conquest for his following friends remain'd;
He reap'd the field, and they but only *glean'd*. *Dryden.*

She went, by hard necessity compell'd,
To *glean* Palæmon's fields. *Thomson's Autumn.*

2. To gather any thing thinly scattered.

Gather
So much as from occasions you may *glean*,
If aught, to us unknown, afflicts him thus. *Shakes. Hamlet.*

That goodness
Of *gleaning* all the land's wealth into one,
Into your own hands, card'nal, by extortion. *Shak. H.*VIII.

They *gleaned* of them in the highways five thousand men. *Judg.* xx. 45.

But Argive chiefs, and Agamemnon's train,
When his refulgent arms flash'd through the shady plain,
Fled from his well-known face with wonted fear;
As when his thund'ring sword and pointed spear
Drove headlong to their ships, and *glean'd* the routed rear. *Dryden's Æn. b.* vi.

In the knowledge of bodies we must be content to *glean* what we can from particular experiments; since we cannot, from a discovery of their real essences, grasp at a time whole sheaves, and in bundles comprehend the nature and properties of whole species together. *Locke.*

GLEAN. *n. s.* [from the verb.] Collection made laboriously by slow degrees.

Plains, meads, and orchards all the day he plies;
The *gleans* of yellow thyme distend his thighs:
He spoils the saffron. *Dryden's Virg. Georg. b.* iv.

GLE'ANER. *n. s.* [from *glean.*]

1. One who gathers after the reapers.

For still the world prevail'd, and its dread laugh,
Which scarce the firm philosopher can scorn,
Should his heart own a *gleaner* in the field. *Thoms. Autumn.*

2. One who gathers any thing slowly and laboriously.

An ordinary coffee-house *gleaner* of the city is an arrant statesman, and as much superior to him, as a man conversant about the court is to a shopkeeper. *Locke.*

GLE'ANING. *n. s.* [from *glean.*] The act of gleaning, or thing gleaned.

There shall be as the shaking of an olive-tree, and as the *gleaning* of grapes when the vintage is done. *Bible.*

The orphan and widow are members of the same common family, and have a right to be supported out of the incomes of it, as the poor Jews had to gather the *gleanings* of the rich man's harvest. *Atterbury's Sermons.*

GLEBE. *n. s.* [*gleba*, Latin.]

1. Turf; soil; ground.

Fertile of corn the *glebe*, of oil and wine,
With herds the pastures throng'd, with flocks the hills. *Milt.*

Mark well the flow'ring almonds in the wood;
If od'rous blooms the bearing branches load,
The *glebe* will answer to the sylvan reign,
Great heats will follow, and large crops of grain. *Dryden.*

Sleeping

Sleeping vegetables lie,
'Till the glad summons of a genial ray
Unbinds the *globe*, and calls them out to day. *Garth.*

2. The land possessed as part of the revenue of an ecclesiastical benefice.

The ordinary living or revenue of a parsonage is of three sorts: the one in land, commonly called the *glebe*; another in tythe, which is a set part of our goods rendered to God; the third, in other offerings bestowed upon God and his church by the people. *Spelman.*

A trespass done on a parson's *glebe* land, which is a freehold, cannot be tried in a spiritual court. *Ayliffe's Parergon.*

Many parishes have not an inch of *glebe*. *Swift.*

GLE'BOUS. *adj.* [from *glebe.*] Turfy. *Dict.*

GLE'BY. *adj.* [from *glebe.*] Turfy; perhaps in the following passage fat or fruitful, if it has indeed any meaning.

Pernicious flatt'ry! thy malignant seeds
In an ill hour, and by a fatal hand
Sadly diffus'd o'er virtue's *gleby* land,
With rising pride amidst the corn appear,
And choke the hopes and harvest of the year. *Prior.*

GLEDE. *n. s.* [ᵹliðaᵹliðe, Saxon.] A kite.

Ye shall not eat the *glede*, the kite, and the vulture. *Deutr.*

GLEE *n. s.* [ᵹliᵹᵹe, Saxon] Joy; merriment; gayety. It anciently signified musick played at feasts. It is not now used, except in ludicrous writing, or with some mixture of irony and contempt.

She marcheth home, and by her takes the knight,
Whom all the people follow with great *glee*. *Fairy Queen.*

Many wayfarers make themselves *glee*, by putting the inhabitants in mind of their privilege; who again foreslow not to baigne them with perfume. *Carew's Survey of Cornwal.*

And his sportive limbs,
This way and that convolv'd, in friskful *glee*
Their frolicks play. *Thomson's Spring.*

Is Blouzelinda dead? Farewel my *glee!*
No happiness is now reserv'd for me. *Gay's Pastorals.*

GLEED. *n. s.* [from ᵹlopan, Saxon, to glow.] A hot glowing coal. A provincial and obsolete word.

GLE'EFUL. *adj.* [*glee* and *full.*] Gay; merry; cheerful.

My lovely Aaron, wherefore look'st thou sad,
When every thing doth make a *gleeful* boast? *Shakespeare.*

GLEEK. *n. s.* [ᵹliᵹᵹe, Saxon.] Musick; or musician.

What will you give us?——No money, but the *gleek:* I will give you the minstrel. *Shakesp. Romeo and Juliet.*

To GLEEK. *v. a.* [ᵹliᵹman, in Saxon, is a mimick or a droll.]

1. To sneer; to gibe; to droll upon.

I can *gleek* upon occasion. *Shakesp. Midſ. Night's Dream.*

I have seen you *gleeking* or galling at this gentleman twice or thrice. *Shakespeare's Henry V.*

2. In Scotland it is still retained, and signifies to fool or spend time idly, with something of mimickry or drollery.

To GLEEN. *v. n.* To shine with heat or polish. I know not the original notion of this word: it may be of the same race with *glow* or with *gleam.*

Those who labour
The sweaty forge, who edge the crooked scythe,
Bend stubborn steel, and harden *gleening* armour,
Acknowledge Vulcan's aid. *Prior.*

GLEET. *n. s.* [It is written by *Skinner glitt*, and derived from ᵹliðan, Saxon, to run softly.] A sanious ooze; a thin ichor running from a sore.

There then lay a hard dry eschar, without either matter or *gleet*. *Wiseman's Surgery.*

To GLEET. *v. n.* [from the noun.]

1. To drip or ooze with a thin sanious liquor.

His thumb being inflamed and swelled, I made an incision into it to the bone: this not only bled, but *gleeted* a few drops. *Wiseman's Surgery.*

2. To run slowly.

Vapours may be raised by the sun in such quantities as are sufficient to make clouds, which are carried up and down the atmosphere, 'till they hit against the sides of the more mountainous places of the globe, and by this concussion are condensed, and so *gleet* down the rocky caverns of these mountains, whose inner parts, being hollow and stony, afford them a bason. *Cheyne's Phil. Princ.*

GLE'ETY. *adj.* [from *gleet.*] Ichory; thinly sanious.

If the flesh lose its ruddiness, and the matter change to be thin and *gleety*, you may suspect it corrupting. *Wiseman.*

GLEN. *n. s.* [*gleann*, Erse.] A valley; a dale; a depression between two hills.

From me his madding mind is start,
And wooes the widow's daughter of the *glen*. *Spenser.*

GLEW. *n. s.* [*gluten*, Latin.] A viscous cement made by dissolving the skins of animals in boiling water, and drying the gelly. See GLUE.

GLIB. *adj.* [from λεῖος. *Skinner.*]

1. Smooth; slippery; so formed as to be easily moved.

Liquid bodies have nothing to sustain their parts, nor any thing to cement them: the parts being *glib* and continually in motion, fall off from one another, which way soever gravity inclines them. *Burnet's Theory of the Earth.*

Habbakkuk brought him a smooth strong rope, compactly twisted together, with a noose that slipt as *glib* as a birdcatcher's gin. *Arbuthnot.*

2. Smooth; voluble.

I want that *glib* and oily art
To speak and purpose not, since what I well intend,
I'll do't before I speak. *Shakespeare's King Lear.*

There was never so much *glib* nonsense put together in well sounding English. *Locke.*

Now Curl his shop from rubbish drains;
Three genuine tomes of Swift's remains:
And then, to make them pass the *glibber*,
Revis'd by Tibbald, Moore, and Cibber. *Swift.*

Be sure he's a fine spoken man;
Do but hear on the clergy how *glib* his tongue ran. *Swift.*

GLIB. *n. s.*

They have another custom from the Scythians, the wearing of mantles and long *glibs*; which is a thick curled bush of hair hanging down over their eyes, and monstrously disguising them. *Spenser on Ireland.*

To GLIB. *v. a.* [from the adjective.] To castrate.

I'll geld them all: fourteen they shall not see,
To bring false generations; they are coheirs,
And I had rather *glib* myself than they
Should not produce fair issue. *Shakesp. Winter's Tale.*

GLI'BLY. *adv.* [from *glib.*] Smoothly; volubly.

Many who would startle at an oath, whose stomachs as well as consciences recoil at an obscenity, do yet slide *glibly* into a detraction. *Government of the Tongue.*

GLI'BNESS. *n. s.* [from *glib.*] Smoothness; slipperiness.

A polish'd ice-like *glibness* doth enfold
The rock. *Chapman's Odyssey.*

The tongue is the most ready for motion of any member, needs not so much as the flexure of a joint, and by access of humours acquires a *glibness* too, the more to facilitate its moving. *Government of the Tongue.*

To GLIDE. *v. n.* [ᵹliðan, Saxon; *glijden*, Dutch.]

1. To flow gently and silently.

By East, among the dusty vallies, *glide*
The silver streams of Jordan's crystal flood. *Fairfax, b. iii.*

Broke by the jutting land on either side,
In double streams the briny waters *glide*. *Dryden's Æn.*

Just before the confines of the wood,
The *gliding* Lethe leads her silent flood. *Dryden's Æn.*

Where stray the Muses, in what lawn or grove?
In those fair fields where sacred Isis *glides*,
Or else where Cam his winding vales divides. *Pope.*

2. To pass gently and without tumult.

Ye *gliding* ghosts, permit me to relate
The mystick wonders of your silent state. *Dryden's Æn.*

3. To move swiftly and smoothly along.

If one of mean affairs
May plod it in a week, why may not I
Glide thither in a day? *Shakespeare's Cymbeline.*

Shoals of fish, with fins and shining scales,
Glide under the green wave. *Milton.*

He trembl'd every limb, and felt a smart
As if cold steel had *glided* through his heart. *Dryd. Fables.*

All things are beheld as in a hasty motion, where the objects only *glide* before the eye and disappear. *Dryden.*

GLIDE. *n. s.* [from the verb.] Lapse; act or manner of passing smoothly.

About his neck
A green and gilded snake had wreath'd itself,
Who, with her head nimble in threats, approach'd
The opening of his mouth; but suddenly
Seeing Orlando it unlink'd itself,
And with indented *glides* did slip away
Into a bush. *Shakespeare's As you like it.*

GLI'DER. *n. s.* [from *glide.*] One that glides.

The glaunce into my heart did glide;
Hey ho the *glider*;
Therewith my soul was sharply gride,
Such wounds soon waxen wider. *Spenser's Pastoral.*

GLIKE. *n. s.* [ᵹliᵹ, Saxon. See GLEEK.] A sneer; a scoff; a flout. Not now in use.

Now where's the bastard's braves, and Charles his *glikes?*
Shakespeare's Henry VI. p. i.

To GLI'MMER. *v. n.* [*glimmer*, Danish, to shine; *glimmen*, Dutch, to glow.]

1. To shine faintly.

The West yet *glimmers* with some streaks of day. *Shakes.*

The truth appears so naked on my side,
That any purblind eye may find it out.
—And on my side it is so well apparel'd,
So clear, so shining, and so evident,
That it will *glimmer* through a blind man's eye. *Shakespeare.*

Oft in *glimmering* bowers and glades
He met her. *Milton.*

See'st thou yon' dreary plain, forlorn and wild,
The seat of desolation, void of light,
Save what the *glimmering* of these livid flames
Casts pale and dreadful? *Milton's Paradise Lost, b. i.*
The sacred influence
Of light appears, and from the walls of heav'n
Shoots far into the bosom of dim night
A *glimmering* dawn. *Milton's Paradise Lost, b. ii.*
Through these sad shades this chaos in my soul,
Some seeds of light at length began to roll;
The rising motion of an infant ray
Shot *glimm'ring* through the cloud, and promis'd day. *Prior.*
Oft by the winds, extinct the signal lies;
Or smother'd in the *glimm'ring* socket dies. *Gay's Trivia.*
When rosy morning *glimmer'd* o'er the dales,
He drove to pasture all the lusty males. *Pope's Odyssey.*

2. To be perceived imperfectly; to appear faintly.

On the way the baggage post-boy, who had been at court, got a *glimmering* who they were. *Wotton.*

The Pagan priesthood was always in the druids; and there was a perceivable *glimmering* of the Jewish rites in it, though much corrupted. *Swift.*

GLI'MMER. *n. s.* [from the verb.]

1. Faint splendour; weak light.
2. A kind of fossil.

The lesser masses that are lodged in sparry and stony bodies, dispersedly, from their shining and glimmering, were an inducement to the writers of fossils to give those bodies the name of mica and *glimmer*. *Woodward on Fossils.*

Stones which are composed of plates, that are generally plain and parallel, and that are flexible and elastick: talc, catsilver, or *glimmer*, of which there are three sorts, the yellow or golden, the white or silvery, and the black. *Woodward.*

GLIMPSE. *n. s.* [*glimmen*, Dutch, to glow.]

1. A weak faint light.

Such vast room in nature,
Only to shine, yet scarce to contribute
Each orb a *glimpse* of light, convey'd so far
Down to this habitable, which returns
Light back to them. *Milt. Par. Lost.*

Thousands of things, which now either wholly escape our apprehensions, or, which our shortsighted reason having got some faint *glimpse* of, we, in the dark, grope after. *Locke.*

2. A quick flashing light.

Light as the lightning *glimpse* they ran? *Milton's P. Lost.*
My thoughtless youth was wing'd with vain desires;
My manhood, long misled by wand'ring fires,
Follow'd false lights; and when their *glimpse* was gone,
My pride struck out new spangles of her own. *Dryden.*

3. Transitory lustre.

If I, celestial fire, in aught
Have serv'd thy will, or gratified thy thought,
One *glimpse* of glory to my issue give;
Grac'd for the little time he has to live. *Dryd. Fables.*

4. Short fleeting enjoyment.

If, while this weary'd flesh draws fleeting breath,
Not satisfy'd with life, afraid of death,
If hap'ly be thy will that I should know
Glimpse of delight, or pause from anxious woe;
From now, from instant now, great fire, dispel
The clouds that press my soul. *Prior.*

5. A short transitory view.

O friends! I hear the tread of nimble feet
Hasting this way, and now by *glimpse* discern
Ithuriel, and Zephon, through the shade. *Milt. Par. Lost.*

Some he punisheth exemplarily in this world, that we might from thence have a taste or *glimpse* of his present justice. *Hakewill on Providence.*

A man, used to such sort of reflections, sees as much at one *glimpse* as would require a long discourse to lay before another, and make out in one entire and gradual deduction. *Locke.*

What should I do! while here I was enchain'd,
No *glimpse* of godlike liberty remain'd. *Dryden's Virgil.*

6. The exhibition of a faint resemblance.

There is no man hath a virtue that he has not a *glimpse* of. *Shakespeare's Troilus and Cressida.*

To GLI'STEN. *v. n.* [*glittan*, German.] To shine; to sparkle with light.

The bleating kind
Eye the bleak heaven, and next the *glistening* earth,
With looks of dumb despair. *Thomson's Winter.*

The ladies eyes *glistened* with pleasure. *Richardson's Pamela.*

To GLI'STER. *v. n.* [*glittun*, German; *glisteren*, Dutch.] To shine; to be bright.

The wars flame most in Summer, and the helmets *glister* brightest in the fairest sunshine. *Spenser on Ireland.*

How he *glisters*
Through my dark rust! And how his piety
Does my deeds make the blacker! *Shakesp. Winter's Tale.*
'Tis better to be lowly born,
And range with humble livers in content,
Than to be perk'd up in a *glistering* grief,
And wear a golden sorrow. *Shakespeare's Henry VIII.*
The golden sun
Gallops the zodiack in his *glist'ring* coach. *Shakespeare.*
All that *glisters* is not gold. *Shakesp. Merch. of Venice.*
You were more the eye and talk
Of the court to-day, than all
Else that *glister'd* in Whitehall. *Ben. Johns. Underwoods.*

When the sun shone upon the shields of gold and brass, the mountains *glistered* therewith, and shined like lamps of fire. *1 Mac. vi. 39.*

Glister'd in one snake, and into fraud
Led Eve, our credulous mother, to the tree
Of prohibition. *Milton's Paradise Lost, b. ix.*

It consisted not of rubies, yet the small pieces of it were of a pleasant redish colour, and *glistered* prettily. *Boyle.*

GLI'STER. *n. s.* [Properly written *clyster*, from κλύζω.] See CLYSTER.

Now enters Bush with new state airs,
His lordship's premier minister;
And who, in all profound affairs,
Is held as needful as his *glister*. *Swift.*

Choler is the natural *glister*, or one excretion whereby nature excludeth another; which, descending daily unto the bowels, extimulates those parts, and excites them unto expulsion. *Brown's Vulgar Errours, b. iii. c. 2.*

To GLI'TTER. *v. n.* [ȝlıtınan, Saxon.]

1. To shine; to exhibit lustre; to gleam.

Steel glosses are more resplendent than the like plates of brass, and so is the *glittering* of a blade. *Bacon's Phys. Rem.*

Before the battle joins, from afar
The field yet *glitters* with the pomp of war. *Dryden's Virg.*
Scarce had'st thou time t' unsheath thy conqu'ring blade;
It did but *glitter*, and the rebels fled. *Granville.*

2. To be specious; to be striking.

Let them on the one hand set the most *glittering* temptations to discord, and on the other the dismal effects of it. *Decay of Piety.*

GLI'TTER. *n. s.* [from the verb.] Lustre; bright show; splendour.

Clad
With what permissive glory since his fall
Was left him, or false *glitter*. *Milton's Paradise Lost, b. x.*

A man has reason not to flourish too much upon the *glitter* of his fortune, for fear there should be too much alloy in it. *Collier on Pride.*

GLI'TTERAND. Shining; sparkling. A participle used by *Chaucer* and the old English poets. This participial termination is still retained in Scotland.

GLI'TTERINGLY. *adv.* [from *glitter*.] With shining lustre.

To GLOAR. *v. a.* [*gloeren*, Dutch.]

1. To squint; to look askew. *Skinner.*
2. In Scotland, to stare; as, *what a* gloarand *quean*.

To GLOAT. *v. n.* [This word I conceive to be ignorantly written for *gloar*.] To cast side glances as a timorous lover.

Teach every grace to smile in your behalf,
And her deluding eyes to *gloat* for you. *Rowe's Ja. Shore.*

GLO'BARD. *n. s.* [from *glow*.] A glow-worm.

GLOBATED. *adj.* [from *globe*.] Formed in shape of a globe; spherical; spheroidical.

GLOBE. *n. s.* [*globe*, French; *globus*, Latin.]

1. A sphere; a ball; a round body; a body of which every part of the surface is at the same distance from the centre.
2. The terraqueous ball.

The youth, whose fortune the vast *globe* obey'd,
Finding his royal enemy betray'd,
Wept at his fall. *Stepney.*

Where God declares his intention to give this dominion, it is plain he meant that he would make a species of creatures that should have dominion over the other species of this terrestrial *globe*. *Locke.*

3. A sphere in which the various regions of the earth are geographically depicted, or in which the constellations are laid down according to their places in the sky.

The astrologer who spells the stars,
Mistakes his *globe*, and in her brighter eye
Interprets heaven's physiognomy. *Cleaveland.*
These are the stars,
But raise thy thought from sense, nor think to find
Such figures there as are in *globes* design'd. *Creech.*

4. A body of soldiers drawn into a circle.

Him round
A *globe* of fiery seraphim inclos'd,
With bright imblazoning, and horrent arms. *Milton.*

GLOBE *Amaranth*, or *everlasting flower*. *n. s.* [*amaranthoides*,

The flowers are small, and cut into four segments, which are collected into squamose heads: from each of these scales is produced a single flower: the ovary in the bottom of the flower becomes a roundish crooked seed, contained in a thin pellicule or skin. *Miller.*

GLOBE *Daisy*. *n. s.* A kind of flower.

GLOBE

GLOBE *Fish.* *n. s.* A kind of orbicular fish.

GLOBE *Ranunculus.* *n. s.* [*helleboro-ranunculus.*]

It hath single circumscribed leaves, like the ranunculus: the cup of the flower consists of five small leaves of the same colour with the flower. *Miller.*

GLOBE *Thistle.* *n. s.*

It hath the whole appearance of a thistle: the leaves are produced alternately: the florets consist of one leaf, which is divided into five segments, and is hollow, and each single floret has a scaly cup: the flowers are collected into a spherical head, which has the common cup or covering. *Miller.*

GLOBO'SE. *adj.* [*globosus*, Latin.] Spherical; round.

Regions, to which
All thy dominion, Adam, is no more
Than what this garden is to all the earth,
And all the sea; from one entire *globose*
Stretch'd into longitude. *Milton's Paradise Lost*, *b.* v.

Then form'd the moon
Globose, and ev'ry magnitude of stars. *Milton's Par. Lost.*

GLOBO'SITY. *n. s.* [from *globose.*] Sphericity; sphericalness.

Why the same eclipse of the sun, which is seen to them that live more easterly, when the sun is elevated six degrees above the horizon, should be seen to them that live one degree more westerly, where the sun is but five degrees above the horizon, and so lower and lower proportionably, 'till at last it appear not at all: no account can be given, but the *globosity* of the earth. *Ray on the Creation.*

GLO'BOUS. *adj.* [*globosus*, Latin. When the accent is intended to be on the last syllable, the word should be written *globose*, when on the first *globous*: I have transferred hither a passage of *Milton*, in which this rule has been neglected.] Spherical; round.

Wide over all the plain, and wider far
Than all this *globose* earth in plain outspread,
Such are the courts of God! *Milton.*

The brazen instruments of death discharge
Horrible flames, and turbid streaming clouds;
Large *globous* irons fly, of dreadful hiss,
Singeing the air. *Phillips.*

GLO'BULAR. *adj.* [*globulus*, Latin.] In form of a small sphere; round; spherical.

The figure of the atoms of all visible fluids seemeth to be *globular*, there being no other figure so well fitted to the making of fluidity. *Grew's Cosmol. Sacr. b.* i. *c.* 2.

GLO'BULARIA. *n. s.* [Lat. *globulaire*, Fr.] A flosculous flower, consisting of many florets, which are divided into several segments, and have one lip. *Miller.*

GLO'BULE. *n. s.* [*globule*, Fr. *globulus*, Lat.] Such a small particle of matter as is of a globular or spherical figure, as the red particles of the blood, which swim in a transparent serum, and are easily discovered by the microscope. These will attract one another when they come within a due distance, and unite like the spheres of quicksilver. *Quincy.*

The hailstones have opaque *globules* of snow in their centre, to intercept the light within the halo. *Newton's Opt.*

Blood consists of red *globules*, swimming in a thin liquor called serum: the red *globules* are elastick, and will break: the vessels which admit the smaller *globule*, cannot admit the greater without a disease. *Arbuthnot on Aliments.*

GLO'BULOUS. *adj.* [from *globule.*] In form of a small sphere; round.

The whiteness of such *globulous* particles proceeds from the air included in the froth. *Boyle.*

To GLO'MERATE. *v. a.* [*glomero*, Latin.] To gather into a ball or sphere.

GLOMERA'TION. *n. s.* [*glomeratio*, Latin.]

1. The act of forming into a ball or sphere.
2. A body formed into a ball.

The rainbow consisteth of a *glomeration* of small drops, which cannot possibly fall but from the air that is very low. *Bacon's Natural History*, N°. 832.

GLO'MEROUS. *adj.* [*glomerosus*, Latin.] Gathered into a ball or sphere.

GLOOM. *n. s.* [ȝlomanȝ, Saxon, twilight.]

1. Imperfect darkness; dismalness; obscurity; defect of light.

Glowing embers through the room,
Teach light to counterfeit a *gloom*. *Milton.*

This the seat,
That we must change for heav'n? This mournful *gloom*,
For that celestial light? *Milton's Paradise Lost*, *b.* i.

The still night, not now, as ere men fell,
Wholsome, and cool, and mild; but with black air
Accompany'd; with damps, and dreadful *gloom*. *Milton.*

Now warm in love, now with'ring in thy bloom,
Lost in a convent's solitary *gloom*. *Pope.*

2. Cloudiness of aspect; heaviness of mind; sullenness.

To GLOOM. *v. n.* [from the noun.]

1. To shine obscurely, as the twilight. This sense is not now in use.

His glist'ring armour made
A little *glooming* light much like a shade. *Fairy Queen.*

Scarcely had Phœbus in the *glooming* East
Yet harnessed his fiery footed team. *Spenser.*

2. To be cloudy; to be dark.
3. To be melancholy; to be sullen.

GLOO'MILY. *adv.* [from *gloomy.*]

1. Obscurely; dimly; without perfect light; dismally.
2. Sullenly; with cloudy aspect; with dark intentions; not cheerfully.

See, he comes: how *gloomily* he looks! *Dryden.*

Gloomily retir'd
The villain spider lives. *Thomson's Summer.*

GLOO'MINESS. *n. s.* [from *gloomy.*]

1. Want of light; obscurity; imperfect light; dismalness.
2. Want of cheerfulness; cloudiness of look; heaviness of mind; melancholy.

Neglect spreads *gloominess* upon their humour, and makes them grow sullen and unconversable. *Collier of the Spleen.*

The *gloominess* in which sometimes the minds of the best men are involved, very often stands in need of such little incitements to mirth and laughter as are apt to disperse melancholy. *Addison's Spectator*, N°. 179.

GLOO'MY. *adj.* [from *gloom.*]

1. Obscure; imperfectly illuminated; almost dark; dismal for want of light.

These were from without
The growing miseries, which Adam saw
Already in part, though hid in *gloomiest* shade,
To sorrow abandon'd. *Milton's Paradise Lost*, *b.* x.

Deep in a cavern dwells the drowsy god,
Whose *gloomy* mansion nor the rising sun,
Nor setting visits, nor the lightsome noon. *Dryden's Fables.*

The surface of the earth is clearer or *gloomier*, just as the sun is bright or more overcast. *Pope's Letters.*

2. Dark of complexion.

That fair field
Of Enna, where Proserpine gathering flow'rs,
Herself a fairer flow'r, by *gloomy* Dis
Was gather'd. *Milton's Paradise Lost*, *b.* iv.

3. Sullen; melancholy; cloudy of look; heavy of heart.

GLO'RIED. *adj.* [from *glory.*] Illustrious; honourable; decorated with glory; dignified with honours.

Old respect,
As I suppose, toward your once *glory'd* friend,
My son now captive, hither hath inform'd
Your younger feet, while mine cast back with age
Came lagging after. *Milton's Agonistes.*

GLORIFICA'TION. *n. s.* [*glorification*, Fr. from *glorify.*] The act of giving glory.

At opening your eyes, enter upon the day with thanksgiving for the preservation of you the last night, with the *glorification* of God for the works of the creation. *Taylor.*

To GLO'RIFY. *v. a.* [*glorifier*, French; *glorifico*, Latin.]

1. To procure honour or praise to one.

Two such silver currents, when they join,
Do *glorify* the banks that bound them in. *Shakesp. K. John.*

Justice is their virtue: that alone
Makes them sit sure, and *glorifies* the throne. *Daniel.*

2. To pay honour or praise in worship.

God is *glorified* when such his excellency, above all things, is with due admiration acknowledged. *Hooker*, *b.* v.

This form and manner of *glorifying* God was not at that time first begun; but received long before, and alleged at that time as an argument for the truth. *Hooker*, *b.* v. *s.* 42.

Good fellow, tell us here the circumstance,
That we for thee may *glorify* the Lord. *Shakesp. Henry* VI.

All nations shall *glorify* thy name. *Ps.* lxxxvi. 9.

This is the perfection of every thing, to attain its true and proper end; and the end of all these gifts and endowments, which God hath given us, is to *glorify* the giver. *Tillotson.*

3. To praise; to honour; to extol.

Whomsoever they find to be most licentious of life, desperate in all parts of disobedience and rebellious disposition, him they set up and *glorify*. *Spenser on Ireland.*

No chymist yet the elixir got,
But *glorifies* his pregnant pot,
If by the way to him befall
Some odoriferous thing, or medicinal. *Donne.*

4. To exalt to glory or dignity.

If God be glorified in him, God shall also *glorify* him in himself, and shall straightway *glorify* him. *Jo* xiii. 32.

Whom he justified, them he also *glorified.* *Rom.* viii. 30.

The soul, being immortal, will, at some time or other, resume its body again in a *glorified* manner. *Ayliffe's Parergon.*

GLO'RIOUS. *adj.* [*gloriosus*, Latin; *glorieux*, French.]

1. Boastful; proud; haughty; ostentatious.

Glorious followers, who make themselves as trumpets of the commendation of those they follow, taint business for want of secrecy. *Bacon.*

They that are *glorious* must needs be factious; for all bravery stands upon comparisons. *Bacon*, *Essay* 55.

2. Noble; illustrious; excellent.

Let

Let them know that thou art Lord, the only God, and *glorious* over the whole world. *Dan.* iii. 22.

Impartial justice holds her equal scales,
'Till stronger virtue does the weight incline;
If over thee thy *glorious* foe prevails,
He now defends the cause that once was thine. *Prior.*

Let us remember we are Cato's friends,
And act like men who claim that *glorious* title. *Addison's Cato.*

GLO'RIOUSLY. *adv.* [from *glorious.*] Nobly; splendidly; illustriously.

They inspire with those celestial flames, which shine so *gloriously* in their works. *Dryden's Dufresnoy.*

Great wits sometimes may *gloriously* offend,
And rise to faults true criticks dare not mend. *Pope.*

GLO'RY. *n. s.* [*gloire*, French; *gloria*, Latin. Among the old poets it was used sometimes as one syllable, *glore*.]

1. Praise paid in adoration.

Glory to God in the highest. *Luke* ii. 14.

2. The felicity of heaven prepared for those that please God.

Thou shalt guide me with thy counsel, and afterwards receive me to thy *glory.* *Psal.* lxxiii. 24.

Then enter into *glory*, and resume
His seat at God's right hand, exalted high
Above all names in heav'n. *Milton's Paradise Lost.*

3. Honour; praise; fame; renown; celebrity.

Think it no *glory* to swell in tyranny. *Sidney.*

Glory is like a circle in the water,
Which never ceaseth to enlarge itself,
'Till by broad spreading it disperse to nought. *Shak. H.* VI.

And with that word and warning soon was dight,
Each soldier longing for near coming *glory.* *Fairfax, b.* i.

Can we imagine that either the ambition of princes, or interest, or gain in private persons, or curiosity and the desire of knowledge, or the *glory* of discoveries, could ever move them in that endless time to try their fortunes upon the sea. *Burnet.*

4. Splendour; magnificence.

Solomon, in all his *glory*, was not arrayed like one of these. *Matt.* vi. 29.

Treated so ill, chas'd from your throne,
Returning, you adorn the town;
And with a brave revenge do show
Their *glory* went and came with you. *Waller.*

Aristotle says, that should a man under ground converse with works of art, and be afterwards brought up into the open day, and see the several *glories* of the heaven and earth, he would pronounce them the works of God. *Addison's Spectator.*

5. Lustre; brightness.

Now sleeping flocks on their soft fleeces lie;
The moon, serene in *glory*, mounts the sky. *Pope's Winter.*

From opening skies may streaming *glories* shine,
And saints embrace thee with a love like mine. *Pope.*

6. A circle of rays which surrounds the heads of saints in picture.

It is not a converting but a crowning grace; such an one as irradiates, and puts a circle of *glory* about the head of him upon whom it descends. *South's Sermons.*

A smile plays with a surprising agreeableness in the eye, breaks out with the brightest distinction, and sits like a *glory* upon the countenance. *Collier of the Aspect.*

7. Pride; boastfulness; arrogance.

By the vain *glory* of men they entered into the world, and therefore shall they come shortly to an end. *Wisd.* xiv. 14.

8. Generous pride.

The success of those wars was too notable to be unknown to your ears, to which all worthy fame hath *glory* to come unto. *Sidney, b.* ii.

To GLO'RY. *v. n.* [*glorior*, Latin.] To boast in; to be proud of.

With like judgment *glorying* when he had happened to do a thing well, as when he had performed some notable mischief. *Sidney, b.* ii.

They were wont, in the pride of their own proceedings to *glory*, that whereas Luther did but blow away the roof, and Zuinglius batter but the walls of popish superstition, the last and hardest work of all remained, which was to raze up the very ground and foundation of popery. *Hooker, b.* v. *s.* 42.

Let them look they *glory* not in mischief,
Nor build their evils on the graves of great men;
For then my guiltless blood must cry against them. *Shakesp.*

Your *glorying* is not good. 1 *Cor.* v. 6.

Thou hast seen mount Atlas,
While storms and tempests thunder on its brow,
And oceans break their billows at its feet,
It stands unmov'd, and *glories* in its height. *Addis. Cato.*

This title is what I most *glory* in, and what most effectually calls to my mind the happiness of that government under which I live. *Addison's Freeholder,* N°. 1.

If others may *glory* in their birth, why may not we, whose parents were called by God to attend on him at his altar? *Atter.*

No one is out of the reach of misfortune; no one therefore should *glory* in his prosperity. *Clarissa.*

To GLOSE. *v. a.* To flatter; to collogue. *Hanmer.* See *To* GLOZE.

GLOSS. *n. s.* [γλῶσσα; *glose*, French.]

1. A scholium; a comment.

They never hear sentence, which mentioneth the word or scripture, but forthwith their *glosses* upon it are the word preached, the scripture explained, or delivered unto us in sermons. *Hooker, b.* v. *s.* 22.

If then all souls, both good and bad, do teach,
With gen'ral voice, that souls can never die;
'Tis not man's flatt'ring *gloss*, but nature's speech,
Which, like God's oracles, can never lie. *Davies.*

Some mutter at certain passages therein, by putting ill *glosses* upon the text, and taking with the left hand what I offer with the right. *Howel.*

All this, without a *gloss* or comment,
He could unriddle in a moment. *Hudibras, p.* i. *cant.* i.

In many places he has perverted my meaning by his *glosses*, and interpreted my words into blasphemy and bawdry, of which they were not guilty. *Dryden's Fables, Preface.*

They give the scandal, and the wise discern;
Their *glosses* teach an age too apt to learn. *Dryden.*

Explaining the text in short *glosses*, was Accursius's method. *Baker's Reflections on Learning.*

Indentures, cov'nants, articles they draw,
Large as the fields themselves, and larger far
Than civil codes with all their *glosses* are. *Pope.*

2. An interpretation artfully specious; a specious representation.

Poor painters oft with silly poets join,
To fill the world with strange but vain conceit;
One brings the stuff, the other stamps the coin,
Which breeds nought else but *glosses* of deceit. *Sidney, b.* ii.

It is no part of my secret meaning to draw you hereby into hatred, or to set upon the face of this cause any fairer *gloss* than the naked truth doth afford. *Hooker, Preface.*

He seems with forged quaint conceit
To set a *gloss* upon his bad intent. *Shakespeare's Henry* VI.

The common *gloss*
Of theologians. *Milton.*

3. Superficial lustre.

His iron coat, all over grown with rust,
Was underneath enveloped with gold,
Whose glistering *gloss* dark'ned with filthy dust. *Fai. Queen.*

You are a sectary,
That's the plain truth: your painted *gloss* discovers,
To men that understand you, words and weakness. *Shakes.*

Golden opinions from all sorts of people,
Which would be worn now in their newest *gloss.* *Shakesp.*

The doubt will be whether it will polish so well; for steel *glosses* are more resplendent than the like plates of brass, and so is the glittering of a blade. *Bacon's Phys. Rem.*

Weeds that the wind did toss
The virgins wore: the youths, woven coats, that cast a faint dim *gloss*,
Like that of oil. *Chapman's Iliads, b.* xviii.

It was the colour of devotion, giving a lustre to reverence, and a *gloss* to humility. *South's Sermons.*

Groves, fields, and meadows, are at any season pleasant to look upon; but never so much as in the opening of the Spring, when they are all new and fresh, with their first *gloss* upon them. *Addison's Spectator,* N°. 412.

To GLOSS. *v. n.* [*gloser*, Fr. from the noun.]

1. To comment.

Thou detain'st Briseis in thy bands,
By priestly *glossing* on the gods commands. *Dryd. Fables.*

2. To make sly remarks.

Her equals first observ'd her growing zeal,
And laughing *gloss'd*, that Abra serv'd so well. *Prior.*

To GLOSS. *v. a.*

1. To explain by comment.

No woman shall succeed in Salique land;
Which Salique land the French unjustly *gloss*
To be the realm of France. *Shakespeare's Henry* V.

In parchment then, large as the fields, he draws
Assurances, big as *gloss'd* civil laws. *Donne.*

2. To palliate by specious exposition or representation.

Is this the paradise, in description whereof so much *glossing* and deceiving eloquence hath been spent? *Hooker's Sermons.*

Do I not reason wholly on your conduct?
You have the art to *gloss* the foulest cause. *Phillips's Briton.*

3. To embellish with superficial lustre.

But thou, who lately of the common strain
Wert one of us, if still thou do'st retain
The same ill habits, the same follies too,
Gloss'd over only with a saint-like show,
Then I resume the freedom which I gave,
Still thou art bound to vice, and still a slave. *Dryden's Pers.*

GLO'SSARY. *n. s.* [*glossarium*, Latin; *glossaire*, French.] A dictionary of obscure or antiquated words.

According to Varro, the most learned of the Romans, when *delubrum* was applied to a place, it signified such a one, *in quo dei simulachrum dedicatum est*; and also in the old *glossaries.* *Stillingfleet.*

I could

I could add another word to the *glossary*. *Baker.*

GLOSSA'TOR. *n. s.* [*glossateur*, French, from *gloss.*] A writer of glosses; a commentator.

The reason why the assertion of a single judge does not prove the existence of judicial acts, is because his office is to pronounce judgment, and not to become an evidence: but why may not the same be said of two judges? Therefore, in this respect, the *glossator's* opinion must be false. *Ayliffe.*

GLO'SSER. *n. s.* [*glossarius*, Latin.]

1. A scholiast; a commentator.
2. A polisher.

GLO'SSINESS. *n. s.* [from *glossy.*] Smooth polish; superficial lustre.

Those grains were as like little cubes as if they had been made by a skilful jeweller, and their surfaces had a smoothness and *glossiness* much surpassing whatever I had observed in marine or common salt. *Boyle.*

GLO'SSOGRAPHER. *n. s.* [γλῶσσα and γράφω.] A scholiast; a commentator.

GLO'SSOGRAPHY. *n. s.* [γλῶσσα and γράφω.] The writing of commentaries.

GLO'SSY. *adj.* [from *gloss.*] Shining; smoothly polished.

There came towards us a person of place: he had on him a gown with wide sleeves, of a kind of water-camblet, of an excellent azure colour, far more *glossy* than ours. *Bacon.*

The rest entire
Shone with a *glossy* scurf. *Milton.*

His surcoat was a bearskin on his back;
His hair hung long behind, and *glossy* raven black. *Dryden.*

Myself will search our planted grounds at home,
For downy peaches and the *glossy* plum. *Dryden's Virgil.*

GLOVE. *n. s.* [ʒlope, Saxon, from *klaffue*, Danish, to divide.] Cover of the hands.

Like an uproar in a town,
Before them every thing went down;
They flew about like chaff i' th' wind;
For haste some left their masks behind,
Some could not stay their *gloves* to find. *Drayton.*

White *gloves* were on his hands, and on his head
A wreath of laurel. *Dryden.*

To GLOVE. *v. a.* [from the noun.] To cover as with a glove.

My limbs,
Weaken'd with grief, being now enrag'd with grief,
Are thrice themselves: hence therefore, thou nice crutch;
A scaly gauntlet now, with joints of steel,
Must *glove* this hand. *Shakespeare's Henry* IV. *p.* i.

The next he preys on is her palm,
That alm'ner of transpiring balm;
So soft, 'tis air but once remov'd;
Tender as 'twere a jelly *glov'd.* *Cleaveland.*

GLO'VER. *n. s.* [from *glove.*] One whose trade is to make or sell gloves.

Does he not wear a great round beard like a *glover's* paring knife? *Shakespeare's Merry Wives of Windsor.*

To GLOUT. *v. n.* [A low word of which I find no etymology.] To pout; to look sullen. It is still used in Scotland.

She lurks in midst of all her den, and streaks
From out a ghastly whirlpool all her necks,
Where, *glowting* round her rock, to fish she falls. *Chapman.*

Glouting with sullen spight, the fury shook
Her clotted locks, and blasted with each look. *Garth.*

To GLOW. *v. n.* [ʒlopan, Saxon; *gloeyen*, Dutch.]

1. To be heated so as to shine without flame.

But sithence silence lesseneth not my fire,
But told it flames, and hidden it does *glow*,
I will reveal what ye so much desire. *Fairy Queen, b.* i.

His goodly eyes,
That o'er the files and musters of the war
Have *glow'd* like plated Mars, now bend, now turn
Their office upon a tawny front. *Shakesp. Ant. and Cleopat.*

Kunigund, wife to the emperor Henry II. to show her innocency, did take seven *glowing* irons, one after another, in her bare hands, and had thereby no harm. *Hakewill.*

Not all parts like, but all alike inform'd
With radiant light, as *glowing* iron with fire. *Milt. Par. L.*

2. To burn with vehement heat.

Nor would you find it easy to compose
The mettled steeds, when from their nostrils flows
The scorching fire that in their entrails *glows. Addis. Ovid.*

How op'ning heav'ns their happy regions show,
And yawning gulphs with flaming vengeance *glow.* *Smith.*

Fires that *glow*,
Shrieks of woe. *Pope.*

3. To feel heat of body.

Did not his temples *glow*
In the same sultry winds and scorching heats? *Addis. Cato.*

The cord slides swiftly through his *glowing* hands. *Gay.*

4. To exhibit a strong bright colour.

With smile that *glow'd*
Celestial rosy red, love's proper hue. *Milton.*

Clad in a gown that *glows* with Tyrian rays. *Dryden.*

A malicious joy,
Whose red and fiery beams cast through your visage
A *glowing* pleasure. *Dryden and Lee's Oedipus.*

From the mingled strength of shade and light,
A new creation rises to my sight;
Such heav'nly figures from his pencil flow,
So warm with life his blended colours *glow*,
Amidst the soft variety I'm lost. *Addison.*

Like th' ethereal *glow'd* the green expanse. *Savage.*

Fair ideas flow,
Strike in the sketch, or in the picture *glow.* *Pope.*

Not the fair fruit that on yon branches *glows*,
With that ripe red th' autumnal sun bestows,
Can move the god. *Pope.*

Each pleasing Blount shall endless smiles bestow,
And fair Belinda's blush for ever *glow.* *Pope.*

Here clearer stars *glow* round the frozen pole. *Pope.*

From her naked limbs of *glowing* white,
In folds loose floating, fell the fainter lawn. *Thomson.*

5. To feel passion of mind, or activity of fancy.

You strive in vain
To hide your thoughts from him, who knew too well
The inward *glowings* of a heart in love. *Addison's Cato.*

Forc'd compliments and formal bows
Will shew thee just above neglect;
The fire with which thy lover *glows*,
Will settle into cold respect. *Prior.*

Did Shadrach's zeal my *glowing* breast inspire
To weary tortures, and rejoice in fire. *Prior.*

Let the gay conscience of a life well spent
Calm ev'ry thought, inspirit ev'ry grace,
Glow in thy heart, and smile upon thy face. *Pope.*

With furies surrounded,
Despairing, confounded,
He trembles, he *glows*,
Amidst Rhodope's snows. *Pope.*

So perish all, whose breasts ne'er learn'd to *glow*
For others good, or melt at others woe. *Pope.*

To praise is always hard,
When real virtue fires the *glowing* bard. *Lewis.*

6. To rage or burn as a passion.

A fire which every windy passion blows;
With pride it mounts, and with revenge it *glows.* *Dryden.*

When crept into aged veins,
Love slowly burns, and long remains;
It *glows*, and with a sullen heat,
Like fire in logs, it warms us long. *Shadwell.*

To GLOW. *v. a.* To make hot so as to shine. Not in use.

On each side her
Stood pretty dimpled boys, like smiling Cupids,
With divers colour'd fans, whose wind did seem
To *glow* the delicate cheeks which they did cool. *Shakesp.*

GLOW. *n. s.* [from the verb.]

1. Shining heat.
2. Vehemence of passion.
3. Brightness or vividness of colour.

The pale complexion of true love,
And the red *glow* of scorn and proud disdain. *Shakespeare.*

A waving *glow* his bloomy beds display,
Blushing in bright diversities of day. *Pope, Epistle* iv.

GLO'WWORM. *n. s.* [*glow* and *worm.*] A small creeping insect with a luminous tail.

The honey bags steal from the humble bees,
And for night-tapers crop their waxen thighs,
And light them at the fiery *glowworm's* eyes. *Shakespeare.*

The *glowworm* shews the mattin to be near,
And 'gins to pale his uneffectual fire. *Shakesp. Hamlet.*

A great light drowneth a smaller that it cannot be seen; as the sun that of a *glowworm.* *Bacon's Natural History.*

The man, who first upon the ground
A *glowworm* spy'd, supposing he had found
A moving diamond, a breathing stone;
For life it had, and like those jewels shone:
He held it dear, 'till by the springing day
Inform'd, he threw the worthless worm away. *Waller.*

To GLOZE. *v. n.* [ʒlepan, Saxon.]

1. To flatter; to wheedle; to insinuate; to fawn.

Man will hearken to his *glozing* lies,
And easily transgress. *Milton's Paradise Lost, b.* iii.

So *gloz'd* the tempter, and his proem tun'd:
Into the heart of Eve his words made way. *Milt. Par. Lost.*

A false *glozing* parasite would call his foolhardiness valour, and then he may go on boldly, because blindly, and by mistaking himself for a lion, come to perish like an ass. *South.*

Now for a *glozing* speech,
Fair protestations, specious marks of friendship. *Phillips.*

2. To comment. This should be *gloss.*

Which Salique land the French unjustly *gloze*
To be the realm of France. *Shakespeare's Henry* V.

GLOZE. *n. s.* [from the verb.]
1. Flattery; insinuation.
Now to plain dealing; lay these *glozes* by. *Shakespeare.*
2. Specious show; gloss.
Precious couches full oft are shaked with a fever;
If then a bodily evil in a bodily *gloze* be not hidden,
Shall such morning dews be an ease to the heat of a love's fire? *Sidney, b.* i.

GLUE. *n. s.* [*glu*, Fr. *gluten*, Lat. *glud*, Welsh.] A viscous body commonly made by boiling the skins of animals to a gelly; any viscous or tenacious matter by which bodies are held one to another; a cement.
Water, and all liquors, do hastily receive dry and more terrestrial bodies proportionable; and dry bodies, on the other side, drink in waters and liquors: so that, as it was well said by one of the ancients of earthly and watery substances, one is a *glue* to another. *Bacon's Natural History*
To build the earth did chance materials chuse,
And through the parts cementing *glue* diffuse. *Blackmore.*
The clearest, driest, and most transparent *glue* is the best. *Moxon's Mech. Exer.*
The flowers of grains, mixed with water, will make a sort of *glue*. *Arbuthnot on Aliments.*

To GLUE. *v. a.* [from the noun.]
1. To join with a viscous cement.
I fear thy overthrow
More than my body's parting with my soul:
My love and fear *glu'd* many friends to thee. *Shakesp. H. VI.*
Whoso teacheth a fool is as one that *glueth* a potsherd together. *Ecclus.* xxii. 7.
The custom of crowning the Holy Virgin is so much in vogue among the Italians, that one often sees in their churches a little tinsel crown, or a circle of stars, *glued* to the canvas over the head of the figure. *Addison on Italy.*
Most wounds, if kept clean, and from the air, the flesh will *glue* together with its own native balm. *Derham.*
2. To hold together.
The parts of all homogeneal hard bodies, which fully touch one another, stick together very strongly; and for explaining how this may be, some have invented hooked atoms, which is begging the question; and others tell us their bodies are *glued* together by rest, that is, by an occult quality, or rather by nothing. *Newton's Opt.*
3. To join; to unite; to inviscate.
Those wasps in a honeypot are so many sensual men, that are plunged in their lusts and pleasures; and when they are once *glued* to them, 'tis a very hard matter to work themselves out. *L'Estrange, Fable* 126.
Intemperance, sensuality, and fleshly lusts, do debase mens minds and clog their spirits; sink us down into sense, and *glue* us to those low and inferior things. *Tillotson's Sermons.*
She curb'd a groan, that else had come;
And pausing, view'd the present in the tomb:
Then to the heart ador'd devoutly *glu'd*
Her lips, and, raising it, her speech renew'd. *Dryden.*
I hear thee, view thee, gaze o'er all thy charms,
And round thy phantom *glue* my clasping arms. *Pope.*

GLU'EBOILER. *n. s.* [*glue* and *boil.*] One whose trade is to make glue.

GLU'ER. *n. s.* [from *glue.*] One who cements with glue.

GLUM. *adj.* [A low cant word formed by corrupting *gloom.*] Sullen; stubbornly grave.
Some, when they hear a story, look *glum*, and cry, Well, what then? *Guardian.*

To GLUT. *v. a.* [*engloutir*, French; *glutio*, Lat. to swallow; γλύζω.]
1. To swallow; to devour.
'Till cram'd and gorg'd, nigh burst
With suck'd and *glutted* offal. *Milton's Paradise Lost, b.* x.
2. To cloy; to fill beyond sufficiency; to sate; to disgust.
The ambassador, making his oration, did so magnify the king and queen, as was enough to *glut* the hearers. *Bacon.*
Love breaks friendship, whose delights
Feed, but not *glut* our appetites. *Denham.*
What way remove
His settled hate, and reconcile his love,
That he may look propitious on our toils,
And hungry graves no more be *glutted* with our spoils. *Dry.*
No more, my friend;
Here let our *glutted* execution end. *Dryden's Æn.*
I found
The fickle ear soon *glutted* with the sound,
Condemn'd eternal changes to pursue,
Tir'd with the last, and eager of the new. *Prior.*
3. To feast or delight even to satiety.
With death's carcase *glut* the grave. *Milton.*
His faithful heart, a bloody sacrifice,
Torn from his breast, to *glut* the tyrant's eyes. *Dryden.*
A sylvan scene, which, rising by degrees,
Leads up the eye below, nor *gluts* the sight
With one full prospect; but invites by many,
To view at last the whole. *Dryden's State of Innocence.*
4. To overfill; to load.
He attributes the ill success of either party to their *glutting* the market, and retailing too much of a bad commodity at once. *Arbuthnot's Art of Polite Lying.*
5. To saturate.
The menstrum, being already *glutted*, could not act powerfully enough to dissolve it. *Boyle.*

GLUT. *n. s.* [from the verb.]
1. That which is gorged or swallowed.
Disgorging foul
Their devilish *glut*, chain'd thunderbolts, and hail
Of iron globes. *Milton's Paradise Lost, b.* vi.
2. Plenty even to loathing and satiety.
So death
Shall be deceiv'd his *glut*; and with us two
Be forc'd to satisfy his rav'nous maw. *Milton's Par. Lost.*
Let him but set the one in balance against the other, and he shall find himself miserable, even in the very *glut* of his delights. *L'Estrange, Fable* 11.
A *glut* of study and retirement in the first part of my life, cast me into this; and this will throw me again into study and retirement. *Pope to Swift.*
3. More than enough; overmuch.
If you pour a *glut* of water upon a bottle, it receives little of it. *Ben. Johnson's Discoveries.*
4. Any thing that fills up a passage.
The water some suppose to pass continually from the bottom of the sea to the heads of springs and rivers, through certain subterranean conduits or channels, until they were by some *glut*, stop, or other means, arrested in their passage. *Woodward's Natural History.*

GLU'TINOUS. *adj.* [*glutinex*, French, from *gluten*, Latin.] Gluey; viscous; tenacious.
The cause of all vivification is a gentle and proportionable heat, working upon a *glutinous* and yielding substance; for the heat doth bring forth spirit in that substance, and the substance being *glutinous*, produceth two effects: the one, that the spirit is detained, and cannot break forth; the other, that the matter, being gentle and yielding, is driven forwards by the motion of the spirits, after some swelling, into shape and members. *Bacon's Natural History*, N°. 900.
Next this marble venom'd seat,
Smear'd with gums of *glutinous* heat. *Milton.*
Nourishment too viscid and *glutinous* to be subdued by the vital force. *Arbuthnot on Aliments.*

GLU'TINOUSNESS. *n. s.* [from *glutinous.*] Viscosity; tenacity.
There is a resistance in fluids, which may arise from their elasticity, *glutinousness*, and the friction of their parts. *Cheyne.*

GLU'TTON. *n. s.* [*glouton*, French, from *glutio*, Latin, to swallow.]
1. One who indulges himself too much in eating.
The Chinese eat horseflesh at this day, and some *gluttons* have used to have catsflesh baked. *Bacon's Natural History.*
Through Macer's gullet she runs down,
When the vile *glutton* dines alone;
And, void of modesty and thought,
She follows Bibo's endless draught. *Prior.*
2. One eager of any thing to excess.
The rest bring home in state the happy pair
To that last scene of bliss, and leave them there;
All those free joys insatiably to prove,
With which rich beauty feasts the *glutton* love. *Cowley.*
Gluttons in murder, wanton to destroy,
Their fatal arts so impiously employ. *Granville.*

To GLU'TTONISE. *v. n.* [from *glutton.*] To play the glutton; to be luxurious.

GLU'TTONOUS. *adj.* [from *glutton.*] Given to excessive feeding; delighted overmuch with food.
When they would smile and fawn upon his debts,
And take down th' interest in their *glutt'nous* maws. *Shakesp.*
The exceeding luxuriousness of this *gluttonous* age, wherein we press nature with overweighty burdens, and finding her strength defective, we take the work out of her hands, and commit it to the artificial help of strong waters. *Raleigh.*
Thou well observe
The rule of not too much, by temperance taught
In what thou eat'st and drink'st; seeking from thence
Due nourishment, no *gluttonous* delight. *Milton's Par. Lost.*

GLU'TTONOUSLY. *adv.* [from *gluttonous*] With the voracity of a glutton.

GLU'TTONY. *n. s.* [*glutonnie*, Fr. from *glutton.*] Excess of eating; luxury of the table.
Their sumptuous *gluttonies* and gorgeous feasts,
On citron tables or Atlantick stone. *Milton's Parad. Reg.*
Well may they fear some miserable end,
Whom *gluttony* and want at once attend. *Dryden's Juven.*
The inhabitants of cold moist countries are generally more fat than those of warm and dry; but the most common cause is too great a quantity of food, and too small a quantity of motion; in plain English, *gluttony* and laziness. *Arbuthnot.*

GLU'Y. *adj.* [from *glue.*]
2. Viscous; tenacious; glutinous.

It is called balsamick mixture, because it is a *gluy* spumous matter. *Harvey on Consumptions.*

With *gluy* wax some new foundations lay
Of virgin combs. *Dryden's Ann. Mirab.*

Whatever is the composition of the vapour, let it have but one quality of being very *gluy* or viscous, and it will mechanically solve all the phænomena of the grotto. *Addison.*

GLYN. *n. s.* [Irish; *gleann*, *glyn*, plur. Erse; *glenn*, Scottish.] A hollow between two mountains.

Though he could not beat out the Irish, yet he did shut them up within those narrow corners and *glyns* under the mountains foot. *Spenser's State of Ireland.*

To GNAR. } *v. n.* [ʒnyrran, Saxon; *knorren*, Dutch.] To
To GNARL. } growl; to murmur; to snarl.

When he 'gan to rear his bristles strong,
And felly *gnar*, until day's enemy
Did him appease. *Fairy Queen, b.* i. *cant.* i.

Thus is the shepherd beaten from thy side,
And wolves are *gnarling* who shall gnaw thee first. *Shakesp.*

Gnarling sorrow hath less power to bite
The man that mocks at it, and sets it light. *Shakesp. R.* II.

The *gnarring* porter durst not whine for doubt;
Still were the furies while their sovereign spoke. *Fairfax.*

GNA'RLED. *adj.* [*gnar*, *nar*, or *nurr*, is in Staffordshire a hard knot of wood which boys drive with sticks.] Knotty.

Merciful heav'n!
Thou rather with thy sharp and sulph'rous bolt
Split'st the unwedgeable and *gnarled* oak,
Than the soft myrtle. *Shak. Measure for Measure.*

To GNASH. *v. a.* [*knaschen*, Dutch.] To strike together; to clash.

The seer, who could not yet his wrath asswage,
Rowl'd his green eyes, that sparkl'd with his rage,
And *gnash'd* his teeth. *Dryden's Virg. Georg.*

To GNASH. *v. n.*

1. To grind or collide the teeth.

He shall *gnash* with his teeth, and melt away. *Ps.* cxii. 10.

There shall be weeping and *gnashing* of teeth. *Mat.* viii.

2. To rage even to collision of the teeth; to fume; to growl.

His great iron teeth he still did grind,
And grimly *gnash*, threatning revenge in vain. *Fai. Queen.*

They *gnashed* upon me with their teeth. *Ps.* xxxv. 16.

They him laid
Gnashing for anguish, and despite and shame,
To find himself not matchless. *Milton's Paradise Lost.*

With boiling rage Atrides burn'd;
And foam betwixt his *gnashing* grinders churn'd. *Dryden.*

GNAT. *n. s.* [ʒnæt, Saxon.]

1. A small winged stinging insect.

Her whip of cricket's bone, the lash of film;
Her waggoner, a small grey-coated *gnat*. *Shak. Rom. and Ju.*

2. Any thing proverbially small.

Ye blind guides, which strain at a *gnat*, and swallow a camel. *Mat.* xxiii. 24.

GNA'TFLOWER. *n. s.* [*gnat* and *flower*.] A flower otherwise called the beeflower.

GNA'TSNAPPER. *n. s.* [*gnat* and *snap*.] A bird so called, because he lives by catching gnats.

They deny that any bird is to be eaten whole, but only the *gnatsnapper*. *Hakewill on Providence.*

To GNAW. *v. a.* [ʒnaʒan, Saxon; *knaghen*, Dutch.]

1. To eat by degrees; to devour by slow corrosion.

To you such scabb'd harsh fruit is giv'n, as raw
Young soldiers at their exercisings *gnaw*. *Dryden's Juvenal.*

2. To bite in agony or rage.

Alas, why *gnaw* you so your nether lip?
Some bloody passion shakes your very frame. *Shak. Othello.*

They *gnawed* their tongues for pain. *Rev.* xvi. 10.

He comely fell, and dying *gnaw'd* the ground. *Dryden.*

3. To wear away by biting.

Gnawing with my teeth my bonds asunder,
I gain'd my freedom. *Shakesp. Comedy of Errours.*

Like rotten fruit I fall, worn like a cloth
Gnawn into rags by the devouring moth. *Sandys.*

A lion, hampered in a net, called to a mouse to help him out of the snare: the mouse *gnawed* the threads to pieces, and set the lion at liberty. *L'Estrange.*

4. To fret; to waste; to corrode.

5. To pick with the teeth.

His bones clean pick'd; his very bones they *gnaw*. *Dryd.*

To GNAW. *v. n.* To exercise the teeth.

I might well, like the spaniel, *gnaw* upon the chain that ties him; but I should sooner mar my teeth than procure liberty. *Sidney.*

See the hell of having a false woman: my bed shall be abused, my coffers ransacked, my reputation *gnawn* at. *Shakes.*

I thought I saw a thousand fearful wrecks,
A thousand men that fishes *gnaw'd* upon. *Shakesp. R.* III.

GNA'WER. *n. s.* [from *gnaw*.] One that gnaws.

GNO'MON. *n. s.* [γνώμων.] The hand or pin of a dial.

The *gnomon* of every dial is supposed to represent the axis of the world, and therefore the two ends or extremities thereof must directly answer to the North and South pole. *Harris.*

There were from great antiquity sun-dials, by the shadow of a style or *gnomon*, denoting the hours of the day. *Brown.*

GNO'MONICKS. *n. s.* [γνωμονικὴ.] A science which makes a part of the mathematicks: it teaches to find the just proportion of shadows for the construction of all kinds of sun and moon dials, and for knowing what o'clock it is by means thereof; as also of a gnomon or stile, that throws off the shadow for this purpose. *Trevoux.*

To GO. *v. n.* pret. *I went*; *I have gone*. [ʒan, Saxon. This was probably changed to *gone*, or *gang*, then contracted to *go*.]

1. To walk; to move step by step.

You know that love
Will creep in service where it cannot *go*. *Shakespeare.*

After some months those muscles become callous; and, having yielded to the extension, the patient makes shift to *go* upon it, though lamely. *Wiseman's Surgery.*

2. To move; not stand still.

Rise, let us be *going*. *Mat.* xxvi. 46.

3. To walk solemnly.

If there be cause for the church to *go* forth in solemn procession, his whole family have such business come upon them that no one can be spared. *Hooker, b.* v. *s.* 41.

4. To walk leisurely, not run.

And must I *go* to him?
—Thou must run to him; for thou hast staid so long, that *going* will scarce serve the turn. *Shakespeare.*

5. To travel; to journey a-foot.

I will only *go* through on my feet. *Num.* xx. 19.

And whosoever shall compel thee to *go* a mile, *go* with him twain. *Mat.* v. 41.

From them I *go*,
This uncouth errand sole. *Milton.*

6. To proceed; to make a progress.

Thus others we with defamation wound,
While they stab us; and so the jest *goes* round. *Dryden.*

7. To remove from place to place.

I am in blood
Stept in so far, that, should I wade no more,
Returning were as tedious as *go* o'er. *Shakesp. Macbeth.*

8. To depart from a place; to move from a place; the opposite of *to come*.

I hope it be not *gone*, to tell my lord
That I kiss aught but him. *Shakespeare's Cymbeline.*

At once, good-night:
Stand not upon the order of your *going*,
But *go* at once. *Shakespeare's Macbeth.*

Ye shall not *go* forth hence. *Gen.* xlii. 15.

And when she had so said she *went* her way. *Jo.* xi. 28.

I will let you *go*, that ye may sacrifice; only you shall not *go* very far away. *Ex.* viii. 28.

Colchester oysters are put into pits, where the sea *goeth* and cometh. *Bacon's Natural History.*

A young tall squire
Did from the camp at first before him *go*. *Cowley's Davideis.*

Then I concur to let him *go* for Greece,
And wish our Egypt fairly rid of him. *Dryden's Cleomenes.*

Go first the master of thy herds to find,
True to his charge, a loyal swain and kind. *Pope's Odyssey.*

9. To move or pass in any manner, or to any end.

Though the vicar be bad, or the parson be evil,
Go not for thy tything thyself to the devil. *Tuss. Husbandry.*

She may *go* to bed when she list; all is as she will. *Shakesp.*

You did wish that I would make her turn;
Sir, she can turn and turn, and yet *go* on. *Shakes. Othello.*

I am glad to see your lordship abroad: I heard say your lordship was sick: I hope your lordship *goes* abroad by advice. *Shakespeare's Henry* IV. *p.* ii.

Go to, let us *go* down, and there confound their language. *Gen.* xi. 7.

Let my Lord *go* amongst us. *Ex.* xxxiv. 9.

The mourners *go* about the streets. *Eccl.* xii. 5.

The sun shall *go* down over the prophets, and the day shall be dark over them. *Mic.* iii. 6.

Put every man his sword by his side, and *go* in and out from gate to gate throughout the camp. *Ex.* xxxii. 27.

The sun, which once did shine alone,
Hung down his head, and wish'd for night,
When he beheld twelve suns for one
Going about the world, and giving light. *Herbert.*

This seen, the rest at awful distance stood,
As if they had been there as servants set,
To stay, or to *go* on, as he thought good,
And not pursue, but wait on his retreat. *Dryd. Ann. Mir.*

Not turning them *going*, 'till you have given them all the satisfaction they are capable of, and so leading them by your answers into farther questions. *Locke.*

History only acquaints us that his fleet *went* up the Elbe, he having carried his arms as far as the banks of that river. *Arbuthnot on Coins.*

The last advice I give you relates to your behaviour when you

you are *going* to be hanged, which, either for robbing your master, for housebreaking, or *going* upon the highway, may very probably be your lot. *Swift's Directions to the Footman.*

Those who come for gold will *go* off with pewter and brass, rather than return empty. *Swift.*

10. To pass in company with others.

Thou shalt again be adorned with thy tabrets, and shalt *go* forth in the dances of them that make merry. *Jer.* xxxi. 4.

Whatever remains in story of Atlas, or his kingdom of old, is so obscured with age or fables, that it may *go* along with those of the Atlantick islands. *Temple.*

11. To proceed in any course of life good or bad.

He *goeth* in company with the workers of iniquity, and walketh with wicked men. *Job* xxxiv. 8.

And the Levites that are *gone* away far from me, when Israel *went* astray, which *went* astray away from me after their idols, they shall even bear their iniquity. *Ezek.* xliv. 10.

12. To proceed in mental operations.

If I had unwarily too far engaged myself for the present publishing it, truely I should have kept it by me 'till I had once again *gone* over it. *Digby on the Soul, Dedication.*

Thus I have *gone* through the speculative consideration of the Divine Providence. *Hale's Origin of Mankind.*

I hope, by *going* over all these particulars, you may receive some tolerable satisfaction about this great subject. *South.*

If we *go* over the laws of Christianity, we shall find that, excepting a very few particulars, they enjoin the very same things, only they have made our duty more clear and certain. *Tillotson, Sermon* 6.

In their primary qualities we can *go* but a very little way. *Locke.*

I *go* over some parts of this argument again, and enlarge a little more upon them. *Locke.*

They are not able all their life-time to reckon, or regularly *go* over any moderate series of numbers. *Locke.*

13. To take any road.

I will *go* along by the highway; I will neither turn to the right hand, nor to the left. *Deutr.* ii. 27.

Who shall bemoan thee? Or who shall *go* aside to ask how thou doest? *Jer.* xv. 5.

His horses *go* about
Almost a mile. *Shakespeare's Macbeth.*

I have endeavoured to escape into the ease and freedom of a private scene, where a man may *go* his own way and his own pace. *Temple.*

14. To march in a hostile or warlike manner.

You were advis'd his flesh was capable
Of wounds and scars, and that his forward spirit
Would lift where most trade of danger rang'd;
Yet did you say *go* forth. *Shakespeare's Henry* IV. *p.* i.

We be not able to *go* up against the people; for they are stronger than we. *Numb.* xiii. 31.

Let us *go* down after the Philistines by night, and spoil them until the morning light. 1 *Sa.* xiv. 36.

Thou art able to *go* against this Philistine to fight with him. 1 *Sa.* xvii. 33.

The remnant of Jacob shall be among the Gentiles as a lion among the beasts of the forest; who, if he *go* through, both treadeth down and teareth in pieces, and none can deliver. *Mic.* v. 8.

15. To change state or opinion for better or worse.

We will not hearken to the king's words to *go* from our religion. 1 *Mac.* ii. 22.

The regard of the publick state, in so great a danger, made all those goodly things, which *went* so to wreck, to be lightly accounted of, in comparison of their lives and liberty. *Knolles.*

They become secretly discontent, and look upon men and matters with an evil eye; and are best pleased when things *go* backward, which is the worst property of a servant of a prince or state. *Bacon, Essay* 37.

All *goes* to ruin, they themselves contrive
To rob the honey, and subvert the hive. *Dryd. Virg. Georg.*

Landed men, as well as others, by their providence and good husbandry, accommodating their expences to their income, keep themselves from *going* backwards in the world. *Locke.*

Cato, we all *go* into your opinion. *Addison's Cato.*

16. To apply one's self.

Seeing himself confronted by so many, like a resolute orator, he *went* not to denial, but to justify his cruel falsehood. *Sidney.*

Because this atheist *goes* mechanically to work, he will not offer to affirm that all the parts of the embryon could, according to his explication, be formed at a time. *Bentley's Sermons.*

17. To have recourse to.

Dare any of you, having a matter against another, *go* to law before the unjust, and not before the saints? 1 *Cor.* vi. 1.

18. To be about to do.

So extraordinary an example, in so degenerate an age, deserves for the rarity, and, I was *going* to say, for the incredibility of it, the attestation of all that knew him, and considered his worth. *Locke.*

19. To shift; to pass life not quite well.

Every goldsmith, eager to engross to himself as much as he could, was content to pay high for it, rather than *go* without. *Locke.*

Cloaths they must have; but if they speak for this stuff, or that colour, they should be sure to *go* without it. *Locke.*

20. To decline; to tend towards death or ruin.

He is far *gone*, and, truly, in my youth,
I suffer'd much extremity for love,
Very near this. *Shakespeare's Hamlet.*

21. To be in party or design.

They with the vanquish'd prince and party *go*,
And leave their temples empty to the foe. *Dryden.*

22. To escape.

Timotheus himself fell into the hands of Dositheus and Sosipater, whom he besought with much craft to let him *go* with his life. 2 *Mac.* xii. 24.

23. To tend to any act.

There be some women, Silvius, had they mark'd him
In parcels as I did, would have *gone* near
To fall in love with him. *Shakesp. As you like it.*

24. To be uttered.

His disciples personally appeared among them, and ascertained the report which had *gone* abroad concerning a life so full of miracles. *Addison on the Christian Religion.*

25. To be talked of; to be known.

It has the greatest town in the island that *goes* under the name of Ano-Caprea, and is in several places covered with a very fruitful soil. *Addison's Remarks on Italy.*

26. To pass; to be received.

Because a fellow of my acquaintance set forth her praises in verse, I will only repeat them, and spare my own tongue, since she *goes* for a woman. *Sidney.*

And the man *went* among men for an old man in the days of Saul. 1 *Sa.* xvii. 12.

A kind imagination makes a bold man have vigour and enterprize in his air and motion: it stamps value upon his face, and tells the people he is to *go* for so much. *Collier.*

Clipping should be finally stopped, and the money which remains should *go* according to its true value. *Locke.*

27. To move by mechanism.

This pope is decrepid, and the bell *goeth* for him: take order that, when he is dead, there be chosen a pope of fresh years. *Bacon's Holy War.*

Clocks will *go* as they are set; but man,
Irregular man's never constant, never certain. *Otway.*

'Tis with our judgments as our watches, none
Go just alike, yet each believes his own. *Pope's Ess. on Crit.*

28. To be in motion from whatever cause.

The weyward sisters, hand in hand,
Posters of the sea and land,
Thus do *go* about, about. *Shakespeare's Macbeth.*

Clipt and washed money *goes* about, when the entire and weighty lies hoarded up. *Waller.*

29. To move in any direction.

Doctor, he is a curer of souls, and you a curer of bodies: if you should fight, you *go* against the hair of your professions. *Shakespeare's Merry Wives of Windsor.*

Thou trustest upon the staff of this bruised reed, even upon Egypt; on which, if a man lean, it will *go* into his hand and pierce it. 2 *Kings* xviii. 21.

Shall the shadow *go* forward ten degrees, or *go* back ten degrees? 2 *Kings* xx. 9.

30. To flow; to pass; to have a course.

The god I am, whose yellow water flows
Around these fields, and fattens as it *goes*,
Tyber my name. *Dryden's Æn.*

31. To have any tendency.

Athenians, know
Against right reason all your counsels *go*;
This is not fair, nor profitable that,
Nor t'other question proper for debate. *Dryden's Pers.*

32. To be in a state of compact or partnership.

As a lion was bestriding an ox that he had newly plucked down, a robber passing by cried out to him, half shares: you should *go* your snip, says the lion, if you were not so forward to be your own carver. *L'Estrange.*

There was a hunting match agreed upon betwixt a lion, an ass, and a fox, and they were to *go* equal shares in the booty. *L'Estrange.*

33. To be regulated by any method; to proceed upon principles.

Where the multitude beareth sway, laws that shall tend to the preservation of that state must make common smaller offices to *go* by lot, for fear of strife and divisions likely to arise. *Hook.*

We are to *go* by another measure. *Sprat's Sermons.*

The principles I there *went* on, I see no reason to alter. *Loc.*

The reasons that they *went* upon were very specious and probable. *Bentley's Sermons.*

34. To

34. To be pregnant.

Great bellied women,
That had not half a week to *go*. *Shakesp. Henry* VIII.
The fruit she *goes* with,
I pray that it good time and life may find. *Shakes. H.* VIII.

Of living creatures some are a longer time in the womb, and some shorter: women *go* commonly nine months, the cow and the ewe about six months. *Bacon's Nat. History.*

Some do *go* with their young the sixth part of a year, or two over or under, that is, about six or nine weeks; and the whelps of these see not 'till twelve days. *Brown.*

And now with second hopes she *goes*,
And calls Lucina to her throws. *Milton.*

35. To pass; not to remain.

She began to afflict him, and his strength *went* from him. *Judg.* xvi. 19.

When our merchants have brought them, if our commodities will not be enough, our money must *go* to pay for them. *Locke.*

36. To pass; not to be retained.

Then he lets me *go*,
And, with his head over his shoulder turn'd,
He seem'd to find his way without his eyes. *Shakes. Hamlet.*
Let *go* the hand of that arch heretick. *Shakes. K. John.*

37. To be expended.

Scholars are close and frugal of their words, and not willing to let any *go* for ornament, if they will not serve for use. *Felton on the Classicks.*

38. To be in order of time or place.

We must enquire farther what is the connexion of that sentence with those that *go* before it, and those which follow it. *Watts's Logick.*

39. To reach or be extended to any degree.

Can another man perceive that I am conscious of any thing, when I perceive it not myself? No man's knowledge here can *go* beyond his experience. *Locke.*

40. To extend to consequences.

It is not one master that either directs or takes notice of these: it *goes* a great way barely to permit them. *L'Estrange.*

41. To reach by effects.

Considering the cheapness, so much money might *go* farther than a sum ten times greater could do now. *Wilkins.*

42. To extend in meaning.

His amorous expressions *go* no further than virtue may allow. *Dryden's Ovid, Preface.*

43. To spread; to be dispersed; to reach farther.

Whose flesh, torn off by lumps, the rav'nous foe
In morsels cut, to make it farther *go*. *Tate's Juven. Sat.*

44. To have influence; to be of weight.

I had another reason to decline it, that ever uses to *go* far with me upon all new inventions or experiments; which is, that the best trial of them is by time, and observing whether they live or no. *Temple.*

'Tis a rule that *goes* a great way in the government of a sober man's life, not to put any thing to hazard that may be secured by industry, consideration, or circumspection. *L'Estr.*

Whatever appears against their prevailing vice *goes* for nothing, being either not applied, or passing for libel and slander. *Swift.*

45. To be rated one with another; to be considered with regard to greater or less worth.

I think, as the world *goes*, he was a good sort of man enough. *Arbuthnot.*

46. To contribute; to conduce; to concur.

The medicines which *go* to the ointments are so strong, that, if they were used inwards, they would kill those that use them. *Bacon's Natural History.*

More parts of the greater wheels *go* to the making one part of their lines. *Glanv. Sceps. c.* 8.

There *goes* a great many qualifications to the compleating this relation: there is no small share of honour and conscience and sufficiency required. *Collier of Friendship.*

I had some thoughts of giving the sex their revenge, by laying together the many vicious characters that prevail in the male world, and shewing the different ingredients that *go* to the making up of such different humours and constitutions. *Addison's Spectator*, N°. 211.

Something better and greater than high birth and quality must *go* toward acquiring those demonstrations of publick esteem and love. *Swift to Pope.*

47. To fall out, or terminate; to succeed.

Your strong possession much more than your right,
Or else it must *go* wrong with you and me. *Shakes. K. John.*
Howe'er the business *goes*, you have made fault
I' th' boldness of your speech. *Shakesp. Winter's Tale.*

I will send to thy father, and they shall declare unto him how things *go* with thee. *Tob.* x. 8.

In many armies, if the matter should be tried by duel between two champions, the victory should *go* on the one side; and yet, if it be tried by the gross, it would *go* on the other side. *Bacon's Collection of Good and Evil.*

It has been the constant observation of all, that if a minister had a cause depending in the court, it was ten to one but it *went* against him. *South's Sermons.*

At the time of the prince's landing, the father, easily foreseeing how things would *go*, went over, like many others, to the prince. *Swift.*

Whether the cause *goes* for me or against me, you must pay me the reward. *Watts's Logick.*

48. To be in any state. This sense is impersonal.

It shall *go* ill with him that is left in his tabernacle. *Job* xx.

He called his name Beriah, because it *went* evil with his house. 1 *Chr.* vii. 23.

49. To proceed in train or consequence.

How *goes* the night, boy?
—The moon is down: I have not heard the clock;
And she *goes* down at twelve.
I take't 'tis later, sir. *Shakespeare's Macbeth.*

I had hope,
When violence was ceas'd, and war on earth,
All would have then *gone* well. *Milton.*

Duration in itself is to be considered as *going* on in one constant, equal, uniform course. *Locke.*

50. *To* Go *about*. To attempt; to endeavour; to set one's self to any business.

O dear father,
It is thy business that I *go about*. *Shakespeare's King Lear.*
I lost him; but so found, as well I saw
He could not lose himself, but *went about*
His father's business. *Paradise Regain'd, b.* ii.

Which answer exceedingly united the vulgar minds to them, who concurred only with them as they saw them like to prevail in what they *went about*. *Clarendon.*

Some men, from a false persuasion that they cannot reform their lives, break off their ill customs, and root out their old vicious habits, never so much as attempt, endeavour, or *go about* it. *South's Sermons.*

Either my book is plainly enough written to be rightly understood by those who peruse it with attention and indifferency, or else I have writ mine so obscurely that it is in vain to *go about* to mend it. *Locke.*

They never *go about*, as in former times, to hide or palliate their vices; but expose them freely to view. *Swift.*

51. *To* Go *aside*. To err; to deviate from the right.

If any man's wife *go aside*, and commit a trespass against him. *Numb.* v. 12.

52. *To* Go *between*. To interpose; to moderate between two.

I did *go between* them, as I said; but more than that, he loved her; for, indeed, he was mad for her. *Shakespeare.*

53. *To* Go *by*. To pass away unnoticed.

Do not you come your tardy son to chide,
That laps'd in time and passion, lets *go by*
Th' important acting of your dread command? *Sh. Hamlet.*
So much the more our carver's excellent,
Which lets *go by* some sixteen years, and makes her
As she liv'd now. *Shakespeare's Winter's Tale.*
What's that to us? The time *goes by*; away. *Shakespeare.*

54. *To* Go *by*. To find or get in the conclusion.

In argument with men a woman ever
Goes by the worse, whatever be her cause. *Milt. Agonistes.*

He's sure to *go by* the worst that contends with an adversary that is too mighty for him. *L'Estrange.*

55. *To* Go *by*. To observe as a rule.

'Tis not to be supposed, that by searching one can positively judge of the size and form of a stone; and indeed the frequency of the fits, and violence of the symptoms, are a better rule to *go by*. *Sharp's Surgery.*

56. *To* Go *down*. To be swallowed; to be received, not rejected.

Nothing so ridiculous, nothing so impossible, but it *goes down* whole with him for truth and earnest. *L'Estrange.*

Folly will not easily *go down* in its own natural form with discerning judges. *Dryden's Aurengzebe, Preface.*

If he be hungry, bread will *go down*. *Locke.*

Ministers are so wise to leave their proceedings to be accounted for by reasoners at a distance, who often mould them into the systems that do not only *go down* very well in the coffeehouse, but are supplies for pamphlets in the present age. *Swift on the present State of Affairs.*

57. *To* Go *in and out*. To do the business of life.

The Lord shall preserve thy *going out* and thy coming *in*. *Ps.*

58. *To* Go *in and out*. To be at liberty.

He shall *go in and out*, and find pasture. *John* x. 9.

59. *To* Go *off*. To die; to go out of life; to decease.

I would the friends we miss were safe arriv'd:
Some must *go off*; and yet, by these I see,
So great a day as this is cheaply bought. *Shakesp. Macbeth.*

In this manner he *went off*, not like a man that departed out of life, but one that returned to his abode. *Tatler*, N°. 86.

60. *To* Go *off*. To depart from a post.

The leaders having charge from you to stand,
Will not *go off* until they hear you speak. *Shakesp. H.* IV.

61. *To* Go *on.* To make attack.

Bold Cethegus,
Whoſe valour I have turn'd into his poiſon,
And prais'd ſo to daring, as he would
Go on upon the gods. *Ben. Johnſon's Catiline.*

62. *To* Go *on.* To proceed.

He found it a great war to keep that peace, but was fain to *go on* in his ſtory. *Sidney, b.* ii.

He that deſires only that the work of God and religion ſhall *go on*, is pleaſed with it, whoever is the inſtrument. *Taylor.*

I have eſcaped many threats of ill fits by theſe motions: if they *go on*, the only poltice I have dealt with is wool from the belly of a fat ſheep. *Temple.*

To look upon the ſoul as *going on* from ſtrength to ſtrength, to conſider that ſhe is to ſhine for ever with new acceſſions of glory, and brighten to all eternity, is agreeable. *Addiſ. Spect.*

Go on chearfully in the glorious courſe you have undertaken. *Addiſon's Spectator*, N° 164.

Copious bleeding is the moſt effectual remedy in the beginning of the diſeaſe; but when the expectoration *goes on* ſucceſsfully, not ſo proper, becauſe it ſometimes ſuppreſſeth it. *Arbuthnot on Diet.*

I have already handled ſome abuſes during the late management, and in convenient time ſhall *go on* with the reſt. *Swift.*

When we had found that deſign impracticable, we ſhould not have *gone on* in ſo expenſive a management of it. *Swift.*

Many clergymen write in ſo diminutive a manner, with ſuch frequent blots and interlineations, that they are hardly able to *go on* without perpetual heſitations, or extraordinary expletives. *Swift.*

I wiſh you health to *go on* with that noble work. *Berkley.*

63. *To* Go *over.* To revolt; to betake himſelf to another party.

In the change of religion, men of ordinary underſtandings don't ſo much conſider the principles as the practice of thoſe to whom they *go over.* *Addiſon on Italy.*

Power, which, according to the old maxim, was uſed to follow, is now *gone over* to money. *Swift.*

64. *To* Go *out.* To go upon any expedition.

You need not have pricked me: there are other men fitter to *go out* than I. *Shakeſpeare's Henry* IV. *p.* ii.

65. *To* Go *out.* To be extinguiſhed.

Think'ſt thou the fiery fever will *go out*,
With titles blown from adulation? *Shakeſpeare's Henry* V.

Spirit of wine burned 'till it *go out* of itſelf, will burn no more. *Bacon's Natural Hiſtory.*

The care of a ſtate, or an army, ought to be as conſtant as the chymiſt's fire, to make any great production; and if it *goes* out for an hour, perhaps the whole operation fails. *Temp.*

The morning, as miſtaken, turns about;
And all her early fires again *go out.* *Dryden's Aurengzebe.*

Let the acquaintance be decently buried, and the flame rather *go out* than be ſmothered. *Collier of Friendſhip.*

My blood runs cold, my heart forgets to heave,
And life itſelf *goes out* at thy diſpleaſure. *Addiſon's Cato.*

And at her felt approach and ſecret might,
Art after art *goes out*, and all is night. *Pope's Dunciad, b.* iii.

66. *To* Go *through.* To perform throughly; to execute.

Finding Pyrocles every way able to *go through* with that kind of life, he was as deſirous for his ſake as for his own to enter into it. *Sidney, b.* ii.

If you can as well *go through* with the ſtatute laws of that land, I will think you have not loſt all your time there. *Spenſer.*

Kings ought not to ſuffer their council to *go through* with the reſolution and direction, as if it depended on them, but take the matter back into their own hands. *Bacon, Eſſay* 21.

He much feared the earl of Antrim had not ſteadineſs of mind enough to *go through* with ſuch an undertaking. *Clarend.*

The amazing difficulty and greatneſs of his account will rather terrify than inform him, and keep him from ſetting heartily about ſuch a taſk, as he deſpairs ever to *go through* with it. *South's Sermons.*

The powers in Germany are borrowing money, in order to *go through* their part of the expence. *Addiſon on the War.*

67. *To* Go *through.* To ſuffer; to undergo.

I tell thee that it is abſolutely neceſſary for the common good that thou ſhouldſt *go through* this operation. *Arbuthnot.*

68. The ſenſes of this word are very indiſtinct: its general notion is motion or progreſſion.

Go to. *interject.* Come, come, take the right courſe. A ſcornful exhortation.

Go to then, O thou far renowned ſon
Of great Apollo; ſhew thy famous might
In medicine. *Fairy Queen, b.* i. *cant.* 5. *ſtan.* 43.

Go to, go to, thou art a fooliſh fellow;
Let me be clear of thee. *Shakeſpeare's Twelfth Night.*

My favour is not bought with words like theſe:
Go to; you'll teach your tongue another tale. *Rowe.*

Go-by. *n. ſ.* Deluſion; artifice; circumvention; over-reach.

Except an apprentice is inſtructed how to adulterate and varniſh, and give you the *go-by* upon occaſion, his maſter may be charged with neglect. *Collier on Pride.*

Go-cart. *n. ſ.* [*go* and *cart.*] A machine in which children are incloſed to teach them to walk, and which they puſh forward without danger of falling.

Young children, who are try'd in
Go-carts, to keep their ſteps from ſliding,
When members knit, and legs grow ſtronger,
Make uſe of ſuch machine no longer. *Prior.*

Goad. *n. ſ.* [ᵹab, Saxon.] A pointed inſtrument with which oxen are driven forward.

Oft in his harden'd hand a *goad* he bears. *Pope.*

To Goad. *v. a.* [from the noun.]

1. To prick or drive with a goad.
2. To incite; to ſtimulate; to inſtigate; to drive forward.

Moſt dangerous
Is that temptation, that doth *goad* us on
To ſin in loving virtue. *Shakeſp. Meaſure for Meaſure.*

Goaded with moſt ſharp occaſions,
Which lay nice manners by, I put you to
The uſe of your own virtues. *Shak. All's well that ends well.*

Of all that breathes the various progeny,
Stung with delight, is *goaded* on by thee. *Dryden's Lucret.*

Goal. *n. ſ.* [*gaule*, French, a long pole ſet up to mark the bounds of the race.]

1. The landmark ſet up to bound a race; the point marked out to which racers run.

As at the Olympian games, or Pythian fields,
Part curb their fiery ſteeds, or ſhun the *goal*
With rapid wheels. *Milton's Paradiſe Loſt, b.* ii.

And the ſlope ſun his upward beam
Shoots againſt the duſky pole,
Pacing toward the other *goal.* *Milton.*

2. The ſtarting poſt.

Haſt thou beheld, when from the *goal* they ſtart,
The youthful charioteers with heaving heart
Ruſh to the race? *Dryden's Virg. Georg.*

3. The final purpoſe; the end to which a deſign tends.

Our poet has always the *goal* in his eye, which directs him in his race: ſome beautiful deſign, which he firſt eſtabliſhes, and then contrives the means, which will naturally conduct him to his end. *Dryden's Ovid, Preface.*

Each individual ſeeks a ſev'ral *goal*;
But heav'n's great view is one, and that the whole. *Pope.*

So man, who here ſeems principal alone,
Perhaps acts ſecond to ſome ſphere unknown;
Touches ſome wheel, or verges to ſome *goal*;
'Tis but a part we ſee, and not a whole.
Pope's Eſſay on Man.

4. It is ſometimes improperly written for *gaol*, or *jail.*

Goar. *n. ſ.* [*goror*, Welſh.] Any edging ſewed upon cloath to ſtrengthen it. *Skinner.*

Goat. *n. ſ.* [ᵹat, Saxon and Scottiſh.] A ruminant animal that ſeems a middle ſpecies between deer and ſheep.

Gall of *goat*, and ſlips of yew. *Shakeſp. Macbeth.*

You may draw naked boys riding and playing with their paper-mills or bubble-ſhells upon *goats*, eagles, or dolphins. *Peacham on Drawing.*

The little bear that rock'd the mighty Jove,
The ſwan whoſe borrow'd ſhape conceal'd his love,
Are grac'd with light; the nurſing *goat*'s repaid
With heaven, and duty rais'd the pious maid. *Creech.*

Go'atbeard. *n. ſ.* [*goat* and *beard.*]

It is a plant with a ſemifloſculous flower, conſiſting of many half florets: theſe with the embryoes are included in one common many leaved flower-cup, not ſcaly, but the ſegments are ſtretched out above the florets: the embryoes afterward become oblong ſeeds incloſed in coats, and have a thick down like a beard adhering to them. *Miller.*

Goa'tsbread. The ſame with Goatsbeard, which ſee.

Goa'tchafer. *n. ſ.* An inſect; a kind of beetle. *Bailey.*

Goa'therd. *n. ſ.* [ᵹat and hẏrb, Saxon, a feeder or tender.] One whoſe employment is to tend goats.

Is not thilk ſame *goatherd* proud,
That ſits on yonder bank,
Whoſe ſtraying herd themſelf doth ſhrowd
Among the buſhes rank? *Spenſer's Paſtorals.*

They firſt gave the *goatherd* good contentment, and the marquis and his ſervant chaſed the kid about the ſtack. *Wotton.*

Goa'tmarjoram. *n. ſ.* The ſame with Goatsbeard, which ſee.

Goa'tsmilk. *n. ſ.* [*goat* and *milk.*]

After the fever and ſuch like accidents are diminiſhed, aſſes and *goatſmilk* may be neceſſary. *Wiſeman's Surgery.*

Goa'tmilker. *n. ſ.* [*goat* and *milker.*] A kind of owl ſo called from ſucking goats. *Bailey.*

Goats *Rue. n. ſ.* [*galega.*]

It hath a perennial root: the leaves grow by pairs, faſtened to a mid-rib, terminating in an odd lobe: the flower is of the papilionaceous kind, conſiſting of a ſtandard, the wings, and the keel: the pointal becomes a long taper pod, which is filled with oblong kidney-ſhaped ſeeds. This plant is propagated for medicinal uſe. *Miller.*

Goat's rue is a native of Italy, and some parts of Spain, where it has the reputation of being a great alexipharmick and sudorifick: the Italians eat it raw and boiled, and make a kind of tea of it; but with us it is of no esteem. *Hill.*

GOA'TSKIN. *n. s.* [*goat* and *skin.*]

They wandered about in sheepskins and *goatskins*, being destitute, afflicted, and tormented. *Hebr.* ii. 37.

Then fill'd two *goatskins*, with her hands divine;
With water one, and one with sable wine. *Pope's Odyssey.*

GOATS-THORN *n. s.* [*goat* and *thorn.*]

It hath a papilinaceous flower, out of which empalement arises the pointal, which afterwards becomes a bicapsular pod filled with kidney-shaped seeds: the leaves grow by pairs on a middle rib, which always end in a thorn. Tournefort says the gum adragant, or dragon, is produced in Crete. *Miller.*

GOA'TISH. *adj.* [from *goat.*] Resembling a goat in any qualities: as, rankness; lust.

An admirable evasion of a whoremaster, man, to lay his *goatish* disposition on the change of a star. *Shak. King Lear.*

The last is notorious for its *goatish* smell, and tufts not unlike the beard of that lecherous animal. *More against Atheism.*

GOB *n. s.* [*gobe*, French.] A small quantity. A low word.

Do'st think I have so little wit as to part with such a *gob* of money? *L'Estrange.*

GO'BBET. *n. s.* [*gobe*, French.] A mouthful; as much as can be swallowed at once.

Therewith she spew'd out of her filthy maw
A flood of poison, horrible and black,
Full of great lumps of flesh and *gobbets* raw. *Fairy Queen.*

By devilish policy art thou grown great,
And, like ambitious Sylla, overgorg'd
With *gobbets* of thy mother's bleeding heart. *Shakesp. H.* VI.

The cooks, slicing it into little *gobbets*, prick it on a prog of iron, and hang it in a furnace. *Sandys's Travels.*

The giant, gorg'd with flesh, and wine, and blood,
Lay stretcht at length, and snoring in his den,
Belching raw *gobbets* from his maw, o'ercharg'd
With purple wine and cruddl'd gore confus'd. *Addison.*

To GO'BBET. *v. a* [from the noun.] To swallow at a mouthful. A low word.

Down comes a kite powdering upon them, and *gobbets* up both together. *L'Estrange, Fable* 4.

To GO'BBLE. *v. a.* [*gober*, to swallow, old French.] To swallow hastily with tumult and noise.

The sheep were so keen upon the acorns, that they *gobbled* up now and then a piece of the coat along with them. *L'Est.*

Of last year's corn in barn great store;
Fat turkeys *gobbling* at the door *Prior.*

The time too precious now to waste,
And supper *gobbled* up in haste,
Again afresh to cards they run. *Swift.*

GO'BBLER. *n. s* [from *gobble.*] One that devours in haste; a gormand; a greedy eater.

GOBETWEEN *n. s.* [*go* and *between.*] One that transacts business by running between two parties.

Even as you came in to me, her assistant, or *go-between*, parted from me: I say I shall be with her between ten and eleven. *Shakespeare's Merry Wives of Windsor.*

GO'BLET *n. s.* [*gobelet*, French.] A bowl, or cup, that holds a large draught.

My figur'd *goblets* for a dish of wood. *Shakesp. Rich.* II.

We love not loaded boards, and *goblets* crown'd;
But free from surfeits our repose is found. *Denham.*

Crown high the *goblets* with a chearful draught;
Enjoy the present hour, adjourn the future thought. *Dryden.*

GO'BLIN. *n. s.* [French; *gobelina*, which *Spenser* has once retained, writing it in three syllables. This word some derive from the *Gibellines* a faction in Italy; so that *elfe* and *goblin* is *Guelph* and *Gibelline*, because the children of either party were terrified by their nurses with the name of the other: but it appears that *elfe* is Welsh, and much older than those factions. *Eilf Uylhon* are *phantoms of the night*, and the Germans likewise have long had spirits among them named *Goboldi*, from which *gobelin* might be derived.]

1. An evil spirit; a walking spirit; a frightful phantom.

Angels and ministers of grace defend us!
Be thou a spirit of health, or *goblin* damn'd,
Bring with thee airs from heav'n, or blasts from hell? *Shak.*

To whom the *goblin*, full of wrath, reply'd,
Art thou that traytor angel? *Milton's Paradise Lost, b.* ii.

Always, whilst he is young be sure to preserve his tender mind from all impressions and notions of spirits and *goblins*, or any fearful apprehensions in the dark. *Locke.*

2. A fairy; an elf.

His son was Elfinel, who overcame
The wicked *gobbelines* in bloody field;
But Elfant was of most renowned fame,
Who of all crystal did Panthea build. *Fairy Queen, b.* ii.

Go, charge my *goblins* that they grind their joints
With dry convulsions; shorten up their sinews
With aged cramps. *Shakespeare's Tempest.*

Mean time the village rouzes up the fire,
While well attested, and as well believ'd,
Heard solemn goes the *goblin* story round. *Thomson's Winter.*

GOD. *n. s.* [ʒoꝺ, Saxon, which likewise signifies *good* The same word passes in both senses with only accidental variations through all the Teutonick dialects.]

1. The Supreme Being.

God is a spirit, and they that worship him must worship him in spirit and in truth. *John* iv. 24.

God above
Deal between thee and me: for ever now
I put myself to thy direction. *Shakespeare's Macbeth.*

The Supreme Being, whom we call *God*, is necessary, self-existent, eternal, immense, omnipotent, omniscient, and best being; and therefore also a being who is and ought to be esteemed most sacred or holy. *Grew's Cosmol. Sacr. b.* i.

2. A false god; an idol.

He that sacrificeth unto any *god*, save unto the Lord only, he shall be utterly destroyed. *Exod.* xxii. 20.

As flies to wanton boys are we to the *gods*,
They kill us for their sport. *Shakespeare's King Lear.*

Strong *god* of arms, whose iron sceptre sways
The freezing North, and Hyperborean seas,
And Scythian colds, and Thracia's Winter coast,
Where stand thy steeds, and thou art honour'd most. *Dryd.*

3. Any person or thing deified or too much honoured.

Whose end is destruction, whose *god* is their belly. *Phil.* iii.

I am not Licio,
Nor a musician as I seem to be;
But one that scorns to live in this disguise,
For such a one as leaves a gentleman,
And makes a *god* of such a cullion. *Shakespeare.*

To GOD. *v. a.* [from the noun.] To deify; to exalt to divine honours.

This last old man,
Lov'd me above the measure of a father;
Nay, *godded* me, indeed. *Shakespeare's Coriolanus.*

GO'DCHILD. *n. s.* [*god* and *child*] A term of spiritual relation; one for whom one became sponsor at baptism, and promised to see educated as a Christian.

GO'DDAUGHTER. *n. s.* [*god* and *daughter.*] A girl for whom one became sponsor in baptism. A term of spiritual relation.

GO'DDESS. *n. s.* [from *god.*] A female divinity.

Hear, nature, hear; dear *goddess*, hear a father! *Shakes.*

A woman I forswore; but I will prove,
Thou being a *goddess*, I forswore not thee:
My vow was earthy, thou a heav'nly love. *Shakespeare.*

I long have waited in the temple nigh,
Built to the gracious *goddess* Clemency;
But rev'rence thou the pow'r. *Dryden's Fables.*

From his seat the *goddess* born arose,
And thus undaunted spoke. *Dryden's Fables.*

When the daughter of Jupiter presented herself among a crowd of *goddesses*, she was distinguished by her graceful stature and superior beauty. *Addison's Freeholder*, N°. 21.

Modesty with-held the *goddess'* train. *Pope's Odyssey.*

GO'DDESS-LIKE. *adj.* [*goddess* and *like.*] Resembling a goddess.

Then female voices from the shore I heard;
A maid amidst them *goddess-like* appear'd. *Pope's Odyssey.*

GO'DFATHER. *n. s.* [*god* and *father.*] The sponsor at the font.

He had a son by her, and the king did him the honour as to stand *godfather* to his child. *Bacon's Henry* VII.

Confirmation, a profitable usage of the church, transcribed from the apostles, consists in the child's undertaking in his own name the baptismal vow; and, that he may more solemnly enter this obligation, bringing some *godfather* with him, not now, as in baptism, as his procurator. *Hammond.*

GO'DHEAD. *n. s.* [from *god.*]

1. Godship; deity; divinity; divine nature.

Be content;
Your low laid son our *godhead* will uplift. *Shakesp. Cymbel.*

At the holy mount
Of heav'n's high-seated top, th' imperial throne
Of *godhead*, fix'd for ever firm and sure,
The filial pow'r arriv'd *Milton's Paradise Lost, b.* vii.

So may thy *godhead* be confest,
So the returning year be blest. *Prior.*

2. A deity in person; a god or goddess.

Were your *godheads* to borrow of men, men would forsake the gods. *Shakespeare's Timon of Athens.*

Adoring first the *genius* of the place,
The nymphs and native *godheads* yet unknown. *Dryd. Æn.*

GO'DLESS *adj* [from *god.*] Without sense of duty to God; atheistical; wicked; irreligious; impious.

Of these two sorts of men, both *godless*, the one has utterly no knowledge of God, and the other studies how to persuade themselves that there is no such thing to be known. *Hooker.*

That *godless* crew
Rebellious. *Milton's Paradise Lost, b.* vi. *l.* 49.

For

For faults not his, for guilt and crimes
Of *godless* men, and of rebellious times,
Him his ungrateful country sent,
Their best Camillus, into banishment. *Dryden.*

GO'DLIKE. *adj.* [*god* and *like.*] Divine; resembling a divinity; supremely excellent.

Thus Adam his illustrious guest besought,
And thus the *godlike* angel answer'd mild. *Milt. Par. Lost.*

Musing and much revolving in his breast,
How best the mighty work he might begin
Of saviour to mankind, and which way first
Publish his *godlike* office now mature. *Paradise Regain'd.*

That prince shall be so wise and *godlike*, as, by established laws of liberty, to secure protection and encouragement to the honest industry of mankind. *Locke.*

GO'DLING. *n. s.* [from *god.*] A little divinity; a diminutive god.

Thy puny *godlings* of inferior race,
Whose humble statues are content with brass. *Dryd. Juven.*

GO'DLINESS. *n. s.* [from *godly.*]

1. Piety to God.

2. General observation of all the duties prescribed by religion.

Virtue and *godliness* of life are required at the hands of the minister of God. *Hooker, b.* v. *s.* 2.

GO'DLY. *adj.* [from *god.*]

1. Pious towards God.

Grant that we may hereafter live a *godly*, righteous, and sober life. *Common Prayer.*

2. Good; righteous; religious.

Help, Lord, for the *godly* man ceaseth, for the faithful fail among the children of men. *Ps.* xii. 1.

GO'DLY. *adv.* Piously; righteously.

The apostle St. Paul teacheth, that every one which will live *godly* in Christ Jesus must suffer persecution. *Hooker, b.* v.

GO'DLYHEAD. *n. s.* [from *godly.*] Goodness; righteousness. An old word.

For this, and many more such outrage,
I crave your *godlyhead* to asswage
The rancorous rigour of his might. *Spenser.*

GO'DMOTHER. *n. s.* [*god* and *mother*] A woman who has become sponsor in baptism. A term of spiritual relation.

GO'DSHIP. *n. s.* [from *god.*] The rank or character of a god; deity; divinity.

Discoursing largely on this theme,
O'er hills and dales their *godships* came. *Prior.*

GO'DSON. *n. s.* [*god* and *son.*] One for whom one has been sponsor at the font.

What, did my father's *godson* seek your life?
He whom my father named? your Edgar? *Shakes. K. Lear.*

GO'DWARD. *adj.* To *Godward* is *toward God.* So we read, *Hac Arethusa tenus*, for *hactenus Arethusa*.

And such trust have we through Christ to *Godward.* 2 *Cor.*

GO'DWIT. *n. s.* [ʒoð, good, and pıta, an animal.] A bird of particular delicacy.

Nor ortelans nor *godwits* crown his board. *Cowley.*

GO'DYELD. }
GO'DYIELD. } *adv.* [corrupted from *God shield* or protect.] A term of thanks. Now not used.

Herein I teach you,
How you should bid *godyeld* us for your pains,
And thank us for your trouble. *Shakespeare's Macbeth.*

GOEL. *adj.* [ʒolen, Saxon.] Yellow. An old word.

In March at the furthest, dry season or wet,
Hop-roots so well chosen let skilful go set;
The *goeler* and younger, the better I love;
Well gutted and pared, the better they prove. *Tuss. Husb.*

GO'ER. *n s.* [from *go.*]

1. One that goes; a runner.

I would they were in Africk both together,
Myself by with a needle, that I might prick
The *goer* back. *Shakespeare's Cymbeline.*

Such a man
Might be a copy to these younger times;
Which, follow'd well, would now demonstrate them
But *goers* backward. *Shakes. All's well that ends well.*

Nothing could hurt either of us so much as the intervening officious impertinence of those *goers* between us, who in England pretend to intimacies with you, and in Ireland to intimacies with me. *Pope to Swift.*

2. A walker; one that has a gait or manner of walking good or bad.

The earl was so far from being a good dancer, that he was no graceful *goer*. *Wotton.*

To GO'GGLE. *v. n.* To look asquint.

Inflam'd all over with disgrace,
To be seen by her in such a place,
Which made him hang his head, and scoul,
And wink and *goggle* like an owl. *Hudibras, p.* ii. *cant.* 1.

Nor sighs, nor groans, nor *goggling* eyes did want. *Dryd.*

GO'GGLE-EYED. *adj.* [ſceʒl eʒen, Saxon.] Squint-eyed; not looking strait.

They are deformed, unnatural, or lame; and very unseemly to look upon, except to men that be *goggle-eyed* themselves. *Ascham's Schoolmaster.*

GO'ING. *n. s.* [from *going.*]

1. The act of walking.

When nobles are their taylors tutors,
No hereticks burnt, but wenches suitors,
Then comes the time, who lives to see't,
That *going* shall be us'd with feet. *Shakes. King Lear.*

2. Pregnancy.

The time of death has a far greater latitude than that of our birth; most women coming, according to their reckoning, within the compass of a fortnight; that is, the twentieth part of their *going*. *Grew's Cosmol. Sacr. b.* iii. *c.* 3.

3. Departure.

Thy *going* is not lonely; with thee goes
Thy husband; him to follow thou art bound. *Milt. P. Lost.*

GOLA. *n. s.* The same with CYMATIUM, which see.

In a cornice the *gola*, or cymatium of the corona, the coping, the modillions or dentelli, make a noble show. *Spect.*

GOLD. *n. s.* [ʒolð, Saxon; *golud*, riches, Welsh. It is called *gold* in our English tongue either of *geel*, as *Scaliger* says, which is in Dutch to shine; or of another Dutch word, which is *gelten*, and signifies in Latin *valere*, in English to be of price or value: hence cometh their ordinary word *gelt*, for money. *Peacham on Drawing.*]

1. *Gold* is the heaviest, the most dense, the most simple, the most ductile, and most fixed of all bodies; not to be injured either by air or fire, and seeming incorruptible. It is soluble by means of sea-salt; but is injured by no other salt, and is most easily of all metals amalgamated with silver. *Gold* is frequently found native, and very rarely in a state of ore. It never constitutes a peculiar ore, but is found most frequently among ore of silver. Native *gold* is seldom found pure, but has almost constantly silver with it, and very frequently copper. *Gold* dust, or native *gold*, in small masses, is mixed among the sand of rivers in many parts of the world. It is found, in the greatest abundance, bedded in masses of hard stone, often at the depth of a hundred and fifty fathoms in the mines of Peru. Pure *gold* is so fixed, that Boerhaave informs us of an ounce of it set in the eye of a glass furnace for two months, without losing a single grain. *Hill on Fossils.*

Gold hath these natures: greatness of weight, closeness of parts, fixation, pliantness or softness, immunity from rust, and the colour or tincture of yellow. *Bacon's Nat. History.*

Ah! Buckingham, now do I ply the touch,
To try if thou be current *gold* indeed. *Shakes. Rich.* III.

We commonly take shape and colour for so presumptive ideas of several species, that, in a good picture, we readily say this is *gold*, and that a silver goblet, only by the different figures and colours represented to the eye by the pencil. *Locke.*

The *gold* fraught vessel, which mad tempests beat,
He sees now vainly make to his retreat. *Dryd. Tyran. Love.*

2. Money.

For me, the *gold* of France did not seduce,
Although I did admit it as a motive
The sooner to effect what I intended. *Shakesp. Henry* V.

Thou, that so stoutly hast resisted me,
Give me thy *gold*, if thou hast any *gold*;
For I have bought it with an hundred blows. *Shakes. H.* VI.

If I want *gold*, steal but a beggar's dog,
And give it Timon, why, the dog coins *gold*. *Shakespeare.*

3. It is used for any thing pleasing or valuable. So among the ancients χρυσῆ ἀφροδίτη; and *animamq; moresque* aureos *educit in astra.* Horace.

The king's a bawcock, and a heart of *gold*,
A lad of life, an imp of fame. *Shakespeare's Henry* V.

GOLD *of Pleasure. n. s.* [*myagrum*,]

It hath a flower of four leaves, placed in form of a cross, out of whose cup arises the pointal, which becomes a turbinated fruit, having one cell, in which is included an oblong seed, and two empty cells at the point. *Miller.*

GO'LDBEATER. *n. s.* [*gold* and *beat.*] One whose occupation is to beat or foliate gold so as to gild other matter.

Our *goldbeaters*, though, for their own profit sake, they are wont to use the finest coined gold they can get, yet they scruple not to employ coined gold; and that the mint-masters are wont to alloy with copper or silver, to make the coin more stiff, and less subject to be wasted by attrition. *Boyle.*

This gilder was a *goldbeater*. *Pope.*

GO'LDBEATER'S *Skin. n. s.* The intestinum rectum of an ox, which goldbeaters lay between the leaves of their metal while they beat it, whereby the membrane is reduced thin, and made fit to apply to cuts or small fresh wounds, as is now the common practice. *Quincy.*

When your gilliflowers blow, if they break the pod, open it with a penknife or lancet at each division, as low as the flower has burst it, and bind it about with a narrow slip of *goldbeater's skin*, which moisten with your tongue, and it will stick together. *Mortimer's Husbandry.*

GO'LDBOUND. *adj.* [*gold* and *bound.*] Encompassed with gold.

Thy air,
Thou other *goldbound* brow, is like the first. *Shakesp. Macb.*

Go'lden. *adj.* [from *gold.*]

1. Made of gold; consisting of gold.

O would to God that the inclusive verge
Of *golden* metal, that must round my brow,
Were red-hot steel to sear me to the brain. *Shakesp. R.* III.

Nine royal knights in equal rank succeed,
Each warrior mounted on a fiery steed,
In *golden* armour glorious to behold;
The rivets of their arms were nail'd with gold. *Dryden.*

2. Shining; bright; splendid; resplendent.

So sweet a kiss the *golden* sun gives not
To those fresh morning drops upon the rose,
Nor shines the silver moon one half so bright
Through the transparent bosom of the deep. *Shakespeare.*

'Tis better to be lowly born,
And range with humble livers in content,
Than to be perk'd up in a glistering grief,
And wear a *golden* sorrow. *Shakespeare's Henry* VIII.

Heaven's *golden* winged herald late he saw
To a poor Galilean virgin sent. *Crashaw.*

To her hard yoke you must hereafter bow,
Howe'er she shines all *golden* to you now. *Dryden.*

And see the guardian angels of the good,
Reclining soft on many a *golden* cloud. *Rowe's Royal Conv.*

3. Yellow; of the colour of gold.

Golden russeting hath a gold coloured coat under a russet hair, and its flesh of a yellow colour. *Mortimer.*

4. Excellent; valuable.

I have bought
Golden opinions from all sort of people,
Which would be worn now in their newest gloss,
Not cast aside so soon. *Shakespeare's Macbeth.*

That verse which they commonly call *golden*, has two substantives and two adjectives, with a verb betwixt them to keep the peace. *Dryden.*

Thence arises that *golden* rule of dealing with others as we would have others deal with us. *Watts's Logick.*

5. Happy; resembling the age of gold.

They say many young gentlemen flock to him every day, and fleet the time carelessly, as they did in the *golden* world. *Shakespeare's As you like it.*

Go'lden *Saxifrage. n. s.* [*chrysosplenium,*]

It hath a perennial fibrose root: the flowercup is divided into four parts: the flower has no visible petals, but eight stamina, or threads, which surround the ovary: the pointal becomes a membraneous vessel, which is forked and bivalve, inclosing many small seeds. It grows wild upon marshy soil, and in shady woods. *Miller.*

Go'ldenly. *adv.* [from *golden.*] Delightfully; splendidly.

My brother Jaques he keeps at school, and report speaks *goldenly* of his profit. *Shakespeare's As you like it.*

Go'ldfinch. *n. s.* [ȝolðꝼinc, Saxon.] A singing bird, so named from his golden colour. This is called in Staffordshire a *proud taylor.*

Of singing birds they have linnets, *goldfinches*, ruddocks, Canary-birds, blackbirds, thrushes, and divers others. *Carew.*

A *goldfinch* there I saw, with gaudy pride
Of painted plumes, that hopp'd from side to side. *Dryden.*

Go'ldfinder. *n. s.* [*gold* and *find.*] One who finds gold. A term ludicrously applied to those that empty jakes.

His empty paunch that he might fill,
He suck'd his vittels through a quill;
Untouch'd it pass'd between his grinders,
Or't had been happy for *goldfinders.* *Swift.*

Go'ldhammer. *n. s.* A kind of bird. *Dict.*

Go'lding. *n. s.* A sort of apple. *Dict.*

Go'ldney. *n. s.* A sort of fish, otherwise called Gilthead, which see. *Dict.*

Go'ldpleasure. *n. s.* An herb. *Dict.*

Go'ldsize. *n. s.* A glue of a golden colour; glue used by gilders.

The gum of ivy is good to put into your *goldsize*, and other colours. *Peacham on Drawing.*

Go'ldsmith. *n. s.* [ȝolð and ꞅmıꞇ, Saxon.]

1. One who manufactures gold.

Neither chain nor *goldsmith* came to me. *Shakespeare.*

2. A banker; one who keeps money for others in his hands.

The *goldsmith* or scrivener, who takes all your fortune to dispose of, when he has beforehand resolved to break the following day, does surely deserve the gallows. *Swift.*

Go'ldylocks. *n. s.* [*coma aurea*, Latin.]

It hath a fibrose perennial root: its numerous leaves are produced alternately on every side the branches: the flowers are yellow, and produced either singly or in an umbel upon the tops of the branches. *Miller.*

Goll. *n. s.* [corrupted, as *Skinner* thinks, from pal or pol, whence pealoan, to handle or manage.] Hands; paws; claws. Used in contempt, and obsolete.

They set hands, and Mopsa put to her golden *golls* among them; and blind fortune, that saw not the colour of them, gave her the preheminence. *Sidney, b.* ii.

Gome. *n. s.* The black and oily grease of a cart-wheel. *Bailey.*

GO'MPHOSIS. n. s. A particular form of articulation.

Gomphosis is the connexion of a tooth to its socket. *Wisem.*

GO'NDOLA. n. s. [*gondole*, French.] A boat much used in Venice; a small boat.

He saw did swim
Along the shore, as swift as glance of eye,
A little *gondelay*, bedecked trim
With boughs and arbours woven cunningly. *Fairy Queen.*

In a *gondola* were seen together Lorenzo and his amorous Jessica. *Shakespeare's Merchant of Venice.*

As with *gondola's* and men, his
Good excellence the duke of Venice
Sails out, and gives the gulph a ring. *Prior.*

Gondoli'er. *n. s.* [from *gondola.*] A boatman; one that rows a gondola.

Your fair daughter,
Transported with no worse nor better guard,
But with a knave of hire, a *gondolier*,
To the gross clasps of a lascivious Moor. *Shakesp. Othello.*

Gone. *part. preter.* [from *go.* See *To* GO.] As,

I need not qualify these remarks with a supposition that I have *gone* upon through the whole course of my papers. *Addis.*

1. Advanced; forward in progress.

I have known sheep cured of the rot, when they have not been far *gone* with it, only by being put into broomlands. *Mort.*

The observator is much the brisker of the two, and, I think, farther *gone* of late in lyes and impudence than his Presbyterian brother. *Swift.*

2. Ruined; undone.

He must know 'tis none of your daughter, nor my sister; we are *gone* else. *Shakespeare's Winter's Tale.*

3. Past.

I'll tell the story of my life,
And the particular accidents *gone* by,
Since I came to this isle. *Shakespeare's Tempest.*

4. Lost; departed.

When her masters saw that the hope of their gains was *gone*, they caught Paul and Silas. *Acts* xvi. 19.

Speech is confined to the living, and imparted to only those that are in presence, and is transient and *gone.* *Holder.*

5. Dead; departed from life.

I mourn Adonis dead and *gone.* *Oldham.*

A dog, that has his nose held in the vapour, loses all signs of life; but carried into the air, or thrown into a lake, recovers, if not quite *gone.* *Addison's Remarks on Italy.*

Go'nfalon. } *n. s.* [*gonfanon*, French; *gunfana*, Islandick,
Go'nfanon. } from *gunn*, a battle, and *fani*, a flag. Mr. *Lye.*

An ensign; a standard.

Ten thousand thousand ensigns high advanc'd,
Standards and *gonfalons*, 'twixt van and rear,
Stream in the air. *Milton's Parad. Lost, b.* v.

Gonorrhoe'a. *n. s.* [γόνος and ῥέω.] A morbid running of venereal hurts.

Rauty mummy or stone mummy grows on the tops of high rocks: they powder and boil it in milk, and then give it to stop *gonorrhœas.* *Woodward on Fossils.*

GOOD. *adj.* comp. *better*, superl. *best.* [ȝoð, Saxon; *goed*, Dutch.]

1. Having such physical qualities as are expected or desired.

God saw every thing that he had made, and behold it was very *good.* *Gen.* i. 31.

Take ye *good* heed unto yourselves. *Deutr.* ii. 4.

A universe of death! which God by curse
Created evil; for evil only *good.* *Milt. Paradise Lost.*

Resolv'd
From an ill cause to draw a *good* effect. *Dryden's Fables.*

Notwithstanding this criticism the verses were *good.* *Spectat.*

A man is no more to be praised upon this account, than because he has a regular pulse and a *good* digestion. *Addison.*

We may as well pretend to obtain the good which we want without God's assistance, as to know what is *good* for us without his direction. *Smalridge's Sermons.*

Ah! ne'er so dire a thirst of glory boast,
Nor in the critick let the man be lost!
Good nature and *good* sense must ever join;
To err is human, to forgive, divine. *Pope's Ess. on Critic.*

2. Proper; fit; convenient.

It is not *good* that the man should be alone. *Gen.* ii. 18.

We thought it *good* to be left at Athens alone. 1 *Thes.* iii. 1.

Amongst a man's peers a man shall be sure of familiarity, and therefore it is *good* a little to keep state: amongst a man's inferiors one shall be sure of reverence, and therefore it is *good* a little to be familiar. *Bacon, Essay* 53.

Let us, if you think *good*, give Martius leave to proceed in his discourse. *Bacon's holy War.*

He concluded, that it was a *good* time to comply with the importunity of the gentlemen of Sussex. *Clarendon, b.* viii.

3. Uncorrupted; undamaged.

He also bartered away plumbs, that would have rotted in a week, for nuts, that would last *good* for his eating a whole year. *Locke.*

4. Wholsome; salubrious.

A man first builds a country seat,
Then finds the walls not *good* to eat. *Prior.*

5. Medicinal; salutary.

The water of Nilus is sweeter than other waters in taste, and it is excellent *good* for the stone and hypochondriack melancholy. *Bacon's Natural History*, N°. 767.

6. Pleasant to the taste.

Eat thou honey, because it is *good*; and the honeycomb, which is sweet. *Prov.* xxiv. 13.

Of herbs and plants some are *good* to eat raw; as lettuce, endive, and purslane. *Bacon's Natural History.*

7. Complete; full.

The Protestant subjects of the abbey make up a *good* third of its people. *Addison on Italy.*

8. Useful; valuable.

All quality, that is *good* for any thing, is originally founded upon merit. *Collier of Envy.*

We discipline betimes those other creatures we would make useful and *good* for somewhat. *Locke.*

9. Sound; not false; not fallacious.

He is resolved now to shew how slight the propositions were which Luther let go for *good*. *Atterbury.*

10. Legal; valid; rightly claimed or held.

According to military custom the place was *good*, and the lieutenant of the colonel's company might well pretend to the next vacant captainship in the same regiment. *Wotton.*

11. Confirmed; attested; valid.

Ha! am I sure she's wrong'd? Perhaps 'tis malice!
Slave, make it clear, make *good* your accusation. *Smith.*

12. Having the qualities desired to a considerable degree; sufficient; not too little.

The king had likewise provided a *good* fleet, and had caused a body of three thousand foot to be embarked on those ships. *Clarendon*, *b.* ii.

13. With *as* preceding. It has a kind of negative or inverted sense; *as good as*, no better than.

Therefore sprang there even of one, and him *as good* as dead, so many as the stars of the sky in multitude. *Heb.* xi.

14. No worse.

He sharply reproved them as men of no courage, which, being many times as *good* as in possession of the victory, had most cowardly turned their backs upon their enemies. *Knolles.*

The master, I am sure, will be as *good* as his word, for his own business. *L'Estrange, Fable* 52.

15. Well qualified; not deficient.

If they had held their royalties by that title, either there must have been but one sovereign over them all, or else every father of a family had been as *good* a prince, and had as *good* a claim to royalty as these. *Locke.*

16. Skilful; ready; dexterous.

Flatter him it may, I confess; as those are generally *good* at flattering who are *good* for nothing else. *South's Sermons.*

I make my way where e'er I see my foe;
But you, my lord, are *good* at a retreat. *Dryd. Span. Fryar.*

17. Happy; prosperous.

Behold how *good* and how pleasant it is for brethren to dwell together in unity. *Ps.* cxxxiii. 1.

Many *good* morrows to my noble lord!
—*Good* morrow, Catesby, you are early stirring. *Shak. R.* III.

Good e'en, neighbours;
Good e'en to you all, *good* e'en to you all. *Shakesp. Coriolan.*

At once *good* night:
Stand not upon the order of your going,
But go at once. *Shakespeare's Macbeth.*

At my window bid *good* morrow. *Milton.*
Good morrow, Portius! Let us once embrace. *Addison.*

18. Honourable.

Silence, the knave's repute, the whore's *good* name,
The only honour of the wishing dame. *Pope.*

19. Cheerful; gay. Joined with any words expressing temper of mind.

That when they are certified of our mind, they may be of *good* comfort, and ever go cheerfully about their own affairs. 2 *Mac.* xi. 26.

Quietness of mind improves into cheerfulness, enough to make me just so *good* humoured as to wish that world well. *Pope to Swift.*

20. Considerable; not small though not very great.

A *good* while ago God made choice that the Gentiles by my mouth should hear the word. *Acts* xv. 7.

It seemeth the plant, having a great stalk and top, doth prey upon the grass a *good* way about, by drawing the juice of the earth from it. *Bacon's Natural History.*

Mirtle and pomgranate, if they be planted, though a *good* space one from the other, will meet. *Peacham on Drawing.*

We may suppose a great many degrees of littleness and lightness in these earthy particles, so as many of them might float in the air a *good* while, like exhalations before they fell down. *Burnet's Theory of the Earth.*

They held a *good* share of civil and military employments during the whole time of the usurpation. *Swift.*

21. Elegant; decent; delicate. With *breeding*.

If the critick has published nothing but rules and observations in criticism, I then consider whether there be a propriety and elegance in his thoughts and words, clearness and delicacy in his remarks, wit and *good* breeding in his raillery. *Addison's Guardian.*

Mankind have been forced to invent a kind of artificial humanity, which is what we express by the word *good* breeding. *Addison's Spectator.*

Those among them, who return into their several countries, are sure to be followed and imitated as the greatest patterns of wit and *good* breeding. *Swift.*

22. Real; serious; earnest.

Love not in *good* earnest, nor no farther in sport neither, than with safety of a pure blush thou may'st in honour come off again. *Shakespeare's As you like it.*

23. Rich; of credit; able to fulfil engagements.

Antonio is a *good* man: my meaning, in saying that he is a *good* man, is to have you understand me that he is sufficient. *Shakespeare's Merchant of Venice.*

24. Having moral qualities, such as are wished; virtuous.

For a *good* man some would even dare to die. *Rom.* v. 7.

The woman hath wrought a *good* work upon me. *Matt.*

Grant the bad what happiness they would,
One they must want, which is to pass for *good*. *Pope.*

25. Kind; soft; benevolent.

Matters being so turned in her, that where at first liking her manners did breed *good* will, now *good* will became the chief cause of liking her manners. *Sidney*, *b.* ii.

Glory to God in the highest, and on earth peace and *good* will towards men. *Lu.* ii. 14.

Without *good* nature man is but a better kind of vermin. *Bacon's Ornam. Ration.*

Here we are lov'd, and there we love;
Good nature now and passion strive
Which of the two should be above,
And laws unto the other give. *Suckling.*

'Tis no wonder if that which affords so little glory to God, hath no more *good* will for men. *Decay of Piety.*

When you shall see him, sir, to die for pity,
'Twere such a thing, 'twould so deceive the world,
'Twould make the people think you were *good* natur'd. *Denh.*

To teach him betimes to love and be *good* natured to others, is to lay early the true foundation of an honest man. *Locke.*

Good sense and *good* nature are never separated, though the ignorant world has thought otherwise. *Dryd. Juven. Dedicat.*

Affability, mildness, tenderness, and a word which I would fain bring back to its original signification of virtue, I mean *good* nature, are of daily use. *Dryden.*

This doctrine of God's *good* will towards men, this command of mens proportionable *good* will to one another, is not this the very body and substance, this the very spirit and life of our Saviour's whole institution? *Spratt's Sermons.*

It was his greatest pleasure to spread his healing wings over every place, and to make every one sensible of his *good* will to mankind. *Calamy's Sermons.*

How could you chide the young *good* natur'd prince,
And drive him from you with so stern an air. *Addis. Cato.*

26. Favourable; loving.

But the men were very *good* unto us, and we were not hurt. 1 *Sa.* xxv. 15.

Truly God is *good* to Israel, even to such as are of a clean heart. *Ps.* lxxiii. 1.

You have *good* remembrance of us always, desiring greatly to see us, as we also to see you. 1 *Thess.* iii. 6.

This idea, thus made, and laid up for a pattern, must necessarily be adequate, being referred to nothing else but itself, nor made by any other original but the *good* liking and will of him that first made this combination. *Locke.*

27. Companionable; sociable; merry. Often used ironically.

It was well known, that Sir Roger had been a *good* fellow in his youth. *Ascham's Schoolmaster.*

Though he did not draw the *good* fellows to him by drinking, yet he eat well. *Clarendon*, *b.* viii.

Not being permitted to drink without eating, will prevent the custom of having the cup often at his nose; a dangerous beginning and preparation to *good* fellowship. *Locke.*

28. It is sometimes used as an epithet of slight contempt, implying a kind of negative virtue or bare freedom from ill.

My *good* man, as far from jealousy as I am from giving him cause. *Shakespeare's Merry Wives of Windsor.*

She had left the *good* man at home, and brought away her gallant. *Addison's Spectator.*

29. In a ludicrous sense.

As for all other *good* women that love to do but little work, how handsome it is to louse themselves in the sunshine, they that have been but a while in Ireland can well witness. *Spenser.*

30.

30. Hearty; earnest; not dubious.

He, that saw the time fit for the delivery he intended, called unto us to follow him, which we both, bound by oath and willing by *good* will, obeyed. *Sidney, b.* ii.

The *good* will of the nation to the present war has been since but too much experienced by the successes that have attended it. *Temple.*

Good will, she said, my want of strength supplies;
And diligence shall give what age denies. *Dryden's Fables.*

31. *In* GOOD *time.* Not too fast.

In good time, replies another, you have heard them dispute against a vacuum in the schools. *Collier on Human Reason.*

32. *In* GOOD *sooth.* Really; seriously.

What, must I hold a candle to my shames?
They in themselves, *good sooth,* are too too light. *Shakesp.*

33. GOOD [*To make.*] To keep; to maintain; not to give up; not to abandon.

There died upon the place all the chieftains, all *making good* the fight without any ground given. *Bacon's Henry* VII.

He forced them to retire in spite of their dragoons, which were placed there to *make good* their retreat. *Clarendon.*

Since we claim a proper interest above others in the preeminent rights of the houshold of faith, then, no doubt, to *make good* that claim, we are proportionably obliged above others to conform to the proper manners and virtues that belong to and become this houshold, and distinguish it from all others. *Spratt's Sermons.*

He without fear a dangerous war pursues;
As honour made him first the danger chuse,
So still he *makes* it *good* on virtue's score. *Dryd. Ann. Mirab.*

34. GOOD [*To make.*] To perform; to confirm.

I farther will maintain
Upon his bad life to *make* all this *good.* *Shakesp. Rich.* II.

While she so far extends her grace,
She *makes* but *good* the promise of her face. *Waller.*

These propositions I shall endeavour to *make good.* *Smalridge.*

35. GOOD [*To make.*] To supply.

Every distinct being has somewhat peculiar to itself, to *make good* in one circumstance what it wants in another. *L'Est.*

GOOD. *n. s.*

1. That which physically contributes to happiness; benefit; advantage; the contrary to evil.

I fear the emperor means no *good* to us. *Shak. Tit. Andr.*

Let me play the lion too: I will roar, that I will do any man's heart *good* to hear me. *Shak. Midsum. Night's Dream.*

He wav'd indifferently 'twixt them, doing neither *good* nor harm. *Shakespeare's Coriolanus.*

Nature in man's heart her laws doth pen,
Prescribing truth to wit, and *good* to will. *Davies.*

This caution will have also this *good* in it, that it will put them upon considering, and teach them the necessity of examining more than they do. *Locke.*

Good is what is apt to cause or increase pleasure, or diminish pain in us; or else to procure or preserve us the possession of any other *good,* or absence of any evil. *Locke.*

Refuse to leave thy destin'd charge too soon,
And for the church's *good* defer thy own. *Prior.*

Works may have more wit than does them *good,*
As bodies perish through excess of blood. *Pope's Ess. on Crit.*

A thirst after truth, and a desire of *good,* are principles which still act with a great and universal force. *Rogers.*

2. Prosperity; advancement.

If he had employ'd
Those excellent gifts of fortune and of nature
Unto the *good,* not ruin of the state. *Ben. Johns. Catiline.*

3. Earnest; not jest.

The good woman never died after this, 'till she came to die for *good* and all. *L'Estrange.*

4. Moral qualities, such as are desirable; virtue; righteousness; piety.

Depart from evil, and do *good.* *Ps.* xxxiv. 14.

Empty of all *good,* wherein consists
Woman's domestick honour, and chief praise. *Milt. P. L.*

By *good,* I question not but *good,* morally so called, *bonum honestum* ought, chiefly at least, to be understood; and that the *good* of profit or pleasure the *bonum utile,* or *jucundum,* hardly come into any account here. *South.*

Nor holds this earth a more deserving knight
For virtue, valour, and for noble blood,
Truth, honour, all that is compriz'd in *good.* *Dryden.*

5. GOOD placed after *had,* with *as,* seems a substantive; but the expression is, I think, vitious; and *good* is rather an adjective elliptically used, or it may be considered as adverbial. See GOOD *adv.*

The pilot must intend some port before he steers his course, or he had *as good leave* his vessel to the direction of the winds, and the government of the waves. *South's Sermons.*

Without good nature and gratitude, men had as *good* live in a wilderness as in a society. *L'Estrange.*

GOOD. *adv.*

1. Well; not ill; not amiss.

2. *As* GOOD. No worse.

Was I to have never parted from thy side,
As good have grown there still a lifeless rib. *Milton.*

Says the cuckow to the hawk, Had you not *as good* have been eating worms now as pigeons? *L'Estrange.*

GOOD. *interjection.* Well! right! It is sometimes used ironically.

Good! my complexion! do'st thou think, though I am caparison'd like a man, I have a doublet and hose in my disposition? *Shakespeare's As you like it.*

GOO'D CONDITIONED. *adj.* Without ill qualities or symptoms. Used both of things and persons, but not elegantly.

No surgeon, at this time, dilates an abscess of any kind by injections, when the pus is *good-conditioned.* *Sharp's Surgery.*

GOOD-NOW. *interjection.*

1. In good time; *a la bonne heure.* A gentle exclamation of intreaty. It is now a low word.

Good-now sit down, and tell me, he that knows,
Why this same watch? *Shakespeare's Hamlet.*

2. A soft exclamation of wonder.

Good-now, good-now, how your devotions jump with mine! *Dryden's Spanish Fryar.*

GO'ODLINESS. *n. s.* [from *goodly.*] Beauty; grace; elegance.

She sung this song with a voice no less beautiful to his ears, than her *goodliness* was full of harmony to his eyes. *Sidney.*

The stateliness of houses, the *goodliness* of trees, when we behold them, delighteth the eye. *Hooker, b.* i.

GO'ODLY. *adj.* [from *good.*]

1. Beautiful; graceful; fine; splendid. Now little in use.

A prince of a *goodly* aspect, and the more *goodly* by a grave majesty, wherewith his mind did deck his outward graces. *Sidn.*

A *goodly* city is this Antium. *Shakesp. Coriolanus.*

Patience and sorrow strove
Which should express her *goodliest:* you have seen
Sunshine and rain at once. Her smiles and tears
Were like a wetter May. *Shakespeare's King Lear.*

Here from gracious England have I offer
Of *goodly* thousands. *Shakespeare's Macbeth.*

But he's something stain'd
With grief, that's beauty's canker, thou might'st call him
A *goodly* person. *Shakespeare's Tempest.*

Rebekah took *goodly* raiment of her eldest son Esau, and put them upon Jacob. *Gen.* xxvii. 15.

There was not among the children of Israel a *goodlier* person than he. 1 *Sa.* ix. 2.

He had not, according to his promise to them in time of his distress, made them any recompence for their *goodly* houses and olive gardens, destroyed in the country by Roscetes in the former wars. *Knolles's History of the Turks.*

The *goodliest* man of men since born
His sons, the fairest of her daughters Eve. *Milton.*

Of the fourth Edward was his noble song;
Fierce, *goodly,* valiant, beautiful and young. *Waller.*

Not long since walking in the field,
My nurse and I, we there beheld
A *goodly* fruit, which, tempting me,
I would have pluck'd. *Waller.*

How full of ornament is all I view
In all its parts! and seems as beautiful as new:
O *goodly* order'd work! O power divine!
Of thee I am, and what I am is thine! *Dryden's Innocence.*

His eldest born, a *goodly* youth to view,
Excell'd the rest in shape and outward shew;
Fair, tall, his limbs with due proportion join'd,
But of a heavy, dull, degen'rate mind. *Dryden's Fables.*

2. Bulky; swelling; affectedly turgid.

Round as a globe, and liquor'd every chink,
Goodly and great he sails behind his link. *Dryden.*

3. Happy; desireable; gay.

England was a peaceable kingdom, and but lately inured to the mild and *goodly* government of the Confessor. *Spenser.*

We have many *goodly* days to see. *Shak. Richard* III.

GOO'DLY. *adv.* Excellently. Obsolete.

There Alma, like a virgin queen most bright,
Doth flourish in all beauty excellent;
And to her guests doth bounteous banquet dight,
Atempered *goodly* well for health and for delight. *F. Queen.*

GOO'DLYHOOD. *n. s.* [from *goodly.*] Grace; goodness. Obsolete.

But mote thy *goodlyhood* forgive it me,
To meet which of the gods I shall thee name. *Fai. Queen.*

GOO'DMAN. *n. s.* [*good* and *man.*]

1. A slight appellation of civility: generally ironical.

Help ho! murther! murther!
—How now, what's the matter? part.
—With you, *goodman* boy, if you please: come, I'll flesh ye. *Shakespeare's King Lear.*

2. A rustick term of compliment; gaffer.

Are you my wife, and will not call me husband? My men should call me lord: I am your *goodman.* *Shakespeare.*

Nay, hear your *goodman* delver. *Shakesp. Hamlet.*

But see the sun-beams bright to labour warn,
And gild the thatch of *goodman* Hodge's barn. *Gay's Past.*

Old

Old *goodman* Dobſon of the green,
Remembers he the trees has ſeen. *Swift.*

Go'odness. *n. ſ.* [from *good.*] Deſirable qualities either moral or phyſicial; kindneſs; favour.

If for any thing he loved greatneſs, it was becauſe therein he might exerciſe his *goodneſs.* *Sidney, b.* ii.

There is in all things an appetite or deſire, whereby they incline to ſomething which they may be; all which perfections are contained under the general name of *goodneſs.* *Hooker.*

All *goodneſs*
Is poiſon to thy ſtomach.
——Yes, that *goodneſs*
Of gleaning all the land's wealth into one,
Into your own hands, cardinal, by extortion:
The *goodneſs* of your intercepted packets
You writ to the pope againſt the king; your *goodneſs,*
Since you provoke me, ſhall be moſt notorious. *Sh. H.* VIII.

There's no *goodneſs* in thy face. *Shak. Ant. and Cleopatra.*

The *goodneſs* of every thing is meaſured by its end and uſe, and that's the beſt thing which ſerves the beſt end and purpoſe. *Tillotſon, Sermon* 1.

All ſeverally made him very particular relations of the ſtrength of the Scots army, the excellent diſcipline that was obſerved in it, and the *goodneſs* of the men. *Clarendon, b.* ii.

No body can ſay that tobacco of the ſame *goodneſs* is riſen in reſpect of itſelf: one pound of the ſame *goodneſs* will never exchange for a pound and a quarter of the ſame *goodneſs.* *Locke.*

Goods. *n. ſ.* [from *good.*]

1. Moveables in a houſe.

That a writ be ſu'd againſt you,
To forfeit all your *goods,* lands, tenements,
Caſtles, and whatſoever. *Shakeſpeare's Henry* VIII.

2. Wares; freight; merchandiſe.

Her majeſty, when the *goods* of our Engliſh merchants were attached by the duke of Alva, arreſted likewiſe the *goods* of the Low Dutch here in England. *Raleigh's Eſſays.*

Sallee, that ſcorn'd all pow'r and laws of men,
Goods with their owners hurrying to their den. *Waller.*

Goo'dy. *n. ſ.* [corrupted from *good wife.*] A low term of civility uſed to mean perſons.

Soft, *goody* ſheep, then ſaid the fox, not ſo;
Unto the king ſo raſh ye may not go. *Hubberd's Tale.*

Swarm'd on a rotten ſtick the bees I ſpy'd,
Which erſt I ſaw when *goody* Dobſon dy'd. *Gay's Paſtorals.*

Plain *goody* would no longer down;
'Twas madam in her grogram gown. *Swift.*

GOOSE. *n. ſ.* plural *geeſe.* [ᵹoꞅ, Saxon; *goes,* Dutch; *gawe,* Erſe, ſing. *gewey,* plural.]

1. A large waterfowl proverbially noted, I know not why, for fooliſhneſs.

Thou cream-faced lown,
Where got'ſt thou that *gooſe* look? *Shakeſp. Macbeth.*

Since I pluckt *geeſe,* play'd truant, and whipt top, I knew not what 'twas to be beaten 'till lately. *Shakeſpeare.*

Smile you my ſpeeches, as I were a fool?
Gooſe, if I had you upon Sarum plain,
I'd drive ye cackling home to Comelot. *Shakeſ. King Lear.*

Birds moſt eaſy to be drawn are waterfowl; as the *gooſe* and ſwan. *Peacham on Drawing.*

Nor watchful dogs, nor the more wakeful *geeſe,*
Diſturb with nightly noiſe the ſacred peace. *Dryd. Fables.*

2. A taylor's ſmoothing iron.

Come in, taylor: here you may roaſt your *gooſe.* *Shakeſp.*

Go'oseberry. *n. ſ.* [*gooſe* and *berry,* becauſe eaten with young geeſe as ſauce.]

The leaves are laciniated or jagged: the whole plant is ſet with prickles: the fruit grows diſperſedly upon the tree, having for the moſt part but one fruit upon a footſtalk, which is of an oval or globular figure, containing many ſmall ſeeds, ſurrounded by a pulpy ſubſtance. The ſpecies are, 1. The common gooſeberry. 2. The large manured gooſeberry. 3. The red hairy gooſeberry. 4. The large white Dutch gooſeberry. 5. The large amber gooſeberry. 6. The large green gooſeberry. 7. The large red gooſeberry. 8. The yellow-leaved gooſeberry. 9. The ſtriped-leaved gooſeberry. *Miller.*

Auguſt has upon his arm a baſket of all manner of ripe fruits; as pears, plums, apples, *gooſeberries.* *Peacham.*

Upon a *gooſeberry* buſh a ſnail I found;
For always ſnails near ſweeteſt fruit abound. *Gay's Paſt.*

Go'osefoot. *n. ſ.* [*chenopodium,*] Wild orach.

The ſeeds are ſingle and globoſe in ſome ſpecies; but in others they are compreſſed: the cup of the flower is quinquefid: the leaves grow alternately upon the ſtalks between the ſeeds. *Miller.*

Go'osegrass. *n. ſ.* Clivers; an herb. See Clivers.

Gooſegraſs, or wild tanſy, is a weed that ſtrong clays are very ſubject to. *Mortimer's Husbandry.*

GO'RBELLY. *n. ſ.* [from ᵹoꞃ, dung, and *belly,* according to *Skinner* and *Junius.* It may perhaps come from *gor,* Welſh, beyond, too much; or, as ſeems to me more likely, may be contracted from *gormand,* or *gormand's bel'y,* the belly of a glutton.] A big paunch; a ſwelling belly. A term of reproach for a fat man.

Go'rbellied. *adj.* [from *gorbelly.*] Fat; bigbellied; having ſwelling paunches.

Hang ye, *gorbellied* knaves, are you undone? No, ye fat chuffs, I would your ſtore were here. *Shakeſp. Henry* IV. *p.* i.

Gord. *n. ſ.* An inſtrument of gaming, as appears from *Beaumont* and *Fletcher.* *Warburton.*

Thy dry bones can reach at nothing now, but *gords* and ninepins. *Beaumont and Fletcher.*

Let vultures gripe thy guts; for *gords* and Fulham holds.
Shakeſpeare's Merry Wives of Windſor.

GORE. *n. ſ.* [ᵹoꞃe, Saxon; *gôr,* Welſh, ſanious matter.]

1. Blood.

A grieſly wound,
From which forth guſh'd a ſtream of *gore* blood thick,
That all her goodly garment ſtain'd around,
And into a deep ſanguine dy'd the graſſy ground. *F. Queen.*

Another's crimes the youth unhappy bore,
Glutting his father's eyes with guiltleſs *gore.* *Dryden's Æn.*

2. Blood clotted or congealed.

The bloody fact
Will be aveng'd; though here thou ſee him die,
Rolling in duſt and *gore.* *Milton's Paradiſe Loſt, b.* xi.

His horrid beard and knotted treſſes ſtood
Stiff with his *gore,* and all his wounds ran blood. *Denham.*

To Gore. *v. a.* [ᵹebeꞃian, Saxon.]

1. To ſtab; to pierce.

Oh, let no noble eye profane a tear
For me, if I be *gor'd* with Mowbray's ſpear. *Shakeſ. R.* II.

No weaker lion's by a ſtronger ſlain;
Nor from his larger tuſks the foreſt boar
Commiſſion takes his brother ſwine to *gore.* *Tate's Juven.*

For arms his men long pikes and jav'lins bore,
And poles with pointed ſteel their foes in battle *gore.* *Dryd.*

2. To pierce with a horn.

Some toſs'd, ſome *gor'd,* ſome trampling down he kill'd.
Dryden's Preface to the Conqueſt of Granada.

He idly butting, feigns
His rival *gor'd* in every knotty trunk. *Thomſon's Spring.*

GORGE. *n. ſ.* [*gorge,* French.]

1. The throat; the ſwallow.

There were birds alſo made ſo finely, that they did not only deceive the ſight with their figures, but the hearing with their ſongs, which the watry inſtruments did make their *gorge* deliver. *Sidney.*

And now how abhorred in my imagination it is! my *gorge* riſes at it. *Shakeſpeare's Hamlet.*

Her delicate tenderneſs will find itſelf abuſed, begin to heave the *gorge,* diſreliſh and abhor the Moor. *Shakeſ. Othello.*

2. That which is gorged or ſwallowed.

And all the way, moſt like a brutiſh beaſt,
He ſpewed up his *gorge,* that all did him deteſt. *Fa. Queen.*

To Gorge. *v. a.* [*gorger,* French.]

1. To fill up to the throat; to glut; to ſatiate.

Thou deteſtable maw, thou womb of death,
Gorg'd with the deareſt morſel of the earth. *Sh. Ro. and Jul.*

Being with his preſence glutted, *gorg'd,* and full. *Shakeſ.*

He that makes his generation meſſes,
To *gorge* his appetite. *Shakeſpeare's King Lear.*

Gorge with my blood thy barbarous appetite. *Dryden.*

I muſt therefore deſire, that they will not *gorge* him either with nonſenſe or obſcenity. *Addiſon's Guardian.*

Nor would his ſlaughter'd army now have lain
On Africk's ſands, diſfigur'd with their wounds,
To *gorge* the wolves and vultures of Numidia. *Addiſ. Cato.*

The giant, *gorg'd* with fleſh, and wine, and blood,
Lay ſtretcht at length, and ſnoring in his den. *Addiſon.*

2. To ſwallow: as, *the fiſh has* gorged *the hook.*

GO'RGEOUS. *adj.* [*gorgias,* old French. *Skinner.*] Fine; ſplendid; glittering in various colours; ſhowy; magnificent.

O, that deceit ſhould dwell
In ſuch a *gorgeous* palace! *Shakeſ. Romeo and Juliet.*

As full of ſpirit as the month of May,
And *gorgeous* as the ſun at Midſummer. *Shakeſp. Hen.* IV.

He bad them look upon themſelves and upon their enemies, themſelves dreadful, their enemies *gorgeous* and brave. *Hayw.*

The *gorgeous* Eaſt, with richeſt hand,
Pours on her kings barbaric, pearl and gold. *Milton.*

With *gorgeous* wings, the marks of ſov'reign ſway,
The two contending princes make their way. *Dryd. Virgil.*

Go'rgeously. *adv.* [from *gorgeous.*] Splendidly; magnificently; finely.

The duke, one ſolemn day, *gorgeouſly* clad in a ſuit all over ſpread with diamonds, loſt one of them of good value. *Wotton.*

Go'rgeousness. *n. ſ.* [from *gorgeous.*] Splendour; magnificence; ſhow.

Go'rget. *n. ſ.* [from *gorge.*] The piece of armour that defends the throat.

He with a palſy fumbling on his *gorget,*
Shakes in and out the rivet. *Shakeſ. Troilus and Creſſida.*

He did oftentimes ſpend the night in the church alone praying, his headpiece, *gorget*, and gauntlets lying by him. *Knolles's Hiſtory of the Turks.*

See how his *gorget* peers above his gown,
To tell the people in what danger he was. *Ben. Johnſ. Cat.*

About his neck a threefold *gorget*,
As rough as trebled leathern target. *Hudibras, p.* i. *cant.* 2.

GO'RGON. *n. ſ.* [γοργὼ.] A monſter with ſnaky hairs, of which the ſight turned beholders to ſtone; any thing ugly or horrid.

Gorgons and hydras, and chimera's dire. *Milton.*

Why did'ſt thou not encounter man for man,
And try the virtue of that *gorgon* face
To ſtare me into ſtature. *Dryden.*

GO'RMAND. *n. ſ.* [*gourmand*, French.] A greedy eater; a ravenous luxurious feeder.

To GO'RMANDIZE. *v. n.* [from *gormand*.] To eat greedily; to feed ravenouſly.

GO'RMANDIZER. *n. ſ.* [from the verb.] A voracious eater.

GORSE. *n. ſ.* [ȝoꞃꞅ, Saxon.] Furz; a thick prickly ſhrub that bears yellow flowers in Winter.

GO'RY. *adj.* [from *gore*.]

1. Covered with congealed blood.

When two boars with rankling malice met,
Their *gory* ſides the freſh wounds fiercely fret. *Spenſer.*

Why do'ſt thou ſhake thy *gory* locks at me?
Thou can'ſt not ſay I did it. *Shakeſp. Macbeth.*

2. Bloody; murtherous; fatal. Not in uſe.

The obligation of our blood forbids
A *gory* emulation 'twixt us twain. *Shak. Troil. and Creſſida.*

GO'SHAWK. *n. ſ.* [ȝoꞅ, gooſe, and hapoc, a hawk.] A hawk of a large kind.

Such dread his awful viſage on them caſt;
So ſeem poor doves at *goſhawks* ſight aghaſt. *Fairfax, b.* iii.

GO'SLING. *n. ſ.* [from *gooſe*.]

1. A young gooſe; a gooſe not yet full grown.

Why do you go nodding and waggling ſo like a fool, as if you were hipſhot? ſays the gooſe to her *goſling*. *L'Eſtrange.*

Nature hath inſtructed even a brood of *goſlings* to ſtick together, while the kite is hovering over their heads. *Swift.*

2. A cat's tail on nut-trees and pines.

GO'SPEL. *n. ſ.* [ȝobeꞃ ꞅpel, or God's or good tidings; εὐαγγέλιον; *ſoſkkel*, *ſkeal ſuach*, happy tidings, Erſe.]

1. God's word; the holy book of the Chriſtian revelation.

Thus may the *goſpel* to the riſing ſun
Be ſpread, and flouriſh where it firſt begun. *Waller.*

How is a good Chriſtian animated and cheered by a ſtedfaſt belief of the promiſes of the *goſpel!* *Bentley's Sermons.*

2. Divinity; theology.

To GO'SPEL. *v. n.* [from the noun.] To fill with ſentiments of religion. This word in *Shakeſpeare*, in whom alone I have found it, is uſed, though ſo venerable in itſelf, with ſome degree of irony: I ſuppoſe from the goſpellers, who had long been held in contempt.

Are you ſo *goſpell'd*
To pray for this good man, and for his iſſue,
Whoſe heavy hand hath bow'd you to the grave? *Shakeſp.*

GO'SPELLER. *n. ſ.* [from *goſpel*.] A name of the followers of *Wicklif*, who firſt attempted a reformation from popery, given them by the Papiſts in reproach, from their profeſſing to follow and preach only the goſpel.

Theſe *goſpellers* have had their golden days,
Have troden down our holy Roman faith. *Rowe's J. Shore.*

GO'SSAMER. *n. ſ.* [*goſſipium*, low Latin.] The down of plants; the long white cobwebs which fly in the air in calm ſunny weather, eſpecially about the time of Autumn. *Hanmer.*

A lover may beſtride the *goſſamour*,
That idles in the wanton Summer air,
And yet not fall, ſo light is vanity. *Shakeſ. Rom. and Juliet.*

Had'ſt thou been aught but *goſſamere*, feathers, air,
So many fathom down precipitating,
Thou'd'ſt ſhiver'd like an egg. *Shakeſp. King Lear.*

Four nimble gnats the horſes were,
Their harneſſes of *goſſamere*. *Drayton's Nymphid.*

The filmy *goſſamer* now flits no more,
Nor halcyons baſk on the ſhort ſunny ſhore. *Dryd. Virgil.*

GO'SSIP. *n. ſ.* [from ȝob and ꞅyb, relation, affinity, Saxon.]

1. One who anſwers for the child in baptiſm.

Go to a *goſſip*'s feaſt and gaude with me,
After ſo long grief ſuch nativity:
—With all my heart, I'll goſſip at this feaſt. *Shakeſpeare.*

At the chriſtening of George duke of Clarence, who was born in the caſtle of Dublin, he made both the earl of Kildare and the earl of Ormond his *goſſips*. *Davies on Ireland.*

2. A tippling companion.

And ſometimes lurk I in a *goſſip*'s bowl,
In very likeneſs of a roaſted crab,
And when ſhe drinks againſt her lips I bob. *Shakeſpeare.*

3. One who runs about tattling like women at a lying-in.

To do the office of a neighbour,
And be a *goſſip* at his labour. *Hudibras, p.* ii. *cant.* 1.

'Tis ſung in ev'ry ſtreet,
The common chat of *goſſips* when they meet. *Dryden.*

To GO'SSIP. *v. n.* [from the noun.]

1. To chat; to prate; to be merry.

Go to a goſſip's feaſt and gaude with me.
—With all my heart, I'll *goſſip* at this feaſt. *Shakeſpeare.*

His mother was a votreſs of my order,
And, in the ſpiced Indian air by night,
Full often hath ſhe *goſſipt* by my ſide. *Shakeſpeare.*

The market and exchange muſt be left to their own ways of talking; and *goſſippings* not be robbed of their ancient privilege. *Locke.*

2. To be a pot-companion.

Nor met with fortune, other than at feaſts,
Full warm of blood, of mirth, of *goſſipping*. *Shak. K. John.*

GO'SSIPRED. *n. ſ.* [*goſſipry*, from *goſſip*.]

Goſſipred or compaternity, by the canon law, is a ſpiritual affinity; and the juror, that was goſſip to either of the parties, might, in former times, have been challenged as not indifferent. *Davies on Ireland.*

GO'STING. *n. ſ.* An herb. *Ainſworth.*

GOT. *pret.* [from the verb *get*.]

Titus Lartius writes, they fought together; but Aufidius *got* off. *Shakeſpeare's Coriolanus.*

If you have ſtrength Achilles' arms to bear,
Though foul Therſites *got* thee, thou ſhalt be
Lov'd and eſteem'd. *Dryden's Juvenal.*

Theſe regions and this realm my wars have *got*;
This mournful empire is the loſer's lot. *Dryd. Innocence.*

When they began to reaſon about the means how the ſea *got* thither, and away back again, there they were preſently in the dark. *Woodward's Natural Hiſtory.*

GOT. *part. paſſ.* of *get*.

Solyman commended them for their valour in their evil haps, in a plot ſo well by them laid, more than he did the victory of others *got* by good fortune, not grounded upon any good reaſon. *Knolles's Hiſtory of the Turks.*

Let him boaſt
His knowledge of good loſt, and evil *got*. *Milt. Par. Loſt.*

A gentle perſuaſion in reaſoning, when the firſt point of ſubmiſſion to your will is *got*, will moſt times do. *Locke.*

If he behaves himſelf ſo when he depends on us for his daily bread, can any man ſay what he will do when he is *got* above the world? *Arbuthnot's Hiſtory of John Bull.*

Thou wert from Ætna's burning entrails torn,
Got by fierce whirlwinds, and in thunder born. *Pope.*

GO'TTEN. *part. paſſ.* of *get*.

Wiſdom cannot be *gotten* for gold. *Job.* xxviii. 15.

Few of them, when they are *gotten* into an office, apply their thoughts to the execution of it. *Temple.*

GOUD. *n. ſ.* Woad: a plant. *Dict.*

GOVE. *n. ſ.* A mow. *Tuſſer.*

To GOVE. *v. n.* To mow; to put in a gove, goff, or mow. An old word.

Load ſafe, carry home, follow time being fair,
Gove juſt in the barn, it is out of deſpair. *Tuſſ. Husbandry.*

To GO'VERN. *v. a.* [*gouverner*, French; *guberno*, Latin.]

1. To rule as a chief magiſtrate.

This inconvenience is more hard to be redreſſed in the governor than the *governed*; as a malady in a vital part is more incurable than in an external. *Spenſer on Ireland.*

Slaves to our paſſions we become, and then
It grows impoſſible to *govern* men. *Waller.*

2. To regulate; to influence; to direct.

The welfare of that is the chief point, which he is to carry always in his eye, and by which he is to *govern* all his counſels, deſigns, and actions. *Atterbury's Sermons.*

3. To manage; to reſtrain.

Go after her, ſhe's deſperate; *govern* her. *Shak. K. Lear.*

4. [In grammar.] To have force with regard to ſyntax: as, *amo governs* the accuſative caſe.

5. To pilot; to regulate the motions of a ſhip.

To GO'VERN. *v. n.* To keep ſuperiority; to behave with haughtineſs.

By that rule,
Your wicked atoms may be working now
To give bad counſel, that you ſtill may *govern*. *Dryden.*

GO'VERNABLE. *adj.* [from *govern*.] Submiſſive to authority; ſubject to rule; obedient; manageable.

The flexibleneſs of the former part of a man's age, not yet grown up to be headſtrong, makes it more *governable* and ſafe. *Locke.*

GO'VERNANCE. *n. ſ.* [from *govern*.]

1. Government; rule; management.

Jonathan took the *governance* upon him at that time, and roſe up inſtead of his brother Judas. 1 *Mac.* ix. 31.

2. Control, as that of a guardian.

Me he knew not, neither his own ill,
'Till through wiſe handling, and fair *governance*,
I him recured to a better will. *Fairy Queen, b.* ii.

What! ſhall king Henry be a pupil ſtill,
Under the ſurly Glo'ſter's *governance*? *Shakeſ. Hen. VI.*

3. Behaviour; manners. Obſolete.

Go'vernante. *n. s.* [*gouvernante*, French.] A lady who has the care of young girls of quality. The more usual and proper word is *governess*.

Go'verness. *n. s.* [*gouverneresse*, old French, from *govern*.]

1. A female invested with authority.

The moon, the *governess* of floods,
Pale in her anger, washes all the air,
That rheumatick diseases do abound. *Shakespeare.*

2. A tutoress; a woman that has the care of young ladies.

He presented himself unto her, falling down upon both his knees, and holding up his hands, as the old *governess* of Danae is painted, when she suddenly saw the golden shower. *Sidn.*

His three younger children were taken from the *governess* in whose hands he put them. *Clarendon, b.* viii.

3. A tutoress; an instructress; a directress.

Great affliction that severe *governess* of the life of man brings upon those souls she seizes on. *More against Atheism.*

Go'vernment. *n. s.* [*gouvernment*, French.]

1. Form of a community with respect to the disposition of the supreme authority.

There seem to be but two general kinds of *government* in the world: the one exercised according to the arbitrary commands and will of some single person; and the other according to certain orders or laws introduced by agreement or custom, and not to be changed without the consent of many. *Temple.*

2. An establishment of legal authority.

There they shall found
Their *government*, and their great senate chuse
Through the twelve tribes, to rule by laws ordain'd. *Milton.*

While he survives, in concord and content
The commons live, by no divisions rent;
But the great monarch's death dissolves the *government*. *Dryd.*

Every one knows, who has considered the nature of *government*, that there must be in each particular form of it an absolute unlimited power. *Addison.*

Where any one person or body of men seize into their hands the power in the last resort, there is properly no longer a *government*, but what Aristotle and his followers call the abuse or corruption of one. *Swift.*

3. Administration of publick affairs.

Safety and equal *government* are things
Which subjects make as happy as their kings. *Waller.*

4. Regularity of behaviour.

You needs must learn, lord, to amend this fault;
Though sometimes it shews greatness, courage, blood,
Yet oftentimes it doth present harsh rage,
Defect of manners, want of *government*,
Pride, haughtiness, opinion and disdain. *Shakes. Hen.* IV.

'Tis *government* that makes them seem divine;
The want thereof makes thee abominable. *Shakes. H.* VI.

5. Manageableness; compliance; obsequiousness.

Thy eyes windows fall,
Like death, when he shuts up the day of life;
Each part depriv'd of supple *government*,
Shall stiff and stark, and cold appear, like death. *Shakesp.*

6. Management of the limbs or body. Obsolete.

Their god
Shot many a dart at me with fierce intent;
But I them warded all with wary *government*. *Fairy Queen.*

7. [In grammar.] Influence with regard to construction.

Go'vernour. *n. s.* [*gouverneur*, French.]

1. One who has the supreme direction.

It must be confessed, that of Christ, working as a creator and a *governour* of the world by providence, all are partakers. *Hooker, b.* v. *s.* 56.

They beget in us a great idea and veneration of the mighty author and *governour* of such stupendous bodies, and excite and elevate our minds to his adoration and praise. *Bentley.*

2. One who is invested with supreme authority in a state.

For the kingdom is the Lord's, and he is the *governour* among the nations. *Ps.* xxii. 28.

The magistrate cannot urge obedience upon such potent grounds as the minister, if so disposed, can urge disobedience: as, for instance, if my *governour* should command me to do a thing, or I must die, or forfeit my estate; and the minister steps in and tells me, that I offend God, and ruin my soul, if I obey that command, 'tis easy to see a greater force in this persuasion. *South's Sermons.*

3. One who rules any place with delegated and temporary authority.

To you, lord *governour*,
Remains the censure of this hellish villain. *Shakes. Othello.*

4. A tutor; one who has care of a young man.

To Eltam will I, where the young king is,
Being ordain'd his special *governour*;
And for his safety there I'll best devise. *Shakesp. Henry* VI.

The great work of a *governour* is to fashion the carriage, and form the mind; to settle in his pupil good habits, and the principles of virtue and wisdom. *Locke.*

5. Pilot; regulator; manager.

Behold also the ships, which though they be so great, and are driven of fierce winds, yet they are turned about with a very small helm, whithersoever the *governour* listeth. *Ja.* iii. 4.

GOUGE. *n. s.* [French.] A chissel having a round edge, for the cutting such wood as is to be rounded or hollowed. *Moxon.*

Go'ujeres. *n s.* [from *gouje*, French, a camp trull.] The French disease. *Hanmer.*

Gourd. *n. s.* [*gouhorde*, French.]

1. It hath a flower consisting of one leaf, of the expanded bell-shape, for the most part so deeply cut that it seems to consist of five distinct leaves: this, like the cucumber, has male and female flowers on the same plant. The fruit of some species are long, of others round, or bottle-shaped, and is commonly divided into six cells, in which are contained many flat oblong seeds. *Miller.*

But I will haste, and from each bough and brake,
Each plant, and juiciest *gourd*, will pluck such choice
To entertain our angel-guest. *Milton's Paradise Lost, b.* v.

Gourd seeds are used in medicine; and they abound so much in oil, that a sweet and pleasant one may be drawn from them by expression: they are of the number of the four greater cold seeds, and are used in emulsions. *Hill's Mat. Med.*

2. A bottle [from *gourt*, old French. *Skinner.*]

The large fruit so called is often scooped hollow, for the purpose of containing and carrying wine, and other liquors: from thence any leathern bottle grew to be called by the same name, and so the word is used by *Chaucer*. *Hanmer.*

Gou'rdiness. *n. s.* [from *gourd.*] A swelling in a horse's leg after a journey. *Farrier's Dict.*

Gou'rnet. *n. s.* A fish. *Ainsworth.*

GOUT. *n. s.* [*goutte*, French.]

1. The arthritis; a periodical disease attended with great pain.

The *gout* is a disease which may affect any membranous part, but commonly those which are at the greatest distance from the heart or the brain, where the motion of the fluids is the slowest, the resistance, friction, and stricture of the solid parts the greatest, and the sensation of pain, by the dilaceration of the nervous fibres, extreme. *Arbuthnot on Diet.*

One that's sick o' th' *gout*, had rather
Groan so in perplexity than be cur'd
By th' sure physician death. *Shakespeare's Cymbeline.*

This very rev'rend lecher, quite worn out
With rheumatisms, and crippled with his *gout*,
Forgets what he in youthful times has done,
And swinges his own vices in his son. *Dryden's Juvenal.*

2. A drop, [*goutte*, French; *gutta*, Latin.] *Gut* for *drop* is still used in Scotland by physicians.

I see thee still,
And on the blade o' th' dudgeon *gouts* of blood,
Which was not so before. *Shakespeare's Macbeth.*

GOUT. *n. s.* [French.] A taste. An affected cant word.

The method which he has published will make these catalogues exceeding useful, and serve for a direction to any one that has a *goût* for the like studies. *Woodward on Fossils.*

Go'utwort. *n. s.* [*gout* and *wort.*] An herb. *Ainsworth.*

Go'uty. *adj.* [from *gout.*]

1. Afflicted or diseased with the gout.

There dies not above one of a thousand of the gout, although I believe that more die *gouty*. *Graunt's Bills of Mortal.*

Knots upon his *gouty* joints appear,
And chalk is in his crippled fingers found. *Dryd. Pers. Sat.*

Most commonly a *gouty* constitution is attended with great acuteness of parts, the nervous fibres, both in the brain and the other extremities, being delicate. *Arbuthnot on Diet.*

2. Relating to the gout.

GOWN. *n. s.* [*gonna*, Italian; *gwn*, Welsh and Erse.]

1. A long upper garment.

They make garments either short, as cloaks, or, as *gowns*, long to the ground. *Abbot's Description of the World.*

If ever I said a loosebodied *gown*, sew me up in the skirts of it, and beat me to death with a bottom of brown thread; I said a *gown*. *Shakesp. Taming of the Shrew.*

In length of train descends her sweeping *gown*,
And by her graceful walk the queen of love is known. *Dry.*

2. A woman's upper garment.

I despise your new *gown*, 'till I see you dressed in it. *Pope.*

3. The long habit of a man dedicated to acts of peace, as divinity, medicine, law.

The benefices themselves are so mean in Irish counties, that they will not yield any competent maintenance for any honest minister, scarcely to buy him a *gown*. *Spenser on Ireland.*

Girt in his Gabin *gown* the hero sat. *Dryden's Æn.*

4. The dress of peace.

He Mars depos'd, and arms to *gowns* made yield;
Successful councils did him soon approve
As fit for close intrigues as open field. *Dryden.*

Go'wned. *adj.* [from *gown.*] Dressed in a gown.

A noble crew about them waited round
Of sage and sober peers, all gravely *gown'd*. *Fairy Queen.*

In velvet white as snow the troop was *gown'd*,
The seams with sparkling emeralds set around. *Dryden.*

Go'wnman. *n. s.* [*gown* and *man.*] A man devoted to the acts of peace; one whose proper habit is a gown.

Let him with pedants
Pore out his life amongst the lazy *gownmen*. *Rowe.*

Thus will that whole bench, in an age or two, be composed of mean, fawning *gownmen*, dependants upon the court for a morsel of bread. *Swift.*

To GRA'BBLE. *v. n.* [probably corrupted from *grapple.*] To grope; to feel eagerly with the hands.

My blood chills about my heart at the thought of these rogues, with their bloody hands *grabbling* in my guts, and pulling out my very entrails. *Arbuthnot's Hist. of John Bull.*

To GRA'BBLE. *v. a.* To lie prostrate on the ground. *Ainsw.*

GRACE. *n. s.* [*grace*, French; *gratia*, Latin; *graace*, Erse.]

1. Favour; kindness.

If the highest love in no base person may aspire to *grace*, then may I hope your beauty will not be without pity. *Sidney.*

O momentary *grace* of mortal men,
Which we more hunt for than the grace of God! *Shakesp.*

Such as were popular,
And well deserving, were advanc'd by *grace*. *Daniel.*

Is this the reward and thanks I am to have for those many acts of *grace* I have lately passed? *King Charles.*

Yet those remov'd,
Such *grace* shall one just man find in his sight,
That he relents, not to blot out mankind. *Milt. Par. Lost.*

Noble pity held
His hand a while, and to their choice gave space
Which they would prove, his valour or his *grace*. *Waller.*

Or each, or all, may win a lady's *grace*;
Then either of you knights may well deserve
A princess born. *Dryden's Fables.*

None of us, who now your *grace* implore,
But held the rank of sovereign queen before. *Dryden.*

With profer'd service I repaid the fair,
That of her *grace* she gave her maid to know
The secret meaning of this moral show. *Dryden.*

2. Favourable influence of God on the human mind.

Prevenient *grace* descending had remov'd
The stony from their hearts, and made new flesh
Regenerate grow instead. *Milton.*

The *grace* of God, that passeth understanding, keep your hearts and minds. *Common Prayer.*

3. Virtue; effect of God's influence.

How Van wants *grace*, who never wanted wit. *Pope.*

4. Pardon.

Bow and sue for *grace*
With suppliant knee. *Milton.*

5. Favour conferred.

I should therefore esteem it great favour and *grace*,
Would you be so kind as to go in my place. *Prior.*

6. Privilege.

But to return and view the chearful skies,
To few great Jupiter imparts this *grace*. *Dryden.*

7. A goddess, by the heathens supposed to bestow beauty.

This forehead, where your verse has said
The loves delighted and the *graces* play'd. *Prior.*

8. Behaviour, considered as decent or unbecoming.

Have I reason or good *grace* in what I do. *Temple.*

They would have ill *grace* in denying it. *Bolingbroke.*

9. Adventitious or artificial beauty; pleasing appearance.

Her purple habit sits with such a *grace*
On her smooth shoulders, and so suits her face. *Dryd. Æn.*

To write and speak correctly gives a *grace*, and gains a favourable attention to what one has to say. *Locke.*

10. Natural excellence.

It doth grieve me, that things of principal excellency should be thus bitten at by men whom God hath endued with *graces*, both of wit and learning, for better purposes. *Hooker.*

To some kind of men,
Their *graces* serve them but as enemies. *Shak. As you like it.*

In his own *grace* he doth exalt himself
More than in your advancement. *Shakes. King Lear.*

The charming Lausus, full of youthful fire,
To Turnus only second in the *grace*
Of manly mien, and features of the face. *Dryden's Æn.*

11. Embellishment; recommendation; beauty.

Set all things in their own peculiar place,
And know that order is the greatest *grace*. *Dryden.*

The flow'r which lasts for little space,
A short liv'd good, and an uncertain *grace*. *Dryden.*

12. Single beauty.

I pass their form and every charming *grace*. *Dryden.*

13. Ornament; flower; highest perfection.

By their hands this *grace* of kings must die,
If hell and treason hold their promises. *Shakes. Henry V.*

14. Virtue; goodness.

Where justice grows, there grows the greater *grace*,
The which doth quench the brand of hellish smart. *Fa. Qu.*

The king-becoming *graces*,
As justice, verity, temp'rance, stableness,
Devotion, patience, courage, fortitude,
I have no relish of them. *Shakespeare's Macbeth.*

The *graces* of his religion prepare him for the most useful discharge of every relation of life. *Rogers.*

15. Virtue physical.

O, mickle is the pow'rful *grace* that lies
In plants, herbs, stones, and their true qualities. *Shakespeare.*

16. The title of a duke; formerly of the king, meaning the same as *your goodness*, or *your clemency*.

Here come I from our princely general,
To know your griefs; to tell you from his *grace*,
That he will give you audience. *Shakesp. Henry IV.*

High and mighty king, your *grace*, and those your nobles here present, may be pleased to bow your ears. *Bacon's H. VII.*

17. A short prayer said before and after meat.

Your soldiers use him as the *grace* 'fore meat,
Their talk at table, and their thanks at end. *Shak. Coriolan.*

While *grace* is saying after meat, do you and your brethren take the chairs from behind the company. *Swift.*

Then chearful healths, your mistress shall have place;
And what's more rare, a poet shall say *grace*. *Pope's Horace.*

GRACE-CUP. *n. s.* [*grace* and *cup.*] The cup or health drank after grace.

The *grace-cup* serv'd, the cloth away,
Jove thought it time to shew his play. *Prior.*

To GRACE. *v. a.* [from the noun.]

1. To adorn; to dignify; to embellish; to recommend; to decorate.

This they study, this they practise, this they *grace* with a wanton superfluity of wit. *Hooker, b. v. s. 2.*

I do not think a braver gentleman,
More daring, or more bold is now alive,
To *grace* this latter age with noble deeds. *Shakesp. Hen. IV.*

Little of this great world can I speak,
And therefore little shall I *grace* my cause,
In speaking for myself. *Shakespeare's Othello.*

There is due from the judge to the advocate some commendation and *gracing*, where causes are well handled. *Bacon.*

Rich crowns were on their royal scutcheons plac'd,
With saphires, diamonds, and with rubies *grac'd*. *Dryden.*

By both his parents of descent divine;
Great Jove and Phœbus *grac'd* his noble line. *Pope's Statius.*

Though triumphs were to generals only due,
Crowns were reserv'd to *grace* the soldiers too. *Pope.*

2. To dignify or raise by an act of favour.

He writes
How happily he lives, how well belov'd,
And daily *graced* by the emperor. *Sh. Two Gent. of Verona.*

Dispose all honours of the sword and gun,
Grace with a nod, and ruin with a frown. *Dryden's Juven.*

3. To favour.

When the guests withdrew,
Their courteous host saluting all the crew,
Regardless pass'd her o'er, nor *grac'd* with kind adieu. *Dryd.*

GRA'CED. *adj.* [from *grace.*]

1. Beautiful; graceful.

He saw this gentleman, one of the properest and best *graced* men that ever I saw, being of a middle age and a mean stature. *Sidney, b. ii.*

2. Virtuous; regular; chaste.

Epicurism and lust
Make it more like a tavern or a brothel,
Than a *grac'd* palace. *Shakesp. King Lear.*

GRA'CEFUL. *adj.* [from *grace.*] Beautiful with dignity.

Amid' the troops, and like the leading god,
High o'er the rest in arms the *graceful* Turnus rode. *Dryden.*

Matchless his pen, victorious was his lance;
Bold in the lists, and *graceful* in the dance. *Pope.*

Yet *graceful* ease, and sweetness void of pride,
Might hide her faults, if belles had faults to hide. *Pope.*

GRA'CEFULLY. *adv.* [from *graceful.*] Elegantly; with pleasing dignity.

Through nature and through art she rang'd,
And *gracefully* her subject chang'd. *Swift.*

Walking is the mode or manner of man, or of a beast; but walking *gracefully* implies a manner or mode super-added to that action. *Watts's Logick.*

GRA'CEFULNESS. *n. s.* [from *graceful.*] Elegance of manner; dignity with beauty.

His neck, his hands, his shoulders, and his breast,
Did next in *gracefulness* and beauty stand,
To breathing figures. *Dryden's Ovid.*

He executed with so much *gracefulness* and beauty, that he alone got money and reputation. *Dryden's Dufresnoy.*

There is a secret *gracefulness* of youth which accompanies his writings, though the staidness and sobriety of age be wanting. *Dryden's Ovid, Preface.*

If hearers are amaz'd from whence
Proceeds that fund of wit and sense,
Which, though her modesty would shroud,
Breaks like the sun behind a cloud;
While *gracefulness* its art conceals,
And yet through ev'ry motion steals. *Swift.*

GRA'CELESS. *adj.* [from *grace.*] Without grace; wicked; hopelessly corrupt; abandoned.

This *graceless* man, for furtherance of his guile,
Did court the handmaid of my lady dear. *Fairy Queen.*

Whose hap shall be to have her,
Will not so *graceless* be, to be ingrate. *Shakespeare.*

In all manner of *graceless* and hopeless characters, some are lost for want of advice, and others for want of heed. *L'Estr.*

Furnish'd for offence, he cross'd the way
Betwixt the *graceless* villain and his prey. *Dryden.*

GRA'CES. *n. s.* *Good graces* for favour is seldom used in the singular.

Demand deliv'ry of her heart,
Her goods and chattels, and good *graces*,
And person up to his embraces. *Hudibras, p.* iii.

GRA'CILE. *adj.* [*gracilis*, Latin.] Slender; small. *Dict.*

GRA'CILENT. *n. s.* [*gracilentus*, Latin.] Lean. *Dict.*

GRACI'LITY. *n. s.* [*gracilitas*, Latin.] Slenderness; smalness. *Dict.*

GRA'CIOUS. *adj.* [*gracieux*, French.]

1. Merciful; benevolent.

Common sense and reason could not but tell them, that the good and *gracious* God could not be pleased, nor consequently worshipped, with any thing barbarous or cruel. *South's Serm.*

To be good and *gracious*, and a lover of knowledge, are two of the most amiable things. *Burnet's Theory of the Earth.*

2. Favourable; kind.

And the Lord was *gracious* unto them, and had compassion on them. 2 *Kings* xiii. 23.

From now reveal
A *gracious* beam of light; from now inspire
My tongue to sing, my hand to touch the lyre. *Prior.*

3. Acceptable; favoured.

Doctrine is much more profitable and *gracious* by example than by rule. *Spenser.*

He made us *gracious* before the kings of Persia, so that they gave us food. 1 *Esdr.* viii. 80.

Goring, who was now general of the horse, was no more *gracious* to prince Rupert than Wilmot had been. *Clarendon.*

4. Virtuous; good.

Kings are no less unhappy, their issue not being *gracious*, than they are in losing them when they have approved their virtues. *Shakespeare's Winter's Tale.*

5. Excellent.

The grievous abuse which hath been of counsels, should rather cause men to study how so *gracious* a thing may again be reduced to that first perfection. *Hooker, b.* i. *s.* 10.

6. Graceful; becoming.

Our womens names are more *gracious* than their Rutilia, that is, red head. *Camden.*

GRA'CIOUSLY. *adv.* [from *gracious.*]

1. Kindly; with kind condescension.

His testimony he *graciously* confirmed, that it was the best of all my tragedies. *Dryden.*

He heard my vows, and *graciously* decreed
My grounds to be restor'd, my former flocks to feed. *Dryd.*

If her majesty would but *graciously* be pleased to think a hardship of this nature worthy her royal consideration. *Swift.*

2. In a pleasing manner.

GRA'CIOUSNESS. *n. s.* [from *gracious.*]

1. Kind condescension.

The *graciousness* and temper of this answer made no impression on them. *Clarendon.*

2. Pleasing manner.

GRADA'TION. *n. s.* [*gradation*, French; *gradus*, Latin.]

1. Regular progress from one degree to another.

The desire of more and more rises by a natural *gradation* to most, and after that to all. *L'Estrange.*

2. Regular advance step by step.

From thence,
By cold *gradation*, and well balanc'd form,
We shall proceed with Angelo. *Shakesp. Meas. for Meas.*

The psalmist very elegantly expresseth to us the several *gradations* by which men at last come to this horrid degree of impiety. *Tillotson, Sermon* 2.

3. Order; arrangement.

'Tis the curse of service;
Preferment goes by letter and affection,
Not, as of old, *gradation*, where each second
Stood heir to th' first. *Shakespeare's Othello.*

4. Regular process of argument.

Certain it is, by a direct *gradation* of consequences from this principle of merit, that the obligation to gratitude flows from, and is enjoined by, the first dictates of nature. *South.*

GRADA'TORY. *n. s.* [*gradus*, Latin.] Steps from the cloisters into the church. *Ainsworth.*

GRA'DIENT. *adj.* [*gradiens*, Latin.] Walking; moving by steps.

Amongst those *gradient* automata, that iron spider is especially remarkable, which, being but of an ordinary bigness, did creep up and down as if it had been alive. *Wilkins.*

GRA'DUAL. *adj.* [*graduel*, French.] Proceeding by degrees; advancing step by step; from one stage to another.

Nobler birth
Of creatures animate with *gradual* life,
Of growth, sense, reason, all summ'd up in man. *Milton.*

Men still suppose a *gradual* natural progress of things; as that, from great, things and persons should grow greater, 'till at length, by many steps and ascents, they come to be at greatest. *South.*

GRA'DUAL. *n. s.* [*gradus*, Latin.] An order of steps.

Before the *gradual* prostrate they ador'd,
The pavement kiss'd, and thus the saint implor'd. *Dryden.*

GRADUA'LITY. *n. s.* [from *gradual.*] Regular progression.

This some ascribe unto the mixture of the elements, others to the *graduality* of opacity and light. *Brown's Vulg. Errours.*

GRA'DUALLY. *adv.* [from *gradual.*] By degrees; in regular progression.

When the moon passes over the fixed stars, and eclipses them, your light vanishes; not *gradually*, like that of the planets, but all at once. *Newton's Opt.*

The Author of our being weans us *gradually* from our fondness of life the nearer we approach towards the end of it. *Swift.*

Human creatures are able to bear air of much greater density in diving, and of much less upon the tops of mountains, provided the changes be made *gradually*. *Arbuthnot.*

To GRA'DUATE. *v. a.* [*graduer*, French; *gradus*, Latin.]

1. To dignify with a degree in the university.

John Tregonwel, *graduated* a doctor and dubbed a knight, did his prince good service. *Carew's Survey of Cornwal.*

Concerning columns and their adjuncts, architects make such a noise as if the terms of architraves, frizes, and cornices were enough to *graduate* a master of this art. *Wotton's Architect.*

2. To mark with degrees.

The places were marked where the spirits stood at the severest cold and greatest heat, and according to these observations he *graduates* his thermometers. *Derham's Physico-Theology.*

3. To raise to a higher place in the scale of metals: a chimical term.

The tincture was capable to transmute or *graduate* as much silver as equalled in weight that gold. *Boyle.*

4. To heighten; to improve.

Not only vitriol is a cause of blackness, but the salts of natural bodies; and dyers advance and *graduate* their colours with salts. *Brown's Vulgar Errours, b.* vi. *c.* 12.

GRA'DUATE. *n. s.* [*gradué*, French, from *gradus*, Latin.] A man dignified with an academical degree.

Of *graduates* I dislike the learned rout,
And chuse a female doctor for the gout. *Bramston.*

GRADUA'TION. *n. s.* [*graduation*, French, from *graduate.*]

1. Regular progression by succession of degrees.

The *graduation* of the parts of the universe is likewise necessary to the perfection of the whole. *Grew's Cosmol. Sacra.*

Of greater repugnancy unto reason is that which he delivers concerning its *graduation*, that heated in fire, and often extinguished in oyl of mars or iron, the loadstone acquires an ability to extract a nail fastened in a wall. *Brown's Vu. Err.*

2. The act of conferring academical degrees.

GRAFF. *n. s.* [See GRAVE.] A ditch; a moat.

Though the fortifications were not regular, yet the walls were good, and the *graff* broad and deep. *Clarendon, b.* viii.

GRAFF. } *n. s.* [*greffe*, French.] A small branch inserted into
GRAFT. } the stock of another tree, and nourished by its sap, but bearing its own fruit; a young cyon.

God gave unto man all kind of seeds and *graffs* of life; as the vegetative life of plants, the sensual of beasts, the rational of man, and the intellectual of angels. *Raleigh.*

It is likely, that as in fruit-trees the *graft* maketh a greater fruit, so in trees that bear no fruit it will make the greater leaves. *Bacon's Natural History*, N°. 475.

'Tis usual now an inmate *graff* to see
With insolence invade a foreign tree. *Dryd. Virg. Georg.*

If you cover the top with clay and horse-dung, in the same manner as you do a *graft*, it will help to heel the sooner. *Mort.*

Now the cleft rind inserted *graffs* receives,
And yields an offspring more than nature gives. *Pope.*

To GRAFF. }
To GRAFT. } *v. a.* [*greffer*, French.]

1. To insert a cyon or branch of one tree into the stock of another.

His growth is but a wild and fruitless plant;
I'll cut his barren branches to the stock,
And *graft* you on to bear. *Dryden's Don Sebastian.*

With his pruning hook disjoin
Unbearing branches from their head,
And *graft* more happy in their stead. *Dryden.*

2. To propagate by insertion or inoculation.

In March is good *graffing* the skilful do know,
So long as the wind in the East do not blow:
From moon being changed, 'till past be the prime,
For *graffing* and cropping is very good time. *Tusser's Husb.*

To have fruit in greater plenty the way is to *graft*, not only upon young stocks, but upon divers boughs of an old tree; for they will bear great numbers of fruit: whereas, if you *graft* but upon one stock, the tree can bear but few. *Bacon.*

Now

Now let me *graff* my pears, and prune the vine. *Dryden.*

3. To insert into a place or body to which it did not originally belong.

And they also, if they bide not still in unbelief, shall be *graffed* in; for God is able to *graff* them in again. *Rom.* xi. 23.

These are th' Italian names which fate will join
With ours, and *graff* upon the Trojan line. *Dryden's Æn.*

4. To fill with an adscititious branch.

We've some old crab-trees here at home, that will not
Be *grafted* to your relish. *Shakespeare's Coriolanus.*
The noble isle doth want her proper limbs;
Her royal stock *graft* with ignoble plants. *Shakesp. R.* III.

5. To join one thing so as to receive support from another.

This resolution against any peace with Spain is a new incident *grafted* upon the original quarrel, by the intrigues of a faction among us. *Swift.*

May one kind grave unite each hapless name,
And *graft* my love immortal on thy fame. *Pope.*

GRA'FTER. *n. s.* [from *graff* or *graft.*] One who propagates fruit by grafting.

I am informed, by the trials of more than one of the most skilful and experienced *grafters* of these parts, that a man shall seldom fail of having cherries borne by his graft the same year in which the insition is made. *Evelyn.*

GRAIL. *n. s.* [from *grêle*, French.] Small particles of any kind.

Hereof this gentle knight unweeting was,
And, lying down upon the sandy *grails*,
Drank of the stream as clear as crystal glass. *Fairy Queen.*

GRAIN. *n. s.* [*graine*, French; *granum*, Latin; *grano*, Italian, has all the following significations.]

1. A single seed of corn.

Look into the seeds of time,
And say which *grain* will grow, and which will not. *Shakes.*

His reasons are as two *grains* of wheat hid in two bushels of chaff. *Shakespeare's Merchant of Venice.*

Let them pronounce the steep Tarpeian death,
Vagabond exile, flaying, pent to linger
But with a *grain* a day, I would not buy
Their mercy at the price of one fair word. *Shak. Coriolanus.*

Many of the ears, being six inches long, had sixty *grains* in them, and none less than forty. *Mortimer's Husbandry.*

2. Corn.

As it ebbs, the seedsman
Upon the slime and ooze scatters his *grain*,
And shortly comes to harvest. *Shakesp. Ant. and Cleopatra.*
Pales no longer swell'd the teeming *grain*,
Nor Phœbus fed his oxen on the plain. *Dryden's Pastorals.*

'Tis a rich soil, I grant you; but oftner covered with weeds than *grain*. *Collier on Fame.*

3. The seed of any fruit.

4. Any minute particle; any single body.

Thou exist'st on many thousand *grains*
That issue out of dust. *Shakesp. Meas. for Measure.*
By intelligence
And proofs as clear as founts in July, when
We see each *grain* of gravel. *Shakespeare's Henry* VIII.

5. The smallest weight, of which in physick twenty make a scruple, and in Troy weight twenty-four make a peny weight; a grain so named because it is supposed of equal weight with a grain of corn.

They began at a known body, a barley-corn, the weight whereof is therefore called a *grain*; which ariseth, being multiplied, to scruples, drachms, ounces and pounds. *Holder.*

The trial being made betwixt lead and lead, weighing severally seven drachms, in the air; the balance in the water weigheth only four drachms and forty-one *grains*, and abateth of the weight in the air two drachms and nineteen *grains*: the balance kept the same depth in the water as abovesaid. *Bacon's Phys. Rem.*

His brain
Outweigh'd his rage but half a *grain*. *Hudibras, p.* i.

6. Any thing proverbially small.

For the whole world before thee is as a little *grain* of the balance. *Wisd.* xi. 22.

The ungrateful person lives to himself, and subsists by the good nature of others, of which he himself has not the least *grain*. *South's Sermons.*

7. GRAIN *of Allowance.* Something indulged or remitted; something above or under the exact weight.

He, whose very best actions must be seen with *grains of allowance*, cannot be too mild, moderate, and forgiving. *Addis.*

I would always give some *grains of allowance* to the sacred science of theology. *Watts's Improvement of the Mind.*

8. The direction of the fibres of wood, or other fibrous matter.

Knots, by the conflux of meeting sap,
Infect the sound pine, and divert his *grain*
Tortive and errant from his course of growth. *Shakesp.*

9. The body of the wood.

The beech, the swimming alder, and the plane,
Hard box, and linden of a softer *grain*. *Dryden.*

10. The body considered with respect to the form or direction of the constituent particles.

The tooth of a sea-horse, in the midst of the solider parts, contains a curdled *grain* which is not to be found in ivory. *Brown's Vulgar Errours, b.* iii. *c.* 23.

Stones of a constitution so compact, and a *grain* so fine, that they bear a fine polish. *Woodward.*

11. Died or stained substance.

How the red roses flush up in her cheeks,
And the pure snow with goodly vermil stain,
Like crimson dy'd in *grain*. *Spenser's Prothalam.*
Over his lucid arms
A military vest of purple flow'd,
Livelier than melibæan, or the *grain*
Of sarra, worn by kings and heroes old. *Milton's P. Lost.*
Come, pensive nun, devout and pure,
All in a robe of darkest *grain*,
Flowing with majestick train. *Milton.*
The third, his feet
Shadow'd from either heel with feather'd mail,
Sky-tinctur'd *grain!* *Milton's Paradise Lost, b.* v.

12. Temper; disposition; inclination; humour.

Your minds, preoccupied with what
You rather must do than what you should do,
Made you against the *grain* to voice him consul. *Shakesp.*
Quoth Hudibras, it is in vain,
I see, to argue 'gainst the *grain*. *Hudibras, p.* ii. *cant.* 2.
Old clients, weary'd out with fruitless care,
Dismiss their hopes of eating, and despair;
Though much against the *grain*, forc'd to retire,
Buy roots for supper, and provide a fire. *Dryden's Juvenal.*

13. The heart; the bottom.

The one being tractable and mild, the other stiff and impatient of a superior, they lived but in cunning concord, as brothers *glued* together, but not united in *grain*. *Hayward.*

14. The form of the surface with regard to roughness and smoothness.

The smaller the particles of those substances are, the smaller will be the scratches by which they continually fret and wear away the glass until it be polished; but be they never so small, they can wear away the glass no otherwise than by grating and scratching it, and breaking the protuberances; and therefore polish it no otherwise than by bringing its roughness to a very fine *grain*, so that the scratches and frettings of the surface become too small to be visible. *Newton's Opt.*

GRA'INED. *adj.* [from *grain.*] Rough; made less smooth.

Though now this *grained* face of mine be hid
In sap consuming Winter's drizzled snow,
Yet hath my night of life some memory. *Shakespeare.*

GRAINS. *n. s.* [without a singular.] The husks of malt exhausted in brewing.

Give them *grains* their fill,
Husks, draff, to drink and swill. *Ben. Johns. New Inn.*

GRA'INY. *adj.* [from *grain.*]

1. Full of corn.
2. Full of grains or kernels.

GRAME'RCY. *interj.* [contracted from *grant me mercy.*] An obsolete expression of surprise.

Gramercy, sir, said he; but mote I weet
What strange adventure do ye now pursue? *Fairy Queen.*
Gramercy, lovely Lucius, what's the news? *Shakesp.*

GRAMI'NEOUS. *adj.* [*gramineus*, Latin.] Grassy. *Gramineous* plants are such as have a long leaf without a footstalk.

GRAMINI'VOROUS. *adj.* [*gramen* and *voro*, Latin.] Grass-eating; living upon grass.

The ancients were versed chiefly in the dissection of brutes, among which the *graminivorous* kind have a party-coloured choroides. *Sharp's Surgery.*

GRA'MMAR. *n. s.* [*grammaire*, French; *grammatica*, Latin; γραμματικη.]

1. The science of speaking correctly; the art which teaches the relations of words to each other.

We make a countryman dumb, whom we will not allow to speak but by the rules of *grammar*. *Dryden's Dufresnoy.*

Men, speaking language according to the *grammar* rules of that language, do yet speak improperly of things. *Locke.*

2. Propriety or justness of speech; speech according to grammar.

Varium & mutabile semper femina, is the sharpest satire that ever was made on woman; for the adjectives are neuter, and animal must be understood to make them *grammar*. *Dryden.*

3. The book that treats of the various relations of words to one another.

GRA'MMAR *School. n. s.* A school in which the learned languages are grammatically taught.

Thou hast most traitorously corrupted the youth of the realm in erecting a *grammar school*. *Shakespeare's Hen.* VI.

The ordinary way of learning Latin in a *grammar school* I cannot encourage. *Locke.*

GRAMMA'RIAN. *n. s.* [*grammairien*, French, from *grammar.*] One who teaches grammar; a philologer.

Many disputes the ambiguous nature of letters hath created among the *grammarians*. *Holder's Elements of Speech.*

They who have called him the torture of *grammarians*, might also have called him the plague of translators. *Dryden.*

GRAMMA'TICAL. *adj.* [*grammatical*, Fr. *grammaticus*, Latin.]

1. Belonging to grammar.

The beauty of virtue still being set before their eyes, and that taught them with far more diligent care than *grammatical* rules. *Sidney, b.* ii.

I shall take the number of consonants, not from the *grammatical* alphabets of any language, but from the diversity of sounds framed by single articulations with appulse. *Holder.*

2. Taught by grammar.

They seldom know more than the *grammatical* contruction, unless born with a poetical genius. *Dryden's Dufresnoy.*

GRAMMA'TICALLY. *adv.* [from *grammatical.*] According to the rules or science of grammar.

When a sentence is distinguished into the nouns, the verbs, pronouns, adverbs, and other particles of speech which compose it, then it is said to be analysed *grammatically*. *Watts.*

As grammar teacheth us to speak properly, so it is the part of rhetorick to instruct how to do it elegantly, by adding beauty to that language that before was naked and *grammatically* true. *Baker's Reflections on Learning.*

GRAMMATICA'STER. n. s. [Latin.] A mean verbal pedant; a low grammarian.

I have not vexed their language with the doubts, the remarks, and eternal triflings of the French *grammaticasters*. *Rymer's Tragedies of the last Age.*

GRA'MPLE. *n. s.* A crab-fish. *Ainsworth.*

GRA'MPUS. *n. s.* A large fish of the cetaceous kind.

GRA'NARY. *n. s.* [*granarium*, Latin.] A storehouse for threshed corn.

Ants, by their labour and industry, contrive the matter so, that corn will keep as dry in their nests as in our *granaries*. *Addison's Guardian*, N°. 156.

The naked nations cloath,
And be th' exhaustless *granary* of a world. *Thomson's Spring.*

GRA'NATE. *n. s.* [from *granum*, Latin.] A kind of marble so called, because it is marked with small variegations like grains. Otherwise GRANITE.

GRAND. *adj.* [*grand*, French; *grandis*, Latin.]

1. Great; illustrious; high in power.

God had planted, that is, made to grow the trees of life and knowledge, plants only proper and becoming the paradise and garden of so *grand* a Lord. *Raleigh's Hist. of the World.*

2. Great; splendid; magnificent.

A voice has flown
To re-enflame a *grand* design. *Young.*

3. Noble; sublime; lofty; conceived or expressed with great dignity.

4. It is used to signify ascent or descent of consanguinity.

GRA'NDAM. *n. s.* [*grand* and *dam* or *dame.*]

1. Grandmother; my father's or mother's mother.

I meeting him, will tell him that my lady
Was fairer than his *grandam*, and as chaste
As may be in the world. *Shakesp. Troilus and Cressida.*

A woman's story, at a Winter's fire,
Authoris'd by her *grandam*. *Shakesp. Macbeth.*

We have our forefathers and great *grandames* all before us, as they were in Chaucer's days. *Dryden's Fables, Pref.*

Thy tygress heart belies thy angel face:
Too well thou shew'st thy pedigree from stone;
Thy *grandame*'s was the first by Pyrrha thrown. *Dryden.*

2. An old withered woman.

The women
Cry'd, one and all, the suppliant should have right,
And to the *grandame* hag adjudg'd the knight. *Dryden.*

GRA'NDCHILD. *n. s.* [*grand* and *child.*] The son or daughter of my son or daughter; one in the second degree of descent.

Augustus Cæsar, out of indignation against his daughters and Agrippa his *grandchild*, would say that they were not his seed, but imposthumes broken from him. *Bacon's Apophthegms.*

These hymns may work on future wits, and so
May great *grandchildren* of thy praises grow. *Donne.*

He hoped his majesty did believe, that he would never make the least scruple to obey the *grandchild* of king James. *Clarend.*

Fair daughter, and thou son and *grandchild* both! *Milton.*

He 'scaping with his gods and reliques fled,
And tow'rds the shore his little *grandchild* led. *Denham.*

GRA'NDAUGHTER. *n. s.* [*grand* and *daughter.*] The daughter of a son or daughter.

GRANDE'E. *n. s.* [*grand*, French; *grandis*, Latin.] A man of great rank, power, or dignity.

They had some sharper and some milder differences, which might easily happen in such an interview of *grandees*, both vehement on the parts which they swayed. *Wotton.*

When a prince or *grandee* manifests a liking to such a thing, men generally set about to make themselves considerable for such things. *South's Sermons.*

Some parts of the Spanish monarchy are rather for ornament than strength: they furnish out viceroyalties for the *grandees*, and posts of honour for the noble families. *Addison.*

GRANDE'VITY. *n. s.* [from *grandævus*, Latin.] Great age; length of life. *Dict.*

GRANDE'VOUS. *adj.* [*grandævus*, Latin.] Long lived; of great age. *Dict.*

GRA'NDEUR. *n. s.* [French.]

1. State; splendour of appearance; magnificence.

As a magistrate or great officer, he locks himself from all approaches by the multiplied formalities of attendance, by the distance of ceremony and *grandeur*. *South's Sermons.*

2. Elevation of sentiment or language.

GRA'NDFATHER. *n. s.* [*grand* and *father.*] The father of my father or mother; the next above my father in the scale of ascent.

One was saying that his great grandfather, and *grandfather*, and father died at sea: said another, that heard him, an' I were as you, I would never come at sea. Why, saith he, where did your great grandfather, and *grandfather*, and father die? He answered, where but in their beds? He answered, an' I were as you, I would never come in bed. *Bacon's Apophth.*

Our grandchildren will see a few rags hung up in Westminsterhall, which cost an hundred millions, whereof they are paying the arrears, and boast that their *grandfathers* were rich and great. *Swift.*

GRANDI'FICK. *adj.* [*grandis* and *facio*, Latin.] Making great. *Dict.*

GRA'NDINOUS. *adj.* [*grando*, Latin.] Full of hail; consisting of hail. *Dict.*

GRA'NDITY. *n. s.* [from *grandis*, Latin.] Greatness; grandeur; magnificence. An old word.

Our poets excel in *grandity* and gravity, smoothness and property, in quickness and briefness. *Camden's Remains.*

GRA'NDMOTHER. *n. s.* [*grand* and *mother.*] The father's or mother's mother.

Thy *grandmother* Lois, and thy mother Eunice. 1 *Tim.* i. 5.

GRA'NDSIRE. *n. s.* [*grand* and *sire.*]

1. Grandfather.

Think'st thou, that I will leave my kingly throne,
Wherein my *grandsire* and my father sat? *Shakesp. Hen.* VI.

Thy *grandsire*, and his brother, to whom fame
Gave, from two conquer'd parts o' th' world, their name. *Denham.*

The wreaths his *grandsire* knew to reap
By active toil and military sweat. *Prior.*

2. Any ancestor, poetically.

Why should a man, whose blood is warm within,
Sit like his *grandsire* cut in alabaster? *Shakesp. Merch. of Ven.*

Above the portal, carv'd in cedar wood,
Plac'd in their ranks, their godlike *grandsires* stood. *Dryden.*

So mimick ancient wits at best,
As apes our *grandsires* in their doublets drest. *Pope.*

GRA'NDSON. *n. s.* [*grand* and *son.*] The son of a son or daughter.

Almighty Jove augment your wealthy store,
Give much to you, and to his *grandsons* more. *Dryden.*

Grandfathers in private families are not much observed to have great influence on their *grandsons*, and, I believe, they have much less among princes. *Swift.*

GRANGE. *n. s.* [*grange*, French.] A farm: generally a farm with a house at a distance from neighbours.

One, when he had got the inheritance of an unlucky old *grange*, would needs sell it; and, to draw buyers, proclaimed the virtues of it: nothing ever thrived on it, saith he; the trees were all blasted, the swine died of the measles, the cattle of the murrain, and the sheep of the rot; nothing was ever reared there, not a duckling or a goose. *Ben. Johnson's Discov.*

At the moated *grange* resides this dejected Mariana. *Shakesp.*

The loose unletter'd hinds,
When for their teeming flocks and *granges* full
In wanton dance they praise the bounteous Pan. *Milton.*

If the church was of their own foundation, they might huse, the incumbent being once dead, whether they would put any other therein, unless, perhaps, the said church had people belonging to it; for then they must still maintain a curate: and of this sort were their *granges* and priories. *Ayliffe.*

GRA'NITE. *n. s.* [*granit*, Fr. from *granum*, Lat. because consisting as it were of grains, or small distinct particles.] A stone composed of separate and very large concretions, rudely compacted together; of great hardness, giving fire with steel; not fermenting with acids, and imperfectly calcinable in a great fire. The hard white granite with black spots, commonly called moor-stone, forms a very firm, and though rude, yet beautifully variegated mass. It is found in immense strata in Ireland, but not used there. In Cornwal and the adjacent counties it is found on the surface of the earth in prodigious masses, and brought in great quantities to London, where it is used for the steps of publick buildings. Hard red granite, variegated with black and white, now called oriental granite, is valuable for its extreme hardness and beauty, and capable of a most elegant polish. It is common in Egypt and Arabia,

and

and is alſo found in the Weſt of England little inferiour. The vulgar opinion of their being caſt out of various fragments of marble, becauſe they appear compoſed of particles or granules of different colours, is eaſily confuted by an accurate inſpection of the ſtructure and formation of thoſe granules, the leaſt and meaneſt of which no human art could ever compoſe, nor fire leave in the ſtate in which we ſee them. A third ſort of granite has a beautiful variegation of colours, red, white, black and yellow, and capable of an elegant poliſh: it is little inferiour in beauty to the oriental granite, and there are immenſe ſtrata of it in Minorca. Detached nodules of it, two or three foot in circumference, are alſo frequent on the ſhores of Guernſey, from whence it is brought as ballaſt, and uſed in paving our ſtreets. *Hill on Foſſils.*

Alabaſter, marble of divers colours, both ſimple and mixed, the opulites, porphyry, and the *granite.* *Woodward.*

There are ſtill great pillars of *granite*, and other fragments of this ancient temple. *Addiſon on Italy.*

Grani'vorous. *adj.* [*granum* and *voro*, Lat.] Eating grain; living upon grain.

Granivorous birds, as a crane, upon the firſt peck of their bills, can diſtinguiſh the qualities of hard bodies, which the ſenſe of men diſcerns not without maſtication. *Brown.*

Panick affords a ſoft demulcent nouriſhment, both for *granivorous* birds and mankind. *Arbuthnot on Aliments.*

Gra'nnam. *n. ſ.* [for *grandam.*] Grandmother. Only uſed in burleſque works.

Oft my kind *grannam* told me, Tim, take warning. *Gay.*

To **GRANT.** *v. a.* [from *garantir*, French, *Junius* and *Skinner*; perhaps, as *Minſhew* thinks, from *gratuito*, or rather from *gratia* or *gratificor.*]

1. To admit that which is not yet proved; to allow; to yield; to concede.

They gather out of Scripture general rules to be followed in making laws; and ſo, in effect, they plainly *grant*, that we ourſelves may lawfully make laws for the church. *Hooker.*

Grant that the fates have firm'd, by their decree,
The Trojan race to reign in Italy. *Dryden's Æn. b.* vii.

Suppoſe, which yet I *grant* not, thy deſire
A moment elder than my rival fire,
Can chance of ſeeing firſt thy title prove? *Dryden.*

If he be one indifferent as to the preſent rebellion, they may take it for *granted* his complaint is the rage of a diſappointed man. *Addiſon's Freeholder.*

2. To beſtow ſomething which cannot be claimed of right.

The God of Iſrael *grant* thee thy petition that thou haſt aſked of him. 1 *Sa.* xvii.

Then hath God alſo to the Gentiles *granted* repentance unto life. *Acts* xiii. 18.

Did'ſt thou not kill this king?
——I grant ye.
—Do'ſt grant me, hedgehog? Then God *grant* me too,
Thou may'ſt be damned for that wicked deed. *Shak. R.* III.

He heard, and *granted* half his prayer;
The reſt the winds diſpers'd. *Pope.*

Grant. *n. ſ.* [from the verb.]

1. The act of granting or beſtowing.

2. The thing granted; a gift; a boon.

Courtiers juſtle for a *grant*,
And when they break their friendſhip plead their want. *Dry.*

3. [In law] A gift in writing of ſuch a thing as cannot aptly be paſſed or conveyed by word only; as rent, reverſions, ſervices, advowſons in groſs, common in groſs, tithes, &c. or made by ſuch perſons as cannot give but by deed, as the king, and all bodies politick; which differences be often in ſpeech neglected, and then is taken generally for every gift whatſoever, made of any thing by any perſon; and he that granteth it is named the grantor, and he to whom it is made the grantee. A thing is ſaid to be in *grant* which cannot be aſſigned without deed. *Cowel.*

All the whole land is the queen's, unleſs there be ſome *grant* of any part thereof, to be ſhewed from her majeſty. *Spenſer's State of Ireland.*

4. Conceſſion; admiſſion of ſomething in diſpute.

But of this ſo large a *grant*, we are content not to take advantage. *Hooker, b.* iii. *ſ.* 11.

This *grant* deſtroys all you have urg'd before. *Dryden.*

Gra'ntable. *adj.* [from *grant.*] That which may be granted.

The office of the biſhop's chancellor was *grantable* for life. *Ayliffe's Parergon.*

Grantee'. *n. ſ.* [from *grant.*] He to whom any grant is made.

To ſmooth the way for popery in Mary's time, the *grantees* were confirmed by the pope in the poſſeſſion of the abby-lands. *Swift.*

Gra'ntor. *n. ſ.* [from *grant.*] He by whom a grant is made.

A *duplex querela* ſhall not be granted under pain of ſuſpenſion of the *grantor* from the execution of his office. *Ayliffe.*

Gra'nulary. *adj.* [from *granule.*] Small and compact; reſembling a ſmall grain or ſeed.

Small-coal, with ſulphur and nitre, proportionably mixed, tempered, and formed into *granulary* bodies, do make up that powder which is in uſe for guns. *Brown's Vulgar Errours.*

To **GRA'NULATE.** *v. n.* [*granuler*, Fr. from *granum*, Latin.] To be formed into ſmall grains.

The juice of grapes, inſpiſſated by heat, *granulates* into ſugar. *Spratt.*

To **Gra'nulate.** *v. a.*

1. To break into ſmall maſſes or granules.

2. To raiſe into ſmall aſperities.

I have obſerved, in many birds, the gullet, before its entrance into the gizzard, to be much dilated, and thick ſet, or as it were *granulated* with a multitude of glandules, each whereof was provided with its excretory veſſel. *Ray.*

Granula'tion. *n. ſ.* [*granulation*, French, from *granulate.*]

1. The act of pouring melted metal into cold water, ſo as it may granulate or congeal into ſmall grains: it is generally done through a colander, or a birchen broom. Gunpowder and ſome ſalts are likewiſe ſaid to be granulated, from their reſemblance to grain or ſeed. *Quincy.*

2. The act of ſhooting or breaking in ſmall maſſes.

Tents in wounds, by reſiſting the growth of the little *granulations* of the fleſh, in proceſs of time harden them, and in that manner produce a fiſtula. *Sharp's Surgery.*

GRA'NULE. *n. ſ.* [from *granum*, Latin.] A ſmall compact particle.

With an excellent microſcope, where the naked eye did ſee but a green powder, the aſſiſted eye could diſcern particular *granules*, ſome blue, and ſome yellow. *Boyle on Colours.*

Gra'nulous. *adj.* [from *granule.*] Full of little grains.

GRAPE. *n. ſ.* [*grappe*, French; *krappe*, Dutch.] The fruit of the vine, growing in cluſters; the fruit from which wine is expreſſed.

And thou ſhalt not glean thy vineyard, neither ſhalt thou gather every *grape* of thy vineyard; thou ſhalt leave them for the poor and ſtranger. *Lev.* xix. 10.

Turn back thine hand, as the *grape* gatherers into the baſkets. *Jer.* vi. 9.

Anacreon, for thy ſake
I of the *grape* no mention make;
Ere my Anacreon by thee fell,
Curſed plant I lov'd thee well. *Cowley.*

Here are the vines in early flow'r diſcry'd,
Here *grapes* diſcolour'd on the ſunny ſide. *Pope's Odyſſey.*

Grape *Hyacinth*, or **Grape** *Flower.* See **Musk.**

Gra'pestone. *n. ſ.* [*grape* and *ſtone.*] The ſtone or ſeed contained in the grape.

When obedient nature knows his will,
A fly, a *grapeſtone*, or a hair can kill. *Prior.*

GRA'PHICAL. *adj.* [γράφω.] Well delineated.

Write with a needle, or bodkin, or knife, or the like, when the fruit or trees are young; for as they grow, ſo the letters will grow more large and *graphical.* *Bacon's Natural Hiſtory.*

Gra'phically. *adv.* [from *graphical.*] In a pictureſque manner; with good deſcription or delineation.

The hyena odorata, or civet cat, is delivered and *graphically* deſcribed by Caſtellus. *Brown's Vulgar Errours, b.* iii.

Gra'pnel. *n. ſ.* [*grapin*, French.]

1. A ſmall anchor belonging to a little veſſel.

2. A grappling iron with which in fight one ſhip faſtens on another.

To **GRA'PPLE.** *v. n.* [*grabbelen*, Dutch; *krappeln*, German.]

1. To contend by ſeizing each other, as wreſtlers.

They muſt be alſo practiſed in all the locks and gripes of wreſtling, as need may often be in fight to tugg or *grapple*, and to cloſe. *Milton.*

Living virtue, all atchievements paſt,
Meets envy, ſtill to *grapple* with at laſt. *Waller.*

Does he think that he can *grapple* with divine vengeance, and endure the everlaſting burnings? *South's Sermons.*

Antæus here and ſtern Alcides ſtrive,
And both the *grappling* ſtatues ſeem to live. *Addiſon.*

2. To conteſt in cloſe fight.

I'll in my ſtandard bear the arms of York,
To *grapple* with the houſe of Lancaſter. *Shakeſp. Hen.* VI.

Sometimes, from fighting ſquadrons of each fleet,
Two *grappling* Ætna's on the ocean meet,
And Engliſh fires with Belgian flames contend. *Dryden.*

To **Gra'pple.** *v. a.*

1. To faſten; to fix; to join indiſſolubly. Now obſolete.

Grapple your minds to ſternage of the navy,
And leave your England as dead midnight ſtill. *Shak. H.* V.

I will put that buſineſs in your boſoms,
Whoſe execution takes your enemy off,
Grapples you to the heart and love of us. *Shakeſp. Macbeth.*

2. To ſeize; to lay faſt hold of.

Gra'pple. *n. ſ.* [from the verb.]

1. Conteſt hand to hand, in which the combatants ſeize each other; the wreſtlers hold.

As when earth's ſon, Antæus, ſtrove
With Jove's Alcides, and, oft foil'd, ſtill roſe

Freſh

Fresh from his fall, and fiercer *grapple* join'd,
Throttled at length in th' air, expir'd and fell. *Milton.*
Or did his genius
Know mine the stronger demon, fear'd the *grapple*,
And, looking round him, found this nook of fate,
To skulk behind my sword. *Dryden's Don Sebastian.*

2. Close fight.

In the *grapple* I boarded them; on the instant they got clear of our ship, so I alone became their prisoner. *Shakesp. Hamlet.*

3. Iron instrument by which one ship fastens on another.

But Cymon soon his crooked *grapples* cast,
Which with tenacious hold his foes embrac'd. *Dryden.*

GRA'PPLEMENT. *n. s.* [from *grapple.*] Close fight; hostile embrace.

They catching hold of him, as down he lent,
Him backward overthrew, and down him stay'd
With their rude hands and griesly *grapplement*. *Fairy Queen.*

GRA'SHOPPER. *n. s.* [*grass* and *hop.*] A small insect that hops in the Summer grass. The *cicada* of the Latins, or *cicala* of the Italians, is often by the poets translated *grashopper*, but improperly.

Her waggon spokes made of long spinners legs,
The cover of the wings of *grashoppers*. *Shakesp. Ro. and Jul.*

Grashoppers eat up the green of whole countries. *Bacon.*

Where silver lakes, with verdant shadows crown'd,
Disperse a grateful chilness all around;
The *grashopper* avoids the untainted air,
Nor in the midst of Summer ventures there. *Addison.*

The women were of such an enormous stature, that we appeared as *grashoppers* before them. *Addison's Spectator.*

GRA'SIER. See GRAZIER.

To GRASP. *v. a* [*graspare*, Italian.]

1. To hold in the hand; to gripe.

O fool that I am, that thought I could *grasp* water and bind the wind. *Sidney, b.* ii.

In his right hand
Grasping ten thousand thunders, which he sent
Before him, such as in their souls infix'd
Plagues. *Milton's Paradise Lost, b.* vi.

Kings, by *grasping* more than they could hold,
First made their subjects, by oppression, bold. *Denham.*

Doom, as they please, my empire not to stand,
I'll *grasp* my sceptre with my dying hand. *Dryd. Ind. Emp.*

2. To seize; to catch at.

This *grasping* of the militia of the kingdom into their own hands, was desired the Summer before. *Clarendon.*

To GRASP. *v. n.*

1. To catch; to endeavour to seize; to try at.

So endless and exorbitant are the desires of men, that they will *grasp* at all, and can form no scheme of perfect happiness with less. *Swift.*

2. To struggle; to strive; to grapple. Not now in use.

See, his face is black and full of blood;
His hands abroad display'd, as one that *graspt*
And tugg'd for life. *Shakespeare's Henry* VI. *p.* ii.

3. To gripe; to encroach.

Like a miser 'midst his store,
Who *grasps* and *grasps* 'till he can hold no more. *Dryden.*

GRASP. *n. s.* [from the verb.]

1. The gripe or seizure of the hand.

Nor wanted in his *grasp*
What seem'd both spear and shield. *Milton's Paradise Lost.*

This hand and sword have been acquainted well;
It should have come before into my *grasp*,
To kill the ravisher. *Dryden's Don Sebastian.*

The left arm is a little defaced, though one may see it held something in its *grasp* formerly. *Addison on Italy.*

2. Possession; hold.

I would not be the villain that thou think'st
For the whole space that's in the tyrant's *grasp*,
And the rich East to boot. *Shakespeare's Macbeth.*

3. Power of seizing.

Within the direful *grasp*
Of savage hunger, or of savage heat. *Milton.*

They looked upon it as their own, and had it even within their *grasp*. *Clarendon, b.* viii.

GRA'SPER. *n. s.* [from *grasp.*] One that grasps, seizes, or catches at.

GRASS. *n. s.* [ᵹꞃæꞅ, Saxon.] The common herbage of the field on which cattle feed; an herb with long narrow leaves.

Ye are grown fat as the heifer at *grass*, and bellow as bulls. *Jer.* l. 11.

The trade of beef for foreign exportation was prejudiced, and almost sunk; for the flesh being young, and only *grass* fed, was thin, light and moist, and not of a substance to endure the salt, or be preserved by it, for long voyages, or a slow consumption. *Temple.*

You'll be no more your former you;
But for a blooming nymph will pass,
Just fifteen, coming Summer's *grass*. *Swift.*

GRASS *of Parnassus. n. s.* [*parnassia*, Latin.]

It hath a rose-shaped flower of five large leaves, and five small at the bottom fringed, of a greenish colour, and planted orbicularly: out of the flower-cup arises the pointal, which turns to an oval membranaceous fruit, having but one cell filled with seeds. This plant grows wild in most meadows, particularly in the North. It is called *parnassia* from mount Parnassus, where it was supposed to grow; and because the cattle feed on it, it obtained the name of grass, though the plant has no resemblance to the grass kind. *Miller.*

To GRASS. *v. n.* [from the noun.] To breed grass; to become pasture.

Land arable, driven, or worn to the proof,
With oats ye may sow it, the sooner to *grass*,
More soon to be pasture, to bring it to pass. *Tuss. Husband.*

GRASS-PLOT. *n. s.* [*grass* and *plot.*] A small level covered with short grass.

Here on this *grass-plot*, in this very place,
Come and sport. *Shakespeare's Tempest.*

The part of your garden next your house should be a parterre for flowers, or *grass-plots* bordered with flowers. *Temple.*

They are much valued by our modern planters, to adorn their walks and *grass-plots*. *Mortimer's Husbandry.*

GRASS-POLY. A species of WILLOW-WORT, which see.

GRA'SSINESS. *n. s.* [from *grassy.*] The state of abounding in grass.

GRA'SSY. *adj.* [from *grass.*] Covered with grass; abounding with grass.

Ne did he leave the mountains bare unseen,
Nor the rank *grassy* fens delights untry'd. *Spenser.*

Rais'd of *grassy* turf
Their table was, and mossy seats had round. *Milt. P. Lost.*

The most in fields, like herded beasts, lie down,
To dews obnoxious, on the *grassy* floor. *Dryd. Ann. Mir.*

GRATE. *n. s.* [*crates*, Latin.]

1. A partition made with bars placed near to one another, or crossing each other: such as are in cloysters or prisons.

I have grated upon my good friends for three reprieves for you, and your couch-fellow, Nim; or else you had look'd through the *grates*, like a geminy of baboons. *Shakespeare.*

Out at a little *grate* his eyes he cast
Upon those bord'ring hills, and open plain. *Daniel's C. W.*

A fan has on it a nunnery of lively black-eyed vestals, who are endeavouring to creep out at the *grates*. *Addison.*

2. The range of bars within which fires are made.

My dear is of opinion that an old fashioned *grate* consumes coals, but gives no heat. *Spectator*, N°. 30.

To GRATE. *v. a.* [*gratter*, French.]

1. To rub or wear any thing by the attrition of a rough body.

Thereat the fiend his gnashing teeth did *grate*. *Fai. Qu.*

Blind oblivion swallow'd cities up,
And mighty states characterless are *grated*
To dusty nothing. *Shakespeare's Troilus and Cressida.*

If the particles of the putty were not made to stick fast in the pitch, they would, by rolling up and down, *grate* and fret the object metal, and fill it full of little holes. *Newton's Opt.*

2. To offend by any thing harsh or vexatious.

Thereat enraged, soon he 'gan upstart,
Grinding his teeth and *grating* his great heart. *Hubb. Tale.*

They have been partial in the gospel, culled and chosen out those softer and more gentle dictates which should less *grate* and disturb them. *Decay of Piety.*

Just resentment and hard usage coin'd
Th' unwilling word; and, *grating* as it is,
Take it, for it is thy due. *Dryden's Don Sebastian.*

This habit of writing and discoursing, wherein I unfortunately differ from almost the whole kingdom, and am apt to *grate* the ears of more than I could wish, was acquired during my apprenticeship in London. *Swift.*

3. To form a sound by collision of asperities or hard bodies.

The *grating* shock of wrathful iron arms. *Shakes. R.* II.

On a sudden open fly,
With impetuous recoil and jarring sound,
Th' infernal doors, and on their hinges *grate*
Harsh thunder, that the lowest bottom shook
Of Erebus. *Milton's Paradise Lost, b.* ii.

To GRATE. *v. n.*

1. To rub hard so as to injure or offend; to offend, as by oppression or importunity.

Wherein have you been galled by the king?
What peer hath been suborn'd to *grate* on you,
That you should seal this lawless bloody book
Of forg'd rebellion with a seal divine? *Shakes. Henry* IV.

I have *grated* upon my good friends for three reprieves for you, or else you had looked through the grates. *Shakespeare.*

Paradoxing is of great use; but the faculty must be so tenderly managed as not to *grate* upon the truth and reason of things. *L'Estrange's Fables.*

This *grated* harder upon, and raised greater tumults and boilings in the hearts of men, than the seeming unreasonableness of former articles. *South's Sermons.*

I never heard him make the least complaint, in a case that would have *grated* sorely on some men's patience, and have filled their lives with discontent. *Locke.*

2. To make a harsh noise, as that of a rough body drawn over another.

We are not so nice as to cast away a sharp knife, because the edge of it may sometimes *grate*. *Hooker, b.* v. *s.* 36.

GRA'TEFUL. *adj.* [*gratus*, Latin.]

1. Having a due sense of benefits; willing to acknowledge and to repay benefits.

A *grateful* mind
By owing owes not, but still pays. *Milton.*

Years of service past,
From *grateful* souls exact reward at last. *Dryden's Fables.*

2. Pleasing; acceptable; delightful; delicious.

Whatsoever is ingrate at first, is made *grateful* by custom; but whatsoever is too pleasing at first, groweth quickly to satiate. *Bacon's Natural History.*

Now golden fruits on loaded branches shine,
And *grateful* clusters swell with floods of wine. *Pope.*

GRA'TEFULLY. *adv.* [from *grateful.*]

1. With willingness to acknowledge and repay benefits; with due sense of obligation.

He, as new wak'd, thus *gratefully* reply'd. *Milton.*

Enough remains for houshold charge beside,
His wife and tender children to sustain,
And *gratefully* to feed his dumb deserving train. *Dryd. Virg.*

In Cyprus long by men and gods obey'd,
The lovers toil she *gratefully* repaid. *Granville.*

2. In a pleasing manner.

Study detains the mind by the perpetual occurrence of something new, which may *gratefully* strike the imagination. *Watts.*

GRA'TEFULNESS. *n. s.* [from *grateful.*]

1. Gratitude; duty to benefactors. Now obsolete.

A Laconian knight, having sometime served him with more *gratefulness* than good courage defended him. *Sidney.*

Blessings beforehand, ties of *gratefulness*,
The sound of glory ringing in our ears. *Herbert.*

2. Quality of being acceptable; pleasantness.

GRA'TER. *n. s.* [*gratoir*, Fr. from *grate.*] A kind of coarse file with which soft bodies are rubbed to powder.

GRATIFICA'TION. *n. s.* [*gratificatio*, Latin.]

1. The act of pleasing.

They are incapable of any design above the present *gratification* of their palates. *South's Sermons.*

2. Pleasure; delight.

How hardly is his will brought to change all its desires and aversions, and to renounce those *gratifications* in which he has been long used to place his happiness? *Rogers's Sermons.*

3. Reward; recompence. A low word.

To GRA'TIFY. *v. a.* [*gratificor*, Latin.]

1. To indulge; to please by compliance.

You steer between the country and the court,
Nor *gratify*, whate'er the great desire,
Nor grudging give what publick needs require. *Dryden.*

2. To delight; to please.

But pride stood ready to prevent the blow;
For who would die to *gratify* a foe? *Dryden's Fables.*

The captive generals to his car are ty'd;
The joyful citizens tumultuous tide
Echoing his glory, *gratify* his pride. *Prior.*

A palled appetite is humorous, and must be *gratified* with sauces rather than food. *Tatler*, N°. 54.

At once they *gratify* their scent and taste,
While frequent cups prolong the rich repast. *Pope.*

A thousand little impertinencies are very *gratifying* to curiosity, though not improving to the understanding. *Addison.*

3. To requite with a gratification: as, I'll *gratify* you for this trouble.

GRA'TINGLY. *adv.* [from *grate.*] Harshly; offensively.

GRA'TIS. *adv.* [Latin.] For nothing; without a recompence.

The people cry you mock'd them; and, of late,
When corn was given them *gratis*, you repin'd. *Shakesp.*

They sold themselves; but thou, like a kind fellow, gav'st thyself away *gratis*, and I thank thee for thee. *Shakespeare.*

Kindred are no welcome clients, where relation gives them a title to have advice *gratis*. *L'Estrange.*

I scorned to take my degree at Utrecht or Leyden, though offered it *gratis* by those universities. *Arbuthnot's John Bull.*

GRA'TITUDE. *n. s.* [*gratitudo*, low Latin.]

1. Duty to benefactors.

Forbid
That our renowned Rome, whose *gratitude*
Tow'rds her deserving children is enroll'd,
Should now eat up her own! *Shakespeare's Coriolanus.*

2. Desire to return benefits.

The debt immense of endless *gratitude*. *Milton.*

Gratitude is properly a virtue, disposing the mind to an inward sense and an outward acknowledgment of a benefit received, together with a readiness to return the same, or the like. *South's Sermons.*

GRATU'ITOUS. *adj.* [*gratuitus*, Latin; *gratuit*, Fr.]

1. Voluntary; granted without claim or merit.

We mistake the *gratuitous* blessings of heaven for the fruits of our own industry. *L'Estrange.*

2. Asserted without proof.

The second motive they had to introduce this *gratuitous* declination of atoms, the same poet gives us. *Ray.*

GRATU'ITOUSLY. *adv.* [from *gratuitous.*]

1. Without claim or merit.

2. Without proof.

I would know whence came this obliquity of direction, which they *gratuitously* tack to matter: this is to ascribe will and choice to these particles. *Cheyne's Phil. Prin.*

GRATU'ITY. *n. s.* [*gratuité*, Fr. from *gratuitous.*] A present or acknowledgment; a free gift.

They might have pretended to comply with Ulysses, and dismissed him with a small *gratuity*. *Notes on the Odyssey.*

He used every year to present us with his almanack, upon the score of some little *gratuity* we gave him. *Swift.*

To GRA'TULATE. *v. a.* [*gratulor*, Latin.]

1. To congratulate; to salute with declarations of joy.

To gratify the good Andronicus,
And *gratulate* his safe return to Rome,
The people will accept whom he admires. *Shakes. Tit. Andr.*

Whither away so fast?
——No farther than the Tower,
To *gratulate* the gentle princes there. *Shakesp. Rich.* III.

Since nature could behold so dire a crime,
I *gratulate* at least my native clime,
That such a land, which such a monster bore,
So far is distant from our Thracian shore. *Dryden's Fables.*

2. To declare joy for.

Yet give thy jealous subjects leave to doubt,
Who this thy 'scape from rumour *gratulate*,
No less than if from peril; and devout,
Do beg thy care unto thy after state. *Ben. Johns. Epigrams.*

GRATULA'TION. *n. s.* [from *gratulatio*, Latin.] Salutations made by expressing joy; expression of joy.

They are the first *gratulations* wherewith our Lord and Saviour was joyfully received at his entrance into the world, by such as in their hearts, arms, and bowels embraced him. *Hook.*

The earth
Gave signs of *gratulation*, and each hill. *Milt. Par. Lost.*

Your enjoyments, according to the standard of a Christian desire, are so compleat that they require no addition: I shall turn my wishes into *gratulations*, and, congratulating their fulness, only wish their continuance. *South.*

GRA'TULATORY. *adj.* [from *gratulate.*] Congratulatory, expressing congratulation.

GRAVE, a final syllable in the names of places, is from the Saxon ȝꞃæꝼ, a grove or cave. *Gibson's Camden.*

GRAVE. *n. s.* [ȝꞃæꝼ, Saxon.] The place in the ground in which the dead are reposited.

Now it is the time of night,
That the *graves*, all gaping wide,
Every one lets forth his spright,
In the church-way paths to glide. *Shakespeare.*

Thou wilt not leave me in the loathsome *grave*. *Milton.*

To walk upon the *graves* of our dead masters,
Is our own security. *Denham's Sophy.*

A flood of waters would overwhelm all those fragments which the earth broke into, and bury in one common *grave* all mankind, and all the inhabitants of the earth. *Burnet.*

GRA'VE-CLOATHS. *n. s.* [*grave* and *cloaths.*] The dress of the dead.

But of such subtle substance and unsound,
That like a ghost he seem'd, whose *grave-cloaths* were unbound. *Spenser's Fairy Queen, b.* xi.

And he that was dead came forth, bound hand and foot with *grave-cloaths*. *Jo.* xi. 44.

GRA'VE-STONE. *n. s.* [*grave* and *stone.*] The stone that is laid over the grave; the monumental stone.

Timon, presently prepare thy *grave*;
Lye where the light foam of the sea may beat
Thy *grave-stone* daily. *Shakespeare's Timon of Athens.*

To GRAVE. *v. a.* preter. *graved*; part. pass. *graven.* [*graver*, French; γϱάφω.]

1. To insculp; to carve a figure or inscription in any hard substance.

Cornice with bossy sculptures *graven*. *Milton.*

Such later vows, oaths, or leagues can never blot out those former *gravings* or characters, which by just and lawful oaths were made upon their souls. *King Charles.*

Thy sum of duty let two words contain;
O! may they *graven* in thy heart remain,
Be humble and be just. *Prior.*

2. To carve or form.

What profiteth the *graven* image, that the maker thereof hath *graven* it? *Heb.* ii. 18.

3. To copy paintings upon wood or metal, in order to be impressed on paper.

The gravers can and ought to imitate the bodies of the colours by the degrees of the lights and ſhadows: 'tis impoſſible to give much ſtrength to what they *grave*, after the works of the ſchools, without imitating in ſome ſort the colour of the objects. *Dryden's Dufreſnoy.*

4. [From *grave.*] To entomb. Not in uſe.

There's more gold:
Do you damn others, and let this damn you:
And ditches *grave* you all! *Shakeſpeare's Timon of Athens.*

5. To clean, caulk, and ſheath a ſhip. *Ainſworth.*

To Grave. *v. n.* To write or delineate on hard ſubſtances.

Thou ſhalt make a plate of pure gold, and *grave* upon it. *Ex.* xxviii. 36.

Grave. *adj.* [*grave*, French; *gravis*, Latin.]

1. Solemn; ſerious; ſober; not gay; not light or trifling.

To th' more mature,
A glaſs that featur'd them; and to the *grave*,
A child that guided dotards. *Shakeſpeare's Cymbeline.*

We ſhould have elſe deſir'd
Your good advice, which ſtill hath been both *grave*
And proſperous, in this day's council. *Shakeſp. Macbeth.*

That *grave* awfulneſs, as in your beſt breed of maſtives, or elegancy and prettineſs, as in your leſſer dogs, are modes of beauty. *More's Antidote againſt Atheiſm.*

Even the *grave* and ſerious characters are diſtinguiſhed by their ſeveral ſorts of gravity. *Dryden's Fables, Preface.*

Youth on ſilent wings is flown;
Graver years come rolling on. *Prior.*

To laugh, were want of goodneſs and of grace;
And to be *grave*, exceeds all pow'r of face. *Pope's Epiſtles.*

Folly-painting humour, *grave* himſelf,
Calls laughter forth. *Thomſon's Winter.*

2. Of weight; not futile; credible. Little uſed.

The Roman ſtate was of all others the moſt celebrated for their virtue, as the *graveſt* of their own writers, and of ſtrangers, do bear them witneſs. *Grew's Coſmol. Sac. b.* iii. *c.* 3.

3. Not ſhowy; not tawdry: as, a *grave* ſuit of cloaths.

4. Not ſharp of ſound; not acute.

Accent, in the Greek names and uſage, ſeems to have regarded the tone of the voice; the acute accent raiſing the voice, in ſome certain ſyllables, to a higher, *i. e.* more acute pitch or tone, and the *grave* depreſſing it lower, and both having ſome emphaſis, *i. e.* more vigorous pronunciation. *Holder's Elements of Speech.*

GRA'VEL. *n. ſ.* [*gravier*, French; *graveel*, Dutch; *gravel*, Armorick.]

1. Hard ſand; ſand conſiſting of very ſmall pebbleſtones.

Gravel conſiſts of flints of all the uſual ſizes and colours, of the ſeveral ſorts of pebbles; ſometimes with a few pyritæ, and other mineral bodies, confuſedly intermixed, and common ſand. *Woodward's Met. Foſſ.*

His armour, all *gilt*, was ſo well handled, that it ſhewed like a glittering ſand and *gravel*, interlaced with ſilver rivers. *Sidney.*

By intelligence,
And proofs as clear as founts in July, when
We ſee each grain of *gravel*. *Shakeſpeare's Henry* VIII.

Providence permitted not the ſtrength of the earth to ſpend itſelf in baſe *gravel* and pebbles, inſtead of quarries of ſtones. *More's Antidote againſt Atheiſm.*

So deep, and yet ſo clear, we might behold
The *gravel* bottom, and that bottom gold. *Dryden.*

The upper garden at Kenſington was at firſt nothing but a *gravel* pit. *Spectator*, N°. 477.

Gravel walks are beſt for fruit-trees. *Mortimer's Husbandry.*

2. [*Gravelle*, French.] Sandy matter concreted in the kidneys.

If the ſtone is brittle it will often crumble, and paſs in the form of *gravel*: if the ſtone is too big to paſs, the beſt method is to come to a ſort of a compoſition or truce with it. *Arbuthn.*

To Gra'vel. *v. a.* [from the noun.]

1. To pave or cover with gravel.

Moſs groweth upon alleys, eſpecially ſuch as lie cold, and upon the North, as in divers terraſſes; and again, if they be much trodden, or if they were at the firſt *gravelled*. *Bacon.*

2. To ſtick in the ſand.

William the Conqueror, when he invaded this iſland, chanced at his arrival to be *gravelled*; and one of his feet ſtuck ſo faſt in the ſand, that he fell to the ground. *Camden.*

3. To puzzle; to ſtop; to put to a ſtand; to embarraſs.

I would kiſs before I ſpoke.
—Nay, you were better ſpeak firſt, and when you were *gravell'd* for lack of matter you might take occaſion to kiſs. *Shak.*

The diſeaſe itſelf will *gravel* him to judge of it; nor can there be any prediction made of it, it is ſo ſharp. *Howel.*

What work do our imaginations make with eternity and immenſity? And how are we *gravelled* by their cutting dilemma's? *Glanv. Scepſ. c.* 13.

Mat, who was here a little *gravell'd*,
Toſt up his noſe, and would have cavill'd. *Prior.*

4. [In horſemanſhip.] To hurt the foot with gravel confined by the ſhoe.

Gra'veless. *adj.* [from *grave.*] Without a tomb; unburied.

By degrees the memory of my womb,
Together with my brave Egyptians all,
By the diſcandying of this pelletted ſtorm,
Lie *graveleſs*. *Shakeſpeare's Antony and Cleopatra.*

Gra'velly. *adj.* [*graveleux*, French, from *gravel.*] Full of gravel; abounding with gravel; conſiſting of gravel.

There are ſome natural ſpring-waters that will inlapidate wood; ſo that you ſhall ſee one piece of wood, whereof the part above the water ſhall continue wood, and the part under the water ſhall be turned into a *gravelly* ſtone. *Bacon's N. Hiſt.*

If you live in a conſumptive air, make choice of the more open, high, dry, and *gravelly* part of it. *Harvey on Conſumpt.*

Gra'vely. *adv.* [from *grave.*]

1. Solemnly; ſeriouſly; ſoberly; without lightneſs or mirth.

Thou ſtand'ſt
Gravely in doubt when to hold them wiſe. *Milton.*

A girl longs to tell her confidant that ſhe hopes to be married in a little time, and aſks her very *gravely* what ſhe would have her to do. *Spectator.* N°. 475.

Wiſdom's above ſuſpecting wiles;
The queen of learning *gravely* ſmiles. *Swift.*

A formal ſtory was very *gravely* carried to his excellency, by ſome zealous members. *Swift.*

2. Without gaudineſs or ſhow.

Gra'veness. *n. ſ.* [from *grave.*] Seriouſneſs; ſolemnity and ſobriety of behaviour.

You no leſs becomes
The light and careleſs livery that it wears,
Than ſettled age his ſables, and his weeds,
Importing health and *graveneſs*. *Shakeſpeare's Hamlet.*

But yet beware of counſels when too full;
Number makes long diſputes and *graveneſs* dull. *Denham.*

Gra'veolent. *adj.* [*graveolens*, Lat.] Strong ſcented. *Dict.*

Gra'ver. *n. ſ.* [*graveur*, French, from *grave.*]

1. One whoſe buſineſs is to inſcribe or carve upon hard ſubſtances; one who copies pictures upon wood or metal to be impreſſed on paper.

If he makes a deſign to be graved, he is to remember that the *gravers* diſpoſe not their colours as the painters do; and that, by conſequence, he muſt take occaſion to find the reaſon of his deſign in the natural ſhadows of the figures, which he has diſpoſed to cauſe the effect. *Dryden's Dufreſnoy.*

2. The ſtile or tool uſed in graving.

With all the care wherewith I tried upon it the known ways of ſoftening *gravers*, I could not ſoften this. *Boyle.*

The toilſome hours in diff'rent labour ſlide,
Some work the file, and ſome the *graver* guide. *Gay's Fan.*

Gravi'dity. *n. ſ.* [*gravidus*, Latin.] Pregnancy; ſtate of being with child.

Women, obſtructed, have not always the forementioned ſymptoms: in thoſe the ſigns of *gravidity* and obſtructions are hard to be diſtinguiſhed in the beginning. *Arbuthnot on Diet.*

Gra'ving. *n. ſ.* [from *grave.*] Carved work.

Skilful to work in gold; alſo to grave any manner of *graving*, and to find out every device which ſhall be put to him. 2 *Chro.* ii. 14.

To GRA'VITATE. *v. n.* [from *gravis*, Latin.] To tend to the center of attraction.

Thoſe who have nature's ſteps with care purſu'd,
That matter is with active force endu'd,
That all its parts magnetick pow'r exert,
And to each other *gravitate*, aſſert. *Blackmore's Creation.*

That ſubtle matter muſt be of the ſame ſubſtance with all other matter, and as much as is comprehended within a particular body muſt *gravitate* jointly with that body. *Bentley.*

Gravita'tion. *n. ſ.* [from *gravitate.*] Act of tending to the centre.

The moſt conſiderable phenomenon belonging to terreſtrial bodies is the general action of *gravitation*, whereby all known bodies, in the vicinity of the earth, do tend and preſs towards its centre. *Bentley's Sermons.*

When the looſe mountain trembles from on high,
Shall *gravitation* ceaſe, if you go by? *Pope's Eſſ. on Man.*

Gra'vity. *n. ſ.* [*gravitas*, Latin; *gravité*, French.]

1. Weight; heavineſs; tendency to the centre.

That quality by which all heavy bodies tend towards the centre of the earth, accelerating their motion the nearer they approach towards it, true philoſophy has ſhewn to be unſolveable by any hypotheſis, and reſolved it into the immediate will of the Creator. Of all bodies, conſidered within the confines of any fluid, there is a twofold *gravity*, true and abſolute, and apparent, vulgar or comparative: abſolute *gravity* is the whole force by which any body tends downwards; but the relative or vulgar is the exceſs of *gravity* in one body above the ſpecifick *gravity* of the fluid, whereby it tends downwards more than the ambient fluid doth. *Quincy.*

Bodies do ſwim or ſink in different liquors, according to the tenacity or *gravity* of thoſe liquors which are to ſupport them. *Brown's Vulgar Errours, b.* vii. *c.* 15.

Though this increaſe of denſity may at great diſtances be exceeding ſlow, yet if the elaſtick tone of this medium be exceeding great, it may ſuffice to impel bodies from the denſer parts of the medium towards the rarer, with all that power which we call *gravity*. *Newton's Opt.*

2. Atrocioufnefs; weight of guilt.

No man could ever have thought this reafonable, that had intended thereby only to punifh the injury committed, according to the *gravity* of the fact. *Hooker, b.* i. *f.* 10.

3. Seriousnefs; folemnity.

There is not a white hair on your face but fhould have his effect of *gravity*. *Shakefpeare's Henry* IV. *p.* i.

Our youths and wildnefs fhall no whit appear,
But all be buried in his *gravity*. *Shakefpeare's Jul. Cæfar.*

For the advocates and council that plead, patience and *gravity* of hearing is an effential part of juftice. *Bacon, Effay* 57.

Great Cato there, for *gravity* renown'd. *Dryden's Æn.*

The emperors often jefted on their rivals or predeceffors, but their mints ftill maintained their *gravity*. *Addifon.*

GRA'VY. *n. f.* The ferous juice that runs from flefh not much dried by the fire.

They ufually boil and roaft their meat until it falls almoft off from the bones; but we love it half raw, with the blood trickling down from it, delicately terming it the *gravy*, which in truth looks more like an ichorous or raw bloody matter. *Harvey on Confumptions.*

There may be a ftronger broth made of vegetables than of any *gravy* foup. *Arbuthnot on Aliments.*

GRAY. *adj.* [ᵹnæᵹ, Saxon; *grau*, Danifh; *graau*, Dutch.]

1. White with a mixture of black.

They left me then, when the *gray* headed even,
Like a fad votarift in palmer's weed,
Rofe from the hindmoft wheels of Phœbus' wain. *Milton.*

Thefe *gray* and dun colours may be alfo produced by mixing whites and blacks, and by confequence differ from perfect whites, not in fpecies of colours, but only in degree of luminoufnefs. *Newton's Opt.*

2. White or hoary with old age.

Living creatures generally do change their hair with age, turning to be *gray*; as is feen in men, though fome earlier and fome later; in horfes, that are dappled and turn white; in old fquirrels that turn grifly, and many others. *Bacon's Nat. Hift.*

Thou haft neither forfaken me now I am become *gray* headed, nor fuffered me to forfake thee in the late days of temptation. *Walton's Life of Bifhop Sanderfon.*

Anon
Gray headed men and grave, with warriors mix'd,
Affemble. *Milton's Paradife Loft, b.* xi.

The reftoration of *gray* hairs to juvenility, and renewing the exhaufted marrow, may be effected. *Glanv. Scepf.*

Gray headed infant! and in vain grown old!
Art thou to learn that in another's gold
Lie charms refiftlefs? *Dryden's Juvenal, Sat.* 13.

We moft of us are grown *gray* headed in our dear mafter's fervice. *Addifon's Spectator*, N°. 517.

Her *gray* hair'd fynods damning books unread,
And Bacon trembling for his brazen head. *Pope's Dunciad.*

3. Dark like the opening or clofe of day; of the colour of afhes.

Our women's names are more gracious than their Cæfilia, that is, *gray* eyed. *Camden's Remains.*

The *gray* ey'd morn fmiles on the frowning night,
Chequ'ring the eaftern clouds with ftreaks of light. *Shakefp.*

I'll fay yon *gray* is not the morning's eye;
'Tis but the pale reflex of Cynthia's brow. *Shak. R. and Jul.*

Soon as the *gray* ey'd morning ftreaks the fkies,
And in the doubtful day the woodcock flies. *Gay's Trivia.*

GRAY. *n. f.* A badger. *Ainfworth.*

GRA'YBEARD. *n. f.* [*gray* and *beard.*] An old man, in contempt.

Youngling, thou can'ft not love fo dear as I.
—*Graybeard*, thy love doth freeze. *Shakefpeare.*
Have I in conqueft ftretcht mine arm fo far,
To be afraid to tell *graybeards* the truth? *Shakef. Jul. Cæf.*

GRA'YHOUND. See GREYHOUND.

GRA'YLING. *n. f.* The umber, a fifh.

The *grayling* lives in fuch rivers as the trout does, and is ufually taken with the fame baits, and after the fame manner: he is of a fine fhape, his flefh white, and his teeth, thofe little ones that he has, are in his throat. He is not fo general a fifh as the trout, nor fo good to eat. *Walton's Angler.*

GRA'YNESS. *n. f.* [from *gray.*] The quality of being gray.

To GRAZE. *v. n.* [from *grafs.*]

1. To eat grafs; to feed on grafs.

The greateft of my pride is to fee my ewes *graze*, and my lambs fuck. *Shakefpeare's As you like it.*

Graze where you will, you fhall not houfe with me. *Shak.*

Leaving in the fields his *grazing* cows,
He fought himfelf fome hofpitable houfe. *Dryden's Fables.*

The more ignoble throng
Attend their ftately fteps, and flowly *graze* along. *Dryden.*

2. To fupply grafs.

Phyficians advife their patients to remove into airs which are plain champaigns, but *grazing*, and not overgrown with heath. *Bacon.*

The fewers muft be kept fo as the water may not ftay too long in the Spring; for then the ground continueth the wet, whereby it will never *graze* to purpofe that year. *Bacon.*

A third fort of *grazing* ground is that near the fea, which is commonly very rich land. *Mortimer's Hufbandry.*

3. To move on devouring.

As every ftate lay next to the other that was oppreffed, fo the fire perpetually *grazed*. *Bacon on the War with Spain.*

4. [From *rafer*, French.] To touch lightly.

Mark then a bounding valour in our Englifh,
That being dead, like to the bullets *grazing*,
Breaks out into a fecond courfe of mifchief,
Killing in relapfe of mortality. *Shakefp. Henry* V.

To GRAZE. *v. a.*

1. To tend grazing cattle; to fet cattle to feed on grafs.

Jacob *graz'd* his uncle Laban's fheep. *Shakefpeare.*

O happy man, faith he, that, lo! I fee
Grazing his cattle in thofe pleafant fields;
If he but know his good! *Daniel's Civil War.*

The chief beheld their chariots from afar;
Their fteeds around,
Free from their harnefs, *graze* the flow'ry ground. *Dryden.*

Grounds *graze* well the next year after plowing. *Mortimer.*

Some *graze* their land 'till Chriftmas, and fome longer. *Mort.*

He hath a houfe and barn in repair, and a field or two to *graze* his cows, with a garden and orchard. *Swift.*

2. To feed upon.

I was at firft as other beafts, that *graze*
The trodden herb, of abject thoughts and low. *Milton.*

This Neptune gave him, when he gave to keep
His fcaly flocks that *graze* the wat'ry deep. *Dryden's Virgil.*

The lambs with wolves fhall *graze* the verdant mead. *Pope.*

GRA'ZIER. *n. f.* [from *graze.*]

All *graziers* prefer their cattle from meaner paftures to better. *Bacon.*

Gentle peace, which filleft the hufbandman's barns, the *grazier's* folds, and the tradefman's fhop. *Howel.*

His confufion increafed when he found the alderman's father to be a *grazier*. *Spectator*, N°. 612.

Of agriculture, the defolation made in the country by engroffing *graziers*, and the great yearly importation of corn from England, are lamentable inftances under what difcouragement it lies. *Swift.*

GREASE. *n. f.* [*graiffe*, French.]

1. The foft part of the fat; the oily or unctuous part of animals.

Greafe, that's fweaten
From the murth'rer's gibbet, throw
Into the flame. *Shakefpeare's Macbeth.*

To take out a fpot of *greafe* they ufe a coal upon brown paper. *Bacon's Natural Hiftory.*

Thou hop'ft, with facrifice of oxen flain,
To compafs wealth, and bribe the god of gain
To give thee flocks and herds, with large increafe;
Fool! to expect them from a bullock's *greafe*. *Dryd. Juv.*

A girdle, foul with *greafe*, binds his obfcene attire. *Dryd.*

2. [In horfemanfhip.] A fwelling and gourdinefs of the legs, which generally happens to a horfe after his journey.

To GREASE. *v. a.* [from the noun.]

1. To fmear or anoint with greafe.

2. To bribe; to corrupt with prefents.

Envy not the ftore
Of the *greas'd* advocate that grinds the poor. *Dryd. Perf.*

GRE'ASINESS. *n. f.* [from *greafe.*] Oilinefs; fatnefs.

Upon the moft of thefe ftones, after they are cut, there appears always, as it were, a kind of *greafinefs* or unctuofity. *Boyle.*

GRE'ASY. *adj.* [from *greafe.*]

1. Oily; fat; unctuous.

The fragments, fcraps, the bits and *greafy* reliques
Of her o'er-eaten faith. *Shakefp.*

2. Smeared with greafe.

Even the lewd rabble
Govern'd their roaring throats, and grumbled pity:
I could have hugg'd the *greafy* rogues; they pleas'd me. *Otw.*

Buy fheep, and fee that they be big-boned, and have a foft, *greafy*, well curled clofe wool. *Mortimer's Hufbandry.*

3. Fat of body; bulky. In reproach.

Let's confult together againft this *greafy* knight. *Shakefpeare.*

GREAT. *adj.* [ᵹneat, Saxon; *groot*, Dutch.]

1. Large in bulk or number.

Judas one of the twelve came, and with a *great* multitude with fwords and ftaves, from the chief priefts and elders of the people. *Mat.* xxvi. 47.

All thefe cities were fenced with high walls, gates and bars, befides unwalled towns a *great* many. *Deutr.* iii. v.

The idea of fo much is pofitive and clear: the idea of *greater* is alfo clear, but it is but a comparative idea. *Locke.*

2. Having any quality in a high degree.

There were they in *great* fear. *Pf.* xiv. 5.

This is a *great* paradox. *Tillotfon.*

3. Considerable in extent or duration.
Thou hast spoken of thy servants house for a *great* while to come. *2 Sa.* vii. 19.
4. Important; weighty.
Many
Have broke their backs with laying manors on them,
For this *great* journey. *Shakespeare's Henry* VIII.
And though this be a *great* truth, if it be impartially considered, yet it is also a great paradox to men of corrupt minds and vitious practices. *Tillotson, Sermon* 6.
5. Chief; principal.
Hear the king's pleasure, cardinal, who commands you
To render up the *great* seal presently. *Shakes. Henry* VIII.
6. Of high rank; of large power.
Such men as he be never at heart's ease,
Whilst they behold a *greater* than themselves. *Sh. Jul. Cæs.*
Of all the *great*, how few
Are just to heaven, and to their promise true! *Pope's Odyss.*
Misfortune made the throne her seat,
And none could be unhappy but the *great*. *Rowe.*
Despise the farce of state,
The sober follies of the wise and *great*. *Pope.*
7. Illustrious; eminent.
O Lord, thou art *great*, and thy name is *great* in might. *Jer.* x. 6.
8. Grand of aspect; of elevated mien.
Such Dido was; with such becoming state,
Amidst the crowd, she walks serenely *great*. *Dryd. Virgil.*
9. Noble; magnanimous.
In her every thing was goodly and stately; yet so, that it might seem that *great* mindedness was but the ancient-bearer to the humbleness. *Sidney.*
10. Swelling; proud.
Solyman perceived that Vienna was not to be won with words, nor the defendants to be discouraged with *great* looks; wherefore he begun to batter the walls. *Knolles.*
11. Familiar; much acquainted. A low word.
Those that would not censure, or speak ill of a man immediately, will talk more boldly of those that are *great* with them, and thereby wound their honour. *Bacon, Essay* 49.
12. Pregnant; teeming.
Their bellies *great*
With swelling vanity, bring forth deceit. *Sandys.*
This fly, for most he stings in heat of day,
From cattle *great* with young keep thou away. *May's Virg.*
13. It is added in every step of ascending or descending consanguinity: as *great* grandson is the son of my grandson.
I dare not yet affirm for the antiquity of our language, that our *great-great-great* grandsires tongue came out of Persia. *Camden's Remains.*
What we call *great-great* grandfather they called forthafader. *Camden's Remainder.*
Their holiday-cloaths go from father to son, and are seldom worn out 'till the second or third generation; so that 'tis common enough to see a countryman in the doublet and breeches of his *great* grandfather. *Addison.*
14. Hard; difficult; grievous. A proverbial expression.
It is no *great* matter to live lovingly with good natured and meek persons. *Taylor's Devotion.*

GREAT. *n. s.* [from the adjective.]
1. The whole; the gross; the whole in a lump.
To let out thy harvest by *great* or by day,
Let this by experience lead thee the way:
By *great* will deceive thee with ling'ring it out,
By day will dispatch. *Tusser's Husbandry for August.*
It were behoveful, for the strength of the navy, that no ships should be builded by the *great*; for by daily experience they are found to be weak and imperfect. *Raleigh's Essays.*
He did at length so many slain forget,
And lost the tale, and took them by the *great*. *Dryden.*
Carpenters, for uniformity, generally make them so, unless they build an house by the *great*, and are agreed for the sum of money. *Moxon's Mech. Exer.*
I set aside one day in a week for lovers, and interpret by the *great* for any gentlewoman who is turned of sixty. *Addison.*

GRE'ATBELLIED. *adj.* [*great* and *belly.*] Pregnant; teeming.
Greatbellied women,
That had not half a week to go, like rams
In the old time of war, would shake the press,
And make 'em reel from before 'em. *Shakesp. Henry* VIII.
A *greatbellied* woman, walking through the city in the day-time, had her child struck out of her womb, and carried half a furlong from her. *Wilkins's Math. Magick.*

To GRE'ATEN. *v. a.* [from *great.*] To aggrandize; to enlarge; to magnify. A word little used.
After they sought to *greaten* themselves in Italy itself, using strangers for the commanders of their armies, the Turks by degrees beat them out of all their goodly countries. *Raleigh.*

GREATHEA'RTED. *adj.* [*great* and *heart.*] High spirited; undejected.
The earl, as *greathearted* as he, declared that he neither cared for his friendship, nor feared his hatred. *Clarendon.*

GRE'ATLY. *adj.* [from *great.*]
1. In a great degree.
Thy sorrow I will *greatly* multiply. *Milton.*
2. Nobly; illustriously.
Yet London, empress of the northern clime,
By an high fate thou *greatly* didst expire. *Dryd. Ann. Mir.*
3. Magnanimously; generously; bravely.
Where are these bold intrepid sons of war,
That *greatly* turn their backs upon the foe,
And to their general send a brave defiance? *Addison's Cato.*

GRE'ATNESS. *n. s.* [from *great.*]
1. Largeness of quantity or number.
2. Comparative quantity.
We can have no positive idea of any space or duration, which is not made up of and commensurate to repeated numbers of feet or yards, or days or years, and whereby we judge of the *greatness* of these sort of quantities. *Locke.*
All absent good does not, according to the *greatness* it has, or is acknowledged to have, cause pain equal to that *greatness*, as all pain causes desire equal to itself; because the absence of good is not always a pain, as the presence of pain is. *Locke.*
3. High degree of any quality.
Zeal, in duties, should be proportioned to the *greatness* of the reward, and the certainty. *Rogers, Sermon* 13.
4. High place; dignity; power; influence; empire.
Farewel, a long farewel to all my *greatness*. *Shakespeare.*
So many
As will to *greatness* dedicate themselves. *Shakesp. Macbeth.*
I beg your *greatness* not to give the law
In other realms; but beaten, to withdraw. *Dryden's Æn.*
Approaching *greatness* met him with her charms
Of pow'r and future state;
He shook her from his arms. *Dryden.*
Themistocles raised the Athenians to their *greatness* at sea, which he thought to be the true and constant interest of that commonwealth. *Swift.*
5. Swelling pride; affected state.
My lord would have you know, that it is not of pride or *greatness* that he cometh not aboard your ships. *Bacon.*
6. Merit; magnanimity; nobleness of mind.
Greatness of mind and nobleness their seat
Build in her loveliest. *Milton.*
7. Grandeur; state; magnificence.
Greatness with Timon dwells in such a draught,
As brings all Brobdignag before your thought. *Pope.*

GREAVE. *n. s.* [ꝗꞃæꝼ, Saxon.] A grove. *Spenser.*

GREAVES. *n. s.* [from *grêves*, French.] Armour for the legs; a sort of boots. It wants the singular number.
He had *greaves* of brass upon his legs. *1 Sa.* xvii. 6.
A shield make for him, and a helm, fair *greaves*, and curets such
As may renown thy workmanship, and honour him as much. *Chapman's Iliads, b.* xviii.

GRE'CISM. *n. s.* [*græcismus*, Latin.] An idiom of the Greek language.

GREE. *n. s.* [*gré*, French, probably from *gratia.*] Good will; favour; good graces.
And falling her before on lowly knee,
To her makes present of his service seen,
Which she accepts with thanks and goodly *gree*. *Fa Queen.*

GREECE. *n. s.* [corrupted from *degrees.*] A flight of steps.
Ev'ry *greece* of fortune
Is smother'd by that below. *Shakespeare.*
After the procession, the king himself remaining seated in the quire, the lord archbishop, upon the *greece* of the quire, made a long oration. *Bacon's Henry* VII.

GRE'EDILY. *adj.* [from *greedy.*] Eagerly; ravenously; voraciously; with keen appetite or desire.
Greedily she engorg'd without restraint. *Milt. Par. Lost.*
He swallow'd it as *greedily*
As parched earth drinks rain. *Denham's Sophy.*
Ev'n deadly plants, and herbs of pois'nous juice,
Wild hunger seeks; and to prolong our breath,
We *greedily* devour our certain death. *Dryd. Indian Emp.*

GRE'EDINESS. *n. s.* [from *greedy.*] Ravenousness; voracity; hunger; eagerness of appetite or desire.
Fox in stealth, wolf in *greediness*. *Shakes. King Lear.*
Thither with all *greediness* of affection are they gone, and there they intend to sup. *Shakespeare's Winter's Tale.*
If thou wert the wolf, thy *greediness* would afflict thee. *Shakespeare's Timon of Athens.*
I with the same *greediness* did seek,
As water when I thirst, to swallow Greek. *Denham.*

GRE'EDY. *adj.* [ꝗæꝺıꝗ, Sax. *graadig*, Dan. *gretig*, Dutch.]
1. Ravenous; voracious; hungry.
As a lion that is *greedy* of his prey. *Ps.* xvii. 12.
Be not unsatiable in any dainty thing, nor too *greedy* upon meats. *Ecclus.* xxxvii. 29.
He made the *greedy* ravens to be Elias's caterers, and bring him food. *King Charles.*

2. Eager;

2. Eager; vehemently desirous. It is now commonly taken in an ill sense.

Greedy to know, as is the mind of man,
Their cause of death, swift to the fire she ran. *Fairfax.*

The ways of every one that is *greedy* of gain. *Prov.*

Stern look'd the fiend, as frustrate of his will,
Not half suffic'd, and *greedy* yet to kill. *Dryden.*

While the reaper fills his *greedy* hands,
And binds the golden sheaves in brittle bands. *Dryd. Virg.*

GREEN. *adj.* [*grun*, German; *groen*, Dutch.]

1. Having a colour formed commonly by compounding blue and yellow; of the colour of the leaves of trees or herbs. The green colour is said to be most favourable to the sight.

The general colour of plants is *green*, which is a colour that no flower is of: there is a greenish primrose, but it is pale, and scarce a *green*. *Bacon's Natural History.*

Groves for ever *green*. *Pope.*

2. Pale; sickly: from whence we call the maid's disease the *green* sickness, or *chlorosis*. Like it is *Sappho's* χλωροτέρη πόιας.

Was the hope drunk
Wherein you drest yourself? Hath it slept since?
And wakes it now to look so *green* and pale
At what it did so freely? *Shakespeare's Macbeth.*

There's never any of these demure boys come to any proof: they fall into a kind of male *green* sickness. *Shak. Henry* IV.

'Till the *green* sickness and love's force betray'd
To death's remorseless arms th' unhappy maid. *Garth.*

3. Flourishing; fresh; undecayed: from trees in Spring.

4. New; fresh: as, a *green* wound.

The door is open, sir; there lies your way:
You may be jogging while your boots are *green*. *Shakesp.*

Griefs are *green*;
And all thy friends, which thou must make thy friends,
Have but their stings and teeth newly ta'en out. *Sh. H.* IV.

In a vault,
Where bloody Tybalt, yet but *green* in earth,
Lies festering in his blood. *Shakes. Romeo and Juliet.*

A man that studieth revenge keeps his own wounds *green*, which otherwise would heal and do well. *Bacon, Essay* 4.

5. Not dry.

If a spark of error have thus far prevailed, falling even where the wood was *green*, and farthest off from any inclination unto furious attempts; must not the peril thereof be greater in men, whose minds are of themselves as dry fewel, apt beforehand unto tumults? *Hooker, Dedication.*

Of fragility the cause is an impotency to be extended, and therefore stone is more fragil than metal, and so dry wood is more fragil than *green*. *Bacon's Natural History.*

If you but consider a piece of *green* wood burning in a chimney, you will readily discern, in the disbanded parts of it, the four elements. *Boyle.*

The *green* do often heat the ripe, and the ripe, so heated, give fire to the *green*. *Mortimer's Husbandry.*

6. Not roasted; half raw.

Under this head we may rank those words which signify different ideas, by a sort of an unaccountable far-fetched analogy, or distant resemblance, that fancy has introduced between one thing and another; as when we say the meat is *green*, when it is half roasted. *Watts's Logick.*

7. Unripe; immature; young; because fruits are green before they are ripe.

My sallad days,
When I was *green* in judgment, cold in blood! *Shakesp.*

O charming youth, in the first op'ning page;
So many graces in so *green* an age. *Dryden.*

You'll find a difference
Between the promise of his *greener* days,
And these he masters now. *Shakesp. Henry* V.

If you would fat *green* geese, shut them up when they are about a month old. *Mortimer's Husbandry.*

Stubble geese at Michaelmas are seen
Upon the spit, next May produces *green*. *King's Cookery.*

GREEN. *n. s.*

1. The green colour; green colour of different shades.

Her mother hath intended,
That, quaint in *green*, she shall be loose enrob'd. *Shakesp.*

But with your presence cheer'd, they cease to mourn;
And walks wear fresher *green* at your return. *Dryden.*

Cinnabar, illuminated by this beam, appears of the same red colour as in daylight; and if at the lens you intercept the *green* making and blue making rays, its redness will become more full and lively. *Newton's Opt.*

Let us but consider the two colours of yellow and blue: if they are mingled together in any considerable proportion, they make a *green*. *Watts's Logick.*

2. A grassy plain.

For this down-trodden equity, we tread
In warlike march these *greens* before your town. *Shakesp.*

O'er the smooth enamell'd *green*,
Where no print of step hath been,
Follow me as I sing. *Milton.*

The young Æmilia, fairer to be seen
Than the fair lilly on the flow'ry *green*. *Dryden's Fables.*

3. Leaves; branches; wreaths.

With *greens* and flow'rs recruit their empty hives,
And seek fresh forage to sustain their lives. *Dryden's Virg.*

Ev'ry brow with chearful *green* is crown'd;
The feasts are doubled, and the bowls go round. *Dryden.*

The fragrant *greens* I seek, my brows to bind. *Dryden.*

To GREEN. *v. a.* [from the noun.] To make green. A low word.

Great Spring before
Green'd all the year; and fruits and blossoms blush'd
In social sweetness on the self-same bough. *Thoms. Spring.*

GRE'ENBROOM. *n. s.* [*cytiso genista*, Latin.]

It hath papilionaceous flowers, which are succeeded by compressed pods, in which are contained many kidney-shaped seeds: the branches of the trees are flexible, and have sometimes single, and other times three leaves joined together. This shrub grows wild upon barren dry heaths. *Miller.*

GRE'ENCLOTH. *n. s.* A board or court of justice held in the counting-house of the king's houshold, for the taking cognizance of all matters of government and justice within the king's court-royal; and for correcting all the servants that shall offend. *Dict.*

For the *greencloth* law, take it in the largest sense, I have no opinion of it. *Bacon's Advice to Villiers.*

GRE'ENEYED. *adj.* [*green* and *eye*.] Having eyes coloured with green.

Doubtful thoughts, and rash-embrac'd despair,
And shudd'ring fear, and *greeney'd* jealousy. *Shakespeare.*

GRE'ENFINCH. *n. s.* A kind of bird.

The chaffinch, *greenfinch*, dormouse, and other small birds, are injurious to some fruits. *Mortimer's Husbandry.*

GREE'NFISH. *n. s.* A kind of fish. *Ainsworth.*

GRE'ENGAGE. *n. s.* A species of PLUM, which see.

GRE'ENHOUSE. *n. s.* [*green* and *house*.] A house in which tender plants are sheltered from the weather.

If the season prove exceeding piercing, which you may know by the freezing of a moistened cloth set in your *greenhouse*, kindle some charcoal. *Evelyn's Kalendar.*

Sometimes our road led us into several hollow apartments among the rocks and mountains, that look like so many natural *greenhouses*, as being always shaded with a great variety of trees and shrubs that never lose their verdure. *Addison.*

A kitchen garden is a more pleasant sight than the finest orangery or artificial *greenhouse*. *Spectator*, N°. 477.

GRE'ENISH. *adj.* [from *green*.] Somewhat green; tending to green.

With goodly *greenish* locks, all loose, unty'd,
As each had been a bride. *Spenser's Prothalam.*

Of this order the green of all vegetables seems to be, partly by reason of the intenseness of their colours, and partly because, when they wither, some of them turn to a *greenish* yellow. *Newton's Opt.*

GRE'ENLY. *adj.* [from *green*.]

1. With a greenish colour.
2. Newly; freshly.
3. Immaturely.
4. Wanly; timidly.

Kate, I cannot look *greenly*, nor gasp out my eloquence; nor have I cunning in protestation. *Shakespeare's Henry* V.

GRE'ENNESS. *n. s.* [from *green*.]

1. The quality of being green; viridity; viridness.

About it grew such sort of trees, as either excellency of fruit, stateliness of growth, continual *greenness*, or poetical fancies have made at any time famous. *Sidney, b.* i.

In a meadow, though the meer grass and *greenness* delights, yet the variety of flowers doth heighten and beautify. *B. Johns.*

My reason, which discourses on what it finds in my phantasy, can consider *greenness* by itself, or mellowness, or sweetness, or coldness, singly and alone by itself. *Digby on Bodies.*

2. Immaturity; unripeness.

This prince, while yet the errors in his nature were excused by the *greenness* of his youth, which took all the fault upon itself, loved a private man's wife. *Sidney, b.* ii.

3. Freshness; vigour.

Take the picture of a man in the *greenness* and vivacity of his youth, and in the latter date and declension of his drooping years, and you will scarce know it to belong to the same person. *South's Sermons.*

4. Newness.

GRE'ENSICKNESS. *n. s.* [*green* and *sickness*.] The disease of maids, so called from the paleness which it produces.

Sour eructations, and a craving appetite, especially of terrestrial and absorbent substances, are the case of girls in the *greensickness*. *Arbuthnot.*

GRE'ENSWARD. } *n. s.* [*green* and *sward*: of the same original
GRE'ENSWORD. } with *swath*.] The turf on which grass grows.

This is the prettiest low-born lass that ever
Ran on the *greensword*. *Shakespeare's Winter's Tale.*

 After

After break their faſt
On *greenſword* ground, a cool and grateful taſte. *Dryden.*

In ſhallow ſoils all is gravel within a few inches; and ſometimes in low ground a thin *greenſward*, and ſloughy underneath; which laſt turns all into bog. *Swift.*

GRE'ENWEED. *n. ſ.* [*green* and *weed*] Dyers weed.

GRE'ENWOOD. *n. ſ.* [*green* and *wood.*] A wood conſidered as it appears in the Spring or Summer. It is ſometimes uſed as one word.

Among wild herbs under the *greenwood* ſhade. *Fairfax.*

It happen'd on a Summer's holiday,
That to the *greenwood* ſhade he took his way;
For Cymon ſhunn'd the church.
Dryden's Cymon and Iphigenia.

To GREET. *v. a.* [*grat:r*, Latin; ʒnetan, Saxon.]

1. To addreſs at meeting.

I think if men, which in theſe places live,
Durſt look in themſelves, and themſelves retrieve,
They would like ſtrangers *greet* themſelves. *Donne.*

I would gladly go,
To *greet* my Pallas with ſuch news below. *Dryden's Æn.*

2. To addreſs in whatever manner.

My noble partner
You *greet* with preſent grace, and great prediction;
To me you ſpeak not. *Shakeſpeare's Macbeth.*

Now, Thomas Mowbray, do I turn to thee,
And mark my *greeting* well; for what I ſpeak,
My body ſhall make good. *Shakeſpeare's Richard* II.

3. To ſalute in kindneſs or reſpect.

My lord, the mayor of London comes to *greet* you.
—God bleſs your grace with health and happy days. *Shakeſ.*

Now the herald lark
Left his ground neſt, high tow'ring to deſcry
The morn's approach, and *greet* her with his ſong. *Milton.*

Once had the early matrons run
To *greet* her of a lovely ſon. *Milton.*

The ſea's our own; and now all nations *greet*,
With bending ſails, each veſſel of our fleet. *Waller.*

Thus pale they meet, their eyes with fury burn:
None *greets*; for none the *greeting* will return;
But in dumb ſurlineſs, each arm'd with care,
His foe profeſt, as brother of the war. *Dryden's Fables.*

4. To congratulate.

His lady, ſeeing all that channel from far,
Approacht in haſte to *greet* his victorie. *Fairy Queen, b.* i.

5. To pay compliments at a diſtance.

The king's a-bed,
And ſent great largeſs to your officers;
This diamond he *greets* your wife withal,
By the name of moſt kind hoſteſs. *Shakeſpeare's Macbeth.*

6. To meet, as thoſe do who go to pay congratulations. Not much in uſe.

Your haſte
Is now urg'd on you.
——We will *greet* the time. *Shakeſpeare's King Lear.*

Such was that face on which I dwelt with joy,
Ere Greece aſſembled ſtem'd the tides to Troy;
But parting then for that deteſted ſhore,
Our eyes, unhappy! never *greeted* more. *Pope's Odyſſey.*

To GREET. *v. n.* To meet and ſalute.

There *greet* in ſilence, as the dead are wont,
And ſleep in peace. *Shakeſp.*

GREE'TER. *n. ſ.* [from the verb.] He who greets.

GRE'ETING. *n. ſ.* [from *greet.*] Salutation at meeting, or compliments at a diſtance.

I from him
Give you all *greetings*, that a king, as friend,
Can ſend his brother. *Shakeſpeare's Winter's Tale.*

GREEZE. *n. ſ.* [Otherwiſe written *greece.* See GREECE, or GRIEZE, or GRICE, from *degrees.*] A flight of ſteps; a ſtep.

In purity of manhood ſtand upright,
And ſay, this man's a flatterer: if one be,
So are they all; for every *greeze* of fortune
Is ſmooth'd by that below: the learned pate,
Ducks to the golden fool. *Shakeſpeare's Timon of Athens.*

GRE'GAL. *adj.* [*grex, gregis*, Lat.] Belonging to a flock. *Dict.*

GREGA'RIOUS. *adj.* [*gregarius*, Latin.] Going in flocks or herds, like ſheep or partridges.

No birds of prey are *gregarious.* *Ray on the Creation.*

GRE'MIAL. *adj.* [*gremium*, Lat.] Pertaining to the lap. *Dict.*

GRENA'DE. *n. ſ.* [from *pomum granatum*, Latin.] A little hollow globe or ball of iron, or other metal, about two inches and a half in diameter, which, being filled with fine powder, is ſet on fire by means of a ſmall fuſee faſtened to the touch-hole: as ſoon as it is kindled, the caſe flies into many ſhatters, much to the damage of all that ſtand near. Theſe granades ſerve to fire cloſe and narrow paſſages, and are often thrown with the hand among the ſoldiers to diſorder their ranks, more eſpecially in thoſe poſts where they ſtand thickeſt; as in trenches, redoubts, and lodgments. *Harr.*

GRE'NADIER. *n. ſ.* [*grenadier*, Fr. from *grenade.*] A tall foot-ſoldier, of whom there is one company in every regiment: ſuch men being employed to throw grenades.

Peace allays the ſhepherd's fear
Of wearing cap of *grenadier.* *Gay's Paſtorals.*

GRENA'DO. *n. ſ.* See GRENADE.

Yet to expreſs a Scot, to play that prize,
Not all thoſe mouth *grenados* can ſuffice. *Cleaveland.*

You may as well try to quench a flaming *grenado* with a ſhell of fair water, as hope to ſucceed. *Watts.*

GREUT. *n. ſ.* A kind of foſſile body.

A ſort of tin-ore, with its *greut*; that is, a congeries of cryſtals, or ſparks of ſpar, of the bigneſs of bayſalt, and of a brown ſhining colour immerſed therein. *Grew's Muſæum.*

GREW. The preterite of *grow.*

The pleaſing taſk he fails not to renew;
Soft and more ſoft at ev'ry touch it *grew.* *Dryden's Fables.*

GREY. *adj.* [*gris*, French. More properly written *gray.*] See GRAY.

This ancient ruffian, ſir, whoſe life I ſpar'd at ſuit of his *grey* beard. *Shakeſpeare's King Lear.*

Our green youth copies what *grey* ſinners act,
When venerable age commends the fact. *Dryden.*

GRE'YHOUND. *n. ſ.* [ʒnigꝺhunꝺ, Saxon.] A tall fleet dog that chaſes in ſight.

Firſt may a truſty *greyhound* transform himſelf into a tyger. *Sidney, b.* i.

So on the downs we ſee, near Wilton fair,
A haſt'ned hare from greedy *greyhounds* go. *Sidney.*

Th' impatient *greyhound*, ſlipt from far,
Bounds o'er the glebe to catch the fearful hare. *Dryden.*

GRICE. *n. ſ.*

1. A little pig. *Gouldman.*

2. A ſtep or *greeze.*

No, not a *grice*;
This a ſtep to love. *Shakeſpeare's Twelfth Night.*

To GRIDE. *v. n.* [*gridare*, Italian.] To cut; to make way by cutting. A word elegant, but not in uſe.

His poignant ſpear he thruſt with puiſſant ſway,
At proud Cymochles, whiles his ſhield was wide,
That through his thigh the mortal ſteel did *gride.* *F. Queen.*

So ſore
The *griding* ſword, with diſcontinuous wound,
Paſs'd through him! *Milton's Paradiſe Loſt, b.* vi.

GRI'DELIN. *adj.* A colour mixed of white and red.

The ladies dreſs'd in rich ſymars were ſeen,
Of Florence ſatten, flower'd with white and green,
And for a ſhade betwixt the bloomy *gridelin.* *Dryden's Fab.*

GRI'DIRON. *n. ſ.* [*grind*, Iſlandick, a grate and *iron.*] A portable grate on which meat is laid to be broiled upon the fire.

He had added two bars to the *gridiron.* *Spectator*, Nº. 570.

GRIEF. *n. ſ.* [from *grieve*; *griff*, Welſh, probably from the Engliſh.]

1. Sorrow; trouble for ſomething paſt.

I will inſtruct my ſorrows to be proud;
For *grief* is proud, and makes his owner ſtout. *Shakeſpeare.*

Wringing of the hands, knocking the breaſt, or wiſhing one's ſelf unborn, are but the ceremonies of ſorrow, the pomp and oſtentation of an effeminate *grief*, which ſpeak not ſo much the greatneſs of the miſery as the ſmallneſs of the mind. *South's Sermons.*

The mother was ſo afflicted at the loſs of a fine boy, who was her only ſon, that ſhe died for *grief* of it. *Addiſon's Spect.*

2. Grievance; harm. [*Grief*, French.]

Be factious for redreſs of all theſe *griefs*,
And I will ſet this foot of mine as far
As who goes fartheſt. *Shakeſpeare.*

The king hath ſent to know
The nature of your *griefs*, and whereupon
You conjure from the breaſt of civil peace
Such bold hoſtility? *Shakeſp. Henry* IV. *p.* i.

3. Pain; diſeaſe.

GRI'EVANCE. *n. ſ.* [from *grief.*]

1. A ſtate of uneaſineſs. Out of uſe.

2. The cauſe of uneaſineſs. Uſed of ſuch cauſes as are the effects of human conduct.

What remedy can be found againſt *grievances*, but to bring religion into countenance, and encourage thoſe who, from the hope of future reward, and dread of future puniſhment, will be moved to juſtice and integrity? *Swift.*

To GRIEVE. *v. a.* [*grever*, French; *griever*, Flemiſh; *gravis*, Latin.] To afflict; to hurt.

For he doth not afflict willingly, nor *grieve* the children of men. *Lu* iii. 33.

Forty years long was I *grieved* with this generation. *Pſal.*

It repented the Lord that he had made man on the earth, and it *grieved* him at his heart. *Gen.* vi. 6.

Griev'd at the thought, he vow'd his whole endeavour
Should be to cloſe thoſe breaches. *Rowe's Ambitious Stepm.*

To GRIEVE. *v. n.* To be in pain for ſomething paſt; to mourn; to ſorrow, as for the death of friends.

Do not you *grieve* at this; I ſhall be ſent for in private to him: look you, he muſt ſeem thus to the world. *Shak. H.* IV.

With equal mind what happens let us bear;
Nor joy nor *grieve* too much for things beyond our care.
Dryden's Fables.

GRIE'VINGLY. *adv.* [from *grieve.*] In sorrow; sorrowfully.
Grievingly, I think,
The peace between the French and us not values
The cost that did conclude it. *Shakesp. Henry* VIII.

GRIE'VOUS. *adj.* [*gravis*, Latin; or from *To grieve.*]
1. Afflictive; painful; hard to be born.
To the flesh, as the apostle himself granteth, all affliction is naturally *grievous*. *Hooker, b.* v. *s.* 48.
Correction is *grievous* unto him that forsaketh the way, and he that hateth reproof shall die. *Prov.* xv. 10.
2. Such as causes sorrow.
To own a great but *grievous* truth, though they may quicken and sharpen the invention, they corrupt the temper. *Watts's Improvement of the Mind.*
3. Expressing a great degree of uneasiness.
He durst not disobey, but sent *grievous* complaints to the parliament of the usage he was forced to submit to. *Clarendon.*
4. Atrocious; heavy.
It was a *grievous* fault,
And grievously hath Cæsar answer'd it. *Shakes. Jul. Cæsar.*
5. Sometimes used adverbially in low language.
He cannot come, my lord; he's *grievous* sick. *Shakesp.*

GRIE'VOUSLY. *adv.* [from *grievous.*]
1. Painfully; with pain.
Wide was the wound, and a large lukewarm flood,
Red as the rose, thence gushed *grievously*. *Fairy Queen.*
2. With discontent; with ill will.
Grittus, perceiving how *grievously* the matter was taken, with the danger he was in, began to doubt. *Knolles.*
3. Calamitously; miserably.
I see how a number of souls are, for want of right information in this point, oftentimes *grievously* vexed. *Hooker, b.* v.
4. Vexatiously; to a great degree of uneasiness.
Houses built in plains are apt to be *grievously* annoyed with mire and dirt. *Ray on the Creation.*

GRIE'VOUSNESS. *n. s.* [from *grievous.*] Sorrow; pain; calamity.
They fled from the swords, from the drawn sword and from the bent bow, and from the *grievousness* of war. *Is.* xxi. 15.

GRI'FFIN. } *n. s.* [This should rather be written *gryfon*, or *gryphon*, gryps, γρὺψ; but it is generally written *griffon.*] A fabled animal, said to be generated between the lion and eagle, and to have the head and paws of the lion, and the wings of the eagle.
GRI'FFON. }
Of all bearing among these winged creatures, the *griffin* is the most ancient. *Peacham on Blazoning.*
Aristeus, a poet of Proconesus, affirmed, that near the one-eyed nations *griffins* defended the mines of gold. *Brown.*

GRIG. *n. s.* [*kricke*, Bavarian, a little duck.]
1. It seems originally to have signified any thing below the natural size.
2. A small eel.
3. A merry creature. [Supposed from *Greek*; *græculus festivus*, Latin.]
Hard is her heart as flint or stone,
She laughs to see me pale;
And merry as a *grig* is grown,
And brisk as bottle-ale. *Swift.*

To GRILL. *v. n.* [*grille*, a grate, French.] To broil on a grate or gridiron.

GRI'LLADE. *n. s.* [from *grill.*] Any thing broiled on the gridiron.

To GRI'LLY. *v. a.* [from *grill.*] This word signifies, as it seems, to harrass; to hurt: as we now say, *to roast a man*, for *to teaze him.*
For while we wrangle here and jar,
W' are *grillied* all at Temple-bar. *Hudibras, p.* iii.

GRIM. *adj.* [ȝrimma, Saxon.]
1. Having a countenance of terrour; horrible; hideous; frightful.
The innocent prey in haste he does forsake,
Which quit from death, yet quakes in every limb,
With change of fear to see the lion look so *grim*. *F. Queen.*
Thou hast a *grim* appearance, and thy face
Bears a command in't. *Shakespeare's Coriolanus.*
Their dear causes
Would to the bleeding and the *grim* alarm
Excite the mortified man. *Shakespeare's Macbeth.*
What if the breath that kindled those *grim* fires,
Awak'd, should blow them into sevenfold rage? *Milton.*
Expert to turn the sway
Of battle, open when and where to close
The ridges of *grim* war. *Milton's Paradise Lost, b.* vi.
He that dares to die,
May laugh at the *grim* face of law and scorn,
The cruel wrinkle of a tyrant brow. *Denham's Sophy.*
Their swarthy hosts would darken all our plains,
Doubling the native horrour of the war,
And making death more *grim*. *Addison's Cato.*
2. Ugly; ill-looking.
Grim visag'd war hath smooth'd his wrinkl'd front. *Shak.*
Venus was like her mother; for her father is but *grim*. *Shak.*

GRI'MACE. *n. s.* [French, from *grim.*]
1. A distortion of the countenance from habit, affectation, or insolence.
He had not spar'd to shew his piques,
Against th' haranguer's politicks,
With smart remarks of leering faces,
And annotations of *grimaces!* *Hudibras, p.* iii.
The favourable opinion and good word of men comes oftentimes at a very easy rate; and by a few demure looks and affected whims, set off with some odd devotional postures and *grimaces*, and such other little arts of dissimulation, cunning men will do wonders. *South's Sermons.*
The buffoon ape, with *grimaces* and gambols, carried it from the whole field. *L'Estrange, Fable* 116.
The French nation is addicted to *grimace*. *Spectator.*
2. Air of affectation.
Vice in a vizard, to avoid *grimace*,
Allows all freedom, but to see the face. *Granville.*

GRIMA'LKIN. *n. s.* [*gris*, French, grey, and *malkin*, or little *Moll.*]
1. Grey little woman; the name of an old cat.
So, poets sing,
Grimalkin, to domestick vermin sworn
An everlasting foe, with watchful eye
Lies nightly brooding o'er a chinky gap,
Protending her fell claws, to thoughtless mice
Sure ruin. *Phillips.*

GRIME. *n. s.* [from *grim.*] Dirt deeply insinuated; sullying blackness not easily cleansed.
Swart, like my shoe, but her face nothing so clean kept; for why? she sweats: a man may go over shoes in the *grime* of it. *Shakespeare's Comedy of Errours.*
Collow is the word by which they denote black *grime* of burnt coals or wood. *Woodward on Fossils.*

To GRIME. *v. a.* [from the noun.] To dirt; to sully deeply.
My face I'll *grime* with filth,
Blanket my loins, elf all my hair in knots. *Shakespeare.*

GRI'MLY. *adv.* [from *grim.*]
1. Horribly; hideously; terribly.
We've landed in ill time: the skies look *grimly*,
And threaten present blusters. *Shakespeare's Winter's Tale.*
So Pluto, seiz'd of Proserpine, convey'd
To hell's tremendous gloom th' affrighted maid;
There *grimly* smil'd, pleas'd with the beauteous prize,
Nor envy'd Jove his sunshine and his skies. *Addison's Cato.*
2. Sourly; sullenly.
The augurs
Say they know not; they cannot tell; look *grimly*,
And dare not speak their knowledge. *Shakes. Ant. and Cleop.*

GRI'MNESS. *n. s.* [from *grim.*] Horror; frightfulness of visage.

To GRIN. *v. n.* [ȝrennian, Saxon; *grinnen*, *grinden*, Dutch, undoubtedly of the same origin with *To grind*, as we now say *to grind the teeth*; *grincer*, French.]
1. To set the teeth together and withdraw the lips.
Small curs are not regarded when they *grin*;
But great men tremble when the lion roars. *Shakesp. H.* VI.
Death, death! oh, amiable, lovely death!
Come *grin* on me, and I will think thou smil'st. *Shakesp.*
What valour were it, when a cur doth *grin*,
For one to trust his hand between his teeth,
When he might spurn him with his foot away? *Shakesp.*
It was no unpleasant entertainment to me to see the various methods with which they have attacked me; some with piteous moans and outcries, others *grinning*, and only shewing their teeth. *Stillingfleet.*
A lion's hide he wears;
About his shoulders hangs the shaggy skin;
The teeth and gaping jaws severely *grin*. *Dryden's Æn.*
They neither could defend, nor can pursue;
But *grinn'd* their teeth, and cast a helpless view. *Dryden.*
Madness, we fancy, gave an ill-tim'd birth
To *grinning* laughter and to frantick mirth. *Prior.*
2. To fix the teeth as in anguish.
I like not such *grinning* honour as sir Walter hath: give me life, which if I can save, so; if not, honour comes unlook'd for, and there's an end. *Shakes. Henry* IV. *p.* i.

GRIN. *n. s.* [from the verb.] The act of closing the teeth and shewing them.
He laughs at him: in's face too.
—O you mistake him; 'twas an humble *grin*,
The fawning joy of courtiers and of dogs. *Dryden.*
The muscles were so drawn together on each side of his face, that he shewed twenty teeth at a *grin*. *Addison's Spectat.*
Deists are effectually beaten in all their combats at the weapons of men, that is, reason and argument; and they would now attack our religion with the talents of a vile animal, that is, *grin* and grimace. *Watts's Improvement of the Mind.*

GRIN. *n. s.* [ȝrin, ȝrinene, Saxon.] A snare; a trap.

Like a birde that hasteth to his *gryn*,
Not knowinge the perile. *Chaucer.*

The *grin* shall take him by the heel, and the robber shall prevail against him. *Job* xviii. 9.

To GRIND. *v. a.* preter. *I ground*; part. pass. *ground.* [ʒrın-ðan, ʒeʒrunðen, ground, Saxon.]

1. To reduce any thing to powder by friction; to comminute by attrition.

And whosoever shall fall on this stone, shall be broken; but on whomsoever it shall fall, it will *grind* him to powder. *Mat.*

He that will have a cake out of the wheat, must needs tarry the *grinding*. *Shakespeare's Troilus and Cressida.*

What relation or affinity is there between a minute body and cogitation, any more than the greatest? Is a small drop of rain any wiser than the ocean? Or do we *grind* inanimate corn into living and rational meal? *Bentley's Sermons.*

2. To sharpen or smooth by rubbing on something hard.

Meeting with time, slack thing, said I,
Thy sithe is dull; whet it, for shame:
No marvel, sir, he did reply,
If it at length deserve some blame;
But where one man would have me *grind* it,
Twenty for one too sharp do find it. *Herbert.*

Against a stump his tusk the monster *grinds*,
And in the sharpen'd edge new vigour finds. *Dryd. Fables.*

That the stomach in animals *grinds* the substances which it receives, is evident from the dissection of animals, which have swallowed metals, which have been found polished on the side next the stomach. *Arbuthnot on Aliments.*

3. To rub one against another.

So up he let him rise; who with grim look,
And count'nance stern, upstanding, 'gan to *grind*
His grated teeth for great disdain. *Fairy Queen, b.* ii.

Harsh sounds, as of a saw when it is sharpened, and *grinding* of one stone against another, make a shivering or horror in the body, and set the teeth on edge. *Bacon's Nat. History.*

4. To harrass; to oppress.

Some merchants and tradesmen, under colour of furnishing the colony with necessaries, may not *grind* them so as shall always keep them in poverty. *Bacon's Advice to Villiers.*

Another way the Spaniards have taken to *grind* the Neapolitans, and yet to take off the odium from themselves. *Addis.*

To GRIND. *v. n.* To perform the act of grinding; to move a mill.

Fetter'd they send thee
Into the common prison, there to *grind*
Among the slaves and asses. *Milton's Agonistes.*

2. To be moved as in the act of grinding.

Shrinking sinews start,
And smeary foam works o'er my *grinding* jaws. *Rowe.*

GRI'NDER. *n. s.* [from *grind.*]

1. One that grinds; one that works in a mill.

2. The instrument of grinding.

His heart a solid rock, to fear unknown,
And harder than the *grinder*'s nether stone. *Sandys.*

Now exhort
Thy hinds to exercise the pointed steel
On the hard rock, and give a wheely form
To the expected *grinder*. *Phillips.*

3. [Ᵹrınð-τoðaρ.] The back teeth; the double teeth.

The teeth are in men of three kinds: sharp, as the fore-teeth; broad, as the back-teeth, which we call the molar-teeth, or *grinders*; and pointed teeth, or canine, which are between both. *Bacon's Natural History.*

He the raging lioness confounds,
The roaring lion with his javelin wounds;
Scatters their whelps, their *grinders* breaks; so they
With the old hunter starve for want of prey. *Sandys.*

The jaw-teeth or *grinders*, in Latin *molares*, are made flat and broad a-top, and withal somewhat uneven and rugged, that, by their knobs and little cavities, they may the better retain, *grind* and commix the aliments. *Ray on the Creation.*

Nature is at a great deal of labour to transmute vegetable into animal substances; therefore herb-eating animals, which don't ruminate, have strong *grinders*, and chew much. *Arbuth.*

4. The teeth, in irony or contempt.

One, who at sight of supper, open'd wide
His jaws before, and whetted *grinders* try'd. *Dryd. Juven.*

Both he brought;
He mouth'd them, and betwixt his *grinders* caught. *Dryden.*

GRI'NDLESTONE. } *n. s.* [from *grind* and *stone*] The stone
GRI'NDSTONE. } on which edged instruments are sharpened.

Such a light and metall'd dance
Saw you never yet in France;
And by the lead-men, for the nonce,
That turn round like *grindlestones*,
Which they dig out fro' the dells,
For their bairns bread, wives and sells. *Ben. Johnson.*

Literature is the *grindstone* to sharpen the coulters, and to whet their natural faculties. *Hammond on Fundamentals.*

Smiths that make hinges brighten them, yet seldom file them; but grind them on a *grindstone* 'till bright. *Moxon.*

GRI'NNER. *n. s.* [from *grin*.] He that grins.

The frightful'st *grinner*
Be the winner. *Addison's Spectator,* Nº. 170.

GRI'NNINGLY. *adv.* [from *grin.*] With a grinning laugh.

GRIP. *n. s.* A small ditch. *Ainsworth.*

To GRIPE. *v. a.* [*greipan*, Gothick; ʒnıpan, Saxon; *grijpen*, Dutch; *gripp*, Scottish.]

1. To hold with the fingers closed; to grasp; to press with the fingers.

He that speaks doth *gripe* the hearer's wrist,
Whilst he that hears makes fearful action
With wrinkl'd brows. *Shakespeare's King John.*

He seiz'd the shining bough with *griping* hold,
And rent away with ease the ling'ring gold. *Dryden's Æn.*

2. [*Gripper*, French.] To catch eagerly; to seize.

A wond'rous way it for this lady wrought,
From lion's claws to pluck the *griped* prey. *Fairy Queen.*

You took occasion to be quickly woo'd
To *gripe* the gen'ral sway into your hands. *Shakes. Hen.* IV.

3. To close; to clutch.

Unlucky Welsted! thy unfeeling master,
The more thou ticklest, *gripes* his hand the faster. *Pope.*

4. To pinch; to press; to squeeze.

And first the dame came rushing through the wood;
And next the famish'd hounds that sought their food,
And *grip'd* her flanks, and oft essay'd their jaws in blood. *Dryden's Fables.*

To GRIPE. *v. n.* To pinch the belly; to give the colick.

Thus full of counsel to the den she went,
Grip'd all the way, and longing for a vent. *Dryden.*

Many people would, with reason, prefer the *griping* of an hungry belly to those dishes which are a feast to others. *Locke.*

Manna, by the bulk, figure, texture and motion of its parts, has a power to produce the sensations of sickness, and sometimes of acute pains or *gripings* in us. *Locke.*

GRIPE. *n. s.* [from the verb.]

1. Grasp; hold; seizure of the hand or paw.

Therefore still on high
He over him did hold his cruel claws,
Threatning with greedy *gripe* to do him dy. *Fairy Queen.*

They put a barren sceptre in my *gripe*,
Thence to be wrench'd with an unlineal hand. *Shak. Macb.*

Should I
Slaver with lips, as common as the stairs
That mount the Capitol; join *gripes* with hands
Made hardy with hourly falshood as with labour. *Shakesp.*

He gave me his hand,
And, with a feeble *gripe*, says, dear, my lord,
Command my service. *Shakespeare's Henry* V.

I fell; and with my weight the helm constrain'd,
Was drawn along, which yet my *gripe* retain'd. *Dryd. Æn.*

2. Squeeze; pressure.

Fir'd with this thought, at once he strain'd the breast;
'Tis true, the harden'd breast resists the *gripe*,
And the cold lips return a kiss unripe. *Dryden's Fables.*

3. Oppression; crushing power.

I take my cause
Out of the *gripes* of cruel men, and give it
To a most noble judge, the king my master. *Shak. H.* VIII.

4. Affliction; pinching distress.

Adam, at the news
Heart-struck with chilling *gripe* of sorrow stood,
That all his senses bound! *Milton's Paradise Lost, b.* xi.

Can'st thou bear cold and hunger? Can these limbs,
Fram'd for the tender offices of love,
Endure the bitter *gripes* of smarting poverty? *Otway.*

5. [In the plural.] Belly-ach; colick.

In the jaundice the choler is wanting; and the icterical have a great sourness and *gripes*, with windiness. *Floyer.*

GRI'PER. *n. s.* [from *gripe.*] Oppressor; usurer; extortioner.

Others pretend zeal, and yet are professed usurers, *gripers*, monsters of men, and harpies. *Burton on Melancholy.*

GRI'PINGLY. *adv.* [from *griping.*] With pain in the guts.

Clysters help, lest the medicine stop in the guts, and work *gripingly*. *Bacon's Natural History.*

GRI'PLE. *n. s.* A greedy snatcher; a griping miser. *Spenser.*

GRI'SAMBER. *n. s.* Used by *Milton* for ambergrise.

Beasts of chase, or fowl of game,
In pastry built, or from the spit, or boil'd,
Grisamber steam'd. *Milton's Paradise Regain'd, b.* ii.

GRISE. *n. s.* [See GREEZE, as it should be written.] A step, or scale of steps.

Let me speak like ourself; and lay a sentence,
Which, as a *grise* or step, may help these lovers
Into your favour. *Shakespeare's Othello.*

GRI'SKIN. *n. s.* [*grisgin*, roast meat, Irish.] The vertebræ of a hog broiled.

GRI'SLY. *adj.* [ʒnyrlu, Saxon.] Dreadful; horrible; hideous; frightful; terrible.

His

His *grisly* locks, long growen and unbound,
Disordered hung about his shoulders round. *Fairy Queen.*

Where I was wont to seek the honey bee,
The *grisly* toadstool grown there might I see. *Spenser.*

My *grisly* countenance made others fly;
None durst come near, for fear of sudden death. *Sh. H.VI.*

Back step'd those two fair angels, half amaz'd
So sudden to behold the *grisly* king;
Yet thus, unmov'd with fear, accost him soon. *Milt. P. L.*

For that damn'd magician, let him be girt
With all the *grisly* legions that troop
Under the sooty flag of Acheron. *Milton.*

The beauteous form of fight
Is chang'd, and war appears a *grisly* sight. *Dryden's Fables.*

In vision thou shalt see his *grisly* face,
The king of terrors, raging in thy race. *Dryd. Innocence.*

Thus the *grisly* spectre spoke again. *Dryden's Fables.*

Close by each other laid, they press'd the ground,
Their manly bosoms pierc'd with many a *griesly* wound. *Dryden's Fables.*

So rushes on his foe the *grisly* bear. *Addison.*

GRIST. *n. s.* [ᵹrist, Saxon.]

1. Corn to be ground.

Get *grist* to the mill to have plenty in store,
Lest miller lack water. *Tusser's Husbandry.*

A mighty trade this lusty miller drove;
Much *grist* from Cambridge to his lot did fall,
And all the corn they us'd at Scholars-hall. *Miller of Tromp.*

2. Supply; provision.

Matter, as wise logicians say,
Cannot without a form subsist;
And form, say I, as well as they,
Must fail, if matter brings no *grist.* *Swift.*

3. GRIST *to Mill,* is profit; gain.

The computation of degrees, in all matrimonial causes, is wont to be made according to the rules of that law, because it brings *grist to* the *mill.* *Ayliffe's Parergon.*

GRI'STLE. *n. s.* [ᵹristle, Saxon.] A cartilage; a part of the body next in hardness to a bone.

No living creatures, that have shells very hard, as oysters, crabs, lobsters, and especially the tortoise, have no bones within them, but only little *gristles.* *Bacon's Nat. History.*

Lest the asperity or hardness of these cartilages should hurt the oesophagus or gullet, which is tender and of a skinny substance, or hinder the swallowing of our meat, therefore these annulary *gristles* are not made round, or intire circles; but where the gullet touches the windpipe, there, to fill up the circle, is only a soft membrane, which may easily give way to the dilatation of the gullet. *Ray on the Creation.*

GRI'STLY. *adj.* [from *gristle.*] Cartilaginous; made of gristle.

At last they spit out pieces of their lungs; it may be small *gristly* bits, that are eaten off from the lung-pipes. *Harvey.*

She has made the back-bone of several vertebræ, as being more fit to bend, more tough, and less in danger of breaking, than if they were all one intire bone without these *gristly* junctures. *More's Antidote against Atheism.*

Fins are made of *gristly* spokes, or rays connected by membranes; so that they may be contracted or extended like womens fans. *Ray on the Creation.*

They have a louder and stronger note than other birds of the same bigness, which have only a *gristly* windpipe. *Grew.*

Each pipe, distinguish'd by its *gristly* rings,
To cherish life aerial pasture brings. *Blackmore's Creation.*

GRIT. *n. s.* [ᵹrytta, ᵹreot, Saxon.]

1. The coarse part of meal.
2. Oats husked, or coarsely ground.
3. Sand; rough hard particles.

Silesian bole, crackling a little betwixt the teeth, yet without the least particle of *grit,* feels as smooth as Castile soap. *Grew's Musæum.*

The sturdy pear-tree here
Will rise luxuriant, and with toughest root
Pierce the obstructing *grit* and restive marle. *Phillips.*

4. *Grits* are fossils found in minute masses, forming together a kind of powder; the several particles of which are of no determinate shape, but seem the rudely broken fragments of larger masses; not to be dissolved or disunited by water, but retaining their figure, and not cohering into a mass. They are opake, and in many species fermenting with acids, and often fouled with heterogene matters. One sort is a fine, dull looking, grey *grit,* which, if wetted with salt-water into mortar or paste, dries almost immediately, and coalesces into a hard stony mass, such as is not easily afterwards disunited by water. This is the *pulvis puteolanus* of the ancients, mixed among their cements used in buildings sunk into the sea; and in France and Italy an ingredient in their harder plaisters, under the name of pozzolane. It is common on the sides of hills in Italy. Another species, which is a coarse, beautifully green, dull *grit,* is the *chrysocolla* of the ancients, which they used in soldering gold, long supposed a lost fossil. It serves the purpose of soldering metals better than borax, and may be had for carriage from the shores of New England. The ferrugineous black glittering *grit,* is the black shining sand employed to throw over writing, found on the shores of Italy. What is commonly used in London is from Genoa. The coarse, glittering, brownish black is nearly of the same nature, but inferior, in all respects. *Hill on Fossils.*

GRI'TTINESS. *n. s.* [from *gritty.*] Sandiness; the quality of abounding in grit.

In fullers-earth he could find no sand by the microscope, nor any *grittiness.* *Mortimer's Husbandry.*

GRI'TTY. *adj.* [from *grit.*] Full of hard particles; consisting of grit.

I could not discern the unevenness of the surface of the powder, nor the little shadows let fall from the *gritty* particles thereof. *Newton's Opt.*

GRI'ZELIN. *adj.* [More properly *gridelin.* See GRIDELIN.]

The Burgundy, which is a *grizelin* or pale red, of all others, is surest to ripen in our climate. *Temple.*

GRI'ZZLE. *n. s.* [from *gris,* gray; *grisaille,* French.] A mixture of white and black; gray.

O thou dissembling cub! what wilt thou be,
When time hath sow'd a *grizzle* on thy face? *Shakespeare.*

GRI'ZZLED. *adj.* [from *grizzle.*] Interspersed with gray.

To the boy Cæsar, send this *grizzled* head. *Shakespeare.*

His beard was *grizzled:* no.
—It was as I have seen it in his life. *Shakesp. Hamlet.*

His hair just *grizzled,*
As in a green old age. *Dryden and Lee's Oedipus.*

Those *grizzled* locks, which nature did provide
In plenteous growth, their asses ears to hide. *Dryd. Juven.*

GRI'ZZLY. *adj.* [from *gris,* gray, French.] Somewhat gray.

Living creatures generally do change their hair with age, turning to be gray and white; as is seen in men, though some earlier, some later; in horses that are dappled, and turn white; and in old squirrels, that turn *grizzly.* *Bacon's Nat. History.*

To GROAN. *v. n.* [ᵹranan, Saxon; *gronen,* Dutch.] To breathe with a hoarse noise, as in pain or agony.

Many an heir
Of these fair edifices, for my wars,
Have I heard *groan* and drop. *Shakespeare's Coriolanus.*

Men *groan* from out of the city, and the soul of the wounded crieth out. *Job.* xxiv. 12.

Repenting and *groaning* for anguish of spirit. *Wisd.* v. 3.

So shall the world go on,
To good malignant, to bad men benign,
Under her own weight *groaning.* *Milton's Paradise Lost.*

Nothing can so peculiarly gratify the noble dispositions of humanity, as for one man to see another so much himself as to sigh his griefs and *groan* his pains. *South.*

On the blazing pile his parent lay,
Or a lov'd brother *groan'd* his life away. *Pope's Odyssey.*

GROAN. *n. s.* [from the verb.]

1. Breath expired with noise and difficulty.

Alas poor country,
Where sighs and *groans,* and shrieks that rend the air,
Are made, not mark'd! *Shakespeare's Macbeth.*

I led to slaughter, and to slaughter leave;
And ev'n from hence their dying *groans* receive. *Dryden.*

2. Any hoarse dead sound.

Such sheets of fire, such bursts of horrid thunder,
Such *groans* of roaring wind and rain, I never
Remember to have heard. *Shakespeare's King Lear.*

GRO'ANFUL. *adj.* [*groan* and *full.*] Sad; agonizing.

Adown he kest it with so puissant wrest,
That back again it did aloft rebound,
And gave against his mother earth a *groanful* sound. *F. Qu.*

GROAT. *n. s.* [*groot,* Dutch; *grosso,* Italian.]

1. A piece valued at four pence.
2. A proverbial name for a small sum.

My mother was wont
To call them woollen vassals, things created
To buy and sell with *groats.* *Shakespeare's Coriolanus.*

I dare lay a *groat,*
A tertian ague is at least your lot. *Dryden's Fables.*

Imagine a person of quality prevailed on to marry a woman much his inferior, and without a *groat* to her fortune. *Swift.*

3. GROATS. Oats that have the hulls taken off. *Ainsworth.*

GRO'CER. *n. s.* [This should be written *grosser,* from *gross,* a large quantity; a *grocer* originally being one who dealt by wholesale; or from *grossus,* a fig, which their present state seems to favour.]

A *grocer* is a man who buys and sells tea, sugar and plumbs and spices for gain. *Watts's Logick.*

But still the offspring of your brain shall prove
The *grocer*'s care, and brave the rage of Jove. *Garth.*

GRO'CERY. *n. s.* [from *grocer.*] Grocers ware, such as tea, sugar; raisins; spice.

His troops, being now in a country where they were not expected, met with many cart-loads of wine, *grocery,* and tobacco. *Clarendon, b.* viii.

GRO'GERAM. } GRO'GRAM. } GRO'GRAN. } *n. s.* [*gros grain*, French; *grossogranus*, low Latin. *Ainsworth.*] Stuff woven with large woof and a rough pile.

Certes they're neatly cloth'd: I of this mind am,
Your only wearing is your *grogeram*. *Donne.*

Natolia affords great store of chamelots and *grograms*. *Sandys.*

Some men will say this habit of John's was neither of camel's skin nor any coarse texture of its hair, but rather some finer weave of camelot, *grogram*, or the like. *Brown's Vul. Err.*

The natural sweetness and innocence of her behaviour shot me through and through, and did more execution upon me in *grogram* than the greatest beauty in town had ever done in brocade. *Addison's Spectator.*

Plain goody would no longer down;
'Twas madam in her *grogram* gown. *Swift.*

GROIN. *n. s.* [Of uncertain derivation.] The part next the thigh.

The fatal dart arrives,
And through the border of his buckler drives;
Pass'd through and pierc'd his *groin*; the deadly wound
Cast from his chariot, roll'd him on the ground. *Dryden.*

GRO'MWELL. *n. s.* [*lithospermum*, Latin.] Gromill or graymill. A plant.

The cup of the flower consists of one leaf, cut into five long narrow segments: the flower, which is, for the most part, small, consists of one leaf, is funnel-shaped, and open at the top: the pointal is incompassed by four embryo's, which become so many roundish hard polished seeds. *Miller.*

GROOM. *n. s.* [*grom*, Dutch.]

1. A boy; a waiter; a servant.

Then called she a *groom*, that forth him led
Into a goodly lodge. *Fairy Queen, b.* i.

From Egypt's king ambassadours they come;
Them many a squire attends, and many a *groom*. *Fairfax.*

Think then, my soul! that death is but a *groom*
Which brings a taper to the outward room. *Donne.*

In the time of Edward VI. lived Sternhold, whom king Henry his father, a little before, had made *groom* of his chamber, for turning of certain of David's psalms into verse. *Peacham on Poetry.*

Would'st thou be touch'd
By the presuming hands of saucy *grooms*? *Dryd. Don Sebast.*

Amid' the fold he rages, nor the sheep
Their shepherds, nor the *grooms* their bulls can keep. *Dryd.*

2. A young man.

I presume for to intreat this *groom*,
And silly maid, from danger to redeem. *Fairfax, b.* ii.

3. A man newly married.

By this the brides are wak'd, their *grooms* are dress'd;
All Rhodes is summon'd to the nuptial feast. *Dryden.*

GROOVE. *n. s.* [from *grave.*]

1. A deep cavern, or hollow in mines.

He might, to avoid idleness, work in a *groove* or mine-pit thereabouts, which at that time was little esteemed. *Boyle.*

2. A channel or hollow cut with a tool.

The screw-plate is a kind of steel well tempered, with several holes in it, each less than other; and in those holes are threads grooved inwards, into which *grooves* fit the respective taps that belong to them. *Moxon's Mech. Exer.*

To GROOVE. *v. a.* [from the noun.] To cut hollow.

The plates of iron fastened at the bottom of the box preserved the balance while it fell, and every joint of it was well *grooved*. *Gulliver's Travels.*

To GROPE. *v. n.* [ᵹꞃapan, Saxon.] To feel where one cannot see.

My sea-gown scarf about me, in the dark
Grop'd I, to find out them. *Shakespeare's Hamlet.*

We *grope* for the wall like the blind, and we *grope* as if we had no eyes. *Is.* lix. 10.

They meet with darkness in the clearest light;
And *grope* at noon, as if involv'd with night. *Sandys.*

A boy was *groping* for eels, and laid his hand upon a snake. *L'Estrange, Fable* 131.

This, no doubt, is better for men than that they should in the dark *grope* after knowledge; as St. Paul tells us all nations did after God. *Locke.*

He heard us in our course,
And with his out-stretch'd arms around him *grop'd*. *Addison.*

O truth divine! enlighten'd by thy ray,
I *grope* and guess no more, but see my way. *Arbuthnot.*

To GROPE. *v. a.* To search by feeling in the dark; to feel without being able to see.

How vigilant to *grope* mens thoughts, and to pick out somewhat whereof they might complain. *Hayward.*

They have left our endeavours to *grope* them out by twilight, and by darkness almost to discover that, whose existence is evidenced by light. *Brown's Vulgar Errours.*

But Strephon, cautious, never meant
The bottom of the pan to *grope*. *Swift.*

GRO'PER. *n. s.* [from *grope.*] One that searches in the dark.

GROSS. *adj.* [*gros*, French; *grosso*, Italian; *crassus*, Latin.]

1. Thick; bulky.

The crows and choughs, that wing the midway air,
Shew scarce so *gross* as beetles. *Shakesp. King Lear.*

There are two *gross* volumes concerning the power of popes. *Baker on Learning.*

2. Shameful; unseemly.

He ripely considered how *gross* a thing it were for men of his quality, wise and grave men, to live with such a multitude, and to be tenants at will under them. *Hooker, Preface.*

They can say that in doctrine, in discipline, in prayers, and in sacraments, the church of Rome hath very foul and *gross* corruptions. *Hooker, b.* iv.

So far hath the natural understanding, even of sundry whole nations, been darkened, that they have not discerned, no, not *gross* iniquity to be sin. *Hooker, b.* i.

3. Intellectually coarse; palpable; impure; unrefined.

To all sense 'tis *gross*
You love my son: invention is asham'd,
Against the proclamation of thy passion,
To say thou do'st not. *Shakesp. All's well that ends well.*

Examples *gross* as earth exhort me. *Shakesp. Hamlet.*

Like *gross* terms,
The prince will in the perfectness of time
Cast off his followers. *Shakesp. Henry* VI. *p.* ii.

Belial came last, than whom a spirit more lewd
Fell not from heaven, or more *gross* to love
Vice for itself. *Milton's Paradise Lost, b.* i.

Is not religion so perfectly good in itself, above all, in its Author, that, without the *grossest* sensuality, we cannot but admire it. *Spratt's Sermons.*

It is a *gross* mistake of some men, to think that our wants only and imperfections do naturally induce us to be beneficent. *Smalridge's Sermons.*

4. Inelegant; disproportionate in bulk.

The sun's oppressive ray the roseat bloom
Of beauty blasting, gives the gloomy hue,
And feature *gross*. *Thomson's Summer.*

5. Thick; not refined; not pure.

It is manifest, that when the eye standeth in the finer medium, and the object is in the *grosser*, things shew greater; but contrariwise, when the eye is placed in the *grosser* medium, and the object in the finer. *Bacon's Natural History.*

Of elements,
The *grosser* feeds the purer; earth the sea,
Earth and the sea feed air. *Milton's Paradise Lost, b.* v.

Light fumes are merry, *grosser* fumes are sad;
Both are the reasonable soul run mad. *Dryden's Fables.*

Or suck the mists in *grosser* air below,
Or dip their pinions in the painted bow. *Pope.*

6. Stupid; dull.

If she doth then the subtile sense excel,
How *gross* are they that drown her in the blood? *Davies.*

And in clear dream and solemn vision,
Tell her of things that no *gross* ear can hear. *Milton.*

Some men give more light and knowledge by the bare stating of the question with perspicuity and justness, than others by talking of it in *gross* confusion for whole hours together. *Watts.*

7. Coarse; rough; opposite to delicate.

Fine and delicate sculptures are helped with nearness, and *gross* with distance. *Wotton's Architecture.*

8. Thick; fat; bulky.

GROSS. *n. s.* [from the adjective.]

1. The main body; the main force.

The Belgians hop'd, that with disorder'd haste
The deep-cut keels upon the sands might run;
Or, if with caution leisurely were past,
Their numerous *gross* might charge us one by one. *Dryden.*

Several casuists are of opinion, that, in a battle, you should discharge upon the *gross* of the enemy, without levelling your piece at any particular person. *Addison's Freeholder.*

The *gross* of the people can have no other prospect in changes and revolutions than of publick blessings. *Addison.*

2. The bulk; the whole not divided into its several parts.

Certain general inducements are used to make saleable your cause in *gross*. *Hooker, Preface.*

There was an opinion in *gross*, that the soul was immortal. *Abbot's Description of the World.*

Remember, son,
You are a general: other wars require you;
For see the Saxon *gross* begins to move. *Dryden's K. Arthur.*

Notwithstanding the decay and loss of sundry trades and manufactures, yet, in the *gross*, we ship off now one third part more of the manufactures, as also lead and tin, than we did twenty years past. *Child's Discourse on Trade.*

3. Not individual, but a body together.

He hath ribbons of all the colours i' th' rainbow; they come to him by the *gross*. *Shakespeare's Winter's Tale.*

I cannot instantly raise up the *gross*
Of full three thousand ducats. *Shakes. Merchant of Venice.*

You see the united design of many persons to make up one figure: after they have separated themselves in many petty divisions, they rejoin one by one into a *gross*. *Dryden.*

4. The chief part; the main mass.

Comets, out of question, have likewise power and effect over the *gross* and mass of things. *Bacon, Essay* 24.

The articulate sounds are more confused, though the *gross* of the sound be greater. *Bacon's Natural History.*

5. The number of twelve dozen. [*Grosse*, French.]

It is made up only of that simple idea of an unite repeated; and repetitions of this kind, joined together, make those distinct simple modes of a dozen, a *gross*, and a million. *Locke.*

GRO'SSLY. *adv.* [from *gross.*]

1. Bulkily; in bulky parts; coarsely: as, *this matter is* grossly *pulverized.*

2. Without subtilty; without art; without delicacy; without refinement; coarsely; palpably.

Such kind of ceremonies as have been so *grossly* and shamefully abused in the church of Rome, where they remain, are scandalous. *Hooker, b.* iv. *s.* 12.

Treason and murder ever kept together,
As two yoke devils sworn to others purpose;
Working so *grossly* in a natural cause,
That admiration did not whoop at them. *Shakesp. Hen.* V.

And thine eyes
See it so *grossly* shown in thy behaviour,
That in their kind they speak it. *Shakespeare.*

What! are we cuckolds ere we have deserv'd it?
—Speak not so *grossly.* *Shakesp. Merchant of Venice.*

What I have said has been forced from me, by seeing a noble sort of poetry so happily restored by one man, and so *grossly* copied by almost all the rest. *Dryden.*

If at any time I speak of light and rays as coloured, or endued with colours, I would be understood to speak not philosophically and properly, but *grossly*, and according to such conceptions as vulgar people, in seeing all these experiments, would be apt to frame. *Newton's Opt.*

While it is so difficult to learn the springs and motives of some facts, it is no wonder they should be so *grossly* misrepresented to the publick by curious inquisitive heads. *Swift.*

GRO'SSNESS. *n. s.* [from *gross.*]

1. Coarseness; not subtilty; thickness; greatness of parts.

The purpose is perspicuous even as substance,
Whose *grossness* little characters sum up. *Shakespeare.*

And I will purge that mortal *grossness* so,
That thou shalt like an airy spirit go. *Shakespeare.*

The cause of the epilepsy from the stomach is the *grossness* of the vapours which rise and enter into the cells of the brain. *Bacon's Natural History*, N°. 966.

Then all this earthy *grossness* quit;
Attir'd with stars we shall for ever sit,
Triumphing over death. *Milton.*

So this being the first colour which vapours begin to reflect, it ought to be the colour of the finest and most transparent skies, in which vapours are not arrived to that *grossness* requisite to reflect other colours. *Newton's Opt.*

For envy'd wit, like Sol eclips'd, was known
Th' opposing body's *grossness*, not its own. *Pope.*

2. Inelegant fatness; unwieldy corpulence.

Wise men, that be over-fat and fleshy, go to sojourn abroad at the temperate diet of some sober man; and so, by little and little, eat away the *grossness* that is in them. *Ascham.*

3. Want of refinement; want of delicacy; intellectual coarseness.

I was three or four times in the thought they were not fairies; and yet the guiltiness of my mind drove the *grossness* of the foppery into a received belief that they were fairies. *Shak.*

Whatever beauties it may want, 'tis free at least from the *grossness* of those faults I mentioned. *Dryden.*

What a *grossness* is there in the mind of that man, who thinks to reach a lady's heart by wounding her ears! *Clarissa.*

GROT. *n. s.* [*grotte*, French; *grotta*, Italian.] A cave; a cavern for coolness and pleasure.

In the remotest wood and lonely *grot*,
Certain to meet that worst of evils, thought. *Prior.*

Awful see the Egerian *grot.* *Pope.*

GROTE'SQUE. *adj.* [*grotesque*, French; *grottesco*, Italian.] Distorted of figure; unnatural; wildly formed.

The champaign head
Of a steep wilderness, whose hairy sides
With thicket overgrown, *grotesque* and wild,
Access deny'd. *Milton's Paradise Lost, b.* iv.

There is yet a lower sort of poetry and painting, which is out of nature; for a farce is that in poetry which *grotesque* is in a picture: the persons and actions of a farce are all unnatural, and the manners false, that is, inconsisting with the characters of mankind: *grotesque* painting is the just resemblance of this. *Dryden's Dufresnoy.*

An hideous figure of their foes they drew,
Nor lines, nor looks, nor shades, nor colours true,
And this *grotesque* design expos'd to publick view. *Dryden.*

Palladian walls, Venetian doors,
Grotesco roofs, and stucco floors. *Pope's Sat. of Horace.*

GRO'TTO. *n. s.* [*grotte*, French; *grotta*, Italian.] A cavern or cave made for coolness. It is not used properly of a dark horrid cavern.

Their careless chiefs to the cool *grotto's* run,
The bow'rs of kings, to shade them from the sun. *Dryden.*

This was found at the entry of the *grotto* in the Peak. *Woodward on Fossils.*

GROVE. *n. s.* [from *grave*] A walk covered by trees meeting above.

I look'd toward Birnam, and anon methought
The wood began to move:
Within this three mile may you see it coming;
I say, a moving *grove.* *Shakespeare's Macbeth.*

Fortunate fields, and *groves*, and flow'ry vales;
Thrice happy isles! *Milton.*

She left the flow'ry field, and waving *grove.* *Blackmore.*

Banish'd from courts and love,
Abandon'd truth seeks shelter in the *grove.* *Granville.*

Can fierce passions vex his breast,
While every gale is peace, and every *grove*
Is melody? *Thomson's Spring.*

To GRO'VEL. *v. n.* [*grufde*, Islandick, flat on the face. It may perhaps come by gradual corruption from *ground feel.*]

1. To lie prone; to creep low on the ground.

The steel-head passage wrought,
And through his shoulder pierc'd; wherewith to ground
He *groveling* fell, all gored in his gushing wound. *Fa. Qu.*

What see'st thou there? king Henry's diadem,
Inchas'd with all the honours of the world!
If so, gaze on, and *grovel* on thy face,
Until thy head be circled with the same. *Shakes. Hen.* IV.

Now they lie
Groveling and prostrate on yon lake of fire. *Milt. Par. Lost.*

Upon thy belly *groveling* thou shalt go. *Milt. Par. Lost.*

Let us then conclude that all painters ought to require this part of excellence: not to do it, is to want courage, and not dare to shew themselves: 'tis to creep and *grovel* on the ground. *Dryden's Dufresnoy.*

2. To be mean; to be without dignity or elevation.

I must disclaim whate'er he can express;
His *groveling* sense will show my passion less. *Dryden.*

Several thoughts may be natural which are low and *groveling.* *Addison's Spectator.*

GROUND. *n. s.* [ᵹꞃunꝺ, Saxon; *grondt*, Danish.]

1. The earth, considered as solid, or as low.

Israel shall go on dry *ground* through the sea. *Ex.* xiv. 16.

From the other hill
To their fix'd station, all in bright array,
The cherubim descended, on the *ground*
Gliding meteorous. *Milt. Par. Lost.*

2. The earth as distinguished from air or water.

I have made man and beast upon the *ground.* *Jer.* xxvii. 5.

There was dew upon all the *ground.* *Judg.* vi. 40.

It light on him as dew falleth on the *ground.* 2 *Sa.* xvii. 12.

Too late young Turnus the delusion found;
Far on the sea, still making from the *ground.* *Dryden's Æn.*

3. Land; country.

The water breaks its bounds,
And overflows the level *grounds.* *Hudibras.*

4. Region; territory.

With these came they, who from the bord'ring flood
Of old Euphrates to the brook that parts
Egypt from Syrian *ground*, had general names
Of Baalim and Ashtaroth. *Milton's Paradise Lost, b.* i.

5. Farm; estate; possession.

Uneasy still within these narrow bounds,
Thy next design is on thy neighbours *grounds*:
His crop invites, to full perfection grown;
Thy own seems thin, because it is thy own. *Dryd. Juven.*

6. The floor or level of the place.

Wherefore should I smite thee to the *ground*? 2 *Sa.* ii. 22.

Dagon was fallen on his face to the *ground.* 1 *Sa.* v. 4.

A multitude sit on the *ground.* *Ma.* xv. 35.

7. Dregs; lees; fæces; that which settles at the bottom of liquors.

Set by them cyder, verjuice, four drink, or *grounds.* *Mort.*

Some insist upon having had particular success in stopping gangrenes, from the use of the *grounds* of strong beer, mixed up with bread or oatmeal. *Sharp's Surgery.*

8. The first stratum of paint upon which the figures are afterwards painted.

We see the limner to begin with a rude draught, and the painter to lay his *grounds* with shadows and darksome colours. *Hakewill on Providence.*

When solid bodies, sensible to the feeling and dark, are placed on light and transparent *grounds*, as, for example, the heavens, the clouds and waters, and every other thing which is in motion, and void of different objects; they ought to be more rough, and more distinguishable, than that with which they are encompassed. *Dryden's Dufresnoy.*

9. The fundamental substance; that by which the additional or accidental parts are supported.

Indeed

Indeed it was but just that the finest lines in nature should be drawn upon the most durable *ground*. *Pope.*

10. The plain song; the tune on which descants are raised.

Get a prayer-book in your hand,
And stand between two churchmen, good my lord;
For on that *ground* I'll build a holy descant. *Shakes. R. III.*

11. First hint; first traces of an invention; that which gives occasion to the rest.

Though jealousy of state th' invention found,
Yet love refin'd upon the former *ground*;
That way the tyrant had reserv'd to fly,
Pursuing hate, now serv'd to bring two lovers nigh. *Dryden.*

12. The first principles of knowledge.

The concords will easily be known, if the fore *grounds* be thoroughly beaten in. *Preface to Accidence.*

Here statesmen, or of them they which can read,
May of their occupation find the *grounds*. *Donne.*

After evening repasts, 'till bed-time, their thoughts will be best taken up in the easy *grounds* of religion, and the story of scripture. *Milton on Education.*

13. The fundamental cause; the true reason; original principle.

He desired the steward to tell him particularly the *ground* and event of this accident. *Sidney.*

Making happiness the *ground* of his unhappiness, and good news the argument of his sorrow. *Sidney, b.* ii.

The use and benefit of good laws all that live under them may enjoy with delight and comfort, albeit the *grounds* and first original causes from whence they have sprung be unknown. *Hooker, b.* i. *s.* 1.

Thou could'st not have discern'd
Fraud in the serpent, speaking as he spake,
No *ground* of enmity between us known. *Mi't. Par. Lost.*

Nor did either of them ever think fit to make any particular relation of the *grounds* of their proceedings, or the causes of their misadventures. *Clarendon, b.* viii.

Sound judgment is the *ground* of writing well. *Roscomm.*

Love once given from her, and plac'd in you,
Would leave no *ground* I ever would be true. *Dryden.*

If it be natural, ought we not to conclude that there is some *ground* and reason for these fears, and that nature hath not planted them in us to no purpose. *Tillotson.*

Upon that prince's death, although the *grounds* of our quarrel with France had received no manner of addition, yet this lord thought fit to alter his sentiments. *Swift.*

The miraculous increase of the professors of Christianity was without any visible *grounds* and causes, and contrary to all human probability and appearance. *Atterbury's Sermons.*

14. The field or place of action.

Here was thy end decreed, when these men rose;
And ev'n with theirs this act thy death did bring,
Or hasten'd at the least upon this *ground*. *Daniel's C. War.*

15. The space occupied by an army as they fight, advance, or retire.

At length the left wing of the Arcadians began to lose *ground*. *Sidney.*

Heartless they fought, and quitted soon their *ground*,
While our's with easy victory were crown'd. *Dryd. Aureng.*

He has lost *ground* at the latter end of the day, by pursuing his point too far, like the prince of Conde at the battle of Senepa. *Dryden's Fables, Preface.*

16. The intervening space between the flyer and pursuer.

Ev'ning mist,
Ris'n from a river, o'er the marish glides,
And gathers *ground* fast at the labourer's heels,
Homeward returning. *Milton's Paradise Lost, b.* xii.

Superiors think it a detraction from their merit to see another get *ground* upon them, and overtake them in the pursuits of glory. *Addison's Spectator.*

Even whilst we speak our conqueror comes on,
And gathers *ground* upon us every moment. *Addison.*

17. The state in which one is with respect to opponents or competitors.

Had'st thou sway'd as kings should do,
Giving no *ground* unto the house of York,
They never then had sprung. *Shakespeare's Henry* VI.
If they get *ground* and 'vantage of the king,
Then join you with them like a rib of steel,
To make them stronger. *Shakespeare's Henry* IV. *p.* ii.

He will stand his *ground* against all the attacks that can be made upon his probity. *Atterbury's Sermons.*

Whatever *ground* we may have gotten upon our enemies, we have gotten none upon our vices, the worst enemies of the two; but are even subdued and led captive by the one, while we triumph so gloriously over the others. *Atterbury's Sermons.*

18. State of progress or recession.

I have known so many great examples of this cure, and heard of its being so familiar in Austria, that I wonder it has gained no more *ground* in other places. *Temple.*

The squirrel is perpetually turning the wheel in her cage: she runs apace, and wearies herself with her continual motion, and gets no *ground*. *Dryden's Dufresnoy.*

19. The foil to set a thing off.

Like bright metal on a sullen *ground*,
My reformation glittering o'er my fault,
Shall shew more goodly, and attract more eyes,
Than that which hath no foil to set it off. *Shakespeare.*

To GROUND. *v. a.* [from the noun.]

1. To fix on the ground.

Wherever she had *grounded* her foot, neither gods nor men could force her to retire. *Rambler.*

2. To found as upon cause or principle.

Wisdom *groundeth* her laws upon an infallible rule of comparison. *Hooker, b.* i. *s.* 8.

It may serve us to *ground* conjectures more approaching to the truth than we have hitherto met with. *Boyle.*

If your own actions on your will you *ground*,
Mine shall hereafter know no other bound. *Dryd. Aurengz.*

Some eminent spirit, having signalized his valour, becomes to have influence on the people, to grow their leader in warlike expeditions; and this is *grounded* upon the principles of nature and common reason, which, where prudence and courage are required, rather incite us to fly to a single person than a multitude. *Swift.*

3. To settle in first principles or rudiments of knowledge.

Being rooted and *grounded* in love. *Eph.* iii. 17.

GROUND. The preterite and part. pass. of *grind.*

He took the calf which they had made, and burnt it in the fire, and *ground* it to powder. *Exo.* xxxii. 20.

How dull and rugged, ere 'tis *ground*
And polish'd, looks a diamond? *Hudibras, p.* iii.

GROUND is much used in composition for that which is next the ground, or near the ground.

GRO'UND-ASH. *n. s.* A saplin of ash taken from the ground; not a branch cut from a tree.

A lance of tough *groundash* the Trojan threw,
Rough in the rind, and knotted as it grew. *Dryden's Æn.*

Some cut the young ashes off about an inch above the ground, which causes them to make very large straight shoots, which they call *groundash*. *Mortimer's Husbandry.*

GRO'UND-BAIT. *n. s.* [from *ground* and *bait.*] A bait made of barley or malt boiled; which, being thrown into the place where you design to angle, sinks to the bottom, and draws the fish to it.

Take the depth of the place where you mean after to cast your *groundbait*, and to fish. *Walton's Angler.*

GRO'UND-FLOOR. *n. s.* [*ground* and *floor.*] The lower story of a house.

GRO'UND-IVY. *n. s.* [*hedera terrestris*, Latin.] Alehoof, or tunhoof.

The shoots trail upon the ground, and emit roots from almost every joint, which fasten themselves into the earth: the leaves are roundish, thick, rough, and crenated on the edges: the helmet of the flower is roundish, bifid, and reflexed: the beard or lower lip is trifid, or cut into three segments; the middle segment is broad and bifid, and the flowers are produced at the joints of the shoots. The species are, first, common groundivy, or gill-go-by-ground; and second, lesser groundivy. *Miller.*

Alehoof or *groundivy* is, in my opinion, of the most excellent use and virtue of any plants among us. *Temple.*

GRO'UND-OAK. *n. s.* [*ground* and *oak.*]

If the planting of oaks were more in use for underwoods, it would spoil the coopers trade for the making of hoops, either of hasel or ash; because one hoop made of the young shoots of a *groundoak*, would outlast six of the best ash. *Mort.*

GRO'UND-PINE. *n. s.* [*chamæpitys*, Latin.]

The leaves are narrow and trifid; the flower labiated: the place of the crest of the flower is supplied with little teeth: the lower lip is divided into three parts, the middle segment being split again into two parts. The flowers rarely grow in whorles, but one or two are produced at the wings of the leaves. *Miller.*

The whole plant has a very singular smell, resembling that of resin; whence its name *groundpine.* It grows on dry and barren hills, and in some places on the ditch-banks by roadsides. It is highly extolled, by the generality of medical writers, as an aperient, cephalick, and nervous medicine; but it is however little used at present. *Hill's Mat. Med.*

GRO'UND-PLATE. *n. s.* [In architecture.] The outermost pieces of timber lying on or near the ground, and framed into one another with mortises and tennons. In these also are mortises made to receive the tennons of the joists, the summer and girders; and sometimes the trimmers for the stair-case and chimney way, and the binding joist. *Harris.*

In the orthographical schemes there should be a true delineation, if it be a timber-building, of the several sizes of the *groundplates*, breast-summers, and beams. *Mortimer's Husb.*

GRO'UND-PLOT. *n. s.*

1. The ground on which any building is placed.

Wretched Gynecia, where can'st thou find any small *groundplot* for hope to dwell upon? *Sidney.*

2. The ichnography of a building.

GROUND-RENT. *n. s.* Rent paid for the privilege of building on another man's ground.

A foot

A foot in front, and thirty-three five ſevenths deep, would bring in a *ground-rent* of five pounds. *Arbuthnot on Coins.*

GROUND-ROOM. *n. ſ.* A room on the level with the ground.

I beſeeched him hereafter to meditate in a *ground-room*; for that otherwiſe it would be impoſſible for an artiſt of any other kind to live near him. *Tatler*, N°. 88.

GRO'UNDEDLY. *adv.* [from *grounded.*] Upon firm principles.

He hath given the firſt hint of ſpeaking *groundedly*, and to the purpoſe, upon this ſubject. *Glanville.*

GRO'UNDLESS. *n. ſ.* [from *ground.*] Void of reaſon; without ground.

But when vain doubt and *groundleſs* fear
Do that dear fooliſh boſom tear. *Prior.*

We have great reaſon to look upon the high pretenſions which the Roman church makes to miracles as *groundleſs*, and to reject her vain and fabulous accounts of them. *Atterbury.*

The party who diſtinguiſh themſelves by their zeal for the preſent eſtabliſhment, ſhould be careful to diſcover ſuch a reverence for religion, as may ſhew how *groundleſs* that reproach is which is caſt upon them, of being averſe to our national worſhip. *Freeholder*, N°. 129.

GRO'UNDLESSLY. *adv.* [from *groundleſs.*] Without reaſon; without cauſe; without juſt reaſon.

Divers perſons have produced the like by ſpirit of vitriol, or juice of lemons; but have *groundleſsly* aſcribed the effect to ſome peculiar quality of thoſe two liquors. *Boyle on Colours.*

GRO'UNDLESSNESS. *n. ſ.* [from *groundleſs.*] Want of juſt reaſon.

He durſt not cite the words either of my book or ſermons, leſt the reader ſhould have diſcovered the notorious falſhood and *groundleſſneſs* of his calumny. *Tillotſon, Sermon* I.

GRO'UNDLING. *n. ſ.* [from *ground.*] A fiſh which keeps at the bottom of the water: hence one of the low vulgar. *Hanm.*

It offends me to the ſoul, to hear a robuſteous perriwigpated fellow tear a paſſion to tatters, to very rags, to ſplit the ears of the *groundlings*. *Shakeſpeare's Hamlet.*

GRO'UNDLY. *adv.* [from *ground.*] Upon principles; ſolidly; not ſuperficially.

A man, *groundly* learned already, may take much profit himſelf, in uſing by epitome to draw other mens works, for his own memory ſake, into ſhorter room. *Aſcham's Schoolm.*

GRO'UNDSEL. *n. ſ.* [ꝗꞃunꝺ and ꞅyle, the baſis, Sax. perhaps from *ſella*, Latin.] The timber or raiſed pavement next the ground.

The window-frame hath every one of its lights rabbetted on its outſide about half an inch into the frame; and all theſe rabbets, but that on the *groundſel*, are grooved ſquare; but the rabbets on the *groundſel* is levelled downwards, that rain or ſnow may the freelier fall off. *Moxon's Mech. Exer.*

GRO'UNDSEL. *n. ſ.* [*ſenecio*, Latin.]

It hath a floſculous flower, conſiſting of many florets, divided into ſeveral ſegments ſitting on the embryo, contained in an empalement conſiſting of one leaf, and divided into many parts, afterwards becoming of a conical figure: the embryo afterward becomes a ſeed, furniſhed with down; at which time the empalement is reflexed, to make way for the ſeeds to eſcape. *Miller.*

GRO'UNDWORK. *n. ſ.* [*ground* and *work.*]

1. The ground; the firſt ſtratum; the firſt part of the whole; that to which the reſt is additional.

A way there is in heav'n's expanded plain,
Which, when the ſkies are clear, is ſeen below,
And mortals by the name of milky know;
The *groundwork* is of ſtars. *Dryden's Fables.*

2. The firſt part of an undertaking; the fundamentals.

The main ſkill and *groundwork* will be to temper them ſuch lectures and explanations, upon every opportunity, as may lead and draw them in willing obedience. *Milton.*

3. Firſt principle; original reaſon.

The *groundwork* thereof is neverthelefs true and certain, however they through ignorance diſguiſe the ſame, or through vanity. *Spenſer's State of Ireland.*

The morals is the firſt buſineſs of the poet, as being the *groundwork* of his inſtruction. *Dryden.*

GROUP. *n. ſ.* [*grouppe*, French; *groppo*, Italian.] A croud; a cluſter; a huddle; a number thronged together.

In a picture, beſides the principal figures which compoſe it, and are placed in the midſt of it, there are leſs *groups* or knots of figures diſpoſed at proper diſtances, which are parts of the piece, and ſeem to carry on the ſame deſign in a more inferior manner. *Dryden's Dufreſnoy.*

I cannot doubt but the poet had here in view the picture of Zetus, in the famous *group* of figures which repreſents the two brothers binding Dirce to the horns of a mad bull. *Addiſ.*

You ſhould try your graving tools
On this odious *group* of fools. *Swift.*

To GROUP. *v. a.* [*groupper*, French.] To put into a croud; To huddle together.

The difficulty lies in drawing and diſpoſing, or, as the painters term it, in *grouping* ſuch a multitude of different objects, preſerving ſtill the juſtice and conformity of ſtyle and colouring. *Prior.*

GROUSE. *n. ſ.* A kind of fowl; a heathcock.

The 'ſquires in ſcorn will fly the houſe
For better game, and look for *grouſe*. *Swift.*

GROUT. *n. ſ.* [ꝗꞃuꞇ, Saxon. In Scotland they call it *groats.*]

1. Coarſe meal; pollard.

King Hardicnute, 'midſt Danes and Saxons ſtout,
Carous'd in nut-brown ale, and din'd on *grout*:
Which diſh its priſtine honour ſtill retains,
And when each prince is crown'd in ſplendour reigns. *King.*

2. That which purges off.

Sweet honey ſome condenſe, ſome purge the *grout*;
The reſt, in cells apart, the liquid nectar ſhout. *Dryden.*

3. A kind of wild apple. [*Agriomelum*, Latin.]

To GROW. *v. n.* preter. *grew*; part. paſſ. *grown.* [ꝗꞃopan, Saxon; *groeyen*, Dutch.]

1. To vegetate; to have vegetable motion; to increaſe by vegetation.

It is not the *growing* of fruit that nouriſheth man; but it is thy word which preſerveth them. *Wiſd.* xvi. 26.

He cauſeth the graſs to *grow* for the cattle, and herb for the ſervice of man. *Pſ.* civ. 14.

2. To be produced by vegetation.

Ye ſhall eat this year ſuch things as *grow* of themſelves. 2 *Kings* xix. 29.

In this country *groweth* abundance of that wood, which ſince is brought into Europe to die red colours. *Abbot.*

A bag, that *groweth* in the fields, at the firſt is hard like a tennis-ball, and white; and after growth of a muſhroom-colour, and full of light duſt. *Bacon's Natural Hiſtory.*

But ſay, where *grows* the tree? from hence how far?
Milton's Paradiſe Loſt, b ix.

In colder regions men compoſe
Poiſon with art; but here it *grows*. *Waller.*

Thoſe tow'rs of oak o'er fertile plains might go,
And viſit mountains where they once did *grow*. *Waller.*

3. To ſhoot in any particular form.

Children, like tender oſiers, take the bow;
And as they firſt are faſhion'd, always *grow*. *Dryden's Juv.*

4. To increaſe in ſtature.

I long with all my heart to ſee the prince;
I hope he is much *grown* ſince laſt I ſaw him. *Shakeſ. R.* III.

The poor man had nothing, ſave one little ew-lamb, which he had bought and reared up; and it *grew* up together with him and with his children. 2 *Sa.* xii. 3.

Thine own things, and ſuch as are *grown* up with thee, can'ſt thou not know. 2 *Eſdr.* iv. 10.

5. To come to manhood from infancy.

Now the prince *groweth* up faſt to be a man, and is of a ſweet and excellent diſpoſition. *Bacon's Advice to Villiers.*

The main thing to be conſidered, in every action of a child, is how it will become him when he is bigger, and whither it will lead him when he is *grown* up. *Locke.*

We are brought into the world children, ignorant and impotent; and we *grow* up in vanity and folly. *Wake.*

6. To iſſue, as plants from a ſoil, or as branches from the main trunk.

They will ſeem not ſtuck into him, but *growing* out of him. *Dryden's Æn. Dedication.*

7. To increaſe in bulk; to become greater, or more numerous.

Bones, after full growth, continue at a ſtay: as for nails, they *grow* continually. *Bacon's Natural Hiſtory.*

Then their numbers ſwell,
And *grow* upon us. *Denham.*

Diviſions *grow* upon us, by neglect of practick duties: as every age degenerated from primitive piety, they advanced in nice enquiries. *Decay of Piety.*

8. To improve; to make progreſs.

Grow in grace, and in the knowledge of our Lord and Saviour Jeſus Chriſt. 2 *Pet.* iii. 18.

As he *grew* forward in years he was trained up to learning, under one Pronapides, who taught the Pelaſgick letter invented by Linus. *Pope's Eſſay on Homer.*

9. To advance to any ſtate.

Nature, as it *grows* again towards earth,
Is faſhion'd for the journey dull and heavy. *Shakeſpeare.*

They doubted whereunto this would *grow*. *Acts* v. 24.

The king, by this time, was *grown* to ſuch an height of reputation for cunning and policy, that every accident and event that went well was laid and imputed to his foreſight. *Bacon.*

But when to ripen'd manhood he ſhall *grow*,
The greedy ſailor ſhall the ſeas forego. *Dryden's Virgil.*

Verſe, or the other harmony of proſe, I have ſo long ſtudied and practiſed, that they are *grown* into a habit, and become familiar to me. *Dryden's Fables, Preface.*

10. To come by degrees; to reach any ſtate gradually.

After they *grew* to reſt upon number, rather competent than vaſt, they *grew* to advantages of place, cunning diverſions, and the like; and they *grew* more ſkilful in the ordering of their battles. *Bacon's Eſſays.*

The treſpaſſes of people are *grown* up to heaven, and their ſins are got beyond all reſtraints of law and authority. *Rogers.*

11. To come forward; to gather ground.

Some ſeeing the end of their government nigh, and troublous practice *growing* up, which may work trouble to the next governour, will not attempt redreſs. *Spenſer on Ireland.*

It was now the beginning of October, and Winter began to *grow* faſt on: great rain, with terrible thunder and lightning, and mighty tempeſts, then fell abundantly. *Knolles.*

12. To be changed from one ſtate to another; to become either better or worſe; to turn.

A good man's fortune may *grow* out at heels. *Shakeſp.*

Hence, hence, and to ſome barbarous climate fly,
Which only brutes in human form does yield,
And man *grows* wild in nature's common field. *Dryden.*

The nymph *grew* pale, and in a mortal fright,
Spent with the labour of ſo long a flight. *Dryden.*

Patient of command
In time he *grew*; and *growing* us'd to hand,
He waited at his maſter's board for food. *Dryden's Æn.*

We may trade and be buſy, and *grow* poor by it, unleſs we regulate our expences. *Locke.*

You will *grow* a thing contemptible, unleſs you can ſupply the loſs of beauty with more durable qualities. *Swift.*

Delos, by being reckoned a ſacred place, *grew* to be a free port, where nations warring traded, as in a neutral country. *Arbuthnot on Coins.*

13. To proceed as from a cauſe.

What will *grow* out of ſuch errours, as maſked under the cloak of divine authority, impoſſible it is that ever the wit of man ſhould imagine, 'till time have brought forth the fruits of them. *Hooker.*

Shall we ſet light by that cuſtom of reading, from whence ſo precious a benefit hath *grown*? *Hooker, b.* v.

Take heed now that ye fail not to do this: why ſhould damage *grow* to the hurt of the king. *Ez.* iv. 22.

Scipio Naſica feared leſt, if the dread of that enemy were taken away, the Romans would *grow* either to idleneſs or civil diſſention. *Abbot.*

The want of trade in Ireland proceeds from the want of people; and this is not *grown* from any ill qualities of the climate or air, but chiefly from ſo many wars. *Temple.*

14. To accrue; to be forthcoming.

Ev'n juſt the ſum that I do owe to you,
Is *growing* to me by Antipholis. *Shakeſp. Com. of Errours.*

15. To adhere; to ſtick together.

Honour and policy, like unſever'd friends,
I' th' war do *grow* together. *Shakeſpeare's Coriolanus.*

The frog's mouth *grows* up, and he continues ſo for at leaſt ſix months without eating. *Walton's Angler.*

In burnings and ſcaldings the fingers would many times *grow* together: the chin would *grow* to the breaſt, and the arms to the ſides, were they not hindered. *Wiſeman's Surgery.*

16. To ſwell: a ſea term.

Mariners are uſed to the tumbling and rolling of ſhips from ſide to ſide, when the ſea is never ſo little *grown*. *Raleigh.*

GRO'WER. *n. ſ.* [from *grow.*] An increaſer.

It will grow to a great bigneſs, being the quickeſt *grower* of any kind of elm. *Mortimer's Husbandry.*

To GROWL. *v. n.* [*grollen*, Flemiſh.]

1. To ſnarl or murmur like an angry cur.

They roam amid' the fury of their heart,
And *growl* their horrid loves. *Thomſon's Spring.*

Dogs in this country are of the ſize of common maſtiffs, and by nature never bark, but *growl* when they are provoked. *Ellis's Voyage.*

2. To murmur; to grumble.

Othello, neighbours—how he would roar about a fooliſh handkerchief! and then he would *growl* ſo manfully. *Gay.*

GROWN. The participle paſſive of *grow.*

1. Advanced in growth.

2. Covered or filled by the growth of any thing.

I went by the field of the ſlothful, and by the vineyard of the man void of underſtanding; and lo, it was all *grown* over with thorns, and nettles had covered the face thereof. *Prov.*

3. Arrived at full growth or ſtature.

I ſaw lately a pair of China ſhoes, which I was told were for a *grown* woman, that would ſcarce have been big enough for one of our little girls. *Locke.*

GROWTH. *n. ſ.* [from *growth.*]

1. Vegetation; vegetable life; increaſe of vegetation.

Deep in the palace, of long *growth* there ſtood
A laurel's trunk, a venerable wood. *Dryden's Æn. b.* vii.

Thoſe trees that have the ſloweſt *growth*, are, for that reaſon, of the longeſt continuance. *Atterbury's Sermons.*

2. Product; thing produced.

Forbidding every bleak unkindly fog
To touch the proſperous *growth* of this tall wood. *Milton.*

Our little world, the image of the great,
Of her own *growth* hath all that nature craves,
And all that's rare, as tribute from the waves. *Waller.*

The trade of a country ariſes from the native *growths* of the ſoil or ſeas. *Temple.*

I had thought, for the honour of our nation, that this ſtory was of Engliſh *growth*, and Chaucer's own. *Dryden.*

3. Increaſe in number, bulk, or frequency.

What I have tried, or thought, or heard upon this ſubject, may go a great way in preventing the *growth* of this diſeaſe, where it is but new. *Temple.*

4. Increaſe of ſtature; advance to maturity.

They ſay my ſon of York
Has almoſt overta'en him in his *growth*. *Shakeſ. Rich.* III.

The ſtag, now conſcious of his fatal *growth*,
To ſome dark covert his retreat had made. *Denham.*

Though an animal arrives at its full *growth* at a certain age, perhaps it never comes to its full bulk 'till the laſt period of life. *Arbuthnot on Aliments.*

5. Improvement; advancement.

It grieved David's religious mind to conſider the *growth* of his own eſtate and dignity, the affairs of religion continuing ſtill in the former manner. *Hooker, b.* iv. *ſ.* 2.

GRO'WTHEAD. } *n. ſ.* [from *groſs* or *great head*; *capito*,
GRO'WTNOL. } Latin.]

1. A kind of fiſh. *Ainſworth.*

2. An idle lazy fellow.

Though ſleeping one hour refreſheth his ſong,
Yet truſt not Hob *growthead* for ſleeping too long. *Tuſſer.*

To GRUB. *v. a.* [*graban*, preter. *grôb*, to dig, Gothick.] To dig up; to deſtroy by digging; to root out of the ground; to eradicate by throwing up out of the ſoil.

A fooliſh heir cauſed all the buſhes and hedges about his vineyard to be *grubbed* up. *L'Eſtrange.*

Foreſt land,
From whence the ſurly ploughman *grubs* the wood. *Dryden.*

The *grubbing* up of woods and trees may be very needful, upon the account of their unthriftineſs. *Mortimer's Husband.*

As for the thick woods, which not only Virgil but Homer mentions, they are moſt of them *grubbed* up, ſince the promontory has been cultivated and inhabited. *Addiſon on Italy.*

GRUB. *n. ſ.* [from *grubbing*, or mining.]

1. A ſmall worm that eats holes in bodies.

There is a difference between a *grub* and a butterfly, and yet your butterfly was a *grub*. *Shakeſpeare's Coriolanus.*

New creatures riſe,
A moving maſs at firſt, and ſhort of thighs;
'Till ſhooting out with legs, and imp'd with wings,
The *grubs* proceed to bees with pointed ſtings. *Dryden.*

Sometimes they are eaten with *grubs*. *Mortimer's Huſband.*

The *grub*,
Oft unobſerv'd, invades the vital core;
Pernicious tenant! and her ſecret cave
Enlarges hourly, preying on the pulp
Ceaſeleſs. *Phillips.*

2. A ſhort thick man; a dwarf. In contempt.

John Romane, a ſhort clowniſh *grub*, would bear the whole carcaſe of an ox, yet never tugged with him. *Carew.*

To GRU'BBLE. *v. n.* [*grubelen*, German, from *grub.*] To feel in the dark.

Thou haſt a colour;
Now let me rowl and *grubble* thee:
Blind men ſay white feels ſmooth, and black feels rough:
Thou haſt a rugged ſkin; I do not like thee. *Dryden.*

GRU'BSTREET. *n. ſ.* Originally the name of a ſtreet in Moorfields in London, much inhabited by writers of ſmall hiſtories, dictionaries, and temporary poems; whence any mean production is called *grubſtreet.*

Χαῖρ' Ἰθακη μεθ' ἄεθλα, μεθ' ἄλγεα πικρὰ
Ἀσπασίως τέον ὖδας ἱκάνομαι.

The firſt part, though calculated only for the meridian of *grubſtreet*, was yet taken notice of by the better ſort. *Arbuthn.*

I'd ſooner ballads write, and *grubſtreet* lays. *Gay.*

To GRUDGE. *v. a.* [from *gruger*, according to *Skinner*, which in French is to grind or eat. In this ſenſe we ſay of one who reſents any thing ſecretly, *he chews it.* *Grwgnach*, in Welſh, is to murmur; to grumble. *Grunigh*, in Scotland, denotes a grumbling moroſe countenance.]

1. To envy; to ſee any advantage of another with diſcontent.

What means this baniſhing me from your counſels? Do you love your ſorrow ſo well, as to *grudge* me part of it? *Sidney.*

'Tis not in thee
To *grudge* my pleaſures, to cut off my train. *Shak. K. Lear.*

He ſtruggles into birth, and cries for aid;
Then helpleſs in his mother's lap is laid:
He creeps, he walks; and, iſſuing into man,
Grudges their life from whence his own began. *Dryden.*

Theſe clamours with diſdain he heard,
Much *grudg'd* the praiſe, but more the rob'd reward. *Dryd.*

Do not, as ſome men, run upon the tilt, and taſte of the ſediments of a *grudging* uncommunicative diſpoſition. *Spectat.*

Let us conſider the ample proviſion of waters, thoſe inexhauſted treaſures of the ocean; and though ſome have *grudged* the great ſhare that it takes of the ſurface of the earth, yet we ſhall propoſe this too, as a conſpicuous mark and character of the wiſdom of God. *Bentley's Sermons.*

I have often heard the Preſbyterians ſay they did not *grudge* us our employments. *Swift.*

2. To give or take unwillingly.

Let me at least a funeral marriage crave,
Nor *grudge* my cold embraces in the grave. *Dryd. Aurengz.*
You steer betwixt the country and the court,
Nor gratify whate'er the great desire,
Nor *grudging* give what publick needs require. *Dryd. Fab.*

They have *grudged* those contributions, which have set our country at the head of all the governments of Europe. *Addison.*

To GRUDGE. *v. n.*

1. To murmur; to repine.

They knew the force of that dreadful curse, whereunto idolatry maketh subject; nor is there cause why the guilty sustaining the same should *grudge* or complain of injustice. *Hook.*

2. To be unwilling; to be reluctant.

Many times they go with as great *grudging* to serve in his majesty's ships, as if it were to be slaves in the gallies. *Raleigh.*

3. To be envious.

Grudge not one against another, brethren, lest ye be condemned. *Ja.* v. 9.

4. To wish in secret. A low word.

E'en in the most sincere advice he gave,
He had a *grudging* still to be a knave. *Dryden's Medal.*

5. To give or have any uneasy remains. I know not whether the word in this sense be not rather *grugeons*, or remains; *grugeons* being the part of corn that remains after the fine meal has passed the sieve.

My Dolabella,
Hast thou not still some *grudgings* of thy fever? *Dryden.*

GRUDGE. *n. s.* [from the verb.]

1. Old quarrel; inveterate malevolence; sullen malice.

Many countries about her were full of wars, which, for old *grudges* to Corinth, were thought still would conclude there. *Sidney, b.* ii.

Two housholds, both alike in dignity,
From ancient *grudge* break to new mutiny,
Where civil blood makes civil hands unclean. *Shakespeare.*

Let me go in to see the generals:
There is some *grudge* between 'em; 'tis not meet
They be alone. *Shakespeare's Julius Cæsar.*

Deep-fester'd hate;
A *grudge* in both, time out of mind, begun,
And mutually bequeath'd from sire to son. *Tate's Juvenal.*

2. Anger; ill-will.

The god of wit, to shew his *grudge*,
Clapt ass's ears upon the judge. *Swift.*

3. Unwillingness to benefit.

4. Envy; odium; invidious censure.

Those to whom you have
With *grudge* preferr'd me. *Ben. Johnson's Catiline.*

4. Remorse of conscience. *Ainsworth.*

5. Some little commotion, or forerunner of a disease. *Ainsw.*

GRU'DGINGLY. *adj.* [from *grudge.*] Unwillingly; malignantly; reluctantly.

Like harpies they could scent a plenteous board;
Then to be sure they never fail'd their lord:
The rest was form, and bare attendance paid;
They drank and eat, and *grudgingly* obey'd. *Dryden.*

GRUEL. *n. s.* [*gruau, gruelle*, French.] Food made by boiling oatmeal in water; any kind of mixture made by boiling ingredients in water.

Finger of birth-strangl'd babe,
Ditch-deliver'd by a drab;
Make the *gruel* thick and slab. *Shakespeare's Macbeth.*

Was ever Tartar fierce or cruel
Upon the strength of water *gruel?* *Prior.*

Gruel made of grain, broths, malt-drink not much hopped, posset-drinks, and in general whatever relaxeth. *Arbuthnot.*

GRUFF. *adj.* [*groff*, Dutch] Sour of aspect; harsh of manners.

Around the fiend, in hideous order, sat
Foul bawling infamy and bold debate,
Gruff discontent, through ignorance misled. *Garth.*

The appellation of honour was such an one the *gruff*, such an one the stocky. *Addison.*

GRU'FFLY. *adv.* [from *gruff.*] Harshly; ruggedly; roughly.

The form of Mars high on a chariot stood,
All sheath'd in arms, and *gruffly* look'd the god. *Dryden.*

GRU'FFNESS. *n. s.* [from *gruff.*] Ruggedness of mien; harshness of look or voice.

GRUM. *adj.* [contracted from *grumble.*] Sour; surly; severe. A low word.

Nic looked sour and *grum*, and would not open his mouth. *Arbuthnot's History of John Bull.*

To GRU'MBLE. *v. n.* [*grommelen, grommen*, Dutch.]

1. To murmur with discontent.

A bridegroom,
A *grumbling* groom, and that the girl shall find. *Shakesp.*

Thou *grumblest* and railest every hour on Achilles, and thou art as full of envy at his greatness as Cerberus is at Proserpina's beauty. *Shakespeare's Troilus and Cressida.*

Th' accurst Philistian stands on th' other side,
Grumbling aloud, and smiles 'twixt rage and pride. *Cowley.*

Suitors, all but one, will depart *grumbling*, because they miss of what they think their due. *South's Sermons.*

Providence has allotted man a competency: all beyond it is superfluous; and there will be *grumbling* without end, if we reckon that we want this, because we have it not. *L'Estr.*

L'Avare, not using half his store,
Still *grumbles* that he has no more. *Prior.*

2. To growl; to gnarl.

The lion, though he sees the toils are set,
Yet, pinch'd with raging hunger, scours away;
Hunts in the face of danger all the day;
At night, with sullen pleasure, *grumbles* o'er his prey. *Dryd.*

3. To make a hoarse rattle.

Thou *grumbling* thunder join thy voice. *Motteux.*

Like a storm
That gathers black upon the frowning sky,
And *grumbles* in the wind. *Rowe's Royal Convert.*

Vapours foul
Dash on the mountains brow, and shake the woods
That *grumbling* wave below. *Thomson's Winter.*

GRU'MBLER. *n. s.* [from *grumble.*] One that grumbles; a murmurer; a discontented man.

The half-pence are good half-pence, and I will stand by it: if I made them of silver, it would be the same thing to the *grumbler*. *Swift.*

GRU'MBLING. *n. s.* [from *grumble.*] A murmuring through discontent; a grudge.

I have serv'd
Without or grudge or *grumblings*. *Shakesp. Tempest.*

GRUME. *n. s.* [*grumeau*, French; *grumus*, Latin.] A thick viscid consistence of a fluid: as the white of an egg, or clotted like cold blood. *Quincy.*

GRU'MLY. *adv.* [from *grum.*] Sullenly; morosely.

GRU'MMEL. *n. s.* [*lithospermum*, Lat] An herb. *Ainsworth.*

GRU'MOUS. *adj.* [from *grume.*] Thick; clotted.

The blood, when let, was black, *grumous*, the red part without a due consistence, the serum saline, and of a yellowish green. *Arbuthnot on Diet.*

GRU'MOUSNESS. *n. s.* [from *grumous.*] Thickness of a coagulated liquor.

The cause may be referred either to the coagulation of the serum, or *grumousness* of the blood. *Wiseman's Surgery.*

GRU'NSEL. *n. s.* [More usually *groundsil*, unless *Milton* intended to preserve the Saxon ʒrunꝺ.] The groundsil; the lower part of the building.

Next came one
Who mourn'd in earnest, when the captive ark
Maim'd his brute image, head and hands lopp'd off
In his own temple, on the *grunsel* edge,
Where he fell flat, and sham'd his worshippers. *Milton.*

To GRUNT. } *v. n.* [*grunnio*, Latin.] To murmur like
To GRU'NTLE. } a hog.

And neigh, and bark, and *grunt*, and roar and burn,
Like horse, hound, hog, bear, fire, at every turn. *Shakesp.*

Lament, ye swine! in *gruntings* spend your grief;
For you, like me, have lost your sole relief. *Gay's Past.*

Thy brinded boars may slumber undismay'd,
Or *grunt* secure beneath the chesnut shade. *Tickel.*

The scolding quean to louder notes doth rise,
To her full pipes the *grunting* hog replies;
The *grunting* hogs alarm the neighbours round. *Swift.*

GRUNT. *n. s.* [from the verb.] The noise of a hog.

Ran cow and calf, and family of hogs,
In panick horrour of pursuing dogs;
With many a deadly *grunt* and doleful squeak,
Poor swine, as if their pretty hearts would break. *Dryden.*

From hence were heard
The *grunts* of bristled boars, and groans of bears,
And herds of howling wolves. *Dryden's Æn.*

GRU'NTER. *n. s.* [from *grunt.*]

1. He that grunts.

2. A kind of fish. [χρομὶς.] *Ainsworth.*

GRU'NTLING. *n. s.* [from *grunt.*] A young hog.

To GRUTCH. *v. n.* [corrupted for the sake of rhyme from *grudge.*] To envy; to repine; to be discontented.

The poor at the enclosure doth *grutch*,
Because of abuses that fall,
Lest some men should have but too much,
And some again nothing at all. *Tusser's Husbandry.*

But what we're born for we must bear,
Our frail condition it is such,
That what to all may happen here,
If't chance to me, I must not *grutch*. *Ben. Johnson.*

GRUTCH. *n. s.* [from the verb.] Malice; ill-will.

In it he melted leaden bullets,
To shoot at foes, and sometimes pullets;
To whom he bore so fell a *grutch*,
He ne'er gave quarter t' any such. *Hudibras, p.* i.

GRY. *n. s.* [γρῦ.] Any thing of little value: as, the paring of the nails. *Dict.*

GUAIA'CUM. *n. s.* [See LIGNUM-VITÆ.]

Guaiacum is attenuant and aperient, and promotes discharges by sweat and urine. It is an excellent medicine in many chronick cases, and was once famous for curing the venereal

venereal disease, which it still does singly in warmer climates, but with us we find it insufficient. We have a resin of it, improperly called gum *guaiacum*, given in the same cases with the famous balsamum polycrestum is made of it. *Hill.*

GUARANTE'E. *n. s.* [*guarant*, French.] A power who undertakes to see stipulations performed.

God, the great *guarantee* for the peace of mankind, where laws cannot secure it, may think it the concern of his providence. *South's Sermons.*

A prince distinguished by being a patron of Protestants, and *guarantee* of the Westphalian treaty. *Addison on the War.*

To GUA'RANTY. *v. a.* [*garantir*, French.] To undertake to secure the performance of any articles.

To GUARD. *v. a.* [*garder*, French, from our word *ward*, the *w* being changed by the French into *g*; as *Galles* for *Wales*.]

1. To watch by way of defence and security.

2. To protect; to defend.

Naked the graces *guarded* you from all
Dangers abroad, and now your thunder shall. *Waller.*
Your pow'r you never use, but for defence,
To *guard* your own or others innocence. *Dryden.*
Fix'd on defence, the Trojans are not slow
To *guard* their shore from an expected foe. *Dryden.*

The port of Genoa is very ill *guarded* against the storms. *Addison on Italy.*

3. To preserve by caution.

One would take care to *guard* one's self against this particular imperfection, because it is that which our nature very strongly inclines us to. *Addison's Spectator.*

4. To provide against objections.

Homer has *guarded* every circumstance with as much caution as if he had been aware of the objection. *Notes on Odyssey.*

5. To adorn with lists, laces, or ornamental borders.

Give him a livery
More *guarded* than his fellows. *Shakesp. Merch. of Venice.*
See a fellow
In a long motley, *guarded* with yellow. *Shak. Henry* VIII.

To GUARD. *v. n.* To be in a state of caution or defence.

There are other nice cases, in which a man must *guard*, if he intends to keep fair with the world, and turn the penny. *Collier on Popularity.*

To *guard* against such mistakes, it is necessary to acquaint ourselves a little with words. *Watts's Logick.*

GUARD. *n. s.* [*garde*, French; *ward*, Teutonick.]

1. A man, or body of men, whose business is to watch by way of defence or prevention.

The *guard* bare them, and brought them back into the guard-chamber. 1 *Kings* xiv. 28.

Up into heav'n, from paradise, in haste
Th' angelick *guards* ascended, mute, and sad,
For man. *Milton's Paradise Lost, b.* x.
With lifted hands, and gazing eyes,
His *guards* behold him soaring through the skies. *Dryden.*

Others are cooped in close by the strict *guards* of those whose interest it is to keep them ignorant. *Locke.*

He must be trusted to his own conduct, since there cannot always be a *guard* upon him, except what you put into his own mind by good principles. *Locke.*

They, usurping arbitrary power, had their *guards* and spies, after the practice of tyrants. *Swift.*

2. A state of caution; a state of vigilance.

The great alteration which he made in the state ecclesiastical, caused him to stand upon his *guard* at home. *Davies.*

Temerity puts a man off his *guard.* *L'Estrange.*

It is wisdom to keep ourselves upon a *guard.* *L'Estrange.*

Now he stood collected and prepar'd;
For malice and revenge had put him on his *guard. Dryden.*

Men are always upon their *guard* against an appearance of design. *Smalridge's Sermons.*

3. Limitation; anticipation of objection; caution of expression.

They have expressed themselves with as few *guards* and restrictions as I. *Atterbury.*

4. An ornamental hem, lace, or border.

5. Part of the hilt of a sword.

GUA'RDAGE. *n. s.* [from *guard.*] State of wardship.

A maid so tender, fair and happy,
Run from her *guardage* to the sooty bosom
Of such a thing as thou. *Shakespeare's Othello.*

GU'ARDER. *n. s.* One who guards. *Ainsworth.*

GUA'RDIAN. *n. s.* [*gardien*, French, from *guard.*]

1. One that has the care of an orphan; one who is to supply the want of parents.

I am sorry for her, as I have just cause, being her uncle and her *guardian.* *Shakesp. Much Ado about Nothing.*

When perjur'd *guardians*, proud with impious gains,
Choak up the streets, too narrow for their trains! *Dryden.*

Hocus, with two other of the *guardians*, thought it their duty to take care of the interest of the three girls. *Arbuthnot.*

2. One to whom the care and preservation of any thing is committed.

I gave you all,
Made you my *guardians*, my depositaries;
But kept a reservation to be follow'd
With such a number. *Shakes. King Lear.*

3. A repository or storehouse. Not used.

Where is Duncan's body?
——Carried to Colmeskill,
The sacred storehouse of his predecessors,
And *guardian* of their bones. *Shakesp. Macbeth.*

GUARDIAN *of the Spiritualties.* He to whom the spiritual jurisdiction of any diocese is committed, during the vacancy of the see. He may be either guardian in law, or *jure magistratus*, as the archbishop is of any diocese within his province; or guardian by delegation, as he whom the archbishop or vicar-general doth for the time depute. *Cowel.*

GUA'RDIAN. *adj.* Performing the office of a kind protector or superintendant.

My charming patroness protects me unseen, like my *guardian* angel; and shuns my gratitude like a fairy, who is bountiful by stealth, and conceals the giver, when she bestows the gift. *Dryden's Dedication to Cleomenes.*

Thus shall mankind his *guardian* care engage,
The promis'd father of the future age. *Pope's Messiah.*
Mean while Minerva, in her *guardian* care,
Shoots from the starry vaults through fields of air. *Pope.*

GUA'RDIANSHIP. *n. s.* [from *guardian.*] The office of a guardian.

The curate stretched his patent for the cure of souls, to a kind of tutelary *guardianship* over goods and chattels. *L'Estr.*

Theseus is the first who established the popular state in Athens, assigning to himself the *guardianship* of the laws, and chief commands in war. *Swift.*

GUA'RDLESS. *adj.* [from *guard.*] Without defence.

So on the *guardless* herd, their keeper slain,
Rushes a tyger in the Lybian plain. *Waller.*

A rich land, *guardless* and undefended, must needs have been a double incitement. *South's Sermons.*

GUA'RDSHIP. *n. s.* [from *guard.*]

1. Care; protection.

How bless'd am I, by such a man led!
Under whose wise and careful *guardship*
I now despise fatigue and hardship. *Swift.*

2. [*Guard* and *ship.*] A king's ship to guard the coast.

GUA'IAVA. } *n. s.*
GUA'VA. }

The flowers consist of five leaves, produced in a circular order, having many stamina or threads surrounding the ovary: the ovary is of a long tubulous figure, which becomes a fleshy fruit, crowned on the top, and containing many small hard seeds. The fruit, says Sir Hans Sloane, is extremely delicious and wholsome. They have only this inconvenience, that, being very astringent, they stop up the belly, if taken in great quantities. *Miller.*

GUBERNA'TION. *n. s.* [*gubernatio*, Lat.] Government; superintendency; superiour direction.

Perhaps there is little or nothing in the government of the kingdoms of nature and grace, but what is transacted by the man Jesus, inhabited by the divine power and wisdom, and employed as a medium or conscious instrument of this extensive *gubernation.* *Watts's Improvement of the Mind.*

GU'DGEON. *n. s.* [*goujon*, French.]

1. A small fish found in brooks and rivers, easily caught, and therefore made a proverbial name for a man easily cheated.

'Tis true, no turbets dignify my boards;
But *gudgeons*, flounders, what my Thames affords. *Pope.*

This he did to draw you in, like so many *gudgeons*, to swallow his false arguments. *Swift.*

2. Something to be caught to a man's own disadvantage; a bait; an allurement: *gudgeons* being commonly used as baits for pike.

But fish not with this melancholy bait,
For this fool's *gudgeon*, this opinion. *Shakes. Merch. of Ven.*

GUE'RDON. *n. s.* [*guerdon*, *gardon*, French.] A reward; a recompense. A word now no longer in use.

He hearken'd, and did stay from further harms,
To gain so goodly *guerdon* as she spake. *Fairy Queen, b.* i.
But to the virgin comes, who all this while
Amazed stands herself so mock'd to see,
By him who has the *guerdon* of his guile,
For so misfeigning her true knight to be. *Fairy Queen, b.* i.

He shall, by thy revenging hand, at once receive the just *guerdon* of all his former villanies. *Knolles.*

Fame is the spur that the clear spirit doth raise
To scorn delights, and live laborious days;
But the fair *guerdon* when we hope to find,
And think to burst out into sudden blaze,
Comes the blind fury with th' abhorred shears,
And slits the thin-spun life. *Milton.*

To GUESS. *v. a.* [*ghissen*, Dutch.]

1. To conjecture; to judge without any certain principles of judgment.

Incapable and shallow innocents!
You cannot *guess* who caus'd your father's death. *Shakesp.*
Let not your ears despise my tongue for ever,
Which shall possess them with the heaviest sound

That ever yet they heard.
—Hum! I *guess* at it. *Shakes. Macbeth.*

He that, by reason of his swift motions, can inform himself of all places and preparations, should he not very often *guess* rightly of things to come, where God pleaseth not to give impediment? *Raleigh's History of the World.*

There issue swarming bands
Of ambush'd men, whom, by their arms and dress,
To be Taxcallan enemies I *guess*. *Dryd. Indian Emperor.*

The same author ventures to *guess* at the particular fate which would attend the Roman government. *Swift.*

Nor can imagination *guess*,
How that ungrateful charming maid
My purest passion has betray'd. *Swift.*

2. To conjecture rightly.

One may *guess* by Plato's writings, that his meaning, as to the inferiour deities, was, that they who would have them might, and they who would not, might let them alone; but that himself had a right opinion concerning the true God. *Stillingfleet's Defence of Disc. on Rom. Idol.*

To Guess. *v. a.* To hit upon by accident; to determine rightly of any thing without certain direction of the judgment.

If Xerxes was able to call every common soldier by his name in his army, it may be *guessed* he got not this wonderful ability by learning his lessons by heart *Locke.*

Guess. *n. s.* [from the verb.] Conjecture; judgment without any positive or certain grounds.

The enemy's in view; draw up your powers:
Hard is the *guess* of their true strength and forces. *Shakesp.*

A poet must confess
His art's like physick, but a happy *guess*. *Dryden.*

It is a wrong way of proceeding to venture a greater good for a less, upon uncertain *guesses*, before a due examination. *Locke.*

We may make some *guess* at the distinction of things, into those that are according to, above, and contrary to reason. *Locke.*

This problem yet, this offspring of a *guess*,
Let us for once a child of truth confess. *Prior.*

Gue'sser. *n. s.* [from *guess*.] Conjecturer; one who judges without certain knowledge.

It is the opinion of divers good *guessers*, that the last fit will not be more violent than advantageous. *Pope.*

If fortune should please but to take such a crochet,
To thee I apply, great Smedley's successor,
To give thee lawn-sleeves, a mitre and rochet,
Whom would'st thou resemble? I leave thee a *guesser*. *Swift.*

Gue'ssingly. *adv.* [from *guessing*.] Conjecturally; uncertainly.

What confed'racy have you with the traytors
Late footed in the kingdom?
——I have a letter *guessingly* set down,
Which came from one that's of a neutral heart,
And not from one oppos'd. *Shakes. King Lear.*

GUEST. *n. s.* [ᵹerꞇ, ᵹyꞅꞇ, Saxon; *gwest*, Welsh.]

1. One entertained in the house of another.

They all murmured, saying, that he was gone to be *guest* with a man that is a sinner. *Lu.* xix. 7.

Methinks a father
Is, at the nuptial of his son, a *guest*
That best becomes the table. *Shakesp. Winter's Tale.*

Tell my royal *guest*
I add to his commands my own request. *Dryden's Æn.*

2. A stranger; one who comes newly to reside.

O desarts, desarts! how fit a *guest* am I for you, since my heart can people you with wild ravenous beasts, which in you are wanting. *Sidney.*

Those happiest smiles
That play'd on her ripe lip, seem'd not to know
What *guests* were in her eyes; which parted thence
As pearls from diamonds dropt. *Shakespeare.*

Gue'stchamber. *n. s.* [*guest* and *chamber*.] Chamber of entertainment.

Where is the *guestchamber*, where I shall eat the passover with my disciples? *Mar.* xiv. 14.

To Guggle. *v. n.* [*gorgoliare*, Italian.] To sound as water running with intermissions out of a narrow mouthed vessel.

Gui'dage. *n. s.* [from *guide*.] The reward given to a guide. *Ainsworth.*

Gui'dance. *n. s.* [from *guide*.] Direction; government.

As to those who lived under the *guidance* of reason alone, without the assistance of supernatural light, it is highly probable that miracles, or a message from the dead, would persuade them. *Atterbury's Sermons.*

Particular application must be left to Christian prudence, under the *guidance* of God's holy spirit, who knows our necessity before we ask, and our ignorance in asking. *Rogers.*

A prince ought not to be under the *guidance* or influence of either faction, because he declines from his office of presiding over the whole to be the head of a party. *Swift.*

To GUIDE. *v. a.* [*guider*, French.]

1. To direct in a way.

When the spirit of truth is come, he will *guide* you into all truth. *Jo.* xvi. 13.

The new light served to *guide* them to their neighbours coffers. *Decay of Piety.*

Whosoever has a faithful friend to *guide* him in the dark passages of life, may carry his eyes in another man's head, and yet see never the worse. *South's Sermons.*

2. To govern by counsel; to instruct.

For thy name's sake lead me and *guide* me. *Ps.* xxxi. 3.

3. To regulate; to superintend.

Women neglect that which St. Paul assigns them as their proper business, the *guiding* of the house. *Decay of Piety.*

Guide. *n. s.* [*guide*, French, from the verb.]

1. One who directs another in his way.

Judas was *guide* to them that took Jesus. *Acts* i. 16.

Thou gavest them a burning pillar of fire, to be a *guide* of the unknown journey. *Wisd.* xviii. 3.

Can knowledge have no bound, but must advance
So far to make us wish for ignorance?
And rather in the dark to grope our way,
Than led by a false *guide* to err by day? *Denham.*

2. One who directs another in his conduct.

While yet but young his father dy'd,
And left him to an happy *guide*. *Waller.*

3. Director; regulator.

Who the *guide* of nature, but only the God of nature? In him we live, move and are. Those things which nature is said to do, are by divine art performed, using nature as an instrument: nor is there any such art or knowledge divine in nature herself working, but in the *guide* of nature's work. *Hooker, b.* i. *s.* 3.

Some truths are not by reason to be tried,
But we have sure experience for our *guide*. *Dryden's Fables.*

Gui'deless. *adj.* [from *guide*.] Without a guide; without a governour or superintendant.

Th' ambitious Swede, like restless billows tost,
Though in his life he blood and ruin breath'd,
To his now *guideless* kingdom peace bequeath'd. *Dryden.*

There fierce winds o'er dusky valleys blow,
Whose every puff bears empty shades away,
Which *guideless* in those dark dominions stray. *Dryden.*

Gui'der. *n. s.* [from *guide*.] Director; regulator; guide.

Our *guider* come! to the Roman camp conduct us. *Shak.*

That person, that being provoked by excessive pain, thrust his dagger into his body, and thereby, instead of reaching his vitals, opened an imposthume, the unknown cause of all his pain, and so stabbed himself into perfect health and ease, surely had great reason to acknowledge chance for his chirurgeon, and providence for the *guider* of his hand. *South.*

GUI'DON. *n. s.* [French.] A standardbearer; a standard. Obsolete.

GUILD. *n. s.* [ᵹılꝺꞅcıp, Saxon, a fellowship, a corporation.] A society; a corporation; a fraternity or company, combined together by orders and laws made among themselves by their prince's licence. Hence the common word *gild* or *guildhall* proceeds, being a fraternity or commonalty of men gathered into one combination, supporting their common charge by mutual contribution. *Cowel.*

Towards three or four o'clock
Look for the news that the *guild* hall affords. *Shak. R.* III.

In woollen cloth it appears, by those ancient *guilds* that were settled in England for this manufacture, that this kingdom greatly flourished in that art. *Hale's Origin of Mankind.*

As when the long-ear'd milky mothers wait
At some sick miser's triple-bolted gate,
For their defrauded absent foals they make
A moan so loud, that all the *guild* awake. *Pope's Dunciad.*

GUILE. *n. s.* [*guille*, *gille*, old French, the same with *wile*.] Deceitful cunning; insidious artifice; mischievous subtilty.

With fawning words he courted her awhile,
And looking lovely, and oft sighing sore,
Her constant heart did court with divers *guile*;
But words and looks, and sighs she did abhor. *Fairy Queen.*

When I have most need to employ a friend,
Deep, hollow, treacherous, and full of *guile*,
Be he to me! This do I beg of heav'n,
When I am cold in zeal to you or yours. *Shak. Rich.* III.

We may, with more successful hope, resolve
To wage by force or *guile* eternal war. *Milt. Parad. Lost.*

Nor thou his malice and false *guile* contemn:
Subtile he needs must be who could seduce
Angels. *Milton's Paradise Lost, b.* ix.

Gui'leful. *adj.* [*guile* and *full*.]

1. Wily; insidious; mischievously artful.

The way not to be inveigled by them that are so *guileful* through skill, is throughly to be instructed in that which maketh skilful against guile. *Hooker, b.* iii. *s.* 8.

Without expence at all,
By *guileful* fair words, peace may be obtain'd. *Shak. H.* VI.

He ſaw his *guileful* act
By Eve, though all unweeting, ſeconded
Upon her huſband. *Milton's Paradiſe Loſt, b.* x.

The *guileful* phantom now forſook the ſhrowd,
And flew ſublime, and vaniſh'd in a cloud. *Dryden's Æn.*

2. Treacherous; ſecretly miſchievous.

I train'd thy brethren to that *guileful* hole,
Where the dead corps of Baſſianus lay. *Shakeſp. Tit. Andr.*

GUI'LEFULLY. *adv.* [from *guileful.*] Inſidiouſly; treacherouſly.

To whom the tempter *guilefully* reply'd. *Milton's P. Loſt.*

GUI'LEFULNESS. *n. ſ.* [from *guileful.*] Secret treachery; tricking cunning.

GUI'LELESS. *adj.* [from *guile.*] Without deceit; without inſidiouſneſs; ſimply honeſt.

GUI'LER. *n. ſ.* [from *guile.* See BEGUILE.] One that betrays into danger by inſidious practices.

But he was wary wiſe in all his way,
And well perceived his deceitful ſleight;
Ne ſuffered luſt his ſafety to betray;
So goodly did beguile the *guiler* of the prey. *Fairy Queen.*

GUILT. *n. ſ.* [ᵹılꞇ, Saxon, originally ſignified the fine or mulct paid for an offence, and afterward the offence itſelf.]

1. The ſtate of a man juſtly charged with a crime; the contrary to innocence.

It was neither *guilt* of crime, nor reaſon of ſtate, that could quench the envy that was upon the king for this execution. *Bacon's Henry* VII.

When theſe two are taken away, the poſſibility of *guilt*, and the poſſibility of innocence, what reſtraint can the belief of the creed lay upon any man? *Hammond on Fundamentals.*

2. A crime; an offence.

Cloſe pent up *guilts*
Rive your concealing continents, and aſk
Theſe dreadful ſummoners grace. *Shakeſ. King Lear.*

GUI'LTILY. *adv.* [from *guilty.*] Without innocence; without clearneſs of conſcience.

Bloody and guilty, *guiltily* awake,
And in a bloody battle end thy days:
Think on lord Haſtings, and deſpair and die. *Shak. R.* III.

GUI'LTINESS. *n. ſ.* [from *guilty.*] The ſtate of being guilty; wickedneſs; conſciouſneſs of crime.

He thought his flight rather to proceed of a fearful *guiltineſs* than of an humble faithfulneſs. *Sidney, b.* ii.

The laſt was I that felt thy tyranny:
O, in the battle think on Buckingham,
And die in terrour of thy *guiltineſs*. *Shakeſp. Richard* III.

I ſhould be guiltier than my *guiltineſs*. *Shakeſpeare.*

GUI'LTLESS. *adj.* [from *guilt.*] Innocent; free from crime.

I am in this commanded to deliver
The noble duke of Clarence to your hands:
I will not reaſon what is meant hereby,
Becauſe I will be *guiltleſs* of the meaning. *Shakeſp. R.* III.

Many worthy and chaſte dames thus,
All *guiltleſs*, meet reproach. *Shakeſpeare's Othello.*

Then ſhall the man be *guiltleſs* from iniquity, and this woman ſhall bear her iniquity. *Num.* v. 31.

Thou, who do'ſt all thou wiſheſt at thy will,
And never willeſt aught but what is right,
Preſerve this *guiltleſs* blood they ſeek to ſpill;
Thine be my kingdom. *Fairfax.*

Guiltleſs of greatneſs, thus he always pray'd,
Nor knew nor wiſh'd he, that thoſe vows he made
On his own head ſhould be at laſt repaid. *Dryden.*

Thou know'ſt how *guiltleſs* firſt I met thy flame,
When love approach'd me under friendſhip's name. *Pope.*

GUI'LTLESSLY. *adv.* [from *guiltleſs.*] Without guilt; innocently.

GUI'LTLESSNESS. *n. ſ.* [from *guiltleſs.*] Innocence; freedom from crime.

A good number, truſting to their number more than to their value, and valuing money higher than equity, felt that *guiltleſſneſs* is not always with eaſe oppreſſed. *Sidney, b.* ii.

I would not have had any hand in his death, of whoſe *guiltleſſneſs* I was better aſſured than any man living could be. *King Charles.*

GUI'LTY. *adj.* [ᵹılꞇıᵹ, Saxon, one condemned to pay a fine for an offence.]

1. Juſtly chargeable with a crime; not innocent.

Is there not a ballad of the king and the beggar?
—The world was *guilty* of ſuch a ballad ſome three ages ſince. *Shakeſpeare's Love's Labour Loſt.*

Mark'd you not
How that the *guilty* kindred of the queen
Look'd pale, when they did hear of Clarence' death? *Shak.*

We are verily *guilty* concerning our brother, in that we ſaw the anguiſh of his ſoul when he beſought us, and we would not hear. *Gen.* xlii. 21.

With mortal hatred I purſu'd his life,
Nor he, nor you, were *guilty* of the ſtrife;
Nor I, but as I lov'd; yet all combin'd,
Your beauty and my impotence of mind. *Dryden.*

Farewel the ſtones
And threſhold, *guilty* of my midnight moans. *Dryden.*

There is no man, that is knowingly wicked, but is *guilty* to himſelf; and there is no man, that carries guilt about him, but he receives a ſting into his ſoul. *Tillotſon's Sermons.*

2. Wicked; corrupt.

All the tumult of a *guilty* world,
Toſt by ungenerous paſſion, ſinks away. *Thomſon's Spring.*

GUI'NEA. *n. ſ.* [from *Guinea*, a country in *Africa* abounding with gold.] A gold coin valued at one and twenty ſhillings.

By the word gold I muſt be underſtood to deſign a particular piece of matter; that is, the laſt *guinea* that was coined. *Locke.*

GUINE'ADROPPER. *n. ſ.* [*guinea* and *drop.*] One who cheats by dropping guineas.

Who now the *guineadropper*'s bait regards,
Trick'd by the ſharper's dice, or juggler's cards. *Gay.*

GUI'NEAHEN. *n. ſ.* A ſmall Indian hen.

GUINE'APEPPER. *n. ſ.* [*capſicum*, Latin.]

The characters are: the flowers conſiſt of one leaf, and are expanded like thoſe of nightſhade: the fruit is ſoft, fleſhy and membraneous, divided into two or more cells, in which are contained many flat kidney-ſhaped ſeeds. *Miller.*

GUI'NEAPIG. *n. ſ.* A ſmall animal with a pig's ſnout.

GUISE. *n. ſ.* [The ſame with *wiſe*; *guiſe*, French; ƿıſa, Saxon, the ƿ or *w* being changed as is common into *g.*]

1. Manner; mien; habit; caſt of behaviour.

His own fire, and maſter of his *guiſe*,
Did often tremble at his horrid view. *Fairy Queen, b.* i.

Thus women know, and thus they uſe the *guiſe*,
T' enchant the valiant and beguile the wiſe. *Fairfax, b.* iv.

Lo you! here ſhe comes: this is her very *guiſe*; and, upon my life, faſt aſleep: obſerve her, ſtand cloſe. *Shakeſp. Macbeth.*

They ſtand a horrid front
Of dreadful length, and dazzling arms, in *guiſe*
Of warriors old, with order'd ſpear and ſhield,
Awaiting what command their mighty chief
Had to impoſe. *Milton's Paradiſe Loſt, b.* i.

By their *guiſe*
Juſt men they ſeem, and all their ſtudy bent
To worſhip God a-right. *Milton's Paradiſe Loſt, b.* xi.

Back, ſhepherds, back;
Here be without duck or nod,
Other trippings to be trod,
Of lighter toes and ſuch court *guiſe*,
As Mercury did firſt deviſe. *Milton.*

Their external ſhapes are notoriouſly accommodated to that law or *guiſe* of life that nature has deſigned them. *More.*

2. Practice; cuſtom; property.

This would not be ſlept;
Old *guiſe* muſt be kept. *Ben. Johnſon.*

The ſwain reply'd, it never was our *guiſe*
To ſlight the poor, or aught humane deſpiſe. *Pope.*

3. External appearance; dreſs.

When I was very young, nothing was ſo much talked of as rickets among children, and conſumptions among young people: after theſe the ſpleen came in play, and then the ſcurvy, which was the general complaint, and both were thought to appear in many various *guiſes*. *Temple.*

The Hugonots were engaged in a civil war, by the ſpecious pretences of ſome, who, under the *guiſe* of religion, ſacrificed ſo many thouſands to their own ambition. *Swift.*

GUITA'R. *n. ſ.* [*ghitara*, Italian; *guiterre*, French.] A ſtringed inſtrument of muſick.

Sallads and eggs, and lighter fare,
Tune the Italian ſpark's *guitar*. *Prior.*

GULCH. } *n. ſ.* [from *gulo*, Latin.] A little glutton.
GU'LCHIN. } *Skinner.*

GULES. *adj.* [perhaps from *geule*, the throat.] Red: a barbarous term of heraldry.

Follow thy drum;
With man's blood paint the ground: *gules*, *gules*:
Religious canons, civil laws are cruel;
Then what ſhould war be? *Shakeſp. Timon of Athens.*

He whoſe ſable arms,
Black as his purpoſe, did the knight reſemble,
When he laid couched in the ominous horſe,
Hath now his dread and black complexion ſmear'd
With heraldry more diſmal; head to foot,
Now he is total *gules*. *Shakeſpeare's Hamlet.*

GULF. *n. ſ.* [*golfo*, Italian.]

1. A bay; an opening into land.

Piſaurius, the Venetian admiral, knowing himſelf unable to encounter with the Turks great fleet at ſea, withdrew himſelf farther off from the iſland Corfu, into the *gulf* of the Adriatick. *Knolles's Hiſtory of the Turks.*

2. An abyſs; an unmeaſurable depth.

Thence turning back, in ſilence ſoft they ſtole,
And brought the heavy corſe with eaſy pace
To yawning *gulf* of deep Avernus' hole;
By that ſame hole, an entrance dark and baſe,
With ſmoak and ſulphur hiding all the place,
Deſcends to hell. *Fairy Queen, b.* i. *cant.* 5.

I know

I know thou'd'st rather
Follow thine enemy in a fiery *gulf*,
Than flatter him in a bower. *Shakespeare's Coriolanus.*

This is the *gulf* through which Virgil's Alecto shoots herself into hell: the fall of waters, the woods that encompass it, are all in the description. *Addison on Italy.*

The sea could not be much narrower than it is, without a great loss to the world; and must we now have an ocean of mere flats and shallows, to the utter ruin of navigation, for fear our heads should turn giddy at the imagination of gaping abysses and unfathomable *gulfs?* *Bentley.*

3. A whirlpool; a sucking eddy.

England his approaches makes as fierce
As waters to the sucking of a *gulf*. *Shakesp. Henry V.*

4. Any thing insatiable.

Scull of dragon, tooth of wolf,
Witches mummy; maw and *gulf*
Of the ravening salt sea shark;
Root of hemlock, digg'd i' th' dark. *Shakesp. Macbeth.*

Gu'lfy. *adj.* [from *gulf.*] Full of gulfs or whirlpools; *vorticosus.*

Rivers arise; whether thou be the son
Of utmost Tweed, or Oose, or *gulfy* Dun. *Milton.*

At their native realms the Greeks arriv'd,
All who the war of ten long years surviv'd,
And 'scap'd the perils of the *gulfy* main. *Pope's Odyssey.*

High o'er a *gulfy* sea the Pharian isle
Fronts the deep roar of disemboguing Nile. *Pope's Odyssey.*

To GULL. *v. a.* [*guiller*, to cheat, old French.] To trick; to cheat; to defraud; to deceive.

If I do not *gull* him into a nay word, and make him a common recreation, do not think I have wit enough to lie straight in my bed. *Shakespeare's Twelfth Night.*

Yet love these sorc'ries did remove, and move
Thee to *gull* thine own mother for my love. *Donne.*

He would have *gull'd* him with a trick,
But Mart was too too politick. *Hudibras, p. ii.*

They are not to be *gulled* twice with the same trick. *L'Estr.*

The Roman people were grosly *gulled* twice or thrice over, and as often enslaved in one century, and under the same pretence of reformation. *Dryden's Æn. Dedication.*

By their designing leaders taught,
The vulgar, *gull'd* into rebellion, arm'd; *Dryden.*

For this advantage age from youth has won,
As not to be out-ridden, though out-run;
By fortune he was now to Venus trin'd,
And with stern Mars in Capricorn was join'd:
Of him disposing in his own abode,
He sooth'd the goddess, while he *gull'd* the god. *Dryden.*

Gull. *n. s.* [from the verb.]

1. A sea-bird.

2. A cheat; a fraud; a trick.

I should think this a *gull*, but that the white-bearded fellow speaks it. *Shakespeare's Much Ado about Nothing.*

Either they have these excellencies they are praised for, or they have not; if they have not, 'tis an apparent cheat and *gull.* *Government of the Tongue.*

3. A stupid animal; one easily cheated.

Being fed by us you us'd us so,
As that ungentle *gull*, the cuckow bird,
Useth the sparrow. *Shakes. Henry IV. p. i.*

Why have you suffer'd me to be imprison'd,
Kept in a dark house, visited by the priest,
And made the most notorious geck and *gull*
That e'er invention plaid on. *Shakesp. Twelfth Night.*

That paltry story is untrue,
And forg'd to cheat such *gulls* as you. *Hudibras, p. ii.*

Gu'llcatcher. *n. s.* [*gull* and *catch.*] A cheat; a man of trick; one who catches silly people.

Here comes my noble *gullcatcher*. *Shakesp. Twelfth Night.*

Gu'ller. *n. s.* [from *gull.*] A cheat; an impostor.

Gu'llery. *n. s.* [from *gull.*] Cheat; imposture. *Ainsworth.*

Gu'llet. *n. s.* [*goulet*, French; *gula*, Latin.] The throat; the passage through which the food passes; the meat-pipe; the œsophagus.

It might be his doom
One day to sing
With *gullet* in string. *Denham.*

Many have the *gullet* or feeding channel which have no lungs or windpipe; as fishes which have gills, whereby the heart is refrigerated; for such thereof as have lungs and respiration are not without wizzon, as whales and cetaceous animals. *Brown's Vulgar Errours, b. iv. c. 8.*

Nature has various tender muscles plac'd,
By which the artful *gullet* is embrac'd. *Blackmore's Creation.*

The liquor in the stomach is a compound of that which is separated from its inward coat, the spittle which is swallowed, and the liquor which distils from the *gullet*. *Arbuthnot.*

To Gu'lly. *v. n.* [corrupted from *gurgle.*] To run with noise.

Gu'llyhole. *n. s.* [from *gully* and *hole.*] The hole where the gutters empty themselves in the subterraneous sewer.

Gulo'sity. *n. s.* [*gulosus*, Latin.] Greediness; gluttony; voracity.

They are very temperate, seldom offending in ebriety, or excess of drink; nor erring in *gulosity*, or superfluity of meats. *Brown's Vulgar Errours, b. iv. c. 10.*

To Gulp. *v. a.* [*golpen*, Dutch.] To swallow eagerly; to suck down without intermission.

He loosens the fish, *gulps* it down, and so soon as ever the morsel was gone wipes his mouth. *L'Estrange.*

I thirsty stand,
And see the double flaggon charge their hand;
See them puff off the froth, and *gulp* amain,
While with dry tongue I lick my lips in vain. *Gay.*

Gulp. *n. s.* [from the verb.] As much as can be swallowed at once.

In deep suspirations we take more large *gulphs* of air to cool our heart, overcharged with love and sorrow. *More.*

As oft as he can catch a *gulp* of air,
And peep above the seas, he names the fair. *Dryden's Fables.*

GUM. *n. s.* [*gummi*, Latin.]

1. A vegetable substance differing from a resin, in being more viscid and less friable, and generally dissolving in aqueous menstruums; whereas resins, being more sulphurous, require a spirituous dissolvent. *Quincy.*

One whose eyes,
Albeit unused to the melting mood,
Drop tears as fast as the Arabian trees
Their medicinal *gum*. *Shakespeare's Othello.*

He ripens spices, fruit, and precious *gum*,
Which from remotest regions hither come. *Waller.*

Her maiden train,
Who bore the vests that holy rites require,
Incense, and od'rous *gums*, and cover'd fire. *Dryd. Fables.*

2. [Goma, Saxon; *gumme*, Dutch.] The fleshy covering that invests and contains the teeth.

From the babe that milks me
I'd pluck my nipple from his boneless *gums*. *Shak. Macbeth.*

Untwists a wire, and from her *gums*
A set of teeth completely comes. *Swift.*

To Gum. *v. a.* [from the noun.] To close with gum; to smear with gum.

The eyelids are apt to be *gummed* together with a viscous humour. *Wiseman's Surgery.*

To prevent the *gumming* of the eyelids cut a piece of sponge, and lay it wet upon the eye. *Wiseman's Surgery.*

Gu'mminess. *n. s.* [from *gummy.*] The state of being gummy; accumulation of gum.

The tendons are involved with a great *gumminess* and collection of matter. *Wiseman's Surgery.*

Gummo'sity. *n. s.* [from *gummous.*] The nature of gum; gumminess.

Sugar and honey make windy liquors, and the elastick fermenting particles are detained by their innate *gummosity*. *Floyer.*

Gu'mmous. *adj.* [from *gum.*] Of the nature of gum.

Observations concerning English amber, and relations about the amber of Prussia, prove that amber is not a *gummous* or resinous substance drawn out of trees by the sun's heat, but a natural fossil. *Woodward's Natural History.*

Gu'mmy. *adj.* [from *gum.*]

1. Consisting of gum; of the nature of gum.

From the utmost end of the head branches there issueth out a *gummy* juice, which hangeth downward like a cord. *Raleigh.*

Nor all the *gummy* stores Arabia yields. *Dryden's Virgil.*

How each arising alder now appears,
And o'er the Po distils her *gummy* tears. *Dryden's Silenus.*

2. Productive of gum.

Late the clouds
Justling, or push'd with winds, rude in their shock,
Tine the slant light'ning; whose thwart flame driv'n down,
Kindles the *gummy* bark of fir and pine. *Milton's Par. Lost.*

3. Overgrown with gum.

The yawning youth, scarce half awake, essays
His lazy limbs and dozy head to raise;
Then rubs his *gummy* eyes, and scrubs his pate. *Dryden.*

GUN. *n. s.* [Of this word there is no satisfactory etymology. Mr. *Lye* observes that *gun* in Iceland signifies *battle*; but when *guns* came into use we had no commerce with Iceland.] The general name for firearms; the instrument from which shot is discharged by fire.

These dread curses, like the sun 'gainst glass,
Or like an overcharged *gun*, recoil
And turn upon thyself. *Shakespeare's Henry VI. p. ii.*

The emperor, smiling, said that never emperor was yet slain with a *gun*. *Knolles's History of the Turks.*

The bullet flying, makes the *gun* recoil. *Cleaveland.*

In vain the dart or glitt'ring sword we shun,
Condemn'd to perish by the slaught'ring *gun*. *Granville.*

Gu'nnel. *n. s.* [corrupted for *gunwale.* See Gunwale.]

Gu'nner. *n. s.* [from *gun.*] Cannonier; he whose employment is to manage the artillery in a ship.

The nimble *gunner*
With lynstock now the devilish cannon touches,
And down goes all before him. *Shakespeare's Henry* V.

They slew the principal *gunners*, and carried away their artillery. *Hayward.*

GU'NNERY. *n. s.* [from *gunner.*] The science of artillery; the art of managing cannon.

GU'NPOWDER. *n. s.* [*gun* and *powder.*] The powder put into guns to be fired. It consists of about twenty parts of nitre, three parts of sulphur, and three of charcoal. The proportions are not exactly kept.

Gunpowder consisteth of three ingredients, saltpetre, small-coal, and brimstone. *Brown's Vulgar Errours, b.* ii.

Burning by *gunpowder* frequently happens at sea. *Wiseman.*

GU'NSHOT. *n. s.* [*gun* and *shot.*] The reach or range of a gun; the space to which a shot can be thrown.

Those who are come over to the royal party are supposed to be out of *gunshot.* *Dryden.*

GU'NSHOT. *adj.* Made by the shot of a gun.

The greater symptoms I have translated to *gunshot* wounds. *Wiseman's Surgery.*

GU'NSMITH. *n. s.* [*gun* and *smith.*] A man whose trade is to make guns.

It is of particular esteem with the *gunsmiths* for stocks. *Mort.*

GU'NSTICK. *n. s.* [*gun* and *stick.*] The rammer; or stick with which the charge is driven.

GU'NSTOCK. *n. s.* [*gun* and *stock.*] The wood to which the barrel of the gun is fixed.

The timber is useful for bows, pullies, screws, mills, and *gunstocks.* *Mortimer's Husbandry.*

GU'NSTONE. *n. s.* [*gun* and *stone.*] The shot of cannon. They used formerly to shoot stones from artillery.

Tell the pleasant prince, this mock of his
Hath turn'd his ball to *gunstones*, and his soul
Shall stand sore charged for the wasteful vengeance
That shall fly with them. *Shakesp. Hen.* V.

GU'NWALE, or GUNNEL *of a Ship.* That piece of timber which reaches on either side of the ship from the half-deck to the forecastle, being the uppermost bend which finisheth the upper works of the hull in that part, and wherein they put the stanchions which support the waste trees; and this is called the *gunwale*, whether there be guns in the ship or no; and the lower part of any port, where any ordnance are, is also termed the *gunwale.* *Harris.*

GURGE. *n. s.* [*gurges*, Latin.] Whirlpool; gulf.

Marching from Eden he shall find
The plain, wherein a black bituminous *gurge*
Boils out from under ground. *Milton's Paradise Lost, b.* xii.

GU'RGION. *n. s.* The coarser part of the meal, sifted from the bran.

To GU'RGLE. *v. n.* [*gorgogliare*, Italian.] To fall or gush with noise, as water from a bottle.

Then when a fountain's *gurgling* waters play,
They rush to land, and end in feasts the day. *Pope.*

GU'RNARD. } *n. s.* [*gournal*, French.] A kind of sea-fish.
GU'RNET. }

If I be not asham'd of my soldiers I am a sowc'd *gurnet:*
I have misus'd the king's press damnably. *Shak. Henry* IV.

To GUSH. *v. n.* [*gosteleu*, Dutch.]

1. To flow or rush out with violence; not to spring in a small stream, but in a large body.

A sea of blood *gush'd* from the gaping wound,
That her gay garments stain'd with filthy gore. *Fai. Queen.*

The covering of this abyss was broken asunder, and the water *gushed* out that made the deluge. *Burnet.*

Incessant streams of thin magnetick rays
Gush from their fountains with impetuous force,
In either pole, then take an adverse course. *Blackmore.*

On either hand the *gushing* waters play,
And down the rough cascade white-dashing fall. *Thomson.*

2. To emit in a copious effluxion.

The gaping wound *gush'd* out a crimson flood. *Dryden.*

Line after line my *gushing* eyes o'erflow,
Led through a sad variety of woe. *Pope.*

GUSH. *n. s.* [from the verb.] An emission of liquor in a large quantity at once; the liquor so emitted.

If a lung-vein be bursted, generally at the first cough a great *gush* of blood is coughed up. *Harvey on Consumpt.*

GU'SSET. *n. s.* [*gousset*, French.] Any thing sewed on to cloath, in order to strengthen it.

GUST. *n. s.* [*goust*, French; *gustus*, Latin.]

1. Sense of tasting.

Destroy all creatures for thy sport or *gust*,
Yet cry, if man's unhappy, God's unjust. *Pope.*

2. Height of perception; height of sensual enjoyment.

They fondly thinking to allay
Their appetite with *gust*, instead of fruit
Chew'd bitter ashes, which th' offended taste
With spattering noise rejected. *Milton's Paradise Lost, b.* x.

Where love is duty on the female side,
On theirs meer sensual *gust*, and sought with surly pride. *Dryden's Fables.*

My sight, and smell, and hearing were employ'd,
And all three senses in full *gust* enjoy'd. *Dryden's Fables.*

3. Love; liking.

To kill, I grant, is sin's extremest *gust*;
But, in defence, by mercy 'tis made just. *Shakesp. Timon.*

Old age shall do the work of taking away both the *gust* and comfort of them. *L'Estrange, Fable* 38.

We have lost, in a great measure, the *gust* and relish of true happiness. *Tillotson's Sermons.*

4. Turn of fancy; intellectual taste.

The principal part of painting is to find what nature has made most proper to this art, and a choice of it may be made according to the *gust* and manner of the ancients. *Dryden.*

5. [From *gustr*, Islandick.] A sudden violent blast of wind.

Some troops pursue the bloody-minded queen,
That led calm Henry, though he were a king,
As doth a sail, fill'd with a fretting *gust*,
Command an argosie to stem the waves. *Shakesp. Hen.* VI.

You may as well forbid the mountain pines
To wag their high tops, and to make a noise,
When they are fretted with the *gusts* of heav'n. *Shakesp.*

Presently come forth swarms and volleys of libels, which are the *gusts* of liberty of speech restrained. *Bacon's H.* VII.

As when fierce northern blasts from th' Alps descend,
From his firm roots with struggling *gusts* to rend
An aged sturdy oak, the rattling sound
Grows loud. *Denham.*

Part stay for passage, 'till a *gust* of wind
Ships o'er their forces in a shining sheet. *Dryd. Ann. Mirab.*

Pardon a weak distemper'd soul, that swells
With sudden *gusts*, and sinks as soon in calms,
The sport of passions. *Addison's Cato.*

6. It is written in *Spenser* vitiously for *justs*, sports.

Full jolly knight he seem'd, and fair did sit,
As one for knightly *gusts* and fierce encounters fit. *Fa. Qu.*

GU'STABLE. *n. s.* [*gusto*, Latin.]

1. To be tasted.

This position informs us of a vulgar errour, terming the gall bitter; whereas there is nothing *gustable* sweeter. *Harvey.*

2. Pleasant to the taste.

A *gustable* thing, seen or smelt, excites the appetite, and affects the glands and parts of the mouth. *Derham.*

GUSTA'TION. *n. s.* [*gusto*, Latin.] The act of tasting.

In it the gullet and conveying parts are only seated, which partake of the nerves of *gustation*, or appertaining unto sapor. *Brown's Vulgar Errours, b.* vii.

GU'STFUL. *adj.* [*gust* and *full.*] Tasteful; well-tasted.

What he defaults from some dry insipid sin, is but to make up for some other more *gustful.* *Decay of Piety.*

GU'STO. *n. s.* [Italian.]

1. The relish of any thing; the power by which any thing excites sensations in the palate.

Pleasant *gustos* gratify the appetite of the luxurious. *Derh.*

2. Intellectual taste; liking.

In reading what I have written, let them bring no particular *gusto* along with them. *Dryden.*

GU'STY. *adj.* [from *gust.*] Stormy; tempestuous.

Once upon a raw and *gusty* day,
The troubled Tyber chafing with his shores. *Sh. Jul. Cæs.*

Or whirl'd tempestuous by the *gusty* wind. *Thomson.*

GUT. *n. s.* [*kutteln*, German.]

1. The long pipe reaching with many convolutions from the stomach to the vent.

This lord wears his wit in his belly, and his *guts* in his head. *Shakespeare's Troilus and Cressida.*

Reveng'd I will be, as sure as his *guts* are made of puddings. *Shakespeare's Merry Wives of Windsor.*

A viol should have a lay of wire-strings below, close to the belly, and then the strings of *guts* mounted upon a bridge, that by this means the upper strings stricken should make the lower resound. *Bacon's Natural History.*

The intestines or *guts* may be inflamed by any acrid or poisonous substance taken inwardly. *Arbuthnot on Diet.*

2. The stomach; the receptacle of food: proverbially.

And cramm'd them 'till their *guts* did ake,
With cawdle, custard, and plum-cake. *Hudibras, p.* ii.

With false weights their servants *guts* they cheat,
And pinch their own to cover the deceit. *Dryden's Juvenal.*

3. Gluttony; love of gormandising.

Apicius, thou did'st on thy *guts* bestow
Full ninety millions; yet, when this was spent,
Ten millions still remain'd to thee; which thou,
Fearing to suffer thirst and famishment,
In poison'd potion drank'st. *Hakewill on Providence.*

To GUT. *v. a.* [from the noun.]

1. To eviscerate; to draw; to exenterate.

The fishermen save the most part of their fish: some are *gutted*, splitted, powdered and dried. *Carew's Sur. of Cornwal.*

2. To plunder of contents.

In Nero's arbitrary time,
When virtue was a guilt, and wealth a crime,

A troop

A troop of cut-throat guards were sent to seize
The rich men's goods, and *gut* their palaces. *Dryd. Juven.*

Tom Brown, of facetious memory, after having *gutted* a proper name of its vowels, used it in his works as free as he pleased. *Spectator*, Nº. 567.

GU'TTATED. *adj.* [from *gutta*, Latin, a drop.] Besprinkled with drops; bedropped. *Dict.*

GU'TTER. *n. s.* [from *guttur*, a throat, Latin.] A passage for water.

These *gutter* tiles are in length ten inches and a half. *Moxon.*

Rocks rise one above another, and have deep *gutters* worn in the sides of them by torrents of rain. *Addison on Italy.*

To GU'TTER. *v. a.* [from the noun.] To cut in small hollows.

Tempests themselves, high seas, and howling winds,
The *gutter'd* rocks, and congregated sands,
Traitors ensteep'd to clog the guiltless keel,
As having sense of beauty, do omit
Their mortal natures, letting safe go by
The divine Desdemona. *Shakespeare's Othello.*

My cheeks are *gutter'd* with my fretting tears. *Sandys.*

First in a place, by nature close, they build
A narrow flooring, *gutter'd*, wall'd, and til'd. *Dryden.*

The *gutter'd* rocks, and mazy-running clefts. *Thomson.*

To GU'TTLE. *v. n.* [from *gut.*] To feed luxuriously; to gormandise. A low word.

His jolly brother, opposite in sense,
Laughs at his thrift; and, lavish of expence,
Quaffs, crams, and *guttles* in his own defence. *Dryden.*

To GU'TTLE. *v. a.* [from *gut.*] To swallow.

The fool spit in his porridge, to try if they'd hiss: they did not hiss, and so he *guttled* them up, and scalded his chops. *L'Estrange.*

GU'TTLER. *n. s.* [from *guttle.*] A greedy eater.

GU'TTULOUS. *adj.* [from *guttula*, Latin.] In the form of a small drop.

Ice is plain upon the surface of the water, but round in hail, which is also a glaciation, and figured in its *guttulous* descent from the air. *Brown's Vulgar Errours, b.* ii.

GU'TTURAL. *adj.* [*gutturalis*, Latin.] Pronounced in the throat; belonging to the throat.

The Hebrews have assigned which letters are labial, which dental, and which *guttural.* *Bacon's Natural History.*

In attempting to pronounce the nasals, and some of the vowels spiritally, the throat is brought to labour, and makes that which we call a *guttural* pronunciation. *Holder.*

GU'TTURALNESS. *n. s.* [from *guttural.*] The quality of being guttural. *Dict.*

GU'TWORT. *n. s.* [*gut* and *wort.*] An herb.

GUY. *n. s.* [from *guide.*] A rope used to lift any thing into the ship. *Skinner.*

To GU'ZZLE. *v. n.* [from *gut*, or *gust*, to *guttle*, or *gustle.*] To gormandise; to feed immoderately; to swallow any liquor greedily.

Well season'd bowls the gossip's spirits raise,
Who while she *guzzles* chats the doctor's praise. *Roscommon.*

They fell to lapping and *guzzling*, 'till they burst themselves. *L'Estrange.*

No more her care shall fill the hollow tray,
To fat the *guzzling* hogs with floods of whey. *Gay.*

To GU'ZZLE. *v. a.* To swallow with immoderate gust.

The Pylian king
Was longest liv'd of any two-legg'd thing,
Still *guzzling* must of wine. *Dryd. Juvenal.*

GU'ZZLER. *n. s.* [from *guzzle.*] A gormandiser; an immoderate eater or drinker.

GYBE. *n. s.* [See GIBE.] A sneer; a taunt; a sarcasm.

Ready in *gybes*, quick answer'd, saucy, and as quarrellous as the weazel. *Shakespeare's Cymbeline.*

To GYBE. *v. n.* To sneer; to taunt.

The vulgar yield an open ear,
And common courtiers love to *gybe* and fleer. *Hubb. Tale.*

GYMNA'STICALLY. *adv.* [from *gymnastick.*] Athletically; fitly for strong exercise.

Such as with agility and vigour have not the use of either, who are not *gymnastically* composed, nor actively use those parts. *Brown's Vulgar Errours b.* iv. *c.* 5.

GYMNA'STICK. *adj.* [γυμναςικὸς; *gymnastique*, French.] Pertaining to athletick exercises; consisting of leaping, wrestling, running, throwing the dart, or quoit.

The Cretans wisely forbid their servants *gymnasticks* as well as arms; and yet your modern footmen exercise themselves daily, whilst their enervated lords are softly lolling in their chariots. *Arbuthnot and Pope's Mart. Scriblerus.*

GY'MNICK. *adj.* [γυμνικὸς; *gymnique*, French.] Such as practise the athletick or gymnastick exercises.

Have they not sword-players, and ev'ry sort
Of *gymnick* artists, wrestlers, riders, runners. *Milton.*

GYMNOSPE'RMOUS. *adj.* [γύμνος and σπέρμα.] Having the seeds naked.

GY'NECOCRASAY. *n. s.* [γυναικοκρατία; *gynecocratie*, French.] Petticoat government; female power.

GYRA'TION. *n. s.* [*gyro*, Latin.] The act of turning any thing about.

This effluvium attenuateth and impelleth the neighbour air, which, returning home, in a *gyration* carrieth with it the obvious bodies into the electrick. *Brown's Vulgar Errours.*

If a burning coal be nimbly moved round in a circle with *gyrations*, continually repeated, the whole circle will appear like fire; the reason of which is, that the sensation of the coal in the several places of that circle remains impressed on the sensorium, until the coal return again to the same place. *Newt.*

GYRE. *n. s.* [*gyrus*, Latin.] A circle described by any thing going in an orbit.

Ne thenceforth his approved skill to ward,
Or strike, or hurlen round in warlike *gyre*,
Remember'd he; ne car'd for his safe guard,
But rudely rag'd. *Fairy Queen, b.* ii. *cant.* 5.

Does the wild haggard tow'r into the sky,
And to the South by thy direction fly?
Or eagle in her *gyres* the clouds embrace? *Sandys.*

He fashion'd those harmonious orbs, that roll
In restless *gyres* about the Artick pole. *Sandys.*

Quick and more quick he spins in giddy *gyres*,
Then falls, and in much foam his soul expires. *Dryden.*

GYVES. *n. s.* [*gevyn*, Welsh.] Fetters; chains for the legs.

The villains march wide betwixt the legs, as if they had *gyves* on. *Shakespeare's Henry* IV. *p.* i.

And knowing this, should I yet stay,
Like such as blow away their lives,
And never will redeem a day,
Enamour'd of their golden *gyves*? *Ben. Johnson's Forest.*

The poor prisoners, ready to take the occasion offered, boldly starting up, break off their chains and *gyves*. *Knolles.*

Do'st thou already single me? I thought
Gyves and the mill had tam'd thee. *Milton's Agonistes.*

But Telamon rush'd in, and hap'd to meet
A rising root, that held his fasten'd feet;
So down he fell, whom sprawling on the ground,
His brother from the wooden *gyves* unbound. *Dryd. Fables.*

To GYVE. *v. a.* [from the noun.] To fetter; to shackle; to enchain; to ensnare.

With as little a web as this, will I ensnare as great a fly as Cassio. Ay, smile upon her, do. I will *gyve* thee in thine own courtship. *Shakespeare's Othello.*

H.

H Is in English, as in other languages, a note of aspiration, sounded only by a strong emission of the breath, without any conformation of the organs of speech, and is therefore by many grammarians accounted no letter. The *h* in English is scarcely ever mute at the beginning of a word, or where it immediately precedes a vowel; as *house*, *behaviour*: where it is followed by a consonant it has no sound, according to the present pronunciation: but anciently, as now in Scotland, it made the syllable guttural; as *right*, *bought*.

HA. *interject.* [*ha*, Latin.]

1. An expression of wonder, surprise, sudden question, or sudden exertion.

You shall look fairer ere I give or hazard:
What says the golden chest? *ha!* let me see. *Shakesp.*
Ha! what art thou! thou horrid headless trunk!
It is my Hastings! *Rowe's Jane Shore.*

2. An expression of laughter.

He saith among the trumpets *ha*, *ha*, and he smelleth the battle afar off. *Job* xxxix. 25.

Ha, *ha*, 'tis what so long I wish'd and vow'd;
Our plots and delusions
Have wrought such confusions,
That the monarch's a slave to the crowd. *Dryd. Albion.*

HAAK. *n. s.* A fish. *Ainsworth.*

HA'BEAS CORPUS. [Latin.] A writ, the which, a man indicted of some trespass, being laid in prison for the same, may have out of the King's Bench, thereby to remove himself thither at his own costs, and to answer the cause there. *Cowel.*

HABERDA'SHER. *n. s.* [This word is ingeniously deduced by *Minshew* from *habt ihr dass*, German, *have you this*, the expression of a shopkeeper offering his wares to sale.] One who sells small wares; a pedlar.

Because these cunning men are like *haberdashers* of small wares, it is not amiss to set forth their shop. *Bacon's Essays.*

A *haberdasher*, who was the oracle of the coffeehouse, declared his opinion. *Addison's Spectator*, N°. 48.

HA'BERDINE. *n. s.* A dried salt cod. *Ainsworth.*

HA'BERGEON. *n. s.* [*haubergeon*, French; *halbergium*, low Lat.] Armour to cover the neck and breast; breastplate; neckpiece; gorget.

And halbert some, and some a *haberion*;
So every one in arms was quickly dight. *Fairfax*, *b.* i.
The shot let fly, and grazing
Upon his shoulder, in the passing,
Lodg'd in Magnano's brass *habergeon*. *Hudibras*, *p.* i.

HABI'LIMENT. *n. s.* [*habilement*, French.] Dress; cloaths; garment.

He the fairest Una found,
Strange lady, in so strange *habiliment*,
Teaching the satyres. *Fairy Queen*, *b.* i. *cant.* 6.
My riches are these poor *habiliments*,
Of which if you should here disfurnish me,
You take the sum and substance that I have. *Shakespeare.*

The clergy should content themselves with wearing gowns and other *habiliments* of Irish drapery. *Swift.*

To HABI'LITATE. *v. n.* [*habiliter*, French.] To qualify; to entitle.

Divers persons in the house of commons were attainted, and thereby not legal, nor *habilitate* to serve in parliament, being disabled in the highest degree. *Bacon's Henry* VII.

HABILITA'TION. *n. s.* [from *habilitate*.] Qualification.

The things formerly spoken of, are but *habilitations* towards arms; and what is *habilitation* without intention and act? *Bacon*, *Essay* 30.

HA'BILITY. *n. s.* [*habilite*, French.] Faculty; power.

HA'BIT. *n. s.* [*habitus*, Latin.]

1. State of any thing: as, *habit* of body.

2. Dress; accoutrement.

I shifted
Into a madman's rags, t' assume a semblance
The very dogs disdain'd; and in this *habit*
Met I my father. *Shakespeare's King Lear.*
If you have any justice, any pity;
If ye be any thing, but churchmen's *habits*. *Shakespeare.*

Both the poets being dressed in the same English *habit*, story compared with story, judgment may be made betwixt them. *Dryden's Fables, Preface.*

The scenes are old, the *habits* are the same
We wore last year. *Dryden's Indian Emperor.*

There are among the statues several of Venus, in different *habits*. *Addison on Italy.*

The clergy are the only set of men who wear a distinct *habit* from others. *Swift.*

3. *Habit* is a power or ability in man of doing any thing, when it has been acquired by frequent doing the same thing. *Locke.*

He hath a better bad *habit* of frowning than the count Palatine. *Shakesp. Merchant of Venice.*

4. Custom; inveterate use.

This is the last fatal step but one, which is, by frequent repetition of the sinful act, to continue and persist in it, 'till at length it settles into a fixed confirmed *habit* of sin; which being properly that which the apostle calls the finishing of sin, ends certainly in death; death not only as to merit, but also as to actual infliction. *South's Sermons.*

No civil broils have since his death arose,
But faction now by *habit* does obey;
And wars have that respect for his repose,
As winds for halcyons when they breed at sea. *Dryden.*

The force of education is so great, that we may mould the minds and manners of the young into what shape we please, and give the impressions of such *habits* as shall ever afterwards remain. *Atterbury's Sermons.*

To HA'BIT. *v. a.* [from the noun.] To dress; to accoutre; to array.

Present yourself and your fair princess
Before Leontes:
She shall be *habited* as it becomes
The partner of your bed. *Shakesp. Winter's Tale.*

Having called to his memory Sir George Villiers, and the cloaths he used to wear, in which at that time he seemed to be *habited*, he thought him to be that person. *Clarendon.*

They *habited* themselves like those rural deities, and imitated them in their rustick dances. *Dryden.*

HA'BITABLE. *adj.* [*habitable*, Fr. *habitabilis*, Lat.] Capable of being dwelt in; capable of sustaining human creatures.

By means of our solitary situation, we know well most part of the *habitable* world, and are ourselves unknown. *Bacon.*

That was her torrid and inflaming time;
This is her *habitable* tropique clime. *Donne.*
Look round the *habitable* world, how few
Know their own good, or knowing it, pursue. *Dryden.*

HA'BITABLENESS. *n. s.* [from *habitable*.] Capacity of being dwelt in.

The cutting of the Equinoctial line decides that controversy of the *habitableness* of the Torrid zone. *More.*

Those ancient problems of the spherical roundness of the earth, the being of antipodes, and of the *habitableness* of the torrid zone, are abundantly demonstrated. *Ray.*

HA'BITANCE. *n. s.* [*habitatio*, Latin.] Dwelling; abode.

What art thou, man, if man at all thou art,
That here in desart hast thine *habitance*?
And these rich heaps of wealth do'st hide apart
From the world's eye, and from her right usance. *Fa. Qu.*

HA'BITANT. *n. s.* [*habitant*, Fr. *habitans*, Latin.] Dweller; one that lives in any place; inhabitant.

Not to earth are those bright luminaries
Officious; but to the earth's *habitant*:
And for the heav'n's wide circuit, let it speak
The maker's high magnificence. *Milton's Paradise Lost.*
Pow'rs celestial to each other's view
Stand still confest, though distant far they lie,
Or *habitants* of earth, or sea, or sky. *Pope's Odyssey.*

HABITA'TION. *n. s.* [*habitation*, French; *habitatio*, Latin.]

1. The act of dwelling; the state of a place receiving dwellers.

Amplitude almoſt immenſe, with ſtars
Numerous, and ev'ry ſtar perhaps a world
Of deſtin'd *habitation*. *Milton's Paradiſe Loſt, b.* vii.

Palaces,
For want of *habitation* and repair,
Diſſolve to heaps of ruins. *Denham's Sophy.*

Rocks and mountains, which in the firſt ages were high and craggy, and conſequently then inconvenient for *habitation*, were by continual deterration brought to a lower pitch. *Woodward's Natural Hiſtory.*

2. Place of abode; dwelling.

Wiſdom, to the end ſhe might ſave many, built her houſe of that nature which is common unto all; ſhe made not this or that man her *habitation*, but dwelt in us. *Hooker, b.* v.

God oft deſcends to viſit men
Unſeen, and through their *habitations* walks
To mark their doings. *Milton's Paradiſe Loſt, b.* xii.

HABITA'TOR. n. ſ. [Latin.] Dweller; inhabitant.

So is his preſence more continued unto the northern inhabitants; and the longeſt day in Cancer is longer unto us than that in Capricorn unto the northern *habitators*. *Brown.*

HABI'TUAL. *adj.* [*habituel*, from *habit*, French.] Cuſtomary; accuſtomed; inveterate; eſtabliſhed by frequent repetition.

Sin, there in pow'r before
Once actual; now in body, and to dwell
Habitual habitant. *Milton's Paradiſe Loſt, b.* x.

Art is properly an *habitual* knowledge of certain rules and maxims. *South.*

By length of time
The ſcurf is worn away of each committed crime:
No ſpeck is left of their *habitual* ſtains;
But the pure ether of the ſoul remains. *Dryden's Æn.*

'Tis impoſſible to become an able artiſt, without making your art *habitual* to you. *Dryden's Dufreſnoy.*

HABI'TUALLY. *adv.* [from *habitual*.] Cuſtomarily; by habit.

Internal graces and qualities of mind ſanctify our natures, and render us *habitually* holy. *Atterbury's Sermons.*

To HABI'TUATE. *v. a.* [*habituer*, French.] To accuſtom; to uſe one's ſelf by frequent repetition.

Men are firſt corrupted by bad counſel and company, and next they *habituate* themſelves to their vicious practices. *Tillot.*

Such as live in a rarer air are *habituated* to the exerciſe of a greater muſcular ſtrength. *Arbuthnot on Air.*

HA'BITUDE. *n. ſ.* [*habitudo*, Latin; *habitude*, French.]

1. Relation; reſpect; ſtate with regard to ſomething elſe.

We cannot conclude this complexion of nations from the vicinity or *habitude* they hold unto the ſun. *Brown's Vul. Err.*

The will of God is like a ſtreight unalterable rule; but the various comportments of the creature, either thwarting this rule, or holding conformity to it, occaſions ſeveral *habitudes* of this rule into it. *Hale's Origin of Mankind.*

It reſults from the very nature and being of things, as they ſtand in ſuch a certain *habitude*, or relation to one another. *South's Sermons.*

As by the objective part of perfect happineſs we underſtand that which is beſt and laſt, and to which all other things are to be referred; ſo by the formal part muſt be underſtood the beſt and laſt *habitude* of man toward that beſt object. *Norr.*

In all the *habitudes* of life
The friend, the miſtreſs, and the wife;
Variety we ſtill purſue. *Swift.*

2. Familiarity; converſe; frequent intercourſe.

His knowledge in the nobleſt uſeful arts,
Was ſuch dead authors could not give;
But *habitudes* with thoſe who live. *Dryden.*

To write well, one muſt have frequent *habitudes* with the beſt company. *Dryden.*

3. Long cuſtom; habit; inveterate uſe.

Mankind is not more liable to deceit than willing to continue in a pleaſing errour, ſtrengthened by a long *habitude*. *Dryden's Dufreſnoy.*

Thy ear, inur'd to charitable ſounds,
And pitying love, muſt feel the hateful wounds
Of jeſt obſcene, and vulgar ribaldry,
The ill-bred queſtion, and the loud reply,
Brought by long *habitude* from bad to worſe;
Muſt hear the frequent oath, the direful curſe. *Prior.*

4. The power of doing any thing acquired by frequent repetition.

It is impoſſible to gain an exact *habitude*, without an infinite number of acts and perpetual practice. *Dryd. Dufreſnoy.*

HA'BNAB. *adv.* [*hap ne hap*, or *nap*; as *would ne would*, *will ne will*; that is, *let it happen or not*.] At random; at the mercy of chance; without any rule or certainty of effect.

He circles draws and ſquares,
With cyphers, aſtral characters;
Then looks 'em o'er to underſtand 'em,
Although ſet down *habnab* at random. *Hudibras, p.* ii.

To HACK. *v. a.* [ƿaccan, Saxon; *hacken*, Dutch; *hacher*, Fr. from acaꞅe, an axe, Saxon.]

1. To cut into ſmall pieces; to chop; to cut ſlightly with frequent or unſkilful blows.

He put on that armour, whereof there was no one piece wanting, though *hacked* in ſome places, bewraying ſome fight not long ſince paſſed. *Sidney.*

What a ſlave art thou, to *hack* thy ſword as thou haſt done, and ſay it was in fight! *Shakeſpeare's Henry* IV. *p.* i.

Richard the ſecond here was *hack'd* to death. *Shak R.* III.
I'll fight 'till from my bones my fleſh be *hackt*. *Shakeſp.*

One flouriſhing branch of his moſt royal root
Is *hackt* down, and his ſummer leaves all faded,
By envy's hand, and murder's bloody axe. *Shakeſ. Rich.* II.

Burn me, *hack* me, hew me into pieces. *Dryden.*

But fate with butchers plac'd thy prieſtly ſtall,
Meek modern faith to murder, *hack* and mawl. *Pope.*

Not the *hack'd* helmet, nor the duſty field,
But purple veſts and flow'ry garlands pleaſe. *Addiſ. Ovid.*

2. To ſpeak unreadily, or with heſitation.

Diſarm them, and let them queſtion; let them keep their limbs whole, and *hack* our Engliſh. *Shakeſpeare.*

To HACK. *v. n.* To hackney; to turn hackney or proſtitute. *Hanmer.*

I could be knighted.—What! thou lieſt. Sir Alice Ford, theſe knights will *hack*, and ſo thou ſhouldſt alter the article of thy gentry. *Shakeſp. Merry Wives of Windſor.*

HA'CKLE. *n. ſ.* Raw ſilk; any filmy ſubſtance unſpun.

Take the *hackle* of a cock or capon's neck, or a plover's top: take off one ſide of the feather, and then take the *hackle* ſilk, gold or ſilver thread, and make theſe faſt at the bent of the hook. *Walton's Angler.*

To HA'CKLE. *v. a.* [from *hack*.] To dreſs flax.

HA'CKNEY. *n. ſ.* [*hacnai*, Welſh; *hackeneye*, Teuton. *haquenée*, French.]

1. A pacing horſe.

2. A hired horſe; hired horſes being uſually taught to pace, or recommended as good pacers.

Light and lewd perſons were as eaſily ſuborned to make an affidavit for money, as poſt-horſes and *hackneys* are taken to hire. *Bacon's Off. of Alienation.*

Who, mounted on a broom, the nag
And *hackney* of a Lapland hag,
In queſt of you came hither poſt,
Within an hour, I'm ſure, at moſt. *Hudibras, p.* iii.

3. A hireling; a proſtitute.

Three kingdoms rung
With his accumulative and *hackney* tongue. *Roſcommon.*

That is no more than every lover
Does from his *hackney* lady ſuffer. *Hudibras.*

Shall each ſpurgall'd *hackney* of the day,
Or each new penſion'd ſycophant, pretend
To break my windows. *Pope, Dial.* 2.

4. Any thing let out for hire.

A wit can ſtudy in the ſtreets;
Not quite ſo well, however, as one mought;
A *hackney* coach may chance to ſpoil a thought. *Pope.*

5. Much uſed; common.

Theſe notions young ſtudents in phyſick derive from their *hackney* authors. *Harvey on Conſumptions.*

To HA'CKNEY. *v. a.* [from the noun.] To practiſe in one thing; to accuſtom to the road.

He is long *hackney'd* in the ways of men. *Shakeſpeare.*

HA'CQUETON. *n. ſ.* [*haquet*, old French, a little horſe.] Some piece of armour.

You may ſee the very faſhion of the Iriſh horſeman in his long hoſe, riding ſhoes of coſtly cordwain, his *hacqueton*, and his habergeon. *Spenſer's State of Ireland.*

HAD. The preterite and part. paſſ. of *have*.

I *had* rather be a country ſervant maid,
Than a great queen with this condition,
To be thus taunted. *Shakeſpeare's Richard* III.

Had we not better leave this Utica,
To arm Numidia in our cauſe? *Addiſon's Cato.*

HA'DDOCK. *n. ſ.* [*hadot*, French.] A ſea-fiſh of the cod kind, but ſmall.

The coaſt is plentifully ſtored with pilchards, herrings, and *haddocks*. *Carew's Survey of Cornwal.*

HAFT. *n. ſ.* [ƿæꝼꞇ, Saxon; *heft*, Dutch, from *To have* or *hold*.] A handle; that part of any inſtrument that is taken into the hand.

This brandiſh'd dagger
I'll bury to the *haft* in her fair breaſt. *Dryd. and Lee's Oedip.*

Theſe extremities of the joints are the *hafts* and handles of the members. *Dryden's Dufreſnoy.*

A needle is a ſimple body, being only made of ſteel; but a ſword is a compound, becauſe its *haft* or handle is made of materials different from the blade. *Watts's Logick.*

To HAFT. *v. a.* [from the noun.] To ſet in a haft. *Ainſw.*

HAG. *n. ſ.* [ƿæᵹeꞅꞅe, a goblin, Saxon; *heckle*, a witch, Dutch.]

1. A fury; a ſhe monſter.

Thus

Thus spoke th' impatient prince, and made a pause,
His foul *hags* rais'd their heads, and clapt their hands;
And all the powers of hell, in full applause,
Flourish'd their snakes, and tost their flaming brands. *Crash.*

2. A witch; an enchantress.

Out of my door, you witch! you *hag*, you baggage, you poulcat, you runnion. *Shakesf. Merry Wives of Windsor.*

3. An old ugly woman.

Such affectations may become the young;
But thou, old *hag*, of threescore years and three,
Is shewing of thy parts in Greek for thee? *Dryden's Juven.*

To HAG. *v. a.* [from the noun.] To torment; to harrass with vain terrour.

That makes them in the dark see visions,
And *hag* themselves with apparitions. *Hudibras, p.* iii.

How are superstitious men *hagged* out of their wits with the fancy of omens, tales, and visions! *L'Estrange.*

HA'GARD. *adj* [*hagard*, French.]

1. Wild; untamed; irreclaimable.

To let them down before that his flights end,
As *hagard* hawk, presuming to contend
With hardy fowl above his able might,
His weary pounces all in vain doth spend,
To truss the prey too heavy for his flight. *Fairy Queen.*

2. [*Hager*, German.] Lean. To this sense I have put the following passage; for so the author ought to have written.

A *hagged* carion of a wolf, and a jolly sort of dog, with good flesh upon's back, fell into company together. *L'Estr.*

3. [*Hage*, Welsh.] Ugly; rugged; deformed; wildly disordered.

She's too disdainful;
I know her spirits are as coy and wild,
As *hagard* as the rock. *Shakespeare.*

Fearful besides of what in fight had pass'd,
His hands and *hagard* eyes to heav'n he cast. *Dryden's Æn.*

Where are the conscious looks, the face now pale,
Now flushing red, the down-cast *hagard* eyes,
Or fixt on earth, or slowly rais'd! *Smith's Phæd. and Hipp.*

HA'GGARD. *n. s.*

1. Any thing wild or irreclaimable.

I will be married to a wealthy widow,
Ere three days pass, which has as long lov'd me
As I have lov'd this proud disdainful *haggard.* *Shakespeare.*

2. A species of hawk.

Does the wild *haggard* tow'r into the sky,
And to the South by thy direction fly? *Sandys.*

I enlarge my discourse to the observation of the aires, the brancher, the ramish hawk, and the *haggard.* *Walton's Angler.*

3. A hag. So *Garth* has used it for want of understanding it.

Beneath the gloomy covert of an yew,
In a dark grot, the baleful *haggard* lay,
Breathing black vengeance, and infecting day. *Garth.*

HA'GGARDLY. *adv.* [from *haggard.*] Deformed; ugly.

For her the rich Arabia sweats her gum;
And precious oils from distant Indies come,
How *haggardly* soe'er she looks at home. *Dryd. Juven.*

HA'GGESS. *n. s.* [from *hog* or *hack.*] A mass of meat, generally pork chopped, and inclosed in a membrane. In Scotland it is commonly made in a sheep's maw of the entrails of the same animal, cut small, with suet and spices.

HA'GGISH. *adj.* [from *hag.*] Of the nature of a hag; deformed; horrid.

He lasted long;
But on us both did *haggish* age steal on,
And wore us out of act. *Shak. All's well that ends well.*

To HA'GGLE. *v. a.* [corrupted from *hackle* or *hack.*] To cut; to chop; to mangle.

Suffolk first died, and York all *haggled* o'er
Comes to him where in gore he lay insteep'd. *Shakes. H.* V.

To HA'GGLE. *v. n.* To be tedious in a bargain; to be long in coming to the price.

HA'GGLER. *n. s.* [from *haggle.*]

1. One that cuts.

2. One that is tardy in bargaining.

HA'GIOGRAPHER. *n. s.* [ἅγιος and γράφω.] A holy writer. The Jews divide the Holy Scriptures of the Old Testament into the law, the prophets, and the *hagiographers.*

HAH. *interject.* An expression of sudden effort.

Her coats tuck'd up, and all her motions just,
She stamps, and then cries *hah!* at ev'ry thrust. *Dryden.*

HAIL. *n. s.* [hagel, Saxon.]

1. Drops of rain frozen in their falling. *Locke.*

As thick as *hail*
Came post on post. *Shakespeare's Macbeth.*

To HAIL. *v. n.* To pour down hail.

My people shall dwell in a peaceable habitation when it shall *hail*, coming down on the forest. *Is.* xxxii. 19.

HAIL. *interj.* [hæl, health, Saxon: *hail*, therefore, is the same as *salve* of the Latins, or ὑγιαίνε of the Greeks, health be to you.] A term of salutation now used only in poetry; health be to you.

Hail, hail, brave friend!
Say to the king the knowledge of the broil
As thou did'st leave it. *Shakespeare's Macbeth.*

Her sick head is bound about with clouds:
It does not look as it would have a *hail*
Or health wish'd in it, as on other morns. *Ben. Johnson.*

The angel *hail*
Bestow'd, the holy salutation us'd
Long after to blest Mary, second Eve. *Milt. Parad. Lost.*

Farewel, happy fields,
Where joy for ever dwells! *hail* horrors! *hail*
Infernal world! and thou profoundest hell
Receive thy new possessor! *Milton' Paradise Lost, b.* i.

All *hail*, he cry'd, thy country's grace and love;
Once first of men below, now first of birds above. *Dryd.*

Hail to the sun! from whose returning light
The chearful soldier's arms new lustre take,
To deck the pomp of battle. *Rowe's Tamerlane.*

To HAIL. *v. a.* [from the noun.] To salute; to call to.

A galley well appointed, with a long boat, drawing near unto the shore, was *hailed* by a Turk, accompanied with a troop of horsemen. *Knolles's History of the Turks.*

Thrice call upon my name, thrice beat your breast,
And *hail* me thrice to everlasting rest. *Dryden.*

HA'ILED. *adj.* [from *hail.*] Struck with hail.

HA'ILSHOT. *n. s.* [*hail* and *shot.*] Small shot scattered like hail.

The master of the artillery did visit them sharply with murdering *hailshot*, from the pieces mounted towards the top of the hill. *Hayward.*

HA'ILSTONE. *n s.* [*hail* and *stone.*] A particle or single ball of hail.

You are no surer, no,
Than is the coal of fire upon the ice,
Or *hailstone* in the sun. *Shakespeare.*

Hard *hailstones* lye not thicker on the plain,
Nor shaken oaks such show'rs of acorns rain. *Dryden.*

HAI'LY. *adj.* [from *hail.*] Consisting of hail.

From whose dark womb a rattling tempest pours,
Which the cold North congeals to *haily* showers. *Pope.*

HAIR. *n. s.* [hæп, Saxon.]

1. One of the common teguments of the body. It is to be found upon all the parts of the body, except the soles of the feet and palms of the hands. When we examine the hairs with a microscope, we find that they have each a round bulbous root, which lies pretty deep in the skin, and which draws their nourishment from the surrounding humours: that each hair consists of five or six others, wrapt up in a common tegument or tube. They grow as the nails do, each part near the root thrusting forward that which is immediately above it, and not by any liquor running along the hair in tubes, as plants grow. *Quincy.*

2. A single hair.

My fleece of woolly *hair* uncurls. *Shakesp. Tit. Andr.*

Shall the difference of *hair* only, on the skin, be a mark of a different internal constitution between a changeling and a drill? *Locke.*

Naughty lady,
These *hairs* which thou do'st ravish from my chin,
Will quicken and accuse thee. *Shakesp. King Lear.*

Much is breeding;
Which, like the courser's *hair*, hath yet but life,
And not a serpent's poison. *Shakesp. Ant. and Cleopatra:*

3. Any thing proverbially small.

If thou tak'st more
Or less than just a pound; if the scale turn
But in the estimation of a *hair*,
Thou diest. *Shakespeare's Merchant of Venice.*

He judges to a *hair* of little indecencies, and knows better than any man what is not to be written. *Dryden.*

4. Course; order; grain; the hair falling in a certain direction.

Mr. doctor, he is a curer of souls, and you a curer of bodies: if you should fight, you go against the *hair* of your profession. *Shakespeare's Merry Wives of Windsor.*

HA'IRBRAINED. *adj.* [This should rather be written *harebrained*, unconstant, unsettled, wild as a *hare.*] Wild; irregular; unsteady.

Let's leave this town; for they are *hairbrain'd* slaves,
And hunger will enforce them be more eager. *Shakes. H.*VI.

HA'IRBREADTH. *n. s.* [*hair* and *breadth.*] A very small distance; the diameter of a hair.

Seven hundred chosen men left-handed could sling stones at an *hairbreadth*, and not miss. *Judg.* xx. 16.

I spoke of most disastrous chances,
Of moving accidents by flood and field;
Of *hairbreadth* 'scapes in th' imminent deadly breach. *Shak.*

HAI'RBEL. *n. s.* The name of a flower; the hyacinth.

HA'IRCLOTH. *n. s.* [*hair* and *cloth.*] Stuff made of hair, very rough and prickly, worn sometimes in mortification.

It is composed of reeds and parts of plants woven together, like a piece of *haircloth.* *Grew's Musæum.*

Hairla'ce. *n. ſ.* [*hair* and *lace*] The fillet with which women tie up their hair.

Worms are commonly reſembled to a woman's *hairlace* or fillet, thence called tenia. *Harvey on Conſumptions.*

If Molly happens to be careleſs,
And but neglects to warm her *hairlace*,
She gets a cold as ſure as death. *Swift.*

Ha'irless. *adj.* [from *hair.*] Without hair.

White beards have arm'd their thin and *hairleſs* ſcalps
Againſt thy majeſty. *Shakeſpeare's Richard* II.

Ha'iriness. *n. ſ.* [from *hairy.*] The ſtate of being covered with hair, or abounding with hair.

Ha'iry. *adj.* [from *hair.*]

1. Overgrown with hair; covered with hair.

She his *hairy* temples then had rounded
With coronet of flowers. *Shakeſ. Midſum. Night's Dream.*

Children are not *hairy*, for that their ſkins are more perſpirable. *Bacon's Natural Hiſtory.*

2. Conſiſting of hair.

Storms have ſhed
From vines the *hairy* honours of their head. *Dryd. Virgil.*

Hake. *n. ſ.* A kind of fiſh.

The coaſt is plentifully ſtored with mackrel and *hake*. *Carew's Survey of Cornwal.*

Ha'kot. *n. ſ.* [from *hake.*] A kind of fiſh. *Ainſworth.*

Hal is derived like *al* from the Saxon ƿealle, *i. e.* a hall, a palace. In Gothick *alh* ſignifies a temple, or any other famous building. *Gibſon's Camden.*

HA'LBERD. *n. ſ.* [*halebarde*, French; *hallebarde*, Dutch, from *barde*, an ax, and *halle*, a court, halberds being the common weapons of guards.] A battle-ax fixed to a long pole.

Advance thy *halberd* higher than my breaſt,
Or I'll ſtrike thee to my foot. *Shakeſpeare's Richard* III.

Our *halberds* did ſhut up his paſſage. *Shakeſp. Henry* VI.

Four knaves in garbs ſuccinct, a truſty band,
Caps on their heads, and *halberds* in their hand,
Draw forth to combat on the velvet plain. *Pope.*

Halberdi'er. *n. ſ.* [*halebardier*, French, from *halberd.*] One who is armed with a halberd.

The dutcheſs appointed him a guard of thirty perſons, *halberdeers*, in a livery of murrey and blue, to attend his perſon. *Bacon's Henry* VII.

The king had only his *halberdeers*, and fewer of them than uſed to go with him. *Clarendon.*

Ha'lcyon. *n. ſ.* [*halcyo*, Latin.] A bird, of which it is ſaid that ſhe breeds in the ſea, and that there is always a calm during her incubation.

Such ſmiling rogues, as theſe, ſooth ev'ry paſſion,
Bring oil to fire, ſnow to their colder moods;
Renege, affirm, and turn their *halcyon* beaks
With ev'ry gale and vary of their maſters. *Shakeſ. K. Lear.*

Amidſt our arms as quiet you ſhall be,
As *halcyons* brooding on a Winter ſea. *Dryden's Ind. Emp.*

Ha'lcyon. *adj.* [from the noun.] Placid; quiet; ſtill; peaceful.

When great Auguſtus made war's tempeſts ceaſe,
His *halcyon* days brought forth the arts of peace. *Denham.*

No man can expect eternal ſerenity and *halcyon* days from ſo incompetent and partial a cauſe, as the conſtant courſe of the ſun in the equinoctial circle. *Bentley's Sermons.*

Hale. *adj.* [This ſhould rather be written *hail*, from *hæl*, health.] Healthy; ſound; hearty; well complexioned.

My ſeely ſheep like well below,
For they been *hale* enough I trow,
And liken their abode. *Spenſer's Paſtorals.*

Some of theſe wiſe partizans concluded the government had hired two or three hundred *hale* men, to be pinioned, if not executed, as repreſentatives of the pretended captives. *Addiſon's Freeholder*, Nº. 7.

His ſtomach too begins to fail;
Laſt year we thought him ſtrong and *hale*,
But now he's quite another thing:
I wiſh he may hold out 'till Spring. *Swift.*

To **Hale.** *v. a.* [*halen*, Dutch; *haler*, French.] To drag by force; to pull violently.

Fly to your houſe;
The plebeians have got your fellow tribune,
And *hale* him up and down. *Shakeſp. Coriolanus.*

My third comfort,
Starr'd moſt unluckily, is from my breaſt
Hal'd out to murder. *Shakeſpeare's Winter's Tale.*

Give diligence that thou mayeſt be delivered from him, leſt he *hale* thee to the judge. *Lu.* xii. 58.

He by the neck hath *hal'd*, in pieces cut,
And ſet me as a mark on every butt. *Sandys.*

Thither by harpy-footed furies *hal'd*,
At certain revolutions, all the damn'd
Are brought. *Milton's Paradiſe Loſt*, *b.* ii.

This ſiniſtrous gravity is drawn that way by the great artery, which then ſubſideth, and *haleth* the heart unto it. *Brown.*

Who would not be diſguſted with any recreation, in itſelf indifferent, if he ſhould with blows be *haled* to it when he had no mind? *Locke.*

In all the tumults at Rome, though the people proceeded ſometimes to pull and *hale* one another about, yet no blood was drawn 'till the time of the Gracchi. *Swift.*

Ha'ler. *n. ſ.* [from *hale.*] He who pulls and hales.

HALF. *n. ſ.* plural. [ƿealf, Saxon, and all the Teutonick dialects. The *l* is often not ſounded.]

1. A moiety; one part of two; an equal part.

An *half* acre of land. 1 *Sa.* xiv. 14.

Many might go to heaven with *half* the labour they go to hell, if they would venture their induſtry the right way. *Ben. Johnſon's Diſcoveries.*

Well choſen friendſhip, the moſt noble
Of virtues, all our joys makes double,
And into *halves* divides our trouble. *Denham.*

Or what but riches is there known
Which man can ſolely call his own;
In which no creature goes his *half*,
Unleſs it be to ſquint and laugh? *Hudibras*, *p.* ii.

No mortal tongue can *half* the beauty tell;
For none but hands divine could work ſo well. *Dryden.*

Of our manufacture foreign markets took off one *half*, and the other *half* were conſumed amongſt ourſelves. *Locke.*

The council is made up *half* out of the noble families, and *half* out of the plebeian. *Addiſon on Italy.*

Half the miſery of life might be extinguiſhed, would men alleviate the general curſe by mutual compaſſion. *Addiſon.*

Her beauty, in thy ſofter *half*
Bury'd and loſt, ſhe ought to grieve. *Prior.*

Natural was it for a prince, who had propoſed to himſelf the empire of the world, not to neglect the ſea, the *half* of his dominions. *Arbuthnot on Coins.*

2. It ſometimes has a plural ſignification when a number is divided.

Had the land ſelected of the beſt,
Half had come hence, and let the world provide the reſt. *Dryden.*

3. It is much uſed in compoſition to ſignify a thing imperfect, as the following examples will ſhow.

Half. *adv.* In part; equally.

I go with love and fortune, two blind guides,
To lead my way; *half* loth, and *half* conſenting. *Dryden.*

Half-blood. *n. ſ.* One not born of the ſame father and mother.

Which ſhall be heir of the two male twins, who, by the diſſection of the mother, were laid open to the world? Whether a ſiſter by the *half-blood* ſhall inherit before a brother's daughter by the whole-blood? *Locke.*

Half-blooded. *adj.* [*half* and *blood.*] Mean; degenerate.

The let alone lies not in your good will.
——Nor in thine, lord.
——*Half-blooded* fellow, yes. *Shakeſ. King Lear.*

Half-cap. *n. ſ.* Cap imperfectly put off, or faintly moved.

After diſtaſteful looks, and theſe hard fractions,
With certain *half-caps* and cold moving nods,
They froze me into ſilence. *Shakeſ. Timon of Athens.*

Ha'lfendeal. *n. ſ.* [*half* and ðæl, Saxon.] Part. *Spenſer.*

Half-faced. *adj.* [*half* and *faced.*] Showing only part of the face; ſmall faced.

Proud incroaching tyranny
Burns with revenging fire, whoſe hopeful colours
Advance, a *half-faced* ſun ſtriving to ſhine. *Shak. Hen.* VI.

This ſame *half-faced* fellow, Shadow; give me this man: he preſents no mark to the enemy: the foeman may with as great aim level at the edge of a penknife. *Shak. Henry* IV.

Half-hatched. *adj.* [*half* and *hatch.*] Imperfectly hatched.

Here, thick as hailſtones pour,
Turnips, and *half-hatch'd* eggs, a mingled ſhow'r,
Among the rabble rain. *Gay's Trivia.*

Half-heard. *adj.* Imperfectly heard; not heard to an end.

Not added years on years my taſk could cloſe;
Back to thy native iſlands might'ſt thou ſail,
And leave *half-heard* the melancholy tale. *Pope's Odyſſey.*

Half-moon. *n. ſ.*

1. The moon in its appearance when at half increaſe or decreaſe.

2. Any thing in the figure of a half moon.

See how in warlike muſter they appear,
In rhombs and wedges, and *half-moons* and wings. *Milton.*

Half-peny. *n. ſ.* plural *half-pence.* [*half* and *peny.*] A copper coin, of which two make a peny.

There ſhall be in England ſeven *half-peny* loaves ſold for a peny. *Shakeſpeare's Henry* VI. *p.* ii.

Bardolph ſtole a lute-caſe, bore it twelve leagues, and ſold it for three *half-pence.* *Shakeſpeare's Henry* V.

I thank you; and ſure, dear friend, my thanks are too dear of a *half-peny.* *Shakeſpeare.*

He cheats for *half-pence*, and he doffs his coat
To ſave a farthing in a ferryboat. *Dryden's Perſ.*

Never admit this pernicious coin, no not ſo much as one ſingle *half-peny.* *Swift.*

You will wonder how Wood could get his majeſty's broad ſeal for ſo great a ſum of bad money, and that the nobility here could not obtain the ſame favour, and make our own *half-pence* as we uſed to do. *Swift.*

HALF-PIKE. *n. ſ.* [*half* and *pike.*] The ſmall pike carried by officers.

The various ways of paying the ſalute with the *half-pike.* *Tatler*, N°. 60.

HALF-PINT. *n. ſ.* [*half* and *pint.*] The fourth part of a quart.

One *half-pint* bottle ſerves them both to dine;
And is at once their vinegar and wine. *Pope's Horace.*

HALF-SCHOLAR. *n. ſ.* Imperfectly learned.

We have many *half-ſcholars* now-a-days, and there is much confuſion and inconſiſtency in the notions and opinions of ſome perſons. *Watts's Improvement of the Mind.*

HALF-SEAS *over.* A proverbial expreſſion for any one far advanced. It is commonly uſed of one half drunk.

I am *half-ſeas o'er* to death;
And ſince I muſt die once, I would be loth
To make a double work of what's half finiſh'd. *Dryden.*

HALF-SIGHTED. *adj.* [*half* and *ſight.*] Seeing imperfectly; having weak diſcernment.

The officers of the king's houſhold had need be provident, both for his honour and thrift: they muſt look both ways, elſe they are but *half-ſighted.* *Bacon's Advice to Villiers.*

HALF-SPHERE. *n. ſ.* [*half* and *ſphere.*] Hemiſphere.

Let night grow blacker with thy plots; and day,
At ſhewing but thy head forth, ſtart away
From this *half-ſphere.* *Ben. Johnſon's Catiline.*

HALF-STRAINED. *adj.* [*half* and *ſtrain.*] Half-bred; imperfect.

I find I'm but a *half-ſtrain'd* villain yet,
But mungril-miſchievous; for my blood boil'd
To view this brutal act. *Dryden's Don Sebaſtian.*

HALF-SWORD. *n. ſ.* Cloſe fight; within half the length of a ſword.

I am a rogue, if I were not at *half-ſword* with a dozen of them two hours together. *Shakeſpeare's Henry* IV. *p.* i.

HALF-WAY. *adv.* [*half* and *way.*] In the midd e.

Fearleſs he ſees, who is with virtue crown'd,
The tempeſt rage, and hears the thunder ſound;
Ever the ſame, let fortune ſmile or frown:
Serenely as he liv'd reſigns his breath;
Meets deſtiny *half-way*, nor ſhrinks at death. *Granville.*

HALF-WIT. *n. ſ.* [*half* and *wit.*] A blockhead; a fooliſh fellow.

Half-wits are fleas, ſo little and ſo light,
We ſcarce could know they live, but that they bite. *Dryden.*

HALF-WITTED. *adj.* [from *half-wit.*] Imperfectly furniſhed with underſtanding.

I would rather have truſted the refinement of our language, as to ſound, to the judgment of the women than of *half-witted* poets. *Swift.*

Jack had paſſed for a poor, well-meaning, *half-witted*, crack-brained fellow: people were ſtrangely ſurpriſed to find him in ſuch a roguery. *Arbuthnot's Hiſt. of John Bull.*

HA'LIBUT. *n. ſ.* A ſort of fiſh. *Ainſworth.*

HA'LIDOM. *n. ſ.* [haliᵹ dom, holy judgment, or haliᵹ and *dame*, for lady.] Our bleſſed lady.

By my *halidom*, quoth he,
Ye a great maſter are in your degree. *Hubberd's Tale.*

HA'LIMASS. *n. ſ.* [haliᵹ and *maſs.*] The feaſt of All-ſouls.

My queen to France; from whence ſet forth in pomp,
She came adorned hither like ſweet May;
Sent back like *halimaſs*, or ſhorteſt day. *Shakeſ. Rich.* II.

HA'LITUOUS. *adj.* [*halitus*, Latin.] Vaporous; fumous.

We ſpeak of the atmoſphere as of a peculiar thin and *halituous* liquor, much lighter than ſpirit of wine. *Boyle.*

HALL. *n. ſ.* [hal, Saxon; *halle*, Dutch.]

1. A court of juſtice.
2. A manour-houſe ſo called, becauſe in it were held courts for the tenants.

Captain Sentry, my maſter's nephew, has taken poſſeſſion of the *hall* houſe, and the whole eſtate. *Addiſon's Spectator.*

3. The publick room of a corporation.

With expedition on the beadle call,
To ſummon all the company to the *hall.* *Garth.*

4. The firſt large room of a houſe.

That light we ſee is burning in my *hall.* *Shakeſpeare.*

Courteſy is ſooner found in lowly ſheds
With ſmoky rafters, than in tap'ſtry *halls*
And courts of princes. *Milton.*

HALLELU'JAH. *n. ſ.* [הללויה] *Praiſe ye the Lord.* A ſong of thankſgiving.

Then ſhall thy ſaints
Unfained *hallelujahs* to Thee ſing,
Hymns of high praiſe. *Milton's Paradiſe Loſt, b.* vi.

Singing thoſe devout hymns and heavenly anthems, in which the church militant ſeems ambitious to emulate the triumphant, and echo back the ſolemn praiſes and *hallelujahs* of the celeſtial choirs. *Boyle.*

HA'LLOO. *interj.* [The original of this word is controverted: ſome imagine it corrupted from *a lui*, to him! others from *allons*, let us go! and *Skinner* from *haller*, to draw.] A word of encouragement when dogs are let looſe on their game.

Some popular chief,
More noiſy than the reſt, but cries *halloo*,
And, in a trice, the bellowing herd come out. *Dryden.*

To HA'LLOO. *v. n.* [*haler*, Fr.] To cry as after the dogs.

A number of country folks *hallooed* and houted after me, as at the arranteſt coward that ever ſhewed his ſhoulders to his enemy. *Sidney, b.* ii.

A cry more tuneable
Was never *halloo'd* to, nor cheer'd with horn. *Shakeſpeare.*

To HA'LLOO. *v. a.*

1. To encourage with ſhouts.

If, whilſt a boy, Jack ran from ſchool,
Fond of his hunting-horn and pole,
Though gout and age his ſpeed detain,
Old John *halloos* his hounds again. *Prior.*

2. To chaſe with ſhouts.

If I fly, Marcius,
Halloo me like a hare. *Shakeſpeare's Coriolanus.*

3. To call or ſhout to.

When we have found the king, he that firſt lights on him,
Halloo the other. *Shakeſpeare's King Lear.*

To HA'LLOW. *v. a.* [halᵹian, haliᵹ, Saxon, holy.]

1. To conſecrate; to make holy.

When we ſanctify or *hallow* churches, it is only to teſtify that we make them places of publick reſort; that we inveſt God himſelf with them, and that we ſever them from common uſes. *Hooker, b.* v. *ſ.* 12.

With us it cannot be endured to hear a man openly profeſs that he putteth fire to his neighbour's houſe, but yet ſo *halloweth* the ſame with prayer, that he hopeth it ſhall not burn. *Hooker, b* v. *ſ.* 29.

Is't Cade that I have ſlain, that monſtrous traitor?
Sword, I will *hallow* thee for this thy deed,
And hang thee o'er my tomb, when I am dead. *Shakeſp.*

My prayers
Are not words duly *hallow'd*, nor my wiſhes
More worth than vanities; yet pray'rs and wiſhes
Are all I can return. *Shakeſpeare's Henry* VIII.

And from work
Now reſting, bleſs'd and *hallow'd* the ſeventh day,
As reſting on that day from all his works,
But not in ſilence holy kept. *Milton.*

Then baniſh'd faith ſhall once again return,
And veſtal fires in *hallow'd* temples burn. *Dryden's Virgil.*

No ſatyr lurks within this *hallow'd* ground;
But nymphs and heroines, kings and gods abound. *Granv.*

2. To reverence as holy; *hallowed* be thy name.

HALLUCINA'TION. *n. ſ.* [*hallucinatio*, Latin.] Errour; blunder; miſtake; folly.

A waſting of fleſh, without cauſe, is frequently termed a bewitched diſeaſe; but queſtionleſs a meer *hallucination* of the vulgar. *Harvey on Conſumptions.*

This muſt have been the *hallucination* of the tranſcriber, who probably miſtook the daſh of the I for a T. *Addiſ. Spect.*

HALM. *n. ſ.* [healm, Saxon.] Straw. Pronounced *hawm.*

HA'LO. *n. ſ.* A red circle round the ſun or moon.

And, if the hail be a little flatted, the light tranſmitted may grow ſo ſtrong, at a little leſs diſtance than that of twenty-ſix degrees, as to form a *halo* about the ſun or moon; which *halo*, as often as the hailſtones are duly figured, may be coloured. *Newton's Opt.*

I ſaw by reflexion, in a veſſel of ſtagnating water, three *halo's*, crowns or rings of colours about the ſun, like three little rainbows, concentrick to his body. *Newton's Opt.*

HA'LSENING. *adj.* [*hals*, German; *haſs*, Scottiſh, the neck.] Sounding harſhly; inharmonious in the throat or tongue.

This ill *halſening* horny name hath, as cornuto in Italy, opened a gap to the ſcoffs of many. *Carew.*

HA'LSER. *n. ſ.* [from halſ, neck, and ſeel, a rope. It is now in marine pronunciation corrupted to *hawſer.*] A rope leſs than a cable.

A beechen maſt then in the hollow baſe
They hoiſted, and with well-wreath'd *halſers* hoiſe
Their white ſails. *Chapman's Odyſſey, b.* ii.

No *halſers* need to bind theſe veſſels here,
Nor bearded anchors; for no ſtorms they fear. *Dryd. Virg.*

To HALT. *v. n.* [healt, Saxon, lame; healtan, to limp.]

1. To limp; to be lame.

And will ſhe yet debaſe her eyes
On me, that *halt* and am miſ-ſhapen thus? *Shakeſ. R.* III.

Thus inborn broils the factions would engage,
Or wars of exil'd heirs, or foreign rage,
'Till *halting* vengeance overtook our age. *Dryden.*

Spenſer himſelf affects the obſolete,
And Sidney's verſe *halts* ill on Roman feet. *Pope.*

2. To ſtop in a march.

I was forced to *halt* in this perpendicular march. *Addiſon.*

3. To heſitate; to ſtand dubious.

How long *halt* ye between two opinions? 1 *Kings* xviii.

4. To fail; to faulter.

Here's a paper written in his hand;
A *halting* ſonnet of his own pure brain,
Faſhion'd to Beatrice. *Shakeſp. Much Ado about Nothing.*

All my familiars watched for my *halting*, ſaying, peradventure he will be enticed, and we ſhall prevail againſt him. *Jer.*

HALT. *adj.* [from the verb.] Lame; crippled.

Bring in hither the poor, the maimed, the *halt*, and the blind. *Lu.* xiv. 21.

HALT. *n. ſ.* [from the verb.]

1. The act of limping; the manner of limping.

2. [*Alte*, French.] A ſtop in a march.

The heav'nly bands
Down from a ſky of jaſper lighted now
In Paradiſe, and on a hill made *halt*. *Milt. Paradiſe Loſt.*

Scouts each coaſt light armed ſcour
Each quarter to deſcry the diſtant foe,
Where lodg'd, or whether fled, or if for fight
In motion, or in *halt*. *Milton's Paradiſe Loſt, b.* vi.

Without any *halt* they marched between the two armies. *Clarendon, b.* viii.

He might have made a *halt* 'till his foot and artillery came up to him. *Clarendon, b.* ii.

HA'LTER. *n. ſ.* [from *halt.*] He who limps.

HA'LTER. *n. ſ.* [healſtre, Saxon, from halſ, the neck.]

1. A rope to hang malefactors.

He's fled, my lord, and all his pow'rs do yield;
And humbly thus, with *halters* on their necks,
Expect your highneſs' doom of life or death. *Shak. H.* VI.

Anſwer was made, it was by the ſword if they ſtood upon defence, and by the *halter* if they yielded; wherefore they made choice to die rather as ſoldiers than as dogs. *Hayward.*

Were I a drowſy judge, whoſe diſmal note
Diſgorgeth *halters*, as a juggler's throat
Doth ribbands. *Cleaveland.*

When the times begin to alter,
None riſe ſo high as from the *halter*. *Hudibras, p.* iii.

He gets renown, who, to the *halter* near,
But narrowly eſcapes, and buys it dear. *Dryden's Juvenal.*

2. A cord; a ſtrong ſtring.

Whom neither *halter* binds nor burthens charge. *Sandys.*

To HA'LTER. *v. a.* [from the noun.] To bind with a cord; to catch in a nooſe.

He might have employed his time in the frivolous delights of catching moles and *haltering* frogs. *Atterbury.*

To HALVE. *v. a.* [from *half*, *halves.*] To divide into two parts.

HALVES. *interj.* [from *half*, *halves* being the plural.] An expreſſion by which any one lays claim to an equal ſhare.

Have you not ſeen how the divided dam
Runs to the ſummons of her hungry lamb?
But when the twin cries *halves*, ſhe quits the firſt. *Cleaveland.*

HAM, whether initial or final, is no other than the Saxon ham, a houſe, farm, or village. *Gibſon's Camden.*

HAM. *n. ſ.* [ham, Saxon; *hamme*, Dutch.]

1. The hip; the hinder part of the articulation of the thigh with the knee.

The *ham* was much relaxed; but there was ſome contraction remaining. *Wiſeman.*

2. The thigh of a hog ſalted.

Who has not learn'd, freſh ſturgeon and *ham* pye
Are no rewards for want and infamy. *Pope's Horace.*

HA'MATED. *adj.* [*hamatus*, Latin.] Hooked; ſet with hooks.

To HA'MBLE. *v. a.* [from *ham.*] To cut the ſinews of the thigh; to hamſtring.

HAME. *n. ſ.* [hama, Saxon.] The collar by which a horſe draws in a waggon.

HA'MLET. *n. ſ.* [ham, Saxon, and *let*, the diminutive termination.] A ſmall village.

Within the ſelf-ſame lordſhip, pariſh, or *hamlet*, lands have divers degrees of value. *Bacon's Off. of Alienation.*

He pitch'd upon the plain
His mighty camp, and, when the day return'd,
The country waſted and the *hamlets* burn'd. *Dryden's Fables.*

HA'MMER. *n. ſ.* [hamer, Saxon; *hammer*, Daniſh.]

1. The inſtrument conſiſting of a long handle and heavy head, with which any thing is forged or driven.

The armourers,
With buſy *hammers* cloſing rivets up,
Give dreadful note of preparation. *Shakeſpeare's Henry* V.

The ſtuff will not work well with a *hammer*. *Bacon.*

It is broken not without many blows, and will break the beſt anvils and *hammers* of iron. *Brown's Vulgar Errours.*

Every morning he riſes freſh to his *hammer* and his anvil. *South's Sermons.*

The ſmith prepares his *hammer* for the ſtroke. *Dryd. Juv.*

2. Any thing deſtructive.

That renowned pillar of truth and *hammer* of hereſies, St. Auguſtine. *Hakewill on Providence.*

To HA'MMER. *v. a.* [from the noun.]

1. To beat with a hammer.

His bones the *hammer'd* ſteel in ſtrength ſurpaſs. *Sandys.*

2. To forge or form with a hammer.

Some *hammer* helmets for the fighting field. *Dryd. Æn.*

Drudg'd like a ſmith, and on the anvil beat,
'Till he had *hammer'd* out a vaſt eſtate. *Dryden's Juvenal.*

I muſt pay with *hammered* money inſtead of milled. *Dryden.*

3. To work in the mind; to contrive by intellectual labour.

Wilt thou ſtill be *hammering* treachery,
To humble down thy huſband and thyſelf? *Shakeſp. H.* VI.

He was nobody that could not *hammer* out of his name an invention by this witcraft, and picture it accordingly. *Camden.*

Some ſpirits, by whom they were ſtirred and guided in the name of the people, *hammered* up the articles. *Hayward.*

To HA'MMER. *v. n.*

1. To work; to be buſy.

Nor need'ſt thou much importune me to that,
Whereon this month I have been *hammering*. *Shakeſpeare.*

I have been ſtudying how to compare
This priſon where I live unto the world;
And, for becauſe the world is populous,
And here is not a creature but myſelf,
I cannot do it; yet I'll *hammer* on't. *Shakeſpeare.*

2. To be in agitation.

Vengeance is in my heart, death in my hand;
Blood and revenge are *hammering* in my head. *Sh. Tit. Andr.*

HA'MMERER. *n. ſ.* [from *hammer.*] He who works with a hammer.

HA'MMERHARD. *n. ſ.* [*hammer* and *hard.*]

Hammerhard is when you harden iron or ſteel with much hammering on it. *Moxon's Mech. Exer.*

HA'MMOCK. *n. ſ.* [hamaca, Saxon.] A ſwinging bed.

Prince Maurice of Naſſau, who had been accuſtomed to *hammocks*, uſed them all his life. *Temple.*

HA'MPER. *n. ſ.* [Suppoſed by *Minſhew* to be contracted from *hand panier*; but *hanaperium* appears to have been a word long in uſe, whence *hanaper*, *hamper.*] A large baſket for carriage.

What powder'd wigs! what flames and darts!
What *hampers* full of bleeding hearts. *Swift.*

To HA'MPER. *v. a.* [The original of this word, in its preſent meaning, is uncertain: *Junius* obſerves that *hamplyns* in Teutonick is a quarrel: others imagine that *hamper* or *hanaper*, being the treaſury to which fines are paid, to *hamper*, which is commonly applied to the law, means originally to fine.]

1. To ſhackle; to entangle in chains.

O looſe this frame, this knot of man untie!
That my free ſoul may uſe her wing,
Which now is pinion'd with mortality,
As an entangl'd, *hamper'd* thing. *Herbert.*

We ſhall find ſuch engines to aſſail,
And *hamper* thee, as thou ſhalt come of force. *Milton.*

What was it but a lion *hampered* in a net! *L'Eſtrange.*

They *hamper* and entangle our ſouls, and hinder their flight upwards. *Tillotſon's Sermons.*

2. To enſnare; to inveigle; to catch with allurements.

She'll *hamper* thee, and dandle thee like a baby. *Shakeſp.*

Wear under vizard-maſks their talents,
And mother wits before their gallants;
Until they're *hamper'd* in the nooze,
Too faſt to dream of breaking looſe. *Hudibras, p.* iii.

3. To complicate; to tangle.

Engend'ring heats, theſe one by one unbind,
Stretch their ſmall tubes, and *hamper'd* nerves unwind. *Blac.*

4. To perplex; to embarraſs by many lets and troubles.

And when th' are *hamper'd* by the laws,
Releaſe the lab'rers for the cauſe. *Hudibras, p.* iii. *cant* 2.

HA'MSTRING. *n. ſ.* [*ham* and *ſtring.*] The tendon of the ham.

A ſtrutting player, whoſe conceit
Lies in his *hamſtring*, doth think it rich
To hear the wooden dialogue, and found
'Twixt his ſtretch'd footing and the ſcaffoldage. *Shakeſp.*

On the hinder ſide it is guarded with the two *hamſtrings*. *Wiſeman's Surgery.*

To HA'MSTRING. *v. a.* preter. and part. paſſ. *hamſtrung.* [from the noun.] To lame by cutting the tendon of the ham.

Hamſtring'd behind, unhappy Gyges dy'd;
Then Phalaris is added to his ſide. *Dryden's Æn.*

HAN for *have*, in the plural. *Spenſer.*

HA'NAPER. *n. ſ.* [*hanaperium*, low Latin.] A treaſury; an exchequer. The clerk of the *hanaper* receives the fees due to the king for the ſeal of charters and patents.

The fines for all original writs were wont to be immediately paid into the *hanaper* of the Chancery. *Bacon.*

HA'NCES. *n. ſ.* [In a ſhip.] Falls of the fife-rails placed on banniſters on the poop and quarter-deck down to the gangway. *Har.*

HANCES. [In architecture.] The ends of elliptical arches; and theſe are the arches of ſmaller circles than the ſcheme, or middle part of the arch. *Harris.*

The ſweep of the arch will not contain above fourteen inches, and perhaps you muſt cement pieces to many of the courſes in the *hance*, to make them long enough to contain fourteen inches. *Moxon's Mech. Exer.*

HAND.

HAND. *n. s.* [hand, hond, Saxon, and in all the Teutonick dialects.]

1. The palm with the fingers; the member with which we hold or use any instrument.

They laid *hands* upon him, and bound him *hand* and foot. *Knolles's History of the Turks.*

So *hand* in *hand* they pass'd, the loveliest pair
That ever since in love's embraces met. *Milt. Parad. Lost.*

They *hand* in *hand*, with wandering steps and slow,
Through Eden took their solitary way. *Milton.*

That wonderful instrument the *hand*, was it made to be idle? *Berkley.*

2. Measure of four inches; a measure used in the matches of horses; a palm.

3. Side, right or left.

For the other side of the court-gate on this *hand*, and that *hand*, were hangings of fifteen cubits. *Ex.* xxxviii. 15.

4. Part; quarter; side.

It is allowed on all *hands*, that the people of England are more corrupt in their morals than any other nation this day under the sun. *Swift.*

5. Ready payment with respect to the receiver.

Of which offer the bassa accepted, receiving in *hand* one year's tribute. *Knolles's History of the Turks.*

These two must make our duty very easy; a considerable reward in *hand*, and the assurance of a far greater recompence hereafter. *Tillotson's Sermons.*

6. Ready payment with regard to the payer.

Let not the wages of any man tarry with thee, but give it him out of *hand*. *Tob.* iv. 14.

7. Rate; price.

Time is the measure of business, as money of wares: business is bought at a dear *hand*, where there is small dispatch. *Bacon, Essay* 26.

8. Terms; conditions.

With simplicity admire and accept the mystery; but at no *hand* by pride, ignorance, interest, or vanity wrest it to ignoble senses. *Taylor's Worthy Communicant.*

It is either an ill sign or an ill effect, and therefore at no *hand* consistent with humility. *Taylor's Rule of living holy.*

9. Act; deed; external action.

Thou sawest the contradiction between my heart and *hand*. *King Charles.*

10. Labour; act of the hand.

Alnaschar was a very idle fellow, that never would set his *hand* to any business during his father's life. *Addison's Spectat.*

I rather suspect my own judgment than I can believe a fault to be in that poem, which lay so long under Virgil's correction, and had his last *hand* put to it. *Addison.*

11. Performance.

Where are these porters,
These lazy knaves? Y'ave made a fine *hand!* fellows,
There's a trim rabble let in. *Shakespeare's Henry* VIII.

12. Power of performance.

Will. Honeycomb has told me, that he had a great mind to try his *hand* at a Spectator, and that he would fain have one of his writing in my works. *Addison's Spectator.*

A friend of mine has a very fine *hand* on the violin. *Addison's Guardian*, N°. 98.

13. Attempt; undertaking.

Out of them you dare take in *hand* to lay open the original of such a nation. *Spenser on Ireland.*

14. Manner of gathering or taking.

As her majesty hath received great profit, so may she, by a moderate *hand*, from time to time reap the like. *Bacon.*

15. Workmanship; power or act of manufacturing or making.

An intelligent being, coming out of the *hands* of infinite perfection, with an aversion or even indifferency to be reunited with its Author, the source of its utmost felicity, is such a shock and deformity in the beautiful analogy of things, as is not consistent with finite wisdom and perfection. *Cheyne.*

16. Manner of acting or performing.

The master saw the madness rise;
His glowing cheeks, his ardent eyes;
And while he heav'n and earth defy'd,
Chang'd his *hand*, and check'd his pride. *Dryden.*

17. Agency; part in action.

God must have set a more than ordinary esteem upon that which David was not thought fit to have an *hand* in. *South.*

18. The act of giving or presenting.

Let Tamar dress the meat in my sight, that I may eat it at her *hand*. 2 *Sa.* xiii. 5.

To-night the poet's advocate I stand,
And he deserves the favour at my *hand*. *Addison.*

19. Act of receiving any thing ready to one's *hand*, when it only waits to be taken.

His power reaches no farther than to compound and divide the materials that are made to his *hand*; but can do nothing towards the making or destroying one atom of what is already in being. *Locke.*

Many, whose greatness and fortune were not made to their *hands*, had sufficient qualifications and opportunities of rising to these high posts. *Addison's Freeholder.*

20. Care; necessity of managing.

Jupiter had a farm a long time upon his *hands*, for want of a tenant to come up to his price. *L'Estrange.*

When a statesman wants a day's defence,
Or envy holds a whole week's war with sense,
Or simple pride for flatt'ry makes demands,
May dunce by dunce be whistled off my *hands*. *Pope.*

21. Discharge of duty.

Let it therefore be required, on both parts, at the *hands* of the clergy, to be in meanness of estate like the apostles; at the *hands* of the laity, to be as they who lived under the apostles. *Hooker, Preface.*

22. Reach; nearness: as, *at hand*, within reach, near, approaching.

Your husband is at *hand*, I hear his trumpet. *Shakesp.*

Cousins, I hope the days are near at *hand*
That chambers will be safe. *Shakespeare's Macbeth.*

He is at *hand*, and Pindarus is come
To do you salutation. *Shakespeare's Julius Cæsar.*

The fight of his mind was like some fights of eyes; rather strong at *hand* than to carry afar off. *Bacon's Henry* VII.

Any light thing that moveth, when we find no wind, sheweth a wind at *hand*. *Bacon's Natural History.*

A very great sound near *hand* hath strucken many deaf. *Bacon's Natural History*, N°. 128.

It is not probable that any body should effect that at a distance, which, nearer *hand*, it cannot perform. *Brown.*

When mineral or metal is to be generated, nature needs not to have at *hand* salt, sulphur, and mercury. *Boyle.*

23. Manual management.

Nor swords at *hand*, nor hissing darts afar,
Are doom'd t' avenge the tedious bloody war. *Dryd. Juven.*

24. State of being in preparation.

Where is our usual manager of mirth?
What revels are in *hand?* Is there no play,
To ease the anguish of a torturing hour? *Shakespeare.*

25. State of being in present agitation.

I look'd upon her with a soldier's eye;
That lik'd, but had a rougher task in *hand*
Than to drive liking to the name of war. *Shakespeare.*

It is indifferent to the matter in *hand* which way the learned shall determine of it. *Locke.*

26. Cards held at a game.

There was never an *hand* drawn, that did double the rest of the habitable world, before this; for so a man may term it, if he shall put to account that which may be hereafter, by the occupation and colonizing of those countries. *Bacon.*

27. That which is used in opposition to another.

He would dispute,
Confute, change *hands*, and still confute. *Hudibras, p.* i.

28. Scheme of action.

Consult of your own ways, and think which *hand*
Is best to take. *Ben. Johnson's Catiline.*

They who thought they could never be secure, except the king were first at their mercy, were willing to change the *hand* in carrying on the war. *Clarendon, b.* viii.

29. Advantage; gain; superiority.

The French king, supposing to make his *hand* by those rude ravages in England, broke off his treaty of peace, and proclaimed hostility. *Hayward.*

30. Competition; contest.

She in beauty, education, blood,
Holds *hand* with any princess of the world. *Shakes. K. Lear.*

31. Transmission; conveyance; agency of conveyance.

The salutation by the *hand* of me Paul. *Col.* iv. 18.

32. Possession; power.

Sacraments serve as the moral instruments of God to that purpose; the use whereof is in our *hands*, the effect in his. *Hooker.*

And though you war, like petty wrangling states,
You're in my *hand*; and when I bid you cease,
You shall be crush'd together into peace. *Dryden.*

Between the landlord and tenant there must be a quarter of the revenue of the land constantly in their *hands*. *Locke.*

It is fruitless pains to learn a language, which one may guess by his temper he will wholly neglect, as soon as an approach to manhood, setting him free from a governour, shall put him into the *hands* of his own inclination. *Locke.*

Vectigales Agri were lands taken from the enemy, and distributed amongst the soldiers, or left in the *hands* of the proprietors under the condition of certain duties. *Arbuthnot.*

33. Pressure of the bridle.

There are no tricks in plain and simple faith;
But hollow men, like horses hot at *hand*,
Make gallant show and promise of their mettle. *Shakesp.*

34. Method of government; discipline; restraint.

Menelaus bare an heavy *hand* over the citizens, having a malicious mind against his countrymen. 2 *Mac.* v. 23.

He kept a strict *hand* on his nobility, and chose rather to advance clergymen and lawyers. *Bacon's Henry* VII.

However

However strict a *hand* is to be kept upon all desires of fancy, yet in recreation fancy must be permitted to speak. *Locke.*

35. Influence; management.

Flattery, the dang'rous nurse of vice,
Got *hand* upon his youth, to pleasures bent. *Daniel.*

36. That which performs the office of a hand in pointing.

The body, though it moves, yet changing perceivable distance with other bodies, as fast as the ideas of our own minds do naturally follow one another, the thing seems to stand still; as is evident in the *hands* of clocks and shadows of sun-dials. *Locke.*

37. Agent; person employed.

The wisest prince, if he can save himself and his people from ruin, under the worst administration, what may not his subjects hope for when he changeth *hands*, and maketh use of the best? *Swift.*

38. Giver, and receiver.

This tradition is more like to be a notion bred in the mind of man, than transmitted from *hand* to *hand* through all generations. *Tillotson, Sermon* 1.

39. An actor; a workman; a soldier.

Your wrongs are known: impose but your commands,
This hour shall bring you twenty thousand *hands*. *Dryden.*

Demetrius appointed the painter guards for his security, pleased that he could preserve that *hand* from the barbarity and insolence of soldiers. *Dryden's Dufresnoy.*

A dictionary containing a natural history requires too many *hands*, as well as too much time, ever to be hoped for. *Locke.*

40. Catch or reach without choice.

The men of Israel smote as well the men of every city as the beast, and all that came to *hand*. *Judg.* xx. 48.

A sweaty reaper from his tillage brought
First fruits, the green ear, and the yellow sheaf,
Uncull'd as came to *hand*. *Milton's Paradise Lost, b.* xi.

41. Form or cast of writing.

Here is th' indictment of the good lord Hastings,
Which in a set *hand* fairly is engross'd;
Eleven hours I've spent to write it over. *Shakesp. Rich.* III.

Solyman shewed him his own letters intercepted, asking him if he knew not that *hand*, if he knew not that seal. *Knoll.*

Being discovered by their knowledge of Mr. Cowley's *hand*, I happily escaped. *Denham, Dedication.*

If my debtors do not keep their day,
Deny their *hands*, and then refuse to pay,
I must attend. *Dryd. Juvenal.*

Whether men write court or Roman *hand*, or any other, there is something peculiar in every one's writing. *Cockburn.*

The way to teach to write, is to get a plate graved with the characters of such *hand* you like. *Locke.*

Constantia saw that the *hand* writing agreed with the contents of the letter. *Addison's Spectator.*

I present these thoughts in an ill *hand*; but scholars are bad penmen: we seldom regard the mechanick part of writing. *Felton on the Classicks.*

They were wrote on both sides, and in a small *hand*. *Arbut.*

42. Hand *over head*. Negligently; rashly; without seeing what one does.

So many strokes of the alarum bell of fear and awaking to other nations, and the facility of the titles, which, *hand over head*, have served their turn, doth ring the peal so much the louder. *Bacon's War with Spain.*

A country fellow got an unlucky tumble from a tree: thus 'tis, says a passenger, when people will be doing things *hand over head*, without either fear or wit. *L'Estrange.*

43. Hand *to* Hand. Close fight.

In single opposition, *hand to hand*,
He did confound the best part of an hour. *Shakesp. H.* IV.

He issues, ere the fight, his dread command,
That slings afar, and poiniards *hand to hand*,
Be banish'd from the field. *Dryden's Fables.*

44. Hand *in* Hand. In union; conjointly.

Had the sea been Marlborough's element, the war had been bestowed there, to the advantage of the country, which would then have gone *hand in hand* with his own. *Swift.*

45. Hand *in* Hand. Fit; pat.

As fair and as good, a kind of *hand in hand* comparison, had been something too fair and too good for any lady in Britany. *Shakespeare's Cymbeline.*

46. Hand *to mouth*. As want requires.

I can get bread from *hand to mouth*, and make even at the year's end. *L'Estrange.*

47. *To bear in* Hand. To keep in expectation; to elude.

A rascally yea forsooth knave, to *bear in hand*, and then stand upon security. *Shakespeare's Henry* IV. *p.* ii.

48. *To be* Hand *and Glove*. To be intimate and familiar.

To Hand. *v. a.* [from the noun.]

1. To give or transmit with the hand.

Judas was not far off, not only because he dipped in the same dish, but because he was so near that our Saviour could *hand* the sop unto him. *Brown's Vulgar Errours.*

Reports, like snowballs, gather still the farther they roll; and when I have once *handed* it to another, how know I how he may improve it? *Government of the Tongue.*

I have been shewn a written prophecy that is *handed* among them with great secrecy. *Addison's Freeholder.*

2. To guide or lead by the hand.

Angels did *hand* her up, who next God dwell;
For she was of that order whence most fell. *Donne.*

By safe and insensible degrees he will pass from a boy to a man, which is the most hazardous step in life: this therefore should be carefully watched, and a young man with great diligence *handed* over it. *Locke.*

3. To seize; to lay hands on.

Let him, that makes but trifles of his eyes,
First *hand* me: on mine own accord, I'll off. *Shakespeare.*

4. To manage; to move with the hand.

'Tis then that with delight I rove
Upon the boundless depth of love:
I bless my chains, I *hand* my oar,
Nor think on all I left on shoar. *Prior.*

5. To transmit in succession; to deliver down from one to another.

They had not only a tradition of it in general, but even of several the most remarkable particular accidents of it likewise, which they *handed* downwards to the succeeding ages. *Woodw.*

I know no other way of securing these monuments, and making them numerous enough to be *handed* down to future ages. *Addison on ancient Medals.*

Arts and sciences consist of scattered theorems and practices, which are *handed* about amongst the masters, and only revealed to the *filii artis*, 'till some great genius appears, who collects these disjointed propositions, and reduces them into a regular system. *Arbuthnot's History of John Bull.*

One would think a story so fit for age to talk of, and infancy to hear, were incapable of being *handed* down to us. *Pope's Essay on Homer.*

Hand is much used in composition for that which is manageable by the hand, as a *handsaw*; or born in the hand, as a *handbarrow*.

Ha'nd-barrow. *n. s.* A frame on which any thing is carried by the hands of two men, without wheeling on the ground.

A *hand-barrow*, wheelbarrow, shovel and spade. *Tusser.*

Set the board whereon the hive standeth on a *hand-barrow*, and carry them to the place you intend. *Mortim. Husbandry.*

Hand-basket. *n. s.* A portable basket.

You must have woollen yarn to tie grafts with, and a small *hand-basket* to carry them in. *Mortimer's Husbandry.*

Hand-bell. *n. s.* A bell rung by the hand.

The strength of the percussion is a principal cause of the loudness or softness of sounds; as in ringing of a *hand-bell* harder or softer. *Bacon's Natural History.*

Hand-breadth. *n. s.* A space equal to the breadth of the hand; a palm.

A border of an *hand-breadth* round about. *Ex.* xxv. 25.

Within were hooks an *hand-breadth*, fastened round about. *Ezek.* xl. 43.

The eastern people determined their *hand-breadth* by the breadth of barley-corns, six making a digit, and twenty-four a *hand's breadth*. *Arbuthnot on Coins.*

Ha'nded. *adj.* [from *hand*.]

1. Having the use of the hand left or right.

Many are right *handed*, whose livers are weakly constituted; and many use the left, in whom that part is strongest. *Brown's Vulgar Errours, b.* iv. *c.* 5.

2. With hands joined.

Into their inmost bow'r
Handed they went. *Milton's Paradise Lost, b.* iv.

Ha'nder. *n. s.* [from *hand*.] Transmitter; conveyor in succession.

They would assume, with wond'rous art,
Themselves to be the whole, who are but part,
Of that vast frame the church; yet grant they were
The *handers* down, can they from thence infer
A right t' interpret? Or would they alone,
Who brought the present, claim it for their own? *Dryden.*

Ha'ndfast. *n. s.* [*hand* and *fast*.] Hold; custody. Obsolete.

If that shepherd be not in *handfast*, let him fly. *Shakesp.*

Ha'ndful. *n. s.* [*hand* and *full*.]

1. As much as the hand can gripe or contain.

In the park I saw a country gentleman at the side of Rosamond's pond, pulling a *handful* of oats out of his pocket, and gathering the ducks about him. *Freeholder*, N°. 44.

2. A palm; a hand's breadth; four inches.

Take one vessel of silver and another of wood, each full of water, and knap the tongs together about an *handful* from the bottom, and the sound will be more resounding from the vessel of silver than that of wood. *Bacon's Natural History.*

The peaceful scabbard where it dwelt,
The rancour of its edge had felt;
For of the lower end two *handful*
It had devour'd, it was so manful. *Hudibras, p.* i.

3. A small number or quantity.

 Being

Being in possession of the town, they had their *handsful* to defend themselves from firing. *Raleigh's Apology.*

He could not, with such a *handful* of men, and without cannon, propose reasonably to fight a battle. *Clarendon.*

HAND-GALLOP. *n. s.* A slow easy gallop, in which the hand presses the bridle to hinder increase of speed.

Ovid, with all his sweetness, has as little variety of numbers and sound as he: he is always upon a *hand-gallop*, and his verse runs upon carpet ground. *Dryden.*

HAND-GUN. *n. s.* A gun wielded by the hand.

They have names given them, some from serpents or ravenous birds, as culverines or colubrines; others in other respects, as cannons, demicannons, *handguns* and muskets. *Camd.*

HA'NDICRAFT. *n. s.* [*hand* and *craft.*] Manual occupation; work performed by the hand.

The nurseries for children of ordinary gentlemen and *handicrafts* are managed after the same manner. *Gulliver's Trav.*

The cov'nants thou shalt teach by candle-light,
When puffing smiths, and ev'ry painful trade
Of *handicrafts*, in peaceful beds are laid. *Dryden's Juvenal.*

Particular members of convents have excellent mechanical genius's, and divert themselves with painting, sculpture, architecture, gardening, and several kinds of *handicrafts*. *Addison.*

HANDICRA'FTSMAN. *n. s.* [*handicraft* and *man.*] A manufacturer; one employed in manual occupation.

O miserable age! virtue is not regarded in *handicraftsmen*. *Shakespeare's Henry VI. p. ii.*

He has simply the best wit of any *handicraftsman* in Athens. *Shakespeare's Midsummer Night's Dream.*

The principal bulk of the vulgar natives are tillers of the ground, free servants, and *handicraftsmen*; as smiths, masons and carpenters. *Bacon, Essay 30.*

The profaneness and ignorance of *handicraftsmen*, small traders, servants, and the like, are to a degree very hard to be imagined greater. *Swift.*

It is the landed man that maintains the merchant and shopkeeper, and *handicraftsman*. *Swift.*

HA'NDILY. *adv.* [from *handy.*] With skill; with dexterity.

HA'NDINESS. *n. s.* [from *handy.*] Readiness; dexterity.

HA'NDIWORK. *n. s.* [*handy* and *work.*] Work of the hand; product of labour; manufacture.

In general they are not repugnant unto the natural will of God, which wisheth to the works of his own hands, in that they are his own *handiwork*, all happiness; although perhaps, for some special cause in our own particular, a contrary determination have seemed more convenient. *Hooker, b. v.*

As proper men as ever trod upon neats-leather have gone upon my *handiwork*. *Shakespeare's Julius Cæsar.*

The heavens declare the glory of God, and the firmament sheweth his *handiwork*. *Ps. xix. 1.*

He parted with the greatest blessing of human nature for the *handiwork* of a taylor. *L'Estrange.*

HA'NDKERCHIEF. *n. s.* [*hand* and *kerchief.*] A piece of silk or linen used to wipe the face, or cover the neck.

She found her sitting in a chair, in one hand holding a letter, in the other her *handkerchief*, which had lately drunk up the tears of her eyes. *Sidney, b. ii.*

He was torn to pieces with a bear: this avouches the shepherd's son, who has not only his innocence, but a *handkerchief* and rings of his, that Paulina knows. *Shak. Winter's Tale.*

They did not make use of *handkerchiefs*, but of the lacinia or border of the garment, to wipe their face. *Arbuthnot.*

To HA'NDLE *v. a.* [*handelen*, Dutch, from *hand.*]

1. To touch; to feel with the hand.

The bodies which we daily *handle* make us perceive, that whilst they remain between them, they hinder the approach of the parts of our hands that press them. *Locke.*

2. To manage; to wield.

That fellow *handles* his bow like a cowkeeper. *Shakespeare.*

3. To make familiar to the hand by frequent touching.

An incurable shyness is the general vice of the Irish horses, and is hardly ever seen in Flanders, because the hardness of the Winters forces the breeders there to house and *handle* their colts six months every year. *Temple.*

4. To treat in discourse.

He left nothing fitting for the purpose
Untouch'd, or slightly *handled* in discourse. *Shakes. R. III.*

I tell thee, I am mad
In Cressid's love: thou answer'st, she is fair;
Pour'st in the open ulcer of my heart
Her eyes, her hair, her cheek, her gait, her voice,
Thou *handlest* in thy discourse. *Shakes. Troilus and Cressida.*

Leaving to the author the exact *handling* of every particular, and labouring to follow the rules of abridgment. *2 Mac.*

Of a number of other like instances we shall speak more, when we *handle* the communication of sounds. *Bacon.*

By Guidus Ubaldus, in his treatise, for the explication of this instrument, the subtleties of it are largely and excellently *handled*. *Wilkins's Dædalus.*

In an argument, *handled* thus briefly, every thing cannot be said. *Atterbury's Sermons, Preface.*

5. To deal with; to practise.

They that *handle* the law know me not. *Jer. ii. 8.*

6. To treat well or ill.

Talbot, my life, my joy, again return'd!
How wert thou *handled*, being prisoner? *Shak. Henry VI.*

They were well enough pleased to be rid of an enemy that had *handled* them so ill. *Clarendon, b. viii.*

7. To practise upon; to do with.

Pray you, my lord, give me leave to question; you shall see how I'll *handle* her. *Shakesp. Meas. for Measure.*

HA'NDLE. *n. s.* [handle, Saxon.]

1. That part of any thing by which it is held in the hand.

No hand of blood and bone
Can gripe the sacred *handle* of our sceptre,
Unless he do prophane, steal, or usurp. *Shakesp. Rich. II.*

Fortune turneth the *handle* of the bottle, which is easy to be taken hold of; and after the belly, which is hard to grasp. *Bacon's Ornam. Ration.*

There is nothing but hath a double *handle*, or at least we have two hands to apprehend it. *Taylor's Rule of living holy.*

A carpenter, that had got the iron work of an ax, begged only so much wood as would make a *handle* to it. *L'Estrange.*

Of bone the *handles* of my knives are made,
Yet no ill taste from thence affects the blade,
Or what I carve; nor is there ever left
Any unsav'ry haut-goust from the haft. *Dryden's Juvenal.*

A beam there was, on which a beechen pail
Hung by the *handle* on a driven nail. *Dryden's Fables.*

2. That of which use is made.

They overturned him in all his interests by the sure but fatal *handle* of his own good nature. *South's Sermons.*

HA'NDLESS. *adj.* [*hand* and *less.*] Without a hand.

Speak, my Lavinia, what accursed hand
Hath made thee *handless*? *Shakesp. Titus Andronicus.*

His mangled Myrmidons,
Noseless, *handless*, hackt and clipt, come to him,
Crying on Hector. *Shakespeare's Troilus and Cressida.*

HA'NDMAID. *n. s.* A maid that waits at hand.

Brave Burgundy, undoubted hope of France!
Stay, let thy humble *handmaid* speak to thee. *Sh. Hen. VI.*

She gave the knight great thanks in little speech,
And said she would his *handmaid* poor remain. *Fairfax.*

I will never set politicks against ethicks, especially for that true ethicks are but as a *handmaid* to divinity and religion. *Bac.*

Heav'n's youngest teamed star
Hath fix'd her polish'd car,
Her sleeping Lord with *handmaid* lamp attending. *Milton.*

Love led them on; and faith, who knew them best
Thy *handmaids*, clad them o'er with purple beams
And azure wings, that up they flew so drest,
And speak the truth of thee on glorious themes
Before the judge. *Milton.*

Those of my family their master slight,
Grown despicable in my *handmaid's* sight. *Sandys.*

By viewing nature, nature's *handmaid*, art,
Makes mighty things from small beginnings great:
Thus fishes first to shipping did impart,
Their tail the rudder, and their head the prow. *Dryden.*

Since he had placed his heart upon wisdom, health, wealth, victory and honour should always wait on her as her *handmaids*. *Addison's Guardian.*

The great master will descend to hear
The humble series of his *handmaid's* care. *Prior.*

Then criticism the muse's *handmaid* prov'd,
To dress her charms and make her more belov'd. *Pope.*

HA'NDMILL. *n. s.* [*hand* and *mill.*] A mill moved by the hand.

Oft the drudging ass is driv'n with toil;
Returning late, and loaden home with gain
Of barter'd pitch, and *handmills* for the grain. *Dryd. Virg.*

HANDS *off.* A vulgar phrase for keep off; forbear.

They cut a stag into parts; but as they were entering upon the dividend, *hands off*, says the lion. *L'Estrange's Fables.*

HA'NDSAILS. *n. s.* Sails managed by the hand.

The seamen will neither stand to their *handsails*, nor suffer the pilot to steer. *Temple.*

HA'NDSAW. *n. s.* Saw manageable by the hand.

My buckler cut through and through, and my sword hack'd like a *handsaw*. *Shakespeare's Henry IV. p. i.*

To perform this work it is necessary to be provided with a strong knife and a small *handsaw*. *Mortimer's Husbandry.*

HA'NDSEL. *n. s.* [*hansel*, a first gift, Dutch.] The first act of using any thing; the first act of sale.

The apostles term it the pledge of our inheritance, and the *hansel* or earnest of that which is to come. *Hooker.*

Thou art joy's *handsel*; heav'n lies flat in thee,
Subject to ev'ry mounter's bended knee. *Herbert.*

To HA'NDSEL. *v. a.* To use or do any thing the first time.

In timorous deer he *handsels* his young paws,
And leaves the rugged bear for firmer claws. *Cowley.*

I'd show you
How easy 'tis to die, by my example,
And *handsel* fate before you. *Dryden.*

HANDSOME.

 HAN

HA'NDSOME. *adj.* [*handſaem*, Dutch, ready, dexterous.]

1. Ready; gainly; convenient.

For a thief it is ſo *handſome*, as it may ſeem it was firſt invented for him. *Spenſer.*

2. Beautiful with dignity; graceful.

A great man entered by force into a peaſant's houſe, and, finding his wife very *handſome*, turned the good man out of his dwelling. *Addiſon's Guardian.*

3. Elegant; graceful.

That eaſineſs and *handſome* addreſs in writing, which is hardeſt to be attained by perſons bred in a meaner way, will be familiar to you. *Felton on the Claſſicks.*

4. Ample; liberal: as, a *handſome* fortune.

5. Generous; noble: as, a *handſome* action

To HA'NDSOME. *v. a.* [from the adjective.] To render elegant or neat.

Him all repute
For his device in *handſoming* a ſuit;
To judge of lace he hath the beſt conceit. *Donne.*

HA'NDSOMELY. *adv.* [from *handſome.*]

1. Conveniently; dexterouſly.

Under it he may cleanly convey any fit pillage that cometh *handſomely* in his way. *Spenſer on Ireland.*

Where the kind nymph, changing her faultleſs ſhape,
Becomes unhandſome, *handſomely* to 'ſcape. *Waller.*

2. Beautifully; gracefully.

3. Elegantly; neatly.

A carpenter, after he hath ſawn down a tree, hath wrought it *handſomely*, and made a veſſel thereof. *Wiſd.* xiii. 11.

4. Liberally; generouſly.

I am finding out a convenient place for an alms-houſe, which I intend to endow very *handſomely* for a dozen ſuperannuated huſbandmen. *Addiſon.*

HA'NDSOMENESS. *n. ſ.* [from *handſome.*] Beauty; grace; elegance.

Accompanying her mourning garments with a doleful countenance, yet neither forgetting *handſomeneſs* in her mourning garments, nor ſweetneſs in her doleful countenance. *Sidney.*

For *handſomeneſs* ſake, it were good you hang the upper glaſs upon a nail. *Bacon's Natural Hiſtory,*

In cloths, cheap *handſomeneſs* doth bear the bell. *Herbert.*

Perſons of the fairer ſex like that *handſomeneſs* for which they find themſelves to be the moſt liked. *Boyle.*

HA'NDVICE. *n. ſ.* [*hand* and *vice.*] A vice to hold ſmall work in. *Moxon's Mech. Exer.*

HA'NDWRITING. *n. ſ.* [*hand* and *writing.*] A caſt or form of writing peculiar to each hand.

That you beat me at the mart, I have your hand to ſhow;
If the ſkin were parchment, and the blows you gave me ink,
Your own *handwriting* would tell you what I think. *Shak.*

To no other cauſe than the wiſe providence of God can be referred the diverſity of *handwritings.* *Cockburn.*

HA'NDY. *adj.* [from *hand.*]

1. Executed or performed by the hand.

Proudly vaunting, that although they were but few, yet they would eaſily overthrow the great numbers of them, if ever they came to *handy* blows. *Knolles's Hiſt. of the Turks.*

Both parties now were drawn ſo cloſe,
Almoſt to come to *handy* blows. *Hudibras, p.* i. *cant.* 3.

2. Ready; dexterous; ſkilful.

She ſtript the ſtalks of all their leaves; the beſt
She cull'd, and them with *handy* care ſhe dreſt. *Dryden.*

The ſervants waſh the platter, ſcour the plate;
And each is *handy* in his way. *Dryden.*

3. Convenient.

The ſtrike-block is a plane ſhorter than the jointer, and is more *handy* than the long jointer. *Moxon's Mech. Exer.*

HA'NDYDANDY. *n. ſ.* A play in which children change hands and places.

See how yond juſtice rails upon yond ſimple thief! Hark in thine ear: change places, and, *handydandy*, which is the juſtice, which is the thief *Shakeſpeare's King Lear.*

Neither croſs and pile, nor ducks and drakes, are quite ſo ancient as *handydandy.* *Arbuthn. and Pope's Mart. Scrib.*

To HANG. *v. a.* preter. and part. paſſ. *hanged* or *hung*, anciently *hong.* [hangan, Saxon.]

1. To ſuſpend; to faſten in ſuch a manner as to be ſuſtained not below, but above.

Strangely viſited people he cures;
Hanging a golden ſtamp about their necks,
Put on with holy prayers. *Shakeſpeare's Macbeth.*

His great army is utterly ruined, he himſelf ſlain in it, and his head and right hand cut off, and *hung* up before Jeruſalem. *South's Sermons.*

2. To place without any ſolid ſupport.

Thou all things haſt of nothing made,
That *hung'ſt* the ſolid earth in fleeting air,
Vein'd with clear ſprings, which ambient ſeas repair. *Sandys.*

3. To choak and kill by ſuſpending by the neck, ſo as that the ligature intercepts the breath and circulation.

He hath commiſſion from thy wife and me
To *hang* Cordelia in the priſon. *Shakeſpeare's King Lear.*

Hanging ſuppoſes human ſoul and reaſon;
This animal's below committing treaſon:
Shall he be *hang'd*, who never could rebel?
That's a preferment for Achitophel. *Dryden.*

Virgil has deſcribed *hanging* more happily than Homer. *Broome's Notes on the Odyſſey.*

4. To diſplay; to ſhow aloft.

This unlucky mole miſled ſeveral coxcombs; and, like the *hanging* out of falſe colours, made ſome of them converſe with Roſalinda in what they thought the ſpirit of her party. *Addiſ.*

5. To let fall below the proper ſituation; to decline.

There is a wicked man that *hangeth* down his head ſadly; but inwardly he is full of deceit. *Eccluſ.* xix. 26.

The beauties of this place ſhould mourn;
Th' immortal fruits and flow'rs at my return
Should *hang* their wither'd head; for ſure my breath
Is now more pois'nous. *Dryden's State of Innocence.*

The roſe is fragrant, but it fades in time;
The violet ſweet, but quickly paſt the prime;
White lilies *hang* their heads, and ſoon decay;
And whiter ſnow in minutes melts away. *Dryden.*

The cheerful birds no longer ſing;
Each drops his head, and *hangs* his wing. *Prior.*

6. To fix in ſuch a manner as in ſome directions to be moveable.

The gates and the chambers they renewed, and *hanged* doors upon them. 1 *Mac.* iv. 57.

7. To adorn by hanging upon.

Hung be the heav'ns with black, yield day to night! *Sh.*

The pavement ever foul with human gore;
Heads and their mangled members *hung* the door. *Dryden.*

8. To furniſh with ornaments or draperies faſtened to the wall.

Muſick is better in chambers wainſcotted than *hanged.* *Bac.*

If e'er my pious father for my ſake
Did grateful off'rings on thy altars make,
Or I increas'd them with my ſilvan toils,
And *hung* thy holy roofs with ſavage ſpoils,
Give me to ſcatter theſe. *Dryden's Æn.*

Sir Roger has *hung* ſeveral parts of his houſe with the trophies of his labours. *Addiſon's Spectator.*

To HANG. *v. n.*

1. To be ſuſpended; to be ſupported above, not below.

Over it a fair portcullis *hong*,
Which to the gate directly did incline,
With comely compaſs and compacture ſtrong. *Fairy Queen.*

2. To depend; to fall looſely on the lower part; to dangle.

A tower full of aſhes had a round inſtrument, which every ſide *hanged* down. 2 *Mac.* xiii. 5.

Upon her ſhoulders wings ſhe wears
Like *hanging* ſleeves, lin'd through with ears. *Hudibras.*

If gaming does an aged ſire entice,
Then my young maſter ſwiftly learns the vice,
And ſhakes in *hanging* ſleeves the little box and dice. *Dry.*

3. To bend forward.

By *hanging* is only meant a poſture of bending forward to ſtrike the enemy. *Addiſon.*

4. To float; to play.

And fall theſe ſayings from that gentle tongue,
Where civil ſpeech and ſoft perſuaſion *hung.* *P*

5. To be ſupported by ſomething raiſed above the ground.

Whatever is placed on the head may be ſaid to *hang*; call *hanging* gardens ſuch as are planted on the top houſe. *Addiſon*

6. To reſt upon by embracing.

She *hung* about my neck, and kiſs on kiſs
She vied. *Shakeſpeare's Taming of the S.*

To-day might I, *hanging* on Hotſpur's neck,
Have talk'd of Monmouth's grave. *Shakeſp. Henry* IV.

Fauſtina is deſcribed in the form of a lady ſitting upon a bed, and two little infants *hanging* about her neck. *Peacham.*

7. To hover; to impend.

With this ſtrange virtue
He hath a heavenly gift of prophecy;
And ſundry bleſſings *hang* about his throne,
That ſpeak him full of grace. *Shakeſpeare's Macbet*

Odious names of diſtinction, which had ſlept while dread of popery *hung* over us, were revived. *Atterbury's Se*

8. To be looſely joined.

Whither go you?
—To ſee your wife: is ſhe at home?
—Ay, and as idle as ſhe may *hang* together, for want of company. *Shakeſpeare's Merry Wives of Windſor.*

9. To drag; to be incommodiouſly joined.

In my Lucia's abſence
Life *hangs* upon me, and becomes a burden. *Addiſ. Cato.*

10. To be compact or united.

In the common cauſe we are all of a piece; we *hang* together. *Dryden's Spaniſh Fryar.*

Your device *hangs* very well together; but is it not liable to the ſame exceptions you made to ſuch explications as have nothing but the writer's imagination to ſupport them? *Addiſon.*

11. To adhere.

A cheerful temper ſhines out in all her converſation

dissipates those apprehensions which *hang* on the timorous or the modest, when admitted to her presence. *Addison.*

Shining landskips, gilded triumphs, and beautiful faces, disperse that gloominess which is apt to *hang* upon the mind in those dark disconsolate seasons. *Addison's Spectator.*

12. To rest.

Sleep shall neither night nor day
Hang upon his penthouse lid. *Shakespeare's Macbeth.*

Two women, the babes *hanging* at their breasts, were cast headlong from the wall. 2 *Mac.* vi. 10.

13. To be in suspense; to be in a state of uncertainty.

Thy life shall *hang* in doubt before thee, and thou shalt fear day and night, and shalt have none assurance of thy life. *Deut.*

14. To be delayed; to linger.

A noble stroke he lifted,
Which *hung* not, but so swift with tempest fell
On the proud crest of Satan. *Milton's Paradise Lost, b.* vi.

She thrice essay'd to speak: her accents *hung*,
And fault'ring dy'd unfinish'd on her tongue. *Dryden.*

15. To be dependant on.

Oh, how wretched
Is that poor man that *hangs* on princes favours. *Shakesp.*

Great queen! whose name strikes haughty monarchs pale,
On whose just sceptre *hangs* Europa's scale. *Prior.*

16. To be fixed or suspended with attention.

Though wond'ring senates *hung* on all he spoke,
The club must hail him master of the joke. *Pope's Epistles.*

17. To have a steep declivity.

Sussex marl shews itself on the middle of the sides of *hanging* grounds. *Mortimer's Husbandry.*

18. To be executed by the halter.

The court forsakes him, and sir Balaam *hangs*. *Pope.*

19. To decline; to tend down.

His neck obliquely o'er his shoulders *hung*,
Press'd with the weight of sleep that tames the strong. *Pope.*

HA'NGER. *n. s.* [from *hang.*] That by which any thing hangs: as, the pot *hangers*.

HA'NGER. *n. s.* [from *hang.*] A short broad sword.

HA'NGER-ON. *n. s.* [from *hang.*] A dependant; one who eats and drinks without payment.

If the wife or children were absent, their rooms were supplied by the umbræ, or *hangers-on*. *Brown's Vulgar Errours.*

They all excused themselves save two, which two he reckoned his friends, and all the rest *hangers-on*. *L'Estrange.*

He is a perpetual *hanger-on*, yet nobody knows how to be without him. *Swift.*

HA'NGING. *n. s.* [from *hang.*] Drapery hung or fastened against the walls of rooms by way of ornament.

A storm, or robbery, call it what you will,
Shook down my mellow *hangings*, nay, my leaves,
And left me bare to weather. *Shakespeare's Cymbeline.*

Like rich *hangings* in an homely house,
So was his will in his old feeble body. *Shakesp. Henry* VI.

Being informed that his breakfast was ready, he drew towards the door, where the *hangings* were held up. *Clarendon.*

Now purple *hangings* cloath the palace walls,
And sumptuous feasts are made in splendid halls. *Dryden.*

Lucas Van Leyden has infected all Europe with his designs for tapestry, which, by the ignorant, are called ancient *hangings*. *Dryden's Dufresnoy.*

Rome oft has heard a cross haranguing,
With prompting priest behind the *hanging*. *Prior.*

HA'NGING. *participial adj.* [from *hang.*]

1. Foreboding death by the halter.

Surely, sir, a good favour you have; but that you have a *hanging* look. *Shakespeare's Measure for Measure.*

What Ethiops lips he has!
How foul a snout, and what a *hanging* face! *Dryd. Juven.*

2. Requiring to be punished by the halter.

HA'NGMAN. *n. s.* [*hang* and *man.*] The publick executioner.

This monster sat like a *hangman* upon a pair of gallows; in his right hand he was painted holding a crown of laurel, and in his left hand a purse of money. *Sidney, b.* ii.

One cried, God bless us! and amen! the other;
As they had seen me with these *hangman's* hands:
Listening their fear, I could not say amen,
When they did say God bless us. *Shakespeare's Macbeth.*

He hath twice or thrice cut Cupid's bowstring, and the little *hangman* dare not shoot at him. *Shakespeare.*

Who makes that noise there? Who are you?
—Your friend, sir, the *hangman*: you must be so good, sir, to rise, and be put to death. *Shakesp. Meas. for Measure.*

Men do not stand
In so ill case, that God hath with his hand
Sign'd kings blank charters to kill whom they hate;
Nor are they vicars, but *hangmen* to fate. *Donne.*

I never knew a critick, who made it his business to lash the faults of other writers, that was not guilty of greater himself; as the *hangman* is generally a worse malefactor than the criminal that suffers by his hand. *Addison's Whig Examiner.*

HANK. *n. s.* [*hank*, Islandick, a chain or coil of rope.]

1. A skein of thread.

2. A tye; a check; an influence. A low word.

Do we think we have the *hank* that some gallants have on their trusting merchants, that, upon peril of losing all former scores, he must still go on to supply? *Decay of Piety.*

To HA'NKER. *v. n.* [*hankeren*, Dutch.] To long importunately; to have an incessant wish.

And now the saints began their reign,
For which th' had yearn'd so long in vain,
And felt such bowel *hankerings*,
To see an empire all of kings. *Hudibras, p.* iii. *cant.* 2.

Among women and children, care is to be taken that they get not a *hankering* after these juggling astrologers and fortunetellers. *L'Estrange's Fables.*

The shepherd would be a merchant, and the merchant *hankers* after something else. *L'Estrange's Fables.*

Do'st thou not *hanker* after a greater liberty in some things? If not, there's no better sign of a good resolution. *Calamy.*

The wife is an old coquette, that is always *hankering* after the diversions of the town. *Addison's Spectator.*

The republick that fell under the subjection of the duke of Florence, still retains many *hankerings* after its ancient liberty. *Addison on Italy.*

HAN'T, for *has not*, or *have not.*

That roguish leer of your's makes a pretty woman's heart ake: you *han't* that simper about the mouth for nothing. *Addis.*

HAP. *n. s.* [*anhap*, in Welsh, is misfortune.]

1. Chance; fortune.

Things casual do vary, and that which a man doth but chance to think well of cannot still have the like *hap*. *Hooker.*

Whether art it were, or heedless *hap*,
As through the flow'ring forest rash she fled,
In her rude hairs sweet flowers themselves did lap,
And flourishing fresh leaves and blossoms did enwrap. *F. Q.*

A fox had the *hap* to fall into the walk of a lion. *L'Estr.*

2. That which happens by chance or fortune.

Curst be good *haps*, and curst be they that build
Their hopes on *haps*, and do not make despair
For all these certain blows the surest shield. *Sidney.*

To have ejected whatsoever that church doth make account of, without any other crime than that it hath been the *hap* thereof to be used by the church of Rome, and not to be commanded in the word of God, might haply have pleased some few men, who, having begun such a course themselves, must be glad to see their example followed. *Hooker, b.* iv.

3. Accident; casual event; misfortune.

Solyman commended them for their valour in their evil *haps*, more than the victory of others got by good fortune. *Knolles.*

Nor feared she among the bands to stray
Of armed men; for often had she seen
The tragick end of many a bloody fray:
Her life had full of *haps* and hazards been. *Fairfax, b.* vi.

HAP-HAZARD. *n. s.* Chance; accident.

The former of these is the most sure and infallible way; but so hard that all shun it, and had rather walk as men do in the dark by *hap-hazard*, than tread so long and intricate mazes for knowledge sake. *Hooker, b.* i. *s.* 7.

We live at *haphazard*, and without any insight into causes and effects. *L'Estrange.*

We take our principles at *hap-hazard* upon trust, and without ever having examined them; and then believe a whole system, upon a presumption that they are true. *Locke.*

To HAP. *v. n.* [from the noun.] To come by accident; to fall out; to happen.

It will be too late to gather provision from abroad, for the furnishing of ships or soldiers, which peradventure may need to be presently employed, and whose want may *hap* to hazard a kingdom. *Spenser on Ireland.*

Run you to the citadel,
And tell my lord and lady what hath *hap'd*. *Shak. Othello.*

In destructions by deluge, the remnant which *hap* to be reserved are ignorant people. *Bacon.*

HA'PLY. *adv.* [from *hap.*]

1. Perhaps; peradventure; it may be.

This love of theirs myself have often seen,
Haply when they have judg'd me fast asleep. *Shakespeare.*

To warn
Us, *haply* too secure, of our discharge
From penalty, because from death releas'd
Some days. *Milton's Paradise Lost, b.* xi.

Then *haply* yet your breast remains untouch'd,
Though that seems strange. *Rowe's Royal Convert.*

Let us now see what conclusions may be found for instruction of any other state, that may *haply* labour under the like circumstances. *Swift on the Dissent. in Athens and Rome.*

2. By chance; by accident.

Leviathan, which God of all his works
Created hugest, that swim the ocean stream,
Him *haply* slumb'ring on the Norway foam,
The pilot of some small night-founder'd skiff
Deeming some island oft, as seamen tell,
With fixed anchor in his scaly rind,
Moors by his side. *Milton's Paradise Lost, b.* i.

HA'PLESS. *adj.* [from *hap.*] Unhappy; unfortunate; luckless; unlucky.

Hapless Ægeon, whom the fates have mark'd
To bear th' extremity of dire mishap! *Shakespeare.*
Here *hapless* Icarus had found his part,
Had not the father's grief restrain'd his art. *Dryden's Æn.*
Did his *hapless* passion equal mine,
I would refuse the bliss. *Smith's Phædra and Hippolitus.*

To HA'PPEN. *v. n.* [from *hap.*]

1. To fall out; to chance; to come to pass.

Bring forth your strong reasons, and shew us what shall *happen.* *Is.* xl. 22.

Say not I have sinned, and what harm hath *happened* unto me. *Eccluf.* v. 4.

If it so fall out that thou art miserable for ever, thou hast no reason to be surprized, as if some unexpected thing had *happened* to thee. *Tillotson's Sermons.*

2. To light; to fall by chance.

I have *happened* on some other accounts relating to mortalities. *Graunt's Bills of Mortality.*

HA'PPILY. *adv.* [from *happy.*]

1. Fortunately; luckily; successfully.

Were she as rough
As are the swelling Adriatick seas,
I come to wive it wealthily in Padua:
If wealthily, then *happily* in Padua. *Shakespeare.*
Preferr'd by conquest, *happily* o'erthrown,
Falling they rise to be with us made one. *Waller.*

Neither is it so trivial an undertaking to make a tragedy end *happily*; for 'tis more difficult to save than kill. *Dryden.*

2. Addressfully; gracefully; without labour.

Form'd by thy converse, *happily* to steer
From grave to gay, from lively to severe. *Pope.*

3. In a state of felicity: as, he lives *happily.*

4. By chance; peradventure. In this sense *happily* is written erroneously for *haply.*

One thing more I shall wish you to desire of them, who *happily* may peruse these two treatises. *Digby.*

HA'PPINESS. *n. s.* [from *happy.*]

1. Felicity; state in which the desires are satisfied.

Happiness is that estate whereby we attain, so far as possibly may be attained, the full possession of that which simply for itself is to be desired, and containeth in it after an eminent sort the contentation of our desires, the highest degree of all our perfection. *Hooker, b.* i.

Oh! *happiness* of sweet retir'd content,
To be at once secure and innocent. *Denham.*

The various and contrary choices that men make in the world, argue that the same thing is not good to every man alike: this variety of pursuits shews, that every one does not place his *happiness* in the same thing. *Locke.*

2. Good luck; good fortune.

3. Fortuitous elegance; unstudied grace.

Certain graces and *happinesses*, peculiar to every language, give life and energy to the words. *Denham.*

Some beauties yet no precepts can declare;
For there's a *happiness* as well as care. *Pope on Criticism.*

HA'PPY. *adj.* [from *hap*; as *lucky* for *luck.*]

1. In a state of felicity; in a state where the desire is satisfied.

At other end Uran did Strephon lend
Her *happy* making hand. *Sidney.*
Am I *happy* in thy news?
—If to have done the thing you gave in charge
Beget you happiness, be *happy* then;
For it is done. *Shakespeare's Richard* III.
Truth and peace, and love, shall ever shine
About the supreme throne
Of him, t' whose *happy* making sight alone,
When once our heav'nly guided soul shall climb. *Milton.*

Though the presence of imaginary good cannot make us *happy*, the absence of it may make us miserable. *Addison.*

2. Lucky; successful; fortunate.

Chymists have been more *happy* in finding experiments than the causes of them. *Boyle.*

Yet in this agony his fancy wrought,
And fear supply'd him with this *happy* thought. *Dryden.*

3. Addressful; ready.

One gentleman is *happy* at a reply, and another excels in a rejoinder. *Swift.*

HA'QUETON. *n. s.* A piece of armour. *Spenser.*

HARA'NGUE. *n. s.* [*harangue*, French. The original of the French word is much questioned: *Menage* thinks it a corruption of *hearing*, English; *Junius* imagines it to be *discours au rang*, to a circle, which the Italian *arringo* seems to favour. Perhaps it may be from *orare*, or *orationare*, *orationer*, *oraner*, *aranger*, *haranguer.*] A speech; a popular oration.

Gray-headed men, and grave, with warriors mix'd,
Assemble, and *harangues* are heard; but soon
In factious opposition. *Milton's Par. Lost, b.* xi.

Nothing can better improve political schoolboys than the art of making plausible or implausible *harangues*, against the very opinion for which they resolve to determine. *Swift.*

A multitude of preachers neglect method in their *harangues*. *Watts's Improvement of the Mind.*

To HARA'NGUE. *v. n.* [*haranguer*, French.] To make a speech; to pronounce an oration.

HARA'NGUER. *n. s.* [from *harangue.*] An orator; a publick speaker: generally with some mixture of contempt.

To HA'RASS. *v. a.* [*harasser*, French, from *harasse*, a heavy buckler, according to *Du Cauge.*] To weary; to fatigue; to tire with labour and uneasiness.

These troops came to the army but the day before, *harassed* with a long and wearisome march. *Bacon's War with Spain.*

Our walls are thinly mann'd, our best men slain;
The rest, an heartless number, spent with watching,
And *harass'd* out with duty. *Dryden's Spanish Fryar.*
Nature oppress'd, and *harass'd* out with care,
Sinks down to rest. *Addison's Cato.*

HA'RASS. *n. s.* [from the verb.] Waste; disturbance.

The men of Judah, to prevent
The *harass* of their land, beset me round. *Milton's Agonist.*

HA'RBINGER. *n. s.* [*herberger*, Dutch, one who goes to provide lodgings or an *harbour* for those that follow.] A forerunner; a precursor.

Make all our trumpets speak, give them all breath,
Those clam'rous *harbingers* of blood and death. *Sh. Macb.*
I'll be myself the *harbinger*, and make joyful
The hearing of my wife with your approach. *Shak. Macb.*
Sin, and her shadow death, and misery,
Death's *harbinger*. *Milt. Par. Lost, b.* ix. *l.* 13.
And now of love they treat, 'till th' evening star,
Love's *harbinger*, appear'd. *Milt. Par. Lost, b.* xi.
Before him a great prophet, to proclaim
His coming, is sent *harbinger*, who all
Invites. *Milton's Paradise Regain'd, b.* i.
As Ormond's *harbinger* to you they run;
For Venus is the promise of the Sun. *Dryden.*

HA'RBOUR. *n. s.* [*herberge*, French; *herberg*, Dutch; *albergo*, Italian.]

1. A lodging; a place of entertainment.

For *harbour* at a thousand doors they knock'd;
Not one of all the thousand but was lock'd. *Dryd. Fables.*
Doubly curs'd
Be all those easy fools who give it *harbour*. *Rowe's J. Shore.*

2. A port or haven for shipping.

Three of your argosies
Are richly come to *harbour* suddenly. *Shakes. Merch. of Ven.*
They leave the mouths of Po,
That all the borders of the town o'erflow;
And spreading round in one continu'd lake,
A spacious hospitable *harbour* make. *Addison on Italy.*

3. An asylum; a shelter; a place of shelter and security.

To HA'RBOUR. *v. n.* [from the noun.] To receive entertainment; to sojourn; to take shelter.

This night let's *harbour* here in York. *Shakes. Henry* VI.
They are sent by me,
That they should *harbour* where their lord would be. *Shakes.*
Southwards they bent their flight,
And *harbour'd* in a hollow rock at night:
Next morn they rose, and set up every sail;
The wind was fair, but blew a mackrel gale. *Dryden.*
Let me be grateful; but let far from me
Be fawning cringe, and false dissembling look,
And servile flattery, that *harbours* oft
In courts and gilded roofs. *Phillips.*

To HA'RBOUR. *v. a.*

1. To entertain; to permit to reside.

My lady bids me tell you, that though she *harbours* you as her uncle, she's nothing allied to your disorders. *Shakespeare.*

Knaves I know, which in this plainness
Harbour more craft, and more corrupter ends,
Than twenty silky ducking observants,
That stretch their duties nicely. *Shakesp. King Lear.*
Let not your gentle breast *harbour* one thought
Of outrage from the king. *Rowe's Royal Convert.*

We owe this old house the same kind of gratitude that we do to an old friend who *harbours* us in his declining condition, nay even in his last extremities. *Pope.*

How people, so greatly warmed with a sense of liberty, should be capable of *harbouring* such weak superstition; and that so much bravery and so much folly can inhabit the same breasts. *Pope.*

2. To shelter; to secure.

Harbour yourself this night in this castle, because the time requires it; and, in truth, this country is very dangerous for murthering thieves to trust a sleeping life among them. *Sidney.*

HA'RBOURAGE. *n. s.* [*herbergage*, Fr. from *harbour.*] Shelter; entertainment.

Let in us, your king, whose labour'd spirits,
Forewearied in this action of swift speed,
Crave *harbourage* within your city walls. *Shakesp. King John.*

HA'RBOURER. *n. s.* [from *harbour.*] One that entertains another.

HA'RBOURLESS. *adj.* [from *harbour.*] Without harbour; without lodging; without shelter.

HARBROUGH for *harbour*. *Spenser.*

HARD. *adj.* [heaɲd, Saxon; *hard*, Dutch.]

1. Firm; resisting penetration or separation; not soft; not easy to be pierced or broken.

Repose you there, while I to the hard house,
More *hard* than is the stone whereof 'tis rais'd;
Which even but now, demanding after you,
Denied me to come in. *Shakespeare's King Lear.*

2. Difficult; not easy to the intellect.

Some diseases, when they are easy to be cured, are *hard* to be known. *Sidney, b.* ii.

The *hard* causes they brought unto Moses; but every small matter they judged themselves. *Ex.* xviii. 26.

When *hard* words, jealousies, and fears,
Set folks together by the ears. *Hudibras, p.* i.

'Tis *hard* to say if Clymene were mov'd
More by his pray'r, whom she so dearly lov'd,
Or more with fury fir'd. *Dryden.*

As for the *hard* words, which I was obliged to use, they are either terms of art, or such as I substituted in place of others that were too low. *Arbuthnot.*

3. Difficult of accomplishment; full of difficulties.

Is any thing too *hard* for the Lord? *Gen.* xviii. 14.

Possess
As lords a spacious world, t' our native heav'n
Little inferior, by my adventure *hard*
With peril great atchiev'd. *Milton's Par. Lost, b.* x.

Long is the way
And *hard*, that out of hell leads up to light:
Our prison strong. *Milton's Paradise Lost, b.* ii.

He now discerned he was wholly to be on the defensive, and that was like to be a very *hard* part too. *Clarendon, b.* viii.

Nervous and tendinous parts have worse symptoms, and are *harder* of cure, than fleshy ones. *Wiseman on Inflammation.*

The love and pious duty which you pay,
Have pass'd the perils of so *hard* a way. *Dryden's Æn.*

4. Painful; distressful; laborious.

Rachael travelled, and she had *hard* labour. *Gen.* xxxv. 16.

Worcester's horse came but to-day;
And now their pride and mettle is asleep,
Their courage with *hard* labour tame and dull,
That not a horse is half of himself. *Shakesp. Henry* IV.

Continual *hard* duty, with little fighting, lessened and diminished his army. *Clarendon, b.* viii.

When Sebastian weeps, his tears
Come *harder* than his blood. *Dryden's Don Sebastian.*

A man obliged to *hard* labour is not reduced to the necessity of having twice as much victuals as one under no necessity to work. *Cheyne's Phil. Princ.*

5. Cruel; oppressive; rigorous.

The bargain of Julius III. may be accounted a very *hard* one. *Brown's Vulgar Errours, b.* iii. *c.* 23.

Whom scarce my sheep, and scarce my painful plough,
The needful aids of human life allow;
So wretched is thy son, so *hard* a mother thou. *Dryden.*

If you thought that *hard* upon you, we would not refuse you half your time. *Dryden's Juven. Dedication.*

It will be a loss to all those, who have their estates in money, of one third of their estates; which will be a very *hard* case upon a great number of people. *Locke.*

No people live with more ease and prosperity than the subjects of little commonwealths; as, on the contrary, there are none who suffer more under the grievances of a *hard* government than the subjects of little principalities. *Addison.*

Rough ungovernable passions hurry men on to say or do very *hard* or offensive things. *Atterbury's Sermons.*

To find a bill that may bring punishment upon the innocent, will appear very *hard.* *Swift.*

6. Sower; rough; severe.

What, have you given him any *hard* words of late? *Shak.*

7. Unfavourable; unkind.

As thou lov'st me, do him not that wrong,
To bear a *hard* opinion of his truth. *Shakespeare.*

Absalom and Achitophel he thinks is a little *hard* on his fanatick patrons. *Dryden's Fables, Preface.*

Some *hard* rumours have been transmitted from t'other side the water, and rumours of the severest kind. *Swift.*

8. Insensible; untouched.

If I by chance succeed
In what I write, and that's a chance indeed,
Know I am not so stupid, or so *hard*,
Not to feel praise, or fame's deserv'd reward. *Dryd. Pers.*

9. Unhappy; vexatious.

It is a very *hard* quality upon our soil or climate, that so excellent a fruit, which prospers among all our neighbours, will not grow here. *Temple.*

10. Vehement; keen; severe: as, a *hard* Winter.

11. Unreasonable; unjust.

It is a little *hard*, that in an affair of the last consequence to the very being of the clergy, this whole reverend body should be the sole persons not consulted. *Swift.*

It is the *hardest* case in the world, that Steele should take up the reports of his faction, and put them off as additional fears. *Swift.*

12. Forced; not easily granted.

If we allow the first couple, at the end of one hundred years, to have left ten pair of breeders, which is no *hard* supposition; there would arise from these, in fifteen hundred years, a greater number than the earth was capable of. *Burnet.*

13. Powerful.

The stag was too *hard* for the horse, and the horse flies for succour to one that's too *hard* for him, and rides the one to death, and outright kills the other. *L'Estrange's Fables.*

Let them consider the vexation they are treasuring up for themselves, by struggling with a power which will be always too *hard* for them. *Addison's Freeholder.*

A disputant, when he finds that his adversary is too *hard* for him, with slyness turns the discourse. *Watts.*

14. Austere; rough, as liquids.

In making of vinegar, set vessels of wine over against the noon sun, which calleth out the more oily spirits, and leaveth the spirit more sour and *hard.* *Bacon's Natural History.*

15. Harsh; stiff; constrained.

Others, scrupulously tied to the practice of the ancients, make their figures *harder* than even the marble itself. *Dryden.*

His diction is *hard*, his figures too bold, and his tropes, particularly his metaphors, insufferably strained. *Dryden.*

16. Not plentiful; not prosperous.

You have got a famous victory: there are bonfires decreed; and, if the times had not been *hard*, my billet should have burnt too. *Dryden's Spanish Fryar.*

17. Avaricious; faultily sparing.

HARD. *adv.* [*hardo*, very old German.]

1. Close; near.

Hard by was a house of pleasure, built for a Summer retiring place. *Sidney.*

They doubted a while what it should be, 'till it was cast up even *hard* before them; at which time they fully saw it was a man. *Sidney.*

A little lowly hermitage it was,
Down in a dale *hard* by a forest's side,
Far from resort of people that did pass
In travel to and fro. *Fairy Queen, b.* i.

Scarce had he said, when *hard* at hand they spie
That quicksand nigh, with water covered. *Fairy Queen.*

When these marshal the way, *hard* at hand comes the master and main exercise. *Shakespeare's Othello.*

Abimeleck went *hard* unto the door of the tower, to burn it with fire. *Judg.* ix. 52.

Hard by a cottage chimney smokes,
From betwixt two aged oaks. *Milton.*

2. Diligently; laboriously; incessantly; vehemently; earnestly; importunately.

Geneura rose in his defence,
And pray'd so *hard* for mercy from the prince,
That to his queen the king th' offender gave. *Dryden.*

An ant works as *hard* as a man who should carry a very heavy load every day four leagues. *Addison's Guardian.*

Whoever my unknown correspondent be, he presses *hard* for an answer, and is earnest in that point. *Atterbury.*

3. Uneasily; vexatiously.

When a man's servant shall play the cur with him, look you it goes *hard.* *Shakes. Two Gentlemen of Verona.*

4. Vehemently; distressfully.

The question is *hard* set, and we have reason to doubt. *Bro.*

A stag, that was *hard* set by the huntsmen, betook himself to a stall for sanctuary. *L'Estrange.*

5. Fast; nimbly.

The Philistines followed *hard* upon Saul. 2 *Sa.* xxxi. 2.

The wolves scampered away as *hard* as they could drive. *L'Estrange's Fables.*

6. With difficulty; in a manner requiring labour.

Solid bodies foreshow rain, as boxes and pegs of wood when they draw and wind *hard.* *Bacon's Natural History.*

7. Tempestuously; boisterously.

When the North wind blows *hard*, and it rains sadly, none but fools sit down in it and cry; wise people defend themselves against it. *Taylor's Rule of living holy.*

HA'RDBOUND. *adj.* [*hard* and *bound.*] Costive.

Just writes to make his barrenness appear,
And strains from *hardbound* brains eight lines a year. *Pope.*

To HA'RDEN. *v. n.* [from *hard.*] To grow hard.

The powder of loadstone and flint, by the addition of whites of eggs and gum-dragon, made into paste, will in a few days *harden* to the hardness of a stone. *Bacon's Natural History.*

To HA'RDEN. *v. a.* [from *hard.*]

1. To make hard; to indurate.

Sure he, who first the passage try'd,
In *harden'd* oak his heart did hide,
And ribs of iron arm'd his side,
Who tempted first the briny flood. *Dryden.*

A piece of the *hardened* marl. *Woodward on Fossils.*

2. To confirm in effrontery; to make impudent.

3. To confirm in wickedness; to make obdurate.

But

But exhort one another daily, leſt any of you be *hardened* through the deceitfulneſs of ſin. *Hebr.* iii. 13.

He ſtiffened his neck, and *hardened* his heart from turning unto the Lord *2 Chro.* xxxvi. 13.

It is a melancholy conſideration, that there ſhould be ſeveral among us ſo *hardened* and deluded as to think an oath a proper ſubject for a jeſt. *Addiſon's Freeholder.*

4. To make inſenſible; to ſtupify.

Our religion ſets before us not the example of a ſtupid ſtoick, who had by obſtinate principles *hardened* himſelf againſt all ſenſe of pain; but an example of a man like ourſelves, that had a tender ſenſe of the leaſt ſuffering, and yet patiently endured the greateſt. *Tillotſon's Sermons.*

Years have not yet *hardened* me, and I have an addition of weight on my ſpirits ſince we loſt him. *Swift to Pope.*

5. To make firm; to endue with conſtancy.

Then ſhould I yet have comfort? yea, I would *harden* myſelf in ſorrow. *Job* vi. 10.

One raiſes the ſoul, and *hardens* it to virtue; the other ſoftens it again, and unbends it into vice. *Dryden.*

HA'RDENER. *n. ſ.* [from *harden.*] One that makes any thing hard.

HARDFA'VOURED. *adj.* [*hard* and *favour.*] Coarſe of feature; harſh of countenance.

When the blaſt of war blows in your ears,
Stiffen the ſinews, ſummon up the blood,
Diſguiſe fair nature with *hardfavour'd* looks,
Then lend the eye a terrible aſpect. *Shakeſp. Henry* V.

The brother a very lovely youth, and the ſiſter *hardfavoured.* *L'Eſtrange.*

When Vulcan came into the world he was ſo *hardfavoured* that both his parents frowned on him. *Dryden.*

HARDHA'NDED. *adj.* [*hard* and *hand.*] Coarſe; mechanick; one that has hands hard with labour.

What are they that do play it?
—*Hardhanded* men that work in Athens here,
Which never labour'd in their minds 'till now. *Shakeſpeare.*

HA'RDHEAD. *n. ſ.* [*hard* and *head.*] Claſh of heads; manner of fighting in which the combatants daſh their heads together.

I have been at *hardhead* with your butting citizens; I have routed your herd, I have diſperſt them. *Dryden's Span. Fryar.*

HARDHE'ARTED. *adj.* [*hard* and *heart.*] Cruel; inexorable; mercileſs; pitileſs; barbarous; inhuman; ſavage; uncompaſſionate.

Hardhearted Clifford, take me from the world;
My ſoul to heav'n. *Shakeſpeare's Henry* VI.

Can you be ſo *hardhearted* to deſtroy
My ripening hopes, that are ſo near to joy? *Dryden.*

John Bull, otherwiſe a good-natured man, was very *hardhearted* to his ſiſter Peg. *Arbuthnot's Hiſt. of John Bull.*

HARDHE'ARTEDNESS. *n. ſ.* [from *hardhearted.*] Cruelty; want of tenderneſs; want of compaſſion.

Hardheartedneſs and cruelty is not only an inhuman vice, but worſe than brutal. *L'Eſtrange.*

How black and baſe a vice ingratitude is, may be ſeen in thoſe vices which it is always in combination with, pride and *hardheartedneſs*, or want of compaſſion. *South's Sermons.*

Hardheartedneſs is an eſſential in the character of a libertine. *Clariſſa.*

HA'RDIHEAD. } *n. ſ.* [from *hardy.*] Stoutneſs; bravery. Ob-
HA'RDIHOOD. } ſolete.

Enflam'd with fury and fierce *hardyhead*,
He ſeem'd in heart to harbour thoughts unkind,
And nouriſh bloody vengeance in his bitter mind. *Fa. Qu.*

If you have this about you,
Boldly aſſault the necromancer's hall,
Where if he be, with dauntleſs *hardihood.* *Milton.*

HA'RDIMENT. *n. ſ.* [from *hardy*, *hardiment*, adv. French.] Courage; ſtoutneſs; bravery.

But full of fire and greedy *hardiment*,
The youthful knight could not for aught be ſtaid. *Fa. Qu.*

On the gentle Severn's ſedgy bank,
In ſingle oppoſition, hand to hand,
He did confound the beſt part of an hour
In changing *hardiment* with great Glendower. *Shak. H.* IV.

Zeal was the ſpring whence flowed her *hardiment.* *Fairf.*

HA'RDINESS. *n. ſ.* [*hardieſſe*, French, from *hardy.*]

1. Hardſhip; fatigue.

They are valiant and hardy; great endurers of cold, hunger, and all *hardineſs.* *Spenſer.*

2. Stoutneſs; courage; bravery.

If with thrice ſuch powers left at home,
Cannot defend our own doors from the dog,
Let us be worried; and our nation loſe
The name of *hardineſs* and policy. *Shakeſp. Henry* V.

Perkin had gathered together a power of all nations, neither in number nor in the *hardineſs* and courage of their perſons contemptible. *Bacon's Henry* VII.

He has the courage of a rational creature, and ſuch an *hardineſs* we ſhould endeavour by cuſtom and uſe to bring children to. *Locke.*

Criminal as you are, you avenge yourſelf againſt the *hardneſs* of one that ſhould tell you of it. *Spectator.*

3. Effrontery; confidence.

HARDLA'BOURED. *adj.* [*hard* and *labour.*] Elaborate; ſtudied; diligently wrought.

How chearfully the hawkers cry
A ſatire, and the gentry buy!
While my *hardlabour'd* poem pines,
Unfold upon the printer's lines. *Swift.*

HA'RDLY. *adv.* [from *hard.*]

1. With difficulty; not eaſily.

For the moſt part it ſo falleth out, touching things which generally are received, that although in themſelves they be moſt certain, yet, becauſe men preſume them granted of all, we are *hardlieſt* able to bring ſuch proof of their certainty as may ſatisfy gainſayers, when ſuddenly and beſides expectation they require the ſame at our hands. *Hooker, b.* v. *ſ.* 2.

There are but a few, and they endued with great ripeneſs of wit and judgment, free from all ſuch affairs as might trouble their meditations, inſtructed in the ſharpeſt and ſubtleſt points of learning; who have, and that very *hardly*, been able to find out but only the immortality of the ſoul. *Hooker.*

God hath delivered a law as ſharp as the two-edged ſword, piercing the very cloſeſt and moſt unſearchable corners of the heart, which the law of nature can *hardly*, human laws by no means, poſſibly reach unto. *Hooker, b.* i.

There are in living creatures parts that nouriſh and repair eaſily, and parts that nouriſh and repair *hardly.* *Bacon.*

The barks of thoſe trees are more cloſe and ſoft than thoſe of oaks and aſhes, whereby the moſs can the *hardlier* iſſue out. *Bacon's Natural Hiſtory.*

Falſe confidence is eaſily taken up, and *hardly* laid down. *South's Sermons.*

The father, mother, daughter they invite;
Hardly the dame was drawn to this repaſt. *Dryden.*

Recov'ring *hardly* what he loſt before,
His right endears it much, his purchaſe more. *Dryden.*

2. Scarcely; ſcant; not lightly.

The fiſh that once was caught, new bait will *hardly* bite.
Fairy Queen, b. ii. *cant.* 1.

They are worn, lord conſul, ſo
That we ſhall *hardly* in our ages ſee
Their banners wave again. *Shakeſpeare's Coriolanus.*

Hardly ſhall you find any one ſo bad, but he deſires the credit of being thought good. *South's Sermons.*

The wand'ring breath was on the wing to part,
Weak was the pulſe, and *hardly* heav'd the heart. *Dryden.*

There is *hardly* a gentleman in the nation who hath not a near alliance with ſome of that body. *Swift.*

3. Grudgingly; as an injury.

If I unwittingly
Have aught committed that is *hardly* borne
By any in this preſence, I deſire
To reconcile me. *Shakeſpeare's Richard* III.

4. Severely; unfavourably.

If there are ſome reaſons inducing you to think *hardly* of our laws, are thoſe reaſons demonſtrative, are they neceſſary, or meer poſſibilities only? *Hooker, Preface.*

5. Rigorouſly; oppreſſively.

Many men believed that he was *hardly* dealt with. *Clarend.*

They are now in priſon, and treated *hardly* enough; for there are fifteen dead within two years. *Addiſon on Italy.*

They have begun to ſay, and to fetch inſtances, where he has in many things been *hardly* uſed. *Swift.*

6. Unwelcomely; harſhly.

Such information, even from thoſe who have authority over them, comes very *hardly* and harſhly to a grown man; and, however ſoftened, goes but ill down. *Locke.*

7. Not ſoftly; not tenderly; not delicately.

Heav'n was her canopy, bare earth her bed;
So *hardly* lodg'd. *Dryden.*

HA'RDMOUTHED. *adj.* [*hard* and *mouth.*] Diſobedient to the rein; not ſenſible of the bit.

'Tis time my *hardmouth'd* courſers to controul,
Apt to run riot, and trangreſs the goal,
And therefore I conclude. *Dryden's Fables.*

But who can youth, let looſe to vice, reſtrain?
When once the *hardmouth'd* horſe has got the rein,
He's paſt thy pow'r to ſtop. *Dryden's Juvenal.*

HA'RDNESS. *n. ſ.* [from *hard.*]

1. Durity; power of reſiſtance in bodies.

Hardneſs is a firm coheſion of the parts of matter that make up maſſes of a ſenſible bulk, ſo that the whole does not eaſily change its figure. *Locke.*

From the various combinations of theſe corpuſcles happen all the varieties of the bodies formed out of them, in colour, taſte, ſmell, *hardneſs*, and ſpecifick gravity. *Woodward.*

2. Difficulty to be underſtood.

I found
This label on my boſom, whoſe containing
Is ſo from ſenſe in *hardneſs*, that I can
Make no collection of it. *Shakeſpeare's Cymbeline.*

3. Difficulty to be accomplished.

It was time now or never to sharpen my intention to pierce through the *hardness* of this enterprize. *Sidney.*

Concerning the duty itself, the *hardness* thereof is not such as needeth much art. *Hooker, b.* v. *s.* 31.

4. Scarcity; penury.

The tenants poor, the *hardness* of the times,
Are ill excuses for a servant's crimes. *Swift.*

5. Obduracy; profligateness.

Every commission of sin introduces unto the soul a certain degree of *hardness*, and an aptness to continue in that sin. *South's Sermons.*

6. Coarseness; harshness of look.

By their virtuous behaviour they compensate the *hardness* of their favour, and by the pulchritude of their souls make up what is wanting in the beauty of their bodies. *Ray.*

7. Keenness; vehemence of weather or seasons.

If the *hardness* of the Winter should spoil them, neither the loss of seed nor labour will be much. *Mortimers Husbandry.*

8. Cruelty of temper; savageness; harshness; barbarity.

We will ask,
That if we fail in our request, the blame
May hang upon your *hardness*. *Shakespeare's Coriolanus.*
They quicken sloth, perplexities unty,
Make roughness smooth, and *hardness* mollify. *Denham.*

9. Stiffness; harshness.

Sculptors are obliged to follow the manners of the painters, and to make many ample folds, which are insufferable *hardnesses*, and more like a rock than a natural garment. *Dryden.*

10. Faulty parsimony; stinginess.

HA'RDOCK. *n. s.* I suppose the same with *burdock.*

Why he was met ev'n now,
Crown'd with rank fumiter and furrow-weeds,
With *hardocks*, hemlock, nettles, cuckoo-flowers. *Shakesp.*

HARDS. *n. s.* The refuse or coarser part of flax.

HA'RDSHIP. *n. s.* [from *hard.*]

1. Injury; oppression.

They are ripe for a peace, to enjoy what we have conquered for them; and so are we, to recover the effects of their *hardships* upon us. *Swift.*

2. Inconvenience; fatigue.

They were exposed to *hardship* and penury. *Sprat's Serm.*
You could not undergo the toils of war,
Nor bear the *hardships* that your leaders bore. *Addis. Cato.*
In journeys or at home, in war or peace,
By *hardships* many, many fall by ease. *Prior.*

HA'RDWARE. *n. s.* [*hard* and *ware.*] Manufactures of metal.

HA'RDWAREMAN. *n. s.* [*hardware* and *man.*] A maker or seller of metalline manufactures.

One William Wood, an *hardwareman*, obtains by fraud a patent in England to coin 108,000 l. in copper to pass in Ireland, leaving us liberty to take or refuse. *Swift.*

HA'RDY. *adj.* [*hardi*, French.]

1. Bold; brave; stout; daring.

Try the imagination of some in cock-fights, to make one cock more *hardy*, and the other more cowardly. *Bacon.*

Recite
The feats of Amazons, the fatal fight
Betwixt the *hardy* queen and hero knight. *Dryd. Fables.*

Who is there *hardy* enough to contend with the reproach which is prepared for those, who dare venture to dissent from the received opinions of their country? *Locke.*

Could thirst of vengeance, and desire of fame,
Excite the female breast with martial flame?
And shall not love's diviner pow'r inspire
More *hardy* virtue, and more gen'rous fire? *Prior.*

2. Strong; hard; firm.

Is a man confident of his present strength? An unwholsome blast may shake in pieces his *hardy* fabrick. *South.*

3. Confident; firm.

HARE and HERE, differing in pronunciation only, signify both an army and a lord. So *Harold* is a general of an army; *Hareman*, a chief man in the army; *Herwin*, a victorious army; which are much like *Stratocles*, *Polemarchus*, and *Hegesistratus* among the Greeks. *Gibson's Camden.*

HARE. *n. s.* [hapa, Saxon; *karh*, Erse.]

1. A small quadruped, with long ears and short tail, that moves by leaps, remarkable for timidity, vigilance, and fecundity; the common game of hunters.

Dismay'd not this
Our captains Macbeth and Banquo?
——Yes,
As sparrows, eagles; or the *hare*, the lion. *Shakesp. Macb.*

We view in the open champaign a brace of swift greyhounds coursing a good stout and well breathed *hare*. *More.*

Your dressings must be with Galen's powder and *hare's* fur. *Wiseman's Surgery.*

Poor is the triumph o'er the timid *hare*. *Thoms. Autumn.*

2. A constellation.

The *hare* appears, whose active rays supply
A nimble force, and hardly wings deny. *Creech.*

To HARE. *v. n.* [*harier*, French.] To fright; to hurry with terrour.

To *hare* and rate them, is not to teach but vex them. *Locke.*

HA'REBELL. *n. s.* [*hare* and *bell.*] A blue flower campaniform.

Thou shalt not lack
The flow'r that's like thy face, pale primrose; nor
The azur'd *harebell*, like thy veins. *Shakesp. Cymbeline.*

HA'REBRAINED. *adj.* [from *hare* the verb and *brain.*] Volatile; unsettled; wild; fluttering; hurried.

That *harebrained* wild fellow begins to play the fool, when others are weary of it. *Bacon's Henry VII.*

HA'REFOOT. *n. s.* [*hare* and *foot.*]

1. A bird. *Ainsworth.*

2. An herb. *Ainsworth.*

HA'RELIP. *n. s.* A fissure in the upper lip with want of substance, a natural defect. *Quincy.*

The blots of nature's hand
Shall not in their issue stand;
Never mole, *harelip*, nor scar,
Shall upon their children be. *Shakes. Mids. Night's Dream.*

The third stitch is performed with pins or needles, as in *harelips*. *Wiseman's Surgery.*

HA'RESEAR. *n. s.* [*bupleurum*, Latin.] A plant.

The characters are: the leaves grow alternately upon the branches, and for the most part surround the stalk, having no footstalk: the seeds are oblong, smooth, and furrowed. *Miller.*

HA'RIER. *n. s.* [from *hare.*] A dog for hunting hares. *Ainsw.*

To HARK. *v. n.* [Contracted from *hearken.*] To listen.

The king,
To me inveterate, *harks* my brother's suit. *Shakespeare.*
Pricking up his ears, to *hark*
If he could hear too in the dark. *Hudibras, p.* iii.

HARK. *interj.* [It is originally the imperative of the verb *hark.*] List! hear! listen!

What harmony is this? My good friends, *hark! Shakes.*

The butcher saw him upon the gallop with a piece of flesh, and called out, *hark* ye, friend, you may make the best of your purchase. *L'Estrange's Fables.*

Hark! methinks the roar that late pursu'd me,
Sinks like the murmurs of a falling wind. *Rowe's Ja. Shore.*
Hark how loud the woods
Invite you forth! *Thomson's Spring.*

HARL. *n. s.*

1. The filaments of flax.

2. Any filamentous substance.

The general sort are wicker hives, made of privet, willow, or *harl*, daubed with cow-dung. *Mortimer's Husbandry.*

HA'RLEQUIN. *n. s.* [This name is said to have been given by *Francis* of France to a busy buffoon, in ridicule of his enemy *Charles le quint*. *Menage* derives it more probably from a famous comedian that frequented M. *Harlay's* house, whom his friends called *Harlequino*, little Harley. *Trev.*] buffoon who plays tricks to divert the populace; a Jack-pudding; a zani.

The joy of a king for a victory must not be like that of a *harlequin* upon a letter from his mistress. *Dryden.*

The man in graver tragick known,
Though his best part long since was done,
Still on the stage desires to tarry;
And he who play'd the *harlequin*,
After the jest still loads the scene,
Unwilling to retire, though weary. *Prior.*

HA'RLOT. *n. s.* [*herlodes*, Welsh, a girl. Others for *horelet*, a little whore. Others from the name of the mother of *William* the Conqueror. *Hurlet* is used in *Chaucer* for a low male drudge.] A whore; a strumpet.

Away, my disposition, and possess me with
Some *harlot's* spirit. *Shakesp. Coriolanus.*
They help thee by such aids as geese and *harlots*. *Ben. Johns.*
The barbarous *harlots* crowd the publick place;
Go, fools, and purchase an unclean embrace. *Dryd. Juven.*

HA'RLOTRY. *n. s.* [from *harlot.*]

1. The trade of a harlot; fornication.

Nor shall,
From Rome's tribunal, thy harangues prevail
'Gainst *harlotry*, while thou art clad so thin. *Dryd. Juven.*

2. A name of contempt for a woman.

A peevish self-will'd *harlotry*,
That no persuasion can do good upon. *Shakesp. Henry IV.*

HARM. *n. s.* [heapm, Saxon.]

1. Injury; crime; wickedness.

2. Mischief; detriment; hurt.

We, ignorant of ourselves,
Beg often our own *harms*, which the wise powers
Deny us for our good. *Shakes. Ant. and Cleopatra.*

They should be suffered to write on: it would keep them out of *harms* way, and prevent them from evil courses. *Swift.*

To HARM. *v. a.* To hurt; to injure.

What sense had I of her stol'n hours or lust?
I saw't not, thought it not, it *harm'd* not me. *Shak. Othello.*
Passions ne'er could grow
To *harm* another, or impeach your rest. *Waller.*

After

After their young are hatched, they brood them under their wings, leſt the cold, and ſometimes the heat, ſhould *harm* them. *Ray on the Creation.*

HA'RMFUL. *adj.* [*harm* and *full.*] Hurtful; miſchievous; noxious; injurious; detrimental.

His dearly loved ſquire
His ſpear of heben-wood behind him bare,
Whoſe *harmful* head, thrice heated in the fire,
Had riven many a breaſt with pike-head ſquare. *Fa. Queen.*

Let no man fear that *harmful* creature leſs, becauſe he ſees the apoſtle ſafe from that poiſon. *Hall.*

The earth brought forth fruit and food for man, without any mixture of *harmful* quality. *Raleigh's Hiſtory.*

For flax and oats will burn the tender field,
And ſleepy poppies *harmful* harveſts yield. *Dryden's Georg.*

HA'RMFULLY. *adv.* [from *harmful.*] Hurtfully; noxiouſly; detrimentally.

A ſcholar is better occupied in playing or ſleeping, than ſpending his time not only vainly, but *harmfully* in ſuch kind of exerciſe. *Aſcham's Schoolmaſter.*

HA'RMFULNESS. *n. ſ.* [from *harmful.*] Hurtfulneſs; miſchievouſneſs; noxiouſneſs.

HA'RMLESS. *adj.* [from *harm.*]

1. Innocent; innoxious; not hurtful.

Touching ceremonies *harmleſs* in themſelves, and hurtful only in reſpect of number, was it amiſs to decree that thoſe things that were leaſt needful, and newlieſt come, ſhould be the firſt that were taken away? *Hooker, b.* iv. *ſ.* 14.

She, like *harmleſs* lightning, throws her eye
On him, her brothers, me, her maſter; hitting
Each object with a joy. *Shakeſpeare's Cymbeline.*

2. Unhurt; undamaged.

The ſhipwright will be careful to gain by his labour, or at leaſt to ſave himſelf *harmleſs*, and therefore ſuit his work ſlightly, according to a ſlight price. *Raleigh's Eſſays.*

HA'RMLESSLY. *adv.* [from *harmleſs.*] Innocently; without hurt; without crime.

He ſpent that day free from worldly trouble, *harmleſsly*, and in a recreation that became a churchman. *Walton.*

Bullets batter the walls which ſtand inflexible, but fall *harmleſsly* into wood or feathers. *Decay of Piety.*

HA'RMLESSNESS. *n. ſ.* [from *harmleſs.*] Innocence; freedom from injury or hurt.

When, through taſteleſs flat humility,
In dough-bak'd men ſome *harmleſſneſs* we ſee,
'Tis but his phlegm that's virtuous, and not he. *Donne.*

Compare the *harmleſſneſs*, the credulity, the tenderneſs, the modeſty, and the ingenuous pliableneſs to virtuous counſels, which is in youth untainted, with the miſchievouſneſs, the ſlyneſs, the craft, the impudence, the falſhood, and the confirmed obſtinacy in an aged long-practiſed ſinner. *South.*

HA'RMONICAL. } *adj.* [ἁρμονικὸς; *harmonique*, French.] Pro-
HA'RMONICK. } portioned to each other; adapted to each other; concordant; muſical.

After every three whole notes, nature requireth, for all *harmonical* uſe, one half note to be interpoſed. *Bacon's N. Hiſt.*

Harmonical ſounds, and diſcordant ſounds, are both active and poſitive; but blackneſs and darkneſs are, indeed, but privatives. *Bacon's Natural Hiſtory.*

So ſwells each wind-pipe; aſs intones to aſs,
Harmonick twang of leather, horn, and braſs. *Pope.*

HARMO'NIOUS. *adj.* [*harmonieux*, French, from *harmony.*]

1. Adapted to each other; having the parts proportioned to each other.

All the wide-extended ſky,
And all th' *harmonius* worlds on high,
And Virgil's ſacred work ſhall dye. *Cowley.*

God has made the intellectual world *harmonious* and beautiful without us; but it will never come into our heads all at once; we muſt bring it home piece-meal. *Locke.*

2. Having ſounds concordant to each other; muſical.

Harmony in wedded pair,
More grateful than *harmonious* ſounds to th' ear. *Milton.*

The verſe of Chaucer is not *harmonious* to us: they who lived with him, and ſome time after him, thought it muſical. *Dryden's Fables, Preface.*

HA'RMONIOUSLY. *adv.* [from *harmonious.*]

1. With juſt adaptation and proportion of parts to each other.

Not chaos-like, together cruſh'd and bruis'd;
But as the world, *harmoniouſly* confus'd:
Where order in variety we ſee,
And where, though all things differ, they agree. *Pope.*

That all theſe diſtances, motions, and quantities of matter ſhould be ſo accurately and *harmoniouſly* adjuſted in this great variety of our ſyſtem, is above the fortuitous hits of blind material cauſes, and muſt certainly flow from that eternal fountain of wiſdom. *Bentley's Sermons.*

2. Muſically; with concord of ſounds.

If we look upon the world as a muſical inſtrument, well-tuned, and *harmoniouſly* ſtruck, we ought not therefore to worſhip the inſtrument, but him that makes the muſick. *Stillingfleet's Def. of Diſc. on Rom. Idol.*

HARMO'NIOUSNESS. *n. ſ.* [from *harmonious.*] Proportion; muſicalneſs.

To HA'RMONIZE. *v. a.* [from *harmony.*] To adjuſt in fit proportions; to make muſical.

Love firſt invented verſe, and form'd the rhime,
The motion meaſur'd, *harmoniz'd* the chime. *Dryden.*

HA'RMONY. *n. ſ.* [ἁρμονία; *harmonie*, French.]

1. The juſt adaptation of one part to another.

The pleaſures of the eye and ear are but the effects of equality, good proportion, or correſpondence; ſo that equality and correſpondence are the cauſes of *harmony.* *Bacon.*

The *harmony* of things,
As well as that of ſounds, from diſcord ſprings. *Denham.*

Sure infinite wiſdom muſt accompliſh all its works with conſummate *harmony*, proportion, and regularity. *Cheyne.*

2. Juſt proportion of ſound; muſical concord.

Harmony is a compound idea, made up of different ſounds united. *Watts's Logick.*

3. Concord; correſpondent ſentiment.

In us both one ſoul,
Harmony to behold in wedded pair!
More grateful than harmonious ſounds to th' ear. *Milton.*

I no ſooner in my heart divin'd,
My heart, which by a ſecret *harmony*
Still moves with thine, join'd in connexion ſweet! *Milton.*

HA'RNESS. *n. ſ.* [*harnois*, French, ſuppoſed from *iern* or *hiern*, Runnick; *hiairn*, Welſh and Erſe, iron.]

1. Armour; defenſive furniture of war.

A goodly knight, all dreſs'd in *harneſs* meet,
That from his head no place appeared to his feet. *F. Queen.*

Doff thy *harneſs*, youth:
I am to-day i' th' vein of chivalry. *Shakeſp. Troil. and Creſſ.*

Of no right, nor colour like to right,
He doth fill fields with *harneſs.* *Shakeſp. Henry* IV. *p.* i.

Were I a great man, I ſhould fear to drink:
Great men ſhould drink with *harneſs* on their throats. *Shak.*

2. The traces of draught horſes, particularly of carriages of pleaſure or ſtate: of other carriages we ſay *geer.*

Or wilt thou ride? Thy horſes ſhall be trapp'd,
Their *harneſs* ſtudded all with gold and pearl. *Shakeſpeare.*

Their ſteeds around,
Free from their *harneſs*, graze the flow'ry ground. *Dryden.*

To HA'RNESS. *v. a.* [from the noun.]

1. To dreſs in armour.

He was *harneſt* light, and to the field goes he. *Shakeſp.*

Full fifty years, *harneſs'd* in rugged ſteel,
I have endur'd the biting Winter's blaſt. *Rowe.*

2. To fix horſes in their traces.

Before the door her iron chariot ſtood,
All ready *harneſſed* for journey new. *Fairy Queen, b.* i.

Harneſs the horſes, and get up the horſemen, and ſtand forth with your helmets. *Jer.* xlvi. 4.

When I plow my ground, my horſe is *harneſſed* and chained to my plough. *Hale's Origin of Mankind.*

To the *harneſſed* yoke
They lend their ſhoulder, and begin their toil. *Thomſon.*

HARP. *n. ſ.* [hearp, Saxon; *harpe*, French. It is uſed through both the Teutonick and Roman dialects, and has been long in uſe.

Romanuſq; lyrâ plaudat tibi, Barbarus harpâ. Ven. Fort.]

1. A lyre; an inſtrument ſtrung with wire and ſtruck with the finger.

Arion, when through tempeſts cruel wreck
He forth was thrown into the greedy ſeas,
Through the ſweet muſick which his *harp* did make,
Allur'd a dolphin him from death to eaſe. *Spenſer.*

They touch'd their golden *harps*, and hyming prais'd
God and his works. *Milton's Paradiſe Loſt, b.* vii.

Nor wanted tuneful *harp*, nor vocal quire,
The muſes ſung, Apollo touch'd the lyre. *Dryden.*

2. A conſtellation.

Next ſhines the *harp*, and through the liquid ſkies
The ſhell, as lighteſt, firſt begins to riſe;
This when ſweet Orpheus ſtruck, to liſt'ning rocks
He ſenſes gave, and ears to wither'd oaks. *Creech's Manilus.*

To HARP. *v. n.* [*harper*, French, from the noun.]

1. To play on the harp.

I heard the voice of harpers *harping* with their harps. *Rev.*

Things without life giving ſound, whether pipe or harp, except they give a diſtinction in the ſounds, how ſhall it be known what is piped or *harped.* 1 *Cor.* xiv. 7.

The helmed cherubim,
And ſworded ſeraphim,
Are ſeen in glitt'ring ranks with wings diſplay'd,
Harping in loud and ſolemn quire,
With unexpreſſive notes to heav'n's new-born heir. *Milton.*

I conceive you *harp* a little too much upon one ſtring. *Collier on Pride.*

2. To touch any paſſion, as the harper touches a ſtring; to dwell on a ſubject.

Gracious duke,
Harp not on that, nor do not baniſh reaſon

For inequality; but let your reaſon ſerve
To make the truth appear. *Shakeſp. Meaſ. for Meaſure.*
Macbeth, beware Macduff!
Beware the thane of Fife: diſmiſs me: enough.
——Whate'er thou art, for thy good caution, thanks:
Thou'ſt *harp'd* my fear aright. *Shakeſpeare's Macbeth.*
He ſeems
Proud and diſdainful, *harping* on what I am,
Not what he knew I was. *Shakeſ. Ant. and Cleopatra.*

HA'RPER. *n. ſ.* [from *harp.*] A player on the harp.
Never will I truſt to ſpeeches penn'd,
Nor to the motion of a ſchoolboy's tongue;
Nor wooe in rhime, like a blind *harper*'s ſong. *Shakeſpeare.*
I'm the god of the harp: ſtop, my faireſt:—in vain;
Nor the harp, nor the *harper*, could fetch her again. *Tickell.*

HA'RPING *Iron. n. ſ.* [from *harpago*, Latin.] A bearded dart with a line faſtened to the handle, with which whales are ſtruck and caught.
The boat which on the firſt aſſault did go,
Struck with a *harping iron* the younger foe;
Who, when he felt his ſide ſo rudely gor'd,
Loud as the ſea that nouriſh'd him he roar'd. *Waller.*

HARPONE'ER. *n. ſ.* [*harponeur*, French, from *harpoon.*] He that throws the harpoon in whaleſiſhing.

HARPO'ON. *n. ſ.* [*harpon*, French.] A harping iron.

HA'RPSICORD. *n. ſ.* A muſical inſtrument.

HA'RPY. *n. ſ.* [*harpyia*, Latin; *harpie*, *harpye*, French.]
The *harpies* were a kind of birds which had the faces of women, and foul long claws, very filthy creatures; which, when the table was furniſhed for Phineus, came flying in, and devouring or carrying away the greater part of the victuals, did ſo defile the reſt that they could not be endured. *Raleigh.*
That an *harpy* is not a centaur is by this way as much a truth, as that a ſquare is not a circle. *Locke.*

2. A ravenous wretch.
I will do you any ambaſſage to the pigmies, rather than hold three words conference with this *harpy*. *Shakeſpeare.*

HA'RQUEBUSS. *n. ſ.* [See ARQUEBUSE.] A handgun.

HA'RQUEBUSSIER. *n. ſ.* [from *harquebuſs.*] One armed with a harquebuſs.
About thirty paces off were placed twenty thouſand nimble *harquebuſſiers*, ranged in length, and but five in a rank. *Knolles.*

HARRIDA'N. *n. ſ.* [corrupted from *haridelle*, a worn-out worthleſs horſe.] A decayed ſtrumpet.
She juſt endur'd the Winter ſhe began,
And in four months a batter'd *harridan*;
Now nothing's left, but wither'd, pale, and ſhrunk,
To bawd for others, and go ſhares with punk. *Swift.*

HA'RROW. *n. ſ.* [*charroue*, French; *harcke*, German, a rake.] A frame of timbers croſſing each other, and ſet with teeth, drawn over ſowed ground to break the clods and throw the earth over the ſeed.
The land with daily care
Is exercis'd, and with an iron war
Of rakes and *harrows*. *Dryden's Georgick.*
Two ſmall *harrows*, that clap on each ſide of the ridge, harrow it right up and down. *Mortimer's Husbandry.*

To HA'RROW. *v. a.* [from the noun.]

1. To break with the harrow.
Friend, *harrow* in time, by ſome manner of means,
Not only thy peaſon, but alſo thy beans. *Tuſſ. Husbandry.*
Can'ſt thou bind the unicorn with his band in the furrow? or will he *harrow* the valleys after thee? *Job* xxxix. 10.
Let the Volſcians
Plow Rome, and *harrow* Italy, I'll never
Be ſuch a goſling to obey inſtinct. *Shakeſp. Coriolanus.*

2. To tear up; to rip up.
I could a tale unfold, whoſe lighteſt word
Would *harrow* up thy ſoul, freeze thy young blood,
Make thy two eyes, like ſtars, ſtart from their ſpheres. *Sh.*
Imagine you behold me bound and ſcourg'd,
My aged muſcles *harrow'd* up with whips;
Or hear me groaning on the rending rack. *Rowe.*

3. To pillage; to ſtrip; to lay waſte. See HARRY, which in Scottiſh is the ſame thing.
As the king did excel in good commonwealth laws, ſo he had in ſecret a deſign to make uſe of them, as well for collecting of treaſure as for correcting of manners; and ſo meaning thereby to *harrow* his people, did accumulate them the rather. *Bacon's Henry* VII.

4. To invade; to haraſs with incurſions. [From hergian, Saxon.]
And he that *harrow'd* hell with heavy ſtowre,
The faulty ſouls from thence brought to his heavenly bowre. *Fairy Queen, b.* i. *cant.* 10.
Moſt glorious Lord of life, that on this day
Did'ſt make thy triumph over death and ſin;
And having *harrow'd* hell, did'ſt bring away
Captivity thence captive, us to win. *Spenſer's Sonnets.*

5. To diſturb; to put into commotion. [This ſhould rather be written *harry*, *harer*, French.]
Moſt like: it *harrows* me with fear and wonder. *Shakeſp.*

HAR

Amaz'd I ſtood, *harrow'd* with grief and care. *Milton.*
Harrow now out and weal away, he cried;
What diſmal day hath ſent this curſed light,
To ſee my lord ſo deadly damnify'd? *Fairy Queen, b.* ii.

HA'RROW. *interj.* An exclamation of ſudden diſtreſs. Now out of uſe.

HA'RROWER. *n. ſ.* [from *harrow.*]

1. He who harrows.

2. A kind of hawk. *Ainſworth.*

To HA'RRY. *v. a.* [*harer*, French.]

1. To teaze; to hare; to ruffle.
Thou muſt not take my former ſharpneſs ill.
—I repent me much
That I ſo *harry'd* him. *Shakeſp. Ant. and Cleopatra.*

2. In Scotland it ſignifies to rob, plunder, or oppreſs: as, *one* harried *a neſt*; that is, he took the young away: as alſo, *he* harried *me out of houſe and home*; that is, he robbed me of my goods, and turned me out of doors. See *To* HARROW.

HARSH. *adj.* [*herviſche*, German, *Skinner.*]

1. Auſtere; roughly ſour.
Our nature here is not unlike our wine;
Some ſorts, when old, continue briſk and fine:
So age's gravity may ſeem ſevere,
But nothing *harſh* or bitter ought t' appear. *Denham.*
Sweet, bitter, ſour, *harſh* and ſalt, are all the epithets we have to denominate that numberleſs variety of reliſhes. *Locke.*
The ſame defect of heat which gives a fierceneſs to our natures, may contribute to that roughneſs of our language, which bears ſome analogy to the *harſh* fruit of colder countries. *Swift to the Lord High Treaſurer.*

2. Rough to the ear.
A name unmuſical to Volſcian ears,
And *harſh* in ſound to thine. *Shakeſp. Coriolanus.*
Age might, what nature never gives the young,
Have taught the ſmoothneſs of thy native tongue;
But ſatire needs not that, and wit will ſhine
Through the *harſh* cadence of a rugged line. *Dryden.*
The unneceſſary conſonants made their ſpelling tedious, and their pronunciation *harſh*. *Dryden.*
Thy lord commands thee now
With a *harſh* voice, and ſupercilious brow,
To ſervile duties. *Dryden's Perſ. Sat.* 5.

3. Crabbed; moroſe; peeviſh.
He was a wiſe man and an eloquent; but in his nature *harſh* and haughty. *Bacon's Henry* VII.
Bear patiently the *harſh* words of thy enemies, as knowing that the anger of an enemy admoniſhes us of our duty. *Taylor.*
No *harſh* reflection let remembrance raiſe;
Forbear to mention what thou can'ſt not praiſe. *Prior.*
A certain quickneſs of apprehenſion inclined him to kindle into the firſt motions of anger; but, for a long time before he died, no one heard an intemperate or *harſh* word proceed from him. *Atterbury's Sermons.*

4. Rugged to the touch.
Black feels as if you were feeling needles points, or ſome *harſh* ſand; and red feels very ſmooth. *Boyle on Colours.*

5. Unpleaſing; rigorous.
With eloquence innate his tongue was arm'd;
Though *harſh* the precept, yet the preacher charm'd. *Dryd.*

HA'RSHLY. *adj.* [from *harſh.*]

1. Sourly; auſterely to the palate, as unripe fruit.

2. With violence; in oppoſition to gentleneſs, unleſs in the following paſſage it rather ſignifies unripely.
'Till, like ripe fruit, thou drop
Into thy mother's lap; or be with eaſe
Gather'd, not *harſhly* pluck'd. *Milton's Paradiſe Loſt, b.* xi.

3. Severely; moroſely; crabbedly.
I would rather he was a man of a rough temper, that would treat me *harſhly*, than of an effeminate nature. *Addiſon.*

4. Ruggedly to the ear.
My wife is in a wayward mood to-day:
I tell you, 'twould ſound *harſhly* in her ears. *Shakeſpeare.*
Get from him why he puts on this confuſion,
Grating ſo *harſhly* all his days of quiet
With turbulent and dang'rous lunacy. *Shakeſp. Hamlet.*
A hollow groan, a murm'ring wind aroſe;
The rings of iron that on the doors were hung,
Sent out a jarring ſound, and *harſhly* rung. *Dryd. Fables.*

HA'RSHNESS. *n. ſ.* [from *harſh.*]

1. Sourneſs; auſtere taſte.
Take an apple and roll it upon a table hard: the rolling doth ſoften and ſweeten the fruit, which is nothing but the ſmooth diſtribution of the ſpirits into the parts; for the unequal diſtribution of the ſpirits maketh the *harſhneſs*. *Bacon.*

2. Roughneſs to the ear.
Neither can the natural *harſhneſs* of the French, or the perpetual ill accent, be ever refined into perfect harmony like the Italian. *Dryden.*
Cannot I admire the height of Milton's invention, and the ſtrength of his expreſſion, without defending his antiquated words, and the perpetual *harſhneſs* of their ſound? *Dryden.*

'Tis not enough no *harſhneſs* gives offence;
The ſound muſt ſeem an echo to the ſenſe. *Pope.*

3. Ruggedneſs to the touch.
Harſhneſs and ruggedneſs of bodies is unpleaſant to the touch *Bacon's Natural Hiſtory.*

4. Crabbedneſs; moroſeneſs; peeviſhneſs.
No, Regan, you ſhall never have my curſe:
Thy tender-hefted nature ſhall not give
Thee o'er to *harſhneſs:* her eyes are fierce, but thine
Do comfort and not burn. *Shakeſp. King Lear.*

HART. *n. ſ.* [heoꞃꞇ, Saxon.] A he-deer of the large kind; the male of the roe.
That inſtant was I turn'd into a *hart,*
And my deſires, like fell and cruel hounds,
E'er ſince purſue me. *Shakeſ. Twelfth Night.*
The deer
And fearful *harts* do wander every where
Amidſt the dogs. *May's Virgil's Georg.*

HA'RTSHORN. *n. ſ.*
Hartſhorn is a drug that comes into uſe as many ways, and under as many forms, as any one in the whole *materia medica.* What is uſed here are the whole horns of the common male deer, which fall off every year. This ſpecies is the fallow deer; but ſome tell us, that the medicinal *hartſhorn* ſhould be that of the true hart or ſtag, called the red deer. The ſalt of *hartſhorn* is a great ſudorifick, and the ſpirit has all the virtues of volatile alkalies: it is uſed to bring people out of faintings by its pungency, holding it under the noſe, and pouring down ſome drops of it in water. *Hill's Mat. Med.*
Ramoſe concretions of the volatile ſalts are obſervable upon the glaſs of the receiver, whilſt the ſpirits of vipers and *hartſhorn* are drawn. *Woodward on Foſſils.*

HA'RTSHORN. *n. ſ.* An herb. *Ainſworth.*

HA'RT-ROYAL. *n. ſ.* A plant. A ſpecies of buckthorn plantain.

HA'RTSTONGUE. *n. ſ.* [*lingua cervina,* Latin.] A plant.
It commonly grows out from the joints of old walls and buildings, where they are moiſt and ſhady. There are very few of them in Europe. *Miller.*
Hartſtongue is propagated by parting the roots, and alſo by ſeed. *Mortimer's Husbandry.*

HA'RTWORT. *n. ſ.* [*tordylium,* Latin.] It is an umbelliferous plant, with a roſe-ſhaped flower, conſiſting of five unequal heart-faſhioned petals, which are placed circularly and reſt on the empalement, which afterward becomes an almoſt round fruit, compoſed of two flat ſeeds, which eaſily caſt off their covering with a raiſed border, which are commonly indented. It is an annual plant, and periſhes ſoon after it has perfected its ſeed. It is found wild in ſeveral parts of England. *Miller.*

HA'RVEST. *n. ſ.* [hæꞃꝼeꞅꞇ, Saxon.]

1. The ſeaſon of reaping and gathering the corn.
As it ebbs, the ſeedſman
Upon the ſlime and ooze ſcatters his grain,
And ſhortly comes to *harveſt.* *Shakeſ. Ant. and Cleopatra.*
With *harveſt* work he is worſe than he was in the Spring. *L'Eſtrange.*

2. The corn ripened, gathered and inned.
From Ireland come I with my ſtrength,
And reap the *harveſt* which that raſcal ſow'd. *Shak. H. VI.*
When the father is too fondly kind,
Such ſeed he ſows, ſuch *harveſt* ſhall he find. *Dryden.*

3. The product of labour.
Let theſe ſmall cotts and hills ſuffice:
Let us the *harveſt* of our labour eat;
'Tis labour makes the coarſeſt diet ſweet. *Dryden's Juven.*

HA'RVEST-HOME. *n. ſ.*

1. The ſong which the reapers ſing at the feaſt made for having inned the harveſt.
Your hay it is mow'd, and your corn is reap'd;
Your barns will be full, and your hovels heap'd;
Come, my boys, come,
Come, my boys, come,
And merrily roar out *harveſt-home.* *Dryden's K. Arthur.*

2. The time of gathering harveſt.
At *harveſt-home,* and on the ſhearing-day,
When he ſhould thanks to Pan and Pales pay,
And better Ceres, trembling to approach
The little barrel. *Dryden's Perſ. Sat. 4.*

3. The opportunity of gathering treaſure.
His wife ſeems to be well favoured: I will uſe it as the key of the cuckoldy rogue's coffer; and there's my *harveſt-home.* *Shakeſpeare's Merry Wives of Windſor.*

HA'RVEST-LORD. *n. ſ.* The head reaper at the harveſt.
Grant *harveſt-lord* more by a peny or two,
To call on his fellows the better to do. *Tuſſ. Husbandry.*

HA'RVESTER. *n. ſ.* [from *harveſt.*] One who works at the harveſt.

HA'RVESTMAN. *n. ſ.* [*harveſt* and *man.*] A labourer in harveſt.
Like to a *harveſtman,* that's taſk'd to mow
Or all, or loſe his hire. *Shakeſpeare's Coriolanus.*

To HASH. *v. n.* [*hacher,* French.] To mince; to chop into ſmall pieces, and mingle.
He rais'd his arm
Above his head, and rain'd a ſtorm
Of blows ſo terrible and thick,
As if he meant to *haſh* her quick. *Hudibras, p. i.*
What have they to complain of but too great variety, tho' ſome of the diſhes be not ſerved in the exacteſt order, and politeneſs; but *haſhed* up in haſte. *Garth.*

HASK. *n. ſ.* This ſeems to ſignify a caſe or habitation made of ruſhes or flags.
Phœbus, weary of his yearly taſk,
Eſtabliſhed hath his ſteeds in lowly lay,
And taken up his inn in fiſhes *haſk.* *Spenſer's Paſtorals.*

HA'SLET. } *n. ſ.* [*haſla,* Iſlandick, a bundle; *haſterel, haſtereau, haſtier,* French.] The heart, liver, and lights of a hog, with the windpipe and part of the throat to it.
HA'RSLET. }

HASP. *n. ſ.* [hæpſ, Saxon, whence in ſome provinces it is yet called *hapſe.*] A claſp folded over a ſtaple, and faſtened on with a padlock.
Have doors to open and ſhut at pleaſure, with *haſps* to them. *Mortimer's Huſbandry.*

To HASP. *v. n.* [from the noun.] To ſhut with a haſp.

HA'SSOCK. *n. ſ.* [*haſeck,* German. *Skinner.*]

1. A thick mat on which men kneel at church.
He found his pariſhioners very irregular; and in order to make them kneel, and join in the reſponſes, he gave every one of them a *haſſock* and common prayer book. *Addiſon.*

2. In Scotland it is applied to any thing made of ruſhes or privet, on which a perſon may ſit: it is therefore probable that *haſſock* and *haſk* are the ſame.

HAST. The ſecond perſon ſingular of *have.*

HASTE. *n. ſ.* [*haſte,* French; *haeſte,* Dutch.]

1. Hurry; ſpeed; nimbleneſs; precipitation.
Spare him, death!
Let not pity with her tears
Keep ſuch diſtance from thine ears:
But O, thou wilt not, canſt not ſpare!
Haſte hath never time to hear. *Craſhaw.*
Our lines reform'd, and not compos'd in *haſte,*
Poliſh'd like marble, would like marble laſt;
But as the preſent, ſo the laſt age writ;
In both we find like negligence and wit. *Waller.*
In as much *haſte* as I am, I cannot forbear giving an example. *Dryden's Dufreſnoy.*
The wretched father, running to their aid
With pious *haſte,* but vain, they next invade. *Dryden.*

2. Paſſion; vehemence.
I ſaid in my *haſte,* all men are liars. *Pſ.* cxvi. 11.

To HASTE. } *v. n.* [*haſter,* French; *haeſten,* Dutch.]
To HA'STEN. }

1. To make haſte; to be in a hurry; to be buſy; to be ſpeedy.
I have not *haſtened* from being a paſtor to follow thee. *Jer.*

2. To move with ſwiftneſs.
'Tis Cinna, I do know him by his gait;
He is a friend. Cinna, where *haſte* you ſo? *Shakeſpeare.*
They were troubled and *haſted* away. *Pſ.* xlviii. 5.
All thoſe things are paſſed away like a ſhadow, and as a poſt that *haſted* by. *Wiſd.* v. 9.
Haſting to pay his tribute to the ſea,
Like mortal life to meet eternity. *Denham.*
Theſe rites perform'd, the prince, without delay,
Haſtes to the nether world, his deſtin'd way. *Dryden's Æn.*
To diſtant Sparta, and the ſpacious waſte
Of ſandy Pyle, the royal youth ſhall *haſte.* *Pope's Odyſſey.*
Soon as the ſun awakes the ſprightly court,
Leave their repoſe, and *haſten* to the ſport. *Prior.*

To HASTE. } *v. a.* To puſh forward; to urge on; to precipitate; to drive to a ſwifter pace.
To HA'STEN. }
Let it be ſo *haſted,* that ſupper be ready at the fartheſt by five of the clock. *Shakeſ. Merry Wives of Windſor.*
All hopes of ſuccour from your arms is paſt;
To ſave us now, you muſt our ruin *haſte.* *Dryden.*
Each ſees his lamp with diff'rent luſtre crown'd;
Each knows his courſe with diff'rent periods bound;
And in his paſſage through the liquid ſpace,
Nor *haſtens,* nor retards his neighbour's race. *Prior.*

HA'STENER. *n. ſ.* [from *haſten.*] One that haſtens or hurries.

HA'STILY. *adj.* [from *haſty.*]

1. In a hurry; ſpeedily; nimbly; quickly.
A voice, that called loud and clear,
Come hither, hither, O come *haſtily!* *Fa. Queen.*
If your grace incline that we ſhould live,
You muſt not, ſir, too *haſtily* forgive. *Waller.*
The next to danger, hot purſu'd by fate,
Half cloth'd, half naked, *haſtily* retire. *Dryden.*

2. Raſhly; precipitately.
Without conſidering conſequences, we *haſtily* engaged in a war which hath coſt us ſixty millions. *Swift.*

3. Paſſionately; with vehemence.

HASTINESS. *n. ſ.* [from *haſty.*]

1. Haſte;

1. Haſte; ſpeed.

A fellow being out of breath, or ſeeming to be for haſte, with humble *haſtineſs* told Baſilius. *Sidney, b.* i.

2. Hurry; precipitation.

There is moſt juſt cauſe to fear, leſt our *haſtineſs* to embrace a thing of ſo perilous conſequence, ſhould cauſe poſterity to feel thoſe evils. *Hooker, Preface.*

The turns of his verſe, his breakings, his propriety, his numbers, and his gravity, I have as far imitated as the poverty of our language, and the *haſtineſs* of my performance, would allow. *Dryden.*

3. Angry teſtineſs; paſſionate vehemence.

HA'STINGS. *n. ſ.* [from *haſty*.] Peas that come early.

The large white and green *haſtings* are not to be ſet 'till the cold is over. *Mortimer's Husbandry.*

HA'STY. *adj.* [*haſtif*, French, from *haſte*; *haeſtig*, Dutch.]

1. Quick; ſpeedy.

Is all the counſel that we two have ſhar'd,
The ſiſters vows, the hours that we have ſpent,
When we have chid the *haſty* footed time
For parting us. *Shakeſ. Midſummer Night's Dream.*

2. Paſſionate; vehement.

He that is ſlow to wrath is of great underſtanding; but he that is *haſty* of ſpirit exalteth folly. *Prov.* xiv. 29.

3. Raſh; precipitate.

Seeſt thou a man that is *haſty* in his words? There is more hope of a fool than of him. *Prov.* xxix. 20.

Be not raſh with thy mouth, and let not thine heart be *haſty* to utter any thing before God. *Eccl.* v. 2.

4. Early ripe.

Beauty ſhall be a fading flower, and as the *haſty* fruit before the Summer. *Iſ.* xxviii. 4.

HA'STY-PUDDING. *n. ſ.* A pudding made of milk and flower, boiled quick together; as alſo of oatmeal and water boiled together.

Sure *haſty-pudding* is thy chiefeſt diſh,
With bullock's liver, or ſome ſtinking fiſh. *Dorſet.*

HAT. *n. ſ.* [hæt, Saxon; *hatt*, German.] A cover for the head.

She's as big as he is; and there's her thrum *hat*, and her muffler too. *Shakeſpeare's Merry Wives of Windſor.*

Out of meer ambition you have made
Your holy *hat* be ſtampt on the king's coin. *Shak. H.* VIII.

His *hat* was like a helmet, or Spaniſh montera. *Bacon.*

Hermes o'er his head in air appear'd,
And with ſoft words his drooping ſpirits cheer'd;
His *hat* adorn'd with wings diſclos'd the god,
And in his hand he bore the ſleep compelling rod. *Dryden.*

HA'TBAND. *n. ſ.* [*hat* and *band*.] A ſtring tied round the hat.

They had hats of blue velvet, with fine plumes of divers colours, ſet round like *hatbands*. *Bacon's New Atlantis.*

Room for the noble gladiator! ſee
His coat and *hatband* ſhew his quality. *Dryden's Juven.*

HA'TCASE. *n. ſ.* [*hat* and *caſe*.] A ſlight box for a hat.

I might mention a *hatcaſe*, which I would not exchange for all the beavers in Great Britain. *Addiſon's Spectator.*

To HATCH. *v. a.* [*hecken*, German, as *Skinner* thinks, from *heghen*, *eghen*, æʒ, egg, Saxon.]

1. To produce young from eggs by the warmth of incubation.

When they have laid ſuch a number of eggs as they can conveniently cover and *hatch*, they give over, and begin to ſit. *Ray on the Creation.*

He kindly ſpreads his ſpacious wing,
And *hatches* plenty for th' enſuing Spring. *Denham.*

The tepid caves, and fens and ſhores,
Their brood as numerous *hatch* from th' eggs, that ſoon
Burſting with kindly rupture, forth diſclos'd
Their callow young. *Milton's Paradiſe Loſt, b.* vii.

2. To quicken the egg by incubation.

Others *hatch* their eggs and tend the birth, 'till it is able to ſhift for itſelf. *Addiſon's Spectator.*

3. To produce by precedent action.

4. To form by meditation; to contrive.

Which thing they very well know, and, I doubt not, will eaſily confeſs, who live to their great both toil and grief, where the blaſphemies of Arrians are renewed by them; who, to *hatch* their hereſy, have choſen thoſe churches as fitteſt neſts where Athanaſius's creed is not heard. *Hooker, b.* v. *ſ.* 42.

He was a man harmleſs and faithful, and one who never *hatched* any hopes prejudicial to the king, but always intended his ſafety and honour. *Hayward.*

5. [From *hacher*, to cut.] To ſhade by lines in drawing or graving.

Who firſt ſhall wound, through others arms, his blood appearing freſh,
Shall win this ſword, ſilver'd and *hatcht*. *Chapm. Iliads.*

Such as Agamemnon and the hand of Greece
Should hold up high in braſs; and ſuch again
As venerable Neſtor, *hatch'd* in ſilver,
Should with a bond of air, ſtrong as the axle-tree
On which heav'n rides, knit all the Grecian ears
To his experienc'd tongue. *Shakeſp. Troil. and Creſſida.*

Thoſe tender hairs, and thoſe *hatching* ſtrokes of the pencil, which make a kind of minced meat in painting, are never able to deceive the ſight. *Dryden's Dufreſnoy.*

To HATCH. *v. n.*

1. To be in the ſtate of growing quick.

He obſerved circumſtances in eggs, whilſt they were *hatching*, which varied. *Boyle.*

2. To be in a ſtate of advance towards effect.

HATCH. *n. ſ.* [from the verb.]

1. A brood excluded from the egg.

2. The act of excluſion from the egg.

3. Diſcloſure; diſcovery.

Something's in his ſoul,
O'er which his melancholy ſits on brood;
And, I do doubt, the *hatch* and the diſcloſe
Will be ſome danger. *Shakeſpeare's Hamlet.*

4. [Hæca, Saxon; *hecke*, Dutch, a bolt.] The half door; the opening over the door.

Something about, a little from the right,
In at the window, or elſe o'er the *hatch*. *Shakeſ. K. John.*

5. [In the plural.] The doors or openings by which they deſcend from one deck or floor of a ſhip to another.

To the king's ſhip, inviſible as thou art,
There ſhalt thou find the mariners aſleep
Under the *hatches*. *Shakeſpeare's Tempeſt.*

There ſhe's hid;
The mariners all under *hatches* ſtow'd. *Shakeſp. Tempeſt.*

So ſeas, impell'd by winds with added pow'r,
Aſſault the ſides, and o'er the *hatches* tow'r. *Dryden.*

A ſhip was faſten'd to the ſhore;
The plank was ready laid for ſafe aſcent,
For ſhelter there the trembling ſhadow bent,
And ſkip'd and ſculk'd, and under *hatches* went. *Dryden.*

6. *To be under* HATCHES. To be in a ſtate of ignominy, poverty, or depreſſion.

He aſſures us how this fatherhood began in Adam, continued its courſe 'till the flood, got out of the ark with Noah, made and ſupported all the kings of the earth, 'till the captivity in Egypt, and then the poor fatherhood was *under hatches*. *Locke.*

7. *Hatches.* Floodgates. *Ainſworth.*

To HA'TCHEL. *v. a.* [*hachelen*, German.] To beat flax ſo as to ſeparate the fibrous from the brittle part.

This aſbeſtos ſeems different from that mentioned by Kircher in his deſcription of China; which he ſays, put into water, moulders like clay, and is a fibrous ſmall excreſcence, like hairs growing upon the ſtones; and for the *hatchelling*, ſpinning, and weaving it, he refers to his *mundus ſubterraneus*. *Woodward on Foſſils.*

HA'TCHEL. *n. ſ.* [from the verb; *hachel*, German.] The inſtrument with which flax is beaten.

HA'TCHELLER. *n. ſ.* [from *hatchel*.] A beater of flax.

HA'TCHET. *n. ſ.* [*hache*, *hachette*, French; *aſcia*, Latin] A ſmall axe.

The *hatchet* is to hew the irregularities of pieces of ſtuff. *Moxon's Mech. Exer.*

His harmful *hatchet* he hent in his hand,
And to the field he ſpeedeth. *Spenſer's Paſtorals.*

Ye ſhall have a hempen caudle then, and the help of a *hatchet*. *Shakeſpeare's Henry* VI. *p.* ii.

Nails, hammers, *hatchets* ſharp, and halters ſtrong,
Swords, ſpears, twice dipt in the dire ſtains
Of brothers blood. *Craſhaw.*

Tyrrheus, the foſter-father of the beaſt,
Then clench'd a *hatchet* in his horny fiſt. *Dryden's Æn.*

Our countryman preſented him with a curious *hatchet*; and aſking him whether it had a good edge, tried it upon the donor. *Addiſon's Freeholder.*

HA'TCHET-FACE. *n. ſ.* An ugly face; ſuch, I ſuppoſe, as might be hewn out of a block by a hatchet.

An ape his own dear image will embrace;
An ugly beau adores a *hatchet-face*. *Dryden.*

HA'TCHMENT. *n. ſ.* [Corrupted from *atchievement*. See ATCHIEVEMEMT.] Armorial eſcutcheon placed over a door at a funeral.

His means of death, his obſcure funeral,
No trophy, ſword, nor *hatchment* o'er his bones,
No noble rites nor formal oſtentation,
Cry to be heard. *Shakeſpeare's Hamlet.*

HA'TCHWAY. *n. ſ.* [*hatches* and *way*.] The way over or through the hatches.

To HATE. *v. a.* [hatian, Saxon.] To deteſt; to abhor; to abominate; to regard with the paſſion contrary to love.

You are, I think, aſſur'd I love you not.
—I am aſſur'd, if I be meaſur'd rightly,
Your majeſty hath no juſt cauſe to *hate* me. *Shak. Hen.* IV.

Do all men kill the thing they do not love?
—*Hates* any man the thing he would not kill?
—Ev'ry offence is not a hate at firſt. *Shakeſpeare.*

Thoſe old inhabitants of thy holy land thou *hateſt* for doing moſt odious works. *Wiſd.* xii. 4.

But whatsoever our jarring fortunes prove,
Though our lords *hate*, methinks we two may love. *Dryden.*

HATE. *n.s.* [ȝate, Saxon.] Malignity; detestation; the contrary to love.

Speak then to me, who neither beg nor fear
Your favours nor your *hate*. *Shakespeare's Macbeth.*

Hate to Mezentius, arm'd five hundred more,
Whom Mincius from his sire Benacus bore. *Dryden's Æn.*

Nausicaa teaches that the afflicted are not always the objects of divine *hate*. *Broome's Notes on the Odyssey.*

HA'TEFUL. *adj.* [*hate* and *full.*]

1. That which causes abhorrence; odious; abominable; detestable.

My name's Macbeth.
—The devil himself could not pronounce a title
More *hateful* to mine ear. *Shakespeare's Macbeth.*

There is no vice more *hateful* to God and man than ingratitude. *Peacham.*

What owe I to his commands
Who hates me, and hath hither thrust me down,
To sit in *hateful* office here confin'd,
Inhabitant of heav'n, and heav'nly born? *Milt. Par. Lost.*

I hear the tread
Of *hateful* steps: I must be viewless now. *Milton.*

But Umbriel, *hateful* gnome! forbears not so;
He breaks the vial whence the sorrows flow. *Pope.*

2. Abhorrent; detesting; malignant; malevolent.

Palamon, compell'd
No more to try the fortune of the field;
And, worse than death, to view with *hateful* eyes
His rival's conquest, and renounce the prize. *Dryden.*

HA'TEFULLY. *adv.* [from *hateful.*]

1. Odiously; abominably.

2. Malignantly; maliciously.

All their hearts stood *hatefully* appaid
Long since. *Chapman's Iliads.*

They shall deal with thee *hatefully*, take away all thy labour, and leave thee naked and bare. *Ezek.* xxiii. 29.

HA'TEFULNESS. *n.s.* [from *hateful.*] Odiousness.

HA'TER. *n.s.* [from *hate.*] One that hates; an abhorrer; a detester.

I of her understood of that most noble constancy in my lord Argalus; which whosoever loves not, shews himself to be a *hater* of virtue, and unworthy to live in the society of mankind. *Sidney.*

Whilst he stood up and spoke,
He was my master, and I wore my life
To spend upon his *haters*. *Shakesp. Ant. and Cleopatra.*

An enemy to God, and a *hater* of all good. *Brown.*

They never wanted so much knowledge as to inform and convince them of the unlawfulness of a man's being a murderer, an *hater* of God, and a covenant-breaker. *South.*

HA'TRED. *n.s.* [from *hate.*] Hate; ill-will; malignity; malevolence; dislike; abhorrence; detestation; abomination; the passion contrary to love.

Hatred is the thought of the pain which any thing present or absent is apt to produce in us. *Locke.*

I wish I had a cause to seek him there,
To oppose his *hatred* fully. *Shakespeare's Macbeth.*

Hatred is the passion of defiance, and there is a kind of aversation and hostility included in its very essence; but then, if there could have been *hatred* in the world when there was scarce any thing odious, it would have acted within the compass of its proper object. *South's Sermons.*

Hatreds are often begotten from slight and almost innocent occasions, and quarrels propagated and continued in the world. *Locke.*

Retain no malice nor *hatred* against any: be ready to do them all the kindness you are able. *Wake's Preparat. for Death.*

She is a Presbyterian of the most rank and virulent kind, and consequently has an inveterate *hatred* to the church. *Swift.*

To HA'TTER. *v. a.* [Perhaps corrupted from *batter.*] To harass; to weary; to wear out with fatigue.

He's *hatter'd* out with pennance. *Dryden.*

HA'TTER. *n.s.* [from *hat.*] A maker of hats.

A *hatter* sells a dozen of hats for five shillings a piece. *Swift.*

HA'TTOCK. *n.s.* [*attock*, Erse.] A shock of corn. *Dict.*

HAU'BERK. *n.s.* [*hauberg*, old French.] A coat of mail; a breastplate.

Him on the *hauberk* struck the princess sore,
That quite disparted all the linked frame,
And pierced to the skin. *Fairy Queen, b.* ii.

Hauberks and helms are hew'd with many a wound;
The mighty maces with such haste descend,
They break the bones, and make the solid armour bend. *Dryden's Knight's Tale.*

To HAVE. *v. a.* pret. and part. pass. *had.* [*haban*, Gothick; ȝabban, Saxon; *hebben*, Dutch; *avoir*, French; *avere*, Ital.]

1. Not to be without.

I have brought him before you, that after examination had I might *have* something to write. *Acts* xxv. 26.

2. To carry; to wear.

Upon the mast they saw a young man, who sat as on horseback, *having* nothing upon him. *Sidney.*

3. To make use of.

I *have* no Levite to my priest. *Judg.* xvii. 13.

4. To possess.

He that gathered much *had* nothing over, and he that gathered little *had* no lack. *Ex.* xvi. 18.

5. To bear; to carry; to be attended with or united to, as an accident or concomitant.

I will never trust a man again for keeping his sword clean; nor believe he can *have* every thing in him, by wearing his apparel neatly. *Shakespeare's All's well that ends well.*

6. To obtain; to enjoy.

Now, O Father, glorify me with thine own self, with the glory which I *had* with thee before the world was. *Jo.* xvii. 5.

7. To take; to receive.

A secret happiness, in Petronius, is called *curiosa felicitas*, and which I suppose he *had* from the *feliciter audere* of Horace. *Dryden.*

8. To be in any state.

Have I need of madmen, that ye have brought this fellow? 1 *Sa.* xxi. 15.

9. To put; to take.

With tossing and raking, and setting on cox,
Grass lately in swathes is meat for an oxe;
That done, go and cart it, and *have* it away. *Tuss. Husb.*

10. To procure; to find.

I would fain *have* any one name to me that tongue, that any one can speak as he should do, by the rules of grammar. *Locke on Education.*

11. Not to neglect; not to omit.

I cannot speak; if my heart be not ready to burst: Well, sweet Jack, *have* a care of thyself. *Shakespeare's Henry* IV.

Your plea is good; but still I say beware:
Laws are explain'd by men; so *have* a care. *Pope.*

12. To hold; to regard.

Of the maid servants shall I be *had* in honour. 2 *Sa.* vi. 22.

The proud *have had* me greatly in derision. *Ps.* cxix. 51.

13. To maintain; to hold opinion.

Sometimes they will *have* them to be natural heat, whereas some of them are crude and cold; and sometimes they will *have* them to be the qualities of the tangible parts, whereas they are things by themselves. *Bacon's Natural History.*

14. To contain.

You have of these pedlars that *have* more in 'em than you'd think, sister. *Shakespeare's Winter's Tale.*

15. To require; to claim.

What would these madmen *have*?
First they would bribe us without pence,
Deceive us without common sense,
And without pow'r enslave. *Dryden.*

16. To be a husband or wife to another.

If I had been married to him, for all he was in woman's apparel, I would not have *had* him. *Shakespeare.*

17. To be engaged, as in a task.

If we maintain things that are established, we *have* to strive with a number of heavy prejudices, deeply rooted in the hearts of men. *Hooker, b.* i. *s.* 1.

The Spaniards captain never *hath* to meddle with his soldiers pay. *Spenser on Ireland.*

You did set your course to treat of the evils which hindered the peace and good ordering of that land, among which that of the inconvenience of the laws was the first which you *had* in hand. *Spenser on Ireland.*

Kings *have* to deal with their neighbours, their wives, their children, their prelates or clergy, their nobles, their merchants and their commons. *Bacon's Essays.*

18. To wish; to desire.

I *had* rather be a door-keeper in the house of my God, than to dwell in the tents of wickedness. *Ps.* lxxxiv. 10.

I would *have* no man discouraged with that kind of life or series of actions, in which the choice of others, or his own necessities, may have engaged him. *Addison.*

19. To buy.

If these trifles were rated only by art and artfulness, we should *have* them much cheaper. *Collier on human Reason.*

20. It is most used in English, as in other European languages, as an auxiliary verb to make the tenses. *Have* the preterperfect, and *had* the preterpluperfect.

If there *had* been words enow between them to *have* expressed provocation, they *had* gone together by the ears. *Cong.*

I have heard one of the greatest genius's this age *has* produced, who *had* been trained up in all the polite studies of antiquity, assure me, upon his being obliged to search into records, that he at last took an incredible pleasure in it. *Addison.*

I *have* not here considered custom as it makes things easy, but as it renders them delightful; and though others *have* made the same reflections, it is impossible they may not *have* drawn those uses from it. *Addison.*

 That

That admirable precept which Pythagoras is said to *have* given to his disciples, and which that philosopher must *have* drawn from the observation I *have* enlarged upon. *Addison.*

The gods *have* placed labour before virtue. *Addison.*

This observation we *have* made on man. *Addison.*

Evil spirits *have* contracted in the body habits of lust and sensuality, malice and revenge. *Addison.*

There torments *have* already taken root in them. *Addison.*

It *has* been finely improved by many divines. *Addison.*

That excellent author *has* shewn how every particular custom and habit of virtue will, in its own nature, produce the heaven, or a state of happiness, in him who shall hereafter practise it. *Addison.*

21. Have *at*, or *with*, is an expression denoting resolution to make some attempt.

He that will caper with me for a thousand marks, let him lend me the money, and *have at* him. *Shak. Henry* IV. *p.* ii.

I can bear my part; 'tis my occupation: *have at* it with you. *Shakespeare's Winter's Tale.*

I never was out at a mad frolick, though this is the maddest I ever undertook: *have with* you, lady mine; I take you at your word. *Dryden's Spanish Fryar.*

HA'VEN. *n. s.* [*haven*, Dutch; *havre*, French.]

1. A port; a harbour; a safe station for ships.

Only love was threatened and promised to him, and so to his cousin, as both the tempest and *haven* of their best years. *Sidney, b.* ii.

Order for sea is given:
They have put forth the *haven.* *Shakesp. Ant. and Cleopat.*

After an hour and a half sailing, we entered into a good *haven*, being the port of a fair city. *Bacon's New Atlantis.*

The queen beheld, as soon as day appear'd,
The navy under sail, the *haven* clear'd. *Denham.*

We may be shipwreckt by her breath:
Love, favour'd once with that sweet gale,
Doubles his haste, and fills his sail,
'Till he arrive, where she must prove
The *haven*, or the rock of love. *Waller.*

2. A shelter; an asylum.

All places, that the eye of heaven visits,
Are to a wise man ports and happy *havens.* *Shakes. R.* II.

Ha'vener. *n. s.* [from *haven.*] An overseer of a port.

These earls and dukes appointed their special officers, as receiver, *havener*, and customer. *Carew's Survey of Cornwal.*

Ha'ver. *n. s.* [from *have.*] Possessor; holder.

Valour is the chiefest virtue, and
Most dignifies the *haver.* *Shakesp. Coriolanus.*

Ha'ver is a common word in the northern counties for oats: as, *haver* bread for oaten bread.

When you would anneal, take a blue stone, such as they make *haver* or oat cakes upon, and lay it upon the cross bars of iron. *Peacham.*

Haught. *adj.* [*haut*, French.]

1. Haughty; insolent; proud; contemptuous; arrogant.

The proud insulting queen,
With Clifford and the *haught* Northumberland,
Have wrought the easy melting king, like wax. *Shakesp.*
No lord of thine, thou *haught* insulting man;
Nor no man's lord. *Shakespeare's Richard* II.

2. High; proudly magnanimous.

His courage *haught*,
Desir'd of foreign foemen to be known,
And far abroad for strange adventures sought. *Fairy Queen.*

Hau'ghtily. *adv.* [from *haughty.*] Proudly; arrogantly; contemptuously.

Her heav'nly form too *haughtily* she priz'd;
His person hated, and his gifts despis'd. *Dryden.*

Ha'ughtiness. *n. s.* [from *haughty.*] Pride; arrogance; the quality of being haughty.

By the head we make known our supplications, our threatnings, our mildness, our *haughtiness*, our love, and our hatred. *Dryden's Dufresnoy.*

HA'UGHTY. *adj.* [*hautaine*, French.]

1. Proud; lofty; insolent; arrogant; contemptuous.

His wife, being a woman of a *haughty* and imperious nature, and of a wit superior to his, quickly resented the disrespect she received from him. *Clarendon, b.* viii.

I shall sing of battles, blood and rage,
And *haughty* souls, that mov'd with mutual hate,
In fighting fields pursu'd and found their fate. *Dryd. Æn.*

2. Proudly great.

Our vanquish'd wills that pleasing force obey:
Her goodness takes our liberty away;
And *haughty* Britain yields to arbitrary sway. *Prior.*

3. Bold; adventurous.

Who now shall give me words and sound
Equal unto this *haughty* enterprize?
Or who shall lend me wings, with which from ground
My lowly verse may loftily arise? *Fairy Queen, b.* ii.

Ha'ving. *n. s.* [from *have.*]

1. Possession; estate; fortune.

My *having* is not much;
I'll make division of my present with you:
Hold, there's half my coffer. *Shakesp. Twelfth Night.*

2. The act or state of possessing.

Of the one side was alleged the *having* a picture, which the other wanted; of the other side, the first striking the shield. *Sidney.*

Thou art not for the fashion of these times,
Where none will sweat but for promotion;
And having that, do choak their service up,
Even with the *having.* *Shakes. As you like it.*

3. Behaviour; regularity. This is still retained in the Scottish dialect.

The gentleman is of no *having*: he kept company with the wild prince and Poinz: he is of too high a region; he knows too much. *Shakes. Merry Wives of Windsor.*

Ha'viour. *n. s.* [for *behaviour.*] Conduct; manners.

Their ill *haviour* garres men misstay
Both of their doctrines and their fay. *Spenser's Pastorals.*

To Haul. *v. a.* [*haler*, French, to draw.] To pull; to draw; to drag by violence. A word which, applied to things, implies violence; and, to persons, aukwardness or rudeness.

Thy Dol, and Helen of thy noble thoughts,
Is in base durance and contagious prison,
Haul'd thither by mechanick dirty hands. *Shakes. Henry* IV.

The youth with songs and rhimes,
Some dance, some *haul* the rope. *Denham.*

Some the wheels prepare,
And fasten to the horses feet; the rest
With cables *haul* along th' unwieldly beast. *Dryden's Æn.*

In his grandeur he naturally chuses to *haul* up others after him whose accomplishments most resemble his own. *Swift.*

Thither they bent, and *haul'd* their ships to land;
The crooked keel divides the yellow sand. *Pope's Odyssey.*

While romp-loving miss
Is *haul'd* about in gallantry robust. *Thomson's Autumn.*

Haul. *n. s.* [from the verb.] Pull; violence in dragging.

The leap, the slap, the *haul*; and shook to notes
Of native musick, the respondent dance. *Thoms. Winter.*

Haum. *n. s.* [or *hame*, or *halm*; þealm, Saxon; *halm*, Dutch and Danish.] Straw.

In champion countrie a pleasure they take
To mow up their *haume* for to brew and to bake:
The *haume* is the straw of the wheat or the rie,
Which once being reaped, they mow by and by. *Tusser.*

Having stripped off the *haum* or binds from the poles, as you pick the hops, stack them up for their security in Winter. *Mortimer's Husbandry.*

Haunch. *n. s.* [*hancke*, Dutch; *hanche*, French; *anca*, Italian.]

1. The thigh; the hind hip.

Hail, groom! didst thou not see a bleeding hind,
Whose right *haunch* earst my stedfast arrow strake?
If thou didst, tell me. *Fairy Queen, b.* ii. *cant.* 3.

To make a man able to teach his horse to stop and turn quick, and to rest on his *haunches*, is of use to a gentleman both in peace and war. *Locke.*

2. The rear; the hind part.

O Westmorland, thou art a Summer bird,
Which ever in the *haunch* of Winter sings
The lifting up of day. *Shakesp. Henry* IV. *p.* ii.

To HAUNT. *v. a.* [*hanter*, French.]

1. To frequent; to be much about any place or person.

A man who for his hospitality is so much *haunted*, that no news stir but come to his ears. *Sidney.*

Now we being brought known unto her, the time that we spent in curing some very dangerous wounds, after once we were acquainted, and acquainted we were sooner than ourselves expected, she continually almost *haunted* us. *Sidney.*

I do *haunt* thee in the battle thus,
Because some tell me that thou art a king. *Shak. Hen.* IV.

She this dang'rous forest *haunts*,
And in sad accents utters her complaints. *Waller.*

Earth now
Secur'd like to heav'n, a seat where gods might dwell,
Or wander with delight, and love to *haunt*
Her sacred shades. *Milton's Paradise Lost, b.* vii.

Celestial Venus *haunts* Idalia's groves;
Diana Cynthus, Ceres Hybla loves. *Pope's Spring.*

2. It is used frequently in an ill sense of one that comes unwelcome.

You wrong me, sir, thus still to *haunt* my house;
I told you, sir, my daughter is dispos'd of. *Shakespeare.*

Oh, could I see my country-seat!
There leaning near a gentle brook,
Sleep, or peruse some ancient book;
And there in sweet oblivion drown
Those cares that *haunt* the court and town. *Swift.*

3. It is eminently used of apparitions or spectres that appear in a particular place.

Foul ſpirits *haunt* my reſting place,
And ghaſtly viſions break my ſleep by night. *Fairfax.*

All theſe the woes of Oedipus have known,
Your fates, your furies, and your *haunted* town. *Pope.*

To Haunt. *v. n.* To be much about; to appear frequently.

I've charged thee not to *haunt* about my doors:
In honeſt plainneſs thou haſt heard me ſay,
My daughter's not for thee. *Shakeſpeare's Othello.*

Where they moſt breed and *haunt*, I have obſerv'd
The air is delicate. *Shakeſpeare's Macbeth.*

Haunt. *n. ſ.* [from the verb.]

1. Place in which one is frequently found.

We ſet toils, nets, gins, ſnares and traps for beaſts and birds in their own *haunts* and walks, and without any ſeal of faith and confidence. *L'Eſtrange.*

To me pertains not, ſhe replies,
To know or care where Cupid flies;
What are his *haunts*, or which his way,
Where he would dwell, or whither ſtray. *Prior.*

A ſcene where, if a god ſhould caſt his ſight,
A god might gaze and wonder with delight!
Joy touch'd the meſſenger of heav'n; he ſtay'd
Entranc'd, and all the bliſsful *haunt* ſurvey'd. *Pope's Odyſſ.*

2. Habit of being in a certain place.

The *haunt* you have got about the courts will one day or another bring your family to beggary. *Arbuthn. John Bull.*

Ha'unter. *n. ſ.* [from *haunt.*] Frequenter; one that is often found in any place.

The ancient Grecians were an ingenious people, of whom the vulgar ſort, ſuch as were *haunters* of theatres, took pleaſure in the conceits of Ariſtophanes. *Wotton on Education.*

O goddeſs, *haunter* of the woodland green,
Queen of the nether ſkies. *Dryden's Fables.*

Ha'vock. *n. ſ.* [*hafog*, Welſh, devaſtation.] Waſte; wide and general devaſtation; mercileſs deſtruction.

Having been never uſed to have any thing of their own, and now being upon ſpoil of others, they make no ſpare of any thing, but *havock* and confuſion of all they meet with. *Spenſer on Ireland.*

Saul made *havock* of the church. *Acts* viii. 3.

Ye gods, what *havock* does ambition make
Among your works! *Addiſon's Cato.*

The Rabbins, to expreſs the great *havock* which has been made of them, tells us, that there were ſuch torrents of holy blood ſhed, as carried rocks of a hundred yards in circumference above three miles into the ſea. *Addiſon's Spectator.*

If it had either air or fuel, it muſt make a greater *havock* than any hiſtory mentions. *Cheyne's Phil. Prin.*

Ha'vock. *interj.* [from the noun.] A word of encouragement to ſlaughter.

Why ſtand theſe royal fronts amazed thus?
Cry *havock*, kings! *Shakeſp. King John.*

Até by his ſide,
Cries *havock!* and lets looſe the dogs of war. *Shakeſpeare.*

To Ha'vock. *v. a.* [from the noun.] To waſte; to deſtroy; to lay waſte.

Whatſoever they leave, the ſoldier ſpoileth and *havocketh* likewiſe; ſo that, between both, nothing is very ſhortly left. *Spenſer's State of Ireland.*

See! with what heat theſe dogs of hell advance,
To waſte and *havock* yonder world, which I
So fair and good created! *Milton's Paradiſe Loſt*, b. x.

Ha'utboy. *n. ſ.* [*haut* and *bois.*] A wind inſtrument.

I ſaw it, and told John of Gaunt he beat his own name; for you might have truſs'd him and all his apparel into an eelſkin: the caſe of a treble *hautboy* was a manſion for him, a court; and now hath he land and beeves. *Shakeſ. Henry IV.*

Now give the *hautboys* breath; he comes, he comes. *Dry.*

Ha'utboy *Strawberry.* See Strawberry.

Haw. *n. ſ.* [ꞅaᵹ, Saxon.]

1. The berry and ſeed of the hawthorn.

Now ſow and go harrow, where ridge ye did draw
The ſeed of the bremble with kernel and *haw.* *Tuſſer.*

Years of ſtore of *haws* and hips commonly portend cold Winters. *Bacon's Natural Hiſtory.*

His quarrel to the hedge was, that his thorns and his brambles did not bring forth raiſins, rather than *haws* and blackberries. *L'Eſtrange.*

2. An excreſcence in the eye.

3. [ꞅaᵹa, Saxon; *haw*, a garden, Daniſh.] A ſmall piece of ground adjoining to an houſe. In Scotland they call it *haugh.*

Upon the *haw* at Plymouth is cut out in the ground the portraiture of two men, with clubs in their hands, whom they term Gog and Magog. *Carew's Survey of Cornwal.*

Ha'wthorn. *n. ſ.* [ꞅæᵹ ðorn, Saxon.] A ſpecies of medlar; the thorn that bears haws.

The great uſe to which it is applied in England is to make hedges and fences; and there are two or three varieties of it about London; but that ſort which produces the ſmalleſt leaves is preferable, becauſe its branches always grow cloſe together. *Miller.*

There is a man haunts the foreſt, that abuſes our young plants with carving Roſalind on their barks; hangs odes upon *hawthorns*, and elegies on brambles. *Shak. As you like it.*

The *hawthorn* fly is all black, and not big. *Walton's Angler.*

Some in their hands, beſide the lance and ſhield,
The boughs of woodbine, or of *hawthorn* held. *Dryden*

Now *hawthorns* bloſſom, now the daiſies ſpring. *Pope*

The *hawthorn* whitens, and the juicy groves
Put forth their buds. *Thomſon's Spring.*

To Haw. *v. n.* [Perhaps corrupted from *hawk* or *hack.*] To ſpeak ſlowly with frequent intermiſſion and heſitation.

'Tis a great way; but yet, after a little humming and *hawing* upon't, he agreed to undertake the job. *L'Eſtrange.*

Hawk. *n. ſ.* [*hæbeg*, Welſh; ꞅaꝼoc, Saxon.]

1. A bird of prey, uſed much anciently in ſport to catch other birds.

Do'ſt thou love hawking? Thou haſt *hawks* will ſoar
Above the morning lark. *Shak. Taming of the Shrew.*

It can be no more diſgrace to a great lord to draw a fair picture, than to cut his *hawk*'s meat. *Peacham on Drawing.*

Whence borne on liquid wing
The ſounding culver ſhoots; or where the *hawk*,
High in the beetling cliff, his airy builds. *Thomſon's Spring.*

2. [*Hoch*, Welſh.] An effort to force phlegm up the throat.

To Hawk. *v. n.* [from *hawk.*]

1. To fly hawks at fowls; to catch birds by means of a hawk.

'Tis his highneſs' pleaſure
You do prepare to ride unto St. Alban's,
Whereas the king and queen do mean to *hawk.* *Shakeſpeare.*

Do'ſt thou love *hawking?* Thou haſt hawks will ſoar
Above the morning lark. *Shakeſpeare.*

One followed ſtudy and knowledge, and another *hawking* and hunting. *Locke.*

He that *hawks* at larks and ſparrows has no leſs ſport, though a much leſs conſiderable quarry, than he that flies at nobler game. *Locke.*

A falc'ner Henry is, when Emma *hawks*;
With her of tarſels and of lures he talks. *Prior.*

2. To fly at; to attack on the wing.

A faulcon tow'ring in her pride of place,
Was by a mouſing owl *hawk'd* at and kill'd. *Shakeſ. Macb.*

Whether upward to the moon they go,
Or dream the Winter out in caves below,
Or *hawk* at flies elſewhere, concerns us not to know. *Dry.*

3. [*Hoch*, Welſh.] To force up phlegm with a noiſe.

Come, ſit, ſit, and a ſong.——Shall we clap into't roundly, without *hawking* or ſpitting, or ſaying we are hoarſe, which are the only prologues to a bad voice. *Shakeſpeare.*

She complained of a ſoreneſs of her throat, and of a ſtinking tough phlegm which ſhe *hawked* up in the mornings. *Wiſeman's Surgery.*

Blood, caſt out of the throat or windpipe, is ſpit out with a *hawking* or ſmall cough; that out of the gums is ſpit out without *hawking*, coughing, or vomiting. *Harvey on Conſumpt.*

4. To ſell by proclaiming it in the ſtreets. [From *hock*, German, a ſaleſman.]

His works were *hawk'd* in ev'ry ſtreet;
But ſeldom roſe above a ſheet. *Swift.*

Ha'wked. *adj.* [from *hawk.*] Formed like a hawk's bill.

Flat noſes ſeem comely unto the Moor, an aquiline or *hawked* one unto the Perſian, a large and prominent noſe unto the Roman. *Brown's Vulgar Errours.*

Ha'wker. *n. ſ.* [from *hock*, German.] One who ſells his wares by proclaiming them in the ſtreet.

I ſaw my labours, which had coſt me ſo much thought and watching, bawled about by common *hawkers*, which I once intended for the weighty conſideration of the greateſt perſon. *Swift's Vindication of Iſaac Bickerſtaff.*

To grace this honour'd day the queen proclaims,
By herald *hawkers*, high heroick games:
She ſummons all her ſons; an endleſs band
Pours forth, and leaves unpeopled half the land. *Pope.*

Ha'wkweed. *n. ſ.*

The characters are: the ſtalks are branched and ſlender, the leaves produced alternately, and the flower conſiſts of many leaves placed in an orbicular order, and open in form of a marigold: the ſeeds are ſlender and angular, or furrowed: the whole plant hath a milky juice. Oxtongue is a ſpecies of this plant. *Miller.*

Ha'wses. *n. ſ.* [of a ſhip.] Two round holes under the ſhip's head or beak, through which the cables paſs when ſhe is at anchor. *Harris.*

HAY. *n. ſ.* [ꞅeᵹ, ꞅiᵹ, Saxon; *hey*, Dutch.] Graſs dried to fodder cattle in Winter.

Make *hay* while the ſun ſhines. *Camden's Remains.*

Make poor men's cattle break their necks;
Set fire on barns and *hay* ſtacks in the night,
And bid the owners quench them with their tears. *Shakeſp.*

We have heats of dungs, and of *hays* and herbs laid up moiſt. *Bacon's New Atlantis.*

The

Or if the earlier season lead
To the tann'd *hay* cock in the mead. *Milton.*
Bring them for food sweet boughs and osiars cut,
Nor all the Winter long thy *hay* rick shut. *May's Virgil.*

Some turners turn long and slender sprigs of ivory, as small as an *hay* stalk. *Moxon's Mech. Exer.*

The best manure for meadows is the bottom of *hay* mows and *hay* stacks. *Mortimer's Husbandry.*

Hay and oats, in the management of a groom, will make ale. *Swift.*

By some *hay* cock, or some shady thorn,
He bids his beads both even song and morn. *Dryden.*
Blouzelinda, in a gamesome mood,
Behind a *hay* cock loudly laughing stood. *Gay's Pastorals.*
The hum of bees inviting sleep sincere,
Into the guiltless breast, beneath the shade,
Or thrown at large amid' the fragrant *hay*. *Thoms. Autumn.*

To dance the HAY. To dance in a ring: probably from dancing round a hay cock.

I will play on the tabor to the worthies,
And let them dance the *hay*. *Shakesp. Love's Labour Lost.*
This maids think on the hearth they see,
When fires well nigh consumed be,
There dancing *hays* by two and three,
Just as your fancy casts them. *Drayton's Nymphid.*
The gum and glist'ning, which with art
And study'd method, in each part
Hangs down the heart,
Looks just as if that day
Snails there had crawl'd the *hay*. *Suckling.*

HAY. *n. s.* [from *haie*, French, a hedge.] A net which incloses the haunt of an animal.

Coneys are destroyed by *hays*, curs, spaniels, or tumblers bred up for that purpose. *Mortimer's Husbandry.*

HA'YMAKER. *n. s.* [*hay* and *make.*] One employed in drying grass for hay.

As to the return of his health and vigour, were you here, you might enquire of his *haymakers*. *Pope to Swift.*

HA'ZARD. *n. s.* [*hazard*, French; *azar*, Spanish; *haski*, Runick, danger.]

1. Chance; accident; fortuitous hap.

I have set my life upon a cast,
And I will stand the *hazard* of the die. *Shakesp. Rich.* III.
I will upon all *hazards* well believe
Thou art my friend, that know'st my tongue so well. *Shak.*

Where the mind does not perceive this connection, there mens opinions are not the product of judgment, but the effects of chance and *hazard*, of a mind floating at all adventures, without choice and without direction. *Locke.*

2. Danger; chance of danger.

We are bound to yield unto our Creator, the father of all mercy, eternal thanks, for that he hath delivered his law unto the world; a law wherein so many things are laid open, as a light which otherwise would have been buried in darkness, not without the *hazard*, or rather not with the *hazard*, but with the certain loss of thousands of souls, most undoubtedly now saved. *Hooker, b.* i.

The *hazard* I have run to see you here, should inform you that I love not at a common rate. *Dryden's Spanish Fryar.*

Men are led on from one stage of life to another in a condition of the utmost *hazard*, and yet without the least apprehension of their danger. *Rogers's Sermons.*

3. A game at dice.

The duke playing at *hazard* at the groom-porter's, in much company, held in a great many hands together, and drew a huge heap of gold. *Swift.*

To HA'ZARD. *v. a.* [*hazarder*, French.] To expose to chance; to put into danger.

They might, by persisting in the extremity of that opinion, *hazard* greatly their own estates, and so weaken that part which their places now give. *Hooker, b.* v.

It was not in his power to adventure upon his own fortune, or bearing a publick charge to *hazard* himself against a man of private condition. *Hayward.*

To HA'ZARD. *v. n.*

1. To try the chance.

I pray you tarry; pause a day or two,
Before you *hazard*; for in chusing wrong,
I lose your company. *Shakesp. Merchant of Venice.*

2. To adventure.

She from her fellow-provinces would go,
Rather than *hazard* to have you her foe. *Waller.*

HA'ZARDABLE. *adj.* [from *hazard.*] Venturesome; liable to chance.

An *hazardable* determination it is, unto fluctuating and indifferent effects, to affix a positive type or period. *Brown.*

HA'ZARDER. *n. s.* [from *hazard.*] He who hazards.

HA'ZARDRY. *n. s.* [from *hazard.*] Temerity; precipitation; rash adventurousness. Obsolete.

Hasty wrath, and heedless *hazardry*,
Do breed repentance late, and lasting infamy.
Fairy Queen.

HA'ZARDOUS. *adj.* [*hazardeux*, Fr. from *hazard.*] Dangerous; exposed to chance.

Grant that our *hazardous* attempt prove vain,
We feel the worst, secur'd from greater pain. *Dryden.*

HA'ZARDOUSLY. *adv.* [from *hazardous.*] With danger or chance.

HAZE. *n. s.* [The etymology unknown.] Fog; mist.

To HAZE. *v. n.* To be foggy or misty.

To HAZE. *v. a.* To fright one. *Ainsworth.*

HA'ZEL. *n. s.* [hæsel, Saxon; *corylus*, Latin.]

It hath male flowers growing at remote distances from the fruit on the same tree: the nuts grow in clusters, and are closely joined together at the bottom, each being covered with an outward husk or cup, which opens at the top, and when the fruit is ripe it falls out: the leaves are roundish and intire. The species are hazelnut, cobnut, and filbert. The red and white filberts are mostly esteemed for their fruit. *Miller.*

Kate, like the *hazel* twig,
Is straight and slender; and as brown in hue
As *hazel* nuts, and sweeter than the kernels. *Shakespeare.*
Her chariot is an empty *hazel* nut. *Shak. Rom. and Jul.*
Why sit we not beneath the grateful shade,
Which *hazels*, intermix'd with elms, have made? *Dryden.*

There are some from the size of a *hazle* nut to that of a man's fist. *Woodward on Fossils.*

HA'ZEL. *adj.* [from the noun.] Light brown; of the colour of hazle.

Chuse a warm dry soil, that has a good depth of light *hazel* mould. *Mortimer's Husbandry.*

HA'ZELLY. *adj.* Of the colour of hazel; a light brown.

Uplands consist either of sand, gravel, chalk, rock or stone, *hazelly* loam, clay, or black mould. *Mortimer's Husbandry.*

HA'ZY. *adj.* [from *haze.*] Dark; foggy; misty.

Our clearest day here is misty and *hazy*; we see not far, and what we do see is in a bad light. *Burnet's Theory of the Earth.*

Oft engender'd by the *hazy* North,
Myriads on myriads, insect armies waft. *Thomson.*

HE. *pronoun.* gen. *him*; plur. *they*; gen. *them.* [*hy*, Dutch; he, Saxon. It seems to have borrowed the plural from ðir, plural ðar, dative ðirum.]

1. The man that was named before.

All the conspirators, save only *he*,
Did that they did in envy of great Cæsar. *Shakespeare.*
If much you note *him*,
You shall offend *him*, and increase his passion;
Feed and regard *him* not. *Shakespeare's Macbeth.*
I am weary of this moon; would *he* would change. *Shakes.*
Adam spoke;
So cheer'd *he* his fair spouse, and she was cheer'd. *Milton.*
When Adam wak'd, *he* on his side
Leaning half rais'd hung over her. *Milton.*
Thus talking, hand in hand along *they* pass'd
On to their blissful bow'rs. *Milton.*
Extol
Him first, *him* last, *him* midst. *Milton.*

2. The man; the person. It sometimes stands without reference to any foregoing word.

He is never poor
That little hath, but *he* that much desires. *Daniel.*

3. Man or male being.

Such mortal drugs I have; but Mantua's law
Is death to any *he* that utters them. *Shakesp. Rom. and Jul.*

Ay, crook-back, here I stand to answer thee, or any *he* the proudest of thy sort. *Shakespeare's Henry* VI. *p.* iii.

Tros and his race the sculptor shall employ,
And *he* the god who built the walls of Troy. *Dryd. Virg.*

4. Male: as, a *he* bear, a *he* goat. It is used where the male and female have not different denominations.

The *he's* in birds have the fairest feathers. *Bacon's N. Hist.*

5. In the two last senses *he* is rather a noun than pronoun.

HEAD. *n. s.* [heafod, heafd, Saxon; *hoofd*, Dutch; *heved*, old English, whence by contraction *head.*]

1. The part of the animal that contains the brain or the organ of sensation or thought.

Vein healing verven, and *head* purging dill. *Spenser.*
Over *head* up-grew
Insuperable height of loftiest shade. *Milton's Parad. Lost.*
My *head* geers off, what filthy work you make. *Dryden.*
The dewy paths of meadows we will tread,
For crowns and chaplets to adorn thy *head*. *Dryden.*

I could still have offers, that some, who hold their *heads* higher, would be glad to accept. *Swift.*

2. Person as exposed to any danger or penalty.

What he gets more of her than sharp words, let it lie on my *head*. *Shakespeare's Merry Wives of Windsor.*

Who of all ages to succeed, but feeling
The evil on him brought by me, will curse
My *head*? ill fare our ancestor impure. *Milt. Parad. Lost.*

3. HEAD *and Ears.* The whole person.

In jingling rhimes well fortify'd and strong,
He fights intrench'd o'er *head and ears* in song. *Granville.*

4. Denomination of any animals.

When Innocent XI. desired the marquis of Carpio to furnish thirty thousand *head* of swine, he could not spare them; but thirty thousand lawyers he had at his service. *Addison.*

The tax upon pasturage was raised according to a certain rate *per head* upon cattle. *Arbuthnot on Coins.*

5. Chief; principal person; one to whom the rest are subordinate; leader; commander.

For their commons, there is little danger from them, except it be where they have great and potent *heads*. *Bacon.*

Your *head* I him appoint;
And by myself have sworn, to him shall bow
All knees in heav'n, and shall confess him lord. *Milton.*

The *heads* of the chief sects of philosophy, as Thales, Anaxagoras, and Pythagoras, did likewise consent to this tradition. *Tillotson's Sermons.*

6. Place of honour; the first place.

Notwithstanding all the justices had taken their places upon the bench, they made room for the old knight at the *head* of them. *Addison's Spectator.*

7. Place of command.

An army of fourscore thousand troops, with the duke of Marlborough at the *head* of them, could do nothing against an enemy. *Addison on the War.*

8. Countenance; presence.

Richard not far from hence hath hid his *head*. *Sh. R.* II.
With Cain go wander through the shade of night,
And never shew thy *head* by day or light. *Shak. Rich.* II.
Ere to-morrow's sun shall shew his *head*. *Dryden.*

9. Understanding; faculties of the mind.

The wenches laid their *heads* together. *L'Estrange.*

A fox and a goat went down a well to drink: the goat fell to hunting which way to get back; oh, says Reynard, never trouble your *head*, but leave that to me. *L'Estrange.*

Work with all the ease and speed you can, without breaking your *head*, and being so very industrious in starting scruples. *Dryden's Dufresnoy.*

The lazy and inconsiderate took up their notions by chance, without much beating their *heads* about them. *Locke.*

If a man shews that he has no religion, why should we think that he beats his *head* and troubles himself to examine the grounds of this or that doctrine. *Locke.*

When in ordinary discourse we say a man has a fine *head*, we express ourselves metaphorically, and speak in relation to his understanding; and when we say of a woman she has a fine head, we speak only in relation to her commode. *Addison.*

We laid our *heads* together, to consider what grievances the nation had suffered under king George. *Addis. Freeholder.*

10. Face; front; fore part.

The gathering crowd pursues;
The ravishers turn *head*, the fight renews. *Dryden.*

11. Resistance; hostile opposition.

Then made he *head* against his enemies,
And Hymner slew. *Fairy Queen, b.* ii.

Sometimes hath Henry Bolingbroke made *head* against my power. *Shakespeare's Henry* IV. *p.* i.

Two valiant gentlemen first making *head* against them, seconded by half a dozen more, made forty of them run away. *Raleigh's Apology.*

Sin having depraved his judgment, and got possession of his will, there is no other principle left him naturally, by which he can make *head* against it. *South's Sermons.*

12. Spontaneous resolution.

The bordering wars in this kingdom were made altogether by voluntaries, upon their own *head*, without any pay or commission from the state. *Davies on Ireland.*

13. State of a deer's horns, by which his age is known.

It was a buck of the first *head*. *Shakesp. Love's Labour Lost.*

The *buck* is called the fifth year a buck of the first *head*. *Shak.*

14. Individual. It is used in numbers or computation.

If there be six millions of people, then there is about four acres for every *head*. *Graunt's Bills of Mortality.*

15. The top of any thing bigger than the rest.

His spear's *head* weighed six hundred shekels of iron. 1 *Sa.*

As high
As his proud *head* is rais'd towards the sky,
So low tow'rds hell his roots descend. *Denham.*

Trees, which have large and spreading *heads*, would lie with their branches up in the water. *Woodward.*

If the buds are made our food, they are called *heads* or tops; so *heads* of asparagus and artichoaks. *Watts's Logick.*

It is an equivocal term; for it signifies the *head* of a nail, or of a pin, as well as of an animal. *Watts's Logick.*

16. Place of chief resort.

The horse took the alarm, and made their escape to Winchester, the *head* quarters. *Clarendon, b.* viii.

17. The fore part of any thing, as of a ship.

By gallies with brazen *heads* she might transport over Indus at once three hundred thousand soldiers.
Raleigh's History of the World.

On oozy ground his gallies moor;
Their *heads* are turn'd to sea, their sterns to shore. *Dryden.*

18. That which rises on the top.

Let it stand in a tub four or five days before it be put into the cask, stirring it twice a day, and beating down the *head* or yeast into it. *Mortimer's Husbandry.*

19. The blade of an axe.

A man fetcheth a stroke with the axe to cut down the tree, and the *head* slippeth from the helve. *Deutr.* xix. 5.

20. Upper part of a bed.

Israel bowed upon the bed's *head*. *Gen.* xlvii. 31.

21. The brain.

As eastern priests in giddy circles run,
And turn their *heads* to imitate the sun. *Pope's Essays.*

22. Dress of the head.

Politick ladies think they gain a great point when they have teazed their husbands to buy them a laced *head*, or a fine petticoat. *Swift.*

23. Principal topicks of discourse.

These *heads* are of a mixed order, and we propose only such as belong to the natural world. *Burnet's Theo. of the Earth.*

These *heads* are set down more fully in the arguments of each chapter. *Burnet's Theory of the Earth.*

'Tis our great interest, and our chief duty, to satisfy ourselves on this *head*, upon which our whole conduct depends.
Atterbury's Sermons, Preface.

24. Source of a stream.

It is the glory of God to give; his very nature delighteth in it: his mercies in the current, through which they would pass, may be dried up, but at the *head* they never fail. *Hooker.*

The current by Gaza is but a small stream, rising between it and the Red sea, whose *head* from Gaza is little more than twenty English miles. *Raleigh's History of the World.*

Some did the song, and some the choir maintain,
Beneath a laurel shade, where mighty Po
Mounts up to woods above, and hides his *head* below. *Dry.*

25. Crisis; pitch.

The indisposition which has long hung upon me, is at last grown to such a *head*, that it must quickly make an end of me, or of itself. *Addison's Spectator.*

26. Power; influence; force; strength; dominion.

Within her breast though calm, her breast though pure,
Motherly cares and fears got *head*, and rais'd
Some troubled thoughts. *Milton's Paradise Regain'd.*

God will not admit of the passionate man's apology, that he has so long given his unruly passions their *head*, that he cannot now govern nor controul them. *South's Sermons.*

27. Body; conflux.

People under command chuse to consult, and after to march in order; and rebels, contrariwise, run upon an *head* together in confusion. *Bacon's Henry* VII.

Let all this wicked crew gather
Their forces to one *head*. *Ben. Johnson's Catiline.*

28. Power; armed force.

My lord, my lord, the French have gather'd *head*. *Shakes.*

At sixteen years,
When Tarquin made a *head* for Rome, he fought
Beyond the mark of others. *Shakespeare's Coriolanus.*

A mighty and a fearful *head* they are,
As ever offer'd foul play in a state. *Shakesp. Henry* IV.

Far in the marches here we heard you were,
Making another *head* to fight again. *Shakesp. Henry* VI.

29. Liberty in running a horse.

He gave his able horse the *head*,
And bounding forward struck his agile heels
Against the panting sides of his poor jade
Up to the rowel-head. *Shakesp. Henry* IV. *p.* ii.

30. It is very improperly applied to roots.

How turneps hide their swelling *heads* below,
And how the closing coleworts upwards grow. *Gay.*

31. HEAD *and Shoulders.* By force; violently.

People that hit upon a thought that tickles them, will be still bringing it in by *head and shoulders*, over and over, in several companies. *L'Estrange.*

They can bring in every odd exception in grammar, every figure of speech, *head and shoulders* by main force, in spite of nature and their subject. *Felton on the Classicks.*

To HEAD. *v. a.* [from the noun.]

1. To lead; to influence; to direct; to govern.

Nor is what has been said of princes less true of all other governours, from him that *heads* an army to him that is master of a family, or of one single servant. *South.*

Abas, who seem'd our friend, is either fled,
Or, what we fear, our enemies does *head*. *Dryd. Aurengz.*

This lord had *headed* his appointed bands,
In firm allegiance to his king's commands. *Prior.*

2. To behead; to kill by taking away the head.

If you *head* and hang all that offend that way but for ten years together, you'll be glad to give out a commission for more heads. *Shakesp. Measure for Measure.*

3. To fit any thing with a head, or principal part.

Headed with flints and feathers bloody dy'd,
Such as the Indians in their quivers hide. *Fairy Queen.*

Of cornel-wood a ſpear upright,
Headed with piercing ſteel, and poliſh'd bright. *Dryden.*

4. To lop trees.

You muſt diſbranch them, leaving only the ſummit entire: unleſs the ſoil be very good, it may be neceſſary to *head* them too. *Mortimer's Huſbandry.*

HE'ADACH. *n. ſ.* [*head* and *ach.*] Pain in the head.

From the cruel *headach*,
Riches do not preſerve. *Sidney, b.* i.

Nothing more expoſes to *headachs*, colds, catarrhs, and coughs, than keeping the head warm. *Locke.*

In the *headach* he orders the opening of the vein of the forehead. *Arbuthnot.*

At ſome dear idle time,
Not plagu'd with *headachs*, or the want of rhyme. *Pope.*

HE'ADBAND. *n. ſ.* [*head* and *band.*]

1. A fillet for the head; a topknot.

The Lord will take away the bonnets, and the *headbands.* *Iſ.* iii. 20.

2. The band at each end of a book.

HE'ADBOROUGH. *n. ſ.* [*head* and *borough.*] A conſtable; a ſubordinate conſtable.

Here lies John Dod, a ſervant of God, to whom he is gone,
Father or mother, ſiſter or brother, he never knew none;
A *headborough* and a conſtable, a man of fame,
The firſt of his houſe, and laſt of his name. *Camden.*

This none are able to break through,
Until they're freed by *head* of *borough.* *Hudibras, p.* i.

HE'ADDRESS. *n. ſ.* [*head* and *dreſs.*]

1. The covering of a woman's head.

There is not ſo variable a thing in nature as a lady's *headdreſs:* I have known it riſe and fall. *Addiſon's Spectator.*

If ere with airy horns I planted heads,
Or diſcompos'd the *headdreſs* of a prude. *Pope.*

2. Any thing reſembling a headdreſs, and prominent on the head.

Among birds the males very often appear in a moſt beautiful *headdreſs*, whether it be a creſt, a comb, a tuft of feathers, or a natural little plume, erected like a kind of pinnacle on the very top of the head. *Addiſon's Spectator.*

HE'ADER. *n. ſ.* [from *head.*]

1. One that heads nails or pins, or the like.

2. The firſt brick in the angle.

If the *header* of one ſide of the wall is toothed as much as the ſtretcher on the outſide, it would be a ſtronger toothing, and the joints of the *headers* of one ſide would be in the middle of the *headers* of the courſe they lie upon of the other ſide, *Moxon's Mech. Exer.*

HE'ADGARGLE. *n. ſ.* [*head* and *gargle.*] A diſeaſe, I ſuppoſe, in cattle.

For the *headgargle* give powder of fenugreek. *Mortimer.*

HE'ADINESS. *n. ſ.* [from *heady.*] Hurry; raſhneſs; ſtubbornneſs; precipitation; obſtinacy.

If any will raſhly blame ſuch his choice of old and unwonted words, him may I more juſtly blame and condemn, either of witleſs *headineſs* in judging, or of headleſs hardineſs in condemning. *Spenſer.*

HE'ADLAND. *n. ſ.* [*head* and *land.*]

1. Promontary; cape.

An heroick play ought to be an imitation of an heroick poem, and conſequently love and valour ought to be the ſubject of it: both theſe ſir William Davenant began to ſhadow; but it was ſo as diſcoverers draw their maps, with *headlands* and promontories. *Dryden.*

2. Ground under hedges.

Now down with the graſs upon *headlands* about,
That groweth in ſhadow ſo rank and ſo ſtout. *Tuſſer.*

HE'ADLESS. *adj.* [from *head.*]

1. Without an head; beheaded.

His ſhining helmet he 'gan ſoon unlace,
And left his *headleſs* body bleeding at the place. *Fairy Queen.*

Were I a man, a duke, and next of blood,
I would remove theſe tedious ſtumbling blocks,
And ſmooth my way upon their *headleſs* necks. *Shak. H.* VI.

On the cold earth lies th' unregarded king,
A *headleſs* carkaſs, and a nameleſs thing. *Denham.*

Prickly ſtubs, inſtead of trees, are found;
Headleſs the moſt, and hideous to behold. *Dryden.*

2. Without a chief.

They reſted not until they had made the empire ſtand *headleſs* about ſeventeen years. *Raleigh's Eſſays.*

3. Obſtinate; inconſiderate; ignorant; wanting intellects: perhaps for *heedleſs.*

If any will raſhly blame ſuch his choice of old unwonted words, him may I more juſtly blame and condemn, either of witleſs headineſs in judging, or of *headleſs* hardineſs in condemning. *Spenſer.*

HE'ADLONG. *adj.*

1. Raſh; thoughtleſs.

2. Sudden; precipitate.

It ſuddenly fell from an exceſs of favour, which, many examples having taught them, never ſtopt his race 'till it came to a *headlong* overthrow. *Sidney, b.* ii.

HE'ADLONG. *adv.* [*head* and *long.*]

1. With the head foremoſt. It is often doubtful whether this word be adjective or adverb.

I'll look no more,
Leſt my brain turn, and the deficient ſight
Topple down *headlong.* *Shakeſ. King Lear.*

Who, while he ſteering view'd the ſtars, and bore
His courſe from Africk to the Latian ſhore,
Fell *headlong* down. *Dryden's Æn. b.* vi.

Headlong from thence the glowing fury ſprings,
And o'er the Theban palace ſpreads her wings. *Pope.*

2. Raſhly; without thought; precipitately.

To give Ahab ſuch warning, as might infallibly have prevented his deſtruction, was eſteemed by him evil; and to puſh him on *headlong* into it, becauſe he was fond of it, was accounted good. *South's Sermons.*

Some aſk for envy'd pow'r, which publick hate
Purſues and hurries *headlong* to their fate;
Down go the titles. *Dryden's Juv. Sat.* x.

3. Haſtily; without delay or reſpite.

Unhappy offspring of my teeming womb!
Dragg'd *headlong* from thy cradle to thy tomb. *Dryden.*

4. It is very negligently uſed by *Shakeſpeare.*

Hence will I drag thee *headlong* by the heels
Unto a dunghill, which ſhall be thy grave. *Shakeſp. H.* VI.

HE'ADMOULD-SHOT. *n. ſ.* [*head, mould,* and *ſhot.*] This is when the ſutures of the ſkull, generally the coronal, ride; that is, have their edges ſhot over one another; which is frequent in infants, and occaſions convulſions and death. *Quincy.*

HE'ADPIECE. *n. ſ.* [*head* and *piece.*]

1. Armour for the head; helmet; morion.

I pulled off my *headpiece*, and humbly intreated her pardon, or knowledge why ſhe was cruel. *Sidney, b.* ii.

The word is giv'n; with eager ſpeed they lace
The ſhining *headpiece*, and the ſhield embrace. *Dryden.*

Another reaſon for this fiction was their wearing a *headpiece*, or martial vizor, that had but one ſight through it. *Broome's Notes on the Odyſſey.*

This champion will not be in ſuch haſte to come into the field, before his great blunderbuſs can be got ready, his old ruſty breaſtplate ſcoured, and his cracked *headpiece* mended. *Swift.*

2. Underſtanding; force of mind.

'Tis done by ſome ſeverals
Of *headpiece* extraordinary, lower meſſes
Perchance are to this buſineſs purblind. *Shak. Winter's Tale.*

Eumenes had the beſt *headpiece* of all Alexander's captains. *Prideaux.*

HE'ADQUARTERS. *n. ſ.* [*head* and *quarters.*] The place of general rendezvous, or lodgment for ſoldiers.

Thoſe ſpirits, poſted upon the out-guards, immediately ſcour off to the brain, which is the *headquarters*, or office of intelligence, and there they make their report. *Collier.*

HE'ADSHIP. *n. ſ.* [from *head.*] Dignity; authority; chief place.

HE'ADSMAN. *n. ſ.* [*head* and *man.*] Executioner; one that cuts off heads.

Rods broke on our aſſociates bleeding backs,
And *headſmen* lab'ring 'till they blunt their ax? *Dryden.*

HE'ADSTALL. *n. ſ.* [*head* and *ſtall.*] Part of the bridle that covers the head.

His horſe near legg'd before, and with a half-cheek'd bit, and a *headſtall* of ſheep's leather, which being reſtrained to keep him from ſtumbling, hath been often burſt, and now repaired with knots. *Shakeſp. Taming of the Shrew.*

HE'ADSTONE. *n. ſ.* [*head* and *ſtone.*] The firſt or capital ſtone.

The ſtone, which the builders refuſed, is become the *headſtone.* *Pſ.* cxviii. 24.

HE'ADSTRONG. *adj.* [*head* and *ſtrong.*] Unreſtrained; violent; ungovernable; reſolute to run his own way: as a horſe whoſe head cannot be held in.

An example, for *headſtrong* and inconſiderate zeal, no leſs fearful than Achitophel for proud and irreligious wiſdom. *Hooker, Dedication.*

How now, my *headſtrong!* where have you been gadding?
—Where I have learnt me to repent the ſin
Of diſobedient oppoſition. *Shakeſ. Romeo and Juliet.*

But ſuch a *headſtrong* potent fault it is,
That it but mocks reproof. *Shakeſp. Twelfth Night.*

He ill aſpires to rule
Cities of men or *headſtrong* multitudes,
Subject himſelf to anarchy within. *Milton's Paradiſe Loſt.*

There's no oppoſing the torrent of a *headſtrong* multitude. *L'Eſtrange.*

Now let the *headſtrong* boy my will controul:
Virtue's no ſlave of man; no ſex confines the ſoul:
I, for myſelf, th' imperial ſeat will gain,
And he ſhall wait my leiſure for his reign. *Dryd. Aurengz.*

Your

Your father's folly took a *headſtrong* courſe;
But I'll rule yours, and teach you love by force. *Dryden.*
I'll try if yet I can reduce to reaſon
This *headſtrong* youth, and make him ſpurn at Cato. *Addiſ.*

Why there it is, you will be both judge and party: I am ſorry thou diſcovereſt ſo much of thy *headſtrong* humour. *Arb.*

Can we forget how the mad *headſtrong* rout
Defy'd their prince to arms, nor made account
Of faith or duty, or allegiance ſworn? *Phillips.*

HE'ADWORKMAN. *n. ſ.* [*head work* and *man.*] The foreman, or chief ſervant over the reſt.

Can Wood be otherwiſe regarded than as the mechanick, the *headworkman*, to prepare his furnace, metal, and ſtamps? *Swift's Addreſs to Parliament.*

HE'ADY. *adj.* [from *head.*]

1. Raſh; precipitate; haſty; violent; ungovernable; hurried on with paſſion.

Take pity of your town and of your people,
While yet the cool and temp'rate wind of grace
O'erblows the filthy and contagious clouds
Of *heady* murther, ſpoil and villany. *Shakeſp. Henry V.*

I am adviſed what I ſay:
Neither diſturb'd with the effect of wine,
Nor, *heady* raſh, provok'd with raging ire;
Albeit my wrongs might make one wiſer mad. *Shakeſpeare.*

I'll forbear,
And am fall'n out with my more *heady* will,
To take the indiſpos'd and ſickly fit
For the ſound man. *Shakeſpeare's King Lear.*

Never came reformation in a flood
With ſuch a *heady* current ſcow'ring faults;
Nor ever hydra-headed wilfulneſs
So ſoon did loſe his ſeat, and all at once,
As in this king. *Shakeſpeare's Henry V.*

Wives, the readieſt helps
To betray *heady* huſbands, rob the eaſy. *Ben. Johnſ. Catil.*

Men, naturally warm and *heady*, are tranſported with the greateſt fluſh of good nature. *Addiſon's Freeholder.*

2. Apt to affect the head.

I was entertained with a ſort of wine which was very *heady*, but otherwiſe ſeemed to be ſack. *Boyle.*

Since hearty beef and mutton will not do,
Here's julep-dance, ptiſan of ſong and ſhow:
Give you ſtrong ſenſe, the liquor is too *heady*;
You're come to farce, that's aſſes milk, already. *Dryden.*

Flow, Welſted! flow, like thine inſpirer, beer;
Heady, not ſtrong; and foaming, though not full. *Pope.*

To HEAL. *v. a.* [*halgan*, Gothick; hælan, Saxon; *heelen*, Dutch.]

1. To cure a perſon; to reſtore from hurt or ſickneſs.

I will reſtore health, and *heal* thee of thy wounds. *Jer.* xxx.

Who would not believe that our Saviour *healed* the ſick, and raiſed the dead, when it was publiſhed by thoſe who themſelves often did the ſame miracles? *Addiſon.*

Phyſicians, by juſt obſervations, grow up to an honourable degree of ſkill in the art of *healing*. *Watts's Imp. of the Mind.*

2. To cure a wound or diſtemper.

Thou haſt no *healing* medicines. *Jer.* xxx. 13.

A fontanel had been made in the ſame leg, which he was forced to *heal* up, by reaſon of the pain. *Wiſeman's Surgery.*

3. To perform the act of making a ſore to cicatrize, after it is cleanſed.

After ſeparation of the eſchar, I deterged and *healed*. *Wiſem.*

4. To reconcile: as, he *healed* all diſſenſions.

To HEAL. *v. n.* To grow well. Uſed of wounds or ſores.

Thoſe wounds *heal* that men do give themſelves. *Shakeſ.*

Abſceſſes will have a greater or leſs tendency to *heal*, as they are higher or lower in the body. *Sharp's Surgery.*

HE'ALER. *n. ſ.* [from *heal.*] One who cures or heals.

I will not be an *healer*. *Iſ.* iii. 7.

HE'ALING. *participial adj.* [from *heal.*] Mild; mollifying; gentle; aſſuaſive: as, he's of a *healing* pacifick temper.

HEALTH. *n. ſ.* [from hæl, Saxon.]

1. Freedom from bodily pain or ſickneſs.

Health is the faculty of performing all actions proper to a human body, in the moſt perfect manner. *Quincy.*

Our father is in good *health*, he is yet alive. *Gen.* xliii. 28.

May be he is not well;
Infirmity doth ſtill neglect all office,
Whereto our *health* is bound. *Shakeſpeare's King Lear.*

2. Welfare of mind; purity; goodneſs; principle of ſalvation.

There is no *health* in us. *Common Prayer.*

The beſt preſervative to keep the mind in *health*, is the faithful admonition of a friend. *Bacon, Eſſay* 28.

3. Salvation ſpiritual and temporal.

My God, my God, why haſt thou forſaken me, and art ſo far from my *health*, and from the words of my complaint? *Pſ.*

4. Wiſh of happineſs in drinking.

Come, love and *health* to all;
I drink to th' general joy of the whole table. *Shakeſpeare's Macbeth.*

He aſked leave to begin two *healths*: the firſt was to the king's miſtreſs, and the ſecond to his wife. *Howel.*

For peace at home, and for the publick wealth,
I mean to crown a bowl to Cæſar's *health*. *Dryden's Perſ.*

HE'ALTHFUL. *adj.* [*health* and *full.*]

1. Free from ſickneſs.

Adam knew no diſeaſe, ſo long as temperance from the forbidden fruit ſecured him: nature was his phyſician, and innocence and abſtinence would have kept him *healthful* to immortality. *South's Sermons.*

2. Well diſpoſed.

Such an exploit have I in hand, Ligarius,
Had you an *healthful* ear to hear it. *Shakeſ. Julius Cæſar.*

3. Wholeſome; ſalubrious.

There be many good and *healthful* airs that do appear by habitation and proofs, that differ not in ſmell from other airs. *Bacon's Natural Hiſtory.*

While they pervert pure nature's *healthful* rules
To loathſome ſickneſs; worthily ſince they
God's image did not reverence in themſelves. *Milt. P. Loſt.*

Our *healthful* food the ſtomach labours thus,
At firſt embracing what it ſtraight doth cruſh. *Dryden.*

4. Salutary; productive of ſalvation.

Pour upon them the *healthful* ſpirit of thy grace. *Com. Prayer.*

HE'ALTHFULLY. *adv.* [from *healthful.*]

1. In health.
2. Wholſomely.

HE'ALTHFULNESS. *n. ſ.* [from *healthful.*]

1. State of being well.
2. Wholſomeneſs; ſalubrious qualities.

You have taſted of that cup whereof I have liberally drank, which I look upon as God's phyſick, having that in *healthfulneſs* which it wants in pleaſure. *King Charles.*

We ventured to make a ſtandard of the *healthfulneſs* of the air from the proportion of acute and epidemical diſeaſes. *Graunt.*

To the winds the inhabitants of Geneva aſcribe the *healthfulneſs* of their air; for as the Alps ſurround them on all ſides, there would be a conſtant ſtagnation of vapours, did not the north wind put them in motion. *Addiſon on Italy.*

HE'ALTHILY. *adv.* [from *healthy.*] Without ſickneſs or pain.

HE'ALTHINESS. *n. ſ.* [from *healthy.*] The ſtate of health.

HE'ALTHLESS. *adj.* [from *health.*] Weak; ſickly; infirm.

He that ſpends his time in ſports, is like him whoſe garment is all made of fringes, and his meat nothing but ſauces; they are *healthleſs*, chargeable, and uſeleſs. *Taylor.*

HE'ALTHSOME. *adj.* [from *health.*] Wholſome; ſalutary.

Shall I not then be ſtifled in the vault,
To whoſe foul mouth no *healthſome* air breathes in,
And there be ſtrangl'd ere my Romeo comes? *Shakeſpeare.*

HE'ALTHY. *adj.* [from *health.*] In health; free from ſickneſs; hale; ſound.

The huſbandman returns from the field, and from manuring his ground, ſtrong and *healthy*, becauſe innocent and laborious. *South's Sermons.*

Gardening or huſbandry, and working in wood, are fit and *healthy* recreations for a man of ſtudy or buſineſs. *Locke.*

Temperance, induſtry, and a publick ſpirit, running thro' the whole body of the people in Holland, hath preſerved an infant commonwealth, of a ſickly conſtitution, through ſo many dangers, as a much more *healthy* one could never have ſtruggled againſt without thoſe advantages. *Swift.*

Air and exerciſe contribute to make the animal *healthy*. *Arb.*

HEAM. *n. ſ.* In beaſts the ſame as the after-birth in women.

HEAP. *n. ſ.* [heap, Saxon; *hoop*, Dutch and Scottiſh.]

1. Many ſingle things thrown together; a pile; an accumulation.

The way to lay the city flat,
And bury all which yet diſtinctly ranges,
In *heaps* and piles of ruin. *Shakeſpeare's Coriolanus.*

The dead were fallen down by *heaps*, one upon another. *Wiſd.* xviii. 23.

Huge *heaps* of ſlain around the body riſe. *Dryden's Æn.*

One may form from it an idea of Venice in its firſt beginnings, when it had only a few *heaps* of earth for its dominions. *Addiſon on Italy.*

2. A crowd; a throng; a rabble.

A cruel tyranny, bathed in the blood of their emperors; a *heap* of vaſſals and ſlaves, no freemen, no inheritance, no ſtirp or ancient families. *Bacon's holy War.*

3. Cluſter; number driven together.

An univerſal cry reſounds aloud;
The ſailors run in *heaps*, a helpleſs crowd. *Dryden.*

To HEAP. *v. a.* [from the noun.]

1. To throw on heaps; to pile; to throw together.

Heap on wood, kindle the fire, conſume the fleſh, and ſpice it well. *Ezek.* xxiv. 10.

2. To accumulate; to lay up.

Though the wicked *heap* up ſilver as the duſt, and raiment as the clay; but the juſt ſhall put it on, and the innocent ſhall divide the ſilver. *Job* xxvii. 16.

How great the credit was, wherein that oracle was preſerved,

served, may be gathered from the vast riches which were there *heaped* up from the offerings of all the Grecian nations. *Temple.*

They who will make profession of painting, must *heap* up treasures out of their reading, and there will find many wonderful means of raising themselves above others. *Dryden.*

3. To add to something else.

For those of old,
And the late dignities *heap'd* up to them,
We rest your hermits. *Shakespeare's Macbeth.*

HE'APER. *n. s.* [from *heap.*] One that makes piles or heaps.

HE'APY. *adj.* [from *heap.*] Lying in heaps.

Where a dim gleam the paly lanthorn throws
O'er the mid pavement, *heapy* rubbish grows. *Gay.*

Scarce his head
Rais'd o'er the *heapy* wreath, the branching elk
Lies slumb'ring sullen in the white abyss. *Thoms. Winter.*

To HEAR. *v. n.* [hyran, Saxon; *hooren*, Dutch.]

1. To enjoy the sense by which sounds are distinguished.

Sound is nothing but a certain modulation of the external air, which, being gathered by the external ear, beats, as is supposed, upon the membrana tympani, which moves the four little bones in the tympanum: in like manner as it is beat by the external air, these little bones move the internal air which is in the tympanum and vestibulum; which internal air makes an impression upon the auditory nerve in the labyrinth and cochlea, according as it is moved by the little bones in the tympanum: so that, according to the various reflexions of the external air, the internal air makes various impressions upon the auditory nerve, the immediate organ of *hearing*; and these different impressions represent different sounds. *Quincy.*

The object of *hearing* is sound, whose variety is so great, that it brings in admirable store of intelligence. *Holder.*

2. To listen; to hearken.

Since 'tis your command, what you so well
Are pleas'd to *hear*, I cannot grieve to tell. *Denham.*

3. To be told; to have an account.

I have *heard* by many of this man. *Acts* ix. 13.

I was bowed down at the *hearing* of it; I was dismayed at the seeing of it. *Is.* xxi. 3.

Prepare to *hear* of such a crime
As tragick poets, since the birth of time,
Ne'er feign'd. *Tate's Juven. Sat.* 15.

This, of eldest parents, leaves us more in the dark, who, by divine institution, has a right to civil power, than those who never *heard* any thing at all of heir or descent. *Locke.*

To HEAR. *v. a.*

1. To perceive by the ear.

The trumpeters and singers were as one sound to be *heard* in praising the Lord. *2 Chro.* v. 13.

2. To give an audience, or allowance to speak.

He sent for Paul, and *heard* him concerning the faith in Christ. *Acts* xxiv. 24.

I must beg the forbearance of censure, 'till I have been *heard* out in the sequel of this discourse. *Locke.*

3. To attend; to listen to; to obey.

Hear the word at my mouth, and give them warning from me. *Ezek.* iii. 17.

4. To attend favourably.

They think they shall be *heard* for their much speaking. *Mat.*

5. To try; to attend judicially.

Hear the causes, and judge righteously. *Deutr.* i. 16.

6. To acknowledge. A Latin phrase.

Or *hear'st* thou rather pure ethereal stream,
Whose fountain who shall tell? *Milton.*

Hear'st thou submissive, but a lowly birth? *Prior.*

HEARD signifies a keeper, and is sometimes initial; as *heard-bearht*, a glorious keeper: sometimes final, as *cyneheard*, a royal keeper. *Gibson's Camden.* It is now written *herd:* as, *cowherd*, a cowkeeper; hyrd, Saxon.

HE'ARER. *n. s.* [from *hear.*] One who attends to any doctrine or discourse delivered orally by another.

And so was she dulled withal, that we could come so near as to hear her speeches, and yet she not perceive the *hearers* of her lamentation. *Sidney, b.* ii.

St. John and St. Mathew, which have recorded these sermons, heard them; and being *hearers*, did think themselves as well respected as the pharisees. *Hooker, b.* v. *s.* 19.

Words, be they never so few, are too many, when they benefit not the *hearer*. *Hooker, b.* v.

The *hearers* will shed tears,
And say, alas, it was a piteous deed! *Shakesp. Henry* VI.

Tell thou the lamentable fall of me,
And send the *hearers* weeping to their beds.
Shakespeare's Richard II.

Plays in themselves have neither hopes nor fears;
Their fate is only in their *hearers* ears. *Ben. Johnson.*

Her *hearers* had no share
In all she spoke, except to stare. *Swift.*

HE'ARING. *n. s.* [from *hear.*]

1. The sense by which sounds are perceived.

Bees are called with sound upon brass, and therefore they have *hearing*. *Bacon's Natural History.*

2. Audience.

The French ambassador upon that instant
Crav'd audience; and the hour, I think, is come
To give him *hearing*. *Shakespeare's Henry* V.

3. Judicial trial.

Agrippa and Bernice entered into the place of *hearing*. *Acts.*

The readers are the jury to decide according to the merits of the cause, or to bring it to another *hearing* before some other court. *Dryden's Fables, Pref.*

Those of different principles may be betrayed to give you a fair *hearing*, and to know what you have to say for yourself.
Addison's Freeholder.

4. Reach of the ear.

If we profess, as Peter did, that we love the Lord, and profess it in the *hearing* of men; charity is prone to hear all things, and therefore charitable men are likely to think we do so. *Hooker, b.* iii.

In our *hearing* the king charged thee, beware that none touch Absalom. *2 Sa.* xviii. 12.

You have been talked of since your travels much,
And that in Hamlet's *hearing*, for a quality
Wherein they say you shine. *Shakespeare's Hamlet.*

The fox had the good luck to be within *hearing*. *L'Estrange.*

To HE'ARKEN. *v. n.* [heancnian, Saxon.]

1. To listen by way of curiosity.

The youngest daughter, whom you *hearken* for,
Her father keeps from access of suitors. *Shakespeare.*

He *hearkens* after prophecies and dreams. *Shakes. R.* III.

They do me too much injury,
That ever said I *hearken'd* for your death:
If it were so, I might have let alone
Th' insulting hand of Douglas over you. *Shakespeare.*

The gaping three-mouth'd dog forgets to snarl;
The furies *hearken*, and their snakes uncurl. *Dryd. Virgil.*

Louder, and yet more loud, I hear the alarms
Of human cries:
I mount the terrass, thence the town survey,
And *hearken* what the fruitful sounds convey. *Dryden.*

He who makes much necessary, will want much; and, wearied with the difficulty of the attainment, will incline to *hearken* after any expedient that offers to shorten his way to it. *Rogers's Sermons.*

2. To attend; to pay regard.

Hearken unto me, thou son of Zippor. *Nu.* xxiii. 18.

Those who put passion in the place of reason, neither use their own, nor *hearken* to other people's reason, any farther than it suits their humour. *Locke.*

There's not a blessing individuals find,
But some way leans and *hearkens* to the kind. *Pope.*

HE'ARKENER. *n. s.* [from *hearken.*] Listener; one that hearkens.

HE'ARSAY. *n. s.* [*hear* and *say.*] Report; rumour; what is not known otherwise than by account from others.

For prey these shepherds two he took,
Whose metal stiff he knew he could not bend
With *hearsay* pictures, or a window look. *Sidney.*

He affirms by *hearsay*, that some giants saved themselves upon the mountain Baris in Armenia. *Raleigh's History.*

All the little scramblers after fame fall upon him, publish every blot in his life, and depend upon *hearsay* to defame him. *Addison's Freeholder.*

HEARSE. *n. s.* [of unknown etymology.]

1. A carriage in which the dead are conveyed to the grave.

2. A temporary monument set over a grave.

To add to your laments,
Wherewith you now bedew king Henry's *hearse*,
I must inform you of a dismal fight. *Shakesp. Henry* VI.

HEART. *n. s.* [heopt, Saxon; *hertz*, German.]

1. The muscle which by its contraction and dilation propels the blood through the course of circulation, and is therefore considered as the source of vital motion. It is supposed in popular language to be the seat sometimes of courage, sometimes of affection.

He with providence and courage so passed over all, that the mother took such spiteful grief at it, that her *heart* brake withal, and she died. *Sidney.*

Thou wouldst have left thy dearest *heart* blood there,
Rather than made that savage duke thine heir,
And disinherited thine only son. *Shakesp. Henry* VI.

Snakes, in my *heart* blood warm'd, that sting my *heart*.
Shakespeare's Richard II.

Our battle is more full of names than your's,
Our men more perfect in the use of arms,
Our armour all as strong, our cause the best;
Then reason wills our *hearts* should be as good. *Shak. H.* IV.

I thank you for my venison, master Shallow.
—Master Page, much good do it your good *heart*. *Shakesp.*

But ſince the brain doth lodge the pow'rs of ſenſe,
How makes it in the *heart* thoſe paſſions ſpring?
The mutual love, the kind intelligence
'Twixt *heart* and brain, this ſympathy doth bring. *Davies.*

We all ſet our *hearts* at reſt, ſince whatever comes from above is for the beſt. *L'Eſtrange.*

The only true zeal is that which is guided by a good light in the head, and that which conſiſts of good and innocent affections in the *heart*. *Spratt's Sermons.*

Preſt with *heart* corroding grief and years,
To the gay court a rural ſhed prefers. *Pope's Odyſſey.*

2. The chief part; the vital part.

Barley being ſteeped in water, and turned upon a dry floor, will ſprout half an inch; and, if it be let alone, much more, until the *heart* be out. *Bacon's Natural Hiſtory.*

3. The inner part of any thing.

Some Engliſhmen did with great danger paſs by water into the *heart* of the country. *Abbot's Deſcription of the World.*

The king's forces are employed in appeaſing diſorders more near the *heart* of the kingdom. *Hayward.*

Generally the inſide or *heart* of trees is harder than the outward parts. *Boyle.*

Here in the *heart* of all the town I'll ſtay,
And timely ſuccour, where it wants, convey. *Dryden.*

If the foundations be bad, provide good piles made of *heart* of oak, ſuch as will reach ground. *Moxon's Mech. Exer.*

4. Perſon; character. Uſed with reſpect to courage or kindneſs.

The king's a bawcock, and a *heart* of gold,
A lad of life, an imp of fame. *Shakeſpeare's Henry* V.

Hey, my *hearts*; cheerly, my *hearts*. *Shakeſp. Tempeſt.*

What ſays my *heart* of elder? Ha! is he dead, bully-ſtale? Is he dead? *Shakeſ. Merry Wives of Windſor.*

5. Courage; ſpirit.

If it pleaſe you to make his fortune known, as I have done Erona's, I will after take *heart* again to go on with his falſehood. *Sidney, b.* ii.

There did other like unhappy accidents happen out of England, which gave *heart* and good opportunity to them to regain their old poſſeſſions. *Spenſer on Ireland.*

Wide was the wound; and a large lukewarm flood,
Red as the roſe, thence guſhed grievouſly,
That when the painim ſpy'd the ſtreaming blood,
Gave him great *heart* and hope of victory. *Fairy Queen.*

Eve, recov'ring *heart*, reply'd. *Milton.*

Having left that city well provided, and in good *heart*, his majeſty removed with his little army to Bewdley. *Clarendon.*

Finding that it did them no hurt, they took *heart* upon't, went up to't, and viewed it. *L'Eſtrange's Fables.*

The expelled nations take *heart*, and when they fly from one country invade another. *Temple.*

6. Seat of love.

Ah! what avails it me the flocks to keep,
Who loſt my *heart* while I preſerv'd my ſheep? *Pope.*

7. Affection; inclination.

Joab perceived that the king's *heart* was towards Abſalom. 2 *Sa.* xiv. 1.

Means how to feel, and learn each other's *heart*,
By th' abbot's ſkill of Weſtminſter is found. *Daniel.*

Nor ſet thy *heart*,
Thus over-fond, on that which is not thine. *Milton.*

'Tis well to be tender; but to ſet the *heart* too much upon any thing, is what we cannot juſtify. *L'Eſtrange.*

A friend makes me a feaſt, and ſets all before me; but I ſet my *heart* upon one diſh alone, and if that happen to be thrown down, I ſcorn all the reſt. *Temple.*

Then mixing pow'rful herbs with magick art,
She chang'd his form who could not change his *heart*. *Dryd.*

What did I not, her ſtubborn *heart* to gain?
But all my vows were anſwer'd with diſdain. *Dryden.*

8. Memory.

Whatſoever was attained to, concerning God and his working in nature, the ſame was delivered over by *heart* and tradition from wiſe men to a poſterity equally zealous. *Raleigh.*

We call the committing of a thing to memory the getting it by *heart*; for it is the memory that muſt tranſmit it to the heart; and it is in vain to expect that the heart ſhould keep its hold of any truth, when the memory has let it go. *South.*

Shall I in London act this idle part?
Compoſing ſongs for fools to get by *heart*. *Pope.*

9. Good-will; ardour of zeal. *To take to heart* any thing, is to be zealous or ſolicitous or ardent about it.

If he take not their cauſes to *heart*, how ſhould there be but in them frozen coldneſs, when his affections ſeem benumbed, from whom theirs ſhould take fire? *Hooker.*

If he would take the buſineſs to *heart*, and deal in it effectually, it would ſucceed well. *Bacon's Henry* VII.

The lady marchioneſs of Hertford engaged her huſband to take this buſineſs to *heart*. *Clarendon, b.* viii.

Amongſt thoſe, who took it moſt to *heart*, ſir John Stawel was the chief. *Clarendon, b.* viii.

Every prudent and honeſt man would join himſelf to that ſide which had the good of their country moſt at *heart*. *Addiſ.*

Learned men have been now a long time ſearching after the happy country from which our firſt parents were exiled: if they can find it, with all my *heart*. *Woodward's Nat. Hiſtory.*

I would not be ſorry to find the Preſbyterians miſtaken in this point, which they have moſt at *heart*. *Swift.*

What I have moſt at *heart* is, that ſome method ſhould be thought on for aſcertaining and fixing our language. *Swift.*

10. Paſſions; anxiety; concern.

Set your *heart* at reſt;
The fairy land buys not the child of me. *Shakeſpeare.*

11. Secret thoughts; receſſes of the mind.

Michal ſaw king David leaping and dancing before the Lord, and ſhe deſpiſed him in her *heart*. 2 *Sa.* vi. 16.

The next generation will in tongue and *heart*, and every way elſe, become Engliſh; ſo as there will be no difference or diſtinction, but the Iriſh ſea, betwixt us. *Davies on Ireland.*

Thou ſaweſt the contradiction between my *heart* and hand. *King Charles.*

Would you have him open his *heart* to you, and aſk your advice, you muſt begin to do ſo with him firſt. *Locke.*

Men, ſome to pleaſure, ſome to buſineſs take;
But every woman is, at *heart*, a rake. *Pope, Epiſtle* ii.

12. Diſpoſition of mind.

Doing all things with ſo pretty a grace, that it ſeemed ignorance could not make him do amiſs, becauſe he had a *heart* to do well. *Sidney.*

13. The heart is conſidered as the ſeat of tenderneſs: a *hard heart* therefore is cruelty.

I've ſeen thee ſtern, and thou haſt oft beheld
Heart hardening ſpectacles. *Shakeſp. Coriolanus.*

Such iron *hearts* we are, and ſuch
The baſe barbarity of human kind. *Rowe's Jane Shore.*

14. *To find in the* HEART. To be not wholly averſe.

For my breaking the laws of friendſhip with you, I could *find in my heart* to aſk you pardon for it, but that your now handling of me gives me reaſon to confirm my former dealing. *Sidney.*

15. Secret meaning; hidden intention.

I will on with my ſpeech in your praiſe,
And then ſhew you the *heart* of my meſſage. *Shakeſpeare.*

16. Conſcience; ſenſe of good or ill.

Every man's *heart* and conſcience doth in good or evil, even ſecretly committed, and known to none but itſelf, either like or diſallow itſelf. *Hooker, b.* i. *ſ.* 9.

17. Strength; power.

Try whether leaves of trees, ſwept together, with ſome chalk and dung mixed, to give them more *heart*, would not make a good compoſt. *Bacon's Natural Hiſtory.*

He keeps a ſabbath of alternate years,
That the ſpent earth may gather *heart* again,
And, better'd by ceſſation, bear the grain. *Dryden's Georg.*

Care muſt be taken not to plow ground out of *heart*, becauſe if 'tis in *heart*, it may be improved by marl again. *Mortimer.*

18. Utmoſt degree.

This gay charm,
Whoſe eye beck'd forth my wars, and call'd thee home,
Whoſe boſom was my crownet, my chief end,
Like a right gipſy, hath, at faſt and looſe,
Beguil'd me to the very *heart* of loſs. *Shakeſpeare.*

19. Life. *For my heart* ſeems ſometimes to ſignify, *if life was at ſtake*; and ſometimes *for tenderneſs.*

I bid the raſcal knock upon your gate,
And could not get him *for my heart* to do it. *Shakeſpeare.*

I gave it to a youth,
A prating boy, that begg'd it as a fee:
I could not for my *heart* deny it him. *Shakeſ. Mer. of Venice.*

Profoundly ſkill'd in the black art,
As Engliſh Merlin for his *heart*. *Hudibras, p.* i.

20. It is much uſed in compoſition for mind, or affection.

HEART-ACH. *n. ſ.* [*heart* and *ach.*] Sorrow; pang; anguiſh of mind.

To die—to ſleep—
No more; and, by a ſleep, to ſay we end
The *heartach*, and the thouſand natural ſhocks
That fleſh is heir to. *Shakeſpeare's Hamlet.*

HEART-BREAK. *n. ſ.* [*heart* and *break*] Overpowering ſorrow.

Better a little chiding than a great deal of *heartbreak*. *Shakeſ.*

HEART-BREAKER. *n. ſ.* A cant name for a woman's curls, ſuppoſed to break the heart of all her lovers.

Like Sampſon's *heartbreakers*, it grew
In time to make a nation rue. *Hudibras, p.* i.

HEART-BREAKING. *adj.* Overpowering with ſorrow.

Thoſe piteous plaints and ſorrowful ſad tine,
Which late you poured forth, as ye did ſit
Beſide the ſilver ſprings of Helicone,
Making your muſick of *heartbreaking* mone. *Spenſer.*

HEART-BREAKING. *n. ſ.* Overpowering grief.

What greater *heartbreaking* and confuſion can there be to one, than to have all his ſecret faults laid open, and the ſentence of condemnation paſſed upon him? *Hakewill.*

HE'ART-BURNED. *adj.* [*heart* and *burn.*] Having the heart inflamed.

How tartly that gentleman looks! I never can see him but I am *heart-burn'd* an hour after. *Shak. Much Ado about Nothing.*

HEART-BURNING. *n. s.* [*heart* and *burn.*]

1. Pain at the stomach, commonly from an acrid humour.

Fine clean chalk is one of the most noble absorbents, and powerfully corrects and subdues the acrid humours in the stomach: this property renders it very serviceable in the cardialgia, or *heart-burning.* *Woodward on Fossils.*

2. Discontent; secret enmity.

In great changes, when right of inheritance is broke, there will remain much *heart-burning* and discontent among the meaner people. *Swift to Pope.*

HEART-DEAR. *adj.* Sincerely beloved.

The time was, father, that you broke your word,
When you were more endear'd to it than now;
When your own Percy, when my *heart-dear* Harry,
Threw many a northward look to see his father
Bring up his pow'rs; but he did long in vain! *Shak. H.* IV.

HEART-EASE. *n. s.* Quiet; tranquillity.

What infinite *heart-ease* must kings neglect,
That private men enjoy? *Shakespeare's Henry* V.

HEART-EASING. *adj.* Giving quiet.

But come, thou goddess fair and free,
In heav'n yclep'd Euphrosyne,
And by men *heart-easing* mirth. *Milton.*

HEART-FELT. *adj.* Felt in the conscience.

What nothing earthly gives, or can destroy,
The soul's calm sun-shine, and the *heart-felt* joy,
Is virtue's prize. *Pope's Essay on Man.*

HEART-PEAS. *n. s.* A plant.

The characters are: it hath a trailing stalk, emitting claspers, whereby it fastens itself to whatever plant stands near it: the flower-cup consists of three leaves, the flower of eight leaves, and are of an anomalous figure: the ovary becomes a fruit like a bladder, divided into three cells, in which are contained round seeds in form of peas, of a black colour, having the figure of an heart of a white colour upon each. *Miller.*

HEART-QUELLING. *adj.* Conquering the affection.

And let fair Venus, that is queen of love,
With her *heart-quelling* son, upon you smile. *Spenser.*

HEART-RENDING. *adj.* Killing with anguish.

Heart-rending news, and dreadful to those few
Who her resemble, and her steps pursue;
That death should licence have to rage among
The fair, the wise, the virtuous, and the young! *Waller.*

HEART-ROBBING. *adj.* Ecstatick; depriving of thought.

Sweet is thy virtue, as thyself sweet art;
For when on me thou shinedst, late in sadness,
A melting pleasance ran through every part,
And me revived with *heart-robbing* gladness. *Spenser.*

HEART-SICK. *adj.*

1. Pained in mind.

If we be *heart-sick*, or afflicted with an uncertain soul, then we are true desirers of relief and mercy. *Taylor.*

2. Mortally ill; hurt in the constitution.

Good Romeo, hide thyself.
—Not I, unless the breath of *heart-sick* groans,
Mist like, infold me from the search of eyes. *Shakespeare.*

HEARTS-EASE. *n. s.* A plant.

Hearts-ease is a sort of violet that blows all Summer, and often in Winter: it sows itself. *Mortimer.*

HEART-SORE. *n. s.* Struck with sorrow.

Wherever he that godly knight may find,
His only *heart-sore* and his only foe. *Fairy Queen, b.* ii.

HEART-STRING. *n. s.* [*string* and *heart.*] The tendons or nerves supposed to brace and sustain the heart.

He was by Jove deprived
Of life himself, and *heart-strings* of an eagle rived. *Fa. Qu.*

How, out of tune on the strings?
—Not so; but yet so false, that he grieves my very *heart-strings.* *Shakespeare's Two Gentlemen of Verona.*

That grates my *heart-strings*: what should discontent him!
Except he thinks I live too long. *Denham's Sophy.*

If thou thinkest thou shalt perish, I cannot blame thee to be sad 'till thy *heart-strings* crack. *Taylor's Rule of living holy.*

There's the fatal wound,
That tears my *heart-strings*; but he shall be found,
My arms shall hold him. *Granville.*

HEART-STRUCK. *adj.*

1. Driven to the heart; infixed for ever in the mind.

Who is with him?
——None but the fool who labours to out-jest
His *heart-struck* injuries. *Shakespeare's King Lear.*

2. Shocked with fear or dismay.

He added not; for Adam, at the news
Heart-struck, with chilling gripe of sorrow stood,
That all his senses bound! *Milton's Paradise Lost, b.* xi.

HEART-SWELLING. *adj.* Rankling in the mind.

Drawn into arms, and proof of mortal fight,
Through proud ambition and *heart-swelling* hate. *Spenser.*

HEART-WHOLE. *adj.*

1. With the affections yet unfixed.

You have not seen me yet, and therefore I am confident you are *heart-whole.* *Dryden's Spanish Fryar.*

Cupid hath clapt him o' th' shoulder; but I'll warrant him *heart-whole.* *Shakespeare's As you like it.*

2. With the vitals yet unimpaired.

HEART-WOUNDED. *adj.* Filled with passion of love or grief.

Mean time the queen, without reflection due,
Heart-wounded, to the bed of state withdrew. *Pope's Odyss.*

HEART-WOUNDING. *adj.* Filling with grief.

With a shriek *heart-wounding* loud she cry'd,
While down her cheeks the gushing torrents ran,
Fast falling on her hands. *Rowe's Jane Shore.*

HE'ARTED. *adj.* It is only used in composition: as, hard *hearted.*

To HE'ARTEN. *v. a.* [from *heart.*]

1. To encourage; to animate; to stir up.

Palladius blaming those that were slow, *heartening* them that were forward, but especially with his own example leading them, made an impression into the squadron. *Sidney.*

My royal father, cheer these noble lords,
And *hearten* those that fight in your defence:
Unsheath your sword, good father; cry, St. George! *Shak.*

This rare man, Tydides, would prepare;
That he might conquer, *hearten'd* him, and taught him tricks. *Chapman's Iliads.*

Thus *hearten'd* well, and flesh'd upon his prey,
The youth may prove a man another day. *Dryden.*

2. To meliorate with manure.

The ground one year at rest; forget not then
With richest dung to *hearten* it again. *May's Virg. Georg.*

HEARTH. *n. s.* The pavement of a room in which a fire is made; the ground under the chimney.

Hoop'd out of Rome: now this extremity
Hath brought me to this *hearth.* *Shakespeare's Coriolanus.*

Cricket, to Windsor chimneys shalt thou leap,
Whereas thou find'st unrak'd, and *hearths* unswept,
There pinch the maids as blue as bilberry. *Shakespeare.*

Good luck befriend thee, son; for at thy birth
The fairy ladies danc'd upon the *hearth.* *Milton.*

The vanquish'd fires withdraw from every place;
Or, full with feeding, sink into a sleep:
Each houshold genius shews again its face,
And from the *hearths* the little lares creep. *Dryden.*

HE'ARTILY. *adv.* [from *hearty.*]

1. Sincerely; actively; diligently; vigorously.

Where his judgment led him to oppose men on a publick account, he would do it vigorously and *heartily*; yet the opposition ended there. *Atterbury's Sermons.*

2. From the heart; fully.

I bear no malice for my death;
But those that sought it, I could wish more Christians;
Be what they will, I *heartily* forgive them. *Shakes. H.* VIII.

If to be sad is to be wise,
I do most *heartily* despise
Whatever Socrates has said,
Or Tully writ, or Wanley read. *Prior.*

3. Eagerly; with desire.

As for my eating *heartily* of the food, know that anxiety has hindered my eating 'till this moment. *Addison's Guardian.*

HE'ARTINESS. *n. s.* [from *hearty.*]

1. Sincerity; freedom from hypocrisy.

This entertainment may a free face put on; derive a liberty from *heartiness*, and well become the agent. *Shakespeare.*

2. Vigour; diligence; strength.

The anger of an enemy represents our faults, or admonishes us of our duty, with more *heartiness* than the kindness of a friend. *Taylor's Rule of living holy.*

HE'ARTLESS. *adj.* [from *heart.*] Without courage; spiritless.

I joyed oft to chase the trembling pricket,
Or hunt the *heartless* hare 'till she were tame. *Spenser.*

Then hopeless, *heartless* 'gan the cunning thief,
Persuade us die, to stint all further strife. *Fairy Queen, b.* i.

What, art thou drawn among these *heartless* hinds?
Turn thee, Benvolio; look upon thy death. *Shakespeare.*

Thousands besides stood mute and *heartless* there,
Men valiant all; nor was I us'd to fear. *Cowley.*

The peasants were accustomed to payments, and grew *heartless* as they grew poor. *Temple.*

Heartless they fought, and quitted soon their ground,
While our's with easy victory were crown'd. *Dryden.*

HE'ARTLESSLY. *adv.* [from *heartless.*] Without courage; faintly; timidly.

HE'ARTLESSNESS. *n. s.* [from *heartless.*] Want of courage or spirit; dejection of mind.

HE'ARTY. *adj.* [from *heart.*]

1. Sincere; undissembled; warm; zealous.

They did not bring that *hearty* inclination to peace, which they hoped they would have done. *Clarendon, b.* viii.

But

But the kind hoſts their entertainment grace
With *hearty* welcome and an open face;
In all they did, you might diſcern with eaſe
A willing mind, and a deſire to pleaſe. *Dryden.*

Every man may pretend to any employment, provided he has been loud and frequent in declaring himſelf *hearty* for the government. *Swift.*

2. In full health.

3. Vigorous; ſtrong.

Whoſe laughs are *hearty*, though his jeſts are coarſe,
And loves you beſt of all things but his horſe. *Pope.*

4. Strong; hard; durable.

Oak, and the like true *hearty* timber, being ſtrong in all poſitions, may be better truſted in croſs and tranſverſe work. *Wotton's Architecture.*

HEARTY-HALE. *adj.* [*heart* and *hale.*] Good for the heart.

Vein-healing verven, and head-purging dill,
Sound ſavory, and baſil *hearty-hale.* *Spenſer.*

HEAT. *n. ſ.* [hæꞇ, hæꞇ, Saxon; *heete*, Daniſh.]

1. The ſenſation cauſed by the approach or touch of fire.

Heat is a very briſk agitation of the inſenſible parts of the object, which produces in us that ſenſation from whence we denominate the object hot; ſo what in our ſenſation is *heat*, in the object is nothing but motion. *Locke.*

The word *heat* is uſed to ſignify the ſenſation we have when we are near the fire, as well as the cauſe of that ſenſation, which is in the fire itſelf; and thence we conclude, that there is a ſort of *heat* in the fire reſembling our own ſenſation: whereas in the fire there is nothing but little particles of matter, of ſuch particular ſhapes as are fitted to impreſs ſuch motions on our fleſh as excite the ſenſe of *heat.* *Watts.*

2. The cauſe of the ſenſation of burning.

The ſword which is made fiery doth not only cut by reaſon of the ſharpneſs which ſimply it hath, but alſo burn by means of that *heat* which it hath from fire. *Hooker, b.* v.

After they came down into the valley, and found the intolerable *heats* which are there, and knew no means of lighter apparel, they were forced to begin the cuſtom of going naked. *Bacon's New Atlantis.*

3. Hot weather.

Mark well the flow'ring almonds in the wood;
The glebe will anſwer to the ſylvan reign;
Great *heats* will follow, and large crops of grain. *Dryden.*

The pope would not comply with the propoſal, as fearing the *heats* might advance too far before they had finiſhed their work, and produce a peſtilence among the people. *Addiſon.*

4. State of any body under the action of the fire.

The *heats* ſmiths take of their iron are a blood-red *heat*, a white flame *heat*, and a ſparkling or welding *heat.* *Moxon.*

5. One violent action unintermitted.

The continual agitations of the ſpirits muſt needs be a weakening of any conſtitution, eſpecially in age; and many cauſes are required for refreſhment betwixt the *heats.* *Dryden.*

6. The ſtate of being once hot.

I'll ſtrike my fortune with him at a *heat*,
And give him not the leiſure to forget. *Dryden's Aurengz.*

7. A courſe at a race, between each of which courſes there is an intermiſſion.

Feign'd zeal, you ſaw, ſet out the ſpeedier pace;
But the laſt *heat*, plain dealing won the race. *Dryden.*

8. Pimples in the face; fluſh.

It has raiſed animoſities in their hearts, and *heats* in their faces, and broke out in their ribbans. *Addiſon's Freeholder.*

9. Agitation of ſudden or violent paſſion; vehemence of action.

They ſeeing what forces were in the city with them, iſſued againſt the tyrant while they were in this *heat*, before practices might be uſed to diſſever them. *Sidney, b.* ii.

The friend hath loſt his friend;
And the beſt quarrels, in the *heat*, are curſt
By thoſe that feel their ſharpneſs. *Shakeſp. King Lear.*

It might have pleaſed in the *heat* and hurry of his rage, but muſt have diſpleaſed in the cool ſedate reflections of his mind. *South's Sermons.*

We have ſpilt no blood but in the *heat* of the battle, or the chaſe. *Atterbury's Sermons.*

One playing at hazard, held in many hands together, and drew a huge heap of gold; but, in the *heat* of play, never obſerved a ſharper, who ſwept it into his hat. *Swift.*

10. Faction; conteſt; party rage.

Our ſtate thinks not ſo: they are in a moſt warlike preparation, and hope to come upon them in the *heat* of their diviſion. *Shakeſpeare's Coriolanus.*

I was ſorry to hear with what partiality and popular *heat* elections were carried. *King Charles.*

What can more gratify the Phrygian foe
Than thoſe diſtemper'd *heats*? *Dryden's Homer.*

11. Ardour of thought or elocution.

Plead it to her
With all the ſtrength and *heats* of eloquence,
Fraternal love and friendſhip can inſpire. *Addiſon's Cato.*

To HEAT. *v. a.* [from the noun.]

1. To make hot; to endue with the power of burning.

He commanded that they ſhould *heat* the furnace one ſeven times more than it was wont to be *heated.* *Dan.* iii. 19.

2. To cauſe to ferment.

Hops lying undried *heats* them, and changes their colour. *Mortimer's Husbandry.*

3. To make the conſtitution feveriſh.

Thou art going to lord Timon's feaſt.
—Ay, to ſee meat fill knaves, and wine *heat* fools. *Shakeſ.*

Whatever increaſeth the denſity of the blood, even without increaſing its celerity, *heats*, becauſe a denſer body is hotter than a rarer. *Arbuthnot on Aliments.*

4. To warm with vehemence of paſſion or deſire.

A noble emulation *heats* your breaſt,
And your own fame now robs you of your reſt. *Dryden.*

5. To agitate the blood and ſpirits with action.

When he was well *heated* the younger champion could not ſtand before him; and we find the elder contended not for the gift, but for the honour. *Dryden's Æn. Dedication.*

HE'ATER. *n. ſ.* [from *heat.*] An iron made hot, and put into a box-iron, to ſmooth and plait linnen.

HEATH. *n. ſ.* [*erica*, Latin.]

1. A plant.

It is a ſhrub of low ſtature: the leaves are ſmall, and abide green all the year: the flower conſiſts of one leaf, is naked, and, for the moſt part, ſhaped like a pitcher: the ovary, which is produced in the bottom of the flower, becomes a roundiſh fruit, divided into four cells, in which are contained many ſmall ſeeds. *Miller.*

In Kent they cut up the *heath* in May, burn it, and ſpread the aſhes. *Mortimer's Husbandry.*

Oft with bolder wing they ſoaring dare
The purple *heath.* *Thomſon's Spring.*

2. A place overgrown with heath.

Say, from whence
You owe this ſtrange intelligence? or why
Upon this blaſted *heath* you ſtop our way
With ſuch prophetick greeting. *Shakeſpeare's Macbeth.*

3. A place covered with ſhrubs of whatever kind.

Some woods of oranges, and *heaths* of roſemary, will ſmell a great way into the ſea. *Bacon's Natural Hiſtory.*

HEATH-COCK. *n. ſ.* [*heath* and *cock.*] A large fowl that frequents heaths.

Cornwall hath quail, rail, partridge, pheaſant, *heath-cock*, and powte. *Carew's Survey of Cornwall.*

HEATH-POUT. *n. ſ.* [*heath* and *pout*] A bird.

Not *heath-pout*, or the rarer bird
Which Phaſis or Ionia yields,
More pleaſing morſels would afford
Than the fat olives of my fields. *Dryden.*

HEATH-PEAS. *n. ſ.* A ſpecies of bitter VETCH, which ſee.

HEATH-ROSE. *n. ſ.* [*heath* and *roſe*] A plant. *Ainſworth.*

HE'ATHEN. *n. ſ.* [*heyden*, German.] The gentiles; the pagans; the nations unacquainted with the covenant of grace.

Deliver us from the *heathen*, that we may give thanks to thy holy name. 1 *Chro.* xvi. 35.

If the opinions of others, whom we think well of, be a ground of aſſent, men have reaſon to be *heathens* in Japan, mahometans in Turkey, papiſts in Spain, and proteſtants in England. *Locke.*

In a paper of morality, I conſider how I may recommend the particular virtues I treat of, by the precepts or examples of the ancient *heathens.* *Addiſon's Spectator.*

HE'ATHEN. *adj.* Gentile; pagan.

It was impoſſible for a *heathen* author to relate theſe things, becauſe, if he had believed them, he would no longer have been a *heathen.* *Addiſon.*

HE'ATHENISH. *adj.* [from *heathen.*]

1. Belonging to the gentiles.

When the apoſtles of our Lord and Saviour were ordained to alter the laws of *heatheniſh* religion, choſen they were, St. Paul excepted; the reſt unſchooled altogether, and unlettered men. *Hooker, b.* iv.

2. Wild; ſavage; rapacious; cruel.

The Moors did tread under their *heatheniſh* feet whatever little they found yet there ſtanding. *Spenſer.*

That execrable Cromwel made a *heatheniſh* or rather inhuman edict againſt the poor epiſcopal clergy, that they ſhould neither preach, pray in publick, baptize, marry, bury, nor teach ſchool. *South's Sermons.*

HE'ATHENISHLY. *adv.* [from *heatheniſh.*] After the manner of heathens.

HE'ATHENISM. *n. ſ.* [from *heathen.*] Gentiliſm; paganiſm.

It ſignifies the acknowledgment of the true God, in oppoſition to *heatheniſm.* *Hammond's Pract. Catech.*

HE'ATHY. *adj.* [from *heath.*] Full of heath.

This ſort of land they order the ſame way with the *heathy* land. *Mortimer's Husbandry.*

To HEAVE. *v. a.* pret. *heaved*, anciently *hove*; part. *heaved*, or *hoven.*

1. To lift; to raiſe from the ground.

So ſtretch'd out huge in length the arch fiend lay,
Chain'd on the burning lake; nor ever hence

Had ris'n, or *heav'd* his head, but that the will
And high permission of all-ruling heaven
Left him at large. *Milton's Paradise Lost, b.* i.

2. To carry.
Now we bear the king
Tow'rd Calais: grant him there; and there being seen,
Heave him away upon your winged thoughts
Athwart the sea. *Shakespeare's Henry* V.

3. To raise; to lift.
So daunted, when the giant saw the knight,
His heavy hand he *heaved* up on high,
And him to dust thought to have batter'd quite. *Fa. Queen.*
Unhappy that I am, I cannot *heave*
My heart into my mouth: I love your majesty
According to my bond, no more nor less. *Shakesp. K. Lear.*
He dy'd in fight;
Fought next my person, as in consort fought,
Save when he *heav'd* his shield in my defence,
And on his naked side receiv'd my wound. *Dryd. Don Seb.*

4. To cause to swell.
The groans of ghosts, that cleave the earth with pain,
And *heave* it up: they pant and stick half way. *Dryden.*
The glittering finny swarms,
That *heave* our friths and croud upon our shores. *Thomson.*

5. To force up from the breast.
Made she no verbal quest?
—Yes, once or twice she *heav'd* the name of father
Pantingly forth, as if it prest her heart. *Shak. King Lear.*
The wretched animal *heav'd* forth such groans,
That their discharge did stretch his leathern coat
Almost to bursting. *Shakesp. As you like it.*

6. To exalt; to elevate.
Poor shadow, painted queen;
One *heav'd* on high, to be hurl'd down below. *Shak. R.* III.

7. To puff; to elate.
The Scots, *heaved* up into high hope of victory, took the English for foolish birds fallen into their net, forsook their hill, and marched into the plain. *Hayward.*

To Heave. *v. n.*

1. To pant; to breathe with pain.
'Tis such as you,
That creep like shadows by him, and do sigh
At each his needless *heavings*; such as you
Nourish the cause of his awaking. *Shakesp. Winter's Tale.*
He *heaves* for breath, which, from his lungs supply'd,
And fetch'd from far, distends his lab'ring side. *Dryden.*

2. To labour.
The church of England had struggled and *heaved* at a reformation ever since Wickliff's days. *Atterbury.*

3. To rise with pain; to swell and fall.
Thou hast made my curdled blood run back,
My heart *heave* up, my hair to rise in bristles. *Dryden.*
The wand'ring breath was on the wing to part;
Weak was the pulse, and hardly *heav'd* the heart. *Dryden.*
No object affects my imagination so much as the sea or ocean: I cannot see the *heaving* of this prodigious bulk of waters, even in a calm, without a very pleasing astonishment.. *Addison's Spectator.*
Frequent for breath his panting bosom *heaves*. *Prior.*
The *heaving* tide
In widen'd circles beats on either side. *Gay's Trivia.*

4. To keck; to feel a tendency to vomit.

Heave. *n. s.* [from the verb.]

1. Lift; exertion or effort upwards.
None could guess whether the next *heave* of the earthquake would settle them on the first foundation, or swallow them. *Dryden's Don Sebastian.*

2. Rising of the breast.
There's matter in these sighs; these profound *heaves*
You must translate; 'tis fit we understand them. *Shakesp.*

3. Effort to vomit.

4. Struggle to rise.
But after many strains and *heaves*,
He got up to his saddle eaves. *Hudibras, p.* i. *cant.* i.

Heave *Offering. n. s.* An offering among the Jews.
Ye shall offer a cake of the first of your dough for an *heave offering*, as ye do the *heave offering* of the threshing floor. *Num.*

HE'AVEN. *n. s.* [heofon, which seems to be derived from heofd, the places over head, Saxon.]

1. The regions above; the expanse of the sky.
A station like the herald Mercury,
New lighted on a *heaven* kissing hill. *Shakes. Hamlet.*
Thy race in time to come
Shall spread the conquests of imperial Rome;
Rome, whose ascending tow'rs shall *heav'n* invade,
Involving earth and ocean in her shade. *Dryden's Æn.*
The words are taken more properly for the air and ether than for the *heavens*, as the best Hebrecians understand them. *Raleigh's History of the World.*
This act, with shouts *heav'n* high, the friendly band
Applaud. *Dryden's Fables.*

2. The habitation of God, good angels, and pure souls departed.
It is a knell
That summons thee to *heaven*, or to hell. *Shakes. Macbeth.*
These, the late
Heav'n banish'd host, left desert utmost hell. *Milton.*
All yet left of that revolted rout,
Heav'n fall'n, in station stood, or just array,
Sublime with expectation. *Milton's Paradise Lost, b.* x.

3. The supreme power; the sovereign of heaven.
Now *heav'n* help him! *Shakespeare's King Lear.*
The will
And high permission of all-ruling *heav'n*
Left him at large. *Milton.*
The prophets were taught to know the will of God, and thereby instruct the people, and enabled to prophesy, as a testimony of their being sent by *heaven*. *Temple.*

4. The pagan gods; the celestials.
Our brows
No more obey the *heavens* than our courtiers. *Shak. Cymbel.*
Take physick, pomp;
Expose thyself to feel what wretches feel,
That thou may'st shake the superflux to them,
And show the *heavens* more just. *Shakes. King Lear.*
They can judge as fitly of his worth,
As I can of those mysteries which *heaven*
Will not have earth to know. *Shakespeare's Coriolanus.*
Heav'ns! what a spring was in his arm, to throw!
How high he held his shield, and rose at ev'ry blow. *Dryd.*

5. Elevation; sublimity.
O, for a muse of fire, that would ascend
The brightest *heav'n* of invention. *Shakesp. Henry* V. *Prol.*

6. It is often used in composition.

Heaven-begot. Begot by a celestial power.
If I am *heav'n-begot*, assert your son
By some sure sign. *Dryden.*

Heaven-born. Descended from the celestial regions; native of heaven.
If a fever fires his sulphurous blood,
In ev'ry fit he feels the hand of God,
And *heav'n-born* flame. *Dryden's Juvenal, Sat.* 13.
Oh *heav'n-born* sisters! source of art!
Who charm the sense, or mend the heart;
Who lead fair virtue's train along,
Moral truth, and mystick song! *Pope.*

Heaven-bred. Produced or cultivated in heaven.
Much is the force of *heav'n-bred* poesy. *Shakespeare.*

Heaven-built. Built by the agency of gods.
My soul inspire,
As when we wrapt Troy's *heav'n-built* walls in fire. *Pope.*
His arms had wrought the destin'd fall
Of sacred Troy, and raz'd her *heav'n-built* wall. *Pope.*

Heaven-directed.

1. Raised towards the sky.
Who taught that *heav'n-directed* spire to rise? *Pope.*

2. Taught by the powers of heaven.
O sacred weapon! left for truth's defence;
To all but *heaven-directed* hands deny'd;
The muse may give it, but the gods must guide. *Pope.*

He'avenly. *adj.* [from *heaven.*]

1. Resembling heaven; supremely excellent.
As the love of heaven makes one *heavenly*, the love of virtue virtuous, so doth the love of the world make one become worldly. *Sidney.*
Not Maro's muse, who sung the mighty man;
Nor Pindar's *heav'nly* lyre, nor Horace when a swan. *Dryd.*

2. Celestial; inhabiting heaven.
Adoring first the genius of the place,
Then earth, the mother of the *heav'nly* race. *Dryd. Æn.*

He'avenly. *adv.*

1. In a manner resembling that of heaven.
In these deep solitudes and awful cells,
Where *heav'nly* pensive contemplation dwells,
And ever-musing melancholy reigns,
What means this tumult in a vestal's veins? *Pope.*

2. By the agency or influence of heaven.
Truth and peace and love shall ever shine
About the supreme throne
Of him, t' whose happy-making sight alone,
Our *heav'nly* guided soul shall climb. *Milton.*

He'avenward. *adv.* [*heaven* and peard, Saxon.] Towards heaven.
I prostrate lay,
By various doubts impell'd, or to obey,
Or to object; at length, my mournful look
Heav'nward erect, determin'd, thus I spoke. *Prior.*

He'avily. *adv.* [from *heavy.*]

1. With great ponderousness.

2. Grievously; afflictively.
Ease must be impracticable to the envious: they lie under a double misfortune; common calamities and common blessings fall *heavily* upon them. *Collier of Envy.*

3. Sorrowfully;

3. Sorrowfully; with an air of dejection.

I came hither to tranſport the tydings,
Which I have *heavily* born. *Shakeſpeare's Macbeth.*
Why looks your grace ſo *heavily* to-day?
—O, I have paſt a miſerable night. *Shakeſpeare's R.* III.

This O'Neil took very *heavily*, becauſe his condition in the army was leſs pleaſant to him. *Clarendon.*

HE'AVINESS. *n. ſ.* [from *heavy.*]

1. Ponderouſneſs; the quality of being heavy; weight.

The ſubject is concerning the *heavineſs* of ſeveral bodies, or the proportion that is required betwixt any weight and the power which may move it. *Wilkins.*

2. Dejection of mind; depreſſion of ſpirit.

We are, at the hearing of ſome, more inclined unto ſorrow and *heavineſs*; of ſome more mollified, and ſoftened in mind. *Hooker, b.* v. *ſ.* 38.

Heavineſs in the heart of man maketh it ſtoop; but a good word maketh it glad. *Prov.* xii. 25.

Ye greatly rejoice; though now for a ſeaſon ye are in *heavineſs*, through manifold temptations. *1 Pet.* i. 6

Againſt ill chances men are ever merry;
But *heavineſs* foreruns the good event. *Shak. Henry* IV.

Let us not burthen our remembrance with
An *heavineſs* that's gone. *Shakeſpeare's Tempeſt.*

3. Inaptitude to motion or thought; ſluggiſhneſs; torpidneſs; dulneſs of ſpirit; languidneſs; languor.

Our ſtrength is all gone into *heavineſs*,
That makes the weight. *Shak. Ant. and Cleopatra.*
What means this *heavineſs* that hangs upon me?
This lethargy that creeps through all my ſenſes? *Add. Cato.*
He would not violate that ſweet receſs,
And found beſides a welcome *heavineſs*,
Which ſeiz'd his eyes. *Dryden.*

A ſenſation of drouſineſs, oppreſſion, *heavineſs*, and laſſitude, are ſigns of a too plentiful meal. *Arbuthn. on Aliment.*

4. Oppreſſion; cruſh; affliction.

5. Deepneſs or richneſs of ſoil.

As Alexandria exported many commodities, ſo it received ſome from other European ports, which, by reaſon of the fatneſs and *heavineſs* of the ground, Egypt did not produce; ſuch as metals, wood, and pitch. *Arbuthnot on Coins.*

HE'AVY. *adj.* [heaƿıᵹ, Saxon.]

1. Weighty; ponderous; tending ſtrongly to the center; contrary to light.

Merſennus tells us, that a little child, with an engine of an hundred double pulleys, might move this earth, though it were much *heavier* than it is. *Wilkins.*

2. Sorrowful; dejected; depreſſed.

Let me not be light;
For a light wife doth make a *heavy* huſband. *Shakeſpeare.*

3. Grievous; oppreſſive; afflictive.

Menelaus bore an *heavy* hand over the citizens, having a malicious mind. *2 Mac.* v. 23.

Let not your ears deſpiſe my tongue for ever,
Which ſhall poſſeſs them with the *heavieſt* ſound
That ever yet they heard. *Shakeſpeare's Macbeth.*

If the cauſe be not good, the king himſelf hath a *heavy* reckoning to make. *Shakeſpeare's Henry* V.

Are you ſo goſpell'd
To pray for this good man, and for his iſſue?
Whoſe *heavy* hand hath bow'd you to the grave,
And beggar'd yours for ever. *Shakeſpeare's Macbeth.*

Chartres, at the levee,
Tells with a ſneer the tydings *heavy*. *Swift.*

4. Wanting alacrity; wanting briſkneſs of appearance.

My *heavy* eyes, you ſay, confeſs
A heart to love and grief inclin'd. *Prior.*

5. Wanting ſpirit or rapidity of ſentiment; unanimated.

A work was to be done, a *heavy* writer to be encouraged, and accordingly many thouſand copies were beſpoke. *Swift.*

6. Wanting activity; indolent; lazy.

Fair, tall, his limbs with due proportion join'd;
But of a *heavy*, dull, degenerate mind. *Dryden's Fables.*

7. Drouſy; dull; torpid.

Peter and they that were with him were *heavy* with ſleep. *Lu.* ix. 33.

8. Slow; ſluggiſh.

But let thy ſpiders, that ſuck up thy venom,
And *heavy* gaited toads lie in their way. *Shakeſp. Rich.* II.

9. Stupid; fooliſh.

This *heavy* headed revel, Eaſt and Weſt
Makes us traduc'd, and tax'd of other nations. *Shakeſp.*

I would not be accounted ſo baſe minded, or *heavy* headed, that I will confeſs that any of them is for valour, power, or fortune better than myſelf. *Knolles's Hiſtory of the Turks.*

10. Burdenſome; troubleſome; tedious.

I put into thy hands what has been the diverſion of ſome of my idle and *heavy* hours. *Locke's Epiſtle to the Reader.*

When alone, your time will not lie *heavy* upon your hands for want of ſome trifling amuſement. *Swift.*

11. Loaded; incumbered; burthened.

Hearing that there were forces coming againſt him, and not willing that they ſhould find his men *heavy* and laden with booty, he returned unto Scotland. *Bacon's Henry* VII.

12. Not eaſily digeſted; not light to the ſtomach.

Such preparations as retain the oil or fat, are moſt *heavy* to the ſtomach, which makes baked meat hard of digeſtion. *Arb.*

13. Rich in ſoil; fertile, as *heavy* lands.

14. Deep; cumberſome, as *heavy* roads.

HE'AVY. *adv.* As an adverb it is only uſed in compoſition; heavily.

Your carriages were *heavy* laden; they are a burden to the weary beaſt. *Iſ.* xlvi. 1.

Come unto me all ye that labour and are *heavy* laden, and I will give you reſt. *Mat.* ii. 28.

HE'BDOMAD. *n. ſ.* [*hebdomas*, Latin.] A week; a ſpace of ſeven days.

Computing by the medical month, the firſt *hebdomad* or ſeptenary conſiſts of ſix days, ſeventeen hours and a half. *Brown.*

HEBDO'MADAL. } *adj.* [from *hebdomas*, Latin.] Weekly;
HEBDO'MADARY. } conſiſting of ſeven days.

As for *hebdomadal* periods, or weeks, in regard of their ſabbaths, they were obſerved by the Hebrews. *Brown.*

To HEBE'TATE. *v. a.* [*hebeto*, Latin; *hebeter*, French.] To dull; to blunt; to ſtupify.

The eye, eſpecially if *hebetated*, might cauſe the ſame perception. *Harvey on Conſumptions.*

Beef may confer a robuſtneſs on the limbs of my ſon, but will *hebetate* and clog his intellectuals. *Arb. and Pope's M. Scrib.*

HEBETA'TION. *n. ſ.* [from *hebetate.*]

1. The act of dulling.

2. The ſtate of being dulled.

HE'BETUDE. *n. ſ.* [*hebetudo*, Latin.] Dulneſs; obtuſeneſs; bluntneſs.

The peſtilent ſeminaries, according to their groſſneſs or ſubtilty, activity or *hebetude*, cauſe more or leſs truculent plagues. *Harvey on the Plague.*

HE'BRAISM. *n. ſ.* [*hebraiſme*, French; *hebraiſmus*, Latin.] A Hebrew idiom.

Milton has infuſed a great many Latiniſms, as well as Græciſms, and ſometimes *Hebraiſms*, into his poem. *Spectator.*

HE'BRAIST. *n. ſ.* [*hebræus*, Latin.] A man ſkilled in Hebrew.

HE'BRICIAN. *n. ſ.* [from *Hebrew.*] One ſkilful in Hebrew.

The words are more properly taken for the air or ether than the heavens, as the beſt *Hebrecians* underſtand them. *Raleigh.*

The nature of the Hebrew verſe, as the meaneſt *Hebrician* knoweth, conſiſts of uneven feet. *Peacham.*

HE'CATOMB. *n. ſ.* [*hecatombe*, French; ἑκατόμβη.] A ſacrifice of an hundred cattle.

In rich mens homes
I bid kill ſome beaſts, but no *hecatombs*;
None ſtarve, none ſurfeit ſo. *Donne.*
One of theſe three is a whole *hecatomb*,
And therefore only one of them ſhall die. *Dryden.*
Her triumphant ſons in war ſucceed,
And ſlaughter'd *hecatombs* around 'em bleed. *Addiſon.*

HE'CTICAL. } *adj.* [*hectique*, French, from ἕξις.]
HE'CTICK. }

1. Habitual; conſtitutional.

This word is joined only to that kind of fever which is ſlow and continual, and ending in a conſumption, is the contrary to thoſe fevers which ariſe from a plethora, or too great fulneſs from obſtruction, becauſe it is attended with too lax a ſtate of the excretory paſſages, and generally thoſe of the ſkin; whereby ſo much runs off as leaves not reſiſtance enough in the contractile veſſels to keep them ſufficiently diſtended, ſo that they vibrate oftener, agitate the fluids the more, and keep them thin and hot. *Quincy.*

A *hectick* fever hath got hold
Of the whole ſubſtance, not to be controul'd. *Donne.*

2. Troubled with a morbid heat.

No *hectick* ſtudent ſcars the gentle maid. *Taylor.*

HE'CTICK. *n. ſ.* An hectick fever.

Like the *hectick* in my blood he rages,
And thou muſt cure me. *Shakeſpeare's Hamlet.*

HE'CTOR. *n. ſ.* [from the name of *Hector*, the great *Homeric* warriour.]

1. A bully; a bluſtering, turbulent, pervicacious, noiſy fellow.

Thoſe uſurping *hectors*, who pretend to honour without religion, think the charge of a lye a blot not to be waſhed out but by blood. *South's Sermons.*

We'll take one cooling cup of nectar,
And drink to this celeſtial *hector*. *Prior.*

To HE'CTOR. *v. a.* [from the noun.] To threaten; to treat with inſolent authoritative terms.

They reckon they muſt part with honour together with their opinion, if they ſuffer themſelves to be *hectored* out of it. *Government of the Tongue.*

The weak low ſpirit, fortune makes her ſlave;
But ſhe's a drudge, when *hector'd* by the brave. *Dryden.*

An honeſt man, when he came home at night, found another fellow domineering in his family, *hectoring* his ſervants, and calling for ſupper. *Arbuthnot's Hiſt. of John Bull.*

To HE'CTOR. *v. n.* To play the bully; to bluster.

They have attacked me, some with piteous moans and outcries, others grinning and only shewing their teeth, others ranting and *hectoring*, others scolding and reviling. *Stillingfleet.*

One would think the *hectoring*, the storming, the sullen, and all the different species of the angry, should be cured. *Spect.*

Don Carlos made her chief director,
That she might o'er the servants *hector*. *Swift.*

HEDERA'CEOUS. *adj.* [*hederaceus*, Lat.] Producing ivy. *Dict.*

HEDGE. *n. s.* [hegge, Saxon.] A fence made round grounds with prickly bushes.

It is a good wood for fire, if kept dry; and is very useful for stakes in *hedges*. *Mortimer's Husbandry.*

The gardens unfold variety of colours to the eye every morning, and the *hedges* breath is beyond all perfume. *Pope.*

Through the verdant maze
Of sweet-briar *hedges* I pursue my walk. *Thomson.*

HEDGE, prefixed to any word, notes something mean, vile, of the lowest class: perhaps from a *hedge*, or *hedge-born man*, a man without any known place of birth.

There are five in the first shew: the pedant, the braggart, the *hedge-priest*, the fool, and the boy. *Shakespeare.*

The clergy do much better than a little *hedge*, contemptible, illiterate vicar can be presumed to do. *Swift.*

A person, who, by his stile and literature, seems to have been the corrector of a *hedge-press* in Little Britain, proceeded gradually to an author. *Swift.*

To HEDGE. *v. a.* [from the noun.]

1. To inclose with a hedge, or fence of wood dry or growing.

Hedge thy possession about with thorns. *Ecclus.* xxviii. 24.

Those alleys must be *hedged* at both ends, to keep out the wind. *Bacon, Essay* 47.

2. To obstruct.

I will *hedge* up thy way with thorns. *Hos.* ii. 6.

3. To incircle for defence.

England, *hedg'd* in with the main,
That water-walled bulwark, still secure
And confident from foreign purposes. *Shakes. King John.*

There's such divinity doth *hedge* a king,
That reason can but peep to what it would. *Shakes. Hamlet.*

4. To shut up within an inclosure.

It must not be paid and exported in ready money; so says our law; but that is a law to *hedge* in the cuckow, and serves for no purpose: for if we export not goods, for which our merchants have money due to them, how can it be paid by bills of exchange? *Locke.*

5. To force into a place already full. This seems to be mistaken for *edge*. *To edge in*, is to put in by the way that requires least room; but *hedge* may signify to thrust in with difficulty, as into a *hedge*.

Bay not me,
I'll not endure it: you forget yourself
To *hedge* me in: I am a soldier. *Shakes. Julius Cæsar.*

When I was hasty, thou delay'dst me longer:
I pr'ythee, let me *hedge* one moment more
Into thy promise; for thy life preserv'd. *Dryden.*

When you are sent on an errand, be sure to *hedge* in some business of your own. *Swift's Directions to the Footman.*

To HEDGE. *v. n.* To shift; to hide the head.

I myself sometimes, hiding mine honour in my necessity, am fain to shuffle, to *hedge*, and to lurch; and yet you rogue will ensconce your rags, your catamountain looks, your red-lettice phrases. *Shakespeare.*

HEDGE-BORN. *adj.* [*hedge* and *born.*] Of no known birth; meanly born.

He then, that is not furnish'd in this sort,
Doth but usurp the sacred name of knight,
And should, if I were worthy to be judge,
Be quite degraded, like a *hedge-born* swain,
That doth presume to boast of gentle blood. *Shak. Hen.* VI.

HEDGE-FUMITORY. *n. s.* A plant. *Ainsworth.*

HEDGE-HOG. *n. s.* [*hedge* and *hog.*]

1. An animal set with prickles, like thorns in an hedge.

Like *hedge-hogs*, which
Lie tumbling in my bare-foot way, and mount
Their pricks at my foot-fall. *Shakespeare's Tempest.*

Few have belief to swallow, or hope enough to experience, the collyrium of Albertus; that is, to make one see in the dark: yet thus much, according unto his receipt, will the right eye of an *hedge-hog*, boiled in oil, and preserved in a brazen vessel, effect. *Brown's Vulgar Errours, b.* i.

The *hedge-hog* hath his backside and flanks thick set with strong and sharp prickles; and besides, by the help of a muscle, can contract himself into a globular figure, and so withdraw his whole under part, head, belly and legs, within his thicket of prickles. *Ray on the Creation.*

2. A term of reproach.

Did'st thou not kill this king?
——I grant ye.
——Do'st grant me, *hedge-hog?* *Shakes. Richard* III.

3. A plant. *Ainsworth.*

4. The globe-fish. *Ainsworth.*

HEDGE-HYSSOP. *n. s.* [*hedge* and *hyssop.*] A species of willow-wort.

Hedge-hyssop is a purging medicine, and a very rough one: externally it is said to be a vulnerary. *Hill's Mat. Medica.*

HEDGE-MUSTARD. *n. s.* A plant.

The flower has four leaves, expanded in a crucial form: the pointal becomes a long, slender, bivalve pod, divided by a partition into two cells, which contain many round seeds. The species are five. *Miller.*

HEDGE-NETTLE. *n. s.* A plant. *Ainsworth.*

HEDGE-NOTE. *n. s.* [*hedge* and *note.*] A word of contempt for low writing.

When they began to be somewhat better bred, they left these *hedge-notes* for another sort of poem, which was also full of pleasant raillery. *Dryden's Juvenal, Dedication.*

HEDGE-PIG. *n. s.* [*hedge* and *pig.*] A young hedge-hog.

Thrice the brinded cat hath mew'd,
Thrice and once the *hedge-pig* whin'd. *Shakes. Macbeth.*

HEDGE-ROW. *n. s.* [*hedge* and *row.*] The series of trees or bushes planted for inclosures.

Sometime walking not unseen
By *hedge-row* elms, on hillocks green. *Milton.*

The fields in the northern side are divided by *hedge-rows* of myrtle. *Berkley to Pope.*

HE'DGE-SPARROW. *n. s.* [*hedge* and *sparrow.*] A sparrow that lives in bushes.

The *hedge-sparrow* fed the cuckoo so long,
That it had its head bit off by its young. *Shakesp. K. Lear.*

HE'DGING-BILL. *n. s.* [*hedge* and *bill.*] A cutting hook used in making hedges.

Comes master Dametas with a *hedging-bill* in his hand, chaffing and swearing. *Sidney.*

HE'DGER. *n. s.* [from *hedge.*] One who makes hedges.

The labour'd ox
In his loose traces from the furrow came,
And the swink'd *hedger* at his supper sat. *Milton.*

He would be laughed at, that should go about to make a fine dancer out of a country *hedger* at past fifty. *Locke.*

To HEED. *v. a.* [hedan, Saxon.] To mind; to regard; to take notice of; to attend.

With pleasure Argus the musician *heeds*;
But wonders much at those new vocal reeds. *Dryden.*

He will no more have clear ideas of all the operations of his mind, than he will have all the particular ideas of any landscape or clock, who will not turn his eyes to it, and with attention *heed* all the parts of it. *Locke.*

HEED. *n. s.* [from the verb.]

1. Care; attention.

With wanton *heed* and giddy cunning,
The melting voice through mazes running. *Milton.*

Take *heed* that, in their tender years, ideas, that have no natural cohesion, come not to be united in their heads. *Locke.*

Thou must take *heed*, my Portius;
The world has all its eyes on Cato's son. *Addison's Cato.*

2. Caution; fearful attention; suspicious watch.

Either wise bearing or ignorant carriage is caught as men catch diseases, one of another; therefore, let men take *heed* of their company. *Shakespeare's Henry* IV. *p.* ii.

Take *heed*, have open eye; for thieves do foot by night:
Take *heed* ere Summer comes, or cuckoo birds affright.
Shakesp. Merry Wives of Windsor.

3. Care to avoid.

We should take *heed* of the neglect or contempt of his worship. *Tillotson's Sermons.*

4. Notice; observation.

Speech must come by hearing and learning; and birds give more *heed*, and mark words more than beasts. *Bacon.*

5. Seriousness; staidness.

He did unseal them; and the first he view'd,
He did it with a serious mind; a *heed*
Was in his countenance. *Shakesp. Henry* VIII.

6. Regard; respectful notice.

It is a way of calling a man a fool, when no *heed* is given to what he says. *L'Estrange.*

HE'EDFUL. *adj.* [from *heed.*]

1. Watchful; cautious; suspicious.

Give him *heedful* note;
For I mine eyes will rivet to his face;
And, after, we will both our judgments join,
In censure of his seeming. *Shakespeare's Hamlet.*

2. Attentive; careful; observing.

I am commanded
To tell the passion of my sovereign's heart;
Where fame, late ent'ring at his *heedful* ears,
Hath plac'd thy beauty's image and thy virtue. *Shak. H.* VI.

To him one of the other twins was bound,
Whilst I had been like *heedful* of the other. *Shakespeare.*

Thou, *heedful* of advice, secure proceed;
My praise the precept is, be thine the deed. *Pope's Odyssey.*

HE'EDFULLY. *adv.* [from *heedful.*] Attentively; carefully; cautiously.

Let the learner maintain an honourable opinion of his instructor,

ſtructor, and *heedfully* liſten to his inſtructions, as one willing to be led. *Watts.*

HE'EDFULNESS. *n. ſ.* [from *heedful.*] Caution; vigilance; attention.

HE'EDILY. *adv.* Cautiouſly; vigilantly. *Dict.*

HE'EDINESS. *n ſ.* Caution; vigilance. *Dict.*

HE'EDLESS. *adj.* [from *heed.*] Negligent; inattentive; careleſs; thoughtleſs; regardleſs; unobſerving.

The *heedleſs* lover does not know
Whoſe eyes they are that wound him ſo. *Waller.*

Heedleſs of verſe, and hopeleſs of the crown,
Scarce half a wit, and more than half a clown. *Dryden.*

Some ideas, which have more than once offered themſelves to the ſenſes, have yet been little taken notice of; the mind being either *heedleſs*, as in children, or otherwiſe employed, as in men. *Locke.*

HE'EDLESSLY. *adv.* [from *heedleſs.*] Careleſly; negligently; inattentively.

Whilſt ye diſcharge the duty of matrimony, ye *heedleſsly* ſlide into ſin. *Arbuthnot and Pope's Mart. Scriblerus.*

HE'EDLESSNESS. *n. ſ.* [from *heedleſs.*] Careleſſneſs; thoughtleſſneſs; negligence; inattention.

In the little harms they ſuffer from knocks and falls, they ſhould not be pitied, but bid do ſo again; which is a better way to cure their *heedleſſneſs.* *Locke.*

HEEL. *n. ſ.* [ƿele, Saxon.]

1. The part of the foot that protuberates behind.

He calls to mind his ſtrength, and then his ſpeed,
His winged *heels*, and then his armed head;
With theſe t' avoid, with that his fate to meet;
But fear prevails, and bids him truſt his feet. *Denham.*

If the luxated bone be diſtorted backward, it lieth over the *heel* bone. *Wiſeman's Surgery.*

2. The whole foot of animals.

Pegaſus appeared hanging off the ſide of a rock, with a fountain running from his *heel.* *Addiſon's Guardian.*

3. The feet, as employed in flight.

Nothing is commoner, in times of danger, than for men to leave their maſters to bears and tygers, and ſhew them a fair pair of *heels* for't. *L'Eſtrange's Fables.*

4. *To be at the* HEELS. To purſue cloſely; to follow hard.

Sir, when comes your book forth?
—Upon the *heels* of my preſentment. *Shakeſp. Timon.*

But is there no ſequel at the *heels* of this
Mother's admiration? *Shakeſp. Hamlet.*

Could we break our way
By force, and at our *heels* all hell ſhould riſe
With blackeſt inſurrection, to confound
Heav'n's pureſt light. *Milton's Paradiſe Loſt, b.* ii.

5. To purſue as an enemy.

The Spaniards fled on towards the North to ſeek their fortunes, being ſtill chaſed by the Engliſh navy at their *heels*, until they were fain to give them over for want of powder. *Bacon.*

Want! hungry want! that hungry meagre fiend,
Is at my *heels*, and chaces me in view. *Otway.*

6. To follow cloſe as a dependent.

Through proud London he came ſighing on,
After th' admired *heels* of Bolingbroke. *Shakeſ. Henry* IV.

7. *To lay by the* HEELS. To fetter; to ſhackle; to put in gyves.

If the king blame me for't, I'll *lay* ye all
By th' heels, and ſuddenly; and on your heads
Clap round fines for neglect. *Shakeſ. Henry* VIII.

One half of man, his mind,
Is, *ſui juris*, unconfin'd,
And cannot be laid by the *heels.* *Hudibras, p.* i. *cant.* 3.

I began to ſmoke that they were a parcel of mummers; and wondered that none of the Middleſex juſtices took care to *lay* ſome of them by the *heels.* *Addiſon's Freeholder.*

8. Any thing ſhaped like a heel.

At the other ſide is a kind of *heel* or knob, to break clots with. *Mortimer's Husbandry.*

9. The back part of a ſtocken: whence the phraſe *to be out at heels*, to be worn out.

I've watch'd and travell'd hard;
Some time I ſhall ſleep out, the reſt I'll whiſtle:
A good man's fortune may grow *out at heels.* *Shak. K. Lear.*

To HEEL. *v. n.* [from the noun.]

1. To dance.

I cannot ſing,
Nor *heel* the high lavolt, nor ſweeten talk. *Shakeſpeare.*

2. To lean on one ſide: as, the ſhip *heels.*

HEE'LER. *n. ſ.* [from *heel.*] A cock that ſtrikes well with his heels.

HE'EL-PIECE. *n. ſ.* [*heel* and *piece.*] A piece fixed on the hinder part of the ſhoe, to ſupply what is worn away.

To HE'EL-PIECE. *v. a.* [*heel* and *piece.*] To put a piece of leather on a ſhoe-heel.

Some blamed Mrs. Bull for new *heel-piecing* her ſhoes. *Arb.*

HEFT. *n. ſ.* [from *heave.*]

1. Heaving; effort.

May be in the cup
A ſpider ſteep'd, and one may drink; depart,
And yet partake no venom; for his knowledge
Is not infected: but if one preſent
Th' abhorr'd ingredient to his eye, make known
How he hath drunk, he cracks his gorge, his ſides
With violent *hefts.* *Shakeſp. Winter's Tale.*

2. [For *haft.*] Handle.

His oily ſide devours both blade and *heft.* *Waller.*

HE'GIRA. *n. ſ.* [Arabick.] A term in chronology, ſignifying the epocha, or account of time, uſed by the Arabians and Turks, who begin their computation from the day that *Mahomet* was forced to make his eſcape from the city of Mecca, which happened on Friday July 16, *A. D.* 622, under the reign of the emperor *Heracleus.* *Harris.*

HE'IFER. *n. ſ.* [ƿeahfore, Saxon.] A young cow.

Who finds the *heifer* dead and bleeding freſh,
And ſees faſt by a butcher with an ax,
But will ſuſpect 'twas he that made the ſlaughter? *Shakeſp.*

A *heifer* will put up her noſe, and ſnuff in the air, againſt rain. *Bacon's Natural Hiſtory.*

For her the flocks refuſe their verdant food,
Nor thirſty *heifers* ſeek the gliding flood. *Pope's Winter.*

HEIGH-HO. *interj.*

1. An expreſſion of ſlight languour and uneaſineſs.

Heigh-ho! an't be not four by the day, I'll be hang'd. *Shak.*

2. It is uſed by *Dryden*, contrarily to cuſtom, as a voice of exultation.

We'll toſs off our ale 'till we cannot ſtand,
And *heigh-ho* for the honour of old England. *Dryden.*

HEIGHT. *n ſ.* [from *high.*]

1. Elevation above the ground; any place aſſigned.

Into what pit thou ſee'ſt,
From what *height* fall'n. *Milton's Paradiſe Loſt, b.* i.

2. Altitude; ſpace meaſured upwards.

Abroad I'll ſtudy thee,
As he removes far off, that great *heights* takes. *Donne.*

There is in Ticinium, in Italy, a church that is in length one hundred feet, in breadth twenty, and in *height* near fifty. *Bacon's Natural Hiſtory.*

An amphitheatre appear'd,
Rais'd in degrees, to ſixty paces rear'd;
That when a man was plac'd in one degree,
Height was allow'd for him above to ſee. *Dryden.*

An amphitheatre's amazing *height*
Here fills the eye with terror and delight. *Addiſon.*

3. Degree of latitude.

Guinea lieth to the North ſea, in the ſame *height* as Peru to the South. *Abbot's Deſcription of the World.*

4. Summit; aſcent; towering eminence.

From Alpine *heights* the father firſt deſcends;
His daughter's huſband in the plain attends. *Dryden's Æn.*

Every man of learning need not enter into their difficulties, nor climb the *heights* to which ſome others have arrived. *Watts.*

5. Elevation of rank; ſtation of dignity.

By him that rais'd me to this careful *height*,
From that contented hap which I enjoy'd,
I never did incenſe his majeſty
Againſt Clarence. *Shakeſpeare's Richard* III.

Ten kings had from the Norman conqu'ror reign'd,
When England to her greateſt *height* attain'd,
Of pow'r, dominion, glory, wealth and ſtate. *Daniel.*

6. The utmoſt degree; full completion.

Putrefaction doth not riſe to its *height* at once. *Bacon.*

Did not ſhe
Of Timna firſt betray me, and reveal
The ſecret, wreſted from me in the *height*
Of nuptial love profeſs'd? *Milton's Agoniſtes.*

Hide me from the face
Of God, whom to behold was then my *height*
Of happineſs! *Milton's Paradiſe Loſt, b.* x.

7. Utmoſt exertion.

Come on, ſir; I ſhall now put you to the *height* of your breeding. *Shakeſp. All's well that ends well.*

8. State of excellence; advance towards perfection.

Social duties are carried to greater *heights*, and enforced with ſtronger motives, by the principles of our religion. *Addiſ.*

To HE'IGHTEN. *v. a.* [from *height.*]

1. To raiſe higher.

2. To improve; to meliorate.

3. To aggravate.

Foreign ſtates gave us their aſſiſtance in reducing our country to a ſtate of peace; and which of them uſed their endeavours to *heighten* our confuſions, and plunge us into all the evils of a civil war? *Addiſon's Freeholder.*

4. To improve by decorations.

As in a room, contrived for ſtate, the height of the roof ſhould bear a proportion to the area; ſo in the *heightenings* of poetry, the ſtrength and vehemence of figures ſhould be ſuited to the occaſion. *Dryden's Span. Fryar, Dedication.*

HE'INOUS. *adj.* [*haineux*, French, from *hain*, hate; or from the Teutonick *hoon*, ſhame.] Atrocious; wicked in a high degree.

To abrogate or innovate the goſpel of Chriſt, if men or angels

angels ſhould attempt, it were moſt *heinous* and accurſed ſacrilege. *Hooker*, *b.* iii. *ſ.* 10.

This is the man ſhould do the bloody deed:
The image of a wicked *heinous* fault
Lives in his eye. *Shakeſpeare's King John.*

As it is a moſt *heinous*, ſo it is a moſt dangerous impiety to deſpiſe him that can deſtroy us. *Tillotſon's Sermons.*

HE'INOUSLY. *adv.* [from *heinous.*] Atrociouſly; wickedly.

HE'INOUSNESS. *n. ſ.* [from *heinous.*] Atrociouſneſs; wickedneſs.

He who can treat offences provoking to God as jeſts and trifles, muſt have very little ſenſe of the *heinouſneſs* of them. *Rogers's Sermons.*

HEIR. *n. ſ.* [*heire*, old Fr. *hæres*, Latin.] One that is inheritor of any thing after the preſent poſſeſſor.

An *heir* ſignifies the eldeſt, who is, by the laws of England, to have all his father's land. *Locke.*

What lady is that?
—The *heir* of Alanſon, Roſaline her name. *Shakeſpeare.*

That I'll give my voice on Richard's ſide,
To bar my maſter's *heirs* in true deſcent,
God knows, I will not do it. *Shakeſp. Richard* III.

Being *heirs* together of the grace of life. 1 *Pet.* iii. 7.

The young extravagant *heir* had got a new ſteward, and was reſolved to look into his eſtate before things grew deſperate. *Swift.*

Sunk is the hero, and his glory loſt,
And I his *heir* in miſery alone. *Pope's Odyſſey.*

The *heirs* to titles and large eſtates have a weakneſs in their eyes, and a tenderneſs in their conſtitutions. *Swift.*

To HEIR. *v. a.* [from the noun.] To inherit.

His ſons in blooming youth were ſnatch'd by fate;
One only daughter *heir'd* the royal ſtate. *Dryden's Æn.*

HE'IRESS. *n. ſ.* [from *heir.*] An inheritrix; a woman that inherits.

An *heireſs* ſhe, while yet alive;
All that was her's to him did give. *Waller.*

Æneas, though he married the *heireſs* of the crown, yet claimed no title to it during the life of his father-in-law. *Dryd.*

HE'IRLESS. *adj.* [from *heir.*] Without an heir; wanting one to inherit after him.

I ſtill think of
The wrong I did myſelf; which was ſo much,
That *heirleſs* it hath made my kingdom. *Shakeſ. Wint. Tale.*

HE'IRSHIP. *n. ſ.* [from *heir.*] The ſtate, character, or privileges of an heir.

A layman appoints an heir or an executor in his will, to build an hoſpital within a year, under pain of being deprived of his *heirſhip*. *Ayliffe's Parergon.*

HE'IRLOOM. *n. ſ.* [*heir* and *ȝeloma*, goods, Sax.] Any furniture or moveable decreed to deſcend by inheritance, and therefore inſeparable from the freehold.

Achilles' ſceptre was of wood,
Tranſmitted to the hero's line;
Thence through a long deſcent of kings
Came an *heirloom*, as Homer ſings. *Swift.*

HELD. The preterite and part. paſſ. of *hold.*

A rich man beginning to fall, is *held* up of friends. *Eccluſ.*

If Minerva had not appeared and *held* his hand, he had executed his deſign. *Dryden.*

HELI'ACAL. *adj.* [*heliaque*, Fr. from ἥλιος.] Emerging from the luſtre of the ſun, or falling into it.

Had they aſcribed the heat of the ſeaſon to this ſtar, they would not have computed from its *heliacal* aſcent. *Brown.*

HE'LIACALLY. *adv.* [from *heliacal.*]

From the riſing of this ſtar, not coſmically, that is, with the ſun, but *heliacally*, that is, its emerſion from the rays of the ſun, the ancients computed their canicular days. *Brown.*

He is tempeſtuous in the Summer, when he riſes *heliacally*; and rainy in the Winter, when he riſes achronically. *Dryden.*

HE'LICAL. *adv.* [*helice*, Fr. from ἕλιξ.] Spiral; with many circumvolutions.

The ſcrew is a kind of wedge, multiplied or continued by a *helical* revolution about a cylinder, receiving its motion not from any ſtroke, but from a vectis at one end of it. *Wilkins.*

HE'LIOID *Parabola*, in mathematicks, or the parabolick ſpiral, is a curve which ariſes from the ſuppoſition of the axis of the common Apollonian parabola's being bent round into the periphery of a circle, and is a line then paſſing through the extremities of the ordinates, which do now converge towards the centre of the ſaid circle. *Harris.*

HELIOCE'NTRICK. *adj.* [*heliocentrique*, Fr. ἥλιος, and κέντρον.]

The *heliocentrick* place of a planet is ſaid to be ſuch as it would appear to us from the ſun, if our eye were fixed in its centre. *Harris.*

HE'LIOSCOPE. *n. ſ.* [*helioſcope*, Fr. ἥλιος and σκοπέω.] A ſort of teleſcope fitted ſo as to look on the body of the ſun, without offence to the eyes. *Harris.*

HE'LIOTROPE. *n. ſ.* [ἥλιος and τρέπω; *heliotrope*, French; *heliotropium*, Latin.] A plant that turns towards the ſun; but more particularly the turnſol, or ſun-flower.

'Tis a common obſervation of flatterers, that they are like the *heliotrope*; they open only towards the ſun, but ſhut and contract themſelves at night, and in cloudy weather. *Government of the Tongue.*

HE'LISPHERICAL. *adj.* [*helix* and *ſphere.*]

The *heliſpherical* line is the rhomb line in navigation, and is ſo called becauſe on the globe it winds round the pole ſpirally, and ſtill comes nearer and nearer to it, but cannot terminate in it. *Harris.*

HE'LIX. *n. ſ.* [*helice*, Fr. ἕλιξ.] A ſpiral line; a circumvolution.

Find the true inclination of the ſcrew, together with the certain quantity of water which every *helix* does contain. *Wilkins's Dædalus.*

HELL. *n. ſ.* [ꝥelle, Saxon.]

1. The place of the devil and wicked ſouls.

For it is a knell
That ſummons thee to heaven, or to *hell*. *Shakeſ. Macbeth.*

If a man were a porter of *hell* gates, he ſhould have old turning the key. *Shakeſpeare's Macbeth.*

Let none admire
That riches grow in *hell*; that ſoil may beſt
Deſerve the precious bane. *Milton.*

Hell's black tyrant trembled to behold
The glorious light he forfeited of old. *Cowley.*

2. The place of ſeparate ſouls, whether good or bad.

I will go down to my ſon mourning to *hell*. *Gen.* vi. 35.

He deſcended into *hell*. *Apoſtles Creed.*

3. Temporal death.

The pains of *hell* came about me; the ſnares of death overtook me. *Pſalm* xviii. 4.

4. The place at a running play to which thoſe who are caught are carried.

Then couples three be ſtraight allotted there;
They of both ends the middle two do fly;
The two that in mid-place, *hell* called were,
Muſt ſtrive with waiting foot, and watching eye,
To catch of them, and them to *hell* to bear,
That they, as well as they, *hell* may ſupply. *Sidney.*

5. The place into which the taylor throws his ſhreds.

This truſty ſquire, he had, as well
As the bold Trojan knight, ſeen *hell*;
Not with a counterfeited paſs
Of golden bough, but true gold lace. *Hudibras, p.* i.

In Covent-garden did a taylor dwell,
Who might deſerve a place in his own *hell*. *King's Cookery.*

6. The infernal powers.

Much danger firſt, much did he ſuſtain,
While Saul and *hell* croſt his ſtrong fate in vain. *Cowley.*

7. It is uſed in compoſition by the old writers more than by the modern.

HELL-BLACK. *adj.* Black as hell.

The ſea, with ſuch a ſtorm as his bare head
In *hell-black* night endur'd, would have boil'd up,
And quench'd the ſtelled fires. *Shakeſp. King Lear.*

HELL-BRED. *adj.* [*hell* and *bred.*] Produced in hell.

Heart cannot think what courage and what cries,
With foul enfouldred ſmoak and flaſhing fire,
The *hell-bred* beaſt threw forth unto the ſkies. *Fairy Queen.*

HELL-BROTH. *n. ſ.* [*hell* and *broth.*] A compoſition boiled up for infernal purpoſes.

Adder's fork, and blind worm's ſting,
Lizard's leg, and owlet's wing;
For a charm of pow'rful trouble,
Like a *hell-broth* boil and bubble. *Shakeſp. Macbeth.*

HELL-DOOMED. *adj.* [*hell* and *doom.*] Conſigned to hell.

And reckon'ſt thou thyſelf with ſpirits of heav'n,
Hell-doom'd! and breath'ſt defiance here and ſcorn,
Where I reign king? *Milton's Paradiſe Loſt, b.* ii.

HELL-GOVERNED. *adj.* Directed by hell.

Earth gape open wide and eat him quick,
As thou do'ſt ſwallow up this good king's blood,
Which his *hell-govern'd* arm hath butcher'd. *Shak. R.* III.

HELL-HATED. *adj.* Abhorred like hell.

Back do I toſs theſe treaſons to thy head,
With the *hell-hated* lie o'erwhelm thy heart. *Shak. K. Lear.*

HELL-HAUNTED. *adj.* [*hell* and *haunt.*] Haunted by the devil.

Fierce Oſmond clos'd me in the bleeding bark,
And bid me ſtand expoſed to the bleak winds,
And Winter's ſtorms, and heav'n's inclemency,
Bound to the fate of this *hell-haunted* grove. *Dryden.*

HELL-HOUND. *n. ſ.* [ꝥelle ꝥunꝺ, Saxon.]

1. Dogs of hell.

Thou had'ſt a Clarence too, and Richard kill'd him:
From forth the kennel of thy womb hath crept
A *hell-hound*, that doth hunt us all to death. *Shakeſp. R.* III.

Now the *hell-hounds* with ſuperior ſpeed
Had reach'd the dame, and, faſt'ning on her ſide,
The ground with iſſuing ſtreams of purple dy'd. *Dryden.*

2. Agent of hell.

I call'd

I call'd
My *hell-hounds* to lick up the draff, and filth,
Which man's polluting sin with taint had shed
On what was pure. *Milton's Paradise Lost, b.* x.

HE'LL-KITE. *n. s.* [*hell* and *kite.*] Kite of infernal breed. The term *hell* prefixed to any word notes detestation.

All my pretty ones?
Did you say all? What, all? Oh, *hell-kite!* all?
What, all my pretty chickens, and their dam,
At one fell swoop? *Shakesp. Macbeth.*

HE'LLEBORE. *n. s.* [*helleborus*, Latin.] Christmas flower.

It hath a digitated leaf: the flower consists of several leaves placed orbicularly, and expanding in form of a rose: in the centre of the flower rises the pointal, encompassed about the base with several little horns between the chives and petals, which turn to a fruit, in which the membranaceous husks are gathered into a little head, ending in an horn, opening longwise, and full of roundish or oval seeds. *Miller.*

HE'LLEBORE *White. n. s.* [*veratrum*, Latin.] A plant.

The flower is naked, consisting of six leaves, expanding in form of a rose: in the middle arises the pointal, surrounded by six threads, which turn to a fruit; in which three membranaceous sheaths are gathered into a little head, and are full of oblong seeds resembling a grain of wheat, and compassed by a leafy wing. *Miller.*

There are great doubts whether any of its species be the true *hellebore* of the ancients. *Miller.*

HE'LLENISM. *n. s.* [ἑλληνισμὸς.] An idiom of the Greek. *Ainsworth.*

HE'LLISH. *adj.* [from *hell.*]

1. Having the qualities of hell; infernal; wicked; detestable.

No benefits shall ever allay that diabolical rancour that ferments in some *hellish* breasts, but that it will foam out at its foul mouth in slander. *South's Sermons.*

Victory and triumph to the son of God,
Now entering his great duel, not of arms,
But to vanquish by wisdom *hellish* wiles. *Paradise Regain'd.*

2. Sent from hell; belonging to hell.

O thou celestial or infernal spirit of love, or what other heavenly or *hellish* title thou list to have, for effects of both I find in myself, have compassion of me. *Sidney, b.* i.

HE'LLISHLY. *adv.* [from *hellish.*] Infernally; wickedly; detestably.

HE'LLISHNESS. *n. s.* [from *hellish.*] Wickedness; abhorred qualities.

HE'LLWARD. *adv.* [from *hell.*] Towards hell.

Be next thy care the sable sheep to place
Full o'er the pit, and *hellward* turn their face. *Pope's Odyss.*

HELM denotes defence: as *Eadhelm*, happy defence; *Sighelm*, victorious defence; *Berthelm*, eminent defence: like *Amyntas* and *Boetius* among the Greeks. *Gibson's Camden.*

HELM. *n. s.* [helm, Saxon, from *helan*, to cover, to protect.]

1. A covering for the head in war; a helmet; a morrion; an headpiece.

France spreads his banners in our noiseless land;
With plumed *helm* thy slay'r begins his threats. *Shakespeare.*
Mnestheus lays hard load upon his *helm.* *Dryden.*

2. The part of a coat of arms that bears the crest.

More might be added of *helms*, crests, mantles, and supporters. *Camden's Remains.*

3. The upper part of the retort.

The vulgar chymists themselves pretend to be able, by repeated cohobations, and other fit operations, to make the distilled parts of a concrete bring its own *caput mortuum* over the *helm.* *Boyle.*

4. [helma, Saxon.] The steerage; the rudder.

They did not leave the *helm* in storms!
And such they are make happy states. *Ben. Johns. Catiline.*
More in prosperity is reason tost
Than ships in storms, their *helms* and anchors lost. *Denh.*
Fair occasion shews the springing gale,
And int'rest guides the *helm*, and honour swells the sail. *Pri.*

5. The station of government.

I may be wrong in some of the means; but that is no material objection against the design: let those who are at the *helm* contrive it better. *Swift.*

6. In the following line it is difficult to determine whether *steersman* or *defender* is intended: I think *steersman.*

You slander
The *helms* o' th' state, who care for you like fathers,
When you curse them as enemies. *Shakesp. Coriolanus.*

To HELM. *v. a.* [from the noun.] To guide; to conduct. *Hanmer.*

The very stream of his life, and the business he hath *helmed*, must give him a better proclamation. *Shakesp. Meas. for Meas.*

HE'LMED. *adj.* [from *helm.*]

1. Furnished with a headpiece.

The *helmed* cherubim
Are seen in glittering ranks with wings display'd. *Milton.*

HE'LMET. *n. s.* [Probably a diminutive of *helm.*] A helm; a headpiece; armour for the head.

I saw him down; thrice up again, and fighting;
From *helmet* to the spur all bleeding o'er. *Shakesp. H.* V.
Put in their hands thy bruising irons of wrath,
That they may crush down with a heavy fall
Th' usurping *helmets* of our adversaries. *Shak. Rich.* III.
Sev'n darts are thrown at once, and some rebound
From his bright shield, some on his *helmet* found. *Dryden.*

HELMI'NTHICK. *adj.* [from ἕλμινθος.] Relating to worms. *Dict.*

To HELP. *v. a.* preter. *helped*, or *holp*; part. *helped*, or *holpen.* [*hilpan*, Gothick; helpan, Saxon.]

1. To assist; to support; to aid.

Let us work as valiant men behoves;
For boldest hearts good fortune *helpeth* out. *Fairfax, b.* ii.

God *helped* him against the Philistines. 2 *Chro.* xxvi. 7.

They *helped* them in all things with silver and gold. 1 *Esdr.*

A man reads his prayers out of a book, as a means to *help* his understanding and direct his expressions. *Stillingfleet.*

This he conceives not hard to bring about,
If all of you should join to *help* him out. *Dryden.*

What I offer is so far from doing any diskindness to the cause these gentlemen are engaged in, that it does them a real service, and *helps* them out with the main thing whereat they stuck. *Woodward's Natural History.*

The god of learning and of light,
Would want a god himself to *help* him out. *Swift.*

2. To remove, or advance by help.

Woe to him that is alone when he falleth; for he hath not another to *help* him up. *Eccl.* iv. 10.

Having never learned any laudable manual art, they have recourse to those foolish or ill ways in use to *help* off their time. *Locke.*

Wherever they are at a stand, *help* them presently over the difficulty without any rebuke. *Locke.*

3. To free from pain or disease.

Help and ease them, but by no means bemoan them. *Locke.*

4. To cure; to heal.

Love doth to her eyes repair,
To *help* him of his blindness. *Shakesp. Two Gent. of Verona.*

5. To remedy; to change for the better.

Cease to lament for that thou can'st not *help*;
And study help for that which thou lament'st. *Shakespeare.*

If they take offence when we give none, it is a thing we cannot *help*, and therefore the whole blame must lie upon them. *Sanderson.*

It is a high point of ill nature to make sport with any man's imperfections, that he cannot *help.* *L'Estrange.*

Those closing skies might still continue bright;
But who can *help* it, if you'll make it night. *Dryden.*
She, betwixt her modesty and pride,
Her wishes, which she could not *help*, would hide. *Dryden.*

It is reckoned ill manners for men to quarrel upon difference in opinion, because that is a thing which no man can *help* in himself. *Swift.*

Those few who reside among us, only because they cannot *help* it. *Swift.*

6. To forbear; to avoid.

He cannot *help* believing, that such things he saw and heard. *Atterbury's Sermons.*

I cannot *help* remarking the resemblance betwixt him and our author in qualities, fame, and fortune. *Pope.*

7. To promote; to forward.

If you make the earth narrower at the bottom than at the top, in fashion of a sugar-loaf reversed, it will *help* the experiment. *Bacon's Natural History.*

8. *To* HELP *to.* To supply with; to furnish with.

Whom they would *help* to a kingdom, those reign; and whom again they would, they displace. 1 *Mac.* viii. 13.

The man that is now with Tiresias can *help* him to his oxen again. *L'Estrange.*

In plenty starving, tantaliz'd in state,
And complaisantly *help'd* to all I hate;
Treated, caress'd, and tir'd, I take my leave. *Pope.*

To HELP. *v. n.*

1. To contribute assistance.

Sir, how come it you
Have *holp* to make this rescue? *Shakes. Coriolanus.*

Discreet followers and servants *help* much to reputation. *Bac.*

Bennet's grave look was a pretence,
And Danby's matchless impudence
Help'd to support the knave. *Dryden.*

A generous present *helps* to persuade as well as an agreeable person. *Garth.*

2. To bring a supply.

Some, wanting the talent to write, made it their care that the actors should *help* out where the muses failed. *Rymer.*

HELP. *n. s.* [from the verb; *hulpe*, Dutch.]

1. Assistance; aid; support; succour.

Muleasses, despairing to recover the city, hardly escaped his enemies hands by the good *help* of his uncle. *Knolles.*

He

He may be beholden to experience and acquired notions, where he thinks he has not the leaſt *help* from them. *Locke.*

So great is the ſtupidity of ſome of thoſe, that they may have no ſenſe of the *help* adminiſtred to them. *Smalridge.*

2. That which forwards or promotes.

Coral is in uſe as an *help* to the teeth of children. *Bacon.*

3. That which gives help.

Though theſe contrivances increaſe the power, yet they proportionably protract the time: that which by ſuch *helps* one man may do in a hundred days, may be done by the immediate ſtrength of a hundred men in one day. *Wilkins.*

Virtue is a friend and an *help* to nature; but it is vice and luxury that deſtroys it, and the diſeaſes of intemperance are the natural product of the ſins of intemperance. *South.*

Another *help* St. Paul himſelf affords us towards the attaining the true meaning contained in his epiſtles. *Locke.*

4. Remedy.

There is no *help* for it, but he muſt be taught accordingly to comply with that faulty way of writing. *Holder on Speech.*

HE'LPER. *n. ſ.* [from *help.*]

1. An aſſiſtant; an auxiliary; an aider; one that helps or aſſiſts.

There was not any left, nor any *helper* for Iſrael. *2 Kings.*

We ought to receive ſuch, that we might be fellow *helpers* to the truth. *3 Jo.* viii.

It is impoſſible for that man to deſpair who remembers that his *helper* is omnipotent. *Taylor's Rule of living holy.*

2. One that adminiſters remedy.

Compaſſion, the mother of tears, is not always a mere idle ſpectator, but an *helper* oftentimes of evils. *More.*

3. A ſupernumerary ſervant.

I live in the corner of a vaſt unfurniſhed houſe: my family conſiſts of a ſteward, a groom, a *helper* in the ſtable, a footman, and an old maid. *Swift to Pope.*

4. One that ſupplies with any thing wanted.

Heaven
Hath brought me up to be your daughter's dower,
As it hath fated her to be my motive
And *helper* to a huſband. *Shak. All's well that ends well.*

HE'LPFUL. *adj.* [*help* and *full.*]

1. Uſeful; that which gives aſſiſtance.

Let's fight with gentle words,
'Till time lend friends, and friends their *helpful* ſwords. *Sh.*
He orders all the ſuccours which they bring;
The *helpful* and the good about him run,
And form an army. *Dryden's Ann. Mirab.*

2. Wholſome; ſalutary.

A ſkilful chymiſt can as well, by ſeparation of viſible elements, draw *helpful* medicines out of poiſon, as poiſon out of the moſt healthful herbs. *Raleigh's Hiſtory of the World.*

HE'LPLESS. *adj.* [from *help.*]

1. Wanting power to ſuccour one's ſelf.

One dire ſhot
Cloſe by the board the prince's main-maſt bore;
All three now *helpleſs* by each other lie. *Dryd. Ann. Mirab.*

Let our enemies rage and perſecute the poor and the *helpleſs*; but let it be our glory to be pure and peaceable. *Rogers.*

2. Wanting ſupport or aſſiſtance.

How ſhall I then your *helpleſs* fame defend?
'Twill then be infamy to ſeem your friend. *Pope.*

3. Irremediable; admitting no help.

Such *helpleſs* harms it's better hidden keep,
Than rip up grief, where it may not avail. *Fairy Queen.*

4. Unſupplied; void.

Naked he lies, and ready to expire,
Helpleſs of all that human wants require. *Dryden.*

HE'LPLESSLY. *adv.* [from *helpleſs.*] Without ſuccour; without ability.

HE'LPLESSNESS. *n. ſ.* [from *helpleſs.*] Want of ſuccour; want of ability.

HELTER-SKELTFR. *adv.* [As *Skinner* fancies, from ꝑeolꞅꞇeꞃ ꞅceaꝺo, the darkneſs of hell; hell, ſays he, being a place of confuſion.] In a hurry; without order; tumultuouſly.

Sir John, I am thy Piſtol, and thy friend;
And *helter-ſkelter* have I rode to England,
And tidings do I bring. *Shakeſpeare's Henry* V.

He had no ſooner turned his back but they were at it *helter-ſkelter*, throwing books at one another's heads. *L'Eſtrange.*

HELVE. *n. ſ.* [ꝑelꝼe, Saxon.] The handle of an axe.

The ſlipping of an axe from the *helve*, whereby another is ſlain, was the work of God himſelf. *Raleigh's Hiſtory.*

To HELVE. *v. a.* [from the noun.] To fit with a helve or handle.

HEM. *n. ſ.* [ꝑem, Saxon.]

1. The edge of a garment doubled and ſewed to keep the threads from ſpreading.

Rowlers muſt be made of even cloth, white and gentle, without *hem*, ſeam, or thread hanging by. *Wiſeman.*

2. [*Hemmen*, Dutch.] The noiſe uttered by a ſudden and violent expiration of the breath.

I would try if I could cry *hem*, and have him. *Shakeſpeare.*

He loves to clear his pipes in good air, and is not a little pleaſed with any one who takes notice of the ſtrength which he ſtill exerts in his morning *hems.* *Addiſon's Spectator.*

3. *interject.* Hem! [Latin.]

To HEM. *v. a.*

1. To cloſe the edge of cloath by a hem or double border ſewed together.

2. To border; to edge.

All the ſkirt about
Was *hem'd* with golden fringe. *Fairy Queen, b.* ii.
Along the ſhoar of ſilver ſtreaming Thames,
Whoſe ruſhy bank, the which his river *hems.* *Spenſer.*

3. To encloſe; to environ; to confine; to ſhut.

So of either ſide, ſtretching itſelf in a narrow length, was it *hemmed* in by woody hills, as if indeed nature had meant therein to make a place for beholders. *Sidney, b.* ii.

What lets us then the great Jeruſalem
With valiant ſquadrons round about to *hem.* *Fairfax, b.* i.
Why, Neptune, haſt thou made us ſtand alone,
Divided from the world for this, ſay they;
Hemm'd in to be a ſpoil to tyranny,
Leaving affliction hence no way to fly? *Daniel's Civ. War.*
I hurry me in haſte away,
And find his honour in a pound,
Hemm'd by a triple circle round,
Chequer'd with ribbons, blue and green. *Pope.*

To HEM. *v. n.* [*hemmen*, Dutch.] To utter a noiſe by violent expulſion of the breath.

HE'MICRANY. *n. ſ.* [ἥμισυ, half, and κράνιον, the ſkull, or head.] A pain that affects only one part of the head at a time. *Quincy.*

HE'MICYCLE. *n. ſ.* [ἡμίκυκλος.] A half round.

HE'MINA. *n. ſ.* An ancient meaſure: now uſed in medicine to ſignify about ten ounces in meaſure. *Quincy.*

HE'MIPLEGY. *n. ſ.* [ἥμισυ, half, and πλήσσω, to ſtrike or ſeize.] A palſy, or any nervous affection relating thereunto, that ſeizes one ſide at a time; ſome partial diſorder of the nervous ſyſtem.

HE'MISPHERE. *n. ſ.* [ἡμισφαίριον; *hemiſphere*, French.] The half of a globe when it is ſuppoſed to be cut through its centre in the plane of one of its greateſt circles.

That place is earth, the ſeat of man; that light
His day, which elſe, as th' other *hemiſphere*,
Night would invade. *Milton's Paradiſe Loſt, b.* iii.
God ſaw the light was good,
And light from darkneſs by the *hemiſphere*
Divided. *Milton's Paradiſe Loſt, b.* vii.
A hill
Of Paradiſe, the higheſt from whoſe top
The *hemiſphere* of earth, in cleareſt ken
Stretch'd out to th' ampleſt reach of proſpect lay. *Milt. P. L.*

The ſun is more powerful in the northern *hemiſphere*, and in the apogeum; for therein his motion is ſlower. *Brown.*

In open proſpect nothing bounds our eye,
Until the earth ſeems join'd unto the ſky;
So in this *hemiſphere* our utmoſt view
Is only bounded by our king and you. *Dryden.*

HEMISPHE'RICAL. } *adj.* [from *hemiſphere.*] Half round;
HEMISPHE'RICK. } containing half a globe.

The thin film of water ſwells above the ſurface of the water it ſwims on, and commonly conſtitutes *hemiſpherical* bodies with it. *Boyle.*

A pyrites, placed in the cavity of another of an *hemiſpherick* figure, in much the ſame manner as an acorn in its cup. *Woodward on Foſſils.*

HE'MISTICK. *n. ſ.* [ἡμιστίχιον; *hemiſtiche*, Fr.] Half a verſe.

He broke off in the *hemiſtick*, or midſt of the verſe; but ſeized, as it were, with a divine fury, he made up the latter part of the *hemiſtick.* *Dryden's Dufreſnoy.*

HE'MLOCK. *n. ſ.* ꝑemloc, Saxon.] An herb.

The leaves are cut into many minute ſegments: the petals of the flower are bifid, heart-ſhaped, and unequal: the flower is ſucceeded by two ſhort chanelled ſeeds. One ſort is ſometimes uſed in medicine, though it is noxious; but the hemlock of the ancients, which was ſuch deadly poiſon, is generally ſuppoſed different. *Miller.*

He was met even now,
As mad as the vext ſea, ſinging aloud;
Crown'd with rank fumiter and furrow-weeds,
With hardocks, *hemlock.* *Shakeſp. King Lear.*

We cannot with certainty affirm, that no man can be nouriſhed by wood or ſtones, or that all men will be poiſoned by *hemlock.* *Locke.*

HE'MORRHAGE. } *n. ſ.* [αἱμοῤῥαγία; *hemorragie*, French.] A
HE'MORRHAGY. } violent flux of blood.

Great *hemorrhagy* ſucceeds the ſeparation. *Ray.*

Twenty days faſting will not diminiſh its quantity ſo much as one great *hemorrhage.* *Arbuthnot on Aliments.*

HE'MORRHOIDS. *n. ſ.* [αἱμοῤῥοιδες; *hemorrhoids*, French.] The piles; the emrods.

I got the *hemorrhoids.* *Swift.*

HE'MORRHOIDAL. *adj.* [*hemorrhoidal*, Fr. from *hemorrhoids.*] Belonging to the veins in the fundament.

Beſides there are hemorrhages from the noſe and *hemorrhoidal* veins, and fluxes of rheum. *Ray on the Creation.*

Emboſt upon the field, a battle ſtood
Of leeches, ſpouting *hemorrhoidal* blood. *Garth's Diſpenſat.*

HEMP. *n. ſ.* [hænep, Saxon; *hampe*, Dutch.] A fibrous plant of which coarſe linen and ropes are made.

It hath digitated leaves oppoſite to one another: the flowers have no viſible petals; it is male and female in different plants. It is propagated in the rich fenny parts of Lincolnſhire in great quantities for its bark, which is uſeful for cordage, cloth, &c. and the ſeed affords an oil uſed in medicine. *Miller.*

Let gallows go for dog; let man go free,
And let not *hemp* his windpipe ſuffocate. *Shakeſ. Hen.* V.

Hemp and flax are commodities that deſerve encouragement, both for their uſefulneſs and profit. *Mortimer's Husbandry.*

HEMP *Agrimony. n. ſ.* A plant.

The common *hemp agrimony* is found wild by ditches and ſides of rivers. *Miller.*

HE'MPEN. *adj.* [from *hemp.*] Made of hemp.

In foul reproach of knighthood's fair degree,
About his neck a *hempen* rope he wears. *Fairy Queen, b.* i.

Behold
Upon the *hempen* tackle ſhip-boys climbing. *Shak. Hen.* V.

Ye ſhall have a *hempen* caudle then, and the help of a hatchet. *Shakeſpeare's Henry* VI. *p.* iii.

I twitch'd his dangling garter from his knee;
He wiſt not when the *hempen* ſtring I drew. *Gay.*

HEN. *n. ſ.* [henne, Saxon and Dutch; *han*, German, a cock.]

1. The female of a houſe-cock.

2. The female of any land-fowl.

The peacock, pheaſant, and goldfinch cocks have glorious colours; the *hens* have not. *Bacon's Natural Hiſtory.*

Whilſt the *hen* bird is covering her eggs, the male generally takes his ſtand upon a neighbouring bough within her hearing, and by that means diverts her with his ſongs during the whole time of her ſitting. *Addiſon's Spectator.*

The wild duck hence,
O'er the rough moſs, and o'er the trackleſs waſte
The heath *hen* flutters. *Thomſon's Spring.*

HEN-DRIVER. *n. ſ.* [*hen* and *driver.*] A kind of hawk.

The *hen-driver* I forbear to name. *Walton's Angler.*

HE'N-HARM. } *n. ſ.* A kind of kite. *Ainſw.* So called
HE'N-HARRIER. } probably from deſtroying chickens.

HEN-HEARTED. *adj.* [*hen* and *heart.*] Daſtardly; cowardly; like a hen. A low word.

HEN-PECKED. *adj.* [*hen* and *pecked.*] Governed by the wife.

A ſtepdame too I have, a curſed ſhe,
Who rules my *hen-peck'd* ſire, and orders me. *Dryd. Virgil.*

The neighbours reported that he was *hen-pecked*, which was impoſſible, by ſuch a mild-ſpirited woman as his wife. *Arbuthn.*

HEN-ROOST. *n. ſ.* [*hen* and *rooſt.*] The place where the poultry reſt.

Many a poor devil ſtands to a whipping poſt for the pilfering of a ſilver ſpoon, or the robbing of a *hen-rooſt*. *L'Eſtr.*

Her houſe is frequented by a company of rogues, whom ſhe encourageth to rob his *hen-rooſts*. *Swift.*

If a man proſecutes gipſies with ſeverity, his *hen-rooſt* is ſure to pay for it. *Addiſon's Spectator.*

They oft have ſally'd out to pillage
The *hen-rooſts* of ſome peaceful village. *Tickell.*

HENS-FEET. *n. ſ.* A kind of plant. *Ainſworth.*

HE'NBANE. *n. ſ.* [*hyoſcyamus*, Latin.] A plant.

The leaves are ſoft and hairy, growing alternately upon the branches: the cup of the flower is ſhort, bell-ſhaped, and divided into five ſegments: the flower conſiſts of one leaf, the bottom part of which is tubeloſe, but is expanded at the top, and divided into five ſegments, having five obtuſe ſtamina: the fruit, which is incloſed within the calyx, reſembles a pot with a cover to it, and is divided by a partition into two cells, which contain many ſmall ſeeds. It is very often found growing upon the ſides of banks and old dunghills. This is a very poiſonous plant. *Miller.*

That to which old Socrates was curs'd,
Or *henbane* juice, to ſwell 'em 'till they burſt. *Dryden.*

HE'NBIT. *n. ſ.* A plant.

In a ſcarcity in Sileſia a rumour was ſpread of its raining millet-ſeed; but it was found to be only the ſeeds of the ivy-leaved ſpeedwell, or ſmall *henbit*. *Derham's Phyſ. Theology.*

HENCE. *adv.* or *interj.* [heonan, Saxon; *hennes*, old Engliſh.]

1. From this place to another.

Diſcharge my follow'rs; let them *hence* away,
From Richard's night to Bolinbroke's fair day. *Shak. R.* II.

Th' Almighty hath not built
Here for his envy; will not drive us *hence*. *Milton's P. L.*

A ſullen prudence drew thee *hence*
From noiſe, fraud and impertinence. *Roſcommon.*

2. Away; to a diſtance.

Be not found here; *hence* with your little ones. *Shak. Macb.*
Hence with denial vain, and coy excuſe. *Milton.*

3. At a diſtance; in other place.

Why ſhould I then be falſe, ſince it is true
That I muſt die here, and live *hence* by truth? *Shakeſpeare.*

All members of our cauſe, both here and *hence*,
That are inſinewed to this action. *Shakeſp. Henry* IV.

4. From this time; in the future.

He who can reaſon well to-day about one ſort of matters, cannot at all reaſon to-day about others, though perhaps a year *hence* he may. *Locke.*

Let not poſterity a thouſand years *hence* look for truth in the voluminous annals of pedants. *Arbuthnot.*

5. For this reaſon; in conſequence of this.

Hence perhaps it is, that Solomon calls the fear of the Lord the beginning of wiſdom. *Tillotſon, Sermon* 1.

6. From this cauſe; from this ground.

By too ſtrong a projectile motion the aliment tends to putrefaction: *hence* may be deduced the force of exerciſe in helping digeſtion. *Arbuthnot on Aliments.*

7. From this ſource; from this original; from this ſtore.

My Flora was my ſun; for as
One ſun, ſo but one Flora was:
All other faces borrowed *hence*
Their light and grace, as ſtars do thence. *Suckling.*

8. *From hence* is a vitious expreſſion, which crept into uſe even among good authors, as the original force of the word *hence* was gradually forgotten.

An ancient author propheſy'd *from hence*,
Behold on Latian ſhores a foreign prince!
From the ſame parts of heav'n his navy ſtands,
To the ſame parts on earth. *Dryden's Æn. b.* vii.

To HENCE. *v. a.* [from the adverb.] To ſend off; to diſpatch to a diſtance. Obſolete.

Go, bawling cur! thy hungry maw go fill
On yon foul flock, belonging not to me;
With that his dog he *henc'd*, his flock he curſt. *Sidney.*

HENCEFO'RTH. *adv.* [heonforð, Saxon.] From this time forward.

Thanes and kinſmen,
Henceforth be earls. *Shakeſpeare's Macbeth.*

Never *henceforth* ſhall I joy again;
Never, oh never, ſhall I ſee more joy. *Shakeſ. Henry* VI.

Happier thou may'ſt be, worthier can'ſt not be;
Taſte this, and be *henceforth* among the gods,
Thyſelf a goddeſs. *Milton's Par. Loſt, b.* v.

I never from thy ſide *henceforth* will ſtray,
'Till day droop. *Milton's Paradiſe Loſt, b.* xi.

If we treat gallant ſoldiers in this ſort,
Who then *henceforth* to our defence will come? *Dryden.*

HENCEFO'RWARD. *adv.* [*hence* and *forward.*] From this time to all futurity.

Henceforward will I bear
Upon my target three fair ſhining ſuns. *Shakeſ. Henry* VI.

Henceforward it ſhall be treaſon for any that calls me other than lord Mortimer. *Shakeſpeare's Henry* VI. *p.* ii.

Pardon, I beſeech you;
Henceforward I am ever rul'd by you. *Shak. Romeo and Jul.*

The royal academy will admit *henceforward* only ſuch who are endued with good qualities. *Dryden's Dufreſnoy.*

HE'NCHMAN. *n. ſ.* [hync, a ſervant, and *man*, *Skinner*; hengſt, a horſe, and *man*, *Spelman.*] A page; an attendant. Obſolete.

Why ſhould Titania croſs her Oberon?
I do but beg a little changeling boy,
To be my *henchman*. *Shakeſpeare's Midſ. Night's Dream.*

Three *henchmen* were for ev'ry knight aſſign'd,
All in rich livery clad, and of a kind. *Dryden.*

To HEND. *v. a.* [hendan, Saxon, from *hendo*, low Latin, which ſeems borrowed from *hand* or *hond*, Teutonick.]

1. To ſeize; to lay hold on.

With that the ſergeants *hent* the young man ſtout,
And bound him likewiſe in a worthleſs chain. *Fairfax, b.* ii.

2. To croud; to ſurround. Perhaps the following paſſage is corrupt, and ſhould be read *hemmed.*

The generous and graveſt citizens
Have *hent* the gates, and very near upon
The duke is entering. *Shakeſp. Meaſ. for Meaſure.*

HE'NDECAGON. *n. ſ.* [ἕνδεκα and γωνία.] A figure of eleven ſides or angles.

HEPA'TICAL. } *adj.* [*hepaticus*, Latin; *hepatique*, French, from
HEPA'TICK. } ἧπαρ.] Belonging to the liver.

If the evacuated blood be florid, it is ſtomach blood; if red and copious, it's *hepatick*. *Harvey on Conſumptions.*

The cyſtick gall is thick, and intenſely bitter; the *hepatick* gall is more fluid, and not ſo bitter. *Arbuthn. on Aliments.*

HEPS. *n. ſ.* Hawthorn-berries, commonly written *hips*. *Ainſw.*

In hard Winters there is obſerved great plenty of *heps* and haws, which preſerve the ſmall birds from ſtarving. *Bacon.*

HEPTACA'PSULAR. *adj.* [ἑπτὰ and *capſula.*] Having ſeven cavities or cells.

HE'PTAGON. *n. ſ.* [*heptagone*, French; ἑπτὰ and γωνία.] A figure with ſeven ſides or angles.

HEPTA'GONAL. *adj.* [from *heptagon.*] Having ſeven angles or ſides.

HE'PTARCHY. *n. ſ.* [*heptarchie*, Fr. ἑπτὰ and ἀρχή.] A ſevenfold government.

In the Saxon *heptarchy* I find little noted of arms, albeit the Germans, of whom they deſcended, uſed ſhields. *Camden.*

England began not to be a people, when Alfred reduced it into

into a monarchy; for the materials thereof were extant before, namely, under the *heptarchy*. *Hale's Origin of Mankind.*

The next returning planetary hour
Of Mars, who shar'd the *heptarchy* of pow'r,
His steps bold Arcite to the temple bent. *Dryden.*

HER. *pron.* [ƿena, ƿen, in Saxon, stood for *their*, or of *them*, which at length became the female possessive.]

1. Belonging to a female; of a she; of a woman:

About his neck
A green and gilded snake had wreath'd itself,
Who with *her* head, nimble in threats, approach'd
The opening of his mouth. *Shakesp. As you like it.*

Still new favourites she chose,
'Till up in arms my passion rose,
And cast away *her* yoke. *Cowley.*

One month, three days, and half an hour,
Judith held the sov'reign pow'r;
Wond'rous beautiful *her* face;
But so weak and small *her* wit,
That she to govern were unfit,
And so Susanna took *her* place. *Cowley.*

2. The oblique case of *she*.

England is so idly king'd,
Her sceptre so fantastically borne,
That fear attends *her* not. *Shakespeare's Henry* V.

She cannot seem deform'd to me,
And I would have *her* seem to others so. *Cowley.*

The moon arose clad o'er in light,
With thousand stars attending on her train;
With *her* they rise, with *her* they set again. *Cowley.*

Should I be left, and thou be lost, the sea,
That bury'd *her* I lov'd, should bury me. *Dryden.*

HERS. *pronoun.* This is used when it refers to a substantive going before: as, such are *her* charms, such charms are *hers*.

This pride of *hers*,
Upon advice, hath drawn my love from her. *Shakespeare.*

Thine own unworthiness,
Will still that thou art mine not *hers* confess. *Cowley.*

Some secret charm did all her acts attend,
And what his fortune wanted, *hers* could mend. *Dryden.*

I bred you up to arms, rais'd you to power,
Indeed to save a crown, not *hers*, but yours. *Dryden.*

HE'RALD. *n. s.* [*herault*, French; *herald*, German.]

1. An officer whose business it is to register genealogies, adjust ensigns armorial, regulate funerals, and anciently to carry messages between princes, and proclaim war and peace.

May none, whose scatter'd names honour my book,
For strict degrees of rank or title look;
'Tis 'gainst the manners of an epigram,
And I a poet here, no *herald* am. *Ben. Johnson's Epigrams.*

When time shall serve, let but the *herald* cry,
And I'll appear again. *Shakesp. King Lear.*

After my death I wish no other *herald*,
No other speaker of my living actions,
But such an honest chronicler as Griffith. *Shakes. Hen.*VIII.

Embassador of peace, if peace you chuse;
Or *herald* of a war, if you refuse. *Dryden's Ind. Emperor.*

Please thy pride, and search the *herald*'s roll,
Where thou shalt find thy famous pedigree. *Dryden.*

2. A precursor; a forerunner; a harbinger.

It is the part of men to fear and tremble,
When the most mighty gods, by tokens, send
Such dreadful *heralds* to astonish us. *Shak. Julius Cæsar.*

It was the lark, the *herald* of the morn. *Shakespeare.*

To HE'RALD *v. a.* [from the noun.] To introduce as an herald. A word not used.

We are sent
To give thee from our royal master thanks;
Only to *herald* thee into his sight,
Not pay thee. *Shakespeare's Macbeth.*

HE'RALDRY. *n. s.* [*herauldrie*, French, from *herald*.]

1. The art or office of a herald.

I am writing of *heraldry*. *Peacham.*

Grant her, besides, of noble blood that ran
In ancient veins, ere *heraldry* began. *Dryden's Juvenal.*

'Twas no false *heraldry*, when madness drew
Her pedigree from those who too much knew. *Denham.*

2. Blazonry.

Metals may blazon common beauties; she
Makes pearls and planets humble *heraldry*. *Cleaveland.*

HERB. *n. s.* [*herbe*, French; *herba*, Latin.]

Herbs are those plants whose stalks are soft, and have nothing woody in them; as grass and hemlock. *Locke.*

In such a night
Medea gather'd the enchanted *herbs*
That did renew old Æson. *Shakesp. Merch. of Venice.*

With sweet-swelling *herbs*
Espoused Eve deck'd first her nuptial bed. *Milton.*

Unhappy, from whom still conceal'd does lie
Of *herbs* and roots the harmless luxury. *Cowley.*

If the leaves are of chief use to us, then we call them *herbs*; as sage and mint. *Watts's Logick.*

Herb eating animals, which don't ruminate, have strong grinders, and chew much. *Arbuthnot on Aliments.*

HERB *Christopher*, or *Bane-berries*. *n. s.* A plant.

The flower consists of five leaves, placed orbicularly in form of a rose: in its centre arises the ovary, which becomes a soft fruit or berry of an oval shape, and filled with seeds in a double row, which for the most part adhere together. *Miller.*

HERBA'CEOUS. *adj.* [from *herba*, Latin.]

1. Belonging to herbs.

Ginger is the root of neither tree nor trunk; but an *herbaceous* plant, resembling the water flower-de-luce. *Brown.*

2. Feeding on vegetables.

Their teeth are fitted to their food; the rapacious to catching, holding, and tearing their prey; the *herbaceous* to gathering and comminution of vegetables. *Derham's Phys. Theology.*

HE'RBAGE. *n. s.* [*herbage*, French.]

1. Herbs collectively; grass; pasture.

Rocks lie cover'd with eternal snow;
Thin *herbage* in the plains, and fruitless fields. *Dryden.*

At the time the deluge came the earth was loaded with *herbage*, and thronged with animals. *Woodward's Nat. Hist.*

2. The tythe and the right of pasture. *Ainsworth.*

HE'RBAL. *n. s.* [from *herb*.] A book containing the names and description of plants.

We leave the description of plants to *herbals*, and other like books of natural history. *Bacon's Natural History.*

Such a plant will not be found in the *herbal* of nature. *Bro.*

As for the medicinal uses of plants, the large *herbals* are ample testimonies thereof. *More's Antid. against Atheism.*

Our *herbals* are sufficiently stored with plants. *Baker.*

HE'RBALIST. *n. s.* [from *herbal*.] A man skilled in herbs.

Herbalists have thus distinguished them, naming that the male whose leaves are lighter, and fruit and apples rounder. *Brown's Vulgar Errours, b.* ii. *c.* 6.

HE'RBAR. *n. s.* [A word, I believe, only to be found in *Spenser*.] Herb; plant.

The roof hereof was arched over head,
And deck'd with flowers and *herbars* daintily. *Fairy Queen.*

HE'RBARIST. *n. s.* [*herbarius*, from *herba*, Latin.] One skilled in herbs.

Herbarists have exercised a commendable curiosity in subdividing plants of the same denomination. *Boyle.*

He was too much swayed by the opinions then current amongst *herbarists*, that different colours or multiplicity of leaves in the flower were sufficient to constitute a specifick difference. *Ray on the Creation.*

As to the fuci, their seed hath been discovered and shewed me first by an ingenious *herbarist*. *Derham's Phys. Theology.*

HE'RBELET. *n. s.* [Diminutive of *herb*, or of *herbula*, Latin.] A small herb.

Even so
These *herbelets* shall, which we upon you strow. *Shakesp.*

HERBE'SCENT. *adj.* [*herbescens*, Latin.] Growing into herbs.

HE'RBID. *adj.* [*herbidus*, Latin.] Covered with herbs.

HE'RBORIST. *n. s.* [from *herb*.] One curious in herbs. This seems a mistake for *herbarist*.

A curious *herborist* has a plant, whose flower perishes in about an hour. *Ray.*

HE'RBOROUGH. *n. s.* [*herberg*, German.] Place of temporary residence. Now written *harbour*.

The German lord, when he went out of Newgate into the cart, took order to have his arms set up in his last *herborough*; said he was taken and committed upon suspicion of treason, no witness appearing against him. *Ben. Johnson's Discoveries.*

HE'RBOUS. *adj.* [*herbosus*, Latin.] Abounding with herbs.

HE'RBULENT. *adj.* [from *herbula*.] Containing herbs. *Dict.*

HE'RBWOMAN. *n. s.* [*herb* and *woman*.] A woman that sells herbs.

I was like to be pulled to pieces by brewer, butcher, and baker; even my *herbwoman* dunned me as I went along. *Arb.*

HE'RBY. *adj.* [from *herb*.] Having the nature of herbs.

No substance but earth, and the procedures of earth, as tile and stone, yieldeth any moss or *herby* substance. *Bacon.*

HERD. *n. s.* [ƿeoꞃꝺ, Saxon.]

1. A number of beasts together. It is peculiarly applied to black cattle. *Flocks* and *herds* are *sheep* and *oxen* or *kine*.

Note a wild and wanton *herd*,
Or race of youthful and unhandled colts,
Fetching mad bounds. *Shakes. Merchant of Venice.*

There find a *herd* of heifers, wand'ring o'er
The neighbouring hill, and drive them to the shore. *Addison.*

2. A company of men, in contempt or detestation.

Survey the world, and where one Cato shines,
Count a degenerate *herd* of Catilines. *Dryden's Juven.*

I do not remember where ever God delivered his oracles by the multitude, or nature truths by the *herd*. *Locke.*

3. It anciently signified a keeper of cattle, and in Scotland it is still used. [ƿẏꞃꝺ, Saxon,] a sense still retained in composition: as *goatherd*.

To HERD. *v. n.* [from the noun.]

1. To run in herds or companies.

Weak women should, in danger, *herd* like deer. *Dryden.*

It

HERO'ICAL. *adj.* [from *hero.*] Befitting an hero; heroick.
Musidorus was famous over all Asia for his *heroical* enterprizes. *Sidney, b.* ii.
Though you have courage in an *heroical* degree, I ascribe it to you as your second attribute. *Dryden's Fables, Dedic.*

HERO'ICALLY. *adv.* [from *heroical.*] After the way of a hero; suitably to an hero.
Not *heroically* in killing his tyrannical cousin. *Sidney, b.* ii.
Free from all meaning, whether good or bad;
And, in one word, *heroically* mad. *Dryden.*

HERO'ICK. *adj.* [from *hero*; *heroique,* French.]
1. Productive of heroes.
Bolingbroke
From John of Gaunt doth bring his pedigree,
Being but the fourth of that *heroick* line. *Shakesp. Hen.* VI.
2. Noble; suitable to an hero; brave; magnanimous; intrepid; enterprising; illustrious.
Not that which justly gives *heroick* name
To person, or to poem. *Milton's Par. Lost, b.* ix.
Verse makes *heroick* virtue live,
But you can life to verses give. *Waller.*
3. Reciting the acts of heroes.
Methinks *heroick* poesy, 'till now,
Like some fantastick fairy land did show. *Cowley.*
I have chosen the most *heroick* subject which any poet could desire: I have taken upon me to describe the motives, the beginning, progress and successes of a most just and necessary war. *Dryden's Ann. Mirab. Preface.*
An *heroick* poem is the greatest which the soul of man is capable to perform: the design of it is to form the mind to heroick virtue by example. *Dryden.*

HERO'ICKLY. *adv.* [from *heroick.*] Suitably to an hero. *Heroically* is more frequent, and more analogical.
Samson hath quit himself
Like Samson, and *heroickly* hath finish'd
A life heroick. *Milton's Agonistes.*

HE'ROINE. *n. s.* [from *hero*; *heroine,* French.] A female hero. Anciently, according to English analogy, *heroess.*
But inborn worth, that fortune can controul,
New-strung, and stiffer bent her softer soul;
The *heroine* assum'd the woman's place,
Confirm'd her mind, and fortify'd her face. *Dryden.*
Then shall the British stage
More noble characters expose to view,
And draw her finish'd *heroines* from you. *Addison.*

HE'ROISM. *n. s.* [*heroisme,* French.] The qualities or character of an hero.
If the Odyssey be less noble than the Iliad, it is more instructive: the Iliad abounds with more *heroism,* this with more morality. *Broome's Notes to the Odyssey.*

HE'RON. *n. s.* [*heron,* French.]
1. A bird that feeds upon fish.
So lords, with sport of stag and *heron* full,
Sometimes we see small birds from nests do pull. *Sidney.*
The *heron,* when she soareth high, sheweth winds. *Bacon.*
2. It is now commonly pronounced *hern.*
The tow'ring hawk let future poets sing,
Who terror bears upon his soaring wing;
Let them on high the frighted *hern* survey,
And lofty numbers paint their airy fray. *Gay.*

HE'RONRY. } *n. s.* [from *heron*; commonly pronounced *hern-*
HE'RONSHAW. } *ry.*] A place where herons breed.
They carry their load to a large *heronry* above three miles. *Derham's Physico-Thelogy.*

HE'RPES. *n. s.* [ἕρπης.] A cutaneous inflammation of two kinds: *miliaris,* or *pustularis,* which is like millet-feed upon the skin; and *exedens,* which is more corrosive and penetrating, so as to form little ulcers, if not timely taken care of. *Quincy.*
A farther progress towards acrimony maketh a *herpes*; and, if the access of acrimony be very great, it maketh an *herpes exedens.* *Wiseman's Surgery.*

HE'RRING. *n. s.* [*hareng,* French; hæring, Saxon.] A small sea-fish.
The coast is plentifully stored with round fish, pilchard, *herring,* mackrel, and cod. *Carew's Survey of Cornwal.*
Buy my *herring* fresh. *Swift.*

HERS. *pron.* The female possessive used when it refers to a substantive going before: as, this is *her* house, this house is *hers.*
How came her eyes so bright? not with salt tears;
If so, my eyes are oftner wash'd than *hers.* *Shakespeare.*
Whom ill fate would ruin, it prefers;
For all the miserable are made *hers.* *Waller.*
I see her rowling eyes;
And panting, lo! the god, the god, she cries;
With words not *hers,* and more than human sound,
She makes th' obedient ghosts peep trembling through the ground. *Roscommon.*

HERSE. *n. s.* [*hersia,* low Latin; supposed to come from herian, to praise.]
1. A temporary monument raised over a grave.
2. The carriage in which corpses are drawn to the grave.
When mourning nymphs attend their Daphnis' *herse,*
Who does not weep that reads the moving verse? *Roscom.*
Crowds of dead in decent pomp are born;
Their friends attend the *herse,* the next relations mourn. *Dryden's Virgil's Georg. b.* iv.
On all the line a sudden vengeance waits,
And frequent *herses* shall besiege your gates. *Pope.*

To HERSE. *v. a.* [from the noun.] To put into an herse.
I would my daughter were dead at my foot, and the jewels in her ear. O, would she were *hers'd* at my foot, and the ducats in her coffin. *Shakesp. Merchant of Venice.*
The Grecians spritefully drew from the darts the corse,
And *hers'd* it, bearing it to fleet. *Chapman's Iliads.*
The house is *hers'd* about with a black wood,
Which nods with many a heavy-headed tree:
Each flower's a pregnant poison, try'd and good;
Each herb a plague. *Crashaw.*

HERSELF. *pronoun.* The female personal pronoun, in the oblique cases reciprocal.
The jealous o'er-worn widow and *herself,*
Since that our brother dubb'd them gentlewomen,
Are mighty gossips in this monarchy. *Shakesp. Rich.* III.
The more she looks, the more her fears increase,
At nearer sight; and she's *herself* the less. *Dryden.*

HE'RSELIKE. *adj.* [*herse* and *like.*] Funereal; suitable to funerals.
Even in the Old Testament, if you listen to David's harp, you shall hear as many *herselike* airs as carols. *Bacon.*

To HE'RY. *v. a.* [herian, Saxon, to praise, to celebrate.] To hallow; to regard as holy. Now no longer in use.
Thenot, now nis the time of merrymake,
Nor Pan to *hery,* nor with love to play;
Like mirth in May is meetest for to make,
Or Summer shade, under the cocked hay. *Spenser's Past.*
Thenceforth it firmly was established,
And for Apollo's honour highly *heried.* *Fairy Queen.*
But were thy years green as now be mine,
Then wouldst thou learn to carol of love,
And *hery* with hymns thy lass's glove. *Spenser.*

HE'SITANCY. *n. s.* [from *hesitate.*] Dubiousness; uncertainty; suspence.
The reason of my *hesitancy* about the air is, that I forgot to try whether that liquor, which shot into crystals exposed to the air, would not have done the like in a vessel accurately stopped. *Boyle.*
Some of them reasoned without doubt or *hesitancy,* and lived and died in such a manner as to shew that they believed their own reasonings. *Atterbury's Sermons.*

To HE'SITATE. *v. a.* [*hæsito,* Latin; *hesiter,* French.] To be doubtful; to delay; to pause; to make difficulty.
A spirit of revenge makes him curse the Grecians in the seventh book, when they *hesitate* to accept Hector's challenge. *Broome's Notes on the Iliad.*
Willing to wound, and yet afraid to strike,
Just hint a fault, and *hesitate* dislike;
Alike reserv'd to blame or to commend,
A tim'rous foe, and a suspicious friend. *Pope.*

HESITA'TION. *n. s.* [from *hesitate.*]
1. Doubt; uncertainty; difficulty made.
I cannot foresee the difficulties and *hesitations* of every one: they will be more or fewer, according to the capacity of each peruser. *Woodward's Natural History.*
2. Intermission of speech; want of volubility.
Many clergymen write in so diminutive a manner, with such frequent blots and interlineations, that they are hardly able to go on without perpetual *hesitations.* *Swift.*

HEST. *n. s.* [hæst, Saxon.] Command; precept; injunction.
If thou be the most kind preserver
Of living wights, the sovereign lord of all,
How falls it then, that, with thy furious fervour,
Thou dost afflict the not deserver,
As him that doth thy lovely *hests* despise. *Spenser.*
Thou wast a spirit too delicate
To act her earthy and abhorr'd commands,
Refusing her grand *hests.* *Shakespeare's Tempest.*

HE'TEROCLITE. *n. s.* [*heteroclite,* Fr. *heteroclitum,* Latin; ἕτερος and κλίνω.]
1. Such nouns as vary from the common forms of declension, by any redundancy, defect, or otherwise. *Clarke's Lat. Gram.*
The *heteroclite* nouns of the Latin should not be touched in the first learning of the rudiments of the tongue. *Watts.*
2. Any thing or person deviating from the common rule.

HETEROCLI'TICAL. *adj.* [from *heteroclite.*] Deviating from the common rule.
Of sins *heteroclitical,* and such as want either name or president, there is oft times a sin, even in their histories. *Brown's Vulgar Errours.*

HE'TERODOX. *adj.* [*heterodoxe,* French; ἕτερος and δόξα.] Deviating from the established opinion; not orthodox.

Partiality

Partiality may be observed in some to vulgar, in others to *heterodox* tenets. *Locke.*

HE'TERODOX. *n. s.* An opinion peculiar.

Not only a simple *heterodox*, but a very hard paradox it will seem, and of great absurdity, if we say attraction is unjustly appropriated unto the loadstone. *Brown's Vulgar Errours.*

HETEROGE'NEAL. *adj.* [*heterogene*, French; ἕτερος and γένος.] Not of the same nature; not kindred.

Let the body adjacent and ambient be not commaterial, but merely *heterogeneal* towards the body that is to be preserved: such are quicksilver and white amber to herbs and flies. *Bacon's Natural History.*

The light, whose rays are all alike refrangible, I call simple, homogeneal, and similar; and that whose rays are some more refrangible than others, I call compound, *heterogeneal*, and dissimilar. *Newton's Opt.*

HETEROGENE'ITY. *n. s.* [*heterogeneité*, Fr. from *heterogeneous.*]

1. Opposition of nature; contrariety or dissimilitude of qualities.

2. Opposite or dissimilar part.

Guaiacum, burnt with an open fire in a chimney, is sequestered into ashes and soot; whereas the same wood, distilled in a retort, does yield far other *heterogeneities*, and is resolved into oil, spirit, vinegar, water and charcoal. *Boyle.*

HETEROGE'NEOUS. *adj.* [ἕτερος and γένος.] Not kindred; opposite or dissimilar in nature.

I have with great care observed the condition of such *heterogeneous* bodies, which I found immersed and included in the mass of this sandstone. *Woodward.*

HETERO'SCIANS. *n. s.* [ἕτερος and σκία.] Those whose shadows fall only one way, as the shadows of us who live north of the Tropick fall at noon always to the North.

To HEW. *v. a.* part. *hewn* or *hewed*. [heapan, Saxon; *hauwen*, Dutch.]

1. To cut with an edged instrument; to hack.

Upon the joint the lucky steel did light,
And made such way that *hew'd* it quite in twain. *Spenser.*

I had purpose
Once more to *hew* thy target from thy brawn,
Or lose my arm for't. *Shakespeare's Coriolanus.*

He was *hewn* in pieces by Hamilton's friends. *Hayward.*

One Vane was so grievously *hewn*, that many thousands have died of less than half his hurts, whereof he was cured. *Hayw.*

2. To chop; to cut.

Scarce can I speak, my choler is so great:
Oh! I could *hew* up rocks and fight with flint. *Shakesp.*

He from deep wells with engines water drew,
And us'd his noble hands the wood to *hew*. *Dryd. Fables.*

3. To fell, as with an ax.

He that depends
Upon your favours, swims with fins of lead,
And *hews* down oaks with rushes. *Shakesp. Coriolanus.*

Brave followers, yonder stands the thorny wood,
Which, by the heav'n's assistance and your strength,
Must by the roots be *hewn* up yet ere night. *Shakes. H. VI.*

Yet shall the axe of justice *hew* him down,
And level with the root his lofty crown. *Sandys.*

He from the mountain *hewing* timber tall,
Began to build a vessel of huge bulk. *Milton's Parad. Lost.*

We'll force the gate where Marcus keeps his guard,
And *hew* down all that would oppose our passage. *Addison.*

4. To form or shape with an axe.

Thou hast *hewed* thee out a sepulchre here, as he that *hewed* him out a sepulchre on high. *Is.* xxii. 16.

Nor is it so proper to *hew* out religious reformations by the sword, as to polish them by fair and equal disputations. *K. Ch.*

This river rises in the very heart of the Alps, and has a long valley that seems *hewn* out on purpose to give its waters a passage amidst so many rocks. *Addison on Italy.*

Next unto bricks are preferred the square *hewn* stone. *Mort.*

5. To form laboriously.

The gate was adamant; eternal frame!
Which, *hew'd* by Mars himself, from Indian quarries came,
The labour of a god. *Dryden's Fables.*

I now pass my days, not studious nor idle, rather polishing old works than *hewing* out new. *Pope to Swift.*

HE'WER. *n. s.* [from *hew.*] One whose employment is to cut wood or stone.

At the building of Solomon's temple there were fourscore thousand *hewers* in the mountains. *Brown's Vulgar Errours.*

HE'XAGON. *n. s.* [*hexagone*, French; ἓξ and γωνία.] A figure of six sides or angles: the most capacious of all the figures that can be added to each other without any interstice; and therefore the cells in honeycombs are of that form.

HEXA'GONAL. *adj.* [from *hexagon.*] Having six sides or corners.

As for the figures of crystal, it is for the most part *hexagonal*, or six-cornered. *Brown's Vulgar Errours.*

Many of them shoot into regular figures; as crystal and bastard diamonds into *hexagonal*. *Ray on the Creation.*

HEXA'GONY. *n. s.* [from *hexagon.*] A figure of six angles.

When I read in St. Ambrose of *hexagonies*, or sexangular cellars of bees, did I therefore conclude that they were mathematicians? *Bramh against Hobbs.*

HEXA'METER. *n. s.* [ἓξ and μέτρον.] A verse of six feet.

The Latin *hexameter* has more feet than the English heroick. *Dryden.*

HEXA'NGULAR. *adj.* [ἓξ and *angulus*, Latin.] Having six corners.

Hexangular sprigs or shoots of crystal, of various sizes, some clear, and others a little soiled. *Woodward on Fossils.*

HEXA'POD. *n. s.* [ἓξ and πόδες.] An animal with six feet.

I take those to have been the *hexapods*, from which the greater sort of beetles come; for that sort of *hexapods* are eaten in America. *Ray on the Creation.*

HEXA'STICK. *n. s.* [ἓξ and στίχος.] A poem of six lines.

HEY. *interj.* [from *high.*] An expression of joy, or mutual exhortation; the contrary to the Latin *hei.*

Shadwell from the town retires,
To bless the wood with peaceful lyrick;
Then *hey* for praise and panegyrick. *Prior.*

HE'YDAY. *interj.* [for *high day*] An expression of frolick and exultation, and sometimes of wonder.

Thou'lt say anon he is some kin to thee,
Thou spend'st such *heyday* wit in praising him. *Shakespeare.*

'Twas a strange riddle of a lady,
Not love, if any lov'd her, *heyday!* *Hudibras, p.* i.

HE'YDAY. *n. s.* A frolick; wildness.

At your age
The *heyday* in the blood is tame, it's humble,
And waits upon the judgment. *Shakespeare's Hamlet.*

HE'YDEGIVES. *n. s.* A wild frolick dance.

But friendly fairys met with many graces,
And light-foot nymphs can chase the ling'ring night
With *heydegives*, and trimly trodden traces. *Spenser.*

HIA'TION. *n. s.* [from *hio*, Latin.] The act of gaping.

Men observing the continual *hiation*, or holding open its mouth, conceive the intention thereof to receive the aliment of air; but this is also occasioned by the greatness of the lungs. *Brown's Vulgar Errours.*

HIA'TUS. *n. s.* [*hiatus*, Latin.]

1. An aperture; a breach.

Those *hiatus's* are at the bottom of the sea, whereby the abyss below open into and communicates with it. *Woodward.*

2. The opening of the mouth by the succession of an initial to a final vowel.

The *hiatus* should be avoided with more care in poetry than in oratory; and I would try to prevent it, unless where the cutting it off is more prejudicial to the sound than the *hiatus* itself. *Pope.*

HIBE'RNAL. *adj.* [*hibernus*, Latin.] Belonging to the Winter.

This star should rather manifest its warming power in the Winter, when it remains conjoined with the sun in its *hibernal* conversion. *Brown's Vulgar Errours.*

HICCIUS DOCCIUS. n. s. [corrupted, I fancy, from *hic est doctus, this* or *here* is the learned man. Used by jugglers of themselves.] A cant word for a juggler; one that plays fast and loose.

An old dull sot, who told the clock
For many years at Bridewell dock,
At Westminster and Hicks's hall,
And *hiccius doccius* play'd in all;
Where, in all governments and times,
H' had been both friend and foe to crimes. *Hudibras, p.* iii.

HICCO'UGH. *n. s.* [*hicken*, Danish.] A convulsion of the stomach producing sobs.

So by an abbey's skeleton of late
I heard an eccho supererogate
Through imperfection, and the voice restore,
As if she had the *hiccough* o'er and o'er. *Cleaveland.*

Sneezing cureth the *hiccough*, and is profitable unto women in hard labour. *Brown's Vulgar Errours.*

If the stomach be hurt, singultus or *hiccough* follows, with vomiting and nausea. *Wiseman's Surgery.*

To HI'CCOUGH. *v. n.* [from the noun.] To sob with convulsion of the stomach.

To HI'CKUP. *v. n.* [corrupted from *hiccough.*] To sob with a convulsed stomach.

Quoth he, to bid me not to love,
Is to forbid my pulse to move,
My beard to grow, my ears to prick up,
Or, when I'm in a fit, to *hickup*. *Hudibras, p.* ii.

HI'CKWALL. } *n. s.* A bird. *Ainsworth.*
HI'CKWAY. }

HID. } *part. pass.* of *hide.*
HI'DDEN. }

Thus fame shall be atchiev'd, renown on earth;
And what most merits fame, in silence *hid*. *Milton.*

Nature and nature's laws lay *hid* in night;
God said, let Newton be, and all was light. *Pope's Epist.*

To HIDE. *v. a.* preter. *hid*; part. pass. *hid* or *hidden*. [hidan, Saxon.] To conceal; to withold or withdraw from sight or knowledge.

Avaunt, and quit my sight; let the earth *hide* thee! *Shak.*

The plenteous board *high-heap'd* with cates divine,
And o'er the foaming bowl the laughing wine. *Pope.*

2. Raised into high piles.

I saw myself the vast unnumber'd store
Of brass, *high-heap'd* amidst the regal dome. *Pope's Odyssey.*

HIGH-HE'ELED. Having the heel of the shoe much raised.

By these embroider'd *high-heel'd* shoes,
She shall be caught as in a noose. *Swift.*

HI'GH-HUNG. Hung aloft.

By the *high-hung* taper's light,
I could discern his cheeks were glowing red. *Dryden.*

HIGH-ME'TTLED. Proud or ardent of spirit.

He fails not in these to keep a stiff rein on a *high-mettled* Pegasus; and takes care not to surfeit here, as he had done on other heads, by an erroneous abundance. *Garth.*

HIGH-MI'NDED. Proud; arrogant.

My breast I'll burst with straining of my courage,
But I will chastise this *high-minded* strumpet. *Shakes. H.VI.*

Because of unbelief they were broken off, and thou standest by faith: be not *high-minded*, but fear. *Rom.* ii. 20.

HIGH-PRI'NCIPLED. Extravagant in notions of politicks.

This seems to be the political creed of all the *high-principled* men I have met with. *Swift.*

HIGH-RE'D. Deeply red.

Oil of turpentine, though clear as water, being digested upon the purely wh te sugar of lead, has in a short time afforded a *high-red* tincture. *Boyle on Colours.*

HIGH-SE'ASONED. Piquant to the palate.

Be sparing also of salt in the seasoning of all his victuals, and use him not to *high-seasoned* meats. *Locke.*

HIGH-SI'GHTED. Always looking upwards.

Let *high-sighted* tyranny range on,
'Till each man drop by lottery;
But if these countrymen bear fire enough,
What need we any spur but our own cause? *Shakespeare.*

HIGH-SPI'RITED. Bold; daring; insolent.

HIGH-STO'MACHED. Obstinate; lofty.

High-stomach'd are they both, and full of ire;
In rage, deaf as the sea, hasty as fire. *Shakespeare.*

HIGH-TA'STED. Gustful; piquant.

Flatt'ry still in sugar'd words betrays,
And poison in *high-tasted* meats conveys. *Denham.*

HIGH-VI'CED. Enormously wicked.

Be as a planetary plague, when Jove
Will o'er some *high-vic'd* city hang his poison
In the sick air. *Shakespeare's Timon of Athens.*

HI'GH-WROUGHT. Accurately finished; nobly laboured.

Thou triumph'st, victor of the *high-wrought* day,
And the pleas'd dame, soft smiling, lead'st away. *Pope.*

HI'GHLAND. *n. s.* [*high* and *land.*] Mountainous region.

The wond'ring moon
Beholds her brother's steeds beneath her own;
The *highlands* smoak'd, cleft by the piercing rays. *Addison.*

Ladies in the *highlands* of Scotland use this discipline to their children in the midst of Winter, and find that cold water does them no harm. *Locke.*

HIGHLA'NDER. *n. s.* [from *highland.*] An inhabitant of mountains.

His cabinet council of *highlanders.* *Addison.*

HI'GHLY. *adv.* [from *high.*]

1. With elevation as to place and situation.

2. In a great degree.

Whatever expedients can allay those heats, which break us into different factions, cannot but be useful to the publick, and *highly* tend to its safety. *Addison's Freeholder.*

It cannot but be *highly* requisite for us to support and enliven our faith, by dwelling often on the same considerations. *Atterbury's Sermons.*

3. Proudly; arrogantly; ambitiously.

What thou wouldst *highly*,
That thou wouldst holily; wouldst not play false,
And yet wouldst wrongly win. *Shakesp. Macbeth.*

4. With esteem; with estimation.

Every man that is among you, not to think of himself more *highly* than he ought to think. *Rom.* xii. 3.

HI'GHMOST. *adj.* [An irregular word.] Highest; topmost.

Now is the sun upon the *highmost* hill
Of this day's journey; and from nine 'till twelve,
Is three long hours. *Shakesp. Romeo and Juliet.*

HI'GHNESS. *n. s.* [from *high.*]

1. Elevation above the surface.

2. The title of princes, anciently of kings.

Most royal majesty,
I crave no more than that your *highness* offer'd. *Shakespeare.*

How long in vain had nature striv'd to frame
A perfect princess, ere her *highness* came? *Waller.*

Beauty and greatness are eminently joined in your royal *highness.* *Dryden.*

3. Dignity of nature; supremacy.

Destruct[illegible]n from God was a terrour to me, and by reason of his *high*[illegible] I could not endure. *Job* xxxi. 23.

HIGHT. [Th[illegible] is an imperfect verb, used only in the preterite tense with a passive signification: hatan, to call, Saxon; *heissen*, to be called, German.]

1. Was named; was called.

The city of the great king *hight* it well,
Wherein eternal peace and happiness doth dwell. *Fa. Queen.*

Within this homestead liv'd, without a peer
For crowing loud, the noble Chanticleer,
So *hight* her cock. *Dryden's Nun's Priest.*

2. It is sometimes used as a participle passive, and signifies called; named. It is now obsolete, except in burlesque writings.

Amongst the rest a good old woman was,
Hight mother Hubberd. *Hubberd's Tale.*

HIGHWA'TER. *n. s.* [*high* and *water.*] The utmost flow of the tide.

They have a good way in Essex of draining of lands that lie below the *highwater*, and that are something above the lowwater mark. *Mortimer's Husbandry.*

HIGHWA'Y. *n. s.* [*high* and *way.*] Great road; publick path.

So few there be
That chuse the narrow path, or seek the right:
All keep the broad *highway*, and take delight
With many rather for to go astray. *Fairy Queen, b.* i.

Two inscriptions give a great light to the histories of Appius, who made the *highway*, and of Fabius the dictator. *Addison.*

Ent'ring on a broad *highway*,
Where power and titles scatter'd lay,
He strove to pick up all he found. *Swift.*

I could mention more trades we have lost, and are in the *highway* to lose. *Child on Trade.*

HI'GHWAYMAN. *n. s.* [*highway* and *man.*] A robber that plunders on the publick roads.

'Tis like the friendship of pickpockets and *highwaymen*, that observe strict justice among themselves. *Bentley's Sermons.*

A remedy like that of giving my money to an *highwayman* before he attempts to take it by force, to prevent the sin of robbery. *Swift.*

HI'GLAPER. *n. s.* An herb. *Ainsworth.*

HILA'RITY. *n. s.* [*hilaritas*, Latin] Merriment; gayety.

Averroes restrained his *hilarity*, and made no more thereof than Seneca commendeth, and was allowable in Cato; that is, a sober incalescence from wine. *Brown's Vulgar Errours.*

HILD, in *Ælrick*'s grammar, is interpreted a lord or lady: so *Hildebert* is a noble lord; *Mahtild*, an heroick lady; and in the same sense is *Wiga* also found. *Gib. Camden.*

HI'LDING. *n. s.* [hild, Saxon, signifies a lord: perhaps *hilding* means originally a *little lord* in contempt, for a man that has only the delicacy or bad qualities of high rank; or a term of reproach abbreviated from *hinderling*, degenerate. *Hughes's Spens.*]

1. A sorry, paltry, cowardly fellow.

He was some *hilding* fellow, that had stol'n
The horse he rode on. *Shakespeare's Henry* IV. *p.* i.

If your lordship find him not a *hilding*, hold me no more in your respect. *Shakes. All's well that ends well.*

You are curb'd from that enlargement by
The consequence o' th' crown, and must not foil
The precious note of it with a base slave,
A *hilding* for a livery, a squire's cloth. *Shak. Cymbeline.*

This idle toy, this *hilding* scorns my power,
And sets us all at naught. *Rowe's Jane Shore.*

2. It is used likewise for a mean woman.

Laura, to his lady, was but a kitchen wench;
Helen and Hero, *hildings* and harlots. *Shak. Rom. and Jul.*

HILL. *n. s.* [hil, Saxon.] An elevation of ground less than a mountain.

My sheep are thoughts, which I both guide and serve;
Their pasture is fair *hills* of fruitless love. *Sidney, b.* ii.

Jerusalem is seated on two *hills*,
Of height unlike, and turned side to side. *Fairfax.*

Three sides are sure imbar'd with crags and *hills*,
The rest is easy, scant to rise espy'd;
But mighty bulkwarks fence the plainer part:
So art helps nature, nature strengtheneth art. *Fairfax, b.* iii.

When our eye some prospect would pursue,
Descending from a *hill*, looks round to view. *Granville.*

A *hill* is nothing but the nest of some metal or mineral, which, by a plastick virtue, and the efficacy of subterranean fires, converting the adjacent earths into their substance, do increase and grow. *Cheyne's Phil. Princ.*

HI'LLOCK. *n. s.* [from *hill.*] A little hill.

Yet weigh this, alas! great is not great to the greater:
What, judge you, doth a *hillock* show by the lofty Olympus!
Sidney, b. i.

Sometime walking not unseen
By hedge-row elms, on *hillocks* green. *Milton.*

This mountain, and a few neighbouring *hillocks* that lie scattered about the bottom of it, is the whole circuit of these dominions. *Addison on Italy.*

HI'LLY. *adj.* [from *hill.*] Full of hills; unequal in the surface.

Towards the *hilly* corners of Druina remain yet her very Aborigenes, fatally thrust amongst an assembly of mountains. *Howel's Vocal Forrest.*

Climbing to a *hilly* steep,
He views his herds in vales afar. *Dryden.*

Lo! how the Norick plains
Rise *hilly*, with large piles of slaughter'd knights. *Phillips.*

Hilly countries afford the most entertaining prospects, tho' aman would chuse to travel through a plain one. *Addison.*

HILT. *n. s.* [hilt, Saxon, from healdan, to hold.] The handle of any thing, particularly of a sword.

Now sits expectation in the air,
And hides a sword from *hilt* unto the point,
With crowns imperial; crowns and coronets,
Promis'd to Harry and his followers. *Shakesp. Henry* V.

Take thou the *hilt*,
And when my face is cover'd, as 'tis now,
Guide thou the sword. *Shakespeare's Julius Cæsar.*

Be his this sword, whose blade of brass displays
A ruddy gleam; whose *hilt*, a silver blaze. *Pope's Odyssey.*

HIM. [him, Saxon.]

1. The oblique case of *he*.

Me he restored unto my office, and *him* he hanged. *Gen.* xli.

2 *Him* was anciently used for *it* in a neutral sense.

HI'MSELF. *pron.* [*him* and *self*.]

1. In the nominative the same as *he*, only more emphatical.

It was a sparing speech of the ancients to say, that a friend is another *himself*; for that a friend is far more than *himself*. *Bacon.*

With shame remembers, while *himself* was one
Of the same herd, *himself* the same had done. *Denham.*

2. In ancient authors it is used neutrally for *itself*.

She is advanc'd
Above the clouds as high as heav'n *himself*. *Shakespeare.*

3. In the oblique cases it has a reciprocal signification.

I perceive it was not altogether your brother's evil disposition made him seek his death; but a provoking merit, set awork by a reproveable badness in *himself*. *Shakesp. K. Lear.*

4. It is sometimes not reciprocal.

Nothing in nature can so peculiarly gratify the noble dispositions of humanity, as for one man to see another so much *himself* as to sigh his griefs, and groan his pains, to sing his joys, and do and feel every thing by sympathy. *South.*

HIN. *n. s.* [הין] A measure of liquids among Jews, containing about ten pints.

With the one lamb a tenth deal of flour, mingled with the fourth part of an *hin* of beaten oil. *Ex.* xxix. 40.

HIND. *adj.* compar. *hinder*; superl. *hindmost*. [hyndan, Saxon.] Backward; contrary in position to the face: as, *hind* legs. See HINDER and HINDMOST.

Bringing its tail to its head, it bends its back so far 'till its head comes to touch its *hind* part, and so with its armour gathers itself into a ball. *Ray on the Creation.*

The stag
Hears his own feet, and thinks they sound like more,
And fears his *hind* legs will o'ertake his fore. *Pope.*

HIND. *n. s.* [hinde, Saxon, from *hinnus*, Latin.]

1. The she to a stag; the female of red deer.

How he slew, with glancing dart amiss,
A gentle *hind*, the which the lovely boy
Did love as life. *Fairy Queen, b.* i.

Can'st thou mark when the *hinds* do calve? *Job* xxxix. 1.

Nor Hercules more lands or labours knew,
Not though the brazen-footed *hind* he slew. *Dryden's Æn.*

2. [hine, Saxon.] A servant.

A couple of Ford's knaves, his *hinds*, were called forth by their mistress, to carry me in the name of foul cloaths to Datchet-lane. *Shakespeare's Merry Wives of Windsor.*

3. [hineman, Saxon.] A peasant; a boor; a mean rustick.

The Dutch, who came like greedy *hinds* before,
To reap the harvest their ripe ears did yield,
Now look like those, when rolling thunders roar,
And sheets of lightning blast the standing field. *Dryden.*

He cloth'd himself in coarse array,
A lab'ring *hind* in shew. *Dryden's Fables.*

HINDBE'RRIES. *n. s.* The same as raspberries. *Ainsworth.*

To HI'NDER. *v. a.* [hindrian, Saxon.] To obstruct; to stop; to let; to impede.

Hinder me not, seeing the Lord hath prospered my way. *Gen.* xxiv. 56.

The whole world shined with clear light, and none were *hindered* in their labour. *Wisd.* xvii. 20.

You minimus of *hindring* knot-grass made;
You bead, you acorn. *Shakespeare's Midſ. Night's Dream.*

If the alms were *hindered* only by intreaty, the hinderer is not tied to restitution, because intreaty took not liberty away from the giver. *Taylor's Rule of living holy.*

This objection *hinders* not but that the heroick action of some commander, enterprised for the Christian cause, and executed happily, may be written. *Dryden's Juv. Dedicat.*

What *hinders* younger brothers, being fathers of families, from having the same right? *Locke.*

HI'NDER. *adj.* [from *hind*.] That which is in a position contrary to that of the face.

These beasts, fighting with any man, stand upon their *hinder* feet, and so this did, being ready to give me a shrewd embracement. *Sidney, b.* i.

As the *hinder* feet of the horse stuck to the mountain, while the body reared up in the air, the poet with great difficulty kept himself from sliding off his back. *Addison's Guardian.*

HI'NDERANCE. *n. s.* [from *hinder*.] Impediment; let; stop; obstruction.

False opinions, touching the will of God to have things done, are wont to bring forth mighty and violent practices against the *hinderances* of them, and those practices new opinions more pernicious than the first; yea, most extremely sometimes opposite to the first. *Hooker, Preface.*

They must be in every Christian church the same, except mere impossibility of so having it be the *hinderance*. *Hooker.*

What *hinderance* have they been to the knowledge of what is well done? *Dryden's Dufresnoy.*

Have we not plighted each our holy oath,
One soul should both inspire, and neither prove
His fellow's *hind'rance* in pursuit of love? *Dryden.*

He must conquer all these difficulties, and remove all these *hinderances* out of the way that leads to justice. *Atterbury.*

HI'NDERER. *n. s.* [from *hinder*.] He or that which hinders or obstructs.

Brakes, great *hinderers* of all plowing, grow. *May.*

HI'NDERLING. *n. s.* [from *hind* or *hinder*.] A paltry, worthless, degenerate animal.

HI'NDERMOST. *adj.* [This word seems to be less proper than *hindmost*.] Hindmost; last; in the rear.

He put the handmaids and their children foremost, and Leah and her children after, and Rachel and Joseph *hindermost*. *Gen.*

Like to an enter'd tide, they all rush by,
And leave you *hindermost*. *Shakesp. Troilus and Cressida.*

HI'NDMOST. *adj.* [*hind* and *most*.] The last; the lag; that which comes in the rear.

'Tis not his wont to be the *hindmost* man,
Whate'er occasion keeps him from us now. *Shakesp. H.* VI.

He met thee by the way, and smote the *hindmost* of thee, even all that were feeble behind. *Deutr.* xxv. 18.

Let him retire, betwixt two ages cast,
The first of this, and *hindmost* of the last,
A losing gamester. *Dryden's Aurengz. Prologue.*

The race by vigour, not by vaunts is won;
So take the *hindmost*, hell—he said, and run. *Pope.*

HINGE. *n. s.* [or *hingle*, from *hangle* or *hang*.]

1. Joints upon which a gate or door turns.

At the gate
Of heav'n arriv'd, the gate self-open'd wide,
On golden *hinges* turning. *Milton's Paradise Lost, b.* v.

Then from the *hinge* their strokes the gates divorce,
And where the way they cannot find, they force. *Denham.*

Heav'n's imperious queen shot down from high;
At her approach the brazen *hinges* fly,
The gates are forc'd. *Dryden's Æn.*

2. The cardinal points of the world, East, West, North, and South.

If when the moon is in the *hinge* at East,
The birth breaks forward from its native rest;
Full eighty years, if you two years abate,
This station gives. *Creech's Manilius.*

And these being *hinges* of the world, create
New powers in stars. *Creech's Manilius.*

3. A governing rule or principle.

The other *hinge* of punishment might turn upon a law, whereby all men, who did not marry by the age of five and twenty, should pay the third part of their revenue. *Temple.*

4. *To be off the* HINGES. To be in a state of irregularity and disorder.

The man's spirit is out of order and *off the hinges*; and 'till that be put into its right frame, he will be perpetually disquieted. *Tillotson, Sermon* 4.

To HINGE. *v. a.* [from the noun.]

1. To furnish with hinges.

2. To bend as an hinge.

Be thou a flatt'rer now, and *hinge* thy knee;
And let his very breath, whom thou'lt observe,
Blow off thy cap. *Shakes. Timon of Athens.*

To HINT. *v. a.* [*enter*, French. *Skinner.*] To bring to mind by a slight mention or remote allusion; to mention imperfectly.

Willing to wound, and yet afraid to strike,
Just *hint* a fault, and hesitate dislike. *Pope.*

In waking whispers, and repeated dreams,
To *hint* pure thought, and warn the favour'd soul. *Thomson.*

To HINT. *at.* To allude to; to touch slightly upon.

Speaking of Augustus's actions, he still remembers that agriculture ought to be some way *hinted* at throughout the whole poem. *Addison on the Georgicks.*

HINT. *n. s.* [from the verb.]

1. Faint notice given to the mind; remote allusion; distant insinuation.

But thou bring'ſt valour too and wit,
Two things that ſeldom fail to *hit*. *Hudibras, p.* i.

This may *hit*, 'tis more than barely poſſible; for friars have free admittance into every houſe. *Dryden's Spaniſh Fryar.*

All human race would fain be wits,
And millions miſs for one that *hits*. *Swift.*

4. To light on.

You've *hit* upon the very ſtring, which touch'd,
Echoes the ſound, and jars within my ſoul;
There lies my grief. *Dryden's Spaniſh Fryar.*

It is much, if men were from eternity, that they ſhould not find out the way of writing before that time: ſure he was a fortunate man, who, after men had been eternally ſo dull as not to find it out, had the luck at laſt to *hit* upon it. *Tillotſon's Sermons.*

There's a juſt medium betwixt eating too much and too little; and this dame had *hit* upon't, when the matter was ſo ordered that the hen brought her every day an egg. *L'Eſtr.*

None of them *hit* upon the art. *Addiſon's Guardian.*

There's but a true and a falſe prediction in any telling of fortune; and a man that never *hits* on the right ſide, cannot be called a bad gueſſer, but muſt miſs out of deſign. *Bentley.*

Hit. *n. ſ.* [from the verb.]

1. A ſtroke.

The king hath laid, that in a dozen paſſes between you and him, he ſhall not exceed you three *hits*. *Shakeſ. Hamlet.*

So he the fam'd Cilician fencer prais'd,
And at each *hit* with wonder ſeem'd amaz'd. *Dryd. Juven.*

2. A lucky chance.

Have all his ventures fail'd? What, not one *hit*? *Shak.*

To ſuppoſe a watch, by the blind *hits* of chance, to perform diverſity of orderly motions, without the regulation of art, this were the more pardonable abſurdity. *Glanville.*

If the rule we judge by be uncertain, it is odds but we ſhall judge wrong; and if we ſhould judge right, yet it is not properly ſkill, but chance; not a true judgment, but a lucky *hit*. *South's Sermons.*

But with more lucky *hit* than thoſe
That uſe to make the ſtars depoſe. *Hudibras, p.* i.

The fiſherman's waiting, and the lucky *hit* it had in the concluſion, tells us, that honeſt endeavours will not fail. *L'Eſt.*

Theſe *hits* of words a true poet often finds, without ſeeking. *Dryden's Dufreſnoy.*

If caſual concourſe did the world compoſe,
And things and *hits* fortuitous aroſe,
Then any thing might come from any thing;
For how from chance can conſtant order ſpring? *Blackmore.*

If at firſt he minds his *hits*,
And drinks champaigne among the wits,
Five deep he toaſts the tow'ring laſſes. *Prior.*

To Hitch. *v. n.* [hiegan, Saxon, or *hocher*, French. *Skinner.*] To catch; to move by jerks. I know not where it is uſed but in the following paſſage.

Whoe'er offends, at ſome unlucky time
Slides in a verſe, or *hitches* in a rhyme;
Sacred to ridicule his whole life long,
And the ſad burthen of ſome merry ſong. *Pope's Horace.*

To Hi'tchel. *v. a.* [See Hatchel.] To beat or comb flax or hemp.

Hi'tchel. *n. ſ.* [*heckel*, German.] The inſtrument with which flax is beaten or combed.

Hithe. *n. ſ.* [hyðe, Saxon.] A ſmall haven to land wares out of veſſels or boats: as *Queenhithe*, and *Lambhithe*, now *Lambeth*.

HI'THER. *adv.* [hiðer, Saxon.]

1. To this place from ſome other.

Cæſar, tempted with the fame
Of this ſweet iſland, never conquered,
And envying the Britons blazed name,
O hideous hunger of dominion, *hither* came. *Fairy Queen.*

Men muſt endure
Their going hence, even as their coming *hither*. *Shakeſp.*

Who brought me *hither*
Will bring me hence, no other guide I ſeek. *Parad. Reg.*

2. It is uſed in oppoſition: *hither* and *thither*, to this place and that.

3. To this end; to this deſign; to this topick of argument: [*huc*, Latin. *Huc refer exitum.*]

Hereupon dependeth whatſoever difference there is between the ſtates of ſaints in glory; *hither* we refer whatſoever belongeth unto the higheſt perfection of man, by way of ſervice towards God. *Hooker, b.* ii. *ſ.* 8.

Hither belong all thoſe texts, which require of us that we ſhould not walk after the fleſh, but after the ſpirit. *Tillotſon.*

Hi'ther. *adj.* ſuperl. *hithermoſt.* Nearer; towards this part.

After theſe,
But on the *hither* ſide, a different ſort,
From the high neighb'ring hills deſcended. *Milton's P. Loſt.*

An eternal duration may be ſhorter or longer upon the *hither* end thereof, namely, that extreme wherein it is finite. *Hale's Origin of Mankind.*

Hi'thermost. *adj.* [of *hither*, adv.] Neareſt on this ſide.

That which is eternal cannot be extended to a greater extent at the *hithermoſt* and concluding extreme. *Hale.*

Hi'therto. *adv.* [from *hither.*]

1. To this time; yet; in any time till now.

More ample ſpirit than *hitherto* was wont,
Here needs me, whiles the famous anceſtries
Of my moſt dreadful ſovereign I recount. *Fairy Queen.*

Hitherto I have only told the reader what ought not to be the ſubject of a picture or of a poem. *Dryden's Dufreſnoy.*

2. At every time till now.

In this we are not their adverſaries, tho' they in the other *hitherto* have been ours. *Hooker, b.* v. *ſ.* 22.

Hitherto, lords, what your commands impos'd
I have perform'd, as reaſon was, obeying. *Milton's Agoniſt.*

Hitherto ſhe kept her love conceal'd,
And with thoſe graces ev'ry day beheld
The graceful youth. *Dryden's Fables.*

He could not have failed to add the oppoſition of ill ſpirits to the good: they have alſo their deſign ever oppoſite to that of heaven, and this alone has *hitherto* been the practice of the moderns. *Dryden's Juven. Dedication.*

We ought to ſtruggle with thoſe natural diſadvantages, and be careful whom we employ, whenever we deſign to correct them, which is a work that has *hitherto* been aſſumed by the leaſt qualified hands. *Swift.*

Hi'therward. } *adv.* [hyðerpeard, Saxon.] This way;
Hi'therwards. } towards this place.

Some parcels of their power are forth already,
And only *hitherward*. *Shakeſpeare's Coriolanus.*

The king himſelf in perſon hath ſet forth,
Or *hitherwards* intended ſpeedily,
With ſtrong and mighty preparation. *Shakeſp. Henry* IV.

A puiſſant and mighty pow'r
Of gallow-glaſſes and ſtout kernes,
Is marching *hitherward* in proud array. *Shakeſ. Henry* VI.

Look now for no enchanting voice, nor fear
The bait of honey'd words; a rougher tongue
Draws *hitherward*. *Milton's Agoniſtes.*

HIVE. *n. ſ.* [hyfe, Saxon.]

1. The habitation or cell of bees.

So bees with ſmoke, and doves with noiſome ſtench,
Are from their *hives* and houſes driv'n away. *Shakeſ. H.* VI.

So wand'ring bees would periſh in the air,
Did not a ſound, proportion'd to their ear,
Appeaſe their rage, invite them to the *hive*. *Waller.*

Bees, of which we are told ſo many wonderful things, have each of them a hole in their *hives*: their honey is their own, and every bee minds her own concerns. *Addiſon's Guardian.*

2. The bees inhabiting a hive.

The commons, like an angry *hive* of bees
That want their leader, ſcatter up and down. *Shak. H.* VI.

3. A company being together.

What modern maſons call a lodge was by antiquity called a *hive* of free maſons; and therefore, when a diſſention happens, the going off is to this day called ſwarming. *Swift.*

To Hive. *v. a.* [from the noun.]

1. To put into hives; to harbour.

Mr. Addiſon of Oxford has been troubleſome to me: after his bees, my latter ſwarm is ſcarcely worth *hiving*. *Dryden.*

When they are fully ſettled, and the cluſter at the biggeſt, *hive* them. *Mortimer's Husbandry.*

2. To contain in hives.

Ambitious now to take exciſe
Of a more fragrant paradiſe,
He at Fuſcara's ſleeve arriv'd,
Where all delicious ſweets are *hiv'd*. *Cleaveland.*

To Hive. *v. n.* To take ſhelter together.

He ſleeps by day
More than the wild cat: drones *hive* not with me,
Therefore I part with him. *Shakeſp. Merchant of Venice.*

In Summer we wander in a paradiſaical ſcene, among groves and gardens; but at this ſeaſon we get into warmer houſes, and *hive* together in cities. *Pope's Letters.*

Hi'ver. *n. ſ.* [from *hive.*] One who puts bees in hives.

Let the *hiver* drink a cup of good beer, and waſh his hands and face therewith. *Mortimer's Husbandry.*

Ho. } *interj.* [*eho!* Latin.] A call; a ſudden exclamation to
Hoa. } give notice of approach, or any thing elſe.

What noiſe there, *ho?* *Shakeſpeare.*
Here dwells my father Jew: *hoa*, who's within? *Shakeſ.*
Stand, *ho!* ſpeak the word along. *Shakeſ. Julius Cæſar.*

When I cried *hoa!*
Like boys, kings would ſtart forth, and cry,
Your will. *Shakeſpeare.*

Ho, ho, come forth and flee. *Zech.* ii. 6.

Ho, ſwain, what ſhepherd owns theſe ragged ſheep? *Dry.*

HOAR. *adj.* [har, Saxon.]

1. White.

A people,
Whom Ireland ſent from loughs and forreſts *hore*. *Fairfax.*

Iſland

Island of bliss, all assaults
Baffling, like thy *hoar* cliffs the loud sea-wave. *Thomson.*

2. Grey with age.
It govern'd was and guided evermore
Through wisdom of a matron grave and *hoar*. *Fai. Queen.*
Now swarms the populace, a countless throng;
Youth and *hoar* age, and man drives man along. *Pope.*

3. White with frost.

HOAR-FROST. *n. s.* [*hoar* and *frost.*] The congelations of dew in frosty mornings on the grass.

When the dew was gone up, behold upon the face of the wilderness there lay a small round thing, as small as the *hoar-frost* on the ground. *Ex.* xvi. 14.

In Farenheit's thermometer, at thirty-two degrees, the water in the air begins to freeze, which is known by *hoar-frosts.* *Arbuthnot on Air.*

HOARD. *n. s.* [hoꞃd, Saxon.] A store laid up in secret; a hidden stock; a treasure.

I have a venturous fairy, that shall seek
The squirrel's *hoard*, and fetch thee thence new nuts. *Shak.*

They might have even starved, had it not been for this providential reserve, this *hoard*, that was stowed in the strata underneath, and now seasonably disclosed. *Woodw. Nat. History.*

To HOARD. *v. n.* To make hoards; to lay up store.
He fear'd not once himself to be in need,
Nor car'd to *hoard* for those whom he did breed. *Fa. Queen.*
Happy always was it for that son,
Whose father for his *hoarding* went to hell? *Shak. Hen.* VI.

To HOARD. *v. a.* To lay in hoards; to husband privily; to store secretly.

The *hoarded* plague of the gods requite your love? *Shak.*

I have just occasion to complain of them, who, because they understand Chaucer, would *hoard* him up as misers do their grandam gold, only to look on it themselves, and hinder others from making use of it. *Dryd. Fab. Preface.*

You *hoard* not health for your own private use,
But on the publick spend the rich produce. *Dryden's Fables.*
The base wretch, who *hoards* up all he can,
Is prais'd, and call'd a careful thrifty man. *Dryden's Juven.*

You will be unsuccessful, if you give out of a great man, who is remarkable for his frugality for the publick, that he squanders away the nation's money; but you may safely relate that he *hoards* it. *Arbuthnot's Art of political Lying.*

A superfluous abundance tempts us to forget God, when it is *hoarded* in our treasures, or considered as a safe, independent provision laid up for many years. *Rogers, Sermon* 2.

HOA'RDER. *n. s.* [from *hoard.*] One that stores up in secret.

Since commodities will be raised, this alteration will be an advantage to nobody but *hoarders* of money. *Locke.*

HO'ARHOUND. *n. s.* [*marrubium*, Latin.] A plant.

It is a verticillate plant with a lip flower, consisting of one leaf, whose upper lip or crest is upright, with two horns; but the under lip or beard is divided into three parts: the pointal is fixed to the hinder part of the flower, and attended by four embryoes, which become so many oblong seeds, inclosed in the flower-cup. *Miller.*

Hoarhound has its leaves and flower-cup covered very thick with a white hoariness: it is famous for the relief it gives in moist asthmas, and in all diseases of the breast and lungs, of which a thick and viscous matter is the cause; but it is now little used. *Hill's Mat. Med.*

HO'ARINESS. *n. s.* [from *hoary.*] The state of being whitish; the colour of old mens hair.
He grows a wolf, his *hoariness* remains,
And the same rage in other members reigns. *Dryden.*

HOARSE. *adj.* [haꞃ, Saxon; *heersch*, Dutch.] Having the voice rough, as with a cold; having a rough sound.

Come, sit, sit, and a song.
——Clap into't roundly, without hawking or spitting, or saying we are *hoarse.* *Shakespeare's As you like it.*

The raven himself is *hoarse*,
That crokes the fatal entrance of Duncan
Under my battlements. *Shakespeare's Macbeth.*
He sped his steps along the *hoarse* resounding shore. *Dry.*
The stock-dove only through the forest cooes,
Mournfully *hoarse.* *Thomson's Summer.*

HO'ARSELY. *adv.* [from *hoarse.*] With a rough harsh voice.
The hounds at nearer distance *hoarsely* bay'd;
The hunter close pursu'd the visionary maid. *Dryden.*

HO'ARSENESS. *n. s.* [from *hoarse.*] Roughness of voice.

The voice is sometimes intercluded by an *hoarseness*, or viscuous phlegm. *Holder.*

She sings them back in my despight!
I had a voice in heav'n, ere sulph'rous steams
Had damp'd it to a *hoarseness.* *Dryden's King Arthur.*

The want of it in the wind-pipe occasions *hoarseness* in the gullet, and difficulty of swallowing. *Arbuthnot on Aliments.*

HO'ARY. *adj.* [haꞃ, haꞃunᵹ, Saxon. See HOAR.]

1. White; whitish.
Thus she rested on her arm reclin'd,
The *hoary* willows waving with the wind. *Addison.*

2. White or grey with age.
A comely palmer, clad in black attire,
Of ripest years, and hairs all *hoary* grey. *Spenser.*

Solyman, marvelling at the courage and majesty of the *hoary* old prince in his so great extremity, dismissed him, and sent him again into the city. *Knolles's History of the Turks.*

Has then my *hoary* head deserv'd no better? *Rowe.*
Then in full age, and *hoary* holiness,
Retire, great preacher, to thy promis'd bliss. *Prior.*

3. White with frost.
Through this distemperature we see
The seasons alter; *hoary* headed frosts
Fall in the fresh lap of the crimson rose. *Shakespeare.*

4. Mouldy; mossy; rusty.

There was brought out of the city into the camp very coarse, *hoary*, moulded bread. *Knolles's History of the Turks.*

HO'BNOB. This is probably corrupted from *hab nab* by a coarse pronunciation. See HAB NAB.

His incensement at this moment is so implacable, that satisfaction can be none, but pangs of death and sepulchre: *hobnob* is his word; give't, or take't. *Shakes. Twelfth Night.*

To HO'BBLE. *v. n.* [to *hop*, to *hopple*, to *hobble.*]

1. To walk lamely or awkwardly upon one leg more than the other; to hitch.

The friar was *hobbling* the same way too, accidentally again. *Dryden's Spanish Fryar.*

Some persons continued a kind of *hobbling* march on the broken arches, but fell through. *Addison's Spectator.*

Was he ever able to walk without leading-strings, without being discovered by his *hobbling.* *Swift.*

2. To move roughly or unevenly. Feet being ascribed to verses, whatever is done with feet is likewise ascribed to them.

Those ancient Romans had a sort of extempore poetry, or untuneable *hobbling* verse. *Dryden.*

While you Pindarick truths rehearse,
She *hobbles* in alternate verse. *Prior.*

HO'BBLE. *n. s.* [from the verb.] Uneven awkward gait.

One of his heels is higher than the other, which gives him a *hobble* in his gait. *Gulliver's Travels.*

HO'BBLER. *n. s.* [from *hobby.*]

For twenty *hobblers* armed, the Irishmen were so called, because they served on hobbies, he paid six-pence a-piece *per diem.* *Davies on Ireland.*

HO'BBLINGLY. *adv.* [from *hobble.*] Clumsily; aukwardly; with a halting gait.

HO'BBY. *n. s.* [*hobereau*, French.]

1. A species of hawk.

They have such a hovering possession of the Valtoline, as an *hobby* hath over a lark. *Bacon.*

The common people will chop like trouts at an artificial fly, and dare like larks under the awe of a painted *hobby.* *L'Estrange's Fables.*

Larks lie dar'd to shun the *hobby*'s flight. *Dryden.*

2. [*Hoppe*, Gothick, a horse; *hobin*, French, a pacing horse.] An Irish or Scottish horse; a pacing horse; a garran.

3. A stick on which boys get astride and ride.

Those grave contenders about opiniative trifles look like aged Socrates upon his boy's *hobby* horse. *Glanv. Sceps. c.* 27.

As young children, who are try'd in
Go-carts, to keep their steps from sliding,
When members knit, and legs grow stronger,
Make use of such machine no longer;
But leap *pro libitu*, and scout
On horse call'd *hobby*, or without. *Prior.*
No *hobby* horse, with gorgeous top,
Could with this rod of Sid compare. *Swift.*

4. A stupid fellow.

I have studied eight or nine wise words to speak to you, which these *hobby* horses must not hear. *Shakespeare.*

HOBGO'BLIN. *n. s.* [according to *Skinner*, for *robgoblins*, from *Robin Goodfellow*, *Hob* being the nickname of *Robin*: but more probably, according to *Wallis* and *Junius*, *hopgoblins empusæ*, because they do not move their feet: whence, says *Wallis*, came the boys play of *fox in the hole*, the fox always hopping on one leg.

Fairies, black, grey, green, and white,
Attend your office and your quality:
Crier *hobgoblin*, make the fairy o-yes. *Shakespeare.*

HO'BIT. *n. s.* A small mortar to shoot little bombs.

HO'BNAIL. *n. s.* [from *hobby* and *nail.*] A nail used in shoing a hobby or little horse; a nail with a thick strong head.

Steel, if thou turn thine edge, or cut not out the burly-bon'd clown in chines of beef, ere thou sleep in thy sheath, I beseech Jove on my knees thou may'st be turn'd into *hobnails.* *Shakespeare's Henry* VI. *p.* iii.

We shall buy maidens as they buy *hobnails*, by the hundred. *Shakespeare's Henry* IV. *p.* i.

HO'BNAILED. *adj.* [from *hobnail*] Set with hobnails.
Would'st thou, friend, who hast two legs alone,
Would'st thou, to run the gantlet, these expose
To a whole company of *hobnail'd* shoes? *Dryden's Juvenal.*

HOCK.

HOCK. *n. s.* [The same with *hough*; hoh, Saxon.] The joint between the knee and the fetlock.

To HOCK. *v. a.* [from the noun.] To disable in the hock.

HOCK. } *n. s.* [from *Hockheim* on the *Maine.*] Old
HO'CKAMORE. } strong Rhenish.

Restor'd the fainting high and mighty,
With brandy, wine, and *aqua vitæ*;
And made 'em stoutly overcome
With bachrach, *hockamore* and mum. *Hudibras, p.* iii.

Wine becomes sharp, as in *hock*, like the vitriolick acidity. *Floyer on the Humours.*

If cyder-royal should become unpleasant, and as unfit to bottle as old *hockamore*, mix one hogshead of that and one of tart new cyder together. *Mortimer's Husbandry.*

HO'CKHERB. *n. s.* [*hock* and *herb.*] A plant; the same with mallows. *Ainsworth.*

To HO'CKLE. *v. a.* [from *hock.*] To hamstring; to cut the sinews about the ham or hough. *Hanmer.*

HOCUS POCUS. [The original of this word is referred by *Tillotson* to a form of the Romish church. *Junius* derives it from *hocced*, Welsh, a cheat, and *poke* or *pocus*, a bag, jugglers using a bag for conveyance. It is corrupted from some words that had once a meaning, and which perhaps cannot be discovered.] A juggle; a cheat.

This gift of *hocus pocussing*, and of disguising matters, is surprising. *L'Estrange.*

HOD. *n. s.* [corrupted perhaps in contempt from *hood*, a hod being carried on the head.] A kind of trough in which a labourer carries mortar to the masons.

A fork and a hook to be tampering in clay,
A lath, hammer, trowel, a *hod* or a tray. *Tuss. Husband.*

HO'DMAN. *n. s.* [*hod* and *man.*] A labourer that carries mortar.

HODMANDO'D. *n. s.* A fish.

Those that cast their shell are the lobster, the crab, the crawfish, and the *hodmandod* or dodman. *Bacon's Nat. History.*

HODGE-PODGE. *n. s.* [*haché poché*, *hochepot*, quasi *hachis en pot*, French.] A medley of ingredients boiled together.

They have made our English tongue a gallimaufrey, or *hodge-podge* of all other speeches. *Spenser.*

It produces excellent corn, whereof the Turks make their trachana and bouhourt, a certain *hodge-podge* of sundry ingredients. *Sandys's Travels.*

HODIE'RNAL. *adj.* [*hodiernus*, Latin.] Of to-day.

HOE. *n. s.* [*houe*, French; *houwe*, Dutch.] An instrument to cut up the earth, of which the blade is at right angles with the handle.

If they come up too thick, they should be thinned with a *hoe*. *Mortimer's Husbandry.*

To HOE. *v. a.* [*houer*, French; *houwen*, Dutch.] To cut or dig with a hoe.

If it be a dry Spring, they must be continually kept with weeding and *hoeing*. *Mortimer's Husbandry.*

HOG. *n. s.* [*hwch*, Welsh.]

1. The general name of swine.

This will raise the price of *hogs*, if we grow all to be pork-eaters. *Shakespeare's Merchant of Venice.*

The *hog*, that plows not nor obeys thy call,
Lives on the labours of this Lord of all. *Pope.*

2. A castrated boar.

3. *To bring* HOGS *to a fair market.* To fail of one's design.

You have brought your *hogs to a fair market.* *Spectator.*

HO'GCOTE. *n. s.* [*hog* and *cote.*] A house for hogs; a hogsty.

Out of a small *hogcote* sixty or eighty load of dung hath been raised. *Mortimer's Husbandry.*

HO'GGEREL. *n. s.* A two year old ewe. *Ainsworth.*

HOGH. *n. s.* [otherwise written *ho*, *how*, or *hough*, from *hoogh*, Dutch.] A hill; rising ground; a cliff. Obsolete.

That well can witness yet unto this day,
The western *hogh*, besprinkl'd with the gore
Of mighty Goëmot. *Fairy Queen, b.* ii.

HOGHE'RD. *n. s.* [*hog* and hyrd, a keeper.] A keeper of hogs.

The terms *hogherd* and cowkeeper are not to be used in our poetry; but there are no finer words in the Greek language. *Broome's Notes on the Odyssey.*

HO'GGISH. *adj.* [from *hog.*] Having the qualities of an hog; brutish; greedy; selfish.

Suspicion Miso had, for the *hoggish* shrewdness of her brain, and Mopsa, for a very unlikely envy. *Sidney.*

HO'GGISHLY. *adv.* [from *hoggish.*] Greedily; selfishly.

HO'GGISHNESS. *n. s.* [from *hoggish.*] Brutality; greediness; selfishness.

HO'GSBEANS. }
HO'GSBREAD. } *n. s.* Plants. *Ainsworth.*
HO'GSMUSHROOMS. }

HO'GSFENNEL. *n. s.* [*hog* and *fennel.*] A plant. *Ainsworth.*

HO'GSHEAD. *n. s.* [*hog* and *head.*]

1. A measure of liquids containing sixty gallons.

Varro tells, that every jugerum of vines yielded six hundred urns of wine: according to this proportion, our acre should yield fifty-five *hogsheads*, and a little more. *Arbuthnot on Coins.*

2. Any large barrel.

Blow strongly with a pair of bellows into a *hogshead*, putting into it before that which you would have preserved; and in the instant that you withdraw the bellows, stop the hole. *Bacon.*

They flung up one of their largest *hogsheads*: I drank it off; for it did not hold half a pint. *Gulliver's Travels.*

HOGSTY'. *n. s.* [*hog* and *sty.*] The place in which swine are shut to be fed.

The families of farmers live in filth and nastiness, without a shoe or stocking to their feet, or a house so convenient as an English *hogsty*. *Swift.*

HOGWA'SH. *n. s.* [*hog* and *wash.*] The draff which is given to swine.

Your butler purloins your liquor, and the brewer sells you *hogwash*. *Arbuthnot's History of John Bull.*

HO'IDEN. *n. s.* [*hoeden*, Welsh; *fœmina levioris famæ*, Latin.] An ill-taught awkward country girl.

To HO'IDEN. *v. n.* [from the noun.] To romp indecently.

Some of them would get a scratch; but we always discovered, upon examining, that they had been *hoidening* with the young apprentices. *Swift.*

To HOISE. } *v. a.* [*hausser*, French.] To raise up on
To HOIST. } high.

'Tis the sport to have the engineer *hoist* up with his own petar. *Shakespeare's Hamlet.*

Join you with me;
We'll quickly *hoist* duke Humphrey from his seat. *Shakesp.*

Hoise sail, and fly;
And in thy flight aloud on Cratis cry. *Chapman's Odyssey.*

Auria had *hoised* sail, and was on his way toward the bay of Naupactus. *Knolles's History of the Turks.*

They loosed the rudder-bands, and *hoised* up the mainsail to the wind, and made toward shore. *Acts* xxvii. 40.

That man which prizeth virtue for itself, and cannot endure to *hoise* and strike his sails, as the divers natures of calms and storms require, must cut his sails of mean length and breadth, and content himself with a slow and sure navigation. *Raleigh.*

What made Absalom kick at all the kindnesses of his father, but because his ambition would needs be fingering the sceptre, and *hoisting* him into his father's throne. *South's Serm.*

We thought for Greece
The sails were *hoisted*, and our fears release. *Dryden's Æn.*

They *hoist* him on the bier, and deal the dole,
And there's an end. *Dryden's Pers.*

What haste she made to *hoist* her purple sails!
And to appear magnificent in flight,
Drew half our strength away. *Dryden's All for Love.*

Their navy swarms upon the coasts: they cry
To *hoist* their anchors, but the gods deny. *Dryden's Æn.*

Seize him, take, *hoist* him up, break off his hold,
And toss him headlong from the temple's wall. *Southern.*

If 'twas an island where they found the shells, they straightways concluded that the whole island lay originally at the bottom of the sea, and that it was *hoisted* up by some vapour from beneath. *Woodward's Natural History.*

HOLD, in the old glossaries, is mentioned in the same sense with *wold*, *i. e.* a governour or chief officer; but in some other place for love, as *holdlic*, lovely. *Gibson's Camden.*

To HOLD. *v. a.* preter. *held*; part. pass. *held* or *holden.* [*haldan*, Gothick; healdan, Saxon; *henden*, Dutch.]

1. To grasp in the hand; to gripe; to clutch.

France, thou may'st *hold* a serpent by the tongue,
A fasting tyger safer by the tooth,
Than keep in peace that hand which thou do'st *hold.* *Shak.*

2. To keep; to retain; to gripe fast.

Too late it was for satyrs to be told,
Or ever hope recover her again;
In vain he seeks, that having cannot *hold.* *Fairy Queen.*

The loops *held* one curtain to another. *Ex.* xxxvi. 12.

Prove all things: *hold* fast that which is good. 2 *Thes.* v.

3. To maintain as an opinion.

Men with assurance *hold* and profess, without ever having examined. *Locke.*

4. To consider as good or bad; to hold in regard.

I as a stranger to my heart and me
Hold thee from this for ever. *Shakesp. King Lear.*

I *hold* him but a fool, that will endanger
His body for a girl that loves him not. *Shakespeare.*

One amongst the fair'st of Greece,
That *holds* his honour higher than his ease. *Shakespeare.*

This makes thee blessed peace so light to *hold*,
Like Summer's flies that fear not Winter's cold. *Fairfax.*

Receive him therefore in the Lord with all gladness, and *hold* such in esteem. *St. Paul.*

He would make us amends, and spend some time with us, if we *held* his company and conference agreeable. *Bacon.*

As he is the father of English poetry, so I *hold* him in the same degree of veneration as the Grecians *held* Homer, or the Romans Virgil. *Dryden's Fables, Preface.*

Ye Latian dames, if any here
'*Hold* your unhappy queen Amata dear!
The orgies and nocturnal rites prepare. *Dryden's Æn.*

5. To have any station.
The star bids the shepherd fold;
Now the top of heav'n doth *hold.* *Milton.*
And now the strand, and now the plain they *held*;
Their ardent eyes with bloody streaks were fill'd. *Dryden.*
Observe the youth who first appears in sight,
And *holds* the nearest station to the light. *Dryden's Æn.*

How pleasant and joyful a thing is it to have a light *held* us forth from heaven to guide our steps. *Cheyne's Phil. Princ.*

6. To possess; to enjoy.
Holding Corioli in the name of Rome,
Even like a fawning greyhound in the leash,
To let him slip at will. *Shakespeare's Coriolanus.*

The castle, *holden* by a garrison of Germans, he commanded to be besieged. *Knolles's History of the Turks.*

Assuredly it is more shame for a man to lose that which he *holdeth*, than to fail in getting that which he never had. *Hayw.*

7. To possess in subordination.
The duke was willing to yield himself unto Solyman as his vassal, and of him to *hold* his seigniory for a yearly tribute. *Knolles's History of the Turks.*

8. To suspend; to refrain.
Death! what do'st? O *hold* thy blow!
What thou do'st, thou do'st not know. *Crashaw.*

9. To stop; to restrain.
We cannot *hold* mortality's strong hand. *Shak. K. John.*
Fell, banning hag! inchantress, *hold* thy tongue. *Shakesp.*

Men in the midst of their own blood, and so furiously assailed, *held* their hands, contrary to the laws of nature and necessity. *Bacon's War with Spain.*

When straight the people, by no force compell'd,
Nor longer from their inclination *held*,
Break forth at once. *Waller.*
Unless thou find occasion, *hold* thy tongue;
Thyself or others, careless talk may wrong. *Denham.*

Hold your laughter, and then divert your fellow-servants. *Swift's Directions to the Footman.*

10. To fix to any condition.
His gracious promise you might,
As cause had call'd you up, have *held* him to. *Shak. Coriol.*

11. To preserve; to keep.
Stay but a little; for my cloud of dignity
Is *held* from falling with so weak a wind,
That it will quickly drop: my day is dim. *Shakes. Hen.* IV.

12. To confine to a certain state.
The most High then shewed signs for then, and *held* still the flood, 'till they were passed over. 2 *Esdr.* xiii. 14.

13. To detain.
Him God hath raised up, having loosed the pains of death, because it was not possible that he should be *holden* of it. *Acts.*

14. To retain; to continue.
These reasons mov'd her star-like husband's heart;
But still he *held* his purpose to depart. *Dryden.*

15. To solemnize; to celebrate.
The queen this day here *holds* her parliament,
But little thinks we shall be of her council. *Shakesp. H.* VI.
He *held* a feast in his house, like the feast of a king. 1 *Sa.*

16. To offer; to propose.
Christianity came into the world with the greatest simplicity of thought and language, as well as life and manners, *holding* forth nothing but piety, charity, and humility, with the belief of the Messiah and of his kingdom. *Temple.*

My account is so far from interfering with Moses, that it *holds* forth a natural and unforced interpretation of his sense. *Woodward's Natural History.*

17. To conserve; not to violate.
Her husband heard it, and *held* his peace. *Numb.* xxx. 7.
She said, and *held* her peace: Æneas went,
Unknowing whom the sacred sibyl meant. *Dryden's Æn.*

18. To manage; to handle intellectually.
Some in their discourse desire rather commendation of wit, in being able to *hold* all arguments, than of judgment in discerning what is true. *Bacon, Essay* 33.

19. To maintain.
Whereupon they also made engines against their engines, and *held* them battle a long season. 1 *Mac.* vi. 52.

20. To form; to plan.
The Pharisees went out, and *held* a counsel against him. *Mat.* xii. 14.

21. To carry on; to continue.
He came to the land's end, where he *holding* his course, in a narrow passage towards the West, for the space of divers days, did at length peaceably pass through the straits. *Abbot.*

22. *To* HOLD *forth.* To offer to exhibit.
Observe the connection of these ideas in the propositions, which those books *hold forth* and pretend to teach as truths. *Locke.*

23. *To* HOLD *in.* To restrain; to govern by the bridle.
I have lately sold my nag, and honestly told his greatest fault, which is, that he became such a lover of liberty that I could scarce *hold* him *in.* *Swift.*

24. *To* HOLD *in.* To restrain in general.
These mens hastiness the warier sort of you doth not commend; ye wish they had *held* themselves longer *in*, and not so dangerously flown abroad. *Hooker, Preface.*

25. *To* HOLD *off.* To keep at a distance.
Although 'tis fit that Cassio have his place;
Yet if you please to *hold* him *off* a while,
You shall by that perceive him. *Shakespeare's Othello.*

The object of sight doth strike upon the pupil of the eye directly, without any interception; whereas the cave of the ear doth *hold off* the sound a little from the organ. *Bacon.*

I am the better acquainted with you for absence, as men are with themselves for affliction: absence does but *hold off* a friend, to make one see him truly. *Pope to Swift.*

26. *To* HOLD *on.* To continue; to protract; to push forward.
They took Barbarossa, *holding on* his course to Africk, who brought great fear upon the country. *Knolles's Hist. of the Turks.*

If the obedience challenged were indeed due to these laws, then did our brethren both begin the quarrel and *hold* it *on.* *Sanderson's Judgment in one View.*

27. *To* HOLD *out.* To extend; to stretch forth.
The king *held out* to Esther the golden sceptre that was in his hand. *Esth.* v. 2.

28. *To* HOLD *out.* To offer; to propose.
Fortune *holds out* these to you, as rewards. *Ben. Johnson.*

29. *To* HOLD *out.* To continue to do or suffer.
He cannot long *hold out* these pangs,
Th' incessant care and labour of his mind. *Shakes. H.* IV.

30. *To* HOLD *up.* To raise aloft.
I should remember him: does he not *hold up* his head, as it were, and strut in his gait? *Shakes. Merry Wives of Windsor.*

The hand of the Almighty visibly *held up*, and prepared to take vengeance. *Locke.*

31. *To* HOLD *up.* To sustain; to support.
There is no man at once either excellently good or extremely evil, but grows either as he *holds* himself *up* in virtue, or lets himself slide to viciousness. *Sidney.*

It followeth, that all which they do in this sort proceedeth originally from some such agent as knoweth, appointeth, *holdeth up*, and actually frameth the same. *Hooker, b.* i. *s.* 3.

The time misorder'd doth in common sense
Crowd us, and crush us to this monstrous form,
To *hold* our safety *up.* *Shakespeare's Henry* IV. *p.* ii.
And so success of mischief shall be born,
And heir from heir shall *hold* his quarrel *up.* *Shakes. H.* IV.

Those princes have *held up* their sovereignty best, which have been sparing in those grants. *Davies on Ireland.*

We have often made one considerably thick piece of marble take and *hold up* another, having purposely caused their flat surfaces to be carefully ground and polished. *Boyle.*

Then do not strike him dead with a denial,
But *hold* him *up* in life, and cheer his soul
With the faint glimmering of a doubtful hope. *Addis. Cato.*

To HOLD. *v. n.*

1. To stand; to be right; to be without exception.
To say that simply an argument, taken from man's authority, doth *hold* no way, neither affirmatively nor negatively, is hard. *Hooker, b.* ii. *s.* 7.

This *holdeth* not in the sea-coasts, because the vapour of the sea, without showers, doth refresh. *Bacon's Natural History.*

The lasting of plants is most in those that are largest of body; as oak, elm, and chestnut, and this *holdeth* in trees; but in herbs it is often contrary. *Bacon's Natnral History.*

When the religion formerly received is rent by discords, and when the holiness of the professors of religion is decayed, and full of scandal, and withal the times be stupid, ignorant, and barbarous, you may doubt the springing up of a new sect; if then also there should arise any extravagant and strange spirit, to make himself author thereof; all which points *held* when Mahomet published his law. *Bacon, Essay* 59.

Nothing can be of greater use and defence to the mind than the discovering of these colours, shewing in what cases they *hold*, and in what they deceive. *Bacon.*

Where outward force constrains, the sentence *holds*;
But who constrains me? *Milton.*

So doth he deal with the testimonies of the fathers, let them be never so express against all sorts of prayers and invocations: they *hold* only of such a sort of prayer. *Stillingfleet.*

The reasons given by them against the worship of images, will equally *hold* against the worship of images amongst Christians. *Stillingfleet's Def. of Disc. on Rom. Idol.*

None of his solutions will *hold* by mere mechanicks. *More.*

This unseen agitation of the minute parts will *hold* in light and spirituous liquors. *Boyle.*

It *holds* in all operative principles whatsoever, but especially in such as relate to morality; in which not to proceed, is certainly to go backward. *South's Sermons.*

The drift of this figure *holds* good in all the parts of the creation. *L'Estrange.*

The

The proverb *holds*, that to be wiſe and love,
Is hardly granted to the gods above. *Dryden's Fables.*
As if th' experiment were made to *hold*
For baſe production, and reject the gold. *Dryden.*
This remark, I muſt acknowledge, is not ſo proper for the colouring as the deſign; but it will *hold* for both. *Dryden.*
Our author offers no reaſon; and when any body does, we ſhall ſee whether it will *hold* or no. *Locke.*
The rule *holds* in land as well as all other commodities. *Loc.*
This ſeems to *hold* in moſt caſes. *Addiſon's Spectator.*
The analogy *holds* good, and preciſely keeps to the ſame properties in the planets and comets. *Cheyne.*
Sanctorius's experiment of perſpiration, being to the other ſecretion as five to three, does not *hold* in this country, except in the hotteſt time of Summer. *Arbuthnot on Aliments.*
In words, as faſhions, the ſame rule will *hold*;
Alike fantaſtick, if too new or old. *Pope on Criticiſm.*
2 To continue unbroken or unſubdued.
Our force by land hath nobly *held*. *Shakeſpeare.*
3. To laſt; to endure.
We ſee, by the peeling of onions, what a *holding* ſubſtance the ſkin is. *Bacon's Natural Hiſtory.*
Never any man was yet ſo old,
But hop'd his life one Winter more might *hold*. *Denham.*
4. To continue.
He did not *hold* in this mind long. *L'Eſtrange.*
5. To refrain.
His dauntleſs heart would fain have *held*
From weeping, but his eyes rebell'd. *Dryden.*
6. To ſtand up for; to adhere.
Through envy of the devil came death into the world, and they that do *hold* of his ſide do find it. *Wiſd.* ii. 24.
They muſt, if they *hold* to their principles, agree that things had their production always as now they have. *Hale.*
When Granada for your uncle *held*,
You was by us reſtor'd, and he expell'd. *Dryden.*
Numbers *hold*
With the fair freckled king and beard of gold:
So vig'rous are his eyes, ſuch rays they caſt,
So prominent his eagle's beak is plac'd. *Dryden's Fables.*
7. To be dependent on.
The other two were great princes, though *holding* of him; men of giant-like both hugeneſs and force. *Sidney, b.* ii.
The mother, if the houſe *holds* of our lady, had rather, yea and will, have her ſon cunning and bold, in making him to live trimly. *Aſcham's Schoolmaſter.*
The great barons had not only great numbers of knights, but even petty barons *holding* under them. *Temple.*
My crown is abſolute, and *holds* of none. *Dryden.*
8. To derive right.
'Tis true, from force the nobleſt title ſprings;
I therefore *hold* from that which firſt made kings. *Dryden.*
9. *To* HOLD *forth.* To harangue; to ſpeak in publick; to ſet forth publickly.
A petty conjurer, telling fortunes, *held forth* in the market-place. *L'Eſtrange's Fables.*
10. *To* HOLD *in.* To reſtrain one's ſelf.
I am full of the fury of the Lord: I am weary with *holding in.* *Jer.* vi. 11.
11. *To* HOLD *in.* To continue in luck.
A duke, playing at hazard, *held in* a great many hands together. *Swift.*
12. *To* HOLD *off.* To keep at a diſtance without cloſing with offers.
Theſe are intereſts important enough, and yet we muſt be wooed to conſider them; nay, that does not prevail neither, but with a perverſe coyneſs we *hold off.* *Decay of Piety.*
13. *To* HOLD *on.* To continue; not to be interrupted.
The trade *held on* for many years after the biſhops became Proteſtants; and ſome of their names are ſtill remembered with infamy, on account of enriching their families by ſuch ſacrilegious alienations. *Swift.*
14. *To* HOLD *on.* To proceed.
He *held on*, however, 'till he was upon the very point of breaking. *L'Eſtrange.*
15. *To* HOLD *out.* To laſt; to endure.
Before thoſe dews that form manna come upon trees in the valleys, they diſſipate, and cannot *hold out.* *Bacon's Nat. Hiſt.*
As there are mountebanks for the natural body, ſo are there mountebanks for the politick body; men that perhaps have been lucky in two or three experiments, but want the grounds of ſcience, and therefore cannot *hold out.* *Bacon's Eſſays.*
Truth, fidelity, and juſtice, are a ſure way of thriving, and will *hold out*, when all fraudulent arts and devices will fail. *Tillotſon's Sermons.*
By an extremely exact regimen a conſumptive perſon may *hold out* for years, if the ſymptoms are not violent. *Arbuthnot.*
16. *To* HOLD *out.* Not to yield; not to be ſubdued.
The great maſter, leaving a ſufficient number of ſoldiers for the keeping of that fort, went with the reſt of his company to a place where the Spaniards, ſore charged by Achimetes, had much ado to *hold out.* *Knolles's Hiſtory of the Turks.*
You think it ſtrange a perſon, obſequious to thoſe he loves, ſhould *hold out* ſo long againſt importunity. *Boyle.*
Nor could the hardeſt ir'n *hold out*
Againſt his blows. *Hudibras.*
I would cry now, my eyes grow womaniſh;
But yet my heart *holds out.* *Dryden's Spaniſh Fryar.*
The citadel of Milan has *held out* formerly, after the conqueſt of the reſt of the dutchy. *Addiſon on Italy.*
As to the *holding out* againſt ſo many alterations of ſtate, it ſometimes proceeds from principles. *Collier on Pride.*
Pronounce your thoughts: are they ſtill fixt
To *hold* it *out*, and fight it to the laſt?
Or are your hearts ſubdu'd at length, and wrought
By time and ill ſucceſs to a ſubmiſſion? *Addiſon's Cato.*
17. *To* HOLD *together.* To be joined.
Thoſe old Gothick caſtles, made at ſeveral times, *hold together* only, as it were, by rags and patches. *Dryd. Dufreſnoy.*
18. *To* HOLD *together.* To remain in union.
Even outlaws and robbers, who break with all the world beſides, muſt keep faith amongſt themſelves, or elſe they cannot *hold together.* *Locke.*
19. *To* HOLD *up.* To ſupport himſelf.
All the wiſe ſayings and advices which philoſophers could muſter up to this purpoſe, have helped only to ſupport ſome few ſtout and obſtinate minds, which, without the aſſiſtance of philoſophy, could have *held up* pretty well of themſelves. *Tillotſon, Sermon* 5.
20 *To* HOLD *up.* Not to be foul weather.
Though nice and dark the point appear,
Quoth Ralph, it may *hold up* and clear. *Hudibras, p.* ii.
21. *To* HOLD *up.* To continue the ſame ſpeed.
When two ſtart into the world together, the ſucceſs of the firſt ſeems to preſs upon the reputation of the latter; for why could not he *hold* up? *Collier of Envy.*
HOLD has the appearance of an interjection; but is the imperative mood. Forbear; ſtop; be ſtill.
Hold, ho! lieutenant—ſir—Montano! Gentlemen,
Have you forgot all ſenſe of place and duty?
The general ſpeaks to you—*hold, hold*, for ſhame! *Shakeſp.*
Hold, hold! are all thy empty wiſhes ſuch!
A good old woman would have ſaid as much. *Dryden's Perſ.*
HOLD. *n. ſ.* [from the verb.]
1. The act of ſeizing; gripe; graſp; ſeizure.
Thoſe bards, Cæſar writeth, delivered no certain truth of any thing; neither is there any certain *hold* to be taken of any antiquity which is received by tradition. *Spenſer on Ireland.*
The wits of the multitude are ſuch, that many things they cannot lay *hold* on at once. *Hooker, Dedication.*
Uzzah put forth his hand to the ark of God, and took *hold* of it; for the oxen ſhook it. 2 *Sa.* vi. 6.
This is to give him liberty and power:
Rather thou ſhould'ſt lay *hold* upon him, ſend him
To deſerv'd death, and a juſt puniſhment. *Ben. Johnſ. Catil.*
Let but them
Find courage to lay *hold* on this occaſion. *Milt. Agoniſtes.*
The devil himſelf, when let looſe upon Job, could not tranſport that patient good man beyond his temper, or make him quit his *hold.* *L'Eſtrange.*
He ſeiz'd the ſhining bough with griping *hold*,
And rent away with eaſe the ling'ring gold. *Dryden's Æn.*
The head is divided into four fingers bending forwards, and one oppoſite to them bending backwards, and of greater ſtrength than any of them ſingly, which we call the thumb, to join with them ſeverally or united, whereby it is fitted to lay *hold* of objects of any ſize or quantity. *Ray on the Creation.*
Yet then, from all my grief, O Lord,
Thy mercy ſet me free,
Whilſt, in the confidence of pray'r,
My ſoul took *hold* on thee. *Addiſon's Spectator.*
We are ſtrangely backward to lay *hold* of this ſafe, this only method of cure. *Atterbury's Sermons.*
He kept his *hold*,
Nor loſt 'till beauty was decay'd and old,
And love was by poſſeſſion pall'd and cold. *Granville.*
2. Something to be held; ſupport.
If a man be upon an high place, without rails or good *hold*, he is ready to fall. *Bacon's Natural Hiſtory.*
3. Catch; power of ſeizing or keeping.
The law hath yet another *hold* on you. *Shakeſpeare.*
Let it conſiſt with ſuch a man's intereſt and ſafety to wrong you, and then it will be impoſſible you can have any *hold* upon him, becauſe there is nothing left to give him a check, or to put in the balance againſt his profit. *Swift.*
4. Priſon; place of cuſtody.
They lay him in *hold*, becauſe it was not declared what was to be done with him. *Hooker, b.* iii.
The priſoner to his *hold* retir'd,
His troop with equal emulation fir'd, *Dryden.*

4. Power;

5. Power; influence.

Rural recreations abroad, and books at home, are the innocent pleasures of a man who is early wise; and gives fortune no more *hold* of him than of necessity he must. *Dryden.*

Fear is that passion which hath the greatest power over us, and by which God and his laws take the surest *hold* of us. *Till.*

6. Custody.

King Richard, he is in the mighty *hold*
Of Bolinbroke. *Shakespeare's Richard* II.

7. HOLD *of a Ship.* All that part which lies between the keelson and the lower deck. *Harris.*

Now a sea into the *hold* was got,
Wave upon wave another sea had wrought. *Dryden's Juv.*

8. A lurking place: as, the *hold* of a wild beast or dear.

9. A fortified place; a fort.

It was his policy to leave no *hold* behind him; but make all plain and waste. *Spenser.*

HO'LDER. *n. s.* [from *hold.*]

1. One that holds or gripes any thing in his hand.

The makers and *holders* of plows are wedded to their own particular way. *Mortimer's Husbandry.*

2. A tenant; one that holds land under another.

In times past not holdings were so plentiful, and *holders* so scarce, as well was the landlord, who could not get one to be his tenant. *Carew's Survey of Cornwal.*

HOLDERFO'RTH. *n. s.* [*hold* and *forth.*] An haranguer; one who speaks in publick.

Whence some tub *holdersforth* have made
In powd'ring tubs the richest trade. *Hudibras, p.* iii.

He was confirmed in this opinion upon seeing the *holderforth.* *Addison's Freeholder.*

HO'LDFAST. *n. s.* [*hold* and *fast.*] Any thing which takes hold; a catch; a hook.

The several sorts of teeth are furnished with *holdfasts* suitable to the stress that they are put to. *Ray on the Creation.*

HO'LDING. *n. s.* [from *hold.*]

1. Tenure; farm.

Holdings were so plentiful, and holders so scarce, as well was the landlord who could not get a tenant. *Carew.*

2. It sometimes signifies the burthen or chorus of a song. *Hanm.*

The *holding* every man shall beat as loud
As his strong sides can volly. *Shakesp. Ant. and Cleopatra.*

HOLE. *n. s.* [*hol*, Dutch; *hole*, Saxon.]

1. A cavity narrow and long, either perpendicular or horizontal.

The earth had not a *hole* to hide this deed. *Shakesp.*

Tickling is most in the soles, and under the arm *holes* and sides. *Bacon.*

A loadstone is so disposed, that it shall draw unto it, on a reclined plane, a bullet of steel, which, as it ascends near to the loadstone, may fall down through some *hole*, and so return to the place whence it began to move. *Wilkins's Dædalus.*

There are the tops of the mountains, and under their roots in *holes* and caverns the air is often detained. *Burnet.*

2. A perforation; a small interstitial vacuity.

Look upon linen that has small *holes* in it: those *holes* appear very black, and men are often deceived in taking *holes* for spots of ink; and painters, to represent *holes*, make use of black. *Boyle on Colours.*

3. A cave; a hollow place.

Upon his bloody finger he doth wear
A precious ring, that lightens all the *hole*. *Shakespeare.*

4. A cell of an animal.

A tortoise spends all his days in a *hole*, with a house upon his head. *L'Estrange.*

I have frighted ants with my fingers, and pursued them as far as another *hole*, stopping all passages to their own nest, and it was natural for them to fly into the next *hole*. *Addison.*

5. A mean habitation. *Hole* is generally used, unless in speaking of manual works, with some degree of dislike.

When Alexander first beheld the face
Of the great cynick, thus he did lament:
How much more happy thou, that art content
To live within this little *hole*, than I
Who after empire, that vain quarry, fly. *Dryden's Juven.*

6. Some subterfuge or shift. *Ainsw.*

HO'LIDAM. *n. s.* [*holy dame.*] Blessed lady. *Hanmer.*

By my *holidam*, here comes Catharine. *Shakespeare.*

HO'LILY. *adv.* [from *holy.*]

1. Piously; with sanctity.

Thou would'st be great,
Art not without ambition; but without
The illness should attend it: what thou would'st highly,
That would'st thou *holily*. *Shakespeare's Macbeth.*

2. Inviolably; without breach.

Friendship, a rare thing in princes, more rare between princes, that so *holily* was observed to the last of those two excellent men. *Sidney, b.* ii.

HO'LINESS. *n. s.* [from *holy.*]

1. Sanctity; piety; religious goodness.

I will not hence and leave my husband here;
And ill it doth beseem your *holiness*
To separate the husband and the wife. *Shakes. Com. of Err.*

Religion is rent by discords, and the *holiness* of the professors is decayed, and full of scandal. *Bacon's Essays.*

Then in full age, and hoary *holiness*,
Retire, great teacher, to thy promis'd bliss. *Prior.*

We see piety and *holiness* ridiculed as morose singularities. *Rogers, Sermon* 15.

2. The state of being hallowed; dedication to religion.

3. The title of the pope.

I here appeal unto the pope,
To bring my whole cause 'fore his *holiness*. *Shakes. H.* VIII.

His *holiness* has told some English gentlemen, that those of our nation should have the privileges. *Addison on Italy.*

HO'LLA. *interj.* [*hola*, French.] A word used in calling to any one at a distance.

List, list! I hear
Some far off *hollow* break the silent air. *Milton.*

To HO'LLA. *v. n.* [from the interjection. This word is now vitiously written *hollo* by the best authors: sometimes *halloo.*] To cry out loudly.

But I will find him when he lies asleep,
And in his ear I'll *holla*, Mortimer! *Shakesp. Henry* IV.

What *halloing* and what stir is this to-day? *Shakespeare.*

HO'LLAND. *n. s.* Fine linen made in Holland.

Some for the pride of Turkish courts design'd,
For folded turbants finest *holland* bear. *Dryden.*

HO'LLOW. *adj.* [from *hole.*]

1. Excavated; having a void space within; not solid.

It is fortune's use
To let the wretched man outlive his wealth,
To view with *hollow* eye and wrinkled brow
An age of poverty. *Shakesp. Merchant of Venice.*

Some search for *hollow* trees, and fell the woods. *Dryden.*

He frets, he fumes, he stares, he stamps the ground;
The *hollow* tow'rs with clamours ring around. *Dryden.*

2. Noisy, like sound reverberated from a cavity.

The southern wind,
Now by his *hollow* whistling in the leaves,
Foretels a tempest. *Shakesp. Henry* IV. *p.* i.

Thence issu'd such a blast and *hollow* roar,
As threaten'd from the hinge to heave the door. *Dryden.*

3. Not faithful; not sound; not what one appears.

Who in want a *hollow* friend doth try,
Directly seasons him his enemy. *Shakesp. Hamlet.*

Hollow church papists are like the roots of nettles, which themselves sting not; but yet they bear all the stinging leaves. *Bacon's Ornam. Ration.*

He seem'd
For dignity compos'd, and high exploit;
But all was false and *hollow*. *Milton's Par. Lost, b.* ii.

What could be expected from him, but knotty and crooked *hollow* hearted dealings? *Howel's Vocal Forrest.*

The *hollow* hearted, disaffected,
And close malignants are detected. *Hudibras, p.* iii.

HO'LLOW. *n. s.*

1. Cavity; concavity.

I've heard myself proclaim'd,
And by the happy *hollow* of a tree
Escap'd the hunt. *Shakesp. King Lear.*

I suppose there is some vault or *hollow*, or isle, behind the wall, and some passage to it. *Bacon's Natural History.*

Against the horse's side his spear
He throws, which trembles with enclosed fear;
Whilst from the *hollows* of his womb proceed
Groans, not his own. *Denham.*

Himself, as in the *hollow* of his hand,
Holding, obedient to his high command,
The deep abyss. *Prior.*

2. Cavern; den; hole.

Who art thou, that lately did'st descend
Into this gaping *hollow* of the earth? *Shak. Titus Andronicus.*

Forests grew
Upon the barren *hollows*, high o'ershading
The haunts of savage beasts. *Prior.*

3. Pit.

A fine genius for gardening thought of forming such an unsightly *hollow* into so uncommon and agreeable a scene. *Addis.*

4. Any opening or vacuity.

He touched the *hollow* of his thigh. *Gen.* xxii. 25.

5. Passage; canal.

The little springs and rills are conveyed through little channels into the main *hollow* of the aqueduct. *Addison on Italy.*

To HO'LLOW. *v. a.* [from the noun.] To make hollow; to excavate.

Trees, rudely *hollow'd*, did the waves sustain,
'Ere ships in triumph plow'd the watry plain. *Dryd. Ovid.*

Multitudes were employed in the sinking of wells, the digging of trenches, and the *hollowing* of trees. *Spectator.*

To HO'LLOW. *v. n.* [This is written by neglect of etymology for *holla*. See HOLLA.] To shout; to hoot.

This

This unseen judge will wait, and in your ear
Will *hollow* rebel, tyrant, murderer. *Dryden's Aurengzebe.*

I pass for a disaffected person and a murderer, for no other reason but because I do not hoot and *hollow*, and make a noise. *Addison's Spectator.*

He with his hounds comes *hollowing* from the stable,
Makes love with nods, and kneels beneath a table. *Pope.*

HO'LLOWLY. *adv.* [from *hollow.*]

1. With cavities.
2. Unfaithfully; insincerely; dishonestly.

O earth, bear witness,
And crown what I profess with kind event,
If I speak true; if *hollowly*, invert
What best is boaded me, to mischief! *Shakesp. Tempest.*

You shall arraign your conscience,
And try your penitence, if it be found,
Or *hollowly* put on. *Shakesp. Measure for Measure.*

HO'LLOWNESS. *n. s.* [from *hollow.*]

1. Cavity; state of being hollow.

If you throw a stone or a dart, they give no sound; no more do bullets, except they happen to be a little hollowed in the casting, which *hollowness* penneth the air. *Bacon's Natur. Hist.*

I have seen earth taken up by a strong wind, so that there remained great empty *hollowness* in the place. *Hakewill.*

An heap of sand or fine powder will suffer no *hollowness* within them, though they be dry substances. *Burnet.*

2. Deceit; insincerity; treachery.

Thy youngest daughter does not love thee least;
Nor are those empty hearted, whose low sound
Reverbs no *hollowness.* *Shakespeare's King Lear.*

People, young and raw, and soft natured, think it an easy thing to gain love, and reckon their own friendship a sure price of any man's: but when experience shall have shewn them the hardness of most hearts, the *hollowness* of others, and the baseness and ingratitude of almost all, they will then find that a friend is the gift of God, and that he only who made hearts can unite them. *South's Sermons.*

HO'LLOWROOT. *n. s.* [*hollow* and *root.*] A plant. *Ainsworth.*

HO'LLY. *n. s.* [holeyn, Saxon.] A plant.

The leaves are set about the edges with long, sharp, stiff prickles: the berries are small, round, and generally of a red colour, containing four triangular striated seeds in each. Of this tree there are several species; some variegated in the leaves, some with yellow berries, and some with white. *Mill.*

Fairest blossoms drop with every blast;
But the brown beauty will like *hollies* last. *Gay.*

Some to the *holly* hedge
Nestling repair, and to the thicket some;
Some to the rude protection of the thorn. *Thomson's Spring.*

HO'LLYHOCK. *n. s.* [holihoc, Saxon, commonly called *holyoak.*] Rosemallow.

It is in every respect larger than the common mallow: its leaves are rougher, and its flowers, which are in some species double, adhere closely to the stalk. They flower in July. *Mill.*

Holyocks far exceed poppies for their durableness, and are very ornamental. *Mortimer's Husbandry.*

HO'LLYROSE. } *n. s.* Plants. *Ainsworth.*
HO'LLYTREE. }

HOLME. *n. s.*

1. *Holme* or *howme*, whether jointly or singly, comes from the Saxon holme, a river island; or if the place be not such, the same word signifies also a hill, or mountain. *Gibson's Camden.*
2. The ilex; the evergreen oak.

Under what tree did'st thou take them companying together? who answered, under a *holm* tree. *Sus.* lviii.

The carver *holme*, the maple seldom inward sound. *Spens.*

HO'LOCAUST. *n. s.* [ὅλος and καίω.] A burnt sacrifice; a sacrifice of which the whole was consumed by fire, and nothing retained by the offerer.

Isaac carried the wood for the sacrifice, which being an *holocaust*, or burnt offering, to be consumed unto ashes, we cannot well conceive a burthen for a boy. *Brown's Vulg. Err.*

Let the eye behold no evil thing, and it is made a sacrifice; let the tongue speak no filthy word, and it becomes an oblation; let the hand do no unlawful action, and you render it a *holocaust.* *Ray on the Creation.*

Eumenes cut a piece from every part of the victim, and by this he made it an *holocaust*, or an entire sacrifice. *Broome.*

HO'LOGRAPH. *n. s.* [ὅλος and γράφω] This word is used in the Scottish law to denote a deed written altogether by the granter's own hand.

HOLP. The old preterite and participle passive of *help.*

His great love, sharp as his spur, hath *holp* him
To's home before us. *Shakespeare's Macbeth.*

HO'LPEN. The old participle passive of *help.*

In a long trunk the sound is *holpen*, though both the mouth and the ear be a handful from the trunk; and somewhat more *holpen* when the hearer is near, than when the speaker. *Bacon.*

HO'LSTER. *n. s.* [heolster, Saxon, a hiding place.] A case for a horseman's pistol.

In's rusty *holsters* put what meat
Into his hose he cou'd not get. *Butler.*

HOLT, whether at the beginning or ending of the name of any place, signifies that it is or hath been woody, from the Saxon holt, a wood; or sometimes possibly from the Saxon hol, *i. e.* hollow, especially when the name ends in *tun* or *dun.* *Gibson.*

HO'LY. *adj.* [haliʒ, Saxon; *heyligh*, Dutch, from hal, healthy, or in a state of salvation.]

1. Good; pious; religious.

See where his grace stands 'tween two clergymen!
And see a book of prayer in his hand,
True ornaments to know a *holy* man. *Shakesp. Rich.* III.

Doubtless
With joy he will embrace you; for he's honourable,
And, doubling that, most *holy.* *Shakes. Cymbeline.*

2. Hallowed; consecrated to divine use.

State, *holy* or unhallow'd, what of that? *Shak. Hen.* VI.

Bare was his hoary head; one *holy* hand
Held forth his laurel crown, and one his sceptre. *Dryden.*

3. Pure; immaculate.

Common sense could tell them, that the good God could not be pleased with any thing cruel; nor the most *holy* God with any thing filthy and unclean. *South's Sermons.*

4. Sacred.

An evil soul producing *holy* witness,
Is like a villain with a smiling cheek. *Shak. Merch. of Ven.*

He has deserv'd it, were it carbuncled
Like *holy* Phœbus' car. *Shakespeare's Ant. and Cleopatra.*

HO'LY-GHOST. *n. s.* [haliʒ and ʒast, Saxon.] The third person of the adorable Trinity.

If strength of persuasion be the light which must guide us, I ask, how shall any one distinguish the inspirations of the *Holy-ghost?* *Locke.*

HO'LY-THURSDAY. *n. s.* The day on which the ascension of our Saviour is commemorated, ten days before Whitsuntide.

HO'LY-WEEK. *n. s.* The week before Easter.

HO'LYDAY. *n. s.* [*holy* and *day.*]

1. The day of some ecclesiastical festival.
2. Anniversary feast.

This victory was so welcome unto the Persians, that in memorial thereof they kept that day as one of their solemn *holydays* for many years after. *Knolles's History of the Turks.*

Rome's *holydays* you tell, as if a guest
With the old Romans you were wont to feast. *Waller.*

3. A day of gayety and joy.

He writes verses, he speaks *holyday*, he smells April and May; he will carry it. *Shak. Merry Wives of Windsor.*

What, have I 'scaped love-letters in the *holyday* time of my beauty, and am I now a subject for them? *Shakespeare.*

4. A time that comes seldom.

Courage is but a *holyday* kind of virtue, to be seldom exercised. *Dryden's Fables, Dedication.*

HO'MAGE. *n. s* [*hommage*, French; *homagium*, low Latin.]

1. Service paid and fealty professed to a sovereign or superior lord.

Call my sovereign yours,
And do him *homage* as obedient subjects. *Shakesp. Hen.* VI.

The chiefs, in a solemn manner, did their *homages*, and made their oaths of fidelity to the earl marshal. *Davies.*

2. Obeisance; respect paid by external action.

The gods great mother, when her heav'nly race
Do *homage* to her. *Denham.*

A tuft of daisies on a flow'ry lay
They saw, and thitherward they bent their way;
To this both knights and dames their *homage* made,
And due obeisance to the daisy paid. *Dryden.*

Go, go, with *homage* yon proud victors meet!
Go, lie like dogs beneath your masters feet. *Dryden.*

To HO'MAGE. *v. a.* [from the noun.] To reverence by external action; to pay honour to; to profess fealty.

HO'MAGER. *n. s.* [*hommager*, Fr. from *homage.*] One who holds by homage of some superior lord.

As I'm Egypt's queen,
Thou blushest, Antony; and that blood of thine
Is Cæsar's *homager.* *Shakesp. Ant. and Cleopatra.*

His subjects, traytors, are received by the duke of Bretagne his *homager.* *Bacon's Henry* VII.

HOME. *n. s.* [ham, Saxon.]

1. His own house; the private dwelling.

I'm now from *home*, and out of that provision
Which shall be needful for your entertainment. *Shakespeare.*

Home is the sacred refuge of our life,
Secur'd from all approaches but a wife. *Dryden.*

When Hector went to see
His virtuous wife, the fair Andromache,
He found her not at *home*; for she was gone. *Dryden.*

Those who have *homes*, when *home* they do repair,
To a last lodging calls their wand'ring friends. *Dryden.*

2. His own country.

How can tyrants safely govern *home*,
Unless abroad they purchase great alliance? *Shakes. H.* VI.

Their determination is to return to their *homes*, and to trouble you no more. *Shakesp. Merchant of Venice.*

With honour to his *home* let Theſeus ride,
With love to friend. *Dryden's Fables.*
At *home* the hateful names of parties ceaſe,
And factious ſouls are weary'd into peace. *Dryden.*

They who paſs through a foreign country, towards their native *home*, do not uſually give up themſelves to the pleaſures of the place. *Atterbury's Sermons.*

3. The place of conſtant reſidence.
Flandria, by plenty made the *home* of war,
Shall weep her crime, and bow to Charles reſtor'd. *Prior.*

4. United to a ſubſtantive, it ſignifies domeſtick.

Let the exportation of *home* commodities be more in value than the importation of foreign. *Bacon's Advice to Villiers.*

HOME. *adv.* [from the noun.]

1. To one's own habitation.

One of Adam's children in the mountains lights on a glittering ſubſtance; *home* he carries it to Adam, who finds it to be hard, to have a bright yellow colour, and exceeding great weight. *Locke.*

2. To one's own country.

3. Cloſe to one's own breaſt or affairs.

He that encourages treaſon lays the foundation of a doctrine, that will come *home* to himſelf. *L'Eſtrange.*

This is a conſideration that comes *home* to our intereſt. *Add.*

Theſe conſiderations, propoſed in general terms, I am ſure, madam, you will, by particular application, bring *home* to your own concern. *Wake's Preparation for Death.*

4. To the point deſigned; to the utmoſt; cloſely; fully.

Crafty enough either to hide his faults, or never to ſhew them, but when they might pay *home*. *Sidney, b.* ii.

In fell motion,
With his prepared ſword he charges *home*
My unprovided body. *Shakeſpeare's King Lear.*

A loyal ſir
To him thou follow'ſt: I will pay thy graces
Home both in word and deed. *Shakeſpeare's Tempeſt.*

Her cauſe and yours
I'll perfect him withal; and he ſhall bring you
Before the duke, and to the head of Angelo
Accuſe him *home* and *home*. *Shakeſp. Meaſure for Meaſure.*

Men of age object too much, adventure too little, and ſeldom drive buſineſs *home* to the full period; but content themſelves with a mediocrity of ſucceſs. *Bacon.*

That cometh up *home* to the buſineſs, and taketh off the objection clearly. *Sanderſon.*

Break through the thick array
Of his throng'd legions, and charge *home* upon him. *Addiſ.*

He makes choice of ſome piece of morality; and in order to preſs this *home*, he makes leſs uſe of the force of reaſoning. *Pope's View of Epick Poems.*

I can only refer the reader to the authors themſelves, who ſpeak very *home* to the point. *Atterbury's Serm. Preface.*

5. United to a ſubſtantive, it implies force and efficacy.

Poiſon may be falſe;
The *home* thruſt of a friendly ſword is ſure. *Dryden.*

I am ſorry to give him ſuch *home* thruſts; for he lays himſelf ſo open, and uſes ſo little art to avoid them, that I muſt either do nothing, or expoſe his weakneſs. *Stillingfleet.*

HOMEBO'RN. *adj.* [*home* and *born.*]

1. Native; natural.

Though to be thus elemented, arm
Theſe creatures from *homeborn* intrinſick harm. *Donne.*

2. Domeſtick; not foreign.

Num'rous bands
With *homeborn* lyes, or tales from foreign lands. *Pope.*

HO'MEBRED. *adj.* [*home* and *bred.*]

1. Native; natural.

God hath taken care to anticipate every man, to draw him early into his church, before other competitors, *homebred* luſts, or vicious cuſtoms of the world, ſhould be able to pretend to him. *Hammond on Fundamentals.*

2. Not poliſhed by travel; plain; rude; artleſs; uncultivated.

Only to me two *homebred* youths belong. *Dryden's Juven.*

3. Domeſtick; not foreign.

But if of danger, which hereby doth dwell,
And *homebred* evil, ye deſire to hear,
I can you tydings tell. *Fairy Queen, cant.* i.

This once happy land,
By *homebred* fury rent, long groan'd. *Phillips.*

HO'MEFELT. *adj.* [*home* and *felt.*] Inward; private.

Yet they in pleaſing ſlumber lull'd the ſenſe,
And in ſweet madneſs robb'd it of itſelf;
But ſuch a ſacred and *homefelt* delight,
Such ſober certainty of waking bliſs,
I never heard 'till now. *Milton.*

Happy next him who to theſe ſhades retires,
Whom nature charms, and whom the muſe inſpires,
Whom humbler joys of *homefelt* quiet pleaſe,
Succeſſive ſtudy, exerciſe, and eaſe. *Pope.*

HO'MELILY. *adv.* [from *homely.*] Rudely; inelegantly.

HO'MELINESS. *n. ſ.* [from *homely.*] Plainneſs; rudeneſs; coarſeneſs.

Homer has opened a great field of raillery to men of more delicacy than greatneſs of genius, by the *homelineſs* of ſome of his ſentiments. *Addiſon's Spectator.*

HO'MELY. *adj.* [from *home.*] Plain; homeſpun; not elegant; not beautiful; not fine; coarſe; rude.

Each place handſome without curioſity, and *homely* without loathſomeneſs. *Sidney.*

Within this wood, out of a rock did riſe
A ſpring of water, mildly tumbling down;
Whereto approached not in any wiſe
The *homely* ſhepherd, nor the ruder clown. *Spenſer.*

Like rich hangings in an *homely* houſe,
So was his will in his old feeble body. *Shakeſp. Henry* VI.

Be plain, good ſon, and *homely* in thy drift:
Riddling confeſſion finds but riddling ſhrift. *Shakeſpeare.*

Home-keeping youth have ever *homely* wits. *Shakeſpeare.*

Our ſtomachs will make what's *homely* ſavoury. *Shakeſp.*

It is for *homely* features to keep home;
They had their name thence. *Milton.*

It is obſerved by ſome, that there is none ſo *homely* but loves a looking-glaſs. *South's Sermons.*

Their *homely* fare diſpatch'd, the hungry band
Invade their trenchers next. *Dryden's Æn. b.* vii.

Now Strephon daily entertains
His Chloe in the *homeli'ſt* ſtrains. *Swift.*

Homely perſons, the more they endeavour to adorn themſelves, the more they expoſe the defects they want to hide. *Clar.*

HO'MELY. *adv.* Plainly; coarſely; rudely.

Thus like the god his father, *homely* dreſt,
He ſtrides into the hall a horrid gueſt. *Dryden's Æn.*

HO'MELYN. *n. ſ.* A kind of fiſh. *Ainſworth.*

HOMEMA'DE. *adj.* [*home* and *made.*] Made at home; not manufactured in foreign parts.

A tax laid on your native product, and *homemade* commodities, makes them yield leſs to the firſt ſeller. *Locke.*

HO'MER. *n. ſ.* A meaſure of about three pints.

An *homer* of barley-ſeed ſhall be valued at fifty ſhekels of ſilver. *Lev.* xxvii. 16.

HO'MESPUN. *adj.* [*home* and *ſpun.*]

1. Spun or wrought at home; not made by regular manufacturers.

Inſtead of *homeſpun* coifs were ſeen
Good pinners, edg'd with colberteen. *Swift.*

2. Not made in foreign countries.

He appeared in a ſuit of Engliſh broad-cloath, very plain, but rich: every thing he wore was ſubſtantial, honeſt, *homeſpun* ware. *Addiſon.*

3. Plain; coarſe; rude; homely; inelegant.

They ſometimes put on, when they go aſhore, long ſleeveleſs coats of *homeſpun* cotton. *Sandys's Travels.*

We ſay, in our *homeſpun* Engliſh proverb, He killed two birds with one ſtone; pleaſed the emperor, by giving him the reſemblance of his anceſtors, and gave him ſuch a reſemblance as was not ſcandalous in that age. *Dryden's Æn. Dedicat.*

Our *homeſpun* authors muſt forſake the field,
And Shakeſpeare to the ſoft Scarlatti yield. *Addiſon.*

HOMESPU'N. *n. ſ.* A coarſe, inelegant, rude, untaught, ruſtick man.

What hempen *homeſpuns* have we ſwaggering here,
So near the cradle of the fairy queen? *Shakeſpeare.*

HO'MESTALL. } *n. ſ.* [ham and ſtede, Saxon.] The place of
HO'MESTEAD. } the houſe.

Both houſe and *homeſtead* into ſeas are born,
And rocks are from their old foundations torn. *Dryden.*

HO'MEWARD. } *adv.* [ham and peard, Saxon.] Towards
HO'MEWARDS. } home; towards the native place; towards the place of reſidence.

Then Urania *homeward* did ariſe,
Leaving in pain their well-fed hungry eyes. *Sidney.*

My affairs
Do even drag me *homeward*. *Shakeſp. Winter's Tale.*

Since ſuch love's natural ſtation is, may ſtill
My love deſcend, and journey down the hill,
Not panting after growing beauties; ſo
I ſhall ebb on with them who *homeward* go. *Donne.*

Look *homeward*, angel now, and melt with ruth;
And, O ye dolphins, waft the hapleſs youth! *Milton.*

Like a long team of ſnowy ſwans on high,
Which clap their wings, and cleave the liquid ſky,
Which *homeward* from their wat'ry paſtures born,
They ſing, and Aſia's lakes their notes return. *Dryd. Æn.*

What now remains,
But that once more we tempt the wat'ry plains,
And, wand'ring *homewards*, ſeek our ſafety hence. *Dryden.*

HO'MICIDE. *n. ſ.* [*homicide*, French; *homicidium*, Latin.]

1. Murder; manquelling.

The apoſtles command to abſtain from blood: conſtrue this according to the law of nature, and it will ſeem, that *homicide* only is forbidden; but conſtrue it in reference to the law of the Jews, about which the queſtion was, and it ſhall eaſily appear to have a clean other ſenſe, and a truer, when we expound it of eating, and not of ſhedding blood. *Hooker, b.* iv.

2. Deſtruction.

2. Destruction. In the following lines it is not proper.

What wonder is't that black detraction thrives!
The *homicide* of names is less than lives. *Dryden.*

3. [*Homicide*, Fr. *homicida*, Lat.] A murderer; a manslayer.

Your beauty, that did haunt me in my sleep,
To undertake the death of all the world,
So might I live one hour in your sweet bosom.
——If I thought that, I tell thee, *homicide*,
These nails should rend that beauty from my cheeks. *Shakesp.*

Hector comes, the *homicide*, to wield
His conqu'ring arms, with corps to strew the field. *Dryden.*

HOMICI'DAL. *adj.* [from *homicide.*] Murderous; bloody.

The troop forth issuing from the dark recess,
With *homicidal* rage, the king oppress. *Pope's Odyssey.*

HOMILE'TICAL. *adj.* [ὁμιλητικὸς.] Social; conversible.

His life was holy, and, when he had leisure for retirements, severe: his virtues active chiefly, and *homiletical*; not those lazy sullen ones of the cloyster. *Atterbury.*

HO'MILY. *n. s.* [*homilie*, French; ὁμιλία.] A discourse read to a congregation.

Homilies were a third kind of readings usual in former times; a most commendable institution, as well then to supply the casual, as now the necessary defect of sermons. *Hooker.*

What tedious *homily* of love have you wearied your parishioners withal, and never cried have patience, good people. *Shakespeare's As you like it.*

If we survey the *homilies* of the ancient church, we shall discern that, upon festival days, the subject of the *homily* was constantly the business of the day. *Hammond's Fundamentals.*

HOMOGE'NEAL. } *adj.* [*homogene*, Fr. ὁμογενὴς.] Having
HOMOGE'NEOUS. } the same nature or principles; suitable to each other.

The means of reduction, by the fire, is but by congregation of *homogeneal* parts. *Bacon's Phys. Rem.*

Ice is a similary body, and *homogeneous* concretion, whose material is properly water. *Brown's Vulgar Errours.*

An *homogeneous* mass of one kind is easily distinguishable from any other; gold from iron, sulphur from alum, and so of the rest. *Woodward's Natural History.*

The light, whose rays are all alike refrangible, I call simple, *homogeneal*, and similar; and that whose rays are some more refrangible than others, I call compound, heterogeneal, and dissimilar. *Newton's Opt.*

HOMOGE'NEALNESS. } *n. s.* [from *homogeneous*, or *homogeneal.*]
HOMOGENE'ITY. } Participation of the same principles or
HOMOGE'NEOUSNESS. } nature; similitude of kind.

The mixtures acquire a greater degree of fluidity and similarity, or *homogeneity* of parts. *Arbuthnot on Aliments.*

Upon this supposition of only different diameters, it is impossible to account for the *homogeneity* or similarity of the secerned liquors. *Cheyne's Phil. Prin.*

HO'MOGENY. *n. s.* [ὁμογενία.] Joint nature.

By the driving back of the principal spirits, which preserve the consistence of the body, their government is dissolved, and every part returneth to his nature or *homogeny.* *Bacon.*

HOMO'LOGOUS. *adj.* [*homologue*, Fr. ὁμόλογος.] Having the same manner or proportions.

HOMO'NYMOUS. *adj.* [*homonyme*, Fr. ὁμώνυμος.] Denominating different things; equivocal; ambiguous.

As words signifying the same thing are called synonymous, so equivocal words, or those which signify several things, are called *homonymous*, or ambiguous; and when persons use such ambiguous words, with a design to deceive, it is called equivocation. *Watts's Logick.*

HOMO'NYMY. *n. s.* [*homonymie*, French; ὁμονυμία.] Equivocation; ambiguity.

HOMO'TONOUS. *adj.* [ὁμότονος.] Equable: said of such distempers as keep a constant tenour of rise, state, and declension. *Quincy.*

HONE. *n. s.* [This word *M. Casaubon* derives from ἀκονή; *Junius* from *hogsaen*, Welsh; *Skinner*, who is always rational, from hæn, Saxon, a stone; hænan, to stone.] A whetstone for a rasor.

A *hone* and a parer, to pare away *grass.* *Tusser's Husband.*

To HONE. *v. n.* [hongian, Saxon.] To pine; to long for any thing.

HO'NEST. *adj.* [*honeste*, French; *honestus*, Latin.]

1. Upright; true; sincere.

What art thou?
—A very *honest* hearted fellow, and as poor as the king. *Sh.*

The way to relieve ourselves from those sophisms, is an *honest* and diligent enquiry into the real nature and causes of things. *Watts's Logick.*

2. Chaste.

Wives may be merry, and yet *honest* too. *Shakespeare.*

3. Just; righteous; giving to every man his due.

4. It is sometimes used criminally for dishonest; base.

I'll devise some *honest* slanders
To stain my cousin with: one doth not know
How much an ill word doth impoison liking. *Shakespeare.*

HO'NESTLY. *adv.* [from *honest.*]

1. Uprightly; justly.

It doth make me tremble,
There should those spirits yet breathe, that when they cannot
Live *honestly*, would rather perish basely. *Ben. Johns. Catil.*

For some time past all endeavours or proposals from private persons to advance the publick service, however *honestly* and innocently designed, have been called flying in the king's face. *Swift.*

2. With chastity; modestly.

HO'NESTY. *n. s.* [*honnesteté*, French; *honestas*, Latin.] Justice; truth; virtue; purity.

Thou shalt not have thy husband's lands.
——Why, then mine *honesty* shall be my dower. *Shakesp.*

Goodness, as that which makes men prefer their duty and their promise before their passions or their interest, and is properly the object of trust, in our language goes rather by the name of *honesty*; though what we call an honest man, the Romans called a good man; and *honesty* in their language, as well as in French, rather signifies a composition of those qualities which generally acquire honour and esteem. *Temple.*

HO'NIED. *adj.* [from *honey.*]

1. Covered with honey.

The bee with *honied* thigh,
That at her flow'ry work doth sing. *Milton.*

2. Sweet; luscious.

When he speaks,
The air, a charter'd libertine, is still;
And the mute wonder lurketh in mens ears,
To steal his sweet and *honied* sentences. *Shakesp. Henry V.*

Look now for no enchanting voice, nor fear
The bait of *honey'd* words; a rougher tongue
Draws hitherward. *Milton's Agonistes.*

HO'NEY. *n. s.* [hunig, Saxon; *honig*, Dutch; *honec*, *honag*, German.]

1. A thick, viscous, fluid substance, of a whitish or yellowish colour, sweet to the taste, soluble in water; and becoming vinous on fermentation, inflammable, liquable by a gentle heat, and of a fragrant smell. We have three kinds of honey: the first and finest is virgin honey, not very firm, and of a fragrant smell: it is the first produce of the swarm, obtained by draining from the combs without pressing. The second is thicker than the first, often almost solid, procured from the combs by pressure: and the worst is the common yellow honey, extracted by heating the combs over the fire, and then pressing them. In the flowers of plants, by certain glands near the basis in the petals, is secreted a sweet juice, which the bee, by means of its probosis or trunk, sucks up, swallows it, flies away with it to the hive, and discharges again from the stomach through the mouth into some of the cells of the comb. The honey thus taken up into the body of the bee, and deposited again into the cells of the comb, is destined for the food of the young offspring; but in hard seasons the bees are sometimes reduced to the necessity of feeding on it themselves, and die of hunger after they have eat it all up. Honey, taken out of the new combs early in the Summer, is vastly preferrable to that taken from the same hive in Autumn. Honey is an excellent pectoral, is detergent, aperient, and diuretick. *Hill's Mat. Med.*

So work the *honey* bees,
Creatures that by a ruling nature teach
The art of order to a peopled kingdom. *Shakes. Hen. V.*

The like contention is found among the Greeks, touching his education and first fostering: some affirm, that he was fed by *honey* bees. *Raleigh's History of the World.*

In ancient time there was a kind of *honey*, which, either of its own nature, or by art, would grow as hard as sugar, and was not so luscious as ours. *Bacon's Natural History.*

When the patient is rich, there's no fear of physicians about him, as thick as wasps to a *honey* pot. *L'Estrange.*

Honey is the most elaborate production of the vegetable kind, being a most exquisite vegetable sope, resolvent of the bile, balsamick and pectoral: *honey* contains no inflammable spirit, before it has felt the force of fermentation; for by distillation it affords nothing that will burn in the fire. *Arbuthn.*

New wine, with *honey* temper'd milk we bring;
Then living waters from the crystal spring. *Pope's Odyssey.*

2. Sweetness; lusciousness.

The king hath found
Matter against him, that for ever mars
The *honey* of his language. *Shakespeare's Henry VIII.*

A *honey* tongue, a heart of gall,
Is fancy's spring, but sorrow's fall. *Shakespeare.*

3. A name of tenderness; sweet; sweetness. [*Mel*; *corculum.*]

Honey, you shall be well desir'd in Cyprus;
I've found great love amongst them. Oh, my sweet,
I prattle out of fashion, and I dote
In mine own comfort. *Shakespeare's Othello.*

Why, *honey* bird, I bought him on purpose for thee: did'st not thou say, thou long'dst for a Christian slave? *Dryden.*

To HO'NEY. *v. n.* [from the noun.] To talk fondly.

Nay, but to live
In the rank sweat of an incestuous bed,
Stew'd in corruption, *honeying* and making love
Over the nasty sty. *Shakespeare's Hamlet.*

HO'NEY-BAG.

HO'NEY-BAG. *n. s.* [*honey* and *bag.*]

The *honey-bag* is the stomach, which they always fill to satisfy, and to spare, vomiting up the greater part of the honey to be kept against Winter. *Grew's Musæum.*

HO'NEY-COMB. *n. s.* [*honey* and *comb.*] The cells of wax in which the bee stores her honey.

All these a milk-white *honey-comb* surround,
Which in the midst the country banquet crown'd. *Dryden.*

HON'EY-COMBED. *adj.* [*honey* and *comb.*] Spoken of a piece of ordnance flawed with little cavities by being ill cast.

A mariner having discharged his gun, which was *honey-combed*, and loading it suddenly again, the powder took fire. *Wiseman.*

HO'NEY-DEW. *n. s.* [*honey* and *dew.*] Sweet dew.

There is a *honey-dew* which hangs upon their leaves, and breeds insects. *Mortimer's Husbandry.*

How *honey-dews* embalm the fragrant morn,
And the fair oak with luscious sweets adorn. *Garth.*

HO'NEY-FLOWER. *n. s.* [*melanthus*, Latin.] A plant.

It hath a perennial root, and the appearance of a shrub: the leaves are like those of burnet; the cup of the flower is divided into several parts: the flower consists of four leaves, and is of an anomalous figure, sometimes in the shape of a fan, and at other times conical: the ovary becomes a fruit, resembling a bladder four cornered, divided into four cells, and pregnant with roundish seeds. This plant produces large spikes of chocolate-coloured flowers in May, in each of which is contained a large quantity of black sweet liquor, from whence it is supposed to derive its name. *Miller.*

HO'NEY-GNAT. *n. s.* [*melio*, Latin; *honey* and *gnat.*] An insect. *Ainsworth.*

HO'NEY-MOON. *n. s.* [*honey* and *moon.*] The first month after marriage, when there is nothing but tenderness and pleasure.

A man should keep his finery for the latter season of marriage, and not begin to dress 'till the *honey-moon* is over. *Addis.*

HO'NEY-SUCKLE. *n. s.* [*caprifolium*, Latin.] Woodbine.

It hath a climbing stalk, which twists itself about whatsoever tree stands near it: the flowers are tubulous and oblong, consisting of one leaf, which opens towards the top, and is divided into two lips; the uppermost of which is subdivided into two, and the lowermost is cut into many segments: the tube of the flowers is bent, somewhat resembling a huntsman's horn. They are produced in clusters, and are very sweet. *Miller* enumerates ten species, of which three grow wild in our hedges.

Bid her steal into the pleached bower,
Where *honey-suckles*, ripen'd by the sun,
Forbid the sun to enter; like to favourites,
Made proud by princes, that advance their pride
Against the power that bred it. *Shakespeare.*

Watch upon a bank
With ivy canopied, and interwove
With flaunting *honeysuckle.* *Milton.*

Then melfoil beat, and *honey-suckles* pound;
With these alluring savours strew the ground. *Dryd. Virgil.*

HO'NEYLESS. *adj.* [from *honey.*] Without honey.

But for your words, they rob the Hybla bees,
And leave them *honeyless.* *Shakesp. Julius Cæsar.*

HO'NEY-WORT. *n. s.* [*cerinthe*, Latin.] A plant.

It hath glaucous deep green leaves, which are, for the most part, beset with prickles: the flowers are cylindrical, consisting of one leaf, in shape like those of comfrey, and are pendulous: each flower turns to the top of the second page of the third leaf following. *Miller.*

HO'NORARY. *adj.* [*honorarius*, Latin.]

1. Done in honour.

There was probably some distinction made among the Romans between such *honorary* arches erected to emperors, and those that were raised to them on the account of a victory, which are properly triumphal arches. *Addison on Italy.*

This monument is only *honorary*; for the ashes of the emperor lie elsewhere. *Addison on Italy.*

2. Conferring honour without gain.

The Romans abounded with these little *honorary* rewards, that, without conferring wealth and riches, gave only place and distinction to the person who received them. *Addis. Guard.*

HO'NOUR. *n. s.* [*honeur*, French; *honor*, Latin.]

1. Dignity; high rank.

2. Reputation; fame.

A man is an ill husband of his *honour*, that entereth into any action, the failing wherein may disgrace him more than the carrying of it through can honour him. *Bacon's Essays.*

3. The title of a man of rank.

Return unto thy lord,
Bid him not fear the separated councils:
His *honour* and myself are at the one;
And at the other is my good friend Catesby. *Shakes. R. III.*

4. Subject of praise.

Thou happy father,
Think that the clearest gods, who make them *honours*
Of man's impossibilities, have preserv'd thee. *Shakesp.*

5. Nobleness of mind; scorn of meanness; magnanimity.

Now shall I see thy love; what motive may
Be stronger with thee than the name of wife?
—That which upholdeth him, that thee upholds,
His *honour*. Oh, thine *honour*, Lewis; thine *honour*. *Shak.*

If by *honour* is meant any thing distinct from conscience, 'tis no more than a regard to the censure and esteem of the world. *Rogers's Sermons.*

6. Reverence; due veneration.

They take thee for their mother,
And every day do *honour* to thy grave. *Shakes. Cymbeline.*

There, my lord,
The high promotion of his grace of Canterbury,
Who holds his state at door, 'mongst pursuivants.
—— Ha! 'tis he, indeed!
Is this the *honour* they do one another? *Shakesp. Hen. VIII.*

This is a duty in the fifth commandment, required towards our prince and our parent, under the name of *honour*; a respect, which, in the notion of it, implies a mixture of love and fear, and, in the object, equally supposes goodness and power. *Rogers's Sermons.*

7. Chastity.

Be she *honour* flaw'd,
I have three daughters, the eldest is eleven;
If this prove true, they'll pay for't. *Shak. Winter's Tale.*

She dwells so securely on the excellency of her *honour*, that the folly of my soul dares not prevent itself: she is too bright to be looked against. *Shakesp. Merry Wives of Windsor.*

8. Dignity of mien.

Two of far nobler shape, erect and tall,
Godlike erect! with native *honour* clad,
In naked majesty, seem'd lords of all. *Milton's Parad. Lost.*

9. Glory; boast.

A late eminent person, the *honour* of his profession for integrity and learning. *Burnet's Theory of the Earth.*

10. Publick mark of respect.

He saw his friends, who whelm'd beneath the waves,
Their fun'ral *honours* claim'd, and ask'd their quiet graves. *Dryden's Æn. b. vi.*

Such discourses, on such mournful occasions as these, were instituted not so much in *honour* of the dead, as for the use of the living. *Atterbury's Sermons.*

Numbers engage their lives and labours, some to heap together a little dirt that shall bury them in the end; others to gain an *honour*, that, at best, can be celebrated but by an inconsiderable part of the world, and is envied and calumniated by more than 'tis truly given. *Wake's Preparation for Death.*

11. Privileges of rank or birth.

Henry the seventh, truly pitying
My father's loss, like a most royal prince,
Restor'd to me my *honours*; and, from ruins,
Made my name once more noble. *Shakesp. Henry VIII.*

12. Civilities paid.

Then here a slave, or if you will a lord,
To do the *honours*, and to give the word. *Pope's Horace.*

13. Ornament; decoration.

The fire then shook the *honours* of his head,
And from his brows damps of oblivion shed. *Dryden.*

My hand to thee, my *honour* on my promise. *Shakesp.*

To HO'NOUR. *v. a.* [*honnorer*, French; *honoro*, Latin.]

1. To reverence; to regard with veneration.

He was called our father, and was continually *honoured* of all men, as the next person unto the king. *Esth.* xvi. 11.

The poor man is *honoured* for his skill, and the rich man is *honoured* for his riches. *Ecclus.* x. 30.

He that is *honoured* in poverty, how much more in riches? *Ecclus.* x. 31.

How lov'd, how *honour'd* once, avails thee not. *Pope.*

2. To dignify; to raise to greatness.

In soothing them, we nourish 'gainst our senate
The cockle of rebellion, insolence, sedition,
Which we ourselves have plow'd for, sow'd and scatter'd,
By mingling them with us, the *honour'd* number. *Shakesp.*

I will harden Pharaoh's heart, that he shall follow after them, and I will be *honoured* upon Pharaoh, and upon all his host, that the Egyptians may know that I am the Lord. *Ex.* xiv.

HO'NOURABLE. *adj.* [*honorable*, French.]

1. Illustrious; noble.

Sir, I'll tell you,
Since I am charg'd in honour, and by him
That I think *honourable.* *Shakespeare's Winter's Tale.*

Who hath taken this counsel against Tyre, the crowning city, whose merchants are princes, whose traffickers are the *honourable* of the earth? *Is.* xxiii. 8.

2. Great; magnanimous; generous.

Think'st thou it *honourable* for a nobleman
Still to remember wrongs. *Shakespeare's Coriolanus.*

3. Conferring honour.

Then warlike kings, who for their country fought,
And *honourable* wounds from battle brought. *Dryden's Æn.*

Many of thoſe perſons, who put this *honourable* taſk on me, were more able to perform it themſelves. *Dryden's Dufreſnoy.*

4. Accompanied with tokens of honour.

Sith this wretched woman overcome,
Of anguiſh, rather than of crime hath been,
Preſerve her cauſe to her eternal doom;
And in the mean, vouchſafe her *honourable* tomb. *Fa. Qu.*

5. Not to be diſgraced.

Here's a Bohemian tartar tarries the coming down of thy fat woman:—let her deſcend, my chambers are *honourable*. *Shak.*

6. Without taint; without reproach.

As he was *honourable* in all his acts, ſo in this, that he took Joppe for an haven. 1 *Mac.* xiv. 5.

Methinks I could not die any where ſo contented as in the king's company, his cauſe being juſt and his quarrel *honourable*. *Shakeſpeare's Henry* V.

7. Honeſt; without intention of deceit.

The earl ſent again to know if they would entertain their pardon, in caſe he ſhould come in perſon, and aſſure it: they anſwered, they did conceive him to be ſo *honourable*, that from himſelf they would moſt thankfully embrace it. *Hayward.*

If that thy bent of love be *honourable*,
Thy purpoſe marriage, ſend me word to-morrow. *Shakeſp.*

8. Equitable.

Ho'nourableness. *n. ſ.* [from *honourable.*] Eminence; magnificence; generoſity.

Ho'nourably. *adv.* [from *honourable.*]

1. With tokens of honour.

The rev'rend abbot,
With all his convent, *honourably* receiv'd him. *Sh. H.* VIII.

2. Magnanimouſly; generouſly.

After ſome ſix weeks diſtance of time, which the king did *honourably* interpoſe, to give ſpace to his brother's interceſſion, he was arraigned of high treaſon, and preſently after condemned. *Bacon's Henry* VII.

3. Reputably; with exemption from reproach.

'Tis juſt, ye gods! and what I well deſerve:
Why did I not more *honourably* ſtarve! *Dryden's Juvenal.*

Ho'nourer. *n. ſ.* [from *honour.*] One that honours; one that regards with veneration.

I muſt not here omit to do juſtice to Mr. Gay, whoſe zeal in your concern is worthy a friend and *honourer*. *Pope.*

Hood, in compoſition, is derived from the Saxon had, in German *heit*, in Dutch *heid*. It denotes quality; character; condition: as, *knighthood*; *childhood*; *fatherhood*. Sometimes it is uſed after the Dutch, as *maidenhead*. Sometimes it is taken collectively: as, *brotherhood*, a confraternity; *ſiſterhood*, a company of ſiſters.

HOOD. *n. ſ.* [hod, Saxon, probably from heafod, head.]

1. The upper covering of a woman's head.

In velvet, white as ſnow, the troop was gown'd;
Their *hoods* and ſleeves the ſame. *Dryden's Fables.*

2. Any thing drawn upon the head, and wrapping round it.

Undertaking ſo to geſture and muffle up himſelf in his *hood*, as the duke's manner was to ride in cold weather, that none ſhould diſcern him. *Wotton.*

The lacerna came, from being a military habit, to be a common dreſs: it had a *hood*, which could be ſeparated or joined to it. *Arbuthnot on Coins.*

3. A covering put over the hawk's eyes, when he is not to fly.

4. An ornamental fold that hangs down the back of a graduate, to mark his degree.

To Hood. *v. a.* [from the noun.]

1. To dreſs in a hood.

The cobler apron'd, and the parſon gown'd,
The friar *hooded*, and the monarch crown'd. *Pope.*

2. To blind, as with a hood.

While grace is ſaying, I'll *hood* mine eyes
Thus with my hat, and ſigh, and ſay, amen. *Shakeſpeare.*

3. To cover.

An hollow cryſtal pyramid he takes,
In firmamental waters dipt above;
Of it a broad extinguiſher he makes,
And *hoods* the flames that to their quarry ſtrove. *Dryden.*

Ho'odman's *Blind. n. ſ.* A play in which the perſon hooded is to catch another, and tell the name; blindman's buff.

What devil was't,
That thus hath cozen'd you at *hoodman blind*? *Shak. Haml.*

To Ho'od-wink. *v. a.* [*hood* and *wink.*]

1. To blind with ſomething bound over the eyes.

They willingly *hood-winking* themſelves from ſeeing his faults, he often abuſed the virtue of courage to defend his foul vice of injuſtice. *Sidney.*

We will bind and *hood-wink* him ſo, that he ſhall ſuppoſe he is carried into the leaguer of the adverſaries. *Shakeſpeare.*

You may
Convey your pleaſures in a ſpacious plenty,
And yet ſeem cold, the time you may ſo *hood-wink*. *Shakeſ.*

Then ſhe who hath been *hood-wink'd* from her birth,
Doth firſt herſelf within death's mirrour ſee. *Davies.*

So have I ſeen, at Chriſtmaſs ſports, one loſt,
And, *hood-wink'd*, for a man embrace a poſt. *Ben. Johnſon.*

Satan is fain to *hood-wink* thoſe that are apt to ſtart. *Decay of Piety.*

Prejudice ſo dexterouſly *hood-winks* mens minds as to keep them in the dark, with a belief that they are more in the light. *Locke.*

Muſt I wed Rodogune?
Fantaſtick cruelty of *hood-wink'd* chance! *Rowe.*

On high, where no hoarſe winds or clouds reſort,
The *hood-wink'd* goddeſs keeps her partial court. *Garth.*

2. To cover; to hide.

Be patient; for the prize, I'll bring thee to,
Shall *hood-wink* this miſchance. *Shakeſpeare's Tempeſt.*

3. To deceive; to impoſe upon.

She delighted in infamy, which often ſhe had uſed to her huſband's ſhame, filling all mens ears, but his, with reproach; while he, *hood-winked* with kindneſs, leaſt of all men knew who ſtruck him. *Sidney.*

HOOF. *n. ſ.* [hof, Saxon; *hoef*, Dutch.] The hard horny ſubſtance on the feet of graminivorous animals.

With the *hoofs* of his horſes ſhall he tread down all thy ſtreets. *Ezek.* xxvi. 11.

The bull and ram know the uſe of their horns as well as the horſe of his *hoofs*. *More's Antidote againſt Atheiſm.*

Ho'ofed. *adj.* [from *hoof.*] Furniſhed with hoofs.

Among quadrupeds, the roe-deer is the ſwifteſt; of all the *hoofed*, the horſe is the moſt beautiful; of all the clawed, the lion is the ſtrongeſt. *Grew's Coſmol. Sac. b.* ii. *c.* 8.

Hoof-bound. *adj.* [*hoof* and *bound.*]

A horſe is ſaid to be *hoof-bound* when he has a pain in the forefeet, occaſioned by the dryneſs and contraction or narrowneſs of the horn of the quarters, which ſtraitens the quarters of the heels, and oftentimes makes the horſe lame. A *hoof-bound* horſe has a narrow heel, the ſides of which come too near one another, inſomuch that the fleſh is kept too tight, and has not its natural extent. *Farrier's Dict.*

HOOK. *n. ſ.* [hoce, Saxon; *hoeck*, Dutch.]

1. Any thing bent ſo as to catch hold: as, a ſhepherd's *hook* and pot *hooks*.

This falling not, for that they had not far enough undermined it, they aſſayed with great *hooks* and ſtrong ropes to have pulled it down. *Knolles.*

2. The curvated wire on which the bait is hung for fiſhes, and with which the fiſh is pierced.

Like unto golden *hooks*,
That from the fooliſh fiſh their baits do hide. *Spenſer.*

My bended *hook* ſhall pierce
Their ſlimy jaws. *Shakeſ. Ant. and Cleopatra.*

Though divine Plato thus of pleaſures thought,
They us with *hooks* and baits, like fiſhes, caught. *Denham.*

3. A ſnare; a trap.

A ſhop of all the qualities that man
Loves woman for, beſides that *hook* of wiving,
Fairneſs, which ſtrikes the eye. *Shakeſp. Cymbeline.*

4. A ſickle to reap corn.

Peaſe are commonly reaped with a *hook* at the end of a long ſtick. *Mortimer's Huſbandry.*

5. An iron to ſeize the meat in the caldron.

About the caldron many cooks accoil'd,
With *hooks* and ladles, as need did require;
The while the viands in the veſſel boil'd. *Fairy Queen, b.* ii.

6. Any inſtrument to cut or lop with.

Not that I'd lop the beauties from his book,
Like ſlaſhing Bentley with his deſperate *hook*. *Pope.*

7. The part of the hinge fixed to the poſt: whence the proverb, *off the hooks*, for in diſorder.

My doublet looks,
Like him that wears it, quite *off* o' *the hooks*. *Cleaveland.*

She was horribly bold, meddling and expenſive, eaſily put *off the hooks*, and monſtrous hard to be pleaſed again. *L'Eſtr.*

While Sheridan is *off the hooks*,
And friend Delany at his books. *Swift.*

8. Hook. [In huſbandry.] A field ſown two years running. *Ainſ.*

9. Hook *or Crook.* One way or other; by any expedient; by any means direct or oblique.

Which he by *hook or crook* had gather'd,
And for his own inventions father'd. *Hudibras, p.* iii.

He would bring him by *hook or crook* into his quarrel. *Dryd.*

To Hook. *v. a.* [from the noun.]

1. To catch with a hook.

The huge jack he had caught was ſerved up for the firſt diſh: upon our ſitting down to it, he gave us a long account how he had *hooked* it, played with it, foiled it, and at length drew it out upon the bank. *Addiſon's Spectator.*

2. To intrap; to enſnare.

3. To draw as with a hook.

But ſhe
I can *hook* to me. *Shakeſpeare's Winter's Tale.*

4. To faſten as with an hook.

5. To be drawn by force or artifice.

There are many branches of the natural law no way reducible to the two tables, unleſs *hooked* in by tedious conſequences. *Norris.*

HO'OKED. *adj.* [from *hook*.] Bent; curvated.

Gryps signifies eagle or vulture; from whence the epithet grypus, for an *hooked* or aquiline nose. *Brown.*

Now thou threaten'st, with unjust decree,
To seize the prize which I so dearly bought:
Mean match to thine; for still above the rest,
Thy *hook'd* rapacious hands usurp the best. *Dryden.*

Caterpillars have claws and feet: the claws are *hooked*, to take the better hold in climbing from twig to twig, and hanging on the backsides of leaves. *Grew's Cosmol. Sac.*

HO'OKEDNESS. *n. s.* [from *hooked*. State of being bent like a hook.

HOOKNO'SED. *adj.* [*hook* and *nose*.] Having the aquiline nose rising in the middle.

I may justly say with the *hook-nosed* fellow of Rome there, Cæsar, I came, saw, and overcame. *Shakes. Henry* IV. *p.* ii.

HOOP. *n. s.* [*hoep*, Dutch.]

1. Any thing circular by which something else is bound, particularly casks or barrels.

Thou shalt prove a shelter to thy friends,
A *hoop* of gold to bind thy brothers in,
That the united vessel of their blood
Shall never leak. *Shakesp. Henry* IV. *p.* ii.

If I knew
What *hoop* would hold us staunch, from edge to edge
O' th' world I would pursue it. *Shakesp. Ant. and Cleopat.*

A quarrel, ho, already! what's the matter?
—About a *hoop* of gold, a paltry ring. *Shak. Merch. of Ven.*

To view so lewd a town, and to refrain,
What *hoops* of iron could my spleen contain! *Dryd. Juven.*

And learned Athens to our art must stoop,
Could she behold us tumbling through a *hoop*. *Pope.*

3. The whalebone with which women extend their petticoats; a farthingale.

A petticoat without a *hoop*. *Swift.*

At coming in you saw her stoop;
The entry brush'd against her *hoop*. *Swift.*

All that *hoops* are good for is to clean dirty shoes, and to keep fellows at distance. *Clarissa.*

2. Any thing circular.

I have seen at Rome an antique statue of time, with a wheel or *hoop* of marble in his hand. *Addison on Italy.*

To HOOP. *v. a.* [from the noun.]

1. To bind or enclose with hoops.

The three *hoop'd* pot shall have ten hoops, and I will make it felony to drink small beer. *Shakespeare's Henry* VI. *p.* ii.

The cask for his majesty's shipping were *hooped* as a wine-cask, or *hooped* with iron. *Raleigh's Essays.*

2. To encircle; to clasp; to surround.

If ever henceforth thou
Shalt *hoop* his body more with thy embraces,
I will devise a death. *Shakesp. Winter's Tale.*

I *hoop* the firmament, and make
This my embrace the zodiack. *Cleaveland.*

That shelly guard, which *hoops* in the eye, and hides the greater part of it, might occasion his mistake. *Grew's Mus.*

To HOOP. *v. n.* [from *wopgan* or *wopyan*, Gothick; or *houper*, French, derived from the Gothick. This word is generally written *whoop*, which is more proper, if we deduce it from the Gothick; and *hoop*, if we derive it from the French.] To shout; to make an outcry by way of call or pursuit.

To HOOP. *v. a.*

1. To drive with a shout.

Dastard nobles
Suffer'd me, by th' voice of slaves, to be
Hoop'd out of Rome. *Shakespeare's Coriolanus.*

2. To call by a shout.

HO'OPER. *n. s.* [from *hoop*, to inclose with hoops.] A cooper; one that hoops tubs.

HO'OPING-COUGH. *n. s.* [or *whooping-cough*, from *hoop*, to shout.] A convulsive cough, so called from its noise; the chine cough.

To HOOT. *v. n.* [*hwt*, Welsh; *huer*, French.]

1. To shout in contempt.

A number of country folks happened to pass thereby, who hollowed and *hooted* after me as at the arrantest coward. *Sidney.*

Matrons and girls shall *hoot* at thee no more. *Dryd. Juv.*

2. To cry as an owl.

Some keep back
The clamorous owl, that nightly *hoots*, and wonders
At our queint sports. *Shakes. Midsum. Night's Dream.*

To HOOT. *v. a.* To drive with noise and shouts.

We lov'd him; but, like beasts,
Our coward nobles gave way to your clusters,
Who did *hoot* him out o' th' city. *Shakesp. Coriolanus.*

The owl of Rome, whom boys and girls will *hoot*!
That were I set up for that wooden god
That keeps our gardens, could not fright the crows,
Or the least bird, from muting on my head. *Ben. Johnson.*

Patridge and his clan may *hoot* me for a cheat and impostor, if I fail in any particular of moment. *Swift.*

HOOT. *n. s.* [*huée*, French, from the verb.] Clamour; shout; noise.

Its assertion would be entertained with the *hoot* of the rabble. *Glanville's Sceps.*

To HOP. *v. n.* [hoppan, Saxon; *hoppen*, Dutch.]

1. To jump; to skip lightly.

I would have thee gone,
And yet no further than a wanton's bird,
That lets it *hop* a little from her hand,
And with a silk thread plucks it back again. *Shakespeare.*

Go, *hop* me over every kennel home;
For you shall *hop* without my custom, sir. *Shakespeare.*

Be kind and curteous to this gentleman,
Hop in his walks, and gambol in his eyes. *Shakespeare.*

The painted birds, companions of the Spring,
Hopping from spray to spray were heard. *Dryden.*

Your Ben and Fletcher, in their first young flight,
Did no Volpone, nor no Arbaces write;
But *hopp'd* about, and short excursions made
From bough to bough, as if they were afraid. *Dryden.*

Why don't we vindicate ourselves by trial ordeal, and *hop* over heated ploughshares blindfold. *Collier on Duelling.*

I am highly delighted to see the jay or the thrush *hopping* about my walks. *Spectator.*

2. To leap on one leg.

Men with heads like dogs, and others with one huge foot alone, whereupon they did *hop* from place to place. *Abbot.*

3. To walk lamely, or with one leg less nimble or strong than the other; to limp; to halt.

The limping smith observ'd the sadden'd feast,
And *hopping* here and there, himself a jest,
Put in his word. *Dryden's Homer.*

4. To move; to play.

Softly feel
Her feeble pulse, to prove if any drop
Of living blood yet in her veins did *hop*. *Fairy Queen, b.* ii.

HOP. *n. s.* [from the verb.]

1. A jump; a light leap.

2. A jump on one leg.

When my wings are on, I can go above a hundred yards at a *hop*, step, and jump. *Addison's Guardian.*

3. A place where meaner people dance. *Ainsworth.*

HOP. *n. s.* [*hop*, Dutch; *lupulus*, Latin.] A plant.

It has a creeping root: the leaves are rough, angular, and conjugated; the stalks climb and twist about whatever is near them; the flowers are male and female on different plants: the male flower consists of a calyx divided into five parts, which surrounds the stamina, but has no petals to the flower: the female plants have their flowers collected into squamose heads, which grow in bunches: from each of the leafy scales is produced an horned ovary, which becomes a single roundish seed. *Miller.*

If *hop* yard or orchard ye mind for to have,
For *hop* poles and crotches in lopping go save. *Tuss. Husb.*

The planting of *hop* yards is profitable for the planters, and consequently for the kingdom. *Bacon's Advice to Villiers.*

Beer hath malt first infused in the liquor, and is afterwards boiled with the *hop*. *Bacon's Natural History.*

Next to thistles are *hop* strings, cut after the flowers are gathered. *Derham's Physico-Theology.*

Have the poles without forks, otherwise it will be troublesome to part the *hop* vines and the poles. *Mortimer's Husband.*

When you water *hops*, on the top of every hill put dissolved dung, which will enrich your *hop* hills. *Mortimer's Husbandry.*

In Kent they plant their *hop* gardens with apple-trees and cherry-trees between. *Mortimer's Husbandry.*

The price of hoeing of *hop* ground is forty shillings an acre. *Mortimer's Husbandry.*

Hop poles, the largest sort, should be about twenty foot long, and about nine inches in compass. *Mortimer's Husband.*

To HOP. *v. a.* [from the noun.]

1. To impregnate with hops.

Brew in March or October, and *hop* it for long keeping. *Mortimer's Husbandry.*

To increase the milk, diminished by flesh-meat, take malt-drink not much *hopped*. *Arbuthnot on Aliments.*

HOPE. *n. s.* [hopa, Saxon; *hope*, Dutch.]

1. Expectation of some good; an expectation indulged with pleasure.

There is *hope* of a tree, if cut down, that it will sprout again. *Job* xiv. 7.

Hope is that pleasure in the mind which every one finds in himself, upon the thought of a profitable future enjoyment of a thing, which is apt to delight him. *Locke.*

When in heav'n she shall his essence see,
This is her sov'reign good, and perfect bliss;
Her longing, wishings, *hopes*, all finish'd be;
Her joys are full, her motions rest in this. *Davies.*

Sweet *hope*! kind cheat! fair fallacy! by thee
We are not where or what we be;
But what and where we would be: thus art thou
Our absent presence, and our future now. *Crashaw.*

Faith

Faith is opposed to infidelity, and *hope* to despair. *Taylor.*

He sought them both, but wish'd his hap might find
Eve separate: he wish'd, but not with *hope*
Of what so seldom chanc'd: when to his wish,
Beyond his *hope*, Eve separate he spies. *Milton's Parad. Lost.*

The Trojan dames
To Pallas' fane in long procession go,
In *hopes* to reconcile their heav'nly foe. *Dryden's Virg. Æn.*

Why not comfort myself with the *hope* of what may be, as torment myself with the fear on't? *L'Estrange.*

To encourage our *hopes* it gives us the highest assurance of most lasting happiness, in case of obedience. *Tillotson.*

The deceased really lived like one that had his *hope* in another life; a life which he hath now entered upon, having exchanged *hope* for sight, desire for enjoyment. *Atterbury.*

Young men look rather to the past age than the present, and therefore the future may have some *hopes* of them. *Swift.*

2. Confidence in a future event, or in the future conduct of any body.

It is good, being put to death by men, to look for *hope* from God, to be raised up again by him. 2 *Mac.* vii. 14.

Blessed is he who is not fallen from his *hope* in the Lord. *Eccluf.* xiv. 2.

I had *hope* of France,
Ev'n as I have of fertile England's soil. *Shakes. Henry* VI.

3. That which gives hope; that on which the hopes are fixed, as an agent by which something desired may be effected.

I might see from far some forty truncheoneers draw to her succour, which were the *hope* of the Strand, where she was quarter'd. *Shakespeare's Henry* VIII.

4. The object of hope.

Thy mother felt more than a mother's pain,
And yet brought forth less than a mother's *hope*;
To wit, an indigested deform'd lump. *Shakes. Henry* VI.

She was his care, his *hope*, and his delight,
Most in his thought, and ever in his sight. *Dryden.*

HOPE. *n. s.* Any sloping plain between the ridges of mountains. *Ainsworth.*

To HOPE. *v. n.* [from the noun.]

1. To live in expectation of some good.

Hope for good success, according to the efficacy of the causes and the instrument; and let the husbandman *hope* for a good harvest. *Taylor's Rule of living holy.*

My muse, by storms long tost,
Is thrown upon your hospitable coast;
And finds more favour by her ill success,
Than she could *hope* for by her happiness. *Dryden.*

Who knows what adverse fortune may befall!
Arm well your mind, *hope* little, and fear all. *Dryden.*

2. To place confidence in futurity.

He shall strengthen your heart, all ye that *hope* in the Lord. *Ps.* xxxi. 24.

To HOPE. *v. a.* To expect with desire.

The sun shines hot; and if we use delay,
Cold-biting Winter mars our *hop'd* for hay. *Shak. Hen.* VI.

So stands the Thracian herdsman with his spear
Full in the gap, and *hopes* the hunted bear. *Dryden's Fables.*

HO'PEFUL. *adj.* [*hope* and *full.*]

1. Full of qualities which produce hope; promising; likely to obtain success; likely to come to maturity; likely to gratify desire, or answer expectation.

He will advance thee:
I know his noble nature, not to let
Thy *hopeful* service perish. *Shakesp. Henry* VIII.

You serve a great and gracious master, and there is a most *hopeful* young prince whom you must not desert. *Bacon.*

What to the old can greater pleasure be,
Than *hopeful* and ingenious youth to see? *Denham.*

They take up a book in their declining years, and grow very *hopeful* scholars by that time they are threescore. *Addison.*

2. Full of hope; full of expectation of success. This sense is now almost confined to Scotland, though it is analogical, and found in good writers.

Men of their own natural inclination *hopeful* and strongly conceited, whatsoever they took in hand. *Hooker, b.* v.

I was *hopeful* the success of your first attempts would encourage you to make trial also of more nice and difficult experiments. *Boyle.*

Whatever ills the friendless orphan bears,
Bereav'd of parents in his infant years,
Still must the wrong'd Telemachus sustain,
If *hopeful* of your aid, he hopes in vain. *Pope's Odyssey.*

HO'PEFULLY. *adv.* [from *hopeful.*]

1. In such a manner as to raise hope; in a promising way.

He left all his female kindred either matched with peers of the realm actually, or *hopefully* with earls sons and heirs. *Wott.*

They were ready to renew the war, and to prosecute it *hopefully*, to the reduction or suppression of the Irish. *Clarendon.*

2. With hope; without despair. This sense is rare.

From your promising and generous endeavours we may *hopefully* expect a considerable enlargement of the history of nature. *Glanv. Sceps. Preface.*

HO'PEFULNESS. *n. s.* [from *hopeful.*] Promise of good; likelihood to succeed.

Set down beforehand certain signatures of *hopefulness*, or characters, whereby may be timely described what the child will prove in probability. *Wotton.*

HO'PELESS. *adj.* [from *hope.*]

1. Without hope; without pleasing expectation.

Are they indifferent, being used as signs of immoderate and *hopeless* lamentation for the dead? *Hooker, b.* iv.

Alas, I am a woman, friendless, *hopeless!* *Shakespeare.*

He watches with greedy hope to find
His wish, and best advantage, us asunder;
Hopeless to circumvent us join'd, where each
To other speedy aid might lend at need. *Milt. Parad. Lost.*

The fall'n archangel, envious of our state,
And *hopeless* to prevail by open force,
Seeks hid advantage. *Dryden's State of Innocence.*

Hopeless of ransom, and condemn'd to lie
In durance, doom'd a ling'ring death to die. *Dryden's Fab.*

2. Giving no hope; promising nothing pleasing.

The *hopeless* word of never to return,
Breathe I against thee upon pain of life. *Shakesp. R.* II.

HO'PER. *n. s.* [from *hope.*] One that has pleasing expectations.

I except all *hopers*, who turn the scale, because the strong expectation of a good certain salary, will outweigh the loss by bad rents. *Swift on the Sacramental Test.*

HO'PINGLY. *adv.* [from *hoping.*] With hope; with expectation of good.

One sign of despair is the peremptory contempt of the condition which is the ground of hope; the going on not only in terrours and amazement of conscience, but also boldly, *hopingly*, and confidently in wilful habits of sin. *Hammond.*

HO'PPER. *n. s.* [from *hop.*] He who hops or jumps on one leg. *Ainsworth.*

HO'PPERS. [commonly called *Scotch hoppers.*] A kind of play in which the actor hops on one leg.

HO'PPER. *n. s.* [so called because it is always *hopping*, or in agitation. It is called in French, for the same reason, *tremie* or *tremue.*]

1. The box or open frame of wood into which the corn is put to be ground.

The salt of the lake Asphaltites shooteth into perfect cubes: sometimes they are pyramidal and plain, like the *hopper* of a mill. *Grew's Cosmol. Sac.*

Granivorous birds have the mechanism of a mill: their maw is the *hopper* which holds and softens the grain, letting it drop by degrees into the stomach. *Arbuthnot on Aliments.*

Just at the *hopper* will I stand,
In my whole life I never saw grist ground,
And mark the clack how justly it will sound. *Betterton.*

2. A basket for carrying seed. *Ainsworth.*

HO'RAL. *adj.* [from *hora*, Latin.] Relating to the hour.

Howe'er reduc'd and plain,
The watch would still a watch remain;
But if the *horal* orbit ceases,
The whole stands still, or breaks to pieces. *Prior.*

HO'RARY. *adj.* [*horaire*, French; *horarius*, Latin.]

1. Relating to an hour.

I'll draw a figure that shall tell you
What you perhaps forgot befell you,
By way of *horary* inspection,
Which some account our worst erection. *Hudibras, p.* ii.

In his answer to an *horary* question, as what hour of the night to set a fox-trap, he has largely discussed, under the character of Reynard, the manner of surprising all sharpers. *Tatler*, N°. 56.

2. Continuing for an hour.

When, from a basket of Summer-fruit, God by Amos foretold the destruction of his people, thereby was declared the propinquity of their desolation, and that their tranquility was of no longer duration than those *horary* or soon decaying fruits of Summer. *Brown's Vulgar Errours.*

HORDE. *n. s.* A clan; a migratory crew of people.

Of lost mankind, in polish'd slavery sunk,
Drove martial *horde* on *horde* with dreadful sweep,
And gave the vanquish'd world another form. *Thoms. Winter.*

HORI'ZON. *n. s.* [ὁρίζων.] The line that terminates the view. The *horizon* is distinguished into sensible and real: the sensible horizon is the circular line which limits the view; the real is that which would bound it, if it could take in the hemisphere. It is falsely pronounced by *Shakespeare hórizon.*

When the morning sun shall raise his car
Above the border of this *horizon*,
We'll forward towards Warwick and his mates. *Shakesp.*

She began to cast with herself from what coast this blazing star should first appear, and at what time it must be upon the *horizon* of Ireland. *Bacon's Henry* VII.

Far in th' *horizon* to the North appear'd,
From skirt to skirt, a fiery region. *Milton's Paradise Lost.*

In his East the glorious lamp was seen,
Regent of day; and all th' *horizon* round
Invested with bright rays. *Milton's Paradise Lost, b.* vii.

The morning lark, the meſſenger of day,
Saluted in her ſong the morning gray;
And ſoon the ſun aroſe with beams ſo bright,
That all th' *horizon* laugh'd to ſee the joyous ſight. *Dryden.*

When the ſea is worked up in a tempeſt, ſo that the *horizon* on every ſide is nothing but foaming billows and floating mountains, it is impoſſible to deſcribe the agreeable horrour that riſes from ſuch a proſpect. *Addiſon's Spectator.*

HORIZO'NTAL. *adj.* [*horizontal*, French, from *horizon.*]

1. Near the horizon.

As when the ſun, new riſen,
Looks through the *horizontal* miſty air,
Shorn of his beams; or from behind the moon,
In dim eclipſe, diſaſtrous twilight ſheds
On half the nations. *Milton's Paradiſe Loſt*, *b.* i.

2. Parallel to the horizon; on a level.

An obeliſk erected, and golden figures placed *horizontal* about it, was brought out of Egypt by Auguſtus. *Brown.*

The problem is reduced to this; what perpendicular height is neceſſary to place ſeveral ranks of rowers in a plane inclined to a *horizontal* line in a given angle? *Arbuthnot on Coins.*

HORIZO'NTALLY. *adv.* [from *horizontal.*] In a direction parallel to the horizon.

As it will not ſink into the bottom, ſo will it neither float above, like lighter bodies; but, being near in weight, lie ſuperficially, or almoſt *horizontally* unto it. *Brown's Vulg. Err.*

The ambient ether is too liquid and empty to impel them *horizontally* with celerity. *Bentley's Sermons.*

HORN. *n. ſ.* [*haurn*, Gothick; ȝorn, Saxon; *horn*, Dutch.]

1. The hard pointed bodies which grow on the heads of ſome graminivorous quadrupeds, and ſerve them for weapons.

No beaſt that hath *horns* hath upper teeth. *Bacon's N. Hiſt.*

Zetus riſes through the ground,
Bending the bull's tough neck with pain,
That toſſes back his *horns* in vain. *Addiſon on Italy.*

All that proceſs is no more ſurpriſing than the eruption of *horns* in ſome brutes, or of teeth and beard in men at certain periods of age. *Bentley's Sermons.*

2. An inſtrument of wind-muſick made of horn.

The ſquire 'gan nigher to approach,
And wind his *horn* under the caſtle-wall,
That with the noiſe it ſhook as it would fall. *Fairy Queen.*

There's a poſt come from my maſter, with his *horn* full of good news. *Shakeſp. Merchant of Venice.*

The goddeſs to her crooked *horn*
Adds all her breath: the rocks and woods around,
And mountains, tremble at th' infernal ſound. *Dryden.*

Fair Aſcanius, and his youthful train,
With *horns* and hounds a hunting match ordain. *Dryden.*

3. The extremity of the waxing or waining moon, as mentioned by poets.

She bleſs'd the bed, ſuch fruitfulneſs convey'd,
That ere ten moons had ſharpen'd either *horn*,
To crown their bliſs, a lovely boy was born. *Dryden.*

The moon
Wears a wan circle round her blunted *horns*. *Thomſon.*

4. The feelers of a ſnail. Whence the proverb, *To pull in the horns*, to repreſs one's ardour.

Love's feeling is more ſoft and ſenſible,
Than are the tender *horns* of cockled ſnails. *Shakeſpeare.*

Aufidius,
Hearing of our Marcius's baniſhment,
Thruſt forth his *horns* again into the world,
Which were inſhell'd when Marcius ſtood for Rome,
And durſt not once peep out. *Shakeſp. Coriolanus.*

5. A drinking cup made of horn.

6. Antler of a cuckold.

If I have *horns* to make one mad,
Let the proverb go with me, I'll be horn mad. *Shakeſpeare.*

Merchants, vent'ring through the main,
Slight pyrates, rocks, and *horns* for gain. *Hudibras, p.* ii.

7. HORN *mad.* Perhaps mad as a cuckold.

I am glad he went not in himſelf: if he had, he would have been *horn mad.* *Shakeſp. Merry Wives of Windſor.*

HORNBE'AK. } *n. ſ.* A kind of fiſh. *Ainſworth.*
HORNFI'SH. }

HO'RNBEAM. *n. ſ.* [*horn* and *boem*, Dutch, for *tree*, from the hardneſs of the timber.]

It hath leaves like the elm or beech-tree: the katkins are placed at remote diſtances from the fruit on the ſame tree, and the outward ſhell of the fruit is winged. This tree was formerly much uſed in hedges for wilderneſſes and orangeries. The timber is very tough and inflexible, and of excellent uſe. *Miller.*

HO'RNBOOK. *n. ſ.* [*horn* and *book*] The firſt book of children, covered with horn to keep it unſoiled.

He teaches boys the *hornbook*. *Shak. Love's Labour Loſt.*

Nothing has been conſidered of this kind out of the ordinary road of the *hornbook* and primer. *Locke.*

To maſter John the Engliſh maid
A *hornbook* gives of ginger-bread;
And that the child may learn the better,
As he can name, he eats the letter. *Prior.*

HO'RNED. *adj.* [from *horn.*] Furniſhed with horns.

As when two rams, ſtirr'd with ambitious pride,
Fight for the rule of the rich fleeced flock,
Their *horned* fronts ſo fierce on either ſide
Do meet, that, with the terrour of the ſhock,
Aſtoniſhed both ſtand ſenſeleſs as a block. *Fairy Queen, b.* i.

O, that I were
Upon the hill of Baſan, to out-roar
The *horned* herd. *Shakeſ. Ant. and Cleopatra.*

Thither all the *horned* hoſt reſorts,
To graze the ranker mead. *Denham.*

Thou king of *horned* floods, whoſe plenteous urn
Suffices fatneſs to the fruitful corn. *Dryden.*

HO'RNER. *n. ſ.* [from *horn.*] One that works in horn, and ſells horns.

The ſkin of a bull's forehead is the part of the hide made uſe of by *horners*, whereupon they ſhave their horns. *Grew.*

HO'RNET. *n. ſ.* [ȝẏrnette, Saxon, from its horns] A very large ſtrong ſtinging fly, which makes its neſt in hollow trees.

Silence, in times of ſuff'ring, is the beſt;
'Tis dangerous to diſturb a *hornet*'s neſt. *Dryden.*

Hornets do miſchief to trees by breeding in them. *Mortim.*

I have often admired how *hornets*, that gather dry materials for building their neſts, have found a proper matter to glue their combs. *Derham's Phyſico-Theology.*

HO'RNFOOT. *n. ſ.* [*horn* and *foot.*] Hoofed.

Mad frantick man,
That did not inly quake!
With *hornfoot* horſes, and braſs wheels,
Jove's ſtorms to emulate. *Hakewill on Providence.*

HO'RNOWL. *n. ſ.* A kind of horned owl. *Ainſworth.*

HO'RNPIPE. *n. ſ.* [*horn* and *pipe.*] A county dance, danced commonly to a horn.

A luſty tabrere,
That to thee many a *hornpipe* play'd,
Whereto they dauncen each one with his maid. *Spenſer.*

There many a *hornpipe* he tun'd to his Phyllis. *Raleigh.*

Let all the quickſilver i' the mine
Run t' the feet-veins, and refine
Your firkhum jerkhum to a dance
Shall fetch the fiddlers out of France,
To wonder at the *hornpipes* here
Of Nottingham and Derbyſhire. *Ben. Johnſon.*

Florinda danced the Derbyſhire *hornpipe* in the preſence of ſeveral friends. *Tatler*, N°. 106.

HO'RNSTONE. *n. ſ.* A kind of blue ſtone. *Ainſworth.*

HO'RNWORK. *n. ſ.* A kind of angular fortification.

HO'RNY. *adj.* [from *horn.*]

1. Made of horn.

2. Reſembling horn.

He thought he by the brook of Cherith ſtood,
And ſaw the ravens with their *horny* beaks
Food to Elijah bringing even and morn. *Milton's Pa. Loſt.*

The *horny* or pellucid coat of the eye doth not lie in the ſame ſuperficies with the white of the eye, but riſeth up above its convexity, and is of an hyperbolical figure. *Ray.*

Rough are her ears, and broad her *horny* feet. *Dryd. Virg.*

The pineal gland was encompaſſed with a kind of *horny* ſubſtance. *Addiſon's Spectat.*

As the ſerum of the blood is reſolvable by a ſmall heat, a greater heat coagulates it ſo as to turn it *horny*, like parchment; but when it is thoroughly putrified, it will no longer concrete. *Arbuthnot on Aliments.*

3. Hard as horn; callous.

Tyrrheus, the foſter-father of the beaſt,
Then clench'd a hatchet in his *horny* fiſt. *Dryden's Æn.*

HORO'GRAPHY. *n. ſ.* [*horographie*, Fr. ὥρα and γράφω.] An account of the hours.

HO'ROLOGE. } *n. ſ.* [*horologium*, Latin.] Any inſtrument that
HO'ROLOGY. } tells the hour: as a clock; a watch; an hour-glaſs.

'Tis evermore the prologue to his ſleep;
He'll watch the *horologe* a double ſet,
If drink rock not his cradle. *Shakeſpeare's Othello.*

Before the days of Jerome there were *horologies*, that meaſured the hours not only by drops of water in glaſſes, called clepſydra, but alſo by ſand in glaſſes, called clepſammia. *Brown.*

HORO'METRY. *n. ſ.* [*horometrie*, French; ὥρα and μετρέω.] The art of meaſuring hours.

It is no eaſy wonder how the *horometry* of antiquity diſcovered not this artifice. *Brown's Vulgar Errours.*

HO'ROSCOPE. *n. ſ.* [*horoſcope*, French; ὡροσκόπος.] The configuration of the planets at the hour of birth.

How unlikely is it, that the many almoſt numberleſs conjunctions of ſtars, which occur in the progreſs of a man's life, ſhould not match and countervail that one *horoſcope* or conjunction which is found at his birth? *Drummond.*

A proportion of the *horoſcope* unto the ſeventh houſe, or oppoſite ſigns every ſeventh year, oppreſſeth living natures. *Bro.*

Him born beneath a boding *horoſcope*,
His fire, the blear-ey'd Vulcan of a ſhop,
From Mars his forge ſent to Minerva's ſchool. *Dryd. Juven.*

Where

The Greek names this the *horoscope*;
This governs life, and this marks out our parts,
Our humours, manners, qualities and arts. *Creech's Manil.*

They underſtood the planets and the zodiack by inſtinct, and fell to drawing ſchemes of their own *horoſcopes* in the ſame duſt they ſprung out of. *Bentley's Sermons.*

HO'RRIBLE. *adj.* [*horrible*, French; *horribilis*, Lat.] Dreadful; terrible; ſhocking; hideous; enormous.

No colour affecteth the eye much with diſpleaſure: there be ſights that are *horrible*, becauſe they excite the memory of things that are odious or fearful. *Bacon's Natural Hiſtory.*

Eternal happineſs and eternal miſery, meeting with a perſuaſion that the ſoul is immortal, are, of all others, the firſt the moſt deſireable, and the latter the moſt *horrible* to human apprehenſion. *South's Sermons.*

HO'RRIBLENESS. *n. ſ.* [from *horrible.*] Dreadfulneſs; hideouſneſs; terribleneſs; fearfulneſs.

HO'RRIBLY. *adv.* [from *horrible.*]

1. Dreadfully; hideouſly.

What hideous noiſe was that!
Horribly loud. *Milton's Agoniſtes.*

2. To a dreadful degree.

The contagion of theſe ill precedents, both in civility and virtue, *horribly* infects children. *Locke.*

HO'RRID. *adj.* [*horridus*, Latin.]

1. Hideous; dreadful; ſhocking.

Oh!
Give colour to my pale cheek with thy blood,
That we the *horrider* may ſeem to thoſe
Which chance to find us. *Shakeſpeare's Cymbeline.*

Not in the legions
Of *horrid* hell can come a devil more damn'd,
In evils to top Macbeth. *Shakeſpeare's Macbeth.*

2. Shocking; offenſive; unpleaſing: in womens cant.

Already I your tears ſurvey,
Already hear the *horrid* things they ſay. *Pope.*

3. Rough; rugged.

Horrid with fern, and intricate with thorn,
Few paths of human feet or tracks of beaſts were worn. *Dry.*

HO'RRIDNESS. *n. ſ.* [from *horrid.*] Hideouſneſs; enormity.

A bloody deſigner ſuborns his inſtrument to take away ſuch a man's life, and the confeſſor repreſents the *horridneſs* of the fact, and brings him to repentance. *Hammond.*

HO'RRIFICK. *adj.* [*horrificus*, Latin.] Cauſing horrour.

His jaws *horrifick*, arm'd with three-fold fate,
Here dwells the direful ſhark. *Thomſon's Summer.*

HORRI'SONOUS. *adj.* [*horriſonus*, Latin.] Sounding dreadfully. *Dict.*

HO'RROUR. *n. ſ.* [*horror*, Latin; *horreur*, French.]

1. Terrour mixed with deteſtation; a paſſion compounded of fear and hate, both ſtrong.

Over them ſad *horrour*, with grim hue,
Did always ſoar, beating his iron wings;
And after him owls and night ravens flew,
The hateful meſſengers of heavy things. *Fairy Queen, b.* ii.

I have ſupt full with *horrours*;
Direneſs, familiar to my ſlaught'rous thoughts,
Cannot once ſtart me. *Shakeſpeare's Macbeth.*

Doubtleſs all ſouls have a ſurviving thought,
Therefore of death we think with quiet mind;
But if we think of being turn'd to nought,
A trembling *horrour* in our ſouls we find. *Davies.*

Me damp *horrour* chill'd
At ſuch bold words, vouch'd with a deed ſo bold. *Milton.*

Deep *horrour* ſeizes ev'ry human breaſt;
Their pride is humbled, and their fear confeſt. *Dryden.*

2. Gloom; drearineſs.

Her gloomy preſence ſaddens all the ſcene,
Shades ev'ry flow'r, and darkens ev'ry green;
Deepens the murmur of the falling floods,
And breathes a browner *horrour* on the woods. *Pope.*

3. [In medicine.] Such a ſhuddering or quivering as precedes an ague-fit; a ſenſe of ſhuddering or ſhrinking. *Quincy.*

All objects of the ſenſes, which are very offenſive, do cauſe the ſpirits to retire; and, upon their flight, the parts are in ſome degree deſtitute, and ſo there is induced in them a trepidation and *horrour*. *Bacon's Natural Hiſtory.*

HORSE. *n. ſ.* [hoꞃꞅ, Saxon.]

1. A neighing quadruped, uſed in war, and draught and carriage.

Duncan's *horſes*, the minions of the race,
Turn'd wild in nature, broke their ſtalls. *Shakeſp. Macbeth.*

A *horſe!* a *horſe!* my kingdom for a *horſe!* *Shak. R.* III.

I would ſell my *horſe*, and buy ten more
Better than he. *Shakeſp. Timon of Athens.*

Thy face, bright centaur, Autumn's heats retain,
The ſofter ſeaſon ſuiting to the man;
Whilſt Winter's ſhivering goat afflicts the *horſe*
With froſt, and makes him an uneaſy courſe. *Creech.*

We call a little *horſe*, ſuch a one as comes not up to the ſize of that idea which we have in our minds to belong ordinarily to *horſes*. *Locke.*

I took *horſe* to the lake of Conſtance, which is formed by the entry of the Rhine. *Addiſon on Italy.*

2. It is uſed in the plural ſenſe, but with a ſingular termination, for horſes, horſemen, or cavalry.

I did hear
The galloping of *horſe*: who was't came by? *Shak. Macb.*

The armies were appointed, conſiſting of twenty-five thouſand *horſe* and foot, for the repulſing of the enemy at their landing. *Bacon's War with Spain.*

If they had known that all the king's *horſe* were quartered behind them, their foot might very well have marched away with their *horſe*. *Clarendon, b.* viii.

Th' Arcadian *horſe*
With ill ſucceſs engage the Latin force. *Dryden's Æn.*

3. Something on which any thing is ſupported: as, a *horſe* to dry linnen on.

4. A wooden machine which ſoldiers ride by way of puniſhment. It is ſometimes called a timber-mare.

5. Joined to another ſubſtantive, it ſignifies ſomething large or coarſe: as, a *horſeface*, a face of which the features are large and indelicate.

To HORSE. *v. a.* [from the noun.]

1. To mount upon a horſe.

He came out with all his clowns, *horſed* upon ſuch cart-jades, and ſo furniſhed, as in good faith I thought with myſelf, if that were thrift, I wiſht none of my friends or ſubjects ever to thrive. *Sidney, b.* ii.

After a great fight there came to the camp of Gonſalvo, the great captain, a gentleman proudly *horſed* and armed: Diego de Mendoza aſked the great captain, Who's this? Who anſwered, It is St. Ermin, who never appears but after the ſtorm. *Bacon's Apophthegms.*

2. To carry one on the back.

3. To ride any thing.

Stalls, bulks, windows
Are ſmother'd, leads fill'd, and ridges *hors'd*
With variable complexions; all agreeing
In earneſtneſs to ſee him. *Shakeſpeare.*

4. To cover a mare.

If you let him out to *horſe* more mares than your own, you muſt feed him well. *Mortimer's Huſbandry.*

HO'RSEBACK. *n. ſ.* [*horſe* and *back.*] The ſeat of the rider; the ſtate of being on a horſe.

I've ſeen the French,
And they can well on *horſeback*. *Shakeſpeare's Hamlet.*

I ſaw them ſalute on *horſeback*,
Beheld them when they lighted. *Shakeſpeare's Henry* VIII.

He fought but one remarkable battle wherein there were any elephants, and that was with Porus, king of India; in which notwithſtanding he was on *horſeback*. *Brown's Vul. Err.*

When manniſh Mevia, that two-handed whore,
Aſtride on *horſeback* hunts the Tuſcan boar. *Dryd. Juvenal.*

If your ramble was on *horſeback*, I am glad of it, on account of your health. *Swift to Gay.*

HORSEBEA'N. *n. ſ.* [*horſe* and *bean.*] A ſmall bean uſually given to horſes.

Only the ſmall *horſebean* is propagated by the plough. *Mort.*

HO'RSEBLOCK. *n. ſ.* [*horſe* and *block.*] A block on which they climb to a horſe.

HORSEBOA'T. *n. ſ.* [*horſe* and *boat.*] A boat uſed in ferrying horſes.

HORSEBO'Y. *n. ſ.* [*horſe* and *boy.*] A boy employed in dreſſing horſes; a ſtableboy.

Some *horſeboys*, being awake, diſcovered them by the fire in their matches. *Knolles's Hiſtory of the Turks.*

HO'RSEBREAKER. *n. ſ.* [*horſe* and *break.*] One whoſe employment it is to tame horſes to the ſaddle.

Under Sagittarius are born chariot-racers, *horſebreakers*, and tamers of wild beaſts. *Creech.*

HORSECHE'SNUT. *n. ſ.* [*horſe* and *cheſnut.*] A plant.

It hath digitated or fingered leaves: the flowers, which conſiſt of five leaves, are of an anomalous figure, opening with two lips: there are male and female upon the ſame ſpike: the female flowers are ſucceeded by nuts, which grow in green prickly huſks. Their whole year's ſhoot is commonly performed in three weeks time, after which it does no more than increaſe in bulk, and become more firm; and all the latter part of the Summer is occupied in forming and ſtrengthening the buds for the next year's ſhoots. *Miller.*

I may bring in the *horſecheſnut*, which grows into a goodly ſtandard. *Mortimer's Huſbandry.*

HO'RSECOURSER. *n. ſ.* [*horſe* and *courſer*. *Junius* derives it from *horſe* and *coſe*, an old Scotch word, which ſignifies to change; and it ſhould therefore, he thinks, be writ *horſecoſer*. The word now uſed in Scotland is *horſecouper*, to denote a jockey, ſeller, or rather changer of horſes. It may well be derived from *courſe*, as he that ſells horſes may be ſuppoſed to *courſe* or exerciſe them.]

1. One that runs horſes, or keeps horſes for the race.

2. A dealer in horſes.

A ſervant to a *horſecourſer* was thrown off his horſe. *Wiſem.*

A Florentine bought a horſe for ſo many crowns, upon

condition to pay half down: the *horſecourſer* comes to him next morning for the remainder. *L'Eſtrange.*

Ho'rsecrab. *n. ſ.* A kind of fiſh. *Ainſworth.*

Horsecu'cumber. *n. ſ.* [*horſe* and *cucumber.*] A plant.

The *horſecucumber* is the large green cucumber, and the beſt for the table, green out of the garden. *Mortimer.*

Ho'rsedung. *n. ſ.* [*horſe* and *dung.*] The excrements of horſes.

Put it into an ox's horn, and, covered cloſe, let it rot in hot *horſedung*. *Peacham on Drawing.*

Horsee'mmet. *n. ſ.* [*horſe* and *emmet.*] Ant of a large kind.

Ho'rseflesh. *n. ſ.* [*horſe* and *fleſh.*] The fleſh of horſes.

The Chineſe eat *horſefleſh* at this day, and ſome gluttons have colts fleſh baked. *Bacon's Natural Hiſtory.*

An old hungry lion would fain have been dealing with a good piece of *horſefleſh* that he had in his eye; but the nag he thought would be too fleet for him. *L'Eſtrange.*

Ho'rsefly. *n. ſ.* [*horſe* and *fly.*] A fly that ſtings horſes, and ſucks their blood.

Ho'rsefoot. *n. ſ.* An herb. The ſame with coltsfoot. *Ainſ.*

Ho'rsehair. *n. ſ.* [*horſe* and *hair.*] The hair of horſes.

His glitt'ring helm, which terribly was grac'd
With waving *horſehair*. *Dryden's Æn.*

Ho'rseheel. *n. ſ.* An herb. *Ainſworth.*

Ho'rselaugh. *n. ſ.* [*horſe* and *laugh.*] A loud violent rude laugh.

A *horſelaugh*, if you pleaſe, at honeſty;
A joke on Jekyl. *Pope.*

Ho'rseleech. *n. ſ.* [*horſe* and *leech.*]

1. A great leech that bites horſes.

The *horſeleech* hath two daughters, crying give, give. *Prov.*

Let us to France; like *horſeleeches*, my boys,
The very blood to ſuck. *Shakeſpeare's Henry* V.

2. A farrier. *Ainſworth.*

Ho'rselitter. *n. ſ.* [*horſe* and *litter.*] A carriage hung upon poles between two horſes, in which the perſon carried lyes along.

He that before thought he might command the waves of the ſea, was now caſt on the ground, and carried in an *horſe-litter*. 2 *Mac.* ix. 8.

Ho'rseman. *n. ſ.* [*horſe* and *man.*]

1. One ſkilled in riding.

A ſkilful *horſeman*, and a huntſman bred. *Dryden's Æn.*

2. One that ſerves in wars on horſeback.

Encounters between *horſemen* on the one ſide, and foot on the other, are ſeldom with extremity of danger; becauſe as *horſemen* can hardly break a battle on foot, ſo men on foot cannot poſſibly chaſe *horſemen*. *Hayward.*

In the early times of the Roman commonwealth, a *horſeman* received yearly *tria millia æris*, and a foot-ſoldier one mille; that is, more than ſix-pence a day to a *horſeman*, and two-pence a day to a foot-ſoldier. *Arbuthnot on Coins.*

3. A rider; a man on horſeback.

With deſcending ſhow'rs of brimſtone fir'd,
The wild Barbarian in the ſtorm expir'd;
Wrapt in devouring flames the *horſeman* rag'd,
And ſpurr'd the ſteed in equal flames engag'd. *Addiſon.*

A *horſeman's* coat ſhall hide
Thy taper ſhape, and comelineſs of ſide. *Prior.*

Ho'rsemanship. *n. ſ.* [from *horſeman.*] The art of riding; the art of managing a horſe.

He vaulted with ſuch eaſe into his ſeat,
As if an angel dropt down from the clouds,
To turn and wind a fiery Pegaſus,
And witch the world with noble *horſemanſhip*. *Shak. H.* IV.

They pleaſe themſelves in terms of hunting or *horſemanſhip*. *Wotton.*

His majeſty, to ſhew his *horſemanſhip*, ſlaughtered two or three of his ſubjects. *Addiſon's Freeholder.*

Peers grew proud, in *horſemanſhip* t' excel;
Newmarket's glory roſe, as Britain's fell. *Pope.*

Ho'rsemarten. *n. ſ.* A kind of large bee. *Ainſworth.*

Ho'rsematch. *n. ſ.* A bird. *Ainſworth.*

Ho'rsemeat. *n. ſ.* [*horſe* and *meat.*] Provender.

Though green peas and beans be eaten ſooner, yet the dry ones that are uſed for *horſemeat* are ripe laſt. *Bac. Nat. Hiſt.*

Ho'rsemint. *n. ſ.* A large coarſe mint.

Ho'rsemuscle. *n. ſ.* A large muſcle.

The great *horſemuſcle*, with the fine ſhell, that breedeth in ponds, do not only gape and ſhut as the oyſters do, but remove from one place to another. *Bacon's Natural Hiſtory.*

Ho'rseplay. *n. ſ.* [*horſe* and *play.*] Coarſe, rough, rugged play.

He is too much given to *horſeplay* in his raillery, and comes to battle like a dictator from the plough. *Dryd. Fab. Preface.*

Ho'rsepond. *n. ſ.* [*horſe* and *pond.*] A pond for horſes.

Horsera'ce. *n. ſ.* [*horſe* and *race.*] A match of horſes in running.

In *horſeraces* men are curious to foreſee that there be not the leaſt weight upon the one horſe more than upon the other. *Bacon's Natural Hiſtory.*

Trajan, in the fifth year of his tribuneſhip, entertained the people with a *horſerace*. *Addiſon on ancient Medals.*

Ho'rseradish. *n. ſ.* [*horſe* and *radiſh.*] A root acrid and biting: a ſpecies of ſcurvygraſs.

Horſeradiſh is increaſed by ſprouts ſpreading from the old roots left in the ground, that are cut or broken off. *Mortimer.*

Stomachicks are the creſſe acrids, as *horſeradiſh* and ſcurvygraſs, infuſed in wine. *Floyer on the Humours.*

Ho'rseshoe. *n. ſ.* [*horſe* and *ſhoe.*]

1. A plate of iron nailed to the feet of horſes.

I was thrown into the Thames, and cool'd glowing hot in that ſurge, like a *horſeſhoe*. *Shakeſp. Merry Wives of Windſor.*

2. An herb. *Ainſworth.*

Horsestea'ler. *n. ſ.* [*horſe* and *ſteal.*] A thief who takes away horſes.

He is not a pickpurſe, nor a *horſeſtealer*; but for his verity in love, I do think him as concave as a covered goblet, or a worm-eaten nut. *Shakeſp. As you like it.*

Ho'rsetail. *n. ſ.* A plant.

Ho'rsetongue. *n. ſ.* An herb. *Ainſworth.*

Ho'rseway. *n. ſ.* [*horſe* and *way.*] A broad way by which horſes may travel.

Know'ſt thou the way to Dover?
—Both ſtile and gate, *horſeway* and footpath. *Shak. K. Lear.*

Horta'tion. *n. ſ.* [*hortatio*, Latin.] The act of exhorting; a hortatory precept; advice or encouragement to ſomething.

Ho'rtative. *n. ſ.* [from *hortor*, Latin.] Exhortation; precept by which one incites or animates.

Generals commonly in their *hortatives* put men in mind of their wives and children. *Bacon, Eſſay* 8.

Ho'rtatory. *adj.* [from *hortor*, Latin.] Encouraging; animating; adviſing to any thing: uſed of precepts, not of perſons; a *hortatory* ſpeech, not a *hortatory* ſpeaker.

Horticu'lture. *n. ſ.* [*hortus* and *cultura*, Latin.] The art of cultivating gardens.

Ho'rtulan. *adj.* [*hortulanus*, Latin.] Belonging to a garden.

This ſeventh edition of my *hortulan* kalendar is yours. *Evelyn's Kalendar.*

Ho'sanna. *n. ſ.* [ὡσαννα.] An exclamation of praiſe to God.

Through the vaſt of heav'n
It ſounded, and the faithful armies rung
Hoſanna to the Higheſt. *Milton's Paradiſe Loſt, b.* vi.

The publick entrance which Chriſt made into Jeruſalem was celebrated with the *hoſanna's* and acclamations of the people. *Fiddes's Sermons.*

HOSE. *n. ſ.* plur. *hoſen.* [hoſa, Saxon; *hoſan*, Welſh; *oſſan*, Erſe, *oſſanen*, plur. *chauſſe*, French.]

1. Breeches.

Guards on wanton Cupid's *hoſe*. *Shakeſpeare.*

Here's an Engliſh taylor come hither for ſtealing out of a French *hoſe*. *Shakeſpeare's Macbeth.*

Theſe men were bound in their coats, *hoſen*, hats, and other garments, and caſt into the midſt of the burning fiery furnace. *Dan.* iii. 21.

He croſs examin'd both our *hoſe*,
And plunder'd all we had to loſe. *Hudibras, p.* ii. *cant.* 3.

2. Stockings; covering for the legs.

He being in love, could not ſee to garter his *hoſe*;
And you, being in love, cannot ſee to put on
Your *hoſe*. *Shakeſ. Two Gentlemen of Verona.*

Will ſhe thy linen waſh, or *hoſen* darn,
And knit thee gloves? *Gay's Paſtorals.*

Ho'sier. *n. ſ.* [from *hoſe.*] One who ſells ſtockings.

You are as arrant a cockney as any *hoſier* in Cheapſide. *Swift to Gay.*

HO'SPITABLE. *adj.* [*hoſpitabilis*, Latin.] Giving entertainment to ſtrangers; kind to ſtrangers.

I'm your hoſt:
With robbers hands my *hoſpitable* favour
You ſhould not ruffle thus. *Shakeſp. King Lear.*

Receive the ſhip-wreck'd on your friendly ſhore;
With *hoſpitable* rites relieve the poor. *Dryden's Æn.*

Ho'spitably. *adv.* [from *hoſpitable.*] With kindneſs to ſtrangers.

Ye thus *hoſpitably* live,
And ſtrangers with good cheer receive. *Prior.*

The former liveth as piouſly and *hoſpitably* as the other. *Swift.*

HO'SPITAL. *n. ſ.* [*hoſpital*, French; *hoſpitalis*, Latin.]

1. A place built for the reception of the ſick, or ſupport of the poor.

They who were ſo careful to beſtow them in a college when they were young, would be ſo good as to provide for them in ſome *hoſpital* when they are old. *Wotton.*

I am about to build an *hoſpital*, which I will endow handſomely for twelve old huſbandmen. *Addiſon's Spectator.*

2. A place for ſhelter or entertainment.

They ſpy'd a goodly caſtle, plac'd
Foreby a river in a pleaſant dale,
Which chuſing for that evening's *hoſpital*,
They thither march'd. *Fairy Queen, b.* ii.

Hospita'lity. *n. ſ.* [*hoſpitalité*, French.] The practice of entertaining ſtrangers.

The

The Lacedemonians forbidding all access of strangers into their coasts, are, in that respect, deservedly blamed, as being enemies to that *hospitality* which, for common humanity sake, all the nations on earth should embrace. *Hooker, b.* i.

My master is of a churlish disposition,
And little recks to find the way to heav'n
By doing deeds of *hospitality*. *Shakesp. As you like it.*

How has this spirit of faction broke all the laws of charity, neighbourhood, alliance, and *hospitality?* *Swift.*

HO'SPITALLER. *n. s.* [*hospitallier*, French; *hospitalarius*, low Latin, from *hospital.*] One residing in an hospital in order to receive the poor or stranger.

The first they reckon such as were granted to the *hospitallers* in *titulum beneficii*. *Ayliffe's Parergon.*

To HO'SPITATE. *v. a.* [*hospitor*, Latin.] To reside under the roof of another.

That always chuses an empty shell, and this *hospitates* with the living animal in the same shell. *Grew's Musæum.*

HOST. *n. s.* [*hoste*, French; *hospes, hospitis*, Latin.]

1. One who gives entertainment to another.

Homer never entertained either guests or *hosts* with long speeches, 'till the mouth of hunger be stopped. *Sidney.*

Here, father, take the shadow of this tree
For your good *host*. *Shakesp. King Lear.*

2. The landlord of an inn.

Time's like a fashionable *host*,
That slightly shakes his parting guest by th' hand;
But with his arms out-stretch'd, as he would fly,
Grasps in the comer. *Shakesp. Troilus and Cressida.*

The frighted friend arose by break of day,
And found the stall where late his fellow lay;
Then of his impious *host* enquiring more,
Was answer'd that his guest was gone before. *Dryden.*

3. [From *hostis*, Latin.] An army; numbers assembled for war.

Let ev'ry soldier hew him down a bough,
And bear't before him; thereby shall we shadow
The numbers of our *host*. *Shakespeare's Macbeth.*

Then through the fiery pillar, and the cloud,
God looking forth, will trouble all his *host*,
And craze your chariot-wheels. *Milton's Paradise Lost, b.* i.

After these came arm'd, with spear and shield,
An *host* so great as cover'd all the field. *Dryden.*

4. Any great number.

Give to a gracious message
An *host* of tongues; but let ill tidings tell
Themselves, when they be felt. *Shakesf. Ant. and Cleopatra.*

5. [*Hostia*, Latin; *hostie*, French.] The sacrifice of the mass in the Romish church; the consecrated wafer.

To HOST. *v. n.* [from the noun.]

1. To take up entertainment.

Go, bear it to the centaur, where we *host*;
And stay there, Dromio, 'till I come to thee. *Shakespeare.*

2. To encounter in battle.

Strange to us it seem'd
At first, that angel should with angel war,
And in fierce *hostings* meet. *Milton's Paradise Lost, b.* vi.

From his loins
New authors of dissension spring; from him
Two branches, that in *hosting* long contend
For sov'reign sway. *Phillips.*

3. To review a body of men; to muster.

Lords have had the leading of their own followers to the general *hostings*. *Spenser on Ireland.*

HO'STAGE. *n. s.* [*ostage*, French.] One given in pledge for security of performance of conditions.

Your *hostages* I have, so have you mine;
And we shall talk before we fight. *Shakesf. Ant. and Cleopat.*

Do this message honourably;
And if he stand on *hostage* for his safety,
Bid him demand what pledge will please him best. *Shakesp.*

He that hath wife and children, hath given *hostages* to fortune; for they are impediments to great enterprises, either of virtue or mischief. *Bacon, Essay* 8.

They who marry give *hostages* to the publick, that they will not attempt the ruin or disturb the peace of it. *Atterbury.*

The Romans having seized a great number of *hostages*, acquainted them with their resolution. *Arbuthnot on Coins.*

HO'STEL. }
HO'STELRY. } *n. s.* [*hostel, hostelerie*, French.] An inn. *Ainsw.*

HO'STESS. *n. s.* [*hostesse*, French, from *host.*] A female host; a woman that gives entertainment.

Fair and noble *hostess*,
We are your guest to-night. *Shakespeare's Macbeth.*

Ye were beaten out of door,
And rail'd upon the *hostess* of the house. *Shakespeare.*

Be as kind an *hostess* as you have been to me, and you can never fail of another husband. *Dryden's Æn. Dedicat.*

HO'STESS-SHIP. *n. s.* [from *hostess.*] The character of an hostess.

It is my father's will I should take on me
The *hostess-ship* o' th' day: you're welcome, sirs. *Shakesp.*

HO'STILE. *adj.* [*hostilis*, Latin.] Adverse; opposite; suitable to an enemy.

He has now at last
Giv'n *hostile* strokes, and that not in the presence
Of dreaded justice, but on the ministers
That do distribute it. *Shakes. Coriolanus.*

Fierce Juno's hate,
Added to *hostile* force, shall urge thy fate. *Dryden's Æn.*

HO'STILITY. *n. s.* [*hostilité*, Fr. from *hostile.*] The practices of an open enemy; open war; opposition in war.

Neither by treason nor *hostility*
To seek to put me down, and reign thyself. *Shakesp. H.* VI.

Hostility being thus suspended with France, preparation was made for war against Scotland. *Hayward.*

What peace can we return,
But, to our pow'r, *hostility* and hate,
Untam'd reluctance and revenge? *Milt. Parad. Lost, b.* ii.

In this bloody dispute we have shewed ourselves fair, nay, generous adversaries; and have carried on even our *hostilities* with humanity. *Atterbury's Sermons.*

HO'STLER. *n. s.* [*hosteller*, from *hostel.*] One who has the care of horses at an inn.

The cause why they are now to be permitted is want of convenient inns for lodging travellers on horseback, and *hostlers* to tend their horses by the way. *Spenser on Ireland.*

HO'STRY. *n. s.* [corrupted from *hostelry.*] A place where the horses of guests are kept.

Swift rivers are with sudden ice constrain'd,
And studded wheels are on its back sustain'd;
An *hostry* now for waggons, which before
Tall ships of burden on its bosom bore. *Dryden's Georg.*

HOT. *adj.* [ꞅat, Saxon; *hat*, Scottish.]

1. Having the power to excite the sense of heat; contrary to cold; fiery.

What is thy name?
——Thou'lt be afraid to hear it.
—No, though thou call'st thyself a *hotter* name
Than any is in hell. *Shakespeare's Macbeth.*

The great breezes which the motion of the air in great circles, such as are under the girdle of the world, produceth, do refrigerate; and therefore, in those parts, noon is nothing so *hot* as about nine in the forenoon. *Bacon's Natural History.*

Hot and cold were in one body fixt;
And soft with hard, and light with heavy mixt. *Dryden.*

Black substances do soonest of all others become *hot* in the sun's light, and burn; which effect may proceed partly from the multitude of refractions in a little room, and partly from easy commotion of so very small corpuscles. *Newton's Opt.*

2. Lustful; lewd.

What *hotter* hours,
Unregister'd in vulgar fame, you have
Luxuriously pick'd out. *Shakes. Ant. and Cleopatra.*

Now the *hot* blooded gods assist me! remember, Jove, thou was't a bull for thy Europa. *Shakesp.*

3. Strongly affected by sensible qualities: in allusion to dogs hunting.

Nor law, nor checks of conscience will he hear,
When in *hot* scent of gain and full career. *Dryden.*

4. Violent; furious; dangerous.

That of Carthagena, where the Spaniards had warning of our coming, and had put themselves in their full strength, was one of the *hottest* services, and most dangerous assaults, that hath been known. *Bacon's War with Spain.*

He resolved to storm; but his soldiers declined that *hot* service, and plied it with artillery. *Clarendon, b.* viii.

To court the cry directs us, when we found
Th' assault so *hot*, as if 'twere only there. *Denham.*

Our army
Is now in *hot* engagement with the Moors. *Dryden.*

5. Ardent; vehement; precipitate.

Come, come, lord Mortimer, you are as slow,
As *hot* lord Percy is on fire to go. *Shakesp. Henry* IV.

Nature to youth *hot* rashness doth dispense,
But with cold prudence age doth recompense. *Denham.*

Achilles is impatient, *hot*, revengeful; Æneas, patient, considerate, and careful of his people. *Dryd. Fables, Preface.*

6. Eager; keen in desire.

It is no wonder that men, either perplexed in the necessary affairs of life, or *hot* in the pursuit of pleasures, should not seriously examine their tenets. *Locke.*

Quoth Ralph, a jointure,
Which makes him have so *hot* a mind t' her. *Hudibras.*

7. Piquant; acrid.

HO'TBED. *n. s.* A bed of earth made hot by the fermentation of dung.

The bed we call a *hotbed* is this: there was taken horsedung, old and well rotted; this was laid upon a bank half a foot high, and supported round about with planks, and upon the top was cast sifted earth two fingers deep. *Bacon's Nat. History.*

Preserve the *hotbed* as much as possible from rain. *Evelyn.*

HOTBRA'INED. *adj.* [*hot* and *brain.*] Violent; vehement; furious.

You

You shall find 'em either *hotbrain'd* youth,
Or needy bankrupts. *Dryden's Spanish Fryar.*

HOTCO'CKLES. *n. s.* [*hautes coquilles*, French.] A play in which one covers his eyes, and guesses who strikes him.

The chytindra is certainly not our *hotcockles*; for that was by pinching, not by striking. *Arbuthn. and Pope's Mar. Scribl.*

As at *hotcockles* once I laid me down,
And felt the weighty hand of many a clown,
Buxoma gave a gentle tap, and I
Quick rose, and read soft mischief in her eye. *Gay's Past.*

HOTHEA'DED. *adj.* [*hot* and *head.*] Vehement; violent; passionate.

One would not make the same person zealous for a standing army and publick liberty; nor a *hotheaded*, crackbrained coxcomb forward for a scheme of moderation. *Arbuthnot.*

HO'THOUSE. *n. s.* [*hot* and *house.*]

1. A bagnio; a place to sweat and cup in.

Now she professes a *hothouse*, which, I think, is a very ill house too. *Shak. Measure for Measure.*

2. A brothel.

Where lately harbour'd many a famous whore,
A purging bill, now fix'd upon the door,
Tells you it is a *hothouse*; so it may,
And still be a whorehouse: th' are synonyma. *Ben. Johnson.*

HO'TLY. *adv.* [from *hot.*]

1. With heat; not coldly.

2. Violently; vehemently.

The stag was in the end so *hotly* pursued, that he was driven to make courage of despair. *Sidney.*

I do contest
As *hotly* and as nobly with thy love,
As ever in ambitious strength I did
Contend against thy valour. *Shak. Coriolanus.*

The enemy, now at hand, began *hotly* to skirmish in divers places with the Christians. *Knolles's History of the Turks.*

Though this controversy be revived, and *hotly* agitated, I doubt whether it be not a nominal dispute. *Boyle.*

3. Lustfully.

Voracious birds, that *hotly* bill and breed,
And largely drink, because on salt they feed. *Dryden.*

HOTMOU'THED. *adj.* [*hot* and *mouth.*] Headstrong; ungovernable.

I fear my people's faith,
That *hotmouth'd* beast that bears against the curb,
Hard to be broken. *Dryden's Spanish Fryar.*

HO'TNESS. *n. s.* [from *hot.*] Heat; violence; fury.

HO'TCHPOTCH. *n. s.* [*haché en poche*, French; or *hachee en pot*, French, as *Camden* has it, as being boiled up in a pot; yet the former corruption is now generally used.] A mingled hash; a mixture.

Such patching maketh Littleton's *hotchpot* of our tongue, and, in effect, brings the same rather to a Babellish confusion than any one entire language. *Camden's Remains.*

A mixture of many disagreeing colours is ever unpleasant to the eye, and a mixture or *hotchpotch* of many tastes is unpleasant to the taste. *Bacon's Natural History.*

Nor limbs, nor bones, nor carcass would remain;
But a mash'd heap, a *hotchpotch* of the slain. *Dryd. Juvenal.*

HO'TSPUR. *n. s.* [*hot* and *spur.*]

1. A man violent, passionate, precipitate and heady.

My nephew's trespass may be well forgot;
It hath the excuse of youth and heat of blood,
A harebrain'd *hotspur*, govern'd by a spleen. *Shakes. H.* IV.

Wars are begun by hairbrained dissolute captains, parasitical fawners, unquiet *hotspurs*, and restless innovators. *Burton.*

2 A kind of pea of speedy growth.

Of such peas as are planted or sown in gardens, the *hotspur* is the speediest of any in growth. *Mortimer's Husbandry.*

HO'TSPURRED. *adj.* [from *hotspur.*] Vehement; rash; heady.

To draw Mars like a young Hippolytus, with an effeminate countenance, or Venus like that *hotspurred* Harpalice in Virgil, this proceedeth from a senseless judgment. *Peacham.*

HOVE. The preterite of *heave.*

HO'VEL. *n. s.* [Diminutive of hoȝe, house, Saxon.]

1. A shed open on the sides, and covered overhead.

So likewise a *hovel* will serve for a roome,
To stacke on the pease, when harvest shall come. *Tusser.*

If you make a large *hovel*, thatched, over some quantity of ground, plank the ground over, and it will breed saltpetre. *Bacon's Natural History.*

Your hay it is mow'd, your corn it is reap'd,
Your barns will be full, and your *hovels* heap'd. *Dryden.*

2. A mean habitation; a cottage.

The men clamber up the acclivities, dragging their kine with them, where they feed them and milk them, and do all the dairy-work in such sorry *hovels* and sheds as they build to inhabit in during the Summer. *Ray on the Creation.*

To HO'VEL. *v. a.* [from the noun.] To shelter in an hovel.

And was't thou fain, poor father,
To *hovel* thee with swine and rogues forlorn,
In short and musty straw? *Shakespeare's King Lear.*

HO'VEN. *part. pass.* [from *heave.*] Raised; swelled; tumefied.

Tom Piper hath *hoven* and puffed up cheeks;
If cheese be so *hoven*, make Cisse to seek creeks. *Tusser.*

To HO'VER. *v. n.* [*hovi*, to hang over, Welsh.]

1. To hang in the air over head, without flying off one way or other.

Some fiery devil *hovers* in the sky,
And pours down mischief. *Shak. King John.*

Ah, my poor princes! ah, my tender babes!
If yet, your gentle souls fly in the air,
And be not fix'd in doom perpetual,
Hover about me with your airy wings,
And hear your mother's lamentation. *Shak. Richard* III.

A *hovering* mist came swimming o'er his sight,
And seal'd his eyes in everlasting night. *Dryden's Æn.*

Great flights of birds are *hovering* about the bridge, and settling upon it. *Addison's Spectator.*

'Till as the earthly part decays and falls,
The captive breaks her prison's mould'ring walls;
Hovers a-while upon the sad remains,
Which now the pile, or sepulchre, contains,
And thence with liberty unbounded flies,
Impatient to regain her native skies. *Prior.*

Some less refin'd, beneath the moon's pale light,
Hover, and catch the shooting stars by night. *Pope.*

2. To stand in suspense or expectation.

The landlord will no longer covenant with him; for that he daily looketh after change and alteration, and *hovereth* in expectation of new worlds. *Spenser on Ireland.*

3. To wander about one place.

We see so warlike a prince at the head of so great an army, *hovering* on the borders of our confederates. *Addison.*

The truth and certainty is seen, and the mind fully possesses itself of it; in the other, it only *hovers* about it. *Locke.*

HOUGH. *n. s.* [hoȝ, Saxon.]

1. The lower part of the thigh.

Blood shall be from the sword unto the belly, and dung of men unto the camel's *hough.* 2 *Esd.* xiii. 36.

2. [*Hue*, French.] An adz; an hoe. See HOE.

Did they really believe that a man, by *houghs* and an ax, could cut a god out of a tree? *Stillingfleet.*

To HOUGH. *v. a.* [from the noun.]

1. To hamstring; to disable by cutting the sinews of the ham.

Thou shalt *hough* their horses. *Jos.* ii. 6.

2. To cut up with an hough or hoe.

3. To hawk. This orthography is uncommon. See *To* HAWK.

Neither could we *hough* or spit from us; much less could we sneeze or cough. *Grew's Cosmol. Sac. b.* i.

HO'ULET. *n. s.* The vulgar name for an owl. The Scots and northern counties still retain it.

HOULT. *n. s.* [holt, Saxon.] A small wood. Obsolete.

Or as the wind, in *hoults* and shady greaves,
A murmur makes among the boughs and leaves. *Fairfax.*

HOUND. *n. s.* [hund, Saxon; *hund*, Scottish] A dog used in the chase.

Hounds and greyhounds, mungrels, spaniels, curs,
Are cleped all by the name of dogs. *Shakespeare's Macbeth.*

Jason threw, but fail'd to wound
The boar, and slew an undeserving *hound*,
And through the dog the dart was nail'd to ground. *Dryd.*

The kind spaniel and the faithful *hound*,
Likest that fox in shape and species found,
Pursues the noted path and covets home. *Prior.*

To HOUND. *v. a.* [from the noun.]

1. To set on the chase.

God is said to harden the heart permissively, but not operatively nor effectively; as he who only lets loose a greyhound out of the slip, is said to *hound* him at the hare. *Bramhall.*

2. To hunt; to pursue.

If the wolves had been *hounded* by tygers, they should have worried them. *L'Estrange.*

HO'UNDFISH. *n. s.* A kind of fish. *Ainsworth.*

HOUNDSTO'NGUE. *n. s.* [*cynoglossum*, Latin.] A plant.

The cup of the flower consists of one leaf, deeply cut into five parts: the flower consists of one leaf, is funnel-shaped, and cut into five segments: the pointal, which arises from the bottom of the flower, changes into a fruit composed of four rough, each for the most part burry cells, and containing a flat seed affixed to a pyramidal and quadrilateral placenta. The proper season to take the roots up is soon after the leaves decay. *Miller.*

HO'UNDTREE. *n. s.* A kind of tree. *Ainsworth.*

HOUP. *n. s.* [*upupa*, Latin.] The puet. *Ainsworth.*

HOUR. *n. s.* [*heure*, French; *hora*, Latin.]

1. The twenty-fourth part of a natural day; the space of sixty minutes.

See the minutes how they run:
How many makes the *hour* full compleat,
How many *hours* bring about the day,
How many days will finish up the year,
How many years a mortal man may live. *Shakesp. H.* VI.

2. A particular time.

Vexation

Vexation almoſt ſtops my breath,
That ſunder'd friends greet in the *hour* of death. *Shakeſp.*
When we can intreat an *hour* to ſerve,
We'll ſpend it in ſome words upon that buſineſs,
If you would grant the time. *Shakeſpeare's Macbeth.*
The conſcious wretch muſt all his arts reveal,
From the firſt moment of his vital breath,
To his laſt *hour* of unrepenting death. *Dryden's Æn.*

3. The time as marked by the clock.
The *hour* runs through the roughest day. *Shakeſpeare.*

Our neighbour let her floor to a genteel man, who kept good *hours*. *Tatler*, Nº. 88.

They are as loud any *hour* of the morning, as our own countrymen at midnight. *Addiſon's Guardian.*

Ho'urglass. *n. ſ.* [*hour* and *glaſs.*]

1. A glaſs filled with ſand, which, running through a narrow hole, marks the time.

Next morning, known to be a morning better by the *hourglaſs* than by the day's clearneſs. *Sidney.*

If a man be in ſickneſs, the time will ſeem longer without a clock or *hourglaſs* than with it; for the mind doth value every moment. *Bacon.*

O, recollect your thoughts!
Shake not his *hourglaſs*, when his haſty ſand
Is ebbing to the laſt. *Dryden's Spaniſh Fryar.*

2. Space of time. A manner of ſpeaking rather affected than elegant.

We, within the *hourglaſs* of two months, have won one town, and overthrown great forces in the field. *Bacon.*

Ho'urly. *adj.* [from *hour.*] Happening or done every hour; frequent; often repeated.

Alcyone
Computes how many nights he had been gone,
Obſerves the waining moon with *hourly* view,
Numbers her age, and wiſhes for a new. *Dryden.*

We muſt live in *hourly* expectation of having thoſe troops recalled, which they now leave with us. *Swift.*

Ho'urly. *adv.* [from *hour.*] Every hour; frequently.

She deſerves a lord,
That twenty ſuch rude boys might tend upon,
And *hourly* call her miſtreſs. *Shak. All's well that ends well.*
Our eſtate may not endure
Hazard ſo near us, as doth *hourly* grow
Out of his lunacies. *Shakeſpeare's Hamlet.*
They with ceaſeleſs cry
Surround me, as thou ſaw'ſt; *hourly* conceiv'd,
And *hourly* born, with ſorrow infinite
To me! *Milton's Paradiſe Loſt, b.* ii.
Great was their ſtrife, which *hourly* was renew'd,
'Till each with mortal hate his rival view'd. *Dryden.*

Hou'rplate. *n. ſ.* [*hour* and *plate.*] The dial; the plate on which the hours pointed by the hand of a clock are inſcribed.

If eyes could not view the hand, and the characters of the *hourplate*, and thereby at a diſtance ſee what o'clock it was, their owner could not be much benefited by that acuteneſs. *Locke.*

HOUSE. *n. ſ.* [ḥuſ, Saxon; *huys*, Dutch; *huſe*, Scottiſh.]

1. A place wherein a man lives; a place of human abode.

Sparrows muſt not build in his *houſe* eaves. *Shakeſpeare.*

Houſes are built to live in, not to look on; therefore let uſe be preferred before uniformity, except where both may be had. *Bacon, Eſſay* 46.

In a *houſe* the doors are moveable, and the rooms ſquare; yet the *houſe* is neither moveable nor ſquare. *Watts.*

2. Any place of abode.
The bees with ſmoke, the doves with noiſome ſtench,
Are from their hives and *houſes* driven away. *Shakeſpeare.*

3. Place in which religious or ſtudious perſons live in common; monaſtery; college.

Theodoſius arrived at a religious *houſe* in the city, where now Conſtantia reſided. *Addiſon's Spectator.*

4. The manner of living; the table.

He kept a miſerable *houſe*, but the blame was laid wholly upon madam. *Swift.*

5. Station of a planet in the heavens, aſtrologically conſidered.

Pure ſpiritual ſubſtances we cannot converſe with, therefore have need of means of communication, which ſome make to be the celeſtial *houſes*: thoſe who are for the celeſtial *houſes* worſhip the planets, as the habitations of intellectual ſubſtances that animate them. *Stillingfleet.*

6. Family of anceſtors, deſcendants, and kindred; race.
The red roſe and the white are on his face,
The fatal colours of our ſtriving *houſes*. *Shakeſ. Henry* VI.
An ignominious ranſom and free pardon
Are of two *houſes*; lawful mercy ſure
Is nothing kin to foul redemption. *Shak. Meaſ. for Meaſure.*

By delaying my laſt fine, upon your grace's acceſſion to the patrimonies of your *houſe*, I may ſeem to have made a forfeiture. *Dryden's Fables, Dedication.*

A poet is not born in ev'ry race;
Two of a *houſe* few ages can afford,
One to perform, another to record. *Dryden's Fables.*

7. A body of the parliament; the lords or commons collectively conſidered.

Nor were the crimes objected againſt him ſo clear, as to give convincing ſatisfaction to the major part of both *houſes*, eſpecially that of the lords. *King Charles.*

To House. *v. a.* [from the noun.]

1. To harbour; to admit to reſidence.

Palladius wiſhed him to *houſe* all the Helots, and make themſelves maſters of the gates. *Sidney.*

Upon the North-ſea a valley *houſeth* a gentleman, who hath worn out his former name. *Carew's Survey of Cornwall.*

Slander lives upon ſucceſſion,
For ever *houſed* where it gets poſſeſſion. *Shakeſpeare.*
Mere cottagers are but *houſed* beggars. *Bacon.*
Oh, can your counſel his deſpair defer,
Who now is *houſed* in his ſepulchre? *Sandys.*

We find them *houſing* themſelves under ground in dens. *South's Sermons.*

In expectation of ſuch times as theſe,
A chapel *hous'd* 'em, truly call'd of eaſe. *Dryden.*

2. To ſhelter; to keep under a roof.

As we *houſe* hot country plants to ſave them, ſo we may *houſe* our own to forward them. *Bacon's Natural Hiſtory.*

Houſe your choiceſt carnations, or rather ſet them under a pent-houſe, to preſerve them in extremity of weather. *Evelyn.*

Wit in northern climates will not blow,
Except, like orange-trees, 'tis *hous'd* from ſnow. *Dryden.*

To House. *v. n.*

1. To take ſhelter; to keep abode; to reſide.
Ne ſuffer it to *houſe* there half a day. *Hubberd's Tale.*
Graze where you will, you ſhall not *houſe* with me. *Shak.*
Summers three times eight, ſave one,
She had told; alas, too ſoon,
After ſo ſhort time of breath,
To *houſe* with darkneſs and with death. *Milton.*

2. To have an aſtrological ſtation in the heavens.
In fear of this, obſerve the ſtarry ſigns'
Where Saturn *houſes*, and where Hermes joins. *Dryden.*
I *houſing* in the lion's hateful ſign,
Bought ſenates and deſerting troops are mine. *Dryden.*

Housebrea'ker. *n. ſ.* [*houſe* and *break.*] Burglar; one who makes his way into houſes to ſteal.

All *houſebreakers* and ſharpers had thief written in their foreheads. *L'Eſtrange.*

Housebrea'king. *n. ſ.* [*houſe* and *break.*] Burglary.

When he hears of a rogue to be tried for robbing or *houſebreaking*, he will ſend the whole paper to the government. *Swift.*

Ho'usedog. *n. ſ.* [*houſe* and *dog.*] A maſtiff kept to guard the houſe.

A very good *houſedog*, but a dangerous cur to ſtrangers, had a bell about his neck. *L'Eſtrange.*

You ſee the goodneſs of the maſter even in the old *houſedog*. *Addiſon's Spectator.*

Ho'usehold. *n. ſ.* [*houſe* and *hold.*]

1. A family living together.
Two *houſholds*, both alike in dignity,
In fair Verona, where we lay our ſcene,
From ancient grudge break to new mutiny,
Where civil blood makes civil hands unclean. *Shakeſpeare.*

A little kingdom is a great *houſhold*, and a great *houſhold* a little kingdom. *Bacon's Advice to Villiers.*

Of God obſerv'd
The one juſt man alive, by his command,
Shall build a wond'rous ark, as thou beheld'ſt,
To ſave himſelf and *houſhold* from amidſt
A world devote to univerſal wreck. *Milt. Parad. Loſt, b.* xi.

He has always taken to himſelf, amongſt the ſons of men, a peculiar *houſhold* of his love, which at all times he has cheriſhed as a father, and governed as a maſter: this is the proper *houſhold* of faith; in the firſt ages of the world, 'twas ſometimes literally no more than a ſingle *houſhold*, or ſome few families. *Spratt's Sermons.*

Great crimes muſt be with greater crimes repaid,
And ſecond funerals on the former laid;
Let the whole *houſhold* in one ruin fall,
And may Diana's curſe o'ertake us all. *Dryden's Fables.*
Learning's little *houſhold* did embark,
With her world's fruitful ſyſtem in her ſacred ark. *Swift.*
In his own church he keeps a ſeat,
Says grace before and after meat;
And calls, without affecting airs,
His *houſhold* twice a day to prayers. *Swift.*

2. Family life; domeſtick management.
An inventory, thus importing
The ſeveral parcels of his plate, his treaſure,
Rich ſtuffs, and ornaments of *houſhold*. *Shakeſp. H.* VIII.

3. It is uſed in the manner of an adjective, to ſignify domeſtick; belonging to the family.

Cornelius called two of his *houſhold* ſervants. *Acts* x. 7.

For nothing lovelier can be found
In woman, than to study *houshold* good;
And good works in her husband to promote. *Milt. Pa. Lost.*

It would be endless to enumerate the oaths and blasphemies among the men, among the women the neglect of *houshold* affairs. *Swift.*

HO'USEHOLDER. *n. s.* [from *household.*] Master of a family.

A certain *householder* planted a vineyard. *Mat.* xxi. 33.

HOU'SEHOLDSTUFF. *n. s.* [*household* and *stuff.*] Furniture of an house; utensils convenient for a family.

In this war that he maketh, he still flieth from his foe, and lurketh in the thick woods, waiting for advantages: his cloke is his bed, yea and his *housholdstuff*. *Spenser on Ireland.*

A great part of the building was consumed, with much costly *housholdstuff*. *Bacon's Henry* VII.

The poor woman had her jest for her *housholdstuff*, and paid her physician with a conceit for his money. *L'Estrange.*

HOU'SEKEEPER. *n. s.* [*house* and *keep.*]

1. Householder; master of a family.

To be said an honest man and a good *housekeeper*, goes as fairly as to say a graceful man and a great scholar. *Shakespeare.*

If I may credit *housekeepers* and substantial tradesmen, all sorts of provisions and commodities are risen excessively. *Locke.*

2. One who lives in plenty.

The people are apter to applaud *housekeepers* than houseraisers. *Wotton.*

3. One who lives much at home.

How do you both? You are manifest *housekeepers.* What are you sewing here? *Shakespeare's Coriolanus.*

4. A woman servant that has care of a family, and superintends the other maid servants.

Merry folks, who want by chance
A pair to make a country-dance,
Call the old *housekeeper*, and get her
To fill a place for want of better. *Swift.*

5. A housedog.

Distinguish the *housekeeper*, the hunter. *Shakes. Macbeth.*

HOU'SEKEEPING. *adj.* [*house* and *keep.*] Domestick; useful to a family.

His house, for pleasant prospect, large scope, and other *housekeeping* commodities, challengeth the pre-eminence. *Carew.*

HO'USEKEEPING. *n. s.* Hospitality; liberal and plentiful table.

I hear your grace hath sworn out *housekeeping*. *Shakespeare.*

His table was one of the last that gave us an example of the old *housekeeping* of an English nobleman: an abundance reigned, which shewed the master's hospitality. *Prior.*

HO'USEL. *n. s.* [ƿuꞅl, Saxon, from *hunsel*, Gothick, a sacrifice, or *hostia*, dimin. *hostiola*, Latin.] The holy eucharist.

To HO'USEL. *v. a.* [from the noun.] To give or receive the eucharist. Both the noun and verb are obsolete.

HO'USELEEK. *n. s.* [*house* and *leek.*] A plant.

The flower consists of several leaves, which are placed orbicularly, and expanded in form of a rose; out of whose flower-cup rises the pointal, which afterwards turns to a fruit, composed, as it were, of many seed-vessels resembling husks, which are collected into a sort of head, and full of small seeds. The species are six. *Miller.*

The acerbs supply their quantity of cruder acids; as juices of apples, grapes, the sorrels, and *houseleek*. *Floyer.*

HO'USELESS. *adj.* [from *house.*] Without abode; wanting habitation.

Poor naked wretches,
How shall your *houseless* heads and unfed sides,
Your loop'd and window'd raggedness, defend you. *Shakes.*

This hungry, *houseless*, suffering, dying Jesus, fed many thousands with five loaves and two fishes. *West.*

HO'USEMAID. *n. s.* [*house* and *maid.*] A maid employed to keep the house clean.

The *housemaid* may put out the candle against the looking-glass. *Swift.*

HO'USEROOM. *n. s.* [*house* and *room.*] Place in a house.

Houseroom, that costs him nothing, he bestows;
Yet still we scribble on, though still we lose. *Dryden's Juv.*

HO'USESNAIL. *n. s.* A kind of snail.

HO'USEWARMING. *n. s.* [*house* and *warm.*] A feast or merry-making upon going into a new house.

HO'USING. *n. s.* [from *house.*]

1. Quantity of inhabited building.

London is supplied with people to increase its inhabitants, according to the increase of *housing*. *Graunt.*

2. [From *houseaux*, *heuses*, or *houses*, French.] Cloath originally used to keep off dirt, now added to saddles as ornamental.

HO'USLING. *adj.* [from *house*] Provided for entertainment at first entrance into a house; housewarming.

His own two hands the holy knot did knit,
That none but death for ever can divide;
His own two hands, for such a turn most fit,
The *housling* fire did kindle and provide. *Fairy Queen, b.* i.

HOUSS. *n. s.* [from *houseaux*, or *houses*, French.] Covering of cloath originally used to keep off dirt, now added to saddles as ornamental; housings. This word, though used by *Dryden*, I do not remember in any other place.

Six lions hides, with thongs together fast,
His upper part defended to his waist;
And where man ended, the continu'd vest,
Spread on his back, the *houss* and trappings of a beast. *Dryd.*

HO'USEWIFE. *n. s.* [*house* and *wife.* This is now frequently written *huswife*, or *hussy.*] The mistress of a family.

You will think it unfit for a good *housewife* to stir in or to busy herself about her housewifry. *Spenser on Ireland.*

I have room enough, but the kind and hearty *housewife* is dead. *Pope to Swift.*

3. A female œconomist.

Fitting is a mantle for a bad man, and surely for a bad *housewife* it is no less convenient; for some of them, that be wandering women, it is half a wardrobe. *Spenser on Ireland.*

Let us sit and mock the good *housewife*, fortune, from her wheel, that her gifts may henceforth be disposed equally. *Shak.*

Farmers in degree,
He a good husband, a good *housewife* she. *Dryden.*

Early *housewives* leave the bed,
When living embers on the hearth are spread. *Dryden.*

The fairest among the daughters of Britain shew themselves good stateswomen as well as good *housewives*. *Addis. Freehold.*

3. One skilled in female business.

He was bred up under the tuition of a tender mother, 'till she made him as good an *housewife* as herself: he could preserve apricocks, and make jellies. *Addison's Spectator.*

HO'USEWIFELY. *adj.* [from *housewife.*] Skilled in the acts becoming a housewife.

HO'USEWIFELY. *adv.* [from *housewife.*] With the œconomy of a housewife.

HO'USEWIFERY. *n. s.* [from *housewife.*]

1. Domestick or female business; management becoming the mistress of a family.

You will think it unfit for a good housewife to stir in or to busy herself about her *housewifery*. *Spenser on Ireland.*

He ordain'd a lady for his prise,
Generally praiseful; fair and young, and skill'd in *housewiferies*. *Chapman's Iliads.*

Little butter was exported abroad, and that discredited by the *housewifery* of the Irish in making it up. *Temple.*

2. Female œconomy.

Learn good works for necessary uses; for St. Paul expresses the obligation of Christian women to good *housewifery*, and charitable provisions for their family and neighbourhood. *Tayl.*

HOW. *adv.* [ƿu, Saxon; *hoe*, Dutch.]

1. In what manner; to what degree.

How long wilt thou refuse to humble thyself before me? *Ex.* x. 3.

How much better is it to get wisdom than gold? and to get understanding rather to be chosen than silver? *Prov.* xvi. 16.

How oft is the candle of the wicked put out? And *how* oft cometh their destruction upon them? *Job* xxi. 17.

O *how* love I thy law: it is my meditation. *Ps.* cxix. 97.

How many children's plaints, and mother's cries!
How many woful widows left to bow
To sad disgrace! *Daniel's Civil War.*

Consider into *how* many differing substances it may be analysed by the fire. *Boyle.*

2. In what manner.

Mark'd you not,
How that the guilty kindred of the queen
Look'd pale, when they did hear of Clarence' death? *Shak.*

Prosecute the means of thy deliverance
By ransom, or *how* else. *Milton's Agonistes.*

We examine the why, the what, and the *how* of things. *L'Estrange.*

'Tis much in our power *how* to live; but not at all when or *how* to die. *L'Estrange.*

It is pleasant to see *how* the small territories of this little republick are cultivated to the best advantage. *Addison on Italy.*

3. For what reason; from what cause.

How now, my love? Why is your cheek so pale?
How chance the roses there do fade so fast? *Shakespeare.*

4. By what means.

How is it thou hast found it so quickly. *Gen.* xxvii. 10.

Men would have the colours of birds feathers, if they could tell *how*; or they will have gay skins instead of gay clothes. *Bacon's Natural History.*

5. In what state.

For *how* shall I go up to my father? *Gen.* xliv. 34.

Whence am I forc'd, and whither am I born?
How, and with what reproach shall I return? *Dryden's Æn.*

6. It is used in a sense marking proportion or correspondence.

Behold, he put no trust in his servants, *how* much less on them that dwell in houses of clay, whose foundation is in the dust. *Job* iv. 19.

A great division fell among the nobility, so much the more dangerous by *how* much the spirits were more active and high. *Hayward.*

By *how* much they would diminish the present extent of the sea, so much they would impair the fertility, and fountains and rivers of the earth. *Bentley's Sermons.*

7. It is much used in exclamation.
How are the mighty fallen! *Sam.*
How doth the city sit solitary as a widow. *Lam.* i. 1.
8. In an affirmative sense, not easily explained; that so it is; that.
Thick clouds put us in some hope of land, knowing *how* that part of the South sea was utterly unknown, and might have islands or continents. *Bacon's New Atlantis.*
HOWBE'IT. } *adv.* [*how be it.*] Nevertheless; notwithstand-
HOWBE. } ing; yet; however. Not now in use.
Siker thou speak'st like a lewd lorrel,
Of heaven to deemen so,
Howbe I am but rude and borrel,
Yet nearer ways I know. *Spenser.*
Things so ordained are to be kept, *howbeit* not necessarily, any longer than 'till there grow some urgent cause to ordain the contrary. *Hooker, b.* iv. *s.* 14.
There is a knowledge which God hath always revealed unto them in the works of nature: this they honour and esteem highly as profound wisdom, *howbeit* this wisdom saveth them not. *Hooker, b.* v. *s.* 22.
There was no army transmitted out of England, *howbeit* the English colonies in Ireland did win ground upon the Irish. *Davies on Ireland.*
HOWD'YE. [Contracted from *how do ye.*] In what state is your health A message of civility.
Years make men more talkative, but less writative; so that I now write no letters but of plain business, or plain *howd'ye's*, to those few I am forced to correspond with. *Pope.*
HOWE'VER. *adv.* [*how* and *ever.*]
1. In whatsoever manner; in whatsoever degree.
This ring he holds
In most rich choice; yet in his idle fire,
To buy his will, it would not seem too dear,
Howe'er repented of. *Shakesp. All's well that ends well.*
To trace the ways
Of highest agents, deem'd *however* wise. *Milton's Par. Lost.*
2. At all events; happen what will; at least.
Our chief end is to be freed from all, if it may be, *however* from the greatest evils; and to enjoy, if it may be, all good, *however* the chiefest. *Tillotson, Sermon* 1.
3. Nevertheless; notwithstanding; yet.
In your excuse your love does little say;
You might *howe'er* have took a fairer way. *Dryden.*
Its views are bounded on all sides by several ranges of mountains, which are *however* at so great a distance, that they leave a wonderful variety of beautiful prospects. *Addison on Italy.*
I do not build my reasoning wholly on the case of persecution, *however* I do not exclude it. *Atterbury.*
Few turn their thoughts to examine how those diseases in a state are bred, that hasten its end; which would, *however*, be a very useful enquiry. *Swift.*
To HOWL. *v. n.* [*huglen*, Dutch; *ululo*, Latin.]
1. To cry as a wolf or dog.
Methought a legion of foul fiends
Environ'd me, and *howled* in mine ears
Such hideous cries, that with the very noise
I trembling wak'd. *Shakespeare's Richard* III.
If wolves had at thy gate *howl'd* that stern time,
Thou should'st have said, Go, porter, turn the key. *Shakes.*
He found him in a desert land, and in the waste *howling* wilderness. *Deutr.* xxxii. 10.
As when a sort of wolves infest the night,
With their wild *howlings* at fair Cynthia's light. *Waller.*
Hard as his native rocks, cold as his sword,
Fierce as the wolves that *howl'd* around his birth;
He hates the tyrant, and the suppliant scorns. *Smith.*
2. To utter cries in distress.
Therefore will I *howl*, and cry out for all Moab. *Jer.* xlviii.
The damned use that word in hell,
Howlings attend it. *Shakesp. Romeo and Juliet.*
Each new morn
New widows *howl*, new orphans cry, new sorrows
Strike heaven on the face, that it resounds
As if it felt with Scotland. *Shakespeare's Macbeth.*
I have words
That would be *howl'd* out in the desart air,
Where hearing should not catch them. *Shakesp. Macbeth.*
The noise grows louder still:
Rattling of armour, trumpets, drums and ataballes;
And sometimes peals of shouts that rend the heav'ns,
Like victory: then groans again, and *howlings*
Like those of vanquish'd men. *Dryden's Spanish Fryar.*
3. To speak with a belluine cry or tone.
Peace, monster, peace! Go tell thy horrid tale
To savages, and *howl* it out in desarts!
Me would'st thou make the accomplice of thy crimes?
A. Phillips's Distrest Mother.
4. It is used poetically of any noise loud and horrid.
HOWL. *n. s.* [from the verb.]
1. The cry of a wolf or dog.
Murther,
Alarm'd by his sentinel the wolf,
Whose *howl's* his watch. *Shakespeare's Macbeth.*
These and the like rumours are no more than the last *howls* of a dog dissected alive. *Swift.*
2. The cry of a human being in horrour.
She raves, she runs with a distracted pace,
And fills with horrid *howls* the publick place. *Dryden's Æn.*
HOWSOE'VER. *adv.* [*how* and *soever.*]
1. In what manner soever. See HOWEVER.
Berosus, who, after Moses, was one of the most ancient, *howsoever* he hath been since corrupted, doth in the substance of all agree. *Raleigh's History of the World.*
2. Although.
The man doth fear God, *howsoever* it seems not in him.
Shakespeare's Much Ado about Nothing.
To HOX. *v. a.* [from hoȝ, Saxon.] To hough; to hamstring.
Thou art a coward,
Which *hoxes* honesty behind, restraining
From course required. *Shakesp. Winter's Tale.*
Lodronius, perceiving the old soldier's meaning, alighted, and with his sword *hoxed* his horse, saying aloud, This day, valiant soldiers, shall you have me both your general and fellow soldier, fighting on foot as one of yourselves. *Knolles.*
HOY. *n. s.* [*hou*, old French.] A large boat sometimes with one deck.
He sent to Germany, strange aid to rear;
From whence eftsoons arrived here three *hoys*
Of Saxons, whom he for his safety employs. *Fairy Queen.*
To define a barge and *hoy*, which are between a boat and a ship, is hard. *Watts's Logick.*
HU'BBUB. *n. s.* [I know not the etymology, unless it be from *up up*, or *hobnob.*] A tumult; a riot.
People pursued the business with all contempt of the government; and in the *hubbub* of the first day there appeared nobody of name or reckoning, but the actors were really of the dregs of the people. *Clarendon.*
An universal *hubbub* wild
Of stunning sounds, and voices all confus'd,
Borne through the hollow dark, assaults his ear
With loudest vehemence. *Milton's Paradise Lost, b.* ii.
Why wolves raise a *hubbub* at her,
And dogs howl when she shines in water. *Hudibras, p.* ii.
HU'CKABACK. *n. s.* A kind of linen on which the figures are raised.
HU'CKLEBACKED. *adj.* [*hocker*, German, a *bunch*, and *back.*] Crooked in the shoulders.
HU'CKLEBONE. *n. s.* [from *hucken*, Dutch, to sit down.] The hipbone.
HU'CKSTER. } *n. s.* [*hock*, German, a pedlar; *hockster*, a she-
HU'CKSTERER. } pedlar.]
1. One who sells goods by retail, or in small quantities; a pedlar.
There cannot be a more ignominious trade than the being *hucksters* to such vile merchandise. *Government of the Tongue.*
God deliver the world from such guides, or rather such *hucksters* of souls, the very shame of religion. *South's Sermons.*
Should thy shoe wrench aside, down, down you fall,
And overturn the scolding *huckster*'s stall,
The scolding *huckster* shall not o'er thee moan,
But pence expect for nuts and pears o'erthrown. *Gay.*
There should be a general confederacy of all the servants in every family, for the publick good, to drive those China *hucksters* from the doors. *Swift.*
Those *hucksterers* or money-jobbers will be found necessary, if this brass money is made current. *Swift.*
2. A trickish mean fellow.
Now the ape wanted his *huckster* man. *Hubb. Tale.*
To HU'CKSTER. *v. n.* [from the noun.] To deal in petty bargains.
They must pay a shilling, for changing their piece into silver, to some *huckstering* fellow who follows that trade. *Swift.*
To HU'DDLE. *v. a.* [probably from *hood.*]
1. To dress up close so as not to be discovered; to mobble.
2. To put on carelesly in a hurry.
At twelve she rose with much ado;
Her cloaths were *huddl'd* on by two. *Prior.*
Now all in haste they *huddle* on
Their hoods, their cloaks, and get them gone. *Swift.*
3. To cover up in haste.
4. To perform in a hurry.
I have given much application to this poem: this is not a play *huddled* up in haste. *Dryden.*
When continu'd rain
The lab'ring husband in his house restrain,
Let him forecast his work with timely care,
Which else is *huddled* when the skies are fair. *Dryd. Virgil.*
5. To throw together in confusion.
Our adversary, *huddling* several suppositions together, and that in doubtful and general terms, makes a medley and confusion. *Locke.*

To HU'DDLE. *v. n.* To come in a crowd or hurry.

Glance an eye of pity on his losses,
That have of late so *huddled* on his back,
Enough to press a royal merchant down. *Shakespeare.*

Brown answered after his blunt and *huddling* manner. *Bacon.*

Thyrsis, whose artful strains have oft delay'd
The *huddling* brook to hear his madrigal,
And sweeten'd every muskrose of the dale. *Milton.*

Their eyes are more imperfect than others; for they will run against things, and, *huddling* forwards, fall from high places. *Brown's Vulgar Errours.*

HU'DDLE. *n. s.* [from the verb.] Crowd; tumult; confusion.

That the Aristotelian philosophy is a *huddle* of words and terms insignificant, has been the censure of the wisest. *Glanv.*

Your carrying business in a *huddle*,
Has forc'd our rulers to new model. *Hudibras, p.* iii.

Nature doth nothing in a *huddle*. *L'Estrange.*

The understanding sees nothing distinctly in things remote, and in a *huddle*. *Locke.*

Several merry answers were made to my question, which entertained us 'till bed-time, and filled my mind with a *huddle* of ideas. *Addison's Spectator.*

HUE. *n. s.* [hiepe, Saxon.]

1. Colour; die.

For never in that land
Face of fair lady she before did view,
Or that dread lyon's look her cast in deadly *hue*. *Fairy Qu.*

For now three months have changed thrice their *hue*. *Fairy Queen, canto* viii.

To add another *hue* unto the rainbow,
Is wasteful and ridiculous excess. *Shakes. King John.*

Flow'rs of all *hue*, and without thorn the rose. *Milton.*

To whom the angel, with a smile that glow'd
Celestial rosy red, love's proper *hue*,
Answer'd. *Milton's Paradise Lost, b.* viii.

Your's is much of the camelion *hue*,
To change the die with distant view. *Dryden.*

2. [*Huée*, French.] A clamour; a legal pursuit; an alarm given to the country.

Hue and cry, villain, go! Assist me, knight, I am undone: fly, run, *hue* and cry! villain, I am undone. *Shakespeare.*

Immediately comes a *hue* and cry after a gang of thieves, that had taken a purse upon the road. *L'Estrange.*

If you should hiss, he swears he'll hiss as high;
And, like a culprit, join the *hue* and cry. *Addison.*

The *hue* and cry went after Jack, to apprehend him dead or alive, wherever he could be found. *Arbuthnot's John Bull.*

HUE'R. *n. s.* [*huer*, French, to cry.] One whose business is to call out to others.

They lie hovering upon the coast, and are directed by a balker or *huer*, who standeth on the cliff-side, and from thence discerneth the course of the pilchard. *Carew's Surv. of Cornw.*

HUFF. *n. s.* [from *hove*, or *hoven*, swelled: he is *huffed up by distempers*. So in some provinces we still say the bread *huffs up*, when it begins to *heave* or ferment: *huff*, therefore, may be ferment. To be in a *huff* is then to be in a *ferment*, as we now speak.]

1. Swell of sudden anger or arrogance.

Quoth Ralpho, honour's but a word
To swear by only in a lord;
In others it is but a *huff*,
To vapour with instead of proof. *Hudibras, p.* ii.

His frowns kept multitudes in awe,
Before the bluster of whose *huff*
All hats, as in a storm, flew off. *Hudibras.*

We have the apprehensions of a change to keep a check upon us in the very *huff* of our greatness. *L'Estrange.*

A Spaniard was wonderfully upon the *huff* about his extraction. *L'Estrange.*

No man goes about to ensnare or circumvent another in a passion, to lay trains, and give secret blows in a present *huff*. *South's Sermons.*

2. A wretch swelled with a false opinion of his own value.

Lewd shallow-brained *huffs* make atheism and contempt of religion the sole badge and character of wit. *South.*

As for you, colonel *huff*-cap, we shall try before a civil magistrate who's the greater plotter. *Dryden's Spanish Fryar.*

To HUFF. *v. a.* [from the noun.]

1. To swell; to puff.

In many wild birds the diaphragm may easily be *huffed* up with air, and blown in at the windpipe. *Grew's Cosmol. Sac.*

2. To hector; to treat with insolence and arrogance, or brutality.

To HUFF. *v. n.* To bluster; to storm; to bounce; to swell with indignation or pride.

This senseless arrogant conceit of theirs made them *huff* at the doctrine of repentance, as a thing below them. *South.*

A *huffing*, shining, flatt'ring, cringing coward,
A cankerworm of peace, was rais'd above him. *Otway.*

A thief and justice, fool and knave,
A *huffing* officer and slave. *Hudibras, p.* ii. *cant.* 3.

Huffing to cowards, fawning to the brave,
To knaves a fool, to cred'lous fools a knave. *Roscommon.*

Now what's his end? O charming glory, say!
What, a fifth act to crown his *huffing* play? *Dryd. Juvenal.*

What a small pittance of reason and truth is mixed with those *huffing* opinions they are swelled with. *Locke.*

When Peg received John's message, she *huffed* and stormed like the devil. *Arbuthnot's History of John Bull.*

HU'FFER. *n. s.* [from *huff*.] A blusterer; a bully.

Nor have I hazarded my art
To be expos'd i' th' end to suffer,
By such a braggadocio *huffer*. *Hudibras, p.* ii. *cant.* 3.

HU'FFISH. *adj.* [from *huff*.] Arrogant; insolent; hectoring.

HU'FFISHLY. *adv.* [from *huffish*.] With arrogant petulance; with bullying bluster.

HU'FFISHNESS. *n. s.* Petulance; arrogance; noisy bluster.

To HUG. *v. a.* [hegian, Saxon, to hedge, to inclose.]

1. To press close in an embrace.

He bewept my fortune,
And *hugg'd* me in his arms. *Shakesp. Richard* III.

What would not he do now to *hug* the creature that had given him so admirable a serenade! *L'Estrange.*

Ev'n in that urn their brother they confess,
And *hug* it in their arms, and to their bosom press. *Dryden.*

King Xerxes was enamoured upon an oak, which he would *hug* and kiss. *Harvey on Consumptions.*

2. To fondle; to treat with tenderness.

I, under fair pretence of friendly ends,
And well-plac'd words of glozing courtesy,
Baited with reasons not unplausible,
Win me into the easy-hearted man,
And *hug* him into snares. *Milton.*

We *hug* deformities, if they bear our names. *Glanville.*

Admire yourself,
And, without rival, *hug* your darling book. *Roscommon.*

Though they know that the flatterer knows the falsehood of his own flatteries, yet they love the impostor, and with both arms *hug* the abuse. *South's Sermons.*

Mark with what joy he *hugs* the dear discovery! *Rowe.*

3. To hold fast.

Age makes us most fondly *hug* and retain the good things of life, when we have the least prospect of enjoying them. *Atterb.*

HUG. *n. s.* [from the noun.] Close embrace.

Why these close *hugs*? I owe my shame to him. *Gay.*

HUGE. *adj.* [*hoogh*, *high*, Dutch.]

1. Vast; immense.

Let the state of the people of God, when they were in the house of bondage, and their manner of serving God in a strange land, be compared with that which Canaan and Jerusalem did afford; and who seeth not what *huge* difference there was between them? *Hooker, b.* iv.

This space of earth is so *huge*, as that it equalleth in greatness not only Asia, Europe and Africa, but America. *Abbot.*

2. Great even to deformity or terribleness.

The patch is kind enough, but a *huge* feeder. *Shakesp.*

Through forrests *huge*, and long untravell'd heaths,
With desolation brown he wanders waste. *Thomson's Spring.*

HU'GELY. *adv.* [from *huge*.]

1. Immensely; enormously.

Who cries out on pride,
That can therein tax any private party?
Doth it not flow as *hugely* as the sea? *Shakes. As you like it.*

2. Greatly; very much.

I am *hugely* bent to believe, that whenever you concern yourselves in our affairs, it is for our good. *Swift.*

HU'GENESS. *n. s.* [from *huge*.] Enormous bulk; greatness.

My mistress exceeds in goodness the *hugeness* of your unworthy thinking. *Shakespeare's Cymbeline.*

HU'GGERMUGGER. *n. s.* [corrupted perhaps from *hug er morcker*, or hug in the dark. *Morcker* in Danish is darkness, whence our *murky*. It is written by Sir *Thomas More*, *hoker moker*. *Hoker*, in *Chaucer*, is *peevish*, *crossgrained*, of which *moker* may be only a ludicrous reduplication. *Hooke* is likewise in German *a corner*, and *moky* is in English *dark*. I know not how to determine.] Secrecy; bye-place.

Now hold in *huggermugger* in their hand,
And all the rest do rob of goods and land. *Hubberd's Tale.*

But if I can but find them out,
Where e'er th' in *huggermugger* lurk,
I'll make them rue their handy-work. *Hudibras, p.* i.

There's a distinction betwixt what's done openly and barefaced, and a thing that's done in *huggermugger*, under a seal of secrecy and concealment. *L'Estrange's Fables.*

HU'GY. *adj.* [See HUGE.] Vast; great; huge.

This *hugy* rock one finger's force
Apparently will move. *Carew's Survey of Cornwal.*

HUKE. *n. s.* [*huque*, French.] A cloak.

As we were thus in conference, there came one that seemed to be a messenger in a rich *huke*. *Bacon's New Atlantis.*

HULK. *n. s.* [*hulcke*, Dutch; hulc, Saxon.]

1. The body of a ship.

There's a whole merchant's venture of Bourdeaux stuff in him: you have not seen a *hulk* better stuffed in the hold. *Shakes.*

The

The custom they had of giving the colour of the sea to the *hulks*, sails, and mariners of their spy-boats, to keep them from being discovered, came from the Veneti. *Arbuthnot.*

They Argo's *hulk* will tax,
And scrape her pitchy sides for wax. *Swift.*
The sooty *hulk*
Steer'd sluggish on. *Thomson's Autumn.*

2. Any thing bulky and unwieldy. This sense is still retained in Scotland: as, a *hulk* of a fellow.

And Harry Monmouth's brawn, the *hulk* sir John,
Is prisoner to your son. *Shakespeare's Henry* IV. *p.* ii.

To Hulk. *v. a.* To exenterate: as, to *hulk* a hare. *Ainsw.*

Hull. *n. s.* [*hulgan*, Gothick, to cover.]

1. The husk or integument of any thing; the outer covering: as, the *hull* of a nut covers the shell. [*Hule*, Scottish.]

2. The body of a ship; the hulk. *Hull* and *hulk* are now confounded; but *hulk* seems originally to have signified not merely the body or hull, but a whole ship of burden, heavy and bulky.

Deep in their *hulls* our deadly bullets light,
And through the yielding planks a passage find. *Dryden.*

So many arts hath the Divine Wisdom put together, only for the *hull* and tackle of a sensible and thinking creature. *Grew's Cosmol. Sac. b.* i. *c.* 5.

To Hull. *v. n.* [from the noun.] To float; to drive to and fro upon the water without sails or rudder.

They saw a sight full of piteous strangeness; a ship, or rather the carcase of the ship, or rather some few bones of the carcase, *hulling* there, part broken, part burned, and part drowned. *Sidney.*

Will you hoist sail, sir? here lies your way.
—No, good swabber, I am to *hull* here a little longer. *Shak.*

He look'd, and saw the ark *hull* on the flood,
Which now abated. *Milton's Parad. Lost, b.* xi.

People walking down upon the shore, saw somewhat come *hulling* toward them. *L'Estrange.*

Hu'lly. *adj.* [from *hull.*] Siliquose; husky. *Ainsworth.*

Hu'lver. *n. s.* Holly.

Save *hulver* and thorn, thereof flail for to make. *Tusser.*

To Hum. *v. a.* [*hommelen*, Dutch.]

1. To make the noise of bees.

The *humming* of bees is an unequal buzzing. *Bacon.*

An airy nation flew,
Thick as the *humming* bees that hunt the golden dew
In Summer's heat. *Dryden's Æn. b.* vi.

So weary bees in little cells repose;
But if night-robbers lift the well-stor'd hive,
An *humming* through their waxen city grows. *Dryden.*

2. To make an inarticulate and buzzing sound.

I think he'll hear me: yet to bite his lip,
And *hum* at good Cominius, much unhearts me. *Shakesp.*

Upon my honour, sir, I heard a *humming*,
And that a strange one too, which did awake me. *Shakesp.*

The cloudy messenger turns me his back,
And *hums*; as who should say, you'll rue. *Shakesp. Macbeth.*

3. To pause in speaking, and supply the interval with an audible emission of breath.

Having pump'd up all his wit,
And *humm'd* upon it, thus he writ. *Hudibras, p.* iii.
I still acquiesce,
And never *humm'd* and haw'd sedition,
Nor snuffled treason. *Hudibras, p.* iii. *cant.* 2.

The man lay *humming* and hawing a good while; but, in the end, he gave up himself to the physicians. *L'Estrange.*

Still *humming* on, their drowsy course they keep,
And lash'd so long, like tops, are lash'd asleep. *Pope.*

4. To sing low.

The musical accents of the Indians, to us, are but inarticulate *hummings*; as are ours to their otherwise tuned organs. *Glanv. Apol.*

Hum half a tune. *Pope.*

5. To applaud. Approbation was commonly expressed in publick assemblies by a hum, about a century ago.

Hum. *n. s.* [from the verb.]

1. The noise of bees or insects.

To black Hecat's summons
The shard-born beetle, with his drowsy *hums*,
Hath rung night's yawning peal. *Shakespeare's Macbeth.*

Nor undelightful is the ceaseless *hum*,
To him who muses through the woods at noon. *Thomson.*

2. The noise of bustling crowds.

From camp to camp, through the foul womb of night,
The *hum* of either army stilly sounds. *Shakesp. Hen.* V.

Tower'd cities please us then,
And the busy *hum* of men. *Milton.*

One theatre there is of vast resort,
Which whilome of requests was call'd the court;
But now the great exchange of news 'tis hight,
And full of *hum* and buz from noon 'till night. *Dryden.*

3. Any low dull noise.

Who sat the nearest, by the words o'ercome,
Slept fast; the distant nodded to the *hum*. *Pope's Dunciad.*

4. A pause with an inarticulate sound.

These shrugs, these *hums* and haws,
When you have said she's goodly, come between,
'Ere you can say she's honest. *Shakes. Winter's Tale.*

Your excuses want some grains to make 'em current: *hum* and ha will not do the business. *Dryden's Spanish Fryar.*

5. In *Hudibrass* it seems used for *ham.*

And though his countrymen the Huns,
Did stew their meat between their *hums*
And the horses backs o'er which they straddle,
And ev'ry man eat up his saddle. *Hudibras, p.* i. *cant.* ii.

6. An expression of applause.

You hear a *hum* in the right place. *Spectator.*

Hum. *interject.* A sound implying doubt and deliberation.

Let not your ears despise the heaviest sound
That ever yet they heard.
—*Hum!* I guess at it. *Shakespeare's Macbeth.*
See sir Robert—*hum!*
And never laugh for all my life to come. *Pope.*

HU'MAN. *adj.* [*humanus*, Latin; *humain*, French.]

1. Having the qualities of a man.

It will not be asked whether he be a gentleman born, but whether he be a *human* creature. *Swift.*

2. Belonging to man.

The king is but a man as I am: the violet smells to him as it doth to me; all his senses have but *human* conditions. *Shakes.*

For man to tell how *human* life began
Is hard; for who himself beginning knew? *Milton's P. L.*
Thee, serpent, subtil'st beast of all the field,
I knew; but not with *human* voice indu'd. *Milt. Par. Lost.*

Intuitive knowledge needs no probation, nor can have any, this being the highest of all *human* certainty. *Locke.*

HUMA'NE. *adj.* [*humaine*, French.] Kind; civil; benevolent; good-natured.

Love of others, if it be not spent upon a few, doth naturally spread itself towards many, and maketh men become *humane* and charitable. *Bacon's Essays.*

Envy, malice, covetousness and revenge are abolished: a new race of virtues and graces, more divine, more moral, more *humane*, are planted in their stead. *Spratt's Sermons.*

Huma'nely. *adv.* [from *humane.*] Kindly; with good-nature.

If they would yield us the superfluity, while it were wholesome, we might guess they relieved us *humanely*. *Shakespeare.*

Hu'manist. *n. s.* [*humaniste*, French.] A philologer; a grammarian.

Huma'nity. *n. s.* [*humanité*, French; *humanitas*, Latin.]

1. The nature of man.

Look to thyself; reach not beyond *humanity*. *Sidney.*

A rarer spirit never did steer *humanity*. *Shakespeare.*

The middle of *humanity* thou never knewest, but the extremity of both ends. *Shakesp. Timon of Athens.*

To preserve the Hebrew intire and uncorrupt, there hath been used the highest caution *humanity* could invent. *Brown.*

2. Humankind; the collective body of mankind.

If he can untie those knots, he is able to teach all *humanity*, and will do well to oblige mankind by his informations. *Glan.*

3. Benevolence; tenderness.

All men ought to maintain peace, and the common offices of *humanity* and friendship in diversity of opinions. *Locke.*

How few, like thee, enquire the wretched out,
And court the offices of soft *humanity?*
Like thee reserve their raiment for the naked,
Reach out their bread to feed the crying orphan,
Or mix their pitying tears with those that weep? *Rowe.*

4. Philology; grammatical studies.

To Hu'manize. *v. a.* [*humaniser*, French.] To soften; to make susceptive of tenderness or benevolence.

Here will I paint the characters of woe,
And here my faithful tears in showers shall flow,
To *humanize* the flints whereon I tread. *Wotton.*

Was it the business of magick to *humanize* our natures with compassion, forgiveness, and all the instances of the most extensive charity? *Addison on the Christian Religion.*

Hu'mankind. *n. s.* [*human* and *kind.*] The race of man; mankind.

Blest with a taste exact, yet unconfin'd;
A knowledge both of books and *humankind*. *Pope.*

Hu'manly. *adv.* [from *human.*]

1. After the notions of men; according to the power of men.

Thus the present happy prospect of our affairs, *humanly* speaking, may seem to promise. *Atterbury.*

2. Kindly; with good-nature. This should be *humanely*.

Though learn'd, well bred; and though well bred, sincere;
Modestly bold, and *humanly* severe. *Pope's Ess. on Criticism.*

Hu'mbird. *n. s.* [from *hum* and *bird.*] The humming bird.

All ages have conceived the wren the least of birds, yet our own plantations have shewed us one far less; that is, the *humbird*, not much exceeding a beetle. *Brown's Vulg. Err.*

HU'MBLE. *adj.* [*humble*, French; *humilis*, Latin.]

1. Not proud; modest; not arrogant.

And mighty proud to *humble* weak does yield. *Fairy Qu.*

Now

Now we have shewn our power,
Let us seem *humbler* after it is done,
Than when it was a doing. *Shakesp. Coriolanus.*
Thy *humble* servant vows obedience,
And faithful service, 'till the point of death. *Shak. H.* VI.

We should be as *humble* in our imperfections and sins as Christ was in the fulness of the spirit, great wisdom, and perfect life. *Taylor's Rule of living holy.*

Chuse you for me; for well you understand
But if an *humble* husband may request,
Provide and order all things for the best. *Dryden.*
Ten thousand trifles light as these,
Nor can my rage nor anger move:
She should be *humble*, who would please;
And she must suffer, who can love. *Prior.*

2. Low; not high; not great.
Th' example of the heav'nly lark,
Thy fellow-poet, Cowley, mark!
Above the skies let thy proud musick sound,
Thy *humble* nest build on the ground. *Cowley.*
Denied what ev'ry wretch obtains of fate,
An *humble* roof and an obscure retreat. *Yalden.*
Ah! prince, hadst thou but known the joys which dwell
With *humbler* fortunes, thou wouldst curse thy royalty. *Rowe.*
Far *humbler* titles suit my lost condition. *Smith.*

To HU'MBLE. *v. a.* [from the adjective.

1. To make humble; to make submissive; to make to bow down with humility.
Take this purse, thou whom the heaven's plagues
Have *humbled* to all strokes. *Shakesp. King Lear.*
The executioner
Falls not the axe upon the *humbled* neck,
But first begs pardon. *Shakesp. As you like it.*

Humble yourselves under the mighty hand of God, that he may exalt you. 1 *Pet.* v. 6.

Hezekiah *humbled* himself for the pride of his heart. 2 *Chro.*

Why do I *humble* thus myself, and suing
For peace, reap nothing but repulse and hate. *Milton.*

Let the sinner put away the evil of his doings, and *humble* himself by a speedy and sincere repentance: let him return to God, and then let him be assured that God will return to him. *Rogers's Sermons.*

2. To crush; to break; to subdue; to mortify.
Yearly injoin'd, some say, to undergo
This annual *humbling* certain number'd days,
To dash their pride, and joy, for man seduc'd. *Milt. P. L.*

We are pleased, by some implicit kind of revenge, to see him taken down and *humbled* in his reputation, who had so far raised himself above us. *Addison's Spectat.*

The mistress of the world, the seat of empire,
The nurse of heroes, the delight of gods,
That *humbled* the proud tyrants of the earth. *Addis. Cato.*

Men that make a kind of insult upon society, ought to be *humbled* as disturbers of the publick tranquillity. *Freeholder.*

Fortune not much of *humbling* me can boast;
Though double tax'd, how little have I lost! *Pope.*

3. To make to condescend.
This would not be to condescend to their capacities, when he *humbles* himself to speak to them, but to lose his design in speaking. *Locke.*

4. To bring down from an height.
In process of time the highest mountains may be *humbled* into valleys; and again, the lowest valleys exalted into mountains. *Hakewill on Providence.*

HU'MBLEBEE. *n. s.* [*hum* and *bee.*] A buzzing wild bee.
The honeybags steal from the *humblebees*,
And for night-tapers crop their waxen thighs. *Shakespeare.*

This puts us in mind once again of the *humblebees* and the tinderboxes. *Atterbury.*

HU'MBLEBEE. *n. s.* A herb. *Ainsworth.*

HU'MBLEBEE *Eater. n. s.* A fly that eats the humblebee. *Ains.*

HU'MBLENESS. *n. s.* [from *humble.*] Humility; absence of pride.
With how true *humbleness*
They look'd down to triumph over pride! *Sidney.*

I am rather with all subjected *humbleness* to thank her excellencies, since the duty thereunto gave me rather heart to save myself, than to receive thanks for a deed which was her only inspiring. *Sidney, b.* i.

It was answered by us all, in all possible *humbleness*; but yet with a countenance, that we knew that he spoke it but merrily. *Bacon's New Atlantis.*

A grain of glory, mixt with *humbleness*,
Cures both a fever and lethargickness. *Herbert.*

HU'MBLER. *n. s.* [from *humble.*] One that humbles or subdues himself or others.

HU'MBLEMOUTHED. *adj.* [*humble* and *mouth.*] Mild; meek.
You are meek and *humblemouth'd*; but your heart
Is cramm'd with arrogancy, spleen and pride. *Shak. H.* VIII.

HU'MBLEPLANT. *n. s.* A species of sensitiveplant.
The *humbleplant* is so called because, as soon as you touch it, it prostrates itself on the ground, and in a short time elevates itself again, is raised in hotbeds. *Mortimer's Husbandry.*

HU'MBLES. *n. s.* Entrails of a deer.

HU'MBLESS. *n. s.* [from *humble.*] Humbleness; humility.
And with meek *humbless*, and afflicted mood,
Pardon for thee, and grace for me intreat. *Spenser.*

HU'MBLY. *adv.* [from *humble.*]

1. Without pride; with humility.
They were us'd to bend,
To send their smiles before them to Achilles,
To come *humbly* as they us'd to creep to holy altars. *Shakes.*
Here the tam'd Euphrates *humbly* glides,
And there the Rhine submits her swelling tides. *Dryden.*
Write him down a slave, who, *humbly* proud,
With presents begs preferments from the crowd. *Dryden.*
In midst of dangers, fears, and death,
Thy goodness I'll adore;
And praise thee for thy mercies past,
And *humbly* hope for more. *Addison's Spectator.*

2. Without height; without elevation.

HU'MDRUM. *adj.* [from *hum*, *drone*, or *humming drone.*] Dull; dronish; stupid.
Shall we, quoth she, stand still *humdrum*,
And see stout Bruin all alone,
By numbers basely overthrown? *Hudibras, p.* i.

I was talking with an old *humdrum* fellow, and, before I had heard his story out, was called away by business. *Addison.*

To HUME'CT. } *v. a.* [*humecto*, Latin; *humecter*, Fr.]
To HUME'CTATE. } To wet; to moisten.

The Nile and Niger do not only moisten and contemperate the air by their exhalations, but refresh and *humectate* the earth by their annual inundations. *Brown's Vulgar Errours.*

Her rivers are wheeled up into small cataracts, and so divided into sluices, to *humectate* the bordering soil, and make it wonderfully productive. *Howel's Vocal Forrest.*

The medicaments are of a cool *humecting* quality, and not too much astringent. *Wiseman's Surgery.*

HUMECTA'TION. *n. s.* [*humectation*, Fr. from *humectate.*] The act of wetting; moistening.

Plates of brass, applied to a blow, will keep it down from swelling: the cause is repercussion, without *humectation*, or entrance of any body. *Bacon's Natural History.*

That which is concreted by exsiccation, or expression of humidity, will be resolved by *humectation*, as earth and clay. *Brown's Vulgar Errours.*

HU'MERAL. *adj.* [*humeral*, Fr. from *humerus*, Latin.] Belonging to the shoulder.

The largest crooked needle should be used, with a ligature, in taking up the *humeral* arteries in amputation. *Sharp.*

HUMICUBA'TION. *n. s.* [*humi* and *cubo*, Latin.] The act of lying on the ground.

Fasting and sackcloth, and ashes and tears, and *humicubations*, used to be companions of repentance. *Bramhall.*

HU'MID. *adj.* [*humide*, French; *humidus*, Lat.] Wet; moist; watery.
Iris there, with *humid* bow,
Waters the odorous banks that blow
Flowers of more mingl'd hue
Than her purpled scarff can shew. *Milton.*
The queen, recover'd, rears her *humid* eyes,
And first her husband on the poop espies. *Dryden.*

If they slip easily, and are of a fit size to be agitated by heat, and the heat is big enough to keep them in agitation, the body is fluid; and if it be apt to stick to things, it is *humid*. *Newton's Opt.*

HUMI'DITY. *n. s.* [*humidité*, Fr. from *humid.*] That quality which we call moisture, or the power of wetting other bodies. It differs very much from fluidity, depending altogether on the congruity of the component particles of any liquor to the pores or surfaces of such particular bodies as it is capable of adhering to. Thus quicksilver is not a moist liquor, in respect to our hands or clothes, and many other things it will not stick to; but it may be called so in reference to gold, tin, or lead, to whose surfaces it will presently adhere. And even water itself, that wets almost every thing, and is the great standard of *humidity*, is not capable of wetting every thing; for it stands and runs easily off in globular drops on the leaves of cabbages, and many other plants; and it will not wet the feathers of ducks, swans, and other water-fowl. *Quincy.*

We'll use this unwholsome *humidity*, this gross watry pumpion: we'll teach him to know turtles from jays. *Shakespeare.*

O blessing-breeding sun, draw from the earth
Rotten *humidity*; below thy sister's orb
Infect the air. *Shakesp. Timon of Athens.*

Young animals have more tender fibres, and more *humidity*, than old animals, which have their juices more exalted and relishing. *Arbuthnot on Diet.*

HUMILIA'TION. *n. s.* [French.]

1. Descent from greatness; act of humility.
The former was an *humiliation* of Deity, the latter an *humiliation* of manhood; for which cause there followed upon the

latter an exaltation of that which was humbled; for with power he created the world, but restored it by obedience. *Hooker, b.* v. *s.* 55.

Thy *humiliation* shall exalt
With thee thy manhood also to this throne. *Milt. Pa. Lost.*

2. Mortification; external expression of sin and unworthiness.

John fared poorly, according unto the apparel he wore, that is, of camel's hair; and the doctrine he preached was *humiliation* and repentance. *Brown's Vulgar Errours.*

With tears
Watering the ground, and with our sighs the air
Frequenting, sent from hearts contrite, in sign
Of sorrow unfeign'd, and *humiliation* meek. *Milt. Pa. Lost.*

3. Abatement of pride.

It may serve for a great lesson of *humiliation* to mankind, to behold the habits and passions of men trampling over interest, friendship, honour, and their own personal safety, as well as that of their country. *Swift.*

HUMI'LITY. *n. s.* [*humilité*, French.]

1. Freedom from pride; modesty; not arrogance.

When we make profession of our faith, we stand; when we acknowledge our sins, or seek unto God for favour, we fall down; because the gesture of constancy becometh us best in the one, in the other the behaviour of *humility*. *Hooker.*

I do not know that Englishman alive,
With whom my soul is any jot at odds,
More than the infant that is born to-night;
I thank my God for my *humility*. *Shakesp. Richard* III.

What the height of a king tempteth to revenge, the *humility* of a Christian teacheth to forgive. *King Charles.*

The *humility* of the style gained them many friends. *Claren.*

There are some that use
Humility to serve their pride, and seem
Humble upon their way, to be the prouder
At their wish'd journey's end. *Denham's Sophy.*

It is an easy matter, when there is no danger of a trial, to extol *humility* in the midst of honours, or to begin a fast after dinner. *South's Sermons.*

As high turrets, for their airy steep,
Require foundations in proportion deep;
And lofty cedars as far upwards shoot,
As to the nether heavens they drive the root;
So low did her secure foundation lye,
She was not humble, but *humility*. *Dryden.*

2. Act of submission.

With these *humilities* they satisfied the young king, and by their bowing and bending avoided the present storm. *Davies.*

HU'MMER. *n. s.* [from *hum.*] An applauder. *Ainsworth.*

HU'MORAL. *adj.* [from *humour.*] Proceeding from the humours.

This sort of fever is comprehended under continual *humoral* fevers. *Harvey on Consumptions.*

HU'MORIST. *n. s.* [*humoristo*, Italian; *humoriste*, French.]

1. One who conducts himself by his own fancy; one who gratifies his own humour.

The wit sinks imperceptibly into an *humorist*. *Spectator.*

The notion of a *humorist* is one that is greatly pleased, or greatly displeased, with little things; his actions seldom directed by the reason and nature of things. *Watts's Logick.*

This *humorist* keeps to himself much more than he wants, and gives a vast refuse of his superfluities to purchase heaven. *Addison's Spectator.*

2. One who has violent and peculiar passions.

By a wise and timous inquisition the peccant humours and *humorists* must be discovered and purged, or cut off: mercy, in such a case, in a king, is true cruelty. *Bacon to Villiers.*

HU'MOROUS. *adj.* [from *humour.*]

1. Full of grotesque or odd images.

Some of the commentators tell us, that Marsya was a lawyer who had lost his cause; others that this passage alludes to the story of the satire Marsyas, who contended with Apollo, which I think is more *humorous*. *Addison on Italy.*

Thy *humorous* vein, thy pleasing folly,
Lies all neglected, all forgot;
And pensive, wav'ring, melancholy,
Thou dread'st and hop'st thou know'st not what. *Prior.*

2. Capricious; irregular; without any rule but the present whim.

I am known to be a *humorous* patrician; said to be something imperfect, in favouring the first complaint; hasty and tinder-like, upon too trivial motion. *Shakesp. Coriolanus.*

Thou fortune's champion, that do'st never fight
But when her *humorous* ladyship is by,
To teach thee safety. *Shakesp. King John.*

He's *humorous* as Winter, and as sudden
As flaws congeal'd in the spring of day. *Shakesp. Hen.* IV.

O, you awake then: come away,
Times be short, are made for play;
The *humorous* moon too will not stay:
What doth make you thus delay? *Ben. Johnson.*

Vast is his courage, boundless is his mind,
Rough as a storm, and *humorous* as the wind. *Dryden.*

He that would learn to pass a just sentence on persons and things, must take heed of a fanciful temper of mind, and an *humorous* conduct in his affairs. *Watts's Logick.*

3. Pleasant; jocular. *Ainsworth.*

HU'MOROUSLY. *adj.* [from *humorous.*]

1. Merrily; jocosely.

A cabinet of medals Juvenal calls, very *humourously*, *concisum argentum in titulos faciesque minutas*. *Addison on Medals.*

We resolve by halves, and unadvisedly; we resolve rashly, sillily, or *humorously*, upon no reasons that will hold. *Calamy.*

It has been *humorously* said, that some have fished the very jakes for papers left there by men of wit. *Swift.*

2. With caprice; with whim.

HU'MOROUSNESS. *n. s.* [from *humorous.*] Fickleness; capricious levity.

HU'MORSOME. *adj.* [from *humour.*]

1. Peevish; petulant.

2. Odd; humorous.

Our science cannot be much improved by masquerades, where the wit of both sexes is altogether taken up in continuing singular and *humorsome* disguises. *Swift.*

HU'MORSOMELY. *adv.* [from *humorsome.*] Peevishly; petulantly.

HU'MOUR. *n. s.* [*humeur*, French; *humor*, Latin.]

1. Moisture.

The aqueous *humour* of the eye will not freeze, which is very admirable, seeing it hath the perspicuity and fluidity of common water. *Ray on the Creation.*

2. The different kind of moisture in man's body, reckoned by the old physicians to be phlegm, blood, choler, and melancholy, which, as they predominated, were supposed to determine the temper of mind.

Believe not these suggestions, which proceed
From anguish of the mind and *humours* black,
That mingle with thy fancy. *Milton's Agonistes.*

3. General turn or temper of mind.

As there is no *humour*, to which impudent poverty cannot make itself serviceable; so were there enow of those of desperate ambition, who would build their houses upon others ruin. *Sidney, b.* ii.

There came with her a young lord, led hither with the *humour* of youth, which ever thinks that good whose goodness he sees not. *Sidney.*

King James, as he was a prince of great judgment, so he was a prince of a marvellous pleasant *humour*: as he was going through Lusen by Greenwich, he asked what town it was; they said Lusen. He asked, a good while after, what town is this we are now in? They said still it was Lusen: said the king, I will be king of Lusen. *Bacon's Apophthegms.*

Examine how your *humour* is inclin'd,
And which the ruling passion of your mind. *Roscommon.*

They, who were acquainted with him, know his *humour* to be such, that he would never constrain himself *Dryden.*

In cases where it is necessary to make examples, it is the *humour* of the multitude to forget the crime, and to remember the punishment. *Addison's Freeholder.*

Good *humour* only teaches charms to last,
Still makes new conquests, and maintains the past. *Pope.*

4. Present disposition.

It is the curse of kings to be attended
By slaves, that take their *humours* for a warrant
To break into the blood-house of life. *Shakesp. K. John.*

Another thought her nobler *humour* fed. *Fairfax, b.* ii.

Their *humours* are not to be won,
But when they are impos'd upon. *Hudibras, p.* iii.

Tempt not his heavy hand;
But one submissive word which you let fall,
Will make him in good *humour* with us all. *Dryden.*

5. Grotesque imagery; jocularity; merriment.

6. Diseased or morbid disposition.

He was a man frank and generous; when well, denied himself nothing that he had a mind to eat or drink, which gave him a body full of *humours*, and made his fits of the gout frequent and violent. *Temple.*

7. Petulance; peevishness.

Is my friend all perfection, all virtue and discretion? Has he not *humours* to be endured, as well as kindnesses to be enjoyed? *South's Sermons.*

8. A trick; a practice.

I like not the *humour* of lying: he hath wronged me in some *humours*: I should have born the humour'd letter to her. *Shakespeare's Merry Wives of Windsor.*

9. Caprice; whim; predominent inclination.

In private, men are more bold in their own *humours*; and in consort, men are more obnoxious to others *humours*; therefore it is good to take both. *Bacon's Essays.*

To HU'MOUR. *v. a.* [from the noun.]

1. To gratify; to sooth by compliance.

If I had a suit to master Shallow, I would *humour* his men; if to his men, I would curry with master Shallow. *Shakesp.*

If I were Brutus now, and he were Cassius,
He should not *humour* me. *Shakesp. Julius Cæsar.*

Obedience

Obedience and subjection were never enjoined by God to *humour* the passions, lusts, and vanities of those who are commanded to obey our governours. *Swift.*

You *humour* me, when I am sick;
Why not when I am splenetick? *Pope.*

Children are fond of something which strikes their fancy most, and sullen and regardless of every thing else, if they are not *humoured* in that fancy. *Watts's Logick.*

2. To fit; to comply with.

To after age thou shalt be writ the man,
That with smooth air could'st *humour* best our tongue. *Milt.*

'Tis my part to invent, and the musicians to *humour* that invention. *Dryden's Preface to Albion.*

Fountainbleau is situated among rocks and woods, that give a fine variety of savage prospects: the king has *humoured* the genius of the place, and only made use of so much art as is necessary to regulate nature. *Addison's Guardian.*

HUMP. *n. s.* [corrupted perhaps from *bump*. See BUMP.] The protuberance formed by a crooked back.

These defects were mended by succeeding matches; the eyes were opened in the next generation, and the *hump* fell. *Tatler*, N°. 74.

HU'MPBACK. *n. s.* [*hump* and *back.*] Crooked back; high shoulders.

The chief of the family was born with an *humpback* and very high nose. *Tatler.*

HUMPBA'CKED. *adj.* Having a crooked back.

To HUNCH. *v. a.* [*husch*, German.]

1. To strike or punch with the fists.

Jack's friends began to *hunch* and push one another: why don't you go and cut the poor fellow down? *Arbuthnot.*

2. [*Hocker*, a crooked back, German.] To crook the back.

Thy crooked mind within *hunch'd* out thy back,
And wander'd in thy limbs: to thy own kind
Make love, if thou can'st find it in the world. *Dryden.*

HUNCHBA'CKED. *adj.* [*hunch* and *back.*] Having a crooked back.

His person deformed to the highest degree, flat-nosed, and *hunchbacked.* *L'Estrange.*

But I more fear Creon!
To take that *hunchback'd* monster in my arms,
Th' excrescence of a man. *Dryd. and Lee's Oedipus.*

The second daughter was peevish, haggard, pale, with saucer-eyes, a sharp nose, and *hunchbacked.* *Arbuthn. Hist. of J. Bull.*

HU'NDRED. *adj.* [hunꝺ, hunꝺreꝺ, Saxon; *honderd*, Dutch.] The number consisting of ten multiplied by ten.

A base, proud, three suited, *hundred* pound, filthy, worsted stocking knave. *Shakespeare's King Lear.*

A *hundred* altars in her temple smoke,
A thousand bleeding hearts her pow'r invoke. *Dryd. Æn.*

Many thousands had seen the transactions of our Saviour, and many *hundred* thousands received an account of them from the mouths of those who were eye-witnesses. *Addison.*

HU'NDRED. *n. s.*

1. A company or body consisting of an hundred.

Very few will take this proposition, that God is pleased with the doing of what he himself commands, for an innate moral principle: whosoever does so, will have reason to think *hundreds* of propositions innate. *Locke.*

Lands, taken from the enemy, were divided into centuries or *hundreds*, and distributed amongst the soldiers. *Arbuthnot.*

2. A canton or division of a county, perhaps once containing an hundred manors. [*Hundredum*, low Latin; *hundrede*, old French.]

Imposts upon merchants do seldom good to the king's revenue; for that that he wins in the *hundred*, he loseth in the shire. *Bacon.*

For justice they had a bench under a tree, where Ket usually sat, and with him two of every *hundred* whence their companies had been raised: here complaints were exhibited. *Hayw.*

HU'NDREDTH. *adj.* [hunꝺreonteogoþa, Saxon.] The ordinal of an hundred; the tenth ten times told.

We shall not need to use the *hundredth* part of that time, which themselves bestow in making invectives. *Hooker.*

If this medium is rarer within the sun's body than at its surface, and rarer there than at the *hundredth* part of an inch from its body, and rarer there than at the orb of Saturn, I see no reason why the increase of density should stop any where. *Newton's Opt.*

HUNG. The *preterite* and *part. pass.* of *hang*.

A wife so *hung* with virtues, such a freight,
What mortal shoulders can support! *Dryden's Juvenal.*

A room that is richly adorned, and *hung* round with a great variety of pictures, strikes the eye at once. *Watts.*

HU'NGER. *n. s.* [hungeɲ, Saxon; *honger*, Dutch.]

1. Desire of food; the pain felt from fasting.

An uneasy sensation at the stomach for food. When the stomach is empty, and the fibres in their natural tension, they draw up so close as to rub against each other, so as to make that sensation: but when they are distended with food, it is again removed; unless when a person fasteth so long as for want of spirits, or nervous fluid, to have those fibres grow too flaccid to corrugate, and then we say a person has fasted away his stomach; and this is occasioned by the attrition of the coats of the stomach against each other. *Quincy.*

Thou shalt serve thine enemies in *hunger* and in thirst. *Deutr.* xxviii. 48.

The sub-acid part of the animal spirits, being cast off by the lower nerves upon the coats of the stomach, vellicates the fibres, and thereby produces the sense we call *hunger.* *Grew.*

Something viscous, fat and oily, remaining in the stomach, destroys the sensation of *hunger.* *Arbuthnot on Aliments.*

2. Any violent desire.

The immaterial felicities we expect, do naturally suggest the necessity of preparing our appetites and *hungers* for them, without which heaven can be no heaven to us. *Decay of Piety.*

To HU'NGER. *v. n.* [from the noun.]

1. To feel the pain of hunger.

Widely they gape, and to the eye they roar,
As if they *hunger'd* for the food they bore. *Cowley.*

2. To desire with great eagerness.

Do'st thou so *hunger* for my empty chair,
That thou wilt needs invest thee with my honours,
Before thy hour be ripe? O, foolish youth,
Thou seek'st the greatness that will overwhelm thee!
Stay but a little. *Shakespeare's Henry* IV. *p.* ii.

My more having, would be as a sauce
To make me *hunger* more. *Shakespeare's Macbeth.*

I content me,
And from the sting of famine fear no harm,
Nor mind it, fed with better thoughts that feed
Me *hung'ring* more to do my father's will. *Milton's P. Lost.*

HU'NGERBIT. } *adj.* [*hunger* and *bit.*] Pained or weak-
HU'NGERBITTEN. } ened with hunger.

His strength shall be *hungerbitten*, and destruction shall be ready at his side. *Job* xviii. 12.

Thyself
Bred up in poverty and straits at home;
Lost in a desert here, and *hungerbit.* *Milton's Parad. Reg.*

HU'NGERLY. *adj.* [from *hunger.*] Hungry; in want of nourishment.

His beard
Grew thin and *hungerly*, and seem'd to ask
His sops as he was drinking. *Shakes. Taming of the Shrew.*

HU'NGERLY. *adv.* With keen appetite.

You have sav'd my longing, and I feed
Most *hungerly* on your sight. *Shak. Timon of Athens.*

They are all but stomachs, and we all but food;
They eat us *hungerly*, and, when they're full,
They belch us. *Shakespeare's Othello.*

HU'NGERSTARVED. *adj.* [*hunger* and *starved.*] Starved with hunger; pinched by want of food.

All my followers to th' eager foe
Turn back, and fly like ships before the wind,
Or lambs pursu'd by *hungerstarved* wolves. *Shakesp. H.* VI.

O'ertake me, if thou can'st; I scorn thy strength:
Go, go, chear up thy *hungerstarved* men. *Shakesp. H.* VI.

As to some holy house th' afflicted came,
Th' *hungerstarv'd*, the naked, and the lame,
Want and diseases, fled before her name. *Dryden.*

HU'NGRED. *adj.* [from *hunger.*] Pinched by want of food.

Odours do in a small degree nourish, and we see men an *hungred* love to smell hot bread. *Bacon's Natural History.*

HU'NGRILY. *adv.* [from *hungry.*] With keen appetite.

Thus much to the kind rural gods we owe,
Who pity'd suff'ring mortals long ago;
When on harsh acorns *hungrily* they fed,
And gave 'em nicer palates, better bread. *Dryden's Juven.*

HU'NGRY. *adj.* [from *hunger.*]

1. Feeling pain from want of food.

That face of his the *hungry* cannibals
Would not have touch'd, would not have stain'd with blood. *Shakespeare's Henry* VI. *p.* iii.

They that talk thus may say that a man is always *hungry*, but that he does not always feel it; whereas hunger consists in that very sensation. *Locke.*

2. Not fat; not fruitful; not prolifick; more disposed to draw from other substances than to impart to them.

Cassius has a lean and *hungry* look. *Shakes. Jul. Cæsar.*

The more fat water will bear soap best; for the *hungry* water doth kill its unctuous nature. *Bacon's Natural History.*

In rushy grounds springs are found at the first and second spit, and sometimes lower in a *hungry* gravel. *Mortimer.*

To this great day of retribution our Saviour refers us, for reaping the fruits that we here sow in the most *hungry* and barren soil. *Smalridge's Sermons.*

HUNKS. *n. s.* [*hunskur*, sordid, Islandick.] A covetous sordid wretch; a miser; a curmudgeon:

The old *hunks* was well served, to be tricked out of a whole hog for the securing of his puddings. *L'Estrange.*

She has a husband, a jealous, covetous, old *hunks.* *Dryden.*

Irus has given all the intimations of being a close *hunks*, worth money. *Addison's Spectator.*

To HUNT. *v. a.* [huntian, Saxon, from hund, a dog.]

1. To chaſe wild animals.

The man that once did ſell the lion's ſkin,
While the beaſt liv'd, was kill'd in *hunting* him. *Shak. H.V.*

Wilt thou *hunt* the prey for the lion, or fill the appetite of the young lions? *Job* xxxviii. 39.

We ſhould ſingle every criminal out of the herd, and *hunt* him down, however formidable and overgrown; and, on the contrary, ſhelter and defend virtue. *Addiſon's Spectator.*

2. To purſue; to follow cloſe.

Evil ſhall *hunt* the violent man to overthrow him. *Pſ.* cxl.

The heart ſtrikes five hundred ſort of pulſes in an hour, and is *hunted* unto ſuch continual palpitations, through anxiety, that fain would it break. *Harvey on Conſumptions.*

3. To ſearch for.

Not certainly affirming any thing, but by conferring of times and monuments, I do *hunt* out a probability. *Spenſer.*

All that is found in books is not rightly deduced from the principles it is pretended to be built upon: ſuch an examen every reader's mind is not forward to make, eſpecially in thoſe who have given themſelves up to a party, and only *hunt* for what may favour and ſupport the tenets of it. *Locke.*

4. To direct or manage hounds in the chace.

He *hunts* a pack of dogs better than any, and is famous for finding hares. *Addiſon's Spectator.*

To Hunt. *v. n.*

1. To follow the chaſe.

When he returns from *hunting*,
I will not ſpeak with him. *Shakeſpeare's King Lear.*

Eſau went to the field to *hunt* for veniſon. *Gen.* xxvii. 5.

One followed ſtudy and knowledge, and another hawking and *hunting*. *Locke.*

On the old pagan tombs maſks, *hunting* matches, and Bacchanals are very common. *Addiſon on Italy.*

2. To purſue or ſearch.

Very much of kin to this is the *hunting* after arguments to make good one ſide of a queſtion, and wholly to neglect and refuſe thoſe which favour the other ſide. *Locke.*

Hunt. *n. ſ.* [from the verb.]

1. A pack of hounds.

The common *hunt*, though from their rage reſtrain'd
By ſov'reign pow'r, her company diſdain'd,
Grinn'd as they paſs'd. *Dryden's Hind and Panther.*

2. A chace.

The *hunt* is up, the morn is bright and gray;
The fields are fragrant, and the woods are green. *Shakeſp.*

3. Purſuit.

I've heard myſelf proclaim'd;
And by the happy hollow of a tree,
Eſcap'd the *hunt*. *Shakeſpeare's King Lear.*

Hu'nter. *n. ſ.* [from *hunt.*]

1. One who chaſes animals for paſtime.

If thoſe Engliſh lords had been good *hunters*, and reduced the mountains, boggs, and woods within the limits of foreſts, chaces and parks, the foreſt law would have driven them into the plains. *Davies on Ireland.*

Down from a hill the beaſt that reigns in woods,
Firſt *hunter* then, purſu'd a gentle brace,
Goodlieſt of all the foreſt, hart and hind. *Milt. Par. Loſt.*

Another's crimes th' unhappy *hunter* bore,
Glutting his father's eyes with guiltleſs gore. *Dryden's Æn.*

This was the arms or device of our old Roman *hunters*; a paſſage of Manilius lets us know the pagan *hunters* had Meleager for their patron. *Addiſon on Italy.*

Bold Nimrod firſt the ſavage chace began,
A mighty *hunter*, and his game was man. *Pope.*

2. A dog that ſcents game or beaſts of prey.

Of dogs, the valu'd file
Diſtinguiſhes the ſwift, the ſlow, the ſubtle,
The houſekeeper, the *hunter*. *Shakeſp. Macbeth.*

Hu'ntinghorn. *n. ſ.* [*hunting* and *horn.*] A bugle; a horn uſed to cheer the hounds.

Whilſt a boy, Jack ran from ſchool,
Fond of his *huntinghorn* and pole. *Prior.*

Hu'ntress. *n. ſ.* [from *hunter.*] A woman that follows the chace.

And thou thrice crowned queen of night, ſurvey
With thy chaſte eye, from thy pale ſphere above,
Thy *huntreſs'* name, that my full life doth ſway. *Shakeſp.*

Shall I call
Antiquity from the old ſchools of Greece,
To teſtify the arms of chaſtity?
Hence had the *huntreſs* Dian her dread bow,
Fair ſilver-ſhafted queen, for ever chaſte. *Milton.*

Let old Arcadia boaſt her ample plain,
Th' immortal *huntreſs*, and her virgin train;
Nor envy Windſor. *Pope's Windſor Foreſt.*

Homer repreſents Diana with her quiver at her ſhoulder; but at the ſame time he deſcribes her as an *huntreſs*. *Broome.*

Hu'ntsman. *n. ſ.* [*hunt* and *man.*]

1. One who delights in the chace.

Like as a *huntſman*, after weary chace,
Seeing the game eſcape from him away,
Sits down to reſt him. *Spenſer's Sonnets.*

Such game, whilſt yet the world was new,
The mighty Nimrod did purſue:
What *huntſman* of our feeble race,
Or dogs, dare ſuch a monſter chace? *Waller.*

2. The ſervant whoſe office it is to manage the chace.

Apply this moral rather to the *huntſman*, that managed the chace, than to the maſter. *L'Eſtrange's Fables.*

Hun'tsmanship. *n. ſ.* [from *huntſman.*] The qualifications of a hunter.

At court your fellows every day
Give th' art of rhiming, *huntſmanſhip*, or play. *Donne.*

Hu'rdle. *n. ſ.* [hyrdel, Saxon.] A texture of ſticks woven together; a crate.

Settle your fine joints 'gainſt Thurſday next,
Or I will drag thee on a *hurdle* thither. *Shakeſpeare.*

The blackſmith was hanged, drawn, and quartered at Tyburn; taking pleaſure upon the *hurdle*, to think that he ſhould be famous in after times. *Bacon's Henry* VII.

The ſled, the tumbril, *hurdles* and the flail,
Theſe all muſt be prepar'd. *Dryden's Georg.*

Hurds. *n. ſ.* The refuſe of hemp or flax. *Ainſworth.*

To HURL. *v. a.* [from *huorlt*, to throw down, Iſlandick; or, according to *Skinner*, from *whirl.*]

1. To throw with violence; to drive impetuouſly.

If heav'ns have any grievous plagues in ſtore,
O, let them keep it 'till thy ſins be ripe,
And then *hurl* down their indignation
On thee. *Shakeſpeare's Richard* III.

He holds vengeance in his hand,
To *hurl* upon their heads that break his law. *Shak. R.* III.

I with my nails digg'd ſtones out of the ground,
To *hurl* at the beholders of my ſhame. *Shakeſ. Henry* VI.

If he thruſt him of hatred, or *hurl* at him by laying of wait. *Num.* xxxv. 20.

They uſe both the right hand and the left in *hurling* ſtones. *Chron.* xii. 2.

Hurl ink and wit,
As madmen ſtones. *Ben. Johnſon.*

His darling ſons,
Hurl'd headlong to partake with us, ſhall curſe
Their frail original and faded bliſs. *Milton's Parad. Loſt.*

She ſtrikes the lute; but if it ſound,
Threatens to *hurl* it on the ground. *Waller.*

Corrupted light of knowledge *hurl'd*
Sin, death, and ignorance o'er all the world. *Denham.*

Young Phaeton,
From Eaſt to North irregularly *hurl'd*,
Firſt ſet himſelf on fire, and then the world. *Dryd. Juven.*

Conjure him far to drive the Grecian train,
And *hurl* them headlong to their fleet and main. *Pope's Iliad.*

2. To utter with vehemence. [*Hurler*, French, to make an howling or hideous noiſe.]

The glad merchant that does view
His ſhip far come from watry wilderneſs,
He *hurls* out vows. *Spenſer.*

Highly they rag'd againſt the Higheſt,
Hurling defiance toward the vault of heav'n. *Milton.*

3. To play at a kind of game.

Hurling taketh its denomination from throwing of the ball, and is of two ſorts; to goals, and to the country: for *hurling* to goals there are fifteen or thirty players, more or leſs, choſen out on each ſide, who ſtrip themſelves, and then join hands in ranks, one againſt another: out of theſe ranks they match themſelves by pairs, one embracing another, and ſo paſs away; every of which couple are to watch one another during this play. *Carew's Survey of Cornwal.*

Hurl. *n. ſ.* [from the verb.] Tumult; riot; commotion.

He in the ſame *hurl* murdering ſuch as he thought would withſtand his deſire, was choſen king. *Knolles.*

Hu'rlbat. *n. ſ.* [*hurl* and *bat.*] Whirlbat. *Ainſworth.*

Hu'rler. *n. ſ.* [from *hurl.*] One that plays at hurling.

The *hurlers* muſt hurl man to man, and not two ſet upon one man at once. *Carew's Survey of Cornwal.*

Hu'rlwind. *n. ſ.* [*hurl* and *wind.*] A whirlwind; a violent guſt. A word not in uſe.

Like ſcatter'd down by howling Eurus blown,
By rapid *hurlwinds* from his manſion thrown. *Sandys.*

Hu'rly. } *n. ſ.* [I have been told that this word owes its
Hu'rlyburly. } original to two neighbouring families named *Hurly* and *Burly*, or *Hurleigh* and *Burleigh*, which filled their part of the kingdom with conteſts and violence. If this account be rejected, the word muſt be derived from *hurl*, *hurly*, and *burly*, a ludicrous reduplication. *Hurlade*, French; *hurlubrelu*, inconſiderately.] Tumult; commotion; buſtle.

Winds take the ruffian billows by the top,
That with the *hurley* death itſelf awakes. *Shakeſp. H.* IV.

Poor diſcontents,
Which gape and rub the elbow at the news
Of *hurlyburly* innovation. *Shakeſ. Henry* IV. *p.* i.

Methinks, I ſee this *hurly* all on foot. *Shakeſp. K. John.*

All places were filled with tumult and *hurlyburly*, every man meaſured the danger by his own fear; and ſuch a pitiful cry was in every place, as in cities preſently to be beſieged. *Knolles.*

HU'RRICANE. } *n. ſ.* [*huracan*, Spaniſh; *ouragan*, French.] A
HU'RRICANO. } violent ſtorm, ſuch as is often experienced in the eaſtern hemiſphere.

Blow winds, and crack your cheeks;
Your cataracts and *hurricanoes* ſpout. *Shakeſp. K. Lear.*

A ſtorm or *hurricano*, though but the force of air, makes a ſtrange havock where it comes. *Burnet's Theory of the Earth.*

A poet who had a great genius for tragedy, made every man and woman too in his plays ſtark raging mad: all was tempeſtuous and bluſtering; heaven and earth were coming together at every word; a mere *hurricane* from the beginning to the end. *Dryden's Dufreſnoy.*

The miniſters of ſtate, who gave us law,
In corners with ſelected friends withdraw;
There, in deaf murmurs, ſolemnly are wiſe,
Whiſp'ring like winds, ere *hurricanes* ariſe. *Dryden.*

So, where our wide Numidian waſtes extend,
Sudden th' impetuous *hurricanes* deſcend,
Wheel through the air, in circling eddies play,
Tear up the ſands, and ſweep whole plains away. *Addiſon.*

To HU'RRY. *v. a.* [heꞃᵹian, to plunder, Saxon: *hurs* was likewiſe a word uſed by the old Germans in urging their horſes to ſpeed; but ſeems the imperative of the verb.] To haſten; to put into precipitation or confuſion; to drive confuſedly.

Your nobles will not hear you; but are gone
To offer ſervice to your enemy;
And wild amazement *hurries* up and down
The little number of your doubtful friends. *Shakeſpeare.*

For whom all this haſte
Of midnight march, and *hurry'd* meeting here? *Milton.*

Impetuous luſt *hurries* him on to ſatisfy the cravings of it. *South's Sermons.*

That *hurry'd* o'er
Such ſwarms of Engliſh to the neighb'ring ſhore. *Dryden.*

A man has not time to ſubdue his paſſions, eſtabliſh his ſoul in virtue, and come up to the perfection of his nature, before he is *hurried* off the ſtage. *Addiſon's Spectator.*

Stay theſe ſudden guſts of paſſion,
That *hurry* you away. *Rowe's Royal Convert.*

If a council be called, or a battle fought, you are not coldly informed, the reader is *hurried* out of himſelf by the poet's imagination. *Pope's Preface to the Iliad.*

To HU'RRY. *v. n.* To move on with precipitation.

Did you but know what joys your way attend,
You would not *hurry* to your journey's end. *Dryd. Aurengz.*

HU'RRY. *n. ſ.* [from the verb.] Tumult; precipitation; commotion.

Among all the horrible *hurries* in England, Ireland was then almoſt quiet. *Hayward.*

It might have pleaſed him in the preſent heat and *hurry* of his rage; but muſt have diſpleaſed him infinitely in the ſedate reflection. *South's Sermons.*

After the violence of the *hurry* and commotion was over, the water came to a ſtate ſomewhat more calm. *Woodw.*

Ambition raiſes a tumult in the ſoul, it inflames the mind, and puts it into a violent *hurry* of thought. *Addiſ. Spectator.*

A long train of coaches and ſix ran through the heart, one after another, in a very great *hurry*. *Addiſon's Guardian.*

I do not include the life of thoſe who are in a perpetual *hurry* of affairs, but of thoſe who are not always engaged. *Addiſ.*

The pavement ſounds with trampling feet,
And the mixt *hurry* barricades the ſtreet. *Gay's Trivia.*

HURST. *n. ſ.* [hẏꞃꞅꞇ, Sax.] A grove or thicket of trees. *Ainſ.*

To HURT. *v. a.* preter. *I hurt*; part. paſſ. *I have hurt*. [hẏꞃꞇ, wounded, Saxon; *heurter*, to ſtrike, French.]

1. To miſchief; to harm.

Virtue may be aſſail'd, but never *hurt*;
Surpriz'd by unjuſt force, but not enthrall'd. *Milton.*

2. To wound; to pain by ſome bodily harm.

My heart is turn'd to ſtone: I ſtrike it, and it *hurts* my hand. *Shakeſpeare's Othello.*

The Adonis of the ſea is ſo called, becauſe it is a loving and innocent fiſh, that *hurts* nothing that has life. *Walton's Angler.*

It breeds contempt
For herds to liſten, or preſume to pry,
When the *hurt* lion groans within his den. *Dryd. Don Seb.*

HURT. *n. ſ.* [from the verb.]

1. Harm; miſchief.

The *hurt* which cometh thereby is greater than the good. *Spenſer's State of Ireland.*

I found it ſtand there uncorrected, as if there had been no *hurt* done. *Baker on Learning.*

2. Wound or bruiſe.

Where is he wounded?
—There will be large cicatrices to ſhew the people: he received ſeven *hurts* i' th' body. *Shakeſpeare's Coriolanus.*

Carter adventured bravely, and received two great *hurts* in his body. *Hayward.*

The pains of ſickneſs and *hurts*, hunger, thirſt and cold, all men feel. *Locke.*

In arms and ſcience 'tis the ſame,
Our rival's *hurts* create our fame. *Prior.*

HU'RTER. *n. ſ.* [from *hurt*.] One that does harm.

HU'RTFUL. *adj.* [*hurt* and *full*.] Miſchievous; pernicious.

Secret neglect of our duty is but only our own hurt: one man's contempt of the common prayer of the church of God may be moſt *hurtful* unto many. *Hooker, b. v.*

The *hurtful* hazle in thy vineyard ſhun,
Nor plant it to receive the ſetting ſun. *Dryden's Georg.*

HU'RTFULLY. *adv.* [from *hurtful*.] Miſchievouſly; pernicioufly.

HU'RTFULNESS. *n. ſ.* [from *hurtful*.] Miſchievouſneſs; perniciouſneſs.

To HU'RTLE. *v. n.* [*heurter*, French; *urtare*, Italian.] To claſh; to ſkirmiſh; to run againſt any thing; to joſtle; to meet in ſhock and encounter. *Hanmer.*

The noiſe of battle *hurtled* in the air. *Shak. Jul. Cæſar.*

Kindneſs, nobler ever than revenge,
And nature ſtronger than his juſt occaſion,
Made him give battle to the lioneſs,
Who quickly fell before him; in which *hurtling*,
From miſerable ſlumber I awak'd. *Shakeſp. As you like it.*

To HU'RTLE. *v. a.* To move with violence or impetuoſity. This is probably the original of *hurl*.

His harmful club he 'gan to *hurtle* high,
And threaten battle to the fairy knight. *Fairy Queen, b.* ii.

HU'RTLEBERRY. *n. ſ.* [*hiort bar*, Daniſh.] Bilberry.

HU'RTLESS. *adj.* [from *hurt*.]

1. Innocent; harmleſs; innoxious; doing no harm.

Unto her home he oft would go,
Where bold and *hurtleſs* many a play he tries,
Her parents liking well it ſhould be ſo;
For ſimple goodneſs ſhined in his eyes. *Sidney.*

She joy'd to make proof of her cruelty
On gentle dame, ſo *hurtleſs* and ſo true. *Fairy Queen.*

Shorter ev'ry gaſp he takes,
And vain efforts and *hurtleſs* blows he makes. *Dryden's Æn.*

2. Receiving no hurt.

HU'RTLESSLY. *adv.* [from *hurtleſs*.] Without harm.

Your neighbours have found you ſo *hurtleſly* ſtrong, that they thought it better to reſt in your friendſhip than make new trial of your enmity. *Sidney.*

HU'RTLESSNESS. *n. ſ.* [from *hurtleſs*.] Freedom from any pernicious quality.

HU'SBAND. *n. ſ.* [*hoſband*, maſter, Daniſh, from *houſe* and *bonda*, Runick, a maſter.]

1. The correlative to wife; a man married to a woman.

Thy *husband* is thy lord, thy life, thy keeper,
Thy head, thy ſovereign. *Shakeſp. Taming of the Shrew.*

Why, woman, your *husband* is in his old lunes again: he ſo takes on yonder with my *husband*, and ſo rails againſt all married mankind. *Shakeſp. Merry Wives of Windſor.*

This careful *husband* had been long away,
Whom his chaſte wife and little children mourn. *Dryden.*

The contract and ceremony of marriage is the occaſion of the denomination or relation of *husband*. *Locke.*

2. The male of animals.

Ev'n though a ſnowy ram thou ſhalt behold,
Prefer him not in haſte, for *husband* to thy fold. *Dryden.*

3. An œconomiſt; a man that knows and practiſes the methods of frugality and profit. Its ſignification is always modified by ſome epithet implying bad or good.

Edward I. ſhewed himſelf a right good *husband*; owner of a lordſhip ill huſbanded. *Davies on Ireland.*

I was conſidering the ſhortneſs of life, and what ill *husbands* we are of ſo tender a fortune. *Collier on Fame.*

4. A tiller of the ground; a farmer.

Husband's work is laborious and hard. *Hubberd's Tale.*

I heard a great *husband* ſay, that it was a common error to think that chalk helpeth arable grounds. *Bacon's Nat. Hiſtory.*

In thoſe fields
The painful *husband* plowing up his ground,
Shall find all fret with ruſt, both pikes and ſhields. *Hakewill.*

If continu'd rain
The lab'ring *husband* in his houſe reſtrain,
Let him forecaſt his work. *Dryden's Georgicks.*

To HU'SBAND. *v. a.* [from the noun.]

1. To ſupply with an huſband.

Think you I am no ſtronger than my ſex,
Being ſo father'd and ſo *husbanded*? *Shak. Julius Cæſar.*

If you ſhall prove
This ring was ever her's, you ſhall as eaſy
Prove that I *husbanded* her bed in Florence,
Where yet ſhe never was. *Shakeſpeare.*

In my right,
By me inveſted, he compeers the beſt.
—That were the moſt, if he ſhould *husband* you. *Shakeſp.*

2. To manage with frugality.

It will be paſtime paſſing excellent,
If it be *husbanded* with modeſty. *Shakeſpeare.*

The

The French, wisely *husbanding* the possession of a victory, kept themselves within their trenches. *Bacon's Henry* VII.

If thou be master-gunner, spend not all
That thou can'st speak at once; but *husband* it,
And give men turns of speech. *Herbert.*

3. To till; to cultivate the ground with proper management.

A farmer cannot *husband* his ground, if he sits at a great rent. *Bacon's Essays.*

HU'SBANDLESS. *adj.* [from *husband.*] Without an husband.

A widow, *husbandless*, subject to fears;
A woman, naturally born to fears. *Shakesp. King John.*

HU'SBANDLY. *adj.* [from *husband.*] Frugal; thrifty.

Bare plots full of galls, if ye plow overthwart;
And compass it then, is a *husbandly* part. *Tuss. Husbandry.*

HU'SBANDMAN. *n. s.* [*husband* and *man.*] One who works in tillage.

This Davy serves you for good uses; he is your servingman, and your *husbandman.* *Shakesp. Henry* IV. *p.* ii.

The mule being more swift in his labour than the ox, more ground was allowed to the mule by the *husbandman.* *Broome.*

HU'SBANDRY. *n. s.* [from *husband.*]

1. Tillage; manner of cultivating land.

He began with a wild method to run over all the art of *husbandry*, especially employing his tongue about well dunging of a field. *Sidney, b.* ii.

Askt if in *husbandry* he ought did know,
To plough, to plant, to reap, to sow. *Hubberd's Tale.*

Husbandry supplieth unto us all things necessary for food. *Spenser's State of Ireland.*

Peace hath from France too long been chas'd;
And all her *husbandry* doth lie on heaps,
Corrupting in its own fertility. *Shakesp. Henry* V.

Her plenteous womb
Expresseth its full tilth and *husbandry.* *Shakespeare.*

The seeds of virtue may, by the *husbandry* of Christian counsel, produce better fruit than the strength of self-nature. *Raleigh's History of the World.*

Husbandry the Spaniards wanting in the valley of Mexico, could not make our wheat bear seed. *Raleigh's H. of the World.*

A family governed with order, will fall naturally to the several trades of *husbandry*, tillage, and pasturage. *Temple.*

Let any one consider the difference between an acre of land sown with wheat, and an acre of the same land lying without any *husbandry* upon it, and he will find that the improvement of labour makes the value. *Locke.*

2. Thrift; frugality; parsimony.

There's *husbandry* in heaven;
The candles are all out. *Shakespeare's Macbeth.*

You have already saved several millions to the publick, and that what we ask is too inconsiderable to break into any rules of the strictest good *husbandry.* *Swift.*

3. Care of domestick affairs.

Lorenzo, I commit into your hands
The *husbandry* and manage of my house. *Shakespeare.*

HUSH. *interj.* [Without etymology.] Silence! be still! no noise!

The king hath done you wrong; but *hush!* 'tis so. *Shak.*

There's something else to do; *hush* and be mute,
Or else our spell is marr'd. *Shakespeare's Tempest.*

HUSH. *adj.* [from the interjection.] Still; silent; quiet.

As we often see, against some storm,
A silence in the heav'ns, the rack stand still,
The bold winds speechless, and the orb below
As *hush* as death. *Shakespeare's Hamlet.*

To HUSH. *v. n.* [from the interjection.] To be still; to be silent.

This frown'd, that fawn'd, the third for shame did blush;
Another seemed envious or coy;
Another in her teeth did gnaw a rush;
But at these strangers presence every one did *hush.* *F. Queen.*

To HUSH. *v. a.* To still; to silence; to quiet; to appease.

Yet can I not of such tame patience boast,
As to be *husht*, and nought at all to say. *Shakesp. Rich.* II.

It was my breath that blew this tempest up,
Upon your stubborn usage of the pope;
But since you are a gentle convertite,
My tongue shall *hush* again this storm of war,
And make fair weather in your blust'ring land. *Sh. K. John.*

Speak softly;
All's *husht* as midnight yet. *Shakespeare's Tempest.*

My love would speak; my duty *hushes* me. *Shakespeare.*

When in a bed of straw we shrink together,
And the bleak winds shall whistle round our heads,
Wilt thou then talk thus to me? Wilt thou then
Hush my cares thus, and shelter me with love? *Otway.*

Hush'd as midnight silence go;
He will not have your acclamations now. *Dryden.*

Her sire at length is kind,
Calms ev'ry storm, and *hushes* ev'ry wind;
Prepares his empire for his daughter's ease,
And for his hatching nephews smooths the seas. *Dryden.*

Upon his rising the court was *hushed*, and a whisper ran. *Addison's Spectator.*

To HUSH *up. v. a.* To suppress in silence; to forbid to be mentioned.

This matter is *hushed up*, and the servants are forbid to talk of it. *Pope.*

HU'SHMONEY. *n. s.* [*hush* and *money.*] A bribe to hinder information; pay to secure silence.

A dext'rous steward, when his tricks are found,
Hushmoney sends to all the neighbours round;
His master, unsuspicious of his pranks,
Pays all the cost, and gives the villain thanks. *Swift.*

HUSK. *n. s.* [*huldsch*, Dutch, or *huysken*, from *huys.*] The outmost integument of fruits.

Do but behold yon poor and starved band,
And your fair shew shall suck away their souls,
Leaving them but the shales and *husks* of men. *Shak. H.* V.

Most seeds, in their growing, leave their *husk* or rind about the root. *Bacon's Natural History.*

Thy food shall be
The fresh brook mussels, withered roots, and *husks*
Wherein the acorn cradled. *Shakespeare's Tempest.*

Fruits of all kinds, in coat
Rough, or smooth rind, or bearded *husks*, or shell
She gathers; tribute large! and on the board
Heaps with unsparing hand. *Milton's Paradise Lost, b.* v.

Some steep their seeds, and some in cauldrons boil
O'er gentle fires; the exuberant juice to drain,
And swell the flatt'ring *husks* with fruitful grain. *Dryden.*

Some when the press, by utmost vigour screw'd,
Has drain'd the pulpous mass, regale their swine
With the dry refuse; thou, more wise, shalt steep
The *husks* in water, and again employ
The pond'rous engine. *Phillips.*

Barley for ptisan was first steeped in water 'till it swelled; afterwards dried in the sun, then beat 'till the *husk* was taken off, and ground. *Arbuthnot on Coins.*

Do not content yourselves with mere words, lest you only amass a heap of unintelligible phrases, and feed upon *husks* instead of kernels. *Watts's Improvement of the Mind.*

To HUSK. *v. a.* [from the noun.] To strip off the outward integument.

HU'SKED. *adj.* [from *husk.*] Bearing an husk; covered with a husk.

HU'SKY. *adj.* [from *husk.*] Abounding in husks; consisting of husks.

Most have found
A *husky* harvest from the grudging ground. *Dryden's Virgil.*

With timely care
Shave the goat's shaggy beard, lest thou too late
In vain should'st seek a strainer, to dispart
The *husky* terrene dregs from purer must. *Phillips.*

HU'SSY. *n. s.* [corrupted from *housewife*: taken in an ill sense.] A sorry or bad woman; a worthless wench. It is often used ludicrously in slight disapprobation.

Get you in, *hussy*, go: now will I personate this hopeful young jade. *Southern's Innocent Adultery.*

HU'STINGS. *n. s.* [hustings, Saxon.] A council; a court held.

To HU'STLE. *v. a.* [perhaps corrupted from *hurtle.*] To shake together.

HU'SWIFE. *n. s.* [corrupted from *housewife.*]

1. A bad manager; a sorry woman. It is common to use *housewife* in a good, and *huswife* or *hussy* in a bad sense.

Bianca,
A *huswife*, that, by selling her desires,
Buys herself bread and cloth. *Shakespeare's Othello.*

2. An œconomist; a thrifty woman.

Why should you want?
The bounteous *huswife*, nature, on each bush
Lays her fulness before you. *Shakespeare.*

To HU'SWIFE. *v. a.* [from the noun.] To manage with œconomy and frugality.

But *huswifing* the little heav'n had lent,
She duly paid a groat for quarter-rent;
And pinch'd her belly, with her daughters two,
To bring the year about with much ado. *Dryden.*

HU'SWIFERY. *n. s.* [from *huswife.*]

1. Management good or bad.

Good *huswifery* trieth
To rise with the cock;
Ill *huswifery* lyeth
'Till nine of the clock. *Tusser.*

2. Management of rural business committed to women.

If cheeses in dairie have Argus his eyes,
Tell Cisley the fault in her *huswifery* lies. *Tuss. Husbandry.*

HUT. *n. s.* [hutte, Saxon; *hute*, French.] A poor cottage.

Our wand'ring saints, in woful state,
To a small cottage came at last,
Where dwelt a good old honest yeoman,
Who kindly did these saints invite
In his poor *hut* to pass the night. *Swift.*

Sore pierc'd by wintry wind,
How many ſhrink into the ſordid *hut*
Of chearleſs poverty. *Thomſon.*

HUTCH. *n. ſ.* [ƿpæcca. Saxon; *huche*, French.] A corn cheſt.

The beſt way to keep them, after they are threſhed, is to dry them well, and keep them in *hutches*, or cloſe caſks. *Mort.*

To HUZZ. *v. n.* [from the ſound.] To buzz; to murmur.

HUZZA'. *interj.* A ſhout; a cry of acclamation.

The *huzzas* of the rabble are the ſame to a bear that they are to a prince. *L'Eſtrange.*

It was an unfair thing in you to keep a parcel of roaring bullies about me day and night, with *huzzas* and hunting horns never let me cool. *Arbuthnot's Hiſtory of John Bull.*

All fame is foreign, but of true deſert;
Plays round the head, but comes not to the heart:
One ſelf-approving hour whole years outweighs
Of ſtupid ſtarers and of loud *huzzas*. *Pope's Eſſay on Man.*

To HUZZA'. *v. n.* [from the interjection.] To utter acclamation.

A caldron of fat beef, and ſtoop of ale,
On the *huzzaing* mob ſhall ſtill prevail. *King's Cookery.*

To HUZZA'. *v. a.* To receive with acclamation.

He was *huzzaed* into the court by ſeveral thouſands of weavers and clothiers. *Addiſon.*

HY'ACINTH. *n. ſ.* [ὑάκινθος; *hyacinthe*, Fr. *hyacinthus*, Lat.]

1. A plant.

It hath a bulbous root: the leaves are long and narrow: the ſtalk is upright and naked, the flowers growing on the upper part in a ſpike: the flowers conſiſt each of one leaf, are naked, tubuloſe, and cut into ſix diviſions at the brim, which are reflexed: the ovary becomes a roundiſh fruit with three angles, which is divided into three cells, which are filled with roundiſh ſeeds. *Miller.*

The ſilken fleece, impurpl'd for the loom,
Rival'd the *hyacinth* in vernal bloom. *Pope's Odyſſey.*

2. The *hyacinth* is the ſame with the *lapis lyncurius* of the ancients. It is a leſs ſhewy gem than any of the other red ones, but not without its beauty, though not gaudy. It is ſeldom ſmaller than a ſeed of hemp, or larger than a nutmeg. It is found of various degrees of deepneſs and paleneſs; but its colour is always a deadiſh red, with a conſiderable admixture of yellow, which even ſometimes ſeems predominant: but its moſt uſual is that mixed red and yellow, which we know by the name of flame-colour. This gem is found in ſeveral parts of Europe; but the fineſt ſort comes from the Eaſt and Weſt Indies. *Hill on Foſſils.*

HYACI'NTHINE. *adj.* [ὑακίνθινος.] Made of hyacinths.

HY'ADES. } *n. ſ.* [ὑάδες.] A watry conſtellation.
HY'ADS. }

Then ſailors quarter'd heav'n, and found a name
For ev'ry fix'd and ev'ry wand'ring ſtar;
The pleiads, *hyads*. *Dryden's Georgicks.*

HY'ALINE. *adj.* [ὑάλινος.] Glaſſy; cryſtalline; made glaſs; reſembling glaſs.

From heav'n-gate not far, founded in view
On the clear *hyaline*, the glaſſy ſea. *Milton's Parad. Loſt.*

HY'BRIDOUS. *adj.* [ὕβρις; *hybrida*, Latin.] Begotten between animals of different ſpecies.

Why ſuch different ſpecies ſhould not only mingle together, but alſo generate an animal, and yet that that *hybridous* production ſhould not again generate, is to me a myſtery. *Ray.*

HYDA'TIDES. *n. ſ.* [from ὕδωρ.] Little tranſparent bladders of water in any part: moſt common in dropſical perſons, from a diſtention or rupture of the lympheducts; for they happen moſtly in parts abounding with thoſe veſſels. *Quincy.*

All the water is contained in little bladders, adhering to the liver and peritoneum, known by the name of *hydatides*. *Wiſem.*

HY'DRA. *n. ſ.* [*hydra*, Latin.] A monſter with many heads ſlain by *Hercules*: whence any multiplicity of evils is termed a *hydra*.

New rebellions raiſe
Their *hydra* heads, and the falſe North diſplays
Her broken league to imp her ſerpent wings. *Milton.*

More formidable *hydra* ſtands within,
Whoſe jaws with iron-teeth ſeverely grin.
Subdue
The *hydra* of the many-headed hiſſing crew. *Dryden's Æn.* *Dryden.*

HY'DRAGOGUES. *n. ſ.* [ὕδωρ and ἄγω; *hydragogue*, Fr.] Such medicines as occaſion the diſcharge of watery humours, which is generally the caſe of the ſtronger cathartícks, becauſe they ſhake moſt forcibly by their vellications the bowels and their appendages, ſo as to ſqueeze out water enough to make the ſtools ſeem to be little elſe. *Quincy.*

HYDRAU'LICAL. } *adj.* [from *hydraulick*.] Relating to the conveyance of water through pipes.
HYDRAU'LICK. }

Among the engines in which the air is uſeful, pumps may be accounted not contemptible ones, and divers other *hydraulical* engines. *Derham's Phyſico-Theology.*

We have employed a virtuoſo to make an *hydraulick* engine, in which a chymical liquor, reſembling blood, is driven through elaſtick channels. *Arbuthn. and Pope's Mart. Scriblerus.*

HYDRAU'LICKS. *n. ſ.* [ὕδωρ, water, and αὐλὸς, a pipe.] The ſcience of conveying water through pipes or conduits.

HYDROCE'LE. *n. ſ.* [ὑδροκήλη; *hydrocele*, Fr.] A watery rupture.

HYDROCE'PHALUS. *n. ſ.* [ὕδωρ and κεφαλή.] A dropſy in the head.

A *hydrocephalus*, or dropſy of the head, is only incurable when the ſerum is extravaſated into the ventricles of the brain. *Arbuthnot on Diet.*

HYDRO'GRAPHER. *n. ſ.* [ὕδωρ and γράφω; *hydrographe*, Fr.] One who draws maps of the ſea.

It may be drawn from the writings of our *hydrographer*. *Boyle.*

HYDRO'GRAPHY. *n. ſ.* [ὕδωρ and γράφω; *hydrographie*, Fr.] Deſcription of the watery part of the terraqueous globe.

HY'DROMANCY. *n. ſ.* [ὕδωρ and μαντεία; *hydromantie*, Fr.] Prediction by water.

Divination was invented by the Perſians: there are four kinds of divination; *hydromancy*, pyromancy, aeromancy, and geomancy. *Ayliffe's Parergon.*

HY'DROMEL. *n. ſ.* [ὕδωρ and μέλι; *hydromel*, Fr.] Honey and water.

Hydromel is a drink prepared of honey, being one of the moſt pleaſant and univerſal drinks the northern part of Europe affords, as well as one of the moſt ancient. *Mortimer's Huſb.*

In fevers the aliments preſcribed by Hippocrates were ptiſans and cream of barley; *hydromel*, that is, honey and water, when there was no tendency to a delirium. *Arbuthnot.*

HYDRO'METER. *n. ſ.* [ὕδωρ and μέτρον] An inſtrument to meaſure the extent of water.

HYDRO'METRY. *n. ſ.* [ὕδωρ and μέτρον.] The act of meaſuring the extent of water.

HYDROPHO'BIA. *n. ſ.* [ὑδροφοβία; *hydrophobie*, Fr.] Dread of water.

Among thoſe diſmal ſymptoms that follow the bite of a mad dog, the dread of water is the moſt remarkable. *Quincy.*

HYDRO'PICAL. } *adj.* [ὑδρωπικός; *hydropique*, French; from
HYDRO'PICK. } *hydrops*, Latin.] Dropſical; diſeaſed with extravaſated water.

Cantharides heats the watery parts of the body; as urine, and *hydropical* water. *Bacon's Nat. Hiſt.*

The world's whole ſap is ſunk:
The general balm th' *hydropick* earth hath drunk;
Whither, as to the bedsfeet, life is ſhrunk,
Dead and interr'd. *Donne.*

Some mens *hydropick* inſatiableneſs learned to thirſt the more, by how much more they drank. *King Charles.*

Hydropical ſwellings, if they be pure, are pellucid. *Wiſem.*

Every luſt is a kind of *hydropick* diſtemper, and the more we drink the more we ſhall thirſt. *Tillotſon's Sermons.*

Hydropick wretches by degrees decay,
Growing the more, the more they waſte away;
By their own ruins they augmented lye,
With thirſt and heat amidſt a deluge fry. *Blackmore.*

One ſort of remedy he uſes in dropſies, *viz.* the water of the *hydropicks*, which is a remedy for the diſeaſe. *Arbuthnot.*

HYDROSTA'TICAL. *adj.* [ὕδωρ and ςατική.] Relating to hydroſtaticks; taught by hydroſtaticks.

A human body forming in ſuch a fluid, will never be reconcilable to this *hydroſtatical* law: there will be always ſomething lighter beneath, and ſomething heavier above; becauſe bone, the heavieſt in ſpecie, will be ever in the midſt. *Bentley.*

HYDROSTA'TICALLY. *adv.* [from *hydroſtatical*] According to hydroſtaticks.

The weight of all bodies around the earth is ever proportional to the quantity of their matter: for inſtance, a pound weight, examined *hydroſtatically*, doth always contain an equal quantity of ſolid maſs. *Bentley's Sermons.*

HYDROSTA'TICKS. *n. ſ.* [ὕδωρ and ςατική; *hydroſtatique*, Fr.] The ſcience of weighing fluids; weighing bodies in fluids.

HYDRO'TICK. *n. ſ.* [ὕδωρ; *hydrotique*, French.] Purger of water or phlegm.

He ſeems to have been the firſt who divided purges into *hydroticks* and purgers of bile. *Arbuthnot on Coins.*

HY'EN. } *n. ſ.* [*hyene*, French; *hyæna*, Latin.] An animal like
HYE'NA. } a wolf, ſaid fabulouſly to imitate human voices.

I will weep when you are diſpoſed to be merry; I will laugh like a *hyen*, when you are inclined to ſleep. *Shakeſpeare.*

A wonder more amazing would we find;
The *hyena* ſhews it, of a double kind:
Varying the ſexes in alternate years,
In one begets, and in another bears. *Dryden's Fables.*

The *hyena* was indeed well joined with the bever, as having alſo a bag in thoſe parts, if thereby we underſtand the *hyena odorata*, or civet cat. *Brown's Vulgar Errours.*

The keen *hyena*, felleſt of the fell. *Thomſon's Summer.*

HYGRO'METER. *n. ſ.* [ὑγρὸς and μετρέω; *hygrometre*, French.] An inſtrument to meaſure the degrees of moiſture.

A ſponge, perhaps, might be a better *hygrometer* than the earth of the river. *Arbuthnot on Air.*

HY'GROSCOPE. *n. ſ.* [ὑγρὸς and σκοπέω; *hygroſcope*, Fr.] An inſtrument to ſhew the moiſture and dryneſs of the air, and to meaſure and eſtimate the quantity of either extreme. *Quincy.*

Moiſture in the air is diſcovered by *hygroſcopes*. *Arbuthnot.*

HYLA'RCHICAL. *adj.* [ὕλη and ἀρχὴ.] Preſiding over matter.

HYM. *n. ſ.* A ſpecies of dog.

Avaunt, you curs!
Maſtiff, greyhound, mungril grim,
Hound or ſpaniel, brache or *hym*;
Or bobtail tike, or trundle tail,
Tom will make him weep and wail. *Shakeſp. King Lear.*

HY'MEN. *n. ſ.* [ὑμὴν.]
1. The god of marriage.
2. The virginal membrane.

HYMENE'AL. } *n. ſ.* [ὑμέναι@.] A marriage ſong.
HYMENE'AN. }

And heav'nly choirs the *hymenean* ſung. *Milt. Par. Loſt.*
For her the ſpouſe prepares the bridal ring;
For her white virgins *hymeneals* ſing. *Pope.*

HYMENE'AL. } *adj.* Pertaining to marriage.
HYMENE'AN. }

The ſuitors heard, and deem'd the mirthful voice
A ſignal of her *hymeneal* choice. *Pope's Odyſſey.*

HYMN. *n. ſ.* [*hymne*, Fr. ὕμν@.] An encomiaſtick ſong, or ſong of adoration to ſome ſuperiour being.

As I earſt, in praiſe of mine own dame,
So now in honour of thy mother dear,
An honourable *hymn* I eke ſhould frame. *Spenſer.*

Our ſolemn *hymns* to ſullen dirges change;
Our bridal flow'rs ſerve for a buried coarſe. *Shakeſpeare.*

When ſteel grows
Soft as the paraſite's ſilk, let *hymns* be made
An overture for the wars. *Shakeſpeare's Coriolanus.*

There is an *hymn* ſung; but the ſubject of it is always the praiſes of Adam, and Noah and Abraham, concluding ever with a thankſgiving for the nativity of our Saviour. *Bacon.*

Farewel, you happy ſhades,
Where angels firſt ſhould practiſe *hymns*, and ſtring
Their tuneful harps, when they to heav'n would ſing. *Dryd.*

To HYMN. *v. a.* [ὑμνέω.] To praiſe in ſong; to worſhip with hymns.

To HYMN. *v. n.* To ſing ſongs of adoration.

They touch'd their golden harps, and *hymning* prais'd
God and his works. *Milton.*

He had not left alive this patient ſaint,
This anvil of affronts, but ſent him hence
To hold a peaceful branch of palm above,
And *hymn* it in the quire. *Dryden's Spaniſh Fryar.*

HY'MNICK. *adj.* [ὕμνος.] Relating to hymns.

He rounds the air, and breaks the *hymnick* notes
In birds, heav'n's choriſters, organick throats;
Which, if they did not die, might ſeem to be
A tenth rank in the heavenly hierarchy. *Donne.*

To HYP. *v. a.* [barbarouſly contracted from *hypochondriack.*] To make melancholy; to diſpirit.

I have been, to the laſt degree, *hypped* ſince I ſaw you. *Spect.*

HY'PALLAGE. *n. ſ.* [ὑπαλλαγὴ.] A figure by which words change their caſes with each other.

HY'PER. *n. ſ.* [A word barbarouſly curtailed by *Prior* from *hypercritick.*] A hypercritick; one more critical than neceſſity requires. *Prior* did not know the meaning of the word.

Criticks I read on other men,
And *hypers* upon them again. *Prior.*

HYPE'RBOLA. *n. ſ.* [*hyperbole*, Fr. ὑπὲρ and βάλλω.] In geometry, a ſection of a cone made by a plane, ſo that the axis of the ſection inclines to the oppoſite leg of the cone, which in the parabola is parallel to it, and in the ellipſis interſects it. The axis of the hyperbolical ſection will meet alſo with the oppoſite ſide of the cone, when produced above the vertex. *Harris.*

Had the velocities of the ſeveral planets been greater or leſs than they are, or had their diſtances from the ſun, or the quantity of the ſun's matter, and conſequently his attractive power been greater or leſs than they are now, with the ſame velocities, they would not have revolved in concentrick circles, but have moved in *hyperbola's* very eccentrick. *Bentley's Serm.*

HY'PERBOLE. *n. ſ.* [*hyperbole*, Fr. ὑπερβολὴ.] A figure in rhetorick by which any thing is increaſed or diminiſhed beyond the exact truth: as, *he runs faſter than lightning. His poſſeſſions are fallen to duſt. He was ſo gaunt, the caſe of a flagellet was a manſion for him.* Shakeſp.

Terms unſquar'd,
Which, from the tongue of roaring Typhon dropt,
Would ſeem *hyperboles*. *Shakeſ. Troilus and Creſſida.*

Taffata phraſes, ſilken terms preciſe,
Three pil'd *hyperboles*, ſpruce affectation,
Figures pedantical, theſe Summer flies,
Have blown me full of maggot oſtentation. *Shakeſpeare.*

They were above the *hyperboles*, that fond poetry beſtows upon its admired objects. *Glanv. Sceſſ. c.* 1.

Hyperboles, ſo daring and ſo bold,
Diſdaining bounds, are yet by rules control'd;
Above the clouds, but yet within our ſight,
They mount with truth, and make a tow'ring flight. *Granv.*

The common people underſtand raillery, or at leaſt rhetorick, and will not take *hyperboles* in too literal a ſenſe. *Swift.*

HYPERBO'LICAL. } *adj.* [*hyperbolique*, French; from *hyperbola.*]
HYPERBO'LICK. }

1. Belonging to the hyperbola; having the nature of an hyperbola.

Cancellated in the middle with ſquares, with triangles before, and behind with *hyperbolick* lines. *Grew's Muſæum.*

The horny or pellucid coat of the eye riſeth up, as a hillock, above the convexity of the white of the eye, and is of an *hyperbolical* or parabolical figure. *Ray on the Creation.*

2. [From *hyperbole.*] Exaggerating or extenuating beyond fact.

It is parabolical, and probably *hyperbolical*, and therefore not to be taken in a ſtrict ſenſe. *Boyle.*

HYPERBO'LICALLY. *adv.* [from *hyperbolical.*]
1. In form of an hyperbola.
2. With exaggeration or extenuation.

Yet may all be ſolved, if we take it *hyperbolically*. *Brown.*

Scylla is ſeated upon a narrow mountain, which thruſts into the ſea a ſteep high rock, and *hyperbolically* deſcribed by Homer as inacceſſible. *Broome's Notes on the Odyſſey.*

HYPERBO'LIFORM. *adj.* [*hyperbola* and *forma.*] Having the form, or nearly the form of the hyperbola.

HYPERBO'REAN. *n. ſ.* [*hyperborëen*, French; *hyperboreus*, Lat.] Northern.

HYPERCRI'TICK. *n. ſ.* [*hypercritique*, Fr. ὑπὲρ and κρίτικος.] A critick exact or captious beyond uſe or reaſon.

Thoſe *hypercriticks* in Engliſh poetry differ from the opinion of the Greek and Latin judges of antiquity, from the Italians and French, and from the general taſte of all ages. *Dryd.*

HYPERCRI'TICAL. *adj.* [from *hypercritick.*] Critical beyond neceſſity or uſe.

We are far from impoſing thoſe nice and *hypercritical* punctilio's, which ſome aſtrologers oblige our gardeners to. *Evelyn.*

Such *hypercritical* readers will conſider my buſineſs was to make a body of refined ſayings, only taking care to produce them in the moſt natural manner. *Swift.*

HYPE'RMETER. *n. ſ.* [ὑπὲρ and μέτρον.] Any thing greater than the ſtandard requires.

When a man riſes beyond ſix foot, he is an *hypermeter*, and may be admitted into the tall club. *Addiſon's Guardian.*

HYPERSARCO'SIS. *n. ſ.* [ὑπερσάρκωσις, ὑπὲρ and σαρκὸς.] The growth of fungous or proud fleſh.

Where the *hyperſarcoſis* was great, I ſprinkled it with precipitate, whereby I more ſpeedily freed the ulcer of its putrefaction. *Wiſeman's Surgery.*

HY'PHEN. *n. ſ.* [ὑφὲν.] A note of conjunction: as, *vir-tue, ever-living.*

HYPNO'TICK. *n. ſ.* [ὕπνος.] Any medicine that induces ſleep.

HYPOCHO'NDRES. *n. ſ.* [*hypocondre*, Fr. ὑποχόνδριον.] The two regions lying on each ſide the cartilago enſiformis, and thoſe of the ribs, and the tip of the breaſt, which have in one the liver, and in the other the ſpleen. *Quincy.*

The blood moving too ſlowly through the celiack and meſenterick arteries, produce various complaints in the lower bowels and *hypochondres*; from whence ſuch perſons are called hypochondriack. *Arbuthnot on Aliments.*

HYPOCHONDRI'ACAL. } *adj.* [*hypocondriaque*, French, from *hypochondres.*]
HYPOCHONDRI'ACK. }

1. Melancholy; diſordered in the imagination.

Socrates laid down his life in atteſtation of that moſt fundamental truth, the belief of one God; and yet he's not recorded either as fool or *hypochondriack*. *Decay of Piety.*

2. Producing melancholy.

Cold ſweats are many times mortal, and always ſuſpected; as in great fears, and *hypochondriacal* paſſions, being a relaxation or forſaking of the ſpirits. *Bacon's Nat. Hiſtory.*

HY'POCIST. *n. ſ.* [ὑπόκισις; *hypociſte*, French.]

Hypociſt is an inſpiſſated juice in large flat maſſes, conſiderably hard and heavy, of a fine ſhining black colour, when broken. It is brought from the Levant, ſometimes from France, and other parts of Europe. The ſtem of the plant, from which it is produced, is thick and fleſhy; and, what is ſingular, much thicker at the top than towards the bottom. The fruits contain a tough glutinous liquor, which are gathered before they are ripe; and the juice is expreſſed, then evaporated over a gentle fire, formed into cakes, and dried in the ſun. It is an aſtringent medicine of conſiderable power. *Hill's Mat. Med.*

HYPO'CRISY. *n. ſ.* [*hypocriſie*, Fr. ὑπόκρισις.] Diſſimulation with regard to the moral or religious character.

Next ſtood *hypocriſy* with holy leer,
Soft ſmiling and demurely looking down;
But hid the dagger underneath the gown. *Dryden's Fables.*

Hypocriſy is much more eligible than open infidelity and vice: it wears the livery of religion, and is cautious of giving ſcandal: nay, continued diſguiſes are too great a conſtraint: men would leave off their vices, rather than undergo the toil of practiſing them in private. *Swift.*

HY'POCRITE. *n. ſ.* [*hypocrite*, French; ὑποκρίτης.] A diſſembler in morality or religion.

He heartily prays some occasion may detain us longer: I dare swear he is no *hypocrite*, but prays from his heart. *Shak.*

A wise man hateth not the law; but he that is an *hypocrite* therein, is as a ship in a storm. *Ecclus.* xxxiii. 3.

Fair *hypocrite*, you seek to cheat in vain;
Your silence argues, you ask time to reign. *Dryden.*

The making religion necessary to interest might increase hypocrisy; but if one in twenty should be brought to true piety, and nineteen be only *hypocrites*, the advantage would still be great. *Swift.*

Beware, ye honest: the third circling glass
Suffices virtue: but may *hypocrites*,
Who slily speak one thing, another think,
Hateful as hell, still pleas'd unwarn'd drink on,
And through intemp'rance grow a while sincere. *Phillips.*

HYPOCRI'TICAL. } HYPOCRI'TICK. } *adj.* [from *hypocrite.*] Dissembling; insincere; appearing differently from the reality.

Now you are confessing your enormities; I know it by that *hypocritical*, down-cast look. *Dryden's Spanish Fryar.*

Whatever virtues may appear in him, they will be esteemed an *hypocritical* imposture on the world; and in his retired pleasures, he will be presumed a libertine. *Roger's Sermons.*

Let others skrew their *hypocritick* face. *Swift.*

HYPOCRI'TICALLY. *adv.* [from *hypocritical.*] With dissimulation; without sincerity; falsely.

Simeon and Levi spake not only falsely, but insidiously, nay *hypocritically*, abusing at once their proselytes and their religion. *Government of the Tongue.*

HYPOGA'STRICK. *adj.* [*hypogastrique*, French; ὑπο and γαςὴρ.] Seated in the lower part of the belly.

The swelling we supposed to rise from an effusion of serum through all the *hypogastrick* arteries. *Wiseman's Surgery.*

HYPOGE'UM. *n. s.* [ὑπο and γῆ.] A name which the ancient architects gave to all the parts of a building that were under ground, as cellars and vaults *Harris.*

HYPO'STASIS. *n. s.* [*hypostase*, French; ὑπόςασις.]

1. Distinct substance.

2 Personality. A term used in the doctrine of the Holy Trinity.

The oneness of our Lord Jesus Christ, referring to the several *hypostases* in the one eternal, indivisible, divine nature, and the eternity of the Son's generation, and his co-eternity and consubstantiality with the Father, are assertions equivalent to those before comprised in the ancient more simple article. *Hammond on Fundamentals.*

HYPOSTA'TICAL. *adj.* [*hypostatique*, French, from *hypostasis.*]

1. Constitutive; constituent as distinct ingredients.

Let our Carneades warn men not to subscribe to the grand doctrine of the chymists, touching their three *hypostatical* principles, 'till they have a little examined it. *Boyle.*

2. Personal; distinctly personal.

HYPOTENU'SE. *n. s.* [*hypotenuse*, Fr. ὑποτείνουσα.] The line that subtends the right angle of a right-angled triangle; the subtense.

The square of the *hypotenuse* in a right-angled triangle, is equal to the squares of the two other sides. *Locke.*

HYPO'THESIS. *n. s.* [*hypothese*, Fr. ὑπόθεσις.] A supposition; a system formed upon some principle not proved.

The mind casts and turns itself restlesly from one thing to another, 'till at length it brings all the ends of a long and various *hypothesis* together; sees how one part coheres with another, and so clears off all the appearing contrarieties that seemed to lie cross, and make the whole intelligible. *South's Serm.*

With imagin'd sovereignty
Lord of his new *hypothesis* he reigns:
He reigns: how long? 'till some usurper rise;
And he too, mighty thoughtful, mighty wise,
Studies new lines, and other circles feigns. *Prior.*

HYPOTHE'TICAL. } HYPOTHE'TICK. } *adj.* [*hypothetique*, Fr. from *hypothesis.*] Including a supposition; conditional.

Conditional or *hypothetical* propositions are those whose parts are united by the conditional particle *if*; as, *if* the sun be fixed, the earth must move. *Watts's Logick.*

HYPOTHE'TICALLY. *adv.* [from *hypothetical.*] Upon supposition; conditionally.

The only part liable to imputation is calling her a goddess; yet this is proposed with modesty and doubt, and *hypothetically*. *Broome's Notes to Pope's Odyssey.*

HYRST, } HURST, } HERST, } Are all from the Saxon hyrst, a wood or grove. *Gibs.*

HY'SSOP. *n. s.* [*hyssope*, Fr. *hyssopus*, Lat.] A verticillate plant, with long narrow leaves: the crest of the flower is roundish, erect, and divided into two parts: the beard is divided into three parts; the middle part is hollowed like a spoon, having a double point, and is somewhat winged: the whorles of the flowers are short, and at the lower part of the stalk are placed at a great distance; but toward the top are closer joined, so as to form a regular spike. It hath been a great dispute, whether the hyssop commonly known is the same which is mentioned in Scripture. *Miller.*

The *hyssop* of Solomon cannot be well conceived to be our common *hyssop*; for that is not the least of vegetables observed to grow upon walls; but rather some kind of capillaries, which only grow upon walls and stony places. *Brown.*

HYSTE'RICAL. } HYSTE'RICK. } *adj.* [*hysterique*, French; ὑςερικός.]

1. Troubled with fits; disordered in the regions of the womb.

In *hysterick* women the rarity of symptoms doth oft strike such an astonishment into spectators, that they report them possessed with the devil. *Harvey on Consumptions.*

Many *hysterical* women are sensible of wind passing from the womb. *Floyer on the Humours.*

2. Proceeding from disorders in the womb.

Parent of vapours, and of female wit,
Who gave th' *hysterick* or poetick fit. *Pope's Ra. of the Lock.*

This terrible scene made too violent an impression upon a woman in her condition, and threw her into a strong *hysterick* fit. *Arbuthn and Pope's Mart. Scribl.*

HYSTE'RICKS. *n. s.* [ὑςερικός.] Fits of women, supposed to proceed from disorders in the womb.

I.

I.

I, Is in English considered both as a vowel and consonant; though, since the vowel and consonant differ in their form as well as sound, they may be more properly accounted two letters.

I vowel has a long sound, as *fine*, *thine*, which is usually marked by an *e* final; and a short sound, as *fin*, *thin*. Prefixed to *e* it makes a diphthong of the same sound with the soft *i*, or double *e*, *ee*: thus *field*, *yield*, are spoken as *feeld*, *yeeld*; except *friend*, which is spoken *frend*. Subjoined to *a* or *e* it makes them long, as *fail*, *neigh*; and to *o* makes a mingled sound, which approaches more nearly to the true notion of a diphthong, or sound composed of the sounds of two vowels, than any other combination of vowels in the English language, as *oil*, *coin*. The sound of *i* before another *i*, and at the end of a word, is always expressed by *y*.

J consonant has invariably the same sound with that of *g* in *giant*; as *jade*, *jet*, *jilt*, *jolt*, *just*.

I. *pronoun personal.* [*ik*, Gothick; ıc, Saxon; *ich*, Dutch.]
I, gen. *me*; plural *we*; gen. *us*.
ıc, *me*, pe, uƿ.

1. The pronoun of the first person, *myself*.

I do not like these several councils, *I*. *Shakesp. Rich.* III.
There is none greater in this house than *I*. *Gen.* xxxix. 9.
Be of good cheer, it is *I*; be not afraid. *Mat.* xiv. 27.

What shall *I* do to be for ever known,
And make the age to come my own?
I shall like beasts or common people dye,
Unless you write my elegy. *Cowley.*

Hence, and make room for *me*. *Cowley.*

When chance of business parts *us* two,
What do our souls, I wonder, do? *Cowley.*

Of that book you have given *us* a large earnest. *Cowley.*

Thus, having pass'd the night in fruitless pain,
I to my longing friends return again. *Dryden's Æn.*

2. *Me* is in the following passage written for *I*.

There is but one man whom she can have, and that is *me*. *Clarissa.*

3. *I* is more than once in *Shakespeare* written for *ay*, or *yes*.

Hath Romeo slain himself? Say thou but *I*,
And that bare vowel, *I*, shall poison more
Than the death-darting eye of cockatrice. *Shakespeare.*

Did your letters pierce the queen?
—*I*, sir; she took 'em and read 'em in my presence,
And now and then an ample tear trill'd down. *Shakespeare.*

To JA'BBER. *v. n.* [*gabberen*, Dutch.] To talk idly; to prate without thinking; to chatter.

We scorn, for want of talk, to *jabber*
Of parties. *Swift.*

JA'BBERER. *n. s.* [from *jabber*.] One who talks inarticulately or unintelligibly.

Out cant the Babylonian labourers
At all their dialects of *jabberers*. *Hudibras, p.* iii.

JA'CENT. *adj.* [*jacens*, Latin.] Lying at length.

So laid, they are more apt in swagging down to pierce than in the *jacent* posture. *Wotton's Architect.*

JACI'NTH. *n. s.* [for *hyacinth*, as *Jerusalem* for *Hierusalem*.]

1. The same with hyacinth.
2. A gem of a deep redish yellow approaching to a flame colour, or the deepest amber. *Woodward's Met. Foss.*

JACK. *n. s.* [Probably by mistake from *Jaques*, which in French is *James*.]

1. The diminutive of *John*. Used as a general term of contempt for saucy or paltry fellows.

I am in estimation:
You will perceive that a *Jack* gardant cannot
Office me from my son Coriolanus. *Shakespeare.*

I have in my mind
A thousand raw tricks of these bragging *Jacks*,
Which I will practise. *Shakes. Merchant of Venice.*

Every *Jack* slave hath his belly-full of fighting, and I must go up and down like a cock that nobody can match. *Shakesp.*

2. The name of instruments which supply the place of a boy, as an instrument to pull off boots.

Foot-boys, who had frequently the common name of *jack* given them, were kept to turn the spit, or to pull off their masters boots; but when instruments were invented for both those services, they were both called *jacks*. *Watts's Logick.*

3. An engine which turns the spit.

The excellencies of a good *jack* are, that the *jack* frame be forged and filed square; that the wheels be perpendicularly and strongly fixed on the squares of the spindles; that the teeth be evenly cut, and well smoothed; and that the teeth of the worm-wheel fall evenly into the groove of the worm. *Moxon.*

The ordinary *jacks*, used for roasting of meat, commonly consist but of three wheels. *Wilkins's Math. Magick.*

Clocks and *jacks*, though the screws and teeth be never so smooth, yet, if not oiled, will hardly move. *Ray.*

A cookmaid, by the fall of a *jack* weight upon her head, was beaten down. *Wiseman's Surgery.*

Some strain in rhyme; the muses on their racks
Scream, like the winding of ten thousand *jacks*. *Pope.*

4. A young pike.

No fish will thrive in a pond where roach or gudgeons are, except *jacks*. *Mortimer's Husbandry.*

5. [*Jacque*, French.] A coat of mail.

The residue were on foot, well furnished with *jack* and skull, pike, dagger, bucklers made of board, and slicing swords, broad, thin, and of an excellent temper. *Hayward.*

6. A cup of waxed leather.

Dead wine, that stinks of the borrachio, sup
From a foul *jack*, or greasy mapple cup. *Dryden's Pers.*

7. A small bowl thrown out for a mark to the bowlers.

'Tis as if one should say, that a bowl equally poised, and thrown upon a plain bowling-green, will run necessarily in a direct motion; but if it be made with a byass, that may decline it a little from a straight line, it may acquire a liberty of will, and so run spontaneously to the *jack*. *Bentley's Sermons.*

8. A part of the musical instrument called a virginal.

In a virginal, as soon as ever the *jack* falleth, and toucheth the string, the sound ceaseth. *Bacon's Natural History.*

9. The male of animals.

A *jack* ass, for a stallion, was bought for three thousand two hundred and twenty-nine pounds three shillings and four pence. *Arbuthnot on Coins.*

10. A support to saw wood on. *Ainsworth.*
11. The colours or ensign of a ship. *Ainsworth.*
12. A cunning fellow who can turn to any thing.

Jack of all trades, show and sound;
An inverse burse, an exchange under ground. *Cleaveland.*

JACK *Boots. n. s.* [from *jack*, a coat of mail.] Boots which serve as armour to the legs.

A man on horseback, in his breeches and *jack boots*, dressed up in a commode and a night-rail. *Spectator.*

JACK *by the Hedge. n. s.* An herb.

Jack by the hedge is an herb that grows wild under hedges, is eaten as other sallads are, and much used in broth. *Mortim.*

JACK *Pudding. n. s.* [*jack* and *pudding.*] A zani; a merry Andrew.

Every *jack pudding* will be ridiculing palpable weaknesses which they ought to cover. *L'Estrange.*

A buffoon is called by every nation by the name of the dish they like best: in French *jean pottage*, and in English *jack pudding*. *Guardian.*

Jack pudding, in his party-colour'd jacket,
Tosses the glove, and jokes at ev'ry packet. *Gay.*

JACK *with a Lantern.* An *ignis fatuus.*

JACKALE'NT. *n. s.* [*Jack in Lent*, a poor starven fellow.] A simple sheepish fellow.

You little *jackalent*, have you been true to us?
—Ay, I'll be sworn. *Shakesp. Merry Wives of Windsor.*

JACKA'L. *n. s.* [*chacal*, French.] A small animal supposed to start prey for the lyon.

The Belgians tack upon our rear,
And raking chase-guns through our sterns they send:
Close by their fireships, like *jackals*, appear,
Who on their lions for the prey attend. *Dryd. Ann. Mirab.*

The

The mighty lyon, before whom stood the little *jackal*, the faithful spy of the king of beasts. *Arbuth. and Pope's M. Scrib.*

JA'CKANAPES. *n. s.* [*jack* and *ape.*]

1. Monkey; an ape.
2. A coxcomb; an impertinent.

Which is he?
—That *jackanapes* with scarfs. *Shakesp.*

People wondered how such a young upstart *jackanapes* should grow so pert and saucy, and take so much upon him. *Arbuth.*

JACKDA'W. *n. s.* [*jack* and *daw.*] A cock daw; a bird taught to imitate the human voice.

To impose on a child to get by heart a long scroll of phrases, without any ideas, is a practice fitter for a *jackdaw* than for any thing that wears the shape of man. *Watts.*

JA'CKET. *n. s.* [*jacquet*, French.]

1. A short coat; a close waistcoat.

In a blue *jacket*, with a cross of red. *Hubberd's Tale.*

And hens, and dogs, and hogs are feeding by;
And here a sailor's *jacket* hangs to dry. *Swift.*

Jack pudding, in his party-colour'd *jacket*,
Tosses the glove, and jokes at ev'ry packet. *Gay.*

2. *To beat one's* JACKET, is to beat the man.

She fell upon the *jacket* of the parson, who stood gaping at her. *L'Estrange.*

JA'COB'*s Ladder. n. s.* The same with Greek valerian.

JA'COB'*s Staff. n. s.*

1. A pilgrim's staff.
2. Staff concealing a dagger.
3. A cross staff; a kind of astrolabe.

JA'COBINE. *n. s.* A pidgeon with a high tuft. *Ainsworth.*

JACTITA'TION. *n. s.* [*jactito*, Latin.] Tossing; motion; restlessness; heaving.

If the patient be surprised with *jactitation*, or great oppression about the stomach, expect no relief from cordials. *Harv.*

JACULA'TION. *n. s.* [*jaculatio*, *jaculor*, Latin.] The act of throwing missive weapons.

So hills amid' the air encounter'd hills,
Hurl'd to and fro with *jaculation* dire. *Milt. Parad. Lost.*

JADE. *n. s.* [The etymology of this word is doubtful: *Skinner* derives it from *gaad*, a goad, or spur.]

1. A horse of no spirit; a hired horse; a worthless nag.

Alas, what wights are these that load my heart!
I am as dull as Winter-starved sheep,
Tir'd as a *jade* in overloaden cart. *Sidney.*

When they should endure the bloody spur,
They fall their crest, and, like deceitful *jades*,
Sink in the tryal. *Shakesp. Julius Cæsar.*

The horsemen sit like fixed candlesticks,
With torchstaves in their hand; and their poor *jades*
Lob down their heads, dropping the head and hips. *Shakes.*

To other regions
France is a stable, we that dwell in't *jades*;
Therefore to th' war. *Shakes. All's well that ends well.*

So have I seen with armed heel
A wight bestride a commonweal,
While still the more he kick'd and spurr'd,
The less the sullen *jade* has stirr'd. *Hudibras, p.* i.

The plain nag came upon the trial to prove those to be *jades* that made sport with him. *L'Estrange.*

False steps but help them to renew their race,
As, after stumbling, *jades* will mend their pace. *Pope.*

2. A sorry woman. A word of contempt noting sometimes age, but generally vice.

Shall these, these old *jades*, past the flower
Of youth, that you have, pass you. *Chapman's Iliads.*

But she, the cunning'st *jade* alive,
Says, 'tis the ready way to thrive,
By sharing female bounties. *Stepney.*

Get in, hussy: now will I personate this young *jade*, and discover the intrigue. *Southerne's Innocent Adultery.*

In di'monds, pearl, and rich brocades,
She shines the first of batter'd *jades*,
And flutters in her pride. *Swift.*

3. A young woman: in irony and slight contempt.

You see now and then some handsome young *jades* among them: the sluts have very often white teeth and black eyes. *Add.*

JADE. *n. s.* A species of stone.

The *jade* is a species of the jasper, and of extreme hardness. Its colour is composed of a pale blueish grey, or ash-colour, and a pale green, not simple and uniform, but intermixed. It appears dull and coarse on the surface, but it takes a very elegant and high polish. It is found in the East Indies, and is much used by the Turks for handles of sabres. It is so highly esteemed by the Indians as to be called the divine stone: they wear it externally as a remedy for the gravel, and an amulet to preserve them from the bite of venomous animals. *Hill's Materia Medica.*

To JADE. *v. a.* [from the noun.

1. To tire; to harass; to dispirit; to weary.

With his banners, and his well-paid ranks,
The ne'er-yet-beaten horse of Parthia
We've *jaded* out o' th' field. *Shakesp. Ant. and Cleopatra.*

It is good in discourse to vary and intermingle speech of the present occasion with arguments; for it is a dull thing to tire and *jade* any thing too far. *Bacon's Essays.*

If fleet dragon's progeny at last
Proves *jaded*, and in frequent matches cast,
No favour for the stallion we retain,
And no respect for the degen'rate strain. *Dryden's Juven.*

The mind once *jaded*, by an attempt above its power, is very hardly brought to exert its force again. *Locke.*

There are seasons when the brain is overtired or *jaded* with study or thinking; or upon some other accounts animal nature may be languid or cloudy, and unfit to assist the spirit in meditation. *Watts's Logick.*

2. To overbear; to crush; to degrade; to harass, as a horse that is ridden too hard.

If we live thus tamely,
To be thus *jaded* by a piece of scarlet,
Farewel nobility. *Shakespeare's Henry* VIII.

3. To employ in vile offices.

The honourable blood
Must not be shed by such a *jaded* groom. *Shakes. Hen.* VI.

4. To ride; to rule with tyranny.

I do not now fool myself, to let imagination *jade* me; for every reason excites to this. *Shakesp. Twelfth Night.*

To JADE. *v. n.* To lose spirit; to sink.

Many offer at the effects of friendship, but they do not last: they are promising in the beginning, but they fail and *jade* and tire in the prosecution. *South's Sermons.*

JA'DISH. *adj.* [from *jade.*]

1. Vitious; bad, as an horse.

That hors'd us on their backs, to show us
A *jadish* trick at last, and throw us. *Hudibras, p.* iii.

When once the people get the *jadish* trick
Of throwing off their king, no ruler's safe. *Southern.*

2. Unchaste; incontinent.

'Tis to no boot to be jealous of a woman; for if the humour takes her to be *jadish*, not all the locks and spies in nature can keep her honest. *L'Estrange.*

To JAGG. *v. a.* [*gagaw*, slits or holes, Welsh.] To cut into indentures; to cut into teeth like those of a saw.

Some leaves are round, some long, some square, and many *jagged* on the sides. *Bacon's Natural History.*

The *jagging* of pinks and gilliflowers is like the inequality of oak-leaves; but they never have any small plain purls. *Bac.*

The banks of that sea must be *jagged* and torn by the impetuous assaults, or the silent underminings of waves; violent rains must wash down earth from the tops of mountains. *Bentl.*

An alder-tree is one among the lesser trees, whose younger branches are soft, and whose leaves are *jagged*. *Watts.*

JAGG. *n. s.* [from the verb.] A protuberance or denticulation.

The figure of the leaves is divided into so many *jaggs* or escallops, and curiously indented round the edges. *Ray.*

Take off all the staring straws, twigs, and *jaggs* in the hive, and make them as smooth as possible. *Mort. Husbandry.*

JA'GGY. *adj.* [from *jagg.*] Uneven; denticulated.

His tow'ring crest was glorious to behold;
His shoulders and his sides were scal'd with gold;
Three tongues he brandish'd when he charg'd his foes;
His teeth stood *jaggy* in three dreadful rows. *Addison.*

Amid' those angles, infinitely strain'd,
They joyful leave their *jaggy* salts behind. *Thoms. Autumn.*

JA'GGEDNESS. *n. s.* [from *jagged.*] The state of being denticulated; unevenness.

First draw rudely your leaves, making them plain with your coal or lead, before you give them their veins or *jaggedness*. *Peacham on Drawing.*

JAIL. *n. s.* [*geol*, French.] A gaol; a prison; a place where criminals are confined. See GAOL. It is written either way; but commonly by latter writers *jail.*

Away with the dotard, to the *jail* with him. *Shakesp.*

A dependant upon him paid six pound ready money, which, poor man, he lived to repent in a *jail*. *Clarendon.*

He sigh'd and turn'd his eyes, because he knew
'Twas but a larger *jail* he had in view. *Dryden.*

One *jail* did all their criminals restrain,
Which now the walls of Rome can scarce contain. *Dryden.*

JA'ILBIRD. *n. s.* [*jail* and *bird.*] One who has been in a jail.

JA'ILER. *n. s.* [from *jail.*] A gaoler; the keeper of a prison.

Seeking many means to speak with her, and ever kept from it, as well because she shunned it, seeing and disdaining his mind, as because of her jealous *jailers*. *Sidney.*

This is as a *jailer*, to bring forth
Some monstrous malefactor. *Shakes. Ant. and Cleopatra.*

His pow'r to hollow caverns is confin'd;
There let him reign, the *jailer* of the wind;
With hoarse commands his breathing subjects call,
And boast and bluster in his empty hall. *Dryden's Æn.*

Palamon, the pris'ner knight,
Restless for woe, arose before the light;
And with his *jailer*'s leave, desir'd to breathe
An air more wholesome than the damp beneath. *Dryden.*

JAKES.

Jakes. *n. s.* [Of uncertain etymology.] A house of office.

I will tread this unbolted villain into mortar, and daub the walls of *jakes* with him. *Shakespeare's King Lear.*

Their sordid avarice rakes
In excrements, and hires the very *jakes*. *Dryden's Juvenal.*

Some have fished the very *jakes* for papers left there by men of wit. *Swift.*

Ja'lap. *n. s.* [*jalap*, French; *jalapium*, low Latin.]

Jalap is a firm and solid root, of a wrinkled surface, and generally cut into slices, heavy and hard to break; of a faintish smell, and of an acrid and nauseous taste. It was not known in Europe 'till after the discovery of America, and had its name *jalapium*, or *jalapa*, from Xalapa, a town in New Spain, in the neighbourhood of which it was discovered; though it is now principally brought from the Madeiras. It is an excellent purgative in all cases where serous humours are to be evacuated. *Hill's Mat. Med.*

Jam. *n. s.* [I know not whence derived.] A conserve of fruits boiled with sugar and water.

Jamb. *n. s.* [*jambe*, French.] Any supporter on either side, as the posts of a door.

No timber is to be laid within twelve inches of the foreside of the chimney *jambs*. *Moxon's Mech. Exer.*

Ia'mbick. *n. s.* [*iambique*, French; *iambicus*, Latin.] Verses composed of iambick feet, or a short and long syllable alternately: used originaly in satire, therefore taken for satire.

In thy felonious heart though venom lies,
It does but touch thy Irish pen, and dies:
Thy genius calls thee not to purchase fame
In keen *iambicks*, but mild anagram. *Dryden.*

To **Ja'ngle.** *v. n.* [*jangler*, French. *Skinner.*] To altercate; to quarrel; to bicker in words.

Good wits will be *jangling*; but, gentiles agree,
This civil war of wits were much better us'd
On Navarre and his book-men. *Shak. Love's Labour Lost.*

So far am I glad it did so sort,
As this their *jangling* I esteem a sport. *Shakespeare.*

There is no errour which hath not some appearance of probability resembling truth, which when men, who study to be singular, find out, straining reason, they then publish to the world matter of contention and *jangling*. *Raleigh.*

To **Ja'ngle.** *v. a.* To make to sound untuneable.

Now see that noble and that sovereign reason,
Like sweet bells *jangled* out of tune and harsh. *Shak. Huml.*

'Ere Gothick forms were known in Greece,
And in our verse 'ere monkish rhimes
Had *jangl'd* their fantastick chimes. *Prior.*

Ja'ngler. *n. s.* [from the verb.] A wrangling, chattering, noisy fellow.

Ja'nizary. *n. s.* [A Turkish word.] One of the guards of the Turkish king.

His grand visier, presuming to invest
The chief imperial city of the West,
With the first charge compel'd in haste to rise;
The standards lost, and *janizaries* slain,
Render the hopes he gave his master vain. *Waller.*

Ja'nnock. *n. s.* [probably a corruption of *bannock.*] Oat-bread. A northern word.

Ja'nty. *adj.* [corrupted from *gentil*, French.] Showy; fluttering.

This sort of woman is a *janty* slattern: she hangs on her cloaths, plays her head, and varies her posture. *Spectator.*

Ja'nuary. *n. s.* [*Januarius*, Latin.] The first month of the year, from *Janus*, to whom it was among the Romans consecrated.

January is clad in white, the colour of the earth at this time, blowing his nails. This month had the name from Janus, painted with two faces, signifying providence. *Peacham.*

Japa'n. *n. s.* [from *Japan* in *Asia*, where figured work was originally done.] Work varnished and raised in gold and colours.

The poor girl had broken a large *japan* glass, of great value, with a stroke of her brush. *Swift.*

To **Japa'n.** *v. a.* [from the noun.]

1. To varnish, and embellish with gold and raised figures.

For not the desk with silver nails,
Nor bureau of expence,
Nor standish well *japan'd*, avails
To writing of good sense. *Swift.*

2. To black shoes. A low phrase.

The god of fire
Among these gen'rous presents joins his part,
And aids with soot the new *japanning* art. *Gay's Trivia.*

Japa'nner. *n. s.* [from *japan.*]

1. One skilled in japan work.

2. A shoeblacker.

The poor have the same itch;
They change their weekly barber, weekly news,
Prefer a new *japanner* to their shoes. *Pope's Horace.*

To **Jar.** *v. n.* [from eoppe, anger, Saxon; or *guerre*, war, French; or *garren*, old Teutonick, to clamour.]

1. To strike together with a kind of short rattle.

A hollow groan, a murm'ring wind arose;
The rings of iron, that on the doors were hung,
Sent out a *jarring* sound, and harshly rung. *Dryden.*

My knees tremble with the *jarring* blow. *Gay.*

2. To strike or sound untuneably.

O, you kind gods!
Cure this great breach in his abused nature:
Th' untun'd and *jarring* senses, O, wind up,
Of this child-changed father. *Shakesp. King Lear.*

I perceive you delight not in musick.
—Not a whit, when it *jars* so. *Shakespeare.*

A string may *jar* in the best master's hand,
And the most skilful archer miss his aim. *Roscommon.*

He keeps his temper'd mind, serene and pure,
And every passion aptly harmoniz'd
Amid' a *jarring* world. *Thomson's Summer.*

3. To clash; to interfere; to act in opposition; to be inconsistent.

At last, though long, our *jarring* notes agree. *Shakesp.*

For orders and degrees
Jar not with liberty, but well consist. *Milt. Parad. Lost.*

Venalus concluded his report:
A *jarring* murmur fill'd the factious court:
As when a torrent rolls with rapid force,
The flood, constrain'd within a scanty space,
Roars horrible. *Dryden's Æn.*

4. To quarrel; to dispute.

When those renowned noble peers of Greece,
Through stubborn pride, among themselves did *jar*,
Forgetful of the famous golden fleece,
Then Orpheus with his harp their strife did bar. *Spenser.*

They must be sometimes ignorant of the means conducing to those ends, in which alone they can *jar* and oppose each other. *Dryden's Juvenal, Dedication.*

Jar. *n. s.* [from the verb.]

1. A kind of rattling vibration of sound.

In *r*, the tongue is held stifly at its whole length, by the force of the muscles; so as when the impulse of breath strikes upon the end of the tongue, where it finds passage, it shakes and agitates the whole tongue, whereby the sound is affected with a trembling *jar*. *Holder's Elements of Speech.*

2. Clash; discord; debate.

He maketh war, he maketh peace again,
And yet his peace is but continual *jar*:
O miserable men, that to him subject are! *Fairy Queen.*

Nath'less, my brother, since we passed are
Unto this point, we will appease our *jar*. *Hubberd's Tale.*

Force would be right; or rather, right and wrong,
Between whose endless *jar* justice presides,
Would lose their names, and so would justice too. *Shakesp.*

3. A state in which a door unfastened may strike the post; half opened.

The chaffering with dissenters, and dodging about this or t'other ceremony, is but like opening a few wickets, and leaving them a *jar*, by which no more than one can get in at a time. *Swift.*

4. [*Giarro*, Italian.] An earthen vessel.

About the upper part of the *jar* there appeared a good number of bubbles. *Boyle.*

He mead for cooling drink prepares,
Of virgin honey in the *jars*. *Dryden.*

Warriors welter on the ground,
Whilst empty *jars* the dire defeat resound. *Garth.*

Ja'rdes. *n. s.* [French.] Hard callous tumours in horses, a little below the bending of the ham on the outside. This distemper in time will make the horse halt, and grow so painful as to cause him to pine away, and become light-bellied. It is most common to managed horses, that have been kept too much upon their haunches. *Farrier's Dict.*

Ja'rgon. *n. s.* [*jargon*, French; *gerigonça*, Spanish.] Unintelligible talk; gabble; gibberish.

Nothing is clearer than mathematical demonstration, yet let one, who is altogether ignorant in mathematicks, hear it, and he will hold it to be plain fustian or *jargon*. *Bramhall.*

From this last toil again what knowledge flows?
Just as much, perhaps, as shows
That all his predecessor's rules
Were empty cant, all *jargon* of the schools. *Prior.*

During the usurpation an infusion of enthusiastick *jargon* prevailed in every writing. *Swift.*

Ja'rgonelle. *n. s.* See **Pear**, of which it is a species.

Ja'shawk. *n. s.* A young hawk. *Ainsworth.*

Ja'smine. *n. s.* [*jasmin*, French. It is often pronounced *jessamine.*]

It hath a funnel-shaped flower, consisting of one leaf, which is cut into several segments at the brim, out of whose cup arises the pointal, which afterward becomes the fruit or pod, which, for the most part, grows double and open lengthwise, discovering the seeds, which are oblong, and have a border round them: these are ranged over each other like slates on a house, and are fastened to the placenta. *Miller.*

Thou, like the harmless bee, may'st freely range;
From *jasmine* grove to grove may'st wander. *Thomson.*

JA'SMINE *Perſian. n. ſ.* A plant. See LILAC, of which it is a ſpecies.

JA'SPER. *n. ſ.* [*jaſpe*, Fr. *iaſpis*, Lat.] A hard ſtone of a bright beautiful green colour, ſometimes clouded with white, found in maſſes of various ſizes and ſhapes. It is capable of a very elegant poliſh, and is found in many parts of the Eaſt Indies, and in Egypt, Africa, Tartary, and China. *Hill's Mat. Med.*

The baſis of *jaſper* is uſually of a greeniſh hue, and ſpotted with red, yellow and white. *Woodward's Met. Foſſ.*

The moſt valuable pillars about Rome are four columns of oriental *jaſper* in St. Paulina's chapel, and one of tranſparent oriental *jaſper* in the vatican library. *Addiſon on Italy.*

IATROLE'PTICK. *adj.* [*iatraleptique*, Fr. ἰατρὸς and ἀλείφω.] That which cures by anointing.

To JA'VEL, or *jable. v. a.* To bemire; to ſoil over with dirt through unneceſſary traverſing and travelling. This word is ſtill retained in Scotland and the northern counties.

JA'VEL. *n. ſ.* [perhaps from the verb.] A wandering fellow.

When as time, flying with wings ſwift,
Expired had the term that thoſe two *javels*
Should render up a reckoning of their travels. *Hubb. Tale.*

JA'VELIN. *n. ſ.* [*javeline*, French.] A ſpear or half pike, which anciently was uſed either by foot or horſe. It had an iron head pointed.

Others, from the wall, defend
With dart and *jav'lin*, ſtones and ſulph'rous fire;
On each hand ſlaughter and gigantick deeds. *Milt. Pa. Loſt.*

She ſhakes her myrtle *jav'lin*; and, behind,
Her Lycian quiver dances in the wind. *Dryden's Æn.*

Flies the *javelin* ſwifter to its mark,
Launch'd from the vigour of a Roman arm? *Addiſ. Cato.*

JA'UNDICE. *n. ſ.* [*jauniſſe*, *jaune*, yellow, Fr.] A diſtemper from obſtructions of the glands of the liver, which prevents the gall being duly ſeparated by them from the blood; and ſometimes, eſpecially in hard drinkers, they are ſo indurated as never after to be opened, and ſtraighten the motion of the blood ſo much through that viſcus as to make it divert with a force great enough into the gaſtrick arteries, which go off from the hepatick, to break through them, and drain into the ſtomach; ſo that vomiting of blood, in this diſtemper, is a fatal ſymptom. *Quincy.*

Why ſhould a man, whoſe blood is warm within,
Sit like his grandſire cut in alabaſter?
Sleep when he wakes, and creep into the *jaundice*
By being peeviſh? *Shakeſp. Merchant of Venice.*

What grief hath ſet the *jaundice* on your cheeks? *Shak.*

Thoſe were thy thoughts, and thou couldſt judge aright,
'Till int'reſt made a *jaundice* in thy ſight. *Dryden.*

The eyes of a man in the *jaundice* make yellow obſervations on every thing; and the ſoul, tinctured with any paſſion, diffuſes a falſe colour over the real appearances of things. *Watts's Improvement of the Mind.*

JA'UNDICED. *adj.* [from *jaundice.*] Infected with the jaundice.

All ſeems infected, that th' infected ſpy,
As all looks yellow to the *jaundic'd* eye. *Pope.*

To JAUNT. *v. n.* [*janter*, French.] To wander here and there; to buſtle about. It is now always uſed in contempt or levity.

I was not made a horſe,
And yet I bear a burthen like an aſs;
Spur-gall'd and tir'd by *jaunting* Bolingbroke. *Shak. R.* II.

JAUNT. *n. ſ.* [from the verb.] Ramble; flight; excurſion. It is commonly uſed ludicrouſly, but ſolemnly by *Milton.*

Our Saviour meek, and with untroubled mind,
After his airy *jaunt*, though hurry'd ſore,
Hungry and cold, betook him to his reſt. *Milt. Par. Reg.*

He ſends me out on many a *jaunt*,
Old houſes in the night to haunt. *Hudibras, p.* iii.

They parted, and away poſts the cavalier in queſt of his new miſtreſs: his firſt *jaunt* is to court. *L'Eſtrange.*

If you are for a merry *jaunt*, I'll try for once who can foot it fartheſt. *Dryden's Spaniſh Fryar.*

Thus much of the ſcheme of my deſign in this part have I run over, and led my reader a long and tedious *jaunt*, in tracing out theſe metallick and mineral bodies. *Woodward.*

JA'UNTINESS. *n. ſ.* [from *jaunty*, or *janty*, corrupted from *gentil*, French. See JANTY.] Airyneſs; flutter; genteelneſs.

A certain ſtiffneſs in my limbs entirely deſtroyed that *jauntineſs* of air I was once maſter of. *Addiſon's Spectator.*

JAW. *n. ſ.* [*joue*, a cheek, French; whence *joowbone*, or *cheekbone*, then *jaw.*]

1. The bone of the mouth in which the teeth are fixed.

A generation whoſe teeth are as ſwords, and their *jaw* teeth as knives, to devour the poor. *Prov.* xxx. 14.

The *jaw* bones, hearts, and galls of pikes are very medicinable. *Walton's Angler.*

Piſo, who probably ſpeaks Ariſtotle's meaning, ſaith that the crocodile doth not only move his upper *jaw*, but that his nether *jaw* is immoveable. *Grew's Muſæum.*

More formidable hydra ſtands within,
Whoſe *jaws* with iron teeth ſeverely grin. *Dryden's Æn.*

2. The mouth.

My tongue cleaveth to my *jaws*, and thou haſt brought me into the duſt of death. *Pſ.* xxii. 15.

My bended hook ſhall pierce their ſlimy *jaws*. *Shakeſpeare.*

A ſmeary foam works o'er my grinding *jaws*,
And utmoſt anguiſh ſhakes my lab'ring frame. *Rowe.*

JAY. *n. ſ.* [named from *his cry. Skinner.*] A bird.

Two ſharp winged ſheers,
Deck'd with diverſe plumes, like painted *jays*,
Were fixed at his back, to cut his airy ways. *Fairy Queen.*

We'll uſe this unwholſome humidity, this groſs wat'ry pumpion—we'll teach him to know turtles from *jays*. *Shakeſ.*

What, is the *jay* more precious than the lark,
Becauſe his feathers are more beautiful? *Shakeſpeare.*

I am highly delighted to ſee the *jay* or the thruſh hopping about my walks. *Spectator.*

Admires the *jay*, the inſects gilded wings,
Or hears the hawk, when Philomela ſings. *Pope.*

JA'ZEL. *n. ſ.* A precious ſtone of an azure or blue colour. *Dict.*

ICE. *n. ſ.* [ıſ, Saxon; *eyſe*, Dutch.]

1. Water or other liquor made ſolid by cold.

You are no ſurer, no,
Than is the coal of fire upon the *ice*,
Or hailſtone in the ſun. *Shakeſpeare's Coriolanus.*

Thou art all *ice*, thy kindneſs freezes. *Shakeſp. R.* III.

If I ſhould aſk whether *ice* and water were two diſtinct ſpecies of things, I doubt not but I ſhould be anſwered in the affirmative. *Locke.*

2. Concreted ſugar.

3. *To break the* ICE. To make the firſt opening to any attempt.

If you *break the ice*, and do this feat,
Atchieve the elder, ſet the younger free
For our acceſs, whoſe hap ſhall be to have her,
Will not ſo graceleſs be to be ingrate. *Shakeſpeare.*

Thus have I *broken the ice* to invention, for the lively repreſentation of floods and rivers neceſſary for our painters and poets. *Peacham on Drawing.*

After he'd a while look'd wiſe,
At laſt *broke* ſilence and the *ice*. *Hudibras, p.* iii.

To ICE. *v. a.* [from the noun.]

1. To cover with ice; to turn to ice.

2. To cover with concreted ſugar.

I'CEHOUSE. *n. ſ.* [*ice* and *houſe.*] A houſe in which ice is repoſited againſt the warm months.

ICHNE'UMON. *n. ſ.* [ἰχνεύμων.] A ſmall animal that breaks the eggs of the crocodile.

ICHNEUMONFLY'. *n. ſ.* A ſort of fly.

The generation of the *ichneumonfly* is in the bodies of caterpillars, and other nymphæ of inſects. *Derham's Phyſico-Theol.*

ICHNO'GRAPHY. *n. ſ.* [ἴχνος and γράφω.] The groundplot.

It will be more intelligible to have a draught of each front in a paper by itſelf, and alſo to have a draught of the groundplot or *ichnography* of every ſtory in a paper by itſelf. *Moxon.*

I'CHOR. *n. ſ.* [ἰχώρ.] A thin watery humour like ſerum. *Quincy.*

Milk, drawn from ſome animals that feed only upon fleſh, will be more apt to turn rancid and putrify, acquiring firſt a ſaline taſte, which is a ſign of putrefaction, and then it will turn into an *ichor*. *Arbuthnot on Aliments.*

I'CHOROUS. *adj.* [from *ichor.*] Sanious; thin; undigeſted.

The lung-growth is imputed to a ſuperficial ſanious or *ichorous* exulceration. *Harvey on Conſumptions.*

The pus from an ulcer of the liver, growing thin and *ichorous*, corrodes the veſſels. *Arbuthnot on Diet.*

ICHTHYO'LOGY. *n. ſ.* [*ichthyologie*, Fr. ἰχθυολογία, from ἰχθὺς and λέγω.] The doctrine of the nature of fiſh.

Some there are, as camels and ſheep, which carry no name in *ichthyology*. *Brown's Vulgar Errours.*

ICHTHYO'PHAGY. *n. ſ.* [ἰχθὺς and φάγω.] Diet of fiſh; the practice of eating fiſh.

I'CICLE. *n. ſ.* [from *ice.*] A ſhoot of ice hanging down from the upper part.

If diſtilled vinegar or aqua-fortis be poured into the powder of loadſtone, the ſubſiding powder, dried, retains ſome magnetical virtue; but if the menſtruum be evaporated to a conſiſtence, and afterwards doth ſhoot into *icicles*, or cryſtals, the loadſtone hath no power upon them. *Brown's Vulgar Err.*

From locks uncomb'd, and from the frozen beard,
Long *icicles* depend, and crackling ſounds are heard. *Dryd.*

The common dropſtone conſiſts principally of ſpar, and is frequently found in form of an *icicle*, hanging down from the tops and ſides of grotto's. *Woodward's Nat. Hiſtory.*

I'CINESS. *n. ſ.* [from *icy.*] The ſtate of generating ice.

I'CON. *n. ſ.* [εἰκών.] A picture or repreſentation.

Boyſardus, in his tract of divination, hath ſet forth the *icons* of theſe ten, yet added two others. *Brown's Vulg. Err.*

Some of our own nation, and many Netherlanders, whoſe names and *icons* are publiſhed, have deſerved good commendation. *Hakewill on Providence.*

ICO'NOCLAST. *n. ſ.* [*iconoclaſte*, French; εικονοκλαςης.] A breaker of images.

ICONO'LOGY. *n. ſ.* [*iconologie*, French; εικὼν and λέγω.] The doctrine of picture or repreſentation.

ICTE'RICAL. *n. ſ.* [*icterique*, French; *icterus*, Latin.]

1. Afflicted with the jaundice.

In the jaundice the choler is wanting, and the *icterical* have a great ſourneſs, and gripes with windineſs. *Floyer.*

2. Good againſt the jaundice.

I'CY. *adj.* [from *ice.*]

1. Full of ice; covered with ice; cold; froſty.

But my poor heart firſt ſet free,
Bound in thoſe *icy* chains by thee. *Shakeſp. Meaſ. for Meaſ.*

Here feel we but the penalty of Adam,
The ſeaſon's difference; as, the *icy* phang,
And churliſh chiding of the Winter's wind. *Shakeſpeare.*

He relates the exceſſive coldneſs of the water they met with in Summer in that *icy* region, where they were forced to winter. *Boyle.*

Bear Britain's thunder, and her croſs diſplay
To the bright regions of the riſing day;
Tempt *icy* ſeas, where ſcarce the waters roll,
Where clearer flames glow round the frozen pole. *Pope.*

2. Cold; free from paſſion.

Thou would'ſt have never learn'd
The *icy* precepts of reſpect. *Shakeſp. Timon.*

3. Frigid; backward.

If thou do'ſt find him tractable to us,
Encourage him, and tell him all our reaſons;
If he be leaden, *icy*, cold, unwilling,
Be thou ſo too. *Shakeſpeare's Richard* III.

I'D. Contracted for *I would.*

IDE'A. *n. ſ.* [*ideé*, French; ἰδέα.] Mental imagination.

Whatſoever the mind perceives in itſelf, or is the immediate object of perception, thought, or underſtanding, that I call *idea*. *Locke.*

The form under which theſe things appear to the mind, or the reſult of our apprehenſion, is called an *idea*. *Watts.*

Happy you that may to the ſaint, your only *idea*,
Although ſimply attir'd, your manly affection utter. *Sidney.*

Our Saviour himſelf, being to ſet down the perfect *idea* of that which we are to pray and wiſh for on earth, did not teach to pray or wiſh for more than only that here it might be with us, as with them it is in heaven. *Hooker, b.* i.

Her ſweet *idea* wander'd through his thoughts. *Fairfax.*

I did infer your lineaments,
Being the right *idea* of your father,
Both in your form and nobleneſs of mind. *Shakeſp. R.* III.

How good, how fair,
Anſwering his great *idea!* *Milton's Paradiſe Loſt, b.* vii.

If Chaucer by the beſt *idea* wrought,
The faireſt nymph before his eyes he ſet. *Dryden.*

IDE'AL. *adj.* [from *idea.*] Mental; intellectual; not perceived by the ſenſes.

There is a two-fold knowledge of material things; one real, when the thing, and the real impreſſion thereof on our ſenſes, is perceived; the other *ideal*, when the image or idea of a thing, abſent in itſelf, is repreſented to and conſidered on the imagination. *Cheyne's Phil. Prin.*

IDE'ALLY. *adv.* [from *ideal.*] Intellectually; mentally.

A tranſmiſſion is made materially from ſome parts, and *ideally* from every one. *Brown's Vulgar Errours.*

IDE'NTICAL. } *adj.* [*identique*, French.] The ſame; imply-
IDE'NTICK. } ing the ſame thing; compriſing the ſame idea.

The beard's th' *identick* beard you knew,
The ſame numerically true. *Hudibras, p.* ii.

There majus is *identical* with magis. *Hale's Origin of Man.*

Thoſe ridiculous *identical* propoſitions, that faith is faith, and rule is a rule, are firſt principles in this controverſy of the rule of faith, without which nothing can be ſolidly concluded either about rule or faith. *Tillotſon's Sermons.*

If this pre-exiſtent eternity is not compatible with a ſucceſſive duration, as we clearly and diſtinctly perceive that it is not, then it remains, that ſome being, though infinitely above our finite comprehenſions, muſt have had an *identical*, invariable continuance from all eternity, which being is no other than God. *Bentley's Sermons.*

IDE'NTITY. *n. ſ.* [*identité*, French; *identitas*, ſchool Latin.] Sameneſs; not diverſity.

There is a fallacy of equivocation from a ſociety in name, inferring an *identity* in nature: by this fallacy was he deceived that drank aqua-fortis for ſtrong water. *Brown's Vulg. Errours.*

Certainly thoſe actions muſt needs be regular, where there is an *identity* between the rule and the faculty. *South's Serm.*

Conſidering any thing as exiſting, at any determined time and place, we compare it with itſelf exiſting at another time, and thereon form the ideas of *identity* and diverſity. *Locke.*

It cuts off the ſenſe at the end of every firſt line, which muſt always rhime to the next following, and conſequently produces too frequent an *identity* in ſound, and brings every couplet to the point of an epigram. *Prior.*

IDES. *n. ſ.* [*ides*, Fr. *idus*, Lat.] A term anciently uſed among the Romans, and ſtill retained in the Romiſh kalendar. It is the 13th day of each month, except in the months of March, May, July and October, in which it is the 15th day, becauſe in theſe four months it was ſix days before the nones, and in the others four days. *Trevoux.*

A ſoothſayer bids you beware the *ides* of March. *Shakeſp.*

IDIO'CRASY. *n. ſ.* [*idiocraſe*, French; ἴδιος and κρᾶσις.] Peculiarity of conſtitution.

IDIOCRA'TICAL. *adj.* [from *idiocraſy.*] Peculiar in conſtitution.

I'DIOCY. *n. ſ.* [ἰδιωτεία.] Want of underſtanding.

I ſtand not upon their *idiocy* in thinking that horſes did eat their bits. *Bacon's Holy War.*

I'DIOM. *n. ſ.* [*idiome*, French; ἰδίωμα.] A mode of ſpeaking peculiar to a language or dialect; the particular caſt of a tongue; a phraſe; phraſeology.

He did romanize our tongue, leaving the words tranſlated as much Latin as he found them; wherein he followed their language, but did not comply with the *idiom* of ours. *Dryden.*

Some that with care true eloquence ſhall teach,
And to juſt *idioms* fix our doubtful ſpeech. *Prior.*

IDIOMA'TICAL. } *adj.* [from *idiom.*] Peculiar to a tongue;
IDIOMA'TICK. } phraſeological.

Since phraſes uſed in converſation contract meanneſs by paſſing through the mouths of the vulgar, a poet ſhould guard himſelf againſt *idiomatick* ways of ſpeaking. *Spectator.*

IDIO'PATHY. *n. ſ.* [*idiopathie*, Fr. ἴδιος and πάθος.] A primary diſeaſe that neither depends on nor proceeds from another. *Quincy.*

IDIOSY'NCRASY. *n. ſ.* [*idioſyncraſe*, Fr. ἴδιος, σύν, and κρᾶσις.] A peculiar temper or diſpoſition not common to another. *Quincy.*

Whether quails, from any *idioſyncraſy* or peculiarity of conſtitution, do innocuouſly feed upon hellebore, or rather ſometimes but medicinally uſe the ſame. *Brown's Vulg. Errours.*

The underſtanding alſo hath its *idioſyncraſies*, as well as other faculties. *Glanv. Scepſ. c.* 15.

I'DIOT. *n. ſ.* [*idiote*, Fr. *idiota*, Latin; ἰδιώτης.] A fool; a natural; a changeling; one without the powers of reaſon.

Life is a tale,
Told by an *idiot*, full of ſound and fury,
Signifying nothing. *Shakeſpeare's Macbeth.*

What elſe doth he herein, than by a kind of circumlocution tell his humble ſuppliants that he holds them *idiots*, or baſe wretches, not able to get relief? *Raleigh's Eſſays.*

By idle boys and *idiots* vilify'd,
Who me and my calamities deride. *Sandys.*

Many *idiots* will believe that they ſee what they only hear. *Dennis.*

I'DIOTISM. *n. ſ.* [*idiotiſme*, French; ἰδιωτισμός.]

1. Peculiarity of expreſſion; mode of expreſſion peculiar to a language.

Scholars ſometimes in common ſpeech, or writing, in their native language, give terminations and *idiotiſms* ſuitable to their native language unto words newly invented. *Hale.*

2. Folly; natural imbecillity of mind.

I'DLE. *adj.* [ẏdel, Saxon.]

1. Lazy; averſe from labour.

For ſhame, ſo much to do, and yet *idle*. *Bull.*

2. Not buſy; at leiſure.

For often have you writ to her; and ſhe in modeſty,
Or elſe for want of *idle* time, could not again reply. *Shak.*

3. Unactive; not employed.

No war or battle's ſound
Was heard the world around,
The *idle* ſpear and ſhield were high up hung. *Milton.*

Children generally hate to be *idle*; all the care then is, that their buſy humour ſhould be conſtantly employed in ſomething of uſe to them. *Locke.*

Suppoſing, among a multitude embarked in the ſame veſſel, there are ſeveral that, in the fury of a tempeſt, will rather periſh than work for their preſervation; would it not be madneſs in the reſt to ſtand *idle*, and rather chuſe to ſink than do more than comes to their ſhare? *Addiſon.*

4. Uſeleſs; vain; ineffectual.

They aſtoniſh'd, all reſiſtance loſt,
All courage; down their *idle* weapons dropp'd. *Milton.*

And threatning France, plac'd like a painted Jove,
Held *idle* thunder in his lifted hand. *Dryden.*

Where was then
The power that guards the ſacred lives of kings?
Why ſlept the lightning and the thunderbolts,
Or bent their *idle* rage on fields and trees,
When vengeance call'd 'em here? *Dryden's Spaniſh Fryar.*

5. Worthleſs; barren; not productive of good.

Suffice it then, thou money god, quoth he,
That all thine *idle* offers I refuſe;
All that I need I have: what needeth me
To covet more than I have cauſe to uſe? *Fairy Queen.*

Of antres vaſt, and deſarts *idle*,
It was my hent to ſpeak. *Shakeſpeare's Othello.*

The murmuring ſurge,
That on th' unnumber'd *idle* pebbles chafes,
Cannot be heard ſo high. *Shakeſp. King Lear.*

He was met even now,
Crown'd with rank fumiter and furrow-weeds,
Darnel, and all the *idle* weeds that grow
In our sustaining corn. *Shakesp. King Lear.*

6. Trifling; of no importance: as, an *idle* story.

This answer is both *idle* in regard of us, and also repugnant to themselves. *Hooker.*

They are not, in our estimation, *idle* reproofs, when the authors of needless innovations are opposed with such negatives, as that of Leo: how are these new devices brought in, which our fathers never knew? *Hooker, b.* ii.

His friend smil'd scornful, and, with proud contempt,
Rejects as *idle* what his fellow dreamt. *Dryden.*

An *idle* reason lessens the weight of the good ones you gave before. *Swift.*

How ill he wishes to recall the precious hours he has spent in trifles, and loitered away in *idle* unprofitable diversions. *Rogers's Sermons.*

To IDLE. *v. n.* [from the adjective.] To lose time in laziness and inactivity.

Yet free from this poetick madness,
Next page he says, in sober sadness,
That she and all her fellow-gods
Sit *idling* in their high abodes. *Prior.*

IDLEHE'ADED. *adj.* [*idle* and *head.*] Foolish; unreasonable.

These *idleheaded* seekers resorted thither. *Carew.*

Upon this loss she fell *idleheaded*, and to this very day stands near the place still. *L'Estrange.*

I'DLENESS. *n. s.* [from *idle.*]

1. Laziness; sloth; sluggishness; aversion from labour.

Nor is excess the only thing by which sin mauls and breaks men in their health, and the comfortable enjoyment of themselves thereby; but many are also brought to a very ill and languishing habit of body by mere *idleness*, and *idleness* is both itself a great sin, and the cause of many more. *South's Serm.*

2. Absence of employment.

All which yet could not make us accuse her, though it made us pine away for spight, to lose any of our time in so troublesome an *idleness*. *Sidney, b.* ii.

To the English court assemble now,
From ev'ry region, apes of *idleness*. *Shakesp. Henry* IV.

He fearing *idleness*, the nurse of ill,
In sculpture exercis'd his happy skill. *Dryden's Ovid.*

Nature being liberal to all without labour, necessity imposing no industry or travel, *idleness* bringeth forth no other fruits than vain thoughts and licentious pleasures. *Raleigh.*

3. Omission of business.

Ten thousand harms, more than the ills I know,
My *idleness* doth hatch. *Shakes. Ant. and Cleopatra.*

4. Unimportance; trivialness.
5. Inefficacy; uselessness.
6. Barrenness; worthlessness.
7. Unreasonableness; want of judgment; foolishness; madness.

There is no heat of affection but is joined with some *idleness* of brain. *Bacon's War with Spain.*

I'DLER. *n. s.* [from *idle.*] A lazy person; a sluggard.

Many of these poor fishermen and *idlers*, that are commonly presented to his majesty's ships, are so ignorant in sea-service as that they know not the name of a rope. *Raleigh.*

Thou sluggish *idler*, dilatory slave. *Irene.*

I'DLY. *adv.* [from *idle.*]

1. Lazily; without employment.

I will slay myself,
For living *idly* here in pomp and ease. *Shakesp. Henry* VI.

2. Foolishly; in a trifling manner.

And modern Asgil, whose capricious thought
Is yet with stores of wilder notions fraught,
Too soon convinc'd, shall yield that fleeting breath,
Which play'd so *idly* with the darts of death. *Prior.*

3. Carelesly; without attention.

This from rumour's tongue
I *idly* heard; if true or false, I know not. *Shakes. K. John.*

But shall we take the muse abroad,
To drop her *idly* on the road?
And leave our subject in the middle,
As Butler did his bear and fiddle? *Prior.*

4. Ineffectually; vainly.

Let this and other allegations, suitable unto it, cease to bark any longer *idly* against the truth, the course and passage whereof it is not in them to hinder. *Hooker.*

I'DOL. *n. s.* [*idole*, French; εἴδωλον; *idolum*, Latin.]

1. An image worshipped as God.

They did sacrifice upon the *idol* altar, which was upon the altar of God. 1 *Mac.* i. 59.

A nation from one faithful man to spring,
Him on this side Euphrates yet residing,
Bred up in *idol* worship. *Milton's Parad. Lost.*

The apostle is there arguing against the gnosticks who joined in the *idol* feasts, and whom he therefore accuses of participating of the *idol* god. *Atterbury.*

2. A counterfeit.

Woe to the *idol* shepherd that leaveth the flock. *Zech.* ii. 17.

3. An image.

Never did art so well with nature strive,
Nor ever *idol* seem'd so much alive;
So like the man, so golden to the sight;
So base within, so counterfeit and light. *Dryden.*

4. A representation.

Men beholding so great excellence,
And rare perfection in mortality,
Do her adore with sacred reverence,
As th' *idol* of her maker's great magnificence. *Fairy Qu.*

5. One loved or honoured to adoration.

He's honoured and lov'd by all;
The soldiers god, and people's *idol*. *Denham's Sophy.*

IDO'LATER. *n. s.* [*idolatre*, French; *idololatra*, Latin.] One who pays divine honours to images; one who worships for God that which is not God.

The state of *idolaters* is two ways miserable: first, in that which they worship they find no succour; and secondly, at his hands, whom they ought to serve, there is no other thing to be looked for but the effects of most just displeasure, the withdrawing of grace, dereliction in this world, and in the world to come confusion. *Hooker.*

An astrologer may be no Christian; he may be an *idolater* or a pagan; but I would hardly think astrology to be compatible with rank atheism. *Bentley's Sermons.*

To IDO'LATRIZE. *v. a.* [from *idolater.*] To worship idols. *Ains.*

IDO'LATROUS. *adj.* [from *idolater.*] Tending to idolatry; comprising idolatry, or the worship of false gods.

Neither may the pictures of our Saviour, the apostles, and martyrs of the church, be drawn to an *idolatrous* use, or be set up in churches to be worshipped. *Peacham on Drawing.*

IDO'LATROUSLY. *adv.* [from *idolatrous.*] In an idolatrous manner.

Not therefore whatsoever idolaters have either thought or done; but let whatsoever they have either thought or done *idolatrously*, be so far forth abhorred. *Hooker.*

IDO'LATRY. *n. s.* [*idolatrie*, Fr. *idololatria*, Lat.] The worship of images; the worship of any thing as God which is not God.

Thou shalt be worshipp'd, kiss'd, lov'd and ador'd;
And, were there sense in his *idolatry*,
My substance should be statued in thy stead. *Shakespeare.*

Idolatry is not only an accounting or worshipping that for God which is not God, but it is also a worshipping the true God in a way wholly unsuitable to his nature; and particularly by the mediation of images and corporeal resemblances. *South's Sermons.*

The kings were distinguished by judgments or blessings, according as they promoted *idolatry*, or the worship of the true God. *Addison's Spectator.*

I'DOLIST. *n. s.* [from *idol.*] A worshipper of images. A poetical word.

I to God have brought
Dishonour, obloquy, and op'd the mouths
Of *idolists* and atheists. *Milton's Agonistes.*

To I'DOLIZE. *v. a.* [from *idol*] To love or reverence to adoration.

Those who are generous, humble, just and wise,
Who not their gold, nor themselves *idolize*. *Denham.*

Parties, with the greatest violation of Christian unity, denominate themselves, not from the grand author and finisher of our faith, but from the first broacher of their *idolized* opinions. *Decay of Piety.*

IDO'NEOUS. *adj.* [*idoneus*, Latin.] Fit; proper; convenient; adequate.

You entangle, and so fix their saline part, by making them corrode some *idoneous* body. *Boyle.*

An ecclesiastical benefice is sometimes void *de jure & facto*, and then it ought to be conferred on an *idoneous* person. *Ayliffe.*

I'DYL. *n. s.* [εἰδύλλιον; *idyllium*, Latin.] A small short poem.

I. E. for *id est*, or *that is*.

That which raises the natural interest of money, is the same that raises the rent of land, *i. e.* its aptness to bring in yearly, to him that manages it, a greater overplus of income above his rent, as a reward to his labour. *Locke.*

JE'ALOUS. *adj.* [*jaloux*, French.]

1. Suspicious in love.

To both these sisters have I sworn my love:
Each *jealous* of the other, as the stung
Are of the adder. *Shakespeare's King Lear.*

Wear your eye thus; not *jealous*, nor secure:
I would not have your free and noble nature,
Out of self-bounty, be abus'd: look to't. *Shak. Othello.*

Mistress Ford, the honest woman, the modest wife, the virtuous creature, that hath the *jealous* fool to her husband. *Shakespeare's Merry Wives of Windsor.*

A *jealous* empress lies within your arms,
Too haughty to endure neglected charms. *Dryd. Aurengz.*

2. Emulous; full of competition.

I could not, without extreme reluctance, resign the theme of your beauty to another hand: give me leave to acquaint the world that I am *jealous* of this subject. *Dryden.*

3. Zealously cautious against dishonour.
I have been very *jealous* for the Lord God of hosts. 1 *Kings*.
4. Suspiciously vigilant.
I am *jealous* over you with godly jealousy. 2 *Cor.* ii. 2.
His apprehensions, as his *jealous* nature had much of sagacity in it, or his restless and mutinous humour, transported him. *Clarendon, b.* viii.
5. Suspiciously careful.
Although he were a prince in military virtue approved, and *jealous* of the honour of the English nation; yet his cruelties and parricides weighed down his virtues. *Bacon's Henry* VII.

They *jealous* of their secrets, fiercely oppos'd
My journey strange, with clamorous uproar
Protesting fate supreme. *Milton's Paradise Lost, b.* x.

How nicely *jealous* is every one of us of his own repute, and yet how maliciously prodigal of other mens. *Dec. of Piety.*
6. Suspiciously fearful.

'Tis doing wrong creates such doubts as these;
Renders us *jealous*, and destroys our peace. *Waller.*

While the people are so *jealous* of the clergy's ambition, I do not see any other method left for them to reform the world, than by using all honest arts to make themselves acceptable to the laity. *Swift.*

JE'ALOUSLY. *adv.* [from *jealous*.] Suspiciously; emulously; with suspicious fear, vigilance, or caution.

JE'ALOUSNESS. *n. s.* [from *jealous*.] The state of being jealous; rivalry; suspicion; suspicious vigilance.
Nor is it hard for thee to preserve me amidst the unjust hatred and *jealousness* of too many, which thou hast suffered to prevail upon me. *King Charles.*

JE'ALOUSY. *n. s.* [*jalousie*, French, from *jealous*.]
1. Suspicion in love.

But gnawing *jealousy*, out of their sight
Sitting alone, his bitter lips did bite. *Fairy Queen.*

The sweet woman leads an ill life with him; he's a very *jealousy* man. *Shakespeare.*

How all the other passions fleet to air,
As doubtful thoughts, and rash embrac'd despair;
And shudd'ring fear, and green-ey'd *jealousy!*
O love, be moderate; allay thy extasy. *Shakespeare.*

Why did you suffer Jachimo,
Slight thing of Italy,
To taint his noble heart and brain
With needless *jealousy?* *Shakespeare's Cymbeline.*

Small *jealousies*, 'tis true, inflame desire;
Too great, not fan, but quite blow out the fire. *Dryden.*

2. Suspicious fear.
The obstinacy in Essex, in refusing to treat with the king, proceeded only from his *jealousy*, that when the king had got him into his hands, he would take revenge upon him. *Clarend.*
3. Suspicious caution, vigilance, or rivalry.

To JEER. *v. n.* [Of uncertain etymology.] To scoff; to flout; to make mock.

The merry world did on a day,
With his trainbands and mates, agree
To meet together where I lay,
And all in sport to *jeer* at me. *Herbert.*

Abstain from dissolute laughter, petulant uncomely jests, loud talking, and *jeering*, which are called indecencies and incivilities. *Taylor's Rule of living holy.*

To JEER. *v. a.* To treat with scoffs.
My children abroad are driven to disavow me, for fear of being *jeered*. *Howel's England's Tears.*

JEER. *n. s.* [from the verb.] Scoff; taunt; biting jest; flout; jibe; mock.

Midas, expos'd to all their *jeers*,
Had lost his art, and kept his ears. *Swift.*

They tipt the forehead in a *jeer*,
As who should say—she wants it here;
She may be handsome, young and rich;
But none will burn her for a witch. *Swift.*

JE'ERER. *n. s.* [from *jeer*.] A scoffer; a scorner; a mocker.

JE'ERINGLY. *adj.* [from *jeering*.] Scornfully; contemptuously; in mock; in scoff.
He *jeeringly* demandeth, whether the sonorous rays are refracted? *Derham's Physico-Theology.*

JE'GGET. *n. s.* A kind of sausage. *Ainsworth.*

JEHO'VAH. *n. s.* [יהוה.] The proper name of God in the Hebrew language.

JEJU'NE. *adj.* [*jejunus*, Latin.]
1. Wanting; empty; vacant.
Gold is the only substance which hath nothing in it volatile, and yet melteth without much difficulty: the melting sheweth that it is not *jejune*, or scarce in spirit. *Bacon.*
2. Hungry; not saturated.
In gross and turbid streams there might be contained nutriment, and not *jejune* or limpid water. *Brown's Vulgar Err.*
3. Dry; unaffecting.
You may look upon an inquiry made up of meer narratives, as somewhat *jejune*. *Boyle.*

JEJU'NENESS. *n. s.* [from *jejune*.]
1. Penury; poverty.
There are three causes of fixation: the even spreading both parts, and the *jejuneness* or extreme comminution of spirits. *Bacon's Natural History.*
2. Dryness; want of matter that can engage the attention.

JE'LLIED. *adj.* [See GELLY.] Glutinous; brought to a state of viscosity.

The kiss that sips
The *jellied* philtre of her lips. *Cleaveland.*

JE'LLY. *n. s.* [*gelatinum*, Latin. See GELLY, which is the proper orthography.]
1. Any thing brought to a state of glutinousness and viscosity.

They, distill'd
Almost to *jelly* with th' effect of fear,
Stand dumb, and speak not to him. *Shakesp. Hamlet.*

2. Sweetmeat made by boiling sugar in the gelly.

The desert came on, and *jellies* brought. *King.*
That *jelly*'s rich, this malmsey healing;
Pray dip your whiskers. *Pope's Sat. of Horace.*

JE'NNETING. *n. s.* [corrupted from *Juneting*, an apple ripe in *June*.] A species of apple soon ripe, and of a pleasant taste. *Mortimer's Husbandry.*

JE'NNET. *n. s.* [See GENNET.] A Spanish horse.

The Spanish king presents a *jennet*,
To shew his love. *Prior.*

To JE'OPARD. *v. a.* [See JEOPARDY.] To hazard; to put in danger. Obsolete.
He had been accused of Judaism, and did boldly *jeopard* his body and life for the religion of the Jews. 2 *Mac.* xiv. 38.

JE'OPARDOUS. *adj.* [from *jeopardy*.] Hazardous; dangerous.

JE'OPARDY. *n. s.* [This word is supposed to be derived from *j'ai perdu*, or *jeu perdu*. *Skinner* and *Junius*.] Hazard; danger; peril. A word not now in use.

And would ye not poor fellowship expel,
Myself would offer you t' accompany,
In this adventure's chanceful *jeopardy*. *Hubberd's Tale.*

Thy rage shall burn thee up, and thou shalt turn
To ashes ere our blood shall quench that fire:
Look to thyself, thou art in *jeopardy*. *Shakesp. K. John.*

This colour will be reprehended or encountered, by imputing to all excellencies in compositions a kind of poverty, or at least a casualty or *jeopardy*. *Bacon.*

To JERK. *v. a.* [ᵹeꞃeccan, Saxon.] To strike with a quick smart blow; to lash. It is sometimes written *yerk*.

I lack iniquity
Sometimes to do me service: nine or ten times
I thought to've *jerk'd* him here under the ribs. *Shakes. Othel.*

Bastings heavy, dry, obtuse,
Only dulness can produce;
While a little gentle *jerking*
Sets the spirits all a working. *Swift.*

To JERK. *v. n.* To strike up; to accost eagerly. This seems to be the meaning in this place, but is mere cant.

Nor blush, should he some grave acquaintance meet;
But, proud of being known, will *jerk* and greet. *Dryden.*

JERK. *n. s.* [from the verb.]
1. A smart quick lash.
Contemn the silly taunts of fleering buffoonry; and the *jerks* of that wit, that is but a kind of confident folly. *Glanv.*
Wit is not the *jerk* or sting of an epigram, nor the seeming contradiction of a poor antithesis; neither is it so much the morality of a grave sentence, affected by Lucan, but more sparingly used by Virgil. *Dryden.*
2. A sudden spring; a quick jolt that shocks or starts.

Well run Tawney, the abbot's churl;
His jade gave him a *jerk*,
As he would have his rider hurl
His hood after the kirk. *Ben. Johnson's Underwoods.*

Lobsters use their tails as fins, wherewith they commonly swim backwards by *jerks* or springs, reaching ten yards at once. *Grew.*

JE'RKEN. *n. s.* [cyꞃꞇelkın, Saxon.] A jacket; a short coat; a close waistcoat.
A man may wear it on both sides, like a leather *jerkin*. *Shak.*
Mistress Line, is not this my *jerkin?* Now is the *jerkin* under the line: now, *jerkin*, you are like to lose your hair, and prove a bald *jerkin*. *Shakespeare's Tempest.*
Unless we should expect that nature should make *jerkins* and stockings grow out of the ground, what could she do better than afford us so fit materials for clothing as the wool of the sheep? *More's Antidote against Atheism.*
Imagine an ambassador presenting himself in a poor frize *jerkin*, and tattered cloaths, certainly he would have but small audience. *South's Sermons.*

Then strip thee of thy carnal *jerkin*,
And give thy outward fellow a ferkin. *Hudibras, p.* ii.

I walked into the sea, in my leathern *jerkin*, about an hour before high water. *Gulliver's Travels.*

JE'RKIN. *n. s.* A kind of hawk. *Ainsworth.* This should be written *gyrkin*.

JE'RSEY. *n. s.* [from the island of *Jersey*, where much yarn is spun.] Fine yarn of wool.

JESS. *n. s.* [*gecte*, French; *getto*, Italian.] Short straps of leather tied about the legs of a hawk, with which she is held on the fist. *Hanmer.*

If I prove her haggard,
Though that my *jesses* were her dear heartstrings,
I'd whistle her off, and let her down the wind
To prey at fortune. *Shakespeare's Othello.*

JE'SSAMINE. *n. s.* [See JASMINE.] A fragrant flower.

Her goodly bosom, like a strawberry bed;
Her neck, like to a bunch of cullambines;
Her breast like lillies, ere their leaves be shed;
Her nipples, like young blossom'd *jessamines.* *Spenser.*

JERU'SALEM *Artichokes. n. s.* Sunflower, of which they are a species.

Jerusalem artichokes are increased by small off-sets, and by quartering the roots. *Mortimer's Husbandry.*

To JEST. *v. n.* [*gesticulor*, Latin.] To divert or make merry by words or actions.

Jest not with a rude man, lest thy ancestors be disgraced. *Eccluſ.* viii. 4.

Fear you the boar, and go so unprovided?
—You may *jest* on; but
I do not like these several councils. *Shakesp. Rich.* III.

JEST. *n. s.* [from the verb.]

1. Any thing ludicrous, or meant only to raise laughter.

But is this true, or is it else your pleasure,
Like pleasant travellers to break a *jest*
Upon the company you overtake? *Shakespeare.*

As for *jest*, there be certain things which ought to be privileged from it; namely, religion, matters of state, and great persons. *Bacon's Essays.*

No man ought to have the less reverence for the principles of religion, or for the holy Scriptures, because idle and profane wits can break *jests* upon them. *Tillotson's Sermons.*

He had turn'd all tragedy to *jest.* *Prior.*

2. The object of jests; laughing-stock.

If I suspect without cause, why then make sport at me; then let me be your *jest*, I deserve it. *Shak. Mer. W. of Windſ.*

3. Manner of doing or speaking feigned, not real; ludicrous, not serious; game, not earnest.

That high All-seer, which I dallied with,
Hath turn'd my feigned prayer on my head,
And giv'n in earnest what I begg'd in *jest.* *Shakesp. R.* III.

When his play-fellows chose him their king, he spoke and did those things in *jest*, which would have become a king in earnest. *Grew's Cosmol.*

JE'STER. *n. s.* [from *jest.*]

1. One given to merriment and pranks.

The skipping king, he rambled up and down
With shallow *jesters*, and rash bavin wits;
Soon kindled, and soon burnt. *Shakesp. Henry* IV.

2. One given to sarcasm.

Now, as a *jester*, I accost you,
Which never yet one friend has lost you. *Swift.*

3. Buffoon; jackpudding.

Another sort of like loose fellows do pass up and down, amongst gentlemen, by the name of *jesters*; but are, indeed, notable rogues, and partakers not only of many stealths, but also privy to many traitorous practices. *Spenser on Ireland.*

JET. *n. s.* [ȝaȝat, Saxon; *get*, Dutch; *gagates*, Latin.]

1. *Jet* is a very beautiful fossil, of a firm and very even structure, and of a smooth surface; found in masses, seldom of a great size, lodged in clay. It is of a fine deep black colour, having a grain resembling that of wood. The ancients recommend *jet* in medicine; but it is now used only in toys. It is confounded with cannal-coal, which has no grain, and is extremely hard; and the *jet* is but moderately so. *Hill.*

Black, forsooth; coal-black, as *jet.* *Shakesp. Henry* VI.

There is more difference between thy flesh and hers, than between *jet* and ivory. *Shakesp. Merchant of Venice.*

The bottom clear,
Now laid with many a fet
Of seed-pearl, ere she bath'd her there,
Was known as black as *jet.* *Drayton.*

One of us in glass is set,
One of us you'll find in *jet.* *Swift.*

Under flowing *jet*,
Of sunny ringlets, or of circling brown,
The neck slight shaded. *Thomson's Summer.*

2. [*Jet*, French.] A spout or shoot of water.

Prodigious 'tis, that one attractive ray
Should this way bend, the next an adverse way!
For should th' unseen magnetick *jets* descend
All the same way, they could not gain their end. *Blackmore's Creation.*

Thus the small *jet*, which hasty hands unlock,
Spurts in the gard'ner's eyes who turns the cock. *Pope.*

3. A yard. Obsolete.

What orchard unrobbed escapes?
Or pullet dare walk in their *jet.* *Tusser's Husbandry.*

To JET. *v. n.* [*jetter*, French.]

1. To shoot forward; to shoot out; to intrude; to jut out.

Think you not how dangerous
It is to *jet* upon a prince's right? *Shakesp. Tit. Andr.*

8

2. To strut; to agitate the body by a proud gait.

Contemplation makes a rare turkey-cock of him: how he *jets* under his advanced plumes. *Shakesp. Twelfth Night.*

3. To jolt; to be shaken. [*Jetter*, French.]

Upon the *jetting* of a hackney-coach she was thrown out of the hinder seat against a bar of iron in the forepart. *Wisem.*

JE'TSAM. } *n. s.* [*jetter*, French.] Goods or other things
JE'TSON. } which, having been cast over board in a storm, or after shipwreck, are thrown upon the shore, and belong to the lord admiral. *Bailey.*

JE'TTY. *adj.* [from *jet.*]

1. Made of jet.

2. Black as jet.

The people about Capo Negro, Cefala, and Madagascar, are of a *jetty* black. *Brown's Vulgar Errours.*

Her hair
Adown her shoulders loosely lay display'd,
And in her *jetty* curls ten thousand Cupids play'd. *Prior.*

Nigrina black, and Merdamante brown,
Vied for his love in *jetty* bow'rs below. *Pope's Dunciad.*

JE'WEL. *n. s.* [*joyaux*, French; *jeweelen*, Dutch.]

1. Any ornament of great value, used commonly of such as are adorned with precious stones.

Here, wear this *jewel* for me; 'tis my picture. *Shakes.*

They found him dead, and cast into the streets,
An empty casket, where the *jewel*, life,
By some damn'd hand was robb'd and ta'en away. *Shakes.*

The pleasure of the religious man is an easy and a portable pleasure, such an one as he carries about in his bosom, without alarming either the eye or envy of the world: a man putting all his pleasures into this one, is like a traveller's putting all his goods into one *jewel.* *South.*

2. A precious stone; a gem.

Jewels too, stones, rich and precious stones,
Stol'n by my daughter! *Shakesp. Merchant of Venice.*

Proud fame's imperial seat
With *jewels* blaz'd, magnificently great. *Pope.*

3. A name of fondness; an appellation of tender regard.

Bid farewel to your sisters.
—Ye *jewels* of our father, with wash'd eyes
Cordelia leaves you. *Shakespeare's King Lear.*

JEWEL-HOUSE, *or Office. n. s.* The place where the regal ornaments are reposited.

The king has made him
Master of the *jewel-house.* *Shakespeare's Henry* VIII.

JE'WELLER. *n. s.* [from *jewel.*] One who trafficks in precious stones.

These grains were as like little dice as if they had been made by a *jeweller.* *Boyle.*

The price of the market to a *jeweller* in his trade is one thing; but the intrinsick worth of a thing to a man of sense is another. *L'Estrange.*

I will turn *jeweller:* I shall then deal in diamonds, and all sorts of rich stones. *Addison.*

JEWS-EARS. *n. s.* [from its resemblance of the human ear. *Skinner.*] A fungus, tough and thin; and naturally, while growing, of a rumpled figure, like a flat and variously hollowed cup; from an inch to two inches in length, and about two thirds of its length in breadth. Its sides are undulated, and in many places run into the hollow, so as to represent in it ridges like those of the human ear. Its substance is tough like leather, and its colour very dark. It is light when dry, of a disagreeable smell and nauseous taste. It generally grows on the lower parts of the trunks of elder-trees, especially where they are decaying. It is not much used by physicians; but the common people cure themselves of sore throats with a decoction of it in milk. *Hill's Mat. Med.*

An herb called *jews-ear* groweth upon the lower parts of elder, and sometimes ashes: in warm water it swelleth, and openeth extremely. *Bacon's Natural History.*

JEWS-MALLOW. *n. s.* [*corchorus*, Latin.]

The leaves are produced alternately at the joints of the stalks: the flower has five leaves, which expand in form of a rose: the pointal of the flower becomes a cylindrical fruit, divided into five cells, filled with angular seeds. *Ranwolf* says it is sown in great plenty about Aleppo as a pot-herb, the Jews boiling the leaves of this plant to eat it with their meat. *Miller.*

JEWS-STONE. *n. s.* An extraneous fossil, being the clavated spine of a very large egg-shaped sea-urchin, petrified by long lying in the earth. It is of a regular figure, oblong and rounded, swelling in the middle, and gradually tapering to each end; generally about three quarters of an inch in length, and half an inch in diameter. It is ridged and furrowed alternately, in a longitudinal direction; and its colour is a pale dusky grey, with a faint cast of dusky redishness. It is found in Syria, lodged in a loose sandy stone, or a marly very hard earth. It is diuretick; but has been falsely recommended as a lithontriptick. *Hill's Mat. Med.*

JEWS-HARP. *n. s.* A kind of musical instrument held between the teeth, which gives a sound by the motion of a broad

spring

ſpring of iron, which, being ſtruck by the hand, plays againſt the breath.

If. *conjunction.* [ᵹıꝼ, Saxon.]

1. Suppoſe that; allowing that. A hypothetical particle.

Abſolute approbation, without any cautions, qualifications, *ifs* or ands. *Hooker, Preface.*

If that rebellion
Came like itſelf, in baſe and abject routs;
I ſay, *if* damn'd commotion ſo appear'd,
In his true, native, and moſt proper ſhape,
You, reverend father, and theſe noble lords,
Had not been here. *Shakeſpeare's Henry* IV.

If they have done this deed, my noble lord.
—*If!* talk'ſt thou to me of *ifs?* Thou art a traitor. *Shak.*

This ſeeing of all things, becauſe we can deſire to ſee all things, he makes a proof that they are preſent to our minds; and *if* they be preſent, they can no ways be preſent but by the preſence of God, who contains them all. *Locke.*

This is only an infallibility upon ſuppoſition, which amounts to this, that *if* a thing be true, it is impoſſible to be falſe. *Tillotſon's Sermons, Preface.*

All of them ſuppoſe the apoſtle to have allowed the Epicurean maxim to be good; *if* ſo be there were no reſurrection. *Atterbury's Sermons, Preface.*

Tiſiphone, that oft haſt heard my pray'r,
Aſſiſt, *if* Oedipus deſerve thy care. *Pope's Statius.*

2. Whether or no.

Uncertain *if* by augury, or chance;
But by this eaſy riſe they all advance. *Dryden.*

She doubts *if* two and two make four:
It can't—it may be—and it muſt;
To which of theſe muſt Alma truſt?
Nay, further yet they make her go,
In doubting *if* ſhe doubts or no. *Prior.*

3. Though I doubt whether; ſuppoſe it be granted that.

Such mechanical circumſtances, *if* I may ſo call them, were not neceſſary to the experiments. *Boyle.*

I'gneous. *adj.* [*igneus*, Latin.] Firy; containing fire; emitting fire; having the nature of fire.

That the fire burns by heat, leaves us ſtill ignorant of the immediate way of *igneous* ſolutions. *Glanv. Scepſ. c.* 20.

Igni'potent. *adj.* [*ignis* and *potens*, Latin.] Preſiding over fire. *Pope's Homer.*

I'GNIS FATUUS. *n. ſ.* [Latin.] Will with the wiſp; Jack with the lanthorn.

Vapours ariſing from putrified waters are uſually called *ignes fatui.* *Newton's Opt.*

To I'GNITE. *v. a.* [from *ignis*, fire, Latin.] To kindle; to ſet on fire.

Take good firm chalk, *ignite* it in a crucible, and then powder it. *Grew's Muſæum.*

Igni'tion. *n. ſ.* [*ignition*, French, from *ignite.*] The act of kindling, or of ſetting on fire.

The laborant ſtirred the kindled nitre, that the *ignition* might be preſently communicated. *Boyle.*

Thoſe black circular lines we ſee on diſhes, and other turned veſſels of wood, are the effects of *ignition*, by the preſſure of an edged ſtick upon the veſſel turned nimbly in the lathe. *Ray.*

Igni'tible. *adj.* [from *ignite.*] Inflammable; capable of being ſet on fire.

Such bodies only ſtrike fire which have ſulphur or *ignitible* parts. *Brown's Vulgar Errours.*

Igni'vomous. *adj.* [*ignivomus*, Latin.] Vomiting fire.

Vulcanos and *ignivomous* mountains are ſome of the moſt terrible ſhocks of the globe. *Derham's Phyſico-Theology.*

IGNO'BLE. *adj.* [*ignoble*, *ignobilis*, Latin.]

1. Mean of birth; not noble; not of illuſtrious race.

As when in tumults riſe th' *ignoble* crowd,
Mad are their motions, and their tongues are loud. *Dryden.*

2. Worthleſs; not deſerving honour. Uſed of things or perſons.

The noble iſle doth want her proper limbs;
Her royal ſtock graft with *ignoble* plants. *Shak. Rich.* III.

Igno'bly. *adv.* [from *ignoble.*] Ignominiouſly; meanly; diſhonourably; reproachfully; diſgracefully.

To theſe, that ſober race of men, whoſe lives
Religious, titled them the ſons of God,
Shall yield up all their virtue, all their fame
Ignobly! *Milton's Paradiſe Loſt, b.* xi.

Here, over-match'd in fight, in heaps they lie;
There ſcatter'd o'er the fields *ignobly* fly. *Dryden's Æn.*

Ignomi'nious. *adj.* [*ignominieux*, French; *ignominioſus*, Lat. from *ignominy.*] Mean; ſhameful; reproachful; diſhonourable. Uſed both of perſons and things.

They with pale fear ſurpriz'd,
Fled *ignominious.* *Milton.*

Cethegus, though a traitor to the ſtate,
And tortur'd, 'ſcap'd this *ignominious* fate. *Dryden's Juven.*

They gave, and ſhe transferr'd the curs'd advice,
That monarchs ſhould their inward ſoul diſguiſe;
By *ignominious* arts, for ſervile ends,
Should compliment their foes, and ſhun their friends. *Prior.*

Nor has this kingdom deſerved to be ſacrificed to one ſingle, rapacious, obſcure, *ignominious* projector. *Swift.*

Ignomi'niously. *adv.* [from *ignominious.*] Meanly; ſcandalouſly; diſgracefully; ſhamefully; reproachfully.

It is ſome allay to the infamy of him who died *ignominiouſly* to be buried privately. *South's Sermons.*

I'GNOMINY. *n. ſ.* [*ignominie*, Fr. *ignominia*, Latin.] Diſgrace; reproach; ſhame; infamy; meanneſs; diſhonour.

Adieu, and take thy praiſe with thee to heav'n;
Thy *ignominy* ſleep with thee in the grave. *Shakeſp. H.* IV.

Strength from truth divided, and from juſt,
Illaudable, nought merits but diſpraiſe
And *ignominy*; yet to glory aſpires,
Vain-glorious, and through infamy ſeeks fame. *Milton.*

Their generals have been received with honour after their defeat, yours with *ignominy* after conqueſt. *Addiſon.*

IGNORA'MUS. *n. ſ.* [Latin.]

1. *Ignoramus* is a word properly uſed by the grand inqueſt impannelled in the inquiſition of cauſes criminal and publick; and written upon the bill, whereby any crime is offered to their conſideration, when they miſlike their evidence as defective, or too weak to make good the preſentment: the effect of which word ſo written is, that all farther inquiry upon that party, for that fault, is thereby ſtopped, and he delivered without farther anſwer. *Cowel.*

2. A fooliſh fellow; a vain uninſtructed pretender. A low word.

Tell an *ignoramus*, in place and power, that he has a wit and an underſtanding above all the world, and he ſhall readily admit the commendation. *South's Sermons.*

I'gnorance. *n. ſ.* [*ignorance*, French; *ignoratio*, Latin.]

1. Want of knowledge; unſkilfulneſs.

If all the clergy were as learned as themſelves are that moſt complain of *ignorance* in others, yet our book of prayer might remain the ſame. *Hooker, b.* v.

Ignorance is the curſe of God,
Knowledge the wing wherewith we fly to heav'n. *Shakeſp.*

Still baniſh your defenders, 'till at length
Your *ignorance* deliver you,
As moſt abated captives, to ſome nation
That won you without blows! *Shakeſpeare's Coriolanus.*

If he have power,
Then veil your *ignorance*; if none, awake
Your dangerous lenity. *Shakeſpeare's Coriolanus.*

If we ſee right, we ſee our woes;
Then what avails it to have eyes?
From *ignorance* our comfort flows,
The only wretched are the wiſe! *Prior.*

2. Want of knowledge diſcovered by external effect. In this ſenſe it has a plural.

Forgive us all our ſins, negligences, and *ignorances.* *C. Pray.*
Puniſh me not for my ſins and *ignorances.* *Tob.* iii. 2.

I'GNORANT. *adj.* [*ignorant*, French; *ignorans*, Latin.]

1. Wanting knowledge; unlearned; uninſtructed; unenlightened.

So fooliſh was I and *ignorant*, I was as a beaſt. *Pſ.* lxxiii. 22.

Thy letters have tranſported me beyond
This *ign'rant* preſent time, and I feel now
The future in the inſtant. *Shakeſpeare's Macbeth.*

In ſuch buſineſs
Action is eloquence, and the eyes of th' *ignorant*
More learned than the ears. *Shakeſpeare's Coriolanus.*

He that doth not know thoſe things which are of uſe for him to know, is but an *ignorant* man, whatever he may know beſides. *Tillotſon's Sermons.*

Fools grant whate'er ambition craves,
And men, once *ignorant*, are ſlaves. *Pope.*

2. Unknown; undiſcovered.

If you know aught, which does behove my knowledge
Thereof to be inform'd, impriſon't not
In *ignorant* concealment. *Shakeſpeare's Winter's Tale.*

3. Without knowledge of ſome particular.

Let not judges be ſo *ignorant* of their own right, as to think there is not left to them, as a principal part of their office, a wiſe application of laws. *Bacon's Eſſays.*

O viſions ill foreſeen! Better had I
Liv'd *ignorant* of future! ſo had borne
My part of evil only. *Milton's Paradiſe Loſt, b.* xi.

4. Unacquainted with. In a good ſenſe.

Ignorant of guilt, I fear not ſhame. *Dryden.*

5. Ignorantly made or done.

His ſhipping,
Poor *ignorant* baubles, on our terrible ſeas
Like egg-ſhells mov'd. *Shakeſpeare.*

I'gnorant. *n. ſ.* One untaught, unlettered, uninſtructed.

Did I for this take pains to teach
Our zealous *ignorants* to preach! *Denham.*

I'gnorantly. *adv.* [from *ignorant.*] Without knowledge; unſkilfully; without information.

The greateſt and moſt cruel foes we have,
Are thoſe whom you would *ignorantly* ſave. *Dryden.*

When a poet, an orator, or a painter has performed admirably,

mirably, we sometimes mistake his blunders for beauties, and are so *ignorantly* fond as to copy after them. *Watts.*

To IGNO'RE. *v. a.* [*ignorer*, French; *ignoro*, Latin.] Not to know; to be ignorant of. This word *Boyle* endeavoured to introduce; but it has not been received.

I *ignored* not the stricter interpretation, given by modern criticks to divers texts, by me alleged *Boyle.*

Philosophy would solidly be established, if men would more carefully distinguish those things that they know from those that they *ignore.* *Boyle.*

IGNO'SCIBLE. *adj.* [*ignoscibilis*, Latin.] Capable of pardon. *Dict.*

JIG. *n. s.* [*giga*, Italian; *geige*, Teutonick, a fiddle.] A light careless dance, or tune.

When Cyrus had overcome the Lydians, that were a warlike nation, instead of their warlike musick, he appointed to them certain lascivious lays and loose *jigs*; by which he so mollified and abated their courage, that they forgot their former fierceness. *Spenser on Ireland.*

As fiddlers still,
Though they be paid to be gone, yet needs will
Thrust one more *jig* upon you. *Donne.*

Posterity shall know that you dare, in these *jig* given times, to countenance a legitimate poem. *Ben. Johnson.*

All the swains that there abide,
With *jigs* and rural dance resort. *Milton.*

The muses blush'd to see their friends exalting
Those elegant delights of *jig* and vaulting. *Fenton.*

They wrote to her friends in the country, that she should dance a *jig* next October in Westminsterhall. *Arbuthnot.*

Another Phœbus, thy own Phœbus reigns,
Joys in my *jigs*, and dances in my chains. *Pope.*

To JIG. *v. n.* [from the noun.] To dance carelesly; to dance. Expressed in contempt.

As for the *jigging* part and figures of dances, I count that little. *Locke.*

JI'G-MAKER. *n. s.* [*jig* and *make.*] One who dances or plays merrily.

Your only *jig-maker!* what should a man do but be merry? *Shakespeare's Hamlet.*

JI'GGUMBOB. *n. s.* [A cant word.] A trinket; a knick-knack; a slight contrivance in machinery.

He rifled all his pokes and fobs
Of gimcracks, whims, and *jiggumbobs.* *Hudibras, p.* iii.

JILT. *n. s.* [*gilia*, Islandick, to intrap in an amour. Mr. *Lye.* Perhaps from *giglot*, by contraction; or *gillet*, or *gillot*, the diminutive of *gill*, the ludicrous name for a woman. 'Tis also called *jillet* in Scotland.]

1. A woman who gives her lover hopes, and deceives him.

Avoid both courts and camps,
Where dilatory fortune plays the *jilt*
With the brave, noble, honest, gallant man,
To throw herself away on fools. *Otway's Orphan.*

2. A name of contempt for a woman.

When love was all an easy monarch's care,
Jilts rul'd the state, and statesmen farces writ. *Pope.*

To JILT. *v. a.* [from the noun.] To trick a man by flattering his love with hopes, and then leaving him for another.

Tell who loves who;
And who is *jilted* for another's sake. *Dryden's Juvenal.*

Tell a man, passionately in love, that he is *jilted*; bring a score of witnesses of the falsehood of his mistress, and it is ten to one but three kind words of hers shall invalidate all their testimonies. *Locke.*

She might have learn'd to cuckold, *jilt*, and sham,
Had Covent-garden been at Surinam. *Congreve.*

To JI'NGLE. *v. n.* [A word made from *jangle*, or copied from the sound intended to be expressed.] To clink; to sound correspondently.

What should the wars do with these *jingling* fools? *Shak.*

With noises
Of roaring, shrieking, howling, *jingling* chains,
We were awak'd. *Shakespeare's Tempest.*

You ne'er with *jingling* words deceive the ear;
And yet, on humble subjects, great appear. *Smith.*

What crowds of these, impenitently bold,
In sounds and *jingling* syllables grown old! *Pope.*

JI'NGLE. *n. s.* [from the verb.]

1. Correspondent sounds.

Vulgar judges are nine parts in ten of all nations, who call conceits and *jingles* wit. *Dryden's Fables, Preface.*

2. Any thing sounding; a rattle; a bell.

If you plant where savages are, do not only entertain them with trifles and *jingles*, but use them justly. *Bacon's Essays.*

ILE. *n. s.* [corrupted from *aisle*, French.] A walk or alley in a church or publick building. Properly *aile.*

Upward the columns shoot, the roofs ascend,
And arches widen, and long *iles* extend. *Pope.*

ILE. *n. s.* [*aisle*, French.] An ear of corn. *Ainsworth.*

ILEUS. *n. s.* [Latin.]

The consequences of inflammation is an *ileus*, commonly called the twisting of the guts; but is really either a circumvolution, or insertion of one part of the gut within the other. *Arbuthnot on Diet.*

I'LEX. *n. s.* [Latin.]

The *ilex*, or great scarlet oak, thrives well in England, is a hardy sort of tree, and easily raised of acorns. The Spaniards have a sort they call enzina; the wood of which, when old, is finely chambletted, as if it were painted, and is useful for stocks of tools, mallet-heads, chairs, axle-trees, wedges, beetles, pins, and pallisadoes for fortifications, being very hard and durable. *Mortimer.*

ILIAC. *adj.* [*iliacus*, Latin.] Relating to the lower bowels.

The *iliac* passion is a kind of convulsion in the belly.

Those who die of the *iliac* passion have their bellies much swelled. *Floyer on the Humours.*

I'LIAC *Passion. n. s.* A kind of nervous cholick, whose seat is the ilium, whereby that gut is twisted, or one part enters the cavity of the part immediately below or above; whence it is also called the volvulus, from *volvo*, to roll.

ILK. *adv.* [ealc, Saxon.] Eke; also. It is still retained in Scotland, and denotes each: as, *ilk ane of you*, every one of you. It also signifies the same; as, *Macintosh of that ilk*, denotes a gentleman whose surname and the title of his estate are the same.

Shepherds, should it not yshend
Your roundels fresh, to hear a doleful verse
Of Rosalind, who knows not Rosalind,
That Colin made? *ilk* can I you rehearse. *Spenser.*

ILL. *adj.* [contracted from EVIL, and retaining all its senses.]

1. Bad in any respect; contrary to good, whether physical or moral; evil. See EVIL.

There's some *ill* planet reigns;
I must be patient, 'till the heavens look
With an aspect more favourable. *Shakes. Winter's Tale.*

Of his own body he was *ill*, and gave
The clergy *ill* example. *Shakespeare's Henry* VIII.

Neither is it *ill* air only that maketh an *ill* seat; but *ill* ways, *ill* markets, and *ill* neighbours. *Bacon's Essays.*

Some, of an *ill* and melancholy nature, incline the company to be sad and ill-disposed: others, of a jovial nature, dispose them to be merry. *Bacon.*

2. Sick; disordered; not in health. I know not that *evil* is ever used in this sense.

You wish me health in very happy season;
For I am on the sudden something *ill.* *Shakes. Henry* IV.

I have known two towns of the greatest consequence lost, by the governours falling *ill* in the time of the sieges. *Temple.*

ILL. *n. s.*

1. Wickedness.

Ill, to man's nature, as it stands perverted, hath a natural motion strongest in continuance. *Bacon.*

Young men to imitate all *ills* are prone;
But are compell'd to avarice alone:
For then in virtue's shape they follow vice. *Dryden's Juv.*

Strong virtue, like strong nature, struggles still,
Exerts itself, and then throws off the *ill.* *Dryden's Aureng.*

2. Misfortune; misery.

Who can all sense of others *ills* escape,
Is but a brute at best in human shape. *Tate's Juvenal.*

Though plung'd in *ills* and exercis'd in care,
Yet never let the noble mind despair;
When prest by dangers, and beset with foes,
The gods their timely succour interpose;
And when our virtue sinks, o'erwhelm'd with grief,
By unforeseen expedients bring relief. *A. Phillips.*

ILL. *adv.*

1. Not well; not rightly in any respect.

Ill at ease, both she and all her train
The scorching sun had borne, and beating rain. *Dryden.*

2. Not easily.

Thou desir'st
The punishment all on thyself! alas!
Bear thine own first; *ill* able to sustain
His full wrath, whose thou feel'st as yet least part,
And my displeasure bear'st so *ill.* *Milton's Paradise Lost.*

Ill bears the sex a youthful lover's fate,
When just approaching to the nuptial state. *Dryden.*

ILL, substantive or adverb, is used in composition to express any bad quality or condition, which may be easily understood by the following examples.

ILL. *substantive.*

Dangerous conjectures in *ill* breeding minds. *Shak. Hamlet.*

I have an *ill* divining soul:
Methinks I see thee, now thou art below,
As one dead in the bottom of a tomb. *Shakespeare.*

No look, no last adieu before he went!
In an *ill* boding hour to slaughter sent. *Dryd. Æn.*

I know
The voice *ill* boding, and the solemn sound. *Phillips.*

He may strew
The wisest prince on earth may be deceived by the craft of *ill* designing men. *Swift's Examiner.*

Your

Your *ill* meaning politician lords,
Under pretence of bridal friends and guests,
Appointed to await me thirty spies,
Who, threat'ning cruel death, constrain'd the bride
To wring from me and tell to them my secret. *Milt. Agon.*

A spy distinguish'd from his airy stand,
To bribe whose vigilance, Ægisthus told
A mighty sum of *ill* persuading gold. *Pope's Odyssey.*

Ill. *adverb.*

There sounded an *ill* according cry of the enemies, and a lamentable noise was carried abroad. *Wisd.* xviii. 10.

My colleague,
Being so *ill* affected with the gout,
Will not be able to be there in person. *Ben. Johns. Catil.*

The danger of the day's but newly gone,
And the examples
Of every minute's instance, present now,
Have put us in these *ill* beseeming arms. *Shakesp. H.* IV.

Lead back thy Saxons to their ancient Elbe:
I would restore the fruitful Kent, the gift
Of Vortigern, or Hengist's *ill* bought aid. *Dryd. K. Arthur.*

We simple toasters take delight
To see our women's teeth look white;
And ev'ry saucy *ill* bred fellow
Sneers at a mouth profoundly yellow. *Prior.*

The ungrateful treason of her *ill* chosen husband overthrows her. *Sidney, b.* ii.

Envy, how carefully does it look? How meagre and *ill* complexioned? It preys upon itself, and exhausts the spirits. *Collier on Envy.*

There grows,
In my most *ill* compos'd affection, such
A stanchless avarice, that, were I king,
I should cut off the nobles for their lands. *Shakes. Macb.*

To what end this *ill* concerted lye,
Palpable and gross? *Dryden's Don Sebastian.*

Our generals at present are such as are likely to make the best use of their numbers, without throwing them away on any *ill* concerted projects. *Addison on the War.*

The second daughter was a peevish, froward, *ill* conditioned creature as ever was. *Arbuthnot's History of John Bull.*

No Persian arras hides his homely walls
With antick vests, which, through their shady fold,
Betray the streaks of *ill* dissembled gold. *Dryd. Virg. Geor.*

You shall not find me, daughter,
After the slander of most step-mothers,
Ill ey'd unto you. *Shakespeare's Cymbeline.*

I see thy sister's tears,
Thy father's anguish, and thy brother's death,
In the pursuit of our *ill* fated loves. *Addison's Cato.*

Others *ill* fated are condemn'd to toil
Their tedious life. *Prior.*

Plain and rough nature, left to itself, is much better than an artificial ungratefulness, and such studied ways of being *ill* fashioned. *Locke.*

Much better, when I find virtue in a fair lodging, than when I am bound to seek it in an *ill* favoured creature, like a pearl in a dunghill. *Sidney.*

Near to an old *ill* favoured castle they meant to perform their unknightly errand. *Sidney, b.* ii.

O, what a world of vile *ill* favour'd faults
Look handsome in three hundred pounds a year! *Shakesp.*

If a man had but an *ill* favoured nose, the deep thinkers would contrive to impute the cause to the prejudice of his education. *Swift.*

I was at her house the hour she appointed.
——And you sped, sir?
——Very *ill* favouredly. *Shakes. Merry Wives of Winds.*

He shook him *ill* favouredly for the time, raging through the very bowels of his country, and plundering all wheresoever he came. *Howel's Vocal Forrest.*

They would not make bold, as every where they do, to destroy *ill* formed and mis-shaped productions. *Locke.*

The fabled dragon never guarded more
The golden fleece, than he his *ill* got store. *Dryd. Juven.*

Bid him employ his care for these my friends,
And make good use of his *ill* gotten power,
By shelt'ring men much better than himself. *Addis. Cato.*

Ill govern'd passions in a prince's breast,
Hazard his private and the publick rest. *Waller.*

That knowledge of theirs is very superficial and *ill* grounded. *Dryden's Dufresnoy.*

Ill grounded passions quickly wear away;
What's built upon esteem can ne'er decay. *Walsh.*

Hither, of *ill* join'd sons and daughters born,
First from the ancient world these giants came. *Milton.*

Nor has he erred above once by an *ill* judged superfluity. *Garth's Ovid.*

Did you never taste delicious drink out of an *ill* looked vessel? *L'Estrange.*

The match had been so *ill* made for Plexirtus, that his ill led life would have tumbled to destruction, had there not come fifty to his defence. *Sidney, b.* ii.

The works are weak, the garrison but thin,
Dispirited with frequent overthrows,
Already wavering on their *ill* mann'd walls. *Dryden.*

He will not hear me out!
Was ever criminal forbid to plead?
Curb their *ill* manner'd zeal. *Dryden.*

These are the product
Of those *ill* mated marriages thou saw'st,
Where good with bad were match'd. *Milt. Parad. Lost.*

It is impossible for the most *ill* minded, avaritious, or cunning clergyman to do the least injustice to the meanest cottager, in any bargain for tythes. *Swift.*

Soon as th' *ill* omen'd rumour reach'd his ear,
Who can describe th' amazement in his face! *Dryden.*

The eternal law of things must not be altered, to comply with his *ill* ordered choice. *Locke.*

When you expose the scene,
Down the *ill* organ'd engines fall,
Off fly the vizards. *Swift.*

For Phthia fix'd is my return;
Better at home my *ill* paid pains to mourn,
Than from an equal here sustain the publick scorn. *Dryden.*

There motly images her fancy strike,
Figures *ill* pair'd, and similies unlike. *Pope's Dunciad.*

Sparta has not to boast of such a woman;
Nor Troy to thank her, for her *ill* plac'd love. *Dryden.*

I shall direct you better, a task for which I take myself not to be *ill* qualified, because I have had more opportunities than many others to observe what sources the follies of women are derived from. *Swift.*

Actions are pleasing or displeasing, either in themselves, or considered as a means to a greater and more desirable end: the eating of a well seasoned dish, suited to a man's palate, may move the mind, by the delight itself that accompanies the eating, without reference to any other end; to which the consideration of the pleasure there is in health and strength may add a new gust, able to make us swallow an *ill* relished potion. *Locke.*

Blushes, *ill* restrain'd, betray
Her thoughts inventive on the bridal day;
The conscious fire the dawning blush survey'd,
And smiling thus bespoke the blooming maid. *Pope's Odyss.*

Behold the fruit of *ill* rewarded pain:
As many months as I sustain'd her hate,
So many years is she condemn'd by fate. *Dryden.*

The god inform'd
This *ill* shap'd body with a daring soul. *Dryden and Lee's Oedipus.*

There was plenty enough, but the dishes were *ill* sorted: whole pyramids of sweetmeats for boys and women; but little of solid meat for men. *Dryden.*

It does not belong to the priest's office to impose this name in baptism: he may refuse to pronounce the same, if the parents give them ludicrous, filthy, or *ill* sounding names. *Ayliffe.*

Ill spirited Wor'ster, did we not send grace,
Pardon and terms of love to all of you? *Shakesp. H.* IV.

From thy foolish heart, vain maid, remove
An useless sorrow, and an *ill* starr'd love. *Prior.*

Ah, why th' *ill* suiting pastime must I try?
To gloomy care my thoughts alone are free:
Ill the gay sports with troubled hearts agree. *Pope's Odyssey.*

Holding of *ill* tasted things in the mouth will make a small salivation. *Grew's Cosmol. b.* ii.

The maid, with downcast eyes, and mute with grief,
For death unfinish'd, and *ill* tim'd relief,
Stood sullen to her suit. *Dryden's Ovid.*

How should opinions, thus settled, be given up, if there be any suspicion of interest or design, as there never fails to be, where men find themselves *ill* treated? *Locke.*

That boldness and spirit which lads get amongst their playfellows at school, has ordinarily a mixture of rudeness and *ill* turned confidence; so that these misbecoming and disingenuous ways of shifting in the world must be unlearned. *Locke.*

Il, before words beginning with *l*, stands for *in.*

Illa'chrymable. *adj.* [*illachrymabilis*, Latin.] Incapable of weeping. *Dict.*

Illa'pse. *n. s.* [*illapsus*, Latin.]

1. Gradual immission or entrance of one thing into another.

As a piece of iron red hot, by reason of the *illapse* of the fire into it, appears all over like fire; so the souls of the blessed, by the *illapse* of the divine essence into them, shall be all over divine. *Norris.*

2. Sudden attack; casual coming.

Life is oft preserved
By the bold swimmer in the swift *illapse*
Of accident disastrous. *Thomson's Summer.*

To ILLA'QUEATE. *v. a.* [*illaqueo*, Latin.] To entangle; to entrap; to ensnare.

I am *illaquated*, but not truly captivated into an assent to your conclusion. *More's Divine Dialogues.*

ILLAQUEA'TION. *n. s.* [from *illaqueate.*]

1. The act of catching or ensnaring.

The word in Mathew doth not only signify suspension, or pendulous *illaqueation*, but also suffocation. *Brown's Vul. Err.*

2. A snare; any thing to catch.

ILLA'TION. *n. s.* [*illatio*, Latin.] Inference; conclusion drawn from premises.

Herein there seems to be a very erroneous *illation* from the indulgence of God unto Cain, concluding an immunity unto himself. *Brown's Vulgar Errours.*

Illation so orders the intermediate ideas as to discover what connection there is in each link of the chain, whereby the extremes are held together. *Locke.*

I'LLATIVE. *adj.* [*illatus*, Latin.] Relating to illation or conclusion.

In common discourse or writing such causal particles as *for*, *because*, manifest the act of reasoning as well as the *illative* particles then and therefore. *Watts.*

ILLA'UDABLE. *adj.* [*illaudabilis*, Latin.] Unworthy of praise or commendation.

Strength from truth divided and from just,
Illaudable, nought merits but dispraise. *Milton's Par. Lost.*

ILLA'UDABLY. *adv.* [from *illaudable.*] Unworthily; without deserving praise.

It is natural for all people to form, not *illaudably*, too favourable a judgment of their own country. *Broome.*

ILLE'GAL. *adj.* [*in* and *legalis*, Latin.] Contrary to law.

No patent can oblige the subject against law, unless an *illegal* patent passed in one kingdom can bind another, and not itself. *Swift.*

ILLEGA'LITY. *n. s.* [from *illegal.*] Contrariety to law.

He wished them to consider what votes they had passed, of the *illegality* of all those commissions, and of the unjustifiableness of all the proceedings by virtue of them. *Clarendon.*

ILLE'GALLY. *adv.* [from *illegal.*] In a manner contrary to law.

ILLE'GIBLE. *adj.* [*in* and *legibilis*, from *lego*, Latin.] What cannot be read.

The secretary poured the ink-box all over the writings, and so defaced them that they were made altogether *illegible*. *Howel.*

ILLEGI'TIMACY. *n. s.* [from *illegitimate.*] State of bastardry.

ILLEGI'TIMATE. *adj.* [*in* and *legitimus*, Latin.] Unlawfully begotten; not begotten in wedlock.

Grieve not at your state;
For all the word is *illegitimate*. *Cleaveland.*

Being *illegitimate*, I was deprived of that endearing tenderness and uncommon satisfaction, which a good man finds in the love and conversation of a parent. *Addison's Spectator.*

ILLEGI'TIMATELY. *adv.* [from *illegitimate.*] Not in wedlock.

ILLEGITIMA'TION. *n. s.* [from *illegitimate.*] The state of one not begotten in wedlock.

Richard III. had a resolution, out of his hatred to both his brethren, to disable their issues, upon false and incompetent pretexts, the one of attainder, the other of *illegitimation*. *Bac.*

ILLE'VIABLE. *adv.* [*lever*, French.] What cannot be levied or exacted.

He rectified the method of collecting his revenue, and removed obsolete and *illeviable* parts of charge. *Hale.*

ILLFA'VOURED. *adj.* Deformed. See the compositions of ILL. *adv.*

ILLFA'VOUREDLY. *adv.* With deformity.

ILLFA'VOUREDNESS. *n. s.* Deformity.

ILLI'BERAL. *adj.* [*illiberalis*, Latin.]

1. Not noble; not ingenuous.

The charity of most men is grown so cold, and their religion so *illiberal*. *King Charles.*

2. Not munificent; not generous; sparing.

Yet subsist they did, and well too: an argument that that earth did not deal out their nourishment with an oversparing or *illiberal* hand. *Woodward's Natural History.*

ILLIBERA'LITY. *n. s.* [*illiberalitas*, Lat. from *illiberal.*] Parsimony; niggardliness; want of munificence.

The *illiberality* of parents, in allowance towards their children, is an harmful error, and acquaints them with shifts. *Bac.*

ILLI'BERALLY. *adv.* [from *illiberal.*] Disingenuously; meanly.

One that had been bountiful only upon surprize and incogitancy, *illiberally* retracts. *Decay of Piety.*

ILLI'CIT. *adj.* [*illicitus*, Latin; *illicite*, French.] Unlawful.

To ILLI'GHTEN. *v. n.* [*in* and *lighten.*] To enlighten; to illuminate. A word, I believe, only in *Raleigh.*

Corporeal light cannot be, because then it would not pierce the air, nor diaphanous bodies; and yet every day we see the air *illightened*. *Raleigh.*

ILLI'MITABLE. *adj.* [*in* and *limes*, Latin.] That which cannot be bounded or limited.

Although in adoration of idols, unto the subtiler heads, the worship perhaps might be symbolical; yet was the idolatry direct in the people, whose credulity is *illimitable*, and who may be made believe that any thing is God. *Brown's Vu. Err.*

With what an awful world-revolving power,
Were first th' unwieldy planets launch'd along
The *illimitable* void! *Thomson's Summer.*

ILLI'MITABLY. *adv.* [from *illimitable.*] Without susceptibility of bounds.

ILLI'MITED. *adj.* [*in* and *limes*, Latin; *illimité*, French.] Unbounded; interminable.

ILLI'MITEDNESS. *n. s.* [from *illimited.*] Exemption from all bounds.

The absoluteness and *illimitedness* of his commission was generally much spoken of. *Clarendon, b.* viii.

ILLI'TERATE. *adj.* [*illiteratus*, Latin.] Unlettered; untaught; unlearned; unenlightened by science.

The duke was *illiterate*, yet had learned at court to supply his own defects, by the drawing unto him of the best instruments of experience. *Wotton.*

Th' *illiterate* writer, empirick like, applies
To minds diseas'd unsafe chance remedies:
The learn'd in schools, where knowledge first began,
Studies with care th' anatomy of man;
Sees virtue, vice, and passions in their cause,
And fame from science, not from fortune draws. *Dryden.*

In the first ages of Christianity not only the learned and the wise, but the ignorant and *illiterate* embraced torments and death. *Tillotson's Sermons.*

ILLI'TERATENESS. *n. s.* [from *illiterate.*] Want of learning; ignorance of science.

Many acquainted with chymistry but by report, have, from the *illiterateness* and impostures of those that pretend skill in it, entertained an ill opinion of the art. *Boyle.*

ILLI'TERATURE. *n. s.* [*in* and *literature.*] Want of learning.

The more usual causes of this deprivation are want of holy orders, *illiterature*, or inability for the discharge of that sacred function, and irreligion. *Ayliffe's Parergon.*

I'LLNESS. *n. s.* [from *ill.*]

1. Badness or inconvenience of any kind, natural or moral.

He that has his chains knocked off, and the prison-doors set open, is perfectly at liberty, though his preference be determined to stay, by the *illness* of the weather. *Locke.*

2. Sickness; malady; disorder of health.

On the Lord's day, which immediately preceded this *illness*, he had received the sacrament. *Atterbury's Sermons.*

Since the account her majesty received of the insolent behaviour of the faction, during her late *illness* at Windsor, she hath been willing to see them deprived of all power to do mischief. *Swift.*

3. Wickedness.

Thou would be great;
Art not without ambition; but without
The *illness* should attend it. *Shakesp. Macbeth.*

ILLNA'TURE. *n. s.* [*ill* and *nature.*] Habitual malevolence; want of humanity.

Illnature inclines a man to those actions that thwart and sour and disturb conversation, and consists of a proneness to do ill turns, attended with a secret joy upon the sight of any mischief that befals another, and of an utter insensibility of any kindness done him. *South's Sermons.*

ILLNA'TURED. *adj.* [from *illnature.*]

1. Habitually malevolent; wanting kindness or goodwill; mischievous.

These ill qualities denominate a person *illnatured*, they being such as make him grievous and uneasy to all whom he deals and associates himself with. *South's Sermons.*

Stay, silly bird, th' *illnatur'd* task refuse;
Nor be the bearer of unwelcome news. *Addison's Ovid.*

It might be one of those *illnatured* beings who are at enmity with mankind, and do therefore take pleasure in filling them with groundless terrors. *Atterbury's Sermons.*

2. *Phillips* applies it to land. Untractable; not yielding to culture.

The fondly studious of increase,
Rich foreign mold on their *illnatur'd* land
Induce. *Phillips.*

ILLNA'TUREDLY. *adv.* [from *illnatured.*] In a peevish, froward manner.

ILLNA'TUREDNESS. *n. s.* [from *illnatured.*] Want of a kindly disposition.

ILLO'GICAL. *adj.* [*in* and *logical.*]

1. Ignorant or negligent of the rules of reasoning.

One of the dissenters appeared to Dr. Sanderson so bold and *illogical* in the dispute, as forced him to say he had never met with a man of more pertinacious confidence, and less abilities. *Walton.*

2. Contrary to the rules of reason.

Reason cannot dispute and make an inference so utterly *illogical*. *Decay of Piety.*

ILLO'GICALLY. *adv.* [from *illogical.*] In a manner contrary to the laws of argument.

To Illu'de. *v. a.* [*illudo*, Latin.] To deceive; to mock; to impose on; to play upon; to torment by some contemptuous artifice of mockery.

Sometimes athwart, sometimes he strook him strait,
And falsed of this blow, t' *illude* him with such bait. *F. Qu.*

In vain we measure this amazing sphere,
While its circumference, scorning to be brought
Ev'n into fancy'd space, *illudes* our vanquish'd thought. *Pri.*

To Illu'me. *v. a.* [*illuminer*, French.]

1. To enlighten; to illuminate.

When yon same star, that's westward from the pole,
Had made his course t' *illume* that part of heav'n,
Where now it burns. *Shakesp. Hamlet.*

2. To brighten; to adorn.

The mountain's brow,
Illum'd with fluid gold, his near approach
Betoken. *Thomson's Summer.*

To Illu'mine. *v. a.* [*illuminer*, French.]

1. To enlighten; to supply with light.

To confirm his words, out flew
Millions of flaming swords, drawn from the thighs
Of mighty cherubims: the sudden blaze
Far round *illumin'd* hell. *Milton's Paradise Lost, b.* i.

What in me is dark,
Illumine! what is low, raise and support! *Milt. Par. Lost.*

2. To decorate; to adorn.

To Cato, Virgil paid one honest line;
O let my country's friends *illumine* mine. *Pope.*

To ILLU'MINATE. *v. a.* [*illuminer*, French; *lumen*, Latin.]

1. To enlighten; to supply with light.

Do thou vouchsafe, with thy love-kindling light,
T' *illuminate* my dim and dulled eyn. *Spenser.*

No painting can be seen in full perfection, but as all nature is *illuminated* by a single light. *Wotton.*

He made the stars,
And set them in the firmament of heav'n,
T' *illuminate* the earth and rule the night. *Milt. Par. Lost.*

Reason our guide, what can she more reply
Than that the sun *illuminates* the sky;
Than that night rises from his absent ray,
And his returning lustre kindles day? *Prior.*

2. To adorn with festal lamps or bonfires.

3. To enlighten intellectually with knowledge or grace.

Satan had no power to abuse the *illuminated* world with his impostures. *Sandys's Travels.*

When he *illuminates* the mind with supernatural light, he does not extinguish that which is natural. *Locke.*

4. To adorn with pictures or initial letters of various colours.

5. To illustrate.

My health is insufficient to amplify these remarks, and to *illuminate* the several pages with variety of examples. *Watts.*

Illumina'tion. *n. s.* [*illuminatio*, Lat. *illumination*, Fr. from *illuminate.*]

1. The act of supplying with light.

2. That which gives light.

The sun is but a body illightened, and an *illumination* created. *Raleigh's History of the World.*

3. Festal lights hung out as a token of joy.

Flow'rs are strew'd, and lamps in order plac'd,
And windows with *illuminations* grac'd. *Dryden's Pers.*

4. Brightness; splendour.

The illuminators of manuscripts borrowed their title from the *illumination* which a bright genius giveth to his work. *Felton on the Classicks.*

5. Infusion of intellectual light; knowledge or grace.

Hymns and psalms are such kinds of prayer as are not conceived upon a sudden; but framed by meditation beforehand, or by prophetical *illumination* are inspired. *Hooker.*

We have forms of prayers imploring God's aid and blessing for the *illumination* of our labours, and the turning them into good and holy uses. *Bacon.*

No holy passion, no *illumination*, no inspiration, can be now a sufficient commission to warrant those attempts which contradict the common rules of peace. *Spratt's Sermons.*

Illu'minative. *adj.* [*illuminatif*, Fr. from *illuminate.*] Having the power to give light.

What makes itself and other things be seen, being accompanied by light, is called fire: what admits the *illuminative* action of fire, and is not seen, is called air. *Digby on Bodies.*

Illumina'tor. *n. s.* [from *illuminate.*]

1. One who gives light.

2. One whose business it is to decorate books with pictures at the beginning of chapters.

Illuminators of manuscripts borrowed their title from the illumination which a bright genius giveth to his work. *Felton.*

Illu'sion. *n. s.* [*illusio*, Latin; *illusion*, Fr.] Mockery; false show; counterfeit appearance; errour.

That, distill'd by magick slights,
Shall raise such artificial sprights,
As, by the strength of their *illusion*,
Shall draw him on to his confusion. *Shakesp. Macbeth.*

There wanted not some about him that would have persuaded him that all was but an *illusion.* *Bacon's Henry* VII.

So oft they fell
Into the same *illusion*; not as man,
Whom they triumph'd, once laps'd. *Milton's Parad. Lost.*

An excuse for uncharitableness, drawn from pretended inability, is of all others the most general and prevailing *illusion.* *Atterbury's Sermons.*

Many are the *illusions* by which the enemy endeavours to cheat men into security, and defeat their title to salvation. *Rogers's Sermons.*

To dream once more I close my willing eyes;
Ye soft *illusions*, dear deceits, arise! *Pope.*

We must use some *illusion* to render a pastoral delightful; and this consists in exposing the best side only of a shepherd's life, and in concealing its miseries. *Pope.*

Illu'sive. *adj.* [from *illusus*, Latin.] Deceiving by false show.

The heathen bards, who idle fables drest,
Illusive dreams in mystick forms exprest. *Blackmore.*

While the fond soul,
Wrapt in gay visions of unreal bliss,
Still paints th' *illusive* form. *Thomson's Spring.*

I'llusory. *adj.* [from *in* and *lusorius*, Latin; *illusoire*, Fr.] Deceiving; fraudulent.

Subtilty, in those who make profession to teach or defend truth, hath passed for a virtue: a virtue indeed, which, consisting for the most part in nothing but the fallacious and *illusory* use of obscure or deceitful terms, is only fit to make men more conceited in their ignorance. *Locke.*

To ILLU'STRATE. *v. n.* [*illustro*, Latin; *illustrer*, Fr.]

1. To brighten with light.

2. To brighten with honour.

Matter to me of glory! whom their hate
Illustrates, when they see all regal pow'r
Giv'n me to quell their pride. *Milton's Paradise Lost.*

Thee she enroll'd her garter'd knights among,
Illustrating the noble list. *Phillips.*

3. To explain; to clear; to elucidate.

They take up popular conceits, and from tradition unjustifiable, or really false, *illustrate* matters of undeniable truth. *Brown's Vulgar Errours.*

Illustra'tion. *n. s.* [*illustration*, Fr. from *illustrate.*] Explanation; elucidation; exposition.

Whoever looks about him will find many living *illustrations* of this emblem. *L'Estrange.*

Space and duration, being ideas that have something very abstruse and peculiar in their nature, the comparing them one with another may perhaps be of use for their *illustration.* *Locke.*

Illu'strative. *adj.* [from *illustrate.*] Having the quality of elucidating or clearing.

They play much upon the simile, or *illustrative* argumentation, to induce their enthymemes unto the people. *Brown.*

Illu'stratively. *adv.* [from *illustrative.*] By way of explanation.

Things are many times delivered hieroglyphically, metaphorically, *illustratively*, and not with reference to action. *Brown's Vulgar Errours.*

ILLU'STRIOUS. *adj.* [*illustris*, Latin; *illustre*, Fr.] Conspicuous; noble; eminent for excellence.

In other languages the most *illustrious* titles are derived from things sacred. *South's Sermons.*

Of ev'ry nation, each *illustrious* name,
Such toys as those have cheated into fame. *Dryden's Juven.*

Illu'striously. *adv.* [from *illustrious.*] Conspicuously; nobly; eminently.

He disdained not to appear at festival entertainments, that he might more *illustriously* manifest his charity. *Atterb. Sermons.*

Enjoy the glory to be great no more;
And carrying with you all the world can boast,
To all the world *illustriously* are lost. *Pope's Spring.*

Illu'striousness. *n. s.* [from *illustrious.*] Eminence; nobility; grandeur.

I'm. Contracted from *I am.*

Im is used commonly, in composition, for *in* before mute letters.

I'MAGE. *n. s.* [*image*, French; *imago*, Latin.]

1. Any corporeal representation, generally used of statues; a statue; a picture.

Whose is this *image* and superscription? *Mat.* xxii. 20.

The one is too like an *image*, and says nothing; and the other too like my lady's oldest son, ever more talking. *Shakes.*

Thy brother I,
Even like a stony *image*, cold and numb. *Shakesp. Tit. And.*

The *image* of a deity may be a proper object for that which is but the *image* of a religion. *South's Sermons.*

Still must I be upbraided with your line;
But your late brother did not prize me less,
Because I could not boast of *images.* *Dryd. Tyrann. Love.*

2. An idol; a false god.

3. A copy; representation; likeness.

Long may'st thou live,
To bear his *image* and renew his glories! *Shakesp. Hen.* VI.

I have

I have bewept a worthy husband's death,
And liv'd by looking on his *images:*
But now two mirrours of his princely semblance
Are crack'd in pieces by malignant death. *Shakesp. R.* III.
The *image* of the jest
I'll shew you here at large. *Shakesp. Mer. Wives of Windf.*
He made us to his *image* all agree;
That *image* is the soul, and that must be,
Or not the maker's *image*, or be free. *Dryden.*

4. Semblance; show; appearance.
Deny to speak with me? They're sick, they're weary,
They have travell'd all night! Mere fetches,
The *images* of revolt. *Shakespeare's King Lear.*
This is the man should do the bloody deed:
The *image* of a wicked heinous fault
Lives in his eye. *Shakespeare's King John.*
The face of things a frightful *image* bears,
And present death in various forms appears. *Dryden's Æn.*

5. An idea; a representation of any thing to the mind; a picture drawn in the fancy.
Outcasts of mortal race! can we conceive
Image of aught delightful, soft, or great? *Prior.*

When we speak of a figure of a thousand angles, we may have a clear idea of the number one thousand angles; but the *image*, or sensible idea, we cannot distinguish by fancy from the *image* of a figure that has nine hundred angles. *Watts.*

To I'MAGE. *v. a.* [from the noun.] To copy by the fancy; to imagine.

How are immaterial substances to be *imaged*, which are such things whereof we can have no notion? *Dryden.*
Image to thy mind
How our forefathers to the Stygian shades
Went quick. *Phillips.*
His ear oft frighted with the *imag'd* voice
Of heav'n, when first it thunder'd. *Prior.*
If fate some future bard shall join
In sad similitude of griefs to mine,
Condemn'd whole years in absence to deplore,
And *image* charms he must behold no more. *Pope.*

I'MAGERY. *n. s.* [from *image.*]

1. Sensible representations; pictures; statues.
Of marble stone was cut
An altar, carv'd with cunning *imagery.* *Fairy Queen.*
When in those oratories might you see
Rich carvings, portraitures, and *imagery*;
Where ev'ry figure to the life express'd
The godhead's pow'r. *Dryden's Knight's Tale.*
Your gift shall two large goblets be
Of silver, wrought with curious *imagery*,
And high emboss'd. *Dryden's Æn.*

2. Show; appearance.
What can thy *imagery* of sorrow mean?
Secluded from the world, and all its care,
Hast thou to grieve or joy, to hope or fear? *Prior.*

All the visionary beauties of the prospect, the paint and *imagery* that attracted our senses, fade and disappear. *Rogers.*

Things of the world fill the imaginative part with beauties and fantastick *imagery.* *Taylor.*

3. Copies of the fancy; false ideas; imaginary phantasms.

It might be a mere dream which he saw; the *imagery* of a melancholick fancy, such as musing men mistake for a reality. *Atterbury's Sermons.*

4. Representations in writing; such descriptions as force the image of the thing described upon the mind.

I wish there may be in this poem any instance of good *imagery.* *Dryden.*

IMA'GINABLE. *adj.* [*imaginable*, Fr. from *imagine.*] Possible to be conceived.

It is not *imaginable* that men will be brought to obey what they cannot esteem. *South's Sermons.*

Men, sunk into the greatest darkness *imaginable*, retain some sense and awe of a Deity. *Tillotson's Sermons.*

IMA'GINANT. *adj.* [*imaginant*, French.] Imagining; forming ideas.

We will enquire what the force of imagination is, either upon the body *imaginant*, or upon another body. *Bacon.*

IMA'GINARY. *adj.* [*imaginaire*, French, from *imagine.*]

1. Fancied; visionary; existing only in the imagination.
False sorrow's eye,
Which, for things true, weeps things *imaginary.* *Shakesp.*
Expectation whirls me round:
Th' *imaginary* relish is so sweet,
That it enchants my sense. *Shakesp. Troilus and Cressida.*

Fortune is nothing else but a power *imaginary*, to which the successes of human actions and endeavours were for their variety ascribed. *Raleigh's History of the World.*
Why wilt thou add, to all the griefs I suffer,
Imaginary ills and fancied tortures? *Addison's Cato.*

IMA'GINATION. *n. s.* [*imaginatio*, Latin; *imagination*, French, from *imagine.*]

1. Fancy; the power of forming ideal pictures; the power of representing things absent to one's self or others.

Imagination I understand to be the representation of an individual thought. *Imagination* is of three kinds: joined with belief of that which is to come; joined with memory of that which is past; and of things present, or as if they were present: for I comprehend in this *imagination* feigned and at pleasure, as if one should imagine such a man to be in the vestments of a pope, or to have wings. *Bacon.*

Our simple apprehension of corporal objects, if present, is sense; if absent, *imagination:* when we would perceive a material object, our fancies present us with its idea. *Glanv. Sceps.*
O whither shall I run, or which way fly
The sight of this so horrid spectacle,
Which erst my eyes beheld, and yet behold!
For dire *imagination* still pursues me. *Milton's Agonistes.*

His *imaginations* were often as just as they were bold and strong. *Dennis.*
Where beams of warm *imagination* play,
The memory's soft figures melt away. *Pope.*

2. Conception; image in the mind; idea.

Sometimes despair darkens all her *imaginations*; sometimes the active passion of love cheers and clears her invention. *Sidn.*
Princes have but their titles for their glories,
An outward honour for an inward toil;
And, for unfelt *imaginations*,
They often feel a world of restless cares. *Shakesp. R.* III.
Better I were distract,
So should my thoughts be sever'd from my griefs;
And woes, by wrong *imaginations*, lose
The knowledge of themselves. *Shakesp. King Lear.*

We are apt to think that space, in itself, is actually boundless; to which *imagination*, the idea of space, of itself leads us. *Locke.*

3. Contrivance; scheme.

Thou hast seen all their vengeance, and all their *imaginations* against me. *Lam.* iii. 60.

IMA'GINATIVE. *adj.* [*imaginatif*, Fr. from *imagine.*] Fantastick; full of imagination.

Witches are *imaginative*, and believe oft times they do that which they do not. *Bacon's Natural History.*

Lay fetters and restraints upon the *imaginative* and fantastick part, because our fancy is usually pleased with the entertainment of shadows and gauds. *Taylor's Rule of living holy.*

To IMA'GINE. *v. a.* [*imaginer*, French; *imaginor*, Latin.]

1. To fancy; to paint in the mind.
Look what notes and garments he doth give thee,
Bring them, I pray thee, with *imagin'd* speed. *Shakespeare.*
Present feats
Are less than horrible *imaginings.* *Shakesp. Macbeth.*

What are our ideas of eternity and immensity but the repeated additions of certain ideas of *imagined* parts of duration and expansion, with the infinity of number, in which we can come to no end of addition? *Locke.*

2. To scheme; to contrive.

They intended evil against thee, they *imagined* a mischievous device. *Ps.* xxi. 11.

IMA'GINER. *n. s.* [from *imagine.*] One who forms ideas.

The juggler took upon him to know that such an one should point in such a place of a garter that was held up; and still he did it, by first telling the *imaginer*, and after bidding the actor think. *Bacon's Natural History.*

IMBE'CILE. *adj.* [*imbecilis*, Latin; *imbecille*, French.] Weak; feeble; wanting strength of either mind or body.

To IMBE'CILE. *v. a.* [from the adjective. This word is corruptly written *embezzle.*] To weaken a stock or fortune by clandestine expences or unjust appropriations.

Princes must in a special manner be guardians of pupils and widows, not suffering their persons to be oppressed, or their states *imbeciled.* *Taylor's Rule of living holy.*

IMBECI'LITY. *n. s.* [*imbecillité*, French.] Weakness; feebleness of mind or body.

A weak and imperfect rule argueth *imbecility* and imperfection. *Hooker, b.* iv.

No *imbecility* of means can prejudice the truth of the promise of God herein. *Hooker.*

We that are strong must bear the *imbecility* of the impotent, and not please ourselves. *Hooker.*

That way we are contented to prove, which, being the worse in itself, is notwithstanding now, by reason of common *imbecility*, the fitter and likelier to be brooked. *Hooker.*
Strength would be lord of *imbecility*,
And the rude son would strike his father dead. *Shakespeare.*

Imbecility, for sex and age, was such as they could not lift up a hand against them. *King Charles.*

When man was fallen, and had abandoned his primitive innocence, a strange *imbecility* immediately seized and laid hold of him. *Woodward's Natural History.*

To IMBI'BE. *v. a.* [*imbibo*, Latin; *imbiber*, French.]

1. To drink in; to draw in.

A pot of ashes will receive more hot water than cold, forasmuch as the warm water *imbibeth* more of the salt. *Brown.*
The torrent merciless *imbibes*
Commissions, perquisites, and bribes. *Swift.*

Illumin'd wide,
The dewy-skirted clouds *imbibe* the sun. *Thomson's Autumn.*

2. To admit into the mind.

Those, that have *imbibed* this error, have extended the influence of this belief to the whole gospel, which they will not allow to contain any thing but promises. *Hammond.*

It is not easy for the mind to put off those confused notions and prejudices it has *imbibed* from custom. *Locke.*

Conversation with foreigners enlarges our minds, and sets them free from many prejudices we are ready to *imbibe* concerning them. *Watts's Improvement of the Mind.*

3. To drench; to soak. This sense, though unusual, perhaps unexampled, is necessary in the English, unless the word *imbue* be adopted, which our writers seem not willing to receive.

Metals, corroded with a little acid, turn into rust, which is an earth tasteless and indissolvable in water; and this earth, *imbibed* with more acid, becomes a metallick salt. *Newton.*

IMBI'BER. *n. s.* [from *imbibe.*] That which drinks or sucks.

Salts are strong *imbibers* of sulphureous steams. *Arbuthnot.*

IMBIBI'TION. *n. s.* [*imbibition*, French, from *imbibe.*] The act of sucking or drinking in.

Most powders grow more coherent by mixture of water than of oil: the reason is the congruity of bodies, which maketh a perfecter *imbibition* and incorporation. *Bacon.*

Heat and cold have a virtual transition, without communication of substance, but in moisture not; and to all madefaction there is required an *imbibition.* *Bacon's Natural History.*

A drop of oil, let fall upon a sheet of white paper, that part of it, which, by the *imbibition* of the liquor, acquires a greater continuity and some transparency, will appear much darker than the rest; many of the incident beams of light being now transmitted, that otherwise would be reflected. *Boyle.*

To IMBI'TTER. *v. a.* [from *bitter.*]

1. To make bitter.

2. To deprive of pleasure; to make unhappy.

Let them extinguish their passions which *imbitter* their lives, and deprive them of their share in the happiness of the community. *Addison's Freeholder.*

Is there any thing that more *imbitters* the enjoyments of this life than shame? *South's Sermons.*

3. To exasperate.

To IMBO'DY. *v. a.* [from *body.*]

1. To condense to a body.

2. To invest with matter.

An opening cloud reveals
An heav'nly form *imbody'd*, and array'd
With robes of light. *Dryden.*

Though assiduity in the most fixed cogitation be no trouble to immaterialised spirits, yet is it more than our *embodied* souls can bear without lassitude. *Glanv. Sceps.*

3. To bring together into one mass or company.

I by vow am so *embodied* yours,
That she which marries you must marry me. *Shakespeare.*

Never since created, man
Met such *imbodied* force, as nam'd with these,
Could merit more than that small infantry
Warr'd on by cranes. *Milton's Paradise Lost, b.* i.

Under their head *embody'd* all in one. *Milt. Par. Lost.*

Then Clausus came, who led a num'rous band
Of troops *embodied*, from the Sabine land. *Dryden's Æn.*

4. To inclose. Improper.

In those strata we shall meet with the same metal or mineral *imbodied* in stone, or lodged in coal, that elsewhere we found in marle. *Woodward's Natural History.*

To IMBO'DY. *v. n.* To unite into one mass; to coalesce

The soul grows clotted by contagion,
Imbodies and imbrutes, 'till she quite lose
The divine property of her first being. *Milton.*

The idea of white, which snow yielded yesterday, and another idea of white from another snow to-day, put together in your mind, *imbody* and run into one. *Locke.*

To IMBO'IL. *v. n.* [from *boil.*] To exestuate; to effervesce; to move with violent agitation like hot liquor in a caldron.

With whose reproach and odious menace,
The knight *imboiling* in his haughty heart,
Knit all his forces, and 'gan soon unbrace
His grasping hold. *Fairy Queen.*

To IMBO'LDEN. *v. a.* [from *bold.*] To raise to confidence; to encourage.

'Tis necessary he should die:
Nothing *imboldens* sin so much as mercy. *Shak. Timon.*

I think myself in better plight for a lender than you are, the which hath something *imboldened* me to this unseasoned intrusion. *Shakes. Merry Wives of Windsor.*

I was the more *imboldened*, because I found I had a soul congenial to his. *Dryden.*

Nor flight was left, nor hopes to force his way;
Imbolden'd by dispair, he stood at bay. *Dryden's Æn.*

Their virtues and superior genius *imboldened* them, in great exigencies of state, to attempt the service of their prince and country out of the common forms. *Swift.*

To IMBO'SOM. *v. a.* [from *bosom.*]

1. To hold on the bosom; to cover fondly with the folds of one's garment; to hide under any cover.

The Father infinite,
By whom in bliss *imbosom'd* sat the son. *Milton's Par. Lost.*

Villages *imbosom'd* soft in trees,
And spiry towns by surging columns mark'd. *Thomson.*

2. To admit to the heart, or to affection.

But glad desire, his late *embosom'd* guest,
Yet but a babe, with milk of sight he nurst. *Sidney.*

Who glad t' *embosom* his affection vile,
Did all she might, more plainly to appear. *Fairy Queen.*

To IMBO'UND. *v. a.* [from *bound.*] To inclose; to shut in.

That sweet breath,
Which was *embounded* in this beauteous clay. *Shak. K. John.*

To IMBO'W. *v. a.* [from *bow.*] To arch; to vault.

Prince Arthur gave a box of diamond sure,
Imbowed with gold and gorgeous ornament. *Fairy Queen.*

Imbowed windows be pretty retiring places for conference: they keep both the wind and sun off. *Bacon.*

Let my due feet never fail
To walk the studious cloister's pale,
And love the high *embowed* roof,
With antick pillar massy proof. *Milton.*

IMBO'WMENT. *n. s.* [from *imbow.*] Arch; vault.

The roof all open, not so much as any *embowment* near any of the walls left. *Bacon's Natural History.*

To IMBO'WER. *v. a.* [from *bower.*] To cover with a bower; to shelter with trees.

And stooping thence to Ham's *embowering* walks,
In spotless peace retir'd. *Thomson.*

To IMBRA'NGLE. *v. a.* To intangle. A low word.

With subtle cobweb cheats
They're catch'd in knotted law, like nets;
In which, when once they are *imbrangled*,
The more they stir, the more they're tangled. *Hudibras.*

IMBRI'CATED. *adj.* [from *imbrex*, Latin.] Indented with concavities; bent and hollowed like a roof or gutter-tile.

IMBRICA'TION. *n. s.* [*imbrex*, Latin.] Concave indenture.

All is guarded with a well made tegument, adorned with neat *imbrications*, and many other fineries. *Derham.*

To IMBRO'WN. *v. a.* [from *brown.*] To make brown; to darken; to obscure; to cloud.

Where the morning sun first warmly smote
The open field, and where the unpierc'd shade
Imbrown'd the noontide bow'rs. *Milton's Paradise Lost.*

The walking crew,
At thy request, support the miry shoe;
The foot grows black that was with dirt *imbrown'd*,
And in thy pocket gingling half-pence sound. *Gay.*

Another age shall see the golden ear
Imbrown the slope, and nod on the parterre. *Pope.*

Imbrown'd with native bronze, lo! Henly stands. *Pope.*

To IMBRU'E. *v. a.* [from *in* and *brue.*]

1. To steep; to soak; to wet much or long.

Thou mad'st many hearts to bleed
Of mighty victors, with wide wounds *embru'd*,
And by thy cruel darts to thee subdu'd. *Spenser.*

There streams a spring of blood so fast
From those deep wounds, as all *embru'd* the face
Of that accursed caitiff. *Daniel's Civil War.*

The merciless Turks, *embrued* with the Christian blood, were weary of slaughter, and began greedily to seek after the spoil. *Knolles's History of the Turks.*

At me, as at a mark, his bow he drew,
Whose arrows in my blood their wings *imbrue.* *Sandys.*

Lucius pities the offenders,
That would *embrue* their hands in Cato's blood. *Addison.*

Lo! these hands in murder are *imbru'd*,
Those trembling feet by justice are pursu'd. *Prior.*

These, where two ways in equal parts divide,
The direful monster from afar descry'd,
Two bleeding babes depending at her side;
Whose panting vitals, warm with life, she draws,
And in their hearts *embrues* her cruel claws. *Pope.*

His virgin sword Ægysthus' veins *imbru'd*;
The murd'rer fell, and blood atton'd for blood. *Pope.*

A good man chuses rather to pass by a verbal injury than *imbrue* his hands in blood. *Clarissa.*

2. To pour; to emit moisture. Obsolete.

Some bathed kisses, and did oft *embrue*
The sugar'd liquor through his melting lips. *Fairy Queen.*

To IMBRU'TE. *v. a.* [from *brute.*] To degrade to brutality.

I, who erst contended
With gods to sit the highest, am now constrain'd
Into a beast; and mix with bestial slime,
This essence to incarnate and *imbrute.* *Milton's Par. Lost.*

To IMBRU'TE. *v. n.* To sink down to brutality.

The soul grows clotted by contagion,
Imbodies and *imbrutes*, 'till she quite lose
The divine property of her first being. *Milton.*

To IMBU'E. *v. a.* [*imbuo*, Latin. This word, which seems wanted in our language, has been proposed by several writers, but not yet adopted by the rest. *Imbu*, French, the participial adj. is only used.] To tincture deep; to imbibe with any liquor or die.

I would render this treatise intelligible to every rational man, however little versed in scholastick learning; among whom I expect it will have a fairer passage, than among those that are deeply *imbued* with other principles. *Digby.*

Cloaths which have once been throughly *embued* with black, cannot well afterwards be dyed into lighter colour. *Boyle.*

Where the mineral matter is great, so as to take the eye, the body appears *imbued* and tinctured with the colour. *Woodw.*

To IMBU'RSE. *v. a.* [*bourse*, French.] To stock with money. This should be *emburse*, from *embourser*, French.

IMITABI'LITY. *n. s.* [*imitabilis*, Latin.] The quality of being imitable.

According to the multifariousness of this *imitability*, so are the possibilities of being. *Norris.*

I'MITABLE. *adj.* [*imitabilis*, Latin; *imitable*, French.]

1. Worthy to be imitated.

How could the most base men, and separate from all *imitable* qualities, attain to honour but by an observant slavish course? *Raleigh's History of the World.*

As acts of parliament are not regarded by most *imitable* writers, I account the relation of them improper for history. *Hayw.*

2. Possible to be imitated.

The characters of men placed in lower stations of life, are more useful, as being *imitable* by greater numbers. *Atterbury.*

To I'MITATE. *v. a.* [*imitor*, Latin; *imiter*, French.]

1. To copy; to endeavour to resemble.

We *imitate* and practise to make swifter motions than any out of your muskets. *Bacon.*

Despise wealth, and *imitate* a god. *Cowley.*

I would caress some stableman of note,
And *imitate* his language and his coat. *Man of Taste.*

2. To counterfeit.

This hand appear'd a shining sword to wield,
And that sustain'd an *imitated* shield. *Dryden's Æn.*

3. To pursue the course of a composition, so as to use parallel images and examples.

For shame! what, *imitate* an ode! *Gay.*

IMITA'TION. *n. s.* [*imitatio*, Latin; *imitation*, French.]

1. The act of copying; attempt to resemble.

Since a true knowledge of nature gives us pleasure, a lively *imitation* of it, either in poetry or painting, must produce a much greater; for both these arts are not only true *imitations* of nature, but of the best nature. *Dryden.*

2. That which is offered as a copy.

3. A method of translating looser than paraphrase, in which modern examples and illustrations are used for ancient, or domestick for foreign.

In the way of *imitation*, the translator not only varies from the words and sense, but forsakes them as he sees occasion; and, taking only some general hints from the original, runs division on the groundwork. *Dryden.*

I'MITATIVE. *adj.* [*imitativus*, Latin.] Inclined to copy.

This temple, less in form, with equal grace,
Was *imitative* of the first in Thrace. *Dryden.*

IMITA'TOR. *n. s.* [Latin; *imitateur*, French.] One that copies another; one that endeavours to resemble another.

Imitators are but a servile kind of cattle, says the poet. *Dry.*

IMMA'CULATE. *adj.* [*immaculatus*, Latin; *immaculé*, Fr.]

1. Spotless; pure; undefiled.

To keep this commandment *immaculate* and blameless, was to teach the gospel of Christ. *Hooker.*

His words are bonds, his oaths are oracles;
His love sincere, his thoughts *immaculate*. *Shakespeare.*

The king, whom catholicks count a saint-like and *immaculate* prince, was taken away in the flower of his age. *Bacon.*

Were but my soul as pure
From other guilts as that, heav'n did not hold
One more *immaculate*. *Denham's Sophy.*

2. Pure; limpid. Improper.

Thou clear, *immaculate*, and silver fountain,
From whence this stream, through muddy passages,
Hath had his current and defil'd himself. *Shakes. Rich.* II.

To IMMA'NACLE. *v. a.* [from *manacle*.] To fetter; to confine.

Thou can'st not touch the freedom of my mind
With all thy charms, although this corporal rind
Thou hast *immanacl'd*. *Milton.*

IMMA'NE. *adj.* [*immanis*, Latin.] Vast; prodigiously great.

I'MMANENT. *adj.* [*immanent*, French; *in* and *maneo*, Latin.] Intrinsick; inherent; internal.

Judging the infinite essence by our narrow selves, we ascribe intellections, volitions, and such like *immanent* actions, to that nature which hath nothing in common with us. *Glanv. Sceps.*

What he wills and intends once, he willed and intended from all eternity; it being grosly contrary to the very first notions we have of the infinite perfections of the Divine Nature to state or suppose any new *immanent* act in God. *South.*

IMMA'NIFEST. *adj.* [*in* and *manifest*.] Not manifest; not plain.

A time not much unlike that which was before time, *immanifest* and unknown. *Brown's Vulgar Errours.*

IMMA'NITY. *n. s.* [*immanitas*, Latin.] Barbarity; savageness.

It was both impious and unnatural,
That such *immanity* and bloody strife
Should reign among professors of one faith. *Shakes. H.* VI.

IMMARCE'SSIBLE. *adj.* [*in* and *marcesco*, Latin.] Unfading. *Dict.*

IMMA'RTIAL. *adj.* [*in* and *martial*.] Not warlike.

My pow'rs are unfit,
Myself *immartial*. *Chapman's Odyssey.*

To IMMA'SK. *v. a.* [*in* and *mask*.] To cover; to disguise.

I have cases of buckram for the nonce, to *immask* our noted outward garments. *Shakespeare's Henry* IV.

IMMATE'RIAL. *adj.* [*immateriel*, Fr. *in* and *materia*, Latin.]

1. Incorporeal; distinct from matter; void of matter.

Angels are spirits *immaterial* and intellectual, the glorious inhabitants of those sacred palaces, where there is nothing but light and immortality; no shadow of matter for tears, discontentments, griefs, and uncomfortable passions to work upon; but all joy, tranquillity, and peace, even for ever and ever, do dwell. *Hooker.*

As then the soul a substance hath alone,
Besides the body, in which she is confin'd;
So hath she not a body of her own,
But is a spirit, and *immaterial* mind. *Davies.*

Those *immaterial* felicities we expect, suggest the necessity of preparing our appetites, without which heaven can be no heaven to us. *Decay of Piety.*

No man that owns the existence of an infinite spirit can doubt of the possibility of a finite spirit; that is, such a thing as is *immaterial*, and does not contain any principle of corruption. *Tillotson's Sermons.*

2. Unimportant; without weight; impertinent; without relation. This sense has crept into the conversation and writings of barbarians; but ought to be utterly rejected.

IMMATE'RIALITY. *n. s.* [from *immaterial*.] Incorporeity; distinctness from body or matter.

When we know cogitation is the prime attribute of a spirit, we infer its *immateriality*, and thence its immortality. *Watts.*

IMMATE'RIALLY. *adv.* [from *immaterial*.] In a manner not depending upon matter.

The visible species of things strike not our senses *immaterially*; but streaming in corporal rays, do carry with them the qualities of the object from whence they flow, and the medium through which they pass. *Brown's Vulgar Errours.*

IMMATE'RIALIZED. *adj.* [from *in* and *materia*, Latin.] Distinct from matter; incorporeal.

Though assiduity in the most fixed cogitation be no trouble to *immaterialized* spirits, yet is it more than our imbodied souls can bear without lassitude. *Glanv. Sceps.*

IMMATE'RIALNESS. *n. s.* [from *immaterial*.] Distinctness from matter.

IMMATE'RIATE. *adj.* [*in* and *materia*, Latin.] Not consisting of matter; incorporeal; without body.

It is a virtue which may be called incorporeal and *immateriate*, whereof there be in nature but few. *Bacon.*

After a long enquiry of things immerse in matter, I interpose some object which is *immateriate*, or less materiate; such as this of sounds. *Bacon.*

IMMATU'RE. *adj.* [*immaturus*, Latin.]

1. Not ripe.

2. Not perfect; not arrived at fulness or completion.

The land enterprize of Panama was an ill measured and *immature* counsel; for it was grounded upon a false account, that the passages were no better fortified than Drake had left them. *Bacon.*

This is your time for faction and debate,
For partial favour, and permitted hate:
Let now your *immature* dissension cease,
Sit quiet. *Dryden.*

3. Hasty; early; come to pass before the natural time.

We are pleased, and call not that death *immature*, if a man lives 'till seventy. *Taylor's Rule of living holy.*

IMMATU'RELY. *adv.* [from *immature*.] Too soon; too early; before ripeness or completion.

IMMATU'RENESS. } *n. s.* [from *immature*.] Unripeness; in-
IMMATU'RITY. } completeness; a state short of completion.

I might reasonably expect a pardon from the ingenious for faults committed in an *immaturity* of age and judgment. *Glan.*

IMMEABI'LITY. *n. s.* [*immeabilis*, Latin.] Want of power to pass.

From this phlegm proceeds white cold tumours, viscidity, and consequently *immeability* of the juices. *Arbuthnot.*

IMME'ASUREABLE. *adj.* [*in* and *measure*.] Immense; not to be measured; indefinitely extensive.

Churches reared up to an height *immeasurable*, and adorned with far more beauty in their restoration than their founders before had given them. *Hooker.*

From the shore
They view'd the vast *immeasurable* abyss,
Outrageous as a sea, dark, wasteful, wild. *Milt. Par. Lost.*
Immeasurable strength they might behold
In me, of wisdom nothing more than mean. *Milt. Agonist.*

What a glorious show are those beings entertained with, that can see such tremendous objects wandering through those *immeasurable* depths of ether? *Addison's Guardian.*

Nor friends are there, nor vessels to convey,
Nor oars to cut th' *immeasurable* way. *Pope's Odyssey.*

IMME'ASURABLY. *adv.* [from *immeasurable.*] Immensely; beyond all measure.

The Spaniards *immeasurably* bewail their dead. *Spenser.*

There ye shall be fed, and fill'd
Immeasurably; all things shall be your prey. *Milt. Pa. Lost.*

IMMECHA'NICAL. *adj.* [*in* and *mechanical.*] Not according to the laws of mechanicks.

We have nothing to do to show any thing that is *immechanical*, or not according to the established laws of nature. *Cheyne.*

IMME'DIACY. *n. s.* [*immediateté*, French, from *immediate.*] Personal greatness; power of acting without dependance. This is a harsh word, and sense peculiar I believe to *Shakespeare.*

He led our pow'rs,
Bore the commission of my place and person;
The which *immediacy* may well stand up,
And call itself your brother. *Shakes. King Lear.*

IMME'DIATE. *adj.* [*immediat*, French; *in* and *medius*, Latin.]

1. Being in such a state with respect to something else as that there is nothing between them; proximate; with nothing intervening.

Moses mentions the *immediate* causes, the rains and the waters; and St. Peter mentions the more remote and fundamental causes, that constitution of the heavens. *Burnet.*

2. Not acting by second causes.

It is much to be ascribed to the *immediate* will of God, who giveth and taketh away beauty at his pleasure. *Abbot.*

3. Instant; present with regard to time. *Prior* therefore should not have written *more* immediate.

Immediate are my needs, and my relief
Must not be tost and turn'd to me in words,
But find supply *immediate.* *Shakesp. Timon.*

Death denounc'd that day,
Which he presumes already vain, and void,
Because not yet inflicted, as he fear'd,
By some *immediate* stroke. *Milton's Paradise Lost.*

But she, howe'er of vict'ry sure,
Contemns the wreath too long delay'd;
And arm'd with more *immediate* pow'r,
Calls cruel silence to her aid. *Prior.*

IMME'DIATELY. *adv.* [from *immediate.*]

1. Without the intervention of any other cause or event.

God's acceptance of it, either *immediately* by himself, or mediately by the hands of the bishop, is that which vests the whole property of a thing in God. *South's Sermons.*

2. Instantly; at the time present; without delay.

Her father hath commanded her to slip
Away with Slender, and with him at Eaton
Immediately to marry. *Shakesp. Merry Wives of Windsor.*

IMME'DIATENESS. *n. s.* [from *immediate.*]

1. Presence with regard to time.
2. Exemption from second or intervening causes.

IMME'DICABLE. *adj.* [*immedicabilis*, Latin.] Not to be healed; incurable.

My griefs ferment and rage,
Nor less than wounds *immedicable*,
Rankle and fester, and gangrene
To black mortification. *Milton's Agonistes.*

IMME'MORABLE. *adj.* [*immemorabilis*, Latin.] Not worth remembering.

IMMEMO'RIAL. *adj.* [*immemorial*, French; *in* and *memoria*, Latin.] Past time of memory; so ancient that the beginning cannot be traced.

By a long *immemorial* practice, and prescription of an aged thorough-paced hypocrisy, they come to believe that for a reality, which, at first practice of it, they themselves knew to be a cheat. *South's Sermons.*

All the laws of this kingdom have some memorials in writing, yet all have not their original in writing; for some obtained their force by *immemorial* usage or custom. *Hale.*

IMME'NSE. *adj.* [*immense*, Fr. *immensus*, Lat.] Unlimited; unbounded; infinite.

O goodness infinite! goodness *immense*!
That all this good of evil shall produce! *Milt. Parad Lost.*

As infinite duration hath no relation unto motion and time, so infinite or *immense* essence hath no relation unto body; but is a thing distinct from all corporeal magnitude, which we mean when we speak of immensity, and of God as of an *immense* being. *Grew's Cosmol.*

IMME'NSELY. *adv.* [from *immense.*] Infinitely; without measure.

We shall find that the void space of our system is *immensely* bigger than all its corporeal mass. *Bentley's Sermons.*

IMME'NSITY. *n. s.* [*immensité*, French.] Unbounded greatness; infinity.

By the power we find in ourselves of repeating, as often as we will, any idea of space, we get the idea of *immensity. Locke.*

He that will consider the *immensity* of this fabrick, and the great variety that is to be found in this inconsiderable part of it which he has to do with, may think that in other mansions of it there may be other and different intelligent beings. *Locke.*

All these illustrious worlds,
And millions which the glass can ne'er descry,
Lost in the wilds of vast *immensity*,
Are suns, are centers. *Blackmore's Creation.*

IMMENSURABI'LITY. *n. s.* [from *immensurable.*] Impossibility to be measured.

IMME'NSURABLE. *adj.* [*in* and *mensurabilis*, Latin.] Not to be measured.

To IMME'RGE. *v. a.* [*immergo*, Latin.] To put under water.

IMME'RIT. *n. s.* [*immerito*, Latin.] Want of worth; want of desert.

When I receive your lines, and find there expressions of a passion, reason and my own *immerit* tell me it must not be for me. *Suckling.*

IMME'RSE. *adj.* [*immersus*, Latin.] Buried; covered; sunk deep.

After long inquiry of things *immerse* in matter, I interpose some object which is immateriate, or less materiate; such as this of sounds, that the intellect may become not partial. *Bac.*

To IMME'RSE. *v. a.* [*immersus*, Latin.]

1. To put under water.
2. To sink or cover deep.

He stood
More than a mile *immers'd* within the wood;
At once the wind was laid. *Dryden.*

They observed that they were *immersed* in their rocks, quarries, and mines, in the same manner as they are at this day found in all known parts of the world. *Woodw. Nat. History.*

3. To keep in a state of intellectual depression.

It is a melancholy reflection, that our country, which, in times of popery, was called the nation of saints, should now have less appearance of religion in it than any other neighbouring state or kingdom; whether they be such as continue still *immersed* in the errours of the church of Rome, or such as are recovered out of them. *Addison's Freeholder.*

We are prone to engage ourselves with the business, the pleasures, and the amusements of this world: we give ourselves up too greedily to the pursuit, and *immerse* ourselves too deeply in the enjoyment of them. *Atterbury's Sermons.*

It is impossible for a man to have a lively hope in another life, and yet be deeply *immersed* in the enjoyments of this. *Atterbury's Sermons.*

IMME'RSION. *n. s.* [*immersio*, Latin; *immersion*, French.]

1. The act of putting any body into a fluid below the surface.

Achilles's mother is said to have dipped him, when he was a child, in the river Styx, which made him invulnerable all over, excepting that part which the mother held in her hand during this *immersion.* *Addison's Guardian.*

2. The state of sinking below the surface of a fluid.
3. The state of being overwhelmed or lost in any respect.

There are many persons, who, through the heat of their lusts and passions, through the contagion of ill example, or too deep an *immersion* in the affairs of life, swerve from the rules of their holy faith; and yet would, upon extraordinary warning, be brought to comply with them. *Atterbury.*

IMMETHO'DICAL. *adj.* [*in* and *methodical.*] Confused; being without regularity; being without method.

M. Bayle compares the answering of an *immethodical* author to the hunting of a duck: when you have him full in your sight he gives you the slip, and becomes invisible. *Addis.*

IMMETHO'DICALLY. *adv.* [from *immethodical.*] Without method.

I'MMINENCE. *n. s.* [from *imminent.*] Any ill impending; immediate or near danger. A word not in use.

I do not speak of flight, of fear, of death;
But dare all *imminence*, that gods and men
Address their dangers in. *Shakesp. Troilus and Cressida.*

I'MMINENT. *adj.* [*imminent*, Fr. *imminens*, Lat.] Impending; at hand; threatning. Always in an ill sense.

What dangers at any time are *imminent*, what evils hang over our heads, God doth know, and not we. *Hooker.*

Three times to-day
You have defended me from *imminent* death. *Shakes. H. VI.*

These she applies for warnings and portents
Of evils *imminent*; and on her knee
Hath begg'd, that I will stay at home to-day. *Shakespeare.*

To them preach'd
Conversion and repentance, as to souls
In prison, under judgments *imminent.* *Milton's Par. Lost.*

Men could not sail without *imminent* danger and inconveniences. *Pope.*

To IMMI'NGLE. *v. a.* [*in* and *mingle.*] To mingle; to mix; to unite.

Some

Some of us, like thee, through stormy life
Toil'd, tempest-beaten, ere we could attain
This holy calm, this harmony of mind,
Where purity and peace immingle charms. *Thoms. Summer.*

IMMINU'TION. *n. s.* [from *imminuo*, Latin.] Diminution; decrease.

These revolutions are as exactly uniform as the earth's are, which could not be, were there any place for chance, and did not a providence continually oversee and secure them from all alteration or *imminution*. *Ray on the Creation.*

IMMISCIBI'LITY. *n. s.* [from *immiscible.*] Incapacity of being mingled.

IMMI'SCIBLE. *adj.* [*in* and *miscible.*] Not capable of being mingled. *Clarissa.*

IMMI'SSION. *n. s.* [*immissio*, Latin.] The act of sending in; contrary to emission.

To IMMI'T. *v. n.* [*immitto*, Latin.] To send in.

To IMMI'X. *v. a.* [*in* and *mix.*] To mingle.

Samson, with these *immixt*, inevitably
Pull'd down the same destruction on himself. *Milton.*

IMMI'XABLE. *adj.* [*in* and *mix*] Impossible to be mingled.

Fill a glass sphere with such liquors as may be clear, of the same colour, and *immixable*. *Wilkins.*

IMMOBI'LITY. *n. s.* [*immobilité*, French, from *immobilis*, Latin.] Unmoveableness; want of motion; resistance to motion.

The course of fluids through the vascular solids must in time harden the fibres, and abolish many of the canals; from whence driness, weakness, *immobility*, and debility of the vital force. *Arbuthnot on Aliments.*

IMMO'DERATE. *adj.* [*immoderé*, Fr. *immoderatus*, Latin.] Excessive; exceeding the due mean.

One means, very effectual for the preservation of health, is a quiet and chearful mind, not afflicted with violent passions, or distracted with *immoderate* cares. *Ray on the Creation.*

IMMO'DERATELY. *adv.* [from *immoderate.*] In an excessive degree.

Immoderately she weeps for Tybalt's death. *Shakespeare.*

It weakened more and more the arch of the earth, sucking out the moisture that was the cement of its parts, drying it *immoderately*, and chapping it. *Burnet's Theory of the Earth.*

IMMODERA'TION. *n. s.* [*immoderation*, Fr. from *immoderate.*] Want of moderation; excess.

IMMO'DEST. *adj.* [*immodeste*, French; *in* and *modest.*]

1. Wanting shame; wanting delicacy or chastity.

She railed at herself, that she should be so *immodest* to write to one that she knew would flout her. *Shakespeare.*

2. Unchaste; impure.

Immodest deeds you hinder to be wrought;
But we proscribe the least *immodest* thought. *Dryden.*

3. Obscene.

'Tis needful that the most *immodest* word
Be look'd upon, and learn'd; which once attain'd,
Comes to no farther use
But to be known and hated. *Shakespeare's Henry IV.*

4. Unreasonable; exorbitant; arrogant.

IMMO'DESTY. *n. s.* [*immodestie*, French, from *immodest.*] Want of modesty; indecency.

It was a piece of *immodesty*. *Pope.*

To IMMOLATE. *v. a.* [*immolo*, Latin; *immoler*, French.] To sacrifice; to kill in sacrifice.

These courtiers of applause being oftentimes reduced to live in want, these costly trifles so ingrossing all that they can spare, that they frequently enough are forced to *immolate* their own desires to their vanity. *Boyle.*

Now *immolate* the tongues, and mix the wine,
Sacred to Neptune and the powers divine. *Pope's Odyssey.*

IMMOLA'TION. *n. s.* [*immolation*, French, from *immolate.*]

1. The act of sacrificing.

In the picture of the *immolation* of Isaac, or Abraham sacrificing his son, Isaac is described as a little boy. *Brown.*

2. A sacrifice offered.

We make more barbarous *immolations* than the most savage heathens. *Decay of Piety.*

IMMO'MENT. *adj.* [*in* and *moment.*] Trifling; of no importance or value. A barbarous word.

I some lady-trifles have reserv'd,
Immoment toys, things of such dignity
As we greet modern friends withal. *Shakesp. Ant. and Cleop.*

IMMO'RAL. *adj.* [*in* and *moral.*] Wanting regard to the laws of natural religion; contrary to honesty; dishonest.

IMMORA'LITY. *n. s.* [from *immoral.*] Dishonesty; want of virtue; contrariety to virtue.

Such men are put into the commission of the peace who encourage the grossest *immoralities*, to whom all the bawds of the ward pay contribution. *Swift.*

IMMO'RTAL. *adj.* [*immortalis*, Latin.]

1. Exempt from death; never to die.

To the king eternal, *immortal*, invisible, the only wise God, be glory for ever. *Tim.* i. 17.

Her body sleeps in Capulet's monument,
And her *immortal* part with angels lives. *Shak. Ro. and Jul.*

There was an opinion in gross, that the soul was *immortal*. *Abbot's Description of the World.*

The Paphian queen,
With gored hand, and veil so rudely torn,
Like terror did among th' *immortals* breed,
Taught by her wound that goddesses may bleed. *Waller.*

2. Never ending; perpetual.

Give me my robe, put on my crown: I have
Immortal longings in me. *Shakes. Ant. and Cleopatra.*

IMMORTA'LITY. *n. s.* [*immortalité*, Fr. from *immortal.*] Exemption from death; life never to end.

This corruptible shall put on incorruption, and this mortal, *immortality*. *Corinth.*

Quaff *immortality* and joy. *Milton.*

He th' *immortality* of souls proclaim'd,
Whom th' oracle of men the wisest nam'd. *Denham.*

His existence will of itself continue for ever, unless it be destroyed; which is impossible, from the immutability of God, and the nature of his *immortality*. *Cheyne's Phil. Princ.*

When we know cogitation is the prime attribute of a spirit, we infer its immateriality, and thence its *immortality*. *Watts.*

IMMO'RTALLY. *adv.* [from the adjective.] So as never to die.

To IMMO'RTALIZE. *v. a.* [*immortaliser*, French, from *immortal.*] To make immortal; to perpetuate; to exempt from death.

Drive them from Orleans, and be *immortaliz'd*. *Shakesp.*

For mortal things desire their like to breed,
That so they may their kind *immortalize*. *Davies.*

To IMMO'RTALIZE. *v. n.* To become immortal. This word is, I think, peculiar to *Pope*.

Fix the year precise,
When British bards begin t' *immortalize*. *Pope.*

IMMO'RTALLY. *adv.* [from *immortal.*] With exemption from death; without end.

There is your crown;
And he that wears the crown *immortally*,
Long guard it yours! *Shakesp. Henry IV.*

What pity 'tis that he cannot wallow *immortally* in his sensual pleasures! *Bentley's Sermons.*

IMMO'VABLE. *adj.* [*in* and *moveable.*]

1. Not to be forced from its place.

We shall not question his removing the earth, when he finds an *immovable* base to place his engine upon. *Brown.*

2. Not liable to be carried away; real in law.

When an executor meddles with the *immovable* estate, before he has seized on the moveable goods, it may be then appealed from the execution of sentence. *Ayliffe's Parergon.*

3. Unshaken; unaffected.

How much happier is he, who, centring on himself, remains *immovable*, and smiles at the madness of the dance about him! *Dryden's Don Sebastian.*

IMMO'VABLY. *adv.* [from *immovable.*] In a state not to be shaken.

Immovably firm to their duty, when they could have no prospect of reward. *Atterbury's Sermons.*

IMMU'NITY. *n. s.* [*immunité*, French; *immunitas*, Latin.]

1. Discharge from any obligation.

Of things harmless whatsoever there is, which the whole church doth observe, to argue for any man's *immunity* from observing the same, it were a point of most insolent madness. *Hooker.*

2. Privilege; exemption.

Granting great *immunities* to the commons, they prevailed so far as to cause Palladius to be proclaimed successor. *Sidney.*

Simon sent to Demetrius, to the end he should give the land an *immunity*, because all that Tryphon did was to spoil. 1 *Mac.* xiii. 34.

The laity invidiously aggravate the rights and *immunities* of the clergy. *Sprat's Sermons.*

3. Freedom.

Common apprehensions entertain the antidotal condition of Ireland, conceiving only in that land an *immunity* from venomous creatures. *Brown's Vulgar Errours.*

But this annex'd condition of the crown,
Immunity from errors, you disown. *Dryden.*

To IMMU'RE. *v. a.* [*in* and *murus*, Lat. *emmurer*, old French, so that it might be written *emmure.*] To inclose within walls; to confine; to shut up; to imprison.

Pity, you ancient stones, these tender babes,
Whom envy hath *immur'd* within your walls! *Shak. R. III.*

One of these three contains her heav'nly picture;
And shall I think in silver she's *immur'd*! *Shakespeare.*

At the first descent on shore he was not *immured* with a wooden vessel, but he did countenance the landing in his long-boat. *Wotton.*

Lysimachus *immured* it with a wall. *Sandys's Travels.*

Though a foul foolish prison her *immure*
On earth, she, when escap'd, is wise and pure. *Denham.*

IMMU'RE. *n. s.* [from the verb.] A wall; an inclosure, as in *Shakespeare*.

Their vow is made
To ransack Troy; within whose strong *immures*
The ravish'd Helen, Menelaus' queen,
With wanton Paris sleeps. *Shakespeare.*

IMMU'SICAL.

IMMU'SICAL. *adj.* [*in* and *muſical.*] Unmuſical; inharmonious.

All ſounds are either muſical, which are ever equal, or *immuſical*, which are ever unequal, as the voice in ſpeaking, and whiſperings. *Bacon's Natural Hiſtory.*

When we conſider the *immuſical* note of all ſwans we ever beheld or heard of, we cannot conſent. *Brown.*

IMMUTABI'LITY. *n. ſ.* [*immutabilitas*, Lat. *immutabilité*, Fr. from *immutable.*] Exemption from change; invariableneſs; unchangeableneſs.

The *immutability* of God they ſtrive unto, by working after one and the ſame manner. *Hooker.*

His exiſtence will of itſelf continue for ever, unleſs it be deſtroyed; which is impoſſible, from the *immutability* of God. *Cheyne's Phil. Princ.*

IMMU'TABLE. *adj.* [*immutabilis*, Latin.] Unchangeable; invariable; unalterable.

By two *immutable* things, in which it was impoſſible for God to lye, we have a ſtrong conſolation. *Heb.* vi.

Thy threat'nings, Lord, as thine, thou may'ſt revoke;
But if *immutable* and fix'd they ſtand,
Continue ſtill thyſelf to give the ſtroke,
And let not foreign foes oppreſs thy land. *Dryden.*

IMMU'TABLY. *adv.* [from *immutable.*] Unalterably; invariably; unchangeably.

His love is like his eſſence, *immutably* eternal. *Boyle.*

IMP. *n. ſ.* [*imp*, Welſh, a ſhoot, a ſprout, a ſprig.]

1. A ſon; the offſpring; progeny.

That noble *imp* your ſon. *Lord Cromwel to King Henry.*

And thou, moſt dreaded *imp* of higheſt Jove,
Fair Venus' ſon. *Fairy Queen, b.* i.

The tender *imp* was weaned from the teat. *Fairfax.*

A lad of life, an *imp* of fame. *Shakeſp. Henry* V.

2. A ſubaltern devil; a puny devil. In this ſenſe 'tis ſtill retained.

Such we deny not to be the *imps* and limbs of Satan. *Hook.*

Him after long debate, irreſolute
Of thoughts revolv'd, his final ſentence choſe,
Fit veſſel, fitteſt *imp* of fraud, in whom
To enter, and his dark ſuggeſtions hide
From ſharpeſt ſight. *Milt. Paradiſe Loſt, b.* ix.

As ſoon as you can hear his knell,
This god on earth turns d——l in hell;
And, lo! his miniſters of ſtate,
Transform'd to *imps*, his levee wait. *Swift.*

To IMP. *v. a.* [*impio*, to engraff, Welſh.] To lengthen or enlarge with any thing adſcititious.

If then we ſhall ſhake off our ſlaviſh yoke,
Imp out our drooping country's broken wings. *Shak. R.* II.

New rebellions raiſe
Their hydra heads, and the falſe North diſplays
Her broken league to *imp* her ſerpent wings. *Milton.*

Help, ye tart ſatyriſts, to *imp* my rage,
With all the ſcorpions that ſhould whip this age. *Cleavel.*

With cord and canvas from rich Hamburgh ſent,
His navy's molted wings he *imps* once more. *Dryden.*

New creatures riſe,
A moving maſs at firſt, and ſhort of thighs;
'Till ſhooting out with legs, and *imp'd* with wings,
The grubs proceed to bees with pointed ſtings. *Dryden.*

The Mercury of heav'n, with ſilver wings
Impt for the flight, to overtake his ghoſt. *Southern.*

To IMPA'CT. *v. a.* [*impactus*, Latin.] To drive cloſe or hard.

They are angular; but of what particular figure is not eaſy to determine, becauſe of their being *impacted* ſo thick and confuſedly together. *Woodward on Foſſils.*

To IMPA'INT. *v. a.* [*in* and *paint.*] To paint; to decorate with colours. Not in uſe.

Never yet did inſurrection want
Such water-colours to *impaint* his cauſe. *Shakeſp. H.* VI.

To IMPA'IR. *v. a.* [*empirer*, to make worſe, French. *Skinner.*] To diminiſh; to injure; to make worſe; to leſſen in quantity, value, or excellence.

To change any ſuch law, muſt needs, with the common ſort, *impair* and weaken the force of thoſe grounds whereby all laws are made effectual. *Hooker.*

Objects divine
Muſt needs *impair*, and weary human ſenſe. *Milt. Pa. Loſt.*

That ſoon refreſh'd him weary'd, and repair'd
What hunger, if aught hunger had *impair'd*,
Or thirſt. *Milton's Paradiſe Regain'd.*

Nor was the work *impair'd* by ſtorms alone,
But felt th' approaches of too warm a ſun. *Pope.*

In years he ſeem'd, but not *impair'd* by years. *Pope.*

To IMPA'IR. *v. n.* To be leſſened or worn out.

Fleſh may *impair*, quoth he; but reaſon can repair. *F. Q.*

IMPA'IR. *n. ſ.* [from the verb.] Diminution; decreaſe.

A loadſtone, kept in undue poſition, that is, not lying on the meridian, or with its poles inverted, receives in longer time *impair* in activity and exchange of faces, and is more powerfully preſerved by ſite than duſt of ſteel. *Brown.*

IMPA'IRMENT. *n. ſ.* [from *impair.*] Diminution; injury.

His poſterity, at this diſtance, and after ſo perpetual *impairment*, cannot but condemn the poverty of Adam's conception, that thought to obſcure himſelf from his Creator in the ſhade of the garden. *Brown's Vulgar Errours, b.* i.

IMPA'LPABLE. *adj.* [*impalpable*, Fr. *in* and *palpable.*] Not to be perceived by touch.

If beaten into an *impalpable* powder, when poured out, it will emulate a liquor, by reaſon that the ſmalneſs of the parts do make them eaſy to be put into motion. *Boyle.*

To IMPA'RADISE. *v. a.* [*imparadiſare*, Italian.] To put in a place or ſtate reſembling paradiſe in felicity.

This *imparadiſed* neighbourhood made Zelmane's ſoul cleave unto her, both through the ivory caſe of her body, and the apparel which did over-cloud it. *Sidney, b.* ii.

All my ſouls be
Imparadis'd in you, in whom alone
I underſtand, and grow, and ſee. *Donne.*

Thus theſe two,
Imparadis'd in one another's arms,
The happier Eden, ſhall enjoy their fill
Of bliſs on bliſs. *Milton's Paradiſe Loſt.*

IMPA'RITY. *n. ſ.* [*imparitas*, *impar*, Latin.]

1. Inequality; diſproportion.

Some bodies are hard, ſome ſoft: the hardneſs is cauſed chiefly by the jejuneneſs of the ſpirits, and their *imparity* with the tangible parts. *Bacon.*

2. Oddneſs; indiviſibility into equal parts.

What verity is there in that numeral conceit, in the lateral diviſion of man, by even and odd; and ſo by parity or *imparity* of letters in mens names, to determine misfortunes on either ſide of their bodies? *Brown's Vulgar Errours.*

To IMPA'RK. *v. a.* [*in* and *park.*] To incloſe with a park; to ſever from a common.

To IMPA'RT. *v. a.* [*impartior*, Latin.]

1. To grant; to give.

High ſtate and honours to others *impart*,
But give me your heart. *Dryden.*

2. To communicate.

Gentle lady,
When firſt I did *impart* my love to you,
I freely told you, all the wealth I had
Ran in my veins. *Shakeſ. Merch. of Venice.*

As in confeſſion the revealing is for the eaſe of a man's heart, ſo ſecret men come to the knowledge of many things, while men rather diſcharge than *impart* their minds. *Bacon.*

Thou to me thy thoughts
Waſt wont, I mine to thee was wont t' *impart.* *Milt. P. L.*

I find thee knowing of thyſelf;
Expreſſing well the ſpirit within thee free,
My image, not *imparted* to the brute. *Milt. Par. Loſt.*

IMPA'RTIAL. *adj.* [*impartial*, Fr. *in* and *partial.*] Equitable; free from regard to party; indifferent; diſintereſted; equal in diſtribution of juſtice; juſt. It is uſed as well of actions as perſons.

Succeſs I hope, and fate I cannot fear:
Alive or dead, I ſhall deſerve a name;
Jove is *impartial*, and to both the ſame. *Dryden's Æn.*

IMPARTIA'LITY. [*n. ſ.* [*impartialité*, French; from *impartial.*] Equitableneſs; juſtice.

A pious and well diſpoſed will gives not only diligence, but alſo *impartiality* to the underſtanding in its ſearch into religion, which is abſolutely neceſſary to give ſucceſs unto our inquiries into truth; it being ſcarce poſſible for that man to hit the mark, whoſe eye is ſtill glancing upon ſomething beſide it. *South's Sermons.*

IMPA'RTIALLY. *adv.* [from *impartial.*] Equitably; with indifferent and unbiaſſed judgment; without regard to party or intereſt; juſtly; honeſtly.

Since the Scripture promiſes eternal happineſs and pardon of ſin, upon the ſole condition of faith and ſincere obedience, it is evident, that he only can plead a title to ſuch a pardon, whoſe conſcience *impartially* tells him that he has performed the required condition. *South's Sermons.*

IMPA'RTIBLE. *adj.* [*impartible*, Fr. from *impart.*] Communicable; to be conferred or beſtowed. This word is elegant, though uſed by few writers.

The ſame body may be conceived to be more or leſs *impartible* than it is active or heavy. *Digby.*

IMPA'SSABLE. *adj.* [*in* and *paſſable.*] Not to be paſſed; not admitting paſſage; impervious.

There are in America many high and *impaſſable* mountains, which are very rich. *Raleigh.*

Over this gulf
Impaſſable, impervious; let us try,
To found a path from hell to that new world. *Milton.*

When Alexander would have paſſed the Ganges, he was told by the Indians that all beyond it was either *impaſſable* marſhes, or ſandy deſarts. *Temple.*

IMPASSIBI'LITY. *n. ſ.* [*impaſſibilité*, Fr. from *impaſſible.*] Exemption from ſuffering; inſuſceptibility of injury from external things.

Two divinities might have pleaded their prerogative of *impassibility*, or at least not have been wounded by any mortal hand. *Dryden's Æn. Dedicat.*

IMPA'SSIBLE. *adj.* [*impassible*, Fr. *in* and *passio*, Latin] Incapable of suffering; exempt from the agency of external causes; exempt from pain.

If the upper soul check what is consented to by the will, in compliance with the flesh, and can then hope that, after a few years of sensuality, that rebellious servant shall be eternally cast off, drop into a perpetual *impassible* nothing, take a long progress into a land where all things are forgotten, this would be some colour. *Hammond.*

Secure of death, I should contemn thy dart,
Though naked, and *impassible* depart *Dryden.*

IMPA'SSIBLENESS. *n. s.* [from *impassible.*] Impassibility; exemption from pain.

How shameless a partiality is it, thus to reserve all the sensualities of this world, and yet cry out for the *impassibleness* of the next? *Decay of Piety.*

IMPA'SSIONED. *adj.* [*in* and *passion.*] Seized with passion.

So, standing, moving, or to height upgrown,
The tempter, all *impassion'd*, thus began. *Milt. Par. Lost.*

IMPA'SSIVE. *adj.* [*in* and *passive.*] Exempt from the agency of external causes.

She told him what those empty phantoms were,
Forms without bodies, and *impassive* air. *Dryden's Æn.*
Pale suns, unfelt at distance, roll away;
And on th' *impassive* ice the lightnings play. *Pope.*

IMPA'STED. *adj.* [*in* and *paste.*] Covered as with paste.

Horridly trickt
With blood of fathers, mothers, daughters, sons,
Bak'd and *impasted* with the parching fires. *Shakesp. Hamlet.*

IMPA'TIENCE. *n. s.* [*impatience*, Fr. *impatientia*, Latin.]

1. Inability to suffer pain; rage under suffering.

All the power of his wits has given way to his *impatience*.
Shakespeare's King Lear.

The experiment I resolved to make was upon thought, and not rashness or *impatience*. *Temple.*

2. Vehemence of temper; heat of passion.

3 Inability to suffer delay; eagerness.

IMPA'TIENT. *adj.* [*impatient*, Fr. *impatiens*, Latin.]

1. Not able to endure; incapable to bear.

Fame, *impatient* of extremes, decays
Not more by envy than excess of praise. *Pope.*

2. Furious with pain; unable to bear pain.

The tortur'd savage turns around,
And flings about his foam, *impatient* of the wound. *Dryden.*

3. Vehemently agitated by some painful passion.

To be *impatient* at the death of a person, concerning whom it was certain he must die, is to mourn because thy friend was not born an angel. *Taylor's Rule of living holy.*

The *impatient* man will not give himself time to be informed of the matter that lies before him. *Addison's Spectator.*

4. Eager; ardently desirous; not able to endure delay.

The mighty Cæsar waits his vital hour,
Impatient for the world, and grasps his promis'd pow'r. *Dry.*
On the seas prepar'd the vessel stands;
Th' *impatient* mariner thy speed demands. *Pope's Odyssey.*

IMPA'TIENTLY. *adv.* [from *impatient.*]

1. Passionately; ardently.

He considered one thing so *impatiently*, that he would not admit any thing else to be worth consideration. *Clarendon.*

2. Eagerly; with great desire.

To IMPA'TRONIZE. *v. a.* [*impatroniser*, Fr. *in* and *patronize.*] To gain to one's self the power of any seigniory. This word is not usual.

The ambition of the French king was to *impatronize* himself of the dutchy. *Bacon's Henry* VII.

To IMPA'WN. *v. a.* [*in* and *pawn.*] To impignorate; to pawn; to give as a pledge; to pledge.

Go to the king, and let there be *impawn'd*
Some surety for a safe return again. *Shakesp. Henry* IV.
Many now in health
Shall drop their blood, in approbation
Of what your reverence shall invite us to;
Therefore take heed how you *impawn* our person,
How you awake our sleeping sword of war. *Shakesp. H.* V.

To IMPE'ACH. *v. a.* [*empecher*, French.]

1. To hinder; to impede This sense is little in use.

Each door he opened without any breach;
There was no bar to stop, nor foe him to *impeach*.
Fairy Queen.

These ungracious practices of his sons did *impeach* his journey to the Holy Land, and vexed him all the days of his life. *Davies.*

If they will *impeach* the purposes of an army, which they have no reason to think themselves able to resist, they put themselves out of all expectation of mercy. *Hayward.*

A defluxion on my throat *impeached* my utterance. *Howel.*

2. To accuse by publick authority.

They were both *impeached* by a house of commons. *Addison.*

Great dissentions were kindled between the nobles and commons on account of Coriolanus, whom the latter had *impeached.* *Swift.*

IMPE'ACH. *n. s.* [from the verb.] Hindrance; let; impediment.

Why, what an intricate *impeach* is this?
If here you hous'd him, here he would have been;
If he were mad, he would not plead so coldly. *Shakespeare.*

IMPEA'CHABLE. *adj.* [from *impeach.*] Accusable; chargeable.

Had God omitted by positive laws to give religion to the world, the wisdom of his providence had been *impeachable.* *Grew's Cosmol.*

IMPE'ACHER. *n. s.* [from *impeach.*] An accuser; one who brings an accusation against another.

Many of our fiercest *impeachers* would leave the delinquent to the merciful indulgence of a Saviour. *Gov. of the Tongue.*

IMPE'ACHMENT. *n. s.* [from *impeach.*]

1. Hindrance; let; impediment; obstruction. Not in use.

Tell us what things, during your late continuance there, are most offensive, and the greatest *impeachment* to the good government thereof. *Spenser on Ireland.*

Turn thee back,
And tell thy king I do not seek him now;
But could be willing to march on to Calais,
Without *impeachment.* *Shakesp. Henry* V.

Neither is this accession of necessity any *impeachment* to Christian liberty, or ensnaring of mens consciences. *Sanders.*

2. Publick accusation; charge preferred.

The king, provok'd to it by the queen,
Devis'd *impeachments* to imprison him. *Shak. Rich.* III.

The lord Somers, though his accusers would gladly have dropped their *impeachment*, was instant with them for the prosecution. *Addison.*

The consequences of Coriolanus's *impeachment* had like to have been fatal to their state. *Swift.*

To IMPE'ARL. *v. a.* [*in* and *pearl.*]

1. To form in resemblance of pearls.

Innumerable as the stars of night,
Or stars of morning, dewdrops, which the sun
Impearls on every leaf, and ev'ry flow'r. *Milton's Par. Lost.*

2. To decorate as with pearls.

The dews of the morning *impearl* every thorn, and scatter diamonds on the verdant mantle of the earth. *Digby to Pope.*

IMPECCABI'LITY. *n. s.* [*impeccabilité*, Fr. from *impeccable.*] Exemption from sin; exemption from failure.

Infallibility and *impeccability* are two of his attributes. *Pope.*

IMPE'CCABLE. *adj.* [*impeccable*, French; *in* and *pecco*, Latin.] Exempt from possibility of sin.

That man pretends he never commits any act prohibited by the word of God, and then that were a rare charm to render him *impeccable*, or that is the means of consecrating every sin of his. *Hammond on Fundamentals.*

To IMPE'DE. *v. a.* [*impedio*, Latin.] To hinder; to let; to obstruct.

All the forces are mustered to *impede* its passage.
Decay of Piety.

The way is open, and no stop to force
The stars return, or to *impede* their course. *Creech.*

IMPE'DIMENT. *n. s.* [*impedimentum*, Latin.] Hindrance; let; impeachment; obstruction; opposition.

The minds of beasts grudge not at their bodies comfort, nor are their senses letted from enjoying their objects: we have the *impediments* of honour, and the torments of conscience. *Sidney.*

What *impediments* there are to hinder it, and which were the speediest way to remove them. *Hooker.*

The life is led most happily wherein all virtue is exercised without *impediment* or let. *Hooker.*

They bring one that was deaf, and had an *impediment* in his speech. *Mar.* vii. 32.

But for my tears,
The moist *impediments* unto my speech,
I had forestall'd this dear and deep rebuke. *Shakesp. H.* IV.
May I never
To this good purpose, that so fairly shews,
Dream of *impediment.* *Shakesp. Ant. and Cleopatra.*
Free from th' *impediments* of light and noise,
Man, thus retir'd, his nobler thoughts employs. *Waller.*

Fear is the greatest *impediment* to martyrdom; and he that is overcome by little arguments of pain, will hardly consent to lose his life with torments. *Taylor's Rule of living holy.*

To IMPE'L. *v. a.* [*impello*, Latin.] To drive on towards a point; to urge forward; to press on.

So Myrrha's mind, *impell'd* on either side,
Takes ev'ry bent, but cannot long abide. *Dryden's Ovid.*
The surge *impell'd* me on a craggy coast. *Pope.*
Propitious gales
Attend thy voyage, and *impel* thy sails. *Pope's Odyssey.*
A mightier pow'r the strong direction sends,
And sev'ral men *impels* to sev'ral ends;
This drives them constant to a certain coast. *Pope.*

IMPE'LLENT. *n. s.* [*impellens*, Latin.] An impulsive power; a power that drives forward.

How

How such a variety of motions should be regularly managed, in such a wilderness of passages, by mere blind *impellents* and material conveyances, I have not the least conjecture. *Glanv.*

To IMPE'ND. *v. n.* [*impendeo*, Lat.] To hang over; to be at hand; to press nearly.

It expresses our deep sorrow for our past sins, and our lively sense of God's *impending* wrath. *Smalridge's Sermons.*

Destruction sure o'er all your heads *impends*;
Ulysses comes, and death his steps attends. *Pope's Odyssey.*
No story I unfold of publick woes,
Nor bear advices of *impending* foes. *Pope's Odyssey.*

IMPE'NDENT. *adj.* [*impendens*, Latin.] Imminent; hanging over; pressing closely.

If the evil feared or *impendent* be a greater sensible evil than the good, it over-rules the appetite to aversation. *Hale.*

Dreadful in arms, on Landen's glorious plain
Place Ormond's duke: *impendent* in the air
Let his keen sabre, comet-like, appear. *Prior.*

IMPE'NDENCE. *n. s.* [from *impendent.*] The state of hanging over; near approach.

Though it be good, yet sometimes it is not safe to be attempted, by reason of the *impendence* of a greater sensible evil. *Hale's Origin of Mankind.*

IMPENETRABI'LITY. *n. s.* [*impenetrabilité*, Fr. from *impenetrable.*]

1. Quality of not being pierceable.

All bodies, so far as experience reaches, are either hard or may be hardened; and we have no other evidence of universal *impenetrability*, besides a large experience, without an experimental exception. *Newton's Opt.*

2. Insusceptibility of intellectual impression.

IMPE'NETRABLE. *adj.* [*impenetrable*, Fr. *impenetrabilis*, Lat.]

1. Not to be pierced; not to be entered by any external force.

With hard'ning cold, and forming heat,
The cyclops did their strokes repeat,
Before th' *impenetrable* shield was wrought. *Dryden.*

2. Impervious; not admitting entrance.

Deep into some thick covert would I run,
Impenetrable to the stars or sun. *Dryden.*

The mind frights itself with any thing reflected on in gross: things, thus offered to the mind, carry the shew of nothing but difficulty in them, and are thought to be wrapped up in *impenetrable* obscurity. *Locke.*

3. Not to be taught; not to be informed.

4. Not to be affected; not to be moved.

It is the most *impenetrable* cur
That ever kept with men.
——Let him alone;
I'll follow him no more with bootless prayers. *Shakespeare.*

Some will never believe a proposition in divinity, if any thing can be said against it: they will be credulous in all affairs of life, but *impenetrable* by a sermon of the gospel. *Taylor.*

IMPE'NETRABLY. *adv.* [from *impenetrable.*] With hardness to a degree incapable of impression.

Blunt the sense, and fit it for a skull
Of solid proof, *impenetrably* dull. *Pope's Dunciad.*

IMPE'NITENCE. } *n. s.* [*impenitence*, Fr. *in* and *penitence.*] Obduracy; want of remorse for crimes; final disregard of God's threatenings or mercy.
IMPE'NITENCY. }

Where one man ever comes to repent, a thousand end their days in final *impenitence*. *South's Sermons.*

Before the revelation of the gospel the wickedness and *impenitency* of the heathens was a much more excuseable thing, because they were in a great measure ignorant of the rewards of another life. *Tillotson's Sermons.*

He will advance from one degree of wickedness and *impenitence* to another, 'till at last he becomes hardened without remorse. *Rogers's Sermons.*

IMPE'NITENT. *adj.* [*impenitent*, Fr. *in* and *penitent.*] Finally negligent of the duty of repentance; obdurate.

Our Lord in anger hath granted some *impenitent* mens requests; as, on the other side, the apostle's suit he hath of favour and mercy not granted. *Hooker.*

They dy'd
Impenitent, and left a race behind
Like to themselves. *Milton.*

When the reward of penitents, and punishment of *impenitents*, is once assented to as true, 'tis impossible but the mind of man should wish for the one, and have dislikes to the other. *Hammond.*

IMPE'NITENTLY. *adv.* [from *impenitent.*] Obdurately; without repentance.

The condition required of us is a constellation of all the gospel graces, every one of them rooted in the heart, though mixed with much weakness, and perhaps with many sins, so they be not wilfully, and *impenitently* lived and died in. *Hamm.*

What crowds of these, *impenitently* bold,
In sounds and jingling syllables grown old,
Still run on poets! *Pope.*

IMPE'NNOUS. *adj.* [*in* and *penna*, Latin.] Wanting wings.

It is generally received an earwigg hath no wings, and is reckoned amongst *impennous* insects; but he that shall with a needle put aside the short and sheathy cases on their back, may draw forth two wings, larger than in many flies. *Brown.*

I'MPERATE. *adj.* [*imperatus*, Latin.] Done with consciousness; done by direction of the mind.

The elicit internal acts of any habit may be quick and vigorous, when the external *imperate* acts of the same habit utterly cease. *South's Sermons.*

Those natural and involuntary actings are not done by deliberation, yet they are done by the energy of the soul and instrumentality of the spirits, as well as those *imperate* acts, wherein we see the empire of the soul. *Hale's Origin of Mank.*

IMPE'RATIVE. *adj.* [*imperatif*, Fr. *imperativus*, Latin.] Commanding; expressive of command.

The verb is formed in a different manner, to signify the intention of commanding, forbidding, allowing, disallowing, intreating; which likewise, from the principal use of it, is called the *imperative* mood. *Clarke's Latin Grammar.*

IMPERCE'PTIBLE. *adj.* [*imperceptible*, Fr. *in* and *perceptible.*] Not to be discovered; not to be perceived; small; subtle; quick or slow so as to elude observation.

Some things are in their nature *imperceptible* by our sense; yea, and the more refined parts of material existence, which, by reason of their subtilty, escape our perception. *Hale.*

In the sudden changes of his subject with almost *imperceptible* connections, the Theban poet is his master. *Dryden.*

The parts must have their outlines in waves, resembling flames, or the gliding of a snake upon the ground: they must be almost *imperceptible* to the touch, and even. *Dryden.*

The alterations in the globe are very slight, and almost *imperceptible*, and such as tend to the benefit of the earth. *Wood.*

IMPERCE'PTIBLENESS. *n. s.* [from *imperceptible.*] The quality of eluding observation.

Many excellent things there are in nature, which, by reason of their subtilty and *imperceptibleness* to us, are not so much as within any of our faculties to apprehend. *Hale.*

IMPERCE'PTIBLY. *adv.* [from *imperceptible.*] In a manner not to be perceived.

Upon reading of a fable we are made to believe we advise ourselves: the moral insinuates itself *imperceptibly*, we are taught by surprize, and become wiser and better unawares. *Add.*

IMPE'RFECT. *adj.* [*imparfait*, Fr. *imperfectus*, Latin.]

1. Not complete; not absolutely finished; defective. Used either of persons or things.

Something he left *imperfect* in the state,
Which, since his coming forth, is thought of,
Which brought the kingdom so much fear and danger,
That his return was most required. *Shakesp.*

Opinion is a light, vain, crude and *imperfect* thing, settled in the imagination; but never arriving at the understanding, there to obtain the tincture of reason. *Ben. Johnson.*

The middle action, which produceth *imperfect* bodies, is fitly called, by some of the ancients, inquination or inconcoction, which is a kind of putrefaction. *Bacon.*

The ancients were *imperfect* in the doctrine of meteors, by their ignorance of gunpowder and fireworks. *Brown.*

There are divers things we agree to be knowledge by the bare light of nature, which yet are so uneasy to be satisfactorily understood by our *imperfect* intellects, that let them be delivered in the clearest expressions, the notions themselves will yet appear obscure. *Boyle.*

A marcor is either *imperfect*, tending to a greater withering, which is curable; or perfect, that is, an intire wasting of the body, excluding all cure. *Harvey on Consumptions.*

The still-born sounds upon the palate hung,
And dy'd *imperfect* on the falt'ring tongue. *Dryden.*

As obscure and *imperfect* ideas often involve our reason, so do dubious words puzzle men. *Locke.*

2. Frail; not completely good.

IMPERFE'CTION. *n. s.* [*imperfection*, Fr. from *imperfect.*] Defect; failure; fault, whether physical or moral; whether of persons or things.

Laws, as all other things human, are many times full of *imperfection*; and that which is supposed behoveful unto men, proveth oftentimes most pernicious. *Hooker.*

The duke had taken to wife Anne Stanhope, a woman for many *imperfections* intolerable; but for pride monstrous. *Hayw.*

Imperfections would not be half so much taken notice of, if vanity did not make proclamation of them. *L'Estrange.*

The world is more apt to censure than applaud, and himself fuller of *imperfections* than virtues. *Addison's Spectator.*

These are rather to be imputed to the simplicity of the age than to any *imperfection* in that divine poet. *Addison.*

IMPE'RFECTLY. *adv.* [from *imperfect.*] Not completely; not fully; not without failure.

Should sinking nations summon you away,
Maria's love might justify your stay;
Imperfectly the many vows are paid,
Which for your safety to the gods were made. *Stepney.*

Those would hardly understand language or reason to any tolerable degree; but only a little and *imperfectly* about things familiar. *Locke.*

IMPE'RFORABLE. *adj.* [*in* and *perforo*, Latin.] Not to be bored through.

IMPE'RFORATE. *adj.* [*in* and *perforatus*, Latin.] Not pierced through; without a hole.

Sometimes children are born *imperforate*; in which case a small puncture, dressed with a tent, effects the cure. *Sharp.*

IMPE'RIAL. *adj.* [*imperial*, French; *imperialis*, Latin.]

1. Royal; possessing royalty.

Aim he took
At a fair vestal, throned in the West;
But I might see young Cupid's fiery shaft
Quench'd in the chaste beams of the wat'ry moon,
And the *imperial* vot'ress passed on
In maiden meditation, fancy free. *Shakespeare.*

2. Betokening royalty; marking sovereignty.

My due from thee is this *imperial* crown,
Which, as immediate from thy place and blood,
Derives itself to me. *Shakesp. Henry* IV.

3. Belonging to an emperor or monarch; regal; royal; monarchical.

The main body of the marching foe
Against th' *imperial* palace is design'd. *Dryd. Ann. Mirab.*
You that are a sov'reign prince, allay
Imperial pow'r with your paternal sway. *Dryden.*
To tame the proud, the fetter'd slave to free,
These are *imperial* arts, and worthy thee. *Dryden's Æn.*

IMPE'RIALIST. *n. s.* [from *imperial.*] One that belongs to an emperour.

The *imperialists* imputed the cause of so shameful a flight unto the Venetians. *Knolles's History of the Turks.*

IMPE'RIOUS. *adj.* [*imperieux*, French; *imperiosus*, Latin.]

1. Commanding; tyrannical; authoritative; haughty; arrogant; assuming command.

If it be your proud will
To shew the power of your *imperious* eyes. *Spenser.*
This *imperious* man will work us all
From princes into pages. *Shakespeare's Henry* VIII.
Not th' *imperious* show
Of the full-fortun'd Cæsar ever shall
Be brooch'd with me. *Shakes. Ant. and Cleopatra.*

He is an *imperious* dictator of the principles of vice, and impatient of all contradiction. *More's Divine Dialogues.*

How much I suffer'd, and how long I strove
Against th' assaults of this *imperious* love! *Dryden.*

Recollect what disorder hasty or *imperious* words from parents or teachers have caused in his thoughts. *Locke.*

2. Powerful; ascendant; overbearing.

A man, by a vast and *imperious* mind, and a heart large as the sand upon the sea-shore, could command all the knowledge of nature and art. *Tillotson's Sermons.*

IMPE'RIOUSLY. *adv.* [from *imperious.*] With arrogance of command; with insolence of authority.

Who's there, that knocketh so *imperiously*? *Shak. H.* VI.

Who can abide, that, against their own doctors, six whole books should, by their fatherhoods of Trent, be under pain of a curse, *imperiously* obtruded upon God and his church. *Hall.*

It is not to insult and domineer, to look disdainfully, and revile *imperiously*, that procures an esteem from any one. *South.*

The sage, transported at th' approaching hour,
Imperiously thrice thunder'd on the floor! *Garth's Dispens.*

IMPE'RIOUSNESS. *n. s.* [from *imperious.*]

1. Authority; air of command.

So would he use his *imperiousness*, that we had a delightful fear and awe, which made us loth to lose our hopes. *Sidney.*

2. Arrogance of command.

Imperiousness and severity is but an ill way of treating men, who have reason of their own to guide them. *Locke.*

IMPE'RISHABLE. *adj.* [*imperissable*, French; *in* and *perish.*] Not to be destroyed.

We find this our empyreal form
Incapable of mortal injury,
Imperishable; and though pierc'd with wound,
Soon closing, and by native vigour heal'd. *Milt. Par. Lost.*

IMPE'RSONAL. *adj.* [*impersonel*, French; *impersonalis*, Lat.] Not varied according to the persons.

IMPE'RSONALLY. *adv.* [from *impersonal.*] According to the manner of an impersonal verb.

IMPERSUA'SIBLE. *adj.* [*in* and *persuasibilis*, Latin.] Not to be moved by persuasion.

Every pious person ought to be a Noah, a preacher of righteousness; and if it be his fortune to have as *impersuasible* an auditory, if he cannot avert the deluge, it will yet be the delivering his own soul, if he cannot benefit other mens. *Decay of Piety.*

IMPE'RTINENCE. } *n. s.* [*impertinence*, French; from *impertinent.*]
IMPE'RTINENCY. }

1. That which is of no present weight; that which has no relation to the matter in hand.

Some tho' they lead a single life, yet their thoughts do end with themselves, and account future times *impertinencies*. *Bac.*

2. Folly; rambling thought.

O, matter and *impertinency* mixt,
Reason and madness! *Shakesp. King Lear*

3. Troublesomeness; intrusion.

It will be said I handle an art no way suitable to my employments or fortune, and so stand charged with intrusion and *impertinency*. *Wotton's Architecture*

We should avoid the vexation and *impertinence* of pedants who affect to talk in a language not to be understood. *Swift*

4. Trifle; thing of no value.

I envy your felicity, delivered from the gilded *impertinencies* of life, to enjoy the moments of a solid contentment. *Evelyn*

Nothing is more easy than to represent as *impertinencies* any parts of learning, that have no immediate relation to the happiness or convenience of mankind. *Addison*

There are many subtle *impertinencies* learnt in the schools, and many painful trifles, even among the mathematical theorems and problems. *Watts's Improvement of the Mind*

IMPE'RTINENT. *adj.* [*impertinent*, Fr. *in* and *pertinens*, Latin.]

1. Of no relation to the matter in hand; of no weight.

The law of angels we cannot judge altogether *impertinent* unto the affairs of the church of God. *Hooker*

The contemplation of things that are *impertinent* to us, and do not concern us, are but a more specious idleness. *Tillotson*

2. Importunate; intrusive; meddling.

'Tis not a sign two lovers are together, when they can be so *impertinent* as to enquire what the world does. *Pope.*

3. Foolish; trifling.

IMPE'RTINENT. *n. s.* A trifler; a meddler; an intruder.

Governours would have enough to do to trouble their head with the politicks of every meddling officious *impertinent*. *L'Estrange's Fables.*

IMPE'RTINENTLY. *adv.* [from *impertinent.*]

1. Without relation to the present matter.

2. Troublesomely; officiously; intrusively.

I have had joy given me as preposterously, and as *impertinently*, as they give it to men who marry where they do not love. *Suckling.*

The blessedest of mortals, now the highest saint in the celestial hierarchy, began to be so *impertinently* importuned, that great part of the liturgy was addressed solely to her. *Howel.*

Why will any man be so *impertinently* officious as to tell me all this is only fancy? If it is a dream, let me enjoy it. *Addis.*

IMPE'RVIOUS. *adj.* [*impervius*, Latin.]

1. Unpassable; impenetrable.

We may thence discern of how close a texture glass is, since so very thin a film proved so *impervious* to the air, that it was forced to break the glass to free itself. *Boyle.*

Lest the difficulty of passing back
Stay his return, perhaps, over this gulf
Impassable, *impervious*; let us try
To found a path from hell to that new world. *Milton.*

The cause of reflexion is not the impinging of light on the solid or *impervious* parts of bodies. *Newton's Opt.*

A great many vessels are, in this state, *impervious* by the fluids. *Arbuthnot.*

From the damp earth *impervious* vapours rise,
Increase the darkness, and involve the skies. *Pope.*

2. Inaccessible. Perhaps improperly used.

A river's mouth *impervious* to the wind,
And clear of rocks. *Pope's Odyssey.*

IMPE'RVIOUSNESS. *n. s.* [from *impervious.*] The state of not admitting any passage.

IMPERTRA'NSIBILITY. *n. s.* [*in* and *pertranseo*, Latin.] Impossibility to be passed through.

I willingly declined those many ingenious reasons given by others; as of the *impertransibility* of eternity, and impossibility therein to attain to the present limit of antecedent ages. *Hale.*

IMPETI'GINOUS. *adj.* [from *impetigo*, Latin.] Scurfy; covered with small scabs.

I'MPETRABLE. *adj.* [*impetrabilis*, from *impetro*, Lat *impetrable*, French.] Possible to be obtained. *Dict.*

To I'MPETRATE. *v. a.* [*impetrer*, Fr. *impetro*, Latin.] To obtain by intreaty. *Dict.*

I'MPETRATION. *n. s.* [*impetration*, Fr. *impetratio*, from *impetro*, Latin.] The act of obtaining by prayer or intreaty.

The blessed sacrament is the mystery of the death of Christ, and the application of his blood, which was shed for the remission of sins, and is the great means of *impetration*, and the meritorious cause of it. *Taylor.*

It is the greatest solemnity of prayer, the most powerful liturgy, and means of *impetration* in this world. *Taylor.*

IMPETUO'SITY. *n. s.* [*impetuosité*, French, from *impetuous.*]

1. Violence; fury; vehemence; force.

I will set upon Aguecheek a notable report of valour, and drive the gentleman into a most hideous opinion of his rage, skill, fury, and *impetuosity*. *Shakesp. Twelfth Night.*

The whole intrigue was contrived by the duke, and so violently pursued by his spirit and *impetuosity*. *Clarendon.*

The

The mind gives not only licence, but incitation to the other passions to take their freest range, and act with the utmost *impetuosity*. *Decay of Piety.*

IMPE'TUOUS. *adj.* [*impetueux*, Fr. from *impetus*, Latin]

1. Violent; forcible; fierce.

Their virtue, like their Tyber's flood,
Rolling its course, design'd their country's good;
But oft the torrent's too *impetuous* speed,
From the low earth tore some polluted weed. *Prior.*

2. Vehement; passionate.

The king, 'tis true, is noble, but *impetuous*. *Rowe.*

IMPE'TUOUSLY. *adv.* [from *impetuous*.] Violently; vehemently.

They view the windings of the hoary Nar;
Through rocks and woods *impetuously* he glides,
While froth and foam the fretting surface hides. *Addison.*

IMPE'TUOUSNESS. *n. s.* [from *impetuous*.] Violence; fury.

I wish all words of this sort might vanish in that breath that utters them; that as they resemble the wind in fury and *impetuousness*, so they might in transientness. *Decay of Piety.*

I'MPETUS. *n. s.* [Latin.] Violent tendency to any point; violent effort.

Why did not they continue their descent 'till they were contiguous to the sun, whither both mutual attraction and *impetus* carried them. *Bentley's Sermons.*

IMPIE'RCEABLE. *adj.* [*in* and *pierce*] Impenetrable; not to be pierced.

Exceeding rage inflam'd the furious beast;
For never felt his *impierceable* breast
So wond'rous force from hand of living wight. *Fa. Queen.*

IMPI'ETY. *n. s.* [*impieté*, French; *impietas*, Latin.]

1. Irreverence to the Supreme Being; contempt of the duties of religion.

To keep that oath were more *impiety*
Than Jeptha's, when he sacrific'd his daughter. *Shak. H. VI.*

2. An act of wickedness; expression of irreligion. In this sense it has a plural.

If they die unprovided, no more is the king guilty of those *impieties* for which they are now visited. *Shakesp. Hen. V.*

Can Juno such *impieties* approve? *Denham.*

We have a melancholy prospect of the state of our religion: such amazing *impieties* can be equalled by nothing but by those cities consumed of old by fire. *Swift's Examiner.*

To IMPI'GNORATE. *v. a.* [*in* and *pignus*, Latin.] To pawn; to pledge.

IMPIGNORA'TION. *n. s.* [from *impignorate*.] The act of pawning or putting to pledge.

To IMPI'NGE. *v. n.* [*impingo*, Latin.] To fall against; to strike against; to clash with.

Things are reserved in the memory by some corporeal exuviæ and material images, which, having *impinged* on the common sense, rebound thence into some vacant cells of the brain. *Glanville's Sceps.*

The cause of reflexion is not the *impinging* of light on the solid or impervious parts of bodies. *Newton's Opt.*

To IMPI'NGUATE. *v. a.* [*in* and *pinguis*, Lat.] To fatten; to make fat.

Frictions also do more fill and *impinguate* the body than exercise; for that in frictions the inward parts are at rest. *Bacon.*

I'MPIOUS. *adj.* [*impius*, Latin.] Irreligious; wicked; profane; without reverence of religion.

That Scripture standeth not the church of God in any stead to direct, but may be let pass as needless to be consulted with, we judge it profane, *impious*, and irreligious to think. *Hooker.*

Cease then this *impious* rage. *Milton.*

Ye gods, destroy that *impious* sex. *Waller.*

Then lewd Auchemolus he laid in dust,
Who stain'd his stepdame's bed with *impious* lust. *Dryden.*

When no female arts his mind could move,
She turn'd to furious hate her *impious* love. *Dryden.*

And *impious* nations fear'd eternal night. *Dryden.*

Shame and reproach is generally the portion of the *impious* and irreligious. *South.*

When vice prevails, and *impious* men bear sway,
The post of honour is a private station. *Addison.*

Since after thee may rise an *impious* line,
Coarse manglers of the human face divine:
Paint on, 'till fate dissolve thy mortal part,
And live and die the monarch of thy art. *Tickel.*

They, *impious*, dar'd to prey
On herds devoted to the god of day. *Pope.*

Grand mistakes in religion proceed from taking literally what was meant figuratively, from which several *impious* absurdities followed, terminating in absolute infidelity. *Forbes.*

I'MPIOUSLY. *adv.* [from *impious*.] Profanely; wickedly.

The Roman wit, who *impiously* divides
His hero and his gods to different sides,
I would condemn. *Granville.*

IMPLACABI'LITY. *n. s.* [from *implacable*.] Inexorableness; irreconcilable enmity; determined malice.

IMPLA'CABLE. *adj.* [*implacabilis*, Lat. *implacable*, Fr.] Not to be pacified; inexorable; malicious; constant in enmity.

His incensement is so *implacable*, that satisfaction can be none but by pangs of death. *Shakesp. Twelfth Night.*

Darah bears a generous mind;
But to *implacable* revenge inclin'd;
A bounteous master, but a deadly foe. *Dryden's Aurengz.*

The French are the most *implacable* and the most dangerous enemies of the British nation. *Addison.*

IMPLA'CABLY. *adv.* [from *implacable*.]

1. With malice not to be pacified; inexorably.

An order was made for disarming all the papists; upon which though nothing was after done, yet it kept up the apprehensions in the people of dangers, and disinclined them from the queen, whom they begun every day more *implacably* to hate, and consequently to disoblige. *Clarendon.*

2. It is once used by *Dryden* in a kind of mixed sense of a tyrant's love.

I love,
And 'tis below my greatness to disown it:
Love thee *implacably*, yet hate thee too. *Dryd. Don Sebast.*

To IMPLA'NT. *v. a.* [*in* and *planto*; Latin.] To infix; to insert; to place; to engraft; to settle; to set; to sow.

How can you him unworthy then decree,
In whose chief part your worths *implanted* be. *Sidney.*

See, Father! what first fruits on earth are sprung,
From thy *implanted* grace in man! *Milton's Parad. Lost.*

No need of publick sanctions this to bind,
Which nature has *implanted* in the mind. *Dryden.*

There grew to the outside of the arytenoides another cartilage, capable of motion, by the help of some muscles that were *implanted* in it. *Ray.*

God, having endowed man with faculties of knowing, was no more obliged to *implant* those innate notions in his mind, than that, having given him reason, hands, and materials, he should build him bridges. *Locke.*

IMPLANTA'TION. *n. s.* [*implantation*, Fr. from *implant*.] The act of setting or planting.

IMPLA'USIBLE. *adj.* [*in* and *plausible*.] Not specious; not likely to seduce or persuade.

Nothing can better improve political school-boys than the art of making plausible or *implausible* harangues against the very opinion for which they resolve to determine. *Swift.*

I'MPLEMENT. *n. s.* [*implementum*, from *impleo*, Latin.]

1. Something that fills up vacancy, or supplies wants.

Unto life many *implements* are necessary; more, if we seek such a life as hath in it joy, comfort, delight, and pleasure. *Hooker.*

2. Tool; instrument of manufacture.

Wood hath coined seventeen thousand pounds, and hath his tools and *implements* to coin six times as much. *Swift.*

It is the practice of the eastern regions for the artists in metals to carry about with them the whole *implements* of trade, to the house where they find employment. *Broome.*

3. Vessels of a kitchen.

IMPLE'TION. *n. s.* [*impleo*, Latin.] The act of filling; the state of being full.

Theophrastus conceiveth, upon a plentiful *impletion*, there may succeed a disruption of the matrix. *Brown's Vulg. Err.*

IMPLE'X. *adj.* [*implexus*, Latin.] Intricate; entangled; complicated.

Every poem is either simple or *implex*: it is called simple when there is no change of fortune in it; *implex*, when the fortune of the chief actor changes from bad to good, or from good to bad. *Spectator.*

To I'MPLICATE. *v. a.* [*impliquer*, Fr. *implico*, Latin.] To entangle; to embarrass; to involve; to infold.

The ingredients of saltpetre do so mutually *implicate* and hinder each other, that the concrete acts but very languidly. *Boyle.*

IMPLICA'TION. *n. s.* [*implicatio*, Lat. *implication*, French, from *implicate*.]

1. Involution; entanglement.

Three principal causes of firmness are the grossness, the quiet contact, and the *implication* of the component parts. *Boyle.*

2. Inference not expressed, but tacitly inculcated.

Though civil causes, according to some men, are of less moment than criminal, yet the doctors are, by *implication*, of a different opinion. *Ayliffe's Parergon.*

IMPLI'CIT. *adj.* [*implicite*, Fr. *implicitus*, Latin.]

1. Entangled; infolded; complicated.

In his woolly fleece
I cling *implicit*. *Pope.*

The humble shrub,
And bush with frizzl'd hair *implicit*. *Thomson.*

2. Inferred; tacitly comprised; not expressed.

In the first establishments of speech there was an *implicit* compact, founded upon common consent, that such and such words should be signs, whereby they would express their thoughts one to another. *South.*

Our express requests are not granted, but the *implicit* desires of our hearts are fulfilled. *Smalridge's Sermons.*

3. Resting

3. Resting upon another; connected with another over which that which is connected to it has no power; trusting without reserve or examination.

There be false peaces or unities, when the peace is grounded but upon an *implicit* ignorance; for all colours will agree in the dark. *Bacon's Essays.*

No longer by *implicit* faith we err,
Whilst every man's his own interpreter. *Denham.*

IMPLI'CITLY. *adv.* [from *implicit.*]

1. By inference comprised though not expressed.

The divine inspection into the affairs of the world doth necessarily follow from the nature and being of God; and he that denies this, doth *implicitly* deny his existence: he may acknowledge what he will with his mouth, but in his heart he hath said there is no God. *Bentley.*

2. By connexion with something else; dependently; with unreserved confidence or obedience.

My blushing muse with conscious fear retires,
And whom they like, *implicitly* admires. *Roscommon.*

Learn not to dispute the methods of his providence; but humbly and *implicitly* to acquiesce in and adore them. *Atterb.*

We *implicitly* follow in the track in which they lead us, and comfort ourselves with this poor reflection, that we shall fare as well as those that go before us. *Rogers's Sermons.*

To IMPLO'RE. *v. a.* [*implorer*, French; *imploro*, Latin.]

1. To call upon in supplication; to solicit.

They ship their oars, and crown with wine
The holy goblet to the pow'rs divine,
Imploring all the gods that reign above. *Pope's Odyssey.*

2. To ask; to beg.

Do not say 'tis superstition, that
I kneel, and then *implore* her blessing. *Shakesp. Winter's Tale.*

IMPLO'RE. *n. s.* [from the verb.] The act of begging; intreaty; solicitation. Not in use.

Urged sore
With piercing words and pitiful *implore*,
Him hasty to arise. *Fairy Queen.*

IMPLO'RER. *n. s.* [from *implore.*] Solicitor.

Meer *implorers* of unholy suits,
Breathing, like sanctified and pious,
The better to beguile. *Shakesp. Hamlet.*

IMPLU'MED. *adj.* [*implumis*, Latin.] Without feathers. *Dict.*

To IMPLY'. *v. a.* [*impliquer*, French; *implico*, Latin.]

1. To infold; to cover; to intangle.

Whose courage stout,
Striving to loose the knot that fast him ties,
Himself in straighter bonds too rash *implies*. *Fairy Queen.*

And Phœbus flying so most shameful sight,
His blushing face in foggy cloud *implies*. *Fairy Queen.*

2. To involve or comprise as a consequence or concomitant.

That it was in use among the Greeks the word triclinium *implieth*. *Brown's Vulgar Errours.*

What follows next is no objection; for that *implies* a fault. *Dryden.*

Bows the strength of brawny arms *imply*,
Emblems of valour, and of victory. *Dryden.*

To IMPO'ISON. *v. a.* [*empoisoner*, French. It might be written *empoison.*]

1. To corrupt with poison.

One doth not know
How much an ill word doth *impoison* liking. *Shakespeare.*

2. To kill with poison. This is rare. See EMPOISON.

A man by his own alms *impoison'd*,
And with his charity slain. *Shak. Coriolanus.*

IMPO'LARILY. *adv.* [*in* and *polar.*] Not according to the direction of the poles.

Being *impolarily* adjoined unto a more vigorous loadstone, it will, in a short time, exchange its poles. *Brown's Vulg. Err.*

IMPOLI'TICAL. } *adj.* [*in* and *politick.*] Imprudent; indiscreet;
IMPO'LITICK. } void of art or forecast.

He that exhorteth to beware of an enemy's policy, doth not give counsel to be *impolitick*; but rather to use all prudent foresight and circumspection, lest our simplicity be over-reacht by cunning slights. *Hooker.*

IMPOLI'TICALLY. } *adv.* [*in* and *political.*] Without art or
IMPO'LITICKLY. } forecast.

IMPO'NDEROUS. *adj.* [*in* and *ponderous.*] Void of perceptible weight.

It produces visible and real effects by *imponderous* and invisible emissions. *Brown's Vulgar Errours.*

IMPORO'SITY. *n. s.* [*in* and *porous.*] Absence of interstices; compactness; closeness.

The porosity or *imporosity* betwixt the tangible parts, and the greatness or smalness of the pores. *Bacon's Nat. History.*

IMPO'ROUS. *adj.* [*in* and *porous.*] Free from pores; free from vacuities or interstices; close of texture; completely solid.

It has its earthly and salinous parts so exactly resolved, that its body is left *imporous*, and not discreted by atomical terminations. *Brown's Vulgar Errours.*

If atoms should descend plumb down with equal velocity, being all perfectly solid and *imporous*, they would never the one overtake the other. *Ray on the Creation.*

To IMPO'RT. *v. a.* [*importo*, Latin.]

1. To carry into any country from abroad: opposed to *export*.

For Elis I would sail with utmost speed,
T' *import* twelve mares, which there luxurious feed. *Pope.*

2. To imply; to infer.

Himself not only comprehended all our necessities, but in such sort also framed every petition as might most naturally serve for many; and doth, though not always require, yet always *import* a multitude of speakers together. *Hooker.*

The name of discipline *importeth* not as they would fain have it construed; but the self-same thing it signifieth, which the name of doctrine doth. *Hooker.*

This question we now asked, *imported*, as that we thought this land a land of magicians. *Bacon.*

3. To produce in consequence.

Something he left imperfect in the state,
Which since his coming forth is thought of, which
Imports the kingdom so much fear and danger,
That his return was most requir'd. *Shakesp. K. Lear.*

4. [*Importer*, *importe*, French. Impersonally.] To be of moment: as, it *imports*, it is of weight or consequence.

Her length of sickness, with what else more serious
Importeth thee to know, this bears. *Shak. Ant. and Cleopatr.*

Let the heat be such as may keep the metal perpetually molten; for that above all *importeth* to the work. *Bacon.*

Number in armies *importeth* not much, where the people is of weak courage. *Bacon's Essays.*

This to attain, whether heav'n move, or earth,
Imports not, if thou reckon right. *Milton's Paradise Lost.*

It may *import* us in this calm to hearken more than we have done to the storms that are now raising abroad. *Temple.*

If I endure it, what *imports* it you? *Dryd. Span. Fryar.*

IMPO'RT. *n. s.* [from the verb.]

1. Importance; moment; consequence.

What occasion of *import*
Hath all so long detain'd you from your wife? *Shakespeare.*

Some business of *import* that triumph wears
You seem to go with. *Dryd. and Lee's Oedipus.*

When there is any dispute, the judge ought to appoint the sum according to the eloquence and ability of the advocate, and in proportion to the *import* of the cause. *Ayliffe.*

2. Tendency.

Add to the former observations made about vegetables a third of the same *import* made in mineral substances. *Boyle.*

3. Any thing imported from abroad.

IMPO'RTABLE. *adj.* [*in* and *portable.*] Unsupportable; not to be endured. A word peculiar to *Spenser*, and accented by him on the first syllable.

Both at once him charge on either side,
With hideous straoks and *importable* power,
That forced him his ground to traverse wide,
And wisely watch to ward that deadly stour. *Fairy Queen.*

IMPO'RTANCE. *n. s.* [French.]

1. Thing imported or implied.

A notable passion of wonder appeared in them; but the wisest beholder, that knew no more but seeing, could not say if the *importance* were joy or sorrow. *Shak. Winter's Tale.*

2. Matter; subject.

It had been pity you should have been put together with so mortal a purpose, as then each bore, upon *importance* of so slight a nature. *Shakespeare's Cymbeline.*

3. Consequence; moment.

We consider
Th' *importance* of Cyprus to the Turks. *Shak. Othello.*

Thy own *importance* know,
Nor bound thy narrow views to things below. *Pope.*

4. Importunity. An improper use peculiar to *Shakespeare.*

Maria writ
The letter at sir Toby's great *importance*;
In recompence whereof he hath married her. *Shakespeare.*

IMPO'RTANT. *adj.* [*important*, French.]

1. Momentous; weighty; of great consequence.

The most *important* and pressing care of a new and vigorous king was his marriage, for mediate establishment of the royal line. *Wotton.*

This superadds treachery to the crime: 'tis the falsifying the most *important* trust. *Decay of Piety.*

O then, what interest shall I make
To save my last *important* stake,
When the most just have cause to quake. *Roscommon.*

The great *important* end that God designs it for, the government of mankind, sufficiently shews the necessity of its being rooted deep in the heart, and put beyond the danger of being torn up by any ordinary violence. *South.*

Examine how the fashionable practice of the world can be reconciled to the *important* doctrine of our religion. *Rogers.*

Important truths still let your fables hold,
And moral mysteries with art unfold. *Granville.*

Th'

Th' *important* hour had paſs'd unheeded by. *Irene.*

2. Momentous; forcible; of great efficacy. This ſeems to be the meaning here.

He fiercely at him flew,
And with *important* outrage him aſſail'd;
Who ſoon prepar'd to field, his ſword forth drew,
And him with equal value countervail'd. *Fairy Queen.*

3. Importunate. A corrupt uſe of the word.

Great France
My mourning and *important* tears hath pitied. *Shakeſpeare.*

IMPORTA'TION. *n. ſ.* [from *import.*] The act or practice of importing, or bringing into a country from abroad.

The king's reaſonable profit ſhould not be neglected upon *importation* and exportation. *Bacon.*

Theſe mines fill the country with greater numbers of people than it would be able to bear, without the *importation* of corn from foreign parts. *Addiſon on Italy.*

The emperor has forbidden the *importation* of their manufactures into any part of the empire. *Addiſon on Italy.*

IMPO'RTER. *n. ſ.* [from *import.*] One that brings in from abroad.

It is impoſſible to limit the quantity that ſhall be brought in, eſpecially if the *importers* of it have ſo ſure a market as the Exchequer. *Swift.*

IMPO'RTLESS. *adj.* [from *import.*] Of no moment or conſequence. This is a word not in uſe, but not inelegant.

We leſs expect
That matter needleſs, of *importleſs* burthen,
Divide thy lips. *Shakeſp. Troilus and Creſſida.*

IMPO'RTUNATE. *adj.* [*importunus*, Latin; *importune*, Fr.] Unſeaſonable and inceſſant in ſolicitations; not to be repulſed.

I was in debt to my *importunate* buſineſs; but he would not hear my excuſe. *Shakeſpeare's Timon.*

They may not be able to bear the clamour of an *importunate* ſuitor. *Smalridge's Sermons.*

A rule reſtrains the moſt *importunate* appetites of our nature. *Rogers's Sermons.*

IMPO'RTUNATELY. *adv.* [from *importunate.*] With inceſſant ſolicitation; pertinaciouſly.

Their pertinacy is ſuch, that when you drive them out of one form, they aſſume another; and are ſo *importunately* troubleſome, as makes many think it impoſſible to be freed from them. *Duppa's Rules of Devotion.*

IMPO'RTUNATENESS. *n. ſ.* [from *importunate.*] Inceſſant ſolicitation.

She with more and more *importunateneſs* craved, which, in all good manners, was either of us to be deſired, or not granted. *Sidney.*

To IMPORTU'NE. *v. a.* [*importuner*, French; *importunus*, Latin. Accented anciently on the ſecond ſyllable.] To teize; to haraſs with ſlight vexation perpetually recurring; to moleſt.

Againſt all ſenſe you do *importune* her. *Shakeſpeare.*

If he eſpied any lewd gaiety in his fellow-ſervants, his maſter ſhould ſtraightways know it, and not reſt free from *importuning*, until the fellow had put away his fault. *Carew.*

The bloom of beauty other years demands,
Nor will be gather'd by ſuch wither'd hands:
You *importune* it with a falſe deſire. *Dryd. Aurengzebe.*

The higheſt ſaint in the celeſtial hierarchy began to be ſo impertinently *importuned*, that a great part of the liturgy was addreſſed ſolely to her. *Howel's Vocal Foreſt.*

Every one hath experimented this troubleſome intruſion of ſome friſking ideas, which thus *importune* the underſtanding, and hinder it from being employed. *Locke.*

We have been obliged to hire troops from ſeveral princes of the empire, whoſe miniſters and reſidents here have perpetually *importuned* the court with unreaſonable demands. *Swift.*

IMPORTU'NE. *adj.* [*importunus*, Latin. It was anciently pronounced with the accent on the ſecond ſyllable.]

1. Conſtantly recurring; troubleſome by frequency.

All that charge did fervently apply,
With greedy malice and *importune* toil;
And planted there their huge artillery,
With which they daily made moſt dreadful battery. *F. Qu.*

Henry, calling himſelf king of England, needed not to have beſtowed ſuch great ſums of treaſure, nor ſo to have buſied himſelf with *importune* and inceſſant labour and induſtry, to compaſs my death and ruin, if I had been ſuch a feigned perſon. *Bacon's Henry VII.*

2. Troubleſome; vexatious.

And th' armies of their creatures all, and ſome
Do ſerve to them, and with *importune* might
War againſt us, the vaſſals of their will. *Spenſer.*

If the upper ſoul can check what is conſented to by the will, in compliance with the fleſh, and can then hope that after a few years of ſenſuality, that *importune* rebellious ſervant ſhall be eternally caſt off, this would be ſome colour for that novel perſuaſion. *Hammond.*

The ſame airs, which ſome entertain with moſt delightful tranſports, to others are *importune.* *Glanv. Scep.*

3. Unſeaſonable; coming, aſking, or happening at a wrong time.

No fair to thine
Equivalent, or ſecond! which compell'd
Me thus, though *importune* perhaps, to come
And gaze and worſhip thee. *Milton's Paradiſe Loſt, b. ix.*

IMPORTU'NELY. *adv.* [from *importune.*]

1. Troubleſomely; inceſſantly.

The palmer bent his ear unto the noiſe,
To weet who called ſo *importunely:*
Again he heard a more efforced voice,
That bad him come in haſte. *Fairy Queen.*

2. Unſeaſonably; improperly.

The conſtitutions that the apoſtles made concerning deacons and widows, are, with much importunity, but very *importunely* urged by the diſciplinarians. *Sanderſon.*

IMPORTU'NITY. *n. ſ.* [*importunitas*, Lat. *importunité*, French, from *importunate.*] Inceſſant ſolicitation.

Overcome with the *importunity* of his wife, a woman of a haughty ſpirit, he altered his former purpoſe. *Knolles.*

Thrice I deluded her, and turn'd to ſport
Her *importunity.* *Milton's Agoniſtes.*

To IMPO'SE. *v. a.* [*impoſer*, French; *impoſitum*, Latin.]

1. To lay on as a burthen or penalty.

If a ſon, ſent by his father, do fall into a lewd action, the imputation, by your rule, ſhould be *impoſed* upon his father. *Shakeſpeare.*

It ſhall not be lawful to *impoſe* toll upon them. *Ezra* vii.

To tyrants others have their country ſold,
Impoſing foreign lords for foreign gold. *Dryd. Æn.*
On impious realms and barb'rous kings *impoſe*
Thy plagues, and curſe them with ſuch ills as thoſe. *Pope.*

2. To enjoin as a duty or law.

What good or evil is there under the ſun, what action correſpondent or repugnant unto the law which God hath *impoſed* upon his creatures, but in or upon it God doth work, according to the law which himſelf hath eternally purpoſed to keep? *Hooker.*

There was a thorough way made by the ſword for the *impoſing* of the laws upon them. *Spenſer on Ireland.*

Thou on the deep *impoſeſt* nobler laws,
And by that juſtice haſt remov'd the cauſe. *Waller.*

Chriſtianity hath hardly *impoſed* any other laws upon us, but what are enacted in our natures, or are agreeable to the prime and fundamental laws of it. *Tillotſon.*

Impoſe but your commands,
This hour ſhall bring you twenty thouſand hands. *Dryden.*

It was neither *impoſed* on me, nor ſo much as the ſubject given me by any man. *Dryden.*

3. To fix on; to impute to.

This cannot be allowed, except we impute that unto the firſt cauſe which we *impoſe* not on the ſecond; or what we deny unto nature, we impute unto nativity itſelf. *Brown.*

4. To obtrude fallaciouſly.

Our poet thinks not fit
T' *impoſe* upon you what he writes for wit. *Dryden.*

5. *To* IMPOSE *on.* To put a cheat on; to deceive.

Phyſicians and philoſophers have ſuffered themſelves to be ſo far *impoſed upon* as to publiſh chymical experiments, which they never tried. *Boyle.*

He that thinks the name centaur ſtands for ſome real being, *impoſes on* himſelf, and miſtakes words for things. *Locke.*

6. [Among printers.] To put the pages on the ſtone, and fit on the chaſes, in order to carry the forms to preſs.

IMPO'SE. *n. ſ.* [from the verb.] Command; injunction. Not in uſe.

According to your ladyſhip's *impoſe*,
I am thus early come. *Shakeſpeare.*

IMPO'SEABLE. *adj.* [from *impoſe.*] To be laid as obligatory on any body.

They were not ſimply *impoſeable* on any particular man, farther than he was a member of ſome church. *Hammond.*

IMPO'SER. *n. ſ.* [from *impoſe.*] One who enjoins; one who lays any thing on another as a hardſhip.

The univerſities ſufferings might be manifeſted to all nations, and the *impoſers* of theſe oaths might repent. *Walton.*

IMPOSI'TION. *n. ſ.* [*impoſition*, French; *impoſitus*, Latin.]

1. The act of laying any thing on another.

The ſecond part of confirmation is the prayer and benediction of the biſhop, made more ſolemn by the *impoſition* of hands. *Hammond.*

2. The act of giving a note of diſtinction.

The firſt *impoſition* of names was grounded, among all nations, upon future good hope conceived of children. *Camden.*

The *impoſition* of the name is grounded only upon the predominancy of that element, whoſe name is aſcribed to it. *Boyle.*

3. Injunction of any thing as a law or duty.

Their determination is to trouble you with no more ſuit; unleſs you may be won by ſome other ſort than your father's *impoſition*, depending on the caſkets. *Shakeſp. Merch. of Venice.*

From *impoſition* of ſtrict laws, to free
Acceptance of large grace; from ſervile fear
To filial; works of law, to works of faith. *Milt. P. Loſt.*

4. Conſtraint; oppreſſion.

The conſtraint of receiving and holding opinions by authority was rightly called *impoſition*. *Locke.*

A greater load has been laid on us than we have been able to bear, and the groſſeſt *impoſitions* have been ſubmitted to, in order to forward the dangerous deſigns of a faction. *Swift.*

Let it not be made, contrary to its own nature, the occaſion of ſtrife, a narrow ſpirit, and unreaſonable *impoſitions* on the mind and practice. *Watts's Improvement of the Mind.*

5. Cheat; fallacy; impoſture.

IMPO'SSIBLE. *adj.* [*impoſſibile*, Fr. *in* and *poſſible.*] Not to be done; not to be attained; impracticable.

Unlawful deſires are puniſhed after the effect of enjoying; but *impoſſible* deſires are puniſhed in the deſire itſelf. *Sidney.*

It was *impoſſible* that the ſtate ſhould continue quiet. 2 *Mac.*

With men this is *impoſſible*; but with God all things are poſſible. *Mat.* xix. 26.

'Twere *impoſſible* for any enterprize to be lawful, if that which ſhould legitimate it is ſubſequent to it. *Decay of Piety.*

Difficult it is, but not *impoſſible*. *Chillingworth.*

It is *impoſſible* the mind ſhould be ſtopped any where in its progreſs in this ſpace, how far ſoever it extends its thoughts. *Locke.*

We cannot believe it *impoſſible* to God to make a creature with more ways to convey into the underſtanding the notice of corporeal things than five. *Locke.*

I my thoughts deceive
With hope of things *impoſſible* to find. *Walſh.*

IMPOSSIBI'LITY. *n. ſ.* [*impoſſibilité*, Fr. from *impoſſible.*]

1. Impracticability; the ſtate of being not feaſible.

Simple Philoclea, it is the *impoſſibility* that doth torment me; for unlawful deſires are puniſhed after the effect of enjoying, but impoſſible deſires in the deſire itſelf. *Sidney.*

Admit all theſe *impoſſibilities* and great abſurdities to be poſſible and convenient. *Whitgifte.*

Let the mutinous winds
Strike the proud cedars 'gainſt the firy ſun,
Murdering *impoſſibility*, to make
What cannot be, ſlight work. *Shakeſp. Coriolanus.*

They confound difficulty with *impoſſibility*. *South.*

Thoſe who aſſert the *impoſſibility* of ſpace exiſting without matter, muſt make body infinite. *Locke.*

When we ſee a man of like paſſions and weakneſs with ourſelves going before us in the paths of duty, it confutes all lazy pretences of *impoſſibility*. *Rogers.*

2. That which cannot be done.

Though men do, without offence, wiſh daily that the affairs, which with evil ſucceſs are paſt, might have fallen out much better; yet to pray that they may have been any other than they are, this being a manifeſt *impoſſibility* in itſelf, the rules of religion do not permit. *Hooker.*

Impoſſibilities! oh no, there's none,
Could I bring thy heart captive home. *Cowley.*

I'MPOST. *n. ſ.* [*impoſt*, *impôt*, French; *impoſitum*, Latin.] A tax; a toll; cuſtom paid.

Taxes and *impoſts* upon merchants do ſeldom good to the king's revenue; for that that he wins in the hundred, he loſeth in the ſhire. *Bacon's Eſſays.*

IMPO'STS. *n. ſ.* [*impoſte*, Fr. *incumba*, Latin.] In architecture, that part of a pillar, in vaults and arches, on which the weight of the whole building lieth. *Ainſworth.*

To IMPO'STHUMATE. *v. n.* [from *impoſthume.*] To form an abſceſs; to gather; to form a cyſt or bag containing matter.

The bruiſe *impoſthumated*, and afterwards turned to a ſtinking ulcer, which made every body ſhy to come near her. *Arbuthnot.*

To IMPO'STHUMATE. *v. a.* To afflict with an impoſthume.

They would not fly that ſurgeon, whoſe lancet threatens none but the *impoſthumated* parts. *Decay of Piety.*

IMPOSTHUMA'TION. *n. ſ.* [from *impoſthumate.*] The act of forming an impoſthume; the ſtate in which an impoſthume is formed.

He that maketh the wound bleed inwards, endangereth malign ulcers and pernicious *impoſthumations*. *Bacon's Eſſays.*

IMPO'STHUME. *n. ſ.* [This ſeems to have been formed by corruption from *impoſtem*, as *South* writes it; and *impoſtem* to have been written erroneouſly for *apoſtem*, ἀπόςημα, an abſceſs.] A collection of purulent matter in a bag or cyſt.

Now the rotten diſeaſes of the South, ruptures, catarrhs, and bladders full of *impoſthumes*, make prepoſterous diſcoveries. *Shakeſpeare's Troilus and Creſſida.*

An error in the judgment is like an *impoſtem* in the head, which is always noiſome, and frequently mortal. *South.*

Fumes cannot tranſude through the bag of an *impoſthume*. *Harvey on Conſumptions.*

IMPO'STOR. *n. ſ.* [*impoſteur*, Fr. from *impoſe*; *impoſitor*, Latin.] One who cheats by a fictitious character.

Shame and pain, poverty and ſickneſs, yea death and hell itſelf, are but the trophies of thoſe fatal conqueſts got by that grand *impoſtor*, the devil, over the deluded ſons of men. *South.*

IMPO'STURE. *n. ſ.* [*impoſture*, Fr. *impoſtura*, Latin.] Cheat; fraud; ſuppoſititiouſneſs; cheat committed by giving to perſons or things a falſe character.

That the foul and angels have nothing to do with groſſer locality is generally opinioned; but who is it that retains not a great part of the *impoſture*, by allowing them a definitive *ubi*, which is ſtill but imagination? *Glanv. Scepſ.*

Open to them ſo many of the interior ſecrets of this myſterious art, without *impoſture* or invidious reſerve. *Evelyn.*

We know how ſucceſsful the late uſurper was, while his army believed him real in his zeal againſt kingſhip; but when they found out the *impoſture*, upon his aſpiring to the ſame himſelf, he was preſently deſerted, and never able to crown his uſurped greatneſs with that title. *South.*

Form new legends,
And fill the world with follies and *impoſtures*. *Irene.*

I'MPOTENCE. } *n. ſ.* [*impotentia*, Latin.]
I'MPOTENCY. }

1. Want of power; inability; imbecillity; weakneſs.

Some were poor by *impotency* of nature; as young fatherleſs children, old decrepit perſons, ideots, and cripples. *Hayw.*

Weakneſs, or the *impotence* of exerciſing animal motion, attends fevers. *Arbuthnot.*

God is a friend and a father, whoſe care ſupplies our wants, and defends our *impotence*, and from whoſe compaſſion in Chriſt we hope for eternal glory hereafter. *Rogers's Sermons.*

This is not a reſtraint or *impotency*, but the royal prerogative of the moſt abſolute king of kings; that he wills to do nothing but what he can; and that he can do nothing which is repugnant to his divine goodneſs. *Bentley.*

2. Ungovernableneſs of paſſion. A Latin ſignification: *animi impotentia.*

Will he, ſo wiſe, let looſe at once his ire,
Belike through *impotence*, or unaware,
To give his enemies their wiſh, and end
Them in his anger, whom his anger ſaves
To puniſh endleſs? *Milton's Paradiſe Loſt.*

Yet all combin'd,
Your beauty and my *impotence* of mind. *Dryden.*

3. Incapacity of propagation.

Dulneſs with obſcenity muſt prove
As hateful, ſure, as *impotence* in love. *Pope.*

I'MPOTENT. *adj.* [*impotent*, Fr. *impotens*, Latin.]

1. Weak; feeble; wanting force; wanting power.

We that are ſtrong muſt bear the imbecillity of the *impotent*, and not pleaſe ourſelves. *Hooker.*

Yet wealth is *impotent*
To gain dominion, or to keep it gain'd. *Milton.*

Although in dreadful whirls we hung,
High on the broken wave,
I knew thou wert not ſlow to hear,
Nor *impotent* to ſave. *Addiſon's Spectator.*

2. Diſabled by nature or diſeaſe.

In thoſe porches lay a great multitude of *impotent* folk, of blind, halt, and withered. *Jo.* v. 3.

There ſat a certain man, *impotent* in his feet, being a cripple from his mother's womb, who never had walked. *Acts* xiv.

I have learn'd that fearful commenting
Is leaden ſervitor to dull delay;
Delay leads *impotent* and ſnail-pac'd beggary. *Shakeſ. R.* III.

3. Without power of reſtraint. [*Animi impotens.*]

With jealous eyes at diſtance ſhe had ſeen,
Whiſp'ring with Jove, the ſilver-footed queen;
Then, *impotent* of tongue, her ſilence broke,
Thus turbulent in rattling tone ſhe ſpoke. *Dryden.*

4. Without power of propagation.

He told beau Prim, who is thought *impotent*, that his miſtreſs would not have him, becauſe he is a ſloven, and had committed a rape. *Tatler.*

I'MPOTENTLY. *adv.* [from *impotent.*] Without power.

Proud Cæſar, 'midſt triumphal cars,
The ſpoils of nations, and the pomp of wars,
Ignobly vain, and *impotently* great,
Shew'd Rome her Cato's figure drawn in ſtate. *Pope.*

To IMPO'UND. *v. a.* [*in* and *pound.* See POUND.]

1. To incloſe as in a pound; to ſhut in; to confine.

The great care was rather how to *impound* the rebels, that none of them might eſcape, than that any doubt was made to vanquiſh them. *Bacon's Henry* VII.

2. To ſhut up in a pinfold.

England
Hath taken and *impounded* as a ſtray
The king. *Shakeſpeare's Henry* V.

Seeing him wander about, I took him up for a ſtray, and *impounded* him, with intention to reſtore him to the right owner. *Dryden's Don Sebaſtian.*

To IMPO'WER. See EMPOWER.

IMPRA'CTICABLE. *adj.* [*impracticable*, Fr. *in* and *practicable.*]

1. Not to be performed; unfeaſible; impoſſible.

Had

Had there not been still remaining bodies, the legitimate offsprings of the antediluvian earth, 'twould have been an extravagant and *impracticable* undertaking to have gone about to determine any thing concerning it. *Woodward's Nat. Hist.*

To preach up the necessity of that which our experience tells us is utterly *impracticable*, were to affright mankind with the terrible prospect of universal damnation. *Rogers's Serm.*

2. Untractable; unmanageable.

That fierce *impracticable* nature
Is govern'd by a dainty-finger'd girl. *Rowe.*

IMPRA'CTICABLENESS. *n. s.* [from *impracticable.*] Impossibility.

I do not know a greater mark of an able minister than that of rightly adapting the several faculties of men, nor is any thing more to be lamented than the *impracticableness* of doing this. *Swift.*

To I'MPRECATE. *v. a.* [*imprecor*, Latin.] To call for evil upon himself or others.

IMPRECA'TION. *n. s.* [*imprecatio*, Lat. *imprecation*, Fr. from *imprecate.*] Curse; prayer by which any evil is wished.

My mother shall the horrid furies raise
With *imprecations*. *Chapman's Odyssey.*

Sir John Hotham, uncursed by any language or *imprecation* of mine, not long after paid his own and his eldest son's heads. *King Charles.*

With *imprecations* thus he fill'd the air,
And angry Neptune heard th' unrighteous pray'r. *Pope.*

I'MPRECATORY. *adj.* [from *imprecate.*] Containing wishes of evil.

To IMPRE'GN. *v. a.* [*in* and *prægno*, Latin.] To fill with young; to fill with any matter or quality.

In her ears the sound
Yet rung of his persuasive words, *impregn'd*
With reason, to her seeming. *Milton's Paradise Lost.*

Th' unfruitful rock itself, *impregn'd* by thee,
Forms lucid stones. *Thomson's Summer.*

IMPRE'GNABLE. *adj.* [*imprenable*, French.]

1. Not to be stormed; not to be taken.

Two giants kept themselves in a castle, seated upon the top of a rock, *impregnable*, because there was no coming to it but by one narrow path, where one man's force was able to keep down an army. *Sidney.*

Let us be back'd with God, and with the seas,
Which he hath given for fence *impregnable*,
And with their helps alone defend ourselves. *Shakes. H. VI.*

Hast thou not him, and all
Which he calls his, inclosed with a wall
Of strength *impregnable?* *Sandys.*

There the capitol thou see'st,
Above the rest lifting his stately head
On the Tarpeian rock, her citadel
Impregnable. *Milton's Paradise Regain'd, b.* iv.

2. Unshaken; unmoved; unaffected.

The man's affection remains wholly unconcerned and *impregnable*; just like a rock, which, being plied continually by the waves, still throws them back again, but is not at all moved. *South's Sermons.*

IMPRE'GNABLY. *adv.* [from *impregnable.*] In such a manner as to defy force or hostility.

A castle strongly seated on a high rock, joineth by an isthmus to the land, and is *impregnably* fortified. *Sandys.*

To IMPRE'GNATE. *v. a.* [*in* and *prægno*, Latin.]

1. To fill with young; to make prolifick.

Hermaphrodites, although they include the parts of both sexes, cannot *impregnate* themselves. *Brown's Vulg. Err.*

Impregnate, from their loins they shed
A slimy juice. *Dryden's Virg. Georg.*

With native earth their blood the monsters mix'd;
The blood, endu'd with animating heat,
Did in the *impregnate* earth new sons beget. *Dryden.*

2. [*Impregner*, French.] To fill; to saturate.

Christianity is of so prolifick a nature, so apt to *impregnate* the hearts and lives of its proselytes, that it is hard to imagine that any branch should want a due fertility. *Decay of Piety.*

IMPREGNA'TION. *n. s.* [from *impregnate.*]

1. The act of making prolifick; fecundation.

They ought to refer matters unto counsellors, which is the first begetting or *impregnation*; but when they are elaborate in the womb of their counsel, and grow ripe to be brought forth, then they take the matter back into their own hands. *Bacon.*

2. That with which any thing is impregnated.

What could implant in the body such peculiar *impregnations*, as should have such power? *Derham's Physico-Theology.*

3. [*Impregnation*, French.] Saturation. *Ainsworth.*

IMPREJU'DICATE. *adj.* [*in*, *præ*, and *judico*, Latin.] Unprejudiced; not prepossessed; impartial.

The solid reason of one man with *imprejudicate* apprehensions, begets as firm a belief as the authority or aggregated testimony of many hundreds. *Brown.*

IMPREPARA'TION. *n. s.* [*in* and *preparation.*] Unpreparedness; want of preparation.

Impreparation and unreadiness when they find in us, they turn it to the soothing up of themselves. *Hooker.*

To IMPRE'SS. *v. a.* [*impressum*, Latin.]

1. To print by pressure; to stamp.

So foul and ugly, that exceeding fear
Their visages *imprest*, when they approached near. *Fa. Qu.*

When God from earth form'd Adam in the East,
He his own image on the clay *imprest*. *Denham.*

The conquering chief his foot *imprest*
On the strong neck of that destructive beast. *Dryd. Ovid.*

2. To fix deep.

We should dwell upon the arguments, and *impress* the motives of persuasion upon our own hearts, 'till we feel the force of them. *Watts.*

3. To force into service. This is generally now spoken and written *press*.

His age has charms in it, his title more,
To pluck the common bosoms on his side,
And turn our *imprest* launces in our eyes
Which do command them. *Shakespeare's King Lear.*

Macbeth shall never vanquish'd be, until
Great Birnam-wood to Dunsinane's high hill
Shall come against him.
——That will never be:
Who can *impress* the forest, bid the tree
Unfix his earth-bound root? *Shakespeare's Macbeth.*

Ormond should contribute all he could for the making those levies of men, and for *impressing* of ships. *Clarendon.*

IMPRE'SS. *n. s.* [from the verb.]

1. Mark made by pressure.

This weak *impress* of love is as a figure
Trench'd in ice, which with an hour's heat
Dissolves to water. *Shakesp. Two Gent. of Verona.*

They having taken the *impresses* of the insides of these shells with that exquisite niceness, as to express even the finest lineaments of them. *Woodward's Nat. History.*

2. Effects upon another substance.

How objects are represented to myself I cannot be ignorant; but in what manner they are received, and what *impresses* they make upon the differing organs of another, he only knows that feels them. *Glanv. Sceps.*

3. Mark of distinction; stamp.

God, surveying the works of the creation, leaves us this general *impress* or character upon them, that they were exceeding good. *South's Sermons.*

4. Device; motto.

To describe emblazon'd shields,
Impresses quaint, caparisons, and steeds,
Bases, and tinsel trappings. *Milton's Paradise Lost, b.* ix.

5. Act of forcing any into service; compulsion; seizure. Now commonly *press*.

Ajax was here the voluntary, and you as under an *impress*. *Shakesp. Troilus and Cressida.*

Why such *impress* of shipwrights, whose sore task
Does not divide the Sunday from the week. *Shakes. Hamlet.*

Your ships are not well mann'd;
Your mariners are muliteers, reapers, people
Ingrost by swift *impress*. *Shakesp. Ant. and Cleopatra.*

IMPRE'SSION. *n. s.* [*impressio*, Latin; *impression*, Fr.]

1. The act of pressing one body upon another.

Sensation is such an *impression* or motion, made in some part of the body, as produces some perception in the understanding. *Locke.*

2. Mark made by pressure; stamp.

Like to a chaos, or unlick'd bear-whelp,
That carries no *impression* like the dam. *Shakesp. Henry* VI.

3. Image fixed in the mind.

Were the offices of religion stript of all the external decencies, they would not make a due *impression* on the mind. *Atter.*

The false representations of the kingdom's enemies had made some *impression* in the mind of the successor. *Swift.*

4. Operation; influence.

The king had made him high sheriff of Sussex, that he might the better make *impression* upon that county. *Clarendon.*

We lie open to the *impressions* of flattery, which we admit without scruple, because we think we deserve it. *Atterbury.*

Universal gravitation is above all mechanism, and proceeds from a divine energy and *impression*. *Bentley's Sermons.*

There is a real knowledge of material things, when the thing itself, and the real action and *impression* thereof on our senses, is perceived. *Cheyne's Phil. Princ.*

5. Edition; number printed at once; one course of printing.

To be distracted with many opinions, makes men to be of the last *impression*, and full of change. *Bacon.*

For ten *impressions*, which his works have had in so many years, at present a hundred books are scarcely purchased once a twelvemonth. *Dryden.*

6. Effect of an attack.

Such a defeat of near two hundred horse, seconded with two thousand foot, may surely endure a comparison with any of the bravest *impressions* in ancient times. *Wotton.*

IMPRE'SSIBLE. *adj.* [*in* and *pressum*, Lat.] What may be impressed.

The differences of *impressible* and not *impressible*, figurable and not figurable, are plebeian notions. *Bacon's Natural Hist.*

IMPRE'SSURE. *n. s.* [from *impress.*] The mark made by pressure; the dent; the impression.

Lean but upon a rush,
The cicatrice and capable *impressure*
Thy palm some moments keeps. *Shakesp. As you like it.*

To IMPRI'NT. *v. a.* [*imprimer*, French.]

1. To mark upon any substance by pressure.

One and the same seal, *imprinted* upon pieces of wax of different colours. *Holder's Elements of Speech.*

Having surveyed the image of God in the soul of man, we are not to omit those characters of majesty that God *imprinted* upon the body. *South's Sermons.*

She amid'st his spacious meadows flows;
Inclines her urn upon his fatten'd lands,
And sees his num'rous herds *imprint* her sands. *Prior.*

2. To stamp words upon paper by the use of types.

3. To fix on the mind or memory.

There is a kind of conveying of effectual and *imprinting* passages, amongst compliments, which is of singular use. *Bac.*

When we set before our eyes a round globe, the idea *imprinted* in our mind is of a flat circle, variously shadowed. *Loc.*

We have all those ideas in our understandings which we can make the objects of our thoughts, without the help of those sensible qualities which first *imprinted* them. *Locke.*

Retention is the power to revive again in our minds those ideas, which, after *imprinting*, have disappeared. *Locke.*

By familiar acquaintance he has got the ideas of those two different things distinctly *imprinted* on his mind. *Locke.*

To IMPRI'SON. *v. a.* [*emprisonner*, Fr. *in* and *prison.*] To shut up; to confine; to keep from liberty.

He *imprison'd* was in chains remediless;
For that Hippolytus' rent corse he did redress. *Fa. Queen.*

Now we are in the street, he first of all,
Improvidently proud, creeps to the wall;
And so *imprison'd* and hemm'd in by me,
Sells for a little state his liberty. *Donne.*

Try to *imprison* the resistless wind;
So swift is guilt, so hard to be confin'd. *Dryden.*

If a man *imprisons* himself in his closet, and employs reason to find out the nature of the corporeal world, without experiments, he will frame a scheme of chimeras. *Watts.*

It is not improbable, that all the virtual heat in the juices of vegetables, metals, and minerals may be owing to the action of the *imprisoned* rays. *Cheyne's Phil. Princ.*

IMPRI'SONMENT. *n. s.* [*emprisonnement*, Fr. from *imprison.*] Confinement; clausure; state of being shut in prison. It may be written *emprisonment.*

His sinews waxen weak and raw,
Through long *imprisonment* and hard constraint. *F. Queen.*

Which shall I first bewail,
Thy bondage or lost sight,
Thou art become, O worst *imprisonment!*
The dungeon of thyself. *Milton's Agonistes.*

From retentive cage
When sullen Philomel escapes, her notes
She varies, and of past *imprisonment*
Sweetly complains. *Phillips.*

Count Serini, still close prisoner in this castle, lost his senses by his long *imprisonment* and afflictions. *Addison.*

It is well if they don't fix the brand of heresy on the man who is leading them out of their long *imprisonment*, and loosing the fetters of their souls. *Watts's Impr. of the Mind.*

IMPROBABI'LITY. *n. s.* [from *improbable.*] Unlikelihood; difficulty to be believed.

The difficulty being so great, and the *improbability* of attempting this successfully, it was but reason that a solid foundation should be laid. *Hammond.*

As to the *improbabilities* of a spirit appearing, I boldly answer him, that a heroick poet is not tied to the bare representation of what is true, or exceeding probable. *Dryden.*

IMPRO'BABLE. *adj.* [*improbable*, Fr. *improbabilis*, Lat. *in* and *probable.*] Unlikely; incredible.

This account of party-patches will appear *improbable* to those who live at a distance from the fashionable world. *Addis.*

IMPRO'BABLY. *adv.* [from *improbable.*]

1. Without likelihood.

2. In a manner not to be approved. Obsolete.

Aristotle tells us, if a drop of wine be put into ten thousand measures of water, the wine being overpowered, will be turned into water: he speaks very *improbably.* *Boyle.*

To IMPRO'BATE. *v. a.* [*in* and *probo*, Latin.] Not to approve. *Ainsworth.*

IMPROBA'TION. *n. s.* [*improbatio*, Latin; *improbation*, French.] Act of disallowing. *Ainsworth.*

IMPRO'BITY. *n. s.* [*improbitas*, *improbus*, Latin.] Want of honesty; dishonesty; baseness.

He was perhaps excommunicable, yea, and cast out for notorious *improbity.* *Hooker.*

We balance the *improbity* of the one with the *improbity* of the other. *L'Estrange.*

To IMPROLI'FICATE. *v. a.* [*in* and *prolifick.*] To impregnate; to fecundate. A word not used.

A difficulty in the doctrine of eggs is how the sperm of the cock *improlificates*, and makes the oval conception fruitful. *Brown's Vulgar Errours.*

IMPRO'PER. *adj.* [*impropre*, Fr. *improprius*, Latin.]

1. Not well adapted; unqualified.

As every science requires a peculiar genius, so likewise there is a genius peculiarly *improper* for every one. *Burnet.*

2. Unfit; not conducive to the right end.

The methods used in an original disease would be very *improper* in a gouty case. *Arbuthnot on Diet.*

3. Not just; not accurate.

He disappear'd, was rarify'd;
For 'tis *improper* speech to say he dy'd:
He was exhal'd. *Dryden.*

IMPRO'PERLY. *adv.* [from *improper.*]

1. Not fitly; incongruously.

2. Not justly; not accurately.

Improperly we measure life by breath;
Such do not truly live who merit death. *Dryd. Juvenal.*

They assuring me of their assistance in correcting my faults where I spoke *improperly*, I was encouraged. *Dryden.*

To IMPRO'PRIATE. *v. a.* [*in* and *proprius*, Latin.]

1. To convert to private use; to seize to himself.

For the pardon of the rest, the king thought it not fit it should pass by parliament; the better, being matter of grace, to *impropriate* the thanks to himself. *Bacon's Henry VII.*

2. To put the possessions of the church into the hands of laicks.

Mrs. Gulston being possessed of the *impropriate* parsonage of Bardwell in Suffolk, did procure from the king leave to annex the same to the vicarage. *Spelman.*

IMPROPRIA'TION. *n. s.* [from *impropriate.*]

An *impropriation* is properly so called when the church land is in the hands of a layman; and an appropriation is when it is in the hands of a bishop, college, or religious house, though sometimes these terms are confounded. *Ayliffe's Parergon.*

Having an *impropriation* in his estate, he took a course to dispose of it for the augmentation of the vicarage. *Spelman.*

IMPROPRIA'TOR. *n. s.* [from *impropriate.*] A layman that has the possession of the lands of the church.

Where the vicar leases his glebe, the tenant must pay the great tythes to the rector or *impropriator.* *Ayliffe's Parerg.*

IMPROPRI'ETY. *n. s.* [*impropriété*, Fr. from *improprius*, Latin.] Unfitness; unsuitableness; inaccuracy; want of justness.

These mighty ones, whose ambition could suffer them to be called gods, would never be flattered into immortality; but the proudest have been convinced of the *impropriety* of that appellation. *Brown's Vulg. Errours.*

Many gross *improprieties*, however authorized by practice, ought to be discarded. *Swift.*

IMPRO'SPEROUS. *adj.* [*in* and *prosperous.*] Unhappy; unfortunate; not successful.

This method is in the design probable, how *improsperous* soever the wickedness of men hath rendered the success of it. *Hammond on Fundamentals.*

Our pride seduces us at once into the guilt of bold, and punishment of *improsperous* rebels. *Decay of Piety.*

Seven revolving years are wholly run,
Since the *improsperous* voyage we begun. *Dryden's Æn.*

IMPRO'SPEROUSLY. *adv.* [from *improsperous.*] Unhappily; unsuccessfully; with ill fortune.

This experiment has been but very *improsperously* attempted. *Boyle.*

IMPRO'VABLE. *adj.* [from *improve.*] Capable of being advanced from a good to a better state; capable of melioration.

Adventures in knowledge are laudable, and the essays of weaker heads afford *improvable* hints unto better. *Brown.*

We have stock enough, and that too of so *improvable* a nature, that is, capable of infinite advancement. *Decay of Piety.*

Man is accommodated with moral principles, *improvable* by the exercise of his faculties. *Hale's Origin of Mankind.*

Animals are not *improvable* beyond their proper genius: a dog will never learn to mew, nor a cat to bark. *Grew's Cosmol.*

I have a fine spread of *improvable* lands, and am already planting woods and draining marshes. *Addison's Spectator.*

IMPRO'VABLENESS. *n. s.* [from *improvable.*] Capableness of being made better.

IMPRO'VABLY. *adv.* [from *improvable.*] In a manner that admits of melioration.

To IMPRO'VE. *v. a.* [*in* and *probus. Quasi probum facere. Skinner.*]

1. To advance any thing nearer to perfection; to raise from good to better. We *amend* a *bad*, but *improve* a *good* thing.

I love not to *improve* the honour of the living by impairing that of the dead. *Denham.*

Heaven seems *improv'd* with a superior ray,
And the bright arch reflects a double day. *Pope.*

2. [*In* and *prove*; *improuver*, Fr. *improbo*, Lat.] To disprove.

Though the prophet Jeremy was unjustly accused, yet doth not that *improve* any thing that I have said. *Whitgifte.*

To IMPRO'VE. *v. n.* To advance in goodness.

We take care to *improve* in our frugality and diligence; virtues which become us, particularly in times of war. *Atterb.*

IMPRO'VEMENT. *n. s.* [from *improve.*]

1. Melioration; advancement of any thing from good to better.

Some virtues tend to the preservation of health, and others to the *improvement* and security of estates. *Tillotson.*

2. Act of improving.

The parts of Sinon, Camilla, and some few others, are *improvements* on the Greek poet. *Addison's Spectator.*

3. Progress from good to better.

There is a design of publishing the history of architecture, with its several *improvements* and decays. *Addison.*

4. Instruction; edification.

I look upon your city as the best place of *improvement:* from the school we go to the university, but from the universities to London. *South.*

5. Effect of melioration.

Love is the greatest of human affections, and friendship the noblest and most refined *improvement* of love. *South.*

IMPRO'VER. *n. s.* [from *improve.*]

1. One that makes himself or any thing else better.

They were the greatest *improvers* of those qualifications with which courts used to be adorned. *Clarendon.*

The first started ideas have been examined, and many effectually confuted by the late *improvers* of this way. *Locke.*

Homer is like a skilful *improver*, who places a beautiful statue so as to answer several vistas. *Pope.*

2. Any thing that meliorates.

Chalk is a very great *improver* of most lands. *Mortimer.*

IMPROVI'DED. *adj.* [*improvisus*, Latin; *imprevu*, Fr.] Unforeseen; unexpected; unprovided against.

She suborned hath
This crafty messenger with letters vain,
To work new woe, and *improvided* scath,
By breaking off the band betwixt us twain. *Fairy Queen.*

IMPRO'VIDENCE. *n. s.* [from *improvident.*] Want of forethought; want of caution.

Men would escape floods by running up to mountains; and though some might perish through *improvidence*, or through the sudden inundation of a deluge, many would escape. *Hale.*

The *improvidence* of my neighbour must not make me inhuman. *L'Estrange.*

IMPRO'VIDENT. *adj.* [*improvidus*, Latin.] Wanting forecast; wanting care to provide.

Improvident soldiers, had your watch been good,
This sudden mischief never could have fall'n. *Shak. H.* VI.

When men well have fed, the blood being warm,
Then are they most *improvident* of harm. *Daniel's Ci. War.*

I shall conclude this digression, and return to the time when that brisk and *improvident* resolution was taken. *Clarendon.*

This were an *improvident* revenge in the young ones, whereby, in defect of provision, they must destroy themselves. *Brown's Vulgar Errours.*

IMPRO'VIDENTLY. *adv.* [from *improvident.*] Without forethought; without care.

Now we are in the street, he first of all,
Improvidently proud, creeps to the wall;
And so imprison'd, and hemm'd in by me,
Sells for a little state his liberty. *Donne.*

IMPROVI'SION. *n. s.* [*in* and *provision.*] Want of forethought.

Her *improvision* would be justly accusable. *Brown.*

IMPRU'DENCE. *n. s.* [*imprudence*, Fr. *imprudentia*, Lat.] Want of prudence; indiscretion; negligence; inattention to interest.

IMPRU'DENT. *adj.* [*imprudent*, Fr. *imprudens*, Lat.] Wanting prudence; injudicious; indiscreet; negligent.

There is no such *imprudent* person as he that neglects God and his soul. *Tillotson.*

I'MPUDENCE. } *n. s.* [*impudence*, Fr. *impudentia*, Lat.] Shame-
I'MPUDENCY. } lessness; immodesty.

I ne'er heard yet
That any of these bolder vices wanted
Less *impudence* to gainsay what they did,
Than to perform it first. *Shakesp. Winter's Tale.*

Nor did Noah's open infirmity justify Cham's *impudency*, or exempt him from that curse of being servant of servants. *King Charles.*

Those clear truths, that either their own evidence forces us us to admit, or common experience makes it *impudence* to deny. *Locke.*

I'MPUDENT. *adj.* [*impudent*, Fr. *impudens*, Latin.] Shameless; wanting modesty.

It is not a confident brow, nor the throng of words that come with such more than *impudent* sawciness from you, can thrust me from a level consideration. *Shakesp. Henry* IV.

When we behold an angel, not to fear,
Is to be *impudent*. *Dryd. Spanish Fryar.*

I'MPUDENTLY. *adv.* [from *impudent.*] Shamelesly; without modesty.

At once assail
With open mouths, and *impudently* rail. *Sandys.*

Why should soft Fabius *impudently* bear
Names gain'd by conquest in the Gallick war?
Why lays he claim to Hercules his strain,
Yet dares be base, effeminate, and vain? *Dryden.*

To IMPU'GN. *v. a.* [*impugner*, Fr. *impugno*, Lat.] To attack; to assault.

Of a strange nature is the suit you follow;
Yet in such rule, that the Venetian law
Cannot *impugn* you. *Shakesp. Merch. of Venice.*

I cannot think myself engaged to discourse of lots, as to their nature, use, and allowableness; and that not only in matters of moment and business, but also of recreation, which is indeed *impugned* by some, though better defended by others. *South's Sermons.*

St. Hierom reporteth, that he saw one of these in his time; but the truth hereof I will not rashly *impugn*, or over-boldly affirm. *Peacham on Drawing.*

IMPU'GNER. *n. s.* [from *impugn.*] One that attacks or invades.

IMPUI'SSANCE. *n. s.* [French] Impotence; inability; weakness; feebleness.

As he would not trust Ferdinando and Maximilian for supports of war, so the *impuissance* of the one, and the double proceeding of the other, lay fair for him for occasions to accept of peace. *Bacon's Henry* VII.

I'MPULSE. *n. s.* [*impulsus*, Latin.]

1. Communicated force; the effect of one body acting upon another.

If these little *impulses* set the great wheels of devotion on work, the largeness and height of that shall not at all be prejudiced by the smalness of its occasion. *South's Sermons.*

Bodies produce ideas in us manifestly by *impulse*. *Locke.*

Bodies, from the *impulse* of a fluid, can only gravitate in proportion to their surfaces, and not according to their quantity of matter, which is contrary to experience. *Cheyne.*

2. Influence acting upon the mind; motive; idea.

Mean time, by Jove's *impulse*, Mezentius arm'd,
Succeeded Turnus. *Dryden's Æn.*

These were my natural *impulses* for the undertaking; but there was an accidental motive, which was full as forcible. *Dry.*

Moses saw the bush burn without being consumed, and heard a voice out of it: this was something, besides finding an *impulse* upon his mind to go to Pharaoh, that he might bring his brethren out of Egypt. *Locke.*

3. Hostile impression.

Like two great rocks against the raging tide,
Unmov'd the two united chiefs abide,
Sustain th' *impulse*, and receive the war. *Prior.*

IMPU'LSION. *n. s.* [*impulsion*, Fr. *impulsus*, Latin.]

1. The agency of body in motion upon body.

The motion in the minute parts of any solid body passeth without sound; for that sound that is heard sometimes is produced only by the breaking of the air, and not by the *impulsion* of the air. *Bacon's Natural History.*

To the *impulsion* there is requisite the force of the body that moveth, and the resistance of the body that is moved; and if the body be too great, it yieldeth too little; and if it be too small, it resisteth too little. *Bacon's Natural History.*

2. Influence operating upon the mind.

But thou didst plead
Divine *impulsion*, prompting how thou might'st
Find some occasion to infest our foes. *Milton's Agonistes.*

IMPU'LSIVE. *adj.* [*impulsif*, Fr. from *impulse.*] Having the power of impulse; moving; impellent.

Nature and duty bind him to obedience;
But those being placed in a lower sphere,
His fierce ambition, like the highest mover,
Has hurried with a strong *impulsive* motion
Against their proper course. *Denham's Sophy.*

What is the fountain or *impulsive* cause of this prevention of sin? It is perfectly free grace. *South's Sermons.*

Poor men! poor papers! we and they
Do some *impulsive* force obey,
And are but play'd with, do not play. *Prior.*

IMPU'NITY. *n. s.* [*impunité*, Fr. *impunitas*, Latin.] Freedom from punishment; exemption from punishment.

In the condition of subjects they will gladly continue, as long as they may be protected and justly governed, without oppression on the one side, or *impunity* on the other. *Davies.*

A general *impunity* would confirm them; for the vulgar will never be brought to believe, that there is a crime where they see no penalty. *Addison's Freeholder.*

Men, potent in the commonwealth, will employ their ill-gotten influence towards procuring *impunity*, or extorting undue favours for themselves or dependents. *Atterbury's Sermons.*

IMPU'RE. *adj.* [*impur*, Fr. *impurus*, Latin.]

1. Contrary to sanctity; unhallowed; unholy.

No more can *impure* man retain and move
In that pure region of a worthy love,
Than earthly substance can unforc'd aspire,
And leave his nature to converse with fire. *Donne.*

Hypocrites austerely talk,
Condemning as *impure* what God has made
Pure, and commands to some, leaves free to all. *Milton.*

2. Unchaste.

2. Unchaſte.

If black ſcandal, or foul-fac'd reproach,
Attend the ſequel of your impoſition,
Your meer enforcement ſhall acquittance me
From all the *impure* blots and ſtains thereof. *Shakeſp. R.* III.

One could not deviſe a more proper hell for an *impure* ſpirit, than that which Plato has touched upon. *Addiſon.*

3. Feculent; foul with extraneous mixtures; droſſy.

IMPU'RELY. *adv.* [from *impure*] With impurity.

IMPU'RENESS. } *n. ſ.* [*impureté*, French; *impuritas*, Lat. from IMPU'RITY. } *impure.*]

1. Want of ſanctity; want of holineſs.
2. Act of unchaſtity.

The foul *impurities* that reigned among the monkiſh clergy. *Atterbury's Sermons.*

3. Feculent admixture.

Cleanſe the alimentary duct by vomiting and clyſters, the *impurities* of which will be carried into the blood. *Arbuthnot.*

To IMPU'RPLE. *v. a.* [*empourprer*, Fr. from *purple.*] To make red; to colour as with purple.

Now in looſe garlands, thick thrown off the bright
Pavement, that like a ſea of jaſper ſhone,
Impurpled with celeſtial roſes, ſmil'd. *Milton.*

IMPU'TABLE. *adj.* [from *impute*]

1. Chargeable upon any one.

That firſt ſort of fooliſhneſs is *imputable* to them. *South:*

2. Accuſable; chargeable with a fault. Not proper.

If the wife departs from her huſband, through any default of his, as on the account of cruelty, then he ſhall be compelled to allow her alimony; for the law deems her to be a dutiful wife as long as the fault lies at his door, and ſhe is in no wiſe *imputable.* *Ayliffe's Parergon.*

IMPU'TABLENESS. *n. ſ.* [from *imputable.*] The quality of being imputable.

'Tis neceſſary to the *imputableneſs* of an action, that it be avoidable. *Norris.*

IMPUTA'TION. *n. ſ.* [*imputation*, Fr. from *impute.*]

1. Attribution of any thing: generally of ill.

Truſt to me, Ulyſſes;
Our *imputation* ſhall be oddly pois'd
In this wild action. *Shakeſp. Troilus and Creſſida.*

If a ſon that is ſent by his father about merchandize, do fall into ſome lewd action, the *imputation* of his wickedneſs, by your rule, ſhould be impoſed upon his father. *Shakeſpeare.*

To uſe intellections and volitions in the infinite eſſence, as hypotheſes, is allowable; but a rigorous *imputation* is derogatory to him, and arrogant in us. *Glanv. Sceps.*

I have formerly ſaid that I could diſtinguiſh your writings from thoſe of any others: 'tis now time to clear myſelf from any *imputation* of ſelf-conceit on that ſubject. *Dryden.*

2. Sometimes of good.

If I had a ſuit to maſter Shallow, I would humour his men with the *imputation* of being near their maſter. *Shakeſpeare.*

3. Cenſure; reproach.

Whatſoever happens they alſo the leaſt feel that ſcourge of vulgar *imputation*, which notwithſtanding they deſerve. *Hooker.*

Let us be careful to guard ourſelves againſt theſe groundleſs *imputations* of our enemies, and to riſe above them. *Addiſon.*

Neither do I reflect upon the memory of his late majeſty, whom I entirely acquit of any *imputation* upon this matter. *Swift.*

4. Hint; reflection.

Anthonio is a good man.
—Have you heard any *imputation* to the contrary?
—No, no; my meaning is to have you underſtand me that he is ſufficient. *Shakeſp. Merchant of Venice.*

IMPUTA'TIVE. *adj.* [from *impute.*] That which may impute. *Ainſworth.*

To IMPU'TE. *v. a.* [*imputer*, Fr. *imputo*, Latin.]

1. To charge upon; to attribute: generally ill; ſometimes good.

It was *imputed* to him for righteouſneſs. *Ro.* iv. 22.

Men in their innovations ſhould follow the example of time, which innovateth but quietly, and by degrees ſcarce to be perceived; for otherwiſe whatſoever is new and unlooked for, ever mends ſome, and pairs others; and he that is holpen takes it for a fortune, and thanks the time; and he that is hurt for a wrong, *imputeth* it to the author. *Bacon's Eſſays.*

I made it by your perſuaſion, to ſatisfy thoſe who *imputed* it to folly. *Temple.*

Impute your dangers to our ignorance. *Dryden.*

This obſcurity cannot be *imputed* to want of language in ſo great a maſter of ſtile. *Locke.*

I have read a book *imputed* to lord Bathurſt, called a diſſertation on parties. *Swift.*

2. To reckon to one what does not properly belong to him.

Thy merit
Imputed ſhall abſolve them who renounce
Their own both righteous and unrighteous deeds. *Milton.*

IMPU'TER. *n. ſ.* [from *impute.*] He that imputes.

IN. *prep.* [*in*, Latin.]

1. Noting the place where any thing is preſent.

In ſchool of love are all things taught we ſee;
There learn'd this maid of arms the ireful guiſe. *Fairfax.*

Is this place here not ſufficient ſtrong
To guard us *in?* *Daniel's Civil War.*

2. Noting the ſtate preſent at any time.

The other is only by error and miſconceit named the ordinance of Jeſus Chriſt: no one proof is yet brought forth, whereby it may clearly appear to be ſo *in* very deed. *Hooker.*

Like one of two contending *in* a prize,
That thinks he hath done well *in* people's eyes. *Shakeſp.*

Sir Edmond Courtney, and the haughty prelate,
With many more confederates, are *in* arms. *Shak. R.* III.

Danger before, and *in*, and after the act,
You needs muſt grant is great. *Daniel's Civil War.*

However it be *in* knowledge, I may truly ſay it is of no uſe at all *in* probabilities; for the aſſent there, being to be determined by the preponderancy, after a due weighing of all the proofs on both ſides, nothing is ſo unfit to aſſiſt the mind *in* that as ſyllogiſm. *Locke.*

In all likelihood I brought all my limbs out of the bed, which, 'tis probable, he has not done off the breach. *Collier.*

God hath made our eternal and temporal intereſts, *in* moſt caſes, very conſiſtent. *Smalridge's Sermons.*

None was ſo little *in* their friendſhips, or ſo much *in* that of thoſe whom they had moſt abuſed. *Letter to Publ. of Dunciad.*

3. Noting the time.

When we would conſider eternity *a parte ante*, what do we but, beginning from ourſelves and the preſent time we are *in*, repeat in our minds the ideas of years or ages paſt, with a proſpect of proceeding in ſuch addition with all the infinity of numbers? *Locke.*

4. Noting power.

To feed mens ſouls, quoth he, is not *in* man. *Hubb. Tale.*

5. Noting proportion.

Let uſury in general be reduced to five *in* the hundred, and let that rate be proclaimed to be free and current. *Bacon.*

I cannot but lament the common courſe, which, at leaſt, nine *in* ten of thoſe who enter into the miniſtry are obliged to enter. *Swift.*

6. Concerning.

I only conſider what he, who is allowed to have carried this argument fartheſt, has ſaid *in* it. *Locke.*

7. For the ſake. A ſolemn phraſe.

Now, *in* the names of all the gods at once,
Upon what meat does this our Cæſar feed,
That he is grown ſo great? *Shakeſ. Julius Cæſar.*

In the name of the people,
And *in* the power of us the tribunes, we
Baniſh him our city. *Shakeſ. Coriolanus.*

Now, *in* the name of honour, ſir, I beg you
That I may ſee your father's death reveng'd. *Dryden.*

8. Noting cauſe.

King Henry, be thy title right or wrong,
Lord Clifford vows to fight *in* thy defence. *Shakeſp. H.* VI.

9. IN *that.* Becauſe.

Some things they do *in that* they are men; *in that* they are wiſe men, and chriſtian men, ſome things; ſome things *in that* they are men miſled, and blinded with error. *Hooker.*

He cannot brook ſuch diſgrace well, as he ſhall run into; *in that* it is a thing of his own ſearch, and againſt my will. *Shakeſpeare's As you like it.*

10. IN *as much.* Since; ſeeing that.

Thoſe things are done voluntarily by us, which other creatures do naturally, *in as much* as we might ſtay our doing of them if we would. *Hooker.*

IN. *adv.*

1. Within ſome place; not out.

How infamous is the falſe, fraudulent, and unconſcionable perſon; eſpecially if he be arrived at that conſummate and robuſt degree of falſhood as to play *in* and out, and ſhow tricks with oaths, the ſacredeſt bonds which the conſcience of man can be bound with. *South's Sermons.*

I fear me, you'll be *in* 'till then. *Shakeſpeare.*

2. Engaged to any affair.

We know the worſt can come: 'tis thought upon:
We cannot ſhift being *in*, we muſt go on. *Daniel.*

Theſe pragmatical flies value themſelves for being *in* at every thing, and are found at laſt to be juſt good for nothing. *L'Eſt.*

3. Placed in ſome ſtate.

Poor rogues talk of court news,
Who loſes and who wins; who's *in*, who's out. *Shakeſp.*

Muſt never patriot then declaim at gin,
Unleſs, good man, he has been fairly *in.* *Pope.*

4. Noting entrance.

Go to thy fellows; bid them cover the table, ſerve *in* the meat, and we will come *in* to dinner. *Shakeſpeare.*

He's too big to go *in* there: what ſhall I do?
——Let me ſee't; I'll *in*, I'll *in*: follow your friend's advice, I'll *in.* *Shakeſpeare's Merry Wives of Windſor.*

In the ſaid cavity lies looſe the ſhell of ſome ſort of bivalve larger than could be introduced *in* at either of thoſe holes. *Woodward on Foſſils.*

5. Into any place.

Is it not more elegible to come *in* with a smooth gale, than to be tossed at sea with a storm. *Collier.*

Next fill the hole with its own earth again,
And trample with thy feet, and tread it *in*. *Dryd. Georg.*

6. Close; home.

The posture of left-handed fencers is so different from that of the right-handed, that you run upon their swords if you push forward; and they are *in* with you, if you offer to fall back without keeping your guard. *Tatler.*

IN has commonly in composition a negative or privative sense, as in the Latin: so, *active* denotes that which *acts*, *inactive* that which does *not act*. *In* before *r* is changed into *r*; as *irregular*: before *l* into *l*; as *illative*: and into *m* before some other consonants; as *improbable*.

INABI'LITY. *n. s.* [*in* and *ability*.] Impuissance; impotence; want of power.

If no natural nor casual *inability* cross their desires, they always delighting to inure themselves with actions most beneficial to others, cannot but gather great experience, and thro' experience the more wisdom. *Hooker.*

Neither ignorance nor *inability* can be pretended; and what plea can we offer to divine justice to prevent condemnation? *Rogers.*

INA'BSTINENCE. *n. s.* [*in* and *abstinence*.] Intemperance; want of power to abstain.

Diseases dire; of which a monstrous crew
Before thee shall appear, that thou may'st know
What misery the *inabstinence* of Eve
Shall bring on man. *Milt. Par. Lost.*

INACCE'SSIBLE. *adj.* [*inaccessible*, Fr. *in* and *accessible*.] Not to be reached; not to be approached.

Whate'er you are,
That in this desart *inaccessible*,
Under the shade of melancholy boughs,
Lose and neglect the creeping hours of time. *Shakespeare.*

Many other hidden parts of nature, even of a far lower form, are *inaccessible* to us. *Hale's Origin of Mankind.*

There shall we clearly see the ends and uses of these things, which here were either too subtile for us to penetrate, or too remote and *inaccessible* for us to come to any distinct view of. *Ray on the Creation.*

This part, which is so noble, is not altogether *inaccessible*; and that an easy way may be found to it, 'tis to consider nature and to copy her. *Dryden.*

INA'CCURACY. *n. s.* [from *inaccurate*.] Want of exactness.

INA'CCURATE. *adj.* [*in* and *accurate*.] Not exact; not accurate. It is used sometimes of persons, but more frequently of performances.

INA'CTION. *n. s.* [*inaction*, Fr. *in* and *action*.] Cessation from labour; forbearance of labour.

The times and amusements past are not more like a dream to me, than those which are present: I lie in a refreshing kind of *inaction*. *Pope.*

INA'CTIVE. *adj.* [*in* and *active*.] Not busy; not diligent; idle; indolent; sluggish.

INA'CTIVELY. *adv.* [from *inactive*.] Idly; without labour; without motion; sluggishly.

In seasons of perfect freedom, mark how your son spends his time; whether he *inactively* loiters it away, when left to his own inclination. *Locke.*

INACTI'VITY. *n. s.* [*in* and *activity*.] Idleness; rest; sluggishness.

A doctrine which manifestly tends to discourage the endeavours of men, to introduce a lazy *inactivity*, and neglect of the ordinary means of grace. *Rogers's Sermons.*

Virtue, conceal'd within our breast,
Is *inactivity* at best. *Swift.*

INA'DEQUATE. *adj.* [*in* and *adæquatus*, Latin.] Not equal to the purpose; defective; falling below the due proportion.

Remorse for vice
Not paid, or paid *inadequate* in price,
What farther means can reason now direct? *Dryden.*

Inadequate ideas are such, which are but a partial or incomplete representation of those archetypes to which they are referred. *Locke.*

INA'DEQUATELY. *adv.* [from *inadequate*.] Defectively; not completely.

These pores they may either exactly fill, or but *inadequately*. *Boyle.*

INADVE'RTENCE. } *n. s.* [*inadvertance*, French; from *inadvertent*.]
INADVE'RTENCY. }

1. Carelessness; negligence; inattention.

There is a vast difference between them; indeed, as vast as between *inadvertency* and deliberation, between surprize and set purpose. *South.*

From an habitual heedless *inadvertency*, men are so intent upon the present that they mind nothing else. *L'Estrange.*

2. Act or effect of negligence.

Many persons have lain under great and heavy scandals, which have taken their first rise only from some *inadvertence* or indiscretion. *Government of the Tongue.*

The productions of a great genius, with many lapses and *inadvertencies*, are infinitely preferrable to the works of an inferior kind of author, which are scrupulously exact. *Addison.*

INADVE'RTENT. *adj.* [*in* and *advertens*, Latin.] Negligent; careless.

INADVE'RTENTLY. *adv.* [from *inadvertent*.] Carelesly; negligently.

Aristotle mentions Telegonus as the son of Circe and Ulysses, who afterwards slew his father with the bone of a fish *inadvertently*. *Broome's Notes on the Odyssey.*

Worthy persons, if *inadvertently* drawn into a deviation, will endeavour instantly to recover their lost ground. *Clarissa.*

INA'LIENABLE. *adj.* [*in* and *alienable*.] That cannot be alienated.

INALIME'NTAL. *adj.* [*in* and *alimental*.] Affording no nourishment.

Dulcoration importeth a degree to nourishment; and the making of things *inalimental* to be become alimental, may be an experiment of great profit for making new victual. *Bacon.*

INAMI'SSIBLE. *adj.* [*inamissible*, French; *in* and *amissum*, Lat.] Not to be lost.

These advantages are *inamissible*. *Hammond.*

INA'NE. *adj.* [*inanis*, Latin.] Empty; void.

We sometimes speak of place in the great *inane*, beyond the confines of the world. *Locke.*

To INA'NIMATE. *v. a.* [*in* and *animo*, Latin.] To animate; to quicken. This word is not in use.

There's a kind of world remaining still,
Though she which did *inanimate* and fill
The world be gone; yet in this last long night
Her ghost doth walk, that is, a glimmering light. *Donne.*

INA'NIMATE. } *adj.* [*inanimatus*, Latin; *inanimé*, French.]
INA'NIMATED. } Void of life; without animation.

The spirits of animate bodies are all in some degree kindled; but *inanimate* bodies have their spirits no whit inflamed. *Bacon's Natural History.*

The golden goddess, present at the pray'r,
Well knew he meant th' *inanimated* fair,
And gave the sign of granting. *Dryden.*

All the ideas of sensible qualities are not inherent in the *inanimate* bodies; but are the effects of their motion upon our nerves. *Bentley.*

They can neither subsist nor be produced by the powers of mechanism; for both require the constant influence of a principle different from that which governs the *inanimated* part of the universe. *Cheyne's Phil. Prin.*

From roofs when Verrio's colours fall,
And leave *inanimate* the naked wall,
Still in thy song should vanquish'd France appear. *Pope.*

INANI'TION. *n. s.* [*inanition*, Fr. *inanis*, Lat.] Emptiness of body; want of fulness in the vessels of the animal.

Weakness which attends fevers proceeds from too great fulness in the beginning, and too great *inanition* in the latter end of the disease. *Arbuthnot on Diet.*

INA'NITY. *n. s.* [from *inanis*, Latin.] Emptiness; void space.

This opinion excludes all such *inanity*, and admits no vacuities but so little ones as no body whatever can come to, but will be bigger than they, and must touch the corporal parts which those vacuities divide. *Digby on Bodies.*

INA'PPETENCY. *n. s.* [*in* and *appetentia*, Latin.] Want of stomach or appetite.

INA'PPLICABLE. *adj.* [*in* and *applicable*.] Not to be put to a particular use.

INAPPLICA'TION. *n. s.* [*inapplication*, Fr. *in* and *application*.] Indolence; negligence.

INA'RABLE. *adj.* [*in* and *aro*, Latin.] Not capable of tillage. *Dict.*

To INA'RCH. *v. a.* [*in* and *arch*.]

Inarching is a method of grafting, which is commonly called grafting by approach. This method of grafting is used when the stock and the tree may be joined: take the branch you would *inarch*, and, having fitted it to that part of the stock where you intend to join it, pare away the rind and wood on one side about three inches in length: after the same manner cut the stock or branch in the place where the graft is to be united, so that they may join equally together that the sap may meet: then cut a little tongue upwards in the graft, and make a notch in the stock to admit it; so that when they are joined the tongue will prevent their slipping, and the graft will more closely unite with the stock. Having thus placed them exactly together, tie them; then cover the place with grafting clay, to prevent the air from entering to dry the wound, or the wet from getting in to rot the stock: you should fix a stake into the ground, to which that part of the stock, as also the graft, should be fastened, to prevent the wind from breaking them asunder. In this manner they are to remain about four months, in which time they will be sufficiently united; and the graft may then be cut from the mother-tree, observing to slope it off close to the stock, and cover the joined parts with fresh grafting clay. The operation is always performed in April or May, and is commonly practised upon oranges, myrtles, jasmines, walnuts firrs, and pines, which will not succeed by common grafting or budding. *Miller.*

INARTI'CULATE. *adj.* [*inarticulé*, Fr. *in* and *articulate.*] Not uttered with diſtinctneſs like that of the ſyllables of human ſpeech.

Obſerve what *inarticulate* ſounds reſemble any of the particular letters. *Wilkins's Math. Magic.*

By the harmony of words we elevate the mind to a ſenſe of devotion; as our ſolemn muſick, which is *inarticulate* poeſy, does in churches. *Dryden.*

INARTI'CULATELY. *adv.* [from *inarticulate.*] Not diſtinctly.

INARTI'CULATENESS. *n. ſ.* [from *inarticulate.*] Confuſion of ſounds; want of diſtinctneſs in pronouncing.

INARTIFI'CIAL. *adj.* [*in* and *artificial.*] Contrary to art.

I have ranked this among the effects; and it may be thought *inartificial* to make it the cauſe alſo. *Decay of Piety.*

INARTIFI'CIALLY. *adv.* [from *inartificial.*] Without art; in a manner contrary to the rules of art.

This lofty humour is clumſily and *inartificially* managed, when its affected by thoſe of a ſelf-denying profeſſion. *Collier.*

INATTE'NTION. *n. ſ.* [*inattention*, Fr. *in* and *attention.*] Diſregard; negligence; neglect.

Perſons keep out of the reach of the reproofs of the miniſtry, or hear with ſuch *inattention* or contempt as renders them of little effect. *Rogers's Sermons.*

We ſee a ſtrange *inattention* to this moſt important proſpect. *Rogers's Sermons.*

Novel lays attract our raviſh'd ears;
But old, the mind with *inattention* hears. *Pope.*

INATTE'NTIVE. *adj.* [*in* and *attentive.*] Careleſs; negligent; regardleſs.

If we indulge the frequent roving of paſſions, we ſhall procure an unſteady and *inattentive* habit. *Watts.*

INAU'DIBLE. *adj.* [*in* and *audible.*] Not to be heard; void of ſound.

Let's take the inſtant by the forward top;
For we are old, and on our quick'ſt decrees
Th' *inaudible* and noiſeleſs foot of time
Steals, ere we can effect them. *Shakeſpeare.*

To INAU'GURATE. *v. a.* [*inauguro*, Latin.] To conſecrate; to inveſt with a new office by ſolemn rites; to begin with good omens; to begin.

Thoſe beginnings of years were propitious to him, as if kings did chuſe remarkable days to *inaugurate* their favours, that they may appear acts as well of the time as of the will. *Wotton.*

INAUGURA'TION. *n. ſ.* [*inauguration*, Fr. *inauguro*, Latin.] Inveſtiture by ſolemn rites.

The royal olive was ſolemnly ſworn, at his *inauguration*, to obſerve theſe things inviolable. *Howel's Vocal Forreſt.*

At his regal *inauguration* his old father reſigned the kingdom to him. *Brown's Vulgar Errours.*

INAURA'TION. *n. ſ.* [*inauro*, Latin.] The act of gilding or covering with gold.

The Romans had the art of gilding after our manner; but ſome ſort of their *inauration*, or gilding, muſt have been much dearer than ours. *Arbuthnot on Coins.*

INAUSPI'CIOUS. *adj.* [*in* and *auſpicious.*] Ill-omened; unlucky; unfortunate.

Oh here
I will ſet up my everlaſting reſt;
And ſhake the yoke of *inauſpicious* ſtars
From this world-wearied fleſh. *Shakeſ. Rom. and Juliet.*

Though heaven's *inauſpicious* eye
Lay black on love's nativity,
Her eye a ſtrong appeal can give;
Beauty, ſmiles, and love ſhall live. *Craſhaw.*

The ſtars feel not the diſeaſes their *inauſpicious* influence produces. *Boyle.*

With *inauſpicious* love a wretched ſwain
Purſu'd the faireſt nymph of all the plain;
She plung'd him hopeleſs in a deep deſpair. *Dryden.*

INBE'ING. *n. ſ.* [*in* and *being.*] Inherence; inſeparableneſs.

When we ſay the bowl is round, the boy is witty, theſe are proper or inherent modes; for they have a ſort of *inbeing* in the ſubſtance itſelf, and do not ariſe from the addition of any other ſubſtance to it. *Watts.*

I'NBORN. *adj.* [*in* and *born.*] Innate; implanted by nature.

Led by ſenſe of good,
Inborn to all, I ſought my needful food. *Dryden.*

All paſſions being *inborn* with us, we are almoſt equally judges of them. *Dryden.*

Some Carolina, to heaven's dictates true,
Thy *inborn* worth with conſcious eyes ſhall ſee,
And ſlight th' imperial diadem for thee. *Addiſon.*

INBRE'ATHED. *adj.* [*in* and *breath.*] Inſpired; infuſed by inſpiration.

Bleſt pair of ſyrens, pledges of heav'n's joy,
Sphere-born harmonious ſiſters, voice and verſe,
Wed your divine ſounds, and mixt power employ,
Dead things with *inbreath'd* ſenſe able to pierce. *Milton.*

I'NBRED. *adj.* [*in* and *bred.*] Produced within; hatched or generated within.

My *inbred* enemy
Forth iſſu'd. *Milton's Paradiſe Loſt, b.* ii.

A man thinks better of his children than they deſerve; but there is an impulſe of tenderneſs, and there muſt be ſome eſteem for the ſetting of that *inbred* affection at work. *L'Eſtr.*

But he unmov'd contemns their idle threat;
And *inbred* worth doth boaſting valour ſlight. *Dryden.*

To INCA'GE. *v. a.* [*in* and *cage.*] To coop up; to ſhut up; to confine in a cage, or any narrow ſpace.

And yet *incaged* in ſo ſmall a verge,
Thy waſte is no whit leſſer than thy lord's. *Shakeſ. R.* II.

It made my impriſonment a pleaſure;
Ay, ſuch a pleaſure as *incaged* birds
Conceive. *Shakeſpeare's Henry* VI.

INCALE'SCENCE. } *n. ſ.* [*incaleſco*, Latin.] The ſtate of growing warm; warmth; incipient heat.
INCALE'SCENCY. }

Averroes reſtrained his hilarity, making no more thereof than Seneca commendeth, and was allowable in Cato; that is, a ſober *incaleſcence*, and regulated eſtuation from wine. *Brown.*

The oil preſerves the ends of the bones from *incaleſcency*, which they, being ſolid bodies, would neceſſarily contract from a ſwift motion. *Ray on the Creation.*

INCANTA'TION. *n. ſ.* [*incantation*, Fr. *incanto*, Lat.] Charms uttered by ſinging; enchantment.

My ancient *incantations* are too weak,
And hell too ſtrong. *Shakeſpeare's Henry* VI.

By Adam's hearkening to his wife, mankind, by that her *incantation*, became the ſubject of labour, ſorrow, and death. *Raleigh's Hiſtory of the World.*

The great wonders of witches, their carrying in the air, and transforming themſelves into other bodies, are reported to be wrought, not by *incantations* or ceremonies, but by anointing themſelves all over, move a man to think that theſe fables are the effects of imagination; for ointments, if laid on any thing thick, by ſtopping of the pores, ſhut in the vapours, and ſend them to the head extremely. *Bacon's Natural Hiſtory.*

The name of a city being diſcovered unto their enemies, their penates and patronal gods might be called forth by charms and *incantations*. *Brown's Vulgar Errours.*

The nuptial rights his outrage ſtrait attends;
The dow'r deſir'd is his transfigur'd friends:
The *incantation* backward ſhe repeats,
Inverts her rod, and what ſhe did, defeats. *Garth.*

The commands which our religion hath impoſed on its followers are not like the abſurd ceremonies of pagan idolatry, the frivolous rites of their initiations and worſhip, that might look like *incantations* and magick, but had no tendency to make mankind the happier. *Bentley's Sermons.*

INCA'NTATORY. *adj.* [from *incanto*, Latin.] Dealing by enchantment; magical.

Fortune-tellers, jugglers, geomancers, and the like *incantatory* impoſtors, daily delude them. *Brown's Vulg. Errours.*

To INCA'NTON. *v. a.* [*in* and *canton.*] To unite to a canton or ſeparate community.

When the cantons of Bern and Zurich propoſed the incorporating Geneva in the cantons, the Roman catholicks, fearing the proteſtant intereſt, propoſed the *incantoning* of Conſtance as a counterpoiſe. *Addiſon on Italy.*

INCAPABI'LITY. } *n. ſ.* [from *incapable.*] Inability natural; diſqualification legal.
INCA'PABLENESS. }

You have nothing to urge but a kind of *incapability* in yourſelf to the ſervice. *Suckling.*

INCA'PABLE. *adj.* [*incapable*, Fr. *in* and *capable.*]

1. Wanting power; wanting underſtanding; unable to comprehend, learn, or underſtand.

Incapable and ſhallow innocents!
You cannot gueſs who caus'd your father's death. *Shakeſp.*

2. Not able to receive any thing.

Wilmot, when he ſaw Goring put in the command, thought himſelf *incapable* of reparation. *Clarendon.*

3. Unable; not equal to any thing.

Is not your father grown *incapable*
Of reaſonable affairs? Is he not ſtupid
With age? *Shakeſ. Winter's Tale.*

4. Diſqualified by law.

Their lands are almoſt entirely taken from them, and they are rendered *incapable* of purchaſing any more. *Swift.*

5. In converſation it is uſual to ſay a man is *incapable* of falſehood, or *incapable* of generoſity, or of any thing good or bad.

INCAPA'CIOUS. *adj.* [*in* and *capacious.*] Narrow; of ſmall content.

Souls that are made little and *incapacious* cannot enlarge their thoughts to take in any great compaſs of times or things. *Burnet.*

INCAPA'CIOUSNESS. *n. ſ.* [from *incapacious.*] Narrowneſs; want of containing ſpace.

To INCAPA'CITATE. *v. a.* [*in* and *capacitate.*]

1. To diſable; to weaken.

Nothing of conſequence ſhould be left to be done in the laſt *incapacitating* hours of life. *Clariſſa.*

2. To

2. To disqualify.

Monstrosity could not *incapacitate* from marriage. *Arbuthn.*

INCAPA'CITY. *n. s.* [*incapacité*, Fr. *in* and *capacity.*] Inability; want of natural power; want of power of body; want of comprehensiveness of mind.

It chiefly proceedeth from natural *incapacity*, and genial indisposition. *Brown's Vulgar Errours.*

Admonition he imputes either to envy, or else ignorance and *incapacity* of estimating his worth. *Govern. of the Tongue.*

The inactivity of the soul is its *incapacity* to be moved with any thing common. *Arbuthnot.*

To INCA'RCERATE. *v. a.* [*incarcero*, Latin.] To imprison; to confine. It is used in the Scots law to denote imprisoning or confining in a gaol; otherwise it is seldom found.

The pestilent contagion may be propagated by those dense bodies, that easily *incarcerate* the infected air; as woollen cloaths. *Harvey on Consumptions.*

INCARCERA'TION. *n. s.* [from *incarcerate.*] Imprisonment; confinement.

To INCA'RN. *v. a.* [*incarno*, Latin.] To cover with flesh.

The flesh will soon arise in that cut of the bone, and make exfoliation of what is necessary, and *incarn* it. *Wiseman.*

To INCA'RN. *v. n.* To breed flesh.

The slough came off, and the ulcer happily *incarned. Wisem.*

To INCA'RNADINE. *v. a.* [*incarnadine*, Fr. *incarnadino*, pale red, Italian.] To dye red. This word I find only once.

Will all great Neptune's ocean wash this blood
Clean from my hand? No, this my hand will rather
The multitudinous sea *incarnardine*,
Making the green one red. *Shakespeare's Macbeth.*

To INCA'RNATE. *v. a.* [*incarner*, Fr. *incarno*, Latin.]

1. To cloath with flesh; to embody with flesh.

I, who erst contended
With gods to sit the highest, am now constrain'd
Into a beast, and mix with bestial slime,
This essence to *incarnate* and imbrute. *Milton.*

INCA'RNATE. *participial adj.* [*incarnat*, Fr. from the verb.]

1. Cloathed with flesh; embodied in flesh.

Undoubtedly even the nature of God itself, in the person of the son, is *incarnate*, and hath taken to itself flesh. *Hooker.*

They say he cried out of women.
—Yes, that he did, and said they were devils *incarnate. Shak.*

A most wise sufficient means of redemption and salvation, by the satisfactory death and obedience of the *incarnate* son of God, Jesus Christ, God blessed for ever. *Sanderson.*

Here shalt thou sit *incarnate*, here shalt reign
Both God and man. *Milton's Paradise Lost, b.* iii.

2. It may be doubted whether *Swift* understood this word.

But he's possest,
Incarnate with a thousand imps. *Swift.*

3. In Scotland *incarnate* is applied to any thing tinged of a deep red colour, from its resemblance to a flesh colour.

INCARNA'TION. *n. s.* [*incarnation*, Fr. from *incarnate.*]

1. The act of assuming body.

We must beware we exclude not the nature of God from *incarnation*, and so make the son of God incarnate not to be very God. *Hooker.*

Upon the annunciation, or our Lady-day, meditate on the *incarnation* of our blessed Saviour. *Taylor's Guide to Devotion.*

2. The state of breeding flesh.

The pulsation under the cicatrix proceeded from the too lax *incarnation* of the wound. *Wiseman's Surgery.*

INCA'RNATIVE. *n. s.* [*incarnatif*, Fr. from *incarn.*] A medicine that generates flesh.

I deterged the abscess, and incarned by the common *incarnative*. *Wiseman's Surgery.*

To INCA'SE. *v. a.* [*in* and *case.*] To cover; to inclose; to inwrap.

Rich plates of gold the folding doors *incase*,
The pillars silver. *Pope's Odyssey.*

INCAU'TIOUS. *adj.* [*in* and *cautious.*] Unwary; negligent; heedless.

His rhetorical expressions may easily captivate any *incautious* reader. *Keil against Burnet.*

INCAU'TIOUSLY. *adv.* [from *incautious.*] Unwarily; heedlessly; negligently.

A species of palsy invades such as *incautiously* expose themselves to the morning air. *Arbuthnot on Air.*

INCE'NDIARY. *n. s.* [*incendiarius*, from *incendo*, Latin; *incendiaire*, French.]

1. One who sets houses or towns on fire in malice or for robbery.

2. One who inflames factions, or promotes quarrels.

Nor could any order be obtained impartially to examine impudent *incendiaries*. *King Charles.*

Incendiaries of figure and distinction, who are the inventers and publishers of gross falshoods, cannot be regarded but with the utmost detestation. *Addison.*

Several cities of Greece drove them out as *incendiaries*, and pests of commonweals. *Bentley's Sermons.*

I'NCENSE. *n. s.* [*incensum*, Latin, a thing burnt; *encens*, French.] Perfumes exhaled by fire in honour of some god or goddess.

Upon such sacrifices, my Cordelia,
The gods themselves throw *incense*. *Shakesp. K. Lear.*

Numa the rites of strict religion knew;
On ev'ry altar laid the *incense* due. *Prior.*

To INCE'NSE. *v. a.* [*incensus*, Latin.] To enkindle to rage; to inflame with anger; to enrage; to provoke; to irritate to anger; to heat; to fire; to make furious; to exasperate.

The world, too saucy with the gods,
Incenses them to send destruction. *Shakesp. Julius Cæsar.*

If 'gainst yourself you be *incens'd*, we'll put you,
Like one that means his proper harm, in manacles. *Shakes.*

He is attended with a desp'rate train;
And what they may *incense* him to, being apt
To have his ear abus'd, wisdom bids fear. *Shakes. K. Lear.*

Tractable obedience is a slave
To each *incensed* will. *Shakesp. Henry* VIII.

Foul idolatries and other faults,
Heap'd to the popular sum, will so *incense*
God as to leave them. *Milton's Paradise Lost, b.* xii.

How could my pious son thy pow'r *incense?*
Or what, alas! is vanquish'd Troy's offence? *Dryden's Æn.*

INCE'NSEMENT. *n. s.* [from *incense.*] Rage; heat; fury.

His *incensement* at this moment is so implacable, that satisfaction can be none but by pangs of death. *Shakespeare.*

INCE'NSION. *n. s.* [*incensio*, Latin.] The act of kindling; the state of being on fire.

Sena loseth its windiness by decocting; and subtile or windy spirits are taken off by *incension* or evaporation. *Bacon.*

INCE'NSOR. *n. s.* [Latin.] A kindler of anger; an inflamer of passions.

Many priests were impetuous and importunate *incensors* of the rage. *Hayward.*

INCE'NSORY. *n. s.* [from *incense.*] The vessel in which incense is burnt and offered. *Ainsworth.*

INCE'NTIVE. *n. s.* [*incentivum*, Latin.]

1. That which kindles.

Their unreasonable severity was not the least *incentive*, that blew up into those flames the sparks of discontent. *K. Charles.*

2. That which provokes; that which encourages; incitement; motive; encouragement; spur. It is used of that which incites, whether to good or ill.

Congruity of opinions, to our natural constitution, is one great *incentive* to their reception. *Glanv. Sceps.*

Even the wisdom of God hath not suggested more pressing motives, more powerful *incentives* to charity, than these, that we shall be judged by it at the last dreadful day. *Atterbury.*

It encourages speculative persons, with all the *incentives* of place, profit, and preferment. *Addison's Freeholder.*

INCE'NTIVE. *adj.* Inciting; encouraging.

Competency is the most *incentive* to industry: too little makes men desperate, and too much careless. *Decay of Piety.*

INCE'PTION. *n. s.* [*inceptio*, Latin.] Beginning.

The *inception* of putrefaction hath in it a maturation. *Bac.*

INCE'PTIVE. *adj.* [*inceptivus*, Latin.] Noting beginning.

An *inceptive* and desitive proposition, as, the fogs vanish as the sun rises; but the fogs have not yet begun to vanish, therefore the sun is not yet risen. *Locke.*

INCE'PTOR. *n. s.* [Latin.] A beginner; one who is in his rudiments.

INCERA'TION. *n. s.* [*incero*, Latin.] The act of covering with wax. *Dict.*

INCE'RTITUDE. *n. s.* [*incertitude*, Fr. *incertitudo*, Lat.] Uncertainty; doubtfulness.

INCE'SSANT. *adj.* [*in* and *cessans*, Latin.] Unceasing; unintermitted; continual; uninterrupted.

Raging wind blows up *incessant* show'rs;
And when the rage allays, the rain begins. *Shakes. H.* VI.

The *incessant* weeping of my wife,
Forc'd me to seek delays. *Shakespeare.*

If, by pray'r
Incessant, I could hope to change the will
Of him who all things can, I would not cease
To weary him with my assiduous cries. *Milt. Parad. Lost.*

In form, a herald of the king she flies,
From peer to peer, and thus *incessant* cries. *Pope's Odyss.*

INCE'SSANTLY. *adv.* [from *incessant.*] Without intermission; continually.

Both his hands most filthy feculent,
Above the water were on high extent,
And fain'd to wash themselves *incessantly*. *Fairy Queen.*

Who reads
Incessantly, and to his reading brings not
A spirit and judgment equal or superior. *Milt. Par. Lost.*

The Christians, who carried their religion through so many persecutions, were *incessantly* comforting one another with the example and history of our Saviour and his apostles. *Addison.*

I'NCEST. *n. s.* [*inceste*, French; *incestum*, Latin.] Unnatural and criminal conjunction of persons within degrees prohibited.

Is't not a kind of *incest* to take life
From thine own sister's shame? *Shakes. Meas. for Measure.*

He who entered in the first act, a young man like Pericles, prince of Tyre, must not be in danger in the fifth act of committing *incest* with his daughter. *Dryden's Dufresnoy.*

Ince'stuous. *adj.* [*incestueux*, French.] Guilty of incest; guilty of unnatural cohabitation.

Hide me, thou bloody hand,
Thou perjure, thou simular of virtue,
That art *incestuous*. *Shakespeare's King Lear.*

We may easily guess with what impatience the world would have heard an *incestuous* Herod discoursing of chastity. *South.*

Ere you reach to this *incestuous* love,
You must divine and human rights remove. *Dryden.*

Ince'stuously. *adv.* [from *incestuous*.] With unnatural love.

Macareus and Canace, son and daughter to Æolus, god of the winds, loved each other *incestuously*. *Dryden.*

INCH. *n. s.* [ince, Saxon; *uncia*, Latin.]

1. A measure of length supposed equal to three grains of barley laid end to end; the twelfth part of a foot.

A foot is the sixth part of the stature of man, a span one eighth of it, and a thumb's breadth or *inch* one seventy-second. *Holder on Time.*

2. A proverbial name for a small quantity.

The plebeians have got your fellow tribune;
They'll give him death by *inches*. *Shakesp. Coriolanus.*

As in lasting, so in length is man,
Contracted to an *inch*, who was a span. *Donne.*

Is it so desirable a condition to consume by *inches*, and lose one's blood by drops? *Collier.*

He should never miss, in all his race,
Of time one minute, or one *inch* of space. *Blackmore.*

The commons were growing by degrees into power and property, gaining ground upon the patricians *inch* by *inch*. *Sw.*

3. A nice point of time.

Beldame, I think, we watch'd you at an *inch*. *Shakesp.*

To Inch. *v. a.* [from the noun.]

1. To drive by inches.

Valiant they say, but very popular;
He gets too far into the soldiers graces,
And *inches* out my master. *Dryden's Cleomenes.*

2. To deal out by inches; to give sparingly. *Ainsw.*

To Inch. *v. n.* To advance or retire a little at a time.

I'nched. *adj.* [with a word of number before it.] Containing inches in length or breadth.

Poor Tom, proud of heart to ride on a bay trotting horse over four *inched* bridges. *Shakespeare's King Lear.*

I'nchipin. *n. s.* Some of the inside of a deer. *Ainsworth.*

I'nchmeal. *n. s.* [*inch* and *meal*.] A piece an inch long.

All th' infections that the sun sucks up
From bogs, fens, flats, on Prospero fall, and make him
By *inchmeal* a disease! *Shakes. Tempest.*

To I'nchoate. *v. a.* [*inchoo*, Latin.] To begin; to commence.

It is neither a substance perfect, nor a substance *inchoate*, or in the way of perfection. *Raleigh's Hist. of the World.*

Inchoa'tion. *n. s.* [*inchoatus*, Lat.] Inception; beginning.

It discerneth of four kinds of causes; forces, frauds, crimes various of stellionate, and the *inchoations* or middle acts towards crimes capital, not actually perpetrated. *Bacon's Henry VII.*

The setting on foot some of those arts in those parts would be looked upon as the first *inchoation* of them, which yet would be but their reviving. *Hale's Origin of Mankind.*

I'nchoative. *adj.* [*inchoative*, Fr. *inchoativus*, Latin.] Inceptive; noting inchoation or beginning.

To Inci'de. *v. a.* [from *incido*, to cut, Latin.]

Medicines are said to *incide* which consist of pointed and sharp particles; as acids, and most salts, by which the particles of other bodies are divided from one another: thus some expectorating medicines are said to *incide* or cut the phlegm. *Quincy.*

The menses are promoted by all saponaceous substances, which *incide* the mucus in the first passages. *Arbuthnot.*

I'ncidence.
I'ncidency. } *n. s.* [*incido*, to fall, Latin; *incidence*, French.]

1. The direction with which one body strikes upon another, and the angle made by that line, and the plane struck upon, is called the angle of *incidence*. In the occursions of two moving bodies, their *incidence* is said to be perpendicular or oblique, as their directions or lines of motion make a straight line or an oblique angle at the point of contact. *Quincy.*

In mirrours there is the like angle of *incidence*, from the object to the glass, and from the glass to the eye. *Bacon.*

In equal *incidences* there is a considerable inequality of refractions, whether it be that some of the incident rays are refracted more and others less constantly, or one and the same ray is by refraction disturbed. *Newton's Opt.*

The permanent whiteness argues, that in like *incidences* of the rays there is no such separation of the emerging rays. *Newt.*

He enjoys his happy state most when he communicates it, and receives a more vigorous joy from the reflexion than from the direct *incidency* of his happiness. *Norris.*

2. [*Incidens*, Latin.] Accident; hap; casualty.

What *incidency* thou do'st guess of harm declare,
Is creeping towards me. *Shakespeare's Winter's Tale.*

INCIDENT. *adj.* [*incident*, Fr. *incidens*, Latin.]

1. Casual; fortuitous; occasional; happening accidentally; falling in beside the main design; happening beside expectation.

As the ordinary course of common affairs is disposed of by general laws, so likewise mens rarer *incident* necessities and utilities should be with special equity considered. *Hooker.*

I would note in children not only their articulate answers, but likewise smiles and frowns upon *incident* occasions. *Wotton.*

In a complex proposition the predicate or subject is sometimes made complex by the pronouns who, which, whose, whom, &c. which make another proposition: as, every man, who is pious, shall be saved: Julius, whose surname was Cæsar, overcame Pompey: bodies, which are transparent, have many pores. Here the whole proposition is called the primary or chief, and the additional proposition is called an *incident* proposition. *Watts.*

2. Happening; apt to happen.

Constancy is such a stability and firmness of friendship as overlooks all those failures of kindness, that through passion, *incident* to human nature, a man may be sometimes guilty of. *South's Sermons.*

I'ncident. *n. s.* [*incident*, Fr. from the adjective.] Something happening beside the main design; casualty.

His wisdom will fall into it as an *incident* to the point of lawfulness. *Bacon's holy War.*

No person, no *incident* in the play, but must be of use to carry on the main design. *Dryden's Dufresnoy.*

Incide'ntal. *adj.* Incident; casual; happening by chance; not intended; not deliberate.

The satisfaction you received from those *incidental* discourses which we have wandered into. *Milton.*

By some religious duties scarce appear to be regarded at all, and by others only as an *incidental* business, to be done when they have nothing else to do. *Rogers's Sermons.*

Incide'ntally. *adv.* [from *incidental*.] Beside the main design; occasionally.

These general rules are but occasionally and *incidentally* mentioned in Scripture, rather to manifest unto us a former than to lay upon us a new obligation. *Sanderson.*

I treat either purposely or *incidentally* of colours. *Boyle.*

I'ncidently. *adv.* [from *incident*.] Occasionally; by the bye; by the way.

It was *incidently* moved amongst the judges what should be done for the king himself, who was attainted; but resolved that the crown takes away defects. *Bacon's Henry VII.*

To Inci'nerate. *v. a.* [*in* and *cineres*, Latin.] To burn to ashes.

By baking, without melting, the heat indurateth, and then maketh fragile; and lastly, it doth *incinerate* and calcinate. *Bacon's Natural History.*

Fire burneth wood, making it first luminous, then black and brittle, and lastly broken and *incinerate*. *Bacon.*

These dregs stick in the capillar insertions of the stomach, and are soon *incinerated* and calcined into such salts which produce coughs. *Harvey on Consumptions.*

Inci'neration. *n. s.* [*incineration*, Fr. from *incinerate*.] The act of burning any thing to ashes.

I observed in the fixt salt of urine, brought by depuration to be very white, a taste not unlike common salt, and very differing from the caustick lixiviate taste of other salts made by *incineration*. *Boyle.*

Incircumspe'ction. *n. s.* [*in* and *circumspection*.] Want of caution; want of heed.

An unexpected way of delusion, whereby he more easily led away the *incircumspection* of their belief. *Brown's Vul. Err.*

Inci'sed. *adj.* [*incisé*, Fr. *incisus*, Latin.] Cut; made by cutting: as, an *incised* wound.

I brought the *incised* lips together. *Wiseman's Surgery.*

Inci'sion. *n. s.* [*incision*, Fr. *incisio*, Latin.]

1. A cut; a wound made with a sharp instrument. Generally used for wounds made by a chirurgeon.

Let us make *incision* for your love,
To prove whose blood is reddest, his or mine. *Shakespeare.*

God help thee, shallow man: God make *incision* in thee, thou art raw. *Shakesp. As you like it.*

The reception of one is as different from the admission of the other, as when the earth falls open under the *incisions* of the plough, and when it gapes to drink in the dew of heaven, or the refreshments of a shower. *South's Sermons.*

A small *incision* knife is more handy than a larger for opening the bag. *Sharp's Surgery.*

2. Division of viscosities by medicines.

Abstersion is a scouring off, or *incision* of the more viscous humours, and making them more fluid, and cutting between them and the part; as is found in nitrous water, which scoureth linen cloth. *Bacon's Nat. Hist.*

Inci'sive. *adj.* [*incisif*, Fr. from *incisus*, Latin.] Having the quality of cutting or dividing.

The colour of many corpuscles will cohere by being precipitated together, and be destroyed by the effusion of very piercing and *incisive* liquors. *Boyle.*

INCI'SOR. *n. s.* [*incisor*, Latin.] Cutter; tooth in the forepart of the mouth.

INCI'SORY. *adj.* [*incisoire*, French.] Having the quality of cutting.

INCI'SURE. *n. s.* [*incisura*, Latin.] A cut; an aperture.

In some creatures it is wide, in some narrow, in some with a deep *incisure* up into the head, for the better catching and holding of prey, and more easy comminuting of hard food. *Derham's Physico-Theology.*

INCITA'TION. *n. s.* [*incitatio*, Latin.] Incitement; incentive; motive; impulse.

Dr. Ridley, in his tract of magnetical bodies, defines magnetical attraction to be a natural *incitation* and disposition conforming unto contiguity, an union of one magnetical body unto another. *Brown's Vulgar Errours.*

The multitude of objects do proportionably multiply both the possibilities and *incitations*. *Governm. of the Tongue.*

The mind gives not only licence, but *incitation* to the other passions to act with the utmost impetuosity. *Decay of Piety.*

To INCI'TE. *v. a.* [*incito*, Lat. *inciter*, Fr.] To stir up; to push forward in a purpose; to animate; to spur; to urge on.

How many now in health
Shall drop their blood, in approbation
Of what your reverence shall *incite* us to? *Shakes. H.* V.

No blown ambition doth our arms *incite*;
But love, dear love, and our ag'd father's right. *Shakespeare.*

Antiochus, when he *incited* Prusias to join in war, set before him the greatness of the Romans, comparing it to a fire, that took and spread from kingdom to kingdom. *Bacon.*

The principles of nature and common reason, which in all difficulties, where prudence or courage are required, do rather *incite* us to fly for assistance to a single person than a multitude. *Swift.*

INCI'TEMENT. *n. s.* [from *incite*.] Motive; incentive; impulse; inciting power.

A marvel it were, if a man of great capacity, having such *incitements* to make him desirous of all furtherances unto his cause, could espy in the whole scripture of God nothing which might breed at the least a probable opinion of likelihood, that divine authority was the same way inclinable. *Hooker.*

A person sent hither by some good providence, to be the occasion and *incitement* of great good to this island. *Milton.*

If thou must reform the stubborn times,
From the long records of distant age
Derive *incitements* to renew thy rage. *Pope's Statius.*

INCI'VIL. *adj.* [*incivil*, Fr.] Unpolished. See UNCIVIL.

INCIVI'LITY. *n. s.* [*incivilité*, Fr. *in* and *civility*.]

1. Want of courtesy; rudeness.

He does offend against that reverence which is due to the common apprehensions of mankind, whether true or not, which is the greatest *incivility*. *Tillotson's Sermons.*

2. Act of rudeness.

Abstain from dissolute laughter, uncomely jests, loud talking and jeering, which, in civil account, are called indecencies and *incivilities*. *Taylor's Rule of living holy.*

INCLE'MENCY. *n. s.* [*inclemence*, Fr. *inclementia*, Latin.] Unmercifulness; cruelty; severity; harshness; roughness.

And though by tempests of the prize bereft,
In heaven's *inclemency* some ease we find:
Our foes we vanquish'd by our valour left. *Dryden.*

INCLE'MENT. *adj.* [*in* and *clemens*, Latin.] Unmerciful; unpitying; void of tenderness; harsh.

Teach us further by what means to shun
Th' *inclement* seasons, rain, ice, hail and snow. *Milton.*

I stand
Naked, defenceless, on a foreign land:
Propitious to my wants, a vest supply,
To guard the wretched from th' *inclement* sky. *Pope.*

INCLI'NABLE. *adj.* [*inclinabilis*, Latin.]

1. Having a propension of will; favourably disposed; willing; tending by disposition.

People are not always *inclinable* to the best. *Spenser.*

A marvel it were, if a man of capacity could espy in the whole scripture nothing which might breed a probable opinion, that divine authority was the same way *inclinable*. *Hooker.*

The gall and bitterness of certain mens writings, who spared him little, made him, for their sakes, the less *inclinable* to that truth which he himself should have honoured. *Hooker.*

Desire,
Inclinable now grown to touch or taste,
Solicited her longing eye. *Milton's Paradise Lost.*

2. Having a tendency.

If such a crust naturally fell, then it was more likely and *inclinable* to fall this thousand years than the last; but if the crust was always gradually nearer and nearer to falling, that plainly evinces that it had not endured eternally. *Bentley.*

INCLINA'TION. *n. s.* [*inclinaison*, *inclination*, Fr. *inclinatio*, Lat.]

1. Tendency towards any point.

The two rays, being equally refracted, have the same *inclination* to one another after refraction which they had before; that is, the *inclination* of half a degree answering to the sun's diameter. *Newton's Opt.*

2. Natural aptness.

Though most of the thick woods are grubbed up since the promontory has been cultivated, there are still many spots of it which shew the natural *inclination* of the soil leans that way. *Addison.*

3. Propension of mind; favourable disposition; incipient desire.

The king was wonderfully disquieted, when he found that the prince was totally aliened from all thoughts of or *inclination* to the marriage. *Clarendon.*

A mere *inclination* to a thing is not properly a willing of that thing; and yet, in matters of duty, men frequently reckon it for such: for otherwise how should they so often plead and rest in the honest and well-inclined disposition of their minds, when they are justly charged with an actual non-performance of the law. *South's Sermons.*

4. Love; affection.

We have had few knowing painters, because of the little *inclination* which princes have for painting. *Dryden.*

5. Disposition of mind.

Bid him
Report the features of Octavia, her years,
Her *inclination*. *Shakesp. Ant. and Cleopatra.*

6. The tendency of the magnetical needle to the East or West.

7. [In pharmacy.] The act by which a clear liquor is poured off from some fæces or sediment by only stooping the vessel, which is also called decantation. *Quincy.*

INCLI'NATORY. *adj.* [from *incline*.] Having a quality of inclining to one or other.

If that *inclinatory* virtue be destroyed by a touch from the contrary pole, that end which before was elevated will then decline. *Brown's Vulgar Errours.*

INCLI'NATORILY. *adv.* [from *inclinatory*.] Obliquely; with inclination to one side or the other; with some deviation from North and South.

Whether they be refrigerated *inclinatorily*, or somewhat equinoxially, that is, toward the eastern or western points, they discover some verticity. *Brown's Vulgar Errours.*

To INCLI'NE. *v. n.* [*inclino*, Latin; *incliner*, Fr.]

1. To bend; to lean; to tend towards any part.

Her house *inclineth* unto death, and her paths unto the dead. *Prov.* ii. 18.

Still to this place
My heart *inclines*, still hither turn my eyes;
Hither my feet unbidden find their way. *Rowe.*

2. To be favourably disposed to; to feel desire beginning.

Doth his majesty
Incline to it, or no?
——He seems indifferent;
Or rather swaying more upon our part. *Shak. H.* V.

To INCLI'NE. *v. a.*

1. To give a tendency or direction to any place or state.

The timely dew of sleep,
Now falling with soft slumb'rous weight, *inclines*
Our eyelids. *Milton.*

Thus far both armies to Belinda yield;
Now to the baron fate *inclines* the field. *Pope.*

A tow'ring structure to the palace join'd;
To this his steps the thoughtful prince *inclin'd*. *Pope.*

2. To turn the desire towards any thing.

3. To bend; to incurvate.

With due respect my body I *inclin'd*,
As to some being of superior kind,
And made my court. *Dryden's Flower and Leaf.*

To INCLI'P. *v. a.* [*in* and *clip*.] To grasp; to inclose; to surround.

Whate'er the ocean pales, or sky *inclips*,
Is thine, if thou wilt ha't. *Shakesp. Ant. and Cleopat.*

To INCLO'ISTER. *v. a.* [*in* and *cloister*.] To shut up in a cloister.

To INCLO'UD. *v. a.* [*in* and *cloud*.] To darken; to obscure.

In their thick breaths,
Rank of gross diet, shall we be *inclouded*,
And forc'd to drink their vapour. *Shakespeare.*

To INCLU'DE. *v. a.* [*includo*, Latin.]

1. To inclose; to shut in.

2. To comprise; to comprehend.

This desire being recommended to her majesty, it liked her to *include* the same within one intire lease. *Bacon.*

The marvellous fable *includes* whatever is supernatural, and especially the machines of the gods. *Pope.*

Instead of enquiring whether he be a man of virtue, the question is only whether he be a whig or a tory; under which terms all good and ill qualities are *included*. *Swift.*

INCLU'SIVE. *adj.* [*inclusif*, French.]

1. Inclosing; encircling.

O, would that the *inclusive* verge
Of golden metal, that must round my brow,
Were red-hot steel, to sear me to the brain. *Shak. R.* III.

2. Comprehended in the sum or number: as, from Wednesday to Saturday *inclusive*; that is, both Wednesday and Saturday taken into the number.

I'll search where ev'ry virtue dwells,
From courts *inclusive* down to cells. *Swift.*

INCLU'SIVELY. *adv.* [from *inclusive.*] The thing mentioned reckoned into the account.

Thus much shall serve for the several periods or growth of the common law, until the time of Edward I. *inclusively. Hale.*

All articulation is made within the mouth, from the throat to the lips *inclusively*; and is differenced partly by the organs used in it, and partly by the manner and degree of articulating. *Holder's Elements of Speech.*

INCOA'GULABLE. *adj.* [*in* and *coagulable.*] Incapable of concretion.

INCOEXI'STENCE. *n. s.* [*in* and *coexistence.*] The quality of not existing together; non-association of existence.

Another more incurable part of ignorance, which sets us more remote from a certain knowledge of the coexistence or *incoexistence* of different ideas in the same subject, is, that there is no discoverable connection between any secondary quality and those primary qualities it depends on. *Locke.*

INCO'G. *adv.* [corrupted by mutilation from *incognito*, Latin.] Unknown; in private.

But if you're rough, and use him like a dog,
Depend upon it, he'll remain *incog.* *Addison.*

INCO'GITANCY. *n. s.* [*incogitantia*, Latin.] Want of thought.

One man's fancies are laws to others, who convey them as such to their succeeders, who afterwards misname all unobsequiousness to their *incogitancy* presumption. *Boyle.*

Next to the stupid and meerly vegetable state of *incogitancy*, we may rank partial and piece-meal consideration. *Dec. of Piety.*

INCO'GITATIVE. *adj.* [*in* and *cogitative.*] Wanting the power of thought.

Purely material beings, as clippings of our beards, and sensible, thinking, perceiving beings, such as we find ourselves, we will call cogitative and *incogitative* beings. *Locke.*

INCO'GNITO. *adv.* [*incognitus*, Latin.] In a state of concealment.

'Twas long ago
Since gods came down *incognito.* *Prior.*

INCOHE'RENCE. } *n. s.* [*in* and *coherence.*]
INCOHE'RENCY. }

1. Want of connection; incongruity; inconsequence; want of dependance of one part upon another.

I find that laying the intermediate ideas naked in their due order, shews the *incoherence* of the argumentations better than syllogisms. *Locke.*

Incoherences in matter, and suppositions without proofs, put handsomely together, are apt to pass for strong reason. *Locke.*

2. Want of cohesion; looseness of material parts.

If plaister be beaten into an impalpable powder, when poured out it will emulate a liquor, by reason that the smalness and *incoherence* of the parts do both make them easy to be put into motion, and makes the pores they intercept so small, that they interrupt not the unity or continuity of the mass. *Boyle.*

INCOHE'RENT. *adj.* [*in* and *coherent.*]

1. Inconsequential; inconsistent; having no dependence of one part upon another.

We have instances of perception whilst we are asleep, and retain the memory of them; but how extravagant and *incoherent* are they, and how little conformable to the perfection of a rational being! *Locke.*

2. Without cohesion; loose; not fixed to each other.

Had the strata of stone become solid, but the matter whereof they consist continued lax and *incoherent*, they had consequently been as pervious as those of marle or gravel. *Woodw.*

INCOHE'RENTLY. *adv.* [from *incoherent.*] Inconsistently; inconsequentially.

The character of Eurylochus is the imitation of a person confounded with fears, speaking irrationally and *incoherently.* *Broome's Notes on the Odyssey.*

INCOLU'MITY. *n. s.* [*incolumitas*, Latin.] Safety; security. A word very little in use.

The parliament is necessary to assert and preserve the national rights of a people, with the *incolumity* and welfare of a country. *Howel.*

INCOMBUSTIBI'LITY. *n. s.* [from *incombustible.*] The quality of resisting fire so that it cannot consume.

The stone in the Appennines is remarkable for its shining quality, and the amianthus for its *incombustibility.* *Ray.*

INCOMBU'STIBLE. *adj.* [*incombustible*, Fr. *in* and *combustible.*] Not to be consumed by fire.

It agrees in this common quality ascribed unto both, of being *incombustible*, and not consumable by fire. *Wilkins.*

INCOMBU'STIBLENESS. *n. s.* [from *incombustible.*] The quality of not being wasted by fire.

I'NCOME. *n. s.* [*in* and *come.*] Revenue; produce of any thing.

Thou who repinest at the plenty of thy neighbour, and the greatness of his *incomes*, consider what are frequently the dismal consequences of all this. *South's Sermons.*

No fields afford
So large an *income* to the village lord. *Dryden's Georg.*

St. Gaul has scarce any lands belonging to it, and little or no *income* but what arises from its trade: the great support of this little state is its linen manufacture. *Addison on Italy.*

Notwithstanding the large *incomes* annexed to some few of her preferments, this church hath in the whole little to subsist on. *Atterbury's Sermons.*

INCOMMENSURABI'LITY. *n. s.* [from *incommensurable.*] The state of one thing with respect to another, when they cannot be compared by any common measure.

INCOMME'NSURABLE. *adj.* [French, from *in*, *con*, and *mensurabilis*, Latin.] Not to be reduced to any measure common to both; not to be measured together, such as that the proportion of one to the other can be told.

Our disputations about vacuum or space, *incommensurable* quantities, the infinite divisibility of matter, and eternal duration, will lead us to see the weakness of our nature. *Watts.*

INCOMME'NSURATE. *adj.* [*in*, *con*, and *mensura*, Latin.] Not admitting one common measure.

The diagonal line and side of a quadrate, which, to our apprehension, are *incommensurate*, are yet commensurable to the infinite comprehension of the divine intellect. *More.*

As all other measures of time are reducible to these three; so we labour to reduce these three, though strictly of themselves *incommensurate* to one another, for civil use, measuring the greater by the less. *Holder on Time.*

If the year comprehend days, it is but as any greater space of time may be said to comprehend a less, though the less space be *incommensurate* to the greater. *Holder on Time.*

To INCO'MMODATE. } *v. a.* [*incommodo*, Lat. *incommoder*,
To INCOMMO'DE. } Fr.] To be inconvenient to; to hinder or embarrass without very great injury.

A gnat, planted upon the horn of a bull, begged the bull's pardon; but rather than *incommode* ye, says he, I'll remove. *L'Estrange.*

Although they sometimes molest and *incommode* the inhabitants of some parts, yet the agent, whereby both the one and the other is effected, is of that indispensable necessity to the earth and to mankind, that they could not subsist without it. *Woodward's Natural History.*

INCOMMO'DIOUS. *adj.* [*incommodus*, Latin.] Inconvenient; vexatious without great mischief.

Things of general benefit, for in this world what is so perfect that no inconvenience doth ever follow it? may by some accident be *incommodious* to a few. *Hooker.*

Mens intentions in speaking are to be understood, without frequent explanations and *incommodious* interruptions. *Locke.*

INCOMMO'DIOUSLY. *adv.* [from *incommodious.*] Inconveniently; not at ease.

INCOMMO'DIOUSNESS. *n. s.* [from *incommodious.*] Inconvenience.

Diseases, disorders, and the *incommodiousness* of external nature, are inconsistent with happiness. *Burnet.*

INCOMMO'DITY. *n. s.* [*incommodité*, Fr. *incommoditas*, Latin.] Inconvenience; trouble.

Declare your opinion, what *incommodity* you have conceived to be in the common law, which I would have thought most free from all such dislike. *Spenser's State of Ireland.*

If iron can be incorporated with flint or stone, without over great charge, or other *incommodity*, the cheapness doth make the compound stuff profitable. *Bacon.*

By considering the region and the winds, one might so cast the rooms, which shall most need fire, that he should little fear the *incommodity* of smoak. *Wotton's Architecture.*

INCOMMUNICABI'LITY. *n. s.* [from *incommunicable.*] The quality of not being impartible.

INCOMMU'NICABLE. *adj.* [*incommunicable*, Fr. *in* and *communicable.*]

1. Not impartible; not to be made the common right, property, or quality of more than one.

They cannot ask more than I can give, may I but reserve to myself the *incommunicable* jewel of my conscience. *K. Charles.*

Only the God of nature perfectly knows her; and light without darkness is the *incommunicable* claim of him that dwells in light inaccessible. *Glanv.*

It was agreed on both sides, that there was one supreme excellency, which was *incommunicable* to any creatures. *Stilling.*

2. Not to be expressed; not to be told.

Neither did he treat them with these peculiarities of favour in the extraordinary discoveries of the gospel only, but also of those *incommunicable* revelations of the divine love, in reference to their own personal interest in it. *South's Sermons.*

INCOMMU'NICABLY. *adv.* [from *incommunicable.*] In a manner not to be imparted or communicated.

To annihilate is both in reason, and by the consent of divines, as *incommunicably* the effect of a power divine, and above nature, as is creation itself. *Hakewill on Providence.*

INCOMMU'NICATING. *adj.* [*in* and *communicating.*] Having no intercourse with each other.

The judgments and administrations of common justice carry a consonancy one to another, whereby both are preserved from that confusion that would ensue, if the administration was by several *incommunicating* hands, or by provincial establishments. *Hale's Common Law.*

INCOMPA'CT. } *adj.* [*in* and *compacted.*] Not joined; not
INCOMPA'CTED. } cohering.

Salt, say they, is the basis of solidity and permanency in

compound

compound bodies, without which the other four elements might be variously blended, but would remain *incompacted*. *Boyle.*

Inco'mparable. *adj.* [*incomparable*, Fr. *in* and *comparable.*] Excellent above compare; excellent beyond all competition.

My heart would not suffer me to omit any occasion, whereby I might make the *incomparable* Pamela see how much extraordinary devotion I bore to her service. *Sidney.*

A most *incomparable* man, breath'd as it were
To an untirable and continuate goodness. *Shakesp. Timon.*
Her words do shew her wit *incomparable.* *Shakes. H.* VI.
Now this mask
Was cried *incomparable*, and th' ensuing night
Made it a fool and beggar. *Shakesp. Henry* VIII.

If I could leave this argument of your *incomparable* beauty, I might turn to one which would equally oppress me with its greatness. *Dryden.*

Inco'mparably. *adv.* [from *incomparable.*]

1. Beyond comparison; without competition.

A founder it had, whom I think *incomparably* the wisest man that ever the French church did enjoy, since the hour it enjoyed him. *Hooker.*

Self-preservation will oblige a man voluntarily to undergo any less evil, to secure himself but from the probability of an evil *incomparably* greater. *South's Sermons.*

2. Excellently; to the highest degree. A low phrase.

There are the heads of Antoninus Pius, the Faustina's, and Marcus Aurelius, all *incomparably* well cut. *Addison on Italy.*

Incompa'ssionate. *adj.* [*in* and *compassionate.*] Void of pity; void of tenderness.

Incompatibi'lity. *n. s.* [properly *incompetibility*, *in* and *competo*, Latin.] Inconsistency of one thing with another.

He overcame that natural *incompatibility*, which hath been noted between the vulgar and the sovereign favour. *Wotton.*

The reason of the stress rests not upon the *incompetibility* of excess of one infinitude above another, either in intension or extension; but the *incompetibility* of any multitude to be infinite. *Hale.*

Incompa'tible. [*incompatible*, French; rather *incompetible*, as it is sometimes written; *in* and *competo*, Lat.] Inconsistent with something else; such as cannot subsist or cannot be possessed together with something else.

Fortune and love have ever been so *incompatible*, that it is no wonder, madam, if, having had so much of the one for you, I have ever found so little of the other for myself. *Suckl.*

May not the outward expressions of love in many good Christians be greater to some other object than to God? Or is this *incompetible* with the sincerity of the love of God? *Hamm.*

The repugnancy of infinitude is equally *incompetible* to continued or successive motion, and depends upon the incompossibility of things successive with infinitude. *Hale.*

We know those colours which have a friendship with each other, and those which are *incompatible*, by mixing together those colours of which we would make trial. *Dryden.*

Sense I have proved to be *incompatible* with mere bodies, even those of the most compound and elaborate textures. *Bent.*

Inco'mpatibly. *adv.* [for *incompetibly*, from *incompatible.*] Inconsistently.

Inco'mpetency. *n. s.* [*incompetence*, Fr. from *incompetent.*] Inability; want of adequate ability or qualification.

Our not being able to discern the motion of a shadow of a dial-plate, or that of the index upon a clock, ought to make us sensible of the *incompetency* of our eyes to discern some motions of natural bodies incomparably slower than these. *Boyle.*

Inco'mpetent. *adj.* [*in* and *competent.*] Not suitable; not adequate; not proportionate. In the civil law it denotes some defect of right to do any thing.

Richard III. had a resolution, out of hatred to his brethren, to disable their issues, upon false and *incompetent* pretexts, the one of attainder, the other of illegitimation. *Bacon's H.* VII.

Every speck does not blind a man, nor does every infirmity make one unable to discern, or *incompetent* to reprove the grosser faults of others. *Government of the Tongue.*

I thank you for the commission you have given me: how I have acquitted myself of it, must be left to the opinion of the world, in spight of any protestation which I can enter against the present age, as *incompetent* or corrupt judges. *Dryden.*

Laymen, with equal advantages of parts, are not the most *incompetent* judges of sacred things. *Dryden.*

An equal attraction on all sides of all matter, is just equal to no attraction at all; and by this means all the motion in the universe must proceed from external impulse alone, which is an *incompetent* cause for the formation of a world. *Bentley.*

Inco'mpetently. *adv.* [from *incompetent.*] Unsuitably; unduly.

Incomple'te. *adj.* [*in* and *complete.*] Not perfect; not finished.

It pleaseth him in mercy to account himself *incomplete* and maimed without us. *Hooker.*

In *incomplete* ideas we are apt to impose on ourselves, and wrangle with others, especially where they have particular and familiar names. *Locke.*

Incomple'teness. *n. s.* [from *incomplete.*] Imperfection; unfinished state.

The *incompleteness* of our seraphick lover's happiness, in his fruitions, proceeds not from their want of satisfactoriness, but of an intire possession. *Boyle.*

Incompli'ance. *n. s.* [*in* and *compliance.*]

1. Untractableness; impracticableness; contradictious temper.

Self-conceit produces peevishness and *incompliance* of humour in things lawful and indifferent. *Tillotson's Sermons.*

2. Refusal of compliance.

Consider the vast disproportion between the worst inconveniences that can attend our *incompliance* with men, and the eternal displeasure of an offended God. *Rogers.*

Incompo'sed. *adj.* [*in* and *composed.*] Disturbed; discomposed; disordered.

Somewhat *incomposed* they are in their trimming, and extraordinary tender of their young ones. *Howel.*

Incompossibi'lity. *n. s.* from *incompossible.*] Quality of being not possible but by the negation or destruction of something; inconsistency with something.

The manifold *incompossibilities* and lubricities of matter cannot have the same fitnesses in any modification. *More.*

Though the repugnancy of infinitude be equally incompetible to continued or successive motion, and depends upon the *incompossibility* of the very nature of things successive or extensive with infinitude, yet that *incompossibility* is more conspicuous in discrete quantity, that ariseth from individuals already actually distinguished. *Hale's Origin of Mankind.*

Incompo'ssible. *adj.* [*in*, *con*, and *possible.*] Not possible together; not possible but by the negation of something else.

Incomprehensibi'lity. *n. s.* [*incomprehensibilité*, Fr. from *incomprehensible.*] Unconceivableness; superiority to human understanding.

Incomprehe'nsible. *adj.* [*incomprehensible*, Fr. *in* and *comprehensible.*]

1. Not to be conceived; not to be fully understood.

His precepts tend to the improving and perfecting the most valuable part of us, and annexing *incomprehensible* rewards as an eternal weight of glory. *Hammond.*

One thing more is *incomprehensible* in this matter. *Locke.*

The laws of vegetation, life, sustenance, and propagation are the arbitrary pleasure of God, and may vary in manners *incomprehensible* to our imaginations. *Bentley.*

2. Not to be contained. Not now used.

Presence every where is the sequel of an infinite and *incomprehensible* substance; for what can be every where but that which can no where be comprehended? *Hooker.*

Incomprehe'nsibleness. *n. s.* [from *incomprehensible.*] Unconceivableness.

I might argue from God's *incomprehensibleness*: if we could believe nothing but what we have ideas of, it would be impossible for us to believe God is incomprehensible. *Watts.*

Incomprehe'nsibly. *adv.* [from *incomprehensible.*] In a manner not to be conceived.

We cannot but be assured that the God, of whom and from whom are all things, is *incomprehensibly* infinite. *Locke.*

Incompre'ssible. *adj.* [*incompressible*, Fr. *in* and *compressible.*] Not capable of being compressed into less space.

Their hardness is the reason why water is *incompressible*, when the air lodged in it is exhausted. *Cheyne's Phil. Prin.*

Imcompressibi'lity. *n. s.* [from *incompressible.*] Incapacity to be squeezed into less room.

Inconcu'rring. *adj.* [*in* and *concur*] Not concurring.

They derive effects not only from *inconcurring* causes, but things devoid of all efficiency. *Brown's Vulgar Errours.*

Inconce'alable. *adj.* [*in* and *conceal.*] Not to be hid; not to be kept secret.

The *inconcealable* imperfections of ourselves will hourly prompt us our corruption, and loudly tell us we are sons of earth. *Brown's Vulgar Errours.*

Inconce'ivable. *adj.* [*inconceivable*, Fr. *in* and *conceivable.*] Incomprehensible; not to be conceived by the mind.

Such are Christ's promises, divine *inconceivable* promises; a bliss to be enjoyed to all eternity, and that by way of return for a weak obedience of some few years. *Hammond.*

It is *inconceivable* to me, that a spiritual substance should represent an extended figure. *Locke.*

How two ethers can be diffused through all space, one of which acts upon the other, and by consequence is reacted upon, without retarding, shattering, dispersing, and confounding one another's motions, is *inconceivable.* *Newton's Opt.*

Inconce'ivably. *adv.* [from *inconceivable.*] In a manner beyond comprehension; to a degree beyond human comprehension.

Does that man take a rational course to preserve himself, who refuses the endurance of those lesser troubles, to secure himself from a condition *inconceivably* more miserable? *South.*

Inconce'ptible. *adj.* [*in* and *conceptible*; *conceptus*, Latin.] Not to be conceived; incomprehensible; inconceivable. A word not used.

It is *inconceptible* how any such man, that hath stood the shock of an eternal duration without corruption, should after be corrupted. *Hale's Origin of Mankind.*

Inconclu'dent. *adj.* [*in* and *concludens*, Latin.] Inferring no consequence.

The depositions of witnesses themselves, as being false, various, contrariant, single, *inconcludent*. *Ayliffe's Parergon.*

Inconclu'sive. *adj.* [*in* and *conclusive.*] Not enforcing any determination of the mind; not exhibiting cogent evidence.

Inconclu'sively. *adv.* [from *inconclusive.*] Without any such evidence as determines the understanding.

Inconclu'siveness. *n. s.* [from *inconclusive.*] Want of rational cogency.

A man, unskilful in syllogism, at first hearing, could perceive the weakness and *inconclusiveness* of a long, artificial, and plausible discourse, wherewith some others, better skilled in syllogism, have been misled. *Locke.*

Inconco'ct. } *adj.* [*in* and *concoct.*] Unripened; immature;
Inconco'cted. } not fully digested.

While the body, to be converted and altered, is too strong for the efficient that should convert it, it is all that while crude and *inconcoct*; and the process is to be called crudity and inconcoction. *Bacon's Natural History.*

I understand, remember, and reason better in my riper years than when I was a child, and had my organical parts less digested and *inconcocted.* *Hale's Orgin of Mankind.*

Inconco'ction. *n. s.* [from *inconcoct.*] The state of being indigested; unripeness; immaturity.

The middle action, which produceth such imperfect bodies, is fitly called inquination, or *inconcoction*, which is a kind of putrefaction. *Bacon's Natural History.*

While the body, to be converted and altered, is too strong for the efficient that should convert it, it is all that while crude and inconcoct; and the process is to be called crudity and *inconcoction.* *Bacon's Natural History.*

Inco'ndite. *adj.* [*inconditus*, Lat.] Irregular; rude; unpolished.

Now sportive youth
Carol *incondite* rhymes with suiting notes,
And quaver inharmonious. *Phillips.*

Incondi'tional. *adj.* [*in* and *conditional.*] Without exception; without limitation; without stipulation.

From that which is but true in a qualified sense, an *inconditional* and absolute verity is inferred. *Brown's Vulgar Errours.*

Incondi'tionate. *adj.* [*in* and *condition.*] Not limited; not restrained by any conditions; absolute.

They ascribe to God, in relation to every man, an eternal, unchangeable, and *inconditionate* decree of election or reprobation. *Boyle.*

Inconfo'rmity. *n. s.* [*in* and *conformity.*] Incompliance with the practice of others.

We have thought their opinion to be, that utter *inconformity* with the church of Rome was not an extremity whereunto we should be drawn for a time, but the very mediocrity itself, wherein they meant we should ever continue. *Hooker.*

Inconfu'sion. *n. s.* [*in* and *confusion.*] Distinctness.

The cause of the confusion in sounds, and the *inconfusion* in species visible, is, for that the sight worketh in right lines, and so there can be no coincidence in the eye; but sounds that move in oblique and arcuate lines, must needs encounter and disturb the one the other. *Bacon.*

Inco'ngruence. *n. s.* [*in* and *congruence.*] Unsuitableness; want of adaptation.

Humidity is but relative, and depends upon the congruity or *incongruence* of the component particles of the liquor to the pores of the bodies it touches. *Boyle.*

Incongru'ity. *n. s.* [*incongruité*, Fr. from *incongruous.*]

1. Unsuitableness of one thing to another.

The fathers make use of this acknowledgment of the *incongruity* of images to the Deity, from thence to prove the *incongruity* of the worship of them. *Stillingfleet.*

2. Inconsistency; inconsequence; absurdity; impropriety.

To avoid absurdities and *incongruities*, is the same law established for both arts: the painter is not to paint a cloud at the bottom of a picture, nor the poet to place what is proper to the end in the beginning of a poem. *Dryden.*

3. Disagreement of parts; want of symmetry.

She, whom after what form soe'er we see,
Is discord and rude *incongruity*;
She, she is dead, she's dead. *Donne.*

Inco'ngruous. *adj.* [*incongru*, Fr. *in* and *congruous.*]

1. Unsuitable; not fitting.

Wiser heathens condemned the worship of God as *incongruous* to a divine nature, and a disparagement to the deity. *Stillingfleet.*

2. Inconsistent; absurd.

Inco'ngruously. *adv.* [from *incongruous.*] Improperly; unfitly.

Inconne'xedly. *adv.* [*in* and *connex.*] Without any connexion or dependance.

Others ascribed hereto, as a cause, what perhaps but casually or *inconnexedly* succeeds. *Brown's Vulgar Errours.*

Inco'nscionable. *adj.* [*in* and *conscionable.*] Void of the sense of good and evil; without influence of conscience.

So *inconscionable* are these common people, and so little feeling have they of God, or their own souls good. *Spenser.*

Inco'nsequence. *n. s.* [*inconsequence*, Fr. *inconsequentia*, Lat.] Inconclusiveness; want of just inference.

This he bestows the name of many fallacies upon: and runs on with shewing the *inconsequence* of it, as though he did in earnest believe it were an impertinent answer. *Stillingfleet.*

Inco'nsequent. *adj.* [*in* and *consequens*, Lat.] Without just conclusion; without regular inference.

The ground he assumes is unsound, and his illation from thence deduced *inconsequent.* *Hakewill on Providence.*

Men rest not in false apprehensions without absurd and *inconsequent* deductions from fallacious foundations, and misapprehended mediums, erecting conclusions no way inferible from their premises. *Brown's Vulgar Errours.*

Inconsi'derable. *adj.* [*in* and *considerable.*] Unworthy of notice; unimportant.

No, I am an *inconsiderable* fellow, and know nothing. *Denham's Sophy.*

The most *inconsiderable* of creatures may at some time or other come to revenge itself upon the greatest. *L'Estrange.*

Casting my eyes upon the ants, continually taken up with a thousand cares, very *inconsiderable* with respect to us, but of the greatest importance for them, they appeared to me worthy of my curiosity. *Addison.*

May not planets and comets perform their motions more freely, and with less resistance, in this ethereal medium than in any fluid, which fills all space adequately without leaving any pores, and by consequence is much denser than quicksilver or gold? And may not its resistance be so small as to be *inconsiderable?* *Newton's Opt.*

If we were under any real fear of the papists, it would be hard to think us so stupid not to be equally apprehensive with others, since we are likely to be the greatest sufferers; but we look upon them to be altogether as *inconsiderable* as the women and children. *Swift.*

Let no sin appear small or *inconsiderable* by which an almighty God is offended, and eternal salvation endangered. *Rogers.*

Inconsi'derableness. *n. s.* [from *inconsiderable.*] Small importance.

To those who are thoroughly convinced of the *inconsiderableness* of this short dying life, in comparison of that eternal state which remains for us in another life, the consideration of a future happiness is the most powerful motive. *Tillotson.*

From the consideration of our own smalness and *inconsiderableness*, in respect of the greatness and splendor of those glorious heavenly bodies, let us with the holy psalmist raise up our hearts. *Ray on the Creation.*

Inconsi'derate. *adj.* [*inconsidere*, Fr. *inconsideratus*, Latin.]

1. Careless; thoughtless; negligent; inattentive; inadvertent.

When thy *inconsiderate* hand
Flings ope this casement, with my trembling name,
Then think this name alive, and that thou thus
In it offend'st my genius. *Donne.*

If you lament it,
That which now looks like justice, will be thought
An *inconsiderate* rashness. *Denham's Sophy.*

It is a very unhappy token of our corruption, that there should be any so *inconsiderate* among us as to sacrifice morality to politicks. *Addison's Freeholder.*

2. Wanting due regard.

He who laid down his life for the redemption of the transgressions, which were under the first Testament, cannot be so *inconsiderate* of our frailties. *Decay of Piety.*

Inconsi'derately. *adv.* [from *inconsiderate.*] Negligently; thoughtlesly; inattentively.

The king, transported with just wrath, *inconsiderately* fighting and precipitating the charge, before his whole numbers came up, was slain in the pursuit. *Bacon.*

Joseph was delighted with Mariamne's conversation, and endeavoured with all his art to set out the excess of Herod's passion for her; but when he still found her cold and incredulous, he *inconsiderately* told her the private orders he left behind. *Addison's Spectator.*

Inconsi'derateness. *n. s.* [from *inconsiderate.*] Carelessness; thoughtlessness; negligence; want of thought; inadvertence; inattention.

If men do know and believe that there is such a being as God, not to demean ourselves towards him, as becomes our relation to him, is great stupidity and *inconsiderateness.* *Tillots.*

Inconsidera'tion. *n. s.* [*inconsideration*, Fr. *in* and *consideration.*] Want of thought; inattention; inadvertence.

S. Gregory reckons uncleanness to be the parent of blindness of mind, *inconsideration*, precipitancy or giddiness in actions, and self-love. *Taylor.*

Inconsi'sting. *adj.* [*in* and *consist.*] Not consistent; incompatible with.

The persons and actions of a farce are all unnatural, and the manners false; that is, *inconsisting* with the characters of mankind. *Dryden's Dufresnoy.*

Inconsi'stence. } *n. s.* [from *inconsistent.*]
Inconsi'stency. }

1. Such opposition as that one proposition infers the negation of the other; such contrariety that both cannot be together.

There

There is a perfect *inconsistency* between that which is of debt, and that which is of free gift. *South's Sermons.*

2. Absurdity in argument or narration; argument or narrative where one part destroys the other; self-contradiction.

3. Incongruity.

Mutability of temper, and *inconsistency* with ourselves, is the greatest weakness of human nature. *Addison.*

If a man would register all his opinions upon love, politicks, religion and learning, what a bundle of *inconsistencies* and contradictions would appear at last? *Swift.*

4. Unsteadiness; changeableness.

INCONSI'STENT. *adj.* [*in* and *consistent.*]

1. Incompatible; not suitable; incongruous.

Finding no kind of compliance, but sharp protestations against the demands, as *inconsistent* with conscience, justice, or religion, the conference broke off. *Clarendon.*

Compositions of this nature, when thus restrained, shew that wisdom and virtue are far from being *inconsistent* with politeness and good humour. *Addison's Freeholder.*

2. Contrary, so as that one infers the negation or destruction of the other.

The idea of an infinite space or duration is very obscure and confused, because it is made up of two parts very different, if not *inconsistent.* *Locke.*

3. Absurd; having parts of which one destroys the other.

INCONSI'STENTLY. *adv.* [from *inconsistent.*] Absurdly; incongruously; with self-contradiction.

INCO'NSOLABLE. *adj.* [*in onsolable*, Fr. *in* and *console.*] Not to be comforted; sorrowful beyond susceptibility of comfort.

Her women will represent to me that she is *inconsolable*, by reason of my unkindness. *Addison.*

They take pleasure in an obstinate grief, in rendering themselves *inconsolable.* *Fiddes's Sermons.*

INCO'NSONANCY. *n.s.* [*in* and *consonancy.*] Disagreement with itself.

INCONSPI'CUOUS. *adj.* [*in* and *conspicuous.*] Indiscernible; not perceptible by the sight.

When an excellent experimenter had taken pains in accucurately filling up a tube of mercury, we found that yet there remained store of *inconspicuous* bubbles. *Boyle.*

INCO'NSTANCY. *n.s.* [*inconstantia*, Lat. *inconstance*, Fr. from *inconstant.*] Unsteadiness; want of steady adherence; mutability of temper or affection.

I have suffered more for their sakes, more than the villanous *inconstancy* of man is able to bear. *Shak. Mer. Wives of Windſ.*

Be made the mark
For all the people's hate, the princess' curses,
And his son's rage, or the old king's *inc nstancy.* *Denham.*

Irresolution on the schemes of life which offer to our choice, and *inconstancy* in pursuing them, are the greatest causes of all our unhappiness. *Addison's Spectator.*

As much *inconstancy* and confusion is there in their mixtures or combinations; for it is rare to find any of them pure and unmixt. *Wo dward's Natural History.*

INCO'NSTANT. *adj.* [*inconstant*, Fr. *inconstans*, Latin]

1. Not firm in resolution; not steady in affection; various of inclination; wanting perseverance.

He is so naturally *inconstant*, that I marvel his soul finds not some way to kill his body. *Sidney.*

2. Changeable; mutable; variable.

O swear not by the moon, th' *inconstant* moon,
That monthly changes in her circled orb,
Lest that thy love prove likewise variable. *Shakespeare.*

INCONSU'MABLE. *adj.* [*in* and *consume.*] Not to be wasted.

By arts were weaved napkins, shirts, and coats, *inconsumable* by fire, and wherein they burnt the bodies of kings. *Brown.*

INCONSU'MPTIBLE. *adj.* [*in* and *consumptus*, Lat.] Not to be spent; not to be brought to an end; not to be destroyed by fire. This seems a more elegant word than *inconsumable.*

Before I give any answer to this objection of pretended *inconsumptible* lights, I would gladly see the effect undoubtedly proved. *Digby on Bodies.*

INCONTE'STABLE. *adj.* [*incontestable*, Fr. *in* and *contest.*] Not to be disputed; not admitting debate; uncontrovertible.

Our own being furnishes us with an evident and *incontestable* proof of a Deity; and I believe no body can avoid the cogency of it, who will carefully attend to it. *Locke.*

INCONTE'STABLY. *adv.* [from *incontestable.*] Indisputably; uncontrovertibly.

INCONTI'GUOUS. *adj.* [*in* and *contiguous.*] Not touching each other; not joined together.

They seemed part of small bracelets, consisting of equally little *incontiguous* beads. *Boyle.*

INCO'NTINENCE. }
INCO'NTINENCY. } *n.s.* [*incontinentia*, Lat. *in* and *continence.*] Inability to restrain the appetites; unchastity.

The cognizance of her *incontinency*
Is this; she hath bought the name of whore thus dearly. *Sh.*

But beauty, like the fair Hesperian tree,
Laden with blooming gold, had need the guard
Of dragon-watch with uninchanted eye,
To save her blossoms, and defend her fruit
From the rash hand of bold *incontinence.* *Milton.*

This is my defence;
I pleas'd myself, I shunn'd *incont nence*,
And, urg'd by strong desires, indulg'd my sense. *Dryden.*

The words *sine veste Dianam* agree better with Livia, who had the fame of chastity, than with either of the Julia's, who were both noted of *incontinency.* *Dryden.*

INCO'NTINENT. *adj.* [*incontinens*, Lat. *in* and *continent.*]

1. Unchaste; indulging unlawful pleasure.

In these degrees have they made a pair of stairs to marriage, which they will climb incontinent, or else be *incontinent* before marriage. *Shakesp. As you like it.*

Men shall be lovers of their own selves, false accusers, *incontinent*, fierce. 2 *Tim.* iii. 3.

2. Shunning delay; immediate. This is a meaning now obsolete.

They ran towards the far rebounded noise,
To weet what wight so loudly did lament;
Unto the place they came *incontinent.* *Fairy Queen.*

Come, mourn with me for what I do lament,
And put on sullen black *inc ntinent.* *Shakesp. Rich.* II.

He says he will return *incontinent.* *Shak. Othello.*

INCO'NTINENTLY. *adv.* [from *incont nent.*]

1. Unchastely; without restraint of the appetites.

2. Immediately; at once. An obsolete sense. *Spenser.*

The cause of this war is no other than that we will not *incontinently* submit ourselves to our neighbours. *Hayward.*

Incontinently I left Madrid, and have been dogged and waylaid through several nations. *Arbuthn. and Pope.*

INCONTROVE'RTIBLE. *adj.* [*in* and *controvertible.*] Indisputable; not to be disputed.

INCONTROVE'RTIBLY. *adv.* [fro *incontrovertible.*] To a degree beyond controversy or dispute.

The Hebrew is *incontrovertibly* the primitive and surest test to rely upon; and to preserve the same uncorrupt, there hath been used the highest caution humanity could invent. *Brown.*

INCONVE'NIENCE. }
INCONVE'NIENCY. } *n.s.* [*inconvenient*, French.]

1. Unfitness; inexpedience.

They plead against the *inconvenience*, not the unlawfulness of popish apparel; and against the *inconvenience*, not the unlawfulness of ceremonies in burial. *Hooker.*

2. Disadvantage; cause of uneasiness; difficulty.

There is a place upon the top of mount Athos above all clouds of rain, or other *inconvenience.* *Raleigh's History.*

Man is liable to a great many *inconveniences* every moment, and is continually unsecure even of life itself. *Tillotson.*

The *inconvenience* of old age makes him incapable of corporal pleasures. *Dryden.*

Would not quickness of sensation be an *inconvenience* to an animal, that must lie still where chance has once placed it? *Locke.*

Consider the disproportion between the worst *inconveniences* that attends incompliance with men, and the eternal displeasure of God. *Rogers.*

We are freed from many *inconveniences*, and we enjoy several advantages. *Atterbury.*

The things of another world, being distant, operate but faintly upon us: to remedy this *inconveniency*, we must frequently revolve their certainty and importance. *Atterbury.*

INCONVE'NIENT. *adj.* [*inconvenient*, Fr. *in* and *conveniens*, Lat.]

1. Incommodious; disadvantageous.

They delight rather to lean to their old customs, though they be more unjust, and more *inconvenient* for the common people. *Spenser on Ireland.*

We are not to look that the church should change her publick laws, although it chance that for some particular men the same be found *inconvenient*, especially when there may be other remedy against particular inconveniences. *Hooker.*

He knows that to be *inconvenient*, which we falsely think convenient for us. *Smalridge's Sermons.*

2. Unfit; inexpedient.

INCONVE'NIENTLY. *adv.* [from *inconvenient.*]

1. Unfitly; incommodiously.

2. Unseasonably. *Ainsworth.*

INCONVE'RSABLE. *adj.* [*in* and *conversable.*] Incommunicative; ill qualified by temper for conversation; unsocial.

He is a person very *inconversable.* *More.*

INCONVE'RTIBLE. *adj.* [*in* and *convertible.*] Not transmutable; incapable of change.

It entereth not the veins, but taketh leave of the permeant parts, and accompanyeth the *inconvertible* portion unto the siege. *Brown's Vulgar Errours.*

INCONVI'NCIBLE. *adj.* [*in* and *convincible.*] Not to be convinced; not capable of conviction.

INCONVI'NCIBLY. *adv.* [from *inconvincible.*] Without admitting conviction.

It is injurious unto knowledge obstinately and *inconvincibly* to side with any one. *Brown's Vulgar Errours.*

INCO'NY. *adj.* [perhaps from *in* and *conn*, to know.]

1. Unlearned; artless.

2. In Scotland it denotes mischievously unlucky: as, he's an *incony* fellow. This seems to be the meaning in *Shakespeare.*

O' my

O' my troth, most sweet jests, most *incony* vulgar wit,
When it comes so smoothly off. *Shakespeare.*

INCO'RPORAL. *adj.* [*in* and *corporal.*] Immaterial; distinct from matter; distinct from body.

Why do'st thou bend thine eye on vacancy,
And with th' *incorporal* air do'st hold discourse? *Shak. Haml.*

Learned men have not resolved us whether light be corporal or *incorporal:* corporal they say it cannot be, because then it would neither pierce the air, nor solid diaphanous bodies, and yet every day we see the air illightened: *incorporal* it cannot be, because sometimes it affecteth the sight with offence. *Ral.*

INCORPORA'LITY. *n. s.* [*incorporalité*, Fr. from *incorporal.*] Immaterialness; distinctness from body.

INCO'RPORALLY. *adv.* [from *incorporal.*] Without matter; immaterially.

To INCO'RPORATE. *v. a.* [*incorporer*, French.]

1. To mingle different ingredients so as they shall make one mass.

A fifteenth part of silver, *incorporate* with gold, will not be recovered, except you put a greater quantity of silver to draw to it the less. *Bacon's Natural History.*

Who the swelling clouds in bladders ties,
To mollify the stubborn clods with rain,
And scatter'd dust *incorporate* again? *Sandys.*

2. To conjoin inseparably.

Villainous thoughts, Roderigo, when
These mutualities so marshal the way,
Hard at hand comes the master and main exercise,
The *incorporate* conclusion. *Shakespeare's Othello.*

By your leaves, you shall not stay alone,
'Till holy church *incorporate* two in one. *Shakes. R. and Ju.*

Upon my knees
I charm you, by that great vow
Which did *incorporate* and make us one. *Shak. Jul. Cæsar.*

3. To form into a corporation, or body politick. In this sense they say in Scotland, the *incorporate* trades in any community.

The apostle affirmeth plainly of all men christian, that be they Jews or Gentiles, bond or free, they are all *incorporated* into one company, they all make but one body. *Hooker.*

The same is *incorporated* with a majoralty, and nameth burgesses to parliament. *Carew's Survey of Cornwal.*

4. To unite; to associate.

It is Casca, one *incorporate*
To our attempts. *Shakesp. Julius Cæsar.*

Your most grave belly was deliberate,
Not rash, like his accusers, and thus answer'd;
True is it, my *incorporate* friends, quoth he,
That I receive the general food at first,
Which you do live upon. *Shakesp. Coriolanus.*

All this learning is ignoble and mechanical among them, and the Confutian only essential and *incorporate* in their government. *Temple.*

The Romans did not subdue a country to put the inhabitants to fire and sword, but to *incorporate* them into their own community. *Addison's Freeholder.*

5. To embody.

Courtesy, that seemed *incorporated* in his heart, would not be persuaded by danger to offer any offence. *Sidney.*

The idolaters, who worshipped their images as gods, supposed some spirit to be *incorporated* therein, and so to make together with it a person fit to receive worship. *Stillingfleet.*

To INCO'RPORATE. *v. n.* To unite into one mass.

Painters colours and ashes do better *incorporate* with oil. *Bacon's Natural History.*

It is not universally true, that acid salts and oils will not *incorporate* or mingle. *Boyle.*

Thy soul
In real darkness of the body dwells,
Shut out from outward light,
T' *incorporate* with gloomy night. *Milton's Agonistes.*

It finds the mind unprepossessed with any former notions, and so easily gains upon the assent, grows up with it, and *incorporates* into it. *South's Sermons.*

INCO'RPORATE. *adj.* [*in* and *corporate.*] Immaterial; unbodied.

Moses forbore to speak of angels, and things invisible and *incorporate.* *Raleigh.*

INCORPORA'TION. *n. s.* [*incorporation*, Fr. from *incorporate.*]

1. Union of divers ingredients in one mass.

Make proof of the *incorporation* of iron with flint; for if it can be incorporated without over great charge, the cheapness of the flint doth make the compound stuff profitable. *Bacon.*

This, with some little additional, may further the intrinsick *incorporation.* *Bacon's Natural History.*

2. Formation of a body politick.

3. Adoption; union; association.

In him we actually are, by our actual *incorporation* into that society which hath him for their head. *Hooker.*

INCORPO'REAL. *adj.* [*incorporalis*, Lat. *incorporel*, Fr. *in* and *corporeal.*] Immaterial; unbodied.

It is a virtue which may be called *incorporeal* and immateriate, whereof there be in nature but few. *Bacon.*

Sense and perception must necessarily proceed from some *incorporeal* substance within us. *Bentley's Sermons.*

INCORPO'REALLY. *adv.* [from *incorporeal.*] Immaterially; without body.

The sense of hearing striketh the spirits more immediately than the other senses, and more *incorporeally* than the smelling. *Bacon's Natural History.*

INCORPORE'ITY. *n. s.* [*in* and *corporeity.*] Immateriality; distinctness from body.

To INCO'RPSE. *v. a.* [*in* and *corpse.*] To incorporate; to unite into one body.

He grew unto his seat,
As he had been *incorps'd* and demy-natur'd
With the brave horse. *Shakespeare's Hamlet.*

INCORRE'CT. *adj.* [*in* and *correct.*] Not nicely finished; not exact; inaccurate; full of faults.

The piece you think is *incorrect:* why take it;
I'm all submission; what you'd have it, make it. *Pope.*

INCORRE'CTLY. *adv.* [from *incorrect.*] Inaccurately; not exactly.

INCORRE'CTNESS. *n. s.* [*in* and *correctness.*] Inaccuracy; want of exactness.

INCO'RRIGIBLE. *adj.* [*incorrigible*, Fr. *in* and *corrigible.*] Bad beyond correction; depraved beyond amendment by any means; erroneous beyond hope of instruction.

The loss is many times irrecoverable, and the inconvenience *incorrigible.* *More's Divine Dialogues.*

What are their thoughts of things, but variety of *incorrigible* error? *L'Estrange.*

Provok'd by those *incorrigible* fools,
I left declaiming in pedantick schools. *Dryden's Juven.*

Whilst we are *incorrigible*, God may in vengeance continue to chastise us with the judgment of war. *Smalridge's Serm.*

The most violent party-men are such as have discovered least sense of religion or morality; and when such are laid aside, as shall be found *incorrigible*, it will be no difficulty to reconcile the rest. *Swift.*

INCORRI'GIBLENESS. *n. s.* [from *incorrigible.*] Hopeless depravity; badness beyond all means of amendment.

What we call penitence becomes a sad attestation of our *incorrigibleness.* *Decay of Piety.*

I would not have chiding used, much less blows, 'till obstinacy and *incorrigibleness* make it absolutely necessary. *Locke.*

INCO'RRIGIBLY. *adv.* [from *incorrigible.*] To a degree of depravity beyond all means of amendment.

Appear *incorrigibly* mad,
They cleanliness and company renounce. *Roscommon.*

INCORRU'PT. } *adj.* [*in* and *corruptus*, Latin; *incorrompu*,
INCORRU'PTED. } French.]

1. Free from foulness or depravation.

Sin, that first
Distemper'd all things, and, of *incorrupt*,
Corrupted. *Milton's Paradise Lost, b.* xi.

2. Pure of manners; honest; good. It is particularly applied to a mind above the power of bribes.

INCORRUPTIBI'LITY. *n. s.* [*incorruptibilité*, Fr. from *incorruptible.*] Insusceptibility of corruption; incapacity of decay.

Philo, in his book of the world's *incorruptibility*, alledgeth the verses of a Greek tragick poet. *Hakewill.*

INCORRU'PTIBLE. *adj.* [*incorruptible*, Fr. *in* and *corruptible.*] Not capable of corruption; not admitting decay.

In such abundance lies our choice,
As leaves a great store of fruit untouch'd,
Still hanging *incorruptible.* *Milton's Paradise Lost, b.* ix.

Our bodies shall be changed into *incorruptible* and immortal substances, our souls be entertained with the most ravishing objects, and both continue happy throughout all eternity. *Wake.*

INCORRU'PTION. *n. s.* [*incorruption*, Fr. *in* and *corruption.*] Incapacity of corruption.

So also is the resurrection of the dead: it is sown in corruption, it is raised in *incorruption.* 1 *Cor.* xv. 42.

INCORRU'PTNESS. *n. s.* [*in* and *corrupt.*]

1. Purity of manners; honesty; integrity.

Probity of mind, integrity, and *incorruptness* of manners, is preferable to fine parts and subtile speculations. *Woodward.*

2. Freedom from decay or degeneration.

To INCRA'SSATE. *v. a.* [*in* and *crassus*, Lat.] To thicken; the contrary to attenuate.

If the cork be too light to sink under the surface, the body of water may be attenuated with spirits of wine; if too heavy, it may be *incrassated* with salt. *Brown's Vulgar Errours.*

Acids dissolve or attenuate, alcalies precipitate or *incrassate.* *Newton's Opt.*

Acids, such as are austere, as unripe fruits, produce too great a stricture of the fibres, *incrassate* and coagulate the fluids; from whence pains and rheumatism. *Arbuthnot.*

INCRASSA'TION. *n. s.* [from *incrassate.*]

1. The act of thickening.

2. The state of growing thick.

Nothing doth conglaciate but water; for the determination of quicksilver is fixation, that of milk coagulation, and that of oil *incrassation.* *Brown's Vulgar Errours.*

INCRA'SSATIVE. *n. s.* [from *incrassate.*] Having the quality of thickening.

The two latter indicate restringents to stench, and *incrassatives* to thicken the blood. *Harvey on Consumpt.*

To INCRE'ASE. *v. n.* [*in* and *cresco*, Lat.] To grow more in number, or greater in bulk; to advance in quantity or value, or in any quality capable of being more or less.

Hear and observe to do it, that it may be well with thee, and that ye may *increase* mightily. *Deutr.* vi. 3.

Profane and vain babbling will *increase* unto ungodliness. 2 *Tim.* ii. 16.

From fifty to threescore he loses not much in fancy, and judgment, the effect of observation, still *increases*. *Dryden.*

Henry, in knots, involving Emma's name
Upon this tree; and, as the tender mark,
Grew with the year, and widen'd with the bark:
Venus had heard the virgin's soft address,
That as the wound the passion might *increase*. *Prior.*

To INCRE'ASE. *v. a.* [See ENCREASE.] To make more or greater.

He hath *increased* in Judah mourning and lamentation. *Sam.*

I will *increase* the famine, and break your staff of bread. *Ezek.* v. 16.

I will *increase* them with men like a flock. *Ezek.* xxxvi.

Hye thee from this slaughter-house,
Lest thou *increase* the number of the dead. *Shakesp. R.* III.

Fishes are more numerous or *increasing* than beasts or birds, as appears by their numerous spawn. *Hale.*

It serves to *increase* that treasure, or to preserve it. *Temple.*

INCRE'ASE. *n. s.* [from the verb.]

1. Augmentation; the state of growing more or greater.

For three years he liv'd with large *increase*
In arms of honour, and esteem in peace. *Dryden.*

Hail, bards triumphant! born in happier days,
Whose honours with *increase* of ages grow,
As streams roll down, enlarging as they flow. *Pope.*

2. Increment; that which is added to the original stock.

3. Produce.

As Hesiod sings, spread waters o'er thy field,
And a most just and glad *increase* 'twill yield. *Denham.*

Those grains which grew produced an *increase* beyond expectation. *Mortimer's Husbandry.*

4. Generation.

Into her womb convey sterility;
Dry up in her the organs of *increase*,
And from her derogate body never spring a babe. *Shakesp.*

5. Progeny.

Him young Thoasa bore, the bright *increase*
Of Phorcys. *Pope's Odyssey.*

6. The state of waxing, or growing full orbed. Used of the moon.

Seeds, hair, nails, hedges and herbs, will grow soonest, if set or cut in the *increase* of the moon. *Bacon's Nat. Hist.*

INCRE'ASER. *n. s.* [from *increase.*] He who increases.

INCREA'TED. *adj.* Not created.

Since the desire is infinite, nothing but the absolute and *increated* Infinite can adequately fill it. *Cheyne's Phil. Princ.*

INCREDIBI'LITY. *n. s.* [*incredibilité*, French.] The quality of surpassing belief.

For objects of *incredibility*, none are so removed from all appearance of truth as those of Corneille's Andromede. *Dryd.*

INCRE'DIBLE. *adj.* [*incredibilis*, Lat.] Surpassing belief; not to be credited.

The ship Argo, that there might want no *incredible* thing in this fable, spoke to them. *Raleigh.*

Presenting things impossible to view,
They wander through *incredible* to true. *Granville.*

INCRE'DIBLENESS. *n. s.* [from *incredible.*] Quality of being not credible.

IECRE'DIBLY. *adv.* [from *incredible.*] In a manner not to be believed.

INCREDU'LITY. *n. s.* [*incredulité*, French.] Quality of not believing; hardness of belief.

He was more large in the description of Paradise, to take away all scruple from the *incredulity* of future ages. *Raleigh.*

INCRE'DULOUS. *adj.* [*incredule*, Fr. *incredulus*, Latin.] Hard of belief; refusing credit.

I am not altogether *incredulous* but there may be such candles as are made of salamander's wool, being a kind of mineral which whiteneth in the burning, and consumeth not. *Bac.*

INCRE'DULOUSNESS. *n. s.* [from *incredulous.*] Hardness of belief; incredulity.

INCRE'MABLE. *adj.* [*in* and *cremo*, Latin.] Not consumable by fire.

If from the skin of the salamander these *incremable* pieces are composed. *Brown's Vulg. Errours.*

I'NCREMENT. *n. s.* [*incrementum*, Latin.]

1. Act of growing greater.

Divers conceptions are concerning its *increment*, or inundation. *Brown's Vulgar Errours.*

2. Increase; cause of growing more.

This stratum is expanded at top, serving as the seminary that furnisheth matter for the formation and *increment* of animal and vegetable bodies. *Woodward.*

3. Produce.

The orchard loves to wave
With Winter winds: the loosen'd roots then drink
Large *increment*, earnest of happy years. *Phillips.*

To I'NCREPATE. *v. a.* [*increpo*, Latin.] To chide; to reprehend.

INCREPA'TION. *n. s.* [*increpatio*, Latin.] Reprehension; chiding.

The admonitions, fraternal or paternal, of his fellow Christians, or of the governours of the church, then more publick reprehensions and *increpations*. *Hammond.*

To INCRU'ST. } *v. a.* [*incrusto*, Latin; *incruster*, French.]
To INCRU'STATE. } To cover with an additional coat adhering to the internal matter.

The finer part of the wood will be turned into air, and the grosser stick baked and *incrustate* upon the sides of the vessel. *Bacon's Natural History.*

Some rivers bring forth spars, and other mineral matter, so as to cover and *incrust* the stones. *Woodward.*

Save but our army; and let Jove *incrust*
Swords, pikes, and guns with everlasting rust. *Pope.*

Any of these sun-like bodies in the centers of the several vortices, are so *incrustated* and weakened as to be carried about in the vortex of the true sun. *Cheyne's Phil. Prin.*

The shield was purchased by Woodward, who *incrusted* it with a new rust. *Arbuthn. and Pope's Mart. Scribl.*

INCRUSTA'TION. *n. s.* [*incrustation*, Fr. from *incrusto*, Latin.] An adherent covering; something superinduced.

Having such a prodigious stock of marble, their chapels are laid over with such a rich variety of *incrustations* as cannot be found in any other part. *Addison on Italy.*

To I'NCUBATE. *v. n.* [*incubo*, Latin.] To sit upon eggs.

INCUBA'TION. *n. s.* [*incubation*, Fr. *incubatio*, Lat.] The act of sitting upon eggs to hatch them.

Whether that vitality was by *incubation*, or how else, is only known to God. *Raleigh's History of the World.*

Birds have eggs enough at first conceived in them to serve them, allowing such a proportion for every year as will serve for one or two *incubations*. *Ray on the Creation.*

When the whole tribe of birds by *incubation* produce their young, it is a wonderful deviation, that some few families should do it in a more novercal way. *Derham.*

As the white of an egg by *incubation*, so can the serum by the action of the fibres be attenuated. *Arbuthnot.*

I'NCUBUS. *n. s.* [Latin; *incube*, Fr.] The night-mare.

The *incubus* is an inflation of the membranes of the stomach, which hinders the motion of the diaphragma, lungs, pulse, and motion, with a sense of a weight oppressing the breast. *Floyer on the Humours.*

To INCU'LCATE. *v. a.* [*inculco*, Latin; *inculquer*, French.] To impress by frequent admonitions; to enforce by constant repetition.

Manifest truth may deserve sometimes to be *inculcated*, because we are too apt to forget it. *Atterbury.*

Homer continually *inculcates* morality, and piety to the gods. *Broome's Notes to Pope's Odyssey.*

INCULCA'TION. *n. s.* [from *inculcate.*] The act of impressing by frequent admonition; admonitory repetition.

INCU'LT. *adj.* [*inculte*, French; *incultus*, Lat.] Uncultivated; untilled.

Her forests huge,
Incult, robust and tall, by nature's hand
Planted of old. *Thomson's Autumn.*

INCU'LPABLE. *adv.* [*in* and *culpabilis*, Lat.] Unblameable; not reprehensible.

Ignorance, so far as it may be resolved into natural inability, is, as to men, at least *inculpable*, and consequently not the object of scorn, but pity. *South.*

INCU'LPABLY. *adj.* [*in* and *culpabilis*, Lat.] Unblameably; without blame.

As to errours or infirmities, the frailty of man's condition has invincibly, and therefore *inculpably*, exposed him. *South.*

INCU'MBENCY. *n. s.* [from *incumbent.*]

1. The act of lying upon another.

2. The state of keeping a benefice.

These fines are only to be paid to the bishop, during his *incumbency* in the same see. *Swift.*

INCU'MBENT. *adj.* [*incumbens*, Latin.]

1. Resting upon; lying upon.

Then with expanded wings he steers his flight
Aloft, *incumbent* on the dusky air,
That felt unusual weight. *Milt. Paradise Lost, b.* i.

The ascending parcels of air, having now little more than the weight of the *incumbent* water to surmount, were able both so to expand themselves as to fill up that part of the pipe which they pervaded, and, by pressing every way against the sides of it, to lift upwards with them what water they found above them. *Boyle.*

With wings expanded wide ourselves we'll rear,
And fly *incumbent* on the dusky air. *Dryden.*
Here the rebel giants lye;
And, when to move th' *incumbent* load they try,
Ascending vapours on the day prevail. *Addison.*
Man is the destin'd prey of pestilence,
And o'er his guilty domes
She draws a close *incumbent* cloud of death. *Thomson.*

2. Imposed as a duty.

All men, truly zealous, will perform those good works that are *incumbent* on all Christians. *Sprat's Sermons.*

There is a double duty *incumbent* upon us in the exercise of our powers. *L'Estrange.*

Thus, if we think and act, we shall shew ourselves duly mindful not only of the advantages we receive from thence, but of the obligations also which are *incumbent* upon us. *Atter.*

INCU'MBENT. *n. s.* [*incumbens*, Latin.] He who is in present possession of a benefice.

In many places the whole ecclesiastical dues are in lay hands, and the *incumbent* lieth at the mercy of his patron. *Swift.*

To INCU'MBER. *v. a.* [*encombrer*, French.] To embarrass.

My cause is call'd, and that long look'd-for day
Is still *incumber'd* with some new delay. *Dryden's Juven.*

To INCU'R. *v. a.* [*incurro*, Latin.] To become liable to a punishment or reprehension.

I have *incurred* displeasure from inferiours for giving way to the faults of others. *Hayward.*

They, not obeying,
Incurr'd, what could they less? the penalty;
And manifold in sin, deserv'd to fall. *Milton's Par. Lost.*
So judge thou still, presumptuous! 'till the wrath,
Which thou *incurr'st* by flying, meet thy flight
Sev'nfold, and scourge that wisdom back to hell. *Milton.*

They had a full persuasive that not to do it were to desert God, and consequently to *incur* damnation. *South.*

2. To occur; to press on the senses.

The motions of the minute parts of bodies are invisible, and *incur* not to the eye; but yet they are to be deprehended by experience. *Bacon's Natural History.*

The mind of man, even in spirituals, acts with corporeal dependance; and so is he helped or hindered in its operations, according to the different quality of external objects that *incur* into the senses. *South's Sermons.*

INCURABI'LITY. *n. s.* [*incurabilité*, Fr. from *incurable.*] Impossibility of cure; utter insusceptibility of remedy.

We'll instantly open a door to the manner of a proper and improper consumption, together with the reason of the *incurability* of the former, and facile cure of the other. *Harvey.*

INCU'RABLE. *adj.* [*incurable*, Fr. *in* and *curable*] Not admitting remedy; not to be removed by medicine; irremediable; hopeless.

Pause not; for the present time's so sick,
That present medicine must be ministred,
Or overthrow *incurable* ensues. *Shakes. King John.*
Stop the rage betime,
Before the wound do grow *incurable*;
For being green, there is great hope of help. *Shakes. H.* VI.

A schirrus is not absolutely *incurable*, because it has been known that fresh pasture has cured it in cattle. *Arbuthnot.*

If idiots and lunaticks cannot be found, *incurables* may be taken into the hospital. *Swift.*

INCU'RABLENESS. *n. s.* [from *incurable.*] State of not admitting any cure.

INCU'RABLY. *adv.* [from *incurable.*] Without remedy.

We cannot know it is or is not, being *incurably* ignorant. *Locke.*

INCU'RIOUS. *adj.* [*in* and *curious.*] Negligent; inattentive.

The Creator did not bestow so much skill upon his creatures, to be looked upon with a careless *incurious* eye. *Derham.*

He seldom at the park appear'd;
Yet, not *incurious*, was inclin'd
To know the converse of mankind. *Swift.*

INCU'RSION. *n. s.* [from *incurro*, Latin.]

1. Attack; mischievous occurrence.

Sins of daily *incursion*, and such as human frailty is unavoidably liable to. *South's Sermons.*

2. [*Incursion*, Fr.] Invasion without conquest; inroad; ravage.

Spain is very weak at home, or very slow to move, when they suffered a small fleet of English to make an hostile invasion, or *incursion*, upon their havens and roads. *Bacon.*

Now the Parthian king hath gather'd all his host
Against the Scythian, whose *incursions* wild
Have wasted Sogdiana. *Milton's Parad. Regain'd.*

The *incursions* of the Goths disordered the affairs of the Roman empire. *Arbuthnot on Coins.*

INCURVA'TION. *n. s.* [from *incurvo*, Latin.]

1. The act of bending or making crooked.

One part moving while the other rests, one would think, should cause an *incurvation* in the line. *Glanv. Sceps.*

2. Flexion of the body in token of reverence.

He made use of acts of worship which God hath appropriated; as *incurvation*, and sacrifice. *Stillingfleet.*

To INCU'RVATE. *v. a.* [*incurvo*, Latin.] To bend; to crook.

Sir Isaac Newton has shewn, by several experiments of rays passing by the edges of bodies, that they are *incurvated* by the action of these bodies. *Cheyne's Phil. Prin.*

INCU'RVITY. *n. s.* [from *incurvus*, Latin.] Crookedness; the state of bending inward.

The *incurvity* of a dolphin must be taken not really, but in appearance, when they leap above water, and suddenly shoot down again: strait bodies, in a sudden motion, protruded obliquely downward, appear crooked. *Brown's Vulgar Errours.*

To I'NDAGATE. *v. a.* [*indago*, Latin.] To search; to beat out.

INDAGA'TION. *n. s.* [from *indagate.*] Search; enquiry; examination.

Paracelsus directs us, in the *indagation* of colours, to have an eye principally upon salts. *Boyle.*

Part hath been discovered by himself, and some by human *indagation.* *Brown's Vulgar Errours.*

INDAGA'TOR. *n. s.* [*indagator*, Latin.] A searcher; an enquirer; an examiner.

The number of the elements of bodies is an enquiry whose truth requires to be searched into by such skilful *indagators* of nature. *Boyle.*

To INDA'RT. *v. a.* [*in* and *dart.*] To dart in; to strike in.

I'll look to like, if looking liking move;
But no more deep will I *indart* mine eye,
Than your consent gives strength to make it fly. *Shakesp.*

To INDE'BT. *v. a.*

1. To put into debt.
2. To oblige; to put under obligation.

INDE'BTED. *participial adj.* [*in* and *debt.*] Obliged by something received; bound to restitution; having incurred a debt. It has *to* before the person to whom the debt is due, and *for* before the thing received.

If the course of politick affairs cannot in any good course go forward without fit instruments, and that which fitteth them be their virtues, let polity acknowledge itself *indebted to* religion, godliness being the chiefest top and well-spring of all true virtues, even as God is of all good things. *Hooker.*

Forgive us our sins; for we forgive every one that is *indebted to* us. *Lu.* xi. 4.

He for himself
Indebted and undone, has nought to bring. *Milton.*
This blest alliance may
Th' *indebted* nation bounteously repay. *Granville.*

Few consider how much we are *indebted to* government, because few can represent how wretched mankind would be without it. *Atterbury's Sermons.*

Let us represent to our souls the love and beneficence *for* which we daily stand *indebted to* God. *Rogers's Sermons.*

We are wholly *indebted for* them *to* our ancestors. *Swift.*

INDE'CENCY. *n. s.* [*indecence*, French.] Any thing unbecoming; any thing contrary to good manners; something wrong, but scarce criminal.

He will in vain endeavour to reform *indecency* in his pupil, which he allows in himself. *Locke.*

INDE'CENT. *adj.* [*indecent*, Fr. *in* and *decent.*] Unbecoming; unfit for the eyes or ears.

'Till these men can prove these things, ordered by our church, to be either intrinsically unlawful or *indecent*, the use of them, as established amongst us, is necessary. *South.*

Characters, where obscene words were proper in their mouths, but very *indecent* to be heard. *Dryden.*

INDE'CENTLY. *adv.* [from *indecent.*] Without decency; in a manner contrary to decency.

INDECI'DUOUS. *adj.* [*in* and *deciduous.*] Not falling; not shed.

We find the statue of the sun framed with rays about the head, which were the *indeciduous* and unshaken locks of Apollo. *Brown's Vul. Err.*

INDECLI'NABLE. *adj.* [*indeclinable*, Fr. *indeclinabilis*, Latin.] Not varied by terminations.

Pondo is an *indeclinable* word, and when it is joined to numbers it signifies *libra.* *Arbuthnot.*

INDECO'ROUS. *adj.* [*indecorus*, Latin.] Indecent; unbecoming.

What can be more *indecorous* than for a creature to violate the commands, and trample upon the authority of that awful excellence to whom he owes his life? *Norris.*

INDECO'RUM. *n. s.* [Latin.] Indecency; something unbecoming.

INDE'ED. *adv.* [*in* and *deed.*]

1. In reality; in truth; in verity.

Yet loving *indeed*, and therefore constant. *Sidney.*

Though such assemblies be had *indeed* for religion's sake, hurtful nevertheless they may prove, as well in regard of their fitness to serve the turn of hereticks, and such as privily will venture to instil their poison into new minds. *Hooker.*

Some, who have not deserved judgment of death, have been for their goods sake caught up and carried streight to the bough: a thing *indeed* very pitiful and horrible. *Spenser.*

2. Above

2. Above common rate.

Then didst thou utter, I am yours for ever;
'Tis grace *indeed*. *Shakespeare.*

Borrows, in mean affairs, his subjects pains;
But things of weight and consequence *indeed*,
Himself doth in his chamber them debate. *Davies.*

Such sons of Abraham, how highly soever they may have the luck to be thought of, are far from being Israelites *indeed*. *South.*

I were a beast, *indeed*, to do you wrong,
I who have lov'd and honour'd you so long. *Dryden.*

3. This is to be granted that. A particle of connection.

This limitation, *indeed*, of our author, will save those the labour who would look for Adam's heir amongst the race of brutes; but will very little contribute to the discovery of one next heir amongst men. *Locke.*

There is nothing in the world more generally dreaded, and yet less to be feared, than death: *indeed*, for those unhappy men whose hopes terminate in this life, no wonder if the prospect of another seems terrible and amazing. *Wake.*

4. It is used sometimes as a slight assertion or recapitulation in a sense hardly perceptible or explicable.

This is *indeed* more criminal in thee. *Shakespeare.*

I said I thought it was confederacy between the juggler and the two servants; tho' *indeed* I had no reason so to think. *Bac.*

Some sons *indeed*, some very few we see,
Who keep themselves from this infection free. *Dryden.*

There is *indeed* no greater pleasure in visiting these magazines of war, after one has seen two or three of them. *Addis.*

5. It is used to note concession in comparisons.

Against these forces were prepared to the number of near one hundred ships; not so great of bulk *indeed*, but of a more nimble motion. *Bacon's War with Spain.*

INDEFA'TIGABLE. *adj.* [*indefatigabilis*, *in* and *defatigo*, Lat.] Unwearied; not tired; not exhausted by labour.

Who shall spread his airy flight,
Upborne with *indefatigable* wings,
Over the vast abrupt. *Milton.*

The ambitious person must rise early and sit up late, and pursue his design with a constant *indefatigable* attendance: he must be infinitely patient and servile. *South.*

INDEFA'TIGABLY. *adv.* [from *indefatigable.*] Without weariness.

A man *indefatigably* zealous in the service of the church and state, and whose writings have highly deserved of both. *Dryd.*

INDEFECTIBI'LITY. *n. s.* [from *indefectible.*] The quality of suffering no decay; of being subject to no defect.

INDEFE'CTIBLE. *adj.* [*in* and *defectus*, Lat.] Unfailing; not liable to defect or decay.

INDEFE'ISIBLE. *adj.* [*indefaisible*, French.] Not to be cut off; not to be vacated; irrevocable.

So *indefeisible* is our estate in those joys, that, if we do not sell it in reversion, we shall, when once invested, be beyond the possibility of ill husbandry. *Decay of Piety.*

INDEFE'NSIBLE. *adj.* [*in* and *defensum*, Lat.] What cannot be defended or maintained.

As they extend the rule of consulting Scripture to all the actions of common life, even so far as to the taking up of a straw, so it is altogether false and *indefensible*. *Sanderson.*

INDE'FINITE. *adj.* [*indefinitus*, Latin; *indefinit*, Fr.]

1. Not determined; not limited; not settled.

Though a position should be wholly rejected, yet that negative is more pregnant of direction than an *indefinite*; as ashes are more generative than dust. *Bacon's Essays.*

Her advancement was left *indefinite*; but thus, that it should be as great as ever any former queen of England had. *Bacon.*

Tragedy and picture are more narrowly circumscribed by place and time than the epick poem: the time of this last is left *indefinite*. *Dryden's Dufresnoy.*

2. Large beyond the comprehension of man, though not absolutely without limits.

Though it is not infinite, it may be *indefinite*; though it is not boundless in itself, it may be so to human comprehension. *Spectator.*

INDE'FINITELY. *adj.* [from *indefinite.*]

1. Without any settled or determinate limitation.

We observe that custom, whereunto St. Paul alludeth, and whereof the fathers of the church in their writings make often mention, to shew *indefinitely* what was done; but not universally to bind for ever all prayers unto one only fashion of utterance. *Hooker.*

We conceive no more than the letter beareth; that is, four times, or *indefinitely* more than thrice. *Brown's Vulg. Err.*

A duty to which all are *indefinitely* obliged, upon some occasions, by the express command of God. *Smalridge.*

2. To a degree indefinite.

If the world be *indefinitely* extended, that is, so far as no human intellect can fancy any bounds of it, then what we see must be the least part. *Ray on the Creation.*

INDEFI'NITUDE. *n. s.* [from *indefinite*] Quantity not limited by our understanding, though yet finite.

They arise to a strange and prodigious multitude, if not *indefinitude*, by their various positions, combinations, and conjunctions. *Hale's Origin of Mankind.*

INDELI'BERATE. } *adj.* [*indeliberé*, Fr. *in* and *deliberate.*] Un-
INDELI'BERATED. } premeditated; done without consideration.

Actions proceeding from blandishments, or sweet persuasions, if they be *indeliberated*, as in children, who want the use of reason, are not presently free actions. *Bramhall.*

The love of God better can consist with the *indeliberate* commissions of many sins, than with an allowed persistance in any one. *Government of the Tongue.*

INDE'LIBLE. *adj.* [*indeleble*, Fr. *indelebilis*, Lat. *in* and *delible*. It should be written *indeleble.*]

1. Not to be blotted out or effaced.

Wilful perpetrations of unworthy actions brands with *indelible* characters the name and memory. *King Charles.*

Thy heedless sleeve will drink the colour'd oil,
And spot *indelible* thy pocket soil. *Gay's Trivia.*

2. Not to be annulled.

All endued with *indelible* power from above to feed, to govern this houshold, and to consecrate pastors and stewards of it to the world's end. *Sprat's Sermons.*

INDE'LICACY. *n. s.* [*in* and *delicacy.*] Want of delicacy; want of elegant decency.

Your papers would be chargeable with worse than *indelicacy*, they would be immoral, did you treat detestable uncleanness as you rally an impertinent self-love. *Addison.*

INDE'LICATE. *adj.* [*in* and *delicate.*] Wanting decency; void of a quick sense of decency.

INDEMNIFICA'TION. *n. s.* [from *indemnify.*]

1. Security against loss or penalty.
2. Reimbursement of loss or penalty.

To INDE'MNIFY. *v. a.* [*in* and *damnify.*]

1. To secure against loss or penalty.
2. To maintain unhurt.

Insolent signifies rude and haughty, *indemnify* to keep safe. *Watts.*

INDE'MNITY. *n. s.* [*indemnite*, French.] Security from punishment; exemption from punishment.

I will use all means, in the ways of amnesty and *indemnity*, which may most fully remove all fears, and bury all jealousies in forgetfulness. *King Charles.*

To INDE'NT. *v. a.* [*in* and *dens*, a tooth, Lat.] To mark any thing with inequalities like a row of teeth; to cut in and out; to make to wave or undulate.

About his neck
A green and gilded snake had wreath'd itself,
Who with her head, nimble in threats, approach'd
The opening of his mouth; but suddenly,
Seeing Orlando, it unlink'd itself,
And with *indented* glides did slip away
Into a bush. *Shakespeare's As you like.*

The serpent then, not with *indented* wave,
Prone on the ground, as since; but on his rear
Circular base of rising folds, that tower'd
Fold above fold, a surging maze! *Milton's Paradise Lost.*

Trent, who, like some earth-born giant, spreads
His thirty arms along the *indented* meads. *Milton.*

The margins on each side do not terminate in a streight line, but are *indented*. *Woodward.*

To INDE'NT. *v. n.* [from the method of cutting counterparts of a contract together, that, laid on each other, they may fit, and any want of conformity may discover a fraud.] To contract; to bargain; to make a compact.

Shall we buy treason, and *indent* with fears,
When they have lost and forfeited themselves? *Shakes. H.* IV.

He descends to the solemnity of a pact and covenant, and has *indented* with us. *Decay of Piety.*

INDE'NT. *n. s.* [from the verb.] Inequality; incisure; indentation.

Trent shall not wind with such a deep *indent*,
To rob me of so rich a bottom here. *Shakesp. Hen.* IV.

INDENTA'TION. *n. s.* [*in* and *dens*, Latin.] An indenture; waving in any figure.

The margins on each side do not terminate in a streight line, but are indented; each *indentation* being continued in a small ridge across the line, to the *indentation* that answers it on the opposite margin. *Woodward on Fossils.*

INDE'NTURE. *n. s.* [from *indent.*] A covenant, so named because the counterparts are indented or cut one by the other.

In Hall's chronicle much good matter is quite marred with *indenture* English. *Ascham's Schoolmaster.*

The critick to his grief will find
How firmly these *indentures* bind. *Swift.*

INDEPE'NDENCE. } *n. s.* [*independance*, Fr. *in* and *dependence.*]
INDEPE'NDENCY. } Freedom; exemption from reliance or control; state over which none has power.

Dreams may give us some idea of the great excellency of a human soul, and some intimations of its *independency* on matter. *Addison's Spectator.*

Let fortune do her worst, whatever she makes us lose, as long as she never makes us lose our honesty and our *independence*. *Pope.*

Give me, I cry'd, enough for me,
My bread and *independency:*
So bought an annual rent or two,
And liv'd juſt as you ſee I do. *Pope.*

INDEPE'NDENT. *adj.* [*independant*, Fr. *in* and *dependent.*]

1. Not depending; not ſupported by any other; not relying on another; not controlled. It is uſed with *on*, *of*, or *from* before the object; of which *on* ſeems moſt proper, ſince we ſay to *depend on*, and conſequently *dependent on.*

Creation muſt needs infer providence, and God's making the world irrefragably proves that he governs it too; or that a being of dependent nature remains nevertheleſs *independent upon* him in that reſpect. *South's Sermons.*

Since all princes of *independent* governments are in a ſtate of nature, the world never was without men in that ſtate. *Locke.*

The town of St. Gaul is a proteſtant republick, *independent of* the abbot, and under the protection of the cantons. *Addiſ.*

2. Not relating to any thing elſe, as to a ſuperiour cauſe or power.

The conſideration of our underſtanding, which is an incorporeal ſubſtance *independent from* matter; and the contemplation of our own bodies, which have all the ſtamps and characters of excellent contrivance; theſe alone do very eaſily guide us to the wiſe Author of all things. *Bentley's Sermons.*

INDEPE'NDENT. *n.ſ.* One who in religious affairs holds that every congregation is a complete church, ſubject to no ſuperiour authority.

We ſhall, in our ſermons, take occaſion to juſtify ſuch paſſages in our liturgy as have been unjuſtly quarrelled at by preſbyterians, *independents*, or other puritan ſectaries. *Sanderſ.*

A very famous *independent* miniſter was head of a college in thoſe times. *Addiſon's Spectator.*

INDEPE'NDENTLY. *adv.* [from *independent.*] Without reference to other things.

Diſpoſe lights and ſhadows, without finiſhing every thing, *independently* the one of the other. *Dryden.*

INDESE'RT. *n.ſ.* [*in* and *deſert.*] Want of merit.

Thoſe who were once looked on as his equals, are apt to think the fame of his merit a reflection on their own *indeſert.* *Addiſon's Spectator.*

INDE'SINENTLY. *adv.* [*indeſinenter*, Fr. *in* and *deſinio*, Latin.] Without ceſſation.

They continue a month *indeſinently.* *Ray on the Creation.*

INDESTRU'CTIBLE. *adj.* [*in* and *deſtructible.*] Not to be deſtroyed.

Glaſs is ſo compact and firm a body, that it is *indeſtructible* by art or nature. *Boyle.*

INDETE'RMINABLE. *adj.* [*in* and *determinable.*] Not to be fixed; not to be defined or ſettled.

There is not only obſcurity in the end, but beginning of the world; that as its period is inſcrutable, ſo is its nativity *indeterminable.* *Brown's Vulgar Errours.*

INDETE'RMINATE. *adj.* [*indeterminé*, Fr. *in* and *determinate.*] Unfixed; not defined; indefinite.

The rays of the ſame colour were by turns tranſmitted at one thickneſs, and reflected at another thickneſs, for an *indeterminate* number of ſucceſſions. *Newton's Opt.*

INDETE'RMINATELY. *adv.* [*in* and *determinately.*] Indefinitely; not in any ſettled manner.

His perſpicacity diſcerned the loadſtone to reſpect the North, when ours beheld it *indeterminately.* *Brown's Vulg. Err.*

The depth of the hold is *indeterminately* expreſſed in the deſcription. *Arbuthnot on Coins.*

INDETE'RMINED. *adj.* [*in* and *determined.*] Unſettled; unfixed.

We ſhould not amuſe ourſelves with floating words of *indetermined* ſignification, which we can uſe in ſeveral ſenſes to ſerve a turn. *Locke.*

INDETERMINA'TION. *n.ſ.* [*in* and *determination.*] Want of determination; want of fixed or ſtated direction.

By contingents I underſtand all things which may be done, and may not be done, may happen, or may not happen, by reaſon of the *indetermination* or accidental concurrence of the cauſes. *Bramhall againſt Hobbes.*

INDEVO'TION. *n.ſ.* [*indevotion*, Fr. *in* and *devotion.*] Want of devotion; irreligion.

Let us make the church the ſcene of our penitence, as of our faults; deprecate our former *indevotion*, and, by an exemplary reverence, redreſs the ſcandal of our profaneneſs. *Decay of Piety.*

INDEVOU'T. *adj.* [*indevot*, Fr. *in* and *devout.*] Not devout; not religious; irreligious.

He prays much, yet curſes more; whilſt he is meek, but *indevout.* *Decay of Piety.*

INDE'X. *n.ſ.* [Latin.]

1. The diſcoverer; the pointer out.

Taſtes are the *indexes* of the different qualities of plants, as well as of all ſorts of aliment. *Arbuthnot on Aliments.*

That which was once the *index* to point out all virtues, does now mark out that part of the world where leaſt of them reſides. *Decay of Piety.*

2. The hand that points to any thing, as to the hour or way.

They have no more inward ſelf-conſciouſneſs of what they do or ſuffer, than the *index* of a watch, of the hour it points to. *Bentley's Sermons.*

3. The table of contents to a book.

In ſuch *indexes*, although ſmall
To their ſubſequent volumes, there is ſeen
The baby figure of the giant maſs
Of things to come, at large. *Shakeſpeare.*

If a book has no *index*, or good table of contents, 'tis very uſeful to make one as you are reading it; and in your *index* to take notice only of parts new to you. *Watts.*

INDEXTE'RITY. *n.ſ.* [*in* and *dexterity.*] Want of dexterity; want of readineſs; want of handineſs.

The *indexterity* of our conſumption-curers demonſtrates their dimneſs in beholding its cauſes. *Harvey on Conſumptions.*

I'NDIAN *Arrow-root.* *n.ſ.* [*marcanta*, Latin.] A root.

It has a flower conſiſting of one leaf, almoſt funnel-ſhaped, opening in ſix parts, three of which are alternately larger than the others: the lower part of the flower-cup afterwards becomes an oval ſhaped fruit, having one cell, with one hard rough ſeed. It was brought from the Spaniſh ſettlements of America into the iſlands of Barbadoes and Jamaica, where it is cultivated as a medicinal plant, it being a ſovereign remedy for curing the bite of waſps, and expelling the poiſon of the manchineel tree. This root the Indians apply to extract the venom of their arrows: after they have dug it up they clean it, maſh it, and lay it as a poultice to the wounded part, and are generally ſucceſsful in the cure. *Miller.*

I'NDIAN *Creſs.* *n.ſ.* [*acriviola*, Latin.] A plant.

The leaves are round, umbillicated, and placed alternately; the ſtalks trailing; the cup of the flower is quinquefid; the flowers conſiſt of five leaves in form of a violet; the ſeeds are roundiſh and rough, three of them ſucceeding each flower. The ſpecies are five. *Miller.*

I'NDIAN *Fig.* *n.ſ.* [*opuntia*, Latin.] A plant.

The characters are: the flower conſiſts of many leaves, which expand in form of a roſe, having a great number of ſtamina in the centre, which grow upon the top of the ovary: the ovary afterwards becomes a fleſhy umbillicated fruit, with a ſoft pulp, incloſing many ſeeds, which are for the moſt part angular. *Miller.*

I'NDIAN *Red.* *n.ſ.* A kind of mineral earth.

Indian red, ſo called by the painters, is a ſpecies of ochre; and is a very fine purple earth, of firm compact texture, and great weight: while in the ſtratum it is of a pure blood colour, and almoſt of a ſtony hardneſs: when dry it is of a fine glowing red, of a rough duſty ſurface, and, when broken, full of white particles, large, ſolid, bright, and glittering. It is alſo called Perſian earth, and is dug in the iſland of Ormuz in the Perſian gulph, and alſo at Bombay. *Hill on Foſſils.*

I'NDICANT. *adj.* [*indicans*, Latin.] Showing; pointing out; that which directs what is to be done in any diſeaſe.

To I'NDICATE. *v. a.* [*indico*, Latin.]

1. To ſhow; to point out.
2. [In phyſick.] To point out a remedy.

INDICA'TION. *n.ſ.* [*indication*, Fr. *indicatio*, from *indico*, Lat.]

1. Mark; token; ſign; note; ſymptom.

The frequent ſtops they make in the moſt convenient places, are a plain *indication* of their weарineſs. *Addiſon's Guardian.*

We think that our ſucceſſes are a plain *indication* of the divine favour towards us. *Atterbury's Sermons.*

2. [In phyſick.] *Indication* is of four kinds: vital, preſervative, curative, and palliative, as it directs what is to be done to continue life, cutting off the cauſe of an approaching diſtemper, curing it whilſt it is actually preſent, or leſſening its effects, or taking off ſome of its ſymptoms before it can be wholly removed. *Quincy.*

Theſe be the things that govern nature principally, and without which you cannot make any true analyſis, and *indication* of the proceedings of nature. *Bacon's Nat. Hiſt.*

The depravation of the inſtruments of maſtication is a natural *indication* of a liquid diet. *Arbuthnot on Aliments.*

3. Diſcovery made; intelligence given.

If a perſon, that had a fair eſtate in reverſion, ſhould be aſſured by ſome ſkilful phyſician, that he would inevitably fall into a diſeaſe that would totally deprive him of his underſtanding and memory; if, I ſay, upon a certain belief of this *indication*, the man ſhould appear overjoyed at the news, would not all that ſaw him conclude that the diſtemper had ſeized him? *Bentley's Sermons.*

INDI'CATIVE. *adj.* [*indicativus*, Lat.]

1. Showing; informing; pointing out.
2. [In grammar.] A certain modification of a verb, expreſſing affirmation or indication.

The verb is formed in a certain manner to affirm, deny, or interrogate; which formation, from the principal uſe of it, is called the *indicative* mood. *Clarke's Lat. Gram.*

INDI'CATIVELY. *adv.* [from *indicative.*] In ſuch a manner as ſhows or betokens.

Theſe images, formed in the brain, are *indicatively* of the ſame ſpecies with thoſe of ſenſe. *Grew's Coſmol.*

To INDICT. See INDITE, and its derivatives.

INDI'CTION. *n. s.* [*indiction*, Fr. *indico*, Latin.]

1. Declaration; proclamation.

After a legation *ad res repetendas*, and a refusal, and a denunciation and *indiction* of a war, the war is left at large. *Bac.*

2. [In chronology.] The *indiction*, instituted by Constantine the great, is properly a cycle of tributes, orderly disposed, for fifteen years, and by it accounts of that kind were kept. Afterwards, in memory of the great victory obtained by Constantine over Mezentius, 8 Cal. Oct. 312, by which an intire freedom was given to Christianity, the council of Nice, for the honour of Constantine, ordained that the accounts of years should be no longer kept by the Olympiads, which 'till that time had been done; but that, instead thereof, the *indiction* should be made use of, by which to reckon and date their years, which hath its epocha *A. D.* 313, Jan. 1.

INDI'FFERENCE. } *n. s.* [*indifference*, French; *indifferentia*,
INDI'FFERENCY. } Latin.]

1. Neutrality; suspension; equipoise or freedom from motives on either side.

In choice of committees it is better to chuse indifferent persons, than to make an *indifferency* by putting in those that are strong on both sides. *Bacon's Essays.*

By an equal *indifferency* for all truth, I mean, not loving it as such, before we know it to be true. *Locke.*

A perfect *indifferency* in the mind, not determinable by its last judgment, would be as great an imperfection as the want of *indifferency* to act, or not to act, 'till determined by the will. *Locke.*

Those who would borrow light from expositors, either consult only those who have the good luck to be thought sound and orthodox, avoiding those of different sentiments; or else with *indifferency* look into the notes of all commentators. *Locke.*

2. Impartiality.

Read the book with *indifferency* and judgment, and thou can'st not but greatly commend it. *Whitgifte.*

3. Negligence; want of affection; unconcernedness.

Indifference cannot but be criminal, when it is conversant about objects which are so far from being of an indifferent nature, that they are of the highest importance. *Addison.*

A place which we must pass through, not only with the *indifference* of strangers, but with the vigilance of those who travel through the country of an enemy. *Rogers.*

Indiff'rence, clad in wisdom's guise,
All fortitude of mind supplies;
For how can stony bowels melt,
In those who never pity felt? *Swift.*

He will let you know he has got a clap with as much *indifferency* as he would a piece of publick news. *Swift.*

The people of England should be frighted with the French king and the pretender once a year: the want of observing this necessary precept, has produced great *indifference* in the vulgar. *Arbuthnot.*

4. State in which no moral or physical reason preponderates; state in which there is no difference.

The choice is left to our discretion, except a principal bond of some higher duty remove the *indifference* that such things have in themselves: their *indifference* is removed, if we take away our own liberty. *Hooker.*

INDI'FFERENT. *adj.* [*indifferent*, Fr. *indifferens*, Latin.]

1. Neutral; not determined to either side.

Doth his majesty
Incline to it or no?
——He seems *indifferent*. *Shakespeare's Henry V.*

Being *indifferent*, we should receive and embrace opinions according as evidence gives the attestation of truth. *Locke.*

Let guilt or fear
Disturb man's rest; Cato knows neither of them:
Indifferent in his choice to sleep or die. *Addison's Cato.*

2. Unconcerned; inattentive; regardless.

One thing was all to you, and your fondness made you *indifferent* to every thing else. *Temple.*

It was a remarkable law of Solon, that any person who, in the civil commotions of the republick, remained neuter, or an *indifferent* spectator of the contending parties, should be condemned to perpetual banishment. *Addison's Freeholder.*

But how *indifferent* soever man may be to eternal happiness, yet surely to eternal misery none can be *indifferent*. *Rogers.*

3. Not to have such difference as that the one is for its own sake preferable to the other.

The nature of things *indifferent* is neither to be commanded nor forbidden, but left free and arbitrary. *Hooker.*

These two customs, which of themselves are *indifferent* in other kingdoms, became exceeding evil in this realm, by reason of the inconveniences which followed thereupon. *Davies.*

Though at first it was free, and in my choice whether or no I should publish these discourses; yet, the publication being once resolved, the dedication was not so *indifferent*. *South.*

This I mention only as my conjecture, it being *indifferent* to the matter in hand which way the learned shall determine. *Loc.*

4. Impartial; disinterested.

Medcalfe was partial to none, but *indifferent* to all; a master for the whole, and a father to every one. *Ascham.*

I am a most poor woman, and a stranger,
Born out of your dominions; having here
No judge *indiff'rent*, and no more assurance
Of equal friendship and proceeding. *Shakesp. Hen. VIII.*

There can hardly be an *indifferent* trial had between the king and the subject, or between party and party, by reason of this general kindred and consanguinity. *Davies.*

5. Passable; having mediocrity; of a middling state; neither good nor worst. This is an improper and colloquial use, especially when applied to persons.

Some things admit of mediocrity:
A counsellor, or pleader at the bar,
May want Messala's pow'rful eloquence,
Or be less read than deep Cassellius;
Yet this *indiff'rent* lawyer is esteem'd. *Roscommon.*

Who would excel, when few can make a test
Betwixt *indiff'rent* writing and the best? *Dryden.*

This has obliged me to publish an *indifferent* collection of poems, for fear of being thought the author of a worse *Prior.*

There is not one of these subjects that would not sell a very *indifferent* paper, could I think of gratifying the publick by such mean and base methods. *Addison.*

6. In the same sense it has the force of an adverb.

I am myself *indifferent* honest; but yet I could accuse me of such things, that it were better that my mother had not borne me. *Shakespeare's Hamlet.*

This will raise a great scum on it, and leave your wine *indifferent* clear. *Mortimer.*

INDI'FFERENTLY. *adv.* [*indifferenter*, Latin.]

1. Without distinction; without preference.

Whiteness is a mean between all colours, having itself *indifferently* to them all, so as with equal facility to be tinged with any of them. *Newton's Opt.*

Were pardon extended *indifferently* to all, which of them would think himself under any particular obligation? *Addison.*

Though a church of England-man thinks every species of government equally lawful, he does not think them equally expedient, or for every country *indifferently*. *Swift.*

2. In a neutral state; without wish or aversion.

Set honour in one eye, and death i' th' other,
And I will look on death *indifferently*. *Shakesp. Jul. Cæs.*

3. Not well; tolerably; passably; middlingly.

A moyle will draw *indifferently* well, and carry great burthens. *Carew.*

I hope it may *indifferently* entertain your lordship at an unbending hour. *Rowe.*

An hundred and fifty of their beds, sown together, kept me but very *indifferently* from the floor. *Gulliver's Travels.*

I'NDIGENCE. } *n. s.* [*indigence*, Fr. *indigentia*, Lat.] Want;
I'NDIGENCY. } penury; poverty.

Where there is happiness, there must not be *indigency*, or want of any due comforts of life. *Burnet's Theo. of the Earth.*

For ev'n that *indigence*, that brings me low,
Makes me myself, and him above to know. *Dryden.*

Athens worshipped God with temples and sacrifices, as if he needed habitation and sustenance; and that the heathens had such a mean apprehension about the *indigency* of their gods, appears from Aristophanes and Lucian. *Bentley.*

INDI'GENOUS. *adj.* [*indigéne*, Fr. *indigena*, Latin.] Native to a country; originally produced or born in a region.

Negroes were all transported from Africa, and are not *indigenous* or proper natives of America. *Brown's Vulg. Err.*

It is wonderful to observe one creature, that is, mankind, *indigenous* to so many different climates. *Arbuthnot.*

I'NDIGENT. *adj.* [*indigent*, French; *indigens*, Latin.]

1. Poor; needy; necessitous.

Charity consists in relieving the *indigent*. *Addison.*

2. In want; wanting.

Rejoice, O Albion, sever'd from the world
By nature's wise indulgence; *indigent*
Of nothing from without. *Phillips.*

3. Void; empty.

Such bodies have the tangible parts *indigent* of moisture. *Bacon's Natural History.*

INDIGE'ST. } *adj.* [*indigeste*, Fr. *indigestus*, Latin.]
INDIGE'STED. }

1. Not separated into distinct orders; not regularly disposed.

This mass, or *indigested* matter, or chaos, created in the beginning, was without the proper form, which it afterwards acquired. *Raleigh's History of the World.*

Before the seas, and this terrestrial ball,
One was the face of nature, if a face;
Rather a rude and *indigested* mass. *Dryden's Ovid.*

2. Not formed, or shaped.

Set a form upon that *indigest* project,
So shapeless and so rude. *Shakesp. King John.*

Hence, heap of wrath, foul *indigested* lump;
As crooked in thy manners as thy shape. *Shakes. H. VI.*

3. Not well considered and methodised.

By irksome deformities, through endless and senseless effusions of *indigested* prayers, they oftentimes disgrace the worthiest part of Christian duty towards God. *Hooker.*

The political creed of the high-principled men sets the protestant succession upon a firmer foundation than all the *indigested* schemes of those who profess revolution principles. *Swift.*

4. Not concocted in the stomach.

Dreams are bred
From rising fumes of *indigested* food. *Dryden.*

5. Not brought to suppuration.

His wound was *indigested* and inflamed. *Wiseman.*

INDIGE'STIBLE. *adj.* [from *in* and *digestible.*] Not conquerable in the stomach; not convertible to nutriment.

Eggs are the most nourishing and exalted of all animal food, and most *indigestible:* no body can digest the same quantity of them as of other food. *Arbuthnot on Diet.*

INDIGE'STION. *n. s.* [*indigestion*, Fr. from *in* and *digestion.*] The state of meats unconcocted.

The fumes of *indigestion* may indispose men to thought, as well as to diseases of danger and pain. *Temple.*

To INDI'GITATE. *v. a.* [*indigito*, Lat.] To point out; to show.

Antiquity expressed numbers by the fingers: the depressing this finger, which in the left hand implied but six, in the right hand *indigitated* six hundred. *Brown's Vulgar Errours.*

As though there were a seminality of urine, we foolishly conceive we behold therein the anatomy of every particle, and can thereby *indigitate* their affections. *Brown's Vulg. Err.*

We are not to *indigitate* the parts transmittent. *Harvey.*

INDIGITA'TION. *n. s.* [from *indigitate.*] The act of pointing out or showing.

Which things I conceive no obscure *indigitation* of providence. *More against Atheism.*

INDI'GN. *adj.* [*indigne*, Fr. *indignus*, Latin.]

1. Unworthy; undeserving.

Where there is a kingdom that is altogether unable or *indign* to govern, is it just for another nation, that is civil or policed, to subdue them? *Bacon's Holy War.*

2. Bringing indignity. This is a word not in use.

And all *indign* and base adversities
Make head against my estimation. *Shakespeare's Othello.*

INDI'GNANT. *adj.* [*indignans*, Latin.] Angry; raging; inflamed at once with anger and disdain.

He scourg'd with many a stroke th' *indignant* waves. *Milt.*

The lustful monster fled, pursued by the valorous and *indignant* Martin. *Arbuth. and Pope's Mart. Scrib.*

What rage that hour did Albion's soul possess,
Let chiefs imagine, and let lovers guess!
He strides *indignant*, and with haughty cries
To single fight the fairy prince defies. *Tickel.*

INDIGNA'TION. *n. s.* [*indignation*, Fr. *indignatio*, Latin.]

1. Anger mingled with contempt or disgust.

Suspend your *indignation* against my brother, 'till you derive better testimony of his intent. *Shak. King Lear.*

From those officers, warm with *indignation* at the insolences of that vile rabble, came words of great contempt. *Clarend.*

But keep this swelling *indignation* down,
And let your cooler reason now prevail. *Rowe.*

2. The anger of a superiour.

There was great *indignation* against Israel. 2 *Kings* iii. 27.

3. The effect of anger.

If heav'ns have any grievous plague in store,
Let them hurl down their *indignation*
On thee, thou troubler of the world. *Shakes. Rich.* III.

INDI'GNITY. *n. s.* [*indignitas*, from *indignus*, Latin; *indignité*, Fr.] Contumely; contemptuous injury; violation of right accompanied with insult.

Bishops and prelates could not but have bleeding hearts to behold a person of so great place and worth constrained to endure so foul *indignities.* *Hooker.*

No emotion of passion transported me, by the *indignity* of his carriage, to say or do any thing unbeseeming myself. *King Charles.*

Man he made, and for him built
Magnificent this world, and earth his seat,
Him lord pronounc'd; and, O *indignity!*
Subjected to his service angel-wings,
And flaming ministers, to watch and tend
Their earthly charge. *Milton's Paradise Lost, b.* ix.

He does not see how that mighty passion for the church can well consist with those *indignities* and that contempt men bestow on the clergy. *Swift.*

To more exalted glories born,
Thy mean *indignities* I scorn. *Pattison.*

I'NDIGO. *n. s.* [*indicum*, Latin.] A plant, by the Americans called anil.

It hath pennated leaves, terminated by a single lobe: the flowers, disposed in a spike, consist of five leaves, and are of the papilionaceous kind; the uppermost petal being larger than the others, rounder, and lightly furrowed on the side: the lower leaves are short, terminating in a point: in the middle of the flower is the style, which afterward becomes a jointed pod, containing one cylindrical seed in one partition, from which indigo is made, which is used in dying for a blue colour. *Miller.*

INDIRE'CT. *adj.* [*indirect*, Fr. *indirectus*, Latin.]

1. Not strait; not rectilinear.

2. Not tending otherwise than collaterally or consequentially to a point.

The tender prince
Would fain have come with me to meet your grace;
But by his mother was perforce with-held.
——Fy, what an *indirect* and peevish course
Is this of her's? *Shakespeare's Richard* III.

3. Not fair; not honest.

Think you, that any means under the sun
Can assecure so *indirect* a course? *Daniel's Civil War.*

Those things which they do know they may, upon sundry *indirect* considerations, let pass; and although themselves do not err, yet may they deceive others. *Hooker.*

O pity and shame! that they who to live well
Enter'd so fair, should turn aside, to tread
Paths *indirect.* *Milt. Par. Lost, b.* xi.

Indirect dealing will be discovered one time or other, and then he loses his reputation. *Tillotson.*

INDIRE'CTION. *n. s.* [*in* and *direction.*]

1. Oblique means; tendency not in a straight line.

And thus do we, of wisdom and of reach,
With windlaces, and with essays of byas,
By *indirections* find directions out. *Shakesp. Hamlet.*

2. Dishonest practice.

I had rather coin my heart than wring
From the hard hands of peasants their vile trash,
By any *indirection.* *Shakespeare's Julius Cæsar.*

INDIRE'CTLY. *adv.* [from *indirect.*]

1. Not in a right line; obliquely.

2. Not in express terms.

Still she suppresses the name Ithaca, which continues his doubts and hopes; and at last she *indirectly* mentions it. *Broome's Notes on the Odyssey.*

3. Unfairly; not rightly.

He bids you then resign
Your crown and kingdom, *indirectly* held
From him the true challenger. *Shakesp. Henry* V.

He that takes any thing from his neighbour, which was justly forfeited, to satisfy his own revenge or avarice, is tied to repentance, but not to restitution: because I took the forfeiture *indirectly*, I am answerable to God for my unhandsome, unjust, or uncharitable circumstances. *Taylor.*

INDIRE'CTNESS. *n. s.* [*in* and *directness.*]

1. Obliquity.

2. Unfairness.

INDISCE'RNIBLE. *adj.* [*in* and *discernible.*] Not perceptible; not discoverable.

Speculation, which, to my dark soul,
Depriv'd of reason, is as *indiscernible*
As colours to my body, wanting sight. *Denham's Sophy.*

INDISCE'RNIBLY. *adv.* [from *indiscernible.*] In a manner not to be perceived.

INDISCE'RPTIBLE. *adj.* [*in* and *discerptible.*] Not to be separated; incapable of being broken or destroyed by dissolution of parts.

INDISCERPTIBI'LITY. *n. s.* [from *indiscerptible.*] Incapability of dissolution.

INDISCO'VERY. *n. s.* [*in* and *discovery.*] The state of being hidden. An unusual word.

The ground of this assertion was the magnifying esteem of the ancients, arising from the *indiscovery* of its head. *Brown.*

INDISCREE'T. *adj.* [*indiscret*, Fr. *in* and *discreet.*] Imprudent; incautious; inconsiderate; injudicious.

Why then
Are mortal men so fond and *indiscreet*,
So evil gold to seek unto their aid;
And having not complain, and having it upbraid. *Fa. Qu.*

If thou be among the *indiscreet*, observe the time; but be continually among men of understanding. *Ecclus.* xxvii. 12.

INDISCREE'TLY. *adv.* [from *indiscreet.*] Without prudence; without consideration; without judgment.

Job on justice hath aspersions flung,
And spoken *indiscreetly* with his tongue. *Sandys.*

Let a great personage undertake an action passionately, let him manage it *indiscreetly*, and he shall have enough to flatter him. *Taylor's Rule of living holy.*

INDISCRE'TION. *n. s.* [*indiscretion*, Fr. *in* and *discretion.*] Imprudence; rashness; inconsideration.

Indiscretion sometimes serves us well,
When our deep plots do fail. *Shakesp. Hamlet.*

His offences did proceed rather from negligence, rashness, or other *indiscretion*, than from any malicious thought. *Hayward.*

Loose papers have been obtained from us by the importunity and divulged by the *indiscretion* of friends, although restrained by promises. *Swift.*

INDISCRI'MINATE. *adj.* [*indiscriminatus*, Latin.] Undistinguishable; not marked with any note of distinction.

INDISCRI'MINATELY. *adv.* [from *indiscriminate.*] Without distinction.

Others use defamatory discourse purely for love of talk, whose

whose speech, like a flowing current, bears away *indiscriminately* whatever lies in its way. *Government of the Tongue.*

Liquors, strong of acid salts, destroy the blueness of the infusion of our wood; and liquors *indiscriminately*, that abound with sulphureous salts, restore it. *Boyle.*

INDISPE'NSABLE. *adj.* [French.] Not to be remitted; not to be spared; necessary.

Rocks, mountains, and caverns, against which these exceptions are made, are of *indispensable* use and necessity, as well to the earth as to man. *Woodward's Natural History.*

INDISPE'NSABLENESS. *n. s.* [from *indispensable.*] State of not being to be spared; necessity.

INDISPE'NSABLY. *adv.* [from *indispensable.*] Without dispensation; without remission; necessarily.

Every one must look upon himself as *indispensably* obliged to the practice of duty. *Addison's Freeholder.*

To INDISPO'SE. *v. a.* [*indisposer*, French.]

1. To make unfit. With *for*.

Nothing can be reckoned good or bad to us in this life, any farther than it prepares or *indisposes* us *for* the enjoyments of another. *Atterbury.*

2. To disincline; to make averse. With *to.*

It has a strange efficacy to *indispose* the heart *to* religion. *South's Sermons.*

3. To disorder; to disqualify for its proper functions.

The soul is not now hindered in its actings by the distemperature of *indisposed* organs. *Glanv. Sceps.*

4. To disorder slightly with regard to health.

Though it weakened, yet it made him rather *indisposed* than sick, and did no ways disable him from studying. *Walton.*

5. To make unfavourable. With *towards.*

The king was sufficiently *indisposed towards* the persons, or the principles of Calvin's disciples. *Clarendon.*

INDISPO'SEDNESS. *n. s.* [from *indisposed.*] State of unfitness or disinclination; depraved state.

It is not any innate harshness in piety that renders the first essays of it unpleasant; that is owing only to the *indisposedness* of our own hearts. *Decay of Piety.*

INDISPOSI'TION. *n. s.* [*indisposition*, Fr. from *indispose.*]

1. Disorder of health; tendency to sickness.

The king did complain of a continual infirmity of body, yet rather as an *indisposition* in health than any set sickness. *Hayward.*

I have known a great fleet lose great occasions, by an *indisposition* of the admiral, while he was neither well enough to exercise, nor ill enough to leave the command. *Temple.*

Wisdom is still looking forward, from the first *indispositions*, into the progress of the disease. *L'Estrange.*

His life seems to have been prolonged beyond its natural term, under those *indispositions* which hung upon the latter part of it. *Addison's Freeholder.*

2. Disinclination; dislike.

The *indisposition* of the church of Rome to reform herself, must be no stay unto us from performing our duty to God. *Hooker.*

The mind, by every degree of affected unbelief, contracts more and more of a general *indisposition* towards believing. *Att.*

INDISPU'TABLE. *adj.* [*in* and *disputable.*] Uncontrovertible; incontestable.

There is no maxim in politicks more *indisputable*, than that a nation should have many honours to reserve for those who do national services. *Addison's Guardian.*

The apostle asserts a clear *indisputable* conclusion, which could admit of no question. *Rogers's Sermons.*

INDISPU'TABLENESS. *n. s.* [from *indisputable.*] The state of being indisputable; certainty.

INDISPU'TABLY. *adv.* [from *indisputable.*]

1. Without controversy; certainly.

The thing itself is questionable, nor is it *indisputably* certain what death she died. *Brown's Vulgar Errours.*

2. Without opposition.

They questioned a duty that had been *indisputably* granted to so many preceding kings. *Howel's Vocal Forest.*

INDISSO'LVABLE. *adj.* [*in* and *dissolvable.*]

1. Indissoluble; not separable as to its parts.

Metals, corroded with a little acid, turn into rust, which is an earth tasteless and *indissolvable* in water; and this earth, imbibed with more acid, becomes a metallick salt. *Newt. Opt.*

2. Not to be broken; binding for ever.

Deposition and degradation are without hope of any remission, and therefore the law stiles them an *indissolvable* bond; but a censure, a dissolvable bond. *Ayliffe's Parergon.*

INDISSOLUBI'LITY. *n. s.* [*indissolubilité*, Fr. from *indissoluble.*] Resistance of a dissolving power; firmness; stableness.

What hoops hold this mass of matter in so close a pressure together, from whence steel has its firmness, and the parts of a diamond their hardness and *indissolubility*. *Locke.*

INDI'SSOLUBLE. *adj.* [*indissoluble*, Fr. *indissolubilis*, Lat. *in* and *dissoluble.*]

1. Resisting all separation of its parts; firm; stable.

When common gold and lead are mingled, the lead may be severed almost unaltered; yet if, instead of the gold, a tantillum of the red elixir be mingled with the saturn, their union will be so *indissoluble*, that there is no possible way of separating the diffused elixir from the fixed lead. *Boyle.*

Ere yet she grew
To this deep-laid *indissoluble* state. *Thomson's Spring.*

2. Binding for ever; subsisting for ever.

Far more comfort it were for us to be joined with you in bands of *indissoluble* love and amity, to live as if our persons being many, our souls were but one. *Hooker.*

There is the supreme and *indissoluble* consanguinity between men, of which the heathen poet saith we are all his generation. *Bacon's holy War.*

They might justly wonder, that men so taught, so obliged to be kind to all, should behave themselves so contrary to such heavenly instructions, such *indissoluble* obligations. *South.*

INDI'SSOLUBLENESS. *n. s.* [from *indissoluble.*] Indissolubility; resistance to separation of parts.

Adam, though consisting of a composition intrinsically dissolvable, might have held, by the Divine Will, a state of immortality and *indissolubleness* of his composition. *Hale.*

INDI'SSOLUBLY. *adv.* [from *indissoluble.*]

1. In a manner resisting all separation.

On they move
Indissolubly firm; nor obvious hill,
Nor strait'ning vale, nor wood, nor stream divide
Their perfect ranks. *Milton's Paradise Lost.*

The remaining ashes, by a further degree of fire, may be *indissolubly* united into glass. *Boyle.*

They willingly unite,
Indissolubly firm; from Dubris south
To northern Orcades. *Phillips.*

2. For ever obligatorily.

INDISTI'NCT. *adj.* [*indistinct*, Fr. *in* and *distinctus*, Latin.]

1. Not plainly marked; confused.

That which is now a horse, even with thought,
The rack dislimns, and makes it *indistinct*
As water is in water. *Shakespeare's Ant. and Cleopatra.*

She warbled in her throat,
And tun'd her voice to many a merry note;
But *indistinct*, and neither sweet nor clear. *Dryden.*

When we speak of the infinite divisibility of matter, we keep a very clear and distinct idea of division and divisibility; but when we come to parts too small for our senses, our ideas of these little bodies become obscure and *indistinct*. *Watts.*

2. Not exactly discerning.

We throw out our eyes for brave Othello,
Ev'n 'till we make the main and th' aerial blue
An *indistinct* regard. *Shakespeare's Othello.*

INDISTI'NCTION. *n. s.* [from *indistinct.*]

1. Confusion; uncertainty.

The *indistinction* of many of the same name, or the misapplication of the act of one unto another, hath made some doubt. *Brown's Vulgar Errours.*

2. Omission of discrimination.

An *indistinction* of all persons, or equality of all orders, is far from being agreeable to the will of God. *Spratt.*

INDISTI'NCTLY. *adv.* [from *indistinct.*]

1. Confusedly; uncertainly.

In its sides it was bounded distinctly, but on its ends confusedly and *indistinctly*, the sight there vanishing by degrees. *Newton's Opt.*

2. Without being distinguished.

Making trial thereof, both the liquors soaked *indistinctly* through the bowl. *Brown's Vulg. Errours.*

INDISTI'NCTNESS. *n. s.* [from *indistinct.*] Confusion; uncertainty; obscurity.

There is unevenness or *indistinctness* in the style of these places, concerning the origin and form of the earth. *Burnet.*

Old age makes the cornea and coat of the crystalline humour grow flatter than before; so that the light, for want of a sufficient refraction, will not converge to the bottom of the eye, but beyond it, and by consequence paint in the bottom of the eye a confused picture; and according to the *indistinctness* of this picture, the object will appear confused. *Newton.*

INDISTU'RBANCE. *n. s.* [*in* and *disturb.*] Calmness; freedom from disturbance.

What is called by the stoicks apathy, and by the scepticks *indisturbance*, seems all but to mean great tranquillity of mind. *Temple.*

INDIVI'DUAL. *adj.* [*individu*, *individuel*, Fr. *individuus*, Lat.]

1. Separate from others of the same species; single; numerically one.

Neither is it enough to consult, *secundum genera*, what the kind and character of the person should be; for the most judgment is shown in the choice of *individuals*. *Bacon.*

They present us with images more perfect than the life in any *individual*. *Dryden's Dufresnoy.*

Must the whole man, amazing thought! return
To the cold marble, or contracted urn?
And never shall those particles agree,
That were in life this *individual* he? *Prior.*

Know all the good that *individuals* find,
Lie in three words, health, peace and competence. *Pope.*

We see each circumstance of art and *individual* of nature summoned together by the extent and fecundity of his imagination. *Pope's Preface to the Iliad.*

It would be wise in them, as *individual* and private mortals, to look back a little upon the storms they have raised, as well as those they have escaped. *Swift.*

The object of any particular idea is called an *individual*: so Peter is an *individual* man, London an *individual* city. *Watts.*

2. Undivided; not to be parted or disjoined.

To give thee being, I lent
Out of my side to thee, nearest my heart,
Substantial life, to have thee by my side
Henceforth an *individual* solace dear. *Milton's Parad. Lost.*

Long eternity shall greet our bliss
With an *individual* kiss. *Milton.*

Under his great vicegerent reign abide
United, as one *individual* soul,
For ever happy. *Milt. Parad. Lost, b.* v.

INDIVIDUA'LITY. *n. s.* [from *individual.*] Separate or distinct existence.

Crambe would tell his instructor, that all men were not singular; that *individuality* could hardly be predicated of any man; for it was commonly said that a man is not the same he was, and that mad men are beside themselves. *Arbuthnot.*

INDIVI'DUALLY. *adv.* [from *individual.*] With separate or distinct existence; numerically.

How should that subsist solitarily by itself, which hath no substance, but *individually* the very same whereby others subsist with it. *Hooker.*

I dare not pronounce him omniscious, that being an attribute *individually* proper to the godhead, and incommunicable to any created substance. *Hakewill on Providence.*

To INDIVIDUATE. *v. a.* [from *individuus*, Latin.] To distinguish from others of the same species; to make single.

Life is *individuated* into infinite numbers, that have their distinct sense and pleasure. *More against Atheism.*

No man is capable of translating poetry, who, besides a genius to that art, is not a master both of his author's language and of his own; nor must we understand the language only of the poet, but his particular turn of thoughts and expression, which are the characters that distinguish and *individuate* him from all other writers. *Dryden.*

INDIVIDUA'TION. *n. s.* [from *individuate.*] That which makes an individual.

What is the principle of *individuation*? Or what is it that makes any one thing the same as it was before? *Watts.*

INDIVIDU'ITY. *n. s.* [from *individuus*, Lat.] The state of being an individual; separate existence.

INDIVI'NITY. *n. s.* [*in* and *divinity.*] Want of divine power. Not in use.

How openly did the oracle betray his *indivinity* unto Crœsus, who being ruined by his amphibology, and expostulating with him, received no higher answer than the excuse of his impotency. *Brown's Vulgar Errours.*

INDIVISIBI'LITY. } *n. s.* [from *indivisible.*] State in which no
INDIVI'SIBLENESS. } more division can be made.

A pestle and mortar will as soon bring any particle of matter to *indivisibility* as the acutest thought of a mathematician. *Locke.*

INDIVI'SIBLE. *adj.* [*indivisible*, Fr. *in* and *divisible.*] What cannot be broken into parts; so small as that it cannot be smaller; having reached the last degree of divisibility.

By atom, no body will imagine we intend to express a perfect *indivisible*, but only the least sort of natural bodies. *Digby.*

Here is but one *indivisible* point of time observed, but one action performed; yet the eye cannot comprehend at once the whole object. *Dryden's Dufresnoy.*

INDIVI'SIBLY. *adv.* [from *indivisible.*] So as it cannot be divided.

INDO'CIBLE. *adj.* [*in* and *docible.*] Unteachable; insusceptible of instruction.

INDO'CIL. *adj.* [*indocile*, Fr. *indocilis*, Latin.] Unteachable; incapable of being instructed.

These certainly are the fools in the text, *indocil*, intractable fools, whose stolidity can baffle all arguments, and is proof against demonstration itself. *Bentley's Sermons.*

INDOCI'LITY. *n. s.* [*indocilité*, Fr. *in* and *docility.*] Unteachableness; refusal of instruction.

To INDO'CTRINATE. *v. a.* [*endoctriner*, old French.] To instruct; to tincture with any science, or opinion.

Under a master that discoursed excellently, and took much delight in *indoctrinating* his young unexperienced favourite, Buckingham had obtained a quick conception of speaking very gracefully and pertinently. *Clarendon.*

They that never peept beyond the common belief, in which their easy understandings were at first *indoctrinated*, are strongly assured of the truth and co-operative excellency of their receptions. *Glanv. Sceps.*

INDOCTRINA'TION. *n. s.* [from *indoctrinate.*] Instruction; information.

Although postulates are very accommodable unto junior *indoctrinations*, yet are these authorities but temporary, and not to be embraced beyond the minority of our intellectuals. *Bro.*

I'NDOLENCE. } *n. s.* [*in* and *doleo*, Latin; *indolence*, French.]
I'NDOLENCY. }

1. Freedom from pain.

As there must be *indolency* where there is happiness, so there must not be indigency. *Burnet's Theory of the Earth.*

2. Laziness; inattention; listlessness.

Let Epicurus give *indolency* as an attribute to his gods, and place in it the happiness of the blest: the divinity which we worship has given us not only a precept against it, but his own example to the contrary. *Dryden.*

The Spanish nation, roused from their ancient *indolence* and ignorance, seem now to improve trade. *Bolingbroke.*

I'NDOLENT. *adj.* [French.]

1. Free from pain. *Ainsworth.*

2. Careless; lazy; inattentive; listless.

Ill fits a chief
To waste long nights in *indolent* repose. *Pope's Iliad.*

I'NDOLENTLY. *adv.* [from *indolent.*]

1. With freedom from pain.

2. Carelesly; lazily; inattentively; listlesly.

While lull'd by sound, and undisturb'd by wit,
Calm and serene you *indolently* sit. *Addison.*

To INDOW. *v. a.* [*indotare*, Latin.] To portion; to enrich with gifts, whether of fortune or nature. See ENDOW.

INDRA'UGHT. *n. s.* [*in* and *draught.*]

1. An opening in the land into which the sea flows.

Ebbs and floods there could be none, when there was no *indraughts*, bays, or gulphs to receive a flood. *Raleigh.*

2. Inlet; passage inwards.

Navigable rivers are so many *indraughts* to attain wealth. *Bacon's Advice to Villiers.*

To INDRE'NCH. *v. a.* [from *drench.*] To soak; to drown.

My hopes lie drown'd; in many fathoms deep
They lie *indrench'd*. *Shakes. Troilus and Cressida.*

INDU'BIOUS. *adj.* [*in* and *dubious.*] Not doubtful; not suspecting; certain.

Hence appears the vulgar vanity of reposing an *indubious* confidence in those antipestilential spirits. *Harvey.*

INDU'BITABLE. *adj.* [*indubitabilis*, Lat. *indubitable*, Fr. *in* and *dubitable.*] Undoubted; unquestionable.

When general observations are drawn from so many particulars as to become certain and *indubitable*, these are jewels of knowledge. *Watts's Improvement of the Mind.*

INDU'BITABLY. *adv.* [from *indubitable.*] Undoubtedly; unquestionably.

If we transport these proportions from audible to visible objects, there will *indubitably* result from either a graceful and harmonious contentment. *Wotton's Architecture.*

The patriarchs were *indubitably* invested with both these authorities. *Spratt's Sermons.*

I appeal to all sober judges, whether our souls may be only a mere echo from clashing atoms; or rather *indubitably* must proceed from a spiritual substance. *Bentley's Sermons.*

INDU'BITATE. *adj.* [*indubitatus*, Latin.] Unquestioned; certain; apparent; evident.

If he stood upon his own title of the house of Lancaster, he knew it was condemned by parliament, and tended directly to the disinherison of the line of York, held then the *indubitate* heirs of the crown. *Bacon's Henry* VII.

I have been tempted to wonder how, among the jealousies of state and court, Edgar Atheling could subsist, being then the apparent and *indubitate* heir of the Saxon line. *Wotton.*

To INDU'CE. *v. a.* [*induire*, Fr. *induco*, Latin.]

1. To persuade; to influence to any thing.

The self-same argument in this kind, which doth but *induce* the vulgar sort to like, may constrain the wiser to yield. *Hook.*

This lady, albeit she was furnished with many excellent endowments both of nature and education, yet would she never be *induced* to entertain marriage with any. *Hayward.*

Desire with thee still longer to converse
Induc'd me. *Milton's Paradise Lost, b.* viii.

Let not the covetous design of growing rich *induce* you to ruin your reputation, but rather satisfy yourself with a moderate fortune; and let your thoughts be wholly taken up with acquiring to yourself a glorious name. *Dryden's Dufresnoy.*

2. To produce by persuasion or influence.

Let the vanity of the times be restrained, which the neighbourhood of other nations have *induced*, and we strive apace to exceed our pattern. *Bacon's Advice to Villiers.*

As this belief is absolutely necessary to all mankind, the evidence for *inducing* it must be of that nature as to accommodate itself to all species of men. *Forbes.*

3. To offer by way of induction, or consequential reasoning.

They play much upon the simile, or illustrative argumentation, to *induce* their enthymemes unto the people, and take up popular conceits. *Brown's Vulgar Errours.*

4. To inculcate; to enforce.

This *induces* a general change of opinion, concerning the person

person or party like to be obeyed by the greatest or strongest part of the people. *Temple.*

5. To cause extrinsically; to produce.

Sour things *induce* a contraction in the nerves, placed in the mouth of the stomach, which is a great cause of appetite. *Bacon.*

Acidity, as it is not the natural state of the animal fluids, but *induced* by aliment, is to be cured by aliment with the contrary qualities. *Arbuthnot on Aliments.*

6. To introduce; to bring into view.

To exprobrate their stupidity, he *induceth* the providence of storks: now, if the bird had been unknown, the illustration had been obscure, and the exprobration not so proper. *Brown.*

The poet may be seen *inducing* his personages in the first Iliad, where he discovers their humours, interests, and designs. *Pope.*

7. To bring on; to superinduce.

Schism is marked out by the apostle as a kind of petrifying crime, which *induces* that induration to which the fearful expectation of wrath is consequent. *Decay of Piety.*

INDU'CEMENT. *n. s.* [from *induce.*] Motive to any thing; that which allures or persuades to any thing.

The former *inducements* do now much more prevail, when the very thing hath ministered farther reason. *Hooker.*

Many *inducements*, besides Scripture, may lead me to that, which if Scripture be against, they are of no value, yet otherwise are strongly effectual to persuade. *Hooker.*

That mov'd me to't,
Then mark th' *inducement*. *Shakesp. Henry* VIII.

He lives
Higher degree of life; *inducement* strong
For us. *Milt. Par. Lost, b.* ix.

My *inducement* hither,
Was not at present here to find my son. *Milton's Agonist.*

Instances occur of oppression, to which there appears no *inducement* from the circumstances of the actors. *Rogers.*

INDU'CER. *n. s.* [from *induce.*] A persuader; one that influences.

To INDU'CT. *v. a.* [*inductus*, Latin.]

1. To introduce; to bring in.

The ceremonies in the gathering were first *inducted* by the Venetians. *Sandys's Travels.*

2. To put into actual possession of a benefice.

If a person thus instituted, though not *inducted*, takes a second benefice, it shall make the first void. *Ayliffe's Parergon.*

INDU'CTION. *n. s.* [*induction*, Fr. *inductio*, Latin.]

1. Introduction; entrance.

These promises are fair, the parties sure,
And our *induction* full of prosp'rous hope. *Shakesp. Hen.* IV.

2. *Induction* is when, from several particular propositions, we infer one general: as, the doctrine of the Socinians cannot be proved from the gospels, it cannot be proved from the acts of the apostles, it cannot be proved from the epistles, nor the book of revelations; therefore it cannot be proved from the New Testament. *Watts's Logick.*

The inquisition by *induction* is wonderful hard; for the things reported are full of fables, and new experiments can hardly be made but with extreme caution. *Bacon's Natural History.*

Mathematical things are only capable of clear demonstration: conclusions in natural philosophy are proved by *induction* of experiments, things moral by moral arguments, and matters of fact by credible testimony. *Tillotson.*

Although the arguing from experiments and observations by *induction* be no demonstration of general conclusions, yet it is the best way of arguing which the nature of things admits of, and may be looked upon as so much the stronger by how much the *induction* is more general; and if no exception occur from phænomena, the conclusion may be general. *Newton's Opt.*

He brought in a new way of arguing from *induction*, and that grounded upon observation and experiments. *Baker.*

3. The act or state of taking possession of an ecclesiastical living.

INDU'CTIVE. *adj.* [from *induct.*]

1. Leading; persuasive. With *to.*

A brutish vice,
Inductive mainly *to* the sin of Eve. *Milt. Par. Lost.*

2. Capable to infer or produce.

Abatements may take away infallible concludency in these evidences of fact, yet they may be probable and *inductive* of credibility, though not of science. *Hale's Origin of Mankind.*

To INDU'E. *v. a.* [*induo*, Latin.]

1. To invest.

One first matter all,
Indu'd with various forms. *Milton's Paradise Lost.*

2. It seems sometimes to be, even by good writers, confounded with *endow* or *indow*, to furnish or enrich with any quality or excellence.

The angel, by whom God *indued* the waters of Bethesda with supernatural virtue, was not seen; yet the angel's presence was known by the waters. *Hooker.*

His pow'rs, with dreadful strength *indu'd*,
She, with her fair hand, still'd into the nostrils of his friend. *Chapman's Iliads.*

To INDU'LGE. *v. a.* [*indulgeo*, Latin.]

1. To fondle; to favour; to gratify with concession; to foster.

The lazy glutton safe at home will keep,
Indulge his sloth, and fatten with his sleep. *Dryd. Pers.*

A mother was wont to *indulge* her daughters with dogs, squirrels, or birds; but then they must keep them well. *Locke.*

To live like those that have their hope in another life, implies that we *indulge* ourselves in the gratifications of this life very sparingly. *Atterbury.*

2. To grant not of right, but favour.

Ancient privileges, *indulged* by former kings to their people, must not, without high reason, be revoked by their successors. *Taylor's Rule of living holy.*

The virgin ent'ring bright, *indulg'd* the day
To the brown cave, and brush'd the dreams away. *Dryden.*

This is what nature's want may well suffice;
But since among mankind so few there are,
Who will conform to philosophick fare,
This much I will *indulge* thee for thy ease,
And mingle something of our times to please. *Dryd. Juv.*

My friend, *indulge* one labour more,
And seek Atrides. *Pope's Odyssey.*

Yet, yet a moment, one dim ray of light
Indulge, dread chaos and eternal night! *Dunciad.*

To INDU'LGE. *v. n.* [A Latinism not in use.] To be favourable; to give indulgence. With *to.*

He must, by *indulging to* any one sort of reproveable discourse himself, defeat all his endeavours against the rest. *Government of the Tongue.*

INDU'LGENCE. } INDU'LGENCY. } *n. s.* [*indu'gence*, Fr. from *indulge.*]

1. Fondness; fond kindness.

Restraint she will not brook;
And left to herself, if evil thence ensue,
She first his weak *indulgence* will accuse. *Milt. Parad. Lost.*

The glories of our isle,
Which yet like golden ore, unripe in beds,
Expect the warm *indulgency* of heaven. *Dryd. K. Arthur.*

2. Forbearance; tenderness; opposite to rigour.

They err, that through *indulgence* to others, or fondness to any sin in themselves, substitute for repentance any thing less. *Hammond on Fundamentals.*

In known images of life, I guess
The labour greater, as th' *indulgence* less. *Pope.*

3. Favour granted.

If all these gracious *indulgences* are without any effect on us, we must perish in our own folly. *Rogers.*

4. Grant of the church of Rome, not defined by themselves.

Thou, that giv'st whores *indulgences* to sin,
I'll canvas thee. *Shakespeare's Henry* VI.

Indulgences, dispenses, pardons, bulls,
The sport of winds. *Milton.*

In purgatory, *indulgences*, and supererogation, the assertors seem to be unanimous in nothing but in reference to profit. *Decay of Piety.*

Leo X. is deservedly infamous for his base prostitution of *indulgences*. *Atterbury.*

INDU'LGENT. *adj.* [*indulgent*, Fr. *indulgens*, Latin.]

1. Kind; gentle.

God has done all for us that the most *indulgent* Creator could do for the work of his hands. *Rogers's Sermons.*

2. Mild; favourable.

Hereafter such in thy behalf shall be
Th' *indulgent* censure of posterity. *Waller.*

3. Gratifying; favouring; giving way to. With *of.*

The feeble old, *indulgent of* their ease. *Dryden's Æn.*

INDU'LGENTLY. *adv.* [from *indulgent.*] Without severity; without censure; without self-reproach; with indulgence.

He that not only commits some act of sin, but lives *indulgently* in it, is never to be counted a regenerate man. *Hamm.*

INDU'LT. } INDU'LTO. } *n. s.* [Ital. and French.] Privilege or exemption.

To I'NDURATE. *v. n.* [*induro*, Latin.] To grow hard; to harden.

Stones within the earth at first are but rude earth or clay; and so minerals come at first of juices concrete, which afterwards *indurate*. *Bacon's Nat. Hist.*

That plants and ligneous bodies may *indurate* under water, without approachment of air, we have experiments in coralline. *Brown's Vulgar Errours.*

To I'NDURATE. *v. a.*

1. To make hard.

A contracted *indurated* bladder is a circumstance sometimes attending on the stone, and indeed an extraordinary dangerous one. *Sharp's Surgery.*

2. To harden the mind; to sear the conscience.

INDURA'TION. *n. s.* [from *indurate.*]

1. The state of growing hard.

This is a notable instance of condensation and *induration*, by burial under earth, in caves, for a long time. *Bacon.*

2. The act of hardening.

3. Obduracy; hardness of heart.

Schism is marked out by the apostle as a kind of petrifying crime, which induces that *induration* to which the fearful expectation of wrath is consequent. *Decay of Piety.*

INDU'STRIOUS. *adj.* [*industrieux*, Fr. *industrius*, Lat.] Diligent; laborious; assiduous. Opposed to *slothful.*

He himself, being excellently learned, and *industrious* to seek out the truth of all things concerning the original of his own people, hath set down the testimony of the ancients truly. *Spenser on Ireland.*

Let our just censures
Attend the true event, and put we on
Industrious soldiership. *Shakespeare's Macbeth.*

His thoughts were low:
To vice *industrious*; but to nobler deeds
Timorous and slothful. *Milton's Paradise Lost.*

2. Designed; done for the purpose.

The *industrious* perforation of the tendons of the second joints of fingers and toes, draw the tendons of the third joints through. *More's Divine Dialogues.*

Observe carefully all the events which happen either by an occasional concurrence of various causes, or by the *industrious* application of knowing men. *Watts's Improv. of the Mind.*

INDU'STRIOUSLY. *adv.* [from *industrious.*]

1. Diligently; laboriously; assiduously.

If *industriously*
I play'd the fool, it was my negligence,
Not weighing well the end. *Shakesp. Winter's Tale.*

Some friends to vice *industriously* defend
These innocent diversions, and pretend
That I the tricks of youth too roughly blame. *Dryd. Juv.*

2. For the set purpose; with design.

Great Britain was never before united in itself under one king, notwithstanding that the uniting had been *industriously* attempted both by war and peace. *Bacon.*

I am not under the necessity of declaring myself, and I *industriously* conceal my name, which wholly exempts me from any hopes and fears. *Swift.*

I'NDUSTRY. *n. s.* [*industrie*, Fr. *industria*, Lat.] Diligence; assiduity.

The sweat of *industry* would dry and die,
But for the end it works to. *Shakespeare's Cymbeline.*

See the laborious bee
For little drops of honey flee,
And there with humble sweets content her *industry*. *Cowl.*

Providence would only initiate mankind into the useful knowledge of her treasures, leaving the rest to employ our *industry*, that we might not live like idle loiterers. *More's Antid.*

To INE'BRIATE. *v. a.* [*inebrio*, Latin.] To intoxicate; to make drunk.

Wine sugared *inebriateth* less than wine pure: sops in wine, quantity for quantity, *inebriates* more than wine of itself. *Bac.*

Fish, entering far in and meeting with the fresh water, as if *inebriated*, turn up their bellies and are taken. *Sandys.*

To INE'BRIATE. *v. n.* To grow drunk; to be intoxicated.

At Constantinople fish, that come from the Euxine sea into the fresh water, do *inebriate* and turn up their bellies, so as you may take them with your hand. *Bacon's Natural Hist.*

INEBRIA'TION. *n. s.* [from *inebriate.*] Drunkenness; intoxication.

That cornelians and bloodstones may be of virtue to those intentions they are applied, experience will make us grant; but not that an amethyst prevents *inebriation*. *Brown.*

INEFFABI'LITY. *n. s.* [from *ineffable.*] Unspeakableness.

INE'FFABLE. *adj.* [*ineffable*, Fr. *ineffabilis*, Lat.] Unspeakable; unutterable; not to be expressed. It is used almost always in a good sense.

To whom the son, with calm aspect, and clear,
Light'ning divine, *ineffable*, serene!
Made answer. *Milton's Paradise Lost, b.* v.

Reflect upon a clear, unblotted, acquitted conscience, and feed upon the *ineffable* comforts of the memorial of a conquered temptation. *South.*

INE'FFABLY. *adv.* [from *ineffable.*] In a manner not to be expressed.

He all his father full express'd,
Ineffably into his face receiv'd. *Milton.*

INEFFE'CTIVE. *adj.* [*ineffectif*, Fr. *in* and *effective.*] That which can produce no effect.

As the body, without blood, is a dead and lifeless trunk; so is the word of God, without the spirit, a dead and *ineffective* letter. *Taylor.*

He that assures himself he never errs, will always err; and his presumptions will render all attempts to inform him *ineffective*. *Glanv. Sceps.*

INEFFE'CTUAL. *adj.* [*in* and *effectual.*] Unable to produce its proper effect; weak; without power.

The publick reading of the Apocrypha they condemn as a thing effectual unto evil: the bare reading even of Scriptures themselves they mislike, as a thing *ineffectual* to do good. *Hook.*

The death of Patrocles, joined to the offer of Agamemnon, which of itself had proved *ineffectual*. *Pope.*

INEFFE'CTUALLY. *adv.* [from *ineffectual.*] Without effect.

INEFFE'CTUALNESS. *n. s.* [from *ineffectual.*] Inefficacy; want of power to perform the proper effect.

St. James speaks of the *ineffectualness* of some mens devotion, Ye ask, and receive not, because ye ask amiss. *Wake.*

INEFFICA'CIOUS. *adj.* [*inefficace*, Fr. *inefficax*, Latin.] Unable to produce effects; weak; feeble.

Is not that better than always to have the rod in hand, and, by frequent use of it, misapply and render *inefficacious* this useful remedy? *Locke.*

INE'FFICACY. *n. s.* [*in* and *efficacia*, Latin.] Want of power; want of effect.

INE'LEGANCE. } *n. s.* [from *inelegant.*] Absence of beauty;
INE'LEGANCY. } want of elegance.

INE'LEGANT. *adj.* [*inelegans*, Lat.]

1. Not becoming; not beautiful: opposite to elegant.

What order, so contriv'd as not to mix
Tastes, not well join'd, *inelegant*, but bring
Taste after taste, upheld with kindliest change. *Milton.*

This very variety of sea and land, hill and dale, which is here reputed so *inelegant* and unbecoming, is indeed extremely charming and agreeable. *Woodward.*

2. Mean; despicable; contemptible.

Modern criticks, having never read Homer, but in low and *inelegant* translations, impute the meanness of the translation to the poet. *Broome's Notes on the Odyssey.*

INE'LOQUENT. *adj.* [*in* and *eloquens*, Latin.] Not persuasive; not oratorical: opposite to *eloquent*.

INE'PT. *adj.* [*ineptus*, Lat.] Unfit; useless; trifling; foolish.

The works of nature, being neither useless nor *inept*, must be guided by some principle of knowledge. *More.*

After their various unsuccesful ways,
Their fruitless labour, and *inept* essays,
No cause of these appearances they'll find,
But power exerted by th' Eternal Mind. *Blackmore*

When the upper and vegetative stratum was once washed off by rains, the hills would have become barren, the strata below yielding only mere sterile matter, such as was wholly *inept* and improper for the formation of vegetables. *Woodward.*

INE'PTLY. *adv.* [*inepté*, Latin.] Triflingly; foolishly; unfitly.

None of them are made foolishly or *ineptly*. *More.*

All things were at first disposed by an omniscient intellect, that cannot contrive *ineptly*. *Glanv. Sceps.*

INE'PTITUDE. *n. s.* [from *ineptus*, Lat.[Unfitness.

The grating and rubbing of axes against the sockets, wherein they are placed, will cause some *ineptitude* or resistency to rotation of the cylinder. *Wilkins.*

An omnipotent agent works infallibly and irresistibly, no *ineptitude* or stubbornness of the matter being ever able to hinder him. *Ray on the Creation.*

There is an *ineptitude* to motion from too great laxity, and an *ineptitude* to motion from too great tension. *Arbuthnot.*

INEQUA'LITY. *n. s.* [*inegalité*, Fr. from *in æqualitas* and *in æqualis*, Latin.]

1. Difference of comparative quantity.

There is so great an *inequality* in the length of our legs and arms, as makes it impossible for us to walk on all four. *Ray.*

2. Unevenness; interchange of higher and lower parts.

The country is cut into so many hills and *inequalities* as renders it defensible. *Addison on Italy.*

The glass seemed as well wrought as the object-glasses use to be; yet when it was quicksilvered, the reflexion discovered innumerable *inequalities* all over the glass. *Newton's Opt.*

If there were no *inequalities* in the surface of the earth, nor in the seasons of the year, we should lose a considerable share of the vegetable kingdom. *Bentley.*

3. Disproportion to any office or purpose; state of not being adequate; inadequateness.

The great *inequality* of all things to the appetites of a rational soul appears from this, that in all worldly things a man finds not half the pleasure in the actual possession that he proposed in the expectation. *South's Sermons.*

4. Change of state; unlikeness of a thing to itself; difference of temper or quality.

In some places, by the nature of the earth, and by the situation of woods and hills, the air is more unequal than in others; and *inequality* of air is ever an enemy to health. *Bacon.*

5. Difference of rank or station.

If so small *inequality* between man and man make in them modesty a commendable virtue, who respecting superiors as superiors, can neither speak nor stand before them without fear. *Hooker.*

INERRABI'LITY. *n. s.* [from *inerrable.*] Exemption from error; infallibility.

I cannot allow their wisdom such a completeness and *inerrability* as to exclude myself from judging. *King Charles.*

INE'RRABLE. *adj.* [*in* and *err.*] Exempt from errour.

We have conviction from reason, or decisions from the *inerrable* and requisite conditions of sense. *Brown's Vulgar Err.*

Infallibility and inerrableness is assumed by the Romish church, without any *inerrable* ground to build it on. *Hamm.*

INE'RRABLENESS. *n. s.* [from *inerrable.*] Exemption from errour.

Infallibility and *inerrableness* is assumed and inclosed by the Romish church, without any inerrable ground to build it on. *Hammond on Fundamentals.*

INE'RRABLY. *adv.* [from *inerrable.*] With security from errour; infallibly.

INE'RRINGLY. *adv.* [*in* and *erring.*] Without errour; without mistake; without deviation.

That divers limners at a distance, without copy, should draw the same picture, is more conceivable, than that matter should frame itself so *inerringly* according to the idea of its kind. *Glanv. Sceps.*

INE'RT. *adj.* [*iners*, Lat.] Dull; sluggish; motionless.

Body alone, *inert* and brute, you'll find;
The cause of all things is by you assign'd. *Blackmore.*

Informer of the planetary train!
Without whose quickening glance their cumb'rous orbs
Were brute unlively mass, *inert* and dead. *Thomson.*

INE'RTLY. *adv.* [from *inert.*] Sluggishly; dully.

Ye pow'rs,
Suspend a while your force *inertly* strong. *Dunciad.*

INESCA'TION. *n. s.* [*in* and *esca*, Lat.] The act of baiting. *Dict.*

INE'STIMABLE. *adj.* [*inestimable*, Fr. *inestimabilis*, Lat.] Too valuable to be rated; transcending all price.

I thought I saw a thousand fearful wrecks,
A thousand men that fishes gnaw'd upon;
Wedges of gold, great anchors, heaps of pearl,
Inestimable stones, unvalu'd jewels. *Shakesp. Rich.* III.

The pope thereupon took advantage, abusing the simplicity of the king to suck out *inestimable* sums of money, to the intolerable grievance of both the clergy and temporality. *Abbot.*

There we shall see a sight worthy dying for, that blessed Saviour, of whom the Scripture does so excellently entertain us, and who does so highly deserve of us upon the score of his infinite perfections, and his *inestimable* benefits. *Boyle.*

And shall this prize, th' *inestimable* prize,
On that rapacious hand for ever blaze! *Pope.*

INE'VIDENT. *adj.* [*inevident*, Fr. *in* and *evident.*] Not plain; obscure. Not in use.

The habit of faith in divinity is an argument of things unseen, and a stable assent unto things *inevident*, upon authority of the divine revealer. *Brown's Vulgar Errours.*

INEVITABI'LITY. *n. s.* [from *inevitable.*] Impossibility to be avoided; certainty.

By liberty, I do understand neither a liberty from sin, misery, servitude, nor violence, but from necessity, or rather necessitation; that is, an universal immunity from all *inevitability* and determination to one. *Bramh. against Hobbs.*

INE'VITABLE. *adj.* [*inevitable*, Fr. *inevitabilis*, Lat.] Unavoidable; not to be escaped.

I had a pass with him: he gives me the stuck in with such a mortal motion, that it is *inevitable*. *Shakesp. Twelfth Night.*

Fate *inevitable*
Subdues us. *Milton.*

Since my *inevitable* death you know,
You safely unavailing pity show. *Dryden's Aurengzebe.*

INE'VITABLY. *adv.* [from *inevitable.*] Without possibility of escape.

The day thou eat'st thereof, my sole command
Transgrest, *inevitably* thou shalt die. *Milton's Par. Lost.*

How *inevitably* does an immoderate laughter end in a sigh? *South's Sermons.*

To look no further than the next line, it will *inevitably* follow, that they can drive to no certain point. *Dryden.*

Inflammations of the bowels oft *inevitably* tend to the ruin of the whole. *Harvey on Consumptions.*

If our sense of hearing were exalted, we should have no quiet or sleep in the silentest nights, and we must *inevitably* be stricken deaf or dead with a clap of thunder. *Bentley.*

INEXCU'SABLE. *adj.* [*inexcusable*, Fr. *inexcusabilis*, Lat. *in* and *excusable.*] Not to be excused; not to be palliated by apology.

It is a temerity, and a folly *inexcusable*, to deliver up ourselves needlesly into another's power. *L'Estrange.*

As we are an island with ports and navigable seas, we should be *inexcusable* if we did not make these blessings turn to account. *Addison's Freeholder.*

Such a favour could only render them more obdurate, and more *inexcusable*: it would inhance their guilt. *Atterbury.*

If learning be not encouraged under your administration, you are the most *inexcusable* person alive. *Swift.*

A fallen woman is the more *inexcusable*, as, from the cradle, the sex is warned against the delusions of men. *Clarissa.*

INEXCU'SABLENESS. *n. s.* [from *inexcusable.*] Enormity beyond forgiveness or palliation.

Their *inexcusableness* is stated upon the supposition that they knew God, but did not glorify him. *South's Sermons.*

INEXCU'SABLY. *adv.* [from *inexcusable.*] To a degree of guilt or folly beyond excuse.

It will *inexcusably* condemn some men, who having received excellent endowments, yet have frustrated the intention. *Brown.*

INEXHA'LABLE. *adj.* [*in* and *exhale.*] That which cannot evaporate.

A new laid egg will not so easily be boiled hard, because it contains a great stock of humid parts, which must be evaporated before the heat can bring the *inexhalable* parts into consistence. *Brown's Vulgar Errours.*

INEXHA'USTED. *adj.* [*in* and *exhausted.*] Unemptied; not possible to be emptied.

So wert thou born into a tuneful strain,
An early, rich, and *inexhausted* vein. *Dryden.*

INEXHA'USTIBLE. *adj.* [*in* and *exhaustible.*] Not to be drawn all away; not to be spent.

Reflect on the variety of combinations which may be made with number, whose stock is *inexhaustible*, and truly infinite. *Locke.*

The stock that the mind has in its power, by varying the idea of space, is perfectly *inexhaustible*, and so it can multiply figures *in infinitum*. *Locke.*

INEXI'STENT. *adj.* [*in* and *existent.*] Not having being; not to be found in nature.

To express complexed significations they took a liberty to compound and piece together creatures of allowable forms into mixtures *inexistent*. *Brown's Vulg. Err.*

We doubt whether these heterogeneities be so much as *inexistent* in the concrete, whence they are obtained. *Boyle.*

INEXI'STENCE. *n. s.* [*in* and *existence.*] Want of being; want of existence.

He calls up the heroes of former ages from a state of *inexistence* to adorn and diversify his poem. *Broome on the Odyss.*

INE'XORABLE. *adj.* [*inexorable*, Fr. *inexorabilis*, Latin.] Not to be intreated; not to be moved by intreaty.

You are more inhuman, more *inexorable*,
Oh ten times more, than tygers of Hyrcania. *Shakesp. H.* VI.

Inexorable dog. *Shak. Merch of Venice.*

The scourge
Inexorable calls to penance. *Milton.*

The guests invited came,
And with the rest th' *inexorable* dame. *Dryden.*

Th' *inexorable* gates were barr'd,
And nought was seen, and nought was heard,
But dreadful gleams, shrieks of woe *Pope's St. Cæcilia.*

We can be deaf to the words of so sweet a charmer, and *inexorable* to all his invitations. *Rogers.*

INEXPE'DIENCE. } *n. s.* [*in* and *expediency.*] Want of fitness;
INEXPE'DIENCY. } want of propriety; unsuitableness to time or place; inconvenience.

It concerneth superiours to look well to the expediency and *inexpediency* of what they enjoin in different things. *Sanderson.*

INEXPE'DIENT. *adj.* [*in* and *expedient.*] Inconvenient; unfit; improper; unsuitable to time or place.

It is not *inexpedient* they should be known to come from a person altogether a stranger to chymical affairs. *Boyle.*

We should be prepared not only with patience to bear, but to receive with thankfulness a repulse, if God should see them to be *inexpedient*. *Smalridge's Sermons.*

INEXPE'RIENCE. *n. s.* [*inexperience*, Fr. *in* and *experience.*] Want of experimental knowledge; want of experience.

Thy words at random argue thine *inexperience*. *Milton.*

Prejudice and self-sufficiency naturally proceed from *inexperience* of the world, and ignorance of mankind. *Addison.*

INEXPE'RIENCED. *adj.* [*inexpertus*, Lat.] Not experienced.

INEXPE'RT. *adj.* [*inexpertus*, Lat. *in* and *expert.*] Unskilful; unskilled.

The race elect advance
Through the wild desert; not the readiest way,
Left ent'ring on the Canaanite alarm'd,
War terrify them *inexpert*. *Milton's Paradise Lost, b.* xii.

In letters and in laws
Not *inexpert*. *Prior.*

INE'XPIABLE. *adj.* [*inexpiable*, French; *inexpiabilis*, Latin.]

1. Not to be atoned.
2. Not to be mollified by atonement.

Love seeks to have love:
My love how could'st thou hope, who took'st the way
To raise in me *inexpiable* hate? *Milton's Agonistes.*

INE'XPIABLY. *adv.* [from *inexpiable.*] To a degree beyond atonement.

Excursions are *inexpiably* bad,
And 'tis much safer to leave out than add. *Roscommon.*

INE'XPLEABLY. *adv.* [*in* and *expleo*, Lat.] Insatiably. A word not in use.

What were these harpies but flatterers, delators, and the *inexpleably* covetous. *Sandys's Travels.*

INE'XPLICABLE. *adj.* [*inexplicable*, Fr. *in* and *explico*, Lat.] Incapable of being explained; not to be made intelligible.

What could such apprehensions breed, but, as their nature is, *inexplicable* passions of mind, desires abhorring what they embrace, and embracing what they abhor? *Hooker.*

To me at least this seems *inexplicable*, if light be nothing else than pression or motion propagated through ether. *Newton.*

None eludes sagacious reason more,
Than this obscure *inexplicable* pow'r. *Blackmore.*

INE'XPLICABLY. *adv.* [from *inexplicable.*] In a manner not to be explained.

INEXPRE'SSIBLE. *adj.* [*in* and *express.*] Not to be told; not to be uttered; unutterable.

Thus when in orbs
Of circuit *inexpressible* they stood,
Orb within orb. *Milton's Paradise Lost, b.* v.

Nothing can ſo peculiarly gratify the noble diſpoſitions of human nature, as for one man to ſee another ſo much himſelf as to ſigh his griefs, and groan his pains, to ſing his joys, and do and feel every thing by ſympathy and ſecret *inexpreſſible* communications. *South's Sermons.*

The true God had no certain name given to him; for Father, and God, and Creator, are but titles ariſing from his works; and God is not a name, but a notion ingrafted in human nature of an *inexpreſſible* being. *Stillingfleet.*

There is an inimitable grace in Virgil's words; and in them principally conſiſts that beauty, which gives ſo *inexpreſſible* a pleaſure to him who beſt underſtands their force: this diction of his is never to be copied. *Dryden.*

INEXPRE'SSIBLY. *adv.* [from *inexpreſſible.*] To a degree or in a manner not to be uttered; unutterably.

God will protect and reward all his faithful ſervants in a manner and meaſure *inexpreſſibly* abundant. *Hammond.*

He began to play upon it: the ſound was exceeding ſweet, and wrought into a variety of tunes that were *inexpreſſibly* melodious. *Addiſon's Spectator.*

INEXPU'GNABLE. *adj.* [*inexpugnable*, Fr. *inexpugnabilis*, Lat.] Impregnable; not to be taken by aſſault; not to be ſubdued.

Why ſhould there be implanted in each ſex ſuch a vehement and *inexpugnable* appetite of copulation? *Ray on the Creation.*

INEXTI'NGUISHABLE. *adj.* [*inextinguible*, Fr. *in* and *extinguo*, Latin.] Unquenchable.

Pillars, ſtatues, and other memorials, are a ſort of ſhadow of an endleſs life, and ſhow an *inextinguiſhable* deſire which all men have of it. *Grew's Coſmol.*

INE'XTRICABLE. *adj.* [*inextricable*, Fr. *inextricabilis*, Latin.] Not to be diſintangled; not to be cleared; not to be ſet free from obſcurity or perplexity.

He that ſhould tye *inextricable* knots, only to baffle the induſtry of thoſe that ſhould attempt to unlooſe them, would be thought not to have ſerved his generation. *Decay of Piety.*

Stopt by awful heights, and gulphs immenſe
Of wiſdom, and of vaſt omnipotence,
She trembling ſtands, and does in wonder gaze,
Loſt in the wild *inextricable* maze. *Blackmore.*

INE'XTRICABLY. *adv.* [from *inextricable.*] To a degree of perplexity not to be diſintangled.

The mechanical atheiſt, though you grant him his laws of mechaniſm, is nevertheleſs *inextricably* puzzled and baffled with the firſt formation of animals. *Bentley's Sermons.*

In vain they ſtrive; th' intangling ſnares deny,
Inextricably firm, the power to fly. *Pope's Odyſſey.*

To INE'YE. *v. n.* [*in* and *eye.*] To inoculate; to propagate trees by the inſition of a bud into a foreign ſtock.

Let ſage experience teach thee all the arts
Of grafting and *ineying.* *Phillips.*

INFALLIBI'LITY. } *n. ſ.* [*infallibilité*, Fr. from *infallible.*] In-
INFA'LLIBLENESS. } errability; exemption from errour.

Infallibility is the higheſt perfection of the knowing faculty, and conſequently the firmeſt degree of aſſent. *Tillotſon.*

INFA'LLIBLE. *adj.* [*infallible*, Fr. *in* and *fallible.*] Privileged from errour; incapable of miſtake; not to be miſled or deceived; certain.

Every cauſe admitteth not ſuch *infallible* evidence of proof, as leaveth no poſſibility of doubt or ſcruple behind it. *Hooker.*

Believe my words;
For they are certain and *infallible.* *Shakeſp. Henry* VI.

The ſucceſs is certain and *infallible*, and none ever yet miſcarried in the attempt. *South's Sermons.*

INFA'LLIBLY. *adv.* [from *infallible.*]

1. Without danger of deceit; with ſecurity from errour.

We cannot be as God *infallibly* knowing good and evil. *Smalridge's Sermons.*

2. Certainly.

Our bleſſed Lord has diſtinctly opened the ſcene of futurity to us, and directed us to ſuch a conduct as will *infallibly* render us happy in it. *Rogers's Sermons.*

To INFA'ME. *v. a.* [*infamer*, Fr. *infamo*, Lat.] To repreſent to diſadvantage; to defame; to cenſure publickly; to make infamous; to brand.

Livia is *infamed* for the poiſoning of her huſband. *Bacon.*

Hitherto obſcur'd, *infam'd*,
And thy fair fruit let hang, as to no end
Created. *Milton's Paradiſe Loſt.*

I'NFAMOUS. *adj.* [*infamé*, *infamant*, Fr. *infamis*, Lat.] Publickly branded with guilt; openly cenſured; of bad nature.

Thoſe that be near, and thoſe that be far from thee, ſhall mock thee, which art *infamous.* *Ezek.* xxii. 5.

Theſe are as ſome *infamous* bawd or whore
Should praiſe a matron; what could hurt her more. *B. Johnſ.*

After times will diſpute it, whether Hotham were more *infamous* at Hull or at Tower-hill. *King Charles.*

Perſons *infamous*, or branded with any note of infamy in any publick court of judicature, are, *ipſo jure*, forbidden to be advocates. *Aylife's Parergon.*

I'NFAMOUSLY. *adv.* [from *infamous.*]

1. With open reproach; with publick notoriety of reproach.

2. Shamefully; ſcandalouſly.

That poem was *infamouſly* bad. *Dryden's Dufreſnoy.*

I'NFAMOUSNESS. } *n. ſ.* [*infamie*, Fr. *infamia*, Lat.] Publick
I'NFAMY. } reproach; notoriety of bad character.

Ye are taken up in the lips of talkers, and are the *infamy* of the people. *Ezek.* xxxvi. 3.

I throw my *infamy* at thee:
I will not ruinate my father's houſe,
Who gave his blood to lime the ſtones together,
And ſet up Lancaſter. *Shakeſpeare's Henry* VI.

The noble iſle doth want her proper limbs,
Her face defac'd with ſcars of *infamy.* *Shakeſp. Rich.* III.

Wilful perpetrations of unworthy actions brand, with moſt indelible characters of *infamy*, the name and memory to poſterity. *King Charles.*

I'NFANCY. *n. ſ.* [*infantia*, Latin.]

1. The firſt part of life. Uſually extended by naturaliſts to ſeven years.

Dare we affirm it was ever his meaning, that unto their ſalvation, who even from their tender *infancy* never knew any other faith or religion than only Chriſtian, no kind of teaching can be available, ſaving that which was ſo needful for the firſt univerſal converſion of Gentiles, hating Chriſtianity? *Hooker.*

Pirithous came t' attend
This worthy Theſeus, his familiar friend:
Their love in early *infancy* began,
And roſe as childhood ripen'd into man. *Dryden.*

The inſenſible impreſſions on our tender *infancies* have very important and laſting conſequences. *Locke.*

2. Civil infancy, extended by the Engliſh law to one and twenty years.

3. Firſt age of any thing; beginning; original; commencement.

In Spain our ſprings, like old mens children, be
Decay'd and wither'd from their *infancy.* *Dryd. Ind. Emp.*

The difference between the riches of Roman citizens in the *infancy* and in the grandeur of Rome, will appear by comparing the firſt valuation of eſtates with the eſtates afterwards poſſeſſed. *Arbuthnot on Coins.*

INFA'NGTHEF, or *hingfangtheft*, or *infangtheof*, is compounded of three Saxon words: the prepoſition, *in*, *fang*, or *fong*, to take or catch, and *thef.* It ſignifies a privilege or liberty granted unto lords of certain manors to judge any thief taken within their fee. *Cowel.*

I'NFANT. *n. ſ.* [*infant*, French; *infans*, Latin.]

1. A child from the birth to the end of the ſeventh year.

It being a part of their virtuous education, ſerveth greatly both to nouriſh in them the fear of God, and to put us in continual remembrance of that powerful grace, which openeth the mouths of *infants* to ſound his praiſe. *Hooker.*

Within the *infant* rind of this ſmall flower
Poiſon hath reſidence, and medicine power. *Shakeſpeare.*

There ſhall be no more thence an *infant* of days, nor an old man that hath not filled his days. *Iſ.* lxv. 20.

Firſt the ſhrill ſound of a ſmall rural pipe,
Was entertainment for the *infant* ſtage. *Roſcommon.*

Young mothers wildly ſtare, with fear poſſeſt,
And ſtrain their helpleſs *infants* to their breaſt. *Dryd. Æn.*

In their tender nonage, while they ſpread
Their ſpringing leaves and lift their *infant* head,
Indulge their childhood. *Dryden's Virg. Georg.*

2. [In law.] A young perſon to the age of one and twenty.

INFA'NTA. *n. ſ.* [Spaniſh.] A princeſs deſcended from the royal blood of Spain.

INFA'NTICIDE. *n. ſ.* [*infanticide*, Fr. *infanticidium*, Lat.] The ſlaughter of the infants by *Herod.*

I'NFANTILE. *adj.* [*infantilis*, Latin.] Pertaining to an infant.

The fly lies all the Winter in theſe balls in its *infantile* ſtate, and comes not to its maturity 'till the following Spring. *Derh.*

I'NFANTRY. *n. ſ.* [*infanterie*, French.] The foot ſoldiers of an army.

The principal ſtrength of an army conſiſteth in the *infantry* or foot; and to make good *infantry* it requireth men bred in ſome free and plentiful manner. *Bacon's Henry* VII.

That ſmall *infantry*,
Warr'd on by cranes. *Milton.*

INFA'RCTION. *n. ſ.* [*in* and *farcio*, Latin.] Stuffing; conſtipation.

An hypocondriack conſumption is occaſioned by an *infarction* and obſtruction of the ſpleen. *Harvey.*

To I'NFATUATE. *v. a.* [*infatuo*, from *in* and *fatuus*, Latin; *infatuer*, French.] To ſtrike with folly; to deprive of underſtanding.

The judgment of God will be very viſible in *infatuating* a people, as ripe and prepared for deſtruction, into folly and madneſs, making the weak to contribute to the deſigns of the wicked; and ſuffering even thoſe, out of a conſcience of their guilt, to grow more wicked. *Clarendon.*

It is the reforming of the vices and ſottiſhneſs that had long overſpread the *infatuated*, gentile world; a prime branch of that deſign of Chriſt's ſending his diſciples. *Hammond.*

The

The people are so universally *infatuated* with the notion, that, if a cow falls sick, it is ten to one but an old woman is clapt up in prison for it. *Addison on Italy.*

The carriage of our atheists or deists is amazing: no dotage so *infatuate*, no phrensy so extravagant as theirs. *Bentley.*

May hypocrites,
That slily speak one thing, another think,
Drink on unwarn'd, 'till, by enchanting cups
Infatuate, they their wily thoughts disclose. *Phillips.*

INFATUA'TION. *n. s.* [from *infatuate.*] The act of striking with folly; deprivation of reason.

Where men give themselves over to the defence of wicked interests and false propositions, it is just with God to smite the greatest abilities with the greatest *infatuations*. *South's Serm.*

INFA'USTING. *n. s.* [from *infaustus*, Lat.] The act of making unlucky. An odd and inelegant word.

As the king did in some part remove the envy from himself, so he did not observe that he did withal bring a kind of malediction and *infausting* upon the marriage, as an ill prognostick. *Bacon's Henry VII.*

INFE'ASIBLE. *adj.* [*in* and *feasible.*] Impracticable.

This is so difficult and *infeasible*, that it may well drive modesty to despair of science. *Glanv. Sceps.*

To INFE'CT. *v. a.* [*infecter*, French; *infectus*, Latin.]

1. To act upon by contagion; to affect with communicated qualities; to hurt by contagion; to taint; to poison; to pollute.

They put such words in the mouths of one of those fantastical mind *infected* people, that children and musicians call lovers. *Sidney.*

Thine eyes, sweet lady, have *infected* mine. *Shak. R. III.*
The nature of bad news *infects* the teller. *Shakespeare.*

Ev'ry day
It would *infect* his speech, that if the king
Should without issue die, he'd carry it so
To make the scepter his. *Shakespeare's Henry VIII.*

Infected minds
To their deaf pillows will discharge their secrets. *Shakesp.*

She speaks poniards, and every word stabs: if her breath were as terrible as her terminations, there were no living near her; she would *infect* to the north-star. *Shakespeare.*

I am return'd your soldier;
No more *infected* with my country's love,
Than when I parted hence. *Shakes. Coriolanus.*

The love-tale
Infected Sion's daughters with like heat,
Whose wanton passions in the sacred porch
Ezekiel saw. *Milton.*

2. To fill with something hurtfully contagious.

Infected be the air whereon they ride,
And damn'd all those that trust them! *Shakes. Macbeth.*

INFE'CTION. *n. s.* [*infection*, Fr. *infectio*, Latin.] Contagion; mischief by communication; taint; poison.

Infection is that manner of communicating a disease by some effluvia, or particles which fly off from distempered bodies, and mixing with the juices of others, occasion the same disorders as in the bodies they came from *Quincy.*

What a strange *infection*
Is fall'n into thy ear! *Shakesp. Cymbeline.*

The blessed gods
Purge all *infections* from our air, whilst you
Do climate here. *Shakes. Winter's Tale.*

Vouchsafe, diffus'd *infection* of a man,
For these known evils but to give me leave,
By circumstance, to curse thy cursed self. *Shakesp. R. III.*

Hence,
Lest that th' *infection* of his fortune take
Like hold on thee. *Shakespeare's King Lear.*

The transmission or emission of the thinner and more airy parts of bodies, as in odours and *infections*, is, of all the rest, the most corporeal; but withal there be a number of those emissions, both wholesome and unwholesome, that give no smell at all. *Bacon's Natural History.*

INFE'CTIOUS. *adj.* [from *infect.*] Contagious; influencing by communicated qualities.

The most *infectious* pestilence upon thee! *Shakespeare.*

In a house,
Where the *infectious* pestilence did reign. *Shakespeare.*

Some known diseases are *infectious*, and others are not: those that are *infectious* are such as are chiefly in the spirits, and not so much in the humours, and therefore pass easily from body to body; such as pestilences and lippitudes. *Bacon.*

Smells may have as much power to do good as to do harm, and contribute to health as well as to diseases; which is too much felt by experience in all that are *infectious*, and by the operation of some poisons, that are received only by the smell. *Temple.*

INFE'CTIOUSLY. *adv.* [from *infectious.*] Contagiously.

The will dotes, that is inclinable
To what *infectiously* itself affects. *Shakes. Troil. and Cressida.*

INFE'CTIOUSNESS. *n. s.* [from *infectious.*] The quality of being infectious; contagiousness.

INFE'CTIVE. *adj.* [from *infect.*] Having the quality of contagion.

True love, well considered, hath an *infective* power. *Sidn.*

INFECU'ND. *n. s.* [*infæcundus*, Latin.] Unfruitful; infertile.

How safe and agreeable a conservatory the earth is to vegetables, is manifest from their rotting, drying, or being rendered *infecund* in the waters, or the air; but in the earth their vigour is long preserved. *Derham's Physico-Theology.*

INFECU'NDITY. *n. s.* [*infæcunditas*, Lat.] Want of fertility; barrenness.

INFELI'CITY. *n. s.* [*infelicité*, Fr. *infelicitas*, Latin.] Unhappiness; misery; calamity.

Whatever is the ignorance and *infelicity* of the present state, we were made wise and happy. *Glanv. Sceps. c. 1.*

Here is our great *infelicity*, that, when single words signify complex ideas, one word can never distinctly manifest all the parts of a complex idea. *Watts.*

To INFE'R. *v. a.* [*inferer*, French; *infero*, Latin.]

1. To bring on; to induce.

Vomits *infer* some small detriment to the lungs. *Harvey.*

2. To *infer* is nothing but, by virtue of one proposition laid down as true, to draw in another as true, *i. e.* to see or suppose such a connection of the two ideas of the *inferred* proposition. *Locke.*

Yet what thou can'st attain, which best may serve
To glorify the Maker, and *infer*
Thee also happier, shall not be with-held
Thy hearing. *Milton's Par. Lost, b. vii.*

Great,
Or bright, *infers* not excellence: the earth,
Though in comparison of heav'n so small,
Nor glistering, may of solid good contain
More plenty than the sun, that barren shines. *Milton.*

One would wonder how, from so differing premisses, they should all *infer* the same conclusion. *Decay of Piety.*

They have more opportunities than other men have of purchasing publick esteem, by deserving well of mankind; and such opportunities always *infer* obligations. *Atterbury.*

3. To offer; to produce.

Full well hath Clifford play'd the orator,
Inferring arguments of mighty force. *Shakes. Hen. VI.*

I'NFERENCE. *n. s.* [*inference*, French, from *infer.*] Conclusion drawn from previous arguments.

Though it may chance to be right in the conclusion, it is yet unjust and mistaken in the method of *inference*. *Glanv.*

These *inferences* or conclusions are the effects of reasoning, and the three propositions, taken all together, are called syllogism or argument. *Watts.*

INFE'RIBLE. *adj.* [from *infer.*] Deducible from premised grounds.

As simple mistakes commonly beget fallacies, so men from fallacious foundations, and misapprehended mediums, erect conclusions no way *inferrible* from their premisses. *Brown.*

INFE'RIORITY. *n. s.* [*inferiorité*, Fr. from *inferiour.*] Lower state of dignity or value.

The language, though not of equal dignity, yet as near approaching to it as our modern barbarism will allow; and therefore we are to rest contented with that only *inferiority* which is not possibly to be remedied. *Dryden.*

INFE'RIOUR. *adj.* [*inferior*, Lat. *inferieur*, French.]

1. Lower in place.

2. Lower in station or rank of life.

A great person gets more by obliging his *inferiour* than by disdaining him. *South.*

3. Lower in value or excellency.

The love of liberty with life is giv'n,
And life itself th' *inferiour* gift of heav'n. *Dryden.*

I have added some original papers of my own, which, whether they are equal or *inferiour* to my other poems, an author is the most improper jndge of. *Dryden.*

4. Subordinate.

General and fundamental truths in philosophy, religion, and human life, conduct our thoughts into a thousand *inferiour* and particular propositions. *Watts.*

INFE'RIOUR. *n. s.* [from the adjective.] One in a lower rank or station than another.

INFE'RNAL. *adj.* [*infernal*, French; *infernus*, Latin.] Hellish; tartarean.

His gigantick limbs, with large embrace,
Infold nine acres of *infernal* space. *Dryden's Æn.*

INFE'RNAL *Stone. n. s.*

Infernal stone, or the lunar caustick, is prepared from an evaporated solution of silver, or from crystals of silver. It is a very powerful caustick, eating away the flesh and even the bones to which it is applied. *Hill's Mat. Med.*

INFE'RTILE. *adj.* [*infertile*, Fr. *in* and *fertile.*] Unfruitful; not productive; without fecundity; infecund.

Ignorance being of itself, like stiff clay, an *infertile* soil, when pride comes to scorch and harden it, it grows perfectly impenetrable. *Government of the Tongue.*

INFERTI'LITY. *n. s.* [*infertilité*, Fr. from *infertile.*] Unfruitfulness; want of fertility.

The ſame diſtemperature of the air that occaſioned the plague, occaſioned alſo the *infertility* or noxiouſneſs of the ſoil, whereby the fruits of the earth became either very ſmall, or very unwholſome. *Hale's Origin of Mankind.*

To INFE'ST. *v. a.* [*infeſter*, Fr. *infeſto*, Latin.] To harraſs; to diſturb; to plague.

They ceaſed not, in the mean while, to ſtrengthen that part which in heart they favoured, and to *infeſt* by all means, under colour of other quarrels, their greateſt adverſaries in this cauſe. *Hooker.*

Although they were a people *infeſted*, and mightily hated of all others, yet was there nothing of force to work the ruin of their ſtate, 'till the time beforementioned was expired. *Hook.*

Unto my feeble breaſt
Come gently; but not with that mighty rage
Wherewith the martial troops thou do'ſt *infeſt*,
And hearts of greateſt heroes do'ſt enrage. *Spenſer.*

They were no mean, diſtreſſed, calamitous perſons that fled to him for refuge; but of ſo great quality, as it was apparent that they came not thither to protect their own fortune, but to *infeſt* and invade his. *Bacon's Henry* VII.

Theſe, ſaid the genius, are envy, avarice, ſuperſtition, love, with the like cares and paſſions that *infeſt* human life. *Addiſon's Spectator.*

No diſeaſe *infeſts* mankind more terrible in its ſymptoms and effects. *Arbuthnot on Diet.*

INFESTI'VITY. *n. ſ.* [*in* and *feſtivity.*] Mournfulneſs; want of cheerfulneſs.

INFE'STRED. *adj.* [*in* and *feſter.*] Rankling; inveterate.

This curſed creature, mindful of that old
Infeſtred grudge, the which his mother felt,
So ſoon as Clarion he did behold,
His heart with vengeful malice inly ſwelt. *Spenſer.*

INFEUDA'TION. *n. ſ.* [*in* and *feudum*, Lat.] The act of putting one in poſſeſſion of a fee or eſtate.

Another military proviſion was conventional and by tenure, upon the *infeudation* of the tenant, and was uſually called knight's ſervice. *Hale's Common Law of England.*

I'NFIDEL. *n. ſ.* [*infidelle*, Fr. *infidelis*, Latin.] An unbeliever; a miſcreant; a pagan; one who rejects Chriſtianity.

Exhorting her, if ſhe did marry, yet not to join herſelf to an *infidel*, as in thoſe times ſome widows chriſtian had done, for the advancement of their eſtate in this world. *Hooker.*

INFIDE'LITY. *n. ſ.* [*infidelité*, French; *infidelitas*, Lat.]

1. Want of faith.

The conſideration of the divine omnipotence and infinite wiſdom, and our own ignorance, are great inſtruments of ſilencing the murmurs of *infidelity*. *Taylor's Rule of living holy.*

2. Diſbelief of Chriſtianity.

One would fancy that infidels would be exempt from that ſingle fault, which ſeems to grow out of the imprudent fervours of religion; but ſo it is, that *infidelity* is propagated with as much fierceneſs and contention, as if the ſafety of mankind depended upon it. *Addiſon's Spectator.*

3. Treachery; deceit.

The *infidelities* on the one part between the two ſexes, and the caprices on the other, the vanities and vexations attending even the moſt refined delights that make up this buſineſs of life, render it ſilly and uncomfortable. *Spectator.*

I'NFINITE. *adj.* [*infini*, French; *infinitus*, Latin.]

1. Unbounded; boundleſs; unlimited; immenſe; having no boundaries or limits to its nature.

Impoſſible it is, that God ſhould withdraw his preſence from any thing, becauſe the very ſubſtance of God is *infinite*. *Hooker.*

What's time, when on eternity we think?
A thouſand ages in that ſea muſt ſink:
Time's nothing but a word; a million
Is full as far from *infinite* as one. *Denham.*

Thou ſov'reign pow'r, whoſe ſecret will controuls
The inward bent and motion of our ſouls!
Why haſt thou plac'd ſuch *infinite* degrees
Between the cauſe and cure of my diſeaſe? *Prior.*

When we would think of *infinite* ſpace or duration, we at firſt make ſome very large idea; as perhaps of millions of ages or miles, which poſſibly we multiply ſeveral times. *Locke.*

Even an angel's comprehenſive thought
Cannot extend as far as thou haſt wrought:
Our vaſt conceptions are by ſwelling brought,
Swallow'd and loſt in *infinite*, to nought. *Dennis.*

2. It is hyperbolically uſed for large; great.

I'NFINITELY. *adv.* [from *infinite.*] Without limits; without bounds; immenſely.

Nothing may be *infinitely* deſired, but that good which indeed is infinite. *Hooker.*

This is Antonio,
To whom I am ſo *infinitely* bound. *Shakeſ. Merch. of Ven.*

The king ſaw that contrariwiſe it would follow, that England, though much leſs in territory, yet ſhould have *infinitely* more ſoldiers of their native forces than thoſe other nations have. *Bacon's Henry* VII.

Infinitely the greater part of mankind have profeſſed to act under a full perſuaſion of this great article. *Rogers.*

I'NFINITENESS. *n. ſ.* [from *infinite.*] Immenſity; boundleſſneſs; infinity.

The cunning of his flattery, the readineſs of his tears, the *infiniteneſs* of his vows, were but among the weakeſt threads of his net. *Sidney.*

Let us always bear about us ſuch impreſſions of reverence, and fear of God, that we may humble ourſelves before his Almightineſs, and expreſs that infinite diſtance between his *infiniteneſs* and our weakneſſes. *Taylor.*

INFINITE'SIMAL. *adj.* [from *infinite.*] Infinitely divided.

INFI'NITIVE. *adj.* [*infinitif*, Fr. *infinitivus*, Latin.] In grammar, the *infinitive* affirms, or intimates the intention of affirming, which is one uſe of the indicative; but then it does not do it abſolutely. *Clarke's Lat. Gram.*

INFI'NITUDE. *n. ſ.* [from *infinite.*]

1. Infinity; immenſity.

Confuſion heard his voice, and wild uproar
Stood rul'd, ſtood vaſt *infinitude* confin'd. *Milt. Par. Loſt.*

Though the repugnancy of *infinitude* be equally incompetible to continued or ſucceſſive motion, or continued quantity, and depends upon the incompoſſibility of the very nature of things ſucceſſive or extenſive with *infinitude*; yet that incompoſſibility is more conſpicuous in diſcrete quantity, that ariſeth from parts actually diſtinguiſhed. *Hale.*

2. Boundleſs number.

We ſee all the good ſenſe of the age cut out, and minced into almoſt an *infinitude* of diſtinctions. *Addiſon's Spectator.*

INFI'NITY. *n. ſ.* [*infinité*, French; *infinitas*, Latin.]

1. Immenſity; boundleſſneſs; unlimited qualities.

There cannot be more *infinities* than one; for one of them would limit the other. *Raleigh's Hiſt. of the World.*

The better, the more deſirable; that therefore muſt be deſirable, wherein there is *infinity* of goodneſs; ſo that if any thing deſirable may be infinite, that muſt needs be the higheſt of all things that are deſired: no good is infinite but only God, therefore he our felicity and bliſs. *Hooker.*

2. Endleſs number. An hyperbolical uſe of the word.

Homer has concealed faults under an *infinity* of admirable beauties. *Broome's Notes on the Odyſſey.*

The liver, being ſwelled, compreſſeth the ſtomach, ſtops the circulation of the juices, and produceth an *infinity* of bad ſymptoms. *Arbuthnot on Diet.*

INFI'RM. *adj.* [*infirme*, French; *infirmus*, Latin.]

1. Weak; feeble; diſabled of body.

Here ſtand I your brave;
A poor, *infirm*, weak, and deſpis'd old man. *Shakeſp.*

That on my head all might be viſited,
Thy frailty, and *infirmer* ſex, forgiv'n;
To me committed, and by me expos'd. *Milt. Par. Loſt.*

2. Weak of mind; irreſolute.

I'll go no more;
I am afraid to think what I have done:
Look out again, I dare not.
——*Infirm* of purpoſe;
Give me the dagger. *Shakeſp. Macbeth.*

3. Not ſtable; not ſolid.

He who fixes upon falſe principles, treads upon *infirm* ground, and ſo ſinks; and he, who fails in his deductions from right principles, ſtumbles upon firm ground, and falls. *South.*

To INFI'RM. *v. a.* [*infirmer*, Fr. *infirmo*, Lat.] To weaken; to ſhake; to enfeeble. Not in uſe.

Some contrary ſpirits will object this as a ſufficient reaſon to *infirm* all thoſe points. *Raleigh's Eſſays.*

The ſpleen is unjuſtly introduced to invigorate the ſiniſter ſide, which, being dilated, would rather *infirm* and debilitate it. *Brown's Vulgar Errours.*

INFI'RMARY. *n. ſ.* [*infirmerie*, French.] Lodgings for the ſick.

Theſe buildings to be for privy lodgings on both ſides, and the end for privy galleries, whereof one ſhould be for an *infirmary*, if any ſpecial perſon ſhould be ſick. *Bacon.*

INFI'RMITY. *n. ſ.* [*infirmité*, French.]

1. Weakneſs of ſex, age, or temper.

Infirmity,
Which waits upon worn times, hath ſomething ſeiz'd
His wiſh'd ability. *Shakeſpeare's Winter's Tal.*

Diſcover thine *infirmity*,
That warranteth by law to be thy privilege:
I am with child, ye bloody homicides. *Shakeſp. Henry* VI.

If he had done or ſaid any thing amiſs, he deſired their worſhips to think it was his *infirmities*. *Shak. Julius Cæſ.*

Are the *infirmities* of the body, pains, and diſeaſes his complaints? His faith reminds him of the day when this corruptible ſhall put on incorruption, and this mortal immortality. *Rogers.*

2. Failing; weakneſs; fault.

A friend ſhould bear a friend's *infirmities*;
But Brutus makes mine greater than they are. *Shakeſpeare.*

Many *infirmities* made it appear more requiſite, that a wiſer man ſhould have the application of his intereſt. *Clarendon.*

3. Diſeaſe;

How difficult is it to preserve a great name, when he that has acquired it, is so obnoxious to such little weaknesses and *infirmities*, as are no small diminution to it, when discovered. *Addison's Spectator.*

3. Disease; malady.

General laws are like general rules of physick, according whereunto, as now, no wise man will desire himself to be cured, if there be joined with his disease some special accident, in regard that thereby others in the same *infirmity*, but without the like accident, may. *Hooker.*

INFI'RMNESS. *n. s.* [from *infirm.*] Weakness; feebleness.

Some experiments may discover the *infirmness* and insufficiency of the peripatetick doctrine. *Boyle.*

To INFI'X. *v. a.* [*infixus*, Latin.] To drive in; to fasten.

And at the point two stings *infixed* are,
Both deadly sharp, that sharpest steel exceeden far. *Fa. Qu.*
I never lov'd myself,
'Till now, *infixed*, I behold myself,
Drawn in the flatt'ring table of her eye. *Shakesp. K. John.*
Immoveable, *infix'd*, and frozen round. *Milton.*
That sting *infix'd* within her haughty mind,
And her proud heart with secret sorrow pin'd. *Dryden.*
Arcite on Emily had fix'd his look:
The fatal dart a ready passage found,
And deep within her heart *infix'd* the wound. *Dryden.*

To INFLA'ME. *v. a.* [*inflammo*, Latin.]

1. To kindle; to set on fire.

Love more clear than yourselves, dedicated to a love, I fear, more cold than yourselves, with the clearness lays a night of sorrow upon me, and with the coldness *inflames* a world of fire within me. *Sidney.*

Its waves of torrent fire *inflam'd* with rage. *Milton.*

2. To kindle desire.

Their lust was *inflamed* towards her. *Susan.* viii.
More *inflam'd* with lust than rage. *Milton.*

3. To exaggerate; to aggravate.

A friend exaggerates a man's virtues, an enemy *inflames* his crimes. *Addison's Spectator.*

4. To heat the body morbidly with obstructed matter.

5. To provoke; to irritate.

A little vain curiosity weighs so much with us, or the church's peace so little, that we sacrifice the one to the whetting and *inflaming* of the other. *Decay of Piety.*

6. To fire with passion.

Satan, with thoughts *inflam'd* of highest design,
Puts on swift wings. *Milton.*

To INFLA'ME. *v. n.* To grow hot, angry, and painful by obstructed matter.

If the vesiculæ are opprest, they *inflame*. *Wiseman.*

INFLA'MER. *n. s.* [from *inflame.*] The thing or person that inflames.

Interest is a great *inflamer*, and sets a man on persecution under the colour of zeal. *Addison's Spectator.*

Assemblies, who act upon publick principles, proceed upon influence from particular leaders and *inflamers*. *Swift.*

INFLAMMABI'LITY. *n. s.* [from *inflammable.*] The quality of catching fire.

This it will do, if the ambient air be impregnate with subtile *inflammabilities*. *Brown's Vulgar Errours.*

Choler is the lightest and most inflammable part of the blood; whence, from its *inflammability*, it is called a sulphur. *Harvey on Consumptions.*

INFLA'MMABLE. *adj.* [French.] Easy to be set on flame; having the quality of flaming.

The juices of olives, almonds, nuts, and pine-apples, are all *inflammable*. *Bacon's Natural History.*

Licetus thinks it possible to extract an *inflammable* oil from the stone asbestus. *Wilkins's Math. Magic.*

Out of water grow all vegetable and animal substances, which consist as well of sulphureous, fat, and *inflammable* parts as of earthy and alcalizate ones. *Newton's Opt.*

Inflammable spirits are subtile volatile liquors, which come over in distillation, miscible with water, and wholly combustible. *Arbuthnot on Aliments.*

INFLA'MMABLENESS. *n. s.* [from *inflammable.*] The quality of easily catching fire.

We may treat of the *inflammableness* of bodies. *Boyle.*

INFLAMMA'TION. *n. s.* [*inflammatio*, Latin; *inflammation*, French.]

1. The act of setting on flame.

2. The state of being in flame.

The flame extendeth not beyond the inflammable effluence, but closely adheres unto the original of its *inflammation*. *Bro.*

Some urns have had inscriptions on them, expressing that the lamps within them were burning when they were first buried; whereas the *inflammation* of fat and viscous vapours doth presently vanish. *Wilkins's Dæd.*

3. [In chirurgery.] *Inflammation* is when the blood is obstructed so as to crowd in a greater quantity into any particular part, and gives it a greater colour and heat than usual. *Quincy.*

If that bright spot stay in his place, it is an *inflammation* of the burning. *Lev.* xiii. 28.

4. The act of exciting fervour of mind.

Prayer kindleth our desire to behold God by speculation; and the mind, delighted with that contemplative sight of God, taketh every where new *inflammations* to pray the riches of the mysteries of heavenly wisdom, continually stirring up in us correspondent desires towards them. *Hooker.*

INFLA'MMATORY. *adj.* [from *inflame.*] Having the power of inflaming.

The extremity of pain often creates a coldness in the extremities: such a sensation is very consistent with an *inflammatory* distemper. *Arbuthnot on Diet.*

An *inflammatory* fever hurried him out of this life in three days. *Pope to Swift.*

To INFLA'TE. *v. a.* [*inflatus*, Latin.]

1. To swell with wind.

That the muscles are *inflated* in time of rest, appears to the very eye in the faces of children. *Ray.*

Vapours are no other than *inflated* vesiculæ of water. *Derh.*

2. To fill with the breath.

With might and main they chas'd the murd'rous fox,
With brazen trumpets and *inflated* box,
To kindle Mars with military sounds,
Nor wanted horns t' inspire sagacious hounds. *Dryden.*

INFLA'TION. *n. s.* [*inflatio*, Lat. from *inflate.*] The state of being swelled with wind; flatulence.

Wind coming upwards, *inflations* and tumours of the belly are signs of a phlegmatick constitution. *Arbuthnot on Diet.*

To INFLE'CT. *v. a.* [*inflecto*, Latin.]

1. To bend; to turn.

What makes them this one way their race direct,
While they a thousand other ways reject?
Why do they never once their course *inflect*? *Blackm.*

Do not the rays of light which fall upon bodies, begin to bend before they arrive at the bodies? And are they not reflected, refracted, and *inflected* by one and the same principle, acting variously in various circumstances? *Newton's Opt.*

2. To change or vary.

3. To vary a noun or verb in its terminations.

INFLE'CTION. *n. s.* [*inflectio*, Latin.]

1. The act of bending or turning.

Neither the divine determinations, persuasions, or *inflexions* of the understanding or will of rational creatures, doth deceive the understanding, pervert the will, or necessitate either to any moral evil. *Hale.*

2. Modulation of the voice.

His virtue, his gesture, his countenance, his zeal, the motion of his body, and the *inflection* of his voice, who first uttereth them as his own, is that which giveth the very essence of instruments available to eternal life. *Hooker.*

3. Variation of a noun or verb.

The same word in the original tongue, by divers *inflections* and variations, makes divers dialects. *Brerewood.*

INFLE'CTIVE. *adj.* [from *inflect.*] Having the power of bending.

This *inflective* quality of the air is a great incumbrance and confusion of astronomical observations. *Derham.*

INFLEXIBI'LITY. } *n. s.* [*inflexibilité*, French, from *inflexible.*]
INFLE'XIBLENESS. }

1. Stiffness; quality of resisting flexure.

2. Obstinacy; temper not to be bent; inexorable pertinacy.

INFLE'XIBLE. *adj.* [French; *inflexibilis*, Latin.]

1. Not to be bent or incurvated.

Such errors as are but acorns in our younger brows, grow oaks in our older heads, and become *inflexible* to the powerful arm of reason. *Brown's Preface to Vul. Err.*

Too great rigidity and elasticity of the fibres makes them *inflexible* to the causes, to which they ought to yield. *Arbuthnot.*

2. Not to be prevailed on; immovable.

The man resolv'd and steady to his trust,
Inflexible to ill, and obstinately just. *Addison.*

A man of an upright and *inflexible* temper, in the execution of his country's laws, can overcome all private fear. *Addison.*

3. Not to be changed or altered.

The nature of things are *inflexible*, and their natural relations unalterable: we must bring our understandings to things, and not bend things to our fancies. *Watts.*

INFLE'XIBLY. *adv.* [from *inflexible.*] Inexorably; invariably; without relaxation or remission.

It should be begun early, and *inflexibly* kept to, 'till there appears not the least reluctancy. *Locke.*

To INFLI'CT. *v. a.* [*infligo*, *inflictus*, Latin; *infliger*, Fr.] To put in act or impose as a punishment.

I know no pain, they can *inflict* upon him,
Will make him say I mov'd him to those arms. *Shakesp.*
Sufficient is this punishment which was *inflicted*. 2 *Cor.* ii.
What the potent victor in his rage
Can else *inflict*. *Milton.*
What heart could wish, what hand *inflict* this dire disgrace? *Dryden's Æn. b.* vi.

By diseases we condemn ourselves to greater torments than have been yet invented by anger or revenge, or *inflicted* by the greatest tyrants upon the worst of men. *Temple.*

INFLI'CTER. *n. s.* [from *inflict*.] He who punishes.

Revenge is commonly not bounded, but extended to the utmost power of the *inflicter*. *Government of the Tongue.*

INFLI'CTION. *n. s.* [from *inflict*.]

1. The act of using punishments.

So our decrees,
Dead to *infliction*, to themselves are dead;
And liberty plucks justice by the nose. *Shakespeare.*

Sin ends certainly in death; death not only as to merit, but also as to actual *infliction*. *South's Sermons.*

2. The punishment imposed.

What, but thy malice, mov'd thee to misdeem
Of righteous Job, than cruelly to afflict him
With all *inflictions*? But his patience won. *Paradise Reg.*

How despicable are the threats of a creature as impotent as ourselves, when compared with the wrath of an Almighty Judge, whose power extends to eternal *inflictions*? *Rogers.*

His severest *inflictions* are in themselves acts of justice and righteousness. *Rogers's Sermons.*

INFLI'CTIVE. *adj.* [*inflictive*, Fr. from *inflict*.] That which is laid on as a punishment.

I'NFLUENCE. *n. s.* [*influence*, Fr. *influo*, Latin.]

1. Power of the celestial aspects operating upon terrestrial bodies and affairs.

The sacred *influence* of light appears. *Milton.*
Comets no rule, no righteous order own;
Their *influence* dreaded, as their ways unknown. *Prior.*

2. Ascendant power; power of directing or modifying.

Incomparable lady, your commandment doth not only give me the will, but the power to obey you; such *influence* hath your excellency. *Sidney.*

God hath his *influence* into the very essence of all things, without which *influence* of Deity supporting them, their utter annihilation could not chuse but follow. *Hooker.*

A wise man shall over-rule his stars, and have a greater *influence* upon his own content than all the constellations and planets of the firmament. *Taylor's Rule of living holy.*

Foreknowledge had no *influence* on their fault. *Milton.*

Religion hath so great an *influence* upon the felicity of men, that it ought to be upheld, not only out of a dread of the divine vengeance in another world, but out of regard to the temporal prosperity of men. *Tillotson.*

Our inconsistency in the pursuit of schemes throughly digested, has a bad *influence* on our affairs. *Addison.*

So astonishing a scene would have present *influence* upon them, but not produce a lasting effect. *Atterbury.*

Where it ought to have greatest *influence*, this obvious indisputable truth is little regarded. *Rogers.*

To I'NFLUENCE. *v. a.* [from the noun.] To act upon with directive or impulsive power; to modify to any purpose; to guide or lead to any end.

By thy kind pow'r and *influencing* care,
The various creatures move, and live, and are. *Milton.*

These experiments succeed after the same manner *in vacuo* as in the open air, and therefore are not *influenced* by the weight or pressure of the atmosphere. *Newton's Opt.*

This standing revelation was attested in the most solemn and credible manner; and is sufficient to *influence* their faith and practice, if they attend. *Atterbury.*

All the restraint men are under is, by the violation of one law, broken through; and the principle which *influenced* their obedience has lost its efficacy on them. *Rogers's Sermons.*

I'NFLUENT. *adj.* [*influens*, Latin.] Flowing in.

The chief intention of chirurgery, as well as medicine, is keeping a just equilibrium between the *influent* fluids and vascular solids. *Arbuthnot on Aliments.*

INFLUE'NTIAL. *adj.* [from *influence*.] Exerting influence or power.

Our now over-shadowed souls may be emblemed by those crusted globes, whose *influential* emissions are interrupted by the interposal of the benighted element. *Glanv. Sceps.*

The inward springs and wheels of the corporal machine, on the most sublimed intellectuals, is dangerously *influential*. *Glan.*

I'NFLUX. *n. s.* [*influxus*, Latin.]

1. Act of flowing into any thing.

If once contracted in a systole, by the *influx* of the spirits, why, the spirits continually flowing in without let, doth it not always remain so? *Ray on the Creation.*

An elastick fibre, like a bow, the more extended, it restores itself with the greater force: if the spring be destroyed, it is like a bag, only passive as to the *influx* of the liquid. *Arbuthn.*

2. Infusion.

There is another life after this; and the *influx* of the knowledge of God, in relation to this everlasting life, is infinitely of moment. *Hale's Origin of Mankind.*

3. Influence; power. In this sense it is now not used.

We will enquire whether there be, in the footsteps of nature, any such transmission and *influx* of immateriate virtues, and what the force of imagination is, either upon the body imaginant, or upon another body. *Bacon's Nat. Hist.*

Adam, in innocence, might have held, by the continued *influx* of the divine will and power, a state of immortality. *Hale.*

These two do not so much concern sea-fish, yet they have a great *influx* upon rivers, ponds, and lakes. *Hale.*

INFLU'XIOUS. *adj.* [from *influx*.] Influential. Not used.

The moon hath an *influxious* power to make impressions upon their humours. *Howel's England's Tears.*

To INFO'LD. *v. a.* [*in* and *fold*.] To involve; to inwrap; to inclose with involutions.

For all the crest a dragon did *infold*
With greedy paws, and over all did spread
His golden wings. *Fairy Queen.*

Noble Banquo, let me *infold* thee,
And hold thee to my heart. *Shakesp. Macbeth.*

But does not nature for the child prepare
The parent's love, the tender nurse's care?
Who, for their own forgetful, seek his good,
Infold his limbs in bands, and fill his veins with food. *Black.*

Wings raise her arms, and wings her feet *infold*. *Pope.*

To INFO'LIATE. *v. a.* [*in* and *folium*, Lat.] To cover with leaves.

Long may his fruitful vine *infoliate* and clasp about him with embracements. *Howel.*

To INFO'RM. *v. a.* [*informer*, Fr. *informo*, Latin.]

1. To animate; to actuate by vital powers.

All alike *inform'd*
With radiant light, as glowing ir'n with fire. *Milton.*

Let others better mold the running mass
Of metals, and *inform* the breathing brass;
And soften into flesh a marble face. *Dryden's Æn.*

As from chaos, huddl'd and deform'd,
The god struck fire, and lighted up the lamps
That beautify the sky; so he *inform'd*
This ill-shap'd body with a daring soul. *Dryd. and Lee's Oed.*

Breath *informs* this fleeting frame. *Prior.*

This sovereign arbitrary soul
Informs, and moves, and animates the whole. *Blackmore.*

While life *informs* these limbs, the king reply'd,
Well to deserve be all my cares employ'd. *Pope's Odyssey.*

2. To instruct; to supply with new knowledge; to acquaint. Before the thing communicated was anciently put *with*; now generally *of*, sometimes *in*: I know not how proper.

The drift is to *inform* their minds *with* some method of reducing the laws into their original causes. *Hooker.*

I have this present evening from my sister
Been well *informed of* them, and with cautions. *Shakesp.*

Our ruin, by thee *inform'd*, I learn. *Milton.*

The long speeches rather confounded than *informed* his understanding. *Clarendon.*

The difficulty arises not from what sense *informs* us *of*, but from wrong applying our notions. *Digby.*

Though I may not be able to *inform* men more than they know, yet I may give them the occasion to consider. *Temple.*

The ancients examined in what consists the beauty of good postures, as their works sufficiently *inform* us. *Dryden.*

He may be ignorant of these truths, who will never take the pains to employ his faculties to *inform* himself *of* them. *Locke.*

To understand his calling in the commonwealth, and of religion, is enough to take up his time: few *inform* themselves *in* these to the bottom. *Locke.*

A more proper opportunity tends to make the narration more *informing* or beautiful. *Broome's Notes on the Iliad.*

I think it necessary, for the interest of virtue and religion, that the whole kingdom should be *informed in* some parts of your character. *Swift.*

3. To offer an accusation to a magistrate.

Tertullus *informed* the governor against Paul. *Acts* xxvi. 1.

To INFO'RM. *v. n.*

1. To give intelligence.

It is the bloody business which *informs*
Thus to mine eyes. *Shakespeare's Macbeth.*

INFO'RMAL. *adj.* [from *inform*.] Offering an information; accusing. A word not used.

These poor *informal* women are no more
But instruments of some more mightier member,
That sets them on. *Shakes. Meas. for Measure.*

INFO'RMANT. *n. s.* [French.]

1. One who gives information or instruction.

He believes the sentence is true, as it is made up of terms which his *informant* understands, though the ideas be unknown to him which his *informant* has under these words. *Watts.*

2. One who exhibits an accusation.

INFORMA'TION. *n. s.* [*informatio*, Lat. from *inform*.]

1. Intelligence given; instruction.

But reason with the fellow,
Lest you should chance to whip your *information*,
And beat the messenger who bids beware
Of what is to be dreaded. *Shak. Coriolanus.*

The active *informations* of the intellect filling the passive reception of the will, like form closing with matter, grew actuate into a third and distinct perfection of practice. *South.*

They gave those complex ideas names, that the things they were continually to give and receive *information* about, might be the easier and quicker understood. *Locke.*

He

He ſhould regard the propriety of his words, and get ſome *information* in the ſubject he intends to handle. *Swift.*

Theſe men have had longer opportunities of *information*, and are equally concerned with ourſelves. *Rogers.*

2. Charge or accuſation exhibited.

3. The act of informing or actuating.

INFO'RMER. *n. ſ.* [from *inform.*]

1. One who gives intelligence.

This writer is either byaſſed by an inclination to believe the worſt, or a want of judgment to chuſe his *informers*. *Swift.*

2. One who diſcovers offenders to the magiſtrate.

There were ſpies and *informers* ſet at work to watch the company. *L'Eſtrange.*

Let no court ſycophant pervert my ſenſe,
Nor ſly *informer* watch theſe words to draw
Within the reach of treaſon. *Pope.*

Informers are a deteſtable race of people, although ſometimes neceſſary. *Swift.*

INFO'RMIDABLE. *adj.* [*in* and *formidabilis*, Lat.] Not to be feared; not to be dreaded.

Of ſtrength, of courage haughty, and of limb
Heroick built, though of terreſtrial mold;
Foe not *informidable*, exempt from wound. *Milton.*

INFO'RMITY. *n. ſ.* [from *informis*, Lat.] Shapeleſſneſs.

From this narrow time of geſtation may enſue a ſmalneſs in the excluſion; but this infereth no *informity*. *Brown.*

INFO'RMOUS. *adj.* [*informe*, Fr. *informis*, Latin.] Shapeleſs; of no regular figure.

That a bear brings forth her young *informous* and unſhapen, which ſhe faſhioneth after by licking them over, is an opinion not only common with us at preſent, but hath been delivered by ancient writers. *Brown's Vulgar Errours.*

INFO'RTUNATE. *adj.* [*infortuné*, Fr. *infortunatus*, Latin.] Unhappy. See UNFORTUNATE, which is commonly uſed.

Perkin, ſeeing himſelf priſoner, and deſtitute of all hopes, having found all either falſe, faint, or *infortunate*, did gladly accept of the condition. *Bacon's Henry* VII.

To INFRA'CT. *v. a.* [*infractus*, Latin.] To break.

Falling faſt, from gradual ſlope to ſlope,
With wild *infracted* courſe and leſſen'd roar,
It gains a ſafer bed. *Thomſon's Summer.*

INFRA'CTION. *n. ſ.* [*infraction*, Fr. *infractio*, Lat.] The act of breaking; breach; violation.

By the ſame gods, the juſtice of whoſe wrath
Puniſh'd the *infraction* of my former faith. *Waller.*

The wolves, pretending an *infraction* in the abuſe of their hoſtages, fell upon the ſheep immediately without their dogs. *L'Eſtrange's Fables.*

INFRA'NGIBLE. *adj.* [*in* and *frangible*.] Not to be broken.

Theſe atoms are ſuppoſed *infrangible*, extremely compacted and hard, which compactedneſs and hardneſs is a demonſtration that nothing could be produced by them, ſince they could never cohere. *Cheyne's Phil. Princ.*

INFRE'QUENCY. *n. ſ.* [*infrequentia*, Latin.] Uncommonneſs; rarity.

The abſence of the gods, and the *infrequency* of objects, made her yield. *Broome's Notes on Pope's Odyſſey.*

INFRE'QUENT. *adj.* [*infrequens*, Lat.] Rare; uncommon.

To INFRI'GIDATE. *v. a.* [*in* and *frigidus*, Lat.] To chill; to make cold.

The drops reached little further than the ſurface of the liquor, whoſe coldneſs did not *infrigidate* thoſe upper parts of the glaſs. *Boyle.*

To INFRI'NGE. *v. a.* [*infringo*, Latin.]

1. To violate; to break laws or contracts.

Thoſe many had not dar'd to do that evil,
If the firſt man that did th' edict *infringe*,
Had anſwer'd for his deed. *Shakeſp. Meaſ. for Meaſ.*

Having *infring'd* the law, I wave my right
As king, and thus ſubmit myſelf to fight. *Waller.*

2. To deſtroy; to hinder.

Homilies, being plain and popular inſtructions, do not *infringe* the efficacy, although but read. *Hooker.*

Bright as the deathleſs gods and happy, ſhe
From all that may *infringe* delight is free. *Waller.*

INFRI'NGEMENT. *n. ſ.* [from *infringe.*] Breach; violation.

The puniſhing of this *infringement* is proper to that juriſdiction againſt which the contempt is. *Clarendon.*

INFRI'NGER. *n. ſ.* [from *infringe.*] A breaker; a violator.

A clergyman's habit ought to be without any lace, under a ſevere penalty to be inflicted on the *infringers* of the provincial conſtitution. *Ayliffe's Parergon.*

INFU'NDIBULIFORM. *n. ſ.* [*infundibulum* and *forma*, Lat.] Of the ſhape of a funnel or tundiſh.

INFU'RIATE. *adj.* [*in* and *furia*, Lat.] Enraged; raging.

At th' other bore, with touch of fire
Dilated and *infuriate*. *Milton.*

Fir'd by the torch of noon to tenfold rage,
Th' *infuriate* hill forth ſhoots the pillar'd flame. *Thomſon.*

INFUSCA'TION. *n. ſ.* [*infuſcatus*, Latin.] The act of darkening or blackening.

To INFU'SE. *v. a.* [*infuſer*, Fr. *infuſus*, Latin.]

1. To pour in; to inſtil.

Thou almoſt mak'ſt me waver in my faith,
To hold opinion with Pythagoras,
That ſouls of animals *infuſe* themſelves
Into the trunks of men. *Shakeſ. Merchant of Venice.*

My early miſtreſs, now my ancient muſe,
That ſtrong Circean liquor ceaſe t' *infuſe*,
Wherewith thou didſt intoxicate my youth. *Denham.*

Why ſhould he deſire to have qualities *infuſed* into his ſon, which himſelf never poſſeſſed? *Swift.*

Meat muſt be with money bought;
She therefore, upon ſecond thought,
Infus'd, yet as it were by ſtealth,
Some ſmall regard for ſtate and wealth. *Swift.*

2. To pour into the mind; to inſpire into.

For when God's hand had written in the hearts
Of our firſt parents all the rules of good,
So that their ſkill *infus'd* ſurpaſs'd all arts
That ever were before, or ſince the flood. *Davies.*

Sublime ideas, and apt words *infuſe*;
The muſe inſtruct my voice, and thou inſpire the muſe. *Roſc.*

He *infus'd*
Bad influence into th' unwary breaſt. *Milton.*

Infuſe into their young breaſts ſuch a noble ardour as will make them renowned. *Milton.*

3. To ſteep in any liquor with a gentle heat; to macerate ſo as to extract the virtues of any thing.

Take violets, and *infuſe* a good pugil of them in a quart of vinegar. *Bacon's Natural Hiſtory.*

4. To make an infuſion with any ingredient; to ſupply, to tincture, to ſaturate with any thing infuſed.

Drink, *infuſed* with fleſh, will nouriſh faſter and eaſier than meat and drink together. *Bacon's Natural Hiſtory.*

5. To inſpire with.

Thou didſt ſmile,
Infuſed with a fortitude from heav'n. *Shakeſp. Tempeſt.*

Infuſe his breaſt with magnanimity,
And make him, naked, foil a man at arms. *Shakeſp. H. VI.*

INFU'SIBLE. *adj.* [from *infuſe.*]

1. Poſſible to be infuſed.

From whom the doctrines being *infuſible* into all, it will be more neceſſary to forewarn all of the danger of them. *Hamm.*

2. Incapable of diſſolution; not fuſible.

Vitrification is the laſt work of fire, and a fuſion of the ſalt and earth, wherein the fuſible ſalt draws the earth and *infuſible* part into one continuum. *Brown's Vulgar Errours.*

INFU'SION. *n. ſ.* [*infuſion*, Fr. *infuſio*, Latin.]

1. The act of pouring in; inſtillation.

Our language has received innumerable elegancies and improvements from that *infuſion* of Hebraiſms, which are derived to it out of the poetical paſſages in holy writ. *Addiſon's Spect.*

2. The act of pouring into the mind; inſpiration.

We participate Chriſt partly by imputation, as when thoſe things which he did and ſuffered for us are imputed to us for righteouſneſs; partly by habitual and real *infuſion*, as when grace is inwardly beſtowed on earth, and afterwards more fully both our ſouls and bodies in glory. *Hooker.*

They found it would be matter of great debate, and ſpend much time; during which they did not deſire their company, nor to be troubled with their *infuſions*. *Clarendon.*

Here his folly and his wiſdom are of his own growth, not the echo or *infuſion* of other men. *Swift.*

3. The act of ſteeping any thing in moiſture without boiling.

Repeat the *infuſion* of the body oftener. *Bacon.*

4. The liquor made by infuſion.

To have the *infuſion* ſtrong, in thoſe bodies which have finer ſpirits, repeat the infuſion of the body oftener. *Bacon.*

INFU'SIVE. *adj.* [from *infuſe.*] Having the power of infuſion, or being infuſed. A word not authoriſed.

Still let my ſong a nobler note aſſume,
And ſing th' *infuſive* force of Spring on man. *Thomſon.*

INGA'TE. *n. ſ.* [*in* and *gate.*] Entrance; paſſage in.

One noble perſon ſtoppeth the *ingate* of all that evil which is looked for, and holdeth in all thoſe which are at his back. *Spenſer on Ireland.*

INGANNA'TION. *n. ſ.* [*ingannare*, Italian.] Cheat; fraud; deception; juggle; deluſion; impoſture; trick; ſlight. A word neither uſed nor neceſſary.

Whoever ſhall reſign their reaſons, either from the root of deceit in themſelves, or inability to reſiſt ſuch trivial *ingannations* from others, are within the line of vulgarity. *Brown.*

INGA'THERING. *n. ſ.* [*in* and *gathering.*] The act of getting in the harveſt.

Thou ſhalt keep the feaſt of *ingathering*, when thou haſt gathered in thy labours out of the field. *Ex.* xxiii. 16.

INGE, in the names of places, ſignifies a meadow, from the Saxon ing, of the ſame import. *Gibſon's Camden.*

To INGE'MINATE. *v. a.* [*ingemino*, Latin.] To double; to repeat.

He would often *ingeminate* the word peace, peace. *Clarendon.*

INGEMINA'TION. *n. ſ.* [*in* and *geminatio*, Latin.] Repetition; reduplication.

INGE'NDERER. *n. s.* [from *ingender.*] He that generates. See ENGENDER.

INGE'NERABLE. *adj.* [*in* and *generate.*] Not to be produced or brought into being.

Divers naturalists esteem the air, as well as other elements, to be *ingenerable* and incorruptible. *Boyle.*

INGE'NERATE. } *adj.* [*ingeneratus*, Latin.]
INGE'NERATED. }

1. Inborn; innate; inbred.

Those virtues were rather feigned and affected things to serve his ambition, than true qualities *ingenerate* in his judgment or nature. *Bacon's Henry VII.*

In divers children their *ingenerate* and seminal powers lie deep, and are of slow disclosure. *Wotton.*

Those noble habits are *ingenerated* in the soul, as religion, gratitude, obedience, and tranquillity. *Hale's Origin of Mank.*

2. Unbegotten. Not commonly used.

Yet shall we demonstrate the same, from persons presumed as far from us in condition as time; that is, our first and *ingenerated* forefathers. *Brown's Vulg. Err.*

INGE'NIOUS. *adj.* [*ingenieux*, Fr. *ingeniosus*, Latin.]

1. Witty; inventive; possessed of genius.

'Tis a per'lous boy,
Bold, quick, *ingenious*, forward, capable:
He's all the mother's from the top to toe. *Shakesp. R.* III.

Our *ingenious* friend Cowley not only has employed much eloquence to persuade that truth in his preface, but has in one of his poems given a noble example of it. *Boyle.*

2. Mental; intellectual. Not in use.

The king is mad: how stiff is my vile sense,
That I stand up, and have *ingenious* feeling
Of my huge sorrows; better I were distract. *Shakespeare.*

INGE'NIOUSLY. *adv.* [from *ingenious.*] Wittily; subtily.

I will not pretend to judge by common fears, or the schemes of men too *ingeniously* politick. *Temple.*

INGE'NIOUSNESS. *n. s.* [from *ingenious.*]

1. Wittiness; subtilty; strength of genius.

The greater appearance of *ingeniousness* there is in the practice I am disapproving, the more dangerous it is. *Boyle.*

INGE'NITE. *adj.* [*ingenitus*, Latin.] Innate; inborn; native; ingenerate.

Aristotle affirms the mind to be at first a mere *rasa tabula*; and that notions are not *ingenite*, and imprinted by the finger of nature, but by the latter and more languid impressions of sense, being only the reports of observation, and the result of so many repeated experiments. *South.*

We give them this *ingenite*, moving force,
That makes them always downward take their course. *Black.*

INGENU'ITY. *n. s.* [*ingenuité*, Fr. from *ingenuous.*]

1. Openness; fairness; candour; freedom from dissimulation.

Such of high quality, or other of particular note, as shall fall under my pen, I shall not let pass without their due character, being part of my professed *ingenuity*. *Wotton.*

My constancy I to the planets give;
My truth, to them who at the court do live;
Mine *ingenuity* and openness
To jesuits; to buffoons my pensiveness. *Donne.*

I know not whether it be more shame or wonder, that men can so put off *ingenuity*, and the native greatness of their kind, as to descend to so base, so ignoble a vice. *Gov. of the Tongue.*

If a child, when questioned for any thing, directly confess, you must commend his *ingenuity*, and pardon the fault, be it what it will. *Locke.*

2. [From *ingenious.*] Wit; invention; genius; subtilty; acuteness.

These are but the frigidities of wit, and become not the genius of manly *ingenuities*. *Brown's Vulg. Errours.*

The ancient atomical hypothesis might have slept for ever, had not the *ingenuity* of the present age recalled it from its urn and silence. *Glanv. Sceps.*

Such sots have neither parts nor wit, *ingenuity* of discourse, nor fineness of conversation, to entertain or delight any one. *South.*

A pregnant instance how far virtue surpasses *ingenuity*, and how much an honest simplicity is preferable to fine parts and subtile speculations. *Woodward.*

INGE'NUOUS. *adj.* [*ingenuus*, Latin.]

1. Open; fair; candid; generous; noble.

Many speeches there are of Job's, whereby his wisdom and other virtues may appear; but the glory of an *ingenuous* mind he hath purchased by these words only, Behold I will lay mine hand upon my mouth; I have spoken once, yet will I not therefore maintain argument: yea twice, howbeit for that cause further I will not proceed. *Hooker.*

Infusing into their young breasts such an *ingenuous* and noble ardour, as would not fail to make many of them renowned. *Milton on Education.*

If an *ingenuous* detestation of this shameful vice be but carefully and early instilled, that is the true and genuine method to obviate dishonesty. *Locke.*

2. Freeborn; not of servile extraction.

Subjection, as it preserves property, peace, and safety, so it will never diminish rights nor *ingenuous* liberties. *K. Charles.*

INGE'NUOUSLY. *adv.* [from *ingenuous.*] Openly; fairly; candidly; generously.

Ingenuously I speak,
No blame belongs to thee. *Shakesp. Timon.*

It was a notable observation of a wise father, and no less *ingenuously* confessed, that those which held and persuaded pressure of consciences were commonly interested. *Bacon.*

I will *ingenuously* confess, that the helps were taken from divines of the church of England. *Dryden.*

INGE'NUOUSNESS. *n. s.* [from *ingenuous.*] Openness; fairness; candour.

I'NGENY. *n. s.* [*ingenium*, Lat.] Genius; wit. Not in use.

Whatever of the production of his *ingeny* comes into foreign parts, is highly valued. *Boyle.*

To INGE'ST. *v. a.* [*ingestus*, Lat.] To throw into the stomach.

Nor will we affirm that iron, *ingested*, receiveth in the belly of the osteridge no alteration. *Brown's Vulg. Errours.*

Some the long funnel's curious mouth extend,
Through which *ingested* meats with ease descend. *Blackm.*

INGE'STION. *n. s.* [from *ingest.*] The act of throwing into the stomach.

It has got room enough to grow into its full dimension, which is performed by the daily *ingestion* of milk and other food, that's in a short time after digested into blood. *Harvey.*

INGLO'RIOUS. *adj.* [*inglorius*, Latin.] Void of honour; mean; without glory.

Left fear return them back to Egypt, chusing
Inglorious life with servitude. *Milton's Paradise Lost, b.* xii.

It was never held *inglorious* or derogatory for a king to be guided by his great council, nor dishonourable for subjects to yield and bow to their king. *Howel.*

Yet though our army brought not conquest home,
I did not from the fight *inglorious* come. *Dryd. Ind. Emp.*

INGLO'RIOUSLY. *adv.* [from *inglorious.*] With ignominy; with want of glory.

This ease the chief o'ercome,
Replenish'd not *ingloriously* at home. *Pope.*

I'NGOT. *n. s.* [*lingot*, French; or from *ingegoten*, melted, Dut.] A mass of metal.

Some others were new driven, and distent
Into great *ingots*, and to wedges square. *Fairy Queen.*

If thou art rich, thou'rt poor;
For like an ass, whose back's with *ingots* bound,
Thou bear'st thy heavy riches but a journey,
And death unloadeth thee. *Shakesp. Meas. for Meas.*

Within the circle arms and tripods lye,
Ingots of gold and silver heap'd on high. *Dryden's Æn.*

Every one of his pieces is an *ingot* of gold, intrinsically and solidly valuable. *Prior.*

To INGRA'FF. *v. a.* [*in* and *graff.*]

1. To propagate trees by insition.

Nor are the ways alike in all
How to *ingraff*, how to inoculate. *May's Virg. Georg.*

2. To plant the sprig of one tree in the stock of another.

3. To plant any thing not native.

All his works on me,
Good or not good, *ingraft*, my merits those
Shall perfect, and for those alone. *Milton.*

As next of kin, Achilles' arms I claim;
This fellow would *ingraft* a foreign name
Upon our stock. *Dryden.*

4. To fix deep; to settle.

For a spur of diligence, we have a natural thirst after knowledge *ingrafted* in us. *Hooker.*

'Tis great pity that the noble Moor
Should hazard such a place as his own second,
With one of an *ingraft* infirmity. *Shakesp. Othello.*

Ingrafted love he bears to Cæsar. *Shakesp. Jul. Cæsar.*

INGRA'FTMENT. *n. s.* [from *ingraft.*]

1. The act of ingrafting.

2. The sprig ingrafted.

INGRA'TE. } *adj.* [*ingratus*, Latin; *ingrat*, French.]
INGRA'TEFUL. }

1. Ungrateful; unthankful.

That we have been familiar,
Ingrate forgetfulness shall poison, rather
Than pity note how much. *Shakesp. Coriolanus.*

And you degen'rate, you *ingrate* revolts,
You bloody Neros. *Shakesp.*

So will fall
He and his faithless progeny: whose fault?
Whose but his own? *Ingrate*; he had of me
All he could have: I made him just and right,
Sufficient to have stood, though free to fall. *Milt. Par. Lost.*

Words! which no ear ever to hear in heav'n
Expected; least of all from thee, *ingrate!* *Milt. Par. Lost.*

Perfidious and *ingrate!*
His stores ye ravage, and usurp his state. *Pope's Odyssey.*

2. Unpleasing to the sense.

The causes of that which is pleasing or *ingrate* to the hearing, may receive light by that which is pleasing and grateful to the sight. *Bacon's Natural History.*

He gives no *ingrateful* food. *Milton.*

To INGRA'TIATE. *v. a.* [*in* and *gratia*, Lat.] To put in favour; to recommend to kindness.

Those

Thoſe have been far from receiving the rewards of ſuch *ingratiatings* with the people. *King Charles.*

Their managers turn water into blood for them, make them ſee armies in the air, and give them their word, the more to *ingratiate* themſelves with them, that they ſignify nothing leſs than future ſlaughter and deſolation. *Addiſon.*

Politicians, who would rather *ingratiate* themſelves with their ſovereign than promote his real ſervice, accommodate his counſels to his inclinations. *Spectator*, Nº. 479.

INGRA'TITUDE. *n. ſ.* [*ingratitude*, French; *in* and *gratitude.*] Retribution of evil for good; unthankfulneſs.

Ingratitude! thou marble-hearted fiend,
More hideous, when thou ſhew'ſt thee in a child,
Than the ſea monſter. *Shakeſpeare's King Lear.*

Ingratitude is abhorred both by God and man, and vengeance attends thoſe that repay evil for good. *L'Eſtrange.*

Nor was it with *ingratitude* return'd,
In equal fires the bliſsful couple burn'd;
One joy poſſeſs'd 'em both, and in one grief they mourn'd. *Dryden.*

INGRE'DIENT. *n. ſ.* [*ingredient*, French; *ingrediens*, Latin.] Component part of a body, conſiſting of different materials. It is commonly uſed of the ſimples of a medicine.

The ointment is made of divers *ingredients*, whereof the hardeſt to come by is the moſs upon the ſkull of a dead man unburied. *Bacon's Nat. Hiſt.* Nº. 998.

So deep the pow'r of theſe *ingredients* pierc'd,
Ev'n to the inmoſt ſeat of mental ſight,
That Adam, now enforc'd to ſhut his eyes,
Sunk down, and all his ſpirits became entranc'd. *Milton.*

By this way of analyſis we may proceed from compounds to *ingredients*, and from motions to the forces producing them; and in general, from effects to their cauſes, and from particular cauſes to more general ones, till the argument end in the more general. *Newton's Opticks.*

I have often wondered, that learning is not thought a proper *ingredient* in the education of a woman of quality or fortune. *Addiſon's Guard.* Nº. 155.

Parts, knowledge, and experience, are excellent *ingredients* in a publick character. *Rogers's Sermons.*

Water is the chief *ingredient* in all the animal fluids and ſolids. *Arbuthnot on Aliments.*

I'NGRESS. *n. ſ.* [*ingres*, French; *ingreſſus*, Latin.] Entrance; power of entrance.

All putrefactions come from the ambient body; either by *ingreſs* of the ſubſtance of the ambient body into the body putrefied; or elſe by excitation of the body putrefied by the body ambient. *Bacon's Nat. Hiſt.* N . 836.

Thoſe air-bladders, by a ſudden ſubſidence, meet again by the *ingreſs* and egreſs of the air. *Arbuthnot on Aliments.*

INGRE'SSION. *n. ſ.* [*ingreſſion*, French; *ingreſſio*, Lat.] The act of entering.

The fire would ſtrain the pores of the glaſs too ſuddenly, and break it all in pieces to get *ingreſſion.* *Digby on Bodies.*

I'NGUINAL. *adj.* [*inguinal*, French; *inguen*, Lat.] Belonging to the groin.

The plague ſeems to be a particular diſeaſe, characteriſed with eruptions in buboes, by the inflammation and ſuppuration of the axillary, *inguinal*, and other glands. *Arbuthnot.*

To INGU'LF. *v. a.* [*in* and *gulf.*]

1. To ſwallow up in a vaſt profundity.

A river large
Paſs'd underneath *ingulph'd.* *Milton.*

The river flows redundant;
Then rowling back, in his capacious lap
Ingulfs their whole militia, quick immerſt. *Philips.*

2. To caſt into a gulf.

If we adjoin to the lords, whether they prevail or not, we *ingulf* ourſelves into aſſured danger. *Hayward.*

Caſt out from God, falls
Into utter darkneſs deep *ingulph'd.* *Milton.*

To INGU'RGITATE. *v. a.* [*ingurgito*, Latin.] To ſwallow down. *Dict.*

INGURGITA'TION. *n. ſ.* [from *ingurgitate.*] Voracity.

INGU'STABLE. *adj.* [*in* and *guſto*, Lat.] Not perceptible by the taſte.

As for their taſte, if the cameleon's nutriment be air, neither can the tongue be an inſtrument thereof; for the body of the element is *inguſtable*, void of all ſapidity, and without any action of the tongue, is, by the rough artery, or wizzen, conducted into the lungs. *Brown's Vulgar Errours, b.* iii.

INHA'BILE. *adj.* [*inhabile*, French; *inhabilis*, Lat.] Unſkilful; unready; unfit; unqualified.

To INHA'BIT. *v. a.* [*habito*, Latin.] To dwell in; to hold as a dweller.

Not all are partakers of that grace whereby Chriſt *inhabiteth* whom he ſaveth. *Hooker.*

They ſhall build houſes and *inhabit* them. *Iſa.* lxv. 21.

She ſhall be *inhabited* of devils. *Baruch* iv. 35.

To INHA'BIT. *v. n.* To dwell; to live.

Learn what creatures there *inhabit.* *Milton.*

They ſay, wild beaſts *inhabit* here;
But grief and wrong ſecure my fear. *Waller.*

INHA'BITABLE. *adj.* [from *inhabit.*]

1. Capable of affording habitation.

The fixed ſtars are all of them ſuns, with ſyſtems of *inhabitable* planets moving about them. *Locke.*

2. [*Inhabitable*, French.] Incapable of inhabitants; not habitable; uninhabitable. Not in uſe.

The frozen ridges of the Alps,
Or any other ground *inhabitable.* *Shakeſpeare's Richard* II.

INHA'BITANCE. *n. ſ.* [from *inhabit.*] Reſidence of dwellers.

So the ruins yet reſting in the wild moors, teſtify a former *inhabitance.* *Carew's Survey of Cornwall.*

INHA'BITANT. *n. ſ.* [from *inhabit.*] Dweller; one that lives or reſides in a place.

In this place they report that they ſaw *inhabitants*, which were very fair and fat people. *Abbot.*

If the fervour of the ſun were the ſole cauſe of blackneſs in any land of negroes, it were alſo reaſonable that *inhabitants* of the ſame latitude, ſubjected unto the ſame vicinity of the ſun, ſhould alſo partake of the ſame hue. *Brown.*

For his ſuppoſed love a third
Lays greedy hold upon a bird,
And ſtands amaz'd to find his dear
A wild *inhabitant* of th' air. *Waller.*

What happier natures ſhrink at with affright,
The hard *inhabitant* contends is right. *Pope.*

INHABITA'TION. *n. ſ.* [from *inhabit.*]

1. Habitation; place of dwelling.

Univerſal groan,
As if the whole *inhabitation* periſh'd. *Milton's Agoniſt.*

2. The act of inhabiting or planting with dwellings; ſtate of being inhabited.

By knowing this place we ſhall the better judge of the beginning of nations, and of the world's *inhabitation.* *Raleigh.*

3. Quantity of inhabitants.

We ſhall rather admire how the earth contained its *inhabitation* than doubt it. *Brown's Vulgar Errours, b.* vi.

INHA'BITER. *n. ſ.* [from *inhabit.*] One that inhabits; a dweller.

The ſame name is given unto the inlanders, or midland *inhabiters*, of this iſland. *Brown's Vulgar Errours.*

Wo to the *inhabiters* of the earth. *Rev.* viii. 13.

They ought to underſtand, that there is not only ſome *inhabiter* in this divine houſe, but alſo ſome ruler. *Derham.*

To INHA'LE. *v. a.* [*inhalo*, Latin.] To draw in with air; to inſpire.

Martin was walking forth to *inhale* the freſh breeze of the evening. *Arbuthnot's and Pope's Mart. Scrib.*

But from the breezy deep the bleſt *inhale*
The fragrant murmurs of the weſtern gale. *Pope's Odyſſey.*

There ſits the ſhepherd on the graſſy turf,
Inhaling healthful the deſcending ſun. *Thomſon's Spring.*

INHARMO'NIOUS. *adj.* [*in* and *harmonious.*] Unmuſical; not ſweet of ſound.

Catullus, though his lines be rough, and his numbers *inharmonious*, I could recommend for the ſoftneſs and delicacy, but muſt decline for the looſeneſs, of his thoughts. *Felton.*

The identity of ſound may appear a little *inharmonious*, and ſhock the ear. *Broome's Notes on the Odyſſey.*

To INHE'RE. *v. n.* [*inhæreo*, Latin.] To exiſt in ſomething elſe.

For, nor in nothing, nor in things
Extreme and ſcattering bright, can love *inhere.* *Donne.*

They do but *inhere* in their ſubject which ſupports them; their being is a dependence on a ſubject. *Digby on Bodies.*

INHE'RENT. *adj.* [*inherent*, French; *inhærens*, Lat.] Exiſting in ſomething elſe, ſo as to be inſeparable from it; innate; inborn.

I will not do't,
Leſt I ſurceaſe to honour mine own truth;
And, my body's action, teach my mind
A moſt *inherent* baſeneſs. *Shakeſpeare's Coriolanus.*

I mean not the authority which is annexed to your office: I ſpeak of that only which is inborn and *inherent* to your perſon. *Dryden's Juvenal.*

The power of drawing iron is one of the ideas of a loadſtone; and a power to be ſo drawn is a part of the complex one of iron; which powers paſs for *inherent* qualities. *Locke.*

Animal oil is various according to principles *inherent* in it. *Arbuthnot on Aliments.*

They will be ſure to decide in favour of themſelves, and talk much of their *inherent* right. *Swift.*

The ideas of ſuch modes can no more be ſubſiſtent, than the idea of redneſs was juſt now found to be *inherent* in the blood, or that of whiteneſs in the brain. *Bentley's Sermons.*

The obligations we are under of diſtinguiſhing ourſelves as much by an *inherent* and habitual, as we are already diſtinguiſhed by an external and relative holineſs. *Bentley's Serm.*

To INHE'RIT. *v. a.* [*enheriter*, French.]

1. To receive or poſſeſs by inheritance.

Treason is not *inherited*, my lord. *Shak. As you like it.*

Why, all delights are vain; but that most vain,
Which with pain purchas'd doth *inherit* pain. *Shakespeare.*

Prince Harry is valiant; for the cold blood he did naturally *inherit* of his father he hath, like lean, steril land, manured with excellent good store of fertile sherris. *Shakesp. Henry* IV.

Blessed are the meek, for they shall *inherit* the earth. *Mat.*

The son can receive from him the portion of good things, and advantages of education naturally due to him, without pire, that was vested in him for the good of others; and therefore the son cannot claim or *inherit* it by a title, which is founded wholly on his own private good. *Locke.*

We must know how the first ruler, from whom any one claims, came by his authority, before we can know who has a right to succeed him in it, and *inherit* it from him. *Locke.*

Unwilling to sell an estate he had some prospect of *inheriting*, he formed delays. *Addison's Spect.* Nº. 198.

2. To possess; to obtain possession of: in *Shakespeare.*

He, that had wit, would think that I had none,
To bury so much gold under a tree,
And never after to *inherit* it. *Shakesp. Titus Andronicus.*

INHE'RITABLE. *adj.* [from *inherit.*] Transmissible by inheritance; obtainable by succession.

A kind of *inheritable* estate accrued unto them. *Carew.*

By the ancient laws of the realm, they were not *inheritable* to him by descent. *Hayward.*

Was the power the same, and from the same original in Moses as it was in David? And was it *inheritable* in one and not in the other? *Locke.*

INHE'RITANCE. *n. s.* [from *inherit.*]

1. Patrimony; hereditary possession.

In the book of Numbers it is writ,
When the son dies let the *inheritance*
Descend unto the daughter. *Shakespeare's Henry* V.

Is there yet any portion or *inheritance* for us in our father's house. *Gen.* xxxi. 14.

Claim our just *inheritance* of old. *Milton.*

Oh dear, unhappy babe! must I bequeath thee
Only a sad *inheritance* of woe?
Gods! cruel gods! can't all my pains atone,
Unless they reach my infant's guiltless head? *Smith.*

2. In *Shakespeare*, possession.

You will rather shew our general lowts
How you can frown, than spend a fawn upon them,
For the *inheritance* of their loves, and safeguard
Of what that want might ruin. *Shakesp. Coriolanus.*

3. The reception of possession by hereditary right.

Men are not proprietors of what they have merely for themselves, their children have a title to part of it, which comes to be wholly theirs, when death has put an end to their parents use of it; and this we call *inheritance.* *Locke.*

INHE'RITOR. *n. s.* [from *inherit.*] An heir; one who receives any thing by succession.

You, like a letcher, out of whorish loins,
Are pleas'd to breed out your *inheritors.* *Shakespeare.*

The sole *inheritor*
Of all perfections that a man may owe. *Shakespears.*

The very conveyances of his lands will hardly lie in this box; and must the *inheritor* himself have no more? *Shakesp.*

Marriage without consent of parents they do not make void, but they mulct it in the *inheritors*; for the children of such marriages are not admitted to inherit above a third part of their parents inheritance. *Bacon's New Atlantis.*

INHE'RITRESS. *n. s.* [from *inheritor.*] An heiress; a woman that inherits.

Having given artificially some hopes to marry Anne, *inheritress* to the duchy of Bretagne. *Bacon's Henry* VII.

INHE'RITRIX. *n. s.* [from *inheritor.*] An heiress. This is now more commonly used, though *inheritress* be a word more analogically English.

Charles the great
Establish'd then this law, to wit, No feme
Should be *inheritrix* in Salike land. *Shakesp. Henry* V.

To INHE'RSE. *v. a.* [*in* and *herse.*] To inclose, in a funeral monument.

See, where he lies, *inhersed* in the arms
Of the most bloody nurser of his harms. *Shak. Henry* VI.

INHE'SION. *n. s.* [*inhæsio*, Latin.] Inherence; the state of existing in something else.

To INHI'BIT. *v. a.* [*inhibeo*, Lat. *inhiber*, French.]

1. To restrain; to hinder; to repress; to check.

Holding of the breath doth help somewhat to cease the hiccough; and vinegar put to the nostrils or gargerised doth it also, for that it is astringent, and *inhibiteth* the motion of the spirits. *Bacon's Nat. Hist.* Nº. 686.

The stars and planets being whirled about with great velocity, would suddenly, did nothing *inhibit* it, be shattered in pieces. *Ray on the Creation.*

Their motions also are excited and *inhibited*, are moderated and managed, by the objects without them. *Bentley's Serm.*

2. To prohibit; to forbid.

All men were *inhibited* by proclamation, at the dissolution, so much as to mention a parliament. *Clarendon.*

Burial may not be *inhibited* or denied to any one. *Ayliffe.*

INHIBI'TION. *n. s.* [*inhibition*, Fr. *inhibitio*, Latin.]

1. Prohibition; embargo.

He might be judged to have imposed an envious *inhibition* on it, because himself has not stock enough to maintain the trade. *Government of the Tongue, s.* 7.

2. [In law.]

Inhibition is a writ to inhibit or forbid a judge from farther proceeding in the cause depending before him. *Inhibition* is most commonly a writ issuing out of a higher court Christian to a lower and inferior, upon an appeal; and prohibition out of the king's court to a court Christian, or to an inferior temporal court. *Cowell.*

To INHO'LD. *v. a.* [*in* and *hold.*] To have inherent; to contain in itself.

It is disputed, whether this light first created be the same which the sun *inholdeth* and casteth forth, or whether it had continuance any longer than till the sun's creation. *Raleigh.*

INHO'SPITABLE. *adj.* [*in* and *hospitable.*] Affording no kindness nor entertainment to strangers.

All places else
Inhospitable appear, and desolate;
Nor knowing us, nor known. *Milton's Par. Lost, b.* xi.

Since toss'd from shores to shores, from lands to lands,
Inhospitable rocks, and barren sands. *Dryden's Virgil.*

INHO'SPITABLY. *adv.* [from *inhospitable.*] Unkindly to strangers.

Of guests he makes them slaves
Inhospitably; and kills their infant males. *Milton's Pa. Lost.*

INHOSPI'TABLENESS. } *n. s.* [*in* and *hospitality*; *inhospitalité*,
INHOSPITA'LITY. } Fr.] Want of hospitality; want of courtesy to strangers.

INHU'MAN. *adj.* [*inhumain*, Fr. *inhumanus*, Latin.] Barbarous; savage; cruel; uncompassionate.

A just war may be persecuted after a very unjust manner; by perfidious breaches of our word, by *inhuman* cruelties, and by assassinations. *Atterbury's Sermons.*

The more these praises were enlarged, the more *inhuman* was the punishment, and the sufferer more innocent. *Gulliver's Travels.*

Princes and peers attend! while we impart
To you the thoughts of no *inhuman* heart. *Pope's Odyssey.*

INHUMA'NITY. *n. s.* [*inhumanité*, French; from *inhuman.*] Cruelty; savageness; barbarity.

Banished
Her mind, beams, state, far from thy weak twigs,
And love with lover hurts is *inhumanity.* *Sidney, b.* i.

The rudeness of those who must make up their want of justice with *inhumanity* and impudence. *King Charles.*

Each social feeling fell,
And joyless *inhumanity* pervades,
And petrifies the heart. *Thomson's Spring, l.* 305.

INHU'MANLY. *adv.* [from *inhuman.*] Savagely; cruelly; barbarously.

O what are these
Death's ministers, not men: who thus deal death
Inhumanly to men; and multiply
Ten thousand fold the sin of him who slew
His brother. *Milton's Par. Lost, b.* xi.

I, who have established the whole system of all true politeness and refinement in conversation, think myself most *inhumanly* treated by my countrymen. *Swift.*

To I'NHUMATE. } *v. a.* [*inhumer*, French; *humo*, Lat.] To
To INHU'ME. } bury; to inter.

Weeping they bear the mangled heaps of slain,
Inhume the natives in their native plain. *Pope's Odyssey.*

To INJE'CT. *v. a.* [*injectus*, Latin.]

1. To throw in; to dart in.

Angels *inject* thoughts into our minds, and know our cogitations. *Glanville's Scep. c.* 24.

2. To throw up; to cast up.

Though bold in open field, they yet surround
The town with walls, and mound *inject* on mound. *Pope.*

INJE'CTION. *n. s.* [*injection*, French; *injectio*, Latin.]

1. The act of casting in.

This salt powdered was, by the repeated *injection* of well-kindled charcoal, made to flash like melted nitre. *Boyle.*

2. Any medicine made to be injected by a syringe, or any other instrument, into any part of the body. *Quincy.*

3. The act of filling the vessels with wax, or any other proper matter, to shew their shapes and ramifications, often done by anatomists. *Quincy.*

INIMITABI'LITY. *n. s.* [from *inimitable.*] Incapacity to be imitated.

Truths must have an eternal existence in some understanding; or rather they are the same with that understanding itself, considered as variously representative, according to the various modes of *inimitability* or participation. *Norris.*

INI'MITABLE. *adj.* [*inimitabilis*, Latin; *inimitable*, French.] Above imitation; not to be copied.

The portal shone, *inimitable* on earth
By model, or by shading pencil drawn. *Milton.*

What is most excellent is most *inimitable.* *Denham.*

And

And imitate the *inimitable* force. *Dryden.*

Virgil copied this circumſtance from the ancient ſculptors, in that *inimitable* deſcription of military fury in the temple of Janus. *Addiſon on ancient Medals.*

INIMI'TABLY. *adv.* [from *inimitable.*] In a manner not to be imitated; to a degree of excellence above imitation.

A man could not have been always blind who thus *inimitably* copies nature. *Pope's Eſſay on Homer.*

Thus terribly adorn'd the figures ſhine,
Inimitably wrought with ſkill divine. *Pope.*

Charms ſuch as thine, *inimitably* great. *Broome.*

To INJO'IN. *v. a.* [*enjoindre*, French; *injungo*, Latin.]

1. To command; to enforce by authority. See ENJOIN.

Laws do not only teach what is good, but they *injoin* it; they have in them a certain conſtraining force. *Hooker, b.* i.

This garden tend, our pleaſant taſk *injoin'd.* *Milton.*

2. In *Shakeſpeare*, to join.

The Ottomites
Steering with due courſe towards the iſle of Rhodes,
Have there *injoin'd* them with a fleet. *Shakeſpeare.*

INI'QUITOUS. *adj.* [*inique*, Fr. from *iniquity.*] Unjuſt; wicked.

INI'QUITY. *n. ſ.* [*iniquitas*, Lat. *iniquité*, French.]

1. Injuſtice; unreaſonableneſs.

There is greater or leſs probability of an happy iſſue to a tedious war, according to the righteouſneſs or *iniquity* of the cauſe for which it was commenced. *Smalridge's Sermons.*

2. Wickedneſs; crime.

Want of the knowledge of God is the cauſe of all *iniquity* amongſt men. *Hooker, b.* v.

Till God at laſt,
Wearied with their *iniquities*, withdraw
His preſence from among them. *Milton's Par. Loſt, b.* xii.

INI'TIAL. *adj.* [*initial*, French; *initialis*, from *initium*, Lat.]

1. Placed at the beginning.

In the editions, which had no more than the *initial* letters, he was made by Keys to hurt the inoffenſive. *Pope.*

2. Incipient; not complete.

Moderate labour of the body conduces to the preſervation of health, and cures many *initial* diſeaſes; but the toil of the mind deſtroys health, and generates maladies. *Harvey.*

The ſchools have uſed a middle term to expreſs this affection, and have called it the *initial* fear of God. *Rogers.*

To INI'TIATE. *v. a.* [*initier*, French; *initio*, Lat.] To enter; to inſtruct in the rudiments of an art; to place in a new ſtate; to put into a new ſociety.

Providence would only *initiate* mankind into the uſeful knowledge of her treaſures, leaving the reſt to employ our induſtry. *More's Antidote againſt Atheiſm.*

To *initiate* his pupil in any part of learning, an ordinary ſkill in the governour is enough. *Locke on Education.*

He was *initiated* into half a dozen clubs before he was one and twenty. *Spectator*, Nº. 576.

No ſooner was a convert *initiated*, but, by an eaſy figure, he became a new man. *Addiſon.*

To INI'TIATE. *v. n.* To do the firſt part; to perform the firſt rite.

The king himſelf *initiates* to the pow'r,
Scatters with quiv'ring hand the ſacred flour,
And the ſtream ſprinkles. *Pope's Odyſſey.*

INI'TIATE. *adj.* [*initié*, Fr. *initiatus*, Lat.] Unpractiſed.

My ſtrange and ſelf-abuſe
Is the *initiate* fear; that wants hard uſe:
We're yet but young. *Shakeſpeare's Macbeth.*

INITIA'TION. *n. ſ.* [*initiatio*, Lat. from *initiate.*] The act of entering of a new comer into any art or ſtate.

The ground of initiating or entering men into Chriſtian life, is more ſummarily compriſed in the form of baptiſm, the ceremony of this *initiation* inſtituted by Chriſt. *Hammond.*

Silence is the firſt thing that is taught us at our *initiation* into ſacred myſteries. *Broome's Notes to the Odyſſey.*

INJUCU'NDITY. *n. ſ.* [*in* and *jucundity.*] Unpleaſantneſs.

INJU'DICABLE. *adj.* [*in* and *judico*, Lat.] Not cognizable by a judge.

INJUDI'CIAL. *adj.* [*in* and *judicial.*] Not according to form of law. *Dict.*

INJUDI'CIOUS. *adj.* [*in* and *judicious.*] Void of judgment; without judgment.

A philoſopher would either think me in jeſt, or very *injudicious*, if I took the earth for a body regular in itſelf, if compared with the reſt of the univerſe. *Burnet.*

A ſharp wit may find ſomething in the wiſeſt man, whereby to expoſe him to the contempt of *injudicious* people. *Tillotſon.*

INJUDI'CIOUSLY. *adv.* [from *injudicious.*] With ill judgment; not wiſely.

Scaliger *injudiciouſly* condemns this deſcription. *Broome.*

INJU'NCTION. *n. ſ.* [from *injoin*; *injunctus*, *injunctio*, Latin.] Command; order; precept.

The inſtitution of God's law is deſcribed as being eſtabliſhed by ſolemn *injunction.* *Hooker, b.* i.

My duty cannot ſuffer
T' obey in all your daughter's hard commands;
Though the *injunction* be to bar my doors,
And let this tyrannous night take hold upon you. *Shakeſp.*

For, ſtill they knew; and ought t' have ſtill remember'd
The high *injunction*, not to taſte that fruit,
Whoever tempted. *Milton's Par. Loſt, b.* x.

The ceremonies of the church are neceſſary as the *injunctions* of lawful authority, the practice of the primitive church, and the general rules of decency. *South.*

2. [In law.] *Injunction* is an interlocutory decree out of the chancery, ſometimes to give poſſeſſion unto the plaintiff for want of appearance in the defendants, ſometimes to the king's ordinary court, and ſometimes to the court-chriſtian, to ſtay proceeding. *Cowell.*

To I'NJURE. *v. a.* [*injurier*, French; *injuria*, Lat.]

1. To hurt unjuſtly; to miſchief undeſervedly; to wrong.

They *injure* by chance in a crowd, and without a deſign; then hate always whom they have once *injured.* *Temple.*

Forgiveneſs to the *injur'd* does belong;
But they ne'er pardon who commit the wrong. *Dryden.*

2. To annoy; to affect with any inconvenience.

Leſt heat ſhould *injure* us, his timely care
Hath unbeſought provided. *Milton.*

I'NJURER. *n. ſ.* [from *injure*, Lat.] He that hurts another unjuſtly; one who wrongs another.

Ill deeds are well turn'd back upon their authors;
And 'gainſt an *injurer*, the revenge is juſt. *Benj. Johnſon.*

The upright judge will countenance right, and diſcountenance wrong, whoever be the *injurer* or the ſufferer. *Atterb.*

INJU'RIOUS. *adv.* [from *injury*; *injurius*, Lat. *injurieux*, Fr.]

1. Unjuſt; invaſive of another's rights.

Till the *injurious* Roman did extort
This tribute from us, we were free. *Shakeſp. Cymbeline.*

Injurious ſtrength would rapine ſtill excuſe,
By off'ring terms the weaker muſt refuſe. *Dryden.*

2. Guilty of wrong or injury.

Yet beauty, though *injurious*, hath ſtrange power,
After offence returning, to regain
Love once poſſeſt. *Milton's Agoniſt. l.* 1003.

3. Miſchievous; unjuſtly hurtful.

Our repentance is not real, becauſe we have not done what we can to undo our fault, or at leaſt to hinder the *injurious* conſequences of it from proceeding. *Tillotſon's Sermons.*

4. Detractory; contumelious; reproachful; wrongful.

A priſon, indeed *injurious*, becauſe a priſon, but elſe well teſtifying affection, becauſe in all reſpects as commodious as a priſon can be. *Sidney, b.* ii.

It is natural for a man, by directing his prayers to an image, to ſuppoſe the being he prays to repreſented by that image: which how *injurious*, how contumelious muſt it be to the glorious nature of God? *South's Sermons.*

If *injurious* appellations were of any advantage to a cauſe, what appellations would thoſe deſerve who thus endeavour to ſow the ſeeds of ſedition. *Swift.*

INJU'RIOUSLY. *adv.* [from *injurious.*] Wrongfully; hurtfully with injuſtice.

Nor ought he to neglect the vindication of his character, when it is *injuriouſly* attacked. *Pope and Gay.*

INJU'RIOUSNESS. *n. ſ.* [from *injurious.*] Quality of being injurious.

Some miſcarriages might eſcape, rather through ſudden neceſſities of ſtate than any propenſity either to *injuriouſneſs* or oppreſſion. *King Charles.*

I'NJURY. *n. ſ.* [*injuria*, Lat. *injure*, Fr.]

1. Hurt without juſtice.

The town of Bouline, and other places, were acquired by juſt title of victory; and therefore in keeping of them no *injury* was offered. *Hayward.*

Riot aſcends above their loftieſt tow'rs,
And *injury* and outrage. *Milton.*

2. Miſchief; detriment.

Many times we do *injury* to a cauſe by dwelling upon trifling arguments. *Watts's Logick.*

3. Annoyance.

Great *injuries* ſuch vermin as mice and rats do in the fields. *Mortimer.*

4. Contumelious language; reproachful appellation.

Caſting off the reſpects fit to be continued between great kings, he fell to bitter invectives againſt the French king; and, by how much he was the leſs able to do, talking ſo much the more, ſpake all the *injuries* he could deviſe of Charles. *Bacon.*

INJU'STICE. *n. ſ.* [*injuſtice*, French; *injuſtitia*, Lat.] Iniquity; wrong.

Cunning men can be guilty of a thouſand *injuſtices* without being diſcovered, or at leaſt without being puniſhed. *Swift.*

INK. *n. ſ.* [*encre*, French; *inchioſtro*, Italian.] The black liquor with which men write.

Mourn boldly my *ink*; for while ſhe looks upon you, your blackneſs will ſhine. *Sidney. b.* ii.

O! ſhe's fallen
Into a pit of *ink*, that the wide ſea
Hath drops too few to waſh her clean again. *Shakeſpeare.*

Write, my queen,
And with mine eyes I'll drink the works you ſend;
Though *ink* be made of gall. *Shakeſp. Cymbeline.*

Like madmen they hurl'd ſtones and *ink.* *Benj. Johnſon.*

Intending

Intending to have try'd
The silver favour which you gave,
In *ink* the shining point I dy'd,
And drench'd it in the sable wave. *Waller.*

Vitriol is the active or chief ingredient in *ink*, and no other salt will strike the colour with galls. *Brown's Vulgar Errours.*

I have found pens blacked almost all over when I had a while carried them about me in a silver *ink* case. *Boyle.*

The secretary poured the *ink* box all over the writings, and so defaced them. *Howel's Vocal Forest.*

He that would live clear of envy must lay his finger upon his mouth, and keep his hand out of the *ink* pot. *L'Estrange.*

I could hardly restrain them from throwing the *ink* bottle at one another's heads. *Arbuthnot's Hist. of John Bull.*

2. *Ink* is used for any liquor with which they write: as, red *ink*; green *ink*.

To INK. *v. a.* [from the noun.] To black or daub with ink: as, *his face is all over* inked.

INKHO'RN. *n. s.* [*ink* and *horn.*] A portable case for the instruments of writing, commonly made of horn.

Bid him bring his pen and *inkhorn* to the jail; we are now to examine those men. *Shakesp. Much ado about Nothing.*

Ere that we will suffer such a prince
To be disgrac'd by an *inkhorn* mate,
We, and our wives and children, all will fight. *Shakesp.*

What is more frequent than to say, a silver *inkhorn*. *Grew.*

I'NKLE. *n. s.* A kind of narrow fillet; a tape.

Incles, caddisses, cambricks, lawns: why he songs them over as they were gods and goddesses. *Shakespeare.*

I twitch'd his dangling garter from his knee:
He wist not when the hempen string I drew,
Now mine I quickly doff of *inkle* blue. *Gay's Pastorals.*

I'NKLING. *n. s.* [This word is derived by *Skinner* from *inklincken*, to sound within. This sense is still retained in Scotland: as, *I heard not an* inkling.] Hint; whisper; intimation.

Our business is not unknown to the senate: they have had *inkling* what we intend to do, which now we'll shew them in deeds. *Shakespeare's Coriolanus.*

We in Europe, notwithstanding all the remote discoveries and navigations of this last age, never heard of any of the least *inkling* or glimpse of this island. *Bacon's New Atlantis.*

They had some *inkling* of secret messages betwen the merquis of Newcastle and young Hotham. *Clarendon, b.* viii.

Aboard a Corinthian vessel he got an *inkling* among the ship's crew of a conspiracy. *L'Estrange's Fables.*

I'NKMAKER. *n. s.* [*ink* and *maker.*] He who makes ink.

I'NKY. *adj.* [from *ink.*]

1. Consisting of ink.

England bound in with the triumphant sea,
Whose rocky shore beats back the envious siege
Of wat'ry Neptune, is bound in with shame,
With *inky* blots and rotten parchment bonds. *Shakespeare.*

2. Resembling ink.

The darkness of the liquor presently began to be discussed, and grow pretty clear and transparent, losing its *inky* blackness. *Boyle on Colours.*

3. Black as ink.

'Tis not alone my *inky* cloak good mother,
Nor customary suits of solemn black,
That can denote me truly. *Shakespeare's Hamlet.*

I'NLAND. *adj.* [*in* and *land.*] Interior; lying remote from the sea.

In this wide *inland* sea, that hight by name,
The idle lake, my wand'ring ship I row. *Fairy Queen.*

Goodly laws, like little *inland* seas, will carry even ships upon their waters. *Spenser's State of Ireland.*

An old religious uncle of mine was, in his youth, an *inland* man. *Shakespeare's As you like it.*

A substitute shines brightly as a king,
Until a king be by; and then his state
Empties itself, as doth an *inland* brook
Into the main of waters. *Shakesp. Merchant of Venice.*

This person did publish a pamphlet printed in England for a general excise, or *inland* duty. *Swift.*

I'NLAND. *n. s.* Interior or midland parts.

Out of these small beginnings, gotten near to the mountains, did they spread themselves into the *Inland.* *Spenser.*

They of those marches shall defend
Our *inland* from the pilferring borderers. *Shakespeare.*

The rest were all
Far to th' *inland* retir'd, about the walls
Of Pandæmonium. *Milton's Par. Lost, b.* x.

I'NLANDER. *n. s.* [from *inland.*] Dweller remote from the sea.

The same name is given unto the *inlanders*, or midland inhabiters of this island. *Brown's Vulgar Errours, b.* vi.

To INLA'PIDATE. *v. a.* [*in* and *lapido*, Lat.] To make stoney; to turn to stone.

Some natural spring waters will *inlapidate* wood; so that you shall see one piece of wood, whereof the part above the water shall continue wood, and the part under the water shall be turned into a kind of gravelly stone. *Bacon.*

To INLA'Y. *v. a.* [*in* and *lay.*]

1. To diversify with different bodies inserted into the ground or substratum.

They are worthy
To *inlay* heav'n with stars. *Shakespeare's Cymbeline.*

Look, how the floor of heav'n
Is thick *inlaid* with patens of bright gold. *Shakespeare.*

A saphire throne, *inlaid* with pure
Amber, and colours of the show'ry arch. *Milton.*

The timber bears a great price with the cabinet makers, when large, for *inlaying.* *Mortimer's Husbandry.*

Here clouded canes 'midst heaps of toys are found,
And *inlaid* tweezer cases strow the ground. *Gay.*

2. To make variety by being inserted into bodies; to variegate.

Sea-girt isles,
That like to rich and various gems *inlay*
The unadorned bosom of the deep. *Milton.*

INLA'Y. *n. s.* [from the verb.] Matter inlaid; wood formed to inlay.

Under foot the violet,
Crocus, and hyacinth, with rich *inlay*,
Broider'd the ground. *Milton's Par. Lost, b.* iv.

To INLA'W. *v. a.* [*in* and *law.*] To clear of outlawry or attainder.

It should be a great incongruity to have them to make laws, who themselves were not *inlawed.* *Bacon's Henry* VII.

I'NLET. *n. s.* [*in* and *let.*] Passage; place of ingress; entrance.

Doors and windows, *inlets* of men and of light, I couple together, because I find their dimensions brought under one. *Wotton.*

She through the porch and *inlet* of each sense
Dropt in ambrosial oils till she reviv'd. *Milton.*

I desire any one to assign any simple idea, which is not received from one of these *inlets.* *Locke.*

A fine bargain indeed, to part with all our commodious ports, which the greater the *inlet* is are so much the better, for the imaginary pleasure of a streight shore. *Bentley.*

Inlets amongst broken lands and islands, rocks and shoals. *Ellis's Voyage.*

I'NLY. *adj.* [from *in.*] Interior; internal; secret.

Didst thou but know the *inly* touch of love,
Thou would'st as soon go kindle fire with snow,
As seek to quench the fire of love with words. *Shakesp.*

I'NLY. *adv.* Internally; within; secretly; in the heart.

Her heart with joy unwonted *inly* swell'd,
As feeling wond'rous comfort in her weaker eld. *Fa. Qu.*

I've *inly* wept,
Or should have spoke ere this. *Shakespeare's Tempest.*

Whereat he *inly* rag'd, and as they talk'd,
Smote him into the midriff with a stone,
That beat out life. *Milton's Par. Lost, b.* xi.

The stubborn only to destroy
These growing thoughts, my mother soon perceiving
By words at times cast forth, *inly* rejoic'd,
And said to me apart. *Milton's Par. Reg. b.* i.

The soldiers shout around with gen'rous rage;
He prais'd their ardor: *inly* pleas'd to see
His host. *Dryden's Knight's Tale.*

I'NMATE. *n. s.* [*in* and *mate.*]

Inmates are those that be admitted to dwell for their money jointly with another man, though in several rooms of his mansion-house, passing in and out by one door. *Cowell.*

So spake the enemy of mankind, inclos'd
In serpent, *inmate* bad! and toward Eve
Address'd his way. *Milton's Par. Lost, b.* ix.

There he dies, and leaves his race
Growing into a nation; and now grown,
Suspected to a sequent king, who seeks
To stop their overgrowth, as *inmate* guests
Too numerous. *Milton's Par. Lost, b.* xii.

Home is the sacred refuge of our life,
Secur'd from all approaches but a wife:
If thence we fly, the cause admits no doubt,
None but an *inmate* foe could force us out. *Dryden's Aur.*

I'NMOST. *adj.* [from *in.*] Deepest within; remotest from the surface.

'Tis you must dig with mattock and with spade,
And pierce the *inmost* centre of the earth. *Shakespeare.*

Rising sighs and falling tears,
That show too well the warm desires,
The silent, slow, consuming fires,
Which on my *inmost* vitals prey,
And melt my very soul away. *Addison on Italy.*

Comparing the quantity of light reflected from the several rings, I found that it was most copious from the first or *inmost*, and in the exterior rings became less and less. *Newton.*

He sends a dreadful groan: the rocks around
Through all their *inmost* hollow caves resound. *Pope.*

I got into the *inmost* court, and I applied my face to the windows. *Gulliver's Travels.*

INN. *n. s.* [inn, Saxon, a chamber.] A house of entertainment for travellers.

How all this is but a fair *inn*,
Of fairer guests which dwell within. *Sidney, b.* ii.

Palmer,

Palmer, quoth he, death is an equal doom
To good and bad, the common *inn* of reſt;
But, after death, the trial is to come,
When beſt ſhall be to them that lived beſt. *Fairy Queen.*
Now day is ſpent,
Therefore with me ye may take up your *inn*. *Fairy Queen.*
The Weſt, that glimmers with ſome ſtreaks of day,
Now ſpurs the lated traveller apace
To gain the timely *inn*. *Shakeſpeare's Macbeth.*
That very hour, and in the ſelf-ſame *inn*,
A poor mean woman was delivered. *Shakeſpeare.*
Like pilgrims to th' appointed place we tend;
The world's an *inn*, and death the journey's end. *Dryden.*

One may learn more here in one day, than in a year's rambling from one *inn* to another. *Locke.*

2. A houſe where ſtudents were boarded and taught: whence we ſtill call the colleges of common law *inns* of court.

Go ſome and pull down the Savoy; others to the *inns* of courts: down with them all. *Shakeſp. Henry* VI.

To INN. *v. n.* [from the noun.] To take up temporary lodging.

In thyſelf dwell;
Inn any where: continuance maketh hell. *Donne.*

To INN. *v. a.* To houſe; to put under cover.

He that ears my land, ſpares my team, and gives me leave to *inn* the crop. *Shakeſp. All's well that ends well.*

Howſoever the laws made in that parliament did bear good fruit, yet the ſubſidy bare a fruit that proved harſh and bitter: all was *inned* at laſt into the king's barn. *Bacon's Henry* VII.

Mow clover or rye-graſs, and make it fit to *inn*. *Mortimer.*

INNA'TE. } INNA'TED. } *adj* [*inné*, Fr. *innatus*, Latin.] Inborn; ingenerate; natural; not ſuperadded; not adſcititious. It is applied to things as well as perſons; but more properly to perſons.

The Druinian hath been cried up for an *innated* integrity, and accounted the uprighteſt dealer on earth. *Howel.*

With eloquence *innate* his tongue was arm'd;
Though harſh the precept, yet the people charm'd. *Dryden.*

Mutual gravitation, or ſpontaneous attraction, cannot poſſibly be *innate* and eſſential to matter. *Bentley's Serm.*

INNA'TENESS. *n. ſ.* [from *innate.*] The quality of being innate.

INNA'VIGABLE. *adj.* [*innavigabilis*, Latin.] Not to be paſſed by failing.

If you ſo hard a toil will undertake,
As twice to paſs th' *innavigable* lake,
Receive my counſel. *Dryden's Æn.*

I'NNER. *adj.* [from *in.*] Interiour; not outward.

But th' elfin knight with wonder all the way
Did feed his eyes, and fill'd his *inner* thought. *Fairy Queen.*
This attracts the ſoul,
Governs the *inner* man, the nobler part;
That other o'er the body only reigns. *Milton's Paradiſe Loſt.*

Many families are eſtabliſhed in the Weſt Indies, and ſome diſcovered in the *inner* parts of America. *Addiſon's Spectator.*

The kidney is a conglomerated gland, which is to be underſtood only of the outer part; for the *inner* part, whereof the papillæ are compoſed, is muſcular. *Grew's Coſmol.*

Thus, ſeiz'd with ſacred fear, the monarch pray'd;
Then to his *inner* court the gueſts convey'd. *Pope.*

INNE'RMOST. *adj.* [from *inner*. It ſeems leſs proper than *inmoſt.*] Remoteſt from the outward part.

The reflected beam of light would be ſo broad at the diſtance of ſix feet from the ſpeculum, where the rings appeared, as to obſcure one or two of the *innermoſt* rings. *Newton.*

INNHO'LDER. *n. ſ.* [*inn* and *hold.*] A man who keeps an inn; an innkeeper.

I'NNINGS. *n. ſ.* Lands recovered from the ſea. *Ainſworth.*

INNKE'EPER. *n. ſ.* [*inn* and *keeper.*] One who keeps lodgings and proviſions for the entertainment of travellers.

Clergymen muſt not keep a tavern, nor a judge be an *innkeeper*. *Taylor's Rule of holy living.*

A factious *innkeeper*, in the reign of Henry VII. was hanged, drawn, and quartered. *Addiſon's Freeholder.*

We were not ſo inquiſitive about the inn as the *innkeeper*; and provided our landlord's principles were ſound, did not take any notice of the ſtaleneſs of his proviſions. *Addiſon.*

I'NNOCENCE. } I'NNOCENCY. } *n. ſ.* [*innocence*, French; *innocentia*, Latin.]

1. Purity from injurious action; untainted integrity.

Simplicity and ſpotleſs *innocence*. *Milton.*

What comfort does overflow the devout ſoul, from a conſcience of its own *innocence* and integrity. *Tillotſon.*

2. Freedom from guilt imputed.

It will help me nothing
To plead mine *innocence*; for that dye is on me
Which makes my whit'ſt part black. *Shakeſ. Henry* VIII.
If truth and upright *innocency* fail me,
I'll to the king my maſter. *Shakeſ. H.* IV.

3. Harmleſſneſs; innoxiouſneſs.

The air was calm and ſerene; none of thoſe tumultuary motions and conflicts of vapours, which the mountains and the winds cauſe in ours: 'twas ſuited to a golden age, and to the firſt *innocency* of nature. *Burnet's Theory of the Earth.*

4. Simplicity of heart, perhaps with ſome degree of weakneſs.

I urge this childhood proof,
Becauſe what follows is pure *innocence*. *Shakeſpeare.*

I'NNOCENT. *adj.* [*innocent*, French; *innocens*, Latin.]

1. Pure from miſchief.

Something
You may deſerve of him through me and wiſdom,
To offer up a weak, poor, *innocent* lamb,
T' appeaſe an angry god. *Shakeſp. Macbeth.*
Wreck on *innocent* frail man his loſs. *Milton.*

2. Free from any particular guilt.

Good madam, keep yourſelf within yourſelf;
The man is *innocent*. *Shakeſ. Ant. and Cleopatra.*
The peaſant, *innocent* of all theſe ills,
With crooked ploughs the fertile fallows tills,
And the round year with daily labour fills. *Dryden.*

3. Unhurtful; harmleſs in effects.

The ſpear
Sung *innocent*, and ſpent its force in air. *Pope.*

I'NNOCENT. *n. ſ.*

1. One free from guilt or harm.

So pure an *innocent* as that ſame lamb. *Fairy Queen.*
Thou haſt kill'd the ſweeteſt *innocent*,
That e'er did lift up eye. *Shakeſp. Othello.*
If murth'ring *innocents* be executing,
Why, then thou art an executioner. *Shakeſ. Henry* VI.

2. A natural; an idiot.

Innocents are excluded by natural defects. *Hooker.*

I'NNOCENTLY. *adv.* [from *innocent.*]

1. Without guilt.

The humble and contented man pleaſes himſelf *innocently* and eaſily, while the ambitious man attempts to pleaſe others ſinfully and difficultly. *South's Sermons.*

2. With ſimplicity; with ſillineſs or imprudence.

3. Without hurt.

Balls at his feet fell *innocently* dead. *Cowley.*

INNO'CUOUS. *adj.* [*innocuus*, Latin.] Harmleſs in effects.

The moſt dangerous poiſons, ſkilfully managed, may be made not only *innocuous*, but of all other medicines the moſt effectual. *Grew's Coſmol.*

INNO'CUOUSLY. *adv.* [from *innocuous.*] Without miſchievous effects.

Whether quails, from any peculiarity of conſtitution, do *innocuouſly* feed upon hellebore, or rather ſometimes but medically uſe the ſame. *Brown's Vulgar Errours.*

INNO'CUOUSNESS. *n. ſ.* [from *innocuous.*] Harmleſſneſs.

The blow which ſhakes a wall, or beats it down, and kills men, hath a greater effect than that which penetrates into a mud wall, and doth little harm; for that *innocuouſneſs* of the effect makes, that, although in itſelf it be as great as the other, yet 'tis little obſerved. *Digby on Bodies.*

To I'NNOVATE. *v. a.* [*innover*, French; *innovo*, Latin.]

1. To bring in ſomething not known before.

Time indeed *innovateth* greatly, but quietly and by degrees. *Bacon.*

Men purſue ſome few principles which they have chanced upon, and care not to *innovate*, which draws unknown inconveniences. *Bacon.*

Former things
Are ſet aſide like abdicated kings;
And every moment alters what is done,
And *innovates* ſome act 'till then unknown. *Dryden.*

Every man cannot diſtinguiſh betwixt pedantry and poetry; every man therefore is not fit to *innovate*. *Dryden.*

2. To change by introducing novelties.

From his attempts upon the civil power he proceeds to *innovate* God's worſhip. *South's Sermons.*

INNOVA'TION. *n. ſ.* [*innovation*, French, from *innovate.*] Change by the introduction of novelty.

The love of things ancient doth argue ſtayedneſs; but levity and want of experience maketh apt unto *innovations*. *Hooker.*

It were good that men in *innovations* would follow the example of time itſelf, which indeed innovateth greatly, but quietly and by degrees. *Bacon's Eſſays.*

Great changes may be made in a government, yet the form continue; but large intervals of time muſt paſs between every ſuch *innovation*, enough to make it of a piece with the conſtitution. *Swift.*

INNOVA'TOR. *n. ſ.* [*innovateur*, French, from *innovate*.]

1. An introductor of novelties.

I attach thee as a traiterous *innovator*,
A foe to th' publick weal. *Shakeſ. Coriolanus.*

Every medicine is an innovation; and he that will not apply new remedies, muſt expect new evils; for time is the greateſt *innovator*: and if time of courſe alter things to the worſe, and wiſdom and counſel ſhall not alter them to the better, what ſhall be the end? *Bacon's Eſſays.*

2. One that makes changes by introducing novelties.

He counſels him to deteſt and perſecute all *innovators* of divine worſhip. *South's Sermons.*

INNO'XIOUS. *adj.* [*innoxius*, Latin.]

1. Free from miſchievous effects.

Innoxious flames are often ſeen on the hair of mens heads and horſes manes. *Digby.*

We may ſafely uſe purgatives, they being benign, and of *innoxious* qualities. *Brown's Vulg. Errours.*

Sent by the better genius of the night,
Innoxious gleaming on the horſe's mane,
The meteor ſits. *Thomſon's Autumn.*

2. Pure from crimes.

Stranger to civil and religious rage,
The good man walk'd *innoxious* through his age. *Pope.*

INNO'XIOUSLY. *adv.* [from *innoxious.*] Harmleſly.

Animals, that can *innoxiouſly* digeſt theſe poiſons, become antidotal to the poiſon digeſted. *Brown's Vulgar Err.*

INNO'XIOUSNESS. *n. ſ.* [from *innoxious.*] Harmleſſneſs.

INNUE'NDO. *n. ſ.* [*innuendo*, from *innuo*, Latin.] An oblique hint.

As if the commandments, that require obedience and forbid murder, were to be indicted for a libellous *innuendo* upon all the great men that come to be concerned. *L'Eſtrange.*

Mercury, though employed on a quite contrary errand, owns it a marriage by an *innuendo*. *Dryden.*

Purſue your trade of ſcandal-picking,
Your hints that Stella is no chicken;
Your *innuendo's*, when you tell us,
That Stella loves to talk with fellows. *Swift.*

INNU'MERABLE. *adj.* [*innumerable*, Fr. *innumerabilis*, Lat.] Not to be counted for multitude.

You have ſent *innumerable* ſubſtance
To furniſh Rome, and to prepare the ways
You have for dignities. *Shakeſpeare's Henry* VIII.

Cover me, ye pines,
Ye cedars! with *innumerable* boughs
Hide me where I may never ſee them more. *Milton.*

In lines, which appear of an equal length, one may be longer than the other by *innumerable* parts. *Locke.*

INNU'MERABLY. *adv.* [from *innumerable.*] Without number.

INNU'MEROUS. *adj.* [*innumerus*, Latin.] Too many to be counted.

'Twould be ſome ſolace yet, ſome little chearing,
In this cloſe dungeon of *innumerous* boughs. *Milton.*

I take the wood,
And in thick ſhelter of *innum'rous* boughs,
Enjoy the comfort gentle ſleep allows. *Pope's Odyſſey.*

To INO'CULATE. *v. a.* [*inoculo*, *in* and *oculus*, Latin.]

1. To propagate any plant by inſerting its bud into another ſtock; to practiſe inoculation. See INOCULATION.

Nor are the ways alike in all
How to ingraff, how to *inoculate*. *May's Virg. Georg.*

Now is the ſeaſon for the budding of the orange-tree: *inoculate* therefore at the commencement of this month. *Evelyn.*

But various are the ways to change the ſtate,
To plant, to bud, to graft, to *inoculate*. *Dryden.*

2. To yield a bud to another ſtock.

Virtue cannot ſo *inoculate* our old ſtock, but we ſhall reliſh of it. *Shakeſpeare's Hamlet.*

Thy ſtock is too much out of date,
For tender plants t' *inoculate*. *Cleaveland.*

Where lilies, in a lovely brown,
Inoculate carnation. *Cleaveland.*

INOCULA'TION. *n. ſ.* [*inoculatio*, Lat. from *inoculate.*]

1. *Inoculation* is practiſed upon all ſorts of ſtone-fruit, and upon oranges and jaſmines. In order to perform it, be provided with a ſharp pen-knife, having a flat haft, and ſome ſound baſs-mat. Having taken off the cuttings from the trees you would propagate, chuſe a ſmooth part of the ſtock; then with your knife make an horizontal cut croſs the rind of the ſtock, and from the middle of that cut make a ſlit downwards about two inches in length in the form of a T; but be careful not to cut too deep, leſt you wound the ſtock: then having cut off the leaf from the bud, leaving the foot-ſtalk remaining, make a croſs cut about half an inch below the eye, and with your knife ſlit off the bud, with part of the wood to it. This done, with your knife pull off that part of the wood which was taken with the bud, obſerving whether the eye of the bud be left to it or not; for all theſe buds which loſe their eyes in ſtripping are good for nothing: then raiſing the bark of the ſtock with the flat haft of your pen-knife clear to the wood, thruſt the bud therein, placing it ſmooth between the rind and the wood of the ſtock, cutting off any part of the rind belonging to the bud which may be too long; and ſo having exactly fitted the bud to the ſtock, tie them cloſely round with baſs-mat, beginning at the under part of the ſlit, and ſo proceed to the top, taking care not to bind round the eye of the bud. The March following cut off the ſtock three inches above the bud, ſloping it, that the wet may paſs off: to this part of the ſtock, above the bud, faſten the ſhoot which proceeds from the bud, and which would be in danger of being blown out; but this muſt continue no longer than one year, after which it muſt be cut off cloſe above the bud, that the ſtock may be covered thereby. *Miller.*

In the ſtem of Elaiana they all met, and came to be ingrafted all upon one ſtock, moſt of them by *inoculation*. *Howel.*

2. The practice of tranſplanting the ſmall-pox, by infuſion of the matter from ripened puſtules into the veins of the uninfected, in hopes of procuring a milder ſort than what frequently comes by infection. *Quincy.*

It is evident, by *inoculation*, that the ſmalleſt quantity of the matter, mixed with the blood, produceth the diſeaſe. *Arbuthn.*

INOCULA'TOR. *n. ſ.* [from *inoculate.*]

1. One that practiſes the inoculation of trees.

2. One who propagates the ſmall-pox by inoculation.

Had John a Gaddeſden been now living, he would have been at the head of the *inoculators*. *Friend's Hiſt. of Phyſick.*

INO'DORATE. *adj.* [*in* and *odoratus*, Lat.] Having no ſcent.

Whites are more *inodorate* than flowers of the ſame kind coloured. *Bacon's Natural Hiſtory.*

INO'DOROUS. *adj.* [*inodorus*, Latin.] Wanting ſcent; not affecting the noſe.

The white of an egg is a viſcuous, unactive, inſipid, *inodorous* liquor. *Arbuthnot on Aliments.*

INOFFE'NSIVE. *adj.* [*in* and *offenſive.*]

1. Giving no ſcandal: giving no provocation.

A ſtranger, *inoffenſive*, unprovoking. *Fleetwood.*

However *inoffenſive* we may be in other parts of our conduct, if we are found wanting in this trial of our love, we ſhall be diſowned by God as traitors. *Rogers's Sermons.*

2. Giving no pain; cauſing no terror.

Should infants have taken offence at any thing, diverting their thoughts, or mixing pleaſant and agreeable appearances with it, muſt be uſed, 'till it be grown *inoffenſive* to them. *Loc.*

3. Harmleſs; hurtleſs; innocent.

For drink the grape
She cruſhes, *inoffenſive* moſt. *Milton.*

With whate'er gall thou ſet'ſt thyſelf to write,
Thy *inoffenſive* ſatires never bite. *Dryden.*

Hark, how the cannon, *inoffenſive* now,
Gives ſigns of gratulation. *Phillips.*

4. Unembarraſſed; without ſtop or obſtruction. A Latin mode of ſpeech.

From hence a paſſage broad,
Smooth, eaſy, *inoffenſive*, down to hell. *Milton's Parad. Loſt.*

INOFFE'NSIVELY. *adv.* [from *inoffenſive.*] Without appearance of harm; without harm.

INOFFE'NSIVENESS. *n. ſ.* [from *inoffenſive.*] Harmleſſneſs; freedom from appearance of harm.

INOFFI'CIOUS. *adj.* [*in* and *officious.*] Not civil; not attentive to the accommodation of others.

INO'PINATE. *adj.* [*inopinatus*, Lat. *inopiné*, Fr.] Not expected.

INOPPORTU'NE. *adj.* [*inopportunus*, Latin.] Unſeaſonable; inconvenient.

INO'RDINACY. *n. ſ.* [from *inordinate.*] Irregularity; diſorder. It is ſafer to uſe *inordination.*

They become very ſinful by the exceſs, which were not ſo in their nature: that *inordinacy* ſets them in oppoſition to God's deſignation. *Government of the Tongue.*

INO'RDINATE. *adj.* [*in* and *ordinatus*, Latin.] Irregular; diſorderly; deviating from right.

Theſe people at firſt were wiſely brought to acknowledge allegiance to the kings of England; but being ſtraight left unto their own *inordinate* life, they forgot what before they were taught. *Spenſer on Ireland.*

Thence raiſe
At laſt diſtemper'd, diſcontented thoughts;
Vain hopes, vain arms, *inordinate* deſires,
Blown up with high conceits engend'ring pride. *Milton.*

From *inordinate* love and vain fear comes all unquietneſs of ſpirit. *Taylor's Guide to Devotion.*

INO'RDINATELY. *adv.* [from *inordinate.*] Irregularly; not rightly.

As ſoon as a man deſires any thing *inordinately*, he is preſently diſquieted in himſelf. *Taylor.*

INO'RDINATENESS. *n. ſ.* [from *inordinate.*] Want of regularity; intemperance of any kind.

INORDINA'TION. *n. ſ.* [from *inordinate.*] Irregularity; deviation from right.

Schoolmen and caſuiſts, having too much philoſophy to clear a lye from that intrinſick *inordination* and deviation from right reaſon, inherent in the nature of it, held that a lye was abſolutely and univerſally ſinful. *South's Sermons.*

INORGA'NICAL. *adj.* [*in* and *organical.*] Void of organs or inſtrumental parts.

We come to the loweſt and the moſt *inorganical* parts of matter. *Locke.*

To INO'SCULATE. *v. n.* [*in* and *oſculum*, Lat.] To unite by appoſition or contact.

This fifth conjugation of nerves is branched to the ball of the eye, and to the præcordia alſo in ſome meaſure, by *inoſculating* with one of its nerves. *Derham's Phyſico-Theology.*

INOSCULA'TION. *n. ſ.* [from *inoſculate.*] Union by conjunction of the extremities.

The almoſt infinite ramifications and *inoſculations* of all the ſeveral ſorts of veſſels may eaſily be detected by glaſſes. *Ray.*

I'NQUEST. *n. s.* [*enqueste*, French; *inquisitio*, Latin.]

1. Judicial enquiry or examination.

What confusion of face shall we be under, when that grand *inquest* begins; when an account of our opportunities of doing good, and a particular of our use or misuse of them is given in? *Atterbury's Sermons.*

2. [In law.] The *inquest* of jurors, or by jury, is the most usual trial of all causes, both civil and criminal, in our realm; for in civil causes, after proof is made on either side, so much as each part thinks good for himself, if the doubt be in the fact, it is referred to the discretion of twelve indifferent men, impanelled by the sheriff for the purpose, and as they bring in their verdict so judgment passes: for the judge saith, the jury finds the fact thus; then is the law thus, and so we judge. For the *inquest* in criminal causes, see JURY. *Cowel.*

3. Enquiry; search; study.

This is the laborious and vexatious *inquest* that the soul must make after science. *South's Sermons.*

INQUI'ETUDE. *n. s.* [*inquietude*, Fr. *inquietudo*, *inquietus*, Lat.] Disturbed state; want of quiet; attack on the quiet.

Having had such experience of his fidelity and observance abroad, he found himself engaged in honour to support him at home from any farther *inquietude*. *Wotton.*

Iron, that has stood long in a window, being thence taken, and by a cork balanced in water, where it may have a free mobility, will bewray a kind of *inquietude* and discontentment 'till it attain the former position. *Wotton.*

The youthful hero, with returning light,
Rose anxious from th' *inquietudes* of night. *Pope's Odyssey.*

To I'NQUINATE. *v. a.* [*inquino*, Latin.] To pollute; to corrupt.

An old opinion it was, that the ibis feeding upon serpents, that venomous food so *inquinated* their oval conceptions, that they sometimes came forth in serpentine shapes. *Brown.*

INQUINA'TION. *n. s.* [*inquinatio*, Lat. from *inquinate.*] Corruption; pollution.

Their causes and axioms are so full of imagination, and so infected with the old received theories, as they are mere *inquinations* of experience, and concoct it not. *Bacon.*

The middle action, which produceth such imperfect bodies, is fitly called by some of the ancients *inquination*, or inconcoction, which is a kind of putrefaction. *Bacon's Nat. Hist.*

INQU'IRABLE. *adj.* [from *inquire.*] That of which inquisition or inquest may be made.

To INQUI'RE. *v. n.* [*enquirer*, French; *inquiro*, Latin.]

1. To ask questions; to make search; to exert curiosity on any occasion.

You have oft *inquir'd*
After the shepherd that complain'd of love. *Shakespeare.*

We will call the damsel, and *inquire* at her mouth. *Gen.*

They began to *inquire* among themselves, which of them it was that should do this thing. *Lu.* xxii. 23.

Inquire for one Saul of Tarsus. *Acts* ix. 11.

You sent Hadoram to king David, to *inquire* of his welfare. *Chron.* xviii. 10.

It is a subject of a very noble inquiry, to *inquire* of the more subtile perceptions; for it is another key to open nature, as well as the house. *Bacon's Nat. Hist.*

It may deserve our best skill to *inquire* into those rules, by which we may guide our judgment. *South's Sermons.*

The step-dame poison for the son prepares;
The son *inquires* into his father's years. *Dryden.*

Under their grateful shade Æneas sat;
His left young Pallas kept, fix'd to his side,
And oft of winds *inquir'd*, and of the tide. *Dryd. Æn.*

They are more in danger to go out of the way, who are marching under a guide that will mislead them, than he that is likelier to be prevailed on to *inquire* after the right way. *Locke.*

To those who *inquired* about me, my lover would answer, that I was an old dependent upon his family. *Swift.*

2. To make examination.

Awful Rhadamanthus rules the state:
He hears and judges each committed crime,
Enquires into the manner, place, and time. *Dryden's Æn.*

To INQUI'RE. *v. a.*

1. To ask about; to seek out: as, he *inquired* the way.

2. To call; to name. Obsolete.

Canute had his portion from the rest,
The which he call'd Canutium, for his hire,
Now Cantium, which Kent we commonly *inquire.* *F. Qu.*

INQUI'RER. *n. s.* [from *inquire.*]

1. Searcher; examiner; one curious and inquisitive.

What satisfaction may be obtained from those violent disputers, and eager *inquirers* in what day of the month the world began? *Brown's Vulgar Errours.*

What's good doth open to th' *inquirers* stand,
And itself offers to th' accepting hand. *Denham.*

Superficial *inquirers* may satisfy themselves that the parts of matter are united by muscles, nerves, and other like ligaments. *Glanv. Sceps.*

This is a question only of *inquirers*, not disputers, who neither affirm nor deny, but examine. *Locke.*

Late *inquirers* by their glasses find,
That ev'ry insect of each different kind,
In its own egg, chear'd by the solar rays,
Organs involv'd and latent life displays. *Blackmore.*

2. One who interrogates; one who questions.

INQUI'RY. *n. s.* [from *inquire.*]

1. Interrogation; search by question.

The men which were sent from Cornelius had made *inquiry* for Simon's house, and stood before the gate. *Acts* x. 17.

2. Examination; search.

This exactness is absolutely necessary in *inquiries* after philosophical knowledge, and in controversies about truth. *Locke.*

As to the *inquiry* about liberty, I think the question is not proper, whether the will be free, but whether a man be free. *Locke.*

I have been engaged in physical *inquiries.* *Locke.*

It is a real *inquiry*, concerning the nature of a bird, or a bat, to make their yet imperfect ideas of it more complete. *Locke.*

Judgment or opinion, in a remoter sense, may be called invention: as when a judge or a physician makes an exact *inquiry* into any cause. *Grew's Cosmol. Sac.*

INQUISI'TION. *n. s.* [*inquisition*, Fr. *inquisitio*, Latin.]

1. Judicial inquiry.

When he maketh *inquisition* for blood, he remembereth them: he forgetteth not the cry of the humble. *Ps.* ix. 12.

We were willing to make a pattern or precedent of an exact *inquisition.* *Bacon's Natural History.*

With much severity, and strict *inquisition*, were punished the adherents and aiders of the late rebels. *Bacon's Hen.* VII.

Though it may be impossible to recollect every failing, yet you are so far to exercise an *inquisition* upon yourself, as, by observing lesser particulars, you may the better discover what the corruption of your nature sways you to. *Taylor.*

By your good leave,
These men will be your judges: we must stand
The *inquisition* of their raillery
On our condition. *Southern.*

2. Examination; discussion.

When *inquisition* was made of the matter, it was found out. 2 *Esth.* xxiii.

3. [In law.] A manner of proceeding in matters criminal, by the office of the judge. *Cowel.*

4. The court established in some countries subject to the pope for the detection of heresy.

One kiss of her's, and but eighteen words,
Put quite down the Spanish *inquisition.* *Corbet.*

INQUI'SITIVE. *adj.* [*inquisitus*, Latin.] Curious; busy in search; active to pry into any thing. With *about*, *after*, *into*, or *of*, and sometimes *into.*

My boy at eighteen years became *inquisitive*
After his brother. *Shakespeare's Comedy of Errours.*

This idleness, together with fear of imminent mischiefs, have been the cause that the Irish were ever the most *inquisitive* people *after* news of any nation in the world. *Davies.*

He is not *inquisitive into* the reasonableness of indifferent and innocent commands. *Taylor's Rule of living holy.*

It can be no duty to write his heart upon his forehead, and to give all the *inquisitive* and malicious world a survey of those thoughts, which is the prerogative of God only to know. *South.*

His old shaking sire,
Inquisitive of fights, still longs in vain
To find him in the number of the slain. *Dryden's Juv.*

Thou, what befits the new lord-mayor,
And what the Gallick arms will do,
Art anxiously *inquisitive* to know. *Dryden.*

A Dutch ambassador, entertaining the king of Siam with the particularities of Holland, which he was *inquisitive* after, told him that the water would, in cold weather, be so hard that men walked upon it. *Locke.*

The whole neighbourhood grew *inquisitive* after my name and character. *Addison's Spectator.*

A wise man is not *inquisitive about* things impertinent. *Broome's Notes on the Odyssey.*

They cannot bear with the impertinent questions of a young *inquisitive* and sprightly genius. *Watts's Improv. of the Mind.*

INQUI'SITIVELY. *adv.* [from *inquisitive.*] With curiosity; with narrow scrutiny.

INQUI'SITIVENESS. *n. s.* [from *inquisitive.*] Curiosity; diligence to pry into things hidden.

Though he thought *inquisitiveness* an uncomely guest, he could not but ask who she was. *Sidney.*

Heights that scorn our prospect, and depths in which reason will never touch the bottom, yet surely the pleasure arising from thence is great and noble; for as much as they afford perpetual matter to the *inquisitiveness* of human reason, and so are large enough for it to take its full scopes and range in. *South.*

Providence, delivering great conclusions to us, designed to excite our curiosity and *inquisitiveness* after the methods by which things were brought to pass. *Burnet.*

Curiosity in children nature has provided, to remove that ignorance they were born with; which, without this busy *inquisitiveness*, will make them dull. *Locke.*

INQUI'SITOR. *n. s.* [*inquisitor*, Latin; *inquisiteur*, French.]

1. One who examines judicially.

In these particulars I have played myself the *inquisitor*, and find nothing contrary to religion or manners, but rather medicinable. *Bacon's Essays.*

Minos, the strict *inquisitor*, appears,
And lives and crimes with his assessors hears. *Dryden.*

2. An officer in the popish courts of inquisition.

To INRA'IL. *v. a.* [*in* and *rail.*] To inclose with rails.

In things indifferent, what the whole church doth think convenient for the whole, the same if any part do wilfully violate, it may be reformed and *inrailed* again, by that general authority whereunto each particular is subject. *Hooker.*

Where fam'd St. Giles's ancient limits spread,
An *inrail'd* column rears its lofty head;
Here to sev'n streets sev'n dials count the day,
And from each other catch the circling ray. *Gay.*

I'NROAD. *n. s.* [*in* and *road.*] Incursion; sudden and desultory invasion.

Many hot *inroads*
They make in Italy. *Shakesp. Ant. and Cleopatra.*

From Scotland we have had in former times some alarms, and *inroads* into the northern parts of this kingdom. *Bacon.*

By proof we feel
Our pow'r sufficient to disturb his heav'n,
And with perpetual *inroads* to alarm,
Though inaccessible his fatal throne. *Milton's Paradise Lost.*

The loss of Shrewsbury exposed all North Wales to the daily *inroads* of the enemy. *Clarendon.*

The country open lay without defence;
For poets frequent *inroads* there had made. *Dryden.*

INSA'NABLE. *adj.* [*insanabilis*, Latin.] Incurable; irremediable.

INSA'NE. *adj.* [*insanus*, Latin.] Mad; making mad.

Were such things here as we do speak about?
Or have we eaten of the *insane* root,
That takes the reason prisoner? *Shakes. Macbeth.*

INSA'TIABLE. *adj.* [*insatiabilis*, Latin; *insatiable*, French.] Greedy beyond measure; greedy so as not to be satisfied.

INSA'TIABLENESS. *n. s.* [from *insatiable.*] Greediness not to be appeased.

Some mens hydropick *insatiableness* had learned to thirst the more, by how much more they drank. *King Charles.*

INSA'TIABLY. *adv.* [from *insatiable.*] With greediness not to be appeased.

They were extremely ambitious, and *insatiably* covetous; and therefore no impression, from argument or miracles, could reach them. *South.*

INSA'TIATE. *adj.* [*insatiatus*, Latin.] Greedy so as not to be satisfied.

When my mother went with child
Of that *insatiate* Edward, noble York,
My princely father, then had wars in France. *Shak. R. III.*

Insatiate to pursue
Vain war with heav'n. *Milton.*

Too oft has pride,
And hellish discord, and *insatiate* thirst
Of others rights, our quiet discompos'd. *Phillips.*

INSATISFA'CTION. *n. s.* [*in* and *satisfaction.*] Want; unsatisfied state.

It is a profound contemplation in nature, to consider of the emptiness or *insatisfaction* of several bodies, and of their appetite to take in others. *Bacon's Natural History.*

INSA'TURABLE. *adj.* [*insaturabilis*, Lat.] Not to be glutted; not to be filled.

To INSCRI'BE. *v. a.* [*inscribo*, Latin; *inscrire*, French.]

1. To write on any thing. It is generally applied to something written on a monument, or on the outside of something.

In all you writ to Rome, or else
To foreign princes, *ego & rex meus*
Was still *inscrib'd.* *Shakespeare's Henry VIII.*

Connatural principles are in themselves highly reasonable, and deducible by a strong process of ratiocination to be most true; and consequently the high exercise of ratiocination might evince their truth, though there were no such originally *inscribed* in the mind. *Hale's Origin of Mankind.*

Ye weeping loves! the stream with myrtles hide,
And with your golden darts, now useless grown,
Inscribe a verse on this relenting stone. *Pope.*

2. To mark any thing with writing: as, I *inscribed* the stone with my name.

3. To assign to a patron without a formal dedication.

One ode, which pleased me in the reading, I have attempted to translate in Pindarick verse: 'tis that which is *inscribed* to the present earl of Rochester. *Dryden.*

4. To draw a figure within another.

In the circle *inscribe* a square. *Notes to Creech's Manilius.*

INSCRI'PTION. *n. s.* [*inscription*, Fr. *inscriptio*, Latin.]

1. Something written or engraved.

This avarice of praise in time to come,
Those long *inscriptions* crowded on the tomb. *Dryden.*

2. Title.

Joubertus by the same title led our expectation, whereby we reaped no advantage, it answering scarce at all the promise of the *inscription.* *Brown's Vulgar Errours.*

3. [In law.] Is an obligation made in writing, whereby the accuser binds himself to undergo the same punishment, if he shall not prove the crime which he objects to the party accused in his accusatory libel, as the defendant himself ought to suffer, if the same be proved. *Ayliffe's Parergon.*

4. Consignment of a book to a patron without a formal dedication.

INSCRU'TABLE. *adj.* [*inscrutabilis*, Lat. *inscrutable*, Fr.] Unsearchable; not to be traced out by inquiry or study.

A jest unseen, *inscrutable*, invisible,
As a weather-cock on a steeple. *Shak. Two Gent. of Verona.*

This king had a large heart, *inscrutable* for good, and was wholly bent to make his kingdom and people happy. *Bacon.*

O how *inscrutable!* his equity
Twins with his power. *Sandys.*

Hereunto they have recourse as unto the oracle of life, the great determinator of virginity, conception, fertility, and the *inscrutable* infirmities of the whole body. *Brown's Vulg. Erro.*

We should contemplate reverently the works of nature and grace, the *inscrutable* ways of providence, and all the wonderful methods of God's dealing with men. *Atterbury.*

To INSCU'LP. *v. a.* [*insculpo*, Latin.] To engrave; to cut.

A coin that bears the figure of an angel
Stamp'd in gold, but that *insculpt* upon. *Shakespeare.*

INSCU'LPTURE. *n. s.* [from *in* and *sculpture.*] Any thing engraved.

Timon is dead,
Entomb'd upon the very hem o' th' sea;
And on the grave-stone this *insculpture*, which
With wax I brought away. *Shakesp. Timon.*

It was usual to wear rings on either hand; but when precious gems and rich *insculptures* were added, the custom of wearing them was translated unto the left. *Brown.*

To INSE'AM. *v. a.* [*in* and *seam.*] To impress or mark by a seam or cicatrix.

Deep o'er his knee *inseam'd* remain'd the scar. *Pope.*

INSECT. *n. s.* [*insecta*, Latin.]

1. *Insects* may be considered together as one great tribe of animals: they are called *insects* from a separation in the middle of their bodies, whereby they are cut into two parts, which are joined together by a small ligature, as we see in wasps and common flies. *Locke.*

Beast, bird, *insect*, or worm, durst enter none. *Milton.*

2. Any thing small or contemptible.

In ancient times the sacred plough employ'd
The kings, and awful fathers of mankind;
And some with whom compar'd, your *insect* tribes
Are but the beings of a Summer's day,
Have held the scale of empire. *Thomson's Spring.*

INSECTA'TOR. *n. s.* [from *insector*, Latin.] One that persecutes or harasses with pursuit. *Dict.*

INSE'CTILE. *adj.* [from *insect.*] Having the nature of insects.

Insectile animals, for want of blood, run all out into legs. *Bac.*

INSECTO'LOGER. *n. s.* [*insect* and λογος.] One who studies or describes insects.

The insect itself is, according to modern *insectologers*, of the ichneumon-fly kind. *Derham's Physico-Theology.*

INSE'CURE. *adj.* [*in* and *secure.*]

1. Not secure; not confident of safety.

He is liable to a great many inconveniences every moment of his life, and is continually *insecure* not only of the good things of this life, but even of life itself. *Tillotson's Serm.*

2. Not safe.

INSECU'RITY. *n. s.* [*in* and *security.*]

1. Uncertainty; want of reasonable confidence.

It may be easily perceived with what *insecurity* of truth we ascribe effects, depending upon the natural period of time, unto arbitrary calculations, and such as vary at pleasure. *Brown.*

2. Want of safety; danger; hazard.

The unreasonableness and presumption, the danger and desperate *insecurity* of those that have not so much as a thought, all their lives long, to advance so far as attrition and contrition, sorrow, and resolution of amendment. *Hammond.*

INSEMINA'TION. *n. s.* [*insemination*, Fr. *insemino*, Lat.] The act of scattering seed on ground.

INSECU'TION. *n. s.* [*insecution*, Fr. *insecutio*, Lat.] Pursuit. Not in use.

Not the king's own horse got more before the wheel
Of his rich chariot, that might still the *insecution* feel,
With the extreme hairs of his tail. *Chapman's Iliads.*

INSE'NSATE. *adj.* [*insense*, French; *insensato*, Italian.] Stupid; wanting thought; wanting sensibility.

Ye be reprobates; obdurate *insensate* creatures. *Hammond.*

So fond are mortal men,
As their own ruin on themselves t' invite,
Insensate left, or to sense reprobate,
And with blindness internal struck. *Milton's Agonistes.*

INSENSIBI'LITY. *n. s.* [*insensibilité*, French, from *insensible.*]

1. Inability to perceive.

Insensibility of slow motions may be thus accounted for: motion cannot be perceived without perception of the parts of space which it left, and those which it next acquires. *Glanv.*

2. Stupidity; dulness of mental perception.

3. Torpor; dulness of corporal sense.

INSE'NSIBLE. *adj.* [*insensible*, French.]

1. Imperceptible; not discoverable by the senses.

What is honour? a word. What is that word honour? air; a trim reckoning. Who hath it? he that died a Wednesday. Doth he feel it? no. Doth he hear it? no. Is it *insensible* then? yea, to the dead: but will it not live with the living? no. Why? detraction will not suffer it. *Shakesp.*

Two small and almost *insensible* pricks were found upon Cleopatra's arm. *Brown's Vulgar Errours.*

The dense and bright light of the circle will obscure the rare and weak light of these dark colours round about it, and render them almost *insensible*. *Newton's Opt.*

2. Slowly gradual.

They fall away,
And languish with *insensible* decay. *Dryden.*

3. Void of feeling either mental or corporal.

I thought
I then was passing to my former state
Insensible, and forthwith to dissolve. *Milton.*

4. Void of emotion or affection.

You grow *insensible* to the conveniency of riches, the delights of honour and praise. *Temple.*

You render mankind *insensible* to their beauties, and have destroyed the empire of love. *Dryden.*

INSE'NSIBLENESS. *n. s.* [from *insensible.*] Absence of perception; inability to perceive.

The *insensibleness* of the pain proceeds rather from the relaxation of the nerves than their obstruction. *Ray.*

INSE'NSIBLY. *adv.* [from *insensible.*]

1. Imperceptibly; in such a manner as is not discovered by the senses.

The planet earth, so stedfast though she seem,
Insensibly three different motions moves. *Milt. Par. Lost.*

The hills rise *insensibly*, and leave the eye a vast uninterrupted prospect. *Addison on Italy.*

2. By slow degrees.

Equal they were form'd,
Save what sin hath impair'd, which yet hath wrought
Insensibly. *Milton.*

Proposals agreeable to our passions will *insensibly* prevail upon our weakness. *Rogers's Sermons.*

Cadenus
Insensibly came on her side. *Swift.*

3. Without mental or corporal sense.

INSEPARABI'LITY. } *n. s.* [from *inseparable.*] The quality of
INSE'PARABLENESS. } being such as cannot be severed or divided.

The parts of pure space are immovable, which follows from their *inseparability*, motion being nothing but change of distance between any two things; but this cannot be between parts that are inseparable. *Locke.*

INSE'PARABLE. *adj.* [*inseparable*, French; *inseparabilis*, Latin.] Not to be disjoined; united so as not to be parted.

Ancient times figure both the incorporation and *inseparable* conjunction of counsel with kings, and the wise and politick use of counsel by kings. *Bacon.*

Thou, my shade,
Inseparable, must with me along;
For death from sin no pow'r can separate. *Milt. Par. Lost.*

Care and toil came into the world with sin, and remain ever since *inseparable* from it. *South's Sermons.*

No body feels pain, that he wishes not to be eased of, with a desire equal to that pain, and *inseparable* from it. *Locke.*

The parts of pure space are *inseparable* one from the other, so that the continuity cannot be separated, neither really nor mentally. *Locke.*

Together out they fly,
Inseparable now the truth and lie;
And this or that unmixt no mortal ear shall find. *Pope.*

INSE'PARABLY. *adv.* [from *inseparable.*] With indissoluble union.

Drowning of metals is, when the baser metal is so incorporate with the more rich as it cannot be separated; as if silver should be *inseparably* incorporated with gold. *Bacon.*

Him thou shalt enjoy,
Inseparably thine. *Milton.*

Atheists must confess, that before that assigned period matter had existed eternally, *inseparably* endued with this principle of attraction; and yet had never attracted nor convened before, during that infinite duration. *Bentley's Sermons.*

To INSE'RT. *v. a.* [*inserer*, Fr. *insero*, *insertum*, Latin.] To place in or amongst other things.

Those words were very weakly *inserted*, where they are so liable to misconstruction. *Stillingfleet.*

With the worthy gentleman's name I will *insert* it at length in one of my papers. *Addison.*

It is the editor's interest to *insert* what the author's judgment had rejected. *Swift.*

Poesy and oratory omit things essential, and *insert* little beautiful digressions, in order to place every thing in the most affecting light. *Watts.*

INSE'RTION. *n. s.* [*insertion*, Fr. *insertio*, Latin.]

1. The act of placing any thing in or among other matter.

The great disadvantage our historians labour under is too tedious an interruption, by the *insertion* of records in their narration. *Felton on the Classicks.*

An ileus, commonly called the twisting of the guts, is either a circumvolution or *insertion* of one part of the gut within the other. *Arbuthnot on Diet.*

2. The thing inserted.

He softens the relation by such *insertions*, before he describes the event. *Broome's Notes on the Odyssey.*

To INSE'RVE. *v. a.* [*inservio*, Latin.] To be of use to an end.

INSE'RVIENT. *adj.* [*inserviens*, Latin.] Conducive; of use to an end.

The providence of God, which disposeth of no part in vain, where there is no digestion to be made, makes not any parts *inservient* to that intention. *Brown.*

To INSHE'LL. *v. a.* [*in* and *shell.*] To hide in a shell.

Aufidius, hearing of our Marcius' banishment,
Thrusts forth his horns again into the world,
Which were *inshell'd* when Marcius stood for Rome,
And durst not once peep out. *Shakesp. Coriolanus.*

To INSHI'P. *v. a.* [*in* and *ship.*] To shut in a ship; to stow; to embark.

See them safely brought to Dover; where, *inshipp'd*,
Commit them to the fortune of the sea. *Shakes. Hen. VI.*

To INSHRI'NE. *v. a.* [*in* and *shrine.*] To inclose in a shrine or precious case.

Warlike and martial Talbot, Burgundy
Inshrines thee in his heart. *Shakespeare's Henry VI.*

Not Babylon,
Equal'd in all its glories, to *inshrine* Belus. *Milton.*

I'NSIDE. *n. s.* [*in* and *side.*] Interiour part; part within. Opposed to the surface or *outside*.

Look'd he o' th' *inside* of the paper?
He did unseal them. *Shakespeare's Henry VIII.*

Shew the *inside* of your purse to the outside of his hand, and no more ado. *Shakespeare's Winter's Tale.*

Here are the outsides of the one, the *insides* of the other, and there's the moiety I promised ye. *L'Estrange.*

As for the *inside* of their nest, none but themselves were concerned in it. *Addison's Guardian.*

INSIDIA'TOR. *n. s.* [Lat.] One who lies in wait. *Dict.*

INSI'DIOUS. *adj.* [*insidieux*, French; *insidiosus*, Latin.] Sly; circumventive; diligent to entrap; treacherous.

Since men mark all our steps, and watch our haltings, let a sense of their *insidious* vigilance excite us so to behave ourselves, that they may find a conviction of the mighty power of Christianity towards regulating the passions. *Atterbury's Sermons.*

They wing their course,
And dart on distant coasts, if some sharp rock,
Or shoal *insidious*, breaks not their career. *Thomson.*

INSI'DIOUSLY. *adv.* [from *insidious.*] In a sly and treacherous manner; with malicious artifice.

The castle of Cadmus was taken, and the city of Thebes itself invested by Phebidas the Lacedemonian, *insidiously* and in violation of league. *Bacon's War with Spain.*

Simeon and Levi spoke not only falsely but *insidiously*, nay hypocritically, abusing their proselytes and their religion, for the effecting their cruel designs. *Government of the Tongue.*

I'NSIGHT. *n. s.* [*insicht*, Dutch. This word had formerly the accent on the first syllable.] Inspection; deep view; knowledge of the interiour parts; thorough skill in any thing.

Hardy shepherd, such as thy merits, such may be her *insight*
Justly to grant thee reward. *Sidney.*

Straightway sent with careful diligence
To fetch a leech, the which had great *insight*
In that disease of grieved conscience,
And well could cure the same; his name was patience. *Spens.*

Now will be the right season of forming them to be able writers, when they shall be thus fraught with an universal *insight* into things. *Milton.*

The use of a little *insight* in those parts of knowledge, which are not a man's proper business, is to accustom our minds to all sorts of ideas. *Locke.*

A garden gives us a great *insight* into the contrivance and wisdom of providence, and suggests innumerable subjects of meditation. *Spectator.*

Due consideration, and a deeper *insight* into things, would soon have made them sensible of their error. *Woodward.*

INSIGNIFI'CANCE. } *n. s.* [*insignificance*, French; from *insigni-*
INSIGNIFI'CANCY. } *ficant.*]

1. Want of meaning; unmeaning terms.

To give an account of all the *insignificancies* and verbal nothings of this philosophy, would be almost to transcribe it. *Glanv. Sceps. c.* 18.

2. Unimportance.

2. Unimportance.

As I was ruminating on that I had seen, I could not forbear reflecting on the *insignificancy* of human art, when set in comparison with the designs of providence. *Addison's Guardian.*

My annals are in mouldy mildews wrought,
With easy *insignificance* of thought. *Garth.*

INSIGNI'FICANT. *adj.* [*in* and *significant.*]

1. Wanting meaning; void of signification.

'Till you can weight and gravity explain,
Those words are *insignificant* and vain. *Blackmore.*

2. Unimportant; wanting weight; ineffectual.

That I might not be vapoured down by *insignificant* testimonies, I presumed to use the great name of your society to annihilate all such arguments. *Glanv. Sceps. Preface.*

Calumny robs the publick of all that benefit that it may justly claim from the worth and virtue of particular persons, by rendering their virtue utterly *insignificant.* *South's Sermons.*

All the arguments to a good life will be very *insignificant* to a man that hath a mind to be wicked, when remission of sins may be had upon such cheap terms. *Tillotson's Sermons.*

Nothing can be more contemptible and *insignificant* than the scum of a people, instigated against a king. *Addison.*

In a hemorrhage from the lungs, no remedy so proper as bleeding, often repeated: stypticks are often *insignificant.* *Arb.*

INSIGNI'FICANTLY. *adv.* [from *insignificant.*]

1. Without meaning.

Birds are taught to use articulate words, yet they understand not their import, but use them *insignificantly,* as the organ or pipe renders the tune, which it understands not. *Hale.*

2. Without importance or effect.

INSINCE'RE. *adj.* [*insincerus,* Lat. *in* and *sincere.*]

1. Not what he appears; not hearty; dissembling; unfaithful.

2. Not sound; corrupted.

Ah why, Penelope, this causeless fear,
To render sleep's soft blessings *insincere?*
Alike devote to sorrow's dire extreme,
The day reflection, and the midnight dream. *Pope.*

INSINCE'RITY. *n. s.* [from *insincere.*] Dissimulation; want of truth or fidelity.

If men should always act under a mask, and in disguise, that indeed betrays design and *insincerity.* *Broome's Notes on the Odyss.*

To INSI'NEW. *v. a.* [*in* and *sinew.*] To strengthen; to confirm.

All members of our cause,
That are *insinewed* to this action. *Shakesp. H. IV.*

INSI'NUANT. *adj.* [French.] Having the power to gain favour.

Men not so quick perhaps of conceit as slow to passions, and commonly less inventive than judicious, howsoever prove very plausible, *insinuant,* and fortunate men. *Wotton.*

To INSI'NUATE. *v. a.* [*insinuer,* Fr. *insinuo,* Latin.]

1. To introduce any thing gently.

The water easily *insinuates* itself into and placidly distends the vessels of vegetables. *Woodward.*

2. To push gently into favour or regard: commonly with the reciprocal pronoun.

There is no particular evil which hath not some appearance of goodness, whereby to *insinuate* itself. *Hooker.*

At the isle of Rhee he *insinuated* himself into the very good grace of the duke of Buckingham. *Clarendon.*

3. To hint; to impart indirectly.

And all the fictions bards pursue
Do but *insinuate* what's true. *Swift.*

4. To instill; to infuse gently.

All the art of rhetorick, besides order and clearness, are for nothing else but to *insinuate* wrong ideas, move the passions, and thereby mislead the judgment. *Locke.*

To INSI'NUATE. *v. n.*

1. To wheedle; to gain on the affections by gentle degrees.

I love no colours; and without all colour
Of base *insinuating* flattery,
I pluck this white rose with Plantagenet. *Shakes. H. VI.*

2. To steal into imperceptibly; to be conveyed insensibly.

Pestilential miasms *insinuate* into the humoral and consistent parts of the body. *Harvey.*

3. I know not whether *Milton* does not use this word, according to its etymology, for, to enfold; to wreath; to wind.

Close the serpent sly
Insinuating, of his fatal guile
Gave proof unheeded. *Milton.*

INSINUA'TION. *n. s.* [*insinuatio,* Lat. *insinuation,* Fr. from *insinuate.*] The power of pleasing or stealing upon the affections.

When the industry of one man hath settled the work, a new man, by *insinuation* or misinformation, may not supplant him without a just cause. *Bacon.*

He had a natural *insinuation* and address, which made him acceptable in the best company. *Clarendon.*

INSI'NUATIVE. *adj.* [from *insinuate.*] Stealing on the affections.

It is a strange *insinuative* power which example and custom have upon us. *Government of the Tongue.*

INSI'NUATOR. *n. s.* [*insinuator,* Lat.] He that insinuates. *Ains.*

INSIPID. *adj.* [*insipider,* French; *insipidus,* Latin.]

1. Without taste; without power of affecting the organs of gust.

Some earths yield, by distillation, a liquor very far from being inodorous or *insipid.* *Boyle.*

This chyle is the natural and alimentary pituita, which the ancients described as *insipid.* *Floyer on the Humours.*

She lays some useful bile aside,
To tinge the chyle's *insipid* tide. *Prior.*

2. Without spirit; without pathos; flat; dull; heavy.

The gods have made your noble mind for me,
And her *insipid* soul for Ptolemy;
A heavy lump of earth without desire,
A heap of ashes that o'er-lays your fire. *Dryd. Cleom.*

Some short excursions of a broken vow
He made indeed, but flat *insipid* stuff. *Dryd. Don Sebast.*

INSIPI'DITY. } *n. s.* [*insipidité,* Fr. from *insipid.*]
INSI'PIDNESS. }

1. Want of taste.

2. Want of life or spirit.

Dryden's lines shine strongly through the *insipidity* of Tate's. *Pope.*

INSI'PIDLY. *adv.* [from *insipid.*] Without taste; dully.

One great reason why many children abandon themselves wholly to silly sports, and trifle away all their time *insipidly,* is because they have found their curiosity baulked. *Locke.*

INSI'PIENCE. *n. s.* [*insipientia,* Latin.] Folly; want of understanding.

To INSI'ST. *v. n.* [*insister,* French; *insisto,* Latin.]

1. To stand or rest upon.

The combs being double, the cells on each side the partition are so ordered, that the angles on one side *insist* upon the centers of the bottom of the cells on the other side. *Ray.*

2. Not to recede from terms or assertions; to persist in.

Upon such large terms, and so absolute,
As our conditions shall *insist* upon,
Our peace shall stand as firm as rocky mountains. *Shakesp.*

3. To dwell upon in discourse.

Were there no other act of hostility but that which we have hitherto *insisted* on, the intercepting of her supplies were irreparably injurious to her. *Decay of Piety.*

INSI'STENT. *adj.* [*insistens,* Latin.] Resting upon any thing.

The breadth of the substruction must be at least double to the *insistent* wall. *Wotton.*

INSITIENCY. *n. s.* [*in* and *sitio,* Latin.] Exemption from thirst.

What is more admirable than the fitness of every creature, for the use we make of him? The docility of an elephant, and the *insitiency* of a camel for travelling in desarts. *Grew.*

INSI'TION. *n. s.* [*insitio,* Latin.] The insertion or ingraffment of one branch into another.

Without the use of these we could have nothing of culture or civility: no tillage or agriculture, no pruning or lopping, grafting or *insition.* *Ray on the Creation.*

INSI'STURE. *n. s.* [from *insist.*] This word seems in *Shakespeare* to signify constancy or regularity.

The heav'ns themselves, the planets, and the centre,
Observe degree, priority, and place,
Insisture, course, proportion, season, form,
Office and custom, in all line of order. *Shakespeare.*

To INSNA'RE. *v. a.* [*in* and *snare.*]

1. To intrap; to catch in a trap, gin, or snare; to inveigle.

Why strewst thou sugar on that bottled spider,
Whose deadly web *insnareth* thee about. *Shakesp. R. III.*

She *insnar'd*
Mankind with her fair looks. *Milton.*

By long experience Durfey may no doubt
Insnare a gudgeon, or perhaps a trout;
Though Dryden once exclaim'd in partial spite;
He fish'd!—because the man attempts to write. *Fenton.*

2. To intangle in difficulties or perplexities.

That which in a great part, in the weightiest causes belonging to this present controversy, hath *insnared* the judgments both of sundry good and of some well learned men, is the manifest truth of certain general principles, whereupon the ordinances that serve for usual practice in the church of God are grounded. *Hooker.*

That the hypocrite reign not, lest the people be *insnared.* *Job* xxxiv. 30.

INSNA'RER. *n. s.* [from *insnare.*] He that insnares.

INSO'CIABLE. *adj.* [*insociable,* French; *insociabilis,* Latin.]

1. Averse from conversation.

If this austere *insociable* life,
Change not your offer made in heat of blood. *Shakesp.*

2. Incapable of connexion or union.

The lowest ledge or row must be merely of stone, closely laid, without mortar, which is a general caution for all parts in building that are contiguous to board or timber, because lime and wood are *insociable.* *Wotton's Architecture.*

INSOBRI'ETY. *n. s.* [*in* and *sobriety.*] Drunkenness; want of sobriety.

He whose conscience upbraids him with profaneness towards God, and *insobriety* towards himself, if he is just to his neighbour, he thinks he has quit scores. *Decay of Piety.*

To

To I'NSOLATE. *v. a.* [*inſolo*, Latin.] To dry in the ſun; to expoſe to the action of the ſun.

INSOLA'TION. *n. ſ.* [*inſolation*, French, from *inſolate.*] Expoſition to the ſun.

We uſe theſe towers for *inſolation*, refrigeration, conſervation, and for the view of divers meteors. *Bacon's Nat. Hiſt.*

If it have not a ſufficient *inſolation* it looketh pale, and attains not its laudable colour: if it be ſunned too long, it ſuffereth a torrefaction. *Brown's Vulgar Errours.*

I'NSOLENCE. } *n. ſ.* [*inſolence*, Fr. *inſolentia*, Latin.] Pride exerted in contemptuous and overbearing treatment of others; petulant contempt.
I'NSOLENCY. }

They could not reſtrain the *inſolency* of O'Neal, who, finding none now to withſtand him, made himſelf lord of thoſe few people that remained. *Spenſer on Ireland.*

Such a nature,
Tickled with good ſucceſs, diſdains the ſhadow
Which he treads on at noon; but I do wonder
His *inſolence* can brook to be commanded
Under Cominius. *Shakeſpeare.*

Flown with *inſolence* and wine. *Milton.*

Publick judgments are the banks and ſhores upon which God breaks the *inſolency* of ſinners, and ſtays their proud waves. *Tillotſon.*

The ſteady tyrant man,
Who with the thoughtleſs *inſolence* of power,
For ſport alone, purſues the cruel chace. *Thomſon.*

The fear of any violence, either againſt her own perſon or againſt her ſon, might deter Penelope from uſing any endeavours to remove men of ſuch *inſolence* and power. *Broome.*

To I'NSOLENCE. *v. a.* [from the noun.] To inſult; to treat with contempt. A very bad word.

The biſhops, who were firſt faulty, *inſolenced* and aſſaulted. *King Charles.*

I'NSOLENT. *adj.* [*inſolent*, Fr. *inſolens*, Latin.] Contemptuous of others; haughty; overbearing.

We have not pillaged thoſe rich provinces which we reſcued: victory itſelf hath not made us *inſolent* maſters. *Atterbury.*

I'NSOLENTLY. *adv.* [*inſolenter*, Latin.] With contempt of others; haughtily; rudely.

What I muſt diſprove,
He *inſolently* talk'd to me of love. *Dryden.*

Not faction, when it ſhook thy regal ſeat,
Not ſenates, *inſolently* loud,
Thoſe echoes of a thoughtleſs crowd,
Could warp thy ſoul to their unjuſt decree. *Dryden.*

Briant, being naturally of an haughty temper, treated him very *inſolently*, and more like a criminal than a priſoner of war. *Addiſon's Guardian.*

INSO'LVABLE. *adj.* [*inſolvable*, Fr. *in* and *ſolve.*]

1. Not to be ſolved; not to be cleared; inextricable; ſuch as admits of no ſolution, or explication.

Spend a few thoughts on the puzzling inquiries concerning vacuums, the doctrine of infinites, indiviſibles and incommenſurables, wherein there appear ſome *inſolvable* difficulties. *Watts's Improvement of the Mind.*

2. That cannot be paid.

INSO'LUBLE. *adj.* [*inſoluble*, French; *inſolubilis*, Latin.]

1. Not to be cleared; not to be reſolved.

Admit this, and what ſhall the Scripture be but a ſnare and a torment to weak conſciences, filling them with infinite ſcrupuloſities, doubts *inſoluble*, and extreme deſpair. *Hooker.*

2. Not to be diſſolved or ſeparated.

Stony matter may grow in any part of a human body; for when any thing *inſoluble* ſticks in any part of the body, it gathers a cruſt about it. *Arbuthnot on Diet.*

INSO'LVENT. *adj.* [*in* and *ſolvo*, Latin.] Unable to pay.

By publick declaration he proclaimed himſelf *inſolvent* of thoſe vaſt ſums he had taken upon credit. *Howel.*

A farmer accuſed his guards for robbing him of oxen, and the emperor ſhot the offenders; but demanding reparation of the accuſer for ſo many brave fellows, and finding him *inſolvent*, compounded the matter by taking his life. *Addiſon.*

An *inſolvent* is a man that cannot pay his debts. *Watts.*

Inſolvent tenant of incumber'd ſpace. *Smart.*

INSO'LVENCY. *n. ſ.* [from *inſolvent.*] Inability to pay debts.

INSOMU'CH. *conj.* [*in ſo much.*] So that; to ſuch a degree that.

It hath ever been the uſe of the conqueror to deſpiſe the language of the conquered, and to force him to learn his: ſo did the Romans always uſe, *inſomuch* that there is no nation but is ſprinkled with their language. *Spenſer.*

To make ground fertile, aſhes excel; *inſomuch* as the countries about Ætna have amends made them, for the miſchiefs the eruptions do. *Bacon's Natural Hiſtory.*

Simonides was an excellent poet, *inſomuch* that he made his fortune by it. *L'Eſtrange.*

They made the ground uneven about their neſt, *inſomuch* that the ſlate did not lie flat upon it, but left a free paſſage underneath. *Addiſon's Guardian.*

To INSPE'CT. *v. a.* [*inſpicio*, *inſpectum*, Latin.] To look into by way of examination.

INSPE'CTION. *n. ſ.* [*inſpection*, French; *inſpectio*, Latin.]

1. Prying examination; narrow and cloſe ſurvey.

With narrow ſearch, and with *inſpection* deep,
Conſider every creature. *Milton.*

Our religion is a religion that dares to be underſtood; that offers itſelf to the ſearch of the inquiſitive, to the *inſpection* of the ſevereſt and the moſt awakened reaſon; for, being ſecure of her ſubſtantial truth and purity, ſhe knows that for her to be ſeen and looked into, is to be embraced and admired, as there needs no greater argument for men to love the light than to ſee it. *South's Sermons.*

2. Superintendence; preſiding care. In the firſt ſenſe it ſhould have *into* before the object, and in the ſecond ſenſe may admit *over*; but authors confound them.

We may ſafely conceal our good deeds from the publick view, when they run no hazard of being diverted to improper ends, for want of our own *inſpection*. *Atterbury.*

We ſhould apply ourſelves to ſtudy the perfections of God, and to procure lively and vigorous impreſſions of his perpetual preſence with us, and *inſpection* over us. *Atterbury.*

The divine *inſpection* into the affairs of the world, doth neceſſarily follow from the nature and being of God; and he that denies this, doth implicitly deny his exiſtence. *Bentley.*

INSPE'CTOR. *n. ſ.* [Latin.]

1. A prying examiner.

With their new light our bold *inſpectors* preſs,
Like Cham, to ſhew their father's nakedneſs. *Denham.*

2. A ſuperintendent.

They may travel under a wiſe *inſpector* or tutor to different parts, that they may bring home uſeful knowledge. *Watts.*

INSPE'RSION. *n. ſ.* [*inſperſio*, Lat.] A ſprinkling. *Ainſw.*

To INSPHE'RE. *v. a.* [*in* and *ſphere.*] To place in an orb or ſphere.

Where thoſe immortal ſhapes
Of bright aereal ſpirits live *inſpher'd*,
In regions mild of calm and ſerene air. *Milton.*

INSPI'RABLE. *adj.* [from *inſpire.*] Which may be drawn in with the breath; which may be infuſed.

To theſe *inſpirable* hurts, we may enumerate thoſe they ſuſtain from their expiration of fuliginous ſteems. *Harvey.*

INSPIRA'TION. *n. ſ.* [from *inſpire.*]

1. The act of drawing in the breath.

In any inflammation of the diaphragm, the ſymptoms are a violent fever, and a moſt exquiſite pain increaſed upon *inſpiration*, by which it is diſtinguiſhed from a pleuriſy, in which the greateſt pain is in expiration. *Arbuthnot.*

2. The act of breathing into any thing.

3. Infuſion of ideas into the mind by a ſuperiour power.

I never ſpoke with her in all my life.
—How can ſhe then call us by our names,
Unleſs it be by *inſpiration?* *Shak. Comedy of Errours.*

Your father was ever virtuous, and holy men at their death have good *inſpirations*. *Shakeſp. Merch. of Venice.*

We to his high *inſpiration* owe,
That what was done before the flood we know. *Denham.*

What the tragedian wrote, the late ſucceſs
Declares was *inſpiration*, and not gueſs. *Denham.*

Inſpiration is when an overpowering impreſſion of any propoſition is made upon the mind by God himſelf, that gives a convincing and indubitable evidence of the truth and divinity of it: ſo were the prophets and the apoſtles *inſpired*. *Watts.*

To INSPI'RE. *v. n.* [*inſpiro*, Latin; *inſpirer*, Fr.] To draw in the breath.

If the *inſpiring* and expiring organ of any animal be ſtopt, it ſuddenly yields to nature, and dies. *Walton.*

To INSPI'RE. *v. a.*

1. To breathe into; to infuſe into the mind; to impreſs upon the fancy.

I have been troubled in my ſleep this night;
But dawning day new comfort hath *inſpir'd*. *Shakeſpeare.*

He knew not his Maker, and he that *inſpired* into him an active ſoul, and breathed in a living ſpirit. *Wiſd.* xv. 11.

Then to the heart *inſpir'd*
Vernal delight. *Milton.*

2. To animate by ſupernatural infuſion.

Nor th' *inſpir'd*
Caſtalian ſpring. *Milton.*

Erato, thy poet's mind *inſpire*,
And fill his ſoul with thy celeſtial fire. *Dryd. Æn.*

The letters are often read to the young religious, to *inſpire* with ſentiments of virtue. *Addiſon.*

3. To draw in with the breath.

By means of ſulphurous coal ſmoaks the lungs are ſtifled and oppreſſed, whereby they are forced to *inſpire* and expire the air with difficulty, in compariſon of the facility of *inſpiring* and expiring the air in the country. *Harvey.*

His baleful breath *inſpiring* as he glides;
Now like a chain around her neck he rides. *Dryden.*

INSPI'RER. *n. ſ.* [from *inſpire.*] He that inſpires.

To the infinite God, the omnipotent creator and preſerver of the world, the moſt gracious redeemer, ſanctifier, and *inſpirer* of mankind, be all honour. *Derham.*

To INSPI'RIT. *v. a.* [*in* and *ſpirit.*] To animate; to actuate; to fill with life and vigour; to enliven; to invigorate; to encourage.

It has pleased God to *inspirit* and actuate all his evangelical methods by a concurrence of supernatural strength, which makes it not only eligible but possible; easy and pleasant for us to do whatever he commands us. *Decay of Piety.*

A discreet use of becoming ceremonies renders the service of the church solemn and affecting, *inspirits* the sluggish, and inflames even the devout worshipper. *Atterbury's Sermons.*

The courage of Agamemnon is *inspirited* by love of empire and ambition. *Pope's Preface to the Iliads.*

Let joy or ease, let affluence or content,
And the gay conscience of a life well spent,
Calm ev'ry thought, *inspirit* ev'ry grace,
Glow in thy heart, and smile upon thy face. *Pope.*

To INSPI'SSATE. *v. a.* [*in* and *spissus*, Lat.] To thicken; to make thick.

Sugar doth *inspissate* the spirits of the wine, and maketh them not so easy to resolve into vapour. *Bacon's Nat. Hist.*

This oil farther *inspissated* by evaporation, turns by degrees into balm. *Arbuthnot on Aliments.*

INSPISSA'TION. *n. s.* [from *inspissate.*] The act of making any liquid thick.

The effect is wrought by the *inspissation* of the air. *Bacon.*

Recent urine will crystallize by *inspissation*, and afford a salt neither acid nor alkaline. *Arbuthnot on Aliments.*

INSTABI'LITY. *n. s.* [*instabilitas*, from *instabilité*, French; *instabilis*, Lat.] Inconstancy; fickleness; mutability of opinion or conduct.

Instability of temper ought to be checked, when it disposes men to wander from one scheme of government to another; since such a fickleness cannot but be fatal to our country. *Addison's Freeholder*, N°. 25.

INSTA'BLE. *adj.* [*instabilis*, Lat.] Inconstant; changing. See UNSTABLE.

To INSTA'LL. *v. a.* [*installer*, French, *in* and *stall.*] To advance to any rank or office, by placing in the seat or stall proper to that condition.

She reigns a goddess now among the saints,
That whilom was the saint of shepherds light,
And is *installed* now in heaven's hight. *Spenser's Past.*

Cranmer is return'd with welcome,
Install'd archbishop of Canterbury. *Shakesp. Henry* VIII.

The king chose him master of the horse, after this he was *installed* of the most noble order. *Wotton.*

INSTALLA'TION. *n. s.* [*installation*, French, from *install.*] The act of giving visible possession of a rank or office, by placing in the proper seat.

Upon the election the bishop gives a mandate for his *installation*. *Ayliffe's Parergon.*

INSTA'LMENT. *n. s.* [from *install.*]

1. The act of installing.

Is it not easy
To make lord William Hastings of our mind,
For the *instalment* of this noble duke
In the seat royal. *Shakespeare's Richard* III.

2. The seat in which one is installed.

Search Windsor-castle, elves,
The several chairs of order look you scour;
Each fair *instalment*, coat and several crest
With loyal blazon evermore be blest! *Shakespeare.*

I'NSTANCE. } *n. s.* [*instance*, French.]
I'NSTANCY. }

1. Importunity; urgency; solicitation.

Christian men should much better frame themselves to those heavenly precepts which our Lord and Saviour with so great *instancy* gave us concerning peace and unity, if we did concur to have the ancient councils renewed. *Hooker*, *b.* i.

2. Motive; influence; pressing argument. Not now in use.

She dwells so securely upon her honour, that folly dares not present itself. Now, could I come to her with any direction in my hand, my desires had *instance* and argument to commend themselves. *Shakesp. Merry Wives of Windsor.*

The *instances* that second marriage move,
Are base respects of thrift, but none of love. *Shakespeare.*

3. Prosecution or process of a suit.

The *instance* of a cause is said to be that judicial process which is made from the contestation of a suit, even to the time of pronouncing sentence in the cause, or till the end of three years. *Ayliffe's Parergon.*

4. Example; document.

Yet doth this accident
So far exceed all *instance*, all discourse,
That I am ready to distrust mine eyes. *Shakespeare.*

In furnaces of copper and brass, where vitriol is often cast in, there riseth suddenly a fly, which sometimes moveth on the walls of the furnace; sometimes in the fire below; and dieth presently as soon as it is out of the furnace: which is a noble *instance*, and worthy to be weighed. *Bacon.*

We find in history *instances* of persons, who, after their prisons have been flung open, have chosen rather to languish in their dungeons, than stake their miserable lives and fortunes upon the success of a revolution. *Addison.*

The greatest saints are sometimes made the most remarkable *instances* of suffering. *Atterbury's Sermons.*

Suppose the earth should be removed nearer to the sun, and revolve for *instance* in the orbit of Mercury, the whole ocean would boil with heat. *Bentley's Sermons.*

The use of *instances* is to illustrate and explain a difficulty; and this end is best answered by such *instances* as are familiar and common. *Baker's Reflections on Learning.*

5. State of any thing.

These seem as if, in the time of Edward the first, they were drawn up into the form of a law in the first *instance*. *Hale.*

6. Occasion; act.

The performances required on our part, are no other than what natural reason has endeavoured to recommend, even in the most severe and difficult *instances* of duty. *Rogers.*

To I'NSTANCE. *v. n.* [from the noun.] To give or offer an example.

As to false citations, that the world may see how little he is to be trusted, I shall *instance* in two or three about which he makes the loudest clamor. *Tillotson.*

In tragedy and satire, this age and the last have excelled the ancients; and I would *instance* in Shakespeare of the former, in Dorset of the latter sort. *Dryden's Juvenal.*

I'NSTANT. *adj.* [*instant*, Fr. *instans*, Latin.]

1. Pressing; urgent; importunate; earnest.

And they were *instant* with loud voices, requiring that he might be crucified. *Luke* xxiii. 23.

Rejoicing in hope; patient in tribulation; continuing *instant* in prayer. *Rom.* xii. 12.

2. Immediate; without any time intervening; present.

Our good old friend bestow
Your needful counsel to our businesses,
Which crave the *instant* use. *Shakesp. King Lear.*

Th' *instant* stroke of death denounc'd to day,
Remov'd far off. *Milton.*

Nor native country thou, nor friend shalt see;
Nor war hast thou to wage, nor year to come;
Impending death is thine, and *instant* doom. *Prior.*

3. Quick; without delay.

Instant without disturb they took alarm. *Milton.*

Griev'd that a visitant so long should wait
Unmark'd, unhonour'd, at a monarch's gate;
Instant he flew with hospitable haste,
And the new friend with courteous air embrac'd. *Pope.*

I'NSTANT. *n. s.* [*instant*, French.]

1. *Instant* is such a part of duration wherein we perceive no succession. *Locke.*

There is scarce an *instant* between their flourishing and their not being. *Hooker*, *b.* v.

I can at any unseasonable *instant* of the night appoint her to look out at her lady's chamber window. *Shakespeare.*

Her nimble body yet in time must move,
And not in *instants* through all places stride;
But she is nigh and far, beneath, above,
In point of time, which thought cannot divide. *Davies.*

At any *instant* of time the moving atom is but in one single point of the line; therefore all but that one point is either future or past, and no other parts are co-existent or contemporary with it. *Bentley's Sermons.*

2. It is used in low and commercial language for a day of the present or current month.

On the twentieth *instant* it is my intention to erect a lion's head. *Addison's Guard.* N°. 98.

INSTANTA'NEOUS. *adj.* [*instantaneus*, Latin.] Done in an instant; acting at once without any perceptible succession; acting with the utmost speed; done with the utmost speed.

This manner of the beginning or ceasing of the deluge doth not at all agree with the *instantaneous* actions of creation and annihilation. *Burnet's Theory of the Earth.*

The rapid radiance *instantaneous* strikes
Th' illumin'd mountain. *Thomson.*

INSTANTA'NEOUSLY. *adv.* [from *instantaneous.*] In an indivisible point of time.

What I had heard of the raining of frogs came to my thoughts, there being reason to conclude that those came from the clouds, or were *instantaneously* generated. *Derham.*

I'NSTANTLY. *adv.* [*instanter*, Latin.]

1. Immediately; without any perceptible intervention of time.

In a great whale, the sense and the affects of any one part of the body *instantly* make a transcursion throughout the whole body. *Bacon's Nat. Hist. cent.* x.

Sleep *instantly* fell on me. *Milton.*

As several winds arise,
Just so their natures alter *instantly*. *May's Virgil.*

2. With urgent importunity.

To INSTA'TE. *v. a.* [*in* and *state.*]

1. To place in a certain rank or condition.

This kind of conquest does only *instate* the victor in these rights of government, which the conquered prince, or that prince to whom the conqueror pretends a right of succession, had. *Hale's Common Law of England.*

Had this glistering monster been born to thy poverty, he could not have been so bad: nor, perhaps, had thy birth *instated* thee in the same greatness, wouldst thou have been better. *South's Sermons.*

The first of them being eminently holy and dear to God, should derive a blessing to his posterity on that account, and prevail at last to have them also accepted as holy, and *instated* in the favour of God. *Atterbury's Sermons.*

2. To invest. Obsolete.

For his possessions,
Although by confiscation they are ours,
We do *instate* and widow you withal. *Shakespeare.*

INSTAURA'TION. *n. s.* [*instauration*, French; *instauratio*, Lat.] Restoration; reparation; renewal.

INSTE'AD *of.* prep. [A word formed by the coalition of *in* and *stead*, place.]

1. In room of; in place of.

Vary the form of speech, and *instead* of the word church make it a question in politicks, whether the monument be in danger. *Swift.*

2. Equal to.

This very consideration to a wise man is *instead* of a thousand arguments, to satisfy him, that, in those times, no such thing was believed. *Tillotson's Sermons.*

To INSTE'EP. *v. a.* [*in* and *steep.*]

1. To soak; to macerate in moisture.

Suffolk first died, and York, all haggled over,
Comes to him where in gore he lay *insteep'd.* *Shakespeare.*

2. Lying under water.

The guttered rocks, and congregated sands,
Traitors *insteep'd* to clog the guiltless keel. *Shak. Othello.*

I'NSTEP. *n. s.* [*in* and *step.*] The upper part of the foot where it joins to the leg.

The caliga was a military shoe with a very thick sole, tied above the *instep* with leather thongs. *Arbuthnot on Coins.*

To I'NSTIGATE. *v. a.* [*instigo*, Lat. *instiguer*, French.] To urge to ill; to provoke or incite to a crime.

INSTIGA'TION. *n. s.* [*instigation*, French; from *instigate.*] Incitement to a crime; encouragement; impulse to ill.

Such *instigations* have been often dropt,
Where I have took them up. *Shakesp. Julius Cæsar.*

Why, what need we
Commune with you of this? But rather follow
Our forceful *instigation.* *Shakesp. Winter's Tale.*

It was partly by the *instigation* of some factious malecontents that bare principal stroke amongst them. *Bacon.*

Shall any man, that wilfully procures the cutting of whole armies to pieces, set up for an innocent? As if the lives that were taken away by his *instigation* were not to be charged upon his account. *L'Estrange's Fables.*

We have an abridgment of all the baseness and villainy that both the corruption of nature and the *instigation* of the devil could bring the sons of men to. *South's Sermons.*

INSTIGA'TOR. *n. s.* [*instigateur*, French; from *instigate.*] Inciter to ill.

That sea of blood is enough to drown in eternal misery the malicious author or *instigator* of its effusion. *K. Charles.*

Either the eagerness of acquiring, or the revenge of missing dignities, have been the great *instigators* of ecclesiastick feuds. *Decay of Piety.*

To INSTI'LL. *v. a.* [*instillo*, Lat. *instiller*, French.]

1. To infuse by drops.

He from the well of life three drops *instill'd.* *Milton.*

2. To insinuate any thing imperceptibly into the mind; to infuse.

Though such assemblies be had indeed for religion's sake, hurtful nevertheless they may easily prove, as well in regard of their fitness to serve the turn of hereticks, and such as privily will soonest adventure to *instil* their poison into mens minds. *Hooker, b.* v.

He had a farther design in all this compassion, to *instil* and insinuate good instruction, by contributing to their happiness in this present life. *Calamy's Sermons.*

Those heathens did in a particular manner *instil* the principle into their children of loving their country, which is far otherwise now-a-days. *Swift's Miscel.*

INSTILLA'TION. *n. s.* [*instillatio*, Lat. from *instil.*]

1. The act of pouring in by drops.
2. The act of infusing slowly into the mind.
3. The thing infused.

They imbitter the cup of life by insensible *instillations.* *Rambler.*

INSTI'NCT. *adj.* [*instinct*, Fr. *instinctus*, Lat.] Moved; animated. A word not in use.

Forth rush'd with whirlwind sound
The chariot of paternal deity,
Flashing thick flames, wheel within wheel undrawn,
Itself *instinct* with spirit, but convoy'd
By four cherubick shapes. *Milton's Par. Lost, b.* vi.

I'NSTINCT. *n. s.* [*instinct*, Fr. *instinctus*, Lat. This word had its accent formerly on the last syllable.] Desire or aversion acting in the mind without the intervention of reason or deliberation; the power determining the will of brutes.

In him they fear your highness' death;
And mere *instinct* of love and loyalty
Makes them thus forward in his banishment. *Shakespeare.*

Thou knowest I am as valiant as Hercules; but beware *instinct*; the lion will not touch the true prince: *instinct* is a great matter. I was a coward on *instinct*: I shall think the better of myself and thee, during my life; I for a valiant lion, and thee for a true prince. *Shakesp. Henry* IV. *p.* i.

But providence or *instinct* of nature seems,
Or reason though disturb'd, and scarce consulted,
To have guided me aright. *Milton's Agonist. l.* 1545.

Nature first pointed out my Portius to me,
And easily taught me by her secret force
To love thy person, e'er I knew thy merit;
Till what was *instinct* grew up into friendship. *Addison.*

The philosopher avers,
That reason guides our deed, and *instinct* theirs.
Instinct and reason how shall we divide? *Prior.*

Reason serves when press'd;
But honest *instinct* comes a volunteer. *Pope.*

INSTI'NCTED. *adj.* [*instinctus*, Lat.] Impressed as an animating power. This, neither musical nor proper, was perhaps introduced by *Bentley.*

What native unextinguishable beauty must be impressed and *instincted* through the whole, which the defedation of so many parts by a bad printer and a worse editor could not hinder from shining forth. *Bentley's Preface to Milton.*

INSTI'NCTIVE. *adj.* [from *instinct.*] Acting without the application of choice of reason; rising in the mind without apparent cause.

Rais'd
By quick *instinctive* motion, up I sprung,
As thitherward endeavouring. *Milton's Par. Lost, b.* viii.

It will be natural that Ulysses's mind should forbode; and it appears that the *instinctive* presage was a favourite opinion of Homer's. *Broome's Notes on the Odyssey.*

INSTI'NCTIVELY. *adv.* [from *instinctive.*] By instinct; by the call of nature.

The very rats
Instinctively had quit it. *Shakespeare's Tempest.*

To I'NSTITUTE. *v. n.* [*instituo*, *institutum*, Lat. *instituer*, Fr.]

1. To fix; to establish; to appoint; to enact; to settle; to prescribe.

God then *instituted* a law natural to be observed by creatures; and therefore, according to the manner of laws, the institution thereof is described as being established by solemn injunction. *Hooker, b.* i.

Here let us breathe, and haply *institute*
A course of learning, and ingenuous studies. *Shakespeare.*

To the production of the effect they are determined by the laws of their nature, *instituted* and imprinted on them by inimitable wisdom. *Hale's Original of Mankind.*

To *institute* a court and country party without materials, would be a very new system in politicks, and what, I believe, was never thought on before. *Swift.*

2. To educate; to instruct; to form by instruction.

If children were early *instituted*, knowledge would insensibly insinuate itself. *Decay of Piety.*

I'NSTITUTE. *n. s.* [*institut*, Fr. *institutum*, Latin.]

1. Established law; settled order.

This law, though custom now directs the course,
As nature's *institute*, is yet in force
Uncancel'd, though disused. *Dryden.*

2. Precept; maxim; principle.

Thou art pale in mighty studies grown,
To make the Stoick *institutes* thy own. *Dryden's Persius.*

INSTITU'TION. *n. s.* [*institution*, Fr. *institutio*, Latin.]

1. Act of establishing.
2. Establishment; settlement.

The *institution* of God's law is described as being established by solemn injunction. *Hooker.*

It became him by whom all things are, to be the way of salvation to all, that the *institution* and restitution of the world might be both wrought with one hand. *Hooker, b.* v.

This unlimited power placed fundamentally in the body of a people, is what legislators have endeavoured, in their several schemes or *institutions* of government, to deposit in such hands as would preserve the people. *Swift.*

3. Positive law.

The holiness of the first fruits and the lump is an holiness, merely of *institution*, outward and nominal; whereas the holiness of the root is an holiness of nature, inherent and real. *Atterbury's Sermons.*

The law and *institution* founded by Moses was to establish religion, and to make mercy and peace known to the whole earth. *Forbes.*

4. Education.

After baptism, when it is in infancy received, succeeds instruction and *institution* in the nature and several branches of that vow, which was made at the font, in a short intelligible manner. *Hammond's Fundamentals.*

It is a necessary piece of providence in the *institution* of our children, to train them up to somewhat in their youth, that may honestly entertain them in their age. *L'Estrange.*

His learning was not the effect of precept or *institution.* *Bentley.*

INSTITU'TIONARY. *adj.* [from *institution.*] Elemental; containing the first doctrines, or principles of doctrine.

That it was not out of fashion Aristotle declareth in his politicks, among the *institutionary* rules of youth. *Brown.*

1. An establisher; one who settles.

I'NSTITUTOR. *n. s.* [*instituteur*, Fr. *institutor*, Latin.]

It might have succeeded a little better, if it had pleased the *institutors* of the civil months of the sun to have ordered them alternately odd and even. *Holder on Time.*

2. Instructor; educator.

The two great aims which every *institutor* of youth should mainly and intentionally drive at. *Walker.*

I'NSTITUTIST. *n. s.* [from *institute.*] Writer of institutes, or elemental instructions.

Green gall the *institutists* would persuade us to be an effect of an over-hot stomach. *Harvey on Consumptions.*

To INSTO'P. *v. a.* [*in* and *stop.*] To close up; to stop.

With boiling pitch another near at hand
The seams *instops.* *Dryden's Ann. Mirab.*

To INSTRU'CT. *v. a.* [*instruo*, Latin; *instruire*, French.]

1. To teach; to form by precept; to inform authoritatively; to educate; to institute; to direct.

Out of heaven he made thee to hear his voice, that he might *instruct* thee. *Deut.* iv. 36.

His God doth *instruct* him to discretion, and doth teach him. *Isa.* xxviii. 26.

They that were *instructed* in the songs of the Lord were two hundred fourscore and eight. 1 *Chron.* xxv. 7.

These are the things wherein Solomon was *instructed* for building of the house of God. 2 *Chron.* iii. 3.

Chenaniah, chief of the Levites, *instructed* about the song, because he was skilful. 1 *Chron.* xv. 22.

She being before *instructed* of her mother. *Matth.* xiv. 8.

Thou approvest the things that are more excellent, being *instructed* out of the law. *Rom.* ii. 18.

Instruct me, for thou knowest. *Milton.*

He ever by consulting at thy shrine
Return'd the wiser, or the more *instruct*
To fly or follow what concern'd him most. *Milton.*

2. To model; to form. Little in use.

They speak to the merits of a cause, after the proctor has prepared and *instructed* the same for a hearing before the judge. *Ayliffe's Parergon.*

INSTRU'CTER. *n. s.* [from *instruct.*] A teacher; an instituter; one who delivers precepts or imparts knowledge.

You have ten thousand *instructors* in Christ. 1 *Cor.* iv. 15.

After the flood arts to Chaldea fell,
The father of the faithful there did dwell,
Who both their parent and *instructor* was. *Denham.*

O thou, who future things can'st represent
As present, heav'nly *instructor!* *Milton's Par. Lost, b.* xi.

Poets, the first *instructors* of mankind,
Brought all things to their native proper use. *Roscommon.*

They see how they are beset on every side, not only with temptations, but *instructors* to vice. *Locke on Education.*

We have precepts of duty given us by our *instructors.* *Rog.*

Several *instructors* were disposed among this little helpless people. *Addison's Guard.* N°. 105.

INSTRU'CTION. *n. s.* [*instructiou*, French; from *instruct.*]

1. The act of teaching; information.

It lies on you to speak,
Not by your own *instruction*, nor by any matter
Which your heart prompts you to, but with such words
As are rooted in your tongue. *Shakespeare's Coriolanus.*

We are beholden to judicious writers of all ages, for those discoveries and discourses they have left behind them for our *instruction.* *Locke.*

2. Precepts conveying knowledge.

Will ye not receive *instruction* to hearken to receive my words? *Jer.* xxxv.

On ev'ry thorn delightful wisdom grows,
In ev'ry stream a sweet *instruction* flows;
But some untaught o'erhear the whisper'ring rill,
In spite of sacred leisure, blockheads still. *Young.*

3. Authoritative information; mandate.

See this dispatch'd with all the haste thou can'st;
Anon I'll give thee more *iustruction.* *Shakespeare.*

INSTRU'CTIVE. *adj.* [from *instruct*; *instructif*, French.] Conveying knowledge.

With variety of *instructive* expressions by speech man alone is endowed. *Holder.*

I would not laugh but in order to instruct; or if my mirth ceases to be *instructive*, it shall never cease to be innocent. *Addison's Spect.* N°. 179.

I'NSTRUMENT. *n. s.* [*instrument*, Fr. *instrumentum*, Lat.]

1. A tool used for any work or purpose.

If he smite him with an *instrument* of iron, so that he die, he is a murderer. *Num.* xxxv. 16.

What artificial frame, what *instrument*,
Did one superior genius e'er invent;
Which to the muscles is preferr'd. *Blackmore on Creation.*

Box is a wood useful for turners and *instrument* makers. *Mortimer.*

2. A frame constructed so as to yield harmonious sounds.

He that striketh an *instrument* with skill, may cause notwithstanding a very pleasant sound, if the string whereon he striketh chance to be capable of harmony. *Hooker, b.* i.

She taketh most delight
In musick, *instruments* and poetry. *Shakespeare.*

In solitary groves he makes his moan,
Nor, mix'd in mirth, in youthful pleasure shares,
But sighs when songs and *instruments* he hears. *Dryden.*

3. A writing containing any contract or order.

He called Edna his wife, and took paper, and did write an *instrument* of covenants, and sealed it. *Tob.* vii. 14.

4. The agent or mean of any thing. It is used of persons as well as things, but of persons very often in an ill sense.

The gods would not have delivered a soul into the body which hath arms and legs, only *instruments* of doing; but that it were intended the mind should employ them. *Sidney.*

If, haply, you my father do suspect,
An *instrument* of this your calling back,
Lay not your blame on me. *Shakesp. Othello.*

All voluntary self-denials and austerities which Christianity commends become necessary, not simply for themselves, but as *instruments* towards a higher end. *Decay of Piety.*

Reputation is the smallest sacrifice those can make us, who have been the *instruments* of our ruin. *Swift's Miscel.*

There is one thing to be considered concerning reason, whether syllogism be the proper *instrument* of it, and the usefullest way of exercising this faculty. *Locke.*

5. One who acts only to serve the purposes of another.

He scarcely knew what was done in his own chamber, but as it pleased her *instruments* to frame themselves. *Sidney, b.* ii.

All the *instruments* which aided to expose the child, were even then lost when it was found. *Shakesp. Winter's Tale.*

In benefits as well as injuries, it is the principal that we are to consider, not the *instrument*; that which a man does by another, is in truth his own act. *L'Estrange.*

The bold are but th' *instruments* of the wise,
They undertake the dangers they advise. *Dryden.*

INSTRUME'NTAL. *adj.* [*instrumental*, French; *instrumentum*, Latin.]

1. Conducive as means to some end; organical.

All second and *instrumental* causes, without that operative faculty which God gave them, would become altogether silent, virtueless, and dead. *Raleigh's Hist. of the World.*

Prayer, which is *instrumental* to every thing, hath a particular promise in this thing. *Taylor's Rule of living holy.*

It is not an essential part of religion, but rather an auxiliary and *instrumental* duty. *Smalridge's Sermons.*

I discern some excellent final causes of conjunction of body and soul; but the *instrumental* I know not, nor what invisible bands and fetters unite them together. *Bentley's Sermons.*

2. Acting to some end; contributing to some purpose; helpful: used of persons and things.

The presbyterian merit is of little weight, when they allege themselves *instrumental* towards the restoration. *Swift.*

3. Consisting not of voices but instruments.

They which, under pretence of the law ceremonial abrogated, require the abrogation of *instrumental* musick, approving nevertheless the use of vocal melody to remain, must shew some reason, wherefore the one should be thought a legal ceremony and not the other. *Hooker, b.* v.

4. Produced by instruments; not vocal.

Oft in bands,
While they keep watch, or nightly rounding walk,
With heav'nly touch of *instrumental* sounds
In full harmonious number join'd, their songs
Divide the night, and lift our thoughts to heav'n. *Milton.*

Sweet voices, mix'd with *instrumental* sounds,
Ascend the vaulted roof, the vaulted roof rebounds. *Dryd.*

INSTRUMENTA'LITY. *n. s.* [from *instrumental.*] Subordinate agency; agency of any thing as means to an end.

Those natural and involuntary actings are not done by deliberation and formal command, yet they are done by the virtue, energy, and influx of the soul, and the *instrumentality* of the spirits. *Hale's Original of Mankind.*

INSTRUME'NTALLY. *adv.* [from *instrumental.*] In the nature of an instrument; as means to an end.

Mens well-being here in this life is but *instrumentally* good, as being the means for him to be well in the next life. *Digby.*

Habitual preparation for the sacrament consists in a standing, permanent habit, or principle of holiness, wrought chiefly by God's spirit, and *instrumentally* by his word, in the heart or soul of man. *South's Sermons.*

INSTRUME'NTALNESS. *n. s.* [from *instrumental.*] Usefulness as means to an end.

The *instrumentalness* of riches to works of charity, has rendered it very political, in every Christian commonwealth, by laws to settle and secure propriety. *Hammond's Fund.*

INSU'FFERABLE. *adj.* [*in* and *sufferable.*]

1. Intolerable; insupportable; intense beyond endurance.

The one is oppressed with constant heat, the other with *insufferable* cold. *Brown's Vulgar Errours, b.* vi.

Though great light be *insufferable* to our eyes, yet the highest degree of darkness does not at all disease them; because that causing no disorderly motion, leaves that curious organ unharmed. *Locke.*

2. Detestable; contemptible.

A multitude of scribblers, who daily pester the world with their *insufferable* stuff, should be discouraged from writing any more. *Dryden's Dedication to Juvenal.*

INSU'FFERABLY. *adv.* [from *insufferable.*] To a degree beyond endurance.

Those heav'nly shapes
Will dazzle now this earthly, with their blaze
Insufferably bright. *Milton's Par. Lost, b.* ix.

There is no person remarkably ungrateful, who was not also *insufferably* proud. *South's Sermons.*

INSUFFI'CIENCE. } *n. s.* [*insufficience*, Fr. *in* and *sufficient.*] In-
INSUFFI'CIENCY. } dequateness to any end or purpose; want of requisite value or power: used of things and persons.

The minister's aptness or *insufficiency*, otherwise than by reading to instruct the flock, standeth in this place as a stranger, with whom our form of common prayer hath nothing to do. *Hooker, b.* v.

The *insufficiency* of the light of nature is, by the light of scripture, so fully supplied, that further light than this hath added, there doth not need unto that end. *Hooker, b.* ii.

We will give you sleepy drinks, that your senses, unintelligent of our *insufficience*, may, though they cannot praise us, as little accuse us. *Shakespeare's Winter's Tale.*

Till experience had discovered their defect and *insufficiency*, I did certainly conclude them to be infallible. *Wilkins.*

Consider the pleas made use of to this purpose, and shew the *insufficiency* and weakness of them. *Atterbury.*

INSUFFI'CIENT. *adj.* [*insufficient*, French; *in* and *sufficient.*] Inadequate to any need, use, or purpose; wanting abilities; incapable; unfit.

The bishop to whom they shall be presented, may justly reject them as incapable and *insufficient.* *Spenser on Ireland.*

We are weak, dependant creatures, *insufficient* to our own happiness, full of wants which of ourselves we cannot relieve, exposed to a numerous train of evils which we know not how to divert. *Rogers's Sermons.*

Fasting kills by the bad state, not by the *insufficient* quantity of fluids. *Arbuthnot on Aliments.*

INSUFFI'CIENTLY. *adv.* [from *insufficient.*] With want of proper ability; not skilfully.

INSUFFLA'TION. [*in* and *sufflo*, Latin.] The act of breathing upon.

Imposition of hands is a custom of parents in blessing their children, but taken up by the apostles instead of that divine *insufflation* which Christ used. *Hammond's Fundamentals.*

I'NSULAR. } *adj.* [*insulaire*, French; *insularis*, Lat.] Belong-
I'NSULARY. } ing to an island.

Druina, being surrounded with the sea, is hardly to be invaded, having many other *insulary* advantages. *Howel.*

I'NSULATED. *adj.* [*insula*, Lat.] Not contiguous on any side.

INSU'LSE. *adj.* [*insulsus*, Lat.] Dull; insipid; heavy. *Dict.*

INSU'LT. *n. s.* [*insultus*, Lat. *insulte*, French.]

1. The act of leaping upon any thing. In this sense it has the accent on the last syllable: the sense is rare.

The bull's *insult* at four she may sustain,
But after ten from nuptial rites refrain. *Dryden's Virgil.*

2. Act of insolence or contempt.

Take the sentence seriously, because railleries are an *insult* on the unfortunate. *Broome's Notes on the Odyssey.*

To INSU'LT. *v. a.* [*insulter*, Fr. *insulto*, Lat.]

1. To treat with insolence or contempt. It is used sometimes with *over*, sometimes without a preposition.

The poet makes his hero, after he was glutted by the death of Hector, and the honour he did his friend by *insulting over* his murderer, to be moved by the tears of king Priam. *Pope.*

2. To trample upon; to triumph over.

It pleas'd the king his master very lately
To strike at me upon his misconstruction;
When he conjunct, and flatt'ring his displeasure,
Tript me behind; being down, *insulted*, rail'd,
And put upon him such a deal of man,
That worthied him. *Shakespeare's King Lear.*

So 'scapes the *insulting* fire his narrow jail,
And makes small outlets into open air. *Dryden.*

Ev'n when they sing at ease in full content,
Insulting o'er the toil they underwent,
Yet still they find a future task remain,
To turn the soil. *Dryden's Virgil.*

INSU'LTER. *n. s.* [from *insult.*] One who treats another with insolent triumph.

Ev'n man, the merciless *insulter* man,
Man, who rejoices in our sex's weakness,
Shall pity thee. *Rowe's Jane Shore.*

INSU'LTINGLY. *adv.* [from *insulting.*] With contemptuous triumph.

Insultingly, he made your love his boast,
Gave me my life, and told me what it cost. *Dryden.*

INSUPERABI'LITY. *n. s.* [from *insuperable.*] The quality of being invincible.

INSU'PERABLE. *adj.* [*insuperabilis*, Latin.] Invincible; insurmountable; not to be conquered; not to be overcome.

This appears to be an *insuperable* objection, because of the evidence that sense seems to give it. *Digby on Bodies.*

Much might be done would we but endeavour; nothing is *insuperable* to pains and patience. *Ray on the Creation.*

And middle natures how they long to join,
Yet never pass th' *insuperable* line. *Pope's Essay on Man.*

INSU'PERABLENESS. *n. s.* [from *insuperable.*] Invincibleness; impossibility to be surmounted.

INSU'PERABLY. *adv.* [from *insuperable.*] Invincibly; insurmountably.

Between the grain and the vein of a diamond there is this difference, that the former furthers, the latter, being so *insuperably* hard, hinders the splitting of it. *Grew's Musæum.*

INSUPPO'RTABLE. *adj.* [*insupportable*, French; *in* and *supportable.*] Intolerable; insufferable; not to be endured.

A disgrace put upon a man in company is *insupportable*; it is heightened according to the greatness, and multiplied according to the number of the persons that hear. *South.*

The baser the enemies are, the more *insupportable* is the insolence *L'Estrange's Fables.*

The thought of being nothing after death is a burden *insupportable* to a virtuous man: we naturally aim at happiness, and cannot bear to have it confined to our present being. *Dryd.*

To those that dwell under or near the Equator, this Spring would be a most pestilent and *insupportable* Summer; and as for those countries that are nearer the Poles, a perpetual Spring will not do their business. *Bentley's Sermons.*

INSUPPO'RTABLENESS. *n. s.* [from *insupportable.*] Insufferableness; the state of being beyond endurance.

Then fell she to so pitiful a declaration of the *insupportableness* of her desires, that Dorus's ears procured his eyes with tears to give testimony how much they suffered for her suffering. *Sidney.*

INSUPPO'RTABLY. *adv.* [from *insupportable.*] Beyond endurance.

But safest he who stood aloof,
When *insupportably* his foot advanc'd,
In scorn of their proud arms and warlike tools,
Spurn'd them to death by troops. *Milton's Agonistes.*

The first day's audience sufficiently convinced me, that the poem was *insupportably* too long. *Dryden.*

INSURMO'UNTABLE. *adj.* [*insurmontable*, Fr. *in* and *surmountable.*] Insuperable; unconquerable.

This difficulty is *insurmountable*, 'till I can make simplicity and variety the same. *Locke.*

Hope thinks nothing difficult; despair tells us, that difficulty is *insurmountable.* *Watts.*

INSURMO'UNTABLY. *adv.* [from *insurmountable.*] Invincibly; unconquerably.

INSURRE'CTION. *n. s.* [*insurgo*, Latin.] A seditious rising; a rebellious commotion.

Between the acting of a dreadful thing,
And the first motion, all the interim is
Like a phantasma, or a hideous dream:
The genius and the mortal instruments
Are then in council; and the state of man,
Like to a little kingdom, suffers then
The nature of an *insurrection.* *Shak. Jul. Cæsar.*

This city of old time hath made *insurrection* against kings, and that rebellion and sedition have been made therein. *Ezra.*

There shall be a great *insurrection* upon those that fear the Lord. 2 *Esd.* xvi. 70.

Insurrections of base people are commonly more furious in their beginnings. *Bacon's Henry* VII.

The trade of Rome had like to have suffered another great stroke by an *insurrection* in Egypt, excited by Achilleus. *Arbuth.*

INSUSURRA'TION. *n. s.* [*insusurro*, Latin.] The act of whispering.

INTA'CTIBLE. *adj.* [*in* and *tactum*, Latin.] Not perceptible to the touch. *Dict.*

INTA'GLIO. *n. s.* [Italian.] Any thing that has figures engraved on it.

We meet with the figures which Juvenal describes on antique *intaglios* and medals. *Addison on Italy.*

INTA'STABLE. *adj.* [*in* and *taste.*] Not raising any sensations in the organs of taste.

Something which is invisible, *intastable*, and intangible, as existing only in the fancy, may produce a pleasure superior to that of sense. *Grew's Cosmol.*

INTEGER. *n. s.* [Latin.] The whole of any thing.

As not only signified a piece of money, but any *integer*; from whence is derived the word *ace*, or unit. *Arbuthnot.*

I'NTEGRAL. *adj.* [*integral*, French; *integer*, Latin.]

1. Whole: applied to a thing considered as comprising all its constituent parts.

A local motion keepeth bodies *integral*, and their parts together. *Bacon's Natural History.*

2. Uninjured; complete; not defective.

No wonder if one remain speechless, though of *integral* principles, who, from an infant, should be bred up amongst mutes, and have no teaching. *Holder.*

3. Not fractional; not broken into fractions.

I'NTEGRAL. *n. s.* The whole made up of parts.

Physicians, by the help of anatomical dissections, have searched into those various meanders of the veins, arteries, nerves, and *integrals* of the human body. *Hale.*

Consider the infinite complications and combinations of several concurrences to the constitution and operation of almost every *integral* in nature. *Hale.*

A mathematical whole is better called *integral*, when the several parts, which make up the whole, are distinct, and each may subsist apart. *Watts.*

INTE'GRITY. *n. s.* [*integrité*, Fr. *integritas*, from *integer*, Lat.]

1. Honesty; uncorrupt mind; purity of manners; uncorruptedness.

Your dishonour
Mangles true judgment, and bereaves the state
Of that *integrity* which should become it. *Shakesp. Coriol.*

Macduff, this noble passion,
Child of *integrity*, hath from my soul
Wip'd the black scruples, reconcil'd my thoughts
To thy good truth and honour. *Shakesp. Macbeth.*

Whoever has examined both parties cannot go far towards the extremes of either, without violence to his *integrity* or understanding. *Swift.*

The libertine, instead of attempting to corrupt our *integrity*, will conceal and disguise his own vices. *Rogers.*

2. Purity; genuine unadulterate state.

Language continued long in its purity and *integrity*. *Hale.*

3. Intireness; unbroken whole.

Take away this transformation, and there is no chasm, nor can it affect the *integrity* of the action. *Broome.*

INTE'GUMENT. *n. s.* [*integumentum*, *intego*, Lat.] Any thing that covers or invelops another.

He could no more live without his frize-coat than without his skin: it is not indeed so properly his coat, as what the anatomists call one of the *integuments* of the body. *Addison.*

I'NTELLECT. *n. s.* [*intellect*, Fr. *intellectus*, Lat.] The intelligent mind; the power of understanding.

All heart they live, all head, all eye, all ear,
All *intellect*, all sense. *Milton.*

All those arts, rarities, and inventions, which vulgar minds gaze at, and the ingenious pursue, are but the reliques of an *intellect* defaced with sin and time. *South's Sermons.*

INTELLE'CTION. *n. s.* [*intellection*, Fr. *intellectio*, Latin.] The act of understanding.

Simple apprehension denotes the soul's naked *intellection* of an object, without either composition or deduction. *Glanv.*

A determinate *intellection* of the modes of being, never hinted by the senses, can realize chimeras. *Glanv. Sceps.*

They will say 'tis not the bulk or substance of the animal spirit, but its motion and agility, that produces *intellection* and sense. *Bentley's Sermons.*

INTELLE'CTIVE. *adj.* [*intellectif*, Fr. from *intellect.*] Having power to understand.

If a man as *intellective* be created, then either he means the whole man, or only that by which he is *intellective*. *Glanv.*

INTELLE'CTUAL. *adj.* [*intellectuel*, French; *intellectualis*, low Latin.]

1. Relating to the understanding; belonging to the mind; transacted by the understanding.

Religion teaches us to present to God our bodies as well as our souls: if the body serves the soul in actions natural and civil, and *intellectual*, it must not be eased in the only offices of religion. *Taylor.*

2. Mental; comprising the faculty of understanding; belonging to the mind.

Logick is to teach us the right use of our reason, or *intellectual* powers. *Watts.*

3. Ideal; perceived by the intellect, not the senses.

In a dark vision's *intellectual* scene,
Beneath a bow'r for sorrow made,
The melancholy Cowley lay. *Cowley.*

A train of phantoms in wild order rose,
And, join'd, this *intellectual* scene compose. *Pope.*

4. Having the power of understanding.

Anaxagoras and Plato term the maker of the world an *intellectual* worker. *Hooker.*

Who would lose,
Though full of pain, this *intellectual* being,
Those thoughts that wander through eternity,
To perish rather, swallow'd up and lost,
In the wide womb of uncreated night,
Devoid of sense and motion? *Milton's Parad. Lost.*

5. Proposed as the object not of the senses but intellect: as, *Cudworth* names his book the *intellectual* system of the universe.

INTELLE'CTUAL. *n. s.* Intellect; understanding; mental powers or faculties. This is little in use.

Her husband not nigh,
Whose higher *intellectual* more I shun. *Milton.*

The fancies of most, like the index of a clock, are moved but by the inward springs of the corporeal machine; which, even on the most sublimed *intellectual*, is dangerously influential. *Glanv. Sceps.*

I have not consulted the repute of my *intellectuals* in bringing their weaknesses into such discerning presences. *Glanv.*

INTE'LLIGENCE. } *n. s.* [*intelligence*, French; *intelligentia*,
INTE'LLIGENCY. } Latin.]

1. Commerce of information; notice; mutual communication; account of things distant or secret.

It was perceived there had not been in the catholicks, either at Armenia or at Seleucia, so much foresight as to provide that true *intelligence* might pass between them of what was done. *Hooker, b. v.*

A mankind witch! hence with her, out of door!
A most *intelligency* bawd! *Shakespeare.*

He furnished his employed men liberally with money, to draw on and reward *intelligences*; giving them also in charge to advertise continually what they found. *Bacon's H. VII.*

The advertisements of neighbour princes are always to be regarded, for that they receive *intelligence* from better authors than persons of inferior note. *Hayward.*

Let all the passages
Be well secur'd, that no *intelligence*
May pass between the prince and them. *Denham's Sophy.*

Those tales had been sung to lull children asleep, before ever Berosus set up his *intelligence* office at Coos. *Bentley.*

2. Commerce of acquaintance; terms on which men live one with another.

Factious followers are worse to be liked, which follow not upon affection to him with whom they range themselves; whereupon commonly ensueth that ill *intelligence* that we see between great personages. *Bacon.*

He lived rather in a fair *intelligence* than any friendship with the favourites. *Clarendon.*

3. Spirit; unbodied mind.

How fully hast thou satisfied me, pure
Intelligence of heav'n, angel! *Milt. Parad. Lost.*

There are divers ranks of created beings intermediate between the glorious God and man, as the glorious angels and created *intelligences*. *Hale.*

They hoped to get the favour of the houses, and by the favour of the houses they hoped for that of the *intelligencies*, and by their favour for that of the supreme God. *Stillingfleet.*

The regularity of motion, visible in the great variety and curiosity of bodies, is a demonstration that the whole mass of matter is under the conduct of a mighty *intelligence*. *Collier.*

Satan, appearing like a cherub to Uriel, the *intelligence* of the sun circumvented him even in his own province. *Dryden.*

4. Understanding; skill.

Heaps of huge words, up hoarded hideously,
They think to be chief praise of poetry;
And thereby wanting due *intelligence*,
Have marr'd the face of goodly poesie. *Spenser.*

INTELLIGE'NCER. *n. s.* [from *intelligence.*] One who sends or conveys news; one who gives notice of private or distant transactions; one who carries messages between parties.

His eyes, being his diligent *intelligencers*, could carry unto him no other news but discomfortable. *Sidney.*

Who hath not heard it spoken
How deep you were within the books of heav'n?
To us, th' imagin'd voice of heav'n itself;
The very opener and *intelligencer*
Between the grace and sanctities of heav'n,
And our dull workings. *Shakesp. Henry IV.*

If they had instructions to that purpose, they might be the best *intelligencers* to the king of the true state of his whole kingdom. *Bacon.*

They are the best sort of *intelligencers*; for they have a way into the inmost closets of princes. *Howel.*

They have news-gatherers and *intelligencers*, who make them acquainted with the conversation of the whole kingdom. *Spectator.*

INTE'LLIGENT. *adj.* [*intelligent*, Fr. *intelligens*, Latin.]

1. Knowing; instructed; skilful.

It is not only in order of nature for him to govern that is the more *intelligent*, as Aristotle would have it; but there is no-

no leſs required for government, courage to protect, and above all honeſty. *Bacon.*

Intelligent of ſeaſons, they ſet forth
Their airy caravan. *Milton.*

He of times,
Intelligent, th' harſh hyperborean ice
Shuns for our equal Winters; when our ſuns
Cleave the chill'd ſoil, he backwards wings his way. *Phillips.*

Trace out the numerous footſteps of the preſence and interpoſition of a moſt wiſe and *intelligent* architect throughout all this ſtupendous fabrick. *Woodward.*

2. Giving information.

Servants, who ſeem no leſs,
Which are to France the ſpies and ſpeculations
Intelligent of our ſtate. *Shakeſ. King Lear.*

INTELLIGE'NTIAL. *adj.* [from *intelligence.*]

1. Conſiſting of unbodied mind.

Food alike thoſe pure
Intelligential ſubſtances require,
As doth your rational. *Milton's Par. Loſt.*

2. Intellectual; exerciſing underſtanding.

In at his mouth
The devil enter'd; and his brutal ſenſe,
His heart or head poſſeſſing, ſoon inſpir'd
With act *intelligential.* *Milton's Paradiſe Loſt.*

INTELLIGIBI'LITY. *n. ſ.* [from *intelligible.*]

1. Poſſibility to be underſtood.

2. The power of underſtanding; intellection. Not proper.

The ſoul's nature conſiſts in *intelligibility.* *Glanv. Sceps.*

INTE'LLIGIBLE. *adj.* [*intelligible*, Fr. *intelligibilis*, Latin.] To be conceived by the underſtanding; poſſible to be underſtood.

We ſhall give ſatisfaction to the mind, to ſhew it a fair and *intelligible* account of the deluge. *Burnet.*

Something muſt be loſt in all tranſlations, but the ſenſe will remain, which would otherwiſe be loſt, or at leaſt be maimed, when it is ſcarce *intelligible.* *Dryden.*

Many natural duties relating to God, ourſelves, and our neighbours, would be exceeding difficult for the bulk of mankind to find out by reaſon; therefore it has pleaſed God to expreſs them in a plain manner, *intelligible* to ſouls of the loweſt capacity. *Watts.*

INTE'LLIGIBLENESS. *n. ſ.* [from *intelligible.*] Poſſibility to be underſtood; perſpicuity.

It is in our ideas that both the rightneſs of our knowledge, and the propriety or *intelligibleneſs* of our ſpeaking, conſiſts. *Locke.*

INTE'LLIGIBLY. *adv.* [from *intelligible.*] So as to be underſtood; clearly; plainly.

The genuine ſenſe, *intelligibly* told,
Shews a tranſlator both diſcreet and bold. *Roſcommon.*

To write of metals and minerals *intelligibly*, is a taſk more difficult than to write of animals. *Woodward's Nat. Hiſt.*

INTE'MERATE. *adj.* [*intemeratus*, Latin.] Undefiled; unpolluted.

INTE'MPERAMENT. *n. ſ.* [*in* and *temperament.*] Bad conſtitution.

Some depend upon the *intemperament* of the part ulcerated, and others upon the continual afflux of lacerative humours. *Harvey on Conſumptions.*

INTE'MPERANCE. } *n. ſ.* [*intemperance*, Fr. *intemperantia*, Lat.]
INTE'MPERANCY. } Want of temperance; want of moderation; exceſs in meat or drink.

Boundleſs *intemperance*
In nature is a tyranny; it hath been
The fall of many kings. *Shakeſp. Macbeth.*

Another law of Lycurgus induced to *intemperancy* and all kind of incontinency. *Hakewill.*

Some, as thou ſaw'ſt, by violent ſtroke ſhall die;
By fire, flood, famine, by *intemperance* more
In meats and drinks, which on the earth ſhall bring
Diſeaſes dire; of which a monſtrous crew
Before thee ſhall appear; that thou may'ſt know
What miſery th' inabſtinence of Eve
Shall bring on men. *Milton's Paradiſe Loſt, b.* xi.

The Lacedemonians trained up their children to hate drunkenneſs and *intemperance*, by bringing a drunken man into their company. *Watts.*

INTE'MPERATE. *adj.* [*intemperant*, Fr. *intemperatus*, Latin.]

1. Immoderate in appetite; exceſſive in meat or drink; drunken; gluttonous.

More women ſhould die than men, if the number of burials anſwered in proportion to that of ſickneſſes; but men, being more *intemperate* than women, die as much by reaſon of their vices, as women do by the infirmity of their ſex. *Graunt.*

Notwithſtanding all their talk of reaſon and philoſophy, and thoſe unanſwerable doubts, which, over their cups or their coffee, they pretend to have againſt Chriſtianity; perſuade but the covetous man not to deify his money, the *intemperate* man to abandon his revels, and I dare undertake that all their giant-like objections ſhall vaniſh. *South.*

2. Paſſionate; ungovernable; without rule.

You are more *intemperate* in your blood
Than thoſe pamper'd animals,
That rage in ſavage ſenſuality. *Shakeſpeare.*

Uſe not thy mouth to *intemperate* ſwearing; for therein is the word of ſin. *Eccluſ.* xxiii. 13.

INTE'MPERATELY. *adv.* [from *intemperate.*]

1. With breach of the laws of temperance.

How groſly do many of us contradict the plain precepts of the Goſpel, by living *intemperately* or unjuſtly? *Tillotſon.*

2. Immoderately; exceſſively.

Do not too many believe no religion to be pure, but what is *intemperately* rigid? Whereas no religion is true that is not peaceable as well as pure. *Spratt's Sermons.*

INTE'MPERATENESS. *n. ſ.* [from *intemperate.*]

1. Want of moderation.

2. Unſeaſonableneſs of weather. *Ainſworth.*

INTE'MPERATURE. *n. ſ.* [from *intemperate.*] Exceſs of ſome quality.

To INTE'ND. *v. a.* [*intendo*, Latin.]

1. To ſtretch out. Obſolete.

The ſame advancing high above his head,
With ſharp *intended* ſting ſo rude him ſmote,
That to the earth him drove, as ſtricken dead;
Ne living wight would have him life behot. *Fairy Queen.*

2. To enforce; to make intenſe.

What ſeems to be the ground of the aſſertion, is the magnified quality of this ſtar, conceived to cauſe or *intend* the heat of this ſeaſon, we find that wiſer antiquity was not of this opinion. *Brown's Vulg. Err.*

By this the lungs are *intended* or remitted. *Hale.*

This vis inertiæ is eſſential to matter, becauſe it neither can be deprived of it, nor *intended* or remitted in the ſame body; but is always proportional to the quantity of matter. *Cheyne.*

Magnetiſm may be *intended* and remitted, and is found only in the magnet and in iron. *Newton's Opt.*

3. To regard; to attend; to take care of.

This they ſhould carefully *intend*, and not when the ſacrament is adminiſtred, imagine themſelves called only to walk up and down in a white and ſhining garment. *Hooker.*

2. To pay regard or attention to. This ſenſe is now little uſed.

They could not *intend* to the recovery of that country of the north. *Spenſer.*

Having no children, ſhe did with ſingular care and tenderneſs *intend* the education of Philip. *Bacon's H.* VII.

The king prayed them to have patience 'till a little ſmoak, that was raiſed in his country, was over; ſlighting, as his manner was, that openly, which nevertheleſs he *intended* ſeriouſly. *Bacon's H.* VII.

Neither was there any queen-mother who might ſhare any way in the government, while the king *intended* his pleaſure. *Bacon's Henry* VII.

Go therefore, mighty pow'rs!
Terror of heav'n, though fallen! *intend* at home,
While here ſhall be our home, what beſt may eaſe
The preſent miſery, and render hell
More tolerable. *Milton's Paradiſe Loſt, b.* ii.

Their beauty they, and we our loves ſuſpend;
Nought can our wiſhes, ſave thy health, *intend.* *Waller.*

4. To mean; to deſign.

The opinion ſhe had of his wiſdom was ſuch, as made her eſteem greatly of his words; but that the words themſelves ſounded ſo, as ſhe could not imagine what they *intended.* *Sidn.*

The gods would not have delivered a ſoul into the body, which hath arms and legs, only inſtruments of doing, but that it were *intended* the mind ſhould employ them. *Sidney.*

Thou art ſworn
As deeply to effect what we *intend*,
As cloſely to conceal what we impart? *Shakeſ. R.* III.

The earl was a very acute and ſound ſpeaker, when he would *intend* it. *Wotton.*

According to this model Horace writ his odes and epods; for his ſatires and epiſtles, being *intended* wholly for inſtruction, required another ſtyle. *Dryden.*

INTE'NDANT. *n. ſ.* [French.] An officer of the higheſt claſs, who overſees any particular allotment of the publick buſineſs.

Nearchus, who commanded Alexander's fleet, and Oneſicrates, his *intendant* general of marine, have both left relations of the Indies. *Arbuthnot.*

INTE'NDIMENT. *n. ſ.* [*entendement*, French.] Attention; patient hearing; accurate examination. This word is only to be found in *Spenſer.*

Be nought hereat diſmay'd,
'Till well ye wot, by grave *intendiment*,
What woman, and wherefore doth me upbraid. *Fa. Queen.*

INTE'NDMENT. *n. ſ.* [*entendement*, French.]

1. Intention; deſign.

Out of my love to you, I came hither to acquaint you withal; that either you might ſtay him from his *intendment*, or brook ſuch diſgrace well as he ſhall run into. *Shakeſpeare.*

All that worſhip for fear, profit, or ſome other by-end, fall more or leſs within the *intendment* of this emblem. *L'Eſtrange.*

To INTE'NERATE. *v. a.* [*in* and *tener*, Latin.] To make tender; to soften. *Bp. Taylor.*

Autumn vigour gives,
Equal, *intenerating*, milky grain. *Phillips.*

INTENERA'TION. *n. s.* [from *intenerate.*] The act of softening or making tender.

In living creatures the noblest use of nourishment is for the prolongation of life, restoration of some degree of youth, and *inteneration* of the parts. *Bacon.*

INTE'NIBLE. *adj.* [*in* and *tenible.*] That cannot hold. It is commonly written *intenable.*

I know I love in vain, strive against hope;
Yet in this captious and *intenible* sieve,
I still pour in the waters of my love. *Shakespeare.*

INTE'NSE. *adj.* [*intensus*, Latin.]

1. Raised to a high degree; strained; forced; not slight; not lax.

To observe the effects of a distillation, prosecuted with so *intense* and unusual a degree of heat, we ventured to come near. *Boyle.*

Sublime or low, unbended or *intense*,
The sound is still a comment to the sense. *Roscommon.*

2. Vehement; ardent.

Hebraisms warm and animate our language, and convey our thoughts in more ardent and *intense* phrases. *Addison.*

3. Kept on the stretch; anxiously attentive.

But in disparity
The one *intense*; the other still remiss,
Cannot well suit with either, but soon prove
Tedious alike. *Milton's Paradise Lost, b.* viii.

INTE'NSELY. *adv.* [from *intense.*] To a great degree.

If an Englishman considers our world, how *intensely* it is heated, he cannot suppose that it will cool again. *Addison.*

INTE'NSENESS. *n. s.* [from *intense.*] The state of being affected to a high degree; force; contrariety to laxity or remission.

The water of standing springs and rivers, that sustains a diminution from the heat above, being evaporated more or less, in proportion to the greater or lesser *intenseness* of heat. *Woodward's Natural History.*

INTE'NSION. *n. s.* [*intension*, Fr. *intensio*, Latin.] The act of forcing or straining any thing; contrariety to remission or relaxation.

Sounds will be carried further with the wind than against the wind; and likewise do rise and fall with the *intension* or remission of the wind. *Bacon's Nat. Hist.*

Faith differs from hope in the extension of its object, and in the *intension* of degree. *Taylor's Rule of living holy.*

INTE'NSIVE. *adj.* [from *intense.*]

1. Stretched or increased with respect to itself.

As his perfection is infinitely greater than the perfection of a man, so it is infinitely greater than the perfection of an angel; and were it not infinitely greater than the perfection of an angel, it could not be infinitely greater than the perfection of a man, because the *intensive* distance between the perfection of an angel and of a man is but finite. *Hale.*

2. Intent; full of care.

Tired with that assiduous attendance and *intensive* circumspection, which a long fortune did require, he was not unwilling to bestow upon another some part of the pains. *Wott.*

INTE'NSIVELY. *adv.* To a greater degree.

God and the good angels are more free than we are, that is, *intensively* in the degree of freedom; but not extensively in the latitude of the object, according to a liberty of exercise, but not of specification. *Bramh. against Hobbs.*

INTE'NT. *adj.* [*intentus*, Latin.] Anxiously diligent; fixed with close application.

Distractions in England made most men *intent* to their own safety. *King Charles.*

When we use but those means which God hath laid before us, it is a good sign that we are rather *intent* upon God's glory than our own conveniency. *Taylor.*

The general himself had been more *intent* upon his command. *Clarendon.*

They on their mirth and dance
Intent. *Milton.*

Of action eager, and *intent* on thought,
The chiefs your honourable danger sought. *Dryden.*

Were men as *intent* upon this as on things of lower concernment, there are none so enslaved to the necessities of life, who might not find many vacancies that might be husbanded to this advantage of their knowledge. *Locke.*

Whilst they are *intent* on one particular part of their theme, they bend all their thoughts to prove or disprove some proposition that relates to that part, without attention to the consequences that may affect another. *Watts.*

Be *intent* and solicitous to take up the meaning of the speaker. *Watts.*

INTE'NT. *n. s.* [from *intend.*] A design; a purpose; a drift; a view formed; meaning.

Although the Scripture of God be stored with infinite variety of matter in all kinds, although it abound with all sorts of laws, yet the principal *intent* of Scripture is to deliver the laws of duties supernatural. *Hooker.*

Whereas commandment was given to destroy all places where the Canaanites had served the gods, this precept had reference unto a special *intent* and purpose, which was that there should be but one place whereunto the people might bring offerings. *Hooker.*

Those that accuse him in his *intent* towards our wives, are a yoke of his discarded men. *Shak. Merry Wives of Windsor.*

I'll urge his hatred more to Clarence;
And, if I fail not in my deep *intent*,
Clarence hath not another day to live. *Shakesp. R.* III.

There is an incurable blindness caused by a resolution not to see; and, to all *intents* and purposes, he who will not open his eyes is for the present as blind as he that cannot. *South.*

He was a miserable creature to all *intents* and purposes. *L'Estrange's Fables.*

This fury fit for her *intent* she chose;
One who delights in wars. *Dryden's Æn.*

The Athenians sent their fleet to Sicily, upon pretence only to assist the Leontines against Syracuse; but with an *intent* to make themselves masters of that island. *Grew.*

Of darkness visible so much be lent,
As half to shew, half veil the deep *intent.* *Dunciad.*

INTE'NTION. *n. s.* [*intention*, French; *intentio*, Latin.]

1. Eagerness of desire; closeness of attention; deep thought; vehemence or ardour of mind.

Intention is when the mind with great earnestness, and of choice, fixes its view on any idea, considers it on every side, and will not be called off by the ordinary solicitation of other ideas. *Locke.*

Effectual prayer is joined with a vehement *intention* of the inferior powers of the soul, which cannot therein long continue without pain: it hath been therefore thought good, by turns, to interpose still somewhat for the higher part of the mind and the understanding to work upon. *Hooker.*

She did course o'er my exteriors with such a greedy *intention*, that the appetite of her eye did seem to scorch me up like a burning-glass. *Shakes. Merry Wives of Windsor.*

In persons possessed with other notions of religion, the understanding cannot quit these but by great examination; which cannot be done without some labour and *intention* of the mind, and the thoughts dwelling a considerable time upon the survey and discussion of each particular. *South's Sermons.*

2. Design; purpose.

Most part of chronical distempers proceed from laxity of the fibres; in which case the principal *intention* is to restore the tone of the solid parts. *Arbuthnot on Aliments.*

3. The state of being intense or strained. This for distinction is more generally and more conveniently written *intension.*

The operations of agents admit of *intention* and remission; but essences are not capable of such variation. *Locke.*

INTE'NTIONAL. *adj.* [*intentionel*, Fr. from *intention.*] Designed; done by design.

The glory of God is the great end which every intelligent being is bound to consult, by a direct and *intentional* service. *Rogers's Sermons.*

INTE'NTIONALLY. *adv.* [from *intentional.*]

1. By design; with fixed choice.

I find in myself that this inward principle doth exert many of its actions *intentionally* and purposely. *Hale.*

2. In will, if not in action.

Whenever I am wishing to write to you, I shall conclude you are *intentionally* doing so to me. *Atterbury to Pope.*

INTE'NTIVE. *adj.* [from *intent.*] Diligently applied; busily attentive.

Where the object is fine and accurate, it conduceth much to have the sense *intentive* and erect. *Bacon's Natural History.*

The naked relation, at least the *intentive* consideration of that, is able still, and at this disadvantage of time, to rend the hearts of pious contemplators. *Brown's Vulg. Errours.*

INT'ENIVELY. *adv.* [from *intentive.*] With application; closely.

INTE'NTLY. *adv.* [from *intent.*] With close attention; with close application; with eager desire.

If we insist passionately or so *intently* on the truth of our beliefs, as not to proceed to as vigorous pursuit of all just, sober, and godly living. *Hammond on Fundamentals.*

The odd paintings of an Indian screen, at first glance, may surprise and please a little; but when you fix your eye *intently* upon them, they appear so extravagantly disproportioned that they give a judicious eye pain. *Atterbury.*

The Chian medal seats him with a volume open, and reading *intently.* *Pope.*

INTE'NTNESS. *n. s.* [from *intent.*] The state of being intent; anxious application.

He is grown more disengaged from his *intentness* on his own affairs. *Swift.*

To INTE'R. *v. a.* [*enterrer*, French.] To cover under ground; to bury.

Within their chiefest temple I'll erect
A tomb, wherein his corps shall be *interr'd.* *Shakes. H.* VI.

The evil that men do lives after them;
The good is oft *interred* with their bones. *Shakes. Jul. Cæs.*

His

His body ſhall be royally *interr'd*,
And the laſt funeral pomps adorn his herſe. *Dryden.*

The aſhes, in an old record of the convent, are ſaid to have been *interred* between the very wall and the altar where they were taken up. *Addiſon on Italy.*

The beſt way is to *inter* them as you furrow peaſe. *Mort.*

INTE'RCALAR. } *adj.* [*intercalaire*, Fr. *intercalaris*, Latin.]
INTE'RCALARY. } Inſerted out of the common order to preſerve the equation of time, as the twenty-ninth of February in a leap-year is an *intercalary* day.

To INTE'RCALATE. *v. a.* [*intercaler*, Fr. *intercalo*, Lat.] To inſert an extraordinary day.

INTERCALA'TION. *n. ſ.* [*intercalation*, Fr. *intercalatio*, Latin.] Inſertion of days out of the ordinary reckoning.

In ſixty-three years there may be loſt almoſt eighteen days, omitting the *intercalation* of one day every fourth year, allowed for this quadrant, or ſix ſupernumeraries. *Brown's Vul. Err.*

To INTERCE'DE. *v. n.* [*interceder*, Fr. *intercedo*, Latin.]

1. To paſs between.

He ſuppoſeth that a vaſt period *interceded* between that origination and the age wherein he lived. *Hale's Origin of Mank.*

Thoſe ſuperficies reflect the greateſt quantity of light, which have the greateſt refracting power, and which *intercede* mediums that differ moſt in their refractive denſities. *Newton.*

2. To mediate; to act between two parties with a view of reconciling differences.

Them the glad ſon
Preſenting, thus to *intercede* began. *Milt. Parad. Loſt.*

Nor was our bleſſed Saviour only our propitiation to die for us, and procure our atonement, but he is ſtill our advocate, continually *interceding* with his Father in behalf of all true penitents. *Calamy.*

I may reſtore myſelf into the good graces of my fair criticks, and your lordſhip may *intercede* with them on my promiſe of amendment. *Dryden.*

Origen denies that any prayer is to be made to them, although it be only to *intercede* with God for us, but only the ſon of God. *Stillingfleet.*

INTERCE'DER. *n. ſ.* [from *intercede.*] One that intercedes; a mediator.

To INTERCEPT. *v. a.* [*intercepter*, Fr. *interceptus*, Latin.]

1. To ſtop and ſeize in the way.

The better courſe ſhould be by planting of garriſons about him, which, whenſoever he ſhall look forth, or be drawn out, ſhall be always ready to *intercept* his going or coming. *Spenſer.*

Who *intercepts* me in my expedition?
——O, ſhe that might have *intercepted* thee,
By ſtrangling thee. *Shakeſpeare's Richard* III.

I then in London, keeper of the king,
Muſter'd my ſoldiers, gather'd flocks of friends,
March'd towards St. Alban's t' *intercept* the queen. *Shakeſp.*

Your *intercepted* packets
You writ to the pope. *Shakeſp. Henry* VIII.

If we hope for things which are at too great a diſtance from us, it is poſſible that we may be *intercepted* by death in our progreſs towards them. *Addiſon's Spectator.*

2. To obſtruct; to cut off; to ſtop from being communicated.

Though they cannot anſwer my diſtreſs,
Yet in ſome ſort they're better than the tribunes;
For that they will not *intercept* my tale. *Shakeſ. Tit. Andr.*

Since death's near, and runs with ſo much force,
We muſt meet firſt, and *intercept* his courſe. *Dryden.*

On barbed ſteeds they rode in proud array,
Thick as the college of the bees in May,
When ſwarming o'er the duſky fields they fly
New to the flow'rs, and *intercept* the ſky. *Dryden.*

Behind the hole I faſtened to the paſteboard, with pitch, the blade of a ſharp knife, to *intercept* ſome part of the light which paſſed through the hole. *Newton's Opt.*

The direful woes,
Which voyaging from Troy the victors bore,
While ſtorms vindictive *intercept* the ſhore. *Pope.*

INTERCE'PTION. *n. ſ.* [*interception*, Fr. *interceptio*, Lat. from *intercept.*] Stoppage in courſe; hindrance; obſtruction.

The pillars, ſtanding at a competent diſtance from the outmoſt wall, will, by *interception* of the ſight, ſomewhat in appearance diminiſh the breadth. *Wotton's Architecture.*

The word in Mathew doth not only ſignify ſuſpenſion, but alſo ſuffocation, ſtrangulation, or *interception* of breath. *Brown.*

INTERCE'SSION. *n. ſ.* [*interceſſion*, Fr. *interceſſio*, Lat.] Mediation; interpoſition; agency between two parties; agency in the cauſe of another, generally in his favour.

Yet loving, indeed, and therefore conſtant, he uſed ſtill the *interceſſion* of diligence and faith, ever hoping becauſe he would not put himſelf into that hell to be hopeleſs, until the time of our being come and captived there brought forth this end. *Sid.*

Can you, when you puſh'd out of your gates the very defender of them, think to front his revenges with the palſied *interceſſion* of ſuch a decay'd dotard as you ſeem to be? *Shakep.*

He maketh *interceſſion* to God againſt Iſrael. *Ro.* xi. 2.

He bare the ſin of many, and made *interceſſion* for the tranſgreſſors. *Iſ.* liii. 12.

Pray not thou for this people, neither make *interceſſion* to me; for I will not hear thee. *Jer.* vii. 16.

To pray to the ſaints to obtain things by their merits and *interceſſions*, is allowed and contended for by the Roman church. *Stillingfleet.*

Your *interceſſion* now is needleſs grown;
Retire, and let me ſpeak with her alone. *Dryd. Aurengz.*

INTERCE'SSOUR. *n. ſ.* [*interceſſeur*, Fr. *interceſſor*, Lat.] Mediator; agent between two parties to procure reconciliation.

Behold the heav'ns! thither thine eyeſight bend;
Thy looks, ſighs, tears, for *interceſſours* ſend. *Fairfax.*

On man's behalf,
Patron or *interceſſour*, none appear'd. *Milt. Par. Loſt.*

When we ſhall hear our eternal doom from our *interceſſour*, it will convince us, that a denial of Chriſt is more than tranſitory words. *South's Sermons.*

To INTERCHA'IN. *v. a.* [*inter* and *chain.*] To chain; to link together.

Two boſoms *interchained* with an oath;
So then two boſoms, and a ſingle troth. *Shakeſpeare.*

To INTERCHA'NGE. *v a.* [*inter* and *change.*]

1. To put each in the place of the other; to give and take mutually; to exchange.

They had left but one piece of one ſhip, whereon they kept themſelves in all truth, having *interchanged* their cares, while either cared for other, each comforting and counſelling how to labour for the better, and to abide the worſe. *Sidney.*

I ſhall *interchange*
My wained ſtate for Henry's regal crown. *Shakeſpeare.*

2. To ſucceed alternately.

His faithful friend and brother Euarchus came ſo mightily to his ſuccour, that, with ſome *interchanging* changes of fortune, they begat of a juſt war, the beſt child peace. *Sidney.*

INTERCHA'NGE. *n. ſ.* [from the verb.]

1. Commerce; permutation of commodities.

Thoſe people have an *interchange* or trade with Elana. *Howel.*

2. Alternate ſucceſſion.

With what delight could I have walk'd thee round?
If I could joy in ought! ſweet *interchange*
Of hill and valley, rivers, woods, and plains. *Milton.*

The original meaſures of time, by help of the lights in the firmament, are perceptible to us by the *interchanges* of light and darkneſs, and ſucceſſion of ſeaſons. *Holder.*

Removes and *interchanges* would often happen in the firſt ages after the flood. *Burnet's Theory of the Earth.*

3. Mutual donation and reception.

Let Diomedes bear him,
And bring us Creſſid hither. Good Diomede,
Furniſh you fairly for this *interchange*. *Shak. Troil. and Creſſ.*

Farewel; the leiſure, and the fearful time,
Cuts off the ceremonious vows of love,
And ample *interchange* of ſweet diſcourſe. *Shakeſp. R.* III.

Since their more mature dignities and royal neceſſities made ſeparation of their ſociety, their encounters, though not perſonal, have been royally attornied with *interchange* of gifts, letters, loving embaſſies. *Shakeſ. Winter's Tale.*

After ſo vaſt an obligation, owned by ſo free an acknowledgment, could any thing be expected but a continual *interchange* of kindneſſes. *South.*

INTERCHA'NGEABLE. *adj.* [from *interchange.*]

1. Given and taken mutually.

So many teſtimonies, *interchangeable* warrants, and counterrolments, running through the hands and reſting in the power of ſo many ſeveral perſons, is ſufficient to argue and convince all manner of falſhood. *Bacon's Off. of Alienation.*

2. Following each other in alternate ſucceſſion.

Juſt under the line they may ſeem to have two Winters and two Summers; but there alſo they have four *interchangeable* ſeaſons, which is enough whereby to meaſure. *Holder.*

All along the hiſtory of the Old Teſtament we find the *interchangeable* providences of God, towards the people of Iſrael, always ſuited to their manners. *Tillotſon.*

INTERCHA'NGEABLY. *adv.* [from *interchangeable.*] Alternately; in a manner whereby each gives and receives.

In theſe two things the Eaſt and Weſt churches did *interchangeably* both confront the Jews and concur with them. *Hook.*

This in myſelf I boldly will defend,
And *interchangeably* hurl down my gage
Upon this overweening traitor's foot. *Shakeſp. R.* II.

Theſe articles were ſigned by our plenipotentiaries, and thoſe of Holland; but not by the French, although it ought to have been done *interchangeably*; and the miniſters here prevailed on the queen to execute a ratification of articles, which only one part had ſigned. *Swift.*

INTERCHA'NGEMENT. *n. ſ.* [*inter* and *change.*] Exchange; mutual transference.

A contract of eternal bond of love,
Confirm'd by mutual joinder of your hands,
Atteſted by the holy cloſe of lips,
Strengthen'd by *interchangement* of your rings. *Shakeſpeare.*

INTERCI'PIENT. *n. s.* [*intercipiens*, Latin.] An intercepting power; something that causes a stoppage.

They commend repellents, but not with much astringency, unless as *intercipients* upon the parts above, lest the matter should thereby be impacted in the part. *Wiseman.*

INTERCI'SION. *n. s.* [*inter* and *cædo*, Lat.] Interruption.

By cessation of oracles we may understand their *intercision*, not abscission, or consummate desolation. *Brown's Vulgar Err.*

To INTERCLU'DE. *v. n.* [*intercludo*, Latin.] To shut from a place or course by something intervening; to intercept.

The voice is sometimes *intercluded* by a hoarseness, or viscuous phlegm cleaving to the aspera arteria. *Holder.*

INTERCLU'SION. *n. s.* [*interclusus*, Latin.] Obstruction; interception.

INTERCOLUMNIA'TION. *n. s* [*inter* and *columna*, Latin.] The space between the pillars.

The distance or *intercolumniation* may be near four of his own diameter, because the materials commonly laid over this pillar were rather of wood than stone. *Wotton.*

To INTERCO'MMON. *v. n.* [*inter* and *common.*] To feed at the same table.

Wine is to be forborn in consumptions, for that the spirits of the wine do prey upon the roscid juice of the body, and *intercommon* with the spirits of the body, and so rob them of their nourishment. *Bacon's Natural History.*

INTERCOMMU'NITY. *n. s.* [*inter* and *community.*] A mutual communication or community; a mutual freedom or exercise of religion.

INTERCO'STAL. *adj.* [*intercostal*, Fr. *inter* and *costa*, Lat.] Placed between the ribs.

The diaphragm seems the principal instrument of ordinary respiration, although to restrained respiration the *intercostal* muscles may concur. *Boyle.*

By the assistance of the inward *intercostal* muscles, in deep suspirations, we take more large gulps of air to cool our heart. *More's Antidote against Atheism.*

I'NTERCOURSE. *n. s.* [*entrecours*, French.]

1. Commerce; exchange.

This sweet *intercourse*
Of looks, and smiles; for smiles from reason flow,
To brute deny'd, and are of love the food. *Milton.*

2. Communication.

The choice of the place requireth many circumstances, as the situation near the sea, for the commodiousness of an *intercourse* with England. *Bacon.*

What an honour is it that God should admit us into such a participation of himself? That he should give us minds capable of such an *intercourse* with the Supreme Mind? *Atterbury.*

INTERCU'RRENCE. *n. s.* [from *intercurro*, Latin.] Passage between.

Consider what fluidity saltpetre is capable of, without the *intercurrence* of a liquor. *Boyle.*

INTERCU'RRENT. *adj.* [*intercurrens*, Lat.] Running between.

If into a phial, filled with good spirit of nitre, you cast a piece of iron, the liquor, whose parts moved placidly before, meeting with particles in the iron, altering the motion of its parts, and perhaps that of some very subtile *intercurrent* matter, those active parts presently begin to penetrate, and scatter abroad particles of the iron *Boyle.*

INTERDE'AL. *n. s.* [*inter* and *deal.*] Traffick; intercourse.

The Gaulish speech is the very British, which is yet retained of the Welshmen and Britons of France; though the alteration of the trading and *interdeal* with other nations has greatly altered the dialect. *Spenser.*

To INTERDI'CT. *v. a.* [*interdire*, Fr. *interdico*, Latin.]

1. To forbid; to prohibit.

Alone I pass'd, through ways
That brought me on a sudden to the tree
Of *interdicted* knowledge. *Milton's Par. Lost, b.* v.
By magick fenc'd, by spells encompass'd round,
No mortal touch'd this *interdicted* ground. *Tickel.*

2. To prohibit from the enjoyment of communion with the church.

An archbishop may not only excommunicate and *interdict* his suffragans, but his vicar-general may do the same. *Ayliffe.*

INTERDI'CT. *n. s.* [from the verb.]

1. Prohibition; prohibiting decree.

Amongst his other fundamental laws, he did ordain the *interdicts* and prohibitions touching entrance of strangers. *Bacon.*

Those are not fruits forbidden, no *interdict*
Defends the touching of these viands pure;
Their taste no knowledge works at least of evil. *Milt. P. L.*
Had he liv'd to see her happy change,
He would have cancell'd that harsh *interdict*,
And join'd our hands himself. *Dryd. Don Sebastian.*

2. A papal prohibition to the clergy to celebrate the holy offices.

Nani carried himself meritoriously against the pope, in the time of the *interdict*, which held up his credit among the patriots. *Wotton.*

INTERDI'CTION. *n. s.* [*interdiction*, Fr. *interdictio*, Lat. from *interdict.*]

1. Prohibition; forbidding decree.

Sternly he pronounc'd
The rigid *interdiction*, which resounds
Yet dreadful in mine ear. *Milton's Paradise Lost, b.* viii.

2. Curse: from the papal *interdict*. An improper use of the word.

The truest issue of thy throne,
By his own *interdiction* stands accurst. *Shakesp. Macbeth.*

INTERDI'CTORY. *adj.* [from *interdict.*] Belonging to an interdiction. *Ainsworth.*

To INTERE'SS. } *v. a.* [*interesser*, French.] To concern; to
To INTERE'ST. } affect; to give share in.

The mystical communion of all faithful men is such as maketh every one to be *interessed* in those precious blessings, which any one of them receiveth at God's hands. *Hooker.*

Our joy,
Although our last not least; to whose young love,
The vines of France and milk of Burgundy,
Strive to be *int'ress'd.* *Shakesp. King Lear.*

To love our native country, and to study its benefit and its glory, to be *interessed* in its concerns, is natural to all men. *Dryden's Æn. Dedicat.*

Scipio, restoring the Spanish bride, gained a great nation to *interest* themselves for Rome against Carthage. *Dryden.*

This was a goddess who used to *interest* herself in marriages. *Addison on Medals.*

Ill successes did not discourage that ambitious and *interested* people. *Arbuthnot on Coins.*

To INTERE'ST. *v. n.* To affect; to move; to touch with passion; to gain the affections: as, this is an *interesting* story.

I'NTEREST. *n. s.* [*interest*, Latin; *interest*, French.]

1. Concern; advantage; good.

O give us a serious comprehension of that one great *interest* of others, as well as ourselves. *Hammond.*

There is no man but God hath put many things into his possession, to be used for the common good and *interest*. *Calam.*

2. Influence over others.

They, who had hitherto preserved them, had now lost their *interest*. *Clarendon.*

Exert, great God, thy *int'rest* in the sky;
Gain each kind pow'r, each guardian deity,
That, conquer'd by the publick vow,
They bear the dismal mischief far away. *Prior.*

Endeavour to adjust the degrees of influence, that each cause might have in producing the effect, and the proper agency and *interest* of each therein. *Watts.*

3. Share; part in any thing; participation: as, this is a matter in which we have *interest*.

4. Regard to private profit.

Wherever *interest* or power thinks fit to interfere, it little imports what principles the opposite parties think fit to charge upon each other. *Swift.*

'Tis *int'rest* calls off all her sneaking train. *Pope.*

5. Money paid for use; usury.

Did he take *interest?*
——No, not take *interest*; not, as you would say,
Directly, *int'rest*; mark what Jacob did. *Shakespeare.*

It is a sad life we lead, my dear, to be so teazed; paying *interest* for old debts, and still contracting new ones. *Arbuthn.*

6. Any surplus of advantage.

With all speed
You shall have your desires with *interest*. *Shakespeare.*

To INTERFE'RE. *v. n.* [*inter* and *ferio*, Latin.]

1. To interpose; to intermeddle.

So cautious were our ancestors in conversation, as never to *interfere* with party disputes in the state. *Swift.*

2. To clash; to oppose each other.

If each acts by an independent power, their commands may *interfere*. *Smalridge's Serm.*

3. A horse is said to *interfere*, when the side of one of his shoes strikes against and hurts one of his fetlocks, or the hitting one leg against another, and striking off the skin. *Farrier's Dict.*

INTE'RFLUENT. *adj.* [*interfluens*, Lat.] Flowing between.

Air may consist of any terrene or aqueous corpuscles, kept swimming in the *interfluent* celestial matter. *Boyle.*

INTERFU'LGENT. *adj.* [*inter* and *fulgens*, Latin.] Shining between.

INTERFU'SED. *adj.* [*interfusus*, Latin.] Poured or scattered between.

The ambient air wide *interfus'd*,
Embracing round this florid earth. *Milton.*

INTERJA'CENCY. *n. s.* [from *interjacens*, Latin.]

1. The act or state of lying between.

England and Scotland is divided only by the *interjacency* of the Tweed, and some desert ground. *Hale.*

2. The thing lying between.

Its fluctuations are but motions, which winds, storms, shoars, and every *interjacency* irregulates. *Brown's Vulg. Err.*

INTERJA'CENT. *adj.* [*interjacens*, Latin.] Intervening; lying between.

The sea itself must be very broad, and void of little islands *interjacent*, else will it yield plentiful argument of quarrel to the kingdoms which it serveth. *Raleigh.*

Through

Through this hole objects that were beyond might be seen distinctly, which would not at all be seen through other parts of the glasses, where the air was *interjacent*. *Newton's Opt.*

INTERJE'CTION. *n. s.* [*interjection*, Fr. *interjectio*, Latin.]

1. A part of speech that discovers the mind to be seized or affected with some passion: such as are in English, *O! alas! ah!* *Clarke's Lat. Gram.*

Their wild natural notes, when they would express their passions, are at the best but like natural *interjections*, to discover their passions or impressions. *Hale's Origin of Mankind.*

2. Intervention; interposition; act of something coming between; act of putting something between.

Laughing causeth a continued expulsion of the breath, with the loud noise which maketh the *interjection* of laughing. *Bacon.*

I'NTERIM. *n. s.* [*interim*, Latin.] Mean time; intervening time.

I a heavy *interim* shall support,
By his dear absence. *Shakespeare's Othello.*

One bird happened to be foraging for her young ones, and in this *interim* comes a torrent that washes away nest, birds, and all. *L'Estrange.*

In this *interim* my women asked what I thought. *Tatler.*

INTERJO'IN. *adj.* [*inter* and *join.*] To join mutually; to intermarry.

So fellest foes,
Whose passions and whose plots have broke their sleep,
To take the one the other, by some chance,
Some trick not worth an egg, shall grow dear friends,
And *interjoin* their issues. *Shakesp. Coriolanus.*

INTE'RIOUR. *adj.* [*interior*, Lat. *interieur*, Fr.] Internal; inner; not outward; not superficial.

The fool-multitude, that chuse by show,
Not learning more than the fond eye doth teach,
Which pry not to th' *interiour*. *Shakespeare.*

The grosser parts, thus sunk down, would harden and constitute the *interiour* parts of the earth. *Burnet.*

INTERKNO'WLEDGE. *n. s.* [*inter* and *knowledge.*] Mutual knowledge.

All nations have *interknowledge* one of another, either by voyage into foreign parts, or by strangers that come to them. *Bacon's New Atlantis.*

To INTERLA'CE. *v. a.* [*entrelasser*, French.] To intermix; to put one thing within another.

Some are to be *interlaced* between the divine readings of the law and prophets. *Hooker.*

Touching reannexing of Bretagne to France, the ambassadors declined any mention thereof; but contrariwise *interlaced*, in their conference, the purpose of their master to match with the daughter of Maximilian. *Bacon's Henry VII.*

They acknowledged what services he had done for the commonwealth, yet *interlacing* some errors, wherewith they seemed to reproach him. *Hayward.*

Your argument is as strong against the use of rhyme in poems as in plays; for the epick way is every where *interlaced* with dialogue. *Dryden.*

INTERLA'PSE. *n. s.* [*inter* and *lapse.*] The flow of time between any two events.

These dregs are calcined into such salts, which, after a short *interlapse* of time, produce coughs. *Harvey.*

To INTERLA'RD. *v. a.* [*entrelarder*, French.]

1. To mix meat with bacon, or fat; to diversify lean with fat.

2. To interpose; to insert between.

Jests should be *interlarded*, after the Persian custom, by ages young and old. *Carew.*

3. To diversify by mixture.

The laws of Normandy were the defloration of the English laws, and a transcript of them, though mingled and *interlarded* with many particular laws of their own, which altered the features of the original. *Hale's Laws of England.*

4. *Philips* has used this word very harshly, and probably did not understand it.

They *interlard* their native drinks with choice
Of strongest brandy. *Philips.*

To INTERLE'AVE. *v. a.* [*inter* and *leave.*] To chequer a book by the insertion of blank leaves.

To INTERLI'NE. *v. a.* [*inter* and *line.*]

1. To write in alternate lines.

When, by *interlining* Latin and English one with another, he has got a moderate knowledge of the Latin tongue, he may then be advanced farther. *Locke.*

2. To correct by something written between the lines.

He cancell'd an old will, and forg'd a new;
Made wealthy at the small expence of signing,
With a wet seal, and a fresh *interlining*. *Dryden's Juven.*

Three things render a writing suspected: the person producing a false instrument, the person that frames it, and the *interlining* and rasing out of words contained in such instruments. *Ayliffe's Parergon.*

The muse invok'd, sit down to write,
Blot out, correct, and *interline*. *Swift.*

INTERLINEA'TION. *n. s.* [*inter* and *lineation.*] Correction made by writing between the lines.

Many clergymen write in so diminutive a manner, with such frequent blots and *interlineations*, that they are hardly able to go on without perpetual hesitations. *Swift.*

To INTERLI'NK. *v. a.* [*inter* and *link.*] To connect chains one to another; to join one in another.

The fair mixture in pictures causes us to enter into the subject which it imitates, and imprints it the more deeply into our imagination and our memory: these are two chains which are *interlinked*, which contain, and are at the same time contained. *Dryden's Dufresnoy.*

INTERLOCU'TION. *n. s.* [*interlocution*, Fr. *interlocutio*, Latin.]

1. Dialogue; interchange of speech.

The plainest and the most intelligible rehearsal of the psalms they savour not, because it is done by *interlocution*, and with a mutual return of sentences from side to side. *Hooker.*

2. Preparatory proceeding in law; an intermediate act before final decision.

These things are called accidental, because some new incident in judicature may emerge upon them, on which the judge ought to proceed by *interlocution*. *Ayliffe's Parergon.*

INTERLO'CUTOR. *n. s.* [*inter* and *loquor*, Latin.] Dialogist; one that talks with another.

Some morose readers shall find fault with my having made the *interlocutors* compliment with one another. *Boyle.*

INTERLO'CUTORY. *adj.* [*interlocutoire*, Fr. *inter* and *loquor*, Lat.]

1. Consisting of dialogue.

When the minister by exhortation raiseth them up, and the people by protestation of their readiness declare he speaketh not in vain unto them; these *interlocutory* forms of speech, what are they else but most effectual, partly testifications, and partly inflammations of all piety? *Hooker.*

There are several *interlocutory* discourses in the holy Scriptures, though the persons speaking are not alternately mentioned or referred to. *Fiddes's Sermons.*

2. Preparatory to decision.

To INTERLO'PE. *v. n.* [*inter* and *loopen*, Dutch, to run.] To run between parties and intercept the advantage that one should gain from the other; to traffick without a proper licence; to forestall; to anticipate irregularly.

The patron is desired to leave off this *interloping* trade, or admit the knights of the industry to their share. *Tatler.*

INTERLO'PER. *n. s.* [from *interlope.*] One who runs into business to which he has no right.

The swallow was a fly-catcher, and was no more an *interloper* upon the spider's right, than the spider was upon the swallow's. *L'Estrange.*

INTERLU'CENT. *adj.* [*interlucens*, Latin.] Shining between. *Dict.*

I'NTERLUDE. *n. s.* [*inter* and *ludus*, Latin.] Something plaid at the intervals of festivity; a farce.

When there is a queen, and ladies of honour attending her, there must sometimes be masques, and revels, and *interludes*. *Bacon's Advice to Villiers.*

The enemies of Socrates hired Aristophanes to personate him on the stage, and, by the insinuations of those *interludes*, conveyed a hatred of him into the people. *Gov. of the Tongue.*

Dreams are but *interludes*, which fancy makes;
When monarch reason sleeps, this mimick wakes. *Dryden.*

INTERLU'ENCY. *n. s.* [*interluo*, Latin.] Water interposited; interposition of a flood.

Those parts of Asia and America, which are now disjoined by the *interluency* of the sea, might have been formerly contiguous. *Hale's Origin of Mankind.*

INTERLU'NAR. } *adj.* [*inter* and *luna*, Lat.] Belonging to the
INTERLU'NARY. } time when the moon, about to change, is invisible.

We add the two Egyptian days in every month, the *interlunary* and prenilunary exemptions. *Brown.*

The sun to me is dark,
And silent as the moon,
When she deserts the night,
Hid in her vacant *interlunar* cave. *Milton.*

INTERMA'RRIAGE. *n. s.* [*inter* and *marriage.*] Marriage between two families, where each takes one and gives another.

Because the many alliances and *intermarriages*, as well as the personal feuds that happen among so small a people, might obstruct the course of justice, they have always a foreigner for this employ. *Addison on Italy.*

To INTERMA'RRY. *v. n.* [*inter* and *marry.*] To marry some of each family with the other.

About the middle of the fourth century, from the building of Rome, it was declared lawful for nobles and plebeians to *intermarry*. *Swift.*

To INTERME'DDLE. *v. n.* [*inter* and *meddle.*] To interpose officiously.

The practice of Spain hath been by war, and by conditions of treaty, to *intermeddle* with foreign states, and declare themselves protectors general of Catholicks. *Bacon.*

Seeing the king was a sovereign prince, the emperor should not *intermeddle* with ordering his subjects, or directing the affairs of his realm. *Hayward.*

There were no ladies, who difpofed themfelves to *intermeddle* in bufinefs. *Clarendon.*

To INTERME'DDLE. *v. a.* [*entremefler*, French.] To intermix; to mingle. This is perhaps mifprinted for *intermelled.*

Many other adventures are *intermeddled*; as the love of Britomert, and the virtuoufnefs of Belphæbe. *Spenfer.*

INTERME'DLER. *n. f.* [from *intermeddle.*] One that interpofes officioufly; one that thrufts himfelf into bufinefs to which he has no right.

There's hardly a greater peft to government and families, than officious tale-bearers, and bufy *intermeddlers. L'Eftrange.*

Our two great allies abroad, and our ftock-jobbers at home, direct her majefty not to change her fecretary or treafurer, who, for the reafons that thefe officious *intermeddlers* demanded their continuance, ought never to have been admitted into the leaft truft. *Swift.*

Shall faucy *intermeddlers* fay,
Thus far, and thus, are you allow'd to punifh? *A. Phillips.*

INTERME'DIACY. *n. f.* [from *intermediate.*] Interpofition; intervention. An unauthorifed word.

In birds the auditory nerve is affected by only the *intermediacy* of the columella. *Derham.*

INTERME'DIAL *adj.* [*inter* and *medius*, Latin.] Intervening; lying between; intervenient.

The love of God makes a man temperate in the midft of feafts, and is active enough without any *intermedial* appetites. *Taylor.*

A gardener prepares the ground, and in all the *intermedial* fpaces he is careful to drefs it. *Evelyn's Kalendar.*

INTERME'DIATE. *adj.* [*intermediat*, Fr. *inter* and *medius*, Lat.] Intervening; interpofed; holding the middle place or degree between two extremes.

Do not the moft refrangible rays excite the fhorteft vibrations for making a fenfation of a deep violet, the leaft refrangible the largeft for making a fenfation of deep red, and the feveral *intermediate* forts of rays, vibrations of feveral *intermediate* bigneffes, to make fenfations of the feveral *intermediate* colours? *Newton's Opt.*

An animal confifts of folid and fluid parts, unlefs one fhould reckon fome of an *intermediate* nature as fat and phlegm. *Arb.*

Thofe general natures, which ftand between the neareft and moft remote, are called *intermediate. Watts.*

INTERME'DIATELY. *adv.* [from *intermediate.*] By way of intervention.

To INTERME'LL. *v. a.* [*entremefler*, Fr.] To mix; to mingle.

By occafion hereof many other adventures are *intermelled*, but rather as accidents than intendments. *Spenfer.*

INTE'RMENT. *n. f.* [*interment*, French; from *inter.*] Burial; fepulchre.

INTERMIGRA'TION. *n. f.* [*intermigration*, Fr. *inter* and *migro*, Lat.] Act of removing from one place to another, fo as that of two parties removing each takes the place of the other.

Men have a ftrange variety in colour, ftature, and humour; and all arifing from the climate, though the continent be but one, as to point of accefs, mutual intercourfe, and poffibility of *intermigrations. Hale's Origin of Mankind.*

INTE'RMINABLE. *adj.* [*interminable*, Fr. *in* and *termino*, Latin.] Immenfe; admitting no boundary.

As if they would confine th' *interminable*,
And tie him to his own prefcript. *Milton's Agoniftes.*

INTE'RMINATE. *adj.* [*interminate*, Fr. *interminatus*, Latin.] Unbounded; unlimited.

Within a thicket I repos'd; when round
I ruffled up fall'n leaves in heaps, and found,
Let fall from heaven, a fleep *interminate. Chapm. Odyff.*

INTERMINA'TION. *n. f.* [*intermination*, Fr. *intermino*, Latin.] Menace; threat.

The threats and *interminations* of the Gofpel, thofe terrors of the Lord, as goads, may drive thofe brutifh creatures who will not be attracted. *Decay of Piety.*

To INTERMI'NGLE. *v. a.* [*inter* and *mingle.*] To mingle; to mix; to put fome things amongft others.

The church in her liturgies hath *intermingled*, with readings out of the New Teftament, leffons taken out of the law and prophets. *Hooker.*

His church he compareth unto a field, where tares, manifeftly known and feen by all men, do grow *intermingled* with good corn. *Hooker.*

My lord fhall never reft:
I'll *intermingle* every thing he does
With Caffio's fuit. *Shakefpeare's Othello.*

Here failing fhips delight the wand'ring eyes;
There trees and *intermingled* temples rife. *Pope.*

To INTERMI'NGLE. *v. n.* To be mixed or incorporated.

INTERMI'SSION. *n. f.* [*intermiffion*, Fr. *intermiffio*, Lat.]

1. Ceffation for a time; paufe; intermediate ftop.

Came a reeking poft,
Deliver'd letters, fpight of *intermiffion*,
Which prefently they read. *Shakefp. King Lear.*

I count *intermiffion* almoft the fame thing as change; for that that hath been intermitted, is after a fort new. *Bacon.*

The water afcends gently, and by *intermiffions*; but it falls continuately, and with force. *Wilkins's Dæd.*

The peafants work on, in the hotteft part of the day, without *intermiffion. Locke.*

2. Intervenient time.

But gentle heav'n
Cut fhort all *intermiffion*: front to front,
Bring thou this fiend of Scotland and myfelf. *Shakefp.*

3. State of being intermitted.

Words borrowed of antiquity, have the authority of years, and out of their *intermiffion* do win to themfelves a kind of grace-like newnefs *Ben. Johnfon.*

4. The fpace between the paroxyfms of a fever, or any fits of pain; reft; paufe of forrow.

Reft or *intermiffion* none I find. *Milton.*

INTERMI'SSIVE. *adj.* [from *intermit.*] Coming by fits; not continual.

Wounds I will lend the French, inftead of eyes,
To weep their *intermiffive* miferies. *Shakefp. Henry VI.*

I reduced Ireland, after fo many *intermiffive* wars, to a perfect paffive obedience. *Howel's England's Tears.*

As though there were any feriation in nature, or juftitiums imaginable in profeffions, whofe fubject is under no *intermiffive* but conftant way of mutation, this feafon is commonly termed the phyficians vacation. *Brown's Vulgar Errours.*

To INTERMI'T. *v. a.* [*intermitto*, Latin.] To forbear any thing for a time; to interrupt.

If nature fhould *intermit* her courfe, and leave altogether, though it were but for a while, the obfervation of her own laws. *Hooker.*

Run to your houfes, fall upon your knees;
Pray to the gods, to *intermit* the plague
That needs muft light on this ingratitude. *Shakefpeare.*

His mifled, lafcivious fon,
Edward the fecond, *intermitted* fo
The courfe of glory. *Daniel's Civ. War.*

The fetting on foot fome of thofe arts that were once well known, would be but the reviving of thofe arts which were long before practifed, though *intermitted* and interrupted by war. *Hale's Origin of Mankind.*

Certain Indians, when a horfe is running in his full career, leap down, gather any thing from the ground, and immediately leap up again, the horfe not *intermitting* his courfe. *Wilkins.*

Speech *intermitted*, thus began. *Milton.*

We are furnifhed with an armour from heaven of firmnefs; but if we are remifs, or fuffer ourfelves to be perfuaded to lay by our arms, and *intermit* our guard, we may be furprifed. *Rogers's Sermons.*

To INTERMI'T. *v. n.* To grow mild between the fits or paroxyfms. Ufed of fevers.

INTERMI'TTENT. *adj.* [*intermittent*, Fr. *intermittens*, Latin.] Coming by fits.

Next to thofe durable pains, fhort *intermittent* or fwift recurrent pains do precipitate patients into confumptions. *Harv.*

To INTERMI'X. *v. a.* [*inter* and *mix.*] To mingle; to join; to put fome things among others.

Her perfuafions fhe *intermixed* with tears, affirming, that fhe would depart from him. *Hayward.*

Reveal
To Adam what fhall come in future days,
As I fhall thee enlighten: *intermix*
My cov'nant in the woman's feed renew'd. *Milt. Par. Loft.*

In yonder fpring of rofes, *intermix'd*
With myrtle, find what to redrefs 'till noon. *Milton.*

I doubt not to perform the part of a juft hiftorian to my royal mafter, without *intermixing* with it any thing of the poet. *Dryden.*

To INTERMI'X. *v. n.* To be mingled together.

INTERMI'XTURE. *n. f.* [*inter* and *mixtura*, Latin.]

1. Mafs formed by mingling bodies.

The analytical preparation of gold or mercury, leave perfons much unfatisfied whether the fubftances they produce be truly the hypoftatical principles, or only fome *intermixtures* of the divided bodies with thofe employed. *Boyle.*

2. Something additional mingled in a mafs.

In this height of impiety there wanted not an *intermixture* of levity and folly. *Bacon's Henry VI.*

INTERMU'NDANE. *adj.* [*inter* and *mundus*, Latin.] Subfifting between worlds, or between orb and orb.

The vaft diftances between thefe great bodies are called *intermundane* fpaces; in which though there may be fome fluid, yet it is fo thin and fubtile, that it is as much as nothing. *Locke.*

INTERMU'RAL. *adj.* [*inter*, *muralis*, *murus*, Lat.] Lying between walls. *Ainfworth.*

INTERMU'TUAL. *adj.* [*inter* and *mutual.*] Mutual; interchanged. *Inter* before *mutual* is improper.

A folemn oath religioufly they take,
By *intermutual* vows protefting there,
This never to reveal, nor to forfake
So good a caufe. *Daniel's Civil War.*

INTE'RN. *adj.* [*interne*, French; *internus*, Latin.] Inward; inteftine; not foreign.

The midland towns are moft flourifhing, which fhews that her riches are *intern* and domeftick. *Howel.*

INTE'RNAL. *adj.* [*internus*, Latin.]
1. Inward; not external.

That ye shall be as gods, since I as man,
Internal man, is but proportion meet. *Milt. Par. Lost.*
Myself, my conscience, and *internal* peace. *Milton.*

Bad comes of setting our hearts upon the shape, colour, and external beauty of things, without regard to the *internal* excellence and virtue of them. *L'Estrange.*

If we think most mens actions to be the interpreters of their thoughts, they have no such *internal* veneration for good rules. *Locke.*

2. Intrinsick; not depending on external accidents; real.

We are to provide things honest; to consider not only the *internal* rectitude of our actions in the sight of God, but whether they will be free from all mark or suspicion of evil. *Rogers.*

INTE'RNALLY. *adv.* [from *internal.*]
1. Inwardly.
2. Mentally; intellectually.

We are symbolically in the sacrament, and by faith and the spirit of God *internally* united to Christ. *Taylor.*

INTERNE'CINE. *adj.* [*internecinus*, Latin.] Endeavouring mutual destruction.

Th' Egyptians worship'd dogs, and for
Their faith made *internecine* war. *Hudibras, p.* i.

INTERNE'CION. *n. s.* [*internecion*, French; *internecio*, Latin.] Massacre; slaughter.

That natural propension of self-love, and natural principle of self-preservation, will necessarily break out into wars and *internecions*. *Hale's Origin of Mankind.*

INTERNU'NCIO. *n. s.* [*internuncius*, Latin.] Messenger between two parties.

INTERPELLA'TION. *n. s.* [*interpellation*, Fr. *interpellatio*, Lat.] A summons; a call upon.

In all extrajudicial acts one citation, monition, or extrajudicial *interpellation* is sufficient. *Ayliffe's Parergon.*

To INTE'RPOLATE. *v. a.* [*interpoler*, Fr. *interpolo*, Latin.]
1. To foist any thing into a place to which it does not belong.

The Athenians were put in possession of Salamis by another law, which was cited by Solon, or, as some think, *interpolated* by him for that purpose. *Pope.*

2. To renew; to begin again; to carry on with intermissions.

This motion of the heavenly bodies themselves seems to be partly continued and unintermitted, as that motion of the first moveable, partly *interpolated* and interrupted. *Hale.*

That individual hath necessarily a concomitant succession of *interpolated* motions; namely, the pulses of the heart, and the successive motions of respiration. *Hale.*

INTERPOLA'TION. *n. s.* [*interpolation*, Fr. from *interpolate.*] Something added or put into the original matter.

I have changed the situation of some of the Latin verses, and made some *interpolations*. *Cromwell to Pope.*

INTERPOLA'TOR. *n. s.* [Latin; *interpolateur*, Fr.] One that foists in counterfeit passages.

You or your *interpolator* ought to have considered. *Swift.*

INTERPO'SAL. *n. s.* [from *interpose.*]
1. Interposition; agency between two persons.

The *interposal* of my lord of Canterbury's command for the publication of this mean discourse, may seem to take away my choice. *South's Sermons.*

2. Intervention.

Our overshadowed souls may be emblemed by crusted globes, whose influential emissions are intercepted by the *interposal* of the benighting element. *Glanv. Sceps.*

To INTERPO'SE. *v. a.* [*interpono*, Latin; *interposer*, Fr.]
1. To thrust in as an obstruction, interruption, or inconvenience.

What watchful cares do *interpose* themselves
Betwixt your eyes and night. *Shakesp. Julius Cæsar.*
Death ready stands to *interpose* his dart. *Milton.*

Human frailty will too often *interpose* itself among persons of the holiest function. *Swift.*

2. To offer as a succour or relief.

The common father of mankind seasonably *interposed* his hand, and rescued miserable man out of the gross stupidity and sensuality whereinto he was plunged. *Woodward.*

3. To place between; to make intervenient.

Some weeks the king did honourably *interpose*, both to give space to his brother's intercession, and to show that he had a conflict with himself what he should do. *Bacon.*

To INTERPO'SE. *v. n.*
1. To mediate: to act between two parties.
2. To put in by way of interruption.

But, *interposes* Eleutherius, this objection may be made indeed almost against any hypothesis. *Boyle.*

INTERPO'SER. *n. s.* [from *interpose.*]
1. One that comes between others.

I will make haste; but 'till I come again,
No bed shall ere be guilty of my stay;
No rest be *interposer* 'twixt us twain. *Shakespeare.*

2. An intervenient agent; a mediator.

INTERPOSI'TION. *n. s.* [*interposition*, Fr. *interpositio*, Lat. from *interpose.*]
1. Intervenient agency.

There never was a time when the *interposition* of the magistrate was more necessary to secure the honour of religion. *Atterbury's Sermons.*

Though warlike successes carry in them often the evidences of a divine *interposition*, yet are they no sure marks of the divine favour. *Atterbury.*

2. Mediation; agency between parties.

The town and abbey would have come to an open rupture, had it not been timely prevented by the *interposition* of their common protectors. *Addison.*

3. Intervention; state of being placed between two.

The nights are so cold, fresh, and equal, by reason of the intire *interposition* of the earth, as I know of no other part of the world of better or equal temper. *Raleigh.*

She sits on a globe that stands in water, to denote that she is mistress of a new world, separate from that which the Romans had before conquered, by the *interposition* of the sea. *Addis.*

4. Any thing interposed.

A shelter, and a kind of shading cool
Interposition, as a Summer's cloud. *Milt. Paradise Regain'd.*

To INTE'RPRET. *v. a.* [*interpreter*, French; *interpretor*, Lat.] To explain; to translate; to decipher; to give a solution; to clear by exposition; to expound.

One, but painted thus,
Would be *interpreted* a thing perplex'd
Beyond self-explication. *Shakes. Cymbeline.*
You should be women,
And yet your beards forbid me to *interpret*
That you are so. *Shakesp. Macbeth.*

He hanged the chief baker, as Joseph had *interpreted* to them. *Gen.* xl. 22.

Pharaoh told them his dream; but there was none that could *interpret* them unto him. *Gen.* xli. 8.

An excellent spirit, knowledge, and understanding, *interpreting* of dreams, and shewing of hard sentences, and dissolving of doubts, were found in the same Daniel. *Dan.* v. 12.

Hear his sighs, though mute!
Unskilful with what words to pray, let me
Interpret for him. *Milton's Paradise Lost, b.* xi.

INTE'RPRETABLE. *adj.* [from *interpret.*] Capable of being expounded or deciphered.

No man's face is actionable: these singularities are *interpretable* from more innocent causes. *Collier.*

INTERPRETA'TION. *n. s.* [*interpretation*, Fr. *interpretatio*, Lat. from *interpret.*]
1. The act of interpreting; explanation.

This is a poor epitome of your's,
Which, by th' *interpretation* of full time,
May shew like all yourself. *Shakes. Coriolanus.*
Look how we can, or sad or merrily,
Interpretation will misquote our looks. *Shakep. H.* IV.

2. The sense given by an interpreter; exposition.

If it be obscure or uncertain what they meant, charity, I hope, constraineth no man, which standeth doubtful of their minds, to lean to the hardest and worst *interpretation* that their words can carry. *Hooker.*

The primitive Christians knew how the Jews, who preceded our Saviour, interpreted these predictions, and the marks by which the Messiah would be discovered; and how the Jewish doctors, who succeeded him, deviated from the *interpretations* of their forefathers. *Addison.*

3. The power of explaining.

We beseech thee to prosper this great sign, and to give us the *interpretation* and use of it in mercy. *Bacon.*

INTE'RPRETATIVE. *adj.* [from *interpret.*] Collected by interpretation.

Though the creed apostolick were sufficient, yet when the church hath erected that additional bulwork against hereticks, the rejecting their additions may justly be deemed an *interpretative* siding with heresies. *Hammond.*

INTE'RPRETATIVELY. *adv.* [from *interpretative.*] As may be collected by interpretation.

By this provision the Almighty *interpretatively* speaks to him in this manner: I have now placed thee in a well furnished world. *Ray on the Creation.*

INTE'RPRETER. *n. s.* [*interprete*, Fr. *interpres*, Latin.]
1. An explainer; an expositor; an expounder.

What we oft do best,
By sick *interpreters*, or weak ones, is
Not ours, or not allow'd: what worst, as oft,
Hitting a grosser quality, is cry'd up
For our best act. *Shakespeare's Henry* VIII.

In the beginning the earth was without form and void; a fluid, dark, confused mass, and so it is understood by *interpreters*, both Hebrew and Christian. *Burnet.*

We think most mens actions to be the *interpreters* of their thoughts. *Locke.*

2. A translator.

Nor word for word be careful to transfer,
With the same faith as an *interpreter*. *Fanshaw.*

How shall any man, who hath a genius for history, undertake such a work with spirit, when he considers that in an age or two he shall hardly be understood without an *interpreter*. *Swift.*

INTERPU'NCTION. *n. s.* [*interpunctio*, Fr. *interpungo*, Latin.] Pointing between words or sentences.

INTERRE'GNUM. *n. s.* [Lat.] The time in which a throne is vacant between the death of a prince and accession of another.

Next ensu'd a vacancy,
Thousand worse passions than possess'd
The *interregnum* of my breast:
Bless me from such an anarchy! *Cowley.*

He would shew the queen my memorial with the first opportunity, in order to have it done in this *interregnum* or suspension of title. *Swift.*

INTERRE'IGN. *n. s.* [*interregne*, Fr. *interregnum*, Latin.] Vacancy of the throne.

The king knew there could not be any *interreign* or suspension of title. *Bacon's Henry* VII.

To INTE'RROGATE. *v. a.* [*interrogo*, Lat. *interroger*, Fr.] To examine; to question.

To INTE'RROGATE. *v. n.* To ask; to put questions.

By his instructions touching the queen of Naples, it seemeth he could *interrogate* touching beauty. *Bacon's Henry* VII.

His proof will easily be retorted by *interrogating*, Shall the adulterer and the drunkard inherit the kingdom of God. *Hammond's Fundamentals.*

INTERROGA'TION. *n. s.* [*interrogation*, Fr. *interrogatio*, Lat.]

1. A question put; an enquiry.

How demurely soever such men may pretend to sanctity, that *interrogation* of God presses hard upon them, shall I count them pure with the wicked balances, and with the bag of deceitful weights? *Government of the Tongue.*

This variety is obtained by *interrogations* to things inanimate; by beautiful digressions, but those short. *Pope.*

2. A note that marks a question: thus ? as, Does *Job* serve God for nought?

INTERRO'GATIVE. *adj.* [*interrogatif*, Fr. *interrogativus*, Lat.] Denoting a question; expressed in a questionary form of words.

INTERRO'GATIVE. *n. s.* A pronoun used in asking questions: as, who? what? which? whether?

INTERRO'GATIVELY. *adv.* [from *interrogative.*] In form of a question.

INTERROGA'TOR. *n. s.* [from *interrogate.*] An asker of questions.

INTE'RROGATORY. *n. s.* [*interrogatoire*, French.] A question; an enquiry.

He with no more civility, though with much more business than those under-fellows had shewed, began in captious manner to put *interrogatories* unto him. *Sidney, b.* ii.

Nor time, nor place,
Will serve long *interrogatories*. *Shakespeare's Cymbeline.*
What earthly name to *interrogatories*
Can task the free breath of a sacred king. *Shakespeare.*

The examination was summed up with one question, Whether he was prepared for death? The boy was frighted out of his wits by the last dreadful *interrogatory*. *Addison.*

INTERRO'GATORY. *adj.* Containing a question; expressing a question.

To INTERRU'PT. *v. a.* [*interrompre*, Fr. *interruptus*, Lat.]

1. To hinder the process of any thing by breaking in upon it.

Rage doth rend
Like *interrupted* waters, and o'erbear
What they are used to bear. *Shakespeare's Coriolanus.*

He might securely enough have engaged his body of horse against their whole inconsiderable army, there being neither tree nor bush to *interrupt* his charge. *Clarendon, b.* ii.

This motion of the heavenly bodies seems partly uninterrupted, as that of the first moveable interpolated and *interrupted*. *Hale.*

2. To hinder one from proceeding by interposition.

Answer not before thou hast heard the cause; neither *interrupt* men in the midst of their talk. *Ecclus.* xi. 8.

3. To divide; to separate.

Seest thou what rage
Transports our adversary, whom no bounds,
Nor yet the main abyss wide *interrupt*, can hold. *Milton.*

INTERRU'PTEDLY. *adv.* [from *interrupted.*] Not in continuity; not without stoppages.

The incident light that meets with a grosser liquor, will have its beams either refracted or imbibed, or else reflected more or less *interruptedly* than they would be, if the body had been unmoistened. *Boyle on Colours.*

INTERRU'PTER. *n. s.* [from *interrupt.*] He who interrupts.

INTERRU'PTION. *n. s.* [*interruption*, Fr. *interruptio*, Latin.]

1. Interposition; breach of continuity.

Places severed from the continent by the *interruption* of the sea. *Hale's Original of Mankind.*

2. Intervention; interposition.

You are to touch the one as soon as you have given a stroke of the pencil to the other, lest the *interruption* of time cause you to lose the idea of one part. *Dryden's Dufresnoy.*

3. Hindrance; stop; let; obstruction.

Bloody England into England gone,
O'erbearing *interruption*, spite of France. *Shakespeare.*

This way of thinking on what we read, will be a rub only in the beginning; when custom has made it familiar, it will be dispatched without resting or *interruption* in the course of our reading. *Locke.*

Amidst the *interruptions* of his sorrow, seeing his penitent overwhelmed with grief, he was only able to bid her be comforted. *Addison's Spect.* N°. 164.

INTERSCA'PULAR. *adj.* [*inter* and *scapula*, Latin.] Placed between the shoulders.

To INTERSCI'ND. *v. a.* [*inter* and *scindo*, Latin.] To cut off by interruption. *Dict.*

To INTERSCRI'BE. *v. a.* [*inter* and *scribo*, Lat.] To write between. *Dict.*

INTERSE'CANT. *adj.* [*intersecans*, Latin.] Dividing any thing into parts.

To INTERSE'CT. *v. a.* [*interseco*, Lat.] To cut; to divide each other mutually.

Perfect and viviparous quadrupeds so stand in their position of proneness, that the opposite joints of neighbour legs consist in the same plane; and a line descending from their navel *intersects* at right angles the axis of the earth. *Brown.*

Excited by a vigorous loadstone, it will somewhat depress its animated extreme, and *intersect* the horizontal circumference. *Brown's Vulgar Errours, b.* ii.

To INTERSE'CT. *v. n.* To meet and cross each other.

The sagittal suture usually begins at that point where these lines *intersect*. *Wiseman's Surgery.*

INTERSE'CTION. *n. s.* [*intersectio*, Lat. from *intersect.*] Point where lines cross each other.

They did spout over interchangeably from side to side in forms of arches, without any *intersection* or meeting aloft, because the pipes were not opposite. *Wotton's Architecture.*

The first star of Aries, in the time of Meton the Athenian, was placed in the very *intersection*, which is now elongated, and moved eastward twenty-eight degrees. *Brown.*

Ships would move in one and the same surface; and consequently must needs encounter, when they either advance towards one another in direct lines, or meet in the *intersection* of cross ones. *Bentley's Sermons.*

To INTERSE'RT. *v. a.* [*intersero*, Lat.] To put in between other things.

If I may *intersert* a short philosophical speculation, the depth of the sea is determined in Pliny to be fifteen furlongs. *Brerewood on Languages.*

INTERSE'RTION. *n. s.* [from *intersert.*] An insertion, or thing inserted between any thing.

These two *intersertions* were clear explications of the apostle's old form, God the father, ruler of all, which contained an acknowledgement of the unity. *Hammond.*

To INTERSPE'RSE. *v. a.* [*interspersus*, Lat.] To scatter here and there among other things.

The possibility of a body's moving into a void space beyond the utmost bounds of body, as well as into a void space *interspersed* amongst bodies, will always remain clear. *Locke.*

It is the editor's interest to insert what the author's judgment had rejected; and care is taken to *intersperse* these additions in such a manner, that scarce any book can be bought without purchasing something unworthy of the author. *Swift.*

INTERSPE'RSION. *n. s.* [from *intersperse.*] The act of scattering here and there.

For want of the *interspersion* of now and then an elegiack or a lyrick ode. *Watts's Improvement of the Mind.*

INTERSTE'LLAR. *adj.* [*inter* and *stellar*, Lat.] Intervening between the stars.

The *interstellar* sky hath so much affinity with the star, that there is a rotation of that as well as of the star. *Bacon.*

I'NTERSTICE. *n. s.* [*interstitium*, Lat. *interstice*, Lat.]

1. Space between one thing and another.

The sun shining through a large prism upon a comb placed immediately behind the prism, his light, which passed through the *interstices* of the teeth fell upon a white paper: the breadths of the teeth were equal to their *interstices*, and seven teeth together with their *interstices* took up an inch in breadth. *Newton's Opticks.*

The force of the fluid will separate the smallest particles which compose the fibres, so as to leave vacant *interstices* in those places where they cohered before. *Arbuthnot.*

2. Time between one act and another.

I will point out the *interstices* of time which ought to be between one citation and another. *Ayliffe's Parergon.*

INTERSTI'TIAL. *adj.* [from *interstice.*] Containing interstices.

In oiled papers, the *interstitial* division being actuated by the accession of oil, becometh more transparent. *Brown.*

INTERTE'XTURE. *n. s.* [*intertexo*, Latin.] Diversification of things mingled or woven one among another.

To INTERTWI'NE. } *v. a.* [*inter* and *twine*, or *twist.*] To unite
To INTERTWI'ST. } by twisting one in another.

Under some concourse of shades,
Whose branching arms thick *intertwin'd* might shield
From dews and damps of night his shelter'd head. *Milton.*

I'NTERVAL. *n. s.* [*intervalle*, Fr. *intervallum*, Latin.]

1. Space between places; interstice; vacuity; space unoccupied; void place; vacancy; vacant space.

With any obstacle let all the light be now stopped which passes through any one *interval* of the teeth, so that the range of colours which comes from thence may be taken away, and you will see the light of the rest of the ranges to be expanded into the place of the range taken away, and there to be coloured. *Newton's Opticks.*

2. Time passing between two assignable points.

The century and half following, to the end of the third Punick war, was a very busy period at Rome; the *intervals* between every war being so short. *Swift.*

3. Remission of a delirium or distemper.

Though he had a long illness, considering the great heat with which it raged, yet his *intervals* of sense being few and short, left but little room for the offices of devotion. *Atterb.*

To INTERVE'NE. *v. n.* [*intervenio*, Lat. *intervenir*, Fr.] To come between things or persons; to be intercepted; to make intervals.

While so near each other thus all day
Our task we chuse, what wonder, if so near,
Looks *intervene*, and smiles. *Milton's Par. Lost, b.* ix.

Esteem the danger of an action, and the possibilities of miscarriage, and every cross accident that can *intervene*, to be either a mercy on God's part, or a fault on ours. *Taylor.*

INTERVE'NE. *n. s.* [from the verb.] Opposition, or perhaps interview. A word out of use.

They had some sharper and some milder differences, which might easily happen in such an *intervene* of grandees, both vehement on the parts which they swayed. *Wotton.*

INTERVE'NIENT. *adj.* [*interveniens*, Lat. *intervenant*, French.] Intercedent; interposed; passing between.

There be *intervenient* in the rise of eight, in tones, two bemolls or half notes. *Bacon's Nat. Hist.* N°. 104.

Many arts were used to discuss new affection: all which notwithstanding, for I omit things *intervenient*, there is conveyed to Mr. Villiers an intimation of the king's pleasure to be sworn his servant. *Wotton.*

INTERVE'NTION. *n. s.* [*intervention*, Fr. *interventio*, Latin.]

1. Agency between persons.

God will judge the world in righteousness by the *intervention* of the man Christ Jesus, who is the Saviour as well as the judge of the world. *Atterbury's Sermons.*

2. Agency between antecedents and consecutives.

In the dispensation of God's mercies to the world, some things he does by himself, others by the *intervention* of natural means, and by the mediation of such instruments as he has appointed. *L'Estrange.*

3. Interposition; the state of being interposed.

Sound is shut out by the *intervention* of that laxe membrane, and not suffered to pass into the inward ear. *Holder.*

To INTERVE'RT. *v. a.* [*interverto*, Lat.] To turn to another course.

The duke *interverted* the bargain, and gave the poor widow of Erpenius for the books five hundred pounds. *Wotton.*

INTERVI'EW. *n. s.* [*entrevue*, French.] Mutual sight; sight of each other. It is commonly used for a formal and appointed meeting or conference.

The day will come, when the passions of former enmity being allayed, we shall with ten times redoubled tokens of reconciled love shew ourselves each towards other the same, which Joseph and the brethren of Joseph were at the time of their *interview* in Egypt. *Hooker.*

His fears were, that the *interview* betwixt
England and France might, through their amity,
Breed him some prejudice. *Shakesp. Henry* VIII.

Such happy *interview*, and fair event
Of love, and youth not lost, songs, garlands, flow'rs,
And charming symphonies, attach'd the heart
Of Adam. *Milton's Par. Lost, b.* xi.

To INTERVO'LVE. *v. a.* [*intervolvo*, Latin.] To involve one within another.

Mystical dance! which yonder starry sphere
Of planets, and of fix'd, in all her wheels
Resembles nearest; mazes intricate,
Eccentrick, *intervolv'd*, yet regular,
Then most, when most irregular, they seem. *Milton.*

To INTERWE'AVE. *v. a.* preter. *interwove*, part. pass. *interwoven*, *interwove*, or *interweaved*. [*inter* and *weave*.] To mix one with another in a regular texture; to intermingle.

Then laid him down
Under the hospitable covert nigh
Of trees thick *interwoven*. *Milton's Par. Lost, b.* ii.

At last
Words *interwove* with sighs found out their way. *Milton.*

I sat me down to watch upon a bank
With ivy canopied, and *interwove*
With flaunting honeysuckle. *Milton.*

None
Can say here nature ends, and art begins,
But mixt like th' elements, and born like twins,
So *interweav'd*, so like, so much the same:
None, this mere nature, that mere art can name. *Denham.*

The proud theatres disclose the scene,
Which *interwoven* Britons seem to raise,
And show the triumph which their shame displays. *Dryden.*

He so *interweaves* truth with probable fiction, that he puts a pleasing falacy upon us. *Dryden.*

It appeared a vast ocean planted with islands, that were covered with fruits and flowers, and *interwoven* with a thousand little shining seas that ran among them. *Addison's Spect.*

It is a confusion of kitchen and parterre, orchard and flower-garden, which lie so mixt and *interwoven* with one another, as to look like a natural wilderness. *Spectat.*

The Supreme Infinite could not make intelligent creatures, without implanting in their natures a most ardent desire, *interwoven* in the substance of their spiritual natures, of being reunited with himself. *Cheyne's Phil. Principles.*

I do not altogether disapprove the *interweaving* texts of scripture through the style of your sermon. *Swift's Miscel.*

To INTERWI'SH. *v. a.* [*inter* and *wish*.] To wish mutually to each other.

The venom of all stepdames, gamester's gall,
What tyrants and their subjects *interwish*,
All ill fall on that man. *Donne.*

INTE'STABLE. *adj.* [*intestabilis*, Latin.] Disqualified to make a will.

A person excommunicated is rendered infamous and *intestable* both actively and passively. *Ayliffe's Parergon.*

INTE'STATE. *adj.* [*intestat*, Fr. *intestatus*, Latin.] Wanting a will; dying without will.

Why should calamity be full of words?
—Windy attorneys to their client woes,
Airy succeeders of *intestate* joys,
Poor breathing orators of miseries. *Shakesp. Richard* III.

Present punishment pursues his maw,
When surfeited and swell'd, the peacock raw,
He bears into the bath; whence want of breath,
Repletions, apoplex, *intestate* death. *Dryden's Juvenal.*

INTE'STINAL. *adj.* [*intestinal*, Fr. from *intestine*.] Belonging to the guts.

The mouths of the lacteals are opened by the *intestinal* tube, affecting a straight instead of a spiral cylinder. *Arbuth.*

INTE'STINE. *adj.* [*intestin*, Fr. *intestinus*, Latin.]

1. Internal; inward; not external.

Of these inward and *intestine* enemies to prayer, there are our past sins to wound us, our present cares to distract us, our distempered passions to disorder us, and a whole swarm of loose and floating imaginations to molest us. *Duppa.*

Intestine war no more our passions wage,
Ev'n giddy factions hear away their rage. *Pope.*

2. Contained in the body.

Intestine stone, and ulcer, cholick pangs,
And moon-struck madness. *Milton's Par. Lost, b.* xi.

A wooden jack, which had almost
Lost, by disuse, the art to roast,
A sudden alteration feels,
Increas'd by new *intestine* wheels. *Swift's Miscel.*

3. Domestick, not foreign. I know not whether the word be properly used in the following example of *Shakespeare*: perhaps for *mortal* and *intestine* should be read *mortal internecine*.

Since the mortal and *intestine* jars
'Twixt thy seditious countrymen and us,
It hath in solemn synods been decreed,
T' admit no traffick to our adverse towns. *Shakespeare.*

But God, or Nature, while they thus contend,
To these *intestine* discords put an end. *Dryden's Ovid.*

She saw her sons with purple deaths expire,
A dreadful series of *intestine* wars,
Inglorious triumphs, and dishonest scars. *Pope.*

INTE'STINE. *n. s.* [*intestinum*, Lat. *intestine*, Fr.] The gut; the bowel: most commonly without a singular.

The *intestines* or guts may be inflamed by an acrid substance taken inwardly. *Arbuthnot on Diet.*

To INTHRALL. *v. a.* [*in* and *thrall*.] To enslave; to shackle; to reduce to servitude. A word now seldom used, at least in prose.

What though I be *inthrall'd*, he seems a knight,
And will not any way dishonour me. *Shakesp. Henry* VI.

The Turk has sought to extinguish the ancient memory of those people which he has subjected and *inthrall'd*. *Raleigh.*

Authors to themselves in all
Both what they judge, and what they choose; for so
I form'd them free, and free they must remain
Till they *inthrall* themselves. *Milton's Par. Lost, b.* ii.

She soothes, but never can *inthrall* my mind:
Why may not peace and love for once be join'd. *Prior.*

INTHRA'LMENT. *n. s.* [from *inthrall*.] Servitude; slavery.

Moses and Aaron, sent from God to claim
His people from *inthralment*, they return
With glory, and spoil, back to their promis'd land. *Milton's Par. Lost.*

To INTHRO'NE. *v. a.* [*in* and *throne.*] To raise to royalty; to seat on a throne.

One, chief, in gracious dignity *inthron'd*,
Shines o'er the rest. *Thomson's Summer, l.* 395.

I'NTIMACY. *n. s.* [from *intimate.*] Close familiarity.

It is in our power to confine our friendships and *intimacies* to men of virtue. *Rogers's Sermons.*

I'NTIMATE. *adj.* [*intimado*, Spanish; *intimus*, Lat.]

1. Inmost; inward; intestine.

They knew not
That what I mention'd was of God, I knew
From *intimate* impulse, and therefore urged on
The marriage. *Milton's Agonist. l.* 221.

Fear being so *intimate* to our natures, it is the strongest bond of laws. *Tillotson's Sermons.*

2. Near; not kept at distance.

Moses was with him in the retirements of the mount, received there his private instructions; and when the multitude were thundered away from any approach, he was honoured with an *intimate* and immediate admission. *South's Sermons.*

3. Familiar; closely acquainted.

United by this sympathetick bond,
You grow familiar, *intimate*, and fond. *Roscommon.*

I'NTIMATE. *n. s.* [*intimado*, Spanish; *intime*, French; *intimus*, Latin.] A familiar friend; one who is trusted with our thoughts.

The design was to entertain his reason with a more equal converse, assign him an *intimate* whose intellect as much corresponded with his as did the outward form. *Gov. Tongue.*

To I'NTIMATE. *v. a.* [*intimer*, French; *intimare*, low Latin.] To hint; to point out indirectly, or not very plainly.

Alexander Van Suchten tells us, that by a way he *intimates*, may be made a mercury of copper, not of the silver colour of other mercuries, but green. *Boyle.*

The names of simple ideas and substances, with the abstract ideas in the mind, *intimate* some real existence, from which was derived their original patern. *Locke.*

'Tis the divinity that stirs within us;
'Tis heav'n itself that points out an hereafter,
And *intimates* eternity to man. *Addison's Cato.*

I'NTIMATELY. *adv.* [from *intimate.*]

1. Closely; with intermixture of parts.

The same œconomy is observed in the circulation of the chyle with the blood, by mixing it *intimately* with the parts of the fluid to which it is to be assimilated. *Arbuthnot.*

2. Nearly; inseparably.

Quality, as it regards the mind, has its rise from knowledge and virtue, and is that which is more essential to us, and more *intimately* united with us. *Addison's Spect.* N°. 219.

3. Familiarly; with close friendship.

INTIMA'TION. *n. s.* [*intimation*, Fr. from *intimate.*] Hint; obscure or indirect declaration or direction.

Let him strictly observe the first stirrings and *intimations*; the first hints and whispers of good and evil that pass in his heart. *South's Sermons.*

Of those that are only probable we have some reasonable *intimations*, but not a demonstrative certainty. *Woodward.*

Besides the more solid parts of learning, there are several little *intimations* to be met with on medals. *Addison.*

I'NTIME. *adj.* Inward; being within the mass; not being external, or on the surface; internal.

As to the composition or dissolution of mixed bodies, which is the chief work of elements, and requires an *intime* application of the agents, water hath the principality and excess over earth. *Digby on Bodies.*

To INTI'MIDATE. *v. a.* [*intimider*, French; *in* and *timidus*, Lat.] To make fearful; to dastardize; to make cowardly.

Now guilt once harbour'd in the conscious breast,
Intimidates the brave, degrades the great. *Irene.*

INTI'RE. *n. s.* [*integer*, Lat. *entier*, French; better written *entire*, which see, and all its derivatives.] Whole; undiminished; broken.

The lawful power of making laws, to command whole politick societies of men, belongeth so properly unto the same *intire* societies, that for any prince to exercise the same of himself, and not either by express commission immediately and personally received from God, or else by authority derived at the first from their consent upon whose persons he imposes laws, it is no better than mere tyranny. *Hooker.*

INTI'RENESS. *n. s.* [from *intire*; better *entireness.*] Wholeness; integrity.

So shall all times find me the same:
You this *intireness* better may fulfil,
Who have the pattern with you still. *Donne.*

I'NTO. *prep.* [*in* and *to.*]

1. Noting entrance with regard to place.

If iron will acquire by mere continuance an habitual inclination to the site it held, how much more may education, being a constant plight and inurement, induce by custom good habits *into* a reasonable creature. *Wotton.*

To give life to that which has yet no being, is to frame a living creature, fashion the parts, and having fitted them together, to put *into* them a living soul. *Locke.*

Water introduces *into* vegetables the matter it bears along with it. *Woodward's Nat. Hist.*

Acrid substances, which pass *into* the capillary tubes, must irritate them into greater contraction. *Arbuthnot on Aliments.*

2. Noting penetration beyond the outside, or some action which reaches beyond the superficies or open part.

To look *into* letters already opened or dropt is held an ungenerous act. *Pope.*

2. Noting a new state to which any thing is brought by the agency of a cause.

They have denominated some herbs solar and some lunar, and such like toys put *into* great words. *Bacon.*

Compound bodies may be resolved *into* other substances than such as they are divided *into* by the fire. *Boyle.*

A man must sin himself *into* a love of other mens sins; for a bare notion of this black art will not carry him so far. *South.*

Sure thou art born to some peculiar fate,
When the mad people rise against the state,
To look them *into* duty; and command
An awful silence with thy lifted hand. *Dryden's Persius.*

It concerns every man that would not trifle away his soul, and fool himself *into* irrecoverable misery, with the greatest seriousness to enquire into these matters. *Tillotson.*

He is not a frail being, that he should be tired *into* compliance by the force of assiduous application. *Smalridge.*

In hollow bottoms, if any fountains chance to rise, they naturally spread themselves *into* lakes, before they can find any issue. *Addison on Italy.*

It would have been all irretrievably lost, was it not by this means collected and brought *into* one mass. *Woodward.*

Why are these positions charged upon me as their sole author; and the reader led *into* a belief, that they were never before maintained by any person of virtue. *Atterbury.*

It is no ways congruous, that God should be always frightening and astonishing men *into* an acknowledgement of the truth, who were made to be wrought upon by calm evidence. *Atterbury's Sermons.*

A man may whore and drink himself *into* atheism; but it is impossible he should think himself *into* it. *Bentley.*

INTO'LERABLE. *adj.* [*intolerabilis*, Lat. *intolerable*, Fr.]

1. Insufferable; not to be endured; not to be born; having any quality in a degree too powerful to be endured.

If we bring into one day's thoughts the evil of many, certain and uncertain, what will be and what will never be, our load will be as *intolerable* as it is unreasonable. *Taylor.*

His awful presence did the croud surprize,
Nor durst the rash spectator meet his eyes;
Eyes that confess'd him born for kingly sway,
So fierce, they flash'd *intolerable* day. *Dryden.*

Some men are quickly weary of one thing: the same study long continued in is as *intolerable* to them, as the appearing long in the same clothes is to a court lady. *Locke.*

From Param's top th' Almighty rode,
Intolerable day proclaim'd the God. *Broome.*

2. Bad beyond sufferance.

INTO'LERABLENESS. *n. s.* [from *intolerable.*] Quality of a thing not to be endured.

INTO'LERABLY. *adv.* [from *intolerable.*] To a degree beyond endurance.

INTO'LERANT. *adj.* [*intolerant*, French.] Not enduring; not able to endure.

Too great moisture affects human bodies with one class of diseases, and too great dryness with another; the powers of human bodies being limited and *intolerant* of excesses. *Arbuth.*

To INTOMB. *v. a.* [*in* and *tomb.*] To inclose in a funeral monument; to bury.

What commandment finally had they for the ceremony of odours used about the bodies of the dead, after which custom notwithstanding our Lord was contented that his own most precious blood should be *intombed.* *Hooker, b.* i.

Is't night's predominance or the day's shame,
That darkness does the face of earth *intomb.* *Shakespeare.*

Mighty hero's more majestick shades,
And youths *intomb'd* before their father's eyes. *Dryden.*

To I'NTONATE. *v. a.* [*intono*, Lat.] To thunder. *Dict.*

INTONA'TION. *n. s.* [*intonation*, Fr. from *intonate.*] The act of thundering. *Dict.*

To INTO'NE. *v. n.* [from *intono*, or rather from *tone*; *intonner*, French.] To make a slow protracted noise.

So swells each wind-pipe; ass *intones* to ass
Harmonick twang. *Pope's Dunciad, b.* ii.

To INTO'RT. *v. a.* [*intortuo*, Lat.] To twist; to wreath; to wring.

The brain is a congeries of glands, that separate the finer parts of the blood, called animal spirits; and a gland is nothing but a canal variously *intorted* and wound up together. *Arbuth.*

With rev'rent hand the king presents the gold,
Which round th' *intorted* horns the gilder roll'd. *Pope.*

To INTO'XICATE. *v. a.* [*in* and *toxicum*, Latin.] To inebriate; to make drunk.

The more a man drinketh of the world, the more it *intoxicateth*; and age doth profit rather in the powers of underſtanding than in the virtues of the will and affections. *Bacon.*

As with new wine *intoxicated* both,
They ſwim in mirth, and fancy that they feel
Divinity within them breeding wings,
Wherewith to ſcorn the earth. *Milton's Par. Loſt, b.* ix.

My early miſtreſs, now my ancient muſe,
That ſtrong Circean liquor ceaſe t' infuſe,
Wherewith thou didſt *intoxicate* my youth. *Denham.*

What part of wild fury was there in the bacchanals which we have not ſeen equall'd, if not exceeded by ſome *intoxicated* zealots? *Decay of Piety.*

Others, after having done fine things, yet ſpoil them by endeavouring to make them better; and are ſo *intoxicated* with an earneſt deſire of being above all others, that they ſuffer themſelves to be deceived. *Dryden's Dufreſnoy.*

Vegetables by fermentation are wrought up to ſpirituous liquors, having quite different qualities from the plant itſelf; for no fruit taken crude has the *intoxicating* quality of wine. *Arbuthnot.*

INTOXICA'TION. *n. ſ.* [from *intoxicate.*] Inebriation; ebriety; the act of making drunk; the ſtate of being drunk.

That king, being in amity with him, did ſo burn in hatred towards him, as to drink of the lees and dregs of Perkin's *intoxication*, who was every where elſe detected. *Bacon.*

Whence can this proceed, but from that beſotting *intoxication* which verbal magick brings upon the mind. *South.*

INTRA'CTABLE. *n. ſ.* [*intractabilis*, Lat. *intraitable*, Fr.]

1. Ungovernable; violent; ſtubborn; obſtinate.

To love them who loves us is ſo natural a paſſion, that even the moſt *intractable* tempers obey its force. *Rogers.*

2. Unmanageable; furious.

By what means ſerpents, and other noxious and more *intractable* kinds, as well as the more innocent and uſeful, got together. *Woodward's Nat. Hiſt. p.* iii.

INTRA'CTABLENESS. *n. ſ.* [from *intractable.*] Obſtinacy; perverſeneſs.

INTRA'CTABLY. *adv.* [from *intractable.*] Unmanageably; ſtubbornly.

INTRANQUI'LITY. *n. ſ.* [*in* and *tranquility.*] Unquietneſs; want of reſt.

Jactations were uſed for amuſement, and allay in conſtant pains, and to relieve that *intranquility* which makes men impatient of lying in their beds. *Temple.*

INTRA'NSITIVE. *v. a.* [*intranſitivus*, Latin.]

[In grammar.] A verb *intranſitive* is that which ſignifies an action, not conceived as having an effect upon any object; as, *curro*, I run. *Clarke's Lat. Gram.*

INTRANSMU'TABLE. *adj.* [*in* and *tranſmutable.*] Unchangeable to any other ſubſtance.

Some of the moſt experienced chemiſts do affirm quickſilver to be *intranſmutable*, and therefore call it liquor æternus. *Ray on the Creation.*

To INTRE'ASURE. *v. a.* [*in* and *treaſure.*] To lay up as in a treaſury.

There is a hiſtory in all mens lives,
Figuring the nature of the times deceas'd;
The which obſerv'd, a man may propheſy,
With a near aim, of the main chance of things
As yet not come to life, which in their ſeeds
And weak beginnings he *intreaſured*. *Shakeſp. Henry* IV.

To INTRE'NCH. *v. n.* [*in* and *trancher*, French.]

1. To invade; to encroach; to cut off part of what belongs to another.

Little I deſire my ſcepter ſhould *intrench* on God's ſovereignty, which is the only king of men's conſciences. *K. Charles.*

That crawling inſect, who from mud began,
Warm'd by my beams, and kindled into man!
Durſt he, who does but for my pleaſure live,
Intrench on love, my great prerogative. *Dryden's Aureng.*

We are not to *intrench* upon truth in any converſation, but leaſt of all with children. *Locke.*

2. To break with hollows.

His face
Deep ſcars of thunder had *intrench'd*, and care
Sat on his faded cheek. *Milton's Par. Loſt, b.* i.

3. To fortify with a trench: as, the allies were *intrenched* in their camp.

INTRE'NCHANT. *adj.* [This word, which is, I believe, found only in *Shakeſpeare*, is thus explained by one of his editors: The *intrenchant* air means the air which ſuddenly encroaches and cloſes upon the ſpace left by any body which had paſſed through it. *Hanmer.* I believe *Shakeſpeare* intended rather to expreſs the idea of indiviſibility or invulnerableneſs, and derived *intrenchant*, from *in* privative, and *trencher*, to cut; *intrenchant* is indeed properly *not cutting*, rather than *not to be cut*; but this is not the only inſtance in which *Shakeſpeare* confounds words of active and paſſive ſignification.] Not to be divided; not to be wounded; indiviſible.

As eaſy may'ſt thou the *intrenchant* air
With thy keen ſword impreſs, as make me bleed. *Shakeſp.*

INTRE'NCHMENT. *n. ſ.* [from *intrench.*] Fortification with a trench.

INTRE'PID. *adj.* [*intrepide*, Fr. *intrepidus*, Latin.] Fearleſs; daring; bold; brave.

Argyle
Calm and *intrepid* in the very throat
Of ſulphurous war, on Teniers dreadful field. *Thomſon.*

INTREPI'DITY. *n. ſ.* [*intrepidité*, Fr.] Fearleſſneſs; courage; boldneſs.

I could not ſufficiently wonder at the *intrepidity* of theſe diminutive mortals, who durſt venture to walk upon my body, without trembling. *Gulliver's Travels.*

INTRE'PIDLY. *adv.* [from *intrepid.*] Fearleſly; boldly; daringly.

He takes the globe for the ſcene; he launches forward *intrepidly*, like one to whom no place is new. *Pope.*

I'NTRICACY. *n. ſ.* [from *intricate.*] State of being entangled; perplexity; involution; complication of facts or notions.

The part of Ulyſſes in Homer's Odyſſey is much admired by Ariſtotle, as perplexing that fable with very agreeable plots and *intricacies*, by the many adventures in his voyage, and the ſubtilty of his behaviour. *Addiſon.*

I'NTRICATE. *adj.* [*intricatus*, Lat.] Entangled; perplexed; involved; complicated; obſcure.

Much of that we are to ſpeak may ſeem to a number perhaps tedious, perhaps obſcure, dark, and *intricate*. *Hooker.*

His ſtile in writing was fit to convey the moſt *intricate* buſineſs to the underſtanding with the utmoſt clearneſs. *Addiſon.*

To I'NTRICATE. [from the adjective.] To perplex; to darken. Not proper, nor in uſe.

Alterations of ſirnames have ſo *intricated*, or rather obſcured, the truth of our pedigrees, that it will be no little hard labour to deduce them. *Camden.*

I'NTRICATELY. *adv.* [from *intricate.*] With involution of one in another; with perplexity.

That variety of factions, into which we are ſo *intricately* engaged, gave occaſion to this diſcourſe. *Swift.*

I'NTRICATENESS. *n. ſ.* [from *intricate.*] Perplexity; involution; obſcurity.

He found ſuch *intricateneſs*, that he could ſee no way to lead him out of the maze. *Sidney.*

INTRI'GUE. *n. ſ.* [*intrigue*, French.]

1. A plot; a private tranſaction in which many parties are engaged: uſually an affair of love.

Theſe are the grand *intrigues* of man,
Theſe his huge thoughts, and theſe his vaſt deſires. *Flatman.*

A young fellow long made love, with much artifice and *intrigue*, to a rich widow. *Addiſon's Gurrd.*

The hero of a comedy is repreſented victorious in all his *intrigues*. *Swift.*

Now love is dwindled to *intrigue*,
And marriage grown a money league. *Swift's Miſcel.*

2. Intricacy; complication. Little in uſe.

Though this vicinity of ourſelves to ourſelves cannot give us the full proſpect of all the *intrigues* of our nature, yet we have much more advantage to know ourſelves, than to know other things without us. *Hale's Originat. of Mankind.*

3. The complication or perplexity of a fable or poem; artful involution of feigned tranſaction.

As theſe cauſes are the beginning of the action, the oppoſite deſigns againſt that of the hero are the middle of it, and form that difficulty or *intrigue* which makes up the greateſt part of the poem. *Pope.*

To INTRI'GUE. *v. n.* [*intriguer*, Fr. from the noun.] To form plots; to carry on private deſigns.

INTRI'GUER. *n. ſ.* [*intrigueur*, Fr. from *intrigue.*] One who buſies himſelf in private tranſactions; one who forms plots; one who perſues women.

I deſire that *intriguers* will not make a pimp of my lion, and convey their thoughts to one another. *Addiſon.*

INTRI'GUINGLY. *adv.* [from *intrigue.*] With intrigue; with ſecret plotting.

INTRI'NSECAL. *adj.* [*intrinſecus*, Lat. *intrinſeque*, French. This word is now generally written *intrinſical*, contrarily to etymology.]

1. Internal; ſolid; natural; not accidental; not merely apparent.

Theſe meaſure the laws of God not by the *intrinſecal* goodneſs and equity of them, but by reluctancy and oppoſition which they find in their own hearts againſt them. *Tillotſon.*

The near and *intrinſecal*, and convincing argument of the being of God, is from human nature itſelf. *Bentley's Sermons.*

2. Intimate; cloſely familiar. Out of uſe.

He falls into *intrinſecal* ſociety with Sir John Graham, who diſſuaded him from marriage, and gave him rather encouragement to woo fortune in court. *Wotton.*

Sir Fulk Greville was a man in appearance *intrinſecal* with him, or at leaſt admitted to his melancholy hours. *Wotton.*

INTRI'NSECALLY.

INTRI'NSECALLY. *adv.* [from *intrinsecal.*]

1. Internally; naturally; really.

A lye is a thing absolutely and *intrinsecally* evil. *South.*

Every one of his pieces is an ingot of gold, *intrinsecally* and solidly valuable. *Prior.*

2. Within; at the inside.

In his countenance no open alteration; but the less he shewed without, the more it wrought *intrinsecally*. *Wotton.*

If once bereaved of motion, it cannot of itself acquire it again; nor till it be thrust by some other body from without, or *intrinsecally* moved by an immaterial self-active substance that can pervade it. *Bentley's Sermons.*

INTRI'NSICK. *adj.* [*intrinsecus*, Latin.]

1. Inward; internal; real; true.

Intrinsick goodness consists in accordance, and sin in contrariety to the secret will of God, as well as to his revealed. *Hammond's Fundamentals.*

2. Not depending on accident; fixed in the nature of the thing.

The difference between worth and merit, strictly taken; that is, a man's *intrinsick*; this, his current value. *Grew.*

His fame, like gold, the more 'tis try'd,
The more shall its *intrinsick* worth proclaim. *Prior.*

Beautiful as a jewel set in gold, which, though it adds little to *intrinsick* value, yet improves the lustre, and attracts the eyes of the beholder. *Rogers's Sermons.*

INTRI'NSECATE. *adj.* [This word seems to have been ignorantly formed between *intricate* and *intrinsecal.*] Perplexed; entangled.

Such smiling rogues as these,
Like rats, oft bite the holy cords in twain
Too *intrinsecate* t' unloose. *Shakesp. King Lear.*

Come, mortal wretch,
With thy sharp teeth this knot *intrinsicate*
Of life at once un,ie. *Shakesp. Antony and Cleopatra.*

To INTRODU'CE. *v. a.* [*introduco*, Lat. *introduire*, Fr.]

1. To conduct or usher into a place, or to a person.

Mathematicians of advanced speculations may have other ways to *introduce* into their minds ideas of infinity. *Locke.*

2. To bring something into notice or practice.

This vulgar error whosoever is able to reclaim, he shall *introduce* a new way of cure, preserving by theory as well as practice. *Brown's Vulgar Errours, b.* iv.

An author who should *introduce* a sport of words upon the stage, would meet with small applause. *Broome.*

3. To produce; to give occasion.

Whatsoever *introduces* habits in children, deserves the care and attention of their governors. *Locke on Education.*

4. To bring into writing or discourse by proper preparatives.

INTRODU'CER. *n. s.* [*introducteur*, Fr. from *introduce.*]

1 One who conducts another to a place or person.

2. Any one who brings any thing into practice or notice.

The beginning of the earl of Essex I must attribute to my lord of Leicester; but yet as an *introducer* or supporter, not as a teacher. *Wotton.*

It is commonly charged upon the army, that the beastly vice of drinking to excess hath been lately, from their example, restored among us; but whoever the *introducers* were, they have succeeded to a miracle. *Swift.*

INTRODU'CTION. *n. s.* [*introduction*, Fr. *introductio*, Latin.]

1. The act of conducting or ushering to any place or person; the state of being ushered or conducted.

2. The act of bringing any new thing into notice or practice.

The archbishop of Canterbury had pursued the *introduction* of the liturgy and the canons into Scotland with great vehemence. *Clarendon.*

3. The preface or part of a book containing previous matter.

INTRODU'CTIVE. *adj.* [*introductif*, French; from *introduce.*] Serving as the means to something else.

The truths of Christ crucified, is the Christian's philosophy, and a good life is the Christian's logick; that great instrumental *introductive* art, that must guide the mind into the former. *South's Sermons.*

INTRODU'CTORY. *adj.* [from *introductus*, Latin.] Previous; serving as a means to something further.

This *introductory* discourse itself is to be but an essay, not a book. *Boyle.*

INTROGRE'SSION. *n. s.* [*introgressio*, Latin.] Entrance; the act of entering.

INTRO'IT. *n. s.* [*introit*, French.] The beginning of the mass; the beginning of publick devotions.

INTROMI'SSION. *n. s.* [*intromissio*, Latin.]

1. The act of sending in.

If sight be caused by *intromission*, or receiving in the form of that which is seen, contrary species or forms should be received confusedly together, which Aristotle shews to be absurd. *Peacham on Drawing.*

All the reason that I could ever hear alleged by the chief factors for a general *intromission* of all sects and persuasions into our communion, is, that those who separate from us are stiff and obstinate, and will not submit to the rules of our church, and that therefore they should be taken away. *South.*

2. [In the Scottish law.] The act of intermeddling with another's effects: as, *he shall be brought to an account for his* intromissions *with such an estate.*

To I'NTROMIT. *v. a.* [*intromitto*, Latin.] To send in; to let in; to admit; to allow to enter; to be the medium by which any thing enters.

Glass in the window *intromits* light without cold to those in the room. *Holder's Elements of Speech.*

Tinged bodies and liquors reflect some sorts of rays, and *intromit* or transmit other sorts. *Newton's Opt.*

To INTROSPE'CT. *v. a.* [*introspectus*, Latin.] To take a view of the inside.

INTROSPE'CTION. *n. s.* [from *introspect.*] A view of the inside.

The actings of the mind or imagination itself, by way of reflection or *introspection* of themselves, are discernible by man. *Hale's Origin of Mankind.*

I was forced to make an *introspection* into my own mind, and into that idea of beauty which I have formed in my own imagination. *Dryden.*

INTROVE'NIENT. *adj.* [*intro* and *venio*, Latin.] Entering; coming in.

Scarce any condition which is not exhausted and obscured, from the commixture of *introvenient* nations, either by commerce or conquest. *Brown's Vulgar Errours.*

To INTRU'DE. *v. n.* [*intrudo*, Latin.]

1. To come in unwelcome by a kind of violence; to enter without invitation or permission.

Thy years want wit, thy wit wants edge
And manners, to *intrude* where I am grac'd. *Shakesp.*

The Jewish religion was yet in possession; and therefore that this might so enter, as not to *intrude*, it was to bring its warrant from the same hand of omnipotence. *South.*

Forgive me, fair one, if officious friendship
Intrudes on your repose, and comes thus late
To greet you with the tidings of success. *Rowe's Ja. Shore.*

Some thoughts rise and *intrude* upon us, while we shun them; others fly from us, when we would hold them. *Watts.*

2. To encroach; to force in uncalled or unpermitted.

Let no man beguile you of your reward, in a voluntary humility, and worshipping of angels, *intruding* into those things which he hath not seen by his fleshly mind. *Col.* ii. 18.

To INTRU'DE. *v. a.* To force without right or welcome.

Not to *intrude* one's self into the mysteries of government, which the prince keeps secret, is represented by the winds shut up in a bull-hide, which the companions of Ulysses would needs be so foolish as to pry into. *Pope.*

INTRU'DER. *n. s.* [from *intrude.*] One who forces himself into company or affairs without right or welcome.

And the hounds
Should drive upon the new transformed limbs,
Unmannerly *intruder* as thou art! *Shak. Titus Andronicus.*

Go, base *intruder!* over-weening slave!
Bestow thy fawning smiles on equal mates. *Shakespeare.*

They were but *intruders* upon the possession, during the minority of the heir: they knew those lands were the rightful inheritance of that young lady. *Davies on Ireland.*

Will you, a bold *intruder*, never learn
To know your basket, and your bread discern? *Dryden.*

She had seen a great variety of faces: they were all strangers and *intruders*, such as she had no acquaintance with. *Locke.*

The whole fraternity of writers rise up in arms against every new *intruder* into the world of fame. *Addison's Freeholder.*

INTRU'SION. *n. s.* [*intrusion*, French; *intrusio*, Latin.]

1. The act of thrusting or forcing any thing or person into any place or state.

It must raise more substantial superstructions, and fall upon very many excellent strains, which have been justled off by the *intrusions* of poetical fictions. *Brown's Vulgar Errours.*

The separation of the parts of one body, upon the *intrusion* of another, and the change from rest to motion upon impulse, and the like, seem to have some connection. *Locke.*

2. Encroachment upon any person or place; unwelcome entrance; entrance without invitation or permission.

I think myself in better plight for a lender than you are, the which hath something emboldened me to this unseasoned *intrusion*; for they say, if money go before, all ways do lie open. *Shakespeare.*

Frogs, lice, and flies, must all his palace fill
With loath'd *intrusion*. *Milton's Paradise Lost.*

How's this, my son? Why this *intrusion?*
Were not my orders that I should be private? *Addis. Cato.*

I may close, after so long an *intrusion* upon your meditations. *Wake's Preparation for Death.*

3. Voluntary and uncalled undertaking of any thing.

It will be said, I handle an art no way suitable either to my employment or fortune, and so stand charged with *intrusion* and impertinency. *Wotton.*

To INTRU'ST. *v. a.* [*in* and *trust.*] To treat with confidence; to charge with any secret commission, or thing of value.

His majesty had a solicitous care for the payment of his debts; though in such a manner, that none of the duke's officers were *intrusted* with the knowledge of it. *Clarendon.*

Receive my counsel, and securely move;
Intrust thy fortune to the pow'rs above. *Dryden's Juven.*
Are not the lives of those, who draw the sword
In Rome's defence, *intrusted* to our care? *Addis. Cato.*

He composed his billet-doux, and at the time appointed went to *intrust* it to the hands of his confidant. *Arbuthnot.*

INTUI'TION. *n. s.* [*intuitus*, *intueor*, Latin.]

1. Sight of any thing. Used commonly of mental view; immediate knowledge.

At our rate of judging, St. Paul had surely passed for a most malicious persecutor; whereas God saw he did it ignorantly in unbelief, and upon that *intuition* had mercy on him. *Government of the Tongue.*

The truth of these propositions we know by a bare simple *intuition* of the ideas, and such propositions are called self-evident. *Locke.*

2. Knowledge not obtained by deduction of reason, but instantaneously accompanying the ideas which are its object.

All knowledge of causes is deductive; for we know none by simple *intuition*, but through the mediation of their effects; for the causality itself is insensible. *Glanv. Sceps.*

Discourse was then almost as quick as *intuition*. *South.*

He their single virtues did survey,
By *intuition* in his own large breast. *Dryden.*

INTU'ITIVE. *adj.* [*intuitivus*, low Latin; *intuitif*, French.]

1. Seen by the mind immediately without the intervention of reason.

Immediate perception of the agreement or disagreement of two ideas, is when, by comparing them together in our minds, we see their agreement or disagreement; this therefore is called *intuitive* knowledge. *Locke.*

Those lofty flights of thought, and almost *intuitive* perception of abstruse notions, those exalted discoveries of mathematical theorems, we sometimes see existent in one and the same person. *Bentley.*

2. Seeing, not barely believing.

Faith, beginning here with a weak apprehension of things not seen, endeth with the *intuitive* vision of God in the world to come. *Hooker.*

3. Having the power of discovering truth immediately without ratiocination.

The rule of ghostly or immaterial natures, as spirits and angels, is their *intuitive* intellectual judgment, concerning the amiable beauty and high goodness of that object, which, with unspeakable joy and delight, doth set them on work. *Hooker.*

The soul receives
Discursive or *intuitive*. *Milton.*

INTUI'TIVELY. *adv.* [*intuitivement*, French.] Without deduction of reason; by immediate perception.

That our love is found and sincere, that it cometh from a pure heart, and a good conscience, and a faith unfeigned, who can pronounce, saving only the searcher of all mens hearts, who alone *intuitively* doth know in this kind who are his. *Hook.*

God Almighty, who sees all things *intuitively*, does not want logical helps. *Baker on Learning.*

INTUME'SCENCE. } *n. s.* [*intumescence*, French; *intumesco*, Lat.]
INTUME'SCENCY. } Swell; tumour; the act or state of swelling.

According to the temper of the terreous parts at the bottom, as they are more hardly or easily moved, they variously begin, continue, or end their *intumescencies*. *Brown.*

This subterranean heat causes a great rarefaction and *intumescence* of the water of the abyss, putting it into very great commotions, and at the same time making the like effort upon the earth, occasions an earthquake. *Woodward's Nat. History.*

INTURGE'SCENCE. *n. s.* [*in* and *turgesco*, Latin.] Swelling; the act or state of swelling.

Not by attenuation of the upper part of the sea, but *inturgescencies* caused first at the bottom, and carrying the upper part of it before them. *Brown's Vulgar Err.*

INTU'SE. *n. s.* [*intusus*, Latin.] Bruise. *Spenser.*

To INTWI'NE. *v. a.* [*in* and *twine*.]

1. To twist, or wreath together.

This opinion, though false, yet *intwined* with a true, that the souls of men do never perish, abated the fear of death in them. *Hooker.*

2. To incompass by circling round it.

The vest and veil divine,
Which wand'ring foliage and rich flow'rs *intwine*. *Dryden.*

To INVA'DE. *v. a.* [*invado*, Latin.]

1. To attack a country; to make an hostile entrance.

He will *invade* them with troops. *Hab.* iii. 16.

Should he *invade* any part of their country, he would soon see that nation up in arms. *Knolles.*

With dang'rous expedition they *invade*
Heav'n, whose high walls fear no assault. *Milton.*
Thy race in times to come
Shall spread the conquests of imperial Rome;
Rome, whose ascending tow'rs shall heav'n *invade*,
Involving earth and ocean in her shade. *Dryden's Æn.*

Encouraged with success, he *invades* the province of philosophy. *Dryden.*

In vain did nature's wise command
Divide the waters from the land,
If daring ships, and men prophane,
Invade th' inviolable main. *Dryden.*

2. To attack; to assail; to assault.

There shall be sedition among men, and *invading* one another; they shall not regard their kings. 2 *Esdr.* xv. 16.

Thou think'st 'tis much, that this contentious storm
Invades us to the skin; so 'tis to thee:
But where the greater malady is fix'd,
The lesser is scarce felt. *Shakesp. King Lear.*

3. To violate with the first act of hostility; to attack, not defend.

Your foes are such, as they, not you, have made;
And virtue may repel, though not *invade*. *Dryden.*

INVA'DER. *n. s.* [from *invado*, Latin.]

1. One who enters with hostility into the possessions of another.

The breath of Scotland the Spaniards could not endure; neither durst they, as *invaders*, land in Ireland. *Bacon.*

Their piety
In sharp contest of battle found no aid
Against *invaders*. *Milton's Paradise Lost.*

That knowledge, like the coal from the altar, serves only to embroil and consume the sacrilegious *invaders*. *Decay of Piety.*

Were he lost, the naked empire
Would be a prey expos'd to all *invaders*. *Denham's Sophy.*

The country about Attica was the most barren of any in Greece, through which means it happened that the natives were never expelled by the fury of *invaders*. *Swift.*

Secure, by William's care, let Britain stand;
Nor dread the bold *invader*'s hand. *Prior.*

Esteem and judgment with strong fancy join,
To call the fair *invader* in;
My darling favourite inclination, too,
All, all conspiring with the foe. *Granville.*

2. An assailant.

3. Encroacher; intruder.

The substance thereof was formerly comprised in that uncompounded style, but afterwards prudently enlarged for the repelling and preventing heretical *invaders*. *Hammond.*

INVALE'SCENCE. *n. s.* [*invalesco*, Latin.] Strength; health; force. *Dict.*

INVA'LID. *adj.* [*invalide*, Fr. *invalidus*, Latin.] Weak; of no weight or cogency.

But this I urge,
Admitting motion in the heav'ns, to shew
Invalid, that which thee to doubt it mov'd. *Milton.*

To INVA'LIDATE. *v. a.* [from *invalid*.] To weaken; to deprive of force or efficacy.

To *invalidate* such a consequence, some things might be speciously enough alledged. *Boyle.*

Tell a man, passionately in love, that he is jilted, bring a score of witnesses of the falshood of his mistress, and it is ten to one but three kind words of her's shall *invalidate* all their testimonies. *Locke.*

INVALI'D. *n. s.* [Fr.] One disabled by sickness or hurts.

What beggar in the *invalides*,
With lameness broke, with blindness smitten,
Wish'd ever decently to die? *Prior.*

INVALI'DITY. *n. s.* [*in* and *validity*; *invalidité*, French.]

1. Weakness; want of cogency.

2. Want of bodily strength. This is no English meaning.

He ordered, that none who could work should be idle; and that none who could not work, by age, sickness, or *invalidity*, should want. *Temple.*

INVA'LUABLE. *adj.* [*in* and *valuable*.] Precious above estimation; inestimable.

The faith it produced would not be so free an act as it ought, to which are annexed all the glorious and *invaluable* privileges of believing. *Atterbury.*

INVA'RIABLE. *adj.* [*in* and *variarus*, Lat. *invariabile*, Fr.] Unchangeable; constant.

Being not able to design times by days, months, or years, they thought best to determine these alterations by some known and *invariable* signs, and such did they conceive the rising and setting of the fixed stars. *Brown's Vulg. Err.*

The rule of good and evil would not then appear uniform and *invariable*, but would seem different, according to mens different complexions and inclinations. *Atterbury.*

INVA'RIABLENESS. *n. s.* [from *invariable*.] Immutability; constancy.

INVA'RIABLY. *adv.* [from *invariable*.] Unchangeably; constantly.

He, who steers his course *invariably* by this rule, takes the surest way to make all men praise him. *Atterbury.*

INVA'SION. *n. s.* [*invasion*, French; *invasio*, Latin.]

1. Hostile entrance upon the rights or possessions of another; hostile encroachment.

We made an *invasion* upon the Cherethites. 1 *Sa.* xxx.

Reason finds a secret grief and remorse from every *invasion* that sin makes upon innocence, and that must render the first entrance and admission of sin uneasy. *South's Sermons.*

The nations of th' Ausonian shore
Shall hear the dreadful rumour, from afar,
Of arm'd *invasion*, and embrace the war. *Dryd. Æn.*

William the Conqueror invaded England about the year 1060, which means this; that taking the duration from our Saviour's time 'till now, for one intire length of time, it shews at what distance this *invasion* was from the two extremes. *Locke.*

2. Attack of an epidemical disease.

What demonstrates the plague to be endemial to Egypt, is its *invasion* and going off at certain seasons. *Arbuthnot.*

INVA'SIVE. *adj.* [from *invade.*] Entering hostilely upon other mens possessions; not defensive.

I must come closer to my purpose, and not make more *invasive* wars abroad, when, like Hannibal, I am called back to the defence of my country. *Dryden.*

Let other monarchs, with *invasive* bands,
Lessen their people, and extend their lands;
By gasping nations hated and obey'd,
Lords of the desarts that their swords had made. *Arbuthnot.*

INVE'CTIVE. *n. s.* [*invective*, Fr. *invectiva*, low Lat.] A censure in speech or writing; a reproachful accusation.

Plain men desiring to serve God as they ought, but being not so skilful as to unwind themselves, where the snares of glosing speech do lie to entangle them, are in mind not a little troubled, when they hear so bitter *invectives* against that which this church hath taught them to reverence as holy, to approve as lawful, and to observe as behoveful for the exercise of Christian duty. *Hooker.*

So desp'rate thieves, all hopeless of their lives,
Breathe out *invectives* 'gainst the officers. *Shakes. H.* VI.

Casting off the respect fit to be continued between kings, even when their blood is hottest, he fell to bitter *invectives* against the French king. *Bacon's H.* VII.

Whilst we condemn others, we may indeed be in the wrong; and then all the *invectives* we make at their supposed errours, fall back with a rebounded force upon our own real ones. *Decay of Piety.*

If we take satyr, in the general signification of the world, for an *invective*, 'tis certain that 'tis almost as old as verse. *Dryd. Juv. Dedication.*

INVE'CTIVE. *adj.* [from the noun.] Satirical; abusive.

Let him rail on; let his *invective* muse
Have four and twenty letters to abuse. *Dryden.*

INVE'CTIVELY. *adv.* Satirically; abusively.

Thus most *invectively* he pierceth through
The body of the country, city, court,
Yea and of this our life; swearing that we
Are meer usurpers, tyrants. *Shakespeare.*

To INVE'IGH. *v. a.* [*inveho*, Latin.] To utter censure or reproach.

I cannot blame him for *inveighing* so sharply against the vices of the clergy in his age. *Dryden.*

He *inveighs* severely against the folly of parties, in retaining scoundrels to retail their lyes. *Arbuthnot.*

INVE'IGHER. *n. s.* [from *inveigh.*] Vehement railer.

One of these *inveighers* against mercury, in a course of seven weeks, could not cure one small herpes in the face. *Wiseman's Surgery.*

To INVE'IGLE. *v. a.* [*invogliare*, Ital. *Minshew*; *aveugler*, or *enaveugler*, French, *Skinner* and *Junius.*] To persuade to something bad or hurtful; to wheedle; to allure; to seduce.

Most false Duessa, royal richly dight,
That easy was to *inveigle* weaker sight,
Was, by her wicked arts and wily skill,
Too false and strong for earthly skill or might. *Fa. Queen.*

Achilles hath *inveigled* his fool from him. *Shakespeare.*

Yet have they many baits and guileful spells,
To *inveigle* and invite th' unwary sense
Of them that pass unweeting by the way. *Milton.*

Both right able
T' *inveigle* and draw in the rabble. *Hudibras.*

Those drops of prettiness, scatteringly sprinkled amongst the creatures, were designed to exalt our conceptions, not *inveigle* or detain our passions. *Boyle.*

I leave the use of garlick to such as are *inveigled* into the gout by the use of too much drinking. *Temple.*

The *inveigling* a woman, before she is come to years of discretion, should be as criminal as the seducing of her before she is ten years old. *Spectator.*

INVE'IGLER. *n. s.* [from *inveigle.*] Seducer; deceiver; allurer to ill.

Being presented to the emperor for his admirable beauty, the prince clapt him up as his *inveigler*. *Sandys.*

To INVE'NT. *v. a.* [*inventer*, French; *invenio*, Latin.]

1. To discover; to find out; to excogitate; to produce something not made before.

The substance of the service of God, so far forth as it hath in it any thing more than the law of reason doth teach, may not be *invented* of men, but must be received from God himself. *Hooker.*

By their count, which lovers books *invent*,
The sphere of Cupid forty years contains. *Spenser.*

Matter of mirth enough, though there were none
She could devise, and thousand ways *invent*
To feed her foolish humour and vain jolliment. *Fa. Queen.*

Woe to them that *invent* to themselves instruments of musick. *Amos* vi. 5.

We may *invent*
With what more forcible we may offend
Our enemies. *Milton.*

In the motion of the bones in their articulations, a twofold liquor is prepared for the inunction of their heads; both which make up the most apt mixture, for this use, that can be *invented* or thought upon. *Ray.*

Ye skilful masters of Machaon's race,
Who nature's mazy intricacies trace,
By manag'd fire and late *invented* eyes. *Blackmore.*

But when long time the wretches thoughts refin'd,
When want had set an edge upon their mind,
Then various cares their working thoughts employ'd,
And that which each *invented*, all enjoy'd. *Creech.*

The ship by help of a screw, *invented* by Archimedes, was launched into the water. *Arbuthnot.*

2. To forge; to contrive falsely; to fabricate.

I never did such things as those men have maliciously *invented* against me. *Susan.* xliii.

Here is a strange figure *invented*, against the plain sense of the words. *Stillingfleet.*

3. To feign; to make by the imagination.

I would *invent* as bitter searching terms,
With full as many signs of deadly hate,
As lean-fac'd envy in her lothsome cave. *Shakespeare.*

Hercules's meeting with pleasure and virtue, was *invented* by Prodicus, who lived before Socrates, and in the first dawnings of philosophy. *Addison's Spectator.*

4. To light on; to meet with.

Far off he wonders what them makes so glad:
Or Bacchus' merry fruit they did *invent*,
Or Cybel's frantick rites have made them mad. *Spenser.*

INVE'NTER. *n. s.* [from *inventeur*, French.]

1. One who produces something new; a deviser of something not known before.

As a translator, he was just; as an *inventer*, he was rich. *Garth.*

2. A forger.

INVE'NTION. *n. s.* [*invention*, French; *inventio*, Latin.]

1. Fiction.

O for a muse of fire, that would ascend
The brightest heaven of *invention!* *Shakes. H.* V. *Prol.*

By improving what was writ before,
Invention labours less, but judgment more. *Roscommon.*

Invention is a kind of muse, which, being possessed of the other advantages common to her sisters, and being warmed by the fire of Apollo, is raised higher than the rest. *Dryden.*

The chief excellence of Virgil is judgment, of Homer is *invention.* *Pope.*

2. Discovery.

Nature hath provided several glandules to separate this juice from the blood, and no less than four pair of channels to convey it into the mouth, which are of a late *invention*, and called *ductus salivales.* *Ray on the Creation.*

3. Excogitation; act of producing something new.

Mine is th' *invention* of the charming lyre;
Sweet notes and heav'nly numbers I inspire. *Dryden.*

4. Forgery.

We hear our bloody cousins, not confessing
Their cruel parricide, filling their hearers
With strange *invention.* *Shakesp. Macbeth.*

If thou can'st accuse,
Do it without *invention* suddenly. *Shakesp. Henry* VI.

5. The thing invented.

The garden, a place not fairer in natural ornaments than artificial *inventions.* *Sidney.*

Th' *invention* all admir'd; and each how he
To be th' inventor miss'd, so easy it seem'd
Once found, which yet unfound most would have thought
Impossible. *Milton's Parad. Lost.*

INVE'NTIVE. *adj.* [*inventif*, Fr. from *invent.*] Quick at contrivance; ready at expedients; having the power of fiction.

Those have the *inventivest* heads for all purposes, and roundest tongues in all matters. *Ascham's Schoolmaster.*

As he had an *inventive* brain, so there never lived any man that believed better thereof, and of himself. *Raleigh.*

Reason, remembrance, wit, *inventive* art,
No nature, but immortal, can impart. *Denham.*

That *inventive* head
Her fatal image from the temple drew,
The sleeping guardians of the castle slew. *Dryden.*

The *inventive* god, who never fails his part,
Inspires the wit, when once he warms the heart. *Dryden.*

INVE'NTOR. *n. s.* [*inventor*, Latin.]

1. A finder out of something new.

We have the statue of your Columbus, that discovered the West Indies, also the *inventor* of ships: your Monk, that was the *inventor* of ordnance, and of gunpowder. *Bacon.*

Studious they appear
Of arts that polish life; *inventors* rare,
Unmindful of their maker. *Milton's Paradise Lost.*
Th' invention all admir'd, and each how he
To be the *inventor* miss'd. *Milton.*

Why are these positions charged upon me as their sole author and *inventor*, and the reader led into a belief that they were never before maintained by any person of virtue? *Atterb.*

2. A contriver; a framer. In an ill sense.

In this upshot, purposes mistook,
Fall'n on th' *inventors* heads. *Shakes. Hamlet.*

INVENTO'RIALLY. *adv.* [from *inventory*, whence perhaps *inventorial.*] In manner of an inventory.

To divide *inventorially*, would dizzy the arithmetick of memory. *Shakespeare's Hamlet.*

INVE'NTORY. *n. s.* [*inventaire*, French; *inventarium*, Latin.] An account or catalogue of moveables.

I found,
Forsooth, an *inventory*, thus importing,
The several parcels of his plate. *Shakesp. H.* VIII.

The leanness that afflicts us, the object of our misery, is as an *inventory* to particularize their abundance: our sufferings is a gain to them. *Shakespeare's Coriolanus.*

Whoe'er looks,
For themselves dare not go, o'er Cheapside books,
Shall find their wardrobe's *inventory.* *Donne.*

It were of much consequence to have such an *inventory* of nature, wherein, as on the one hand, nothing should be wanting, so nothing repeated on the other. *Grew's Musæum.*

In Persia the daughters of Eve are reckoned in the *inventory* of their goods and chattels; and it is usual, when a man sells a bale of silk, to toss half a dozen women into the bargain. *Spectator.*

He gave me an *inventory* of her goods and estate. *Spectator.*

To I'NVENTORY. *v. a.* [*inventorier*, Fr.] To register; to place in a catalogue.

I will give out divers schedules of my beauty: it shall be *inventoried*, and every particle and utensil labell'd to my will. *Shakes. Twelfth Night.*

A man looks on the love of his friend as one of the richest possessions: the philosopher thought friends were to be *inventoried* as well as goods. *Gov. of the Tongue.*

INVE'NTRESS. *n. s.* [*inventrice*, Fr. from *inventor.*] A female that invents.

The arts, with all their retinue of lesser trades, history and tradition tell us when they had their beginning; and how many of their inventors and *inventresses* were deified. *Burnet.*

Cecilia came,
Inventress of the vocal frame:
The sweet enthusiast, from her sacred store,
Enlarg'd the former narrow bounds. *Dryden.*

INVE'RSE. *adj.* [*inverse*, Fr. *inversus*, Latin.] Inverted; reciprocal: opposed to *direct.* It is so called in proportion, when the fourth term is so much greater than the third, as the second is less than the first; or so much less than the third as the second is greater than the first.

Every part of matter tends to every part of matter with a force, which is always in a direct proportion of the quantity of matter, and an *inverse* duplicate proportion of the distance. *Garth.*

INVE'RSION. *n. s.* [*inversion*, Fr. *inversio*, Latin.]

1. Change of order or time, so as that the last is first, and first last.

If he speaks truth, it is upon design, and a subtle *inversion* of the precept of God, to do good that evil may come of it. *Brown's Vulg. Errours.*

'Tis just the *inversion* of an act of parliament; your lordship first signed it, and then it was passed amongst the lords and commons. *Dryden.*

2. Change of place, so as that each takes the room of the other.

To INVE'RT. *v. a.* [*inverto*, Latin.]

1. To turn upside down; to place in contrary method or order to that which was before.

With fate *inverted*, shall I humbly woo?
And some proud prince, in wild Numidia born,
Pray to accept me, and forget my scorn? *Waller.*
Ask not the cause why sullen Spring
So long delays her flow'rs to bear,
And Winter storms *invert* the year. *Dryden.*

Poesy and oratory omit things essential, and *invert* times and actions, to place every thing in the most affecting light. *Watts.*

2. To place the last first.

Yes, every poet is a fool;
By demonstration Ned can show it:
Happy, could Ned's *inverted* rule
Prove every fool to be a poet. *Prior.*

3. To divert; to turn into another channel; to imbezzle. Instead of this *convert* or *intervert* is now commonly used.

Solyman charged him bitterly with *inverting* his treasures to his own private use, and having secret intelligence with his enemies. *Knolles's History of the Turks.*

INVE'RTEDLY. *adv.* [from *inverted.*] In contrary or reversed order.

Placing the forepart of the eye to the hole of the window of a darkened room, we have a pretty landskip of the objects abroad, *invertedly* painted on the paper, on the back of the eye. *Derham's Physico-Theology.*

To INVE'ST. *v. a.* [*investir*, Fr. *investio*, Latin.]

1. To dress; to clothe; to array. When it has two accusatives it has *in* or *with* before the thing.

Their gesture sad,
Invest in lank lean cheeks and war-worn coats,
Presented them unto the gazing moon,
So many horrid ghosts. *Shakesp. Henry* V.
Thou *with* a mantle didst *invest*
The rising world of waters. *Milton.*
Let thy eyes shine forth in their full lustre;
Invest them *with* thy loveliest smiles, put on
Thy choicest looks. *Denham's Sophy.*

2. To place in possession of a rank or office.

When we sanctify or hallow churches, that which we do is only to testify that we make places of publick resort, that we *invest* God himself *with* them, and that we sever them from common uses. *Hooker.*

After the death of the other archbishop he was *invested in* that high dignity, and settled in his palace at Lambeth. *Claren.*

The practice of all ages, and all countries, hath been to do honour to those who are *invested with* publick authority. *Atter.*

3. To adorn; to grace.

Honour must,
Not accompanied, *invest* him only;
But signs of nobleness, like stars, shall shine
On all deservers. *Shakespeare's Macbeth.*
The foolish, over-careful fathers for this engross'd
The canker'd heaps of strong atchieved gold;
For this they have been thoughtful to *invest*
Their sons with arts and martial exercises. *Shakespeare.*
Some great potentate,
Or of the thrones above; such majesty
Invests him coming. *Milt. Parad. Lost.*

4. To confer; to give.

If there can be found such an inequality between man and man, as there is between man and beast, or between soul and body, it *investeth* a right of government. *Bacon.*

5. To inclose; to surround so as to intercept succours or provisions: as, the enemy *invested* the town.

INVE'STIENT. *adj.* [*investiens*, Latin.] Covering; clothing.

The shells served as plasms or moulds to this sand, which, when consolidated and freed from its *investient* shell, is of the same shape as the cavity of the shell. *Woodward.*

INVE'STIGABLE. *adj.* [from *investigate.*] To be searched out; discoverable by rational disquisition.

Finally, in such sort they are *investigable*, that the knowledge of them is general; the world hath always been acquainted with them. *Hooker.*

In doing evil, we prefer a less good before a greater, the greatness whereof is by reason *investigable*, and may be known. *Hooker.*

To INVE'STIGATE. *v. a.* [*investigo*, Latin.] To search out; to find out by rational disquisition.

Investigate the variety of motions and figures made by the organs for articulation. *Holder of Speech.*

From the present appearances *investigate* the powers and forces of nature, and from these account for future observations. *Cheyne's Phil. Princ.*

INVESTIGA'TION. *n. s.* [*investigation*, Fr. *investigatio*, Latin.]

1. The act of the mind by which unknown truths are discovered.

Not only the *investigation* of truth, but the communication of it also, is often practised in such a method as neither agrees precisely to synthetick or analytick. *Watts.*

Progressive truth, the patient force of thought
Investigation calm, whose silent powers
Command the world. *Thomson's Summer.*

2. Examination.

Your travels I hear much of: my own shall never more be in a strange land, but a diligent *investigation* of my own territories: I mean no more translations, but something domestick, fit for my own country. *Pope to Swift.*

INVE'STITURE. *n. s.* [French.]

1. The right of giving possession of any manor, office, or benefice.

He had refused to yield up to the pope the *investiture* of bishops, and collation of ecclesiastical dignities within his dominions. *Raleigh's Essays.*

2. The act of giving possession.

INVE'STMENT. *n. s.* [*in* and *vestment.*] Dress; cloaths; garment; habit.

Ophelia, do not believe his vows; for they are brokers,
Not of that die which their *investments* shew. *Shakes. Ham.*

You, my lord archbishop,
Whose see is by a civil peace maintained,
Whose beard the silver hand of peace hath touch'd,
Whose learning and good letters peace hath tutor'd,
Whose white *investments* figure innocence,
The dove, and every blessed spirit of peace;
Wherefore do you so ill translate yourself,
Out of the speech of peace, that bears such grace,
Into the harsh and boist'rous tongue of war? *Shak. H.* IV.

INVE'TERACY. *n. s.* [*inveteratio*, Latin.]

1. Long continuance of any thing bad; obstinacy confirmed by time.

The *inveteracy* of the people's prejudices compelled their rulers to make use of all means for reducing them. *Addison.*

2. [In physick.] Long continuance of a disease.

INVE'TERATE. *adj.* [*inveteratus*, Latin.]

1. Old; long established.

The custom of Christians was then, and had been a long time, not to wear garlands, and therefore that undoubtedly they did offend who presumed to violate such a custom by not observing that thing; the very *inveterate* observation whereof was a law, sufficient to bind all men to observe it, unless they could shew some higher law, some law of Scripture, to the contrary. *Hooker.*

It is an *inveterate* and received opinion, that cantharides, applied to any part of the body, touch the bladder and exulcerate it. *Bacon's Natural History.*

2. Obstinate by long continuance.

It is not every sinful violation of conscience that can quench the spirit; but it must be a long *inveterate* course and custom of sinning, that at length produces and ends in such a cursed effect. *South's Sermons.*

He who writes satire honestly is no more an enemy to the offender, than the physician to the patient when he prescribes harsh remedies to an *inveterate* disease. *Dryden.*

In a well-instituted state the executive power will never let abuses grow *inveterate*, or multiply so far that it will be hard to find remedies. *Swift.*

To INVE'TERATE. *v. a.* [*inveterer*, Fr. *invetero*, Latin.] To harden or make obstinate by long continuance.

The vulgar conceived, that now there was an end given, and a consummation to superstitious prophecies, and to an ancient tacit expectation, which had by tradition been infused and *inveterated* into mens minds. *Bacon.*

Let not atheists lay the fault of their sins upon human nature, which have their prevalence from long custom and *inveterated* habit. *Bentley's Sermons.*

INVE'TERATENESS. *n. s.* [from *inveterate.*] Long continuance of any thing bad; obstinacy confirmed by time.

As time hath rendered him more perfect in the art, so hath the *inveterateness* of his malice made him more ready in the execution. *Brown's Vulg. Errours.*

Neither the *inveterateness* of the mischief, nor the prevalency of the fashion, shall be any excuse for those who will not take care about the meaning of their words. *Locke.*

INVETERA'TION. *n. s.* [*inveteratio*, Latin.] The act of hardening or confirming by long continuance.

INVI'DIOUS. *adj.* [*invidiosus*, Latin.]

1. Envious; malignant.

I shall open to them the interior secrets of this mysterious art, without imposture or *invidious* reserve. *Evelyn.*

2. Likely to incur or to bring hatred. This is the more usual sense.

Agamemnon found it an *invidious* affair to give the preference to any one of the Grecian heroes. *Broome.*

Not to be further tedious, or rather *invidious*, these are a few causes which have contributed to the ruin of our morals. *Swift.*

INVI'DIOUSLY. *adv.* [from *invidious.*]

1. Malignantly; enviously.

The clergy murmur against the privileges of the laity; the laity *invidiously* aggravate the immunities of the clergy. *Sprat.*

2. In a manner likely to provoke hatred.

INVI'DIOUSNESS. *n. s.* [from *invidious.*] Quality of provoking envy or hatred.

To INVI'GORATE. *v. a.* [*in* and *vigour.*] To endue with vigour; to strengthen; to animate; to enforce.

The spleen is introduced to *invigorate* the sinister side, which, dilated, would rather infirm and debilitate. *Brown.*

I have lived in a reign when the prince, instead of *invigorating* the laws, or giving them their proper course, assumed a power of dispensing with them. *Addison.*

No one can enjoy health, without he feel a lightsome and *invigorating* principle, which spurs him to action. *Spectator.*

Christian graces and virtues they cannot be, unless fed, *invigorated*, and animated by a principle of universal charity. *Atterbury's Sermons.*

Gentle warmth
Discloses well the earth's all teeming womb,
Invigorating tender seeds. *Phillips.*

INVIGORA'TION. *n. s.* [from *invigorate.*]

1. The act of invigorating.

2. The state of being invigorated.

I find in myself an appetitive faculty, which is always in actual exercise, in the very height of activity and *invigoration.* *Norris.*

INVI'NCIBLE. *adj.* [*invincible*, French; *invincibilis*, Latin.] Insuperable; unconquerable; not to be subdued.

I would have thought her spirits had been *invincible* against all assaults of affection. *Shakespeare.*

Should he invade any part of their country, he would soon see that *invincible* nation with their united forces up in arms. *Knolles's History of the Turks.*

The spirit remains *invincible*. *Milton.*

That mistake, which is the consequence of *invincible* errour, scarce deserves the name of wrong judgment. *Locke.*

If an atheist had had the making of himself, he would have framed a constitution that could have kept pace with his insatiable lust, been *invincible* by intemperance, and have held out a thousand years in a perpetual debauch. *Bentley's Sermons.*

INVI'NCIBLENESS. *n. s.* [from *invincible.*] Unconquerableness; insuperableness.

INVI'NCIBLY. *adv.* [from *invincible.*] Insuperably; unconquerably.

Ye have been fearless in his righteous cause;
And as ye have receiv'd, so have ye done
Invincibly. *Milton.*

Neither invitations nor threats avail with those who are *invincibly* impeded, to apply them to their benefit. *Dec. of Piety.*

INVI'OLABLE. *adj.* [*inviolable*, French; *inviolabilis*, Latin.]

1. Not to be profaned; not to be injured.

Thou, be sure, shalt give account
To him who sent us, whose charge is to keep
This place *inviolable*, and these from harm. *Milt. Par. Lost.*

In vain did nature's wise command
Divide the waters from the land,
If daring ships, and men prophane,
Invade the *inviolable* main;
Th' eternal fences overleap,
And pass at will the boundless deep. *Dryden.*

Ye lamps of heav'n! he said, and lifted high
His hands, now free; thou venerable sky!
Inviolable pow'rs! ador'd with dread,
Be all of you adjur'd. *Dryden's Æn.*

This birthright, when our author pleases, must and must not be sacred and *inviolable.* *Locke.*

2. Not to be broken.

The prophet David thinks, that the very meeting of men together, and their accompanying one another to the house of God, should make the bond of their love insoluble, and tie them in a league of *inviolable* amity. *Hooker.*

See, see, they join, embrace, and seem to kiss,
As if they vow'd some league *inviolable.* *Shakesp. H.* VI.

3. Insusceptible of hurt or wound.

Th' *inviolable* saints
In cubick phalanx firm advanc'd intire. *Milton.*

INVI'OLABLY. *adv.* [from *inviolable.*] Without breach; without failure.

The true profession of Christianity *inviolably* engages all its followers to do good to all men. *Spratt's Sermons.*

Meer acquaintance you have none: you have drawn them all into a nearer line; and they who have conversed with you, are for ever after *inviolably* yours. *Dryden.*

INVI'OLATE. *adj.* [*inviolate*, Fr. *inviolatus*, Lat.] Unhurt; uninjured; unprofaned; unpolluted; unbroken.

His fortune of arms was still *inviolate.* *Bacon's H.* VII.

But let *inviolate* truth be always dear
To thee; even before friendship, truth prefer. *Denham.*

If the past
Can hope a pardon, by those mutual bonds
Nature has seal'd between us, which though I
Have cancell'd, thou hast still preserv'd *inviolate:*
I beg thy pardon. *Denham's Sophy.*

My love your claim *inviolate* secures;
'Tis writ in fate, I can be only yours. *Dryden's Aurengz.*

In all the changes of his doubtful state,
His truth, like heav'n's, was kept *inviolate.* *Dryden.*

I'NVIOUS. *adj.* [*invius*, Latin.] Impassable; untrodden.

If nothing can oppugn his love,
And virtue *invious* ways can prove,
What may not he confide to do,
That brings both love and virtue too. *Hudibras.*

INVISIBI'LITY. *n. s.* [*invisibilité*, Fr. from *invisible.*] The state of being invisible; imperceptibleness to sight.

They may be demonstrated to be innumerable, substituting their smalness for the reason of their *invisibility.* *Ray.*

INVI'SIBLE. *adj.* [*invisible*, Fr. *invisibilis*, Latin.] Not perceptible by the sight; not to be seen.

He was *invisible* that hurt me so;
And none *invisible*, but spirits, can go. *Sidney.*

The threaden sails,
Borne with th' *invisible* and creeping wind,
Drew the huge bottoms to the furrow'd sea. *Shakesp. H.* V.

'Tis

'Tis wonderful,
That an *invisible* instinct should frame them
To loyalty unlearn'd, honour untaught,
Civility not seen from others. *Shakesp. Cymbeline.*

To us *invisible*, or dimly seen,
In these thy lowest works. *Milton.*

He that believes a God, believes such a being as hath all perfections; among which this is one, that he is a spirit, and consequently that he is *invisible*, and cannot be seen. *Tillotson.*

It seems easier to make one's self *invisible* to others, than to make another's thoughts visible to me, which are not visible to himself. *Locke.*

INVI'SIBLY. *adv.* [from *invisible.*] Imperceptibly to the sight.

Age by degrees *invisibly* doth creep,
Nor do we seem to die, but fall asleep. *Denham.*

To INVI'SCATE. *v. a.* [*in* and *viscus*, Latin.] To lime; to intangle in glutinous matter.

The cameleon's food being flies, it hath in the tongue a mucous and slimy extremity, whereby, upon a sudden emission, it *inviscates* and intangleth those insects. *Brown.*

INVITA'TION. *n. s.* [*invitation*, Fr. *invitatio*, Lat.] The act of inviting, bidding, or calling to any thing with ceremony and civility.

That other answer'd with a lowly look,
And soon the gracious *invitation* took. *Dryden.*

INVI'TATORY. *adj.* [from *invito*, Latin.] Using invitation; containing invitation.

To INVITE. *v. a.* [*invito*, Latin; *inviter*, French.]

1. To bid; to ask to any place, particularly to one's own house, with intreaty and complaisance.

If thou be *invited* of a mighty man, withdraw thyself. *Ecclus.* i. 39.

He comes *invited* by a younger son. *Milton.*

When much company is *invited*, then be as sparing as possible of your coals. *Swift.*

2. To allure; to persuade.

A war upon the Turks is more worthy than upon any other Gentiles, though facility and hope of success might *invite* some other choice. *Bacon.*

Nor art thou such
Created, or such place hast here to dwell,
As may not oft *invite*, though spirits of heav'n,
To visit thee. *Milton's Paradise Lost*, b. v.

The liberal contributions such teachers met with, served still to *invite* more labourers into that work. *Decay of Piety.*

Shady groves, that easy sleep *invite*,
And after toilsome days a soft repose at night. *Dryd. Virgil.*

To INVI'TE. *v. n.* [*invito*, Latin.] To ask or call to any thing pleasing.

All things *invite*
To peaceful counsels. *Milton.*

INVI'TER. *n. s.* [from *invite.*] He who invites.

They forcibly cut out abortive votes, such as their *inviters* and encouragers most fancied. *King Charles.*

Honour was the aim of the guests, and interest was the scope of the *inviter*. *Smalridge's Sermons.*

Wines and cates the table grace,
But most the kind *inviter's* chearful face. *Pope's Odyss.*

INVI'TINGLY. *adv.* [from *inviting.*] In such a manner as invites or allures.

If he can but dress up a temptation to look *invitingly*, the business is done. *Decay of Piety.*

To INU'MBRATE. *v. a.* [*inumbro*, Latin.] To shade; to cover with shades. *Dict.*

INU'NCTION. *n. s.* [*inungo*, *inunctus*, Latin.] The act of smearing or anointing.

The wise Author of nature hath placed on the rump two glandules, which the bird catches hold upon with her bill, and squeezes out an oily liniment, fit for the *inunction* of the feathers, and causing their filaments to cohere. *Ray.*

INUNDA'TION. *n. s.* [*inundation*, French; *inundatio*, Latin.]

1. The overflow of waters; flood; deluge. *Inundation*, says *Cowley*, implies less than deluge.

Her father counts it dangerous,
That she should give her sorrow so much sway;
And in his wisdom hastes our marriage,
To stop the *inundation* of her tears. *Shak. Rom. and Juliet.*

The same *inundation* was not past forty foot in most places; so that although it destroyed man and beast generally, yet some few wild inhabitants of the woods escaped. *Bacon.*

All fountains of the deep,
Broke up, shall heave the ocean to usurp
Beyond all bounds, 'till *inundation* rise
Above the highest hills. *Milton's Paradise Lost*, b. xi.

This *inundation* unto the Egyptians happeneth when it is Winter unto the Ethiopians. *Brown's Vulg. Errours.*

Your care about your banks infers a fear
Of threatening floods, and *inundations* near. *Dryden.*

The hero next assail'd proud Doway's head,
And spite of confluent *inundations* spread
With unexampled valour did succeed. *Blackmore.*

No swelling *inundation* hides the grounds,
But crystal currents glide within their bounds. *Gay.*

2. A confluence of any kind.

Many good towns, through that *inundation* of the Irish, were utterly wasted. *Spenser.*

To I'NVOCATE. *v. a.* [*invoco*, Latin.] To invoke; to implore; to call upon; to pray to.

Poor key-cold figure of a holy king!
Be't lawful, that I *invocate* thy ghost,
To hear the lamentations of poor Anne. *Shakes. Rich.* III.

If Dagon be thy god,
Go to his temple, *invocate* his aid
With solemnest devotion. *Milton's Agonistes.*

Here rather let me drudge, and earn my bread,
'Till vermin or the draff of servile food
Consume me, and oft *invocated* death
Hasten the welcome end of all my pains. *Milton's Agonist.*

INVOCA'TION. *n. s.* [*invocation*, French; *invocatio*, Latin.]

1. The act of calling upon in prayer.

Is not the name of prayer usual to signify even all the service that ever we do unto God? And that for no other cause, as I suppose, but to shew that there is in religion no acceptable duty, which devout *invocation* of the name of God doth not either presuppose or infer. *Hooker.*

2. The form of calling for the assistance or presence of any being.

My *invocation* is
Honest and fair, and in his mistress' name. *Shakes.*

The proposition of Gratius is contained in a line, and that of *invocation* in half a line. *Wase.*

I will strain myself to breath out this one *invocation*. *Howel.*

The whole poem is a prayer to fortune, and the *invocation* is divided between the two deities. *Addison on Italy.*

I'NVOICE. *n. s.* [This word is perhaps corrupted from the French word *envoyez*, send.] A catalogue of the freight of a ship, or of the articles and price of goods sent by a factor.

To INVO'KE. *v. a.* [*invoco*, Latin; *invoquer*, French.] To call upon; to implore; to pray to.

The power I will *invoke* dwells in her eyes. *Sidney.*

One peculiar nation to select
From all the rest, of whom to be *invok'd*. *Milton's P. Lost.*

The skilful bard,
Striking the Thracian harp, *invokes* Apollo,
To make his hero and himself immortal. *Prior.*

To INVO'LVE. *v. a.* [*involvo*, Latin.]

1. To inwrap; to cover with any thing circumfluent.

Leave a singed bottom all *involv'd*
With stench and smoke. *Milton.*

No man could miss his way to heaven for want of light; and yet so vain are they as to think they oblige the world by *involving* it in darkness. *Decay of Piety.*

In a cloud *involv'd*, he takes his flight,
Where Greeks and Trojans mix'd in mortal fight. *Dryden.*

2. To imply; to comprise.

We cannot demonstrate these things so as to shew that the contrary necessarily *involves* a contradiction. *Tillotson.*

3. To entwist; to join.

He knows his end with mine *involv'd*. *Milton.*

4. To take in; to catch.

The gath'ring number, as it moves along,
Involves a vast involuntary throng. *Pope.*

Sin we should hate altogether; but our hatred of it may *involve* the person which we should not hate at all. *Sprat.*

One death *involves*
Tyrants and slaves. *Thomson's Summer.*

5. To intangle.

This reference of the name to a thing whereof we have no idea, is so far from helping at all, that it only serves the more to *involve* us in difficulties. *Locke.*

As obscure and imperfect ideas often *involve* our reason, so do dubious words puzzle mens reason. *Locke.*

6. To complicate; to make intricate.

Some *involv'd* their snaky folds. *Milton.*

Syllogism is of necessary use, even to the lovers of truth, to shew them the fallacies that are often concealed in florid, witty, or *involved* discourses. *Locke.*

7. To blend; to mingle together confusedly.

Earth with hell mingle and *involve*. *Milton.*

INVO'LUNTARILY. *adv.* [from *involuntary.*] Not by choice; not spontaneously.

INVO'LUNTARY. *adj.* [*in* and *voluntarius*, Latin; *involontaire*, French.]

1. Not having the power of choice.

The gath'ring number, as it moves along,
Involves a vast *involuntary* throng,
Who gently drawn, and struggling less and less,
Roll in her vortex, and her pow'r confess. *Dunciad*, b. iv.

2. Not chosen; not done willingly.

The forbearance of that action, consequent to such command of the mind, is called voluntary; and whatsoever action is performed without such a thought of the mind, is called *involuntary*. *Locke.*

But

But why? ah tell me, ah too dear!
Steals down my cheek th' *involuntary* tear. *Pope.*

INVOLU'TION. *n. s.* [*involutio*, Latin.]

1. The act of involving or inwrapping.

2. The state of being entangled; complication.

All things are mixed, and causes blended by mutual *involutions.* *Glanville's Sceps. c.* 23.

3. That which is wrapped round any thing.

Great conceits are raised of the *involution* or membranous covering called the silly-how, sometimes found about the heads of children. *Brown's Vulgar Errours, b.* v.

To INU'RE. *v. a.* [*in* and *ure.*]

1. To habituate; to make ready or willing by practice and custom; to accustom. It had anciently *with* before the thing practised, now *to.*

Because they insist so much, and so proudly insult thereon, we must a little *inure* their ears *with* hearing how others, whom they more regard, are in this case accustomed to use the self-same language with us. *Hooker, b.* v.

If there might be added the right helps of true art and learning, there would be as much difference, in maturity of judgment, between men *therewith inured*, and that which now men are, as between men that are now and innocents. *Hooker, b.* i. *s.* 6.

That it may no painful work endure,
It *to* strong labour can itself *inure.* *Hubberd's Tale.*

England was a peaceable kingdom, and but lately *inured to* the mild and goodly government of the Confessor. *Spenser.*

The forward hand, *inur'd to* wounds, makes way
Upon the sharpest fronts of the most fierce. *Daniel.*

Then cruel, by their sports *to* blood *enur'd*
Of fighting beasts, and men to beasts expos'd. *Milton.*

To *inure*
Our prompt obedience. *Milton's Par. Lost, b.* viii.

They, who had been most *inured to* business, had not in their lives ever undergone so great fatigue for twenty days together. *Clarendon, b.* viii.

We may *inure* ourselves by custom *to* bear the extremities of weather without injury. *Addison's Guard.* N°. 102.

2. To bring into use; to practise again.

The wanton boy was shortly well recur'd
Of that his malady;
But he soon after fresh again *inur'd*
His former cruelty. *Spenser.*

INU'REMENT. *n. s.* [from *inure.*] Practice; habit; use; custom; frequency.

If iron will acquire by mere continuance a secret appetite, and habitual inclination to the site it held, then how much more may education, being nothing else but a constant plight and *inurement*, induce by custom good habits into a reasonable creature. *Wotton.*

To INU'RN. *v. a.* [*in* and *urn.*] To intomb; to bury.

The sepulchre
Wherein we saw thee quietly *inurn'd*,
Hath op'd its ponderous and marble jaws
To cast thee up again. *Shakespeare's Hamlet.*

Amidst the tears of Trojan dames *inurn'd*,
And by his loyal daughters truly mourn'd. *Dryden.*

INU'STION. *n. s.* [*inustio*, Lat.] The act of burning.

INU'TILE. *adj.* [*inutile*, Fr. *inutilis*, Lat.] Useless; unprofitable.

To refer to heat and cold is a compendious and *inutile* speculation. *Bacon's Nat. Hist.* N°. 839.

INUTI'LITY. *n. s.* [*inutilité*, Fr. *inutilitas*, Lat.] Uselessness; unprofitableness.

INVU'LNERABLE. *adj.* [*invulnerable*, Fr. *invulnerabilis*, Lat.] Not to be wounded; secure from wound.

Our cannon's malice vainly shall be spent
Against th' *invulnerable* clouds of heav'n. *Shakespeare.*

Nor vainly hope
To be *invulnerable* in those bright arms,
That mortal dint none can resist. *Milton.*

Vanessa, though by Pallas taught,
By love *invulnerable* thought,
Searching in books for wisdom's aid,
Was in the very search betray'd. *Swift's Miscel.*

To INWA'LL. *v. a.* [*in* and *wall.*] To inclose with a wall.

Three such towns in those places with the garrisons, would be so augmented as they would be able with little to *inwall* themselves strongly. *Spenser on Ireland.*

I'NWARD. } *adv.* [inpeарð, Saxon.]
I'NWARDS. }

1. Towards the internal parts; within.

The parts of living creatures that be more *inwards* nourish more than the outward flesh. *Bacon's Nat. Hist.*

The medicines which go to these magical ointments are so strong, that if they were used *inwards* they would kill; and therefore they work potently, though outwards. *Bacon.*

Cœlestial light shine *inward.* *Milton.*

2. With inflexion or incurvity; concavely.

He stretches out his arm in sign of peace, with his breast bending *inward.* *Dryden's Dufresnoy.*

3. Into the mind or thoughts.

Looking *inward* we are stricken dumb; looking upward we speak and prevail. *Hooker, b.* v.

I'NWARD. *adj.*

1. Internal; placed not on the outside but within.

Though the lord of the liberty do pain himself all he may to yield equal justice unto all, yet can there not but great abuses lurk in so *inward* and absolute a privilege. *Spenser.*

He could not rest, but did his stout heart eat,
And waste his *inward* gall with deep despight. *Fa. Qu.*

To each *inward* part
It shoots invisible. *Milton.*

Sickness, contributing no less than old age to the shaking down this scaffolding of the body, may discover the *inward* structure more plainly. *Pope.*

2. Reflecting; deeply thinking.

With outward smiles their flatt'ry I receiv'd;
But bent and *inward* to myself again
Perplex'd, these matters I revolv'd, in vain. *Prior.*

3. Intimate; domestick.

All my *inward* friends abhorred me. *Job* xix. 19.

4. Seated in the mind.

Princes have but their titles for their glories,
An outward honour for an *inward* toil;
And for unfelt imaginations,
They often feel a world of restless cares. *Shakespeare.*

I'NWARD. *n. s.*

1. Any thing within, generally the bowels. Seldom has this sense a singular.

Then sacrificing, laid
The *inwards*, and their fat, with incense strew'd
On the cleft wood, and all due rites perform'd. *Milton.*

They esteem them most profitable, because of the great quantity of fat upon their *inwards.* *Mortimer's Husb.*

2. Intimate; near acquaintance.

Sir, I was an *inward* of his; a sly fellow was the duke; and I know the cause of his withdrawing. *Shakespeare.*

I'NWARDLY. *adv.* [from *inward.*]

1. In the heart; privately.

That which *inwardly* each man should be, the church outwardly ought to testify. *Hooker, b.* v.

I bleed *inwardly* for my lord. *Shakespeare.*

Mean time the king, though *inwardly* he mourn'd,
In pomp triumphant to the town return'd,
Attended by the chiefs. *Dryden's Knight's Tale.*

2. In the parts within; internally.

Let Benedick, like covered fire,
Consume away in sighs, waste *inwardly.* *Shakespeare.*

Cantharides he prescribes both outwardly and *inwardly.* *Arbuthnot on Coins.*

3. With inflexion or concavity.

I'NWARDNESS. *n. s.* [from *inward.*] Intimacy; familiarity.

You know, my *inwardness* and love
Is very much unto the prince and Claudio. *Shakespeare.*

To INWE'AVE. preter. *inwove* or *inweaved*, part. pass. *inwove* or *inwoven.* [*in* and *weave.*]

1. To mix any thing in weaving so that it forms part of the texture.

A fair border, wrought of sundry flowers,
Inwoven with an ivy winding trail. *Spenser.*

Down they cast
Their crowns, *inwove* with amaranth and gold. *Milton.*

And o'er soft palls of purple grain unfold
Rich tap'stry, stiffen'd with *inwoven* gold. *Pope's Odyssey.*

2. To intwine; to complicate.

The roof
Of thickest covert was *inwoven* shade. *Milton's Par. Lost.*

To INWO'OD. *v. a.* [*in* and *wood.*] To hide in woods.

He got out of the river, *inwooded* himself so as the ladies lost the marking his sportfulness. *Sidney, b.* ii.

To INWRA'P. *v. a.* [*in* and *wrap.*]

1. To cover by involution; to involve.

And over them Arachne high did lift
Her cunning web, and spread her subtil net,
Inwrapped in foul smoak. *Fairy Queen, b.* ii.

This, as an amber drop, *inwraps* a bee, }
Covering discovers your quick soul; that we }
May in your through-shine front our hearts thoughts see. } *Donne.*

2. To perplex; to puzzle with difficulty or obscurity.

The case is no sooner made than resolv'd: if it be made not *inwraped*, but plainly and perspicuously. *Bacon.*

3. It is doubtful whether the following examples should not be *enrap* or *inrap*, from *in* and *rap*, *rapio*, Latin, to ravish or transport.

This pearl she gave me I do feel't and see't;
And though 'tis wonder that *enwraps* me thus,
Yet 'tis not madness. *Shakespeare's Twelfth Night.*

For if such holy song
Enwrap our fancy long,
Time will run back, and fetch the age of gold. *Milton.*

INWRO'UGHT. *adj.* [*in* and *wrought.*] Adorned with work.

Camus,

Camus, reverend sir, went footing slow,
His mantle hairy and his bonnet sedge,
Inwrought with figures dim, and on the edge
Like to that sanguine flower inscrib'd with woe. *Milton.*

To INWRE'ATHE. *v. a.* [*in* and *wreath.*] To surround as with a wreath.

Bind their resplendent locks *inwreath'd* with beams. *Milton.*

Nor less the palm of peace *inwreathes* thy brow. *Thomson.*

JOB. *n. s.* [A low word now much in use, of which I cannot tell the etymology.]

2. A low mean lucrative busy affair.

1. Petty, piddling work; a piece of chance work.

He was now with his old friends in the state of a poor disbanded officer after peace, like an old favourite of a cunning minister after the *job* is over. *Arbuthnot.*

No cheek is known to blush, no heart to throb,
Save when they lose a question, or a *job*. *Pope.*

Such patents as these never were granted with a view of being a *job*, for the interest of a particular person to the damage of the publick. *Swift.*

3. A sudden stab with a sharp instrument.

To JOB. *v. a.*

1. To strike suddenly with a sharp instrument.

As an ass with a galled back was feeding in a meadow, a raven pitched upon him, and there sat *jobbing* of the sore. *L'Estrange.*

2. To drive in a sharp instrument.

Let peacocke and turkey leave *jobbing* their bex. *Tusser.*

The work would, where a small irregularity of stuff should happen, draw or *job* the edge into the stuff. *Moxon.*

To JOB. *v. n.* To play the stockjobber; to buy and sell as a broker.

The judge shall *job*, the bishop bite the town,
And mighty dukes pack cards for half a crown. *Pope.*

JOB's *tears.* *n. s.* An herb. *Ains.*

JO'BBER. *n. s.* [from *job.*]

1. A man who sells stock in the publick funds,

So cast it in the southern seas,
And view it through a *jobber's* bill;
Put on what spectacles you please,
Your guinea's but a guinea still. *Swift's Miscel.*

2. One who does chancework.

JOBBERNO'WL. *n. s.* [most probably from *jobbe*, Flemish, dull, and *nowl*, þnol, Saxon, a head.] Loggerhead; blockhead.

And like the world, men's *jobbernowls*
Turn round upon their ears, the poles. *Hudibras, p.* iii.

JO'CKEY. *n. s.* [from *Jack*, the diminutive of *John*, comes *Jackey*, or, as the Scotch, *jockey*, used for any boy, and particularly for a boy that rides race-horses.

1. A fellow that rides horses in the race.

These were the wise ancients, who heaped up greater honours on Pindar's *jockies* than on the poet himself. *Addison.*

2. A man that deals in horses.

3. A cheat; a trickish fellow.

To JO'CKEY. *v. a.* [from the noun.]

1. To justle by riding against one.

2. To cheat; to trick.

JOCO'SE. *adj.* [*jocosus*, Latin.] Merry; waggish; given to jest.

If the subject be sacred, all ludicrous turns, and *jocose* or comical airs, should be excluded, lest young minds learn to trifle with the awful solemnities of religion. *Watts.*

JOCO'SELY. *adv.* [from *jocose.*] Waggishly; in jest; in game.

Spondanus imagines that Ulysses may possibly speak *jocosely*, but in truth Ulysses never behaves with levity. *Broome.*

JOCO'SENESS. } JOCO'SITY. } *n. s.* [from *jocose.*] Waggery; merriment.

A laugh there is of contempt or indignation, as well as of mirth or *jocosity*. *Brown's Vulgar Errours, b.* vii.

JO'CULAR. *adj.* [*jocularis*, Latin.] Used in jest; merry; jocose; waggish; not serious.

These *jocular* slanders are often as mischievous as those of deepest design. *Government of the Tongue, s.* 5.

The satire is a dramatick poem; the stile is partly serious, and partly *jocular*. *Dryden.*

JO'CULARITY. *n. s.* [from *jocular.*] Merriment; disposition to jest.

The wits of those ages were short of these of ours; when men could maintain immutable faces, and persist unalterably at the efforts of *jocularity*. *Brown's Vulgar Errours, b.* vii.

JOCU'ND. *adj.* [*jocundus*, Lat.] Merry; gay; airy; lively.

There's comfort yet; then be thou *jocund*. *Shakespeare.*

No *jocund* health, that Denmark drinks to day,
But the great cannon to the clouds shall tell. *Shakespeare.*

They on their mirth and dance
Intent, with *jocund* musick charm his ear;
At once with joy and fear his heart rebounds. *Milton.*

Alexis shun'd his fellow swains
Their rural sports, and *jocund* strains. *Prior.*

JOCU'NDLY. *adv.* [from *jocund.*] Merrily; gaily.

He has no power of himself to leave it; but he is ruined *jocundly* and pleasantly, and damned according to his heart's desire. *South's Sermons.*

To JOG. *v. a.* [*schocken*, Dutch.] To push; to shake by a sudden impulse; to give notice by a sudden push.

Now leaps he upright, *jogs* me and cries, Do you see
Yonder well-favour'd youth? *Donne.*

This said, he *jogg'd* his good steed nigher,
And steer'd him gently toward the squire. *Hudibras, p.* i.

I was pretty well pleased while I expected, till fruition *jogged* me out of my pleasing slumber, and I knew it was but a dream. *Norris's Miscel.*

Sudden I *jogg'd* Ulysses, who was laid
Fast by my side. *Pope's Odyssey.*

To JOG. *v. n.* To move by succussation; to move with small shocks like those of a low trot.

The door is open, Sir, there lies good way,
You may be *jogging* while your boots are green. *Shakesp.*

Jog on, *jog* on the foot-path way,
And merrily heat the stile-a,
A merry heart goes all the day,
Your sad tires in a mile-a. *Shakesp. Winter's Tale.*

Here lieth one, who did most truly prove
That he could never die while he could move;
So hung his destiny, never to rot
While he might still *jog* on and keep his trot. *Milton.*

Away they trotted together: but as they were *jogging* on, the wolf spy'd a bare place about the dog's neck. *L'Estrange.*

Thus they *jog* on, still tricking, never thriving,
And murd'ring plays, which they miscal reviving. *Dryden.*

JOG. *n. s.* [from the verb.]

1. A push; a slight shake; a sudden interruption by a push or shake; a hint given by a push.

As a leopard was valuing himself upon his party-coloured skin, a fox gave him a *jog*, and whispered him, that the beauty of the mind was above that of a painted outside. *L'Estrange.*

Nick found the means to slip a note into Lewis's hands, which Lewis as slily put into John's pocket, with a pinch or a *jog* to warn him what he was about. *Arbuthnot.*

A letter when I am inditing,
Comes Cupid, and gives me a *jog*,
And I fill all the paper with writing
Of nothing but sweet Molly Mogg. *Swift's Miscel.*

2. A rub; a small stop; an irregularity of motion.

How that which penetrates all bodies without the least *jog* or obstruction, should impress a motion on any, is inconceivable. *Glanville's Sceps.*

JO'GGER. *n. s.* [from *jog.*] One who moves heavily and dully.

They, with their fellow *joggers* of the plough. *Dryden.*

To JO'GGLE. *v. n.* To shake.

In the head of man, the base of the brain is parallel to the horizon; by which there is less danger of the two brains *joggling*, or slipping out of their place. *Derham.*

JO'HNAPPLE. *n. s.*

A *johnapple* is a good relished sharp apple the Spring following, when most other fruit is spent: they are fit for the cyder plantations. *Mortimer's Husb.*

To JOIN. *v. a.* [*joindre*, French.]

1. To add one to another in continuity.

Wo unto them that *join* house to house, that lay field to field. *Isa.* lviii.

Join them one to another into one stick. *Ezek.* xxxvii. 17.

The wall was *joined* together unto the half. *Neh.* iv. 6.

2. To couple; to combine.

In this faculty of repeating and *joining* together its ideas, the mind has great power. *Locke.*

3. To unite in league or marriage.

One only daughter heirs my crown and state,
Whom not our oracles, nor heav'n, nor fate,
Nor frequent prodigies permit to *join*
With any native of the Ausonian line. *Dryden's Æn.*

4. To dash together; to collide; to encounter.

When they *joined* battle, Israel was smitten. 1 *Sam.* iv. 2.

They should with resolute minds set down themselves to endure, until they might *join* battle with their enemies. *Knolles's Hist. of the Turks.*

5. To associate.

Go near, and *join* thyself to this chariot. *Acts* vii. 29.

Thou shalt not be *joined* with them in burial. *Isa.* xiv. 20.

6. To unite in one act.

Our best notes are treason to his fame,
Join'd with the loud applause of publick voice. *Dryden.*

Thy tuneful voice with numbers *join*,
Thy words will more prevail than mine. *Dryden.*

7. To unite in concord.

Be perfectly *joined* together in the same mind. 1 *Cor.* i. 10.

8. To act in concert with.

Know your own int'rest, Sir, where'er you lead,
We jointly vow to *join* no other head. *Dryden's Aureng.*

To

To JOIN. *v. n.*

1. To grow to; to adhere; to be continuous.

Justus's house *joined* hard to the synagogue. *Acts* xviii. 7.

2. To close; to clash.

Look you, all you that kiss my lady peace at home, that our armies *join* not in a hot day. *Shakesp. Henry* IV.

Here's the earl of Wiltshire's blood,
Whom I encounter'd, as the battles *join'd*. *Shakespeare.*

3. To unite with in marriage, or any other league.

Should we again break thy commandments, and *join* in affinity with the people? *Ezra* ix. 14.

4. To become confederate.

When there falleth out any war, they *join* unto our enemies, and fight against us. *Exod.* i. 10.

Let us make peace with him, before he *join* with Alexander against us. 1 *Mac.* x. 4.

Ev'n you yourself
Join with the rest; you are arm'd against me. *Dryden.*

Any other may *join* with him that is injured, and assist him in recovering satisfaction. *Locke.*

JO'INDER. *n. s.* [from *join.*] Conjunction; joining.

A contract of eternal bond of love,
Confirm'd by mutual *joinder* of your hands. *Shakespeare.*

JO'INER. *n. s.* [from *join.*] One whose trade is to make utensils of wood joined.

The people wherewith you plant ought to be smiths, carpenters, and *joiners*. *Bacon's Essays.*

It is counted good workmanship in a *joiner* to bear his hand curiously even. *Moxon's Mech. Exercise.*

JO'INERY. *n. s.* [from *joiner.*]

Joinery is an art whereby several pieces of wood are so fitted and joined together by strait lines, squares, miters, or any bevel, that they shall seem one entire piece. *Moxon.*

JOINT. *n. s.* [*junctura*, Lat. *jointure*, French.]

1. Articulation of limbs; juncture of moveable bones in animal bodies.

Dropsies and asthmas, and *joint* racking rheums. *Milton.*

I continued well, till I felt the same pain in the same *joint*. *Temple.*

2. Hinge; junctures which admit motion of the parts.

The coach, the cover whereof was made with such *joints* that as they might, to avoid the weather, pull it up close when they lifted; so when they would, they might remain as discovered and open-sighted as on horseback. *Sidney.*

3. [In Joinery; *jointe*, Fr.]

Strait lines, in joiners language, is called a *joint*, that is, two pieces of wood are shot, that is, plained. *Moxon.*

4. A knot or commissure in a plant.

5. One of the limbs of an animal cut up by the butcher.

In bringing up a *joint* of meat, it falls out of your hand. *Swift.*

6. *Out of* JOINT. Luxated; slipped from the socket, or correspondent part where it naturally moves.

Jacob's thigh was *out of joint*. *Gen.* xxiii. 25.

My head and whole body was sore hurt, and also one of my arms and legs put *out of joint*. *Herbert.*

7. *Out of* JOINT. Thrown into confusion and disorder; confused; full of disturbance.

The time is *out of joint*, oh cursed spight!
That ever I was born to set it right. *Shakespeare.*

JOINT. *adj.*

1. Shared among many.

Entertain no more of it,
Than a *joint* burthen laid upon us all. *Shakespeare.*

Though it be common in respect of some men, it is not so to all mankind; but is the *joint* property of this country, or this parish. *Locke.*

2. United in the same possession: as we say, *jointheirs* or *coheirs*, *jointheiresses* or *coheiresses*.

The sun and man did strive,
Joint tenants of the world, who should survive. *Donne.*

Pride then was not; nor arts, that pride to aid;
Man walk'd with beast *joint* tenant of the shade. *Pope.*

3. Combined; acting together in consort.

On your *joint* vigour now,
My hold of this new kindom all depends. *Milton.*

In a war carried on by the *joint* force of so many nations, France could send troops. *Addison on the State of the War.*

To JOINT. *v. a.* [from the noun.]

1. To join together in confederacy.

The times
Made friends of them, *jointing* their force 'gainst Cæsar. *Shak.*

2. To form many parts into one.

Against the steed he threw
His forceful spear, which hissing as it flew,
Pierc'd through the yielding planks of *jointed* wood. *Dryd.*

3. To form in articulations.

The fingers are *jointed* together for motion, and furnished with several muscles. *Ray on the Creation.*

4. To divide a joint; to cut or quarter into joints.

He *joints* the neck; and with a stroke so strong
The helm flies off; and bears the head along. *Dryden.*

JO'INTED. *adj.* [from *joint.*] Full of joints, knots, or commissures.

Three cubits high
The *jointed* herbage shoots. *Philips.*

JO'INTER. [from *joint.*] A sort of plane.

The *jointer* is somewhat longer than the fore-plane, and hath its sole perfectly strait: its office is to follow the fore-plane, and shoot an edge perfectly strait, when a joint is to be shot. *Moxon's Mech. Exercise.*

JO'INTLY. *adv.* [from *joint.*]

1. Together; not separately.

I began a combat first with him particularly, and after his death with the others *jointly*. *Sidney, b.* ii.

Because all that are of the church cannot *jointly* and equally work; the first thing in polity required is a difference of persons in the church. *Hooker, b.* iii.

The generous prince told him he could lay no claim to his gratitude, but desired they might go to the altar together, and *jointly* return their thanks to whom only it was due. *Addison's Freeholder*, N°. 49.

2. In a state of union or co-operation.

His name a great example stands, to show
How strangely high endeavours may be blest,
Where piety and valour *jointly* go. *Dryden.*

JO'INTRESS. *n. s.* [from *jointure.*] One who holds any thing in jointure.

Our queen,
Th' imperial *jointress* of this warlike state,
We've taken now to wife. *Shakesp. Hamlet.*

JOINTSTO'OL. *n. s.* [*joint* and *stool.*] A stool made not merely by insertion of the feet, but by inserting one part in another.

He rides the wild mare with the boys, and jumps upon *jointstools*, and wears his boot very smooth like unto the sign of the leg. *Shakespeare's Henry* IV. *p.* ii.

Could that be eternal which they had seen a rude trunk, and perhaps the other piece of it a *jointstool*. *South's Sermons.*

He used to lay chairs and *jointstools* in their way, that they might break noses by falling. *Arbuthnot.*

JO'INTURE. *n. s.* [*jointure*, French.] Estate settled on a wife to be enjoyed after her husband's decease.

The *jointure* that your king must make,
With her dow'ry shall be counterpois'd. *Shakesp.*

The old countess of Desmond, who lived in 1589, and many years since, was married in Edward the fourth's time, and held her *jointure* from all the earls of Desmond since then. *Raleigh's Hist. of the World.*

There's a civil question us'd of late,
Where lies my *jointure*, where your own estate? *Dryden.*

What's property? You see it alter,
Or, in a mortgage, prove a lawyer's share,
Or, in a *jointure*, vanish from the heir. *Pope.*

JOIST. *n. s.* [from *joindre*, French.] The secondary beam of a floor.

Some wood is not good to use for beams or *joists*, because of the brittleness. *Mortimer's Husbandry.*

The kettle to the top was hoist,
And there stood fasten'd to a *joist*. *Swift.*

To JOIST. *v. a.* [from the noun.] To fit in the smaller beams of a flooring.

JOKE. *n. s.* [*jocus*, Latin.] A jest; something not serious.

Link towns to towns with avenues of oak,
Inclose whole downs in walls, 'tis all a *joke!*
Inexorable death shall level all. *Pope.*

Why should publick mockery in print, or a merry *joke* upon a stage, be a better test of truth than severe railing sarcasms and publick persecutions? *Watts's Improv. of the Mind.*

To JOKE. *v. n.* [*jocor*, Latin.] To jest; to be merry in words or actions.

Our neighbours tell me oft, in *joking* talk,
Of ashes, leather, oat-meal, bran, and chalk. *Gay.*

JO'KER. *n. s.* [from *joke.*] A jester; a merry fellow.

Thou mad'st thy first appearance in the world like a dry *joker*, buffoon, or jack-pudding. *Dennis.*

JOLE. *n. s.* [*gueule*, French; crol, Saxon.]

1. The face or cheek. It is seldom used but in the phrase *cheek by jole.*

Follow! nay, I'll go with thee cheek by *jole*. *Shakesp.*

And by him in another hole,
Afflicted Ralpho, cheek by *jole*. *Hudibras.*

A man, who has digested all the fathers, lets a pure English divine go cheek by *jole* with him. *Collier on Pride.*

Your wan complexion, and your thin *joles*, father. *Dryden.*

2. The head of a fish.

A salmon's belly, Helluo, was thy fate;
The doctor call'd, declares all help too late:
Mercy! cries Helluo, mercy on my soul!
Is there no hope? alas! then bring the *jowl*. *Pope.*

Red-speckled trouts, the salmon's silver *jole*,
The jointed lobster, and unscaly soale. *Gay's Trivia.*

To JOLL. *v. a.* [from *joll*, the head.] To beat the head against any thing; to clash with violence.

Howso'ever

Howsoe'er their hearts are sever'd in religion, their heads are both one: they may *joll* horns together like any deer i' th' herd. *Shakespeare.*

The tortoises envied the easiness of the frogs, 'till they saw them *jolled* to pieces and devoured for want of a buckler. *L'Est.*

Jo'llily. *adv.* [from *jolly.*] In a disposition to noisy mirth.

The goodly empress, *jollily* inclin'd,
Is to the welcome bearer wond'rous kind. *Dryden's Pers.*

Jo'lliment. *n. s.* [from *jolly.*] Mirth; merriment; gaiety.

Matter of mirth enough, though there were none,
She could devise, and thousand ways invent
To feed her foolish humour, and vain *jolliment.* *Fa. Queen.*

Jo'lliness. } *n. s.* [from *jolly.*]
Jo'llity. }

1. Gaiety; elevation of spirit.

He with a proud *jollity* commanded him to leave that quarrel only for him, who was only worthy to enter into it. *Sidney.*

2. Merriment; festivity.

With joyance bring her, and with *jollity.* *Spenser.*

There shall these pairs of faithful lovers be
Wedded, with Theseus, all in *jollity.* *Shakespeare.*

The brazen throat of war had ceas'd to roar;
All now was turn'd to *jollity* and game,
To luxury and riot, feast and dance. *Milton's Parad. Lost.*

Good men are never so surprised as in the midst of their *jollities*, nor so fatally overtaken and caught as when the table is made the snare. *South's Sermons.*

With branches we the fanes adorn, and waste
In *jollity* the day ordain'd to be the last. *Dryden's Æn.*

My heart was filled with melancholy to see several dropping in the midst of mirth and *jollity.* *Addison's Spectator.*

JO'LLY. *adj.* [*joli*, French; *jovialis*, Latin.]

1. Gay; merry; airy; cheerful; lively; jovial.

Like a *jolly* troop of huntsmen, come
Our lusty English. *Shakesp. King John.*

O nightingale!
Thou with fresh hope the lover's heart do'st fill,
While the *jolly* hours lead on propitious May. *Milton.*

All my griefs to this are *jolly*;
Nought so sad as melancholy. *Burton.*

Ev'n ghosts had learn'd to groan;
But free from punishment, as free from sin,
The shades liv'd *jolly*, and without a king. *Dryd. Juven.*

This gentle knight, inspir'd by *jolly* May,
Forsook his easy couch at early day. *Dryden.*

A shepherd now along the plain he roves,
And with his *jolly* pipe delights the groves. *Prior.*

2. Plump; like one in high health.

He catches at an apple of Sodom, which though it may entertain his eye with a florid, *jolly* white and red, yet, upon the touch, it shall fill his hand only with stench and foulness. *South.*

To JOLT. *v. n.* [I know not whence derived.] To shake as a carriage on rough ground.

In such a contrivance every little unevenness of the ground will cause such a *jolting* of the chariot as to hinder the motion of its sails. *Wilkins.*

Violent motion, as *jolting* in a coach, may be used in this case. *Arbuthnot on Diet.*

A coach and six horses is the utmost exercise you can bear, and how glad would you be, if it could waft you in the air to avoid *jolting.* *Swift to Gay.*

To Jolt. *v. a.* To shake one as a carriage does.

Jolt. *n. s.* [from the verb.] Shock; violent agitation.

The symptoms are, bloody water upon a sudden *jolt* or violent motion. *Arbuthnot on Diet.*

The first *jolt* had like to have shaken me out; but afterwards the motion was easy. *Gulliver's Travels.*

Jo'lthead. *n. s.* [I know not whence derived.] A great head; a dolt; a blockhead.

Fie on thee, *jolthead*, thou can'st not read. *Shakespeare.*

Had he been a dwarf, he had scarce been a reasonable creature; for he must then have either had a *jolthead*, and so there would not have been body and blood enough to supply his brain with spirits; or he must have had a small head, and so there would not have been brain enough for his business. *Grew.*

Jonqui'lle. *n. s.* [*jonquille*, French.] A species of daffodil. The flowers of this plant, of which there are single and double kinds, are greatly esteemed for their strong sweet scent, though few ladies can bear the smell of them, it being so powerful as to overcome their spirits. *Miller.*

Nor gradual bloom is wanting,
Nor hyacinths of purest virgin white,
Low bent and blushing inward; nor *jonquilles*
Of potent fragrance. *Thomson's Spring.*

Jo'rden. *n. s.* [ȝoŋ, *stercus*, and ben, *receptaculum.*] A pot.

They will allow us ne'er a *jorden*, and then we leak in your chimney; and your chamberlye breeds fleas like a loach. *Shak.*

This China *jorden* let the chief o'ercome
Replenish, not ingloriously at home. *Pope's Dunciad.*

The copper-pot can boil milk, heat porridge, hold small-beer, or, in case of necessity, serve for a *jorden.* *Swift.*

Jo'seph's *Flowers.* *n. s.* A plant. *Ainsworth.*

To Jo'stle. *v. a.* [*jouster*, French.] To justle; to rush against.

Jot. *n. s.* [ἰῶτα.] A point; a tittle; the least quantity assignable.

As superfluous flesh did rot,
Amendment ready still at hand did wait,
To pluck it out with pincers fiery hot,
That soon in him was left no one corrupt *jot.* *Fa. Queen.*

Go, Eros, send his treasure after, do it;
Detain no *jot*, I charge thee. *Shakesp. Ant. and Cleopat.*

Let me not stay a *jot* from dinner; go, get it ready. *Shakes.*

This nor hurts him nor profits you a *jot*;
Forbear it therefore; give your cause to heav'n. *Shakesp.*

This bond doth give thee here no *jot* of blood;
The words expresly are a pound of flesh. *Shakespeare.*

I argue not
Against heav'n's hand, or will; nor bate one *jot*
Of heart or hope; but still bear up and steer
Right onwards. *Milton.*

You might, with every *jot* as much justice, hang me up, because I'm old, as beat me because I'm impotent. *L'Estrange.*

A man may read the discourses of a very rational author, and yet acquire not one *jot* of knowledge. *Locke.*

The final event will not be one *jot* less the consequence of our own choice and actions, for God's having from all eternity foreseen and determined what that event shall be. *Rogers.*

JO'VIAL. *adj.* [*jovial*, French; *jovialis*, Latin.]

1. Under the influence of Jupiter.

The fixed stars are astrologically differenced by the planets, and are esteemed martial or *jovial*, according to the colours whereby they answer these planets. *Brown's Vulg. Err.*

2. Gay; airy; merry.

My lord, sleek o'er your rugged looks,
Be bright and *jovial* 'mong your guests. *Shakesp. Macb.*

Our *jovial* star reign'd at his birth. *Shakesp. Cymbeline.*

Some men, of an ill and melancholy nature, incline the company, into which they come, to be sad and ill-disposed; and contrariwise, others of a *jovial* nature dispose the company to be merry and cheerful. *Bacon's Natural History.*

His odes are some of them panegyrical, others moral, the rest *jovial* or bacchanalian. *Dryden.*

Perhaps the jest that charm'd the sprightly crowd,
And made the *jovial* table laugh so loud,
To some false notion ow'd its poor pretence. *Prior.*

Jo'vially. *adv.* [from *jovial.*] Merrily; gaily.

Jo'vialness. *n. s.* [from *jovial.*] Gaiety; merriment.

Jo'uisance. *n. s.* [*rejouissance*, French.] Jollity; merriment; festivity.

Colin, my dear, when shall it please thee sing,
As thou wert wont, songs of some *jouisance*;
Thy muse too long slumbereth in sorrowing,
Lulled asleep through love's misgovernance. *Spenser.*

Jo'urnal. *adj.* [*journale*, French; *giornale*, Italian.] Daily; quotidian. Out of use.

Now 'gan the golden Phœbus for to steep
His fiery face in billows of the West,
And his faint steeds water'd in ocean deep,
Whilst from their *journal* labours they did rest. *Fa. Queen.*

Ere twice the sun has made his *journal* greeting
To th' under generation, you shall find
Your safety manifested. *Shakes. Meas. for Measure.*

So sick I am not, yet I am not well;
But not so citizen a wanton, as
To seem to die ere sick; so, please you, leave me:
Stick to your *journal* course; the breach of custom
Is breach of all. *Shakespeare's Cymbeline.*

Jo'urnal. *n. s.* [*journal*, French; *giornale*, Italian.]

1. A diary; an account kept of daily transactions.

Edward kept a most judicious *journal* of all the principal passages of the affairs of his estate. *Hayward on Edw. VI.*

Time has destroyed two noble *journals* of the navigation of Hanno and of Hamilcar. *Arbuthnot on Coins.*

2. Any paper published daily.

Jo'urnalist. *n. s.* [from *journal.*] A writer of journals.

JO'URNEY. *n. s.* [*journee*, French.]

1. The travel of a day.

When Duncan is asleep,
Whereto the rather shall this day's hard *journey*
Soundly invite him. *Shakespeare's Macbeth.*

Scarce the sun
Hath finish'd half his *journey.* *Milton.*

2. Travel by land; a voyage or travel by sea.

So are the horses of the enemy,
In general *journey* bated and brought low. *Shakes. H. IV.*

Before the light of the gospel, mankind travelled like people in the dark, without any certain prospect of the end of their *journey*, or of the way that led to it. *Rogers.*

He for the promis'd *journey* bids prepare
The smooth hair'd horses and the rapid car. *Pope's Odyss.*

3. Passage from place to place.

Some, having a long *journey* from the upper regions, would float up and down a good while. *Burnet's Theory of the Earth.*

Light of the world, the ruler of the year,
Still as thou do'ft thy radiant *journies* run,
Through every diftant climate own,
That in fair Albion thou haft feen
The greateft prince, the brighteft queen. *Prior.*

To JO'URNEY. *v. n.* [from the noun.] To travel; to pafs from place to place.

Gentlemen of good efteem
Are *journeying* to falute the emperor. *Shakespeare.*

We are *journeying* unto the place, of which the Lord faid, I will give it you. *Numb.* x. 29.

Make the two trumpets, that thou mayeft ufe them for the *journeying* of the camps. *Numb.* x. 2.

Since fuch love's natural ftation is, may ftill
My love defcend, and *journey* down the hill;
Not panting after growing beauties, fo
I fhall ebb on with them who homeward go. *Donne.*

I have *journeyed* this morning, and it is now the heat of the day; therefore your lordfhip's difcourfes had need content my ears very well, to make them intreat my eyes to keep open. *Bacon's Holy War.*

Over the tent a cloud
Shall reft by day, a fiery gleam by night,
Save when they *journey.* *Milton's Par. Loft, b.* xii.

Having heated his body by *journeying*, he took cold upon the ground. *Wifeman's Surgery.*

JO'URNEYMAN. *n. f.* [*journée*, a day's work, Fr. and *man.*] A hired workman.

They were called *journeymen* that wrought with others by the day, though now by ftatute it be extended to thofe likewife that convenant to work in their occupation with another by the year. *Cowel.*

Players have fo ftrutted and bellowed, that I have thought fome of nature's *journeymen* had made men, and not made them well. *Shakespeare's Hamlet.*

I intend to work for the court myfelf, and will have *journeymen* under me to furnifh the reft of the nation. *Addifon.*

Says Frog to Bull, this old rogue will take the management of the young lord's bufinefs into his hands: in that cafe what muft become of us and our families? We muft ftarve or turn *journeymen* to old Lewis Baboon. *Arbuthnot's John Bull.*

JO'URNEYWORK. *n. f.* [*journee*, French, and *work.*] Work performed for hire.

See how your foldier wears his cage
Of iron, like the captive Turk,
And as the guerdon of his rage!
See how your glimmering peers do lurk,
Or at the beft work *journeywork.* *Cleaveland.*

Did no committee fit, where he
Might cut out *journeywork* for thee?
And fet thee a tafk with fubornation,
To ftitch up fale and fequeftration. *Hudibras.*

Her family fhe was forced to hire out at *journeywork* to her neighbours. *Arbuthnot's Hiftory of John Bull.*

JOUST. *n. f.* [*jouft*, French.] Tilt; tournament; mock fight. It is now written lefs properly *juft.*

Bafes, and tinfel trappings, gorgeous knights
At *jouft* and tournament. *Milton's Parad. Loft, b.* ix.

To JOUST. *v. n.* [*joufter*, French.] To run in the tilt.

All who fince
Joufted in Afpramont or Montalban. *Milton.*

JO'WLER. *n. f.* [perhaps corrupted from *howler*, as making a hideous noife after the game, whom the reft of the pack follow as their leader.] A kind of hunting dog or beagle.

See him drag his feeble legs about,
Like hounds ill-coupled: *jowler* lugs him ftill
Through hedges, ditches, and through all this ill. *Dryden.*

JO'WTER. *n. f.* [perhaps corrupted from *jolter.*]

Plenty of fifh is vented to the fifh-drivers, whom we call *jowters.* *Carew.*

JOY. *n. f.* [*joye*, French; *gioia*, Italian.]

1. The paffion produced by any happy accident; gladnefs; exultation.

Joy is a delight of the mind, from the confideration of the prefent, or affured approaching poffeffion of a good. *Locke.*

There appears much *joy* in him; even fo much, that *joy* could not fhew itfelf modeft enough without a badge of bitternefs. *Shakespeare.*

There fhould not be fuch heavinefs in their deftruction, as fhall be *joy* over them that are perfuaded to falvation. 2 *Efdr.*

The lightfome paffion of *joy* was not that trivial, vanifhing, fuperficial thing, that only gilds the apprehenfion, and plays upon the furface of the foul. *South's Sermons.*

2. Gaiety; merriment; feftivity.

The roofs with *joy* refound;
And hymen, iö hymen, rung around. *Dryden.*

3. Happinefs; felicity.

My lord Baffanio, and my gentle lady,
I wifh you all the *joy* that you can wifh. *Shakespeare.*

Come, love and health to all;
Then I'll fit down: give me fome wine:
I drink to the general *joy* of the whole table. *Shakesp.*

Almeyda fmiling came,
Attended with a train of all her race,
Whom in the rage of empire I had murder'd;
But now, no longer foes, they gave me *joy*
Of my new conqueft. *Dryden's Don Sebaftian.*

The bride,
Lovely herfelf, and lovely by her fide,
A bevy of bright nymphs, with fober grace,
Came glitt'ring like a ftar, and took her place:
Her heav'nly form beheld, all wifh'd her *joy*;
And little wanted, but in vain, their wifhes all employ. *Dry.*

4. A term of fondnefs.

Now our *joy*,
Although our laft, yet not our leaft young love,
What fay you? *Shakef. King Lear.*

To JOY. *v. n.* [from the noun.] To rejoice; to be glad; to exult.

Sometimes I *joy*, when glad occafion fits,
And mafk in mirth like to a comedy;
Soon after, when my joy to forrow flits,
I will make my woes a tragedy. *Spenfer.*

I cannot *joy*, until I be refolv'd
Where our right valiant father is become. *Shakef. H.* VI.

He will *joy* over thee with finging. *Zeph.* iii. 17.

I will rejoice in the Lord, I will *joy* in the God of my falvation. *Heb.* iii. 18.

Exceedingly the more *joyed* we for the joy of Titus, becaufe his fpirit was refrefhed by you. 2 *Cor.* vii. 13.

They laugh, we weep; they *joy* while we lament. *Fairf.*

No man imparteth his joys to his friend, but he *joyeth* the more; and no man imparteth his griefs, but he grieveth the lefs. *Bacon's Effays.*

Well then, my foul, *joy* in the midft of pain;
Thy Chrift, that conquer'd hell, fhall from above
With greater triumph yet return again,
And conquer his own juftice with his love. *Wotton.*

Joy thou,
In what he gives to thee this paradife,
And thy fair Eve. *Milton's Paradife Loft, b.* viii.

Their chearful age with honour youth attends,
Joy'd that from pleafure's flav'ry they are free. *Denham.*

To JOY. *v. a.*

1. To congratulate; to entertain kindly.

Like us they love or hate; like us they know
To *joy* the friend, or grapple with the foe. *Prior.*

2. To gladden; to exhilarate.

She went to Pamela, meaning to delight her eyes and *joy* her thoughts with the converfation of her beloved fifter. *Sidney.*

My foul was *joy'd* in vain;
For angry Neptune rouz'd the raging main. *Pope.*

3. [*Jouir de*, French.] To enjoy; to have happy poffeffion.

Let us hence,
And let her *joy* her raven-colour'd love. *Shakefp. Tit. Andr.*

I might have liv'd, and *joy'd* immortal blifs,
Yet willingly chofe rather death with thee. *Milton.*

Th' ufurper *joy'd* not long
His ill-got crown. *Dryden's Spanifh Fryar.*

JOYA'NCE. *n. f.* [*joiant*, old French.] Gaiety; feftivity.

Bring home with you the glory of her gain;
With *joyance* bring her, and with jollity. *Spenfer.*

There him refts in riotous fuffifance,
Of all his gladfulnefs and kingly *joyance.* *Spenfer.*

JO'YFUL. *adj.* [*joy* and *full.*]

1. Full of joy; glad; exulting.

They bleffed the king, and went unto their tents *joyful* and glad of heart. 1 *Kings* viii. 66.

My foul fhall be *joyful* in my God. *If.* lxi. 10.

2. Sometimes it has *of* before the caufe of joy.

Six brave companions from each fhip we loft:
With fails outfpread we fly th' unequal ftrife,
Sad for their lofs, but *joyful of* our life. *Pope's Odyffey.*

JO'YFULLY. *adj.* [from *joyful.*] With joy; gladly.

If we no more meet 'till we meet in heav'n,
Then *joyfully*, my noble lord of Bedford,
And my kind kinfmen, warriours all, adieu. *Shakefp. H.* V.

Never did men more *joyfully* obey,
Or fooner underftood the fign to flie:
With fuch alacrity they bore away,
As if to praife them all the ftates ftood by. *Dryden.*

The good Chriftian confiders pains only as neceffary paffages to a glorious immortality; that, through this dark fcene of fancied horror, fees a crown and a throne, and everlafting bleffings prepared for him, *joyfully* receives his fummons, as he has long impatiently expected it. *Wake.*

JO'YFULNESS. *n. f.* [from *joyful.*] Gladnefs; joy.

Thou fervedft not the Lord thy God with *joyfulnefs*, and with gladnefs of heart, for the abundance of all things. *Deutr.*

JO'YLESS. *adj.* [from *joy.*]

1. Void of joy; feeling no pleafure.

A little joy enjoys the queen thereof;
For I am fhe, and altogether *joylefs.* *Shakefp. R.* III.

With

With down-cast eyes the *joyless* victor sat,
Revolving in his alter'd soul
The various turns of chance below;
And now and then a sigh he stole,
And tears began to flow. *Dryd. Alexander's Feast.*

2. It has sometimes *of* before the object.
With two fair eyes his mistress burns his breast;
He looks and languishes, and leaves his rest:
Forsakes his food, and, pining for the lass,
Is *joyless of* the grove, and spurns the growing grass. *Dryd.*

3. Giving no pleasure.
A *joyless*, dismal, black, and sorrowful issue:
Here is the babe, as loathsome as a toad. *Shakesp. Tit. And.*
Here love his golden shafts employs; here lights
His constant lamp, and waves his purple wings;
Reigns here, and revels: not in the bought smiles
Of harlots, loveless, *joyless*, unendear'd,
Casual fruition. *Milton's Paradise Lost.*

The pure in heart shall see God; and if any others could so invade this their inclosure, as to take heaven by violence, it surely would be a very *joyless* possession. *Decay of Piety.*

He forgets his sleep, and loaths his food,
That youth, and health, and war are *joyless* to him. *Addison.*

JO'YOUS. *adj.* [*joyeux*, French.]

1. Glad; gay; merry.
Most *joyous* man, on whom the shining sun
Did shew his face, myself I did esteem,
And that my falser friend did no less *joyous* deem. *Fa. Queen.*
Joyous the birds; fresh gales and gentle airs
Whisper'd it. *Milton.*
Then *joyous* birds frequent the lonely grove,
And beasts, by nature stung, renew their love. *Dryden.*
Fast by her flow'ry bank the sons of Arcas,
Fav'rites of heav'n, with happy care protect
Their fleecy charge, and *joyous* drink her wave. *Prior.*

2. Giving joy.
They all as glad as birds of *joyous* prime,
Thence led her forth, about her dancing round. *F. Queen.*

3. It has *of* sometimes before the cause of joy.
Round our death-bed ev'ry friend should run,
And *joyous of* our conquest early won;
While the malicious world with envious tears
Should grudge our happy end, and wish it theirs. *Dryden.*

IPECACUA'NHA. *n. s.* [An Indian plant.]

Ipecacuanha is a small irregularly contorted root, rough, dense, and firm. One sort is of a dusky greyish colour on the surface, and of a paler grey when broken, which is brought from Peru: the other sort is a smaller root, resembling the former; but it is of a deep dusky brown, or blackish colour on the outside, and white when broken, brought from the Brasils. The grey ought to be preferred in medicinal use, because the brown, being stronger, is apt to operate more roughly. *Ipecacuanha* was in the middle of the last century first brought into Europe, and became celebrated for the cure of dysenteries, a virtue discovered in it by the Indians; but after a few years it sunk into oblivion, being given in two large doses. *Hill's Mat. Med.*

IRA'SCIBLE. *adj.* [*irascibilis*, low Latin; *irascible*, French.] Partaking of the nature of anger.

The *irascible* passions follow the temper of the heart, and the concupiscible distractions the crasis of the liver. *Brown.*

I know more than one instance of *irascible* passions subdued by a vegetable diet. *Arbuthnot on Aliments.*

We are here in the country surrounded with blessings and pleasures, without any occasion of exercising our *irascible* faculties. *Digby to Pope.*

IRE. *n. s.* [Fr. *ira*, Latin.] Anger; rage; passionate hatred.
She lik'd not his desire;
Fain would be free, but dreaded parents *ire*. *Sidney.*
If I digg'd up thy forefathers graves,
And hung their rotten coffins up in chains,
It could not slake mine *ire*, nor ease my heart. *Shak. H. VI.*
Or Neptune's *ire*, or Juno's, that so long
Perplex'd the Greek and Cytherea's son. *Milton's Par. Lost.*
The sentence, from thy head remov'd, may light
On me, sole cause to thee of all this woe;
Me! me! only just object of his *ire*. *Milton's Parad. Lost.*
For this th' avenging pow'r employs his darts,
And empties all his quiver in our hearts;
Thus will persist, relentless in his *ire*,
'Till the fair slave be render'd to her sire. *Dryden.*

I'REFUL. *adj.* [*ire* and *full*.] Angry; raging; furious.
The *ireful* bastard Orleans, that drew blood
From thee, my boy, I soon encounter'd. *Shakes. H. VI.*
By many hands your father was subdu'd;
But only slaughter'd by the *ireful* arm
Of unrelenting Clifford. *Shakesp. Henry VI.*
There learn'd this maid of arms the *ireful* guise. *Fairfax.*
In midst of all the dome misfortune sat,
And gloomy discontent and fell debate,
And madness laughing in his *ireful* mood. *Dryden.*

I'REFULLY. *adv.* [from *ire*.] With ire; in an angry manner.

I'RIS *n. s.* [Latin.]

1. The rainbow.
Beside the solary *iris*, which God shewed unto Noah, there is another lunary, whose efficient is the moon. *Brown.*

2. Any appearance of light resembling the rainbow.
When both bows appeared more distinct, I measured the breadth of the interior *iris* 2 gr. 10′; and the breadth of the red, yellow, and green in the exterior *iris*, was to the breadth of the same colours in the interior 3 to 2. *Newton's Opt.*

3. The circle round the pupil of the eye.

4. The flower-de-luce.
Iris all hues, roses and jessamine. *Milton.*

To IRK. *v. a.* [*yrk*, work, Islandick.] This word is used only impersonally, *it irks me*; *mihi pœnæ est*, it gives me pain; or, I am weary of it. Thus the authors of the Accidence say, *tædet*, it *irketh*.
Come, shall we go and kill us venison?
And yet it *irks* me, the poor dappled fools
Should, in their own confines, with forked heads,
Have their round haunches gor'd. *Shakespeare.*
It *irks* his heart he cannot be reveng'd. *Shakes. H. VI.*

I'RKSOME. *adj.* [from *irk*.] Wearisome; tedious; troublesome; toilsome; tiresome; unpleasing.
I know she is an *irksome* brawling scold. *Shakespeare.*
Since that thou can'st talk of love so well,
Thy company, which erst was *irksome* to me,
I will endure. *Shak. As you like it.*
Where he may likeliest find
Truce to his restless thoughts, and entertain
The *irksome* hours, 'till his great chief return. *Milton.*
For not to *irksome* toil, but to delight
He made us, and delight to reason join'd. *Milton.*

There is nothing so *irksome* as general discourses, especially when they turn chiefly upon words. *Addison's Spectator.*

Frequent appeals from hence have been very *irksome* to that illustrious body. *Swift.*

I'RKSOMELY. *adv.* [from *irksome*.] Wearisomely; tediously.

I'RKSOMENESS. *n. s.* [from *irksome*.] Tediousness; wearisomeness.

I'RON. *n. s.* [*haiarn*, Welsh; ịreṇn, ịṛen, Saxon; *iorn*, Erse.]

1. A metal common to all parts of the world, plentiful in most, and of a small price, though superior in real value to the dearest. Though the lightest of all metals, except tin, it is considerably the hardest; and, when pure, naturally malleable, but in a less degree than gold, silver, lead, or copper: when wrought into steel, or when in the impure state from its first fusion, in which it is called cast iron, it is scarce malleable; and the most ductile iron, heated and suddenly quenched in cold water, loses much of this quality. Iron is more capable of rust than any other metal, is very sonorous, and requires the strongest fire of all the metals to melt it, and is with difficulty amalgamated with mercury. Most of the other metals are brittle, while they are hot; but this is most malleable as it approaches nearest to fusion. It consists of a vitriolick salt, a vitrifiable earth, and a peculiar bituminous matter. The specifick gravity of iron is to water as 7632 is to 1000. It is the only known substance that is attracted by the loadstone. Iron is not only soluble in all the stronger acids, but even in common water. Pure iron has been found in some places but very rarely. Iron has greater medicinal virtues than any of the other metals. *Hill.*
Nor airless dungeon, nor strong links of *iron*,
Can be retentive to the strength of spirit. *Shakesp. Jul. Cæs.*

If he smite him with an instrument of *iron*, so that he die, he is a murderer. *Num.* xxxv. 16.

The power of drawing *iron* is one of the ideas of a loadstone, and a power to be so drawn is a part of that of *iron*. *Locke.*

In a piece of *iron* ore, of a ferruginous colour, are several thin plates, placed parallel to each other. *Woodward.*

There are incredible quantities of *iron* flag in various parts of the forest of Dean. *Woodward on Fossils.*

Iron stone lies in strata. *Woodward on Fossils.*

I treated of making *iron* work, and steel work in general. *Moxon's Mech. Exer.*

2. Any instrument or utensil made of iron: as, a flat *iron*, box *iron*, or smoothing *iron*.
Irons of a doit, doublets that hangmen would
Bury with those that wore them, these base slaves,
Ere yet the fight be done, pack up. *Shakesp. Coriolanus.*
O Thou! whose captain I account myself,
Look on my forces with a gracious eye:
Put in their hands thy bruising *irons* of wrath,
That they may crush down with a heavy fall
Th' usurping helmets of our adversaries. *Shak. R. III.*
His feet they hurt with fetters: he was laid in *irons*. *Ps.*

Can'st thou fill his skin with barbed *irons*, or his head with fish-spears? *Job* xli. 7.
For this your locks in paper-durance bound?
For this with tort'ring *irons* wreath'd around? *Pope.*

3. Chain; shackle; manacle: as, he was put in *irons*.
The *iron* entered into his soul. *Psalms. Common Prayer.*

I'RON. *adj.*
1. Made of iron.
In *iron* walls they deem'd me not secure. *Shakesp. H.* VI.
Get me an *iron* crow, and bring it straight
Unto my cell. *Shakesp. Romeo and Juliet.*
Some are of an iron red, shining, and polite; others not polite, but as if powdered with *iron* dust. *Woodward.*
Poll-cats and weesels do a great deal of injury to warrens: the way of taking them is in hutches, and *iron* traps. *Mortim.*
2. Resembling iron in colour.
A piece of stone of a dark *iron* grey colour, but in some parts of a ferruginous colour. *Woodward on Fossils.*
Some of them are of an *iron* red, and very bright. *Woodw.*
3. Harsh; severe; rigid; miserable; calamitous: as, the *iron* age, for an age of hardship and wickedness. These ideas may be found more or less in all the following examples.
Three vigorous virgins, waiting still behind,
Assist the throne of th' *iron* scepter'd king. *Crashaw.*
O sad virgin, that thy power
Might bid the soul of Orpheus sing
Such notes as warbled to the string,
Drew *iron* tears from Pluto's cheek,
And made hell grant what love did seek. *Milton.*
In all my *iron* years of wars and dangers,
From blooming youth down to decaying age,
My fame ne'er knew a stain of dishonour. *Rowe.*
Jove crush the nations with an *iron* rod,
And ev'ry monarch be the scourge of God. *Pope's Odyssey.*
4. Indissoluble; unbroken.
Rash Elpenor, in an evil hour,
Dry'd an immeasurable bowl, and thought
T' exhale his surfeit by irriguous sleep,
Imprudent: him death's *iron* sleep opprest. *Phillips.*
5. Hard; impenetrable.
I will converse with *iron* witted fools,
And unrespective boys: none are for me,
That look into me with consid'rate eyes. *Shakesp. R.* III.

To I'RON. *v. a.* [from the noun.]
1. To smooth with an iron.
2. To shackle with irons.

IRO'NICAL. *adj.* [*ironique*, Fr. from *irony*.] Expressing one thing and meaning another; speaking by contraries.
In this fallacy may be comprised all *ironical* mistakes, or expressions receiving inverted significations. *Brown.*
I take all your *ironical* civilities in a literal sense, and shall expect them to be literally performed. *Swift.*

IRO'NICALLY. *adv.* [from *ironical*.] By the use of irony.
Socrates was pronounced by the oracle of Delphos to be the wisest man of Greece, which he would turn from himself *ironically*, saying, there could be nothing in him to verify the oracle, except this, that he was not wise, and knew it; and others were not wise, and knew it not. *Bacon.*
The dean, *ironically* grave,
Still shunn'd the fool, and lash'd the knave. *Swift.*

IRONMO'NGER. *n. s.* [*iron* and *monger*.] A dealer in iron.

I'RONWOOD. *n. s.* A kind of wood extremely hard, and so ponderous as to sink in water. It grows in America. *Rob. Cruso.*

I'RONWORT. *n. s.* [*sideritis*, Latin.] It is a plant with a labiated flower, consisting of one leaf, whose upper lip or beard is divided into three parts: out of the flower-cup rises the pointal, attended, as it were, by four embryoes; which afterward turn to so many oblong seeds, shut up in an husk, which before was the flower-cup: to these marks must be added, the flowers growing in whorles at the wings of the leaves, which are cut like a crest, and differ from the other leaves of the plant. *Mill.*

I'RONY. *adj.* [from *iron*.] Made of iron; partaking of iron.
The force they are under is real, and that of their fate but imaginary: it is not strange if the *irony* chains have more solidity than the contemplative. *Hammond's Fundamentals.*
Some springs of Hungary, highly impregnated with vitriolick salts, dissolve the body of one metal, suppose iron, put into the spring; and deposite, in lieu of the *irony* particles carried off, coppery particles. *Woodward on Fossils.*

I'RONY. *n. s.* [*ironie*, Fr. εἰρωνεία.] A mode of speech in which the meaning is contrary to the words: as, *Bolingbroke was a holy man.*
So grave a body, upon so solemn an occasion, should not deal in *irony*, or explain their meaning by contraries. *Swift.*

IRRA'DIANCE. } *n. s.* [*irradiance*, French; *irradio*, Latin.]
IRRA'DIANCY. }
1. Emission of rays or beams of light upon any object.
The principal affection is its translucency; the *irradiancy* and sparkling, found in many gems, is not discoverable in this. *Brown's Vulgar Errours.*
2. Beams of light emitted.
Love not the heav'nly spirits? Or do they mix
Irradiance! virtual, or immediate touch? *Milt. Par. Lost.*

To IRRA'DIATE. *v. a.* [*irradio*, Latin.]
1. To adorn with light emitted upon it; to brighten.
When he thus perceives that these opacous bodies do not hinder the eye from judging light to have an equal plenary diffusion through the whole place it *irradiates*, he can have no difficulty to allow air, that is diaphanous, to be every where mingled with light. *Digby on Bodies.*
It is not a converting but a crowning grace; such an one as *irradiates* and puts a circle of glory about the head of him upon whom it descends. *South.*
2. To enlighten intellectually; to illumine; to illuminate.
Celestial light
Shine inward, and the mind through all her pow'rs
Irradiate; there plant eyes: all mist from thence
Purge and disperse. *Milton's Paradise Lost, b.* iii.
3. To animate by heat or light.
Ethereal or solar heat must digest, influence, *irradiate*, and put those more simple parts of matter into motion. *Hale.*
4. To decorate with shining ornaments.
No weeping orphan saw his father's store
Our shrines *irradiate*, or imblaze the floor. *Pope.*

IRRADIA'TION. *n. s.* [*irradiation*, Fr. from *irradiate*.]
1. The act of emitting beams of light.
If light were a body it should drive away the air, which is likewise a body, wherever it is admitted; for within the whole sphere of the *irradiation* of it, there is no point but light is found. *Digby on Bodies.*
The generation of bodies is not effected by *irradiation*, or answerably unto the propagation of light; but herein a transmission is made materially from some parts, and ideally from every one. *Brown's Vulgar Errours.*
2. Illumination; intellectual light.
The means of derivation and immediate union of these intelligible objects to the understanding, are sometimes divine and supernatural, as by immediate *irradiation* or revelation. *Hale's Origin of Mankind.*

IRRA'TIONAL. *adj.* [*irrationalis*, Latin.]
1. Void of reason; void of understanding; without the discoursive faculty.
Thus began
Outrage from lifeless things; but discord first,
Daughter of sin, among th' *irrational*
Death introduc'd. *Milton's Paradise Lost.*
He hath eat'n, and lives,
And knows, and speaks, and reasons and discerns;
Irrational 'till then. *Milt. Paradise Lost, b.* ix.
2. Absurd; contrary to reason.
Since the brain is only a part transmittent, and that humours oft are precipitated to the lungs before they arrive to the brain, no kind of benefit can be effected from so *irrational* an application. *Harvey on Consumptions.*
I shall quietly submit, not wishing so *irrational* a thing as that every body should be deceived. *Pope.*

IRRATIONA'LITY. *n. s.* [from *irrational*.] Want of reason.

IRRA'TIONALLY. *adv.* [from *irrational*.] Without reason; absurdly.

IRRECLA'IMABLE. *adj.* [*in* and *reclaimable*.] Not to be reclaimed; not to be changed to the better.
As for obstinate, *irreclaimable*, professed enemies, we must expect their calumnies will continue. *Addison's Freeholder.*

IRRECONCI'LABLE. *adj.* [*irreconciliable*, Fr. *in* and *reconcilable*.]
1. Not to be reconciled; not to be appeased.
Wage eternal war,
Irreconcilable to our grand foe. *Milton.*
A weak unequal faction may animate a government; but when it grows equal in strength, and *irreconcilable* by animosity, it cannot end without some crisis. *Temple.*
There are no factions, though *irreconcilable* to one another, that are not united in their affection to you. *Dryden.*
2. Not to be made consistent. It has *with* or *to*.
As she was strictly virtuous herself, so she always put the best construction upon the words and actions of her neighbours, except where they were *irreconcilable to* the rules of honesty and decency. *Arbuthn. Hist. of John Bull.*
Since the sense I oppose is attended with such gross *irreconcilable* absurdities, I presume I need not offer any thing farther in support of the one, or in disproof of the other. *Rogers.*
This essential power of gravitation or attraction is *irreconcilable with* the atheist's own doctrine of a chaos. *Bentley.*
All that can be transmitted from the stars is wholly unaccountable, and *irreconcilable to* any system of science. *Bentley.*

IRRECONCI'LABLENESS. *n. s.* [from *irreconcilable*.] Impossibility to be reconciled.

IRRECONCI'LABLY. *adv.* [from *irreconcilable*.] In a manner not admitting reconciliation.

IRRECONCI'LED. *adj.* [*in* and *reconciled*.] Not atoned.
A servant dies in many *irreconciled* iniquities. *Shakes. H.* V.

IRRECO'VERABLE. *adj.* [*in* and *recoverable*.]
1. Not to be regained; not to be restored or repaired.
Time, in a natural sense, is *irrecoverable*: the moment just fled by us, it is impossible to recall. *Rogers.*
2. Not to be remedied.
The *irrecoverable* loss of so many livings of principal value. *Hooker.*
It concerns every man, that would not trifle away his soul, and fool himself into *irrecoverable* misery, with the greatest seriousness to enquire. *Tillotson's Sermons.*

IRRECO'VERABLY. *adv.* [from *irrecoverable.*] Beyond recovery; past repair.

O dark, dark, dark amid' the blaze of noon;
Irrecov'rably dark, total eclipse,
Without all hope of day. *Milton's Agonistes.*

The credit of the Exchequer is *irrecoverably* lost by the last breach with the bankers. *Temple.*

IRREDU'CIBLE. *adj.* [*in* and *reducible.*] Not to be brought or reduced.

These observations seem to argue the corpuscles of air to be *irreducible* into water. *Boyle.*

IRREFRAGABI'LITY. *n. s.* [from *irrefragable.*] Strength of argument not to be refuted.

IRREFRA'GABLE. *adj.* [*irrefragabilis*, school Latin; *irrefragable*, Fr] Not to be confuted; superior to argumental opposition.

Strong and *irrefragable* the evidences of Christianity must be: they who resisted them would resist every thing. *Atterbury.*

The danger of introducing unexperienced men was urged as an *irrefragable* reason for working by slow degrees. *Swift.*

IRREFRA'GABLY. *adv.* [from *irrefragable.*] With force above confutation.

That they denied a future state is evident from St. Paul's reasonings, which are of no force but only on that supposition, as Origen largely and *irrefragably* proves. *Atterbury.*

IRREFU'TABLE. *adj.* [*irrefutabilis*, Latin.] Not to be overthrown by argument.

IRRE'GULAR. *adj.* [*irregulier*, Fr. *irregularis*, Latin.]

1. Deviating from rule, custom, or nature.

The am'rous youth
Obtain'd of Venus his desire,
Howe'er *irregular* his fire. *Prior.*

2. Immethodical; not confined to any certain rule or order.

This motion seems excentrique and *irregular*, yet not well to be resisted or quieted. *King Charles.*

Regular
Then most, when most *irregular* they seem. *Milton.*

The numbers of pindariques are wild and *irregular*, and sometimes seem harsh and uncouth. *Cowley.*

3. Not being according to the laws of virtue. A soft word for *vitious.*

IRREGULA'RITY. *n. s.* [*irregularité*, Fr. from *irregular.*]

1. Deviation from rule.

2. Neglect of method and order.

This *irregularity* of its unruly and tumultuous motion might afford a beginning unto the common opinion. *Brown.*

As these vast heaps of mountains are thrown together with so much *irregularity* and confusion, they form a great variety of hollow bottoms. *Addison on Italy.*

3. Inordinate practice.

Religion is somewhat less in danger of corruption, while the sinner acknowledges the obligations of his duty, and is ashamed of his *irregularities.* *Rogers's Sermons.*

IRRE'GULARLY. *adv.* [from *irregular.*] Without observation of rule or method.

Phaeton,
By the wild courses of his fancy drawn,
From East to West *irregularly* hurl'd,
First set on fire himself, and then the world. *Dryden jun.*

Your's is a soul *irregularly* great,
Which wanting temper, yet abounds with heat. *Dryden.*

It may give some light to those whose concern for their little ones makes them so *irregularly* bold as to consult their own reason, in the education of their children, rather than to rely upon old custom. *Locke.*

To IRRE'GULATE. *v. a.* [from *in* and *regula*, Latin.] To make irregular; to disorder.

Its fluctuations are but motions subservient, which winds, shelves, and every interjacency *irregulates.* *Brown's Vulg. Err.*

IRRE'LATIVE. *adj.* [*in* and *relativus*, Latin.] Having no reference to any thing; single; unconnected.

Separated by the voice of God, things in their species came out in uncommunicated varieties, and *irrelative* seminalities. *Brown's Vulgar Errours.*

IRRELI'GION. *n. s.* [*irreligion*, Fr. *in* and *religion.*] Contempt of religion; impiety.

The weapons with which I combat *irreligion* are already consecrated. *Dryden.*

We behold every instance of prophaneness and *irreligion*, not only committed, but defended and gloried in. *Rogers.*

IRRELI'GIOUS. *adj.* [*irreligieux*, Fr. *in* and *religious.*]

1. Contemning religion; impious.

The issue of an *irreligious* Moor. *Shakesp. Tit. Andron.*

Whoever sees these *irreligious* men,
With burthen of a sickness weak and faint,
But hears them talking of religion then,
And vowing of their souls to ev'ry saint. *Davies.*

Shame and reproach is generally the portion of the impious and *irreligious.* *South's Sermons.*

2. Contrary to religion.

Wherein that Scripture standeth not the church of God in any stead, or serveth nothing at all to direct, but may be let pass as needless to be consulted with, we judge it profane, impious, and *irreligious* to think. *Hooker.*

Might not the queen's domesticks be obliged to avoid swearing, and *irreligious* profane discourse? *Swift.*

IRRELI'GIOUSLY. *adv.* [from *irreligious.*] With impiety; with irreligion.

IRRE'MEABLE. *adj.* [*irremeabilis*, Latin.] Admitting no return.

The keeper charm'd, the chief without delay
Pass'd on, and took th' *irremeable* way. *Dryden.*

IRREME'DIABLE. *adj.* [*irremediable*, Fr. *in* and *remediable.*] Admitting no cure; not to be remedied.

They content themselves with that which was the *irremediable* error of former times, or the necessity of the present hath cast upon them. *Hooker.*

A steddy hand, in governing of military affairs, is more requisite than in times of peace, because an error committed in war may prove *irremediable.* *Bacon.*

Whatever he consults you about, unless it lead to some fatal and *irremediable* mischief, be sure you advise only as a friend. *Locke.*

IRREME'DIABLY. *adv.* [from *irremediable.*] Without cure.

It happens to us *irremediably* and inevitably, that we may perceive these accidents are not the fruits of our labour, but gifts of God. *Taylor's Worthy Communicant.*

IRREMI'SSIBLE. *adj.* [*in* and *remitto*, Lat. *irremissible*, French.] Not to be pardoned.

IRREMI'SSIBLENESS. *n. s.* [from *irremissible.*] The quality of being not to be pardoned.

Thence arises the aggravation and *irremissibleness* of the sin. *Hammond on Fundamentals.*

IRREMO'VABLE. *adj.* [*in* and *remove.*] Not to be moved; not to be changed.

He's *irremovable*,
Resolv'd for flight. *Shakesp. Winter's Tale.*

IRRENO'WNED. *adj.* [*in* and *renown.*] Void of honour.

For all he did was to deceive good knights,
And draw them from pursuit of praise and fame
To sluggish sloth and sensual delights,
And end their days with *irrenowned* shame. *Fairy Queen.*

IRRE'PARABLE. *adj.* [*irreparabilis*, Lat. *irreparable*, Fr.] Not to be recovered; not to be repaired.

Irreparable is the loss, and patience says it is not past her cure. *Shakesp. Tempest.*

Toil'd with loss *irreparable.* *Milton.*

It is an *irreparable* injustice we are guilty of, when we are prejudiced by the looks of those whom we do not know. *Addis.*

The story of Deucalion and Pyrrha teaches, that piety and innocence cannot miss of the divine protection, and that the only loss *irreparable* is that of our probity. *Garth.*

IRRE'PARABLY. *adv.* [from *irreparable.*] Without recovery; without amends.

Such adventures befall artists *irreparably.* *Boyle.*

The cutting off that time industry and gifts, whereby she would be nourished, were *irreparably* injurious to her. *Dec. of Piety.*

IRREPLE'VIABLE. *adj.* [*in* and *replevy.*] Not to be redeemed. A law term.

IRREPREHE'NSIBLE. *adj.* [*irreprehensible*, Fr. *irreprehensibilis*, Latin.] Exempt from blame.

IRREPREHE'NSIBLY. *adv.* [from *irreprehensible.*] Without blame.

IRREPRESE'NTABLE. *adj.* [*in* and *represent.*] Not to be figured by any representation.

God's *irrepresentable* nature doth hold against making images of God. *Stillingfleet.*

IRREPRO'ACHABLE. *adj.* [*in* and *reproachable*] Free from blame; free from reproach.

He was a serious sincere Christian, of an innocent, *irreproachable*, nay, exemplary life. *Atterbury.*

Their prayer may be, that they may raise up and breed as *irreproachable* a young family as their parents have done. *Pope.*

IRREPRO'ACHABLY. *adv.* [from *irreproachable.*] Without blame; without reproach.

IRREPRO'VEABLE. *adj.* [*in* and *reproveable.*] Not to be blamed; irreproachable.

IRRESISTIBI'LITY. *n. s.* [from *irresistible.*] Power or force above opposition.

The doctrine of *irresistibility* of grace, in working whatsoever it works, if it be acknowledged, there is nothing to be affixt to gratitude. *Hammond on Fundamentals.*

IRRESI'STIBLE. *adj.* [*irresistible*, Fr. *in* and *resistible.*] Superiour to opposition.

Fear doth grow from an apprehension of the Deity, indued with *irresistible* power to hurt; and is of all affections, anger excepted, the unaptest to admit conference with reason. *Hook.*

In mighty quadrate join'd
Of union *irresistible.* *Milton.*

Fear of God is inward acknowledgment of an holy just Being, armed with almighty and *irresistible* power. *Tillotson.*

There can be no difference in the subjects, where the application is almighty and *irresistible*, as in creation. *Rogers.*

Won by the charm
Of goodness *irresistible*, she blush'd consent. *Thomson.*

IRRESI'STIBLY. *adv.* [from *irresistible.*] In a manner not to be opposed.

God *irresistibly* sways all manner of events on earth. *Dryden.*

Fond of pleasing and endearing ourselves to those we esteem, we are *irresistibly* led into the same inclinations and aversions with them. *Rogers.*

IRRESI'STLESS. *adj.* [A barbarous ungrammatical conjunction of two negatives] Irresistible; resistless.

Those radiant eyes, whose *irresistless* flame
Strikes envy dumb, and keeps sedition tame,
They can to gazing multitudes give law,
Convert the factious, and the rebel awe. *Granville.*

IRRE'SOLUBLE. *adj.* [*in* and *resolubilis*, Latin.] Not to be broken; not to be dissolved.

In factitious sal armoniac the common and urinous salts are so well mingled, that both in the open fire and in subliming vessels they rise together as one salt, which seems in such vessels *irresoluble* by fire alone. *Boyle.*

IRRE'SOLUBLENESS. *n. s.* [from *irresoluble.*] Resistance to separation of the parts.

Quercetanus has this confession of the *irresolubleness* of diamonds. *Boyle.*

IRRESO'LVEDLY. *adv.* [*in* and *resolved.*] Without settled determination.

Divers of my friends have thought it strange to hear me speak so *irresolvedly* concerning those things, which some take to be the elements, and others the principles of all mixed bodies. *Boyle.*

IRRE'SOLUTE. *adj.* [*irresolu*, Fr. *in* and *resolute.*] Not constant in purpose; not determined.

Were he evil us'd, he would outgo
His father, by as much as a performance
Does an *irresolute* purpose. *Shakesp. Henry* VIII.

Him, after long debate, *irresolute*
Of thoughts revolv'd, his final sentence chose
Fit vessel, fittest imp of fraud, in whom
To enter. *Milton's Paradise Lost, b.* ix.

To make reflections upon what is past, is the part of ingenious but *irresolute* men. *Temple.*

So Myrrha's mind, impell'd on either side,
Takes ev'ry bent, but cannot long abide;
Irresolute on which she should rely,
At last unfix'd in all, is only fix'd to die. *Dryden.*

IRRE'SOLUTELY. *adv.* [from *irresolute.*] Without firmness of mind; without determined purpose.

IRRESOLU'TION. *n. s.* [*irresolution*, Fr. *in* and *resolution.*] Want of firmness of mind.

It hath most force upon things that have the lightest motion, and therefore upon the spirits of men, and in them upon such affections as move lightest; as upon men in fear, or men in *irresolution.* *Bacon's Natural History.*

Irresolution on the schemes of life, which offer themselves to our choice, and inconstancy in pursuing them, are the greatest causes of all our unhappiness. *Addison.*

IRRESPE'CTIVE. *adj.* [*in* and *respective.*] Having no regard to any circumstances.

Thus did the Jew, by persuading himself of his particular *irrespective* election, think it safe to run into all foul sins. *Hammond on Fundamentals.*

According to this doctrine, it must be resolved wholly into the absolute *irrespective* will of God. *Rogers's Sermons.*

IRRESPE'CTIVELY. *adv.* [from *irrespective.*] Without regard to circumstances.

He is convinced, that all the promises belong to him absolutely and *irrespectively.* *Hammond on Fundamentals.*

IRRETRIE'VABLE. *adj.* [*in* and *retrieve.*] Not to be repaired; irrecoverable; irreparable.

IRRETRIE'VABLY. *adv.* [from *irretrievable.*] Irreparably; irrecoverably.

It would not defray the charge of the extraction, and therefore must have been all *irretrievably* lost, and useless to mankind, was it not by this means collected. *Woodward.*

IRRE'VERENCE. *n. s.* [*irreverentia*, Lat. *irreverence*, Fr. *in* and *reverence.*]

1. Want of reverence; want of veneration; want of respect.

Having seen our scandalous *irreverence* towards God's worship in general, 'tis easy to make application to the several parts of it. *Decay of Piety.*

They were a sort of attributes, with which it was a matter of religion to salute them on all occasions, and which it was an *irreverence* to omit. *Pope.*

2. State of being disregarded.

The concurrence of the house of peers in that fury, can be imputed to no one thing more than to the *irreverence* and scorn the judges were justly in, who had been always looked upon there as the oracles of the law. *Clarendon.*

IRRE'VERENT. *adj.* [*irreverent*, Fr. *in* and *reverent.*] Not paying due homage or reverence; not expressing or conceiving due veneration or respect.

As our fear excludeth not that boldness which becometh saints, so, if our familiarity with God do not savour of fear, it draweth too near that *irreverent* confidence wherewith true humility can never stand. *Hooker.*

Knowledge men sought for, and covered it from the vulgar sort as jewels of inestimable price, fearing the *irreverent* construction of the ignorant and irreligious. *Raleigh.*

Witness the *irreverent* son
Of him who built the ark; who, for the shame
Done to his father, heard his heavy curse,
Servant of servants, on his vitious race. *Milt. Par. Lost.*

Swearing, and the *irreverent* using the name of God in common discourse, is another abuse of the tongue. *Ray.*

If an *irreverent* expression or thought too wanton are crept into my verses, through my inadvertency, let their authors be answerable for them. *Dryden.*

IRRE'VERENTLY. *adv.* [from *irreverent.*] Without due respect or veneration.

'Tis but an ill essay of reverence and godly fear to use the gospel *irreverently.* *Government of the Tongue.*

IRREVE'RSIBLE. *adj.* [*in* and *reverse.*] Not to be recalled; not to be changed.

The sins of his chamber and his closet shall be produced before men and angels, and an eternal *irreversible* sentence be pronounced. *Rogers's Sermons.*

IRREVE'RSIBLY. *adv.* [from *irreversible.*] Without change.

The title of fundamentals, being ordinarily confined to the doctrines of faith, hath occasioned that great scandal in the church, at which so many myriads of solifidians have stumbled, and fallen *irreversibly*, by conceiving heaven a reward of true opinions. *Hammond on Fundamentals.*

IRRE'VOCABLE. *adj.* [*irrevocabilis*, Latin; *irrevocable*, French.] Not to be recalled; not to be brought back; not to be reversed.

Give thy hand to Warwick,
And, with thy hand, thy faith *irrevocable*,
That only Warwick's daughter shall be thine. *Shakesp.*

Firm and *irrevocable* is my doom,
Which I have past upon her. *Shakes. As you like it.*

That which is past is gone and *irrevocable*, therefore they do but trifle that labour in past matters. *Bacon's Essays.*

The second, both for piety renown'd,
And puissant deeds, a promise shall receive
Irrevocable, that his regal throne
For ever shall endure. *Milton's Paradise Lost.*

By *her irrevocable* fate,
War shall the country waste and change the state. *Dryden.*

The other victor flame a moment stood,
Then fell, and lifeless left th' extinguish'd wood;
For ever lost, th' *irrevocable* light
Forsook the black'ning coals, and sunk to night. *Dryden.*

Each sacred accent bears eternal weight,
And each *irrevocable* word is fate. *Pope.*

IRRE'VOCABLY. *adv.* [from *irrevocable.*] Without recall.

If air were kept out four or five minutes, the fire would be *irrevocably* extinguished. *Boyle.*

To I'RRIGATE. *v. a.* [*irrigo*, Latin.] To wet; to moisten; to water.

The heart, which is one of the principal parts of the body, doth continually *irrigate*, nourish, keep hot, and supple all the members. *Ray on the Creation.*

A bulky charger near their lips,
With which, in often interrupted sleep,
Their frying blood compels to *irrigate*
Their dry furr'd tongues. *A. Phillips.*

IRRIGA'TION. *n. s.* [from *irrigate.*] The act of watering or moistening.

Help of ground is by watering and *irrigation.* *Bacon.*

IRRI'GUOUS. *adj.* [from *irrigate.*]

1. Watery; watered.

The flow'ry lap
Of some *irriguous* valley spreads her store. *Milton.*

2. Dewy; moist. *Phillips* seems to have mistaken the Latin phrase *irriguus sopor.*

Rash Elpenor
Dry'd an immeasurable bowl, and thought
T' exhale his surfeit by *irriguous* sleep:
Imprudent! him death's iron sleep opprest. *Phillips.*

IRRI'SION. *n. s.* [*irrisio*, Lat. *irrision*, French.] The act of laughing at another.

This person, by his indiscreet and unnatural *irrision*, and exposing of his father, incurs his indignation and curse. *Woodward's Natural History.*

To I'RRITATE. *v. a.* [*irrito*, Latin; *irriter*, French.]

1. To provoke; to teaze; to exasperate.

The earl, speaking to the freeholders in imperious language, did not *irritate* the people. *Bacon's Henry* VII.

His power at court could not qualify him to go through with that difficult reformation, whilst he had a superior in the church, who, having the reins in his hand, could slacken them according to his own humour and indiscretion, and was thought to be the more remiss to *irritate* his cholerick disposition. *Clarendon.*

2. To

2. To fret; to put into motion or diſorder by any irregular or unaccuſtomed contact; to ſtimulate; to vellicate.

Cold maketh the ſpirits vigorous, and *irritateth* them. *Bacon.*

3. To heighten; to agitate; to enforce.

Air, if very cold, *irritateth* the flame, and maketh it burn more fiercely, as fire ſcorcheth in froſty weather. *Bacon.*

When they are collected, the heat becometh more violent and *irritate*, and thereby expelleth ſweat. *Bacon's Nat. Hiſt.*

Rous'd
By daſh of clouds, or *irritating* war
Of fighting winds, while all is calm below,
They furious ſpring. *Thomſon's Summer.*

IRRITA'TION. *n. ſ.* [*irritatio*, Latin; *irritation*, French; from *irritate.*]

1. Provocation; exaſperation.

2. Stimulation; vellication.

Violent affections and *irritations* of the nerves, in any part of the body, is cauſed by ſomething acrimonious. *Arbuthnot.*

IRRU'PTION. *n. ſ.* [*irruption*, Fr. *irruptio*, Latin.]

1. The act of any thing forcing an entrance.

I refrain, too ſuddenly,
To utter what will come at laſt too ſoon;
Leſt evil tidings, with too rude *irruption*,
Hitting thy aged ear, ſhould pierce too deep. *Milton.*

There are frequent inundations made in maritime countries by the *irruption* of the ſea. *Burnet.*

A full and ſudden *irruption* of thick melancholick blood into the heart puts a ſtop to its pulſation. *Harvey.*

2. Inroad; burſt of invaders into any place.

Notwithſtanding the *irruptions* of the barbarous nations, one can ſcarce imagine how ſo plentiful a ſoil ſhould become ſo miſerably unpeopled. *Addiſon on Italy.*

IS. [ıſ, Saxon. See To BE.]

1. The third perſon ſingular of *to be*: I am, thou art, he *is*.

He that *is* of God, heareth God's words. *Jo.* viii. 47.

Be not afraid of them, for they cannot do evil; neither *is* it in them to do good. *Jer.* x. 5.

My thought, whoſe murther yet *is* but fantaſtical,
Shakes ſo my ſingle ſtate of man, that function
Is ſmother'd in ſurmiſe; and nothing *is*,
But what *is* not. *Shakeſpeare's Macbeth.*

2. It is ſometimes expreſſed by *'s*.

There'*s* ſome among you have beheld me fighting. *Shakeſp.*

ISABE'LLA *Colour. n. ſ.* A kind of colour. *Ainſw.*

ISCHIA'DICK. *adj.* [ἰσχίον, ἰσχιαδικὸς; *iſchiadique*, Fr.] In anatomy, an epithet given to the veins of the foot that terminate in the crural. *Harris.*

I'SCHURY. *n. ſ.* [ἰσχȣρία, ἴσχω and ȣ̓ρον, urine; *iſchurie*, Fr. *iſchuria*, Latin.] A ſtoppage of urine, whether by gravel or other cauſe.

ISCHURE'TICK. *n. ſ.* [*iſchuretique*, Fr. from *iſchury.*] Such medicines as force urine when ſuppreſſed.

ISH. [ıſc, Saxon.]

1. A termination added to an adjective to expreſs diminution, a ſmall degree, or incipient ſtate of any quality: as, *bluiſh*, tending to blue; *brightiſh*, ſomewhat bright.

2. It is likewiſe ſometimes the termination of a gentile or poſſeſſive adjective: as, *Swediſh*, *Daniſh*; the *Daniſh* territories, or territories of the Danes.

3. It likewiſe notes participation of the qualities of the ſubſtantive to which it is added: as *fool*, *fooliſh*; *man*, *manniſh*; *rogue*, *roguiſh*.

I'SICLE. *n. ſ.* [More properly *icicle*, from *ice*; but *ice* ſhould rather be written *iſe*; ıſſ, Saxon.] A pendent ſhoot of ice.

Do you know this lady?
——The moon of Rome; chaſte as the *iſicle*
That's curdled by the froſt from pureſt ſnow
Hanging on Dian's temple. *Shakeſpeare.*

The froſts and ſnows her tender body ſpare;
Thoſe are not limbs for *iſicles* to tear. *Dryden.*

ISINGL'ASS. *n. ſ.* [from *ice*, or *iſe*, and *glaſs*; that is, matter congealed into glaſs; *ichthyocolla*, Latin.]

Iſinglaſs is a tough, firm, and light ſubſtance, of a whitiſh colour, and in ſome degree tranſparent, much reſembling glue, but cleanlier and ſweeter. We uſually receive it in twiſted pieces, of a roundiſh figure like a ſtaple, which the druggiſts divide into thin ſhreds like ſkins, that eaſily diſſolve. The fiſh from which *iſinglaſs* is prepared is one of the cartilaginous kind, and a ſpecies of ſturgeon: it grows to eighteen and twenty feet in length, and in its general figure greatly reſembles the ſturgeon. It is frequent in the Danube, the Boriſthenes, the Volga, and many other of the larger rivers of Europe. From the inteſtines of this fiſh the *iſinglaſs* is prepared by boiling. The greateſt quantity of *iſinglaſs* is made in Ruſſia. It is an excellent agglutinant and ſtrengthener, and often preſcribed in gellies and broths. The wine-coopers find it efficacious for clearing wines. *Hill's Mat. Med.*

The cure of putrefaction requires an incraſſating diet, as all viſcid broths, hartſhorn, ivory, and *iſinglaſs*. *Floyer.*

Some make it clear by reiterated fermentations, and others by additions, as *iſinglaſs*. *Mortimer's Huſbandry.*

I'SINGLASS *Stone. n. ſ.* This is a foſſil which is one of the pureſt and ſimpleſt of the natural bodies. It is found in broad maſſes, compoſed of a multitude of extremely thin plates or flakes. The maſſes are of a browniſh or rediſh colour; but when the plates are ſeparated, they are perfectly colourleſs, and more bright and pellucid than the fineſt glaſs. It is found in Muſcovy, Perſia, the iſland of Cyprus, in the Alps and Apennines, and the mountains of Germany. The ancients made their windows of it, inſtead of glaſs. It is alſo ſometimes uſed for glaſs before pictures, and for horn in lanthorns. *Hill's Mat. Med.*

I'SLAND. *n. ſ.* [*inſula*, Latin; *iſola*, Italian; *ealand*, Erſe. It is pronounced *iland.*] A tract of land ſurrounded by water.

He will carry this *iſland* home in his pocket, and give it his ſon for an apple.——And ſowing the kernels of it in the ſea, bring forth more *iſlands*. *Shakeſpeare's Tempeſt.*

Within a long receſs there lies a bay,
An *iſland* ſhades it from the rolling ſea,
And forms a port. *Dryden.*

Some ſafer world in depth of woods embrac'd,
Some happier *iſland* in the wat'ry waſte. *Johnſon.*
Iſland of bliſs! amid' the ſubject ſeas. *Thomſon.*

I'SLANDER. *n. ſ.* [from *iſland*. Pronounce *ilander.*] An inhabitant of a country ſurrounded by water.

We, as all *iſlanders*, are lunares, or the moon's men. *Camd.*

Your dinner, and the generous *iſlanders*
By you invited, do attend your preſence. *Shakeſp. Othello.*

There are many bitter ſayings againſt *iſlanders* in general, repreſenting them as fierce, treacherous, and unhoſpitable: thoſe who live on the continent have ſuch frequent intercourſe with men of different religions and languages, that they become more kind than thoſe who are the inhabitants of an iſland. *Addiſon's Freeholder.*

A race of rugged mariners are theſe,
Unpoliſh'd men, and boiſt'rous as their ſeas;
The native *iſlanders* alone their care,
And hateful he that breathes a foreign air. *Pope's Odyſſey.*

ISLE. *n. ſ.* [*iſle*, French; *inſula*, Latin. Pronounce *ile.*]

1. An iſland; a country ſurrounded by water.

Is it not an eaſy matter
To make lord William Haſtings of our mind,
For the inſtalment of this noble duke
In the ſeat royal of this famous *iſle?* *Shakeſp. R.* III.

The dreadful fight
Betwixt a nation and two whales I write:
Seas ſtain'd with gore I ſing, advent'rous toil,
And how theſe monſters did diſarm an *iſle*. *Waller.*

2. [Written, I think, corruptly for *aile*, from *aile*, French, from *ala*, Latin, the *aile* being probably at firſt only a wing or ſide walk. It may come likewiſe from *allee*, French, a walk.] A long walk in a church, or publick building.

O'er the twilight groves and duſky caves,
Long ſounding *iſles* and intermingled graves,
Black melancholy ſits. *Pope.*

ISOPERIME'TRICAL. *n. ſ.* [ἴσ☉, πέρι, and μέτρον.] In geometry, are ſuch figures as have equal perimeters or circumferences, of which the circle is the greateſt. *Harris.*

ISO'SCELES. *n. ſ.* [*iſoſcele*, Fr. or *equiangular triangle.*] That which hath only two ſides equal. *Harris.*

I'SSUE. *n. ſ.* [*iſſue*, French.]

1. The act of paſſing out.

2. Exit; egreſs; or paſſage out.

Unto the Lord belong the *iſſues* from death. *Pſ.* lxviii. 20.

Keep thy heart with all diligence; for out of it are the *iſſues* of life. *Prov.* iv. 23.

Let us examine what bodies touch a moveable whilſt in motion, as the only means to find an *iſſue* out of this difficulty. *Digby on Bodies.*

We might have eaſily prevented thoſe great returns of money to France; and if it be true the French are ſo impoveriſhed, in what condition muſt they have been, if that *iſſue* of wealth had been ſtopped? *Swift.*

3. Event; conſequence.

Spirits are not finely touch'd,
But to fine *iſſues*. *Shakeſp. Meaſ. for Meaſure.*

If I were ever fearful
To do a thing, where I the *iſſue* doubted,
Whereof the execution did cry out
Againſt the non-performance, 'twas a fear
Which oft infects the wiſeſt. *Shak. Winter's Tale.*

But let the *iſſue* correſpondent prove
To good beginnings of each enterprize. *Fairfax.*

If things were caſt upon this *iſſue*, that God ſhould never prevent ſin 'till man deſerved it, the beſt would ſin, and ſin for ever. *South's Sermons.*

The wittieſt ſayings and ſentences will be found the *iſſues* of chance, and nothing elſe but ſo many lucky hits of a roving fancy. *South's Sermons.*

Our preſent condition is better for us in the *iſſue*, than that uninterrupted health and ſecurity that the atheiſt deſires. *Bent.*

4. Termination;

4. Termination; conclusion.

He hath preserved Argalus alive, under pretence of having him publickly executed after these wars, of which they hope for a soon and prosperous *issue*. *Sidney.*

What *issue* of my love remains for me!
How wild a passion works within my breast!
With what prodigious flames am I possest! *Dryden.*

Homer, at a loss to bring difficult matters to an *issue*, lays his hero asleep, and this solves the difficulty. *Broome.*

5. Sequel deduced from premises.

I am to pray you not to strain my speech
To grosser *issues*, nor to larger reach,
Than to suspicion. *Shakespeare's Othello.*

6. A fontanel; a vent made in a muscle for the discharge of humours.

This tumour in his left arm was caused by strict binding of his *issue*. *Wiseman.*

7. Evacuation.

A woman was diseased with an *issue* of blood. *Mat.* ix. 20.

8. Progeny; offspring.

O nation miserable!
When shalt thou see thy wholsome days again?
Since that the truest *issue* of thy throne,
By his own interdiction stands accurst. *Shakesp. Macbeth.*

Nor where Abassin kings their *issue* guard,
Mount Amara, though this by some suppos'd
True paradise, under the Æthiop line
By Nilus' head. *Milton's Paradise Lost.*

This old peaceful prince, as heav'n decreed,
Was bless'd with no male *issue* to succeed. *Dryden's Æn.*

The frequent productions of monsters, in all the species of animals, and strange *issues* of human birth, carry with them difficulties, not possible to consist with this hypothesis. *Locke.*

9. [In law.] *Issue* hath divers applications in the common law: sometimes used for the children begotten between a man and his wife; sometimes for profits growing from an amercement, fine, or expences of suit; sometime for profits of lands or tenements; sometime for that point of matter depending in suit, whereupon the parties join and put their cause to the trial of the jury. *Issue* is either general or special: general *issue* seemeth to be that whereby it is referred to the jury to bring in their verdict, whether the defendant have done any such thing as the plaintiff layeth to his charge. The special *issue* then must be that, where special matter being alleged by the defendant for his defence, both the parties join thereupon, and so grow rather to a demurrer, if it be *quæstio juris*, or to trial by the jury, if it be *quæstio facti*. *Cowel.*

To I'ssue. *v. n.* [from the noun; *isser*, Fr. *uscire*, Italian.]

1. To come out; to pass out of any place.

Waters *issued* out from under the threshold of the house. *Ezek.* xlvii. 1.

From the utmost end of the head branches there *issueth* out a gummy juice. *Raleigh's History of the World.*

Waters *issu'd* from a cave. *Milton.*

Ere Pallas *issu'd* from the thunderer's head,
Dulness o'er all possess'd her ancient right. *Pope.*

2. To make an eruption.

Three of master Ford's brothers watch the door with pistols, that none should *issue* out, otherwise you might slip away. *Shakespeare.*

See that none hence *issue* forth a spy. *Milton.*

Haste, arm your Ardeans, *issue* to the plain;
With faith to friend, assault the Trojan train. *Dryden.*

At length there *issu'd*, from the grove behind,
A fair assembly of the female kind. *Dryden.*

A buzzing noise of bees his ears alarms;
Straight *issue* through the sides assembling swarms. *Dryden.*

Full for the port the Ithacensians stand,
And furl their sails, and *issue* on the land. *Pope's Odyssey.*

3. To proceed as an offspring.

Of thy sons that shall *issue* from thee, which thou shalt beget, shall they take away. 2 *Kings* xx. 18.

4. To be produced by any fund.

These altarages *issued* out of the offerings made to the altar, and were payable to the priesthood. *Ayliffe's Parergon.*

5. To run out in lines.

It would be tried in pipes, being made with a belly towards the lower end, and then *issuing* into a straight concave again. *Bacon's Natural History.*

To I'ssue. *v. a.*

1. To send out; to send forth.

A weak degree of heat is not able either to digest the parts or to *issue* the spirits. *Bacon's Nat. Hist.*

2. To send out judicially or authoritatively. This is the more frequent sense.

If the council *issued* out any order against them, or if the king sent a proclamation for their repair to their houses, some nobleman published a protestation. *Clarendon.*

Deep in a rocky cave he makes abode,
A mansion proper for a mourning god:
Here he gives audience, *issuing* out decrees
To rivers, his dependent deities.

In vain the master *issues* out commands,
In vain the trembling sailors ply their hands;
The tempest unforeseen prevents their care. *Dryden.*

They constantly wait in court to make a due return of what they have done, and to receive such other commands as the judge shall *issue* forth. *Ayliffe's Parergon.*

I'ssueless. *adj.* [from *issue*.] Without offspring; without descendants.

Carew, by virtue of this entail, succeeded to Hugh's portion, as dying *issueless*. *Carew's Survey of Cornwal.*

I have done sin;
For which the heav'ns, taking angry note,
Have left me *issueless*. *Shakesp. Winter's Tale.*

I'sthmus. *n. s.* [*isthmus*, Latin.] A neck of land joining the peninsula to the continent.

There is a castle strongly seated on a high rock, which joineth by an *isthmus* to the land, and is impregnably fortified. *Sandys's Travels.*

The north side of the Assyrian empire stretcheth northward to that *isthmus* between the Euxine and the Caspian seas. *Brerewood on Languages.*

O life, thou nothing's younger brother!
Thou weak built *isthmus*, that do'st proudly rise
Up betwixt two eternities,
Yet can'st not wave nor wind sustain;
But broken and o'erwhelm'd the ocean meets again. *Cowley.*

Our church of England stands as Corinth between two seas, and there are some busy in cutting the *isthmus*, to let in both at once upon it. *Stillingfleet.*

Cleomenes thinking it more adviseable to fortify, not the *isthmus*, but the mountains, put his design in execution. *Creech.*

Plac'd on this *isthmus* of a middle state,
A being darkly wise, and rudely great. *Pope.*

IT. *pronoun.* [hit, Saxon.]

1. The neutral demonstrative. Used in speaking of things.

Nothing can give that to another which *it* hath not itself. *Bramh. against Hobbs.*

Will our great anger learn to stoop so low?
I know *it* cannot. *Cowley.*

Tell me, O tell, what kind of thing is wit,
Thou who master art of *it*. *Cowley.*

His son, *it* may be, dreads no harm;
But kindly waits his father's coming home. *Flatman.*

The time will come, *it* will, when you shall know
The rage of love. *Dryden.*

How can I speak? or how, sir, can you hear?
Imagine that which you would most deplore,
And that which I would speak, is *it* or more. *Dryden.*

A mind so furnished, what reason has *it* to acquiesce in *its* conclusions! *Locke.*

The glory which encompassed them covered the place, and darted *its* rays with so much strength, that the whole fabrick began to melt. *Addison's Freeholder.*

If we find a greater good in the present constitution, than would have accrued either from the total privation of *it*, or from other frames and structures, we may then reasonably conclude, that the present constitution proceeded from an intelligent and good being, that formed *it* that particular way out of choice. *Bentley's Sermons.*

2. *It* is used absolutely for the state of a person or affair.

How is *it* with our general?
——Even so
As with a man by his own alms impoison'd,
And with his charity slain. *Shakespeare's Coriolanus.*

3. *It* is used for the thing; the matter; the affair.

It's come to pass,
That tractable obedience is a slave
To each incensed will. *Shakesp. Henry* VIII.

4. *It* is sometimes expressed by *'t*.

He rallied, and again fell to *'t*;
For catching foe by nearer foot,
He lifted with such might and strength,
As would have hurl'd him thrice his length. *Hudibras.*

The design, *it* seems, is to avoid the dreadful imputation of pedantry. *Swift.*

5. *It* is used ludicrously after neutral verbs, to give an emphasis.

If Abraham brought all with him, it is not probable that he meant to walk *it* back again for his pleasure. *Raleigh.*

The Lacedemonians, at the straights of Thermopylæ, when their arms failed them, fought *it* out with their nails and teeth. *Dryden.*

I have often seen people lavish *it* profusely in tricking up their children, and yet starve their minds. *Locke.*

A mole courses *it* not on the ground, like the rat or mouse, but lives under the earth. *Addison's Spectator.*

Whether the charmer sinner *it*, or saint *it*,
If folly grows romantick, I must paint it. *Pope.*

6. Sometimes applied familiarly, ludicrously, or rudely to persons.

Let us after him,
Whose care is gone before to bid us welcome:
It is a peerless kinsman. *Shakespeare's Macbeth.*

Do

Do, child, go to *it* grandam, child:
Give grandam kingdom, and *its* grandam will
Give *it* up him. *Shakesp. King John.*

7. *It* is ſometimes uſed of the firſt or ſecond perſon, ſometimes of more. This mode of ſpeech, though uſed by good authors, and ſupported by the *il y a* of the French, has yet an appearance of barbariſm.

Who was't came by?
—'*Tis* two or three, my lord, that bring you word
Macduff is fled to England. *Shakeſ. Macbeth.*

City,
'*Tis* I, that made thy widows. *Shakeſp. Coriolanus.*

'*Tis* theſe that early taint the female ſoul. *Pope.*

ITCH. *n. ſ.* ȝıcþa, Saxon.]

1. A cutaneous diſeaſe extremely contagious, which overſpreads the body with ſmall puſtules filled with a thin ſerum, and raiſed as microſcopes have diſcovered by a ſmall animal. It is cured by ſulphur.

Luſt and liberty
Creep in the minds and marrows of our youths,
That 'gainſt the ſtream of virtue they may ſtrive,
And drown themſelves in riot, *itches*, blains. *Shak. Timon.*

The Lord will ſmite thee with the ſcab and with the *itch*, whereof thou can'ſt not be healed. *Deutr.* xxviii. 27.

As if divinity had catch'd
The *itch*, on purpoſe, to be ſcratch'd. *Hudibras.*

2. The ſenſation of uneaſineſs in the ſkin, which is eaſed by rubbing.

3. A conſtant teazing deſire.

A certain *itch* of meddling with other people's matters, puts us upon ſhifting. *L'Eſtrange.*

He had ſtill pedigree in his head, and an *itch* of being thought a divine king. *Dryden.*

From ſervants company a child is to be kept, not by prohibitions, for that will but give him an *itch* after it, but by other ways. *Locke.*

At half mankind when gen'rous Manly raves,
All know 'tis virtue; for he thinks them knaves:
When univerſal homage Umbra pays,
All ſee 'tis vice, and *itch* of vulgar praiſe. *Pope.*

To ITCH. *v. n.* [from the noun.]

1. To feel that uneaſineſs in the ſkin which is removed by rubbing.

A troubleſome *itching* of the part was occaſioned by want of tranſpiration. *Wiſeman's Surgery.*

My right eye *itches*; ſome good luck is near;
Perhaps my Amaryllis may appear. *Dryden.*

2. To long; to have continual deſire. This ſenſe appears in the following examples, though ſome of them are equivocal.

Maſter Shallow, you have yourſelf been a great fighter, though now a man of peace.——Mr. Page, though now I be old, and of peace, if I ſee a ſword out, my finger *itches* to make one. *Shakeſpeare.*

Caſſius, you yourſelf
Are much condemn'd to have an *itching* palm,
To ſell and mart your offices for gold. *Shak. Julius Cæſar.*

The *itching* ears, being an epidemick diſeaſe, give fair opportunity to every mountebank. *Decay of Piety.*

All ſuch have ſtill an *itching* to deride,
And fain would be upon the laughing ſide. *Pope.*

I'TCHY. *adj.* [from *itch.*] Infected with the itch.

I'TEM. *adv.* [Latin.] Alſo. A word uſed when any article is added to the former.

I'TEM. *n.ſ.*

1. A new article.

I could have looked on him without the help of admiration, though the catalogue of his endowments had been tabled by his ſide, and I to peruſe him by *items*. *Shakeſpeare.*

If this diſcourſe have not concluded our weakneſs, I have one *item* more of mine: if knowledge can be found, I muſt loſe that which I thought I had, that there is none. *Glanv.*

2. A hint; an innuendo.

To I'TERATE. *v. a.* [*itero*, Latin.]

1. To repeat; to utter again; to inculcate by frequent mention.

We covet to make the pſalms eſpecially familiar unto all: this is the very cauſe why we *iterate* the pſalms oftner than any other part of Scripture beſides; the cauſe wherefore we inure the people together with their miniſter, and not the miniſter alone to read them, as other parts of Scripture he doth. *Hook.*

If the one may monthly, the other may daily be *iterated.* *Hooker.*

In the firſt ages God gave laws unto our fathers, and their memories ſerved inſtead of books; whereof the imperfections being known to God, he relieved the ſame by often putting them in mind: in which reſpect we ſee how many times one thing hath been *iterated* into the beſt and wiſeſt. *Hooker.*

The king, to keep a decency towards the French king, ſent new ſolemn ambaſſadors to intimate unto him the decree of his eſtates, and to *iterate* his motion that the French would deſiſt from hoſtility. *Bacon's Henry* VII.

There be two kinds of reflections of ſounds; the one at diſtance, which is the echo, wherein the original is heard diſtinctly, and the reflection alſo diſtinctly: the other in concurrence, when the ſound reflecting, returneth immediately upon the original, and ſo *iterateth* it not, but amplifieth it. *Bacon's Natural Hiſtory.*

2. To do over again.

Aſhes thoroughly burnt, and well reverberated by fire, after the ſalt thereof hath been drawn out by *iterated* decoctions. *Brown's Vulgar Errours.*

Adam took no thought,
Eating his fill; nor Eve to *iterate*
Her former treſpaſs fear'd, the more to ſooth
Him with her lov'd ſociety. *Milt. Par. Loſt, b.* ix.

I'TERANT. *adj.* [*iterans*, Latin.] Repeating.

Waters being near, make a current echo; but being farther off, they make an *iterant* echo. *Bacon's Nat. Hiſtory.*

ITERA'TION. *n. ſ.* [*iteration*, French; *iteratio*, Latin.] Repetition; recital over again.

Truth tir'd with *iteration*
As true as ſteel, as plantage to the moon. *Shakeſpeare.*

My huſband!
——Ay, 'twas he that told me firſt.
—— My huſband!
——What needs this *iteration*, woman?
I ſay, thy huſband. *Shakeſpeare's Othello.*

Iterations are commonly loſs of time; but there is no ſuch gain of time, as to iterate often the ſtate of the queſtion; for it chaſeth away many a frivolous ſpeech. *Bacon's Eſſays.*

In all theſe reſpects it hath a peculiar property to engage the receiver to perſevere in all piety, and is farther improved by the frequent *iteration* and repetition. *Hammond.*

ITI'NERANT. *adj.* [*itinerant*, French.] Wandering; not ſettled.

It ſhould be my care to ſweeten and mellow the voices of *itinerant* tradeſmen, as alſo to accommodate their cries to their reſpective wares. *Addiſon's Spectator.*

ITI'NERARY. *n.ſ.* [*itineraire*, French; *itinerarium*, Latin.] A book of travels.

The clergy are ſufficiently reproached, in moſt *itineraries*, for the univerſal poverty one meets with in this plentiful kingdom. *Addiſon on Italy.*

ITI'NERARY. *adj.* [*itineraire*, Fr. *itinerarius*, Lat.] Travelling; done on a journey; done during frequent change of place.

He did make a progreſs from Lincoln to the northern parts, though it were rather an *itinerary* circuit of juſtice than a progreſs. *Bacon's Henry* VII.

ITSE'LF. *pronoun.* [*it* and *ſelf.*] The neutral reciprocal pronoun applied to things.

Who then ſhall blame
His peſter'd ſenſes to recoil and ſtart,
When all that is within him does condemn
Itſelf for being there? *Shakeſp. Macbeth.*

Borrowing of foreigners, in *itſelf*, makes not the kingdom rich or poor. *Locke.*

JU'BILANT. *adj.* [*jubilans*, Lat.] Uttering ſongs of triumph.

The planets liſt'ning ſtood,
While the bright pomp aſcended *jubilant.* *Milt. Par. Loſt.*

JUBILA'TION. *n. ſ.* [*jubilation*, Fr. *jubilatio*, Lat. The act of declaring triumph.

JU'BILEE. *n.ſ.* [*jubilé*, Fr. *jubilum*, from *jubilo*, low Latin.] A publick feſtivity; a time of rejoicing; a ſeaſon of joy.

Angels utt'ring joy, heav'n rung
With *jubilee*, and loud hoſanna's fill'd
Th' eternal regions. *Milton's Paradiſe Loſt.*

Joy was then a maſculine and a ſevere thing: the recreation of the judgment, or rejoicing, the *jubilee* of reaſon. *South.*

The town was all a *jubilee* of feaſts. *Dryden.*

JUCU'NDITY. *n. ſ.* [*jucunditas*, *jucundus*, Latin.] Pleaſantneſs; agreeableneſs.

The new or unexpected *jucundities*, which preſent themſelves, will have activity enough to excite the earthieſt ſoul, and raiſe a ſmile from the moſt compoſed tempers. *Brown.*

JUDAS *Tree. n. ſ.* [*ſiliquaſtrum*, Latin.] A plant.

It hath a papilionaceous flower, whoſe wings are placed above the ſtandard: the head is compoſed of two petals; the pointal, which riſes in the centre of the flower-cup, and is encompaſſed with the ſtamina, afterward becomes a long flat pod, containing ſeveral kidney-ſhaped ſeeds: to which may be added roundiſh leaves, growing alternately on the branches.

Judas tree yields a fine purpliſh, bright, red bloſſom in the Spring, and is increaſed by layers. *Mortimer's Huſbandry.*

To JUDA'IZE. *v. n.* [*judaiſer*, Fr. *judaizo*, low Latin.] To conform to the manner of the Jews.

Paul *judaiz'd* with Jews, was all to all. *Sandys.*

JUDGE. *n. ſ.* [*juge*, French; *judex*, Latin.]

1. One who is inveſted with authority to determine any cauſe or queſtion, real or perſonal.

Shall not the *judge* of all the earth do right? *Geneſis.*

A father of the fatherleſs, and a *judge* of the widows is God in his holy habitation. *Pſ.* lxviii. 5.

Thou art *judge*
Of all things made, and judgeſt only right. *Milton.*

It is not ſufficient to imitate nature in every circumſtance dully: it becomes a painter to take what is moſt beautiful, as being the ſovereign *judge* of his own art. *Dryden.*

2. One

2. One who presides in a court of judicature.
My lord Bassanio gave his ring away
Unto the *judge* that begg'd it. *Shakespeare's Merch. of Venice.*
A single voice; and that not past me, but
By learned approbation of the *judges*. *Shakesp. H.* VIII.
3. One who has skill sufficient to decide upon the merit of any thing.
How dares your pride,
As in a listed field to fight your cause,
Unask'd the royal grant; nor marshal by,
As knightly rites require, nor *judge* to try. *Dryden.*
A perfect *judge* will read each piece of wit,
With the same spirit that its author writ. *Pope.*

To JUDGE. *v. n.* [*juger*, French; *judico*, Latin.]
1. To pass sentence.
My wrong be upon thee; the Lord *judge* between thee and me. *Genesis.*
Ye *judge* not for man, but for the Lord, who is with you in the judgment. 2 *Chro.* xix. 6.
2. To form or give an opinion.
Beshrew me, but I love her heartily;
For she is wise, if I can *judge* aright. *Shakespeare.*
Ye *judge* after the flesh; I judge no man. *Jo.* viii. 15.
Authors to themselves,
Both what they *judge* and what they chuse. *Milton.*
If I did not know the originals, I should never be able to *judge*, by the copies, which was Virgil, and which Ovid. *Dryd.*
Whether it be a divine revelation or no, reason must *judge*, which can never permit the mind to reject a greater evidence, to embrace what is less evident. *Locke.*
He proceeds in his inquiry into sciences, resolved to *judge* of them freely. *Locke.*
3. To discern; to distinguish.
How doth God know? Can he *judge* through the dark cloud? *Job* xxii. 13.
Judge in yourselves: is it comely a woman pray unto God uncovered? 1 *Cor.* xi. 13.
How properly the tories may be called the whole body of the British nation, I leave to any one's *judging*. *Addison.*

To JUDGE. *v. a.*
1. To pass sentence upon; to examine authoritatively; to determine finally.
Chaos shall *judge* the strife. *Milton.*
Then those, whom form of laws
Condemn'd to die, when traitors *judg'd* their cause. *Dryden.*
2. To pass severe censure; to doom severely.
He shall *judge* among the heathen; he shall fill the places with the dead bodies. *Ps.* cx. 6.
Judge not, that ye be not *judged*. *Matthew.*
Let no man *judge* you in meat or drink. 2 *Col.* 16.

JU'DGER. *n. s.* [from *judge*.] One who forms judgment; or passes sentence.
The vulgar threatened to be their oppressers, and *judgers* of their judges. *King Charles.*
They who guide themselves meerly by what appears, are ill *judgers* of what they have not well examined. *Digby.*

JU'DGMENT. *n. s.* [*jugement*, French]
1. The power of discerning the relations between one term or one proposition and another.
O *judgment!* thou art fled to brutish beasts,
And men have lost their reason. *Shak. Julius Cæsar.*
The faculty, which God has given man to supply the want of certain knowledge, is *judgment*, whereby the mind takes any proposition to be true or false, without perceiving a demonstrative evidence in the proofs. *Locke.*
Judgment is that whereby we join ideas together by affirmation or negation; so, this tree is high. *Watts.*
2. Doom; the right or power of passing judgment.
If my suspect be false, forgive me, God;
For *judgment* only doth belong to thee. *Shakes. H.* VI.
3. The act of exercising judicature.
They gave *judgment* upon him. 2 *Kings* xxv. 6.
When thou, O Lord, shalt stand disclos'd
In majesty severe,
And sit in *judgment* on my soul,
O how shall I appear. *Addison's Spectator.*
4. Determination; decision.
Where distinctions or identities are purely material, the *judgment* is made by the imagination, otherwise by the understanding. *Glanv. Sceps.*
We shall make a certain *judgment* what kind of dissolution that earth was capable of. *Burnet's Theory of the Earth.*
Reason ought to accompany the exercise of our senses, whenever we would form a just *judgment* of things proposed to our inquiry. *Watts.*
5. The quality of distinguishing propriety and impropriety; criticism.
Judgment, a cool and slow faculty, attends not a man in the rapture of poetical composition. *Dennis.*
'Tis with our *judgments* as our watches, none
Go just alike; yet each believes his own. *Pope.*
6. Opinion; notion.
I see mens *judgments* are
A parcel of their fortunes, and things outward
Draw the inward quality after them,
To suffer all alike. *Shakes. Ant. and Cleopatra.*
When she did think my master lov'd her well,
She, in my *judgment*, was as fair as you. *Shakespeare.*
7. Sentence against a criminal.
When he was brought again to th' bar, to hear
His knell rung out, his *judgment*, he was stirr'd
With agony. *Shakesp. Henry* VIII.
The chief priests informed me, desiring to have *judgment* against him. *Acts* xxv. 15.
On Adam last this *judgment* he pronounc'd. *Milton.*
8. Condemnation. This is a theological use.
The *judgment* was by one to condemnation; but the free gift is of many offences unto justification. *Rom* v. 16.
The precepts, promises, and threatenings of the Gospel will rise up in *judgment* against us, and the articles of our faith will be so many articles of accusation. *Tillotson.*
9. Punishment inflicted by providence, with reference to some particular crime.
This *judgment* of the heavens that makes us tremble,
Touches us not with pity. *Shakes. King Lear.*
We cannot be guilty of greater uncharitableness, than to interpret afflictions as punishments and *judgments*: it aggravates the evil to him who suffers, when he looks upon himself as the mark of divine vengeance. *Addison's Spectator.*
10. Distribution of justice.
The Jews made insurrection against Paul, and brought him to the *judgment* seat. *Acts* xviii. 12.
Your dishonour
Mangles true *judgment*, and bereaves the state
Of that integrity which should become it. *Shakes. Coriol.*
In *judgments* between rich and poor, consider not what the poor man needs, but what is his own. *Taylor.*
A bold and wise petitioner goes strait to the throne and *judgment* seat of the monarch. *Arbuthn. and Pope's Mart. Scrib.*
11. Judiciary laws; statutes.
If ye hearken to these *judgmeuts*, and keep and do them, the Lord thy God shall keep unto thee the covenant. *Deutr.*
12. The last doom.
The dreadful *judgment* day
So dreadful will not be as was his sight. *Shakes. Hen.* VI.

JU'DICATORY. *n. s.* [*judico*, Latin.]
1. Distribution of justice.
No such crime appeared as the lords, the supreme court of *judicatory*, would judge worthy of death. *Clarendon.*
2. Court of justice.
Human *judicatories* give sentence on matters of right and wrong, but inquire not into bounty and beneficence. *Atterb.*

JU'DICATURE. *n. s.* [*judicature*, Fr. *judico*, Latin.] Power of distributing justice.
The honour of the judges in their *judicature* is the king's honour. *Bacon's Advice to Villiers.*
If he should bargain for a place of *judicature*, let him be rejected with shame. *Bacon.*
In *judicatures* to take away the trumpet, the scarlet, the attendance, makes justice naked as well as blind. *South's Sermons.*

JUDI'CIAL. *adj.* [*judicium*, Latin.]
1. Practised in the distribution of publick justice.
What government can be without *judicial* proceedings?
And what judicature without a religious oath? *Bentley's Serm.*
2. Inflicted on as a penalty.
The resistance of those will cause a *judicial* hardness. *South.*

JUDI'CIALLY. *adv.* [from *judicial*.] In the forms of legal justice.
It will behove us to think that we see God still looking on, and weighing all our thoughts, words, and actions in the balance of infallible justice, and passing the same judgment which he intends hereafter *judicially* to declare. *Grew's Cosmol.*

JUDI'CIARY. *adj.* [*judiciaire*, Fr. *judiciarius*, Latin.] Passing judgment upon any thing.
Before weight be laid upon notions of *judiciary* astrologers, the influence of constellations ought, by severe experiments, to be made out. *Boyle.*

JUDI'CIOUS. *adj.* [*judicieux*, French.] Prudent; wise; skilful in any matter or affair.
For your husband,
He's noble, wise, *judicious*, and best knows
The fits o' th' season. *Shakes. Macbeth.*
Love hath his seat
In reason, and is *judicious*. *Milton.*
To each favour meaning we apply,
And palate call *judicious*. *Milton.*
We are beholden to *judicious* writers of all ages for those discoveries they have left behind them. *Locke.*

JUDI'CIOUSLY. *adv.* [from *judicious*.] Skilfully; wisely; with just determination.
So bold, yet so *judiciously* you dare,
That your least praise is to be regular. *Dryden.*

Longinus

Longinus has *judiciously* preferred the sublime genius that sometimes errs to the middling or indifferent one, which makes few faults, but seldom rises to excellence. *Dryden.*

JUG. *n. s.* [*jugge*, Danish.] A large drinking vessel with a gibbous or swelling belly.

You'd rail upon the hostess of the house,
Because she bought stone *jugs* and no seal'd quarts. *Shak.*
He fetch'd 'em drink,
Fill'd a large *jug* up to the brink. *Swift's Miscel.*

To JU'GGLE. *v. n.* [*jougler* or *jongler*, Fr. *jocari*, Lat.]

1. To play tricks by slight of hand; to show false appearances of extraordinary performances.

The ancient miracle of Memnon's statue seems to be a *juggling* of the Ethiopian priests. *Digby on Bodies.*

2. To practise artifice or imposture.

Be these *juggling* fiends no more believ'd,
That palter with us in a double sense. *Shakesp. Macbeth.*
Is't possible the spells of France should *juggle*
Men into such strange mockeries? *Shakesp. Henry* VIII.
They ne'er forswore themselves, nor lied,
Disdain'd to stay for friends consents;
Nor *juggl'd* about settlements. *Hudibras, p.* iii.

JU'GGLE. *n. s.* [from the verb.]

1. A trick by legerdemain.
2. An imposture; a deception.

The notion was not the invention of politicians, and a *juggle* of state to cozen the people into obedience. *Tillotson.*

JU'GGLER. *n. s.* [from *juggle.*]

1. One who practises slight of hand; one who deceives the eye by nimble conveyance.

They say this town is full of cozenage,
As nimble *jugglers* that deceive the eye,
Drug-working sorcerers that change the mind,
Disguised cheaters, prating mountebanks,
And many such like libertines of sin. *Shakespeare.*

I saw a *juggler* that had a pair of cards, and would tell a man what card he thought. *Bacon's Nat. Hist.*

Aristæus was a famous poet, that flourished in the days of Crœsus, and a notable *juggler.* *Sandys's Travels.*

Fortune-tellers, *jugglers*, and imposters, do daily delude them. *Brown's Vulgar Errous, b.* i.

The *juggler* which another's slight can show,
But teaches how the world his own may know. *Garth.*

One who is managed by a *juggler* fancies he has money in hand; but let him grasp it never so carefully, upon a word or two it increases or dwindles. *Addison's Freeholder*, N°. 18.

What magick makes our money rise,
When dropt into the southern main;
Or do these *jugglers* cheat us? *Swift's Miscel.*

2. A cheat; a trickish fellow.

O me, you *juggler*; oh, you canker blossom,
You thief of love; what, have you come by night,
And stoll'n my love's heart from him? *Shakespeare.*
I sing no harm
To officer, *juggler*, or justice of peace. *Donne.*

JU'GGLINGLY. *adv.* [from *juggle.*] In a deceptive manner.

JU'GULAR. *adj.* [*jugulum*, Latin.] Belonging to the throat.

A gentleman was wounded into the internal *jugular*, through his neck. *Wiseman's Surgery.*

JUICE. *n. s.* [*jus*, French; *juys*, Dutch.]

1. The liquor, sap, or water of plants and fruits.

If I define wine, I must say, wine is a *juice* not liquid, or wine is a substance; for *juice* includes both substance and liquid. *Watts's Logick, p.* i.

Unnumber'd fruits,
A friendly *juice* to cool thirst's rage contain. *Thomson.*

2. The fluid in animal bodies.

Juice in language is less than blood; for if the words be but becoming and signifying, and the sense gentle, there is *juice*: but where that wanteth, the language is thin, scarce covering the bone. *Benj. Johnson's Discovery.*

An animal whose *juices* are unsound can never be nourished; unsound *juices* can never repair the fluids. *Arbuthnot.*

JUI'CELESS. *adj.* [from *juice.*] Dry; without moisture; without juice.

Divine Providence has spread her table every-where; not with a *juiceless* green carpet, but with succulent herbage and nourishing grass. *More's Antidote against Atheism.*

When Boreas' spirit blusters sore,
Beware th' inclement heav'ns; now let thy hearth
Crackle with *juiceless* boughs. *Philips.*

JU'ICINESS. *n. s.* [from *juice.*] Plenty of juice; succulence.

JU'ICY. *adj.* [from *juice.*] Moist; full of juice.

Earth being taken out of watery woods, will put forth herbs of a fat and *juicy* substance. *Bacon's Nat. Hist.*

Each plant and *juiciest* gourd will pluck. *Milton.*

The musk's surpassing worth! that, in its youth,
Its tender nonage, loads the spreading boughs
With large and *juicy* offspring. *Philips.*

To JUKE. *v. n.* [*jucher*, French.]

1. To perch upon any thing: as, birds.
2. *Juking*, in Scotland, denotes still any complaisance by bending of the head.

Two asses travelled; the one laden with oats, the other with money: the money-merchant was so proud of his trust, that he went *juking* and tossing of his head. *L'Estrange.*

J'UJUB. } *n. s.* [*zizyphus*, Lat.] A plant whose flower con-
JU'JUBES. } sists of several leaves, which are placed circularly, and expand in form of a rose; out of whose empalement rises the pointal, which afterwards becomes an oblong fleshy fruit, shaped like an olive, including an hard shell divided into cells, each containing an oblong nut or kernel. The fruit is like a small plum, but it has little flesh upon the stone. *Mill.*

JU'LAP. *n. s.* [A word of Arabick original; *julapium*, low Lat. *julep*, Fr.]

Julap is an extemporaneous form of medicine, made of simple and compound water sweetened, and serves for a vehicle to other forms not so convenient to take alone. *Quincy.*

Behold this cordial *julap* here,
That flames and dances in his crystal bounds
With spirits of balm and fragrant syrups mixt. *Milton.*

If any part of the after-birth be left, endeavour the bringing that away; and by good sudorificks and cordials expel the venom, and contemperate the heat and acrimony by *julaps* and emulsions. *Wiseman's Surgery.*

JU'LUS. *n. s.*

1. *July flower.* See CLOVE-GILLIFOWER and GILLIFLOWER.
2. *Julus*, among botanists, denotes those long worm-like tufts or palms, as they are called in willows, which at the beginning of the year grow out, and hang pendular down from hazels, walnut-trees, &c. *Miller.*

JU'LY. *n. s.* [*Julius*, Lat. *juillet*, Fr.] The month anciently called *quintilis*, or the fifth from March, named *July* in honour of *Julius Cæsar*; the seventh month from January.

July I would have drawn in a jacket of light yellow, eating cherries, with his face and bosom sun-burnt. *Peacham.*

JU'MART. *n. s.* [French.]

Mules and *jumarts*, the one from the mixture of an ass and a mare, the other from the mixture of a bull and a mare, are frequent. *Locke.*

To JU'MBLE. *v. a.* [in *Chaucer*, *jombre*, from *combler*, French, *Skinner.*] To mix violently and confusedly together.

Persons and humours may be *jumbled* and disguised; but nature, like quicksilver, will never be killed. *L'Estrange.*

A verbal concordance leads not always to texts of the same meaning; and one may observe, how apt that is to *jumble* together passages of scripture, and thereby disturb the true meaning of holy scripture. *Locke.*

Writing is but just like dice,
And lucky mains make people wise;
And *jumbled* words, if fortune throw them,
Shall, well as Dryden, form a poem. *Prior.*

Is it not a firmer foundation for tranquillity, to believe that all things were at first created, and are continually ordered for the best, than that the whole universe is mere bungling and blundering; all ill-favouredly cobled and *jumbled* together by the unguided agitation and rude shuffles of matter. *Bentley's Sermons.*

How tragedy and comedy embrace,
How farce and epick get a *jumbled* race. *Pope's Dunciad.*

That the universe was formed by a fortuitous concourse of atoms, I will no more believe, than that the accidental *jumbling* of the alphabet would fall into a most ingenious treatise of philosophy. *Swift.*

To JU'MBLE. *v. n.* To be agitated together.

They will all meet and *jumble* together into a perfect harmony. *Swift.*

JU'MBLE. *n. s.* [from the verb.] Confused mixture; violent and confused agitation.

Had the world been coagmented from that supposed fortuitous *jumble*, this hypothesis had been tolerable. *Glanville.*

What *jumble* here is made of ecclesiastical revenues, as if they were all alienated with equal justice. *Swift.*

JU'MENT. *n. s.* [*jument*, Fr. *jumentum*, Lat.] Beast of burthen.

Juments, as horses, oxen, and asses, have no eructation, or belching. *Brown's Vulgar Errours, b.* i.

To JUMP. *v. n.* [*gumpen*, Dutch.]

1. To leap; to skip; to move forward without step or sliding.

Not the worst of the three but *jumps* twelve foot and an half by the square. *Shakespeare's Winter's Tale.*

Here, upon this bank and shelve of time,
We'd *jump* the life to come. *Shakesp. Macbeth.*

The herd come *jumping* by me,
And fearless, quench their thirst, while I look on,
And take me for their fellow-citizen. *Dryden.*

So have I seen from Severn's brink
A flock of geese *jump* down together,
Swim where the bird of Jove would sink,
And swimming never wet a feather. *Swift.*

Candidates petition the emperor to entertain the court with a dance on the rope; and whoever *jumps* the highest succeeds in the office. *Gulliver's Travels.*

2. To

2. To leap ſuddenly.

One Peregrinus *jumped* into a fiery furnace at the Olympick games, only to ſhew the company how far his vanity could carry him. *Collier.*

We ſee a little, preſume a great deal, and ſo *jump* to the concluſion. *Spectator*, N°. 626.

3. To jolt.

The noiſe of the prancing horſes, and of the *jumping* chariots. *Nah.* iii. 2.

4. To agree; to tally; to join.

Do not embrace me till each circumſtance
Of place, time, fortune, do cohere and *jump*
That I am Viola. *Shakeſp. Twelfth Night.*

In ſome ſort it *jumps* with my humour. *Shakeſpeare.*

But though they *jump* not on a juſt account,
Yet do they all confirm a Turkiſh fleet. *Shakeſp. Othello.*

Becauſe I will not *jump* with common ſpirits,
And rank me with the barb'rous nations. *Shakeſpeare.*

Herein perchance he *jumps* not with Lipſius. *Hakewill.*

Never did truſty ſquire with knight,
Or knight with ſquire, e'er *jump* more right;
Their arms and equipage did fit,
As well as virtues, parts, and wit. *Hudibras, p.* i.

This ſhews how perfectly the rump
And commonwealth in nature *jump:*
For as a fly that goes to bed,
Reſts with his tail above his head;
So in this mungrel ſtate of ours,
The rabble are the ſupreme powers. *Hudibras, p.* iii.

Good wits *jump*, and mine the nimbler of the two. *More.*

Good now, how your devotions *jump* with mine. *Dryd.*

I am happier for finding our judgments *jump* in the notion. *Pope to Swift.*

JUMP. *adv.* Exactly; nicely. Obſolete.

Otherwiſe one man could not excel another, but all ſhould be either abſolutely good, as hitting *jump* that indiviſible point or center wherein goodneſs conſiſteth; or elſe miſſing it, they ſhould be excluded out of the number of well doers. *Hooker.*

But ſince ſo *jump* upon this bloody queſtion,
You from the Polack wars, and you from England,
Are here arriv'd. *Shakeſpeare's Hamlet.*

Myſelf the while to draw the Moor apart,
And bring him *jump*, when he may Caſſio find
Soliciting his wife. *Shakeſpeare's Othello.*

JUMP. *n. ſ.* [from the verb.]

1. The act of jumping; a leap; a ſkip.

The ſureſt way for a learner is, not to advance by *jumps* and large ſtrides; let that, which he ſets himſelf to learn next, be as nearly conjoined with what he knows already, as is poſſible. *Locke.*

2. A lucky chance.

Do not exceed
The preſcript of this ſcrowl: our fortune lies
Upon this *jump*. *Shakeſp. Antony and Cleopatra.*

3. [*Jupe*, French.] A waiſtcoat; a kind of looſe or limber ſtays worn by ſickly ladies.

The weeping caſſock ſcar'd into a *jump*,
A ſign the preſbyter's worn to the ſtump. *Cleaveland.*

JU'NCATE. *n. ſ.* [*juncade*, French; *gioncata*, Italian.]

1. Cheeſecake; a kind of ſweetmeat of curds and ſugar.

2. Any delicacy.

A goodly table of pure ivory,
All ſpread with *juncates*, fit to entertain
The greateſt prince. *Spenſer, Sonnet* 77.

With ſtories told of many a feat,
How fairy Mab the *juncates* eat. *Milton.*

3. A furtive or private entertainment. It is now improperly written *junket* in this ſenſe, which alone remains much in uſe. See JU'NKET.

JU'NCOUS. *adj.* [*junceus*, Lat.] Full of bulruſhes.

JU'NCTION. *n. ſ.* [*jonction*, French.] Union; coalition.

Upon the *junction* of the two corps, our ſpies diſcovered a great cloud of duſt. *Addiſon.*

JU'NCTURE. *n. ſ.* [*junctura*, Latin.]

1. The line at which two things are joined together.

Beſides thoſe groſſer elements of bodies, ſalt, ſulphur, and mercury, there may be ingredients of a more ſubtile nature, which being extremely little, may eſcape unheeded at the *junctures* of the diſtillatory veſſels, though never ſo carefully luted. *Boyle.*

2. Joint; articulation.

She has made the back-bone of ſeveral vertebræ, as being leſs in danger of breaking than if they were all one entire bone without thoſe griſtly *junctures*. *More.*

All other animals have tranſverſe bodies; and though ſome do raiſe themſelves upon their hinder legs to an upright poſture, yet they cannot endure it long, neither are the figures or *junctures*, or order of their bones, fitted to ſuch a poſture. *Hale's Originat. of Mankind.*

3. Union; amity.

Nor are the ſobereſt of them ſo apt for that devotional compliance and *juncture* of hearts, which I deſire to bear in thoſe holy offices to be performed with me. *K. Charles.*

4. A critical point or article of time.

By this profeſſion in that *juncture* of time, they bid farewel to all the pleaſures of this life. *Addiſon.*

When any law does not conduce to the publick ſafety, but in ſome extraordinary *junctures*, the very obſervation of it would endanger the community, that law ought to be laid aſleep. *Addiſon's Freeholder*, N°. 16.

JUNE. *n. ſ.* [*Juin*, Fr. *Junius*, Lat.] The ſixth month from January.

June is drawn in a mantle of dark green. *Peacham.*

JU'NIOR. *adj.* [*junior*, Lat.] One younger than another.

The fools my *juniors* by a year,
Are tortur'd with ſuſpenſe and fear,
Who wiſely thought my age a ſcreen,
When death approach'd to ſtand between. *Swift.*

According to the nature of men of years, I was repining at the riſe of my *juniors*, and unequal diſtribution of wealth. *Tatler*, N°. 100.

JU'NIPER. *n. ſ.* [*juniperus*, Lat.] A plant.

The leaves of the *juniper* are long, narrow, and prickly; the male flowers are, in ſome ſpecies, produced at remote diſtances from the fruit on the ſame tree; but in other ſpecies they are produced on different trees from the fruit: the firſt is a ſoft pulpy berry, containing three ſeeds in each. *Miller.*

Some of our common *juniper* ſhrubs are males and ſome females, of the ſame ſpecies. The male ſhrubs produce, in April and May, a ſmall kind of juli with apices on them, very large, and full of farina; the females produce none of theſe juli, but only the berries, which do not ripen till the ſecond year, and then do not immediately fall off; ſo that it is no uncommon thing to ſee the berries of three different years at once on the ſame tree. The ſhrub is very common with us on heaths and barren hills, but the berries uſed medicinally in our ſhops are brought from Germany, where it is greatly more abundant. The berries are powerful attenuants, diureticks, and carminative. *Hill.*

A clyſter may be made of the common decoctions, or of mallows, bay, and *juniper* berries, with oil of linſeed. *Wiſem.*

JUNK. *n. ſ.* [probably an Indian word.]

1. A ſmall ſhip of China.

America, which have now but *junks* and canoes, abounded then in tall ſhips. *Bacon's New Atlantis.*

2. Pieces of old cable. *Ainſ.*

JU'NKET. *n. ſ.* [properly *juncate*. See JUNCATE.]

1. A ſweetmeat.

You know, there wants no *junkets* at the feaſt. *Shakeſp.*

2. A ſtolen entertainment.

To JU'NKET. *v. n.* [from the noun.]

1. To feaſt ſecretly; to make entertainments by ſtealth.

Whatever good bits you can pilfer in the day, ſave them to *junket* with your fellow ſervants at night. *Swift.*

2. To feaſt.

Job's children *junketed* and feaſted together often, but the reckoning coſt them dear at laſt. *South's Sermons.*

The apoſtle would have no revelling or *junketing*. *South.*

JU'NTO. *n. ſ.* [Italian.] A cabal; a kind of men combined in any ſecret deſign.

Would men have ſpent toilſome days and watchful nights in the laborious queſt of knowledge preparative to this work, at length come and dance attendance for approbation upon a *junto* of petty tyrants, acted by party and prejudice, who denied fitneſs from learning, and grace from morality. *South.*

From this time began an intrigue between his majeſty and a *junto* of miniſters, which had like to have ended in my deſtruction. *Gulliver's Travels.*

I'VORY. *n. ſ.* [*ivoire*, French; *ebur*, Lat.]

Ivory is a hard, ſolid, and firm ſubſtance, of a fine white colour, and capable of a very good poliſh: it is the dens exertus of the elephant, who carries on each ſide of his jaws a tooth of ſix or ſeven feet in length, of the thickneſs of a man's thigh at the baſe, and almoſt entirely ſolid; the two ſometimes weighing three hundreed and thirty pounds: theſe *ivory* tuſks are hollow from the baſe to a certain height, and the cavity is filled with a compact medullary ſubſtance, ſeeming to have a great number of glands in it. The fineſt *ivory* is brought from the Eaſt-Indies, where great quantity of it is not taken immediately from the head of the animal, but found buried in the earth. The *ivory* of the iſlands of Ceylon and of Achem do not become yellow in the wearing as all other *ivory* does, and it therefore bears a greater price than of the Guinea coaſt. The preparations of *ivory* have the ſame reſtorative virtues with thoſe of the hartſhorn. *Hill.*

There is more difference between thy fleſh and hers, than between jet and *ivory*. *Shakeſp. Merchant of Venice.*

Draw Erato with a ſweet and lovely countenance, bearing a heart with an *ivory* key. *Peacham.*

From their *ivory* port the cherubim
Forth iſſu'd. *Milton.*

Two gates the ſilent houſe of ſleep adorn,
Of poliſh'd *iv'ry* this, that of tranſparent horn:
True viſions through tranſparent horn ariſe,
Through poliſh'd *iv'ry* paſs deluding lies. *Dryden's Æn.*

Juppo'n. *n. ſ.* [*juppon*, French.] A ſhort cloſe coat.
Some wore a breaſt-plate and a light *juppon*,
Their horſes cloath'd with rich capariſon. *Dryden.*

Ju'rat. *n. ſ.* [*juratus*, Lat. *jura juré*, Fr.] A magiſtrate in ſome corporations.

Ju'ratory, *adj.* [*juratoire*, Fr. *juro*, Lat.] Giving an oath.
A contumacious perſon may be compelled to give *juratory* caution *de parendo juri*. *Ayliffe's Parergon.*

Juri'dical. *adj.* [*juridicus*, Lat. *juridique*, Fr.]
1. Acting in the diſtribution of juſtice.
2. Uſed in courts of juſtice.
According to a *juridical* account and legal ſignification, time within memory, by the ſtatute of Weſtminſter, was ſettled in the beginning of the reign of king Richard the firſt. *Hale's Hiſt. of the Common Law of England.*

Juri'dically. *adj.* [from *juridical.*] With legal authority; according to forms of juſtice.

Ju'risconsult. *n. ſ.* [*juris conſultus*, Latin.] One who gives his opinion in caſes of law.
There is mention made, in a deciſion of the *juriſconſult* Javolemus, of a Britannick fleet. *Arbuthnot on Coins.*

Jurisdi'ction. *n. ſ.* [*juriſdictio*, Lat., *juriſdiction*, Fr.]
1. Legal authority; extent of power.
Sometimes the practice of ſuch *juriſdiction* may ſwerve through error even in the very beſt, and for other reſpects, where leſs integrity is. *Hooker, b.* v.
Without the king's aſſent or knowledge,
You wrought to be a legate; by which power
You maim'd the *juriſdiction* of all biſhops. *Shakeſpeare.*
All perſons exerciſing eccleſiaſtical *juriſdiction* ſhould have the king's arms in their ſeals of office. *Hayward.*
This place exempt
From heav'n's high *juriſdiction*. *Milton.*
As Adam had no ſuch power as gave him ſovereign *juriſdiction* over mankind. *Locke.*
This cuſtom in a popular ſtate, of impeaching particular men, may ſeem to be nothing elſe but the people's chuſing to exerciſe their own *juriſdiction* in perſon. *Swift.*
2. Diſtrict to which any authority extends.

Jurispru'dence. *n. ſ.* [*juriſprudence*, Fr. *juriſprudentia*, Lat.] The ſcience of law.

Ju'rist. *n. ſ.* [*juriſte*, Fr. *jura*, Lat.] A civil lawyer; a man who profeſſes the ſcience of the law; a civilian.
This is not to be meaſured by the principles of *juriſts*. *Bac.*

Ju'ror. *n. ſ.* [*juro*, Lat.] One that ſerves on the jury.
Were the *jurors* picked out of choice men, this would be as bad; for the evidence will be as deceitful as the verdict. *Spenſer's State of Ireland.*
I ſhall find your lordſhip judge and *juror*,
You are ſo merciful, I ſee your end,
'Tis my undoing. *Shakeſp. Henry* VIII.
I ſing no harm, good ſooth! to any wight,
Officer, jugler, or juſtice of peace,
Juror, or judge. *Donne.*
About noon the *jurors* went together, and becauſe they could not agree, they were ſhut in. *Hayward.*

Ju'ry. *n. ſ.* [*jurata*, Lat. *juré*, Fr.]
Jury, a company of men, as twenty-four or twelve, ſworn to deliver a truth upon ſuch evidence as ſhall be delivered them touching the matter in queſtion. There be three manners of trials in England: one by parliament, another by battle, and the third by aſſiſe or *jury*. The trial by aſſiſe, be the action civil or criminal, publick or private, perſonal or real, is referred for the fact to a *jury*, and as they find it, ſo paſſeth the judgment. This *jury* is uſed not only in circuits of juſtices errant, but alſo in other courts, and matters of office, as, if the eſcheatour make inquiſition in any thing touching his office, he doth it by a *jury* of inqueſt: if the coroner inquire how a ſubject found dead came to his end, he uſeth an inqueſt: the juſtices of peace in their quarter-ſeſſions, the ſheriff in his county and turn, the bailiff of a hundred, the ſteward of a court-leet or court-baron, if they inquire of any offence, or decide any cauſe between party and party, they do it by the ſame manner: ſo that where it is ſaid, that all things be triable by parliament, battle, or aſſize; aſſize, in this place, is taken for a *jury* or inqueſt, empanelled upon any cauſe in a court where this kind of trial is uſed. This *jury*, though it appertain to moſt courts of the common law, yet it is moſt notorious in the half year courts of the juſtices errants, commonly called the great aſſizes, and in the quarter-ſeſſions, and in them it is moſt ordinarily called a *jury*, and that in civil cauſes; whereas in other courts it is often termed an inqueſt. In the general aſſize, there are uſually many *juries*, becauſe there be ſtore of cauſes, both civil and criminal, commonly to be tried, whereof one is called the grand *jury*, and the reſt petit *juries*. The grand *jury* conſiſts ordinarily of twenty-four grave and ſubſtantial gentlemen, or ſome of them yeomen, choſen indifferently out of the whole ſhire by the ſheriff, to conſider of all bills of indictment preferred to the court; which they do either approve by writing upon them theſe words, *billa vera*, or diſallow by writing *ignoramus*. Such as they do approve, if they touch life and death, are farther referred to another *jury* to be conſidered of, becauſe the caſe is of ſuch importance; but others of lighter moment are, upon their allowance, without more work, fined by the bench, except the party traverſe the indictment, or challenge it for inſufficiency, or remove the cauſe to a higher court by *certiorari*; in which two former caſes it is referred to another *jury*, and in the latter tranſmitted to the higher. Thoſe that paſs upon civil cauſes real, are all, or ſo many as can conveniently be had, of the ſame hundred, where the land or tenement in queſtion doth lie, and four at the leaſt; and they, upon due examination, bring in their verdict either for the demandant or tenant: according unto which, judgment paſſeth afterward in the court where the cauſe firſt began; and the reaſon hereof is, becauſe theſe juſtices of aſſize are, in this caſe, for the eaſe of the countries only to take the verdict of the *jury* by the virtue of the writ called *niſi prius*, and ſo return it to the court where the cauſe is depending. *Cowell.*
The *jury*, paſſing on the priſoner's life,
May in the ſworn twelve have a thief or two
Guiltier than him they try. *Shakeſp. Meaſ. for Meaſure.*
How innocent I was,
His noble *jury* and foul cauſe can witneſs. *Shakeſp. H.* IV.
Clodius was acquitted by a corrupt *jury*, that had palpably taken ſhares of money before they gave up their verdict. *Bac.*

Ju'ryman. *n. ſ.* [*jury* and *man.*] One who is impannelled on a jury.
The hungry judges ſoon the ſentence ſign,
And wretches hang that *jurymen* may dine. *Pope.*
No judge was known, upon or off the bench, to uſe the leaſt inſinuation, that might affect the intereſts of any one ſingle *juryman*, much leſs of a whole jury. *Swift's Miſcel.*

Ju'rymast. *n. ſ.* So the ſeamen call whatever they ſet up in the room of a maſt loſt in a fight, or by a ſtorm; being ſome great yard which they put down into the ſtep of that loſt maſt, faſtening it into the partners, and fitting to it the miſſen or ſome leſſer yard with ſails and ropes, and with it make a hard ſhift to ſail. *Harris.*

JUST. *adj.* [*juſte*, Fr. *juſtus*, Latin.]
1. Upright; incorrupt; equitable in the diſtribution of juſtice.
Take it, while yet 'tis praiſe, before my rage
Unſafely *juſt*, break looſe on this bad age. *Dryden.*
2. Honeſt; without crime in dealing with others.
Juſt balances, *juſt* weights, and a *juſt* ephaph. *Lev.* xix.
Men are commonly ſo *juſt* to virtue and goodneſs, as to praiſe it in others, even when they do not practiſe it themſelves. *Tillotſon's Sermons.*
Juſt of thy word, in ev'ry thought ſincere,
Who knew no wiſh but what the world might hear. *Pope.*
3. Exact; proper; accurate.
Boileau's numbers are excellent, his expreſſions noble, his thoughts *juſt*, his language pure, his ſatyr pointed, and his ſenſe cloſe. *Dryden's Juv.*
Theſe ſcenes were wrought,
Embelliſh'd with good morals and *juſt* thought. *Granville.*
Juſt precepts thus from great examples giv'n,
She drew from them what they deriv'd from heav'n. *Pope.*
Juſt to the tale, as preſent at the fray,
Or taught the labours of the dreadful way. *Pope.*
Once on a time La Mancha's knight, they ſay,
A certain bard encount'ring on the way,
Diſcours'd in terms as *juſt*, with looks as ſage,
As ere could Dennis of the laws o' th' ſtage. *Pope.*
Though the ſyllogiſm be irregular, yet the inferences are *juſt* and true. *Watts's Logick.*
4. Virtuous; innocent; pure.
Noah was a *juſt* man, and perfect. *Gen.* vi. 9.
How ſhould man be *juſt* with God? *Job* ix. 2.
A *juſt* man falleth ſeven times and riſeth. *Prov.* xxiv. 16.
He ſhall be recompenſed at the reſurrection of the *juſt*. *Mat.* xiv. 14.
The juſt th' unjuſt to ſerve. *Milton.*
5. True; not forged; not falſely imputed; well grounded.
Crimes were laid to his charge too many, the leaſt whereof being *juſt*, had bereaved him of eſtimation and credit. *Hooker.*
Me though *juſt* right
Did firſt create your leader. *Milton.*
6. Equally retributed.
He received a *juſt* recompence of reward. *Heb.* ii. 2.
Whoſe damnation is *juſt*. *Rom.* iii. 8.
As Heſiod ſings, ſpread water o'er thy fields,
And a moſt *juſt* and glad increaſe it yields. *Denham.*
7. Complete without ſuperfluity or defect.
He was a comely perſonage, a little above *juſt* ſtature, well and ſtrait limbed, but ſlender. *Bacon's Henry* VII.
8. Regular; orderly.
When all
The war ſhall ſtand ranged in its *juſt* array,
And dreadful pomp; then will I think on thee. *Addiſon.*

9. Exactly proportioned.

The prince is here at hand: pleaseth your lordship
To meet his grace, *just* distance 'tween our armies? *Shak.*

10. Full; of full dimensions.

His soldiers had divers skirmishes with the Numidians, so that once the skirmish was like to have come to a *just* battle. *Knolles's History of the Turks.*

There is not any one particular abovementioned, but would take up the business of a *just* volume. *Hale's Orig. of Mank.*

There seldom appeared a *just* army in the civil wars. *Dutchess of Newcastle.*

11. Exact in retribution.

See nations slowly wise, and meanly *just*,
To bury'd merit raise the tardy bust. *Vanity of Human Wishes.*

JUST. *adv.*

1. Exactly; nicely; accurately.

The god Pan guided my hand *just* to the heart of the beast. *Sidney.*

They go about to make us believe that they are *just* of the same opinion, and that they only think such ceremonies are not to be used when they are unprofitable, or when as good or better may be established. *Hooker.*

There, ev'n *just* there he stood; and as she spoke,
Where last the spectre was, she cast her look. *Dryden.*

A few seem to understand him right; *just* as when our Saviour said, in an allegorical sense, except ye eat the flesh of the son of man, and drink his blood, ye have no life in you. *Bentley's Sermons.*

'Tis with our judgments as our watches, none
Go *just* alike; yet each believes his own. *Pope.*

2. Merely; barely.

It is the humour of weak and trifling men to value themselves upon *just* nothing at all. *L'Estrange.*

The nereids swam before
To smooth the seas; a soft etesian gale
But *just* inspir'd and gently swell'd the sail. *Dryden.*

Give me, ye gods, the product of one field,
That so I neither may be rich nor poor;
And having *just* enough, not covet more. *Dryden.*

3. Nearly.

Being spent with age, and *just* at the point of death, Democritus called for loaves of new bread to be brought, and with the steam of them under his nose prolonged his life. *Temple.*

JUST. *n. s.* [*jouste*, French.] Mock encounter on horseback; tilt; tournament.

None was either more grateful to the beholders, or more noble in itself, than *justs*, both with sword and launce. *Sidney.*

What news from Oxford? hold those *justs* and triumphs? *Shakespeare's Richard* II.

Among themselves the tourney they divide,
In equal squadrons rang'd on either side;
Then turn'd their horses heads, and man to man,
And steed to steed oppos'd, the *justs* began. *Dryden.*

To JUST. *v. n.* [*jouster*, French.]

1. To engage in a mock fight; to tilt.

2. To push; to drive; to justle.

JU'STICE. *n. s.* [*justice*, French; *justitia*, Latin.]

1. The virtue by which we give to every man what is his due.

O that I were judge, I would do *justice*. 2 *Sam.* xv. 4.

The king-becoming graces,
As *justice*, verity, temp'rance, stableness,
I have no relish of them. *Shakesp. Macbeth.*

The nature and office of *justice* being to dispose the mind to a constant and perpetual readiness to render to every man his due, it is evident, that if gratitude be a part of *justice*, it must be conversant about something that is due to another. *Loc.*

2. Vindicative retribution; punishment.

This shews you are above
Yon *justices*, that these our nether crimes
So speedily can venge. *Shakesp. King Lear.*

He executed the *justice* of the Lord. *Deut.* xxxiii. 21.

Lest *justice* overtake us. *Is.* lix. 9.

Examples of *justice* must be made, for terror to some; examples of mercy, for comfort to others: the one procures fear, and the other love. *Bacon's Advice to Villiers.*

3. Right; assertion of right.

Draw thy sword,
That if my speech offend a noble heart,
Thy arm may do thee *justice*. *Shakesp. King Lear.*

4. [*Justiciarius*, Lat.] One deputed by the king to do right by way of judgment. *Cowel.*

And thou, Esdras, ordain judges and *justices*, that they may judge in all Syria. 1 *Esdr.* viii. 23.

5. JU'STICE *of the King's Bench.* [*justiciarius de Banquo Regis.*] Is a lord by his office, and the chief of the rest; wherefore he is also called *capitalis justiciarius Angliæ*. His office especially is to hear and determine all pleas of the crown; that is, such as concern offences committed against the crown, dignity, and peace of the king; as treasons, felonies, mayhems, and such like: but it is come to pass, that he with his assistants heareth all personal actions, and real also, if they be incident to any personal action depending before them. *Cowel.*

Give that whipster his errand,
He'll take my lord chief *justice*' warrant. *Prior.*

6. JU'STICE *of the Common Pleas.* [*justiciarius Communium Placitorum.*] Is a lord by his office, and is called *dominus justiciarius communium placitorum.* He with his assistants originally did hear and determine all causes at the common law; that is, all civil causes between common persons, as well personal as real; for which cause it was called the court of common pleas, in opposition to the pleas of the crown, or the king's pleas, which are special, and appertaining to him only. *Cowel.*

7. JU'STICE *of the Forest.* [*justiciarius Forestæ.*] Is a lord by his office, and hath the hearing and determining of all offences within the king's forest, committed against venison or vert: of these there be two, whereof the one hath jurisdiction over all the forests on this side Trent, and the other of all beyond. *Cowel.*

8. JU'STICES *of Assise.* [*justiciarii ad capiendas Assisas.*] Are such as were wont, by special commission, to be sent into this or that country to take assises; the ground of which polity was the ease of the subjects: for whereas these actions pass always by jury, so many men might not, without great hinderance, be brought to London; and therefore justices, for this purpose, were by commission particularly authorised and sent down to them. *Cowel.*

9. JU'STICES *in Eyre.* [*justiciarii itinerantes.*] Are so termed of the French *erre*, *iter*. The use of these, in ancient time, was to send them with commission into divers counties, to hear such causes especially as were termed the pleas of the crown, and therefore I must imagine they were sent abroad for the ease of the subjects, who must else have been hurried to the king's bench, if the cause were too high for the country court. They differed from the justices of Oyer and Terminer, because they were sent upon some one or few especial cases, and to one place; whereas the justices in eyre were sent through the provinces and countries of the land, with more indefinite and general commission. *Cowel.*

10. JU'STICES *of Gaol Delivery.* [*justiciarii ad Gaolas deliberandas.*] Are such as are sent with commission to hear and determine all causes appertaining to such as for any offence are cast into gaol, part of whose authority is to punish such as let to mainprise those prisoners, that by law be not bailable. These by likelihood, in ancient time, were sent to countries upon several occasions; but afterward justices of assise were likewise authorised to this. *Cowel.*

11. JU'STICES *of Nisi Prius* are all one now-a-days with justices of assise; for it is a common adjournment of a cause, in the common pleas, to put it off to such a day: *nisi prius justiciarii venerint ad eas partes ad capiendas assisas*; and upon this clause of adjournment they are called justices of *nisi prius*, as well as justices of assise, by reason of the writ or action that they have to deal in. *Cowel.*

12. JU'STICES *of Peace.* [*justiciarii ad Pacem.*] Are they that are appointed by the king's commission, with others, to attend the peace of the country where they dwell; of whom some, upon especial respect, are made of the quorum, because some business of importance may not be dealt in without the presence of them, or one of them. *Cowel.*

The *justice*,
In fair round belly with good capon lin'd,
With eyes severe, and beard of formal cut,
Full of wise saws and modern instances,
And so he plays his part. *Shakes. As you like it.*

Thou hast appointed *justices* of the peace to call poor men before them, about matters they were not able to answer. *Shakespeare's Henry* VI.

The *justices* of peace are of great use: anciently they were conservators of the peace; these are the same, saving that several acts of parliament have enlarged their jurisdiction. *Bacon's Advice to Villiers.*

I sing no harm
To officer, juggler, or *justice* of peace. *Donne.*

To JU'STICE. *v. a.* [from the noun.] To administer justice to any. A word not in use.

As for the title of proscription, wherein the emperor hath been judge and party, and hath *justiced* himself, God forbid but that it should endure an appeal to a war. *Bacon.*

Whereas one Styward, a Scot, was apprehended, for intending to poison the young queen of Scots, the king delivered him to the French king, to be *justiced* by him at his pleasure. *Hayward.*

JU'STICEMENT. *n. s.* [from *justice.*] Procedure in courts.

JU'STICER. *n. s.* [from *To justice.*] Administrator of justice. An old word.

He was a singular good *justicer*; and if he had not died in the second year of his government, was the likeliest person to have reformed the English colonies. *Davies on Ireland.*

JU'STICESHIP. *n. s.* [from *justice.*] Rank or office of justice. *Swift.*

JUSTI'CIABLE. *adj.* [from *justice.*] Proper to be examined in courts of justice.

JU'STIFIABLE. *adj.* [from *justify.*] Defensible by law or reason; conformable to justice.

Just are the ways of God,
And *justifiable* to men. *Milton's Agonistes.*

Although some animals in the water do carry a *justifiable* resemblance to some at land, yet are the major part which bear their names unlike. *Brown's Vulgar Errours.*

JU'STIFIABLENESS. *n. s.* [from *justifiable.*] Rectitude; possibility of being fairly defended.

Men, jealous of the *justifiableness* of their doings before God, never think they have human strength enough. *King Charles.*

JU'STIFIABLY. *adv.* [from *justifiable.*] Rightly; so as to be supported by right.

A man may more *justifiably* throw cross and pile for his opinions, than take them up by such measures. *Locke.*

JUSTIFICA'TION. *n. s.* [*justification*, French; *justificatio*, low Latin.]

1. Defence; maintenance; vindication; support; absolution from guilt.

I hope, for my brother's *justification*, he wrote this but as an essay of my virtue. *Shakesp. King Lear.*

Among theological arguments, in *justification* of absolute obedience, was one of a singular nature. *Swift.*

2. Deliverance by pardon from sins past. *Clarke.*

In such righteousness
To them by faith imputed, they may find
Justification towards God, and peace
Of conscience. *Milton's Parad. Lost, b.* xii.

'Tis the consummation of that former act of faith by this latter, or, in the words of St. Paul and St. James, the consummation of faith by charity and good works, that God accepteth in Christ to *justification*, and not the bare aptness of faith to bring forth works, if those works, by the fault of a rebellious infidel, will not be brought forth. *Hammond.*

JUSTIFICA'TOR. *n. s.* [from *justify.*] One who supports, defends, vindicates, or justifies.

JU'STIFIER. *n. s.* [from *justify.*] One who justifies; one who defends or absolves; one who frees from sin by pardon.

That he might be just, and the *justifier* of him which believeth in Jesus. *Ro.* iii. 26.

To JU'STIFY. *v. a.* [*justifier*, French; *justifico*, low Latin.]

1. To clear from imputed guilt; to absolve from an accusation.

The law hath judg'd thee, Eleanor;
I cannot *justify*, whom law condemns. *Shakes. H.* VI.

They say, behold a man gluttonous, a friend of publicans and sinners; but wisdom is *justified* of her children. *Mat.* xi.

How can man be *justified* with God? Or how can he be clean that is born of a woman? *Job* xxv. 4.

There is an exquisite subtilty, and the same is unjust; and there is a wise man that *justifieth* in judgment. *Ecclus.* x. 25.

You're neither *justify'd*, nor yet accus'd. *Dryden.*

2. To maintain; to defend; to vindicate.

When we began in courteous manner to lay his unkindness unto him, he seeing himself confronted by so many, like a resolute orator, went not to denial, but to *justify* his cruel falshood. *Sidney.*

What she did, whatever in itself,
Her doing seem'd to *justify* the deed. *Milt. Par. Lost.*

My unwilling flight the gods inforce,
And that must *justify* our sad divorce. *Denham.*

Yet still thy fools shall stand in thy defence,
And *justify* their author's want of sense. *Dryden.*

Let others *justify* their missions as they can, we are sure we can *justify* that of our fathers by an uninterrupted succession. *Atterbury's Sermons.*

3. To free from past sin by pardon.

By him all that believe are *justified* from all things, from which ye could not be *justified* by the law of Moses. *Acts* xiii.

To JU'STLE. *v. n.* [from *just*, *jouster*, French.] To encounter; to clash; to rush against each other.

While injury of chance
Puts back leave-taking, *justles* roughly by
All time of pause, rudely beguiles our lips
Of all rejoindure. *Shakes. Troilus and Cressida.*

The chariots shall rage in the streets, they shall *justle* one against another in the broad ways. *Nah.* ii. 4.

Argo pass'd
Through Bosphorus, betwixt the *justling* rocks. *Milton.*

Late the clouds
Justling, or push'd with winds, rude in their shock,
Tine the slant lightning. *Milton's Paradise Lost.*

Not one starry spark,
But gods meet gods, and *justle* in the dark. *Lee.*

Courtiers therefore *justle* for a grant;
And, when they break their friendship, plead their want. *Dryden's Knight's Tale.*

Murmuring noises rise in every street;
The more remote run stumbling with their fear,
And, in the dark, men *justle* as they meet. *Dryden.*

When elephant 'gainst elephant did rear
His trunk, and castles *justled* in the air,
My sword thy way to victory had shown. *Dryden.*

Was there not one who had set bars and doors to it, and said hitherto shall thou come, but no farther, and here shall thy proud waves be staid; then might we well expect such vicissitudes, such *justlings* and clashings in nature. *Woodw.*

I thought the dean had been too proud
To *justle* here among a crowd. *Swift.*

To JU'STLE. *v. a.* To push; to drive; to force by rushing against it.

Private and single abilities should not *justle* out and deprive the church of the joint abilities of many learned and godly men. *King Charles.*

Many excellent strains have been *justled* off by their intrusions. *Brown's Vulgar Errours.*

The surly commons shall respect deny,
And *justle* peerage out with property. *Dryden.*

It is not to be imagined that the incongruous alphabets and abuses of writing can ever be *justled* out of their possession of all libraries. *Holder.*

Running in the dark, a man may *justle* a post. *Collier of the Eagerness of Desire.*

Absent good, though thought on, not making any part of unhappiness in its absence, is *justled* out, to make way for the removal of those uneasinesses we feel. *Locke.*

We *justled* one another out, and disputed the post for a great while. *Addison's Guardian.*

JU'STLY. *adv.* [from *just.*]

1. Uprightly; honestly; in a just manner.

Nothing can *justly* be despised, that cannot *justly* be blamed: where there is no choice, there can be no blame. *South.*

With ignominy scourg'd, in open sight:
Next view the Tarquin kings; th' avenging sword
Of Brutus *justly* drawn, and Rome restor'd. *Dryden.*

The goddess, studious of her Grecians fate,
Taught them in laws and letters to excel,
In acting *justly*, and in writing well. *Prior.*

2. Properly; exactly; accurately.

Their artful hands instruct the lute to sound,
Their feet assist their hands, and *justly* beat the ground. *Dryden.*

JU'STNESS. *n. s.* [from *just.*]

1. Justice; reasonableness; equity. *Justness* is properly applied to things, and *justice* to persons; though we now say the *justice* of a cause, as well as of a judge.

It maketh unto the right of the war against him, whose success useth commonly to be according to the *justness* of the cause for which it is made. *Spenser on Ireland.*

We may not think the *justness* of each act
Such and no other than event doth form it. *Shakespeare.*

2. Accuracy; exactness; propriety.

I value the satisfaction I had in seeing it represented with all the *justness* and gracefulness of action. *Dryden.*

I appeal to the people, was the usual saying of a very excellent dramatick poet, when he had any dispute with particular persons about the *justness* and regularity of his productions. *Addison's Guardian.*

To JUT. *v. n.* [This word is supposed to be corrupted from *jet*, perhaps from *shoot.*] To push or shoot into prominences; to come out beyond the main bulk.

Insulting tyranny begins to *jut*
Upon the innocent and awless throne. *Shakesp. R.* III.

All the projected or *jutting* parts should be very moderate, especially the cornices of the lower orders. *Wotton.*

The land, if not restrain'd, had met your way,
Projected out a neck, and *jutted* to the sea. *Dryden.*

A port secure for ships to ride,
Broke by the *jutting* land on either side;
In double streams the briny waters glide. *Dryden.*

It seems to *jut* out of the structure of the poem, and be independent of it. *Broome's Notes on the Odyssey.*

To JU'TTY. *v. a.* [from *jut.*] To shoot out beyond.

Then lend the eye a terrible aspect;
Let it pry through the portage of the head
Like a brass cannon: let the brow o'erwhelm it
As fearfully, as doth a galled rock
O'erhang and *jutty* his confounded base,
Swill'd with the wild and wasteful ocean. *Shakes. H.* V.

JU'VENILE. *adj.* [*juvenilis*, Latin.] Young; youthful.

Learning hath its infancy when it is almost childish; then its youth, when it is luxuriant and *juvenile*; then its strength of years, when it is solid; and lastly, its old age, when it waxeth dry and exhaust. *Bacon's Essays.*

JUVENI'LITY. *n. s.* [from *juvenile.*] Youthfulness.

The restauration of grey heirs to *juvenility*, and renewing the exhausted marrow, may be effected without a miracle. *Glanv. Sceps. c.* 21.

Customary strains and abstracted *juvenilities* have made it difficult to commend and speak credibly in dedications. *Glanv. Sceps. Preface.*

Ju'xtaposition. *n. s.* [*juxtaposition*, French; *juxta* and *positio*. Latin.] Apposition; the state of being placed by each other.

Nor can it be a difference, that the parts of solid bodies are held together by hooks, since the coherence of these will be of difficult conception; and we must either suppose an infinite number of them holding together, or at last come to parts that are united by a meer *juxtaposition*. *Glanv Sceps.*

I'vy. *n. s.* [ıꝼıᵹ, Saxon; *hedera*, Latin.] A plant.

The characters are: it is a parasitick plant, sending forth roots or fibres from its branches, by which it is fastened to either trees, walls, or plants which are near it, and from thence receives a great share of its nourishment: the leaves are angular; the flowers, for the most part, consist of six leaves, and are succeeded by round black berries, which grow in round bunches, each of which, for the most part, contains four seeds. *Miller.*

A gown made of the finest wool;
A belt of straw, and *ivy* buds,
With coral clasps and amber studs;
And if these pleasures may thee move,
Come live with me and be my love. *Raleigh.*

Direct
The clasping *ivy* where to climb. *Milt. Parad. Lost.*

Jy'mold. *adj.* [See Gimal.]

Their poor jades
Lob down their heads, dropping the hide and hips;
And in their pale dull mouths the *jymold* bit
Lies, foul with chew'd grass, still and motionless.
Shakespeare's Henry V.

K.

K.

K. A letter borrowed by the English from the Greek alphabet. It has before all the vowels one invariable ſound: as, *keen*, *ken*, *kill*; but is not much in uſe, except after *c* at the end of words: as, *knock*, *clock*, *crack*, *back*, *brick*, *ſtick*, *pluck*, *check*, which were written anciently with *e* final: as, *clocke*, *checke*, *tricke*. It is alſo in uſe between a vowel and the ſilent *e* final: as, *cloke*, *broke*, *brake*, *pike*, *duke*, *eke*. It likewiſe ends a word after a diphthong: as, *look*, *break*, *ſhock*, *beek*. The Engliſh never uſe *c* at the end of a word. *K* is ſilent in the preſent pronunciation before *n*: as, *knife*, *knee*, *knell*.

Ka'lendar. *n. ſ.* [now written *calendar*.] An account of time.

Let this pernicious hour
Stand as accurſed in the *kalendar*. *Shakeſpeare's Macbeth.*

Ka'li. *n. ſ.* [an Arabick word.] Sea-weed, of the aſhes of which glaſs was made, whence the word *alkali*.

The aſhes of the weed *kali* is ſold to the Venetians for their glaſs works. *Bacon.*

Kam. *adj.* Crooked.

Kam, in Erſe, is ſquint-eyed, and applied to any thing awry: clean *kam* ſignifies crooked, athwart, awry, croſs from the purpoſe. *A-ſchembo*, Italian, hence our Engliſh *a-kimbo*. Clean *kam* is, by vulgar pronunciation, brought to *kim kam*.

The blood he hath loſt, he dropt it for his country:
And what is left, to loſe it by his country,
Were to us all that do't and ſuffer it,
A brand to th' end o' th' world.
—This is clean *kam*.
—Meerly awry. *Shakeſpeare.*

To Kaw. *v. n.* [from the ſound.] To cry as a raven, crow, or rook. See Caw.

Jack-daws *kawing* and fluttering about the neſts, ſet all their young ones a gaping; but having nothing in their empty mouths but noiſe and air, leave them as hungry as before. *Locke.*

Kaw. *n. ſ.* [from the verb.] The cry of a raven or crow.

The daſtard crow that to the wood made wing,
With her loud *kaws* her craven-kind doth bring,
Who, ſafe in numbers, cuff the noble bird. *Dryden.*

Kayle. *n. ſ.* [*quille*, French.]

1. Ninepin; kettlepins, of which ſkittles ſeems a corruption.

And now at *keels* they try a harmleſs chance,
And now their cur they teach to fetch and dance. *Sidney.*

The reſidue of the time they wear out at coits, *kayles*, or the like idle exerciſes. *Carew's Survey of Cornwall.*

2. A kind of play ſtill retained in Scotland, in which nine holes ranged in three's are made in the ground, and an iron bullet rolled in among them.

To Keck. *v. n.* [*kecken*, Dutch.] To heave the ſtomach; to reach at vomiting.

All thoſe diets do dry up humours and rheums, which they firſt attenuate, and while the humour is attenuated it troubleth the body a great deal more; and therefore patients muſt not *keck* at them at the firſt. *Bacon's Nat. Hiſt.* N°. 68.

The faction, is it not notorious?
Keck at the memory of glorious. *Swift's Miſcel.*

To Ke'ckle *a cable*. To defend a cable round with rope. *Ainſworth.*

Ke'cksy. *n. ſ.* [commonly *kex*, *cigue*, French; *cicuta*, Latin. *Skinner.*] *Skinner* ſeems to think *keckſy* or *kex* the ſame as hemlock. It is uſed in Staffordſhire both for hemlock, and any other hollow jointed plant.

Nothing teems
But hateful docks, rough thiſtles, *keckſies*, burs,
Loſing both beauty and utility. *Shakeſp. Henry* V.

Ke'cky. *adj.* [from *kex*.] Reſembling a kex.

An Indian ſceptre, made of a ſort of cane, without any joint, and perfectly round, conſiſteth of hard and blackiſh cylinders, mixed with a ſoft *kecky* body; ſo as at the end cut tranſverſly, it looks as a bundle of wires. *Grew.*

To Kedge. *v. a.* [*kaghe*, a ſmall veſſel, Dutch.]

In bringing a ſhip up or down a narrow river, when the wind is contrary to the tide, they ſet the fore-ſail, or fore-top-ſail and mizzen, and ſo let her drive with the tide. The ſails are to flat her about, if ſhe comes too near the ſhore. They alſo carry out an anchor in the head of the boat, with a hawſer that comes from the ſhip; which anchor, if the ſhip comes too near the ſhore, they let fall in the ſtream, and ſo wind her head about it; then weigh the anchor again when ſhe is about, which is called *kedging*, and from this uſe the anchor a kedger. *Harris.*

Ke'dger. *n. ſ.* [from *kedge*.] A ſmall anchor uſed in a river. See Kedge.

Kee, the provincial plural of *cow*, properly *kine*.

A laſs that Cic'ly hight had won his heart,
Cic'ly the weſtern laſs that tends the *kee*. *Gay's Paſt.*

Ke'dlack. *n. ſ.* A weed that grows among corn; charnock. *Tuſſer.*

Keel. *n. ſ.* [cœle, Saxon; *kiel*, Dutch; *quille*, Fr.] The bottom of the ſhip.

Portunus
Heav'd up his lighten'd *keel*, and ſunk the ſand,
And ſteer'd the ſacred veſſel. *Dryden.*

Her ſharp bill ſerves for a *keel* to cut the air before her; her tail ſhe uſeth as her rudder. *Grew's Coſmol. b.* i.

Your cables burſt, and you muſt quickly feel
The waves impetuous ent'ring at your *keel*. *Swift.*

Keels, the ſame with *kayles*, which ſee.

To Keel. *v. a.* [cælan, Saxon.] This word, which is preſerved in *Shakeſpeare*, probably ſignifies *to cool*, though *Hanmer* explains it otherwiſe.

To *keel* ſeems to mean to drink ſo deep as to turn up the bottom of the pot, like turning up the *keel* of a ſhip. *Hanmer.*

While greaſy Joan doth *keel* the pot. *Shakeſpeare.*

Ke'elfat. *n. ſ.* [cœlan, Saxon, *to cool*, and *fat* or *vat*, a veſſel.] Cooler; tub in which liquor is let to cool.

Ke'elson. *n. ſ.* The next piece of timber in a ſhip to her keel, lying right over it next above the floor timber. *Harris.*

To Ke'elhale. *v. a.* [*keel* and *hale*.] To puniſh in the ſeamens way, by dragging the criminal under water on one ſide of the ſhip and up again on the other.

Keen. *adj.* [cene, Saxon; *kuhn*, German; *koen*, Dutch.]

1. Sharp; well edged; not blunt.

Come thick night
That my *keen* knife ſee not the wound it makes. *Shakeſp.*
Here is my *keen*-edged ſword,
Deck'd with fine flower-de-luces on each ſide. *Shakeſp.*
To me the cries of fighting fields are charms,
Keen be my ſabre, and of proof my arms. *Dryden.*
A ſword *keen*-edg'd within his right he held,
The warlike emblem of the conquer'd field. *Dryden.*

2. Severe; piercing.

The winds
Blow moiſt, and *keen*, ſhattering the graceful locks
Of theſe fair ſpreading trees; which bids us ſeek
Some better ſhroud. *Milton's Par. Loſt, b.* x.

The cold was very ſupportable; but as it changed to the north-weſt, or north, it became exceſſively *keen*. *Ellis.*

3. Eager; vehement.

Never did I know
A creature, that did bear the ſhape of man,
So *keen* and greedy to confound a man. *Shakeſpeare.*
Keen diſpatch of real hunger. *Milton.*

The ſheep were ſo *keen* upon the acrons, that they gobbled up a piece of the coat. *L'Eſtrange.*

Thoſe curs are ſo extremely hungry, that they are too *keen* at the ſport, and worry their game. *Tatler*, N°. 62.

This was a proſpect ſo very inviting, that it could not be eaſily withſtood by any who have ſo *keen* an appetite for wealth. *Swift's Miſcel.*

4. Acrimonious; bitter of mind.

Good father cardinal, cry thou, amen,
To my *keen* curses. *Shakesp. King John.*

I have known some of these absent officers as *keen* against Ireland, as if they had never been indebted to her. *Swift.*

To KEEN. *v. a.* [from the adjective.] To sharpen. An unauthorised word.

Nor when cold Winter *keens* the brightening flood,
Wou'd I weak shivering linger on the brink. *Thomson.*

KE'ENLY. *adj.* [from *keen.*] Sharply; vehemently; eagerly; bitterly.

KE'ENNESS. *n. s.* [from *keen.*]

1. Sharpness; edge.

No, not the hangman's ax bears half the *keenness*
Of thy sharp envy. *Shakesp. Merchant of Venice.*

2. Rigor of weather; piercing cold.

3. Asperity; bitterness of mind.

That they might keep up the *keenness* against the court, till the coming together of both houses, his lordship furnished them with informations, which might be wrested to the king's disadvantage. *Clarendon.*

The sting of every reproachful speech is the truth of it; and to be conscious is that which gives an edge, and *keenness* to the invective. *South's Sermons.*

4. Eagerness; vehemence.

To KEEP. *v. a.* [cepan, Saxon; *kepen*, old Dutch.]

1. To retain; not to lose.

I *kept* the field with the death of some, and flight of others. *Sidney, b.* ii.

We have examples in the primitive church of such as by fear being compelled to sacrifice to strange gods repented, and *kept* still the office of preaching the gospel. *Whitgift.*

Keep in memory what I preached unto you. 1 *Cor.* xv. 2.

This charge I *keep* till my appointed day
Of rend'ring up. *Milton.*

His loyalty he *kept*, his love, his zeal. *Milton.*

You have lost a child; but you have kept one child, and are likely to do so long. *Temple's Miscel.*

If we would weigh, and *keep* in our minds, what we are considering, that would instruct us when we should, or should not, branch into distinctions. *Locke.*

2. To have in custody.

The crown of Stephanus, first king of Hungary, was always *kept* in the castle of Vicegrade. *Knolles.*

She *kept* the fatal key. *Milton.*

3. To preserve; not to let go.

These men of war that could *keep* rank, came with a perfect heart to Hebron. 1 *Chron.* xii. 38.

The Lord God merciful and gracious, *keeping* mercy for thousands, forgiving iniquity. *Exod.* xxxiv. 7.

I spared it greatly, and have *kept* me a grape of the cluster, and a plant of a great people. 2 *Esdr.* ix. 21.

4. To preserve in a state of security.

We passed by where the duke *keeps* his gallies. *Addison.*

5. To protect; to guard.

Behold I am with thee to *keep* thee. *Gen.* xxviii.

6. To guard from flight.

Paul dwelt with a soldier that *kept* him. *Acts* xxviii. 16.

7. To detain.

But what's the cause that *keeps* you here with me?
—That I may know what *keeps* me here with you. *Dryden.*

8. To hold for another.

A man delivers money or stuff to *keep.* *Exod.* xxii. 7.

Reserv'd from night, and *kept* for thee in store. *Milton.*

9. To reserve; to conceal.

Some are so close and reserved, as they will not shew their wares but by a dark light; and seem always to *keep* back somewhat. *Bacon's Essays*, N°. 27.

10. To tend.

God put him in the garden of Eden to *keep* it. *Gen.* ii. 15.

While in her girlish age she *kept* sheep on the moor, it chanced that a merchant saw and liked her. *Carew.*

Count it thine
To till and *keep*, and of the fruit to eat. *Milton.*

11. To preserve in the same tenour or state.

To know the true state, I will *keep* this order. *Bacon.*

Take this at least, this last advice my son,
Keep a stiff rein, and move but gently on:
The coursers of themselves will run too fast,
Your art must be to moderate their haste. *Addison's Ovid.*

12. To regard; to attend.

While the stars and course of heav'n I *keep*,
My weary'd eyes were seiz'd with fatal sleep. *Dryden.*

If that idea be steadily *kept* to, the distinction will easily be conceived. *Locke.*

13. To not suffer to fail.

My mercy will I *keep* for him for ever. *Psal.* lxxxix.

Shall truth fail to *keep* her word? *Milton.*

14. To hold in any state.

Ingenuous shame, and the apprehensions of displeasure, are the only true restraints: these alone ought to hold the reins, and *keep* the child in order. *Locke on Education.*

Men are guilty of many faults in the exercise of this faculty of the mind, which *keep* them in ignorance. *Locke.*

Happy souls! who *keep* such a sacred dominion over their inferior and animal powers, that the sensitive tumults never rise to disturb the superior and better operations of the reasoning mind. *Watts's Improvement of the Mind.*

15. To retain by some degree of force in any place or state.

Plexirtus, said he, this wickedness is found by thee; no good deeds of mine have been able to *keep* it down in thee. *Sidney, b.* ii.

It is hardly to be thought that any governor should so much malign his successor, as to suffer an evil to grow up which he might timely have *kept* under; or perhaps nourish it with coloured countenance of such sinister means. *Spenser.*

What old acquaintance! could not all this flesh
Keep in a little life? Poor Jack, farewel. *Shakespeare.*

Venus took the guard of noble Hector's corse,
And *kept* the dogs off: night and day applying sovereign force
Of rosy balms, that to the dogs were horrible in taste. *Chapman's Iliad.*

The Chinese sail where they will; which sheweth that their law of *keeping* out strangers is a law of pusillanimity and fear. *Bacon's New Atlantis.*

And those that cannot live from him asunder,
Ungratefully shall strive to *keep* him under. *Milton.*

If any ask me what wou'd satisfy,
To make life easy, thus I would reply:
As much as *keeps* out hunger, thirst, and cold. *Dryden.*

Matters, recommended by our passions, take possession of our minds, and will not be *kept* out. *Locke.*

Prohibited commodities should be *kept* out, and useless ones impoverish us by being brought in. *Locke.*

An officer with one of these unbecoming qualities, is looked upon as a proper person to *keep* off impertinence and solicitation from his superior. *Addison's Spectator.*

And if two boots *keep* out the weather,
What need you have two hides of leather. *Prior.*

We have it in our power to *keep* in our breaths, and to suspend the efficacy of this natural function. *Cheyne.*

16. To continue any state or action.

The house of Ahaziah had no power to *keep* still the kingdom. 2 *Chron.* xxii. 9.

Men gave ear, waited, and *kept* silence at my counsel. *Job* xxix. 21.

Auria made no stay, but still *kept* on his course, and with a fair gale came directly towards Carone. *Knolles.*

It was then such a calm, that the ships were not able to *keep* way with the gallies. *Knolles's Hist. of the Turks.*

The moon that distance *keeps* till night. *Milton.*

An heap of ants on a hillock will more easily be *kept* to an uniformity in motion than these. *Glanville's Scep.*

He dy'd in fight:
Fought next my person; as in consort fought:
Kept pace for pace, and blow for blow. *Dryden.*

He, being come to the estate, *keeps* on a very busy family; the markets are weekly frequented, and the commodities of his farm carried out and sold. *Locke.*

Invading foes, without resistance,
With ease I make to *keep* their distance. *Swift.*

17. To preserve in any state.

My son, *keep* the flower of thine age sound. *Ecclus.* xxvi.

18. To practise; to use habitually.

I rule the family very ill, and *keep* bad hours. *Pope.*

19. To copy carefully.

Her servants eyes were fix'd upon her face,
And as she mov'd or turn'd, her motions view'd,
Her measures *kept*, and step by step pursu'd. *Dryden.*

20. To observe any time.

This shall be for a memorial; and you shall *keep* it a feast to the Lord. *Exod.* xii. 14.

That day was not in silence holy *kept.* *Milton.*

21. To observe; not to violate.

It cannot be,
The king should *keep* his word in loving us;
He will suspect us still, and find a time
To punish this offence in other faults. *Shakespeare.*

Sworn for three years term to live with me,
My fellow scholars; and to *keep* those statutes
That are recorded in this schedule here. *Shakespeare.*

Lord God, there is none like thee: who *keepest* covenant and mercy with thy servants. 1 *Kings* viii. 23.

Lord God of Israel, *keep* with thy servant that thou promisedst him. 1 *Kings* viii. 25.

Obey and *keep* his great command. *Milton.*

His promise Palamon accepts; but pray'd
To *keep* it better than the first he made. *Dryden.*

My debtors do not *keep* their day,
Deny their hands and then refuse to pay. *Dryden's Juv.*

My wishes are,
That Ptolemy may *keep* his royal word. *Dryden.*

22. To maintain; to support with necessaries of life.
Much more affliction than already felt
They cannot well impose, nor I sustain,
If they intend advantage of my labours,
The work of many hands, which earns my *keeping*. *Milt.*

23. To have in the house.
Base tyke, call'st thou me host? I scorn the term; nor shall my Nell *keep* lodgers. *Shakespeare's Henry* V.

24. Not to intermit.
Keep a sure watch over a shameless daughter, lest she make thee a laughing-stock to thine enemies, and a bye-word in the city. *Ecclus.* xli. 11.
Not *keeping* strictest watch as she was warn'd. *Milton.*

25. To maintain; to hold.
They were honourably brought to London, where every one of them *kept* house by himself. *Hayward.*
Twelve Spartan virgins, noble, young, and fair,
To the pompous palace did resort;
Where Menelaus *kept* his royal court. *Dryden.*

26. To remain in; not to leave a place.
I pry'thee, tell me, doth he *keep* his bed. *Shakespeare.*

27. Not to reveal; not to betray.
A fool cannot *keep* counsel. *Ecclus.* viii. 17.
Great are thy virtues, though *kept* from man. *Milton.*
If he were wise, he would *keep* all this to himself. *Tillots.*

28. To restrain; to with-hold.
If any rebel or vain spirit of mine
Did, with the least affection of a welcome,
Give entertainment to the might of it;
Let heav'n for ever *keep* it from my head. *Shakespeare.*
Some obscure passages in the inspir'd volume *keep* from the knowledge of divine mysteries. *Boyle on Scripture.*
If the God of this world did not blind their eyes, it would be impossible, so long as men love themselves, to *keep* them from being religious. *Tillotson's Sermons.*
There is no virtue children should be excited to, nor fault they should be *kept* from, which they may not be convinced of by reasons. *Locke on Education.*
If a child be constantly *kept* from drinking cold liquor whilst he is hot, the custom of forbearing will preserve him. *Locke.*
By this they may *keep* them from little faults. *Locke.*

29. To debar from any place.
Ill fenc'd for heav'n to *keep* out such a foe. *Milton.*

30. *To* KEEP *back.* To reserve; to with-hold.
Whatsoever the Lord shall answer, I will declare: I will *keep* nothing *back* from you. *Jer.* xlii. 4.

31. *To* KEEP *back.* To with-hold; to restrain.
Keek back thy servant from presumptuous sins. *Psal.* xix.

32. *To* KEEP *company.* To frequent any one; to accompany.
Heav'n doth know, so shall the world perceive,
That I have turn'd away my former self,
So will I those that *kept* me *company.* *Shakesp. Henry* IV.
Why should he call her whore? Who *keeps* her *company?*
What place? what time? *Shakesp. Othello.*
What mean'st thou, bride! this *company* to *keep?*
To sit up, till thou fain would sleep? *Donne.*
Neither will I wretched thee
In death forsake, but *keep* thee *company.* *Dryden.*

33. *To* KEEP *company with.* To have familiar intercourse.
A virtuous woman is obliged not only to avoid immodesty, but the appearance of it; and she could not approve of a young woman *keeping company with* men, without the permission of father or mother. *Broome's Notes on the Odyssey.*

34. *To* KEEP *in.* To conceal; not to tell.
I perceive in you so excellent a touch of modesty, that you will not extort from me what I am willing to *keep in.* *Shak.*
Syphax, your zeal becomes importunate:
I've hitherto permitted it to rave,
And talk at large; but learn to *keep* it *in,*
Lest it should take more freedom than I'll give it. *Addison.*

35. *To* KEEP *in.* To restrain; to curb.
If thy daughter be shameless, *keep* her *in* straightly, lest she abuse herself through over-much liberty. *Ecclus.* xxvi. 13.
It will teach them to *keep in,* and so master their inclinations. *Locke on Education.*

36. *To* KEEP *off.* To bear to distance; not to admit.

37. *To* KEEP *off.* To hinder.
A superficial reading, accompanied with the common opinion of his invincible obscurity, has *kept off* some from seeking in him the coherence of his discourse. *Locke.*

38. *To* KEEP *up.* To maintain without abatement.
Land *kept up* its price, and sold for more years purchase than corresponded to the interest of money. *Locke.*
This restraint of their tongues will *keep up* in them the respect and reverence due to their parents. *Locke.*
Albano *keeps up* its credit still for wine. *Addison.*
This dangerous dissension among us we *keep up* and cherish with much pains. *Addison's Freeholder,* N°. 34.
The ancients were careful to coin money in due weight and fineness, and *keep it up* to the standard. *Arbuthnot.*

39. *To* KEEP *up.* To continue; to hinder from ceasing.
You have enough to keep you alive, and to *keep up* and improve your hopes of heaven. *Taylor's holy living.*
In joy, that which *keeps up* the action is the desire to continue it. *Locke.*
Young heirs, from their own reflecting upon the estates they are born to, are of no use but to *keep up* their families, and transmit their lands and houses in a line to posterity. *Addison's Spect.* N°. 123.
During his studies and travels he *kept up* a punctual correspondence with Eudoxus. *Addison.*

40. *To* KEEP *under.* To oppress; to subdue.
O happy mixture! whereby things contrary do so qualify and correct the one the danger of the other's excess, that neither boldness can make us presume, as long as we are *kept under* with the sense of our own wretchedness; nor, while we trust in the mercy of God through Christ Jesus, fear be able to tyrannize over us. *Hooker, b.* v.
Truth may be smothered a long time, and *kept under* by violence; but it will break out at last. *Stillingfleet.*
To live like those that have their hope in another life, implies, that we *keep under* our appetites, and do not let them loose into the enjoyments of sense. *Atterbury's Sermons.*

To KEEP. *v. n.*

1. To remain by some labour or effort in a certain state.
With all our force we *kept* aloof to sea,
And gain'd the island where our vessels lay. *Pope's Odys.*
A man that cannot fence will *keep* out of bullies and gamesters company. *Locke on Education.*

2. To continue in any place or state; to stay.
She would give her a lesson for walking so late, that should make her *keep* within doors for one fortnight. *Sidney.*
What! *keep* a week away? seven days and nights?
Eightscore hours? and lovers absent hours.
Oh weary reckoning. *Shakespeare's Othello.*
I think, it is our way,
If we will *keep* in favour with the king,
To be her men, and wear her livery. *Shakesp. Rich.* III.
Thou shalt *keep* fast by my young men, until they have ended. *Ruth* ii. 21.
The necessity of *keeping* well with the maritime powers, will persuade them to follow our measures. *Temple.*
On my better hand Ascanius hung,
And with unequal paces tript along:
Creusa *kept* behind. *Dryden's Æneis.*
The goddess born in secret pin'd;
Nor visited the camp, nor in the council join'd;
But *keeping* close, his gnawing heart he fed
With hopes of vengeance. *Dryden's Homer.*
And while it *keeps* there, it *keeps* within our author's limitation. *Locke.*
There are cases in which a man must guard, if he intends to *keep* fair with the world, and turn the penny. *Collier.*
The endeavours Achilles used to meet with Hector, the contrary endeavours of the Trojan to *keep* out of reach are the intrigue. *Pope's View of Epick Poetry.*

3. To remain unhurt; to last.
Disdain me not, although I be not fair:
Doth beauty *keep* which never sun can burn,
Nor storms do turn? *Sidney, b.* i.
Grapes will *keep* in a vessel half full of wine, so that the grapes touch not the wine. *Bacon's Nat. Hist.*
If the malt be not thoroughly dried, the ale it makes will not *keep.* *Mortimer's Husbandry.*

4. To dwell; to live constantly.
A breath thou art,
Servile to all the skiey influences,
That do this habitation, where thou *keep'st,*
Hourly afflict. *Shakesp. Measure for Measure.*
Knock at the study, where, they say, he *keeps,*
To ruminate strange plots of dire revenge. *Shakespeare.*

5. To adhere strictly.
Did they *keep* to one constant dress they would sometimes be in fashion, which they never are. *Addison's Spect.*
It is so whilst we *keep* to our rule; but when we forsake that, we go astray. *Baker's Reflections on Learning.*

6. *To* KEEP *on.* To go forward.
So chearfully he took the doom;
Nor shrunk, nor stept from death,
But, with unalter'd pace, *kept on.* *Dryden.*

7. *To* KEEP *up.* To continue undismayed.
He grew sick of a consumption; yet he still *kept up,* that he might free his country. *Dryden's Life of Cleomenes.*

8. The general idea of this word is care, continuance, or duration.

KEEP. *n. s.* [from the verb.]

1. Custody; guard.
Pan, thou god of shepherds all,
Which of our lambkins takest *keep;*
And when our flocks into mischance doth fall,
Doest save from mischief the unwary sheep. *Spenser.*

The prison strong,
Within whose *keep* the captive knights were laid:
Was one partition of the palace-wall. *Dryden.*

2. Guardianship; restraint.

Youth is least looked into when they stand in most need of good *keep* and regard. *Ascham.*

KE'EPER. *n. s.* [from *keep.*]

1. One who holds any thing for the use of another.

The good old man having neither reason to dissuade, nor hopes to persuade, received the things with the mind of a *keeper*, not of an owner. *Sidney.*

2. One who has prisoners in custody.

The *keeper* of the prison, call to him. *Shakespeare.*

Io now
With horns exalted stands, and seems to lowe:
A noble charge; her **keeper** by her side
To watch her walks his hundred eyes apply'd. *Dryden.*

A pleasant beverage he prepar'd before,
Of wine and water mix'd, with added store
Of opium; to his *keeper* this he brought,
Who swallowed unaware the sleepy draught. *Dryden.*

3. One who has the care of parks, or beasts of chase.

There is an old tale goes, that Herne the hunter,
Sometime a *keeper* here in Windsor forest,
Doth all the Winter-time, at still of midnight,
Walk round about an oak with ragged horns. *Shakesp.*

The first fat buck of all the season's sent,
And *keeper* takes no fee in compliment. *Dryden.*

4. One that has the superintendence or care of any thing.

Hilkiah went unto Hildah, *keeper* of the wardrobe. 2 *King.*

KE'EPER *of the great seal.* [*custos magni sigilli*, Latin.] Is a lord by his office, and called lord *keeper* of the great seal of England, *&c.* and is of the king's privy-council, under whose hands pass all charters, commissions, and grants of the king, strengthened by the great or broad seal, without which seal all such instruments by law are of no force; for the king is, in interpretation and intendment of law, a corporation, and therefore passeth nothing firmly, but under the great seal. This lord *keeper*, by the statute of 5 Eliz. c. 18. hath the like jurisdiction, and all other advantages, as hath the lord chancellor of England. *Cowell.*

KE'EPERSHIP. *n. s.* [from *keeper.*] Office of a keeper.

The common gaol of the shire is kept at Launceston: this *keepership* is annexed to the constableship of the castle. *Carew's Survey of Cornwall.*

KEG. *n. s.* [*caque*, French.] A small barrel, commonly used for a fish barrel.

KELL. *n. s.* A sort of pottage. *Ainsf.* It is so called in Scotland, being a soupe made with shreded greens.

KELL. *n. s.* The omentum; that which inwraps the guts.

The very weight of bowels and *kell*, in fat people, is the occasion of a rupture. *Wiseman's Surgery.*

KELP. *n. s.* A salt produced from calcined sea-weed.

In making alum, the workmen use the ashes of a sea-weed called *kelp*, and urine. *Boyle on Colours.*

KE'LSON. *n. s.* [more properly *keelson.*] The wood next the keel.

We have added close pillars in the royal ships, which being fastened from the *kelson* to the beams of the second deck, keep them from settling, or giving way. *Raleigh.*

KE'LTER. *n. s.* [He is not in *kelter*, that is, he is not ready; from *kilter*, to gird, Danish. *Skinner.*]

To KEMB. *v. a.* [cœmban, Saxon; *kammen*, German: now written, perhaps less properly, *to comb.*] To separate or disentangle by a denticulated instrument.

Yet are the men more loose than they,
More *kemb'd* and bath'd, and rubb'd and trim'd,
More sleek. *Benj. Johnson.*

Thy head and hair are sleek;
And then thou *kemb'st* the tuzzes on thy cheek. *Dryden.*

To KEN. *v. a.* [cennan, Saxon; *kennan*, Dutch, to know.]

1. To see at a distance; to descry.

At once as far as angels *ken*, he views
The dismal situation, waste and wild. *Milton's Par. Lost.*

The next day about evening we saw, within a *kenning*, before us thick clouds, which did put us in some hope of land. *Bacon's New Atlantis.*

If thou *ken'st* from far,
Among the Pleiads, a new-kindled star;
'Tis she that shines in that propitious light. *Dryden.*

We *ken* them from afar, the setting sun
Plays on their shining arms. *Addison.*

2. To know.

'Tis he, I *ken* the manner of his gate. *Shakesp.*

Now plain I *ken* whence love his rise begun:
Sure he was born some bloody butcher's son,
Bred up in shambles. *Gay's Past.*

KEN. *n. s.* [from the verb.] View; reach of sight.

Lo! within a *ken*, our army lies. *Shakesp. Henry* IV.

When from the mountain top Pisanio shew'd thee,
Thou wast within a *ken*. *Shakesp. Cymbeline.*

It was a hill
Of paradise the highest; from whose top
The hemisphere of earth, in clearest *ken*,
Stretch'd out to th' amplest reach of prospect, lay. *Milton.*

He soon
Saw within *ken* a glorious angel stand. *Milton.*

Rude, as their ships, was navigation then;
No useful compass or meridian known:
Coasting they kept the land within their *ken*,
And knew the North but when the pole-star shone. *Dryd.*

When we consider the reasons we have to think, that what lies within our *ken* is but a small part of the universe, we shall discover an huge abyss of ignorance. *Locke.*

KE'NNEL. *n. s.* [*chenil*, French.]

1. A cot for dogs.

A dog sure, if he could speak, had wit enough to describe his *kennel*. *Sidney.*

From forth the *kennel* of thy womb hath crept
A hell-hound, that doth hunt us all to death. *Shakesp.*

The seditious remain within their station, which, by reason of the nastiness of the beastly multitude, might be more fitly termed a *kennel* than a camp. *Hayward.*

2. A number of dogs kept in a kennel.

A little herd of England's tim'rous deer,
Maz'd with a yelping *kennel* of French curs. *Shakespeare.*

3. The hole of a fox, or other beast.

4. [*Kennel*, Dutch; *chenal*, Fr. *canalis*, Latin.] The watercourse of a street.

Bad humours gather to a a bile; or, as divers *kennels* flow to one sink, so in short time their numbers increased. *Hayw.*

He always came in so dirty, as if he had been dragged through the *kennel* at a boarding-school. *Arbuthnot.*

To KE'NNEL. *v. n.* [from *kennel.*] To lie; to dwell: used of beasts, and of man in contempt.

Yet, when they list, would creep,
If ought disturb'd their noise, into her womb,
And *kennel* there; yet there still bark'd and howl'd
Within, unseen. *Milton's Par. Lost, b.* ii.

The dog *kennelled* in a hollow tree, and the cock roosted upon the boughs. *L'Estrange's Fables.*

KEPT. pret. and part. pass. of *keep.*

KERCHE'IF. *n. s.* [*covrecheif*, *Chaucer*; *couvre*, to cover, and *chef*, the head; and hence a handkercheif to wipe the face or hands.]

1. A head dress.

I see how thine eye would emulate the diamond; thou hast the right arched bent of the brow, that becomes the tire vailant.

—A plain *kerchief*, Sir John; my brows become nothing else. *Shakesp. Merry Wives of Windsor.*

The proudest *kerchief* of the court shall rest
Well satisfy'd of what they love the best. *Dryden.*

2. Any cloath used in dress.

O! what a time have you chose out, brave Caius,
To wear a *kerchief*. *Shakesp. Julius Cæsar.*

Every man had a large *kercheif* folded about the neck. *Hayward.*

KERCHE'IFED. }
KERCHE'IFT. } *adj.* [from *kercheif.*] Dressed; hooded.

The evening comes
Kercheift in a comely cloud,
While racking winds are piping loud. *Milton.*

KERF. *n. s.* [ceorfan, Saxon, *to cut.*]

The sawn-away slit between two pieces of stuff is called a *kerf*. *Moxon's Mech. Exercise.*

KE'RMES. *n. s.*

Kermes is a roundish body, of the bigness of a pea, and of a brownish red colour, covered when most perfect with a purplish grey dust. It contains a multitude of little distinct granules, soft, and when crushed yield a scarlet juice. It is found adhering to a kind of holm oak, and till lately was generally understood to be a vegetable excrescence; but we now know it to be the extended body of an animal parent, filled with a numerous offspring, which are the little red granules. *Hill.*

KERN. *n. s.* [an Irish word.] Irish foot soldier; an Irish boor.

Out of the fry of these rake-hell horseboys, growing up in knavery and villainy, are their *kearn* supplied. *Spenser.*

No sooner justice had with valour arm'd,
Compell'd these skipping *kernes* to trust their heels,
But the Norweyan lord, surveying advantage,
Began a fresh assault. *Shakespeare's Macbeth.*

If in good plight these Northern *kerns* arrive,
Then does fortune promise fair. *Philips's Briton.*

KERN. *n. s.* A hand-mill consisting of two pieces of stone, by which corn is ground. It is still used in some parts of Scotland.

To KERN. *v. n.* [probably from *kernel*, or, by change of a vowel, corrupted from *corn.*]

1. To harden as ripened corn.

When the price of corn falleth, men break no more ground than will supply their own turn, wherethrough it falleth out that an ill *kerned* or saved harvest soon emptieth their old store. *Carew's Survey of Cornwall.*

2. To

2. To take the form of grains; to granulate.

The principal knack is in making the juice, when sufficiently boiled, to *kern* or granulate. *Grew.*

KE'RNEL. *n. s.* [cyрnel, a gland, Saxon; *karne*, Dutch; *cerneau*, French.]

The edible ſubſtance contained in a ſhell.

As brown in hue
As hazle nuts, and ſweeter than the *kernels*. *Shakeſpeare.*

There can be no *kernel* in this light nut; the ſoul of this man is his clothes. *Shakeſp. All's well that ends well.*

The *kernel* of the nut ſerves them for bread and meat, and the ſhells for cups. *More.*

2. Any thing included in a huſk or integument.

The *kernel* of a grape, the fig's ſmall grain,
Can cloath a mountain, and o'erſhade a plain. *Denham.*

Oats are ripe when the ſtraw turns yellow and the *kernel* hard. *Mortimer's Husbandry.*

3. The ſeeds of pulpy fruits.

I think he will carry this iſland home in his pocket, and give it his ſon for an apple.—And ſowing the *kernels* of it in the ſea, bring forth more iſlands. *Shakeſ. Tempeſt.*

The apple incloſed in wax was as freſh as at the firſt putting in, and the *kernels* continued white. *Bacon's Nat. Hiſt.*

4. The central part of any thing upon which the ambient ſtrata are concreted.

A ſolid body in the bladder makes the *kernel* of a ſtone. *Arb.*

5. Knobby concretions in childrens fleſh.

To KE'RNEL. *v. n.* [from the noun.] To ripen to kernels.

In Staffordſhire, garden-rouncivals ſown in the fields *kernel* well, and yield a good increaſe. *Mortimer's Husbandry.*

KE'RNELLY. *adj.* [from *kernel.*] Full of kernels; having the quality or reſemblance of kernels.

KE'RNELWORT. *n. ſ.* An herb. *Ainſworth.*

KE'RSEY. *n. ſ.* [*karſaye*, Dutch; *cariſée*, French.] Coarſe ſtuff.

Taffata phraſes, ſilken terms preciſe,
I do forſwear them; and I here proteſt,
Henceforth my wooing mind ſhall be expreſt
In ruſſet yeas, and honeſt *kerſey* noes. *Shakeſpeare.*

His lackey with a linnen ſtock on one leg, and a *kerſey* boot-hoſe on the other. *Shakeſ. Taming of the Shrew.*

The ſame wool one man felts it into a hat, another weaves it into cloth, and another into *kerſey* or ſerge. *Hale.*

Thy *kerſey* doublet ſpreading wide,
Drew Cic'ly's eye aſide. *Gay.*

KEST. The preter tenſe of *caſt*. It is ſtill uſed in Scotland.

Only that noiſe heav'ns rolling circles *keſt*. *Fairfax.*

KE'STREL. *n. ſ.* A little kind of baſtard hawk. *Hanmer.*

In his *keſtrel* kind,
A pleaſing vein of glory, vain did find,
To which his flowing tongue, and troublous ſprit,
Gave him great aid. *Fairy Queen.*

Kites and *keſtrels* have a reſemblance with hawks. *Bacon.*

KETCH. *n. ſ.* [from *caicchio*, Italian, a barrel.] A heavy ſhip.

I wonder
That ſuch a *ketch* can with his very bulk
Take up the rays o' th' beneficial ſun,
And keep it from the earth. *Shak. Henry* VIII.

KE'TTLE. *n. ſ.* [cetl, Saxon; *ketel*, Dutch.] A veſſel in which liquor is boiled. In the kitchen the name of *pot* is given to the boiler that grows narrower towards the top, and of *kettle* to that which grows wider. In authors they are confounded.

The fire thus form'd, ſhe ſets the *kettle* on;
Like burniſh'd gold the little ſeether ſhone. *Dryden.*

KE'TTLEDRUM. *n. ſ.* [*kettle* and *drum.*] A drum of which the head is ſpread over a body of braſs.

As he drains his draughts of Rheniſh down,
The *kettledrum* and trumpet thus bray out
The triumph of his pledge. *Shakeſp. Hamlet.*

KEY. *n. ſ.* [cœȝ, Saxon.]

1. An inſtrument formed with cavities correſpondent to the wards of a lock, by which the bolt of a lock is puſhed forward or backward.

If a man were porter of hellgate, he ſhould have old turning the *key*. *Shakeſp. Macbeth.*

Fortune, that arrant whore,
Ne'er turns the *key* to th' poor. *Shak. King Lear.*

Poor *key* cold figure of a holy king!
Pale aſhes of the houſe of Lancaſter. *Shakeſ. Rich.* III.

The glorious ſtandard laſt to heav'n they ſpread,
With Peter's *keys* ennobled and his crown. *Fairfax.*

Yet ſome there be, that by due ſteps aſpire
To lay their juſt hands on that golden *key*,
That opes the palace of eternity. *Milton.*

Conſcience is its own counſellor, the ſole maſter of its own ſecrets; and it is the privilege of our nature, that every man ſhould keep the *key* of his own breaſt. *South's Sermons.*

He came, and knocking thrice, without delay
The longing lady heard, and turn'd the *key*. *Dryden.*

I keep her in one room, I lock it;
The *key*, look here, is in this pocket. *Prior.*

2. An inſtrument by which ſomething is ſcrewed or turned.

Hide the *key* of the jack. *Swift.*

3. An explanation of any thing difficult.

An emblem without a *key* to't, is no more than a tale of a tub. *L'Eſtrange.*

Theſe notions, in the writings of the ancients darkly delivered, receive a clearer light when compared with this theory, which repreſents every thing plainly, and is a *key* to their thoughts. *Burnet's Theory of the Earth.*

Thoſe who are accuſtomed to reaſon have got the true *key* of books. *Locke.*

4. The parts of a muſical inſtrument which are ſtruck with the fingers.

Pamela loves to handle the ſpinnet, and touch the *keys*. *Pam.*

5. [In muſick.] Is a certain tone whereto every compoſition, whether long or ſhort, ought to be fitted; and this key is ſaid to be either flat or ſharp, not in reſpect of its own nature, but with relation to the flat or ſharp third, which is joined with it. *Harris.*

Hippolita, I woo'd thee with my ſword,
And won thy love, doing thee injuries;
But I will wed thee in another *key*,
With pomp, with triumph, and with revelling. *Shakeſp.*

But ſpeak you with a ſad brow? Or do you play the flouting Jack? Come, in what *key* ſhall a man take you to go in the ſong? *Shak. Much Ado about Nothing.*

Not know my voice! Oh, time's extremity!
Haſt thou ſo crack'd and ſplitted my poor tongue
In ſev'n ſhort years, that here my only ſon
Knows not my feeble *key* of untun'd cares? *Shakeſpeare.*

6. [*Kaye*, Dutch; *quai*, French.] A bank raiſed perpendicular for the eaſe of lading and unlading ſhips.

A *key* of fire ran along the ſhore,
And lighten'd all the river with a blaze. *Dryden.*

KE'YAGE. *n. ſ.* [from *key.*] Money paid for lying at the key. *Ainſworth.*

KEYHO'LE. *n. ſ.* [*key* and *hole.*] The perforation in the door or lock through which the key is put.

Make doors faſt upon a woman's wit, and it will out at the caſement; ſhut that, and 'twill out at the *keyhole*. *Shakeſpeare.*

I looked in at the *keyhole*, and ſaw a well-made man. *Tatler.*

I keep her in one room; I lock it;
The key, look here, is in this pocket;
The *keyhole* is that left? Moſt certain. *Prior.*

KEYSTO'NE. *n. ſ.* [*key* and *ſtone.*] The middle ſtone of an arch.

If you will add a *keyſtone* and chaptrels to the arch, let the breadth of the upper part of the *keyſtone* be the height of the arch. *Moxon's Mech. Exer.*

KIBE. *n. ſ.* [from *kerb*, a cut, German, *Skinner*; from *kibwe*, Welſh, *Minſhew.*] An ulcerated chilblain; a chap in the heel cauſed by the cold.

If 'twere a *kibe*, 'twould put me to my ſlipper. *Shakeſp.*

The toe of the peaſant comes ſo near the heel of our courtier, that it galls his *kibe*. *Shakeſpeare's Hamlet.*

One boaſt of the cure, calling them a few *kibes*. *Wiſeman.*

KI'BED. *adj.* [from *kibe.*] Troubled with kibes: as *kibed* heels.

To KICK. *v. a.* [*kauchen*, German; *calco*, Latin.] To ſtrike with the foot.

He muſt endure and digeſt all affronts, adore the foot that *kicks* him, and kiſs the hand that ſtrikes him. *South.*

It anger'd Turenne once upon a day,
To ſee a footman *kick'd* that took his pay. *Pope.*

Another, whoſe ſon had employments at court, that valued not, now and then, a *kicking* or a caning. *Swift.*

To KICK. *v. n.* To beat the foot in anger or contempt.

Wherefore *kick* ye at my ſacrifice, which I have commanded? 1 *Sa.* ii. 29.

Jeſhurun waxed fat and *kicked*. *Deutr.* xxxii. 15.

The doctrines of the holy Scriptures are terrible enemies to wicked men, and this is that which makes them *kick* againſt religion, and ſpurn at the doctrines of that holy book. *Tillotſ.*

KICK. *n. ſ.* [from the verb.] A blow with the foot.

What, are you dumb? Quick, with your anſwer, quick,
Before my foot ſalutes you with a *kick*. *Dryd. Juvenal.*

KI'CKER. *n. ſ.* [from *kick.*] One who ſtrikes with his foot.

KI'CKSHAW. *n. ſ.* [This word is ſuppoſed, I think with truth, to be only a corruption of *quelque choſe*, ſomething; yet *Milton* ſeems to have underſtood it otherwiſe; for he writes it *kickſhoe*, and ſeems to think it uſed in contempt of dancing.]

1. Something uncommon; fantaſtical; ſomething ridiculous.

Shall we need the monſieurs of Paris to take our hopeful youth into their ſlight and prodigal cuſtodies, and ſend them over back again transformed into mimicks, apes, and *kickſhoes*? *Milton.*

2. A diſh ſo changed by the cookery that it can ſcarcely be known.

Some pigeons, a couple of ſhort-legged hens, a joint of mutton, and any pretty little tiny *kickſhaws*. *Shakeſ. H.* IV.

In wit, as well as war, they give us vigour;
Creſſy was loſt by *kickſhaws* and ſoup-meagre. *Fenton.*

KI'CKSY-WICKSEY. *n. ſ.* [from *kick* and *wince.*] A made word in ridicule and diſdain of a wife. *Hanmer.*

He

He wears his honour in a box, unseen,
That hugs his *kickſy-wickſey* here at home,
Spending his manly marrow in her arms. *Shakeſpeare.*

KID. *n. ſ.* [*kid*, Daniſh.]

1. The young of a goat.

Leaping like wanton *kids* in pleaſant ſpring. *Fa. Queen.*

There was a herd of goats with their young ones, upon which ſight ſir Richard Graham tells, he would ſnap one of the *kids*, and carry him cloſe to their lodging. *Wotton.*

Sporting the lion ramp'd, and in his paw
Dandled the *kid*. *Milton.*

So *kids* and whelps their ſires and dams expreſs;
And ſo the great I meaſur'd by the leſs. *Dryden's Virgil.*

2. [From *cidwlen*, Welſh, a faggot.] A bundle of heath or furze.

To KID. *v. a.* [from the noun] To bring forth kids.

KI'DDER. *n. ſ.* An ingroſſer of corn to enhance its price. *Ainſ.*

To KIDNA'P. *v. a.* [from *kind*, Dutch, a child, and *nap*.] To ſteal children; to ſteal human beings.

KIDNA'PPER. *n. ſ.* [from *kidnap*.] One who ſteals human beings.

The man compounded with the merchant, upon condition that he might have his child again; for he had ſmelt it out, that the merchant himſelf was the *kidnapper*. *L'Eſtrange.*

Theſe people lye in wait for our children, and may be conſidered as a kind of *kidnappers* within the law. *Spectator.*

KI'DNEY. *n. ſ.* [Etymology unknown.]

1. Theſe are two in number, one on each ſide: they have the ſame figure as kidneybeans: their length is four or five fingers, their breadth three, and their thickneſs two: the right is under the liver, and the left under the ſpleen. The uſe of the kidneys is to ſeparate the urine from the blood, which, by the motion of the heart and arteries, is thruſt into the emulgent branches, which carry it to the little glands, by which the ſeroſity being ſeparated, is received by the orifice of the little tubes, which go from the glands to the pelvis, and from thence it runs by the ureters into the bladder. *Quincy.*

A youth laboured under a complication of diſeaſes, from his meſentery and *kidneys*. *Wiſeman's Surgery.*

2. Race; kind: in ludicrous language.

Think of that, a man of my *kidney*; think of that, that am as ſubject to heat as butter; a man of continual diſſolution and thaw. *Shakeſp. Merry Wives of Windſor.*

There are millions in the world of this man's *kidney*, that take up the ſame reſolution without noiſe. *L'Eſtrange.*

KI'DNEYBEAN. *n. ſ.* [ſo named from its ſhape.]

It hath a papilionaceous flower, out of whoſe empalement riſes the pointal, which becomes a long pod, incloſing ſeveral ſeeds, which are ſhaped almoſt like a kidney. it has pinnated leaves, conſiſting of an unequal number of lobes. *Miller.*

Kidneybeans are a ſort of cod ware, that are very pleaſant wholeſome food. *Mortimer's Husbandry.*

KI'DNEYVETCH. } *n. ſ.* Plants. *Ainſworth.*
KI'DNEYWORT. }

KI'LDERKIN. *n. ſ.* [*kindekin*, a baby, Dutch.] A ſmall barrel.

Make in the *kilderkin* a great bung-hole of purpoſe. *Bacon.*

A tun of man in thy large bulk is writ;
But ſure thou'rt but a *kilderkin* of wit. *Dryden.*

To KILL. *v. a.* [Anciently *To quell*; cpellan, Saxon; *kelen*, Dutch]

1. To deprive of life; to put to death as an agent.

Dar'ſt thou reſolve to *kill* a friend of mine?
—Pleaſe you, I'd rather *kill* two enemies. *Shakeſ. R.* III.

Ye have brought us forth into this wilderneſs, to *kill* this whole aſſembly with hunger. *Ex.* xvi. 3.

There was *killing* of young and old, making away of men, women, and children. 2 *Mac.* v. 13.

2. To deſtroy animals for food.

We're mere uſurpers, tyrants, and what's worſe,
To fright the animals, and to *kill* them up
In their aſſign'd and native dwelling place. *Shakeſpeare.*

Thou ſhalt *kill* of thy herd, and of thy flock. *Deutr.* xii.

Shall I take my bread, and my fleſh that I have *kill'd* for my ſhearers? 1 *Sa.* xxv. 11.

3. To deprive of life as a cauſe or inſtrument.

The medicines which go to the magical ointments, if they were uſed inwards, would *kill* thoſe that uſe them; and therefore they work potently, though outwards. *Bacon.*

4 To deprive of vegetative or other motion, or active qualities.

Try with oil, or barm of drink, ſo they be ſuch things as *kill* not the bough. *Bacon's Natural Hiſtory.*

Catharticks of mercurials mix with all animal acids, as appears by *killing* it with ſpittle. *Floyer on the Humours.*

KI'LLER. *n. ſ.* [from *kill*.] One that deprives of life.

What ſorrow, what amazement, what ſhame was in Amphialus, when he ſaw his dear foſter-father find him the *killer* of his only ſon! *Sidney.*

Wilt thou for the old lion hunt, or fill
His hungry whelps? and for the *killer* kill,
When couch'd in dreadful dens? *Sandys.*

So rude a time,
When love was held ſo capital a crime,
That a crown'd head could no compaſſion find,
But dy'd, becauſe the *killer* had been kind. *Waller.*

KI'LLOW. *n. ſ.* [This ſeems a corruption of *coal* and *low*, a flame, as ſoot is thereby produced.]

An earth of a blackiſh or deep blue colour, and doubtleſs had its name from *kollow*, by which name, in the North, the ſmut or grime on the backs of chimneys is called. *Woodward.*

KILN. *n. ſ.* [cyln, Saxon] A ſtove; a fabrick formed for admitting heat, in order to dry or burn things contained in it.

What ſhall I do? I'll creep up into the chimney.—— There they always uſe to diſcharge their birding-pieces: creep into the *kiln* hole. *Shakeſp. Merry Wives of Windſor.*

After the putting forth in ſprouts, and the drying upon the *kiln*, there will be gained a buſhel in eight of malt. *Bacon.*

Phyſicians chuſe lime which is newly drawn out of the *kiln*, and not ſlacked. *Moxon's Mech. Exer.*

To KI'LNDRY. *v. a.* [*kiln* and *dry*.] To dry by means of a kiln.

The beſt way is to *kilndry* them. *Mortimer's Husbandry.*

KILT for *killed*. *Spenſer.*

KI'MBO. *adj.* [*a ſchembo*, Italian.] Crooked; bent; arched.

The *kimbo* handles ſeem with bears-foot carv'd,
And never yet to table have been ſerv'd. *Dryden's Virgil.*

He obſerved them edging towards one another to whiſper; ſo that John was forced to ſit with his arms a *kimbo*, to keep them aſunder. *Arbuthnot's Hiſtory of John Bull.*

KIN. *n. ſ.* [cynne, Saxon.]

1. Relation either of conſanguinity or affinity.

You muſt uſe them with fit reſpects, according to the bonds of nature; but you are of *kin*, and ſo a friend to their perſons, not to their errours. *Bacon's Advice to Villiers.*

Th' unhappy Palamon,
Whom Theſeus holds in bonds, and will not free,
Without a crime, except his *kin* to me. *Dryden.*

2. Relatives; thoſe who are of the ſame race.

Tumultuous wars
Shall *kin* with *kin*, and kind with kind confound. *Shakeſp.*

The father, mother, and the *kin* beſide,
Were overborn by fury of the tide. *Dryden.*

3. A relation; one related.

Then is the ſoul from God; ſo pagans ſay,
Which ſaw by nature's light her heavenly kind,
Naming her *kin* to God, and God's bright ray,
A citizen of heav'n, to earth confin'd. *Davies.*

4. The ſame generical claſs, though perhaps not the ſame ſpecies; thing related.

The burſt,
And the ear-deaf'ning voice of the oracle,
Kin to Jove's thunder, ſo ſurpriz'd my ſenſe,
That I was nothing. *Shakeſp. Winter's Tale.*

The odour of the fixed nitre is very languid; but that which it diſcovers, being diſſolved in a little hot water, is altogether differing from the ſtink of the other, being of *kin* to that of other alcalizate ſalts. *Boyle.*

5. A diminutive termination from *kind*, a child, Dutch: as, *manikin*, *minikin*.

KIND. *adj.* [from cynne, relation, Saxon.]

1. Benevolent; filled with general good-will.

By the *kind* gods, 'tis moſt ignobly done
To pluck me by the beard. *Shak. King Lear.*

Some of the ancients, like *kind* hearted men, have talked much of annual refrigeriums, or intervals of puniſhment to the damned, as particularly on the great feſtivals of the reſurrection and aſcenſion. *South's Sermons.*

2. Favourable; beneficent.

He is *kind* to the unthankful and evil. *Lu.* vi. 35.

KIND. *n. ſ.* [cynne, Saxon.]

1. Race; generical claſs. *Kind* in Teutonick Engliſh anſwers to *genus*, and *ſort* to *ſpecies*; though this diſtinction, in popular language, is not always obſerved.

Thus far we have endeavoured in part to open of what nature and force laws are, according to their *kinds*. *Hooker.*

As when the total *kind*
Of birds, in orderly array on wing,
Came ſummon'd over Eden, to receive
Their names of Thee. *Milton's Parad. Loſt, b.* vi.

That both are animalia,
I grant; but not rationalia;
For though they do agree in *kind*,
Specifick difference we find. *Hudibras, p.* i.

God and nature do not principally concern themſelves in the preſervation of particulars, but of *kinds* and companies. *South's Sermons.*

He with his wife were only left behind
Of periſh'd man; they two were human *kind*. *Dryden.*

I inſtance ſome acts of virtue common to Heathens and Chriſtians; but I ſuppoſe them to be performed by Chriſtians, after a more ſublime manner than ever they were among the Heathens; and even when they do not differ in *kind* from moral virtues, yet differ in the degrees of perfection. *Atterb.*

He,

He, with a hundred arts refin'd,
Shall ſtretch thy conqueſts over half the *kind*. *Pope.*

2. Particular nature.

No human laws are exempt from faults, ſince thoſe that have been looked upon as moſt perfect in their *kind*, have been found, upon enquiry, to have ſo many. *Baker.*

3. Natural ſtate.

He did, by edict, give the goods of all the priſoners unto thoſe that had taken them, either to take them in *kind*, or compound for them. *Bacon's Henry* VII.

The tax upon tillage was often levied in *kind* upon corn, and called *decumæ*, or tithes. *Arbuthnot on Coins.*

4. Nature; natural determination.

The ſkilful ſhepherd peel'd me certain wands,
And in the doing of the deed of *kind*,
He ſtuck them up before the fulſome ewes. *Shakeſpeare.*
Some of you, on pure inſtinct of nature,
Are led by *kind* t' admire your fellow-creature. *Dryden.*

5. Manner; way.

Send me your priſoners with the ſpeedieſt means,
Or you ſhall hear in ſuch a *kind* from me
As will diſpleaſe you. *Shakeſ. Henry* IV.

This will encourage induſtrious improvements, becauſe many will rather venture in that *kind* than take five in the hundred. *Bacon's Eſſays.*

6. Sort. It has a ſlight and unimportant ſenſe.

Diogenes was aſked, in a *kind* of ſcorn, what was the matter that philoſophers haunted rich men, and not rich men philoſophers? He anſwered, becauſe the one knew what they wanted, the other did not. *Bacon.*

To KI'NDLE. *v. a.*

1. To ſet on fire; to light; to make to burn.

He will take thereof, and warm himſelf; yea, he *kindleth* it and baketh bread. *Iſ.* xliv. 15.

I was not forgetful of thoſe ſparks, which ſome mens diſtempers formerly ſtudied to *kindle* in parliaments. *K. Charles.*

If the fire burns vigorouſly, it is no matter by what means it was at firſt *kindled*: there is the ſame force and the ſame refreſhing virtue in it, *kindled* by a ſpark from a flint, as if it were *kindled* from the ſun. *South's Sermons.*

2. To inflame the paſſions; to exaſperate; to animate; to heat; to fire the mind.

I've been to you a true and humble wife;
At all times to your will conformable:
Ever in fear to *kindle* your diſlike. *Shakeſ. Henry* VIII.

He hath *kindled* his wrath againſt me, and counteth me as one of his enemies. *Job* xix. 11.

Thus one by one *kindling* each other's fire,
'Till all inflam'd, they all in one agree. *Daniel's Civ. War.*
Each was a cauſe alone, and all combin'd
To kindle vengeance in her haughty mind. *Dryden.*

To KI'NDLE. *v. n.* [*cinnu*, Welſh; cyndelan, Saxon.]

1. To catch fire.

When thou walkeſt through the fire, thou ſhalt not be burnt, neither ſhall the flame *kindle* upon thee. *Iſ.* xliii. 2.

2. [From cennan, to bring forth, Saxon.]

Are you native of this place?
—As the coney that you ſee dwells where ſhe is *kindled. Shak.*

KI'NDLER. *n. ſ.* [from *kindle.*] One that lights; one who inflames.

Now is the time that rakes their revels keep,
Kindlers of riot, enemies of ſleep. *Gay.*

KI'NDLY. *adv.* [from *kind.*]

1. Benevolently; favourably; with good will.

Sir Thurio borrows his wit from your ladyſhip's looks, and ſpends what he borrows *kindly* in your company. *Shakeſpeare.*

I ſometime lay here in Corioli,
At a poor man's houſe: he us'd me *kindly. Shakeſp. Coriol.*

Be *kindly* affectioned one to another, with brotherly love, in honour prefering one another. *Ro.* xii. 10.

His grief ſome pity, others blame;
The fatal cauſe all *kindly* ſeek. *Prior.*
Who, with leſs deſigning ends,
Kindlier entertain their friends;
With good words, and count'nance ſprightly,
Strive to treat them all politely? *Swift.*

KI'NDLY. *adj.* [from *kind*; probably from *kind* the ſubſtantive.]

1. Homogeneal; congeneal; kindred; of the ſame nature.

This competency I beſeech God I may be able to digeſt into *kindly* juice, that I may grow thereby. *Hammond.*

Theſe ſoft fires
Not only enlighten, but with *kindly* heat,
Of various influence, foment and warm,
Temper or nouriſh. *Milton's Parad. Loſt, b.* iv.

2. The foregoing ſenſe ſeems to have been originally implied by this word; but following writers, inattentive to its etymology, confounded it with *kind.*

3. Bland; mild; ſoftening.

Through all the living regions do'ſt thou move,
And ſcatter'ſt, where thou goeſt, the *kindly* ſeeds of love. *Dryden.*

Ye heav'ns, from high the dewy nectar pour,
And in ſoft ſilence ſhed the *kindly* ſhow'r! *Pope.*

KI'NDNESS. *n. ſ.* [from *kind.*] Benevolence; beneficence; good will; favour; love.

If there be *kindneſs*, meekneſs, or comfort in her tongue, then is not her huſband like other men. *Eccluſ.* xxxvi. 23.

Old Lelius profeſſes he had an extraordinary *kindneſs* for ſeveral young people. *Collier of Friendſhip.*

Ever bleſt be Cytherea's ſhrine,
Since thy dear breaſt has felt an equal wound,
Since in thy *kindneſs* my deſires are crown'd. *Prior.*

Love and inclination can be produced only by an experience or opinion of *kindneſs* to us. *Rogers's Sermons.*

KI'NDRED. *n. ſ.* [from *kin*; cynrene, Saxon.]

1. Relation by birth or marriage; cognation; affinity.

Like her, of equal *kindred* to the throne,
You keep her conqueſts, and extend your own. *Dryden.*

2. Relation; ſort.

His horſe hipp'd with an old mothy ſaddle, and the ſtirrups of no *kindred. Shakeſp. Taming of the Shrew.*

3. Relatives.

I think there is no man ſecure
But the queen's *kindred. Shakeſp. Richard* III.
Nor needs thy juſter title the foul guilt
Of Eaſtern kings, who, to ſecure their reign,
Muſt have their brothers, ſons, and *kindred* ſlain. *Denham.*

KI'NDRED. *adj.* Congeneal; related; cognate.

From Tuſcan Coritum he claim'd his birth;
But after, when exempt from mortal earth,
From thence aſcended to his *kindred* ſkies
A god. *Dryden.*

KINE. *n. ſ.* plur. from *cow.*

To milk the *kine*,
E'er the milk-maid fine
Hath open'd her eyne. *Ben. Johnſon.*
A field I went, amid' the morning dew,
To milk my *kine*. *Gay.*

KING. *n. ſ.* [A contraction of the Teutonick word *cuning*, or *cyning*, the name of ſovereign dignity. In the primitive tongue it ſignifies ſtout or valiant, the kings of moſt nations being, in the beginning, choſen by the people on account of their valour and ſtrength. *Verſtegan.*]

1. Monarch; ſupreme governour.

The great *king* of *kings*,
Hath in the table of his law commanded,
That thou ſhalt do no murder. *Shakeſ. R.* III.
A ſubſtitute ſhines brightly as a *king*,
Until a *king* be by; and then his ſtate
Empties itſelf, as doth an inland brook
Into the main of waters. *Shak. Merch. of Venice.*
True hope is ſwift, and flies with ſwallows wings;
Kings it makes gods, and meaner creatures *kings*. *Shakeſp.*
The *king* becoming graces,
As juſtice, verity, temp'rance, ſtableneſs,
Bounty, perſev'rance, mercy, lowlineſs,
Devotion, patience, courage, fortitude,
I have no reliſh of them. *Shakeſpeare's Macbeth.*
Thus ſtates were form'd; the name of *king* unknown,
'Till common int'reſt plac'd the ſway in one;
'Twas virtue only, or in arts or arms,
Diffuſing bleſſings, or averting harms,
The ſame which in a ſire the ſons obey'd,
A prince the father of a people made. *Pope.*

2. It is taken by *Bacon* in the feminine: as *prince* alſo is.

Ferdinand and Iſabella, *kings* of Spain, recovered the great and rich kingdom of Granada from the Moors. *Bacon.*

3. A card with the picture of a king.

The *king* unſeen
Lurk'd in her hand, and mourn'd his captive queen. *Pope.*

4. KING *at Arms*, or of heralds, a principal officer at arms, that has the pre-eminence of the ſociety; of whom there are three in number, viz. Garter, Norroy, and Clarencieux. *Phillips.*

A letter under his own hand was lately ſhewed me by ſir William Dugdale, *king at arms*. *Walton.*

To KING. *v. a.* [from the noun.]

1. To ſupply with a king.

England is ſo idly *king'd*,
Her ſceptre ſo fantaſtically borne,
By a vain, giddy, ſhallow, humorous youth,
That fear attends her not. *Shakeſpeare's Henry* V.

2. To make royal; to raiſe to royalty.

Sometimes am I a king;
Then treaſon makes me wiſh myſelf a beggar,
And ſo I am: then cruſhing penury
Perſuades me, I was better when a king;
Then am I *king'd* again. *Shakeſpeare's Richard* II.

KI'NGAPPLE. *n. ſ.* A kind of apple.

The *kingapple* is preferred before the jenneting. *Mortimer.*

KI'NGCRAFT. *n. ſ.* [*king* and *craft.*] The act of governing. A word commonly uſed by king *James*.

KI'NGCUP. *n. ſ.* [*king* and *cup.*] A flower
June is drawn in a mantle of dark graſs green, and upon his head a garland of bents, *kingcups*, and maidenhair. *Peach.*
Fair is the *kingcup* that in meadow blows,
Fair is the daiſy that beſide her grows. *Gay.*

KI'NGDOM. *n. ſ.* [from *king.*]
1. The dominion of a king; the territories ſubject to a monarch.
You're welcome,
Moſt learned, reverend ſir, into our *kingdom.* *Shakeſp.*
Moſes gave unto them the *kingdom* of Sihon, king of the Amorites, and the *kingdom* of Og, king of Baſhan. *Num.* xxxii.
2. A different claſs or order of beings. A word chiefly uſed among naturaliſts.
The animal and vegetable *kingdoms* are ſo nearly joined, that if you take the loweſt of one, and the higheſt of the other, there will ſcarce be perceived any difference. *Locke.*
3. A region; a tract.
The wat'ry *kingdom* is no bar
To ſtop the foreign ſpirits; but they come,
As o'er a brook, to ſee fair Portia. *Shakeſp. Merch. of Ven.*

KI'NGFISHER. *n. ſ.* A ſpecies of bird.
When dew refreſhing on the paſture fields
The moon beſtows, *kingfiſhers* play on ſhore. *May's Virgil.*
Bitterns, herons, ſea-gulls, *kingfiſhers*, and water-rats, are great enemies to fiſh. *Mortimer's Husbandry.*

KI'NGLIKE. } *adj.* [from *king.*]
KI'NGLY. }
1. Royal; ſovereign; monarchical.
There we'll ſit,
Ruling in large and ample empery,
O'er France, and all her almoſt *kingly* dukedoms. *Shakeſp.*
Yet this place
Had been thy *kingly* ſeat, and here thy race,
From all the ends of peopled earth, had come
To rev'rence thee. *Dryden's State of Innocence.*
In Sparta, a *kingly* government, though the people were perfectly free, the adminiſtration was in the two kings and the ephori. *Swift.*
The cities of Greece, when they drove out their tyrannical kings, either choſe others from a new family, or aboliſhed the *kingly* government, and became free ſtates. *Swift.*
2. Belonging to a king.
Why lieſt thou with the vile
In loathſome beds, and leav'ſt the *kingly* couch
A watch-caſe to a common 'larum-bell? *Shakeſp. H.* IV.
Then ſhalt thou give me with thy *kingly* hand,
What huſband in thy power I will command. *Shakeſpeare.*
3. Noble; auguſt.
He was not born to live a ſubject life, each action of his bearing in it majeſty, ſuch a *kingly* entertainment, ſuch a *kingly* magnificence, ſuch a *kingly* heart for enterprizes. *Sidney.*
I am far better born than is the king;
More like a king, more *kingly* in my thoughts. *Shakeſp.*

KI'NGLY. *adv.* With an air of royalty; with ſuperiour dignity.
Adam bow'd low; he, *kingly*, from his ſtate
Inclin'd not. *Milt. Parad. Loſt.*
His hat, which never vail'd to human pride,
Walker with rev'rence took, and laid aſide;
Low bow'd the reſt, he, *kingly*, did but nod. *Dunciad.*

KINGSE'VIL. *n. ſ.* [*king* and *evil.*] A ſcrofulous diſtemper, in which the glands are ulcerated, commonly believed to be cured by the touch of the king.
Sore eyes are frequently a ſpecies of the *kingſevil*, and take their beginning from vicious humours inflaming the tunica adnata. *Wiſeman's Surgery.*

KI'NGSHIP. *n. ſ.* [from *king.*] Royalty; monarchy.
They deſigned and propoſed to me the new modelling of ſovereignty and *kingſhip*, without any reality of power, or without any neceſſity of ſubjection and obedience. *K. Charles.*
We know how ſucceſsful the late uſurper was, while his army believed him real in his zeal againſt *kingſhip*; but when they found out the impoſture, upon his aſpiring to the ſame himſelf, he was preſently deſerted and oppoſed by them, and never able to crown his uſurped greatneſs with the addition of that title which he paſſionately thirſted after. *South.*

KI'NGSPEAR. *n. ſ.* A plant.
The ſtalk is round, ſmooth, ſtrong, and branchy; the leaves like thoſe of a leek, but ſtronger and narrower: the flowers are divided commonly as far as the baſis, naked, ſtellated, and embracing the ovary like a calyx: the apex of the ovary puts forth ſix ſtamina, and a long tube from the centre, which becomes a roundiſh fruit, carnous, triangular, divided into three partitions incloſing triangular ſeeds. *Miller.*

KI'NGSTONE. *n. ſ.* A fiſh. *Ainſworth.*

KI'NSFOLK. *n. ſ.* [*kin* and *folk.*] Relations; thoſe who are of the ſame family.
Thoſe lords, ſince their firſt grants of thoſe lands, have beſtowed them amongſt their *kinsfolks.* *Spenſer.*
My *kinsfolk* have failed, and my familiar friends forgotten me. *Job* xix. 14.

KI'NSMAN. *n. ſ.* [*kin* and *man.*] A man of the ſame race or family.
The jury he made to be choſen out of their neareſt *kinſmen*, and their judges he made of their own fathers. *Spenſer.*
Both fair, and both of royal blood they ſeem'd,
Whom *kinſmen* to the crown the heralds deem'd. *Dryden.*
Let me ſtand excluded from my right,
Robb'd of my *kinſman*'s arms, who firſt appear'd in fight. *Dryden's Fables.*
There is a branch of the Medicis in Naples: the head of it has been owned as a *kinſman* by the great duke, and 'tis thought will ſucceed to his dominions. *Addiſon on Italy.*

KI'NSWOMAN. *n. ſ.* [*kin* and *woman.*] A female relation.
A young noble lady, near *kinſwoman* to the fair Helen, queen of Corinth, was come thither. *Sidney.*
The duke was as much in love with wit as he was with his *kinſwoman.* *Dennis's Letters.*

KIRK. *n ſ.* [cyrce, Saxon; κυριακκὴ.] An old word for a church, yet retained in Scotland.
Home they haſten the poſts to dight,
And all the *kirk* pillars ere day-light,
With hawthorn buds, and ſweet eglantine. *Spenſer.*
Nor is it all the nation hath theſe ſpots,
There is a church as well as *kirk* of Scots. *Cleaveland.*
What one party thought to rivet by the Scots, that the other contemns, deſpiſing the *kirk* government and diſcipline of the Scots. *King Charles.*

KI'RTLE. *n. ſ.* [cyrtel, Saxon.] An upper garment; a gown.
All in a *kirtle* of diſcoloured ſay
He clothed was. *Fairy Queen.*
What ſtuff wilt thou have a *kirtle* of? Thou ſhalt have a cap to-morrow. *Shakeſpeare's Henry* IV.
Thy gowns, thy ſhoes, thy beds of roſes,
Thy cap, thy *kirtle*, and thy poeſies,
Soon break, ſoon wither, ſoon forgotten,
In folly ripe, in reaſon rotten. *Raleigh.*

To KISS. *v. a.* [*cuſan*, Welſh; κύω.]
1. To touch with the lips.
But who thoſe ruddy lips can miſs,
Which bleſſed ſtill themſelves do *kiſs.* *Sidney.*
He took
The bride about the neck, and *kiſt* her lips
With ſuch a clamorous ſmack, that at the parting
All the church echo'd. *Shak. Taming of the Shrew.*
Their lips were four red roſes on a ſtalk,
And in their ſummer beauty *kiſs'd* each other. *Shak. R.* III.
2. To treat with fondneſs.
The hearts of princes *kiſs* obedience,
So much they love it; but to ſtubborn ſpirits,
They ſwell and grow as terrible as ſtorms. *Shak. H.* VIII.
3. To touch gently.
The moon ſhines bright: in ſuch a night as this,
When the ſweet wind did gently *kiſs* the trees,
And they did make no noiſe. *Shakeſ. Merch. of Venice.*

KISS. *n. ſ.* [from the verb.] Salute given by joining lips.
What ſenſe had I of her ſtol'n hours or luſt?
I found not Caſſio's *kiſſes* on her lips. *Shakeſ. Othello.*
Upon my livid lips beſtow a *kiſs*:
O envy not the dead, they feel not bliſs! *Dryden.*

KI'SSER. *n. ſ.* [from *kiſs.*] One that kiſſes.

KI'SSINGCRUST. *n. ſ.* [*kiſſing* and *cruſt.*] Cruſt formed where one loaf in the oven touches another.
Theſe bak'd him *kiſſingcruſts*, and thoſe
Brought him ſmall beer. *King's Cookery.*

KIT. *n. ſ.* [*kitte*, Dutch.]
1. A large bottle. *Skinner.*
2. A ſmall diminutive fiddle.
'Tis kept in a caſe fitted to it, almoſt like a dancing-maſter's *kit.* *Grew's Muſæum.*
3. A ſmall wooden veſſel, in which Newcaſtle ſalmon is ſent up to town.

KI'TCHEN. *n. ſ.* [*kegin*, Welſh; *keg*, Flemiſh; cycene, Sax. *cuiſine*, French; *cucina*, Italian; *kyſhen*, Erſe.] The room in a houſe where the proviſions are cooked.
Theſe being culpable of this crime, or favourers of their friends, which are ſuch by whom their *kitchens* are ſometimes amended, will not ſuffer any ſuch ſtatute to paſs. *Spenſer.*
Can we judge it a thing ſeemly for any man to go about the building of an houſe to the God of heaven, with no other appearance than if his end were to rear up a *kitchen* or a parlour for his own uſe? *Hooker.*
He was taken into ſervice in his court to a baſe office in his *kitchen*; ſo that he turned a broach that had worn a crown. *Bac.*
We ſee no new built palaces aſpire,
No *kitchens* emulate the veſtal fire. *Pope.*

KI'TCHENGARDEN. *n. ſ.* [*kitchen* and *garden.*] Garden in which eſculent plants are produced.
Gardens, if planted with ſuch things as are fit for food, are called *kitchengardens.* *Bacon.*
A *kitchengarden* is a more pleaſant ſight than the fineſt orangery. *Spectator.*

KI'TCHENMAID. *n. ſ.* [*kitchen* and *maid.*] A cookmaid.

KI'TCHENSTUFF. *n. ſ.* [*kitchen* and *ſtuff.*] The fat of meat ſcummed off the pot, or gathered out of the dripping-pan.

As a thrifty wench fcrapes *kitchenftuff*,
And barreling the droppings and the fnuff
Of wafting candles, which in thirty year,
Reliquely kept, perchance buys wedding cheer. *Donne.*
Inftead of *kitchenftuff* fome cry
A gofpel preaching miniftry. *Hudibras.*

KI'TCHENWENCH. *n. f.* [*kitchen* and *wench.*] Scullion; maid employed to clean the inftruments of cookery.
Laura to his lady was but a *kitchenwench.* *Shakefpeare.*
Roafting and boiling leave to the *kitchenwench.* *Swift.*

KI'TCHENWORK. *n. f.* [*kitchen* and *work.*] Cookery; work done in the kitchen.

KITE. *n. f.* [cyta, Saxon.]
1. A bird of prey that infefts the farms, and fteals the chickens.
Ravenous crows and *kites*
Fly o'er our heads. *Shakefpeare's Julius Cæfar.*
More pity that the eagle fhould be mew'd,
While *kites* and buzzards prey at liberty. *Shakef. R. III.*
The heron, when fhe foareth high, fo as fometimes fhe is feen to pafs over a cloud, fheweth winds; but *kites*, flying aloft, fhew fair and dry weather. *Bacon.*
A leopard and a cat feem to differ juft as a *kite* doth from an eagle. *Grew.*
2. A name of reproach denoting rapacity.
Detefted *kite!* thou lieft. *Shakef. King Lear.*
3. A fictitious bird made of paper.
A man may have a great eftate conveyed to him; but if he will madly burn, or childifhly make paper *kites* of his deeds, he forfeits his title with his evidence. *Gov. of the Tongue.*

KI'TESFOOT. *n. f.* A plant. *Ainfworth.*

KI'TTEN. *n. f.* [*katteken*, Dutch.] A young cat.
That a mare will fooner drown than an horfe is not experienced, nor is the fame obferved in the drowning of whelps and *kittens.* *Brown's Vulg. Err.*
It was fcratched in playing with a *kitten.* *Wifeman.*
Helen was juft flipt into bed;
Her eyebrows on the toilet lay,
Away the *kitten* with them fled,
As fees belonging to her prey. *Prior.*

To KI'TTEN. *v. n.* [from the noun.] To bring forth young cats.
So it would have done
At the fame feafon, if your mother's cat
Had *kitten'd*, though yourfelf had ne'er been born. *Shakefp.*
The eagle timbered upon the top of a high oak, and the cat *kittened* in the hollow trunk of it. *L'Eftrange.*

To KLICK. *v. n.* [from *clack.*]
1. To make a fmall fharp noife.
2. In Scotland it denotes to pilfer or fteal away fuddenly with a fnatch.

To KNAB. *v. a.* [*knappen*, Dutch; *knaap*, Erfe.] To bite. Perhaps properly to bite fomething brittle, that makes a noife when it is broken; fo as that *knab* and *knap* may be the fame.
I had much rather lie *knabbing* crufts, without fear, in my own hole, than be miftrefs of the world with cares. *L'Eftran.*
An afs was wifhing, in a hard Winter, for a little warm weather, and a mouthful of frefh grafs to *knab* upon. *L'Eftr.*

KNACK. *n. f.* [*cnec*, Welfh, fly knavery; cnapunge, fkill, Sax.]
1. A little machine; a petty contrivance; a toy.
When I was young, I was wont
To load my fhe with *knacks:* I would have ranfack'd
The pedlar's filken treafury, and have pour'd it
To her acceptance. *Shakefp. Winter's Tale.*
For thee, fond boy,
If I may ever know thou do'ft but figh
That thou no more fhalt fee this *knack*, as never
I mean thou fhalt, we'll bar thee from fuccefs. *Shakefp.*
This cap was moulded on a porringer,
A velvet difh; fie, fie, 'tis lewd and filthy:
Why 'tis a cockle, or a walnut fhell,
A *knack*, a toy, a trick, a baby's cap. *Shakefpeare.*
But is't not prefumption to write verfe to you,
Who make the better poems of the two?
For all thefe pretty *knacks* that you compofe,
Alas, what are they but poems in profe! *Denham.*
He expounded both his pockets,
And found a watch, with rings and lockets;
A copper-plate, with almanacks
Engrav'd upon't, with other *knacks.* *Hudibras.*
2. A readinefs; an habitual facility; a lucky dexterity.
I'll teach you the *knacks*
Of eating of flax,
And out of their nofes
Draw ribbands and pofies. *Ben. Johnfon's Gypfies.*
The *knack* of faft and loofe paffes with foolifh people for a turn of wit; but they are not aware all this while of the defperate confequences of an ill habit. *L'Eftrange.*
There is a certain *knack* in the art of converfation that gives a good grace to many things, by the manner and addrefs of handling them. *L'Eftrange.*
Knaves, who in full affemblies have the *knack*
Of turning truth to lies, and white to black. *Dryden.*
My author has a great *knack* at remarks: in the end he makes another, about our refining in controverfy, and coming nearer and nearer to the church of Rome. *Atterbury.*
The dean was famous in his time,
And had a kind of *knack* at rhime. *Swift.*
3. A nice trick.
For how fhould equal colours do the *knack?*
Cameleons who can paint in white and black? *Pope.*

To KNACK. *v. n.* [from the noun.] To make a fharp quick noife, as when a ftick breaks.

KNA'CKER. *n. f.* [from *knack.*]
1. A maker of fmall work.
One part for plow-wright, cartwright, *knacker*, and fmith. *Mortimer's Husbandry.*
2. A ropemaker. [*Reftio*, Latin.] *Ainfworth.*

KNAG. *n. f.* [*knag*, a wart, Danifh. It is retain'd in Scotland.] A hard knot in wood.

KNA'GGY. *adj.* [from *knag.*] Knotty; fet with hard rough knots.

KNAP. *n. f.* [*cnap*, Welfh, a protuberance, or a broken piece; cnæp, Saxon, a protuberance.] A protuberance; a fwelling prominence.
You fhall fee many fine feats fet upon a *knap* of ground, environed with higher hills round about it, whereby the heat of the fun is pent in, and the wind gathereth as in troughs. *Bacon.*

To KNAP. *v. a.* [*knappen*, Dutch.]
1. To bite; to break fhort.
He *knappeth* the fpear in funder. *Common Prayer.*
He will *knap* the fpears a-pieces with his teeth. *More.*
2. [*Knaap*, Erfe.] To ftrike fo as to make a fharp noife like that of breaking.
Knap a pair of tongs fome depth in a veffel of water, and you fhall hear the found of the tongs. *Bacon's Natural Hift.*

To KNAP. *v. n.* To make a fhort fharp noife.
I reduced fhoulders fo foon, that the ftanders-by heard them *knap* in before they knew they were out. *Wifeman's Surgery.*

To KNA'PPLE. *v. n.* [from *knap.*] To break off with a fharp quick noife. *Ainfworth.*

KNA'PSACK. *n. f.* [from *knappen*, to eat.] The bag which a foldier carries on his back; a bag of provifions.
The conftitutions of this church fhall not be repealed, 'till I fee more religious motives than foldiers carry in their *knapfacks.* *King Charles.*
If you are for a merry jaunt, I'll try for once who can foot it fartheft: there are hedges in Summer, and barns in Winter to be found: I with my *knapfack*, and you with your bottle at your back: we'll leave honour to madmen, and riches to knaves, and travel 'till we come to the ridge of the world. *Dryden's Spanifh Fryar.*

KNA'PWEED. *n. f.* [*jacea*, Latin.]
This is one of the headed plants deftitute of fpines: the cup is fquamofe; the borders of the leaves are equal, being neither ferrated nor indented: the florets round the border of the head are barren; but thofe placed in the center are fucceeded each by one feed, having a down adhering to it. There are fifty fpecies of this plant, thirteen of which grow wild in England, and the reft are exoticks. *Miller.*

KNARE. *n. f.* [*knor*, German.] A hard knot.
A cake of fcurf lies baking on the ground,
And prickly ftubs inftead of trees are found;
Or woods with knots and *knares* deform'd and old,
Headlefs the moft, and hideous to behold. *Dryden.*

KNAVE. *n. f.* [cnapa, Saxon.]
1. A boy; a male child.
2. A fervant. Both thefe are obfolete.
For as the moon the eye doth pleafe
With gentle beams not hurting fight,
Yet hath fir fun the greater praife,
Becaufe from him doth come her light;
So if my man muft praifes have,
What then muft I that keep the *knave?* *Sidney.*
He eats and drinks with his domeftick flaves;
A verier hind than any of his *knaves.* *Dryden.*
3. A petty rafcal; a fcoundrel; a difhoneft fellow.
Moft men rather brook their being reputed *knaves*, than for their honefty be accounted fools; *knave*, in the mean time, paffing for a name of credit. *South's Sermons.*
When both plaintiff and defendant happen to be crafty *knaves*, there's equity againft both. *L'Eftrange.*
An honeft man may take a *knave*'s advice;
But idiots only may be cozen'd twice. *Dryden.*
See all our fools afpiring to be *knaves.* *Pope.*
4. A card with a foldier painted on it.
For 'twill return, and turn t' account,
If we are brought in play upon't,
Or but by cafting *knaves* get in,
What pow'r can hinder us to win? *Hudibras.*

KNA'VERY. *n. f.* [from *knave.*]
1. Difhonefty; tricks; petty villainy.
Here's no *knavery!* See, to beguile the old folks, how the young folks lay their heads together. *Shakefpeare.*
If I thought it were not a piece of honefty to acquaint the king withal, I would do't; I hold it the more *knavery* to conceal it. *Shakefp. Winter's Tale.*

Here's the folly of the ass in trusting the fox, and here's the *knavery* of the fox in betraying the ass. *L'Estrange.*

The cunning courtier should be slighted too,
Who with dull *knavery* makes so much ado;
'Till the shrewd fool, by thriving too too fast,
Like Æsop's fox, becomes a prey at last. *Dryden.*

2. Mischievous tricks or practices. In the following passage it seems a general term for any thing put to an ill use, or perhaps for trifling things of more cost than use.

We'll revel it as bravely as the best,
With amber bracelets, beads, and all this *knav'ry*. *Shakesp.*

KNA'VISH. *adj.* [from *knave.*]

1. Dishonest; wicked; fraudulent.

'Tis foolish to conceal it at all, and *knavish* to do it from friends. *Pope's Letters.*

2. Waggish; mischievous.

Here she comes curst and sad;
Cupid is a *knavish* lad,
Thus to make poor females mad. *Shakesp.*

KNA'VISHLY. *adv.* [from *knavish.*]

1. Dishonestly; fraudulently.
2. Waggishly; mischievously.

To KNEAD. *v. a.* [cnæban, Saxon; *kneden*, Dutch.] To beat or mingle any stuff or substance. It is seldom applied in popular language but to the act of making bread.

Here's yet in the word hereafter, the *kneading*, the making of the cakes, and the heating of the oven. *Shakespeare.*

It is a lump, where all beasts *kneaded* be;
Wisdom makes him an ark where all agree. *Donne.*

Thus *kneaded* up with milk the new made man
His kingdom o'er his kindred world began;
'Till knowledge misapply'd, misunderstood,
And pride of empire, sour'd his balmy blood. *Dryden.*

One paste of flesh on all degrees bestow'd,
And *kneaded* up alike with moist'ning blood. *Dryden.*

Prometheus, in the *kneading* up of the heart, seasoned it with some furious particles of the lion. *Addison's Spectator.*

No man ever reapt his corn,
Or from the oven drew his bread,
Ere hinds and bakers yet were born,
That taught them both to sow and *knead*. *Prior.*

The cake she *kneaded* was the sav'ry meat. *Prior.*

KNE'ADINGTROUGH. *n. s.* [*knead* and *trough.*] A trough in which the paste of bread is worked together.

Frogs shall come into thy *kneadingtroughs*. *Ex.* viii. 3.

KNEE. *n. s.* [cneop, Saxon; *knee*, Dutch.]

1. The joint of the leg where the leg is joined to the thigh.

Thy royal father
Was a most sainted king: the queen that bore thee,
Oftner upon her *knees* than on her feet,
Died every day she liv'd. *Shakespeare's Macbeth.*

I have reserved to myself seven thousand, who have not bowed the *knee* to Baal. *Ro.* xi. 4.

Scotch skink is a kind of strong nourishment, made of the *knees* and sinews of beef long boiled. *Bacon.*

I beg and clasp thy *knees*. *Milton.*

Weary'd with length of ways, worn out with toil,
To lay down, and leaning on her *knees*,
Invok'd the cause of all her miseries;
And cast her languishing regards above,
For help from heav'n, and her ungrateful Jove. *Dryden.*

Disdainful of Campania's gentle plains,
When for them she must bend the servile *knee*. *Thomson.*

2. A *knee* is a piece of timber growing crooked, and so cut that the trunk and branch make an angle. *Moxon's Mech. Exer.*

Such dispositions are the fittest timber to make great politicks of: like to *knee* timber, that is good for ships that are to be tossed; but not for building houses, that shall stand firm. *Bacon.*

To KNEE. *v. a.* [from the noun.] To supplicate by kneeling.

Go you that banish'd him, a mile before his tent, fall down, and *knee* the way into his mercy. *Shakesp. Coriolanus.*

Return with her!
Why, the hot-blooded France, that dow'rless took
Our youngest born: I could as well be brought
To *knee* his throne, and squire-like pension beg. *Shakes.*

KNEED. *adj.* [from *knee.*]

1. Having knees: as *in-kneed*, or *out-kneed*.
2. Having joints: as *kneed* grass.

KNE'EDEEP. *adj.* [*knee* and *deep.*]

1. Rising to the knees.
2. Sunk to the knees.

The country peasant meditates no harm,
When clad with skins of beasts to keep him warm;
In winter weather unconcern'd he goes,
Almost *kneedeep*, through mire in clumsey shoes. *Dryden.*

KNE'EHOLM. *n. s.* An herb. *Ainsworth.*

KNE'EPAN. *n. s.* [*knee* and *pan.*] A little round bone about two inches broad, pretty thick, a little convex on both sides, and covered with a smooth cartilage on its foreside. It is soft in children, but very hard in those of riper years: it is called patella or mola. Over it passes the tendon of the muscles which extend the leg, to which it serves as a pully. *Quincy.*

The *kneepan* must be shewn, with the knitting thereof, by a fine shadow underneath the joint. *Peacham on Drawing.*

To KNEEL. *v. n.* [from *knee.*] To perform the act of genuflection; to bend the knee.

When thou do'st ask me blessing, I'll *kneel* down,
And ask of thee forgiveness. *Shak. King Lear.*

Ere I was risen from the place that shew'd
My duty *kneeling*, came a reeking post,
Stew'd in his haste, half breathing, panting forth
From Goneril, his mistress, salutation. *Shak. King Lear.*

A certain man *kneeling* down to him, said, Lord, have mercy upon my son; for he is lunatick. *Mat.* xvii. 14.

As soon as you are dressed, *kneel* and say the Lord's prayer. *Taylor's Guide to Devotion.*

KNE'ETRIBUTE. *n. s.* [*knee* and *tribute.*] Genuflection; worship or obeisance shown by kneeling.

Receive from us
Kneetribute yet unpaid, prostration vile. *Milton.*

KNEL. *n. s.* [*cnil*, Welsh, a funeral pile; cnyllan, to ring, Sax.] The sound of a bell rung at a funeral.

I would not wish them to a fairer death,
And so his *knell* is knoll'd. *Shakespeare.*

Sea nymphs hourly ring his *knell*:
Hark, now I hear them. *Shak. Tempest.*

When he was brought again to th' bar, to hear
His *knell* rung out, his judgment, he was stirr'd
With such an agony, he sweat extremely. *Shak. H.* VIII.

All these motions, which we saw,
Are but as ice, which crackles at a thaw:
Or as a lute, which in moist weather rings
Her *knell* alone, by cracking of her strings. *Donne.*

Unhappy slave, and pupil to a bell,
Which his hours work, as well as hours do tell;
Unhappy 'till the last, the kind releasing *knell*. *Cowley.*

At dawn poor Stella danc'd and sung;
The am'rous youth around her bow'd:
At night her fatal *knell* was rung;
I saw, and kiss'd her in her shrowd. *Prior.*

KNEW. The preterite of *know*.

KNIFE. *n. s.* plur. *knives*. [cnıf, Sax. *kniff*, Danish.] An instrument edged and pointed, wherewith meat is cut, and animals killed.

Come, thick night,
And pall thee in the dunnest smoke of hell,
That my keen *knife* see not the wound it makes. *Shakesp.*

Blest powers, forbid thy tender life
Should bleed upon a barbarous *knife*. *Crashaw.*

The sacred priests with ready *knives* bereave
The beast of life, and in full bowls receive
The streaming blood. *Dryden's Æn.*

Ev'n in his sleep he starts, and fears the *knife*,
And, trembling, in his arms takes his accomplice wife. *Dryd.*

Pain is not in the *knife* that cuts us; but we call it cutting in the *knife*, and pain only in ourselves. *Watts.*

KNIGHT. *n. s.* [cnıht, Sax. *knecht*, Germ. a servant, or pupil.]

1. A man advanced to a certain degree of military rank. It was anciently the custom to knight every man of rank or fortune, that he might be qualified to give challenges, to fight in the lists, and to perform feats of arms. In England knighthood confers the title of *sir*: as, *sir* Thomas, *sir* Richard. When the name was not known, it was usual to say *sir* knight.

That same *knight*'s own sword this is of yore,
Which Merlin made. *Spenser.*

Sir *knight*, if *knight* thou be,
Abandon this forestalled place. *Spenser.*

When every case in law is right,
No squire in debt, and no poor *knight*. *Shak. King Lear.*

Pardon, goddess of the night,
Those that slew thy virgin *knight*;
For the which, with songs of woe,
Round about her tomb they go. *Shakesp.*

This *knight*; but yet why should I call him *knight*,
To give impiety to this rev'rent stile. *Daniel's Civil War.*

No squire with *knight* did better fit
In parts, in manners, and in wit. *Hudibras.*

2. Among us the order of gentlemen next to the nobility, except the baronets.

The *knight* intends to make his appearance. *Addison.*

3. A champion.

He suddenly unties the poke,
Which out of it sent such a smoke,
As ready was them all to choke,
So grievous was the pother;
So that the *knights* each other lost,
And stood as still as any post. *Drayton.*

Did I for this my country bring
To help their *knight* against their king,
And raise the first sedition? *Denham.*

KNIGHT *Errant.* [*chevalier errant.*] A wandering knight; one who went about in quest of adventures.

Like a bold *knight errant* did proclaim
Combat to all, and bore away the dame. *Denham.*

The ancient *errant knights*
Won all their mistresses in fights;
They cut whole giants into fritters,
To put them into am'rous twitters. *Hudibras.*

KNIGHT *Errantry.* [from *knight errant.*] The character or manners of wandering knights.

That which with the vulgar passes for courage is a brutish sort of *knight errantry*, seeking out needless encounters. *Norris.*

KNIGHT *of the Post.* A hireling evidence.

There are *knights of the post*, and holy cheats enough, to swear the truth of the broadest contradictions, where pious frauds shall give them an extraordinary call. *South's Sermons.*

KNIGHT *of the Shire.* One of the representatives of a county in parliament: he formerly was a military knight, but now any man having an estate in land of six hundred pounds a year is qualified.

To KNIGHT. *v. a.* [from the noun.] To create one a knight, which is done by the king, who gives the person kneeling a blow with a sword, and bids him rise up *sir.*

Favours came thick upon him: the next St. George's day he was *knighted.* *Wotton.*

The lord protector *knighted* the king; and immediately the king stood up, took the sword from the lord protector, and dubbed the lord mayor of London knight. *Hayward.*

The hero William, and the martyr Charles,
One *knighted* Blackmore, and one pension'd Quarles. *Pope.*

KNI'GHTLY. *adj.* [from *knight.*] Befitting a knight; beseeming a knight.

Let us take care of your wound, upon condition that a more *knightly* combat shall be performed between us. *Sidney.*

How dares your pride presume against my laws?
As in a listed field to fight your cause:
Unask'd the royal grant, no marshal by,
As *knightly* rites require, nor judge to try. *Dryden.*

KNI'GHTHOOD. *n. s.* [from *knight.*] The character or dignity of a knight.

For that same knight's own sword this is of yore,
Which Merlin made by his almighty art,
For that his nourfling, when he *knighthood* swore,
Therewith to doen his foes eternal smart. *Fairy Queen.*

Speak truly on thy *knighthood*, and thine oath,
And so defend thee heaven and thy valour. *Shak. R. II.*

Is this the sir, who some waste wife to win,
A *knighthood* bought, to go a wooing in. *Ben. Johnson.*

If you needs must write, write Cæsar's praise,
You'll gain at least a *knighthood*, or the bays. *Pope.*

KNI'GHTLESS. *adj.* [from *knight.*] Unbecoming a knight. Obsolete.

Arise, thou cursed miscreant,
That hast with *knightless* guile, and treacherous train,
Fair knighthood foully shamed. *Fairy Queen.*

To KNIT. *v. n.* preter. *knit* or *knitted.* [cnittan, Saxon.]

1. To make or unite by texture without a loom.

Sleep, that *knits* up the ravell'd sleeve of care,
The birth of each day's life, sore labour's bath,
Balm of hurt minds. *Shakespeare's Macbeth.*

A thousand Cupids in those curls do sit;
Those curious nets thy slender fingers *knit.* *Waller.*

2. To tye.

Send for the county; go tell him of this;
I'll have this knot *knit* up to-morrow morning. *Shakespeare.*

3. To join; to unite.

His gall did grate for grief and high disdain,
And, *knitting* all his force, got one hand free. *Fa. Queen.*

These, mine enemies, are all *knit* up
In their distractions: they are in my power. *Shakespeare.*

O let the vile world end,
And the premised flames of the last day
Knit earth and heav'n together. *Shakesp. Henry VI.*

Lay your highness'
Command upon me; to the which my duties
Are with a most indissoluble tye
For ever *knit.* *Shakesp. Macbeth.*

This royal hand and mine are newly *knit*,
And the conjunction of our inward souls
Married in league, coupled and link'd together
With all religious strength of sacred vows.
Shakespeare's King John.

By the simplicity of Venus' doves,
By that which *knitteth* souls, and prospers loves. *Shakesp.*

If ye be come peaceably, mine heart shall be *knit* unto you. 1 *Chro.* xii. 17.

That their hearts might be comforted, being *knit* together in love. *Col.* ii. 2.

He doth fundamentally and mathematically demonstrate the firmest *knittings* of the upper timbers, which make the roof. *Wotton's Architect.*

Pride and impudence, in faction *knit*,
Usurp the chair of wit! *Ben. Johnson's New Inn.*

Ye *knit* my heart to you by asking this question. *Bacon.*

These two princes were agreeable to be joined in marriage, and thereby *knit* both realms into one. *Hayward.*

Come, *knit* hands, and beat the ground
In a light fantastick round. *Milton.*

God gave several abilities to several persons, that each might help to supply the publick needs, and, by joining to fill up all wants, they be *knit* together by justice, as the parts of the world are by nature. *Taylor's Rule of living holy.*

Nature cannot *knit* the bones while the parts are under a discharge. *Wiseman's Surgery.*

3. To contract.

What are the thoughts that *knit* thy brow in frowns,
And turn thy eyes so coldly on thy prince. *Addison's Cato.*

4. To tie up.

He saw heaven opened, as it had been a great sheet *knit* at the four corners, and let down to the earth. *Acts* x. 11.

To KNIT. *v. n.*

1. To weave without a loom.

A young shepherdess *knitting* and singing: her voice comforted her hands to work, and her hands kept time to her voice's musick. *Sidney.*

Make the world distinguish Julia's son
From the vile offspring of a trull, that sits
By the town-wall, and for her living *knits.* *Dryden.*

2. To join; to close; to unite.

Our sever'd navy too
Have *knit* again, and float, threat'ning most sea-like. *Shak.*

KNIT. *n. s.* [from the verb.] Texture.

Let their heads be sleekly comb'd, their blue coats brush'd, and their garters of an indifferent *knit.* *Shakespeare.*

KNI'TTER. *n. s.* [from *knit.*] One who weaves or knits.

The spinsters and the *knitters* in the sun,
And the free maids that weave their thread with bo[illegible]
Do use to chant it. *Shakespeare's Twelfth Night.*

KNI'TTINGNEEDLE. *n. s.* [*knit* and *needle.*] A wire which women use in knitting.

He gave her a cuff on the ear, she would prick him with her *knittingneedle.* *Arbuthnot's Hist. of John Bull.*

KNI'TTLE. *n. s.* [from *knit.*] A string that gathers a purse round. *Ainsworth.*

KNOB. *n. s.* [cnæp, Saxon; *knoop*, Dutch.] A protuberance; any part bluntly rising above the rest.

Just before the entrance of the right auricle of the heart is a remarkable *knob* or bunch, raised up from the subjacent fat; by the interposition whereof the blood falling down by the descending vein is diverted into the auricle. *Ray.*

KNO'BBED. *adj.* [from *knob.*] Set with knobs; having protuberances.

The horns of a roe deer of Greenland are pointed at the top, and *knobbed* or tuberous at the bottom. *Grew.*

KNO'BBINESS. *n. s.* [from *knobby.*] The quality of having knobs.

KNO'BBY. *adj.* [from *knob.*]

1. Full of knobs.

2. Hard; stubborn.

The informers continued in a *knobby* kind of obstinacy, resolving still to conceal the names of the authors. *Howel.*

To KNOCK. *v. n.* [cnucian, Saxon; *cnoce*, a blow, Welsh.]

1. To clash; to be driven suddenly together.

Any hard body thrust forwards by another body contiguous, without *knocking*, giveth no noise. *Bacon's Nat. Hist.*

They may say, the atoms of the chaos being variously moved according to this catholick law, must needs *knock* and interfere. *Bentley's Sermons.*

2. To beat, as at a door for admittance.

Villain, I say *knock* me at this gate,
And rap me well; or I'll knock your knave's pate. *Shak.*

Whether to *knock* against the gates of Rome,
Or rudely visit them in parts remote,
To fright them, ere destroy. *Shakespeare's Coriolanus.*

I bid the rascal *knock* upon your gate,
And could not get get him for my heart to do it. *Shakesp.*

For harbour at a thousand doors they *knock'd*,
Not one of all the thousand but was lock'd. *Dryden.*

Knock at your own breast, and ask your soul,
If those fair fatal eyes edg'd not your sword. *Dryden.*

3. *To* KNOCK *under.* A common expression, that denotes when a man yields or submits.

To KNOCK. *v. a.*

1. To affect or change in any respect by blows.

How do you mean removing him?
—Why, by making him incapable of Othello's place; *knocking* out his brains. *Shakespeare's Othello.*

He that has his chains *knocked* off, and the prison doors set open to him, is perfectly at liberty. *Locke.*

Time was, a sober Englishman would *knock*
His servants up, and rise by five o'clock;
Instruct his family in ev'ry rule
And send his wife to church, his son to school. *Dryden.*

2. To dash together; to strike; to collide with a sharp noise.

So when the cook saw my jaws thus *knock* it,
She would have made a pancake of my pocket. *Cleaveland.*

At him he lanch'd his spear, and pierc'd his breast;
On the hard earth the Lycian *knock'd* his head,
And lay supine; and forth the spirit fled. *Dryden.*

'Tis

'Tis the ſport of ſtateſmen,
When heroes *knock* their knotty heads together,
And fall by one another. *Rowe.*

3. *To* KNOCK *down.* To fell by a blow.

He began to *knock down* his fellow citizens with a great deal of zeal, and to fill all Arabia with an unnatural medley of religion and bloodſhed. *Addiſon's Freeholder*, N°. 50.

A man who is groſs in a woman's company, ought to be *knocked down* with a club. *Clariſſa.*

4. *To* KNOCK *on the head.* To kill by a blow; to deſtroy.

He betook himſelf to his orchard, and walking there was *knocked on the head* by a tree. *South's Sermons.*

Exceſs, either with an apoplexy, *knocks* a man *on the head*; or with a fever, like fire in a ſtrong-water-ſhop, burns him down to the ground. *Grew's Coſmol.*

KNOCK. *n. ſ.* [from the verb.]

1. A ſudden ſtroke; a blow.

Some men never conceive how the motion of the earth ſhould wave him from a *knock* perpendicularly directed from a body in the air above. *Brown's Vulgar Err. b.* vii.

Ajax belabours there an harmleſs ox,
And thinks that Agamemnon feels the *knocks*. *Dryden.*

2. A loud ſtroke at a door for admiſſion.

Guiſcard, in his leathern frock,
Stood ready, with his thrice-repeated *knock*:
Thrice with a doleful ſound the jarring grate
Rung deaf and hollow. *Dryden's Boccace.*

KNO'CKER. *n. ſ.* [from *knock*.]

1. He that knocks.
2. The hammer which hangs at the door for ſtrangers to ſtrike.

Shut, ſhut the door, good John! fatigu'd, I ſaid,
Tie up the *knocker*, ſay I'm ſick, I'm dead. *Pope.*

To KNOLL. *v. a.* [from *knell*.] To ring the bell, generally for a funeral.

Had I as many ſons as I have hairs,
I would not wiſh them to a fairer death,
And ſo his knell is *knoll'd*. *Shakeſpeare's Macbeth.*

To KNOLL. *v. n.* To ſound as a bell.

If ever you have look'd on better days,
If ever been where bells have *knoll'd* to church. *Shakeſp.*

KNOLL. *n. ſ.* A little hill. *Ainſ.*

KNOP. *n. ſ.* [A corruption of *knap*.] Any tufty top. *Ainſ.*

KNOT. *n. ſ.* [cnotta, Saxon; *knot*, German; *knutte*, Dutch; *knotte*, Erſe.]

1. A complication of a cord or ſtring not eaſily to be diſentangled.

He found that reaſon's ſelf now reaſons found
To faſten *knots*, which fancy firſt had bound. *Sidney.*

As the fair veſtal to the fountain came,
Let none be ſtartled at a veſtal's name,
Tir'd with the walk, ſhe laid her down to reſt;
And to the winds expos'd her glowing breaſt,
To take the freſhneſs of the morning air,
And gather'd in a *knot* her flowing hair. *Addiſon.*

2. Any figure of which the lines frequently interſect each other.

Garden *knots*, the frets of houſes, and all equal figures, pleaſe; whereas unequal figures are but deformities. *Bacon.*

Our ſea-wall'd garden, the whole land,
Is full of weeds, her faireſt flowers choked up,
Her *knots* diſorder'd. *Shakeſp. Rich.* II.

It fed flow'rs worthy of paradiſe, which not nice art
In beds and curious *knots*, but nature boon,
Pour'd forth profuſe on hill and dale, and plain. *Milton.*

Their quarters are contrived into elegant *knots*, adorned with the moſt beautiful flowers. *More.*

Henry in *knots* involving Emma's name,
Had half-expreſs'd, and half-conceal'd his flame
Upon this tree; and as the tender mark
Grew with the year, and widen'd with the bark,
Venus had heard the virgin's ſoft addreſs,
That, as the wound, the paſſion might increaſe. *Prior.*

3. Any bond of aſſociation or union.

Confirm that amity
With nuptial *knot*, if thou vouchſafe to grant
That virtuous lady Bona. *Shakeſp. Henry* VI.

Richmond aims
At young Elizabeth, my brother's daughter,
And by that *knot* looks proudly on the crown. *Shakeſp.*

I would he had continued to his country
As he began, and not unknit himſelf
The noble *knot* he made. *Shakeſpeare's Coriolanus.*

Why left you wife and children,
Thoſe precious motives, thoſe ſtrong *knots* of love. *Shak.*

Not all that Saul could threaten or perſuade,
In this cloſe *knot*, the ſmalleſt looſeneſs made. *Cowley.*

4. A hard part in a piece of wood cauſed by the protuberance of a bough, and conſequently by a tranſverſe direction of the fibres. A joint in an herb.

Taking the very refuſe among thoſe which ſerved to no uſe, being a crooked piece of wood, and full of *knots*, he hath carved it diligently, when he had nothing elſe to do. *Wiſd.*

Such *knots* and croſſneſs of grain is objected here, as will hardly ſuffer that form, which they cry up here as the only juſt reformation, to go on ſo ſmoothly here as it might do in Scotland. *King Charles.*

5. A confederacy; an aſſociation; a ſmall band.

Oh you panderly raſcals! there's a *knot*, a gang, a conſpiracy againſt me. *Shakeſ. Merry Wives of Windſor.*

What is there here in Rome that can delight thee?
Where not a ſoul, without thine own foul *knot*,
But fears and hates thee. *Ben. Johnſon's Catiline.*

A *knot* of good fellows borrowed a ſum of money of a gentleman upon the king's highway. *L'Eſtrange.*

I am now with a *knot* of his admirers, who make requeſt that you would give notice of the window where the knight intends to appear. *Addiſon's Spectator.*

6. Difficulty; intricacy.

A man ſhall be perplexed with *knots* and problems of buſineſs, and contrary affairs, where the determination is dubious, and both parts of the contrariety ſeem equally weighty; ſo that, which way ſoever the choice determines, a man is ſure to venture a great concern. *South's Sermons.*

7. Any intrigue, or difficult perplexity of affairs.

When the diſcovery was made that the king was living, which was the *knot* of the play untied, the reſt is ſhut up in the compaſs of ſome few lines, becauſe nothing then hindered the happineſs of Toriſmond and Leonora. *Dryden's Dufreſn.*

8. A cluſter; a collection.

The way of fortune is like the milky way in the ſky, which is a meeting or *knot* of a number of ſmall ſtars, not ſeen aſunder, but giving light together. *Bacon's Eſſays.*

In a picture, beſides the principal figures which compoſe it, and are placed in the midſt of it, there are leſs groups or *knots* of figures diſpoſed at proper diſtances, which are parts of the piece, and ſeem to carry on the ſame deſign in a more inferior manner. *Dryden's Dufreſnoy.*

To KNOT. *v. a.* [from the noun.]

1. To complicate in knots.

Happy we who from ſuch queens are freed,
That were always telling beads:
But here's a queen when ſhe rides abroad
Is always *knotting* threads. *Sidley.*

2. To intangle; to perplex.
3. To unite.

The party of the papiſts in England are become more *knotted*, both in dependence towards Spain, and amongſt themſelves. *Bacon's War with Spain.*

To KNOT. *v. n.*

1. To form buds, knots, or joints in vegetation.

Cut hay when it begins to *knot*. *Mortimer's Huſbandry.*

2. To knit knots for fringes.

KNO'TBERRYBUSH. *n. ſ.* A plant. *Ainſ.*

KNO'TGRASS. *n. ſ.* [*knot* and *graſs*.] A plant.

KNO'TTED. *adj.* [from *knot*.] Full of knots.

The *knotted* oaks ſhall ſhow'rs of honey weep. *Dryden.*

KNO'TTINESS. *n. ſ.* [from *knotty*.] Fulneſs of knots; unevenneſs; intricacy; difficulty.

Virtue was repreſented by Hercules naked, with his lion's ſkin and knotted club: by his oaken club is ſignified reaſon ruling the appetite; the *knottineſs* thereof, the difficulty they have that ſeek after virtue. *Peacham on Drawing.*

KNO'TTY. *adj.* [from *knot*.]

1. Full of knots.

I have ſeen tempeſts, when the ſcolding winds
Have riv'd the *knotty* oaks. *Shakeſp. Julius Cæſar.*

The timber in ſome trees more clean, in ſome more *knotty*: try it by ſpeaking at one end, and laying the ear at the other; for if it be *knotty*, the voice will not paſs well. *Bacon.*

The *knotty* oaks their liſt'ning branches bow. *Roſcommon.*

One with a brand yet burning from the flame,
Arm'd with a *knotty* club another came. *Dryden's Æn.*

Where the vales with violets once were crown'd,
Now *knotty* burrs and thorns diſgrace the ground:
Come, ſhepherds, come, and ſtrew with leaves the plain;
Such funeral rites your Daphnis did ordain. *Dryden.*

2. Hard; rugged.

Valiant fools
Were made by nature for the wiſe to work with:
They are their tools; and 'tis the ſport of ſtateſmen,
When heroes knock their *knotty* heads together,
And fall by one another. *Rowe's Ambitious Stepmother.*

3. Intricate; perplexed; difficult; embaraſſed.

King Henry, in the very entrance of his reign, when the kingdom was caſt in his arms, met with a point of great difficulty, and *knotty* to ſolve, able to trouble and confound the wiſeſt kings. *Bacon's Henry* VII.

Princes exerciſed ſkill in putting intricate queſtions; and he that was the beſt at the untying of *knotty* difficulties, carried the prize. *L'Eſtrange.*

Some on the bench the *knotty* laws untie. *Dryden.*

They compliment, they ſit, they chat,
Fight o'er the wars, reform the ſtate;
A thouſand *knotty* points they clear,
'Till ſupper and my wife appear. *Prior.*

To KNOW. *v. a.* preter. *I knew*, *I have known.* [cnapan Saxon.]

1. To perceive with certainty, whether intuitive or diſcurſive.

O, that a man might *know*
The end of this day's buſineſs ere it come! *Shakeſpeare.*

The memorial of virtue is immortal, becauſe it is *known* with God and with men. *Wiſd.* iv. 1.

The gods all things *know*. *Milton.*

Not from experience, for the world was new,
He only from their cauſe their natures *knew*. *Denham.*

We doubt not, neither can we properly ſay we think we admire and love you above all other men: there is a certainty in the propoſition, and we *know* it. *Dryden.*

When a man makes uſe of the name of any ſimple idea, which he perceives is not underſtood, or is in danger to be miſtaken, he is obliged by the laws of ingenuity, and the end of ſpeech, to declare his meaning, and make *known* what idea he makes it ſtand for. *Locke.*

2. To be informed of; to be taught.

Ye ſhall be healed, and it ſhall be *known* to you why his hand is not removed from you. 1 *Sa.* vi. 3.

Led on with a deſire to *know*
What nearer might concern him. *Milton.*

One would have thought you had *known* better things than to expect a kindneſs from a common enemy. *L'Eſtrange.*

3. To diſtinguiſh.

Numeration is but the adding of one unit more, and giving to the whole a new name, whereby to *know* it from thoſe before and after, and diſtinguiſh it from every ſmaller or greater multitude of units. *Locke.*

4. To recogniſe.

What a monſtrous fellow art thou, thus to rail on me, that is neither *known* of thee, nor *knows* thee? *Shakeſpeare.*

They told what things were done in the way, and how he was *known* of them in breaking of bread. *Lu.* xxiv. 35.

At nearer view he thought he *knew* the dead,
And call'd the wretched man to mind. *Flatman.*

Tell me how I may *know* him. *Milton.*

5. To be no ſtranger to.

What are you?
—A moſt poor man, made tame to fortune's blows,
Who, by the art of *known* and feeling ſorrows,
Am pregnant to good pity. *Shak. King Lear.*

6. To converſe with another ſex.

And Adam *knew* Eve his wife. *Gen.* iv. 4.

7. To ſee with approbation.

They have reigned, but not by me; they have ſet a ſeigniory over themſelves, but I *knew* nothing of it. *Hoſea.*

To KNOW. *v. n.*

1. To have clear and certain perception; not to be doubtful.

I *know* of a ſurety that the Lord hath ſent his angel, and delivered me out of the hand of Herod. *Acts* xii. 11.

2. Not to be ignorant.

When they *know* within themſelves they ſpeak of that they do not well *know*, they would nevertheleſs ſeem to others to *know* of that which they may not well ſpeak. *Bacon's Eſſays*, N°. 27.

Not to *know* of things remote, but know
That which before us lies in daily life,
Is the prime wiſdom. *Milton.*

In the other world there is no conſideration that will ſting our conſciences more cruelly than this, that we did wickedly, when we *knew* to have done better; and choſe to make ourſelves miſerable, when we underſtood the way to have been happy. *Tillotſon's Sermons.*

They might underſtand thoſe excellencies which they blindly valued, ſo as not to be farther impoſed upon by bad pieces, and to *know* when nature was well imitated by the moſt able maſters. *Dryden's Dufreſnoy.*

3. To be informed.

The prince and Mr. Poins will put on two of our jerkins and aprons, and ſir John muſt not *know* of it. *Shakeſpeare's Henry* IV.

There is but one mineral body, that we *know* of, heavier than common quickſilver. *Boyle.*

4. *To* KNOW *for.* To have knowledge of. A colloquial expreſſion.

He ſaid the water itſelf was a good healthy water; but for the party that own'd it, he might have more diſeaſes than he *knew for.* *Shakeſp. Henry* IV.

5. *To* KNOW *of.* In *Shakeſpeare*, is to take cogniſance of; to examine.

Fair Hermia, queſtion your deſires;
Know of your youth, examine well your blood,
Whether, if you yield not to your father's choice,
You can endure the livery of a nun,
For ay to be in ſhady cloiſter mew'd. *Shakeſpeare.*

KNO'WABLE. *adj.* [from *know.*] Cognoſcible; poſſible to be diſcovered or underſtood.

Theſe are reſolved into a confeſſed ignorance, and I ſhall not purſue them to their old aſylum; and yet it may be, there is more *knowable* in theſe than in leſs acknowledged myſteries. *Glanv. Sceſ.*

'Tis plain, that under the law of works is comprehended alſo the law of nature, *knowable* by reaſon, as well as the law given by Moſes. *Locke.*

Theſe two arguments are the voices of nature, the unanimous ſuffrages of all real beings and ſubſtances created, that are naturally *knowable* without revelation. *Bentley.*

KNO'WER. *n. ſ.* [from *know.*] One who has ſkill or knowledge.

If we look on a vegetable as made of earth, we muſt have the true theory of the nature of that element, or we miſerably fail of our ſcientifical aſpirings; and while we can only ſay 'tis cold and dry, we are pitiful *knowers.* *Glanv.*

I know the reſpect and reverence which in this addreſs I ought to appear in before you, who are a general *knower* of mankind and poetry. *Southern.*

KNO'WING. *adj.* [from *know.*]

1. Skilful; well inſtructed; remote from ignorance.

You have heard, and with a *knowing* ear,
That he, which hath our noble father ſlain,
Purſu'd my life. *Shak. Hamlet.*

The *knowingeſt* of theſe have of late reformed their hypotheſis. *Boyle.*

What makes the clergy glorious is to be *knowing* in their profeſſion, unſpotted in their lives, active and laborious in their charges. *South.*

The neceſſity of preparing for the offices of religion was a leſſon which the mere light and dictates of common reaſon, without the help of revelation, taught all the *knowing* and intelligent part of the world. *South's Sermons.*

Gio Bellino, one of the firſt who was of any conſideration at Venice, painted very drily, according to the manner of his time: he was very *knowing* both in architecture and perſpective. *Dryden's Dufreſnoy.*

All animals of the ſame kind, which form a ſociety, are more *knowing* than others. *Addiſon's Guardian.*

2. Conſcious; intelligent.

Could any but a *knowing* prudent Cauſe
Begin ſuch motions and aſſign ſuch laws?
If the Great Mind had form'd a different frame,
Might not your wanton wit the ſyſtem blame? *Blackmore.*

KNO'WING. *n. ſ.* [from *know.*] Knowledge.

Let him be ſo entertain'd as ſuits gentlemen of your *knowing* to a ſtranger of his quality. *Shakeſpeare.*

KNO'WINGLY. *adv.* [from *knowing.*] With ſkill; with knowledge.

He *knowingly* and wittingly brought evil into the world. *More's Divine Dialogues.*

They who before were rather fond of it than *knowingly* admired it, might defend their inclination by their reaſon. *Dryden's Dufreſnoy.*

To the private duties of the cloſet he repaired, as often as he entered upon any buſineſs of conſequence: I ſpeak *knowingly.* *Atterbury's Sermons.*

KNO'WLEDGE. *n. ſ.* [from *know.*]

1. Certain perception; indubitable apprehenſion.

Knowledge, which is the higheſt degree of the ſpeculative faculties, conſiſts in the perception of the truth of affirmative or negative propoſitions. *Locke.*

2. Learning; illumination of the mind.

Ignorance is the curſe of God,
Knowledge the wing wherewith we fly to heav'n. *Shakeſp.*

3. Skill in any thing.

Do but ſay to me what I ſhould do,
That in your *knowledge* may by me be done,
And I am preſt unto it. *Shak. Merchant of Venice.*

4. Acquaintance with any fact or perſon.

The dog ſtraight fawned upon his maſter for old *knowledge.* *Sidney.*

That is not forgot,
Which ne'er I did remember; to my *knowledge*
I never in my life did look on him. *Shakeſp. Rich.* II.

5. Cogniſance; notice.

Why have I found grace in thine eyes, that thou ſhouldſt take *knowledge* of me, ſeeing I am a ſtranger? *Ruth* ii. 10.

A ſtate's anger ſhould not take
Knowledge either of fools or women. *Ben. Johnſon's Catil.*

6. Information; power of knowing.

I pulled off my headpiece, and humbly entreated her pardon, or *knowledge* why ſhe was cruel. *Sidney.*

To KNO'WLEDGE. *v. a.* [not in uſe.] To acknowledge; to avow.

The prophet Hoſea tells us that God ſaith of the Jews, they have reigned, but not by me; which proveth plainly, that there are governments which God doth not avow: for though they be ordained by his ſecret providence, yet they are not *knowledged* by his revealed will. *Bacon's holy War.*

To KNU'BBLE. *v. a.* [*knipler*, Daniſh.] To beat. *Skinner.*

KNU'CKLE. *n. ſ.* [cnucle, Saxon; *knockle*, Dutch.]

1. The joints of the fingers protuberant when the fingers cloſe.

Thus often at the Temple-ſtairs we've ſeen
Two tritons, of a rough athletick mien,
Sourly diſpute ſome quarrel of the flood,
With *knuckles* bruis'd, and face beſmear'd in blood. *Garth.*

2. The knee joint of a calf.

We find alſo that Scotch ſkinck, which is a pottage of ſtrong nouriſhment, is made with the knees and ſinews of beef, but long boiled: jelly alſo, which they uſed for a reſtorative, is chiefly made of *knuckles* of veal. *Bacon's Nat. Hiſt.*

3. The articulation or joint of a plant.

Divers herbs have joints or *knuckles*, as it were ſtops in their germination; as gillyflowers, pinks, fennel, and corn. *Bacon's Natural Hiſtory.*

To KNU'CKLE. *v. n.* [from the noun.] To ſubmit: I ſuppoſe from an odd cuſtom of ſtriking the under ſide of the table with the knuckles, in confeſſion of an argumental defeat.

KNU'CKLED. *adj.* [from *knuckle.*] Jointed.

The reed or cane is a watry plant, and groweth not but in the water: it hath theſe properties, that it is hollow, and it is *knuckled* both ſtalk and root; that, being dry, it is more hard and fragile than other wood; that it putteth forth no boughs, though many ſtalks out of one root. *Bacon's Nat. History.*

KNUFF. *n. ſ.* [perhaps corrupted from *knave*, or the ſame with *chuff.*] A lout. An old word preſerved in a rhyme of prediction.

The country *knuffs*, Hob, Dick, and Hick,
With clubs and clouted ſhoon,
Shall fill up Duſſendale
With ſlaughtered bodies ſoon. *Hayward.*

KNUR. } *n. ſ.* [*knor*, German.] A knot; a hard ſub-
KNURLE. } ſtance.

The ſtony nodules found lodged in the ſtrata, are called by the workmen *knurs* and knots. *Woodward's Met. Foſſ.*

KONED for *knew.* *Spenſer.*

To KYD. *v. n.* [corrupted probably from cuð, Saxon.] To know.

But ah, unjuſt and worthleſs Colin Clout,
That *kydſt* the hidden kinds of many a weed;
Yet *kydſt* not one to cure thy ſore heart root,
Whoſe rankling wound as yet doth riſely bleed. *Spenſer.*

L.

A

DICTIONARY

OF THE

ENGLISH LANGUAGE:

IN WHICH

The WORDS are deduced from their ORIGINALS,

AND

ILLUSTRATED in their DIFFERENT SIGNIFICATIONS

BY

EXAMPLES from the beſt WRITERS.

TO WHICH ARE PREFIXED,

A HISTORY of the LANGUAGE,

AND

AN ENGLISH GRAMMAR.

By SAMUEL JOHNSON, A. M.

IN TWO VOLUMES.

VOL. II.

Cum tabulis animum cenſoris ſumet honeſti:
Audebit quæcunque parum ſplendoris habebunt,
Et ſine pondere erunt, et honore indigna ferentur.
Verba movere loco; quamvis invita recedant,
Et verſentur adhuc intra penetralia Veſtæ:
Obſcurata diu populo bonus eruet, atque
Proferet in lucem ſpecioſa vocabula rerum,
Quæ priſcis memorata Catonibus atque Cethegis,
Nunc ſitus informis premit et deſerta vetuſtas. HOR.

LONDON,
Printed by W. STRAHAN,
For J. and P. KNAPTON; T. and T. LONGMAN; C. HITCH and L. HAWES;
A. MILLAR; and R. and J. DODSLEY.
MDCCLV.

L.

L, A liquid consonant, which preserves always the same sound in English. In the Saxon it was aspirated a hlaf, *loaf*; hlæfdig, *lady*.

At the end of a monosyllable it is always doubled; as, *shall*; *still*; *full*, except after a diphthong; as, *fail*; *feel*; *veal*; *cool*. In a word of more syllables it is written single; as, *channel*; *canal*; *tendril*. It is sometimes put before *e*, and sounded feebly after it; as *bible*; *title*.

LA. *interject.* [corrupted by an effeminate pronunciation from *lo.*] See; look; behold.

> *La* you! if you speak ill of the devil,
> How he takes it at heart. *Shakes. Twelfth Night.*

LA'BDANUM. *n. s.* A resin of the softer kind, of a strong and not unpleasant smell, and an aromatick, but not agreeable taste. This juice exsudates from a low spreading shrub, of the cistus kind, in Crete, and the neighbouring islands; and the Grecian women make balls of it with a small admixture of ambergrease, by way of a perfume. It was formerly used externally in medicine, but is now neglected. *Hill.*

To LA'BEFY. *v. a.* [*labefacio*, Latin.] To weaken; to impair. *Dict.*

LA'BEL. *n. s.* [*labellum*, Latin.]

1. A small slip or scrip of writing.

> When wak'd, I found
> This *label* on my bosom; whose containing
> Is so from sense in hardness, that I can
> Make no collection of it. *Shakespeare's Cymbeline.*

2. Any thing appendant to a larger writing.

On the *label* of lead, the heads of St. Peter and St. Paul are impressed from the papal seal. *Ayliffe's Parergon.*

3. [In law.] A narrow slip of paper or parchment affixed to a deed or writing, in order to hold the appending seal. So also any paper, annexed by way of addition or explication to any will or testament, is called a label or codicil. *Harris.*

> God join'd my heart to Romeo's; thou our hands;
> And ere this hand by thee to Romeo seal'd,
> Shall be the *label* to another deed,
> Or my true heart with treacherous revolt
> Turn to another, this shall slay them both. *Shakespeare.*

LA'BENT. *adj.* [*labens*, Lat.] Sliding; gliding; slipping. *Dict.*

LA'BIAL. *adj.* [*labialis*, Latin.] Uttered by the lips.

The Hebrews have assigned which letters are *labial*, which dental, and which guttural. *Bacon's Natural History.*

Some particular affection of sound in its passage to the lips, will seem to make some composition in any vowel which is *labial.* *Holder's Elements of Speech.*

LA'BIATED. *adj.* [*labium*, Latin.] Formed with lips.

LA'BIODENTAL. *adj.* [*labium* and *dentalis.*] Formed or pronounced by the co-operation of the lips and teeth.

The dental consonants are very easy; and first the *labiodentals f, v*, also the linguadentals *th, dh.* *Hold. Elm. of Sp.*

LABO'RANT. *n. s.* [*laborans*, Lat.] A chemist. Not in use.

I can shew you a sort of fixt sulphur, made by an industrious *laborant.* *Boyle.*

LA'BORATORY. *n. s.* [*laboratoire*, French.] A chemist's workroom.

It would contribute to the history of colours, if chemists would in their *laboratory* take a heedful notice, and give us a faithful account, of the colours observed in the steam of bodies, either sublimed or distilled. *Boyle on Colours.*

The flames of love will perform those miracles they of the furnace boast of, would they employ themselves in this *laboratory.* *Decay of Piety.*

LABO'RIOUS. *adj.* [*laborieux*, French; *laboriosus*, Latin.]

1. Diligent in work; assiduous.

That which makes the clergy glorious, is to be knowing in their professions, unspotted in their lives, active and *laborious* in their charges, bold and resolute in opposing seducers, and daring to look vice in the face; and lastly, to be gentle, courteous, and compassionate to all. *South's Serm.*

> To his *laborious* youth consum'd in war,
> And lasting age, adorn'd and crown'd with peace. *Prior.*

2. Requiring labour; tiresome; not easy.

> A spacious cave within its farmost part,
> Was hew'd and fashion'd by *laborious* art,
> Through the hill's hollow sides. *Dryd. Æn.* 6.
> Do'st thou love watchings, abstinence, and toil,
> *Laborious* virtues all? learn them from Cato. *Add. Cato.*

LABO'RIOUSLY. *adv.* [from *laborious.*] With labour; with toil.

The folly of him, who pumps very *laboriously* in a ship, yet neglects to stop the leak. *Decay of Piety.*

> I chuse *laboriously* to bear
> A weight of woes, and breathe the vital air. *Pope's Odys.*

LABO'RIOUSNESS. *n. s.* [from *laborious.*]

1. Toilsomeness; difficulty.

The parallel holds in the gainlessness as well as the *laboriousness* of the work; those wretched creatures, buried in earth and darkness, were never the richer for all the ore they digged; no more is the insatiate miser. *Decay of Piety.*

2. Diligence; assiduity.

LA'BOUR, *n. s.* [*labeur*, French; *labor*, Latin.]

1. The act of doing what requires a painful exertion of strength, or wearisome perseverance; pains; toil; travail; work.

If I find her honest, I lose not my *labour*; if she be otherwise, it is *labour* well bestowed. *Shakes. M. W. of Windsor.*

I sent to know your faith, lest the tempter have tempted you, and our *labour* be in vain. 1 *Thes.* iii. 5.

2. Work to be done.

Being a *labour* of so great difficulty, the exact performance thereof we may rather wish than look for. *Hooker.*

> You were wont to say,
> If you had been the wife of Hercules
> Six of his *labours* you'd have done, and sav'd
> Your husband so much sweat. *Shakespeare's Coriolanus.*

3. Exercise; motion with some degree of violence.

Moderate *labour* of the body conduces to the preservation of health, and curing many initial diseases; but the toil of the mind destroys health, and generates maladies. *Harvey.*

4. Childbirth; travail.

> Sith of womens *labours* thou hast charge,
> And generation goodly doest enlarge,
> Incline thy will to effect our wishful vow. *Spens. Epith.*
> Not knowing 'twas my *labour*, I complain
> Of sudden shootings, and of grinding pain;
> My throws come thicker, and my cries encreas'd,
> Which with her hand the conscious nurse suppress'd. *Dryd.*

Not one woman of two hundred dies in *labour.* *Graunt.*

His heart is in continual *labour*; it even travails with the obligation, and is in pangs 'till it be delivered. *South's Serm.*

To LABOUR. *v. n.* [*laboro*, Latin.]

1. To toil; to act with painful effort.

> When shall I come to th' top of that same hill?
> —You do climb up it now; look how we *labour.* *Shakes.*
> For your highness' good I ever *labour'd*,
> More than mine own. *Shakespear's Hen.* VIII.
> Who is with him?
> —None but the fool, who *labours* to out-jest
> His heart-struck injuries. *Shakespeare's K. Lear.*

Let more work be laid upon the men, that they may *labour* therein. *Exod.* v. 9.

2. To do work; to take pains.

Epaphras saluteth you, always *labouring* fervently for you in prayers, that ye may stand perfect. *Col.* iv. 12.

A *labouring* man that is given to drunkenness shall not be rich. *Eccluf.* xix. 1.

That in the night they may be a guard to us, and *labour* on the day. *Neh.* iv. 22.

Yet is there no end of all his labours; neither saith he, for whom do I *labour.* *Eccl.* iv. 8.

As a man had a right to all he could employ his labour upon, so he had no temptation to *labour* for more than he could make use of. *Locke.*

3. To move with difficulty.

The stone that *labours* up the hill,
Mocking the labourer's toil, returning still,
Is love. *Granville.*

4. To be diseased with. [*Morbo laborare*, Latin.]

They abound with horse,
Of which one want our camp doth only *labour*,
And I have found 'em coming. *Ben. Johnson's Catiline.*

I was called to another, who in childbed *laboured* of an ulcer in her left hip. *Wiseman.*

5. To be in distress; to be pressed.

To this infernal lake the fury flies,
Here hides her hated head, and frees the *lab'ring* skies. *Dryd.*
Trumpets and drums shall fright her from the Throne,
As sounding cymbals aid the *lab'ring* moon. *Dryd. Aur.*

This exercise will call down the favour of heaven upon you, to remove those afflictions you now *labour* under from you. *Wake's Preparation for Death.*

6. To be in child-birth; to be in travail.

There lay a log unlighted on the earth,
When she was *lab'ring* in the throws of birth;
For th' unborn chief the fatal sisters came,
And rais'd it up, and toss'd it on the flame. *Dryd. Ovid.*
Here, like some furious prophet, Pindar rode,
And seem'd to *labour* with th' inspiring God. *Pope.*

He is so touch'd with the memory of her benevolence and protection, that his soul *labours* for an expression enough to represent it. *Notes on the Odyssey.*

To La'bour. *v. a.*

1. To work at; to move with difficulty; to form with labour; to prosecute with effect.

To use brevity, and avoid much *labouring* of the work, is to be granted to him that will make an abridgment. 2 *Mac.*

The matter of the ceremonies had wrought, for the most part, only upon light-headed, weak men, whose satisfaction was not to be *laboured* for. *Clarendon.*

The pains of famish'd Tantalus shall feel,
And Sisyphus that *labours* up the hill,
The rowling rock in vain, and curst Ixion's wheel. *Dryd.*
Had you requir'd my helpful hand,
Th' artificer and art you might command,
To *labour* arms for Troy. *Dryden's Æneis.*

An eager desire to know something concerning him, has occasioned mankind to *labour* the point under these disadvantages, and turn on all hands to see if there were any thing left which might have the least appearance of information. *Pope's Essay on Homer.*

2. To beat; to belabour.

Take, shepherd, take a plant of stubborn oak,
And *labour* him with many a sturdy stroak. *Dryden's Virg.*

La'bourer. *n. s.* [*laboureur*, French.]

1. One who is employed in coarse and toilsome work.

If a state run most to noblemen and gentlemen, and that the husbandmen be but as their work-folks and *labourers*, you may have a good cavalry, but never good stable foot. *Bacon.*

The sun but seem'd the *lab'rer* of the year,
Each waxing moon supply'd her wat'ry store,
To swell those tides, which from the line did bear
Their brimful vessels to the Belgian shore. *Dryden.*

Labourers and idle persons, children and striplings, old men and young men, must have divers diets. *Arbuth. on Aliments.*

Not balmy sleep to *lab'rers* faint with pain,
Not show'rs to larks, or sun-shine to the bee,
Are half so charming, as thy sight to me. *Pope's Autumn.*
Yet hence the poor are cloth'd, the hungry fed,
Health to himself, and to his infants bread,
The *lab'rer* bears. *Pope, Ep.* iv. *l.* 167.

The prince cannot say to the merchant, I have no need of thee; nor the merchant to the *labourer*, I have no need of thee. *Swift's Miscel.*

2. One who takes pains in any employment.

Sir, I am a true *labourer*; I earn that I eat; get that I wear; owe no man hate; envy no man's happiness. *Shakes.*

The stone that labours up the hill,
Mocking the *lab'rer*'s toil, returning still,
Is love. *Granville.*

La'boursome. *adj.* [from *labour.*] Made with great labour and diligence.

Forget
Your *laboursome* and dainty trims, wherein
You made great Jove angry. *Shakespeare's Cymbeline.*
He hath, my lord, by *laboursome* petition,
Wrung from me my slow leave. *Shakespeare's Hamlet.*

La'bra. *n. s.* [Spanish.] A lip. *Hanmer.*

Word of denial in thy *labras* here;
Word of denial, froth and scum thou liest. *Shakespeare.*

La'byrinth. *n. s.* [*labyrinthus*, Latin.] A maze; a place formed with inextricable windings.

Suffolk, stay;
Thou may'st not wander in that *labyrinth*;
There Minotaurs, and ugly treasons lurk. *Shakespeare.*
Words, which would tear
The tender *labyrinth* of a maid's soft ear. *Donne.*
My clamours tear
The ear's soft *labyrinth*, and cleft the air. *Sandy's Paraph.*

The earl of Essex had not proceeded with his accustomed wariness and skill; but run into *labyrinths*, from whence he could not disentangle himself. *Clarendon, b.* viii.

My soul is on her journey; do not now
Divert, or lead her back, to lose herself
I' th' maze and winding *labyrinths* o' th' world. *Denham.*

Lac. *n. s.*

Lac is usually distinguished by the name of a gum, but improperly, because it is inflammable and not soluble in water. We have three sorts of it, which are all the product of the same tree. 1. The stick *lac*. 2. The seed *lac*. 3. The shell *lac*. Authors leave us uncertain whether this drug belongs to the animal or the vegetable kingdom. *Hill.*

LACE. *n. s.* [*lacet*, French; *laqueus*, Latin.]

1. A string; a cord.

There the fond fly entangled, struggled long,
Himself to free thereout; but all in vain:
For striving more, the more in *laces* strong
Himself he tied, and wrapt his winges twain
In limy snares, the subtil loops among. *Spenser.*

2. A snare; a gin.

The king had snared been in love's strong *lace*. *Fairfax.*

3. A platted string, with which women fasten their clothes.

O! cut my *lace*, lest my heart cracking, it
Break too. *Shakespeare's Winter's Tale.*
Doll ne'er was call'd to cut her *lace*,
Or throw cold water in her face. *Swift.*

4. Ornaments of fine thread curiously woven.

Our English dames are much given to the wearing of costly *laces*; and, if they be brought from Italy, they are in great esteem. *Bacon's Advice to Villiers.*

5. Textures of thread, with gold or silver.

He wears a stuff, whose thread is coarse and round,
But trimm'd with curious *lace*. *Herbert.*

6. Sugar. A cant word.

If haply he the sect pursues,
That read and comment upon news;
He takes up their mysterious face,
He drinks his coffee without *lace*. *Prior.*

To Lace. *v. a.* [from the noun.]

1. To fasten with a string run through eilet holes.

I caused a fomentation to be made, and put on a *laced* sock, by which the weak parts were strengthened. *Wiseman.*

At this, for new replies he did not stay,
But *lac'd* his crested helm, and strode away. *Dryden.*
These glitt'ring spoils, now made the victor's gain,
He to his body suits; but suits in vain:
Messapus' helm he finds among the rest,
And *laces* on, and wears the waving crest *Dryd. Æneis.*

Like Mrs. Primly's great belly; she may *lace* it down before, but it burnishes on her hips. *Congr. Way of the World.*

When Jenny's stays are newly *lac'd*,
Fair Alma plays about her waist. *Prior.*

2. To adorn with gold or silver textures sewed on.

It is but a night-gown in respect of yours; cloath of gold and coats, and *lac'd* with silver. *Shakes. Much ado about Not.*

3. To embellish with variegations.

Look, love, what envious streaks
Do *lace* the severing clouds in yonder East;
Night's candles are burnt out, and jocund day
Stands tiptoe on the misty mountains tops. *Shakespeare.*
Then clap four slices of pilaster on't,
That, *lac'd* with bits of rustick, makes a front. *Pope.*

4. To beat; whether from the form which *L'Estrange* uses, or by corruption of *lash*.

Go you, and find me out a man that has no curiosity at all, or I'll *lace* your coat for ye. *L'Estrange.*

Laced *Mutton*. An old word for a whore.

Ay, Sir, I, a lost mutton, gave your letter to her a *lac'd mutton*, and she gave me nothing for my labour. *Shakes.*

La'ceman. *n. s.* [*lace* and *man.*] One who deals in lace.

I met with a nonjuror, engaged with a *laceman*, whether the late French king was most like Augustus Cæsar, or Nero. *Addison's Spectator*, N°. 404.

La'cerable. *adj.* [from *lacerate.*] Such as may be torn.

Since the lungs are obliged to a perpetual commerce with the air, they must necessarily lie open to great damages, because of their thin and *lacerable* composure. *Harvey.*

To LA'CERATE. *v. a.* [*lacero*, Latin.] To tear; to rend; to separate by violence.

And my sons *lacerate* and rip up, viper like, the womb that brought them forth. *Howel's England's Tears.*

The heat breaks through the water, so as to *lacerate* and lift up great bubbles too heavy for the air to buoy up, and causeth boiling. *Derham's Physico-Theology.*

Here

Here *lacerated* friendſhip claims a tear. *Va. of human Wiſhes.*

LACERA'TION. *n. ſ.* [from *lacerate.*] The act of tearing or rending; the breach made by tearing.

The effects are, extenſion of the great veſſels, compreſſion of the leſſer, and *lacerations* upon ſmall cauſes. *Arbuth.*

LA'CERATIVE. *adj.* [from *lacerate.*] Tearing; having the power to tear.

Some depend upon the intemperament of the part ulcerated, others upon the continual afflux of *lacerative* humours. *Harvey on Conſumptions.*

LA'CHRYMAL. *adj.* [*lachrymal*, French.] Generating tears.

It is of an exquiſite ſenſe, that, upon any touch, the tears might be ſqueezed from the *lachrymal* glands, to waſh and clean it. *Cheyne's Philoſophical Principles.*

LA'CHRYMARY. *adj.* [*lachryma*, Latin.] Containing tears.

How many dreſſes are there for each particular deity? what a variety of ſhapes in the ancient urns, lamps, and *lachrymary* veſſels. *Addiſon's Travels through Italy.*

LACHRYMA'TION. *n. ſ.* [from *lachryma.*] The act of weeping, or ſhedding tears.

LA'CHRYMATORY. *n. ſ.* [*lachrimatoire*, French.] A veſſel in which tears are gathered to the honour of the dead.

LACI'NIATED. *adj.* [from *lacinia*, Lat.] Adorned with fringes and borders.

To LACK. *v. a.* [*laecken*, to leſſen, Dutch.] To want; to need; to be without.

Every good and holy deſire, though it *lack* the form, hath notwithſtanding in itſelf the ſubſtance, and with him the force of prayer, who regardeth the very moanings, groans, and ſighs of the heart. *Hooker, b.* v. *l.* 348.

A land wherein thou ſhalt eat bread without ſcarceneſs; thou ſhalt not *lack* any thing in it. *Deut.* viii. 9.

One day we hope thou ſhalt bring back,
Dear Bolingbroke, the juſtice that we *lack.* *Daniel.*
Intreat they may; authority they *lack.* *Daniel.*

To LACK. *v. n.*

1. To be in want.

The lions do *lack* and ſuffer hunger. *Common Prayer.*

2. To be wanting.

Peradventure there ſhall *lack* five of the fifty righteous; wilt thou deſtroy all the city for lack of five? *Gen.* viij. 28.

There was nothing *lacking* to them: David recovered all. 1 *Sam.* xxx. 19.

That which was *lacking* on your part, they have ſupplied. 1 *Cor.* xvi. 17.

LACK. *n. ſ.* [from the verb.]

1. Want; need; failure.

In the ſcripture there neither wanteth any thing, the *lack* whereof might deprive us of life. *Hooker, b.* i. *p.* 41.

Many that are not mad
Have ſure more *lack* of reaſon. *Shakeſ. Meaſ. for Meaſ.*

He was not able to keep that place three days, for *lack* of victuals. *Knolles's Hiſtory of the Turks.*

The trenchant blade, toledo truſty,
For want of fighting was grown ruſty,
And eat into itſelf, for *lack*
Of ſomebody to hew and hack. *Hudibras, p.* i. *c.* 1.

2. *Lack*, whether noun or verb, is now almoſt obſolete.

LA'CKBRAIN. *n. ſ.* [*lack* and *brain.*] One that wants wit.

What a *lackbrain* is this? Our plot is as good a plot as ever was laid. *Shakeſpeare's Henry* IV. *p.* i.

LA'CKER. *n. ſ.* A kind of varniſh, which, ſpread upon a white ſubſtance, exhibits a gold colour.

To LA'CKER. *v. a.* [from the noun.] To do over with lacker.

What ſhook the ſtage, and made the people ſtare?
Cato's long wing, flower'd gown, and *lacker'd* chair. *Pope.*

LA'CKEY. *n. ſ.* [*lacquais*, French.] An attending ſervant; a foot-boy.

They would ſhame to make me
Wait elſe at door: a fellow counſellor,
'Mong boys, and grooms, and *lackeys!* *Shakeſ. Hen.* VIII.

Though his youthful blood be fir'd with wine,
He's cautious to avoid the coach and ſix,
And on the *lackeys* will no quarrel fix. *Dryden's Juvenal.*

Lacqueys were never ſo ſaucy and pragmatical as they are now-a-days. *Addiſon's Spectator*, N°. 481.

To LA'CKEY. *v. a.* [from the noun.] To attend ſervilely. I know not whether *Milton* has uſed this word very properly.

This common body,
Like to a vagabond flag upon the ſtream,
Goes to, and back, *lacqueying* the varying tide,
To rot itſelf with motion. *Shakeſp. Ant. and Cleopatra.*

So dear to heav'n is ſaintly chaſtity,
That when a ſoul is found ſincerely ſo,
A thouſand liveried angels *lackey* her,
Driving far off each thing of ſin and guilt. *Milton.*

To LA'CKEY. *v. n.* To act as a foot-boy; to pay ſervile attendance.

Oft have I ſervants ſeen on horſes ride,
The free and noble *lacquey* by their ſide. *Sandys's Par.*

Our Italian tranſlator of the Æneis is a foot poet; he *lackeys* by the ſide of Virgil, but never mounts behind him. *Dryd. Ded. Æn.*

LA'CKLINEN. *adj.* [*lack* and *linen.*] Wanting ſhirts.

I ſcorn you, ſcurvy companion; what? your poor, baſe, raſcally, cheating, *lacklinen* mate; away, you mouldy rogue, away; I'm made for your maſter. *Shakſpeare's Henry* IV.

LA'CKLUSTRE. *adj.* [*lack* and *luſtre.*] Wanting brightneſs.

And then he drew a dial from his poke,
And looking on it with *lackluſtre* eye,
Says very wiſely, it is ten a clock. *Shakeſpeare.*

LACO'NICK. *adj.* [*laconicus*, Lat. *laconique*, Fr.] Short; brief; from *Lacones*, the Spartans, who uſed few words.

I grow *laconick* even beyond laconiciſm; for ſometimes I return only yes, or no, to queſtionary or petitionary epiſtles of half a yard long. *Pope to Swift.*

LA'CONISM. *n. ſ.* [*laconiſme*, French; *laconiſmus*, Latin.] A conciſe ſtile: called by *Pope laconiciſm.* See LACONICK.

As the language of the face is univerſal, ſo it is very comprehenſive: no *laconiſm* can reach it. It is the ſhorthand of the mind, and crowds a great deal in a little room. *Collier of the Aſpect.*

LA'CONICALLY. *adv.* [from *laconick.*] Briefly; conciſely.

Alexander Nequam, a man of great learning, and deſirous to enter into religion there, writ to the abbot *laconically.* *Camden's Remains.*

LA'CTARY. *adj.* [*lactis*, Lat.] Milky; full of juice like milk.

From *lactary*, or milky plants, which have a white and lacteous juice diſperſed through every part, there ariſe flowers blue and yellow. *Brown's Vulgar Errors, b.* vi. *c.* 10.

LA'CTARY. *n. ſ.* [*lactarium*, Latin.] A dairy houſe.

LACTA'TION. *n. ſ.* [*lacto*, Latin.] The act or time of giving ſuck.

LA'CTEAL. *adj.* [from *lac*, Latin.] Conveying chyle.

As the food paſſes, the chyle, which is the nutritive part, is ſeparated from the excrementitious by the *lacteal* veins; and from thence conveyed into the blood. *Locke.*

LA'CTEAL. *n. ſ.* The veſſel that conveys chyle.

The mouths of the *lacteals* may permit aliment, acrimonious or not, ſufficiently attenuated, to enter in people of lax conſtitutions, whereas their ſphincters will ſhut againſt them in ſuch as have ſtrong fibres. *Arbuthnot on Aliments.*

LACTE'OUS. *adj.* [*lacteus*, Latin.]

1. Milky.

Though we leave out the *lacteous* circle, yet are there more by four than Philo mentions. *Brown's Vulgar Errors.*

2. Lacteal; conveying chyle.

The lungs are ſuitable for reſpiration, and the *lacteous* veſſels for the reception of the chyle. *Bentley's Serm.*

LACTES'CENCE. *n. ſ.* [*lacteſco*, Latin.] Tendency to milk.

This *lacteſcence* does commonly enſue, when wine, being impregnated with gums, or other vegetable concretions, that abound with ſulphureous corpuſcles, fair water is ſuddenly poured upon the ſolution. *Boyle on Colours.*

LACTES'CENT. *adj.* [*lacteſcens*, Latin.] Producing Milk.

Amongſt the pot-herbs are ſome *lacteſcent* plants, as lettuce and endive, which contain a wholeſome juice. *Arbuth.*

LACTI'FEROUS. *adj.* [*lac* and *fero.*] What conveys or brings milk.

He makes the breaſts to be nothing but glandules, made up of an infinite number of little knots, each whereof hath its excretory veſſel, or *lactiferous* duct. *Ray on the Creation.*

LAD. *n. ſ.* [leobe, Saxon, which commonly ſignifies people, but ſometimes, ſays Mr. *Lye*, a boy.]

1. A boy; a ſtripling, in familiar language.

We were
Two *lads*, that thought there was no more behind,
But ſuch a day to-morrow as to-day,
And to be boy eternal. *Shakeſpeare's Winter's Tale.*

The poor *lad* who wants knowledge, muſt ſet his invention on the rack, to ſay ſomething where he knows nothing. *Locke.*

Too far from the ancient forms of teaching ſeveral good grammarians have departed, to the great detriment of ſuch *lads* as have been removed to other ſchools. *Watts.*

2. A boy, in paſtoral language.

For grief whereof the *lad* would after joy,
But pin'd away in anguiſh, and ſelf-will'd annoy. *Fa. Qu.*

The ſhepherd *lad*,
Whoſe offspring on the throne of Judah ſat
So many ages. *Milton's Par. Reg. b.* ii. *l.* 439.

LA'DDER. *n. ſ.* [hlaðne, Saxon.]

1. A frame made with ſteps placed between two upright pieces.

Whoſe compoſt is rotten, and carried in time,
And ſpread as it ſhould be, thrift's *ladder* may clime. *Tuſſ.*

Now ſtreets grow throng'd, and buſy as by day,
Some run for buckets to the hallow'd quire;
Some cut the pipes, and ſome the engines play,
And ſome more bold mount *ladders* to the fire. *Dryden.*

I ſaw a ſtage erected about a foot and a half from the ground, capable of holding four of the inhabitants with two or three *ladders* to mount it. *Gulliver's Travels.*

Eaſy

Easy in words thy stile, in sense sublime;
'Tis like the *ladder* in the patriarch's dream,
Its foot on earth, its height above the skies. *Prior.*

2. Any thing by which one climbs.

Then took she help to her of a servant near about her husband, whom she knew to be of a hasty ambition; and such a one, who wanting true sufficiency to raise him, would make a *ladder* of any mischief. *Sidney, b.* ii.

I must climb her window,
The *ladder* made of cords. *Shakes. Two Gent. of Verona.*

Northumberland, thou *ladder*, by the which
My cousin Bolingbroke ascends my throne. *Shakes.*

Lowliness is young ambition's *ladder*,
Whereto the climber upward turns his face. *Shakes.*

3. A gradual rise.

Endow'd with all these accomplishments, we leave him in the full career of success, mounting fast towards the top of the *ladder* ecclesiastical, which he hath a fair probability to reach. *Swift.*

LADE. *n. s.*

Lade is the mouth of a river, and is derived from the Saxon labe, which signifies a purging or discharging; there being a discharge of the waters into the sea, or into some greater river. *Gibson's Camden.*

To LADE. *v. a.* preter. and part. passive, *laded* or *laden.* [from hlaben, Saxon.] It is now commonly written *load.*

1. To load; to freight; to burthen.

And they *laded* their asses with corn, and departed thence. *Gen.* xlii. 26.

The experiment which sheweth the weights of several bodies in comparison with water, is of use in *lading* of ships, and showing what burthen they will bear. *Bacon's Ph. Rem.*

The vessels, heavy *laden*, put to sea
With prosp'rous winds; a woman leads the way. *Dryden.*

Though the peripatetick doctrine does not satisfy, yet it is as easy to account for the difficulties he charges on it, as for those his own hypothesis is *laden* with. *Locke.*

2. [hlaban, to draw, Saxon.] To heave out; to throw out.

He chides the sea that sunders him from them,
Saying, he'll *lade* it dry to have his way. *Shakes.*

They never let blood; but say, if the pot boils too fast there is no need of *lading* out any of the water, but only of taking away the fire; and so they allay all heats of the blood by abstinence, and cooling herbs. *Temple.*

If there be springs in the slate marl, there must be help to *lade* or pump it out. *Mortimer's Husband.*

LA'DING. *n. s.* [from *lade.*] Weight; burthen.

Some we made prize, while others burnt and rent
With their rich *lading* to the bottom went. *Waller.*

The storm grows higher and higher, and threatens the utter loss of the ship: there is but one way to save it, which is, by throwing its rich *lading* overboard. *South's Serm.*

It happened to be foul weather, so that the mariners cast their whole *lading* overboard to save themselves. *L'Estrange.*

Why should he sink where nothing seem'd to press?
His *lading* little, and his ballast less. *Swift.*

LA'DLE. *n. s.* [hlæble, Saxon, from hlaban; *leaugh*, Erse.]

1. A large spoon; a vessel with a long handle, used in throwing out any liquid.

Some stirr'd the molten ore with *ladles* great. *Fa. Qu.*

When the materials of glass have been kept long in fusion, the mixture casts up the superfluous salt, which the workmen take off with *ladles.* *Boyle.*

A *laddle* for our silver dish
Is what I want, is what I wish. *Prior.*

2. The receptacles of a mill wheel, into which the water falling turns it.

LA'DLE-FUL. *n. s.* [*ladle* and *full.*]

If a footman be going up with a dish of soup, let the cook with a *ladle-ful* dribble his livery all the way up stairs. *Sw.*

LA'DY. *n. s.* [hlæfbiᵹ, Saxon.]

1. A woman of high rank: the title of *lady* properly belongs to the wives of knights, of all degrees above them, and to the daughters of earls, and all of higher ranks.

I am much afraid, my *lady*, his mother, play'd false with a smith. *Shakespeare's Merch. of Verona.*

I would thy husband were dead; I would make thee my *lady.*

——I your *lady*, Sir John? alas, I should be a pitiful *lady.* *Shakes. Merry Wives of Windsor.*

I am sorry my relation to so deserving a *lady*, should be any occasion of her danger and affliction. *K. Charles.*

2. An illustrious or eminent woman.

O foolish fairy's son, what fury mad
Hath thee incens'd to haste thy doleful fate?
Were it not better I that *lady* had,
Than that thou hadst repented it too late? *Fairy Qu.*

I love and hate her; for she's fair and royal,
And that she hath all courtly parts more exquisite
Than *lady ladies*; winning from each one
The best she hath, and she of all compounded
Out-sells them all. *Shakespeare's Cymbeline.*

Before Homer's time this great *lady* was scarce heard of. *Ral.*

May every *lady* an Evadne prove,
That shall divert me from Aspasia's love. *Waller.*

Shou'd I shun the dangers of the war,
With scorn the Trojans wou'd reward my pains,
And their proud *ladies* with their sweeping trains. *Dryden.*

We find on medals the representations of *ladies*, that have given occasion to whole volumes on the account only of a face. *Addison on ancient Medals.*

Of all these bounds, even from this line to this,
With shadowy forests, and with champaigns rich'd,
With plenteous rivers, and wide-skirted meads,
We make thee *lady.* *Shakespeare's King Lear.*

4. A word of complaisance used of women.

Say, good Cæsar,
That I some *lady* trifles have reserv'd,
Immoment toys, things of such dignity
As we greet modern friends withal. *Shakes. Ant. and Cl.*

I hope I may speak of women without offence to the *ladies.* *Guardian.*

LA'DY-BEDSTRAW. *n. s.* [Gallium.] It is a plant of the stellate kind; the leaves are neither rough nor knappy, and produced at the joints of the stalks, five or six in number, in a radiant form: the flower consists of one leaf, expanded toward the upper part, and divided into several segments; each of these flowers is succeeded by two dry seeds. *Miller.*

LA'DY-BIRD.
LA'DY-COW. } *n. s.* A small red insect vaginopennous.
LA'DY-FLY.

Fly *lady-bird*, north, south, or east or west,
Fly where the man is found that I love best. *Gay's Past.*

This *lady-fly* I take from off the grass,
Whose spotted back might scarlet red surpass. *Gay.*

LA'DY-DAY. *n. s.* [*lady* and *day.*] The day on which the annunciation of the blessed virgin is celebrated.

LA'DY-LIKE. *adj.* [*lady* and *like.*] Soft; delicate; elegant.

Her tender constitution did declare,
Too *lady-like* a long fatigue to bear. *Dry. Hind and Panth.*

LA'DY-MANTLE. *n. s.* [Alchimilla.] The leaves are serrated, the cup of the flower is divided into eight segments, expanded in form of a star; the flowers are collected into bunches upon the tops of the stalks; each seed vessel generally contains two seeds. *Miller.*

LA'DYSHIP. *n. s.* [from *lady.*] The title of a lady.

Madam, he sends your *ladyship* this ring. *Shakespeare.*

If they be nothing but mere statesmen,
Your *ladyship* shall observe their gravity,
And their reservedness, their many cautions,
Fitting their persons. *Benj. Johnson's Catiline.*

I the wronged pen to please,
Make it my humble thanks express
Unto your *ladyship* in these. *Waller.*

'Tis Galla; let her *ladyship* but peep. *Dryden's Juv.*

LA'DY'S-SLIPPER. *n. s.* [Calceolus] It hath an anomalous flower, consisting of six dissimilar leaves, four of which are placed in form of a cross, the other two pass the middle, one of which is bifid, and rests on the other, which is swelling, and shaped like a shoe; the empalement becomes a fruit, open on three sides, to which adhere the valves, pregnant with very small seeds like dust. *Miller.*

LA'DY'S-SMOCK. *n. s.* [Cardamine.] The flower consists of four leaves succeeded by narrow pods, which when ripe roll up, and cast forth their seeds: the leaves for the most part are winged. The first sort is sometimes used in medicine; the third sort is a very beautiful plant, continuing a long time in flower: they are preserved in botanick gardens, and some of them merit a place in some shady part of every curious garden, for their odd manner of casting forth their seeds on the slightest touch when the pods are ripe. *Miller.*

When dazies pied, and violets blue,
And *lady's-smocks* all silver white,
Do paint the meadows much bedight. *Shakespeare.*

See here a boy gathering lilies and *lady-smocks*, and there a girl cropping culverkeys and cowslips, all to make garlands. *Walton's Angler.*

Lady's-smocks have small stringy roots that run in the ground, and comes up in divers places. *Mortimer's Husbandry.*

LAG. *adj.* [læng, Saxon, long; *lagg*, Swedish, the end.]

1. Coming behind; falling short.

I could be well content
To entertain the *lag* end of my life
With quiet hours. *Shakespeare's Henry* IV.

The slowest footed who come *lag*, supply the show of a reer-ward. *Carew's Survey.*

I am some twelve or fourteen moonshines
Lag of a brother. *Shakespeare's King Lear.*

2. Sluggish; slow; tardy. It is retained in Scotland.

He, poor man, by your first order died,
And that a winged Mercury did bear;
Some tardy cripple had the countermand,
That came too *lag* to see him buried. *Shakes. Rich.* III.

We know your thoughts of us, that laymen are
Lag souls, and rubbish of remaining clay,

Which

Which heav'n, grown weary of more perfect work,
Set upright with a little puff of breath,
And bid us paſs for men. *Dryden's Don Sebaſtian.*

3. Laſt; long delayed.

Pack to their old play-fellows; there I take
They may, *cum privilegio*, wear away
The *lag* end of their lewdneſs, and be laugh'd at. *Shak.*

Lag. *n. ſ.*

1. The loweſt claſs; the rump; the fag end.

The reſt of your foes, O gods, the ſenators of Athens, together with the common *lag* of people, what is amiſs in them, make ſuitable for deſtruction. *Shakeſ. Tim. of Athens.*

2. He that comes laſt, or hangs behind.

The laſt, the *lag* of all the race. *Dryd. Virg. Æneis.*
What makes my ram the *lag* of all the flock. *Pope.*

To Lag. *v. n.*

1. To loiter; to move ſlowly.

She paſs'd, with fear and fury wild;
The nurſe went *lagging* after with the child. *Dryden.*
The remnant of his days he ſafely paſt,
Nor found they *lagg'd* too ſlow, nor flow'd too faſt. *Prior.*

2. To ſtay behind; not to come in.

Behind her far away a dwarf did *lag*. *Fairy Queen.*
I ſhall not *lag* behind, nor err
The way, thou leading. *Milton's Paradiſe Loſt, b. x.*
The knight himſelf did after ride,
Leading Crowdero by his ſide,
And tow'd him, if he *lagg'd* behind,
Like boat againſt the tide and wind. *Hud. p. i. c. 3.*
If he finds a fairy *lag* in light,
He drives the wretch before, and laſhes into night. *Dryd.*
She hourly preſs'd for ſomething new;
Ideas came into her mind
So faſt, his leſſons *lagg'd* behind. *Swift.*

La'gger. *n. ſ.* [from *lag*.] A loiterer; an idler; one that loiters behind.

La'ical. *adj.* [*laïque*, French; *laicus*, Latin; λαός.] Belonging to the laity, or people as diſtinct from the clergy.

In all ages the clerical will flatter as well as the *laical*. *Camden.*

Laid. Preterite participle of *lay*.

Money *laid* up for the relief of widows and fatherleſs children. *2 Mac.* iii. 10.

A ſcheme which was writ ſome years ſince, and *laid* by to be ready on a fit occaſion. *Swift.*

Lain. Preterite participle of *lye*.

Mary ſeeth two angels in white, ſitting, the one at the head, and the other at the feet, where the body of Jeſus had *lain*. *John* xx. 12.

The parcels had *lain* by, before they were opened, between four and five years. *Boyle.*

Lair. *n. ſ.* [*lai*, in French, ſignifies a wild ſow, or a foreſt: the derivation is eaſy in either ſenſe; or from *leger*, Dutch.] The couch of a boar, or wild beaſt.

Out of the ground uproſe,
As from his *lair*, the wild beaſt, where he wons
In foreſt wild, in thicket, brake or den. *Milton's P. Loſt.*
But range the foreſt, by the ſilver ſide
Of ſome cool ſtream, where nature ſhall provide
Green graſs and fatt'ning clover for your fare,
And moſſy caverns for your noon-tide *lair*. *Dryd. Virg.*

Laird. *n. ſ.* [hlaford, Saxon.] The lord of a manor in the Scottiſh dialect.

Shrive but their title, and their moneys poize,
A *laird* and twenty pence pronounc'd with noiſe,
When conſtru'd but for a plain yeoman go,
And a good ſober two pence, and well ſo. *Cleaveland.*

La'ity. *n. ſ.* [λαός.]

1. The people, as diſtinguiſhed from the clergy.

An humble clergy is a very good one, and an humble *laity* too, ſince humility is a virtue that equally adorns every ſtation of life. *Swift's Sentiments of a Ch. of Engl. Man.*

2. The ſtate of a layman.

The more uſual cauſe of this deprivation is a mere *laity*, or want of holy orders. *Ayliffe's Parergon.*

Lake. *n. ſ.* [*lac*, French; *lacus*, Latin.]

1. A large diffuſion of inland water.

He adds the running ſprings and ſtanding *lakes*,
And bounding banks for winding rivers makes. *Dry. Ovid.*

2. Small plaſh of water.

3. A middle colour, betwixt ultramarine and vermilion, yet it is rather ſweet than harſh. *Dryden.*

LAMB. *n. ſ.* [*lamb*, Gothick and Saxon.]

1. The young of a ſheep.

I'm young; but ſomething
You may deſerve of him through me, and wiſdom,
To offer up a weak, poor, innocent *lamb*,
T' appeaſe an angry god. *Shakeſpeare's Macbeth.*
The *lamb*, thy riot dooms to bleed to day,
Had he thy knowledge would he ſkip and play? *Pope.*

2. Typically, the Saviour of the world.

Thou *Lamb* of God that takeſt away the ſins of the world, have mercy upon us. *Common Prayer.*

La'mbkin. *n. ſ.* [from *lamb*.] A little lamb.

'Twixt them both they not a *lambkin* left,
And when lambs fail'd, the old ſheeps lives they reſt. *Hubberd's Ta e.*
Pan, thou god of ſhepherds all,
Which of our tender *lambkins* takeſt, keep. *Spenſ. Paſt.*
Clean as young *lambkins*, or the gooſe's down,
And like the goldfinch in her Sunday gown. *Gay.*

La'mbative. *adj.* [from *lambo*, to lick.] Taken by licking.

In affections both of lungs and weazon, phyſicians make uſe of ſyrups, and *lambative* medicines. *Brown's Vul. Errors.*

Lam'bative. *n. ſ.* A medicine taken by licking with the tongue.

I ſtitch'd up the wound, and applied aſtringents, with compreſs and retentive bandage, then put him into bed, and let him blood in the arm, adviſing a *lambative*, to be taken as neceſſity ſhould require. *Wiſeman's Surgery.*

Lambs-wool. *n. ſ.* [*lamb* and *wool*.] Ale mixed with the pulp of roaſted apples.

A cup of *lambs-wool* they drank to him there.
Song of the King and the Miller.

La'mbent. *adj.* [*lambens*, Lat.] Playing about; gliding over without harm.

From young Iülus head
A *lambent* flame aroſe, which gently ſpread
Around his brows, and on his temples fed. *Dryd. Æneis.*
His brows thick fogs, inſtead of glories, grace,
And *lambent* dulneſs played around his face. *Dryden.*

Lamdoi'dal. *n. ſ.* [λάμβδα and εἶδος.] Having the form of the letter lamda or Λ.

The courſe of the longitudinal ſinus down through the middle of it, makes it adviſeable to trapan at the lower part of the os parietale, or at leaſt upon the *lamdoidal* ſuture. *Sharp's Surgery.*

LAME. *adj.* [laam, lama, Saxon; *lam*, Dutch.]

1. Crippled; diſabled in the limbs.

Who reproves the *lame*, muſt go upright. *Daniel.*

A greyhound, of a mouſe colour, *lame* of one leg, belongs to a lady. *Arbuth. and Pope's Mart. Scrib.*

2. Hobbling; not ſmooth: alluding to the feet of a verſe.

Our authors write,
Whether in proſe, or verſe, 'tis all the ſame;
The proſe is fuſtian, and the numbers *lame*. *Dry. Perſ.*

3. Imperfect; unſatisfactory.

Shrubs are formed into ſundry ſhapes, by moulding them within, and cutting them without; but they are but *lame* things, being too ſmall to keep figure. *Bacon.*

Swift, who could neither fly nor hide,
Came ſneaking to the chariot ſide;
And offer'd many a *lame* excuſe,
He never meant the leaſt abuſe. *Swift.*

To Lame. *v. a.* [from the adjective.] To make lame; to cripple.

I never heard of ſuch another encounter, which *lames* report to follow it, and undoes deſcription to do it. *Shakeſp.*

The ſon and heir
Affronted once a cock of noble kind,
And either *lam'd* his legs, or ſtruck him blind. *Dryd.*

If you happen to let the child fall, and *lame* it, never confeſs. *Swift.*

L'amellated. *adj.* [*lamella*, Latin.] Covered with films or plates.

The *lamellated* antennæ of ſome inſects are ſurpriſingly beautiful, when viewed through a microſcope. *Derham.*

Lame'ly. *adj.* [from *lame*.]

1. Like a cripple; without natural force or activity.

Thoſe muſcles become callous, and, having yielded to the extenſion, the patient makes ſhift to go upon it, though *lamely*. *Wiſeman's Surgery.*

2. Imperfectly; without a full or complete exhibition of all the parts.

Look not ev'ry lineament to ſee,
Some will be caſt in ſhades, and ſome will be
So *lamely* drawn, you ſcarcely know 'tis ſhe. *Dryden.*

La'meness. *n. ſ.* [from *lame*.]

1. The ſtate of a cripple; loſs or inability of limbs.

Let blindneſs, *lameneſs* come; are legs and eyes
Of equal value to ſo great a prize? *Dryden's Juv.*
Lameneſs kept me at home *Digby to Pope.*

2. Imperfection; weakneſs.

If the ſtory move, or the actor help the *lameneſs* of it with his performance, either of theſe are ſufficient to effect a preſent liking. *Dryden's Spaniſh Friar.*

To LAMENT. *v. n.* [*lamentor*, Latin; *lamenter*, French.] To mourn; to wail; to grieve; to expreſs ſorrow.

The night has been unruly where we lay;
And chimneys were blown down: and, as they ſay,
Lamentings heard i' th' air, ſtrange ſcreams of death. *Shak.*
Ye ſhall weep and *lament*, but the world ſhall rejoice. *John.*

Jeremiah *lamented* for Joſiah, and all the ſinging-men and women ſpake of Joſiah in their lamentations. *2 Chron.*

In their wailing they shall take up a lamentation for thee, and *lament* over thee. *Ezek.* xxvii. 32.

Far less I now *lament* for one whole world
Of wicked sons destroy'd, than I rejoice
For one man found so perfect and so just,
That God vouchsafes to raise another world
From him. *Milton's Par. Lost*, *b.* xi. *l.* 874.

To LA'MENT. *v. a.* To bewail; to mourn; to bemoan; to sorrow for.

Come, now tow'rds Chertsey with your holy load,
And still, as you are weary of this weight,
Rest you, while I *lament* king Henry's corse. *Shakespeare.*

The pair of sages praise;
One pity'd, one contemn'd the woful times,
One laugh'd at follies, one *lamented* crimes. *Dryden.*

LA'MENT. *n. s.* [*lamentum*, Latin, from the verb.]

1. Sorrow audibly expressed; lamentation; grief uttered in complaints or cries.

Long ere our approaching heard within
Noise, other than the sound of dance, or song!
Torment, and loud *lament*, and furious rage. *Milton.*

The loud *laments* arise,
Of one distress'd, and mastiffs mingled cries. *Dryden.*

2. Expression of sorrow.

To add to your *laments*,
Wherewith you now bedew king Henry's hearse,
I must inform you of a dismal fight. *Shakes. Henry* VI.

LA'MENTABLE. *adj.* [*lamentabilis*, Latin; *lamentable*, French, from *lament*.]

1. To be lamented; causing sorrow.

The *lamentable* change is from the best;
The worst returns to laughter. *Shakes. King Lear.*

2. Mournful; sorrowful; expressing sorrow.

A *lamentable* tune is the sweetest musick to a woful mind. *Sidney.*

The victors to their vessels bear the prize,
And hear behind loud groans, and *lamentable* cries. *Dryd.*

3. Miserable, in a ludicrous or low sense; pitiful; despicable.

This bishop, to make out the disparity between the heathens and them, flies to this *lamentable* refuge. *Stillingfleet.*

LA'MENTABLY. *adv.* [from *lamentable*.]

1. With expressions or tokens of sorrow; mournfully.

The matter in itself lamentable, *lamentably* expressed by the old prince, greatly moved the two princes to compassion. *Sidney*, *b.* ii.

2. So as to cause sorrow.

Our fortune on the sea is out of breath,
And sinks most *lamentably*. *Shakes. Ant. and Cleopatra.*

3. Pitifully; despicably.

LAMENTA'TION. *n. s.* [*lamentatio*, Latin.] Expression of sorrow; audible grief.

Be't lawful that I invocate thy ghost,
To hear the *lamentations* of poor Anne. *Shakes. R.* III.

His sons buried him, and all Israel made great *lamentation* for him. 1 *Mac.* ii. 10.

LAMEN'TER. *n. s.* [from *lament*.] He who mourns or laments.

Such a complaint good company must pity, whether they think the *lamenter* ill or not. *Spectator*, N°. 429.

LA'MENTINE. *n. s.* A fish called a sea-cow or manatee, which is near twenty feet long, the head resembling that of a cow, and two short feet, with which it creeps on the shallows and rocks to get food; but has no fins: the flesh is commonly eaten. *Bailey.*

LA'MINA. *n. s.* [Lat.] Thin plate; one coat laid over another.

LA'MINATED. *adj.* [from *lamina*.] Plated: used of such bodies whose contexture discovers such a disposition as that of plates lying over one another.

From the apposition of different coloured gravel arises, for the most part, the *laminated* appearance of a stone. *Sharp.*

To LAMM. *v. a.* To beat soundly with a cudgel. *Dict.*

LA'MMAS. *n. s.* [This word is said by *Bailey*, I know not on what authority, to be derived from a custom, by which the tenants of the archbishop of York were obliged, at the time of mass, on the first of August, to bring a lamb to the altar. In Scotland they are said to wean lambs on this day. It may else be corrupted from lattermath.] The first of August.

In 1578 was that famous *lammas* day, which buried the reputation of Don John of Austria. *Bacon.*

LAMP. *n. s.* [*lampe*, French; *lampas*, Latin.]

1. A light made with oil and a wick.

O thievish night,
Why should'st thou, but for some felonious end,
In thy dark lanthorn thus close up the stars
That nature hung in heaven, and fill'd their *lamps*
With everlasting oil, to give due light
To the misled and lonely traveller? *Milton.*

In *lamp* furnaces I used spirit of wine instead of oil, and with the same flame has melted foliated gold. *Boyle.*

2. Any kind of light, in poetical language, real or metaphorical.

Thy gentle eyes send forth a quick'ning spirit,
And feed the dying *lamp* of life within me. *Rowe.*

Cynthia, fair regent of the night,
O may thy silver *lamp* from heaven's high bow'r,
Direct my footsteps in the midnight hour. *Gay.*

LA'MPASS. *n. s.* [*lampas*, French.] A lump of flesh, about the bigness of a nut, in the roof of a horse's mouth, which rises above the teeth. *Farrier's Dict.*

His horse possest with the glanders, troubled with the *lampass*, infected with the fashions. *Shakespeare.*

LA'MPBLACK. *n. s.* [*lamp* and *black*.] It is made by holding a torch under the bottom of a bason, and as it is furred strike it with a feather into some shell, and grind it with gum water. *Peacham on Drawing.*

LAM'PING. *adj.* [λαμπέδων.] Shining; sparkling.

Happy lines, on which with starry light
Those *lamping* eyes will deign sometimes to look. *Spenser.*

LAMPO'ON. *n. s.* [*Bailey* derives it from *lampons*, a drunken song. It imports, *let us drink*, from the old French *lamper*, and was repeated at the end of each couplet at carousals. *Trev.*] A personal satire; abuse; censure written not to reform but to vex.

They say my talent is satire; if so, it is a fruitful age: they have sown the dragon's teeth themselves, and it is but just they should reap each other in *lampoons*. *Dryden.*

Make satire a *lampoon*. *Pope.*

To LAMPO'ON. *v. a.* [from the noun.] To abuse with personal satire.

LAMPO'ONER. *n. s.* [from *lampoon*.] A scribbler of personal satire.

We are naturally displeased with an unknown critick, as the ladies are with a *lampooner*, because we are bitten in the dark. *Dryden's Æn.*

The squibs are those who are called libellers, *lampooners*, and pamphleteers. *Tatler*, N°. 88.

LA'MPREY. *n. s.* [*lamproye*, French; *lampreye*, Dutch.]

Many fish much like the eel frequent both the sea and fresh rivers; as, the lamprel, *lamprey*, and lamperne. *Walton.*

LA'MPRON. *n. s.* A kind of sea fish.

These rocks are frequented by *lamprons*, and greater fishes, that devour the bodies of the drowned. *Notes on the Odyssey.*

LANCE. *n. s.* [*lance*, French; *lancea*, Latin.] A long spear, which, in the heroick ages, seems to have been generally thrown from the hand, as by the Indians at this day. In later times the combatants thrust them against each other on horseback.

He carried his *lances* which were strong, to give a lancely blow. *Sidney.*

Plate sin with gold,
And the strong *lance* of justice hurtless breaks:
Arm it in rags, a pigmy's straw doth pierce it. *Shakes.*

They shall hold the bow and the *lance*. *Jer.* l. 42.

To LANCE. *v. a.* [from the noun.]

1. To pierce; to cut.

In fell motion,
With his prepared sword he charges home
My unprovided body, *lanc'd* my arm. *Shakespeare.*

In their cruel worship they *lance* themselves with knives. *Glanville's Scep. c.* 16.

Th' infernal minister advanc'd,
Seiz'd the due victim, and with fury *lanc'd*
Her back, and piercing through her inmost heart,
Drew backward. *Dryden's Theod. and Honoria.*

2. To open chirurgically; to cut in order to a cure.

We do *lance*
Diseases in our bodies. *Shakes. Ant. and Cleopatra.*

Fell sorrow's tooth doth never rankle more
Than when it bites, but *lanceth* not the sore. *Shakes.*

That differs as far from our usual severities, as the *lancings* of a physician do from the wounds of an adversary. *D. of Pi.*

Lance the sore,
And cut the head; for till the core is found
The secret vice is fed. *Dryden's Georg. l.* 691.

The shepherd stands,
And when the *lancing* knife requires his hands,
Vain help, with idle pray'rs, from heav'n demands. *Dry.*

LA'NCELY. *adj.* [from *lance*.] Suitable to a lance. Not in use.

He carried his lances, which were strong, to give a *lancely* blow. *Sidney*, *b.* i.

LANCEPE'SADE. *n. s.* [*lance spezzate*, French.] The officer under the corporal: not now in use among us.

To th' Indies of her arm he flies,
Fraught both with east and western prize,
Which, when he had in vain essay'd,
Arm'd like a dapper *lancepesade*
With Spanish pike, he broach'd a pore. *Cleaveland.*

LA'NCET. *n. s.* [*lancette*, French.] A small pointed chirurgical instrument.

I gave vent to it by an apertion with a *lancet*, and discharged white matter. *Wiseman's Surgery.*

It differeth from a vein, which in an apparent blue runneth along the body, and if dexterously pricked with a *lancet* emitteth a red drop. *Brown's Vulgar Errors. b.* iii.

Hippocrates saith, blood-letting should be done with broad *lancets*

lancets or ſwords, in order to make a large orifice: the manner of opening a vein then was by ſtabbing or pertuſion, as in horſes. *Arbuthnot on ancient Coins.*

To LANCH. *v. a.* [*lancer*, French. This word is too often written *launch*: it is only a vocal corruption of *lance.*] To dart; to caſt as a lance; to throw; to let fly.

See whoſe arm can *lanch* the ſurer bolt,
And who's the better Jove. *Dryd. and Lee's Oedipus.*

Me, only me, the hand of fortune bore,
Unbleſt to tread that interdicted ſhore:
When Jove tremendous in the ſable deeps,
Launch'd his red light'ning at our ſcatter'd ſhips. *Pope.*

LANCINA'TION. *n. ſ.* [from *lancino*, Latin.] Tearing; laceration.

To LA'NCINATE. *v. a.* [*lancino*, Latin.] To tear; to rend; to lacerate.

LAND. *n. ſ.* [lanꝺ, Gothick, Saxon, and ſo all the Teutonick dialects.]

1. A country; a region; diſtinct from other countries.

All the nations of Scythia, like a mountain flood, did overflow all Spain, and quite drowned and waſhed away whatſoever reliques there were left of the *land-bred* people. *Spenſer's State of Ireland.*

Thy ambition,
Thou ſcarlet ſin, robb'd this bewailing *land*
Of noble Buckingham. *Shakeſpeare's Henry* VIII.

What had he done to make him fly the *land?* *Shakeſ.*

The chief men of the *land* had great authority; though the government was monarchical, it was not deſpotick. *Broome's Notes on the Odyſſey.*

2. Earth; diſtinct from water.

The princes delighting their conceits with confirming their knowledge, ſeeing wherein the ſea-diſcipline differed from the *land-ſervice*, they had pleaſing entertainment. *Sidney.*

He to-night hath boarded a *land-carrack*;
If it prove lawful prize, he's made for ever. *Shakeſpeare.*

By *land* they found that huge and mighty country. *Abbot.*

With eleven thouſand *land-ſoldiers*, and twenty-ſix ſhips of war, we within two months have won one town. *Bacon.*

Neceſſity makes men ingenious and hardy; and if they have but *land-room* or ſea-room, they find ſupplies for their hunger. *Hale's Origin of Mankind.*

Yet, if thou go'ſt by *land*, tho' grief poſſeſs
My ſoul ev'n then, my fears would be the leſs:
But ah! be warn'd to ſhun the wat'ry way. *Dryden.*

They turn their heads to ſea, their ſterns to *land*,
And greet with greedy joy th' Italian ſtrand. *Dryden.*

I writ not always in the proper terms of navigation, or *land-ſervice.* *Dryden's Æneis.*

The French are to pay the ſame duties at the dry ports through which they paſs by *land-carriage*, as we pay upon importation or exportation by ſea. *Add. Freeholder.*

The Phœnicians carried on a *land-trade* to Syria and Meſopotamia, and ſtopt not ſhort, without puſhing their trade to the Indies. *Arbuthnot on Coins.*

The ſpecies brought by *land-carriage* were much better than thoſe which came to Egypt by ſea. *Arbuthnot.*

3. Ground; ſurface of the place. Unuſual.

Beneath his ſteely caſque he felt the blow,
And roll'd, with limbs relax'd, along the *land.* *Pope.*

4. An eſtate real and immoveable.

To forfeit all your goods, *lands*, and tenements,
Caſtles, and goods whatſoever, and to be
Out of the king's protection. *Shakeſ. Henry* VIII.

He kept himſelf within the bounds of loyalty, and enjoyed certain *lands* and towns in the borders of Polonia. *Knolles.*

This man is freed from ſervile hands,
Of hope to riſe, or fear to fall:
Lord of himſelf, though not of *lands*,
And having nothing, yet hath all. *Wotton.*

5. Nation; people.

Theſe anſwers in the ſilent night receiv'd,
The king himſelf divulg'd, the *land* believ'd. *Dryden.*

6. Urine. [hlonꝺ, Saxon.] As

Probably this was a coarſe expreſſion in the cant ſtrain, formerly in common uſe, but ſince laid aſide and forgotten, which meant the taking away a man's life. For *land* or *lant* is an old word for urine, and to ſtop the common paſſages and functions of nature is to kill. *Hanmer.*

You are abuſed, and by ſome putter on,
That will be damn'd for't; would I knew the villain,
I would *land-damn* him. *Shakeſ. Winter Tale.*

To LAND. *v. a.* [from the noun.] To ſet on ſhore.

You ſhall hear
The legions, now in Gallia, ſooner *landed*
In our not fearing Britain. *Shakeſ. Cymbeline.*

I told him of the army that was *landed*;
He laughed at it. *Shakeſpeare's King Lear.*

He who rules the raging wind,
To thee, O ſacred ſhip, be kind,
Thy committed pledge reſtore,
And *land* him ſafely on the ſhore. *Dryden's Horace.*

Another Typhis ſhall new ſeas explore,
Another Argo *land* the chiefs upon th' Iberian ſhore. *Dry.*

To LAND. *v. n.* To come to ſhore.

Let him *land*,
And ſolemnly ſee him ſet on to London. *Shakeſ. Hen.* V.

Land ye not, none of you, and provide to be gone from this coaſt within ſixteen days. *Bacon's New Atlantis.*

I *land*, with luckleſs omens; then adore
Their gods. *Dryden's Æneis.*

LAND-FORCES. *n. ſ.* [*land* and *force.*] Warlike powers not naval; ſoldiers that ſerve on land.

We behold in France the greateſt *land-forces* that have ever been known under any chriſtian prince. *Temple.*

LAN'DED. *adj.* [from *land.*] Having a fortune, not in money but in land.

A landleſs knight makes thee a *landed* ſquire. *Shakeſ.*

Men, whoſe living lieth together in one ſhire, are commonly counted greater *landed* than thoſe whoſe livings are diſperſed. *Bacon's Collection of Good and Evil.*

Cromwell's officers, who were for levelling lands while they had none, when they grew *landed* fell to crying up magna charta. *Temple.*

A houſe of commons muſt conſiſt, for the moſt part, of *landed* men. *Addiſon's Freeholder,* Nº. 20.

LA'NDFALL. *n. ſ.* [*land* and *fall.*] A ſudden tranſlation of property in land by the death of a rich man.

LAND'FLOOD. *n. ſ.* [*land* and *flood.*] Inundation.

Apprehenſions of the affections of Kent, and all other places, looked like a *landflood*, that might roll they knew not how far. *Clarendon.*

LA'NDHOLDER. *n. ſ.* [*land* and *holder.*] One whoſe fortune is in land.

Money, as neceſſary to trade, may be conſidered as in his hands that pays the labourer and *landholder*; and if this man want money, the manufacture is not made, and ſo the trade is loſt. *Locke.*

LA'NDJOBBER. *n. ſ.* [*land* and *job.*] One who buys and ſells lands for other men.

If your maſter be a miniſter of ſtate, let him be at home to none but his *land-jobbers*, or his inventor of new funds. *Swift's Directions to the Steward.*

LA'NDGRAVE. *n. ſ.* [*land* and *grave*, a count, German.] A German title of dominion.

LA'NDING.
LA'NDING-PLACE. } *n. ſ.* [from *land.*] The top of ſtairs.

Let the ſtairs to the upper rooms be upon a fair, open newel, and a fair *landing-place* at the top. *Bacon.*

The *landing-place* is the uppermoſt ſtep of a pair of ſtairs, *viz.* the floor of the room you aſcend upon. *Moxon.*

There is a ſtair-caſe that ſtrangers are generally carried to ſee, where the eaſineſs of the aſcent, the diſpoſition of the lights, and the convenient *landing*, are admirably well contrived. *Addiſon's Remarks on Italy.*

What the Romans called veſtibulum was no part of the houſe, but the court and *landing-place* between it and the ſtreet. *Arbuthnot on Coins.*

LA'NDLADY. *n. ſ.* [*land* and *lady.*]

1. A woman who has tenants holding from her.
2. The miſtreſs of an inn.

If a ſoldier drinks his pint, and offers payment in Wood's halfpence, the *landlady* may be under ſome difficulty. *Swift.*

LA'NDLESS. [from *land.*] Without property; without fortune.

Young Fortinbras,
Of unimproved mettle, hot and full,
Hath in the ſkirts of Norway, here and there,
Shark'd up a liſt of *landleſs* reſolutes. *Shakeſ. Hamlet.*

A *landleſs* knight hath made a landed ſquire. *Shakeſ.*

LA'NDLOCKED. *adj.* [*land* and *lock.*] Shut in, or incloſed with land.

There are few natural parts better *landlocked*, and cloſed on all ſides, than this ſeems to have been. *Addiſ. on Italy.*

LA'NDLOPER. *n. ſ.* [*land* and *loopen*, Dutch.] A landman; a term of reproach uſed by ſeamen of thoſe who paſs their lives on ſhore.

LA'NDLORD. *n. ſ.* [*land* and *lord*]

1. One who owns land or houſes, and has tenants under him.

This regard ſhall be had, that in no place, under any *landlord*, there ſhall be many of them placed together, but diſperſed. *Spenſer's State of Ireland.*

The univerſal *landlord.* *Shakeſ. Ant. and Cleopatra.*

It is a generous pleaſure in a *landlord*, to love to ſee all his tenants look fat, ſleek, and contented. *Clariſſa.*

2. The maſter of an inn.

Upon our arrival at the inn, my companion fetched out the jolly *landlord*, who knew him by his whiſtle. *Addiſon.*

LA'NDMARK. *n. ſ.* [*land* and *mark.*] Any thing ſet up to preſerve the boundaries of lands.

I' th' midſt, an altar, as the *land-mark*, ſtood,
Ruſtick, of graſſy ſod. *Milton's Par. Loſt*, *b.* xi. *l.* 432.

Then *land-marks* limited to each his Right;
For all before was common as the light. *Dryden.*

Though they are not ſelf-evident principles, yet if they have

have been made out from them by a wary and unquestionable deduction, they may serve as *land-marks*, to shew what lies in the direct way of truth, or is quite besides it. *Locke.*

LA'NDSCAPE. *n. s.* [*landschape*, Dutch.]

1. A region; the prospect of a country.

Lovely seem'd
That *landschape!* and of pure, now purer air,
Meets his approach. *Milton's Par. Lost, b.* iv. *l.* 153.

He scarce uprisen,
Shot parallel to th' earth his dewy ray,
Discov'ring in wide *landscape* all the east
Of paradise, and Eden's happy plains. *Milton.*

Straight mine eye hath caught new pleasures,
Whilst the *landscape* round it measures,
Russet lawns and fallows grey,
Where the nibbling flocks do stray. *Milton.*

We are like men entertained with the view of a spacious *landscape*, where the eye passes over one pleasing prospect into another. *Addison.*

2. A picture, representing an extent of space, with the various objects in it.

As good a poet as you are, you cannot make finer *landscapes* than those about the king's house. *Add. Guard.*

Oft in her glass the musing shepherd spies
The wat'ry *landscape* of the pendant woods,
And absent trees, that tremble in the floods. *Pope.*

LAND-TAX. *n. s.* [*land* and *tax.*] Tax laid upon land and houses.

If mortgages were registered, *land-taxes* might reach the lender to pay his proportion. *Locke.*

LAND-WAITER. *n. s.* [*land* and *waiter.*] An officer of the customs, who is to watch what goods are landed.

Give a guinea to a knavish *land-waiter*, and he shall connive at the merchant for cheating the queen of an hundred. *Swift's Examiner*, N°. 27.

LA'NDWARD. *adv.* [from *land.*] Towards the land.

They are invincible by reason of the overpouring mountains that back the one, and slender fortification of the other to *landward.* *Sandys's Journey.*

LANE. *n. s.* [*laen*, Dutch; lana, Saxon.]

1. A narrow way between hedges.

All flying
Through a straight *lane*, the enemy full-hearted
Struck down some mortally. *Shakes. Cymbeline.*

I know each *lane*, and every alley green,
Dingle or bushy dell, of this wild wood,
And every bosky bourn. *Milton.*

Through a close *lane* as I pursu'd my journey. *Otway.*

A pack-horse is driven constantly in a narrow *lane* and dirty road. *Locke.*

2. A narrow street; an alley.

There is no street, not many *lanes*, where there does not live one that has relation to the church. *Sprat's Sermons.*

3. A passage between men standing on each side.

The earl's servants stood ranged on both sides, and made the king a *lane.* *Bacon's Henry* VII.

LA'NERET. *n. s.* A little hawk.

LA'NGUAGE. *n. s.* [*language*, French; *lingua*, Latin.]

1. Human speech.

We may define *language*, if we consider it more materially, to be letters, forming and producing words and sentences; but if we consider it according to the design thereof, then *language* is apt signs for communication of thoughts. *Holder.*

2. The tongue of one nation as distinct from others.

O! good my lord, no Latin;
I am not such a truant since my coming,
As not to know the *language* I have liv'd in. *Shakes.*

He not from Rome alone, but Greece,
Like Jason, brought the golden fleece;
To him that *language*, though to none
Of th' others, as his own was known. *Denham.*

3. Stile; manner of expression.

Though his *language* should not be refin'd,
It must not be obscure and impudent. *Roscommon.*

Others for *language* all their care express,
And value books, as women, men, for dress:
Their praise is still — the stile is excellent;
The sense, they humbly take upon content. *Pope.*

LA'NGUAGED. *adj.* [from the noun.]

Having various languages.

He wand'ring long a wider circle made,
And many *languag'd* nations has survey'd. *Pope.*

LA'NGUAGE-MASTER. *n. s.* [*language* and *master.*] One whose profession is to teach languages.

The third is a sort of *language-master*, who is to instruct them in the stile proper for a minister. *Spectator*, N°. 305.

LA'NGUET. *n. s.* [*languette*, French.] Any thing cut in the form of a tongue.

LA'NGUID. *adj.* [*languidus*, Latin.]

1. Faint; weak; feeble.

Whatever renders the motion of the blood *languid*, disposeth to an acid acrimony; what accelerates the motion of the blood, disposeth to an alkaline acrimony. *Arbuthnot.*

No space can be assigned so vast, but still a larger may be imagined; no motion so swift or *languid*, but a greater velocity or slowness may still be conceived. *Bentley's Serm.*

2. Dull; heartless.

I'll hasten to my troops,
And fire their *languid* souls with Cato's virtue. *Addison.*

LA'NGUIDLY. *adv.* [from *languid.*] Weekly; feebly.

The menstruum work'd as *languidly* upon the coral, as it did before they were put into the receiver. *Boyle.*

LAN'GUIDNESS. *n. s.* [from *languid.*] Weakness; feebleness; want of strength.

To LA'NGUISH. *v. n.* [*languir*, French; *langueo*, Latin.]

1. To grow feeble; to pine away; to lose strength.

Let her *languish*
A drop of blood a-day; and, being aged,
Die of this folly. *Shakespeare's Cymbeline.*

We and our fathers do *languish* of such diseases. 2 *Esdr.*

What can we expect, but that her *languishings* should end in death. *Decay of Piety.*

His sorrows bore him off; and softly laid
His *languish'd* limbs upon his homely bed. *Dryden's Æn.*

2. To be no longer vigorous in motion; not to be vivid in appearance.

The troops with hate inspir'd,
Their darts with clamour at a distance drive,
And only keep the *languish'd* war alive. *Dryden's Æn.*

3. To sink or pine under sorrow, or any slow passion.

What man who knows
What woman is, yea, what she cannot chuse
But must be, will his free hours *languish* out
For assur'd bondage. *Shakespeare's Cymbeline.*

The land shall mourn, and every one that dwelleth therein *languish.* *Hos.* iv. 3.

I have been talking with a suitor here,
A man that *languishes* in your displeasure. *Shakes. Othello.*

I was about fifteen when I took the liberty to chuse for myself, and have ever since *languished* under the displeasure of an inexorable father. *Addison's Spectator*, N°. 181.

Let Leonora consider, that, at the very time in which she *languishes* for the loss of her deceased lover, there are persons just perishing in a shipwreck. *Addison's Spect.* N°. 163.

4. To look with softness or tenderness.

What poems think you soft, and to be read
With *languishing* regards, and bending head? *Dryden.*

LA'NGUISH. *n. s.* [from the verb.] Soft appearance.

And the blue *languish* of soft Allia's eye. *Pope.*

Then forth he walks,
Beneath the trembling *languish* of her beam,
With soften'd soul. *Thomson's Spring, l.* 1035

LA'NGUISHINGLY. *adv.* [from *languishing.*]

1. Weakly; feebly; with feeble softness.

Leave such to tune their own dull rhimes, and knov
What's roundly smooth, or *languishingly* slow. *Pope.*

2. Dully; tediously.

Alas! my Dorus, thou seest how long and *languishingly* the weeks are past over since our last talking. *Sidney.*

LA'NGUISHMENT. *n. s.* [*languissemment*, French; from *languish.*]

1. State of pining.

By that count, which lovers books invent,
The sphere of Cupid forty years contains;
Which I have wasted in long *languishment*,
That seem'd the longer for my greater pains. *Spenser.*

2. Softness of mein.

Humility it expresses, by the stooping or bending of the head; *languishment*, when we hang it on one side. *Dryden.*

LA'NGUOR. *n. s.* [*languor*, Latin; *langueur*, French.] *Languor* and lassitude signifies a faintness, which may arise from want or decay of spirits, through indigestion, or too much exercise; or from an additional weight of fluids, from a diminution of secretion by the common discharges. *Quincy.*

Well hoped I, and fair beginnings had,
That he my captive *languor* should redeem. *Spens. Fa. Q.*

For these, these tribunes, in the dust I write
My heart's deep *languor*, and my soul's sad tears. *Shakes.*

Academical disputation gives vigour and briskness to the mind thus exercised, and relieves the *languor* of private study and meditation. *Watts's Improvement of the Mind.*

To isles of fragrance, lily-silver'd vales
Diffusing *languor* in the panting gales. *Dunciad.*

LA'NGUOROUS. *adj.* [*languoreux*, Fr.] Tedious; melancholy.

Dear lady, how shall I declare thy case,
Whom late I left in *languorous* constraint. *Spens. Fa. Qu.*

To LA'NIATE. *v. a.* [*lanio*, Latin.] To tear in pieces; to rend; to lacerate.

LA'NIFICE. *n. s.* [*lanificium*, Latin.] Woollen manufacture.

The moth breedeth upon cloth and other *lanifices*, especially if they be laid up dankish and wet. *Bacon.*

LA'NIGEROUS. *adj.* [*laniger*, Latin.] Bearing wool.

LANK. *adj.* [*lancke*, Dutch.]

1. Loose; not filled up; not stiffened out; not fat; not plump; slender.

The commons hast thou rack'd; the clergy's bags
Are *lank* and lean with thy extortions. *Shakespeare.*

Name not Winterface, whose skin's slack,
Lank, as an unthrift's purse. *Donne.*

We let down into the receiver a great bladder well tied at the neck, but very *lank*, as not containing above a pint of air, but capable of containing ten times as much. *Boyle.*

Moist earth produces corn and grass, but both
Too rank and too luxuriant in their growth.
Let not my land so large a promise boast,
Lest the *lank* ears in length of stem be lost. *Dryden.*

Now, now my bearded harvest gilds the plain.
Thus dreams the wretch, and vainly thus dreams on,
Till his *lank* purse declares his money gone. *Dryden.*

Meagre and *lank* with fasting grown,
And nothing left but skin and bone;
They just keep life and soul together. *Swift.*

2. *Milton* seems to use this word for faint; languid.

He, piteous of her woes, rear'd her *lank* head,
And gave her to his daughters to imbathe
In nectar'd lavers strew'd with asphodil. *Milton.*

LA'NKNESS. *n. s.* [from *lank.*] Want of plumpness.

LA'NNER. *n. s.* [*lanier*, Fr. *lannarius*, Lat.] A species of hawk.

LA'NSQUENET. *n. s.* [*lance* and *knecht*, Dutch.]

1. A common foot-soldier.

2. A game at cards.

LA'NTERN. *n. s.* [*lanterne*, French; *laterna*, Latin: it is by mistake often written lanthorn.] A transparent case for a candle.

God shall be my hope,
My stay, my guide, my *lanthorn* to my feet. *Shakes.*

Thou art our admiral; thou bearest the *lanthorn* in the poop, but 'tis in the nose of thee; thou art the knight of the burning lamp. *Shakes. Henry IV. p.* i.

A candle lasteth longer in a *lanthorn* than at large. *Bacon.*

Amongst the excellent acts of that king, one hath the pre-eminence, the erection and institution of a society, which we call Solomon's house; the noblest foundation that ever was, and the *lanthorn* of this kingdom. *Bacon's Atlantis.*

O thievish night,
Why shouldst thou, but for some felonious end,
In thy dark *lanthorn* thus close up the stars,
That nature hung in heav'n, and fill'd their lamps
With everlasting oil, to give due light
To the misled and lonely traveller. *Milton.*

Vice is like a dark *lanthorn*, which turns its bright side only to him that bears it, but looks black and dismal in another's hand. *Govern. Tong.*

Judge what a ridiculous thing it were, that the continued shadow of the earth should be broken by sudden miraculous eruptions of light, to prevent the art of the *lantern-maker*. *More's Divine Dialogues.*

There are at Paris, Madrid, Lisbon, Rome, great hospitals, in the walls of which are placed machines in the shape of large *lanthorns*, with a little door in the side of them. *Addis.*

Our ideas succeed one another in our minds, not much unlike the images in the inside of a *lanthorn*, turned round by the heat of a candle. *Locke.*

2. A lighthouse; a light hung out to guide ships.

Caprea, where the *lanthorn* fix'd on high
Shines like a moon through the benighted Sky,
While by its beams the wary sailor steers. *Addison.*

LA'NTERN *jaws.* A term used of a thin visage, such as if a candle were burning in the mouth might transmit the light.

Being very lucky in a pair of long *lanthorn-jaws*, he wrung his face into a hideous grimace. *Addison's Spect.* N°. 173.

LA'NUGINOUS. *adj.* [*lanuginosus*, Latin.] Downy; covered with soft hair.

LAP. *n. s.* [læppe, Saxon; *lappe*, German.]

1. The loose part of a garment, which may be doubled at pleasure.

If a joint of meat falls on the ground, take it up gently, wipe it with the *lap* of your coat, and then put it into the dish. *Swift's Directions to a Footman.*

2. The part of the cloaths that is spread horizontally over the knees as one sits down, so as any thing may lie in it.

It feeds each living plant with liquid sap,
And fills with flowers fair Flora's painted *lap*. *Spenser.*

Upon a day, as love lay sweetly slumb'ring
All in his mothers *lap*,
A gentle bee, with his loud trumpet murm'ring,
About him flew by hap. *Spenser.*

I'll make my haven in a lady's *lap*,
And 'witch sweet ladies with my words and looks. *Shakes.*

She bids you
All on the wanton rushes lay you down,
And rest your gentle head upon her *lap*,
And she will sing the song that pleaseth you. *Shakes.*

Let us rear
The higher our opinion, that our stirring
Can from the *lap* of Egypt's widow pluck
The ne'er-lust-wearied Antony. *Shakes. Ant. and Cleopatra.*

Heav'n's almighty fire
Melts on the bosom of his love, and pours
Himself into her *lap* in fruitful show'rs. *Crashaw.*

Men expect that religion should cost them no pains, and that happiness should drop into their *laps*. *Tillotson.*

He struggles into breath, and cries for aid;
Then, helpless, in his mother's *lap* is laid.
He creeps, he walks, and issuing into man,
Grudges their life from whence his own began:
Retchless of laws, affects to rule alone,
Anxious to reign, and restless on the throne. *Dryden.*

To LAP. *v. a.* [from the noun.]

1. To wrap or twist round any thing.

He hath a long tail, which, as he descends from a tree, he *laps* round about the boughs, to keep himself from falling. *Grew's Museum.*

About the paper, whose two halves were painted with red and blue, and which was stiff like thin pasteboard, I *lapped* several times a slender thread of very black silk. *Newton.*

2. To involve in any thing.

As through the flow'ring forest rash she fled,
In her rude hairs sweet flowers themselves did *lap*,
And flourishing fresh leaves and blossoms did enwrap. *Spens.*

The thane of Cawder 'gan a dismal conflict,
Till that Bellona's bridegroom, *lapt* in proof,
Confronted him. *Shakespeare's Macbeth.*

When we both lay in the field,
Frozen almost to death, how he did *lap* me,
Ev'n in his garments, and did give himself,
All thin and naked, to the numb cold night. *Shakespeare.*

Ever against eating cares,
Lap me in soft Lydian airs. *Milton.*

Indulgent fortune does her care employ,
And smiling, broods upon the naked boy;
Her garment spreads, and *laps* him in the folds,
And covers with her wings from nightly colds. *Dryden.*

Here was the repository of all the wise contentions for power between the nobles and commons, *lapt* up safely in the bosom of a Nero and a Caligula. *Swift.*

To LAP. *v. n.* To be spread or twisted over any thing.

The upper wings are opacous; at their hinder ends, where they *lap* over, transparent, like the wing of a fly. *Grew.*

To LAP. *v. n.* [lappian, Saxon; *lappen*, Dutch.] To feed by quick reciprocations of the tongue.

The dogs by the river Nilus' side being thirsty, *lap* hastily as they run along the shore. *Digby on bodies.*

They had soups served up in broad dishes, and so the fox fell to *lapping* himself, and bade his guest heartily welcome. *L'Estrange, Fab.* 31.

The tongue serves not only for tasting, but for mastication and deglutition, in man, by licking; in the dog and cat kind, by *lapping*. *Ray on Creation.*

To LAP. *v. a.* To lick up.

For all the rest
They'll take suggestion, as a cat *laps* milk. *Shakespeare.*

Upon a bull
Two horrid lyons rampt, and seis'd, and tugg'd off, bellowing still,
Both men and dogs came; yet they tore the hide, and *lapt* their fill. *Chapman's Iliad, b.* xviii.

LA'PDOG. *n. s.* [*lap* and *dog.*] A little dog, fondled by ladies in the lap.

One of them made his court to the *lap-dog*, to improve his interest with the lady. *Collier.*

These if the laws did that exchange afford,
Would save their *lap-dog* sooner than their lord. *Dryden.*

Lap-dogs give themselves the rowsing shake,
And sleepless lovers just at twelve awake. *Pope.*

LA'PFUL. *n. s.* [*lap* and *full.*] As much as can be contained in the lap.

One found a wild vine, and gathered thereof wild goards his *lapful*, and shred them into the pot of pottage. 2 *Kings.*

Will four per cent. increase the number of lenders? if it will not, then all the plenty of money these conjurers bestow upon us, is but like the gold and silver which old women believe other conjurers bestow by whole *lapfulls* on poor credulous girls. *Locke.*

LA'PICIDE. *n. s.* [*lapicida*, Latin.] A stonecutter. *Dict.*

LA'PIDARY. *n. s.* [*lapidaire*, Fr.] One who deals in stones or gems.

As a cock was turning up a dunghil, he espied a diamond: well (says he) this sparkling foolery now to a *lapidary* would have been the making of him; but, as to any use of mine, a barley-corn had been worth forty on't. *L'Estrange.*

Of all the many sorts of the gem kind reckoned up by the *lapidaries*, there are not above three or four that are original. *Woodward's Nat. Hist.*

To LA'PIDATE. *v. a.* [*lapido*, Latin.] To stone; to kill by stoning. *Dict.*

LAPIDA'TION. *n. s.* [*lapidatio*, Lat. *lapidation*, Fr.] A stoning.

LAPI'DEOUS. *adj.* [*lapideus*, Latin.] Stony; of the nature of stone.

There might fall down into the *lapideous* matter, before it was concreted into a stone, some small toad, which might remain there imprisoned, till the matter about it were condensed. *Ray on Creation.*

LAPIDE'SCENCE. *n. s.* [*lapidesco*, Latin.] Stony concretion.

Of lapis ceratites, or cornu fossile, in subterraneous cavities, there are many to be found in Germany, which are but the *lapidescencies*, and putrefactive mutations, of hard bodies. *Brown's Vulgar Errors, b.* iii. *c.* 22.

LAPIDE'SCENT. *adj.* [*lapidescens*, Latin.] Growing or turning to stone.

LAPIDIFICA'TION. [*lapidification*, French.] The act of forming stones.

Induration or *lapidification* of substances more soft, is another degree of condensation. *Bacon's Natural History.*

LAPIDI'FICK. *adj.* [*lapidifique*, French.] Forming stones.

The atoms of the *lapidifick*, as well as saline principle, being regular, do concur in producing regular stones. *Grew.*

LA'PIDIST. *n. s.* [from *lapides*, Latin.] A dealer in stones or gems.

Hardness, wherein some stones exceed all other bodies, being exalted to that degree, that art in vain endeavours to counterfeit it, the factitious stores of chemists in imitation being easily detected by an ordinary *lapidist*. *Ray on Creation.*

LA'PIS. *n. s.* [Latin.] A stone.

LA'PIS *Lazuli.*

The *lapis lazuli*, or azure stone, is a copper ore, very compact and hard, so as to take a high polish, and is worked into a great variety of toys. It is found in detached lumps, usually of the size of a man's fist, of an elegant blue colour, beautifully variegated with clouds of white, and veins of a shining gold colour: that of Asia and Africa is much superior to the Bohemian or German kind: it has been used in medicine, but the present practice takes no notice of it: to it the painters are indebted for their beautiful ultra-marine colour, which is only a calcination of *lapis lazuli*. *Hill.*

LA'PPER. *n. s.* [from *lap*.]

1. One who wraps up.

They may be *lappers* of linen, and bailiffs of the manor. *Swift's Consideration on Two Bills.*

2. One who laps or licks.

LA'PPET. *n. s.* [diminutive of *lap*.] The parts of a head dress that hang loose.

How naturally do you apply your hands to each other's *lappets*, and ruffles, and mantuas. *Swift.*

LAPSE. *n. s.* [*lapsus*, Latin.]

1. Flow; fall; glide.

Round I saw
Hill, dale, and shady woods, and sunny plains,
And liquid *lapse* of murm'ring streams. *Milton.*

Notions of the mind are preserved in the memory, notwithstanding *lapse* of time. *Hale's Original of Mankind.*

2. Petty error; small mistake.

These are petty errors and minor *lapses*, not considerably injurious unto truth. *Brown's Vulgar Errours, b.* vi. *c.* 13.

The weakness of human understanding all will confess; yet the confidence of most practically disowns it; and it is easier to persuade them of it from others *lapses* than their own. *Glanville's Scep. c.* 9.

This scripture may be usefully applied as a caution to guard against those *lapses* and failings, to which our infirmities daily expose us. *Rogers's Sermon.*

It hath been my constant business to examine whether I could find the smallest *lapse* in stile or propriety through my whole collection, that I might send it abroad as the most finished piece. *Swift.*

3. Translation of right from one to another.

In a presentation to a vacant church, a layman ought to present within four months, and a clergyman within six, otherwise a devolution, or *lapse* of right, happens. *Ayliffe.*

To LAPSE. *v. n.* [from the noun.]

1. To glide slowly; to fall by degrees.

This disposition to shorten our words, by retrenching the vowels, is nothing else but a tendency to *lapse* into the barbarity of those northern nations from whom we are descended, and whose languages labour all under the same defect. *Swift's Letter to the Lord Treasurer.*

2. To fail in any thing; to slip.

I have ever narrified my friends,
Of whom he's chief, with all the size that verity
Would without *lapsing* suffer. *Shakes. Coriolanus.*

To *lapse* in fulness
Is sorer than to lie for need; and falshood
Is worse in kings than beggars. *Shakes. Cymbeline.*

3. To slip by inadvertency or mistake.

Homer, in his characters of Vulcan and Thersites, has *lapsed* into the burlesque character, and departed from that serious air essential to an epick poem. *Add. Spectator.*

Let there be no wilful perversion of another's meaning; no sudden seizure of a *lapsed* syllable to play upon it. *Watts.*

3. To lose the proper time.

Myself stood out;
For which if I be *lapsed* in this place,
I shall pay dear. *Shakespeare's Twelfth Night.*

As an appeal may be deserted by the appellant's *lapsing* the term of law, so it may also be deserted by a lapse of the term of a judge. *Ayliffe's Parergon.*

4. To fall by the negligence of one proprietor to another.

If the archbishop shall not fill it up within six months ensuing, it *lapses* to the king. *Ayliffe's Parergon.*

5. To fall from perfection, truth or faith.

Once more I will renew
His *lapsed* pow'rs, though forfeit, and inthrall'd
By sin to foul exorbitant desires. *Milton's Paradise Lost.*

Indeed the charge seems designed as an artifice of diversion, a sprout of that fig-tree which was to hide the nakedness of *lapsed* Adam. *Decay of Piety.*

All publick forms suppose it the most principal, universal, and daily requisite to the *lapsing* state of human corruption. *Decay of Piety.*

These were looked on as *lapsed* persons, and great severities of penance were prescribed them, as appears by the canons of Ancyra. *Stillingfleet's Disc. on Romish Idolatry.*

LA'PWING. *n. s.* [*lap* and *wing*.] A clamorous bird with long wings.

Ah! but I think him better than I say,
And yet would herein others eyes were worse:
Far from her nest the *lapwing* cries away;
My heart prays for him, though my tongue do curse. *Shak.*

And how in fields the *lapwing* Tereus reigns,
The warbling nightingale in woods complains. *Dryden.*

LA'PWORK. *n. s.* [*lap* and *work*.] Work in which one part is interchangeably wrapped over the other.

A basket made of porcupine quills: the ground is a packthread caul woven, into which, by the Indian women, are wrought, by a kind of *lap-work*, the quills of porcupines, not split, but of the young ones intire; mixed with white and black in even and indented waves. *Grew's Musæum.*

LA'RBOARD. *n. s.*

The left-hand side of a ship, when you stand with your face to the head. *Harris.*

Or when Ulysses on the *larboard* shunn'd
Charybdis, and by the other whirlpool steer'd. *Milton.*

Tack to the *larboard*, and stand off to sea,
Veer starboard sea and land. *Dryden.*

LA'RCENY. *n. s.* [*larcin*, Fr. *latrocinium*, Lat.] Petty theft.

Those laws would be very unjust, that should chastize murder and petty *larceny* with the same punishment. *Spectat.*

LARCH. *n. s.* [Larix.]

The leaves, which are long and narrow, are produced out of little tubercles, in form of a painter's pencil, as in the cedar of Libanus, but fall off in winter; the cones are small and oblong, and, for the most part, have a small branch growing out of the top; these are produced at remote distances from the male flowers, on the same tree: the male flowers are, for the most part, produced on the under side of the branches, and, at their first appearance, are very like small cones. *Miller.*

Some botanical criticks tell us, the poets have not rightly followed the traditions of antiquity, in metamorphosing the sisters of Phaëton into poplars, who ought to have been turned into *larch* trees; for that it is this kind of tree which sheds a gum, and is commonly found on the banks of the Po. *Addison on Italy.*

LARD. *n. s.* [*lardum*, Latin; *lard*, French.]

1. The grease of swine.

So may thy pastures with their flow'ry feasts,
As suddenly as *lard*, fat thy lean beasts. *Donne.*

2. Bacon; the flesh of swine.

By this the boiling kettle had prepar'd,
And to the table sent the smoaking *lard*;
On which with eager appetite they dine,
A sav'ry bit, that serv'd to relish wine. *Dryden's Ovid.*

The sacrifice they sped;
Chopp'd off their nervous thighs, and next prepar'd
T' involve the lean in cauls, and mend with *lard*. *Dryden.*

To LARD. *v. a.* [*larder*, French; from the noun.]

1. To stuff with bacon.

The *larded* thighs on loaded altars laid. *Dryd. Homer.*

No man *lards* salt pork with orange peel,
Or garnishes his lamb with spitch-cockt eel. *King.*

2. To fatten.

Now Falstaff sweats to death,
And *lards* the lean earth as he walks along. *Shakesp.*

Brave soldier, doth he lie
Larding the plain. *Shakespeare's Henry* V.

3. To mix with something else by way of improvement.

I found, Horatio,
A royal knavery; an exact command,
Larded with many several sorts of reasons. *Shakes. Hamlet.*

Let no alien interpose
To *lard* with wit thy hungry Epsom prose. *Dryden.*
He *lards* with flourishes his long harangue,
'Tis fine, sayst thou. *Dryd.*

Swearing by heaven; the poets think this nothing, their plays are so much *larded* with it. *Collier's View of the Stage.*

LA'RDER. *n. s.* [*lardier*, old French; from *lard.*] The room where meat is kept or salted.

This similitude is not borrowed of the *larder* house, but out of the school house. *Ascham's Schoolmaster.*

Flesh is ill kept in a room that is not cool; whereas in a cool and wet *larder* it will keep longer. *Bacon.*

So have I seen in *larder* dark,
Of veal a lucid loin. *Dorset.*

Old age,
Morose, perverse in humour, diffident
The more he still abounds, the less content:
His *larder* and his kitchen too observes,
And now, lest he should want hereafter, starves. *King.*

LA'RDERER. [*larder.*] One who has the charge of the larder.

LA'RDON. *n. s.* [French.] A bit of bacon.

LARGE. *adj.* [*large*, French; *largus*, Latin.]

1. Big; bulky.

Charles II. asked me, What could be the reason, that in mountainous countries the men were commonly *larger*, and yet the cattle of all sorts smaller. *Temple.*

Great Theron fell,
Great Theron, *large* of limbs, of giant height. *Dryden.*

Warwick, Leicester, and Buckingham, bear a *large* boned sheep of the best shape and deepest staple. *Mortimer's Husb.*

2. Wide; extensive.

Their former *large* peopling was an effect of the countries impoverishing. *Carew's Survey of Cornwall.*

Let them dwell in the land, and trade therein; for it is *large* enough for them. *Gen.* xxxiv. 21.

There he conquered a thousand miles wide and *large*. *Abbot's Description of the World.*

3. Liberal; abundant; plentiful.

Thou shalt drink of thy sister's cup deep and *large*. *Ezek.*

Vernal suns and showers
Diffuse their warmest, *largest* influence. *Thomson's Autumn.*

4. Copious; diffuse.

Skippon gave a *large* testimony under his hand, that they had carried themselves with great civility. *Clarendon, b.* viii.

I might be very *large* upon the importance and advantages of education, and say a great many things which have been said before. *Felton on the Classicks.*

5. *At* LARGE. Without restraint.

If you divide a cane into two, and one speak at the one end, and you lay your ear at the other, it will carry the voice farther than in the air *at large*. *Bacon's Nat. History.*

Thus incorporeal spirits to smallest forms
Reduc'd their shapes immense; and were at *large*,
Though without number still. *Milton's Paradise Lost.*

The children are bred up in their father's way; or so plentifully provided for, that they are left *at large*. *Sprat.*

Your zeal becomes importunate;
I've hitherto permitted it to rave
And talk *at large*; but learn to keep it in,
Lest it should take more freedom than I'll give it. *Addis.*

6. *At* LARGE. Diffusely.

Discover more *at large* what cause that was,
For I am ignorant, and cannot guess. *Shakesp. Henry* VI.

It does not belong to this place to have that point debated *at large*. *Watts.*

LA'RGELY. *adv.* [from *large.*]

1. Widely; extensively.

2. Copiously; diffusely.

Where the author treats more *largely*, it will explain the shorter hints and brief intimations. *Watts's Imp. on the Mind.*

3. Liberally; bounteously.

How he lives and eats:
How *largely* gives; how splendidly he treats. *Dryden.*

Those, who in warmer climes complain,
From Phœbus' rays they suffer pain,
Must own, that pain is *largely* paid
By gen'rous wines beneath the shade. *Swift.*

4. Abundantly.

They their fill of love, and love's disport
Took *largely*; of their mutual guilt the seal. *Milton.*

LA'RGENESS. *n. s.* [from *large.*]

1. Bigness; bulk.

London excels any other city in the whole world, either in *largeness*, or number of inhabitants. *Sprat's Sermons.*

Nor must Bumastus, his old honours lose,
In length and *largeness* like the dugs of cows. *Dryden.*

2. Greatness; elevation.

There will be occasion for *largeness* of mind and agreeableness of temper. *Collier of Friendship.*

3. Extension; amplitude.

They which would file away most from the *largeness* of that offer, do in more sparing terms acknowledge little less. *Hooker, b.* v. *s.* 27.

The ample proposition that hope makes
In all designs begun on earth below,
Fails in the promised *largeness*. *Shakesp. Troil. and Cres.*

Knowing best the *largeness* of my own heart toward my people's good and just contentment. *King Charles.*

Shall grief contract the *largeness* of that heart,
In which nor fear nor anger has a part? *Waller.*

Man as far transcends the beasts in *largeness* of desire, as dignity of nature and employment. *Glanville's Apology.*

If the *largeness* of a man's heart carry him beyond prudence, we may reckon it illustrious weakness. *L'Estrange.*

4. Wideness.

Supposing that the multitude and *largeness* of rivers ought to continue as great as now; we can easily prove, that the extent of the ocean could be no less. *Bentley's Sermons.*

LA'RGESS. *n. s.* [*largesse*, Fr.] A present; a gift; a bounty.

Our coffers with too great a court,
And liberal *largess*, are grown somewhat light. *Shakesp.*

He left me; having assigned a value of about two thousand ducats, for a bounty to me and my fellows: for they give great *largesses* where they come. *Bacon's New Atlantis.*

A pardon to the captain, and a *largess*
Among the soldiers, had appeas'd their fury. *Denham.*

The paltry *largess* too severely watch'd,
That no intruding guests usurp a share. *Dryden's Juv.*

I am enamoured of Irus, whose condition will not admit of such *largesses*. *Addison's Spectator.*

LA'RGITION. *n. s.* [*largitio*, Lat.] The act of giving. *Dict.*

LARK. *n. s.* [lapence, Saxon; *lerk*, Danish; *lavrack*, Scottish.] A small singing bird.

t was the *lark*, the herald of the morn. *Shakespeare.*

Look up a height, the shrill-gorg'd *lark* so far
Cannot be seen or heard. *Shakespeare's King Lear.*

Th' example of the heav'nly *lark*,
Thy fellow poet, Cowley, mark. *Cowley.*

Mark how the *lark* and linnet sing;
With rival notes
They strain their warbling throats,
To welcome in the spring. *Dryden.*

LA'RKER. *n. s.* [from *lark.*] A catcher of larks. *Dict.*

LA'RKSPUR. *n. s.*

Its flower consists of many dissimilar petals, with the uppermost contracted, which ends in a tail, and receives another bifid petal, which also ends in a tail; in the middle rises a pointal, which becomes a fruit of many pods collected into a head, and filled with seeds generally angular. *Miller.*

LA'RVATED. *adj.* [*larvatus*, Latin.] Masked. *Dict.*

LA'RUM. *n. s.* [from *alarum* or *alarm.*]

1. Alarm; noise noting danger.

Utterers of secrets he from thence debarr'd,
His *larum* bell might loud and wide be heard,
When cause requir'd, but never out of time,
Early and late it rung, at evening and at prime. *Fa. Qu.*

The peaking cornute her husband dwelling in a continual *larum* of jealousy, comes to me in the instant of our encounter. *Shakespeare's Merry Wives of Windsor.*

How far off lie these armies?
—Within a mile and half.
—Then shall we hear their *larum*, and they ours. *Shakes.*

She is become formidable to all her neighbours, as she puts every one to stand upon his guard, and have a continual *larum* bell in his ears. *Howell's Vocal Forest.*

2. An instrument that makes a noise at a certain hour.

Of this nature was that *larum*, which, though it were but three inches big, yet would both wake a man, and of itself light a candle for him at any set hour. *Wilkins.*

I see men as lusty and strong that eat but two meals a day, as others that have set their stomachs, like *larums*, to call on them for four or five. *Locke on Education.*

The young Æneas all at once let down,
Stunn'd with his giddy *larum* half the town. *Dunciad.*

LARY'NGOTOMY. *n. s.* [λάρυγξ and τέμνω; *laryngotomie*, Fr.] An operation where the fore-part of the larynx is divided to assist respiration, during large tumours upon the upper parts; as in a quinsey. *Quincy.*

LA'RYNX. *n. s.* [λάρυγξ.] The upper part of the trachea, which lies below the root of the tongue, before the pharynx. *Quincy.*

There are thirteen muscles for the motion of the five cartilages of the *larynx*. *Derham Physico-Theology.*

LASCI'VIENT. *adj.* [*lasciviens*, Lat.] Frolicksome; wantoning.

LASCI'VIOUS. *adj.* [*lascivus*, Latin.] Leud; lustful.

In what habit will you go along?
—Not like a woman; for I would prevent
The loose encounters of *lascivious* men. *Shakespeare.*

He on Eve
Began to cast *lascivious* eyes; she him
As wantonly repaid; in lust they burn. *Milton's Par. Lost.*

Notwithstanding all their talk of reason and philosophy, and those unanswerable difficulties which, over their cups, they pretend to have against christianity; persuade but the covetous man not to deify his money, the *lascivious* man to throw off his leud amours, and all their giant-like objections against christianity shall presently vanish. *South's Sermons.*

2. Wanton;

2. Wanton; soft; luxurious.

Grim visaged war hath sooth'd his wrinkl'd front;
And now, instead of mounting barbed steeds,
To fright the souls of fearful adversaries,
He capers nimbly in a lady's chamber,
To the *lascivious* pleasing of a lute. *Shakesp. Rich.* III.

LASCI'VIOUSNESS. *n. s.* [from *lascivious.*] Wantonness; looseness.

The reason pretended by Augustus was the *lasciviousness* of his elegies, and his art of love. *Dryd. Preface to Ovid.*

LASCI'VIOUSLY. *adv.* [from *lascivious.*] Leudly; wantonly; loosely.

LASH. *n. s.* [The most probable etymology of this word seems to be that of *Skinner*, from *schlagen*, Dutch, to strike; whence *slash* and *lash.*]

1. A stroke with any thing pliant and tough.

From hence are heard the groans of ghosts, the pains
Of sounding *lashes*, and of dragging chains. *Dryden's Æn.*
Rous'd by the *lash* of his own stubborn tail,
Our lion now will foreign foes assail. *Dryden.*

2. The thong or point of the whip which gives the cut or blow.

Her whip of cricket's bone, her *lash* of film,
Her waggoner a small grey-coated gnat. *Shakespeare.*

I observed that your whip wanted a *lash* to it. *Addis. Spect.*

3. A leash, or string in which an animal is held; a snare: out of use.

The farmer they leave in the *lash*,
With losses on every side. *Tusser's Husbandry.*

4. A stroke of satire; a sarcasm.

The moral is a *lash* at the vanity of arrogating that to ourselves which succeeds well. *L'Estrange.*

To LASH. *v. a.* [from the noun.]

1. To strike with any thing pliant; to scourge.

Lucagus to *lash* his horses bends,
Prone to the wheels. *Dryden.*
Lets whip these stragglers o'er the seas again,
Lash hence these over-weening rags of France. *Shakesp.*

Let men out of their way *lash* on ever so fast, they are not at all the nearer their journey's end. *South's Serm.*

He charg'd the flames, and those that disobey'd
He *lash'd* to duty with his sword of light. *Dryden.*
And limping death, *lash'd* on by fate,
Comes up to shorten half our date. *Dryden's Horace.*
Stern as tutors, and as uncles hard,
We *lash* the pupil, and defraud the ward. *Dryden's Pers.*
Leaning on his lance he mounts his car,
His fiery coursers *lashing* through the air. *Garth's Ovid.*

2. To move with a sudden spring or jirk.

The club hung round his ears, and batter'd brows;
He falls; and *lashing* up his heels, his rider throws. *Dryd.*

3. To beat; to strike with a sharp sound.

The winds grow high,
Impending tempests charge the sky;
The lightning flies, the thunder roars,
And big waves *lash* the frighted shoars. *Prior.*

4. To scourge with satire.

Could pension'd Boileau *lash* in honest strain,
Flatt'rers and bigots ev'n in Louis' reign. *Pope's Horace.*

5. To tie any thing down to the side or mast of a ship.

To LASH. *v. n.* To ply the whip.

They *lash* aloud, each other they provoke,
And lend their little souls at every stroke. *Dryden's Æn.*
Gentle or sharp, according to thy choice,
To laugh at follies, or to *lash* at vice. *Dryden's Persius.*
Wheels clash with wheels, and bar the narrow street;
The *lashing* whip resounds. *Gay's Trivia.*

LASHER. *n. s.* [from *lash.*] One that whips or lashes.

LASS. *n. s.* [from *lad* is formed *laddess*, by contraction *lass. Hickes.*] A girl; a maid; a young woman: used now only of mean girls.

Now was the time for vig'rous lads to show
What love or honour could invite them to;
A goodly theatre, where rocks are round
With reverend age, and lovely *lasses* crown'd. *Waller.*

A girl was worth forty of our widows; and an honest, downright, plain-dealing *lass* it was. *L'Estrange.*

They sometimes an hasty kiss
Steal from unwary *lasses*; they with scorn,
And neck reclin'd, resent. *Philips.*

LA'SSITUDE. *n. s.* [*lassitudo*, Latin; *lassitude*, French.] Weariness; fatigue.

Lassitude is remedied by bathing, or anointing with oil and warm water; for all *lassitude* is a kind of contusion and compression of the parts; and bathing and anointing give a relaxation or emollition. *Bacon's Natural History.*

Assiduity in cogitation is more than our embodied souls can bear without *lassitude* or distemper. *Glanville, Scep.* 14.

She lives and breeds in the air; for the largeness and lightness of her wings and tail sustain her without *lassitude*. *More's Antidote against Atheism.*

Do not over-fatigue the spirits, lest the mind be seized with a *lassitude*, and thereby be tempted to nauseate, and grow tired. *Watts's Improvement of the Mind.*

From mouth and nose the briny torrent ran,
And lost in *lassitude* lay all the man. *Pope's Odyssey.*

Lassitude generally expresses that weariness which proceeds from a distempered state; and not from exercise, which wants no remedy but rest: it proceeds from an increase of bulk, from a diminution of proper evacuation, or from too great a consumption of the fluid necessary to maintain the spring of the solids, as in fevers; or from a vitiated secretion of that juice, whereby the fibres are not supplied. *Quincy.*

LA'SSLORN. *n. s.* [*lass* and *lorn.*] Forsaken by his mistress.

Brown groves,
Whose shadow the dismissed batchelor loves,
Being *lasslorn.* *Shapespeare's Tempest.*

LAST. *n. s.* [latest, Saxon; *laetste*, Dutch.]

1. Latest; that which follows all the rest in time.

I feel my end approach, and thus embrac'd,
Am pleas'd to die; but hear me speak my *last.* *Dryden.*
Here, *last* of Britons, let your names be read;
Are none, none living? let me praise the dead. *Pope.*
Wit not alone has shone on ages past,
But lights the present, and shall warm the *last.* *Pope.*

2. Hindmost; which follows in order of place.

3. Beyond which there is no more.

Unhappy slave, and pupil to a bell,
Unhappy to the *last* the kind releasing knell. *Cowley.*
The swans, that on Cayster often try'd
Their tuneful songs, now sung their *last*, and dy'd. *Addis.*
O! may fam'd Brunswick be the *last*,
The *last*, the happiest British king,
Whom thou shalt paint, or I shall sing. *Addison.*
But, while I take my *last* adieu,
Heave thou no sigh, nor shed a tear. *Prior.*

4. Next before the present, as *last* week.

5. Utmost.

Fools ambitiously contend
For wit and pow'r; their *last* endeavours bend
T' outshine each other. *Dryden's Lucretius.*

6. *At* LAST. In conclusion; at the end.

Gad, a troop shall overcome him: but he shall overcome at the *last.* *Gen.* xlix. 19.

Thus weather-cocks, that for a while
Have turn'd about with ev'ry blast,
Grown old, and destitute of oil,
Rust to a point, and fix at *last.* *Freind.*

7. *The* LAST; the end.

All politicians chew on wisdom past,
And blunder on in business to the *last.* *Pope.*

LAST. *adv.*

1. The last time; the time next before the present.

How long is't now since *last* yourself and I
Were in a mask. *Shakespeare's Romeo and Juliet.*
When *last* I dy'd, and, dear! I die
As often as from thee I go,
I can remember yet that I
Something did say, and something did bestow. *Donne.*

2. In conclusion.

Pleas'd with his idol, he commends, admires,
Adores; and *last*, the thing ador'd desires. *Dryden.*

To LAST. *v. n.* [læstan, Saxon.] To endure; to continue; to persevere.

All more *lasting* than beautiful. *Sidney.*

I thought it agreeable to my affection to your grace, to prefix your name before the essays: for the Latin volume of them, being in the universal language, may *last* as long as books *last.* *Bacon's Essays.*

With several degrees of *lasting*, ideas are imprinted on the memory. *Locke.*

These are standing marks of facts delivered by those who were eye-witnesses to them, and which were contrived with great wisdom to *last* till time should be no more. *Addison.*

LAST. *n. s.* [læst, Saxon.]

1. The mould on which shoes are formed.

The cobler is not to go beyond his *last.* *L'Estrange's Fab.*

A cobler produced several new grins, having been used to cut faces over his *last.* *Addison's Spectator*, N°. 174.

Should the big *last* extend the shoe too wide,
Each stone would wrench th' unwary step aside. *Gay.*

2. [LAST, German.] A load; a certain weight or measure.

LA'STERY. *n. s.* A red colour.

The bashful blood her snowy cheeks did spread,
That her became as polish'd ivory,
Which cunning craftsman's hand hath overlaid,
With fair vermilion, or pure *lastery.* *Spens. Fairy Queen.*

LASTA'GE. *n. s.* [*lestage*, French; *lastagie*, Dutch; hlæst, Saxon, a load.]

1. Custom paid for freightage.

2. The ballast of a ship.

LA'STING. *participial adj.* [from *last.*]

1. Continuing; durable.

Every violence offered weakens and impairs, and renders the body less durable and *lasting*. *Ray on Creation.*

2. Of long continuance; perpetual.

White parents may have black children, as negroes sometimes have *lasting* white ones. *Boyle on Colours.*

The grateful work is done,
The seeds of discord sow'd, the war begun:
Frauds, fears and fury, have possess'd the state,
And fix'd the causes of a *lasting* hate. *Dryden's Æn.*

A sinew cracked seldom recovers its former strength, and the memory of it leaves a *lasting* caution in the man, not to put the part quickly again to any robust employment. *Locke.*

LA'STINGLY. *adv.* [from *lasting*.] Perpetually.

LA'STINGNESS. *n. s.* [from *lasting*.] Durableness; continuance.

All more lasting than beautiful, but that the consideration of the exceeding *lastingness* made the eye believe it was exceeding beautiful. *Sidney.*

Consider the *lastingness* of the motions excited in the bottom of the eye by light. *Newton's Opticks.*

LA'STLY. *adv.* [from *last*.]

1. In the last place.

I will justify the quarrel; secondly, balance the forces; and, *lastly*, propound variety of designs for choice, but not advise the choice. *Bacon's War with Spain.*

2. In the conclusion; at last.

LATCH. *n. s.* [*letse*, Dutch; *laccio*, Italian.] A catch of a door moved by a string, or a handle.

The *latch* mov'd up. *Gay's Pastorals.*

Then comes rosy health from her cottage of thatch,
Where never physician had lifted the *latch*. *Smart.*

To LATCH. *v. a.* [from the noun.]

1. To fasten with a latch.

He had strength to reach his father's house: the door was only *latched*; and, when he had the latch in his hand, he turned about his head to see his pursuer. *Locke.*

2. To fasten; to close, perhaps in this place: unless it rather signifies to *wash* from *lather*.

But hast thou yet *latch'd* the Athenian's eyes
With the love juice, as I did bid thee do? *Shakesp.*

LA'TCHES. *n. s.*

Latches or laskets, in a ship, are small lines like loops, fastened by sewing into the bonnets and drablers of a ship, in order to lace the bonnets to the courses, or the drablers to the bonnets. *Harris.*

LA'TCHET. *n. s.* [*lacet*, Fr.] The string that fastens the shoe.

There cometh one mightier than I, the *latchet* of whose shoes I am not worthy to unloose. *Mark* i. 7.

LATE. *adj.* [læt, Saxon; *laet*, Dutch.]

1. Contrary to early; slow; tardy; long delayed.

My hasting days flie on with full career,
But my *late* spring no bud nor blossom sheweth. *Milton.*
Just was the vengeance, and to *latest* days
Shall long posterity resound thy praise. *Pope's Odyssey.*

2. Last in any place, office, or character.

All the difference between the *late* servants, and those who staid in the family, was, that those latter were finer gentlemen. *Addison's Spectator*, N°. 107.

3. The deceased; as the works of the *late* Mr. Pope.

4. Far in the day or night.

LATE. *adv.*

1. After long delays; after a long time.

O boy! thy father gave thee life too soon,
And hath bereft thee of thy life too *late*. *Shakesp. H.* VI.
Second Silvius after these appears,
Silvius Æneas, for thy name he bears;
For arms and justice equally renown'd,
Who *late* restor'd in Alba shall be crown'd. *Dryd. Æn.*
He laughs at all the giddy turns of state,
When mortals search too soon, and fear too *late*. *Dryden.*

The *later* it is before any one comes to have these ideas, the *later* also will it be before he comes to those maxims. *Locke.*

I might have spar'd his life,
But now it is too *late*. *Philips's Distrest Mother.*

2. In a latter season.

To make roses, or other flowers, come *late*, is an experiment of pleasure; for the antients esteemed much of the rosa sera. *Bacon's Natural History.*

There be some flowers which come more early, and others which come more *late*, in the year. *Bacon's Nat. Hist.*

3. Lately; not long ago.

They arrived in that pleasant isle,
Where sleeping *late*, she left her other knight. *Fairy Qu.*

Men have of *late* made use of a pendulum, as a more steady regulator. *Locke.*

The goddess with indulgent cares,
And social joys, the *late* transform'd repairs. *Pope's Odys.*
From fresh pastures, and the dewy field,
The lowing herds return, and round them throng
With leaps and bounds the *late* imprison'd young. *Pope.*

4. Far in the day or night.

Was it so *late*, friend, ere you went to bed,
That you do lie so *late*?
—Sir, we were carousing till the second cock. *Shakesp.*
Late the nocturnal sacrifice begun;
Nor ended, till the next returning sun. *Dryden's Æn.*

LA'TED. *adj.* [from *late*.] Belated; surprised by the night.

I am so *lated* in the world, that I
Have lost my way for ever. *Shakes. Ant. and Cleopatra.*
The west glimmers with some streaks of day:
Now spurs the *lated* traveller apace
To gain the timely inn. *Shakespeare's Macbeth.*

LA'TELY. *adv.* [from *late*.] Not long ago.

Paul found a certain Jew named Aquila, *lately* come from Italy. *Acts* xviii. 1.

LA'TENESS. *n. s.* [from *late*.] Time far advanced.

Lateness in life might be improper to begin the world with. *Swift to Gay.*

LA'TENT. *adj.* [*latens*, Latin.] Hidden; concealed; secret.

If we look into its retired movements, and more secret *latent* springs, we may there trace out a steady hand producing good out of evil. *Woodward's Natural History.*

Who drinks, alas! but to forget; nor sees,
That melancholy sloth, severe disease,
Mem'ry confus'd, and interrupted thought,
Death's harbingers lie *latent* in the draught. *Prior.*

What were Wood's visible costs I know not, and what were his *latent* is variously conjectured. *Swift.*

LA'TERAL. *adj.* [*lateral*, French; *latera*, Latin.]

1. Growing out on the side; belonging to the side.

Why may they not spread their *lateral* branches till their distance from the centre of gravity depress them. *Ray.*

The smallest vessels, which carry the blood by *lateral* branches, separate the next thinner fluid or serum; the diameters of which *lateral* branches are less than the diameters of the blood-vessels. *Arbuthnot on Aliments.*

2. Placed, or acting in a direction perpendicular to a horizontal line.

Forth rush the levant, and the ponent winds
Eurus and Zephyr, with their *lateral* noise,
Sirocco and Libecchio. *Milton's Paradise Lost, b.* x.

LATERA'LITY. *n. s.* [from *lateral*.] The quality of having distinct sides.

We may reasonably conclude a right and left *laterality* in the ark, or naval edifice of Noah. *Brown's Vulgar Errours.*

LA'TERALLY. *n. s.* [from *lateral*.] By the side; side-wise.

The days are set *laterally* against the columns of the golden number. *Holder on Time.*

LA'TEWARD. *adv.* [*late* and peaꞃo, Saxon.] Somewhat late.

LATH. *n. s.* [laꞇꞇa, Saxon; *late*, *latte*, French.] A small long piece of wood used to support the tiles of houses.

With dagger of *lath*. *Shakespeare's Twelfth Night.*

Penny-royal and orpin they use in the country to trim their houses; binding it with a *lath* or stick, and setting it against a wall. *Bacon's Natural History*, N°. 29.

Laths are made of heart of oak, for outside work, as tiling and plaistering; and of fir for inside plaistering, and pantile lathing. *Moxon's Mechanical Exercises.*

The god who frights away,
With his *lath* sword, the thieves and birds of prey. *Dryd.*

To LATH. *v. a.* [*latter*, Fr. from the noun.] To fit up with laths.

A small kiln consists of an oaken frame, *lathed* on every side. *Mortimer's Husbandry.*

The plaisterers work is commonly done by the yard square for *lathing*. *Mortimer's Husbandry.*

LATH. *n. s.* [læð, Saxon. It is explained by *Du Cange*, I suppose from *Spelman*, *Portio comitatus major tres vel plures hundredas continens*: this is apparently contrary to Spenser, in the following example.] A part of a county.

If all that tything failed, then all that *lath* was charged for that tything; and if the *lath* failed, then all that hundred was demanded for them; and if the hundred, then the shire, who would not rest till they had found that undutiful fellow, which was not amesnable to law. *Spenser's Ireland.*

The fee-farms reserved upon charters granted to cities and towns corporate, and the blanch rents and *lath* silver answered by the sheriffs. *Bacon's Office of Alienation.*

LATHE. *n. s.* The tool of a turner, by which he turns about his matter so as to shape it by the chizel.

Those black circular lines we see on turned vessels of wood, are the effects of ignition, caused by the pressure of an edged stick upon the vessel turned nimbly in the *lathe*. *Ray.*

To LA'THER. *v. n.* [leþan, Saxon.] To form a foam.

Chuse water pure,
Such as will *lather* cold with soap. *Baynard.*

To LA'THER. *v. a.* To cover with foam of water and soap.

LA'THER. *n. s.* [from the verb.] A foam or frothe made commonly by beating soap with water.

LA'TIN. *adj.* [*Latinus.*] Written or spoken in the language of the old Romans.

Augustus himself could not make a new *Latin* word. *Locke.*

LA'TIN. *n. s.* An exercise practised by school-boys, who turn English into Latin.

In learning farther his syntaxis, he shall not use the common order in schools for making of *Latins*. *Ascham.*

LA'TINISM. [*Latinisme*, French; *latinismus*, low Latin.] A Latin idiom; a mode of speech peculiar to the Latin.

Milton has made use of frequent transpositions, *Latinisms*, antiquated words and phrases, that he might the better deviate from vulgar and ordinary expressions. *Addison's Rem.*

LA'TINIST. *n. s.* [from *Latin*.] One skilled in Latin.

LATI'NITY. *n. s.* [*Latinité*, French; *latinitas*, Latin.] Purity of Latin stile; the Latin tongue.

If Shakespeare was able to read Plautus with ease, nothing in *Latinity* could be hard to him. *Dennis's Letters.*

To LA'TINIZE. [*Latiniser*, French; from *Latin*.] To use words or phrases borrowed from the Latin.

I am liable to be charged that I *latinize* too much. *Dryd.*

He uses coarse and vulgar words, or terms and phrases that are *latinized*, scholastick, and hard to be understood. *Watts.*

LATISH. *adj.* [from *late*.] Somewhat late.

LATIRO'STROUS. *adj.* [*latus* and *rostrum*, Lat.] Broad-beaked.

In quadrupeds, in regard of the figure of their heads the eyes are placed at some distance; in *latirostrous* and flat-billed birds they are more laterally seated. *Brown's Vulg. Errours.*

LA'TITANCY. *n. s.* [from *latitans*, Latin.] Delitescence; the state of lying hid.

In vipers she has abridged their malignity by their secession or *latitancy*. *Brown's Vulgar Errours, b.* iii. *c.* 16.

LA'TITANT. *adj.* [*latitans*, Latin.] Delitescent; concealed; lying hid.

This is evident in snakes and lizzards, *latitant* many months in the year, which containing a weak heat in a copious humidity, do long subsist without nutrition. *Brown.*

Force the small *latitant* bubbles of air to disclose themselves and break. *Boyle.*

It must be some other substance *latitant* in the fluid matter, and really distinguishable from it. *More.*

LATITA'TION. *n. s.* [from *latito*, Latin.] The state of lying concealed.

LA'TITUDE. *n. s.* [*latitude*, French; *latitudo*, Latin.]

1. Breadth; width; in bodies of unequal dimensions the shorter axis, in equal bodies the line drawn from right to left.

Whether the exact quadrat, or the long square, be the better, I find not well determined; though I must prefer the latter, provided the length do not exceed the *latitude* above one third part. *Wotton's Architecture.*

2. Room; space; extent.

There is a difference of degrees in men's understandings, to so great a *latitude*, that one may affirm, that there is a greater difference between some men and others, than between some men and beasts. *Locke.*

3. The extent of the earth or heavens, reckoned from the equator to either pole.

4. A particular degree, reckoned from the equator.

Another effect the Alps have on Geneva is, that the sun here rises later and sets sooner than it does to other places of the same *latitude*. *Addison's Remarks on Italy.*

5. Unrestrained acceptation; licentious or lax interpretation.

In such *latitudes* of sense, many that love me and the church well, may have taken the covenant. *King Charles.*

Then, in comes the benign *latitude* of the doctrine of goodwill, and cuts asunder all those hard, pinching cords. *South.*

6. Freedom from settled rules; laxity.

In human actions there are no degrees, and precise natural limits described, but a *latitude* is indulged. *Taylor.*

I took this kind of verse, which allows more *latitude* than any other. *Dryden.*

7. Extent; diffusion.

Albertus, bishop of Ratisbon, for his great learning, and *latitude* of knowledge, sirnamed Magnus; besides divinity, hath written many tracts in philosophy. *Brown.*

Mathematicks, in its *latitude*, is usually divided into pure and mixed. *Wilkins's Mathematical Magick.*

I pretend not to treat of them in their full *latitude*; it suffices to shew how the mind receives them, from sensation and reflection. *Locke.*

LA'TITUDINARIAN. *adj.* [*latitudinaire*, French; *latitudinarius*, low Latin.] Not restrained; not confined; thinking or acting at large.

Latitudinarian love will be expensive, and therefore I would be informed what is to be gotten by it. *Collier on Kindness.*

LA'TITUDINARIAN. *n. s.* One who departs from orthodoxy.

LA'TRANT. *adj.* [*latrans*, Latin.] Barking.

Thy care be first the various gifts to trace,
The minds and genius of the *latrant* race. *Tickell.*

LATRI'A. [λατρεία; *latrie*, Fr.] The highest kind of worship. distinguished by the papists from *dulia*, or inferior worship.

The practice of the catholick church makes genuflections, prostrations, supplications, and other acts of *latria* to the cross. *Stillingfleet on Romish Idolatry.*

LA'TTEN. *n. s.* [*leton*, French; *latoen*, Dutch; *lattwn*, Welsh.] Brass; a mixture of copper and calaminaris stone.

To make lamp-black, take a torch or link, and hold it under the bottom of a *latten* bason, and, as it groweth black within, strike it with a feather into some shell. *Peacham.*

LA'TTER. *adj.* [This is the comparative of *late*, though universally written with *tt*, contrary to analogy, and to our own practice in the superlative *latest*. When the thing of which the comparison is made is mentioned, we use *later*; as, *this fruit is* later *than the rest*; but *latter* when no comparison is expressed; as, *those are* latter *fruits*.

—— —— *Volet usus*
Quem penes arbitrium est, & vis, & norma loquendi.]

1. Happening after something else.

2. Modern; lately done or past.

Hath not navigation discovered, in these *latter* ages, whole nations at the bay of Soldania. *Locke.*

3. Mentioned last of two.

The difference between reason and revelation, and in what sense the *latter* is superior. *Watts.*

LA'TTERLY. *adv.* [from *latter*.] Of late; in the last part of life: a low word lately hatched.

LA'TTICE. *n. s.* [*lattis*, French; by *Junius* written *lettice*, and derived from *lett* men, a hindring iron, or iron stop; by *Skinner* imagined to be derived from *latte*, Dutch, a lath, or to be corrupted from *nettice* or *network*: I have sometimes derived it from *let* and *eye*; *leteyes*, that which *lets* the *eye*. It may be deduced from *laterculus*.] A reticulated window; a window made with sticks or irons crossing each other at small distances.

My good window of *lattice* fare thee well; thy casement I need not open, I look through thee. *Shakespeare.*

The mother of Sisera looked out at a window, and cried through the *lattess*. *Judg.* v. 28.

Up into the watch-tower get,
And see all things despoil'd of fallacies:
Thou shalt not peep through *lattices* of eyes,
Nor hear through labyrinths of ears, nor learn
By circuit or collections to discern. *Donne.*

The trembling leaves through which he play'd,
Dappling the walk with light and shade,
Like *lattice* windows, give the spy
Room but to peep with half an eye. *Cleaveland.*

To LA'TTICE. *v. a.* [from the noun.] To decussate; to mark with cross parts like a lattice.

LAVA'TION. *n. s.* [*lavatio*, Latin.] The act of washing.

Such filthy stuff was by loose lewd varlets sung before the chariot on the solemn day of her *lavation*. *Hakewill.*

LA'VATORY. *n. s.* [from *lavo*, Latin.] A wash; something in which parts diseased are washed.

Lavatories, to wash the temples, hands, wrists, and jugulars, do potently profligate, and keep off the venom. *Harvey.*

LAUD. *n. s.* [*laus*, Latin.]

1. Praise; honour paid; celebration.

Doubtless, O guest, great *laud* and praise were mine,
Reply'd the swain, for spotless faith divine:
If, after social rites, and gifts bestow'd,
I stain'd my hospitable hearth with blood. *Pope's Odyssey.*

2. That part of divine worship which consists in praise.

We have certain hymns and services, which we say daily, of *laud* and thanks to God for his marvellous works. *Bacon.*

In the book of Psalms, the *lauds* make up a very great part of it. *Government of the Tongue.*

To LAUD. *v. a.* [*laudo*, Latin.] To praise; to celebrate.

O thou almighty and eternal Creator, having considered the heavens the work of thy fingers, the moon and the stars which thou hast ordained, with all the company of heaven, we *laud* and magnify thy glorious name. *Bentley's Sermons.*

LA'UDABLE. *adj.* [*laudabilis*, Latin.]

1. Praise-worthy; commendable.

I'm in this earthly world, where to do harm
Is often *laudable*; but to do good, sometime
Accounted dang'rous folly. *Shakespeare's Macbeth.*

Affectation endeavours to correct natural defects, and has always the *laudable* aim of pleasing, though it always misses it. *Locke.*

2. Healthy; salubrious.

Good blood, and a due projectile motion or circulation, are necessary to convert the aliment into *laudable* animal juices. *Arbuthnot on Aliments.*

LAUDABLENESS. *n. s.* [*laudable*.] Praise-worthiness.

LA'UDABLY. *adv.* [from *laudable*.] In a manner deserving praise.

Obsolete words may be *laudably* revived, when either they are sounding or significant. *Dryden's Dedication to Juvenal.*

LA'UDANUM. *n. s.* [A cant word, from *laudo*, Latin.] A soporifick tincture.

To LAVE. *v. a.* [*lavo*, Latin.]

1. To wash; to bathe.

Unsafe, that we must *lave* our honours
In these so flatt'ring streams. *Shakespeare's Macbeth.*

But as I rose out of the *laving* stream,
Heav'n open'd her eternal doors, from whence
The spirit descended on me like a dove. *Paradise Reg.*

With roomy decks, her guns of mighty strength,
Whose low-laid mouths each mounting billow *laves*,
Deep in her draught, and warlike in her length,
She seems a sea-wasp flying on the waves. *Dryden.*

2. [*Lever*, French.] To throw up; to lade; to draw out.

Though

Though hills were set on hills,
And seas met seas to guard thee, I would through:
I'd plough up rocks, steep as the Alps, in dust,
And *lave* the Tyrrhene waters into clouds,
But I would reach thy head. *Benj. Johnson's Catiline.*

Some stow their oars, or stop the leaky sides,
Another bolder yet the yard bestrides,
And folds the sails; a fourth with labour *laves*
Th' intruding seas, and waves ejects on waves. *Dryden.*

To LAVE. *v. n.* To wash himself; to bathe.

In her chaste current oft the goddess *laves*,
And with celestial tears augments the waves. *Pope.*

To LAVE'ER. *v. n.* To change the direction often in a course.

How easy 'tis when destiny proves kind,
With full-spread sails to run before the wind:
But those that 'gainst stiff gales *laveering* go,
Must be at once resolv'd, and skilful too. *Dryden.*

LA'VENDER. *n. s.*

It is one of the verticillate plants, whose flower consists of one leaf, divided into two lips; the upper lip, standing upright, is roundish, and, for the most part, bifid; but the under lip is cut into three segments, which are almost equal: these flowers are disposed in whorles, and are collected into a slender spike upon the top of the stalks. *Miller.*

The whole *lavender* plant has a highly aromatick smell and taste, and is famous as a cephalick, nervous, and uterine medicine. *Hill's Materia Medica.*

And then again he turneth to his play,
To spoil the pleasures of that paradise:
The wholesome sage, and *lavender* still grey,
Rank smelling rue, and cummin good for eyes. *Spenser.*

LA'VER. *n. s.* [*lavoir*, French; from *lave.*] A washing vessel.

Let us go find the body where it lies
Soak'd in his enemies blood, and from the stream
With *lavers* pure, and cleansing herbs, wash off
The clodded gore. *Milton's Agonistes, l.* 1727.

He, piteous of her woes, rear'd her lank head,
And gave her to his daughters, to imbathe
In nectar'd *lavers* strew'd with asphodil. *Milton.*

Young Aretus from forth his bridal bow'r
Brought the full *laver* o'er their hands to pour,
And canisters of consecrated flour. *Pope's Odyssey.*

To LAUGH. *v. n.* [hlahan, Saxon; *lachen*, German and Dutch; *lach*, Scottish.]

1. To make that noise which sudden merriment excites.

You saw my master wink and *laugh* upon you. *Shakesp.*

There's one did *laugh* in's sleep, and one cried, Murther!
They wak'd each other. *Shakespeare's Macbeth.*

At this fusty stuff
The large Achilles, on his prest-bed lolling,
From his deep chest *laughs* out a loud applause. *Shakesp.*

Laughing causeth a continued expulsion of the breath with the loud noise, which maketh the interjection of *laughing*, shaking of the breast and sides, running of the eyes with water, if it be violent. *Bacon's Natural History.*

2. [In poetry.] To appear gay, favourable, pleasant, or fertile.

Entreat her not the worse, in that I pray
You use her well; the world may *laugh* again,
And I may live to do you kindness, if
You do it her. *Shakespeare's Henry* VI. *p.* i.

Then *laughs* the childish year with flowrets crown'd. *Dry.*

The plenteous board, high-heap'd with cates divine,
And o'er the foaming bowl the *laughing* wine. *Pope.*

3. *To* LAUGH *at.* To treat with contempt; to ridicule.

Presently prepare thy grave;
Lie where the light foam of the sea may beat
Thy grave-stone daily; make thine epitaph,
That death in me *at* others lives may *laugh*. *Shakesp.*

'Twere better for you, if 'twere not known in council; you'll be *laugh'd at*. *Shakesp. Merry Wives of Windsor.*

The dissolute and abandoned, before they are aware of it, are often betrayed *to laugh at* themselves, and upon reflection find, that they are merry at their own expence. *Addison's Freeholder*, N°. 45.

No wit to flatter left of all his store;
No fool *to laugh at*, which he valued more. *Pope.*

To LAUGH. *v. a.* To deride; to scorn.

Be bloody, bold and resolute; *laugh* to scorn
The pow'r of man. *Shakespeare's Macbeth.*

A wicked soul shall make him to be *laughed* to scorn of his enemies. *Ecclus.* vi. 4.

LAUGH. *n. s.* [from the verb.] The convulsion caused by merriment; an inarticulate expression of sudden merriment.

Me gentle Delia beckons from the plain,
Then hid in shades, eludes her eager swain;
But feigns a *laugh*, to see me search around,
And by that *laugh* the willing fair is found. *Pope's Spring.*

LA'UGHABLE. *adj.* [from *laugh.*] Such as may properly excite laughter.

Nature hath fram'd strange fellows in her time:
Some that will evermore peep through their eye
And *laugh* like parrots at a bagpiper;
And others of such vinegar aspect,
That they'll not show their teeth in way of smile,
Though Nestor swear the jest be *laughable*. *Shakespeare.*

Casaubon confesses his author Persius was not good at turning things into a pleasant ridicule; or, in other words, that he was not a *laughable* writer. *Dryden's Juvenal.*

LA'UGHER. *n. s.* [from *laugh.*] A man fond of merriment.

I am a common *laugher*. *Shakesp. Julius Cæsar.*

Some sober men cannot be of the general opinion, but the *laughers* are much the majority. *Pope.*

LA'UGHINGLY. *adv.* [from *laughing.*] In a merry way; merrily.

LA'UGHINGSTOCK. *n. s.* [*laugh* and *stock.*] A butt; an object of ridicule.

The forlorn maiden, whom your eyes have seen
The *laughingstock* of fortune's mockerie. *Spens. Fa. Qu.*

Pray you let us not be *laughingstocks* to other mens humours. *Shakespeare's Merry Wives of Windsor.*

Supine credulous frailty exposes a man to be both a prey and *laughingstock* at once. *L'Estrange's Fables.*

LA'UGHTER. *n. s.* [from *laugh.*] Convulsive merriment; an inarticulate expression of sudden merriment.

To be worst,
The lowest, most dejected thing of fortune,
Stands still in esperance; lives not in fear.
The lamentable change is from the best,
The worst returns to *laughter*. *Shakespeare's King Lear.*

The act of *laughter*, which is a sweet contraction of the muscles of the face, and a pleasant agitation of the vocal organs, is not merely voluntary, or totally within the jurisdiction of ourselves. *Brown's Vulgar Errours, b.* vii.

We find not that the *laughter* loving dame
Mourn'd for Anchises. *Waller.*

Pain or pleasure, grief or *laughter*. *Prior.*

LA'VISH. *adj.* [Of this word I have been able to find no satisfactory etymology.]

1. Prodigal; wasteful; indiscreetly liberal.

His jolly brother, opposite in sense,
Laughs at his thrift; and *lavish* of expence,
Quaffs, crams, and guttles, in his own defence. *Dryd.*

The dame has been too *lavish* of her feast,
And fed him till he loaths. *Rowe's Jane Shore.*

2. Scattered in waste; profuse.

3. Wild; unrestrained.

Bellona's bridegroom, lapt in proof,
Confronted him,
Curbing his *lavish* spirit. *Shakespeare's Macbeth.*

To LAVISH. *v. a.* [from the adjective.] To scatter with profusion.

Should we thus lead them to a field of slaughter,
Might not th' impartial world with reason say,
We *lavish'd* at our deaths the blood of thousands. *Addis.*

LA'VISHER. *n. s.* [from *lavish.*] A prodigal; a profuse man.

LA'VISHLY. *adv.* [from *lavish.*] Profusely; prodigally.

My father's purposes have been mistook;
And some about him have too *lavishly*
Wrested his meaning and authority. *Shakesp. Henry* IV.

Then laughs the childish year with flowrets crown'd,
And *lavishly* perfumes the fields around. *Dryden.*

Praise to a wit is like rain to a tender flower; if it be moderately bestowed, it chears and revives; but if too *lavishly*, overcharges and depresses him. *Pope.*

LA'VISHMENT. } *n. s.* [from *lavish.*] Prodigality; profusion.
LA'VISHNESS. }

First got with guile, and then preserv'd with dread,
And after spent with pride and *lavishness*. *Fairy Queen.*

To LAUNCH. *v. n.* [It is derived by *Skinner* from *lance*, because a ship is pushed into water with great force.]

1. To force into the sea.

Launch out into the deep, and let down your nets for a draught. *Luke* v. 4.

So short a stay prevails;
He soons equips the ship, supplies the sails,
And gives the word to *launch*. *Dryden.*

For general history, Raleigh and Howel are to be had. He who would *launch* farther into the ocean, may consult Whear. *Locke.*

2. To rove at large; to expatiate.

From hence that gen'ral care and study springs,
That *launching* and progression of the mind. *Davies.*

Whoever pursues his own thoughts, will find them *launch* out beyond the extent of body into the infinity of space. *Locke.*

In our language Spenser has not contented himself with this submissive manner of imitation: he *launches* out into very flow'ry paths, which still conduct him into one great road. *Prior's Preface to Solomon.*

He had not acted in the character of a suppliant, if he had *launched* out into a long oration. *Broome's Odyssey.*

I have *launched* out of my subject on this article. *Arbuth.*

To LANCH. *v. a.*

1. To p sh to sea.

All art is used to sink episcopacy, and *launch* presbytery, in England. *King Charles.*

With stays and cordage last he rigg'd the ship,
And roll'd on leavers, *launch'd* her in the deep. *Pope.*

2. To dart from the hand. This perhaps, for distinction sake, might better be written lanch.

The King of Heav'n, obscure on high,
Bar'd his red arm, and *launching* from the sky
His writhen bolt, not shaking empty smoke,
Down to the deep abyss the flaming fellow strook. *Dryd.*

LAUND. *n. s.* [*lande*, French; *lawn*, Welsh.] Lawn a plain extended between woods. *Hanmer.*

Under this thick-grown brake we'll shroud ourselves,
For through this *laund* anon the deer will come;
And in this covert will we make our stand,
Culling the principal of all the deer. *Shakes. Henry VI.*

LA'UNDRESS. *n. s.* [*lavandiere*, French: *Skinner* imagines that *lavanderesse* may have been the old word.] A woman whose employment is to wash cloaths.

The countess of Richmond would often say, On condition the princes of Christendom would march against the Turks, she would willingly attend them, and be their *laundress*. *Camden.*

Take up these cloaths here quickly; carry them to the *laundress* in Datchet mead. *Shakes. Merry Wives of Windsor.*

The *laundress* must be sure to tear her smocks in the washing, and yet wash them but half. *Swift.*

LA'UNDRY. *n. s.* [as if *lavanderie.*]

1. The room in which clothes are washed.

The affairs of the family ought to be consulted, whether they concern the stable, dairy, the pantry, or *laundry*. *Swif.t*

2. The act or state of washing.

Chalky water is too fretting, as appeareth in *laundry* of cloaths, which wear out apace. *Bacon's Natural History.*

LAVO'LTA. *n. s.* [*la volte*, French.] An old dance, in which was much turning and much capering. *Hanmer.*

I cannot sing,
Nor heel the high *lavolt*; nor sweeten talk;
Nor play at subtle games. *Shakes. Troilus and Cressida.*

LA'UREATE. *adj.* [*laureatus*, Lat.] Decked or invested with a laurel.

Bid Amaranthus all his beauty shed,
And daffodillies fill their cups with tears,
To strew the *laureate* hearse where Lycid lies, *Milton.*
Soft on her lap her *laureate* son reclines. *Dunciad.*

LAUREA'TION. *n. s.* [from *laureate.*] It denotes, in the Scottish universities, the act or state of having degrees conferred, as they have in some of them a flowery crown, in imitation of laurel among the antients.

LA'UREL. *n. s.* [*laurus*, Lat. *laurier*, French.] A tree, called also the cherry bay.

It hath broad thick shining ever-green leaves, somewhat like those of the bay tree; the cup of the flower is hollow, and funnel-shaped, spreading open at the top, and is divided into five parts: the flower consists of five leaves, which expand in form of a rose, having many stamina in the centre; the fruit, which is like that of the cherry tree, is produced in bunches, and the stone is longer and narrower than that of the cherry. *Miller.*

The *laurus* or *laurel* of the antients is affirmed by naturalists to be what we call the bay tree. *Ainsworth.*

The *laurel*, meed of mighty conquerors,
And poets sage. *Spenser's Fairy Queen.*

The *laurel* or cherry-bay, by cutting away the side branches, will rise to a large tree. *Mortimer's Husbandry.*

LA'URELED. *adj.* [from *laurel.*] Crowned or decorated with laurel.

Hear'st thou the news? my friend! th' express is come
With *laurell'd* letters from the camp to Rome. *Dryden.*
Then future ages with delight shall see
How Plato's, Bacon's, Newton's, looks agree;
Or in fair series *laurell'd* bards be shown
A Virgil there, and here an Addison. *Pope.*

LAW. *n. s.* [laᵹa, Saxon; *loi*, French; *lawgh*, Erse.]

1. A rule of action.

Unhappy man! to break the pious *laws*
Of nature, pleading in his children's cause. *Dryden.*

2. A decree, edict, statute, or custom, publickly established as a rule of justice.

He hath resisted *law*,
And therefore *law* shall scorn him further trial
Than the severity of publick power. *Shakes. Coriolanus.*
Thou art a robber,
A *law-breaker*, a villain; yield thee, thief. *Shakespeare.*

Our nation would not give *laws* to the Irish, therefore now the Irish gave *laws* to them. *Davies on Ireland.*

One *law* is split into two. *Baker Reflect. on Learning.*

3. Judicial process.

When every case in *law* is right. *Shakes. King Lear.*
Who has a breast so pure,
But some uncleanly apprehensions
Keep leets and *law* days, and in sessions sit,
With meditations lawful. *Shakespeare's Othello.*

Tom Touchy is a fellow famous for taking the *law* of every body: there is not one in the town where he lives that he has not sued at a quarter-sessions. *Addison's Spectator.*

4. Conformity to law; any thing lawful.

In a rebellion,
When what's not meet, but what must be, was *law*,
Then were they chosen. *Shakespeare's Coriolanus.*

5. An established and constant mode or process; a fixed correspondence of cause and effect.

I dy'd, whilst in the womb he stay'd,
Attending Nature's *law*. *Shakespeare's Cymbeline.*

LA'WFUL. *adj.* [*law* and *full.*] Agreeable to law; conformable to law; allowed legal by law; legitimate.

It is not *lawful* for thee to have her. *Mat.* xiv. 4.

Gloster's bastard son was kinder to his father, than my daughters, got 'tween the *lawful* sheets. *Shakes. King Lear.*

LA'WFULLY. *adv.* [from *lawful.*] Legally; agreeably to law.

This bond is forfeit;
And *lawfully* by this the Jew may claim
A pound of flesh. *Shakesp. Merchant of Venice.*

Though it be not against strict justice for a man to do those things which he might otherwise *lawfully* do, albeit his neighbour doth take occasion from thence to conceive in his mind a false belief, yet Christian charity will, in many cases, restrain a man. *South's Sermons.*

I may be allowed to tell your lordship, the king of poets, what an extent of power you have, and how *lawfully* you may exercise it. *Dryden's Dedication to Juvenal.*

LA'WFULNESS. *n. s.* [from *lawful.*] Legality; allowance of law.

I think it were an error to speak further, till I may see some sound foundation laid of the *lawfulness* of the action. *Bacon's Holy War.*

LA'WGIVER. *n. s.* [*law* and *giver.*] Legislator; one that makes laws.

Solomon we esteem as the *lawgiver* of our nation. *Bacon.*

A law may be very reasonable in itself, although one does not know the reason of the *lawgivers.* *Swift.*

L'AWGIVING. *adj.* [*law* and *giving.*] Legislative.

Lawgiving heroes, fam'd for taming brutes,
And raising cities with their charming lutes. *Waller.*

LA'WLESS. *adj.* [from *law.*]

1. Unrestrained by any law; not subject to law.

The necessity of war, which among human actions is the most *lawless*, hath some kind of affinity with the necessity of law. *Raleigh's Essays.*

The *lawless* tyrant, who denies
To know their God, or message to regard,
Must be compell'd. *Milton's Paradise Lost, b.* xii.
Orpheus did not, as poets feign, tame savage beasts,
But men as *lawless*, and as wild as they. *Roscommon.*
Not the gods, nor angry Jove will bear
Thy *lawless* wand'ring walks in open air. *Dryd. Æn.*
Blind as the Cyclops, and as blind as he,
They own'd a *lawless* savage liberty,
Like that our painted ancestors so priz'd,
Ere empire's arts their breasts had civiliz'd. *Dryden.*
He Meteor-like, flames *lawless* through the void,
Destroying others, by himself destroy'd. *Pope.*

2. Contrary to law; illegal.

Take not the quarrel from his powerful arms,
He needs no indirect nor *lawless* course
To cut off those that have offended him. *Shakes. R.* III.
We cite our faults,
That they may hold excus'd our *lawless* lives. *Shakesp.*
Thou the first, lay down thy *lawless* claim;
Thou of my blood who bear'st the Julian name. *Dryden.*

LA'WLESLY. *adv.* [from *lawless.*] In a manner contrary to law.

Fear not, he bears an honourable mind,
And will not use a woman *lawlesly.* *Shakespeare.*

LA'WMAKER. *n. s.* [*law* and *maker.*] Legislator; one who makes laws; a lawgiver.

Their judgment is, that the church of Christ should admit no *lawmakers* but the evangelists. *Hooker, b.* iii.

LAWN. *n. s.* [*land*, Danish; *lawn*, Welsh; *lande*, French.]

1. An open space between woods.

Betwixt them *lawns*, or level downs, and flocks,
Grazing the tender herb, were interpos'd. *Milt. Pa. Lost.*

His mountains were in a few years shaded with young trees, that gradually shot up into groves, woods, and forests, intermixed with walks, and *lawns*, and gardens. *Addison's Spectator*, N°. 58.

Stern beasts in trains that by his truncheon fell,
Now grisly forms shoot o'er the *lawns* of hell. *Pope.*
Intersper'd in *lawns* and opening glades,
Thin trees arise that shun each other's shades. *Pope.*

2. [*Linon*, French.] Fine linen, remarkable for being used in the sleeves of bishops.

Should'st thou bleed,
To stop the wounds my finest *lawn* I'd tear,
Wash them with tears, and wipe them with my hair. *Prior.*

From high life high characters are drawn,
A saint in crape is twice a saint in *lawn*. *Pope.*
What awe did the slow solemn knell inspire:
The duties by the *lawn* rob'd prelate pay'd,.
And the last words, that dust to dust convey'd! *Tickell.*

LA'WSUIT. *n. s.* [*law* and *suit.*] A process in law; a litigation.

The giving the priest a right to the tithe would produce *lawsuits* and wrangles; his necessary attendance on the courts of justice would leave his people without a spiritual guide. *Swift's Proposal.*

LAW'YER. *n. s.* [from *law.*] Professor of law; advocate; pleader.

It is like the breath of an unfeed *lawyer*, you gave me nothing for it. *Shakespeare's King Lear.*

Is the law evil, because some *lawyers* in their office swerve from it? *Whitgift.*

I have entered into a work touching laws, in a middle term, between the speculative and reverend discourses of philosophers, and the writings of *lawyers*. *Bacon's Holy War.*

The nymphs with scorn beheld their foes,
When the defendant's council rose;
And, what no *lawyer* ever lack'd,
With impudence own'd all the fact. *Swift.*

LAX. *adj.* [*laxus*, Latin.]

1. Loose; not confined; not closely joined.

Inhabit *lax*, ye pow'rs of heav'n! *Milton's Par. Lost.*

In mines, those parts of the earth which abound with strata of stone, suffer much more than those which consist of gravel, and the like *laxer* matter, which more easily give way. *Woodward.*

2. Vague; not rigidly exact.

Dialogues were only *lax* and moral discourses. *Baker.*

3. Loose in body, so as to go frequently to stool; *laxative* medicines are such as promote that disposition. *Quincy.*

4. Slack; not tense.

By a branch of the auditory nerve that goes between the ear and the palate, they can hear themselves, though their outward ear be stopt by the *lax* membrane to all sounds that come that way. *Holder's Elements of Speech.*

LAX. *n. s.* A looseness; a diarrhœa. *Dict.*

LAXA'TION. *n. s.* [*laxatio*, Latin.]

1. The act of loosening or slackening.
2. The state of being loosened or slackened.

LA'XATIVE. *adj.* [*laxatif*, French; *laxo*, Latin.] Having the power to ease costiveness.

Omitting honey, which is of a *laxative* power itself; the powder of some loadstones in this doth rather constipate and bind, than purge and loosen the belly. *Brown's Vulg. Err.*

The oil in wax is emollient, *laxative*, and anodyne. *Arbuthnot on Aliments.*

LA'XATIVE. *n. s.* A medicine slightly purgative; a medicine that relaxes the bowels without stimulation.

Nought profits him to save abandon'd life,
Nor vomits upward aid, nor downward *laxative*. *Dryd.*

LA'XATIVENESS. *n. s.* [*laxative.*] Power of easing costiveness.

LA'XITY. *n. s.* [*laxitas*, Latin.]

1. Not compression; not close cohesion.

The former causes could never beget whirlpools in a chaos of so great a *laxity* and thinness. *Bentley's Sermons.*

2. Contrariety to rigorous precision.
3. Looseness; not costiveness.

If sometimes it cause any *laxity*, it is in the same way with iron unprepared, which will disturb some bodies, and work by purge and vomit. *Brown's Vulgar Errours.*

4. Slackness; contrariety to tension.

Laxity of a fibre, is that degree of cohesion in its parts which a small force can alter, so as to increase its length beyond what is natural. *Quincy.*

In consideration of the *laxity* of their eyes, they are subject to relapse. *Wiseman's Surgery.*

5. Openness; not closeness.

Hold a piece of paper close by the flame of a candle, and by little and little remove it further off, and there is upon the paper some part of that which I see in the candle, and it grows still less and less as I remove; so that if I would trust my sense, I should believe it as very a body upon the paper as in the candle, though infeebled by the *laxity* of the channel in which it flows. *Digby on Bodies.*

LA'XNESS. *n. s.* Laxity; not tension; not precision; not costiveness.

For the free passage of the sound into the ear, it is requisite that the tympanum be tense, and hard stretched; otherwise the *laxness* of that membrane will certainly dead and damp the sound. *Holder's Elements of Speech.*

LAY. Preterite of *lye.*

O! would the quarrel *lay* upon our heads,
And that no man might draw short breath to day,
But I and Harry Monmouth. *Shakesp. Henry IV.*

He was familiarly acquainted with him at such time as he *lay* embassador at Constantinople. *Knolles's Hist. of the Turks.*

When Ahab had heard those words he fasted, and *lay* in sackcloth. *1 Kings* xxi. 27.

I try'd whatever in the Godhead *lay*. *Dryden.*

He rode to rouze the prey,
That shaded by the fern in harbour *lay*,
And thence dislodged. *Dryden's Knight's Tale.*

Leaving Rome, in my way to Sienna, I *lay* the first night at a village in the territories of the antient Veii. *Addison.*

How could he have the retiredness of the cloister, to perform all those acts of devotion in, when the burthen of the reformation *lay* upon his shoulders? *Francis Atterbury.*

The presbyterians argued, that if the pretender should invade those parts where the numbers and estates of the dissenters chiefly *lay*, they would sit still. *Swift.*

To LAY. *v. a.* [lecȝan, Saxon; *leggen*, Dutch.]

1. To place along.

Seek not to be judge, being not able to take away iniquity, lest at any time thou fear the person of the mighty, and *lay* a stumbling-block in the way of thy uprightness. *Ecclus.*

2. To beat down corn or grass.

Another ill accident is *laying* of corn with great rains in harvest. *Bacon's Natural History.*

Let no sheep there play,
Nor frisking kids the flowery meadows *lay*. *May's Virgil.*

3. To keep from rising; to settle; to still.

I'll use th' advantage of my power,
And *lay* the summer's dust with showers of blood. *Shakes.*

It was a sandy soil, and the way had been full of dust; but an hour or two before a refreshing fragrant shower of rain had *laid* the dust. *Ray on Creation.*

4. To fix deep.

Schismaticks, outlaws, or criminal persons, are not fit to *lay* the foundation of a new colony. *Bacon's Adv. to Villiers.*

I *lay* the deep foundations of a wall,
And Enos, nam'd from me, the city call. *Dryden.*

Men will be apt to call it pulling up the old foundations of knowledge; I persuade myself, that the way I have pursued *lays* those fouudations surer. *Locke.*

5. To put; to place.

Then he offered it to him again; then he put it by again; but, to my thinking, he was very loth to *lay* his fingers on it. *Shakespeare's Julius Cæsar.*

They shall *lay* hands on the sick, and recover. *Mark.*

They, who so state a question, do no more but separate and disentangle the parts of it, one from another, and *lay* them, when so disentangled, in their due order. *Locke.*

We to thy name our annual rites will pay,
And on thy altars sacrifices *lay*. *Pope's Statius.*

6. To bury; to interr.

David fell on sleep, and was *laid* unto his fathers, and saw corruption. *Acts* xiii. 36.

7. To station or place privily.

Lay thee an ambush for the city behind thee. *Jos.* viii. 2.

The wicked have *laid* a snare for me. *Psal.*

Lay not wait, O! wicked man, against the dwelling of the righteous. *Prov.* xxiv. 15.

8. To spread on a surface.

The colouring upon those maps should be *laid* on so thin, as not to obscure or conceal any part of the lines. *Watts.*

9. To paint; to enamel.

The pictures drawn in our minds are *laid* in fading colours; and, if not sometimes refreshed, vanish and disappear. *Locke.*

10. To put into any state of quiet.

They bragged, that they doubted not but to abuse, and *lay* asleep, the queen and council of England. *Bacon.*

11. To calm; to still; to quiet; to allay.

Friends, loud tumults are not *laid*
With half the easiness that they are rais'd. *B. Johnson.*

Thus pass'd the night so foul, till morning fair
Came forth with pilgrim steps in amice grey,
Who with her radiant finger still'd the roar
Of thunder, chas'd the clouds and *laid* the winds. *Milton.*

After a tempest, when the winds are *laid*,
The calm sea wonders at the wrecks it made. *Waller.*

I fear'd I should have found
A tempest in your soul, and came to *lay* it. *Denham.*

At once the wind was *laid*, the whisp'ring sound
Was dumb, a rising earthquake rock'd the ground. *Dryd.*

12. To prohibit a spirit to walk.

The husband found no charm to *lay* the devil in a petticoat, but the rattling of a bladder with beans in it. *L'Estr.*

13. To set on the table.

I *laid* meat unto them. *Hos.* xi. 4.

14. To propagate plants by fixing their twigs in the ground.

The chief time of *laying* gillyflowers is in July, when the flowers are gone. *Mortimer's Husbandry.*

15. To wager.

But since you will be mad, and since you may
Suspect my courage, if I should not *lay*;
The pawn I proffer shall be full as good. *Dryden's Virg.*

16. To reposit any thing.

The sparrow hath found an house, and the swallow a nest, for herself, where she may *lay* her young. *Psal.* lxxxiv. 3.

17. To exclude eggs.

After the egg *lay'd*, there is no further growth or nourishment from the female. *Bacon's Natural History.*

A hen mistakes a piece of chalk for an egg, and sits upon it; she is insensible of an increase or diminution in the number of those she *lays*. *Addison's Spectator*, N°. 120.

18. To apply with violence.

Lay siege against it, and build a fort against it, and cast a mount against it. *Ezek.* iv. 2.

Never more shall my torn mind be heal'd,
Nor taste the gentle comforts of repose!
A dreadful band of gloomy cares surround me,
And *lay* strong siege to my distracted soul. *Phillips.*

19. To apply nearly.

She *layeth* her hands to the spindle, and her hands hold the distaff. *Prov.* xxxi. 19.

It is better to go to the house of mourning than to go to the house of feasting; for that is the end of all men, and the living will *lay* it to his heart. *Eccl.* vii. 2.

The peacock *laid* it extremely to heart, that, being Juno's darling bird, he had not the nightingale's voice. *L'Estrange.*

He that really *lays* these two things to heart, the extreme necessity that he is in, and the small possibility of help, will never come coldly to a work of that concernment. *Duppa.*

20. To add; to conjoin.

Wo unto them that *lay* field to field. *Isa.* v. 8.

21. To put in any state.

Till us death *lay*
To ripe and mellow; we're but stubborn clay. *Donne.*

If the sinus lie distant, *lay* it open first, and cure that apertion before you divide that in ano. *Wiseman's Surgery.*

The wars for some years have *laid* whole countries waste. *Addison's Spectator*, N°. 198.

22. To scheme; to contrive.

Every breast she did with spirit inflame,
Yet still fresh projects *lay'd* the grey-ey'd dame. *Chapman.*

Homer is like his Jupiter, has his terrors, shaking Olympus; Virgil, like the same power in his benevolence, counselling with the gods, *laying* plans for empires. *Pope.*

Don Diego and we have *laid* it so, that before the rope is well about thy neck, he will break in and cut thee down. *Arbuth.*

23. To charge as a payment.

A tax *laid* upon land seems hard to the landholder, because it is so much money going out of his pocket. *Locke.*

24. To impute; to charge.

Preoccupied with what
You rather must do, that what you should do,
Made you against the grain to voice him consul,
Lay the fault on us. *Shakespeare.*

How shall this bloody deed be answered?
It will be *laid* to us, whose providence
Should have kept short, restrain'd, and out of haunt,
This mad young man. *Shakespeare's Hamlet.*

We need not *lay* new matter to his charge. *Shakes.*

Men groan from out of the city, yet God *layeth* not folly to them. *Job* xxiv. 12.

Let us be glad of this, and all our fears
Lay on his providence. *Paradise Regain'd, b.* i.

The writers of those times *lay* the disgraces and ruins of their country upon the numbers and fierceness of those savage nations that invaded them. *Temple.*

They *lay* want of invention to his charge; a capital crime. *Dryden's Æneis.*

You represented it to the queen as wholly innocent of those crimes which were *laid* unjustly to its charge. *Dryden.*

They *lay* the blame on the poor little ones. *Locke.*

There was eagerness on both sides; but this is far from *laying* a blot upon Luther. *Atterbury.*

25. To impose; to enjoin.

The weariest and most loathed life
That age, ach, penury, imprisonment,
Can *lay* on nature, is a paradise
To what we fear of death. *Shakesp. Meas. for Meas.*

Thou shalt not be to him as an usurer, neither shalt thou *lay* upon him usury. *Exod.* xx. 25.

The Lord shall *lay* the fear of you, and the dread of you, upon all the land. *Deut.* xi. 25.

It seemed good to the Holy Ghost, and to us, to *lay* upon you no greater burden. *Acts* xv. 28.

Whilst you *lay* on your friend the favour, acquit him of the debt. *Wycherley.*

A prince who never disobey'd,
Not when the most severe commands were *laid*,
Nor want, nor exile, with his duty weigh'd. *Dryden.*

You see what obligation the profession of Christianity *lays* upon us to holiness of life. *Tillotson's Sermons.*

These words were not spoken to Adam; neither, indeed, was there any grant in them made to Adam, but a punishment *laid* upon Eve. *Locke.*

Neglect the rules each verbal critick *lays*,
For not to know some trifles is a praise. *Pope.*

26. To exhibit; to offer.

It is not the manner of the Romans to deliver any man to die, before that he which is accused have the accusers face to face, and have licence to answer for himself concerning the crime *laid* against him. *Acts* xxv. 16.

Till he *lays* his indictment in some certain country, we do not think ourselves bound to answer an indefinite charge. *Francis Atterbury.*

27. To throw by violence.

He bringeth down them that dwell on high; the lofty city he *layeth* it low, even to the ground. *Isa.* xxvi. 5.

Brave Cæneus *laid* Ortygius on the plain,
The victor Cæneus was by Turnus slain. *Dryden's Æn.*

He took the quiver, and the trusty bow
Achates us'd to bear; the leaders first
He *laid* along, and then the vulgar pierc'd. *Dryden.*

28. To place in comparison.

Lay down by those pleasures the fearful and dangerous thunders and lightnings, and then there will be found no comparison. *Raleigh.*

29. *To* LAY *apart.* To reject; to put away.

Lay apart all filthiness. *James* i. 21.

30. *To* LAY *aside.* To put away; not to retain.

Let us *lay aside* every weight, and the sin which doth so easily beset us. *Heb.* xii. 1.

Amaze us not with that majestick frown,
But *lay aside* the greatness of your crown. *Waller.*

Roscommon first, then Mulgrave rose, like light;
The Stagyrite, and Horace, *laid aside*,
Inform'd by them, we need no foreign guide. *Granville.*

Retention is the power to revive again in our minds those ideas which, after imprinting, have disappeared, or have been *laid aside* out of sight. *Locke.*

When by just vengeance guilty mortals perish,
The gods behold their punishment with pleasure,
And *lay* the uplifted thunder-bolt *aside*. *Addison's Cato.*

31. *To* LAY *away.* To put from one; not to keep.

Queen Esther *laid away* her glorious apparel, and put on the garments of anguish. *Esther* xiv. 2.

32. *To* LAY *before.* To expose to view; to shew; to display.

I cannot better satisfy your piety, than by *laying before* you a prospect of your labours. *Wake's Prepar. for Death.*

That treaty hath been *laid before* the house of commons. *Swift's Preface to Remarks on the Barrier Treaty.*

Their office it is to *lay* the business of the nation *before* him. *Addison's Freeholder*, N°. 46.

33. *To* LAY *by.* To reserve for some future time.

Let every one *lay by* him in store, as God hath prospered him. *1 Cor.* xvi. 2.

34. *To* LAY *by.* To put from one; to dismiss.

Let brave spirits that have fitted themselves for command, either by sea or land, not be *laid by* as persons unnecessary for the time. *Bacon's Advice to Villiers.*

She went away, and *laid by* her veil. *Gen.* xxxviii. 19.

Did they not swear to live and die
With Essex, and straight *laid* him *by*. *Hudibras.*

For that look, which does your people awe,
When in your throne and robes you give 'em law,
Lay it *by* here, and give a gentler smile. *Waller.*

Darkness, which fairest nymphs disarms,
Defends us ill from Mira's charms;
Mira can *lay* her beauty *by*,
Take no advantage of the eye,
Quit all that Lely's art can take,
And yet a thousand captives make. *Waller.*

Then he *lays by* the publick care,
Thinks of providing for an heir;
Learns how to get, and how to spare. *Denham.*

The Tuscan king,
Laid by the lance, and took him to the sling. *Dryden.*

Where Dædalus his borrow'd wings *laid by*,
To that obscure retreat I chuse to fly. *Dryden's Juvenal.*

My zeal for you must *lay* the father *by*,
And plead my country's cause against my son. *Dryden.*

Fortune, conscious of your destiny,
E'en then took care to *lay* you softly *by*;
And wrapp'd your fate among her precious things,
Kept fresh to be unfolded with your king's. *Dryden.*

Dismiss your rage, and *lay* your weapons *by*,
Know I protect them, and they shall not die. *Dryden.*

When their displeasure is once declared, they ought not presently to *lay by* the severity of their brows, but restore their children to their former grace with some difficulty. *Locke.*

35. *To* LAY *down.* To deposit as a pledge, equivalent, or satisfaction.

I *lay down* my life for the sheep. *John* x. 15

For her, my Lord,
I dare my life *lay down*, and will do't, Sir,
Please you t' accept it, that the queen is spotless
I' th' eyes of heaven. *Shakespeare's Winter's Tale.*

36. To

36. *To* LAY *down*. To quit; to resign.
The soldier being once brought in for the service, I will not have him to *lay down* his arms any more. *Spens. Ireland.*
Ambitious conquerors, in their mad career,
Check'd by thy voice, *lay down* the sword and spear.
Blackmore's Creation, *b.* ii.
The story of the tragedy is purely fiction; for I take it up where the history has *laid* it down. *Dryden's Don Sebastian.*
37. *To* LAY *down*. To commit to repose.
I will *lay* me *down* in peace and sleep. *Psal.* xlviii.
And they *lay* themselves *down* upon cloaths laid to pledge, by every altar. *Amos* ii. 8.
We *lay* us *down*, to sleep away our cares; night shuts up the senses. *Glanville's Scep.*
Some god conduct me to the sacred shades,
Or lift me high to Hæmus' hilly crown,
Or in the plains of Tempe *lay* me *down*. *Dryden's Virg.*
38. *To* LAY *down*. To advance as a proposition.
I have *laid down*, in some measure, the description of the old known world. *Abbot's Descrip. of the World.*
Kircher *lays* it *down* as a certain principle, that there never was any people so rude, which did not acknowledge and worship one supreme deity. *Stillingfleet on Rom. Idolatry.*
I must *lay down* this for your encouragement, that we are no longer now under the heavy yoke of a perfect unsinning obedience. *Wake's Preparation for Death.*
Plato *lays* it *down* as a principle, that whatever is permitted to befal a just man, whether poverty or sickness, shall, either in life or death, conduce to his good. *Addison's Spect.*
From the maxims *laid down* many may conclude, that I had a mind the world should think there had been occasion given by some late abuses among men of that calling. *Swift.*
39. *To* LAY *for*. To attempt by ambush, or insidious practices.
He embarked himself at Marseilles, after a long and dangerous journey, being not without the knowledge of Solyman hardly *laid for* at sea by Cortug-ogli, a famous pirate. *Knolles.*
40. *To* LAY *forth*. To diffuse; to expatiate.
O bird! the delight of gods and of men! and so he *lays* himself *forth* upon the gracefulness of the raven. *L'Estrange.*
41. *To* LAY *forth*. To place when dead in a decent posture.
Embalm me,
Then *lay* me *forth*; although unqueen'd, yet like
A queen, and daughter to a king, interr me. *Shakespeare.*
42. *To* LAY *hold of*. To seize; to catch.
Then shall his father and his mother *lay hold on* him, and bring him out. *Deut.* xxi. 19.
Favourable seasons of aptitude and inclination, be heedfully *laid hold of*. *Locke.*
43. *To* LAY *in*. To store; to treasure.
Let the main part of the ground employed to gardens or corn be to a common stock; and *laid in*, and stored up, and then delivered out in proportion. *Bacon's Essays.*
An equal stock of wit and valour
He had *laid in*, by birth a taylor. *Hudibras, p.* i.
They saw the happiness of a private life, but they thought they had not yet enough to make them happy, they would have more, and *laid in* to make their solitude luxurious. *Dryd.*
Readers, who are in the flower of their youth, should labour at those accomplishments which may set off their persons when their bloom is gone, and to *lay in* timely provisions for manhood and old age. *Addison's Guardian.*
44. *To lay on*. To apply with violence.
We make no excuses for the obstinate: blows are the proper remedies; but blows *laid on* in a way different from the ordinary. *Locke on Education.*
45. *To* LAY *open*. To shew; to expose.
Teach me, dear creature, how to think and speak,
Lay open to my earthy gross conceit,
Smother'd in errours, feeble, shallow, weak,
The folded meaning of your word's deceit. *Shakespeare.*
A fool *layeth open* his folly. *Prov.* xiii. 16.
46. *To* LAY *over*. To incrust; to cover; to decorate superficially.
Wo unto him that saith to the wood, awake; to the dumb stone, arise, it shall teach: behold, it is *laid over* with gold and silver, and there is no breath at all in the midst of it.
Hab. ii. 19.
47. *To* LAY *out*. To expend.
Fathers are wont to lay up for their sons,
Thou for thy son art bent to *lay out* all. *Milton.*
Tycho Brahe *laid out*, besides his time and industry, much greater sums of money on instruments than any man we ever heard of. *Boyle.*
The blood and treasure that's *laid out*,
Is thrown away, and goes for nought. *Hudibras.*
If you can get a good tutor, you will never repent the charge; but will always have the satisfaction to think it the money, of all other, the best *laid out*. *Locke.*
I, in this venture, double gains pursue,
And *laid out* all my stock to purchase you. *Dryden.*
My father never at a time like this
Would *lay out* his great soul in words, and waste
Such precious moments. *Addison's Cato.*
A melancholy thing to see the disorders of a houshold that is under the conduct of an angry stateswoman, who *lays out* all her thoughts upon the publick, and is only attentive to find out miscarriages in the ministry. *Addison's Freeholder.*
When a man spends his whole life among the stars and planets, or *lays out* a twelve-month on the spots in the sun, however noble his speculations may be, they are very apt to fall into burlesque. *Addison on ancient Medals.*
Nature has *laid out* all her art in beautifying the face; she has touched it with vermilion, planted in it a double row of ivory, and made it the seat of smiles and blushes. *Addison.*
48. *To* LAY *out*. To display; to discover.
He was dangerous, and takes occasion to *lay out* bigotry, and false confidence, in all its colours. *Atterbury.*
49. *To* LAY *out*. To dispose; to plan.
The garden is *laid out* into a grove for fruits, a vineyard, and an allotment for olives and herbs. *Notes on the Odyssey.*
50. *To* LAY *out*. With the reciprocal pronoun, to exert; to put forth.
No selfish man will be concerned to *lay out* himself for the good of his country. *Smalridge.*
51. *To* LAY *to*. To charge upon.
When we began, in courteous manner, *to lay* his unkindness unto him, he, seeing himself confronted by so many, like a resolute orator, went not to denial, but to justify his cruel falshood. *Sidney.*
52. *To* LAY *to*. To apply with vigour.
We should now *lay to* our hands to root them up, and cannot tell for what. *Oxford Reasons against the Covenant.*
Let children be hired to *lay to* their bones,
From fallow as needeth, to gather up stones. *Tusser.*
53. *To* LAY *to*. To harrass; to attack.
The great master having a careful eye over every part of the city, went himself unto the English station, which was then hardly *laid to* by the Bassa Mustapha. *Knolles.*
Whilst he this, and that, and each man's blow
Doth eye, defend, and shift, being *laid to* sore;
Backwards he bears. *Daniel's Civil War.*
54. *To* LAY *together*. To collect; to bring into one view.
If we *lay* all these things *together*, and consider the parts, rise, and degrees of his sin, we shall find that it was not for nothing. *South's Sermons.*
Many people apprehend danger for want of taking the true measure of things, and *laying* matters rightly *together*. *L'Estr.*
My readers will be very well pleased, to see so many useful hints upon this subject *laid together* in so clear and concise a manner. *Addison's Guardian*, N°. 96.
One series of consequences will not serve the turn, but many different and opposite deductions must be examined, and *laid together*, before a man can come to make a right judgment of the point in question. *Locke.*
55. *To* LAY *under*. To subject to.
A Roman soul is bent on higher views,
To civilize the rude unpolish'd world,
And *lay* it *under* the restraint of laws. *Addison's Cato.*
56. *To* LAY *up*. To confine.
In the East-Indies, the general remedy of all subject to the gout, is rubbing with hands till the motion raise a violent heat about the joints: where it was chiefly used, no one was ever troubled much, or *laid up* by that disease. *Temple.*
57. *To* LAY *up*. To store; to treasure.
St. Paul did will them of the church of Corinth, every man to *lay up* somewhat by him upon the Sunday, and to reserve it in store, till himself did come thither, to send it to the church of Jerusalem for relief of the poor there.
Hooker, *b.* iv. *sect.* 13.
Those things which at the first are obscure and hard, when memory hath *laid* them up for a time, judgment afterwards growing explaineth them. *Hooker*, *b.* v. *sect.* 22.
That which remaineth over, *lay up* to be kept until the morning. *Exod.* xvi. 23.
The king must preserve the revenues of his crown without diminution, and *lay up* treasure in store against a time of extremity. *Bacon's Advice to Villiers.*
Fathers are wont to *lay up* for their sons,
Thou for thy son art bent to lay out all. *Milton.*
The whole was tilled, and the harvest *laid up* in several granaries. *Temple.*
I will *lay up* your words for you till time shall serve. *Dryd.*
This faculty of *laying up*, and retaining ideas, several other animals have to a great degree, as well as man. *Locke.*
What right, what true, what fit, we justly call,
Let this be all my care; for this is all:
To *lay* this harvest *up*, and hoard with haste
What every day will want, and most, the last. *Pope.*
58. *To* LAY *upon*. To importune; to request with earnestness and incessantly. Obsolete.
All the people *laid* so earnestly *upon* him to take that war in

in hand, that they ſaid they would never bear arms more againſt the Turks, if he omitted that occaſion. *Knolles.*

To Lay. *v. n.*

1. To bring eggs.

Hens will greedily eat the herb which will make them *lay* the better. *Mortimer's Huſbandry.*

2. To contrive.

Which mov'd the king,
By all the apteſt means could be procur'd,
To *lay* to draw him in by any train. *Daniel's Civil War.*

3. *To* Lay *about.* To ſtrike on all ſides; to act with great diligence and vigour.

At once he wards and ſtrikes, he takes and pays,
Now forc'd to yield, now forcing to invade,
Before, behind, and round *about* him *lays. Fa. Queen.*
And *laid about* in fight more buſily,
Than th' Amazonian dame Pentheſile. *Hudibras.*

In the late ſucceſsful rebellion, how ſtudiouſly did they *lay about* them, to caſt a ſlur upon the king. *South's Sermons.*

He provides elbow-room enough for his conſcience to *lay about*, and have its full play in. *South's Sermons.*

4. *To* Lay *at.* To ſtrike; to endeavour to ſtrike.

Fiercely the good man did *at* him *lay*,
The blade oft groaned under the blow. *Spenſer's Paſtoral.*
The ſword of him that *layeth at* him cannot hold. *Job.*

5. *To* Lay *in for.* To make overtures of oblique invitation.

I have *laid in* for theſe, by rebating the ſatire, where juſtice would allow it, from carrying too ſharp an edge. *Dryd.*

6. *To* Lay *on.* To ſtrike; to beat.

His heart *laid on* as if it try'd,
To force a paſſage through his ſide. *Hudibras.*
Anſwer, or anſwer not, 'tis all the ſame,
He *lays* me *on*, and makes me bear the blame. *Dryden.*

7. *To* Lay *on.* To act with vehemence.

My father has made her miſtreſs
Of the feaſt, and ſhe *lays* it *on. Shakeſ. Winter's Tale.*

8. *To* Lay *out.* To take meaſures.

Thoſe ants knew ſome days after they had nothing to fear, and began to *lay* out their corn in the ſun. *Addiſ. Guard.*

I made ſtrict enquiry wherever I came, and *laid out* for intelligence of all places, where the intrails of the earth were laid open. *Woodward.*

Lay. *n. ſ.* [from the verb.]

1. A row; a ſtratum.

A viol ſhould have a *lay* of wire-ſtrings below, as cloſe to the belly as the lute, and then the ſtrings of guts mounted upon a bridge as in ordinary viols, that the upper ſtrings ſtrucken might make the lower reſound. *Bacon.*

Upon this they lay a layer of ſtone, and upon that a *lay* of wood. *Mortimer's Huſbandry.*

2. A wager.

It is eſteemed an even *lay*, whether any man lives ten years longer: I ſuppoſe it is the ſame, that one of any ten might die within one year. *Graunt's Bills of Mortality.*

Lay. *n. ſ.* [ley, leag, Saxon; *ley*, Scottiſh.] Graſſy ground; meadow; ground unplowed, and kept for cattle: more frequently, and more properly, written *lea.*

A tuft of daiſies on a flow'ry *lay*
They ſaw. *Dryden's Flower and Leaf.*

The plowing of *layes* is the firſt plowing up of graſs ground for corn. *Mortimer's Huſbandry.*

Lay. *n. ſ.* [*lay*, French. It is ſaid originally to ſignify *ſorrow* or *complaint*, and then to have been transferred to poems written to expreſs ſorrow. It is derived by the French from *leſſus*, Latin, a funeral ſong; but it is found likewiſe in the Teutonick dialect: ley, leoð, Saxon; *leey*, Daniſh.] A ſong; a poem.

To the maiden's ſounding timbrels ſung,
In well attuned notes, a joyous *lay. Spenſ. Fairy Queen.*
Soon he ſlumber'd, fearing not be harm'd,
The whiles with a loud *lay*, ſhe thus him ſweetly charm'd.
Spenſer's Fairy Queen, b. ii.

This is a moſt majeſtick viſion, and
Harmonious charming *lays. Shakeſpeare's Tempeſt.*

Nor then the ſolemn nightingale
Ceas'd warbling, but all night tun'd her ſoft *lays. Milton.*

If Jove's will
Have link'd that amorous power to thy ſoft *lay*,
Now timely ſing. *Milton.*

He reach'd the nymph with his harmonious *lay*,
Whom all his charms could not incline to ſtay. *Waller.*

On Ceres let him call, and Ceres praiſe,
With uncouth dances, and with country *lays. Dryd. Virg.*

Ev'n gods incline their raviſh'd ears,
And tune their own harmonious ſpheres
To his immortal *lays. Dennis.*

Lay. *adj.* [*laicus*, Latin; λαὸς.] Not clerical; regarding or belonging to the people as diſtinct from the clergy.

All this they had by law, and none repin'd,
The pref'rence was but due to Levi's kind:
But when ſome *lay* preferment fell by chance,
The Gourmands made it their inheritance. *Dryden.*

Lay perſons, married or unmarried, being doctors of the civil law, may be chancellors, officials, &c. *Ayliffe's Parerg.*

It might well ſtartle
Our *lay* unlearned faith. *Rowe's Ambitious Step Mother.*

La'yer. *n. ſ.* [from *lay.*]

1. A ſtratum, or row; a bed; one body ſpread over another.

A *layer* of rich mould beneath, and about this natural earth to nouriſh the fibres. *Evelyn's Kalendar.*

The terreſtrial matter is diſpoſed into ſtrata or *layers*, placed one upon another, in like manner as any earthy ſediment, ſettling down from a flood in great quantity, will naturally be. *Woodward's Natural Hiſtory.*

2. A ſprig of a plant.

Many trees may be propagated by *layers:* this is to be performed by ſlitting the branches a little way, and laying them under the mould about half a foot; the ground ſhould be firſt made very light, and, after they are laid, they ſhould have a little water given them: if they do not comply well in the laying of them down, they muſt be pegged down with a hook or two; and if they have taken ſufficient root by the next winter, they muſt be cut off from the main plants, and planted in the nurſery: ſome twiſt the branch, or bare the rind; and if it be out of the reach of the ground, they faſten a tub or baſket near the branch, which they fill with good mould, and lay the branch in it. *Miller.*

Tranſplant alſo carnation ſeedlings, give your *layers* freſh earth, and ſet them in the ſhade for a week. *Evelyn's Kal.*

3. A hen that lays eggs.

The oldeſt are always reckoned the beſt ſitters, and the youngeſt the beſt *layers. Mortimer's Huſbandry.*

La'yman. *n. ſ.* [*lay* and *man.*]

1. One of the people diſtinct from the clergy.

Laymen will neither admoniſh one another themſelves, nor ſuffer miniſters to do it. *Government of the Tongue.*

Since a truſt muſt be, ſhe thought it beſt
To put it out of *laymens* pow'r at leaſt,
And for their ſolemn vows prepar'd a prieſt. *Dryden.*

Where can be the grievance, that an eccleſiaſtical landlord ſhould expect a third part value for his lands, his title as antient, and as legal, as that of a *layman*, who is ſeldom guilty of giving ſuch beneficial bargains. *Swift.*

2. An image.

You are to have a *layman* almoſt as big as the life for every figure in particular, beſides the natural figure before you. *Dryden's Dufreſnoy.*

La'ystall. *n. ſ.* An heap of dung.

Scarce could he footing find in that foul way,
For many corſes, like a great *lay-ſtall*
Of murdered men, which therein ſtrewed lay. *Fa. Qu.*

La'zar. *n. ſ.* [from *Lazarus* in the goſpel.] One deformed and nauſeous with filthy and peſtilential diſeaſes.

They ever after in moſt wretched caſe,
Like loathſome *lazars*, by the hedges lay. *Fairy Queen.*

I'll be ſworn and ſworn upon't, ſhe never ſhrowded any but *lazars. Shakeſpeare's Troil. and Creſſida.*

I am weary with drawing the deformities of life, and *lazars* of the people, where every figure of imperfection more reſembles me. *Dryden's Aurengzebe.*

Life he labours to refine
Daily, nor of his little ſtock denies
Fit alms, to *lazars*, merciful, and meek. *Philips.*

Lazar-house. } *n. ſ.* [*lazaret*, French; *lazzeretto*, Italian;
Lazare'tto. } from *lazar.*] A houſe for the reception of the diſeaſed; an hoſpital.

A place
Before his eyes appear'd, ſad, noiſome, dark,
A *lazar-houſe* it ſeem'd, where were laid
Numbers of all diſeas'd. *Milton's Paradiſe Loſt, b.* xi.

La'zarwort. *n. ſ.* A plant.

La'zily. *adv.* [from *lazy.*] Idly; ſluggiſhly; heavily.

Watch him at play, when following his own inclinations; and ſee whether he be ſtirring and active, or whether he *lazily* and liſtleſly dreams away his time. *Locke.*

The eaſtern nations view the riſing fires,
Whilſt night ſhades us, and *lazily* retires. *Creech.*

La'ziness. *n. ſ.* [from *lazy.*] Idleneſs; ſluggiſhneſs; heavineſs to action.

That inſtance of fraud and *lazineſs*, the unjuſt ſteward, who pleaded that he could neither dig nor beg, would quickly have been brought both to dig and to beg too, rather than ſtarve. *South's Sermons.*

My fortune you have reſcued, not only from the power of others, but from my own modeſty and *lazineſs. Dryden.*

La'zing. *adj.* [from *lazy.*] Sluggiſh; idle.

The hands and the feet mutinied againſt the belly: they knew no reaſon, why the one ſhould be *lazing*, and pampering itſelf with the fruit of the other's labour. *L'Eſtrange.*

The ſot cried, *Utinam hoc eſſet laborare*, while he lay *lazing* and lolling upon his couch. *South's Sermons.*

La'zuli. *n. ſ.*

The ground of this ſtone is blue, veined and ſpotted with white,

white, and a gliſtering or metallick yellow: it appears to be compoſed of, firſt, a white ſparry, or cryſtalline matter; ſecondly, flakes of the golden or yellow talc; thirdly, a ſhining yellow ſubſtance; this fumes off in the calcination of the ſtone, and caſts a ſulphureous ſmell; fourthly, a bright blue ſubſtance, of great uſe among the painters, under the name of ultramarine; and when rich, is found, upon trial, to yield about one-ſixth of copper, with a very little ſilver. *Woodward's Metallick Foſſils.*

LA'ZY. *adj.* [This word is derived by a correſpondent, with great probability, from *a l'aiſe*, French; but it is however Teutonick: *liſer* in Daniſh, and *loſigh* in Dutch, have the ſame meaning; and *Spelman* gives this account of the word: Dividebantur antiqui Saxones, ut teſtatur Nithardus, in tres ordines; Edhilingos, Frilingos & Lazzos; hoc eſt nobiles, ingenuos & ſerviles: quam & nos diſtinctionem diu retinuimus. Sed Ricardo autem ſecundo pars ſervorum maxima ſe in libertatem vindicavit; ſic ut hodie apud Anglos rarior inveniatur ſervus, qui mancipium dicitur. Reſtat nihilominus antiquæ appellationis commemoratio. Ignavos enim hodie *lazie* dicimus.]

1. Idle; ſluggiſh; unwilling to work.

Our ſoldiers, like the night-owl's *lazy* flight,
Or like a *lazy* thraſher with a flail,
Fall gently down, as if they ſtruck their friends. *Shakeſp.*

Wicked condemned men will ever live like rogues, and not fall to work, but be *lazy*, and ſpend victuals. *Bacon.*

Whoſe *lazy* waters without motion lay. *Roſcommon.*

The *lazy* glutton ſafe at home will keep,
Indulge his ſloth, and batten with his ſleep. *Dryden.*

Like Eaſtern kings a *lazy* ſtate they keep,
And cloſe confin'd in their own palace ſleep. *Pope.*

What amazing ſtupidity is it, for men to be negligent of ſalvation themſelves? to ſit down *lazy* and unactive. *Rogers.*

2. Slow; tedious.

The ordinary method for recruiting their armies, was now too dull and *lazy* an expedient to reſiſt this torrent. *Clarendon.*

LD. is a contraction of *lord.*

LEA. *n. ſ.* [ley, Saxon, a fallow; leaȝ, Saxon, a paſture.] Ground incloſed, not open.

Greatly agaſt with this pittious plea;
Him reſted the good man on the *lea.* *Spenſ. Paſtorals.*

Ceres, moſt bounteous lady, thy rich *leas*
Of wheat, rye, barley, fetches, oats and peas. *Shakeſ.*

Her fallow *leas*
The darnel, hemlock, and rank fumitory
Doth root upon. *Shakeſpeare's Henry V.*

Dry up thy harrow'd veins, and plough-torn *leas*,
Whereof ingrateful man with liqu'riſh draughts,
And morſels unctuous, greaſes his pure mind. *Shakeſp.*

Such court guiſe,
As Mercury did firſt deviſe,
With the mincing Dryades,
On the lawns, and on the *leas.* *Milton.*

LEAD. *n. ſ.* [læð, Saxon.]

1. *Lead* is the heavieſt metal except gold; for, though it is conſiderably lighter than quickſilver, as this wants malleability, it ought not to be reckoned in the claſs of metals. *Lead* is the ſofteſt of all the metals, and very ductile, though leſs ſo than gold: it is very little ſubject to ruſt, and the leaſt ſonorous of all the metals except gold. The ſpecifick gravity of *lead* is to that of water as 11322 to 1000. *Lead*, when kept in fuſion over a common fire, throws up all other bodies, except gold, that are mixed, all others being lighter, except Mercury, which will not bear that degree of heat: it afterwards vitrifies with the baſer metals, and carries them off, in form of ſcoriæ, to the ſides of the veſſel. The weakeſt acids are the beſt ſolvents for *lead*: it diſſolves very readily in aqua fortis diluted with water, as alſo in vinegar. Gold, or ſilver, or copper, become brittle on being mixed with *lead* in fuſion; and, if *lead* and tin be melted together, the tin is thrown up to the ſurface in little duſty globes. *Lead* is found in various countries, but abounds particularly in England, in ſeveral kinds of ſoils and ſtones. The ſmoke of the *lead* works at Mendip in Somerſetſhire is a prodigious annoyance, and ſubjects both the workmen, and the cattle that graze about them, to a mortal diſeaſe; trees that grow near them have their tops burnt, and their leaves and outſides diſcoloured and ſcorched. *Hill.*

Thou art a ſoul in bliſs, but I am bound
Upon a wheel of fire; that mine own tears
Do ſcald like molten *lead.* *Shakeſpeare's King Lear.*

Of *lead*, ſome I can ſhew you ſo like ſteel, and ſo unlike common *lead* ore, that the workmen call it ſteel ore. *Boyle.*

Lead is employed for the refining of gold and ſilver by the cupel; hereof is made common ceruſs with vinegar; of ceruſs, red *lead*; of plumbum uſtum, the beſt yellow ochre; of *lead*, and half as much tin, ſolder for *lead.* *Grew.*

2. [In the plural.] Flat roof to walk on.

Stalls, bulks, windows,
Are ſmother'd up, *leads* fill'd, and ridges hors'd
With variable complexions; all agreeing
In earneſtneſs to ſee him. *Shakeſpeare's Coriolanus.*

I would have the tower two ſtories, and goodly *leads* upon the top, raiſed with ſtatues interpoſed. *Bacon.*

To LEAD. *v. a.* [from the noun.] To fit with lead in any manner.

He faſhioneth the clay with his arm, he applieth himſelf to *lead* it over; and he is diligent to make clean the furnace. *Eccluſ.* xxxviii. 30.

There is a traverſe placed in a loft, at the right hand of the chair, with a privy door, and a carved window of glaſs *leaded* with gold and blue, where the mother ſitteth. *Bacon.*

To LEAD. *v. a.* preter. *I led.* [læðan, Saxon; *leiden*, Dutch.]

1. To guide by the hand.

There is a cliff, whoſe high and bending head
Looks fearfully on the confined deep:
Bring me but to the very brim of it,
And I'll repair the miſery, thou doſt bear,
With ſomething rich about me: from that place
I ſhall no *leading* need. *Shakeſp. King Lear.*

Doth not each on the ſabbath looſe his ox or his aſs from the ſtall, and *lead* him away to watering? *Luke* xiii. 15.

They thruſt him out of the city, and *led* him unto the brow of the hill. *Luke* iv. 29.

2. To conduct to any place.

Save to every man his wife and children, that they may *lead* them away, and depart. 1 *Sam.* xxx. 22.

Then brought he me out of the way, and *led* me about the way without unto the utter gate. *Ezek.* xlvii. 2.

He maketh me to lie down in green paſtures; he *leadeth* me beſide the ſtill waters. *Pſal.* xxiii. 2.

3. To conduct as head or commander.

Would you *lead* forth your army againſt the enemy, and ſeek him where he is to fight? *Spenſer on Ireland.*

He turns head againſt the lion's armed jaws;
And being no more in debt to years than thou,
Leads antient lords, and rev'rend biſhops, on
To bloody battles. *Shakeſpeare's Henry* IV. *p.* i.

I wonder much,
Being men of ſuch great *leading* as you are,
That you foreſee not what impediments
Drag back our expedition. *Shakeſp. Henry* IV. *p.* i.

If thou wilt have
The *leading* of thy own revenges, take
One half of my commiſſion, and ſet down
As beſt thou art experienc'd. *Shakeſpeare's Coriolanus.*

He *led* me on to mightieſt deeds,
Above the nerve of mortal arm,
Againſt the uncircumcis'd, our enemies:
But now hath caſt me off. *Milton's Agoniſtes.*

Chriſt took not upon him fleſh and blood, that he might conquer and rule nations, *lead* armies, or poſſeſs places. *South.*

He might muſter his family up, and *lead* them out againſt the Indians, to ſeek reparation upon any injury. *Locke.*

4. To introduce by going firſt.

Which may go out before them, and which may go in before them, and which may *lead* them out, and which may bring them in. *Numb.* xxvii. 17.

His guide, as faithful from that day,
As Heſperus that *leads* the ſun his way. *Fairfax, b.* i.

5. To guide; to ſhow the method of attaining.

Human teſtimony is not ſo proper to *lead* us into the knowledge of the eſſence of things, as to acquaint us with the exiſtence of things. *Watts's Logick.*

6. To draw; to entice; to allure.

Appoint him a meeting, give him a ſhew of comfort, and *lead* him on with a fine baited delay. *Shakeſpeare.*

The lord Cottington, being a maſter of temper, knew how to *lead* him into a miſtake, and then drive him into choler, and then expoſe him. *Clarendon.*

7. To induce; to prevail on by pleaſing motives.

What I did, I did in honour,
Led by th' impartial conduct of my ſoul. *Shakeſ. Hen.* IV.

He was driven by the neceſſities of the times, more than *led* by his own diſpoſition, to any rigour of actions. *K. Charles.*

What I ſay will have little influence on thoſe whoſe ends *lead* them to wiſh the continuance of the war. *Swift.*

8. To paſs; to ſpend in any certain manner.

The ſweet woman *leads* an ill life with him. *Shakeſp.*

So ſhalt thou *lead*
Safeſt thy life, and beſt prepar'd endure
Thy mortal paſſage when it comes. *Milton's Par. Loſt.*

Him, fair Lavinia, thy ſurviving wife
Shall breed in groves, to *lead* a ſolitary life. *Dryden.*

Luther's life was *led* up to the doctrines he preached, and his death was the death of the righteous. *Fr. Atterbury.*

Celibacy, as then practiſed in the church of Rome, was commonly forced, taken up under a bold vow, and *led* in all uncleanneſs. *Francis Atterbury.*

This diſtemper is moſt incident to ſuch as *lead* a ſedentary life. *Arbuthnot on Aliments.*

To LEAD. *v. n.*

1. To go firſt, and ſhow the way.

I will *lead* on ſoftly, according as the cattle that goeth before me, and the children be able to endure. *Gen.* xxxiii.

2. To

2. To conduct as a commander.

Cyrus was beaten and slain under the *leading* of a woman, whose wit and conduct made a great figure in antient story. *Temple.*

3. To shew the way, by going first.

He left his mother a countess by patent, which was a new *leading* example, grown before somewhat rare, since the days of queen Mary. *Wotton.*

The way of maturing of tobacco must be from the heat of the earth or sun; we see some *leading* of this in muskmelons sown upon a hot-bed dunged below. *Bacon.*

The vessels heavy-laden put to sea
With prosp'rous gales, and woman *leads* the way. *Dryden.*

LEAD. *n. s.* [from the verb.] Guidance; first place: a low despicable word.

Yorkshire takes the *lead* of the other countries. *Herring.*

LEADEN. *adj.* [leaden, Saxon.]

1. Made of lead.

This tiger-footed rage, when it shall find
The harm of unskann'd swiftness, will, too late,
Tye *leaden* pounds to 's heels. *Shakespeare's Coriolanus.*

O murth'rous slumber!
Lay'st thou the *leaden* mace upon my boy,
That plays thee musick. *Shakes. Julius Cæsar.*

A *leaden* bullet shot from one of these guns against a stone wall, the space of twenty-four paces from it, will be beaten into a thin plate. *Wilkins's Mathematical Magick.*

2. Heavy; unwilling; motionless.

If thou do'st find him tractable to us,
Encourage him, and tell him all our reasons:
If he be *leaden*, icy, cold, unwilling,
Be thou so too. *Shakespeare's Rich.* III.

3. Heavy; dull.

I'll strive with troubled thoughts to take a nap;
Lest *leaden* slumber poize me down to-morrow,
When I should mount with wings of victory. *Shakesp.*

LEADER. *n. s.* [from *lead.*]

1. One that leads, or conducts.

2. Captain; commander.

In my tent
I'll draw the form and model of our battle,
Limit each *leader* to his several charge,
And part in just proportion our small strength. *Shakesp.*

I have given him for a *leader* and commander to the people. *Isa.* lv. 4.

Those who escaped by flight excused their dishonour, not without a sharp jest against some of their *leaders*, affirming, that, as they had followed them into the field, so it was good reason they should follow them out. *Hayward.*

When our Lycians see
Our brave examples, they admiring say,
Behold our gallant *leaders*. *Denham.*

The brave *leader* of the Lycian crew. *Dryden.*

3. One who goes first.

Nay keep your way, little gallant; you were wont to be a follower now you are a *leader*. *Shakespeare.*

4. One at the head of any party or faction: as the detestable Wharton was the *leader* of the whigs.

The understandings of a senate are enslaved by three or four *leaders*, set to get or to keep employments. *Swift.*

LE'ADING. *participial adj.* Principal.

In organized bodies, which are propagated by seed, the shape is the *leading* quality, and most characteristical part, that determines the species. *Locke.*

Mistakes arise from the influence of private persons upon great numbers stiled *leading* men and parties. *Swift.*

LEADING-STRINGS. *n. s.* [*lead* and *string.*] Strings by which children, when they learn to walk, are held from falling.

Sound may serve such, ere they to sense are grown,
Like *leading-strings*, 'till they can walk alone. *Dryden.*

Was he ever able to walk without *leading-strings*, or swim without bladders, without being discovered by his hobbling and his sinking? *Swift.*

LE'ADMAN. *n. s.* [*lead* and *man.*] One who begins or leads a dance.

Such a light and mettl'd dance
Saw you never,
And by *leadmen* for the nonce,
That turn round like grindle stones. *Benj. Johnson.*

LE'ADWORT. *n. s.* [*lead* and *wort.*]

This flower consists of one leaf, which is shaped like a funnel, and cut into several segments at the top, out of whose fistulous flower-cup rises the pointal, which afterward becomes one oblong seed, for the most part sharp-pointed, which ripens in the flower-cup. *Miller.*

LEAF. *n. s. leaves*, plural. [leap, Saxon; *leaf*, Dutch.]

1. The green deciduous parts of plants and flowers.

This is the state of man; to-day he puts forth
The tender *leaves* of hopes, to-morrow blossoms. *Shakes.*

A man shall seldom fail of having cherries borne by his graft the same year in which his incision is made, if his graft have blossom buds; whereas if it were only *leaf* buds, it will not bear fruit till the second season. *Boyle.*

Those things which are removed to a distant view, ought to make but one mass; as the *leaves* on the trees, and the billows in the sea. *Dryden's Dufresnoy.*

2. A part of a book, containing two pages.

Happy ye *leaves*, when as those lilly hands
Shall handle you. *Spenser.*

Peruse my *leaves* through ev'ry part,
And think thou seest my owner's heart
Scrawl'd o'er with trifles. *Swift.*

3. One side of a double door.

The two *leaves* of the one door were folding. 1 *Kings.*

4. Any thing foliated, or thinly beaten.

Eleven ounces two pence sterling ought to be of so pure silver, as is called *leaf* silver, and then the melter must add of other weight seventeen pence halfpenny farthing. *Camden.*

Leaf gold, that flies in the air as light as down, is as truly gold as that in an ingot. *Digby on Bodies.*

To LEAF. *v. n.* [from the noun.] To bring leaves; to bear leaves.

Most trees sprout, and fall off the *leaves* at autumn; and if not kept back by cold, would *leaf* about the solstice. *Brown's Vulgar Errours, b.* ii.

LEAFLESS. *adj.* [from *leaf.*] Naked of leaves.

Bare honesty without some other adornment, being looked on as a *leafless* tree, nobody will take himself to its shelter. *Government of the Tongue.*

Where doves in flocks the *leafless* trees o'er shade,
And lonely woodcocks haunt the wat'ry glade. *Pope.*

LE'AFY. *adj.* [from *leaf.*] Full of leaves.

The frauds of men were ever so,
Since summer was first *leafy*. *Shakespeare.*

What chance, good lady, hath bereft you thus?
—Dim darkness, and this *leafy* labyrinth. *Milton.*

O'er barren mountains, o'er the flow'ry plain,
The *leafy* forest, and the liquid main,
Extends thy uncontroul'd and boundless reign. *Dryd.*

Her *leafy* arms with such extent were spread,
That hosts of birds, that wing the liquid air,
Perch'd in the boughs. *Dryden's Flower and Leaf.*

So when some swelt'ring travellers retire
To *leafy* shades, near the cool sunless verge
Of Paraba, Brasilian stream; her tail
A grisly hydra suddenly shoots forth. *Philips.*

LEAGUE. *n. s.* [*ligue*, French; *ligo*, Latin.]

1. A confederacy; a combination.

You peers, continue this united *league*:
I every day expect an embassage
From my Redeemer, to redeem me hence.
And now in peace my soul shall part to heav'n,
Since I have made my friends at peace on earth. *Shakesp.*

We come to be informed by yourselves,
What the conditions of that *league* must be. *Shakesp.*

Thou shalt be in *league* with the stones of the field; and the beasts of the field shall be at peace with thee. *Job* v. 23.

Go break thy *league* with Baasha, that he may depart from me. 2 *Chron.* xvi. 3.

It is a great error, and a narrowness of mind, to think, that nations have nothing to do one with another, except there be either an union in sovereignty, or a conjunction in pacts or *leagues*: there are other bands of society and implicit confederations. *Bacon's Holy War.*

I, a private person, whom my country
As a *league* breaker gave up bound, presum'd
Single rebellion, and did hostile acts. *Milton's Agonistes.*

Oh Tyrians, with immortal hate
Pursue this race: let there be
'Twixt us and them no *league* nor amity. *Denham.*

To LEAGUE. *v. n.* To unite; to confederate.

Where fraud and falshood invade society, the band presently breaks, and men are put to a loss where to *league* and to fasten their dependances. *South's Sermons.*

LEAGUE. *n. s.* [*lieuë*, French.]

1. A league; *leuca*, Latin; from *lech*, Welsh; a stone that was used to be erected at the end of every league. *Camden.*

2. A measure of length, containing three miles.

Ere the ships could meet by twice five *leagues*,
We were encount'red by a mighty rock. *Shakespeare.*

Ev'n Italy, though many a *league* remote,
In distant echo's answer'd. *Addison.*

LE'AGUED. *adj.* [from *league.*] Confederated.

And now thus *leagu'd* by an eternal bond,
What shall retard the Britons bold designs. *Philips.*

LE'AGUER. *n. s.* [*beleggeren*, Dutch.] Siege; investment of a town.

We will bind and hoodwink him so, that he shall suppose no other but that he is carried into the *leaguer* of the adversaries, when we bring him to our own tents. *Shakespeare.*

LEAK. *n. s.* [*leck*, *leke*, Dutch.] A breach or hole which lets in water.

There will be always evils, which no art of man can cure; breaches and *leaks* more than man's wit hath hands to stop. *Hooker.*

The

The water rushes in, as it doth usually in the *leak* of a ship. *Wilkins's Mathematical Magick.*

Whether she sprung a *leak* I cannot find,
Or whether she was over set with wind,
Or that some rock below her bottom rent,
But down at once with all her crew she went. *Dryden.*

To LEAK. *v. n.*

1. To let water in or out.

They will allow us ne'er a jordan, and then we *leak* in your chimney. *Shakespeare.*

The water, which will perhaps by degrees *leak* into several parts, may be emptied out again. *Wilkins's Math. Magick.*

His feet should be washed every day in cold water; and have his shoes so thin, that they might *leak*, and let in water. *Locke.*

2. To drop through a breach.

Golden stars hung o'er their heads,
And seemed so crowded, that they burst upon 'em,
And dart at once their baleful influence
In *leaking* fire. *Dryden's and Lee's Oedipus.*

LE'AKAGE. *n. s.* [from *leak.*] Allowance made for accidental loss in liquid measures.

LE'AKY. *adj.* [from *leak.*]

1. Battered or pierced, so as to let water in or out.

Thou'rt so *leaky*,
That we must leave thee to thy sinking; for
Thy dearest quit thee. *Shakesp. Antony and Cleopatra.*

If you have not enjoy'd what youth could give,
But life sunk through you like a *leaky* sieve,
Accuse yourself, you liv'd not while you might. *Dryden.*

2. Loquacious; not close.

Women are so *leaky*, that I have hardly met with one that could not hold her breath longer than she could keep a secret. *L'Estrange.*

To LEAN. *v. n.* preter. *leaned* or *leant.* [hlinan, Saxon; *lenen*, Dutch.]

1. To incline against; to rest against.

Lean thine aged back against mine arm,
And in that case I'll tell thee my disease. *Shakespeare.*

Security is expressed among the medals of Gordianus, by a lady *leaning* against a pillar, a scepter in her hand, before an altar. *Peacham on Drawing.*

The columns may be allowed somewhat above their ordinary length, because they *lean* unto so good supporters. *Wott.*

Upon his iv'ry sceptre first he *leant*,
Then shook his head, that shook the firmament. *Dryden.*

Oppress'd with anguish, panting and o'erspent,
His fainting limbs against an oak he *leant*. *Dryden's Æn.*

If he be angry, all our other dependencies will profit us nothing; every other support will fail under us when we come to *lean* upon it, and deceive us in the day when we want it most. *Rogers's Sermons.*

Then *leaning* o'er the rails he musing stood. *Gay.*

Mid the central depth of black'ning woods,
High rais'd in solemn theatre around
Leans the huge elephant. *Thomson's Summer.*

2. To propend; to tend towards.

They delight rather to *lean* to their old customs, though they be more unjust, and more inconvenient. *Spenser.*

Trust in the Lord with all thine heart; and *lean* not unto thine own understanding. *Prov.* iii. 5.

A desire *leaning* to either side, biasses the judgment strangely. *Watts's Improvement of the Mind.*

3. To be in a bending posture.

She *leans* me out at her mistress's chamber window, bids me a thousand times good night. *Shakespeare.*

Wearied with length of ways, and worn with toil,
She laid her down; and *leaning* on her knees,
Invok'd the cause of all her miseries. *Dryden.*

The gods came downward to behold the wars,
Sharp'ning their sights, and *leaning* from their stars. *Dryd.*

LEAN. *adj.* [hlæne, Saxon.]

1. Not fat; meagre; wanting flesh; bare-boned.

You tempt the fury of my three attendants,
Lean famine, quartering steel, and climbing fire. *Shakesp.*

Lean raw-bon'd rascals! who would e'er suppose,
They had such courage and audacity! *Shakespeare.*

Lean look'd prophets whisper fearful change. *Shakes.*

I would invent as bitter searching terms,
With full as many signs of deadly hate,
As *lean*-fac'd envy in her loathsome cave. *Shakespeare.*

Seven other kine came up out of the river, ill-favoured and *lean*-fleshed. *Gen.* xli. 3.

Let a physician beware how he purge after hard frosty weather, and in a *lean* body, without preparation. *Bacon.*

And fetch their precepts from the cynic tub,
Praising the *lean*, and sallow, abstinence. *Milton.*

Swear that Adrastus, and the *lean*-look'd prophet,
Are joint conspirators. *Dryd. and Lee's Oedipus.*

Lean people often suffer for want of fat, as fat people may by obstruction of the vessels. *Arbuthnot on Aliments.*

No laughing graces wanton in my eyes;
But hagger'd grief, *lean* looking sallow care,
Dwell on my brow. *Rowe's Jane Shore.*

2. Not unctuous; thin; hungry.

There are two chief kinds of terrestrial liquors, those that are fat and light, and those that are *lean* and more earthy, like common water. *Burnet's Theory of the Earth.*

3. Low; poor; in opposition to great or rich.

That which combin'd us was most great, and let not
A *leaner* action rend us. *Shakes. Ant. and Cleopatra.*

LEAN. *n. s.* That part of flesh which consists of the muscle without the fat.

With razors keen we cut our passage clean
Through rills of fat, and deluges of *lean*. *Farquhar.*

LE'ANLY. *adv.* [from *lean.*] Meagerly; without plumpness.

LE'ANNESS. *n. s.* [from *lean.*]

1. Extenuation of body; want of flesh; meagreness.

If thy *leanness* loves such food,
There are those, that, for thy sake,
Do enough. *Benj. Johnson's Forest.*

The symptoms of too great fluidity are excess of universal secretions, as of perspiration, sweat, urine, liquid dejectures, *leanness*, and weakness. *Arbuthnot on Aliments.*

2. Want of bulk.

The poor king Reignier, whose large style
Agrees not with the *leanness* of his purse. *Shakespeare.*

To LEAP. *v. n.* [hleapan, Saxon; *loup*, Scottish.]

1. To jump; to move upward or progressively without change of the feet.

If I could win a lady at leap-frog, or by vaulting into my saddle with my armour on, I should quickly *leap* into a wife. *Shakespeare's Henry* V.

A man *leapeth* better with weights in his hands than without; for that the weight, if it be proportionable, strengtheneth the sinews by contracting them. In *leaping* with weights the arms are first cast backwards and then forwards with so much the greater force; for the hands go backward before they take their rise. *Bacon's Nat. Hist.*

In a narrow pit
He saw a lion, and *leap'd* down to it. *Cowley's Davideis.*

Thrice from the ground she *leap'd*, was seen to wield
Her brandish'd lance. *Dryden's Æn.*

2. To rush with vehemence.

God changed the spirit of the king into mildness, who in a fear *leaped* from his throne, and took her in his arms, till she came to herself again. *Esth.* xv. 8.

After he went into the tent, and found her not, he *leaped* out to the people. *Judith* xiv. 17.

He ruin upon ruin heaps,
And on me, like a furious giant, *leaps*. *Sandys.*

Strait *leaping* from his horse he rais'd me up. *Rowe.*

3. To bound; to spring.

Rejoice ye in that day, and *leap* for joy. *Luke* vi. 23.

I am warm'd, my heart
Leaps at the trumpet's voice, and burns for glory. *Addison.*

4. To fly; to start.

He parted frowning from me, as if ruin
Leap'd from his eyes: so looks the chafed lion
Upon the daring huntsman that has gall'd him;
Then makes him nothing. *Shakes. Henry* VIII.

Out of his mouth go burning lamps, and sparks of fire *leap* out. *Job* xli. 19.

To LEAP. *v. a.*

1. To pass over, or into, by leaping.

Every man is not of a constitution to *leap* a gulf for the saving of his country. *L'Estrange.*

As one condemn'd to *leap* a precipice,
Who sees before his eyes the depth below,
Stops short. *Dryden's Spanish Friar.*

She dares pursue, if they dare *lead*:
As their example still prevails,
She tempts the stream, or *leaps* the pales. *Prior.*

2. To compress; as beasts.

Too soon they must not feel the sting of love:
Let him not *leap* the cow. *Dryden's Georg.*

LEAP. *n. s.* [from the verb.]

1. Bound; jump; act of leaping.

2. Space passed by leaping.

After they have carried their riders safe over all *leaps*, and through all dangers, what comes of them in the end but to be broken-winded. *L'Estrange.*

3. Sudden transition.

Wickedness comes on by degrees, as well as virtue; and sudden *leaps* from one extreme to another are unnatural. *L'Estrange's Fables.*

The commons wrested even the power of chusing a king intirely out of the hands of the nobles; which was so great a *leap*, and caused such a convulsion in the state, that the constitution could not bear. *Swift.*

4. An assault of an animal of prey.

The cat made a *leap* at the mouse. *L'Estrange.*

5. Embrace of animals.

How she cheats her bellowing lovers eye;
The rushing *leap*, the doubtful progeny. *Dryden's Æn.*

6. Hazard,

6. Hazard, or effect of leaping.

Methinks, it were an easy *leap*
To pluck bright honour from the pale-fac'd moon. *Shak.*
You take a precipice for no *leap* of danger,
And woo your own destruction. *Shakespeare's Henry* VIII.
Behold that dreadful downfal of a rock,
Where yon old fisher views the waves from high!
'Tis the convenient *leap* I mean to try. *Dryd. Theocritus.*

LEAP-FROG. *n. s.* [*leap* and *frog.*] A play of children, in which they imitate the jump of frogs.

If I could win a lady at *leap-frog*, I should quickly leap into a wife. *Shakespeare's Henry* V.

LEAP-YEAR. *n. s.*

Leap-year or bissextile is every fourth year, and so called from its *leaping* a day more that year than in a common year: so that the common year hath 365 days, but the *leap-year* 366; and then February hath 29 days, which in common years hath but 28. To find the *leap-year* you have this rule:

Divide by 4; what's left shall be
For *leap-year* 0; for past 1, 2, 3. *Harris.*

That the sun consisteth of 365 days and almost six hours, wanting eleven minutes; which six hours omitted will, in process of time, largely deprave the compute; and this is the occasion of the bissextile or *leap-year*. *Brown's Vulg. Err.*

To LEARN. *v. a.* [leoрnian, Saxon.]

1. To gain the knowledge or skill of.

Learn a parable of the fig-tree. *Mat.* xxiv. 32.

He, in a shorter time than was thought possible, *learned* both to speak and write the Arabian tongue. *Knolles.*

Learn, wretches! *learn* the motions of the mind,
And the great moral end of humankind. *Dryd. Persius.*
You may rely upon my tender care,
To keep him far from perils of ambition:
All he can *learn* of me, will be to weep! *A. Philips.*

2. To teach. [It is observable, that in many of the European languages the same word signifies to learn and to teach; to gain or impart knowledge.]

He would *learn*
The lion stoop to him in lowly-wise,
A lesson hard. *Spenser's Fairy Queen, b.* i.
You taught me language, and my profit on't
Is, I know not how to curse: the red plague rid you,
For *learning* me your language. *Shakesp. Tempest.*
A thousand more mischances than this one,
Have *learn'd* me how to brook this patiently. *Shakes.*
Hast thou not *learn'd* me how
To make perfumes? *Shakespeare's Cymbeline.*

Ye might *learn* in us not to think of men above that which is written. 1 *Cor.* iv. 6.

To LEARN. *v. n.* To take pattern.

Take my yoke upon you, and *learn* of me; for I am meek and lowly. *Mat.* xi. 29.

In imitation of sounds, that man should be the teacher is no part of the matter; for birds will *learn* one of another. *Bacon's Natural History*, N°. 237.

LEARNED. *adj.* [from *learn.*]

1. Versed in science and literature.

It is indifferent to the matter in hand, which way the *learned* shall determine of it. *Locke.*

Some by old words to fame have made pretence:
Such labour'd nothings, in so strange a style,
Amaze th' unlearn'd, and make the *learned* smile. *Pope.*
The *learned* met with free approach,
Although they came not in a coach. *Swift.*

The best account is given of them by their own authors: but I trust more to the table of the *learned* bishop of Bath. *Arbuthnot on Coins.*

2. Skilled; skilful; knowing.

Though train'd in arms, and *learn'd* in martial arts,
Thou chusest not to conquer men but hearts. *Granville.*

3. Skilled in scholastick knowledge.

Till a man can judge whether they be truths or no, his understanding is but little improved: and thus men of much reading are greatly *learned*, but may be little knowing. *Locke.*

LEARNEDLY. *adv.* [from *learned.*] With knowledge; with skill.

Much
He spoke, and *learnedly*, for life; but all
Was either pitied in him, or forgotten. *Shakes. H.* VIII.

The apostle seemed in his eyes but *learnedly* mad. *Hooker.*

Ev'ry coxcomb swears as *learnedly* as they. *Swift.*

LEARNING. *n. s.* [from *learn.*]

1. Literature; skill in languages or sciences; generally scholastick knowledge.

Learning hath its infancy, when it is almost childish; then its youth, when luxuriant and juvenile; then its strength of years, when solid; and, lastly, its old age, when dry and exhaust. *Bacon's Essays.*

To tongue or pudding thou hast no pretence,
Learning thy talent is, but mine is sense. *Prior.*

As Moses was learned in all the wisdom of the Egyptians, so it is manifest from this chapter, that St. Paul was a great master in all the *learning* of the Greeks. *Bentley's Sermons.*

2. Skill in any thing good or bad.

An art of contradiction by way of scorn, a *learning* wherewith we were long sithence forewarned, that the miserable times whereunto we are fallen should abound. *Hooker.*

LE'ARNER. *n. s.* [from *learn.*] One who is yet in his rudiments; one who is acquiring some new art or knowledge.

The late *learners* cannot so well take the ply, except it be in some minds that have not suffered themselves to fix. *Bacon.*

Nor can a *learner* work so cheap as a skilful practised artist can. *Graunt's Bills of Mortality.*

LEASE. *n. s.* [*laisser*, French. *Spelman.*]

1. A contract by which, in consideration of some payment, a temporary possession is granted of houses or lands.

Why, cousin, wer't thou regent of the world,
It were a shame to let this land by *lease*. *Shakespeare.*
Lords of the world have but for life their *lease*,
And that too, if the lessor please, must cease. *Denham.*

I have heard a man talk with contempt of bishops *leases*, as on a worse foot than the rest of his estate. *Swift.*

2. Any tenure.

Our high-plac'd Macbeth
Shall live the *lease* of nature. *Shakespeare's Macbeth.*
Thou to give the world increase,
Short'ned hast thy own life's *lease*. *Milton.*

To LEASE. *v. a.* [from the noun.] To let by lease.

Where the vicar *leases* his glebe, the tenant must pay the great tithes to the rector or impropriator, and the small tithes to the vicar. *Ayliffe's Parergon.*

To LEASE. *v. n.* [*lesen*, Dutch.] To glean; to gather what the harvest men leave.

She in harvest us'd to *lease*;
But harvest done, to chare-work did aspire,
Meat, drink, and two-pence, was her daily hire. *Dryden.*

LE'ASER. *n. s.* [from *lease.*] Gleaner; gatherer after the reaper.

There was no office which a man from England might not have; and I looked upon all who were born here as only in the condition of *leasers* and gleaners. *Swift.*

LEASH. *n. s.* [*lesse*, French; *letse*, Dutch; *laccio*, Italian.] A leather thong, by which a falconer holds his hawk, or a courser leads his greyhound. *Hanmer.*

Holding Corioli in the name of Rome,
Even like a fawning greyhound in the *leash*,
To let him slip at will. *Shakespeare's Coriolanus.*
What I was, I am;
More straining on, for plucking back; not following
My *leash* unwillingly. *Shakespeare's Winter's Tale.*

The ravished soul being shewn such game, would break those *leashes* that tie her to the body. *Boyle.*

2. A tierce; three.

I am sworn brother to a *leash* of drawers, and can call them all by their Christian names. *Shakes. Henry* IV.

Some thought when he did gabble
Th'ad heard three labourers of Babel,
Or Cerberus himself pronounce
A *leash* of languages at once. *Hudibras, p.* i.

3. A band wherewith to tie any thing in general.

Thou art a living comedy; they are a *leash* of dull devils. *Dennis's Letters.*

To LEASH. *v. a.* [from the noun.] To bind; to hold in a string.

Then should the warlike Harry, like himself,
Assume the port of Mars; and, at his heels,
Leasht in like hounds, should famine, sword, and fire,
Crouch for employment. *Shakes. Henry* V.

LE'ASING. *n. s.* [leaſe, Saxon.] Lies; falshood.

O ye sons of men, how long will ye have such pleasure in vanity, and seek after *leasing*? *Psal.* iv. 2.

He 'mongst ladies would their fortunes read
Out of their hands, and merry *leasings* tell. *Hub. Tale.*
He hates foul *leasings* and vile flattery,
Two filthy blots in noble gentery. *Hubbard's Tale.*
That false pilgrim which that *leasing* told,
Was indeed old Archimago. *Spens. Fairy Queen.*
I have ever narrified my friends
With all the size that verity
Would without lapsing suffer: nay, sometimes,
Like to a bowl upon a subtle ground
I've tumbl'd past the throw; and in his praise
Have almost stampt the *leasing*. *Shakes. Coriolanus.*
As folks, quoth Richard, prone to *leasing*,
Say things at first, because they're pleasing;
Then prove what they have once asserted,
Nor care to have their lie deserted:
Till their own dreams at length deceive them,
And oft repeating they believe them. *Prior.*
Trading free shall thrive again,
Nor *leasings* leud affright the swain. *Gay's Pastorals.*

LEAST. *adj.* the superlative of *little.* [læſt, Saxon. This word *Wallis* would persuade us to write *lest*, that it may be analogous

analogous to *less*; but surely the profit is not worth the change.] Little beyond others; smallest.

I am not worthy of the *least* of all the mercies shewed to thy servant. *Gen.* xxxii. 10.

A man can no more have a positive idea of the greatest than he has of the *least* space. *Locke.*

LEAST. *adv.* In the lowest degree; in a degree below others; less than any other way.

He resolv'd to wave his suit,
Or for a while play *least* in sight. *Hudibras, p.* i.

Ev'n that avert; I chuse it not;
But taste it as the *least* unhappy lot. *Dryd. Knight's Tale.*

No man more truly knows to place a right value on your friendship, than he who *least* deserves it on all other accounts than his due sense of it. *Pope's Letters.*

At LEAST. } To say no more; not to demand or affirm
At LEASTWISE. } more than is barely sufficient at the lowest degree.

Upon the mast they saw a young man, *at least* if he were a man, who sate as on horseback. *Sidney.*

Every effect doth after a sort contain, *at leastwise* resemble, the cause from which it proceedeth. *Hooker, b.* i.

The remedies, if any, are to be proposed from a constant course of the milken diet, continued *at least* a year. *Temple.*

A fiend may deceive a creature of more excellency than himself, *at least* by the tacit permission of the omniscient Being. *Dryden's Dedication to Juvenal.*

Let useful observations be *at least* some part of the subject of your conversation. *Watts's Improvement of the Mind.*

LE'ASY. *adj.* [This word seems formed from the same root with *loisir*, French, or *loose*.] Flimsy; of weak texture.

He never leaveth, while the sense itself be left loose and *leasy*. *Ascham's Schoolmaster.*

LE'ATHER. *n. s.* [leðeɲ, Saxon; *leaâr*, Erse.]

8. Dressed hides of animals.

He was a hairy man, and girt with a girdle of *leather* about his loins. 2 *Kings* i. 8.

The shepherd's homely curds,
His cold thin drink out of his *leather* bottle;
Is far beyond a prince's delicates. *Shakes. Henry* VI.

And if two boots keep out the weather,
What need you have two hides of *leather*. *Prior.*

2. Skin; ironically.

Returning sound in limb and wind,
Except some *leather* lost behind. *Swift.*

LE'ATHERCOAT. *n. s.* [*leather* and *coat*.] An apple with a tough rind.

There is a dish of *leathercoats* for you. *Shakes. H.* IV.

LE'ATHERDRESSER. *n. s.* [*leather* and *dresser*.] He who dresses leather.

He removed to Cumæ; and by the way was entertained at the house of one Tychius, a *leather-dresser*. *Pope.*

LEATHER-MOUTHED. *adj.* [*leather* and *mouth*.]

By a *leather-mouthed* fish, I mean such as have their teeth in their throat; as, the chub or cheven. *Walton's Angler.*

LE'ATHERY. *adj.* [from *leather*.] Resembling leather.

Wormius calls this crust a *leathery* skin. *Grew's Musæum.*

LE'ATHERN. *adj.* [from *leather*.] Made of leather.

I saw her hand; she has a *leathern* hand,
A free-stone colour'd hand: I verily did think
That her old gloves were on. *Shakesp. As you like it.*

The wretched animal heav'd forth such groans,
That their discharge did stretch his *leathern* coat
Almost to bursting. *Shakes. As you like it.*

In silken or in *leathern* purse retain
A splendid shilling. *Philips.*

LE'ATHERSELLER. *n. s.* [*leather* and *seller*.] He who deals in leather, and vends it.

LEAVE. *n. s.* [leaꝼe, Saxon; from lyꝼan, to grant.]

1. Grant of liberty; permission; allowance.

By your *leave*, Ireneus, notwithstanding all this your careful foresight, methinks I see an evil lurk unespied. *Spenser.*

When him his dearest Una did behold,
Disdaining life, desiring *leave* to dye. *Spenser.*

I make bold to press upon you.
—You're welcome; give us *leave*, drawer. *Shakespeare.*

The days
Of Sylla's sway, when the free sword took *leave*
To act all that it would. *Benj. Johnson's Cataline.*

Thrice happy snake! that in her sleeve
May boldly creep, we dare not give
Our thoughts so unconfin'd a *leave*. *Waller.*

No friend has *leave* to bear away the dead. *Dryden.*

Offended that we fought without his *leave*,
He takes this time his secret hate to shew. *Dryden.*

One thing more I crave *leave* to offer about syllogism, before I leave it. *Locke.*

I must have *leave* to be grateful to any who serves me, let him be never so obnoxious to any party: nor did the tory party put me to the hardship of asking this *leave*. *Pope.*

3. Farewel; adieu.

Take *leave* and part, for you must part forthwith. *Shak.*

Evils that take *leave*,
On their departure, most of all shew evil. *Shakesp.*

There is further compliment of *leave* taking between France and him. *Shakespeare's King Lear.*

Here my father comes;
A double blessing is a double grace;
Occasion smiles upon a second *leave*. *Shakesp. Hamlet.*

But my dear nothings, take your *leave*,
No longer must you me deceive. *Suckling.*

Many stars may be visible in our hemisphere, that are not so at present; and many which are at present shall take *leave* of our horizon, and appear unto southern habitations. *Brown's Vulgar Errours, b.* iv. *c.* 13.

To LEAVE. *v. a.* pret. *I left*; *I have left*. [Of the derivation of this word the etymologists give no satisfactory account.]

1. To quit; to forsake.

A man shall *leave* his father and his mother, and cleave to his wife. *Gen.* ii. 24.

When they were departed from him, they *left* him in great diseases. 2 *Chron.* xxiv. 25.

If they love lees, and *leave* the lusty wine,
Envy them not their palates with the swine. *B. Johnson.*

2. To desert; to abandon.

He that is of an unthankful mind, will *leave* him in danger that delivered him. *Ecclus.* xxix. 17.

3. To have remaining at death.

There be of them that have *left* a name behind them. *Ecclus.* xliv. 8.

4. Not to deprive of.

They still have *left* me the providence of God, and all the promises of the gospel, and my charity to them too. *Taylor.*

5. To suffer to remain.

If it be done without order, the mind comprehendeth less that which is set down; and besides, it *leaveth* a suspicion, as if more might be said than is expressed. *Bacon.*

These things must be *left* uncertain to farther discoveries in future ages. *Abbot's Description of the World.*

Who those are, to whom this right by descent belongs, he *leaves* out of the reach of any one to discover from his writings. *Locke.*

6. Not to carry away.

They encamped against them, and destroyed the increase of the earth, and *left* no sustenance for Israel. *Judg.* vi. 4.

He shall eat the fruit of thy cattle; which also shall not *leave* thee either corn, wine, or oil. *Deut.* xxviii. 48.

Vastius gave strict commandment, that they should *leave* behind them unnecessary baggage. *Knolles's History.*

7. To fix as a token or remembrance.

This I *leave* with my reader, as an occasion for him to consider, how much he may be beholden to experience. *Locke.*

8. To bequeath; to give as inheritance.

That peace thou *leav'st* to thy imperial line,
That peace, Oh happy shade, be ever thine. *Dryden.*

9. To give up; to resign.

Thou shalt not glean thy vineyard; thou shalt *leave* them for the poor and stranger. *Lev.* xix. 10.

If a wise man were *left* to himself, and his own choice, to wish the greatest good to himself he could devise; the sum of all his wishes would be this, That there were just such a being as God is. *Tillotson, Serm.* 1.

10. To permit without interposition.

Whether Esau were a vassal, I *leave* the reader to judge. *Locke.*

11. To cease to do; to desist from.

Let us return, lest my father *leave* caring for the asses, and take thought for us. 1 *Sam.* ix. 5.

12. *To* LEAVE *off*. To desist from; to forbear.

If, upon any occasion, you bid him *leave off* the doing of any Thing, you must be sure to carry the point. *Locke.*

In proportion as old age came on, he *left off* fox-hunting. *Addison's Spectator*, Nº. 115.

13. *To* LEAVE *off*. To forsake.

He began to *leave off* some of his old acquaintance, his roaring and bullying about the streets: he put on a serious air. *Arbuthnot's History of John Bull.*

14. *To* LEAVE *out*. To omit; to neglect.

My good Camillo;
I am so fraught with curious business, that
I *leave out* ceremony. *Shakesp. Winter's Tale.*

Shun they to treat with me too?
No good lady,
You may partake: I have told 'em who you are.
I should be loth to be *left out*, and here too. *Ben. Johnson.*

What is set down by order and division doth demonstrate, that nothing is *left out* or omitted, but all is there. *Bacon.*

Befriend till utmost end
Of all thy dues be done, and none *left out*,
Ere nice morn on the Indian steep
From her cabin'd loop-hole peep. *Milton.*

We ask, if those subvert
Reason's establish'd maxims, who assert
That we the world's existence may conceive,
Though we one atom *out* of matter *leave*. *Blackmore.*

I always

I always thought this paſſage *left out* with a great deal of judgment, by Tucca and Varius, as it ſeems to contradict a part in the ſixth Æneid. *Addiſon on Italy.*

To LEAVE. *v. n.*

1. To ceaſe; to deſiſt.

She is my eſſence, and I *leave* to be,
If I be not by her fair influence
Foſter'd, illumin'd, cheriſh'd, kept alive. *Shakeſpeare.*

And ſince this buſineſs ſo far fair is done,
Let us not *leave* till all our own be won. *Shakeſ. H. IV.*

He began at the eldeſt, and *left* at the youngeſt. *Geneſ.*

2. *To* LEAVE *off.* To deſiſt.

Grittus, hoping that they in the caſtle would not hold out, *left off* to batter or undermine it, wherewith he perceived he little prevailed. *Knolles's Hiſt. of the Turks.*

But when you find that vigorous heat abate,
Leave off, and for another ſummons wait. *Roſcommon.*

3. *To* LEAVE *off.* To ſtop.

Wrongs do not *leave off* there where they begin,
But ſtill beget new miſchiefs in their courſe. *Daniel.*

To LEAVE. *v. a.* [from *levy*; *lever*, French.] To levy; to raiſe: a corrupt word, made, I believe, by *Spenſer*, for a rhyme.

An army ſtrong ſhe *leav'd*,
To war on thoſe which him had of his realm bereav'd.
Spenſer's Fairy Queen, b. ii.

LE'AVED. *adj.* [from *leaves*, of *leaf.*]

1. Furniſhed with foliage.

2. Made with leaves or folds.

I will looſe the loins of kings, to open before him the two *leaved* gates. *Iſa.* xlv. 1.

LE'AVEN. *n. ſ.* [*levain*, French; *levare*, Latin.]

1. Ferment mixed with any body to make it light; particularly uſed of ſour dough mixed in a maſs of bread.

It ſhall not be baken with *leaven*. *Lev.* vi. 17.

All fermented meats and drinks are eaſilieſt digeſted; and thoſe unfermented, by barm or *leaven*, are hardly digeſted. *Floyer.*

2. Any mixture which makes a general change in the maſs.

Many of their propoſitions ſavour very ſtrong of the old *leaven* of innovations. *King Charles.*

To LE'AVEN. *v. a.* [from the noun.]

1. To ferment by ſomething mixed.

You muſt tarry the *leav'ning*. *Shakeſ. Troil. and Creſſida.*

Whoſoever eateth *leavened* bread, that ſoul ſhall be cut off. *Exod.* xii. 17.

Breads we have of ſeveral grains, with divers kinds of *leavenings*, and ſeaſonings; ſo that ſome do extremely move appetites. *Bacon's Atlantis.*

2. To taint; to imbue.

That cruel ſomething unpoſſeſt,
Corrodes and *leavens* all the reſt. *Prior.*

LE'AVER. *n. ſ.* [*leave.*] One who deſerts or forſakes.

Let the world rank me in regiſter
A maſter-*leaver*, and a fugitive. *Shakeſpeare.*

LEAVES. *n. ſ.* The plural of leaf.

Parts fit for the nouriſhment of man in plants are, ſeeds, roots, and fruits; for *leaves* they give no nouriſhment at all. *Bacon's Natural Hiſtory.*

LE'AVINGS. *n. ſ.* [from *leave.*] Remnant; relicks; offal: it has no ſingular.

My father has this morning call'd together,
To this poor hall, his little Roman ſenate,
The *leavings* of Pharſalia. *Addiſon's Cato.*

Then who can think we'll quit the place,
Or ſtop and light at Cloe's head,
With ſcraps and *leavings* to be fed. *Swift.*

LE'AVY. *adj.* [from *leaf.*] Full of leaves; covered with leaves.

Strephon, with *leavy* twigs of laurel tree,
A garland made on temples for to wear,
For he then choſen was the dignity
Of village lord that Whitſontide to bear. *Sidney.*

Now, near enough: your *leavy* ſcreens throw down,
And ſhow like thoſe you are. *Shakeſpeare's Macbeth.*

To LECH. *v. a.* [*lecher*, French.] To lick over. *Hanmer.*

Haſt thou yet *leched* the Athenian's eyes
With the love juice. *Shakeſp. Midſummer Night's Dream.*

LE'CHER. *n. ſ.* [Derived by *Skinner* from *luxure*, old French: *luxuria* is uſed in the middle ages in the ſame ſenſe.] A whore-maſter.

I will now take the *leacher*; he's at my houſe; he cannot 'ſcape me. *Shakeſ. Merry Wives of Windſor.*

You, like a *letcher*, out of whoriſh loins
Are pleas'd to breed out your inheritors. *Shakeſpeare.*

The *lecher* ſoon transforms his miſtreſs; now
In Io's place appears a lovely cow. *Dryden.*

The ſleepy *leacher* ſhuts his little eyes,
About his churning chaps the frothy bubbles riſe. *Dryden.*

She yields her charms
To that fair *letcher*, the ſtrong god of arms. *Pope's Odyſ.*

To LE'CHER. *v. n.* [from the noun.] To whore.

Die for adultery? no. The wren goes to't, and the ſmall gilded fly does *letcher* in my ſight. *Shakeſp. King Lear.*

Gut eats all day, and *letchers* all the night. *B. Johnſon.*

LECH'EROUS. *adj.* [from *lecher.*] Leud; luſtful.

The ſapphire ſhould grow foul, and loſe its beauty, when worn by one that is *lecherous*; the emerald ſhould fly to pieces, if it touch the ſkin of any unchaſte perſon. *Derham.*

LE'CHEROUSLY. *adv.* [from *lecherous.*] Leudly; luſtfully.

LE'CHEROUSNESS. *n. ſ.* [from *lecherous.*] Leudneſs.

LE'CHERY. *n. ſ.* [from *lecher.*] Leudneſs; luſt.

The reſt welter with as little ſhame in open *lechery*, as ſwine do in the common mire. *Aſcham's Schoolmaſter.*

Againſt ſuch leudſters, and their *lechery*,
Thoſe that betray them do no treachery. *Shakeſpeare.*

LE'CTION. *n. ſ.* [*lectio*, Lat.] A reading; a variety in copies.

Every critick has his own hypotheſis: if the common text be not favourable to his opinion, a various *lection* ſhall be made authentick. *Watts's Logick.*

LE'CTURE. *n. ſ.* [*lecture*, French.]

1. A diſcourſe pronounced upon any ſubject.

Mark him, while Dametas reads his ruſtick *lecture* unto him, how to feed his beaſts before noon, and where to ſhade them in the extreme heat. *Sidney, b.* ii.

Wrangling pedant,
When in muſick we have ſpent an hour,
Your *lecture* ſhall have leiſure for as much. *Shakeſp.*

When letters from Ceſar were given to Ruſticus, he refuſed to open them till the philoſopher had done his *lectures.* *Taylor's Holy Living.*

Virtue is the ſolid good, which tutors ſhould not only read *lectures* and talk of, but the labour and art of education ſhould furniſh the mind with, and faſten there. *Locke.*

Numidia will be bleſt by Cato's *lectures.* *Addiſon's Cato.*

2. The act or practice of reading; peruſal.

In the *lecture* of holy ſcripture, their apprehenſions are commonly confined unto the literal ſenſe of the text. *Browne.*

3. A magiſterial reprimand.

To LE'CTURE. *v. a.* [from the noun.]

1. To inſtruct formally.

2. To inſtruct inſolently and dogmatically.

LE'CTURER. *n. ſ.* [from *lecture.*] An inſtructor; a teacher by way of lecture; a preacher in a church hired by the pariſh to aſſiſt the rector or vicar.

If any miniſter refuſed to admit into his church a *lecturer* recommended by them, and there was not one orthodox or learned man recommended, he was preſently required to attend upon the committee. *Clarendon.*

LE'CTURESHIP. *n. ſ.* [from *lecture.*] The office of a lecturer.

He got a *lectureſhip* in town of ſixty pounds a year, where he preached conſtantly in perſon. *Swift.*

LED. part. pret. of *lead.*

Then ſhall they know that I am the Lord your God, which cauſed them to be *led* into captivity among the heathen. *Ezek.* xxxix. 28.

The leaders of this people cauſed them to err, and they that are *led* of them are deſtroyed. *Iſa.* ix. 16.

As in vegetables and animals, ſo in moſt other bodies, not propagated by ſeed, it is the colour we moſt fix on, and are moſt *led* by. *Locke.*

LEDGE. *n. ſ.* [*leggen*, Dutch, to lie.]

1. A row; layer; ſtratum.

The loweſt *ledge* or row ſhould be merely of ſtone, cloſely laid, without mortar: a general caution for all parts in building contiguous to board. *Wotton's Architecture.*

2. A ridge riſing above the reſt.

The four parallel ſticks riſing above five inches higher than the handkerchief, ſerved as *ledges* on each ſide. *Gulliver.*

3. Any prominence, or riſing part.

Beneath a *ledge* of rocks his fleet he hides,
The bending brow above, a ſafe retreat provides. *Dryden.*

LEDHORSE. *n. ſ.* [*led* and *horſe.*] A ſumpter horſe.

LEE. *n. ſ.* [*lie*, French.]

1. Dregs; ſediment; refuſe.

My cloaths, my ſex, exchang'd for thee,
I'll mingle with the people's wretched *lee.* *Prior.*

2. [Sea term; ſuppoſed by *Skinner* from *l'eau*, French.] It is generally that ſide which is oppoſite to the wind, as the *lee* ſhore is that the wind blows on. To be under the *lee* of the ſhore, is to be cloſe under the weather ſhore. A *leeward* ſhip is one that is not faſt by a wind, to make her way ſo good as ſhe might. To lay a ſhip by the *lee*, is to bring her ſo that all her ſails may lie againſt the maſts and ſhrowds flat, and the wind to come right on her broadſide, ſo that ſhe will make little or no way. *Dict.*

If we, being ſtorm-beaten in the bay of Biſcay, had had a port under our *lee*, that we might have kept our tranſporting ſhips with our men of war, we had taken the Indian fleet, and the Azores. *Raleigh's Apology.*

The Hollanders were wont to ride before Dunkirk with the wind at north weſt, making a *lee* ſhore in all weathers. *Raleigh's Eſſays.*

Unprovided of tackling and victualling, they are forced to ſea by a ſtorm; yet better do ſo than venture ſplitting and ſinking on a *lee* ſhore. *King Charles.*

Him,

Him, haply flumb'ring on the Norway foam,
The pilot of fome fmall night-founder'd fkiff,
Deeming fome ifland, oft, as feamen tell,
With fixed anchor in his fcaly rind,
Moors by his fide under the *lee*, while night
Invefts the fea. *Milton's Paradife Loft, b.* i.

Batter'd by his *lee* they lay,
The paffing winds through their torn canvafs play. *Dryden.*

LEECH. *n. f.* [læc, Saxon.]

1. A phyfician; a profeffor of the art of healing: whence we ftill ufe cowleech.

A *leech*, the which had great infight
In that difeafe of grieved confcience,
And well could cure the fame; his name was patience.
Spenfer's Fairy Queen, b. i.

Her words prevail'd, and then the learned *leach*
His cunning hand 'gan to his wounds to lay,
And all things elfe the which his art did teach. *Fa. Qu.*

Phyfick is their bane.
The learned *leaches* in defpair depart,
And fhake their heads, defponding of their art. *Dryden.*

Wife *leeches* will not vain receipts obtrude:
Deaf to complaints they wait upon the ill,
Till fome fafe crifis. *Dryden.*

The hoary wrinkled *leech* has watch'd and toil'd,
Tried every health reftoring herb and gum,
And wearied out his painful fkill in vain. *Rowe's J. Shore.*

A fkilful *leach*,
They fay, had wrought this bleffed deed;
This *leach* Arbuthnot was yclept. *Gay's Paftorals.*

2. A kind of fmall water ferpent, which faftens on animals, and fucks the blood: it is ufed to draw blood where the lancet is lefs fafe, whence perhaps the name.

I drew blood by *leeches* behind his ear. *Wifeman's Surg.*

Sticking like *leeches*, till they burft with blood,
Without remorfe infatiably. *Rofcommon.*

To LEECH. *v. a.* [from the noun.] To treat with medicaments.

LE'ECHCRAFT. *n. f.* [*leech* and *craft*.] The art of healing.

We ftudy fpeech, but others we perfuade:
We *leechcraft* learn, but others cure with it. *Davies.*

LEEF. *adj.* [*lieve*, *leve*, Dutch.] Kind; fond.

Whilome all thefe were low and *leefe*,
And lov'd their flocks to feed;
They never ftrove to be the chief,
And fimple was their weed. *Spenfer's Paftorals.*

LEEK. *n. f.* [leac, Saxon; *loock*, Dutch; *leechk*, Erfe.]

Its flower confifts of fix pedals, and is fhaped, as it were, like a bell; in the center arifes the pointal, which afterward becomes a roundifh fruit, divided into three cells, which contain roundifh feeds: to thefe notes may be added, the ftamina are generally broad and flat, ending in three capillaments, of which the middle one is furnifhed with a chive; the flowers are alfo gathered into almoft globular bunches: the roots are long, cylindrical, and coated, the coats ending in plain leaves. *Miller.*

Know'ft thou Fluellen? — Yes.
—Tell him I'll knock his *leek* about his pate,
Upon St. David's day. *Shakefpeare's Henry* V.

Leek to the Welfh, to Dutchmen butter's dear. *Gay.*

We ufe acrid plants inwardly and outwardly in gangreens; in the fcurvy, water-creffes, horfe-radifh, garlick, or *leek* pottage. *Floyer on Humours.*

LEER. *n. f.* [hleane, facies, Saxon.]

1. An oblique view.

I fpy entertainment in her; fhe gives the *leer* of invitation. *Shakefpeare's Merry Wives of Windfor.*

Afide the devil turn'd
For envy, yet with jealous *leer* malign
Ey'd them afkance. *Milton's Par. Loft, b.* iv.

2. A laboured caft of countenance.

Damn with faint praife, concede with civil *leer*. *Pope.*

I place a ftatefman full before my fight;
A bloated monfter in all his geer,
With fhamelefs vifage, and perfidious *leer*. *Swift.*

To LEER. *v. n.* [from the noun.]

1. To look obliquely; to look archly.

I will *leer* upon him as he comes by; and do but mark the countenance that he will give me. *Shakefp. Henry* IV.

I wonder whether you tafte the pleafure of independency, or whether you do not fometimes *leer* upon the court. *Swift.*

2. To look with a forced countenance.

Bertran has been taught the arts of courts,
To gild a face with fmiles, and *leer* a man to ruin. *Dryd.*

LEES. *n. f.* [*lie*, French.] Dregs; fediment: it has feldom a fingular.

This proceeded by reafon of the old humour of thofe countries, where the memory of King Richard was fo ftrong, that it lay like *lees* in the bottom of mens hearts; and if the veffel was but ftirred, it would come up. *Bacon's Henry* VII.

If they love *lees*, and leave the lufty wine,
Envy them not their palates with the fwine. *B. Johnfon.*

Thofe *lees* that trouble it refine
The agitated foul of generous wine. *Dryden.*

To LEESE. *v. a.* [*lefen*, Dutch.] To lofe: an old word.

Then fell to thy profit both butter and cheefe,
Who buieth it fooner the more he fhall *leefe*. *Tuffer.*

No caufe, nor client fat, will Chev'ril *leefe*,
But as they come on both fides he takes fees;
And pleafeth both: for while he melts his greafe
For this, that wins for whom he holds his peace. *B. Johnf.*

How in the port our fleet dear time did *leefe*,
Withering like prifoners, which lie but for fees. *Donne.*

LEET. *n. f.*

Leete, or *leta*, is otherwife called a law-day. The word feemeth to have grown from the Saxon leðe, which was a court of jurifdiction above the wapentake or hundred, comprehending three or four of them, otherwife called thirfhing, and contained the third part of a province or fhire: thefe jurifdictions, one and other, be now abolifhed, and fwallowed up in the county court. *Cowell.*

Who has a breaft fo pure,
But fome uncleanly apprehenfions
Keep *leets* and law-days, and in feffions fit
With meditations lawful. *Shakefpeare's Othello.*

You would prefent her at the *leet*,
Becaufe fhe bought ftone jugs, and no feal'd quarts. *Shak.*

LE'EWARD. *adj.* [lee and peaɲð, Saxon.]

1. Towards the wind. See LEE.

The claffice were called long fhips, the onerariæ round, becaufe of their figure approaching towards circular: this figure, though proper for the ftowage of goods, was not the fitteft for failing, becaufe of the great quantity of *leeward* way, except when they failed full before the wind. *Arbuth.*

Let no ftatefman dare,
A kingdom to a fhip compare;
Left he fhould call our commonweal
A veffel with a double keel;
Which juft like ours, new rigg'd and man'd,
And got about a league from land,
By change of wind to *leeward* fide,
The pilot knew not how to guide. *Swift.*

LEFT. participle preter. of *leave*.

Alas, poor lady! defolate and *left*;
I weep myfelf to think upon thy words. *Shakefpeare.*

Had fuch a river as this been *left* to itfelf, to have found its way out from among the Alps, whatever windings it had made, it muft have formed feveral little feas. *Addifon.*

Were I *left* to myfelf, I would rather aim at inftructing than diverting; but if we will be ufeful to the world, we muft take it as we find it. *Addifon's Spectator*, Nº. 179.

LEFT. *adj.* [*lufte*, Dutch; *lævus*, Latin.] Siniftrous; not right.

That there is alfo in men a natural prepotency in the right, we cannot with conftancy affirm, if we make obfervation in children, who permitted the freedom of both hands, do ofttimes confine it unto the *left*, and are not without great difficulty reftrained from it. *Brown's Vulgar Errours, b.* iv.

The right to Pluto's golden palace guides,
The *left* to that unhappy region tends,
Which to the depth of Tartarus defcends. *Dryden's Æn.*

The gods of greater nations dwell around,
And, on the right and *left*, the palace bound;
The commons where they can. *Dryden.*

A raven from a wither'd oak,
Left of their lodging was oblig'd to croak:
That omen lik'd him not. *Dryden.*

The *left* foot naked when they march to fight,
But in a bull's raw hide they fheathe the right. *Dryden.*

The man who ftruggles in the fight,
Fatigues *left* arm as well as right. *Prior.*

LEFT-HANDED. *adj.* [*left* and *hand*.] Ufing the left-hand rather than right.

The limbs are ufed moft on the right-fide, whereby cuftom helpeth; for we fee, that fome are *left-handed*, which are fuch as have ufed the left-hand moft. *Bacon's Nat. Hift.*

For the feat of the heart and liver on one fide, whereby men become *left-handed*, it happeneth too rarely to countenance an effect fo common: for the feat of the liver on the left-fide is very monftrous. *Brown's Vulgar Errours.*

LEFT-HANDEDNESS. *n. f.* [from *left-handed*.] Habitual ufe of the left-hand.

Although a fquint *left-handednefs*
B' ungracious; yet we cannot want that hand. *Donne.*

LEG. *n. f.* [*leg*, Danifh; *leggur*, Iflandick.]

1. The limb by which we walk; particularly that part between the knee and the foot.

They hafte; and what their tardy feet deny'd,
The trufty ftaff, their better *leg*, fupply'd. *Dryden.*

Purging comfits, and ants eggs,
Had almoft brought him off his *legs*. *Hudibras.*

Such intrigues people cannot meet with, who have nothing but *legs* to carry them. *Addifon's Guardian.*

2. An

2. An act of obeisance.

At court, he that cannot make a *leg*, put off his cap, kiss his hand, and say nothing, has neither *leg*, hands, lip, nor cap. *Shakesp. All's well that ends well.*

Their horses never give a blow,
But when they make a *leg*, and bow. *Hudibras, p.* iii.

If the boy should not put off his hat, nor make *legs* very gracefully, a dancing-master will cure that defect. *Locke.*

He made his *leg*, and went away. *Swift.*

3. To stand on his own legs; to support himself.

Persons of their fortune and quality could well have stood upon their own *legs*, and needed not to lay in for countenance and support. *Collier of Friendship.*

4. That by which any thing is supported on the ground: as, the *leg* of a table.

LE'GACY. *n. s.* [*legatum*, Latin.]

Legacy is a particular thing given by last will and testament. *Cowell.*

If there be no such thing apparent upon record, they do as if one should demand a *legacy* by force and virtue of some written testament, wherein there being no such thing specified, he pleadeth that there it must needs be, and bringeth arguments from the love or good-will which always the testator bore him; imagining, that these, or the like proofs, will convict a testament to have that in it, which other men can no-where by reading find. *Hooker, b.* iii.

Go you to Cæsar's house;
Fetch the will hither, and we shall determine
How to cut off some charge in *legacies*. *Shakesf. J. Cæsar.*

Good counsel is the best *legacy* a father can leave a child. *L'Estrange's Fables.*

When he thought you gone
T' augment the number of the bless'd above,
He deem'd 'em *legacies* of royal love;
Nor arm'd, his brothers portions to invade,
But to defend the present you had made. *Dryden.*

When the heir of this vast treasure knew,
How large a *legacy* was left to you,
He wisely ty'd it to the crown again. *Dryden.*

Leave to thy children tumult, strife, and war,
Portions of toil, and *legacies* of care. *Prior.*

LE'GAL. *adj.* [*legal*, French; *leges*, Latin.]

1. Done or conceived according to law.

Whatsoever was before, was before time of memory; and what is since is, in a *legal* sense, within the time of memory. *Hale's Hist. of the Common Law of England.*

2. Lawful; not contrary to law.

His merits
To save them, not their own, though *legal*, works. *Milt.*

LEGA'LITY. *n. s.* [*legalité*, French.] Lawfulness.

To LE'GALIZE. *v. a.* [*legaliser*, French; from *legal.*] To authorize; to make lawful.

If any thing can *legalize* revenge, it should be injury from an extremely obliged person: but revenge is so absolutely the peculiar of heaven, that no consideration can impower, even the best men, to assume the execution of it. *South's Sermons.*

LE'GALLY. *adv.* [from *legal.*] Lawfully; according to law.

A prince may not, much less may inferior judges, deny justice, when it is *legally* and competently demanded. *Taylor.*

LE'GATARY. *n. s.* [*legataire*, French; from *legatum*, Latin.] One who has a legacy left.

An executor shall exhibit a true inventory of goods, taken in the presence of fit persons, as creditors and *legataries* are, unto the ordinary.

LEGATINE. *adj.* [from *legate.*] Made by a legate.

When any one is absolved from excommunication, it is provided by a *legatine* constitution, that some one shall publish such absolution. *Ayliffe's Parergon.*

2. Belonging to a legate of the Roman see.

All those you have done of late,
By your power *legatine* within this kingdom,
Fall in the compass of a præmunire. *Shakespeare.*

LE'GATE. *n. s.* [*legatus*, Latin; *legat*, French; *legato*, Italian.]

1. A deputy; an ambassador.

The *legates* from th' Ætolian prince return:
Sad news they bring, that after all the cost,
And care employ'd, their embassy is lost. *Dryden. Æneis.*

2. A kind of spiritual embassador from the pope; a commissioner deputed by the pope for ecclesiastical affairs.

Look where the holy *legate* comes apace,
To give us warrant from the hand of heav'n. *Shakesp.*

Upon the *legate*'s summons, he submitted himself to an examination, and appeared before him. *Atterbury.*

LEGATE'E. *n. s.* [from *legatum*, Lat.] One who has a legacy left him.

If he chance to 'scape this dismal bout,
The former *legatees* are blotted out. *Dryden's Juvenal.*

My will is, that if any of the above-named *legatees* should die before me, that then the respective legacies shall revert to myself. *Swift.*

LEGA'TION. *n. s.* [*legatio*, Latin.] Deputation; commission; embassy.

It will be found, that after a *legation* ad res repetendas, and a refusal, and a denunciation or indiction of a war, the war is no more confined to the place of the quarrel, but is left at large. *Bacon's War with Spain.*

In the attiring and ornament of their bodies the duke had a fine and unaffected politeness, and upon occasion costly, as in his *legations*. *Wotton.*

LEGA'TOR. *n. s.* [from *lego*, Latin.] One who makes a will, and leaves legacies.

Suppose debate
Betwixt pretenders to a fair estate,
Bequeath'd by some *legator*'s last intent. *Dryden.*

LE'GEND. *n. s.* [*legenda*, Latin.]

1. A chronicle or register of the lives of saints.

Legends being grown in a manner to be nothing else but heaps of frivolous and scandalous vanities, they have been even with disdain thrown out, the very nests which bred them abhorring them. *Hooker, b.* v.

There are in Rome two sets of antiquities, the christian and the heathen; the former, though of a fresher date, are so embroiled with fable and *legend*, that one receives but little satisfaction. *Addison's Remarks on Italy.*

2. Any memorial or relation.

And in this *legend* all that glorious deed
Read, whilst you arm you; arm you whilst you read. *Fairfax, b.* i.

3. An incredible unauthentick narrative.

Who can show the *legends*, that record
More idle tales, or fables so absurd. *Blackmore.*

It is the way and means of attaining to heaven, that makes profane scorners so willingly let go the expectation of it. It is not the articles of the creed, but the duty to God and their neighbour, that is such an inconsistent incredible *legend*. *Bentley's Sermons.*

4. Any inscription; particularly on medals or coins.

Compare the beauty and comprehensiveness of *legends* on ancient coins. *Addison on Medals.*

LE'GER. *n. s.* [from *legger*, Dutch. To lie or remain in a place.] Any thing that lies in a place; as, a leger ambassador; a resident; one that continues at the court to which he is sent; a leger-book, a book that lies in the compting-house.

Lord Angelo, having affairs to heav'n,
Intends you for his swift ambassador,
Where you shall be an everlasting *leiger*. *Shakespeare.*

I've giv'n him that,
Which, if he take, shall quite unpeople her
Of *leidgers* for her sweet. *Shakespeare's Cymbeline.*

If *legier* ambassadors or agents were sent to remain near the courts of princes, to observe their motions, and to hold correspondence with them, such were made choice of as were vigilant. *Bacon's Advice to Villiers.*

Who can endear
Thy praise too much? thou art heav'ns *leiger* here,
Working against the states of death and hell. *Herbert.*

He withdrew not his confidence from any of those who attended his person, who, in truth, lay *leiger* for the covenant, and kept up the spirits of their countrymen by their intelligence. *Clarendon, b.* ii.

I call that a *ledger* bait, which is fixed, or made to rest, in one certain place, when you shall be absent; and I call that a walking bait which you have ever in motion. *Walton.*

LE'GERDEMAIN. *n. s.* [contracted perhaps from *legereté de main*, French.] Slight of hand; juggle; power of deceiving the eye by nimble motion; trick; deception; knack.

He so light was at *legerdemain*,
That what he touch'd came not to light again. *Hubberd.*

Of all the tricks and *legerdemain* by which men impose upon their own souls, there is none so common as the plea of a good intention. *South's Sermons.*

LEG'ERITY. *n. s.* [*legereté*, French.] Lightness; nimbleness; quickness. A word not in use.

When the mind is quicken'd,
The organs though defunct and dead before,
Break up their drowsy grave, and newly move
With casted slough and fresh *legerity*. *Shakespeare.*

LE'GGED. *adj.* [from *leg.*] Having legs; furnished with legs.

LE'GIBLE. *n. s.* [*legibilis*, Latin.]

1. Such as may be read.

You observe some clergymen with their heads held down within an inch of the cushion, to read what is hardly *legible*. *Swift.*

2. Apparent; discoverable.

People's opinions of themselves are *legible* in their countenances. Thus a kind imagination makes a bold man have vigour and enterprize in his air and motion; it stamps value and significancy upon his face. *Collier.*

LE'GIBLY. *adv.* [from *legible.*] In such a manner as may be read.

LE'GION. [*legio*, Latin.]

1. A body of Roman soldiers, consisting of about five thousand.

The most remarkable piece in Antoninus's pillar is, the figure of Jupiter Pluvius sending rain on the fainting army of Marcus Aurelius, and thunderbolts on his enemies, which is the greatest confirmation possible of the story of the Christian *legion*. *Addison.*

2. A military force.

She to foreign realms
Sends forth her dreadful *legions*. *Philips.*

3. Any great number.

Not in the *legions*
Of horrid hell, can come a devil more damn'd. *Shakesp.*

The partition between good and evil is broken down; and where one sin has entered, *legions* will force their way through the same breach. *Rogers's Sermons.*

LE'GIONARY. *adj.* [from *legion.*]

1. Relating to a legion.
2. Containing a legion.
3. Containing a great indefinite number.

Too many applying themselves betwixt jest and earnest, make up the *legionary* body of error. *Brown's Vulg. Errours.*

LEGISLA'TION. *n. s.* [from *legislator*, Lat.] The act of giving laws.

Pythagoras joined *legislation* to his philosophy, and, like others, pretended to miracles and revelations from God, to give a more venerable sanction to the laws he prescribed. *Littleton on the Conversion of St. Paul.*

LEGISLA'TIVE. *adj.* [from *legislator.*] Giving laws; lawgiving.

Their *legislative* frenzy they repent,
Enacting it should make no precedent. *Denham.*

The poet is a kind of lawgiver, and those qualities are proper to the *legislative* style. *Dryden.*

LEGISLA'TOR. *n. s.* [*legislator*, Latin; *legislatour*, French.] A lawgiver; one who makes laws for any community.

It spoke like a *legislator*: the thing spoke was a law. *South.*

Heroes in animated marble frown,
And *legislators* seem to think in stone. *Pope.*

LEGISLA'TURE. *n. s.* [from *legislator*, Latin.] The power that makes laws.

Without the concurrent consent of all three parts of the *legislature*, no law is or can be made. *Hale's Com. Law.*

In the notion of a *legislature* is implied a power to change, repeal, and suspend laws in being, as well as to make new laws. *Addison's Freeholder*, N°. 16.

By the supreme magistrate is properly understood the legislative power; but the word magistrate seeming to denote a single person, and to express the executive power, it came to pass that the obedience due to the *legislature* was, for want of considering this easy distinction, misapplied to the administration. *Swift's Sentiments of a Ch. of England Man.*

LEGI'TIMACY. *n. s.* [from *legitimate.*]

1. Lawfulness of birth.

In respect of his *legitimacy*, it will be good. *Ayliffe.*

2. Genuineness; not spuriousness.

The *legitimacy* or reality of these marine bodies vindicated, I now inquire by what means they were hurried out of the ocean. *Woodward's Natural History.*

LEGI'TIMATE. *adj.* [from *legitimus*, Lat. *legitime*, French.] Born in marriage; lawfully begotten.

Legitimate Edgar, I must have your land;
Our father's love is to the bastard Edmund. *Shakespeare.*

An adulterous person is tied to make provision for the children begotten in unlawful embraces, that they may do no injury to the *legitimate*, by receiving a common portion. *Taylor's Rule of Holy Living.*

To LEGI'TIMATE. *v. a.* [*legitimer*, Fr. from the adjective.]

1. To procure to any the rights of legitimate birth.

Legitimate him that was a bastard. *Ayliffe's Parergon.*

2. To make lawful.

It would be impossible for any enterprize to be lawful, if that which should *legitimate* it is subsequent to it, and can have no influence to make it good or bad. *Decay of Piety.*

LEGI'TIMATELY. *adv.* [from *legitimate.*] Lawfully; genuinely.

By degrees he rose to Jove's imperial seat,
Thus difficulties prove a soul *legitimately* great. *Dryden.*

LEGITIMA'TION. *n. s.* [*legitimation*, French; from *legitimate.*]

1. Lawful birth.

I have disclaim'd my land;
Legitimation, name, and all is gone:
Then, good my mother, let me know my father. *Shakesp.*

From whence will arise many questions of *legitimation*, and what in nature is the difference betwixt a wife and a concubine. *Locke.*

2. The act of investing with the privileges of lawful birth.

LE'GUME. } *n. s.* [*legume*, French; *legumen*, Lat.] Seeds
LEGU'MEN. } not reaped, but gathered by the hand; as, beans: in general, all larger seeds; pulse.

Some *legumens*, as peas or beans, if newly gathered and distilled in a retort, will afford an acid spirit. *Boyle.*

In the spring fell great rains, upon which ensued a most destructive mildew upon the corn and *legumes*. *Arbuthnot.*

LEGU'MINOUS. *adj.* [*legumineux*, French; from *legumen.*] Belonging to pulse; consisting of pulse.

The properest food of the vegetable kingdom is taken from the farinaceous seeds: as oats, barley, and wheat; or of some of the siliquose or *leguminous*; as, peas or beans. *Arbuthnot.*

LE'ISURABLY. *adv.* [from *leisurable.*] At leisure; without tumult or hurry.

Let us beg of God, that when the hour of our rest is come, the patterns of our dissolution may be Jacob, Moses, Joshua, and David, who *leisurably* ending their lives in peace, prayed for the mercies of God to come upon their posterity. *Hooker, b. v.*

LE'ISURABLE. *adj.* [from *leisure.*] Done at leisure; not hurried; enjoying leisure.

A relation inexcuseable in his works of *leisurable* hours, the examination being as ready as the relation. *Brown.*

LE'ISURE. *n. s.* [*loisir*, French.]

1. Freedom from business or hurry; vacancy of mind; power to spend time according to choice.

A gentleman fell very sick, and a friend said to him, Send for a physician; but the sick man answered, It is no matter; for if I die, I will die at *leisure*. *Bacon's Apophthegms.*

Where ambition and avarice have made no entrance, the desire of *leisure* is much more natural than of business and care. *Temple.*

O happy youth!
For whom thy fates reserve so fair a bride:
He sigh'd, and had no *leisure* more to say,
His honour call'd his eyes another way. *Dryden's Ovid.*

You enjoy your quiet in a garden, where you have not only the *leisure* of thinking, but the pleasure to think of nothing which can discompose your mind. *Dryden.*

2. Convenience of time.

We'll make our *leisures* to attend on yours. *Shakes.*

They summon'd up their meiny, strait took horse;
Commanded me to follow, and attend
The *leisure* of their answer. *Shakesp. King Lear.*

I shall leave with him that very rational and emphatical rebuke of Tully, To be considered at his *leisure*. *Locke.*

3. Want of leisure. Not used.

More than I have said, loving countrymen;
The *leisure* and enforcement of the time
Forbids to dwell on. *Shakespeare's Richard* III.

LE'ISURELY. *adj.* [from *leisure.*] Not hasty; deliberate; done without hurry.

He was the wretchedst thing when he was young,
So long a growing, and so *leisurely*,
That, if the rule were true, he should be gracious. *Shakespeare.*

The earl of Warwick, with a handful of men, fired Leith and Edinburgh, and returned by a *leisurely* march. *Hayward.*

The bridge is human life: upon a more *leisurely* survey of it, I found that it consisted of threescore and ten intire arches. *Addison's Spectator*, N°. 159.

LE'ISURELY. *adv.* [from *leisure.*] Not in a hurry; slowly.

The Belgians hop'd, that with disorder'd haste,
Our deep-cut keels upon the sands might run;
Or if with caution *leisurely* we past,
Their numerous gross might charge us one by one. *Dryd.*

We descended very *leisurely*, my friend being careful to count the steps. *Addison's Freeholder*, N. 47.

LE'MAN. *n. s.* [Generally supposed to be *laimant*, the lover, French; but imagined by *Junius*, with almost equal probability, to be derived from *leef*, Dutch, or *leof*, Saxon, *beloved* and *man*. This etymology is strongly supported by the antient orthography, according to which it was written *leveman.*] A sweetheart; a gallant; or a mistress. *Hanmer.*

Hold for my sake, and do him not to dye;
But vanquish'd, thine eternal bondslave make,
And me thy worthy meed unto thy *leman* take. *Fa. Qu.*

A cup of wine,
That's brisk and fine, }
And drink unto the *leman* mine. *Shakes. Henry* IV. }

LE'MMA. *n. s.* [λῆμμα; *lemme*, French.] A proposition previously assumed.

LE'MON. *n. s.* [*limon*, French; *limonium*, low Latin.]

1. The fruit of the lemon-tree.

The juice of *lemons* is more cooling and astringent than that of oranges. *Arbuthnot on Aliments.*

The dyers use it for dying of bright yellows and *lemon* colours. *Mortimer's Husbandry.*

Bear me, Pomona!
To where the *lemon* and the piercing lime,
With the deep orange, glowing through the green,
Their lighter glories blend. *Thomson's Sermons.*

2. The tree that bears lemons.

The *lemon* tree hath large stiff leaves; the flower consists of many leaves, which expand in form of a rose: the fruit is almost of an oval figure, and divided into several cells, in which are lodged hard seeds, surrounded by a thick fleshy substance, which, for the most part, is full of an acid juice. There are many varieties of this tree, and the fruit is yearly imported from Lisbon in great plenty. *Miller.*

LEMONA'DE. *n. s.* [from *lemon.*] Liquor made of water, sugar, and the juice of lemons.

Thou, and thy wife, and children, should walk in my gardens, buy toys, and drink *lemonade.* *Arbuth. J. Bull.*

To LEND. *v. a.* [lænan, Saxon; *leenen*, Dutch.]

1. To afford, on condition of repayment.

Thou shalt not give him thy money upon usury, nor *lend* him thy victuals for increase. *Lev.* xxv. 37.

They dare not give, and e'en refuse to *lend*,
To their poor kindred, or a wanting friend. *Dryden.*

2. To suffer to be used on condition that it be restored.

In common worldly things 'tis call'd ungrateful
With dull unwillingness to pay a debt,
Which, with a bounteous hand, was kindly *lent*;
Much more to be thus opposite with heav'n. *Shakesp.*

I'll *lend* it thee, my dear, but have no power to give it from me. *Shakesp. All's well that ends well.*

The fair blessing we vouchsafe to send;
Nor can we spare you long, though often we may *lend.*
Dryden to the Dutchess of Ormond.

3. To afford; to grant in general.

Covetousness, like the sea, receives the tribute of all rivers, though far unlike it in *lending* any back again. *Decay of Piety.*

Painting and poesy are two sisters so like, that they *lend* to each other their name and office: one is called a dumb poesy, and the other a speaking picture. *Dryden's Dufresnoy.*

From thy new hope, and from thy growing store,
Now *lend* assistance, and relieve the poor. *Dryden's Pers.*

Cato, *lend* me for a while thy patience,
And condescend to hear a young man speak. *Addison.*

Cephisa, thou
Wilt *lend* a hand to close thy mistress' eyes. *A. Philips.*

LE'NDER. *n. s.* [from *lend.*]

1. One who lends any thing.

2. One who makes a trade of putting money to interest.

Let the state be answered some small matter, and the rest left to the *lender*; if the abatement be but small, it will not discourage the *lender*: he that took before ten in the hundred, will sooner descend to eight than give over this trade. *Bacon's Essays.*

Whole droves of *lenders* croud the bankers doors
To call in money. *Dryden's Spanish Friar.*

Interest would certainly encourage the *lender* to venture in such a time of danger. *Addison's Freeholder*, N°. 20.

LENGTH. *n. s.* [from leng, Saxon.]

1. The extent of any thing material from end to end; the longest line that can be drawn through a body.

There is in Ticinum a church that is in *length* one hundred feet, in breadth twenty, and in heighth near fifty: it reporteth the voice twelve or thirteen times. *Bacon.*

2. Horizontal extension.

Mezentius rushes on his foes,
And first unhappy Acron overthrows;
Stretch'd at his *length* he spurns the swarthy ground. *Dryd.*

3. A certain portion of space or time.

Large *lengths* of seas and shores
Between my father and my mother lay. *Shakesp. K. John.*

To get from th' enemy, and Ralph, free;
Left danger, fears, and foes, behind,
And beat, at least three *lengths*, the wind. *Hudibras.*

Time glides along with undiscover'd haste,
The future but a *length* beyond the past. *Dryden's Ovid.*

What *length* of lands, what oceans have you pass'd,
What storms sustain'd, and on what shores been cast? *Dryd.*

4. Extent of duration.

Having thus got the idea of duration, the next thing is to get some measure of this common duration, whereby to judge of its different *lengths.* *Locke.*

5. Long duration or protraction.

May heav'n, great monarch, still augment your bliss
With *length* of days, and every day like this. *Dryden.*

Such toil requir'd the Roman name,
Such *length* of labour for so vast a frame. *Dryden's Æn.*

In *length* of time it will cover the whole plain, and make one mountain with that on which it now stands. *Addison.*

6. Reach or expansion of any thing.

I do not recommend to all a pursuit of sciences, to those extensive *lengths* to which the moderns have advanced them.
Watts's Improvement of the Mind, p. i.

7. Full extent; uncontracted state.

If Lætitia, who sent me this account, will acquaint me with the worthy gentleman's name; I will insert it at *length* in one of my papers. *Addison's Spectator*, N°. 40.

8. Distance.

He had marched to the *length* of Exeter, which he had some thought of besieging. *Clarendon, b.* viii.

9. End; latter part of any assignable time.

Churches purged of things burdensome, all was brought at the *length* unto that wherein now we stand. *Hooker, b.* iv.

A crooked stick is not straitened unless it be bent as far on the clear contrary side, that so it may settle itself at the *length* in a middle state of evenness between them both. *Hooker.*

10. *At* LENGTH. [It was formerly written *at the length.*] At last; in conclusion.

At length, at length, I have thee in my arms,
Though our malevolent stars have struggled hard,
And held us long asunder. *Dryden's King Arthur.*

To LE'NGTHEN. *v. a.* [from *length.*]

1. To draw out; to make longer; to elongate.

Relaxing the fibres, is making them flexible, or easy to be *lengthened* without rupture. *Arbuthnot on Aliments.*

Falling dews with spangles deck'd the glade,
And the low sun had *lengthen'd* ev'ry shade. *Pope.*

2. To protract; to continue.

Break off thy sins by righteousness, and thine iniquities by shewing mercy to the poor; if it may be a *lengthening* of thy tranquillity. *Dan.* iv. 27.

Frame your mind to mirth and merriment,
Which bars a thousand harms, and *lengthens* life. *Shakes.*

It is in our power to secure to ourselves an interest in the divine mercies that are yet to come, and to *lengthen* the course of our present prosperity. *Atterbury's Sermons.*

3. To protract pronunciation.

The learned languages were less constrained in the quantity of every syllable, besides helps of grammatical figures for the *lengthening* or abbreviation of them. *Dryden.*

4. *To* LE'NGTHEN *out.* [The particle *out* is only emphatical.] To protract; to extend.

What if I please to *lengthen out* his date
A day, and take a pride to cozen fate. *Dryden's Aur.*

I'd hoard up every moment of my life,
To *lengthen out* the payment of my tears. *Dryden.*

It *lengthens out* every act of worship, and produces more lasting and permanent impressions in the mind, than those which accompany any transient form of words. *Addison.*

To LE'NGTHEN. *v. n.* To grow longer; to increase in length.

One may as well make a yard, whose parts *lengthen* and shrink, as a measure of trade in materials, that have not always a settled value. *Locke.*

Still 'tis farther from its end;
Still finds its error *lengthen* with its way. *Prior.*

LE'NGTHWISE. *adv.* [*length* and *wise.*] According to the length.

LE'NIENT. *adj.* [*leniens*, Latin.]

1. Assuasive; softening; mitigating.

Consolatories writ
With study'd argument, and much persuasion sought,
Lenient of grief and anxious thought. *Milton's Agonistes.*

In this one passion man can strength enjoy;
Time, that on all things lays his *lenient* hand,
Yet tames not this; it sticks to our last sand. *Pope.*

2. Laxative; emollient.

Oils relax the fibres, are *lenient*, balsamick, and abate acrimony in the blood. *Arbuthnot on Aliments.*

LE'NIENT. *n. s.* An emollient, or assuasive application.

I dressed it with *lenients.* *Wiseman's Surgery.*

To LE'NIFY. *v. a.* [*lenifier*, old French; *lenio*, Latin.] To assuage; to mitigate.

It is used for squinancies and inflammations in the throat, whereby it seemeth to have a mollifying and *lenifying* virtue.
Bacon's Natural History, N°. 554.

All soft'ning simples, known of sov'reign use,
He presses out, and pours their noble juice;
These first infus'd, to *lenify* the pain,
He tugs with pincers, but he tugs in vain. *Dryden.*

LE'NITIVE. *adj.* [*lenitif*, Fr. *lenio*, Lat.] Assuasive; emollient.

Some plants have a milk in them; the cause may be an inception of putrefaction: for those milks have all an acrimony, though one would think they should be *lenitive.* *Bacon.*

There is aliment *lenitive* expelling the fœces without stimulating the bowels; such are animal oils. *Arbuthnot.*

LE'NITIVE *n. s.*

1. Any thing applied to ease pain.

2. A palliative.

There are *lenitives* that friendship will apply, before it would be brought to decretory rigours. *South's Sermons.*

LE'NITY. *n. s.* [*lenitas*, Lat.] Mildness; mercy; tenderness; softness of temper.

Henry gives consent,
Of meer compassion, and of *lenity*,
To ease your country. *Shakespeare's Henry* VI.

Lenity must gain
The mighty men, and please the discontent. *Daniel.*

Albeit so ample a pardon was proclaimed touching treason, yet could not the boldness be beaten down either with severity, or with *lenity* be abated. *Hayward.*

These jealousies
Have but one root, the old imprison'd king,

Whose

Whose *lenity* first pleas'd the gaping crowd:
But when long try'd, and found supinely good,
Like Æsop's log, they leapt upon his back. *Dryden.*

LENS. *n. s.*
A glass spherically convex on both sides, is usually called a *lens*; such as is a burning-glass, or spectacle-glass, or an object glass of a telescope. *Newton's Opticks.*
According to the difference of the *lenses*, I used various distances. *Newton's Opticks.*

LENT. part. pass. from *lend.*
By Jove the stranger and the poor are sent,
And what to those we give, to Jove is *lent*. *Pope's Odys.*

LENT. *n. s.* [lencten, the spring, Saxon.] The quadragesimal fast; a time of abstinence.
Lent is from springing, because it falleth in the spring; for which our progenitors, the Germans, use glent. *Camden.*

LE'NTEN. *adj.* [from *lent.*] Such as is used in lent; sparing.
My lord, if you delight not in man, what *lenten* entertainment the players shall receive from you. *Shakesp. Hamlet.*
She quench'd her fury at the flood,
And with a *lenten* sallad cool'd her blood.
Their commons, though but coarse, were nothing scant.
Dryden's Hind and Panther.

LE'NTICULAR. *adj.* [*lenticulaire*, French.] Doubly convex; of the form of a lens.
The crystalline humour is of a *lenticular* figure, convex on both sides. *Ray on Creation.*

LE'NTIFORM. *adj.* [*lens* and *forma*, Latin.] Having the form of a lens.

LE'NTIGINOUS. *adj.* [from *lentigo.*] Scurfy; furfuraceous.

LENTI'GO. *n. s.* [Latin.] A freckly or scurfy eruption upon the skin; such especially as is common to women in childbearing. *Quincy.*

LE'NTIL. *n. s.* [*lens*, Latin; *lentille*, French.]
It hath a papilionaceous flower, the pointal of which becomes a short pod, containing orbicular seeds, for the most part convex; the leaves are conjugated, growing to one midrib, and are terminated by tendrils. *Miller.*
The Philistines were gathered together, where was a piece of ground full of *lentiles*. 2 *Sam.* xxiii. 11.

LE'NTISCK. *n. s.* [*lentiscus*, Latin; *lentisque*, French.]
Lentisk wood is of a pale brown colour, almost whitish, resinous, of a fragrant smell and acrid taste: it is the wood of the tree which produces the mastich, and is esteemed astringent and balsamick in medicine. *Hill's Mat. Medica.*
Lentisck is a beautiful evergreen, the mastich or gum of which is of use for the teeth or gums. *Mortimer's Husb.*

LE'NTITUDE. *n. s.* [from *lentus*, Latin.] Sluggishness; slowness. *Dict.*

LE'NTNER. *n. s.* A kind of hawk.
I should enlarge my discourse to the observation of the haggard, and the two sorts of *lentners*. *Walton's Angler.*

LE'NTOR. *n. s.* [*lentor*, Latin; *lenteur*, French.]
1. Tenacity; viscosity.
Some bodies have a kind of *lentor*, and more depectible nature than others. *Bacon.*
2. Slowness; delay.
The *lentor* of eruptions, not inflammatory, points to an acid cause. *Arbuthnot on Diet.*
3. [In physick.] It expresses that sizy, viscid, coagulated part of the blood, which, in malignant fevers, obstructs the capillary vessels. *Quincy.*

LE'NTOUS. *adj.* [*lentus*, Latin.] Viscous; tenacious; capable to be drawn out.
In this spawn of a *lentous* and transparent body, are to be discerned many specks which become black, a substance more compacted and terrestrious than the other; for it riseth not in distillation. *Brown's Vulgar Errours, b.* iii.

LE'OD. *n. s.*
Leod signifies the people; or, rather, a nation, country, *&c.* Thus, *leodgar* is one of great interest with the people or nation. *Gibson's Camden.*

LE'OF. *n. s.*
Leof denotes love; so *leofwin* is a winner of love; *leofstan*, best beloved: like these Agapetus, Erasmus, Philo, Amandus, *&c.* *Gibson's Camden.*

LE'ONINE. *adj.* [*leoninus*, Latin.]
1. Belonging to a lion; having the nature of a lion.
2. Leonine verses are those of which the end rhymes to the middle, so named from *Leo* the inventor: as,
Gloria factorum *temere conceditur* horum.

LE'OPARD. *n. s.* [*leo* and *pardus*, Latin.] A spotted beast of prey.
Sheep run not half so tim'rous from the wolf,
Or horse or oxen from the *leopard*,
As you fly from your oft-subdued slaves. *Shakesp. Hen.* VI.
A *leopard* is every way, in shape and actions, like a cat: his head, teeth, tongue, feet, claws, tail, all like a cat's: he boxes with his fore-feet, as a cat doth her kittens; leaps at the prey, as a cat at a mouse; and will also spit much after the same manner: so that they seem to differ, just as a kite doth from an eagle. *Grew's Musæum.*
Before the king tame *leopards* led the way,
And troops of lions innocently play. *Dryden.*

LE'PER. *n. s.* [*lepra*, *leprosus*, Latin.] One infected with a leprosy.
I am no loathsome *leper*; look on me. *Shakespeare.*
The *leper* in whom the plague is, his cloaths shall be rent. *Lev.* xiii. 45.
The number of their *lepers* was very great. *Hakewill.*

LE'PEROUS. *adj.* [Formed from *leprous*, to make out a verse.] Causing leprosy; infected with leprosy; leprous.
Upon my secure hour thy uncle stole,
With juice of cursed hebenon in a viol,
And in the porches of mine ears did pour
The *leperous* distilment. *Shakespeare's Hamlet.*

LE'PORINE. *adj.* [*leporinus*, Lat.] Belonging to a hare; having the nature of a hare.

LEPRO'SITY. *n. s.* [from *leprous.*] Squamous disease.
If the crudities, impurities, and *leprosities* of metals were cured, they would become gold. *Bacon's Nat. Hist.*

LE'PROSY. *n. s.* [*lepra*, Latin; *lepre*, French.] A loathsome distemper, which covers the body with a kind of white scales.
Itches, blains,
Sow all the Athenian bosoms, and their crop
Be general *leprosy*. *Shakesp. Timon of Athens.*
It is a plague of *leprosy*. *Lev.* xiii. 3.
Between the malice of my enemies and other mens mistakes, I put as great a difference as between the itch of novelty and the *leprosy* of disloyalty. *King Charles.*
Authors, upon the first entrance of the pox, looked upon it so highly infectious, that they ran away from it as much as the Jews did from the *leprosy*. *Wiseman's Surgery.*

LE'PROUS. *adj.* [*lepra*, Latin; *lepreux*, French.] Infected with a leprosy.
The silly amorous sucks his death,
By drawing in a *leprous* harlot's breath. *Donne.*

LERE. *n. s.* [læꝛe, Saxon; *leere*, Dutch.] A lesson; lore; doctrine. This sense is still retained in Scotland.
The kid pitying his heaviness,
Asked the cause of his great distress;
And also who, and whence, that he were,
Though he that had well ycond his *lere*,
Thus melled his talk with many a teare. *Spenser.*

LE'RRY. [from *lere.*] A rating; a lecture. rustick word.

LESS. A negative or privative termination. [leaꝛ, Saxon; *loos*, Dutch.] Joined to a substantive, it implies the absence or privation of the thing expressed by that substantive: as, a *witless* man, a man without wit; *childless*, without children; *fatherless*, deprived of a father; *pennyless*, wanting money.

LESS. *adj.* [leaꝛ, Saxon.] The comparative of little: opposed to greater.
Mary, the mother of James the *less*. *Mar.* xv. 40.
Yet could he not his closing eyes withdraw,
Though *less* and *less* of Emily he saw. *Dryden.*
He that thinks he has a positive idea of infinite space will find, that he can no more have a positive idea of the greatest than he has of the least space; for in this latter we are capable only of a comparative idea of smallness, which will always be *less* than any one whereof we have the positive idea. *Locke.*
All the ideas that are considered as having parts, and are capable of increase by the addition of any equal or *less* parts, affords us, by their repetition, the idea of infinity. *Locke.*
'Tis *less* to conquer, than to make wars cease,
And, without fighting, awe the world to peace. *Hallifax.*

LESS. *n. s.* Not so much; opposed to more.
They gathered some more, some *less*. *Exod.* xvi. 17.
Thy servant knew nothing of this, *less* or more. 1 *Sam.*

LESS. *adv.* In a smaller degree; in a lower degree.
This opinion presents a *less* merry, but not *less* dangerous, temptation to those in adversity. *Decay of Piety.*
The less space there is betwixt us and the object, and the more pure the air is, by so much the more the species are preserved and distinguished; and, on the contrary, the more space of air there is, and the *less* it is pure, so much the more the object is confused and embroiled. *Dryden.*
Their learning lay chiefly in flourish; they were not much wiser than the *less* pretending multitude. *Collier on Pride.*
The less they themselves want to receive from others, they will be *less* careful to supply the necessities of the indigent.
Smalridge's Sermons.
Happy, and happy still, she might have prov'd,
Were she *less* beautiful, or *less* belov'd. *Pope's Statius.*

LE'SSEE. *n. s.* The person to whom a lease is given.

To LESSEN. *v. a.* [from *less.*]
1. To diminish in bulk.
2. To diminish in degree of any quality.
Kings may give
To beggars, and not *lessen* their own greatness. *Denham.*

Though charity alone will not make one happy in the other world, yet it ſhall *leſſen* his puniſhment. *Calamy's Serm.*

Collect into one ſum as great a number as you pleaſe, this multitude, how great ſoever, *leſſens* not one jot the power of adding to it, or brings him any nearer the end of the inexhauſtible ſtock of number. *Locke.*

This thirſt after fame betrays him into ſuch indecencies as are a *leſſening* to his reputation, and is looked upon as a weakneſs in the greateſt characters. *Addiſon's Spectator.*

Nor are the pleaſures which the brutal part of the creation enjoy, ſubject to be *leſſened* by the uneaſineſs which ariſes from fancy. *Atterbury's Sermons.*

3. To degrade; to deprive of power or dignity.

Who ſeeks
To *leſſen* thee, againſt his purpoſe ſerves
To manifeſt the more thy might. *Milton's Par. Loſt.*

St. Paul choſe to magnify his office, when ill men conſpired to *leſſen* it. *Atterbury Sermons.*

To LE'SSEN. *v. n.* To grow leſs; to ſhrink; to be diminiſhed.

All government may be eſteemed to grow ſtrong or weak, as the general opinion in thoſe that govern is ſeen to *leſſen* or increaſe. *Temple.*

The objection *leſſens* very much, and comes to no more than this, there was one witneſs of no good reputation. *Atterbury's Sermons.*

LE'SSER. *adj.* A barbarous corruption of *leſs*, formed by the vulgar from the habit of terminating comparatives in *er*; afterwards adopted by poets, and then by writers of proſe.

What great deſpite doth fortune to thee bear,
Thus lowly to abaſe thy beauty bright,
That it ſhould not deface all other *leſſer* light. *Fa. Qu.*

It is the *leſſer* blot, modeſty finds,
Women to change their ſhapes than men their minds.
Shakeſpeare's Two Gentlemen of Verona.

The mountains, and higher parts of the earth, grow *leſſer* and *leſſer* from age to age: ſometimes the roots of them are weakened by ſubterraneous fires, and ſometimes tumbled by earthquakes into thoſe caverns that are under them. *Burnet's Theory of the Earth.*

Cain, after the murder of his brother, cries out, Every man that findeth me ſhall ſlay me. By the ſame reaſon may a man, in the ſtate of nature, puniſh the *leſſer* breaches of that law. *Locke.*

Any heat whatſoever promotes the aſcent of mineral matter, but more eſpecially of that which is ſubtile, and is conſequently moveable more eaſily, and with a *leſſer* power. *Woodward's Natural Hiſtory.*

The larger here, and there the *leſſer* lambs,
The new-fall'n young herd bleating for their dams. *Pope.*

LE'SSER. *adv.* [formed by corruption from *leſs*.]

Some ſay he's mad; others, that *leſſer* hate him,
Do call it valiant fury. *Shakeſpeare's Macbeth.*

LE'SSES. *n. ſ.* [*laiſſées*, French.] The dung of beaſts left on the ground.

LE'SSON. *n. ſ.* [*leçon*, French; *lectio*, Latin.]

1. Any thing read or repeated to a teacher, in order to improvement.

I but repeat that *leſſon*
Which I have learn'd from thee. *Denham's Sophy.*

2. Precept; notion inculcated.

This days enſample hath this *leſſon* dear
Deep written in my heart with iron pen,
That bliſs may not abide in ſtate of mortal men. *Fa. Qu.*

Be not jealous over the wife of thy boſom, and teach her not an evil *leſſon* againſt thyſelf. *Eccluſ.* ix. 1.

3. Portions of ſcripture read in divine ſervice.

Notwithſtanding ſo eminent properties, whereof *leſſons* are happily deſtitute; yet *leſſons* being free from ſome inconveniences whereunto ſermons are more ſubject, they may, in this reſpect, no leſs take, than in other they muſt give the hand which betokeneth pre-eminence. *Hooker, b.* v.

4. Tune pricked for an inſtrument.

Thoſe good laws were like good *leſſons* ſet for a flute out of tune; of which *leſſons* little uſe can be made, till the flute be made fit to be played on. *Davies on Ireland.*

5. A rating lecture.

She would give her a *leſſon* for walking ſo late, that ſhould make her keep within doors for one fortnight. *Sidney.*

To LE'SSON. *v. a.* [from the noun.] To teach; to inſtruct.

Even in kind love, I do conjure thee,
To *leſſon* me. *Shakeſp. Two Gentlemen of Verona.*

Well haſt thou *leſſon'd* us, this ſhall we do. *Shakeſp.*

Children ſhould be ſeaſoned betimes, and *leſſoned* into a contempt and deteſtation of this vice. *L'Eſtrange's Fables.*

LE'SSOR. *n. ſ.* One who lets any thing to farm, or otherwiſe, by leaſe.

Lords of the world have but for life their leaſe,
And that too, if the *leſſor* pleaſe, muſt ceaſe. *Denham.*

If he demiſes the glebe to a layman, the tenant muſt pay the ſmall tithes to the vicar, and the great tithes to the *leſſor*. *Ayliffe's Parergon.*

LEST. *conj.* [from the adjective *leaſt*.] That not.

Forty ſtripes he may give him, and not exceed; *leſt* if he ſhould exceed, then thy brother ſhould ſeem vile. *Deut.* xxv.

King Luitprand brought hither the corps, *leſt* it might be abuſed by the barbarous nations. *Addiſon on Italy.*

LE'STERCOCK. *n. ſ.*

Upon the north coaſt, for want of good harbours they have a device of two ſticks filled with corks, and croſſed flatlong, out of whoſe midſt there riſeth a thread, and at the ſame hangeth a ſail; to this engine, termed a *leſtercock*, they tie one end of their boulter, ſo as the wind coming from the ſhore filleth the ſail, and the ſail carrieth the boulter into the ſea, which, after the reſpite of ſome hours, is drawn in again by a cord faſtened at the nearer end. *Carew on Cornwall.*

To LET. *v. a.* [lætan, Saxon.]

1. To allow; to ſuffer; to permit.

Nay, nay, quoth he, *let* be your ſtrife and doubt. *Fairf.*

Where there is a certainty and an uncertainty, *let* the uncertainty go, and hold to that which is certain. *Bp. Sanderſon.*

On the croud he caſt a furious look,
And wither'd all their ſtrength before he ſpoke;
Back on your lives, *let* be, ſaid he, my prey,
And let my vengeance take the deſtin'd way. *Dryden.*

Remember me; ſpeak, Raymond, will you *let* him?
Shall he remember Leonora. *Dryden's Spaniſh Friar.*

We muſt not *let* go manifeſt truths, becauſe we cannot anſwer all queſtions about them. *Collier.*

One who fixes his thoughts intently on one thing, ſo as to take but little notice of the ſucceſſion of ideas in his mind, *lets* ſlip out of his account a good part of that duration. *Locke.*

A ſolution of mercury in aqua fortis being poured upon iron, copper, tin, or lead, diſſolves the metal, and *lets* go the mercury. *Newton's Opticks.*

2. A ſign of the optative mood uſed before the firſt and imperative before the third perſon. Before the firſt perſon ſingular it ſignifies reſolution; fixed purpoſe, or ardent wiſh.

Let me die with the Philiſtines. *Judges.*

Here is her picture: *let* me ſee; I think,
If I had ſuch a tire, this face of mine
Were full as lovely as in this of her's. *Shakeſpeare.*

3. Before the firſt perſon plural, *let* implies exhortation.

Riſe; *let* us go. *Mark.*

4. Before the third perſon, ſingular or plural, *let* implies permiſſion or precept.

Let the ſoldiers ſeize him for one of the aſſaſſinates. *Dryd.*

5. Before a thing in the paſſive voice, *let* implies command.

Let not the objects which ought to be contiguous be ſeparated, and *let* thoſe which ought to be ſeparated be apparently ſo to us; but *let* this be done by a ſmall and pleaſing difference. *Dryden's Dufreſnoy.*

6. *Let* has an infinitive mood after it without the particle *to*.

But one ſubmiſſive word which you *let* fall,
Will make him in good humour with us all. *Dryden.*

The ſeventh year thou ſhalt *let* it reſt, and lie ſtill. *Exod.*

7. To leave.

They did me too much injury,
That ever ſaid I hearken'd for your death.
If it were ſo, I might have *let* alone
Th' inſulting hand of Douglas over you. *Shakeſpeare.*

The publick outrages of a deſtroying tyranny are but childiſh appetites, *let* alone till they are grown ungovernable. *L'Eſtrange's Fables.*

Let me alone to accuſe him afterwards. *Dryd. Sp. Friar.*

This is of no uſe, and had been better *let* alone: he is fain to reſolve all into preſent poſſeſſion. *Locke.*

Neſtor, do not *let* us alone till you have ſhortened our necks, and reduced them to their antient ſtandard. *Addiſon.*

This notion might be *let* alone and deſpiſed as a piece of harmleſs unintelligible enthuſiaſm. *Rogers's Sermons.*

8. To more than permit.

There's a letter for you, Sir, if your name be Horatio, as I am *let* to know it is. *Shakeſpeare's Hamlet.*

9. To put to hire; to grant to a tenant.

Solomon had a vineyard at Baal Hamon; he *let* the vineyard unto keepers. *Cant.* viii. 11.

Nothing deadens ſo much the compoſition of a picture, as figures which appertain not to the ſubject: we may call them figures to be *let*. *Dryden's Dufreſnoy.*

She *let* her ſecond floor to a very genteel youngiſh man. *Tatler*, N°. 88.

A law was enacted, prohibiting all biſhops, and other eccleſiaſtical corporations, from *letting* their lands for above the term of twenty years. *Swift.*

10. To ſuffer any thing to take a courſe which requires no impulſive violence.

She *let* them down by a cord through the window. *Joſh.*

Launch out into the deep, and *let* down your nets for a draught. *Luke* v. 4.

Let

Let down thy pitcher, I pray thee, that I may drink. *Gen.* xxiv. 14.

My heart sinks in me while I hear him speak,
And every slacken'd fibre drops its hold;
Like nature *letting* down the springs of life:
So much the name of father awes me still. *Dryden.*

From this point of the story, the poet is *let* down to his traditional poverty. *Pope's Essay on Homer.*

You must *let* it down, that is, make it softer by tempering it. *Moxon's Mechanical Exercises.*

11. To permit to take any state or course.

Finding an ease in not understanding, he *let* loose his thoughts wholly to pleasure. *Sidney, b.* ii.

Let reason teach impossibility in any thing, and the will of man doth *let* it go. *Hooker, b.* i.

The beginning of strife is as when one *letteth* out water. *Prov.* xvii. 14.

As terebration doth meliorate fruit, so doth pricking vines or trees after they be of some growth, and thereby *letting* forth gum or tears. *Bacon's Natural History.*

And if I knew which way to do't,
Your honour safe, I'd *let* you out. *Hudibras.*

The *letting* out our love to mutable objects doth but enlarge our hearts, and make them the wider marks for fortune to be wounded. *Boyle.*

He was *let* loose among the woods as soon as he was able to ride on horseback, or carry a gun. *Addison's Spectator.*

12. *To* LET *blood*, is elliptical for *to let out blood.* To free it from confinement; to suffer it to stream out of the vein.

Be rul'd by me;
Let's purge this choler without *letting blood. Shakespeare.*

Hippocrates *let* great quantities of *blood*, and opened several veins at a time. *Arbuthnot on Coins.*

13. *To* LET *blood*, is used with a dative of the person whose blood is let.

Tell him, Catesby,
His antient knot of dangerous adversaries
To-morrow are *let blood* at Pomfret castle. *Shakespeare.*

As terebration doth meliorate fruit, so doth *letting* plants *blood*, as pricking vines, thereby letting forth tears. *Bacon.*

14. *To* LET *in.* To admit.

Let in your king, whose labour'd spirits,
Sore wearied in this action of swift speed,
Crave harbourage within your city walls. *Shakespeare.*

Roscetes presented his army before the gates of the city, in hopes that the citizens would raise some tumult, and *let* him *in.* *Knolles's History of the Turks.*

What boots it at one gate to make defence,
And at another to *let in* the foe,
Effeminately vanquish'd. *Milton's Agonistes.*

The more tender our spirits are made by religion, the more easy we are to *let in* grief, if the cause be innocent. *Taylor's Rule of Holy Living.*

They but preserve the ashes, thou the flame,
True to his sense, but truer to his fame,
Fording his current, where thou find'st it low,
Let'st in thine own to make it rise and flow. *Denham.*

To give a period to my life, and to his fears, you're welcome; here's a throat, a heart, or any other part, ready to *let in* death, and receive his commands. *Denham.*

It is the key that *lets* them *into* their very heart, and enables them to command all that is there. *South's Sermons.*

There are pictures of such as have been distinguished by their birth or miracles, with inscriptions, that *let* you *into* the name and history of the person represented. *Addison.*

Most historians have spoken of ill success, and terrible events, as if they had been *let into* the secrets of providence, and made acquainted with that private conduct by which the world is governed. *Addison's Spectator,* N°. 483.

These are not mysteries for ordinary readers to be *let into.* *Addison's Spectator,* N°. 221.

As soon as they have hewn down any quantity of the rocks, they *let in* their springs and reservoirs among their works. *Addison on Italy.*

As we rode through the town, I was *let into* the characters of all the inhabitants; one was a dog, another a whelp, and another a cur. *Addison's Freeholder.*

15. *To* LET *in.* To procure admission.

They should speak properly and correctly, whereby they may *let* their thoughts *into* other mens minds the more easily. *Locke.*

16. *To* LET *off.* To discharge. Originally used of an arrow dismissed from the gripe, and therefore suffered to fly off the string; now applied to guns.

Charging my pistol only with powder, I first cautioned the emperor not to be afraid, and then *let* it *off* in the air. *Swift.*

17. *To* LET *out.* To lease out; to give to hire or farm.

18. *To* LET. [lettan, Saxon.] To hinder; to obstruct; to oppose.

Their senses are not *letted* from enjoying their objects: we have the impediments of honour, and the torments of conscience. *Sidney.*

To glorify him in all things, is to do nothing whereby the name of God may be blasphemed; nothing whereby the salvation of Jew or Grecian, or any in the church of Christ, may be *let* or hindered. *Hooker, b.* i.

Leave, ah leave off, whatever wight thou be,
To *let* a weary wretch from her due rest,
And trouble dying soul's tranquillity. *Fairy Queen.*

Wherefore do ye *let* the people from their works; go you unto your burdens. *Exod.* v. 4.

The mystery of iniquity doth already work; only he who now *letteth* will *let*, until he be taken out of the way. 2 *Thess.*

I will work, and who will *let* it. *Isa.* xliii. 11.

And now no longer *letted* of his prey,
He leaps up at it with enrag'd desire,
O'erlooks the neighbours with a wide survey,
And nods at every house his threatening fire. *Dryden.*

19. *To* LET, when it signifies *to permit* or *leave*, has *let* in the preterite and part. passive; but when it signifies *to hinder*, it has *letted*; as, *multa me impedierunt, many things have letted me.* *Introduction to Grammar.*

To LET. *v. n.* To forbear; to withold himself.

After king Ferdinando had taken upon him the person of a fraternal ally to the king, he would not *let* to counsel the king. *Bacon's Henry* VII.

LET. *n. s.* [from the verb.] Hindrance; obstacle; obstruction; impediment.

The secret *lets* and difficulties in public proceedings are innumerable and inevitable. *Hooker, b.* i.

Solyman without *let* presented his army before the city of Belgrade. *Knolles's History of the Turks.*

It had been done e'er this, had I been consul;
We had had no stop, no *let.* *Benj. Johnson's Catiline.*

Just judge, two *lets* remove; that free from dread,
I may before thy high tribunal plead. *Sandys on Job.*

To these internal dispositions to sin add the external opportunities and occasions concurring with them, and removing all *lets* and rubs out of the way, and making the path of destruction plain before the sinner's face; so that he may run his course freely. *South.*

LET, the termination of diminutive words, from lyte, Saxon, *little, small.*

LETHA'RGICK. *adj.* [*lethargique*, Fr. from *lethargy.*] Sleepy, beyond the natural power of sleep.

Vengeance is as if minutely proclaimed in thunder from heaven, to give men no rest in their sins, till they awake from the *lethargick* sleep, and arise from so dead, so mortiferous a state. *Hammond's Fundamentals.*

Let me but try if I can wake his pity
From his *lethargick* sleep. *Denham's Sophy.*

A lethargy demands the same cure and diet as an apoplexy from a phlegmatick case, such being the constitution of the *lethargick.* *Arbuthnot on Diet.*

LETHA'RGICKNESS. *n. s.* [from *lethargick.*] Sleepiness; drowsiness.

A grain of glory mixt with humbleness,
Cures both a fever, and *lethargickness.* *Herbert.*

LE'THARGY. *n. s.* [ληθαργία; *lethargie*, Fr.] A morbid drowsiness; a sleep from which one cannot be kept awake.

The *lethargy* must have his quiet course;
If not, he foams at mouth, and by and by
Breaks out to savage madness. *Shakespeare's Othello.*

Though his eye is open, as the morning's,
Towards lusts and pleasures; yet so fast a *lethargy*
Has seiz'd his powers towards publick cares and dangers,
He sleeps like death. *Denham's Sophy.*

Europe lay then under a deep *lethargy*; and was no otherwise to be rescued from it, but by one that would cry mightily. *Atterbury.*

A *lethargy* is a lighter sort of apoplexy, and demands the same cure and diet. *Arbuthnot on Diet.*

LE'THARGIED. *adj.* [from the noun.] Laid asleep; entranced.

His motion weakens, or his discernings
Are *lethargied.* *Shakespeare's King Lear.*

LE'THE. *n. s.* [λήθη.] Oblivion; a draught of oblivion.

The conquering wine hath steept our sense
In soft and delicate *lethe.* *Shakes. Ant. and Cleopatra.*

Lethe, the river of oblivion, rolls
Her wat'ry labyrinth, which who so drinks
Forgets both joy and grief. *Milton.*

LE'TTER. *n. s.* [from *let.*]

1. One who lets or permits.
2. One who hinders.
3. One who gives vent to any thing; as a blood letter.

LE'TTER. *n. s.* [*lettre*, French; *litera*, Latin.]

1. One of the elements of syllables.

A superscription was written over him in *letters* of Greek, Latin, and Hebrew. *Luke* xxiii. 38.

Thou whoreson Zed! thou unnecessary *letter!* *Shakes.*

2. A written message; an epistle.

They use to write it on the top of *letters*. *Shakespeare.*

I have a *letter* from her
Of such contents as you will wonder at. *Shakespeare.*

When a Spaniard would write a *letter* by him, the Indian would marvel how it should be possible, that he, to whom he came, should be able to know all things. *Abbot.*

The asses will do very well for trumpeters, and the hares will make excellent *letter* carriers. *L'Estrange's Fables.*

The stile of *letters* ought to be free, easy, and natural; as near approaching to familiar conversation as possible: the two best qualities in conversation are, good humour and good breeding; those *letters* are therefore certainly the best that shew the most of these two qualities. *Walsh.*

Mrs. P. B. has writ to me, and is one of the best *letter* writers I know; very good sense, civility, and friendship, without any stiffness or constraint. *Swift.*

3. The literal or expressed meaning.

Touching translations of holy scripture, we may not disallow of their painful travels herein, who strictly have tied themselves to the very original *letter*. *Hooker, b.* v.

In obedience to human laws, we must observe the *letter* of the law, without doing violence to the reason of the law, and the intention of the lawgiver. *Taylor's holy living.*

Those words of his must be understood not according to the bare rigour of the *letter*, but according to the allowances of expression. *South's Sermons.*

What! since the pretor did my fetters loose,
And left me freely at my own dispose,
May I not live without controul and awe,
Excepting still the *letter* of the law? *Dryden's Persius.*

4. *Letters* without the singular: learning.

The Jews marvelled, saying, How knoweth this man *letters*, having never learned? *John* vii. 15.

5. Any thing to be read.

Good laws are at best but a dead *letter*. *Addis. Freeholder.*

6. Type with which books are printed.

The iron ladles that *letter* founders use to the casting of printing *letters*, are kept constantly in melting metal. *Moxon.*

To LE'TTER. *v. a.* [from *letter*.] To stamp with letters.

I observed one weight *lettered* on both sides; and I found on one side, written in the dialect of men, and underneath it, calamities; on the other side was written, in the language of the gods, and underneath, blessings. *Addison.*

LE'TTERED. *adj.* [from *letter*.] Literate; educated to learning.

A martial man, not sweetened by a *lettered* education, is apt to have a tincture of sourness. *Collier on Pride.*

LE'TTUCE. *n. s.* *lactuca*, Latin.]

The *lettuce* hath a fibrous root, which is, for the most part, annual; the leaves are smooth, and grow alternately upon the branches; the stalks are, for the most part, tender, slender, and stiff, and commonly terminate in a sort of umbel; the cup of the flower is oblong, slender, and scaly; the seeds are oblong, depressed, and generally terminate in a point: the species are, common or garden *lettuce*; cabbage *lettuce*; Silesia *lettuce*; white and black cos; white cos; red capuchin *lettuce*. *Miller.*

Fat colworts, and comforting purseline,
Cold *lettice*, and refreshing rosemarine. *Spenser.*

Lettuce is thought to be poisonous, when it is so old as to have milk. *Bacon's Natural History.*

The medicaments proper to diminish milk, are *lettice*, purslane, endive. *Wiseman's Surgery.*

LE'VANT. *adj.* [*levant*, French.] Eastern.

Thwart of those, as fierce
Forth rush the *levant*, and the ponent winds,
Eurus and Zephyr. *Milton's Paradise Lost, b.* x.

LEVA'NT. *n. s.* The east, particularly those coasts of the Mediterranean east of Italy.

LEVA'TOR. n. s. [Lat.] A chirurgical instrument, whereby depressed parts of the skull are lifted up.

Some surgeons bring out the bone in the bore; but it will be safer to raise it up with your *levator*, when it is but lightly retained in some part. *Wiseman's Surgery.*

LEUCOPHLE'GMACY. *n. s.* [from *leucophlegmatick*.] Paleness, with viscid juices and cold sweatings.

Spirits produce debility, flatulency, fevers, *leucophlegmacy*, and dropsies. *Arbuthnot on Aliments.*

LEUCOPHLEGMA'TICK. *adj.* [λευκὸς and φλέγμα.] Having such a constitution of body where the blood is of a pale colour, viscid, and cold, whereby it stuffs and bloats the habit, or raises white tumours in the feet, legs, or any other parts; and such are commonly asthmatick and dropsical. *Quincy.*

Asthmatic persons have voracious appetites, and for want of a right sanguification are *leucophlegmatick*. *Arbuthnot.*

LE'VEE. n. s. [French.]

1. The time of rising.

2. The concourse of those who croud round a man of power in a morning.

The servile rout their careful Cæsar praise;
Him they extol, they worship him alone,
They croud his *levees*, and support his throne. *Dryden.*

Woud'st thou be first minister of state?
To have thy *levees* crouded with resort,
Of a depending, gaping, servile court. *Dryden's Juvenal.*

None of her Sylvan subjects made their court,
Levees and couchees pass'd without resort. *Dryden.*

LE'VEL. *adj.* [læfel, Saxon.]

1. Even; not having one part higher than another.

The garden, seated on the *level* floor,
She left behind, and locking ev'ry door,
Thought all secure. *Dryden's Boccace.*

Be *level* in preferments, and you will soon be as *level* in your learning. *Bentley.*

2. Even with any thing else; in the same line with any thing.

Our navy is addressed, our pow'r collected,
Our substitutes in absence well invested,
And ev'ry thing lies *level* to our wish. *Shakesp. Henry* IV.

There is a knowledge which is very proper to man, and lies *level* to human understanding; and that is, the knowledge of our Creator, and of the duty we owe to him. *Tillotson's Sermons.*

To LE'VEL. *v. a.* [from the adjective.]

1. To make even; to free from inequalities.

2. To reduce to the same height with something else.

Reason can never assent to the admission of those brutish appetites which would over-run the soul, and *level* its superior with its inferior faculties. *Decay of Piety.*

Behold the law
And rule of beings in your maker's mind:
And thence, like limbecks, rich ideas draw,
To fit the *levell'd* use of humankind. *Dryden.*

3. To lay flat.

We know by experience, that all downright rains do evermore dissever the violence of outrageous winds, and beat down and *level* the swelling and mountainous billows of the sea. *Raleigh.*

He will thy foes with silent shame confound,
And their proud structures *level* with the ground. *Sandys.*

With unresisted might the monarch reigns,
He *levels* mountains, and he raises plains;
And not regarding diff'rence of degree,
Abas'd your daughter, and exalted me. *Dryden.*

4. To bring to equality of condition.

5. To point in taking aim; to aim.

One to the gunners on St. Jago's tow'r,
Bid 'em for shame,
Level their canon lower. *Dryden's Spanish Friar.*

6. To direct to any end.

The whole body of puritans was drawn to be abettors of all villainy by a few men, whose designs from the first were *levelled* to destroy both religion and government. *Swift.*

To LE'VEL. *v. n.*

1. To aim at; to bring the gun or arrow to the same direction with the mark.

The glory of God, and the good of his church, was the thing which the apostles aimed at, and therefore ought to be the mark whereat we also *level*. *Hooker, b.* iv.

2. To conjecture; to attempt to guess.

I pray thee overname them; and as thou namest them I will describe them; and, according to my description, *level* at my affection. *Shakes. Merchant of Venice.*

3. To be in the same direction with a mark.

He to his engine flew,
Plac'd near at hand in open view,
And rais'd it till it *levell'd* right,
Against the glow-worm tail of kite. *Hudibras, p.* ii.

4. To make attempts; to aim.

Ambitious York did *level* at thy crown. *Shakespeare.*

LE'VEL. *n. s.* [from the adjective.]

1. A plane; a surface without protuberances or inequalities.

After draining of the *level* in Northamptonshire, innumerable mice did upon a sudden arise. *Hale's Original of Mank.*

Those bred in a mountainous country oversize those that dwell on low *levels*. *Sandys's Travels.*

2. Rate; standard.

Love of her made us raise up our thoughts above the ordinary *level* of the world, so as great clerks do not disdain our conference. *Sidney.*

It might perhaps advance their minds so far
Above the *level* of subjection, as
T' assume to them the glory of that war. *Daniel.*

The praises of military men inspired me with thoughts above my ordinary *level*. *Dryden.*

3. A state of equality.

The time is not far off when we shall be upon the *level*; I am resolved to anticipate the time, and be upon the *level* with them now: for he is so that neither seeks nor wants them. *Atterbury to Pope.*

Providence,

Providence, for the most part, set us upon a *level*, and observes a kind of proportion in its dispensations towards us. *Addison's Spectator*, N°. 255.

I suppose, by the stile of old friend, and the like, it must be somebody there of his own *level*; among whom his party have, indeed, more friends than I could wish. *Swift.*

4. An instrument whereby masons adjust their work.

The *level* is from two to ten feet long, that it may reach over a considerable length of the work: if the plumb-line hang just upon the perpendicular, when the *level* is set flat down upon the work, the work is level; but if it hangs on either side the perpendicular, the floor or work must be raised on that side, till the plumb-line hang exactly on the perpendicular. *Moxon's Mechanical Exercises.*

5. Rule: borrowed from the mechanick level.

Be the fair *level* of thy actions laid,
As temp'rance wills, and prudence may persuade,
And try if life be worth the liver's care. *Prior.*

6. The line of direction in which any missive weapon is aimed.

I stood i' th' *level*
Of a full charg'd confederacy, and gave thanks
To you that choked it. *Shakespeare's Henry* VIII.

As if that name,
Shot from the deadly *level* of a gun,
Did murther her. *Shakesp. Romeo and Juliet.*

Thrice happy is that humble pair,
Beneath the *level* of all care,
Over whose heads those arrows fly,
Of sad distrust and jealousy. *Waller.*

7. The line in which the sight passes.

Fir'd at first sight with what the muse imparts,
In fearless youth we tempt the heights of arts;
While from the bounded *level* of our mind
Short views we take, nor see the lengths behind. *Pope.*

LE'VELLER. *n. s.* [from *level.*]

1. One who makes any thing even.
2. One who destroys superiority; one who endeavours to bring all to the same state of equality.

You are an everlasting *leveller*; you won't allow encouragement to extraordinary merit. *Collier on Pride.*

LE'VELNESS. *n. s.* [from *level.*]

1. Evenness; equality of surface.
2. Equality with something else.

The river Tiber is expressed lying along, for so you must remember to draw rivers, to express their *levelness* with the earth. *Peacham.*

LE'VEN. *n. s.* [*levain*, French.]

1. Ferment; that which being mixed in bread makes it rise and ferment.
2. Any thing capable of changing the nature of a greater mass; any thing that tinctures the whole.

The matter fermenteth upon the old *leven*, and becometh more acrid. *Wiseman's Surgery.*

As to the pestilential *levains* conveyed in goods, it is a safe opinion. *Arbuthnot on Air.*

LE'VER. *n. s.* [*levier*, French.]

The second mechanical power, is a balance supported by a hypomochlion; only the centre is not in the middle, as in the common balance, but near one end; for which reason it is used to elevate or raise a great weight; whence comes the name *lever*. *Harris.*

Have you any *leavers* to lift me up again, being down. *Shakespeare's Henry* IV.

Some draw with cords, and some the monster drive
With rolls and *levers*. *Denham.*

In a *leaver*, the motion can be continued only for so short a space, as may be answerable to that little distance betwixt the fulciment and the weight; which is always by so much lesser, as the disproportion betwixt the weight and the power is greater, and the motion itself more easy. *Wilkins's Magick.*

Some hoisting *leavers*, some the wheels prepare. *Dryd.*

You may have a wooden *lever*, forked at the ends. *Mort.*

LE'VERET. [*leivre*, French.] A young hare.

Their travels o'er that silver field does show,
Like track of *leverets* in morning snow. *Waller.*

LEVE'T. *n. s.* [from *lever*, French.] A blast on the trumpet; probably that by which the soldiers are called in the morning.

He that led the cavalcade,
Wore a sowgelder's flagellet,
On which he blew as strong a *levet*;
As well-fee'd lawyer on his breviate. *Hudibras.*

LEVEROOK. *n. s.* [lapepe, Saxon.] This word is retained in Scotland, and denotes the lark.

The smaller birds have their particular seasons; as, the *leverook*. *Walton's Angler.*

If the lufft faa 'twill smoore aw the *leverooks*. *Scotch Prov.*

LE'VIABLE. *adj.* [from *levy.*] That may be levied.

The sums which any agreed to pay, and were not brought in, were to be *leviable* by course of law. *Bacon's Henry* VII.

LEVI'ATHAN. n. s. [לויתן.] A water animal mentioned in the book of *Job*. By some imagined the crocodile, but in poetry generally taken for the whale.

We may, as bootless, spend our vain command
Upon th' enraged soldiers in their spoil,
As send our precepts to th' *leviathan*,
To come ashore. *Shakespeare's Henry* V.

Canst thou draw out *leviathan* with an hook? *Job.*

More to embroil the deep; *leviathan*,
And his unwieldy train, in dreadful sport
Tempest the loosen'd brine. *Thomson's Winter.*

To LE'VIGATE. *v. a.* [*lævigo*, Latin.]

1. To rub or grind to an impalpable powder.
2. To mix till the liquor becomes smooth and uniform.

The chyle is white, as consisting of salt, oil, and water, much *levigated* or smooth. *Arbuthnot on Aliment.*

LEVIGA'TION. *n. s.* [from *levigate.*]

Levigation is the reducing of hard bodies, as coral, tutty, and precious stones, into a subtile powder, by grinding upon marble with a muller; but unless the instruments are extremely hard, they will so wear as to double the weight of the medicine. *Quincy.*

LE'VITE. *n. s.* [*levita*, Latin, from *Levi.*]

1. One of the tribe of Levi; one born to the office of priesthood among the Jews.

In the Christian church, the office of deacons succeeded in the place of the *levites* among the Jews, who were as ministers and servants to the priests. *Ayliffe's Parergon.*

2. A priest: used in contempt.

LEVI'TICAL. *adj.* [from *levite.*] Belonging to the levites; making part of the religion of the Jews.

By the *levitical* law, both the man and the woman were stoned to death; so heinous a crime was the sin of adultery. *Ayliffe's Parergon.*

LE'VITY. *n. s.* [*levitas*, Latin.]

1. Lightness; not heaviness: the quality by which any body has less weight than another.

He gave the form of *levity* to that which ascended; to that which descended, the form of gravity. *Raleigh.*

This bubble, by reason of its comparative *levity* to the fluidity that encloses it, would necessarily ascend to the top. *Bentley's Sermons.*

2. Inconstancy; changeableness.

They every day broached some new thing; which restless *levity* they did interpret to be their growing in spiritual perfection. *Hooker.*

Where wigs with wigs, with sword-knots sword-knots strive,
Beaus banish beaus, and coaches coaches drive,
This erring mortals *levity* may call. *Pope.*

3. Unsteadiness; laxity of mind.

I unbosom'd all my secrets to thee;
Not out of *levity*, but over-pow'r'd
By thy request. *Milton's Agonistes.*

4. Idle pleasure; vanity.

He never employed his omnipotence out of *levity* or ostentation, but as the necessities of men required. *Calamy.*

5. Trifling gaiety; want of seriousness.

Our graver business frowns at this *levity*. *Shakespeare.*

Hopton abhorred the licence, and the *levities*, with which he saw too many corrupted. *Clarendon, b.* viii.

That spirit of religion and seriousness vanished, and a spirit of *levity* and libertinism, infidelity and prophaneness, started up in the room of it. *Atterbury's Sermons.*

To LE'VY. *v. a.* [*lever*, French.]

1. To raise; to bring together men.

He resolved to finish the conquest of Ireland, and to that end *levied* a mighty army. *Davies on Ireland.*

2. To raise money.

Levy a tribute unto the Lord of the men of war. *Numb.*

Instead of a ship, he should *levy* upon his county such a sum of money. *Clarendon.*

3. To make war. This sense, though *Milton*'s, seems improper.

They live in hatred, enmity, and strife,
Among themselves, and *levy* cruel wars. *Milton.*

LE'VY. *n. s.* [from the verb.]

1. The act of raising money or men.

They have already contributed all their superfluous hands, and every new *levy* they make must be at the expence of their farms and commerce. *Addison's State of the War.*

2. War raised.

Treason has done his worst: nor steel, nor poison,
Malice domestick, foreign *levy*, nothing
Can touch him further! *Shakespeare's Macbeth.*

LEWD. *adj.* [læpede, Saxon.]

1. Lay; not clerical. Obsolete.

For *lewyd* men this book I writ. *Bishop Grosthead.*

So these great clerks their little wisdom shew
To mock the *lewd*, as learn'd in this as they. *Davies.*

2. Wicked; bad; naughty.

If some be admitted into the ministry, either void of learning, or *lewd* in life, are all the rest to be condemned? *Whitgift.*

Before

Before they did oppress the people, only by colour of a *lewd* custom, they did afterwards use the same oppressions by warrant. *Davies on Ireland.*

3. Lustful; libidinous.

He is not lolling on a *lewd* love bed,
But on his knees at meditation. *Shakespeare's Rich.* III.
Then *lewd* Anchemolus he laid in dust,
Who stain'd his stepdam's bed with impious lust. *Dryden.*

LE'WDLY. *adj.* [from *lewd.*]

1. Wickedly; naughtily.

A sort of naughty persons, *lewdly* bent,
Have practis'd dangerously against your state. *Shakesp.*

2. Libidinously; lustfully.

He lov'd fair lady Eltred, *lewdly* lov'd,
Whose wanton pleasures him too much did please,
That quite his heart from Guendeline remov'd. *Spenser.*
So *lewdly* dull his idle works appear,
The wretched texts deserve no comments here. *Dryden.*

LE'WDNESS. *n. s.* [from *lewd.*] Lustful licentiousness.

Suffer no *lewdness*, nor indecent speech,
Th' apartment of the tender youth to reach. *Dryd. Juv.*

Damianus's letter to Nicholas is an authentick record of the *lewdnesses* committed under the reign of celibacy. *Atterbury.*

LE'WDSTER. *n. s.* [from *lewd.*] A lecher; one given to criminal pleasures.

Against such *lewdsters*, and their lechery,
Those that betray them do no treachery. *Shakespeare.*

LE'WIS D'OR. *n. s.* [French.] A golden French coin, in value twelve livres, now settled at seventeen shillings. *Dict.*

LEXICO'GRAPHER. *n. s.* [λεξικὸν and γράφω; *lexicographe*, French.] A writer of dictionaries; a harmless drudge, that busies himself in tracing the original, and detailing the signification of words.

Commentators and *lexicographers* acquainted with the Syriac language, have given these hints in their writings on scripture. *Watts's Improvement of the Mind.*

LEXICO'GRAPHY. *n. s.* [λεξικὸν and γράφω.] The art or practice of writing dictionaries.

LE'XICON. *n. s.* [λεξικὸν.] A dictionary; a book teaching the signification of words.

Though a linguist should pride himself to have all the tongues that Babel cleft the world into, yet if he had not studied the solid things in them as well as the words and *lexicons*, yet he were nothing so much to be esteemed a learned man as any yeoman competently wise in his mother dialect only. *Milton.*

LEY. *n. s.*

Ley, *lee*, *lay*, are all from the Saxon leaȝ, a field or pasture, by the usual melting of the letter ȝ or g. *Gibson's Cam.*

LI'ABLE. *n. s.* [*liable*, from *lier*, old French.] Obnoxious; not exempt; subject.

But what is strength without a double share
Of wisdom? vast, unwieldy, burthensome,
Proudly secure, yet *liable* to fall
By weakest subtleties. *Milton's Agonistes.*

The English boast of Spenser and Milton, who neither of them wanted genius or learning; and yet both of them are *liable* to many censures. *Dryden's Juvenal.*

This, or any other scheme, coming from a private hand, might be *liable* to many defects. *Swift.*

LI'AR. *n. s.* [from *lie.* This word would analogically be *lier*; but this orthography has prevailed, and the convenience of distinction from *lier*, he who lies down, is sufficient to confirm it.] One who tells falshood; one who wants veracity.

She's like a *liar*, gone to burning hell!
'Twas I that kill'd her. *Shakespeare's Othello.*
He approves the common *liar*, fame,
Who speaks him thus at Rome. *Shakesp. Ant. and Cleop.*

I do not reject his observation as untrue, much less condemn the person himself as a *liar*, whensoever it seems to be contradicted. *Boyle.*

Thy better soul abhors a *liar*'s part,
Wise is thy voice, and noble is thy heart. *Pope's Odyssey.*

LI'ARD. *adj.*

1. Mingled roan. *Markham.*

2. *Liard* in Scotland denotes gray-haired: as, he's a *liard* old man.

LIBA'TION. *n. s.* [*libatio*, Latin.]

1. The act of pouring wine on the ground in honour of some deity.

In digging new earth pour in some wine, that the vapour of the earth and wine may comfort the spirits, provided it be not taken for a heathen sacrifice, or *libation* to the earth. *Bacon's Natural History.*

2. The wine so poured.

They had no other crime to object against the Christians, but that they did not offer up *libations*, and the smoke of sacrifices, to dead men. *Stillingfleet on Rom. Idolatry.*

The goblet then she took, with nectar crown'd,
Sprinkling the first *libations* on the ground. *Dryden's Æn.*

LI'BBARD. *n. s.* [*liebard*, German; *leopardus*, Lat.] A leopard.

Make the *libbard* stern,
Leave roaring, when in rage he for revenge did yearn.
Spenser's Fairy Queen, b. i.
The *libbard*, and the tiger, as the mole
Rising, the crumbled earth above them threw. *Milton.*

The torrid parts of Africk are by Piso resembled to a *libbard*'s skin, the distance of whose spots represent the dispersness of habitations, or towns of Africk. *Brerewood.*

LI'BEL. *n. s.* [*libellus*, Latin; *libelle*, French.]

1. A satire; defamatory writing; a lampoon:

Are we reproached for the name of Christ? that ignominy serves but to advance our future glory; every such *libel* here becomes panegyrick there. *Decay of Piety.*

Good heav'n! that sots and knaves should be so vain,
To wish their vile resemblance may remain!
And stand recorded, at their own request,
To future days, a *libel* or a jest. *Dryden.*

2. [In the civil law.] A declaration or charge in writing against a person in court.

To LI'BEL. *v. n.* [from the noun.] To spread defamation; generally written or printed.

Sweet scrauls to fly about the streets of Rome:
What's this but *libelling* against the senate? *Shakespeare.*
He, like a privileg'd spy, whom nothing can
Discredit, *libels* now 'gainst each great man. *Donne.*

To LI'BEL. *v. a.* To satirise; to lampoon;

Is then the peerage of England any thing dishonoured when a peer suffers for his treason? if he be *libelled*, or any way defamed, he has his scandalum magnatum to punish the offender. *Dryden.*

But what so pure which envious tongues will spare?
Some wicked wits have *libelled* all the fair. *Pope.*

LI'BELLER. *n. s.* [from *libel.*] A defamer by writing; a lampooner.

Our common *libellers* are as free from the imputation of wit, as of morality. *Dryden's Juvenal.*

The squibs are those who, in the common phrase, are called *libellers* and lampooners. *Tatler.*

The common *libellers*, in their invectives, tax the church with an insatiable desire of power and wealth, equally common to all bodies of men. *Swift.*

LI'BELLOUS. *n. s.* [from *libel.*] Defamatory.

It was the most malicious surmise that had ever been brewed, howsoever countenanced by a *libellous* pamphlet. *Wotton.*

LI'BERAL. *adj.* [*liberalis*, Latin; *liberal.* French.]

1. Not mean; not low in birth; not low in mind.

2. Becoming a gentleman.

3. Munificent; generous; bountiful; not parcimonious.

Her name was Mercy, well known over all
To be both gracious and eke *liberal.* *Spens. Fa. Queen.*
Sparing would shew a worse sin than ill doctrine.
Men of his way should be most *liberal*,
They're set here for examples. *Shakesp. Henry* VIII.
Needs must the pow'r
That made us, and for us this ample world,
Be infinitely good, and of his good
As *liberal* and free, as infinite. *Milton.*

There is no art better than to be *liberal* of praise and commendation to others, in that wherein a man's self hath any perfection. *Bacon's Essays.*

The *liberal* are secure alone;
For what we frankly give, for ever is our own. *Granville.*

Several clergymen, otherwise little fond of obscure terms, are, in their sermons, very *liberal* of all those which they find in ecclesiastical writers, as if it were our duty to understand them. *Swift.*

LIBERA'LITY. *n. s.* [*liberalitas*, Latin; *liberalité*, Fr.] Munificence; bounty; generosity; generous profusion.

Why should he despair, that knows to court
With words, fair looks, and *liberality?* *Shakespeare.*
Such moderation with thy bounty join,
That thou may'st nothing give that is not thine;
That *liberality* is but cast away,
Which makes us borrow what we cannot pay. *Denham.*

LIBERA'LLY. *adv.* [from *liberal.*] Bounteously; bountifully; largely.

If any of you lack wisdom, let him ask of God, that giveth to all men *liberally*, and upbraideth not. *James* i. 5.

LI'BERTINE. *n. s.* [*libertin*, French.]

1. One unconfined; one at liberty.

When he speaks,
The air, a charter'd *libertine*, is still;
And the mute wonder lurketh in men's ears,
To steal his sweet and honied sentences. *Shakesp. Hen.* V.

2. One who lives without restraint or law.

Man, the lawless *libertine*, may rove
Free and unquestion'd. *Rowe's Jane Shore.*

Want of power is the only bound that a *libertine* puts to his views upon any of the sex. *Clarissa.*

2. One

2. One who pays no regard to the precepts of religion.

They say this town is full of couzenage,
As nimble jugglers, that deceive the eye;
Disguised cheaters, prating mountebanks,
And many such like *libertines* of sin. *Shakespeare.*

That word may be applied to some few *libertines* in the audience. *Collier's View of the Stage.*

3. [In law; *libertinus*, Lat.] A freedman; or rather, the son of a freedman.

Some persons are forbidden to be accusers on the score of their sex, as women; others on the score of their age, as pupils and infants; others on the score of their conditions, as *libertines* against their patrons. *Ayliffe's Parergon.*

LI'BERTINE. *adj.* [*libertin*, French.] Licentious; irreligious.

There are men that marry not, but chuse rather a *libertine* and impure single life, than to be yoked in marriage. *Bacon.*

Might not the queen make diligent enquiry, if any person about her should happen to be of *libertine* principles or morals. *Swift's Project for Advancement of Religion.*

LI'BERTINISM. *n. s.* [from *libertine*.] Irreligion; licentiousness of opinions and practice.

That spirit of religion and seriousness vanished all at once, and a spirit of liberty and *libertinism*, of infidelity and profaneness, started up in the room of it. *Atterbury's Sermons.*

LI'BERTY. *n. s.* [*liberté*, French; *libertas*, Latin.]

1. Freedom, as opposed to slavery.

My master knows of your being here, and hath threatened to put me into everlasting *liberty*, if I tell you of it; for he swears, he'll turn me away. *Shakespeare.*

O *liberty!* thou goddess, heav'nly bright!
Profuse of bliss, and pregnant with delight,
Eternal pleasures in thy presence reign. *Addison.*

2. Freedom, as opposed to necessity.

Liberty is the power in any agent to do, or forbear, any particular action, according to the determination, or thought of the mind, whereby either of them is preferred to the other. *Locke.*

As it is in the motions of the body, so it is in the thoughts of our minds: where any one is such, that we have power to take it up, or lay it by, according to the preference of the mind, there we are at *liberty*. *Locke.*

3. Privilege; exemption; immunity.

His majesty gave not an intire country to any, much less did he grant jura regalia, or any extraordinary *liberties*. *Davies.*

4. Relaxation of restraint.

5. Leave; permission.

I shall take the *liberty* to consider a third ground, which, with some men, has the same authority. *Locke.*

LIBI'DINOUS. *n. s.* [*libidinosus*, Latin.] Lewd; lustful.

None revolt from the faith; because they must not look upon a woman to lust after her, but because they are much more restrained from the perpetration of their lusts. If wanton glances and *libidinous* thoughts had been permitted by the gospel, they would have apostatized nevertheless. *Bentley.*

LIBI'DINOUSLY. *adv.* [from *libidinous*.] Lewdly; lustfully.

LI'BRAL. *adj.* [*libralis*, Latin.] Of a pound weight. *Dict.*

LIBRA'RIAN. *n. s.* [*librarius*, Latin.]

1. One who has the care of a library.

2. One who transcribes or copies books.

Charybdis thrice swallows, and thrice refunds, the waves: this must be understood of regular tides. There are indeed but two tides in a day, but this is the error of the *librarians*. *Broome's Notes on the Odyssey.*

LI'BRARY. *n. s.* [*librarie*, Fr.] A large collection of books, publick or private.

Then as they 'gan his *library* to view,
And antique registers for to avise,
There chanced to the prince's hand to rise
An ancient book, hight Briton's monuments. *Fa. Qu.*

Make choice of all my *library*,
And so beguile thy sorrow. *Shakesp. Titus Andronicus.*

I have given you the *library* of a painter, and a catalogue of such books as he ought to read. *Dryden's Dufresnoy.*

To LI'BRATE. *v. a.* [*libro*, Latin.] To poise; to balance; to hold in equipoise.

LIBRA'TION. *n. s.* [*libratio*, Latin; *libration*, French.]

1. The state of being balanced.

This is what may be said of the balance, and the *libration*, of the body. *Dryden's Dufresnoy.*

Their pinions still
In loose *librations* stretch'd, to trust the void
Trembling refuse. *Thomson's Spring.*

2. [In astronomy.]

Libration is the balancing motion or trepidation in the firmament, whereby the declination of the sun, and the latitude of the stars, change from time to time. Astronomers likewise ascribe to the moon a *libratory* motion, or motion of trepidation, which they pretend is from east to west, and from north to south, because that, at full moon, they sometimes discover parts of her disk which are not discovered at other times. These kinds are called, the one a *libration* in longitude, and the other a *libration* in latitude. Besides this, there is a third kind, which they call an apparent *libration*, and which consists in this, that when the moon is at her greatest elongation from the south, her axis being then almost perpendicular to the plane of the ecliptick, the sun must enlighten towards the north pole of the moon some parts which he did not before, and that, on the contrary, some parts of those which he enlightened towards the opposite pole are obscured; and this produces the same effect which the *libration* in latitude does. *Dict. Trev.*

Those planets which move upon their axis, do not all make intire revolutions; for the moon maketh only a kind of *libration*, or a reciprocated motion on her own axis. *Grew.*

LI'BRATORY. *adj.* [from *libro*, Lat.] Balancing; playing like a balance.

LICE, the plural of *louse*.

Red blisters rising on their paps appear,
And flaming carbuncles, and noisome sweat,
And clammy dews, that loathsome *lice* beget;
Till the slow creeping evil eats his way. *Dryden's Virg.*

LI'CEBANE. *n. s.* [*lice* and *bane*.] A plant.

LICENSE. *n. s.* [*licentia*, Latin; *licence*, French.]

1. Exorbitant liberty; contempt of legal and necessary restraint.

Some of the wiser seeing that a popular *licence* is indeed the many-headed tyranny, prevailed with the rest to make Musidorus their chief. *Sidney.*

Taunt my faults
With such full *licence*, as both truth and malice
Have power to utter. *Shakesp. Ant. and Cleopatra.*

They baul for freedom in their senseless moods,
And still revolt when truth would set them free;
Licence they mean, when they cry liberty. *Milton.*

The privilege that ancient poets claim,
Now turn'd to *license* by too just a name. *Roscommon.*

Though this be a state of liberty, yet it is not a state of *licence*; though man, in that state, have an uncontroulable liberty to dispose of his person or possessions, yet he has not liberty to destroy himself. *Locke.*

2. A grant of permission.

They sent some to bring them a *licence* from the senate. *Judith* xi. 14.

Those few abstract names that the schools forged, and put into the mouths of their scholars, could never yet get admittance into common use, or obtain the *licence* of publick approbation. *Locke.*

We procured a *licence* of the duke of Parma to enter the theatre and gallery. *Addison on Italy.*

3. Liberty; permission.

It is not the manner of the Romans to deliver any man to die, before that he which is accused have the accusers face to face, and have *licence* to answer for himself. *Acts.*

To LI'CENSE. *v. a.* [*licencier*, French.]

1. To set at liberty.

He would play well, and willingly, at some games of greatest attention, which shewed, that when he listed he could *license* his thoughts. *Wotton.*

2. To permit by a legal grant.

Wit's titans brav'd the skies,
And the press groan'd with *licens'd* blasphemies. *Pope.*

LI'CENSER. *n. s.* [from *license*.] A granter of permission; commonly a tool of power.

LICE'NTIATE. *n. s.* [*licentiatus*, low Latin.]

1. A man who uses license.

The *licentiates* somewhat licentiously, least they should prejudice poetical liberty, will pardon themselves for doubling or rejecting a letter, if the sense fall aptly. *Camden.*

2. A degree in Spanish universities.

A man might, after that time, sue for the degree of a *licentiate* or master in this faculty. *Ayliffe's Parergon.*

To LICE'NTIATE. *v. a.* [*licentier*, French.] To permit; to encourage by license.

We may not hazard either the stifling of generous inclinations, or the *licentiating* of any thing that is coarse. *L'Estrange.*

LICE'NTIOUS. *n. s.* [*licencieux*, French; *licentiosus*, Latin.]

1. Unrestrained by law or morality.

Later ages pride, like corn-fed steed,
Abus'd her plenty, and fat swoln encrease,
To all *licentious* lust, and gan exceed
The measure of her mean, and natural first need. *Fa. Qu.*

How would it touch thee to the quick,
Should'st thou but hear I were *licentious?*
And that this body, consecrate to thee,
With ruffian lust should be contaminate. *Shakespeare.*

2. Presumptuous; unconfined.

The Tyber, whose *licentious* waves,
So often overflow'd the neighbouring fields,
Now runs a smooth and inoffensive course. *Roscommon.*

LICE'NTIOUSLY. *adv.* [from *licentious*.] With too much liberty; without just restraint.

The licentiates somewhat *licentiously*, least they should prejudice poetical liberty, will pardon themselves for doubling or rejecting a letter. *Camden's Remains.*

LICE'NTIOUSNESS. *n. s.* [from *licentious.*] Boundless liberty; contempt of just restraint.

One error is so fruitful, as it begetteth a thousand children, if the *licentiousness* thereof be not timely restrained. *Ral.*

This custom has been always looked upon, by the wisest men, as an effect of *licentiousness*, and not of liberty. *Swift.*

During the greatest *licentiousness* of the press, the character of the queen was insulted. *Swift.*

LICH. *n. s.* [lice, Saxon.] A dead carcase; whence *lichwake*, the time or act of watching by the dead; *lichgate*, the gate through which the dead are carried to the grave; *Lichfield*, the field of the dead, a city in Staffordshire, so named from martyred christians. *Salve magna parens. Lichwake* is still retained in Scotland in the same sense.

LI'CHOWL. *n. s.* [*lich* and *owl.*] A sort of owl, by the vulgar supposed to fortetel death.

To LICK. *v. a.* [licean, Saxon; *lecken*, Dutch.]

1. To pass over with the tongue.

Æsculapius went about with a dog and a she-goat, both which he used much in his cures; the first for *licking* all ulcered wounds, and the goat's milk for the diseases of the stomach and lungs. *Temple.*

A bear's a savage beast;
Whelp'd without form, until the dam
Has *lick'd* it into shape and frame. *Hudibras, p. i.*

He with his tepid rays the rose renews,
And *licks* the drooping leaves, and dries the dews. *Dryden.*

I have seen an antiquary *lick* an old coin, among other trials, to distinguish the age of it by its taste. *Addison.*

2. To lap; to take in by the tongue.

At once pluck out
The multitudinous tongue; let them not *lick*
The sweet which is their poison. *Shakespeare's Coriolanus.*

3. *To* LICK *up.* To devour.

Now shall this company *lick up* all that are round about us, as the ox *licketh up* the grass. *Numb.* xxii. 4.

When luxury has *lick'd up* all thy pelf,
Curs'd by thy neighbours, thy trustees, thyself:
Think how posterity will treat thy name. *Pope's Horace.*

LICK. *n. s.* [from the verb.] A blow; rough usage: a low word.

He turned upon me as round as a chafed boar, and gave me a *lick* across the face. *Dryden.*

LI'CKERISH. } *adj.* [liccena, a glutton, Saxon.]
LI'CKEROUS. }

1. Nice in the choice of food; squeamish.

Voluptuous men sacrifice all substantial satisfactions to a *liquorish* palate. *L'Estrange.*

2. Eager; greedy.

Then is never tongue-tied, where fit commendation, whereof womankind is so *lickerish*, is offered unto it. *Sidney.*

Strephon, fond boy, delighted, did not know
That it was love that shin'd in shining maid;
But *lick'rous*, poison'd, fain to her would go. *Sidney.*

Certain rare manuscripts, sought in the most remote parts by Erpenius, the most excellent linguist, had been left to his widow, and were upon sale to the jesuits, *liquorish* chapmen of all such ware. *Wotton.*

In vain he profer'd all his goods to save
His body, destin'd to that living grave;
The *liquorish* hag rejects the pelf with scorn,
And nothing but the man would serve her turn. *Dryden.*

In some provinces they were so *liquorish* after man's flesh, that they would suck the blood as it run from the dying man. *Locke.*

3. Nice; delicate; tempting the appetite.

Wouldst thou seek again to trap me here
With *lickerish* baits, fit to ensnare a brute? *Milton.*

LICKERI'SHNESS. *n. s.* [from *lickerish.*] Niceness of palate.

LICORICE. *n. s.* [γλυκύῤῥιζα; *liquoricia*, Italian; *glycyrrhzza*, Latin.] A root of sweet taste.

Liquorice hath a papilionaceous flower; the pointal which arises from the empalement becomes a short pod, containing several kidney-shaped seeds; the leaves are placed by parts joined to the mid-rib, and are terminated by an odd lobe. *Miller.*

Liquorice root is long and slender, externally of a dusky reddish brown, but within of a fine yellow, full of juice, void of smell, and of a taste sweeter than sugar, it grows wild in many parts of France, Italy, Spain, and Germany. This root is excellent in coughs, and all disorders of the lungs. The inspissated juice of this root is brought to us from Spain and Holland; from the first of which places it obtained the name of Spanish juice. *Hill's Materia Medica.*

LICTOR. *n. s.* [Latin.] A beadle that attended the consuls to apprehend or punish criminals.

Saucy *lictors*
Will catch at us like strumpets. *Shakes. Ant. and Cleopatra.*

Proconsuls to their provinces
Hasting, or on return, in robes of state,
Lictors and rods the ensigns of their power. *Milton.*

Democritus could feed his spleen, and shake
His sides and shoulders till he felt 'em ake;
Though in his country-town no *lictors* were,
Nor rods, nor ax, nor tribune. *Dryden's Juvenal.*

LID. [hlid, Saxon; *lied*, German.]

1. A cover; any thing that shuts down over a vessel; a lid, cover, or stopple that enters the mouth.

Hope, instead of flying off with the rest, stuck so close to the *lid* of the cup, that it was shut down upon her. *Addison.*

2. The membrane that, when we sleep or wink, is drawn over the eye.

Do not for ever with thy veiled *lids*,
Seek for thy noble father in the dust. *Shakesp. Hamlet.*

Our eyes have *lids*, our ears still ope we keep. *Davies.*

The fields fair eyes saw her, and saw no more,
But shut their flow'ry *lids* for ever night,
And winter strew'd her way. *Crashaw.*

That eye dropp'd sense distinct and clear,
As any muse's tongue could speak;
When from its *lid* a pearly tear
Ran trickling down her beauteous cheek. *Prior.*

The rod of Hermes
To sleep could mortal eye-*lids* fix,
And drive departed souls to Styx:
That rod was just a type of Sid's,
Which o'er a British senate's *lids*
Could scatter opium full as well,
And drive as many souls to hell. *Swift.*

LIE. *n. s.* [*lie*, French.] Any thing impregnated with some other body; as, soap or salt.

Chamber-*lie* breeds fleas like a loach. *Shakespeare.*

All liquid things concocted by heat become yellow; as, *lye*, wort, &c. *Peacham on Drawing.*

LIE. *n. s.* [lige, Saxon.]

1. A criminal falshood.

My name's Macbeth.
—The devil himself could not pronounce a title
More hateful to mine ear.
—No; nor more fearful.
—Thou liest, abhorred tyrant; with my sword
I'll prove the *lie* thou speak'st. *Shakespeare's Macbeth.*

A *lye* is properly an outward signification of something contrary to, or at least beside, the inward sense of the mind; so that when one thing is signified or expressed, and the same thing not meant, or intended, that is properly a *lye*. *South.*

Truth is the object of our understanding, as good is of our will; and the understanding can no more be delighted with a *lye*, than the will can chuse an apparent evil. *Dryden.*

When I hear my neighbour speak that which is not true, and I say to him, this is not true, or this is false, I only convey to him the naked idea of his error; this is the primary idea: but if I say it is a *lie*, the word *lie* carries also a secondary idea; for it implies both the falshood of the speech, and my reproach and censure of the speaker. *Watts's Logick.*

2. A charge of falshood.

That *lie* shall lye so heavy on my sword,
That it shall render vengeance and revenge;
Till thou the *lie* giver, and that *lie*, rest
In earth as quiet as thy father's skull. *Shakes. Rich.* II.

It is a contradiction to suppose, that whole nations of men should unanimously give the *lie* to what, by the most invincible evidence, every one of them knew to be true. *Locke.*

Men will give their own experience the *lye*, rather than admit of any thing disagreeing with these tenets. *Locke.*

3. A fiction.

The cock and fox, the fool and knave imply;
The truth is moral, though the tale a *lie*. *Dryden.*

To LIE. *v. n.* [leogan, Saxon; *liegen*, Dutch.]

1. To utter criminal falshood.

I know not where he lodges; and for me to devise a lodging, and say, he lies here, or he lies there, were to *lie* in mine own throat. *Shakespeare's Othello.*

If a soul *lye* unto his neighbour in that which was delivered him to keep, he shall restore that which was delivered. *Levit.* vi. 1.

Should I *lye* against my right? *Job* xxxiv. 6.

Inform us, will the emp'ror treat?
Or do the prints and papers *lye*? *Pope.*

To LIE. *v. n.* pret. *I lay*; *I have lain* or *lien.* [liegan, Saxon; *liggen*, Dutch.]

1. To rest horizontally, or with very great inclination against something else.

2. To rest; to lean upon.

Death *lies* on her like an untimely flow'r;
Upon the sweetest flow'r of all the field. *Shakespeare.*

Lie heavy on him, earth, for he
Laid many a heavy load on thee. *Epitaph on Vanbrugh.*

3. To

3. To be repofited in the grave.

All the kings of the nations *lie* in glory, every one in his own houfe. *Ifa.* xiv. 18.

I will *lie* with my fathers, and thou fhalt carry me out of Egypt, and bury me in your burying place. *Gen.* xlvii. 30.

4. To be in a ftate of decumbiture.

How many good young princes would do fo; their fathers *lying* fo fick as yours at this time is. *Shakef. Henry* IV.

My little daughter *lieth* at the point of death; I pray thee come and lay thy hands on her, that fhe may be healed. *Mark* v. 23.

5. To pafs the time of fleep.

The watchful traveller,
That by the moon's miftaken light did rife,
Lay down again, and clos'd his weary eyes. *Dryden.*
Forlorn he muft, and perfecuted flie;
Climb the fteep mountain, in the cavern *lie.* *Prior.*

6. To be laid up or repofited.

I have feen where copperas is made great variety of them, divers of which I have yet *lying* by me. *Boyle.*

7. To remain fixed.

The Spaniards have but one temptation to quarrel with us, the recovering of Jamaica, for that has ever *lien* at their hearts. *Temple.*

8. To refide.

If thou doeft well, fhalt thou not be accepted? and if thou doeft not well, fin *lieth* at the door. *Gen.* iv. 7.

9. To be placed or fituated.

We have gone through deferts, where there *lay* no way. *Wifd.* v. 7.

I fly
To thofe happy climes that *lie*,
Where day never fhuts his eye,
Up in the broad fields of the fky. *Milton.*
There *lies* our way, and that our paffage home. *Dryd.*

Envy *lies* between beings equal in nature, though unequal in circumftances. *Collier of Envy.*

The bufinefs of a tutor, rightly employed, *lies* out of the road. *Locke on Education.*

What *lies* beyond our pofitive idea towards infinity, *lies* in obfcurity, and has the undeterminate confufion of a negative idea. *Locke.*

10. To prefs upon.

Thy wrath *lieth* hard upon me, and thou haft afflicted me with all thy waves. *Pfal.* lxxxviii. 7.

He that commits a fin fhall find
The preffing guilt *lie* heavy on his mind,
Though bribes or favour fhall affert his caufe. *Creech.*

Shew the power of religion, in abating that particular anguifh which feems to *lie* fo heavy on Leonora. *Addifon.*

11. To be troublefome or tedious.

Suppofe kings, befides the entertainment of luxury, fhould have fpent their time, at leaft what *lay* upon their hands, in chemiftry, it cannot be denied but princes may pafs their time advantageoufly that way. *Temple.*

I would recommend the ftudies of knowledge to the female world, that they may not be at a lofs how to employ thofe hours that *lie* upon their hands. *Addifon's Guardian.*

12. To be judicially fixed.

If he fhould intend his voyage towards my wife, I would turn her loofe to him; and what he gets more of her than fharp words, let it *lie* on my head. *Shakefpeare.*

13. To be in any particular ftate.

If money go before, all ways do *lie* open. *Shakefpeare.*

The highways *lie* wafte, the wayfaring man ceafeth. *Ifa.*

The feventh year thou fhalt let it reft and *lie* ftill. *Exod.*

Do not think that the knowledge of any particular fubject cannot be improved, merely becaufe it has *lain* without improvement. *Watts's Improvement of the Mind.*

14. To be in a ftate of concealment.

Many things in them *lie* concealed to us, which they who were concerned underftood at firft fight. *Locke.*

15. To be in prifon.

Your imprifonment fhall not be long;
I will deliver you, or elfe *lye* for you. *Shakefp. Rich.* III.

16. To be in a bad ftate.

Why will you *lie* pining and pinching yourfelf in fuch a lonefome, ftarving courfe of life. *L'Eftrange's Fables.*

The generality of mankind *lie* pecking at one another, till one by one they are all torn to pieces. *L'Eftrange's Fab.*

Are the gods to do your drudgery, and you *lie* bellowing with your finger in your mouth? *L'Eftrange's Fables.*

17. To be in a helplefs or expofed ftate.

To fee a hated perfon fuperior, and to *lie* under the anguifh of a difadvantage, is far enough from diverfion. *Collier.*

It is but a very fmall comfort, that a plain man, *lying* under a fharp fit of the ftone for a week, receives from this fine fentence. *Tillotfon's Sermons.*

As a man fhould always be upon his guard againft the vices to which he is moft expofed, fo we fhould take a more than ordinary care not to *lie* at the mercy of the weather in our moral conduct. *Addifon's Freeholder.*

The maintenance of the clergy is precarious, and collected from a moft miferable race of farmers, at whofe mercy every minifter *lies* to be defrauded. *Swift.*

18. To confift.

The image of it gives me content already; and I truft it will grow to a moft profperous perfection.

—It *lies* much in your holding up; hafte you fpeedily to Angelo. *Shakefpeare's Meafure for Meafure.*

He that thinks that diverfion may not *lie* in hard labour, forgets the early rifing, and hard riding of huntfmen. *Locke.*

19. To be in the power; to belong to.

He fhews himfelf very malicious if he knows I deferve credit, and yet goes about to blaft it, as much as in him *lies.* *Stillingfleet on Idolatry.*

Do'ft thou endeavour, as much as in thee *lies*, to preferve the lives of all men. *Duppa's Rules for Devotion.*

Mars is the warrior's god; in him it *lies*
On whom he favours to confer the prize. *Dryden.*

20. To be charged in any thing; as, an action lieth againft one.

21. To coft; as, it lies me in more money.

22. *To* LIE *at.* To importune; to teaze.

23. *To* LIE *by.* To reft; to remain ftill.

Ev'ry thing that heard him play,
Ev'n the billows of the fea,
Hung their heads, and then *lay by*;
In fweet mufick is fuch art,
Killing care, and grief of heart,
Fall afleep, or hearing die. *Shakefp. Henry* VIII.

24. *To* LIE *down.* To reft; to go into a ftate of repofe.

The leopard fhall *lie down* with the kid. *Ifa.* xi. 6.

The needy fhall *lie down* in fafety. *Ifa.* xiv. 30.

25. *To* LIE *down.* To fink into the grave.

His bones are full of the fin of his youth, which fhall *lie down* with him in the duft. *Job* xx. 11.

26. *To* LIE *in.* To be in childbed.

As for all other good women that love to do but little work, how handfome it is to *lie in* and fleep, or to loufe themfelves in the fun-fhine, they that have been but a while in Ireland can well witnefs. *Spenfer on Ireland.*

You confine yourfelf moft unreafonably. Come; you muft go vifit the lady that *lies in.* *Shakef. Coriolanus.*

She had *lain in*, and her right breaft had been apoftemated. *Wifeman's Surgery.*

The doctor has practifed both by fea and land, and therefore cures the green ficknefs and *lyings in.* *Spectator.*

When Florimel defign'd to *lie* privately *in*;
She chofe with fuch prudence her pangs to conceal,
That her nurfe, nay her midwife, fcarce heard her once fqueal. *Prior.*

Hyfterical affections are contracted by accidents in *lying in.* *Arbuthnot on Diet.*

27. *To* LIE *under.* To be fubject to.

A generous perfon will *lie under* a great difadvantage. *Smalridge's Sermons.*

This miftake never ought to be imputed as a fault to Dryden, but to thofe who fuffered fo noble a genius to *lie under* the neceffity of it. *Pope's Notes on the Iliad.*

Europe *lay* then *under* a deep lethargy, and was no otherwife to be refcued but by one that would cry mightily. *Atterb.*

28. *To* LIE *upon.* To become an obligation or duty.

Thefe are not places merely of favour, the charge of fouls *lies upon* them; the greateft account whereof will be required at their hands. *Bacon's Advice to Villiers.*

It fhould *lie upon* him to make out how matter, by undirected motion, could at firft neceffarily fall, without ever erring or mifcarrying, into fuch a curious formation of human bodies. *Bentley's Sermons.*

29. *To* LIE *with.* To converfe in bed.

Pardon me, Baffanio,
For by this ring fhe *lay with* me. *Shakefpeare.*

LIEF. *adj.* [leof, Saxon; *lief*, Dutch.] Dear; beloved.

My *liefeft* lord, fhe thus beguiled had,
For he was flefh; all flefh doth frailty breed. *Fa. Qu.*
You, with the reft,
Caufelefs have laid difgraces on my head;
And with your beft endeavour have ftirr'd up
My *liefeft* liege to be mine enemy. *Shakefp. Henry* VI.

LIEF. *adv.* Willingly.

If I could fpeak fo wifely under an arreft, I would fend for certain of my creditors; and yet to fay the truth, I had as *lief* have the foppery of freedom, as the morality of imprifonment. *Shakefp. Meafure for Meafure.*

LIEGE. *adj.* [*lige*, French; *ligio*, Italian; *ligius*, low Latin.]

1. Bound by fome feudal tenure; fubject: whence *liegeman* for fubject.

2. Sovereign. [This fignification feems to have accidentally rifen from the former, the lord of *liege men*, being by miftake called *liege lord.*]

Did not the whole realm acknowledge Henry VIII, of famous memory, for their king and *liege* lord. *Spenfer.*

So

My lady *liege*, said he,
What all your sex desire is sovereignty. *Dryden.*

So much of it as is founded on the law of nature, may be stiled natural religion; that is to say, a devotedness unto God our *liege* lord, so as to act in all things according to his will. *Grew's Cosmology.*

LIEGE. *n. s.* Sovereign; superior lord.

O pardon me, my *liege*! but for my tears
I had forestall'd this dear and deep rebuke. *Shakespeare.*
The other part reserv'd I by consent,
For that my sovereign *liege* was in my debt. *Shakespeare.*
You with your best endeavour have stirred up
My liefest *liege* to be mine enemy. *Shakespeare.*
The natives, dubious whom
They must obey, in consternation wait
Till rigid conquest will pronounce their *liege*. *Philips.*

LI'EGEMAN. *n. s.* [from *liege* and *man*.] A subject.

This *liegeman* 'gan to wax more bold,
And when he felt the folly of his lord,
In his own kind, he 'gan himself unfold. *Fairy Queen.*

Sith then the ancestors of those that now live, yielded themselves then subjects and *liegemen*, shall it not tye their children to the same subjection? *Spenser on Ireland.*

Stand, ho! who is there?
—Friends to this ground, and *liegemen* to the Dane. *Shak.*

LI'EGER. *n. s.* [from *liege*.] A resident ambassador.

His passions and his fears
Lie *liegers* for you in his breast, and there
Negotiate your affairs. *Denham's Sophy.*

LI'EN, the participle of *lie*.

One of the people might lightly have *lien* with thy wife. *Gen.* xxvi. 10.

LIENTE'RICK. *adj.* [from *lientery*.] Pertaining to a lientery.

There are many medicinal preparations of iron, but none equal to the tincture made without acids; especially in obstructions, and to strengthen the tone of the parts; as in *lienterick* and other like cases. *Grew's Musæum.*

LI'ENTERY. *n. s.* [from λεῖον, *læve*, smooth, and ἔντερον, *intestinum*, gut; *lienterie*, French.] A particular looseness, or diarrhœa, wherein the food passes so suddenly through the stomach and guts, as to be thrown out by stool with little or no alteration. *Quincy.*

LI'ER. *n. s.* [from *to lie*.] One that rests or lies down; or remains concealed.

There were *liers* in ambush against him behind the city. *Jos.* viii. 14.

LIEU. *n. s.* [French.] Place; room; it is only used with *in*: *in lieu*, instead.

God, of his great liberality, had determined, in *lieu* of man's endeavours, to bestow the same by the rule of that justice which best beseemeth him. *Hooker, b.* i.

In *lieu* of such an increase of dominion, it is our business to extend our trade. *Addison's Freeholder.*

LIEVE. *adv.* [See LIEF.] Willingly.

Speak the speech, I pray you, as I pronounced it to you, trippingly on the tongue: but if you mouth it, as many of our players do, I had as *lieve* the town crier had spoke my lines. *Shakespeare's Hamlet.*

Action is death to some sort of people, and they would as *lieve* hang as work. *L'Estrange.*

LIEUTE'NANCY. *n. s.* [*lieutenance*, French; from *lieutenant*.]

1. The office of a lieutenant.

If such tricks as these strip you out of your *lieutenancy*, it had been better you had not kissed your three fingers so oft. *Shakespeare's Othello.*

2. The body of lieutenants.

The list of undisputed masters, is hardly so long as the list of the *lieutenancy* of our metropolis. *Felton on the Classicks.*

LIEUTE'NANT. *n. s.* [*lieutenant*, French.]

1. A deputy; one who acts by vicarious authority.

Whither away so fast?
—No farther than the tower,
To gratulate the gentle princes there.
—We'll enter all together,
And in good time here the *lieutenant* comes. *Shakespeare.*

I must put you in mind of the lords *lieutenants*, and deputy *lieutenants*, of the counties: their proper use is for ordering the military affairs, in order to oppose an invasion from abroad, or a rebellion or sedition at home. *Bacon.*

Killing, as it is considered in itself without all undue circumstances, was never prohibited to the lawful magistrate, who is the vicegerent or *lieutenant* of God, from whom he derives his power of life and death. *Bramhall against Hobbes.*

Sent by our new *lieutenant*, who in Rome,
And since from me, has heard of your renown:
I come to offer peace. *Philips's Briton.*

2. In war, one who holds the next rank to a superior of any denomination; as, a general has his lieutenant generals, a colonel his lieutenant colonel, and a captain simply his lieutenant.

It were meet that such captains only were employed as have formerly served in that country, and been at least *lieutenants* there. *Spenser on Ireland.*

According to military custom the place was good, and the *lieutenant* of the colonel's company might well pretend to the next vacant captainship. *Wotton.*

The earl of Essex was made *lieutenant* general of the army; the most popular man of the kingdom, and the darling of the sword men. *Clarendon.*

His *lieutenant*, engaging against his positive orders, being beaten by Lysander, Alcibiades was again banished. *Swift.*

Canst thou so many gallant soldiers see,
And captains and *lieutenants* slight for me. *Gay.*

LIEUTE'NANTSHIP. *n. s.* [from *lieutenant*.] The rank or office of lieutenant.

LIFE. *n. s.* plural *lives*. [lifian, to live, Saxon.]

1. Union and co-operation of soul with body.

On thy *life* no more.
—My *life* I never held but as a pawn
To wage against thy foes; nor fear to lose it,
Thy safety being the motive. *Shakespeare's King Lear.*
She shews a body rather than a *life*,
A statue than a breather. *Shakes. Ant. and Cleopatra.*

Let the waters bring forth abundantly the moving creature that hath *life*. *Gen.* i. 20.

The identity of the same man consists in nothing but a participation of the same continued *life*, by constantly fleeting particles of matter, in succession vitally united to the same organized body. *Locke.*

So peaceful shalt thou end thy blissful days,
And steal thyself from *life* by slow decays. *Pope.*

2. Present state.

O *life*, thou nothing's younger brother!
So like, that we may take the one for t'other!
Dream of a shadow! a reflection made
From the false glories of the gay reflected bow,
Is more a solid thing than thou!
Thou weak built isthmus, that do'st proudly rise
Up betwixt two eternities;
Yet canst not wave nor wind sustain,
But, broken and o'erwhelm'd, the ocean meets again. *Cowley.*

When I consider *life* 'tis all a cheat,
Yet fool'd by hope men favour the deceit,
Live on, and think to-morrow will repay;
To-morrow's falser than the former day;
Lies more; and when it says we shall be blest
With some new joy, takes off what we possest.
Strange cozenage! none would live past years again,
Yet all hope pleasure in what yet remain;
And from the dregs of *life* think to receive
What the first sprightly running could not give:
I'm tir'd of waiting for this chemick gold,
Which fools us young, and beggars us when old. *Dryden.*

Howe'er 'tis well that while mankind
Through *life*'s perverse meanders errs,
He can imagin'd pleasures find,
To combat against real cares. *Prior.*

3. Enjoyment, or possession of terrestrial existence.

Then avarice 'gan through his veins to inspire
His greedy flames, and kindle *life* devouring fire. *Fa. Qu.*
Their complot is to have my *life*:
And, if my death might make this island happy,
And prove the period of their tyranny,
I would expend it with all willingness. *Shakespeare.*
Nor love thy *life*, nor hate; but what thou liv'st
Live well, how long or short permit to heav'n. *Milton.*
Untam'd and fierce the tyger still remains,
And tires his *life* with biting on his chains. *Prior.*

He entreated me not to take his *life*, but exact a sum of money. *Notes on the Odyssey.*

4. Blood, the supposed vehicle of life.

His gushing entrails smoak'd upon the ground,
And the warm *life* came issuing through the wound. *Pope.*

5. Conduct; manner of living with respect to virtue or vice.

Henry and Edward, brightest sons of fame,
And virtuous Alfred, a more sacred name;
After a *life* of glorious toils endur'd,
Clos'd their long glories with a sigh. *Pope.*
I'll teach my family to lead good *lives*. *Mrs. Barker.*

6. Condition; manner of living with respect to happiness and misery.

Such was the *life* the frugal Sabines led;
So Remus and his brother god were bred. *Dryden's Virg.*

7. Continuance of our present state.

And some have not any clear ideas of the greatest part of them all their *lives*. *Locke.*

The administration of this bank is for *life*, and partly in the hands of the chief citizens. *Addison on Italy.*

8. The living form; resemblance exactly copied.

Galen hath explained this point unto the *life*. *Brown.*

That is the best part of beauty which a picture cannot express, no, nor the first sight of the *life*. *Bacon's Essays.*

Let him visit eminent persons of great name abroad, that he may tell how the *life* agreeth with the fame. *Bacon.*

He that would be a master, must draw by the *life* as well as copy from originals, and join theory and experience together. *Collier of the Entertainment of Books.*

9. Exact resemblance.

I believe no character of any person was ever better drawn to the *life* than this. *Denham.*

Rich carvings, portraiture, and imag'ry,
Where ev'ry figure to the *life* express'd
The Godhead's pow'r. *Dryden's Knight's Tale.*

He saw in order painted on the wall
The wars that fame around the world had blown,
All to the *life*, and ev'ry leader known. *Dryden's Æn.*

10. General state of man.

Studious they appear
Of arts that polish *life*; inventors rare!
Unmindful of their Maker. *Milton's Par. Lost.*

All that cheers or softens *life*,
The tender sister, daughter, friend, and wife. *Pope.*

11. Common occurrences; human affairs; the course of things.

This I know, not only by reading of books in my study, but also by experience of *life* abroad in the world. *Ascham.*

Not to know at large of things remote
From use, obscure and subtile; but to know
That which before us lies in daily *life*,
Is the prime wisdom. *Milton's Paradise Lost.*

12. Living person.

Why should I play the Roman fool, and die
On my own sword? whilst I see *lives* the gashes
Do better upon them. *Shakespeare's Macbeth.*

13. Narrative of a life past.

Plutarch, that writes his *life*,
Tells us, that Cato dearly lov'd his wife. *Pope.*

14. Spirit; briskness; vivacity; resolution.

The Helots bent thitherward with a new *life* of resolution, as if their captain had been a root out of which their courage had sprung. *Sidney.*

They have no notion of *life* and fire in fancy and in words; and any thing that is just in grammar and in measure is as good oratory and poetry to them as the best. *Felton.*

Not with half the fire and *life*,
With which he kiss'd Amphytrion's wife. *Prior.*

15. Animated existence; animal being.

Full nature swarms with *life*. *Thomson.*

Li'feblood. *n. s.* [*life* and *blood.*] The blood necessary to life; the vital blood.

This sickness doth infect
The very *lifeblood* of our enterprise. *Shakes. Henry* IV.

How could'st thou drain the *lifeblood* of the child. *Shak.*

They loved with that calm and noble value which dwells in the heart, with a warmth like that of *lifeblood*. *Spectator.*

Money, the *lifeblood* of the nation,
Corrupts and stagnates in the veins,
Unless a proper circulation
Its motion and its heat maintains. *Swift.*

His forehead struck the ground,
Lifeblood and life rush'd mingled through the wound. *Dryd.*

Lifeeverlasting. An herb. *Ainsworth.*

Li'fegiving. *n. s.* [*life* and *giving.*] Having the power to give life.

His own heat,
Kindled at first from heaven's *lifegiving* fire. *Spenser.*

He sat devising death
To them who liv'd; nor on the virtue thought
Of that *lifegiving* plant. *Milton's Paradise Lost.*

Lifegua'rd. *n. s.* [*life* and *guard.*] The guard of a king's person.

Li'feless. *adj.* [from *life.*]

1. Dead; deprived of life.

The other victor-flame a moment stood,
Then fell, and *lifeless* left th' extinguish'd wood. *Dryden.*

I who make the triumph of to-day,
May of to-morrow's pomp one part appear,
Ghastly with wounds, and *lifeless* on the bier. *Prior.*

2. Unanimated; void of life.

Was I to have never parted from thy side?
As good have grown there still a *lifeless* rib! *Milt. P. L.*

Thus began
Outrage from *lifeless* things. *Milton's Paradise Lost.*

The power which produces their motions, springs from something without themselves: if this power were suspended, they would become a *lifeless*, unactive heap of matter. *Cheyne.*

And empty words she gave, and sounding strain,
But senseless, *lifeless!* idol void and vain. *Pope's Dunciad.*

3. Without power, force, or spirit.

Hopeless and helpless doth Ægeon wend,
But to procrastinate his *lifeless* end. *Shakespeare.*

Unknowing to command, proud to obey
A *lifeless* king, a royal shade I lay. *Prior.*

Li'felessly. *adv.* [from *lifeless.*] Without vigour; frigidly; jejunely.

Li'felike. *n. s.* [*life* and *like.*] Like a living person.

Minerva, *lifelike*, on embodied air
Impress'd the form of Ipthema the fair. *Pope's Odyssey.*

Li'festring. *n. s.* [*life* and *string.*] Nerve; strings imagined to convey life.

These lines are the veins, the arteries,
The undecaying *lifestrings* of those hearts
That still shall pant, and still shall exercise
The motion spirit and nature both impart. *Daniel's Mus.*

Li'fetime. *n. s.* [*life* and *time.*] Continuance or duration of life.

Jordain talked prose all his *life-time*, without knowing what it was. *Addison on ancient Medals.*

Lifewe'ary. *adj.* [*life* and *weary.*] Wretched; tired of living.

Let me have
A dram of poison, such soon speeding geer
As will disperse itself through all the veins,
That the *lifeweary* taker may fall dead. *Shakespeare*

To Lift. *v. a.* [*lyffta*, Swedish; *loffter*, Danish.]

1. To raise from the ground; to heave; to elevate; to hold on high.

Filial ingratitude!
Is it not as this mouth should tear this hand
For *lifting* food to't. *Shakespeare's King Lear.*

Your guests are coming;
Lift up your countenance, as 'twere the day
Of celebration of that nuptial. *Shakesp. Winter Tale.*

Propp'd by the spring, it *lifts* aloft the head,
But of a sickly beauty soon to shed,
In summer living, and in winter dead. *Dryden.*

2. To bear; to support. Not in use.

So down he fell, that th' earth him underneath
Did groan, as feeble so great load to *lift*. *Fairy Queen.*

3. To rob; to plunder.

So weary bees in little cells repose,
But if night robbers *lift* the well-stor'd hive,
An humming through their waxen city grows. *Dryden.*

4. To exalt; to elevate mentally.

My heart was *lift* up in the ways of the Lord. 2 *Chron.*

Of Orpheus now no more let poets tell,
To bright Cæcilia greater pow'r is given,
His numbers rais'd a shade from hell,
Hers *lift* the soul to heav'n. *Pope's St. Cæcilia.*

5. To raise in fortune.

The eye of the Lord *lifted* up his head from misery. *Eccluf.*

6. To raise in estimation.

Neither can it be thought, because some lessons are chosen out of the Apocrypha, that we do offer disgrace to the word of God, or *lift* up the writings of men above it. *Hooker.*

7. To exalt in dignity.

See to what a godlike height
The Roman virtues *lift* up mortal man. *Addison's Cato.*

8. To elevate; to swell with pride.

Lifted up with pride. *Tim.* iii. 6.

Our successes have been great, and our hearts have been too much *lifted* up by them, so that we have reason to humble ourselves. *Atterbury's Sermons.*

9. *Up* is sometimes emphatically added to *lift*.

He *lift up* his spear against eight hundred, whom he slew at one time. 2 *Sam.* xxiii. 8.

Arise, *lift up* the lad, and hold him in thine hand. *Genesis.*

To Lift. *v. n.* To strive to raise by strength.

Pinch cattle of pasture while summer doth last,
And *lift* at their tailes 'yer a winter be past. *Tusser's Hush.*

The mind, by being engaged in a task beyond its strength, like the body strained by *lifting* at a weight too heavy, has often its force broken. *Locke.*

Lift. *n. s.* [from the verb.] The act of lifting; the manner of lifting.

In the *lift* of the feet, when a man goeth up the hill, the weight of the body beareth most upon the knees. *Bacon.*

In races, it is not the large stride, or high *lift*, that makes the speed. *Bacon's Essays.*

The goat gives the fox a *lift*, and out he springs. *L'Estr.*

2. [In Scottish.] The sky: for in a starry night they say, *How clear the* lift *is!*

3. Effect; struggle. *Dead lift* is an effort to raise what with the whole force cannot be moved; and figuratively any state of impotence and inability.

Myself and Trulla made a shift
To help him out at a *dead lift*. *Hudibras, p.* i.

Mr. Doctor had puzzled his brains
In making a ballad, but was at a stand.
For you freely must own, you were at a *dead lift*. *Swift.*

4. *Lift*, in Scotland, denotes a load or surcharge of any thing; as also, if one be disguised much with liquor, they say, *He has got a great* lift.

5. *Lifts* of a sail are ropes to raise or lower them at pleasure.

Li'fter. *n. s.* [from *lift.*] One that lifts.

Thou, O Lord, art my glory, and the *lifter* up of mine head. *Psal.* iii. 3.

To Lig. *v. n.* [*leggen*, Dutch.] To lie.

Thou kenst the great care
I have of thy health and thy welfare,
Which many wild beasts *liggen* in wait,
For to entrap in thy tender state. *Spenser's Pastorals.*

LI'GAMENT. *n. s.* [*ligamentum*, from *ligo*, Latin; *ligament*, French.]

Ligament is a white and solid body, softer than a cartilage, but harder than a membrane; they have no conspicuous cavities, neither have they any sense, lest they should suffer upon the motion of the joint: their chief use is to fasten the bones, which are articulated together for motion, lest they should be dislocated with exercise. *Quincy.*

Be all their *ligaments* at once unbound,
And their disjointed bones to powder ground. *Sandys.*

The incus situate between the two former is one way joined to the malleus, the other end being a process is fixed with a *ligament* to the stapes. *Holder's Elements of Speech.*

2. [In popular or poetical language.] Any thing which connects the parts of the body.

Though our *ligaments* betimes grow weak,
We must not force them till themselves they break. *Denh.*

3. Bond; chain; entanglement.

Men sometimes, upon the hour of departure, do speak and reason above themselves; for then the soul, beginning to be freed from the *ligaments* of the body, reasons like herself, and discourses in a strain above mortality. *Addison's Spectator.*

Ligame'ntal. } *n. s.* [from *ligament.*] Composing a ligament.
Ligame'ntous. }

The urachos or *ligamental* passage is derived from the bottom of the bladder, whereby it dischargeth the watery and urinary part of its aliment. *Brown's Vulgar Errours.*

The clavicle is inserted into the first bone of the sternon, and bound in by a strong *ligamentous* membrane. *Wiseman.*

Liga'tion. *n. s.* [*ligatio*, Latin.]

1. The act of binding.

2. The state of being bound.

The slumber of the body seems to be but the waking of the soul: it is the *ligation* of sense, but the liberty of reason. *Addison's Spectator*, N°. 487.

Li'gature. *n. s.* [*ligature*, French; *ligatura*, Latin.]

1. Any thing bound on; bandage.

He deludeth us also by philters, *ligatures*, charms, and many superstitious ways in the cure of diseases. *Brown.*

If you slit the artery, and thrust into it a pipe, and cast a strait *ligature* upon that part of the artery; notwithstanding the blood hath free passage through the pipe, yet will not the artery beat below the *ligature*; but do but take off the *ligature* it will beat immediately. *Ray on Creation.*

The many *ligatures* of our English dress check the circulation of the blood. *Spectator*, N°. 576.

I found my arms and legs very strongly fastened on each side to the ground; I likewise felt several slender *ligatures* across my body, from my arm-pits to my thighs. *Gulliver's Trav.*

2. The act of binding.

The fatal noose performed its office, and with most strict *ligature* squeezed the blood into his face. *Arbuth. J. Bull.*

Any stoppage of the circulation will produce a dropsy, as by strong *ligature*, or compression. *Arbuthnot on Diet.*

3. The state of being bound.

Sand and gravel grounds easily admit of heat and moisture, for which they are not much the better, because they let it pass too soon, and contract no *ligature*. *Mortimer's Husb.*

LIGHT. *n. s.* [leoht, Saxon.]

1. That quality or action of the medium of sight by which we see.

Light is propagated from luminous bodies in time, and spends about seven or eight minutes of an hour in passing from the sun to the earth. *Newton's Opticks.*

2. Illumination of mind; instruction; knowledge.

Of those things which are for direction of all the parts of our life needful, and not impossible to be discerned by the *light* of nature itself, are there not many which few mens natural capacity hath been able to find out. *Hooker, b.* i.

Light may be taken from the experiment of the horse-tooth ring, how that those things which assuage the strife of the spirits, do help diseases contrary to the intention desired. *Bacon's Natural History*, N°. 968.

I will place within them as a guide
My umpire conscience, whom if they will hear
Light after *light* well us'd they shall attain,
And to the end persisting safe arrive. *Milton's Par. Lost.*

I opened Ariosto in Italian, and the very first two lines gave me *light* to all I could desire. *Dryden.*

If this internal *light*, or any proposition which we take for inspired, be conformable to the principles of reason, or to the word of God, which is attested revelation, reason warrants it. *Locke.*

The ordinary words of language, and our common use of them, would have given us *light* into the nature of our ideas, if considered with attention. *Locke.*

The books of Varro concerning navigation are lost, which no doubt would have given us great *light* in those matters. *Arbuthnot on Coins.*

3. The part of a picture which is drawn with bright colours, or in which the light is supposed to fall.

Never admit two equal *lights* in the same picture; but the greater *light* must strike forcibly on those places of the picture where the principal figures are; diminishing as it comes nearer the borders. *Dryden's Dufresnoy.*

4. Reach of knowledge; mental view.

Light, and understanding, and wisdom, like the wisdom of the gods, was found in him. *Dan.* v. 11.

We saw as it were thick clouds, which did put us in some hope of land, knowing how that part of the South sea was utterly unknown, and might have islands or continents that hitherto were not come to *light*. *Bacon's Nat. Hist.*

They have brought to *light* not a few profitable experiments. *Bacon's Natural History.*

5. Point of view; situation; direction in which the light falls.

Frequent consideration of a thing wears off the strangeness of it; and shews it in its several *lights*, and various ways of appearance, to the view of the mind. *South.*

It is impossible for a man of the greatest parts to consider any thing in its whole extent, and in all its variety of *lights*. *Addison's Spectator*, N°. 409.

An author who has not learned the art of ranging his thoughts, and setting them in proper *lights*, will lose himself in confusion. *Addison's Spectator*, N°. 291.

6. Explanation.

I have endeavoured, throughout this discourse, that every former part might give strength unto all that follow, and every latter bring some *light* unto all before. *Hooker, b.* i.

We should compare places of scripture treating of the same point: thus one part of the sacred text could not fail to give *light* unto another. *Locke's Essay on St. Paul's Epistles.*

7. Any thing that gives light; a pharos; a taper.

That *light* we see is burning in my hall;
How far that little candle throws his beams,
So shines a good deed in a naughty world. *Shakespeare.*

Then he called for a *light*, and sprang in, and fell down before Paul. *Acts* xvi. 29.

I have set thee to be a *light* of the Gentiles, for salvation unto the ends of the earth. *Acts* xiii. 47.

Let them be for signs,
For seasons, and for days, and circling years;
And let them be for *lights*, as I ordain
Their office in the firmament of heav'n,
To give light on the earth. *Milton's Par. Lost.*

I put as great difference between our new *lights* and ancient truths, as between the sun and an evanid meteor. *Glanville's Scep.*

Several *lights* will not be seen,
If there be nothing else between;
Men doubt because they stand so thick i' th' sky,
If those be stars that paint the galaxy. *Cowley.*

I will make some offers at their safety, by fixing some marks like *lights* upon a coast, by which their ships may avoid at least known rocks. *Temple.*

He still must mourn
The sun, and moon, and ev'ry starry *light*,
Eclips'd to him, and lost in everlasting night. *Prior.*

Light. *adj.* [leoht, Saxon.]

1. Not tending to the center with great force; not heavy.

Hot and cold were in one body fixt,
And soft with hard, and *light* with heavy mixt. *Dryden.*

These weights did not exert their natural gravity till they were laid in the golden balance, insomuch that I could not guess which was *light* or heavy whilst I held them in my hand. *Addison's Spectator*, N°. 463.

2. Not burdensome; easy to be worn, or carried, or lifted; not onerous.

Horse, oxen, plough, tumbrel, cart, waggon, and wain,
The *lighter* and stronger the greater thy gaine. *Tusser.*

It will be *light*, that you may bear it
Under a cloke that is of any length. *Shakespeare.*

A king that would not feel his crown too heavy, must wear it every day; but if he think it too *light*, he knoweth not of what metal it is made. *Bacon's Essays.*

3. Not afflictive; easy to be endured.

Every *light* and common thing incident into any part of man's life. *Hooker, b.* ii.

Light suff'rings give us leisure to complain,
We groan, but cannot speak, in greater pain. *Dryden.*

4. Easy to be performed; not difficult; not valuable.

Forgive
If fictions *light* I mix with truth divine,
And fill these lines with other praise than thine. *Fairfax.*

Well pleas'd were all his friends, the task was *light*,
The father, mother, daughter, they invite. *Dryden.*

5. Easy to be acted on by any power.

Apples of a ripe flavour, fresh and fair,
Mellow'd by winter from their cruder juice,
Light of digestion now, and fit for use. *Dryden's Juvenal.*

6. Not heavily armed.

Paulus Bachitius, with a company of *light* horſemen, lay cloſe in ambuſh, in a convenient place for that purpoſe. *Knol.*

7. Active; nimble.

He ſo *light* was at legerdemain,
That what he touch'd came not to light again. *Spenſer.*

Aſahel was as *light* of foot as a wild roe. 2 *Sam.* ii. 18.

There Stamford came, for his honour was lame
Of the gout three months together;
But it prov'd, when they fought, but a running gout,
For heels were *lighter* than ever. *Denham.*

Youths, a blooming band;
Light bounding from the earth at once they riſe,
Their feet half viewleſs quiver in the ſkies. *Pope's Odyſ.*

8. Unencumbered; unembarraſſed; clear of impediments.

Unmarried men are beſt maſters, but not beſt ſubjects; for they are *light* to run away. *Bacon.*

9. Slight; not great.

A *light* error in the manner of making the following trials was enough to render ſome of them unſucceſsful. *Boyle.*

10. Not craſs; not groſs.

In the wilderneſs there is no bread, nor water, and our ſoul loatheth this *light* bread. *Num.* xxi. 5.

Light fumes are merry, groſſer fumes are ſad,
Both are the reaſonable ſoul run mad. *Dryd. Nun's Tale.*

11. Eaſy to admit any influence; unſteady; unſettled; looſe.

Falſe of heart, *light* of ear, bloody of hand. *Shakeſpeare.*

Theſe *light* vain perſons ſtill are drunk and mad
With ſurfeitings, and pleaſures of their youth. *Davies.*

They are *light* of belief, and great liſteners after news. *Howell.*

There is no greater argument of a *light* and inconſiderate perſon, than prophanely to ſcoff at religion. *Tillotſon's Serm.*

12. Gay; airy; without dignity or ſolidity; trifling.

Seneca cannot be too heavy, nor Plautus too *light*. *Shakeſ.*

13. Not chaſte; not regular in conduct.

Let me not be *light*,
For a *light* wife doth make a heavy huſband. *Shakeſpeare.*

14. [From *light*, *n. ſ.*] Bright; clear.

As ſoon as the morning was *light*, the men were ſent away. *Gen.* xliv. 3.

The horſes ran up and down with their tails and mains on a *light* fire. *Knolles.*

15. Not dark; tending to whiteneſs.

In painting, the light and a white colour are but one and the ſame thing: no colour more reſembles the air than white, and by conſequence no colour which is *lighter*. *Dryden.*

Two cylindric bodies with annular ſulci, found with ſharks teeth, and other ſhells, in a *light* coloured clay. *Woodward.*

LIGHT. *adv.* [for *lightly*, by colloquial corruption.] Lightly; cheaply.

Shall we ſet *light* by that cuſtom of reading, from whence ſo precious a benefit hath grown. *Hooker, b.* v.

To LIGHT. *v. a.* [from *light*, *n. ſ.*]

1. To kindle; to inflame; to ſet on fire.

Swinging coals about in the wire, throughly *lighted* them. *Boyle.*

This truth ſhines ſo clear, that to go about to prove it, were to *light* a candle to ſeek the ſun. *Glanville's Scep.*

The maids, who waited her commands,
Ran in with *lighted* tapers in their hands. *Dryden.*

Be witneſs gods, and ſtrike Jocaſta dead,
If an immodeſt thought, or low deſire,
Inflam'd my breaſt ſince firſt our loves were *lighted*. *Dryden and Lee's Oedipus.*

Abſence might cure it, or a ſecond miſtreſs
Light up another flame, and put out this. *Addiſon's Cato.*

2. To give light to; to guide by light.

A beam that falls,
Freſh from the pure glance of thine eye,
Lighting to eternity. *Craſhaw.*

Ah hopeleſs, laſting flames! like thoſe that burn
To *light* the dead, and warm th' unfruitful urn. *Pope.*

3. To illuminate.

The ſun was ſet, and veſper to ſupply
His abſent beams, had *lighted* up the ſky. *Dryden.*

4. *Up* is emphatically joined to *light*.

No ſun was *lighted* up the world to view. *Dryd. Ovid.*

5. [From the adjective.] To lighten; to eaſe of a burthen.

Land ſome of our paſſengers,
And *light* this weary veſſel of her load. *Fairy Queen.*

To LIGHT. *v. n.* [*lickt*, by chance, Dutch.]

1. To happen; to fall upon by chance.

No more ſettled in valour than diſpoſed to juſtice, if either they had *lighted* on a better friend, or could have learned to make friendſhip a child, and nothe the father of virtue. *Sidney.*

The prince, by chance, did on a lady *light*,
That was right fair, and freſh as morning roſe. *Fa. Qu.*

Haply, your eye ſhall *light* upon ſome toy
You have deſire to purchaſe. *Shakeſpeare.*

As in the tides of people once up, there want not ſtirring winds to make them more rough; ſo this people did *light* upon two ringleaders. *Bacon's Henry* VIIth.

Of late years, the royal oak did *light* upon count Rhodophil. *Howel's Vocal Foreſt.*

The way of producing ſuch a change on colours may be eaſily enough *lighted* on, by thoſe converſant in the ſolutions of mercury. *Boyle on Colours.*

He ſought by arguments to ſooth her pain;
Nor thoſe avail'd: at length he *lights* on one,
Before two moons their orb with light adorn,
If heav'n allow me life, I will return. *Dryden.*

Truth, *light* upon this way, is of no more avail to us than error; for what is ſo taken up by us, may be falſe as well as true; and he has not done his duty, who has thus ſtumbled upon truth in his way to preferment. *Locke.*

Whoſoever firſt *lit* on a parcel of that ſubſtance we call gold, could not rationally take the bulk and figure to depend on its real eſſence. *Locke.*

As wily reynard walk'd the ſtreets at night,
On a tragedian's maſk he chanc'd to *light*,
Turning it o'er, he mutter'd with diſdain,
How vaſt a head is here without a brain. *Addiſon.*

A weaker man may ſometimes *light* on notions which have eſcaped a wiſer. *Watts's Improvement of the Mind.*

2. [Aliȝhtan, Saxon.] To deſcend from a horſe or carriage.

When Naaman ſaw him running after him, he *lighted* down from the chariot to meet him. 2 *Kings* v. 21.

I ſaw 'em ſalute on horſeback,
Beheld them when they *lighted*, how they clung
In their embracement. *Shakeſp. Henry* VIII.

Rebekah lifted up her eyes, and when ſhe ſaw Iſaac, ſhe *lighted* off the camel. *Gen.* xxiv. 64.

The god laid down his feeble rays,
Then *lighted* from his glittering coach. *Swift.*

3. To fall in any particular direction.

The wounded ſteed curvets; and, rais'd upright,
Lights on his feet before: his hoofs behind
Spring up in air aloft, and laſh the wind. *Dryden's Æn.*

4. To fall; to ſtrike on.

He at his foe with furious rigour ſmites,
That ſtrongeſt oak might ſeem to overthrow;
The ſtroke upon his ſhield ſo heavy *lights*,
That to the ground it doubleth him full low. *Fairy Qu.*

At an uncertain lot none can find themſelves grieved on whomſoever it *lighteth*. *Hooker, b.* i.

They ſhall hunger no more; neither ſhall the ſun *light* on them, nor any heat. *Rev.* vii. 16.

On me, me only, as the ſource and ſpring
Of all corruption, all the blame *lights* due. *Milt. Pa. L.*

A curſe *lights* upon him preſently after: his great army is utterly ruined, he himſelf ſlain in it, and his head and right hand cut off, and hung up before Jeruſalem. *South's Serm.*

5. To ſettle; to reſt.

I plac'd a quire of ſuch enticing birds,
That ſhe will *light* to liſten to their lays. *Shakeſpeare.*

Then as a bee which among weeds doth fall,
Which ſeem ſweet flow'rs, with luſtre freſh and gay,
She *lights* on that, and this, and taſteth all,
But pleas'd with none, doth riſe and ſoar away. *Davis.*

Plant trees and ſhrubs near home, for them to pitch on at their ſwarming, that they may not be in danger of being loſt for want of a *lighting* place. *Mortimer's Huſbandry.*

To LI'GHTEN. *v. n.* [ꝉiꝫ, liȝt, Saxon.]

1. To flaſh, with thunder.

This dreadful night,
That thunders, *lightens*, opens graves, and roars
As doth the lion. *Shakeſpeare's Julius Cæſar.*

Although I joy in thee,
I have no joy of his contract to night;
It is too raſh, too unadvis'd, too ſudden,
Too like the light'ning, which doth ceaſe to be
Ere one can ſay it *lightens*. *Shakeſp. Romeo and Juliet.*

The lightning that *lighteneth* out of the one part under heaven, ſheweth unto the other part. *Luke* xvii. 24.

2. To ſhine like lightning.

Yet looks he like a king: behold his eye,
As bright as is the eagle's, *lightens* forth
Controlling majeſty. *Shakeſp. Richard* II.

3. To fall or light. [from *light*.]

O Lord, let thy mercy *lighten* upon us, as our truſt is in thee. *Common Prayer.*

To LI'GHTEN. *v. a.* [from *light*.]

1. To illuminate; to enlighten.

Upon his bloody finger he doth wear
A precious ring, that *lightens* all the hole. *Shakeſpeare.*

O light, which mak'ſt the light which makes the day,
Which ſett'ſt the eye without, and mind within;
Lighten my ſpirit with one clear heav'nly ray,
Which now to view itſelf doth firſt begin. *Davies.*

A key of fire ran all along the ſhore,
And *lighten'd* all the river with a blaze. *Dryden.*

Nature from the ſtorm
Shines out afreſh; and through the *lighten'd* air
A higher luſtre, and a clearer calm,
Diffuſive tremble. *Thomſon's Summer.*

2. To exonerate; to unload.

The mariners were afraid, and caſt forth the wares that were in the ſhip into the ſea, to *lighten* it of them. *Jon.* i. 7.

3. To make leſs heavy.

Long ſince with woe
Nearer acquainted, now I feel by proof,
That fellowſhip in pain divides not ſmart,
Nor *lightens* aught each man's peculiar load. *Parad. Reg.*

Strive
In offices of love how we may *lighten*
Each other's burden. *Milt. Pa. Loſt.*

4. To exhilarate; to cheer.

A truſty villain, very oft,
When I am dull with care and melancholy,
Lightens my humour with his merry jeſts. *Shakeſpeare.*

The audience are grown weary of continued melancholy ſcenes; and few tragedies ſhall ſucceed in this age, if they are not *lightened* with a courſe of mirth. *Dryd. Span. Friar.*

LI'GHTER. *n. ſ.* [from *light*, to make *light*.] A heavy boat into which ſhips are lightened or unloaded.

They have cock boats for paſſengers, and *lighters* for burthen. *Carew's Survey of Cornwall.*

He climb'd a ſtranded *lighter's* height,
Shot to the black abyſs, and plung'd downright. *Pope.*

LI'GHTERMAN. *n. ſ.* [*lighter* and *man*.] One who manages a lighter.

Where much ſhipping is employed, whatever becomes of the poor merchant, multitudes of people will be certain gainers; as ſhipwrights, butchers, carmen, and *lightermen*. *Child's Diſcourſe on Trade.*

LIGHTFI'NGERED. *adj.* [*light* and *finger*.] Nimble at conveyance; thieviſh.

LI'GHTFOOT. *adj.* [*light* and *foot*.] Nimble in running or dancing; active.

And eke the *lightfoot* maids that keep the deer. *Spenſer.*
Him ſo far had born his *lightfoot* ſteed,
Pricked with wrath and fiery fierce diſdain,
That him to follow was but fruitleſs pain. *Fairy Queen.*
And all the troop of *lightfoot* Naïades
Flock all about to ſee her lovely face. *Spenſer's Fa. Qu.*

LIGHTFO'OT. *n. ſ.* Veniſon. A cant word.

LIGHTHE'ADED. *ad.* [*light* and *head*.]

1. Unſteady; looſe; thoughtleſs; weak.

The Engliſh liturgy, how piouſly and wiſely ſoever framed, had found great oppoſition; the ceremonies had wrought only upon *lightheaded*, weak men, yet learned men excepted againſt ſome particulars. *Clarendon.*

2. Delirious; diſordered in the mind by diſeaſe.

LIGHTHE'ADEDNESS. *n. ſ.* Deliriouſneſs; diſorder of the mind.

LIGHTHE'ARTED. *adj.* [*light* and *heart*.] Gay; merry; airy; cheerful.

LIGHTHO'USE. *n. ſ.* [*light* and *houſe*.] An high building, at the top of which lights are hung to guide ſhips at ſea.

He charged himſelf with the riſque of ſuch veſſels as carried corn in winter; and built a pharos or *lighthouſe*. *Arbuth.*

Build two poles to the meridian, with immenſe *lighthouſes* on the top of them. *Arbuthnot and Pope.*

LIGHTLE'GGED. *adj.* [*light* and *leg*.] Nimble; ſwift.

Lightlegged Pas has got the middle ſpace. *Sidney.*

LI'GHTLESS. *adj.* [from *light*.] Wanting light; dark.

LI'GHTLY. *adv.* [from *light*.]

1. Without weight.

This grave partakes the fleſhly birth,
Which cover *lightly*, gentle earth. *Benj. Johnſon.*

2. Without deep impreſſion.

The ſoft ideas of the cheerful note,
Lightly receiv'd, were eaſily forgot. *Prior.*

3. Eaſily; readily; without difficulty; of courſe.

If they write or ſpeak publickly but five words, one of them is *lightly* about the dangerous eſtate of the church of England in reſpect of abuſed ceremonies. *Hooker, b.* iv.

Believ't not *lightly* that your ſon
Will not exceed the common, or be caught
With cautelous baits and practice. *Shakeſp. Coriolanus.*

Short Summer *lightly* has a forward ſpring. *Shakeſp.*

The traitor in faction *lightly* goeth away with it. *Bacon.*

4. Without reaſon.

Flatter not the rich; neither do thou willingly or *lightly* appear before great perſonages. *Taylor's Guide.*

Let every man that hath a calling be diligent in purſuance of its employment, ſo as not *lightly*, or without reaſonable occaſion, to neglect it. *Taylor's Holy Living.*

5. Without affliction; cheerfully.

Bid that welcome
Which comes to puniſh us, and we puniſh it,
Seeming to bear it *lightly*. *Shakeſp. Ant. and Cleopatra.*

6. Not chaſtly.

If I were *lightly* diſpoſed, I could ſtill perhaps have offers, that ſome, who hold their heads higher, would be glad to accept. *Swift's Story of an injured Lady.*

7. Nimbly; with agility; not heavily or tardily.

Methought I ſtood on a wide river's bank;
When on a ſudden, Toriſmond appear'd,
Gave me his hand, and led me *lightly* o'er;
Leaping and bounding on the billows heads,
Till ſafely we had reach'd the farther ſhore. *Dryden.*

8. Gaily; airily; with levity; without heed or care.

LIGHTMI'NDED. *adj.* [*light* and *mind*.] Unſettled; unſteady.

He that is haſty to give credit is *lightminded*. *Eccl.* xix. 4.

LI'GHTNESS. *n. ſ.* [from *light*.]

1. Levity; want of weight; abſence of weight.

Some are for maſts of ſhips, as fir and pine, becauſe of their length, ſtraightneſs, and *lightneſs*. *Bacon's Nat. Hiſt.*

Suppoſe many degrees of littleneſs and *lightneſs* in particles, ſo as many might float in the air a good while before they fell. *Burnet's Theory of the Earth.*

2. Inconſtancy; unſteadineſs.

For, unto knight there is no greater ſhame,
Than *lightneſs* and inconſtancy in love. *Fairy Queen.*

Of two things they muſt chuſe one; namely, whether they would, to their endleſs diſgrace, with ridiculous *lightneſs*, diſmiſs him, whoſe reſtitution they had in ſo importunate manner deſired, or elſe condeſcend unto that demand. *Hooker.*

As I blow this feather from my face,
Obeying with my wind when I do blow,
And yielding to another when it blows,
Commanded always by the greateſt guſt;
Such is the *lightneſs* of you common men. *Shakeſpeare.*

3. Unchaſtity; want of conduct in women.

Is it the diſdain of my eſtate, or the opinion of my *lightneſs*, that have emboldened ſuch baſe fancies towards me? *Sidney, b.* ii.

Can it be,
That modeſty may more betray our ſenſe,
Than woman's *lightneſs*. *Shakeſp. Meaſure for Meaſure.*

4. Agility; nimbleneſs.

LI'GHTNING. *n. ſ.* [from *lighten*, *lightening*, *lightning*.]

1. The flaſh that attends thunder.

Lightning is a great flame, very bright, extending every way to a great diſtance, ſuddenly darting upwards, and there ending, ſo that it is only momentaneous. *Muſchenbrock.*

Senſe thinks the *lightning* born before the thunder;
What tells us then they both together are? *Davies.*

Salmoneus, ſuff'ring cruel pains I found
For emulating Jove; the rattling ſound
Of mimick thunder, and the glitt'ring blaze
Of pointed *lightnings*, and their forky rays. *Dryd. Æn.*

No warning of the approach of flame,
Swiftly, like ſudden death, it came;
Like travellers by *lightning* kill'd,
I burnt the moment I beheld. *Granville.*

2. Mitigation; abatement.

How oft when men are at the point of death,
Have they been merry? which their keepers call
A *lightning* before death. *Shakeſp. Romeo and Juliet.*

We were once in hopes of his recovery, upon a kind meſſage from the widow; but this only proved a *lightning* before death. *Addiſon's Spectator*, N°. 517.

LIGHTS. *n. ſ.* [ſuppoſed to be called ſo from their lightneſs in proportion to their bulk.] The lungs; the organs of breathing.

The complaint was chiefly from the *lights*, a part as of no quick ſenſe, ſo no ſeat for any ſharp diſeaſe. *Hayward.*

LI'GHTSOME. *adj.* [from *light*.]

1. Luminous; not dark; not obſcure; not opake.

Neither the ſun, nor any thing ſenſible is that light itſelf, which is the cauſe that things are *lightſome*, though it make itſelf, and all things elſe, viſible; but a body moſt enlightened, by whom the neighbouring region, which the Greeks call æther, the place of the ſuppoſed element of fire, is effected and qualified. *Raleigh.*

White walls make rooms more *lightſome* than black. *Bac.*

Equal poſture, and quick ſpirits, are required to make colours *lightſome*. *Bacon's Nat. Hiſtory.*

The Sun
His courſe exalted through the Ram had run
Through Taurus, and the *lightſome* realms of love. *Dryd.*

2. Gay; airy; having the power to exhilarate.

It ſuiteth ſo fitly with that *lightſome* affection of joy, wherein God delighteth when his ſaints praiſe him. *Hooker.*

The *lightſome* paſſion of joy was not that which now often uſurps the name; that trivial, vaniſhing, ſuperficial thing, that only gilds the apprehenſion, and plays upon the ſurface of the ſoul. *South's Sermons.*

LI'GHTSOMENESS. *n. ſ.* [from *lightſome*.]

1. Luminouſneſs; not opacity; not obſcurity; not darkſomeneſs.

It is to our atmosphere that the variety of colours, which are painted on the skies, the *lightsomeness* of our air, and the twilight, are owing. *Cheyne's Philosophical Principles.*

2. Cheerfulness; merriment; levity.

LIGNA'LOES. *n. s.* [*lignum aloes*, Latin.] Aloes wood.

The vallies spread forth as gardens by the river's side, as the trees of *lignaloes* which the Lord hath planted, and as cedar trees beside the water. *Num.* xxiv. 6.

LI'GNEOUS. *adj.* [*ligneus*, Latin; *ligneux*, French.] Made of wood; wooden; resembling wood.

It should be tried with shoots of vines, and roots of red roses; for it may be they, being of a more *ligneous* nature, will incorporate with the tree itself. *Bacon's Nat. Hist.*

Ten thousand seeds of the plant harts-tongue, hardly make the bulk of a pepper-corn: now the covers, and the true body of each seed, the parenchymous and *ligneous* part of both, and the fibres of those parts, multiplied one by another, afford a hundred thousand millions of formed atoms, but how many more we cannot define. *Grew's Cosmol.*

LIGNUMVITÆ. n. s. [Lat.] Guiacum; a very hard wood.

It hath pinnated leaves; the flower consists of several petals, which are placed orbicularly, and expand in form of a rose; the pointal of the flower, which arises from the center of the calyx, becomes a fleshy, roundish, stony fruit, or the stony seeds are surrounded with a thin pulp. *Miller.*

LI'GURE. *n. s.* A precious stone.

The third row a *ligure*, an agate, and an amethyst. *Exod.*

LIKE. *adj.* [lic, Saxon; *liik*, Dutch.]

1. Resembling; having resemblance.

Whom art thou *like* in thy greatness. *Ezek.* xxxi. 2.

His son, or one of his illustrious name,
How *like* the former, and almost the same. *Dryd. Æn.*

As the earth was designed for the being of men, why might not all other planets be created for the *like* uses, each for their own inhabitants. *Bentley's Sermons.*

This plan, as laid down by him, looks *liker* an universal art than a distinct logick. *Baker's Reflect. on Learning.*

2. Equal; of the same quantity.

More clergymen were impoverished by the late war, than ever in the *like* space before. *Sprat's Sermons.*

3. [For *likely*.] Probable; credible.

The trials were made, and it is *like* that the experiment would have been effectual. *Bacon's Natural History.*

4. Likely; in a state that gives probable expectations. This is, I think, an improper, though frequent, use.

If the duke continues these favours towards you, you are *like* to be much advanced. *Shakespeare's Twelfth Night.*

He is *like* to die for hunger, for there is no more bread. *Jer.* xxxviii. 9.

The yearly value thereof is already increased double of that it was within these few years, and is *like* daily to rise higher, till it amount to the price of our land in England. *Davies.*

Hopton resolved to visit Waller's quarters, that he might judge whether he were *like* to pursue his purpose. *Clarendon.*

Many were not easy to be governed, nor *like* to conform themselves to strict rules. *Clarendon, b.* viii.

If his rules of reason be not better suited to the Mind than his rules for health are fitted to our bodies, he is not *like* to be much followed. *Baker's Reflections on Learning.*

LIKE. *n. s.* [This substantive is seldom more than the adjective used elliptically; *the like* for the *like thing*, or *like person*.]

1. Some person or thing resembling another.

He was a man, take him for all in all,
I shall not look upon his *like* again. *Shakesp. Hamlet.*

Every *like* is not the same, O Cæsar. *Shakes. Jul. Cæsar.*

Though there have been greater fleets for number, yet for the bulk of the ships never the *like*. *Bacon's War with Spain.*

Albeit an eagle did bear away a lamb in her talons, yet a raven endeavouring to do the *like* was held entangled. *Hayw.*

One offers, and in offering makes a stay;
Another forward sets, and doth no more;
A third the *like*. *Daniel's Civil War.*

His desire
By conversation with his *like* to help,
Or solace his defects. *Milton's Paradise Lost, b.* viii.

Two *likes* may be mistaken. *L'Estrange's Fab.*

She'd study to reform the men,
Or add some grains of folly more,
To women than they had before;
This might their mutual fancy strike,
Since ev'ry being loves its *like*. *Swift.*

2. Near approach; a state like to another state. A sense common, but not just.

Report being carried secretly from one to another in my ship, had *like* to have been my utter overthrow. *Raleigh.*

LIKE. *adv.*

1. In the same manner; in the same manner as.

The joyous nymphs, and lightfoot fairies,
Which thither came to hear their musick sweet;
Now hearing them so heavily lament,
Like heavily lamenting from them went. *Spenser.*

Like as a father pitieth his children, so the Lord pitieth them that fear him. *Psal.* ciii. 13.

Are we proud and passionate, malicious and revengeful? Is this to be *like*-minded with Christ, who was meek and lowly? *Tillotson's Sermons.*

What will be my confusion, when he sees me
Neglected, and forsaken *like* himself. *Philips's Dist. Mother.*

They roar'd *like* lions caught in toils, and rag'd:
The man knew what they were, who heretofore
Had seen the like lie murther'd on the shore. *Waller.*

2. In such a manner as befits.

Be strong, and quit yourselves *like* men. 1 *Sam.* iv. 9.

3. Likely; probably. A popular use not analogical.

I like the work well, ere it be demanded,
As *like* enough it will, I'd have it copied. *Shakespeare.*

To LIKE. *v. a.* [lican, Saxon; *liiken*, Dutch.]

1. To chuse with some degree of preference.

As nothing can be so reasonably spoken as to content all men, so this speech was not of them all *liked*. *Knolles.*

He gave such an account as made it appear that he *liked* the design. *Clarendon, b.* viii.

We *like* our present circumstances well, and dream of no change. *Atterbury's Sermons.*

2. To approve; to view with approbation, not fondness.

He stayed behind to bring the shepherds with whom he meant to confer to breed the better Zelmane's *liking*, which he only regarded. *Sidney, b.* i.

Though they did not *like* the evil he did, yet they *liked* him that did the evil. *Sidney, b.* ii.

He grew content to mark their speeches, then to marvel at such wit in shepherds, after to *like* their company. *Sidney.*

He proceeded from looking to *liking*, and from *liking* to loving. *Sidney.*

For several virtues
I have *lik'd* several women; never any
With so full soul. *Shakespeare's Tempest.*

I look'd upon her with a soldier's eye;
That *liked*, but had a rougher task in hand
Than to drive *liking* to the name of love. *Shakespeare.*

Scarce any man passes to a *liking* of sin in others, but by first practising it himself. *South's Sermons,*

Beasts can *like*, but not distinguish too,
Nor their own *liking* by reflection know. *Dryden.*

3. To please; to be agreeable to. Now disused.

Well hoped he, ere long that hardy guest,
If ever covetous hand, or lustful eye,
Or lips he laid on thing that *lik'd* him best,
Should be his prey. *Spenser's Fairy Queen, b.* ii.

Say, my fair brother now, if this device
Do *like* you, or may you to *like* entice. *Hubberd's Tale.*

This desire being recommended to her majesty, it *liked* her to include the same within one entire lease. *Bacon.*

He shall dwell where it *liketh* him best. *Deut.* xxiii. 16.

There let them learn, as *likes* them, to despise
God and Messiah. *Milton's Paradise Lost, b.* vi.

To LIKE. *v. n.*

1. To be pleased with, with *of* before the thing approved. Obsolete.

Of any thing more than *of* God they could not by any means *like*, as long as whatsoever they knew besides God, they apprehended it not in itself without dependancy upon God. *Hooker, b.* i.

The young soldiers did with such cheerfulness *like of* this resolution, that they thought two days a long delay. *Knolles.*

It is true, there are limits to be set betwixt the boldness and rashness of a poet; but he must understand those limits who pretends to judge, as well as he who undertakes to write: and he who has no *liking* to the whole, ought in reason to be excluded from censuring of the parts. *Dryden.*

2. To chuse; to list; to be pleased.

The man *likes* not to take his brother's wife. *Deut.* xxv. 7.

He that has the prison doors set open is perfectly at liberty, because he may either go or stay, as he best *likes*. *Locke.*

LI'KELIHOOD.
LI'KELINESS. } *n. s.* [from *likely*.]

1. Appearance; shew. Obsolete.

What of his heart perceive you in his face,
By any *likelihood* he show'd to-day?
—That with no man here he is offended. *Shakespeare.*

2. Resemblance; likeness. Obsolete.

The mayor and all his brethren in best sort,
Like to the senators of antique Rome,
Go forth and fetch their conqu'ring Cæsar in.
As by a low, but loving *likelihood*,
Were now the general of our gracious empress,
As in good time he may, from Ireland coming,
How many would the peaceful city quit,
To welcome him. *Shakespeare's Henry* V.

There is no *likelihood* between pure light and black darkness, or between righteousness and reprobation. *Raleigh.*

3. Probability; verisimilitude; appearance of truth.

As it noteth one such to have been in that age, so had there

there been moe, it would by *likelihood* as well have noted many. *Hooker*, *b.* ii.

Many of *likelihood* informed me of this before, which hung so tottering in the balance, that I could neither believe nor misdoubt. *Shakespeare's All's well that ends well.*

It never yet did hurt,
To lay down *likelihood*, and forms of hope. *Shakespeare.*

As there is no *likelihood* that the place could be so altered, so is there no probability that these rivers were turned out of their courses. *Raleigh's Hist. of the World.*

Where things are least to be put to the venture, as the eternal interests of the other world ought to be; there every, even the least, probability, or *likelihood* of danger, should be provided against. *South's Sermons.*

There are predictions of our Saviour recorded by the Evangelists, which were not completed till after their deaths, and had no *likelihood* of being so when they were pronounced by our blessed Saviour. *Addison on the Christian Religion.*

Thus, in all *likelihood*, would it be with a libertine, who should have a visit from the other world: the first horror it raised would go off, as new diversions come on. *Atterbury.*

LI'KELY. *adj.* [from *like.*]

1. Such as may be liked; such as may please. Obsolete.

These young companions make themselves believe they love at the first looking of a *likely* beauty. *Sidney.*

Sir John, they are your *likeliest* men; I would have you served with the best. *Shakesp. Henry* IV. *p.* ii.

2. Probable; such as may in reason be thought or believed; such as may be thought more reasonably than the contrary.

LI'KELY. *adv.* Probably; as may reasonably be thought.

While man was innocent, he was *likely* ignorant of nothing that imported him to know. *Glanville's Scep.*

To LI'KEN. *v. a.* [from *like.*] To represent as having resemblance; to compare.

The prince broke your head for *likening* him to a singing man of Windsor. *Shakesp. Henry* IV. *p.* ii.

For who, though with the tongue
Of angels, can relate? or to what things
Liken on earth conspicuous, that may lift
Human imagination to such heighth
Of God-like power? *Milton's Paradise Lost*, *b.* vi.

LI'KENESS. *n. s.* [from *like.*]

1. Resemblance; similitude.

They all do live, and moved are
To multiply the *likeness* of their kind. *Spenser.*

A translator is to make his author appear as charming as he can, provided he maintains his character, and makes him not unlike himself. Translation is a kind of drawing after the life, where there is a double sort of *likeness*, a good one and a bad one. *Dryden.*

In such cases there will be found a better *likeness*, and a worse; and the better is constantly to be chosen. *Dryden.*

2. Form; appearance.

Never came trouble to my house in the *likeness* of your grace; for trouble being gone, comfort should remain. *Shak.*

It is safer to stand upon our guard against an enemy in the *likeness* of a friend, than to embrace any man for a friend in the *likeness* of an enemy. *L'Estrange.*

3. One who resembles another.

Poor Cupid, sobbing, scarce could speak,
Indeed mamma, I did not know ye:
Alas! how easy my mistake?
I took you for your *likeness* Cloe. *Prior.*

LI'KEWISE. *adv.* [*like* and *wise.*] In like manner; also; moreover; too.

Jesus said unto them, I also will ask you one thing, which if ye tell me, I *likewise* will tell you by what authority I do these things. *Mat.* xxi. 24.

So was it in the decay of the Roman empire, and *likewise* in the empire of Almaigne, after Charles the Great, every bird taking a feather. *Bacon's Essays.*

Spirit of vitriol poured to pure unmixed serum, coagulates it as if it had been boiled. Spirit of sea-salt makes a perfect coagulation of the serum *likewise*, but with some different phænomena. *Arbuthnot on Aliments.*

LI'KING. *adj.* [Perhaps because plumpness is agreeable to the sight.] Plump; in a state of plumpness.

I fear my lord the king, who hath appointed your meat and your drink; for why should he see your faces worse *liking*, than the children which are of your sort. *Dan.* i. 10.

LI'KING. *n. s.* [from *like.*]

1. Good state of body; plumpness.

I'll repent, and that suddenly, while I am in some *liking*; I shall be out of heart shortly, and then I shall have no strength to repent. *Shakespeare's Henry* IV.

Their young ones are in good *liking*; they grow up with corn. *Job* xxxix. 4.

Cappadocian slaves were famous for their lustiness; and, being in good *liking*, were set on a stall when exposed to sale, to shew the good habit of their body. *Dryden's Notes to Pers.*

2. State of trial.

The royal soul, that, like the lab'ring moon,
By charms of art was hurried down;
Forc'd with regret to leave her native sphere,
Came but awhile on *liking* here. *Dryden.*

3. Inclination.

Why do you longer feed on loathed light,
Or *liking* find to gaze on earthly mold. *Fairy Queen.*

LI'LACH. *n. s.* [*lilac*, *lilâs*, French.] A tree.

The white thorn is in leaf, and the *lilach* tree. *Bacon.*

LI'LIED. *adj.* [from *lily.*] Embellished with lilies.

Nymphs and shepherds dance no more
By sandy Ladon's *lillied* banks. *Milton.*

LI'LY. *n. s.* [*lilium*, Latin.]

The *lily* hath a bulbous root, consisting of several fleshy scales adhering to an axis; the stalk is greatly furnished with leaves; the flower is composed of six leaves, and is shaped somewhat like a bell: in some species the petals are greatly reflexed, but in others but little; from the centre of the flower rises the pointal, which becomes an oblong fruit, commonly triangular, divided into three cells, and full of compressed seeds, which are bordered, lying upon each other in a double row. There are thirty-two species of this plant, including white *lilies*, orange *lilies*, red *lilies*, and martagons of various sorts. *Miller.*

Oh! had the monster seen those *lily* hands
Tremble, like aspen leaves, upon a lute,
And make the silken strings delight to kiss them;
He would not then have touch'd them for his life. *Shakesp.*

Shipwreck'd upon a kingdom where no pity!
No friends! no hope! no kindred weep for me!
Almost no grave allow'd me! like the *lily*,
That once was mistress of the field, and flourish'd,
I'll hang my head, and perish. *Shakesp. Henry* VIII.

Arnus, a river of Italy, is drawn like an old man, by his right side a lion, holding forth in his right paw a red *lily*, or flower-de-luce. *Peacham on Drawing.*

Take but the humblest *lily* of the field;
And if our pride will to our reason yield;
It must by sure comparison be shown,
That on the regal seat great David's son,
Array'd in all his robes, and types of pow'r,
Shines with less glory than that simple flow'r. *Prior.*

Go, gentle gales, and bear my sighs along:
For her the feather'd quires forget their song,
For her the *lilies* hang their heads, and die. *Pope.*

LILY-DAFFODIL. *n. s.* [*lilio-narcissus.*] A foreign flower.

LILY-HYACINTH. *n. s.* [*lilio-hyacinthus.*]

It hath a *lily* flower, composed of six leaves, shaped like the flower of hyacinth, whose pointal becomes a globular pointed fruit, three-cornered, and divided into three cells, in which are contained many seeds, almost round: the roots are scaly, and shaped like those of the *lily*. There are three species of this plant; one with a blue flower, another white, and a third red. *Miller.*

LILY *of the Valley*, or *May lily.* *n. s.* [*lilium convallium.*]

The flower consists of one leaf, is shaped like a bell, and divided at the top into six segments; the ovary becomes a soft globular fruit, containing several round seeds. It is very common in shady woods. *Miller.*

Lily of the valley has a strong root that runs into the ground. *Mortimer's Husbandry.*

LILYLI'VERED. *adj.* [*lily* and *liver.*] Whitelivered; cowardly.

A knave, a rascal, an eater of broken meats; a base, proud, shallow, beggarly, three-suited, hundred pound, filthy worsted-stocking knave; a *lilylivered*, action-taking knave. *Shakespeare's King Lear.*

LI'MATURE. *n. s.* [*limatura*, Lat.] Filings of any metal; the particles rubbed off by a file.

LIMB. *n. s.* [lim, Saxon and Scottish; *lem*, Danish.]

1. A member; a jointed or articulated part of animals.

A second Hector, for his grim aspect,
And large proportion of his strong knit *limbs*. *Shakesp.*

O! that I had her here, to tear her *limb* meal. *Shakesp.*

Now am I come each *limb* to survey,
If thy appearance answer loud report. *Milton's Agonistes.*

2. [*Limbe*, French; *limbus*, Latin.] An edge; a border. A philosophical word.

By farther moving the prisms about, the colours again emerged out of the whiteness, the violet and the blue at its inward *limb*, and at its outward *limb* the red and yellow. *Newton's Opticks.*

To LIMB. *v. a.* [from the noun.]

1. To supply with limbs.

As they please,
They *limb* themselves, and colour, shape, and size
Assume, as likes them best, condense, or rare. *Milton.*

2. To tear asunder; to dismember.

LI'MBECK. *n. s.* [corrupted by popular pronunciation from *alembick.*] A still.

Her cheeks, on which this streaming nectar fell,
Still'd through the *limbeck* of her diamond eyes. *Fairfax.*

All

All others from all things draw all that's good,
Life, soul, form, spirit, where they being have;
I, by love's *limbeck*. *Donne.*

Fires of Spain, and the line,
Whose countries *limbecks* to our bodies be,
Canst thou for gain bear? *Donne.*

Call up, unbound,
In various shapes, old Proteus from the sea,
Drain'd through a *limbeck* to his naked form. *Milton.*

The earth, by secret conveyances, lets in the sea, and sends it back fresh, her bowels serving for a *limbeck*. *Howell.*

He first survey'd the charge with careful eyes,
Yet judg'd, like vapours that from *limbecks* rise,
It would in richer showers descend again. *Dryden.*

The warm *limbeck* draws
Salubrious waters from the nocent brood. *Philips.*

Li'mbed. *adj.* [from *limb.*] Formed with regard to limbs.

A steer of five years age, large *limb'd*, and fed,
To Jove's high altars Agamemnon led. *Pope's Iliad.*

Li'mber. *adj.* Flexible; easily bent; pliant; lithe.

You put me off with *limber* vows. *Shakespeare.*

I wonder how, among these jealousies of court and state, Edward Atheling could subsist, being then the apparent and indubitate heir of the Saxon line: but he had tried, and found him a prince of *limber* virtues; so as though he might have some place in his caution, yet he reckoned him beneath his fear. *Wotton.*

At once came forth whatever creeps the ground,
Insect, or worm: those wav'd their *limber* fans
For wings; and smallest lineaments exact
In all the liveries deck'd of Summer's pride. *Milton.*

She durst never stand at the bay, having nothing but her long soft *limber* ears to defend her. *More on Atheism.*

The muscles were strong on both sides of the aspera arteria, but on the under side, opposite to that of the œsophagus, very *limber*. *Ray on Creation.*

At last the ulcer is covered over with a *limber* callus. *Harv.*

Li'mberness. *n. s.* [from *limber.*] Flexibility; pliancy.

Li'mbo. *n. s.* [*Eo quod sit* limbus *inferorum. Du Cange.*]

1. A region bordering upon hell, in which there is neither pleasure nor pain. Popularly hell.

No, he is in tartar *limbo*, worse than hell,
A devil in an everlasting garment hath him,
One whose hard heart is button'd up with steel. *Shakesp.*

Oh what a sympathy of woe is this!
As far from help as *limbo* is from bliss. *Shakesp.*

All these up-whirl'd aloft
Fly o'er the backside of the world far off,
Into a *limbo* large, and broad, since call'd
The paradise of fools. *Milton's Paradise Lost, b.* iii.

2. Any place of misery and restraint.

For he no sooner was at large,
But Trulla straight brought on the charge;
And in the self-same *limbo* put
The knight and squire, where he was shut. *Hudibras.*

Friar, thou art come off thyself, but poor I am left in *limbo*. *Dryden's Spanish Friar.*

Lime. *n. s.* [lim, ȝelyman, Saxon, to glue.]

1. A viscous substance drawn over twigs, which catches and entangles the wings of birds that light upon it.

Poor bird! thoud'st never fear the net or *lime*,
The pitfall, nor the gin. *Shakespeare's Macbeth.*

You must lay *lime*, to tangle her desires,
By wailful sonnets, whose composed rhimes
Should be full fraught with serviceable vows. *Shakesp.*

Monster, come put some *lime* upon your fingers, and away with the rest. *Shakespeare's Tempest.*

Jollier of this state
Than are new-benefic'd ministers, he throws,
Like nets or *lime* twigs, whereso'er he goes,
His title of barrister on every wench. *Donne.*

A poor thrush was taken with a bush of *lime* twigs. *L'Estrange's Fables.*

Then toils for beasts, and *lime* for birds were found,
And deep-mouth'd dogs did forest walks surround. *Dryden.*

Or court a wife, spread out his wily parts
Like nets, or *lime* twigs, for rich widows hearts. *Pope.*

2. Matter of which mortar is made: so called because used in cement.

There are so many species of *lime* stone, that we are to understand by it in general any stone that, upon a proper degree of heat, becomes a white calx, which will make a great ebullition and noise on being thrown into water, falling into a loose white powder at the bottom. The *lime* we have in London is usually made of chalk, which is weaker than that made of stone. *Hill's Materia Medica.*

They were now, like sand without *lime*, ill bound together, especially as many as were English, who were at a gaze, looking strange one upon another, not knowing who was faithful to their side. *Bacon's Henry* VII.

As when a lofty pile is rais'd,
We never hear the workmen prais'd,
Who bring the *lime*, or place the stones,
But all admire Inigo Jones. *Swift.*

Lime is commonly made of chalk, or of any sort of stone that is not sandy, or very cold; as freestone, *&c. Mortimer.*

Lime *tree*, or Linden. *n. s.*
[Lind, Saxon.] The linden tree.

The flower consists of several leaves, placed orbicularly, in the form of a rose, having a long narrow leaf growing to the footstalk of each cluster of flowers, from whose cup rises the pointal, which becomes testiculated, of one capsule, containing an oblong seed. The timber is used by carvers and turners. These trees continue sound many years, and grow to a considerable bulk. Sir Thomas Brown mentions one, in Norfolk, sixteen yards in circuit. *Millar.*

Go, gentle gales! and bear my sighs along.
For her the *limes* their pleasing shades deny,
For her the lilies hang their heads, and die. *Pope.*

4. A species of lemon. [*lime*, French.]

Bear me, Pomona! to thy citron groves;
To where the lemon and the piercing *lime*,
With the deep orange glowing through the green,
Their lighter glories blend. *Thomson's Summer.*

To Lime. *v. a.* [from *lime.*]

1. To entangle; to ensnare.

Oh bosom, black as death!
Oh *limed* soul, that, struggling to be free,
Art more engaged. *Shakespeare's Hamlet.*

Example, that so terrible shows in the wreck of maidenhood, cannot, for all that, dissuade succession, but that they are *limed* with the twigs that threaten them. *Shakespeare.*

The bird that hath been *limed* in a bush,
With trembling wings misdoubeth ev'ry bush;
And I, the hapless male to one sweet bird,
Have now the fatal object in my eye,
Where my poor young was *lim'd*, was caught, and kill'd. *Shakespeare's Henry* VI.

2. To smear with lime.

Myself have *lim'd* a bush for her,
And place a quire of such enticing birds,
That she will light to listen to their lays. *Shakespeare.*

Those twigs in time will come to be *limed*, and then you are all lost if you do but touch them. *L'Estrange.*

3. To cement.

I will not ruinate my father's house,
Who gave his blood to *lime* the stones together,
And set up Lancaster. *Shakesp. Henry* VI.

4. To manure ground with lime.

The reason why they did so was, because of the encouragement which that abatement of interest gave to landlords and tenants, to improve by draining, marling, and *liming*. *Child.*

All sorts of pease love *limed* or marled land. *Mortimer.*

Li'mekiln. *n. s.* [*lime* and *kiln.*] Kiln where stones are burnt to lime.

The counter gate is as hateful to me, as the reek of a *lime kiln*. *Shakesp. Merry Wives of Windsor.*

They were found in a *lime kiln*, and having passed the fire, each is a little vitrified. *Woodward.*

Limestone. *n. s.* [*lime* and *stone.*] The stone of which lime is made.

Fire stone and *lime stone*, if broke small, and laid on cold lands, must be of advantage. *Mortimer's Husbandry.*

Lime-water. *n. s.*

Lime water, made by pouring water upon quick lime, with some other ingredients to take off its ill flavour, is of great service internally in all cutaneous eruptions, and diseases of the lungs. *Hill's Materia Medica.*

He tried an experiment on wheat infused in *lime water* alone, and some in brandy and *lime water* mixed, and had from each grain a great increase. *Mortimer's Husbandry.*

Li'mit. *n. s.* [*limite*, French; *limitor*, Latin.] Bound; border; utmost reach.

The whole *limit* of the mountain round about shall be most holy. *Exod.* xliii. 12.

To Li'mit. *v. a.* [*limiter*, French, from the noun.] To confine with certain bounds; to restrain; to circumscribe; not to leave at large.

They tempted God, and *limited* the Holy One of Israel. *Psal.* lxxviii. 41.

Thanks I must you con,
That you are thieves profest;
For there is boundless theft
In *limited* professions. *Shakesp. Timon of Athens.*

If a king come in by conquest, he is no longer a *limited* monarch. *Swift.*

2. To restrain from a lax or general signification; as, *the universe is here* limited *to this earth.*

Limita'neous. *adj.* [from *limit.*] Belonging to the bounds. *Dictionary.*

LI'MITARY. *adj.* [from *limit.*] Placed at the boundaries as a guard or superintendant.

Then, when I am thy captive, talk of chains,
Proud *limitary* cherub! *Milton's Paradise Lost.*

LIMITA'TION. *n. s.* [*limitation*, French; *limitatio*, Latin.]

1. Restriction; circumscription.

Limitation of each creature, is both the perfection and the preservation thereof. *Hooker, b.* v.

Am I yourself,
But, as it were, in sort of *limitation.* *Shakesp. Jul. Cæsar.*

I despair, how this *limitation* of Adam's empire to his line and posterity, will help us to one heir. This *limitation*, indeed, of our author, will save those the labour, who would look for him amongst the race of brutes; but will very little contribute to the discovery amongst men. *Locke.*

If a king come in by conquest, he is no longer a limited monarch; if he afterwards consent to *limitations*, he becomes immediately king de jure. *Swift.*

2. Confinement from a lax or undeterminate import.

The cause of error is ignorance; what restraints and *limitations* all principles have in regard of the matter whereunto they are applicable. *Hooker, b.* v.

LI'MMER. *n. s.* A mongrel. *Ains.*

To LIMN. *v. a.* [*enluminer*, French, to adorn books with pictures.] To draw; to paint any thing.

Mine eye doth his effigies witness,
Most truly *limn'd*, and living in your face. *Shakespeare.*
Emblems *limned* in lively colours. *Peacham.*

How are the glories of the field spun, and by what pencil are they *limned* in their unaffected bravery? *Glanville.*

LI'MNER. *n. s.* [corrupted from *enlumineur*, a decorator of books with initial pictures.] A painter; a picture-maker.

That divers *limners* at a distance, without either copy or design, should draw the same picture to an undistinguishable exactness, is more conceivable than that matter, which is so diversified, should frame itself so inerringly, according to the idea of its kind. *Glanville's Scept.*

Poets are *limners* of another kind,
To copy out ideas in the mind;
Words are the paint by which their thoughts are shown,
And nature is their object to be drawn. *Granville.*

LI'MOUS. *adj.* [*limosus*, Latin.] Muddy; slimy.

That country became a gained ground by the muddy and *limous* matter brought down by the Nilus, which settled by degrees unto a firm land. *Brown's Vulgar Errours.*

They esteemed this natural melancholick acidity to be the *limous* or slimy fœculent part of the blood. *Floyer.*

LIMP. *adj.* [*limpio*, Italian.]

1. Vapid; weak.

The chub eats waterish, and the flesh of him is not firm, *limp* and tasteless. *Walton's Angler.*

2. It is used in some provinces, and in Scotland, for *limber*, flexile.

To LIMP. *v. n.* [*limpen*, Saxon.] To halt; to walk lamely.

An old poor man,
Who after me hath many a weary step
Limp'd in pure love. *Shakesp. As you like it.*

Son of sixteen,
Pluck the lin'd crutch from thy old *limping* sire. *Shakesp.*

How far
The substance of my praise doth wrong this shadow
In underprising it; so far this shadow
Doth *limp* behind the substance. *Shakespeare.*

When Plutus, which is riches, is sent from Jupiter, he *limps* and goes slowly; but when he is sent by Pluto, he runs, and is swift of foot. *Bacon.*

Limping death, lash'd on by fate,
Comes up to shorten half our date. *Dryden's Horace.*

The *limping* smith observ'd the sadden'd feast,
And hopping here and there put in his word. *Dryden.*

Can syllogism set things right?
No: majors soon with minors fight:
Or both in friendly consort join'd,
The consequence *limps* false behind. *Prior.*

LI'MPET. *n. s.* A kind of shell fish. *Ainsworth.*

LI'MPID. *adj.* [*limpide*, French; *limpidus*, Lat.] Clear; pure; transparent.

The springs which were clear, fresh, and *limpid*, become thick and turbid, and impregnated with sulphur as long as the earthquake lasts. *Woodward's Natural History.*

The brook that purls along
The vocal grove, now fretting o'er a rock,
Gently diffus'd into a *limpid* plain. *Thomson's Summer.*

LI'MPIDNESS. *n. s.* [from *limpid.*] Clearness; purity.

LI'MPINGLY. *adv.* [from *limp.*] In a lame halting manner.

LI'MY. *adj.* [from *lime.*]

1. Viscous; glutinous.

Striving more, the more in laces strong
Himself he tied, and wrapt his winges twain
In *limy* snares the subtil loops among. *Spenser.*

2. Containing lime.

A human skull covered with the skin, having been buried in some *limy* soil, was tanned, or turned into a kind of leather. *Grew's Musæum.*

To LIN. *v. n.* [ablinnan, Saxon.] To stop; to give over.

Unto his foe he came,
Resolv'd in mind all suddenly to win,
Or soon to lose before he once would *lin.* *Fairy Queen.*

LI'NCHPIN. *n. s.* [*linch* and *pin.*] An iron pin, that keeps the wheel on the axle-tree. *Dict.*

LI'NCTUS. *n. s.* [from *lingo*, Latin.] Medicine licked up by the tongue.

LINDEN. *n. s.* [lınd, Saxon.] The lime tree. See LIME.

Hard box, and *linden* of a softer grain. *Dryden.*

Two neighb'ring trees, with walls encompass'd round,
One a hard oak, a softer *linden* one. *Dryden.*

LINE. *n. s.* [*linea*, Latin.]

1. Longitudinal extension.

Even the planets, upon this principle, must gravitate no more towards the Sun; so that they would not revolve in curve *lines*, but fly away in direct tangents, till they struck against other planets. *Bentley's Sermons.*

2. A slender string.

Well sung the Roman bard; all human things,
Of dearest value, hang on slender strings;
O see the then sole hope, and in design
Of heav'n our joy, supported by a *line.* *Waller.*

A *line* seldom holds to strein, or draws streight in length, above fifty or sixty feet. *Moxon's Mechanical Exercises.*

3. A thread extended to direct any operations.

We as by *line* upon the ocean go,
Whose paths shall be familiar as the land. *Dryden.*

4. The string that sustains the angler's hook.

Victorious with their *lines* and eyes,
They make the fishes and the men their prize. *Waller.*

5. Lineaments, or marks in the hand or face.

Long is it since I saw him,
But time hath nothing blurr'd those *lines* of favour
Which then he wore. *Shakespeare's Cymbeline.*

I shall have good fortune; go to, here's a simple *line* of life; here's a small trifle of wives. *Shakespeare.*

Here, while his canting drone-pipe scan'd
The mystic figures of her hand,
He tipples palmestry, and dines
On all her fortune-telling *lines.* *Cleaveland.*

6. Delineation; sketch.

You have generous thoughts turned to such speculations: but this is not enough towards the raising such buildings as I have drawn you here the *lines* of, unless the direction of all affairs here were wholly in your hands. *Temple.*

The inventors meant to turn such qualifications into persons as were agreeable to his character, for whom the *line* was drawn. *Pope's Essay on Homer.*

7. Contour; outline.

Oh lasting as those colours may they shine,
Free as thy stroke, yet faultless as thy *line!* *Pope.*

8. As much as is written from one margin to the other: a verse.

In the preceding *line*, Ulysses speaks of Nausicaa, yet immediately changes the words into the masculine gender. *Broome's Notes on the Odyssey.*

In many *lines* these few epistles tell
What fate attends. *Garth.*

9. Rank.

10. Work thrown up; trench.

Now snatch an hour that favours thy designs,
Unite thy forces, and attack their *lines.* *Dryden's Æn.*

11. Method; disposition.

The heavens themselves, the planets, and this center,
Observe degree, priority, and place,
Insisture, course, proportion, season, form,
Office and custom, in all *line* of order. *Shakespeare.*

12. Extension; limit.

Eden stretch'd her *line*
From Auran eastward to the royal tow'rs
Of great Seleucia. *Milton's Paradise Lost, b.* iv.

13. Equator; equinoctial circle.

When the sun below the *line* descends,
Then one long night continued darkness joins. *Creech.*

14. Progeny; family, ascending or descending.

He chid the sisters
When first they put the name of king upon me,
And bade them speak to him; then prophet like,
They hail'd him father to a *line* of kings. *Shakespeare.*

He sends you this most memorable *line*,
In ev'ry branch truly demonstrative,
Willing you overlook this pedigree. *Shakesp. Henry* V.

Some *lines* were noted for a stern, rigid virtue, savage, haughty, parsimonious and unpopular; others were sweet and affable. *Dryden.*

His empire, courage, and his boasted *line*,
Were all prov'd mortal. *Roscommon.*

A golden

A golden bowl
The queen commanded to be crown'd with wine,
The bowl that Belus us'd, and all the Tyrian *line*. *Dryd.*

The years
Ran ſmoothly on, productive of a *line*
Of wiſe heroick kings. *Philips.*

15. A *line* is one tenth of an inch. *Locke.*

16. [In the plural.] A letter; as, I read your *lines*.

17. Lint or flax.

To LINE. *v. a.* [ſuppoſed by *Junius* from *linum*, linings being made of linen.]

1. To cover on the inſide.

A box *lined* with paper to receive the mercury that might be ſpilt. *Boyle.*

2. To put any thing in the inſide.

The charge amounteth very high for any one man's purſe, except *lined* beyond ordinary, to reach unto. *Carew.*

Her women are about her: what if I do *line* one of their hands. *Shakeſp. Cymbeline.*

He, by a gentle bow, divin'd
How well a cully's purſe was *lin'd*. *Swift.*

3. To guard within.

Notwithſtanding they had *lined* ſome hedges with muſqueteers, they were totally diſperſed. *Clarendon, b.* viii.

4. To ſtrengthen by inner works.

Line and new repair our towns of war
With men of courage, and with means defendant. *Shakeſ.*

5. To cover.

Son of ſixteen,
Pluck the *lin'd* crutch from thy old limping ſire. *Shakeſp.*

6. To double; to ſtrengthen.

Who *lin'd* himſelf with hope,
Eating the air, on promiſe of ſupply. *Shakeſpeare.*

My brother Mortimer doth ſtir
About his title, and hath ſent for you
To *line* his enterpriſe. *Shakeſp. Henry* IV. *p.* i.

The two armies were aſſigned to the leading of two generals, both of them rather courtiers, and aſſured to the ſtate, than martial men; yet *lined* and aſſiſted with ſubordinate commanders of great experience and valour. *Bacon.*

7. To impregnate, applied to animals generating.

Thus from the Tyrian paſtures *lin'd* with Jove
He bore Europa, and ſtill keeps his love. *Creech.*

LI'NEAGE. *n. ſ.* [*linage*, French.] Race; progeny; family, aſcending or deſcending.

Both the *lineage* and the certain ſire
From which I ſprung, from me are hidden yet. *Fa. Qu.*

Joſeph was of the houſe and *lineage* of David. *Luke* ii. 4.

The Tirſan cometh forth with all his generation or *lineage*, the males before him, and the females following him; and if there be a mother from whoſe body the whole *lineage* is deſcended, there is a traverſe where ſhe ſitteth. *Bacon.*

Men of mighty fame,
And from th' immortal gods their *lineage* came. *Dryden.*

No longer ſhall the widow'd land bemoan
A broken *lineage*, and a doubtful throne,
But boaſt her royal progeny's increaſe,
And count the pledges of her future peace. *Addiſon.*

This care was infuſed into them by God himſelf, in order to aſcertain the deſcent of the Meſſiah, and to prove that he was, as the prophets had foretold, of the tribe of Judah, and of the *lineage* of David. *Atterbury's Sermons.*

LI'NEAL. *adj.* [*linealis*, from *linea*, Latin.]

1. Compoſed of lines; delineated.

When any thing is mathematically demonſtrated weak, it is much more mechanically weak; errors ever occurring more eaſily in the management of groſs materials than *lineal* deſigns. *Wotton's Architecture.*

2. Deſcending in a direct genealogy.

To re-eſtabliſh, de facto, the right of *lineal* ſucceſſion to paternal government, is to put a man in poſſeſſion of that government which his fathers did enjoy, and he by *lineal* ſucceſſion had a right to. *Locke.*

3. Claimed by deſcent.

Peace be to France, if France in peace permit
Our juſt and *lineal* ent'rance to our own. *Shakeſ. K. John.*

4. Allied by direct deſcent.

Queen Iſabel, his grandmother,
Was *lineal* of the lady Ermengere. *Shakeſpeare's Henry* V.

O that your brows my laurel had ſuſtain'd!
Well had I been depos'd if you had reign'd:
The father had deſcended for the ſon;
For only you are *lineal* to the throne. *Dryden.*

LI'NEALLY. *adv.* [from *lineal*.] In a direct line.

If he had been the perſon upon whom the crown had *lineally* and rightfully deſcended, it was good law. *Clarendon.*

LI'NEAMENT. *n. ſ.* [*lineament*, French; *lineamentum*, Latin.] Feature; diſcriminating mark in the form.

When that my mother went with child
Of that inſatiate Edward, noble York
Found that the iſſue was not his begot:
Which well appeared in his *lineaments*,
Being nothing like the noble duke, my father. *Shakeſp.*

In companions
There muſt needs be a like proportion
Of *lineaments*, of manners, and of ſpirit. *Shakeſpeare.*

Six wings he wore, to ſhade
His *lineaments* divine. *Milton's Paradiſe Loſt, b.* v.

Man he ſeems
In all his *lineaments*, though in his face
The glimpſes of his father's glory ſhine. *Paradiſe Reg.*

There are not more differences in mens faces, and the outward *lineaments* of their bodies, than there are in the makes and tempers of their minds; only there is this difference, that the diſtinguiſhing characters of the face, and the *lineaments* of the body, grow more plain with time, but the peculiar phyſiognomy of the mind is moſt diſcernible in children. *Locke.*

Advance religion and morals, by tracing ſome few *lineaments* in the character of a lady, who hath ſpent all her life in the practice of both. *Swift.*

The utmoſt force of boiling water is not able to deſtroy the ſtructure of the tendereſt plant: the *lineaments* of a white lily will remain after the ſtrongeſt decoction. *Arbuthnot.*

LI'NEAR. *adj.* [*linearis*, Latin.] Compoſed of lines; having the form of lines.

Where-ever it is freed from the ſand ſtone, it is covered with *linear* ſtriæ, tending towards ſeveral centers, ſo as to compoſe flat ſtellar figures. *Woodward on Foſſils.*

LINEA'TION. *n. ſ.* [*lineatio*, from *linea*.] Draught of a line or lines.

There are in the horney ground two white *lineations*, with two of a pale red. *Woodward.*

LI'NEN. *n. ſ.* [*linum*, Latin.] Cloth made of hemp or flax.

Here is a baſket, he may creep in; throw foul *linen* upon him, as if going to bucking. *Shakeſp. M. Wives of Windſor.*

Unſeen, unfelt, the fiery ſerpent ſkims
Between her *linen* and her naked limbs. *Dryden's Æn.*

LI'NEN. *adj.* [*lineus*, Latin.]

1. Made of linen.

A *linen* ſtock on one leg, and a kerſey boot hoſe on the other, gartered with a red and blue liſt. *Shakeſpeare.*

2. Reſembling linen.

Death of thy ſoul! thoſe *linen* cheeks of thine
Are counſellors to fear. What ſoldiers, whey-face? *Shak.*

LINENDR'APER. *n. ſ.* [*linen* and *draper*.] He who deals in linen.

LING. *n. ſ.* [*ling*, Iſlandick.]

1. Heath. This ſenſe is retained in the northern counties; yet *Bacon* ſeems to diſtinguiſh them.

Heath, and *ling*, and ſedges. *Bacon's Natural Hiſtory.*

2. [*Linghe*, Dutch.] A kind of ſea fiſh.

When harveſt is ended take ſhipping, or ride,
Ling, ſalt fiſh, and herring, for lent to provide. *Tuſſer.*

Our Engliſh bring from thence good ſtore of fiſh, but eſpecially our deepeſt and thickeſt *ling*, which are therefore called iſland *lings*. *Abbot's Deſcript. of the World.*

LING. The termination notes commonly diminution; as, kit*ling*, and is derived from *klein*, German, *little*; ſometimes a quality; as, firſt*ling*, in which ſenſe *Skinner* deduces it from *langen*, old Teutonick, to belong.

To LI'NGER. *v. n.* [from lenʒ, Saxon, *long*.]

1. To remain long in languor and pain.

Like wretches, that have *linger'd* long,
We'll ſnatch the ſtrongeſt cordial of our love. *Dryden.*

Better to ruſh at once to ſhades below,
Than *linger* life away, and nouriſh woe. *Pope's Odyſſey.*

2. To heſitate; to be in ſuſpenſe.

Perhaps thou *ling'reſt*, in deep thoughts detain'd
Of th' enterprize ſo hazardous and high. *Paradiſe Reg.*

3. To remain long. In an ill ſenſe.

Let order die,
And let this world no longer be a ſtage
To feed contention in a *ling'ring* act. *Shakeſp. Henry* IV.

Ye breth'ren of the lyre, and tuneful voice,
Lament his lot; but at your own rejoice.
Now live ſecure, and *linger* out your days;
The gods are pleas'd alone with Purcel's lays. *Dryden.*

Your very fear of death ſhall make ye try
To catch the ſhade of immortality;
Wiſhing on earth to *linger*, and to ſave
Part of its prey from the devouring grave. *Prior.*

4. To remain long without any action or determination.

We have *lingered* about a match between Anne Page and my couſin Slender, and this day we ſhall have our anſwer. *Shakeſp. Merry Wives of Windſor.*

5. To wait long in expectation or uncertainty.

I muſt ſollicit
All his concerns as mine:
And if my eyes have pow'r, he ſhould not ſue
In vain, nor *linger* with a long delay. *Dryden's Cleomenes.*

6. To be long in producing effect.

She doth think, ſhe has ſtrange *ling'ring* poiſons. *Shakeſp.*

To LI'NGER. *v. a.* To protract; to draw out to length. Out of use.

I can get no remedy against this consumption of the purse. Borrowing only *lingers* and *lingers* it out, but the disease is incurable. *Shakesp. Henry* IV. *p.* i.

She *lingers* my desires. *Shakespeare.*

Let your brief plagues be mercy,
And *linger* not our sure destructions on. *Shakespeare.*

LI'NGERER. *n. s.* [from *linger.*] One who lingers.

LI'NGERINGLY. *adj.* [from *lingering.*] With delay; tediously.

Of poisons, some kill more gently and *lingeringly*, others more violently and speedily, yet both kill. *Hale.*

LI'NGET. *n. s.* [from *languet*; *lingot*, French.] A small mass of metal.

Other matter hath been used for money, as among the Lacedemonians, iron *lingets* quenched with vinegar, that they may serve to no other use. *Camden.*

LI'NGO. *n. s.* [Portuguese.] Language; tongue; speech. A low cant word.

I have thoughts to learn somewhat of your *lingo*, before I cross the seas. *Congreve's Way of the World.*

LINGUA'CIOUS. *ad.* [*linguax*, Latin.] Full of tongue; loquacious; talkative.

LINGUADE'NTAL. *adj.* [*lingua* and *dens*, Latin.] Uttered by the joint action of the tongue and teeth.

The *linguadentals f, v*, as also the *linguadentals th, dh*, he will soon learn. *Holder's Elements of Speech.*

LI'NGUIST. *n. s.* [from *lingua.*] A man skilful in languages.

Though a *linguist* should pride himself to have all the tongues that Babel cleft the world into, yet, if he had not studied the solid things in them, as well as the words and lexicons, he were nothing so much to be esteemed a learned man, as any yeoman or tradesman competently wise in his mother dialect only. *Milton on Education.*

Our *linguist* received extraordinary rudiments towards a good education. *Addison's Spectator.*

LI'NGWORT. *n. s.* An herb.

LI'NIMENT. *n. s.* [*liniment*, French; *linimentum*, Lat.] Ointment; balsam; unguent.

The nostrils, and the jugular arteries, ought to be anointed every morning with this *liniment* or balsam. *Harvey.*

The wise author of nature hath provided on the rump two glandules, which the bird catches hold upon with her bill, and squeezes out an oily pap or *liniment*, fit for the inunction of the feathers. *Ray on Creation.*

LI'NING. *n. s.* [from *line.*]

1. The inner covering of any thing; the inner double of a garment.

Was I deceived, or did a sable cloud
Turn forth her silver *lining* on the night. *Milton.*

The folds in the gristle of the nose is covered with a *lining*, which differs from the facing of the tongue. *Grew's Cosmol.*

The gown with stiff embroid'ry shining,
Looks charming with a slighter *lining*. *Prior.*

2. That which is within.

The *lining* of his coffers shall make coats
To deck our soldiers for these Irish wars. *Shakespeare.*

LINK. *n. s.* [*gelencke*, German.]

1. A single ring of a chain.

The Roman state, whose course will yet go on
The way it takes, cracking ten thousand curbs
Of more strong *links* asunder, than can ever
Appear in your impediment. *Shakespeare's Coriolanus.*

The moral of that poetical fiction, that the uppermost *link* of all the series of subordinate causes, is fastened to Jupiter's chair, signifies an useful truth. *Hale.*

Truths hang together in a chain of mutual dependance; you cannot draw one *link* without attracting others. *Glanville.*

While she does her upward flight sustain,
Touching each *link* of the continued chain,
At length she is oblig'd and forc'd to see
A first, a source, a life, a deity. *Prior.*

2. Any thing doubled and closed together.

Make a *link* of horse hair very strong, and fasten it to the end of the stick that springs. *Mortimer's Husbandry.*

3. A chain; any thing connecting.

Nor airless dungeon, nor strong *links* of iron,
Can be retentive to the strength of spirit. *Shakespeare.*

I feel
The *link* of nature draw me; flesh of flesh,
Bone of my bone thou art. *Milton's Par. Lost, b.* ix.

Fire, flood and earth, and air, by this were bound,
And love, the common *link*, the new creation crown'd. *Dryden's Knight's Tale.*

4. Any single part of a series or chain of consequences; a gradation in ratiocination; a proposition joined to a foregoing and following proposition.

The thread and train of consequences in intellective ratiocination is often long, and chained together by divers *links*, which cannot be done in imaginative ratiocination by some attributed to brutes. *Judge Hale.*

5. A series: this sense is improper. *Addison* has used *link* for chain.

Though I have here only chosen this single *link* of martyrs, I might find out others among those names which are still extant, that delivered down this account of our Saviour in a successive tradition. *Addison on the Christian Religion.*

6. [From λύχνος.] A torch made of pitch and hards.

O, thou art an everlasting bonefire light; thou hast saved me a thousand marks in *links* and torches, walking with thee in the night betwixt tavern and tavern. *Shakesp. Henry* IV.

Whereas history should be the torch of truth, he makes her in divers places a fulginous *link* of lies. *Howel.*

Round as a globe, and liquor'd every chink,
Goodly and great he sails behind his *link*. *Dryden.*

One that bore a *link*
On a sudden clapp'd his flaming cudgel,
Like Linstock, to the horse's touch-hole. *Hudibras, p.* ii.

7. Perhaps in the following passage it may mean lamp-black.

There was no *link* to colour Peter's hat;
And Walter's dagger was not come from sheathing. *Shak.*

To LINK. *v. a.* [from the noun.]

1. To complicate; as, the links of a chain.

Descending tread us down
Thus drooping; or with *linked* thunderbolts
Transfix us to the bottom of this gulph. *Milt. Par. Lost.*

Against eating cares,
Lap me in soft Lydian airs;
Married to immortal verse,
Such as the meeting soul may pierce
In notes, with many a winding bought
Of *linked* sweetness long drawn out. *Milton.*

2. To unite; to conjoin in concord.

They're so *link'd* in friendship,
That young prince Edward marries Warwick's daughter. *Shakespeare's Henry* VI. *p.* iii.

3. To join.

Link towns to towns with avenues of oak,
Inclose whole downs in walls, 'tis all a joke. *Pope's Hor.*

So from the first eternal order ran,
And creature *link'd* to creature, man to man. *Pope.*

4. To join by confederacy or contract.

They make an offer of themselves into the service of that enemy, with whose servants they *link* themselves in so near a bond. *Hooker, b.* ii.

Be advised for the best,
Ere thou thy daughter *link* in holy band
Of wedlock, to that new unknown guest. *Fairy Queen.*

Blood in princes *link'd* not in such sort,
As that it is of any pow'r to tye. *Daniel's Civil War.*

5. To connect.

New hope to spring
Out of despair; joy, but with fear yet *link'd*. *Milton.*

God has *linkt* our hopes and our duty together. *Dec. of Pi.*

So gracious hath God been to us, as to *link* together our duty and our interest, and to make those very things the instances of our obedience, which are the natural means and causes of our happiness. *Tillotson's Sermons.*

6. To unite or concatenate in a regular series of consequences.

These things are *linked*, and, as it were, chained one to another: we labour to eat, and we eat to live, and we live to do good; and the good which we do is as seed sown, with reference unto a future harvest. *Hooker, b.* i.

Tell me, which part it does necessitate?
Ill chuse the other; there I'll *link* th' effect;
A chain, which fools to catch themselves project! *Dryd.*

By which chain of ideas thus visibly *linked* together in train, *i. e.* each intermediate idea agreeing on each side with those two, it is immediately placed between, the ideas of men and self-determination appear to be connected. *Locke.*

LI'NKBOY. *n. s.* [*link* and *boy.*] A boy that carries a torch to accommodate passengers with light.

What a ridiculous thing it was, that the continued shadow of the earth should be broken by sudden miraculous disclusions of light, to prevent the officiousness of the *linkboy*. *More's Divine Dialogues.*

Though thou art tempted by the *linkman*'s call,
Yet trust him not along the lonely wall. *Gay.*

In the black form of cinder wench she came.
O may no *linkboy* interrupt their love. *Gay's Trivia.*

LI'NNET. *n. s.* [*linot*, French.] A small singing bird.

The swallows make use of celandine, the *linnet* of euphragia, for the repairing of their sight. *More's Antidote.*

Is it for thee the *linnet* pours his throat? *Pope.*

LINSE'ED. *n. s.* [*semen lini*, Latin.] The seed of flax, which is much used in medicine.

The joints may be closed with a cement of lime, *linseed* oil, and cotton. *Mortimer's Husbandry.*

LI'NSEYWOOLSEY. *adj.* [*linen* and *wool.*] Made of linen and wool mixed. Vile; mean; of different and unsuitable parts.

A lawless *linseywoolsie* brother,
Half of one order, half another. *Hudibras, p.* i.

Peel'd, patch'd and pyebald, *linseywoolsey* brothers,
Grave mummers! sleeveless some, and shirtless others. *Pope's Dunciad, b.* iii.

LI'NSTOCK.

LI'NSTOCK. *n. s.* [*lunte* or *lente*, Teutonick, *lint* and *stock.*] A staff of wood with a match at the end of it, used by gunners in firing cannon. *Hanmer.*

The nimble gunner
With *lynstock* now the devilish cannon touches,
And down goes all before him. *Shakesp. Henry V.*

The distance judg'd for shot of ev'ry size,
The *linstocks* touch, the pond'rous ball expires. *Dryden.*

LINT. *n. s.* [*linteum*, Latin; *llin*, Welsh and Erse.]

1. The soft substance commonly called flax.

2. Linen scraped into soft woolly substance to lay on sores.

I dressed them up with unguentum basilici cum vitello ovi, upon pledgits of *lint*. *Wiseman's Surgery.*

LI'NTEL. *n. s.* [*linteaux*, from *linteal*, French.] That part of the door frame that lies cross the door posts over head.

Take a bunch of hysop, and dip it in the blood that is in the bason, and strike the *lintel* and the two side posts. *Exod.*

When you lay any timber on brick work, as *lintels* over windows, lay them in loam, which is a great preserver of timber. *Moxon's Mechanical Exercises.*

Silver the *lintals* deep projecting o'er,
And gold the ringlets that command the door. *Pope's Odyss.*

LI'ON. *n. s.* [*lion*, French; *leo*, Latin.] The fiercest and most magnanimous of fourfooted beasts.

King Richard's sirname was Cor-de-Lion, for his *lion*-like courage. *Camden's Remains.*

Dismay'd not this
Our captains Macbeth and Banquo? — Yes,
As sparrows, eagles, or the hare, the *lion*. *Shakespeare.*

Be *lion* mettled; proud, and take no care
Who chafes, who frets, or where conspirers are;
Macbeth shall never vanquish'd be. *Shakes. Macbeth.*

The sphinx, a famous monster in Egypt, had the face of a virgin, and the body of a *lion*. *Peacham on Drawing.*

They rejoice
Each with their kind, *lion* with lioness;
So fitly them in pairs thou hast combin'd. *Milt. Pa. Lost.*

The *lion* for the honours of his skin,
The squeezing crab, and stinging scorpion shine
For aiding heaven, when giants dar'd to brave
The threat'ned stars. *Creech's Manilius.*

See *lion* hearted Richard,
Piously valiant, like a torrent swell'd
With wintry tempests, that disdains all mounds,
Breaking away impetuous, and involves
Within its sweep trees, houses, men, he press'd,
Amidst the thickest battle. *Philips.*

LI'ONESS. *n. s.* [feminine of *lion.*] A she lion.

Under which bush's shade, a *lioness*
Lay couching head on ground, with catlike watch
When that the sleeping man should stir. *Shakespeare.*

The furious *lioness*,
Forgetting young ones, through the fields doth roar. *May.*

The greedy *lioness* the wolf pursues,
The wolf the kid, the wanton kid the browze. *Dryden.*

If we may believe Pliny, lions do, in a very severe manner, punish the adulteries of the *lioness*. *Ayliffe's Parergon.*

LI'ONLEAF. *n. s.* [*leontopetalon*, Latin.]

It hath a thick tuberose perennial root; the flower is naked, and consists of five or six petals, which expand in form of a rose, garnished with five stamina; in the middle of the flower arises the pointal, which afterward becomes a bladder, containing many spherical seeds. *Miller.*

LI'ON'S-MOUTH.
LI'ON'S-PAW.
LI'ON'S-TAIL.
LI'ON'S-TOOTH. } *n. s.* [from *lion.*] The name of an herb.

LIP. *n. s.* [lippe, Saxon.]

1. The outer part of the mouth, the muscles that shoot beyond the teeth, which are of so much use in speaking, that they are used for all the organs of speech.

Those happiest smiles
That play'd on her ripe *lip*, seem'd not to know
What guests were in her eyes. *Shakesp. King Lear.*

No falshood shall defile my *lips* with lies,
Or with a vail of truth disguise. *Sandys's Paraph. on Job.*

Her *lips* blush deeper sweets. *Thomson's Spring.*

2. The edge of any thing.

In many places is a ridge of mountains some distance from the sea, and a plain from their roots to the shore; which plain was formerly covered by the sea, which bounded against those hills as its first ramparts, or as the ledges or *lips* of its vessel. *Burnet's Theory of the Earth.*

In wounds, the *lips* sink and are flaccid; a gleet followeth, and the flesh within withers. *Wiseman's Surgery.*

3. To make a lip; to hang the lip in sullenness and contempt.

A letter for me! It gives me an estate of seven years health; in which time I will make a *lip* at the physician. *Shakespeare's Coriolanus.*

To LIP. *v. a.* [from the noun.] To kiss. Obsolete.

A hand, that kings
Have *lipt*, and trembled kissing. *Shakesp. Ant. and Cleop.*

Oh! 'tis the fiend's arch mock,
To *lip* a wanton, and suppose her chaste. *Shakespeare.*

LIPLA'BOUR. *n. s.* [*lip* and *labour.*] Action of the lips without concurrence of the mind; words without sentiments.

Fasting, when prayer is not directed to its own purposes, is but *liplabour*. *Taylor's Rule of holy living.*

LIPO'THYMOUS. *adj.* [λείπω and θυμός.] Swooning; fainting.

If the patient be surprised with a *lipothymous* languor, and great oppression about the stomach and hypochonders, expect no relief from cordials. *Harvey on the Plague.*

LIPO'THYMY. *n. s.* [λειποθυμία.] Swoon; fainting fit.

The senators falling into a *lipothymy*, or deep swooning, made up this pageantry of death with a representing of it unto life. *Taylor's worthy Communicant.*

In *lipothymys* or swoonings, he used the frication of this finger with saffron and gold. *Brown's Vulgar Errours.*

LI'PPED. *adj.* [from *lip.*] Having lips.

LI'PPITUDE. *n. s.* [*lippitude*, Fr. *lippitudo*, Latin.] Blearedness of eyes.

Diseases that are infectious are, such as are in the spirits and not so much in the humours, and therefore pass easily from body to body; such are pestilences and *lippitudes*. *Bac.*

LI'PWISDOM. *n. s.* [*lip* and *wisdom.*] Wisdom in talk without practice.

I find that all is but *lipwisdom*, which wants experience; I now, woe is me, do try what love can do. *Sidney, b. i.*

LI'QUABLE. *adj.* [from *liquo*, Latin.] Such as may be melted.

LI'QUATION. *n. s.* [from *liquo*, Latin.]

1. The art of melting.

2. Capacity to be melted.

The common opinion hath been, that crystal is nothing but ice and snow concreted, and by duration of time, congealed beyond *liquation*. *Brown's Vulgar Errours, b. ii.*

To LI'QUATE. *v. n.* [*liquo*, Latin.] To melt; to liquefy.

If the salts be not drawn forth before the clay is baked, they are apt to *liquate*. *Woodward on Fossils.*

LIQUEFA'CTION. *n. s.* [*liquefactio*, Lat. *liquefaction*, French.] The act of melting; the state of being melted.

Heat dissolveth and melteth bodies that keep in their spirits, as in divers *liquefactions*; and so doth time in honey, which by age waxeth more liquid. *Bacon's Natural History.*

The burning of the earth will be a true *liquefaction* or dissolution of it, as to the exterior region. *Burnet.*

LI'QUEFIABLE. *adj.* [from *liquefy.*] Such as may be melted.

There are three causes of fixation, the even spreading of the spirits and tangible parts, the closeness of the tangible parts, and the jejuneness or extreme comminution of spirits; the two first may be joined with a nature *liquefiable*, the last not. *Bacon's Natural History, N°. 799.*

To LI'QUEFY. *v. a.* [*liquefier*, French; *liquefacio*, Latin.] To melt; to dissolve.

That degree of heat which is in lime and ashes, being a smothering heat, is the most proper, for it doth neither *liquefy* nor rarefy; and that is true maturation. *Bacon's Nat. Hist.*

To LIQUEFY. *v. n.* To grow limpid.

The blood of St. Januarius *liquefied* at the approach of the saint's head. *Addison's Remarks on Italy.*

LIQUE'SCENCY. *n. s.* [*liquescentia*, Latin.] Aptness to melt.

LIQUE'SCENT. *n. s.* [*liquescens*, Latin.] Melting.

LI'QUID. *adj.* [*liquide*, French; *liquidus*, Latin.]

1. Not solid; not forming one continuous substance; fluid.

Gently rolls the *liquid* glass. *Daniel.*

2. Soft; clear.

Her breast, the sug'red nest
Of her delicious soul, that there does lie,
Bathing in streams of *liquid* melody. *Crashaw.*

3. Pronounced without any jar or harshness.

The many *liquid* consonants give a pleasing sound to the words, though they are all of one syllable. *Dryden's Æn.*

Let Carolina smooth the tuneful lay,
Lull with Amelia's *liquid* name the nine,
And sweetly flow through all the royal line. *Pope's Horace.*

4. Dissolved, so as not to be obtainable by law.

If a creditor should appeal to hinder the burial of his debtor's corpse, his appeal ought not to be received, since the business of burial requires a quick dispatch, though the debt be entirely *liquid*. *Ayliffe's Parergon.*

LI'QUID. *n. s.* Liquid substance; liquor.

Be it thy choice, when Summer heats annoy,
To sit beneath her leafy canopy,
Quaffing rich *liquids*. *Philips.*

To LI'QUIDATE. *v. a.* [from *liquid.*] To clear away; to lessen debts.

LIQUI'DITY. *n. s.* [from *liquid.*] Subtilty.

The spirits, for their *liquidity*, are more incapable than the fluid medium, which is the conveyer of sounds, to persevere in the continued repetition of vocal airs. *Glanville's Scep.*

LI'QUIDNESS. *n. s.* [from *liquid.*] Quality of being liquid; fluency.

Oil of annifeeds, in a cool place, thickened into the consistence of white butter, which, with the least heat, resumed its former *liquidness*. *Boyle.*

LIQUOR. *n. s.* [*liquor*, Latin; *liqueur*, French.]

1. Any thing liquid: it is commonly used of fluids inebriating, or impregnated with something, or made by decoction.

Nor envy'd them the grape
Whose heads that turbulent *liquor* fills with fumes. *Milton.*

Sin taken into the soul, is like a *liquor* poured into a vessel; so much of it as it fills, it also seasons. *South's Sermons.*

2. Strong drink; in familiar language.

To LIQUOR. *v. a.* [from the noun.] To drench or moisten.

Cart wheels squeak not when they are *liquored.* *Bacon.*

LIRICO'NFANCY. *n. s.* A flower.

LISNE. *n. s.* A cavity; a hollow.

In the *lisne* of a rock at Kingscote in Gloucestershire, I found a bushel of petrified cockles, each near as big as my fist. *Judge Hale's Originat. of Mankind.*

To LISP. *v. n.* [ƿlirp, Saxon.] To speak with too frequent appulses of the tongue to the teeth or palate, like children.

Come, I cannot cog, and say, thou art this and that, like a many of these *lisping* hawthorn buds, that come like women in mens apparel, and smell like Bucklersbury in simpling time. *Shakespeare's Merry Wives of Windsor.*

Scarce had she learnt to *lisp* a name
Of martyr, yet she thinks it shame
Life should so long play with that breath,
Which spent can buy so brave a death. *Crashaw.*

They ramble not to learn the mode,
How to be drest, or how to *lisp* abroad. *Cleaveland.*

Appulse partial, giving some passage to breath, is made to the upper teeth, and causes a *lisping* sound, the breath being strained through the teeth. *Holder's Elements of Speech.*

As yet a child, nor yet a fool to fame,
I *lisp'd* in numbers, for the numbers came. *Pope.*

LISP. *n. s.* [from the verb.] The act of lisping.

I overheard her answer, with a very pretty *lisp*, O! Strephon, you are a dangerous creature. *Tatler*, N°. 60.

LI'SPER. *n. s.* [from *lisp.*] One who lisps.

LIST. *n. s.* [*liste*, French.]

1. A roll; a catalogue.

He was the ablest emperor of all the *list.* *Bacon.*

Some say the loadstone is poison, and therefore in the *lists* of poisons we find it in many authors. *Brown's Vulg. Errours.*

Bring next the royal *list* of Stuarts forth,
Undaunted minds, that rul'd the rugged north. *Prior.*

2. [*Lice*, French.] Inclosed ground in which tilts are run, and combats fought.

The ocean, overpeering of his *list*,
Eats not the flats with more impetuous haste
Than young Laertes in a riotous head
O'er-bears your officers. *Shakespeare's Hamlet.*

She within *lists* my ranging mind hath brought,
That now beyond myself I will not go. *Davies.*

Till now alone the mighty nations strove,
The rest, at gaze, without the *lists* did stand;
And threat'ning France, plac'd like a painted Jove,
Kept idle thunder in his lifted hand. *Dryden.*

Paris thy son, and Sparta's king advance,
In measur'd *lists* to toss the weighty lance;
And who his rival shall in arms subdue,
His be the dame, and his the treasure too. *Pope's Iliad.*

3. [Lyrtan, Saxon.] Desire; willingness; choice.

Alas, she has no speech!
—Too much;
I find it still when I have *list* to sleep. *Shakesp. Othello.*

Nothing of passion or peevishness, or *list* to contradict, shall have any bias on my judgment. *King Charles.*

He saw false reynard where he lay full low;
I need not swear he had no *list* to crow. *Dryden.*

4. [*Licium*, Latin; *lisse*, French.] A strip of cloth.

A linen stock on one leg, and a kersey boot hose on the other, gartered with a red and blue *list.* *Shakespeare.*

Instead of a *list* of cotton, or the like filtre, we made use of a siphon of glass. *Boyle.*

A *list* the cobler's temples ties,
To keep the hair out of his eyes. *Swift.*

5. A border.

They thought it better to let them stand as a *list*, or marginal border, unto the Old Testament. *Hooker*, *b.* v.

To LIST. *v. n.* [lyrtan, Saxon.] To chuse; to desire; to be disposed; to incline.

Let other men think of your devices as they *list*, in my judgment they be mere fansies. *Whitgift.*

Unto them that add to the word of God what them *listeth*, and make God's will submit unto their will, and break God's commandments for their own tradition's sake, unto them it seemeth not good. *Hooker*, *b.* ii.

They imagine, that laws which permit them not to do as they would, will endure them to speak as they *list.* *Hooker.*

To fight in field, or to defend this wall,
Point what you *list*, I nought refuse at all. *Fairy Queen.*

Now by my mother's son, and that's myself,
It shall be moon, or star, or what I *list.* *Shakespeare.*

Kings, lords of times, and of occasions, may
Take their advantage when, and how, they *list.* *Daniel.*

When they *list*, into the womb
That bred them they return; and howl, and gnaw
My bowels, their repast. *Milton's Paradise Lost.*

To LIST. *v. a.* [from *list*, a roll.]

1. To enlist; to enrol or register.

For a man to give his name to Christianity in those days, was to *list* himself a martyr, and to bid farewel not only to the pleasures, but also to the hopes of this life. *South.*

They *list* with women each degen'rate name,
Who dares not hazard life for future fame. *Dryden's Æn.*

2. To retain and enrol soldiers.

The lords would, by *listing* their own servants, persuade the gentlemen in the town to do the like. *Clarendon*, *b.* viii.

The king who raised this wall appointed a million of soldiers, who were *listed* and paid for the defence of it against the Tartars. *Temple.*

Two hundred horse he shall command;
Though few, a warlike and well-chosen band,
These in my name are *listed.* *Dryden.*

3. [From *list*; enclosed ground.] To enclose for combats.

How dares your pride presume against my laws,
As in a *listed* field to fight your cause?
Unask'd the royal grant. *Dryden's Knight's Tale.*

4. [From *list*, a shred or border.] To sew together, in such a sort as to make a particoloured shew.

Some may wonder at such an accumulation of benefits, like a kind of embroidering or *listing* of one favour upon another. *Wotton's Life of Buckingham.*

5. [Contracted from *listen.*] To hearken to; to listen; to attend.

Then weigh, what loss your honour may sustain,
If with too credent ear you *list* his songs;
Or lose your heart, or your chaste treasure open
To his unmaster'd importunity. *Shakesp. Hamlet.*

I, this found I better know:
List! I would I could hear mo. *Benj. Johnson.*

LI'STED. *adj.* Striped; particoloured in long streaks.

Over his head beholds
A dewy cloud, and in the cloud a bow
Conspicuous, with three *listed* colours gay,
Betok'ning peace from God, and cov'nant new. *Milton.*

As the show'ry arch
With *listed* colours gay, or, azure, gules,
Delights, and puzzles the beholder's eyes. *Philips.*

To LISTEN. *v. a.* To hear; to attend. Obsolete.

Lady, vouchsafe to *listen* what I say. *Shakespeare.*

One cried, God bless us! and, amen! the other;
As they had seen me with these hangman's hands,
Listening their fear I could not say, amen. *Shakespeare.*

He, that no more must say, is *listened* more
Than they whom youth and ease have taught to glose.
Shakespeare's Richard II.

The wonted roar was up amidst the woods,
And filled the air with barbarous dissonance,
At which I ceas'd and *listen'd* them a while. *Milton.*

To LI'STEN. *v. n.* To hearken; to give attention.

Listen to me, and if you speak me fair,
I'll tell you news. *Shakesp. Taming of the Shrew.*

Antigonus used often to go disguised, and *listen* at the tents of his soldiers; and at a time heard some that spoke very ill of him: whereupon he said, If you speak ill of me, you should go a little farther off. *Bacon's Apophthegms.*

Listen, O isles, unto me, and hearken, ye people. *Isa.* xlix.

When we have occasion to *listen*, and give a more particular attention to some sound, the tympanum is drawn to a more than ordinary tension. *Holder's Elements of Speech.*

On the green bank I sat, and *listen'd* long;
Nor till her lay was ended could I move,
But wish'd to dwell for ever in the grove. *Dryden.*

He shall be receiv'd with more regard,
And *listen'd* to, than modest truth is heard. *Dryden.*

To this humour most of our late comedies owe their success: the audience *listens* after nothing else. *Addison.*

LI'STNER. *n. s.* [from *listen.*] One that hearkens: a hearkener.

They are light of belief, and great *listners* after news. *Howell.*

Listeners never hear well of themselves. *L'Estrange.*

If she constantly attends the tea, and be a good *listener*, she may make a tolerable figure, which will serve to draw in the young chaplain. *Swift.*

The hush word, when spoke by any brother in a lodge, was a warning to the rest to have a care of *listeners.* *Swift.*

LI'STLESS. *adj.* [from *list.*]

1. Without inclination; without any determination to one thing more than another.

Intemperance and sensuality clog mens spirits, make them gross, *listless*, and unactive. *Tillotson's Sermons.*

If your care to wheat alone extend,
Let Maja with her sisters first descend,

Before you truſt in earth your future hope,
Or elſe expect a *liſtleſs*, lazy, crop. *Dryden's Virg.*
Lazy lolling ſort
Of ever *liſtleſs* loit'rers, that attend
No cauſe, no truſt. *Pope.*
I was *liſtleſs* and deſponding. *Gulliver.*

2. Careleſs; heedleſs.
The ſick for air before the portal gaſp,
Or idle in their empty hives remain,
Benum'd with cold, and *liſtleſs* of their gain. *Dryden.*

LI'STLESLY. *adv.* [from *liſtleſs.*] Without thought; without attention.

To know this perfectly, watch him at play, and ſee whether he be ſtirring and active, or whether he lazily and *liſtleſly* dreams away his time. *Locke on Education.*

LI'STLESNESS. *n. ſ.* [from *liſtleſs.*] Inattention; want of deſire.

It may be the palate of the ſoul is indiſpoſed by *liſtleſneſs* or ſorrow. *Taylor.*

LIT, the preterite of *light*; whether *to light* ſignifies *to happen*, or *to ſet on fire*, or *guide with light.*
Believe thyſelf, thy eyes,
That firſt inflam'd, and *lit* me to thy love,
Thoſe ſtars, that ſtill muſt guide me to my joy. *Southern.*
I *lit* my pipe with the paper. *Addiſon's Spectator.*

LI'TANY. *n. ſ.* [λιτάνεια; *litanie*, French.] A form of ſupplicatory prayer.

Supplications, with ſolemnity for the appeaſing of God's wrath, were, of the Greek church, termed *litanies* and rogations of the latin. *Hooker, b.* v.

Recollect your ſins that you have done that week, and all your life-time; and recite humbly and devoutly ſome penitential *litanies*. *Taylor's Guide to Devotion.*

LI'TERAL. *adj.* [*literal*, French; *litera*, Latin.]

1. According to the primitive meaning, not figurative.

Through all the writings of the antient fathers, we ſee that the words, which were, do continue; the only difference is, that whereas before they had a *literal*, they now have a metaphorical uſe, and are as ſo many notes of remembrance unto us, that what they did ſignify in the letter, is accompliſhed in the truth. *Hooker, b.* iv.

A foundation, being primarily of uſe in architecture, hath no other *literal* notation but what belongs to it in relation to an houſe, or other building, nor figurative, but what is founded in that, and deduced from thence. *Hammond.*

2. Following the letter, or exact words.

The fitteſt for publick audience are ſuch as, following a middle courſe between the rigour of *literal* tranſlations and the liberty of paraphraſts, do with greater ſhortneſs and plainneſs deliver the meaning. *Hooker, b.* v.

3. Conſiſting of letters; as, the *literal* notation of numbers was known to Europeans before the cyphers.

LI'TERAL. *n. ſ.* Primitive or literal meaning.

How dangerous it is in ſenſible things to uſe metaphorical expreſſions unto the people, and what abſurd conceits they will ſwallow in their *literals*, an example we have in our profeſſion. *Brown's Vulgar Errours, b.* iv.

LI'TERALLY. *adv.* [from *literal.*]

1. According to the primitive import of words; not figuratively.

That a man and his wife are one fleſh, I can comprehend the meaning of; yet *literally* taken, it is a thing impoſſible. *Swift.*

2. With cloſe adherence to words.

Endeavouring to turn his Niſus and Euryalus as cloſe as I was able, I have performed that epiſode too *literally*; that giving more ſcope to Mezentius and Lauſus, that verſion, which has more of the majeſty of Virgil, has leſs of his conciſeneſs. *Dryden.*

So wild and ungovernable a poet cannot be tranſlated *literally*; his genius is too ſtrong to bear a chain. *Dryden.*

LITERA'LITY. *n. ſ.* [from *literal.*] Original meaning.

Not attaining the true deuteroſcopy and ſecond intention of the words, they are fain to omit their ſuperconſequences, coherences, figures, or tropologies, and are not ſometimes perſuaded by fire beyond their *literalities*. *Brown.*

LITERA'TI. n. ſ. [Italian.] The learned.

I ſhall conſult ſome *literati* on the project ſent me for the diſcovery of the longitude. *Spectator*, Nº. 581.

LI'TERATURE. *n. ſ.* [*literatura*, Latin.] Learning; ſkill in letters.

This kingdom hath been famous for good *literature*; and if preferment attend deſervers, there will not want ſupplies. *Bacon's Advice to Villiers.*

When men of learning are acted by a knowledge of the world, they give a reputation to *literature*, and convince the world of its uſefulneſs. *Addiſon's Freeholder*, Nº. 377.

LI'THARGE. *n. ſ.* [*litharge*, French; *lithargyrum*, Latin.]

Litharge is properly lead vitrified, either alone or with a mixture of copper. This recrement is of two kinds, *litharge* of gold, and *litharge* of ſilver. It is collected from the furnaces where ſilver is ſeparated from lead, or from thoſe where gold and ſilver are purified by means of that metal. The *litharge* ſold in the ſhops is produced in the copper works, where lead has been uſed to purify that metal, or to ſeparate ſilver from it. It is uſed in ointments and plaiſters, and is drying, abtergent, and ſlightly aſtrictive. *Hill's Mat. Med.*

I have ſeen ſome parcels of glaſs adhering to the teſt or cupel as well as the gold or *litharge*. *Boyle.*

If the lead be blown off from the ſilver by the bellows, it will, in great part, be collected in the form of a darkiſh powder; which, becauſe it is blown off from ſilver, they call *litharge* of ſilver. *Boyle.*

LITHE. *adj.* [liðe, Saxon.] Limber; flexible; pliant; eaſily bent.

Th' unwieldy elephant,
To make them mirth, us'd all his might, and wreath'd
His *lithe* proboſcis. *Milton's Paradiſe Loſt.*

LI'THENESS. *n. ſ.* [from *lithe.*] Limberneſs; flexibility.

LI'THER. *adj.* [from *lithe.*] Soft; pliant.
Thou antick, death,
Two Talbots winged through the *lither* ſky,
In thy deſpight ſhall 'ſcape mortality. *Shakeſpeare.*

[Lyðeɲ, Saxon.] Bad; ſorry; corrupt. It is in the work of Robert of Glouceſter written *luther.*

LITHO'GRAPHY. *n. ſ.* [λίθος and γραφω.] The art or practice of engraving upon ſtones.

LI'THOMANCY. *n. ſ.* [λίθος and μαντεία.] Prediction by ſtones.

As ſtrange muſt be the *lithomancy*, or divination, from this ſtone, whereby Helenus the prophet foretold the deſtruction of Troy. *Brown's Vulgar Errours, b.* ii.

LITHONTRI'PTICK. *adj.* [λίθος and τρίβω; *lithontriptique*, French.] Any medicine proper to diſſolve the ſtone in the kidneys or bladder.

LITHO'TOMIST. *n. ſ.* [λίθος and τέμνω.] A chirurgeon who extracts the ſtone by opening the bladder.

LITHO'TOMY. *n. ſ.* [λίθος and τέμνω.] The art or practice of cutting for the ſtone.

LI'TIGANT. *n. ſ.* [*litigans*, Latin; *litigant*, French.] One engaged in a ſuit of law.

The caſt *litigant* ſits not down with one croſs verdict, but recommences his ſuit. *Decay of Piety.*

The *litigants* tear one another to pieces for the benefit of ſome third intereſt. *L'Eſtrange's Fables.*

LI'TIGANT. *adj.* Engaged in a juridical conteſt.

Judicial acts are thoſe writings and matters which relate to judicial proceedings, and are ſped in open court at the inſtance of one or both of the parties *litigant*. *Ayliffe's Parerg.*

To LI'TIGATE. *v. a.* [*litigo*, Latin.] To conteſt in law; to debate by judicial proceſs.

To LI'TIGATE. *v. n.* To manage a ſuit; to carry on a cauſe.

The appellant, after the interpoſition of an appeal, ſtill *litigates* in the ſame cauſe. *Ayliffe's Parergon.*

LITIGA'TION. *n. ſ.* [*litigatio*, Latin; from *litigate.*] Judicial conteſt; ſuit of law.

Never one clergyman had experience of both *litigations*, that hath not confeſſed, he had rather have three ſuits in Weſtminſter-hall, than one in the arches. *Clarendon.*

LITI'GIOUS. *adj.* [*litigieux*, French.]

1. Inclinable to law-ſuits; quarrelſome; wrangling.
Soldiers find wars, and lawyers find out ſtill
Litigious men, who quarrels move. *Donne.*

His great application to the law, had not infected his temper with any thing poſitive or *litigious*. *Addiſon.*

2. Diſputable; controvertible.

In *litigious* and controverſed cauſes, the will of God is to have them to do whatſoever the ſentence of judicial and final deciſion ſhall determine. *Hooker.*

No fences parted fields, nor marks, nor bounds,
Diſtinguiſh'd acres of *litigious* grounds. *Dryden's Georg.*

LITI'GIOUSLY. *adv.* [from *litigious.*] Wranglingly.

LITI'GIOUSNESS. *n. ſ.* [from *litigious.*] A wrangling diſpoſition.

LI'TTER. *n. ſ.* [*litiere*, French.]

1. A kind of vehiculary bed; a carriage capable of containing a bed hung between two horſes.
To my *litter* ſtrait;
Weakneſs poſſeſſeth me. *Shakeſp. King John.*

He was carried in a rich chariot *litterwiſe*, with two horſes at each end. *Bacon's New Atlantis.*

The drowſy frighted ſteeds,
That draw the *litter* of cloſe curtain'd ſleep. *Milton.*
Here modeſt matrons in ſoft *litters* driv'n,
In ſolemn pomp appear. *Dryden's Æn.*
Litters thick beſiege the donor's gate,
And begging lords and teeming ladies wait
The promis'd dole. *Dryden's Juvenal.*

2. The ſtraw laid under animals, or on plants.
To crouch in *litter* of your ſtable planks. *Shakeſpeare.*
Take off the *litter* from your kernel beds. *Evelyn.*
Their *litter* is not toſs'd by ſows unclean. *Dryd. Virg.*

3. A brood of young.

I do here walk before thee like a sow that hath overwhelmed all her *litter* but one. *Shakespeare's Henry* IV.

Reflect upon that numerous *litter* of strange, senseless opinions, that crawl about the world. *South's Serm.*

A wolf came to a sow, and very kindly offered to take care of her *litter*. *L'Estrange's Fables.*

Full many a year his hateful head had been
For tribute paid, nor since in Cambria seen:
The last of all the *litter* 'scap'd by chance,
And from Geneva first infested France. *Dryden.*

4. Any number of things thrown sluttishly about.

Strephon, who found the room was void,
Stole in, and took a strict survey
Of all the *litter* as it lay. *Swift.*

5. A birth of animals.

Fruitful as the sow that carry'd
The thirty pigs at one large *litter* farrow'd. *Dryd. Juv.*

To LI'TTER. *v. a.* [from the noun.]

1. To bring forth: used of beasts, or of human beings in abhorrence or contempt.

Then was this iland,
Save for the son that she did *litter* here,
A freckled whelp, hag-born, not honour'd with
A human shape. *Shakespeare's Tempest.*

My father named me Autolicus, being *littered* under Mercury, who, as I am, was likewise a snapper up of unconsidered trifles. *Shakespeare's Winter's Tale.*

The whelps of bears are, at first *littering*, without all form or fashion. *Hakewill on Providence.*

We might conceive that dogs were created blind, because we observe they were *littered* so with us. *Brown.*

2. To cover with things negligently, or sluttishly scattered about.

They found
The room with volumes *litter'd* round. *Swift.*

3. To cover with straw.

He found a stall where oxen stood,
But for his ease well *litter'd* was the floor. *Dryden.*

4. To supply cattle with bedding.

LI'TTLE. *adj.* [comp. *less*, superlat. *least*; *leitels*, Gothick; lyzel, Saxon.]

1. Small in quantity.

The coast of Dan went out too *little* for them. *Josh.* xix.

2. Not great; small; diminutive; of small bulk.

He sought to see Jesus, but could not for the press, because he was *little* of stature. *Luke* xix. 3.

His son, being then very *little*, I considered only as wax, to be moulded as one pleases. *Locke.*

3. Of small dignity, power, or importance.

When thou wast *little* in thine own sight, wast thou not made the head of the tribes. 1 *Sam.* xv. 17.

All that is past ought to seem *little* to thee, because it is so in itself. *Taylor's Guide to Devotion.*

4. Not much; not many.

5. Some; not none.

I leave him to reconcile these contradictions, which may plentifully be found in him, by any one who will but read with a *little* attention. *Locke.*

LITTLE. *n. s.*

1. A small space.

Much was in *little* writ; and all convey'd
With cautious care, for fear to be betray'd. *Dryden.*

2. A small part; a small proportion.

He that despiseth little things, shall perish by *little* and *little*. *Ecclus.*

The poor remnant of human seed which remained in their mountains, peopled their country again slowly, by *little* and *little*. *Bacon's New Atlantis.*

By freeing the precipitated matter from the rest by filtration, and diligently grinding the white precipitate with water, the mercury will *little* by *little* be gathered into drops. *Boyle.*

I gave thee thy master's house, and the house of Israel and Judah; and if that had been too *little*, I would have given such and such things. 2 *Sam.* xii. 8.

They have much of the poetry of Mecænas, but *little* of his liberality. *Dryden's Preface to All for Love.*

Nor grudge I thee the much that Grecians give,
Nor murm'ring take the *little* I receive. *Dryden's Homer.*

There are many expressions, which carrying with them no clear ideas, are like to remove but *little* of my ignorance. *Locke.*

3. A slight affair.

As if 'twere *little* from their town to chase,
I through the seas pursued their exil'd race. *Dryden's Æn.*

I view with anger and disdain,
How *little* gives thee joy or pain:
A print, a bronze, a flow'r, a root. *Prior.*

4. Not much.

These they are fitted for, and *little* else. *Cheyne.*

LI'TTLE. *adv.*

1. In a small degree.

The received definition of names should be changed as *little* as possible. *Watts's Logick.*

2. In a small quantity.

3. In some degree, but not great.

Where there is too great a thinness in the fluids, subacid substances are proper, though they are a *little* astringent. *Arbuthnot on Aliments.*

4. Not much.

The tongue of the just is as choice silver; the heart of the wicked is *little* worth. *Prov.* x. 20.

Finding him *little* studious, she chose rather to endue him with conversative qualities of youth; as, dancing and fencing. *Wotton.*

That poem was infamously bad; this parallel is *little* better. *Dryden's Dufresnoy.*

Several clergymen, otherwise *little* fond of obscure terms, yet in their sermons were very liberal of all those which they find in ecclesiastical writers. *Swift.*

LI'TTLENESS. *n. s.* [from *little*.]

1. Smalness of bulk.

All trying, by a love of *littleness*,
To make abridgments, and to draw to less;
Even that nothing which at first we were. *Donne.*

We may suppose a great many degrees of *littleness* and lightness in these earthy particles, so as many of them might float in the air. *Burnet's Theory of the Earth.*

2. Meanness; want of grandeur.

The English and French, in verse, are forced to raise their language with metaphors, by the pompousness of the whole phrase, to wear off any *littleness* that appears in the particular parts. *Addison's Remarks on Italy.*

3. Want of dignity.

The angelick grandeur, by being concealed, does not awaken our poverty, nor mortify our *littleness* so much, as if it was always displayed. *Collier of Envy.*

LI'TTORAL. *v. a.* [*littoris*, Latin.] Belonging to the shore.

LI'TURGY. *n. s.* [λιτουργία; *liturgie*, Fr.] Form of prayers; formulary of publick devotions.

We dare not admit any such form of *liturgy*, as either appointeth no scripture at all, or very little to be read in the church. *Hooker, b.* v.

The blessedest of mortal wights began to be importuned, so that a great part of divine *liturgy* was addressed solely to her. *Howell.*

It is the greatest solemnity of prayer, the most powerful *liturgy* and means of impetration in this world. *Taylor.*

To LIVE. *v. n.* [lyfian, lyfigan, Saxon.]

1. To be in a state of animation; to be not dead.

She shall be
A pattern to all princes *living* with her,
And all that shall succeed. *Shakespeare's Henry* VIII.

Is't night's predominance, or the day's shame,
That darkness does the face of earth intomb,
When *living* day should kiss it? *Shakespeare's Macbeth.*

To save the *living*, and revenge the dead,
Against one warrior's arms all Troy they led. *Dryden.*

2. To pass life in any certain manner with regard to habits; good or ill, happiness or misery.

O death, how bitter is the remembrance of thee to a man that *liveth* at rest. *Ecclus.* xli. 1.

Dr. Parker, in his sermon before them, touched them so near for their *living*, that they went near to touch him for his life. *Hayward.*

The condition required of us is a conjuncture of all gospel graces rooted in the heart, though mixed with much weakness, and perhaps with many sins, so they be not wilfully *lived* and died in. *Hammond.*

A late prelate, of a remarkable zeal for the church, were religions to be tried by lives, would have *lived* down the pope, and the whole consistory. *Atterbury.*

If we act by several broken views, we shall *live* and die in misery. *Addison's Spectator*, N°. 162.

If we are firmly resolved to *live* up to the dictates of reason, without any regard to wealth and reputation, we may go through life with steadiness and pleasure. *Addison.*

3. To continue in life.

Our high-plac'd Macbeth
Shall *live* the lease of nature, and pay his breath
To time and mortal custom. *Shakespeare.*

See the minutes how they run;
How many makes the hour full complete,
How many hours bring about the day,
How many days will finish up the year,
How many years a mortal man may *live*. *Shakespeare.*

The way to *live* long must be, to use our bodies so as is most agreeable to the rules of temperance. *Ray on Creation.*

4. To live emphatically; to be in a state of happiness.

What greater curse could envious fortune give,
Than just to die when I began to *live*. *Dryden.*

5. To

5. To be exempt from death, temporal or spiritual.

My statutes and judgments, if a man do, he shall *live* in them. *Lev.* xviii. 5.

He died for us, that whether we wake or sleep, we should *live* together with him. 1 *Thes.* v. 10.

6. To remain undestroyed.

It was a miraculous providence that could make a vessel, so ill manned, *live* upon sea; that kept it from being dashed against the hills, or overwhelmed in the deeps. *Burnet.*

Mark how the shifting winds from west arise,
And what collected night involves the skies!
Nor can our shaken vessels *live* at sea,
Much less against the tempest force their way. *Dryden.*

7. To continue; not to be lost.

Mens evil manners *live* in brass, their virtues
We write in water. *Shakespeare's Henry* VIII.

Sounds which address the ear are lost and die
In one short hour; but that which strikes the eye
Lives long upon the mind; the faithful sight
Engraves the knowledge with a beam of light. *Watts.*

The tomb with manly arms and trophies grace.
There high in air memorial of my name
Fix the smooth oar, and bid me *live* to fame. *Pope.*

8. To converse; to cohabit.

The shepherd swains shall dance and sing,
For thy delight each May morning.
If these delights thy mind may move,
Then *live* with me, and be my love. *Shakespeare.*

9. To feed.

Those animals that *live* upon other animals have their flesh more alkalescent than those that *live* upon vegetables. *Arbut.*

10. To maintain one's self.

A most notorious thief; *lived* all his life-time of spoils and robberies. *Spenser.*

They which minister about holy things, *live* of the things of the temple. 1 *Cor.* ix. 13.

His treasure and goods were all seized upon, and a small portion thereof appointed for his poor wife to *live* upon. *Knolles's Hist. of the Turks.*

The number of soldiers can never be great in proportion to that of people, no more than the number of those that are idle in a country, to that of those who *live* by labour. *Temple.*

He had been most of his time in good service, and had something to *live* on now he was old. *Temple.*

11. To be in a state of motion or vegetation.

In a spacious cave of *living* stone,
The tyrant Æolus, from his airy throne,
With pow'r imperial curbs the struggling winds. *Dryden.*

Cool groves and *living* lakes
Give after toilsome days a soft repose at night. *Dryden.*

12. To be unextinguished.

Pure oil and incense on the fire they throw:
These gifts the greedy flames to dust devour,
Then on the *living* coals red wine they pour. *Dryden.*

LIVE. *adj.* [from *alive.*]

1. Quick; not dead.

If one man's ox hurt another that he die, they shall sell the *live* ox, and divide the money. *Exod.* xxi. 35.

2. Active; not extinguished.

A louder sound was produced by the impetuous eruptions of the halituous flames of the saltpetre upon casting of a *live* coal upon it. *Boyle.*

LI'VELESS. *adv.* [from *live.*] Wanting life; rather lifeless.

Description cannot suit itself in words,
To demonstrate the life of such a battle,
In life so *liveless* as it shews itself. *Shakes. Henry* V.

LI'VELIHOOD. *n. s.* [It appears to me corrupted from *livelode.*] Support of life; maintenance; means of living.

Ah! luckless babe! born under cruel star,
And in dead parents baleful ashes bred;
Full little weenest thou what sorrows are,
Left thee for portion of thy *livelihood.* *Fairy Queen.*

That rebellion drove the lady from thence, to find a *livelihood* out of her own estate. *Clarendon, b.* viii.

He brings disgrace upon his character, to submit to the picking up of a *livelihood* in that strolling way of canting and begging. *L'Estrange.*

It is their profession and *livelihood* to get their living by those practices, for which they deserve to forfeit their lives. *South's Sermons.*

They have been as often banished out of most other places; which must very much disperse a people, and oblige them to seek a *livelihood* where they can find it. *Addison's Spect.*

Trade employs multitudes of hands, and furnishes the poorest of our fellow subjects with the opportunities of gaining an honest *livelihood:* the skilful or industrious find their account in it. *Addison's Freeholder,* N°. 42.

LI'VELINESS. *n. s.* [from *lively.*]

1. Appearance of life.

That *liveliness* which the freedom of the pencil makes appear, may seem the living hand of nature. *Dryden's Dufres.*

2. Vivacity; sprightliness.

Extravagant young fellows, that have *liveliness* and spirit, come sometimes to be set right, and so make able and great men; but tame and low spirits very seldom attain to any thing. *Locke on Education.*

LI'VELODE. *n. s.* [*live* and *lode,* from *lead;* the means of leading life.] Maintenance; support; livelihood.

She gave like blessing to each creature,
As well of worldly *livelode* as of life,
That there might be no difference nor strife. *Hubberd.*

LI'VELONG. *adj.* [*live* and *long.*] Tedious; long in passing.

Many a time, and oft,
Have you climb'd up to walls and battlements,
Your infants in your arms; and there have sate
The *livelong* day, with patient expectation
To see great Pompey pass. *Shakesp. Julius Cæsar.*

The obscur'd bird clamour'd the *livelong* night. *Shakes.*

Young and old come forth to play,
On a sun-shine holiday,
Till the *livelong* day-light fail. *Milton.*

Seek for pleasure to destroy
The sorrows of this *livelong* night. *Prior.*

How could she sit the *livelong* day,
Yet never ask us once to play? *Swift.*

2. Lasting; durable.

Thou, in our wonder and astonishment,
Hast built thyself a *livelong* monument. *Milton.*

LI'VELY. *adj.* [*live* and *like.*]

1. Brisk; vigorous; vivacious.

But wherefore comes old Manoa in such haste,
With youthful steps? much *livelier* than ere while
He seems; supposing here to find his son,
Or of him bringing to us some glad news? *Milton's Ag.*

2. Gay; airy.

Form'd by thy converse, happily to steer
From grave to gay, from *lively* to severe. *Pope.*

3. Representing life.

Since a true knowledge of nature gives us pleasure, a *lively* imitation of it in poetry or painting must produce a much greater. *Dryden's Dufresnoy.*

4. Strong; energetick.

His faith must be not only living, but *lively* too; it must be brightened and stirred up by a particular exercise of those virtues specifically requisite to a due performance of this duty. *South's Sermons.*

The colours of the prism are manifestly more full, intense and *lively,* than those of natural bodies. *Newton's Opticks.*

Imprint upon their minds, by proper arguments and reflections, a *lively* persuasion of the certainty of a future state. *Atterbury's Sermons.*

LI'VELILY. } *adv.*
LI'VELY. }

1. Briskly; vigorously.

They brought their men to the slough, who discharging *lively* almost close to the face of the enemy, did much amaze them. *Hayward.*

2. With strong resemblance of life.

That part of poetry must needs be best, which describes most *lively* our actions and passions, our virtues and our vices. *Dryden's Pref. to his State of Innocence.*

LI'VER. *n. s.* [from *live.*]

1. One who lives.

Be thy affections undisturb'd and clear,
Guided to what may great or good appear,
And try if life be worth the *liver*'s care. *Prior.*

2. One who lives in any particular manner with respect to virtue or vice, happiness or misery.

The end of his descent was to gather a church of holy christian *livers* over the whole world. *Hammond's Fund.*

If any loose *liver* have any goods of his own, the sheriff is to seize thereupon. *Spenser on Ireland.*

Here are the wants of children, of distracted persons, of sturdy wandering beggars and loose disorderly *livers,* at one view represented. *Atterbury.*

3. [From lifere, Saxon.] One of the entrails.

With mirth and laughter let old wrinkles come:
And let my *liver* rather heat with wine,
Than my heart cool with mortifying groans. *Shakespeare.*

Reason and respect
Make *livers* pale, and lustihood dejected. *Shakespeare.*

LI'VERCOLOUR. *adj.* [*liver* and *colour.*] Dark red.

The uppermost stratum is of gravel; then clay of various colours, purple, blue, red, *livercolour.* *Woodward.*

LI'VERGROWN. *adj.* [*liver* and *grown.*] Having a great liver.

I inquired what other casualties was most like the rickets, and found that *livergrown* was nearest. *Graunt.*

LI'VERWORT. *n. s.* [*liver* and *wort.*] A plant.

That sort of *liverwort* which is used to cure the bite of mad dogs, grows on commons, and open heaths, where the grass is short, on declivities, and on the sides of pits. This spreads

spreads on the surface of the ground, and, when in perfection, is of an ash colour; but, as it grows old, it alters, and becomes of a dark colour. *Miller.*

LI'VERY. *n. s.* [from *livrer*, French.]

1. The act of giving or taking possession.

You do wrongfully seize Hereford's right,
Call in his letters patents that he hath
By his attorneys general to sue
His *livery*, and deny his offered homage. *Shakesp.*

2. Release from wardship.

Had the two houses first sued out their *livery*, and once effectually redeemed themselves from the wardship of the tumults, I should then suspect my own judgment. *K. Charles.*

2. The writ by which possession is obtained.

3. The state of being kept at a certain rate.

What *livery* is, we by common use in England know well enough, namely, that it is an allowance of horse meat; as they commonly use the word stabling, as to keep horses at *livery*; the which word, I guess, is derived of *livering* or *delivering* forth their nightly food; so in great houses, the *livery* is said to be served up for all night, that is, their evening allowance for drink: and *livery* is also called the upper weed which a serving man wears; so called, I suppose, for that it was delivered and taken from him at pleasure: so it is apparent, that, by the word *livery*, is there meant horse meat, like as by the coigny is understood man's meat. Some say it is derived of coin, for that they used in their coignies not only to take meat but money; but I rather think it is derived of the Irish, the which is a common use amongst landlords of the Irish to have a common spending upon their tenants, who being commonly but tenants at will, they used to take of them what victuals they list; for of victuals they were wont to make a small reckoning. *Spenser on Ireland.*

4. The cloaths given to servants.

My mind for weeds your virtue's *livery* wears. *Sidney.*

Perhaps they are by so much the more loth to forsake this argument, for that it hath, though nothing else, yet the name of scripture, to give it some kind of countenance more than the pretext of *livery* coats affordeth. *Hooker.*

I think, it is our way,
If we will keep in favour with the king,
To be her men, and wear her *livery*. *Shakesp. Rich.* III.

Yet do our hearts wear Timon's *livery*,
That see I by our faces. *Shakesp. Timon of Athens.*

Ev'ry lady cloath'd in white,
And crown'd with oak and laurel ev'ry knight,
Are servants to the leaf, by *liveries* known
Of innocence. *Dryden's Flower and Leaf.*

On others int'rest her gay *liv'ry* flings,
Int'rest that waves on party-colour'd wings;
Turn'd to the sun she casts a thousand dyes,
And as she turns the colours fall or rise. *Dunciad.*

If your dinner miscarries, you were teized by the footmen coming into the kitchen; and to prove it true, throw a ladleful of broth on one or two of their *liveries*. *Swift.*

5. A particular dress; a garb worn as a token or consequence of any thing.

Of fair Urania, fairer than a green,
Proudly bedeck'd in April's *livery*. *Sidney.*

Mistake me not for my complexion
The shadow'd *livery* of the burning sun,
To whom I am a neighbour, and near bred. *Shakesp.*

At once came forth whatever creeps the ground,
Insect, or worm: those wav'd their limber fans,
For wings, and smallest lineaments exact,
In all the *liveries* deck'd of summer's pride,
With spots of gold and purple, azure, green. *Milton.*

Now came still evening on, and twilight grey
Had in her sober *livery* all things clad. *Milt. Pa. Lost.*

LI'VERYMAN. *n. s.* [*livery* and *man.*]

1. One who wears a livery; a servant of an inferior kind.

The witnesses made oath, that they had heard some of the *liverymen* frequently railing at their mistress. *Arbuthnot.*

2. [In London.] A freeman of some standing in a company.

LIVES. *n. s.* [the plural of life.]

So short is life, that every peasant strives,
In a farm house, or field, to have three *lives*. *Donne.*

LI'VID. *adj.* [*lividus*, Latin; *livide*, French.] Discoloured, as with a blow; black and blue.

It was a pestilent fever, not seated in the veins or humours, for that there followed no carbuncles, no purple or *livid* spots, the mass of the blood not being tainted. *Bacon.*

Upon my *livid* lips bestow a kiss:
O envy not the dead, they feel not bliss! *Dryden.*

They beat their breasts with many a bruising blow,
Till they turn'd *livid*, and corrupt the snow. *Dryden.*

LIVI'DITY. *n. s.* [*lividilé*, French; from *livid.*] Discolouration, as by a blow.

The signs of a tendency to such a state, are darkness or *lividity* of the countenance. *Arbuthnot on Aliments.*

LI'VING. *n. s.* [from *live.*]

1. Support; maintenance; fortune on which one lives.

The Arcadians fought as in unknown place, having no succour but in their hands; the Helots, as in their own place, fighting for their *livings*, wives, and children. *Sidney.*

All they did cast in of their abundance; but she of her want did cast in all that she had, even all her *living*. *Mark.*

2. Power of continuing life.

There is no *living* without trusting some body or other, in some cases. *L'Estrange's Fables.*

2. Livelihood.

For ourselves we may a *living* make. *Hubberd's Tale.*

Then may I set the world on wheels, when she can spin for her *living*. *Shakespeare.*

Isaac and his wife, now dig for your life,
Or shortly you'll dig for your *living*. *Denham.*

Actors must represent such things as they are capable to perform, and by which both they and the scribbler may get their *living*. *Dryden's Dufresnoy.*

3. Benefice of a clergyman.

Some of our ministers having the *livings* of the country offered unto them, without pains, will, neither for any love of God, nor for all the good they may do, by winning souls to God, be drawn forth from their warm nests. *Spenser.*

The parson of the parish preaching against adultery, Mrs. Bull told her husband, that they would join to have him turned out of his *living* for using personal reflections. *Arbuth.*

LI'VINGLY. *adv.* [from *living.*] In the living state.

In vain do they scruple to approach the dead, who *livingly* are cadaverous, or fear any outward pollution, whose temper pollutes themselves. *Brown's Vulgar Errours, b.* iv.

LI'VRE. *n. s.* [French.] The sum by which the French reckon their money, equal nearly to our shilling.

LIXI'VIAL. *adj.* [from *lixivium*, Latin.]

1. Impregnated with salts like a lixivium.

The symptoms of the excretion of the bile vitiated, were a yellowish colour of the skin, and a *lixivial* urine. *Arbuth.*

2. Obtained by lixivium.

Helmont conjectured, that *lixivial* salts do not pre-exist in their alcalizate form. *Boyle.*

LI'XIVIATE. *adj.* [*lixivieux*, French; from *lixivium.*] Making a lixivium.

In these the salt and *lixiviated* serosity, with some portion of choler, is divided between the guts and the bladder. *Brown's Vulgar Errours, b.* iii.

Lixiviate salts, to which pot ashes belong, by piercing the bodies of vegetables, dispose them to part readily with their tincture. *Boyle.*

LIXI'VIUM. *n. s.* [Lat.] Lye; water impregnated with salt of whatsoever kind; a liquor which has the power of extraction.

I made a *lixivium* of fair water and salt of wormwood, and having frozen it with snow and salt, I could not discern any thing more like to wormwood than to several other plants. *Boyle.*

LI'ZARD. *n. s.* [*lisarde*, French; *lacertus*, Latin.] An animal resembling a serpent, with legs added to it.

There are several sorts of *lizards*; some in Arabia of a cubit long. In America they eat *lizards*; it is very probable likewise that they were eaten sometimes in Arabia and Judæa, since Moses ranks them among the unclean creatures. *Calmet.*

Thou'rt like a foul mis-shapen stigmatick,
Mark'd by the destinies to be avoided,
As venomous toads, or *lizards* dreadful stings. *Shakesp.*

Adder's fork, and blind worm's sting,
Lizard's leg, and owlet's wing. *Shakespeare's Macbeth.*

LIZA'RDITAL. *n. s.* A plant.

LIZA'RDSTONE. *n. s.* [*lizard* and *stone.*] A kind of stone.

L.L.D. *n. s.* [*legum doctor.*] A doctor of the canon and civil laws.

LO. *interject.* [la, Saxon.] Look; see; behold. It is a word used to recall the attention generally to some object of sight; sometimes to something heard, but not properly; often to something to be understood.

Lo! within a ken our army lies. *Shakespeare.*

Now must the world point at poor Catharine,
And say, *lo!* there is mad Petruchio's wife. *Shakespeare.*

Lo! I have a weapon,
A better never did itself sustain
Upon a soldier's thigh. *Shakespeare's Othello.*

Thou did'st utter,
I am yours for ever.
—Why *lo* you now, I've spoke to the purpose twice. *Shak.*

For *lo!* he sung the world's stupenduous birth. *Roscom.*

Lo! heav'n and earth combine
To blast our bold design. *Dryden's Albion.*

LOACH. *n. s.* [*loche*, French.]

The *loach* is a most dainty fish; he breeds and feeds in little and clear swift brooks or rills, and lives there upon the gravel, and in the sharpest streams: he grows not to be above a finger long, and no thicker than is suitable to that length: he is of the shape of an eel, and has a beard of wattels like a barbel: he has two fins at his sides, four at his belly, and one at his tail, dappled with many black or brown spots: his

his mouth, barbel-like, under his nose. This fish is usually full of eggs or spawn, and is by Gesner, and other learned physicians, commended for great nourishment, and to be very grateful both to the palate and stomach of sick persons, and is to be fished for with a very small worm, at the bottom, for he very seldom or never rises above the gravel. *Walton's Angler.*

LOAD. *n. s.* [hlade, Saxon.]

1. A burthen; a freight; lading.

Then on his back he laid the precious *load*,
And sought his wonted shelter. *Dryden's Nun's Tale.*

2. Any thing that depresses.

How a man can have a quiet and cheerful mind under a great burden and *load* of guilt, I know not, unless he be very ignorant. *Ray on Creation.*

3. As much drink as one can bear.

There are those that can never sleep without their *load*, nor enjoy one easy thought, till they have laid all their cares to rest with a bottle. *L'Estrange.*

To LOAD. *v. a.* [hladan, Saxon.]

1. To burden; to freight.

At last, *laden* with honour's spoils,
Returns the good Andronicus to Rome. *Shakespeare.*

Your carriages were heavy *loaden*; they are a burden to the beast. *Isa.* xlvi. 1.

2. To encumber; to embarrass.

He that makes no reflexions on what he reads, only *loads* his mind with a rhapsody of tales, fit in winter nights for the entertainment of others. *Locke.*

3. To charge a gun.

A mariner having discharged his gun, and *loading* it suddenly again, the powder took fire. *Wiseman.*

4. To make heavy by something appended or annexed.

Thy dreadful vow, *loaden* with death, still sounds
In my stunn'd ears. *Addison's Cato.*

LOAD. *n. s.* [more properly *lode*, as it was anciently written from lædan, Saxon, to lead.] The leading vein in a mine.

The tin lay couched at first in certain strakes amongst the rocks, like the veins in a man's body, from the depth whereof the main *load* spreadeth out his branches, until they approach the open air. *Carew's Survey of Cornwall.*

Their manner of working in the *load* mines, is to follow the *load* as it lieth. *Carew's Survey of Cornwall.*

LO'ADER. *n. s.* [from *load.*] He who *loads.*

LO'ADSMAN. *n. s.* [*lode* and *man.*] He who leads the way; a pilot.

LO'ADSTAR. *n. s.* [more properly as it is in *Maundeville*, *lodestar*, from lædan, to lead.] The polestar; the cynosure; the leading or guiding star.

She was the *loadstar* of my life; she the blessing of mine eyes; she the overthrow of my desires, and yet the recompence of my overthrow. *Sidney.*

My Helice, the *loadstar* of my life. *Spenser.*

O happy fair!
Your eyes are *loadstars*, and your tongue sweet air;
More tuneable than lark to shepherd's ear
When wheat is green, when hawthorn buds appear. *Shak.*

That clear majesty
Which standeth fix'd, yet spreads her heavenly worth,
Lodestone to hearts, and *lodestar* to all eyes. *Davies.*

LO'ADSTONE. *n. s.* [properly *lodestone* or *lædingstone.* See LOADSTAR.] The magnet; the stone on which the mariners compass needle is touched to give it a direction north and south.

The *loadstone* is a peculiar and rich ore of iron, found in large masses, of a deep iron-grey where fresh broken, and often tinged with a brownish or reddish colour: it is very heavy, and considerably hard, and its great character is that of affecting iron. This ore of iron is found in England, and in most other places where there are mines of that metal. *Hill's Materia Medica.*

The use of the *loadstone* was kept as secret as any of the other mysteries of the art. *Swift.*

LOAF. *n. s.* [from hlaf or laf, Saxon.]

1. A mass of bread as it is formed by the baker: a loaf is thicker than a cake.

Easy it is
Of a cut *loaf* to steal a shive, we know. *Shakespeare.*

The bread and bread corn in the town sufficed not for six days: hereupon the soldiers entered into proportion; and, to give example, the lord Clinton limited himself to a *loaf* a day. *Hayward.*

With equal force you may break a *loaf* of bread into more and less parts than a lump of lead of the same bigness. *Digby.*

2. Any mass into which a body is wrought.

Your wine becomes so limpid, that you may bottle it with a piece of *loaf* sugar in each bottle. *Mort.*

LOAM. *n. s.* [lim, laam, Saxon; *limus*, Latin; from λίμνη, a fen, *Junius.*] Fat, unctuous, tenacious, earth; marl.

The purest treasure
Is spotless reputation; that away,
Men are but gilded *loam* or painted clay. *Shakespeare.*

Alexander returneth to dust; the dust is earth; of earth we make *loam*; and why of that *loam* might they not stop a beer barrel? *Shakespeare's Hamlet.*

To LOAM. *v. a.* [from the noun.] To smear with loam, marl, or clay; to clay.

The joist ends, and girders which be in the walls, must be *loamed* all over, to preserve them from the corroding of the mortar. *Moxon's Mechanical Exercises.*

LO'AMY. *adj.* [from *loam.*] Marly.

The mellow earth is the best, between the two extremes of clay and sand, especially if it be not *loamy* and binding. *Bacon's Nat. Hist.* N°. 665.

Auricula seedlings best like a *loamy* sand, or light moist earth; yet rich and shaded. *Evelyn's Kalendar.*

LOAN. *n. s.* [hlæn, Saxon.] Any thing lent; any thing given to another, on condition of return or repayment.

The better such ancient revenues shall be answered and paid, the less need her majesty ask subsidies, fifteens, and *loans.* *Bacon.*

You're on the fret,
Because, in so debauch'd and vile an age,
Thy friend and old acquaintance dares disown
The gold you lent him, and forswear the *loan.* *Dryden.*

LOATH. *adj.* [lað, Saxon.] Unwilling; disliking; not ready; not inclined.

These fresh and delightful brooks, how slowly they slide away, as *loth* to leave the company of so many things united in perfection. *Sidney.*

With lofty eyes, half *loth* to look so low,
She thanked them in her disdainful wise,
Ne other grace vouchsafed them to show
Of princess worthy. *Fairy Queen, b.* i.

When he heard her answers *loth*, he knew
Some secret sorrow did her heart distrain. *Fairy Queen.*

To speak so indirectly, I am *loth*;
I'd say the truth; but to accuse him so,
That is your part. *Shakesp. Meas. for Measure.*

Long doth she stay, as *loth* to leave the land,
From whose soft side she first did issue make,
She tastes all places, turns to ev'ry hand,
Her flow'ry banks unwilling to forsake. *Davies.*

Then wilt thou not be *loth*
To leave this paradise, but shalt possess
A paradise within thee, happier far! *Milton's Par. Lost.*

To pardon willing, and to punish *loth*;
You strike with one hand, but you heal with both:
Lifting up all that prostrate lie, you grieve
You cannot make the dead again to live. *Waller.*

When Æneas is forced to kill Lausus, the poet shews him compassionate, and is *loth* to destroy such a master-piece of nature. *Dryden's Dufresnoy.*

As some faint pilgrim standing on the shore,
First views the torrent he would venture o'er;
And then his inn upon the farther ground,
Loth to wade through, and *lother* to go round:
Then dipping in his staff does trial make
How deep it is; and, sighing, pulls it back. *Dryden.*

I know you shy to be oblig'd;
And still more *loath* to be oblig'd by me. *Southern.*

To LOATHE. *v. a.* [from the noun.]

1. To hate; to look on with abhorrence.

Parthenia had learned both liking and misliking, loving and *loathing.* *Sidney.*

They with their filthiness
Polluted this same gentle soil long time,
That their own mother *loath'd* their beastliness. *Fa. Qu.*

The fish in the river shall die, and the river stink; and the Egyptians shall *loath* to drink of the water. *Exod.* vii. 18.

How am I caught with an unwary oath,
Not to reveal the secret which I *loath!* *Waller.*

For thee the lion *loaths* the taste of blood,
And roaring hunts his female through the wood. *Dryden.*

Why do I stay within this hated place,
Where every object shocks my *loathing* eyes. *Rowe.*

Now his exalted spirit *loaths*
Incumbrances of food and cloaths. *Swift.*

2. To consider with the disgust of satiety.

Loathing the honey'd cakes, I long for bread. *Cowley.*

Our appetite is extinguished with the satisfaction, and is succeeded by *loathing* and satiety. *Rogers's Sermons.*

3. To see food with dislike.

Loathing is a symptom well known to attend disorders of the stomach; and the cure must have regard to the cause. *Quincy.*

To LOATHE. *v. n.* To create disgust; to cause abhorrence.

Where I was wont to seek the honey bee,
The grisly toadstool grown there might I see,
And *loathing* paddocks lording on the same. *Spenser.*

Lo'ather. *n. s.* [from *loath.*] One that loaths.

Lo'athful. *adj.* [*loath* and *full.*]

1. Abhorring; hating.

Which he did with *loathful* eyes behold.
He would no more endure. *Hubberd's Tale.*

2. Abhorred; hated.

Above the reach of *loathful* sinful lust,
Whose base effect, through cowardly distrust
Of his weak wings, dare not to heaven flie. *Spenser.*

Lo'athingly. *adv.* [from *loathe.*] In a fastidious manner.

Lo'athly. *adj.* [from *loath.*] Hateful; abhorred; exciting hatred.

An huge great dragon, horrible in sight,
Bred in the *loathly* lakes of Tartary,
With murd'rous ravin. *Fairy Queen, b.* i.

The people fear me; for they do observe
Unfather'd heirs, and *loathly* births of nature. *Shakesp.*

Sour-ey'd disdain, and discord shall bestow
The union of your bed with weeds so *loathly*,
That you shall hate it. *Shakespeare's Tempest.*

Lo'athly. *adv.* [from *loath.*] Unwillingly; without liking or inclination.

The upper streams make such haste to have their part of embracing, that the nether, though *lothly*, must needs give place unto them. *Sidney.*

Lothly opposite I stood
To his unnat'ral purpose. *Shakespeare's King Lear.*

This shews that you from nature *lothly* stray,
That suffer not an artificial day. *Donne.*

Lo'athness. *n. s.* [from *loath.*] Unwillingness.

The fair soul herself
Weigh'd between *lothness* and obedience,
Which end the beam should bow. *Shakesp. Tempest.*

Pray you, look not sad,
Nor make replies of *lothness*. *Shakesp. Ant. and Cleopatra.*

Should we be taking leave,
As long a term as yet we have to live,
The *lothness* to depart would grow. *Shakesp. Cymbeline.*

After they had sat about the fire, there grew a general silence and *lothness* to speak amongst them; and immediately one of the weakest fell down in a swoon. *Bacon's Nat. Hist.*

Lo'athsome. *adj.* [from *loath.*]

1. Abhorred; detestable.

The fresh young fly
Did much disdain to subject his desire
To *loathsome* sloth, or hours in ease to waste. *Spenser.*

While they pervert pure nature's healthful rules
To *loathsome* sickness. *Milton's Par. Lost, b.* xi.

If we consider man in such a *loathsome* and provoking condition, was it not love enough that he was permitted to enjoy a being. *South's Sermons.*

2. Causing satiety or fastidiousness.

The sweetest honey
Is *loathsome* in its own deliciousness,
And in the taste confounds the appetite. *Shakespeare.*

Lo'athsomeness. *n. s.* [from *loathsome.*] Quality of raising hatred.

The catacombs must have been full of stench and *loathsomeness*, if the dead bodies that lay in them were left to rot in open nitches. *Addison.*

Loaves, plural of *loaf.*

Democritus, when he lay a dying, caused *loaves* of new bread to be opened, and he poured a little wine into them; and so kept himself alive with the odour till a feast was past. *Bacon's Nat. Hist.* N°. 934.

Lob. *n. s.*

1. Any one heavy, clumsy, or sluggish.

Farewel, thou *lob* of spirits, I'll be gone,
Our queen and all her elves come here anon. *Shakesp.*

2. Lob's pound; a prison. Probably a prison for idlers, or sturdy beggars.

Crowdero, whom in irons bound,
Thou basely threw'st into *lob*'s pound. *Hudibras.*

3. A big worm.

For the trout the dew worm, which some also call the *lob* worm, and the brandling are the chief. *Walton's Angler.*

To Lob. *v. a.* To let fall in a slovenly or lazy manner.

The horsemen sit like fixed candlesticks,
And their poor jades
Lob down their heads, dropping the hide and hips. *Shakes.*

Lo'bby. *n. s.* [*laube*, German.] An opening before a room.

His *lobbies* fill with 'tendance,
Rain sacrificial whisp'rings in his ear,
Make sacred even his stirrop. *Shakesp. Tim. of Athens.*

Before the duke's rising from the table, he stood expecting till he should pass through a kind of *lobby* between that room and the next, where were divers attending him. *Wotton.*

Try your back stairs, and let the *lobby* wait,
A stratagem in war is no deceit. *King's Horace.*

Lobe. *n. s.* [*lobe*, French; λοβὸς.] A division; a distinct part: used commonly for a part of the lungs.

Nor could the *lobes* of his rank liver swell
To that prodigious mass, for their eternal meal. *Dryden.*

Air bladders form lobuli, which hang upon the bronchia like bunches of grapes; these lobuli constitute the *lobes*, and the *lobes* the lungs. *Arbuthnot on Aliments.*

Lo'bster. *n. s.* [lobꞅteꞃ, Saxon.] A crustaceous fish.

Those that cast their shell, are the *lobster*, the crab, and craw-fish. *Bacon's Nat. Hist.* N°. 732.

It happeneth often that a *lobster* hath the great claw of one side longer than the other. *Brown's Vulgar Errours.*

LO'CAL. *adj.* [*local*, French; *locus*, Latin.]

1. Having the properties of place.

By ascending, after that the sharpness of death was overcome, he took the very *local* possession of glory, and that to the use of all that are his, even as himself before had witnessed, I go to prepare a place for you. *Hooker, b.* v.

A higher flight the vent'rous goddess tries,
Leaving material worlds, and *local* skies. *Prior.*

2. Relating to place.

The circumstance of *local* nearness in them unto us, might haply enforce in us a duty of greater separation from them than from those other. *Hooker, b.* iv.

Where there is only a *local* circumstance of worship, the same thing would be worshipped, supposing that circumstance changed. *Stillingfleet.*

3. Being in a particular place.

Dream not of their fight,
As of a duel, or the *local* wounds
Of head, or heel. *Milton's Par. Lost, b.* xiii.

How is the change of being sometimes here, sometimes there, made by *local* motion in vacuum, without a change in the body moved? *Digby on Bodies.*

Loca'lity. *n. s.* [from *local.*] Existence in place; relation of place, or distance.

That the soul and angels are devoid of quantity and dimension, and that they have nothing to do with grosser *locality*, is generally opinioned. *Glanville's Scep.*

Loca'lly, *adj.* [from *local.*] With respect to place.

Whether things, in their natures so divers as body and spirit, which almost in nothing communicate, are not essentially divided, though not *locally* distant, I leave to the readers. *Glanville's Scep.*

Loca'tion. *n. s.* [*locatio*, Latin.] Situation with respect to place; act of placing; state of being placed.

To say that the world is somewhere, means no more than that it does exist; this, though a phrase borrowed from place, signifying only its existence, not *location.* *Locke.*

Loch. *n. s.* A lake. Scottish.

A lake or *loch*, that has no fresh water running into it, will turn into a stinking puddle. *Cheyne's Phil. Principles.*

Lock. *n. s.* [loc, Saxon, in both senses.]

1. An instrument composed of springs and bolts, used to fasten doors or chests.

No gate so strong, no *lock* so firm and fast,
But with that piercing noise flew open quit or brast. *F. Qu.*

We have *locks* to safeguard necessaries,
And pretty traps to catch the petty thieves. *Shakespeare.*

As there are *locks* for several purposes, so are there several inventions in *locks*, in contriving their wards or guards. *Moxon.*

2. The part of the gun by which fire is struck.

A gun carries powder and bullets for seven charges and discharges: under the breech of the barrel is one box for the powder; a little before the *lock*, another for the bullets; behind the cock a charger, which carries the powder to the further end of the *lock.* *Grew's Musæum.*

3. A hug; a grapple.

They must be practised in all the *locks* and gripes of wrestling, as need may often be in fight to tugg or grapple, and to close. *Milton on Education.*

4. Any inclosure.

Sergesthus, eager with his beak to press
Betwixt the rival gally and the rock,
Shuts up th' unwieldy centaur in the *lock.* *Dryden's Æn.*

5. A quantity of hair or wool hanging together.

Well might he perceive the hanging of her hair in *locks*, some curled, and some forgotten. *Sidney.*

A goodly cypress, who bowing her fair head over the water, it seemed she looked into it, and dressed her green *locks* by that running river. *Sidney.*

His grizly *locks*, long growen and unbound,
Disordered hung about his shoulders round. *Fairy Qu.*

The bottom was set against a *lock* of wool, and the sound was quite deaded. *Bacon.*

They nourish only a *lock* of hair on the crown of their heads. *Sandys's Travels.*

A *lock* of hair will draw more than a cable rope. *Grew.*

Behold the *locks* that are grown white
Beneath a helmet in your father's battles. *Addison's Cato.*

Two *locks* graceful hung behind
In equal curls, and well-conspir'd, to deck
With shining ringlets her smooth iv'ry neck. *Pope.*

6. A tuft.

I suppose this letter will find thee picking of daisies, or smelling to a *lock* of hay. *Addison's Spectator.*

To Lock. *v. a.* [from the noun.]

1. To shut or fasten with locks.

The garden, seated on the level floor,
She left behind, and *locking* ev'ry door,
Thought all secure. *Dryden.*

2. To shut up or confine, as with locks.

I am *lockt* in one of them;
If you do love me, you will find me out. *Shakespeare.*

We do *lock*
Our former sample in our strong-barr'd gates. *Shakesp.*

Then seek to know those things which make us blest,
And having found them, *lock* them in thy breast. *Denham.*

The frighted dame
The log in secret *lock'd.* *Dryden's Ovid.*

If the door to a council be kept by armed men, and all such whose opinions are not liked kept out, the freedom of those within are infringed, and all their acts as void as if they were *locked* in. *Dryden's Æn.*

One conduces to the poets completing of his work; the other slackens his pace, and *locks* him up like a knight-errant in an enchanted castle. *Dryden's Dedicat. to the Æn.*

The father of the gods
Confin'd their fury to those dark abodes,
And *lock'd* 'em safe within, oppress'd with mountain loads. *Dryden's Æn.*

If one third of the money in trade were *locked* up, must not the landholders receive one third less. *Locke.*

Always *lock* up a cat in a closet where you keep your china plates, for fear the mice may steal in and break them. *Swift.*

Your wine *lock'd* up,
Plain milk will do the feat. *Pope's Horace.*

3. To close fast.

Death blasts his bloom, and *locks* his frozen eyes. *Gay.*

To Lock. *v. n.*

1. To become fast by a lock.

For not of wood, nor of enduring brass,
Doubly disparted it did *lock* and close,
That when it *locked*, none might through it pass. *Fa. Qu.*

2. To unite by mutual insertion.

Either they *lock* into each other, or slip one upon another's surface; as much of their surfaces touches as makes them cohere. *Boyle.*

Lo'cker. *n. s.* [from *lock.*] Any thing that is closed with a lock; a drawer.

I made *lockers* or drawers at the end of the boat. *R. Crusoe.*

Lo'cket. *n. s.* [*loquet*, French.] A small lock; any catch or spring to fasten a necklace, or other ornament.

Where knights are kept in narrow lists,
With wooden *lockets* 'bout their wrists. *Hudibras, p.* ii.

Lo'ckram. *n. s.* A sort of coarse linen. *Hanmer.*

The kitchen malkin pins
Her richest *lockram* 'bout her reeky neck,
Clamb'ring the walls to eye him. *Shakesp. Coriolanus.*

Lo'ckron. *n. s.* A kind of ranunculus.

Locomo'tion. *n. s.* [*locus* and *motus*, Lat.] Power of changeing place.

All progression, or animal *locomotion*, is performed by drawing on, or impelling forward, some part which was before at quiet. *Brown's Vulgar Errours.*

Locomo'tive. *adj.* [*locus* and *moveo*, Lat.] Changing place; having the power of removing or changing place.

I shall consider the motion, or *locomotive* faculty of animals. *Derham's Physico-Theol.*

In the night too oft he kicks,
Or shows his *locomotive* tricks. *Prior.*

An animal cannot well be defined from any particular, organical part, nor from its *locomotive* faculty, for some adhere to rocks. *Arbuthnot on Aliments.*

Lo'cust. *n. s.* [*locusta*, Latin.]

The Hebrews had several sorts of *locusts*, which are not known among us: the old historians and modern travellers remark, that *locusts* are very numerous in Africk, and many places of Asia; that sometimes they fell like a cloud upon the country, and eat up every thing they meet with. Moses describes four sorts of *locusts*. Since there was a prohibition against using *locusts*, it is not to be questioned but that these creatures were commonly eaten in Palestine, and the neighbouring countries. *Calmet.*

To-morrow will I bring the *locusts* into thy coast. *Exod.*

Air replete with the steams of animals rotting, has produced pestilential fevers; such have likewise been raised by great quantities of dead *locusts*. *Arbuthnot on Air.*

Locust-tree. *n. s.*

The *locust-tree* hath a papilionaceous flower, from whose calyx arises the pointal, which afterwards becomes an unicapsular hard pod, including roundish hard seeds, which are surrounded with a fungous stringy substance. *Miller.*

Lodestar. See Loadstar.

Lodestone. See Loadstone.

To Lodge. *v. a.* [logian, Saxon; *loger*, French.]

1. To place in a temporary habitation.

When he was come to the court of France, the king stiled him by the name of the duke of York; *lodged* him, and accommodated him, in great state. *Bacon's Henry VII.*

2. To afford a temporary dwelling; to supply with harbour for a night.

Ev'ry house was proud to *lodge* a knight. *Dryden.*

3. To place; to plant.

When on the brink the foaming boar I met,
And in his side thought to have *lodg'd* my spear,
The desp'rate savage rush'd within my force,
And bore me headlong with him down the rock. *Otway.*

He *lodg'd* an arrow in a tender breast,
That had so often to his own been prest. *Addison's Ovid.*

In viewing again the ideas that are *lodged* in the memory, the mind is more than passive. *Locke.*

4. To fix; to settle.

By whose fell working I was first advanc'd,
And by whose pow'r I well might *lodge* a fear
To be again displac'd. *Shakespeare.*

I can give no reason,
More than a *lodg'd* hate, and a certain loathing
I bear Antonio. *Shakespeare's Merch. of Venice.*

5. To place in the memory.

This cunning the king would not understand, though he *lodged* it, and noted it, in some particulars. *Bacon's H.* VII.

6. To harbour or cover.

The deer is *lodg'd*, I've track'd her to her covert;
Rush in at once. *Addison's Cato.*

7. To afford place to.

The memory can *lodge* a greater store of images, than all the senses can present at one time. *Cheyne's Phil. Principles.*

8. To lay flat.

Though bladed corn be *lodg'd*, and trees blown down,
Though castles topple on their warders heads. *Shakesp.*

We'll make foul weather with despised tears;
Our sighs, and they, shall *lodge* the Summer corn,
And make a dearth in this revolting land. *Shakespeare.*

To Lodge. *v. n.*

1. To reside; to keep residence.

Care keeps his watch in ev'ry old man's eye,
And where care *lodgeth*, sleep will never lie. *Shakesp.*

Something holy *lodges* in that breast,
And with these raptures moves the vocal air
To testify his hidden residence. *Milton.*

And dwells such rage in softest bosom then?
And *lodge* such daring souls in little men? *Pope.*

2. To take a temporary habitation.

Why commands the king,
That his chief followers *lodge* in towns about him,
While he himself keepeth in the cold field? *Shakesp.*

I know not where he *lodges*; and for me to devise a lodging, and say, he lies here, or he lies there, were to lie in mine own throat. *Shakespeare's Othello.*

Thy father is a man of war, and will not *lodge* with the people. 2 *Sam.* xvii. 8.

3. To take up residence at night.

My lords
And soldiers, stay and *lodge* by me this night. *Shakesp.*

Oh, that I had in the wilderness a *lodging* place of wayfaring men, that I might leave my people. *Jer.* ix. 4.

Here thou art but a stranger travelling to thy country; it is therefore a huge folly to be afflicted, because thou hast a less convenient inn to *lodge* in by the way. *Taylor.*

4. To lie flat.

Long cone wheat they reckon in Oxfordshire best for rank clays; and its straw makes it not subject to *lodge*, or to be mildewed. *Mortimer's Husbandry.*

Lodge. *n. s.* [*logis*, French.]

1. A small house in a park or forest.

He brake up his court, and retired himself, his wife and children, into a certain forest thereby, which he calleth his desart, wherein he hath built two fine *lodges*. *Sidney.*

I found him as melancholy as a *lodge* in a warren. *Shak.*

He and his lady both are at the *lodge*,
Upon the north side of this pleasant chace. *Shakespeare.*

Thus at their shady *lodge* arriv'd, both stood,
Both turn'd, and under open sky ador'd
The God that made both sky, air, earth. *Milton.*

Whenever I am turned out, my *lodge* descends upon a low-spirited family. *Swift.*

2. Any small house; as, the porter's lodge.

Lo'dgement. *n. s.* [from *lodge*; *logement*, French.]

1. Accumulation, or collocation in a certain place.

The curious *lodgement* and inosculation of the auditory nerves. *Derham.*

An oppressed diaphragm from a mere *lodgement* of extravasated matter. *Sharp's Surgery.*

2. Possession of the enemy's work.

The military pedant is making *lodgements*, and fighting battels, from one end of the year to the other. *Addison.*

Lo'dger.

Lo'dger. *n. s.* [from *lodge.*]
1. One who lives in rooms hired in the house of another.
Base tyke, call'st thou me host? now, I scorn the term; nor shall my Nell keep *lodgers.* *Shakespeare's Henry* V.
There were in a family, the man and his wife, three children, and three servants or *lodgers.* *Graunt's Bills.*
Those houses are soonest infected that are crowded with multiplicity of *lodgers*, and nasty families. *Harvey.*
The gentlewoman begged me to step; for that a *lodger* she had taken in was run mad. *Tatler*, N°. 88.
Sylla was reproached by his fellow *lodger*, that whilst the fellow *lodger* paid eight pounds one shilling and fivepence halfpeny for the uppermost story, he paid for the rest twenty-four pounds four shillings and fourpence halfpeny. *Arbuthnot.*
2. One that resides in any place.
Look in that breast, most dirty dear;
Say, can you find but one such *lodger* there? *Pope.*

Lo'dging. *n. s.* [from *lodge.*]
1. Temporary habitation; rooms hired in the house of another.
I will in Cassio's *lodging* lose this napkin,
And let him find it. *Shakespeare's Othello.*
Let him change his *lodging* from one end of the town to another, which is a great adamant of acquaintance. *Bacon.*
At night he came
To his known *lodgings*, and his country dame. *Dryden.*
He desired his sister to bring her away to the *lodgings* of his friend. *Addison's Guardian*, N°. 155.
Wits take *lodgings* in the sound of Bow. *Pope.*
2. Place of residence.
Fair bosom fraught with virtue's richest treasure,
The nest of love, the *lodging* of delight,
The bower of bliss, the paradise of pleasure,
The sacred harbour of that heavenly spright. *Spenser.*
3. Harbour; covert.
The hounds were uncoupled; and the stag thought it better to trust to the nimbleness of his feet, than to the slender fortification of his *lodging.* *Sidney.*
4. Convenience to sleep on.
Their feathers serve to stuff our beds and pillows, yielding us soft and warm *lodging.* *Ray on Creation.*

Loft. *n. s.* [*lloft*, Welsh; or from *lift.*]
1. A floor.
There is a traverse placed in a *loft* above. *Bacon.*
2. The highest floor.
To lull him in his slumber soft,
A trickling stream from high rock tumbling down,
And ever drizzling rain upon the *loft*,
Mixt with a murmuring wind. *Fairy Queen*, *b.* i.
3. Rooms on high.
Passing through the spheres of watchful fire,
And hills of snow, and *lofts* of piled thunder. *Milton.*
A weasel once made shift to slink
In at a corn *loft*, through a chink. *Pope.*

Lo'ftily. *adv.* [from *lofty.*]
1. On high; in an elevated place.
2. Proudly; haughtily.
They speak wickedly concerning oppression; they speak *loftily.* *Psal.* lxxiii. 8.
3. With elevation of language or sentiment; sublimely.
My lowly verse may *loftily* arise,
And lift itself unto the highest skies. *Fairy Queen.*

Lo'ftiness. *n. s.* [from *lofty.*]
1. Height; local elevation.
2. Sublimity; elevation of sentiment.
Three poets in three distant ages born;
The first in *loftiness* of thought surpass'd,
The next in majesty; in both the last. *Dryden.*
3. Pride; haughtiness.
Augustus and Tiberius had *loftiness* enough in their temper, and affected to make a sovereign figure. *Collier.*

Lo'fty. *adj.* [from *loft*, or *lift.*]
1. High; hovering; elevated in place.
See *lofty* Lebanon his head advance,
See nodding forests on the mountains dance. *Pope's Messiah.*
2. Sublime; elevated in sentiment.
He knew
Himself to sing and build the *lofty* rhyme. *Milton.*
3. Proud; haughty.
Man, the tyrant of our sex, I hate,
A lowly servant, but a *lofty* mate. *Dryden's Knight's Tale.*
Lofty and sour to them that lov'd him not;
But to those men that sought him, sweet as Summer. *Shak.*

Log. *n. s.* [The original of this word is not known. *Skinner* derives it from liȝȝan, Saxon, to lie; *Junius* from *logge*, Dutch, sluggish; perhaps the Latin *lignum*, is the true original.] A shapeless bulky piece of wood.
Would the light'ning had
Burnt up those *logs* that thou'rt injoin'd to pile. *Shakesp.*
The worms with many feet are bred under *logs* of timber, and many times in gardens, where no *logs* are. *Bacon.*
Some *log*, perhaps, upon the waters swam,
An useless drift, which rudely cut within,
And hollow'd first a floating trough became,
And cross some riv'let passage did begin. *Dryden.*
The frighted dame
The *log* in secret lock'd. *Dryden's Ovid.*
2. An Hebrew measure, which held a quarter of a cab, and consequently five-sixths of a pint. According to Dr. Arbuthnot it was a liquid measure, the seventy-second part of the bath or ephah, and twelfth part of the hin. *Calmet.*
A meat offering, mingled with oil, and one *log* of oil. *Lev.* xiv. 10.

Lo'garithms. *n. s.* [*logarithme*, Fr. λόγος and ἀριθμος.]
Logarithms, which are the indexes of the ratio's of numbers one to another, were first invented by Napier lord Merchison, a Scottish baron, and afterwards completed by Mr. Briggs, Savilian professor at Oxford. They are a series of artificial numbers, contrived for the expedition of calculation, and proceeding in an arithmetical proportion, as the numbers they answer to do in a geometrical one: for instance,

0	1	2	3	4	5	6	7	8	9
1	2	4	8	16	32	64	128	256	512

Where the numbers above, beginning with (0), and arithmetically proportional, are called *logarithms.* The addition and subtraction of *logarithms* answers to the multiplication and division of the numbers they correspond with; and this saves an infinite deal of trouble. In like manner will the extraction of roots be performed, by dissecting the *logarithms* of any numbers for the square root, and trisecting them for the cube, and so on. *Harris.*

Lo'ggats. *n. s.*
Loggats is the ancient name of a play or game, which is one of the unlawful games enumerated in the thirty-third statute of Henry VIII. It is the same which is now called kittlepins, in which boys often make use of bones instead of wooden pins, throwing at them with another bone instead of bowling. *Hanmer.*
Did these bones cost no more the breeding, but to play at *loggats* with them. *Shakespeare's Hamlet.*

Lo'ggerhead. *n. s.* [*logge*, Dutch, *stupid* and *head*, or rather from *log*, a heavy motionless mass, as *blockhead.*] A dolt; a blockhead; a thickscul.
Where hast been, Hal?
With three or four *loggerheads*, amongst three or fourscore hogsheads. *Shakespeare's Henry* IV.
Says this *loggerhead*, what have we to do to quench other peoples fires. *L'Estrange.*
To fall to Loggerheads. } To scuffle; to fight without wea-
To go to Loggerheads. } pons.
A couple of travellers that took up an ass, *fell to loggerheads* which should be his master. *L'Estrange.*

Lo'ggerheaded. *adj.* [from *loggerhead.*] Dull; stupid; doltish.
You *loggerheaded* and unpolish'd groom, what! no attendance? *Shakesp. Taming of the Shrew.*

LO'GICK. *n. s.* [*logique*, French; *logica*, Latin, from λόγος.] The art of reasoning.
Logick is the art of using reason well in our inquiries after truth, and the communication of it to others. *Watts's Logick.*
Talk *logick* with acquaintance,
And practise rhetorick in your common talk. *Shakespeare.*
By a *logick* that left no man any thing which he might call his own, they no more looked upon it as the case of one man, but the case of the kingdom. *Clarendon.*
Here foam'd rebellious *logick*, gagg'd and bound,
There stript fair rhetorick languish'd on the ground. *Pope.*

Lo'gical. *adj.* [from *logick.*]
1. Pertaining to logick; taught in logick.
The heretick complained greatly of St. Augustine, as being too full of *logical* subtilties. *Hooker*, *b.* iii.
Those who in a *logical* dispute keep in general terms, would hide a fallacy. *Dryden's Pref. to Ann. Mirab.*
We ought not to value ourselves upon our ability, in giving subtile rules, and finding out *logical* arguments, since it would be more perfection not to want them. *Baker.*
2. Skilled in logick; furnished with logick.
A man who sets up for a judge in criticism, should have a clear and *logical* head. *Addison's Spect.* N°. 291.

Lo'gically. *adv.* [from *logical.*] According to the laws of logick.
How can her old good man
With honour take her back again?
From hence I *logically* gather,
The woman cannot live with either. *Prior.*

Logi'cian. *n. s.* [*logicien*, French; *logicus*, Latin.] A teacher or professor of logick; a man versed in logick.
If a man can play the true *logician*, and have as well judgment as invention, he may do great matters. *Bacon.*
If we may believe our *logicians*, man is distinguished from all other creatures by the faculty of laughter. *Addison.*
Each staunch polemick stubborn as a rock,
Each fierce *logician* still expelling Locke,
Came whip and spur. *Dunciad*, *b.* iv.

A *logician*

A *logician* might put a caſe that would ſerve for an exception. *Swift.*

The Arabian phyſicians were ſubtile men, and moſt of them *logicians*; accordingly they have given method, and ſhed ſubtilty upon their author. *Baker.*

Lo'gman. *n. ſ.* [*log* and *man.*] One whoſe buſineſs is to carry logs.

For your ſake
Am I this patient *logman.* *Shakeſpeare's Tempeſt.*

Lo'gomachy. *n. ſ.* [λογομαχία.] A contention in words; a contention about words.

Forced terms of art did much puzzle ſacred theology with diſtinctions, cavils, quidditics; and ſo transformed her to a meer kind of ſophiſtry and *logomachy.* *Howel.*

Lo'gwood. *n. ſ.*

Logwood is of a very denſe and firm texture; it is brought to us in very large and thick blocks or logs, and is the heart only of the tree which produces it. It is very heavy, and remarkably hard, and of a deep, ſtrong, red colour. It grows both in the Eaſt and Weſt Indies, but no where ſo plentifully as on the coaſt of the bay of Campeachy. It has been long known by the dyers, and was but lately introduced in medicine, and is found to be an excellent aſtringent. *Hill's Mat. Med.*

To make a light purple, mingle ceruſe with *logwood* water. *Peacham on Drawing.*

Lo'hock. *n. ſ.*

Lohock is an Arabian name for thoſe forms of medicines which are now commonly called Eclegma's, lambatives, or linctus's. *Quincy.*

Lohocks and pectorals were preſcribed, and veneſection repeated. *Wiſeman's Surgery.*

Loin. *n. ſ.* [*llwyn*, Welſh.]

1. The back of an animal carved out by the butcher.

2. *Loins*; the reins.

My face I'll grime with filth,
Blanket my *loins.* *Shakeſpeare's King Lear.*

Thou ſlander of thy heavy mother's womb!
Thou loathed iſſue of thy father's *loins.* *Shakeſp. Rich.* III.

Virgin mother, hail!
High in the love of heav'n! yet from my *loins*
Thou ſhalt proceed, and from thy womb the ſon
Of God moſt high. *Milton's Par. Loſt, b.* xii.

A multitude! like which the populous north
Pour'd never from her frozen *loins*, to paſs
Rhene, or the Danaw, when her barbarous ſons
Came like a deluge on the ſouth. *Milton.*

To Lo'iter. *v. n.* [*loteren*, Dutch.] To linger; to ſpend time careleſsly; to idle.

Sir John, you *loiter* here too long, being you are to take ſoldiers up in the countries. *Shakeſpeare.*

Whence this long delay?
You *loiter*, while the ſpoils are thrown away. *Dryden.*

Mark how he ſpends his time, whether he unactively *loiters* it away. *Locke.*

If we have gone wrong, let us redeem the miſtake; if we have *loitered*, let us quicken our pace, and make the moſt of the preſent opportunity. *Rogers's Sermons.*

Lo'iterer. *n. ſ.* [from *loiter.*] A lingerer; an idler; a lazy wretch; one who lives without buſineſs; one who is ſluggiſh and dilatory.

Give gloves to thy reapers a largeſs to cry,
And daily to *loiterers* have a good eye. *Tuſſer's Huſb.*

The poor, by idleneſs or unthriftineſs, are riotous ſpenders, vagabonds, and *loiterers.* *Hayward.*

Where haſt thou been, thou *loiterer*?
Though my eyes cloſ'd, my arms have ſtill been open'd,
To ſearch if thou wert come. *Otway.*

Providence would only enter mankind into the uſeful knowledge of her treaſures, leaving the reſt to employ our induſtry, that we live not like idle *loiterers* and truants. *More.*

Ever liſtleſs *loit'rers*, that attend
No cauſe, no truſt, no duty, and no friend. *Pope.*

To Loll. *v. n.* [Of this word the etymology is not known. Perhaps it might be contemptuouſly derived from *lollard*, a name of great reproach before the reformation; of whom one tenet was, that all trades not neceſſary to life are unlawful.]

1. To lean idly; to reſt lazily againſt any thing.

So hangs, and *lolls*, and weeps upon me; ſo ſhakes and pulls me. *Shakeſpeare's Othello.*

He is not *lolling* on a lewd love bed,
But on his knees at meditation. *Shakeſp. Rich.* III.

Cloſe by a ſoftly murm'ring ſtream,
Where lovers us'd to *loll* and dream. *Hudibras, p.* i.

To *loll* on couches, rich with cytron ſteds,
And lay your guilty limbs in Tyrian beds. *Dryden.*

Void of care he *lolls* ſupine in ſtate,
And leaves his buſineſs to be done by fate. *Dryd. Perſ.*

But wanton now, and *lolling* at our eaſe,
We ſuffer all the invet'rate ills of peace. *Dryden.*

A lazy, *lolling* ſort
Of ever liſtleſs loit'rers. *Dunciad, b.* iv.

2. To hang out. Uſed of the tongue hanging out in wearineſs or play.

The triple porter of the Stygian ſeat,
With *lolling* tongue lay fawning at thy feet. *Dryden.*

With harmleſs play amidſt the bowls he paſs'd,
And with his *lolling* tongue aſſay'd the taſte. *Dryden.*

To Loll. *v. a.* To put out: uſed of the tongue exerted.

All authors to their own defects are blind;
Hadſt thou but, Janus-like, a face behind,
To ſee the people, when ſplay mouths they make,
To mark their fingers pointed at thy back,
Their tongues *loll'd* out a foot. *Dryden's Perſius.*

By Strymon's freezing ſtreams he ſat alone,
Trees bent their heads to hear him ſing his wrongs,
Fierce tygers couch'd around, and *loll'd* their fawning tongues. *Dryden's Virgil.*

By the wolf were laid the martial twins;
Intrepid on her ſwelling dugs they hung,
The foſter-dam *loll'd* out her fawning tongue. *Dryden.*

Lomp. *n. ſ.* A kind of roundiſh fiſh.

Lone. *adj.* [contracted from *alone.*]

1. Solitary.

Here the *lone* hour a blank of life diſplays. *Savage.*

Thus vaniſh ſceptres, coronets and balls,
And leave you in *lone* woods, or empty walls. *Pope.*

2. Single; without company.

No *lone* houſe in Wales, with a mountain and a rookery, is more contemplative than this court. *Pope.*

Lo'neliness. *n. ſ.* [from *lonely.*] Solitude; want of company; diſpoſition to avoid company.

The huge and ſportful aſſembly grew to him a tedious *lonelineſs*, eſteeming nobody ſound ſince Daiphantus was loſt. *Sidney.*

I ſee
The myſtery of your *lonelineſs*, and find
Your ſalt tears head. *Shakeſpeare.*

Lonely. *adj.* [from *lone.*] Solitary; addicted to ſolitude.

I go alone,
Like to a *lonely* dragon; that his fen
Makes fear'd and talk'd of more than ſeen. *Shakeſp.*

Why thus cloſe up the ſtars
That nature hung in heav'n, and fill'd their lamps
With everlaſting oil, to give due light
To the miſled and *lonely* traveller. *Milton.*

Time has made you dote, and vainly tell
Of arms imagin'd, in your *lonely* cell. *Dryden's Æn.*

When, faireſt princeſs,
You *lonely* thus from the full court retire,
Love and the graces follow to your ſolitude. *Rowe.*

Lo'neness. *n. ſ.* [from *lone.*] Solitude; diſlike of company.

If of court life you knew the good,
You would leave *loneneſs.* *Donne.*

I can love
Her who loves *loneneſs* beſt. *Donne.*

Lo'nesome. *adj.* [from *lone.*] Solitary; diſmal.

You either muſt the earth from reſt diſturb,
Or roll around the heavens the ſolar orb;
Elſe what a dreadful face will nature wear?
How horrid will theſe *loneſome* ſeats appear? *Blackmore.*

Long. *adj.* [*long*, French; *longus*, Latin.]

1. Not ſhort.

He talked a *long* while, even till break of day. *Acts* xx.

He was deſirous to ſee him of a *long* ſeaſon. *Luke* xxiii.

2. Having one of its geometrical dimenſions in a greater degree than either of the other.

His branches became *long* becauſe of the waters. *Ezek.*

We made the trial in a *long* necked phial left open at the top. *Boyle.*

3. Of any certain meaſure in length.

Women eat their children of a ſpan *long.* *Lam.* ii. 20.

4. Not ſoon ceaſing, or at an end.

Man goeth to his *long* home. *Eccl.* xii. 5.

Honour thy father and thy mother, that thy days may be *long* upon the land. *Exod.* xx. 12.

The phyſician cutteth off a *long* diſeaſe. *Eccluſ.* x. 10.

5. Dilatory.

Death will not be *long* in coming, and the covenant of the grave is not ſhewed unto thee. *Eccluſ.* xiv. 12.

6. [From the verb, *to long.*] Longing; deſirous; or perhaps, long continued, from the diſpoſition to continue looking at any thing deſired.

Praying for him, and caſting a *long* look that way, he ſaw the galley leave the purſuit. *Sidney.*

By ev'ry circumſtance I know he loves;
Yet he but doubts, and parlies, and caſts out
Many a *long* look-for ſuccour. *Dryden.*

7. Reaching to a great distance.

If the way be too *long* for thee. *Deut.* xiv. 24.

They are old by reason of the very *long* journey. *Jos.* ix.

8. In musick and pronunciation.] Protracted; as, a long note, a long syllable.

LONG. *adv.*

1. To a great length.

The marble brought, erects the spacious dome,
Or forms the pillars *long*-extended rows
On which the planted grove and pensile garden grows.
Prior.

2. Not for a short time.

With mighty barres of *long*-enduring brass. *Fairfax.*

When the trumpet soundeth *long*, they shall come up to the mount. *Exod.* xix. 13.

The martial Ancus
Furbish'd the rusty sword again,
Resum'd the *long*-forgotten shield. *Dryden.*

One of these advantages, that which Corneille has laid down, is the making choice of some signal and *long*-expected day, whereon the action of the play is to depend. *Dryden on Dramatick Poesy.*

So stood the pious prince unmov'd, and *long*
Sustain'd the madness of the noisy throng. *Dryden's Æn.*

The muse resumes her *long*-forgotten lays,
And love, restor'd, his ancient realm surveys. *Dryden.*

No man has complained that you have discoursed too *long* on any subject, for you leave us in an eagerness of learning more. *Dryden.*

Persia left for you
The realm of Candahar for dow'r I brought,
That *long*-contended prize for which you fought. *Dryden.*

It may help to put an end to that *long*-agitated and unreasonable question, whether man's will be free or no? *Locke.*

Heav'n restores
To thy fond wish the *long*-expected shores. *Pope's Odyssey.*

3. In the comparative, it signifies for more time; and in the superlative, for most time.

When she could not *longer* hide him, she took for him an ark of bullrushes. *Exod.* ii. 3.

Eldest parents signifies either the eldest men and women that have had children, or those who have *longest* had issue. *Locke.*

4. Not soon.

Not *long* after there arose against it a tempestuous wind. *Acts* xxvii. 14.

5. At a point of duration far distant.

If the world had been eternal, those would have been found in it, and generally spread *long* ago, and beyond the memory of all ages. *Tillotson's Sermons.*

Say, that you once were virtuous *long* ago?
A frugal, hardy people. *Philips's Briton.*

6. [For *along*; *au long*, Fr.] All along; throughout.

Them among
There sat a man of ripe and perfect age,
Who did them meditate all his life *long*. *Fairy Queen.*

Some say, that ever 'gainst that season comes,
Wherein our Saviour's birth is celebrated,
The bird of dawning singeth all night *long*,
And then they say no spirit walks abroad.
The nights are wholesome, then no planets strike,
No fairy takes, no witch hath power to charm,
So hallow'd and so gracious is the time. *Shakesp. Hamlet.*

He fed me all my life *long* to this day. *Gen.* xlviii. 15.

Forty years *long* was I grieved with this generation. *Psal.*

LONG. *v. n.* [ȝelanȝ, a fault, Saxon.] By the fault; by the failure. A word now out of use, but truly English.

Respective and wary men had rather seek quietly their own, and wish that the world may go well, so it be not *long* of them, than with pains and hazard make themselves advisers for the common good. *Hooker, b.* v.

Maine, Bloys, Poictiers, and Tours are won away,
Long all of Somerset, and his delay. *Shakesp. Henry* VI.

Mistress, all this coyl is *long* of you. *Shakespeare.*

If we owe it to him that we know so much, it is perhaps *long* of his fond adorers that we know so little more. *Glanv.*

To LONG. *v. n.* [*gelangen*, German, to ask. *Skinner.*] To desire earnestly; to wish with eagerness continued, with *for* or *after* before the thing desired.

Fresh expectation troubled not the land
With any *long'd for* change, or better state. *Shakespeare.*

And thine eyes shall look, and fail with *longing* for them. *Deut.* xxviii. 32.

If erst he wished, now he *longed* sore. *Fairfax, b.* i.

The great master perceived, that Rhodes was the place the Turkish tyrant *longed after*. *Knolles's Hist. of the Turks.*

If the report be good, it causeth love,
And *longing* hope, and well assured joy. *Davies.*

His sons, who seek the tyrant to sustain,
And *long for* arbitrary lords again,
He dooms to death deserv'd. *Dryden's Æn.*

Glad of the gift, the new made warrior goes,
And arms among the Greeks, and *longs for* equal foes. *Dryd.*

Else whence this pleasing hope, this fond desire,
This *longing* after immortality? *Addison's Cato.*

There's the tie that binds you;
You *long* to call him father: Marcia's charms
Work in your heart unseen, and plead for Cato. *Addison.*

Nicomedes *longing* for herrings, was supplied with fresh ones by his cook, though at a great distance from the sea. *Arbuthnot on Coins.*

Through stormy seas
I courted dangers, and I *long'd* for death. *A. Philips.*

LONGANIMITY. *n. s.* [*longanimitas*, Latin; *longanimité*, Fr.] Forbearance; patience of offences.

It had overcome the patience of Job, as it did the meekness of Moses, and surely had mastered any but the *longanimity* and lasting sufferance of God. *Brown's Vulg. Errours.*

That innocent and holy matron had rather go clad in the snowy white robes of meekness and *longanimity*, than in the purple mantle of blood. *Howell's England's Tears.*

LO'NGBOAT. *n. s.* The largest boat belonging to a ship.

At the first descent on shoar, he did countenance the landing in his *longboat*. *Wotton.*

They first betray their masters, and then, when they find the vessel sinking, save themselves in the *longboat*. *L'Estrange.*

LONGE'VITY. *n. s.* [*longævus*, Latin.] Length of life.

That those are countries suitable to the nature of man, and convenient to live in, appears from the *longevity* of the natives. *Ray on Creation.*

The instances of *longevity* are chiefly amongst the abstemious. *Arbuthnot on Aliments.*

LONGI'MANOUS. *adj.* [*longuemain*, French; *longimanus*, Lat.] Long-handed; having long hands.

The villainy of this Christian exceeded the persecution of heathens, whose malice was never so *longimanous* as to reach the soul of their enemies, or to extend unto the exile of their elysiums. *Brown's Vulgar Errours, b.* vii.

LONGI'METRY. *n. s.* [*longus* and μετρέω; *longimetrie*, French.] The art or practice of measuring distances.

Our two eyes are like two different stations in *longimetry*, by the assistance of which the distance between two objects is measured. *Cheyne's Phil. Principles.*

LO'NGING. *n. s.* [from *long.*] Earnest desire; continual wish.

When within short time I came to the degree of uncertain wishes, and that those wishes grew to unquiet *longings*, when I would fix my thoughts upon nothing, but that within little varying they should end with Philoclea. *Sidney.*

I have a woman's *longing*,
An appetite that I am sick withal,
To see great Hector in the weeds of peace. *Shakespeare.*

The will is left to the pursuit of nearer satisfactions, and to the removal of those uneasinesses which it then feels in its want of, and *longings* after, them. *Locke.*

LO'NGINGLY. *adv.* [from *longing.*] With incessant wishes.

To his first bias *longingly* he leans,
And rather would be great by wicked means. *Dryden.*

LO'NGISH. *adj.* [from *long.*] Somewhat long.

LO'NGITUDE. *n. s.* [*longitude*, French; *longitudo*, Latin.]

1. Length; the greatest dimension.

The ancients did determine the *longitude* of all rooms, which were longer than broad, by the double of their latitude. *Wotton's Architect.*

The variety of the alphabet was in mere *longitude* only; but the thousand parts of our bodies may be diversified by situation in all the dimensions of solid bodies; which multiplies all over and over again, and overwhelms the fancy in a new abyss of unfathomable number. *Bentley's Sermons.*

This universal gravitation is an incessant and uniform action by certain and established laws, according to quantity of matter and *longitude* of distance, that it cannot be destroyed nor impaired. *Bentley's Sermons.*

2. The circumference of the earth measured from any meridian.

Some of Magellanus's company were the first that did compass the world through all the degrees of *longitude*. *Abbot.*

3. The distance of any part of the earth to the east or west of any place.

To conclude;
Of *longitudes*, what other way have we,
But to mark when and where the dark eclipses be? *Donne.*

His was the method of discovering the *longitude* by bomb vessels. *Arbuth. and Pope's Mart. Scrib.*

4 The position of any thing to east or west.

The *longitude* of a star is its distance from the first point of numeration toward the east, which first point, unto the ancients, was the vernal equinox. *Brown's Vulg. Errours.*

LONGITU'DINAL. *adj.* [from *longitude*; *longitudinal*, French.] Measured by the length; running in the longest direction.

Longitudinal is opposed to transverse: these vesiculæ are distended, and their *longitudinal* diameters straitened, and so the length of the whole muscle shortened. *Cheyne.*

Lo'ngly. *adv.* [from *long.*] Longingly; with great liking.

Master, you look'd so *longly* on the maid,
Perhaps, you mark not what's the pith of all. *Shakesp.*

Lo'ngsome. *adj.* [from *long.*] Tedious; wearisome by its length.

They found the war so churlish and *longsome*, as they grew then to a resolution, that, as long as England stood in state to succour those countries, they should but consume themselves in an endless war. *Bacon's War with Spain.*

When chill'd by adverse snows, and beating rain,
We tread with weary steps the *longsome* plain. *Prior.*

Lo'ngsuffering. *adj.* [*long* and *suffering.*] Patient; not easily provoked.

The Lord God, merciful and gracious, *longsuffering*, and abundant in goodness. *Exod.* xxxiv. 6.

Lo'ngsuffering. *n. s.* Patience of offence; clemency.

We infer from the mercy and *longsuffering* of God, that they were themselves sufficiently secure of his favour. *Rogers.*

Lo'ngtail. *n. s.* [*long* and *tail.*] Cut and long tail: a canting term for, one or another.

He will maintain you like a gentlewoman.
—Aye, that I will come cut and *longtail* under the degree of a squire. *Shakespeare's Merry Wives of Windsor.*

Lo'ngways. *adv.* [This and many other words so terminated are corrupted from *wise.*] In the longitudinal direction.

This island stands as a vast mole, which lies *longways*, almost in a parallel line to Naples. *Addison on Italy.*

Lo'ngwinded. *adj.* [*long* and *wind.*] Long-breathed; tedious.

My simile you minded,
Which, I confess, is too *longwinded.* *Swift.*

Lo'ngwise. *adv.* [*long* and *wise.*] In the longitudinal direction.

They make a little cross of a quill, *longwise* of that part of the quill which hath the pith, and crosswise of that piece of the quill without pith. *Bacon.*

He was laid upon two beds, the one joined *longwise* unto the other, both which he filled with his length. *Hakewill.*

Loo. *n. s.* A game at cards.

A secret indignation, that all those affections of the mind should be thus vilely thrown away upon a hand at *loo.* *Addis.*

In the fights of *loo.* *Pope.*

Lo'obily. *adj.* [*looby* and *like.*] Aukward; clumsy.

The plot of the farce was a grammar school, the master setting his boys their lessons, and a *loobily* country fellow putting in for a part among the scholars. *L'Estrange.*

Loof. *n. s.* It is that part aloft of the ship which lies just before the chess-trees, as far as the bulk head of the castle. *Sea Dictionary.*

To Loof. *v. a.* To bring the ship close to a wind.

Lo'oby. *n. s.* [Of this word the derivation is unsettled. *Skinner* mentions *lapp*, German, *foolish*; and *Junius*, *llabe*, a clown, Welsh, which seems to be the true original.] A lubber; a clumsy clown.

The vices trace
From the father's scoundrel race.
Who could give the *looby* such airs?
Were they masons, were they butchers? *Swift.*

Lo'ofed. *adj.* [from *aloof.*] Gone to a distance.

She once being *looft*, Antony
Claps on his sea-wing, like a doating mallard,
Leaving the fight. *Shakesp. Ant. and Cleopatra.*

To Look. *v. n.* [locan, Saxon.]

1. To direct the eye to or from any object.

Your queen died, she was more worth such gazes
Than what you *look* on now. *Shakesp. Winter's Tale.*

The gods *look* down, and the unnat'ral scene
They laugh at. *Shakespeare' Coriolanus.*

Abimelech *looked* out at a window, and saw Isaac. *Gen.*

Mine iniquities have taken hold upon me, so that I am not able to *look* up. *Psal.* xl. 12.

He was ruddy, and of a beautiful countenance, and goodly to *look* to. 1 *Sam.* xvi. 12.

The fathers shall not *look* back to their children. *Jer.*

He had *looked* round about on them with anger. *Mark* iii.

The state would cast the eye, and *look* about to see, whether there were any head under whom it might unite. *Bacon.*

Fine devices of arching water without spilling, be pretty things to *look* on, but nothing to health. *Bacon's Essays.*

Froth appears white, whether the sun be in the meridian, or anywhere between it and the horizon, and from what place soever the beholders *look* upon it. *Boyle on Colours.*

They'll rather wait the running of the river dry, than take pains to *look* about for a bridge. *L'Estrange.*

Thus pond'ring, he *look'd* under with his eyes,
And saw the woman's tears. *Dryden's Knight's Tale.*

Bertran; if thou dar'st, *look* out
Upon yon slaughter'd host. *Dryden's Spanish Friar.*

I cannot, without some indignation, *look* on an ill copy of an excellent original; much less can I behold with patience Virgil and Homer abused to their faces, by a botching interpreter. *Dryden.*

Intellectual being, in their constant endeavours after true felicity, can suspend this prosecution in particular cases, till they have *looked* before them, and informed themselves, whether that particular thing lie in their way to their main end. *Locke.*

There may be in his reach a book, containing pictures and discourses capable to delight and instruct him, which yet he may never take the pains to *look* into. *Locke.*

Towards those who communicate their thoughts in print, I cannot but *look* with a friendly regard, provided there is no tendency in their writings to vice. *Addison's Freeholder.*

A solid and substantial greatness of soul *looks* down with a generous neglect on the censures and applauses of the multitude. *Addison's Spectator*, N°. 255.

I have nothing left but to gather up the reliques of a wreck, and *look* about me to see how few friends I have left. *Pope to Swift.*

The optick nerves of such animals as *look* the same way with both eyes, as of men, meet before they come into the brain; but the optick nerves of such animals as do not *look* the same way with both eyes, as of fishes, do not meet. *Newton's Opticks.*

2. To have power of seeing.

Fate sees thy life lodg'd in a brittle glass,
And *looks* it through, but to it cannot pass. *Dryden.*

3. To direct the intellectual eye.

In regard of our deliverance past, and our danger present and to come, let us *look* up to God, and every man reform his own ways. *Bacon's New Atlantis.*

We are not only to *look* at the bare action, but at the reason of it. *Stillingfleet.*

The man only saved the pigeon from the hawk, that he might eat it himself; and if we *look* well about us, we shall find this to be the case of most mediations. *L'Estrange.*

They will not *look* beyond the received notions of the place and age, nor have so presumptuous a thought as to be wiser than their neighbours. *Locke.*

Every one, if he would *look* into himself, would find some defect of his particular genius. *Locke.*

Change a man's view of things; let him *look* into the future state of bliss or misery, and see there God, the righteous Judge, ready to render every man according to his deeds. *Locke.*

4. To expect.

Being once chaft, he speaks
What's in his heart; and that is there, which *looks*
With us to break his neck. *Shakespeare's Coriolanus.*

If he long deferred the march, he must *look* to fight another battle before he could reach Oxford. *Clarendon.*

5. To take care; to watch.

I *look* that ye bind them fast. *Shakespeare.*

He that gathered a hundred bushels of apples, had thereby a property in them: he was only to *look* that he used them before they spoiled, else he robbed others. *Locke.*

6. To be directed with regard to any object.

Let thine eyes *look* right on, and let thine eyelids *look* straight before thee. *Prov.* iv. 25.

7. To have any particular appearance.

I took the way,
Which through a path, but scarcely printed, lay;
And *look'd* as lightly press'd by fairy feet. *Dryden.*

That spotless modesty of private and publick life, that generous spirit, which all other Christians ought to labour after, should *look* in us as if they were natural. *Spratt's Serm.*

Piety, as it is thought a way to the favour of God; and fortune, as it *looks* like the effect either of that, or at least of prudence and courage, beget authority. *Temple.*

Cowards are offensive to my sight;
Nor shall they see me do an act that *looks*
Below the courage of a Spartan king. *Dryd. Cleomenes.*

Should I publish any favours done me by your lordship, I am afraid it would *look* more like vanity than gratitude. *Addis.*

Something very noble may be discerned, but it *looketh* cumbersome. *Felton on the Classicks.*

Late, a sad spectacle of woe, he trod
The desart sands, and now he *looks* a god. *Pope's Odyss.*

From the vices and follies of others, observe how such a practice *looks* in another person, and remember that it *looks* as ill, or worse, in yourself. *Watts.*

8. To seem.

To complain of want, and yet refuse all offers of a supply, *looks* very sullen. *Burnet's Theory of the Earth.*

This makes it *look* the more like truth, nature being frugal in her principles, but various in the effects thence arising. *Cheyne's Philosophical Principles.*

9. To have any air, mien, or manner.

Nay *look* not big, nor stamp, nor stare, nor fret,
I will be master of what is mine own. *Shakespeare.*

What haste looks through his eyes?
So should he *look* that seems to speak things strange. *Shak.*

Give me your hand, and trust me you *look* well, and bear your years very well. *Shakespeare's Henry* IV.

Can

Can these, or such, be any aids to us?
Look they as they were built to shake the world,
Or be a moment to our enterprize? *Benj. Johnson.*

Though I cannot tell what a man says; if he will be sincere, I may easily know what he *looks*. *Collier.*

It will be his lot to *look* singular in loose and licentious times, and to become a by-word. *Atterbury's Sermons.*

10. To form the air in any particular manner, in regarding or beholding.

I welcome the condition of the time,
Which cannot *look* more hideously on me,
Than I have drawn it in my fantasy. *Shakesp. Henry IV.*

That which was the worst now least afflicts me:
Blindness, for had I sight, confus'd with shame,
How could I once *look* up, or heave the head. *Milton.*

These *look* up to you with reverence, and would be animated by the sight of him at whose soul they have taken fire in his writings. *Swift to Pope.*

11. *To* LOOK *about one.* To be alarmed; to be vigilant.

It will import those men who dwell careless *to look about* them; to enter into serious consultation, how they may avert that ruin. *Decay of Piety.*

If you find a wasting of your flesh, then *look* about you, especially if troubled with a cough. *Harvey on Consumptions.*

John's cause was a good milch cow, and many a man subsisted his family out of it: however, John began to think it high time *to look about* him. *Arbuthnot's Hist. of J. Bull.*

12. *To* LOOK *after.* To attend; to take care of; to observe with care, anxiety, or tenderness.

Mens hearts failing them for fear, and for *looking after* those things which are coming on the earth. *Luke* xxi. 26.

Politeness of manners, and knowledge of the world, should principally be *looked* after in a tutor. *Locke on Education.*

A mother was wont to indulge her daughters, when any of them desired dogs, squirrels, or birds; but then they must be sure to *look* diligently *after* them, that they were not ill used. *Locke on Education.*

My subject does not oblige me to *look after* the water, or point forth the place whereunto it is now retreated. *Woodw.*

13. *To* LOOK *for.* To expect.

Phalantus's disgrace was engrieved, in lieu of comfort, of Artesia, who telling him she never *looked for* other, bad him seek some other mistress. *Sidney.*

Being a labour of so great difficulty, the exact performance thereof we may rather wish than *look for.* *Hooker, b.* v.

Thou
Shalt feel our justice, in whose easiest passage
Look for no less than death. *Shakesp. Winter's Tale.*

If we sin wilfully after that we have received the knowledge of the truth, there remaineth no more sacrifice for sins, but a certain fearful *looking for* of judgment. *Heb.* x.

In dealing with cunning persons, it is good to say little to them, and that which they least *look for.* *Bacon's Essays.*

This mistake was not such as they *looked for*; and, though the error in form seemed to be consented to, yet the substance of the accusation might be still insisted on. *Clarendon.*

Inordinate anxiety, and unnecessary scruples in confession, instead of setting you free, which is the benefit to be *looked for* by confession, perplex you the more. *Taylor.*

Look now for no enchanting voice, nor fear
The bait of honied words. *Milton.*

Drown'd in deep despair,
He dares not offer one repenting prayer:
Amaz'd he lies, and sadly *looks* for death. *Dryden's Juv.*

I must with patience all the terms attend,
Till mine is call'd; and that long *look'd for* day
Is still encumber'd with some new delay. *Dryden's Juv.*

This limitation of Adam's empire to his line, will save those the labour who would *look for* one heir amongst the race of brutes, but will very little contribute to the discovery of one amongst men. *Locke.*

14. *To* LOOK *into.* To examine; to sift; to inspect closely; to observe narrowly.

His nephew's levies to him appear'd
To be a preparation 'gainst the Polack;
But better *look'd into*, he truly found
It was against your highness. *Shakesp. Hamlet.*

The more frequently and narrowly we *look into* the works of nature, the more occasion we shall have to admire their beauty. *Atterbury's Sermons.*

It is very well worth a traveller's while to *look into* all that lies in his way. *Addison on Italy.*

15. *To* LOOK *on.* To respect; to regard; to esteem; to consider; to view; to think on.

Ambitious men, if they be checked in their desires, become secretly discontent, and *look upon* men and matters with an evil eye. *Bacon's Essays.*

I *looked on* Virgil as a succinct, majestick writer; one who weighed not only every thought, but every word and syllable. *Dryden.*

If a harmless maid
Should ere a wife become a nurse,
Her friends would *look on* her the worse. *Prior.*

16. *To* LOOK *on.* To consider.

He *looked upon* it as morally impossible, for persons infinitely proud to frame their minds to an impartial consideration of a religion that taught nothing but self-denial and the cross. *South's Sermons.*

Do we not all profess to be of this excellent religion? but who will believe that we do so, that shall *look upon* the actions, and consider the lives of the greatest part of Christians. *Tillotson's Sermons.*

In the want and ignorance of almost all things, they *looked upon* themselves as the happiest and wisest people of the universe. *Locke on human Understanding.*

Those prayers you make for your recovery are to be *looked upon* as best heard by God, if they move him to a longer continuance of your sickness. *Wake's Prepar. for Death.*

17. *To* LOOK *on.* To be a mere idle spectator.

I'll be a candle-holder, and *look on.* *Shakespeare.*

Some come to meet their friends, and to make merry; others come only to *look on.* *Bacon's Apophth.*

18. *To* LOOK *over.* To examine; to try one by one.

Look o'er the present and the former time,
If no example of so vile a crime
Appears, then mourn. *Dryden's Juvenal.*

A young child, distracted with the number and variety of his play-games, tired his maid ever day to *look* them *over.* *Locke on Education.*

19. *To* LOOK *out.* To search; to seek.

When the thriving tradesman has got more than he can well employ in trade, his next thoughts are to *look out* for a purchase. *Locke.*

Where the body is affected with pain or sickness, we are forward enough to *look out* for remedies, to listen greedily to every one that suggests them and immediately to apply them. *Atterbury's Sermons.*

Where a foreign tongue is elegant, expressive, and compact, we must *look out* for words as beautiful and comprehensive as can be found. *Felton on the Classicks.*

The curious are *looking out*, some for flattery, some for ironies, in that poem; the sour folks think they have found out some. *Swift to Pope.*

20. *To* LOOK *out.* To be on the watch.

Is a man bound to *look out* sharp to plague himself? *Collier.*

21. *To* LOOK *to.* To watch; to take care of.

There is not a more fearful wild fowl than your lion living; and we ought to *look to* it. *Shakespeare.*

Who knocks so loud at door?
Look to the door there, Francis. *Shakes. Henry IV.*

Let this fellow be *looked to*: let some of my people have a special care of him. *Shakespeare's Twelfth Night.*

Uncleanly scruples fear not you; *look to*'t. *Shakesp.*

Know the state of thy flocks, and *look* well *to* thy herds. *Prov.* xxvii. 33.

When it came once among our people, that the state offered conditions to strangers that would stay, we had work enough to get any of our men to *look to* our ship. *Bacon.*

If any took sanctuary for case of treason, the king might appoint him keepers to *look to* him in sanctuary. *Bacon.*

The dog's running away with the flesh, bids the cook *look* better *to* it another time. *L'Estrange.*

For the truth of the theory I am in nowise concerned; the composer of it must *look to* that. *Woodward.*

22. *To* LOOK *to.* To behold.

To LOOK. *v. a.*

1. To seek; to search for.

Looking my love, I go from place to place,
Like a young fawn that late hath lost the hind,
And seek each where. *Spenser.*

My father is here *look'd* for every day,
To pass assurance of a dower. *Shakespeare.*

2. To turn the eye upon.

Let us *look* one another in the face. 2 *Kings* xiv. 8.

3. To influence by looks.

Such a spirit must be left behind!
A spirit fit to start into an empire,
And *look* the world to law. *Dryden's Cleomenes.*

4. *To* LOOK *out.* To discover by searching.

Casting my eye upon so many of the general bills as next came to hand, I found encouragement from them to *look out* all the bills I could. *Graunt's Bills of Mortality.*

Whoever has such treatment when he is a man, will *look out* other company, with whom he can be at ease. *Locke.*

LOOK. *interj.* [properly the imperative mood of the verb: it is sometimes *look ye.*] See! lo! behold! observe.

Look, where he comes, and my good man too; he's as far from jealousy as I am from giving him cause. *Shakesp.*

Look you, he must seem thus to the world: fear not your advancement. *Shakespeare.*

Look, when the world hath fewest barbarous people, but such as will not marry, except they know means to live, as it is almost everywhere at this day, except Tartary, there is no danger of inundations of people. *Bacon's Essays.*

Look you! we that pretend to be subject to a constitution, must not carve out our own quality; for at this rate a cobler may make himself a lord. *Collier on Pride.*

LOOK. *n. s.*

1. Air of the face; mien; cast of the countenance.

Thou cream-fac'd lown,
Where got'st thou that goose *look?* *Shakespeare.*

Thou wilt save the afflicted people, but wilt bring down high *looks.* *Psal.* xviii. 27.

Them gracious heav'n for nobler ends design'd,
Their *looks* erected, and their clay refin'd. *J. Dryden, jun.*

And though death be the king of terrors, yet pain, disgrace, and poverty, have frightful *looks*, able to discompose most men. *Locke.*

2. The act of looking or seeing.

Then on the croud he cast a furious *look*,
And wither'd all their strength. *Dryden.*

When they met they made a surly stand,
And glar'd, like angry lions, as they pass'd,
And wish'd that ev'ry *look* might be their last. *Dryden.*

LO'OKER. *n. s.* [from *look.*]

1. One that looks.

2. LO'OKER *on.* Spectator, not agent.

Shepherds poor pipe, when his harsh sound testifies anguish, into the fair *looker on*, pastime not passion enters. *Sidney.*

Such labour is then more necessary than pleasant, both to them which undertake it, and for the *lookers on.* *Hooker.*

My business in this state
Made me a *looker on* here in Vienna;
Where I have seen corruption boil and bubble
Till it o'er-run the stew. *Shakesp. Meas. for Measure.*

Did not this fatal war affront thy coast,
Yet fattest thou an idle *looker on.* *Fairfax, b.* i.

The Spaniard's valour lieth in the eye of the *looker on*; but the English valour lieth about the soldier's heart: a valour of glory and a valour of natural courage are two things. *Bac.*

The people love him;
The *lookers on*, and the enquiring vulgar,
Will talk themselves to action. *Denham's Sophy.*

He wish'd he had indeed been gone,
And only to have stood a *looker on.* *Addison's Ovid.*

LOOKING-GLASS. *n. s.* [*look* and *glass.*] Mirror; a glass which shews forms reflected.

Command a mirror hither straight,
That it may shew me what a face I have.
—Go some of you and fetch a *looking-glass.* *Shakespeare.*

There is none so homely but loves a *looking-glass.* *South.*

We should make no other use of our neighbours faults, than we do of a *looking-glass* to mend our own manners by. *L'Estrange.*

The surface of the lake of Nemi is never ruffled with the least breath of wind, which perhaps, together with the clearness of its waters, gave it formerly the name of Diana's *looking-glass.* *Addison on Italy.*

LOOM. *n. s.* [from *glomus*, a bottom of thread, *Minshow. Lome* is a general name for a tool or instrument, *Junius.*] The frame in which the weavers work their cloath.

He must leave no uneven thread in his *loom*, or by indulging to any one sort of reproveable discourse himself, defeat all his endeavours against the rest. *Governm. of the Tongue.*

Minerva, studious to compose
Her twisted threads, the web she strung,
And o'er a *loom* of marble hung. *Addison.*

A thousand maidens ply the purple *loom*,
To weave the bed, and deck the regal room. *Prior.*

To LOOM. *v. n.* [leoman, Saxon.] To appear at sea. *Skinner.*

LOOM. *n. s.* A bird.

A *loom* is as big as a goose; of a dark colour, dappled with white spots on the neck, back, and wings; each feather marked near the point with two spots: they breed in Farr Island. *Grew's Musæum.*

LOON. *n. s.* [This word, which is now used only in Scotland, is the English word *lown.*] A sorry fellow; a scoundrel; a rascal.

Thou cream-fac'd *loon*!
Where got'st thou that goose look? *Shakesp. Macbeth.*

The false *loon*, who could not work his will
By open force, employ'd his flatt'ring skill:
I hope, my lord, said he, I not offend;
Are you afraid of me that are your friend? *Dryden.*

This young lord had an old cunning rogue, or, as the Scots call it, a false *loon* of a grandfather, that one might call a Jack of all trades. *Arbuthnot's Hist. of J. Bull.*

LOOP. *n. s.* [from *loopen*, Dutch, to run.] A double through which a string or lace is drawn; an ornamental double or fringe.

Nor any skill'd in *loops* of sing'ring fine,
Might in their diverse cunning ever dare
With this, so curious network, to compare. *Spenser.*

Make me to see't, or at least so prove it,
That the probation bear no hinge, nor *loop*,
To hang a doubt on. *Shakespeare's Othello.*

Bind our crooked legs in hoops
Made of shells, with silver *loops.* *Benj. Johnson.*

An old fellow shall wear this or that sort of cut in his cloaths with great integrity, while all the rest of the world are degenerated into buttons, pockets, and *loops.* *Addison.*

LO'OPED. *adj.* [from *loop.*] Full of holes.

Poor naked wretches, wheresoe'er you are,
That 'bide the pelting of this pitiless storm!
How shall your houseless heads and unfed sides,
Your *loop'd* and window'd raggedness, defend you
From seasons such as these. *Shakesp. King Lear.*

LO'OPHOLE. *n. s.* [*loop* and *hole.*]

1. Aperture; hole to give a passage.

The Indian herdsman shunning heat,
Shelters in cool, and tends his pasturing herds;
At *loopholes* cut through thickest shade. *Milton's Par. Lost.*

Ere the blabbing Eastern scout
The nice morn on the Indian steep,
From her cabin'd *loophole* peep. *Milton.*

Walk not near yon corner house by night; for there are blunderbusses planted in every *loophole*, that go off at the squeaking of a fiddle. *Dryden's Spanish Friar.*

2. A shift; an evasion.

Needless, or needful, I not now contend,
For still you have a *loophole* for a friend. *Dryden.*

LO'OPHOLED. *adj.* [from *loophole.*] Full of holes; full of openings, or void spaces.

This uneasy *loophol'd* gaol,
In which y' are hamper'd by the fetlock,
Cannot but put y' in mind of wedlock. *Hudibras, p.* ii.

LOORD. *n. s.* [*loerd*, Dutch; from *lourdant*, French; *lurdan*, Erse; a heavy, stupid, or witless fellow. *D. Trevoux* derives *lourdant* from *lorde* or *lourde*, a village in Gascoigny, the inhabitants of which were formerly noted robbers, say they. But dexterity in robbing implies some degree of subtilty, from which the Gascoigns are so far removed, that, at this day, they are aukward and heavy to a proverb. The Erse imports some degree of knavery, but then it is used in a ludicrous sense, as in English, you pretty rogue; though in general it denotes reproachful heaviness, or stupid laziness. *Spenser's* Scholiast says, *loord* was wont, among the old Britons, to signify a lord; and therefore the Danes, that usurped their tyranny here in Britain, were called, for more dread than dignity, *lurdans*, i. e. lord Danes, whose insolence and pride was so outrageous in this realm, that if it fortuned a Briton to be going over a bridge, and saw the Dane set foot upon the same, he must return back till the Dane was clean over, else he must abide no less than present death: but being afterward expelled, the name of *lurdane* became so odious unto the people whom they had long oppressed, that, even at this day, they use for more reproach to call the quartan ague the fever *lurdane.* So far the Scholiast, but erroneously. From *Spenser's* own words, it signifies something of stupid dulness rather than magisterial arrogance. *Macbean.*] A drone.

Siker, thou's but a lazy *loord*,
And rekes much of thy swinke,
That with fond terms and witless words
To bleer mine eyes do'st think. *Spenser's Pastorals.*

To LOOSE. *v. a.* [leʃan, Saxon.]

1. To unbind; to untie any thing fastened.

The shoes of his feet I am not worthy to *loose.* *Acts.*

Canst thou *loose* the bands of Orion. *Job* xxxviii. 31.

Who is worthy to *loose* the seals thereof. *Rev.* v. 2.

This is to cut the knot when we cannot *loose* it. *Burnet.*

2. To relax.

The joints of his loins were *loosed.* *Dan.* v. 6.

3. To unbind any one bound.

Loose and bring him to me. *Luke* xix. 30.

He *loosed*, and set at liberty, four or five kings of the people of that country, that Berok kept in chains. *Abbot.*

4. To free from imprisonment.

Loose those appointed to death. *Psal.* cii. 20.

The captive hasteneth that he may be *loosed.* *Isaiah.*

5. To free from any obligation.

Art thou *loosed* from a wife, seek not a wife. 1 *Cor.* vii.

6. To free from any thing that shackles the mind.

Ay; there's the man, who, *loos'd* from lust and pelf,
Less to the pretor owes than to himself. *Dryden's Persius.*

7. To free from any thing painful.

Woman, thou art *loosed* from thy infirmity. *Luke* xiii. 12.

8. To disengage.

When heav'n was nam'd, they *loos'd* their hold again,
Then sprung she forth, they follow'd her amain. *Dryden.*

To LOOSE. *v. n.* To set sail; to depart by loosing the anchor.

Ye should have hearkened, and not have *loosed* from Crete. *Acts* xxvii. 21.

The emperor *loosing* from Barcelona, came to the port of Mago, in the island of Minorca. *Knolles's Hist. of the Turks.*

Loosing thence by night, they were driven by contrary winds back into his port. *Raleigh.*

Loose. *adj.* [from the verb.]

1. Unbound; untied.

If he should intend his voyage towards my wife, I would turn her *loose* to him; and what he gets more of her than sharp words, let it lie on my head. *Shakespeare.*

Lo! I see four men *loose* walking. *Dan.* iii. 25.

2. Not fast; not fixed.

Those few that clashed might rebound after the collision; or if they cohered, yet by the next conflict might be separated again, and so on in an eternal vicissitude of fast and *loose*, though without ever consociating into the bodies of planets. *Bentley's Sermons.*

3. Not tight: as, a loose robe.

4. Not crouded; not close.

With extended wings a host might pass,
With horse and chariots, rank'd in *loose* array. *Milton.*

5. Wanton; not chaste.

Fair Venus seem'd unto his bed to bring
Her, whom he waking evermore did ween
To be the chastest flower that ay did spring
On earthly branch, the daughter of a king,
Now a *loose* leman to vile service bound. *Fairy Queen.*

When *loose* epistles violate chaste eyes,
She half consents who silently denies. *Dryden's Ovid.*

6. Not close; not concise; lax.

If an author be *loose* and diffuse in his stile, the translator needs only regard the propriety of the language. *Felton.*

7. Vague; indeterminate.

It is but a *loose* thing to speak of possibilities, without the particular designs; so is it to speak of lawfulness without the particular cases. *Bacon's holy War.*

It seems unaccountable to be so exact in the quantity of liquor where a small error was of little concern, and to be so *loose* in the doses of powerful medicines. *Arbuthnot.*

8. Not strict; not rigid.

Because conscience, and the fear of swerving from that which is right, maketh them diligent observers of circumstances, the *loose* regard whereof is the nurse of vulgar folly. *Hooker, b.* v.

9. Unconnected; rambling.

I dare venture nothing without a strict examination; and am as much ashamed to put a *loose* indigested play upon the publick, as I should be to offer brass money in a payment. *Dryden's Dedication to his Spanish Friar.*

Vario spends whole mornings in running over *loose* and unconnected pages, and with fresh curiosity is ever glancing over new words and ideas, and yet treasures up but little knowledge. *Watts's Improvement of the Mind, p.* i.

10. Lax of body; not costive.

What hath a great influence upon the health, is going to stool regularly: people that are very *loose* have seldom strong thoughts, or strong bodies. *Locke on Education.*

11. Disengaged; not enslaved.

Their prevailing principle is, to sit as *loose* from those pleasures, and be as moderate in the use of them, as they can. *Atterbury's Sermons.*

12. Disengaged from obligation.

Now I stand
Loose of my vow; but who knows Cato's thoughts. *Addis.*

13. Free from confinement.

They did not let prisoners *loose* homeward. *Isa.* xiv. 17.

Wish the wildest tempests *loose*;
That thrown again upon the coast,
I may once more repeat my pain. *Prior.*

14. Remiss; not attentive.

15. *To break* Loose. To gain liberty.

If to *break loose* from the conduct of reason, and to want that restraint of examination which keeps us from chusing the worse, be liberty, madmen and fools are only the freemen. *Locke.*

Like two black storms on either hand,
Our Spanish army and the Indians stand;
This only space betwixt the clouds is clear,
Where you, like day, *broke loose* from both appear. *Dryd.*

16. *To let* Loose. To set at liberty; to set at large; to free from any restraint.

And *let* the living bird *loose* into the open field. *Lev.* xiv. 7.

We ourselves make our fortunes good or bad; and when God *lets loose* a tyrant upon us, or a sickness, if we fear to die, or know not to be patient, the calamity sits heavy upon us. *Taylor's holy Living.*

In addition and division, either of space or duration, it is the number of its repeated additions or divisions that alone remains distinct, as will appear to any one who will *let* his thoughts *loose* in the vast expansion of space, or divisibility of matter. *Locke.*

If one way of improvement cannot be made a recreation, they must be *let loose* to the childish play they fancy; which they should be weaned from, by being made surfeit of it. *Locke on Education.*

Loose. *n. s.* [from the verb.]

1. Liberty; freedom from restraint.

Come, and forsake thy cloying store,
And all the busy pageantry
That wise men scorn, and fools adore:
Come, give thy soul a *loose*, and taste the pleasures of the poor. *Dryden's Horace.*

Lucia, might my big swoln heart
Vent all its griefs, and give a *loose* to sorrow,
Marcia could answer thee in sighs. *Addison's Cato.*

The fiery Pegasus disdains
To mind the rider's voice, or hear the reins;
When glorious fields and opening camps he views,
He runs with an unbounded *loose*. *Prior.*

Poets should not, under a pretence of imitating the antients, give themselves such a *loose* in lyricks, as if there were no connection in the world. *Felton on the Classicks.*

2. Dismission from any restraining force.

Air at large maketh no noise, except it be sharply percussed; as in the sound of a string, where air is percussed by a hard and stiff body, and with a sharp *loose*. *Bacon.*

Lo'osely. *adv.* [from *loose.*]

1. Not fast; not firmly.

I thought your love eternal: was it ty'd
So *loosely*, that a quarrel could divide? *Dryden's Aureng.*

2. Without bandage.

Her golden locks for haste were *loosely* shed
About her ears. *Fairy Queen, b.* i.

3. Without union or connection.

He has eminently, and within himself, all degrees of perfection that exist *loosely* and separately in all second beings. *Norris's Miscellany.*

4. Irregularly.

In this age, a bishop, living *loosely*, was charged that his conversation was not according to the apostles lives. *Camden's Remains.*

5. Negligently; carelessly.

We have not *loosely* through silence permitted things to pass away as in a dream. *Hooker.*

The chiming of some particular words in the memory, and making a noise in the head, seldom happens but when the mind is lazy, or very *loosely* and negligently employed. *Locke.*

6. Unsolidly; meanly; without dignity.

A prince should not be so *loosely* studied, as to remember so weak a composition. *Shakes. Henry* IV. *p.* ii.

7. Unchastly.

The stage how *loosely* does Astræa tread,
Who fairly puts all characters to bed. *Pope.*

To Lo'osen. *v. n.* [from *loose.*] To part.

When the polypus appears in the throat, extract it that way; it being more ready to *loosen* when pulled in that direction than by the nose. *Sharp's Surgery.*

To Lo'osen. *v. a.* [from *loose.*]

1. To relax any thing tied.

2. To make less coherent.

After a year's rooting, then shaking doth the tree good, by *loosening* of the earth. *Bacon's Natural History.*

3. To separate a compages.

She breaks her back, the *loosen'd* sides give way,
And plunge the Tuscan soldiers in the sea. *Dryden's Æn.*

4. To free from restraint.

It resolves those difficulties which the rules beget; it *loosens* his hands, and assists his understanding. *Dryden's Dufresnoy.*

5. To make not costive.

Fear *looseneth* the belly; because the heat retiring towards the heart, the guts are relaxed in the same manner as fear also causeth trembling. *Bacon's Nat. History,* N . 41.

Lo'oseness. *n. s.* [from *loose.*]

1. State contrary to that of being fast or fixed.

The cause of the casting of skin and shell should seem to be the *looseness* of the skin or shell, that sticketh not close to the flesh. *Bacon's Nat. Hist.*

2. Latitude; criminal levity.

A general *looseness* of principles and manners hath seized on us like a pestilence, that walketh not in darkness, but wasteth at noon-day. *Atterbury's Sermons.*

3. Irregularity; neglect of laws.

He endeavoured to win the common people, both by strained curtesy and by *looseness* of life. *Hayward.*

4. Lewdness; unchastity.

Courtly court he made still to his dame,
Pour'd out in *looseness* on the grassy ground,
Both careless of his health and of his fame. *Fairy Qu.*

5. Diarrhœa; flux of the belly.

Taking

Taking cold moveth *looseness* by contraction of the skin and outward parts. *Bacon's Natural History.*

In pestilent diseases, if they cannot be expelled by sweat, they fall likewise into *looseness.* *Bacon's Nat. Hist.*

Fat meats, in phlegmatick stomachs, procure *looseness* and hinder retention. *Arbuthnot on Aliments.*

LOOSESTRIFE. *n. s.* [*lysimachia*, Lat.] An herb.

The leaves are entire, oblong, and produced sometimes by pairs, or three or four at each joint of the stalk: the flower consists of one leaf, which expands in a circular order, and is cut into several segments at the top; the fruit is globular, and open at the top, inclosing many seeds fixed to the placenta: it produces large spikes of fine yellow flowers in July, and is prescribed in medicine. *Miller.*

To LOP. *v. a.* [It is derived by *Skinner* from *laube*, German, a leaf.]

1. To cut the branches of trees.

Gentle niece, what stern ungentle hands
Have *lopp'd*, and hew'd, and made thy body bare
Of her two branches, those sweet ornaments. *Shakesp.*

Like to pillars,
Or hollow'd bodies, made of oak or fir,
With branches *lopp'd* in wood, or mountain fell'd. *Milt.*

The plants, whose luxury was *lopp'd*,
Or age with crutches underprop'd. *Cleaveland.*

The oak, growing from a plant to a great tree, and then *lopped*, is still the same oak. *Locke.*

The hook she bore, instead of Cynthia's spear,
To *lop* the growth of the luxuriant year. *Pope.*

2. To cut any thing.

The gardener may *lop* religion as he please. *Howel.*

So long as there's a head,
Hither will all the mountain spirits fly;
Lop that but off. *Dryden's Sp. Friar.*

All that denominated it paradise was *lopped* off by the deluge, and that only left which it enjoyed in common with its neighbour countries. *Woodward's Nat. Hist.*

I'm sure in needless bonds it poets ties,
Procrustus like, the ax or wheel applies,
To *lop* the mangled sense, or stretch it into size. *Smith.*

LOP. *n. s.* [from the verb.]

1. That which is cut from trees.

Or siker thy head very tottie is,
So on thy corbe shoulder it leans amiss;
Now thyself hath lost both *lop* and top,
As my budding branch thou would'st crop. *Spenser.*

Nor should the boughs grow too big, because they give opportunity to the rain to soak into the tree, which will quickly cause it to decay, so that you must cut it down, or else both body and *lop* will be of little value. *Mortimer.*

2. [*Loppa*, Swedish.] A flea.

LOPE. pret. of *leap.* Obsolete. This is retained in Scotland.

With that sprang forth a naked swain,
With spotted wings like peacock's train,
And laughing *lope* to a tree. *Spenser's Pastorals.*

LO'PPER. *n. s.* [from *lop.*] One that cuts trees.

LO'PPERED. *adj.* Coagulated; as, *loppered* milk. *Ainsworth.* And thus it is still called in Scotland.

LOQUA'CIOUS. *adj.* [*loquax*, Latin.]

1. Full of talk; full of tongue.

To whom sad Eve,
Confessing soon; yet not before her judge
Bold, or *loquacious*, thus abash'd reply'd. *Milt. Pa. Lost.*

In council she gives licence to her tongue,
Loquacious, brawling, ever in the wrong. *Dryden.*

2. Speaking.

Blind British bards, with volant touch
Traverse *loquacious* strings, whose solemn notes
Provoke to harmless revels. *Philips.*

3. Blabbing; not secret.

LOQUA'CITY. *n. s.* [*loquacitas*, Latin.] Too much talk.

Why *loquacity* is to be avoided, the wise man gives sufficient reason for, In the multitude of words there wanteth not sin. *Ray on Creation.*

Too great *loquacity*, and too great taciturnity by fits. *Arb.*

LORD. *n. s.* [hlaford, Saxon.]

1. Monarch; ruler; governour.

Man over man
He made not *lord.* *Milton.*

Of Athens he was *lord.* *Dryden's Knight's Tale.*

We have our author's only arguments to prove, that heirs are *lords* over their brethren. *Locke.*

They call'd their *lord* Actæon to the game,
He shook his head in answer to the name. *Addison.*

O'er love, o'er fear, extends his wide domain,
Unconquer'd *lord* of pleasure and of pain. *Va. of hu. Wishes.*

2. Master; supreme person.

But now I was the *lord*
Of this fair mansion, master of my servants,
Queen o'er myself; and even now, but now,
This house, these servants, and this same myself
Are yours, my lord. *Shakesp. Merchant of Venice.*

3. A tyrant; an oppressive ruler.

Now being assembled into one company, rather without a *lord* than at liberty to accomplish their misery, they fall to division. *Hayward.*

'Tis death to fight, but kingly to controul
Lord-like at ease, with arbitrary pow'r,
To peel the chiefs, the people to devour. *Dryden.*

4. A husband.

I oft in bitterness of soul deplor'd
My absent daughter, and my dearer *lord.* *Pope's Odyssey.*

5. One who is at the head of any business; an overseer.

Grant harvest *lord* more by a peny or two,
To call on his fellows the better to doo. *Tusser's Husb.*

6. A nobleman.

Thou art a *lord*, and nothing but a *lord.* *Shakespeare.*

7. A general name for a peer of England.

Nor were the crimes objected against him so clear, as to give convincing satisfaction to the major part of both houses, especially that of the *lords.* *King Charles.*

8. A baron.

9. An honorary title applied to offices; as, lord chief justice, lord mayor, and lord chief baron.

To LORD. *v. n.* To domineer; to rule despotically.

Unrighteous lord of love! what law is this,
That me thou makest thus tormented be?
The whiles she *lordeth* in licentious bliss
Of her free will, scorning both thee and me. *Spenser.*

I see them *lording* it in London streets. *Shakespeare.*

Those huge tracts of ground they *lorded* over begat wealth, wealth ushered in pride. *Howel's Vocal Forest.*

They had by this possess'd the tow'rs of Gath,
And *lorded* over them whom now they serve. *Milton's Ag.*

I should choose rather to be tumbled into the dust in blood, bearing witness to any known truth of our lord, than by a denial of truths, through blood and perjury, wade to a scepter, and *lord* it in a throne. *South's Sermons.*

But if thy passions *lord* it in thy breast,
Art thou not still a slave? *Dryden's Persius.*

The valour of one man th' afflicted throne
Imperial, that once *lorded* o'er the world,
Sustain'd. *Philips.*

The civilizers! the disturbers say,
The robbers, the corrupters of mankind!
Proud vagabonds! who make the world your home,
And *lord* it where you have no right. *Philips's Briton.*

LO'RDING. *n. s.* [from *lord.*] Lord in contempt or ridicule.

I'll question you
Of my lord's tricks, and yours, when you were boys.
You were pretty *lordings* then? *Shakesp. Winter's Tale.*

To *lordings* proud I tune my lay,
Who feast in bower or hall;
Though dukes they be, to dukes I say,
That pride will have a fall. *Swift.*

LO'RDLING. *n. s.* A diminutive lord.

Traulus, of amphibious breed,
By the dam from *lordlings* sprung,
By the sire exhal'd from dung. *Swift.*

LO'RDLINESS. *n. s.* [from *lordly.*]

1. Dignity; high station.

Thou vouchsafest here to visit me,
Doing the honour of thy *lordliness*
To one so weak. *Shakesp. Ant. and Cleopatra.*

2. Pride; haughtiness.

LO'RDLY. *adj.* [from *lord.*]

1. Befiting a lord.

Lordly sins require *lordly* estates to support them. *South.*

2. Proud; haughty; imperious; insolent.

So bad a peer—
—As who, my lord?
—Why, as yourself, my lord?
An't like your *lordly*, lord protectorship? *Shakespeare.*

Of me as of a common enemy,
So dreaded once, may now exasperate them,
I know not: lords are *lordiest* in their wine. *Milt. Agon.*

Expect another message more imperious,
More *lordly* thund'ring than thou well wilt bear. *Milton.*

Ev'ry rich and *lordly* swain,
With pride wou'd drag about her chain. *Swift.*

LO'RDLY. *adv.* Imperiously; despotically; proudly.

So when a tyger sucks the bullock's blood,
A famish'd lion, issuing from the wood,
Roars *lordly* fierce, and challenges the food. *Dryden.*

LO'RDSHIP. *n. s.* [from *lord.*]

1. Dominion; power.

Let me never know that any base affection should get any *lordship* in your thoughts. *Sidney.*

It being set upon such an insensible rising of the ground, it gives the eye *lordship* over a good large circuit. *Sidney.*

They which are accounted to rule over the Gentiles, exercise *lordship* over them, and their great ones exercise authority upon them. *Mark x. 42.*

There

There is *lordſhip* of the fee, wherein the maſter doth much joy, when he walketh about the line of his own poſſeſſions. *Wotton's Architecture.*

Needs muſt the *lordſhip* there from virtue ſlide. *Fairfax.*

2. Seigniory; domain.

How can thoſe grants of the kings be avoided, without wronging of thoſe lords which had thoſe lands and *lordſhips* given them? *Spenſer on Ireland.*

What lands and *lordſhips* for their owner know
My quondam barber, but his worſhip now. *Dryden.*

3. Title of honour uſed to a nobleman not a duke.

I aſſure your *lordſhip*,
The extreme horrour of it almoſt turn'd me
To air, when firſt I heard it. *Benj. Johnſon's Cataline.*

I could not anſwer it to the world, if I gave not your *lordſhip* my teſtimony of being the beſt huſband now living. *Dry.*

4. Titulary compellation of judges, and ſome other perſons in authority and office.

Lore. *n. ſ.* [from læꞃan, to learn.] Leſſon; doctrine; inſtruction.

And, for the modeſt *lore* of maidenhood
Bids me not ſojourn with theſe armed men.
Oh whither ſhall I fly? *Fairfax.*

The law of nations, or the *lore* of war. *Fairfax.*

Calm region once,
And full of peace; now toſt, and turbulent!
For underſtanding rul'd not; and the will
Heard not her *lore!* but in ſubjection now
To ſenſual appetite. *Milton's Paradiſe Loſt, b.* ix.

The ſubtile fiend his *lore*
Soon learn'd, now milder, and thus anſwer'd ſmooth. *Milt.*

Lo! Rome herſelf, proud miſtreſs now no more
Of arts, but thund'ring againſt heathen *lore.* *Pope.*

Lore. [leoꞃan, Saxon.] Loſt; deſtroyed.

Lo'rel. *n. ſ.* [from leoꞃan, Saxon.] An abandoned ſcoundrel. Obſolete.

Siker thou ſpeak'ſt like a lewd *lorell*
Of heaven to deemen ſo:
How be I am but rude and borrell,
Yet nearer ways I know. *Spenſer's Paſtorals.*

To Lo'ricate. *v. a.* To plate over.

Nature hath *loricated*, or plaiſtered over, the ſides of the tympanum in animals with ear-wax, to ſtop and entangle any inſects that ſhould attempt to creep in there. *Ray.*

Lo'rimer. }
Lo'riner. } *n. ſ.* [*lormier*, French.] Bridlecutter.

Lo'riot. *n. ſ.* A kind of bird.

Lorn. pret. paſſ. of loꞃan, Saxon.] Forſaken; loſt.

Who after that he had fair Una *lorn*,
Through light miſdeeming of her loyalty. *Fairy Queen.*

To Lose. *v. a.* [leoꞃan, Saxon.]

1. To forfeit by unlucky conteſt; the contrary to win.

The lighten'd courſers ran;
They ruſh'd, and won by turns, and *loſt* the day. *Dryden.*

2. To be deprived of.

He *loſt* his right hand with a ſhot, and, inſtead thereof, ever after uſed a hand of iron. *Knolles's Hiſt. of the Turks.*

Who conquer'd him, and in what fatal ſtrife
The youth, without a wound, could *loſe* his life. *Dryden.*

3. To ſuffer deprivation of.

The fear of the Lord goeth before obtaining of authority; but roughneſs and pride is the *loſing* thereof. *Eccluſ.* x. 21.

If ſalt have *loſt* his favour, wherewith ſhall it be ſalted? *Matt.* v. 13.

4. To poſſeſs no longer; contrary to keep.

They have *loſt* their trade of woollen drapery. *Graunt.*

No youth ſhall equal hopes of glory give,
The Trojan honour and the Roman boaſt,
Admir'd when living, and ador'd when *loſt.* *Dryden.*

We ſhould never quite *loſe* ſight of the country, though we are ſometimes entertained with a diſtant proſpect of it. *Addiſon's Eſſay on the Georgicks.*

5. To have any thing gone ſo as that it cannot be found, or had again.

But if to honour *loſt* 'tis ſtill decreed
For you my bowl ſhall flow, my flocks ſhall bleed;
Judge and aſſert my right, impartial Jove. *Pope's Odyſſey.*

When men are openly abandoned, and *loſt* to all ſhame, they have no reaſon to think it hard, if their memory be reproached. *Swift.*

6. To bewilder.

I will go *loſe* myſelf,
And wander up and down to view the city. *Shakeſpeare.*

Nor are conſtant forms of prayer more likely to flat and hinder the ſpirit of prayer and devotion, than unpremeditated and confuſed variety to diſtract and *loſe* it. *King Charles.*

When the mind purſues the idea of infinity, it uſes the ideas and repetitions of numbers, which are ſo many diſtinct ideas, kept beſt by number from running into a confuſed heap, wherein the mind *loſes* itſelf. *Locke.*

7. To deprive of.

How ſhould you go about to *loſe* him a wife he loves with ſo much paſſion. *Temple.*

8. To kill; to deſtroy.

9. To throw away; to employ ineffectually.

He has merit, good nature, and integrity, that are too often *loſt* upon great men, or at leaſt are not all three a match for flattery. *Pope's Letters.*

10. To miſs; to part with, ſo as not to recover.

Theſe ſharp encounters, where always many more men are *loſt* than are killed or taken priſoners, put ſuch a ſtop to Middleton's march, that he was glad to retire. *Clarendon.*

To Lose. *v. n.*

1. Not to win.

We'll hear poor rogues
Talk of court news, and we'll talk with them too,
Who *loſes*, and who wins; who's in, who's out. *Shakeſp.*

2. To decline; to fail.

Wiſdom in diſcourſe with her
Loſes diſcount'nanc'd, and like folly ſhews. *Milton.*

Lo'seable. *adj.* [from *loſe.*] Subject to privation.

Conſider whether motion, or a propenſity to it, be an inherent quality belonging to atoms in general, and not *loſeable* by them. *Boyle.*

Lo'sel. *n. ſ.* [from loꞅian, to periſh.] A ſcoundrel; a ſorry worthleſs fellow. A word now obſolete.

Such *loſels* and ſcatterlings cannot eaſily, by any ſheriff, be gotten, when they are challenged for any ſuch fact. *Spenſer.*

A *loſel* wand'ring by the way,
One that to bounty never caſt his mind,
Ne thought of honour ever did aſſay
His baſer breaſt. *Fairy Queen, b.* ii.

And *loſels* lifted high, where I did look,
I mean to turn the next leaf of the book. *Hubberd's Tale*

Be not with work of *loſels* wit defamed,
Ne let ſuch verſes poetry be named. *Hubberd's Tale.*

By Cambridge a towne I do know,
Whoſe loſſes by *loſſels* doth ſhew
More heere then is needful to tell. *Tuſſer's Huſbandry.*

A groſs hag!
And, *loſel*, thou art worthy to be hang'd,
That wilt not ſtay her tongue. *Shakeſp. Winter's Tale.*

Lo'ser. *n. ſ.* [from *loſe.*] One that is deprived of any thing; one that forfeits any thing; one that is impaired in his poſſeſſion or hope; the contrary to winner or gainer.

With the *loſers* let it ſympathize,
For nothing can ſeem foul to thoſe that win. *Shakeſp.*

No man can be provident of his time that is not prudent in the choice of his company; and if one of the ſpeakers be vain, tedious, and trifling, he that hears, and he that anſwers, are equal *loſers* of their time. *Taylor's holy Living.*

Loſers and malecontents, whoſe portion and inheritance is a freedom to ſpeak. *South's Sermons.*

It cannot laſt, becauſe that act ſeems to have been carried on rather by the intereſt of particular countries, than by that of the whole, which muſt be a *loſer* by it. *Temple.*

A bull with gilded horns,
Shall be the portion of the conquering chief,
A ſword and helm ſhall chear the *loſer*'s grief. *Dryden.*

Loss. *n. ſ.* [from *loſe.*]

1. Forfeiture; the contrary to gain.

The only gain he purchaſed was to be capable of *loſs* and detriment for the good of others. *Hooker, b.* v.

An evil natured ſon is the diſhonour of his father that begat him; and a fooliſh daughter is born to his *loſs.* *Eccluſ.*

The abatement of price of any of the landholder's commodities, leſſens his income, and is a clear *loſs.* *Locke.*

2. Miſs.

If he were dead, what would betide of me?
—No other harm but *loſs* of ſuch a lord.
—The *loſs* of ſuch a lord includes all harms. *Shakeſp.*

3. Deprivation.

4. Deſtruction.

Her fellow ſhips from far her *loſs* deſcry'd;
But only ſhe was ſunk, and all were ſafe beſide. *Dryden.*

There ſucceeded an abſolute victory for the Engliſh, with the ſlaughter of above two thouſand of the enemy, with the *loſs* but of one man, though not a few hurt. *Bacon.*

5. Fault; puzzle.

Not the leaſt tranſaction of ſenſe and motion in man, but philoſophers are at a *loſs* to comprehend. *South's Serm.*

Reaſon is always ſtriving, and always at a *loſs*, while it is exerciſed about that which is not its proper object. *Dryden.*

A man may ſometimes be at a *loſs* which ſide to cloſe with. *Baker's Refl. on Learning.*

6. Uſeleſs application.

It would be *loſs* of time to explain any farther our ſuperiority to the enemy in numbers of men and horſe. *Addiſon.*

Lost. *participial adj.* [from *loſe.*] No longer perceptible.

In ſeventeen days appear'd your pleaſing coaſt,
And woody mountains, half in vapours *loſt.* *Pope's Odyſ.*

Lot. *n. ſ.* [*hlaut*, Gothick; hlot, Saxon; *lot*, Dutch.]

1. Fortune; ſtate aſſigned.

Kala at length concluded my ling'ring *lot*:
Diſdain me not, although I be not fair,

Who is an heir of many hundred sheep,
Doth beauty keep which never sun can burn,
Nor storms do turn. *Sidney, b. i.*

Our own *lot* is best; and by aiming at what we have not, we lose what we have already. *L'Estrange's Fables.*

Prepar'd I stand; he was but born to try
The *lot* of man, to suffer and to die. *Pope's Odyssey.*

2. A die, or any thing used in determining chances.

Aaron shall cast *lots* upon the two goats; one *lot* for the Lord, and the other *lot* for the scape-goat. *Lev.* xvi. 8.

Their tasks in equal portions she divides,
And where unequal, there by *lots* decides. *Dryden's Virg.*

Ulysses bids his friends to cast *lots*, to shew, that he would not voluntarily expose them to so imminent danger. *Notes on the Odyssey.*

3. It seems in *Shakespeare* to signify a lucky or wished chance.

If you have heard your general talk of Rome,
And of his friends there, it is *lots* to blanks
My name hath touch'd your ears; it is Menenius. *Shakes.*

4. A portion; a parcel of goods as being drawn by lot: as, what *lot* of silks had you at the sale?

5. Proportion of taxes: as, to pay scot and *lot*.

Lote *tree* or *nettle tree. n. s.* [Celtis.] See Lotos.

The leaves of the *lote* tree are like those of the nettle; the flowers consist of five leaves, expanded in form of a rose, containing many short stamina in the bosom: the fruit, which is a roundish berry, grows single in the bosom of its leaves. The fruit of this tree is not so tempting to us, as it was to the companions of Ulysses: the wood is durable, and used to make pipes for wind instruments: the root is proper for hafts of knives, and was highly esteemed by the Romans for its beauty and use. *Miller.*

LO'TOS. n. s. [Latin.] See Lote.

The trees around them all their food produce,
Lotos, the name divine, nectareous juice. *Pope's Odyssey.*

Lo'tion. *n. s.* [*lotio*, Latin; *lotion*, French.]

A *lotion* is a form of medicine compounded of aqueous liquids, used to wash any part with; from lavo, to wash. *Quincy.*

In *lotions* in women's cases, he orders two potions of hellebore macerated in two cotylæ of water. *Arbuthnot on Coins.*

Lo'ttery. *n. s.* [*lotterie*, Fr. from *lot.*] A game of chance; a sortilege; distribution of prizes by chance; a play in which lots are drawn for prizes.

Let high-sighted tyranny range on,
Till each man drop by *lottery*. *Shakesp. Julius Cæsar.*

The *lottery* that he hath devised in these three chests of gold, silver, and lead, will never be chosen by any but whom you shall rightly love. *Shakes. Merchant of Venice.*

Every warriour may be said to be a soldier of fortune, and the best commanders to have a kind of *lottery* for their work. *South's Sermons.*

Fortune, that with malicious joy
Does man, her slave, oppress,
Still various and unconstant still,
Promotes, degrades, delights in strife,
And makes a *lottery* of life. *Dryden's Horace.*

Lo'vage. *n. s* [*levisticum*, Latin.]

The lobes of the *lovage* leaves are cut about their borders like those of parsley; the flower consists, for the most part, of five leaves, which expand in form of a rose; each of these flowers are succeeded by two oblong, gibbose, furrowed seeds, which on one side have a leafy border. This plant is often used in medicine. *Miller.*

LOUD. *adj.*

1. Noisy; striking the ear with great force.

Contending on the Lesbian shore,
His prowess Philomelides confess'd,
And *loud* acclaiming Greeks the victor bless'd. *Pope.*

The numbers soft and clear,
Gently steal upon the ear;
Now *louder*, and yet *louder* rise,
And fill with spreading sounds the skies. *Pope's St. Cæcilia.*

2. Clamorous; turbulent.

She is *loud* and stubborn; her feet abide not in her house. *Prov.* vii. 11.

Lo'udly. *adv.* [from *loud.*]

1. Noisily; so as to be heard far.

The soldier that philosopher well blam'd,
Who long and *loudly* in the schools declaim'd. *Denham.*

2. Clamourously.

I read above fifty pamphlets, written by as many presbyterian divines, *loudly* disclaiming toleration. *Swift.*

Lo'udness. *n. s.* Noise; force of sound; turbulence; vehemence or furiousness of clamour.

Had any disaster made room for grief, it would have moved according to prudence, and the proportions of the provocation: it would not have sallied out into complaint or *loudness*. *South's Sermons.*

To LOVE. *v. a.* [lufian, Saxon.]

1. To regard with passionate affection, as that of one sex to the other.

Good shepherd, tell this youth what 'tis to *love*.
—It is to be made all of sighs and tears;
It is to be made all of faith and service;
It is to be all made of fantasy,
All made of passion, and all made of wishes;
All adoration, duty, and obedience;
All humbleness, all patience, all impatience,
All purity, all trial, all observance. *Shakesp. As you like it.*

I could not *love* I'm sure
One who in love were wise. *Cowley.*

The jealous man wishes himself a kind of deity to the person he *loves*; he would be the only employment of her thoughts. *Addison's Spectator*, N. 170.

2. To regard with the affection of a friend.

None but his brethren he, and sisters, knew,
Whom the kind youth prefer'd to me,
And much above myself I *lov'd* them too. *Cowley.*

3. To regard with parental tenderness.

He that loveth me shall be *loved* of my father, and I will *love* him, and will manifest myself to him. *John* xiv. 21.

4. To be pleased with.

Fish used to salt water delight more in fresh: we see that salmons and smelts *love* to get into rivers, though against the stream. *Bacon's Nat. Hist.* N°. 703.

Wit, eloquence, and poetry,
Arts which I *lov'd*. *Cowley.*

He *lov'd* my worthless rhimes. *Cowley.*

5. To regard with reverent unwillingness to offend.

Love the Lord thy God with all thine heart. *Deut.* vi. 5.

Love. *n. s.* [from the verb.]

1. The passion between the sexes.

Hearken to the birds *love*-learned song,
The dewie leaves among! *Spenser's Epithalam.*

While idly I stood looking on,
I found th' effect of *love* in idleness. *Shakespeare.*

My tales of *love* were wont to weary you;
I know you joy not in a *love* discourse. *Shakespeare.*

What! have I 'scaped *love* letters in the holiday-time of my beauty, and am I now a subject for them? *Shakespeare.*

I look'd upon her with a soldier's eye,
That lik'd, but had a rougher task in hand
Than to drive liking to the name of *love*. *Shakespeare.*

What need a vermil-tinctur'd lip for that,
Love-darting eyes, or tresses like the morn. *Milton.*

Love quarrels oft in pleasing concord end,
Not wedlock treachery, endang'ring life. *Milton's Agon.*

A *love* potion works more by the strength of charm than nature. *Collier on Popularity.*

You know y' are in my pow'r by making *love*. *Dryden.*

Let mutual joys our mutual trust combine,
And *love*, and *love*-born confidence be thine. *Pope.*

Cold is that breast which warm'd the world before,
And these *love*-darting eyes must roll no more. *Pope.*

2. Kindness; good-will; friendship.

Death grin on me, and I will think thou smil'st,
And kiss me as thy wife; misery's *love*,
O come to me! *Shakespeare's King John.*

What love, think'st thou, I sue so much to get?
My *love* till death, my humble thanks, my prayers;
That *love* which virtue begs, and virtue grants. *Shakesp.*

God brought Daniel into favour and tender *love* with the prince. *Dan.* i. 9.

The one preach Christ of contention, but the other of *love*. *Phil.* i. 17.

By this shall all men know that ye are my disciples, if ye have *love* one to another. *Rom.* xiii. 35.

Unwearied have we spent the nights,
Till the Ledean stars, so fam'd for *love*,
Wonder'd at us from above. *Cowley.*

3. Courtship.

Demetrius
Made *love* to Nedar's daughter Helena,
And won her soul. *Shakes. Midsummer Night's Dream.*

If you will marry make your *loves* to me,
My lady is bespoke. *Shakespeare's King Lear.*

I to your assistance do make *love*,
Masking the business from the common eye. *Shakespeare.*

The enquiry of truth, which is the *love*-making or wooing of it; the knowledge of truth, the preference of it; and the belief of truth, the enjoying of it, is the sovereign good of human nature. *Bacon's Essays.*

4. Tenderness; parental care.

No religion that ever, was so fully represents the goodness of God, and his tender *love* to mankind, which is the most powerful argument to the love of God. *Tillotson's Sermons.*

5. Liking; inclination to: as, the *love* of one's country.

6. Object beloved.

Open the temple gates unto my *love*. *Spenser.*

If that the world and love were young,
And truth in every shepherd's tongue;
These pretty pleasures might me move,
To live with thee, and be thy *love*. *Shakespeare.*

The banish'd never hopes his *love* to see. *Dryden.*
The lover and the *love* of human kind. *Pope.*

7. Lewdness.
He is not lolling on a lewd *love* bed,
But on his knees at meditation. *Shakesp. Rich.* III.

8. Unreasonable liking.
The *love* to sin makes a man sin against his own reason. *Taylor's holy living.*
Men in *love* with their opinions may not only suppose what is in question, but allege wrong matter of fact. *Locke.*

9. Fondness; concord.
Come *love* and health to all!
Then I'll sit down: give me some wine; fill full. *Shak.*
Shall I come unto you with a rod, or in *love*, and in the spirit of meekness? *1 Cor.* iv. 21.

10. Principle of union.
Love is the great instrument of nature, the bond and cement of society, the spirit and spring of the universe: *love* is such an affection as cannot so properly be said to be in the soul, as the soul to be in that: it is the whole man wrapt up into one desire. *South's Sermons.*

11. Picturesque representation of love.
The lovely babe was born with ev'ry grace:
Such was his form as painters, when they show
Their utmost art, on naked *loves* bestow. *Dryden's Ovid.*

12. A word of endearment.
'Tis no dishonour, trust me, *love*, 'tis none;
I would die for thee. *Dryden's Don Sebastian.*

13. Due reverence to God.
I know that you have not the *love* of God in you. *John.*
Love is of two sorts, of friendship and of desire; the one betwixt friends, the other betwixt lovers; the one a rational, the other a sensitive *love*: so our *love* of God consists of two parts, as esteeming of God, and desiring of him. *Hammond.*
The *love* of God makes a man chaste without the laborious arts of fasting, and exterior disciplines; he reaches at glory without any other arms but those of *love*. *Taylor.*

14. A kind of thin silk stuff. *Ainf.*
This leaf held near the eye, and obverted to the light, appeared so full of pores, with such a transparency as that of a sieve, a piece of cypress, or *lovehood*. *Boyle on Colours.*

LO'VEAPPLE. *n. s.*
The *loveapple* has a flower consisting of one leaf, which expands in a circular order; the style afterwards becomes a roundish, soft, fleshy fruit, divided into several cells, which contain many flat seeds. *Millar.*

LO'VEKNOT. *n. s.* [*love* and *knot.*] A complicated figure, by which affection interchanged is figured.

LO'VELETTER. *n. s.* [*love* and *letter.*] Letter of courtship.
The children are educated in the different notions of their parents: the sons follow the father, while the daughters read *loveletters* and romances to their mother. *Addison's Spect.*

LO'VELILY. *adv.* [from *lovely.*] Amiably; in such a manner as to excite love.
Thou look'st
Lovelily dreadful. *Otway's Venice Preserv'd.*

LO'VELINESS. *n. s.* [from *lovely.*] Amiableness; qualities of mind or body that excite love.
Carrying thus in one person the only two bands of goodwill, *loveliness* and lovingness. *Sidney.*
When I approach
Her *loveliness*, so absolute she seems,
That what she wills to do, or say,
Seems wisest, virtuousest, discreetest, best. *Milt. Pa. Lost.*
If there is such a native *loveliness* in the sex, as to make them victorious when they are in the wrong, how resistless is their power when they are on the side of truth? *Addison.*

LO'VELORN. *adj.* [*love* and *lorn.*] Forsaken of one's love.
The *love-lorn* nightingale,
Nightly to thee her sad song mourneth well. *Milton.*

LO'VELY. *adj.* [from *love.*] Amiable; exciting love.
The breast of Hecuba,
When she did suckle Hector, look'd not *lovelier*
Than Hector's forehead. *Shakespeare's Coriolanus.*
Saul and Jonathan were *lovely* and pleasant in their lives, and in their death they were not divided. *2 Sam.* i. 23.
The flowers which it had press'd
Appeared to my view,
More fresh and *lovely* than the rest,
That in the meadows grew. *Denham.*
The Christian religion gives us a more *lovely* character of God than any religion ever did. *Tillotson's Sermons.*
The fair
With cleanly powder dry their hair;
And round their *lovely* breast and head
Fresh flow'rs their mingl'd odours shed. *Prior.*

LO'VEMONGER. *n. s.* [*love* and *monger.*] One who deals in affairs of love.
Thou art an old *lovemonger*, and speakest skilfully. *Shak.*

LO'VER. *n. s.* [from *love.*]
1. One who is in love.
Love is blind, and *lovers* cannot see
The pretty follies that themselves commit. *Shakespeare.*
Let it be never said, that he whose breast
Is fill'd with love, should break a *lover*'s rest. *Dryden.*

2. A friend; one who regards with kindness.
Your brother and his *lover* have embrac'd. *Shakesp.*
I tell thee, fellow,
Thy general is my *lover*: I have been
The book of his good act, whence men have read
His fame unparallel'd haply amplified. *Shakespeare.*

3. One who likes any thing.
To be good and gracious, and a *lover* of knowledge, are amiable things. *Burnet's Theory of the Earth.*

LO'OVER. *n. s.* [from *l'ouvert*, French, *an opening.*] An opening for the smoke to go out at in the roof of a cottage. *Spens.*

LO'VESECRET. *n. s.* [*love* and *secret.*] Secret between lovers.
What danger, Arimant, is this you fear?
Or what *lovesecret* which I must not hear. *Dryden's Aur.*

LO'VESICK. *adj.* [*love* and *sick.*] Disordered with love; languishing with amorous desire.
See, on the shoar inhabits purple spring,
Where nightingales their *lovesick* ditty sing. *Dryden.*
To the dear mistress of my *lovesick* mind,
Her swain a pretty present has design'd. *Dryden's Virg.*
Of the reliefs to ease a *lovesick* mind,
Flavia prescribes despair. *Granville.*

LO'VESOME. *adj.* [from *love.*] Lovely. A word not used.
Nothing new can spring
Without thy warmth, without thy influence bear,
Or beautiful or *lovesome* can appear. *Dryden's Lucretius.*

LO'VESONG. *n. s.* [*love* and *song.*] Song expressing love.
Poor Romeo is already dead!
Stabb'd with a white wench's black eye,
Run through the ear with a *lovesong*. *Shakespeare.*
Lovesong weeds and satyrick thorns are grown,
Where seeds of better arts were early sown. *Donne.*

LO'VESUIT. *n. s.* [*love* and *suit.*] Courtship.
His *lovesuit* hath been to me
As fearful as a siege. *Shakespeare's Cymbeline.*

LO'VETALE. *n. s.* [*love* and *tale.*] Narrative of love.
The *lovetale*
Infected Sion's daughters with like heat;
Whose wanton passions in the sacred porch
Ezekiel saw. *Milton's Paradise Lost, b.* i.
Cato's a proper person to entrust
A *lovetale* with. *Addison's Cato.*

LO'VETHOUGHT. *n. s.* [*love* and *thought.*] Amorous fancy.
Away to sweet beds of flowers,
Lovethoughts lie rich when canopied with bowers. *Shakesp.*

LO'VETOY. *n. s.* [*love* and *toy.*] Small presents given by lovers.
Has this amorous gentleman presented himself with any *lovetoys*, such as gold snuff-boxes. *Arbuth. and Pope's Ma. Sc.*

LO'VETRICK. *n. s.* [*love* and *trick.*] Art of expressing love.
Other disports than dancing jollities;
Other *lovetricks* than glancing with the eyes. *Donne.*

LOUGH. *n. s.* [*loch*, Irish, a lake.] A lake; a large inland standing water.
A people near the northern pole that won,
Whom Ireland sent from *loughes* and forests hore,
Divided far by sea from Europe's shore. *Fairfax.*
Lough Ness never freezes. *Phil. Trans.*

LO'VING. *participial adj.* [from *love.*]
1. Kind; affectionate.
So *loving* to my mother,
That he permitted not the winds of heav'n
To visit her face too roughly. *Shakesp. Hamlet.*
This earl was of great courage, and for this cause much loved of his soldiers, to whom he was no less *loving* again. *Hayward.*

2. Expressing kindness.
The king took her in his arms till she came to herself, and comforted her with *loving* words. *Esth.* xv. 8.

LO'VINGKINDNESS. Tenderness; favour; mercy. A scriptural word.
Remember, O Lord, thy tender mercies, and thy *loving-kindnesses*. *Psal.* xxv. 6.
He has adapted the arguments of obedience to the imperfection of our understanding, requiring us to consider him only under the amiable attributes of goodness and *loving-kindness*, and to adore him as our friend and patron. *Rogers.*

LO'VINGLY. *adv.* [from *loving.*] Affectionately; with kindness.
The new king, having no less *lovingly* performed all duties to him dead than alive, pursued on the siege of his unnatural brother, as much for the revenge of his father, as for the establishing of his own quiet. *Sidney, b.* ii.
It is no great matter to live *lovingly* with good-natured and meek persons; but he that can do so with the froward and perverse, he only hath true charity. *Taylor.*

LO'VINGNESS. *n. s.* [from *loving.*] Kindness; affection.

Carrying thus in one person the only two bands of good-will, lovelineſs and *lovingneſs*. *Sidney, b.* i.

LOUIS D'OR. *n. ſ.* [French.] A golden coin of France, valued at about ſeventeen ſhillings.

If he is deſired to change a *louis d'or*, he muſt conſider of it. *Spectator*, Nº. 305.

To LOUNGE. *v. n.* [*lunderen*, Dutch.] To idle; to live lazily.

LO'UNGER. *n. ſ.* [from *lounge*.] An idler.

LOURGE. *n. ſ.* [*longurio*, Latin.] A tall gangrel. *Ainſ.*

LOUSE. *n. ſ.* plural *lice*. [lur, Saxon; *luys*, Dutch.] A ſmall animal, of which different ſpecies live on the bodies of men, beaſts, and perhaps of all living creatures.

There were *lice* upon man and beaſt. *Exod.* viii. 18.

Frogs, *lice*, and flies, muſt all his palace fill
With loath'd intruſion. *Milton.*

It is beyond even an atheiſt's credulity and impudence to affirm, that the firſt men might proceed out of the tumours of leaves of trees, as maggots and flies are ſuppoſed to do now, or might grow upon trees; or perhaps might be the *lice* of ſome prodigious animals, whoſe ſpecies is now extinct. *Bentley's Sermons.*

Not that I value the money the fourth part of the ſkip of a *louſe*. *Swift.*

To LOUSE. *v. a.* [from the noun.] To clean from lice.

As for all other good women, that love to do but little work, how handſome it is to *louſe* themſelves in the ſunſhine, they that have been but a while in Ireland can well witneſs. *Spenſer on Ireland.*

You ſat and *lous'd* him all the ſun-ſhine day. *Swift.*

LOUSEWORT. *n. ſ.* The name of a plant; called alſo *rattle* and *cock's-comb*.

There are four different kinds of this plant, which grow wild, and in ſome low meadows are very troubleſome; eſpecially one ſort with yellow flowers, which riſes to be a foot high or more, and is often in ſuch plenty as to be the moſt predominant plant; but it is very bad food for cattle. *Miller.*

LO'USILY. *adv.* [from *louſe*.] In a paltry, mean, and ſcurvy way.

LO'USINESS. *n. ſ.* [from *louſy*.] The ſtate of abounding with lice.

LO'USY. *adj.* [from *louſe*.]

1. Swarming with lice; over-run with lice.

Let him be daub'd with lace, live high and whore,
Sometimes be *louſy*, but be never poor. *Dryden's Juv.*

Sweetbriar and gooſeberry are only *louſy* in dry times, or very hot places. *Mortimer's Huſbandry.*

2. Mean; low born; bred on the dunghil.

I pray you now remembrance on the *louſy* knave mine hoſt.

A *louſy* knave, to have his gibes and his mockeries. *Shakeſp.*

LOUT. *n. ſ.* [*loete*, old Dutch. Mr. *Lye*.] A mean aukward fellow; a bumpkin; a clown.

Pamela, whoſe noble heart doth diſdain, that the truſt of her virtue is repoſed in ſuch a *lout*'s hands, had yet, to ſhew an obedience, taken on ſhepherdiſh apparel. *Sidney.*

This *lowt*, as he exceeds our lords, the odds
Is, that we ſcarce are men, and you are gods. *Shakeſp.*

I have need of ſuch a youth,
That can with ſome diſcretion do my buſineſs;
For 'tis no truſting to yon fooliſh *lout*. *Shakeſpeare.*

Thus wail'd the *louts* in melancholy ſtrain. *Gay's Paſt.*

To LOUT. *v. n.* [hlutan, to bend, Saxon.] To pay obeiſance; to bend; to bow; to ſtoop. Obſolete. It was uſed in a good ſenſe. In Scotland they ſay, a fellow with *lowtan* or *luttan* ſhoulders; that is, one who bends forwards; his ſhoulders or back.

He fair the knight ſaluted, *louting* low,
Who fair him quitted, as that courteous was. *Fa. Qu.*

Under the ſand-bag he was ſeen,
Louting low, like a for'ſter green. *Ben. Johnſon's Underw.*

The palmer, grey with age, with count'nance *lowting* low,
His head ev'n to the earth before the king did bow. *Drayton.*

To LOWT. *v. a.* This word ſeems in *Shakeſpeare* to ſignify, to overpower.

I am *lowted* by a traitor villain,
And cannot help the noble chevalier. *Shakeſp. Henry* VI.

LO'UTISH. *adj.* [from *lout*.] Clowniſh; bumpkinly.

This *loutiſh* clown is ſuch, that you never ſaw ſo ill-favoured a viſar; his behaviour ſuch, that he is beyond the degree of ridiculous. *Sidney.*

LO'URISHLY. *adv.* [from *lout*.] With the air of a clown; with the gait of a bumpkin.

LOW. *adj.*

1. Not high.

2. Not riſing far upwards.

It became a ſpreading vine of *low* ſtature. *Ezek.* xvii. 6.

3. Not elevated in ſituation.

O mighty Cæſar! do'ſt thou lye ſo *low*?
Are all thy conqueſts, glories, triumphs, ſpoils,
Shrunk to this little meaſure? *Shakeſp. Julius Cæſar.*

Whatſoever is waſhed away from them is carried down into the *lower* grounds, and into the ſea, and nothing is brought back. *Burnet's Theory of the Earth.*

4. Deſcending far downwards; deep.

5. Not deep; not ſwelling high; ſhallow: uſed of water.

As two men were walking by the ſea-ſide at *low* water, they ſaw an oyſter, and they both pointed at it together. *L'Eſtrange.*

It is *low* ebb ſure with his accuſer, when ſuch peccadillo's are put in to ſwell the charge. *Atterbury.*

6. Not of high price: as, corn is *low*.

7. Not loud; not noiſy.

As when in open air we blow,
The breath, though ſtrain'd, ſounds flat and *low*:
But if a trumpet take the blaſt,
It lifts it high, and makes it laſt. *Waller.*

The theatre is ſo well contrived, that, from the very deep of the ſtage, the *loweſt* ſound may be heard diſtinctly to the fartheſt part of the audience; and yet, if you raiſe your voice as high as you pleaſe, there is nothing like an echo to cauſe confuſion. *Addiſon on Italy.*

8. In latitudes near to the line.

They take their courſe either high to the north, or *low* to the ſouth. *Abbot's Deſcript. of the World.*

9. Not riſing to ſo great a ſum as ſome other accumulation of particulars.

Who can imagine, that in ſixteen or ſeventeen hundred years time, taking the *lower* chronology, that the earth had then ſtood, mankind ſhould be propagated no farther than Judæa. *Burnet's Theory of the Earth.*

10. Late in time: as, the *lower* empire.

11. Dejected; depreſſed.

To be worſt,
The *loweſt*, moſt dejected, thing of fortune,
Stands ſtill in eſperance. *Shakeſpeare.*

His ſpirits are ſo *low* his voice is drown'd,
He hears as from afar, or in a ſwoon,
Like the deaf murmur of a diſtant ſound. *Dryden.*

Though he before had gall and rage,
Which death or conqueſt muſt aſſwage;
He grows diſpirited and *low*,
He hates the fight, and ſhuns the foe. *Prior.*

12. Impotent; ſubdued.

To keep them all quiet, he muſt keep them in greater awe and leſs ſplendor; which power he will uſe to keep them as *low* as he pleaſes, and at no more coſt than makes for his own pleaſure. *Graunt's Bills of Mortality.*

13. Not elevated in rank or ſtation; abject.

He wooes both high and *low*, both rich and poor. *Shakeſp.*

Try in men of *low* and mean education, who have never elevated their thoughts above the ſpade. *Locke.*

14. Diſhonourable; betokening meanneſs of mind: as, *low* tricks.

15. Not ſublime; not exalted in thought or diction.

He has not ſo many thoughts that are *low* and vulgar, but, at the ſame time, has not ſo many thoughts that are ſublime and noble. *Addiſon's Spectator*, Nº. 279.

In compariſon of theſe divine writers, the nobleſt wits of the heathen world are *low* and dull. *Felton on the Claſſicks.*

16. Reduced; in poor circumſtances; as, I am *low* in the world.

LOW. *adv.*

1. Not aloft; not at a high price; meanly: it is chiefly uſed in compoſition.

Proud of their numbers and ſecure in ſoul,
The confident and over-luſty French:
Do the *low*-rated Engliſh play at dice? *Shakeſp. Hen.* V.

This is the pretrieſt *low*-born laſs, that ever
Ran the greenſord; nothing ſhe does or ſeems,
But ſmacks of ſomething greater than herſelf,
Too noble for this place. *Shakeſpeare's Winter's Tale.*

There under Ebon ſhades and *low*-brow'd rocks,
As ragged as thy locks,
In dark Cimmerian deſert ever dwell. *Milton.*

My eyes no object met
But *low*-hung clouds, that dipt themſelves in rain,
To ſhake their fleeces on the earth again. *Dryden.*

No luxury found room
In *low*-rooft houſes, and bare walls of lome. *Dryden.*

Vaſt yellow offſprings are the German's pride;
But hotter climates narrower frames obtain,
And *low*-built bodies are the growth of Spain. *Creech.*

Whenever I am turned out, my lodge deſcends upon a *low*-ſpirited creeping family. *Swift.*

We wand'ring go through dreary waſtes,
Where round ſome mould'ring tow'r pale ivy creeps,
And *low*-brow'd rocks hang nodding o'er the deeps. *Pope.*

Corruption, like a general flood,
Shall deluge all; and av'rice creeping on,
Spread like a *low*-born miſt, and blot the ſun. *Pope.*

2. In times near our own.

In that part of the world which was firſt inhabited, even as *low* down as Abraham's time, they wandered with their flocks and herds. *Locke.*

3. With a depreſſion of the voice.

Lucia, ſpeak *low*, he is retir'd to reſt. *Addiſon's Cato.*

4. In

4. In a ſtate of ſubjection.

How comes it that, having been once ſo *low* brought, and thoroughly ſubjected, they afterwards lifted up themſelves ſo ſtrongly again. *Spenſer on Ireland.*

To Low. *v. a.* [from the adjective.] To ſink; to make low. Probably miſprinted for *lower*.

The value of guineas was *lowed* from one-and-twenty ſhillings and ſixpence to one-and-twenty ſhillings. *Swift.*

To Low. *v. n.* [hlopan, Saxon. The adjective *low*, not high, is pronounced *lo*; the verb *low*, to *bellow*, *lou*.] To bellow as a cow.

Doth the wild aſs bray when he has graſs? or *loweth* the ox over his fodder? *Job* vi. 5.

The maids of Argos, who, with frantick cries,
And imitated *lowings*, fill'd the ſkies. *Roſcommon.*

Fair Io grac'd his ſhield, but Io now,
With horns exalted ſtands, and ſeems to *low*. *Dryden.*

Had he been born ſome ſimple ſhepherd's heir,
The *lowing* herd, or fleecy ſheep his care. *Prior.*

Lo'wbell. *n. ſ.* [*laeye*, Dutch; leg, Saxon; or *log*, Iſlandick, a flame, and *bell*.] A kind of fowling in the night, in which the birds are wakened by a bell, and lured by a flame into a net. *Lowe* denotes a flame in Scotland; and *to lowe*, to flame.

Lowe. *n. ſ.*

Lowe, *loe*, comes from the Saxon hleap, a hill, heap, or barrow; and ſo the Gothick *hlaiw* is a monument or barrow. *Gibſon's Camden.*

To Lo'wer. *v. a.* [from *low*.]

1. To bring low; to bring down by way of ſubmiſſion.

As our high veſſels paſs their wat'ry way,
Let all the naval world due homage pay;
With haſty reverence their top-honours *lower*,
Confeſſing the aſſerted power. *Prior.*

The ſuppliant nations
Bow to its enſigns, and with *lower'd* ſails
Confeſs the ocean's queen. *Smith's Phædrus and Hippolytus.*

2. To ſuffer to ſink down.

When the water of rivers iſſues out of the apertures with more than ordinary rapidity, it bears along with it ſuch particles of looſe matter as it met with in its paſſage through the ſtone, and it ſuſtains thoſe particles till its motion begins to remit, when by degrees it *lowers* them, and lets them fall. *Woodward's Nat. Hiſt.*

3. To leſſen; to make leſs in price or value.

The kingdom will loſe by this *lowering* of intereſt, if it makes foreigners withdraw any of their money. *Locke.*

Some people know it is for their advantage to *lower* their intereſt. *Child on Trade.*

To Lower. *v. n.* To grow leſs; to fall; to ſink.

The preſent pleaſure,
By revolution *low'ring*, does become
The oppoſite of itſelf. *Shakeſp. Ant. and Cleopatra.*

To Lo'wer. *v. n.* [It is doubtful what was the primitive meaning of this word: if it was originally applied to the appearance of the ſky, it is no more than to *grow low*, as the ſky ſeems to do in dark weather: if it was firſt uſed of the countenance, it may be derived from the Dutch *loeren*, to look aſkance.]

1. To appear dark, ſtormy, and gloomy; to be clouded.

Now is the winter of our diſcontent
Made glorious Summer by this ſon of York;
And all the clouds that *lower'd* upon our houſe,
In the deep boſom of the ocean buried. *Shakeſp. Rich.* III.

The *low'ring* ſpring, with laviſh rain,
Beats down the ſlender ſtem and bearded grain. *Dryden.*

When the heavens are filled with clouds, and all nature wears a *lowering* countenance, I withdraw myſelf from theſe uncomfortable ſcenes. *Addiſon's Spectator*, N°. 83.

The dawn is overcaſt, the morning *low'rs*,
And heavily in clouds brings on the day. *Addiſon's Cato.*

If on Swithin's feaſt the welkin *lours*,
And ev'ry penthouſe ſtreams with haſty ſhow'rs,
Twice twenty days ſhall clouds their fleeces drain. *Gay.*

2. To frown; to pout; to look ſullen.

There was Diana when Actæon ſaw her, and one of her fooliſh nymphs, who weeping, and withal *lowering*, one might ſee the workman meant to ſet forth tears of anger. *Sidney.*

He mounts the throne, and Juno took her place,
But ſullen diſcontent ſat *low'ring* on her face;
Then, impotent of tongue, her ſilence broke,
Thus turbulent in rattling tone ſhe ſpoke. *Dryden.*

Lo'wer. *n. ſ.* [from the verb.]

1. Cloudineſs; gloomineſs.

2. Cloudineſs of look.

Philoclea was jealous for Zelmane, not without ſo mighty a *lower* as that face could yield. *Sidney, b.* ii.

Lo'weringly. *adv.* [from *lower*.] With cloudineſs; gloomily.

Lo'wermost. *adj.* [from *low*, *lower*, and *moſt*.] Loweſt.

Plants have their ſeminal parts uppermoſt, living creatures have them *lowermoſt*. *Bacon's Nat. Hiſt.*

It will alſo happen, that the ſame part of the pipe which was now *lowermoſt*, will preſently become higher, ſo that the water does aſcend by deſcending; aſcending in compariſon to the whole inſtrument, and deſcending in reſpect of its ſeveral parts. *Wilkins's Dædalus.*

Lo'wland. *n. ſ.* [*low* and *land*.] The country that is low in reſpect of neighbouring hills; the marſh.

What a devil's he?
His errand was to draw the *lowland* damps,
And noiſome vapours, from the foggy fens,
Then breathe the baleful ſtench with all his force. *Dryd.*

No nat'ral cauſe ſhe found from brooks or bogs,
Or marſhy *lowlands*, to produce the fogs. *Dryden.*

Lo'wlily. *adv.* [from *lowly*.]

1. Humbly; without pride.

2. Meanly; without dignity.

Lo'wliness. *n. ſ.* [from *lowly*.]

1. Humility; freedom from pride.

Lowlineſs is young ambition's ladder,
Whereto the climber upward turns his face. *Shakeſpeare.*

The king-becoming graces,
As juſtice, verity, temp'rance, ſtableneſs,
Bounty, perſev'rance, mercy, *lowlineſs*,
Devotion, patience, courage, fortitude;
I have no reliſh of them. *Shakeſpeare's Macbeth.*

Eve,
With *lowlineſs* majeſtick, from her ſeat,
And grace, that won who ſaw to wiſh her ſtay,
Roſe. *Milton's Par. Loſt, b.* viii.

If with a true Chriſtian *lowlineſs* of heart, and a devout fervency of ſoul, we perform them, we ſhall find, that they will turn to a greater account to us, than all the warlike preparations in which we truſt. *Atterbury's Sermons.*

2. Meanneſs; want of dignity; abject depreſſion.

They continued in that *lowlineſs* until the time that the diviſion between the two houſes of Lancaſter and York aroſe. *Spenſer's State of Ireland.*

The *lowlineſs* of my fortune has not yet brought me to flatter vice; and it is my duty to give teſtimony to virtue. *Dryden's Preface to Aurengzebe.*

Lo'wly. *adj.* [from *low*.]

1. Humble; meek; mild.

Take my yoke upon you, and learn of me; for I am meek and *lowly* in heart. *Matt.* xi. 29.

He did bend to us a little, and put his arms abroad: we of our parts ſaluted him in a very *lowly* and ſubmiſſive manner, as looking that from him we ſhould receive ſentence of life or death. *Bacon's New Atlantis.*

With cries they fill'd the holy fane;
Then thus with *lowly* voice Ilioneus began. *Dryden.*

The heavens are not pure in his ſight, and he charges even his angels with folly; with how *lowly* a reverence muſt we bow down our ſouls before ſo excellent a being, and adore a nature ſo much ſuperior to our own. *Rogers's Sermons.*

2. Mean; wanting dignity; not great.

For from the natal hour diſtinctive names,
One common right the great and *lowly* claims. *Pope.*

3. Not lofty; not ſublime.

For all who read, and reading not diſdain,
Theſe rural poems, and their *lowly* ſtrain,
The name of Varus oft inſcrib'd ſhall ſee. *Dryd. Silenus.*

Lo'wly. *adv.* [from *low*.]

1. Not highly; meanly; without grandeur; without dignity.

I will ſhew myſelf highly fed, and *lowly* taught; I know my buſineſs is but to the court. *Shakeſpeare.*

'Tis better to be *lowly* born,
And range with humble livers in content,
Than to be perk'd up in a gliſt'ring grief,
And wear a golden ſorrow. *Shakeſp. Henry* VIII.

2. Humbly; meekly; modeſtly.

Heav'n is for thee too high
To know what paſſes there; be *lowly* wiſe:
Think only what concerns thee, and thy being. *Milton.*

Another crowd
Preferr'd the ſame requeſt, and *lowly* bow'd. *Pope.*

Lown. *n. ſ.* [*liun*, Iriſh; *loen*, Dutch, a ſtupid drone.] A ſcoundrel; a raſcal.

King Stephen was a worthy peer,
His breeches coſt him but a crown,
He thought them ſixpence all too dear,
And therefore call'd the taylor *lown*. *Shakeſpeare.*

Lo'wness. *n. ſ.* [from *low*.

1. Abſence of height; ſmall diſtance from the ground.

They know
By th' height, the *lowneſs*, or the mean, if dearth,
Or foizon follow. *Shakeſp. Ant. and Cleopatra.*

The *lowneſs* of the bough where the fruit cometh, maketh the fruit greater, and to ripen better; for you ſhall even ſee, in apricots upon a wall, the greateſt fruits towards the bottom. *Bacon's Nat. Hiſt.* N°. 432.

In our Gothick cathedrals, the narrowneſs of the arch makes it riſe in height, the *lowneſs* often opens it in breadth. *Addiſon's Remarks on Italy.*

2. Meanneſs of condition, whether mental or external.

Nothing could have ſubdu'd nature
To ſuch a *lowneſs*, but his unkind daughter. *Shakeſpeare.*

Now

Now I must
To the young man send humble treaties,
And palter in the shift of *lowness*. *Shakespeare.*

3. Want of rank; want of dignity.

The name of servants has of old been reckoned to imply a certain meanness of mind, as well as *lowness* of condition. *South's Sermons.*

4. Want of sublimity; contrary to loftiness.

A transcendent height, as *lowness* me,
Makes her not see, or not show. *Donne.*

His style is accommodated to his subject, either high or low; if his fault be too much *lowness*, that of Persius is the hardness of his metaphors. *Dryden.*

5. Submissiveness.

The people were in such *lowness* of obedience as subjects were like to yield, who had lived almost four-and-twenty years under so politick a king as his father. *Bacon.*

6. Depression; dejection.

Hence proceeded that poverty and *lowness* of spirit to which a kingdom may be subject, as well as a particular person. *Swift.*

LOWTHO'UGHTED. *adj.* [*low* and *thought.*] Having the thoughts with-held from sublime or heavenly meditations; mean of sentiment; narrow mindedness.

Above the smoak and stir of this dim spot,
Which men call earth, and with *lowthoughted* care,
Strive to keep up a frail and feverish being *Milton.*

O grace serene! Oh virtue heav'nly fair!
Divine oblation of *lowthoughted* care!
Fresh blooming hope, gay daughter of the sky,
And faith our early immortality! *Pope.*

LOWSPIRITED. *adj.* [*low* and *spirit.*] Dejected; depressed; not lively; not vivacious; not spritely.

Severity carried to the highest pitch breaks the mind; and then, in the place of a disorderly young fellow, you have a *lowspirited* moped creature. *Locke.*

LOXODROMICK. *n. s.* [λοξὸς and δρόμος; *loxodromus*, Lat.]

Loxodromick is the art of oblique sailing by the rhomb, which always makes an equal angle with every meridian; that is, when you sail neither directly under the equator, nor under one and the same meridian, but across them: hence the table of rhumbs, or the transverse tables of miles, with the table of longitudes and latitudes, by which the sailor may practically find his course, distance, latitude, or longitude, is called *loxodromick*. *Harris.*

LO'YAL. *adj.* [*loyal*, Fr.]

1. Obedient; true to the prince.

Of Gloster's treachery,
And of the *loyal* service of his son,
When I inform'd him, then he call'd me sot. *Shakesp.*

The regard of duty in that most *loyal* nation overcame all other difficulties. *Knolles.*

Loyal subjects often seize their prince,
Yet mean his sacred person not the least offence. *Dryden.*

2. Faithful in love; true to a lady, or lover.

Hail wedded love! by thee
Founded in reason *loyal*, just, and pure. *Milton.*

There Laodamia with Evadne moves,
Unhappy both! but *loyal* in their loves. *Dryden's Æn.*

LO'YALIST. *n. s.* [from *loyal.*] One who professes uncommon adherence to his king.

The cedar, by the instigation of the *loyalists*, fell out with the homebians. *Howel's Vocal Forest.*

LO'YALLY. *adv.* [from *loyal.*] With fidelity; with true adherence to a king.

The circling year I wait, with ampler stores,
And fitter pomp, to hail my native shores;
Then by my realms due homage would be paid,
For wealthy kings are *loyally* obey'd. *Pope's Odyssey.*

LO'YALTY. *n. s.* [*loiaulté*, French.]

1. Firm and faithful adherence to a prince.

Though *loyalty*, well held, to fools does make
Our faith meer folly; yet he that can endure
To follow with allegiance a fall'n lord,
Does conquer him that did his master conquer. *Shakesp.*

To day shalt thou behold a subject die
For truth, for duty, and for *loyalty*. *Shakesp. Rich.* III.

Commissions flaw'd the heart
Of all their *loyalties*. *Shakespeare's Henry* VIII.

He had never had any veneration for the court, but only such *loyalty* to the king as the law required. *Clarendon.*

Abdiel faithful found
Unshaken, unseduc'd, unterrify'd,
His *loyalty* he kept. *Milton.*

2. Fidelity to a lady, or lover.

LO'ZENGE. *n. s.* [*losenge*, French.] Of unknown etymology.

1. A rhomb.

The best builders resolve upon rectangular squares, as a mean between too few and too many angles; and through the equal inclination of the sides, they are stronger than the rhomb or *losenge*. *Wotton's Architecture.*

2. *Lozenge* is a form of a medicine made into small pieces, to be held or chewed in the mouth till melted or wasted.

3. A cake of preserved fruit: both these are so denominated from the original form, which was rhomboidal.

LP. a contraction for *lordship*.

LU'BBARD. *n. s.* [from *lubber.*] A lazy sturdy fellow.

Yet their wine and their victuals those curmudgeon *lubbards*
Lock up from my sight, in cellars and cupboards. *Swift.*

LU'BBER. *n. s.* [of this word the best derivation seems to be from *lubbed*, said by *Junius* to signify in Danish *fat.*] A sturdy drone; an idle, fat, bulky losel; a booby.

For tempest and showers deceiveth a many,
And ling'ring *lubbers* loose many a penie. *Tusser's Husb.*

These chase the smaller shoals of fish from the main sea into the havens, leaping up and down, puffing like a fat *lubber* out of breath. *Carew's Survey of Cornwall.*

They clap the *lubber* Ajax on the shoulder,
As if his feet were on brave Hector's breast,
And great Troy shrinking. *Shakesp. Troil. and Cressida.*

A notable *lubber* thou reportest him to be. *Shakesp.*

Tell how the drudging goblin sweat;
His shadowy flail hath thresh'd the corn,
That ten day labourers could not end;
Then lies him down the *lubber* fend. *Milton.*

Venetians do not more uncouthly ride,
Than did your *lubber* state mankind bestride. *Dryden.*

How can you name that superannuated *lubber*? *Congreve.*

LU'BBERLY. *adj.* [from *lubber.*] Lazy and bulky.

I came at Eaton to marry Mrs. Anne Page; and she's a great *lubberly* boy. *Shakespeare.*

LU'BBERLY. *adv.* Aukwardly; clumsily.

Merry andrew on the low rope copies *lubberly* the same tricks which his master is so dexterously performing on the high. *Dryden's Dedication.*

LU. *n. s.* A game at cards.

Ev'n mighty pam who kings and queens o'erthrew,
And mow'd down armies in the fights of *lu*. *Pope.*

To LU'BRICATE. *v. a.* [from *lubricus*, Lat.] To make smooth or slippery; to smoothe.

There are aliments which, besides this *lubricating* quality, stimulate in a small degree. *Arbuthnot on Aliments.*

The patient is relieved by the mucilaginous and the saponaceous remedies, some of which *lubricate*, and others both *lubricate* and stimulate. *Sharp's Surgery.*

To LU'BRICITATE. *v. n.* [from *lubricus*, Latin.] To smooth; to make slippery.

LUBRI'CITY. *n. s.* [*lubricus*, Latin; *lubricité*, French.]

1. Slipperiness; smoothness of surface.

2. Aptness to glide over any part, or to facilitate motion.

Both the ingredients are of a lubricating nature; the mucilage adds to the *lubricity* of the oil, and the oil preserves the mucilage from inspissation. *Ray on Creation.*

3. Uncertainty; slipperiness; instability.

The manifold impossibilities and *lubricities* of matter cannot have the same conveniences in any modification. *More.*

He that enjoyed crowns, and knew their worth, excepted them not out of the charge of universal vanity; and yet the politician is not discouraged at the inconstancy of human affairs, and the *lubricity* of his subject. *Glanville's Apology.*

A state of tranquillity is never to be attained, but by keeping perpetually in our thoughts the certainty of death, and the *lubricity* of fortune. *L'Estrange's Fables.*

4. Wantonness; lewdness.

From the letchery of these fauns, he thinks that satyr is derived from them, as if wantonness and *lubricity* were essential to that poem which ought in all to be avoided. *Dryden.*

LU'BRICK. *adj.* [*lubricus*, Latin.]

1. Slippery; smooth on the surface.

A throng
Of short thick sobs, whose thund'ring volleys float
And roul themselves over her *lubrick* throat,
In panting murmurs. *Crashaw.*

2. Uncertain; unsteady.

I will deduce him from his cradle through the deep and *lubrick* waves of state, till he is swallowed in the gulph of fatality. *Wotton.*

2. Wanton; lewd. [*lubrique*, French.]

Why were we hurry'd down
This *lubrick* and adult'rate age;
Nay, added fat pollutions of our own,
T' encrease the steaming ordures of the stage. *Dryden.*

LU'BRICOUS. *adj.* [*lubricus*, Latin.]

1. Slippery; smooth.

The parts of water being voluble and *lubricous* as well as fine, it easily insinuates itself into the tubes of vegetables, and by that means introduces into them the matter it bears along with it. *Woodward's Nat. Hist.*

2. Uncertain.

The judgment being the leading power, if it be stored with *lubricous* opinions instead of clearly conceived truths, and peremptorily resolved in them, the practice will be as irregular as the conceptions. *Glanville's Scep.*

Lubrifica'tion. *n. s.* [*lubricus* and *fio*, Latin.] The act of smoothing.

A twofold liquor is prepared for the inunction and *lubrification* of the heads of the bones; an oily one, furnished by the marrow; a mucilaginous, supplied by certain glandules seated in the articulations. *Ray on Creation.*

Lubrifa'ction. *n. s.* [*lubricus* and *facio*, Latin.] The act of lubricating or smoothing.

The cause is *lubrifaction* and relaxation, as in medicines emollient; such as milk, honey, and mallows. *Bacon.*

Luce. *n. s.* [perhaps from *lupus*, Latin.] A pike full grown.

They give the dozen white *luces* in their coat. *Shakesp.*

Lu'cent. *adj.* [*lucens*, Latin.] Shining; bright; splendid.

I meant the day-star should not brighter rise,
Nor lend like influence from his *lucent* seat. *Benj. Johnson.*
A spot like which perhaps
Astronomer in the sun's *lucent* orb,
Through his glaz'd optick tube yet never saw. *Milton.*

LU'CID. *n. s.* [*lucidus*, Latin; *lucide*, French.]

1. Shining; bright; glittering.

Over his *lucid* arms
A military vest of purple flow'd;
Livelier than Melibœan. *Milton.*

It contracts it, preserving the eye from being injured by too vehement and *lucid* an object, and again dilates it for the apprehending objects more remote in a fainter light. *Ray.*

If at the same time a piece of white paper, or a white cloth, or the end of one's finger, be held at the distance of about a quarter of an inch, or half an inch, from that part of the glass where it is most in motion, the electrick vapour which is excited by the friction of the glass against the hand will, by dashing against the white paper, cloth, or finger, be put into such an agitation as to emit light, and make the white paper, cloth, or finger, appear *lucid* like a glow-worm. *Newton's Opticks.*

The pearly shell its *lucid* globe unfold,
And Phœbus warm the rip'ning ore to gold. *Pope.*

2. Pellucid; transparent.

On the fertile banks
Of Abbana and Pharphar, *lucid* streams. *Milt. Par. Lost.*

On the transparent side of a globe, half silver and half of a transparent metal, we saw certain strange figures circularly drawn, and thought we could touch them, till we found our fingers stopped by that *lucid* substance. *Gulliver's Trav.*

3. Bright with the radiance of intellect; not darkened with madness.

The long dissentions of the two houses, which, although they had had *lucid* intervals and happy pauses, yet they did ever hang over the kingdom, ready to break forth. *Bacon.*

Some beams of wit on other souls may fall,
Strike through and make a *lucid* interval;
But Shadwell's genuine night admits no ray,
His rising fogs prevail upon the day. *Dryden.*

I believed him in a *lucid* interval, and desired he would please to let me see his book. *Tatler.*

A few sensual and voluptuous persons may, for a season, eclipse this native light of the soul; but can never so wholly smother and extinguish it, but that, at some *lucid* intervals, it will recover itself again, and shine forth to the conviction of their conscience. *Bentley's Sermons.*

Luci'dity. *n. s.* [from *lucid.*] Splendor; brightness. *Dict.*

Luci'ferous. *adj.* [*lucifer*, Latin.] Giving light; affording means of discovery.

The experiment is in itself not ignoble, and *luciferous* enough, as shewing a new way to produce a volatile salt. *Boyle.*

Luci'fick. *adj.* [*lux* and *facio*, Latin.] Making light; producing light.

When made to converge, and so mixed together; though their *lucifick* motion be continued, yet by interfering, that equal motion, which is the colorifick, is interrupted. *Grew.*

Luck. *n. s.* [*geluck*, Dutch.]

1. Chance; accident; fortune; hap; casual event.

He forc'd his neck into a nooze,
To shew his play at fast and loose;
And when he chanc'd t' escape, mistook
For art and subtlety, his *luck*. *Hudibras.*

Some such method may be found by human industry or *luck*, by which compound bodies may be resolved into other substances than they are divided into by the fire. *Boyle.*

2. Fortune, good or bad.

Glad of such *luck* the luckless lucky maid,
A long time with that savage people staid,
To gather breath in many miseries. *Spenser.*
Farewel, good Salisbury, and good *luck* go with thee. *Shakespeare's Henry V.*
I did demand what news from Shrewsbury.
He told me, that rebellion had ill *luck*,
And that young Harry Percy's spur was cold. *Shakespeare.*

That part of mankind who have had the justice, or the *luck*, to pass, in common opinion, for the wisest, have followed a very different scent. *Temple.*

Such, how highly soever they may have the *luck* to be thought of, are far from being Israelites indeed. *South.*

The guests are found too num'rous for the treat,
But all, it seems, who had the *luck* to eat,
Swear they ne'er tasted more delicious meat. *Tate's Juv.*

Lu'ckily. *adv.* [from *lucky.*] Fortunately; by good hap.

It is the pencil thrown *luckily* full upon the horse's mouth, to express the foam, which the painter with all his skill could not form. *Dryden's Dufresnoy.*

It happens *luckily* for the establishment of a new race of kings upon the British throne, that the first of this royal line has all high qualifications. *Addison.*

Lu'ckiness. *n. s.* [from *lucky.*] Good fortune; good hap; casual happiness.

He who sometimes lights on truth, is in the right but by chance; and I know not whether the *luckiness* of the accident will excuse the irregularity of his proceeding. *Locke.*

Lu'ckless. *adj.* [from *luck.*] Unfortunate; unhappy.

Glad of such luck, the *luckless* lucky maid,
A long time with that savage people staid,
To gather breath in many miseries. *Fairy Queen.*
Never shall my thoughts be base,
Though *luckless*, yet without disgrace. *Suckling.*
What else but his immoderate lust of pow'r,
Pray'rs made and granted in a *luckless* hour? *Dryden.*

Lu'cky. *n. s.* [from *luck*; *geluckig*, Dutch.] Fortunate; happy by chance.

But I more fearful, or more *lucky* wight,
Dismay'd with that deformed, dismal sight,
Fled fast away. *Fairy Queen, b. x.*
Perhaps some arm more *lucky* than the rest,
May reach his heart, and free the world from bondage. *Addison's Cato.*

Lu'crative. *adj.* [*lucratif*, French; *lucrativus*, Lat.] Gainful; profitable; bringing money.

The trade of merchandize being the most *lucrative*, may bear usury at a good rate; other contracts not so. *Bacon.*

The disposition of Ulysses inclined him to pursue the more dangerous way of living by war, than the more *lucrative* method of life by agriculture. *Notes on the Odyssey.*

Lu'cre. *n. s.* [*lucrum*, Latin.] Gain; profit; pecuniary advantage. In an ill sense.

Malice and *lucre* in them
Have laid this woe here. *Shakesp. Cymbeline.*
They all the sacred mysteries of heav'n
To their own vile advantages shall turn,
Of *lucre*, and ambition. *Milton's Par. Lost, b. xii.*
A soul supreme in each hard instance try'd,
Above all pain, all anger, and all pride,
The rage of pow'r, the blast of publick breath,
The lust of *lucre*, and the dread of death. *Pope.*

What can be thought of the procuring letters by fraud, and the printing them merely for *lucre?* *Pope.*

Lucri'ferous. *adj.* [*lucrum* and *fero*, Latin.] Gainful; profitable.

Silver was afterwards separated from the gold, but in so small a quantity, that the experiment, the cost and pains considered, was not *lucriferous*. *Boyle.*

Lucri'fick. *adj.* [*lucrum* and *facio*, Latin.] Producing gain. *Dict.*

Lu'ctation. *n. s.* [*luctor*, Latin.] Struggle; effort; contest.

To Lu'cubrate. *n. s.* [*lucubror*, Lat.] To watch; to study by night.

Lucubra'tion. *n. s.* [*lucubratio*, Latin.] Study by candlelight; nocturnal study; any thing composed by night.

Thy *lucubrations* have been perused by several of our friends. *Tatler, N° 78.*

Lucubra'tory. *adj.* [*lucubratorius*, from *lucubror*, Latin.] Composed by candle-light.

You must have a sober dish of coffee, and a solitary candle at your side, to write an epistle *lucubratory* to your friend. *Pope.*

Lu'culent. *adj.* [*luculentus*, Latin.]

1. Clear; transparent; lucid. This word is perhaps not used in this sense by any other writer.

And *luculent* along
The purer rivers flow. *Thomson's Winter, l. 715.*

2. Certain; evident.

They are against the obstinate incredulity of the Jews, the most *luculent* testimonies that Christian religion hath. *Hooker.*

L'UDICROUS. *adj.* [*ludicer*, Lat.] Burlesque; merry; sportive; exciting laughter.

Plutarch quotes this as an instance of Homer's judgment, in closing a *ludicrous* scene with decency and instruction. *Notes on the Odyssey.*

Lu'dicrously. *adv.* [from *ludicrous.*] Sportively; in burlesque; in a manner that may excite laughter.

Lu'dicrousness. *n. s.* [from *ludicrous.*] Burlesque; sportiveness; merry cast or manner; ridiculousness.

Ludifica'tion. *n. s.* [*ludificor*, Latin.] The act of mocking, or making sport with another. *Dict.*

LUFF. *n. s.* [in Scotland.] The palm of the hand; as, clap me arles in my *luff*.

To LUFF. *v. n.* [or *loof*.] To keep close to the wind. Sea term.

Contract your swelling sails, and *luff* to wind. *Dryden.*

To LUG. *v. a.* [aluccan, Saxon, to pull; *luga*, Swedish, the hollow of the hand.]

1. To hall or drag; to pull with rugged violence.

You gods! why this
Will *lug* your priests and servants from your sides. *Shakesp.*

Thy bear is safe, and out of peril,
Though *lugg'd* indeed, and wounded very ill. *Hudibras.*

When savage bears agree with bears,
Shall secret ones *lug* saints by th' ears. *Hudibras, p.* iii.

See him drag his feeble legs about
Like hounds ill coupled: Jowler *lugs* him still
Through hedges. *Dryden.*

Whose pleasure is to see a strumpet tear
A cynick's beard, and *lug* him by the hair. *Dryden.*

Either every single animal spirit must convey a whole representation, or else they must divide the image amongst them, and so *lug* off every one his share. *Collier.*

2. *To* LUG *out.* To draw a sword, in burlesque language.

But buff and beltmen never know these cares,
No time, nor trick of law, their action bars;
They will be heard, or they *lug out* and cut. *Dryden.*

To LUG. *v. n.* To drag; to come heavily: perhaps only misprinted for *lags*.

My flagging soul flies under her own pitch,
Like fowl in air, too damp, and *lugs* along,
As if she were a body in a body. *Dryden.*

LUG. *n. s.*

1. A kind of small fish.

They feed on salt unmerchantable pilchards, tag worms, *lugs*, and little crabs. *Carew's Survey of Cornwall.*

2. [In Scotland.] An ear.

3. *Lug*, a land measure; a pole or perch.

That ample pit, yet far renown'd
For the large leap which Debon did compel
Ceaulin to make, being eight *lugs* of ground. *Fa. Qu.*

LU'GGAGE. *n. s.* [from *lug*.] Any thing cumbrous and unweildy that is to be carried away; any thing of more weight than value.

Come bring your *luggage* nobly on your back. *Shakesp.*

What do you mean
To doat thus on such *luggage*? *Shakespeare's Tempest.*

Think not thou to find me slack, or need
Thy politick maxims, or that cumbersome
Luggage of war there shewn me. *Milton's Par. Regain'd.*

How durst thou with that sullen *luggage*
O' th' self, old ir'n, and other baggage,
T' oppose thy lumber against us? *Hudibras, p.* i.

The mind of man is too light to bear much certainty among the ruffling winds of passion and opinion; and if the *luggage* be prized equally with the jewels, none will be cast out till all be shipwrecked. *Glanv.*

A lively faith will bear aloft the mind,
And leave the *luggage* of good works behind. *Dryden.*

I am gathering up my *luggage*, and preparing for my journey. *Swift to Pope.*

LUGU'BRIOUS. *adj.* [*lugubre*, French; *lugubris*, Lat.] Mournful; sorrowful.

A demure, or rather a *lugubrious* look, a sad or whining tone, makes up the sum of many mens humiliations. *Decay of Piety.*

LUKEWARM. *adj.* [The original of this word is doubted. *Warmth*, in Saxon, is pleoð; in old Frisick *blij*; in Dutch *lewte*; whence probably our *luke*, to which *warm* may be added, to determine, by the first word, the force of the second; as we say, *boiling hot*.]

1. Moderately or mildly warm; so warm as to give only a pleasing sensation.

A dreary corse, whose life away did pass,
All wallow'd in his own, yet *lukewarm* blood,
That from his wound yet welled fresh alas! *Fairy Queen.*

May you a better feast never behold,
You knot of mouth friends; smoke and *lukewarm* water
Is your perfection. *Shakesp. Timon of Athens.*

Bathing the body in *lukewarm* water is of great advantage to contemperate hot and sharp humours. *Wiseman's Surgery.*

Whence is it but from this attractive power that water, which alone distils with a gentle *lukewarm* heat, will not distil from salt of tartar without a great heat? *Newton's Opticks.*

2. Indifferent; not ardent; not zealous.

If some few continue stedfast, it is an obedience so *lukewarm* and languishing, that it merits not the name of passion. *Dryden.*

This sober conduct is a mighty virtue
In *lukewarm* patriots. *Addison's Cato.*

LU'KEWARMLY. *adv.* [from the adjective.]

1. With moderate warmth.

2. With indifference.

LU'KEWARMNESS. *n. s.* [from *lukewarm*.]

1. Moderate or pleasing heat.

2. Indifference; want of ardour.

Some kind of zeal counts all merciful moderation *lukewarmness*. *King Charles.*

The defect of zeal is *lukewarmness*, or coldness in religion; the excess is inordinate heat and spiritual fury. *Sprat.*

Go dry your chaff and stubble, give fire to the zeal of your faction, and reproach them with *lukewarmness*. *Swift.*

To LULL. *v. a.* [*lulu*, Danish; *lallo*, Latin.]

1. To compose to sleep by a pleasing sound.

There trickled softly down
A gentle stream, whose murmuring wave did play
Emongst the pumy stones, and made a sound
To *lull* him soft a sleep, that by it lay. *Fairy Queen, b.* ii.

Such sweet compulsion doth in musick lie,
To *lull* the daughters of necessity. *Milton.*

These *lull'd* by nightingales embracing slept. *Milton.*

2. To compose; to quiet; to put to rest.

To find a foe it shall not be his hap,
And peace shall *lull* him in her flow'ry lap. *Milton.*

No more these scenes my meditations aid,
Or *lull* to rest the visionary maid. *Pope.*

By the vocal woods and waters *lull'd*,
And lost in lonely musing in a dream. *Thomson's Spring.*

LU'LLABY. *n. s.* [*lallus*, Latin. Quem nutricum fuisse deum contendit Turnebus, from *lull*: it is observable that the nurses call sleep *by, by*; *lullaby* is therefore *lull to sleep*.] A song to still babes.

Only that noise heav'ns rolling circles kest,
Sung *lullaby*, to bring the world to rest. *Fairfax.*

Philomel, with melody,
Sing in your sweet *lullaby*;
Lulla, lulla, lullaby; lulla, lulla, lullaby. *Shakespeare.*

If you will let your lady know I am here to speak with her; and bring her along with you, it may make my bounty further.
—Marry, Sir, *lullaby* to your bounty till I come again. *Shak.*

Drinking is the *lullaby* used by nurses to still crying children. *Locke on Education.*

LUMBA'GO. *n. s.* [*lumbi*, Lat. the loins.]

Lumbago's are pains very troublesome about the loins, and small of the back, such as precede ague fits and fevers: they are most commonly from fullness and acrimony, in common with a disposition to yawnings, shudderings, and erratick pains in other parts, and go off with evacuation, generally by sweat, and other critical discharges of fevers. *Quincy.*

LU'MBER. *n. s.* [loma, geloma, Saxon, housholdstuff; *lommering*, the dirt of an house, Dutch.] Any thing useless or cumbersome; any thing of more bulk than value.

The very bed was violated
By the coarse hands of filthy dungeon villains,
And thrown amongst the common *lumber*. *Otway.*

One son at home
Concerns thee more than many guests to come.
If to some useful art he be not bred,
He grows mere *lumber*, and is worse than dead. *Dryden.*

Thy neighbour has remov'd his wretched store,
Few hands will rid the *lumber* of the poor. *Dryden's Juv.*

If God intended not the precise use of every single atom, that atom had been no better than a piece of *lumber*. *Grew.*

The poring scholiasts mark;
Wits, who, like owls, see only in the dark;
A *lumber*-house of books in ev'ry head. *Pope's Dunciad.*

To LU'MBER. *v. a.* [from the noun.] To heap like useless goods irregularly.

In Rollo we must have so much stuff *lumbered* together, that not the least beauty of tragedy can appear. *Rymer.*

To LU'MBER. *v. n.* To move heavily, as burthened with his own bulk.

First let them run at large,
Nor *lumber* o'er the meads, nor cross the wood. *Dryden.*

LU'MINARY. *n. s.* [*luminare*, Latin; *luminaire*, French.]

1. Any body which gives light.

The great *luminary*
Dispenses light from far. *Milton.*

2. Any thing which gives intelligence.

Sir John Graham, I know not upon what *luminaries* he espied in his face, dissuaded him from marriage. *Wotton.*

3. Any one that instructs mankind.

The circulation of the blood, and the weight and spring of the air, had been reserved for a late happy discovery by two great *luminaries* of this island. *Bentley's Sermons.*

LUMINA'TION. *n. s.* [from *lumen*.] Emission of light. *Dict.*

LU'MINOUS. *n. s.* [*lumineux*, French.]

1. Shining; emitting light.

Fire burneth wood, making it first *luminous*, then black and brittle, and lastly, broken and incinerate. *Bacon.*

Its first convex divides
The *luminous* inferior orbs inclos'd,
From chaos. *Milton.*

How came the sun to be *luminous*? Not from the necessity of natural causes. *Bentley's Sermons.*

2. Enlightened.

Earth may, induſtrious of herſelf, fetch day,
Travelling eaſt; and with her part averſe
From the ſun's beam, meet night; her other part,
Still *luminous* by his ray. *Milton's Paradiſe Loſt*, *b.* viii.

3. Shining; bright.

The moſt *luminous* of the priſmatick colours are the yellow and orange: theſe affect the ſenſes more ſtrongly than all the reſt together. *Newton's Opticks.*

LUMP. *n. ſ.* [*lompe*, Dutch.]

1. A ſmall maſs of any matter.

The weed kal is by the Egyptians uſed firſt for fuel, and then they cruſh the aſhes into *lumps* like a ſtone, and ſo ſell them to the Venetians. *Bacon's Nat. Hiſt.*

Without this various agitation of the water, how could *lumps* of ſugar or ſalt caſt into it be ſo perfectly diſſolved in it, that the *lumps* themſelves totally diſappear? *Boyle.*

An Ombite wretch is pris'ner made;
Whoſe fleſh torn off by *lumps*, the rav'nous foe
In morſels cut. *Tate.*

Ev'ry fragrant flow'r, and od'rous green,
Were ſorted well, with *lumps* of amber laid between. *Dry.*

To conceive thus of the ſoul's intimate union with an infinite being, and by that union receiving of ideas, leads one into as groſs thoughts, as a country-maid would have of an infinite butter-print, the ſeveral parts whereof being applied to her *lump* of butter, left on it the figure or idea there was preſent need of. *Locke.*

2. A ſhapeleſs maſs.

Hence, heap of wrath, foul indigeſted *lump*;
As crooked in thy manners as thy ſhape. *Shak. Henry* VI.

Bluſh, bluſh, thou *lump* of foul deformity. *Shakeſpeare.*

Why might not there have been, in this great maſs, huge *lumps* of ſolid matter, which, without any form or order, might be jumbled together. *Keil againſt Burnet.*

3. Maſs undiſtinguiſhed.

All mens honours
Lie like one *lump* before him, to be faſhion'd
Into what pinch he pleaſe. *Shakeſpeare's Henry* VIII.

It is rare to find any of theſe metals pure; but copper, iron, gold, ſilver, lead, and tin, all promiſcuouſly in one *lump*. *Woodward's Nat. Hiſt.*

4. The whole together; the groſs.

If my readers will not go to the price of buying my papers by retail, they may buy them in the *lump*. *Addiſon.*

Other epidemical vices are rife and predominant only for a ſeaſon, and muſt not be aſcribed to human nature in the *lump*. *Bentley's Sermons.*

The principal gentlemen of ſeveral counties are ſtigmatized in a *lump*, under the notion of being papiſts. *Swift.*

To LUMP. *v. a.* To take in the groſs, without attention to particulars.

The expences ought to be *lumped* together. *Ayliffe's Par.*

Boccalini, in his political balance, after laying France in one ſcale, throws Spain into the other, which wanted but very little of being a counterpoiſe: the Spaniards upon this reckoned, that if Spain of itſelf weighed ſo well, they could not fail of ſucceſs when the ſeveral parts of the monarchy were *lumped* in the ſame ſcale. *Addiſon.*

LU'MPFISH. [*lump* and *fiſh*; *lumpus*, Lat.] A ſort of fiſh.

LU'MPING. *adj.* [from *lump.*] Large; heavy; great. A low word.

Nick, thou ſhalt have a *lumping* pennyworth. *Arbuthnot.*

LU'MPISH. *adj.* [from *lump.*] Heavy; groſs; dull; unactive; bulky.

Out of the earth was formed the fleſh of man, and therefore heavy and *lumpiſh*. *Raleigh's Hiſt. of the World.*

Sylvia is *lumpiſh*, heavy, melancholy. *Shakeſpeare.*

Love is all ſpirit: fairies ſooner may
Be taken tardy, when they night tricks play,
Than we; we are too dull and *lumpiſh*. *Suckling.*

Little terreſtrial particles ſwimming in it after the groſſeſt were ſunk down, which, by their heavineſs and *lumpiſh* figure, made their way more ſpeedily. *Burnet.*

How dull and how inſenſible a beaſt
Is man, who yet wou'd lord it o'er the reſt?
Philoſophers and poets vainly ſtrove
In every age the *lumpiſh* maſs to move. *Dryden.*

LU'MPISHLY. *adv.* [from *lumpiſh.*] With heavineſs; with ſtupidity.

LU'MPISHNESS. *n. ſ.* [from the adjective.] Stupid heavineſs.

LU'MPY. *adj.* [from *lump.*] Full of lumps; full of compact maſſes.

One of the beſt ſpades to dig hard *lumpy* clays, but too ſmall for light garden mould. *Mortimer's Huſbandry.*

LU'NACY. *n. ſ.* [from *luna*, the moon.] A kind of madneſs influenced by the moon; madneſs in general.

Love is merely madneſs, and deſerves as well a dark houſe and a whip as madmen do; and the reaſon why they are not ſo puniſhed and cured is, that the *lunacy* is ſo ordinary, that the whippers are in love too. *Shakeſp. As you like it.*

Your kindred ſhun your houſe,
As beaten hence by your ſtrange *lunacy*. *Shakeſpeare.*

There is difference of *lunacy*: I had rather be mad with him, that, when he had nothing, thought all the ſhips that came into the haven his, than with you, who, when you have ſo much coming in, think you have nothing. *Suckling.*

LU'NAR. } *adj.* [*lunaire*, Fr. *lunaris*, Latin.] Relating to the
LU'NARY. } moon; under the dominion of the moon.

They that have reſolved that theſe years were but *lunary* years, *viz.* of a month, or Egyptian years, are eaſily confuted. *Raleigh's Hiſt. of the World.*

They have denominated ſome herbs ſolar and ſome *lunar*, and ſuch like toys put into great words. *Bacon's Nat. Hiſt.*

The figure of its ſeed much reſembles a horſhoe, which Baptiſta Porta hath thought too low a ſignification, and raiſed the ſame unto a *lunary* repreſentation. *Brown's Vulg. Errours.*

We upon our globe's laſt verge ſhall go,
And view the ocean leaning on the ſky;
From thence our rolling neighbours we ſhall know,
And on the *lunar* world ſecurely pry. *Dryden.*

LU'NARY. *n. ſ.* [*lunaria*, Latin; *lunaire*, Fr] Moonwort.

Then ſprinkles ſhe the juice of rue
With nine drops of the midnight dew,
From *lunary* diſtilling. *Drayton's Nymphid.*

LU'NATED. *adj.* [from *luna.*] Formed like a half moon.

LU'NATICK. *adj.* [*lunaticus*, Latin.] Mad; having the imagination influenced by the moon.

Bedlam beggars, from low farms,
Sometimes with *lunatick* bans, ſometimes with prayers,
Enforce their charity. *Shakeſpeare.*

LU'NATICK. *n. ſ.* A madman.

The *lunatick*, the lover, and the poet,
Are of imagination all compact:
One ſees more devils than vaſt hell can hold;
The madman. *Shakeſp. Midſummer Night's Dream.*

I dare enſure any man well in his wits, for one in the thouſand that he ſhall not die a *lunatick* in Bedlam within theſe ſeven years; becauſe not above one in about one thouſand five hundred have done ſo. *Graunt's Bills.*

See the blind beggar dance, the cripple ſing,
The ſot a hero, *lunatick* a king. *Pope.*

The reſidue of the yearly profits ſhall be laid out in purchaſing a piece of land, and in building thereon an hoſpital for the reception of idiots and *lunaticks*. *Swift.*

LUNA'TION. *n. ſ.* [*lunaiſon*, French; *luna*, Latin.] The revolution of the moon.

If the *lunations* be obſerved for a cycle of nineteen years, which is the cycle of the moon, the ſame obſervations will be verified for ſucceeding cycles for ever. *Holder on Time.*

LUNCH. } *n. ſ.* [*Minſhaw* derives it from *louja*, Spaniſh;
LU'NCHEON. } *Skinner* from *kleinken*, a ſmall piece, Teutonick. It probably comes from *clutch* or *clunch.*] As much food as one's hand can hold.

When hungry thou ſtood'ſt ſtaring, like an oaf,
I ſlic'd the *luncheon* from the barley loaf;
With crumbled bread I thicken'd well the meſs. *Gay.*

LUNE. *n. ſ.* [*luna*, Latin.]

1. Any thing in the ſhape of an half moon.

2. Fits of lunacy or frenzy, mad freaks. The French ſay of a man who is but fantaſtical or whimſical, *Il a des lunes.* *Hanmer.*

Beſtrew them
Theſe dangerous, unſafe *lunes* i' th' king;
He muſt be told on't, and he ſhall: the office
Becomes a woman beſt. *Shakeſp. Winter's Tale.*

3. A laiſh: as, the *lune* of a hawk.

LUNE'TTE. *n. ſ.* [French.] A ſmall half moon.

Lunette is a covered place made before the courtine, which conſiſts of two faces that form an angle inwards, and is commonly raiſed in foſſes full of water, to ſerve inſtead of a fauſſe braye, and to diſpute the enemy's paſſage: it is ſix toiſes in extent, of which the parapet is four. *Trevoux.*

LUNGS. *n. ſ.* [lungen, Saxon; *long*, Dutch.] The lights; the part by which breath is inſpired and expired.

More would I, but my *lungs* are waſted ſo,
That ſtrength of ſpeech is utterly denied me. *Shakeſpeare.*

The bellows of his *lungs* begin to ſwell,
Nor can the good receive, nor bad expel. *Dryden.*

Had I a hundred mouths, a hundred tongues,
And throats of braſs inſpir'd with iron *lungs*;
I could not half thoſe horrid crimes repeat,
Nor half the puniſhments thoſe crimes have met. *Dryden.*

LUNGED. *adj.* [from *lungs.*] Having lungs; having the nature of lungs; drawing in and emitting air: as, the lungs in an animal body.

The ſmith prepares his hammer for the ſtroke,
While the *lung'd* bellows hiſſing fire provoke. *Dryden.*

LUNG-GROWN. *adj.* [*lung* and *grown.*]

The lungs ſometimes grow faſt to the ſkin that lines the breaſt within; whence ſuch as are detained with that accident are *lung-grown*. *Harvey on Conſumptions.*

LU'NGWORT. *n. ſ.* [*pulmonaria*, Lat.]
The flower conſiſts of one leaf, which is ſhaped like a funnel, whoſe upper part is cut into ſeveral ſegments; from its fiſtulous flower-cup, which is for the moſt part pentagonal, riſes the pointal encompaſſed by four embrios, which afterwards become ſo many ſeeds incloſed in the flower-cup. *Miller.*

LUNISO'LAR. *adj.* [*luniſolaire*, French; *luna* and *ſolaris*, Lat.] Compounded of the revolution of ſun and moon.

LUNT. *n. ſ.* [*lonte*, Dutch.] The matchcord with which guns are fired.

LU'PINE. *n. ſ.* [*lupin*, French; *lupinus*, Latin.] A kind of pulſe.
It has a papilionaceous flower, out of whoſe empalement riſes the pale, which afterward turns into a pod filled with either plain or ſpherical ſeeds: the leaves grow like fingers upon the foot ſtalks. *Miller.*
When Protogenes would undertake any excellent piece, he uſed to diet himſelf with peas and *lupines*, that his invention might be quick and refined. *Peacham on Drawing.*

Where ſtalks of *lupines* grew,
Th' enſuing ſeaſon, in return, may bear
The bearded product of the golden year. *Dryden's Georg.*

Protogenes, drawing the picture of Jalyſus, took no other nouriſhment than *lupines* mixed with water, for fear of clogging his imagination by the luxury of his food. *Dryden.*

LURCH. *n. ſ.* [This word is derived by *Skinner* from *l'ourche*, a game of draughts, much uſed, as he ſays, among the Dutch; *ourche* he derives from *arca*; ſo that, I ſuppoſe, thoſe that are loſt are left in *lorche*, in the *lurch* or *box*; whence the uſe of the word.]

To leave in the LURCH. To leave in a forlorn or deſerted condition; to leave without help.

Will you now to peace incline,
And languiſh in the main deſign,
And *leave* us *in the lurch*. *Denham.*

But though th' art of a different church,
I will not *leave* thee *in the lurch*. *Hudibras, p.* i.

Have a care how you keep company with thoſe that, when they find themſelves upon a pinch, will *leave* their friends *in the lurch*. *L'Eſtrange's Fables.*
Can you break your word with three of the honeſteſt beſt-meaning perſons in the world? It is baſe to take advantage of their ſimplicity and credulity, and *leave* them *in the lurch* at laſt. *Arbuthnot's Hiſt. of J. Bull.*
Flirts about town had a deſign to caſt us out of the faſhionable world, and *leave* us *in the lurch*, by ſome of their late refinements. *Addiſon's Guardian.*

To LURCH. *v. n.* [*loeren*, Dutch; or rather from the noun.]
1. To ſhift; to play tricks.
I myſelf, ſometimes leaving the fear of heav'n on my left-hand, and hiding mine honour in my neceſſity, am fain to ſhuffle, to hedge, and to *lurch*. *Shakeſpeare.*
2. To lie in wait: we now rather uſe *lurk*.
While the one was upon wing, the other ſtood *lurching* upon the ground, and flew away with the fiſh. *L'Eſtrange.*

To LURCH. *v. a.* [*lurcor*, Latin.]
1. To devour; to ſwallow greedily.
Too far off from great cities may hinder buſineſs; or too near *lurcheth* all proviſions, and maketh every thing dear. *Bacon's Eſſays.*
2. To defeat; to diſappoint. A word now uſed only in burleſque. [from the game *lurch*.]

He waxed like a ſea;
And, in the brunt of ſeventeen battles ſince,
He *lurcht* all ſwords o' th' garland. *Shakeſp. Coriolanus.*

God never deſigned the uſe of them to be continual; by putting ſuch an emptineſs in them, as ſhould ſo quickly fail and *lurch* the expectation. *South's Sermons.*
This is a ſure rule, that will never deceive or *lurch* the ſincere communicant. *South's Sermons.*
3. To ſteal privily; to filch; to pilfer.

LU'RCHER. *n. ſ.* [from *lurch*.]
1. One that watches to ſteal, or to betray or entrap.
I cannot repreſent thoſe worthies more naturally than under the ſhadow of a pack of dogs, made up of finders, *lurchers*, and ſetters. *Tatler*, N°. 59.

His thefts ſome tradeſman ſpies,
Swift from his play the ſcudding *lurcher* flies;
Whilſt ev'ry honeſt tongue ſtop thief reſounds. *Gay.*

2. [*Lurco*, Latin.] A glutton; a gormandizer. Not uſed.

LURE. *n. ſ.* [*leurre*, French; *lore*, Dutch.]
1. Something held out to call a hawk.

My faulcon now is ſharp and paſſing empty,
And, till ſhe ſtoop, ſhe muſt not be full-gorg'd,
For then ſhe never looks upon her *lure*. *Shakeſpeare.*

This *lure* ſhe caſt abroad, thinking that this fame and belief would draw, at one time or other, ſome birds to ſtrike upon it. *Bacon's Henry* VII.
A great eſtate to an heir, is as a *lure* to all the birds of prey round about to ſeize on him. *Bacon.*

A falc'ner Henry is, when Emma hawks;
With her of tarſels, and of *lures* he talks. *Prior.*

2. Any enticement; any thing that promiſes advantage.

How many have with a ſmile made ſmall account
Of beauty, and her *lures*, eaſily ſcorn'd
All her aſſaults, on worthier things intent. *Milt. Par. Reg.*
This ſtiffneck'd pride, nor art nor force can bend,
Nor high-flown hopes to reaſon's *lure* deſcend. *Denham.*

To LURE. *v. n.* [from the noun.] To call hawks.
Standing near one that *lured* loud and ſhrill, I had ſuddenly an offence, as if ſomewhat had broken, or been diſlocated in my ear, and immediately after a loud ringing. *Bacon.*

To LURE. *v. a.* To attract; to entice; to draw.

As when a flock
Of ravenous fowl, though many a league remote,
Againſt the day of battle, to a field
Where armies lie encamp'd, come flying, *lur'd*
With ſcent of living carcaſes. *Milton's Par. Loſt.*

A man ſpent one day in labour, that he might paſs the other at eaſe; and *lured* on by the pleaſure of this bait, when he was in vigour he would provide for as many days as he could. *Temple.*

Should you *lure*
From this dark haunt, beneath the tangled roots
Of pendant trees, the monarch of the brook,
Behoves you then to ply your fineſt art. *Thomſon's Spring.*
Volumes on ſhelter'd ſtalls expanded lie,
And various ſcience *lures* the learned eye. *Gay's Trivia.*

LU'RID. *adj.* [*luridus*, Latin.] Gloomy; diſmal.

Slow ſettling o'er the *lurid* grove,
Unuſual darkneſs broods. *Thomſon's Summer.*

To LURK. *v. n.* [probably *lurch* and *lurk* are the ſame word. See LURCH.] To lie in wait; to lie hidden; to lie cloſe.

Far in land a ſavage nation dwelt,
That never taſted grace, nor goodneſs felt;
But like wild beaſts, *lurking* in loathſome den,
And flying faſt as roebuck through the fen,
All naked. *Fairy Queen, b.* ii.

Milbrook *lurketh* between two hills, a village of ſome eighty houſes, and borrowing his name from a mill and little brook running there through. *Carew's Survey of Cornwall.*

They lay not to live by their worke,
But theeviſhly loiter and *lurke*. *Tuſſer's Huſbandry.*

If ſinners entice, conſent not; if they ſay, let us lay wait for blood, let us *lurk* privily for the innocent. *Prov.* i. 11.

The wife, when danger or diſhonour *lurks*,
Safeſt, and ſeemlieſt by her huſband ſtays. *Milton.*

See
The *lurking* gold upon the fatal tree:
Then rend it off. *Dryden's Æn.*

The king unſeen
Lurk'd in her hand, and mourn'd his captive queen;
He ſprings to vengeance. *Pope.*

I do not *lurk* in the dark: I am not wholly unknown to the world: I have ſet my name at length. *Swift.*

LU'RKER. *n. ſ.* [from *lurk*.] A thief that lies in wait.

LU'RKINGPLACE. *n. ſ.* [*lurk* and *place*.] Hiding place; ſecret place.
Take knowledge of all the *lurkingplaces* where he hideth himſelf. 1 *Sam.* xxiii. 23.

LU'SCIOUS. *adj.* [from *delicious*, ſay ſome; but *Skinner* more probably derives it from *luxurious*, corruptly pronounced.]
1. Sweet, ſo as to nauſeate.
2. Sweet in a great degree.
The food that to him now is as *luſcious* as loches, ſhall ſhortly be as bitter as coloquintida. *Shakeſp. Othell.*

With brandiſh'd blade ruſh on him, break his glaſs,
And ſhed the *luſcious* liquor on the ground. *Milton.*
Blown roſes hold their ſweetneſs to the laſt,
And raiſins keep their *luſcious* native taſte. *Dryden.*

3. Pleaſing; delightful.
He will bait him in with the *luſcious* propoſal of ſome gainful purchaſe. *South's Sermons.*

LU'SCIOUSLY. *adv.* [from *luſcious*.] Sweet to a great degree.

LU'SCIOUSNESS. *n. ſ.* [from *luſcious*.] Immoderate ſweetneſs.
Can there be greater indulgence in God, than to embitter ſenſualities whoſe *luſciouſneſs* intoxicates us, and to clip wings which carry us from him. *Decay of Piety.*
Peas breed worms by reaſon of the *luſciouſneſs* and ſweetneſs of the grain. *Mortimer's Huſbandry.*

LU'SERN. *n. ſ.* *lupus cervarius*, Latin.] A lynx.

LUSH. *adj.* Of a dark, deep, full colour, oppoſite to pale and faint; from *louſche*. *Hanmer.*
How *luſh* and luſty the graſs looks? how green? *Shak.*

LUSK. *adj.* [*luſche*, French.] Idle; lazy; worthleſs. *Dict.*

LU'SKISH. *adj.* [from *luſk*.] Somewhat inclinable to lazineſs or indolence.

LU'SKISHLY. *adv.* [from *luſkiſh*.] Lazily; indolently.

LU'SKISHNESS. *adv.* [from *luſkiſh*.] A diſpoſition to lazineſs. *Spenſer.*

LUSO'RIOUS. *adj.* [*luſorius*, Latin.] Uſed in play; ſportive.

15 U

Things

Things more open to exception, yet unjustly condemned as unlawful; such as the *lusorious* lots, dancing and stage-plays. *Bishop Sanderson.*

Lu'sory. *adj.* [*lusorius*, Latin.] Used in play.

There might be many entertaining contrivances for the instruction of children in geometry and geography, in such alluring and *lusory* methods, which would make a most agreeable and lasting impression. *Watts's Improvement of the Mind.*

LUST. *n. s.* [lurt, Saxon; *lust*, Dutch.]

1. Carnal desire.

This our court, infected with their manners,
Shews like a riotous inn, Epicurism and *lust*
Make it more like a tavern or a brothel,
Than a grac'd palace. *Shakespeare's King Lear.*

Lust, and rank thoughts. *Shakespeare's Cymbeline.*

They are immoderately given to the *lust* of the flesh, making no conscience to get bastards. *Abbot.*

When a temptation of *lust* assaults thee, do not resist it by disputing with it, but flie from it, that is, think not at all of it. *Taylor's holy Living.*

2. Any violent or irregular desire.

I will divide the spoil; my *lust* shall be satisfied upon them. *Exod.* xv. 9.

The ungodly, for his own *lust*, doth persecute the poor: let them be taken in the crafty wiliness they imagined. *Psal.*

Virtue was represented by Hercules: he is drawn offering to strike a dragon; by the dragon are meant all manner of *lusts*. *Peacham on Drawing.*

All weigh our acts, and whate'er seems unjust,
Impute not to necessity, but *lust*. *Dryden's Ind. Emp.*

The *lust* of lucre. *Pope.*

3. Vigour; active power. Not used.

Trees will grow greater, and bear better fruit, if you put salt, or lees of wine, or blood, to the root: the cause may be, the increasing the *lust* or spirit of the root. *Bacon.*

To Lust. *v. n.*

1. To desire carnally.

Inconstant man, that loveth all he saw,
And *lusted* after all that he did love. *Roscommon.*

2. To desire vehemently.

Giving sometimes prodigally; not because he loved them to whom he gave, but because he *lusted* to give. *Sidney.*

The Christian captives in chains could no way move themselves, if they should unadvisedly *lust* after liberty. *Knolles.*

3. To list; to like. Out of use.

Their eyes swell with fatness; and they do even what they *lust*. *Psal.* lxxiii. 7.

4. To have irregular dispositions.

The mixed multitude fell a *lusting*; and the children of Israel also wept, and said, Who shall give us flesh to eat? *Num.* xi. 4.

The spirit that dwelleth in us *lusteth* to envy. *Jam.* iv. 5.

Lu'stful. *adj.* [*lust* and *full.*]

1. Libidinous; having irregular desires.

Turning wrathful fire to *lustful* heat,
With beastly sin thought her to have defil'd. *Fairy Qu.*

There is no man that is intemperate or *lustful*, but besides the guilt likewise stains and obscures his soul. *Tillotson.*

2. Provoking to sensuality; inciting to lust.

Thence his *lustful* orgies he enlarg'd. *Milton.*

Lu'stfully. *adv.* [from *lustful.*] With sensual concupiscence.

Lu'stfulness. *n. s.* [from *lustful.*] Libidinousness.

Lu'stihed. } *n. s.* [from *lusty.*] Vigour; sprightliness; corporal ability. Not now in use.
Lu'stihood. }

A goodly personage,
Now in his freshest flower of *lustyhed*,
Fit to inflame fair lady with love's rage. *Fa. Qu.*

Reason and respect
Make livers pale, and *lustihood* dejected. *Shakespeare.*

I'll prove it on his body;
Despight his nice fence, and his active practice,
His May of youth and bloom of *lustyhood*. *Shakespeare.*

Lu'stily. *adv.* [from *lusty.*] Stoutly; with vigour; with mettle.

I determine to fight *lustily* for him. *Shakesp. Henry* V.

Now, gentlemen,
Let's tune, and to it *lustily* a while. *Shakespeare.*

Barbarossa took upon him that painful journey, which the old king *lustily* performed. *Knolles.*

He has fought *lustily* for her, and deserves her. *Southern.*

Lu'stiness. *n. s.* [from *lusty.*] Stoutness; sturdiness; strength; vigour of body.

Fresh Clarion being ready dight,
He with good speed began to take his flight,
Over the fields in his frank *lustiness*. *Spenser's Muiopotmos.*

Where there is so great a prevention of the ordinary time, it is the *lustiness* of the child; but when it is less, it is some indisposition of the mother. *Bacon's Nat. Hist.* N°. 353.

Cappadocian slaves were famous for their *lustiness*, and being in good liking, were set on a stall to shew the good habit of their body, and made to play tricks before the buyers, to shew their activity and strength. *Dryden's Persius.*

Lu'stless. *adj.* [from *lust.*] Not vigorous; weak. *Spenser.*

Lu'stral. *adj.* [*lustrale*, French; *lustralis*, Latin.] Used in purification.

His better parts by *lustral* waves refin'd,
More pure, and nearer to æthereal mind. *Garth.*

Lustra'tion. *n. s.* [*lustration*, French; *lustratio*, Lat.] Purification by water.

Job's religious care,
His sons assembles, whose united prayer,
Like sweet perfumes, from golden censors rise;
He with divine *lustrations* sanctifies. *Sandys's Paraphrase.*

That spirits are corporeal seems a conceit derogative unto himself, and such as he should rather labour to overthrow; yet thereby he establisheth the doctrine of *lustrations*, amulets, and charms. *Brown's Vulgar Errours, b.* i.

What were all their *lustrations* but so many solemn purifyings, to render both themselves and their sacrifices acceptable to their gods. *South's Sermons.*

Should Io's priest command
A pilgrimage to Meroe's burning sand;
Through desarts they wou'd seek the secret spring,
And holy water for *lustration* bring. *Dryden's Juvenal.*

By ardent pray'r, and clear *lustration*,
Purge the contagious spots of human weakness;
Impure no mortal can behold Apollo. *Prior.*

Lu'stre. *n. s.* [*lustre*, French.]

1. Brightness; splendour; glitter.

You have one eye left to see some mischief on him.
—Lest it see more prevent it; out, vile gelly; where is thy *lustre* now? *Shakespeare's King Lear.*

To the soul time doth perfection give,
And adds fresh *lustre* to her beauty still. *Davies.*

The scorching sun was mounted high,
In all its *lustre*, to the noonday sky. *Addison's Ovid.*

Pass but some fleeting years, and these poor eyes,
Where now without a boast some *lustre* lies;
No longer shall their little honours keep,
But only be of use to read or weep. *Prior.*

All nature laughs, the groves are fresh and fair,
The sun's mild *lustre* warms the vital air. *Pope.*

2. A sconce with lights.

Ridotta sips, and dances till she see
The doubling *lustres* dance as quick as she. *Pope's Horace.*

3. Eminence; renown.

His ancestors continued about four hundred years, rather without obscurity than with any great *lustre*. *Wotton.*

I used to wonder how a man of birth and spirit could endure to be wholly insignificant and obscure in a foreign country, when he might live with *lustre* in his own. *Swift.*

4. [From *lustre*, Fr. *lustrum*, Latin.] The space of five years.

Both of us have closed the tenth *lustre*, and it is high time to determine how we shall play the last act of the farce. *Bolingbroke to Swift.*

Lu'string. *n. s.* [from *lustre.*] A shining silk; commonly pronounced *lutestring*.

Lu'strous. *adj.* [from *lustre.*] Bright; shining; luminous.

Noble heroes, my sword and yours are kin, good sparks and *lustrous*. *Shakesp. All's well that ends well.*

The more *lustrous* the imagination is, it filleth and fixeth the better. *Bacon's Nat. Hist.* N°. 956.

Lu'stwort. *n. s.* [*lust* and *wort.*] An herb.

Lu'sty. *adj.* [*lustig*, Dutch.] Stout; vigorous; healthy; able of body.

This *lusty* lady came from Persia late,
She with the Christians had encounter'd oft. *Fairy Qu.*

If *lusty* love should go in quest of beauty,
Where should he find it fairer than in Blanch? *Shakesp.*

We yet may see the old man in a morning,
Lusty as health, come ruddy to the field,
And there pursue the chase. *Otway.*

Lu'tanist. *n. s.* [from *lute.*] One who plays upon the lute.

Luta'rious. *adj.* [*lutarius*, Latin.] Living in mud; of the colour of mud.

A scaly tortoise-shell, of the *lutarious* kind. *Grew.*

LUTE. *n. s.* [*luth*, *lut*, French.]

1. A stringed instrument of musick.

Orpheus with his *lute* made trees,
And the mountain tops that freeze,
Bow themselves when he did sing. *Shakesp. Henry* VIII.

May must be drawn with a sweet and amiable countenance, upon his head a garland of roses, in one hand a *lute*. *Peacham on Drawing.*

In a sadly pleasing strain
Let the warbling *lute* complain. *Pope's St. Cæcilia.*

A *lute* string will bear a hundred weight without rupture, but at the same time cannot exert its elasticity. *Arbuthnot.*

Lands of singing, or of dancing slaves,
Love-whisp'ring woods, and *lute* resounding waves. *Dunc.*

2. [From *lut*, French; *lutum*, Lat.] A composition like clay, with which chemists close up their vessels.

Some temper *lute*, some spacious vessels move,
These furnaces erect, and those approve. *Garth.*

To LUTE. *v. a.* [from the noun.] To close with lute, or chemists clay.

Take a vessel of iron, and let it have a cover of iron well *luted*, after the manner of the chemists. *Bacon's Nat. Hist.*

Iron may be so heated, that, being closely *luted* in a glass, it shall constantly retain the fire. *Wilkins's Math. Magick.*

LU'TULENT. *adj.* [*lutulentus*, Latin.] Muddy; turbid.

To LUX. } *v. a.* [*luxer*, French; *luxo*, Latin.] To put
To LU'XATE. } out of joint; to disjoint.

He complained of extremity of pain, and suspected his hip *luxated*. *Wiseman's Surgery.*

Consider well the *luxated* joint, and which way it slipped out; for it requireth to be returned in the same manner. *Wiseman's Surgery.*

Descending careless from his couch, the fall
Lux'd his joint neck, and spinal marrow bruis'd. *Philips.*

LUXA'TION. *n. s.* [from *luxo*, Latin.]
1. The act of disjointing.
2. Any thing disjointed.

The undue situation, or connexion of parts, in fractures and *luxations*, are to be rectified by chirurgical means. *Floyer.*

LUXE. n. s. [French, *luxius*, Lat.] Luxury; voluptuousness.

The pow'r of wealth I try'd,
And all the various *luxe* of costly pride. *Prior.*

LUXU'RIANCE. } *n. s.* [from *luxurians*, Latin.] Exuberance;
LUXU'RIANCY. } abundant or wanton plenty or growth.

A fungus prevents healing only by its *luxuriancy*. *Wiseman.*

Flowers grow up in the garden in the greatest *luxuriancy* and profusion. *Spectator*, N°. 47.

While through the parting robe th' alternate breast
In full *luxuriance* rose. *Thomson's Summer.*

LUXU'RIANT. *adj.* [*luxurians*, Lat.] Exuberant; superfluously plenteous.

A fluent and *luxuriant* speech becomes youth well, but not age. *Bacon's Essays.*

The mantling vine gently creeps *luxuriant*. *Milton.*

If the fancy of Ovid be *luxuriant*, it is his character to be so. *Dryden's Pref. to Ovid's Epistles.*

Prune the *luxuriant*, th' uncouth refine,
But show no mercy to an empty line. *Pope.*

To LUXU'RIATE. *v. n.* [*luxurior*, Latin.] To grow exuberantly; to shoot with superfluous plenty.

LUXU'RIOUS. *adj.* [*luxurieux*, Fr. *luxuriosus*, Latin.]
1. Delighting in the pleasures of the table.
2. Administring to luxury.

The *luxurious* board. *Anon.*

3. Lustful; libidinous.

She knows the heat of a *luxurious* bed:
Her blush is guiltiness, not modesty. *Shakespeare.*

I grant him bloody,
Luxurious, avaricious, false, deceitful. *Shakespeare.*

4. Voluptuous; enslaved to pleasure.

Those whom last thou saw'st
In triumph, and *luxurious* wealth, are they
First seen in acts of prowess eminent,
And great exploits; but of true virtue void. *Milton.*

Luxurious cities, where the noise
Of riot ascends above their loftiest tow'rs. *Milton.*

5. Softening by pleasure.

Repel the Tuscan foes, their city seize,
Protect the Latians in *luxurious* ease. *Dryden.*

6. Luxuriant; exuberant.

Till more hands
Aid us, the work under our labour grows
Luxurious by restraint. *Milton's Par. Lost, b.* ix.

LUXU'RIOUSLY. *adv.* [from *luxurious.*] Deliciously; voluptuously.

Hotter hours you have
Luxuriously pick'd out. *Shakespeare.*

Where mice and rats devour'd poetick bread,
And with heroick verse *luxuriously* were fed. *Dryden.*

He never supt in solemn state;
Nor day to night *luxuriously* did join. *Dryden.*

LU'XURY. *n. s.* [*luxuré*, old French; *luxuria*, Latin.]
1. Voluptuousness; addictedness to pleasure.

Egypt with Assyria strove
In wealth and *luxury*. *Milton.*

Riches expose a man to pride and *luxury*, and a foolish elation of heart. *Addison's Spectator*, N°. 464.

2. Lust; lewdness.

Urge his hateful *luxury*,
His bestial appetite in change of lust,
Which stretch'd unto their servants, daughters, wives.
Shakespeare's Richard III.

3. Luxuriance; exuberance.

Young trees of several kinds set contiguous in a fruitful ground, with the very *luxury* of the trees will incorporate. *Bacon's Nat. Hist.* N°. 479.

4. Delicious fare.

He cut the side of the rock for a garden, and by laying on it earth, furnished out a kind of *luxury* for a hermit. *Addison.*

LY. *v. n.* [A very frequent termination both of names of places and of adjectives and adverbs: when *ly* terminates the name of a place, it is derived from leag, Saxon, a field; when it ends an adjective or adverb, it is contracted from *lich*, *like*; as, *beastly*, *beastlike*; *plainly*, *plainlike*.]

LYCA'NTHROPY. *n. s.* [*lycantropie*, French; λύκος and ἄνθρωπος.] A kind of madness, in which men have the qualities of wild beasts.

He sees like a man in his sleep, and grows as much the wiser as the man that dreamt of a *lycanthropy*, and was for ever after wary not to come near a river. *Taylor.*

LYEKE. *adj.* for *like*. *Spenser.*

LY'ING, the participle of *lie*, whether it signifies to *be recumbent*, or *to speak falsely*, or otherwise.

They will have me whipt for speaking true, thou wilt have me whipt for *lying*, and sometimes I am whipt for holding my peace. *Shakespeare's King Lear.*

Many tears and temptations befal me by the *lying* in wait of the Jews. *Acts* xx. 19.

LYMPH. *n. s.* [*lymphe*, French; *lympha*, Lat.] Water; transparent colourless liquor.

When the chyle passeth through the mesentery, it is mixed with the *lymph*, the most spirituous and elaborated part of the blood. *Arbuthnot on Aliments.*

LY'MPHATED. *adj.* [*lymphatus*, Latin.] Mad. *Dict.*

LY'MPHATICK. *n. s.* [*lymphatique*, Fr. from *lympha*, Latin.]

The *lymphaticks* are slender pellucid tubes, whose cavities are contracted at small and unequal distances: they are carried into the glands of the mesentery, receiving first a fine thin lymph from the *lymphatick* ducts, which dilutes the chylous fluid. *Cheyne's Phil. Principles.*

Upon the death of an animal, the spirits may sink into the veins, or *lymphaticks* and glandules. *Floyer.*

LY'MPHEDUCT. *n. s.* [*lympha* and *ductus*, Latin.] A vessel which conveys the lymph.

The glands,
All artful knots, of various hollow threads;
Which *lympheducts*, an art'ry, nerve, and vein,
Involv'd and close together wound, contain. *Blackmore.*

LYNX. n. s. [Latin.] A spotted beast, remarkable for speed and sharp sight.

He that has an idea of a beast with spots, has but a confused idea of a leopard, it not being thereby sufficiently distinguished from a *lynx*. *Locke.*

What modes of sight betwixt each wide extreme,
The mole's dim curtain, and the *linx*'s beam. *Pope.*

LYRE. *n. s.* [*lyre*, French; *lyra*, Latin.] A harp; a musical instrument to which poetry is, by poetical writers, supposed to be sung.

With other notes then to th' Orphean *lyre*. *Milton.*

My softest verse, my darling *lyre*,
Upon Euphelia's toilet lay. *Prior.*

He never touched his *lyre* in such a truly chromatick manner as upon that occasion. *Arbuth. and Pope's Mart. Scrib.*

LYR'ICAL. } *adj.* [*lyricus*, Latin; *lyrique*, French.] Pertaining
LY'RICK. } to an harp, or to odes or poetry sung to an harp; singing to an harp.

All his trophies hung and acts enroll'd
In copious legend, or sweet *lyrick* song. *Milton's Agonist.*

Somewhat of the purity of English, somewhat of more equal thoughts, somewhat of sweetness in the numbers; in one word, somewhat of a finer turn, and more *lyrical* verse, is yet wanting. *Dryden.*

The lute neglected, and the *lyrick* muse,
Love taught my tears in sadder notes to flow,
And tun'd my heart to elegies of woe. *Pope.*

LY'RICK. *n. s.* A poet who writes songs to the harp.

The greatest conqueror in this nation, after the manner of the old Grecian *lyricks*, did not only compose the words of his divine odes, but set them to musick himself. *Addison.*

LY'RIST. [*lyristes*, Latin.] A musician who plays upon the harp.

His tender theme the charming *lyrist* chose
Minerva's anger, and the direful woes
Which voyaging from Troy the victors bore. *Pope.*

M.

M Has, in English, one unvaried sound, by compression of the lips; as, *mine*, *tame*, *camp*: it is never mute.

MACARO'ON. *n. ſ.* [*macarone*, Italian.]

1. A coarſe, rude, low fellow; whence *macaronick* poetry, in which the language is purpoſely corrupted.

Like a big wife, at ſight of lothed meat,
Ready to travail; ſo I ſigh and ſweat,
To hear this *macaroon* talk on in vain. *Donne.*

2. [*Macaron*, French, from μάκαρ.] A kind of ſweet biſcuit, made of flower, almonds, eggs, and ſugar.

MACAW-TREE. *n. ſ.*

The *macaw-tree* is a ſpecies of the *palm-tree*, and is very common in the Caribbee iſlands, where the negroes pierce the tender fruit, whence iſſues a pleaſant liquor, which they are very fond of; and the body of the tree affords a ſolid timber, with which they make javelins, arrows, &c. and is ſuppoſed by ſome to be a ſort of ebony. *Miller.*

MACA'W. *n. ſ.* A bird in the Weſt-Indies.

MACE. *n. ſ.* [maʒʒa, Saxon; *maça*, Spaniſh.]

1. An enſign of authority worn before magiſtrates.

He mightily upheld that royal *mace*
Which now thou bear'ſt. *Fairy Queen, b.* ii.
Death with his *mace* petrifick ſmote. *Milton.*

2. [*Maſſue*, French; *maſſa*, Latin.] A heavy blunt weapon; a club of metal.

O murth'rous ſlumber!
Lay'ſt thou thy leaden *mace* upon my boy
That plays thee muſick? *Shakeſp. Julius Cæſar.*

The Turkiſh troops breaking in with their ſcymitars and heavy iron *maces*, made a moſt bloody execution. *Knolles.*

With his *mace* their monarch ſtruck the ground;
With inward trembling earth receiv'd the wound,
And riſing ſtreams a ready paſſage found. *Dryden.*

The mighty *maces* with ſuch haſte deſcend,
They break the bones, and make the ſolid armour bend.
Dryden's Knight's Tale.

3. [*Macis*, Latin.] A kind of ſpice.

The nutmeg is incloſed in a threefold covering, of which the ſecond is *mace*: it is a thin and flat membranaceous ſubſtance, of an oleaginous, and a yellowiſh colour: it has an extremely fragrant, aromatick, and agreeable ſmell, and a pleaſant, but acrid and oleaginous taſte. *Mace* is carminative, ſtomachick, and aſtringent. *Hill's Mat. Med.*

Water, vinegar, and honey, is a moſt excellent ſudorifick: it is more effectual with a little *mace* added to it. *Arbuthnot.*

MACEA'LE. *n. ſ.* [*mace* and *ale.*] Ale ſpiced with mace.

I preſcribed him a draught of *maceale*, with hopes to diſpoſe him to reſt. *Wiſeman's Surgery.*

MA'CEBEARER. *n. ſ.* [*mace* and *bear.*] One who carries the mace before perſons in authority.

I was placed at a quadrangular table, oppoſite to the *macebearer*. *Spectator*, Nº. 617.

To MA'CERATE. *v. a.* [*macero*, Latin; *macerer*, French.]

1. To make lean; to wear away.

Recurrent pains of the ſtomach, megrims, and other recurrent head-aches, *macerate* the parts, and render the looks of patients conſumptive and pining. *Harvey on Conſumptions.*

2. To mortify; to harraſs with corporal hardſhips.

Covetous men are all fools: for what greater folly can there be, or madneſs, than for ſuch a man to *macerate* himſelf when he need not? *Burton on Melancholy.*

Out of an exceſs of zeal they practiſe mortifications; whereby they *macerate* their bodies, and impair their health.
Fiddes's Sermons.

3. To ſteep almoſt to ſolution, either with or without heat.

In lotions in womens caſes, he orders two portions of hellebore *macerated* in two cotylæ of water. *Arbuthnot.*

MACERA'TION. *n. ſ.* [*maceration*, French; from *macerate.*]

1. The act of waſting, or making lean.

2. Mortification; corporal hardſhip.

3. *Maceration* is an infuſion either with or without heat, wherein the ingredients are intended to be almoſt wholly diſſolved. *Quincy.*

The ſaliva ſerves for a *maceration* and diſſolution of the meat into a chyle. *Ray on Creation.*

MA'CHINAL. *adj.* [from *machina*, Latin.] Relating to machines. *Dict.*

To MA'CHINATE. *v. a.* [*machinor*, Latin; *machiner*, Fr.] To plan; to contrive.

MACHINA'TION. *n. ſ.* [*machinatio*, Lat. *machination*, French; from *machinate.*] Artifice; contrivance; malicious ſcheme.

If you miſcarry,
Your buſineſs of the world hath ſo an end,
And *machination* ceaſes. *Shakeſpeare's King Lear.*

O from their *machinations* free,
That would my guiltleſs ſoul betray;
From thoſe who in my wrongs agree,
And for my life their engines lay. *Sandys's Paraphraſe.*

Some one intent on miſchief, or inſpir'd
With dev'liſh *machination*, might deviſe
Like inſtrument, to plague the ſons of men
For ſin; on war, and mutual ſlaughter bent. *Milton.*

Be fruſtrate all ye ſtratagems of hell,
And deviliſh *machinations* come to nought. *Milt. Par. Reg.*

How were they zealous in reſpect to their temporal governors? Not by open rebellion, not by private *machinations*; but in bleſſing and ſubmitting to their emperors, and obeying them in all things but their idolatry. *Spratt's Sermons.*

MACHI'NE. *n. ſ.* [*machina*, Latin; *machine*, French. This word is pronounced *maſheen.*]

1. Any complicated piece of workmanſhip.

We are led to conceive this great *machine* of the world to have been once in a ſtate of greater ſimplicity, as to conceive a watch to have been once in its firſt materials. *Burnet.*

In a watch's fine *machine*,
The added movements which declare
How full the moon, how old the year,
Derive their ſecundary pow'r
From that which ſimply points the hour. *Prior.*

2. An engine.

In the hollow ſide,
Selected numbers of their ſoldiers hide;
With inward arms the dire *machine* they load,
And iron bowels ſtuff the dark abode. *Dryden.*

3. Supernatural agency in poems.

The marvellous fable includes whatever is ſupernatural, and eſpecially the *machines* of the gods. *Pope.*

MACHI'NERY. *n. ſ.* [from *machine.*]

1. Enginery; complicated workmanſhip; ſelf-moved engines.

2. The *machinery* ſignifies that part which the deities, angels, or demons, act in a poem. *Pope's Rape of the Lock.*

MA'CHINIST. *n. ſ.* [*machiniſte*, French; from *machina*, Latin.] A conſtructor of engines or machines.

MA'CILENCY. *n. ſ.* [from *macilent.*] Leanneſs. *Dict.*

MA'CILENT. *adj.* [*macilentus*, Latin.] Lean.

MA'CKEREL. *n. ſ.* [*mackereel*, Dutch; *maquereau*, French.] A ſea-fiſh.

Some fiſh are gutted, ſplit, and kept in pickle; as whiting and *mackerel*. *Carew's Survey of Cornwall.*

Law ordered that the Sunday ſhould have reſt;
And that no nymph her noiſy food ſhould ſell,
Except it were new milk or *mackarel*. *King's Art of Cookery.*

Sooner ſhall cats diſport in water clear,
And ſpeckled *mackrels* graze the meadows fair,
Than I forget my ſhepherds wonted love. *Gay's Paſtorals.*

MACKEREL-GALE ſeems to be, in *Dryden's* cant, a ſtrong breeze, ſuch, I ſuppoſe, as is deſired to bring *mackerel* freſh to market.

They put up every ſail,
The wind was fair, but blew a *mackrel gale*. *Dryden.*

MA'CROCOSM. *n. ſ.* [*macrocoſme*, French; μακρὸς and κόσμος.] The whole world, or viſible ſyſtem, in oppoſition to the microcoſm, or world of man.

MACTA'TION. *n. s.* [*mactatus*, Latin.] The act of killing for sacrifice.

MACULA. *n. s.* [Latin.]

1. A spot.

And lastly, the body of the sun may contract some spots or *maculæ* greater than usual, and by that means be darkened. *Burnet's Theory of the Earth.*

2. [In physick.] Any spots upon the skin, whether those in fevers or scorbutick habits.

To MA'CULATE. *v. a.* [*maculo*, Lat.] To stain; to spot.

MACULA'TION. *n. s.* [from *maculate.*] Stain; spot; taint.

I will throw my glove to death himself,
That there's no *maculation* in thy heart. *Shakespeare.*

MA'CULE. *n. s.* [*macula*, Latin.] A spot; a stain.

MAD. *adj.* [ȝemaad, Saxon; *matto*, Italian.]

1. Disordered in the mind; broken in the understanding; distracted.

Alack, Sir, he is *mad.*
—'Tis the time's plague when madmen lead the blind. *Shakespeare's King Lear.*

The poets sung,
Thy mother from the sea was sprung;
But they were *mad* to make thee young. *Denham.*

We must bind our passions in chains, lest like *mad*-folks they break their locks and bolts, and do all the mischief they can. *Taylor's Worthy Communicant.*

A bear, enrag'd at the stinging of a bee, ran like *mad* into the bee-garden, and over-turn'd all the hives. *L'Estrange.*

Madmen ought not to be *mad*;
But who can help his frenzy? *Dryden's Span. Fryar.*

2. Over-run with any violent or unreasonable desire; with *on*, *after*, *of*, perhaps better *for*, before the object of desire.

It is the land of graven images, and they are *mad* upon their idols. *Jer.* l. 38.

The world is running *mad* after farce, the extremity of bad poetry, or rather the judgment that is fallen upon dramatick writing. *Dryden's Pref. to Cleomenes.*

The people are not so very *mad* of acorns, but that they could be content to eat the bread of civil persons. *Rymer.*

3. Enraged; furious.

Holy writ represents St. Paul as making havock of the church, and persecuting that way unto the death, and being exceedingly *mad* against them. *Decay of Piety.*

To MAD. *v. a.* [from the adjective.] To make mad; to make furious; to enrage.

O villain! cried out Zelmane, *madded* with finding an unlooked-for rival. *Sidney, b.* ii.

Had I but seen thy picture in this plight,
It would have *madded* me. *Shakesp. Titus Andronicus.*

This will witness outwardly,
As strongly as the conscience do's within,
To th' *madding* of her lord. *Shakesp. Cymbeline.*

This musick *mads* me, let it sound no more;
For though it have help'd madmen to their wits,
In me, it seems, it will make wisemen mad. *Shakespeare.*

This *mads* me, that perhaps ignoble hands
Have overlaid him, for they cou'd not conquer. *Dryden.*

To MAD. *v. n.* To be mad; to be furious.

The *madding* wheels
Of brazen chariots rag'd: dire was the noise
Of conflict! *Milton's Par. Lost, b.* vi.

She, mixing with a throng
Of *madding* matrons, bears the bride along. *Dryden.*

MAD. *n. s.* [maðu, Saxon.] An earth worm. *Ainf.*

MA'DAM. *n. s.* [*ma dame*, French, my dame.] The term of compliment used in address to ladies of every degree.

Certes, *madam*, ye have great cause of plaint. *Spenser.*

Madam, once more you look and move a queen!
Philips's Distrest Mother.

MA'DBRAIN. } *adj.* [*mad* and *brain.*] Disordered in the
MA'DBRAINED. } mind; hotheaded.

I give my hand oppos'd against my heart,
Unto a *madbrain* Rudesby, full of spleen. *Shakespeare.*

He let fall his book,
And as he stoop'd again to take it up,
This *madbrain'd* bridegroom took him such a cuff,
That down fell priest and book. *Shakespeare.*

This fell tempest shall not cease to rage,
Until the golden circuit on my head,
Like to the glorious sun's transparent beams,
Do calm the fury of this *madbrain'd* flaw. *Shakespeare.*

MA'DCAP. *n. s.* [*mad* and *cap*; either taking the *cap* for the head, or alluding to the caps put upon distracted persons by way of distinction.] A madman; a wild hotbrained fellow.

That last is Biron, the merry *madcap* lord;
Not a word with him but a jest. *Shakespeare.*

Where is his son,
The nimble-footed *madcap* prince of Wales,
And his comrades, that daft the world aside,
And bid it pass. *Shakespeare's Henry* IV.

To MA'DDEN. *v. n.* [from *mad.*] To become mad; to act as mad.

The dog-star rages, nay 'tis past a doubt,
All Bedlam or Parnassus is let out;
Fire in each eye, and papers in each hand,
They rave, recite, and *madden* round the land. *Pope.*

To MA'DDEN. *v. a.* To make mad.

Such *mad'ning* draughts of beauty,
As for a while overwhelm'd his raptur'd thought. *Thomson.*

MA'DDER. *n. s.* [mæðeɲe, Saxon.]

The flower of the *madder* consists of one single leaf, which is cut into four or five segments, and expanded at the top; the flower-cup afterwards becomes a fruit, composed of two juicy berries closely joined together, containing seed for the most part, hollowed like a navel; the leaves are rough, and surround the stalks in whorles. *Miller.*

Madder is cultivated in vast quantities in Holland: what the Dutch send over for medicinal use is the root, which is only dried; but the greatest quantity is used by the dyers, who have it sent in coarse powder. *Hill.*

MADE, participle preterite of *make.*

Neither hath this man sinned, nor his parents; but that the works of God should be *made* manifest. *John* ix. 3.

MADEFA'CTION. *n. s.* [*madefacio*, Latin.] The act of making wet.

To all *madefaction* there is required an imbibition. *Bacon.*

To MA'DEFY. *v. a.* [*madefio*, Latin.] To moisten; to make wet.

MADGEHOWLET. *n. s.* An owl. *Ainf.*

MA'DHOUSE. *n. s.* [*mad* and *house.*] A house where madmen are cured or confined.

A fellow in a *madhouse* being asked how he came there? why, says he, the mad-folks abroad are too many for us, and so they have mastered all the sober people, and cooped them up here. *L'Estrange.*

MA'DLY. *adv.* [from *mad.*] Without understanding; furiously.

He wav'd a torch aloft, and *madly* vain,
Sought godlike worship from a servile train. *Dryden.*

MA'DMAN. *n. s.* [*mad* and *man.*] A man deprived of his understanding.

They shall be like *madmen*, sparing none, but still sporting. *2 Esd.* xvi. 71.

He that eagerly pursues any thing, is no better than a *madman.* *L'Estrange.*

He who ties a *madman*'s hands, or takes away his sword, loves his person while he disarms his frenzy. *South's Sermons.*

MA'DNESS. *n. s.* [from *mad.*]

1. Distraction; loss of understanding; perturbation of the faculties.

Why, woman, your husband is in his old tunes again: he so rails against all married mankind, so curses all Eve's daughters, and so buffets himself on the forehead, that any *madness* I ever yet beheld seemed but tameness and civility to this distemper. *Shakesp. Merry Wives of Windsor.*

There are degrees of *madness* as of folly, the disorderly jumbling ideas together, in some more, some less. *Locke.*

2. Fury; wildness; rage.

The power of God sets bounds to the raging of the sea, and restrains the *madness* of the people. *King Charles.*

He rav'd with all the *madness* of despair,
He roar'd, he beat his breast, and tore his hair. *Dryden.*

MADRI'ER. *n. s.*

Madrier, in war, a thick plank armed with iron plates, having a cavity sufficient to receive the mouth of the petard when charged, with which it is applied against a gate, or other thing intended to be broken down. *Bailey.*

MA'DRIGAL. *n. s.* [*madrigal*, Spanish and French, from *mandra*, Latin; whence it was written anciently *mandriale*, Italian.] A pastoral song.

A *madrigal* is a little amorous piece, which contains a certain number of unequal verses, not tied to the scrupulous regularity of a sonnet, or subtilty of an epigram: it consists of one single rank of verses, and in that differs from a canzonet, which consists of several strophes, which return in the same order and number. *Bailey.*

Waters, by whose falls
Birds sing melodious *madrigails.* *Shakespeare.*

His artful strains have oft delay'd
The huddling brook to hear his *madrigal.* *Milton.*

Their tongue is light and trifling in comparison of the English; more proper for sonnets, *madrigals*, and elegies, than heroick poetry. *Dryden.*

MA'DWORT. *n. s.* [*mad* and *wort.*] An herb.

MÆRE. *adv.* It is derived from the Saxon mæɲ, famous, great, noted: so *ælmere* is all famous; *æthelmere*, famous for nobility. *Gibson's Camden.*

To MA'FFLE. *v. n.* To stammer. *Ainf.*

MAFFLER. *n. s.* [from the verb.] A stammerer. *Ainf.*

MAGAZI'NE. *n. s.* [*magazine*, French, from the Arabick *machsan*, a treasure.]

1. A storehouse, commonly an arsenal or armoury, or repository of provisions.

If it should appear fit to bestow shipping in those harbours, it shall be very needful that there be a *magazine* of all necessary provisions and munitions. *Raleigh's Essays.*

Plain heroick magnitude of mind;
Their armories and *magazines* contemns. *Milton's Agonist.*

Some o'er the publick *magazines* preside,
And some are sent new forage to provide. *Dryden's Virg.*

Useful arms in *magazines* we place,
All rang'd in order, and dispos'd with grace. *Pope.*

His head was so well stored a *magazine*, that nothing could be proposed which he was not master of. *Locke.*

2. Of late this word has signified a miscellaneous pamphlet, from a periodical miscellany named the *Gentleman's Magazine*, by *Edward Cave*.

MAGE. *n. s.* [*magus*, Latin.] A magician. *Spenser.*

MA'GGOT. *n. s.* [*magrod*, Welsh; *millepeda*, Latin; maðu, Saxon.]

1. A small grub, which turns into a fly.

Out of the sides and back of the common caterpillar we have seen creep out small *maggots*. *Ray on Creation.*

From the sore although the insect flies,
It leaves a brood of *maggots* in disguise. *Garth's Dispens.*

2. Whimsy; caprice; odd fansy.

Taffata phrases, silken terms precise,
Three-pil'd hyperboles, spruce affectation,
Figures pedantical, these summer flies,
Have blown me full of *maggot* ostentation:
I do forswear them.
Henceforth my wooing mind shall be exprest
In russet yeas, and honest kersy noes. *Shakespeare.*

To reconcile our late dissenters,
Our breth'ren though by other venters,
Unite them and their diff'rent *maggots*,
As long and short sticks are in faggots. *Hudibras, p.* iii.

She pricked his *maggot*, and touched him in the tender point; then he broke out into a violent passion. *Arbuthnot.*

MA'GGOTINESS. *n. s.* [from *maggotty*.] The state of abounding with maggots.

MA'GGOTTY. *adv.* [from *maggot*.]

1. Full of maggots.

2. Capricious; whimsical.

To pretend to work out a neat scheme of thoughts with a *maggotty* unsettled head, is as ridiculous as to think to write strait in a jumbling coach. *Norris's Miscel.*

MA'GICAL. *n. s.* [from *magick*.] Acting, or performed by secret and invisible powers, either of nature, or the agency of spirits.

I'll humbly signify what, in his name,
That *magical* word of war, we have effected. *Shakesp.*

They beheld unveiled the *magical* shield of your Ariosto, which dazzled the beholders with too much brightness; they can no longer hold up their arms. *Dryden.*

By the use of a looking-glass, and certain attire made of cambrick, upon her head, she attained to an evil art and *magical* force in the motion of her eyes. *Tatler,* N°. 110.

MA'GICALLY. *adv.* [from *magical*.] According to the rites of magick.

In the time of Valens, divers curious men, by the falling of a ring *magically* prepared, judged that one Theodorus should succeed in the empire. *Camden.*

MA'GICK. *n. s.* [*magia*, Latin.]

1. The art of putting in action the power of spirits: it was supposed that both good and bad spirits were subject to magick; yet magick was in general held unlawful; sorcery; enchantment.

She once being looft,
The noble ruin of her *magick*, Antony,
Claps on his sea-wing. *Shakesp. Ant. and Cleopatra.*

What charm, what *magick*, can over-rule the force of all these motives. *Rogers.*

2. The secret operations of natural powers.

The writers of natural *magick* do attribute much to the virtues that come from the parts of living creatures, as if they did infuse some immaterial virtue into the part severed. *Bacon's Nat. Hist.*

MA'GICK. *adj.* Acting or doing by powers superior to the known power of nature; incantating; necromantick.

Upon the corner of the moon
There hangs a vap'rous drop, profound;
I'll catch it ere it come to ground:
And that distill'd by *magick* slights
Shall raise such artificial sprights,
As by the strength of their illusion,
Shall draw him on to his confusion. *Shakesp. Macbeth.*

And the brute earth would lend her nerves, and shake
Till all thy *magick* structures rear'd so high,
Were shatter'd into heaps. *Milton.*

Like castles built by *magick* art in air,
That vanish at approach, such thoughts appear. *Granville.*

MAGI'CIAN. *n. s.* [*magicus*, Latin.] One skilled in magick; an enchanter; a necromancer.

What black *magician* conjures up this fiend,
To stop devoted charitable deeds. *Shakesp. Rich.* III.

An old *magician*, that did keep
Th' Hesperian fruit, and made the dragon sleep;
Her potent charms do troubled souls relieve,
And, where she lists, makes calmest souls to grieve. *Waller.*

There are millions of truths that a man is not concerned to know; as, whether Roger Bacon was a mathematician, or a *magician*. *Locke.*

MAGISTE'RIAL. *adj.* [from *magister*, Latin.]

1. Such as suits a master.

Such a frame of government is paternal, not *magisterial*. *King Charles.*

He bids him attend as if he had the rod over him; and uses a *magisterial* authority while he instructs him. *Dryden.*

2. Lofty; arrogant; proud; insolent; despotick.

We are not *magisterial* in opinions, nor, dictator like, obtrude our notions on any man. *Brown's Vulgar Errours.*

Pretences go a great way with men that take fair words, and *magisterial* looks, for current payment. *L'Estrange.*

Those men are but trapanned who are called to govern, being invested with authority, but bereaved of power; which is nothing else but to mock and betray them into a splendid and *magisterial* way of being ridiculous. *South's Serm.*

3. Chemically prepared, after the manner of a magistery.

Of corals are chiefly prepared the powder ground upon a marble, and the *magisterial* salt, to good purpose in some fevers: the tincture is no more than a solution of the *magisterial* salt. *Grew's Musæum.*

MAGISTE'RIALLY. *n. s.* [from *magisterial*.] Arrogantly; with an air of authority.

A downright advice may be mistaken, as if it were spoken *magisterially*. *Bacon's Advice to Villiers.*

Over their pots and pipes, claiming and engrossing all these wholly to themselves; *magisterially* censuring the wisdom of all antiquity, scoffing at all piety, and new modelling the world. *South's Sermons.*

MAGISTE'RIALNESS. *n. s.* [from *magisterial*.] Haughtiness; airs of a master.

Peremptoriness is of two sorts; the one a *magisterialness* in matters of opinion, the other a positiveness in relating matters of fact: in the one we impose upon mens understandings, in the other on their faith. *Government of the Tongue.*

MA'GISTERY. *n. s.* [*magisterium*, Latin.]

Magistery is a term made use of by chemists to signify sometimes a very fine powder, made by solution and precipitation; as of bismuth, lead, &c. and sometimes resins and resinous substances; as those of jalap, scamony, &c. but the most genuine acceptation is to express that preparation of any body, wherein the whole, or most part, is, by the addition of somewhat, changed into a body of quite another kind; as when iron or copper is turned into crystals of Mars or Venus. *Quincy.*

Paracelsus extracteth the *magistery* of wine, exposing it unto the extremity of cold; whereby the aqueous parts will freeze, but the spirit be uncongealed in the centre. *Brown.*

The *magistery* of vegetables consists but of the more soluble and coloured parts of the plants that afford it. *Boyle.*

MA'GISTRACY. *n. s.* [*magistratus*, Latin.] Office or dignity of a magistrate.

You share the world, her *magistracies*, priesthoods,
Wealth, and felicity, amongst you, friends. *B. Johnson.*

He had no other intention but to disswade men from *magistracy*, or undertaking the publick offices of state. *Browne.*

Some have disputed even against *magistracy* itself. *Atterbury.*

Duelling is not only an usurpation of the divine prerogative, but it is an insult upon *magistracy* and good government. *Clarissa.*

MA'GISTRALLY. *adv.* [*magistralis*, low Latin.] Despotically; authoritatively; magisterially.

What a presumption is this for one, who will not allow liberty to others, to assume to himself such a license to controul so *magistrally*. *Bishop Bramhall against Hobbes.*

MA'GISTRATE. *n. s.* [*magistratus*, Latin.] A man publickly invested with authority; a governour; an executor of the laws.

They chuse their *magistrate*!
And such a one as he, who puts his shall,
His popular shall, against a graver bench
Than ever frown'd in Greece. *Shakesp. Coriolanus.*

I treat here of those legal punishments which *magistrates* inflict upon their disobedient subjects. *Decay of Piety.*

MAGNA'LITY. *n. s.* [*magnalia*, Latin.] A great thing; something above the common rate. Not used.

Too greedy of *magnalities*, we make but favourable experiments concerning welcome truths. *Brown's Vulgar Errours.*

MAGNANI'MITY. *n. s.* [*magnanimité*, French; *magnanimus*, Latin.] Greatness of mind; bravery; elevation of soul.

With deadly hue, an armed corse did lye,
In whose dead face he read great *magnanimity*. *Fa. Qu.*

Let but the acts of the ancient Jews be but indifferently weighed, from whose *magnanimity*, in causes of most extreme hazard, those strange and unwonted resolutions have grown, which, for all circumstances, no people under the roof of heaven did ever hitherto match. *Hooker, b.* v.

They had enough reveng'd, having reduc'd
Their foe to misery beneath their fears,
The rest was *magnanimity* to remit,
If some convenient ransom was propos'd. *Milton's Agonist.*

Exploding many things under the name of trifles, is a very false proof either of wisdom or *magnanimity*, and a great check to virtuous actions with regard to fame. *Swift.*

MAGNA'NIMOUS. *adj.* [*magnanimus*, Latin.] Great of mind; elevated in sentiment; brave.

To give a kingdom hath been thought
Greater and nobler done, and to lay down
Far more *magnanimous*, than to assume. *Milton's Par. Reg.*
In strength
All mortals I excell'd, and great in hopes,
With youthful courage and *magnanimous* thoughts
Of birth from heaven foretold, and high exploits. *Milton.*

Magnanimous industry is a resolved assiduity and care, answerable to any weighty work. *Grew's Cosmol.*

MAGNA'NIMOUSLY. *adv.* [from *magnanimous.*] Bravely; with greatness of mind.

A complete and generous education fits a man to perform justly, skilfully, and *magnanimously*, all the offices of peace and war. *Milton on Education.*

MA'GNET. *n. s.* [*magnes*, Latin.] The lodestone; the stone that attracts iron.

Two *magnets*, heav'n and earth, allure to bliss,
The larger *loadstone* that, the nearer this. *Dryden.*

It may be reasonable to ask, whether obeying the *magnet* be essential to iron? *Locke.*

MAGNE'TICAL. } *adj.* [from *magnet.*]
MAGNE'TICK. }

1. Relating to the magnet.

Review this whole *magnetick* scheme. *Blackmore.*

Water is nineteen times lighter, and by consequence nineteen times rarer, than gold; and gold is so rare as very readily, and without the least opposition, to transmit the *magnetick* effluvia, and easily to admit quicksilver into its pores, and to let water pass through it. *Newton's Opticks.*

2. Having powers correspondent to those of the magnet.

The magnet acts upon iron through all dense bodies not *magnetick*, nor red hot, without any diminution of its virtue; as through gold, silver, lead, glass, water. *Newton's Opt.*

3. Attractive; having the power to draw things distant.

The moon is *magnetical* of heat, as the sun is of cold and moisture. *Bacon's Nat. Hist.*

She should all parts to reunion bow;
She, that had all *magnetick* force alone,
To draw and fasten hundred parts in one. *Donne.*
They, as they move tow'rds his all-chearing lamp,
Turn swift their various motions, or are turn'd
By his *magnetick* beam. *Milton's Par. Lost, b.* iii.

4. *Magnetick* is once used by *Milton* for *magnet.*

Draw out with credulous desire, and lead
At will the manliest, resolutest breast,
As the *magnetick* hardest iron draws. *Milton's Par. Reg.*

MA'GNETISM. *n. s.* [from *magnet.*] Power of the loadstone; power of attraction.

Many other *magnetisms*, and the like attractions through all the creatures of nature. *Brown's Vulgar Errours, b.* ii.

By the *magnetism* of interest our affections are irresistably attracted. *Glanville's Scep.*

MAGNIFI'ABLE. *adj.* [from *magnify.*] To be extolled or praised. Unusual.

Number, though wonderful in itself, and sufficiently *magnifiable* from its demonstrable affection, hath yet received adjections from the multiplying conceits of men. *Brown.*

MAGNI'FICAL. } *adj.* [*magnificus*, Latin.] Illustrious; grand;
MAGNI'FICK. } great; noble.

The house that is to be builded for the Lord must be exceeding *magnifical* of fame and glory throughout all countries. 1 *Chron.* xxii. 5.

Thrones, dominations, princedoms, virtues, pow'rs!
If these *magnifick* titles yet remain,
Not merely titular. *Milton's Par. Lost, b.* v.
O parent! these are thy *magnifick* deeds;
Thy trophies! *Milton's Par. Lost, b.* x.

MAGNI'FICENCE. *n. s.* [*magnificentia*, Lat.] Grandeur of appearance; splendour.

This desert soil
Wants not her hidden lustre, gems, and gold,
Nor want we skill or art, from whence to raise
Magnificence. *Milton's Par. Lost, b.* ii.
Not Babylon,
Nor great Alcairo, such *magnificence*
Equall'd in all their glories to inshrine
Belus or Serapis, their gods; or seat
Their kings, when Egypt with Assyria strove
In wealth and luxury. *Milton's Par. Lost, b.* i.

One may observe more splendour and *magnificence* in particular persons houses in Genoa, than in those that belong to the publick. *Addison on Italy.*

MAGNI'FICENT. *adj.* [*magnificus*, Latin.]

1. Grand in appearance; splendid; pompous.

Man he made, and for him built
Magnificent this world. *Milton's Par. Lost, b.* ix.

It is suitable to the *magnificent* harmony of the universe, that the species of creatures should, by gentle degrees, ascend upward from us toward his perfection, as we see they gradually descend from us downwards. *Locke.*

Immortal glories in my mind revive,
When Rome's exalted beauties I descry,
Magnificent in piles of ruin lie. *Addison.*

2. Fond of splendour; setting greatness to shew.

If he were *magnificent*, he spent much with an aspiring intent: if he spared, he heaped much with an aspiring intent. *Sidney, b.* ii.

MAGNI'FICENTLY. *adv.* [from *magnificent.*] Pompously; splendidly.

Beauty a monarch is,
Which kingly power *magnificently* proves,
By crouds of slaves and peopled empire's loves. *Dryden.*

We can never conceive too highly of God; so neither too *magnificently* of nature, his handy-work. *Grew's Cosmol.*

MAGNI'FICO. *n. s.* [Italian.] A grandee of Venice.

The duke himself, and the *magnificoes*
Of greatest port, have all proceeded with him. *Shakesp.*

MA'GNIFIER. *n. s.* [from *magnify.*]

1. One that praises; an encomiast; an extoller.

The primitive *magnifiers* of this star were the Egyptians, who notwithstanding chiefly regarded it in relation to their river Nilus. *Brown's Vulgar Errours, b.* iv.

2. A glass that encreases the bulk of any object.

To MA'GNIFY. *v. a.* [*magnifico*, Latin.]

1. To make great; to exaggerate; to amplify; to extol.

The ambassador, making his oration, did so *magnify* the king and queen, as was enough to glut the hearers. *Bacon.*

2. To exalt; to elevate; to raise in estimation.

Greater now in thy return,
Than from the giant-angels: thee that day
Thy thunders *magnify'd*, but to create
Is greater than created to destroy. *Milt. Par. Lost, b.* vii.

3. To raise in pride or pretension.

He shall exalt and *magnify* himself above every god. *Dan.*

If ye will *magnify* yourselves against me, know now that God hath overthrown me. *Job* xix. 5.

He shall *magnify* himself in his heart. *Dan.* viii. 25.

4. To encrease the bulk of any object to the eye.

How these red globules would appear, if glasses could be found that could *magnify* them a thousand times more, is uncertain. *Locke.*

By true reflection I would see my face?
Why brings the fool a *magnifying* glass? *Granville.*

The greatest *magnifying* glasses in the world are a man's eyes, when they look upon his own person. *Pope.*

As things seem large which we through mists descry,
Dulness is ever apt to *magnify*. *Pope's Essay on Criticism.*

5. A cant word for *to have effect.*

My governess assured my father I had wanted for nothing; that I was almost eaten up with the green-sickness: but this *magnified* but little with my father. *Spectator*, N°. 432.

MA'GNITUDE. *n. s.* [*magnitudo*, Latin.]

1. Greatness; grandeur.

With plain heroick *magnitude* of mind,
And celestial vigour arm'd,
Their armories and magazines contemns. *Milt. Agonist.*

2. Comparative bulk.

This tree hath no extraordinary *magnitude*, touching the trunk or stem; it is hard to find any one bigger than the rest. *Raleigh's Hist. of the World.*

Never repose so much upon any man's single counsel, fidelity, and discretion, in managing affairs of the first *magnitude*, that is, matters of religion and justice, as to create in yourself, or others, a diffidence of your own judgment. *K. Charles.*

When I behold this goodly frame, this world,
Of heav'n and earth consisting; and compute
Their *magnitudes*; this earth a spot, a grain,
An atom, with the firmament compar'd. *Milt. Par. Lost.*

Convince the world that you're devout and true;
Whatever be your birth, you're sure to be
A peer of the first *magnitude* to me. *Dryden's Juv.*

Conceive these particles of bodies to be so disposed amongst themselves, that the intervals of empty spaces between them may be equal in *magnitude* to them all; and that these particles may be composed of other particles much smaller, which have as much empty space between them as equals all the *magnitudes* of these smaller particles. *Newton's Opticks.*

MA'GPIE. *n. f.* [from *pie*, *pica*, Latin, and *mag*, contracted from *Margaret*, as *phil* is ufed to a *fparrow*, and *poll* to a *parrot*.] A bird fometimes taught to talk.

Augurs, that underftood relations, have
By *magpies* and by choughs, and rooks brought forth
The fecret'ft man of blood. *Shakefp. Macbeth.*

Diffimulation is expreffed by a lady wearing a vizard of two faces, in her right-hand a *magpie*, which Spenfer defcribed looking through a lattice. *Peacham on Drawing.*

So have I feen in black and white,
A prating thing, a *magpie* height,
Majeftically ftalk;
A ftately, worthlefs animal,
That plies the tongue, and wags the tail,
All flutter, pride, and talk. *Swift.*

MA'GYDARE. *n. f.* [*magudaris*, Lat.] An herb. *Ainf.*

MAID. } MAI'DEN. } *n. f.* [mæden, mæȝden, Saxon, *maegd*, Dutch.]

1. An unmarried woman; a virgin.

Your wives, your daughters,
Your matrons, and your *maids*, could not fill up
The ciftern of my luft. *Shakefpeare's Macbeth.*

This is a man old, wrinkl'd, faded, wither'd,
And not a *maiden*, as thou fay'ft he is. *Shakefpeare.*

I am not folely led
By nice direction of a *maiden*'s eyes. *Shakefpeare.*

She employed the refidue of her life to repairing of highways, building of bridges, and endowing of *maidens*. *Carew.*

Your deluded wife had been a *maid*;
Down on the bridal bed a *maid* fhe lay,
A *maid* fhe rofe at the approaching day. *Dryden's Juv.*

Let me die, fhe faid,
Rather than lofe the fpotlefs name of *maid*. *Dryden.*

2. A woman fervant.

My *maid* Neriffa and myfelf, mean time,
Will live as maids and widows. *Shakefp. Merch. of Venice.*

Old Tancred vifited his daughter's bow'r;
Her cheek, for fuch his cuftom was, he kifs'd,
Then blefs'd her kneeling, and her *maids* difmifs'd. *Dryd.*

Her clofet and the gods fhare all her time,
Except when, only by fome *maids* attended,
She feeks fome fhady folitary grove. *Rowe.*

A thoufand *maidens* ply the purple loom,
To weave the bed, and deck the regal room. *Prior.*

3. Female.

If fhe bear a *maid* child. *Lev.* xii. 5.

MAID. *n. f.* A fpecies of fkate fifh.

MA'IDEN. *adj.*

1. Confifting of virgins.

Nor was there one of all the nymphs that rov'd
O'er Mænalus, amid the *maiden* throng
More favour'd once. *Addifon's Ovid's Metamorph.*

2. Frefh; new; unufed; unpolluted.

He flefhed his *maiden* fword. *Shakefpeare.*

When I am dead, ftrew me o'er
With *maiden* flowers, that all the world may know
I was a chafte wife to my grave. *Shakefp. Henry* VIII.

By this *maiden* bloffom in my hand
I fcorn thee and thy fafhion. *Shakefp Henry* VI.

MA'IDENHAIR. *n. f.* [*maiden* and *hair*.] This plant is a native of the fouthern parts of France and in the Mediterranean, where it grows on rocks, and old ruins, from whence it is brought for medicinal ufe.

June is drawn in a mantle of dark grafs green, upon his head a garland of bents, king's-cup, and *maidenhair*. *Peach.*

MA'IDENHEAD. }
MA'IDENHODE. } *n. f.* [from *maiden*.]
MA'IDENHOOD. }

1. Virginity; virgin purity; freedom from contamination.

And, for the modeft lore of *maidenhood*,
Bids me not fojourn with thefe armed men.
Oh whither fhall I fly? what fecret wood
Shall hide me from the tyrant? or what den. *Fairfax.*

She hated chambers, clofets, fecret mewes,
And in broad fields preferv'd her *maidenhead*. *Fairfax.*

Example, that fo terrible fhews in the wreck of *maidenhood*, cannot for all that diffuade fucceffion, but that they are limed with the twigs that threaten them. *Shakefpeare.*

Maidenhood fhe loves, and will be fwift
To aid a virgin. *Milton.*

2. Newnefs; frefhnefs; uncontaminated ftate. This is now become a low word.

The devil and mifchance look big
Upon the *maidenhead* of our affairs, *Shakefp. Henry* IV.

Some who attended with much expectation, at their firft appearing have ftained the *maidenhead* of their credit with fome negligent performance. *Wotton.*

Hope's chafte kifs wrongs no joys *maidenhead*,
Then fpoufal rites prejudge the marriage-bed. *Crafhaw.*

MA'IDENLIP. *n. f.* An herb. *Ainf.*

MA'IDENLY. *adj.* [*maiden* and *like*.] Like a maid; gentle, modeft, timorous, decent.

'Tis not *maidenly*;
Our fex as well as I may chide you for it. *Shakefpeare.*

Come, you virtuous afs, and bafhful fool; muft you be blufhing? what a *maidenly* man at arms are you become? *Shakefpeare's Henry* IV. *p.* ii.

MA'IDHOOD. *n. f.* [from *maid*.] Virginity.

Cefario,
By *maidhood*, honour, and every thing,
I love thee. *Shakefpeare's Twelfth Night.*

MA'IDMARIAN. *n. f.* [*puer ludius*, Latin.] A kind of dance, fo called from a buffoon dreffed like a man, who plays tricks to the populace.

A fet of morrice-dancers danced a *maidmarian* with a tabor and pipe. *Temple.*

MA'IDPALE. *adj.* [*maid* and *pale*.] Pale like a fick virgin.

Change the complection of her *maidpale* peace
To fcarlet indignation. *Shakefp.*

MAIDSE'RVANT. *n. f.* A female fervant.

It is perfectly right what you fay of the indifference in common friends, whether we are fick or well; the very *maidfervants* in a family have the fame notion. *Swift.*

MAJE'STICAL. }
MAJE'STICK. } *adj.* [from *majefty*.]

1. Auguft; having dignity; grand; imperial; regal; great of appearance.

They made a doubt
Prefence *majeftical* would put him out:
For, quoth the king, an angel fhalt thou fee,
Yet fear not thou, but fpeak audacioufly. *Shakefpeare.*

Get the ftart of the *majeftick* world,
And bear the palm alone. *Shakefp. Julius Cæfar.*

We do it wrong, being fo *majeftical*,
To offer it the fhew of violence. *Shakefp. Hamlet.*

In his face
Sate meeknefs, heighten'd with *majeftick* grace. *Denham.*

A royal robe he wore with graceful pride,
Embroider'd fandals glitter'd as he trod,
And forth he mov'd, *majeftick* as a god. *Pope's Odyffey.*

2. Stately; pompous; fplendid.

It was no mean thing which he purpofed; to perform a work fo *majeftical* and ftately was no fmall charge. *Hooker.*

3. Sublime; elevated; lofty.

Which paffage doth not only argue an infinite abundance, both of artizans and materials, but likewife of magnificent and *majeftical* defires in every common perfon. *Wotton.*

The leaft portions muft be of the epick kind; all muft be grave, *majeftical*, and fublime. *Dryden.*

MAJE'STICALLY. *adv.* [from *majeftical*.] With dignity; with grandeur.

From Italy a wand'ring ray
Of moving light illuminates the day;
Northward fhe bends, *majeftically* bright,
And here fhe fixes her imperial light. *Granville.*

So have I feen in black and white
A prattling thing, a magpie height,
Majeftically ftalk;
A ftately, worthlefs animal,
That plies the tongue, and wags the tail,
All flutter, pride, and talk. *Swift.*

M'AJESTY. *n. f.* [*majeftas*, Latin.]

1. Dignity; grandeur; greatnefs of appearance; an appearance awful and folemn.

The voice of the Lord is full of *majefty*. *Pfal.* xxix. 4.

The Lord reigneth; he is clothed with *majefty*. *Pfal.* xciii.

Amidft
Thick clouds and dark, doth heav'n's all-ruling fire
Chufe to refide, his glory unobfcur'd,
And with the *majefty* of darknefs round
Covers his throne. *Milton's Par. Loft, b.* ii.

Great, without pride, in fober *majefty*. *Pope.*

2. Power; fovereignty.

Thine, O Lord, is the power and *majefty*. 1 *Chron.* xxix.

To the only wife God be glory and *majefty*. *Jude* v. 25.

He gave Nebuchadnezzar thy father *majefty*. *Dan.* v. 18.

3. Dignity; elevation.

The firft in loftinefs of thought furpafs'd,
The next in *majefty*. *Dryden.*

4. The title of kings and queens.

Moft royal *majefty*,
I crave no more than what your highnefs offer'd,
Nor will you tender lefs. *Shakefp. King Lear.*

I have a garden opens to the fea,
From whence I can your *majefty* convey
To fome nigh friend. *Waller.*

He, who had been always believed a creature of the queen, vifited her *majefty* but once in fix weeks. *Clarendon.*

I walk in awful ftate above
The *majefty* of heaven. *Dryden.*

MAIL. *n. f.* [*maille*, Fr. *maglia*, Italian, from *maille*, the mefh of a net. *Skinner*.] A quo fonte derivantur multa virorum nomina pr. ut *mailhir*, long or *meiler*, breich-vail clypeatus, vulgo broch-weel. Hy-vad, Howel boldly armed. *Rowland.*

1. A coat of fteel network worn for defence.

 Some

Some shirts of *mail*, some coats of plate put on,
Some don'd a curace, some a corslet bright. *Fairfax*, b. i.

Being advised to wear a privy coat, the duke gave this answer, That against any popular fury, a shirt of *mail* would be but a silly defence. *Wotton.*

Some wore coat-armour, imitating scale,
And next their skin were stubborn shirts of *mail*;
Some wore a breast-plate. *Dryden's Knight's Tale.*

2. Any armour.

We stript the lobster of his scarlet *mail.* *Gay.*

3. A postman's bundle; a bag. [*male*, *malette*, French.]

To Mail. *v. a.* [from the noun.] To arm defensively; to cover, as with armour.

The *mailed* Mars shall on his altar sit
Up to the ears in blood. *Shakesp. Henry* IV. *p.* i.

I am thy married wife,
And thou a prince, protector of this land;
Methinks I should not thus be led along,
Mail'd up in shame, with papers on my back. *Shakesp.*

To MAIM. *v. a.* [*maitan*, Gothick, to cut off; *mehaigner*, to maim, old French; *mehaina*, Armorick; *mancus*, Lat.] To deprive of any necessary part; to cripple by loss of a limb.

You wrought to be a legate; by which power
You *maim'd* the jurisdiction of all bishops. *Shakespeare.*

The multitude wondered when they saw the dumb to speak, the *maimed* to be whole, and the lame to walk; and they glorified God. *Matth.* xv. 31.

Maim. *n. s.* [from the verb.]

1. Privation of some essential part; lameness, produced by a wound or amputation.

Surely there is more cause to fear, least the want thereof be a *maim*, than the use a blemish. *Hooker*, *b.* v.

Humphry, duke of Glo'ster, scarce himself,
That bears so shrewd a *maim*; two pulls at once;
A lady banish'd, and a limb lopt off? *Shakesp. Henry* VI.

2. Injury; mischief.

Not so deep a *maim*,
As to be cast forth in the common air,
Have I deserved. *Shakesp. Rich.* II.

3. Essential defect.

A noble author esteems it to be a *maim* in history, that the acts of parliament should not be recited. *Hayward.*

Main. *adj.* [*magne*, old French; *magnus*, Latin.]

1. Principal; chief; leading.

In every grand or *main* publick duty which God requireth at the hands of his church, there is, besides that matter and form wherein the essence thereof consisteth, a certain outward fashion, whereby the same is in decent manner administered. *Hooker*, *b.* iv.

There is a history in all mens lives,
Figuring the nature of the times deceased;
The which observ'd a man may prophesy,
With a near aim, of the *main* chance of things
As yet not come to life. *Shakesp. Henry* IV.

He is superstitious grown of late,
Quite from the *main* opinion he had once
Of fantasy, of dreams, and ceremonies. *Shakespeare.*

There arose three notorious and *main* rebellions, which drew several armies out of England. *Davies on Ireland.*

The nether flood,
Which now divided into four *main* streams,
Runs diverse. *Milton's Par. Lost*, *b.* iv.

I should be much for open war, O peers,
If what was urg'd
Main reason to persuade immediate war,
Did not dissuade me most. *Milton's Par. Lost*, *b.* ii.

All creatures look to the *main* chance, that is, food and propagation. *L'Estrange's Fables.*

Our *main* interest is to be as happy as we can, and as long as possible. *Tillotson's Sermons.*

Nor tell me in a dying father's tone,
Be careful still of the *main* chance, my son;
Put out the principal in trusty hands;
Live on the use, and never dip thy lands. *Dryden's Pers.*

Whilst they have busied themselves in various learning, they have been wanting in the one *main* thing. *Baker.*

Nor is it only in the *main* design, but they have followed him in every episode. *Pope's Pref. to the Iliad.*

2. Violent; strong; overpowering; vast.

Think, you question with a Jew.
You may as well go stand upon the beach,
And bid the *main* flood bate his usual height. *Shakesp.*

Seest thou what rage
Transports our adversary, whom no bounds,
Nor yet the *main* abyss,
Wide interrupt, can hold? *Milton's Par. Lost*, *b.* iii.

3. Gross; containing the chief part.

We ourself will follow
In the *main* battle, which on either side
Shall be well winged with our chiefest horse. *Shakespeare.*

All abreast
Charg'd our *main* battle's front. *Shakesp. Henry* VI.

4. Important; forcible.

This young prince, with a train of young noblemen and gentlemen, but not with any *main* army, came over to take possession of his new patrimony. *Davies on Ireland.*

That, which thou aright
Believ'st so *main* to our success, I bring. *Milt. Par. Lost.*

Main. *n. s.*

1. The gross; the bulk; the greater part.

The *main* of them may be reduced to language, and an improvement in wisdom, by seeing men. *Locke.*

2. The sum; the whole; the general.

They allowed the liturgy and government of the church of England as to the *main.* *King Charles.*

These notions concerning coinage have, for the *main*, been put into writing above twelve months. *Locke.*

3. The ocean.

A substitute shines brightly as a king,
Until a king be by; and then his state
Empties itself, as doth an inland brook
Into the *main* of waters. *Shakesp. Merchant of Venice.*

Where's the king?
Bids the wind blow the earth into the sea;
Or swell the curled waters 'bove the *main*,
That things might change. *Shakespeare's King Lear.*

He fell, and struggling in the *main*,
Cry'd out for helping hands, but cry'd in vain. *Dryden.*

Say, why should the collected *main*
Itself within itself contain?
Why to its caverns should it sometimes creep,
And with delighted silence sleep
On the lov'd bosom of its parent deep? *Prior.*

4. Violence; force.

He 'gan advance
With huge force, and insupportable *main*,
And towards him with dreadful fury prance. *Fa. Qu.*

With might and *main*
He hasted to get up again. *Hudibras*, *p.* i.

With might and *main* they chac'd the murd'rous fox,
With brazen trumpets, and inflated box. *Dryden.*

5. [From *manus*, Latin.] A hand at dice.

Were it good,
To set the exact wealth of all our states
All at one cast; to set so rich a *main*
In the nice hazard of one doubtful hour. *Shakespeare.*

To pass our tedious hours away,
We throw a merry *main.* *Earl Dorset's Song.*

Writing is but just like dice,
And lucky *mains* make people wise:
That jumbled words, if fortune throw them,
Shall, well as Dryden, form a poem. *Prior.*

6. The continent.

In 1589 we turned challengers, and invaded the *main* of Spain. *Bacon's War with Spain.*

7. A hamper. *Ains.*

Ma'inland. *n. s.* [*main* and *land.*] Continent.

Ne was it island then, ne was it pays'd
Amid the ocean waves,
But was all desolate, and of some thought,
By sea to have been from the Celtick *mainland* brought. *Fairy Queen*, *b.* ii.

Those whom Tyber's holy forests hide,
Or Circe's hills from the *mainland* divide. *Dryden's Æn.*

Ma'inly. *adv.* [from *main.*]

1. Chiefly; principally.

A brutish vice,
Inductive *mainly* to the sin of Eve. *Milton's Par. Lost.*

They are *mainly* reducible to three. *More.*

The metallick matter now found in the perpendicular intervals of the strata, was originally lodged in the bodies of those strata, being interspersed amongst the matter, whereof the said strata *mainly* consist. *Woodward's Nat. Hist.*

2. Greatly; powerfully.

It was observed by one, that himself came hardly to a little riches, and very easily to great riches: for when a man's stock is come to that, that he can expect the prime of markets, and overcome those bargains, which, for their greatness, are few mens money, and be partner in the industries of younger men, he cannot but increase *mainly.* *Bacon.*

Ma'inmast. *n. s.* [*main* and *mast.*] The chief or middle mast.

One dire shot,
Close by the board the prince's *mainmast* bore. *Dryden.*

A Dutchman, upon breaking his leg by a fall from a *mainmast*, told the standers by, it was a mercy it was not his neck. *Spectator*, N°. 574.

Ma'inpernable. *adj.* Bailable; that may be admitted to give surety.

MA'INPERNOR. *n. s.* Surety; bail.

He enforced the earl himself to fly, till twenty-six noblemen became *mainpernors* for his appearance at a certain day; but he making default, the uttermost advantage was taken against his sureties. *Davies on Ireland.*

MA'INPRISE. *n. s.* [*main* and *pris*, French.] Delivery into the custody of a friend, upon security given for appearance; bail.

Sir William Bremingham was executed for treason, though the earl of Desmond was left to *mainprize.* *Davies.*

Give its poor entertainer quarter;
And, by discharge or *mainprise*, grant
Deliv'ry from this base restraint. *Hudibras, p.* ii.

To MA'INPRISE. *v. a.* To bail.

MA'INSAIL. *n. s.* [*main* and *sail.*] The sail of the mainmast.

They committed themselves unto the sea, and hoisted up the *mainsail* to the wind, and made toward shore. *Acts* xxvii.

MA'INSHEET. *n. s.* [*main* and *sheet.*] The sheet or sail of the mainmast.

Strike, strike the top-sail; let the *mainsheet* fly,
And furl your sails. *Dryden.*

MA'INYARD. *n. s.* [*main* and *yard.*] The yard of the mainmast.

With sharp hooks they took hold of the tackling which held the *mainyard* to the mast, then rowing they cut the tackling, and brought the *mainyard* by the board. *Arbuthnot.*

To MAINTA'IN. *v. a.* [*maintenir*, French.]

1. To preserve; to keep.

The ingredients being prescribed in their substance, *maintain* the blood in a gentle fermentation, reclude oppilations, and mundify it. *Harvey.*

This place, these pledges of your love, *maintain.* *Dryd.*

2. To defend; to hold out; to make good.

God values no man more or less, in placing him high or low, but every one as he *maintains* his post. *Grew's Cosmol.*

3. To vindicate; to justify.

If any man of quality will *maintain* upon Edward earl of Glo'ster, that he is a manifold traitor, let him appear. *Shak.*

These possessions being unlawfully gotten, could not be *maintained* by the just and honourable law of England. *Davies.*

Maintain
My right, nor think the name of mother vain. *Dryden.*

Lord Roberts was full of contradiction in his temper, and of parts so much superior to any in the company, that he could too well *maintain* and justify those contradictions. *Clarendon.*

It is hard to *maintain* the truth. *South.*

4. To continue; to keep up.

Maintain talk with the duke, that my charity be not of him perceived. *Shakespeare's King Lear.*

Some did the song, and some the choir *maintain*,
Beneath a laurel shade. *Dryden.*

5. To keep up; to support the expence of.

I seek not to wax great by others waining;
Sufficeth, that I have *maintains* my state,
And sends the poor well pleased from my gate. *Shakesp.*

What concerns it you if I wear pearl and gold? I thank my good father I am able to *maintain* it. *Shakespeare.*

6. To support with the conveniences of life.

It was St. Paul's choice to *maintain* himself by his own labour. *Hooker.*

If a woman *maintain* her husband, she is full of anger and much reproach. *Ecclus.* xxv. 22.

It is hard to maintain the truth, but much harder to be *maintained* by it. Could it ever yet feed, cloath, or defend its assertors? *South.*

7. To preserve from failure.

Here ten thousand images remain
Without confusion, and their rank *maintain.* *Blackmore.*

To MAINTA'IN. *v. n.* To support by argument; to assert as a tenet.

In tragedy and satire I *maintain* against some of our modern criticks, that this age and the last have excelled the ancients. *Dryden's Juvenal.*

MAINTA'INABLE. *adj.* [from *maintain.*] Defensible; justifiable.

Being made lord lieutenant of Bulloine, the walls sore beaten and shaken, and scarce *maintainable*, he defended the place against the dauphin. *Hayward.*

MAINTA'INER. *n. s.* [from *maintain.*] Supporter; cherisher.

He dedicated the work to Sir Philip Sidney, a special *maintainer* of all learning. *Spenser's Pastorals.*

The *maintainers* and cherishers of a regular devotion, a true and decent piety. *South's Sermons.*

MA'INTENANCE. *n. s.* [*maintenant*, French.]

1. Supply of the necessaries of life; sustenance; sustentation.

It was St. Paul's own choice to maintain himself by his labour, whereas in living by the churches *maintenance*, as others did, there had been no offence committed. *Hooker, b.* i.

God assigned Adam *maintenance* of life, and then appointed him a law to observe. *Hooker, b.* i.

Those of better fortune not making learning their *maintenance*, take degrees with little improvement. *Swift.*

2. Support; protection; defence.

They knew that no man might in reason take upon him to determine his own right, and according to his own determination proceed in *maintenance* thereof. *Hooker, b.* i.

The beginning and cause of this ordinance amongst the Irish was for the defence and *maintenance* of their lands in their posterity. *Spenser on Ireland.*

3. Continuance; security from failure.

Whatsoever is granted to the church for God's honour, and the *maintenance* of his service, is granted for and to God. *South's Sermons.*

MA'INTOP. *n. s.* [*main* and *top.*] The top of the mainmast.

From their *maintop* joyful news they hear
Of ships, which by their mould bring new supplies. *Dryd.*

Dictys could the *maintop*-mast bestride,
And down the ropes with active vigour slide. *Addison.*

MA'JOR. *adj.* [*major*, Latin.]

1. Greater in number, quantity, or extent.

They bind none, no not though they be many, saving only when they are the *major* part of a general assembly, and then their voices being more in number, must oversway their judgments who are fewer. *Hooker, b.* iv.

The true meridian is a *major* circle passing through the poles of the world and the zenith of any place, exactly dividing the east from the west. *Brown's Vulg. Errours.*

In common discourse we denominate persons and things according to the *major* part of their character: he is to be called a wise man who has but few follies. *Watts's Logick.*

2. Greater in dignity.

Fall Greek, fall fame, honour, or go, or stay,
My *major* vow lies here. *Shakesp. Troil. and Cressida.*

MA'JOR. *n. s.*

1. The officer above the captain; the lowest field officer.

2. A mayor or head officer of a town. Obsolete.

3. The first proposition of a syllogism, containing some generality.

The *major* of our author's argument is to be understood of the material ingredients of bodies. *Boyle.*

4. MAJOR-*general.* The general officer of the second rank.

Major-general Ravignan returned with the French king's answer. *Tatler*, N°. 53.

5. MAJOR-*domo. n. s.* [*majeur-dome*, French.] One who holds occasionally the place of master of the house.

MAJORA'TION. *n. s.* [from *major.*] Encrease; enlargement.

There be five ways of *majoration* of sounds: enclosure simple; enclosure with dilatation; communication; reflection concurrent; and approach to the sensory. *Bacon's Nat. Hist.*

MAJO'RITY. *n. s.* [from *major.*]

1. The state of being greater.

It is not plurality of parts without *majority* of parts that maketh the total greater. *Grew's Cosmol.*

2. The greater number. [*majorité*, French.]

It was highly probable the *majority* would be so wise as to espouse that cause which was most agreeable to the publick weal, and by that means hinder a sedition. *Addison.*

As in senates so in schools,
Majority of voices rules. *Prior.*

Decent executions keep the world in awe; for that reason the *majority* of mankind ought to be hanged every year. *Arbuthnot's Hist. of J. Bull.*

3. [From *majores*, Latin.] Ancestry.

Of evil parents an evil generation, a posterity not unlike their *majority*; of mischievous progenitors, a venemous and destructive progeny. *Brown's Vulgar Errours, b.* iii.

4. Full age; end of minority.

During the infancy of Henry the IIId, the barons were troubled in expelling the French: but this prince was no sooner come to his *majority*, but the barons raised a cruel war against him. *Davies on Ireland.*

5. First rank. Obsolete.

Douglas, whose high deeds,
Whose hot incursions, and great name in arms,
Holds from all soldiers chief *majority*,
And military title capital. *Shakesp. Henry* IV.

6. The office of a major.

MAIZE, or *Indian Wheat. n. s.*

The whole *maize* plant has the appearance of a reed; the male flowers are produced at remote distances from the fruit on the same plant, growing generally in a spike upon the top of the stalk; the female flowers are produced from the wings of the leaves, and are surrounded by three or four leaves, which closely adhere to the fruit until it is ripe: this plant is propagated in England only as a curiosity, but in America it is the principal support of the inhabitants, and consequently propagated with great care. *Miller.*

Maize affords a very strong nourishment, but more viscous than wheat. *Arbuthnot on Aliments.*

To Make. *v. a.* [macan, Saxon; *machen*, German; *maken*, Dutch.]

1. To create.

Let us *make* man in our image. *Gen.* i. 26.

The Lord hath *made* all things for himſelf. *Prov.* xvi. 4.

Remember'ſt thou
Thy *making*, while the maker gave thee being. *Milton.*

2. To form of materials.

He faſhioned it with a graving tool, after he had *made* it a molten calf. *Exod.* xxxii. 4.

God hath *made* of one blood all nations of men. *Acts.*

We have no other meaſure, ſave one of the moon, but are artificially *made* out of theſe by compounding or dividing them. *Holder on Time.*

3. To compoſe: as, materials or ingredients.

One of my fellows had the ſpeed of him;
Who, almoſt dead for breath, had ſcarcely more
Than would *make* up his meſſage. *Shakeſp. Macbeth.*

The heav'n, the air, the earth, and boundleſs ſea,
Make but one temple for the deity. *Waller.*

A pint of ſalt of tartar, expoſed unto a moiſt air, will *make* far more liquor than the former meaſure will contain. *Brown's Vulgar Errours, b.* ii.

4. To form by art what is not natural.

There laviſh nature, in her beſt attire,
Pours forth ſweet odours, and alluring ſights;
And art with her contending, doth aſpire
T' excel the natural with *made* delights. *Spenſer.*

5. To produce as the agent.

She may give ſo much credit to her own laws, as to *make* their ſentence weighter than any bare and naked conceit to the contrary. *Hooker, b.* v.

If I ſuſpect without cauſe, why then *make* ſport at me; then let me be your jeſt. *Shakeſp. Merry Wives of Windſor.*

Thine enemies *make* a tumult. *Pſal.* lxxxiii. 2.

When their hearts were merry they ſaid, Call for Sampſon, that he may *make* us ſport. *Judg.* xvi. 25.

Give unto Solomon a perfect heart to build the palace for the which I have *made* proviſion. 1 *Chron.* xxix. 19.

Why *make* ye this ado, and weep? the damſel is not dead. *Mark* v. 39.

He *maketh* interceſſion to God againſt Iſrael. *Rom.* xi. 2.

Thou haſt ſet ſigns and wonders in the land of Egypt, and haſt *made* thee a name. *Jer.* xxxii. 20.

Should we then *make* mirth? *Ezek.* xxi. 10.

Joſhua *made* peace, and *made* a league with them to let them live. *Joſh.* ix. 15.

Both combine
To *make* their greatneſs by the fall of man. *Dryden.*

Egypt, mad with ſuperſtition grown,
Makes gods of monſters. *Tate's Juvenal.*

6. To produce as a cauſe.

Wealth *maketh* many friends; but the poor is ſeparated from his neighbour. *Prov.* xix. 4.

A man's gift *maketh* room for him, and bringeth him before great men. *Prov.* xviii. 16.

The child who is taught to believe any occurrence to be a good or evil omen, or any day of the week lucky, hath a wide inroad *made* upon the ſoundneſs of his underſtanding. *Watts.*

7. To do; to perform; to practiſe; to uſe.

Though ſhe appear honeſt to me, yet in other places ſhe enlargeth her mirth ſo far, that there is ſhrewd conſtruction *made* of her. *Shakeſp. Merry Wives of Windſor.*

She *made* haſte, and let down her pitcher. *Gen.* xxiv. 46.

Thou haſt *made* an atonement for it. *Exod.* xxix. 36.

I will judge his houſe for ever, becauſe his ſons *made* themſelves vile, and he reſtrained them not. 1 *Sam.* iii. 13.

We *made* prayer unto our God. *Neh.* iv. 9.

He ſhall *make* a ſpeedy riddance of all in the land. *Zeph.*

They all began to *make* excuſe. *Luke* xiv. 18.

It hath pleaſed them of Macedonia and Achaia to *make* a certain contribution for the poor. *Rom.* xv. 26.

Make full proof of thy miniſtry. 2 *Tim.* iv. 5.

The Venetians, provoked by the Turks with divers injuries, both by ſea and land, reſolved, without delay, to *make* war likewiſe upon him. *Knolles's Hiſt. of the Turks.*

Such muſick as before was never *made*,
But when of old the ſons of morning ſung. *Milton.*

All the actions of his life were ripped up and ſurveyed, and all malicious gloſſes *made* upon all he had ſaid, and all he had done. *Clarendon.*

Says Carneades, ſince neither you nor I love repetitions, I ſhall not now *make* any of what elſe was urged againſt Themiſtius. *Boyle.*

The Phœnicians *made* claim to this man as theirs, and attributed to him the invention of letters. *Hale.*

What hope, O Pantheus! whether can we run?
Where *make* a ſtand? and what may yet be done? *Dryd.*

While merchants *make* long voyages by ſea
To get eſtates, he cuts a ſhorter way. *Dryden's Juv.*

To what end did Ulyſſes *make* that journey? Æneas undertook it by the expreſs commandment of his father's ghoſt. *Dryden's Dedication to the Æneis.*

He that will *make* a good uſe of any part of his life, muſt allow a large portion of it to recreation. *Locke.*

Make ſome requeſt, and I,
Whate'er it be, with that requeſt comply. *Addiſon.*

Were it permitted, he ſhould *make* the tour of the whole ſyſtem of the ſun. *Arbuthnot and Pope's Mart. Scrib.*

8. To cauſe to have any quality.

I will *make* your cities waſte. *Lev.* xxvi. 31.

Her huſband hath utterly *made* them void on the day he heard them. *Num.* xxx. 12.

When he had made a convenient room, he ſet it in a wall, and *made* it faſt with iron. *Wiſd.* xiii. 15.

Jeſus came into Cana, where he *made* the water wine. *John* iv. 46.

He was the more inflamed with the deſire of battle with Waller, to *make* even all accounts. *Clarendon, b.* viii.

I bred you up to arms, rais'd you to power,
Permitted you to fight for this uſurper;
All to *make* ſure the vengeance of this day,
Which even this day has ruin'd. *Dryden's Spaniſh Fryar.*

In reſpect of actions within the reach of ſuch a power in him, a man ſeems as free as it is poſſible for freedom to *make* him. *Locke.*

9. To bring into any ſtate or condition.

I have *made* thee a god to Pharaoh. *Exod.* vii. 1.

Joſeph *made* ready his chariot, and went up to meet Iſrael. *Gen.* xlvi. 29.

Who *made* thee a prince and a judge over us? *Exod.* ii.

Ye have troubled me to *make* me to ſtink among the inhabitants. *Gen.* xxxiv. 30.

He *made* himſelf of no reputation, and took upon him the form of a ſervant. *Phil.* ii. 7.

He ſhould be *made* manifeſt to Iſrael. *John* i. 31.

Though I be free from all men, yet have I *made* myſelf ſervant unto all, that I might gain the more. 1 *Cor.* ix. 19.

He hath *made* me a by-word of the people, and aforetime I was as a tabret. *Job* xvii. 6.

Make ye him drunken; for he magnified himſelf againſt the Lord. *Jer.* xlviii. 26.

Joſeph was not willing to *make* her a publick example. *Matt.* i. 19.

By the aſſiſtance of this faculty we have all thoſe ideas in our underſtandings, which, though we do not actually contemplate, yet we can bring in ſight, and *make* appear again, and be the objects of our thoughts. *Locke.*

The Lacedemonians trained up their children to hate drunkenneſs by bringing a drunken man into their company, and ſhewing them what a beaſt he *made* of himſelf. *Watts.*

10. To form; to ſettle.

Thoſe who are wiſe in courts
Make friendſhips with the miniſters of ſtate,
Nor ſeek the ruins of a wretched exile. *Rowe.*

11. To hold; to keep.

Deep in a cave the ſybil *makes* abode. *Dryden.*

12. To ſecure from diſtreſs; to eſtabliſh in riches or happineſs.

He hath given her his monumental ring, and thinks himſelf *made* in the unchaſte compoſition. *Shakeſpeare.*

This is the night,
That either *makes* me, or foredoes me quite. *Shakeſp.*

Each element his dread command obeys,
Who *makes* or ruins with a ſmile or frown,
Who as by one he did our nation raiſe,
So now he with another pulls us down. *Dryden.*

13. To ſuffer; to incur.

The loſs was private that I *made*;
'Twas but myſelf I loſt; I loſt no legions. *Dryden.*

He accuſeth Neptune unjuſtly, who *makes* ſhipwreck a ſecond time. *Bacon.*

14. To commit.

She was in his company at Page's houſe, and what they *made* there I know not. *Shakeſpeare.*

I will neither plead my age nor ſickneſs in excuſe of the faults which I have *made*. *Dryden.*

15. To compel; to force; to conſtrain.

That the ſoul in a ſleeping man ſhould be this moment buſy a thinking, and the next moment in a waking man not remember thoſe thoughts, would need ſome better proof than bare aſſertion to *make* it be believed. *Locke.*

They ſhould be *made* to riſe at their early hour; but great care ſhould be taken in waking them, that it be not done haſtily. *Locke.*

16. To intend; to purpoſe to do.

He may aſk this civil queſtion, friend!
What doſt thou *make* a ſhipboard? to what end? *Dryden.*

Gomez; what *mak'ſt* thou here with a whole brotherhood of city-bailiffs? *Dryden's Spaniſh Fryar.*

17. To raiſe as profit from any thing.

He's in for a commodity of brown pepper; of which he *made* five marks ready money. *Shakeſpeare.*

Did

Did I *make* a gain of you by any of them I sent. 2 *Cor.*

If Auletes, who was a negligent prince, *made* so much, what must now the Romans *make*, who govern it so wisely. *Arbuthnot on Coins.*

If it is meant of the value of the purchase, it was very high; it being hardly possible to *make* so much of land, unless it was reckoned at a very low price. *Arbuthnot.*

18. To reach; to tend to; to arrive at.

Acosta recordeth, they that sail in the middle can *make* no land of either side. *Brown's Vulgar Errours, b.* vi.

I've *made* the port already,
And laugh securely at the lazy storm. *Dryden.*

They ply their shatter'd oars
To nearest land, and *make* the Libyan shoars. *Dryden.*

Did I but purpose to embark with thee,
While gentle zephyrs play in prosp'rous gales;
But would forsake the ship, and *make* the shoar,
When the winds whistle, and the tempests roar? *Prior.*

19. To gain.

The wind came about, and settled in the west for many days, so as we could *make* little or no way. *Bacon.*

I have *made* way
To some Philistian lords, with whom to treat. *Milton.*

Now mark a little why Virgil is so much concerned to make this marriage, it was to *make* way for the divorce which he intended afterwards. *Dryden's Æn.*

20. To force; to gain by force.

Rugged rocks are interpos'd in vain;
He *makes* his way o'er mountains, and contemns
Unruly torrents, and unforded streams. *Dryden's Virg.*

The stone wall which divides China from Tartary, is reckoned nine hundred miles long, running over rocks, and *making* way for rivers through mighty arches. *Temple.*

21. To exhibit.

When thou *makest* a dinner, call not thy friends but the poor. *Luke* xiv. 12.

22. To pay; to give.

He shall *make* amends for the harm that he hath done. *Lev.*

23. To put; to place.

You must *make* a great difference between Hercules's labours by land, and Jason's voyage by sea for the golden fleece. *Bacon's War with Spain.*

24. To turn to some use.

Whate'er they catch,
Their fury *makes* an instrument of war. *Dryden's Æn.*

25. To incline; to dispose.

It is not requisite they should destroy our reason, that is, to *make* us rely on the strength of nature, when she is least able to relieve us. *Brown's Vulgar Errours, b.* iv.

26. To prove as an argument.

Seeing they judge this to *make* nothing in the world for them. *Hooker, b.* ii.

You conceive you have no more to do than, having found the principal word in a concordance, introduce as much of the verse as will serve your turn, though in reality it *makes* nothing for you. *Swift.*

27. To represent; to show.

He is not that goose and ass that Valla would *make* him. *Baker's Reflections on Learning.*

28. To constitute.

Our desires carry the mind out to absent good, according to the necessity which we think there is of it, to the *making* or encrease of our happiness. *Locke.*

29. To amount to.

Whatsoever they were, it *maketh* no matter to me: God accepteth no man's person. *Gal.* ii. 16.

30. To mould; to form.

Lye not erect but hollow, which is in the *making* of the bed; or with the legs gathered up, which is the more wholesome. *Bacon's Nat. Hist.*

Some undeserved fault
I'll find about the *making* of the bed. *Shakespeare.*

They mow fern green, and burning of them to ashes, *make* the ashes up into balls with a little water. *Mortimer.*

31. *To* MAKE *away*. To kill; to destroy.

He will not let slip any advantage to *make away* him whose just title, enobled by courage and goodness, may one day shake the seat of a never-secure tyranny. *Sidney, b.* ii.

The duke of Clarence, lieutenant of Ireland, was, by practice of evil persons about the king his brother, called thence away, and soon after, by sinister means, was clean *made away*. *Spenser on Ireland.*

He may have a likely guess,
How these were they that *made away* his brother. *Shakesp.*

Trajan would say of the vain jealousy of princes that seek to *make away* those that aspire to their succession, that there was never king that did put to death his successor. *Bacon.*

My mother I slew at my very birth, and since have *made away* two of her brothers, and happily to make way for the purposes of others against myself. *Hayward.*

Give poets leave to *make* themselves *away*. *Roscommon.*

What multitude of infants have been *made away* by those who brought them into the world. *Addison.*

32. *To* MAKE *away*. To transfer.

Debtors,
When they never mean to pay,
To some friend *make* all *away*. *Waller.*

33. *To* MAKE *account*. To reckon; to believe.

They *made* no *account* but that the navy should be absolutely master of the seas. *Bacon's War with Spain.*

34. *To* MAKE *account of*. To esteem; to regard.

35. *To* MAKE *free with*. To treat without ceremony.

The same who have *made free with* the greatest names in church and state, and exposed to the world the private misfortunes of families. *Dunciad.*

36. *To* MAKE *good*. To maintain; to defend; to justify.

The grand master, guarded with a company of most valiant knights, drove them out again by force, and *made good* the place. *Knolles's Hist. of the Turks.*

When he comes to *make good* his confident undertaking, he is fain to say things that agree very little with one another. *Boyle.*

I'll either die, or I'll *make good* the place. *Dryden.*

As for this other argument, that by pursuing one single theme they gain an advantage to express, and work up, the passions, I wish any example he could bring from them could *make* it *good*. *Dryden on dramatick Poesy.*

I will add what the same author subjoins to *make good* his foregoing remark. *Locke on Education.*

37. *To* MAKE *good*. To fulfil; to accomplish.

This letter doth *make good* the friar's words. *Shakesp.*

38. *To* MAKE *light of*. To consider as of no consequence.

They *made light of* it, and went their ways. *Matt.* xxii. 5.

39. *To* MAKE *love*. To court; to play the gallant.

How happy each of the sexes would be, if there was a window in the breast of every one that *makes* or receives *love*. *Addison's Guardian*, N. 106.

40. *To* MAKE *merry*. To feast; to partake of an entertainment.

A hundred pound or two, to *make merry* withal? *Shakesp.*

The king, to make demonstration to the world, that the proceedings against Sir William Stanley, imposed upon him by necessity of state, had not diminished the affection he bare to his brother, went to Latham, to *make merry* with his mother and the earl. *Bacon's Henry* VIIth.

A gentleman and his wife will ride to *make merry* with his neighbour, and after a day those two go to a third; in which progress they encrease like snowballs, till through their burthensome weight they break. *Carew's Survey of Cornwall.*

41. *To* MAKE *much of*. To cherish; to foster.

The king hearing of their adventure, suddenly falls to take pride in *making much of* them, extolling them with infinite praises. *Sidney, b.* ii.

The bird is dead
That we have *made* so *much on!* *Shakesp. Cymbeline.*

It is good discretion not to *make* too *much of* any man at the first. *Bacon's Essays.*

The easy and the lazy *make much of* the gout; and yet *making much of* themselves too, they take care to carry it presently to bed, and keep it warm. *Temple.*

42. *To* MAKE *of*. *What to make of*, is, how to understand.

That they should have knowledge of the languages and affairs of those that lie at such a distance from them, was a thing we could not tell what to *make of*. *Bacon.*

I past the summer here at Nimmeguen, without the least remembrance of what had happened to me in the spring, till about the end of September, and then I began to feel a pain I knew not what to *make of*, in the same joint of my other foot. *Temple.*

There is another statue in brass of Apollo, with a modern inscription on the pedestal, which I know not what to *make of*. *Addison on Italy.*

I desired he would let me see his book: he did so, smiling: I could not *make* any thing *of* it. *Tatler.*

Upon one side of the pillar were huge pieces of iron sticking out, cut into strange figures, which we knew not what to *make of*. *Gulliver's Travels.*

43. *To* MAKE *of*. To produce from; to effect.

I am astonished, that those who have appeared against this paper have *made* so very little *of* it. *Addison.*

44. *To* MAKE *of*. To consider; to account; to esteem.

Makes she no more *of* me than of a slave? *Dryden.*

45. *To* MAKE *of*. To cherish; to foster.

Xaycus was wonderfully beloved, and *made of*, by the Turkish merchants, whose language he had learned. *Knolles.*

46. *To* MAKE *over*. To settle in the hands of trustees.

Widows, who have tried one lover,
Trust none again till th' have *made over*. *Hudibras, p.* iii.

The wise betimes *make over* their estates.
Make o'er thy honour by a deed of trust,
And give me seizure of the mighty wealth. *Dryden.*

47. *To* MAKE *over.* To transfer.

The second mercy *made over* to us by the second covenant, is the promise of pardon. *Hammond.*

Age and youth cannot be *made over*: nothing but time can take away years, or give them. *Collier.*

My waist is reduced to the depth of four inches by what I have already *made over* to my neck. *Addison's Guard.*

Moor, to whom that patent was *made over*, was forced to leave off coining. *Swift.*

48. *To* MAKE *out.* To clear; to explain; to clear to one's self.

Make out the rest,—I am disorder'd so,
I know not farther what to say or do. *Dryd. Indian Emp.*

Antiquaries *make out* the most ancient medals from a letter with great difficulty to be discerned upon the face and reverse. *Felton on the Classicks.*

It may seem somewhat difficult to *make out* the bills of fare for some suppers. *Arbuthnot on Coins.*

49. *To* MAKE *out.* To prove; to evince.

There is no truth which a man may more evidently *make out* to himself, than the existence of a God. *Locke.*

Though they are not self-evident principles, yet what may be *made out* from them by a wary deduction, may be depended on as certain and infallible truths. *Locke.*

Men of wit and parts, but of short thoughts and little meditation, are apt to distrust every thing for fiction that is not the dictate of sense, or *made out* immediately to their senses. *Burnet's Theory of the Earth.*

We are to vindicate the just providence of God in the government of the world, and to endeavour, as well as we can, upon an imperfect view of things, to *make out* the beauty and harmony of all the seeming discords and irregularities of the divine administration. *Tillotson's Sermons.*

Scaliger hath *made out*, that the history of Troy was no more the invention of Homer than of Virgil. *Dryden.*

In the passages from our own d... of the reasonings which *make out* both my propositions are already suggested. *Atterbury's Sermons.*

I dare engage to *make* it *out*, that, instead of contributing equal to the landed men, they will have their full principal and interest at six per Cent. *Swift's Miscel.*

50. *To* MAKE *sure of.* To consider as certain.

They *made* as *sure of* health and life, as if both of them were at their dispose. *Dryden.*

51. *To* MAKE *sure of.* To secure to one's possession.

But whether marriage bring joy or sorrow,
Make sure of this day, and hang to-morrow. *Dryden.*

52. *To* MAKE *up.* To get together.

How will the farmer be able to *make up* his rent at quarter-day? *Locke.*

53. *To* MAKE *up.* To reconcile; to repair.

This kind of comprehension in scripture being therefore received, still there is no doubt how far we are to proceed by collection before the full and complete measure of things necessary be *made up*. *Hooker, b.* i.

I knew when seven justices could not *make up* a quarrel. *Shakespeare's As you like it.*

54. *To* MAKE *up.* To repair.

I sought for a man among them that should *make up* the hedge, and stand in the gap before me for the land. *Ezek.*

55. To compose, as of ingredients.

These are the lineaments of this vice of flattery, which sure do together *make up* a face of most extreme deformity. *Government of the Tongue.*

He is to encounter an enemy *made up* of wiles and stratagems; an old serpent, and a long experienced deceiver. *South's Sermons.*

Zeal should be *made up* of the largest measures of spiritual love, desire, hope, hatred, grief, indignation. *Sprat.*

Oh he was all *made up* of love and charms;
Whatever maid could wish, or man admire. *Addison.*

Harlequin's part is *made up* of blunders and absurdities. *Addison's Remarks on Italy.*

Vines, figs, oranges, almonds, olives, myrtles, and fields of corn, *make up* the most delightful little landskip imaginable. *Addison on Italy.*

Old mould'ring urns, racks, daggers, and distress,
Make up the frightful horror of the place. *Garth.*

The parties among us are *made up* on one side of moderate whigs, and on the other of presbyterians. *Swift.*

56. *To* MAKE *up.* To shape.

A catapotium is a medicine swallowed solid, and most commonly *made up* in pills. *Arbuthnot on Coins.*

57. *To* MAKE *up.* To supply; to repair.

Whatsoever, to *make up* the doctrine of man's salvation, is added as in supply of the scripture's insufficiency, we reject it. *Hooker, b.* ii.

I borrowed that celebrated name for an evidence to my subject, that so what was wanting in my proof might be *made up* in the example. *Glanville's Scep.*

Thus think the crowd, who, eager to engage,
Take quickly fire, and kindle into rage,
Who ne'er consider, but without a pause
Make up in passion what they want in cause. *Dryden.*

If they retrench any the smaller particulars in their ordinary expence, it will easily *make up* the halfpenny a-day which we have now under consideration. *Addison's Spect.*

This wisely she *makes up* her time,
Mis-spent when youth was in its prime. *Granville.*

There must needs be another state to *make up* the inequalities of this, and to salve all irregular appearances. *Atterbury.*

If his romantick disposition transport him so far as to expect little or nothing from this, he might however hope, that the principals would *make* it *up* in dignity and respect. *Swift.*

58. *To* MAKE *up.* To clear.

The reasons you allege, do more conduce
To the hot passion of distemper'd blood,
Than to *make up* a free determination
'Twixt right and wrong. *Shakesp. Troil. and Cressida.*

Though all at once cannot
See what I do deliver out to each,
Yet I can *make* my audit *up*, that all
From me do back receive the flow'r of all,
And leave me but the bran. *Shakespeare's Coriolanus.*

He was to *make up* his accounts with his lord, and by an easy undiscoverable cheat he could provide against the impending distress. *Rogers's Sermons.*

59. *To* MAKE *up.* To accomplish; to conclude; to complete.

Is not the lady Constance in this troop?
—I know she is not; for this match *made up*,
Her presence would have interrupted much. *Shakespeare.*

On Wednesday the general account is *made up* and printed, and on Thursday published. *Graunt's Bill of Mortality.*

This life is a scene of vanity, that soon passes away, and affords no solid satisfaction but in the consciousness of doing well, and in the hopes of another life: this is what I can say upon experience, and what you will find to be true when you come to *make up* the account. *Locke.*

To MAKE. *v. n.*

1. To tend; to travel; to go any way; to rush.

Oh me, lieutenant! what villains have done this?
—I think, that one of them is hereabouts,
And cannot *make* away. *Shakespeare's Othello.*

I do beseech your majesty *make* up,
Lest your retirement do amaze your friends. *Shakespeare.*

The earl of Lincoln resolved to *make* on where the king was, to give him battle, and marched towards Newark. *Bacon's Henry* VII.

There *made* forth to us a small boat, with about eight persons in it. *Bacon's New Atlantis.*

Warily provide, that while we *make* forth to that which is better, we meet not with that which is worse. *Bacon's Essays.*

A wonderful erroneous observation that *maketh* about, is commonly received contrary to experience. *Bacon.*

Make on, upon the heads
Of men, struck down like piles, to reach the lives
Of those remain and stand. *Benj. Johnson's Cataline.*

The Moors, terrified with the hideous cry of the soldiers *making* toward land, were easily beaten from the shore. *Knolles.*

When they set out from mount Sinai they *made* northward unto Rishmah. *Brown's Vulgar Errours, b.* vi.

Some speedy way for passage must be found;
Make to the city by the postern gate. *Dryden.*

The bull
His easier conquest proudly did forego;
And *making* at him with a furious bound,
From his bent forehead aim'd a double wound. *Dryden.*

Too late young Turnus the delusion found
Far on the sea, still *making* from the ground. *Dryden.*

A man of a disturbed brain seeing in the street one of those lads that used to vex him, stepped into a cutler's shop, and seizing on a naked sword *made* after the boy. *Locke.*

Seeing a country gentleman trotting before me with a spaniel by his horse's side, I *made* up to him. *Addison's Freehold.*

The French king *makes* at us directly, and keeps a king by him to set over us. *Addison.*

A monstrous boar rusht forth; his baleful eyes
Shot glaring fire, and his stiff-pointed bristles
Rose high upon his back; at me he *made*,
Whetting his tusks. *Smith's Phædra and Hippolitus.*

2. To contribute.

Whatsoever *makes* nothing to your subject, and is improper to it, admit not unto your work. *Dryden.*

Blinded he is by the love of himself to believe that the right is wrong, and wrong is right, when it *makes* for his own advantage. *Swift's Miscel.*

2. To operate; to act as a proof or argument, or cause.

Where neither the evidence of any law divine, nor the ſtrength of any invincible argument, otherwiſe found out by the light of reaſon, nor any notable publick inconvenience doth *make* againſt that which our own laws eccleſiaſtical have inſtituted for the ordering of theſe affairs; the very authority of the church itſelf ſufficeth. *Hooker.*

That which ſhould *make* for them muſt prove, that men ought not to make laws for church regiment, but only keep thoſe laws which in ſcripture they find made. *Hooker.*

It is very needful to be known, and *maketh* unto the right of the war againſt him. *Spenſer.*

Let us follow after the things which *make* for peace. *Rom.*

Perkin Warbeck finding that time and temporizing, which, whilſt his practices were covert, *made* for him, did now, when they were diſcovered, rather *make* againſt him, reſolved to try ſome exploit upon England. *Bacon's Henry* VII.

I obſerved a thing that may *make* to my preſent purpoſe. *Boyle.*

It *makes* to this purpoſe, that the light conſerving ſtones in Italy muſt be ſet in the ſun for ſome while before they retain light. *Digby on Bodies.*

What avails it me to acknowledge, that I have not been able to do him right in any line; for even my own confeſſion *makes* againſt me. *Dryden's Ded. to the Æn.*

3. To concur.

Antiquity, cuſtom, and conſent, in the church of God, *making* with that which law doth eſtabliſh, are themſelves moſt ſufficient reaſons to uphold the ſame, unleſs ſome notable publick inconvenience enforce the contrary. *Hooker.*

4. To ſhew; to appear; to carry appearance.

Joſhua and all Iſrael *made* as if they were beaten before them, and fled. *Joſh.* viii. 15.

It is the unanimous opinion of your friends, that you *make* as if you hanged yourſelf, and they will give it out that you are quite dead. *Arbuthnot's Hiſt. of John Bull.*

5. *To* MAKE *away with.* To deſtroy; to kill; to make away. This phraſe is improper.

The women of Greece were ſeized with an unaccountable melancholy, which diſpoſed ſeveral of them to *make away with* themſelves. *Addiſon's Spect.* Nº. 231.

6. *To* MAKE *for.* To advantage; to favour.

Compare with indifferency theſe diſparities of times, and we ſhall plainly perceive, that they *make for* the advantage of England at this preſent time. *Bacon's War with Spain.*

None deny there is a God, but thoſe for whom it *maketh* that there were no God. *Bacon's Eſſays.*

I was aſſur'd, that nothing was deſign'd
Againſt thee but ſafe cuſtody and hold;
That *made for* me, I knew that liberty
Would draw thee forth to perilous enterprizes. *Milton.*

7. *To* MAKE *up.* To compenſate; to be inſtead.

Have you got a ſupply of friends to *make up* for thoſe who are gone? *Swift to Pope.*

MAKE. *n. ſ.* [from the verb.] Form; ſtructure; nature.

Thoſe mercurial ſpirits, which were only lent the earth to ſhew men their folly in admiring it, poſſeſs delights of a nobler *make* and nature, which antedate immortality. *Glanville.*

Upon the deceaſe of a lion the beaſts met to chuſe a king: ſeveral put up, but one was not of *make* for a king; another wanted brains or ſtrength. *L'Eſtrange.*

Is our perfection of ſo frail a *make*,
As ev'ry plot can undermine and ſhake. *Dryden.*

Several lies are produced in the loyal ward of Portſoken of ſo feeble a *make*, as not to bear carriage to the Royal Exchange. *Addiſon's Freeholder,* Nº. 7.

It may be with ſuperior ſouls as with gigantick, which exceed the due proportion of parts, and, like the old heroes of that *make*, commit ſomething near extravagance. *Pope.*

MAKE. *n. ſ.* [maca, ȝemaca, Saxon.] Companion; favourite friend.

The elf therewith aſtonied,
Upſtarted lightly from his looſer *make*,
And his unſteady weapons 'gan in hand to take. *Fa. Qu.*

Bid her therefore herſelf ſoon ready make,
To wait on love amongſt his lovely crew;
Where every one that miſſeth then her *make*,
Shall be by him amearſt with penance due. *Spenſer.*

For ſince the wiſe town,
Has let the ſports down,
Of May games and morris,
The maids and their *makes*,
At dancing and wakes,
Had their napkins and poſies,
And the wipers for their noſes. *Benj. Johnſon's Owls.*

MA'KEBATE. *n. ſ.* [*make* and *debate.*] Breeder of quarrels.

Love in her paſſions, like a right *makebate*, whiſpered to both ſides arguments of quarrel. *Sidney.*

Outrageous party-writers are like a couple of *makebates*, who inflame ſmall quarrels by a thouſand ſtories. *Swift.*

MA'KER. *n. ſ.* [from *make.*]

1. The Creator.

Both in him, in all things, as is meet,
The univerſal *Maker* we may praiſe. *Milton's Par. Loſt*

This the divine Cecilia found,
And to her *Maker*'s praiſe confin'd the ſound. *Pope.*

Such plain roofs as piety could raiſe,
And only vocal with the *Maker*'s praiſe. *Pope.*

The power of reaſoning was given us by our *Maker* to purſue truths. *Watts's Logick.*

2. One who makes any thing.

Every man in Turky is of ſome trade; Sultan Achmet was a *maker* of ivory rings. *Notes on the Odyſſey.*

I dare promiſe her boldly what few of her *makers* of viſits and compliments dare to do. *Pope's Letters.*

3. One who ſets any thing in its proper ſtate.

You be indeed *makers* or marrers of all mens manners within the realm. *Aſcham's Schoolmaſter.*

MA'KEPEACE. *n. ſ.* [*make* and *peace.*] Peacemaker; reconciler.

To be a *makepeace* ſhall become my age. *Shakeſp.*

MA'KEWEIGHT. *n. ſ.* [*make* and *weight.*] Any ſmall thing thrown in to make up weight.

Me lonely ſitting, nor the glimmering light
Of *makeweight* candle, nor the joyous taſk
Of loving friend delights. *Philips.*

MALACHI'TE. *n. ſ.*

This ſtone is ſometimes intirely green, but lighter than that of the nephritick ſtone, ſo as in colour to reſemble the leaf of the mallow, μαλάχη, from which it has its name; though ſometimes it is veined with white, or ſpotted with blue or black. *Woodward's Meth. Foſſils.*

MA'LADY. *n. ſ.* [*maladie*, French.] A diſeaſe; a diſtemper; a diſorder of body; ſickneſs.

Better it is to be private
In ſorrow's torments, than ty'd to the pomp of a palace,
Nurſe inward *maladies*, which have not ſcope to be breath'd out. *Sidney, b.* i.

Wiſe phyſicians firſt require, that the *malady* be known thoroughly, afterwards teach how to cure and redreſs it. *Spenſer's State of Ireland.*

Say, can you faſt? your ſtomachs are too young:
And abſtinence engenders *maladies*. *Shakeſpeare.*

An uſual draught, or accidental violence of motion, has removed that *malady* that has baffled the ſkill of phyſicians. *South's Sermons.*

Love's a *malady* without a cure;
Fierce love has pierc'd me with his fiery dart,
He fires within, and hiſſes at my heart. *Dryden.*

MALA'NDERS. *n. ſ.* [from *mal andare*, Italian, *to go ill.*] A dry ſcab on the paſtern of horſes.

MA'LAPERT. *adj.* [*mal* and *pert.*] Saucy; quick with impudence; ſprightly without reſpect or decency.

Peace, maſter marquis, you are *malapert*;
Your fire-new ſtamp of honour is ſcarce current. *Shakeſp.*

If thou dar'ſt tempt me further, draw thy ſword.
—What, what? nay, then, I muſt have an ounce or two of this *malapert* blood from you. *Shakeſp. Twelfth Night.*

Are you growing *malapert*? Will you force me make uſe of my authority? *Dryden's Spaniſh Fryar.*

MA'LAPERTNESS. *n. ſ.* [from *malapert.*] Livelineſs of reply without decency; quick impudence; ſaucineſs.

MA'LAPERTLY. *adv.* [from *malapert.*] Impudently; ſaucily.

To MALA'XATE. *v. a.* [μαλάττω.] To ſoften, or knead to ſoftneſs, any body.

MALAXA'TION. *n. ſ.* [from *malaxate.*] The act of ſoftening.

MALE. *adj.* [*male*, French; *maſculus*, Lat.] Of the ſex that begets young; not female.

Which ſhall be heir of the two *male* twins, who, by the diſſection of the mother, were laid open to the world? *Locke.*

You are the richeſt perſon in the commonwealth; you have no *male* child; your daughters are all married to wealthy patricians. *Swift's Examiner,* Nº. 27.

MALE. *n. ſ.* The he of any ſpecies.

In moſt the *male* is the greater, and in ſome few the female. *Bacon's Nat. Hiſt.* Nº. 852.

There be more *males* than females, but in different proportions. *Graunt's Bills of Mortality.*

MALE, in compoſition, ſignifies *ill*, from *male*, Latin; *male*, old French.

MALEADMINITRA'TION. *n. ſ.* Bad management of affairs.

From the practice of the wiſeſt nations, when a prince was laid aſide for *maleadminiſtration*, the nobles and people did reſume the adminiſtration of the ſupreme power. *Swift.*

A general canonical denunciation, is that which is made touching ſuch a matter as properly belongs to the eccleſiaſtical court, for that a ſubject denounces his ſuperior, or ſome criminal prelate, for *maleadminiſtration*, or a wicked life. *Ayliffe's Parergon.*

MALECONTE'NT. } *adj.* [*male* and *content.*] Diſcontented; diſſatiſfied.
MALECONTE'NTED. }

Brother Clarence, how like you our choice,
That you ſtand penſive, as half *malecontent*. *Shakeſpeare.*

Poor

Poor Clarence! Is it for a wife
That thou art *malecontent?* I will provide thee. *Shakesp.*

The king, for the better securing his state against mutinous and *malecontented* subjects, who might have their refuge in Scotland, sent a solemn ambassage unto James III. to conclude a peace. *Bacon's Henry* VII.

They cannot signalize themselves as *malecontents*, without breaking through all the softer virtues. *Addison's Freeholder.*

The usual way in despotick governments is to confine the *malecontent* to some castle. *Addison's Freeholder.*

MALECONTE'NTEDLY. *adv.* [from *malecontent.*] With discontent.

MALECONTE'NTEDNESS. *n. s.* [from *malecontent.*] Discontentedness; want of affection to government.

They would ascribe the laying down my paper to a spirit of *malecontentedness*. *Spectator*, N. 445.

MALEDI'CTED. *adj.* [*maledictus*, Latin.] Accursed. *Dict.*

MALEDI'CTION. *n. s.* [*malediction*, French; *maledictio*, Lat.] Curse; execration; denunciation of evil.

Then let my life long time on earth maintained be,
To wretched me, the last, worst *malediction*. *Sidney.*

The true original cause thereof, divine *malediction*, laid by the sin of man upon these creatures which God hath made for the use of man, was above the reach of their natural capacity. *Hooker, b.* i.

In Spain they stayed near eight months, during all which time Buckingham lay under millions of *maledictions*; which yet, upon the prince's safe arrival in the west, did vanish into praises. *Wotton.*

MALEFA'CTION. *n. s.* [*male* and *facio*, Latin.] A crime; an offence.

Guilty creatures at a play
Have, by the very cunning of the scene,
Been struck so to the soul, that presently
They have proclaim'd their *malefactions*. *Shakesp. Hamlet.*

MALEFA'CTOR. *n. s.* [*male* and *facio*, Latin.] An offender against law; a criminal; a guilty person.

A jaylor to bring forth
Some monstrous *malefactor*. *Shakesp. Ant. and Cleopatra.*

Fear his word,
As much as *malefactors* do your sword. *Roscommon.*

It is a sad thing when men shall repair to the ministry, not for preferment but refuge; like *malefactors* flying to the altar, only to save their lives. *South's Sermons.*

If their barking dog disturb her ease,
Th' unmanner'd *malefactor* is arraign'd. *Dryden's Juv.*

The *malefactor* goat was laid
On Bacchus' altar, and his forfeit paid. *Dryden.*

MALE'FICK. } *adj.* [*maleficus*, Latin.] Mischievous; hurtful.
MALE'FIQUE. } *Dict.*

MALEPRA'CTICE. *n. s.* [*male* and *practice.*] Practice contrary to rules.

MALE'VOLENCE. *n. s.* [*malevolentia*, Latin.] Ill will; inclination to hurt others; malignity.

The son of Duncan
Lives in the English court; and is receiv'd
Of the most pious Edward with such grace,
That the *malevolence* of fortune nothing
Takes from his high respect. *Shakesp. Macbeth.*

MALE'VOLENT. *adj.* [*malevolus*, Latin.] Ill-disposed towards others; unfavourable; malignant.

I have thee in my arms,
Though our *malevolent* stars have struggled hard,
And held us long asunder. *Dryden's King Arthur.*

MALE'VOLENTLY. *adv.* [from *malevolence.*] Malignly; malignantly.

The oak did not only resent his fall, but vindicate him from those aspersions that were *malevolently* cast upon him. *Howel's Vocal Forest.*

MA'LICE. *n. s.* [*malice*, French; *malitia*, Latin.]

1. Badness of design; deliberate mischief.

God hath forgiven me many sins of *malice*, and therefore surely he will pity my infirmities. *Taylor's holy living.*

2. Ill intention to any one; desire of hurting.

Duncan is in his grave;
Malice domestick, foreign levy, nothing
Can touch him further! *Shakespeare's Macbeth.*

To MA'LICE. *v. a.* [from the noun.] To regard with ill will. Obsolete.

The cause why he this fly so *maliced*,
Was that his mother which him bore and bred,
The most fine-fingered workman on the ground,
Arachne, by his means, was vanquished. *Spenser.*

MALI'CIOUS. *adj.* [*malicieux*, French; *malitiosus*, Latin.] Ill-disposed to any one; intending ill; malignant.

We must not stint
Our necessary actions in the fear
To cope *malicious* censurers; which ever,
As rav'nous fishes do a vessel follow
That is new trimm'd. *Shakespeare's Henry* VIII.

I grant him bloody,
Sudden, *malicious*, smacking of ev'ry sin
That has a name. *Shakesp. Macbeth.*

Stand up, O Lord, and be not merciful unto them that offend of *malicious* wickedness. *Psal.* lix. 5.

Thou know'st what *malicious* foe,
Envying our happiness, and of his own
Despairing, seeks to work us woe and shame. *Milton.*

The air appearing so *malicious* in this morbifick conspiracy, exacts a more particular regard. *Harvey on Consumptions.*

MALI'CIOUSLY. *adv.* [from *malicious.*] With malignity; with intention of mischief.

An intrigue between his majesty and a junto of ministers *maliciously* bent against me, broke out, and had like to have ended in my utter destruction. *Gulliver's Travels.*

MALI'CIOUSNESS. *n. s.* [from *malicious.*] Malice; intention of mischief to another.

Not out of envy or *maliciousness*,
Do I forbear to crave your special aid. *Herbert.*

MALI'GN. *adj.* [*maligne*, French; *malignus*, Latin: the *g* is mute or liquescent.]

1. Unfavourable; ill-disposed to any one; malicious.

Witchcraft may be by a tacit operation of *malign* spirits. *Bacon's Nat. Hist.*

If in the constellations war were sprung,
Two planets, rushing from aspect *malign*
Of fiercest opposition, in mid sky,
Should combat, and their jarring spheres confound. *Milt.*

Of contempt, and the *malign* hostile influence it has upon government, every man's experience will inform him. *South.*

2. Infectious; fatal to the body; pestilential.

He that turneth the humours back, and maketh the wound bleed inwards, endangereth *malign* ulcers and pernicious impostumations. *Bacon's Essays.*

To MALI'GN. *v. a.* [from the adjective.]

1. To regard with envy or malice.

The people practise what mischiefs and villanies they will against private men, whom they *malign*, by stealing their goods, or murdering them. *Spenser on Ireland.*

It is hardly to be thought that any governor should so *malign* his successor, as to suffer an evil to grow up which he might timely have kept under. *Spenser on Ireland.*

Strangers conspired together against him, and *maligned* him in the wilderness. *Ecclus.* xlv. 18.

If it is a pleasure to be envied and shot at, to be *maligned* standing, and to be depised falling; then is it a pleasure to be great, and to be able to dispose of mens fortunes. *South.*

2. To mischief; to hurt; to harm.

MALI'GNANCY. *n. s.* [from *malignant.*]

1. Malevolence; malice; unfavourableness.

My stars shine darkly over me; the *malignancy* of my fate might, perhaps, distemper yours; therefore I crave your leave, that I may bear my evils alone. *Shakespeare.*

2. Destructive tendency.

The infection doth produce a bubo, which, according to the degree of its *malignancy*, either proves easily curable, or else it proceeds in its venom. *Wiseman's Surgery.*

MALI'GNANT. *adj.* [*malignant*, French.]

1. Malign; envious; unpropitious; malicious; mischievous; intending or effecting ill.

O *malignant* and ill-boading stars!
Now art thou come unto a feast of death. *Shakespeare.*

Not friended by his wish to your high person,
His will is most *malignant*, and it stretches
Beyond you to your friends. *Shakespeare's Henry* VIII.

To good *malignant*, to bad men benign. *Milton.*

They have seen all other notions besides their own represented in a false and *malignant* light; whereupon they judge and condemn at once. *Watts's Improvement of the Mind.*

2. Hostile to life: as, *malignant* fevers.

They hold, that the cause of the gout, is a *malignant* vapour that falls upon the joint; that the swelling is a kindness in nature, that calls down humours to damp the malignity of the vapours, and thereby assuage the sharpness of the pain. *Temple's Miscel.*

Let the learn'd begin
Th' enquiry, where disease could enter in;
How those *malignant* atoms forc'd their way,
What in the faultless frame they found to make their prey?
Dryden to the duchess of Ormond.

MALI'GNANT. *n. s.*

1. A man of ill intention; malevolently disposed.

Occasion was taken, by certain *malignants*, secretly to undermine his great authority in the church of Christ. *Hooker.*

2. It was a word used of the defenders of the church and monarchy by the rebel sectaries in the civil wars.

MALI'GNANTLY. *adv.* [from *malignant.*] With ill intention; maliciously; mischievously.

Now arriving
At place of potency, and sway o' th' state,
If he should still *malignantly* remain

Fast foe to the Plebeians, your voices might
Be curses to yourselves. *Shakespeare's Coriolanus.*

MALI'GNER. *n. s.* [from *malign.*] One who regards another with ill will.

Such as these are philosophy's *maligners*, who pronounce the most generous contemplations, needless unprofitable subtleties. *Glanville's Apology.*

I thought it necessary to justify my character in point of cleanliness, which some of my *maligners* call in question. *Gulliver's Travels.*

2. Sarcastical censurer.

MALI'GNITY. *n. s.* [*malignité*, French.]

1. Malice; maliciousness.

Deeds are done which man might charge aright
On stubborn fate, or undiscerning might,
Had not their guilt the lawless soldiers known,
And made the whole *malignity* their own. *Tickell.*

2. Contrariety to life; destructive tendency.

Whether any tokens of poison did appear, reports are various; his physicians discerned an invincible *malignity* in his disease. *Hayward.*

No redress could be obtained with any vigour proportionable to the *malignity* of that far-spread disease. *K. Charles.*

3. Evilness of nature.

This shows the high *malignity* of fraud, that in the natural course of it tends to the destruction of common life, by destroying trust and mutual confidence. *South's Sermons.*

MALI'GNLY. *adv.* [from *malign.*] Enviously; with ill will; mischievously.

Lest you think I railly more than teach,
Or praise *malignly* arts I cannot reach;
Let me for once presume t' instruct the times. *Pope.*

MA'LKIN. *n. s.* [from *mal*, of *Mary*, and *kin*, the diminutive termination.] A kind of mop made of clouts for sweeping ovens; thence a frightful figure of clouts dressed up; thence a dirty wench. *Hanmer.*

The kitchen *malkin* pins
Her richest lockram 'bout her reechy neck,
Clamb'ring the walls to eye him. *Shakesp. Coriolanus.*

MALL. *n. s.* [*malleus*, Lat. a hammer.]

1. A stroke; a blow.

With mighty *mall*,
The monster merciless him made to fall. *Fairy Queen.*
Give that rev'rend head a *mall*
Or two, or three, against a wall. *Hudibras, p.* ii.

2. A kind of beater or hammer. [*mail*, French.]

He took a *mall*, and after having hollowed the handle, and that part which strikes the ball, he enclosed in them several drugs. *Addison's Spect.* N°. 195.

3. A walk where they formerly played with malls and balls. *Moll* is, in Islandick, an area or walk spread with shells.

This the beau monde shall from the *mall* survey,
And hail with musick its propitious ray. *Pope.*

To MALL. *v. a.* [from the noun.] To beat or strike with a mall.

MA'LLARD. *n. s.* [*malart*, French.] The drake of the wild duck.

Antony
Claps on his sea-wing, like a doating *mallard*,
Leaving the fight in height. *Shak. Ant. and Cleopatra.*

The birds that are most easy to be drawn are *mallard*, shoveler, and goose. *Peacham on Drawing.*

Arm your hook with the line, and cut so much of a brown *mallard*'s feather as will make the wings. *Walton's Angler.*

MALLEABI'LITY. *n. s.* [from *malleable.*] Quality of enduring the hammer; quality of spreading under the hammer.

Supposing the nominal essence of gold to be a body of such a peculiar colour and weight, with the *malleability* and fusibility, the real essence is that constitution on which these qualities and their union depend. *Locke.*

MA'LLEABLE. *adj.* [*malleable*, French; from *malleus*, Latin, a hammer.] Capable of being spread by beating: this is a quality possessed in the most eminent degree by gold, it being more ductile than any other metal; and is opposite to friability or brittleness. *Quincy.*

Make it more strong for falls, though it come not to the degree to be *malleable.* *Bacon.*

The beaten soldier proves most manful,
That like his sword endures the anvil;
And justly 's held more formidable,
The more his valour's *malleable.* *Hudibras, p.* ii.

If the body is compact, and bends or yields inward to pression without any sliding of its parts, it is hard and elastick, returning to its figure with a force rising from the mutual attraction of its parts: if the parts slide upon one another, the body is *malleable* or soft. *Newton's Opticks.*

MA'LLEABLENESS. *n. s.* [from *malleable.*] Quality of enduring the hammer; malleability; ductility.

The bodies of most use that are sought for out of the earth are the metals, which are distinguished from other bodies by their weight, fusibility, and *malleableness.* *Locke.*

To MA'LLEATE. *v. a.* [from *malleus*, Latin.] To hammer; to forge or shape by the hammer.

He first found out the art of melting and *malleating* metals, and making them useful for tools. *Derham.*

MALLET. *n. s.* [*malleus*, Latin.] A wooden hammer.

The vessel soddered up was warily struck with a wooden *mallet*, and thereby compressed. *Boyle.*

Their left-hand does the calking iron guide,
The rattling *mallet* with the right they lift. *Dryden.*

MA'LLOWS. *n. s.* [*malva*, Latin; mælepe, Saxon.]

The *mallow* has a fibrous root; the leaves are round or angular: the flower consists of one leaf, is of the expanded bell-shaped kind, and cut into five segments almost to the bottom: from the centre rises a pyramidal tube, for the most part loaded wtth many small threads or filaments: from the centre of the flower-cup rises the pointal in the tube, which becomes the fruit, and this is flat, round, and sometimes pointed, wrapt, for the most part, within the flower-cup, and divided into several cells so disposed round the axle, that each little lodge appears most artificially jointed within the corresponding striæ or channels: the seed is often shaped like a kidney: the species are six, of which the first is found wild, and used in medicine. *Miller.*

Shards or *mallows* for the pot,
That keep the loosen'd body sound. *Dryden.*

MA'LMSEY. *n. s.*

1. A sort of grape. See VINE.

2. A kind of wine.

White-handed mistress, one sweet word with thee.
—Honey, and milk, and sugar, there is three.
—Nay then two treys; and if you grow so nice,
Metheglin, wort, and *malmsey.* *Shakespeare.*

MALT. *n. s.* [mealt, Saxon; *mout*, Dutch.] Grain steeped in water and fermented, then dried on a kiln.

Beer hath *malt* first infused in the liquor, and is afterwards boiled with the hop. *Bacon's Nat. Hist.* N°. 308.

MA'LTDUST. *n. s.* [*malt* and *dust.*]

Malt-dust is an enricher of barren land, and a great improver of barley. *Mortimer's Husbandry.*

MALTFLOOR. *n. s.* [*malt* and *floor.*] A floor to dry malt.

Empty the corn from the cistern into the *malt*-floor. *Mort.*

To MALT. *v. n.*

1. To make malt.

2. To be made malt.

To house it green it will mow-burn, which will make it *malt* worse. *Mortimer's Husbandry.*

MA'LTDRINK. *n. s.* [*malt* and *drink.*]

All *maltdrinks* may be boiled into the consistence of a slimy syrup. *Floyer on the Humours.*

MA'LTHORSE. *n. s.* [*malt* and *horse.*] It seems to have been, in *Shakespeare*'s time, a term of reproach for a dull dolt.

You peasant swain, you whoreson, you *malthorse* drudge. *Shakespeare's Taming of the Shrew.*

Mome, *malthorse*, capon, coxcomb, idiot, patch. *Shak.*

MA'LTMAN. }
MALTSTER. } *n. s.* [from *malt.*] One who makes malt.

Sir Arthur the *maltster!* how fine it will sound! *Swift.*

Tom came home in the chariot by his lady's side; but he unfortunately taught her to drink brandy, of which she died; and Tom is now a journeyman *maltster.* *Swift.*

MALVA'CEOUS. *adj.* [*malva*, Latin.] Relating to mallows.

MALVERSA'TION. *n. s.* [French.] Bad shifts; mean artifices; wicked and fraudulent tricks.

MAM. }
MAMMA'. } *n. s.* [*mamma*, Latin: this word is said to be found for the compellation of *mother* in all languages; and is therefore supposed to be the first syllables that a child pronounces.] The fond word for mother.

Poor Cupid sobbing scarce could speak;
Indeed, *mamma*, I did not know ye:
Alas! how easy my mistake?
I took you for your likeness Cloe. *Prior.*

Little masters and misses are great impediments to servants; the remedy is to bribe them, that they may not tell tales to papa and *mamma.* *Swift's Rules to Servants.*

MAMME'E *tree. n. s.*

The *mammee tree* hath a rosaceous flower, which consists of several leaves placed in a circular order, from whose cup arises the pointal, which afterwards becomes an almost spherical fleshy fruit, containing two or three seeds inclosed in hard rough shells. *Miller.*

MA'MMET. *n. s.* [from *mam* or *mamma.*] A puppet, a figure dressed up. *Hanmer.*

Kate; this is no world
To play with *mammets*, and to tilt with lips. *Shakesp.*

MA'MMIFORM. *adj.* [*mammiforme*, French; *mamma* and *forma*, Latin.] Having the shape of paps or dugs.

MAMMI'LLARY. *adj.* [*mammillaire*, Fr. *mammillaris*, Latin.] Belonging to the paps or dugs.

MA'MMOCK. *n. s.* A large shapeless piece.

The ice was broken into large *mammocks.* *James's Voyage.*

To MA'MMOCK. *v. a.* [from the noun.] To tear; to break; to pull to pieces.

I saw him run after a gilded butterfly; and he did so set his teeth, and did tear it! Oh, I warrant, how he *mammockt* it! *Shakespeare's Coriolanus.*

MA'MMON. *n. s.* [Syriack.] Riches.

MAN. *n. s.* [man, mon, Saxon.]

1. Human being.

The king is but a *man* as I am; the violet smells to him as it doth to me; the element shews to him as it doth to me, all his senses have but human conditions. *Shakesp.*

All the west bank of Nilus is possessed by an idolatrous, *man*-eating nation. *Brerewood on Languages.*

A creature of a more exalted kind
Was wanted yet, and then was *man* design'd,
Conscious of thought. *Dryden's Ovid.*

Nature in *man* capacious souls hath wrought,
And given them voice expressive of their thought;
In *man* the God descends, and joys to find
The narrow image of his greater mind. *Creech's Manilius.*

A combination of the ideas of a certain figure, with the powers of motion, and reasoning joined to substance, make the ordinary idea of a *man*. *Locke.*

On human actions reason though you can,
It may be reason, but it is not *man*. *Pope's Epistles.*

2. Not a woman.

Bring forth *men* children only!
For thy undaunted metal should compose
Nothing but males. *Shakespeare's King Lear.*

I had not so much of *man* in me,
But all my mother came into mine eyes,
And gave me up to tears. *Shakespeare's Henry V.*

Every *man* child shall be circumcised. *Gen.* xvii. 10.

Ceneus, a woman once, and once a *man*,
But ending in the sex she first began. *Dryden's Æn.*

A long time since the custom began, among people of quality, to keep *men* cooks of the French nation. *Swift.*

3. Not a boy.

The nurse's legends are for truths receiv'd,
And the *man* dreams but what the boy believ'd. *Dryden.*

4. A servant; an attendant; a dependant.

Now thanked be the great god Pan,
Which thus preserves my loved life,
Thanked be I that keep a *man*,
Who ended hath this bloody strife:
For if my *man* must praises have,
What then must I that keep the knave? *Sidney, b.* i.

My brother's servants
Were then my fellows, now they are my *men*. *Shakesp.*

Such gentlemen as are his majesty's own sworn servants should be preferred to the charge of his majesty's ships; choice being made of *men* of valour and capacity rather than to employ other mens *men*. *Raleigh's Essays.*

I and my *man* will presently go ride
Far as the Cornish mount. *Cowley.*

5. A word of familiarity bordering on contempt.

You may partake of any thing we say:
We speak no treason, *man*. *Shakesp. Richard III.*

6. It is used in a loose signification like the French *on*, one, any one.

This same young sober-blooded boy doth not love me, nor a *man* cannot make him laugh. *Shakesp. Henry IV.*

A *man* in an instant may discover the assertion to be impossible. *More's Divine Dialogues.*

He is a good-natured man, and will give as much as a *man* would desire. *Stillingfleet.*

By ten thousand of them a *man* shall not be able to advance one step in knowledge. *Tillotson's Sermons.*

Our thoughts will not be directed what objects to pursue, nor be taken off from those they have once fixed on; but run away with a *man*, in pursuit of those ideas they have in view. *Locke.*

A *man* would expect to find some antiquities; but all they have to show of this nature is an old rostrum of a Roman ship. *Addison.*

A *man* might make a pretty landscape of his own plantation. *Addison.*

7. One of uncommon qualifications.

Manners maketh *man*. *William of Wickham.*

I dare do all that may become a *man*;
Who dares do more is none.
—What beast was't then
That made you break this enterprise to me?
When you durst do it, then you were a *man*;
And, to be more than what you were, you would
Be so much more the *man*. *Shakespeare's Macbeth.*

He tript me behind, being down, insulted, rail'd,
And put upon him such a deal of *man*,
That worthied him. *Shakespeare's King Lear.*

Will reckons he should not have been the *man* he is, had not he broke windows, and knocked down constables, when he was a young fellow. *Addison's Spect.* N°. 105.

8. A human being qualified in any particular manner.

Thou art but a youth, and he a *man* of war from his youth. 1 *Sam.* xvii. 33.

9. Individual.

In matters of equity between *man* and *man*, our Saviour has taught us to put my neighbour in the place of myself, and myself in the place of my neighbour. *Watts's Logick.*

10. Not a beast.

Thy face, bright Centaur, autumn's heats retain,
The softer season suiting to the *man*. *Creech's Manilius.*

11. Wealthy or independant person: to this sense some refer the following passage of *Shakespeare*, others to the sense next foregoing.

There would this monster make a *man*; any strange beast there makes a *man*. *Shakespeare's Tempest.*

What poor man would not carry a great burthen of gold to be made a *man* for ever. *Tillotson's Sermons.*

12. When a person is not in his senses, we say, he is not his own *man*. *Ains.*

13. A moveable piece at chess or draughts.

14. MAN *of war*. A ship of war.

A Flemish *man of war* lighted upon them, and overmastered them. *Carew's Survey of Cornwall.*

To MAN. *v. a.* [from the noun.]

1. To furnish with men.

Your ships are not well *mann'd*;
Your mariners are muliteers, or reapers. *Shakespeare.*

A navy, to secure the seas, is *mann'd*;
And forces sent. *Daniel's Civil War.*

It hath been agreed, that either of them should send certain ships to sea well *manned*, and apparelled to fight. *Hayward.*

Their ships go as long voyages as any, and are for their burdens as well *manned*. *Raleigh's Essays.*

He had *manned* it with a great number of tall soldiers, more than for the proportion of the castle. *Bacon.*

They *man* their boats, and all their young men arm. *Waller.*

The Venetians could set out thirty men of war, a hundred gallies, and ten galeases; though I cannot conceive how they could *man* a fleet of half the number. *Addison on Italy.*

Timoleon forced the Carthaginians out, though they had *manned* out a fleet of two hundred men of war. *Arbuthnot.*

2. To guard with men.

See, how the surly Warwick *mans* the wall. *Shakesp.*

There stands the castle by yond tuft of trees,
Mann'd with three hundred men. *Shakesp. Richard II.*

The summons take of the same trumpet's call,
To sally from one port, or *man* one publick wall. *Tate.*

3. To fortify; to strengthen.

Advise how war may be best upheld,
Mann'd by her two main nerves, iron and gold,
In all her equipage. *Milton.*

Theodosius having *mann'd* his soul with proper reflexions, exerted himself in the best manner he could, to animate his penitent. *Addison's Spect.* N°. 164.

4. To tame a hawk.

Another way I have to *man* my haggard,
To make her come, and know her keeper's call;
That is, to watch her. *Shakespeare.*

5. To attend; to serve; to wait on.

Thou whoreson mandrake, thou art fitter to be worn in my cap than to wait at my heels: I was never *manned* with agate till now. *Shakespeare's Henry IV.*

They distill their husbands land
In decoctions, and are *mann'd*
With ten empyricks in their chamber,
Lying for the spirit of amber. *Benj. Johnson's Forest.*

6. To direct in hostility; to point; to aim. An obsolete word.

Man but a rush against Othello's breast,
And he retires. *Shakespeare's Othello.*

MA'NACLES. *n. s.* [*manicles*, French, *manicæ* from *manus*, Latin.] Chain for the hands; shackles.

For my sake wear this glove;
It is a *manacle* of love. *Shakespeare's Cymbeline.*

Thou
Must, as a foreign recreant, be led
With *manacles* along our street. *Shakespeare's Coriolanus.*

Such a person
Could fetch your brother from the *manacles*
Of the all-holding law. *Shakesp. Meas. for Measure.*

Doctrine unto fools is as fetters on the feet, and like *manacles* on the right-hand. *Ecclus.* xxi. 19.

The bounds of the law good men count their ornament and protection; others, their *manacles* and oppression. *King Charles.*

To MA'NACLE. *v. a.* [from the noun.] To chain the hands; to shackle.

We'll bait thy bears to death,
And *manacle* the bearward in their chains. *Shakespeare.*

I'll *manacle* thy neck and feet together. *Shakespeare.*

Is it thus you use this monarch, to *manacle* and shackle him hand and foot. *Arbuthnot and Pope's Mart. Scrib.*

To MA'NAGE. *v. a.* [*menager*, French.]

1. To conduct; to carry on.

The fathers had *managed* the charge of idolatry against the heathens. *Stillingfleet.*

Let her at leaſt the vocal braſs inſpire,
And tell the nations in no vulgar ſtrain,
What wars I *manage*, and what wreaths I gain. *Prior.*

2. To train a horſe to graceful action.

He rode up and down gallantly mounted, *managing* his horſe, and charging and diſcharging his lance. *Knolles.*

They vault from hunters to the *manag'd* ſteed. *Young.*

3. To govern; to make tractable.

Let us ſtick to our point, and we will *manage* Bull I'll warrant you. *Arbuthnot's Hiſt. of John Bull.*

4. To wield; to move or uſe eaſily.

Long tubes are cumberſome, and ſcarce to be eaſily *managed.* *Newton.*

5. To huſband; to make the object of caution.

There is no more to *manage!* If I fall,
It ſhall be like myſelf; a ſetting ſun
Should leave a track of glory in the ſkies. *Dryden.*

The leſs he had to loſe, the leſs he car'd,
To *manage* loathſome life, when love was the reward. *Dryd.*

6. To treat with caution or decency: this is a phraſe merely Gallick; not to be imitated.

Notwithſtanding it was ſo much his intereſt to *manage* his proteſtant ſubjects in the country, he made over his principality to France. *Addiſon on Italy.*

To MA'NAGE. *v. n.* To ſuperintend affairs; to tranſact.

Leave them to *manage* for thee, and to grant
What their unerring wiſdom ſees thee want. *Dryden.*

MANA'GE. *v. a.* [*meſnage*, *menage*, French.]

1. Conduct; adminiſtration.

To him put
The *manage* of my ſtate. *Shakeſpeare's Tempeſt.*

This might have been prevented,
With very eaſy arguments of love,
Which now the *manage* of two kingdoms muſt
With fearful, bloody iſſue arbitrate. *Shakeſp. K. John.*

For the rebels which ſtand out in Ireland,
Expedient *manage* muſt be made, my liege,
Ere further leiſure yield them further means. *Shakeſpeare.*

Young men, in the conduct and *manage* of actions, embrace more than they can hold, and ſtir more than they can quiet. *Bacon's Eſſays.*

The plea of a good intention will ſerve to ſanctify the worſt actions; the proof of which is but too manifeſt from that ſcandalous doctrine of the jeſuits concerning the direction of the intention, and likewiſe from the whole *manage* of the late rebellion. *South's Sermons.*

Whenever we take a ſtrong biaſs, it is not out of a moral incapacity to do better, but for want of a careful *manage* and diſcipline to ſet us right at firſt. *L'Eſtrange's Fables.*

2. Uſe; inſtrumentality.

To think to make gold of quickſilver is not to be hoped; for quickſilver will not endure the *manage* of the fire. *Bacon.*

3. Government of a horſe.

In thy ſlumbers
I heard thee murmur tales of iron wars,
Speak terms of *manage* to the bounding ſteed. *Shakeſp.*

The horſe you muſt draw in his career with his *manage* and turn, doing the curvetto. *Peacham.*

MA'NAGEABLE. *adj.* [from *manage.*]

1. Eaſy in the uſe; not difficult to be wielded or moved.

The conditions of weapons and their improvement are, that they may ſerve in all weathers; and that the carriage may be light and *manageable.* *Bacon's Eſſays.*

Very long tubes are, by reaſon of their length, apt to bend, and ſhake by bending ſo as to cauſe a continual trembling in the objects, whereas by contrivance the glaſſes are readily *manageable.* *Newton's Opticks.*

2. Governable; tractable.

MA'NAGEABLENESS. *n. ſ.* [from *manageable.*]

1. Accommodation to eaſy uſe.

This diſagreement may be imputed to the greater or leſs exactneſs or *manageableneſs* of the inſtruments employed. *Boyle.*

2. Tractableneſs; eaſineſs to be governed.

MA'NAGEMENT. *n. ſ.* [*menagement*, French.]

1. Conduct; adminiſtration.

Mark with what *management* their tribes divide;
Some ſtick to you, and ſome to t'other ſide. *Dryden.*

An ill argument introduced with deference, will procure more credit than the profoundeſt ſcience with a rough, inſolent, and noiſy *management.* *Locke on Education.*

The wrong *management* of the earl of Godolphin was the only cauſe of the union. *Swift's Miſcel.*

2. Practice; tranſaction; dealing.

He had great *managements* with eccleſiaſticks in the view of being advanced to the pontificate. *Addiſon on Italy.*

MA'NAGER. *n. ſ.* [from *manage.*]

1. One who has the conduct or direction of any thing.

A ſkilful *manager* of the rabble, ſo long as they have but ears to hear, needs never enquire whether they have any underſtanding. *South's Sermons.*

The *manager* opens his ſluice every night, and diſtributes the water into the town. *Addiſon.*

An artful *manager*, that crept between
His friend and ſhame, and was a kind of ſcreen. *Pope.*

2. A man of frugality; a good huſband.

A prince of great aſpiring thoughts: in the main, a *manager* of his treaſure, and yet bountiful from his own motion, wherever he diſcerns merit. *Temple's Miſcel.*

The moſt ſevere cenſor cannot but be pleaſed with the prodigality of Ovid's wit; though he could have wiſhed, that the maſter of it had been a better *manager.* *Dryden.*

MA'NAGERY. *n. ſ.* [*menagerie*, French.]

1. Conduct; direction; adminiſtration.

They who moſt exactly deſcribe that battle, give ſo ill an account of any conduct or diſcretion in the *managery* of that affair, that poſterity would receive little benefit in the moſt particular relation of it. *Clarendon, b.* viii.

2. Huſbandry; frugality.

The court of Rome has, in other inſtances, ſo well atteſted its good *managery*, that it is not credible crowns are conferred gratis. *Decay of Piety.*

3. Manner of uſing.

No expert general will bring a company of raw, untrained men into the field, but will, by little bloodleſs ſkirmiſhes, inſtruct them in the manner of the fight, and teach them the ready *managery* of their weapons. *Decay of Piety.*

MANA'TION. *n. ſ.* [*manatio*, Latin.] The act of iſſuing from ſomething elſe.

MA'NCHE. *n. ſ.* [French.] A ſleeve.

MA'NCHET. *n. ſ.* [*michet*, French. *Skinner.*] A ſmall loaf of fine bread.

Take a ſmall toaſt of *manchet*, dipped in oil of ſweet almonds. *Bacon.*

I love to entertain my friends with a frugal collation; a cup of wine, a diſh of fruit, and a *manchet.* *More's Dial.*

MANCHINE'EL *tree.* *n. ſ.* [*mancanilla*, Latin.]

The *manchineel tree* has male flowers, or katkins, which are produced at remote diſtances from embrios, which become round fleſhy fruit, in which is contained a rough woody nut, incloſing four or five flat ſeeds: it is a native of the Weſt Indies, and grows equal to the ſize of an oak: its wood, which is ſawn out into planks, and brought to England, is of a beautiful grain, will poliſh well and laſt long, and is therefore much eſteemed in cabinet-makers work: in cutting down thoſe trees, the juice of the bark, which is of a milky colour, muſt be burnt out before the work is begun; for its nature is ſo corroſive, that it will raiſe bliſters on the ſkin, and burn holes in linen; and if it ſhould happen to flie into the eyes of the labourers, they are in danger of loſing their ſight: the fruit is of the colour and ſize of the golden pippen, by which many Europeans have been deceived; ſome of whom have greatly ſuffered, and others loſt their lives by eating it, which will corrode the mouth and throat: the leaves of theſe trees alſo abound with a milky juice of the ſame nature, ſo that the cattle never ſhelter themſelves under them, and ſcarcely will any vegetable grow under their ſhade; yet the goats eat this fruit without any injury. *Miller.*

To MA'NCIPATE. *v. a.* [*mancipo*, Latin.] To enſlave; to bind; to tie.

Although the regular part of nature is ſeldom varied, yet the meteors, which are in themſelves more unſtable, and leſs *mancipated* to ſtated motions, are oftentimes employed to various ends. *Hale's Origin of Mankind.*

MANCIPA'TION. *n. ſ.* [from *mancipate.*] Slavery; involuntary obligation.

MA'NCIPLE. *n. ſ.* [*manceps*, Latin.] The ſteward of a community; the purveyor: it is particularly uſed of the purveyor of a college.

Their *manciple* fell dangerouſly ill,
Bread muſt be had, their griſt went to the mill:
This ſimkin moderately ſtole before,
Their ſteward ſick, he robb'd them ten times more.
Betterton's Miller of Trompington.

MANDA'MUS. *n. ſ.* [Latin.] A writ granted by the king, ſo called from the initial word.

MANDARI'N. *n. ſ.* A Chineſe nobleman or magiſtrate.

MA'NDATARY. *n. ſ.* [*mandataire*, Fr. from *mando*, Latin.]

He to whom the pope has, by virtue of his prerogative, and his own proper right, given a *mandate* for his benefice. *Ayliffe's Parergon.*

MA'NDATE. *n. ſ.* [*mandatum*, Latin.]

1. Command.

Her force is not any where ſo apparent as in expreſs *mandates* or prohibitions, eſpecially upon advice and conſultation going before. *Hooker, b.* i.

The neceſſity of the times caſt the power of the three eſtates upon himſelf, that his *mandates* ſhould paſs for laws, whereby he laid what taxes he pleaſed. *Howell's Vocal Foreſt.*

2. Precept; charge; commiſſion, ſent or tranſmitted.

Who

Who knows,
If the scarce bearded Cæsar have not sent
His powerful *mandate* to you. *Shakesp. Ant. and Cleopatra.*
This Moor,
Your special *mandate*, for the state affairs,
Hath hither brought. *Shakespeare's Othello.*
He thought the *mandate* forg'd, your death conceal'd. *Dryd.*
This dream all powerful Juno sends, I bear
Her mighty *mandates*, and her words you hear:
Haste, arm your Ardeans. *Dryden's Æn.*

MANDA'TOR. n. s. [Latin.] Director.

A person is said to be a client to his advocate, but a master and *mandator* to his proctor. *Ayliffe's Parergon.*

MA'NDATORY. *adj.* [*mandare*, Latin.] Preceptive; directory.

MA'NDIBLE. *n. s.* [*mandibula*, Latin.] The jaw; the instrument of manducation.

He saith, only the crocodile moveth the upper jaw, as if the upper *mandible* did make an articulation with the cranium. *Grew's Musæum.*

MANDI'BULAR. *n. s.* [from *mandibula*, Latin.] Belonging to the jaw.

MANDI'LION. *n. s.* [*mandiglione*, Italian.] A soldier's coat. *Skinner.* A loose garment; a sleeveless jacket. *Ainf.*

MA'NDREL. *n. s.* [*mandrin*, French.]

Mandrels are made with a long wooden shank, to fit stiff into a round hole that is made in the work, that is to be turned; this *mandrel* is called a shank, or *pin-mandrel:* and if the hole the shank is to fit into be very small, and the work to be fastened on it pretty heavy, then turners fasten a round iron shank or pin, and fasten their work upon it. *Moxon's Mechanical Exercises.*

MA'NDRAKE. *n. s.* [*mandragoras*, Lat. *mandragôre*, Fr.]

The flower of the *mandrake* consists of one leaf in the shape of a bell, and is divided at the top into several parts; the pointal afterwards becomes a globular soft fruit, in which are contained many kidney-shaped seeds: the roots of this plant is said to bear a resemblace to the human form. The reports of tying a dog to this plant, in order to root it up, and prevent the certain death of the person who dares to attempt such a deed, and of the groans emitted by it when the violence is offered, are equally fabulous. *Miller.*

Among other virtues, *mandrakes* has been falsely celebrated for rendering barren women fruitful: it has a soporifick quality, and the ancients used it when they wanted a narcotick of the most powerful kind. *Hill's Mat. Med.*

Would curses kill, as doth the *mandrake*'s groan,
I would invent as bitter searching terms,
As curst, as harsh, and horrible to hear. *Shakespeare.*
Not poppy, nor *mandragora*,
Nor all the drowsy syrups of the world,
Shall ever med'cine thee to that sweet sleep. *Shakespeare.*
And shrieks like *mandrakes*, torn out of the earth,
That living mortals, hearing them, run mad. *Shakesp.*
Give me of thy sons *mandrakes*. *Gen.* xxx. 14.
Go, and catch a falling star,
Get with child a *mandrake* root. *Donne.*

To MA'NDUCATE. *v. a.* [*manduco*, Lat.] To chew; to eat.

MANDUCA'TION. *n. s.* [*manducatio*, Latin.] Eating.

Manducation is the action of the lower jaw in chewing the food, and preparing it in the mouth before it is received into the stomach. *Quincy.*

As he who is not a holy person does not feed upon Christ, it is apparent that our *manducation* must be spiritual, and therefore so must the food, and consequently it cannot be natural flesh. *Taylor's Worthy Communicant.*

MANE. *n. s.* [*maene*, Dutch.] The hair which hangs down on the neck of horses, or other animals.

Dametas was tossed from the saddle to the *mane* of the horse, and thence to the ground. *Sidney, b.* ii.

A currie comb, *maine* comb, and whip for a jade. *Tusser.*

The weak wanton Cupid
Shall from your neck unloose his am'rous fold;
And, like a dew-drop from the lion's *mane*,
Be shook to air. *Shakesp. Troil. and Cressida.*

The horses breaking loose, ran up and down with their tails and *manes* on a light-fire. *Knolles's Hist. of the Turks.*

A lion shakes his dreadful *mane*,
And angry grows. *Waller.*
For quitting both their swords and reins,
They grasp'd with all their strength the *manes*. *Hudibras.*

MA'NEATER. *n. s.* [*man* and *eat.*] A cannibal; an anthropophagite; one that feeds upon human flesh.

MA'NED. *adj.* [from the noun.] Having a mane.

MANES. n. s. [Latin.] Ghost; shade; that which remains of man after death.

Hail, O ye holy *manes!* hail again
Paternal ashes. *Dryden's Virg.*

MA'NFUL. *adj.* [*man* and *full.*] Bold; stout; daring.

A handful
It had devour'd 'twas so *manful*. *Hudibras.*

MA'NFULLY. *adv.* [from *manful.*] Boldly; stoutly.

Artimesia behaved herself *manfully* in a great fight at sea, when Xerxes stood by as a coward. *Abbot.*

I slew him *manfully* in fight,
Without false 'vantage, or base treachery. *Shakespeare.*

He that with this Christian armour *manfully* fights against, and repels, the temptations and assaults of his spiritual enemies; he that keeps his conscience void of offence, shall enjoy peace here, and for ever. *Ray on Creation.*

MA'NFULNESS. *n. s.* [from *manful.*] Stoutness; boldness.

MANGCO'RN. *n. s.* [*mengen*, Dutch, to mingle.] Corn of several kinds mixed: as, wheat and rye.

MA'NGANESE. *n. s.* [*mangunesia*, low Latin.]

Manganese is extremely well known by name, though the glassmen use it for many different substances, that have the same effect in clearing the foul colour of their glass: it is properly an iron ore of a poorer sort; the most perfect sort is of a dark iron grey, very heavy but brittle. *Hill.*

Manganese is rarely found but in an iron vein. *Woodward.*

MANGE. *n. s.* [*de mangeaison*, French.] The itch or scab in cattle.

The sheep died of the rot, and the swine of the *mange*. *Benj. Johnson.*

Tell what crisis does divine
The rot in sheep, or *mange* in swine. *Hudibras, p.* i.

MA'NGER. *n. s.* [*mangeoire*; French.] The place or vessel in which animals are fed with corn.

She brought forth her first-born son, and laid him in a *manger.* *Luke* ii. 7.

A churlish cur got into a *manger*, and there lay growling to keep the horses from their provender. *L'Estrange's Fab.*

MA'NGINESS. *n. s.* [from *mangy.*] Scabbiness; infection with the mange.

To MA'NGLE. *v. a.* [*mangelen*, Dutch, to be wanting; *mancus*, Latin.] To lacerate; to cut or tear piece-meal; to butcher.

Cassio, may you suspect
Who they should be, that thus have *mangled* you? *Shak.*
Your dishonour
Mangles true judgment, and bereaves the state
Of that integrity which should become it. *Shakespear.*
Thoughts my tormentors arm'd with deadly stings,
Mangle my apprehensive tenderest parts,
Exasperate, exulcerate, and raise
Dire inflammation, which no cooling herb,
Or medicinal liquor can asswage. *Milton's Agonistes.*
The triple porter of the Stygian seat,
With lolling tongue, lay fawning at thy feet,
And, seiz'd with fear, forgot his *mangled* meat. *Dryden.*
What could swords or poison, racks or flame,
But *mangle* and disjoint this brittle frame!
More fatal Henry's words; they murder Emma's fame. *Prior.*

It is hard, that not one gentleman's daughter should read or understand her own natural tongue; as any one may find, who can hear them when they are disposed to *mangle* a play or a novel, where the least word out of the common road disconcerts them. *Swift to a young Lady.*

They have joined the most obdurate consonants without one intervening vowel, only to shorten a syllable; so that most of the books we see now-a-days, are full of those *manglings* and abbreviations. *Swift's Let. to the Ld. Treasurer.*

Inextricable difficulties occur by *mangling* the sense, and curtailing authors. *Baker's Reflections on Learning.*

MA'NGLER. *n. s.* [from *mangle.*] A hacker; one that destroys bunglingly.

Since after thee may rise an impious line,
Coarse *manglers* of the human face divine;
Paint on, till fate dissolve thy mortal part,
And live and die the monarch of thy art. *Tickell.*

MA'NGO. *n. s.* [*mangostan*, Fr.] A fruit of the isle of Java, brought to Europe pickled.

The fruit with the husk, when very young, makes a good preserve, and is used to pickle like *mangoes*. *Mortimer.*

What lord of old wou'd bid his cook prepare
Mangoes, potargo, champignons, cavare. *King.*

MA'NGY. *adj.* [from *mange.*] Infected with the mange; scabby.

Away, thou issue of a *mangy* dog!
I swoon to see thee. *Shakesp. Timon of Athens.*

MANHA'TER. *n. s.* [*man* and *hater.*] Misanthrope; one that hates mankind.

MA'NHOOD. *n. s.* [from *man.*]

1. Human nature.

In Seth was the church of God established; from whom Christ descended, as touching his *manhood*. *Raleigh.*

Not therefore joins the son
Manhood to Godhead, with more strength to foil
Thy enemy. *Milton's Par. Lost, b.* xii.

2. Virility; not womanhood.

'Tis in my pow'r to be a sovereign now,
And, knowing more, to make his *manhood* bow. *Dryden.*

3. Virility; not childhood.

Tetchy

Tetchy and wayward was thy infancy;
Thy ſchool-days frightful, deſp'rate, wild and furious;
Thy prime of *manhood* daring, bold and venturous. *Shak.*

By fraud or force the ſuitor train deſtroy,
And ſtarting into *manhood*, ſcorn the boy. *Pope's Odyſſey.*

4. Courage; bravery; reſolution; fortitude.

Nothing ſo hard but his valour overcame; which he ſo guided with virtue, that although no man was ſpoken of but he for *manhood*, he was called the courteous Amphialus. *Sidney.*

MANI'AC. } *adj.* [*maniacus*, Lat.] Raging with madneſs;
MANI'ACAL. } mad to rage.

Epilepſies and *maniacal* lunacies uſually conform to the age of the moon. *Grew's Coſmol. b.* iii.

MA'NIFEST. *adj.* [*manifeſtus*, Latin.]

1. Plain; open; not concealed; not doubtful; apparent.

They all concur as principles, they all have their forcible operations therein, although not all in like apparent and *manifeſt* manner. *Hooker, b.* i.

That which may be known of God is *manifeſt* in them; for God hath ſhewed it unto them. *Rom.* i. 19.

He was fore-ordained before the foundation of the world, but was *manifeſt* in theſe laſt times for you. 1 *Pet.* i. 20.

He full
Reſplendent all his father *manifeſt*
Expreſs'd. *Milton's Paradiſe Loſt, b.* x.

Thus *manifeſt* to fight the God appear'd. *Dryden's Æn.*

I ſaw, I ſaw him *manifeſt* in view,
His voice, his figure, and his geſture knew. *Dryden.*

2. Detected, with *of*.

Caliſtho there ſtood *manifeſt of* ſhame,
And turn'd a bear, the northern ſtar became. *Dryden.*

MANIFE'ST. *n. ſ.* [*manifeſte*, Fr. *manifeſto*, Italian.] Declaration; publick proteſtation.

You authentick witneſſes I bring,
Of this my *manifeſt*: that never more
This hand ſhall combat on the crooked ſhore. *Dryden.*

To MANIFE'ST. *v. a.* [*manifeſter*, Fr. *manifeſto*, Lat.] To make appear; to make publick; to ſhew plainly; to diſcover.

Thy life did *manifeſt*, thou lov'dſt me not;
And thou wilt have me die aſſured of it. *Shakeſpeare.*

He that loveth me I will love him, and *manifeſt* myſelf to him. *John* xiv. 21.

He was pleaſed himſelf to aſſume, and *manifeſt* his will in, our fleſh, and ſo not only as God from heaven, but God viſible on earth, to preach reformation among us. *Hammond.*

This perverſe commotion
Muſt *manifeſt* thee worthieſt to be heir
Of all things. *Milton's Par. Loſt, b.* vi.

Were he not by law withſtood,
He'd *manifeſt* his own inhuman blood. *Dryden's Juv.*

It may be part of our employment in eternity, to contemplate the works of God, and give him the glory of his wiſdom *manifeſted* in the creation. *Ray on Creation.*

MANIFESTA'TION. *n. ſ.* [*manifeſtation*, Fr. from *manifeſt.*] Diſcovery; publication; clear evidence.

Though there be a kind of natural right in the noble, wiſe and virtuous, to govern them which are of ſervile diſpoſition; nevertheleſs, for *manifeſtation* of this their right, the aſſent of them who are to be governed ſeemeth neceſſary. *Hooker.*

As the nature of God is excellent, ſo likewiſe is it to know him in thoſe glorious *manifeſtations* of himſelf in the works of creation and providence. *Tillotſon's Sermons.*

The ſecret manner in which acts of mercy ought to be performed, requires this publick *manifeſtation* of them at the great day. *Atterbury's Sermons.*

MANIFE'STIBLE. *adj.* [properly *manifeſtable.*] Eaſy to be made evident.

This is *manifeſtible* in long and thin plates of ſteel perforated in the middle, and equilibrated. *Brown's Vulg. Err.*

MA'NIFESTLY. *adv.* [from *manifeſt.*] Clearly; evidently; plainly.

We ſee *manifeſtly*, that ſounds are carried with wind. *Bac.*

Sects, in a ſtate, ſeem to be tolerated becauſe they are already ſpread, while they do not *manifeſtly* endanger the conſtitution. *Swift.*

MA'NIFESTNESS. *n. ſ.* [from *manifeſt.*] Perſpicuity; clear evidence.

MANIFE'STO. *n. ſ.* [Italian.] Publick proteſtation; declaration.

It was propoſed to draw up a *manifeſto*, ſetting forth the grounds and motives of our taking arms. *Addiſon.*

MA'NIFOLD. *adj.* [*many* and *fold.*] Of different kinds; many in number; multiplied; complicated.

When his eyes did her behold,
Her heart did ſeem to melt in pleaſures *manifold.* *Fa. Qu.*

Terror of the torments *manifold*,
In which the damned ſouls he did behold. *Spenſer.*

If that the king
Have any way your good deſerts forgot,
Which he confeſſeth to be *manifold*,
He bids you name your griefs. *Shakeſp. Henry* IV.

If any man of quality will maintain upon Edward earl of Glo'ſter, that he is a *manifold* traitor, let him appear. *Shak.*

They receive *manifold* more in this preſent time, and in the world to come life everlaſting. *Luke* xviii. 30.

To repreſent to the life the *manifold* uſe of friendſhip, ſee how many things a man cannot do himſelf. *Bacon's Eſſays.*

They not obeying,
Incurr'd, what cou'd they leſs? the penalty;
And *manifold* in ſin deſerv'd to fall. *Milton's Par. Loſt.*

My ſcope in this experiment is *manifold.* *Boyle on Colours.*

We are not got further than the borders of the mineral kingdom, ſo very ample is it, ſo various and *manifold* its productions. *Woodward's Nat. Hiſt.*

MANIFO'LDED. *adj.* [*many* and *fold.*] Having many complications or doubles.

His puiſſant arms about his noble breaſt,
And *manifolded* ſhield, he bound about his wriſt. *Fa. Qu.*

MA'NIFOLDLY. *adv.* [from *manifold.*] In a manifold manner.

They were *manifoldly* acknowledged the ſavers of that country. *Sidney, b.* ii.

MANI'GLIONS. *n. ſ.* [in gunnery.] Two handles on the back of a piece of ordnance, caſt after the German form. *Bailey.*

MA'NIKIN. *n. ſ.* [*manniken*, Dutch.] A little man.

This is a dear *manikin* to you, Sir Toby.
—I have been dear to him, lad, ſome two thouſand ſtrong. *Shakeſpeare's Twelfth Night.*

MA'NIPLE. *n. ſ.* [*manipulus*, Latin.]

1. A handful.

2. A ſmall band of ſoldiers.

MANI'PULAR. *adj.* [from *manipulus*, Lat.] Relating to a maniple.

MANKI'LLER. *n. ſ.* [*man* and *killer.*] Murderer.

To kill *mankillers* man has lawful pow'r,
But not th' extended licence to devour. *Dryden's Fables.*

MANKI'ND. *n. ſ.* [*man* and *kind.*]

1. The race or ſpecies of human beings.

Plato witneſſeth, that ſoon after *mankind* began to increaſe, they built many cities. *Raleigh's Hiſt. of the World.*

All *mankind* alike require their grace,
All born to want; a miſerable race. *Pope's Odyſſey.*

2. Reſembling man not woman in form or nature.

A *mankind* witch! hence with her, out o' door:
A moſt intelligency bawd! *Shakeſp. Winter's Tale.*

MA'NLIKE. *adj.* [*man* and *like.*] Having the completion of man.

Such a right *manlike* man, as nature often erring, yet ſhews ſhe would fain make. *Sidney, b.* ii.

MA'NLESS. *adj.* [*man* and *leſs.*] Without men; not manned.

Sir Walter Raleigh was wont to ſay, the Spaniards were ſuddenly driven away with ſquibs; for it was no more but a ſtratagem of fire-boats *manleſs*, and ſent upon the armada at Calais by the favour of the wind in the night, that put them in ſuch terror, as they cut their cables. *Bacon.*

MA'NLINESS. *n. ſ.* [from *manly.*] Dignity; bravery; ſtoutneſs.

Young maſter, willing to ſhew himſelf a man, lets himſelf looſe to all irregularities; and thus courts credit and *manlineſs* in the caſting off the modeſty he has till then been kept in. *Locke.*

MA'NLY. *adj.* [from *man.*] Manlike; becoming a man; firm; brave; ſtout; undaunted; undiſmayed.

As did Æneas old Anchiſes bear,
So I bear thee upon my *manly* ſhoulders. *Shakeſpeare.*

Let's briefly put on *manly* readineſs,
And meet i' th' hall together. *Shakeſpeare's Macbeth.*

I'll ſpeak between the change of man and boy
With a reed voice; and turn two mincing ſteps
Into a *manly* ſtride. *Shakeſp. Merchant of Venice.*

Serene and *manly*, harden'd to ſuſtain
The load of life, and exercis'd in pain. *Dryden's Juv.*

See great Marcellus! how inur'd in toils,
He moves with *manly* grace. *Dryden's Æn.*

MA'NLY. *adv.* [from *man.*] With courage like a man.

MA'NNA. *n. ſ.*

Manna is properly a gum, and is honey-like juice concreted into a ſolid form, ſeldom ſo dry but it adheres more or leſs to the fingers in handling: its colour is whitiſh, yellowiſh, or browniſh, and it has in taſte the ſweetneſs of ſugar, and with it a ſharpneſs that renders it very agreeable: we are ſupplied with *manna* from Calabria and Sicily, which is the product of two different trees, but which are of the ſame genus, being both varieties of the aſh: when the heats of ſummer are free from rain, the leaves, the trunks, and branches of both theſe trees, exſudate a white honey juice, which concretes into what we call *manna*, forming itſelf as it runs, and according to its different quantity, into ſmall roundiſh drops, or long flakes: what flows out of the leaves of theſe trees is all natural, but the Italians procure a forced kind by wounding the trunks and branches: the fineſt *manna* of all is that which oozes naturally out of the leaves in Auguſt, after the ſeaſon of collecting the common *manna* is over: the French have another ſort of *manna*, produced from the

the larch tree, of a very different genus of the ash, and the very tree which produces oil of turpentine; this is called Briançon *manna*, from the country where it is produced: our black thorn, or sloe tree, sometimes yield a true *manna* from the ribs of the leaves in Autumn, but it is in a very small quantity: there is another sort called the *manna Persia*, produced from a small prickly shrub about four or five feet high, growing in Egypt, Armenia, Georgia, and Persia. The Hebrews, who had been acquainted with the last mentioned sort of *manna*, when they found a miraculous food in the desert resembling it, did not scruple to call it *manna*: this was a conjecture the more natural to them, as they saw plainly that this descended from the heavens in form of a dew, and concreted into the globules in which they found it; and the received opinion at that time was, that the Oriental *manna* was formed in the same manner; that it was a dew from the clouds concreted on the plant, none supposing, in those early times, that it was the natural juice of the shrub upon which it was found: it is however evident, that this was not of the nature of *manna*, because it melted away as the sun grew hot, whereas *manna* hardens in that heat. It is but lately that the world were convinced of the mistake of *manna* being an aërial produce, by an experiment being made by covering a tree with sheets in the *manna* season, and the finding as much *manna* on it afterwards as on those which were open to the air and dew. *Manna* is celebrated, both by the ancients and moderns, as a gentle and mild cathartick. *Hill.*

It would be well inquired, whether *manna* doth fall but upon certain herbs, or leaves only. *Bacon's Nat. Hist.*

The *manna* in heaven will suit every man's palate. *Locke.*

MA'NNER. *n.s.* [*maniere*, French.]

1. Form; method.

In my divine Emilia make me blest.
Find thou the *manner*, and the means prepare,
Possession, more than conquest, is my care. *Dryden.*

2. Custom; habit; fashion.

As the *manner* of some is. *New Testament.*

3. Certain degree.

It is in a *manner* done already;
For many carriages he hath dispatch'd
To the sea-side. *Shakesp. King John.*

The bread is in a *manner* common. 1 *Sam.* xxi. 5.

If the envy be general in a *manner* upon all the ministers of an estate, it is truly upon the state itself. *Bacon's Essays.*

This universe we have possest, and rul'd
In a *manner* at our will, th' affairs of earth. *Paradise Reg.*

Antony Augustinus does in a *manner* confess the charge. *Baker's Reflections on Learning.*

4. Sort; kind.

All *manner* of men assembled here in arms against God's peace and the king's: we charge you to repair to your dwelling-places. *Shakespeare Henry VI. p.* i.

A love that makes breath poor, and speech unable,
Beyond all *manner* of so much I love you. *Shakespeare.*

What *manner* of men were they whom ye slew? *Judges.*

The city may flourish in trade, and all *manner* of outward advantages. *Atterbury.*

5. Mien; cast of the look.

Air and *manner* are often more expressive than words. *Clarissa.*

Some men have a native dignity in their *manner*, which will procure them more regard by a look, than others can obtain by the most imperious commands. *Clarissa.*

6. Peculiar way.

If I melt into melancholy while I write, I shall be taken in the *manner*; and I sit by one too tender to these impressions. *Donne's Letters.*

It can hardly be imagined how great a difference was in the humour, disposition, and *manner*, of the army under Essex, and the other under Waller. *Clarendon, b.* viii.

Some few touches of your lordship, which I have endeavoured to express after your *manner*, have made whole poems of mine to pass with approbation. *Dryden's Juv.*

As man is known by his company, so a man's company may be known by his *manner* of expressing himself. *Swift.*

7. Way; sort.

The temptations of prosperity insinuate themselves after a gentle, but very powerful, *manner*. *Atterbury.*

8. Character of the mind.

His princes are as much distinguished by their *manners* as by their dominions; and even those among them, whose characters seem wholly made up of courage, differ from one another as to the particular kinds. *Addison.*

9. *Manners* in the plural. General way of life; morals; habits.

The kinds of musick have most operation upon *manners*: as, to make them warlike; to make them soft and effeminate. *Bacon's Nat. Hist.* N°. 114.

Every fool carries more or less in his face the signature of his *manners*, though more legible in some than others. *L'Estrange's Fables.*

We bring our *manners* to the blest abodes,
And think what pleases us must please the gods. *Dryden.*

10. [In the plural.] Ceremonious behaviour; studied civility.

The time will not allow the compliment,
Which very *manners* urge. *Shakesp. King Lear.*

These bloody accidents must excuse my *manners*,
That so neglected you. *Shakespeare's Othello.*

Our griefs and not our *manners* reason now. *Shakespeare.*

Ungracious wretch,
Fit for the mountains and the barbarous caves,
Where *manners* ne'er were preach'd. *Shakespeare.*

Dear Kate, you and I cannot be confined within the weak list of a country's fashion: we are the makers of *manners*, Kate. *Shakespeare's Henry V.*

Good *manners* bound her to invite
The stranger dame to be her guest that night. *Dryden.*

None but the careless and the confident would rush rudely into the presence of a great man: and shall we, in our applications to the great God, take that to be religion, which the common reason of mankind will not allow to be *manners*? *South's Sermons.*

Your passion bends
Its force against your nearest friends;
Which *manners*, decency, and pride,
Have taught you from the world to hide. *Swift.*

MA'NNERLINESS. *n.s.* [from *mannerly*.] Civility; ceremonious complaisance.

Others out of *mannerliness* and respect to God, though they deny this universal soul of the universe, yet have devised several systems of the universe. *Hale's Origin of Mankind.*

MA'NNERLY. *adj.* [from *manner*.] Civil; ceremonious; complaisant.

Tut, tut; here is a *mannerly* forbearance. *Shakespeare.*

Let me have
What thou think'st meet, and is most *mannerly*. *Shakesp.*

Fools make a mock at sin, affront the God whom we serve, and vilify religion; not to oppose them, by whatever *mannerly* names we may palliate the offence, is not modesty but cowardice, and a traiterous desertion of our allegiance to Christ. *Rogers's Sermons.*

MA'NNERLY. *adv.* Civilly; without rudeness.

When we've supp'd,
We'll *mannerly* demand thee of thy story. *Shakespeare.*

MA'NNIKIN. *n.s.* [*man* and *klein*, German.] A little man; a dwarf.

MA'NNISH. *adj.* [from *man*.] Having the appearance of a man; bold; masculine; impudent.

Nature had proportioned her without any fault, yet altogether seemed not to make up that harmony that Cupid delights in; the reason whereof might seem a *mannish* countenance, which overthrew that lovely sweetness, the noblest power of womankind, far fitter to prevail by parley than by battle. *Sidney.*

A woman, impudent and *mannish* grown,
Is not more loath'd than an effeminate man. *Shakespeare.*

When *mannish* Mevia, that two-handed whore,
Astride on horseback hunts the Tuscan boar. *Dryden.*

MANOR. *n.s.* [*manoir*, old French; *manerium*, low Latin; *maner*, Armorick.]

Manor signifies, in common law, a rule or government which a man hath over such as hold land within his fee. Touching the original of these *manors*, it seems, that, in the beginning, there was a certain compass or circuit of ground granted by the king to some men of worth, for him and his heirs to dwell upon, and to exercise some jurisdiction, more or less, within that compass, as he thought good to grant; performing him such services, and paying such yearly rent for the same, as he by his grant required: and that afterward this great man parcelled his land to other meaner men, injoining them again such services and rents as he thought good; and by that means, as he became tenant to the king, so the inferiors became tenants to him: but those great men, or their posterity, have alienated these mansions and lands so given them by their prince, and many for capital offences have forfeited them to the king; and thereby they still remain in the crown, or are bestowed again upon others. But whosoever possesses these *manors*, the liberty belonging to them is real and predial, and therefore remains, though the owners be changed. In these days, a *manor* rather signifies the jurisdiction and royalty incorporeal, than the land or site: for a man may have a *manor* in gross, as the law terms it, that is, the right and interest of a court-baron, with the perquisites thereto belonging. *Cowel.*

My parks, my walks, my *manors* that I had,
Ev'n now forsake me; and of all my lands
Is nothing left me. *Shakespeare's Henry VI.*

Kinsmen of mine,
By this so sicken'd their estates, that never
They shall abound as formerly. O many

Have broke their backs with laying *manors* on them
For this great journey. *Shakespeare's Rich.* II.

MANQUE'LLER. *n. s.* [man and cwellan, Saxon.] A murderer; a mankiller; a manslayer.

This was not Kayne the *manqueller*, but one of a gentler spirit and milder sex, to wit, a woman. *Carew.*

MANSE. *n. s.* [*mansio*, Latin.] A parsonage house.

MA'NSION. *n. s.* [*mansio*, Latin.]

1. Place of residence; abode; house.

All these are but ornaments of that divine spark within you, which being descended from heaven, could not elsewhere pick out so sweet a *mansion*. *Sidney.*

A fault no less grievous, if so be it were true, than if some king should build his *mansion*-house by the model of Solomon's palace. *Hooker, b.* v.

To leave his wife, to leave his babes,
His *mansion*, and his titles in a place,
From whence himself does fly? he loves us not. *Shakesp.*

Thy *mansion* wants thee, Adam, rise
First man, of men innumerable ordain'd;
First father! call'd by thee, I come thy guide
To the garden of bliss, thy seat prepar'd. *Milton.*

A *mansion* is provided thee; more fair
Than this, and worthy heav'n's peculiar care,
Not fram'd of common earth. *Dryden.*

2. Residence; abode.

These poets near our princes sleep,
And in one grave their *mansions* keep. *Denham.*

MANSLA'UGHTER. *n. s.* [*man* and *slaughter*.]

1. Murder; destruction of the human species.

The whole pleasure of that book standeth in open *manslaughter* and bold bawdry. *Ascham's Schoolmaster.*

To overcome in battle, and subdue
Nations, and bring home spoils, with infinite
Manslaughter, shall be held the highest pitch
Of human glory. *Milton's Par. Lost, b.* xi.

2. [In law.] The act of killing a man not wholly without fault, though without malice.

MANSLA'YER. *n. s.* [*man* and *slay*.] Murderer; one that has killed another.

Cities for refuge for the *manslayer*. *Num.* xxxv. 6.

MANSU'ETE. *adj.* [*mansuetus*, Lat.] Tame; gentle; not ferocious; not wild.

This holds not only in domestick and *mansuete* birds; for then it might be thought the effect of cicuration or institution, but also in the wild. *Ray on Creation.*

MA'NSUETUDE. *n. s.* [*mansuetude*, French; *mansuetudo*, Lat.] Tameness; gentleness.

The angry lion did present his paw,
Which by consent was given to *mansuetude*;
The fearful hare her ears, which by their law
Humility did reach to fortitude. *Herbert.*

MA'NTEL. *n. s.* [*mantel*, old Fr.] Work raised before a chimney to conceal it, whence the name, which originally signifies a cloak.

From the Italians we may learn how to raise fair *mantels* within the rooms, and how to disguise the shafts of chimnies. *Wotton's Architecture.*

If you break any china on the *mantletree* or cabinet, gather up the fragments. *Swift.*

MANTELE'T. *n. s.* [*mantelet*, French.]

1. A small cloak worn by women.

2. [In fortification.] A kind of moveable penthouse, made of pieces of timber sawed into planks, which being about three inches thick, are nailed one over another to the height of almost six feet: they are generally cased with tin, and set upon little wheels; so that in a siege they may be driven before the pioneers, and serve as blinds to shelter them from the enemy's small-shot: there are other *mantelets* covered on the top, whereof the miners make use to approach the walls of a town or castle. *Harris.*

MANTI'GER. *n. s.* [*man* and *tiger*.] A large monkey or baboon.

Near these was placed, by the black prince of Monomotapas's side, the glaring cat-a-mountain, and the man-mimicking *mantiger*. *Arbuth. and Pope.*

MA'NTLE. *n. s.* [*mantell*, Welsh.] A kind of cloak or garment thrown over the rest of the dress.

We, well-cover'd with the night's black *mantle*,
At unawares may beat down Edward's guard,
And seize himself. *Shakespeare's Henry* VI.

Poor Tom drinks the green *mantle* of the standing pool. *Shakespeare's King Lear.*

The day begins to break, and night is fled,
Whose pitchy *mantle* over-veil'd the earth. *Shakespeare.*

Their actions were covered and disguised with *mantles*, very usual in times of disorder, of religion and justice. *Hayward's Edward* VI.

The herald and children are cloathed with *mantles* of water green sattin; but the herald's *mantle* is streamed with gold. *Bacon's New Atlantis.*

Before the sun,
Before the heav'ns thou wert, and at the voice
Of God, as with a *mantle*, didst invest
The rising world of waters dark and deep,
Won from the void and formless infinite. *Milton.*

By which the beauty of the earth appears,
The divers-colour'd *mantle* which she wears. *Sandys.*

Upon loosening of his *mantle* the eggs fell from him at unawares, and the eagle was a third time defeated. *L'Estrange.*

Dan Pope for thy misfortune griev'd,
With kind concern and skill has weav'd
A silken web; and ne'er shall fade
Its colours: gently has he laid
The *mantle* o'er thy sad distress,
And Venus shall the texture bless. *Prior.*

A spacious veil from his broad shoulders flew,
That set the unhappy Phaeton to view;
The flaming chariot and the steeds it shew'd,
And the whole fable in the *mantle* glow'd. *Addison.*

To MA'NTLE. *v. a.* [from the noun.] To cloke; to cover; to disguise.

As the morning steals upon the night,
Melting the darkness; so their rising senses
Begin to chace the ign'rant fumes, that *mantle*
Their clearer reason. *Shakespeare's Tempest.*

I left them
I' th' filthy *mantled* pool beyond your cell,
There dancing up to th' chins. *Shakespeare's Tempest.*

To MA'NTLE. *v. n.* [The original of the signification of this word is not plain. *Skinner* considers it as relative to the expansion of a *mantle*: as, *the hawk* mantleth; she spreads her wings like a *mantle*.]

1. To spread the wings as a hawk in pleasure.

The swan with arched neck,
Between her white wings *mantling*, rows
Her state with oary feet. *Milton's Par. Lost, b.* viii.

2. To joy; to revel.

My frail fancy fed with full delight
Doth bathe in bliss, and *mantleth* most at ease;
Ne thinks of other heaven, but how it might
Her heart's desire with most contentment please. *Spenser.*

3. To be expanded; to spread luxuriantly.

The pair that clad
Each shoulder broad, came *mantling* o'er his breast
With regal ornament. *Milton's Par. Lost, b.* v.

The *mantling* vine
Lays forth her purple grape, and gently creeps
Luxuriant. *Milton's Par. Lost, b.* iv.

I saw them under a green *mantling* vine,
That crawls along the side of yon small hill,
Plucking ripe clusters. *Milton.*

You'll sometimes meet a fop, of nicest tread,
Whose *mantling* peruke veils his empty head. *Gay.*

He with the Nais went to dwell,
Leaving the nectar'd feasts of Jove;
And where his mazy waters flow,
He gave the *mantling* vine, to grow
A trophy to his love. *Fenton's Ode to Lord Gower.*

4. To gather any thing on the surface; to froth.

There are a sort of men, whose visages
Do cream and *mantle* like a standing pond;
And do a wilful stillness entertain,
With purpose to be drest in an opinion
Of wisdom, gravity, profound conceit. *Shakespeare.*

It drinketh fresh, flowereth, and *mantleth* exceedingly. *Bacon's Nat. Hist.* N°. 46.

From plate to plate your eye-balls roll,
And the brain dances to the *mantling* bowl. *Pope's Horace.*

5. To ferment; to be in sprightly agitation.

When *mantling* blood
Flow'd in his lovely cheeks; when his bright eyes
Sparkl'd with youthful fires; when ev'ry grace
Shone in the father, which now crowns the son. *Smith.*

MA'NTUA. *n. s.* [this is perhaps corrupted from *manteau*, Fr.] A lady's gown.

Not Cynthia, when her *mantua*'s pinn'd awry,
E'er felt such rage, resentment, and despair,
As thou, sad virgin! for thy ravish'd hair. *Pope.*

How naturally do you apply your hands to each other's lappets, ruffles, and *mantua* s. *Swift.*

MA'NTUAMAKER. *n. s.* [*mantua* and *maker*.] One who makes gowns for women.

By profession a *mantuamaker*: I am employed by the most fashionable ladies. *Addison's Guardian.*

MA'NUAL. *adj.* [*manualis*, Latin; *manuel*, French.]

1. Performed by the hand.

The speculative part of painting, without the assistance of *manual* operation, can never attain to that perfection which is its object. *Dryden's Dufresnoy.*

2. Used by the hand.

The treasurer obliged himself to expiate the injury, to procure some declaration under his majesty's sign *manual*. *Clarendon.*

MA'NUAL. *n. s.* A small book, such as may be carried in the hand.

This *manual* of laws, stiled the confessor's laws, contains but few heads. *Hale's Common Law of England.*

In those prayers which are recommended to the use of the devout persons of your church, in the *manuals* and offices allowed them in our own language, they would be careful to have nothing they thought scandalous. *Stillingfleet.*

MANU'BIAL. *adj.* [*manubiæ*, Lat.] Belonging to spoil; taken in war. *Dict.*

MANU'BRIUM. n. s. [Latin.] A handle.

Though the sucker move easily enough up and down in the cylinder by the help of the *manubrium*, yet if the *manubrium* be taken off, it will require a considerable strength to move it. *Boyle.*

MANUDU'CTION. *n. s.* [*manuductio*, Latin.] Guidance by the hand.

We find no open tract, or constant *manuduction*, in this labyrinth. *Preface to Brown's Vulgar Errours.*

That they are carried by the *manuduction* of a rule, is evident from the constant steadiness and regularity of their motion. *Glanvile.*

This is a direct *manuduction* to all kind of sin, by abusing the conscience with undervaluing persuasions concerning the malignity and guilt even of the foulest. *South's Sermons.*

MANUFA'CTURE. *n. s.* [*manus* and *facio*, Latin; *manufacture*, French.]

1. The practice of making any piece of workmanship.
2. Any thing made by art.

Heav'n's pow'r is infinite: earth, air, and sea,
The *manufacture* mass the making pow'r obey. *Dryden.*

The peasants are clothed in a coarse kind of canvass, the *manufacture* of the country. *Addison on Italy.*

To MANUFA'CTURE. *v. a.* [*manufacturer*, French.] To make by art and labour; to form by workmanship.

MANUFA'CTURER. *n. s.* [*manufacturier*, French; *manufacturus*, Lat.] A workman; an artificer.

In the practices of artificers and the *manufacturers* of various kinds, the end being proposed, we find out ways of composing things for the several uses of human life. *Watts.*

To MANUMI'SE. *v. a.* [*manumitto*, Latin.] To set free; to dismiss from slavery.

A constant report of a danger so eminent run through the whole castle, even into the deep dungeons, by the compassion of certain *manumised* slaves. *Knolles's Hist. of the Turks.*

He presents
To thee renown'd for piety and force,
Poor captives *manumis'd*, and matchless horse. *Waller.*

MANUMI'SSION. *n. s.* [*manumission*, Fr. *manumissio*, Lat.] The act of giving liberty to slaves.

Slaves wore iron rings until their *manumission* or preferment. *Brown's Vulgar Errours, b.* iv.

The pileus was somewhat like a night-cap, as the symbol of liberty, and therefore given to slaves at their *manumission*. *Arbuthnot on Coins.*

To MANUMI'T. *v. a.* [*manumitto*, Latin.] To release from slavery.

Help to *manumit* and release him from those servile drudgeries to vice, under which those remain who live without God. *Government of the Tongue.*

Thou wilt beneath the burthen bow,
And glad receive the *manumitting* blow
On thy shav'd slavish head. *Dryden's Juvenal.*

MANU'RABLE. *adj.* [from *manure.*] Capable of cultivation.

This book gives an account of the *manurable* lands in every manor. *Hale's Origin of Mankind.*

MANU'RANCE. *n. s.* [from *manure.*] Agriculture; cultivation. An obsolete word, worthy of revival.

Although there should none of them fall by the sword, yet they being kept from *manurance*, and their cattle from running abroad, by this hard restraint they would quickly devour one another. *Spenser on Ireland.*

To MANU'RE. *v. a.* [*manouvrer*, French.]

1. To cultivate by manual labour.

They mock our scant *manuring*, and require
More hands than ours to lop their wanton growth. *Milt.*

2. To dung; to fatten with composts.

Fragments of shells, reduced by the agitation of the sea to powder, are used for the *manuring* of land. *Woodward.*

Revenge her slaughter'd citizens,
Or share their fate: the corps of half her senate
Manure the fields of Thessaly, while we
Sit here, deliberating in cold debates. *Addison's Cato.*

MANU'RE. *n. s.* [from the verb.] Soil to be laid on lands; dung or compost to fatten land.

When the Nile from Pharian fields is fled,
The fat *manure* with heav'nly fire is warm'd. *Dryden.*

Mud makes an extraordinary *manure* for land that is sandy. *Mortimer's Husbandry.*

MANU'REMENT. *n. s.* [from *manure.*] Cultivation; improvement.

The *manurement* of wits is like that of soils, where before the pains of tilling or sowing, men consider what the mould will bear. *Wotton on Education.*

MANU'RER. *n. s.* [from the verb.] He who manures land; a husbandman.

MA'NUSCRIPT. *n. s.* [*manuscrit*, Fr. *manuscriptum*, Latin.] A book written, not printed.

A collection of rare *manuscripts*, exquisitely written in Arabick, and sought in the most remote parts by the diligence of Erpenius, the most excellent linguist, were upon sale to the jesuits. *Wotton.*

Her majesty has perused the *manuscript* of this opera, and given it her approbation. *Dryden's Dedication to K. Arthur.*

MA'NY. *adj.* comp. *more*, superl. *most.* [mænig, Saxon.]

1. Consisting of a great number; numerous; more than few.

Our enemy, and the destroyers of our country, slew *many* of us. *Judg.* xvi. 24.

When *many* atoms descend in the air, the same cause which makes them be *many*, makes them be light in proportion to their multitude. *Digby on the Soul.*

The apostles never give the least directions to Christians to appeal to the bishop of Rome for a determination of the *many* differences which, in those times, happened among them. *Tillotson's Sermons.*

2. Marking number indefinite.

Both men and women, as *many* as were willing-hearted, brought bracelets. *Exod.* xxxv. 22.

3. Powerful; with *too*, and in low language.

They come to vie power and expence with those that are too high, and too *many*, for them. *L'Estrange's Fables.*

MA'NY. *n. s.* [This word is remarkable in the Saxon for its frequent use, being written with twenty variations: mænegeo, mænegeo, mænigeo, mænigo, mænigu, mænio, mænıu, mænýgeo, manegeo, manigu, manige, manigo, menegeo, menego, menegu, menigeo, menigo, menigu, menio, menıu.]

1. A multitude; a company; a great number; people.

After him the rascal *many* ran,
Heaped together in rude rabblement. *Fairy Queen.*

O thou fond *many!* with what loud applause
Did'st thou beat heav'n with blessing Bolingbroke. *Shakesp.*

I had a purpose now
To lead our *many* to the holy land;
Lest rest and lying still might make them look
Too near into my state. *Shakesp. Henry* IV.

A care-craz'd mother of a *many* children. *Shakespeare.*

The vulgar and the *many* are fit only to be led or driven, but by no means fit to guide themselves. *South's Sermons.*

There parting from the king the chiefs divide,
And wheeling East and West, before their *many* ride. *Dryd.*

He is liable to a great *many* inconveniences every moment of his life. *Tillotson's Sermons.*

Seeing a great *many* in rich gowns, he was amazed to find that persons of quality were up so early. *Addison's Freeholder.*

2. *Many*, when it is used before a singular noun, seems to be a substantive.

Thou art a collop of my flesh,
And for thy sake have I shed *many* a tear. *Shakespeare.*

He is beset with enemies, the meanest of which is not without *many* and *many* a way to the wreaking of a malice. *L'Estrange's Fables.*

Broad were their collars too, and every one
Was set about with *many* a costly stone. *Dryden.*

Many a child can have the distinct clear ideas of two and three long before he has any idea of infinite. *Locke.*

3. *Many* is used much in composition.

MANYCO'LOURED. *adj.* [*many* and *colour.*] Having many colours.

Hail *manycoloured* messenger, that ne'er
Do'st disobey the voice of Jupiter. *Shakesp. Tempest.*

He hears not me, but on the other side
A *manycolour'd* peacock having spy'd,
Leaves him and me. *Donne.*

The hoary majesty of spades appears;
Puts forth one manly leg, to sight reveal'd,
The rest his *manycoloured* robe conceal'd. *Pope.*

MANYCO'RNERED. *adj.* [*many* and *corner.*] Polygonal; having many corners.

Search those *manycorner'd* minds,
Where woman's crooked fancy turns and winds. *Dryden.*

MANYHE'ADED. *adj.* [*many* and *head.*] Having many heads.

Some of the wiser seeing that a popular licence is indeed the *manyheaded* tyranny, prevailed with the rest to make Musidorus their chief. *Sidney, b.* iii.

The proud Duessa came
High mounted on her *manyheaded* beast. *Fairy Queen.*

The *manyheaded* beaſt hath broke,
Or ſhaken from his head, the royal yoke. *Denham.*
Thoſe were the preludes of his fate,
That form'd his manhood to ſubdue
The hydra of the *manyheaded* hiſſing crew. *Dryden.*

MANYLA'NGUAGED. *adj.* [*many* and *language.*] Having many languages.

Seek Atrides on the Spartan ſhore;
He, wand'ring long, a wider circle made,
And *manylanguag'd* nations has ſurvey'd. *Pope's Odyſſey.*

MANYPE'OPLED. *adj.* [*many* and *people.*] Numerouſly populous.

He from the *manypeopl'd* city flies;
Contemns their labours, and the drivers cries. *Sandys.*

MANYTI'MES, an adverbial phraſe. Often; frequently.

They are Roman catholick in the device and legend, which are both of them *manytimes* taken out of the ſcriptures. *Addiſon on ancient Medals.*

MAP. *n. ſ.* [*mappa*, low Latin.] A geographical picture on which lands and ſeas are delineated according to the longitude and latitude.

Zelmane earneſtly entreated Dorus, that he would beſtow a *map* of his little world upon her, that ſhe might ſee whether it were troubled with ſuch unhabitable climes of cold deſpairs, and hot rages, as her's was. *Sidney.*

I will take the *map* of Ireland, and lay it before me, and make mine eyes my ſchoolmaſters, to give my underſtanding to judge of your plot. *Spenſer on Ireland.*

Old coins are like ſo many *maps* for explaining the ancient geography. *Addiſon on ancient Coins.*

O'er the *map* my finger taught to ſtray,
Croſs many a region marks the winding way;
From ſea to ſea, from realm to realm I rove,
And grow a mere geographer by love. *Tickell.*

To MAP. *v. a.* [from the noun.] To delineate; to ſet down.

I am near to the place where they ſhould meet, if Piſanio have *mapp'd* it right. *Shakeſpeare's Cymbeline.*

MAPLE *tree. n. ſ.*

The *maple tree* hath jagged or angular leaves; the ſeeds grow two together in hard-winged veſſels: there are ſeveral ſpecies, of which the greater *maple* is falſly called the ſycamore tree: the common *maple* is a tree frequent in hedgerows. *Miller.*

The platane round,
The carver holme, the *mapple* ſeldom inward ſound. *Spenſ.*

Of the rotteneſt *maple* wood burnt to aſhes they make a ſtrong lye. *Mortimer's Huſbandry.*

MA'PPERY. *n. ſ.* [from *map.*] The art of planning and deſigning. *Hanmer.*

The ſtill and mental parts,
That do contrive how many hands ſhall ſtrike
When fitneſs calls them on;
They call this bedwork, *mapp'ry*, cloſet war. *Shakeſpeare.*

To MAR. *v. a.* [amyrran, Saxon.] To injure; to ſpoil; to hurt; to miſchief; to damage. Obſolete.

Loſs is no ſhame, nor to be leſs than foe,
But to be leſſer than himſelf, doth *mar*
Both looſer's lot, and victor's praiſe alſo. *Fairy Queen.*

The maſter may here only ſtumble, and perchance fall in teaching, to the *marring* and maiming of the ſcholar in learning. *Aſcham's Schoolmaſter.*

When prieſts are more in words than matter,
When brewers *marr* their malt with water. *Shakeſpeare.*

I pray you *mar* no more trees with writing ſongs in their barks.

—I pray you *mar* no more of my verſes with reading them ill-favouredly. *Shakeſpeare's As you like it.*

Beware thine honour, be not then diſgrac'd,
Take care thou *mar* not when thou think'ſt to mend. *Fairf.*

Aumarle became the man that all did *mar*,
Whether through indiſcretion, chance, or worſe. *Daniel.*

The ambition to prevail in great things is leſs harmful than that other, to appear in every thing; for that breeds confuſion, and *marrs* buſineſs, when great in dependencies. *Bacon's Eſſays.*

O! could we ſee how cauſe from cauſe doth ſpring!
How mutually they link'd and folded are:
And hear how oft one diſagreeing ſtring
The harmony doth rather make than *marr!* *Davies.*

Ire, envy, and deſpair,
Marr'd all his borrow'd viſage, and betray'd
Him counterfeit. *Milton's Par. Loſt.*

Had ſhe been there, untimely joy through all
Mens hearts diffus'd, had *marr'd* the funeral. *Waller.*

Mother!
Tis much unſafe my ſire to diſobey:
Not only you provoke him to your coſt,
But mirth is *marr'd*, and the good cheer is loſt. *Dryden.*

MARANATHA. n. ſ. [Syriack.] It ſignifies, the Lord comes, or, the Lord is come: it was a form of the denouncing or anathematizing among the Jews. St. Paul pronounces, If any love not the Lord Jeſus Chriſt, let him be *anathema maranatha*, which is as much as to ſay, May'ſt thou be devoted to the greateſt of evils, and to the utmoſt ſeverity of God's judgments; may the Lord come quickly to take vengeance of thy crimes. *Calmet.*

MARA'SMUS. *n. ſ.* [μαρασμὸς, from μαραίνω.] A conſumption, in which perſons waſte much of their ſubſtance. *Quincy.*

Pining atrophy,
Maraſmus, and wide-waſting peſtilence. *Milt. Par. Loſt.*

A *maraſmus* imports a conſumption following a fever; a conſumption or withering of the body, by reaſon of a natural extinction of the native heat, and an extenuation of the body, cauſed through an immoderate heat. *Harvey.*

MA'RBLE. *n. ſ.* [*marbre*, French; *marmor*, Latin.]

1. Stone uſed in ſtatues and elegant buildings, capable of a bright poliſh, and in a ſtrong heat calcining into lime.

He plies her hard, and much rain wears the *marble.* *Shakeſpeare's Henry VI.*

Whole as the *marble*, founded as the rock. *Shakeſp.*

Thou *marble* hew'ſt, ere long to part with breath;
And houſes rear'ſt, unmindful of thy death. *Sandys.*

Some dry their corn infected with the brine,
Then grind with *marbles*, and prepare to dine. *Dryden.*

The two flat ſides of two pieces of *marble* will more eaſily approach each other, between which there is nothing but water or air, than if there be a diamond between them; not that the parts of the diamond are more ſolid, but becauſe the parts of water being more eaſily ſeparable, give way to the approach of the two pieces of *marble.* *Locke.*

2. Little balls of marble with which children play.

Marbles taught him percuſſion, and the laws of motion; nut-crackers the uſe of the leaver. *Arbuthnot and Pope.*

3. A ſtone remarkable for the ſculpture or inſcription; as, the Oxford *marbles.*

MA'RBLE. *adj.*

1. Made of marble.

Pygmalion's fate reverſt is mine,
His *marble* love took fleſh and blood,
All that I worſhipp'd as divine,
That beauty, now 'tis underſtood,
Appears to have no more of life,
Than that whereof he fram'd his wife. *Waller.*

2. Variegated, or red like *marble.*

Shall I ſee far-fetched inventions? ſhall I labour to lay *marble* colours over my ruinous thoughts? or rather, though the pureneſs of my virgin-mind be ſtained, let me keep the true ſimplicity of my word. *Sidney, b. ii.*

The appendix ſhall be printed by itſelf, ſtitched, and with a *marble* cover. *Swift.*

To MA'RBLE. *v. a.* [*marbrer*, French, from the noun.] To variegate, or vein like *marble.*

A ſheet of very well ſleeked *marbled* paper did not caſt any of its diſtinct colours upon the wall with an equal diffuſion. *Boyle on Colours.*

Marian
Marbled with ſage the hard'ning cheeſe ſhe preſs'd;
And yellow butter Marian's ſkill profeſs'd. *Gay's Paſtorals.*

MARBLEHE'ARTED. *adj.* [*marble* and *heart.*] Cruel; inſenſible; hard-hearted.

Ingratitude! thou *marblehearted* fiend,
More hideous, when thou ſhew'ſt thee in a child,
Than the ſea monſter. *Shakeſpeare's King Lear.*

MA'RCASITE. *n. ſ.*

The term *marcaſite* has been very improperly uſed by ſome for biſmuth, and by others for zink: the more accurate writers however always expreſs a ſubſtance different from either of theſe by it, ſulphureous and metallick. The *marcaſite* is a ſolid hard foſſil, of an obſcurely and irregularly foliaceous ſtructure, of a bright glittering appearance, and naturally found in continued beds among the veins of ores, or in the fiſſures of ſtone: the variety of forms this mineral puts on is almoſt endleſs: as it is generally found among the ores of metals, it is frequently impregnated with particles of them, and of other foſſile bodies, and thence aſſumes various colours and degrees of hardneſs. There are however only three diſtinct ſpecies of it; one of a bright gold colour, another of a bright ſilver, and a third of a dead white: the ſilvery one ſeems to be peculiarly meant by the writers on the *Materia Medica*. *Marcaſite* is very frequent in the mines of Cornwall, where the workmen call it mundick, but more ſo in Germany, where they extract vitriol and ſulphur from it, beſides which it contains a quantity of arſenick. *Hill.*

The writers of minerals give the name pyrites and *marcaſites* indifferently to the ſame ſort of body: I reſtrain the name of pyrites wholly to the nodules, or thoſe that are found lodged in ſtrata that are ſeparate: the *marcaſite* is part of the matter that either conſtitutes the ſtratum, or is lodged in the perpendicular fiſſures. *Woodward Met. Foſſils.*

The acid ſalt diſſolved in water is the ſame with oil of ſulphur per campanam, and abounding much in the bowels of the earth, and particularly in *marcaſites*, unites itſelf to the other ingredients of the *marcaſite*, which are bitumen, iron, copper,

copper, and earth, and with them compounds alum, vitriol, and sulphur: with the earth alone it compounds alum; with the metal alone, or metal and earth together, it compounds vitriol; and with the bitumen and earth it compounds sulphur: whence it comes to pass, that *marcasites* abound with those three minerals. *Newton's Opticks.*

Here *marcasites* in various figures wait,
To ripen to a true metallick state. *Garth's Dispensatory.*

MARCH. *n. s.* [from *Mars.*] The third month of the year.

March is drawn in tawny, with a fierce aspect, a helmet upon his head, to shew this month was dedicated to Mars. *Peacham on Drawing.*

To MARCH. *v. n.* [*marcher*, French, for *varicare*, *Menage*, from *Mars*, *Junius.*]

1. To move in military form.

Well *march* we on,
To give obedience where 'tis truly ow'd. *Shakespeare.*

He *marched* in battle array with his power against Arphaxad. *Jud.* i. 13.

Maccabeus *marched* forth, and slew five-and-twenty thousand persons. 2 *Mac.* xii. 26.

My father, when some days before his death
He ordered me to *march* for Utica,
Wept o'er me. *Addison's Cato.*

2. To walk in a grave, deliberate, or stately manner.

Plexirtus finding that if nothing else, famine would at last bring him to destruction, thought better by humbleness to creep where by pride he could not *march*. *Sidney, b.* ii.

Doth York intend no harm to us,
That thus he *marcheth* with thee arm in arm. *Shakesp.*

Our bodies, ev'ry footstep that they make,
March towards death, until at last they die. *Davies.*

Like thee appear,
Like thee, great son of Jove, like thee,
When clad in rising majesty,
Thou *marchest* down o'er Delos' hills. *Prior.*

The power of wisdom *march'd* before. *Pope's Odyssey.*

To MARCH. *v. n.*

1. To put in military movement.

Cyrus *marching* his army for divers days over mountains of snow, the dazzling splendor of its whiteness prejudiced the sight of very many of his soldiers. *Boyle on Colours.*

2. To bring in regular procession.

March them again in fair array,
And bid them form the happy day;
The happy day design'd to wait
On William's fame, and Europe's fate. *Prior.*

MARCH. *n. s.* [*marcher*, French.]

1. Movement; journey of soldiers.

These troops came to the army harrassed with a long and wearisome *march*, and cast away their arms and garments, and fought in their shirts. *Bacon's War with Spain.*

Who should command, by his Almighty nod,
These chosen troops, unconscious of the road,
And unacquainted with th' appointed end,
Their *marches* to begin, and thither tend. *Blackmore.*

Their *march* begins in military state. *Van. of hu. Wishes.*

2. Grave and solemn walk.

Waller was smooth, but Dryden taught to join
The varying verse, the full resounding line,
The long majestick *march*, and energy divine. *Pope.*

3. Deliberate or laborious walk.

We came to the roots of the mountain, and had a very troublesome *march* to gain the top of it. *Addison on Italy.*

4. Signals to move.

The drums presently striking up a *march*, they make no longer stay, but forward they go directly towards Neostat. *Knolles's Hist. of the Turks.*

5. *Marches*, without singular. [*marcu*, Gothick; mearc, Saxon; *marche*, French.] Borders; limits; confines.

They of those *marches*
Shall be a wall sufficient to defend
Our inland from the pilferring borderers. *Shakespeare.*

The English colonies were enforced to keep continual guards upon the borders and *marches* round them. *Davies.*

It is not fit that a king of an island should have any *marches* or borders but the four seas. *Davies on Ireland.*

MA'RCHER. *n. s.* [from *marcheur*, French.] President of the marches or borders.

Many of our English lords made war upon the Welshmen at their own charge; the lands which they gained they held to their own use; they were called lords *marchers*, and had royal liberties. *Davies on Ireland.*

MA'RCHIONESS. *n. s.* [feminine, formed by adding the English female termination to the Latin *marchio.*] The wife of a marquis.

The king's majesty
Does purpose honour to you, no less flowing
Than *marchioness* of Pembroke. *Shakesp. Henry* VIII.

From a private gentlewoman he made me a *marchioness*, and from a *marchioness* a queen, and now he intends to crown my innocency with the glory of martyrdom. *Bacon's Apophth.*

The lady *marchioness*, his wife, sollicited very diligently the timely preservation of her husband. *Clarendon, b.* viii.

MA'RCHPANE. *n. s.* [*massepane*, French.] A kind of sweet bread, or biscuit.

Along whose ridge such bones are met,
Like comfits round in *marchpane* set. *Sidney, b.* ii.

MA'RCID. *adj.* [*marcidus*, Latin.] Lean; pining; withered.

A burning colliquative fever, the softer parts being melted away, the heat continuing its adustion upon the drier and fleshy parts, changes into a *marcid* fever. *Harvey on Cons.*

He on his own fish pours the noblest oil;
That to your *marcid* dying herbs assign'd,
By the rank smell and taste betrays its kind. *Dryden.*

MA'RCOUR. *n. s.* [*marcor*, Latin.] Leanness; the state of withering; waste of flesh.

Considering the exolution and languor ensuing the action of venery in some, the extenuation and *marcour* in others, it much abridgeth our days. *Brown's Vulgar Errours, b.* iii.

A *marcour* is either imperfect, tending to a lesser withering, which is curable; or perfect, that is, an entire wasting of the body, excluding all means of cure. *Harvey on Cons.*

MARE. *n. s.* [mane, Saxon.]

1. The female of a horse.

A pair of coursers born of heav'nly breed,
Whom Circe stole from her celestial sire,
By substituting *mares*, produc'd on earth,
Whose wombs conceiv'd a more than mortal birth. *Dryd.*

2. [From *mara*, the name of a spirit imagined by the nations of the north to torment sleepers.] A kind of torpor or stagnation, which seems to press the stomach with a weight; the night hag.

Mab, his merry queen by night,
Bestrides young folks that lie upright,
In elder times the *mare* that hight,
Which plagues them out of measure. *Drayton's Nymphid.*

Mushrooms cause the incubus, or the *mare* in the stomach. *Bacon's Nat. Hist.* N°. 546.

MA'RESCHAL. *n. s.* [*mareschal*, French, derived by *Junius* from *mare*, the female of an horse.] A chief commander of an army.

O William, may thy arms advance,
That he may lose Dinant next year,
And so be *mareschal* of France. *Prior.*

MA'RGARITE. *n. s.* [*margarita*, Latin; *marguerite*, French.] A pearl.

Silver is the second metal, and signifies purity; among the planets it holdeth with luna, among precious stones with the *margarite* or pearl. *Peacham on Blazoning.*

MA'RGARITES. *n. s.* An herb. *Ains.*

MARGE. }
MA'RGENT. } *n. s.* [*margo*, Latin; *marge*, French.]
MA'RGIN. }

1. The border; the brink; the edge; the verge.

He drew his flaming sword, and struck
At him so fiercely, that the upper *marge*
Of his sevenfold shield away it took. *Fairy Queen, b.* ii.

Never since
Met we on hill, in dale, forest, or mead,
Or on the beached *margent* of the sea. *Shakespeare.*

An airy crowd came rushing where he stood,
Which fill'd the *margin* of the fatal flood. *Dryden's Æn.*

2. The edge of a page left blank, or fill'd with a short note.

As much love in rhime,
As would be cramm'd up in a sheet of paper
Writ on both sides the leaf, *margent* and all. *Shakespeare.*

Reconcile those two places, which both you and the *margins* of our bibles acknowledge to be parallel. *Hammond.*

He knows in law, nor text, nor *margent*. *Swift.*

3. The edge of a wound or sore.

All the advantage to be gathered from it is only from the evenness of its *margin*, the purpose will be as fully answered by keeping that under only. *Sharp's Surgery.*

MA'RGINAL. *n. s.* [*marginal*, French, from *margin.*] Placed, or written on the margin.

We cannot better interpret the meaning of these words than pope Leo himself expoundeth them, whose speech concerning our Lord's ascension may serve instead of a *marginal* gloss. *Hooker, b.* v.

What remarks you find worthy of your riper observation note with a *marginal* star, as being worthy of your second year's review. *Watts's Logick.*

MA'RGINATED. *adj.* [*marginatus*, Lat. from *margin.*] Having a margin.

MA'RGRAVE. *n. s.* [*marck* and *graff*, German.] A title of sovereignty in Germany; in its original import, keeper of the marches or borders.

MA'RIETS. *n. s.* A kind of violet. *Dict.*

MA'RIGOLD. *n. s.* [*Mary* and *gold.*] A yellow flower, devoted, I suppose, to the virgin.

The *marigold* hath a radiated discous flower; the petals of them are, for the most part, crenated, the seeds crooked and rough; those which are uppermost long, and those within short: the leaves are long, intire, and, for the most part, succulent. *Miller.*

Your circle will teach you to draw truly all spherical bodies. The most of flowers; as, the rose and *marigold. Peach.*

The *marigold*, whose courtier's face
Echoes the sun, and doth unlace
Her at his rise. *Cleaveland.*

Fair is the gilliflower, of gardens sweet,
Fair is the *marigold*, for pottage meet. *Gay's Pastorals.*

To MA'RINATE. *v. a.* [*mariner*, French.] To salt fish, and then preserve them in oil or vinegar.

Why am I styl'd a cook, if I'm so loath
To *marinate* my fish, or season broth. *King's Cookery.*

MARI'NE. *adj.* [*marinus*, Latin.] Belonging to the sea.

The king was desirous that the ordinances of England and France, touching *marine* affairs, might be reduced into one form. *Hayward.*

Vast multitudes of shells, and other *marine* bodies, are found lodged in all sorts of stone. *Woodward.*

No longer Circe could her flame disguise,
But to the suppliant God *marine* replies. *Garth's Ovid.*

MARI'NE. *n. s.* [*la marine*, French.]

1. Sea-affairs.

Nearchus, who commanded Alexander's fleet, and Onesicrates his intendant-general of *marine*, have both left relations of the state of the Indies at that time. *Arbuthnot.*

2. A soldier taken on shipboard to be employed in descents upon the land.

MA'RINER. *n. s.* [from *mare*, Latin; *marinier*, French.] A seaman; a sailor.

The merry *mariner* unto his word
Soon hearkened, and her painted boat straightway
Turn'd to the shore. *Fairy Queen, b.* ii.

Your ships are not well mann'd,
Your *mariners* are muliteers, or reapers. *Shakespeare.*

We oft deceive ourselves, as did that *mariner* who, mistaking them for precious stones, brought home his ship fraught with common pebbles from the remotest Indies. *Glanville's Scep.*

His busy *mariners* he hastes,
His shatter'd sails with rigging to restore. *Dryden.*

What *mariner* is not afraid,
To venture in a ship decay'd. *Swift's Miscel.*

MA'RJORAM. *n. s.* [*marjorana*, Lat. *marjolaine*, Fr.] A fragrant plant of many kinds; the bastard kind only grows here.

The nymphs of the mountains would be drawn upon their heads garlands of honeysuckles, woodbine, and sweet *marjoram. Peacham on Drawing.*

MA'RISH. *n. s.* [*marais*, French; *merrc*, Saxon; *maersche*, Dutch.] A bog; a fen; a swamp; watry ground; a marsh; a morass; a more.

The flight was made towards Dalkeith; which way, by reason of the *marish*, the English horse were least able to pursue. *Hayward.*

When they had avenged the blood of their brother, they turned again to the *marish* of Jordan. 1 *Mac.* ix. 42.

Lodronius, carried away with the breaking in of the horsemen, was driven into a *marish*; where, after being sore wounded, and fast in the mud, he had done the uttermost. *Knolles's Hist. of the Turks.*

His limbs he coucheth in the cooler shades;
Oft, when heaven's burning eye the fields invades,
To *marishes* resorts. *Sandys's Paraphrase.*

From the other hill
To their fix'd station, all in bright array,
The cherubim descended; on the ground
Gliding meteorous, as ev'ning mist
Ris'n from a river, o'er the *marish* glides,
And gathers ground fast at the labourer's heel. *Milton.*

MA'RISH. *adj.* Morish; fenny; boggy; swampy.

It hath been a great endangering to the health of some plantations, that they have built along the sea and rivers, in *marish* and unwholesome grounds. *Bacon's Essays.*

The fen and quamire so *marish* by kind,
Are to be drained. *Tusser's Husbandry.*

MA'RITAL. *n. s.* [*maritus*, Latin; *marital*, French.] Pertaining to a husband; incident to a husband.

If any one retains a wife that has been taken in the act of adultery, he hereby incurs the guilt of the crime of bawdry. But because repentance does, for the most part, consist in the mind, and since Christian charity, as well as *marital* affection, easily induces a belief thereof, this law is not observed. *Ayliffe's Parergon.*

It has been determined by some unpolite professors of the law, that a husband may exercise his *marital* authority so far, as to give his wife moderate correction. *Art of Tormenting.*

MA'RITATED. *adj.* [from *maritus*, Latin.] Having a husband. *Dict.*

MARI'TIMAL. } *adj.* [*maritimus*, Latin; *maritime*, Fr.]
MA'RITIME. }

1. Performed on the sea; marine.

I discoursed of a *maritimal* voyage, and the passages and incidents therein. *Raleigh's Essays.*

2. Relating to the sea; naval.

At the parliament at Oxford, his youth, and want of experience in *maritime* service, had somewhat been shrewdly touched. *Wotton's Buckingham.*

3. Bordering on the sea.

The friend, the shores *maritimal*
Sought for his bed, and found a place upon which play'd
The murmurring billows. *Chapman's Iliads.*

Ercoco, and the less *maritime* kings
Monbaza and Quiloa. *Milton's Par. Lost, b.* xi.

Neptune upbraided them with their stupidity and ignorance, that a *maritime* town should neglect the patronage of him who was the god of the seas. *Addison's Freeholder.*

MARK. *n. s.* [*marc*, Welsh; *mearc*, Saxon; *mercke*, Dutch; *marque*, French.]

1. A token by which any thing is known.

Once was proclaimed throughout all Ireland, that all men should mark their cattle with an open several *mark* upon their flanks or buttocks, so as if they happened to be stolen they might appear whose they were. *Spenser on Ireland.*

In the present form of the earth there are certain *marks* and indications of its first state; with which, if we compare those things that are recorded in sacred history, we may discover what the earth was in its first original. *Burnet.*

The urine is a lixivium of the salts in a human body, and the proper *mark* of the state and quantity of such salts; and therefore very certain indications for the choice of diet may be taken from the state of urine. *Arbuthnot on Aliments.*

2. A token; an impression.

But cruel fate, and my more cruel wife,
To Grecian swords betray'd my sleeping life:
These are the monuments of Helen's love,
The shame I bear below, the *marks* I bore above. *Dryden.*

'Twas then old soldiers cover'd o'er with scars,
The *marks* of Pyrrhus, or the Punick wars,
Thought all past services rewarded well,
If to their share at least two acres fell. *Dryden's Juvenal.*

At present there are scarce any *marks* left of a subterraneous fire; for the earth is cold, and over-run with grass and shrubs. *Addison on Italy.*

3. A proof; an evidence.

As the confusion of tongues was a *mark* of separation, so the being of one language is a *mark* of union. *Bacon.*

The Argonauts sailed up the Danube, and from thence passed into the Adriatick, carrying their ship Argo upon their shoulders; a *mark* of great ignorance in geography among the writers of that time. *Arbuthnot on Coins.*

4. Notice taken.

5. Conveniency of notice.

Upon the north sea bordereth Stow, so called, per eminentiam, as a place of great and good *mark* and scope. *Carew's Survey of Cornwall.*

6. Any thing at which a missile weapon is directed.

France was a fairer *mark* to shoot at than Ireland, and could better reward the conqueror. *Davies on Ireland.*

Be made the *mark*
For all the people's hate, the prince's curses. *Denham.*

7. The evidence of a horse's age.

At four years old cometh the *mark* of tooth in horses, which hath a hole as big as you may lay a pea within it; and weareth shorter and shorter every year, till at eight years old the tooth is smooth. *Bacon's Nat. Hist.* N. 754.

8. [*Marque*, French.] Licence of reprisals.

9. [*Marc*, French.] A sum of thirteen shillings and fourpence.

We give thee for reward a thousand *marks. Shakespeare.*

Thirty of these pence make a mancus, which some think to be all one with a *mark*, for that manca and mancusa is translated, in ancient books, by marca. *Camden's Remains.*

Upon every writ for debt or damage, amounting to forty pounds or more, a noble is paid to fine; and so for every hundred *marks* more a noble. *Bacon.*

10. A character made by those who cannot write their names.

Here are marriage vows for signing;
Set your *marks* that cannot write. *Dryden's King Arthur.*

To MARK. *v. a.* [*merken*, Dutch; *mearcan*, Saxon; *marquer*, French.]

1. To impress with a token, or evidence.

Will it not be received,
When we have *mark'd* with blood those sleepy two
Of his own chamber, and us'd their very daggers,
That they have don't. *Shakesp. Macbeth.*

For our quiet possession of things useful, they are naturally *marked* where there is need. *Grew's Cosmol.*

2. To distinguish as by a mark.

That which was once the index to point out all virtues, does now *mark* out that part of the world where leaſt of them reſides. *Decay of Piety.*

3. To note; to take notice of.

Alas, poor country!
Where ſighs, and groans, and ſhrieks, that rend the air,
Are made, not *mark'd!* *Shakeſp. Macbeth.*

Mark them which cauſe diviſions contrary to the doctrine which ye have learned, and avoid them. *Rom.* xvi. 17.

Now ſwear, and call to witneſs
Heav'n, hell, and earth, I *mark* it not from one
That breaths beneath ſuch complicated guilt. *Smith.*

To MARK. *v. n.* To note; to take notice.

Men *mark* when they hit, and never *mark* when they miſs, as they do alſo of dreams. *Bacon's Eſſays.*

Mark a little why Virgil is ſo much concerned to make this marriage; it is to make way for the divorce which he intended afterwards. *Dryden's Æn.*

MAR'KER. *n. ſ.* [*marqueur*, French, from *mark*.]

1. One that puts a mark on any thing.
2. One that notes, or takes notice.

MA'RKET. *n. ſ.* [anciently written *mercat*, of *mercatus*, Lat.]

1. A publick time of buying and ſelling.

It were good that the privilege of a *market* were given, the rather to enable them to their defence; for there is nothing doth ſooner cauſe civility than many *market* towns, by reaſon the people repairing often thither will learn civil manners. *Spenſer on Ireland.*

Miſtreſs, know yourſelf, down on your knees,
And thank heav'n, faſting, for a good man's love:
For I muſt tell you friendly in your ear,
Sell when you can, you are not for all *markets.* *Shakeſp.*

They counted our life a paſtime, and our time here a *market* for gain. *Wiſd.* xv. 12.

If one buſhel of wheat and two buſhels of barley will, in the *market*, be taken one for another, they are of equal worth. *Locke.*

2. Purchace and ſale.

With another year's continuance of the war, there will hardly be money left in this kingdom to turn the common *markets*, or pay rents. *Temple.*

The precious weight
Of pepper and Sabæan incenſe take,
And with poſt-haſte thy running *market* make,
Be ſure to turn the penny. *Dryden's Perſius.*

3. Rate; price. [*marché*, French.]

'Twas then old ſoldiers, cover'd o'er with ſcars,
Thought all paſt ſervices rewarded well,
If, to their ſhare, at leaſt two acres fell,
Their country's frugal bounty; ſo of old
Was blood and life at a low *market* ſold. *Dryden's Juv.*

To MA'RKET. *v. n.* To deal at a market; to buy or ſell; to make bargains.

MA'RKET-BELL. *n. ſ.* [*market* and *bell.*] The bell to give notice that trade may begin in the market.

Enter, go in, the *marketbell* is rung. *Shakeſp. Henry* VI.

MA'RKET-CROSS. *n. ſ.* [*market* and *croſs.*] A croſs ſet up where the market is held.

Theſe things you have articulated,
Proclaim'd at *marketcroſſes*, read in churches,
To face the garment of rebellion
With ſome fine colour. *Shakeſpeare's Henry* IV.

MA'RKET-DAY. *n. ſ.* [*market* and *day.*] The day on which things are publickly bought and ſold.

Fool that I was, I thought imperial Rome,
Like Mantua, where on *marketdays* we come,
And thither drive our lambs. *Dryden's Virgil.*

He ordered all the Lucqueſe to be ſeized that were found on a *marketday* in one of his frontier towns. *Addiſon on Italy.*

MA'RKET-FOLKS. *n. ſ.* [*market* and *folks.*] People that come to the market.

Poor *marketfolks*, that come to ſell their corn. *Shakeſp.*

MA'RKET-MAN. *n. ſ.* [*market* and *man.*] One who goes to the market to ſell or buy.

Be wary how you place your words,
Talk like the vulgar ſort of *marketmen*,
That come to gather money for their corn. *Shakeſpeare.*

The *marketman* ſhould act as if his maſter's whole eſtate ought to be applied to that ſervant's buſineſs. *Swift.*

MA'RKET-MAID. *n. ſ.* [*market* and *maid.*] A woman that goes to buy or ſell.

You are come
A *marketmaid* to Rome, and have prevented
The oſtentation of our love. *Shakeſp. Ant. and Cleopatra.*

MA'RKET-PLACE. *n. ſ.* [*market* and *place.*] Place where the market is held.

The king, thinking he had put up his ſword, becauſe of the noiſe, never took leiſure to hear his anſwer, but made him priſoner, meaning the next morning to put him to death in the *marketplace.* *Sidney, b.* ii.

The gates he order'd all to be unbarr'd,
And from the *marketplace* to draw the guard. *Dryden.*

Behold the *marketplace* with poor o'erſpread,
The man of Roſs divides the weekly bread. *Pope.*

MA'RKET-PRICE. } *n. ſ.* [*market* and *price* or *rate.*] The price
MA'RKET-RATE. } at which any thing is currently ſold.

Money governs the world, and the *marketprice* is the meaſure of the worth of men as well as of fiſhes. *L'Eſtrange.*

He that wants a veſſel, rather than loſe his market will not ſtick to have it at the *marketrate.* *Locke.*

MA'RKET-TOWN. *n. ſ.* A town that has the privilege of a ſtated market; not a village.

Nothing doth ſooner cauſe civility in any country than *markettowns*, by reaſon that people repairing often thither will learn civil manners of the better ſort. *Spenſer.*

No, no, the pope's mitre my maſter Sir Roger ſeized, when they would have burnt him at our *markettown.* *Gay.*

MA'RKETABLE. *adj.* [from *market.*]

1. Such as may be ſold; ſuch for which a buyer may be found.

A plain fiſh, and no doubt *marketable.* *Shakeſpeare.*

2. Current in the market.

The pretorian ſoldiers arrived to that impudence, that after the death of Pertinax they made open port ſale of the empire, as if it had been of common *marketable* wares. *Decay of Piety.*

The *marketable* value of any quantities of two commodities are equal, when they will exchange one for another. *Locke.*

MA'RKMAN. } *n. ſ.* [*mark* and *man.*] A man ſkilful to hit a
MA'RKSMAN. } mark.

In ſadneſs, couſin, I do love a woman.
—I aim'd ſo near when I ſuppos'd you lov'd.
—A right good *markſman.* *Shakeſp. Romeo and Juliet.*

Whom nothing can procure,
When the wide world runs bias from his will,
To writhe his limbs, and ſhare, not mend the ill.
This is the *markſman*, ſafe and ſure,
Who ſtill is right, and prays to be ſo ſtill. *Herbert.*

An ordinary *markſman* may know certainly when he ſhoots leſs wide at what he aims. *Dryden's Ded. to the Sp. Fryar.*

MARL. *n. ſ.* [*marl*, Welſh; *mergel*, Dutch; *marga*, Latin; *marle*, *marne*, Fr. in Saxon, meɲʒ is marrow, with an alluſive ſignification, *marl* being the fatneſs of the earth.]

Marl is a kind of clay, which is become fatter, and of a more enriching quality, by a better fermentation, and by its having lain ſo deep in the earth as not to have ſpent or weakened its fertilizing quality by any product. *Marl* is ſuppoſed to be much of the nature of chalk, and is believed to be fertile from its ſalt and oily quality. *Quincy.*

We underſtand by the term *marls* ſimple native earths, leſs heavy than the boles or clays, not ſoft and unctuous to the touch, nor ductile while moiſt, dry and crumbly between the fingers, and readily diffuſible in water. *Hill.*

Marl is the beſt compoſt, as having moſt fatneſs, and not heating the ground too much. *Bacon's Nat. Hiſt.* Nº. 596.

Uneaſy ſteps
Over the burning *marl*, not like thoſe ſteps
On heaven's azure. *Milton's Par. Loſt, b.* i.

To MARL. *v. a.* [from the noun.] To manure with marl.

Thoſe improvements by *marling*, liming, and draining, have been been made ſince money was at five and ſix per cent. *Child's Diſcourſe of Trade.*

Sandy land *marled* will bear good white or blue peaſe. *Mortimer's Huſbandry.*

To MARL. *v. a.* [from *marline.*] To faſten the ſails with marline. *Ainſ.*

MA'RLINE. *n. ſ.* [meaɲn, *Skinner.*] Long wreaths of untwiſted hemp dipped in pitch, with which the ends of cables are guarded againſt friction.

Some the gall'd ropes with dawby *marline* bind,
Or ſearcloth maſts with ſtrong tarpawling coats. *Dryden.*

MA'RLINESPIKE. *n. ſ.* A ſmall piece of iron for faſtening ropes together, or to open the bolt rope when the ſail is to be ſewed in it. *Bailey.*

MA'RLPIT. *n. ſ.* [*marl* and *pit.*] Pit out of which marl is dug.

Several others, of different figures, were found; part of them in a rivulet, the reſt in a *marlpit* in a field. *Woodward.*

MA'RLY. *adj.* [from *marl.*] Abounding with marl.

The oak thrives beſt on the richeſt clay, and will penetrate ſtrangely to come at a *marly* bottom. *Mortimer.*

MA'RMALADE. } *n. ſ.* [*marmelade*, Fr. *marmelo*, Portugueſe,
MA'RMALET. } a quince.]

Marmalade is the pulp of quinces boiled into a conſiſtence with ſugar: it is ſubaſtringent, and grateful to the ſtomach. *Quincy.*

MARMORA'TION. *n. ſ.* [*marmor*, Latin.] Incruſtation with marble. *Dict.*

MARMO'REAN. *adj.* [*marmoreus*, Lat.] Made of marble. *Dict.*

MA'RMOSET. *n. ſ.* [*marmouſet*, French.] A ſmall monkey.

I will inſtruct thee how
To ſnare the nimble *marmozet.* *Shakeſpeare's Tempeſt.*

MARMOT.

MARMOT. } *n. s.* [Italian.]
MARMOTTO.

The *marmotto*, or mus alpinus, as big or bigger than a rabbit, which absconds all winter, doth live upon its own fat. *Ray on Creation.*

MA'RQUETRY. *n. s.* [*marqueterie*, French.] Checquered work; work inlaid with variegation.

MA'RQUIS. *n. s.* [*marquis*, French; *marchio*, Lat. *margrave*, German.]

1. In England one of the second order of nobility, next in rank to a duke.

Peace, master *marquis*, you are malapert;
Your fire-new stamp of honour is scarce current. *Shakesp.*

None may wear ermine but princes, and there is a certain number of ranks allowed to dukes, *marquisses*, and earls, which they must not exceed. *Peacham on Drawing.*

2. *Marquis* is used by *Shakespeare* for *marchioness*. [*marquise*, Fr.]

You shall have
Two noble partners with you: the old duchess
Of Norfolk, and the lady *marquess* Dorset. *Shakespeare.*

MA'RQUISATE. *n. s.* [*marquisat*, French.] The seigniory of a marquis.

MA'RRER. *n. s.* [from *mar.*] One who spoils or hurts any thing.

You be indeed makers, or *marrers*, of all mens manners within the realm. *Ascham's Schoolmaster.*

MA'RRIAGE. *n. s.* [*mariage*, French; *maritagium*, low Latin, from *maritus.*] The act of uniting a man and woman for life.

The *marriage* with his brother's wife
Has crept too near his conscience. *Shakesp. Henry* VIII.

If that thy bent of love be honourable,
Thy purpose *marriage*, send me word to-morrow. *Shakesp.*

The French king would have the disposing of the *marriage* of Bretagne, with an exception, that he should not marry her himself. *Bacon.*

Some married persons, even in their *marriage*, do better please God than some virgins in their state of virginity: they, by giving great example of conjugal affection, by preserving their faith unbroken, and by educating children in the fear of God, please God in a higher degree than those virgins whose piety is not answerable to their opportunities. *Taylor.*

I propose that Palamon shall be
In *marriage* join'd with beauteous Emily. *Dryden.*

MA'RRIAGE is often used in composition.

Neither her worthiness, which in truth was great, nor his own suffering for her, which is wont to endear affection, could fetter his fickleness; but, before the *marriage*-day appointed, he had taken to wife Baccha, of whom she complained. *Sidney, b.* ii.

I by the honour of my *marriage*-bed,
After young Arthur, claim this land for mine. *Shakesp.*

Thou shalt come into the *marriage* chamber. *Tob.* vi. 16.

There on his arms and once lov'd portrait lay,
Thither our fatal *marriage*-bed convey. *Denham.*

To these whom death again did wed,
This grave's the second *marriage*-bed:
For though the hand of fate could force
'Twixt soul and body a divorce,
It could not sever man and wife,
Because they both liv'd but one life. *Crashaw.*

Give me, to live and die,
A spotless maid, without the *marriage*-tie. *Dryden.*

In a late draught of *marriage*-articles, a lady stipulated with her husband, that she shall be at liberty to patch on which side she pleases. *Addison's Spect.* N°. 81.

Virgin awake! the *marriage*-hour is nigh. *Pope.*

MA'RRIAGEABLE. *adj.* [from *marriage.*]

1. Fit for wedlock; of age to be married.

Every wedding, one with another, produces four children, and consequently that is the proportion of children which any *marriageable* man or woman may be presumed shall have. *Graunt's Bills of Mortality.*

I am the father of a young heiress, whom I begin to look upon as *marriageable*. *Spect.* N°. 237.

When the girls are twelve years old, which is the *marriageable* age, their parents take them home. *Swift.*

2. Capable of union.

They led the vine
To wed her elm; she spous'd about him twines
Her *marriageable* arms, and with her brings
Her dow'r, th' adopted clusters to adorn
His barren leaves. *Milton's Par. Lost, b.* v.

MA'RRIED. *adj.* [from *marry.*] Conjugal; connubial.

Thus have you shun'd the *marry'd* state. *Dryden.*

MA'RROW. *n. s.* [mer̄g, Saxon; *smerr*, Erse; *smergh*, Scottish.]

All the bones of the body which have any considerable thickness have either a large cavity, or they are spongious, and full of little cells: in both the one and the other there is an oleagenous substance, called *marrow*, contained in proper vesicles or membranes, like the fat: in the larger bones this fine oil, by the gentle heat of the body, is exhaled through the pores of its small bladders, and enters some narrow passages, which lead to some fine canals excavated in the substance of the bone, that the *marrow* may supple the fibres of the bones, and render them less apt to break. *Quincy.*

Would he were wasted, *marrow*, bones, and all,
That from his loins no hopeful branch may spring. *Shak.*

The skull hath brains as a kind of *marrow* within it: the back-bone hath one kind of *marrow*, and other bones of the body hath another: the jaw-bones have no *marrow* severed, but a little pulp of *marrow* diffused. *Bacon.*

Pamper'd and edify'd their zeal
With *marrow* puddings many a meal. *Hudibras, p.* ii.

He bit the dart, and wrench'd the wood away,
The point still buried in the *marrow* lay. *Addison's Ovid.*

MA'RROW, in the Scottish dialect, to this day, denotes a fellow, companion, or associate; as also equal match, *he met with his* marrow.

Though buying and selling doth wonderful wel,
Yet chopping and changing I cannot commend
With theef of his *marrow* for fear of il end. *Tusser.*

MARR'OWBONE. *n. s.* [*bone* and *marrow.*]

1. Bone boiled for the marrow.

2. In burlesque language, the knees.

Upon this he fell down upon his *marrowbones*, and begged of Jupiter to give him a pair of horns. *L'Estrange's Fables.*

Down on your *marrowbones*, upon your allegiance; and make an acknowledgement of your offences; for I will have ample satisfaction. *Dryden's Spanish Fryar.*

MARR'OWFAT. *n. s.* A kind of pea.

MARRO'WLESS. *adj.* [from *marrow.*] Void of marrow.

Avaunt!
Thy bones are *marrowless*, thy blood is cold;
Thou hast no speculation in those eyes,
Which thou dost glare with. *Shakesp. Macbeth.*

To MARRY. *v. a.* [*marier*, French; *maritor*, Latin.]

1. To join a man and woman.

What! shall the curate controul me? Tell him, that he shall *marry* the couple himself. *Gay's What d'ye call it.*

2. To dispose of in marriage.

When Augustus consulted with Mecænas about the marriage of his daughter Julia, Mecænas took the liberty to tell him, that he must either *marry* his daughter to Agrippa, or take away his life; there was no third way, he had made him so great. *Bacon's Essays*, N°. 28.

3. To take for husband or wife.

You'd think it strange if I should *marry* her. *Shakesp.*

Go in to thy brother's wife, and *marry* her. *Gen.* xxxviii.

As a mother shall she meet him, and receive him as a wife *married* of a virgin. *Ecclus.* xv. 2.

To MA'RRY. *v. n.* To enter into the conjugal state.

He hath my good will,
And none but he, to *marry* with Nan Page. *Shakespeare.*

Let them *marry* to whom they think best. *Num.* xxxvi. 6.

Virgil concludes with the death of Turnus; for after that difficulty was removed, Æneas might *marry*, and establish the Trojans. *Dryden's Dufresnoy.*

MARSH, } are derived from the Saxon mer̄rc, a fen, or fenny
MARS, } place. *Gibson's Camden.*
MAS, }

MARSH. *n. s.* [mer̄rc, Saxon. See MARISH.] A fen; a bog; a swamp; a watry tract of land.

In their courses make that round,
In meadows, and in *marshes* found,
Of them so call'd the fayry ground,
Of which they have the keeping. *Drayton's Nymphid.*

Worms, for colour and shape, alter even as the ground out of which they are got; as the *marsh* worm and the flag worm. *Walton's Angler.*

We may see in more conterminous climates great variety in the people thereof; the up-lands in England yield strong, sinewy, hardy men; the *marsh*-lands, men of large and high stature. *Hale's Origin of Mankind.*

Your low meadows and *marsh*-lands you need not lay up till April, except the Spring be very wet, and your *marshes* very poachy. *Mortimer's Husbandry.*

MARSH-MALLOW. *n. s.* [*althæa*, Lat.] It is in all respects like the mallow, but its leaves are generally more soft and woolly. *Miller.*

MARSH-MARIGOLD. *n. s.* [*populago*, Lat.] This flower consists of several leaves, which are placed circularly, and expand in form of a rose, in the middle of which rises the pointal, which afterward becomes a membranaceous fruit, in which there are several cells, which are, for the most part, bent downwards, collected into little heads, and are full of seeds. *Miller.*

And set soft hyacinths with iron-blue,
To shade *marsh-marigolds* of shining hue. *Dryden.*

MA'RSHAL. *n. s.* [*mareschal*, Fr. *mareschallus*, low Lat. from *marscale*, old French; a word compounded of *mare*, which, in old French, signified a horse, and *scale*, a sort of servant; one that has the charge of horses.]

1. The chief officer of arms.

The duke of Suffolk claims
To be high steward; next the duke of Norfolk
To be earl *marshal*. *Shakespeare.*

2. An officer who regulates combats in the lists.

Dares their pride presume against my laws,
As in a listed field to fight their cause?
Unask'd the royal grant; no *marshal* by,
As kingly rites require, nor judge to try. *Dryden.*

3. Any one who regulates rank or order at a feast, or any other assembly.

Through the hall there walked to and fro
A jolly yeoman, *marshal* of the same,
Whose name was Appetite; he did bestow
Both guests and meats, whenever in they came,
And knew them how to order without blame. *Fa. Queen.*

4. An harbinger; a pursuivant; one who goes before a prince to declare his coming, and provide entertainment.

Her face, when it was fairest, had been but as a *marshal* to lodge the love of her in his mind, which now was so well placed as it needed no further help of outward harbinger. *Sidney.*

To MA'RSHAL. *v. a.* [from the noun.]

1. To arrange; to rank in order.

Multitude of jealousies, and lack of some predominant desire, that should *marshal* and put in order all the rest, maketh any man's heart hard to find or sound. *Bacon.*

It is as unconceivable how it should be the directrix of such intricate motions, as that a blind man should *marshal* an army. *Glanville's Scep.*

Anchises look'd not with so pleas'd a face,
In numb'ring o'er his future Roman race,
And *marshalling* the heroes of his name,
As, in their order, next to light they came. *Dryden.*

2. To lead as an harbinger.

Art thou but
A dagger of the mind, a false creation.
Thou *marshal'st* me the way that I was going. *Shakesp.*

MA'RSHALLER. *n. s.* [from *marshal.*] One that arranges; one that ranks in order.

Dryden was the great refiner of English poetry, and the best *marshaller* of words. *Trapp's Pref. to the Æneis.*

MA'RSHALSEA. *n. s.* [from *marshal.*] The prison in Southwark belonging to the marshal of the king's houshold.

MA'RSHALSHIP. *n. s.* [from *marshal.*] The office of a marshal.

MARSHE'LDER. *n. s.* A gelderrose, of which it is a species.

MARSHRO'CKET. *n. s.* A species of watercresses.

MA'RSHY. *adj.* [from *marsh.*]

1. Boggy; wet; fenny; swampy.

Though here the *marshy* grounds approach your fields,
And there the soil a stony harvest yields. *Dryden's Virg.*

It is a distemper of such as inhabit *marshy*, fat, low, moist soils, near stagnating water. *Arbuthnot on Diet.*

2. Produced in marshes.

Feed
With delicates of leaves and *marshy* weed. *Dryden.*

MART. *n. s.* [contracted from *market.*]

1. A place of publick traffick.

Christ could not suffer that the temple should serve for a place of *mart*, nor the apostle of Christ that the church should be made an inn. *Hooker, b.* v.

If any born at Ephesus
Be seen at Syracusan *marts* and fairs,
He dies. *Shakespeare.*

Ezechiel, in the description of Tyre, and the exceeding trade that it had with all the East as the only *mart* town, reciteth both the people with whom they commerce, and also what commodities every country yielded. *Raleigh.*

Many may come to a great *mart* of the best horses. *Temple's Miscel.*

The French, since the accession of the Spanish monarchy, supply with cloth the best *mart* we had in Europe. *Addison.*

2. Bargain; purchase and sale.

I play a merchant's part,
And venture madly on a desperate *mart*. *Shakesp.*

3. Letters of *mart*. See MARK.

To MART. *v. a.* [from the noun.] To traffick; to buy or sell.

Sooth when I was young I wou'd have ransack'd
The pedlar's silken treasury, you've let him go,
And nothing *marted* with him. *Shakesp. Winter's Tale.*

Cassius, you yourself,
Do sell and *mart* your offices for gold
To undeservers. *Shakesp. Julius Cæsar.*

If he shall think it fit,
A saucy stranger in his court to *mart*,
As in a stew. *Shakespeare's Cymbeline.*

MA'RTEN. } MA'RTERN. } *n. s.* [*marte*, *martre*, Fr. *martes*, Lat.]

1. A large kind of weesel whose fur is much valued.

2. [*Martelet*, Fr.] A kind of swallow that builds in houses; a martlet.

A churchwarden, to express St. Martin's in the Fields, caused to be engraved, on the communion cup, a *martin*, a bird like a swallow, sitting upon a mole-hill between two trees. *Peacham on Blazoning.*

MA'RTIAL. *adj.* [*martial*, Fr. *martialis*, Latin.]

1. Warlike; fighting; given to war; brave.

Into my feeble breast
Come gently, but not with that mighty rage
Wherewith the *martial* troopes thou dost infest,
And hearts of great heroes dost enrage. *Fairy Queen.*

The queen of *martials*,
And Mars himself conducted them. *Chapman's Iliad.*

It hath seldom been seen, that the far southern people have invaded the northern, but contrariwise; whereby it is manifest, that the northern tract of the world is the more *martial* region. *Bacon's Essays.*

His subjects call'd aloud for war;
But peaceful kings o'er *martial* people set,
Each other's poize and counterbalance are. *Dryden.*

2. Having a warlike show; suiting war.

See
His thousands, in what *martial* equipage
They issue forth! Steel bows and shafts their arms,
Of equal dread in flight or in pursuit. *Milton's Par. Reg.*

When our country's cause provokes to arms,
How *martial* musick ev'ry bosom warms. *Pope.*

3. Belonging to war; not civil; not according to the rules or practice of peaceable government.

Let his neck answer for it, if there is any *martial* law in the world. *Shakespeare's Henry V.*

They proceeded in a kind of *martial* justice with their enemies, offering them their law before they drew their sword. *Bacon's holy War.*

4. Borrowing qualities from the planet Mars.

The natures of the fixed stars are astrologically differenced by the planets, and esteemed *martial* or jovial according to the colours whereby they answer these planets. *Brown.*

5. Having parts or properties of iron, which is called *Mars* by the chemists.

MA'RTIALIST. *n. s.* [from *martial.*] A warrior; a fighter.

Many brave adventrous spirits fell for love of her; amongst others the high-hearted *martialist*, who first lost his hands, then one of his chiefest limbs, and lastly his life. *Howell.*

MA'RTINGAL. *n. s.* [*martingale*, French.] It is a broad strap made fast to the girths under the belly of a horse, and runs between the two legs to fasten the other end, under the nose-band of the bridle. *Harris.*

MARTI'NMAS. *n. s.* [*martin* and *mass.*] The feast of St. Martin; the eleventh of November, commonly corrupted to *martilmass* or *martlemass*.

Martilmas beefe doth bear good tacke,
When countrey-folke do dainties lacke. *Tusser's Husb.*

MA'RTINET. } MA'RTLET. } *n. s.* [*martinet*, French.] A kind of swallow.

This guest of Summer,
The temple-haunting *martlet* does approve
By his lov'd mansionry, that heaven's breath
Smells wooingly here. No jutting frieze,
Buttrice, nor coigne of vantage, but this bird
Hath made his pendant bed, and procreant cradle.
Where they most breed and haunt, I have observ'd
The air is delicate. *Shakespeare's Macbeth.*

As in a drought the thirsty creatures cry,
And gape upon the gather'd clouds for rain;
Then first the *martlet* meets it in the sky,
And with wet wings joys all the feather'd train. *Dryden.*

MA'RTNETS. *n. s.* They are small lines fastened to the leetch of the sail, to bring that part of the leetch which is next to the yard-arm close up to the yard, when the sail is to be furled. *Bailey.*

MA'RTYR. *n. s.* [μάρτυρ; *martyr*, French.] One who by his death bears witness to the truth.

Prayers and tears may serve a good man's turn; if not to conquer as a soldier, yet to suffer as a *martyr*. *King Charles.*

Thus could not the mouths of worthy *martyrs* be silenced. *Brown.*

Nearer heav'n his virtues shone more bright,
Like rising flames expanding in their height,
The *martyr*'s glory crown'd the soldier's fight. *Dryden.*

To be a *martyr* signifies only to witness the truth of Christ; but the witnessing of the truth was then so generally attended with persecution, that martyrdom now signifies not only to witness, but to witness by death. *South's Sermons.*

The first *martyr* for Christianity was encouraged, in his last moments, by a vision of that divine person for whom he suffered. *Addison on the Christian Religion.*

Socrates,

Socrates,
Truth's early champion, *martyr* for his God. *Thomson.*

To MA'RTYR. *v. a.* [from the noun.]

1. To put to death for virtue.
2. To murder; to destroy.

You could not beg for grace.
Hark wretches, how I mean to *martyr* you:
This one hand yet is left to cut your throats. *Shakespeare.*

If to every common funeral,
By your eyes *martyr'd*, such grace were allow'd,
Your face would wear not patches, but a cloud. *Suckling.*

MA'RTYRDOM. *n. s.* [from *martyr.*] The death of a martyr; the honour of a martyr.

If an infidel should pursue to death an heretick professing Christianity only for Christian profession sake, could we deny unto him the honour of *martyrdom?* *Hooker, b.* v.

Now that he hath left no higher degree of earthly honour, he intends to crown their innocency with the glory of *martyrdom.* *Bacon.*

Herod, whose unblest
Hand, O! what dares not jealous greatness? tore
A thousand sweet babes from their mother's breast,
The blooms of *martyrdom.* *Crashaw.*

What mists of providence are these,
So saints, by supernatural pow'r set free,
Are left at last in *martyrdom* to die. *Dryden.*

MARTYRO'LOGY. *n. s.* [*martyrologe*, Fr. *martyrologium*, Lat.] A register of martyrs.

In the Roman *martyrology* we find at one time many thousand martyrs destroyed by Dioclesian, being met together in a church, rather than escape by offering a little incense at their coming out. *Stillingfleet.*

MARTYRO'LOGIST. *n. s.* [*martyrologiste*, French.] A writer of martyrology.

MA'RVEL. *n. s.* [*merveille*, French.] A wonder; any thing astonishing. Little in use.

A *marvel* it were, if a man could espy, in the whole scripture, nothing which might breed a probable opinion, that divine authority was the same way inclinable. *Hooker.*

I am scarce in breath, my lord.
—No *marvel*, you have so bestir'd your valour; you cowardly rascal! *Shakespeare's King Lear.*

No *marvel*
My lord protector's hawks do towre so well. *Shakespeare.*

MARVEL *of Peru.* A flower. *Ainf.*

To MA'RVEL. *v. n.* [*merveille*, French.] To wonder; to be astonished. Disused.

You make me *marvel.* *Shakespeare.*

Harry, I do not only *marvel* where thou spendest thy time, but also how thou art accompanied. *Shakespeare.*

—The army *marvelled* at it. *Shakespeare's Coriolanus.*

The countries *marvelled* at thee for thy songs, proverbs, and parables. *Ecclus.* xlvii. 17.

MA'RVELLOUS. *adj.* [*merveilleux*, French.]

1. Wonderful; strange; astonishing.

She has a *marvellous* white hand, I must confess. *Shakesp.*

This is the Lord's doing; it is *marvellous* in our eyes. *Psal.* cxviii. 23.

2. Surpassing credit.

The *marvellous* fable includes whatever is supernatural, and especially the machines of the gods. *Pope's Pref. to the Iliad.*

3. *The marvellous* is used, in works of criticism, to express any thing exceeding natural power, opposed to *the probable.*

MA'RVELLOUSLY. *adv.* [from *marvellous.*] Wonderfully; strangely;

You look not well, seignior Antonio;
You have too much respect upon the world;
They lose it that do buy it with much care.
Believe me, you are *marvellously* chang'd. *Shakespeare.*

The encouragement of his two late successes, with which he was *marvellously* elated. *Clarendon, b.* viii.

MA'RVELLOUSNESS. *n. s.* [from *marvellous.*] Wonderfulness; strangeness; astonishingness.

MA'SCULINE. *adj.* [*masculin*, Fr. *masculinus*, Latin.]

1. Male; not female.

Pray God, she prove not *masculine* ere long! *Shakesp.*

His long beard noteth the air and fire, the two *masculine* elements exercising their operation upon nature being the feminine. *Peacham on Drawing.*

O! why did God,
Creator wise! that peopl'd highest heav'n
With spirits *masculine*, create at last
This novelty on earth, this fair defect
Of nature? *Milton's Par. Lost, b.* x.

2. Resembling man; virile; not soft; not effeminate.

You find something bold and *masculine* in the air and posture of the first figure, which is that of virtue. *Addison.*

3. [In grammar.] It denotes the gender appropriated to the male kind in any word, though not always expressing sex.

MA'SCULINELY. *adv.* [from *masculine.*] Like a man.

Aurelia tells me, you have done most *masculinely*,
And play the orator. *Benj. Johnson's Catiline.*

MA'SCULINENESS. *n. s.* [from *masculine.*] Mannishness, male figure or behaviour.

MASH. *n. s.* [*masche*, Dutch.]

1. The space between the threads of a net, commonly written *mesh.*

To defend one's self against the stings of bees, have a net knit with so small *mashes*, that a bee cannot get through. *Mortimer's Husbandry.*

2. Any thing mingled or beaten together into an undistinguished or confused body. [from *mischen*, Dutch, to mix, or *mascher*, French.]
3. A mixture for a horse.

Put half a peck of ground malt into a pale, then put to it as much scalding water as will wet it well; stir it about for half an hour till the water is very sweet, and give it the horse lukewarm: this *mash* is to be given to a horse after he has taken a purge, to make it work the better; or in the time of great sickness, or after hard labour. *Farrier's Dict.*

When mares foal, they feed them with *mashes*, and other moist food. *Mortimer's Husbandry.*

To MASH. *v. a.* [*mascher*, French.]

1. To beat into a confused mass.

The pressure would be intolerable, and they would even *mash* themselves and all things else apieces. *More.*

To break the claw of a lobster, clap it between the sides of the dining-room door: thus you can do it without *mashing* the meat. *Swift's Directions to the Footman.*

2. To mix malt and water together in brewing.

What was put in the first *mashing*-tub draw off, as also that liquor in the second *mashing*-tub. *Mortimer's Husbandry.*

MASK. *n. s.* [*masque*, French.]

1. A cover to disguise the face; a visor.

Now love pulled off his *mask*, and shewed his face unto her, and told her plainly that she was his prisoner. *Sidney.*

Since she did neglect her looking-glass,
And throw her sun-expelling *mask* away;
The air hath starv'd the roses in her cheeks,
And pitch'd the lily tincture of her face. *Shakespeare.*

Could we suppose that a *mask* represented never so naturally the general humour of a character, it can never suit with the variety of passions that are incident to every single person in the whole course of a play. *Addison on Italy.*

2. Any pretence or subterfuge.

Too plain thy nakedness of soul espy'd,
Why dost thou strive the conscious shame to hide,
By *masks* of eloquence, and veils of pride? *Prior.*

3. A festive entertainment, in which the company is masked.

Will you prepare for this *masque* to-night. *Shakespeare.*

4. A revel; a piece of mummery; a wild bustle.

They in the end agreed,
That at a *masque* and common revelling,
Which was ordain'd, they should perform the deed. *Daniel.*

This thought might lead me through this world's vain *mask*,
Content, though blind, had I no other guide. *Milton.*

5. A dramatick performance, written in a tragick stile without attention to rules or probability.

Thus I have broken the ice to invention, for the lively representation of floods and rivers necessary for our painters and poets in their picturs, poems, comedies, and *masks.* *Peacham.*

To MASK. *v. a.* [*masquer*, French.]

1. To disguise with a mask or visor.

What will grow out of such errors as go *masked* under the cloke of divine authority, impossible it is that ever the wit of man should imagine, till time have brought forth the fruits of them. *Hooker.*

'Tis not my blood
Wherein thou see'st me *masked.* *Shakesp. Coriolanus.*

Him he knew well, and guess'd that it was she;
But being *mask'd* he was not sure. *Shakespeare.*

The old Vatican Terence has, at the head of every scene, the figures of all the persons, with their particular disguises; and I saw in the Villa di Mattheio an antique statue *masked*, which was perhaps designed for Gnatho in the eunuch, for it agrees exactly with the figure he makes in the manuscript. *Addison.*

2. To cover; to hide.

I to your assistance do make love,
Masking the business from the common eye,
For sundry weighty reasons. *Shakesp. Macbeth.*

As when a piece of wanton lawn,
A thin aerial vail is drawn
O'er beauty's face, seeming to hide,
More sweetly shows the blushing bride:
A soul whose intellectual beams
No mists do *mask*, no lazy steams. *Crashaw.*

To MASK. *v. n.*

1. To revel; to play the mummer.

Thy gown? Why, ay; come, taylor, let us see't;
What *masking* stuff's here! *Shakespeare.*

Masking habits, and a borrow'd name,
Contrive to hide my plenitude of shame. *Prior.*

2. To be disguised any way.

MA'SKER. *n. s.* [from *mask.*] One who revels in a mask; a mummer.

Tell false Edward,
That Lewis of France is sending over *maskers*,
To revel it with him and his new bride. *Shakespeare.*

Let the scenes abound with light, and let the *maskers* that are to come down from the scene have some motions upon the scene before their coming down. *Bacon.*

The *maskers* come late, and I think will stay,
Like fairies, till the cock crow them away. *Donne.*

MA'SON. *n. s.* [*maçon*, French; *machio*, low Latin.] A builder with stone.

Many find a reason very wittily before the thing be true; that the materials being left rough, are more manageable in the *mason's* hand than if they had been smooth. *Wotton.*

A *mason* that makes a wall meets with a stone that wants no cutting, and places it in his work. *More.*

MA'SONRY. *n. s.* [*maçonerie*, Fr.] The craft or performance of a mason.

MASQUERA'DE. *n. s.* [from *masque.*]

1. A diversion in which the company is masked.

What guards the purity of melting maids,
In courtly balls, and midnight *masquerades*,
Safe from the treach'rous friend, and daring spark,
The glance by day, the whisper in the dark. *Pope.*

2. Disguise.

I was upon the frolick this evening, and came to visit thee in *masquerade*. *Dryden's Spanish Fryar.*

Truth, of all things the plainest and sincerest, is forced to gain admittance to us in disguise, and court us in *masquerade*. *Felton on the Classicks.*

To MASQUERA'DE. *v. n.* [from the noun.]

1. To go in disguise.

A freak took an ass in the head, and away he goes into the woods, *masquerading* up and down in a lion's skin. *L'Estrange's Fables.*

2. To assemble in masks.

I find that our art hath not gained much by the happy revival of *masquerading* among us. *Swift.*

MASQUERA'DER. *n. s.* [from *masquerade.*] A person in a mask.

The most dangerous sort of cheats are but *masqueraders* under the vizor of friends. *L'Estrange.*

MASS. *n. s.* [*masse*, Fr. *massa*, Latin.]

1. A body; a lump; a continuous quantity.

If it were not for these principles the bodies of the earth, planets, comets, sun, and all things in them, would grow cold and freeze, and become inactive *masses*. *Newton's Opt.*

Some passing into their pores, others adhering in lumps or *masses* to their outsides, so as wholly to cover and involve it in the *mass* they together constituted. *Woodward's Nat. Hist.*

2. A large quantity.

Thy sumptuous buildings, and thy wife's attire,
Have cost a *mass* of publick treasury. *Shakesp. Henry VI.*

He had spent a huge *mass* of treasure in transporting his army. *Davies on Ireland.*

3. Bulk; vast body.

The Creator of the world would not have framed so huge a *mass* of earth but for some reasonable creatures to have their habitation. *Abbot's Description of the World.*

This army of such *mass* and charge,
Led by a delicate and tender prince. *Shakesp. Hamlet.*

He discovered to me the richest mines which the Spaniards have, and from whence all the *mass* of gold that comes into Spain is drawn. *Raleigh's Essays.*

4. Congeries; assemblage indistinct.

The whole knowlege of groupes, of the lights and shadows, and of those *masses* which Titian calls a bunch of grapes, is, in the prints of Rubens, exposed clearly to the sight. *Dryden.*

At distance, through an artful glass,
To the mind's eye things well appear;
They lose their forms, and make a *mass*
Confus'd and black, if brought too near. *Prior.*

Where flowers grow, the ground at a distance seems covered with them, and we must walk into it before we can distinguish the several weeds that spring up in such a beautiful *mass* of colours. *Addison's Freeholder.*

5. Gross body; the general.

Comets have power over the gross and *mass* of things; but they are rather gazed upon than wisely observed in their effects. *Bacon's Essays.*

Where'er thou art, he is; th' eternal mind
Acts through all places; is to none confin'd:
Fills ocean, earth, and air, and all above,
And through the universal *mass* does move. *Dryden.*

The *mass* of the people have opened their eyes, and will not be governed by Clodius and Curio at the head of their myrmidons. *Swift.*

If there is not a sufficient quantity of blood and strength of circulation, it may infect the whole *mass* of the fluids. *Arbuthnot on Aliments.*

6. [*Missa*, Latin.] The service of the Romish church.

Burnished gold is that manner of gilding which we see in old parchment and *mass* books, done by monks and priests, who were very expert herein. *Peacham on Drawing.*

He infers, that then Luther must have been unpardonably wicked in using *masses* for fifteen years. *Atterbury.*

To MASS. *v. n.* [from the noun.] To celebrate mass.

All their *massing* furniture almost they took from the law, least having an altar and a priest they should want vestments. *Hooker, b. iv.*

To MASS. *v. a.* [from the noun.] It seems once to have signified to thicken; to strengthen.

They feared the French might, with filling or *massing* the house, or else by fortifying, make such a piece as might annoy the haven. *Hayward.*

MA'SSACRE. *n. s.* [*massacre*, French, from *mazzare*, Italian.]

1. Carnage; slaughter; butchery; indiscriminate destruction.

Of whom such *massacre*
Make they, but of their brethren, men of men. *Milton.*

Slaughter grows murder, when it goes too far,
And makes a *massacre* what was a war. *Dryd. Ind. Emp.*

2. Murder.

The tyrannous and bloody act is done;
The most arch deed of piteous *massacre*,
That ever yet this land was guilty of. *Shakesp. Rich. III.*

To MA'SSACRE. *v. a.* [*massacrer*, French, from the noun.] To butcher; to slaughter indiscriminately.

I'll find a day to *massacre* them all,
And raze their faction, and their family. *Shakespeare.*

Christian religion, now crumbled into fractions, may, like dust, be irrecoverably dissipated, if God do not countermine us, or we recover so much sobriety as to forbear to *massacre* what we pretend to love. *Decay of Piety.*

After the miserable slaughter of the Jews, at the destruction of Jerusalem, they were scattered into all corners, oppressed and detested, and sometimes *massacred* and extirpated. *Atterb.*

MA'SSICOT. *n. s.* [French.]

Massicot is ceruss calcined by a moderate degree of fire; of this there are three sorts, the white, the yellow, and that of a golden colour, their difference arising from the different degrees of fire applied in the operation. White *massicot* is of a yellowish white, and is that which has received the least calcination; yellow *massicot* has received more, and gold-coloured *massicot* still more; all of them should be an impalpable powder, weighty and high-coloured: they are used in painting. *Trevoux.*

MA'SSINESS. } *n. s.* [from *massy, massive.*] Weight; bulk;
MA'SSIVENESS. } ponderousness.

It was more notorious for the daintiness of the provision which he served in it, than for the *massiness* of the dish. *Hakewill on Providence.*

MA'SSIVE. } *adj.* [*massif*, French.] Heavy; weighty; pon-
MA'SSY. } derous; bulky; continuous.

If you would hurt,
Your swords are now too *massy* for your strength,
And will not be uplifted. *Shakespeare's Tempest.*

Perhaps these few stones and sling, used with invocation of the Lord of Hosts, may countervail the *massive* armour of the uncircumcised Philistine. *Government of the Tongue.*

No sideboards then with gilded plate were press'd,
No sweating slaves with *massive* dishes dress'd. *Dryden.*

The more gross and *massive* parts of the terrestrial globe, the strata of stone, owe their present order to the deluge. *Woodward's Nat. Hist.*

If these liquors or glasses were so thick and *massy* that no light could get through them, I question not but that they would, like all other opaque bodies, appear of one and the same colour in all positions of the eye. *Newton's Opticks.*

Th' intrepid Theban hears the bursting sky,
Sees yawning rocks in *massy* fragments fly,
And views astonish'd from the hills afar,
The floods descending, and the wat'ry war. *Pope's Statius.*

Swift the signal giv'n,
They start away, and sweep the *massy* mound
That runs around the hill. *Thomson's Spring.*

MAST. *n. s.* [*mast, mât*, French; mæꞅꞇ, Saxon.]

1. The beam or post raised above the vessel, to which the sail is fixed.

Ten *masts* attach'd make not the altitude
That thou hast perpendicularly fallen. *Shakesp. King Lear.*

He dropp'd his anchors, and his oars he ply'd;
Furl'd every sail, and drawing down the *mast*,
His vessel moor'd. *Dryden's Homer.*

2. The fruit of the oak and beech.

The oaks bear *masts*, the briars scarlet hips:
The bounteous housewife, nature, on each bush
Lays her full mess before you. *Shakesp. Timon of Athens.*

Trees that bear *mast*, and nuts, are more lasting than those that bear fruits; as oaks and beeches last longer than apples and pears. *Bacon's Nat. Hist.* N°. 583.

When sheep fed like men upon acorns, a shepherd drove his flock into a little oak wood, and up he went to shake them down some *masts*. *L'Estrange's Fables.*

The breaking down an old frame of government, and erecting a new, seems like the cutting down an old oak and planting a young one: it is true, the grandson may enjoy the shade and the *mast*, but the planter, besides the pleasure of imagination, has no other benefit. *Temple's Miscel.*

As a savage boar,
With forest *mast* and fat'ning marshes fed,
When once he sees himself in toils inclos'd,
Whets his tusks. *Dryden's Æn.*

Wond'ring dolphins o'er the palace glide;
On leaves and *mast* of mighty oaks they brouze,
And their broad fins entangle in the boughs. *Dryden.*

MA'STED. *adj.* [from *mast*.] Furnished with masts.

MA'STER. *n. s.* [*meester*, Dutch; *maistre*, French; *magister*, Latin.]

1. One who has servants; opposed to man or servant.

But now I was the lord
Of this fair mansion, *master* of my servnats,
Queen o'er myself; and even now, but now,
This house, these servants, and this same myself
Are yours my lord. *Shakesp. Merchant of Venice.*

Take up thy *master*. *Shakespeare's King Lear.*

My lord Bassanio gave his ring away
Unto the judge that begg'd it;
The boy, his clerk, begg'd mine;
And neither man nor *master* would take aught
But the two rings. *Shakesp. Merchant of Venice.*

2. A director; a governor.

If thou be made the *master* of a feast, be among them as one of the rest. *Ecclus.* xxxii. 1.

My friend, my genius, come along,
Thou *master* of the poet, and the song. *Pope.*

3. Owner; proprietor.

An orator, who had undertaken to make a panegyrick on Alexander the Great, and who had employed the strongest figures of his rhetorick in the praise of Bucephalus, would do quite the contrary to that which was expected from him; because it would be believed, that he rather took the horse for his subject than the *master*. *Dryden's Dufresnoy.*

4. A lord; a ruler.

Wisdom and virtue are the proper qualifications in the *master* of a house. *Guardian*, N°. 165.

There Cæsar, grac'd with both Minerva's, shone,
Cæsar, the world's great *master*, and his own. *Pope.*

Excuse
The pride of royal blood, that checks my soul:
You know, alas! I was not born to kneel,
To sue for pity, and to own a *master*. *Philips.*

5. Chief; head.

Chief *master*-gunner am I of this town,
Something I must do to procure me grace. *Shakespeare.*

As a wise *master*-builder I have laid the foundation, and another buildeth thereon. 1 *Cor.* iii. 10.

The best sets are the heads got from the very tops of the root; the next are the runners, which spread from the *master* roots. *Mortimer's Husbandry.*

6. Possessor.

When I have thus made myself *master* of a hundred thousand drachms, I shall naturally set myself on the foot of a prince, and will demand the grand vizier's daughter in marriage. *Addison's Spectator*, N°. 547.

The duke of Savoy may make himself *master* of the French dominions on the other side of the Rhone. *Addison.*

7. Commander of a trading ship.

An unhappy *master* is he that is made cunning by many shipwrecks; a miserable merchant, that is neither rich nor wise, but after some bankrouts. *Ascham's Schoolmaster.*

A sailor's wife had chesnuts in her lap;
Her husband's to Aleppo gone, *master* o' th' Tyger. *Shakes.*

8. One uncontrouled.

Let ev'ry man be *master* of his time
Till seven at night. *Shakespeare's Macbeth.*

Great, and increasing; but by sea
He is an absolute *master*. *Shakesp. Antony and Cleopatra.*

9. A compellation of respect.

Master doctor, you have brought those drugs. *Shakesp.*

Stand by, my *masters*, bring him near the king. *Shakes.*

Masters play here, I will content your pains,
Something that's brief; and bid, good morrow, general.
Shakespeare's Othello.

10. A young gentleman.

If gaming does an aged sire entice,
Then my young *master* swiftly learns the vice. *Dryden.*

Master lay with his bedchamber towards the south sun; miss lodged in a garret, exposed to the north wind. *Arbuth.*

Where there are little *masters* and misses in a house, they are great impediments to the diversions of the servants; the only remedy is to bribe them, that they may not tell tales. *Swift's Rules to Servants.*

11. One who teaches; a teacher.

Very few men are wise by their own counsel, or learned by their own teaching; for he that was only taught by himself had a fool to his *master*. *Benj. Johnson's Discovery.*

To the Jews join the Egyptians, the first *masters* of learning. *South's Sermons.*

Masters and teachers should not raise difficulties to their scholars; but smooth their way, and help them forwards. *Locke.*

12. A man eminently skilful in practice or science.

The great mocking *master* mock'd not then,
When he said, Truth was buried here below. *Davies.*

Spenser and Fairfax, great *masters* of our language, saw much farther into the beauties of our numbers than those who followed. *Dryden.*

A man must not only be able to judge of words and style, but he must be a *master* of them too; he must perfectly understand his author's tongue, and absolutely command his own. *Dryden.*

He that does not pretend to painting, is not touched at the commendation of a *master* in that profession. *Collier.*

No care is taken to improve young men in their own language, that they may thoroughly understand, and be *masters* of it. *Locke on Education.*

13. A title of dignity in the universities; as, master of arts.

To MA'STER. *v. a.* [from the noun.]

1. To be a master to; to rule; to govern.

Ay, good faith,
And rather father thee, than *master* thee. *Shakespeare.*

2. To conquer; to overpower; to subdue.

Thrice blessed they that *master* so their blood,
To undergo such maiden pilgrimage. *Shakespeare.*

The princes of Germany did not think him sent to command the empire, who was neither able to rule his insolent subjects in England, nor *master* his rebellious people of Ireland. *Davies on Ireland.*

Then comes some third party, that *masters* both plaintiff and defendant, and carries away the booty. *L'Estrange.*

Honour burns in me, not so fiercely bright,
But pale as fires when *master'd* by the light. *Dryden.*

Obstinacy and wilful neglects must be *mastered*, even though it cost blows. *Locke on Education.*

A man can no more justly make use of another's necessity, than he that has more strength can seize upon a weaker, *master* him to his obedience, and, with a dagger at his throat, offer him death or slavery. *Locke.*

The reformation of an habitual sinner is a work of time and patience; evil customs must be *mastered* and subdued by degrees. *Calamy's Sermons.*

3. To execute with skill.

I do not take myself to be so perfect in the transactions and privileges of Bohemia, as to be fit to handle that part: and I will not offer at that I cannot *master*. *Bacon.*

MA'STERDOM. *n. s.* [from *master*.] Dominion; rule. Not in use.

You shall put
This night's great business into my dispatch,
Which shall to all our nights and days to come
Give solely sovereign sway and *masterdom*. *Shakesp. Macb.*

MASTER-HAND. *n. s.* The hand of a man eminently skilful.

Musick resembles poetry, in each
Are nameless graces which no methods teach,
And which a *master-hand* alone can reach. *Pope.*

MASTER-JEST. *n. s.* Principal jest.

Who shall break the *master-jest*,
And what, and how, upon the rest. *Hudibras, p.* iii.

MASTER-KEY. *n. s.* The key which opens many locks, of which the subordinate keys open each only one.

This *master-key*
Frees every lock, and leads us to his person. *Dryden.*

MASTER-LEAVER. *n. s.* One that leaves or deserts his master.

Oh Antony,
Nobler than my revolt is infamous,
Forgive me in thine own particular;
But let the world rank me in register
A *master-leaver*, and a fugitive. *Shakes. Ant. and Cleopatra.*

MASTER-SINEW. *n. s.*

The *master-sinew* is a large sinew that surrounds the hough, and divides it from the bone by a hollow place, where the wind-galls are usually seated, which is the largest and most visible sinew in a horse's body; this oftentimes is relaxed or restrained. *Farrier's Dict.*

MASTER-STRING. *n. s.* Principal string.

He touch'd me
Ev'n on the tend'rest point; the *master-string*
That makes most harmony or discord to me.
I own the glorious subject fires my breast. *Rowe.*

MASTER-STROKE. *n. s.* Capital performance.

Ye skilful masters of Machaon's race,
Who nature's mazy intricacies trace;
Tell how your search has here eluded been,
How oft amaz'd, and ravish'd you have seen,
The conduct, prudence, and stupendous art,
And *master-strokes* in each mechanick part. *Blackmore.*

MA'STERLESS. *adj.* [from *master*.]

1. Wanting a master or owner.

When all was past took up his forlorn weed,
His silver shield now idle *masterless*. *Fairy Queen.*
The foul opinion
You had of her pure honour, gains, or loses,
Your sword or mine; or *masterless* leaves both
To who shall find them. *Shakespeare's Cymbeline.*

2. Ungoverned; unsubdued.

MA'STERLINESS. *n. s.* [from *masterly*.] Eminent skill.

MA'STERLY. *adv.* With the skill of a master.

Thou dost speak *masterly*
Young though thou art. *Shakespeare.*

I read a book; I think it very *masterly* written. *Swift.*

MA'STERLY. *adj.* [from *master*.]

1. Suitable to a master; artful; skilful.

As for the warmth of fansy, the *masterly* figures, and the copiousness of imagination, he has exceeded all others. *Dryd.*

That clearer strokes of *masterly* design,
Of wise contrivance, and of judgment shine,
In all the parts of nature we assert,
Than in the brightest works of human art. *Blackmore.*

A man either discovers new beauties, or receives stronger impressions from the *masterly* strokes of a great author every time he peruses him. *Addison's Spect.* N°. 409.

2. Imperious; with the sway of a master.

MA'STERPIECE. *n. s.* [*master* and *piece*.]

1. Capital performance; any thing done or made with extraordinary skill.

This is the *masterpiece*, and most excellent part, of the work of reformation, and is worthy of his majesty's pains. *Davies on Ireland.*

'Tis done; and 'twas my *masterpiece*, to work
My safety, 'twixt two dangerous extremes:
Scylla and Charybdis. *Denham's Sophy.*

Let those consider this who look upon it as a piece of art, and the *masterpiece* of conversation, to deceive, and make a prey of a credulous and well-meaning honesty. *South.*

This wond'rous *masterpiece* I fain would see;
This fatal Helen, who can wars inspire. *Dryden's Aureng.*

The fifteenth is the *masterpiece* of the whole metamorphoses. *Dryden.*

In the first ages, when the great souls, and *masterpieces* of human nature, were produced, men shined by a noble simplicity of behaviour. *Addison.*

2. Chief excellence.

Beating up of quarters was his *masterpiece*. *Clarendon.*

Dissimulation was his *masterpiece*; in which he so much excelled, that men were not ashamed with being deceived but twice by him. *Clarendon, b.* viii.

MA'STERSHIP. *n. s.* [from *master*.]

1. Dominion; rule; power.

2. Superiority; pre-eminence.

For Python slain he Pythian games decreed,
Where noble youths for *mastership* should strive,
To quoit, to run, and steeds and chariots drive. *Dryden.*

3. Chief work.

Two youths of royal blood, renown'd in fight,
The *mastership* of heav'n in face and mind. *Dryden.*

4. Skill; knowledge.

You were used
To say extremity was the trier of spirits;
That when the sea was calm all boats alike
Shew'd *mastership* in floating. *Shakesp. Coriolanus.*

5. A title of ironical respect.

How now, Signior Launce? what news with your *mastership*? *Shakesp. Two Gentlemen of Verona.*

MASTER-TEETH. *n. s.* [*master* and *teeth*.] The principal teeth.

Some living creatures have their *master-teeth* indented one within another like saws; as lions and dogs. *Bacon.*

MA'STERWORT. *n. s.* [*master*, and ꝩẏꞃꞇ, Saxon.]

The *masterwort* is a plant with a rose and umbellated flower, consisting of several petals, which are sometimes heart-shaped, and sometimes intire, ranged in a circle, and resting on the empalement; which afterward becomes a fruit, composed of two seeds, which are plain, almost oval, gently streaked and bordered, and generally casting their cover; to these marks must be added, that their leaves are winged, and pretty large: the root is used in medicine. *Miller.*

Masterwort is raised of seeds, or runners from the roots. *Mortimer's Husbandry.*

MASTERY. *n. s.* [*maistrise*, French, from *master*.]

1. Dominion; rule.

If divided by mountains, they will fight for the *mastery* of the passages of the tops, and for the towns that stand upon the roots. *Raleigh's Essays.*

2. Superiority; pre-eminence.

If a man strive for *masteries*, yet is he not crowned except he strive lawfully. 2 *Tim.* ii. 5.

This is the case of those that will try *masteries* with their superiors, and bite that which is too hard. *L'Estrange.*

Good men I suppose to live in a state of mortification, under a perpetual conflict with their bodily appetites, and struggling to get the *mastery* over them. *Atterbury.*

3. Skill.

Chief *mast'ry* to dissect,
With long and tedious havock, fabled knights,
In battles feign'd. *Milton's Par. Lost, b.* ix.

He could attain to a *mastery* in all languages, and sound the depths of all arts and sciences. *Tillotson's Serm.*

To give sufficient sweetness, a *mastery* in the language is required: the poet must have a magazine of words, and have the art to manage his few vowels to the best advantage. *Dry.*

4. Attainment of skill or power.

The learning and *mastery* of a tongue being unpleasant in itself, should not be cumbered with any other difficulties. *Locke on Education.*

MA'STFUL. *adj.* [from *mast*.] Abounding in mast, or fruit of oak, beech or chesnut.

Some from seeds inclos'd on earth arise,
For thus the *mastful* chesnut mates the skies. *Dryden.*

MASTICA'TION. *n. s.* [*masticatio*, Lat.] The act of chewing.

In birds there is no *mastication*, or comminution of the meat in the mouth; but in such as are not carnivorous it is immediately swallowed into the crop or craw, and thence transferred into the gizzard. *Ray on the Creation.*

Mastication is a necessary preparation of solid aliment, without which there can be no good digestion. *Arbuthnot.*

MA'STICATORY. *n. s.* [*masticatoire*, French.] A medicine to be chewed only, not swallowed.

Remember *masticatories* for the mouth. *Bacon.*

Salivation and *masticatories* evacuate considerably; salivation many pints of phlegm in a day, and very much by chewing tobacco. *Floyer on Humours.*

MA'STICH. *n. s.* [*mastic*, French.]

1. A kind of gum gathered from trees of the same name in Scio.

We may apply intercipients upon the temples of *mastich*; frontals may also be applied. *Wiseman's Surgery.*

2. A kind of mortar or cement.

As for the small particles of brick and stone, the least moistness would join them together, and turn them into a kind of *mastich*, which those insects could not divide. *Addison.*

MA'STICOT. *n. s.* [*marum*, Latin.] See MASSICOT.

Grind your *masticot* with a small quantity of saffron in gum water. *Peacham on Drawing.*

Masticot is very light, because it is a very clear yellow, and very near to white. *Dryden's Dufresnoy.*

MA'STIFF. *n. s.* *mastives*, plural. [*mastin*, French; *mastino*, Italian.] A dog of the largest size; a bandog; dogs kept to watch the house.

As savage bull, whom two fierce *mastives* bait,
When rancour doth with rage him once engore,
Forgets with wary ward them to await,
But with his dreadful horns them drives afore. *Fairy Qu.*

When rank Thersites opes his *mastiff* jaws,
We shall hear musick, wit, and oracle. *Shakespeare.*

When we knock at a farmer's door, the first answer shall be his vigilant *mastiff*. *More's Antidote against Atheism.*

Soon as Ulysses near th' enclosure drew,
With open mouths the furious *mastives* flew. *Pope's Odys.*

Let the *mastiffs* amuse themselves about a sheep's skin stuffed with hay, provided it will keep them from worrying the flock. *Swift.*

MA'STLESS. *adj.* [from *mast*.] Bearing no mast.

Her shining hair, uncomb'd, was loosely spread,
A crown of *mastless* oak adorn'd her head. *Dryden.*

MA'STLIN. *n. s.* [from *mesler*, French, to mingle, or rather corrupted from *miscellane*.] Mixed corn; as, wheat and rye.

The tother for one lofe hath twaine
Of *mastlin*, of rie and of wheat. *Tusser's Husb.*

MAT. *n. s.* [meatte, Saxon; *matte*, German; *matta*, Lat.] A texture of sedge, flags, or rushes.

The women and children in the west of Cornwall make *mats* of a small and fine kind of bents there growing, which serve to cover floors and walls. *Carew's Survey of Cornwall.*

In the worst inn's worst room, with *mat* half hung,
The floors of plaister, and the walls of dung. *Pope.*

To MAT. *v. a.* [from the noun.]

1. To cover with mats.

Keep the doors and windows of your conservatories well *matted*, and guarded from the piercing air. *Evelyn's Kalendar.*

2. To twist together; to join like a mat.

I on a fountain light,
Whose brim with pinks was platted;
The banks with daffadillies dight,
With grass like sleave was *matted*. *Drayt. Qu. of Cynthia.*

Sometimes beneath an ancient oak,
Or on the *matted* grass he lies;
No god of sleep he did invoke,
The stream that o'er the pebbles flies,
With gentle slumber crowns his eyes. *Dryden.*

He look'd a lion with a gloomy stare,
And o'er his eye-brows hung his *matted* hair. *Dryden.*

The spleen consisteth of muscular fibres, all *matted*, as in the skin, but in more open work. *Grew's Cosmol.*

MA'TADORE. *n. s.* [*matador*, a murderer, Spanish.] A hand of cards so called from its efficacy against the adverse player.

Now move to war her sable *matadores*,
In show like leaders of the swarthy Moors. *Pope.*

MA'TACHIN. n. s. [French.] An old dance.

Who ever saw a *matachin* dance to imitate fighting: this was a fight that did imitate the *matachin*; for they being but three that fought, every one had two adversaries striking him who struck the third. *Sidney.*

MATCH. *n. s.* [*meche*, French; *miccia*, Italian; probably from *mico*, to shine, Latin: surely not, as *Skinner* conjectures, from the Saxon maca, a companion, because a match is companion to a gun.] Any thing that catches fire; generally a card, rope, or small chip of wood dipped in melted sulphur.

Try them in several bottles *matches*, and see which of them last longest without stench. *Bacon.*

He made use of her trees as of *matches* to set Druina a fire. *Howel's Vocal Forest.*

Being willing to try something that would not cherish much fire at once, and would keep fire much longer than a coal, we took a piece of *match*, such as soldiers use. *Boyle.*

2. [From μάχη, a fight, or from maca, Saxon, one equal to another.] A contest; a game; any thing in which there is contest or opposition.

Shall we play the wantons with our woes,
And make some pretty *match* with shedding tears? *Shakesp.*
The goat was mine, by singing fairly won.
A solemn *match* was made; he lost the prize. *Dryden.*

3. [From maca, Saxon.] One equal to another; one able to contest with another.

Government mitigates the inequality of power among particular persons, and makes an innocent man, though of the lowest rank, a *match* for the mightiest of his fellow-subjects. *Addison's Freeholder.*

The old man has met with his *match*. *Spectator.*

The natural shame that attends vice, makes them zealous to encourage themselves by numbers, and form a party against religion: it is with pride they survey their increasing strength, and begin to think themselves a *match* for virtue. *Rogers.*

4. One that suits or tallies with another.

5. A marriage.

The *match*
Were rich and honourable; besides, the gentleman
Is full of virtue, bounty, worth, and qualities,
Beseeming such a wife as your fair daughter. *Shakespeare.*

Love doth seldom suffer itself to be confined by other *matches* than those of its own making. *Boyle.*

With him she strove to join Lavinia's hand,
But dire portents the purpos'd *match* withstand. *Dryden.*

6. One to be married.

She inherited a fair fortune of her own, and was very rich in a personal estate, and was looked upon as the richest *match* of the West. *Clarendon, b.* viii.

To MATCH. *v. a.* [from the noun.]

1. To be equal to.

No settled senses of the world can *match*
The pleasure of that madness. *Shakesp. Winter's Tale.*
O thou good Kent, how shall I live and work
To *match* thy goodness? life will be too short,
And every measure fail me. *Shakesp. King Lear.*

2. To shew an equal.

No history or antiquity can *match* his policies and his conduct. *South's Sermons.*

3. To equal; to oppose.

Eternal might
To *match* with their inventions they presum'd
So easy, and of his thunder made a scorn. *Milton.*

What though his heart be great, his actions gallant,
He wants a crown to poise against a crown,
Birth to *match* birth, and power to balance power. *Dryden.*

The shepherd's kalendar of Spenser is not to be *matched* in any modern language. *Dryden.*

4. To suit; to proportion.

Let poets *match* their subject to their strength,
And often try what weight they can support. *Roscommon.*
Mine have been still
Match'd with my birth; a younger brother's hopes. *Rowe.*

Employ their wit and humour in chusing and *matching* of patterns and colours. *Swift's Miscel.*

5. To marry; to give in marriage.

Great king,
I would not from your love make such a stray,
To *match* you where I hate. *Shakesp. King Lear.*
Thou dost protest thy love, and would'st it show
By *matching* her, as she would *match* her foe. *Donne.*

Them willingly they would have still retain'd,
And *match'd* unto the prince. *Daniel's Civil War.*

When a man thinks himself *matched* to one who should be a comfort to him, instead thereof he finds in his bosom a beast. *South's Sermons.*

A senator of Rome, while Rome surviv'd,
Would not have *match'd* his daughter with a king. *Addison.*

To MATCH. *v. n.*

1. To be married.

A thing that may luckily fall out to him that hath the blessing to *match* with some heroical-minded lady. *Sidney, b.* ii.

I hold it a sin to *match* in my kindred. *Shakespear.*

Let tigers *match* with hinds, and wolves with sheep,
And every creature couple with his foe. *Dryd. Sp. Fryar.*
All creatures else are much unworthy thee,
They *match'd*, and thou alone art left for me. *Dryden.*

2. To suit; to be proportionate; to tally.

MA'TCHABLE. *adj.* [from *match.*]

1. Suitable; equal; fit to be joined.

Ye, whose high worths surpassing Paragon,
Could not on earth have found one fit for mate,
Ne but in heaven *matchable* to none,
Why did ye stoop unto so lowly state? *Spenser, Sonnet* 66.

2. Correspondent.

Those at land that are not *matchable* with any upon our shores, are of those very kinds which are found no where but in the deepest parts of the sea. *Woodward's Nat. Hist.*

MA'TCHLESS. *adj.* [from *match.*] Without an equal.

This happy day two lights are seen,
A glorious saint, a *matchless* queen. *Waller.*
Much less, in arms, oppose thy *matchless* force,
When thy sharp spurs shall urge thy foaming horse. *Dryd.*

MA'TCHLESSLY. *n. s.* In a manner not to be equalled.

MA'TCHLESSNESS. *n. s.* [from *matchless.*] State of being without an equal.

MA'TCHMAKER. *n. s.* [*match* and *make.*]

1. One who contrives marriages.

You came to him to know
If you should carry me, or no;
And would have hir'd him and his imps,
To be your *matchmakers* and pimps. *Hudibras, p.* iii.

2. One who makes matches to burn.

MATE. *n. s.* [maca, Saxon; *maet*, Dutch.]

1. A husband or wife.

I that am frail flesh and earthly wight,
Unworthy match for such immortal *mate*,
Myself well wote, and mine unequal fate. *Fairy Queen.*

2. A companion, male or female.

Go, base intruder! over-weening slave!
Bestow thy fawning smiles on equal *mates*. *Shakespeare.*
My competitor
In top of all design, my *mate* in empire,
Friend and companion in the front of war. *Shakespeare.*
You knew me once no *mate*
For you; there sitting where you durst not soar. *Milton.*
Damon, behold yon breaking purple cloud;
Hear'st thou not hymns and songs divinely loud:
There mounts Amyntas, the young cherubs play
About their godlike *mate*, and sing him on his way. *Dryd.*
Leave thy bride alone:
Go, leave her with her maiden *mates* to play
At sports more harmless, till the break of day. *Dryden.*

3. The male or female of animals.

Part single, or with *mate*;
Graze the sea-weed their pasture, and through groves
Of coral stray. *Milton's Par. Lost, b.* vii.

Pliny tells us, that elephants know no copulation with any other than their own proper *mate*. *Ayliffe's Parergon.*

4. One that sails in the same ship.

What vengeance on the passing fleet she pour'd,
The master frighted, and the *mates* devour'd. *Roscommon.*

5. One that eats at the same table.

6. The second in subordination; as, the master's *mate*; the chirurgeon's *mate*.

To MATE. *v. a.* [from the noun.]

1. To match; to marry.

Ensample make of him your hapless joy,
And of myself now *mated* as you see,
Whose prouder vaunt, that proud avenging boy,
Did soon pluck down, and curb'd my liberty. *Fairy Qu.*
The hind, that would be *mated* by the lion,
Must die for love. *Shakesp. All's well that ends well.*

2. To be equal to.

Some from seeds inclos'd on earth arise,
For thus the mastful chesnut *mates* the skies. *Dryden.*
Parnassus is its name; whose forky rise
Mounts through the clouds, and *mates* the lofty skies:
High on the summit of this dubious cliff,
Deucalion wafting moor'd his little skiff. *Dryden.*

3. To oppoſe; to equal.

I i' th' way of loyalty and truth,
Dare *mate* a ſounder man than Surrey can be,
And all that love his follies. *Shakeſpeare's Henry* VIII.

4. [*Matter*, French; *matar*, Spaniſh.] To ſubdue; to confound; to cruſh.

That is good deceit
Which *mates* him firſt, that firſt intends deceit. *Shakeſp.*

The great effects that may come of induſtry and perſeverance who knoweth not? For audacity doth almoſt bind and *mate* the weaker ſort of minds. *Bacon's Nat. Hiſt.*

My ſenſe ſhe 'as *mated*, and amaz'd my ſight. *Shakeſp.*

Why this is ſtrange; go call the abbeſs hither;
I think you are all *mated*, or ſtark mad. *Shakeſpeare.*

MATE'RIAL. *adj.* [*materiel*, French; *materialis*, Latin.]

1. Conſiſting of matter; corporeal; not ſpiritual.

When we judge, our minds we mirrors make,
And as thoſe glaſſes which *material* be,
Forms of *material* things do only take,
For thoughts or minds in them we cannot ſee. *Davies.*

That theſe trees of life and knowlege were *material* trees, though figures of the law and the goſpel, it is not doubted by the moſt religious and learned writers. *Raleigh.*

2. Important; momentous; eſſential.

We muſt propoſe unto all men certain petitions incident, and very *material* in cauſes of this nature. *Hooker, b.* v.

Hold them for catholicks or hereticks, it is not a thing either one way or another, in this preſent queſtion, *material*. *Hooker, b.* iv.

What part of the world ſoever we fall into, the ordinary uſe of this very prayer hath, with equal continuance, accompanied the ſame, as one of the principal and moſt *material* duties of honour done to Chriſt. *Hooker, b.* v.

It may diſcover ſome ſecret meaning and intent therein, very *material* to the ſtate of that government. *Spenſer.*

The queſtion is not, whether you allow or diſallow that book, neither is it *material*. *Whitgiſt.*

He would not ſtay at your petitions made;
His buſineſs more *material*. *Shakeſp. Winter's Tale.*

Neither is this a queſtion of words, but infinitely *material* in nature. *Bacon's Nat. Hiſt.* N°. 98.

I paſs the reſt, whoſe ev'ry race and name,
And kinds are leſs *material* to my theme. *Dryden's Virg.*

As for the more *material* faults of writing, though I ſee many of them, I want leiſure to amend them. *Dryden.*

I ſhall, in the account of ſimple ideas, ſet down only ſuch as are moſt *material* to our preſent purpoſe. *Locke.*

In this *material* point, the conſtitution of the Engliſh government far exceeds all others. *Swift.*

MATE'RIALS. *n. ſ.* [this word is ſcarcely uſed in the ſingular; *materiaux*, French.] The ſubſtance of which any thing is made.

The Weſt-Indians, and many nations of the Africans, finding means and *materials*, have been taught, by their own neceſſities, to paſs rivers in a boat of one tree. *Raleigh.*

Intending an accurate enumeration of medical *materials*, the omiſſion hereof affords ſome probability it was not uſed by the ancients. *Brown's Vulg. Errours, b.* i.

David, who made ſuch rich proviſion of *materials* for the building of the temple, becauſe he had dipt his hands in blood, was not permitted to lay a ſtone in that ſacred pile. *South.*

That lamp in one of the heathen temples the art of man might make of ſome ſuch *material* as the ſtone aſbeſtus, which being once enkindled will burn without being conſumed. *Wilk.*

The *materials* of that building very fortunately ranged themſelves into that delicate order, that it muſt be a very great chance that parts them. *Tillotſon.*

Simple ideas, the *materials* of all our knowlege, are ſuggeſted to the mind only by ſenſation and reflection. *Locke.*

Such a fool was never found,
Who pull'd a palace to the ground,
Only to have the ruins made
Materials for an houſe decay'd. *Swift's Miſcel.*

MATE'RIALIST. *n. ſ.* [from *material.*] One who denies ſpiritual ſubſtances.

He was bent upon making Memmius a *materialiſt*. *Dryd.*

MATE'RIALITY. *n. ſ.* [*materialité*, Fr. from *material.*] Corporeity; material exiſtence; not ſpirituality.

Conſidering that corporeity could not agree with this univerſal ſubſiſtent nature, abſtracting from all *materiality* in his ideas, and giving them an actual ſubſiſtence in nature, he made them like angels, whoſe eſſences were to be the eſſence, and to give exiſtence to corporeal individuals; and ſo each idea was embodied in every individual of its ſpecies. *Digby.*

MATE'RIALLY. *adv.* [from *material.*]

1. In the ſtate of matter.

I do not mean, that any thing is ſeparable from a body by fire that was not *materially* pre-exiſtent in it. *Boyle.*

2. Not formally.

Though an ill intention is certainly ſufficient to ſpoil and corrupt an act in itſelf *materially* good, yet no good intention whatſoever can rectify or infuſe a moral goodneſs into an act otherwiſe evil. *South's Sermons.*

3. Importantly; eſſentially.

All this concerneth the cuſtoms of the Iriſh very *materially*; as well to reform thoſe which are evil, as to confirm and continue thoſe which are good. *Spenſer on Ireland.*

MATE'RIALNESS. *n. ſ.* [from *material.*] State of being material; importance.

MATE'RIATE. } *adj.* [*materiatus*, Latin.] Conſiſting of matter.
MATE'RIATED. }

After long enquiry of things immerſe in matter, interpoſe ſome ſubject which is immateriate or leſs *materiate*, ſuch as this of ſounds, to the end that the intellect may be rectified, and become not partial. *Bacon's Nat. Hiſt.* N°. 114.

MATERIA'TION. *n. ſ.* [from *materia*, Lat.] The act of forming matter.

Creation is the production of all things out of nothing; a formation not only of matter but of form, and a *materiation* even of matter itſelf. *Brown.*

MATE'RNAL. *adj.* [*materne*, Fr. *maternus*, Lat.] Motherly; befitting or pertaining to a mother.

The babe had all that infant care beguiles,
And early knew his mother in her ſmiles:
At his firſt aptneſs the *maternal* love
Thoſe rudiments of reaſon did improve. *Dryden.*

MATE'RNITY. *n. ſ.* [*maternité*, French, from *maternus*, Lat.] The character or relation of a mother.

MAT-FELON. *n. ſ.* [*matter*, to kill, and *felon*, a thief.] A ſpecies of knap-weed growing wild.

MATHEMA'TICAL } *adj.* [*mathematicus*, Lat.] Conſidered according to the doctrine of the mathematicians.
MATHEMA'TICK. }

The Eaſt and Weſt,
Upon the globe, a *mathematick* point
Only divides: thus happineſs and miſery,
And all extremes, are ſtill contiguous. *Denham's Sophy.*

It is as impoſſible for an aggregate of finites to comprehend or exhauſt one infinite, as it is for the greateſt number of *mathematick* points to amount to, or conſtitute a body. *Boyle.*

I ſuppoſe all the particles of matter to be ſituated in an exact and *mathematical* evenneſs. *Bentley's Serm.*

MATHEMA'TICALLY. *adv.* [from *mathematick.*] According to the laws of the mathematical ſciences.

We may be *mathematically* certain, that the heat of the ſun is according to the denſity of the ſun-beams, and is reciprocally proportional to the ſquare of the diſtance from the body of the ſun. *Bentley's Sermons.*

MATHEMATI'CIAN. *n. ſ.* [*mathematicus*, Lat. *mathematicien*, French.] A man verſed in the mathematicks.

One of the moſt eminent *mathematicians* of the age aſſured me, that the greateſt pleaſure he took in reading Virgil was in examining Æneas's voyage by the map. *Addiſon's Spect.*

MATHEMA'TICKS. *n. ſ.* [μαθηματικη.] That ſcience which contemplates whatever is capable of being numbered or meaſured; and it is either pure or mixt: pure conſiders abſtracted quantity, without any relation to matter; mixt is interwoven with phyſical conſiderations. *Harris.*

The *mathematicks* and the metaphyſicks
Fall to them, as you find your ſtomach ſerves you. *Shak.*

See myſtery to *mathematicks* fly. *Pope.*

MA'THES. *n. ſ.* An herb. *Ainſ.*

MATHE'SIS. *n. ſ.* [μάθησις.] The doctrine of mathematicks.

Mad *Matheſis* alone was unconfin'd. *Pope.*

MA'TIN. *adj.* [*matine*, French; *matutinus*, Latin.] Morning; uſed in the morning.

Up roſe the victor angels, and to arms
The *matin* trumpet ſung. *Milton's Par. Loſt, b.* vi.

I waſte the *matin* lamp in ſighs for thee;
Thy image ſteals between my god and me. *Pope.*

MA'TIN. *n. ſ.* Morning.

The glow-worm ſhews the *mattin* to be near,
And gins to pale his uneffectual fire. *Shakeſpeare.*

MA'TINS. *n. ſ.* [*matines*, French.] Morning worſhip.

The winged choriſters began
To chirp their *mattins*. *Cleaveland.*

By the pontifical, no altar is conſecrated without reliques: the vigils are celebrated before them, and the nocturn and *mattins*, for the ſaints whoſe the reliques are. *Stillingfleet.*

That he ſhould raiſe his mitred creſt on high,
And clap his wings, and call his family
To ſacred rites; and vex th' etherial powers
With midnight *mattins*, at uncivil hours. *Dryden.*

MA'TRASS. *n. ſ.* [*matras*, French.]

Matraſs is the name of a chemical glaſs veſſel made for digeſtion or diſtillation, being ſometimes bellied, and ſometimes riſing gradually taper into a conical figure. *Quincy.*

Protect from violent ſtorms, and the too parching darts of the ſun, your pennached tulips and ranunculus's, covering them with *matraſſes*. *Evelyn's Kalendar.*

MA'TRICE. *n. s.* [*matrix*, Latin.]

1. The womb; the cavity where the fœtus is formed.

If the time required in vivification be of any length, the spirit will exhale before the creature be mature, except it be enclosed in a place where it may have continuance of the heat, and closeness that may keep it from exhaling; and such places are the wombs and *matrices* of the females. *Bacon.*

2. A mould; that which gives form to something inclosed.

Stones that carry a resemblance of cockles, were formed in the cavities of shells; and these shells have served as *matrices* or moulds to them. *Woodward.*

MA'TRICIDE. *n. s.* [*matricidium*, Latin.]

1. Slaughter of a mother.

Nature compensates the death of the father by the *matricide* and murther of the mother. *Brown's Vulg. Errours.*

2. [*Matricida*, Latin; *matricide*, Fr.] A mother killer. *Ainſ.*

To MATRI'CULATE. *v. a.* [from matricula: a matrix, quod ea velut matrice contineantur militum nomina. *Ainſ.*] To enter or admit to a membership of the universities of England; to enlist; to enter into any society by setting down the name.

He, after some trial of his manners and learning, thought fit to enter himself of that college, and after to *matriculate* him in the university. *Walton's Life of Sanderson.*

MATRI'CULATE. *n. s.* [from the verb.] A man matriculated.

Suffer me, in the name of the *matriculates* of that famous university, to ask them some plain questions. *Arbuthnot.*

MATRI'CULATION. *n. s.* [from *matriculate.*] The act of matriculating.

A scholar absent from the university for five years, is struck out of the *matriculation* book; and, upon his coming de novo to the university, ought to be again matriculated. *Ayliffe.*

MATRIMO'NIAL. *adj.* [*matrimonial*, Fr. from *matrimonium*, Latin.] Suitable to marriage; pertaining to marriage; connubial; nuptial; hymeneal.

If he relied upon that title, he could be but a king at curtesy, and have rather a *matrimonial* than a regal power, the right remaining in his queen. *Bacon's Henry* VII.

So spake domestick Adam in his care,
And *matrimonial* love. *Milton's Par. Lost, b.* ix.

Since I am turn'd the husband, you the wife;
The *matrimonial* victory is mine,
Which, having fairly gain'd, I will resign. *Dryden.*

MATRIMO'NIALLY. *adv.* [from *matrimonial.*] According to the manner or laws of marriage.

He is so *matrimonially* wedded unto his church, that he cannot quit the same, even on the score of going unto a religious house. *Ayliffe's Parergon.*

MA'TRIMONY. *n. s.* [*matrimonium*, Lat.] Marriage; the nuptial state; the contract of man and wife; nuptials.

If any know cause why this couple should not be joined in holy *matrimony*, they are to declare it. *Common Prayer.*

MA'TRIX. *n. s.* [Lat. *matrice*, Fr.] Womb; a place where any thing is generated or formed.

If they be not lodged in a convenient *matrix*, they are not excited by the efficacy of the sun. *Brown's Vulgar Err.*

MA'TRON. *n. s.* [*matrone*, French; *matrona*, Latin.]

1. An elderly lady.

Come, civil night,
Thou sober-suited *matron*, all in black. *Shakespeare.*

Your wives, your daughters,
Your *matrons* and your maids, could not fill up
The cistern of my lust. *Shakespeare's Macbeth.*

She was in her early bloom, with a discretion very little inferior to the most experienced *matrons*. *Tatler*, Nº. 53.

2. An old woman.

A *matron* sage
Supports with homely food his drooping age. *Pope's Odyſ.*

MA'TRONAL. *adj.* [*matronalis*, Latin.] Suitable to a matron; constituting a matron.

He had heard of the beauty and virtuous behaviour of the queen of Naples, the widow of Ferdinando the younger, being then of *matronal* years of seven and twenty. *Bacon.*

MA'TRONLY. *adj. matron* and *like.*] Elderly; ancient.

The *matronly* wife plucked out all the brown hairs, and the younger the white. *L'Estrange's Fables.*

MATROSS. *n. s.*

Matrosses, in the train of artillery, are a sort of soldiers next in degree under the gunners, who assist about the guns in traversing, spunging, firing, and loading them: they carry firelocks, and march along with the store-waggons as a guard, and as assistants, in case a waggon should break. *Bailey.*

MA'TTER. *n. s.* [*matiere*, French; *materia*, Latin.]

1. Body; substance extended.

If then the soul another soul do make,
Because her pow'r is kept within a bound,
She must some former stuff or *matter* take,
But in the soul there is no *matter* found. *Davies.*

It seems probable to me, that God in the beginning formed *matter* in solid, massy, hard, impenetrable, moveable particles, of such sizes and figures, and with such other properties, and in such proportion to space, as most conduced to the end for which he formed them; and that those primitive particles being solids are incomparably harder than any porous bodies compounded of them, even so very hard as never to wear or break in pieces, no ordinary power being able to divide what God himself made one in the first creation. *Newt.*

Some have dimensions of length, breadth, and depth, and have also a power of resistance, or exclude every thing of the same kind from being in the same place: this is the proper character of *matter* or body. *Watts's Logick.*

2. Materials; that of which any thing is composed.

The upper regions of the air perceive the collection of the *matter* of tempests before the air here below. *Bacon.*

3. Subject; thing treated.

The subject or *matter* of laws in general is thus far forth constant, which *matter* is that for the ordering whereof laws were instituted. *Hooker, b.* i.

I have words to speak in thy ear will make thee dumb; yet are they much too light for the *matter*. *Shakesp. Hamlet.*

Son of God, Saviour of men! Thy name
Shall be the copious *matter* of my song. *Milt. Par. Lost.*

It is *matter* of the greatest astonishment to observe the common boldness of men. *Decay of Piety.*

I shall turn
Full fraught with joyful tiding of these works,
New *matter* of his praise, and of our songs. *Dryden.*

He grants the deluge to have come so very near the *matter*, that but very few escaped. *Tillotson.*

This is so certain in true philosophy, that it is *matter* of astonishment to me how it came to be doubted. *Cheyne.*

Be thou the copious *matter* of my song. *Phillips.*

4. The whole; the very thing supposed.

5. Affair; business: in a familiar sense.

To help the *matter*, the alchemists call in many vanities out of astrology. *Bacon's Nat. Hist.*

Matters succeeded so well with him, that every-body was in admiration to see how mighty rich he was grown. *L'Estr.*

Never was any thing gotten by sensuality and sloth in *matter* of profit or reputation. *L'Estrange's Fables.*

A fawn was reasoning the *matter* with a stag, why he should run away from the dogs. *L'Estrange's Fables.*

Some young female seems to have carried *matters* so far, that she is ripe for asking advice. *Spectator.*

If chance herself should vary,
Observe how *matters* would miscarry. *Prior.*

6. Cause of disturbance.

Where art thou? What's the *matter* with thee? *Shak.*

What's the *matter*, you dissentious rogues,
That rubbing the poor itch of your opinion,
Make yourselves scabs. *Shakesp. Coriolanus.*

7. Subject of suit or complaint.

Slender, I broke your head; what *matter* have you against me?

—Marry, Sir, I have *matter* in my head against you. *Shak.*

If the craftsmen have a *matter* against any man, the law is open; let them implead one another. *Acts* xix. 38.

In armies, if the *matter* should be tried by duel between two champions, the victory should go on the one side; and yet if tried by the gross, it would go on the other. *Bacon.*

8. Import; consequence; importance; moment.

If I had had time to have made new liveries, I would have bestowed the thousand I borrowed of you: but it is no *matter*, this poor shew doth better. *Shakesp. Henry* IV.

And please yourselves this day;
No *matter* from what hands you have the play. *Dryden.*

A prophet some, and some a poet cry,
No *matter* which, so neither of them lye,
From steepy Othrys' top to Pilus drove
His herd. *Dryden.*

Pleas'd or displeas'd, no *matter* now 'tis past;
The first who dares be angry breaths his last. *Granville.*

9. Thing; object; that which has some particular relation, or is subject to particular consideration.

The king of Armenia had in his company three of the most famous men for *matters* of arms. *Sidney, b.* ii.

Plato reprehended a young man for entering into a dissolute house; the young man said, Why for so small a *matter*? Plato replied, But custom is no small *matter*. *Bacon.*

Many times the things deduced to judgment may be meum and tuum, when the reason and consequence thereof may trench to point of estate. I call *matter* of estate not only the parts of sovereignty, but whatsoever introduceth any great alteration, or dangerous precedent. *Bacon's Essays.*

It is a maxim in state, that all countries of new acquest, till they be settled, are rather *matters* of burden than of strength. *Bacon's War with Spain.*

10. Question considered.

Upon the whole *matter*, it is absurd to think that conscience can be kept in order without frequent examination. *South.*

11. Space or quantity nearly computed.

Away he goes to the market-town, a *matter* of seven miles off, to enquire if any had seen his ass. *L'Estrange.*

I have thoughts to tarry a small *matter* in town, to learn somewhat of your lingo. *Congreve's Way of the World.*

12. Purulent running; that which is formed by suppuration.

In an inflamed tubercle in the great angle of the left eye, the *matter* being suppurated I opened it. *Wiseman's Surgery.*

13. *Upon the* MATTER. A low phrase now out of use, importing, considering the whole; with respect to the main; nearly.

In their superiors it quencheth jealousy, and layeth their competitors asleep; so that *upon the matter*, in a great wit deformity is an advantage to rising. *Bacon's Essays.*

Upon the matter, in these prayers I do the same thing I did before, save only that what before I spake without book I now read. *Bishop Sanderson.*

The elder, having consumed his whole fortune, when forced to leave his title to his younger brother, left *upon the matter* nothing to support it. *Clarendon.*

Waller, with Sir William Balfour, exceeded in horse, but were, *upon the matter*, equal in foot. *Clarendon, b.* viii.

If on one side there are fair proofs, and no pretence of proof on the other, and that the difficulties are most pressing on that side which is destitute of proof, I desire to know, whether this be not *upon the matter* as satisfactory to a wise man as a demonstration. *Tillotson's Sermons.*

To MA'TTER. *v. n.* [from the noun.]

1. To be of importance; to import.

It *matters* not, so they deny it all;
And can but carry the lye constantly. *Benj. Johnson's Catal.*

It *matters* not how they were called, so we know who they are. *Locke.*

If Petrarch's muse did Laura's wit rehearse;
And Cowley flatter'd dear Orinda's verse;
She hopes from you—Pox take her hopes and fears,
I plead her sex's claim: what *matters* hers? *Prior.*

2. To generate matter by suppuration.

Deadly wounds inward bleed, each slight sore *mattereth.* *Sidney, b.* i.

The herpes beneath *mattered*, and were dried up with common epuloticks. *Wiseman's Surgery.*

To MA'TTER. *v. a.* [from the noun.] To regard; not to neglect: as, *I* matter *not that calumny.*

MATTERY. *adj.* [from *matter.*] Purulent; generating matter.

The putrid vapours colliquate the phlegmatick humours of the body, which transcending to the lungs, causes their *mattery* cough. *Harvey on Consumptions.*

MA'TTOCK. *n. s.* [mattuc, Saxon.]

1. A kind of toothed instrument to pull up wood.

Give me that *mattock*, and the wrenching iron. *Shakesp.*

2. A pickax.

You must dig with *mattock* and with spade,
And pierce the inmost centre of the earth. *Shakespeare.*

The Turks laboured with *mattocks* and pick-axes to dig up the foundation of the wall. *Knolles's Hist. of the Turks.*

To destroy mountains was more to be expected from earthquakes than corrosive waters, and condemneth the judgment of Xerxes, that wrought through mount Athos with *mattocks.* *Brown's Vulgar Errours, b.* vii.

MA'TTRESS. *n. s.* [*matras*, French; *attras*, Welsh.] A kind of quilt made to lie upon.

Their *mattresses* were made of feathers and straw, and sometimes of furs from Gaul. *Arbuthnot.*

Nor will the raging fever's fire abate,
With golden canopies and beds of state;
But the poor patient will as soon be found
On the hard *mattress*, or the mother ground. *Dryden.*

MATURA'TION. *n. s.* [from *maturo*, Latin.]

1. The act of ripening; the state of growing ripe.

One of the causes why grains and fruits are more nourishing than leaves is, the length of time in which they grow to *maturation.* *Bacon's Nat. Hist.* N°. 466.

There is the *maturation* of fruits, the *maturation* of drinks, and the *maturation* of impostumes; as also other *maturations* of metals. *Bacon's Nat. Hist.* N°. 312.

We have no heat to spare in Summer; it is very well if it be sufficient for the *maturation* of fruits. *Bentley's Serm.*

2. [In physick.] *Maturation*, by some physical writers, is applied to the suppuration of excrementitious or extravasated juices into matter, and differs from concoction or digestion, which is the raising to a greater perfection the alimentary and natural juices in their proper canals. *Quincy.*

MA'TURATIVE. *adj.* [from *maturo*, Latin.]

1. Ripening; conducive to ripeness.

Between the tropicks and the equator their second Summer is hotter, and more *maturative* of fruits than the former. *Brown's Vulgar Errours, b.* iv.

2. Conducive to the suppuration of a sore.

Butter is *maturative*, and is profitably mixed with anodynes and suppuratives. *Wiseman's Surgery.*

MATU'RE. *adj.* [*maturus*, Latin.]

1. Ripe; perfected by time.

When once he was *mature* for man:
In Britain where was he,
That could stand up his parallel,
Or rival object be? *Shakespeare's Cymbeline.*

Their prince is a man of learning and virtue, *mature* in years and experience, who has seldom any vanity to gratify. *Addison on Italy.*

Mature the virgin was of Egypt's race,
Grace shap'd her limbs, and beauty deck'd her face. *Prior.*

How shall I meet, or how accost the sage,
Unskill'd in speech, nor yet *mature* of age. *Pope's Odyss.*

2. Brought near to completion.

This lies glowing, and is *mature* for the violent breaking out. *Shakespeare's Coriolanus.*

Here i' th' sands
Thee I'll rake up; and in the *mature* time,
With this ungracious paper strike the sight
Of the death-practis'd duke. *Shakesp. King Lear.*

3. Well-disposed; fit for execution; well-digested.

To MATU'RE. *v. a.* [*maturo*, Latin.] To ripen; to advance to ripeness.

Pick an apple with a pin full of holes, not deep, and smear it a little with sack, to see if the virtual heat of the wine will not *mature* it. *Bacon's Nat. Hist.*

Love indulg'd my labours past,
Matures my present, and shall bound my last. *Pope.*

MATU'RELY. *adv.* [from *mature.*]

1. Ripely; completely.

2. With counsel well-digested.

A prince ought *maturely* to consider, when he enters on a war, whether his coffers be full, and his revenues clear of debts. *Swift.*

3. Early; soon.

We are so far from repining at God, that he hath not extended the period of our lives to the longevity of the antediluvians; that we give him thanks for contracting the days of our trial, and receiving us more *maturely* into those everlasting habitations above. *Bentley's Sermons.*

MATU'RITY. *n. s.* [*maturité*, French; *maturitas*, Lat.] Ripeness; completion.

It may not be unfit to call some of young years to train up for those weighty affairs, against the time of greater *maturity.* *Bacon's Advice to Villiers.*

Impatient nature had taught motion
To start from time, and cheerfully to fly
Before, and seize upon *maturity.* *Crashaw.*

Various mortifications must be undergone, many difficulties and obstructions conquered, before we can arrive at a just *maturity* in religion. *Rogers's Sermons.*

MA'UDLIN. *adj.* [*Maudlin* is the corrupt appellation of *Magdelen*, who being drawn by painters with swoln eyes, and disordered look, a drunken countenance, seems to have been so named from a ludicrous resemblance to the picture of *Magdelen.*] Drunk; fuddled.

And the kind *maudling* crowd melts in her praise. *Southern's Spartan Dame.*

And largely, what she wants in words, supplies
With *maudlin* eloquence of trickling eyes. *Roscommon.*

MA'UDLIN. *n. s.* [*ageratum*, Latin.] A plant.

The flowers of the *maudlin* are digested into loose umbels, but in other respects it is very like the costmary. The species are three. *Miller.*

MA'UGRE. *adj.* [*malgré*, French.] In spite of; notwithstanding. It is now out of use.

Maugre all the world, will I keep safe;
Or some of you shall smoke for it in Rome. *Shakespeare.*

Maugre thy strength, place, youth, and eminence;
Thy valour, and thy heart; thou art a traitor. *Shakesp.*

I through the ample air in triumph high
Shall lead hell captive; *maugre* hell! and show
The pow'rs of darkness bound. *Milton's Par. Lost, b.* x.

Maugre all which, 'twas to stand fast,
As long as monarchy should last. *Hudibras, p.* i.

He prophesied of the success of his gospel; which, after his death, immediately took root, and spread itself every-where, *maugre* all opposition or persecution. *Burnet.*

MA'VIS. *n. s.* [*mauvis*, French.] A thrush. An old word.

The world that cannot deem of worthy things,
When I do praise her, say I do but flatter;
So doth the cuckow, when the *mavis* sings,
Begins his witless note apace to clear. *Spenser's Sonnet.*

In birds, kites have a resemblance with hawks, and blackbirds with thrushes and *mavises.* *Bacon's Nat. Hist.*

To MAUL. *v. a.* [from *malleus*, Latin.] To beat; to bruise; to hurt in coarse or butcherly manner.

Will he who saw the soldier's mutton fist,
And saw thee *maul'd*, appear within the list,
To witness truth? *Dryden's Juvenal.*

Once ev'ry week poor Hannibal is *maul'd*,
The theme is given, and strait the council's call'd,
Whether he should to Rome directly go. *Dryden's Juv.*

I had some repute for prose;
And, till they drove me out of date,
Could *maul* a minister of state. *Swift's Miscel.*
But fate with butchers plac'd thy priestly stall,
Meek modern faith to murder, hack and *maul.* *Pope.*

MAUL. *n. s.* [*malleus*, Latin.] A heavy hammer.

A man that beareth false witness is a *maul*, a sword, and sharp arrow. *Prov.* xxv. 18.

MAUND. *n. s.* [mand, Saxon; *mande*, Fr.] A hand-basket.

To MA'UNDER. *v. n.* [*maudire*, French.] To grumble; to murmur.

He made me many visits, *maundring* as if I had done him a discourtesy in leaving such an opening. *Wiseman's Surgery.*

MA'UNDERER. *n. s.* [from *maunder.*] A murmurer; a grumbler.

MAUNDY-THURSDAY. *n. s.* [derived by *Spelman* from *mande*, a hand-basket, in which the king was accustomed to give alms to the poor.] The Thursday before Good-friday.

MAUSO'LEUM. n. s. [Latin; *mausolée*, French. A name which was first given to a stately monument erected by his queen Artimesia to her husband Mausolus, king of Caria.] A pompous funeral monument.

MAW. *n. s.* [maga, Saxon; *maeghe*, Dutch.]

1. The stomach of animals, and of human beings, in contempt.

So oft in feasts with costly changes clad,
To crammed *maws* a sprat new stomach brings. *Sidney.*

We have heats of dungs, and of bellies and *maws* of living creatures, and of their bloods. *Bacon.*

Though plenteous, all too little seems,
To stuff this *maw*, this vast unhidebound corps. *Milton.*
The serpent, who his *maw* obscene had fill'd,
The branches in his curl'd embraces held. *Dryden.*

2. The craw of birds.

Granivorous birds have the mechanism of a mill; their *maw* is the hopper which holds and softens the grain, letting it down by degrees into the stomach, where it is ground by two strong muscles; in which action they are assisted by small stones, which they swallow for the purpose. *Arbuthnot.*

MA'WKISH. *adj.* [perhaps from *maw.*] Apt to give satiety; apt to cause loathing.

Flow, Welsted! flow, like thine inspirer beer,
So sweetly *mawkish*, and so smoothly dull. *Pope.*

MA'WKISHNESS. *n. s.* [from *mawkish.*] Aptness to cause loathing.

MA'WMET. *n. s.* [or *mammet*, from *mam* or *mother.*] A puppet, anciently an idol.

MA'WMISH. *adj.* [from *mawm* or *mawmet.*] Foolish; idle; nauseous.

It is one of the most nauseous, *mawmish* mortifications, for a man of sense to have to do with a punctual, finical fop. *L'Estrange.*

MAW-WORM. *n. s.* [*maw* and *worm.*]

Ordinary gut-worms loosen, and slide off from, the intern tunick of the guts, and frequently creep into the stomach for nutriment, being attracted thither by the sweet chyle; whence they are called stomach or *maw-worms.* *Harvey on Cons.*

MA'XILLAR. } *adj.* [*maxillaris*, Latin.] Belonging to the
MA'XILLARY. } jaw-bone.

The greatest quantity of hard substance continued is towards the head; there is the skull, the teeth, and the *maxillary* bones. *Bacon's Nat. Hist.* N°. 74.

MA'XIM. *n. s.* [*maxime*, French; *maximum*, Lat.] An axiom; a general principle; a leading truth.

This *maxim* out of love I teach. *Shakespeare.*

It is a *maxim* in state, that all countries of new acquest, till settled, are rather matters of burden than of strength. *Bacon's War with Spain.*

Yet, as in duty bound, they serve him on;
Nor ease, nor wealth, nor life itself regard,
For 'tis their *maxim*, love is love's reward. *Dryden.*

That the temper, the sentiments, the morality of men, is influenced by the example and disposition of those they converse with, is a reflexion which has long since passed into proverbs, and been ranked among the standing *maxims* of human wisdom. *Roger's Sermons.*

MAY, auxiliary verb, preterite *might.* [magan, Saxon; *moghen*, Dutch.]

1. To be at liberty; to be permitted; to be allowed; as, you *may* do for me [*per me licet*] all you can.

He that is sent out to travel with the thoughts of a man, designing to improve himself, *may* get into the conversation of persons of condition. *Locke on Education.*

2. To be possible; with the words *may be.*

Be the workmen what they *may be*, let us speak of the work. *Bacon's Essays.*

3. To be by chance.

It *may be*, I shall otherwise bethink me. *Shakesp.*
How old *may* Phillis *be*, you ask,
Whose beauty thus all hearts engages?
To answer is no easy task,
For she has really two ages. *Prior.*

4. To have power.

This also tendeth to no more but what the king *may* do: for what he *may* do is of two kinds; what he *may* do as just, and what he *may* do as possible. *Bacon.*

Make the most of life you *may.* *Bourne.*

5. A word expressing desire.

May you live happily and long for the service of your country. *Dryden's Dedicat. to the Æneis.*

MAY-be. Perhaps.

May-be, that better reason will asswage
The rash revenger's heart, words well dispos'd
Have secret pow'r t' appease inflamed rage. *Fairy Queen.*
May-be, the am'rous count solicits her
In the unlawful purpose. *Shakesp. All's well that ends well.*
'Tis nothing yet, yet all thou hast to give;
Then add those *may-be* years thou hast to live. *Dryden.*

What they offer is bare *may-be* and shift, and scarce ever amounts to a tolerable reason. *Creech.*

MAY. *n. s.* [*Maius*, Latin.] The fifth month of the year; the confine of Spring and Summer; the early or gay part of life.

On a day, alack the day!
Love, whose month is ever *May*,
'Spied a blossom passing fair,
Playing in the wanton air. *Shakesp. Love's Labour lost.*
Maids are *May* when they are maids,
But the sky changes when they are wives. *Shakesp.*
My liege
Is in the very *May*-morn of his youth,
Ripe for exploits. *Shakespeare's Henry* V.
I'll prove it on his body, if he dare;
Despight his nice fence, and his active practice,
His *May* of youth, and bloom of lustihood. *Shakesp.*

May must be drawn with a sweet and amiable countenance, clad in a robe of white and green, embroidered with daffidils, hawthorns, and blue-bottles. *Peacham.*

Hail! bounteous *May*, that do'st inspire
Mirth and youth, and warm desire;
Woods and groves are of thy dressing,
Hill and dale doth boast thy blessing. *Milton.*

To MAY. *v. n.* [from the noun.] To gather flowers on *May* morning.

When merry May first early calls the morn,
With merry maids a *maying* they do go. *Sidney.*
Cupid with Aurora playing,
As he met her once a *maying.* *Milton.*

MAY-BUG. *n. s.* [*May* and *bug.*] A chaffer. *Ains.*

MAY-DAY. *n. s.* [*May* and *day.*] The first of *May.*

'Tis as much impossible,
Unless we swept them from the door with cannons,
To scatter 'em, as 'tis to make 'em sleep
On *May-day* morning. *Shakespeare.*

MAY-FLOWER. *n. s.* [*May* and *flower.*] A plant.

The plague, they report, hath a scent of the *May-flower.* *Bacon's Nat. Hist.*

MAY-FLY. *n. s.* [*May* and *fly.*] An insect.

He loves the *May-fly*, which is bred of the cod-worm or caddis. *Walton's Angler.*

MAY-GAME. *n. s.* [*May* and *game.*] Diversion; sport; such as are used on the first of *May.*

The king this while, though he seemed to account of the designs of Perkin but as a *May-game*, yet had given order for the watching of beacons upon the coasts. *Bacon.*

Like early lovers, whose unpractis'd hearts
Were long the *May-game* of malicious arts,
When once they find their jealousies were vain,
With double heat renew their fires again. *Dryden.*

MAY-LILY. *n. s.* The same with *lily of the valley.*

MAY-POLE. *n. s.* [*May* and *pole.*] Pole to be danced round in *May.*

Amid the area wide she took her stand,
Where the tall *May-pole* once o'er-look'd the strand. *Pope.*

MAY-WEED. *n. s.* [*May* and *weed.*] A species of chamomile, called also stinking chamomile, which grows wild. *Miller.*

The *Maie-weed* doth burne, and the thistle doth freat,
The fitches pul downward both rie and the wheat. *Tusser.*

MA'YOR. *n. s.* [*major*, Lat.] The chief magistrate of a corporation, who, in London and York, is called *Lord Mayor.*

My Lord, the *mayor* of London comes to greet you. *Shakespeare's Rich.* III.

When the king once heard it; out of anger,
He sent command to the lord *mayor* strait
To stop the rumour. *Shakespeare's Henry* VIII.

The *mayor* of this town locked up the gates of the city. *Knolles's Hist. of the Turks.*

Wou'd'st thou not rather chuse a small renown,
To be the *mayor* of some poor, paltry town. *Dryden.*

MA'YORALTY. *n. s.* [from *mayor.*] The office of a mayor.

It is incorporated with a *mayoralty*, and nameth burgesses to the parliament. *Carew's Survey of Cornwall.*

There was a sharp prosecution against Sir William Capel, for misgovernment in his *mayoralty.* *Bacon's Henry* VII.

MA'YORESS. *n. s.* [from *mayor.*] The wife of the mayor.

MA'ZARD. *n. s.* [*maschoire*, French.] A jaw. *Hanmer.*

Now my lady Worm's chapless, and knockt about the *mazard* with a sexton's spade. *Shakesp. Hamlet.*

Where thou might'st stickle without hazard
Of outrage to thy hide and *mazard.* *Hudibras, p.* i.

MAZE. *n. s.* [*missen*, Dutch, to mistake; mase, a whirlpool, *Skinner.*]

1. A labyrinth; a place of perplexity and winding passages.

He, like a copious river, pour'd his song
O'er all the *mazes* of enchanted ground. *Thomson.*

2. Confusion of thought; uncertainty; perplexity.

He left in himself nothing but a *maze* of longing, and a dungeon of sorrow. *Sidney, b.* ii.

While they study how to bring to pass that religion may seem but a matter made, they lose themselves in the very *maze* of their own discourses, as if reason did even purposely forsake them, who of purpose forsake God, the author thereof. *Hooker, b.* v.

I have thrust myself into this *maze*,
Haply to wive and thrive as best I may. *Shakespeare.*

To MAZE. *v. a.* [from the noun.] To bewilder; to confuse.

Much was I maz'd to see this monster kind,
In hundred forms to change his fearful hue. *Spenser.*

MA'ZY. *adj.* [from *maze.*] Perplexed; confused.

The Lapithæ to chariots add the state
Of bits and bridles, taught the steed to bound,
To run the ring, and trace the *mazy* round. *Dryden.*

MA'ZER. *n. s.* [*maeser*, Dutch, a knot of maple.] A maple cup.

Then, lo! Perigot, the pledge which I plight,
A *mazer* ywrought of the maple ware,
Wherein is enchased many a fair sight
Of bears and tygers that make fierce war. *Spenser's Past.*

Virgil observes, like Theocritus, a just decorum, both of the subject and the persons, as particularly in the third pastoral, where one of his shepherds describes a bowl, or *mazer*, curiously carved. *Dryden's Virgil.*

M. D. *Medicinæ doctor*, doctor of physick.

ME,

1. The oblique case of *I.*

Me, only *me*, the hand of fortune bore,
Unblest to tread an interdicted shore. *Pope's Odyssey.*
For *me* the fates severely kind, ordain
A cool suspense. *Pope.*

2. *Me* is sometimes a kind of ludicrous expletive.

He thrusts *me* himself into the company of three or four gentlemanlike dogs, under the duke's table. *Shakespeare.*

He presently, as greatness knows itself,
Steps *me* a little higher than his vow
Made to my father, while his blood was poor. *Shakesp.*

I, having been acquainted with the smell before, knew it was Crab, and goes *me* to the fellow that whips the dogs. *Shakesp. Two Gentlemen of Verona.*

I followed *me* close, came in foot and hand, and, with a thought, seven of the eleven I paid. *Shakesp. Henry* IV.

3. It is sometimes used ungrammatically for *I*; as, *methinks.*

Me rather had, my heart might feel your love,
Than my unpleas'd eye see your courtesy. *Shakespeare.*

ME'ACOCK. *n. s.* [*mes coq. Skinner.*] An uxorious or effeminate man.

ME'ACOCK. *adj.* Tame; timorous; cowardly.

'Tis a world to see,
How tame, when men and women are alone,
A *meacock* wretch can make the curstest shrew. *Shakesp.*

MEAD. *n. s.* [mæδo, Saxon; *meethe*, Dutch; *meth*, German; *hydromeli*, Lat.] A kind of drink made of water and honey.

Though not so solutive a drink as *mead*, yet it will be more grateful to the stomach. *Bacon.*

He sheers his over-burden'd sheep;
Or *mead* for cooling drink prepares,
Of virgin honey in the jars. *Dryden.*

MEAD. }
ME'ADOW. } *n. s.* [mæde, Sax.] Ground somewhat watery, not plowed, but covered with grass and flowers.

Where al thing in common do rest,
Corne feeld with the pasture and *mead*,
Yet what doth it stand you in stead? *Tusser's Husb.*

A band select from forage drives
A herd of beeves, fair oxen, and fair kine,
From a fat *meadow* ground. *Milton's Par. Lost, b.* x.

Paints her, 'tis true, with the same hand which spreads,
Like glorious colours, through the flow'ry *meads*,
When lavish nature with her best attire
Cloaths the gay spring, the season of desire. *Waller.*

Yet ere to-morrow's sun shall shew his head,
The dewy paths of *meadows* we will tread,
For crowns and chaplets to adorn thy bed. *Dryden.*

MEADOW-SAFFRON. *n. s.* [*colchicum*, Lat.] A plant.

The *meadow-saffron* hath a flower consisting of one leaf, shaped like a lily, rising in form of a small tube, and is gradually widened into six segments: it has likewise a solid, bulbous root, covered with a membranous skin. *Miller.*

MEADOW-SWEET. *n. s.* [*ulmaria*, Lat.] A plant.

The *meadow-sweet* hath a flower composed of several leaves placed in a circular order, and expanding in form of a rose, out of whose empalement rises the pointal, which becomes a fruit composed of many little membranous crooked husks gatherd into an head, each of which generally contains one seed. *Miller.*

ME'AGER. *adj.* [*maigre*, French; *macer*, Latin.]

1. Lean; wanting flesh; starven.

Thou art so lean and *meagre* waxen late,
That scarce thy legs uphold thy feeble gate. *Hubberd.*

Now will the canker sorrow eat my bud,
And chase the native beauty from his cheek,
And he will look as hollow as a ghost,
As dim and *meagre* as an ague's fit. *Shakesp. King John.*

Meager were his looks,
Sharp misery had worn him to the bones. *Shakespeare.*

Whatsoever their neighbour gets, they lose, and the very bread that one eats makes t'other *meager.* *L'Estrange.*

The reeking entrails
He to his *meagre* mastiffs made a prey. *Dryden.*

Fierce famine with her *meagre* face,
And fevers of the fiery race,
In swarms th' offending wretch surround,
All brooding on the blasted ground:
And limping death, lash'd on by fate,
Comes up to shorten half our date. *Dryden.*

2. Poor; hungry.

Canaan's happy land, when worn with toil,
Requir'd a Sabbath year to mend the *meagre* soil. *Dryden.*

To ME'AGER. *v. a.* [from the noun.] To make lean.

It cannot be, that I should be so shamefully betrayed, and as a man *meagered* with long watching and painful labour, laid himself down to sleep. *Knolles's Hist. of the Turks.*

ME'AGERNESS. *n. s.* [from *meager.*]

1. Leanness; want of flesh.

2. Scantness; bareness.

Poynings, the better to make compensation of the *meagerness* of his service in the wars by acts of peace, called a parliament. *Bacon's Henry* VII.

MEAK. *n. s.* A hook with a long handle.

A *meake* for the pease, and to swing up the brake. *Tuss.*

MEAL. *n. s.* [male, Saxon, repast or portion.]

1. The act of eating at a certain time.

Boaz said unto her at *meal* time, Come eat, and dip thy morsel. *Ruth* ii. 14.

The quantity of aliment necessary to keep the animal in a due state of vigour, ought to be divided into *meals* at proper intervals. *Arbuthnot on Aliments.*

2. A repast.

What strange fish
Hath made his *meal* on thee? *Shakesp. Tempest.*

Give them great *meals* of beef, and iron and steel, they will eat like wolves, and fight like devils. *Shakesp. Henry* V.

They made m' a miser's feast of happiness,
And cou'd not furnish out another *meal.* *Dryden.*

3. A part; a fragment.

That yearly rent is still paid into the hanaper, even as the former casualty itself was wont to be, in parcel *meal*, brought in, and answered there. *Bacon.*

4. [Mælepe, Saxon; *meel*, Dutch; *mahlen*, to grind, German.] The flower or edible part of corn.

In the bolting and sifting of near fourteen years of such power and favour, all that came out could not be expected to be pure and fine *meal*, but must have a mixture of padar and bran in this lower age of human fragility. *Wotton.*

An old weazel conveys himself into a *meal*-tub for the mice to come to her, since she could not go to them. *L'Estrange's Fables.*

To MEAL. *v. a.* [*meler*, French.] To sprinkle; to mingle.

Were he *meal'd*
With that which he corrects, then were he tyrannous. *Shakespeare's Meas. for Measure.*

ME'ALMAN. *n. s.* [*meal* and *man.*] One that deals in meal.

ME'ALY. *adj.* [from *meal.*]

1. Having the taste or soft insipidity of meal; having the qualities of meal.

The *mealy* parts of plants dissolved in water make too viscid an aliment. *Arbuthnot on Aliments.*

2. Besprinkled, as with meal.

With four wings, as all farinaceous and *mealy*-winged animals, as butterflies and moths. *Brown's Vulgar Errours.*

Like a gay insect, in his summer shine,
The fop light fluttering spreads his *mealy* wings. *Thomson.*

MEALY-MOUTHED. *adj.* [imagined by *Skinner* to be corrupted from *mild-mouthed* or *mellow-mouthed*: but perhaps from the sore mouths of animals, that, when they are unable to comminute their grain, must be fed with meal.] Soft mouthed; unable to speak freely.

She was a fool to be *mealy-mouthed* where nature speaks so plain. *L'Estrange.*

MEALYMO'UTHEDNESS. *n. s.* [from the adjective.] Bashfulness; restraint of speech.

MEAN. *adj.* [mæne, Saxon.]

1. Wanting dignity; of low rank or birth.

She was stricken with most obstinate love to a young man but of *mean* parentage, in her father's court, named Antiphilus; so *mean*, as that he was but the son of her nurse, and by that means, without other desert, became known of her. *Sidney, b.* ii.

This fairest maid of fairer mind;
By fortune *mean*, in nature born a queen. *Sidney.*

Let pale-fac'd fear keep with the *mean*-born man,
And find no harbour in a royal heart. *Shakesp. Henry* VI.

True hope is swift, and flies with swallow wings;
Kings it makes gods, and *meaner* creatures, kings. *Shak.*

2. Low-minded; base; ungenerous; spiritless.

The shepherd knows not thunder from a tabor,
More than I know the sound of Marcius' tongue
From every *meaner* man. *Shakespeare's Coriolanus.*

Can you imagine I so *mean* could prove,
To save my life by changing of my love? *Dryden.*

We fast not to please men, nor to promote any *mean*, worldly interest. *Smalridge's Sermons.*

3. Contemptible; despicable.

The Roman legions, and great Cæsar found
Our fathers no *mean* foes. *Philips.*

I have sacrificed much of my own self-love, in preventing not only many *mean* things from seeing the light, but many which I thought tolerable. *Pope.*

4. Low in the degree of any property; low in worth; low in power.

Some things are good, yet in so *mean* a degree of goodness, that many are only not disproved nor disallowed of God for them. *Hooker, b.* ii.

The lands be not holden of her majesty in chief, but by a *mean* tenure in soccage, or by knight's service at the most. *Bacon's Office of Alienation.*

By this extortion he suddenly grew from a *mean* to a mighty estate, insomuch that his ancient inheritance being not one thousand marks yearly, he became able to dispend ten thousand pounds. *Davies on Ireland.*

To peaceful Rome new laws ordain;
Call'd from his *mean* abode a sceptre to sustain. *Dryden.*

5. [*Moyen*, French.] Middle; moderate; without excess.

He saw this gentleman, one of the properest and best-graced men that ever I saw, being of middle age and a *mean* stature. *Sidney, b.* ii.

Now read with them those organick arts which enable men to discourse and write, and according to the fittest style of lofty, *mean*, or lowly. *Milton on Education.*

6. Intervening; intermediate.

In the *mean* while the heaven was black with clouds and wind, and there was a great rain. 1 *Kings* xviii. 45.

There is French wheat, which is bearded, and requireth the best soil, recompensing the same with a profitable plenty; and not wheat, so termed because it is unbearded, is contented with a *meaner* earth, and contenting with a suitable gain. *Carew on Cornwall.*

MEAN. *n. s.* [*moyen*, French.]

1. Mediocrity; middle rate; medium.

Oft 'tis seen,
Our *mean* securities, and our mere defects
Prove our commodities. *Shakesp. King Lear.*

Temperance with golden square,
Betwixt them both can measure out a *mean*. *Shakesp.*

There is a *mean* in all things, and a certain measure wherein the good and the beautiful consist, and out of which they never can depart. *Dryden's Dufresnoy.*

But no authority of gods or men
Allow of any *mean* in poesie. *Roscommon.*

Against her then her forces prudence joins,
And to the golden *mean* herself confines. *Denham.*

2. Measure; regulation.

The rolling sea resounding soft,
In his big base them fitly answered,
And on the rock the waves breaking aloft,
A solemn *mean* unto them measured. *Fairy Queen.*

3. Interval; interim; mean time.

But sith this wretched woman overcome,
Of anguish rather than of crime hath been,
Reserve her cause to her eternal doom,
And in the *mean* vouchsafe her honourable tomb. *Fairy Queen.*

4. Instrument; measure; that which is used in order to any end.

Pamela's noble heart would needs gratefully make known the valiant *mean* of her safety. *Sidney, b.* i.

As long as that which Christians did was good, and no way subject to just reproof, their virtuous conversation was a *mean* to work the Heathens conversion unto Christ. *Hooker.*

It is no excuse unto him who, being drunk, committeth incest, and alledgeth that his wits were not his own; in as much as himself might have chosen whether his wits should by that *mean* have been taken from him. *Hooker, b.* i.

He tempering goodly well
Their contrary dislikes with loved *means*,
Did place them all in order, and compell
To keep themselves within their sundry reigns,
Together link'd with adamantine chains. *Spenser.*

I'll devise a *mean* to draw the Moor
Out of the way, that your converse and business
May be more free. *Shakespeare's Othello.*

No place will please me so, no *mean* of death,
As here by Cæsar and by you cut off. *Shakespeare.*

Nature is made better by no *mean*,
But nature makes that *mean*; so over that art
Which, you say, adds to nature, is an art
That nature makes. *Shakesp. Winter's Tale.*

Your doctrine leads them to look on this end as essential, and on the *means* as indifferent. *Lord Bolingbrooke to Swift.*

5. It is often used in the plural, and by some not very grammatically with an adjective singular.

The more base art thou,
To make such *means* for her as thou hast done,
And leave her on such slight conditions. *Shakespeare.*

By this *means* he had them the more at vantage, being tired and harrassed with a long march. *Bacon's Henry* III.

Because he wanted *means* to perform any great action, he made *means* to return the sooner. *Davies on Ireland.*

Strong was their plot,
Their parties great, *means* good, the season fit,
Their practice close, their faith suspected not. *Daniel.*

By this *means* not only many helpless persons will be provided for, but a generation will be bred up not perverted by any other hopes. *Sprat's Sermons.*

Who is there that hath the leisure and *means* to collect all the proofs concerning most of the opinions he has, so as safely to conclude that he hath a clear and full view. *Locke.*

A good character, when established, should not be rested in as an end, but only employed as a *means* of doing still farther good. *Atterbury's Sermons.*

It renders us careless of approving ourselves to God by religious duties, and, by that *means*, securing the continuance of his goodness. *Atterbury's Sermons.*

6. *By all* MEANS. Without doubt; without hesitation; without fail.

7. *By no* MEANS. Not in any degree; not at all.

The wine on this side of the lake is *by no means* so good as that on the other. *Addison on Italy.*

8. *Means* are likewise used for revenue; fortune; probably from *desmenes*.

Your *means* are very slender, and your waste is great. *Shakespeare's Henry* IV.

Rust sword; cool blushes; and, parolles, live
Safest in shame! being fool'd, by fool'ry thrive;
There's place and *means* for every man alive. *Shakesp.*

For competence of life I will allow you,
That lack of *means* enforce you not to evil;
And, as we hear you do reform yourselves,
Give you advancement. *Shakespeare's Henry* IV.

Essex did not build or adorn any house; the queen perchance spending his time, and himself his *means*. *Wotton.*

9. MEAN-TIME. } In the intervening time: sometimes an
MEAN-WHILE. } adverbial mode of speech.

Mean-while
The world shall burn, and from her ashes spring
New heav'n and earth. *Milton's Par. Lost, b.* iii.

Mean-time the rapid heav'ns rowl'd down the light,
And on the shaded ocean rush'd the night. *Dryden.*

Mean-time her warlike brother on the seas,
His waving streamers to the winds displays. *Dryden.*

Mean time, in shades of night Æneas lies;
Care seiz'd his soul, and sleep forsook his eyes. *Dryden.*

Mean-while I'll draw up my Numidian troops,
And, as I see occasion, favour thee. *Addison's Cato.*

The Roman legions were all recalled to help their country against the Goths; *mean-time* the Britons, left to shift for themselves, and daily harrassed by cruel inroads from the Picts, were forced to call in the Saxons for their defence. *Swift.*

To MEAN. *v. n.* [*meenen*, Dutch.] To have in the mind; to intend; to purpose.

When your children shall say, What *mean* you by this service? ye shall say, It is the passover. *Exod.* xii. 26.

These delights if thou canst give,
Mirth, with thee I *mean* to live. *Milton.*

To MEAN. *v. a.*

1. To purpose; to intend; to design.

Ye thought evil against me; but God *meant* it unto good, to save much people alive. *Gen.* l. 20.

And life more perfect have attain'd than fate
Meant me, by venturing higher than my lot. *Milton.*

I practis'd it to make you taste your cheer
With double pleasure, first prepar'd by fear:
So loyal subjects often seize their prince,
Yet *mean* his sacred person not the least offence. *Dryden.*

2. To intend; to hint covertly; to underſtand.

I more eaſily forſake an argument on which I could delight to dwell; I *mean* your judgment in your choice of friends. *Dryden's Aurengzebe.*

Whatever was *meant* by them, it could not be that Cain, as elder, had a natural dominion over Abel. *Locke.*

MEA'NDER. *n. ſ.* [*Meander* is a river in Phrygia remarkable for its winding courſe.] Maze; labyrinth; flexuous paſſage; ſerpentine winding; winding courſe.

Phyſicians, by the help of anatomical diſſections, have ſearched into thoſe various *meanders* of the veins, arteries, and integrals of the body. *Hale's Origin of Mankind.*

'Tis well, that while mankind
Through fate's perverſe *meander* errs,
He can imagin'd pleaſures find,
To combat againſt real cares. *Prior.*

While ling'ring rivers in *meanders* glide,
They ſcatter verdant life on either ſide;
The vallies ſmile, and with their flow'ry face,
And wealthy births confeſs the floods embrace. *Blackmore.*

Law is a bottomleſs pit: John Bull was flattered by the lawyers, that his ſuit would not laſt above a year; yet ten long years did Hocus ſteer his cauſe through all the *meanders* of the law, and all the courts. *Arbuthnot.*

MEA'NDROUS. *adj.* [from *meander.*] Winding; flexuous.

ME'ANING. *n. ſ.* [from *mean.*]

1. Purpoſe; intention.

I am no honeſt man, if there be any good *meaning* toward you. *Shakeſpeare's King Lear.*

2. Habitual intention.

Some whoſe *meaning* hath at firſt been fair,
Grow knaves by uſe, and rebels by deſpair. *Roſcommon.*

3. The ſenſe; the thing underſtood.

The *meaning*, not the name, I call: for thou,
Not of the Muſes nine. *Milton's Par. Loſt, b.* vii.

Theſe loſt the ſenſe their learning to diſplay,
And thoſe explain'd the *meaning* quite away. *Pope.*

No word more frequently in the mouths of men than conſcience; and the *meaning* of it is, in ſome meaſure, underſtood: however, it is a word extremely abuſed by many, who apply other *meanings* to it which God Almighty never intended. *Swift's Miſcel.*

ME'ANLY. *adv.* [from *mean.*]

1. Moderately; not in a great degree.

Dr. Metcalfe, maſter of St. John's College, a man *meanly* learned himſelf, but not *meanly* affectioned to ſet forward learning in others. *Aſcham's Schoolmaſter.*

In the reign of Domitian, poetry was but *meanly* cultivated, but painting eminently flouriſhed. *Dryden's Dufreſnoy.*

2. Without dignity; poorly.

It was the winter wild,
While the heav'n-born child,
All *meanly* wrapt in the rude manger lies. *Milton.*

The Perſian ſtate will not endure a king
So *meanly* born. *Denham's Sophy.*

3. Without greatneſs of mind; ungenerouſly.

Would you *meanly* thus rely
On power, you know I muſt obey. *Prior.*

4. Without reſpect.

Our kindred, and our very names, ſeem to have ſomething deſireable in them: we cannot bear to have others think *meanly* of them. *Watts's Logick.*

ME'ANNESS. *n. ſ.* [from *mean.*]

1. Want of excellence.

The miniſter's greatneſs or *meanneſs* of knowledge to do other things, ſtandeth in this place as a ſtranger, with whom our form of common prayer hath nothing to do. *Hooker.*

This figure is of a later date by the *meanneſs* of the workmanſhip. *Addiſon on Italy.*

2. Want of dignity; low rank; poverty.

No other nymphs have title to mens hearts,
But as their *meanneſs* larger hopes imparts. *Waller.*

Poverty, and *meanneſs* of condition, expoſe the wiſeſt to ſcorn, it being natural for men to place their eſteem rather upon things great than good. *South's Sermons.*

3. Lowneſs of mind.

The name of ſervants has of old been reckoned to imply a certain *meanneſs* of mind, as well as lowneſs of condition. *South's Sermons.*

4. Sordidneſs; niggardlineſs.

MEANT, perf. and part. paſſ. of *to mean.*

By Silvia if thy charming ſelf be *meant*;
If friendſhip be thy virgin vows extent:
O! let me in Aminta's praiſes join;
Her's my eſteem ſhall be, my paſſion thine. *Prior.*

MEASE. *n. ſ.* [probably a corruption of meaſure: as, a *meaſe* of herrings is five hundred. *Ainſ.*

ME'ASLES. *n. ſ.* [*morbilli*, Latin.]

Meaſles are a critical eruption in a fever, well known in the common practice, and bear this name, which is a diminutive of morbus, becauſe it hath been accounted a ſpecies of ſuch malignant and peſtilential fevers, to which comparatively this is ſo in a much inferior degree. *Quincy.*

My lungs
Coin words till their decay, againſt thoſe *meaſles*,
Which we diſdain ſhould tetter us, yet ſeek
The very way to catch them. *Shakeſpeare's Coriolanus.*

Before the plague of London, inflammations of the lungs were riſe and mortal, as likewiſe the *meaſles*. *Arbuthnot.*

2. A diſeaſe of ſwine.

One, when he had an unlucky old grange, would needs ſell it, and proclaimed the virtues of it; nothing ever thrived on it, no owner of it ever died in his bed; the ſwine died of the *meaſles*, and the ſheep of the rot. *B. Johnſon's Diſcovery.*

3. A diſeaſe of trees.

Fruit-bearers are often infected with the *meaſles*, by being ſcorched with the ſun. *Mortimer's Huſbandry.*

ME'ASLED. *adj.* [from *meaſles.*] Infected with the meaſles.

Thou vermin wretched,
As e'er in *meaſled* pork was hatched;
Thou tail of worſhip, that doſt grow
On rump of juſtice as of cow. *Hudibras, p.* i.

ME'ASLY. *adj.* [from *meaſles.*] Scabbed with the meaſles.

Laſt trotted forth the gentle ſwine,
To eaſe her againſt the ſtump,
And diſmally was heard to whine,
All as ſhe ſcrubb'd her *meaſly* rump. *Swift.*

ME'ASURABLE. *adj.*

1. Such as may be meaſured; ſuch as may admit of computation.

God's eternal duration is permanent and indiviſible, not *meaſurable* by time and motion, nor to be computed by number of ſucceſſive moments. *Bentley's Sermons.*

2. Moderate; in ſmall quantity.

ME'ASURABLENESS. *n. ſ.* [from *meaſurable.*] Quality of admitting to be meaſured.

ME'ASURABLY. *adv.* [from *meaſurable.*] Moderately.

Wine *meaſurably* drunk, and in ſeaſon, bringeth gladneſs of the heart. *Eccluſ.* xxxi. 28.

ME'ASURE. *n. ſ.* [*meſure*, French; *menſura*, Latin.]

1. That by which any thing is meaſured.

A taylor's news,
Who ſtood with ſhears and *meaſure* in his hand,
Standing on ſlippers, which his nimble haſte
Had falſely thruſt upon contrary feet,
Told of many a thouſand. *Shakeſp. King John.*

A concave *meaſure*, of known and denominated capacity, ſerves to meaſure the capaciouſneſs of any other veſſel. *Holder.*

All magnitudes are capable of being meaſured; but it is the application of one to another which makes actual *meaſures*. *Holder on Time.*

When Moſes ſpeaks of *meaſures*, for example, of an ephah, he preſumes they knew what *meaſure* he meant: that he himſelf was ſkilled in weights and *meaſures*, arithmetick and geometry, there is no reaſon to doubt. *Arbuthnot on Coins.*

2. The rule by which any thing is adjuſted or proportioned.

God's goodneſs is the *meaſure* of his providence. *More.*

I expect, from thoſe that judge by firſt ſight and raſh *meaſures*, to be thought fond or inſolent. *Glanville's Scep.*

3. Proportion; quantity ſettled.

Meaſure is that which perfecteth all things, becauſe every thing is for ſome end; neither can that thing be available to any end, which is not proportionable thereunto; and to proportion as well exceſſes as defects are oppoſite. *Hooker.*

I enter not into the particulars of the law of nature, or its *meaſures* of puniſhment; yet it is certain there is ſuch a law. *Locke.*

4. A ſtated quantity: as, a meaſure of wine.

Be large in mirth, anon we'll drink a *meaſure*
The table round. *Shakeſpeare's Macbeth.*

5. Sufficient quantity.

I'll never pauſe again,
Till either death hath clos'd theſe eyes of mine,
Or fortune given me *meaſure* of revenge. *Shakeſpeare.*

6. Allotment; portion allotted.

Good Kent, how ſhall I live aud work
To match thy goodneſs? life will be too ſhort,
And ev'ry *meaſure* fail me. *Shakeſp. King Lear.*

We will not boaſt of things without our *meaſure*, but according to the meaſure of the rule which God hath diſtributed to us, a *meaſure* to reach even unto you. 2 *Cor.* x. 13.

If elſe thou ſeek'ſt
Ought, not ſurpaſſing human *meaſure*, ſay. *Milton.*

Our religion ſets before us not the example of a ſtupid ſtoick, who had, by obſtinate principles, hardened himſelf againſt all pain beyond the common *meaſures* of humanity, but an example of a man like ourſelves. *Tillotſon's Sermons.*

7. Degree.

I have laid down, in ſome *meaſure*, the deſcription of the old world. *Abbot's Deſcription of the World.*

There is a great *meaſure* of diſcretion to be uſed in the performance of confeſſion, ſo that you neither omit it when your own

own heart may tell you that there is ſomething amiſs, nor over-ſcrupulouſly purſue it when you are not conſcious to yourſelf of notable failings. *Taylor's Guide to a Penitent.*

The rains were but preparatory in ſome *meaſure*, and the violence and conſummation of the deluge depended upon the diſruption of the great abyſs. *Burnet's Theory of the Earth.*

8. Proportionate time; muſical time.

Amaryllis breathes thy ſecret pains,
And thy fond heart beats *meaſure* to thy ſtrains. *Prior.*

9. Motion harmonically regulated.

My legs can keep no *meaſure* in delight,
When my poor heart no meaſure keeps in grief:
Therefore no dancing, girl, ſome other ſport. *Shakeſp.*

As when the ſtars in their æthereal race,
At length have roll'd around the liquid ſpace,
From the ſame point of heav'n their courſe advance,
And move in *meaſures* of their former dance. *Dryden.*

10. A ſtately dance. This ſenſe is, I believe, obſolete.

Wooing, wedding, and repenting, is as a Scotch jig, a *meaſure* and a cinque pace; the firſt ſuit is hot and haſty, like a Scotch jig, and full as fantaſtical; the wedding mannerly, modeſt as a *meaſure*, full of ſtate and anchentry. *Shakeſpeare.*

Now are our brows bound with victorious wreaths,
Our ſtern alarms chang'd to merry meetings,
Our dreadful marches to delightful *meaſures*. *Shakeſpeare.*

11. Moderation; not exceſs.

O love, be moderate, allay thy ecſtaſy;
In *meaſure* rein thy joy, ſcant this exceſs;
I feel too much thy bleſſing, make it leſs,
For fear I ſurfeit. *Shakeſp. Merchant of Venice.*

Hell hath enlarged herſelf, and opened her mouth without *meaſure*. *Iſa.* vi. 14.

12. Limit; boundary. In the ſame ſenſe is

Μέτρον

Τρεῖς ἐτίων δεκάδας τριάδιας δύο, μέτρον ἔθηκαν
Ἡμετέρης Βιοτῆς μάντιες αἰθέριοι.
Ἀρκῦμαι τȣ́τοισιν.

Lord, make me to know mine end, and the *meaſure* of my days what it is, that I may know how frail I am. *Pſal.*

13. Any thing adjuſted.

He only lived according to nature, the other by ill cuſtoms, and *meaſures* taken by other mens eyes and tongues. *Taylor's holy living.*

Chriſt reveals to us the *meaſures* according to which God will proceed in diſpenſing his rewards. *Smalridge's Sermons.*

14. Syllables metrically numbered; metre.

I addreſſed them to a lady, and affected the ſoftneſs of expreſſion, and the ſmoothneſs of *meaſure*, rather than the height of thought. *Dryden.*

The numbers themſelves, though of the heroick *meaſure*, ſhould be the ſmootheſt imaginable. *Pope.*

15. Tune; proportionate notes.

The joyous nymphs and light-foot fairies,
Which thither came to hear their muſick ſweet,
And to the *meaſures* of their melodies
Did learn to move their nimble-ſhifting feet. *Spenſer.*

16. Mean of action; mean to an end.

His majeſty found what wrong *meaſures* he had taken in the conferring that truſt, and lamented his error. *Clarendon.*

17. To have hard *meaſure*; to be hardly dealt by.

To Me'asure. *v. a.* [*meſurer*, French; *menſuro*, Latin.]

1. To compute the quantity of any thing by ſome ſettled rule.

Archidamus having received from Philip, after the victory of Cheronea, proud letters, writ back, that if he *meaſured* his own ſhadow he would find it no longer than it was before his victory. *Bacon's Apophth.*

2. To paſs through; to judge of extent by marching over.

A true devoted pilgrim is not weary
To *meaſure* kingdoms with his feeble ſteps. *Shakeſpeare.*

I'll tell thee all my whole device
At the park-gate; and therefore haſte away,
For we muſt *meaſure* twenty miles to-day. *Shakeſpeare.*

The veſſel ploughs the ſea,
And *meaſures* back with ſpeed her former way. *Dryden.*

3. To judge of quantity or extent, or greatneſs.

Great are thy works, Jehovah; infinite
Thy pow'r! What thought can *meaſure* thee, or tongue
Relate thee? *Milton's Par. Loſt, b.* vii.

4. To adjuſt; to proportion.

To ſecure a contented ſpirit, *meaſure* your deſires by your fortunes, not your fortunes by your deſires. *Taylor.*

Silver is the inſtrument as well as meaſure of commerce; and 'tis by the quantity of ſilver he gets for any commodity in exchange that he *meaſures* the value of the commodity he ſells. *Locke.*

5. To mark out in ſtated quantities.

What thou ſeeſt is that portion of eternity which is called time, *meaſured* out by the ſun, and reaching from the beginning of the world to its conſummation. *Addiſon's Spectator.*

6. To allot or diſtribute by meaſure.

With what meaſure you mete, it ſhall be *meaſured* to you again. *Matth.* vii. 2.

Me'asureless. *adj.* [from *meaſure.*] Immenſe; immeaſureable.

He ſhut up the *meaſureleſs* content. *Shakeſpeare.*

Me'asurement. *n. ſ.* [from *meaſure.*] Menſuration; act of meaſuring.

Me'asurer. *n. ſ.* [from *meaſure.*] One that meaſures.

Me'asuring. *adj.* [from *meaſure.*] It is applied to a caſt not to be diſtinguiſhed in its length from another but by meaſuring.

When luſty ſhepherds throw
The bar by turns, and none the reſt out-go
So far, but that the beſt are *meas'ring* caſts,
Their emulation and their paſtime laſts. *Waller.*

Meat. *n. ſ.* [*met*, French.]

1. Fleſh to be eaten.

To his father he ſent ten ſhe aſſes laden with corn, and bread, and *meat*, for his father by the way. *Gen.* xlv. 23.

Carnivoræ, and birds of prey, are no good *meat*; but the reaſon is, rather the cholerick nature of thoſe birds than their feeding upon fleſh; for pewets and ducks feed upon fleſh, and yet are good *meat*. *Bacon's Nat. Hiſt.* N°. 859.

There was a multitude of exciſes; as, the vectigal macelli, a tax upon *meat*. *Arbuthnot.*

2. Food in general.

Never words were muſick to thine ear,
And never *meat* ſweet-favour'd in thy taſte,
Unleſs I ſpake or carv'd. *Shakeſp. Comedy of Errours.*

Meats for the belly, and the belly for *meats*; but God ſhall deſtroy both. 1 *Cor.* vi. 13.

Me'ated. *adj.* [from *meat.*] Fed; foddered.

Strong oxen and horſes, wel ſhod and wel clad,
Wel *meated* and uſed. *Tuſſer's Huſb.*

Meathe. *n. ſ.* [*medd*, Welſh, unde *mede*, meddwi ebrius ſum.] Drink.

For drink the grape
She cruſhes, inoffenſive muſt, and *meathes*
From many a berry. *Milton's Par. Loſt, b.* v.

Me'azling. *part.* generally called *mizzling*. See Mizzle.

The air feels more moiſt when the water is in ſmall than in great drops; in *meazling* and ſoaking rain, than in great ſhowers. *Arbuthnot on Air.*

Mecha'nical. } *adj.* [*mechanicus*, Lat. *mechanique*, French;
Mecha'nick. } from μηχανὴ.]

1. Mean; ſervile; of mean occupation.

Know you not, being *mechanical*, you ought not walk upon a labouring day, without the ſign of your profeſſion? *Shak.*

Hang him, *mechanical* ſalt-butter rogue; I will ſtare him out of his wits; I will hew him with my cudgel. *Shakeſp.*

Mechanick ſlaves,
With greaſy aprons, rules, and hammers, ſhall
Uplift us to the view. *Shakeſp. Ant. and Cleopatra.*

To make a god, a hero, or a king,
Deſcend to a *mechanick* dialect. *Roſcommon.*

2. Conſtructed by the laws of mechanicks.

Many a fair precept in poetry is, like a ſeeming demonſtration in mathematicks, very ſpecious in the diagram, but failing in the *mechanick* operation. *Dryden.*

The main buſineſs of natural philoſophy, is to argue from phenomena without feigning hypotheſes, and to deduce cauſes from effects till we come to the very firſt cauſe, which certainly is not *mechanical*; and not only to unfold the mechaniſm of the world, but chiefly to reſolve theſe, and ſuch like queſtions. *Newton's Opticks.*

3. Skilled in mechanicks.

Mecha'nick. *n. ſ.* A manufacturer; a low workman.

Do not bid me
Diſmiſs my ſoldiers, or capitulate
Again with Rome's *mechanicks*. *Shakeſp. Coriolanus.*

A third proves a very heavy philoſopher, who poſſibly would have made a good *mechanick*, and have done well enough at the uſeful philoſophy of the ſpade or the anvil. *South.*

Mecha'nicks. *n. ſ.* [*mechanica*, Latin.]

Dr. Wallis defines *mechanicks* to be the geometry of motion, a mathematical ſcience, which ſhews the effects of powers, or moving forces, ſo far as they are applied to engines, and demonſtrates the laws of motion. *Harris.*

The rudiments of geography, with ſomething of *mechanicks*, may be eaſily conveyed into the minds of acute young perſons. *Watts's Improvement of the Mind.*

Salmoneus was a great proficient in *mechanicks*, and inventor of a veſſel which imitated thunder. *Broome.*

Mecha'nically. *adv.* [from *mechanick.*] According to the laws of mechaniſm.

They ſuppoſe even the common animals that are in being, to have been formed *mechanically* among the reſt. *Ray.*

Later philoſophers feign hypotheſes for explaining all things *mechanically*, and refer other cauſes to metaphyſicks. *Newton.*

MECHA'NICALNESS. *n. s.* [from *mechanick.*]
1. Agreeableness to the laws of mechanism.
2. Meanness.

MECHANI'CIAN. *n. s.* [*mechanicien*, French.] A man professing or studying the construction of machines.

Some were figured like male, others like female screws, as *mechanicians* speak. *Boyle.*

MECHA'NISM. *n. s. mechanisme*, French.]
1. Action according to mechanick laws.

After the chyle has passed through the lungs, nature continues her usual *mechanism*, to convert it into animal substances. *Arbuthnot on Aliments.*

He acknowledges nothing besides matter and motion; so that all must be performed either by *mechanism* or accident, either of which is wholly unaccountable. *Bentley.*

2. Construction of parts depending on each other in any complicated fabrick.

MECHO'ACAN. *n. s.*

Mechoacan is a large root, twelve or fourteen inches long, and of the thickness of a man's wrist, usually divided into two branches at the bottom: what we see of it is commonly cut transversely into slices for the conveniency of drying it: its first introduction into Europe was about two hundred and twenty years ago: it is brought from the province of *Mechoacan* in South America, from whence it has its name: the plant which affords it is a species of bindweed, and its stalks, which are angular, and full of a resinous milky juice, climb upon every thing which stands near them: the root in powder is a gentle and mild purgative. *Hill's Mat. Med.*

MECO'NIUM. *n. s.* [μηκώνιον.]
1. Expressed juice of *poppy.*
2. The first excrement of children.

Infants new-born have a *meconium*, or sort of dark-coloured excrement in the bowels. *Arbuthnot on Diet.*

ME'DAL. *n. s.* [*medaille*, Fr. probably from *metallum*, Lat.]
1. An ancient coin.

The Roman *medals* were their current money: when an action deserved to be recorded on a coin, it was stampt, and issued out of the mint. *Addison's Guard.* N°. 96.

2. A piece stamped in honour of some remarkable performance.

MEDA'LLICK. *n. s.* [from *medal.*] Pertaining to medals.

You will never, with all your *medallick* eloquence, persuade Eugenius, that it is better to have a pocketful of Otho's than of Jacobus's. *Addison on ancient Medals.*

MEDA'LLION. *n. s.* [*medaillon*, Fr.] A large antique stamp or medal.

Medalions, in respect of the other coins, were the same as modern medals in respect of modern money. *Addison.*

MEDA'LLIST. *n. s.* [*medailliste*, Fr.] A man skilled or curious in medals.

In the language of a *medallist*, you are not to look upon a cabinet of medals as a treasure of money, but of knowledge. *Addison on ancient Medals.*

To ME'DDLE. *v. n.* [*middelen*, Dutch.]
1. To have to do: in this sense it is always followed by *with.*

It is reported that cassia, when gathered, is put into the skins of beasts newly flayed, which breeding worms, they devour the pith and marrow, and so make it hollow; but *meddle* not *with* the back, because it is bitter. *Bacon.*

With the power of it upon the spirits of men we will only *meddle.* *Bacon's Nat. Hist.* N°. 945.

I have thus far been an upright judge, not *meddling with* the design nor disposition. *Dryden.*

2. To interpose; to act in any thing.

For my part, I'll not *meddle* nor make any farther. *Shak.*

In every turn of state, without *meddling* on either side, he has always been favourable to merit. *Dryden.*

The civil lawyers have pretended to determine concerning the succession of princes; but, by our author's principles, have *meddled* in a matter that belongs not to them. *Locke.*

What hast thou to do to *meddle* with the affairs of my family? to dispose of my estate, old boy? *Arbuthnot.*

3. To interpose or intervene importunely or officiously.

Why should'st thou *meddle* to thy hurt. 2 *Kings* xiv. 10.

It is an honour for a man to cease from strife: but every fool will be *meddling.* *Prov.* xx. 3.

This *meddling* priest longs to be found a fool. *Rowe.*

Let me shake off th' intrusive cares of day,
And lay the *meddling* senses all aside. *Thomson's Winter.*

To MEDDLE. *v. a.* [from *mesler*, Fr.] To mix; to mingle. Obsolete.

A *meddled* state of the orders of the gospel, and the ceremonies of popery, is not the best way to banish popery. *Hooker, b.* iv.

He that had well ycon'd his lere,
Thus *medled* his talk with many a teare. *Spenser.*

ME'DDLER. *n. s.* [from *meddle.*] One who busies himself with things in which he has no concern.

Do not drive away such as bring thee information, as *meddlers*, but accept of them in good part. *Bacon.*

This may be applied to those that assume to themselves the merits of other mens services, *meddlers*, boasters, and impertinents. *L'Estrange.*

ME'DDLESOME. *adj.* Intermeddling: as, a *meddlesome, busy body.* *Ains.*

MEDIA'STINE. n. s. [French; *mediastinum*, Latin.] The fimbriated body about which the guts are convolved.

None of the membranes which invest the inside of the breast but may be the seat of this disease, the *mediastine* as well as the pleura. *Arbuthnot on Diet.*

To ME'DIATE. *v. n.* [from *medius*, Latin.]
1. To interpose as an equal friend to both parties; to act indifferently between contending parties; to intercede.

The corruption of manners in the world, we shall find owing to some *mediating* schemes that offer to comprehend the different interests of sin and religion. *Rogers.*

2. To be between two.

By being crowded, they exclude all other bodies that before *mediated* between the parts of their body. *Digby.*

To MEDI'ATE. *v. a.*
1. To form by mediation.

The earl made many professions of his desire to interpose, and *mediate* a good peace between the nations. *Clarendon.*

I possess chemists and corpuscularians of advantages by the confederacy I am *mediating* between them. *Boyle.*

2. To limit by something in the middle.

They styled a double step, that is, the space from the elevation of one foot to the same foot set down again, *mediated* by a step of the other foot a pace equal to five feet. *Holder on Time.*

ME'DIATE. *adj.* [*mediat*, French; *medius*, Latin.]
1. Interposed; intervening.

Soon the *mediate* clouds shall be dispell'd;
The sun shall soon be face to face beheld. *Prior.*

2. Middle; between two extremes.

Anxious we hover in a *mediate* state,
Betwixt infinity and nothing. *Prior.*

2. Acting as a means. Unusual.

The most important care of a new and vigorous king, was his marriage for *mediate* establishment of the royal line. *Wotton's Life of Buckingham.*

ME'DIATELY. *adv.* [from *mediate.*] By a secondary cause; in such a manner that something acts between the first cause and the last effect.

God worketh all things amongst us *mediately* by secondary means; the which means of our safety being shipping and sea-forces, are to be esteemed as his gifts, and then only available and beneficial when he vouchsafeth his grace to use them aright. *Raleigh's Essays.*

Pestilent contagion is propagated immediately by conversing with infected persons, and *mediately* by pestilent seminaries propagated through the air. *Harvey on Consumptions.*

MEDIA'TION. *n. s.* [*mediation*, French, from *medius*, Lat.]
1. Interposition; intervention; agency between two parties, practised by a common friend.

Some nobler token I have kept apart
For Livia and Octavia, to induce
Their *mediation.* *Shakesp. Antony and Cleopatra.*

Noble offices thou may'st effect
Of *mediation*, after I am dead,
Between his greatness and thy other brethren. *Shakespeare.*

The king sought unto them to compose those troubles between him and his subjects; they accordingly interposed their *mediation* in a round and princely manner. *Bacon.*

2. Agency; an intervenient power.

The passions have their residence in the sensitive appetite: for inasmuch as man is a compound of flesh as well as spirit, the soul, during its abode in the body, does all things by the *mediation* of these passions. *South's Serm.*

It is utterly unconceivable, that inanimate brute matter, without the *mediation* of some immaterial being, should operate upon other matter without mutual contact. *Bentley.*

3. Intercession; entreaty for another.

MEDIA'TOR. *n. s.* [*mediateur*, French.]
1. One that intervenes between two parties.

You had found by experience the trouble of all mens confluence, and for all matters to yourself, as a *mediator* between them and their sovereign. *Bacon's Advice to Villiers.*

2. An intercessor; an entreater for another; one who uses his influence in favour of another.

It is against the sense of the law, to make saints or angels to be *mediators* between God and them. *Stillingfleet.*

3. One of the characters of our blessed Saviour.

Man's friend, his *mediator*, his design'd,
Both ransom and redeemer voluntary. *Milton.*

MEDIATO'RIAL. } *adj.* [from *mediator.*] Belonging to a mediator.
ME'DIATORY. }

All other effects of Christ's *mediatorial* office are accounted for from the truth of his resurrection. *Fiddes's Sermons.*

MEDIA'TORSHIP. *n. s.* [from *mediator.*] The office of a mediator.

MEDIA'TRIX. *n. s.* [*medius*, Lat.] A female mediator. *Ains.*

MEDIC. *n. s.* [*medica*, Latin.] A plant.

The *medic* hath a papilionaceous or buttterfly flower, out of which empalement rises the pointal, which afterward becomes an intorted pod, sometimes like a ram's horn, in which are lodged kidney-shaped seeds. *Miller.*

ME'DICAL. *adj.* [*medicus*, Lat.] Physical; relating to the art of healing; medicinal.

In this work attempts will exceed performances, it being composed by snatches of time, as *medical* vacation would permit. *Brown's Vulgar Errours.*

ME'DICALLY. *adv.* [from *medical.*] Physically; medicinally.

That which promoted this consideration, and *medically* advanced the same, was the doctrine of Hippocrates. *Browne.*

ME'DICAMENT. *n. s.* [*medicament*, Fr. *medicamentum*, Latin.] Any thing used in healing; generally topical applications.

Admonitions, fraternal or paternal, then more publick reprehensions; and, upon the unsuccessfulness of these milder *medicaments*, the use of that stronger physick, the censures. *Hammond's Fundamentals.*

A cruel wound was cured by scalding *medicaments*, after it was putrified; and the violent swelling and bruise of another was taken away by scalding it with milk. *Temple's Miscel.*

MEDICAME'NTAL. *adj.* [*medicamenteux*, Fr. from *medicament.*] Relating to medicine, internal or topical.

MEDICAME'NTALLY. *n. s.* [from *medicamental.*] After the manner of medicine; with the power of medicine.

The substance of gold is invincible by the powerfullest action of natural heat; and that not only alimentally in a substantial mutation, but also *medicamentally* in any corporeal conversion. *Brown's Vulgar Errours, b.* ii.

To ME'DICATE. *v. a.* [*medico*, Lat.] To tincture or impregnate with any thing medicinal.

The fumes, steams, and stenches of London, do so *medicate* and impregnate the air about it, that it becomes capable of little more. *Graunt's Bills of Mortality.*

To this may be ascribed the great effects of *medicated* waters. *Arbuthnot on Aliments.*

She secured the whiteness of my hand by *medicated* gloves. *Rambler.*

MEDICA'TION. *n. s.* [from *medicate.*]

1. The act of tincturing or impregnating with medicinal ingredients.

The watering of the plant with an infusion of the medicine may have more force than the rest, because the *medication* is oft renewed. *Bacon's Nat. Hist.*

2. The use of physick.

He adviseth to observe the times of the equinoxes and solstices, and to declare *medication* ten days before and after. *Brown's Vulgar Errours, b.* iv.

MEDI'CINABLE. *adj.* [*medicinalis*, Lat.] Having the power of physick.

Old oil is more clear and hot in *medicinable* use. *Bacon.*

Accept a bottle made of a serpentine stone, which gives any wine infused therein for four and twenty hours the taste and operation of the Spaw water, and is very *medicinable* for the cure of the spleen. *Wotton.*

The jaw-bones, hearts, and galls of pikes are *medicinable*. *Walton's Angler.*

MEDICI'NAL. *adj.* [*medicinalis*, Latin: this word is now commonly pronounced *medicinal*, with the accent on the second syllable; but more properly, and more agreeably to the best authorities, *medicinal.*]

1. Having the power of healing; having physical virtue.

Come with words as *medicinal* as true,
Honest as either; to purge him of that humour
That presses him from sleep. *Shakesp. Winter's Tale.*

Thoughts my tormentors arm'd with deadly stings,
Mangle my apprehensive tenderest parts;
Exasperate, exulcerate and raise
Dire inflammation, which no cooling herb
Nor *medicinal* liquor can asswage. *Milton's Agonistes.*

The second causes took the swift command,
The *medicinal* head, the ready hand;
All but eternal doom was conquer'd by their art. *Dryden.*

2. Belonging to physick.

Learn'd he was in *med'cinal* lore,
For by his side a pouch he wore,
Replete with strange hermetick powder,
That wounds nine miles point-blank with solder. *Butler.*

Such are called *medicinal-days* by some writers, wherein no crisis or change is expected, so as to forbid the use of medicines: but it is most properly used for those days wherein purging, or any other evacuation, is more conveniently complied with. *Quincy.*

Medicinal-hours are those wherein it is supposed that medicines may be taken, commonly reckoned in the morning fasting, about an hour before dinner, about four hours after dinner, and going to bed; but times are to be governed by the symptoms and aggravation of the distemper. *Quincy.*

MEDICI'NALLY. *adv.* [from *medicinal.*] Physically.

The witnesses that leech-like liv'd on blood,
Sucking for them were *med'cinally* good. *Dryden.*

ME'DICINE. *n. s.* [*medicine*, Fr. *medicina*, Latin. It is generally pronounced as if only of two syllables, *med'cine.*] Physick; any remedy administered by a physician.

O, my dear father! restauration, hang
Thy *medicine* on my lips; and let this kiss
Repair those violent harms. *Shakesp. King Lear.*

Let's make us *medicines* of our great revenge,
To cure this deadly grief. *Shakespeare's Macbeth.*

A merry heart doth good like a *medicine*; but a broken spirit drieth the bones. *Prov.* xvii. 22.

I wish to die, yet dare not death endure;
Detest the *med'cine*, yet desire the cure. *Dryden.*

To ME'DICINE. *v. a.* [from the noun.] To operate as physick. Not used.

Not all the drowsy syrups of the world,
Shall ever *medicine* thee to that sweet sleep
Which thou owedst yesterday. *Shakespeare.*

MEDI'ETY. *n. s.* [*medieté*, Fr. *medietas*, Lat.] Middle state; participation of two extremes; half.

They contained no fishy composure, but were made up of man and bird; the human *mediety* variously placed not only above but below. *Brown's Vulgar Errours.*

MEDIO'CRITY. *n. s.* [*mediocrité*, French; *mediocritas*, Lat.]

1. Small degree; middle rate; middle state.

Men of age seldom drive business home to the full period, but content themselves with a *mediocrity* of success. *Bacon.*

There appeared a sudden and marvellous conversion in the duke's case, from the most exalted to the most depressed, as if his expedition had been capable of no *mediocrities*. *Wotton.*

He likens the *mediocrity* of wit to one of a mean fortune, who manages his store with great parsimony; but who, with fear of running into profuseness, never arrives to the magnificence of living. *Dryden's State of Innocence.*

Getting and improving our knowledge in substances only by experience and history, is all that the weakness of our faculties in this state of *mediocrity*, while we are in this world, can attain to. *Locke.*

2. Moderation; temperance. Obsolete.

Lest appetite, in the use of food, should lead us beyond that which is meet, we owe, in this case, obedience to that law of reason which teacheth *mediocrity* in meats and drinks. *Hooker, b.* i.

When they urge us to extreme opposition against the church of Rome, do they mean we should be drawn unto it only for a time, and afterwards return to a *mediocrity*. *Hooker.*

To ME'DITATE. *v. a.* [*mediter*, French; *meditor*, Lat.] To plan; to scheme; to contrive.

Blessed is the man that doth *meditate* good things in wisdom, and that reasoneth of holy things by his understanding. *Ecclus.* xiv. 20.

Some affirmed that I *meditated* a war; God knows, I did not then think of war. *King Charles.*

Like a lion that unheeded lay,
Dissembling sleep, and watchful to betray,
With inward rage he *meditates* his prey. *Dryden.*

Before the memory of the flood was lost, men *meditated* the setting up a false religion at Babel. *Forbes.*

2. To think on; to revolve in the mind.

Them among
There set a man of ripe and perfect age,
Who did them *meditate* all his life long. *Fairy Queen.*

To ME'DITATE. *v. n.* To think; to muse; to contemplate; to dwell on with intense thought. It is commonly used of pious contemplation.

His delight is in the law of the Lord, and in his law doth he *meditate* night and day. *Psal.* i. 2.

I will *meditate* also of all thy work, and talk of all thy doings. *Psal.* lxxvii. 12.

Meditate till you make some act of piety upon the occasion of what you *meditate*; either get some new arguments against a sin, or some new encouragements to virtue. *Taylor.*

To worship God, to study his will, to *meditate* upon him, and to love him; all these being great pleasure and peace. *Tillotson's Sermons.*

MEDITA'TION. *n. s.* [*meditation*, Fr. *meditatio*, Latin.]

1. Deep thought; close attention; contrivance; contemplation.

I left the *meditations* wherein I was, and spake to her in anger. 2 *Esd.* x. 5.

Some thought and *meditation* are necessary; and a man may possibly be so stupid as not to have God in all his thoughts, or to say in his heart, there is none. *Bentley.*

2. Thought employed upon sacred objects.

His name was heavenly contemplation;
Of God and goodness was his *meditation*. *Fairy Qu. b.* i.

'Tis most true,
That musing *meditation* most affects
The pensive secresy of desert cell. *Milton.*

Thy thoughts to nobler *meditations* give,
And study how to die, not how to live. *Granville.*

3. A series of thoughts, occasioned by any object or occurrence.

ME'DITATIVE. *adj.* [from *meditate.*]

1. Addicted to meditation. *Ainf.*

2. Expressing intention or design.

MEDITERRA'NE.
MEDITERRA'NEAN. } *adj.* [*medius* and *terra*; *mediterranée*, Fr.]
MEDITERRA'NEOUS.

1. Encircled with land.

In all that part that lieth on the north side of the *mediterrane* sea, it is thought not to be the vulgar tongue. *Brerewood.*

2. Inland; remote from the sea.

It is found in mountains and *mediterraneous* parts; and so it is a fat and unctuous sublimation of the earth. *Brown.*

We have taken a less height of the mountains than is requisite, if we respect the *mediterraneous* mountains, or those that are at a great distance from the sea. *Burnet.*

ME'DIUM. *n. s.* [*medium*, Latin.]

1. Any thing intervening.

Whether any other liquors, being made *mediums*, cause a diversity of sound from water, it may be tried. *Bacon.*

I must bring together
All these extremes; and must remove all *mediums*,
That each may be the other's object. *Denham.*

Seeing requires light and a free *medium*, and a right line to the objects; we can hear in the dark, immured, and by curve lines. *Holder.*

He, who looks upon the soul through its outward actions, often sees it through a deceitful *medium*, which is apt to discolour the object. *Addison's Spect.* N°. 257.

The parts of bodies on which their colours depend, are denser than the *medium* which pervades their interstices. *Newt.*

Against filling the heavens with fluid *mediums*, unless they be exceeding rare, a great objection arises from the regular and very lasting motions of the planets and comets in all manner of courses through the heavens. *Newton's Opticks.*

2. Any thing used in ratiocination, in order to a conclusion; the middle term in an argument, by which propositions are connected.

This cannot be answered by those *mediums* which have been used. *Dryden's Juvenal.*

We, whose understandings are short, are forced to collect one thing from another, and in that process we seek out proper *mediums*. *Baker's Reflections on Learning.*

3. The middle place or degree; the just temperature between extremes.

The just *medium* of this case lies betwixt the pride and the abjection, the two extremes. *L'Estrange.*

ME'DLAR. *n. s.* [*mespilus*, Latin.]

1. A tree.

The leaves of the *medlar* are either whole, and shaped like those of the laurel, as in the manured sorts; or laciniated, as in the wild sorts: the flower consists of five leaves, which expand in form of a rose: the fruits are umbilicated, and are not eatable till they decay; and have, for the most part, five hard seeds in each. *Miller.*

2. The fruit of that tree.

You'll be rotten ere you be half ripe,
And that's the right virtue of the *medlar*. *Shakespeare.*

Now will he sit under a *medlar* tree,
And wish his mistress were that kind of fruit,
Which maids call *medlars*. *Shakesp. Romeo and Juliet.*

I was fain to forswear it; they would else have married me to the rotten *medlar*. *Shakespeare.*

October is drawn in a garment of yellow and carnation; with a basket of services, *medlars*, and chesnuts. *Peacham.*

No rotten *medlars*, whilst there be
Whole orchards in virginity. *Cleaveland.*

Men have gather'd from the hawthorn's branch
Large *medlars*, imitating regal crowns. *Philips.*

To MEDLE. } *v. a.* To mingle. *Spenser.*
To MEDLY.

ME'DLY. *n. s.* [from *meddle* for *mingle*.] A mixture; a miscellany; a mingled mass. It is commonly used with some degree of contempt.

Some imagined that the powder in the armory had taken fire; others, that troops of horsemen approached: in which *medly* of conceits they bare down one upon another, and jostled many into the tower ditch. *Hayward.*

Love is a *medley* of endearments, jars,
Suspicions, quarrels, reconcilements, wars;
Then peace again. *Walsh.*

They count their toilsome marches, long fatigues,
Unusual fastings, and will bear no more
This *medley* of philosophy and war. *Addison's Cato.*

Mahomet began to knock down his fellow citizens, and to fill all Arabia with an unnatural *medley* of religion and bloodshed. *Freeholder*, N°. 50.

There are that a compounded fluid drain
From different mixtures: the blended streams,
Each mutually correcting each, create
A pleasurable *medley*. *Philips.*

ME'DLEY. *adj.* Mingled; confused.

I'm strangely discompos'd;
Qualms at my heart, convulsions in my nerves,
Within my little world make *medley* war. *Dryden.*

MEDU'LLAR. } *adj.* [*medullaire*, Fr. from *medulla*, Latin.]
MEDU'LLARY. } Pertaining to the marrow.

These little emissaries, united together at the cortical part of the brain, make the *medullar* part, being a bundle of very small, thread-like chanels or fibres. *Cheyne's Phil. Principles.*

The back, for the security of that *medullary* substance that runs down its cavity, is bent after the manner of the catenarian curve. *Cheyne's Phil. Principles.*

MEED. *n. s.* [meb, Saxon; *miete*, Teutonick.] Reward; recompence. Now rarely used.

He knows his *meed*, if he be spide,
To be a thousand deaths, and shame beside. *Hubberd.*

Whether in beauties glory did exceed,
A rosy garland was the victor's *meede*. *Fairy Queen.*

Thanks to men
Of noble minds is honourable *meed*. *Shakespeare.*

He must not float upon his wat'ry bier
Unwept, and welter to the parching wind,
Without the *meed* of some melodious tear. *Milton.*

If so a cloak and vesture be my *meed*
Till his return, no title shall I plead. *Pope's Odyssey.*

2. Present; gift.

Plutus, the god of gold,
Is but his steward: no *meed* but he repays
Seven-fold above itself. *Shakesp. Timon of Athens.*

MEEK. *adj.* [*minkr*, Islandick.] Mild of temper; not proud; not rough; not easily provoked; soft; gentle.

Moses was very *meek* above all men. *Numb.* xii. 3.

But he her fears to cease,
Sent down the *meek*-ey'd peace. *Milton.*

We ought to be very cautious and *meek*-spirited, till we are assured of the honesty of our ancestors. *Collier.*

To ME'EKEN. *v. a.* [from *meek.*] To make meek; to soften. This word I have found no where else.

The glaring lion saw, his horrid heart
Was *meeken'd*, and he join'd his sullen joy. *Thomson.*

ME'EKLY. *adv.* [from *meek.*] Mildly; gently; not ruggedly; not proudly.

Be therefore, O my dear lords, pacify'd,
And this mis-seeming discord *meekly* lay aside. *Fairy Qu.*

No pride does with your rising honours grow,
You *meekly* look on suppliant crowds below. *Stepney.*

ME'EKNESS. *n. s.* [from *meek.*] Gentleness; mildness; softness of temper.

That pride and *meekness* mixt by equal part,
Do both appear t' adorn her beauty's grace. *Hubberd.*

You sign your place and calling, in full seeming,
With *meekness* and humility; but your heart
Is cramm'd with arrogancy, spleen and pride. *Shakesp.*

When his late distemper attack'd him, he submitted to it with great *meekness* and resignation, as became a Christian. *Atterbury's Sermons.*

MEER. *adj.* See MERE. Simple; unmixed.

MEER. *n. s.* [See MERE.] A lake; a boundary.

ME'ERED. *adj.* Relating to a boundary; *meer* being a boundary, or mark of division. *Hanmer.*

What, although you fled! why should he follow you?
The itch of his affection should not then
Have nickt his captainship; at such a point,
When half to half the world oppos'd, he being
The *meered* question. *Shakesp. Ant. and Cleopatra.*

MEET. *adj.* [of obscure etymology.] Fit; proper; qualified. Now rarely used.

Ah! my dear love, why do you sleep thus long,
When *meeter* were that you should now awake? *Spenser.*

If the election of the minister should be committed to every parish, would they chuse the *meetest*. *Whitgift.*

I am a tainted wether of the flock,
Meetest for death. *Shakesp. Merchant of Venice.*

To be known shortens my laid intent,
My boon I make it, that you know me not,
Till time and I think *meet*. *Shakesp. King Lear.*

What, at any time have you heard her say?
—That, Sir, which I will not report after her.
—You may to me, and 'tis most *meet* you should. *Shak.*

York is *meetest* man
To be your regent in the realm of France. *Shakespeare.*

I am in your hand; do with me as seemeth good and *meet* unto you. *Jer.* xxvi. 14.

The eye is very proper and *meet* for seeing. *Bentley.*

2. MEET *with*. Even with. [from *meet*, the verb.] A low expression.

Niece, you tax Signior Benedick too much; but he'll be *meet with* you. *Shakespeare.*

To MEET. *v. a.* pret. *I met*; *I have met*; particip. *met*. [metan, Saxon, to find; *moeten*, Dutch.]

1. To come face to face; to encounter.

Met'st thou my posts? *Shakespeare.*

His daughter came out to *meet* him with timbrels and dances. *Judges* xi. 34.

Ahimelech was afraid at the *meeting* of David. 1 *Sam.* xxi.

2. To join another in the same place.

When shall we three *meet* again,
In thunder, light'ning, or in rain? *Shakesp. Macbeth.*

Well, send him word to *meet* us in the field. *Shakesp.*

16 H I knew

3

I knew not, till I *met*
My friends, at Ceres' now deserted seat. *Dryden.*
Not look back to see,
When what we love we never must *meet* again. *Dryden.*

3. To close one with another.
The nearer you come to the end of the lake, the mountains on each side grow higher, till at last they *meet*. *Addison.*

4. To find; to be treated with; to light on.
Had I a hundred mouths, a hundred tongues,
I could not half those horrid crimes repeat,
Nor half the punishments those crimes have *met*. *Dryden.*
Of vice or virtue, whether blest or curst,
Which *meets* contempt, or which compassion first. *Pope.*
To me no greater joy,
Than that your labours *meet* a prosp'rous end. *Granville.*

5. To assemble from different parts.
Their choice nobility and flower
Met from all parts to solemnize this feast. *Milton.*

To MEET. *v. n.*
1. To encounter; to close face to face.
2. To encounter in hostility.
3. To assemble; to come together.
They appointed a day to *meet* in together. 2 *Mac.* xiv. 21.
The materials of that building happily *met* together, and very fortunately ranged themselves into that delicate order, that it must be a very great chance that parts them. *Tillotson.*
4. *To* MEET *with*. To light on; to find.
When he cometh to experience of service abroad, he maketh as worthy a soldier as any nation he *meeteth with*. *Spenser.*
We *met with* many things worthy of observation. *Bacon.*
A little sum you mourn, while most have *met*
With twice the loss, and by as vile a cheat. *Creech.*
Hercules' *meeting with* pleasure and virtue, was invented by Prodicus, who lived before Socrates. *Addison.*
What a majesty and force does one *meet with* in these short inscriptions: are not you amazed to see so much history gathered into so small a compass? *Addison on ancient Medals.*
5. *To* MEET *with*. To join.
Falstaff at that oak shall *meet with* us. *Shakespeare.*
6. *To* MEET *with*. To encounter; to engage.
He, that hath suffered this disordered spring,
Hath now himself *met with* the fall of leaf. *Shakespeare.*
Royal mistress,
Prepare to *meet with* more than brutal fury
From the fierce prince. *Rowe's Ambitious Step-mother.*
7. A latinism. To obviate; *occurrere objecto.*
Before I proceed farther, it is good to *meet with* an objection, which if not removed, the conclusion of experience from the time past to the present will not be sound. *Bacon.*
8. To advance half way.
He yields himself to the man of business with reluctancy, but offers himself to the visits of a friend with facility, and all the *meeting* readiness of desire. *South.*
Our *meeting* hearts
Consented soon, and marriage made us one. *Rowe.*
9. To unite; to join: as, these rivers *meet* at such a place and join.

ME'ETERS. *n. s.* [from *meet.*] One that accosts another.
There are beside
Lascivious *meeters*, to whose venom'd sound
The open ear of youth doth always listen. *Shakespeare.*

ME'ETING. *n. s.* [from *meet.*]
1. An assembly; a convention.
If the fathers and husbands of those, whose relief this your *meeting* intends, were of the houshold of faith, then their relicts and children ought not to be strangers to the good that is done in it, if they want it. *Sprat's Sermons.*
Since the ladies have been left out of all *meetings* except parties at play, our conversation hath degenerated. *Swift.*
2. A congress.
Let's be revenged on him; let's appoint him a *meeting*, and lead him on with a fine baited delay. *Shakespeare.*
3. A conventicle; an assembly of Dissenters.
4. A conflux: as, the meeting of two rivers.

MEETING-HOUSE. *n. s.* [*meeting* and *house.*] Place where Dissenters assemble to worship.
His heart misgave him that the churches were so many *meeting-houses*; but I soon made him easy. *Addison.*

ME'ETLY. [from the adjective.] Fitly; properly.

ME'ETNESS. *n. s.* [from *meet.*] Fitness; propriety.

ME'GRIM. *n. s.* [from *Hemicrany, migrain, megrim*, ἡμικρανία.] Disorder of the head.
In every *megrim* or vertigo there is an obtenebration joined with a semblance of turning round. *Bacon's Nat. Hist.*
There screen'd in shades from day's detested glare,
Spleen sighs for ever on her pensive bed,
Pain at her side, and *megrim* at her head. *Pope.*

To MEINE. *v. a.* To mingle. *Ains.*

ME'INY. *n. s.* [menȝu, Saxon. See MANY. *Mesnie*, Fr.] A retinue; domestick servants.
They summon'd up their *meiny*; strait took horse;
Commanded me to follow, and attend. *Shakespeare.*

MELANAGO'GUES. *n. s.* [from μέλανος and ἄγω.] Such medicines as are supposed particularly to purge off black choler.

MELANCHO'LICK. *adj.* [from *melancholy.*] Disordered with melancholy; fanciful; hypochondriacal; gloomy.
The king found himself in the head of his army, after so many accidents and *melancholick* perplexities. *Clarendon.*
If he be mad, or angry, or *melancholick*, or sprightly, he will paint whatsoever is proportionable to any one. *Dryden.*
The commentators on old Ari-
Stotle, 'tis urg'd, in judgment vary:
They to their own conceits have brought
The image of his general thought:
Just as the *melancholick* eye
Sees fleets and armies in the sky. *Prior.*

MELANCHO'LY. *n. s.* [*melancolie*, Fr. from μέλας and χολή.]
1. A disease, supposed to proceed from a redundance of black bile; but it is better known to arise from too heavy and too viscid blood: its cure is in evacuation, nervous medicines, and powerful stimuli. *Quincy.*
2. A kindness of madness, in which the mind is always fixed on one object.
I have neither the scholar's *melancholy*, which is emulation; nor the musician's, which is fantastical; nor the courtier's, which is proud; nor the soldier's, which is ambitious; nor the lawyer's, which is politick; nor the lady's, which is nice; nor the lover's, which is all these; but it is a *melancholy* of mine own, compounded of many simples, extracted from many objects, and, indeed, the sundry contemplation of my travels, in which my often rumination wraps me in a most humorous sadness. *Shakesp. As you like it.*
3. A gloomy, pensive, discontented temper.
He protested unto them, that he had only been to seek solitary places by an extreme *melancholy* that had possessed him. *Sidney, b.* ii.
All these gifts come from him; and if we murmur here, we may at the next *melancholy* be troubled that God did not make us angels. *Taylor's holy Living.*
This *melancholy* flatters, but unmans you;
What is it else but penury of soul,
A lazy frost, a numbness of the mind? *Dryden.*

MELANCHO'LY. *adj.* [*melancolique*, French.]
1. Gloomy; dismal.
Think of all our miseries
But as some *melancholy* dream, which has awak'd us
To the renewing of our joys. *Denham's Sophy.*
If in the *melancholy* shades below,
The flames of friends and lovers cease to glow;
Yet mine shall sacred last, mine undecay'd,
Burn on through death, and animate my shade. *Pope.*
2. Diseased with melancholy; fanciful; habitually dejected.
How now, sweet Frank; art thou *melancholy*. *Shakesp.*
He observes Lamech more *melancholy* than usual, and imagines it to be from a suspicion he has of his wife Adah, whom he loved. *Locke.*

MELICE'RIS. *n. s.* [μελικηρὶς.]
Meliceris is a tumour inclosed in a cystis, and consisting of matter like honey: it gathers without pain, and gives way to pressure, but returns again. If the matter forming it resembles milk curds, the tumour is called atheroma; if like honey, *meliceris*; and if composed of fat, or a suety substance, steatomata. *Sharp's Surgery.*

ME'LILOT. *n. s.* [*melilot*, Fr. *melilotus*, Latin.] A plant.
The *melilot* hath a papilionaceous flower, out of whose empalement arises the pointal, which afterward becomes a naked capsule, that is, not hid in the empalement, as in trefoil, pregnant with one or two roundish seeds: the leaves grow by threes on the foot-stalks, and the flowers are produced in a spike. *Miller.*

To MELI'ORATE. *v. a.* [*meliorer*, Fr. from *melior.*] To better; to improve.
Grafting *meliorates* the fruit; for that the nourishment is better prepared in the stock than in the crude earth. *Bacon.*
But when we graft, or buds inoculate,
Nature by art we nobly *meliorate*. *Denham.*
A man ought by no means to think, that he should be able so much as to alter or *meliorate* the humour of an ungrateful person by any acts of kindness. *South's Sermons.*
Castration serves to *meliorate* the flesh of those beasts that suffer it. *Graunt.*
Much labour is requir'd in trees.
Well must the ground be digg'd, and better dress'd,
New soil to make, and *meliorate* the rest. *Dryden's Virg.*

MELIORA'TION. *n. s.* [*melioration*, Fr. from *meliorate.*] Improvement; act of bettering.
For the *melioration* of musick there is yet much left, in this point of exquisite consorts, to try. *Bacon.*

MELIO'RITY. *n. s.* [from *melior.*] State of being better.
Men incline unto them which are softest, and least in their way, in despight of them that hold them hardest to it; so that this colour of *meliority* and pre-eminence is a sign of weakness. *Bacon's Collection of Good and Evil.*

The

The order and beauty of the inanimate parts of the world, the discernable ends of them, the *meliority* above what was necessary to be, do evince, by a reflex argument, that it is the workmanship not of blind mechanism, but of an intelligent and benign agent. *Bentley.*

To MELL. *v. n.* [*meler, se meler*, Fr.] To mix; to meddle. Obsolete.

With fathers fits not with such things to *mell*. *Spenser.*
Here is a great deal of good matter
Lost for lack of telling.
Now I see thou dost but clatter,
Harm may come of *melling*. *Spenser's Pastorals.*

MELLI'FEROUS. *adj.* Productive of honey. *Dict.*

MELLIFICA'TION. *n. s.* [*mellifico*, Latin.] The art or practice of making honey; production of honey.

In judging of the constitution of the air, many things besides the weather ought to be observed: in some countries, the silence of grashoppers, and want of *mellification* in bees. *Arbuthnot on Air.*

MELLI'FLUENCE. *n. s.* [*mel* and *fluo*, Latin.] A honied flow; a flow of sweetness.

MELLI'FLUENT. } *adj.* [*mel* and *fluo*, Latin.] Flowing with
MELLI'FLUOUS. } honey; flowing with sweetness.

A *mellifluous* voice, as I am a true knight. *Shakespeare.*

As all those things which are most *mellifluous* are soonest changed into choler and bitterness, so are our vanities and pleasures converted into the bitterest sorrows and repentances. *Raleigh's Hist. of the World.*

Innumerous songsters, in the freshening shade
Of new-sprung leaves, their modulations mix
Mellifluous. *Thomson's Spring, l.* 605.

ME'LLOW. *adj.* [meaрpa, soft, Saxon, *Skinner*: more nearly from *mollis, molle, mollow, mellow*; though *r* is indeed easily changed into *l* in common speech.]

1. Soft with ripeness; full ripe.

A storm, or robbery, call it what you will,
Shook down my *mellow* hangings, nay, my leaves. *Shak.*

An apple in my hand works different effects upon my senses: my eye tells me it is green; my nose, that it hath a *mellow* scent; and my taste, that it is sweet. *Digby.*

A little longer,
And nature drops him down without your sin,
Like *mellow* fruit, without a winter storm. *Dryden.*

2. Soft in sound.

Of seven smooth joints a *mellow* pipe I have,
Which with his dying breath Damætas gave. *Dryden.*

3. Soft; unctuous.

Camomile sheweth *mellow* grounds fit for wheat. *Bacon.*

4. Drunk; melted down with drink.

Greedy of physicians frequent fees,
From female *mellow* praise he takes degrees. *Roscommon.*
In all thy humours, whether grave or *mellow*,
Thou'rt such a testy, touchy, pleasant fellow;
Hast so much wit, and mirth, and spleen about thee,
There is no living with thee, nor without thee. *Addison.*

To ME'LLOW. *v. a.* [from the noun.]

1. To ripen; to mature; to soften by ripeness; to ripen by age.

Lord Aubrey Vere
Was done to death, and more than so, my father;
Even in the downfal of his *mellow'd* years. *Shakespeare.*
The royal tree hath left us royal fruit,
Which *mellow'd* by the stealing hours of time,
Will well become the seat of majesty. *Shakesp. Rich.* III.
On foreign mountains may the sun refine
The grape's soft juice, and *mellow* it to wine. *Addison.*

2. To soften.

They plow in the wheat stubble in December; and if the weather prove frosty to *mellow* it, they do not plow it again till April. *Mortimer's Husb.*

3. To mature to perfection.

This episode is not only now the most pleasing entertainment of the Æneis, but was so accounted in his own age, and before it was *mellowed* into that reputation which time has given it. *Dryden.*

To ME'LLOW. *v. n.* To be matured; to ripen.

Though no stone tell thee what I was, yet thou
In my grave's inside see'st, what thou art now;
Yet thou'rt not yet so good, till us death lay
To ripe and *mellow* there, we're stubborn clay. *Donne.*

ME'LLOWNESS. *n. s.* [from *mellow.*]

1. Maturity of fruits; ripeness; softness by maturity.

My reason can consider greenness, *mellowness*, sweetness, or coldness, singly, and without relation to any other quality that is painted in me by the same apple. *Digby of Bodies.*

The Spring, like youth, fresh blossoms doth produce,
But Autumn makes them ripe, and fit for use:
So age a mature *mellowness* doth set
On the green promises of youthful heat. *Denham.*

2. Maturity; full age.

MELOCO'TON. *n. s.* [*melocotone*, Spanish; *malum cotoneum*, Latin.] A quince. Obsolete.

In apricots, peaches, or *melocotones* upon a wall, the greatest fruits are towards the bottom. *Bacon.*

MELO'DIOUS. *adj.* [from *melody.*] Musical; harmonious.

Fountains! and ye that warble, as ye flow,
Melodious murmurs! warbling tune his praise. *Milton.*
And oft with holy hymns he charm'd their ears;
A musick more *melodious* than the spheres. *Dryden.*

MELO'DIOUSLY. *adv.* [from *melodious.*] Musically; harmoniously.

MELO'DIOUSNESS. *n. s.* [from *melodious.*] Harmoniousness; musicalness.

ME'LODY. *n. s.* [μελωδία.] Musick; harmony of sound.

The prophet David having singular knowledge not in poetry alone but in musick also, judged them both to be things most necessary for the house of God, left behind him for that purpose a number of divinely indited poems, and was farther the author of adding unto poetry *melody* in publick prayer, *melody* both vocal and instrumental, for the raising up of mens hearts, and the sweetening of their affections towards God. *Hooker, b.* v.

Singing and making *melody* in your hearts to the Lord. *Eph.* v. 19.

Why rather, sleep, liest thou in smoky cribs,
And husht with buzzing night flies to thy slumber;
Than in the perfum'd chambers of the great,
And lull'd with sounds of sweetest *melody*. *Shakespeare.*
Lend me your songs, ye nightingales: Oh pour
The mazy-running soul of *melody*
Into my varied verse. *Thomson's Spring, l.* 570.

ME'LON. *n. s.* [*melon*, Fr. *melo*, Latin.]

1. A plant.

The flower of the *melon* consists of one leaf, which is of the expanded bell shape, cut into several segments, and exactly like those of the cucumber: some of these flowers are barren, not adhering to the embrio; others are fruitful, growing upon the embrio, which is afterwards changed into a fruit, for the most part of an oval shape, smooth or wrinkled, and divided into three seminal apartments, which seem to be cut into two parts, and contain many oblong seeds. *Miller.*

2. The fruit.

We remember the fish which we did eat in Egypt freely; the cucumbers and the *melons*. *Num.* xi. 5.

MELON-THI'STLE. *n. s.* [*melocactus*, Latin.]

The whole plant of the *melon-thistle* hath a singular appearance, is very succulent, and hath many angles, which are beset with sharp thorns. *Miller.*

To MELT. *v. a.* [mylтan, Saxon.]

1. To dissolve; to make liquid; commonly by heat.

How they would *melt* me out of my fat drop by drop, and liquor fishermens boots with me! *Shakespeare.*

When the *melting* fire burneth, the fire causeth the waters to boil. *Isa.* lxiv. 2.

This price, which is given above the value of the silver in our coin, is given only to preserve our coin from being *melted* down. *Locke.*

Will a goldsmith give one ounce and a quarter of coined silver for one ounce of bullion, when, by putting it into his *melting* pot, he can make it bullion? *Locke.*

The rock's high summit in the temple's shade,
Nor heat could *melt*, nor beating storm invade. *Pope.*

If your butter when *melted* tastes of brass, it is your master's fault, who will not allow you a silver saucepan. *Swift.*

2. To dissolve; to break in pieces.

To take in pieces this frame of nature, and *melt* it down into its first principles; and then to observe how the divine wisdom wrought all these things into that beautiful composition; is a kind of joy, which pierceth the mind. *Burnet.*

3. To soften to love or tenderness.

The mighty master smil'd to see
That love was in the next degree:
'Twas but a kindred sound to move,
For pity *melts* the mind to love. *Dryd. Alexander's Feast.*
Alas! thy story *melts* away my soul. *Addison's Cato.*

4. To waste away.

Thou would'st have plung'd thyself
In general riot, *melted* down thy youth
In different beds of lust. *Shakesp. Timon of Athens.*

To MELT. *v. n.*

1. To become liquid; to dissolve; to be made fluid.

Let them *melt* away as waters which run continually. *Psal.*

The rose is fragrant, but it fades in time;
The violet sweet, but quickly past the prime;
While lilies hang their heads and soon decay,
And whiter snow in minutes *melts* away. *Dryden.*

2. To be softened to pity, or any gentle passion; to grow tender, mild, or gentle.

I *melt*, and am not
Of stronger earth than others. *Shakespeare's Coriolanus.*
Dighton and Forrest;
Albeit, they were flesht villains, bloody dogs,
Melting with tenderness and mild compassion,
Wept like two children in their death's sad story. *Shakesp.*
This said; the mov'd assistants *melt* in tears. *Dryden.*

Melting

Melting into tears, the pious man
Deplor'd so sad a sight. *Dryden.*

3. To be dissolved; to lose substance.

Whether are they vanish'd?
Into the air: and what seem'd corporal
Melted as breath into the wind. *Shakespeare's Macbeth.*

Beauty is a witch,
Against whose charms faith *melteth* into blood. *Shakesp.*

4. To be subdued by affliction.

My soul *melteth* for heaviness: strengthen thou me. *Psal.*

ME'LTER. *n. s.* [from *melt.*] One that melts metals.

Miso and Mopsa, like a couple of foreswat *melters*, were getting the pure silver of their bodies out of the ore of their garments. *Sidney, b.* ii.

This the author attributes to the remissness of the former *melters*, in not exhausting the ore. *Derham's Physico-Theol.*

ME'LTINGLY. *adv.* [from *melting.*] Like something melting.

Zelmane lay upon a bank, with her face so bent over Ladon, that her tears falling into the water, one might have thought she began *meltingly* to be metamorphosed to the running river. *Sidney, b.* ii.

ME'LWEL. *n. s.* A kind of fish. *Ains.*

ME'MBER. *n. s.* [*membre*, French; *membrum*, Latin.]

1. A limb; a part appendant to the body.

The tongue is a little *member*, and boasteth great things. *Jam.* iii. 5.

2. A part of a discourse or period; a head; a clause.

Where the respondent limits or distinguishes any proposition, the opponent must prove his own proposition according to that *member* of the distinction in which the respondent denied it. *Watts's Improvement of the Mind.*

3. Any part of an integral.

In poetry as in architecture, not only the whole but the principal *members*, and every part of them, should be great. *Addison's Spect.* N°. 267.

4. One of a community.

My going to demand justice upon the five *members*, my enemies loaded with obloquies. *King Charles.*

Mean as I am, yet have the Muses made
Me free, a *member* of the tuneful trade. *Dryden.*

Sienna is adorned with many towers of brick, which, in the time of the commonwealth, were erected to such of the *members* as had done any considerable service to their country. *Addison on Italy.*

ME'MBRANE. *n. s.* [*membrane*, Fr. *membrana*, Latin.]

A *membrane* is a web of several sorts of fibres, interwoven together for the covering and wrapping up some parts: the fibres of the *membranes* give them an elasticity, whereby they can contract, and closely grasp, the parts they contain, and their nervous fibres give them an exquisite sense, which is the cause of their contraction; they can, therefore, scarcely suffer the sharpness of medicines, and are difficultly united when wounded. *Quincy.*

The chorion, a thick *membrane* obscuring the formation, the dam doth after tear asunder. *Brown's Vulgar Errours.*

They obstacle find none
Of *membrane*, joint, or limb, exclusive bars:
Easier than air with air, if spirits embrace,
Total they mix. *Milton.*

The inner *membrane* that involved the several liquors of the egg remained unbroken. *Boyle.*

MEMBRANA'CEOUS. }
MEMBRA'NEOUS. } *adj.* [*membraneux*, Fr. from *membrana*, Lat.] Consisting of membranes.
ME'MBRANOUS. }

Lute-strings, which are made of the *membraneous* parts of the guts strongly wreathed, swell so much as to break in wet weather. *Boyle.*

Great conceits are raised of the involution or *membranous* covering called the silly-how. *Brown's Vulgar Errours.*

Such birds as are carnivorous have no gizzard, or musculous, but a *membranous* stomach; that kind of food being torn into small flakes by the beak, may be easily concocted by a *membraneous* stomach. *Ray on Creation.*

Anodyne substances, which take off contractions of the *membranous* parts, are diuretick. *Arbuthnot on Aliments.*

Birds of prey have *membranaceous*, not muscular stomachs. *Arbuthnot on Aliments.*

MEME'NTO. n. s. [Latin.] A memorial notice; a hint to awaken the memory.

Our gracious master, for his learning and piety, is not only a precedent to his own subjects, but to foreign princes; yet he is still but a man, and seasonable *memento* may be useful. *Bacon's Advice to Villiers.*

Is not the frequent spectacle of other peoples deaths a *memento* sufficient to make you think of your own? *L'Estrange.*

MEMO'IR. *n. s.* [*memoire*, French.]

1. An account of transactions familiarly written.

Be our great master's future charge
To write his own *memoirs*, and leave his heirs
High schemes of government and plans of wars. *Prior.*

2. Hint; notice; account of any thing.

There is not in any author a computation of the revenues of the Roman empire, and hardly any *memoirs* from whence it might be collected. *Arbuthnot on Coins.*

ME'MORABLE. *adj.* [*memorable*, Fr. *memorabilis*, Lat.] Worthy of memory; not to be forgotten.

Nothing I so much delight to recount, as the *memorable* friendship that grew betwixt the two princes. *Sidney.*

From this desire, that main desire proceeds,
Which all men have surviving fame to gain,
By tombs, by books, by *memorable* deeds,
For she that this desires doth still remain. *Davies.*

Dares Ulysses for the prize contend,
In sight of what he durst not once defend;
But basely fled that *memorable* day,
When I from Hector's hands redeem'd the flaming prey. *Dryden's Ovid.*

ME'MORABLY. *adv.* [from *memorable.*] In a manner worthy of memory.

MEMORANDUM. n. s. [Latin.] A note to help the memory.

I resolved to new pave every street within the liberties, and entered a *memorandum* in my pocket-book accordingly. *Guardian*, N°. 166.

Nature's fair table-book, our tender souls,
We scrawl all o'er with old and empty rules,
Stale *memorandums* of the schools. *Swift's Miscel.*

MEMO'RIAL. *adj.* [*memorial*, Fr. *memorialis*, Latin.]

1. Preservative of memory.

Thy master now lies thinking in his bed
Of thee and me, and sighs, and takes my glove,
And gives *memorial* dainty kisses to it. *Shakespeare.*

May I, at the conclusion of a work, which is a kind of monument of Pope's partiality to me, place the following lines as an inscription *memorial* of it. *Broome.*

The tomb with manly arms and trophies raise;
There high in air *memorial* of my name
Fix the smooth oar, and bid me live to fame. *Pope.*

2. Contained in memory.

The case is the same with the *memorial* possessions of the greatest part of mankind: a few useful things mixed with many trifles fill up their memories. *Watts.*

MEMO'RIAL. *n. s.*

1. A monument; something to preserve memory.

All churches have had their names; some as *memorials* of peace, some of wisdom, some in memory of the trinity itself, some of Christ under sundry titles; of the blessed Virgin not a few; many of one apostle, saint, or martyr; many of all. *Hooker.*

A *memorial* unto Israel, that no stranger offer incense before the Lord. *Num.* xvi. 43.

All the laws of this kingdom have some monuments or *memorials* thereof in writing, yet all of them have not their original in writing; for some of those laws have obtained their force by immemorial usage. *Hale.*

In other parts like deeds deserv'd
Memorial, where the might of Gabriel fought. *Milton.*

Reflect upon a clear, unblotted, acquitting conscience, and feed upon the ineffable comforts of the *memorial* of a conquered temptation. *South's Sermons.*

Medals are so many monuments consigned over to eternity, that may last when all other *memorials* of the same age are worn out or lost. *Addison on ancient Medals.*

2. Hint to assist the memory.

He was a prince sad, serious, and full of thoughts and secret observations, and full of notes and *memorials* of his own hand touching persons. *Bacon's Henry* VII.

Memorials written with king Edward's hand shall be the ground of this history. *Hayward.*

MEMO'RIALIST. *n. s.* [from *memorial.*] One who writes memorials.

I must not omit a memorial setting forth, that the *memorialist* had, with great dispatch, carried a letter from a certain lord to a certain lord. *Spectator*, N°. 629.

MEMORI'ZE. *v. a.* [from *memory.*] To record; to commit to memory by writing.

They neglect to *memorize* their conquest of the Indians, especially in those times in which the same was supposed. *Spenser on Ireland.*

Let their names that were bravely lost be rather *memorized* in the full table of time; for my part, I love no ambitious pains in an eloquent description of miseries. *Wotton.*

MEMORY. *n. s.* [*memoire*, Fr. *memoria*, Latin.]

1. The power of retaining or recollecting things past; retention; reminiscence; recollection.

Memory is the power to revive again in our minds those ideas which after imprinting have disappeared, or have been laid aside out of sight. *Locke.*

The *memory* is perpetually looking back, when we have nothing present to entertain us: it is like those repositories in animals that are filled with stores of food, on which they may ruminate, when their present pasture fails. *Addison's Spectator.*

2. Exemption

2. Exemption from oblivion.

That ever-living man of *memory*,
Henry the Fifth! *Shakesp. Henry* VI.

3. Time of knowledge.

Thy request think now fulfill'd, that ask'd
How first this world, and face of things, began,
And what, before thy *memory*, was done. *Milton.*

4. Memorial; monumental record.

Be better suited;
These weeds are *memories* of those worser hours:
I pr'ythee put them off. *Shakesp. King Lear.*

A swan in *memory* of Cycnus shines;
The mourning sisters weep in wat'ry signs. *Addison.*

5. Reflection; attention. Not in use.

When Duncan is asleep, his two chamberlains
Will I with wine and wassel so convince,
That *memory*, the warder of the brain,
Shall be a fume. *Shakespeare's Macbeth.*

MEN, the plural of *man.*

Wits live obscurely *men* know not how; or die obscurely *men* mark not when. *Ascham.*

For *men*, there are to be considered the valour and number: the old observation is not untrue, that the Spaniards valour lieth in the eye of the looker-on; but the English valour lieth about the soldiers heart. *Bacon's War with Spain.*

He thought fit that the king's affairs should entirely be conducted by the soldiers and *men* of war. *Clarendon, b.* viii.

MEN-PLE'ASER. *n. s.* [*men* and *pleaser.*] One too careful to please others.

Servants be obedient to them that are your masters: not with eye-service, as *men-pleasers*; but as the servants of Christ, doing the will of God from the heart. *Eph.* vi. 6.

To ME'NACE. *v. a.* [*menacer*, Fr.] To threaten; to threat.

Who ever knew the heavens *menace* so? *Shakespeare.*

Your eyes do *menace* me: why look you pale?
Who sent you hither? *Shakespeare's Richard* III.

My master knows not but I am gone hence,
And fearfully did *menace* me with death,
If I did stay to look on his intents. *Shakespeare.*

From this league
Peep'd harms that *menac'd* him. *Shakesp. Henry* VIII.

What shou'd he do? 'Twas death to go away,
And the god *menac'd* if he dar'd to stay. *Dryden's Fables.*

ME'NACE. *n. s.* [*menace*, Fr. from the verb.] Threat.

He that would not believe the *menace* of God at first, it may be doubted whether, before an ocular example, he believed the curse at last. *Brown's Vulgar Errours, b.* i.

The Trojans view the dusty cloud from far,
And the dark *menace* of the distant war. *Dryden's Æneis.*

ME'NACER. *n. s.* [*menaceur*, Fr. from *menace.*] A threatener; one that threats.

Hence *menacer*! nor tempt me into rage:
This roof protects thy rashness. But begone! *Philips.*

MENA'GE. n. s. [French.] A collection of animals.

I saw here the largest *menage* that I met with any-where. *Addison on Italy.*

ME'NAGOGUE. *n. s.* [μῆνες and ἄγω.] A medicine that promotes the flux of the menses.

To MEND. *v. a.* [*emendo*, Latin.]

1. To repair from breach or decay.

They gave the money to the workmen to repair and *mend* the house. *2 Chron.* xxxiv. 10.

2. To correct; to alter for the better.

The best service they could do to the state, was to *mend* the lives and manners of the persons who composed it. *Temple's Miscel.*

You need not despair, by the assistance of his growing reason, to master his timorousness, and *mend* the weakness of his constitution. *Locke on Education.*

Though in some lands the grass is but short, yet it *mends* garden herbs and fruit. *Mortimer's Husbandry.*

Their opinion of Wood, and his project, is not *mended*. *Swift.*

3. To help; to advance.

Whatever is new is unlooked for; and ever it *mends* some, and impairs others: and he that is holpen takes it for a fortune, and he that is hurt for a wrong. *Bacon.*

If, to avoid succession in eternal existence, they recur to the punctum stans of the schools, they will thereby very little *mend* the matter, or help us to a more positive idea of infinite duration. *Locke.*

4. To improve; to increase.

Death comes not at call; justice divine
Mends not her slowest pace, for pray'r, or cries. *Milton.*

When upon the sands the traveller,
Sees the high sea come rolling from afar,
The land grow short, he *mends* his weary pace,
While death behind him covers all the place. *Dryden.*

He saw the monster *mend* his pace; he springs,
As terror had increas'd his feet with wings. *Dryden.*

To MEND. *v. n.* To grow better; to advance in any good; to be changed for the better.

Name a new play and he's the poet's friend;
Nay, show'd his faults—but when wou'd poets *mend?*
Pope's Essay on Criticism.

ME'NDABLE. *adj.* [from *mend.*] Capable of being mended. A low word.

MENDA'CITY. *n. s.* [from *mendax*, Latin.] Falsehood.

In this delivery there were additional *mendacities*; for the commandment forbid not to touch the fruit, and positively said, Ye shall surely die; but she, extenuating, replied, Lest ye die. *Brown's Vulgar Errours, b.* i.

ME'NDER. *n. s.* [from *mend.*] One who makes any change for the better.

What trade art thou? A trade that I may use with a safe conscience; a *mender* of bad souls. *Shakesp. Julius Cæsar.*

ME'NDICANT. *adj.* [*mendicans*, Latin.] Begging; poor to a state of beggary.

Be not righteous over-much, is applicable to those who, out of an excess of zeal, practise mortifications, whereby they macerate their bodies; or to those who voluntarily reduce themselves to a poor, and perhaps *mendicant*, state. *Fiddes's Sermons.*

ME'NDICANT. *n. s.* [*mendicant*, Fr.] A beggar; one of some begging fraternity in the Romish church.

To ME'NDICATE. *v. a.* [*mendico*, Lat. *mendier*, Fr] To beg; to ask alms.

MENDI'CITY. *n. s.* [*mendicitas*, Lat. *mendicité*, Fr.] The life of a beggar.

MENDS for *amends.*

Let her be as she is: If she be fair, 'tis the better for her; and if she be not, she has the *mends* in her own hands. *Shak.*

ME'NIAL. *adj.* [from *meiny* or *many*; mени, Saxon, or *mesnie*, old French.]

1. Belonging to the retinue, or train of servants.

Two *menial* dogs before their master press'd;
Thus clad, and guarded thus, he seeks his kingly guest. *Dryden's Æneis.*

2. *Swift* seems not to have known the meaning of this word.

The women attendants perform only the most *menial* offices. *Gulliver's Travels.*

ME'NIAL. *n. s.* One of the train of servants.

MENI'NGES. *n. s.* [μενιγξ.] The *meninges* are the two membranes that envelope the brain, which are called the pia mater and dura mater; the latter being the exterior involucrum, is, from its thickness, so denominated. *Dict.*

The brain being exposed to the air groweth fluid, and is thrust forth by the contraction of the *meninges*. *Wiseman.*

MENO'LOGY. *n. s.* [μηνολόγιον; *menologe*, French.] A register of months.

In the Roman martyrology we find, at one time, many thousand martyrs destroyed by Dioclesian: the *menology* saith they were twenty thousand. *Stillingfleet.*

ME'NOW. *n. s.* commonly *minnow.* A fish. *Ainf.*

ME'NSAL. *adj.* [*mensalis*, Lat.] Belonging to the table; transacted at table. A word yet scarcely naturalised.

Conversation either mental or *mensal.* *Clarissa.*

ME'NSTRUAL. *adj.* [*menstrual*, Fr. *menstruus*, Latin.]

1. Monthly; happening once a month; lasting a month.

She turns all her globe to the sun, by moving in her *menstrual* orb, and enjoys night and day alternately, one day of her's being equal to about fourteen days and nights of ours. *Bentley's Sermons.*

2. Pertaining to a menstruum. [*menstrueux*, Fr.]

The dissents of the *menstrual* or strong waters hinder the incorporation, as well as those of the metal. *Bacon.*

ME'NSTRUOUS. *adj.* [*menstruus*, Lat.] Having the catamenia.

O thou of late belov'd,
Now like a *menstruous* woman art remov'd. *Sandys's Par.*

Many, from being women, have proved men at the first point of their *menstruous* eruptions. *Brown.*

ME'NSTRUUM. *n. s.* [This name probably was derived from some notion of the old chemists about the influence of the moon in the preparation of dissolvents.]

All liquors are called *menstruums* which are used as dissolvents, or to extract the virtues of ingredients by infusion, decoction. *Quincy.*

Inquire what is the proper *menstruum* to dissolve metal, what will touch upon the one and not upon the other, and what several *menstrua* will dissolve any metal. *Bacon's Physical Rem.*

White metalline bodies must be excepted, which, by reason of their excessive density, seem to reflect almost all the light incident on their first superficies, unless by solution in *menstruums* they be reduced into very small particles, and then they become transparent. *Newton's Opticks.*

MENSURABI'LITY. *n. s.* [*mensurabilité*, French.] Capacity of being measured.

ME'NSURABLE. *adj.* [*mensura*, Latin.] Measurable; that may be measured.

We measure our time by law and not by nature. The solar month is no periodical motion, and not easily *mensurable*, and the months unequal among themselves, and not to be measured by even weeks or days. *Holder.*

MEʹNSURAL. *adj.* [from *mensura*, Latin.] Relating to measure.

To MEʹNSURATE. *v. a.* [from *mensura*, Latin.] To measure; to take the dimension of any thing.

MENSURAʹTION. *n. s.* [from *mensura*, Lat.] The act or practice of measuring; result of measuring.

After giving the *mensuration* and argumentation of Dr. Cumberland, it would not have been fair to have suppressed those of another prelate. *Arbuthnot on Coins.*

MEʹNTAL. *adj.* [*mentale*, French; *mentis*, Lat.] Intellectual; existing in the mind.

What a *mental* power
This eye shoots forth? How big imagination
Moves in this lip? To the dumbness of the gesture
One might interpret. *Shakesp. Timon of Athens.*

So deep the pow'r of these ingredients pierc'd,
Ev'n to the inmost seat of *mental* sight,
That Adam now enforc'd to close his eyes,
Sunk down, and all his spirits became entranc'd. *Milton.*

The metaphor of taste would not have been so general, had there not been a very great conformity between the *mental* taste and that sensitive taste that affects the palate. *Addison's Spect.* Nº. 409.

If the ideas be not innate, there was a time when the mind was without those principles; for where the ideas are not, there can be no knowledge, no assent, no *mental* or verbal propositions about them. *Locke.*

She kindly talk'd, at least three hours,
Of plastick forms, and *mental* pow'rs. *Prior.*

Those inward representations of spirit, thought, love, and hatred, are pure and *mental* ideas, belonging especially to the mind, and carry nothing of shape or sense in them. *Watts's Logick.*

MEʹNTALLY. *adv.* [from *mental.*] Intellectually; in the mind; not practically, but in thought or meditation.

If we consider the heart the first principle of life, and *mentally* divide it into its constituent parts, we find nothing but what is in any muscle of the body. *Bentley.*

MEʹNTION. *n. s.* [*mention*, Fr. *mentio*, Latin.] Oral or written expression, or recital of any thing.

Think on me when it shall be well with thee; and make *mention* of me unto Pharaoh, and bring me out of this house. *Gen.* xl. 14.

The Almighty introduces the proposal of his laws rather with the *mention* of some particular acts of kindness, than by reminding mankind of his severity. *Rogers's Sermons.*

To MEʹNTION. *v. a.* [*mentionner*, Fr. from the noun.] To write or express in words or writing.

I will *mention* the loving-kindnesses of the Lord, and the praises of the Lord. *Isa.* lxiii. 7.

These *mentioned* by their names were princes in their families. 1 *Chron.* iv. 38.

The rest of the acts of Jehoshaphat are written in the book of Jehu, who is *mentioned* in the book of Kings. 2 *Chron.*

All his transgressions shall not be *mentioned*. *Ezek.* xviii.

MEPHIʹTICAL. *adj.* [*mephitis*, Lat.] Ill savoured; stinking.

Mephitical exhalations are poisonous or noxious steams issuing out of the earth, from what cause soever. *Quincy.*

MERAʹCIOUS. *adj.* [*meracus*, Latin.] Strong; racy.

MEʹRCABLE. *adj.* [*mercor*, Lat.] To be sold or bought. *Dict.*

MEʹRCANTANT. *n. s.* [*mercatante*, Ital.] This word in *Shakespeare* seems to signify a foreigner, or foreign trader.

What is he?
— A *mercantant*, or else a pedant.
I know not what but formal in apparel. *Shakespeare.*

MEʹRCANTILE. *adj.* Trading; commercial.

The expedition of the Argonauts was partly *mercantile*, partly military. *Arbuthnot on Coins.*

Let him travel and fulfil the duties of the military or *mercantile* life; let prosperous or adverse fortune call him to the most distant parts of the globe, still let him carry on his knowledge, and the improvement of his soul. *Watts.*

MEʹRCAT. *n. s.* [*mercatus*, Latin.] Market; trade.

With irresistible majesty and authority our Saviour removed the exchange, and drove the *mercat* out of the temple. *Sprat.*

MEʹRCATURE. *n. s.* [*mercatura*, Latin.] The practice of buying and selling.

MEʹRCENARINESS. *n. s.* [from *mercenary.*] Venality; respect to hire or reward.

To forego the pleasures of sense, and undergo the hardships that attend a holy life, is such a kind of *mercenariness*, as none but a resigned, believing soul is likely to be guilty of; if fear itself, and even the fear of hell, may be one justifiable motive of mens actions. *Boyle.*

MEʹRCENARY. *adj.* [*mercenaire*, Fr. *mercenarius*, Lat.] Venal; hired; sold for money; acting only for hire.

Many of our princes, woe the while!
Lie drown'd, and soked in *mercenary* blood. *Shakespeare.*

Divers Almains, who served in the garisons, being merely *mercenary*, did easily incline to the strongest. *Haywood.*

The appellation of servant imports a *mercenary* temper, and denotes such an one as makes his reward both the sole motive and measure of his obedience. *South's Sermons.*

'Twas not for nothing I the crown resign'd;
I still must own a *mercenary* mind. *Dryden's Aurengzebe.*

MEʹRCENARY. *n. s.* [*mercenaire*, Fr.] A hireling; one retained or serving for pay.

He a poor *mercenary* serves for bread;
For all his travel, only cloth'd and fed. *Sandys's Paraph.*

MEʹRCER. *n. s.* [*mercier*, French.] One who sells silks.

The draper and *mercer* may measure religion as they please, and the weaver may cast her upon what loom he please. *Howel's England's Tears.*

MEʹRCERY. *n. s.* [*mercerie*, Fr. from *mercer.*] Trade of mercers; dealing in silks.

The *mercery* is gone from out of Lombard-street and Cheapside into Paternoster-row and Fleet-street. *Graunt.*

To MEʹRCHAND. *v. n.* [*marchander*, French.] To transact by traffick.

Ferdinando *merchanded* with France for the restoring Roussiglion and Perpignan, oppignerated to them. *Bacon.*

MEʹRCHANDISE. *n. s.* [*marchandise*, French.]

1. Traffick; commerce; trade.

If a son, that is sent by his father about *merchandise*, fall into some leud action, his wickedness, by your rule, should be imposed upon his father. *Shakesp. Henry* V.

If he pay thee to the utmost farthing, thou hast forgiven nothing: it is *merchandise*, and not forgiveness, to restore him that does as much as you can require. *Taylor.*

2. Wares; any thing to be bought or sold.

Fair when her breast, like a rich laden bark
With precious *merchandise*, she forth doth lay. *Spenser.*

Thou shalt not sell her at all for money; thou shalt not make *merchandise* of her. *Deut.* xxi. 14.

As for any *merchandise* you have brought, ye shall have your return in *merchandise* or in gold. *Bacon.*

So active a people will always have money, whilst they can send what *merchandises* they please to Mexico. *Addison.*

To MEʹRCHANDISE. *v. n.* To trade; to traffick; to exercise commerce.

The Phœnicians, of whose exceeding *merchandising* we read so much in ancient histories, were Canaanites, whose very name signifies merchants. *Brerewood on Languages.*

MEʹRCHANT. *n. s.* [*marchand*, French.] One who trafficks to remote countries.

France hath flaw'd the league, and hath attach'd
Our *merchants* goods at Bourdeaux. *Shakesp. Henry* VIII.

The Lord hath given a commandment against the *merchant* city to destroy the strong holds thereof. *Isa.* xxiii. 11.

The most celebrated *merchants* in the world were situated in the island of Tyre. *Addison's Freeholder*, Nº. 42.

MEʹRCHANTLY. } *adj.* [from *merchant.*] Like a merchant.
MEʹRCHANTLIKE. } *Ainsw.*

MEʹRCHANT-MAN. *n. s.* [*merchant* and *man.*] A ship of trade.

Pirates have fair winds and a calm sea, when the just and peaceful *merchant-man* hath them. *Taylor.*

In the time of Augustus and Tiberius, the southern coasts of Spain sent great fleets of *merchant-men* to Italy. *Arbuthnot.*

MEʹRCHANTABLE. *adj.* [*mercabilis*, Lat. from *merchant.*] Fit to be bought or sold.

Why they placed this invention in the beaver, beside the medical and *merchantable* commodity of castor, or parts conceived to be bitten away, might be the sagacity of that animal. *Brown's Vulgar Errours, b.* iii.

MEʹRCIABLE. *adj.* [from *mercy.*] This word in *Spenser* signifies *merciful.*

Nought but well mought him betight:
He is so meek, wise, *merciable*,
And with his word his work is convenable. *Spenser's Past.*

MEʹRCIFUL. *adj.* [*mercy* and *full.*] Compassionate; tender; kind; unwilling to punish; willing to pity and spare.

Be *merciful*, O Lord, unto thy people thou hast redeemed. *Deut.* xxi. 8.

MEʹRCIFULLY. *adv.* [from *merciful.*] Tenderly; mildly; with pity; with compassion.

Make the true use of those afflictions which his hand, *mercifully* severe, hath been pleased to lay upon thee. *Atterbury.*

MEʹRCIFULNESS. *n. s.* [from *merciful.*] Tenderness; willingness to spare.

The band that ought to knit all these excellencies together is a kind *mercifulness* to such a one, as is in his soul devoted to such perfections. *Sidney.*

Use the means ordinary and lawful, among which *mercifulness* and liberality is one, to which the promise of secular wealth is most frequently made. *Hammond.*

MEʹRCILESS. *adj.* [from *mercy.*] Void of mercy; pitiless; hard hearted; cruel; severe.

His mother *merciless*,
Most *merciless* of women Wyden hight,
Her other son fast sleeping did oppress,
And with most cruel hand him murdered pitiless. *Fa. Qu.*

The foe is *merciless*, and will not pity. *Shakespeare.*

Think not their rage so desperate t' essay
An element more *merciless* than they. *Denham.*
What God so mean,
So *merciless* a tyrant to obey! *Dryden's Juvenal.*

Whatever ravages a *merciless* distemper may commit, she shall have one man as much her admirer as ever. *Pope.*

The torrent *merciless* imbibes
Commissions, perquisites, and bribes. *Swift.*

MERCI'LESSLY. *adv.* [from *merciless.*] In a manner void of pity.

ME'RCILESSNESS. *n. s.* [from *merciless.*] Want of pity.

ME'RCURIAL. *adj.* [*mercurialis*, Lat.]

1. Formed under the influence of mercury; active; sprightly.

I know the shape of 's leg: This is his hand,
His foot *mercurial*, his martial thigh,
The brawns of Hercules. *Shakesp. Cymbeline.*

This youth was such a *mercurial*, as could make his own part, if at any time he chanced to be out. *Bacon's Hen.* VII.

Tully considered the dispositions of a sincere, more ignorant, and less *mercurial* nation, by dwelling on the pathetick part. *Swift's Miscel.*

2. Consisting of quicksilver.

MERCURIFICA'TION. *adj.* [from *mercury.*] The act of mixing any thing with quicksilver.

I add the ways of *mercurification.* *Boyle.*

MERCURY. *n. s.* [*mercurius*, Latin.]

1. The chemist's name for quicksilver is *mercury.* *Hill.*

The gall of animals and *mercury* kill worms; and the water in which *mercury* is boiled has this effect. *Arbuthnot.*

2. Sprightly qualities.

Thus the *mercury* of man is fix'd,
Strong grows the virtue with his nature mix'd;
The dross cements what else were too refin'd,
And in one int'rest body acts with mind. *Pope.*

3. A news-paper. *Ainf.*

4. It is now applied, in cant phrase, to the carriers of news and pamphlets.

ME'RCURY. *n. s.* [*mercurialis*, Latin.] A plant.

The leaves of the *mercury* are crenated, and grow by pairs opposite: the cup of the flower consists of one leaf, which expands and is cut into three segments; these are male and female in different places: the flowers of the male grow in long spikes, and consist of many stamina and apices, which are loaded with farina: the ovary of the female plant becomes a testiculated fruit, having a single round seed in each cell. *Miller.*

Herb *mercury* is of an emollient nature, and is eaten in the manner of spinach, which, when cultivated in a garden, it greatly excels. *Hill's Mat. Med.*

ME'RCY. *n. s.* [*merci*, French, contracted from *misericordia*, Latin.]

1. Tenderness; goodness; pity; willingness to save; clemency; mildness; unwillingness to punish.

Oh heav'n have *mercy* on me!
—I say, amen.
And have you *mercy* too? *Shakespeare.*

Mercy is not strain'd;
It droppeth, as the gentle rain from heav'n,
Upon the place beneath. It is twice bless'd;
It blesseth him that gives and him that takes. *Shakesp.*

Arise, and have *mercy* upon Zion. *Psal.* cii. 13.

Thou, O God, art gracious, long-suffering, and in *mercy* ordering all. *Wisd.* xv. 1.

Examples of justice must be made for terror to some; examples of *mercy* for comfort to others: the one procures fear, and the other love. *Bacon's Advice to Villiers.*

Good heav'n, whose darling attribute we find
Is boundless grace, and *mercy* to mankind,
Abhors the cruel. *Dryden.*

We adore his undeserved *mercy* towards us, that he made us the chief of the visible creation. *Bentley's Sermons.*

2. Pardon.

'Twere a paper lost,
As offer'd *mercy* is. *Shakespeare's Cymbeline.*

Cry *mercy* lords,
That you have ta'en a tardy sluggard here. *Shakespeare.*

I cry thee *mercy* with all my heart, for suspecting a friar of the least good-nature. *Dryden's Spanish Friar.*

3. Discretion; power of acting at pleasure.

Condition!
What good condition can a treaty find
I' th' part that is at *mercy?* *Shakespeare's Coriolanus.*

The most authentick record of so ancient a family should lie at the *mercy* of every infant who flings a stone. *Pope.*

A lover is ever complaining of cruelty while any thing is denied him; and when the lady ceases to be cruel, she is, from the next moment, at his *mercy.* *Swift.*

MERCY-SEAT. *n. s.* [*mercy* and *seat.*]

The *mercy-seat* was the covering of the ark of the covenant, in which the tables of the law were deposited: it was of gold, and at its two ends were fixed the two cherubims, of the same metal, which with their wings extended for-

wards, seemed to form a throne for the majesty of God, who in scripture is represented as sitting between the cherubims, and the ark was his footstool: it was from hence that God gave his oracles to Moses, or to the high-priest that consulted him. *Calmet.*

Make a *mercy-seat* of pure gold. *Exod.* xxv. 17.

MERE. *adj.* [*merus*, Latin.] That or this only; such and nothing else; this only.

This avarice
Strikes deeper, grows with more pernicious root
Than Summer-teeming lust; and it hath been
The sword of our slain kings: yet do not fear,
Scotland hath foisons to fill up your will
Of your *mere* own. *Shakespeare's Macbeth.*

I have engag'd myself to a dear friend,
Engag'd my friend to his *mere* enemy,
To feed my means. *Shakesp. Merchant of Venice.*

The *mere* Irish were not admitted to the benefit of the laws of England, until they had purchased charters of denization. *Davies on Ireland.*

From *mere* success nothing can be concluded in favour of any nation upon whom it is bestowed. *Atterbury.*

What if the head, the eye, or ear repin'd,
To serve *mere* engines to the ruling mind. *Pope.*

Let Eastern tyrants from the light of heav'n
Seclude their bosom slaves, meanly possess'd
Of a *mere*, lifeless, violated form. *Thomson's Spring.*

MERE or *mer*, whether in the beginning, middle, or end, always signify the same with the Saxon meꞃe, a pool or lake. *Gibson's Camden.*

MERE. *n. s.* [meꞃe, Saxon.]

1. A pool; commonly a large pool or lake: as, *Winander mere.*

I may say nothing of *meres* stored both with fish and fowl. *Camden's Remains.*

2. A boundary.

The mislayer of a *mere*-stone is to blame: but it is the unjust judge that is the capital remover of land-marks, who defineth amiss of lands. *Bacon.*

ME'RELY. *adv.* [from *mere.*] Simply; only; thus and no other way; for this and for no other end or purpose.

Which thing we ourselves would grant, if the use thereof had been *merely* and only mystical. *Hooker, b.* v.

These external manners of laments
Are *merely* shadows to the unseen grief,
That swells with silence in the tortur'd soul. *Shakesp.*

It is below reasonable creatures to be conversant in such diversions as are *merely* innocent, and have nothing else to recommend them. *Addison's Spect.* N. 93.

Above a thousand bought his almanack *merely* to find what he said against me. *Swift.*

Prize not your life for other ends
Than *merely* to oblige your friends. *Swift.*

MERETRICIOUS. *adj.* [*meretricius*, *meretrix*, Latin.] Whorish; such as is practised by prostitutes; alluring by false show.

Our degenerate understandings having suffered a sad divorce from their dearest object, defile themselves with every *meretricious* semblance, that the variety of opinion presents them with. *Glanville's Scep.*

Not by affected, *meretricious* arts,
But strict harmonious symmetry of parts. *Roscommon.*

MERETRI'CIOUSLY. *adv.* [from *meretricious.*] Whorishly; after the manner of whores.

MERETRI'CIOUSNESS. *n. s.* [from *meretricious.*] False allurement like those of strumpets.

MERIDIAN. *n. s.* [*meridien*, French; *meridies*, Lat.]

1. Noon; mid-day.

He promis'd in his East a glorious race,
Now sunk from his *meridian*, sets apace. *Dryden.*

2. The line drawn from North to South, which the Sun crosses at noon.

The true *meridian* is a circle passing through the poles of the world, and the zenith or vertex of any place, exactly dividing the East from the West. *Brown's Vulg. Errours, b.* ii.

The Sun or Moon, rising or setting, our idea represents bigger than when on the *meridian.* *Watts's Logick.*

3. The particular place or state of any thing.

All other knowledge merely serves the concerns of this life, and is fitted to the *meridian* thereof: they are such as will be of little use to a separate soul. *Hale.*

4. The highest point of glory or power.

I've touch'd the highest point of all my greatness,
And from that full *meridian* of my glory
I haste now to my setting. *Shakesp. Henry* VIII.

Your full majesty at once breaks forth
In the *meridian* of your reign. *Waller.*

MERI'DIAN. *adj.*

1. At the point of noon.

Sometimes tow'rds Eden, which now in his view
Lay pleasant, his griev'd look he fixes sad;

Sometimes

Sometimes tow'rds heav'n, and the full blazing Sun,
Which now sat high in his *meridian* tow'r. *Milton.*

2. Extended from North to South.

Compare the *meridian* line afforded by magnetical needles with one mathematically drawn, and observe the variation of the needle, or its declination from the true *meridian* line. *Boyle.*

3. Raised to the highest point.

MERI'DIONAL. *adj.* [*meridional*, French.]

1. Southern.

In the southern coast of America or Africa, the southern point varieth toward the land, as being disposed that way by the *meridional* or proper hemisphere. *Brown's Vulgar Errours.*

2. Southerly; having a southern aspect.

All offices that require heat, as kitchens, stillatories, and stoves, would be *meridional.* *Wotton's Architect.*

MERIDIONA'LITY. *n. s.* [from *meridional.*] Position in the South; aspect towards the South.

MERI'DIONALLY. *adv.* [from *meridional.*] With a southern aspect.

The Jews, not willing to lie as their temple stood, do place their bed from North to South, and delight to sleep *meridionally.* *Brown's Vulgar Errours, b.* ii.

ME'RIT. *n. s.* [*meritum*, Latin; *merite*, French.]

1. Desert; excellence deserving honour or reward.

You have the captives; use them
As we shall find their *merits* and our safety
May equally determine. *Shakesp. King Lear.*

She deem'd I well deserv'd to die,
And made a *merit* of her cruelty. *Dryden.*

Roscommon, not more learn'd than good,
With manners gen'rous as his noble blood;
To him the wit of Greece and Rome was known,
And ev'ry author's *merit* but his own. *Pope.*

She valu'd nothing less
Than titles, figure, shape, and dress;
That *merit* should be chiefly plac'd
In judgment, knowledge, wit, and taste. *Swift.*

2. Reward deserved.

Those laurel groves, the *merits* of thy youth,
Which thou from Mahomet didst greatly gain,
While bold assertor of resistless truth,
Thy sword did godlike liberty maintain. *Prior.*

3. Claim; right.

As I am studious to promote the honour of my native country, I put Chaucer's *merits* to the trial, by turning some of the Canterbury tales into our language. *Dryden.*

When a point hath been well examined, and our own judgment settled, after a large survey of the *merits* of the cause, it would be a weakness to continue fluttering. *Watts.*

To ME'RIT. *v. a.* [*meriter*, French.]

1. To deserve; to have a right to claim any thing as deserved.

Amply have *merited* of me, of all
Th' infernal empire. *Milton's Par. Lost, b.* x.

A man at best is uncapable of *meriting* any thing from God. *South's Sermons.*

2. To deserve; to earn: it is used generally of good, but sometimes of ill.

Whatsoever jewels I have *merited*, I am sure I have received none, unless experience be a jewel; that I have purchased at an infinite rate. *Shakesp. Merry Wives of Windsor.*

If such rewards to vanquish'd men are due,
What prize may Nisus from your bounty claim,
Who *merited* the first rewards, and fame? *Dryden.*

MERITO'RIOUS. *adj.* [*meritoire*, Fr. from *merit.*] Deserving of reward; high in desert.

Instead of so great and *meritorious* a service, in bringing all the Irish to acknowledge the king for their liege, they did great hurt. *Spenser on Ireland.*

The war that hath such a foundation will not only be reputed just, but holy and *meritorious.* *Raleigh's Essays.*

A most sufficient means of redemption and salvation, by the satisfactory and *meritorious* death and obedience of the incarnate Son of God, Jesus Christ, God blessed for ever. *Bishop Sanderson.*

This is not only the most prudent, but the most *meritorious* charity, which we can practice. *Addison's Spect.*

MERITO'RIOUSLY. *adv.* [from *meritorious.*] In such a manner as to deserve reward.

He carried himself *meritoriously* in foreign employments in time of the interdict, which held up his credit among the patriots. *Wotton.*

MERITO'RIOUSNESS. *n. s.* [from *meritorious.*] The act or state of deserving well.

There was a full persuasion of the high *meritoriousness* of what they did, but still there was no law of God to ground it upon, and consequently it was not conscience. *South.*

ME'RITOT. *n. s.* [*oscillum*, Lat.] A kind of play. *Ains.*

ME'RLIN. *n. s.* A kind of hawk.

Not yielding over to old age his country delights, he was at that time following a *merlin.* *Sidney.*

ME'RMAID. *n. s.* [*mer*, the sea, and *maid.*] A sea woman; an animal with a woman's head and fish's tail.

I'll drown more sailors than the *mermaid* shall. *Shakesp.*

Thou remembrest,
Since once I sat upon a promontory,
And heard a *mermaid* on a dolphin's back
Uttering such dulcet and harmonious breath,
That the rude sea grew civil at her song. *Shakespeare.*

Did sense persuade Ulysses not to hear
The *mermaids* songs, which so his men did please,
That they were all persuaded, through the ear,
To quit the ship and leap into the seas? *Davies.*

Few eyes have escaped the picture of a *mermaid*: Horace his monster, with woman's head above and fishy extremity below, answers the shape of the ancient syrens that attempted upon Ulysses. *Brown's Vulgar Errours, b.* v.

MERMAID'S TRUMPET. *n. s.* A kind of fish. *Ains.*

ME'RRILY. *adv.* [from *merry.*]

1. Gaily; civily; cheerfully; with mirth; with gaiety; with laughter.

Merrily, *merrily*, shall we live now,
Under the blossom that hangs on the bough. *Shakesp.*

When men come to borrow of your masters, they approach sadly, and go away *merrily.* *Shakesp. Timon of Athens.*

You have ended my business, and I will *merrily* accompany you home. *Shakespeare's Coriolanus.*

A paisan of France thinks of no more than his coarse bread and his onions, his canvass clothes and wooden shoes, labours contentedly on working days, and dances or plays *merrily* on holidays. *Temple's Miscel.*

Merrily sing, and sport, and play,
For 'tis Oriana's nuptial day. *Granville.*

ME'RRIMAKE. *n. s.* [*merry* and *make.*] A festival; a meeting for mirth.

Thenot now nis the time of *merrymake*,
Nor Pan to herie, nor with love to play,
Sike mirth in May is meetest for to make,
Or Summer shade, under the cocked hay. *Spenser's Past.*

The knight did not forbear,
Her honest mirth and pleasure to partake,
But when he saw her gibe, and toy, and geare,
And pass the bounds of modest *merrimake*,
Her dalliance he despised. *Fairy Queen, b.* ii.

To ME'RRIMAKE. *v. a.* To feast; to be jovial.

With thee 'twas Marian's dear delight
To moil all day, and *merrimake* at night. *Gay's Pastorals.*

ME'RRIMENT. *n. s.* [from *merry.*] Mirth; gaiety; cheerfulness; laughter.

Who when they heard that piteous strained voice,
In haste forsook their rural *merriment.* *Fairy Queen, b.* i.

A number of *merriments* and jests, wherewith they have pleasantly moved much laughter at our manner of serving God. *Hooker, b.* v.

Methought it was the sound
Of riot and ill-managed *merriment.* *Milton.*

ME'RRINESS. *n. s.* [from *merry.*] Mirth; merry disposition.

The stile shall give us cause to climb in the *merriness.* *Shak.*

ME'RRY. *adj.*

1. Laughing; loudly cheerful; gay of heart.

They drank and were *merry* with him. *Gen.* xliii. 34.

The vine languisheth, all the *merry*-hearted sigh. *Isa.* xxiv.

Some that are of an ill and melancholy nature, incline the company into which they come to be sad and ill-disposed; and others that are of a jovial nature, do dispose the company to be *merry* and cheerful. *Bacon's Nat. Hist.*

Man is the *merriest* species of the creation; all above and below him are serious. *Addison.*

2. Causing laughter.

You kill'd her husband, and for that vile fault
Two of her brothers were condemn'd to death;
My hand cut off, and made a *merry* jest. *Shakespeare.*

3. Prosperous.

In my small pinnace I can sail,
Contemning all the blust'ring roar;
And running with a *merry* gale,
With friendly stars my safety seek,
Within some little winding creek,
And see the storm ashore. *Dryden.*

To make MERRY. To junket; to be jovial.

They trod the grapes and *made merry*, and went into the house of their God. *Judg.* ix. 27.

A fox 'spy'd a bevy of jolly, gossiping wenches *making merry* over a dish of pullets. *L'Estrange.*

MERRY-A'NDREW. *n. s.* A buffoon; a zany; a jack-pudding.

He would be a statesman because he is a buffoon; as if there went no more to the making of a counsellor than the faculties of a *merry-andrew* or tumbler. *L'Estrange.*

The first who made the experiment was a *merry-andrew.* *Spectator, N°.* 599.

MERRY-THOUGHT.

MERRYTHOUGHT. *n. s.* [*merry* and *thought.*] A forked bone on the body of fowls; so called because boys and girls pull in play at the two sides, the longest part broken off betokening priority of marriage.

Let him not be breaking *merrythoughts* under the table with my cousin. *Eachard's Contempt of the Clergy.*

MESERA'ICK. *n. s.* [μεσάραιον: *mesaraique*, Fr. analogy requires it *mesaraick.*] Belonging to the mysentery.

It taketh leave of the permeant parts at the mouths of the *meseraicks*, and accompanieth the inconvertible portion into the siege. *Brown's Vulgar Errours.*

The most subtile part of the chyle passeth immediately into the blood by the absorbent vessels of the guts, which discharge themselves into the *meseraick* veins. *Arbuthnot.*

ME'RSION. *n. s.* [*mersio*, Lat.] The act of sinking, or thrusting over head. *Ains.*

MESE'EMS, impersonal verb. [*me* and *seems*, or *it seems to me*: for this word it is now too common to use *methinks* or *methought*, an ungrammatical word.] I think; it appears to me; methinks.

Alas, of ghosts I hear the gastly cries;
Yet there, *meseems*, I hear her singing loud. *Sidney.*
Meseemed by my side a royal maid,
Her dainty limbs full softly down did lay. *Fairy Queen.*

To that general subjection of the land *meseems* that the custom or tenure can be no bar nor impeachment. *Spenser.*

ME'SENTERY. *n. s.* [μεσεντέριον; *mesentere*, Fr.] That round which the guts are convolved.

When the chyle passeth through the *mesentery*, it is mixed with the lymph. *Arbuthnot on Aliments.*

MESENTE'RICK. *adj.* [*mesenterique*, French, from *mesentery.*] Relating to the mesentery.

They are carried into the glands of the *mesentery*, receiving a fine lymph from the lymphatick ducts, which dilutes this chylous fluid, and scours its containing vessels, which, from the *mesenterick* glands, unite in large channels, and pass directly into the common receptacle of the chyle. *Cheyne.*

MESH. *n. s.* [*maesche*, Dutch; *mache*, old French: it were therefore better written, as it is commonly pronounced, *mash.*] The interstice of a net; the space between the threads of a net.

The drovers hang square nets athwart the tide, thorough which the shoal of pilchard passing, leave many behind entangled in the *meashes*. *Carew's Survey of Cornwall.*

Such a hare is madness the youth, to skip o'er the *meshes* of good counsel the cripple. *Shakesp. Merchant of Venice.*

He spreads his subtle nets from sight,
With twinkling glasses to betray
The larks that in the *meshes* light. *Dryden.*
With all their mouths the nerves the spirits drink,
Which through the cells of the fine strainers sink:
These all the channel'd fibres ev'ry way,
For motion and sensation, still convey:
The greatest portion of th' arterial blood,
By the close structure of the parts withstood,
Whose narrow *meshes* stop the grosser flood. *Blackmore.*

To MESH. *v. a.* [from the noun.] To catch in a net; to ensnare.

The flies by chance *mesht* in her hair,
By the bright radiance thrown
From her clear eyes, rich jewels were,
They so like diamonds shone. *Drayton.*

ME'SHY. *adj.* [from *mesh.*] Reticulated; of net-work.

Some build his house, but thence his issue barre,
Some make his *meashy* bed, but reave his rest. *Carew.*
Caught in the *meshy* snare, in vain they beat
Their idle wings. *Thomson.*

ME'SLIN. *n. s.* [from *mesler*, French, to mix; or rather corruptly pronounced for *miscellane*. See MASLIN.] Mixed corn: as, wheat and rie.

What reason is there which should but induce, and therefore much less enforce, us to think, that care of old dissimilitude between the people of God and the heathen nations about them, was any more the cause of forbidding them to put on garments of sundry stuff, than of charging them withal not to sow their fields with *meslin*. *Hooker, b.* iv.

If worke for the thresher ye mind for to have,
Of wheat and of *mestlin* unthreshed go save. *Tusser.*

MESOLEU'CYS. *n. s.* [μεσόλευκ☉.] A precious stone, black, with a streak of white in the middle. *Dict.*

MESO'LOGARITHMS. *n. s.* [μέσ☉, λόγ☉, and ἀριθμ☉.] The logarithms of the cosines and tangents, so denominated by *Kepler*. *Harris.*

MESO'MELAS. *n. s.* [μεσομέλας.] A precious stone with a black vein parting every colour in the midst. *Bailey.*

ME'SPISE. *n. s.* [probably misprinted for *mesprise*; *mespris*, Fr.] Contempt; scorn.

Mammon was much displeas'd, yet note he chose
But bear the rigour of his bold *mespise*,
And thence him forward led, him further to entice.
Fairy Queen, b. ii.

MESS. *n. s.* [*mes*, old French; *messo*, Italian; *missus*, Latin; *mes*, Gothick; meſe, Saxon, a dish.] A dish; a quantity of food sent to table together.

The bounteous huswife, nature, on each bush
Lays her full *mess* before you. *Shakesp. Timon of Athens.*
Now your traveller,
He and his toothpick at my worship's *mess*. *Shakespeare.*
I had as lief you should tell me of a *mess* of porridge.
Shakespeare's Merry Wives of Windsor.
Herbs, and other country *messes*,
Which the neat-handed Phillis dresses. *Milton.*

Had either of the crimes been cooked to their palates, they might have changed *messes*. *Decay of Piety.*

From him he next receives it thick or thin,
As pure a *mess* almost as it came in. *Pope.*

To MESS. *v. n.* To eat; to feed.

ME'SSAGE. *n. s.* [*message*, Fr.] An errand; any thing committed to another to be told to a third.

She doth display
The gate with pearls and rubies richly dight,
Through which her words so wise do make their way,
To bear the *message* of her spright. *Spenser, Sonnet* 81.
May one, that is a herald and a prince,
Do a fair *message* to his kingly ears! *Shakespeare.*
She is fair, and, fairer than that word,
Of wond'rous virtues; sometimes from her eyes
I did receive fair speechless *messages*. *Shakespeare.*
Gently hast thou told
Thy *message*, which might else in telling wound,
And in performing end us. *Milton's Par. Lost, b.* xi.

Let the minister be low, his interest inconsiderable, the word will suffer for his sake; the *message* will still find reception according to the dignity of the messenger. *South.*

The welcome *message* made, was soon receiv'd;
'Twas to be wish'd and hop'd, but scarce believ'd. *Dryden.*

ME'SSENGER. *n. s.* [*messager*, French.] One who carries an errand; one who comes from another to a third; one who brings an account or foretoken of any thing; an harbinger; a forerunner.

Came running in, much like a man dismaid,
A *messenger* with letters, which his message said. *Fa. Qu.*
Yon grey lines,
That fret the clouds, are *messengers* of day. *Shakespeare.*
Run after that same peevish *messenger*,
The duke's man. *Shakespeare.*

The earl dispatched *messengers* one after another to the king, with an account of what he heard and believed he saw, and yet thought not fit to stay for an answer. *Clarendon.*

Joy touch'd the *messenger* of heav'n; he stay'd
Entranc'd, and all the blissful haunt survey'd. *Pope.*

MESSI'AH. *n. s.* [from the Hebrew.] The Anointed; the Christ; the Saviour of the world; the Prince of peace.

Great and publick opposition the magistrates made against Jesus the man of Nazareth, when he appeared as the *Messiah*. *Watts's Improvement of the Mind.*

MESSI'EURS. n. s. [Fr. plural of *monsieur.*] Sirs; gentlemen.

ME'SSMATE. *n. s.* [*mess* and *mate.*] One who eats at the same table.

ME'SSUAGE. *n. s.* [*messuagium*, law Latin; formed perhaps *mesnage* by mistake of the *n* in court-hand for *u*, they being written alike, *mesnage* from *maison*, French.] The house and ground set apart for houshold uses.

MET, the preterite and part. of *meet.*

A set of very well-meaning gentlemen in England, not to be *met* with in other countries, take it for granted they can never be in the wrong so long as they can oppose ministers of state. *Addison's Freeholder*, Nº. 48.

METAGRA'MMATISM. *n. s.* [μετὰ and γράμμα.]

Anagrammatism, or *metagrammatism*, is a dissolution of a name truly written into its letters, as its elements, and a new connexion of it by artificial transposition, without addition, substraction, or change of any letter into different words, making some perfect sense applicable to the person named.
Camden's Remains.

META'BASIS. n. s. [Greek.] In rhetorick, a figure by which the orator passes from one thing to another. *Dict.*

META'BOLA. *n. s.* [μεταβολή.] In medicine, a change of time, air, or disease.

METACA'RPUS. *n. s.* [μετακάρπιον.] In anatomy, a bone of the arm made up of four bones, which are joined to the fingers. *Dict.*

The conjunction is called synarthrosis; as in the joining of the carpus to the *metacarpus*. *Wiseman's Surgery.*

METACA'RPAL. *adj.* [from *metacarpus.*] Belonging to the metacarpus. *Dict.*

It will facilitate the separation in the joint, when you cut the finger from the *metacarpal* bone. *Sharp's Surgery.*

ME'TAL. *n. s.* [*metal*, French; *metallum*, Latin.]

We understand by the term *metal* a firm, heavy, and hard substance, opake, fusible by fire, and concreting again when cold

cold into a solid body such as it was before, which is malleable under the hammer, and is of a bright, glossy, and glittering substance where newly cut or broken. The *metals* are six in number: 1. gold; 2. silver; 3. copper; 4. tin; 5. iron; and, 6. lead; of which gold is the heaviest, lead the second in weight, then silver, then copper, and iron is the lightest except tin: some have added mercury or quicksilver to the number of *metals*; but as it wants malleability, the criterion of *metals*, it is more properly ranked among the semi *metals*. *Hill's Mat. Med.*

Metallists use a kind of terrace in their vessels for fining *metals*, that the melted *metal* run not out. *Moxon.*

2. Courage; spirit. In this sense it is more frequently written *mettle*. See METTLE.

Being glad to find their companions had so much *metal*, after a long debate the major part carried it. *Clarendon.*

3. Upon this signification the following ambiguity is founded.

Both kinds of *metal* he prepar'd,
Either to give blows or to ward;
Courage and steel both of great force,
Prepar'd for better or for worse. *Hudibras, p. i.*

METALE'PSIS. *n. s.* [μετάληψις.] A continuation of a trope in one word through a succession of significations. *Bailey.*

META'LLICAL. } *adj.* [from *metallum*, Lat. *metallique*, French.]
META'LLICK. } Partaking of metal; containing metal; consisting of metal.

The antients observing in that material a kind of *metallical* nature, or fusibility, seem to have resolved it to nobler use; an art now utterly lost. *Wotton's Architecture.*

The lofty lines abound with endless store
Of min'ral treasure, and *metallick* oar. *Blackmore.*

METALLI'FEROUS. *adj.* [*metallum* and *fero*, Latin.] Producing metals. *Dict.*

META'LLINE. *adj.* [from *metal*.]

1. Impregnated with metal.

Metalline waters have virtual cold in them; put therefore wood or clay into smith's water, and try whether it will not harden. *Bacon's Nat. Hist.* N°. 84.

2. Consisting of metal.

Though the quicksilver were brought to a very close and lovely *metalline* cylinder, not interrupted by interspersed bubbles, yet having caused the air to be again drawn out of the receiver, several little bubbles disclosed themselves. *Boyle.*

ME'TALLIST. *n. s.* [from *metal*; *metalliste*, Fr.] A worker in metals; or skilled in metals.

Metallists use a kind of terrace in their vessels for fining metals, that the melted metal run not out; it is made of quick lime and ox blood. *Moxon's Mech. Exercises.*

ME'TALLOGRAPHY. *n. s.* [*metallum* and γράφω.] An account or description of metals. *Dict.*

META'LLURGIST. *n. s.* [*metallum* and ἔργον.] A worker in metals.

META'LLURGY. *n. s.* [*metallum* and ἔργον.] The art of working metals, or separating them from their ore.

To METAMO'RPHOSE. *v. a.* [*metamorphoser*, Fr. μεταμορφόω.] To change the form or shape of any thing.

Thou, Julia, thou hast *metamorphos'd* me;
Made me neglect my studies, lose my time. *Shakespeare.*

They became degenerate and *metamorphosed* like Nebuchadnezzar, who, though he had the face of a man, had the heart of a beast. *Davies on Ireland.*

The impossibility to conceive so great a prince and favourite so suddenly *metamorphosed* into travellers, with no greater train, was enough to make any man unbelieve his five senses. *Wotton's Buckingham.*

From such rude principles our form began;
And earth was *metamorphos'd* into man. *Dryden's Ovid.*

METAMO'RPHOSIS. *n. s.* [*metamorphose*, Fr. μεταμόρφωσις.]

1. Transformation; change of shape.

His whole oration stood upon a short narration, what was the causer of this *metamorphosis*. *Sidney.*

Obscene talk is grown so common, that one would think we were fallen into an age of *metamorphosis*, and that the brutes did not only poetically but really speak. *Gov. Tongue.*

The fifteenth book is the master-piece of the whole *metamorphoses*. *Dryden.*

What! my noble colonel in *metamorphosis*! On what occasion are you transformed? *Dryden's Spanish Fryar.*

There are probable machines in epick poems, where the gods are no less actors than the men; but the less credible sort, such as *metamorphoses*, are far more rare. *Pope's Odyssey.*

2. It is applied, by *Harvey*, to the changes an animal undergoes, both in its formation and growth; and by several to the various shapes some insects in particular pass through, as the silk-worm, and the like. *Quincy.*

ME'TAPHOR. *n. s.* [*metaphore*, Fr. μεταφορα.] The application of a word to an use to which, in its original import, it cannot be put: as, he *bridles* his anger; he *deadens* the sound; the spring *awakes* the flowers. A metaphor is a simile comprized in a word; the spring putting in action the powers of vegetation, which were torpid in the *winter*, as the powers of a sleeping animal are excited by awaking him.

The work of tragedy is on the passions, and in a dialogue; both of them abhor strong *metaphors*, in which the epopœa delights. *Dryden's Ded. to Virgil's Æneis.*

METAPHO'RICAL. } *adj.* [*metaphorique*, Fr. from *metaphor*.]
METAPHO'RICK. } Not literal; not according to the primitive meaning of the word; figurative.

The words which were do continue; the only difference is, that whereas before they had a literal, they now have a *metaphorical* use. *Hooker.*

METAPHRA'SE. *n. s.* [μετάφρασις.] A mere verbal translation from one language into another.

This translation is not so loose as paraphrase, nor so close as *metaphrase*. *Dryden.*

METAPHRA'ST. *n. s.* [*metaphraste*, Fr. μεταφράστης.] A literal translator; one who translates word for word from one language into another.

METAPHY'SICAL. } *adj.*
METAPHY'SICK. }

1. Versed in metaphysicks; relating to metaphysicks.

2. In *Shakespeare* it means supernatural or preternatural.

Hie thee hither,
To chastise with the valour of my tongue
All that impedes thee from the golden round,
Which fate, and *metaphysical* aid, doth seem
To have crown'd thee withal. *Shakesp. Macbeth.*

METAPHY'SICK. } *n. s.* [*metaphysique*, Fr. μεταφυσικὴ.] On-
METAPHY'SICKS. } tology; the doctrine of the general affections of substances existing.

The mathematicks and the *metaphysicks*,
Fall to them as you find your stomach serves you. *Shakesp.*
Call her the *metaphysicks* of her sex,
And say she tortures wits, as quartans vex
Physicians. *Cleaveland.*

If sight be caused by intromission, or receiving in, the form of contrary species should be received confusedly together, which how absurd it is, Aristotle shews in his *metaphysicks*. *Peacham on Drawing.*

See physick beg the Stagyrite's defence!
See *metaphysick* call for aid on sense! *Pope's Dunciad.*

The topicks of ontology or *metaphysick*, are cause, effect, action, passion, identity, opposition, subject, adjunct, and sign. *Watts's Logick.*

META'PHYSIS. *n. s.* [μετάφυσις.] Transformation; metamorphosis. *Dict.*

ME'TAPLASM. *n. s.* [μεταπλασμὸς.] A figure in rhetorick, wherein words or letters are transposed contrary to their natural order. *Dict.*

META'STASIS. *n. s.* [μετάστασις.] Translation or removal.

His disease was a dangerous asthma; the cause a *metastasis*, or translation of tartarous humours from his joints to his lungs. *Harvey on Consumptions.*

METATA'RSAL. *adj.* [from *metatarsus*.] Belonging to the metatarsus.

The bones of the toes, and part only of the *metatarsal* bones, may be carious; in which case cut off only so much of the foot as is disordered. *Sharp's Surgery.*

METATA'RSUS. *n. s.* [μέτα and ταρσὸς.] The middle of the foot, which is composed of five small bones connected to those of the first part of the foot. *Dict.*

The conjunction is called synarthrosis, as in the joining the tarsus to the *metatarsus*. *Wiseman's Surgery.*

META'THESIS. *n. s.* [μετάθεσις.] A transposition.

To METE. *v. a.* [*metior*, Latin.] To measure; to reduce to measure.

I will divide Shechem, and *mete* the valley of Succoth. *Psal.*

To measure any distance by a line, apply some known measure wherewith to *mete* it. *Holder.*

Though you many ways pursue
To find their length, you'll never *mete* the true,
But thus; take all that space the sun
Metes out, when every daily round is run. *Creech.*

ME'TEWAND. } *n. s.* [*mete* and *yard*, or *wand*.] A staff of a cer-
ME'TEYARD. } tain length wherewith measures are taken.

A true touchstone, a sure *metewand* lieth before their eyes. *Ascham's Schoolmaster.*

Ye shall do no unrighteousness in *meteyard*, weight, or measure. *Lev.* xix. 35.

To METEMPSYCHO'SE. *v. a.* [from *metempsychosis*.] To translate from body to body. A word not received.

The souls of usurers after their death, Lucian affirms to be *metempsychosed*, or translated into the bodies of asses, and there remain certain years, for poor men to take their pennyworth out of their bones. *Peacham on Blazoning.*

METEMPSYCHO'SIS. *n. s.* [μετεμψύχωσις.] The transmigration of souls from body to body.

From the opinion of *metempsychosis*, or transmigration of the souls of men into the bodies of beasts, most suitable unto their human condition, after his death Orpheus the musician became a swan. *Brown's Vulgar Errours, b.* iii.

ME'TEOR. *n. s.* [*meteore*, Fr. μετέωρα.] Any bodies in the air or sky that are of a flux and transitory nature.

Look'd

Look'd he or red, or pale, or ſad, or merrily?
What obſervation mad'ſt thou in this caſe,
Of his heart's *meteors* tilting in his face? *Shakeſpeare.*

She began to caſt with herſelf from what coaſt this blazing ſtar muſt riſe upon the horizon of Ireland; for there had the like *meteor* ſtrong influence before. *Bacon's Henry* VII.

These burning fits but *meteors* be,
Whoſe matter in thee ſoon is ſpent:
Thy beauty, and all parts which are in thee,
Are an unchangeable firmament. *Donne.*

Then flaming *meteors*, hung in air, were ſeen,
And thunders rattled through a ſky ſerene. *Dryden's Æn.*

Why was I rais'd the *meteor* of the world,
Hung in the ſkies, and blazing as I travell'd,
Till all my fires were ſpent; and then caſt downward
To be trod out by Cæſar? *Dryden's All for Love.*

O poet, thou hadſt been diſcreeter,
Hanging the monarch's hat ſo high,
If thou hadſt dubb'd thy ſtar a *meteor*,
Which did but blaze, and rove, and die. *Prior.*

METEOROLO'GICAL. *adj.* [from *meteorology.*] Relating to the doctrine of meteors.

Many others are conſiderable in *meteorological* divinity. *Brown's Vulgar Errours, b.* vii.

Make diſquiſition whether theſe unuſual lights be new-come gueſts, or old inhabitants in heaven, or *meteorological* impreſſions not tranſcending the upper region, or whether to be ranked among celeſtial bodies. *Howel's Vocal Foreſt.*

METEORO'LOGIST. *n. ſ.* [from *meteorology.*] A man ſkilled in meteors, or ſtudious of them.

The *meteorologiſts* obſerve, that amongſt the four elements which are the ingredients of all ſublunary creatures, there is a notable correſpondency. *Howel's Vocal Foreſt.*

METEORO'LOGY. *n. ſ.* [μετέωρα and λέγω.] The doctrine of meteors.

In animals we deny not a natural *meteorology*, or innate preſentation of wind and weather *Brown's Vulgar Errours.*

METE'OROUS. *adj.* [from *meteor.*] Having the nature of a meteor.

From the o'er hill
To their fixt ſtation, all in bright array,
The cherubim deſcended, on the ground
Gliding *meteorous*, as ev'ning miſt,
Ris'n from a river. *Milton's Par. Loſt, b.* xii.

ME'TER. *n. ſ.* [from *mete.*] A meaſurer: as, a coal-*meter*, a land-*meter*.

METHE'GLIN. *n. ſ.* [*meddyglyn*, Welſh, from *medd* and *glyn*, glutinare ait Minſhew, vel a medclyg medicus & llyn potus quia potus medicinalis.] Drink made of honey boiled with water and fermented.

White handed miſtreſs, one ſweet word with thee.
—Honey, and milk, and ſugar, there is three.
—Nay then two treys; and if you grow ſo nice,
Metheglin, wort, and malmſey. *Shakeſpeare.*

T' allay the ſtrength and hardneſs of the wine,
And with old Bacchus new *metheglin* join. *Dryden.*

ME'THINKS, verb imperſonal. [*me* and *thinks.* This is imagined to be a Norman corruption, the French being apt to confound *me* and *I.*] I think; it ſeems to me; meſeems. See MESEEMS, which is more ſtrictly grammatical, though leſs in uſe. *Methinks* was uſed even by thoſe who uſed likewiſe *meſeems.*

In all ages poets have been had in ſpecial reputation, and, *methinks*, not without great cauſe; for, beſides their ſweet inventions, and moſt witty lays, they have always uſed to ſet forth the praiſes of the good and virtuous. *Spenſer on Ireland.*

If he chooſe out ſome expreſſion which does not vitiate the ſenſe, I ſuppoſe he may ſtretch his chain to ſuch a latitude; but by innovation of thoughts, *methinks*, he breaks it. *Dryd.*

There is another circumſtance, which, *methinks*, gives us a very high idea of the nature of the ſoul, in regard to what paſſes in dreams, that innumerable multitude and variety of ideas which then ariſe in her. *Addiſon's Spect.* N°. 487.

Methinks already I your tears ſurvey. *Pope.*

ME'THOD. *n. ſ.* [*methode*, Fr. μέθοδος.]

Method, taken in the largeſt ſenſe, implies the placing of ſeveral things, or performing ſeveral operations in ſuch an order as is moſt convenient to attain ſome end. *Watts.*

To ſee wherein the harm which they feel conſiſteth, the ſeeds from which it ſprang, and the *method* of curing it, belongeth to a ſkill the ſtudy whereof is full of toil, and the practice beſet with difficulties. *Hooker, b.* v.

If you will jeſt with me know my aſpect,
And faſhion your demeanour to my looks,
Or I will beat this *method* in your ſconce. *Shakeſpeare.*

It will be in vain to talk to you concerning the *method* I think beſt to be obſerved in ſchools. *Locke on Education.*

Notwithſtanding a faculty be born with us, there are ſeveral *methods* for cultivating and improving it, and without which it will be very uncertain. *Addiſon's Spect.* N°. 409.

METHO'DICAL. *adj.* [*methodique*, Fr. from *method.*] Ranged or proceeding in due or juſt order.

The obſervations follow one another without that *methodical* regularity requiſite in a proſe author. *Addiſon's Spect.*

He can take a body to pieces, and diſpoſe of them where he pleaſes; to us, perhaps, not without the appearance of irretrievable confuſion; but, with reſpect to his own knowlege, into the moſt regular and *methodical* repoſitories. *Rogers.*

Let me appear, great Sir, I pray,
Methodical in what I ſay. *Addiſon's Roſamon.*

METHO'DICALLY. *adv.* [from *methodical.*] According to method and order.

All the rules of painting are *methodically*, conciſely, and clearly delivered in this treatiſe. *Dryden's Dufreſnoy.*

To begin *methodically*, I ſhould enjoin you travel; for abſence doth remove the cauſe, removing the object. *Suckling.*

To ME'THODISE. *v. a.* [from *method.*] To regulate; to diſpoſe in order.

Reſolv'd his unripe vengeance to defer,
The royal ſpy retir'd unſeen,
To brood in ſecret on his gather'd ſpleen,
And *methodize* revenge. *Dryden's Boccace.*

The man who does not know how to *methodiſe* his thoughts, has always a barren ſuperfluity of words; the fruit is loſt amidſt the exuberance of leaves. *Spectator*, N°. 476.

One who brings with him any obſervations which he has made in his reading of the poets, will find his own reflections *methodized* and explained, in the works of a good critick. *Addiſon's Spect.* N°. 291.

Thoſe rules of old diſcover'd, not deviſ'd,
Are nature ſtill, but nature *methodiſ'd.* *Pope.*

ME'THODIST. *n. ſ.* [from *method.*]

1. A phyſician who practiſes by theory.

Our warieſt phyſicians, not only chemiſts but *methodiſts*, give it inwardly in ſeveral conſtitutions and diſtempers. *Boyle.*

2. One of a new kind of puritans lately ariſen, ſo called from their profeſſion to live by rules and in conſtant method.

METHO'UGHT, the preterite of *methinks.* See METHINKS and MESEEMS. I thought; it appeared to me. I know not that any author has *meſeemed*, though it is more grammatical, and deduced analogically from *meſeems.*

Methought, a ſerpent eat my heart away,
And you ſat ſmiling at his cruel prey. *Shakeſpeare.*

Since I ſought
By pray'r th' offended deity t' appeaſe;
Kneel'd, and before him humbl'd all my heart,
Methought, I ſaw him placable, and mild,
Bending his ear: perſuaſion in me grew
That I was heard with favour; peace return'd
Home to my breaſt; and to my memory
His promiſe, "That thy ſeed ſhall bruiſe our foe." *Milt.*

In theſe
I found not what, *methought*, I wanted ſtill. *Milton.*

Methought I ſtood on a wide river's bank,
Which I muſt needs o'erpaſs, but knew not how. *Dryden.*

METONY'MICAL. *adj.* [from *metonymy.*] Put by metonymy for ſomething elſe.

METONY'MICALLY. *adv.* [from *metonymical.*] By metonymy; not literally.

The diſpoſition of the coloured body, as that modifies the light, may be called by the name of a colour *metonymically*, or efficiently; that is, in regard of its turning the light that rebounds from it, or paſſes through it, into this or that particular colour. *Boyle on Colours.*

METO'NYMY. *n. ſ.* [*metonymie*, Fr. μετωνυμία.] A rhetorical figure, by which one word is put for another, as the matter for the materiate; *he died by ſteel*, that is, by a ſword.

They differ only as cauſe and effect, which by a *metonymy* uſual in all ſorts of authors, are frequently put one for another. *Tillotſon.*

METOPO'SCOPY. *n. ſ.* [*metopoſcopie*, Fr. μέτωπον and σκεπτω.] The ſtudy of phyſiognomy; the art of knowing the characters of men by the countenance.

ME'TRE. *n. ſ.* [*metrum*, Latin; μέτρον.] Speech confined to a certain number and harmonick diſpoſition of ſyllables; verſe; meaſure; numbers.

For the *metre* ſake, ſome words be driven awry which require a ſtraighter placing in plain proſe. *Aſcham's Schoolmaſter.*

He taught his Romans in much better *metre*,
To laugh at fools. *Pope.*

ME'TRICAL. *adj.* [*metricus*, Latin; *metrique*, Fr.] Pertaining to metre or numbers.

METRO'POLIS. *n. ſ.* [*metropolis*, Latin; *metropole*, French; μήτηρ and πόλις.] The mother city; the chief city of any country or diſtrict.

His eye diſcovers unaware
The goodly proſpect of ſome foreign land,
Firſt ſeen: or ſome renown'd *metropolis*,
With gliſtering ſpires and pinnacles adorn'd. *Milton.*

Reduc'd in careful watch
Round their *metropolis.* *Milton's Par. Loſt, b.* x.

We ſtopped at Pavia, that was once the *metropolis* of a kingdom, but at preſent a poor town. *Addiſon on Italy.*

METROPO'LITAN.

Metropo'litan. *n. s.* [*metropolitanus*, Latin.] A bishop of the mother church; an archbishop.

He was promoted to Canterbury upon the death of Dr. Bancroft, that *metropolitan*, who understood the church excellently, and countenanced men of the greatest parts in learning. *Clarendon.*

Metropo'litan. *adj.* Belonging to a metropolis.

Their patriarch, of a covetous desire to enrich himself, had forborn to institute *metropolitan* bishops. *Raleigh.*

Metropoli'tical. *adj.* [from *metropolis.*] Chief or principal of cities.

He fearing the power of the Christians was gone as far as Gratia, the *metropolitical* city of Stiria. *Knolles.*

METTLE. *n. s.* [corrupted from *metal*, but commonly written so when the metaphorical sense is used.]

1. Spirit; spritelinefs; courage.

What a blunt fellow is this grown to be?
He was quick *mettle* when he went to school. *Shakespeare.*

I had rather go with sir priest than sir knight: I care not who knows so much of my *mettle*. *Shakesp. Twelfth Night.*

Upon this heaviness of the king's forces, interpreted to be fear and want of *mettle*, divers resorted to the seditious. *Hayward's Edw.* VI.

He had given so frequent testimony of signal courage in several actions, that his *mettle* was never suspected. *Clarendon.*

'Tis more to guide than spur the muse's steed,
Restrain his fury, than provoke his speed;
The winged courser, like a gen'rous horse,
Shows most true *mettle* when you check his course. *Pope.*

2. Substance: this at least should be *metal.*

Oh thou! whose self-same *mettle*,
Whereof thy proud child, arrogant man, is puft,
Engenders the black toad, and adder blue. *Shakespeare.*

Me'ttled. *adj.* [from *mettle.*] Spritely; courageous; full of ardour; full of fire.

Such a light and *metall'd* dance
Saw you never. *Benj. Johnson.*

Nor would you find it easy to compose
The *mettled* steeds, when from their nostrils flows
The scorching fire that in their entrails glows. *Addison.*

Me'ttlesome. *adj.* [from *mettle.*] Spritely; lively; gay; brisk; airy; fiery; courageous.

Their force differs from true spirit, as much as a vicious from a *mettlesome* horse. *Tatler*, N°. 61.

Me'ttlesomely. *adv.* [from *mettlesome.*] With spritelinefs.

Mew. *n. s.* [*mue*, French.]

1. A cage; an inclosure; a place where any thing is confined.

Forth-coming from her darksom *mew*,
Where she all day did hide her hated hew. *Fairy Queen.*

There then she does transform to monstruous hues,
And horribly mis-shapes with ugly sights,
Captiv'd eternally in iron *mews*,
And darksom dens, where Titan his face never shews. *Fairy Queen, b.* ii.

Her lofty hand would of itself refuse
To touch the dainty needle or nice thread;
She hated chambers, closets, secret *mews*,
And in broad fields preserv'd her maidenhead. *Fairfax.*

2. [Mæp, Saxon.] A sea-fowl.

Among the first sort we reckon coots, sanderlings, and *meawes*. *Carew.*

The vessel sticks, and shews her open'd side,
And on her shatter'd mast the *mews* in triumph ride. *Dryd.*

To Mew. *v. a.* [from the noun.]

1. To shut up; to confine; to imprison; to inclose.

He in dark corners *mew'd*,
Mutter'd of matters as their books them shew'd. *Hubberd.*

Unto the bush her eye did sudden glance,
In which vain Braggadocio was *mewed*,
And saw it stir. *Fairy Queen, b.* ii.

Why should your fears, which, as they say, attend
The steps of wrong, then move you to *mew* up
Your tender kinsman. *Shakesp. King John.*

Fair Hermia, question your desires;
Know of your youth, examine well your blood,
Whether if you yield not to your father's choice,
You can endure the livery of a nun;
For aye to be in shady cloister *mew'd*,
To live a barren sister all your life,
Chanting faint hymns to the cold, fruitless moon. *Shakesp.*

More pity that the eagle should be *mew'd*,
While kites and buzzards prey at liberty. *Shakespeare.*

Feign them sick,
Close *mew'd* in their sedans, for fear of air. *Dryden's Juv.*

It is not possible to keep a young gentleman from vice by a total ignorance of it, unless you will all his life *mew* him up in a closet, and never let him go into company. *Locke.*

2. To shed the feathers. It is, I believe, used in this sense, because birds are, by close confinement, brought to shed their feathers.

I should discourse of hawks, and then treat of their ayries, *mewings*, cutting, and renovation of their feathers. *Walton.*

The sun hath *mew'd* his beams from off his lamp,
And majesty defac'd the royal stamp. *Cleaveland.*

Nine times the moon had *mew'd* her horns, at length
With travel weary, unsupply'd with strength,
And with the burden of her womb opprest,
Sabean fields afford her needful rest. *Dryden.*

3. [*Miauler*, French.] To cry as a cat.

Let Hercules himself do what he may,
The cat will *mew*, the dog will have his day. *Shakesp.*

They are not improveable beyond their own genius: a dog will never learn to *mew*, nor a cat to bark. *Grew's Cos.*

To Mewl. *v. n.* [*miauler*, French.] To squall as a child.

The infant
Mewling and puking in the nurse's arms. *Shakespeare.*

Meze'reon. *n. s.* A species of spurge lawrel.

Mezereon is common in our gardens, and on the Alps and Pyrenean mountains: every part of this shrub is acrid and pungent, and inflames the mouth and throat. *Hill.*

MEZZOTINTO. *n. s.* [Italian.] A kind of graving, so named as nearly resembling paint, the word importing half-painted: it is done by beating the whole into asperity with a hammer, and then rubbing it down with a stone to the resemblance intended.

Meynt. *adv.* Mingled. Obsolete.

The salt Medway, that trickling streams
Adown the dales of Kent,
Till with the elder brother Thames
His brackish waves be *meynt*. *Spenser's Pastorals.*

Mi'asm. *n. s.* [from μιαίνω, inquino, to infect.] Such particles or atoms as are supposed to arise from distempered, putrefying, or poisonous bodies, and to affect people at a distance.

The plague is a malignant fever, caused through pestilential *miasms* insinuating into the humoral and consistent parts of the body. *Harvey on Consumptions.*

Mice, the plural of *mouse.*

Mice that mar the land. 1 *Sam.* vi. 5.

Micha'elmass. *n. s.* [*Michael* and *mass.*] The feast of the archangel *Michael*, celebrated on the twenty-ninth of September.

They compounded to furnish ten oxen after *Michaelmass* for thirty pounds price. *Carew.*

To MICHE. *v. n.* To be secret or covered; to lie hid. *Hanmer.*

Marry this is *miching* malken; it means mischief. *Shak.*

Mi'cher. *n. s.* [from *miche.*] A lazy loiterer, who skulks about in corners and by-places, and keeps out of sight; a hedge-creeper. *Hanmer.*

Mich or *Mick* is still retained in the cant language for an indolent, lazy fellow.

How tenderly her tender hands between
In ivory cage she did the *micher* bind. *Sidney.*

Shall the blessed sun of heav'n prove a *micher*, and eat blackberries? a question not to be asked. Shall the son of England prove a thief, and take purses? a question to be asked. *Shakespeare's Henry* IV, *p.* i.

Mi'ckle. *adj.* [micel, Saxon.] Much; great. Obsolete. In Scotland it is pronounced *muckle.*

This reade is rife that oftentime
Great cumbers fall unsoft:
In humble dales is footing fast,
The trode is not so tickle,
And though one fall through heedless haste,
Yet is his miss not *mickle*. *Spenser's Pastorals.*

Many a little makes a *mickle*. *Camden's Remains.*

If I to-day die with Frenchmens rage,
To-morrow I shall die with *mickle* age *Shakesp. Henry* VI.

O, *mickle* is the pow'rful grace, that lies
In plants, herbs, stones, and their true qualities. *Shakesp.*

All this tract that fronts the falling sun,
A noble peer, of *mickle* trust and power,
Has in his charge. *Milton.*

Microco'sm. *n. s.* [μίκρος and κόσμος.] The little world. Man is so called as being imagined, by some fanciful philosophers, to have in him something analogous to the four elements.

You see this in the map of my *microcosm*. *Shak. Coriolanus.*

She to whom this world must itself refer,
As suburbs, or the *microcosm* of her;
She, she is dead; she's dead, when thou know'st this,
Thou know'st how lame a creeple this world is. *Donne.*

As in this our *microcosm*, the heart
Heat, spirit, motions gives to every part:
So Rome's victorious influence did disperse
All her own virtues through the universe. *Denham.*

Philosophers say, that man is a *microcosm*, or little world, resembling in miniature every part of the great; and the body natural may be compared to the body politick. *Swift.*

Mi'crography. *n. s.* [μικρὸς and γράφω.] The description of the parts of such very small objects as are discernable only with a microscope.

The

The honey-bag is the ſtomach, which they always fill to ſatisfy and to ſpare, vomiting up the greater part of the honey to be kept againſt winter: a curious deſcription and figure of the ſting ſee in Mr. Hook's *micrography*. *Grew's Muſæum.*

MI'CROSCOPE. *n. ſ.* [μίκρος and σκοπέω; *microſcope*, Fr.] An optick inſtrument, contrived various ways to give to the eye a large appearance of many objects which could not otherwiſe be ſeen.

If the eye were ſo acute as to rival the fineſt *microſcopes*, and to diſcern the ſmalleſt hair upon the leg of a gnat, it would be a curſe, and not a bleſſing, to us; it would make all things appear rugged and deformed; the moſt finely poliſhed cryſtal would be uneven and rough; the ſight of our own ſelves would affright us; the ſmootheſt ſkin would be beſet all over with ragged ſcales and briſtly hairs. *Bentley.*

The critick eye, that *microſcope* of wit,
Sees hairs and pores, examines bit by bit. *Dunciad, b.* iv.

MICRO'METER. *n. ſ.* [μίκρος and μέτρον; *micrometre*, French.] An inſtrument contrived to meaſure ſmall ſpaces.

MICROSCO'PICAL. } *n. ſ.* [from *microſcope*.]
MICROSCO'PICK. }

1. Made by a microſcope.

Make *microſcopical* obſervations of the figure and bulk of the conſtituent parts of all fluids. *Arbuthnot and Pope.*

2. Aſſiſted by a microſcope.

Evading even the *microſcopic* eye!
Full nature ſwarms with life. *Thomſon's Summer.*

3. Reſembling a miſcroſcope.

Why has not man a *microſcopick* eye?
For this plain reaſon, Man is not a fly.
Say what the uſe, were finer opticks given,
T' inſpect a mite, not comprehend the heav'n? *Pope.*

MID. *adj.* [contracted from *middle*, or derived from *mid*, Dutch.]

1. Middle; equally between two extremes.

No more the mounting larks, while Daphne ſings,
Shall, lifting in *mid* air, ſuſpend their wings. *Pope.*
Ere the *mid* hour of night, from tent to tent,
Unweary'd, through th' num'rous hoſt he paſt. *Rowe.*

2. It is much uſed in compoſition.

MID-COURSE. *n. ſ.* [*mid* and *courſe*.] Middle of the way.

Why in the Eaſt
Darkneſs ere day's *mid-courſe?* and morning light,
More orient in yon weſtern cloud, that draws
O'er the blue firmament a radiant white. *Milton.*

MID-DAY. *n. ſ.* [*mid* and *day*.] Noon; meridian.

Who ſhoots at the *mid-day* ſun, though he be ſure he ſhall never hit the mark, yet as ſure he is he ſhall ſhoot higher than he who aims but at a buſh. *Sidney, b.* ii.

His ſparkling eyes, replete with awful fire,
More dazzled and drove back his enemies,
Than *mid-day* ſun fierce bent againſt their faces. *Shakeſp.*
Who have before, or ſhall write after thee,
Their works, though toughly laboured, will be
Like infancy or age to man's firm ſtay,
Or early or late twilights to *mid-day.* *Donne.*
Did he not lead you through the *mid-day* ſun,
And clouds of duſt? Did not his temples glow
In the ſame ſultry winds and ſcorching heats? *Addiſon.*

MI'DDEST, ſuperl. of *mid*, *middeſt*, *midſt*.]

Yet the ſtout fairy 'mongſt the *middeſt* crowd,
Thought all their glory vain in knightly view. *Fa. Qu.*

MI'DDLE. *adj.* [middle, Saxon.]

1. Equally diſtant from the two extremes.

The loweſt virtues draw praiſe from the common people; the *middle* virtues work in them aſtoniſhment; but of the higheſt virtues they have no ſenſe. *Bacon's Eſſays.*

A *middle* ſtation of life, within reach of thoſe conveniencies which the lower orders of mankind muſt neceſſarily want, and yet without embarraſſment of greatneſs. *Rogers.*

To deliver all his fleet to the Romans, except ten *middle-ſized* brigantines. *Arbuthnot on Coins.*

I like people of *middle* underſtanding and *middle* rank. *Sw.*

2. Intermediate; intervening.

Will, ſeeking good, finds many *middle* ends. *Davies.*

3. Middle finger; the long finger.

You firſt introduce the *middle* finger of the left-hand. *Sharp.*

MI'DDLE. *n. ſ.*

1. Part equally diſtant from two extremities; the part remote from the verge.

There come people down by the *middle* of the land. *Judg.*
With roof ſo low that under it
They never ſtand, but lie or ſit;
And yet ſo foul, that whoſo is in,
Is to the *middle* leg in priſon. *Hudibras, p.* i.

2. The time that paſſes, or events that happen, between the beginning and end.

The cauſes and deſigns of an action are the beginning; the effects of theſe cauſes, and the difficulties that are met with in the execution of theſe deſigns, are the *middle*; and the unravelling and reſolution of theſe difficulties are the end. *Dryden and Lee's Oedipus.*

MIDDLE-AGED. *adj.* [*middle* and *age*.] Placed about the middle of life.

A *middle-aged* man, that was half grey, half brown, took a fancy to marry two wives. *L'Eſtrange's Fables.*

The *middle-aged* ſupport faſting the beſt, becauſe of the oily parts abounding in the blood. *Arbuthnot on Aliments.*

I found you a very young man, and left you a *middle-aged* one: you knew me a *middle-aged* man, and now I am an old one. *Swift to Pope.*

MI'DDLEMOST. *adj.* [from *middle*.] Being in the middle.

Why have not ſome beaſts more than four feet, ſuppoſe ſix, and the *middlemoſt* ſhorter than the reſt. *More.*

The outmoſt fringe vaniſhed firſt, and the *middlemoſt* next, and the innermoſt laſt. *Newton's Opticks.*

The outward ſtars, with their ſyſtems of planets, muſt neceſſarily have deſcended toward the *middlemoſt* ſyſtem of the univerſe, whither all would be moſt ſtrongly attracted from all parts of a finite ſpace. *Bentley's Sermons.*

MI'DDLING. *adj.* [from *middle*.]

1. Of middle rank.

A *middling* ſort of a man, left well enough to paſs by his father, could never think he had enough ſo long as any man had more. *L'Eſtrange's Fables.*

2. Of moderate ſize; having moderate qualities of any kind.

The bigneſs of a church ought to be no greater than that unto which the voice of a preacher of *middling* lungs will eaſily extend. *Graunt's Bills of Mortality.*

Longinus preferred the ſublime genius that ſometimes errs, to the *middling* or indifferent one, which makes few faults, but ſeldom riſes to any excellence. *Dryden.*

Middling his head, and prone to earth his view. *Tickell.*

MI'DLAND. *adj.* [*mid* and *land*.]

1. That which is remote from the coaſt.

The ſame name is given to the inlanders, or *midland* inhabitants of this iſland, by Cæſar. *Brown's Vulgar Errours.*

The *midland* towns abounding in wealth, ſhews that her riches are intern and domeſtick. *Howel's Vocal Foreſt.*

The various dialects of the Engliſh in the North and Weſt, render their expreſſions many times unintelligible to the other, and both ſcarce intelligible to the *midland*. *Hale.*

2. In the midſt of the land; mediterranean.

There was the Plymouth ſquadron now come in,
Which twice on Biſcay's working bay had been,
And on the *midland* ſea the French had aw'd. *Dryden.*

MIDGE. *n. ſ.* [mieʒe, Saxon.] A gnat.

MID-HEAVEN. *n. ſ.* [*mid* and *heaven*.] The middle of the ſky.

But the hot hell that always in him burns,
Though in *mid-heaven*, ſoon ended his delight. *Milton.*

MI'DLEG. *n. ſ.* [*mid* and *leg*.] Middle of the leg.

He had fifty attendants, young men all, in white ſatten, looſe coats to the *midleg*, and ſtockings of white ſilk. *Bacon.*

MI'DMOST. *adj.* [from *mid*, or contracted from *middlemoſt*: this is one of the words which have not a comparative, though they ſeem to have a ſuperlative degree.] The middle.

Now van to van the foremoſt ſquadrons meet,
The *midmoſt* battles haſting up behind. *Dryden.*
Hear himſelf repine
At fate's unequal laws; and at the clue,
Which, mercileſs in length, the *midmoſt* ſiſter drew. *Dry.*
What dulneſs dropt among her ſons impreſt,
Like motion, from one circle to the reſt:
So from the *midmoſt* the nutation ſpreads
Round, and more round o'er all the ſea of heads. *Pope.*

MI'DNIGHT. *n. ſ.* [*mid* and *night*. *Milton* ſeems to have accented this laſt ſyllable.] The noon of night; the depth of night; twelve at night.

To be up after *midnight*, and to go to bed then, is early; ſo that to go to bed after *midnight*, is to go to bed betimes. *Shakeſpeare's Twelfth Night.*

How now, you ſecret, black and *midnight* hags?
What is't you do? *Shakeſpeare's Macbeth.*

I hope my *midnight* ſtudies, to make our countries flouriſh in myſterious and beneficent arts, have not ungratefully affected your intellects. *Bacon.*

By night he fled, and at *midnight* returned
From compaſſing the earth; cautious of day. *Milton.*

After this time came on the *midnight* of the church, wherein the very names of the councils were forgotten, and men did only dream of what had paſt. *Stillingfleet.*

Some ſolitary cloiſter will I chuſe,
Coarſe my attire, and ſhort ſhall be my ſleep,
Broke by the melancholy *midnight* bell. *Dryden's Sp. Fryar.*

In all that dark *midnight* of popery there were ſtill ſome gleams of light, ſome witneſſes that aroſe to give teſtimony to the truth. *Atterbury.*

They can tell preciſely what altitude the dog-ſtar had at *midnight* or midnoon in Rome when Julius Cæſar was ſlain. *Watts's Logick.*

MI'DRIFF. *n. ſ.* [midhrife, Saxon.] The diaphragm.

The *midriff* divides the trunk of the body into two cavities, the thorax and abdomen: it is compoſed of two muſcles; the

the first and superior of these arises from the sternum, and the ends of the last ribs on each side: its fibres, from this semicircular origination, tend towards their centre, and terminate in a tendon or aponeurosis, which hath always been taken for the nervous part of the *midriff*. The second and inferior muscle comes from the vertebræ of the loins by two productions, of which that on the right side comes from the first, second, and third vertebræ of the loins; that on the left side is somewhat shorter; and both these productions join and make the lower part of the *midriff*, which joins its tendons with the tendon of the other, so as that they make but one membrane, or rather partition. *Quincy.*

Whereat he inly rag'd, and as they talk'd,
Smote him into the *midriff* with a stone
That beat out life. *Milton's Par. Lost, b.* xi.

In the gullet, where it perforateth the *midriff*, the carneous fibres of that muscular part are inflected. *Ray.*

MID-SEA. *n. s.* [*mid* and *sea.*] The Mediterranean sea.

Our Tyrrhene Pharos, that the *mid-sea* meets
With its embrace, and leaves the land behind. *Dryden.*

MI'DSHIPMAN. *n. s.* [from *mid*, *ship*, and *man.*]

Midshipmen are officers aboard a ship, whose station, when they are on duty, is some on the quarter-deck, others on the poop, &c. Their business is to mind the braces, to look out, and to give about the word of command from the captain and other superior officers: they also assist on all occasions, both in sailing the ship, and in storing and rummaging the hold. They are usually young gentlemen, who having served their time as volunteers, are now upon their preferment. *Harris.*

MIDST. *n. s.* Middle.

All is well when nothing pleases but God, being thankful in the *midst* of his afflictions. *Taylor's Guide to Devotion.*

Arise, ye subtle spirits, that can spy
When love is enter'd in a female's eye;
You that can read it in the *midst* of doubt,
And in the *midst* of frowns can find it out. *Dryden.*

MIDST. *adj.* [contracted from *middest*, the superlative of *mid.*] Midmost; being in the middle.

On earth join all ye creatures to extol
Him first, Him last, Him *midst*, and without end. *Milton.*

In the Slighted Maid, there is nothing in the first act but what might have been said or done in the fifth; nor any thing in the *midst* which might not have been placed in the beginning. *Dryden's Dufresnoy.*

MIDSTRE'AM. *n. s.* [*mid* and *stream.*] Middle of the stream.

The *midstream's* his; I creeping by the side,
And shoulder'd off by his impetuous tide. *Dryden.*

MI'DSUMMER. *n. s.* [*mid* and *summer.*] The summer solstice, popularly reckoned to fall on June the twenty-fourth.

However orthodox my sentiments relating to publick affairs may be while I am now writing, they may become criminal enough to bring me into trouble before *Midsummer*. *Swift.*

At eve last *Midsummer* no sleep I sought. *Gay's Past.*

MI'DWAY. *n. s.* [*mid* and *way.*] The part of the way equally distant from the beginning and end.

No *midway* 'twixt these extremes at all. *Shakespeare.*

He were an excellent man that were made in the *midway* between him and Benedick; the one is too like an image, and says nothing; and the other too like my lady's eldest son, evermore tattling. *Shakesp. Much ado about nothing.*

Pity and shame! that they, who to live well
Stood so fair, should turn aside to tread
Paths indirect, or in the *midway* faint! *Milton's Par. Lost.*

The hare laid himself down about *midway*, and took a nap; for I can fetch up the tortoise when I please. *L'Estrange's Fables.*

How didst thou arrive at this place of darkness, when so many rivers of the ocean lie in the *midway*. *Broome's Notes on the Odyssey.*

MI'DWAY. *adj.* Middle between two places.

How fearful
And dizzy 'tis, to cast one's eyes so low!
The crows and choughs that wing the *midway* air,
Shew scarce so gross as beetles. *Shakespeare.*

MI'DWAY. *adv.* In the middle of the passage.

With dry eyes, and with an open look,
She met his glance *midway*. *Dryden's Boccace.*

MI'DWIFE. *n. s.* [This is derived, both by *Skinner* and *Junius*, from mið or *meed*, a reward, and pıf, Saxon.] A woman who assists women in childbirth.

When man doth die, our body, as the womb,
And as a *midwife*, death directs it home. *Donne.*

Without a *midwife* these their throws sustain,
And bowing, bring their issue forth with pain. *Sandys.*

There saw I how the secret felon wrought,
And treason lab'ring in the traitor's thought,
And *midwife* time the ripen'd plot to murder brought. *Dryden's Knight's Tale.*

I had as clear a notion of the relation of brothers between them, as if I had all the skill of a *midwife*. *Locke.*

But no man, sure! e'er left his house
And saddl'd ball with thoughts so wild,
To bring a *midwife* to his spouse,
Before he knew she was with child. *Prior.*

MI'DWIFERY. *n. s.* [from *midwife.*]

1. Assistance given at childbirth.
2. Act of production; help to production; co-operation in production.

So hasty fruits, and too ambitious flow'rs,
Scorning the *midwifry* of rip'ning show'rs,
In spight of frosts, spring from th' unwilling earth. *Stepney.*

There was never any thing propounded for publick good, that did not meet with opposition; arising from the humour of such as would have nothing brought into the world but by their own *midwifry*. *Child's Discourse on Trade.*

3. Trade of a midwife.

MI'DWINTER. *n. s.* [*mid* and *winter.*] The winter solstice.

Begin when the slow waggoner descends,
Nor cease your sowing till *Midwinter* ends. *Dryden.*

MIEN. *n. s.* [*mine*, French.] Air; look; manner.

In her alone that owns this book is seen
Clorinda's spirit, and her lofty *mien*. *Waller.*

What can have more the figure and *mien* of a ruin than craggs, rocks, and cliffs. *Burnet's Theory of the Earth.*

One, in whom an outward *mien* appear'd,
And turn superior to the vulgar herd. *Prior.*

What winning graces, what majestick *mien*,
She moves a goddess, and she looks a queen. *Pope.*

MIGHT, the preterite of *may*.

Matters of such consequence should be in plain words, as little liable as *might* be to doubt. *Locke.*

MIGHT. *n. s.* [mıȝht, Saxon.] Power; strength; force.

What so strong,
But wanting rest, will also want of *might*. *Spenser.*

Quoth she, great grief will not be told,
And can more easily be thought than said;
Right so, quoth he, but he that never would,
Could never; will to *might* gives greatest aid. *Fa. Qu.*

An oath of mickle *might*. *Shakesp. Henry* V.

Wherefore should not strength and *might*
There fail, where virtue fails. *Milton's Par. Lost, b.* vi.

With *might* and main they chac'd the murd'rous fox,
With brazen trumpets and inflated box. *Dryden.*

This privilege the clergy in England formerly contended for with all *might* and main. *Ayliffe's Parergon.*

MI'GHTILY. *adv.* [from *mighty.*]

1. With great power; powerfully; efficaciously; forcibly.

With whom ordinary means will prevail, surely the power of the word of God, even without the help of interpreters, in God's church worketh *mightily*, not unto their confirmation alone which are converted, but also to their conversion which are not. *Hooker, b.* v.

2. Vehemently; vigorously; violently.

Do as adversaries do in law, strive *mightily*, but eat and drink as friends. *Shakespeare.*

3. In a great degree; very much. This is a sense scarcely to be admitted but in low language.

Therein thou wrong'st thy children *mightily*. *Shakesp.*

There's ne'er a one of you but trusts a knave,
That *mightily* deceives you. *Shakesp. Titus Andronicus.*

An ass and an ape conferring grievances: the ass complained *mightily* for want of horns, and the ape for want of a tail. *L'Estrange's Fables.*

These happening nearer home made so lasting impressions upon their minds, that the tradition of the old deluge was *mightily* obscured, and the circumstances of it interwoven and confounded with those of these later deluges. *Woodward.*

I was *mightily* pleased with a story applicable to this piece of philosophy. *Spectator,* Nº. 578.

MI'GHTINESS. *n. s.* [from *mighty.*] Power; greatness; height of dignity.

Think you see them great,
And follow'd with gen'ral throng and sweat
Of thousand friends; then in a moment see,
How soon this *mightiness* meets misery! *Shak. Henry* VIII.

Will't please your *mightiness* to wash your hands? *Shak.*

MI'GHTY. *adj.* [from *might.*]

1. Powerful; strong.

Nimrod began to be a *mighty* one in the earth. *Gen.* x. 8.
Great is truth, and *mighty* above all things. 1 *Esd.* iv. 41.
He is wise in heart and *mighty* in strength. *Job* ii. 1.

2. Excellent, or powerful in any act.

The *mighty* master smil'd. *Dryden.*

MI'GHTY. *adv.* In a great degree. Not to be used but in very low language.

Lord of his new hypothesis he reigns:
He reigns; How long? Till some usurper rise,
And he too *mighty* thoughtful, *mighty* wise:
Studies new lines. *Prior.*

MIGRA'TION. *n. s.* [*migratio*, *migro*, Lat.] Act of changing place.

Aristotle

Ariſtotle diſtinguiſheth their times of generation, latitancy, and *migration*, ſanity, and venation. *Brown's Vulgar Errours.*

Although ſuch alterations, tranſitions, *migrations* of the centre of gravity, and elevations of new iſlands, had actually happened, yet theſe ſhells could never have been repoſed thereby in the manner we find them. *Woodward's Nat. Hiſt.*

MILCH. *adj.* [from *milk.*] Giving milk.

Herne doth, at ſtill of midnight,
Walk round about an oak, with ragged horns;
And then he blaſts the tree, and takes the cattle,
And makes *milch* kine yield blood. *Shakeſpeare.*

When ſhe ſaw Pyrrhus make malicious ſport,
In mincing with his ſword her huſband's limbs,
The inſtant burſt of clamour that ſhe made,
Would have made *milch* the burning eyes of heav'n. *Shak.*

The beſt mixtures of water in ponds for cattle, to make them more *milch*, fatten, or keep them from murrain, may be chalk and nitre. *Bacon's Nat. Hiſt.* N°. 778.

Not above fifty-one have been ſtarved, excepting infants at nurſe, cauſed rather by careleſſneſs and infirmity of the *milch* women. *Graunt's Bills of Mortality.*

With the turneps they feed ſheep, *milch*-cows, or fatting cattle. *Mortimer's Huſbandry.*

MILD. *adj.* [milde, Saxon.]

1. Kind; tender; good; indulgent; merciful; compaſſionate; clement; ſoft; not ſevere; not cruel.

The execution of juſtice is committed to his judges, which is the ſeverer part; but the *milder* part, which is mercy, is wholly left in the king. *Bacon's Advice to Villiers.*

If that *mild* and gentle god thou be,
Who doſt mankind below with pity ſee. *Dryden.*

It teaches us to adore him as a *mild* and merciful being, of infinite love to his creatures. *Rogers's Sermons.*

2. Soft; gentle; not violent.

The roſy morn reſigns her light,
And *milder* glory to the noon. *Waller.*

Nothing reſerv'd or ſullen was to ſee,
But ſweet regards, and pleaſing ſanctity;
Mild was his accent, and his action free. *Dryden.*

Sylvia's like autumn ripe, yet *mild* as May,
More bright than noon, yet freſh as early day. *Pope.*

The folding gates diffus'd a ſilver light,
And with a *milder* gleam refreſh'd the ſight. *Addiſon.*

3. Not acrid; not corroſive; not acrimonious; demulcent; aſſuaſive; mollifying; lenitive.

Their qualities are changed by rendering them acrimonious or *mild.* *Arbuthnot on Aliments.*

4. Not ſharp; mellow; ſweet; having no mixture of acidity.

The Iriſh were tranſplanted from the woods and mountains into the plains, that, like fruit trees, they might grow the *milder*, and bear the better and ſweeter fruit. *Davies.*

Suppoſe your eyes ſent equal rays
Upon two diſtant pots of ale,
Not knowing which was *mild* or ſtale. *Prior.*

MI'LDERNAX. *n. ſ.* Cannabum nauticum. *Ainſ.*

MI'LDEW. *n. ſ.* [milbeape, Saxon.]

Mildew is a diſeaſe that happens in plants, and is cauſed by a dewy moiſture which falls on them, and continuing, for want of the ſun's heat, to draw it up, by its acrimony corrodes, gnaws, and ſpoils, the inmoſt ſubſtance of the plant, and hinders the circulation of the nutritive ſap; upon which the leaves begin to fade, and the bloſſoms and fruit are much prejudiced: or, *mildew* is rather a concrete ſubſtance, which exſudes through the pores of the leaves. What the gardeners commonly call *mildew* is an inſect, which is frequently found in great plenty, preying upon this exſudation. Others ſay, that *mildew* is a thick, clammy vapour, exhaled in the Spring and Summer from the plants, bloſſoms, and even the earth itſelf, in cloſe, ſtill weather, where there is neither ſun enough to draw it upwards to any conſiderable height, nor wind of force ſtrong enough to diſperſe it: it condenſes and falls on plants, and with its thick, clammy ſubſtance ſtops the pores, and by that means prevents perſpiration. Miller thinks the true cauſe of the *mildew* appearing moſt upon plants which are expoſed to the Eaſt, is a dry temperature in the air when the wind blows from that point, which ſtops the pores of the plants, and prevents their perſpiration; whereby the juices of the plants are concreted upon the ſurface of their leaves, which being of a ſweetiſh nature, inſects are inticed thereto, where finding proper nutriment they depoſite their eggs, and multiply ſo faſt as to cover the whole ſurfaces of the plants, and, by corroding the veſſels, prevent the motion of the ſap. It is obſervable, that whenever a tree has been greatly affected by this *mildew*, it ſeldom recovers it in two or three years, and many times never is intirely clear from it after. *Hill.*

Down fell the *mildew* of his ſugred words. *Fairfax.*

The *mildew* cometh by cloſeneſs of air; and therefore in hills, or champain grounds, it ſeldom cometh. *Bacon.*

Soon blaſting *mildews* black'ned all the grain. *Dryden.*

To MI'LDEW. *v. a.* To taint with mildew.

Here is your huſband, like a *mildew'd* ear,
Blaſting his wholeſome brother. *Shakeſp. Hamlet.*

He *mildews* the white wheat, and hurts the poor creatures of the earth. *Shakeſp. King Lear.*

Morals ſnatch from Plutarch's tatter'd page,
A *mildew'd* Bacon, or Stagyra's ſage. *Gay's Trivia.*

MI'LDLY. *adv.* [from *mild.*]

1. Tenderly; not ſeverely.

Prince, too *mildly* reigning,
Ceaſe thy ſorrow and complaining. *Dryden.*

2. Gently; not violently.

The air once heated maketh the flame burn more *mildly*, and ſo helpeth the continuance. *Bacon's Nat. Hiſt.* N°. 375.

MI'LDNESS. *n. ſ.* [from *mild.*]

1. Gentleneſs; tenderneſs; mercy; clemency.

This milky gentleneſs and courſe of yours;
You are much more at taſk for want of wiſdom,
Than prais'd for harmful *mildneſs.* *Shakeſp. King Lear.*

The ſame majeſtick *mildneſs* held its place;
Nor loſt the monarch in his dying face. *Dryden.*

His probity and *mildneſs* ſhows
His care of friends and ſcorn of foes. *Addiſon.*

I ſaw with what a brow you brav'd your fate;
Yet with what *mildneſs* bore your father's hate. *Dryden.*

2. Contrariety to acrimony.

MILE. *n. ſ.* [*mille paſſus*, Latin.] The uſual meaſure of roads in England, one thouſand ſeven hundred and ſixty yards, or, five thouſand two hundred and eighty feet.

We muſt meaſure twenty *miles* to-day. *Shakeſpeare.*

Within this three *mile* may you ſee it coming,
A moving grove. *Shakeſpeare's Macbeth.*

When the enemy appeared, the foot and artillery was four *miles* behind. *Clarendon, b.* ii.

Millions of *miles*, ſo rapid is their race,
To cheer the earth they in few moments paſs. *Blackmore.*

MI'LESTONE. *n. ſ.* [*mile* and *ſtone.*] Stone ſet to mark the miles.

MI'LFOIL. *n. ſ.* [*millefolium*, Latin.] A plant, the ſame with yarrow.

Milfoil and honey-ſuckles pound,
With theſe alluring favours ſtrew the ground. *Dryden.*

MI'LIARY. *adj.* [*milium* millet, Latin; *miliaire*, Fr.] Small; reſembling a millet ſeed.

The ſcarf-ſkin is compoſed of ſmall ſcales, between which the excretory ducts of the *miliary* glands open. *Cheyne.*

MI'LIARY *fever.* A fever that produces ſmall eruptions.

MI'LICE. *n. ſ.* [French.] Standing force. A word innovated by *Temple*, but unworthy of reception.

The two-and-twentieth of the prince's age is the time aſſigned by their conſtitutions for his entering upon the publick charges of their *milice.* *Temple's Miſcel.*

MI'LITANT. *adj.* [*militans*, Latin; *militante*, Fr.]

1. Fighting; proſecuting the buſineſs of a ſoldier.

Againſt foul fiends they aid us *militant*;
They for us fight; they watch and duly ward,
And their bright ſquadrons round about us plant. *Fa. Q.*

2. Engaged in warfare with hell and the world. A term applied to the church of Chriſt on earth, as oppoſed to the church triumphant.

Then are the publick duties of religion beſt ordered, when the *militant* church doth reſemble, by ſenſible means, that hidden dignity and glory wherewith the church triumphant in heaven is beautified. *Hooker, b.* v.

The ſtate of a Chriſtian in this world is frequently compared to a warfare: and this alluſion has appeared ſo juſt, that the character of *militant* has obtained as the common diſtinction of that part of Chriſt's church ſojourning here in this world from that part of the family at reſt. *Rogers.*

MI'LITAR. } *adj.* [*militaris*, Latin; *militaire*, Fr. *Militar*
MI'LITARY. } is now wholly out of uſe.]

1. Engaged in the life of a ſoldier; ſoldierly.

In the time of Severus and Antoninus, many, being ſoldiers, had been converted unto Chriſt, and notwithſtanding continued ſtill in that *military* courſe of life. *Hooker, b.* ii.

He will maintain his argument as well as any *military* man in the world. *Shakeſp. Henry* V.

2. Suiting a ſoldier; pertaining to a ſoldier; warlike.

Although he were a prince in *militar* virtue approved, yet his cruelties weighed down his virtues. *Bacon's Henry* VII.

Numbers numberleſs
The city gates out-pour'd, light-armed troops
In coats of mail and *military* pride. *Milton's Par. Reg.*

The wreaths his grandſire knew to reap
By active toil, and *military* ſweat,
Pining incline their ſickly leaves. *Prior.*

3. Effected by ſoldiers.

He was with general applauſe, and great cries of joy, in a kind of *militar* election or recognition, ſaluted king. *Bacon.*

MILITIA.

MILITIA. *n. s.* [Latin.] The trainbands; the standing force of a nation.

Let any prince think soberly of his forces, except his *militia* be good and valiant soldiers. *Bacon's Essays*, N°. 30.

The *militia* was so settled by law, that a sudden army could be drawn together. *Clarendon.*

Unnumbered spirits round thee fly,
The light *militia* of the lower sky. *Pope's Rape of the Lock.*

MILK. *n. s.* [meelc, Saxon; *melck*, Dutch.]

1. The liquor with which animals feed their young from the breast.

Come to my woman's breasts,
And take my *milk* for gall, you murthering ministers!
Where-ever in your sightless substances
You wait on nature's mischief. *Shakesp. Macbeth.*

I fear thy nature,
It is too full o' th' *milk* of human kindness
To catch the nearest way. *Shakesp. King Lear.*

Milk is the occasion of many tumours of divers kinds. *Wiseman's Surgery.*

When *milk* is dry'd with heat,
In vain the milkmaid tugs an empty teat. *Dryden.*

I concluded, if the gout continued, to confine myself wholly to the *milk* diet. *Temple's Miscel.*

Broths and *milk*-meats are windy to stomachs troubled with acid ferments. *Floyer on the Humours.*

2. Emulsion made by contusion of seeds.

Pistachoes, so they be good and not musty, joined with almonds in almond *milk*, or made into a *milk* of themselves, like unto almond *milk*, are an excellent nourisher. *Bacon.*

To MILK. *v. a.* [from the noun.]

1. To draw milk from the breast by the hand.

Capacious chargers all around were laid
Full pails, and vessels of the *milking* trade. *Pope's Odyssey.*

2. To suck.

I have given suck, and know
How tender 'tis to love the babe that *milks* me. *Shakesp.*

MI'LKEN. *adj.* [from *milk.*] Consisting of milk.

The remedies are to be proposed from a constant course of the *milken* diet, continued at least a year. *Temple.*

MI'LKER. *n. s.* [from *milk.*] One that milks animals.

His kine with swelling udders ready stand,
And lowing for the pail invite the *milker*'s hand. *Dryden.*

MI'LKINESS. *n. s.* [from *milky.*] Softness like that of milk; approach to the nature of milk.

Would I could share thy balmy, even temper,
And *milkiness* of blood. *Dryden's Cleomenes.*

The saltness and oylinefs of the blood absorbing the acid of the chyle, it loses its *milkiness*. *Floyer on the Humours.*

MI'LKLIVERED. *adj.* [*milk* and *liver.*] Cowardly; timorous; faint-hearted.

Milklivered man!
That bear'st a cheek for blows, a head for wrongs. *Shak.*

MI'LKMAID. *n. s.* [*milk* and *maid.*] Woman employed in the dairy.

When milk is dry with heat,
In vain the *milkmaid* tugs an empty teat. *Dryden's Virg.*

A lovely *milkmaid* he began to regard with an eye of mercy. *Addison's Freeholder*, N°. 44.

MI'LKMAN. *n. s.* [*milk* and *man.*] A man who sells milk.

MI'LKPAIL. *n. s.* [*milk* and *pail.*] Vessel into which cows are milked.

That very substance which last week was grazing in the field, waving in the *milkpail*, or growing in the garden, is now become part of the man. *Watts's Impr. of the Mind.*

MI'LKPAN. *n. s.* [*milk* and *pan.*] Vessel in which milk is kept in the dairy.

Sir Fulke Grevil had much and private access to Queen Elizabeth, and did many men good; yet he would say merrily of himself, that he was like Robin Goodfellow; for when the maids spilt the *milkpans*, or kept any racket, they would lay it upon Robin: so what tales the ladies about the queen told her, or other bad offices that they did, they would put it upon him. *Bacon's Apophth.*

MILKPO'TTAGE. *n. s.* [*milk* and *pottage.*] Food made by boiling milk with water and oatmeal.

For breakfast and supper, milk and *milkpottage* are very fit for children. *Locke.*

MI'LKSCORE. *n. s.* [*milk* and *score.*] Account of milk owed for, scored on a board.

He ordered the lord high treasurer to pay off the debts of the crown, particularly a *milkscore* of three years standing. *Addison's Freeholder*, N . 36.

He is better acquainted with the *milkscore* than his steward's accounts. *Addison's Spect.* N°. 482.

MI'LKSOP. *n. s.* [*milk* and *sop.*] A soft, mild, effeminate, feeble-minded man.

Of a most notorious thief, which lived all his life-time of spoils, one of their bards in his praise will say, that he was none of the idle *milksops* that was brought up by the fire-side, but that most of his days he spent in arms, and that he did never eat his meat before he had won it with his sword. *Spenser on Ireland.*

A *milksop*, one that never in his life
Felt so much cold as over shoes in snow. *Shak. Rich.* III.

We have as good passions as yourself; and a woman was never designed to be a *milksop*. *Addison's Spect.*

But give him port and potent sack;
From *milksop* he starts up mohack. *Prior.*

MI'LKTOOTH. *n. s.* [*milk* and *tooth.*]

Milkteeth are those small teeth which come forth before when a foal is about three months old, and which he begins to cast about two years and a half after, in the same order as they grew. *Farrier's Dict.*

MI'LKTHISTLE. *n. s.* [*milk* and *thistle*: plants that have a white juice are named milky.] An herb.

MI'LKTREFOIL. *n. s.* An herb.

MI'LKVETCH. *n. s.* [*astragalus*, Latin.]

The *milkvetch* hath a papilionaceous flower, consisting of the standard, the keel, and the wings; out of the flower-cup arises the pointal covered with a sheath, which becomes a bicapsular pod filled with kidney-shaped seeds: the leaves grow by pairs along the middle rib, with an odd one at the end. *Miller.*

MI'LKWEED. *n. s.* [*milk* and *wood.*] A plant.

MI'LKWHITE. *adj.* [*milk* and *white.*] White as milk.

She a black silk cap on him begun
To set, for foil of his *milkwhite* to serve. *Sidney.*

Then will I raise aloft the *milkwhite* rose,
With whose sweet smell the air shall be perfum'd. *Shakesp.*

Where the bull and cow are both *milkwhite*,
They never do beget a cole-black calf. *Shakespeare.*

The bolt of Cupid fell,
It fell upon a little western flower;
Before *milkwhite*, now purple with love's wound;
And maidens call it love in idleness. *Shakespeare.*

A *milkwhite* goat for you I did provide;
Two *milkwhite* kids run frisking by her side. *Dryden.*

MI'LKWORT. *n. s.* [*milk* and *wort.*]

Milkwort is a bell-shaped flower, consisting of one leaf, whose brims are expanded, and cut into several segments; from the centre arises the pointal, which afterward becomes a round fruit or husk, opening from the top downwards, and filled with small seeds. *Miller.*

MI'LKWOMAN. *n. s.* [*milk* and *woman.*] A woman whose business is to serve families with milk.

Even your *milkwoman* and your nursery-maid have a fellow-feeling. *Arbuthnot's Hist. of John Bull.*

MI'LKY. *adj.* [from *milk.*]

1. Made of milk.

2. Resembling milk.

Not tasteful herbs that in these gardens rise,
Which the kind soil with *milky* sap supplies,
Can move the god. *Pope.*

Some plants upon breaking their vessels yield a *milky* juice. *Arbuthnot on Aliments.*

3. Yielding milk.

Perhaps my passion he disdains,
And courts the *milky* mothers of the plains. *Roscommon.*

4. Soft; gentle; tender; timorous.

Has friendship such a faint and *milky* heart,
It turns in less than two nights. *Shakespeare.*

This *milky* gentleness and course of yours,
You are much more at task for want of wisdom,
Than prais'd for harmful mildness. *Shakesp. King Lear.*

MILKY-WAY. *n. s.* [*milky* and *way.*] The galaxy.

The *milky-way*, or via lactea, is a broad white path or track, encompassing the whole heavens, and extending itself in some places with a double path, but for the most part with a single one. Some of the ancients, as Aristotle, imagined that this path consisted only of a certain exhalation hanging in the air; but, by the telescopical observations of this age, it hath been discovered to consist of an innumerable quantity of fixed stars, different in situation and magnitude, from the confused mixture of whose light its whole colour is supposed to be occasioned. It passes through the constellations of Cassiopeia, Cygnus, Aquila, Perseus, Andromeda, part of Ophiucus and Gemini, in the northern hemisphere; and in the southern it takes in part of Scorpio, Sagittarius, Centaurus, the Argo Navis and the Ara. The galaxy hath usually been the region in which new stars have appeared; as that in Cassiopeia, which was seen in A. D. 1572; that in the breast of the Swan, and another in the knee of Serpentarius; which have appeared for a while, and then become invisible again. *Harris.*

Nor need we with a prying eye survey
The distant skies to find the *milky-way*:
It forcibly intrudes upon our sight. *Creech's Manilius.*

How many stars there must be, a naked eye may give us some faint glimpse, but much more a good telescope, directed towards that region of the sky called the *milky-way*. *Cheyne.*

MILL. *n. s.* [μύλη; *mola*, Lat. *melin*, Welsh; myln, Saxon; *moulin*, Fr. *molen*, Dutch.] An engine or fabrick in which corn is ground to meal, or any other body is comminuted.

The table, and we about it, did all turn round by water which ran under, and carried it about as a *mill*. *Sidney.*

More water glideth by the *mill*
Than wots the miller of. *Shakesp. Titus Andronicus.*

Olives ground in *mills* their fatness boast. *Dryden.*

A miller had his arm and scapula torn from his body by a rope twisted round his wrist, and suddenly drawn up by the *mill*. *Sharp's Surgery.*

To MILL. *v. a.* [from the noun; μυλεῖν; *mila*, Islandick.]
1. To grind; to comminute.
2. To beat up chocolate.
3. To stamp coin in the mints.

It would be better for your *milled* medals, if they carried the whole legend on their edges; but at the same time that they are lettered on the edges, they have other inscriptions on the face and the reverse. *Addison.*

Wood's halfpence are not *milled*, and therefore more easily counterfeited. *Swift.*

MI'LL-COG. *n. s.* [*mill* and *cog*.] The denticulations on the circumference of wheels, by which they lock into other wheels.

The timber is useful for *mill-cogs*. *Mortimer's Husbandry.*

MI'LL-DAM. *n. s.* [*mill* and *dam*.] The mound, by which the water is kept up to raise it for the mill.

A layer of lime and of earth is a great advantage in the making heads of ponds and *mill-dams*. *Mortimer.*

MI'LL-HORSE. *n. s.* Horse that turns a mill.

His impressa was a *mill-horse*, still bound to go in one circle. *Sidney, b.* ii.

MILLMO'UNTAINS. *n. s.* An herb. *Ainf.*

MI'LL-TEETH. *n. s.* [*mill* and *teeth*.] The grinders; *dentes molares*, double teeth.

The best instruments for cracking bones and nuts are grinders or *mill-teeth*. *Arbuthnot on Aliments.*

MILLENA'RIAN. *n. s.* [from *millenarius*, Lat. *millenaire*, Fr.] One who expects the millennium.

MI'LLENARY. *adj.* [*millenaire*, Fr. *millenarius*, Latin.] Consisting of a thousand.

The *millenary* sestertium, in good manuscripts, is marked with a line cross the top thus HS. *Arbuthnot on Coins.*

MI'LLENIST. *n. s.* [from *mille*, Lat.] One that holds the millennium.

MILLE'NNIUM. *n. s.* [Latin.] A thousand years; generally taken for the thousand years, during which, according to an ancient tradition in the church, grounded on a doubtful text in the Apocalypse, our blessed Saviour shall reign with the faithful upon earth after the resurrection, before the final completion of beatitude.

We must give a full account of that state called the *millennium*. *Burnet's Theory of the Earth.*

MILLE'NNIAL. *adj.* [from *millennium*, Lat.] Pertaining to the millennium.

To be kings and priests unto God, is the characteristick of those that are to enjoy the *millennial* happiness. *Burnet.*

MI'LLEPEDES. *n. s.* [*millepieds*, French; *mille* and *pes*, Latin.] Wood-lice, so called from their numerous feet.

If pheasants and partridge are sick give them *millepedes* and earwigs, which will cure them. *Mortimer's Husbandry.*

MI'LLER. *n. s.* [from *mill*.] One who attends a mill.

More water glideth by the mill
Than wots the *miller* of. *Shakespeare.*

Gillius, who made enquiry of *millers* who dwelt upon its shore, received answer, that the Euripus ebbed and flowed four times a day. *Brown's Vulgar Errours, b.* vii.

MI'LLER. *n. s.* A fly. *Ainf.*

MILLER'S-THUMB. *n. s.* [*miller* and *thumb*.] A small fish found in brooks, called likewise a bulhead.

MILLE'SIMAL. *adj.* [*millesimus*, Latin.] Thousandth; consisting of thousandth parts.

To give the square root of the number two, he laboured long in *millesimal* fractions, till he confessed there was no end. *Watts's Improvement of the Mind.*

MI'LLET. *n. s.* [*milium*, Lat. *mil* and *millet*, Fr.]
1. A plant.

The *millet* hath a loose divided panicle, and each single flower hath a calyx, consisting of two leaves, which are instead of petals, to protect the stamina and pistillum of the flower, which afterwards becomes an oval, shining seed. This plant was originally brought from the eastern countries, where it is still greatly cultivated, from whence we are annually furnished with this grain, which is by many persons much esteemed for puddings. *Miller.*

In two ranks of cavities is placed a roundish studd, about the bigness of a grain of *millet*. *Woodward on Fossils.*

Millet is diarrhetick, cleansing, and useful, in diseases of the kidneys. *Arbuthnot on Aliments.*

2. A kind of fish.

Some fish are gutted, split, and kept in pickle; as whiting, mackerel, *millet*. *Carew's Survey of Cornwall.*

MI'LLINER. *n. s.* [I believe from *Milaner*, an inhabitant of Milan, as a Lombard is a banker.] One who sells ribands and dresses for women.

He was perfumed like a *milliner*;
And, 'twixt his finger and his thumb, he held
A pouncet box, which ever and anon
He gave his nose. *Shakesp. Henry IV. p.* i.

The mercers and *milliners* complain of her want of publick spirit. *Tatler,* N°. 52.

MI'LLION. *n. s.* [*million*, Fr. *milliogne*, Italian.]
1. The number of an hundred myriads, or ten hundred thousand.

Within thine eyes sat twenty thousand deaths,
In thy hands clutch'd as many *millions*, in
Thy lying tongue both numbers. *Shakespeare.*

2. A proverbial name for any very great number.

That the three angles of a triangle are equal to two right ones, is a truth more evident than many of those propositions that go for principles; and yet there are *millions* who know not this at all. *Locke.*

There are *millions* of truths that a man is not concerned to know. *Locke.*

She found the polish'd glass, whose small convex
Enlarges to ten *millions* of degrees
The mite, invisible else. *Philips.*

Midst thy own flock, great shepherd, be receiv'd;
And glad all heav'n with *millions* thou hast sav'd. *Prior.*

MI'LLIONTH. *adj.* [from *million*.] The ten hundred thousandth.

The first embrion of an ant is supposed to be as big as that of an elephant; which nevertheless can never arrive to the *millionth* part of the other's bulk. *Bentley's Sermons.*

MI'LLSTONE. *n. s.* [*mill* and *stone*.] The stone by which corn is comminuted.

No man shall take the nether or the upper *millstone* to pledge. *Deut.* xxiv. 6.

Æsop's beasts saw farther into a *millstone* than our mobile. *L'Estrange's Fables.*

MILT. *n. s.* [*mildt*, Dutch.]
1. The sperm of the male fish.

You shall scarce take a carp without a *melt*, or a female without a roe or spawn. *Walton's Angler.*

2. [Milt, Saxon.] The spleen.

To MILT. *v. a.* [from the noun.] To impregnate the roe or spawn of the female fish.

MILTER. *n. s.* [from *milt*.] The he of any fish, the she being called spawner.

The spawner and *milter* labour to cover their spawn with sand. *Walton's Angler.*

MI'LTWORT. *n. s.* An herb. *Ainf.*

MIME. *n. s.* [*mime*, Fr. μῖμος; *mimus*, Latin.] A buffoon who practises gesticulations, either representative of some action, or merely contrived to raise mirth.

Think'st thou, *mime*, this is great? *Benj. Johnson.*

To MIME. *v. n.* To play the mime.

Think'st thou, mime, this is great? or that they strive
Whose noise shall keep thy *miming* most alive,
Whilst thou dost raise some player from the grave,
Out-dance the babion, or out-boast the brave. *B. Johnson.*

MI'MER. *n. s.* [from *mime*.] A mimick; a buffoon.

Jugglers and dancers, anticks, mummers, *mimers*. *Milton's Samson Agonistes.*

MI'MICAL. *adj.* [*mimicus*, Latin.] Imitative; befitting a mimick; acting the mimick.

Man is of all creatures the most *mimical* in gestures, styles, speech, fashion, or accents. *Wotton on Education.*

A *mimical* daw would needs try the same experiment; but his claws were shackled. *L'Estrange's Fables.*

Singers and dancers entertained the people with light songs and *mimical* gestures, that they might not go away melancholy from serious pieces of the theatre. *Dryden's Juvenal.*

MI'MICALLY. *adv.* [from *mimical*.] In imitation; in a mimical manner.

MI'MICK. *n. s.* [*mimicus*, Latin.]
1. A ludicrous imitator; a buffoon who copies another's act or manner so as to excite laughter.

Like poor Andrew I advance,
False *mimick* of my master's dance:
Around the cord a while I sprawl,
And thence, though slow, in earnest fall. *Prior.*

2. A mean or servile imitator.

Of France the *mimick*, and of Spain the prey. *Anon.*

MI'MICK. *adj.* [*mimicus*, Latin.] Imitative.

The busy head with *mimick* art runs o'er
The scenes and actions of the day before. *Swift's Miscel.*

To MI'MICK. *v. a.* [from the noun.] To imitate as a buffoon; to ridicule by a burlesque imitation.

Morpheus express'd
The shape of man, and imitated best;
The walk, the words, the gesture, could supply,
The habit *mimick*, and the mien belye. *Dryden.*

Who wou'd with care some happy fiction frame;
So *mimicks* truth, it looks the very same. *Granville.*

MI'MICKRY. *n. s.* [from *mimick.*] Burlesque imitation.

By an excellent faculty in *mimickry*, my correspondent tells me he can assume my air, and give my taciturnity a slyness which diverts more than any thing I could say. *Spectator.*

MIMO'GRAPHER. *n. s.* [*mimus* and γράφω.] A writer of farces. *Dict.*

MINA'CIOUS. *adj.* [*minax*, Lat.] Full of threats.

MINA'CITY. *n. s.* [from *minax*, Latin.] Disposition to use threats.

MI'NATORY. *adj.* [*minor*, Latin.] Threatening.

The king made a statute monitory and *minatory*, towards justices of peace, that they should duly execute their office, inviting complaints against them. *Bacon's Henry* VII.

To MINCE. *v. a.* [contracted, as it seems, from *minish*, or from *mincer*; *mince*, French, small.]

1. To cut into very small parts.

She saw Pyrrhus make malicious sport,
In *mincing* with his sword her husband's limbs. *Shakesp.*

With a good chopping-knife *mince* the two capons as small as ordinary *minced* meat. *Bacon's Nat. Hist.*

What means the service of the church so imperfectly, and by halves, read over? What makes them *mince* and mangle that in their practice, which they could swallow whole in their subscriptions? *South's Sermons.*

Revive the wits;
But murder first, and *mince* them all to bits. *Dunciad.*

2. To mention any thing scrupulously, by a little at a time; to palliate; to extenuate.

I know no ways to *mince* it in love, but directly to say I love you. *Shakespeare's Henry* V.

Think it a bastard, whom the oracle
Hath doubtfully pronounc'd thy throat shall cut,
And *mince* it. *Shakesp. Timon of Athens.*

Behold yon simpering dame, whose face between her forks presages snow; that *minces* virtue, and does shake the head to hear of pleasure's name. *Shakesp. King Lear.*

Iago,
Thy honesty and love doth *mince* this matter,
Making it light to Cassio. *Shakespeare's Othello.*

These gifts,
Saving your *mincing*, the capacity
Of your soft cheveril conscience would receive,
If you might please to stretch it. *Shakesp. Henry* VIII.

I'll try to force you to your duty:
For so it is, howe'er you *mince* it,
Ere we part, I shall evince it. *Hudibras, p.* ii.

Siren; now *mince* the sin,
And mollify damnation with a phrase.
Say you consented not to Sancho's death,
But barely not forbade it. *Dryden's Spanish Fryar.*

If, to *mince* his meaning, I had either omitted some part of what he said, or taken from the strength of his expression, I certainly had wronged him. *Dryden.*

These, seeing no where water enough to effect a general deluge, were forced to *mince* the matter, and make only a partial one of it, restraining it to Asia. *Woodward.*

To MINCE. *v. n.*

1. To walk nicely by short steps; to act with appearance of scrupulousness and delicacy; to affect nicety.

By her side did sit the bold Sansloy,
Fit mate for such a *mincing* minion,
Who in her looseness took exceeding joy. *Fairy Queen.*

I'll turn two *mincing* steps
Into a manly stride. *Shakesp. Merchant of Venice.*

A harlot form soft sliding by,
With *mincing* step, small voice, and languid eye. *Dunciad.*

2. To speak small and imperfectly.

The reeve, miller, and cook, are as much distinguished from each other, as the *mincing* lady prioress and the broad-speaking wife of Bath. *Dryden's Fables.*

MI'NCINGLY. *adv.* [from *mince.*] In small parts; not fully.

Justice requireth nothing *mincingly*, but all with pressed, and heaped, and even over-enlarged measure. *Hooker, b.* i.

MIND. *n. s.* [ȝemino, Saxon.]

1. The intelligent power.

I am a very foolish, fond old man;
I fear I am not in my perfect *mind*. *Shakesp. King Lear.*

This word being often used for the soul giving life, is attributed abusively to madmen, when we say that they are of a distracted *mind*, instead of a broken understanding: which word, *mind*, we use also for opinion; as, I am of this or that *mind*: and sometimes for mens conditions or virtues; as, he is of an honest *mind*, or a man of a just *mind*: sometimes for affection; as, I do this for my *mind*'s sake: sometimes for the knowledge of principles, which we have without discourse: oftentimes for spirits, angels, and intelligences: but as it is used in the proper signification, including both the understanding agent and passible, it is described to be a pure, simple, substantial act, not depending upon matter, but having relation to that which is intelligible, as to his first object: or more at large thus; a part or particle of the soul, whereby it doth understand, not depending upon matter, nor needing any organ, free from passion coming from without, and apt to be dissevered as eternal from that which is mortal. *Raleigh.*

2. Liking; choice; inclination; propension; affection.

Our question is, whether all be sin which is done without direction by scripture, and not whether the Israelites did at any time amiss, by following their own *minds* without asking counsel of God. *Hooker, b.* ii.

We will consider of your suit:
And come some other time to know our *mind*. *Shakespeare.*

Being so hard to me that brought your *mind*,
I fear she'll prove as hard to you in telling her *mind*. *Shakespeare.*

I will have nothing else but only this;
And now methinks I have a *mind* to it. *Shakespeare.*

Be of the same *mind* one towards another. *Rom.* xii. 16.

Hast thou a wife after thy *mind*? forsake her not. *Ecclus.*

They had a *mind* to French Britain; but they have let fall their bit. *Bacon's War with Spain.*

Sudden *mind* arose
In Adam, not to let th' occasion pass,
Given him by this great conference, to know
Of things above this world. *Milton's Par. Lost, b.* v.

Waller coasted on the other side of the river, but at such a distance that he had no *mind* to be engaged. *Clarendon.*

He had a great *mind* to do it. *Clarendon.*

All the arguments to a good life will be very insignificant to a man that hath a *mind* to be wicked, when remission of sins may be had upon such cheap terms. *Tillotson's Sermons.*

Suppose that after eight years peace he hath a *mind* to infringe any of his treaties, or invade a neighbouring state, what opposition can we make? *Addison.*

3. Thoughts; sentiments.

Th' ambiguous god,
In these mysterious words, his *mind* exprest,
Some truths reveal'd, in terms involv'd the rest. *Dryden.*

4. Opinion.

The earth was not of my *mind*,
If you suppose as fearing you, it shook. *Shakespeare.*

These men are of the *mind*, that they have clearer ideas of infinite duration than of infinite space, because God has existed from all eternity; but there is no real matter coextended with infinite space. *Locke.*

The gods permitting traitors to succeed,
Become not parties in an impious deed;
And, by the tyrant's murder, we may find,
That Cato and the gods were of a *mind*. *Granville.*

5. Memory; remembrancy.

The king knows their disposition; a small touch will put him in *mind* of them. *Bacon's Advice to Villiers.*

When he brings
Over the earth a cloud, will therein set
His triple-coloured bow, whereon to look,
And call to *mind* his covenant. *Milton's Par. Lost, b.* xi.

These, and more than I to *mind* can bring,
Menalcas has not yet forgot to sing. *Dryden.*

The cavern's mouth alone was hard to find,
Because the path disus'd was out of *mind*. *Dryden.*

They will put him in *mind* of his own waking thoughts, ere these dreams had as yet made their impressions on his fancy. *Atterbury's Sermons.*

A wholesome law time out of *mind*;
Had been confirm'd by fate's decree. *Swift's Miscel.*

To MIND. *v. a.* [from the noun.]

1. To mark; to attend.

His mournful plight is swallowed up unwares,
Forgetful of his own that *minds* another's cares. *Fa. Qu.*

Not then mistrust, but tender love injoins,
That I should *mind* thee oft; and *mind* thou me! *Milton.*

If, in the raving of a frantick muse,
And *minding* more his verses than his way,
Any of these should drop into a well. *Roscommon.*

Cease to request me; let us *mind* our way;
Another song requires another day. *Dryden.*

He is daily called upon by the word, the ministers, and inward suggestions of the holy spirit, to attend to those prospects, and *mind* the things that belong to his peace. *Rogers.*

2. To put in mind; to remind.

Let me be punished, that have *minded* you
Of what you should forget. *Shakesp. Winter's Tale.*

I desire to *mind* those persons of what Saint Austin hath said. *Burnet's Theory of the Earth.*

This *minds* me of a cobbling colonel of famous memory. *L'Estrange.*

I shall only *mind* him, that the contrary supposition, if it could be proved, is of little use. *Locke.*

To MIND. *v. n.* To incline; to be disposed.

When one of them *mindeth* to go into rebellion, he will convey away all his lordships to feoffees in trust. *Spenser.*

MI'NDED. *adj.* [from *mind.*] Disposed; inclined; affected.

We come to know
How you stand *minded* in the weighty diff'rence
Between the king and you. *Shakesp. Henry* VIII.

Whose fellowship therefore unmeet for thee,
Good reason was thou freely should'st dislike,
And be so *minded* still. *Milton's Par. Lost, b.* viii.

If men were *minded* to live virtuously, to believe a God would be no hindrance to any such design, but very much for its advancement. *Tillotson's Sermons.*

Pyrrhus is nobly *minded*; and I fain
Would live to thank him. *Philips.*

MI'NDFUL. *adj.* [*mind* and *full.*] Attentive; having memory.

I acknowledge the usefulness of your directions, and I promise you to be *mindful* of your admonitions. *Hammond.*

MI'NDFULLY. *adv.* [from *mindful.*] Attentively.

MI'NDFULNESS. *n. s.* [from *mindful.*] Attention; regard.

MI'NDLESS. *adj.* [from *mind.*]

1. Inattentive; regardless.

Cursed Athens, *mindless* of thy worth,
Forget now thy great deeds, when neighbour states,
But for thy sword and fortune, trod upon them. *Shakesp.*

As the strong eagle in the silent wood,
Mindless of warlike rage, and hostile care,
Plays round the rocky cliff, or crystal flood. *Prior.*

2. Not endued with a mind; having no intellectual powers.

Pronounce thee a gross lowt, a *mindless* slave,
Or else a hovering temporizer. *Shakesp. Winter's Tale.*

God first made angels bodiless, pure, *minds*;
Then other things, which *mindless* bodies be:
Last, he made man. *Davies.*

MIND-STRICKEN. *adj.* [*mind* and *stricken.*] Moved; affected in his mind.

He had been so *mind-stricken* by the beauty of virtue in that noble king, though not born his subject, he ever professed himself his servant. *Sidney, b.* ii.

MINE, pronoun possessive. [myn, Saxon; *mein*, German; *mien*, French; *meus*, Latin. It was anciently the practice to use *my* before a consonant and *mine* before a vowel, which euphony still requires to be observed. *Mine* is always used when the substantive precedes: as, *this is* my *cat*; *this cat is* mine.] Belonging to me.

The devil himself could not pronounce a title
More hateful to *mine* ear. *Shakespear's Macbeth.*

Thou art a soul in bliss, but I am bound
Upon a wheel of fire; that *mine* own tears
Do scald like molten lead. *Shakesp. King Lear.*

When a wise man gives thee better counsel, give me *mine* again. *Shakespeare's King Lear.*

If thou be'st slain, and with no stroke of *mine*,
My wife and children's ghosts will haunt me still. *Shakespeare.*

A friend of *mine* is come to me, and I have nothing to set before him. *Luke* xi. 6.

That palm is *mine*. *Dryden.*

MINE. *n. s.* [*mine*, French; *mwyn* or *mwn*, Welsh, from *maen lapis*, in the plural *meini.*]

1. A place or cavern in the earth which contains metals or minerals.

Though streighter bounds your fortune did confine,
In your large heart was found a wealthy *mine*. *Waller.*

A workman, to avoid idleness, worked in a groove or *mine*-pit thereabouts, which was little esteemed. *Boyle.*

A *mine*-digger may meet with a gem, which he knows not what to make of. *Boyle.*

The heedless *mine*-man aims only at the obtaining a quantity of such a metal as may be vendible. *Boyle.*

2. A cavern dug under any fortification that it may sink for want of support, or, in modern war, that powder may be lodged in it, which being fired at a proper time, whatever is over it may be blown up and destroyed.

By what eclipse shall that sun be defac'd?
What *mine* hath erst thrown down so fair a tower?
What sacrilege hath such a saint disgrac'd? *Sidney, b.* ii.

Build up the walls of Jerusalem, which you have broken down, and fill up the *mines* that you have digged. *Whitgift.*

Others to a city strong
Lay siege, encamp'd; by batt'ry, scale and *mine*,
Assaulting. *Milton's Par. Lost, b.* xi.

To MINE. *v. n.* [from the noun.] To dig mines or burrows; to form any hollows underground.

The ranging stork in stately beeches dwells;
The climbing goats on hills securely feed;
The *mining* coneys shroud in rocky cells. *Wotton*

Of this various matter the terrestrial globe consists, from its surface down to the greatest depth we ever dig or *mine*. *Woodward's Nat. Hist.*

To MINE. *v. a.* To sap; to ruin by mines; to destroy by slow degrees, or secret means.

It will but skin and film the ulcerous place,
While rank corruption *mining* all within,
Infects unseen. *Shakespeare's Hamlet.*

They *mined* the walls, laid the powder, and rammed the mouth; but the citizens made a countermine. *Hayward.*

The slow fever *mines* the constitution *Bolingbroke.*

MI'NER. *n. s.* [*mineur*, Fr. from *mine.*]

1. One that digs for metals.

By me kings palaces are push'd to ground,
And *miners* crush'd beneath their mines are found. *Dryden.*

2. One who makes military mines.

As the bombardeer levels his mischief at cities, the *miner* busies himself in ruining private houses. *Tatler.*

MI'NERAL. *n. s.* [*minerale*, Lat.] Fossile body; matter dug out of mines. All metals are minerals, but all minerals are not metals.

She did confess, she had
For you a mortal *mineral*; which, being took,
Should by the minute feed on life, and ling'ring
By inches waste you. *Shakespeare's Cymbeline.*

The *minerals* of the kingdom, of lead, iron, copper, and tin, are of great value. *Bacon's Advice to Villiers.*

Part hidden veins digg'd up, nor hath this earth
Entrails unlike, of *mineral* and stone. *Milton's Par. Lost.*

Minerals; nitre with vitriol; common salt with alum; and sulphur with vitriol. *Woodward.*

MI'NERAL. *adj.* Consisting of fossile bodies.

By experience upon bodies in any mine, a man may conjecture at the metallick or *mineral* ingredients of any mass found there. *Woodward's Nat. Hist.*

MI'NERALIST. *adj.* [from *mineral.*] One skilled or employed in minerals.

A mine-digger may meet with a gem or a mineral, which he knows not what to make of till he shews it a jeweller or a *mineralist*. *Boyle.*

The metals and minerals which are lodged in the perpendicular intervals do still grow, to speak in the *mineralist*'s phrase, or receive additional increase. *Woodward.*

MINERA'LOGIST. *n. s.* [*mineralogie*, French; from *mineral* and λόγ☉.] One who discourses on minerals.

Many authors deny it, and the exactest *mineralogists* have rejected it. *Brown's Vulgar Errours, b.* ii.

MINER'ALOGY. *n. s.* [from *mineral* and λόγ☉.] The doctrine of minerals.

MINE'VER. *n. s.* A skin with specks of white. *Ains.*

To MI'NGLE. *v. a.* To mix; to join; to compound; to unite with something so as to make one mass.

Wo unto them that are mighty to drink wine, and men of strength to *mingle* strong drink. *Isa.* v. 22.

Lament with me! with me your sorrows join,
And *mingle* your united tears with mine! *Walsh.*

The best of us appear contented with a *mingled*, imperfect virtue. *Rogers's Sermons.*

Our sex, our kindred, our houses, and our very names, we are ready to *mingle* with ourselves, and cannot bear to have others think meanly of them. *Watts's Logick.*

He wooes the bird of Jove
To *mingle* woes with his. *Thomson's Spring, l.* 1035.

To MI'NGLE. *v. n.* To be mixed; to be united with.

Ourself will *mingle* with society,
And play the humble host. *Shakespeare's Macbeath.*

Alcimus had defiled himself wilfully in the times of their *mingling* with the Gentiles. 2 *Mac.* xiv. 13.

Nor priests, nor statesmen,
Could have completed such an ill as that,
If women had not *mingled* in the mischief. *Rowe.*

She, when she saw her sister nymphs, suppress'd
Her rising fears, and *mingled* with the rest. *Addison.*

MI'NGLE. *n. s.* [from the verb.] Mixture; medley; confused mass.

Trumpeters,
With brazen din blast you the city's ear,
Make *mingle* with our rattling tabourines. *Shakespeare.*

Neither can I defend my Spanish Fryar; though the comical parts are diverting, and the serious moving, yet they are of an unnatural *mingle*. *Dryden's Dufresnoy.*

MI'NGLER. *n. s.* [from the verb.] He who mingles.

MI'NIATURE. *n. s.* [*miniature*, French.]

1. Representation in a small compass; representation less than the reality.

The water, with twenty bubbles, not content to have the picture of their face in large, would in each of these bubbles set forth the *miniature* of them. *Sidney, b.* ii.

If the ladies should once take a liking to such a diminutive race, we should see mankind epitomized, and the whole species in *miniature*: in order to keep our posterity from dwindling, we have instituted a tall club. *Addison's Guard.*

The hidden ways
Of nature would'st thou know? how first she frames
All things in *miniature*? thy specular orb
Apply to well dissected kernels: lo!
Strange forms arise, in each a little plant
Unfolds its boughs: observe the slender threads
Of first beginning trees, their roots, their leaves,
In narrow seeds describ'd. *Philips.*

2. Gay

2. *Gay* has improperly made it a ſubſtantive.

Here ſhall the pencil bid its colours flow,
And make a *miniature* creation grow. *Gay.*

MI'NIKIN. *adj.* 1. Small; diminutive. Uſed in ſlight contempt.

Sleepeſt, or wakeſt thou, jolly ſhepherd,
Thy ſheep be in the corn;
And for one blaſt of thy *minikin* mouth,
Thy ſheep ſhall take no harm. *Shakeſp. King Lear.*

MI'NIKIN. *n. ſ.* A ſmall ſort of pins.

MI'NIM. *n. ſ.* [from *minimus*, Lat.]

1. A ſmall being; a dwarf.

Not all
Minims of nature; ſome of ſerpent-kind,
Wond'rous in length, and corpulence, involv'd
Their ſnaky folds, and added wings. *Milton's Par. Loſt.*

2. This word is applied, in the northern counties, to a ſmall ſort of fiſh, which they pronounce *mennim*. See MINNOW.

MI'NIMUS. *n. ſ.* [Latin.] A being of the leaſt ſize.

Get you gone, you dwarf,
You *minimus* of hind'ring knot graſs made;
You bead, you acorn. *Shakeſpeare.*

MI'NION. *n. ſ.* [*mignon*, French.] A favourite; a darling; a low dependant; one who pleaſes rather than benefits. A word of contempt, or of ſlight and familiar kindneſs.

Minion, ſaid ſhe; indeed I was a pretty one in thoſe days; I ſee a number of lads that love you. *Sidney, b.* ii.

They were made great courtiers, and in the way of *minions*, when advancement, the moſt mortal offence to envy, ſtirred up their former friend to overthrow them. *Sidney.*

One, who had been a ſpecial *minion* of Andromanas, hated us for having diſpoſſeſſed him of her heart *Sidney, b.* ii.

Go rate thy *minions*;
Becomes it thee to be thus bold in terms
Before thy ſovereign. *Shakeſpeare's Henry* VI.

Duncan's horſes,
Beauteous and ſwift, the *minions* of the race,
Turn'd wild in nature. *Shakeſpeare's Macbeth.*

His company muſt do his *minions* grace,
Whilſt I at home ſtarve for a merry look. *Shakeſpeare.*

Edward ſent one army into Ireland; not for conqueſt, but to guard the perſon of his *minion* Piers Gaveſton. *Davies.*

If a man ſhould launch into the hiſtory of human nature, we ſhould find the very *minions* of princes linked in conſpiracies againſt their maſter. *L'Eſtrange's Fables.*

The drowſy tyrant by his *minions* led,
To regal rage devotes ſome patriot's head. *Swift.*

MI'NIOUS. *adj.* [from *minium*, Latin.] Of the colour of red lead or vermilion.

Some conceive, that the Red Sea receiveth a red and *minious* tincture from ſprings that fall into it. *Brown.*

To MI'NISH. *v. a.* [from *diminiſh*; *minus*, Latin.] To leſſen; to lop; to impair.

Ye ſhall not *miniſh* ought from your bricks of your daily taſk. *Exod.* v. 19.

They are *miniſhed* and brought low through oppreſſion. *Pſal.* cvii. 39.

Another law was to bring in the ſilver of the realm to the mint, in making all clipt, *miniſhed*, or impaired coins of ſilver, not to be current in payments. *Bacon's Henry* VII.

MI'NISTER. *n. ſ.* [*miniſter*, Latin; *miniſtre*, Fr.]

1. An agent; one who is employed to any end; one who acts not by any inherent authority, but under another.

You, whom virtue hath made the princeſs of felicity, be not the *miniſter* of ruin. *Sidney, b.* ii.

Rumble thy belly full; ſpit fire, ſpout rain,
Nor rain, wind, thunder, fire, are my daughters;
I tax not you, you elements, with unkindneſs:
But yet I call you ſervile *miniſters*,
That have with two pernicious daughters join'd
Your high-engender'd battles, 'gainſt a head
So old and white as this. *Shakeſp. King Lear.*

Th' infernal *miniſter* advanc'd,
Seiz'd the due victim. *Dryden's Theodore* and *Honoria.*

Other ſpirits govern'd by the will,
Shoot through their tracks, and diſtant muſcles fill;
This ſovereign, by his arbitrary nod,
Reſtrains or ſends his *miniſters* abroad. *Blackmore.*

2. One who is employed in the adminiſtration of government.

Kings muſt be anſwerable to God, but the *miniſters* to kings, whoſe eyes, ears, and hands they are, muſt be anſwerable to God and man. *Bacon.*

3. One who ſerves at the altar; one who performs ſacerdotal functions.

Epaphras, a faithful *miniſter* of Chriſt. 1 *Col.* i. 7.

The *miniſters* are always preaching, and the governours putting forth edicts againſt dancing and gaming. *Addiſon.*

The *miniſters* of the goſpel are eſpecially required to ſhine as lights in the world, becauſe the diſtinction of their ſtation renders their conduct more obſervable; and the preſumption of their knowledge, and the dignity of their office, gives a peculiar force and authority to their example. *Rogers.*

4. A delegate; an official.

If wrongfully
Let God revenge; for I may never lift
An angry arm againſt his *miniſter.* *Shakeſp. Rich.* II.

5. An agent from a foreign power, without the dignity of an ambaſſador.

To MI'NISTER. *v. a.* [*miniſtro*, Latin.] To give; to ſupply; to afford.

All the cuſtoms of the Iriſh would *miniſter* occaſion of a moſt ample diſcourſe of the original and antiquity of that people. *Spenſer on Ireland.*

Now he that *miniſtereth* ſeed to the ſower, both *miniſter* bread for your food and multiply your ſeed ſown. 2 *Cor.* ix.

The wounded patient bears
The artiſt's hand that *miniſters* the cure. *Otway's Orphan.*

To MI'NISTER. *v. n.*

1. To attend; to ſerve in any office.

Certain of them had the charge of the *miniſtering* veſſels, to bring them in and out by tale. 1 *Chron.* ix. 28.

They which *miniſter* about holy things, live of the things of the temple. 1 *Cor.* ix. 13.

At table Eve
Miniſter'd naked, and their flowing cups
With pleaſant liquors crown'd. *Milton's Par. Loſt, b.* v.

2. To give medicines.

Can'ſt thou not *miniſter* to a mind diſeas'd,
Pluck from the memory a rooted ſorrow,
Raze out the written troubles of the brain? *Shak. Macb.*

3. To give ſupplies of things needful; to give aſſiſtance; to contribute; to conduce.

Others *miniſtered* unto him of their ſubſtance. *Luke* viii. 3.

He who has a ſoul wholly void of gratitude, ſhould ſet his ſoul to learn of his body; for all the parts of that *miniſter* to one another. *South's Sermons.*

There is no truth which a man may more evidently make out than the exiſtence of a God; yet he that ſhall content himſelf with things as they *miniſter* to us pleaſures and paſſions, and not make enquiry a little farther into their cauſes and ends, may live long without any notion of ſuch a being. *Locke.*

Thoſe good men, who take ſuch pleaſure in relieving the miſerable for Chriſt's ſake, would not have been leſs forward to *miniſter* unto Chriſt himſelf. *Atterbury.*

Faſting is not abſolutely good, but relatively, and as it *miniſters* to other virtues. *Smalridge's Sermons.*

4. To attend on the ſervice of God.

Whether propheſy, let us propheſy according to the proportion of faith; or miniſtry, let us wait on our *miniſtring.* *Rom.* xii. 7.

MINISTE'RIAL. *adj.* [from *miniſter.*]

1. Attendant; acting at command.

Underſtanding is required in a man; courage and vivacity in the lion; ſervice, and *miniſterial* officiouſneſs, in the ox. *Brown's Vulgar Errours.*

From eſſences unſeen, celeſtial names,
Enlight'ning ſpirits, and *miniſterial* flames,
Lift we our reaſon to that ſovereign cauſe,
Who bleſs'd the whole with life. *Prior.*

2. Acting under ſuperior authority.

For the *miniſterial* officers in court there muſt be an eye unto them. *Bacon's Advice to Villiers.*

Abſtinence, the apoſtle determines, is of no other real value in religion, than as a *miniſterial* cauſe of moral effects; as it recalls us from the world, and gives a ſerious turn to our thoughts. *Rogers's Sermons.*

3. Sacerdotal; belonging to the eccleſiaſticks or their office.

Theſe ſpeeches of Jerom and Chryſoſtom plainly allude unto ſuch *miniſterial* garments as were then in uſe. *Hooker.*

4. Pertaining to miniſters of ſtate, or perſons in ſubordinate authority.

MI'NISTERY. *n. ſ.* [*miniſterium*, Lat.] Office; ſervice. This word is now contracted to *miniſtry*, but uſed by *Milton* as four ſyllables.

They that will have their chamber filled with a good ſcent, make ſome odoriferous water be blown about it by their ſervants mouths that are dextrous in that *miniſtery.* *Digby.*

This temple to frequent
With *miniſteries* due, and ſolemn rites. *Milton, b.* xii.

MI'NISTRAL. *adj.* [from *miniſter.*] Pertaining to a miniſter.

MI'NISTRANTS. *adj.* [from *miniſter.*] Attendant; acting at command.

Him thrones, and pow'rs,
Princedoms, and dominations *miniſtrant*,
Accompany'd to heav'n-gate. *Milton's Par. Loſt, b.* x.

Miniſtrant to their queen with buſy care,
Four faithful handmaids the ſoft rites prepare. *Pope.*

MINISTRA'TION. *n. s.* [from *ministro*, Latin.]

1. Agency; intervention; office of an agent delegated or commissioned by another.

God made him the instrument of his providence to me, as he hath made his own land to him, with this difference, that God, by his *ministration* to me, intends to do him a favour. *Taylor's living holy.*

Though sometimes effected by the immediate fiat of the divine will, yet I think they are most ordinarily done by the *ministration* of angels. *Hale's Origin of Mankind.*

2. Service; office; ecclesiastical function.

If the present *ministration* be more glorious than the former, the minister is more holy. *Atterbury's Sermons.*

MI'NIUM. *n. s.* [Latin.]

Melt lead in a broad earthen vessel unglazed, and stir it continually till it be calcined into a grey powder; this is called the calx of lead; continue the fire, stirring it in the same manner, and it becomes yellow; in this state it is used in painting, and is called masticot or massicot; after this put it into a reverberatory furnace, and it will calcine further, and become of a fine red, which is the common *minium* or red lead: among the ancients *minium* was the name for cinnabâr: the modern *minium* is used externally, and is excellent in cleansing and healing old ulcers. *Hill's Mat. Med.*

MI'NISTRY. *n. s.* [contracted from *ministery*; *ministerium*, Lat.]

1. Office; service.

So far is an indistinction of all persons, and, by consequence, an anarchy of all things, so far from being agreeable to the will of God, declared in his great houshold, the world, and especially in all the *ministries* of his proper household the church, that there was never yet any time, I believe, since it was a number, when some of its members were not more sacred than others. *Sprat's Sermons.*

2. Office of one set apart to preach; ecclesiastical function.

Their *ministry* perform'd, and race well run,
Their doctrine and their story written left,
They die. *Milton's Par. Lost, b.* xii.

Saint Paul was miraculously called to the *ministry* of the gospel, and had the whole doctrine of the gospel from God by immediate revelation; and was appointed the apostle of the Gentiles for propagating it in the heathen world. *Locke.*

3. Agency; interposition.

The natural world he made after a miraculous manner; but directs the affairs of it ever since by standing rules, and the ordinary *ministry* of second causes. *Atterbury.*

The poets introduced the *ministry* of the gods, and taught the separate existence of human souls. *Bentley's Sermons.*

4. Business.

He safe from loud alarms,
Abhorr'd the wicked *ministry* of arms. *Dryden's Æn.*

5. Persons employed in the publick affairs of a state.

I converse in full freedom with many considerable men of both parties; and if not in equal number, it is purely accidental, as happening to have made acquaintance at court more under one *ministry* than another. *Swift.*

MI'NNOCK. *n. s.* Of this word I know not the precise meaning. It is not unlikely that *minnock* and *minx* are originally the same word.

An ass's nole I fixed on his head;
Anon his Thisbe must be answered,
And forth my *minnock* comes. *Shakespeare.*

MI'NNOW. *n. s.* [*menue*, French.] A very small fish; a pink: a corruption of *minim*, which see.

Hear you this triton of the *minnows*? *Shakespeare.*

The *minnow*, when he is in perfect season, and not sick, which is only presently after spawning, hath a kind of dappled or waved colour, like a panther, on his sides, inclining to a greenish and sky-colour, his belly being milk-white, and his back almost black or blackish: he is a sharp biter at a small worm in hot weather, and in the Spring they make excellent *minnow* tansies; for being washed well in salt, and their heads and tails cut off, and their guts taken out, being fried with yolks of eggs, primroses and tansy. *Walton's Angler.*

The nimble turning of the *minnow* is the perfection of *minnow* fishing. *Walton's Angler.*

MI'NOR. *adj.* [Latin.]

1. Petty; inconsiderable.

If there are petty errours and *minor* lapses, not considerably injurious unto faith, yet is it not safe to contemn inferiour falsities. *Brown's Vulgar Errours, b.* v.

2. Less; smaller.

They altered this custom from cases of high concernment to the most trivial debates, the *minor* part ordinarily entering their protest. *Clarendon.*

The difference of a third part in so large and collective an account is not strange, if we consider how differently they are set forth in *minor* and less mistakeable numbers. *Browne's Vulgar Errours.*

MI'NOR. *n. s.*

1. One under age; one whose youth cannot yet allow him to manage his own affairs.

King Richard the Second, the first ten years of his reign, was a *minor*. *Davies on Ireland.*

He and his muse might be *minors*, but the libertines are full grown. *Collier's View of the Stage.*

Long as the year's dull circle seems to run,
When the brisk *minor* pants for twenty-one. *Pope.*

The noblest blood of England having been shed in the grand rebellion, many great families became extinct, or supported only by *minors*. *Swift.*

A *minor* or infant cannot be said to be contumacious, because he cannot appear as a defendant in court, but by his guardian. *Ayliffe's Parergon.*

2. The second or particular proposition in the syllogism.

The second or *minor* proposition was, that this kingdom hath cause of just fear of overthrow from Spain. *Bacon.*

He supposed that a philosopher's brain was like a forest, where ideas are ranged like animals of several kinds; that the major is the male, the *minor* the female, which copulate by the middle term, and engender the conclusion. *Arbuthnot.*

To MI'NORATE. *v. a.* [from *minor*, Lat.] To lessen; to diminish. A word not yet admitted into the language.

This it doth not only by the advantageous assistance of a tube, but by shewing in what degrees distance *minorates* the object. *Glanville's Sceps.*

MINORA'TION. *n. s.* [from *minorate*.] The act of lessening; diminution; decrease. A word not admitted.

Bodies emit virtue without abatement of weight, as is most evident in the loadstone, whose efficiences are communicable without a *minoration* of gravity. *Brown's Vulgar Errours.*

We hope the mercies of God will consider our degenerated integrity unto some *minoration* of our offences. *Brown.*

MINO'RITY. *n. s.* [*minorité*, Fr. from *minor*, Latin.]

1. The state of being under age.

I mov'd the king, my master, to speak in the behalf of my daughter, in the *minority* of them both. *Shakespeare.*

He is young, and his *minority*
Is put into the trust of Richard Gloster. *Shakespeare.*

These changes in religion should be staid, until the king were of years to govern by himself: this the people apprehending worse than it was, a question was raised, whether, during the king's *minority*, such alterations might be made or no. *Hayward's Edw.* VI.

Henry the Eighth, doubting he might die in the *minority* of his son, procured an act to pass, that no statute made during the *minority* of the king should bind him or his successors, except it were confirmed by the king at his full age. But the first act that passed in king Edward the Sixth's time, was a repeal of that former act; at which time nevertheless the king was minor. *Bacon's Henry* VII.

If there be evidence, that it is not many ages since nature was in her *minority*, this may be taken for a good proof that she is not eternal. *Burnet's Theory of the Earth.*

Their counsels are warlike and ambitious, though something tempered by the *minority* of their king. *Temple.*

2. The state of being less.

From this narrow time of gestation may ensue a *minority*, or smallness in the exclusion. *Brown's Vulgar Errours, b.* iii.

3. The smaller number: as, the *minority* held for that question in opposition to the majority.

MI'NOTAUR. *n. s.* [*minotaure*, French; *minos* and *taurus*.] A monster invented by the poets, half man and half bull, kept in Dædalus's labyrinth.

Thou may'st not wander in that labyrinth,
There *minotaurs*, and ugly treasons lurk. *Shakespeare.*

MI'NSTER. *n. s.* [mynꝼꞇeꞃe, Saxon.] A monastery; an ecclesiastical fraternity; a cathedral church. The word is yet retained at York and Lichfield.

MI'NSTREL. *n. s.* [*menestril*, Spanish; *menestrallus*, low Latin.] A musician; one who plays upon instruments.

Hark how the *minstrels* 'gin to shrill aloud
Their merry musick that resounds from far,
The pipe, the tabor, and the trembling croud,
That well agree withouten breach or jar. *Spenser's Epithal.*

I will give you the *minstrel*.
—Then I will give you the serving creature. *Shakespeare.*

I to the vulgar am become a jest;
Esteemed as a *minstrel* at a feast. *Sandys's Paraphrase.*

These fellows
Were once the *minstrels* of a country show;
Follow'd the prizes through each paltry town,
By trumpet-cheeks and bloated faces known. *Dryden.*

Often our seers and poets have confess'd,
That musick's force can tame the furious beast;
Can make the wolf, or foaming boar restrain
His rage; the lion drop his crested mane,
Attentive to the song; the lynx forget
His wrath to man, and lick the *minstrel*'s feet. *Prior.*

MI'NSTRELSEY. *n. s.* [from *minstrel*.]

1. Musick; instrumental harmony.

Apollo's self will envy at his play,
And all the world applaud his *minstrelsey*. *Davies.*

That

That loving wretch that swears,
'Tis not the bodies marry, but the minds,
Which he in her angelick finds,
Would swear as justly, that he hears,
In that day's rude hoarse *minstrelsey*, the spheres. *Donne.*

I began,
Wrapt in a pleasing fit of melancholy,
To meditate my rural *minstrelsy*,
Till fancy had her fill. *Milton.*

2. A number of musicians.

Ministring spirits train'd up in feast, and song!
Such hast thou arm'd the *minstrelsey* of heav'n. *Milton.*

MINT. *n. s.* [minte, Saxon; *menthe*, Fr. *mentha*, Latin.] A plant.

The *mint* is a verticillate plant with labiated flowers, consisting of one leaf, whose upper-lip is arched, and the under-lip divided into three parts; but both of them are so cut, that the flower seems to be divided into four parts, the two lips scarcely appearing: these flowers are collected into thick whorles in some species, but in others they grow in a spike; each flower having four seeds succeeding it, which are inclosed in the flower-cup: it hath a creeping root, and the whole plant has a strong aromatick scent. *Miller.*

Then rubb'd it o'er with newly-gather'd *mint*,
A wholesome herb, that breath'd a grateful scent. *Dryden.*

MINT. *n. s.* [*munte*, Dutch; mynetian, *to coin*, Saxon.]

1. The place where money is coined.

What is a person's name or face, that receives all his reputation from the *mint*, and would never have been known had there not been medals. *Addison on ancient Medals.*

2. Any place of invention.

A man in all the world's new fashion planted,
That hath a *mint* of phrases in his brain. *Shakespeare.*

As the *mints* of calumny are at work, a great number of curious inventions are issued out, which grow current among the party. *Addison's Freeholder*, N°. 7.

To MINT. *v. a.* [from the noun.]

1. To coin; to stamp money.

Another law was, to bring in the silver of the realm to the mint, in making all clipped coins of silver not to be current in payments, without giving any remedy of weight; and so to set the mint on work, and to give way to new coins of silver which should be then *minted*. *Bacon's Henry* VII.

2. To invent; to forge.

Look into the titles whereby they hold these new portions of the crown, and you will find them of such natures as may be easily *minted*. *Bacon's War with Spain.*

MI'NTAGE. *n. s.* [from *mint.*]

1. That which is coined or stamped.

Its pleasing poison
The visage quite transforms of him that drinks,
And the inglorious likeness of a beast
Fixes instead, unmoulding reasons *mintage*
Character'd in the face. *Milton.*

2. The duty paid for coining. *Ains.*

MI'NTER. *n. s.* [from *mint.*] Coiner.

Sterling ought to be of so pure silver as is called leaf silver, and the *minter* must add other weight, if the silver be not pure. *Camden's Remains.*

MI'NTMAN. *n. s.* [*mint* and *man.*] One skilled in coinage.

He that thinketh Spain to be some great over-match for this estate, is no good *mintman*; but takes greatness of kingdoms according to their bulk and currency, and not after their intrinsick value. *Bacon's War with Spain.*

MI'NTMASTER. *n. s.* [*mint* and *master.*]

1. One who presides in coinage.

That which is coined, as *mintmasters* confessed, is allayed with about a twelfth part of copper. *Boyle.*

2. One who invents.

The great *mintmasters* of these terms, the schoolmen and metaphysicians, have wherewithal to content him. *Locke.*

MI'NUET. *n. s.* [*menuet*, French.] A stately regular dance.

The tender creature could not see his fate,
With whom she'd danc'd a *minuet* so late. *Stepney.*

John Trot has the assurance to set up for a *minuet* dancer. *Spectator*, N°. 308.

MI'NUM. *n. s.*

1. [With printers.] A small sort of printing letter.

2. [With musicians.] A note of slow time, two of which make a semibrief, as two crotchets make a minum; two quavers a crotchet, and two semiquavers a quaver. *Bailey.*

Oh, he's the courageous captain of compliments; he fights as you sing pricksongs, keeps time, distance, and proportion; rests his *minum*, one, two, and the third in your bosom. *Shakespeare's Romeo and Juliet.*

MINU'TE. *adj.* [*minutus*, Lat.] Small; little; slender; small in bulk; small in consequence.

Some *minute* philosophers pretend,
That with our days our pains and pleasures end. *Denham.*

Such an universal superintendency has the eye and hand of providence over all, even the most *minute* and inconsiderable things. *South's Sermons.*

Into small parts the wond'rous stone divide,
Ten thousand of *minutest* size express
The same propension which the large possess. *Blackmore.*

The serum is attenuated by circulation, so as to pass into the *minutest* channels, and become fit nutriment for the body. *Arbuthnot on Aliments.*

In all divisions we should consider the larger and more immediate parts of the subject, and not divide it at once into the more *minute* and remote parts. *Watts's Logick.*

MI'NUTE. *n. s.* [*minutum*, Latin.]

1. The sixtieth part of an hour.

This man so complete,
Who was enroll'd 'mongst wonders, and when we,
Almost with list'ning ravish'd, could not find
His hour of speech a *minute*. *Shakesp. Henry* VIII.

2. Any small space of time.

They walk'd about me ev'ry *minute* while;
And if I did but stir out of my bed,
Ready they were to shoot me to the heart. *Shakespeare.*

The speed of gods
Time counts not, though with swiftest *minutes* wing'd. *Milton's Par. Lost, b.* x.

Gods! that the world should turn
On *minutes* and on moments. *Denham's Sophy.*

Experience does every *minute* prove the sad truth of this assertion. *South's Sermons.*

Tell her, that I some certainty may bring;
I go this *minute* to attend the king. *Dryden's Aurengzebe.*

3. The first draught of any agreement in writing; this is common in the Scottish law: as, have you made a *minute* of that contract?

To MI'NUTE. *v. a.* [*minuter*, French.] To set down in short hints.

I no sooner heard this critick talk of my works, but I *minuted* what he had said, and resolved to enlarge the plan of my speculations. *Spectator*, N°. 428.

MI'NUTE-BOOK. *n. s.* [*minute* and *book.*] Book of short hints.

MI'NUTE-GLASS. *n. s.* [*minute* and *glass.*] Glass of which the sand measures a minute.

MINU'TELY. *adv.* [from *minúte.*] To a small point; exactly; to the least part; nicely.

In this posture of mind it was impossible for him to keep that slow pace, and observe *minutely* that order of ranging all he said, from which results an obvious perspicuity. *Locke.*

Change of night and day,
And of the seasons ever stealing round,
Minutely faithful. *Thomson's Summer, l.* 40.

MI'NUTELY. *adv.* [from *mínute*, the substantive.]

1. Every minute; with very little time intervening.

What is it but a continued perpetuated voice from heaven, resounding for ever in our ears? As if it were *minutely* proclaimed in thunder from heaven, to give men no rest in their sins, no quiet from Christ's importunity till they arise from so mortiferous a state. *Hammond's Fundamentals.*

2. In the following passage it seems rather to be an adjective, as *hourly* is both the adverb and adjective.

Now *minutely* revolts upbraid his faith-breach,
Those he commands, move only in command,
Nothing in love. *Shakespeare's Macbeth.*

MINU'TENESS. *n. s.* [from *minúte.*] Smallness; exility; inconsiderableness.

The animal spirit and insensible particles never fall under our senses by reason of their *minuteness*. *Bentley's Sermons.*

MI'NUTE-WATCH. *n. s.* [*minute* and *watch.*] A watch in which minutes are more distinctly marked than in common watches which reckon by the hour.

Casting our eyes upon a *minute-watch*, we found that from the beginning of the pumping, about two minutes after the coals had been put in glowing, to the total disappearing of the fire, there had passed but three minutes. *Boyle.*

MINX. *n. s.* [contracted, I suppose, from *minnock.*] A young, pert, wanton girl.

Lewd *minx*!
Come, go with me apart. *Shakespeare.*

Some torches bore, some links,
Before the proud virago *minx*. *Hudibras, p.* ii.

She, when but yet a tender *minx*, began
To hold the door, but now sets up for man. *Dryden.*

MI'RACLE. *n. s.* [*miracle*, Fr. *miraculum*, Latin.]

1. A wonder; something above human power.

Nothing almost sees *miracles*
But misery. *Shakespeare's King Lear.*

Virtuous and holy, chosen from above,
To work exceeding *miracles* on earth. *Shakesp. Henry* VI.

Be not offended, nature's *miracle*,
Thou art allotted to be ta'en by me. *Shakesp. Henry* VI.

2. [In theology.] An effect above human or natural power, performed in attestation of some truth.

The *miracles* of our Lord are peculiarly eminent above the lying wonders of demons, in that they were not made out of vain ostentation of power, and to raise unprofitable amazement; but for the real benefit and advantage of men, by feeding

feeding the hungry, healing all ſorts of diſeaſes, ejecting of devils, and reviving the dead. *Bentley's Sermons.*

MIRA'CULOUS. *adj.* [*miraculeux*, Fr. from *miracle.*] Done by miracle; produced by miracle; effected by power more than natural.

Arithmetical progreſſion might eaſily demonſtrate how faſt mankind would increaſe, overpaſſing as *miraculous*, though indeed natural, that example of the Iſraelites, who were multiplied in two hundred and fifteen years from ſeventy unto ſix hundred thouſand able men. *Raleigh's Eſſays.*

Reſtore this day, for thy great name,
Unto his ancient and *miraculous* right. *Herbert.*

Why this ſtrength
Mirac'lous yet remaining in thoſe locks?
His might continues in thee not for naught. *Milton's Ag.*

At the firſt planting of the Chriſtian religion in the world, God was pleaſed to accompany it with a *miraculous* power. *Tillotſon.*

MIRA'CULOUSLY. *adv.* [from *miraculous.*] By miracle; by power above that of nature.

It was a ſingular providence of God, to draw thoſe northern heathen nations down into thoſe Chriſtian parts, where they might receive Chriſtianity, and to mingle nations ſo remote *miraculouſly*, to make one blood and kindred of all people, and each to have knowledge of him. *Spenſer on Ireland.*

Turnus was to be ſlain that very day; and Æneas, wounded as he was, could not have engaged him in ſingle combat, unleſs his hurt had been *miraculouſly* healed. *Dryden.*

MIRA'CULOUSNESS. *n. ſ.* [from *miraculous.*] The ſtate of being effected by miracle; ſuperiority to natural power.

MIRADO'R. n. ſ. [Spaniſh, from *mirar*, to look.] A balcony; a gallery whence ladies ſee ſhews.

Mean time your valiant ſon, who had before
Gain'd fame, rode round, to ev'ry *mirador*;
Beneath each lady's ſtand a ſtop he made,
And bowing, took th' applauſes which they paid. *Dryden.*

MIRE. *n. ſ.* [*moer*, Dutch.] Mud; dirt at the bottom of water.

He his rider from her lofty ſteed
Would have caſt down, and trod in dirty *mire*. *Fa. Qu.*

Here's that, which is too weak to be a ſinner, honeſt water, which ne'er left man i' th' *mire*. *Shak. Timon of Athens.*

I'm Ralph himſelf, your truſty ſquire,
Wh' has dragg'd your donſhip out o' th' *mire*. *Hudibras.*

I appeal to any man's reaſon, whether it be not better that there ſhould be a diſtinction of land and ſea, than that all ſhould be *mire* and water. *More's Antidote againſt Atheiſm.*

Now plung'd in *mire*, now by ſharp brambles torn. *Roſcommon.*

To MIRE. *v. a.* [from the noun.] To whelm in the mud; to ſoil with mud.

Why had I not, with charitable hand,
Took up a beggar's iſſue at my gates?
Who ſmeered thus, and *mir'd* with infamy,
I might have ſaid no part of it is mine. *Shakeſpeare.*

MIRE. *n. ſ.* [*myr*, Welſh; mýra, Saxon; *mier*, Dutch.] An ant; a piſmire.

MI'RINESS. *n. ſ.* [from *miry.*] Dirtineſs; fullneſs of mire.

MI'RKSOME. *n. ſ.* [*morck*, dark, Daniſh. In the derivatives of this ſet, no regular orthography is obſerved: it is common to write *murky*, to which the reſt ought to conform.] Dark; obſcure.

Through *mirkſome* air her ready way ſhe makes. *F. Qu.*

MI'RROR. *n. ſ.* [*miroir*, French; *mirar*, Spaniſh, to look.]

1. A looking-glaſs; any thing which exhibits repreſentations of objects by reflection.

And in his waters which your *mirror* make,
Behold your faces as the cryſtal bright. *Spenſer's Epith.*

That pow'r which gave me eyes the world to view,
To view myſelf infus'd an inward light,
Whereby my ſoul, as by a *mirror* true,
Of her own form may take a perfect ſight. *Davies.*

Leſs bright the moon,
But oppoſite in levell'd Weſt was ſet
His *mirror*, with full face borrowing her light
From him. *Milton's Par. Loſt*, b. vii.

Miroir of poets, *mirroir* of our age,
Which her whole face beholding on thy ſtage,
Pleas'd and diſpleas'd with her own faults, endures
A remedy like thoſe whom muſick cures. *Waller.*

By chance he ſpy'd a *mirroir* while he ſpoke,
And gazing there beheld his alter'd look;
Wond'ring, he ſaw his features and his hue,
So much were chang'd, that ſcarce himſelf he knew. *Dryden's Knight's Tale.*

Late as I rang'd the cryſtal wilds of air,
In the clear *mirroir* of thy ruling ſtar,
I ſaw, alas! ſome dread event impend. *Pope.*

2. It is uſed for pattern; for that on which the eye ought to be fixed; an exemplar; an archetype.

The works of nature are no leſs exact, than if ſhe did both behold and ſtudy how to expreſs ſome abſolute ſhape or *mirror* always preſent before her. *Hooker*, b. i.

O goddeſs, heavenly bright,
Mirrour of grace and majeſty divine. *Fairy Queen*, b. i.

How far'ſt thou, *mirror* of all martial men? *Shakeſp.*

Mirroir of ancient faith in early youth. *Dryden.*

MIRROR-STONE. *n. ſ.* [*ſelenites*, Lat.] A kind of tranſparent ſtone. *Ainſ.*

MIRTH. *n. ſ.* [myrhþe, Saxon.] Merriment; jollity; gaiety; laughter.

To give a kingdom for a *mirth*, to ſit,
And keep the turn of tippling with a ſlave. *Shakeſpeare.*

Be large in *mirth*, anon we'll drink a meaſure
The table round. *Shakeſpeare's Macbeth.*

His eye begets occaſion for his wit;
For every object that the one doth catch,
The other turns to a *mirth*-moving jeſt. *Shakeſpeare.*

Moſt of the appearing *mirth* in the world is not *mirth* but art: the wounded ſpirit is not ſeen, but walks under a diſguiſe. *South's Sermons.*

With genial joy to warm the ſoul,
Bright Helen mix'd a *mirth*-inſpiring bowl. *Pope's Odyſſey.*

MI'RTHFUL. *adj.* [*mirth* and *full.*] Merry; gay; cheerful.

No ſimple word,
That ſhall be utter'd at our *mirthful* board,
Shall make us ſad next morning. *B. Johnſon, Epigr.* 101.

The feaſt was ſerv'd; the bowl was crown'd;
To the king's pleaſure went the *mirthful* round. *Prior.*

MI'RTHLESS. *adj.* [from *mirth.*] Joyleſs; cheerleſs.

MI'RY. *adj.* [from *mire.*]

1. Deep in mud; muddy.

Thou ſhould'ſt have heard how her horſe fell, and ſhe under her horſe: thou ſhould'ſt have heard in how *miry* a place, how ſhe was bemoiled. *Shakeſp. Taming of the Shrew.*

All men who lived lazy lives, and died natural deaths, by ſickneſs or by age, went into vaſt caves under-ground, all dark and *miry*, full of noiſome creatures, and there grovel'ed in endleſs ſtench and miſery. *Temple.*

Deep, through a *miry* lane ſhe pick'd her way,
Above her ancle roſe the chalky clay. *Gay's Trivia.*

So have I ſeen ill-coupled hounds
Drag diff'rent ways in *miry* grounds. *Swift.*

2. Conſiſting of mire.

Shall thou and I ſit round about ſome fountain,
Looking all downwards to behold our cheeks,
How they are ſtain'd like meadows, yet not dry,
With *miry* ſlime left on them by a flood? *Shakeſpeare.*

MIS, an inſeparable particle uſed in compoſition to mark an ill ſenſe, or depravation of the meaning: as, *chance*, luck; *miſchance*, ill luck; *computation*, reckoning; *miſcomputation*, falſe reckoning; *to like*, to be pleaſed; *to miſlike*, to be offended; from *mes* in Teutonick and French, uſed in the ſame ſenſe. Of this it is difficult to give all the examples; but thoſe that follow will ſufficiently explain it.

MISACCEPTA'TION. *n. ſ.* [*mis* and *acceptation.*] The act of taking in a wrong ſenſe.

MISADVE'NTURE. *n. ſ.* [*meſaventure*, Fr. *mis* and *adventure.*]

1. Miſchance; misfortune; ill luck; bad fortune.

Your looks are pale and wild, and do import
Some *miſadventure*. *Shakeſp. Romeo and Juliet.*

When a commander, either upon neceſſity or *miſadventure*, falleth into danger, it much advanceth both his reputation and enterprize, if bravely he behaveth himſelf. *Hayward.*

The body conſiſted, after all the loſſes and *miſadventures*, of no leſs than ſix thouſand foot. *Clarendon*, b. viii.

Diſtinguiſh betwixt actions of *miſadventure* and of deſign. *L'Eſtrange's Fables.*

The trouble of a *miſadventure* now and then, that reaches not his innocence or reputation, may not be an ill way to teach him more caution. *Locke on Education.*

2. [In law.] Manſlaughter. *Ainſ.*

MISADVE'NTURED. *adj.* [from *miſadventure.*] Unfortunate.

From forth the fatal loins of theſe two foes,
A pair of ſtarcroſt lovers take their life;
Whoſe *miſadventur'd* piteous overthrows
Do with their death bury their parents ſtrife. *Shakeſp.*

MISADVI'SED. *adj.* [*mis* and *adviſed.*] Ill directed.

MISA'IMED. *adj.* [*mis* and *aim.*] Not aimed rightly.

The idle ſtroke enforcing furious way,
Miſſing the mark of his *miſaimed* ſight,
Did fall to ground. *Fairy Queen*, b. i.

MI'SANTHROPE. } *n. ſ.* [*miſanthrope*, French; μισάνθρωπος.]
MISA'NTHROPOS. } A hater of mankind.

I am *miſanthropos*, and hate mankind. *Shakeſpeare.*

Alas, poor dean! his only ſcope
Was to be held a *miſanthrope*;
This into gen'ral odium drew him. *Swift's Miſcel.*

MISA'NTHROPY. *n. ſ.* [*miſanthropie*, Fr. from *miſanthrope.*] Hatred of mankind.

MISAPPLICA'TION. *n. ſ.* [*mis* and *application.*] Application to a wrong purpoſe.

The indiſtinction of many in the community of name, or the *miſapplication* of the act of one unto another, hath made ſome doubt thereof. *Brown's Vulgar Errours*, b. v.

The

The vigilance of those who preside over these charities is so exemplary, that persons disposed to do good can entertain no suspicions of the *misapplication* of their bounty. *Atterbury.*

It is our duty to be provident for the future, and wisely to guard against whatever may lead us into *misapplications* of it. *Roger's Sermons.*

To MISAPPLY'. *v. a.* [*mis* and *apply.*] To apply to wrong purposes.

Virtue itself turns vice, being *misapplied*,
And vice sometime by action's dignified. *Shakespeare.*

The holy treasure was to be reserved, and issued for holy uses, and not *misapplied* to any other ends. *Howel.*

He that knows, that whiteness is the name of that colour he has observed in snow, will not *misapply* that word as long as he retains that idea. *Locke.*

To MISAPPRE'HEND. *v. a.* [*mis* and *apprehend,*] Not to understand rightly.

That your reasonings may lose none of their force by my *misapprehending* or misrepresenting them, I shall give the reader your arguments. *Locke.*

MISAPPREHE'NSION. *n. s.* [*mis* and *apprehension.*] Mistake; not right apprehension.

It is a good degree of knowledge to be acquainted with the causes of our ignorance: and what we have to say under this head, will equally concern our *misapprehensions* and errors. *Glanville's Scep.*

To MISASCRI'BE. *v. a.* [*mis* and *ascribe.*] To ascribe falsly.

That may be *misascribed* to art which is the bare production of nature. *Boyle.*

To MISASSI'GN. *v. a.* [*mis* and *assign*] To assign erroneously.

We have not *misassigned* the cause of this phenomenon. *Boyle.*

To MISBECO'ME. *v. a.* [*mis* and *become.*] Not to become; to be unseemly; not to suit.

Either she has a possibility in that which I think impossible, or else impossible loves need not *misbecome* me. *Sidney.*

What to the dauphin from England?
—Scorn and defiance, slight regard, contempt,
And any thing that may not *misbecome*
The mighty sender. *Shak. Henry* V.

That boldness which lads get amongst their play-fellows, has such a mixture of rudeness and an ill-turn'd confidence, that those *misbecoming* and disingenuous ways of shifting in the world must be unlearned to make way for better principles. *Locke.*

Portius, thou may'st rely upon my conduct;
Thy father will not act what *misbecomes* him. *Addison.*

MISBEGO'T. } *adj.* [*begot* or *begotten* with *mis.*] Unlawfully
MISBEGO'TTEN. } or irregularly begotten.

Contaminated, base,
And *misbegotten* blood, I spill of thine. *Shakesp. Henry* VI.

Your words have taken such pains, as if they labour'd
To bring man-slaughter into form, set quarrelling
Upon the head of valour; which, indeed,
Is valour *misbegot*, and came into the world
When sects and factions were but newly born. *Shakesp.*

The *misbegotten* infant grows,
And, ripe for birth, distends with deadly throes
The swelling rind, with unavailing strife,
To leave the wooden womb, and pushes into life. *Dryden.*

To MISBEHA'VE. *v. n.* [*mis* and *behave.*] To act ill or improperly.

MISBEHA'VED, *adj.* [*mis* and *behaved.*] Untaught; ill-bred; uncivil.

Happiness courts thee in her best array;
But, like a *misbehav'd* and sullen wench,
Thou pout'st upon thy fortune and thy love. *Shakespeare.*

MISBEHA'VIOUR. *n. s.* [*mis* and *behaviour.*] Ill conduct; bad practice.

The *misbehaviour* of particular persons does not at all affect their cause, since a man may act laudably in some respects, who does not so in others. *Addison's Freeholder.*

MISBELI'EF. *n. s.* [*mis* and *belief.*] False religion; a wrong belief.

MISBELI'EVER. *n. s.* [*mis* and *believer.*] One that holds a false religion, or believes wrongly.

Yes, if I drew it with a curst intent
To take a *misbeliever* to my bed,
It must be so. *Dryden's Don Sebastian.*

To MISCA'LCULATE. *v. a.* [*mis* and *calculate.*] To reckon wrong.

After all the care I have taken, there may be, in such a multitude of passages, several misquoted, misinterpreted, and *miscalculated.* *Arbuthnot on Coins.*

To MISCA'L. *v. a.* [*mis* and *call.*] To name improperly.

My heart will sigh when I *miscal* it so. *Shak. Rich.* II.

The third act, which connects propositions and deduceth conclusions from them, the schools call discourse; and we shall not *miscal* it if we name it reason. *Glanville's Scep.*

What you *miscal* their folly is their care. *Dryden.*

MISCA'RRIAGE. *n. s.* [*mis* and *carriage.*]

1. Unhappy event of our undertaking; failure; ill conduct.

Resolutions of future reforming do not always satisfy justice, nor prevent vengeance for former *miscarriages* *King Charles.*

When a counsellor, to save himself,
Would lay *miscarriages* upon his prince,
Exposing him to publick rage and hate,
O, 'tis an act as infamously base,
As, should a common soldier sculk behind,
And thrust his general in the front of war. *Dryd. Sp. Fr.*

If the neglect or abuse of the liberty he had, to examine what would really make for his happiness, misleads him, the *miscarriages* that follow on it must be imputed to his own election. *Locke.*

A great part of that time which the inhabitants of the former earth had to spare, and whereof they made so ill use, was now employed in digging and plowing; and the excess of fertility which contributed so much to their *miscarriages*, was retracted and cut off. *Woodward's Nat. Hist. p.* ii.

Your cures aloud you tell,
But wisely your *miscarriages* conceal. *Garth's Dispensatory.*

How, alas! will he appear in that awful day, when even the failings and *miscarriages* of the righteous shall not be concealed, though the mercy of God be magnified in their pardon. *Rogers's Sermons.*

2. Abortion; act of bringing forth before the time.

There must be flying and death, as well as *miscarriages* and abortions; for there died many women with child. *Graunt's Bills of Mortality.*

To MISCA'RRY. *v. n.* [*mis* and *carry.*]

1. To fail; not to have the intended event; not to succeed; to be lost in an enterprise; not to reach the effect intended.

Have you not heard of Frederick, the great soldier, who *miscarried* at sea? *Shakespeare's Measure for Measure.*

Our sister's man is certainly *miscarried.* *Shakespeare.*

Is it concluded he shall be protector?
—It is determin'd, not concluded yet:
But so it must be if the king *miscarry.* *Shakesp. Rich.* III.

If you *miscarry*,
Your business of the world hath so an end,
And machination ceases. *Shakesp. King Lear.*

Sweet Bassanio, my ships have all *miscarried*, my creditors grow cruel, my estate is very low. *Shak. Merchant of Venice.*

I could mention some projects which I have brought to maturity, and others which have *miscarried.* *Addison's Guard.*

No wonder that this expedient should so often *miscarry*, which requires so much art and genius to arrive at any perfection in it. *Swift's Miscel.*

2. To have an abortion.

Give them a *miscarrying* womb and dry breasts. *Hos.* ix. 14.

So many politick conceptions so elaborately formed and wrought, and grown at length ripe for a delivery, do yet, in the issue, *miscarry* and prove abortive. *South's Sermons.*

His wife *miscarried*; but the abortion proved a female fœtus. *Pope and Arbuthnot's Mart. Scrib.*

You have proved yourself more tender of another's embrios, than the fondest mothers are of their own; for you have preserved every thing that I *miscarried* of. *Pope.*

MISCELLA'NE. *n. s.* [*miscellaneus*, Lat. This is corrupted into *mastlin* or *mestlin.*] Mixed corn: as, wheat and rye.

It is thought to be of use to make some *miscellane* in corn; as if you sow a few beans with wheat, your wheat will be the better. *Bacon's Nat. Hist.* N°. 670.

MISCELLA'NEOUS. *adj.* [*miscellaneus*, Latin.] Mingled; composed of various kinds.

Being *miscellaneous* in many things, he is to be received with suspicion; for such as amass all relations must err in some, and without offence be unbelieved in many. *Browne.*

And what the people but a herd confus'd,
A *miscellaneous* rabble, who extol
Things vulgar, and well weigh'd scarce worth the praise. *Milton's Par. Reg. b.* ii.

MISCELLA'NEOUSNESS. *n. s.* [from *miscellaneous.*] Composition of various kinds.

MI'SCELLANY. *adj.* [*miscellaneus*, Latin.] Mixed of various kinds.

The power of Spain consisteth in a veteran army, compounded of *miscellany* forces of all nations. *Bacon.*

MI'SCELLANY. *n. s.* A mass formed out of various kinds.

I must acquit myself of the presumption of having lent my name to recommend any *miscellanies* or works of other men. *Pope.*

When they have join'd their pericranies,
Out skips a book of *miscellanies.* *Swift.*

To MISCA'ST. *v. a.* [*mis* and *cast.*] To take a wrong account of.

Men *miscast* their days; for in their age they deduce the account not from the day of their birth, but the year of our Lord wherein they were born. *Brown's Vulgar Errours.*

MISCHA'NCE.

Mischa'nce. *n. s.* [*mis* and *chance.*] Ill luck; ill fortune; misfortune; mishap.

The lady Cecropia sent him to excuse the *mischance* of her beasts ranging in that dangerous sort. *Sidney, b.* i.

Extreme dealing had driven her to put herself with a great lady, by which occasion she had stumbled upon such *mischances* as were little for the honour of her family. *Sidney, b.* ii.

View these letters, full of bad *mischance*.
France is revolted. *Shakesp. Henry* VI. *p.* i.

Sleep rock thy brain,
And never come *mischance* between us twain. *Shakespeare.*

Nothing can be a reasonable ground of despising a man but some fault chargeable upon him; and nothing can be a fault that is not naturally in a man's power to prevent; otherwise, it is a man's unhappiness, his *mischance* or calamity, but not his fault. *South's Sermons.*

MI'SCHIEF. *n. s.* [*meschef*, old French.]

1. Harm; hurt; whatever is ill and injuriously done.

The law in that case punisheth the thought; for better is a *mischief* than an inconvenience. *Spenser on Ireland.*

Come you murth'ring ministers!
Wherever in your sightless substances
You wait on nature's *mischief*. *Shakespeare's Macbeth.*

Thy tongue deviseth *mischiefs*. *Psal.* lii. 2.

Was I the cause of *mischief*, or the man,
Whose lawless lust the fatal war began? *Dryden's Æn.*

Come not thou with *mischief*-making beauty,
To interpose between us, look not on him. *Rowe.*

2. Ill consequence; vexatious affair.

States call in foreigners to assist them against a common enemy; but the *mischief* was, these allies would never allow that the common enemy was subdued. *Swift.*

To Mi'schief. *v. a.* [from the noun.] To hurt; to harm; to injure.

If the greatest inward heat be not sweetened by meekness, or not governed by prudence, can it bring to our souls any benefit? rather it *mischiefs* them. *Sprat's Sermons.*

Mi'schiefmaker. *n. s.* [from *mischief* and *make.*] One who causes mischief.

Mi'schievous. *adj.* [from *mischief.*]

1. Harmful; hurtful; destructive; noxious; pernicious; injurious; wicked.

This false, wily, doubling disposition is intolerably *mischievous* to society. *South's Sermons.*

I'm but a half-strain'd villain yet;
But mongrel *mischievous*. *Dryden.*

He had corrupted or deluded most of his servants, telling them that their master was run mad; that he had disinherited his heir, and was going to settle his estate upon a parish-boy; that if he did not look after their master he would do some very *mischievous* thing. *Arbuthnot's Hist. of John Bull.*

2. Spiteful; malicious. *Ainsworth.*

Mi'schievously. *adv.* [from *mischief.*] Noxiously; hurtfully; wickedly.

Nor was the cruel destiny content
To sweep at once her life and beauty too;
But like a harden'd felon took a pride
To work more *mischievously* slow,
And plundered first, and then destroy'd. *Dryden.*

Mi'schievousness. *n. s.* [from *mischievous.*] Hurtfulness; perniciousness; wickedness.

Compare the harmlessness, the tenderness, the modesty, and the ingenuous pliableness, which is in youth, with the *mischievousness*, the slyness, the craft, the impudence, the falshood, and the confirmed obstinacy found in an aged, long-practised sinner. *South's Sermons.*

Mi'scible. *adj.* [from *misceo*, Latin.] Possible to be mingled.

Acid spirits are subtile liquors which come over in distillations, not inflammable, *miscible* with water. *Arbuthnot.*

Miscita'tion. *n. s.* [*mis* and *citation.*] Unfair or false quotation.

Being charged with *miscitation* and unfair dealing, it was requisite to say something; for honesty is a tender point. *Collier's View of the Stage.*

To Misci'te. *v. a.* [*mis* and *cite.*] To quote wrong.

Miscla'im. *n. s.* [*mis* and *claim.*] Mistaken claim.

Error, *misclaim* and forgetfulness, become suitors for some remission of extreme rigour. *Bacon.*

Miscomputa'tion. *n. s.* [*mis* and *computation.*] False reckoning.

It was a general misfortune and *miscomputation* of that time, that the party had so good an opinion of their own reputation and interest. *Clarendon.*

To Misconce'ive. *v. a.* [*mis* and *conceive.*] To mis-judge; to have a false notion of.

Ne let false whispers, breeding hidden fears,
Break gentle sleep with *misconceived* doubt. *Spenser.*

Our endeavour is not so much to overthrow them with whom we contend, as to yield them just and reasonable causes of those things, which, for want of due consideration heretofore, they *misconceived.* *Hooker, b.* v.

Misconceived Joan of Arc hath been
A virgin from her tender infancy. *Shakesp. Henry* VI.

Misconce'it. } *n. s.* [*mis* and *conceit*, and *conception.*] False
Misconce'ption. } opinion; wrong notion.

The other which instead of it we are required to accept, is only by error and *misconceit* named the ordinance of Jesus Christ; no one proof as yet brought forth, whereby it may clearly appear to be so in very deed. *Hooker.*

It cannot be that our knowledge should be other than an heap of *misconception* and error. *Glanville's Scep.*

Great errors and dangers result out of a *misconception* of the names of things. *Harvey on Consumptions.*

It will be a great satisfaction to see those pieces of most ancient history, which have been chiefly preserved in scripture, confirmed anew, and freed from those *misconceptions* or misrepresentations which made them sit uneasy upon the spirits even of the best men. *Burnet's Theory of the Earth.*

Misco'nduct. *n. s.* [*mis* and *conduct.*] Ill behaviour; ill management.

They are industriously proclaimed and aggravated by such as are guilty or innocent of the same slips or *misconducts* in their own behaviour. *Addison's Spect.* N°. 256.

It highly concerned them to reflect, how great obligations both the memory of their past *misconduct*, and their present advantages, laid on them, to walk with care and circumspection. *Rogers's Sermons.*

To Miscondu'ct. *v. a.* [*mis* and *conduct.*] To manage amiss; to carry on wrong.

Misconje'cture. *n. s.* [*mis* and *conjecture.*] A wrong guess.

I hope they will plausibly receive our attempts, or candidly correct our *misconjectures*. *Brown's Vulgar Errours.*

To Misconje'cture. *v. a.* [*mis* and *conjecture.*] To guess wrong.

Misconstru'ction. *n. s.* [*mis* and *construction.*] Wrong interpretation of words or things.

It pleas'd the king his master very lately
To strike at me upon his *misconstruction*,
When he conjunct, and flatt'ring his displeasure,
Tript me behind. *Shakespeare's King Lear.*

Others conceive the literal acceptation to be a *misconstruction* of the symbolical expression. *Brown's Vulgar Err.*

Those words were very weakly inserted where they are so liable to *misconstruction*. *Stillingfleet.*

To Misco'nstrue. *v. a.* [*mis* and *construe.*] To interpret wrong.

That which by right exposition buildeth up Christian faith, being *misconstrued* breedeth error; between true and false construction the difference reason must shew. *Hooker, b.* iii.

We would have had you heard
The manner and the purpose of his treasons;
That you might well have signified the same
Unto the citizens, who, haply, may
Misconstrue us in him. *Shakesp. Rich.* III.

Many of the unbelieving Israelites would have *misconstrued* this story of mankind. *Raleigh.*

Do not, great Sir, *misconstrue* his intent,
Nor call rebellion what was prudent care,
To guard himself by necessary war. *Dryden's Aurengzebe.*

A virtuous emperor was much afflicted to find his actions *misconstrued* and defamed by a party. *Addison.*

Misconti'nuance. *n. s.* [*mis* and *continuance.*] Cessation; intermission.

To Misco'unsel. *v. a.* [*mis* and *counsel.*] To advise wrong.

Every thing that is begun with reason
Will come by ready means unto his end,
But things *miscounseled* must needs miswend. *Spenser.*

To Misco'unt. *v. a.* [*mescounter*, French, *mis* and *count.*] To reckon wrong.

Mi'screance. } *n. s.* [from *mescreance* or *mescroiance*, suspicion,
Mi'screancy. } French.] Unbelief; false faith; adherence to a false religion.

If thou wilt renounce thy *miscreance*,
And my true liegeman yield thyself for ay,
Life will I grant thee for thy valiance. *Spenser.*

The more usual causes of deprivation are murther, manslaughter, heresy, *miscreancy*, atheism, simony. *Ayliffe.*

MI'SCREANT. *n. s.* [*mescreant*, French.]

1. One that holds a false faith; one who believes in false gods.

Their prophets justly condemned them as an adulterous seed, and a wicked generation of *miscreants*, which had forsaken the living God. *Hooker, b.* v.

2. A vile wretch.

Now by Apollo, king,
Thou swear'st thy gods in vain.
—O vassal! *miscreant!* *Shakespeare's King Lear.*

If extraordinary lenity proves ineffectual, those *miscreants* ought to be made sensible that our constitution is armed with force. *Addison's Freeholder*, N°. 50.

MISCREA'TE. } adj. [*mis* and *created.*] Formed unnaturally or
MISCRE'ATED. } illegitimately; made as by a blunder of nature.

Then made he head against his enemies,
And Ymner slew or Logris *miscreate*. *Fa. Qu. b.* ii.
Estsoons he took that *miscreated* fair,
And that false other sprite, on whom he spread
A seeming body of the subtile air. *Spenser.*
God forbid, my lord,
That you should fashion, wrest, or bow your reading;
With opening titles *miscreate*, whose right
Suits not in native colours with the truth. *Shakespeare.*

MISDE'ED. *n. s.* [*mis* and *deed.*] Evil action.

O God,
If thou wilt be aveng'd on my *misdeeds*,
Yet execute thy wrath on me alone. *Shakesp. Rich.* III.
Evils, which our own *misdeeds* have wrought. *Milton.*
Chas'd from a throne, abandon'd, and exil'd
For foul *misdeeds*, were punishments too mild. *Dryden.*

To MISDE'EM. *v. a.* [*mis* and *deem.*] To judge ill of; to mistake.

All unweeting an enchanter bad
His sense abus'd, and made him to *misdeem*
My loyalty, not such as it did seem. *Fairy Queen, b.* i.
Besides, were we unchangeable in will,
And of a wit that nothing could *misdeem*;
Equal to God, whose wisdom shineth still
And never errs, we might ourselves esteem. *Davies.*

To MISDEME'AN. *v. a.* [*mis* and *demean.*] To behave ill.

From frailty
And want of wisdom, you, that best should teach us,
Have *misdemean'd* yourself. *Shakesp. Henry* VIII.

MISDEME'ANOR. *n. s.* [*mis* and *demean.*] Offence; ill behaviour; something less than an atrocious crime.

The house of commons have only power to censure the members of their own house, in point of election or *misdemeanors*, in or towards that house. *Bacon.*

It is no real disgrace to the church merely to lose her privileges, but to forfeit them by her fault or *misdemeanor*. *South.*

These could never have touched the head, or stopped the source of these unhappy *misdemeanors*, for which the punishment was sent. *Woodward's Nat. Hist. p.* ii.

MISDEVO'TION. *n. s.* [*mis* and *devotion.*] Mistaken piety.

A place, where *misdevotion* frames
A thousand prayers to saints, whose very names
The church knew not, heav'n knows not yet. *Donne.*

MISDI'ET. *n. s.* [*mis* and *diet.*] Improper food.

A dropsy through his flesh did flow,
Which by *misdiet* daily greater grew. *Fairy Queen, b.* i.

To MISDISTI'NGUISH. *v. a.* [*mis* and *distinguish.*] To make wrong distinctions.

If we imagine a difference where there is none, because we distinguish where we should not, it may not be denied that we *misdistinguish*. *Hooker, b.* iii.

To MISDO'. *v. a.* [*mis* and *do.*] To do wrong; to commit a crime; to offend.

Afford me place to shew what recompence
T'wards thee I intend for what I have *misdone*. *Milton.*

To MISDO'. *v. n.* To commit faults.

Try the erring soul
Not wilfully *misdoing*, but unaware
Misled. *Paradise Regain'd, b.* i.

The worst is, to think ourselves safe so long as we keep our injuries from the knowledge of men, and out of our own view, without any awe of that all-seeing eye that observes all our *misdoings*. *L'Estrange.*

I have *misdone*, and I endure the smart,
Loth to acknowledge, but more loth to part. *Dryden.*

MISDO'ER. *n. s.* [from *misdo.*] An offender; a criminal; a malefactor.

Were they not contained in duty with a fear of law, which inflicteth sharp punishments to *misdoers*, no man should enjoy any thing. *Spenser on Ireland.*

To MISDO'UBT. *v. a.* [*mis* and *doubt.*] To suspect of deceit or danger.

If she only *misdoubted* me, I were in heaven; for quickly I would bring sufficient assurance. *Sidney, b.* ii.

I do not *misdoubt* my wife, but I would be loth to turn them both together; a man may be too confident. *Shakesp.*

The bird that hath been limed in a bush,
With trembling wings *misdoubteth* ev'ry bush;
And I, the hapless male to one sweet bird,
Have now the fatal object in my eye,
Where my poor young was lim'd, was caught, and kill'd.
Shakespeare's Henry VI. *p.* iii.

If you *misdoubt* me that I am not she,
I know not how I shall assure you farther. *Shakespeare.*
To believe his wiles my truth can move,
Is to *misdoubt* my reason or my love. *Dryden.*

MISDO'UBT. *n. s.* [*mis* and *doubt.*]

1. Suspicion of crime or danger.

He cannot so precisely weed this land,
As his *misdoubts* present occasion;
His foes are so enrooted with his friends,
That, plucking to unfix an enemy,
He doth unfasten so and shake a friend. *Shakesp. Henry* IV.

2. Irresolution; hesitation.

York, steel thy fearful thoughts,
And change *misdoubt* to resolution. *Shakesp. Henry* VI.

MISE. n. s. [French.] Issue. Law term. *Dict.*

To MISEMPLO'Y. *v. a.* [*mis* and *employ.*] To use to wrong purposes.

Their frugal fathers gains they *misemploy*,
And turn to point and pearl, and ev'ry female toy. *Dryd.*

Some taking things upon trust, *misemploy* their power by lazily enslaving their minds to the dictates of others. *Locke.*

That vain and foolish hope, which is *misemployed* on temporal objects, produces many sorrows. *Addison's Spect.*

They grew dissolute and prophane; and by *misemploying* the advantages which God had thrown into their lap, provoked him to withdraw them. *Atterbury.*

MISEMPLO'YMENT. *n. s.* [*mis* and *employment.*] Improper application.

An improvident expence, and *misemployment* of their time and faculties. *Hale's Origin of Mankind.*

MI'SER. *n. s.* [*miser*, Latin.]

1. A wretched person; one overwhelmed with calamity.

Do not disdain to carry with you the woful words of a *miser* now despairing; neither be afraid to appear before her, bearing the base title of the sender. *Sidney, b.* ii.

I wish that it may not prove some ominous foretoken of misfortune to have met with such a *miser* as I am. *Sidney.*

Fair son of Mars, that seek with warlike spoil
And great atchievements, great yourself to make,
Vouchsafe to stay your steed for humble *miser*'s sake.
Fairy Queen, b. ii.

2. A wretch; a mean fellow.

Decrepit *miser!* base ignoble wretch!
I am descended of a gentler blood. *Shakesp. Henry* VI.

3. A wretch covetous to extremity; one who in wealth makes himself miserable by the fear of poverty.

Though she be dearer to my soul than rest
To weary pilgrims, or to *misers* gold,
Rather than wrong Castalio I'd forget her. *Otway's Orphan.*
No silver saints by dying *misers* giv'n,
Here brib'd the rage of ill-requited heav'n;
But such plain roofs as piety could raise,
And only vocal with the Maker's praise. *Pope.*

MI'SERABLE. *adj.* [*miserable*, French; *miser*, Latin.]

1. Unhappy; calamitous; wretched.

O nation *miserable*,
With an untitled tyrant, bloody scepter'd!
When shalt thou see thy wholesome days again? *Shakesp.*
Most *miserable* is the desire that's glorious. *Shakespeare.*
What's more *miserable* than discontent? *Shakespeare.*

It is probable that there will be a future state, and then how *miserable* is the voluptuous unbeliever left in the lurch. *South's Sermons.*

What hopes delude thee, *miserable* man? *Dryden's Æn.*

2. Wretched; worthless.

Miserable comforters are ye all. *Job* xvi. 2.

3. Culpably parsimonious; stingy.

MI'SERABLENESS. *n. s.* [from *miserable.*] State of misery.

MI'SERABLY. *adv.* [from *miserable.*]

1. Unhappily; calamitously.

Of the five employed by him, two of them quarrelled, one of which was slain, and the other hanged for it; the third drowned himself; the fourth, though rich, came to beg his bread; and the fifth was *miserably* stabbed to death. *South.*

2. Wretchedly; meanly.

As the love I bear you makes me thus invite you, so the same love makes me ashamed to bring you to a place, where you shall be so, not spoken by ceremony but by truth, *miserably* entertained. *Sidney. b.* ii.

3. Covetously. *Ainsworth.*

MI'SERY. *n. s.* [*miseria*, Latin; *misere*, French.]

1. Wretchedness; unhappiness.

My heart is drown'd with grief,
My body round engirt with *misery*. *Shakesp. Henry* VI.

Happiness, in its full extent, is the utmost pleasure we are capable of, and *misery* the utmost pain. *Locke.*

2. Calamity; misfortune; cause of misery.

When we our betters see bearing our woes,
We scarcely think our *miseries* our foes. *Shakespeare.*
The gods from heav'n survey the fatal strife,
And mourn the *miseries* of human life. *Dryden's Æn.*

3. [From *miser.*] Covetousness; avarice. Not in use.

He look'd upon things precious, as they were
The common muck o' th' world: he covets less
Than *misery* itself would give. *Shakesp. Coriolanus.*

In a fabrick of forty thousand pounds charge, I wish thirty pounds laid out before in an exact model; for a little *misery* may easily breed some absurdity of greater charge. *Wotton.*

MISESTE'EM. *n. s.* [*mis* and *esteem.*] Disregard; slight.

To MISFA'SHION. *v. a.* [*mis* and *fashion.*] To form wrong.

A thing in reason impossible, thorough their *misfashioned* preconceit, appeared unto them no less certain, than if nature had written it in the very foreheads of all the creatures of God. *Hakewill on Providence.*

To MISFO'RM. *v. a.* [*mis* and *form.*] To put in an ill form.

His monstrous scalp down to his teeth it tore,
And that *misformed* shape misshaped more. *Spenser.*

MISFO'RTUNE. *n. s.* [*mis* and *fortune.*] Calamity; ill luck; want of good fortune.

Fortune thus 'gan say, misery and *misfortune* is all one,
And of *misfortune*, fortune hath only the gift. *Sidney.*
What world's delight, or joy of living speech,
Can heart so plung'd in sea of sorrows deep,
And heaped with so huge *misfortunes* reach? *Fa. Qu.*
Consider why the change was wrought,
You'll find it his *misfortune*, not his fault. *Addison.*

To MISGI'VE. *v. a.* [*mis* and *give.*] To fill with doubt; to deprive of confidence. It is used always with the reciprocal pronoun.

As Henry's late presaging prophesy
Did glad my heart with hope of this young Richmond;
So doth my heart *misgive me* in these conflicts
What may befal him, to his harm or ours. *Shakespeare.*
This is strange! Who hath got the right Anne?
My heart *misgives me*. *Shakesp. Merry Wives of Windsor.*
Yet oft his heart divine of something ill,
Misgave him. *Milton.*

If a conscience thus qualified and informed, be not the measure by which a man may take a true estimate of his absolution, the sinner is left in the plunge of infinite doubts, suspicions, and *misgivings*, both as to the measures of his present duty, and the final issues of his future reward. *South.*

His heart *misgave* him, that these were so many meeting-houses; but, upon communicating his suspicions, I soon made him easy. *Addison's Freeholder*, N°. 47.

To MISGO'VERN. *v. a.* [*mis* and *govern.*] To govern ill; to administer unfaithfully.

Solyman charged him bitterly, that he had *misgoverned* the state, and inverted his treasures to his own private use. *Knolles's Hist. of the Turks.*

MISGO'VERNED. *adj.* [from *misgovern.*] Rude; uncivilised.

Rude, *misgovern'd* hands, from window tops,
Threw dust and rubbish on king Richard's head. *Shakesp.*

MISGO'VERNANCE. *n. s.* [*mis* and *governance.*] Irregularity.

Thy muse too long slumbereth in sorrowing,
Lulled asleep through love's *misgovernance*. *Spenser's Past.*

MISGO'VERNMENT. *n. s.* [*mis* and *government.*]

1. Ill administration of publick affairs.

Men lay the blame of those evils whereof they know not the ground, upon publick *misgovernment*. *Raleigh's Essays.*

2. Ill management.

Men are miserable, if their education hath been so undisciplined, as to leave them unfurnished of skill to spend their time; but most miserable, if such *misgovernment* and unskilfulness make them fall into vicious company. *Taylor.*

3. Irregularity; inordinate behaviour.

There is not chastity enough in language
Without offence to utter them: thus, pretty lady,
I am sorry for thy much *misgovernment*. *Shakespeare.*

MISGU'IDANCE. *n. s.* [*mis* and *guidance.*] False direction.

The Nicene council fixed the equinox the twenty-first of March for the finding out of Easter; which has caused the *misguidance* from the sun which we lie under in respect of Easter, and the moveable feasts. *Holder on Time.*

Whosoever deceives a man, makes him ruin himself; and by causing an error in the great guide of his actions, his judgment, he causes an error in his choice, the *misguidance* of which must naturally engage him to his destruction. *South.*

To MISGUI'DE. *v. a.* [*mis* and *guide.*] To direct ill; to lead the wrong way.

Hunting after arguments to make good one side of a question, and wholly to neglect those which favour the other, is wilfully to *misguide* the understanding; and is so far from giving truth its due value, that it wholly debases it. *Locke.*

Misguided prince! no longer urge thy fate,
Nor tempt the hero to unequal war. *Prior.*
Of all the causes which conspire to blind
Man's erring judgment, and *misguide* the mind,
What the weak head with strongest bias rules,
Is pride, the never-failing vice of fools. *Pope.*

MISHA'P. *n. s.* [*mis* and *hap.*] Ill chance; ill luck; calamity.

To tell you what miserable *mishaps* fell to the young prince of Macedon his cousin, I should too much fill your ears with strange horrours. *Sidney, b.* ii.

Since we are thus far entered into the consideration of her *mishaps*, tell me, have there been any more such tempests wherein she hath thus wretchedly been wrecked. *Spenser.*

Sir knight, take to you wonted strength,
And master these *mishaps* with patient might. *Fa. Queen.*
Rome's readiest champions, repose you here,
Secure from worldly chances and *mishaps*. *Shakespeare.*
It cannot be
But that success attends him: if *mishap*,
Ere this he had return'd, with fury driv'n
By his avengers; since no place like this
Can fit his punishment, or your revenge. *Milton's P. Lost.*
If the worst of all *mishaps* hath fallen,
Speak; for he could not die unlike himself. *Denham.*

MI'SHMASH. *n. s.* *Ains.* A low word. A mingle or hotch-potch.

To MISINFE'R. *v. a.* [*mis* and *infer.*] To infer wrong.

Nestorius teaching rightly, that God and man are distinct natures, did thereupon *misinfer*, that in Christ those natures can by no conjunction make one person. *Hooker, b.* v.

To MISINFO'RM. *v. a.* [*mis* and *inform.*] To deceive by false accounts.

Some belonged to a man of great dignity, and not as that wicked Simon had *misinformed*. 2 *Mac.* iii. 11.

By no means trust to your servants, who mislead you, or *misinform* you; the reproach will lie upon yourself. *Bacon.*

Bid her well beware,
Lest by some fair-appearing good surpriz'd,
She dictate false; and *misinform* the will
To do what God expresly hath forbid. *Milton's Par. Lost.*

MISINFORMA'TION. *n. s.* [from *misinform.*] False intelligence; false accounts.

Let not such be discouraged as deserve well, by *misinformation* of others, perhaps out of envy or treachery. *Bacon.*

The vengeance of God, and the indignation of men, will join forces against an insulting baseness, when backed with greatness, and set on by *misinformation*. *South's Sermons.*

To MISINTE'RPRET. *v. a.* [*mis* and *interpret.*] To explain to a wrong sense.

The gentle reader rests happy to hear the worthiest works *misinterpreted*, the clearest actions obscured, and the innocentest life traduced. *Benj. Johnson.*

After all the care I have taken, there may be several passages misquoted and *misinterpreted*. *Arbuthnot on Coins.*

To MISJO'IN. *v. a.* [*mis* and *join.*] To join unfitly or improperly.

In reason's absence mimick fancy wakes
To imitate her; but *misjoining* shapes,
Wild work produces oft, and most in dreams;
Ill-matching words, and deeds, long past, or late. *Milton.*
Luther, more mistaking what he read,
Misjoins the sacred body with the bread. *Dryden.*

To MISJU'DGE. *v. a.* [*mis* and *judge.*] To form false opinions; to judge ill.

Where we *misjudge* the matter, a miscarriage draws pity after it; but when we are transported by pride, our ruin lies at our own door. *L'Estrange.*

You *misjudge*;
You see through love, and that deludes your sight;
As, what is straight, seems crooked through the water.
Dryden's All for Love.

By allowing himself in what is innocent, he breeds offence to his weak and *misjudging* neighbour. *Atterbury's Sermons.*

Insensate!
Too long *misjudging* have I thought thee wise,
But sure relentless folly steels thy breast. *Pope.*

To MISLA'Y. *v. a.* [*mis* and *lay.*] To lay in a wrong place.

Mean time my worthy wife, our arms *mislay'd*,
And from beneath my head my sword convey'd. *Dryden.*

The fault is generally *mislaid* upon nature; and there is often a complaint of want of parts, when the fault lies in want of a due improvement. *Locke.*

If the butler be the tell-tale, *mislay* a spoon, so as he may never find it. *Swift's Rules to Servants.*

MISLA'YER. *n. s.* [from *mislay.*] One that puts in the wrong place.

The *mislayer* of a mere-stone is to blame: but the unjust judge is the capital remover of land-marks, when he defineth amiss of lands. *Bacon's Essays.*

To MISLE'AD. *v. a.* [*mis* and *lead.*] To guide a wrong way; to betray to mischief or mistake.

Take, oh take those lips away,
That so sweetly were forsworn;
And those eyes, the break of day,
Lights that do *mislead* the morn. *Shakespeare.*
Those we love,
That are *misled* upon your cousin's part. *Shakesp. Henry* IV.
Poor *misled* men: your states are yet worthy pity.
If you would hear, and change your savage minds,
Leave to be mad. *Benj. Johnson's Cataline.*

Trust not to your servants who *mislead* or misinform you. *Bacon's Advice to Villiers.*

O thieviſh night,
Why ſhould'ſt thou but for ſome felonious end,
In thy dark lanthorn thus cloſe up the ſtars,
That nature hung in heav'n, and fill'd their lamps
With everlaſting oil, to give due light
To the *miſled* and lonely traveller? *Milton.*

What can they teach and not *miſlead:*
Ignorant of themſelves, of God much more? *Milton.*

Thou who haſt taught me to forgive the ill,
And recompenſe, as friends, the good *miſled*;
If mercy be a precept of thy will,
Return that mercy on thy ſervant's head. *Dryden.*

The imagination, which is of ſimple perception, doth never of itſelf, and directly, *miſlead* us; yet it is the almoſt fatal means of our deception. *Glanville's Scep.*

Whatever neceſſity determines to the purſuit of real bliſs, the ſame neceſſity eſtabliſhes ſuſpence, and ſcrutiny of each ſucceſſive deſire, whether the ſatisfaction of it does not interfere with our true happineſs, and *miſlead* us from it. *Locke.*

'Tis hard to ſay, if greater want of ſkill
Appear in writing or in judging ill:
But of the two leſs dang'rous is th' offence
To tire our patience, than *miſlead* our ſenſe. *Pope.*

MISLE'ADER. *n. ſ.* [from *miſlead.*] One that leads to ill.

When thou doſt hear I am as I have been,
Approach me, and thou ſhalt be as thou waſt,
The tutor and the feeder of my riots;
Till then I baniſh thee on pain of death,
As I have done the reſt of my *miſleaders.* *Shakeſpeare.*

They have diſclaimed and abandoned thoſe heretical phantaſies touching our Saviour, wherein by their *miſleaders* they had been anciently plunged. *Brerewood on Languages.*

To MISLI'KE. *v. a.* [*mis* and *like.*] To diſapprove; to be not pleaſed with; to diſlike.

It was hard to ſay, whether he more liked his doings, or *miſliked* the effect of his doings. *Sidney.*

Tertullian was not deceived in the nature of the place; but Aquinas, who *miſliked* this opinion, followed a worſe. *Raleigh's Hiſt. of the World.*

Judge not the preacher, for he is thy judge:
If thou *miſlike* him, thou conceiv'ſt him not. *Herbert.*

MISLI'KE. *n. ſ.* [from the verb.] Diſapprobation; diſtaſte.

Setting your ſcorns and your *miſlike* aſide,
Tell me ſome reaſon, why the lady Gray
Should not become my wife. *Shakeſp. Henry* VI.

Their angry geſtures with *miſlike* diſcloſe,
How much his ſpeech offends their noble ears. *Fairfax.*

MISLI'KER. *n. ſ.* [from *miſlike.*] One that diſapproves.

Open flatterers of great men, privy *miſlikers* of good men, fair ſpeakers with ſmiling countenances. *Aſcham.*

MI'SLEN. *n. ſ.* [corrupted from *miſcellane.*] Mixed corn: as, wheat and rie.

They commonly ſow thoſe lands with wheat, *miſlen*, and barley. *Mortimer's Huſbandry.*

To MI'SLE. *v. n.* [from *miſt.*] To rain in imperceptible drops, like a thick miſt: properly *miſtle.*

Ynough, thou mourned haſt,
Now ginnes to *mizzle*, hie we homeward faſt. *Spenſer.*

The very ſmall drops of a *miſling* rain deſcending through a freezing air, do each of them ſhoot into one of thoſe figured icicles. *Grew's Coſmol. b.* i.

This cold precipitates the vapours either in dews, or, if the vapours more copiouſly aſcend, they are condenſed into *miſling*, or into ſhowers of ſmall rain, falling in numerous, thick, ſmall drops. *Derham's Phyſico-Theol.*

In *miſling* days when I my threſher heard,
With nappy beer I to the barn repair'd. *Gay's Paſtorals.*

To MISLI'VE. *v. n.* [*mis* and *live.*] To live ill.

Should not thilke God, that gave him that good,
Eke cheriſh his child if in his ways he ſtood,
For if he *miſlive* in leudneſs and luſt,
Little boots all the wealth and the truſt. *Spenſer's Paſt.*

To MI'SMANAGE. *v. a.* [*mis* and *manage.*] To manage ill.

The debates of moſt princes councils would be in danger to be *miſmanaged*, ſince thoſe who have a great ſtroke in them are not always perfectly knowing in the forms of ſyllogiſm. *Locke.*

MI'SMANAGEMENT. *n. ſ.* [*mis* and *management.*] Ill management; ill conduct.

It is *miſmanagement* more than want of abilities, that men have reaſon to complain of in thoſe that differ from them. *Locke.*

The falls of fav'rites, projects of the great,
Of old *miſmanagements*, taxations new,
All neither wholly falſe, nor wholly true. *Pope.*

To MISMA'RK. *v. a.* [*mis* and *mark.*] To mark with the wrong token.

Things are *miſmarked* in contemplation and life for want of application or integrity. *Collier on human Reaſon.*

To MISMA'TCH. *v. a.* [*mis* and *match.*] To match unſuitably.

What at my years forſaken! had I
Ugly, or old, *miſmatcht* to my deſires,
My natural defects had taught me
To ſet me down contented. *Southern's Spartan Dame.*

To MISNA'ME. *v. a.* [*mis* and *name.*] To call by the wrong name.

They make one man's fancies, or perhaps failings, confining laws to others, and convey them as ſuch to their ſucceeders, who are bold to *miſname* all unobſequiouſneſs to their incogitancy, preſumption. *Boyle on Colours.*

MISNO'MER. *n. ſ.* [French.] In law, an indictment, or any other act vacated by a wrong name.

To MISOBSE'RVE. *v. a.* [*mis* and *obſerve.*] Not to obſerve accurately.

They underſtand it as early as they do language; and, if I *miſobſerve* not, they love to be treated as rational creatures ſooner than is imagined. *Locke on Education.*

MISO'GAMIST. *n. ſ.* [μισῶ and γάμος.] A marriage hater.

MISO'GYNY. *n. ſ.* [μισῶ and γυνή.] Hatred of women.

To MISO'RDER. *v. a.* [*mis* and *order.*] To conduct ill; to manage irregularly.

If the child miſs either in forgetting a word, or *miſordering* the ſentence, I would not have the maſter frown. *Aſcham.*

Yet few of them come to any great age, by reaſon of their *miſordered* life when they were young. *Aſcham.*

The time *miſorder'd* doth in common ſenſe
Crowd us, and cruſh us to this monſtrous form,
To hold our ſafety up. *Shakeſp. Henry* IV. *p.* ii.

MISO'RDER. *n. ſ.* [from the verb.] Irregularity; diſorderly proceedings.

When news was brought to Richard the ſecond, that his uncles, who ſought to reform the *miſorders* of his counſellors, were aſſembled in a wood near unto the court, merrily demanded of one Sir Hugh a Linne, who had been a good military man, but was then ſomewhat diſtraught of his wits, what he would adviſe him to do? Iſſue out, quoth Sir Hugh, and ſlay them every mother's ſon; and when thou haſt ſo done, thou haſt killed all the faithful friends thou haſt in England. *Camden's Remains.*

MISO'RDERLY. *adj.* [from *miſorder.*] Irregular.

His over-much fearing of you drives him to ſeek ſome *miſorderly* ſhift, to be helped by ſome other book, or to be prompted by ſome other ſcholar. *Aſcham's Schoolmaſter.*

To MISPE'L. *v. a.* [*mis* and *ſpell.*] To ſpell wrong.

She became a profeſt enemy to the arts and ſciences, and ſcarce ever wrote a letter to him without wilfully *miſpelling* his name. *Spectator*, N°. 635.

To MISPEND. *v. a.* preterite and part. paſſive *miſpent.* [*mis* and *ſpend.*]

1. To ſpend ill; to waſte; to conſume to no purpoſe; to throw away.

What a deal of cold buſineſs doth a man *miſpend* the better part of life in? In ſcattering compliments, tendering viſits, gathering and venting news. *Benj. Johnſon's Diſcovery.*

Firſt guilty conſcience does the mirrour bring,
Then ſharp remorſe ſhoots out her angry ſting;
And anxious thoughts, within themſelves at ſtrife,
Upbraid the long *miſpent*, luxurious life. *Dryden.*

I this writer's want of ſenſe arraign,
Treat all his empty pages with diſdain,
And think a grave reply *miſpent* and vain. *Blackmore.*

He who has lived with the greateſt care will find, upon a review of his time, that he has ſomething to redeem; but he who has *miſpent* much has ſtill a greater concern. *Rogers.*

Wiſe men retrieve, as far as they are able, every *miſpent* or unprofitable hour which has ſlipped from them. *Rogers.*

2. To waſte, with the reciprocal pronoun.

Now let the arched knife their thirſty limbs
Diſſever, for the genial moiſture due
To apples, otherwiſe *miſpends itſelf*
In barren twigs. *Philips.*

MISPE'NDER. *n. ſ.* [from *miſpend.*] One who ſpends ill or prodigally.

I very much ſuſpect the excellency of thoſe mens parts who are diſſolute, and careleſs *miſpenders* of their time. *Norris's Miſcel.*

MISPERSUA'SION. *n. ſ.* [*mis* and *perſuaſion.*] Wrong notion; falſe opinion.

Some *miſperſuaſions* concerning the Divine Attributes tend to the corrupting mens manners. *Decay of Piety.*

To MISPLA'CE. *v. a.* [*mis* and *place.*] To put in a wrong place.

I'll have this crown of mine cut from my ſhoulders,
Before I'll ſee the crown ſo foul *miſplac'd.* *Shakeſpeare.*

What little arts govern the world! we need not
An armed enemy or corrupted friend,
When ſervice but *miſplac'd*, or love miſtaken,
Performs the work. *Denham's Sophy.*

Is a man betrayed by ſuch agents as he employs? He *miſplaced* his confidence, took hypocriſy for fidelity, and ſo relied upon the ſervices of a pack of villains. *South's Sermons.*

Shall we repine at a little *misplaced* charity; we, who could no way foresee the effect? *Atterbury's Sermons.*

To MISPO'INT. *v. a.* [*mis* and *point.*] To confuse sentences by wrong punctuation.

To MISPRI'SE. *v. a.* Sometimes it signifies mistaken, from the French verb *mesprendre*; sometimes undervalued or disdained, from the French verb *mepriser*. *Hanmer.* It is in both senses wholly obsolete.

1. To mistake.

You spend your passion on a *mispris'd* mood;
I am not guilty of Lysander's blood. *Shakespeare.*

2. To slight; to scorn; to despise.

He's so much in the heart of the world, and especially of my own people who best know him, that I am altogether *misprised*. *Shakesp. As you like it.*

Pluck indignation on thy head;
By the *misprising* of a maid, too virtuous
For the contempt of empire. *Shakespeare.*

MISPRI'SION. *n. s.* [from *misprise.*]

1. Scorn; contempt.

Here take her hand,
Proud scornful boy, unworthy this good gift!
That doth in vile *misprision* shackle up
My love, and her desert. *Shakespeare.*

2. Mistake; misconception.

Thou hast mistaken quite,
And laid thy love juice on some true love's sight;
Of thy *misprision* must perforce ensue
Some true love turn'd, and not a false turn'd true. *Shakesp.*

We feel such or such a sentiment within us, and herein is no cheat or *misprision*; it is truly so, and our sense concludes nothing of its rise. *Glanville's Scep.*

3. [In common law.] It signifies neglect, negligence, or oversight. *Misprision* of treason is the concealment, or not disclosing, of known treason; for the which the offenders are to suffer imprisonment during the king's pleasure, lose their goods and the profits of their lands during their lives. *Misprision* of felony, is the letting any person, committed for treason or felony, or suspicion of either, to go before he be indicted. *Cowel.*

To MISPROPO'RTION. *v. a.* [*mis* and *proportion.*] To join without due proportion.

MISPRO'UD. *adj.* [*mis* and *proud.*] Viciously proud. Obsolete.

Now I fall, thy tough commixtures melt,
Impairing Henry, strength'ning *misproud* York. *Shakesp.*

To MISQUO'TE. *v. a.* [*mis* and *quote.*] To quote falsly.

Look how we can, or sad, or merrily,
Interpretation will *misquote* our looks. *Shakesp. Henry IV.*

After all the care I have taken, there may be several passages *misquoted*. *Arbuthnot on Coins.*

To MISRECI'TE. *v. a.* [*mis* and *recite.*] To recite not according to the truth.

He *misrecites* the argument, and denies the consequence, which is clear. *Bishop Bramhall against Hobbes.*

To MISRE'CKON. *v. a.* [*mis* and *reckon.*] To reckon wrong; to compute wrong.

Whoever finds a mistake in the sum total, must allow himself out, though after repeated trials he may not see in which article he has *misreckoned*. *Swift.*

To MISRELA'TE. *v. a.* [*mis* and *relate.*] To relate inaccurately or falsly.

To satisfy me that he *misrelated* not the experiment, he brought two or three small pipes of glass, which gave me the opportunity of trying it. *Boyle.*

MISRELA'TION. *n. s.* [from *misrelate.*] False or inaccurate narrative.

Mine aim was only to press home those things in writing, which had been agitated between us by word of mouth; a course much to be preferred before verbal conferences, as being less subject to mistakes and *misrelations*, and wherein paralogisms are more quickly detected. *Bishop Bramhall.*

To MISREME'MBER. *v. a.* [*mis* and *remember.*] To mistake by trusting to memory.

If I much *misremember* not, I had such a spirit from peas kept long enough to lose their verdure. *Boyle.*

To MISREPO'RT. *v. a.* [*mis* and *report.*] To give a false account of; to give an account disadvantageous and false.

His doctrine was *misreported*, as though he had everywhere preached this, not only concerning the Gentiles, but also touching the Jews. *Hooker, b.* iv.

A man that never yet
Did, as he vouches, *misreport* your grace. *Shakespeare.*

The wrong judgment that misleads us, and makes the will often fasten on the worse side, lies in *misreporting* upon the various comparisons of these. *Locke.*

MISREPO'RT. *n. s.* [from the verb.] False account; false and malicious representation.

We defend him not,
Only desire to know his crime: 'tis possible
It may be some mistake or *misreport*,
Some false suggestion, or malicious scandal. *Denham.*

As by flattery a man is usually brought to open his bosom to his mortal enemy, so by detraction, and a slanderous *misreport* of persons, he is often brought to shut the same even to his best and truest friends. *South's Sermons.*

To MISREPRESE'NT. *v. a.* [*mis* and *represent.*] To represent not as it is; to falsify to disadvantage: *mis* often signifies not only error, but malice or mischief.

Two qualities necessary to a reader before his judgment should be allowed are, common honesty and common sense; and that no man could have *misrepresented* that paragraph, unless he were utterly destitute of one or both. *Swift.*

While it is so difficult to learn the springs of some facts, and so easy to forget the circumstances of others, it is no wonder they should be so grosly *misrepresented* to the publick by curious and inquisitive heads, who proceed altogether upon conjectures. *Swift.*

MISREPRESENTA'TION. *n. s.* [from *misrepresent.*]

1. The act of misrepresenting.

They have prevailed by *misrepresentations*, and other artifices, to make the successor look upon them as the only persons he can trust. *Swift.*

2. Account maliciously false.

Since I have shewn him his foul mistakes and injurious *misrepresentations*, it will become him publickly to own and retract them. *Atterbury.*

MISRU'LE. *n. s.* [*mis* and *rule.*] Tumult; confusion; revel; unjust domination.

In the portal plac'd, the heav'n-born maid,
Enormous riot, and *misrule* survey'd. *Pope.*
And through his airy hall the loud *misrule*
Of driving tempest, is for ever heard. *Thomson.*

MISS. *n. s.* [contracted from *mistress*. *Bailey.*]

1. The term of honour to a young girl.

Where there are little masters and *misses* in a house, they are great impediments to the diversions of the servants. *Sw.*

2. A strumpet; a concubine; a whore; a prostitute.

All women would be of one piece,
The virtuous matron and the *miss*. *Hudibras, p.* iii.
This gentle cock, for solace of his life,
Six *misses* had besides his lawful wife. *Dryden.*

To MISS. *v. a.* [*missen*, Dutch and German.] *Missed* preter. *mist* part.

1. Not to hit by the mind; to mistake.

Nor can I *miss* the way, so strongly drawn
By this new-felt attraction, and instinct. *Milton.*

2. Not to hit by manual aim.

The life you boasted to your jav'lin giv'n,
Prince, you have *miss'd*. *Pope.*

3. To fail of obtaining.

If she desired above all things to have Orgalus, Orgalus feared nothing but to *miss* Parthenia. *Sidney.*

So may I, blind fortune leading me,
Miss that, which one unworthier may attain;
And die with grieving. *Shakesp. Merchant of Venice.*
Where shall a maid's distracted heart find rest,
If she can *miss* it in her lover's breast? *Dryden.*

When a man *misses* his great end, happiness, he will acknowledge he judged not right. *Locke.*

4. To discover something to be unexpectedly wanting.

Without him I found a weakness, and a mistrustfulness of myself, as one strayed from his best strength, when at any time I *missed* him. *Sidney.*

In vain have I kept all that this fellow hath in the wilderness, so that nothing was *missed*. 1 *Sam.* xxv. 21.

5. To be without.

We cannot *miss* him; he does make our fire,
Fetch in our wood. *Shakespeare's Tempest.*

6. To omit.

She would never *miss* one day,
A walk so fine, a sight so gay. *Prior.*

7. To perceive want of.

My redoubl'd love and care,
May ever tend about thee to old age
With all things grateful chear'd, and so supply'd,
That what by me thou hast lost thou least shalt *miss*. *Milt.*

He who has a firm, sincere friend, may want all the rest without *missing* them. *South's Sermons.*

To MISS. *v. n.*

1. To fly wide; not to hit.

Flying bullets now
To execute his rage, appear too slow,
They *miss* or sweep but common souls away. *Waller.*

2. Not to succeed.

The general root of superstition is, that men observe when things hit, and not when they *miss*; and commit to memory the one, and forget and pass over the other. *Bacon.*

3. To fail; to mistake.

4. To be lost; to be wanting.

My lord,
Upon my lady's *missing*, came to me
With his sword drawn. *Shakesp. Cymbeline.*

16 P

Thy

Thy shepherds we hurt not, neither was there ought *missing* unto them. 1 *Sam.* xxv. 7.

For a time caught up to God, as once
Moses was in the mount, and *missing* long,
And the great Thisbite, who on fiery wheels
Rode up to heaven, yet once again to come. *Milt. Par. R.*

5. To miscarry; to fail.

Th' invention all admir'd, and each, how he
To be th' inventor *miss'd*, so easy it seem'd,
Once found, which yet unfound most would have thought
Impossible. *Milton's Par. Lost, b.* v.

6. To fail to obtain, learn, or find: sometimes with *of* before the object.

Grittus *missing* of the Moldavian fell upon Maylat. *Knolles.*

The moral and relative perfections of the Deity are easy to be understood by us; upon the least reflection we cannot *miss* of them. *Atterbury's Sermons.*

Miss. *n. s.* [from the verb.]

1. Loss; want.

In humble dales is footing fast,
The trode is not so tickle,
And though one fall through heedless haste,
Yet is his *misse* not mickle. *Spenser's Pastorals.*

I could have better spar'd a better man.
Oh, I should have a heavy *miss* of thee,
If I were much in love with vanity. *Shakesp. Henry* IV.

If these papers have that evidence in them, there will be no great *miss* of those which are lost, and my reader may be satisfied without them. *Locke.*

2. Mistake; errour.

He did without any great *miss* in the hardest points of grammar. *Ascham's Schoolmaster.*

Mi'ssal. *n. s.* [*missale*, Lat. *missel*, Fr.] The mass book.

By the rubrick of the *missal*, in every solemn mass, the priest is to go up to the middle of the altar. *Stillingfleet.*

To Missa'y. *v. n.* [*mis* and *say.*] To say ill or wrong.

Their ill haviour garres men *missay*,
Both of their doctrine and their fay. *Spenser's Past.*

Diggon Davie, I bid her godday,
Or Diggon her is, or I *missay*. *Spenser's Past.*

We are not dwarfs, but of equal stature, if Vives *missay* not. *Hakewill on Providence.*

To Misse'em. *v. n.* [*mis* and *seem.*]

1. To make false appearance.

Foul Duessa meet,
Who with her witchcraft and *misseeming* sweet
Inveigled her to follow her desires unmeet. *Fairy Queen.*

2. To misbecome. Obsolete both.

Never knight I saw in such *misseeming* plight. *Fa. Qu.*

To Misse'rve. *v. a.* [*mis* and *serve.*] To serve unfaithfully.

Great men, who *misserved* their country, were fined very highly. *Arbuthnot on Coins.*

To Missha'pe. *v. a.* part. *misshaped* and *misshapen.* [*mis* and *shape.*] To shape ill; to form ill; to deform.

A rude *misshapen*, monstruous rabblement. *Fa. Qu.*

His monstruous scalp down to his teeth it tore,
And that misformed shape, *misshaped* more. *Fairy Queen.*

Him then she does transform to monstruous hues,
And horribly *misshapes* with ugly sights,
Captiv'd eternally in iron mews. *Fairy Queen, b.* ii.

This *misshaped* knave,
His mother was a witch. *Shakespeare's Tempest.*

And will she yet debase her eyes on me,
On me that halt and am *misshapen* thus. *Shak. Rich.* III.

Let the *misshaped* trunk that bears this head
Be round impaled with a glorious crown. *Shakespeare.*

Pride will have a fall: the beautiful trees go all to the wreck here, and only the *misshapen* and despicable dwarf is left standing. *L'Estrange.*

Pluto hates his own *misshapen* race,
Her sister furies fly her hideous face. *Dryden's Æn.*

They make bold to destroy ill-formed and *misshaped* productions. *Locke.*

The Alps broken into so many steps and precipices, form one of the most irregular, *misshapen* scenes in the world. *Addis.*

We ought not to believe that the banks of the ocean are really deformed, because they have not the form of a regular bulwark; nor that the mountains are *misshapen*, because they are not exact pyramids or cones. *Bentley's Sermons.*

Some figures monstrous and *misshap'd* appear
Consider'd singly, or beheld too near,
Which but proportion'd to their site or place,
Due distance reconciles to form and grace. *Pope.*

2. In *Shakespeare*, perhaps, it once signifies ill directed: as, *to shape a course.*

Thy wit, that ornament to shape and love,
Misshapen in the conduct of them both,
Like powder in a skill-less soldiers flask,
Is set on fire. *Shakesp. Romeo and Juliet.*

Mi'ssile. *adj.* [*missilis*, Lat.] Thrown by the hand; striking at distance.

We bend the bow, or wing the *missile* dart. *Pope.*

Mi'ssion. *n. s.* [*missio*, Latin.]

1. Commission; the state of being sent by supreme authority.

Her son tracing the desart wild,
All his great work to come before him set,
How to begin, how to accomplish best,
His end of being on earth, and *mission* high. *Milt. Pa. Reg.*

The divine authority of our *mission*, and the powers vested in us by the high-priest of our profession, Christ Jesus, are publickly disputed and denied. *Atterbury.*

2. Persons sent on any account, usually to propagate religion.

In these ships there should be a *mission* of three of the brethren of Solomon's house, to give us knowledge of the sciences, manufactures, and inventions of all the world, and bring us books and paterns; and that the brethren should stay abroad till the new *mission*. *Bacon's New Atlantis.*

3. Dismission; discharge. Not in use.

In Cesar's army, somewhat the soldiers would have had, yet only demanded a *mission* or discharge, though with no intention it should be granted, but thought to wrench him to their other desires; whereupon with one cry they asked *mission*. *Bacon's Apophth.*

4. Faction; party. Not in use.

Glorious deeds, in these fields of late,
Made emulous *missions* 'mongst the gods themselves,
And drove great Mars to faction. *Shakespeare.*

Mi'ssionary. } *n. s.* [*missionaire*, French.] One sent to propagate religion.
Mi'ssioner. }

You mention the presbyterian *missionary*, who hath been persecuted for his religion. *Swift.*

Like mighty *missioner* you come,
Ad partes infidelium. *Dryden.*

Mi'ssive. *adj.* [*missive*, French.]

1. Such as may be sent.

The king grants a licence under the great seal, called a congé d'eslire, to elect the person he has nominated by his letters *missive*. *Ayliffe's Parergon.*

2. Used at distance.

In vain with darts a distant war they try,
Short, and more short, the *missive* weapons fly. *Dryden.*

MI'SSIVE. *n. s.* [French.]

1. A letter sent: it is retained in Scotland in that sense.

Great aids came in to him; partly upon *missives*, and partly voluntaries from many parts. *Bacon's Henry* VII.

2. A messenger.

Rioting in Alexandria, you
Did pocket up my letters; and with taunts
Did gibe my *missive* out of audience. *Shakespeare.*

While wrapt in the wonder of it came *missives* from the king, who all hail'd me thane of Cawder. *Shakesp. Macbeth.*

Misspe'ak. *v. a.* [*mis* and *speak.*] To speak wrong.

It is not so; thou hast *misspoke*, misheard;
Tell o'er thy tale again. *Shakesp. King Lear.*

A mother delights to hear
Her early child *misspeak* half-utter'd words. *Donne.*

Mist. *n. s.* [mıꞅꞇ, Saxon.]

1. A low thin cloud; a small thin rain not perceived in single drops.

Old Chaucer, like the morning star,
To us discovers day from far;
His light those *mists* and clouds dissolv'd
Which our dark nation long involv'd. *Denham.*

And *mists* condens'd to clouds obscure the sky,
And clouds dissolv'd, the thirsty ground supply. *Roscommon.*

As a *mist* is a multitude of small but solid globules, which therefore descend; so a vapour, and therefore a watry cloud, is nothing else but a congeries of very small and concave globules, which therefore ascend to that height, in which they are of equal weight with the air, where they remain suspended, till by some motion in the air, being broken, they descend in solid drops; either small, as in a *mist*, or bigger, when many of them run together, as in rain. *Grew.*

But hov'ring *mists* around his brows are spread,
And night with sable shades involves his head. *Dryden.*

A cloud is nothing but a *mist* flying high in the air, as a *mist* is nothing but a cloud here below. *Locke.*

2. Any thing that dims or darkens.

My peoples eyes were once blinded with such *mists* of suspicion, they are soon misled into the most desperate actions. *King Charles.*

His passion cast a *mist* before his sense,
And either made or magnify'd th' offence. *Dryden.*

To Mist. *v. a.* [from the noun.] To cloud; to cover with a vapour or steam.

Lend me a looking-glass;
If that her breath will *mist* or stain the stone,
Why then she lives. *Shakesp. King Lear.*

Mista'kable. *adj.* [from *mistake.*] Liable to be conceived wrong.

It is not strange to see the difference of a third part in so large an account, if we consider how differently they are set forth in minor and less *mistakable* numbers. *Brown.*

To MISTA'KE. *v. a.* [*mis* and *take.*] To conceive wrong; to take something for that which it is not.

The towns, neither of the one side nor the other, willingly opening their gates to strangers, nor strangers willingly entering for fear of being *mistaken*. *Sidney.*

These did truly apprehend a great affinity between their practice of invocation of saints and the heathen idolatry, or else there was no danger one should be *mistaken* for the other. *Stillingfleet.*

This if neglected will make the reader very much *mistake*, and misunderstand his meaning, and render the sense very perplexed. *Locke.*

Fancy passes for knowlege, and what is prettily said is *mistaken* for solid. *Locke.*

Fools into the notion fall,
That vice or virtue there is none at all:
Ask your own heart, and nothing is so plain,
'Tis to *mistake* them costs the time and pain. *Pope.*

To MISTA'KE. *v. n.* To err; not to judge right.

Seeing God found folly in his angels; mens judgments, which inhabit these houses of clay, cannot be without their *mistakings*. *Raleigh's Hist. of the World.*

Seldom any one *mistakes* in his names of simple ideas, or applies the name red to the idea green. *Locke.*

Servants *mistake*, and sometimes occasion misunderstanding, among friends. *Swift.*

MISTA'EN. pret. and part. pass. of *mistake* for *mistaken*, and so retained in Scotland.

This dagger hath *mista'en*; for lo! the sheath
Lies empty on the back of Mountague,
The point missheathed in my daughter's bosom. *Shakesp.*

To be MISTA'KEN. To err.

England is so idly king'd.
—You are too much *mistaken* in this king:
Question, your grace, the late embassadors,
How modest in exception, and withal
How terrible in constant resolution. *Shakesp. Henry* V.
Mistaken Brutus thought to break their yoke,
But cut the bond of union with that stroke. *Waller.*

MISTA'KE. *n. s.* [from the verb.] Misconception; error.

He never shall find out fit mate; but such
As some misfortune brings him, or *mistake*. *Milton.*

Infallibility is an absolute security of the understanding from all possibility of *mistake* in what it believes. *Tillotson.*

Those terrors are not to be charged upon religion, which proceed either from the want of religion, or superstitious *mistakes* about it. *Bentley's Sermons.*

MISTA'KINGLY. *adv.* [from *mistaking.*] Erroneously; falsly.

The error is not in the eye, but in the estimative faculty, which *mistakingly* concludes that colour to belong to the wall which does indeed belong to the object. *Boyle on Colours.*

To MISTA'TE. *v. a.* [*mis* and *state.*] To state wrong.

They *mistate* the question, when they talk of pressing ceremonies. *Bishop Sanderson.*

To MISTE'ACH. *v. a.* [*mis* and *teach.*] To teach wrong.

Such guides shall be set over the several congregations as will be sure to *misteach* them. *Bishop Sanderson.*

The extravagances of the lewdest life are the more consummate disorders of a *mistaught* or neglected youth. *L'Estrange's Fables.*

To MISTE'L. *v. a.* [*mis* and *tell.*] To tell unfaithfully or inaccurately.

To MISTE'MPER. *v. a.* [*mis* and *temper.*] To temper ill; to disorder.

This inundation of *mistemper'd* humour
Rests by you only to be qualified. *Shakesp. King John.*

MI'STER. *adj.* [from *mestier*, trade, French.] What *mister*, what *kind* of.

The redcross knight toward him crossed fast,
To weet what *mister* wight was so dismay'd,
There him he finds all senseless and aghast. *Spenser.*

To MISTE'RM. *v. a.* [*mis* and *term.*] To term erroneously.

Hence banished, is banish'd from the world;
And world exil'd is death. That banished
Is death *misterm'd*. *Shakesp. Romeo and Juliet.*

To MISTHI'NK. *v. a.* [*mis* and *think.*] To think ill; to think wrong.

How will the country, for these woful chances,
Misthink the king, and not be satisfy'd. *Shakespeare.*
We, the greatest, are *misthought*
For things that others do. *Shakesp. Ant. and Cleopatra.*
Thoughts! which how found they harbour in thy breast,
Adam! *Misthought* of her to thee so dear? *Milton.*

To MISTI'ME. *v. a.* [*mis* and *time.*] Not to time right; not to adapt properly with regard to time.

MI'STINESS. *n. s.* [from *misty.*] Cloudiness; state of being overcast.

The speedy depredation of air upon watry moisture, and version of the same into air, appeareth in the sudden vanishing of vapours from glass, or the blade of a sword, such as doth not at all detain or imbibe the moisture, for the *mistiness* scattereth immediately. *Bacon's Nat. Hist.* N°. 91.

MI'STION. *n. s.* [from *mistus*, Latin.] The state of being mingled.

In animals many actions are mixt, and depend upon their living form as well as that of *mistion*, and though they wholly seem to retain unto the body, depart upon disunion. *Browne.*

Both bodies do, by the new texture resulting from their *mistion*, produce colour. *Boyle on Colours*

MISTLETOE. *n. s.* [mẏ[illegible]telτan, Saxon; *mistel*, Danish, *birdlime*, and τan, *a twig.*] A plant.

The flower of the *mistletoe* consists of one leaf, which is shaped like a bason, divided into four parts, and beset with warts; the ovary which is produced in the female flowers is placed in a remote part of the plant from the male flowers, and consists of four shorter leaves; this becomes a round berry full of a glutinous substance, inclosing a plain heart-shaped seed: this plant is always produced from seed, and is not to be cultivated in the earth, as most other plants, but will always grow upon trees; from whence the ancients accounted it a super-plant, who thought it to be an excrescence on the tree without the seed being previously lodged there, which opinion is now generally confuted. The manner of its propagation is as follows, *viz.* the *misletoe* thrush, which feeds upon the berries of this plant in winter when it is ripe, doth open the seed from tree to tree; for the viscous part of the berry, which immediately surrounds the seed, doth sometimes fasten it to the outward part of the bird's beak, which, to get disengaged of, he strikes his beak at the branches of a neighbouring tree, and so leaves the seed sticking by this viscous matter to the bark, which, if it lights upon a smooth part of the tree, will fasten itself, and the following winter put out and grow: the trees which this plant doth most readily take upon are the apple, the ash, and some other smooth rind trees: it is observable, that whenever a branch of an oak tree hath any of these plants growing upon it, it is cut off, and preserved by the curious in their collections of natural curiosities. *Miller.*

If snowe do continue, sheepe hardly that fare
Crave *mistle* and ivie for them for to spare. *Tusser's Husb.*
A barren and detested vale, you see it is:
The trees, though Summer, yet forlorn and lean,
O'ercome with moss, and baleful *misselto*. *Shakespeare.*

Misseltoe groweth chiefly upon crab trees, apple trees, sometimes upon hazles, and rarely upon oaks; the *misseltoe* whereof is counted very medicinal: it is ever green Winter and Summer, and beareth a white glistering berry; and it is a plant utterly differing from the plant upon which it groweth. *Bacon.*

All your temples strow
With laurel green, and sacred *misletoe*. *Gay's Trivia.*

MI'STLIKE. *adj.* [*mist* and *like.*] Resembling a mist.

Good Romeo, hide thyself.
—Not I, unless the breath of heart-sick groans,
Mistlike infold me from the search of eyes. *Shakespeare.*

MISTO'LD, particip. pass. of *mistell.*

MISTO'OK, particip. pass. of *mistake.*

Look nymphs, and shepherds look,
What sudden blaze of majesty,
Too divine to be *mistook*. *Milton.*

MI'STRESS. *n. s.* [*maistresse*, *maîtresse*, French.]

1. A woman who governs: correlative to subject or to servant.

Here stood he in the dark, his sharp sword out,
Mumbling of wicked charms, conj'ring the moon
To stand 's auspicious *mistress*. *Shakesp. King Lear.*
Let us prepare
Some welcome for the *mistress* of the house. *Shakespeare.*
Like the lily,
That once was *mistress* of the field and flourish'd,
I'll hang my head and perish. *Shakesp. Henry* VIII.
He'll make your Paris louvre shake for it,
Were it the *mistress* court of mighty Europe. *Shakespeare.*
I will not charm my tongue; I'm bound to speak;
My *mistress* here lies murther'd in her bed. *Shakesp. Othello.*
The late queen's gentlewoman! a knight's daughter!
To be her *mistress' mistress!* the queen's queen. *Shakesp.*

Rome now is *mistress* of the whole world, sea and land, to either pole. *Benj. Johnson's Catiline.*

Wonder not, sov'reign *mistress!* if perhaps
Thou can'st, who art sole wonder; much less arm
Thy looks, the heav'n of mildness, with disdain. *Milton.*
Those who assert the lunar orb presides
O'er humid bodies, and the ocean guides;
Whose waves obsequious ebb, or swelling run
With the declining or encreasing moon;
With reason seem her empire to maintain
As *mistress* of the rivers and the main. *Blackmore.*

What a miserable spectacle, for a nation that had been *mistress* at sea so long! *Arbuthnot on Coins.*

2. A woman who possesses faculties uninjured.

There had she enjoyed herself while she was *mistress* of herself, and had no other thoughts but such as might arise out of quiet senses. *Sidney, b.* ii.

Ages

Ages to come, that shall your bounty hear,
Will think you *mistress* of the Indies were;
Though streighter bounds your fortune did confine,
In your large heart was found a wealthy mine. *Waller.*

3. A woman skilled in any thing.

A letter desires all young wives to make themselves *mistresses* of Wingate's Arithmetick. *Addison's Spect.* N°. 92.

4. A woman teacher.

Erect publick schools, provided with the best and ablest masters and *mistresses*. *Swift.*

5. A woman beloved and courted.

They would not suffer the prince to confer with, or very rarely to see, his *mistress*, whom they pretended he should forthwith marry. *Clarendon.*

Nice honour still engages to requite
False *mistresses* and proud with slight for slight. *Granville.*

6. A term of contemptuous address.

Look you, pale *mistress*,
Do you perceive the ghastness of her eye? *Shakespeare.*

7. A whore; a concubine.

MISTRU'ST. *n. s.* [*mis* and *trust.*] Diffidence; suspicion; want of confidence.

He needs not our *mistrust*, since he delivers
Our offices, and what we have to do,
To the direction just. *Shakesp. Macbeth.*

Not then *mistrust*, but tender love, injoins
That I should mind thee oft; and mind thou me! *Milton.*

To MISTRU'ST. *v. a.* [*mis* and *trust.*] To suspect; to doubt; to regard with diffidence.

Will any man alledge those mentioned human infirmities, as reasons why these things should be *mistrusted* or doubted of. *Hooker, b.* ii.

By a divine instinct, mens minds *mistrust*
Ensuing danger; as by proof we see,
The waters swell before a boisterous storm. *Shakespeare.*

Fate her own book *mistrusted* at the fight,
On that side war, on this a single fight. *Cowley.*

The relation of a Spartan youth, that suffered a fox concealed under his robe to tear out his bowels, is *mistrusted* by men of business. *Brown.*

The gen'rous train complies,
Nor fraud *mistrusts* in virtue's fair disguise. *Pope's Odyssey.*

MISTRU'STFUL. *adj.* [*mistrust* and *full.*] Diffident; doubting.

I hold it cowardice
To rest *mistrustful*, where a noble heart
Hath pawn'd an open hand in sign of love. *Shakespeare.*

Here the *mistrustful* fowl no harm suspects,
So safe are all things which our king protects. *Waller.*

MISTRU'STFULNESS. *n. s.* [from *mistrustful.*] Diffidence; doubt.

Without him I found a weakness, and a *mistrustfulness* of myself, as one strayed from his best strength, when at any time I mist him. *Sidney, b.* ii.

MISTRU'STFULLY. *adv.* [from *mistrustful.*] With suspicion; with mistrust.

MISTRU'STLESS. *adj.* [from *mistrust.*] Confident; unsuspecting.

Where he doth in stream *mistrustless* play,
Veil'd with night's robe, they stalk the shore abroad.
Carew's Survey of Cornwall.

MI'STY. *adj.* [from *mist.*]

1. Clouded; overspread with mists.

The morrow fair with purple beams
Dispers'd the shadows of the *misty* night. *Fairy Queen.*

Loud howling wolves arouse the jades,
That drag the tragick melancholy night;
Who with their drowsy, slow, and flagging wings
Clip dead mens graves; and from their *misty* jaws
Breathe foul contagious darkness in the air. *Shakespeare.*

Parents overprize their children, while they behold them through the vapours of affection which alter the appearance, as things seem bigger in *misty* mornings. *Wotton.*

Now smoaks with show'rs the *misty* mountain ground,
And floated fields lie undistinguish'd round. *Pope.*

2. Obscure; dark; not plain.

To MISUNDERSTA'ND. *v. a.* [*mis* and *understand.*] To misconceive; to mistake.

The words of Tertullian, as they are by them alledged, are *misunderstood*. *Hooker, b.* ii.

He failed in distinguishing these two regions, both called Eden, and he altogether *misunderstood* two of the four rivers. *Raleigh's Hist. of the World.*

In vain do men take sanctuary in such *misunderstood* expressions as these; and from a false persuasion that they cannot reform their lives never go about it. *South.*

This if it be neglected, will make the reader very much mistake and *misunderstand* his meaning. *Locke.*

Were they only designed to instruct the three succeeding generations, they are in no danger of being *misunderstood*.
Addison on ancient Medals.

The example of a good man is the best direction we can follow in the performance of our duty; the most exact rules and precepts are subject to be *misunderstood*; some at least will mistake their meaning. *Rogers's Sermons.*

MISUNDERSTA'NDING. *n. s.* [from *misunderstand.*]

1. Difference; disagreement.

There is a great *misunderstanding* betwixt the corpuscular philosophers and the chemists. *Boyle.*

Servants mistake, and sometimes occasion *misunderstandings* among friends. *Swift's Miscel.*

2. Error; misconception.

Sever the construction of the injury from the point of contempt, imputing it to *misunderstanding* or fear. *Bacon.*

MISU'SAGE. *n. s.* [from *misuse.*]

1. Abuse; ill use.

2. Bad treatment.

To MISU'SE. *v. a.* [*mesuser*, Fr. *mis* and *use.*] To treat or use improperly; to abuse.

You *misuse* the rev'rence of your place,
As a false favourite doth his prince's name
In deeds dishon'rable. *Shakesp. Henry* IV.

It hath been their custom shamefully to *misuse* the fervent zeal of men to religious arms, by converting the monies that have been levied for such wars to their own services. *Raleigh.*

Bacchus, that first from out the purple grape
Crush'd the sweet poison of *misused* wine. *Milton.*

Machiavel makes it appear, that the weakness of Italy, which was once so strong, was caused by the corrupt practices of the papacy, in depraving and *misusing* religion.
South's Sermons.

MISU'SE. *n* [from the verb.] Bad use; bad treatment.

Upon whose dead corpse there was such *misuse*,
Such beastly, shameless transformation,
By those Welshwomen done, as may not be
Without much shame retold. *Shakesp. Henry* IV.

How much names taken for things mislead the understanding, the attentive reading of philosophical writers would discover, and that in words little suspected of any such *misuse*. *Locke.*

We have reason to humble ourselves before God by fasting and prayer, lest he should punish the *misuse* of our mercies, by stopping the course of them. *Atterbury's Sermons.*

To MISWE'EN. *v. n.* [*mis* and *ween.*] To misjudge; to distrust.

Latter times things more unknown shall show,
Why then should witless man so much *misween.* *Fa. Qu.*

To MISWE'ND. *v. n.* [*mis* and *wendan*, Saxon.] To go wrong.

Every thing begun with reason,
Will come by ready means unto his end:
But things miscounselled must needs *miswend.* *Hubberd.*

In this maze still wand'red and *miswent*,
For heaven decreed to conceal the same,
To make the miscreant more to feel his shame. *Fairfax.*

MI'SY. *n. s.* A kind of mineral.

Misy contains no cupreous vitriol but only that of iron: it is a very beautiful mineral, of a fine bright yellow colour, and of a loose and friable structure, and much resembles the golden marcasites. *Hill's Mat. Med.*

MITE. *n. s.* [*mite*, French; *mijt*, Dutch; *midas*, Lat.]

1. A small insect found in cheese or corn; a weevil.

Virginity breeds *mites*, much like a cheese, consumes itself to the very paring, and so dies with feeding its own stomach.
Shakespeare's All's well that ends well.

The polish'd glass, whose small convex
Enlarges to ten millions of degrees,
The *mite* invisible else, of nature's hand
Least animal. *Philips.*

The idea of two is as distinct from the idea of three, as the magnitude of the whole earth is from that of a *mite*. *Locke.*

2. The twentieth part of a grain.

The Seville piece of eight contains thirteen pennyweight twenty-one grains and fifteen *mites*, of which there are twenty in the grain, of sterling silver, and is in value forty-three English pence and eleven hundredths of a penny. *Arbuthnot.*

3. Any thing proverbially small; the third part of a farthing.

Though any man's corn they do bite,
They will not allow him a *mite*. *Tusser's Husb.*

Are you defrauded, when he feeds the poor,
Our *mite* decreases nothing of your store. *Dryden.*

Did I e'er my *mite* with-hold
From the impotent and old. *Swift's Miscel.*

4. A small particle.

Put blue-bottles into an ant-hill they will be stained with red, because the ants thrust in their stings, and instil into them a small *mite* of their stinging liquor, which hath the same effect as oil of vitriol. *Ray on Creation.*

MITE'LLA. *n. s.* A plant.

The *mitella* hath a perennial root; the cup of the flower consists of one leaf, and is divided into five parts; the flower consists of five leaves, which expand in form of a rose; the ovary

ovary becomes a roundish fruit, which terminates in a point, gaping at the top, in form of a bishop's mitre, and full of roundish seeds. *Miller.*

MI'THRIDATE. *n. s.* [*mithridate*, Fr.]

Mithridate is one of the capital medicines of the shops, consisting of a great number of ingredients, and has its name from its inventor Mithridates, king of Pontus. *Quincy.*

But you of learning and religion,
And virtue, and such ingredients, have made
A *mithridate*, whose operation
Keeps off, or cures, what can be done or said. *Donne.*

MI'THRIDATE *mustard. n. s.* [*thlaspi*, Latin.]

The flower of the *mithridate* consists of four leaves placed in form of a cross, out of whose cup rises the pointal, which afterward becomes a smooth roundish fruit, having commonly a leafy border, and slit on the upper side, divided into two cells by an intermediate partition placed obliquely with respect to the valves, and furnished with smooth roundish seeds; to which may be added the undivided leaves, which distinguish it from cresses. *Miller.*

MI'TIGANT. *adj.* [*mitigans*, Lat.] Lenient; lenitive.

To MI'TIGATE. *v. a.* [*mitigo*, Lat. *mitiger*, Fr.]

1. To soften; to make less rigorous.

We could greatly wish, that the rigour of their opinion were allayed and *mitigated*. *Hooker*, *b.* v.

2. To alleviate; to make mild; to assuage.

Mishaps are master'd by advice discreet,
And counsel *mitigates* the greatest smart. *Fairy Queen.*

All it can do is, to devise how that which must be endured may be *mitigated*, and the inconveniences thereof countervailed as near as may be, that, when the best things are not possible, the best may be made of those that are. *Hooker.*

3. To mollify; to make less severe.

I undertook
Before thee: and, not repenting, this obtain
Of right, that I may *mitigate* their doom,
On me deriv'd. *Milton's Par. Lost*, *b.* x.

4. To cool; to moderate.

A man has frequent opportunity of *mitigating* the fierceness of a party, of softening the envious, quieting the angry, and rectifying the prejudiced. *Addison's Spectator.*

MITIGA'TION. *n. s.* [*mitigatio*, Lat. *mitigation*, Fr. from *mitigate.*] Abatement of any thing penal, harsh, or painful.

The king would not have one penny abated of that granted to him by parliament, because it might encourage other countries to pray the like release or *mitigation*. *Bacon.*

They caused divers subjects to be indicted of sundry crimes; and when the bills were found they committed them, and suffered them to languish long in prison, to extort from them great fines and ransoms, which they termed compositions and *mitigations*. *Bacon's Henry* VII.

MI'TRE. *n. s.* [*mitre*, Fr. *mitra*, Latin.]

1. An ornament for the head.

Nor Pantheus, thee, thy *mitre* nor the bands
Of awful Phœbus, sav'd from impious hands. *Dryden.*

2. A kind of episcopal crown.

Bishopricks or burning, *mitres* or faggots, have been the rewards of different persons, according as they pronounced these consecrated syllables, or not. *Watts.*

MI'TRE. } *n. s.* [Among workmen.] A kind of joining two
MI'TER. } boards together. *Miller*

MI'TRED. *adj.* [*mitre*, Fr. from *mitre.*] Adorned with a mitre.

Shall the loud herald our success relate,
Or *mitred* priest appoint the solemn day? *Prior.*

Mitred abbots, among us, were those that were exempt from the diocesan's jurisdiction, as having within their own precincts episcopal authority, and being lords in parliament were called abbots sovereign. *Ayliffe's Parergon.*

MI'TTENT. *adj.* [*mittens*, Lat.] Sending forth; emitting.

The fluxion proceedeth from humours peccant in quantity or quality, thrust forth by the part *mittent* upon the inferior weak parts. *Wiseman's Surgery.*

MI'TTENS. *n. s.* [*mitaines*, French.]

1. Coarse gloves for the Winter.

December must be expressed with a horrid aspect, as also January clad in Irish rug, holding in furred *mittens* the sign of Capricorn. *Peacham on Drawing.*

2. Gloves that cover the arm without covering the fingers.

3. To handle one without *mittens*. To use one roughly. A low phrase. *Ainſ.*

MI'TTIMUS. [Latin.] A warrant by which a justice commits an offender to prison.

To MIX. *v. a.* [*mischen*, Dutch; *misceo*, Latin.]

1. To unite different bodies into one mass; to put various ingredients together.

Ephraim hath *mixed* himself among the people. *Hos.* vii. 8.

A *mixed* multitude went up with them, and flocks and herds. *Exod.* xii. 38.

He sent out of his mouth a blast of fire, and out of his lips a flaming breath, and out of his tongue he cast out sparks and tempests; and they were all *mixt* together. 2 *Esdr.*

2. To form of different faiths.

I have chosen an argument, *mixt* of religious and civil considerations; and likewise *mixt* between contemplative and active. *Bacon's holy War.*

3. To join; to mingle.

Brothers, you *mix* your sadness with some fear;
This is the English not the Turkish court. *Shakespeare.*

MI'XEN. *n. s.* [mixen, Saxon.] A dunghil; a laystal.

MI'XTION. *n. s.* [*mixtion*, Fr. from *mix.*] Mixture; confusion of one body with another.

Others perceiving this rule to fall short, have pieced it out by the *mixtion* of vacuity among bodies, believing it is that which makes one rarer than another. *Digby on Bodies.*

Though we want a proper name, yet are they not to be lightly past over as elementary or subterraneous *mixtions*. *Brown's Vulgar Errours*, *b.* ii.

MI'XTLY. *adv.* [from *mix.*] With coalition of different parts into one.

MI'XTURE. *n. s.* [*mixtura*, Latin.]

1. The act of mixing; the state of being mixed.

O happy *mixture*, wherein things contrary do so qualify and correct the one the danger of the other's excess, that neither boldness can make us presume, as well as we are kept under with the sense of our own wretchedness; nor, while we trust in the mercy of God through Christ Jesus, fear be able to tyrannize over us! *Hooker*, *b.* v.

Those liquors are expelled out of the body which, by their *mixture*, convert the aliment into an animal liquid. *Arbuth.*

I, by baleful furies led,
With monstrous *mixture* stain'd my mother's bed. *Pope.*

2. A mass formed by mingled ingredients.

Come vial--What if this *mixture* do not work at all? *Shakespeare's Romeo and Juliet.*

3. That which is added and mixed.

Neither can God himself be otherwise understood, than as a mind free and disentangled from all corporeal *mixtures*, perceiving and moving all things. *Stillingfleet.*

Cicero doubts whether it were possible for a community to exist, that had not a prevailing *mixture* of piety in its constitution. *Addison's Freeholder*, Nº. 29.

While we live in this world, where good and bad men are blended together, and where there is also a *mixture* of good and evil wisely distributed by God, to serve the ends of his providence. *Atterbury's Sermons.*

MI'ZMAZE. *n. s.* [A cant word, formed from *maze* by reduplication.] A maze; a labyrinth.

Those who are accustomed to reason have got the true key of books, and the clue to lead them through the *mizmaze* of variety of opinions and authors to truth. *Locke.*

MI'ZZEN. *n. s.* [*mezaen*, Dutch.]

The *mizzen* is a mast in the stern or back back of a ship: in some large ships there are two such masts, that standing next the main mast is called the main *mizzen*, and the other near the poop the bonaventure *mizzen*: the length of a *mizzen* mast is half that of the main mast, or the height of it is the same with that of the maintop mast from the quarterdeck, and the length of the *mizzen* topmast is half that. *Bail.*

A commander at sea had his leg fractured by the fall of his *mizzen* topmast. *Wiseman's Surgery.*

MI'ZZY. *n. s.* A bog; a quagmire. *Ainſ.*

MNEMO'NICKS. *n. s.* [μνημονικὴ.] The act of memory.

MO. *adj.* [ma, Saxon; *mae*, Scottish.] Making greater number; more.

Calliope and muses *mo*,
Soon as your oaken pipe begins to sound
Their ivory lutes lay by. *Spenser.*

With oxbows and oxyokes, with other things *mo*,
For oxteem and horseteem in plough for to go. *Tusser.*

MO. *adv.* Further; longer.

Sing no more ditties, sing no *mo*
Of dumps so dull and heavy;
The frauds of men were ever so,
Since Summer was first leafy. *Shakespeare.*

To MOAN. *v. a.* [from mænan, Saxon, to grieve.] To lament; to deplore.

To MOAN. *v. n.* To grieve; to make lamentation.

The gen'rous band redressive search'd
Into the horrors of the gloomy jail,
Unpity'd and unheard', where misery *moans*. *Thomson.*

MOAN. *n. s.* [from the verb.] Lamentation; audible sorrow; grief expressed in words or cries.

I have disabled mine estate,
By shewing something a more swelling port,
Than my faint means would grant continuance;
Nor do I now make *moan* to be abridg'd'
From such a noble rate. *Shakesp. Merchant of Venice.*

The fresh stream ran by her, and murmur'd her *moans*;
The salt tears fell from her, and soft'ned the stones.' *Shak.*

Sullen *moans*,
Hollow groans,
And cries of tortur'd ghosts. *Pope's St. Cæcilia.*

MOAT. *n. s.* [*motte*, French, a mound; *mota*, low Latin.] A canal of water round a house or castle for defence.

The

The castle I found of good strength, having a great *moat* round about it, the work of a noble gentleman, of whose unthrifty son he had bought it. *Sidney, b.* ii.

The fortress thrice himself in person storm'd;
Your valour bravely did th' assault sustain,
And fill'd the *moats* and ditches with the slain. *Dryden.*
No walls were yet, nor fence, nor *mote*, nor mound,
Nor drum was heard. *Dryden's Ovid.*

To MOAT. *v. a.* [*motter*, French, from the noun.] To surround with canals by way of defence.

I will presently to St. Luke's; there at the *moated* Grange resides this dejected Mariana. *Shakesp. Meas. for Measure.*

An arm of Lethe, with a gentle flow,
The palace *moats*, and o'er the pebbles creeps,
And with soft murmurs calls the coming sleeps. *Dryden.*

He sees he can hardly approach greatness, but, as a *moated* castle, he must first pass the mud and filth with which it is encompassed. *Dryden's Pref. to Aurengzebe.*

MOB. *n. s.* [contracted from *mobile*, Latin.] The croud; a tumultuous rout.

Parts of different species jumbled together, according to the mad imagination of the dawber; a very monster in a Bartholomew-fair, for the *mob* to gape at. *Dryden.*

Dreams are but interludes, which fancy makes,
When monarch reason sleeps, this mimick wakes;
Compounds a medley of disjointed things,
A court of coblers, and a *mob* of kings. *Dryden.*

A cluster of *mob* were making themselves merry with their betters. *Addison's Freeholder*, Nº. 44.

MOB. *n. s.* A kind of female head-dress.

To MOB. *v. a.* [from the noun.] To harrass, or overbear by tumult.

MO'BBISH. *adj.* [from *mob.*] Mean; done after the manner of the mob.

To MOBLE. *v. a.* [sometimes written *mable*, perhaps by a ludicrous allusion to the French *je m' habille.*] To dress grossly or inelegantly.

But who, oh! hath seen the *mobled* queen,
Run barefoot up and down. *Shakesp. Hamlet.*

MO'BBY. *n. s.* An American drink made of potatoes.

MO'BILE. *n. s.* [*mobile*, French.] The populace; the rout; the mob.

Long experience has found it true of the unthinking *mobile*, that the closer they shut their eyes the wider they open their hands. *South's Sermons.*

The *mobile* are uneasy without a ruler, they are restless with one. *L'Estrange's Fables.*

MOBI'LITY. *n. s.* [*mobilité*, Fr. *mobilitas*, Latin.]

1. Nimbleness; activity.

Mobility is the power of being moved. *Locke.*

Iron, having stood long in a window, being thence taken, and by a cork balanced in water, where it may have a free *mobility*, will bewray a kind of inquietude. *Wotton.*

The present age hath attempted perpetual motions, whose revolutions might out-last the exemplary *mobility*, and outmeasure time itself. *Brown's Vulgar Errours, b.* v.

The Romans had the advantage by the bulk of their ships, and the fleet of Antiochus in the swiftness and *mobility* of theirs, which served them in great stead in the flight. *Arbuth.*

You tell, it is ingenite, active force,
Mobility, or native power to move
Words, which mean nothing. *Blackmore.*

2. [In cant language.] The populace.

She singled you out with her eye as commander in chief of the *mobility*. *Dryden's Don Sebastian.*

3. Fickleness; inconstancy. *Ains.*

MO'CHO-STONE. *n. s.* [from *Mocha*, therefore more properly *Mocha-stone.*]

Mocho-stones are nearly related to the agat kind, of a clear horny grey, with declinations representing mosses, shrubs, and branches, in black, brown, or red, in the substance of the stone. *Woodward.*

To MOCK. *v. a.* [*mocquer*, French; *moccio*, Welsh.]

1. To deride; to laugh at; to ridicule.

All the regions
Do seemingly revolt; and who resist
Are *mock'd* for valiant ignorance,
And perish constant fools. *Shakespeare's Coriolanus.*
Many thousand widows,
Shall this his mock, *mock* out of their dear husbands;
Mock mothers from their sons, *mock* castles down. *Shakesp.*
We'll dishorn the spirit,
And *mock* him home to Windsor. *Shakespeare.*

Others had trial of cruel *mockings* and scourgings. *Heb.* xi.

I am as one *mocked* of his neighbour; the just, upright man is *mocked* to scorn. *Job* xii. 4.

2. To deride by imitation; to mimick in contempt.

I long, till Edward fall by war's mischance,
For *mocking* marriage with a dame of France. *Shakespeare.*

3. To defeat; to elude.

My father is gone into his grave,
And with his spirit sadly I survive,
To *mock* the expectations of the world;
To frustrate prophecies, and to raze out
Rotten opinion. *Shakespeare's Henry* IV. *p.* ii.

4. To fool; to tantalize; to play on contemptuously.

He will not
Mock us with his blest sight, then snatch him hence,
Soon we shall see our hope return. *Milton's Par. Reg.*
Why do I overlive?
Why am I *mock'd* with death, and lengthen'd out
To deathless pain? *Milton's Par. Lost, b.* x.
Heav'n's fuller influence *mocks* our dazzl'd sight,
Too great its brightness, and too strong its light. *Prior.*

To MOCK. *v. n.* To make contemptuous sport.

Pluck down my officers, break my decrees;
For now a time is come to *mock* at form. *Shakespeare.*

A stallion horse is as a *mocking* friend; he neigheth under every one. *Ecclus.* xxiii. 6.

A reproach unto the heathen, and a *mocking* to all countries. *Ezek.* xxii. 4.

After I have spoken, *mock* on. *Job* xxi. 3.

When thou *mockest*, shall no man make thee ashamed? *Job* xi. 3.

MOCK. *n. s.* [from the verb.]

1. Ridicule; act of contempt; fleer; sneer; gibe; flirt.

Tell the pleasant prince this *mock* of his
Hath turn'd his balls to gun-stones. *Shakesp. Henry* V.
Oh, 'tis the spight of hell, the fiend's arch *mock*,
To lip a wanton, and suppose her chaste. *Shakespeare.*

Fools make a *mock* at sin. *Prov.* xiv. 9.

What shall be the portion of those who have affronted God, derided his word, and made a *mock* of every thing that is sacred? *Tillotson's Sermons.*

Colin makes *mock* at all her piteous smart,
A lass that Cic'ly hight, had won his heart. *Gay.*

2. Imitation; mimickry.

Now reach a strain, my lute,
Above her *mock*, or be for ever mute. *Crashaw.*

MOCK. *adj.* False; counterfeit; not real.

The *mock* astrologer, El astrologo fingido. *Dryden.*

That superior greatness and *mock* majesty, which is ascribed to the prince of fallen angels, is admirably preserved. *Spect.*

MO'CKABLE. *adj.* [from *mock.*] Exposed to derision.

Those that are good manners at the court, are as ridiculous in the country, as the behaviour of the country is most *mockable* at court. *Shakesp. As you like it.*

MOCK-PRI'VET. } *n. s.* Plants. *Ainsworth.*
MOCK-WI'LLOW. }

MO'CKEL. *adj.* [the same with *mickle.* See MICKLE. This word is variously written *mickle*, *mickel*, *mochil*, *mochel*, *muckle.*] Much; many.

The body bigg, and mightily pight,
Thoroughly rooted, and wond'rous height,
Whilom had been the king of the field,
And *mockell* mast to the husband did yield. *Spenser.*

MO'CKER. *n. s.* [from *mock.*]

1. One who mocks; a scorner; a scoffer; a derider.

Our very priests must become *mockers*, if they shall encounter such ridiculous subjects as you are. *Shakespeare.*

Let them have a care how they intrude upon so great and holy an ordinance, in which God is so seldom mocked but it is to the *mocker*'s confusion. *South's Sermons.*

2. A deceiver; an elusory impostor.

MO'CKERY. *n. s.* [*mocquerie*, Latin.]

1. Derision; scorn; sportive insult.

The forlorn maiden, whom your eyes have seen
The laughing-stock of fortune's *mockeries*,
Am the only daughter of a king and queen. *Fa. Qu.*

Why should publick *mockery* in print be a better test of truth than severe railing sarcasms. *Watts.*

2. Ridicule; contemptuous merriment.

A new method they have of turning things that are serious into *mockery*; an art of contradiction by way of scorn, wherewith we were long sithence forewarned. *Hooker, b.* v.

3. Sport; subject of laughter.

What cannot be preserv'd when fortune takes,
Patience her injury a *mockery* makes. *Shakesp. Othello.*

Of the holy place they made a *mockery*. 2 *Mac.* viii. 17.

4. Vanity of attempt; delusory labour; vain effort.

It is as the air, invulnerable;
And our vain blows malicious *mockery*. *Shakesp. Hamlet.*

5. Imitation; counterfeit appearance; vain show.

To have done, is to hang quite out of fashion,
Like rusty mail in monumental *mockery*. *Shakespeare.*
What though no friends in sable weeds appear,
Grieve for an hour, perhaps, then mourn a year,
And bear about the *mockery* of woe
To midnight dances. *Pope's Miscel*

MO'CKING-BIRD. *n. s.* [*mocking* and *bird.*] An American bird which imitates the note of other birds.

MO'CKINGLY. *adv.* [from *mockery.*] In contempt; petulantly; with insult.

Mo'cking-stock. *n. s.* [*mocking* and *stock.*] A but for merriment.

Mo'dal. *adj.* [*modale*, Fr. *modalis*, Latin.] Relating to the form or mode, not the essence.

When we speak of faculties of the soul, we assert not with the schools their real distinction from it, but only a *modal* diversity. *Glanville's Sceps.*

Moda'lity. *n. s.* [from *modal.*] Accidental difference; modal accident.

The motions of the mouth by which the voice is discriminated, are the natural elements of speech; and the application of them in their several compositions, or words made of them, to signify things, or the *modalities* of things, and so to serve for communication of notions, is artificial. *Holder.*

MODE. *n. s.* [*mode*, Fr. *modus*, Latin.]

1. Form; external variety; accidental discrimination; accident.

A *mode* is that which cannot subsist in and of itself, but is always esteemed as belonging to, and subsisting by, the help of some substance, which, for that reason, is called its subject. *Watts's Logick, p.* i.

Few allow *mode* to be called a being in the same perfect sense as a substance is, and some *modes* have evidently more of real entity than others. *Watts's Logick.*

2. Gradation; degree.

What *modes* of sight betwixt each wide extreme,
The mole's dim curtain, and the linx's beam;
Of smell, the headlong lioness between,
And hound sagacious on the tainted green. *Pope.*

3. Manner; method; form; fashion.

Our Saviour beheld
A table richly spread, in regal *mode*,
With dishes pil'd. *Milton's Par. Reg. b.* ii.

The duty itself being resolved upon, the *mode* of doing it may easily be found. *Taylor's Guide to a Penitent.*

4. State; appearance.

My death
Changes the *mode*; for what in me was purchas'd,
Falls upon thee in a much fairer sort,
For thou the garland wear'st successively. *Shakespeare.*

5. [*Mode*, French.] Fashion; custom.

There are certain garbs and *modes* of speaking, which vary with the times; the fashion of our clothes being not more subject to alteration than that of our speech. *Denham.*

We are to prefer the blessings of Providence before the splendid curiosities of *mode* and imagination. *L'Estrange.*

They were invited from all parts; and the favour of learning was the humour and *mode* of the age. *Temple.*

As we see on coins the different faces of persons, we see too their different habits and dresses, according to the *mode* that prevailed. *Addison on ancient Medals.*

If faith itself has diff'rent dresses worn,
What wonder *modes* in wit should take their turn? *Pope.*

MO'DEL. *n. s.* [*modele*, French; *modulus*, Latin.]

1. A representation in miniature of something made or done.

I'll draw the form and *model* of our battle;
Limit each leader to his several charge,
And part in just proportion our small strength. *Shakesp.*

You have the *models* of several ancient temples, though the temples and the gods are perished. *Addison.*

2. A copy to be imitated.

A fault it would be if some king should build his mansion-house by the *model* of Solomon's palace. *Hooker, b.* v.

They cannot see sin in those means they use, with intent to reform to their *models* what they call religion. *K. Charles.*

3. A mould; any thing which shows or gives the shape of that which it incloses.

Nothing can we call our own but death;
And that small *model* of the barren earth,
Which serves as paste and cover to our bones. *Shakesp.*

4. Standard; that by which any thing is measured.

As he who presumes steps into the throne of God, so he that despairs measures providence by his own little contracted *model.* *South's Sermons.*

5. In *Shakespeare* it seems to have two unexampled senses. Something formed or produced.

I have commended to his goodness
The *model* of our chaste loves, his young daughter. *Shak.*

6. Something small and diminutive; which, perhaps, is likewise the meaning of the example affixed to the third sense.

England! *model* to thy inward greatness,
Like little body with a mighty heart. *Shakespeare.*

To **Mo'del.** *v. a.* [*modeler*, French.] To plan; to shape; to mould; to form; to delineate.

When they come to *model* heav'n,
And calculate the stars, how they will wield
The mighty frame. *Milton's Par. Lost, b.* viii.

The government is *modelled* after the same manner with that of the Cantons, as much as so small a community can imitate those of so large an extent. *Addison on Italy.*

Mode'ller. *n. s.* [from *model.*] Planner; schemer; contriver.

Our great *modellers* of gardens have their magazines of plants to dispose of. *Spectat.* Nº. 414.

MO'DERATE. *adj.* [*moderatus*, Lat. *moderé*, Fr.]

1. Temperate; not excessive.

Sound sleep cometh of *moderate* eating, but pangs of the belly are with an insatiable man. *Ecclus.* xxxi. 20.

2. Not hot of temper.

A number of *moderate* members managed with so much art as to obtain a majority, in a thin house, for passing a vote, that the king's concessions were a ground for a future settlement. *Swift.*

3. Not luxurious; not expensive.

There's not so much left as to furnish out
A *moderate* table. *Shakesp. Timon of Athens.*

4. Not extreme in opinion; not sanguine in a tenet.

These are tenets which the *moderatest* of the Romanists will not venture to affirm. *Smalridge.*

Fix'd to one part, but *mod'rate* to the rest. *Pope.*

5. Placed between extremes; holding the mean.

Quietly consider the trial that hath been thus long had of both kinds of reformation; as well this *moderate* kind, which the church of England hath taken, as that other more extreme and rigorous, which certain churches elsewhere have better liked. *Hooker, b.* iv.

6. Of the middle rate.

More *moderate* gifts might have prolong'd his date,
Too early fitted for a better state. *Dryden.*

To **Mo'derate.** *v. a.* [*moderor*, Latin; *moderer*, Fr.]

1. To regulate; to restrain; to still; to pacify; to quiet; to repress.

With equal measure she did *moderate*
The strong extremities of their rage. *Spenser.*

By its astringent quality it *moderates* the relaxing quality of warm water. *Arbuthnot on Aliments.*

2. To make temperate.

Ye swarthy nations of the torrid zone,
How well to you is this great bounty known?
For frequent gales from the wide ocean rise
To fan your air, and *mod*[illegible] your skies. *Blackmore.*

Mo'derately. *adv.* [from *moderate.*]

1. Temperately; mildly.

2. In a middle degree.

Each nymph but *moderately* fair,
Commands with no less rigor here. *Waller.*

Blood in a healthy state, when let out, its red part should congeal strongly and soon, in a mass *moderately* tough, and swim in the serum. *Arbuthnot on Aliments.*

Mo'derateness. *n. s.* [from *moderate.*] State of being moderate; temperateness.

Modera'tion. *n. s.* [*moderatio*, Latin.]

1. Forbearance of extremity; the contrary temper to party violence; state of keeping a due mean betwixt extremes.

Was it the purpose of these churches, which abolished all popish ceremonies, to come back again to the middle point of evenness and *moderation*? *Hooker, b.* iv.

A zeal in things pertaining to God, according to knowledge, and yet duly tempered with candor and prudence, is the true notion of that much talked of, much misunderstood virtue, *moderation.* *Atterbury's Sermons.*

In *moderation* placing all my glory,
While tories call me whig, and whigs a tory. *Pope.*

2. Calmness of mind; equanimity. [*moderation*, Fr.]

Equally inur'd
By *moderation* either state to bear,
Prosperous, or adverse. *Milt. Par. Lost, b.* xi.

3. Frugality in expence. *Ainsworth.*

Modera'tor. *n. s.* [*moderator*, Lat. *moderateur*, Fr.]

1. The person or thing that calms or restrains.

Angling was, after tedious study, a calmer of unquiet thoughts, a *moderator* of passions, and a procurer of contentedness. *Walton's Angler.*

2. One who presides in a disputation, to restrain the contending parties from indecency, and confine them to the question.

Sometimes the *moderator* is more troublesome than the actor. *Bacon's Essays.*

How does Philopolis seasonably commit the opponent with the respondent, like a long-practised *moderator*? *More.*

The first person who speaks when the court is set, opens the case to the judge, chairman, or *moderator* of the assembly, and gives his own reasons for his opinion. *Watts.*

MO'DERN. *n. s.* [*moderne*, Fr. from *modernus*, low Latin, supposed a casual corruption of *hodiernus.* Vel potius ab adverbio *modò*, modernus, ut a *die* diurnus. *Ains.*]

1. Late; recent; not ancient; not antique.

Some of the ancient, and likewise divers of the *modern* writers, that have laboured in natural magick, have noted a sympathy between the sun and certain herbs. *Bacon.*

The glorious parallels then downward bring
To *modern* wonders, and to Britain's king. *Prior.*

2. In

2. In *Shakespeare*, vulgar; mean; common.

Trifles, such as we present *modern* friends withal. *Shakesp.*

The justice
With eyes severe and beard of formal cut,
Full of wise saws and *modern* instances. *Shakespeare.*

We have our philosophical persons to make *modern* and familiar things supernatural and causeless. *Shakespeare.*

Mo'derns. *n. s.* Those who have lived lately, opposed to the ancients.

There are *moderns* who, with a slight variation, adopt the opinion of Plato. *Boyle on Colours.*

Some by old words to fame have made pretence;
Ancients in phrase, mere *moderns* in their sense! *Pope.*

Mo'dernism. *n. s.* [from *modern.*] Deviation from the ancient and classical manner. A word invented by *Swift.*

Scribblers send us over their trash in prose and verse, with abominable curtailings and quaint *modernisms.* *Swift.*

To Mo'dernise. *v. a.* [from *modern.*] To adapt ancient compositions to modern persons or things; to change ancient to modern language.

MO'DEST. *adj.* [*modeste*, Fr. *modestus*, Latin.]

Mo'dernness. *n. s.* [from *modern.*] Novelty.

1. Not arrogant; not presumptuous; not boastful; bashful.

Of boasting more than of a tomb afraid;
A soldier should be *modest* as a maid. *Young.*

2. Not impudent; not forward.

Resolve me with all *modest* haste, which way
Thou might'st deserve, or they impose this usage. *Shakesp.*

Her face, as in a nymph, display'd
A fair fierce boy, or in a boy betray'd
The blushing beauties of a *modest* maid. *Dryden's Ovid.*

3. Not loose; not unchaste.

Mrs. Ford, the honest woman, the *modest* wife, the virtuous creature, that hath the jealous fool to her husband. *Shakesp. Merry Wives of Windsor.*

4. Not excessive; not extreme; moderate; within a mean.

There appears much joy in him, even so much that joy could not shew itself *modest* enough without a badge of bitterness. *Shakesp. Much ado about nothing.*

During the last four years, by a *modest* computation, there have been brought into Brest above six millions sterling in bullion. *Addison's State of the War.*

Mo'destly. *adv.* [from *modest.*]

1. Not arrogantly; not presumptuously.

Though learn'd, well bred; and though well bred, sincere,
Modestly bold, and humanly severe. *Pope.*

I may *modestly* conclude, that whatever errors there may be in this play, there are not those which have been objected to it. *Dryden's Don Sebastian.*

First he *modestly* conjectures,
His pupil might be tir'd with lectures:
Which help'd to mortify his pride,
Yet gave him not the heart to chide. *Swift's Miscel.*

2. Not impudently; not forwardly; with modesty.

I, your glass,
Will *modestly* discover to yourself
That of yourself, which yet you know not of. *Shakesp.*

3. Not loosely; not lewdly.

4. Not excessively; with moderation.

Mo'desty. *n. s.* [*modestie*, Fr. *modestas*, Latin.]

1. Not arrogance; not presumptuousness.

They cannot, with *modesty*, think to have found out absolutely the best which the wit of men may devise. *Hooker.*

2. Not impudence; not forwardness.

3. Moderation; decency.

A lord will hear you play;
But I am doubtful of your *modesties*,
Lest over eying of his odd behaviour,
You break into some merry passion. *Shakespeare.*

4. Chastity; purity of manners.

Would you not swear,
All you that see her, that she were a maid,
By these exterior shews? But she is more,
Her blush is guiltiness, not *modesty.* *Shakespeare.*

Of the general character of women, which is *modesty*, he has taken a most becoming care; for his amorous expressions go no farther than virtue may allow. *Dryden.*

Talk not to a lady in a way that *modesty* will not permit her to answer. *Clarissa.*

Modesty-piece. *n. s.*

A narrow lace which runs along the upper part of the stays before, being a part of the tucker, is called the *modesty-piece.* *Addison's Guard.* N°. 118.

Mo'dicum. *n. s.* [Latin.] Small portion; pittance.

What *modicums* of wit he utters: his evasions have ears thus long. *Shakesp. Troil. and Cressida.*

Though hard their fate,
A cruise of water, and an ear of corn,
Yet still they grudg'd that *modicum.* *Dryden.*

Modifi'able. *adj.* [from *modify.*] That may be diversified by accidental differences.

It appears to be more difficult to conceive a distinct, visible image in the uniform, invariable, essence of God, than in variously *modifiable* matter; but the manner how I see either still escapes my comprehension. *Locke.*

Mo'difiable. *adj.* [from *modify.*] Diversifiable by various modes.

Modifica'tion. *n. s.* [*modification*, French.] The act of modifying any thing, or giving it new accidental differences of form or mode.

The chief of all signs is human voice, and the several *modifications* thereof by the organs of speech, *viz.* the letters of the alphabet, formed by the several motions of the mouth. *Holder's Elements of Speech.*

The phænomena of colours in refracted or reflected light, are not caused by new *modifications* of the light variously impressed, according to the various terminations of the light and shadow. *Newton's Opticks.*

If these powers of cogitation, volition and sensation, are neither inherent in matter as such, nor acquirable to matter by any motion and *modification* of it, it necessarily follows that they proceed from some cogitative substance, some incorporeal inhabitant within us, which we call spirit. *Bentley.*

To Mo'dify. *v. a.* [*modifier*, French.]

1. To change the form or accidents of any thing; to shape.

Yet there is that property in all letters, of aptness to be conjoined in syllables and words through the voluble motions of the organs, that they *modify* and discriminate the voice without appearing to discontinue it. *Holder*

The middle parts of the broad beam of white light which fell upon the paper, did, without any confine of shadow to *modify* it, become coloured all over with one uniform colour, the colour being always the same in the middle of the paper as at the edges. *Newton's Opticks.*

2. To soften; to moderate.

After all this discanting and *modifying* upon the matter, there is hazard on the yielding side. *L'Estrange.*

Of his grace
He *modifies* his first severe decree,
The keener edge of battle to rebate. *Dryden.*

Modi'llon. *n. s.* [French; *modiolus*, Lat.]

Modillons, in architecture, are little brackets which are often set under the corinthian and composite orders, and serve to support the projecture of the larmier or drip: this part must be distinguished from the great model, which is the diameter of the pillar; for, as the proportion of an edifice in general depends on the diameter of the pillar, so the size and number of the *modillons*, as also the interval between them, ought to have due relation to the whole fabrick. *Harris.*

The *modillons* or dentelli make a noble show by their graceful projections. *Spectator*, N°. 415.

Mo'dish. *adj.* [from *mode.*] Fashionable; formed according to the reigning custom.

But you, perhaps, expect a *modish* feast,
With am'rous songs, and wanton dances grac'd. *Dryd.*

Hypocrisy, at the fashionable end of the town, is very different from hypocrisy in the city; the *modish* hypocrite endeavours to appear more vitious than he really is, the other kind of hypocrite more virtuous. *Addison's Spect.* N°. 399.

Mo'dishly. *adv.* [from *modish.*] Fashionably.

Young children should not be much perplexed about putting off their hats, and making legs *modishly.* *Locke.*

Mo'dishness. *n. s.* [from *modish.*] Affectation of the fashion.

To Mo'dulate. *v. a.* [*modulor*, Latin.] To form sound to a certain key, or to certain notes.

The nose, lips, teeth, palate, jaw, tongue, weasan, lungs, muscles of the chest, diaphragm, and muscles of the belly, all serve to make or *modulate* the sound. *Grew's Cosmol.*

Could any person so *modulate* her voice as to deceive so many. *Broome's Notes on the Odyssey.*

Echo propagates around
Each charm of *modulated* sound. *Anon.*

Modula'tion. *n. s.* [from *modulate*; *modulation*, Fr.]

1. The act of forming any thing to certain proportion.

The number of the simple original minerals have not been rightly fixt: the matter of two or more kinds being mixed together, and by the different proportion and *modulation* of that matter variously diversified, have been reputed all different kinds. *Woodward.*

The speech, as it is a sound resulting from the *modulation* of the air, has most affinity to the spirit, but, as it is uttered by the tongue, has immediate cognation with the body, and so is the fittest instrument to manage a commerce between the invisible powers of human souls cloathed in flesh. *Government of the Tongue.*

2. Sound modullated; agreeable harmony.

Innumerous songsters, in the freshening shade,
Their *modulations* mix, mellifluous. *Thomson's Spring.*

Mo'dulator.

MO'DULATOR. *n. s.* [from *modulate.*] He who forms sounds to a certain key; a tuner; that which modulates.

The tongue is the grand instrument of taste, the faithful judge of all our nourishment, the artful *modulator* of our voice, and the necessary servant of mastication. *Derham.*

MO'DULE. *n. s.* [*modulus*, Latin.] An empty representation; a model.

My heart hath one poor string to stay it by,
Which holds but till thy news be uttered;
And then, all this thou seest, is but a clod
And *module* of confounded royalty. *Shakesp. King John.*

MO'DUS. *n. s.* [Latin.] Something paid as a compensation for tithes on the supposition of being a moderate equivalent.

One terrible circumstance of this bill, is turning the tithe of flax and hemp into what the lawyers call a *modus*, or a certain sum in lieu of a tenth part of the product. *Swift.*

MO'DWALL. *n. s.* A bird. *Ainf.*

MOE. *adj.* [ma, Saxon. See MO.] More; a greater number.

The chronicles of England mention no *moe* than only six kings bearing the name of Edward since the conquest, therefore it cannot be there should be more. *Hooker, b.* ii.

MO'HAIR. *n. s.* [*mohere*, *moire*, Fr.] Thread or stuff made of camels or other hair.

She, while her lover pants upon her breast,
Can mark the figures on an Indian chest,
And when she sees her friend in deep despair,
Observes how much a chintz exceeds *mohair.* *Pope.*

MO'HOCK. *n. s.* The name of a cruel nation of America given to ruffians who infested, or rather were imagined to infest, the streets of London.

From milk-sop he starts up *mohock.* *Prior.*
Who has not trembled at the *mohock*'s name? *Gay.*

Thou hast fallen upon me with the rage of a mad dog, or a *mohock*. *Dennis.*

MOI'DERED. *adj.* Crazed. *Ainf.*

MO'IDORE. *n. s.* [*moede*, Fr.] A Portugal coin, rated at one pound seven shillings.

MO'IETY. *n. s.* [*moitié*, French, from *moien*, the middle.] Half; one of two equal parts.

This company being divided into two equal *moieties*, the one before, the other since the coming of Christ; that part which, since the coming of Christ, partly hath embraced, and partly shall embrace, the Christian religion, we term as by a more proper name, the church of Christ. *Hooker, b.* iii.

The death of Antony
Is not a single doom, in that name lay
A *moiety* of the world. *Shakesp. Ant. and Cleopatra.*

Say, that she were gone,
Given to the fire, a *moiety* of my rest
Might come to me. *Shakesp. Winter's Tale.*

Touch'd with human gentleness and love,
Forgive a *moiety* of the principal. *Shakespeare.*

The militia was settled, a *moiety* of which should be nominated by the king, and the other *moiety* by the parliament. *Cl.*

As this is likely to produce a cessation of arms among one half of our island, it is reasonable that the more beautiful *moiety* of his majesty's subjects should establish a truce. *Addis.*

To MOIL. *v. a.* [*mouiller*, French.]

1. To dawb with dirt.

All they which were left were *moiled* with dirt and mire by reason of the deepness of the rotten way. *Knolles.*

2. To weary.

No more tug one another thus, nor *moil* yourselves, receive
Prize equal. *Chapman's Iliad.*

To MOIL. *v. n.* [*mouiller*, French.]

1. To labour in the mire.

Moil not too much under-ground, for the hope of mines is very uncertain. *Bacon's Essays.*

2. To toil; to drudge.

They toil and *moil* for the interest of their masters, that in requital break their hearts; and the freer they are of their flesh, the more scandalous is the bondage. *L'Estrange.*

Oh the endless misery of the life I lead! cries the *moiling* husband; to spend all my days in ploughing. *L'Estrange.*

Now he must *moil*, and drudge, for one he loaths. *Dry.*

With thee 'twas Marian's dear delight
To *moil* all day, and merry-make at night. *Gay's Past.*

MOIST. *adj.* [*moiste*, *moite*, French.]

1. Wet, not dry; wet, not liquid; wet in a small degree.

Why were the *moist* in number so outdone,
That to a thousand dry they are but one. *Blackmore.*

Many who live well in a dry air, fall into all the diseases that depend upon a relaxation in a *moist* one. *Arbuthnot.*

Nor yet, when *moist* Arcturus clouds the sky,
The woods and fields their pleasing toils deny. *Pope.*

2. Juicy; succulent. *Ainf.*

To MOIST. } *v. a.* [from *moist.*] To make damp; to make
To MOISTEN. } wet to a small degree; to damp.

Write till your ink be dry; and with your tears
Moist it again; and frame some feeling line. *Shakespeare*

His breasts are full of milk, and his bones are *moistened* with marrow. *Job* xxi. 24.

A pipe a little *moistened* on the inside, so as there be no drops left, maketh a more solemn sound than if the pipe were dry. *Bacon's Nat. Hist.* N°. 230.

When torrents from the mountains fall no more, the swelling river is reduced into his shallow bed, with scarce water to *moisten* his own pebbles. *Dryden's Æn.*

MO'ISTENER. *n. s.* [from *moisten.*] The person or thing that moistens.

MO'ISTNESS. *n. s.* [from *moist.*] Dampness; wetness in a small degree.

Pleasure both kinds take in the *moistness* and density of the air. *Bacon's Nat. Hist.* N°. 823.

The small particles of brick or stone the least *moistness* would join together. *Addison's Guard.*

MO'ISTURE. *n. s.* [*moiteur*, Fr. from *moist.*] Small quantity of water or liquid.

Sometimes angling to a little river near hand, which, for the *moisture* it bestowed upon roots of some flourishing trees, was rewarded with their shadow. *Sidney.*

All my body's *moisture*
Scarce serves to quench my furnace-burning heat. *Shak.*

Set such plants as require much *moisture* upon sandy, dry grounds. *Bacon's Nat. Hist.* N°. 526.

While dryness *moisture*, coldness heat resists,
All that we have, and that we are, subsists. *Denham.*

If some penurious source by chance appear'd
Scanty of waters, when you scoop'd it dry,
And offer'd the full helmet up to Cato,
Did he not dash th' untasted *moisture* from him. *Addison.*

MOKES *of a net.* The meshes. *Ainf.*

MO'KY. *adj.* Dark: as, *moky* weather. *Ainf.* It seems a corruption of murky: and in some places they call it muggy, dusky.

MOLE. *n. s.* [mœl, Saxon; *mole*, Fr. *mola*, Lat.]

1. A *mole* is a formless concretion of extravasated blood, which grows unto a kind of flesh in the uterus, and is called a false conception. *Quincy.*

2. A natural spot or discolouration of the body.

To nourish hair upon the *moles* of the face, is the perpetuation of a very antient custom. *Brown's Vulgar Errours.*

Such in painting are the warts and *moles*, which adding a likeness to the face, are not therefore to be omitted. *Dryden.*

That Timothy Trim and Jack were the same person, was proved, particularly by a *mole* under the left pap. *Arbuthnot.*

The peculiarities in Homer are marks and *moles*, by which every common eye distinguishes him. *Pope.*

3. [From *moles*, Lat. *mole*, Fr.] A mound; a dyke.

Sion is streightened on the north side by the sea-ruined wall of the *mole*. *Sandys.*

With asphaltick slime the gather'd beach
They fasten'd; and the *mole* immense wrought on
Over the foaming deep high-arch'd; a bridge
Of length prodigious. *Milton's Par. Lost, b.* x.

The great quantities of stones dug out of the rock could not easily conceal themselves, had they not been consumed in the *moles* and buildings of Naples. *Addison on Italy.*

Bid the broad arch the dang'rous flood contain,
The *mole* projected break the roaring main. *Pope.*

4. A little beast that works under-ground.

Tread softly, that the blind *mole* may not
Hear a foot fall; we now are near his cell. *Shakespeare.*

What is more obvious than a *mole*, and yet what more palpable argument of Providence? *More.*

Moles have perfect eyes, and holes for them through the skin, not much bigger than a pin's head. *Ray on the Creation.*

Thy arts of building from the bee receive;
Learn of the *mole* to plow, the worm to weave. *Pope.*

MO'LEBAT. *n. s.* A fish. *Ainf.*

MO'LECAST. *n. s.* [*mole* and *cast.*] Hillock cast up by a mole.

In Spring let the *molecasts* be spread, because they hinder the mowers. *Mortimer's Husbandry.*

MO'LECATCHER. *n. s.* [*mole* and *catcher.*] One whose employment is to catch moles.

Get *moulecatcher* cunningly moule for to kill,
And harrow and cast abroad every hill. *Tusser's Husb.*

MO'LEHILL. *n. s.* [*mole* and *hill.*] Hillock thrown up by the mole working underground.

You feed your solitariness with the conceits of the poets, whose liberal pens can as easily travel over mountains as *molehills*. *Sidney.*

The rocks, on which the salt-sea billows beat,
And Atlas' tops, the clouds in height that pass,
Compar'd to his huge person *molehills* be. *Fairfax.*

A churchwarden, to express Saint Martin's in the Fields, caused to be engraved a martin sitting upon a *molehill* between two trees. *Peacham on Blazoning.*

Our politician having baffled conscience, must not be nonplused with inferior obligations; and, having leapt over such mountains, lie down before a *molehill.* *South's Sermons.*

Mountains, which to your Maker's view
Seem leſs than *molehills* do to you. *Roſcommon.*
Strange ignorance! that the ſame man who knows
How far yond' mount above this *molehill* ſhows,
Should not perceive a difference as great
Between ſmall incomes and a vaſt eſtate! *Dryden's Juv.*

To MOLE'ST. *v. a.* [*moleſter*, Fr. *moleſtus*, Lat.] To diſturb; to trouble; to vex.

If they will firmly perſiſt concerning points which hitherto have been diſputed of, they muſt agree that they have *moleſted* the church with needleſs oppoſition. *Hooker, b.* iii.

No man ſhall meddle with them, or *moleſt* them in any matter. 1 *Mac.* x. 35.

Pleaſure and pain ſignify whatſoever delights or *moleſts* us. *Locke.*

Both are doom'd to death;
And the dead wake not to *moleſt* the living. *Rowe.*

MOLESTA'TION. *n. ſ.* [*moleſtia*, Latin, from *moleſt.*] Diſturbance; uneaſineſs cauſed by vexation.

Though uſeleſs unto us, and rather of *moleſtation*, we refrain from killing ſwallows. *Brown's Vulgar Errours.*

An internal ſatisfaction and acquieſcience, or diſſatisfaction and *moleſtation* of ſpirit, attend the practice of virtue and vice reſpectively. *Norris's Miſcel.*

MOLE'STER. *n. ſ.* [from *moleſt.*] One who diſturbs.

MO'LETRACK. *n. ſ.* [*mole* and *track.*] Courſe of the mole under-ground.

The pot-trap is a deep earthen veſſel ſet in the ground, with the brim even with the bottom of the *moletracks*. *Mort.*

MO'LEWARP. *n. ſ.* [*mole* and *weoppan*, Saxon.] A mole.

The *molewarp*'s brains mixt therewith all,
And with the ſame the piſmire's gall. *Drayton's Nymphid.*

MO'LLIENT. *adj.* [*molliens*, Latin.] Softening.

MO'LLIFIABLE. *adj.* [from *mollify.*] That may be ſoftened.

MOLLIFICA'TION. *n. ſ.* [from *mollify.*]

1. The act of mollifying or ſoftening.

For induration or *mollification*, it is to be inquired what will make metals harder and harder, and what will make them ſofter and ſofter. *Bacon.*

2. Pacification; mitigation.

Some *mollification*, ſweet lady. *Shakeſpeare.*

MO'LLIFIER. *n. ſ.* [from *mollify.*]

1. That which ſoftens; that which appeaſes.

The root hath a tender, dainty heat; when, when it cometh above ground to the ſun and air, vaniſheth; for it is a great *mollifier*. *Bacon's Nat. Hiſt.* N°. 863.

2. He that pacifies or mitigates.

To MO'LLIFY. *v. a.* [*mollio*, Latin; *mollir*, Fr.]

1. To ſoften; to make ſoft.

2. To aſſwage.

Neither herb, nor *mollifying* plaiſter, reſtored them to health. *Wiſd.* xvi. 12.

Sores have not been cloſed, neither bound up, neither *mollified* with ointment. *Iſa.* i. 6.

3. To appeaſe; to pacify; to quiet.

Thinking her ſilent imaginations began to work upon ſomewhat, to *mollify* them, as the nature of muſick is to do, I took up my harp. *Sidney, b.* ii.

He brought them to theſe ſavage parts,
And with ſweet ſcience *mollify'd* their ſtubborn hearts. *Fairy Queen, b.* ii.

The crone, on the wedding-night, finding the knight's averſion, ſpeaks a good word for herſelf, in hope to *mollify* the ſullen bridegroom. *Dryden.*

4. To qualify; to leſſen any thing harſh or burdenſome.

They would, by yielding to ſome things, when they refuſed others, ſooner prevail with the houſes to *mollify* their demands, than at firſt to reform them. *Clarendon, b.* viii.

Cowley thus paints Goliah:
The valley, now, this monſter ſeem'd to fill,
And we, methought, look'd up to him from our hill;
where the two words, ſeem'd and methought, have *mollified* the figure. *Dryden's Pref. to his State of Innocence.*

MO'LTEN. part. paſſ. from *melt.*

Braſs is *molten* out of the ſtone. *Job* xxviii. 2.

In a ſmall furnace made of a temperate heat; let the heat be ſuch as may keep the metal *molten*, and no more. *Bacon.*

Love's myſtick form the artizans of Greece
In wounded ſtone, or *molten* gold expreſs. *Prior.*

MO'LY. *n. ſ.* [*moly*, Latin; *moly*, French.]

The *molly* hath pinnated leaves, like thoſe of the lentiſcus, but are terminated by an odd lobe: the flower expands in the form of a roſe, and the fruit reſembles a grain of pepper. *Miller.*

Moly, or wild garlick, is of ſeveral ſorts; as the great *moly* of Homer, the Indian *moly*, the *moly* of Hungary, ſerpent's *moly*, the yellow *moly*, Spaniſh purple *moly*, Spaniſh ſilver-capped *moly*, Dioſcorides's *moly*, the ſweet *moly* of Montpelier: the roots are tender, and muſt be carefully defended from froſts: as for the time of their flowering, the *moly* of Homer flowers in May, and continues till July, and ſo do all the reſt except the laſt, which is late in September: they are hardy, and will thrive in any ſoil. *Mortimer's Huſb.*

The ſovereign plant he drew,
And ſhew'd its nature, and its wond'rous pow'r,
Black was the root, but milky white the flow'r;
Molly the name. *Pope's Odyſſey.*

MOLO'SSES. } *n. ſ.* [*mellazzo*, Italian.] Treacle; the ſpume or
MOLA'SSES. } ſcum of the juice of the ſugar-cane.

MOME. *n. ſ.* A dull, ſtupid blockhead, a ſtock, a poſt: this owes its original to the French word *momon*, which ſignifies the gaming at dice in maſquerade, the cuſtom and rule of which is, that a ſtrict ſilence is to be obſerved; whatſoever ſum one ſtakes another covers, but not a word is to be ſpoken; from hence alſo comes our word *mum* for ſilence. *Hanmer.*

Mome, malthorſe, capon, coxcomb, idiot, patch!
Either get thee from the door, or ſit down at the hatch. *Shakeſpeare's Comedy of Errours.*

MO'MENT. *n. ſ.* [*moment*, Fr. *momentum*, Latin.]

1. Conſequence; importance; weight; value.

We do not find that our Saviour reproved them of error, for thinking the judgment of the ſcribes to be worth the objecting, for eſteeming it to be of any *moment* or value in matters concerning God. *Hooker, b.* ii.

I have ſeen her die twenty times upon far poorer *moment*. *Shakeſpeare's Antony and Cleopatra.*

What towns of any *moment* but we have? *Shakeſp.*

It is an abſtruſe ſpeculation, but alſo of far leſs *moment* and conſequence to us than the others; ſeeing that without this we can evince the exiſtence of God. *Bentley's Sermons.*

2. Force; impulſive weight; actuating power.

The place of publick prayer is a circumſtance in the outward form, which hath *moment* to help devotion. *Hooker.*

Can theſe or ſuch be any aid to us?
Look they as they were built to ſhake the world?
Or be a *moment* to our enterprize? *Benj. Johnſon.*

Touch with lighteſt *moment* of impulſe
His free-will, to her own inclining left
In even ſcale. *Milton's Par. Loſt, b.* x.

He is a capable judge; can hear both ſides with an indifferent ear; is determined only by the *moments* of truth, and ſo retracts his paſt errors. *Norris's Miſcel.*

3. An indiviſible particle of time.

If I would go to hell for an eternal *moment*, or ſo, I could be knighted. *Shakeſp. Merry Wives of Windſor.*

The flighty purpoſe never is o'ertook,
Unleſs the deed go with it: from this *moment*
The very firſtlings of my heart ſhall be
The firſtlings of my hand. *Shakeſp. Macbeth.*

The imaginary reaſoning of brutes is not a diſtinct reaſoning, but performed in a phyſical *moment*. *Hale.*

Yet thus receiving and returning bliſs
In this great *moment*, in this golden now,
When ev'ry trace of what, or when, or how,
Shou'd from my ſoul by raging love be torn. *Prior.*

MOME'NTALLY. *adv.* [from *momentum*, Latin.] For a moment.

Air but *momentally* remaining in our bodies, hath no proportionable ſpace for its converſion, only of length enough to refrigerate the heart. *Brown's Vulgar Errours, b.* iii.

MOMENTA'NEOUS. } *adj.* [*momentanée*, Fr. *momentaneus*, Lat.]
MO'MENTANY. } Laſting but a moment.

Small difficulties, when exceeding great good is ſure to enſue; and, on the other ſide, *momentary* benefits, when the hurt which they draw after them is unſpeakable, are not at all to be reſpected. *Hooker, b.* i.

Flame above is durable and conſiſtent; but with us it is a ſtranger and *momentany*. *Bacon's Nat. Hiſt.* N°. 31.

MO'MENTARY. *adj.* [from *moment.*] Laſting for a moment; done in a moment.

Momentary as a ſound,
Swift as a ſhadow, ſhort as any dream. *Shakeſpeare.*

Scarce could the ſhady king
The horrid ſum of his intentions tell,
But ſhe, ſwift as the *momentany* wing
Of light'ning, or the words he ſpoke, left hell. *Craſhaw.*

Swift as thought the flitting ſhade
Through air his *momentary* journey made. *Dryden.*

Onions, garlick, pepper, ſalt and vinegar, taken in great quantities, excite a *momentary* heat and fever. *Arbuthnot.*

MOME'NTOUS. *adj.* [from *momentum*, Latin.] Important; weighty; of conſequence.

Great Anne, weighing th' events of war
Momentous, in her prudent heart thee choſe. *Philips.*

If any falſe ſtep be made in the more *momentous* concerns of life, the whole ſcheme of ambitious deſigns is broken. *Add.*

MO'MMERY.

MO'MMERY. *n. s.* [or *mummery*, from *mummer*, *momerie*, Fr.] An entertainment in which maskers play frolicks. See MOME.

All was jollity,
Feasting and mirth, light wantonness and laughter,
Piping and playing, minstrelsy and masking,
Till life fled from us like an idle dream,
A shew of *mommery* without a meaning. *Rowe.*

MO'NACHAL. *adj.* [*monacal*, Fr. *monachalis*, Lat. μοναχικὸς.] Monastick; relating to monks, or conventual orders.

MO'NACHISM. *n. s.* [*monachisme*, Fr.] The state of monks; the monastick life.

MO'NAD. } *n. s.* [μονὰς.] An indivisible thing.
MO'NADE. }

Disunity is the natural property of matter, which of itself is nothing else but an infinite congeries of physical *monads*. *More's Divine Dialogues.*

MO'NARCH. *n. s.* [*monarch*, Fr. μόναρχος.]

1. A governor invested with absolute authority; a king.

I was
A morsel for a *monarch*. *Shakesp. Ant. and Cleopatra.*
Your brother kings and *monarchs* of the earth
Do all expect that you should rouse yourself. *Shakespeare.*

The father of a family or nation, that uses his servants like children, and advises with them in what concerns the commonweal, and thereby is willingly obeyed by them, is what the schools mean by a *monarch*. *Temple's Miscel.*

2. One superior to the rest of the same kind.

The *monarch* oak, the patriarch of the trees,
Three centuries he grows, and three he stays
Supreme in state, and in three more decays. *Dryden.*
With ease distinguish'd is the regal race,
One *monarch* wears an open, honest face;
Shap'd to his size, and godlike to behold,
His royal body shines with specks of gold. *Dryden's Virg.*
Return'd with dire remorseless sway,
The *monarch* savage rends the trembling prey. *Pope's Odyss.*

3. President.

Come, thou *monarch* of the vine,
Plumpy Bacchus, with pink eyne,
In thy vats our cares be drown'd. *Shakesp. Ant. and Cleop.*

MONA'RCHAL. *adj.* [from *monarch*.] Suiting a monarch; regal; princely; imperial.

Satan, whom now transcendent glory rais'd
Above his fellows, with *monarchal* pride,
Conscious of highest worth, unmov'd thus spake. *Milton.*

MONA'RCHICAL. *adj.* [*monarchique*, Fr. μοναρχικὸς, from *monarch*.] Vested in a single ruler.

That storks will only live in free states, is a pretty conceit to advance the opinion of popular policies, and from antipathies in nature to disparage *monarchical* government. *Brown's Vulgar Errours, b.* iii.

The decretals resolve all into a *monarchical* power at Rome. *Baker's Reflections on Learning.*

To MO'NARCHISE. *v. n.* [from *monarch*.] To play the king.

Allowing him a breath, a little scene
To *monarchize*, be fear'd, and kill with looks. *Shakesp.*

MO'NARCHY. *n. s.* [*monarchie*, Fr. μοναρχία.]

1. The government of a single person.

While the *monarchy* flourished, these wanted not a protector. *Atterbury's Sermons.*

2. Kingdom; empire.

I past
Unto the kingdom of perpetual night.
The first that there did greet my stranger soul,
Was my great father-in-law, renowned Warwick,
Who cried aloud, What scourge for perjury
Can this dark *monarchy* afford false Clarence. *Shakespeare.*
This small inheritance
Contenteth me, and 's worth a *monarchy*. *Shakespeare.*

MO'NASTERY. *n. s.* [*monastere*, Fr. *monasterium*, Lat.] House of religious retirement; convent. It is usually pronounced, and often written, *monastry*.

Then courts of kings were held in high renown;
There, virgins honourable vows receiv'd,
But chaste as maids in *monasteries* liv'd. *Dryden.*

In a *monastery* your devotions cannot carry you so far toward the next world, as to make this lose the sight of you. *Pope.*

MONA'STICK. } *adj.* [*monastique*, Fr. *monasticus*, Latin.] Re-
MONA'STICAL. } ligiously recluse; pertaining to a monk.

I drave my suitor to forswear the full stream of the world, and to live in a nook merely *monastick*. *Shak. As you like it.*

The silicious and hairy vests of the strictest orders of friers derive the institution of their *monastick* life from the example of John and Elias. *Brown's Vulgar Errours, b.* v.

When young, you led a life *monastick*,
And wore a vast ecclesiastick;
Now in your age you grow fantastick. *Denham.*

MONA'STICALLY. *adv.* [from *monastick*.] Reclusely; in the manner of a monk

I have a dozen years more to answer for, all *monastically* passed in this country of liberty and delight. *Swift.*

MO'NDAY. *n. s.* [from *moon* and *day*.] The second day of the week.

MO'NEY. *n. s.* [*monnoye*, French; *moneta*, Latin. It has properly no plural except when money is taken for a single piece; but monies was formerly used for sums.] Metal coined for the purposes of commerce.

Importune him for *monies*; be not ceast
With slight denial. *Shakesp. Timon of Athens.*
The jealous wittolly knave hath masses of *money*. *Shakesp.*
You need my help, and you say,
Shylock, we would have *monies*. *Shakespeare.*
I will give thee the worth of it in *money*. 1 *Kings* xxi. 2.
Wives the readiest helps
To betray heady husbands, rob the easy,
And lend the *monies* on return of lust. *Benj. Johnson.*

Money differs from uncoined silver, in that the quantity of silver in each piece of *money* is ascertained by the stamp it bears, which is a publick voucher. *Locke.*

My discourse to the hen-peck'd has produced many correspondents; such a discourse is of general use, and every married man's *money*. *Addison's Spect.* N° 482.

People are not obliged to receive any *monies*, except of their own coinage by a publick mint. *Swift.*

Those hucksterers or *money* jobbers will be found necessary, if this brass money is made current in the exchequer. *Swift.*

MO'NEYBAG. *n. s.* [*money* and *bag*.] A large purse.

Look to my house; I am right loth to go;
There is some ill a brewing towards my rest,
For I did dream of *moneybags* to-night. *Shakespeare.*

My place was taken up by an ill-bred puppy, with a *moneybag* under each arm. *Addison's Guard.* N°. 106.

MO'NEYBOX. *n. s.* [*money* and *box*.] A till.

MO'NEYCHANGER. *n. s.* [*money* and *change*.] A broker in money.

The userers or *moneychangers* being a scandalous employment at Rome, is a reason for the high rate of interest. *Arbuthnot.*

MO'NEYED. *adj.* [from *money*.] Rich in money: often used in opposition to those who are possessed of lands.

Invite *moneyed* men to lend to the merchants, for the continuing and quickening of trade. *Bacon's Essays.*

If exportation will not balance importation, away must your silver go again, whether *moneyed* or not *moneyed*; for where goods do not, silver must pay for the commodities you spend. *Locke.*

Several turned their money into those funds, merchants as well as other *moneyed* men. *Swift.*

With these measures fell in all *monied* men; such as had raised vast sums by trading with stocks and funds, and lending upon great interest. *Swift.*

MO'NEYER. *n. s.* [*monnoyer-eur*, Fr. from *money*.]

1. One that deals in money; a banker.

2. A coiner of money.

MO'NEYLESS. *adj.* [from *money*.] Wanting money; penniless.

The strong expectation of a good certain salary will outweigh the loss by bad rents received out of lands in *moneyless* time. *Swift.*

MO'NEYMATTER. *n. s.* [*money* and *matter*.] Account of debtor and creditor.

What if you and I Nick should enquire how *moneymatters* stand between us? *Arbuthnot's Hist. of John Bull.*

MO'NEYSCRIVENER. *n. s.* [*money* and *scrivener*.] One who raises money for others.

Suppose a young unexperienced man in the hands of *moneyscriveners*; such fellows are like your wire-drawing mills, if they get hold of a man's finger, they will pull in his whole body at last. *Arbuthnot's Hist. of John Bull.*

MO'NEYWORT. *n. s.* A plant.

MO'NEYSWORTH. *n. s.* [*money* and *worth*.] Something valueable; something that will bring money.

There is either money or *moneysworth* in all the controversies of life; for we live in a mercenary world, and it is the price of all things in it. *L'Estrange.*

MO'NGCORN. *n. s.* [manᵹ, Saxon, and *corn*.] Mixed corn: as, wheat and rie.

MO'NGER. *n. s.* [manᵹeɲe, Saxon, a trader; from manᵹian, Saxon, to trade.] A dealer; a seller. It is used after the name of any commodity to express a seller of that commodity: as, a *fishmonger*; and sometimes a medler in any thing: as, a *whoremonger*; a *newsmonger*.

Th' impatient states *monger*
Could now contain himself no longer. *Hudibras, p.* iii.

MO'NGREL. *adj.* [as *mongcorn*, from manᵹ, Saxon, or *mengen*, to mix, Dutch.] Of a mixed breed.

This zealot
Is of a *mongrel*, divers kind,
Clerick before, and lay behind. *Hudibras, p.* i.
Ye *mongrel* work of heav'n, with human shapes,
That have but just enough of sense to know
The master's voice. *Dryden's Don Sebastian.*
I'm but a half-strain'd villain yet.
But *mongrel* mischievous. *Dryden.*

Base,

Baſe, groveling, worthleſs wretches;
Mongrels in faction; poor faint-hearted traitors. *Addiſon.*

His friendſhip ſtill to few confin'd,
Were always of the middling kind;
No fools of rank, or *mongrel* breed,
Who fain wou'd paſs for lords indeed. *Swift's Miſcel.*

Mo'niment. *n. ſ.* [from *moneo*, Lat.] It ſeems here to ſignify inſcription.

Some others were driven and diſtent
Into great ingots and to wedges ſquare,
Some in round plates withouten *moniment*. *Fairy Queen.*

To Mo'nish. *v. a.* [*moneo*, Lat.] To admoniſh, of which it is a contraction.

Moniſh him gently, which ſhall make him both willing to amend, and glad to go forward in love. *Aſcham's Schoolmaſter.*

Mo'nisher. *n. ſ.* [from *moniſh.*] An admoniſher; a monitor.

Moni'tion. *n. ſ.* [*monitio*, Latin; *monition*, Fr.]

1. Information; hint.

We have no viſible *monition* of the returns of any other periods, ſuch as we have of the day, by ſucceſſive light and darkneſs. *Holder on Time.*

2. Instruction; document.

Unruly ambition is deaf, not only to the advice of friends, but to the counſels and *monitions* of reaſon itſelf. *L'Eſtrange.*

After ſage *monitions* from his friends,
His talents to employ for nobler ends,
He turns to politicks his dang'rous wit. *Swift.*

Mo'nitor. *n. ſ.* [Latin.] One who warns of faults, or informs of duty; one who gives uſeful hints. It is uſed of an upper ſcholar in a ſchool commiſſioned by the maſter to look to the boys in his abſence.

You need not be a *monitor* to the king; his learning is eminent: be but his ſcholar, and you are ſafe. *Bacon.*

It was the privilege of Adam innocent to have theſe notions alſo firm and untainted, to carry his *monitor* in his boſom, his law in his heart, and to have ſuch a conſcience as might be its own caſuiſt. *South's Sermons.*

We can but divine who it is that ſpeaks; whether Perſius himſelf, or his friend and *monitor*, or a third perſon. *Dryden.*

The pains that come from the neceſſities of nature, are *monitors* to us to beware of greater miſchiefs. *Locke.*

Mo'nitory. *adj.* [*monitoire*, Fr. *monitorius*, Lat.] Conveying uſeful inſtruction; giving admonition.

Loſſes, miſcarriages, and diſappointments, are *monitory* and inſtructive. *L'Eſtrange's Fables.*

He is ſo taken up ſtill, in ſpite of the *monitory* hint in my eſſay, with particular men, that he neglects mankind. *Pope.*

Mo'nitory. *n. ſ.* Admonition; warning.

A king of Hungary took a biſhop in battle, and kept him priſoner; whereupon the pope writ a *monitory* to him, for that he had broken the privilege of holy church. *Bacon.*

MONK. *n. ſ.* [monec, Saxon; *monachus*, Latin; μοναχὸς.] One of a religious community bound by vows to certain obſervances.

'Twould prove the verity of certain words,
Spoke by a holy *monk*. *Shakeſpeare's Henry* VIII.

Abdemeleck, as one weary of the world, gave over all, and betook himſelf to a ſolitary life, and became a melancholy Mahometan *monk*. *Knolles's Hiſt. of the Turks.*

The droniſh *monks*, the ſcorn and ſhame of manhood,
Rouſe and prepare once more to take poſſeſſion,
And neſtle in their ancient hives again. *Rowe.*

Monks, in ſome reſpects, agree with regulars, as in the ſubſtantial vows of religion; but in other reſpects, *monks* and regulars differ; for that regulars, vows excepted, are not tied up to ſo ſtrict a rule of life as *monks* are. *Ayliffe's Parergon.*

Mo'nkey. *n. ſ.* [*monikin*, a little man.]

1. An ape; a baboon; a jackanapes. An animal bearing ſome reſemblance of man.

One of them ſhewed me a ring that he had of your daughter for a *monkey*: Tubal, it was my turquoiſe; I would not have given it for a wilderneſs of *monkeys*. *Shakeſpeare.*

More new-fangled than an ape; more giddy in my deſires than a *monkey*. *Shakeſp. As you like it.*

Other creatures, as well as *monkeys*, deſtroy their young ones by ſenſeleſs fondneſs. *Locke on Education.*

With glittering gold and ſparkling gems they ſhine,
But apes and *monkeys* are the gods within. *Granville.*

2. A word of contempt, or ſlight kindneſs.

This is the *monkey*'s own giving out; ſhe is perſuaded I will marry her. *Shakeſpeare's Othello.*

Poor *monkey*! how wilt thou do for a father? *Shakeſp.*

Mo'nkery. *n. ſ.* [from *monk.*] The monaſtick life.

Neither do I meddle with their evangelical perfection of vows, nor the dangerous ſervitude of their raſh and impotent votaries, nor the inconveniences of their *monkery*. *Hall.*

Mo'nkhood. *n. ſ.* [*monk* and *hood.*] The character of a monk.

He had left off his *monkhood* too, and was no longer obliged to them. *Atterbury.*

Mo'nkish. *adj.* [from *monk.*] Monaſtick; pertaining to monks; taught by monks.

Thoſe publick charities are a greater ornament to this city than all its wealth, and do more real honour to the reformed religion, than redounds to the church of Rome from all thoſe *monkiſh* and ſuperſtitious foundations of which ſhe vainly boaſts. *Atterbury's Sermons.*

Riſe, riſe, Roſcommon, ſee the Blenheim muſe,
The dull conſtraint of *monkiſh* rhyme refuſe. *Smith.*

Monk's-hood. *n. ſ.* A plant. *Ainſ.*

Monk's-rhubarb. *n. ſ.* A ſpecies of dock: its roots are uſed in medicine.

Mo'nochord. *n. ſ.* [μόνος and χορδή.]

1. An inſtrument of one ſtring: as, the trumpet marine. *Har.*

2. A kind of inſtrument anciently of ſingular uſe for the regulating of ſounds: the ancients made uſe of it to determine the proportion of ſounds to one another: when the chord was divided into two equal parts, ſo that the terms were as one to one, they called them uniſons; but if they were as two to one, they called them octaves or diapaſons; when they were as three to two, they called them fifths or diapentes; if they were as four to three, they called them fourths or diateſſerons; if the terms were as five to four, they called it diton, or a tierce major; but if the terms were as ſix to five, then they called it a demi-diton, or a tierce minor; and, laſtly, if the terms were as twenty-four to twenty-five, they called it a demiton or dieze: the *monochord* being thus divided, was properly that which they called a ſyſtem, of which there were many kinds, according to the different diviſions of the *monochord*. *Harris.*

Mon'ocular. } *adj.* [μόνος and *oculus.*] One-eyed; having
Mono'culous. } only one eye.

He was well ſerved who, going to cut down an antient white hawthorn tree, which, becauſe ſhe budded before others, might be an occaſion of ſuperſtition, had ſome of the prickles flew into his eyes, and made him *monocular*. *Howel.*

Thoſe of China repute all the reſt of the world *monoculous*. *Glanville's Scep.*

Mo'nody. *n. ſ.* [μονῳδία; *monodie*, Fr.] A poem ſung by one perſon not in dialogue.

Mono'gamist. *n. ſ.* [μόνος and γάμος; *monogame*, Fr.] One who diſallows ſecond marriages.

Mono'gamy. *n. ſ.* [*monogamie*, Fr. μόνος and γαμέω.] Marriage of one wife.

Mo'nogram. *n. ſ.* μόνος and γράμμα; *monogramme*, Fr.] A cypher; a character compounded of ſeveral letters.

Mo'nologue. *n. ſ.* [μόνος and λόγος; *monologue*, Fr.] A ſcene in which a perſon of the drama ſpeaks by himſelf; a ſoliloquy.

He gives you an account of himſelf, and of his returning from the country, in *monologue*; to which unnatural way of narration Terence is ſubject in all his plays. *Dryden.*

Mo'nomachy. *n. ſ.* [μονομαχία; μόνος and μάχη.] A duel; a ſingle combat.

Mo'nome. *n. ſ.* [*monome*, Fr.] In algebra, a quantity that has but one denomination or name; as, ab, aab, aaab. *Harris.*

Monope'talous. *adv.* [*monopetale*, Fr. μόνος and πέταλον.] It is uſed for ſuch flowers as are formed out of one leaf, howſoever they may be ſeemingly cut into many ſmall ones, and thoſe fall off together. *Quincy.*

Mono'polist. *n. ſ.* [*monopoleur*, French.] One who by engroſſing or patent obtains the ſole power or privilege of vending any commodity.

To Mono'polize. *v. a.* [μόνος and πωλέω; *monopoler*, Fr.] To have the ſole power or privilege of vending any commodity.

He has ſuch a prodigious trade, that if there is not ſome ſtop put, he will *monopolize*; nobody will ſell a yard of drapery, or mercery ware, but himſelf. *Arbuthnot.*

Mono'poly. *n. ſ.* [μονοπωλία; *monopole*, Fr. μόνος and πωλέω.] The excluſive privilege of ſelling any thing.

Doſt thou call me fool, boy?

—All thy other titles haſt thou given away; that thou waſt born with.

—Lords and great men will not let me; if I had a *monopoly* on't they would have part on't. *Shakeſp. King Lear.*

One of the moſt oppreſſive *monopolies* imaginable; all others can concern only ſomething without us, but this faſtens upon our nature, yea upon our reaſon. *Go. of the Tongue.*

Shakeſpeare rather writ happily than knowingly and juſtly; and Johnſon, who by ſtudying Horace, had been acquainted with the rules, yet ſeemed to envy to poſterity that knowledge, and to make a *monopoly* of his learning. *Dryden's Juv.*

Mono'ptote. *n. ſ.* [μόνος and πτῶσις.] Is a noun uſed only in ſome one oblique caſe. *Clarke's Latin Grammar.*

Mono'stich. *n. ſ.* [μονόστιχον.] A compoſition of one verſe.

Monosylla'bical. *adj.* [from *monoſyllable.*] Conſiſting of words of one ſyllable.

MONOSY'LLABLE. *n. ſ.* [*monoſyllabe*, Fr. μόνος and συλλαβή.] A word of only one ſyllable.

My name of Ptolemy!
It is ſo long it aſks an hour to write it:
I'll change it into Jove or Mars!
Or any other civil *monoſyllable*,
That will not tire my hand. *Dryden's Cleomenes.*

Theſe,

These, although not insensible how much our language was already over-stocked with *monosyllables*, yet, to save time and pains, introduced that barbarous custom of abbreviating words, to fit them to the measure of their verses. *Swift.*

Monosyllable lines, unless artfully managed, are stiff or languishing; but may be beautiful to express melancholy. *Pope.*

MONOSY'LLABLED. *adj.* [*monosyllabe*, Fr. from *monosyllable*.] Consisting of one syllable.

Nine taylors, if rightly spell'd,
Into one man are *monosyllabled*. *Cleaveland.*

MONO'TONY. *n. s.* [μονοτονία; μόνος and τόνος; *monotonie*, Fr.] Uniformity of sound; want of variety in cadence.

I could object to the repetition of the same rhimes within four lines of each other as tiresome to the ear through their *monotony*. *Pope's Letters.*

MO'NSIEUR. n. s. [French.] A term of reproach for a Frenchman.

A Frenchman his companion;
An eminent *monsieur*, that, it seems, much loves
A Gallian girl. *Shakespeare's Cymbeline.*

MONSO'ON. *n. s.* [*monson*, *mongon*, Fr.]

Monsoons are shifting trade winds in the East Indian ocean, which blow periodically; some for half a year one way, others but for three months, and then shift and blow for six or three months directly contrary. *Harris.*

The *monsoons* and trade winds are constant and periodical even to the thirtieth degree of latitude all around the globe, and seldom transgress or fall short of those bounds. *Ray.*

MO'NSTER. *n. s.* [*monstre*, Fr. *monstrum*, Latin.]

1. Something out of the common order of nature.

It ought to be determined whether *monsters* be really a distinct species; we find, that some of these monstrous productions have none of those qualities that accompany the essence of that species from whence they derive. *Locke.*

2. Something horrible for deformity, wickedness, or mischief.

If she live long,
And, in the end, meet the old course of death,
Women will all turn *monsters*. *Shakesp. King Lear.*

All human virtue
Finds envy never conquer'd but by death:
The great Alcides ev'ry labour past,
Had still this *monster* to subdue at last. *Pope.*

To MO'NSTER. *v. a.* [from the noun.] To put out of the common order of things. Not in use.

Her offence
Must be of such unnatural degreee
That *monsters* it. *Shakesp. King Lear.*

I had rather have one scratch my head i' th' sun,
When the alarum were struck, than idly sit
To hear my nothings *monster'd*. *Shakesp. Coriolanus.*

MONSTRO'SITY. } *n. s.* [from *monstrous*.] The state of being
MONSTRU'OSITY. } monstrous, or out of the common order of the universe. *Monstrosity* is more analogous.

This is the *monstruosity* in love, that the will is infinite, and the execution confin'd. *Shakesp. Troil. and Cressida.*

Such a tacit league is against such routs and shoals of people, as have utterly degenerated from nature, as have in their very body and frame of estate a *monstrosity*. *Bacon.*

We read of monstrous births, but we often see a greater *monstrosity* in educations: thus, when a father has begot a man, he trains him up into a beast. *South's Sermons.*

By the same law *monstrosity* could not incapacitate from marriage, witness the case of hermaphrodites. *Arbuthnot and Pope.*

MO'NSTROUS. *adj.* [*monstrueux*, Fr. *monstrosus*, Latin.]

1. Deviating from the stated order of nature.

Every thing that exists has its particular constitution; and yet some *monstrous* productions have few of those qualities which accompany the essence of that species from whence they derive their originals. *Locke.*

2. Strange; wonderful. Generally with some degree of dislike.

Is it not *monstrous* that this player here
But in a fiction, in a dream of passion,
Could force his soul so to his conceit,
That, from her working, all his visage wan'd. *Shakesp.*

O *monstrous!* but one halfpenny worth of bread to this intolerable deal of sack. *Shakespeare.*

3. Irregular; enormous.

No *monstrous* height, or breadth, or length appear,
The whole at once is bold and regular. *Pope.*

4. Shocking; hateful.

This was an invention given out by the Spaniards, to save the *monstrous* scorn their nation received. *Bacon.*

MONSTROUS. *adv.* Exceedingly; very much. A cant term.

Oil of vitriol and petroleum, a dram of each, turn into a mouldy substance, there residing a fair cloud in the bottom, and a *monstrous* thick oil on the top. *Bacon.*

She was easily put off the hooks, and *monstrous* hard to be pleased again. *L'Estrange.*

Add, that the rich have still a gibe in store,
And will be *monstrous* witty on the poor. *Dryden's Juv.*

MO'NSTROUSLY. *adv.* [from *monstrous*.]

1. In a manner out of the common order of nature; shockingly; terribly; horribly.

He walks;
And that self chain about his neck,
Which he forswore most *monstrously* to have. *Shakespeare.*

Tiberius was bad enough in his youth, but superlatively and *monstrously* so in his old age. *South's Sermons.*

2. To a great or enormous degree.

These truths with his example you disprove,
Who with his wife is *monstrously* in love. *Dryden's Juv.*

MO'NSTROUSNESS. *n. s.* [from *monstrous*.] Enormity; irregular nature or behaviour.

See the *monstrousness* of man,
When he looks out in an ungrateful shape! *Shakespeare.*

MO'NTANT. n. s. [French.] A term in fencing.

Vat be all you, one, two, tree, four, come for?
—To see thee fight, to see thee pass thy puncto, thy stock, thy traverse, thy distance, thy *montant*. *Shakesp.*

MONTE'RO. n. s. [Spanish.] A horseman's cap.

His hat was like a helmet, or Spanish *montero*. *Bacon.*

MONTE'TH. *n. s.* [from the name of the inventor.] A vessel in which glasses are washed.

New things produce new words, and thus *Monteth*
Has by one vessel sav'd his name from death. *King.*

MONTH. *n. s.* [monað, Saxon.] A space of time either measured by the sun or moon: the lunar month is the time between the change and change, or the time in which the moon comes to the same point: the solar month is the time in which the sun passes through a sign of the zodiack: the calendar months, by which we reckon time, are unequally of thirty or one-and-thirty days, except February, which is of twenty-eight, and in leap year of twenty-nine.

Till the expiration of your *month*,
Sojourn with my sister. *Shakesp. King Lear.*

From a *month* old even unto five years old. *Lev.* xxvii. 6.

Months are not only lunary, and measured by the moon, but also solary, and determined by the motion of the sun, in thirty degrees of the ecliptick. *Brown's Vulgar Errours, b.* iv.

As many *months* as I sustain'd her hate,
So many years is she condemn'd by fate
To daily death. *Dryden's Theo. and Honoria.*

MONTH's *mind. n. s.* Longing desire.

You have a *month's mind* to them. *Shakespeare.*

For if a trumpet found, or drum beat,
Who has not a *month's mind* to combat? *Hudibras, p.* i.

MO'NTHLY. *adj.* [from *month*.]

1. Continuing a month; performed in a month.

I would ask concerning the *monthly* revolutions of the moon about the earth, or the diurnal ones of the earth upon its own axis, whether these have been finite or infinite. *Bentley.*

2. Happening every month.

The youth of heav'nly birth I view'd,
For whom our *monthly* victims are renew'd. *Dryden.*

MO'NTHLY. *adv.* Once in a month.

If the one may very well *monthly*, the other may as well even daily, be iterated. *Hooker, b.* v.

O swear not by the moon, th' inconstant moon,
That changes *monthly* in her circled orb;
Lest that thy love prove likewise variable. *Shakespeare.*

MONTO'IR. n. s. [French.] In horsemanship, a stone as high as the stirrups, which Italian riding-masters mount their horses from, without putting their foot in the stirrup. *Dict.*

MONTRO'SS. *n. s.* An under gunner, or assistant to a gunner, engineer, or fire-master. *Dict.*

MO'NUMENT. *n. s.* [*monument*, Fr. *monumentum*, Latin.]

1. Any thing by which the memory of persons or things is preserved; a memorial.

In his time there remained the *monument* of his tomb in the mountain Jasius. *Raleigh's Hist. of the World.*

He is become a notable *monument* of unprosperous disloyalty. *King Charles.*

So many grateful altars I would rear
Of grassy turf; and pile up every stone
Of lustre from the brook; in memory,
Or *monument* to ages: and thereon
Offer sweet-smelling gums. *Milton's Par. Lost, b.* xi.

Of ancient British art
A pleasing *monument*, not less admir'd
Than what from Attick or Etruscan hands
Arose. *Philips.*

Collect the best *monuments* of our friends, their own images in their writings. *Pope to Swift.*

2. A tomb; a cenotaph; something erected in memory of the dead.

On your family's old *monument*
Hang mournful epitaphs, and do all rites
That appertain unto a burial. *Shakespeare.*

The flowers which in the circling valley grow,
Shall on his *monument* their odours throw. *Sandys's Paraph.*

In a heap of slain,
Two youthful knights they found beneath a load opprest

Of slaughter'd foes, whom first to death they sent,
The trophies of their strength, a bloody *monument*. *Dryd.*
With thee on Raphael's *monument* I mourn,
Or wait inspiring dreams at Maro's urn. *Pope's Miscel.*

MONUME'NTAL. *adj.* [from *monument*.] Memorial; preserving memory.

When the sun begins to fling
His flaring beams, me, goddess, bring
To arched walks of twilight groves,
And shadows brown that Sylvan loves,
Of pine or *monumental* oak. *Milton.*

The destruction of the earth was the most *monumental* proof that could have been given to all the succeeding ages of mankind. *Woodward's Nat. Hist. p.* ii.

The polish'd pillar different sculptures grace,
A work outlasting *monumental* brass. *Pope.*

2. Raised in honour of the dead; belonging to a tomb.

Perseverance keeps honour bright:
To have done, is to hang quite out of fashion,
Like rusty mail in *monumental* mockery. *Shakespeare.*
I'll not scar that whiter skin of her than snow,
And smooth as *monumental* alabaster. *Shakesp. Othello.*
Therefore if he needs must go,
And the fates will have it so,
Softly may he be possest
Of his *monumental* rest. *Crashaw.*

MOOD. *n. s.* [*mode*, Fr. *modus*, Latin.]

1. The form of an argument.

Mood is the regular determination of propositions according to their quantity and quality, *i. e.* their universal or particular affirmation or negation. *Watts's Logick.*

Aristotle reduced our loose reasonings to certain rules, and made them conclude in *mode* and figure. *Baker on Learning.*

2. Stile of musick.

They move
In perfect phalanx, to the Dorian *mood*
Of flutes, and soft recorders. *Milton's Par. Lost, b.* i.
Their sound seems a tune
Harsh, and of dissonant *mood* from his complaint. *Milton.*

3. The change the verb undergoes in some languages, as the Greek, Latin, and French, to signify various intentions of the mind, is called *mood*. *Clarke's Lat. Grammar.*

4. [From *mod*, Gothick; moꝺ, Saxon; *moed*, Dutch; and generally in all Teutonick dialects.] Temper of mind; state of mind as affected by any passion; disposition.

The trembling ghosts, with sad amazed *mood*,
Chattering their iron teeth, and staring wide
With stony eyes. *Fairy Queen, b.* i.
The kingly beast upon her gazing stood,
With pity calm'd, down fell his angry *mood*. *Fairy Qu.*
Eyes,
Albeit unused to the melting *mood*,
Drop tears as fast as the Arabian trees
Their medicinal gum. *Shakesp. Othello.*
Clorinda changed to ruth her warlike *mood*,
Few silver drops her vermil cheeks depaint. *Fairfax.*

Solyman, in a melancholy *mood*, walked up and down in his tent a great part of the night. *Knolles.*

She was in fittest *mood*
For cutting corns, or letting blood. *Hudibras, p.* ii.
These two kids t' appease his angry *mood*
I bear, of which the furies give him good. *Dryden.*
He now profuse of tears,
In suppliant *mood* fell prostrate at our feet. *Addison.*

5. Anger; rage; heat of mind. *Mod*, in Gothick, signifies habitual temper.

That which we move for our better instruction's sake, turneth into anger and choler in them; yet in their *mood* they cast forth somewhat wherewith, under pain of greater displeasure, we must rest contented. *Hooker, b.* v.

MO'ODY. *adj.* [from *mood*.]

1. Angry; out of humour.

How now, *moody*?
What is't thou canst demand? *Shakesp. Tempest.*
Chide him rev'rently,
When you perceive his blood inclin'd to mirth;
But being *moody*, give him line and scope,
Till that his passions, like a whale on ground,
Confound themselves with working. *Shakesp. Henry* IV.
Every peevish, *moody* malecontent
Shall set the senseless rabble in an uproar? *Rowe.*

2. Mental; intellectual: moꝺ in Saxon signifies the mind.

Give me some musick; musick, *moody* food
Of us that trade in love. *Shakesp. Antony and Cleopatra.*

MOON. *n. s.* [μηνη; *mena*, Gothick; mena, Saxon; *mona*, Islandick; *maane*, Danish; *mane*, German; *maen*, Dutch.]

1. The changing luminary of the night, called by poets Cynthia or Phœbe.

The *moon* shines bright: 'twas such a night as this,
When the sweet wind did gently kiss the trees,
And they did make no noise. *Shakespeare.*
O swear not by the *moon*, th' inconstant *moon*,
That monthly changes in her circled orb,
Lest that thy love prove likewise variable. *Shakespeare.*

Diana hath her name from moisten, which is the property of the *moon*, being by nature cold and moist, and is feigned to be a goddess huntress. *Peacham.*

Ye *moon* and stars bear witness to the truth! *Dryden.*

2. A month. *Ains.*

3. [In fortification.] It is used in composition to denote a figure resembling a crescent: as, a half *moon*.

MOON-BEAM. *n. s.* [*moon* and *beam*.] Rays of lunar light.

The division and quavering, which please so much in musick, have an agreement with the glittering of light, as the *moon-beams* playing upon a wave. *Bacon's Nat. Hist.*

On the water the *moon-beams* played, and made it appear like floating quicksilver. *Dryden on Dramatick Poesy.*

MOON-CALF. *n. s.* [*moon* and *calf*.]

1. A monster; a false conception: supposed perhaps anciently to be produced by the influence of the moon.

How cam'st thou to be the siege of this *moon-calf*. *Shak.*

2. A dolt; a stupid fellow.

The potion works not on the part design'd,
But turns his brain, and stupifies his mind;
The sotted *moon-calf* gapes. *Dryden's Juvenal.*

MOON-EYED. *adj.* [*moon* and *eye*.]

1. Having eyes affected by the revolutions of the moon.

2. Dim eyed; purblind. *Ains.*

MOONFE'RN.] *n. s.* A plant. *Ains.*

MOON-FISH. *n. s.*

Moon-fish is so called, because the tail fin is shaped like a half moon, by which, and his odd trussed shape, he is sufficiently distinguished. *Grew's Musæum.*

MO'ONLESS. *adj.* [from *moon*.] Not enlightened by the moon.

Assisted by a friend, one *moonless* night,
This Palamon from prison took his flight. *Dryden.*

MO'ONLIGHT. *n. s.* [*moon* and *light*.] The light afforded by the moon.

Their bishop and his clergy, being departed from them by *moonlight*, to choose in his room any other bishop, had been altogether impossible. *Hooker.*

Thou hast by *moonlight* at her window sung,
With feigning voice, verses of feigning love. *Shakespeare.*

MO'ONLIGHT. *adj.* Illuminated by the moon.

If you will patiently dance in our round,
And see our *moonlight* revels, go with us. *Shakespeare.*
What beck'ning ghost along the *moonlight* shade
Invites my steps, and points to yonder glade? *Pope.*

MOON-SEED. *n. s.* [*menispermum*, Latin.]

The *moon-seed* hath a rosaceous flower, consisting of several small leaves, which are placed round the embrio in a circular order: the pointal, which is divided into three parts at the top, afterward becomes the fruit or berry, in which is included one flat seed, which is, when ripe, hollowed like the appearance of the moon. *Miller.*

MO'ONSHINE. *n. s.* [*moon* and *shine*.]

1. The lustre of the moon.

Pinch him, and burn him, and turn him about,
Till candles, and starlight, and *moonshine* be out. *Shakesp.*
I, by the *moonshine*, to the windows went:
And, ere I was aware, sigh'd to myself. *Dryd. Span. Fr.*

2. [In burlesque.] A month.

I am some twelve or fourteen *moonshines*
Lag of a brother. *Shakespeare's King Lear.*

MO'ONSHINE. } *adj.* [*moon* and *shine*.] Illuminated by the moon:
MO'ONSHINY. } both seem a popular corruption of *moonshining*.

Fairies, black, grey, green, and white,
You *moonshine* revellers, and shades of night. *Shakespeare.*

Althought it was a fair *moonshine* night, the enemy thought not fit to assault them. *Clarendon, b.* viii.

I went to see them in a *moonshiny* night. *Addison.*

MO'ONSTONE. *n. s.* A kind of stone. *Ains.*

MO'ONSTRUCK. *adj.* [*moon* and *struck*.] Lunatick; affected by the moon.

Demoniack phrensy, moaping melancholy,
And *moonstruck* madness. *Milton's Par. Lost, b.* xi.

MOON-TREFOIL. *n. s.* [*medicago*, Latin.] A plant.

The *moon-trefoil* hath a papilionaceous flower, out of whose empalement arises the pointal, which afterwards becomes a plain orbiculated fruit, shaped like an half moon. *Miller.*

MO'ONWORT. *n. s.* [*moon* and *wort*.] Stationflower; honesty.

The flower of the *moonwort* consists of four leaves in form of a cross; the ovary which arises in the centre of the flower becomes a compressed perfectly-smooth fruit, divided into two cells, and filled with seeds. *Miller.*

MO'ONY. *adj.* [from *moon*.] Lunated; having a crescent for the standard resembling the moon.

Encount'ring fierce
The Solymean sultan, he o'erthrew
His *moony* troops, returning bravely smear'd
With Panim blood. *Philips.*
The Soldan galls th' Illyrian coast;
But soon the miscreant *moony* host
Before the victor-cross shall fly. *Fenton.*

MOOR. *n. s.* [*moer*, Dutch; *modder*, Teutonick, clay.]

1. A marsh; a fen; a bog; a tract of low and watry grounds.

While in her girlifh age fhe kept fheep on the *moor*, it chanced that a London merchant paffing by faw her, and liked her, begged her of her poor parents, and carried her to his home. *Carew's Survey of Cornwall.*

In the great level near Thorny, feveral trees of oak and fir ftand in firm earth below the *moor*. *Hale.*

Let the marfh of Elfham Bruges tell,
What colour were their waters that fame day,
And all the *moor* 'twixt Elverfham and Dell. *Fairy Qu.*

2. [*Maurus*, Latin.] A negro; a black-a-moor.

I fhall anfwer that better than you can the getting up of the negro's belly; the *moor* is with child by you. *Shakefp.*

To Moor. *v. a.* [*morer*, French.] To faften by anchors or otherwife.

Three more fierce Eurus in his angry mood
Dafh'd on the fhallows of the moving fand,
And in mid ocean left them *moor'd* at hand. *Dryden.*

To Moor. *v. n.* To be fixed; to be ftationed.

Æneas gain'd Cajeta's bay:
At length on oozy ground his gallies *moor*,
Their heads are turn'd to fea, their fterns to fhore. *Dryd.*

My veffel, driv'n by a ftrong guft of wind,
Moor'd in a Chian creek. *Addifon's Ovid.*

He vifited the top of Taurus and the famous Ararat, where Noah's ark firft *moor'd*. *Arbuthnot and Pope's Mart. Scrib.*

To blow a Moor. [at the fall of a deer, corrupted from *a mort*, French.] To found the horn in triumph, and call in the whole company of hunters. *Ainf.*

Mo'orcock. *n. f.* [*moor* and *cock*.] The male of the moorhen.

Mo'orhen. *n. f.* [*moor* and *hen*.] A fowl that feeds in the fens, without web feet.

Water fowls, as fea-gulls and *moorhens*, when they flock and fly together from the fea towards the fhores, forefhew rain and wind. *Bacon's Nat. Hift.* N°. 823.

Mo'orish. *n. f.* [from *moor*.] Fenny; marfhy; watry.

In the great level near Thorny, feveral oaks and firs have lain there till covered by the inundation of the frefh and falt waters, and *moorifh* earth exaggerated upon them. *Hale.*

Along the *moorifh* fens
Sighs the fad genius of the coming ftorm. *Thomfon.*

Mo'orland. *n. f.* [*moor* and *land*.] Marfh; fen; watry ground.

In the fouth part of Staffordfhire they go to the north for feed corn, and they of the north to the fouth, except in the *moorlands*. *Mortimer's Hufbandry.*

Or like a bridge that joins a marifh
To *moorlands* of a different parifh. *Swift.*

Mo'orstone. *n. f.* A fpecies of granite.

The third ftratum is of great rocks of *moorftone* and fandy earth. *Woodward on Foffils.*

Mo'ory. *adj.* [from *moor*.] Marfhy; fenny; watry.

The duft the fields and paftures covers,
As when thick mifts arife from *moory* vales. *Fairfax.*

In Effex, *moory*-land is thought the moft proper. *Mortimer.*

Moose. *n. f.* The large American deer; the biggeft of the fpecies of deer.

To Moot. *v. a.* [from motian, mot, gemot, *meeting together*, Saxon, or perhaps, as it is a law term, from *mot*, French.] To plead a mock caufe; to ftate a point of law by way of exercife, as was commonly done in the inns of court at appointed times.

Moot *cafe* or *point*. A point or cafe unfettled and difputable, fuch as may properly afford a topick of difputation.

In this *moot cafe* your judgment to refufe,
Is prefent death. *Dryden's Juvenal.*

Would you not think him crack'd, who would require another to make an argument on a *moot point*, who underftands nothing of our laws? *Locke on Education.*

Let us drop both our pretences; for I believe it is a *moot point*, whether I am more likely to make a mafter Bull, or you a mafter Strut. *Arbuthnot's Hift. of John Bull.*

Mo'oted. *adj.* Plucked up by the root. *Ainf.*

Mo'oter. *n. f.* [from *moot*.] A difputer of moot points.

Mop. *n. f. moppa*, Welfh; *mappa*, Latin.]

1. Pieces of cloth, or locks of wool, fixed to a long handle, with which maids clean the floors.

Such is that fprinkling which fome carelefs quean
Flirts on you from her *mop*, but not fo clean.
You fly, invoke the gods; then turning, ftop
To rail; fhe finging ftill whirls on her *mop*. *Swift.*

2. [Perhaps corrupted from *mock*.] A wry mouth made in contempt.

Each one, tripping on his toe,
Will be here with *mop* and mow. *Shakefp. Tempeft.*

To Mop. *v. a.* [from the noun.] To rub with a mop.

To Mop. *v. n.* [from *mock*.] To make wry mouths in contempt.

Five fiends have been in poor Tom at once; of luft, as Obidicut; Hobbididen, prince of dumbnefs; Mahu, of ftealing; Mohu, of murder; and Flibbertigibbet, of *mopping* and mowing, who fince poffeffes chamber-maids. *Shakefp.*

An afs fell a *mopping* and braying at a lion. *L'Eftrange.*

To MOPE. *v. n.* [Of this word I cannot find a probable etymology.] To be ftupid; to drowfe; to be in a conftant day-dream; to be fpiritlefs, unactive and inattentive; to be ftupid and delirious.

What a wretched and peevifh fellow is this king of England, to *mope* with his fat-brain'd followers. *Shakefpeare.*

Eyes without feeling, feeling without fight,
Ears without hands or eyes, fmelling fans all,
Or but a fickly part of one true fenfe
Could not fo *mope*. *Shakefpeare's Hamlet.*

Ev'n in a dream, were we divided from them,
And were brought *moping* hither. *Shakefp. Tempeft.*

Inteftine ftone, and ulcer, cholick pangs,
Demoniack phrenfy, *moping* melancholy,
And moon-ftruck madnefs. *Milton's Par. Loft, b.* xi.

The bufy craftfman and o'erlabour'd hind,
Forget the travel of the day in fleep;
Care only wakes, and *moping* penfivenefs;
With meagre difcontented looks they fit,
And watch the wafting of the midnight taper. *Rowe.*

To Mope. *v. a.* To make fpiritlefs; to deprive of natural powers.

They fay there are charms in herbs, faid he, and fo threw a handful of grafs; which was fo ridiculous, that the young thief took the old man to be *moped*. *L'Eftrange.*

Severity breaks the mind; and then in the place of a diforderly young fellow, you have a low-fpirited *moped* creature. *Locke on Education.*

Mo'pe-eyed. *adj.* Blind of one eye. *Ainf.*

Mo'ppet. } *n. f.* [perhaps from *mop*.] A puppet made of rags,
Mo'psey. } as a mop is made; a fondling name for a girl.

Our fovereign lady: made for a queen?
With a globe in one hand, and a fceptre in t'other?
A very pretty *moppet*! *Dryden's Spanifh Fryar.*

Mo'pus. *n. f.* [A cant word from *mope*.] A drone; a dreamer.

I'm grown a mere *mopus*; no company comes
But a rabble of tenants. *Swift's Mifcel.*

MO'RAL. *adj.* [*moral*, Fr. *moralis*, Latin.]

1. Relating to the practice of men towards each other, as it may be virtuous or criminal; good or bad.

Keep at the leaft within the compafs of *moral* actions, which have in them vice or virtue. *Hooker, b.* ii.

Laws and ordinances pofitive he diftinguifheth from the laws of the two tables, which were *moral*. *Hooker, b.* iii.

In *moral* actions divine law helpeth exceedingly the law of reafon to guide man's life, but in fupernatural it alone guideth. *Hooker, b.* i.

Now, brandifh'd weapons glitt'ring in their hands,
Mankind is broken loofe from *moral* bands;
No rights of hofpitality remain,
The gueft, by him who harbour'd him, is flain. *Dryden.*

2. Reafoning or inftructing with regard to vice and virtue.

France fpreads his banners in our noifelefs land,
With plumed helm thy flay'r begins his threats,
Whilft thou, a *moral* fool, fit'ft ftill and crieft. *Shakefp.*

2. Popular; fuch as is known or admitted in the general bufinefs of life.

We have found it, with a *moral* certainty, the feat of the Mofaical abyfs. *Burnet's Theory of the Earth.*

Mathematical things are capable of the ftricteft demonftration; conclufions in natural philofophy are capable of proof by an induction of experiments; things of a *moral* nature by *moral* arguments, and matters of fact by credible teftimony. *Tillotfon's Sermons.*

A *moral* univerfality, is when the predicate agrees to the greateft part of the particulars which are contained under the univerfal fubject. *Watts's Logick.*

Mo'ral. *n. f.*

1. Morality; practice or doctrine of the duties of life: this is rather a French than Englifh fenfe.

Their *moral* and œconomy,
Moft perfectly they made agree. *Prior.*

2. The doctrine inculcated by a fiction; the accommodation of a fable to form the morals.

Get you fome diftill'd carduus benedictus, and lay it to your heart; it is the only thing for a qualm.

—Benedictus? why benedictus? you have fome *moral* in this benedictus.

—*Moral!* No, by my troth I have no moral meaning; I meant plain holy thiftle. *Shakefp. Much ado about nothing.*

Left behind to expound the meaning or *moral* of his figns and tokens. *Shakefp. Taming of the Shrew.*

The *moral* is the firft bufinefs of the poet, as being the ground-work of his inftruction; this being formed, he contrives fuch a defign or fable as may be moft fuitable to the *moral*. *Dryden's Dufrefnoy.*

I found a *moral* firft, and then ftudied for a fable, but could do nothing that pleafed me. *Swift to Gay.*

To Mo'ral. *v. n.* [from the adjective.] To moralife; to make moral reflections.

When I did hear
The motley fool thus *moral* on the time,
My lungs began to crow like chanticleer,
That fools fhould be fo deep contemplative. *Shakefpeare.*

Mo'ralist.

Mo'ralist. *n. s.* [*moraliste*, French.] One who teaches the duties of life.

The advice given by a great *moralist* to his friend was, that he should compose his passions; and let that be the work of reason, which would certainly be the work of time. *Addison.*

Mora'lity. *n. s.* [*moralité*, Fr. from *moral.*]

1. The doctrine of the duties of life; ethicks.

The system of *morality*, to be gathered out of the writings of ancient sages, falls very short of that delivered in the gospel. *Swift's Miscel.*

A necessity of sinning is as impossible in *morality*, as any the greatest difficulty can be in nature. *Baker on Learning.*

2. The form of an action which makes it the subject of reward, or punishment.

The *morality* of an action is founded in the freedom of that principle, by virtue of which it is in the agent's power, having all things ready and requisite to the performance of an action, either to perform or not perform it. *South's Sermons.*

To Mo'ralize. *v. a.* [*moraliser*, French.]

1. To apply to moral purposes; to explain in a moral sense.

He 'as left me here behind to expound the meaning or moral of his signs and tokens.

—I pray thee *moralize* them. *Shak. Taming of the Shrew.*

Did he not *moralize* this spectacle?

—O yes, into a thousand similies. *Shakespeare.*

This fable is *moralized* in a common proverb. *L'Estrange.*

2. In *Spenser* it seems to mean, to furnish with manners or examples.

Fierce warres and faithful loves shall *moralize* my song.
Fairy Queen, b. i.

3. In *Prior*, who imitates the foregoing line, it has a sense not easily discovered, if indeed it has any sense.

High as their trumpets tune his lyre he strung,
And with his prince's arms he *moraliz'd* his song. *Prior.*

To Mo'ralize. *v. n.* To speak or write on moral subjects.

Morali'zer. *n. s.* [from *moralize.*] He who moralizes.

Mo'rally. *adv.* [from *moral.*]

1. In the ethical sense.

By good, good *morally* so called, bonum honestum, ought chiefly to be understood; and that the good of profit or pleasure, the bonum utile or jucundum, hardly come into any account here. *South's Sermons.*

Because this, of the two brothers killing each other, is an action *morally* unnatural; therefore, by way of preparation, the tragedy would have begun with heaven and earth in disorder, something physically unnatural. *Rymer.*

2. According to the rules of virtue.

To take away rewards and punishments, is only pleasing to a man who resolves not to live *morally*. *Dryden.*

3. Popularly; according to the common occurrences of life; according to the common judgment made of things.

It is *morally* impossible for an hypocrite to keep himself long upon his guard. *L'Estrange.*

The concurring accounts of many such witnesses render it *morally*, or, as we might speak, absolutely impossible that these things should be false. *Atterbury's Sermons.*

Mo'rals. *n. s.* [without a singular.] The practice of the duties of life; behaviour with respect to others.

Some, as corrupt in their *morals* as vice could make them, have yet been solicitous to have their children soberly, virtuously, and piously brought up. *South's Sermons.*

Learn then what *morals* criticks ought to show:
'Tis not enough wit, art, and learning join;
In all you speak, let truth and candor shine. *Pope.*

Mora'ss. *n. s.* [*marais*, French.] Fen; bog; moor.

Landschapes point out the faireft and most fruitful spots, as well as the rocks, and wildernesses, and *morasses* of the country. *Watts's Improvement of the Mind.*

Nor the deep *morass*
Refuse, but through the shaking wilderness
Pick your nice way. *Thomson's Autumn, l.* 480.

Mo'rbid. *n. s.* [*morbidus*, Latin.] Diseased; in a state contrary to health.

Though every human constitution is *morbid*, yet are there diseases consistent with the common functions of life. *Arbuth.*

Mo'rbidness. *n. s.* [from *morbid.*] State of being diseased.

Morbi'fical. } *n. s.* [*morbus* and *facio*, Lat. *morbifique*, Fr.]
Morbi'fick. } Causing diseases.

The air appearing so malicious in this *morbifick* conspiracy, exacts a more particular regard; wherefore initiate consumptives must change their air. *Harvey on Consumptions.*

This disease is cured by the critical resolution, concoction, and evacuation of the *morbifick* matter. *Arbuthnot.*

Morbo'se. *n. s.* [*morbosus*, Latin.] Proceeding from disease; not healthy.

Malphighi, under galls, comprehends all preternatural and *morbose* tumours and excrescencies of plants. *Ray on Creation.*

Morbo'sity. *n. s.* [from *morbosus*, Lat.] Diseased state. A word not in use.

The inference is fair, from the organ to the action, that they have eyes, therefore some sight was designed, if we except the casual impediments or *morbosities* in individuals. *Brown.*

Morda'cious. *adj. mordax*, Latin.] Biting; apt to bite.

Morda'city. *n. s.* [*mordacitas*, *mordacité*, Fr. from *mordax*, Latin.] Biting quality.

It is to be inquired, whether there be any menstruum to dissolve any metal that is not fretting or corroding, and openeth the body by sympathy, and not by *mordacity*, or violent penetration. *Bacon's Physical Remains.*

Mo'rdicant. *n. s.* [*mordeo*, Lat. *mordicant*, Fr.] Biting; acrid.

He presumes, that the *mordicant* quality of bodies must proceed from a fiery ingredient; whereas the light and inflammable parts must be driven away by that time the fire has reduced the body to ashes. *Boyle.*

Mordica'tion. *n. s.* [from *mordicant.*] The act of corroding or biting.

Another cause is *mordication* of the orifices, especially of the mesentery veins; as any thing that is sharp and biting doth provoke the part to expel, and mustard provoketh sneezing. *Bacon's Nat. Hist.* N°. 37.

MORE. *adj.* [mare, Saxon, the comparative of *some* or *great.*]

1. In greater number; in greater quantity; in greater degree.

Wrong not that wrong with *more* contempt. *Shakesp.*

Their riches were *more* than that they might dwell together. *Gen.* xxxvi. 7.

Let *more* work be laid upon the men, that they may labour. *Exod.* v. 9.

2. Greater. Now out of use.

The *more* part advised to depart. *Acts* xxvi. 12.

More. *adv.*

1. To a greater degree.

He loved Rachel *more* than Leah. *Gen.* xxix. 30.

The spirits of animate bodies are all, in some degree, *more* or less kindled. *Bacon's Nat. Hist.* N°. 601.

Some were of opinion, that feeling *more* and *more* in himself the weight of time, he was not unwilling to bestow upon another some part of the pains. *Wotton.*

The *more* the kindled combat rises higher,
The *more* with fury burns the blazing fire. *Dryden's Æn.*

As the blood passeth through narrower channels, the redness disappears *more* and *more*. *Arbuthnot on Aliments.*

The *more* God has blessed any man with estate or quality, just so much less in proportion is the care he takes in the education of his children. *Swift's Miscel.*

2. The particle that forms the comparative degree.

I am fall'n out with my *more* headier will,
To take the indispos'd and sickly fit
For the sound man. *Shakespeare's King Lear.*

May you long live a happy instrument for your king and country: happy here, and *more* happy hereafter. *Bacon.*

The advantages of learning are *more* lasting than those of arms. *Collier on Pride.*

3. Again; a second time.

Little did I think I should ever have business of this kind on my hands *more*. *Tatler*, N°. 83.

4. Longer; yet continuing; with the negative particle.

Cassius is no *more*! Oh, setting sun!
As in thy red rays thou dost sink to-night,
So in his red blood Cassius' day is set. *Shakespeare.*

More. *n. s.* [A kind of comparative from *some* or *much.*]

1. A greater quantity; a greater degree. Perhaps some of these examples which are adduced under the adverb, with *the* before *more*, should be placed here.

These kind of knaves in this plainness
Harbour *more* craft, and *more* corrupter ends
Than twenty silky ducking observants. *Shakesp. K. Lear.*

Were I king,
I should cut off the nobles for their lands;
And my *more* having would be as a sauce
To make me hunger more. *Shakespeare's Macbeth.*

An heroick poem requires some great action of war; and as much or *more* of the active virtue than the suffering. *Dryd.*

The Lord do so, and much *more*, to Jonathan. 1 *Sam.*

From hence the greatest part of ills descend,
When lust of getting *more* will have no end. *Dryden.*

They that would have *more* and *more* can never have enough; no, not if a miracle should interpose to gratify their avarice. *L'Estrange's Fables.*

A mariner having let down a large portion of his sounding line, he reaches no bottom, whereby he knows the depth to be so many fathoms and *more*; but how much that *more* is, he hath no distinct notion. *Locke.*

2. Greater thing; other thing.

They, who so state a question, do no *more* but separate the parts of it one from another, and lay them so in their due order. *Locke.*

3. Second time; longer time.

4. It is doubtful whether the word, in some cases, be a noun or adverb.

The dove returned not again unto him any *more*. *Gen.* viii.

Pr'ythee be satisfy'd; he shall be aided,
Or I'll no *more* be king. *Dryden's Cleomenes.*

Delia, the queen of love, let all deplore!
Delia, the queen of beauty, is now no *more*. *Walsh.*

MORE'L. *n. f.* [*folanum*, Latin.]

1. The *morel* is a plant, of which there are feveral fpecies: one fort has a black fruit, the root of which is a foot long, waving, of a darkifh white colour and ftringy; its ftalk, which is full of pith, rifes to the height of a foot and an half, of a greenifh caft and angular form, divided into feveral branches, with alternate leaves, oblong, pointed, undulated, of a darkifh green and fhining colour: the flowers proceed from the branches, a little below the leaves: they grow from five to about eight in a bunch, of an inch and an half: each flower is white, of a fingle leaf, cut in form of a bafin, divided into five parts as far as the middle, being long, pointed, and arranged like a ftar: when the flower fheds there fucceeds a fpherical fruit, pretty hard, at firft green like an olive, then black, full of a limpid juice and a great number of feeds. There is a fort of *morel* that has a red fruit; and likewife another that has a yellow fruit. *Trevoux.*

Spungy *morels* in ftrong ragoufts are found,
And in the foup the flimy fnail is drown'd. *Gay's Trivia.*

2. A kind of cherry.

Morel is a black cherry, fit for the confervatory before it be thorough ripe, but it is bitter eaten raw. *Mortimer.*

MO'RELAND. *n. f.* [moplanð, Saxon; mop, a mountain, and lanð.] A mountainous or hilly country: a tract of Staffordfhire is called the *Morlands*.

MOREO'VER. *n. f.* [*more* and *over.*] Beyond what has been mentioned; befides; likewife; alfo; over and above.

Moreover, he hath left you all his walks. *Shakefp.*
He did hold me dear
Above this world; adding thereto, *moreover*,
That he would wed me, or elfe die my lover. *Shakefp.*
Moreover by them is thy fervant warned. *Pfal.* xix. 11.

MORGLA'Y. *n. f.* A deadly weapon. *Ainf.* *Glaive* and *morte*, French, and *glay môhr*, Erfe, a two-handed broad-fword, which fome centuries ago was the highlander's weapon.

MORI'GEROUS. *adj.* [*morigerus*, Lat.] Obedient; obfequious.

MO'RION. *n. f.* [Fr.] A helmet; armour for the head; a cafque.

For all his majefty's fhips a proportion of fwords, targets, *morions*, and cuiras of proof fhould be allowed. *Raleigh.*

Polifh'd fteel that caft the view afide,
And crefted *morions* with their plumy pride. *Dryden.*

MORI'SCO. *n. f.* [*morifco*, Spanifh.] A dancer of the morris or moorifh dance.

I have feen
Him caper upright like a wild *morifco*,
Shaking the bloody darts, as he his bells. *Shak. Henry* VI.

MO'RKIN. *n. f.* [Among hunters.] A wild beaft, dead through ficknefs or mifchance. *Bailey.*

MO'RLING. } *n. f.* [*mort*, French.] Wool plucked from a
MO'RTLING. } dead fheep. *Ainf.*

MORMO. n. f. [ἡ μορμὼ.] Bugbear; falfe terrour.

MORN. *n. f.* [manne, Saxon.] The firft part of the day; the morning. *Morn* is not ufed but by the poets.

The cock, that is the trumpet to the *morn*,
Doth with his lofty and fhrill-founding throat,
Awake the god of day. *Shakefpeare's Hamlet.*
I was of late as petty to his ends,
As is the *morn* dew on the myrtle leaf
To his grand fea. *Shakefp. Ant. and Cleopatra.*
Can you forget your golden beds,
Where you might fleep beyond the *morn*. *Lee.*
Friendfhip fhall ftill thy evening feafts adorn,
And blooming peace fhall ever blefs thy *morn*. *Prior.*

MO'RNING. *n. f.* [*morgen*, Teutonick; but our *morning* feems rather to come from *morn*.] The firft part of the day, from the firft appearance of light to the end of the firft fourth part of the fun's daily courfe.

One mafter Brook hath fent your worfhip a *morning*'s draught of fack. *Shakefp. Merry Wives of Windfor.*

By the fecond hour in the *morning*
Defire the earl to fee me. *Shakefp. Richard* III.
She looks as clear
As *morning* rofes newly wafh'd with dew. *Shakefpeare.*

Your goodnefs is as a *morning* cloud, and as the early dew it goeth away. *Hof.* vi. 5.

Let us go down after the Philiftines by night, and fpoil them until the *morning* light. 1 *Sam.* xiv. 36.

Morning by *morning* fhall it pafs over. *Ifa.* xxviii. 19.

What fhall become of us before night, who are weary fo early in the *morning*? *Taylor's Guide to Devotion.*

The *morning* is the proper part of the day for ftudy. *Dryd.*

The twining jeffamine and blufhing rofe,
With lavifh grace their *morning* fcents difclofe. *Prior.*
All the night they ftem the liquid way,
And end their voyage with the *morning* ray. *Pope's Odyffey.*

MO'RNING-GOWN. *n. f.* A loofe gown worn before one is formally dreffed.

Seeing a great many in rich *morning-gowns*, he was amazed to find that perfons of quality were up fo early. *Addifon.*

MO'RNING-STAR. *n. f.* The planet Venus when fhe fhines in the morning.

Bright as doth the *morning-ftar* appear
Out of the Eaft, with flaming locks bedight,
To tell the dawning day is drawing near. *Fairy Qu.*

MORO'SE. *adj.* [*morofus*, Latin.] Sour of temper; peevifh; fullen.

Without thefe precautions, the man degenerates into a cynick, the woman into a coquette; the man grows fullen and *morofe*, the woman impertinent. *Addifon's Spectator.*

Some have deferved cenfure for a *morofe* and affected taciturnity, and others have made fpeeches, though they had nothing to fay. *Watts's Improvement of the Mind.*

MORO'SELY. *adv.* [from *morofe.*] Sourly; peevifhly.

Too many are as *morofely* pofitive in their age, as they were childifhly fo in their youth. *Gov. of the Tongue.*

MORO'SENESS. *n. f.* [from *morofe.*] Sournefs; peevifhnefs.

Learn good humour, never to oppofe without juft reafon; he fhould abate fome degrees of pride and *morofenefs*. *Watts.*

MORO'SITY. *n. f.* [*morofitas*, Lat. from *morofe.*] Morofenefs; fournefs; peevifhnefs

Why then be fad,
But entertain no *morofity*, brothers, other
Than a joint burthen laid upon us. *Shakefpeare.*
Some *morofities*
We muft expect, fince jealoufy belongs
To age, of fcorn, and tender fenfe of wrongs. *Denham.*

The pride of this man, and the popularity of that; the levity of one, and the *morofity* of another. *Clarendon.*

MO'RRIS. } *n. f.* [that is *moorifh* or *morifco-dance.*]
MO'RRIS-DANCE. }

1. A dance in which bells are gingled, or ftaves or fwords clafhed, which was learned by the Moors, and was probably a kind of Pyrrhick or military dance.

The queen ftood in fome doubt of a Spanifh invafion, though it proved but a *morris-dance* upon our waves. *Wotton.*

One in his catalogue of a feigned library, fets down this title of a book, The *morris-dance* of hereticks. *Bacon.*

The founds and feas, with all their finny drove,
Now to the moon in wavering *morrice* move. *Milton.*

I took delight in pieces that fhewed a country village, *morrice-dancing*, and peafants together by the ears. *Peacham.*

Four reapers danced a *morrice* to oaten pipes. *Spectator.*

2. *Nine mens* MORRIS. A kind of play with nine holes in the ground.

The folds ftand empty in the drowned field,
And crows are fatted with the murrain flock;
The *nine mens morris* is filled up with mud. *Shakefpeare.*

MO'RRIS-DANCER. *n. f.* [*morris* and *dance.*] One who dances *a la morefco*, the moorifh dance.

There went about the country a fet of *morrice-dancers*, compofed of ten men, who danced a maid marian and a tabor and pipe. *Temple.*

MO'RPHEW. *n. f.* [*morphee*, French.] A fcurf on the face.

MO'RROW. *n. f.* [mongen, Saxon; *morghen*, Dutch; *morphæa*, low Latin; *morfea*, Italian. The original meaning of *morrow* feems to have been *morning*, which being often referred to on the preceding day, was underftood in time to fignify the whole day next following.]

1. The day after the prefent day.

I would not buy
Their mercy at the price of one fair word;
To have 't with faying, good *morrow*. *Shakefp. Coriolanus.*
Thou
Canft pluck night from me, but not lend a *morrow*. *Shak.*
The Lord did that thing on the *morrow*. *Exod.* ix. 6.
Peace, good reader, do not weep,
Peace, the lovers are afleep;
They, fweet turtles, folded lie,
In the laft knot that love could tie:
Let them fleep, let them fleep on,
Till this ftormy night be gone,
And the eternal *morrow* dawn,
Then the curtains will be drawn,
And they waken with the light,
Whofe day fhall never fleep in night. *Crafhaw.*
Beyond the Indies does this *morrow* lie. *Cowley.*

2. *To* MO'RROW. [This is an idiom of the fame kind, fuppofing *morrow* to mean originally *morning*: as, *to night*; *to day.*] On the day after this current day.

To morrow comes; 'tis noon; 'tis night;
This day like all the former flies;
Yet on he runs to feek delight
To morrow, till to night he dies. *Prior.*

3. *To morrow* is fometimes, I think improperly, ufed as a noun.

We by *to morrow* draw out all our ftore,
Till the exhaufted well can yield no more. *Cowley.*
To morrow is the time when all is to be rectified. *Spectat.*

MORSE. *n. f.* A fea-horfe.

That which is commonly called a fea-horfe is properly called a *morfe*, and makes not out that fhape. *Brown.*

It feems to have been a tufk of the *morfe* or waltron, called by fome the fea-horfe. *Woodward on Foffils.*

Mo'rsel. *n. s.* [*morsellus*, low Latin, from *morsus.*]

1. A piece fit for the mouth; a mouthful.

Yet cam'st thou to a *morsel* of this feast,
Having fully din'd before. *Shakesp. Coriolanus.*

I was
A *morsel* for a monarch. *Shakesp. Ant. and Cleopatra.*

And me his parent would full soon devour
For want of other prey, but knows that I
Should prove a bitter *morsel*, and his bane. *Milton.*

Every *morsel* to a satisfied hunger, is only a new labour to a tired digestion. *South's Sermons.*

He boils the flesh,
And lays the mangled *morsels* in a dish. *Dryden.*

A wretch is pris'ner made,
Whose flesh torn off by lumps, the rav'nous foe
In *morsels* cut, to make it farther go. *Tate's Juvenal.*

A letter to the keeper of the lion requested that it may be the first *morsel* put into his mouth. *Addison.*

2. A piece; a meal.

On these herbs, and fruits and flow'rs,
Feed first; on each beast next, and fish and fowl;
No homely *morsels!* *Milton's Par. Lost, b.* x.

A dog crossing a river with a *morsel* of flesh in his mouth, saw, as he thought, another dog under the water, upon the very same adventure. *L'Estrange's Fables.*

3. A small quantity. Not proper.

Of the *morsels* of native and pure gold, he had seen some weighed many pounds. *Boyle.*

Mo'rsure. *n. s.* [*morsure*, Fr. *morsura*, Latin.] The act of biting.

MORT. *n. s.* [*morte*, French.]

1. A tune sounded at the death of the game.

To be making practis'd smiles,
As in a looking-glass, and to sigh as 'twere
The *mort* o' th' deer; oh that is entertainment
My bosom likes not. *Shakesp. Winter's Tale.*

2. [*Morgt*, Islandick.] A great quantity. Not in elegant use.

Mo'rtal. *adj.* [*mortalis*, Lat. *mortel*, Fr.]

1. Subject to death; doomed sometime to die.

Nature does require
Her times of preservation, which, perforce,
I her frail son amongst my breth'ren *mortal*
Must give my attendance to. *Shakesp. Henry* VIII.

This corruptible must put on incorruption, and this *mortal* must put on immortality. 1 *Cor.* xv. 53.

Heav'nly powers, where shall we find such love!
Which of ye will be *mortal* to redeem
Man's mortal crime; and just, th' unjust to save. *Milton.*

Know,
The day thou eat'st thereof, my sole command
Transgrest, inevitably thou shalt die;
From that day *mortal:* and this happy state
Shalt lose. *Milton's Par. Lost, b.* viii.

2. Deadly; destructive; procuring death.

Come all you spirits
That tend on *mortal* thoughts, unsex me here,
And fill me from the crown to th' toe, top full
Of cruelty. *Shakespeare's Macbeth.*

The *mortalest* poisons practised by the West Indians, have some mixture of the blood, fat, or flesh of man. *Bacon.*

The fruit
Of that forbidden tree, whose *mortal* taste
Brought death into the world, and all our woe. *Milton.*

Some circumstances have been great discouragers of trade, and others are absolutely *mortal* to it. *Temple.*

Hope not, base man! unquestion'd hence to go,
For I am Palamon, thy *mortal* foe. *Dryden.*

3. Bringing death.

Safe in the hand of one disposing pow'r,
Or in the natal, or the *mortal* hour. *Pope's Essay on Man.*

4. Human; belonging to man.

They met me in the day of success; and I have learned by the perfected report, they have more in them than *mortal* knowledge. *Shakespeare's Macbeth.*

Macbeth
Shall live the lease of nature, pay his breath
To time and *mortal* custom. *Shakespeare's Macbeth.*

The voice of God
To *mortal* ear is dreadful; They beseech,
That Moses might report to them his will,
And terror cease. *Milton's Par. Lost, b.* xii.

Success, the mark no *mortal* wit,
Or surest hand can always hit. *Butler.*

No one enjoyment but is liable to be lost by ten thousand accidents, out of all *mortal* power to prevent. *South's Serm.*

5. Extreme; violent. A low word.

The birds were in a *mortal* apprehension of the beetles, till the sparrow reasoned them into understanding. *L'Estrange.*

The nymph grew pale and in a *mortal* fright,
Spent with the labour of so long a flight;
And now despairing, cast a mournful look
Upon the streams. *Dryden.*

Mo'rtal. *n. s.*

1. Man; human being.

Warn poor *mortals* left behind. *Tickel.*

2. This is often used in ludicrous language.

I can behold no *mortal* now;
For what's an eye without a brow? *Prior.*

Morta'lity. *n. s.* [from *mortal.*]

1. Subjection to death; state of a being subject to death.

I point out mistakes in life and religion, that we might guard against the springs of error, guilt, and sorrow, which surround us in every state of *mortality*. *Watts's Logick.*

2. Death.

I beg *mortality*,
Rather than life preserv'd with infamy. *Shakespeare.*

Gladly would I meet
Mortality my sentence. *Milton's Par. Lost, b.* x.

3. Power of destruction.

Mortality and mercy in Vienna
Live in thy tongue and heart. *Shakesp. Meas. for Measure.*

4. Frequency of death.

The rise of keeping those accounts first began in the year 1592, being a time of great *mortality*. *Graunt.*

5. Human nature.

A single vision so transports them, that it makes up the happiness of their lives; *mortality* cannot bear it often. *Dryd.*

Take these tears, *mortality*'s relief,
And till we share your joys, forgive our grief. *Pope.*

Mo'rtally. *adv.* [from *mortal.*]

1. Irrecoverably; to death.

In the battle of Landen you were not only dangerously, but, in all appearance, *mortally* wounded. *Dryden.*

2. Extremely; to extremity.

Adrian *mortally* envied poets, painters, and artificers, in works wherein he had a vein to excel. *Bacon's Essays.*

Know all, who wou'd pretend to my good grace,
I *mortally* dislike a damning face. *Granville.*

Mo'rtar. *n. s.* [*mortarium*, Lat. *mortier*, Fr.]

1. A strong vessel in which materials are broken by being pounded with a pestle.

Except you could bray Christendom in a *mortar*, and mould it into a new paste, there is no possibility of an holy war. *Bacon's holy War.*

The action of the diaphragm and muscles serves for the comminution of the meat in the stomach by their constant agitation upwards and downwards, resembling the pounding of materials in a *mortar*. *Ray on Creation.*

2. A short wide cannon out of which bombs are thrown.

Those arms which for nine centuries had brav'd
The wrath of time on antique stone engrav'd,
Now torn by *mortars* stand yet undefac'd
On nobler trophies by thy valour rais'd. *Granville.*

Mo'rtar. *n. s.* [*morter*, Dutch; *mortier*, French.] Cement made of lime and sand with water, and used to join stones or bricks.

Mortar, in architecture, is a preparation of lime and sand mixed up with water, serving as a cement, and used by masons and bricklayers in building of walls of stone and brick. Wolfius observes, that the sand should be dry and sharp, so as to prick the hands when rubbed, yet not earthy, so as to foul the water it is washed in: he also finds fault with masons and bricklayers as committing a great error, in letting their lime slacken and cool before they make up their *mortar*, and also in letting their *mortar* cool and die before they use it; therefore he advises, that if you expect your work to be well done, and to continue long, to work up the lime quick, and but a little at a time, that the *mortar* may not lie long before it be used.

I will tread this unbolted villain into *mortar*, and daub the wall of a jakes with him. *Shakesp. King Lear.*

They had brick for stone, and slime for *mortar*. *Gen.* xi. 3.

Lime hot out of the kiln mixed soft with water, putting sand to it, will make better *mortar* than other. *Mortimer.*

Mo'rtgage. *n. s.* [*mort* and *gage*, French.]

1. A dead pledge; a thing put into the hands of a creditor.

Th' estate runs out, and *mortgages* are made,
Their fortune ruin'd, and their fame betray'd. *Dryden.*

The Romans do not seem to have known the secret of paper credit, and securities upon *mortgages*. *Arbuthnot.*

The broker,
Bent on some *mortgage*, to avoid reproach,
He seeks bye-streets, and saves th' expensive coach. *Gay.*

2. The state of being pledged.

The land is given in *mortgage* only, with full intention to be redeemed within one year. *Bacon's Office of Alienation.*

To Mo'rtgage. *v. a.* [from the noun.] To pledge; to put to pledge; to make over to a creditor as a security.

Let men contrive how they disentangle their *mortgaged* souls. *Decay of Piety.*

They make the widows *mortgag'd* ox their prey. *Sandys.*

Their not abating of their expensive way of living, has forced them to *mortgage* their best manors. *Arbuthnot.*

Mortgage'e.

MORTGAGE'E. *n.ſ.* [from *mortgage.*] He that takes or receives a mortgage.

An act may paſs for publick regiſtries of land, by which all purchaſers or *mortgagees* may be ſecured of all monies they lay out. *Temple's Miſcel.*

MO'RTGAGER. *n.ſ.* [from *mortgage.*] He that gives a mortgage.

MORTI'FEROUS. *adj.* [*mortifer*, Latin.] Fatal; deadly; deſtructive.

What is it but a continued perpetuated voice from heaven, to give men no reſt in their ſins, no quiet from Chriſt's importunity, till they awake from the lethargick ſleep, and ariſe from ſo dead, ſo *mortiferous* a ſtate, and permit him to give them life. *Hammond's Fundamentals.*

Theſe murmurings, like a *mortiferous* herb, are poiſonous even in their firſt ſpring. *Government of the Tongue, ſ.* 10.

MORTIFICA'TION. *n.ſ.* [*mortification*, Fr. from *mortify.*]

1. The ſtate of corrupting, or loſing the vital qualities; gangrene.

It appeareth in the gangrene, or *mortification* of fleſh, either by opiates, or intenſe colds. *Bacon's Nat. Hiſt.* N°. 333.

My griefs ferment and rage,
Nor leſs than wounds immedicable,
Rankle and feſter, and gangrene,
To black *mortification.* *Milton's Agoniſt. l.* 617.

2. Deſtruction of active qualities.

Inquire what gives impediment to union or reſtitution, which is called *mortification*; as when quickſilver is mortified with turpentine. *Bacon's Phyſical Remains.*

3. The act of ſubduing the body by hardſhips and macerations.

A diet of ſome fiſh is more rich and alkaleſcent than that of fleſh, and therefore very improper for ſuch as practiſe *mortification.* *Arbuthnot on Aliments.*

4. Humiliation; ſubjection of the paſſions.

The *mortification* of our luſts has ſomething in it that is troubleſome, yet nothing that is unreaſonable. *Tillotſon.*

5. Vexation; trouble.

It is one of the moſt vexatious *mortifications* of a ſtudious man, to have his thoughts diſordered by a tedious viſit. *L'Eſtrange.*

We had the *mortification* to loſe the ſight of Munich, Augſburg, and Ratiſbon. *Addiſon on Italy.*

To MO'RTIFY. *v. a.* [*mortifier*, French.]

1. To deſtroy vital qualities.

2. To deſtroy active powers, or eſſential qualities.

What gives impediment to union or reſtitution is called mortification, as when quickſilver is *mortified* with turpentine or ſpittle. *Bacon.*

He *mortified* pearls in vinegar, and drunk them up. *Hakew.*

Oil of tartar per deliquium has a great faculty to find out and *mortify* acid ſpirits. *Boyle.*

3. To ſubdue inordinate paſſions.

The breath no ſooner left his father's body,
But that his wildneſs *mortified* in him,
Seem'd to die too. *Shakeſp. Henry* V.

Their dear cauſes
Would to the bleeding and the grim alarm
Excite the *mortified* man. *Shakeſp. Macbeth.*

Suppreſs thy knowing pride,
Mortify thy learned luſt,
Vain are thy thoughts, while thou thyſelf art duſt. *Prior.*

He modeſtly conjectures,
His pupil might be tir'd with lectures,
Which help'd to *mortify* his pride. *Swift.*

4. To macerate or harraſs the body to compliance with the mind.

We *mortify* ourſelves with fiſh, and think we fare coarſely if we abſtain from fleſh. *Brown's Vulgar Errours.*

Mortify'd he was to that degree,
A poorer than himſelf he would not ſee. *Dryden.*

5. To humble; to depreſs; to vex.

Let my liver rather heat with wine,
Than my heart cool with *mortifying* groans. *Shakeſpeare.*

He is controuled by a nod, *mortified* by a frown, and tranſported by a ſmile. *Addiſon's Guard.* N°. 113.

How often is the ambitious man *mortified* with the very praiſes he receives, if they do not riſe ſo high as he thinks they ought. *Addiſon's Spect.* N°. 256.

To MO'RTIFY. *v. n.*

1. To gangrene; to corrupt.

Try it with capon laid abroad, to ſee whether it will *mortify* and become tender ſooner; or with dead flies with water caſt upon them, to ſee whether it will putrefy. *Bacon.*

2. To be ſubdued; to die away.

MO'RTISE. *n.ſ.* [*mortaiſe*, *mortoiſe*, Fr.] A hole cut into wood that another piece may be put into it and form a joint.

A fuller blaſt ne'er ſhook our battlements;
If it hath ruffian'd ſo upon the ſea,
What ribs of oak, when mountains melt on them,
Can hold the *mortiſe.* *Shakeſp. Othello.*

Under one ſkin are parts variouſly mingled, ſome with cavities, as *morteſſes* to receive, others with tenons to fit cavities. *Ray.*

To MO'RTISE. *v. a.*

1. To cut with a mortiſe; to join with a mortiſe.

'Tis a maſſy wheel,
To whoſe huge ſpoke ten thouſand leſſer things
Are *mortis'd* and adjoin'd. *Shakeſpeare's Hamlet.*

The walls of ſpiders legs are made,
Well *mortiſed* and finely laid. *Drayton's Nymphid.*

2. It ſeems in the following paſſage improperly uſed.

The one half of the ſhip being finiſhed, and by help of a ſcrew launched into the water, the other half was joined by great braſs nails *mortiſed* with lead. *Arbuthnot on Coins.*

MO'RTMAIN. *n.ſ.* [*morte* and *main*, Fr.] Such a ſtate of poſſeſſion as makes it unalienable; whence it is ſaid to be in a *dead hand*, in a hand that cannot ſhift away the property.

It were meet that ſome ſmall portion of lands were allotted, ſince no more *mortmains* are to be looked for. *Spenſer.*

MO'RTPAY. *n.ſ.* [*mort* and *pay.*] Dead pay; payment not made.

This parliament was merely a parliament of war, with ſome ſtatutes conducing thereunto; as the ſevere puniſhing of *mortpayes*, and keeping back of ſoldiers wages. *Bacon.*

MO'RTRESS. *n.ſ.* [from *mortier de ſageſſe. Skinner.*] A diſh of meat of various kinds beaten together.

A *mortreſs* made with the brawn of capons, ſtamped, ſtrained, and mingled with like quantity of almond butter, is excellent to nouriſh the weak. *Bacon's Nat. Hiſt.*

MO'RTUARY. *n.ſ.* [*mortuaire*, Fr. *mortuarium*, Latin.] A gift left by a man at his death to his pariſh church, for the recompence of his perſonal tythes and offerings not duly paid in his life-time. *Harris.*

MOSA'ICK. *adj.* [*moſaique*, French, ſuppoſed corrupted from *muſæus*, Latin.]

Moſaick is a kind of painting in ſmall pebbles, cockles, and ſhells of ſundry colours; and of late days likewiſe with pieces of glaſs figured at pleaſure; an ornament in truth, of much beauty, and long life, but of moſt uſe in pavements and floorings. *Wotton's Architecture.*

Each beauteous flow'r,
Iris all hues, roſes, and jeſſamin,
Rear'd high their flouriſh'd heads between, and wrought
Moſaick. *Milton's Par. Loſt, b.* iv.

The moſt remarkable remnant of it is a very beautiful *moſaick* pavement, the fineſt I have ever ſeen in marble; the parts are ſo well joined together, that the whole piece looks like a continued picture. *Addiſon on Italy.*

MO'SCHATEL. *n.ſ.* [*moſchatellina*, Lat.] A plant.

The *moſchatel* hath a flower conſiſting of one leaf, which is divided at the brim into many parts, from whoſe cup ariſes the pointal, fixed like a nail in the middle of the flower, which becomes a ſoft ſucculent berry, in which are contained many flat ſeeds. *Miller.*

MOSQUE. *n.ſ.* [*moſquée*, French; *moſchit*, Turkiſh.] A Mahometan temple.

MOSS. *n.ſ.* [*muſcus*, Lat. meoȝ, Saxon.] A plant.

Though *moſs* was formerly ſuppoſed to be only an excreſcence produced from the earth and trees, yet it is no leſs a perfect plant than thoſe of greater magnitude, having roots, flowers, and ſeeds, yet cannot be propagated from ſeeds by any art: the botaniſts diſtinguiſh it into many ſpecies: it chiefly flouriſhes in cold countries, and in the winter ſeaſon, and is many times very injurious to fruit trees: the only remedy in ſuch caſes, is to cut down part of the trees, and plough up the ground between thoſe left remaining; and in the Spring, in moiſt weather, you ſhould with an iron inſtrument ſcrape off the *moſs.* *Miller.*

Moſs is a kind of mould of the earth and trees; but it may be better ſorted as a rudiment of germination. *Bacon.*

Houſes then were caves, or homely ſheds,
With twining oziers fenc'd, and *moſs* their beds. *Dryden.*

Such *moſſes* as grow upon walls, roofs of houſes, and other high places, have ſeeds that, when ſhaken out of their veſſels, appear like vapour or ſmoke. *Ray on Creation.*

The cleft tree
Offers its kind concealment to a few,
Their food its inſects, and its *moſs* their neſts. *Thomſon.*

To MOSS. *v. a.* [from the noun.] To cover with moſs.

An oak whoſe boughs were *moſs'd* with age,
And high top bald with dry antiquity. *Shakeſpeare.*

Will theſe *moſs'd* trees,
That have out-liv'd the eagle page thy heels,
And ſkip when thou point'ſt out. *Shakeſpeare.*

MO'SSINESS. *n.ſ.* [from *moſſy.*] The ſtate of being covered or overgrown with moſs.

The herbs withered at the top, ſheweth the earth to be very cold, and ſo doth the *moſſineſs* of trees. *Bacon.*

MO'SSY. *adj.* [from *moſs.*] Overgrown with moſs; covered with moſs.

Old trees are more *moſſy* far than young; for that the ſap is not ſo frank as to riſe all to the boughs, but tireth by the way, and putteth out moſs. *Bacon's Nat. Hiſt.*

The *moſſy* fountains and the Sylvan ſhades
Delight no more. *Pope's Meſſiah.*

MOST. *adj.* the ſuperlative of *more.* [mæſt, Saxon; *meeſt*, Dutch.] Conſiſting of the greateſt number; conſiſting of the greateſt quantity.

Garden fruits which have any acrimony in them, and *moſt* ſorts of berries, will produce diarrhœas. *Arbuthnot.*

He thinks *moſt* ſorts of learning flouriſhed among them, and I, that only ſome ſort of learning was kept alive by them. *Pope.*

MOST. *adv.* [*maiſh*, Gothick; mæſt, Saxon; *meeſt*, Dutch; *meſt*, Daniſh.]

1. The particle noting the ſuperlative degree.

Competency of all other proportions is the *moſt* incentive to induſtry; too little makes men deſperate, and too much careleſs. *Decay of Piety.*

The faculties of the ſupreme ſpirit *moſt* certainly may be enlarged without bounds. *Cheyne's Phil. Principles.*

2. In the greateſt degree.

Coward dogs
Moſt ſpend their mouths, when what they ſeem to threaten
Runs far before them. *Shakeſpeare.*

He for whoſe only ſake,
Or *moſt* for his, ſuch toils I undertake. *Dryden's Æn.*

Whilſt comprehended under that conſciouſneſs, the little finger is as much a part of itſelf as what is *moſt* ſo. *Locke.*

That which will *moſt* influence their carriage will be the company they converſe with, and the faſhion of thoſe about them. *Locke on Education.*

MOST. [this is a kind of ſubſtantive, being, according to its ſignification, ſingular or plural.]

1. The greateſt number: in this ſenſe it is plural.

Many of the apoſtles immediate diſciples ſent or carried the books of the four evangeliſts to *moſt* of the churches they had planted. *Addiſon on the Chriſtian Religion.*

Gravitation not being eſſential to matter, ought not to be reckoned among thoſe laws which ariſe from the diſpoſition of bodies, ſuch as *moſt* of the laws of motion are. *Cheyne.*

2. The greateſt value: in this ſenſe ſingular.

The report of this repulſe flying to London, the *moſt* was made of that which was true, and many falſities added. *Hayw.*

A covetous man makes the *moſt* of what he has, and of what he can get, without regard to Providence or Nature. *L'Eſtrange's Fables.*

3. The greateſt degree; the greateſt quantity.

A Spaniard will live in Iriſh ground a quarter of a year, or ſome months at the *moſt.* *Bacon.*

MO'STICK. *n. ſ.* A painter's ſtaff on which he leans his hand when he paints. *Ainſ.*

MO'STLY. *adv.* [from *moſt.*] For the greateſt part.

This image of God, namely, natural reaſon, if totally or *moſtly* defaced, the right of government doth ceaſe. *Bacon.*

MO'STWHAT. *n. ſ.* [*moſt* and *what.*] For the moſt part. Obſolete.

God's promiſes being the ground of hope, and thoſe promiſes being but ſeldom abſolute, *moſtwhat* conditionate, the Chriſtian grace of hope muſt be proportioned and attemperate to the promiſe; if it exceed that temper and proportion, it becomes a tympany of hope. *Hammond.*

M TA'TION. *n. ſ.* Act of moving. *Dict.*

MOTE. *n. ſ.* [mot, Saxon; *atomus*, Lat.] A ſmall particle of matter; any thing proverbially little.

You found his *mote*, the king your *mote* did ſee;
But I a beam do find in each of three. *Shakeſpeare.*

The little *motes* in the ſun do ever ſtir, though there be no wind. *Bacon's Nat. Hiſt.* N°. 879.

MOTE for *might.* Obſolete.

Moſt ugly ſhapes,
Such as dame Nature ſelf *mote* fear to ſee,
Or ſhame, that ever ſhould ſo foul defects
From her moſt cunning hand eſcaped be. *Fairy Queen.*

MOTH. *n. ſ.* [moð, Saxon.] A ſmall winged inſect that eats cloths and hangings.

All the yarn Penelope ſpun in Ulyſſes's abſence, did but fill Ithaca full of *moths.* *Shakeſpeare's Coriolanus.*

Every ſoldier in the wars ſhould do as every ſick man in his bed, waſh every *moth* out of his conſcience. *Shakeſp.*

He as a rotten thing conſumeth, as a garment that is *moth* eaten. *Job* xiii. 28.

Let *moths* through pages eat their way,
Your wars, your loves, your praiſes be forgot,
And make of all an univerſal blot. *Dryden's Juv.*

MO'THER. *n. ſ.* [moðor, Saxon; *moder*, Daniſh; *moeder*, Dutch.]

1. A woman that has born a child; correlative to ſon or daughter.

Let thy *mother* rather feel thy pride, than fear
Thy dangerous ſtoutneſs. *Shakeſpeare's Coriolanus.*

Come ſit down every *mother*'s ſon,
And rehearſe your parts. *Shakeſpeare.*

I had not ſo much of man in me,
But all my *mother* came into mine eyes,
And gave me up to tears. *Shakeſp. Henry* V.

2. That which has produced any thing.

Alas, poor country! It cannot
Be call'd our *mother*, but our grave. *Shakeſpeare.*

The reſemblance of the conſtitution and diet of the inhabitants to thoſe of their *mother* country, occaſion a great affinity in the popular diſeaſes. *Arbuthnot on Air.*

The ſtrongeſt branch leave for a ſtandard, cutting off the reſt cloſe to the body of the *mother* plant. *Mortimer's Huſb.*

3. That which has preceded in time: as, a *mother* church to chapels.

4. That which requires reverence and obedience.

The good of *mother* church, as well as that of civil ſociety, renders a judicial practice neceſſary. *Ayliffe's Parergon.*

5. Hyſterical paſſion; ſo called, as being imagined peculiar to women.

This ſtopping of the ſtomach might be the *mother*; foraſmuch as many were troubled with *mother* fits, although few returned to have died of them. *Graunt's Bills.*

6. A familiar term of addreſs to an old woman; or to a woman dedicated to religious auſterities.

7. MOTHER *in law.* A huſband's or wife's mother. *Ainſ.*

I am come to ſet at variance the daughter in law againſt the *mother in law.* *Matth.* x. 35.

8. [*Moeder*, Dutch, from *modder*, mud.] A thick ſubſtance concreting in liquors; the lees or ſcum concreted.

If the body be liquid, and not apt to putrefy totally, it will caſt up a *mother*, as the *mothers* of diſtilled waters. *Bacon.*

Potted fowl, and fiſh come in ſo faſt,
That ere the firſt is out the ſecond ſtinks,
And mouldy *mother* gathers on the brinks. *Dryden.*

9. [More properly *modder*; *modde*, Dutch.] A young girl. Now totally obſolete.

A fling for a *mother*, a bow for a boy,
A whip for a carter. *Tuſſer's Huſbandry.*

MO'THER. *adj.* Had at the birth; native.

For whatſoever *mother* wit or art
Could work, he put in proof. *Hubberd's Tale.*

Where did you ſtudy all this goodly ſpeech?
—It is extempore, from my *mother* wit. *Shakeſpeare.*

Boccace, living in the ſame age with Chaucer, had the ſame genius, and followed the ſame ſtudies: both writ novels, and each of them cultivated his *mother* tongue. *Dryden.*

Cecilia came,
Inventreſs of the vocal frame,
Enlarg'd the former narrow bounds,
And added length to ſolemn ſounds,
With nature's *mother* wit, and arts unknown before. *Dryd.*

To MO'THER. *v. n.* To gather concretion.

They oint their naked limbs with *mother'd* oil. *Dryden.*

MO'THER *of pearl.* A kind of coarſe pearl; the ſhell in which pearls are generated.

His mortal blade
In ivory ſheath, ycarv'd with curious ſlights,
Whoſe hilt was burniſh'd gold, and handle ſtrong
Of *mother-pearl.* *Fairy Qu. b.* i.

They were made of onyx, ſometimes of *mother of pearl.* *Hakewill on Providence.*

MO'THERHOOD. *n. ſ.* [from *mother.*] The office or character of a mother.

Thou ſhalt ſee the bleſſed mother-maid
Exalted more for being good,
Than for her intereſt of *motherhood.* *Donne.*

MO'THERLESS. *adj.* [from *mother.*] Deſtitute of a mother; orphan of a mother.

I might ſhew you my children, whom the rigour of your juſtice would make complete orphans, being already *motherleſs.* *Waller's Speech to the Houſe of Commons.*

My concern for the three poor *motherleſs* children obliges me to give you this advice. *Arbuthnot's Hiſt. of J. Bull.*

MO'THERLY. *adj.* [from *mother* and *like.*] Belonging to a mother; ſuitable to a mother.

They can owe no leſs than child-like obedience to her that hath more than *motherly* power. *Hooker, b.* v.

They termed her the great mother, for her *motherly* care in cheriſhing her brethren whilſt young. *Raleigh.*

Within her breaſt though calm, her breaſt though pure,
Motherly cares and fears got head, and rais'd
Some troubled thoughts. *Milton's Par. Reg. b.* ii.

When I ſee the *motherly* airs of my little daughters when playing with their puppets, I cannot but flatter myſelf that their huſbands and children will be happy in the poſſeſſion of ſuch wives and mothers. *Addiſon's Spect.* N°. 500.

Though ſhe was a truly good woman, and had a ſincere *motherly* love for her ſon John, yet there wanted not thoſe who endeavoured to create a miſunderſtanding between them. *Arb.*

MO'THERLY. *adv.* [from *mother.*] In manner of a mother.

Th' air doth not *motherly* sit on the earth,
To hatch her seasons, and give all things birth. *Donne.*

MOTHER *of thyme. n. s.* [*serpyllum*, Latin.] It hath trailing branches, which are not so woody and hard as those of thyme, but in every other respect is the same. *Miller.*

MO'THERWORT. *n. s.* [*cardiaca*, Latin.] A plant.

The flower of the *motherwort* consists of one leaf, and is of the lip kind, whose upper lip is imbricated and much longer than the under one, which is cut into three parts; from the flower-cup arises the pointal, fixed like a nail in the hinder part of the flower, attended by four embrios which become angular seeds, occupying the flower-cup. *Miller.*

MO'THERY. *adj.* [from *mother.*] Concreted; full of concretions; dreggy; feculent: used of liquors.

MOTHMU'LLEIN. *n. s.* [*blattaria*, Latin.] A plant.

The leaves of the *mothmullein* are placed alternately upon the branches; the cup of the flower consists of one leaf, which is divided into five segments; the flower consists of one leaf, which spreads open, and is divided also into five segments: they are produced in long spikes, and are succeeded by round vessels, which are divided into cells, and contain many small seeds in each. *Miller.*

MO'THWORT. *n. s.* [*moth* and *wort.*] An herb.

MO'THY. *adj.* [from *moth.*] Full of moths.

His horse hipp'd with an old *mothy* saddle, the stirrups of no kindred. *Shakespeare's Taming of the Shrew.*

MO'TION. *n. s.* [*motion*, French; *motio*, Latin.]

1. The act of changing place.
2. Manner of moving the body; port; gait.

Virtue too, as well as vice, is clad
In flesh and blood so well, that Plato had
Beheld, what his high fancy once embrac'd,
Virtue with colours, speech and *motion* grac'd. *Waller.*

3. Change of posture; action.

Encourag'd thus she brought her younglings nigh,
Watching the *motions* of her patron's eye. *Dryden.*

4. Tendency of the mind; thought.

Let a good man obey every good *motion* rising in his heart, knowing that every such *motion* proceeds from God. *South.*

5. Proposal made.

He compassed a *motion* of the prodigal son, and married a tinker's wife within a mile where my land lies. *Shakesp.*

What would you with me?
—Your father and my uncle have made *motions*; if it be my luck, so; if not, happy man be his dole. *Shakespeare.*

If our queen and this young prince agree,
I'll join my younger daughter, and my joy,
To him forthwith, in holy wedlock bands.
—Yes, I agree, and thank you for your *motion*. *Shakesp.*

6. Impulse communicated.

Whether that *motion*, vitality and operation, were by incubation, or how else, the manner is only known to God. *Ral.*

Carnality within raises all the combustion without: this is the great wheel to which the clock owes it *motion*. *Dec. of Pi.*

Love awakes the sleepy vigour of the soul,
And brushing o'er adds *motion* to the pool. *Dryden.*

To MO'TION. *v. a.* [from the noun.] To propose.

MO'TIONLESS. *adj.* [from *motion.*] Wanting motion; being without motion.

We cannot free the lady that sits here,
In stony fetters fixt, and *motionless*. *Milton.*

Ha! Do I dream? Is this my hop'd success?
I grow a statue, stiff and *motionless*. *Dryden's Aurengzebe.*

Should our globe have had a greater share
Of this strong force, by which the parts cohere;
Things had been bound by such a pow'rful chain,
That all would fix'd and *motionless* remain. *Blackmore.*

MO'TIVE. *adj.* [*motivus*, Latin.]

1. Causing motion; having moment.

Shall every *motive* argument used in such kind of conferences be made a rule for others still to conclude the like by, concerning all things of like nature, when as probable inducements may lead them to the contrary? *Hooker, b.* iv.

2. Having the power to move; having power to change place; having power to pass foremost to motion.

The nerves serve for the conveyance of the *motive* faculty from the brain; the ligatures for the strengthening of them, that they may not flag in motion. *Wilkins.*

We ask you whence does *motive* vigour flow? *Blackmore.*

That fancy is easily disproved from the *motive* power of souls embodied, and the gradual increase of men and animals. *Bentl.*

MO'TIVE. *n. s.* [*motif*, French.]

1. That which determines the choice; that which incites the action.

Hereof we have no commandment, either in nature or scripture, which doth exact them at our hands; yet those *motives* there are in both, which draw most effectually our minds unto them. *Hooker, b.* ii.

Why in that rawness left you wife and children,
Those precious *motives*, those strong knots of love,
Without leave-taking? *Shakespeare's Macbeth.*

What can be a stronger *motive* to a firm trust on our Maker, than the giving us his son to suffer for us. *Addison.*

The *motive* for continuing in the same state is only the present satisfaction in it; the *motive* to change is always some uneasiness. *Locke.*

2. Mover.

Heaven brought me up to be my daughter's dower;
As it hath fated her to be my *motive*
And helper to a husband. *Shakesp. All's well that ends well.*

Her wanton spirits look out
At every joint, and *motive* of her body. *Shakespeare.*

MO'TLEY. *adj.* [supposed to be corrupted from *medley*, perhaps from *mothlike* coloured, spotted or variegated like a garden *moth.*] Mingled of various colours.

The *motley* fool thus moral'd on the time,
My lungs began to crow like chanticleer,
That fools should be so deep contemplative. *Shakespeare.*

They that come to see a fellow
In a long *motley* coat, guarded with yellow,
Will be deceiv'd. *Shakespeare's Henry* VIII.

Expence and after-thought, and idle care,
And doubts of *motley* hue, and dark despair. *Dryden.*

Enquire from whence this *motley* style
Did first our Roman purity defile. *Dryden's Persius.*

Traulus, of amphibious breed,
Motley fruit of mungril seed;
By the dam from lordlings sprung,
By the sire exhal'd from dung. *Swift.*

MO'TOR. *n. s.* [*moteur*, Fr. from *moveo*, Latin.] A mover.

Those bodies being of a congenerous nature do readily receive the impressions of their *motor*, and, if not fettered by their gravity, conform themselves to situations, wherein they best unite unto their animator. *Brown's Vulgar Errours, b.* ii.

MO'TORY. *adj.* [*motorius*, Latin.] Giving motion.

The bones, were they dry, could not, without great difficulty, yield to the plucks and attractions of the *motory* muscles. *Ray on Creation.*

MO'TTO. *n. s.* [*motto*, Italian.] A sentence added to a device, or prefixed to any thing written.

It may be said to be the *motto* of human nature, rather to suffer than to die. *L'Estrange's Fables.*

We ought to be meek-spirited, till we are assured of the honesty of our ancestors; for covetousness and circumvention make no good *motto* for a coat. *Collier.*

It was the *motto* of a bishop eminent for his piety and good works in king Charles the second's reign, *Inservi Deo & lætare*, Serve God and be chearful. *Addison's Freeholder.*

To MOVE. *v. a.* [*moveo*, Latin.]

1. To put out of one place into another; to put in motion.

Sinai itself was *moved* at the presence of God. *Psal.* lxviii.

At this my heart trembleth, and is *moved* out of his place. *Job* xxvii. 1.

2. To give an impulse to.

The pretext of piety is but like the hand of a clock, set indeed more conspicuously, but directed wholly by the secret *movings* of carnality within. *Decay of Piety.*

3. To propose; to recommend.

If the first consultation be not sufficient, the will may *move* a review, and require the understanding to inform itself better. *Bishop Bramhall against Hobbes.*

They are to be blamed alike, who *move* and who decline war upon particular respects. *Hayward's Edw.* VI.

They find a great inconvenience in *moving* their suits by an interpreter. *Davies on Ireland.*

To Indamora you my suit must *move*. *Dryden.*

The will being the power of directing our operative faculties to some action, for some end, cannot at any time be *moved* towards what is judged at that time inattainable. *Locke.*

4. To persuade; to prevail on the mind.

A thousand knees,
Ten thousand years together, naked, fasting,
Upon a barren mountain, and still Winter
In storm perpetual, could not *move* the gods
To look that way thou wert. *Shakesp. Winter's Tale.*

Grittus offered the Transylvanians money; but minds desirous of revenge were not *moved* with gold. *Knolles.*

Sometimes the possibility of preferment prevailing with the credulous, expectation of less expence with the covetous, opinion of ease with the fond, and assurance of remoteness with the unkind parents, have *moved* them without discretion, to engage their children in adventures of learning, by whose return they have received but small contentment. *Wotton.*

Could any power of sense the Roman *move*
To burn his own right hand? *Davies.*

That which *moves* a man to do any thing, must be the apprehension and expectation of some good from the thing which he is about to do. *South's Sermons.*

When she saw her reasons idly spent,
And could not *move* him from his fix'd intent,
She flew to rage. *Dryden's Æn.*

But when no female arts his mind could *move*,
She turn'd to furious hate her impious love. *Dryden's Æn.*
What can thy mind to this long journey *move*,
Or need'st thou absence to renew thy love? *Dryden.*

4. To affect; to touch pathetically; to stir passion.
If he see aught in you that makes him like,
That any thing he sees, which *moves* his liking,
I can with ease translate it to my will. *Shakesp. K. John.*
It was great ign'rance, Gloster's eyes being out,
To let him live; where he arrives he *moves*
All hearts against us. *Shakespeare's King Lear.*
Should a shipwreck'd sailor sing his woe,
Wou'd'st thou be *mov'd* to pity, or bestow
An alms? *Dryden's Persius.*

Images are very sparingly to be introduced; their proper place is in poems and orations, and their use is to *move* pity or terror, compassion and resentment. *Felton on the Classicks.*

O let thy sister, daughter, handmaid, *move*
Or all those tender names. *Pope.*

5. To make angry.
From those bloody hands
Throw your distemper'd weapons to the ground,
And hear the sentence of your *moved* prince. *Shakespeare.*

They have *moved* me to jealousy. *Deut.* xxxii. 21.

6. To put into commotion.

When they were come to Bethlehem, all the city was *moved* about them. *Ruth* i. 19.

7. To conduct regularly in motion.
They, as they *move*
Their starry dance in numbers that compute
Days, months, and years, tow'rds his all cheering lamp,
Turn swift their various motions. *Milton.*

To Move. *v. n.*

1. To go from one place to another.
I look'd toward Birnam, and anon, methought,
The wood began to *move*.
Within this three mile may you see it coming;
I say a *moving* grove. *Shakespeare's Macbeth.*

In him we live, *move*, and have our being. *Acts* xvii. 28.

Every *moving* thing that liveth shall be meat for you. *Gen.*

On the green bank I sat and listen'd long,
Nor till her lay was ended could I *move*,
But wish'd to dwell for ever in the grove. *Dryden.*

The senses represent the earth as immoveable; for though it do *move* in itself, it rests to us who are carriedwith it. *Glan.*

This saying, that God is the place of spirits, being literal, makes us conceive that spirits *move* up and down, and have their distances and intervals in God, as bodies have in space. *Locke.*

When we are come to the utmost extremity of body, what is there that can put a stop, and satisfy the mind, that it is at the end of space, when it is satisfied that body itself can *move* into it? *Locke.*

Any thing that *moves* round about in a circle in less time than our ideas are wont to succeed one another in our minds, is not perceived to *move*, but seems to be a perfect entire circle of that matter. *Locke.*

The goddess *moves*
To visit Paphos, and her blooming groves. *Pope's Odyssey.*

2. To walk; to bear the body.
See great Marcellus! how inur'd in toils
He *moves* with manly grace, how rich with regal spoils.
Dryden's Æn.

3. To go forward.
Through various hazards and events we *move*
To Latium. *Dryden's Æn.*

4. To change the posture of the body in ceremony.

When Haman saw Mordecai that he stood not up, nor *moved* for him, he was full of indignation. *Esth.* v. 9.

Mo'veable. *adj.* [from *move.*]

1. Capable of being moved; not fixed; portable; such as may be carried from place to place.

In the vast wilderness, when the people of God had no settled habitation, yet a *moveable* tabernacle they were commanded of God to make. *Hooker, b.* v.

When he made his prayer, he found the boat he was in *moveable* and unbound, the rest remained still fast. *Bacon.*

Any heat whatsoever promotes the ascent of mineral matter, which is subtile, and is consequently *moveable* more easily. *Woodward's Nat. Hist. p.* iv.

Any who sees the Teverone must conclude it to be one of the most *moveable* rivers in the world, that is so often shifted out of one channel into another. *Addison on Italy.*

2. Changing the time of the year.

The lunar month is natural and periodical, by which the *moveable* festivals of the Christian church are regulated. *Holder.*

Mo'veables. *n. s.* [*meubles*, Fr.] Goods; furniture; distinguished from real or immoveable possessions: as, lands or house.

We seize
The plate, coin, revenues, and *moveables*,
Whereof our uncle Gaunt did stand posses'd. *Shakesp.*

Let him that moved you hither,
Remove you hence; I knew you at the first
You were a *moveable*.
—Why, what's a *moveable?*
—A join'd stool. *Shakesp. Taming of the Shrew.*

Surveys rich *moveables* with curious eye,
Beats down the price, and threatens still to buy. *Dryden.*

Mo'veableness. *n. s.* [from *moveable.*] Mobility; possibility to be moved.

Mo'veably. *adv.* [from *moveable.*] So as it may be moved.

His back-piece is composed of eighteen plates, *moveably* joined together by as many intermediate skins. *Grew.*

Mo'veless. *adj.* Unmov'd; not to be put out of the place.

The lungs, though untouched, will remain *moveless* as to any expansion or contraction of their substance. *Boyle.*

The Grecian phalanx, *moveless* as a tow'r,
On all sides batter'd, yet resists his power. *Pope's Iliad.*

Mo'vement. *n. s.* [*mouvement*, French.]

1. Manner of moving.

What farther relieves descriptions of battles, is the art of introducing pathetick circumstances about the heroes, which raise a different *movement* in the mind, compassion and pity. *Pope's Essay on Homer.*

Under workmen are expert enough at making a single wheel in a clock, but are utterly ignorant how to adjust the several parts, or regulate the *movement*. *Swift.*

2. Motion.

Mo'vent. *adj.* [*movens*, Latin.] Moving.

If it be in some part *movent*, and in some part quiescent, it must needs be a curve line, and so no radius. *Grew's Cos.*

Mo'vent. *n. s.* [*movens*, Lat.] That which moves another.

That there is a motion which makes the vicissitudes of day and night, sense may assure us; but whether the sun or earth be the common *movent*, cannot be determined but by a further appeal. *Glanville's Scep.*

Mo'ver. *n. s.* [from *move.*]

1. The person or thing that gives motion.
O thou eternal *mover* of the heav'ns,
Look with a gentle eye upon this wretch. *Shakespeare.*

The strength of a spring were better assisted by the labour of some intelligent *mover*, as the heavenly orbs are supposed to be turned. *Wilkins's Math. Magick.*

2. Something that moves, or stands not still.
You as the soul, as the first *mover*, you
Vigour and life on ev'ry part bestow. *Waller.*
So orbs from the first *mover* motion take,
Yet each their proper revolutions make. *Dryden.*

3. A proposer.
See here these *movers*, that do prize their honours
At a crack'd drachm; cushions, leaden spoons,
Ere yet the fight be done, pack up. *Shakesp. Coriolanus.*

If any question be moved concerning the doctrine of the church of England expressed in the thirty-nine articles, give not the least ear to the *movers* thereof. *Bacon.*

Mo'ving. *participial adj.* [from *move.*] Pathetick; touching; adapted to affect the passions.

Great Jupiter,
The *moving* pray'r of Æacus did grant,
And into men and women turn'd the ant. *Blackmore.*

Mo'vingly. *adj.* [from *moving.*] Pathetically; in such a manner as to seize the passions.

The choice and flower of all things profitable in other books, the Psalms do both more briefly and more *movingly* express, by reason of that poetical form wherewith they are written. *Hooker, b.* v.

I would have had them writ more *movingly*. *Shakesp.*

His air, his voice, his looks, and honest soul,
Speak all so *movingly* in his behalf,
I dare not trust myself to hear him talk. *Addison's Cato.*

Mought. for *might*. Obsolete.

Mould. *n. s.* [*moegel*, Swedish.]

1. A kind of concretion on the top or outside of things kept, motionless and damp; now discovered by microscopes to be perfect plants.

All *moulds* are inceptions of putrefaction, as the *moulds* of pies and flesh, which *moulds* turn into worms. *Bacon.*

Moss is a kind of *mould* of the earth and trees, but may be better sorted as a rudiment of germination. *Bacon.*

Another special affinity is between plants and *mould*, or putrefaction; for all putrefaction, if it dissolve not in arefaction, will, in the end, issue into plants. *Bacon's Nat. Hist.*

The malt made in Summer is apt to contract *mould*. *Mort.*

A hermit, who has been shut up in his cell in a college, has contracted a sort of *mould* and rust upon his soul, and all his airs have aukwardness in them. *Watts.*

2. [*Molb*, Saxon.] Earth; soil; ground in which any thing grows.

Those *moulds* that are of a bright chesnut or hazelly colour are accounted the best; next to that, the dark grey and russet *moulds* are accounted best; the light and dark ash-colour are reckoned the worst, such as are usually found on common or heathy

heathy ground: the clear tawny is by no means to be approved, but that of a yellowish colour is reckoned the worst of all; this is commonly found in wild and waste parts of the country, and for the most part produces nothing but goss, furz, and fern. All good lands after rain, or breaking up by the spade, will emit a good smell; that being always the best that is neither too unctuous or too lean, but such as will easily dissolve; of a just consistence between sand and clay. *Miller.*

Though worms devour me, though I turn to *mould*,
Yet in my flesh I shall his face behold. *Sandys's Paraph.*

The black earth, every-where obvious on the surface of the ground, we call *mould.* *Woodward.*

3. Matter of which any thing is made.

When the world began,
One common mass compos'd the *mould* of man. *Dryden.*
Nature form'd me of her softest *mould*,
Enfeebled all my soul with tender passions,
And sunk me even below my weak sex. *Addison's Cato.*

4 [*Molde*, Spanish; *moule*, French.] The matrix in which any thing is cast; in which any thing receives its form.

If the liturgies of all the ancient churches be compared, it may be easily perceived they had all one original *mould.* *Hooker, b.* v.

A dangerous president were left for the casting of prayers into certain poetical *moulds.* *Hooker, b.* v.

French churches all cast according unto that *mould* which Calvin had made. *Hooker.*

My wife comes foremost; then the honour'd *mould*
Wherein this trunk was fram'd. *Shakesp. Coriolanus.*
New honours come upon him,
Like our strange garments cleave not to their *mould*,
But with the end of use. *Shakesp. Macbeth.*

You may have fruit in more accurate figures, according as you make the *moulds.* *Bacon's Nat. Hist.* N°. 502.

The liquid ore he drain'd
Into fit *moulds* prepar'd; from which he form'd
First his own tools: then what might else be wrought
Fusile, or grav'n in metal. *Milton's Par. Lost, b.* xi.

We may hope for new heavens and a new earth, more pure and perfect than the former; as if this was a refiner's fire, to purge out the dross and coarse parts, and then cast the mass again into a new and better *mould.* *Burnet.*

Sure our souls were near allied, and thine
Cast in the same poetick *mould* with mine. *Dryden.*
Here in fit *moulds* to Indian nations known,
Are cast the several kinds of precious stone. *Blackmore.*

4. Cast; form.

No mates for you,
Unless you were of gentler, milder *mould.* *Shakespeare.*

William earl of Pembroke was a man of another *mould*, and making, and of another fame, being the most universally beloved of any man of that age; and, having a great office in the court, he made the court itself better esteemed, and more reverenced in the country. *Clarendon.*

Learn
What creatures there inhabit, of what *mould*,
Or substance, how endu'd, and what their pow'r,
And where their weakness. *Milton's Par. Lost, b.* ii.
So must the writer, whose productions should
Take with the vulgar, be of vulgar *mould.* *Waller.*
From their main-top joyful news they hear
Of ships, which by their *mould* bring new supplies. *Dryd.*
Hans Carvel, impotent and old,
Married a lass of London *mould.* *Prior.*

5. The suture or contexture of the skull. *Ainf.*

To MOULD. *v. a.* [from the noun.] To contract concreted matter; to gather mould.

In woods, in waves, in wars she wants to dwell,
And will be found with peril and with pain;
Ne can the man that *moulds* in idle cell
Unto her happy mansion attain. *Fairy Queen, b.* ii.

There be some houses wherein sweet meats will relent, and baked meats will *mould*, more than in others. *Bacon.*

To MOULD. *v. a.* To cover with mould; to corrupt by mould.

Very coarse, hoary, *moulded* bread the soldiers thrust upon their spears, railing against Ferdinand, who made no better provision. *Knolles's Hist. of the Turks.*

To MOULD. *v. a.* [from the noun.]

1. To form; to shape; to model.

I feel
Of what coarse metal ye are *moulded.* *Shakesp. Henry* VIII.
Here is the cap your worship did bespeak;
Why this was *moulded* on a poringer,
A velvet dish; fie, fie, 'tis lewd. *Shakespeare.*

The king had taken such liking of his person, that he resolved to make him a master-piece, and to *mould* him platonically to his own idea. *Wotton's Buckingham.*

Did I request thee, Maker! from my clay
To *mould* me man? *Milton's Par. Lost, b.* x.

He forgeth and *mouldeth* metals, and builds houses. *Hale.*

By the force of education we may *mould* the minds and manners of youth into what shape we please, and give them the impressions of such habits as shall ever afterwards remain. *Atterbury's Sermons.*

Then rose the seed of chaos, and of night,
Of dull and venal a new world to *mould*,
And bring Saturnian days of lead and gold. *Dunciad, b.* iv.

A faction in England, under the name of puritan, *moulded* up their new schemes of religion with republican principles in government. *Swift.*

For you alone he stole
The fire that forms a manly soul;
Then, to compleat it ev'ry way,
He *moulded* it with female clay. *Swift's Miscel.*

Fabellus would never learn any moral lessons till they were *moulded* into the form of some fiction or fable like those of Æsop. *Watts's Improvement of the Mind, p.* i.

2. To knead: as, to *mould* bread. *Ainf.*

MO'ULDABLE. *adj.* [from *mould.*] What may be moulded.

The differences of figurable and not figurable, *mouldable* and not *mouldable*, are plebeian notions. *Bacon's Nat. Hist.*

MO'ULDER. *n. f.* [from *mould.*] He who moulds.

To MO'ULDER. *v. n.* [from *mould.*] To be turned to dust; to perish in dust; to be diminished.

If he had sat still, the enemies army would have *mouldered* to nothing, and been exposed to any advantage he would take. *Clarendon, b.* viii.

Whatsoever *moulders*, or is washed away, is carried down into the lower grounds, and nothing ever brought back again. *Burnet's Theory of the Earth.*

Those formed stones despoiled of their shells, and exposed upon the surface of the ground, in time decay, wear, and *moulder* away, and are frequently found defaced, and broken to pieces. *Woodward's Nat. Hist. p.* v.

To them by smiling Jove 'twas giv'n,
Great William's glories to recall,
When statues *moulder*, and when arches fall. *Prior.*

Finding his congregation *moulder* every Sunday, and hearing what was the occasion of it, he resolved to give his parish a little Latin in his turn. *Addison's Spect.* N°. 221.

To MO'ULDER. *v. a.* [from *mould.*] To turn to dust; to crumble.

The natural histories of Switzerland talk of the fall of those rocks when their foundations have been *mouldered* with age, or rent by an earthquake. *Addison on Italy.*

With nodding arches, broken temples spread,
The very tombs now vanish'd like their dead;
Some felt the silent stroke of *mould'ring* age,
Some, hostile fury. *Pope.*

MO'ULDINESS. *n. f.* [from *mouldy.*] The state of being mouldy.

Flesh, fish, and plants, after a *mouldiness*, rottenness, or corrupting, will fall to breed worms. *Bacon's Nat. Hist.*

MO'ULDING. *n. f.* [from *mould.*] Ornamental cavities in wood or stone.

Hollow *mouldings* are required in the work. *Moxon.*

MO'ULDWARP. *n. f.* [molb and peoppan, Saxon.] A mole; a small animal that throws up the earth.

Above the reach of loathful sinful lust,
Whose base effect through cowardly distrust
Of his own wings, dare not to heaven flie,
But like a *mouldwarp* in the earth doth lie. *Spenser.*

While they play the *mouldwarps*, unsavory damps distemper their heads with annoyance only for the present. *Carew.*

With gins we betray the vermin of the earth, namely, the fichat and the *mouldwarp.* *Walton's Angler.*

MO'ULDY. *adj.* [from *mould.*] Overgrown with concretions.

Is thy name *mouldy?*
—Yea.
—'Tis the more time thou wert us'd.
—Ha, ha, ha; most excellent: things that are *mouldy* lack use. Well said, Sir John. *Shakesp. Henry* IV.

The marble looks white and fresh, as being exposed to the winds and salt sea-vapours, that by continually fretting it preserves itself from that *mouldy* colour which others contract. *Addison's Remarks on Italy.*

To MOULT. *v. n.* [*muyten*, Dutch.] To shed or change the feathers; to lose feathers.

Some birds upon *moulting* turn colour, as Robin-red-breasts, after their *moulting*, grow to be red again by degrees. *Bacon.*

Time shall *moult* away his wings,
E'er he shall discover
In the wide whole world again
Such a constant lover. *Suckling.*
The widow'd turtle hangs her *moulting* wings,
And to the woods in mournful murmur sings. *Garth.*

To MOUNCH. } *v. a.* [*mouch*, to eat much. *Ainf.* This word
To MAUNCH. } is retained in Scotland, and denotes the obtunded action of toothless gums on a hard crust, or any thing eatable: it seems to be a corruption of the French word *manger. Macbean.*]

A sailor's wife had chesnuts in her lap,
And *mouncht*, and *mouncht*, and *mouncht.* *Shakesp. Macbeth.*

MOUND.

MOUND. *n. s.* [mundian, Saxon, to defend.] Any thing raised to fortify or defend: usually a bank of earth and stone.

His broad branches laden with rich fee,
Did stretch themselves without the utmost bound
Of this great garden, compass'd with a *mound*. *Fairy Qu.*

The sea's a thief, whose liquid surge resolves
The *mounds* into salt tears. *Shakesp. Timon of Athens.*

God had thrown
That mountain as his garden *mound*, high rais'd. *Milton.*

Such as broke through all *mounds* of law, such as laughed at the sword of vengeance which divine justice brandished in their faces. *South's Sermons.*

Nor cold shall hinder me with horns and hounds
To thrid the thickets, or to leap the *mounds*. *Dryden.*

The state of Milan is like a vast garden sorrounded by a noble *mound*-work of rocks and mountains. *Addison.*

To MOUND. *v. a.* [from the noun.] To fortify with a mound.

MOUNT. *n. s.* [*mont*, French; *mons*, Latin.]

1. A mountain; a hill.

Jacob offered sacrifice upon the *mount*. *Gen.* xxxi. 54.

Behold yon mountain's hoary height,
Made higher with new *mounts* of snow. *Dryden.*

2. An artificial hill raised in a garden, or other place.

He might see what *mounts* they had in short time cast, and what a number there was of brave and warlike soldiers. *Knolles's Hist. of the Turks.*

3. A publick treasure; a bank. Now obsolete.

These examples confirmed me in a resolution to spend my time wholly in writing; and to put forth that poor talent God hath given me, not to particular exchanges, but to banks or *mounts* of perpetuity, which will not break. *Bacon.*

To MOUNT. *v. n.* [*monter*, French.]

1. To rise on high.

Doth the eagle *mount* up at thy command, and make her nest on high? *Job* iii. 27.

I'll strive, with troubl'd thoughts, to take a nap;
Lest leaden slumber poize me down to-morrow,
When I should *mount* with wings of victory. *Shakespeare.*

A base ignoble mind,
That *mounts* no higher than a bird can soar. *Shakespeare.*

The fire of trees and houses *mounts* on high,
And meets half-way new fires that show'r from sky. *Cowley.*

If the liturgy should be offered to them, it would kindle jealousy, and as the first range of that ladder which should serve to *mount* over all their customs. *Clarendon.*

Ambitious meteors set themselves upon the wing, taking every occasion of drawing upward to the sun; not considering, that they have no more time allowed them in their *mounting* than the single revolution of a day; and that when the light goes from them, they are of necessity to fall. *Dryd.*

2. To tower; to be built up to great elevation.

Though his excellency *mount* up to the heavens, and his head reach unto the clouds, yet he shall perish. *Job* xx. 6.

3. To get on horseback.

He
Like a full acorn'd boar, a churning on,
Cry'd, oh! and *mounted*. *Shakespeare's Cymbeline.*

4. [For *amount*.] To rise in value.

Bring then these blessings to a strict account,
Make fair deductions, see to what they *mount*. *Pope.*

To MOUNT. *v. a.*

1. To raise aloft; to lift on high.

The fire that *mounts* the liquor till 't runs o'er,
Seeming to augment, wastes it. *Shakespeare.*

What power is it which *mounts* my love so high,
That makes me see, and cannot feed mine eye? *Shakesp.*

The air is so thin, that a bird has therein no feeling of her wings, or any resistance of air to *mount* herself by. *Ral.*

2. To ascend; to climb.

Shall we *mount* again the rural throne,
And rule the country kingdoms, once our own? *Dryden.*

3. To place on horseback.

Three hundred horses, in high stables fed,
Of these he chose the fairest and the best,
To *mount* the Trojan troop. *Dryden's Æn.*

Clear reason, acting in conjunction with a well-disciplined, but strong and vigorous fancy, seldom fail to attain their end: fancy without reason, is like a horse without a rider; and reason without fancy is not well *mounted*. *Grew's Cos. b.* ii.

4. To embellish with ornaments.

5. *To* MOUNT *guard*. To do duty and watch at any particular post.

6. *To* MOUNT *a cannon*. To set a piece on its wooden frame for the more easy carriage and management in firing it.

MO'UNTAIN. *n. s.* [*montaigne*, French.] A large hill; a vast protuberance of the earth.

I had been drowned; a death that I abhor; for the water swells a man, and what a thing should I have been when I had been swelled? I should have been a *mountain* of mummy. *Shakespeare's Merry Wives of Windsor.*

She did corrupt frail nature with some bribe,
To make an envious *mountain* on my back,
Where sits deformity to mock my body. *Shakespeare.*

From Acmon's hands a rolling-stone there came,
So large, it half deserv'd a *mountain*'s name! *Dryden.*

MO'UNTAIN. *adj.* [*montanus*, Latin.] Found on the mountains; pertaining to the mountains; growing on the mountains.

Now for our *mountain* sport, up to yond hill,
Your legs are young. *Shakespeare's Cymbeline.*

You may as well forbid the *mountain* pines
To wag their high tops, and to make a noise,
When they are fretted with the gusts of heav'n. *Shakesp.*

MOUNTAINE'ER. *n. s.* [from *mountain.*]

1. An inhabitant of the mountains.

A few *mountaineers* may escape, enough to continue human race; and yet illiterate rusticks, as *mountaineers* always are. *Bentley's Sermons.*

Amiternian troops, of mighty fame,
And *mountaineers*, that from Severus came. *Dryden's Æn.*

2. A savage; a free booter; a rustick.

Yield, rustick *mountaineer*. *Shakesp. Cymbeline.*

No savage, fierce banditti, or *mountaineer*,
Will dare to soil her virgin purity. *Milton.*

MO'UNTAINET. *n. s.* [from *mountain.*] A hillock; a small mount. Elegant, but not in use.

Her breasts sweetly rose up like two fair *mountainets* in the pleasant vale of Tempe. *Sidney.*

MO'UNTAINOUS. *adj.* [from *mountain.*]

1. Hilly; full of mountains.

The ascent of the land from the sea to the foot of the mountains, and the height of the mountains from the bottom to the top, are to be computed, when you measure the height of a mountain, or of a *mountainous* land, in respect of the sea. *Burnet's Theory of the Earth.*

2. Large as mountains; huge; bulky.

What custom wills in all things, shou'd we do't,
Mountainous error wou'd be too highly heapt
For truth to o'erpeer. *Shakespeare.*

On earth, in air, amidst the seas and skies,
Mountainous heaps of wonders rise;
Whose tow'ring strength will ne'er submit
To reason's batteries, or the mines of wit. *Prior.*

3. Inhabiting mountains.

In destructions by deluge and earthquake, the remnant which hap to be reserved are ignorant and *mountainous* people, that can give no account of the time past. *Bacon's Essays.*

MO'UNTAINOUSNESS. *n. s.* [from *mountainous.*] State of being full of mountains.

Armenia is so called from the *mountainousness* of it. *Brerewood on Learning.*

MO'UNTAIN-PARSLEY. *n. s.* [*oreosolinum*, Lat.] A plant.

The *mountain-parsley* hath a rose-shaped umbellated flower, consisting of several leaves, placed in a circular order, resting on the empalement, which afterwards becomes a fruit composed of two seeds, which are oval, plain, large, streaked and bordered, and sometimes cast off their cover; the leaves are like parsley. *Miller.*

MO'UNTAIN-ROSE. *n. s.* [*chamærhododendron*, Lat.] A plant.

The *mountain-rose* hath a tubulous flower, consisting of one leaf, shaped somewhat like a funnel; from whose cup arises the pointal, fixed like a nail in the hinder part of the flower, which afterwards becomes an oblong fruit, divided into five cells, in which are contained many very small seeds. *Miller.*

MO'UNTANT. *adj.* [*montans*, Lat.] Rising on high.

Hold up, you sluts,
Your aprons *mountant*; you're not oathable,
Although, I know, you'll swear. *Shak. Timon of Athens.*

MO'UNTEBANK. *n. s.* [*montare* in *banco*, Italian.]

1. A doctor that mounts a bench in the market, and boasts his infallible remedies and cures.

I bought an unction of a *mountebank*
So mortal, that but dip a knife in it,
Where it draws blood, no cataplasm so rare,
Can save the thing from death. *Shakesp. Hamlet.*

She, like a *mountebank*, did wound
And stab herself with doubts profound,
Only to shew with how small pain
The sores of faith are cur'd again. *Hudibras, p.* i.

But Æschylus, says Horace in some page,
Was the first *mountebank* that trod the stage. *Dryden.*

It looks so like a *mountebank* to boast of infallible cures. *Baker's Reflections on Learning.*

2. Any boastful and false pretender.

As nimble jugglers, that deceive the eye,
Disguised cheaters, prating *mountebanks*,
And many such like libertines of sin. *Shakespeare.*

There are *mountebanks*, and smatterers in state. *L'Estrange.*

Nothing so impossible in nature but *mountebanks* will undertake. *Arbuthnot's Hist. of John Bull.*

To MO'UNTEBANK. *v. a.* [from the noun.] To cheat by false boasts or pretences.

I'll *mountebank* their loves,
Cog their hearts from them. *Shakespeare's Coriolanus.*

MO'UNTENANCE. *n. s.* Amount of a thing. *Spenser.*

Mo'unter. *n. s.* [from *mount.*] One that mounts:
Though they to the earth were thrown,
Yet quickly they regain'd their own,
Such nimbleness was never shown;
They were two gallant *mounters*. *Drayton's Nymphid.*
Few bankers will to heav'n be *mounters*. *Swift.*

Mo'unty. *n. s.* [*montée*, French.] The rise of a hawk.
The sport which Basilius would shew to Zemane, was the *mounty* at a heron, which getting up on his waggling wings with pain, as though the air next to the earth were not fit to fly through, now diminished the sight of himself. *Sidney.*

To Mourn. *v. n.* [muꞃnan, Saxon.]
1. To grieve; to be sorrowful.
Abraham came to *mourn* for Sarah, and to weep. *Genes.*
I *mourn* in my complaint. *Psal.* lv. 2.
This day is holy; *mourn* not, nor weep. *Neh.* viii. 9.
The people shall *mourn* over it. *Hos.* x. 5.
My vineyard being desolate, *mourneth* unto me. *Jer.* xii.
They made an appointment to *mourn* with him, and to comfort him. *Job* ii. 11.
They rejoice at the presence of the sun, and *mourn* at the absence thereof. *Bacon's Nat. Hist.* N°. 493.
2. To wear the habit of sorrow.
We *mourn* in black; why *mourn* we not in blood? *Shak.*
Friends in sable weeds appear,
Grieve for an hour, perhaps they *mourn* a year;
They bear about the mockery of woe
To midnight dances, and the puppet-show. *Pope.*
3. To preserve appearance of grief.
The days of *mourning* for my father are at hand, then will I slay Jacob. *Gen.* xxvii. 41.
Feign thyself to be a mourner, and put on *mourning* apparel. 2 *Sam.* xiv. 2.
Publish it that she is dead;
Maintain a *mourning* ostentation,
Hang mournful epitaphs. *Shakesp. Much about nothing.*

To Mourn. *v. a.*
1. To grieve for; to lament.
The muse that *mourns* him now his happy triumph sung. *Dryden.*
Portius himself oft falls in tears before me,
As if he *mourn'd* his rival's ill success. *Addison's Cato.*
2. To utter in a sorrowful manner.
The love-lorn nightingale
Nightly to thee her sad song *mourneth* well. *Milton.*

Mourne. *n. s.* [*morne*, French.] The round end of a staff; the part of a lance to which the steel part is fixed, or where it is taken off.
He carried his lances, which though strong to give a lancely blow indeed, yet so were they coloured with hooks near the *mourne*, that they prettily represented sheep hooks. *Sidney.*

Mo'urner. *n. s.* [from *mourn.*]
1. One that mourns; one that grieves.
The kindred of the queen must die at Pomfret.
—Indeed I am no *mourner* for that news,
Because they have been still my adversaries. *Shakespeare.*
To cure thy woe, she shews thy fame;
Lest the great *mourner* should forget
That all the race whence Orange came,
Made virtue triumph over fate. *Prior.*
2. One who follows a funeral in black.
A woman that had two daughters buried one, and *mourners* were provided to attend the funeral. *L'Estrange's Fables.*
He lives to be chief *mourner* for his son;
Before his face his wife and brother burns. *Dryden.*
3. Something used at funerals.
The *mourner* eugh and builder oak were there. *Dryden.*

Mo'urnful. *adj.* [*mourn* and *full.*]
1. Having the appearance of sorrow.
No funeral rites, nor man in *mournful* weeds,
Nor mournful bell shall ring her burial. *Shakespeare.*
The winds within the quiv'ring branches play'd,
And dancing trees a *mournful* musick made. *Dryden.*
2. Causing sorrow.
Upon his tomb
Shall be engrav'd the sack of Orleans;
The treach'rous manner of his *mournful* death. *Shakesp.*
3. Sorrowful; feeling sorrow.
The *mournful* fair,
Oft as the rolling years return,
With fragrant wreaths and flowing hair,
Shall visit her distinguish'd urn. *Prior.*
4. Betokening sorrow; expressive of grief.
No *mourful* bell shall ring her burial. *Shakespeare.*
On your family's old monument
Hang *mournful* epitaphs. *Shakespeare.*

Mo'urnfully. *adv.* [from *mournful.*] Sorrowfully; with sorrow.
Beat the drum, that it speak *mournfully*. *Shakespeare.*

Mo'urnfulness. *n. s.* [from *mournful.*]
1. Sorrow; grief.
2. Show of grief; appearance of sorrow.

Mo'urning. *n. s.* [from *mourn.*]
1. Lamentation; sorrow.
Wo is me, who will deliver me in those days? the beginning of sorrows and great *mournings*. 2 *Esdr.* xvi. 18.
2. The dress of sorrow.
They through the master-street the corps convey'd,
The houses to their tops with black were spread,
And ev'n the pavements were with *mourning* hid. *Dryden.*

Mo'urningly. *adv.* [from *mourning.*] With the appearance of sorrowing.
The king spoke of him admiringly and *mourningly*. *Shak.*

Mouse. plural *mice*. *n. s.* [muꞅ, Saxon; *mus*, Latin.] The smallest of all beasts; a little animal haunting houses and corn fields, destroyed by cats.
The eagle England being in prey,
To her unguarded nest the weazel Scot
Comes sneaking, and so sucks her princely eggs;
Playing the *mouse* in absence of the cat. *Shakespeare.*
These shall be unclean; the weasle, the *mouse*, and the tortoise. *Lev.* xi. 29.
Where *mice* and rats devour'd poetick bread,
And with heroick verse luxuriously were fed. *Dryden.*
This structure of hair I have observed in the hair of cats, rats, and *mice*. *Derham's Physico-Theol.*

To Mouse. *v. n.* [from the noun.]
1. To catch mice.
An eagle tow'ring, in his pride of place
Was by a *mousing* owl hawk'd and kill'd. *Shakespeare.*
2. I suppose it means, in the following passage, sly; insidious; or predatory; rapacious; interested.
A whole assembly of *mousing* saints, under the mask of zeal and good nature, lay many kingdoms in blood. *L'Estrange.*

Mo'use-ear. *n. s.* [*myosotis*, Lat.]
The *mouse-ear* hath the whole appearance of chick-weed; but the flower is larger, and the fruit shaped like an ox's horn, gaping at the top, and full of small round seeds. *Miller.*

Mo'usehunt. *n. s.* [*mouse* and *hunt.*] Mouser; one that hunts mice.
You have been a *mouse-hunt* in your time,
But I will watch you. *Shakesp. Romeo and Juliet.*

Mo'use-hole. *n. s.* [*mouse* and *hole.*] Small hole; hole at which a mouse only may run in.
He puts the prophets in a *mouse hole*: the last man ever speaks the best reason. *Dryden and Lee's Oedipus.*
He can creep in at a *mouse-hole*, but he soon grows too big ever to get out again. *Stillingfleet.*

Mo'user. *n. s.* [from *mouse.*] One that catches mice.
Puss, a madam, will be a *mouser* still. *L'Estrange.*
When you have fowl in the larder, leave the door open, in pity to the cat, if she be a good *mouser*. *Swift.*

Mo'usetail. *n. s.* An herb.

Mo'use-trap. *n. s.* [*mouse* and *trap.*] A snare or gin in which mice are taken.
Many analogal motions in animals, I have reason to conclude, in their principle are not simply mechanical, although a *mouse-trap*, or Architas dove, moved mechanically. *Hale.*
Madam,
With her own hand the *mouse-trap* baited. *Prior.*

MOUTH. *n. s.* [muð, Saxon.]
1. The aperture in the head of any animal at which the food is received.
The dove came in; and lo, in her *mouth* was an olive leaf. *Gen.* viii. 11.
There can be no reason given, why a visage somewhat longer, or a wider *mouth*, could not have consisted with a soul. *Locke.*
2. The opening; that at which any thing enters; the entrance; the part of a vessel by which it is filled and emptied.
He came and lay at the *mouth* of the haven, daring them to fight. *Knolles's Hist. of the Turks.*
Set a candle lighted in the bottom of a bason of water, and turn the *mouth* of a glass over the candle, and it will make the water rise. *Bacon's Nat. Hist.* N°. 889.
The *mouth* is low and narrow; but, after having entered pretty far in, the grotto opens itself in an oval figure. *Addison.*
The navigation of the Arabick gulf being more dangerous toward the bottom than the *mouth*, Ptolemy built Berenice at the entry of the gulf. *Arbuthnot on Coins.*
3. The instrument of speaking.
Riotous madness,
To be entangled with these *mouth*-made vows,
Which break themselves in swearing. *Shakespeare.*
Either our history shall with full *mouth*
Speak freely of our acts; or else our grave,
Like Turkish mute, shall have a tongueless *mouth*,
Not worshipp'd with a waxen epitaph. *Shakesp. Henry V.*
We will call the damsel, and inquire at her *mouth*. *Gen.* xxiv. 57.
Every body's *mouth* will be full on it for the first four days, and in four more the story will talk itself asleep. *L'Estrange.*
In the innocent age of the world, it was in every body's *mouth* that the son was about to marry. *L'Estrange.*

Having frequently in our *mouths* the name eternity, we think we have a positive idea of it. *Locke.*

There is a certain sentence got into every man's *mouth*, that God accepts the will for the deed. *South's Sermons.*

4. A speaker; a rhetorician; the principal orator. In burlesque language.

Every coffee-house has some particular statesman belonging to it, who is the *mouth* of the street where he lives. *Add.*

5. Cry; voice.

Coward dogs
Most spend their *mouths*, when what they seem to threaten
Runs far before them. *Shakespeare's Henry* V.

The boar
Deals glancing wounds; the fearful dogs divide,
All spend their *mouth* aloft, but none abide. *Dryden.*

You don't now thunder in the capitol,
With all the *mouths* of Rome to second thee. *Addison.*

6. Distortion of the mouth; wry face, in this sense, is said to *make mouths.*

Persevere, counterfeit sad looks,
Make *mouths* upon me when I turn my back. *Shakespeare.*

Against whom make ye a wide *mouth*, and draw out the tongue? *Isa.* lvii. 4.

Why they should keep running asses at Coleshill, or how making *mouths* turns to account in Warwickshire more than any other parts of England, I cannot comprehend. *Addison.*

7. *Down in the* MOUTH. Dejected; clouded in the countenance.

But, upon bringing the net ashore, it proved to be only one great stone, and a few little fishes: upon this disappointment they were *down in the mouth.* *L'Estrange.*

To MOUTH. *v. n.* [from the noun.] To speak big; to speak in a strong and loud voice; to vociferate.

Nay, an thou'lt *mouth*
I'll rant as well as thou. *Shakespeare's Hamlet.*

When Progne's or Thyestes' feast they write,
And for the *mouthing* actor verse indite;
Thou neither like a bellows swell'st thy face,
Nor canst thou strain thy throat. *Dryden's Persius.*

I'll bellow out for Rome, and for my country,
And *mouth* at Cæsar till I shake the senate. *Addison.*

To MOUTH. *v. a.*

1. To utter with a voice affectedly big; to roll in the mouth with tumult.

Speak the speech as I pronounced it, trippingly on the tongue: but if you *mouth* it, I had as lieve the town-crier had spoke my lines. *Shakespeare's Hamlet.*

Twitch'd by the sleeve he *mouths* it more and more,
Till with white froth his gown is slaver'd o'er. *Dryden.*

2. To chew; to eat; to grind in the mouth.

Corne carried let such as be poore go and glean,
And after thy cattel to *mouth* it up clean. *Tusser's Husb.*

Death lines his dead chaps with steel,
The swords of soldiers are his teeth, his phangs;
And now he feasts *mouthing* the flesh of men. *Shakesp.*

3. To seize in the mouth.

He keeps them, like an apple, in the corner of his jaw; first *mouth'd* to be last swallow'd. *Shakesp. Hamlet.*

Lucilius never fear'd the times;
Mutius and Lupus both by name he brought,
He *mouth'd* them, and betwixt his grinders caught. *Dryden.*

4. To form by the mouth.

In regard the cub comes forth involved in the chorion, a thick membrane obscuring the formation, and which the dam doth after tear asunder; the beholder at first sight imputes the ensuing form to the *mouthing* of the dam. *Br. Vulgar Err.*

MO'UTHED. *adj.* [from *mouth.*]

1. Furnished with a mouth.

One tragick sentence if I dare deride,
Which Betterton's grave action dignify'd,
Or well *mouth'd* Booth with emphasis proclaims. *Pope.*

2. In composition, foul *mouthed* or contumelious; mealy *mouthed* or bashful; and a hard *mouthed* horse, or a horse not obedient to the bit.

MO'UTH-FRIEND. *n. s.* [*mouth* and *friend.*] One who professes friendship without intending it.

May you a better feast never behold,
You knot of *mouth-friends:* smoke and lukewarm water
Is your perfection. *Shakespeare.*

MO'UTHFUL. *n. s.* [*mouth* and *full.*]

1. What the mouth contains at once.

2. Any proverbially small quantity.

A goat going out for a *mouthful* of fresh grass, charged her kid not to open the door till she came back. *L'Estrange.*

You to your own Aquinum shall repair,
To take a *mouthful* of sweet country air. *Dryden's Juv.*

MO'UTH-HONOUR. *n. s.* [*mouth* and *honour.*] Civility outwardly expressed without sincerity.

Honour, love, obedience, troops of friends,
I must not look to have; but in their stead,
Curses not loud but deep, *mouth-honour*, breath. *Shakesp.*

MO'UTHLESS. *adj.* [from *mouth.*] Without a mouth.

MOW. *n. s.* [mope, Saxon, a heap.] A loft or chamber where hay or corn is laid up: hay in *mow*, is hay laid up in a house; hay in *rick*, is hay heaped together in a field.

Learne skilfullie how
Each grain for to laie by itself on a *mow*. *Tusser's Husb.*

Where'er I gad, I Blouzelind shall view,
Woods, dairy, barn, and *mows* our passion knew. *Gay.*

Beans when moist give in the *mow*. *Mortimer's Husb.*

To MOW. *v. a.* preter. *mowed*, part. *mown.* [mapan, Saxon. *Mow* the noun is pronounced as *now*; *mow* verb as *mo.*]

1. To cut with a scythe.

Of all the seed that in my youth was sowne,
Was nought but brakes and brambles to be *mown*. *Spenser.*

The care you have
To *mow* down thorns that would annoy our foot,
Is worthy praise. *Shakesp. Henry* VI. *p.* iii.

Forth he goes,
Like to a harvest man, that's task'd to *mow*
Or all, or lose his hire. *Shakesp. Coriolanus.*

It was the latter growth after the king's *mowings*. *Amos* vii.

Whatever
The scythe of time *mows* down, devour unspar'd. *Milton.*

Beat, roll and *mow* carpet-walks and cammomile. *Evelyn.*

2. To cut down with speed and violence.

He will *mow* down all before him, and leave his passage poll'd. *Shakespeare's Coriolanus.*

What valiant foemen, like to autumn's corn,
Have we *mow'd* down. *Shakesp. Henry* VI.

Thou and I, marching before our troops,
May taste fate to 'em; *mow* 'em out a passage,
Begin the noble harvest of the field. *Dryden's All for Love.*

Stands o'er the prostrate wretch, and as he lay,
Vain tales inventing, and prepar'd to pray,
Mows off his head. *Dryden's Æn.*

To MOW. *v. a.* [from the noun.] To put in a mow.

To MOW. *v. n.* To gather the harvest.

Gold, though the heaviest metal, hither swims:
Ours is the harvest where the Indians *mow*,
We plough the deep, and reap what others sow. *Waller.*

MOW. *n. s.* [probably corrupted from *mouth*; *moue*, French.] Wry mouth; distorted face. This word is now out of use, but retained in Scotland.

The very abjects came together against me unawares, making *mows* at me. *Psal.* xxxv. 15. *Common Prayer.*

Apes and monkeys,
'Twixt two such she's, would chatter this way, and
Contemn with *mows* the other. *Shakesp. Cymbeline.*

Those that would make *mowes* at him while my father lived, give twenty ducats apiece for his picture in little. *Shakesp.*

To MOW. *v. n.* [from the noun.] To make mouths; to distort the face.

Some Smithfield ruffian takes up some new *mowing* with the mouth, some wrenching with the shoulder, some fresh, new oath, that is not stale, but will run round in the mouth. *Ascham's Schoolmaster.*

Mohu, of murder; and Flibbertigibbet, of mopping and *mowing*. *Shakespeare's King Lear.*

For every trifle are they set upon me;
Sometimes like apes that *mow* and chatter at me,
And after bite me. *Shakespeare's Tempest.*

To MO'WBURN. *v. n.* [*mow* and *burn.*] To ferment and heat in the mow for want of being dry.

House it not green, lest it *mowburn*. *Mortimer's Husb.*

MO'WER. *n. s.* [from *mow.*] One who cuts with a scythe.

Set *mowers* a mowing, where medow is grown. *Tusser.*

The strawy Greeks, ripe for his edge,
Fall down before him like the *mower's* swath. *Shakesp.*

All else cut off,
As Tarquin did the poppy-heads, or *mowers*
A field of thistles. *Benj. Johnson's Catiline.*

Mowers and reapers, who spend the most part of the hot Summer days exposed to the sun, have the skin of their hands of a darker colour than before. *Boyle.*

MO'XA. *n. s.* An Indian moss, used in the cure of the gout by burning it on the part aggrieved. *Temple.*

MO'YLE. *n. s.* A mule; an animal generated between the horse and the ass.

Ordinary husbandmen should quit breeding of horses, and betake themselves to *moyles*; a beast which will fare hardly, live very long, draw indifferently well, carry great burthens, and hath also a pace swift and easy enough. *Carew.*

'Twould tempt a *moyle* to fury. *May.*

MUCH. *adj.* [*mycker*, Swedish; *mucho*, Spanish.] Large in quantity; long in time; many in number.

Let us know
If 'twill tie up thy discontented sword,
And carry back to Sicily *much* tall youth,
That else must perish here. *Shakesp. Antony and Cleopatra.*

Thou shalt carry *much* seed out, and shalt gather but little in; for the locust shall consume it. *Deut.* xxiv. 38.

I am well served, to take so *much* pains for one resolved to make away with himself. *L'Estrange.*

You

You were pressed for the sea-service, and got off with *much* ado. *Swift's Rules to Servants.*

MUCH. *adv.*

1. In a great degree; by far.

Isaac, thou art *much* mightier than we. *Gen.* xxvi. 16.

Excellent speech becometh not a fool, *much* less do lying lips a prince. *Prov.* xvii. 17.

We have had fathers of our flesh which corrected us, and we gave them reverence; shall we not *much* rather be in subjection unto the Father of spirits, and live? *Heb.* xii. 9.

If they escaped not who refused him that spoke on earth, *much* more shall not we escape, if we turn away from him that speaketh from heaven. *Heb.* xii. 25.

Somewhat aw'd, I shook with holy fear,
Yet not so *much* but that I noted well
Who did the most in song and dance excel. *Dryden.*

2. To a certain degree.

He charged them that they should tell no man: but the more he charged them, so *much* the more a great deal they published it. *Mark* vii. 36.

3. To a great degree.

So spake, so wish'd *much* humbled Eve, but fate
Subscrib'd not. *Milt.*

To thee thy *much*-afflicted mother flies,
And on thy succour and thy faith relies. *Dryden.*

Your *much*-lov'd fleet shall soon
Besiege the petty monarchs of the land. *Dryden.*

If his rules of reason be not better than his rules for health, he is not like to be *much* followed. *Baker's Ref. on Learning.*

Oh *much* experienc'd man! *Pope's Odyssey.*

Sad from my natal hour my days have ran,
A *much* afflicted, much enduring man. *Pope's Odyssey.*

3. Often, or long.

You pine, you languish, love to be alone,
Think *much*, speak little, and in speaking, sigh. *Dryden.*

Homer shall last, like Alexander, long,
As *much* recorded, and as often sung. *Granville.*

4. Nearly.

All left the world *much* as they found it, ever unquiet, subject to changes and revolutions. *Temple.*

MUCH. *n. s.*

1. A great deal; multitude in number; abundance in quantity.

They gathered against Moses and Aaron, and said, Ye take too *much* upon you. *Num.* xvi. 3.

Nor grudge I thee the *much* the Grecians give,
Nor murm'ring take the little I receive. *Dryden's Iliad.*

They have *much* of the poetry of Mecænas, but little of his liberality. *Dryden's Pref. to All for Love.*

The fate of love is such,
That still it sees too little or too *much.* *Dryden.*

Much suff'ring heroes next their honours claim;
Those of less noisy and less guilty fame,
Fair virtue's silent train. *Pope's Temple of Fame.*

2. More than enough; a heavy service or burthen.

Thou think'st it *much* to tread the ooze
Of the salt deep. *Shakespeare's Tempest.*

He thought not *much* to clothe his enemies. *Milton.*

This gracious act the ladies all approve,
Who thought it *much* a man should die for love,
And with their mistress join'd in close debate. *Dryden.*

3. Any assignable quantity or degree.

The waters covered the chariots and horsemen; there remained not so *much* as one. *Exod.* xiv. 28.

We will cut wood out of Lebanon as *much* as thou shalt need. 2 *Chron.* ii. 16.

The matter of the universe was created before the flood; and if any more was created, then there must be as *much* annihilated to make room for it. *Burnet's Theory of the Earth.*

Who is there of whom we can with any rational assurance, or perhaps so *much* as likelihood, affirm, here is a man whose nature is renewed, whose heart is changed. *South's Sermons.*

4. An uncommon thing; something strange.

It was *much* that one that was so great a lover of peace should be happy in war. *Bacon's Henry* VII.

It is *much*, if men were from eternity, that they should not find out the way of writing all that long duration which had past before that time. *Tillotson's Sermons.*

5. *To make* MUCH *of.* To treat with regard; to fondle; to pamper.

Though he knew his discourse was to entertain him from a more streight parley, yet he durst not but kiss his rod, and gladly make *much* of that entertainment which she allotted unto him. *Sidney, b.* ii.

The king understanding of their adventure, suddenly falls to take a pride in making *much* of them, extolling them with infinite praises. *Sidney, b.* ii.

When thou camest first,
Thou stroak'd'st, and mad'st *much* of me; and would'st give me
Water with berries in't. *Shakespeare's Tempest.*

MUCH *at one.* Of equal value; of equal influence.

Then prayers are vain as curses, *much at one*
In a slave's mouth, against a monarch's pow'r. *Dryden.*

MU'CHWHAT. *adv.* [*much* and *what.*] Nearly.

The motion being conveyed from the brain of man to the fancy of another, it is there received; and the same kind of strings being moved, and *muchwhat* after the same manner as in the first imaginant. *Glanville's Scep. c.* 24.

The bigness of her body and bill, as likewise the form of them, is *muchwhat* as swallows. *More's Antidote ag. Atheism.*

If we will disbelieve every thing, because we cannot certainly know all things, we shall do *muchwhat* as wisely as he who would not use his legs because he had no wings to fly. *Locke.*

Unless he can prove cælibatum a man or a woman, this Latin will be *muchwhat* the same with a solecism. *Atterbury.*

MU'CHEL. *adj.* for *muckle* or *mickle.* [mycel, Saxon.] Much.

He had in arms abroad won *muchel* fame,
And fill'd far lands with glory of his might. *Fairy Queen.*

MU'CID. *n. s.* [*mucidus*, Lat. *mucre*, Fr.] Slimy; musty.

MU'CIDNESS. *n. s.* [from *mucid.*] Sliminess; mustiness. *Ains.*

MU'CILAGE. *n. s.* [*mucilage*, French.] A slimy or viscous body; a body with moisture sufficient to hold it together.

Dissolution of gum tragacanth, and oil of sweet almonds, do commingle, the oil remaining on the top till they be stirred, and make the *mucilage* somewhat more liquid. *Bacon.*

Your alaternus seed move with a broom, that the seeds clog not together, unless you will separate it from the *mucilage*, for then you must a little bruise it wet. *Evelyn.*

Both the ingredients improve one another; for the *mucilage* adds to the lubricity of the oil, and the oil preserves the *mucilage* from inspissation. *Ray on the Creation.*

MUCILA'GINOUS. *adj.* [*mucilagineux*, French, from *mucilage.*] Slimy; viscous; soft with some degree of tenacity.

There is a twofold liquor prepared for the inunction and lubrification of the heads or ends of the bones: an oily one, furnished by the marrow; and a *mucilaginous*, supplied by certain glandules seated in the articulations. *Ray on Creation.*

There is a sort of magnetism in all, not *mucilaginous* but resinous gums, even in common rosin. *Grew's Cosmol.*

MUCILA'GINOUS *glands.*

Mucilaginous glands are of two sorts; some are small, and in a manner milliary glands, because glandules are placed all upon the same surface of the membranes which lie over the articulations; the other sort are conglomerated, or many glandules collected and planted one upon another, so as to make a bulk appear conspicuously. *Quincy.*

MUCILA'GINOUSNESS. *n. s.* [from *mucilaginous.*] Sliminess; viscosity.

MUCK. *n. s.* [meox, Saxon; *myer*, Islandick.]

1. Dung for manure of grounds.

Hale out thy *mucke*, and plow out thy ground. *Tusser.*

It is usual to help the ground with *muck*, and likewise to recomfort with *muck* put to the roots; but to water it with *muck* water, which is like to be more forcible, is not practised. *Bacon's Nat. Hist.* N°. 403.

The swine may see the pearl, which yet he values but with the ordinary *muck.* *Glanville's Apology.*

There are, who
Rich foreign mold, on their ill-natur'd land
Induce laborious, and with fat'ning *muck*
Besmear the roots. *Philips.*

Morning insects that in *muck* begun,
Shine, buzz and fly-blow in the setting sun. *Pope.*

2. Any thing low, mean, and filthy.

Reward of worldly *muck* doth foully blend,
And low abase the high heroick spirit
That joys for crowns. *Fairy Queen, b.* ii.

3. *To run a* MUCK, signifies, I know not from what derivation, to run madly and attack all that we meet.

Frontless and satire-proof he scow'rs the streets,
And *runs an* Indian *muck* at all he meets. *Dryden.*

Satire's my weapon, but I am too discreet
To *run a muck*, and tilt at all I meet. *Pope's Horace.*

To MUCK. *v. a.* [from the noun.] To manure with muck; to dung.

Thy garden plot lately wel trenched and *muckt*
Would now be twifallowed. *Tusser.*

MU'CKENDER. *n. s.* [*mouchoir*, French; *mocadero*, Spanish; *muccinium*, low Latin.] A handkerchief.

For thy dull fancy a *muckender* is fit,
To wipe the slabberings of thy snotty wit. *Dorset.*

To MU'CKER. *v. n.* [from *muck.*] To scramble for money; to hoard up; to get or save meanly: a word used by *Chaucer*, and still retained in conversation.

MU'CKERER. *n. s.* [from *mucker.*] One that muckers.

MU'CKHILL. *n. s.* [*muck* and *hill.*] A dunghil.

Old Euclio in Plautus, as he went from home, seeing a crowscrat upon the *muck-hill*, returned in all haste, taking it for an ill sign his money was digged up. *Burton.*

MU'CKINESS. *n. s.* [from *mucky.*] Nastiness; filth.
MU'CKLE. *adj.* [mycel, Saxon.] Much.
MU'CKSWEAT. *n. s.* [*muck* and *sweat*: in this low word, *muck* signifies wet, moist.] Profuse sweat.
MU'CKWORM. *n. s.* [*muck* and *worm.*]
1. A worm that lives in dung.
2. A miser; a curmudgeon.

Worms suit all conditions;
Misers are *muckworms*, silkworms beaus,
And death-watches physicians. *Swift's Miscel.*

MU'CKY. *adj.* [from *muck.*] Nasty; filthy.

Mucky filth his branching arms annoys,
And with uncomely weeds the gentle wave accloys. *Fairy Queen.*

MU'COUS. *adj.* [*mucosus*, Latin.] Slimy; viscous.

The salamander being cold in the fourth, and moist in the third degree, and having also a *mucous* humidity above and under the skin, may a while endure the flame. *Brown.*

About these the nerves and other vessels make a fine web, covered over with a *mucous* substance, to moisten these papillæ pyramidales. *Cheyne's Philosophical Principles.*

MU'COUSNESS. *n. s.* [from *mucous.*] Slime; viscosity.
MU'CRO. n. s. [Latin.] A point.

The *mucro* or point of the heart inclineth unto the left, by this position it giving way unto the ascension of the midriff. *Brown's Vulgar Errours, b.* iv.

MU'CRONATED. *n. s.* [*mucro*, Latin.] Narrowed to a sharp point.

Gems are here shot into cubes consisting of six sides, and *mucronated* or terminating in a point. *Woodward.*

MU'CULENT. *adj.* [from *mucus*, Lat.] Viscous; slimy. *Dict.*
MU'CUS. n. s. [Latin.] Is most properly used for that which flows from the papillary processes through the os cribriforme into the nostrils; but it is also used for any slimy liquor or moisture, as that which daubs over and guards the bowels and all the chief passages in the body; and it is separated by the mucilaginous glands. *Quincy.*

In the action of chewing, the *mucus* mixeth with the aliment: the *mucus* is an humour different from the spittle, and the great quantity of air which it contains helps to dissolve the aliment. *Arbuthnot on Aliments.*

MUD. *n. s.* [*modder*, Dutch.] The slime and uliginous matter at the bottom of still water.

The purest spring is not so free from *mud*,
As I am clear from treason. *Shakesp. Henry* VI. *p.* iii.

Water in *mud* doth putrefy, as not able to preserve itself. *Bacon's Nat. Hist.* N°. 696.

The channel was dried up, and the fish left dead and sticking in the *mud*. *L'Estrange.*

The force of the fluid will separate the smallest particles, so as to leave vacant interstices, which will be again filled up by particles carried on by the succeeding fluid, as a bank by the *mud* of the current, which must be reduced to that figure which gives least resistance to the current. *Arbuthnot.*

A fountain in a darksome wood,
Nor stain'd with falling leaves nor rising *mud*. *Addison.*

To MUD. *v. a.* [from the noun.]
1. To bury in the slime or mud.

I wish
Myself were *mudded* in that oozy bed,
Where my son lies. *Shakespeare's Tempest.*

2. To make turbid; to pollute with dirt; to dash with dirt; to fowl by stirring up the sediment.

I shall not stir in the waters which have been already *mudded* by so many contentious enquiries. *Glanville's Scep.*

MU'DDILY. *adv.* [from *muddy.*] Turbidly; with foul mixture.

Lucilius writ not only loosely and *muddily*, with little art, and much less care, but also in a time which was not yet sufficiently purged from barbarism. *Dryden.*

MU'DDINESS. *n. s.* [from *muddy.*] Turbidness; foulness caused by mud, dregs, or sediment.

Our next stage brought us to the mouth of the Tiber: the season of the year, the *muddiness* of the stream, with the many green trees hanging over it, put me in mind of the delightful image that Virgil has given when Æneas took the first view of it. *Addison's Remarks on Italy.*

Turn the bottle upside down; by this means you will not lose one drop, and the froth will conceal the *muddiness*. *Sw.*

To MU'DDLE. *v. a.* [from *mud.*]
1. To make turbid; to foul; to make muddy.

The neighbourhood told him, he did ill to *muddle* the water and spoil the drink. *L'Estrange's Fables.*

Yet let the goddess smile or frown,
Bread we shall eat, or white or brown;
And in a cottage, or a court,
Drink fine champagne, or *muddl'd* port. *Prior.*

2. To make half drunk; to cloud or stupify.

I was for five years often drunk, always *muddled*; they carried me from tavern to tavern. *Arbuth. Hist. of J. Bull.*

Epicurus seems to have had his brains so *muddled* and confounded, that he scarce ever kept in the right way, though the main maxim of his philosophy was to trust to his senses, and follow his nose. *Bentley's Sermons.*

MU'DDY. *adj.* [from *mud.*]
1. Turbid; foul with mud.

A woman mov'd is like a fountain troubled,
Muddy, ill-seeming, thick, bereft of beauty. *Shakespeare.*

Her garments, heavy with their drink,
Pull'd the poor wretch from her melodious lay
To *muddy* death. *Shakespeare's Hamlet.*

Carry it among the whitsters in Datchet mead, and there empty it in the *muddy* ditch close by the Thames. *Shakesp.*

Who can a pure and crystal current bring
From such a *muddy* and polluted spring? *Sandys's Paraph.*

I strove in vain th' infected blood to cure,
Streams will run *muddy* where the spring's impure. *Roscom.*

Till by the fury of the storm full blown,
The *muddy* bottom o'er the clouds is thrown. *Dryden.*

Out of the true fountains of science painters and statuaries are bound to draw, without amusing themselves with dipping in streams which are often *muddy*, at least troubled; I mean the manner of their masters after whom they creep. *Dryden.*

2. Impure; dark; gross.

There's not the smallest orb which thou behold'st,
But in his motion like an angel sings,
Still quiring to the young ey'd cherubims;
Such harmony is in immortal sounds;
But whilst this *muddy* vesture of decay
Doth grosly close us in, we cannot hear it. *Shakespeare.*

If you chuse, for the composition of such ointment, such ingredients as do make the spirits a little more gross or *muddy*, thereby the imagination will fix the better. *Bacon.*

2. A bird so called. *Ains.*
3. Soiled with mud.

His passengers
Expos'd in *muddy* weeds, upon the miry shore. *Dryden.*

4. Dark; not bright.

The black
A more inferior station seeks,
Leaving the fiery red behind,
And mingles in her *muddy* cheeks. *Swift's Miscel.*

5. Cloudy; dull.

Do'st think I am so *muddy*, so unsettl'd,
To appoint myself in this vexation. *Shak. Winter's Tale.*

Yet I,
A dull and *muddy* mettled rascal, peak,
Like John-a-dreams, unpregnant of my cause,
And can say nothing. *Shakespeare's Hamlet.*

To MU'DDY. *v. a.* [from *mud.*] To make muddy; to cloud; to disturb.

The people *muddied*
Thick and unwholesome in their thoughts and whispers. *Shakespeare's Hamlet.*

Excess, either with an apoplexy, knocks a man on the head; or with a fever, like fire in a strong-water-shop, burns him down to the ground; or if it flames not out, charks him to a coal; *muddies* the best wit, and makes it only to flutter and froth high. *Grew's Cosmol. b.* iii.

MU'DSUCKER. *n. s.* [*mud* and *suck.*] A sea fowl.

In all water-fowl, their legs and feet correspond to that way of life; and in *mudsuckers*, two of the toes are somewhat joined, that they may not easily sink. *Derham.*

MUDWA'LL. *n. s.* [*mud* and *wall.*]
1. A wall built without mortar, by throwing up mud and suffering it to dry.

If conscience contract rust or soil, a man may as well expect to see his face in a *mudwall*, as that such a conscience should give him a true report of his condition. *South's Serm.*

2. A bird so called. *Ains.*

MUDWA'LLED. *adj.* [*mud* and *wall.*] Having a mudwall.

As folks from *mudwall'd* tenement
Bring landlords pepper-corn for rent;
Present a turkey, or a hen,
To those might better spare them ten. *Prior.*

To MUE. *v. a.* [*muer*, Fr.] To moult; to change feathers.
MUFF. *n. s.* [*muff*, Swedish.] A soft cover for the hands in Winter.

Feel but the difference soft and rough,
This a gantlet, that a *muff*. *Cleaveland.*

What! no more favours, not a ribbon more,
Not fan, not *muff*. *Suckling.*

The lady of the spotted *muff* began. *Dryden.*

A child that stands in the dark upon his mother's *muff*, says he stands upon something, he knows not what. *Locke.*

To MU'FFLE. *v. a.* [from *moufle*, French, a winter glove.]
1. To cover from the weather.

His *muffled* feature speaks him a recluse,
His ruins prove him a religious house. *Cleaveland.*

You must be *muffled* up like ladies. *Dryden.*

The face lies *muffled* up within the garment. *Addison.*

2. To blindfold.

Alas that love, whose view is *muffled* still,
Should without eyes see pathways to his ill. *Shakespeare.*

We've

We've caught the woodcock, and will keep him *muffled.* *Shakesp. All's well that ends well.*

Our underſtandings lie grovelling in this lower region, *muffled* up in miſts and darkneſs. *Glanville's Scep.*

Loſs of ſight is the miſery of life, and uſually the forerunner of death: when the malefactor comes once to be *muffled*, and the fatal cloth drawn over his eyes, we know that he is not far from his execution. *South's Sermons.*

Bright Lucifer
That night his heav'nly form obſcur'd with tears;
And ſince he was forbid to leave the ſkies,
He *muffled* with a cloud his mournful eyes. *Dryden.*

One *muffled* up in the infallibility of his ſect, will not enter into debate with a perſon that will queſtion any of thoſe things which to him are ſacred. *Locke.*

3. To conceal; to involve.

This is one of the ſtrongeſt examples of a perſonation that ever was: although the king's manner of ſhewing things by pieces, and by dark lights, hath ſo *muffled* it, that it hath left it almoſt as a myſtery. *Bacon's Henry VII.*

No *muffling* clouds, nor ſhades infernal, can
From his inquiry hide offending man. *Sandys's Paraph.*

The thoughts of kings are like religious groves,
The walks of *muffled* gods. *Dryden's Don Sebaſtian.*

They were in former ages *muffled* up in darkneſs and ſuperſtition. *Arbuthnot's Hiſt. of John Bull.*

To Mu'ffle. *v. n.* [*maffelen, moffelen*, Dutch.] To ſpeak inwardly; to ſpeak without clear and diſtinct articulation.

The freedom or apertneſs and vigour of pronouncing, as in the Bocca Romana, and giving ſomewhat more of aſpiration; and the cloſeneſs and *muffling*, and lazineſs of ſpeaking, render the ſound of ſpeech different. *Holder.*

Mu'ffler. *n. ſ.* [from *muffle.*]

1. A cover for the face.

Fortune is painted with a *muffler* before her eyes, to ſignify to you that fortune is blind. *Shakeſp. Henry V.*

Mr. Hales has found out the beſt expedients for preventing immediate ſuffocation from tainted air, by breathing through *mufflers* which imbibe theſe vapours. *Arbuthnot on Air.*

2. A part of a woman's dreſs by which the face was covered.

There is no woman's gown big enough for him; otherwiſe he might put on a hat, a *muffler*, and a handkerchief, and ſo eſcape. *Shakeſp. Merry Wives of Windſor.*

The Lord will take away your tinkling ornaments, chains, bracelets, and *mufflers.* *Iſa.* iii. 19.

Mufti. *n. ſ.* [a Turkiſh word.] The high prieſt of the Mahometans.

MUG. *n. ſ.* [*Skinner* derives it from *mwgl*, Welſh, warm.] A cup to drink in.

Ah Bowzybee, why didſt thou ſtay ſo long?
The *mugs* were large, the drink was wond'rous ſtrong. *Gay.*

Mu'ggy. }
Mu'ggish. } *adj.* [A cant word.] Moiſt; damp; mouldy.

Cover with ſtones, or *muggy* ſtraw, to keep it moiſt. *Mortimer's Huſbandry.*

Mu'ghouse. *n. ſ.* [*mug* and *houſe.*] An alehouſe; a low houſe of entertainment.

Our ſex has dar'd the *mughouſe* chiefs to meet,
And purchas'd fame in many a well fought ſtreet. *Tickell.*

Mu'gient. *adj.* [*mugiens*, Latin.] Bellowing.

That a bittern maketh that *mugient* noiſe or bumping, by putting its bill into a reed, or by putting the ſame in water or mud, and after a while retaining the air, but ſuddenly excluding it again, is not eaſily made out. *Brown.*

Mu'gwort. *n. ſ.* [mugpyꞃꞇ, Saxon; *artemiſia*, Lat.]

The flowers and fruit of the *mugwort* are very like thoſe of the wormwood, but grow erect upon the branches: the flowers are of a purpliſh colour, and the leaves terminate in ſharp points cut into many ſegments; they are of a dark green on the upper ſide, and hoary on the under ſide. *Miller.*

Some of the moſt common ſimples with us in England are comfry, bugle, Paul's-betony, and *mugwort.* *Wiſeman.*

MULA'TTO. n. ſ. [Spaniſh; *mulat*, French, from *mulus*, Lat.] One begot between a white and a black, as a mule between different ſpecies of animals.

Mu'lberry. }
Mu'lberry *tree.* } *n. ſ.* [moꞃbeꞃıᵹ, Saxon; *morus*, Lat.]

The *mulberry tree* hath large, rough, roundiſh leaves; the male flowers, or katkins, which have a calyx conſiſting of four leaves, are ſometimes produced upon ſeparate trees, at other times at remote diſtances from the fruit on the ſame tree: the fruit is compoſed of ſeveral protuberances, to each of which adhere four ſmall leaves; the ſeeds are roundiſh, growing ſingly in each protuberance; it is planted for the delicacy of the fruit. The white *mulberry* is commonly cultivated for its leaves to feed ſilkworms, in France and Italy, though the Perſians always make uſe of the common black *mulberry* for that purpoſe. *Miller.*

Morton, archbiſhop of Canterbury, was content to uſe *mor* upon a *tun*; and ſometimes a *mulberry tree*, called morus in Latin, out of a tun. *Camden's Remains.*

The ripeſt *mulberry*,
That will not hold the handling. *Shakeſp. Coriolanus.*

A body black, round, with ſmall grain like tubercles on the ſurface; not very unlike a *mulberry.* *Woodward's Foſſils.*

Mulct. *n. ſ.* [*mulcta*, Latin.] A fine; a penalty: uſed commonly of pecuniary penalty.

Becauſe this is a great part, and Euſebius hath yet ſaid nothing, we will, by way of *mulct* or pain, lay it upon him. *Bacon's holy War.*

Look humble upward, ſee his will diſcloſe
The forfeit firſt, and then the fine impoſe;
A *mulct* thy poverty could never pay,
Had not eternal wiſdom found the way. *Dryden.*

To Mulct. *v. a.* [*mulcto*, Lat. *mulcter*, Fr.] To puniſh with fine or forfeiture.

Marriage without conſent of parents they do not make void, but they *mulct* it in the inheritors; for the children of ſuch marriages are not admitted to inherit above a third part of their parents inheritance. *Bacon's New Atlantis.*

Mule. *n. ſ.* [*mule, mulet*, Fr. *mula*, Latin.] An animal generated between a he aſs and a mare, or ſometimes between a horſe and a ſhe aſs.

You have among you many a purchas'd ſlave,
Which, like your aſſes, and your dogs, and *mules*,
You uſe in abject and in ſlaviſh part. *Shakeſpeare.*

Five hundred aſſes yearly took the horſe,
Producing *mules* of greater ſpeed and force. *Sandys.*

Thoſe effluvia in the male ſeed have the greateſt ſtroke in generation, as is demonſtrable in a *mule*, which doth more reſemble the parent, that is, the aſs, than the female. *Ray.*

Twelve young *mules*, a ſtrong laborious race. *Pope.*

Mulete'er. *n. ſ.* [*muletier*, Fr. *mulio*, Lat.] Mule-driver; horſe-boy.

Baſe *muleteers*,
Like peaſant foot-boys, do they keep the walls,
And dare not take up arms like gentlemen. *Shakeſpeare.*

Your ſhips are not well mann'd,
Your mariners are *muleteers*, reapers. *Shakeſpeare.*

Mulie'brity. *n. ſ.* [*muliebris*, Lat.] Womanhood; the contrary to virility; the manners and character of woman.

To Mull. *v. a.* [*mollitus*, Latin.]

1. To ſoften and diſpirit, as wine is when burnt and ſweetened. *Hanmer.*

Peace is a very apoplexy, lethargy
Mull'd, deaf, ſleepy, inſenſible. *Shakeſp. Coriolanus.*

2. To heat any liquor, and ſweeten and ſpice it.

Drink new cyder *mull'd*, with ginger warm. *Gay.*

Mu'llar. *n. ſ.* [*mouleur*, French.] A ſtone held in the hand with which any powder is ground upon a horizotal ſtone. It is now often called improperly *mullet.*

The beſt grinder is the porphyry, white or green marble, with a *mullar* or upper ſtone of the ſame, cut very even without flaws or holes; you may make a *mullar* alſo of a flat pebble, by grinding it ſmooth at a grind-ſtone. *Peacham.*

Mulle'in. *n. ſ.* [*verbaſcum*, Lat.] A plant.

The flower of the *mullein* conſiſts of one leaf, which expands in a circular form, and is cut into ſeveral ſegments; out of the centre ariſes the pointal, which afterward becomes an oval-pointed fruit, divided into two cells by a middle partition filled with ſmall angular ſeeds. *Miller.*

Mu'llet. *n. ſ.* [*mullus*, Lat. *mulet*, Fr.] A ſea fiſh.

Of carps and *mullets* why prefer the great?
Yet for ſmall turbots ſuch eſteem profeſs. *Pope's Horace.*

Mull'grubs. *n. ſ.* Twiſting of the guts. *Ainſ.*

Mu'llock. *n. ſ.* Rubbiſh. *Ainſ.*

Mulse. *n. ſ.* Wine boiled and mingled with honey. *Dict.*

Multa'ngular. [*multus* and *angulus*, Lat.] Many cornered; having many corners; polygonal.

Multa'ngularly. *adv.* [from *multangular.*] Polygonally; with many corners.

Granates are *multangularly* round. *Grew's Coſmol. b.* i.

Multa'ngularness. [from *multangular.*] The ſtate of being polygonal, or having many corners.

Multica'psular. *adj.* [*multus* and *capſula*, Latin.] Divided into many partitions or cells. *Dict.*

Multica'vous. *adj.* [*multus* and *cavus*, Lat.] Full of holes. *Dict.*

Multifa'rious. *adj.* [*multifarius*, Lat.] Having great multiplicity; having different reſpects; having great diverſity in itſelf.

There is a *multifarious* artifice in the ſtructure of the meaneſt animal. *More's Divine Dialogues.*

When we conſider this ſo *multifarious* congruity of things in reference to ourſelves, how can we with-hold from inferring, that that which made both dogs and ducks made them with a reference to us? *More's Antidotes againſt Atheiſm.*

His ſcience is not moved by the guſts of fancy and humour, which blow up and down the *multifarious* opinioniſts. *Glanville to Albius.*

We could not think of a more comprehensive expedient, whereby to assist the frail and torpent memory through so *multifarious* and numerous an employment. *Evelyn's Kalend.*

MULTIFA'RIOUSLY. *adv.* [from *multifarious.*] With multiplicity.

If only twenty-four parts may be so *multifariously* placed, as to make many millions of differing rows: in the supposition of a thousand parts, how immense must that capacity of variation be? *Bentley's Sermons.*

MULTIFA'RIOUSNESS. *n. s.* [from *multifarious.*] Multiplied diversity.

According to the *multifariousness* of this imitability, so are the possibilities of being. *Norris's Miscel.*

MULTI'FIDOUS. *adj.* [*multifidus*, Latin.] Having many partitions; cleft into many branches.

These animals are only excluded without sight which are multiparous and *multifidous*, which have many at a litter, and have feet divided into many portions. *Brown.*

MU'LTIFORM. *adj.* [*multiformis*, Lat.] Having various shapes or appearances.

Ye that in quaterion run
Perpetual circle, *multiform.* *Milton.*

The best way to convince is proving, by ocular demonstration, the *multiform* and amazing operations of the air-pump and the load-stone. *Watts.*

MULTIFO'RMITY. *n. s.* [*multiformis*, Lat.] Diversity of shapes or appearances subsisting in the same thing.

MULTILA'TERAL. *adj.* [*multus* and *lateralis*, Latin.] Having many sides. *Dict.*

MULTI'LOQUOUS. *adj.* [*multiloquus*, Latin.] Very talkative. *Dict.*

MULTINO'MINAL. *adj.* [*multus* and *nomen*, Lat.] Having many names. *Dict.*

MULTI'PAROUS. *n. s.* [*multiparus*, Lat.] Bringing many at a birth.

Double formations do often happen to *multiparous* generations, more especially that of serpents, whose conceptions being numerous, and their eggs in chains, they may unite into various shapes, and come out in mixed formations. *Brown.*

Animals feeble and timorous are generally *multiparous*; or if they bring forth but few at once, as pigeons, they compensate that by their often breeding. *Ray on the Creation.*

MULTIPE'DE. *n. s.* [*multipeda*, Latin.] An insect with many feet; a sow or wood-louse. *Bailey.*

MU'LTIPLE. *adj.* [*multiplex*, Latin.] A term in arithmetick, when one number contains another several times: as, nine is the *multiple* of three, containing it three times. Manifold.

MU'LTIPLIABLE. *adj.* [*multipliable*, Fr. from *multiply.*] Capable to be multiplied.

MULTIPLI'ABLENESS. *n. s.* [from *multipliable.*] Capacity of being multiplied.

MULTIPLICA'BLE. *adj.* [from *multiplico*, Latin.] Capable of being arithmetically multiplied.

MULTIPLICA'ND. *n. s.* [*multiplicandus*, Latin.] The number to be multiplied in arithmetick.

Multiplication hath the *multiplicand*, or number to be multiplied; the multiplier, or number given, by which the *multiplicand* is to be multiplied, and the product, or number produced by the other two. *Cocker's Arithmetick.*

MULTIPLICA'TE. *n. s.* [from *multiplico*, Latin.] Consisting of more than one.

In this *multiplicate* number of the eye, the object seen is not multiplied, and appears but one, though seen with two or more eyes. *Derham's Physico-Theol.*

MULTIPLICA'TION. *n. s.* [*multiplication*, Fr. *multiplicatio*, Lat.]

1. The act of multiplying or increasing any number by addition or production of more of the same kind.

Although they had divers stiles for God, yet under many appellations they acknowledged one divinity; rather conceiving thereby the evidence or acts of his power in several ways than a *multiplication* of essence, or real distractions of unity in any one. *Brown's Vulgar Errours, b.* i.

2. [In arithmetick.]

Multiplication is the increasing of any one number by another, so often as there are units in that number, by which the one is increased. *Cocker's Arithmetick.*

A man had need be a good arithmetician to understand this author's works: his description runs on like a *multiplication* table. *Addison on ancient Medals.*

MULTIPLICA'TOR. *n. s.* [*multiplicateur*, Fr. from *multiplico*, Lat.] The number by which another number is multiplied.

MULTILPI'CITY. *n. s.* [*multiplicité*, French.]

1. More than one of the same kind.

Had they discoursed rightly but upon this one principle, that God was a being infinitely perfect, they could never have asserted a *multiplicity* of gods: for, can one God include in him all perfection, and another God include in him all perfections too? Can there be any more than all? And if this all be in one, can it be also in another? *South's Sermons.*

Company, he thinks, lessens the shame of vice, by sharing it; and abates the torrent of a common odium, by deriving it into many channels; and therefore if he cannot wholly avoid the eye of the observer, he hopes to distract it at least by a *multiplicity* of the object. *South's Sermons.*

2. State of being many.

You equal Donne in the variety, *multiplicity*, and choice of thoughts. *Dryden's Dedication to Juvenal.*

MULTIPLI'CIOUS. *n. s.* [*multiplex*, Latin.] Manifold. Not used.

Amphisbæna is not an animal of one denomination; for properly that animal is not one, but *multiplicious* or many, which hath a duplicity or gemination of principal parts. *Brown.*

MULTIPLI'ER. *n. s.* [from *multiply.*]

1. One who multiplies or increases the number of any thing.

Broils and quarrels are alone the great accumulators and *multipliers* of injuries. *Decay of Piety.*

2. The multiplicator in arithmetick.

Multiplication hath the multiplicand, the *multiplier*, or number given, by which the multiplicand is to be multiplied. *Cocker's Arithmetick.*

To MU'LTIPLY. *v. a.* [*multiplier*, Fr. *multiplico*, Lat.]

1. To increase in number; to make more by generation, accumulation, or addition.

He clappeth his hands amongst us, and *multiplieth* his words against God. *Job* xxxiv. 37.

He shall not *multiply* horses. *Deut.* xvii. 16.

His birth to our just fear gave no small cause,
But his growth now to youth's full flower displaying
All virtue, grace, and wisdom, to atchieve
Things highest, greatest, *multiplies* my fears. *Milton.*

2. To perform the process of arithmetical multiplication.

From one stock of seven hundred years, *multiplying* still by twenty, we shall find the product to be one thousand three hundred forty-seven millions three hundred sixty-eight thousand four hundred and twenty. *Brown's Vulgar Err. b.* vi.

To MU'LTIPLY. *v. n.*

1. To grow in number.

The *multiplying* brood of the ungodly shall not thrive. *Wisd.* iv. 3.

2. To increase themselves.

The *multiplying* villanies of nature
Do swarm upon him. *Shakespeare's Macbeth.*

We see the infinitely fruitful and productive power of this way of sinning; how it can increase and *multiply* beyond all bounds and measures of actual commission. *South's Sermons.*

MULTI'POTENT. *adj.* [*multus* and *potens*, Lat.] Having manifold power; having power to do many different things.

By Jove *multipotent*,
Thou should'st not bear from me a Greekish member. *Shakespeare's Troil. and Cressida.*

MULTIPRE'SENCE. *n. s.* [*multus* and *præsentia*, Latin.] The power or act of being present in more places than one at the same time.

This sleeveless tale of transubstantiation was surely brought into the world, and upon the stage, by that other fable of the *multipresence* of Christ's body. *Hall.*

MULTI'SCIOUS. *adj.* [*multiscius*, Latin.] Having variety of knowledge.

MULTISILI'QUOUS. *adj.* [*multus* and *siliqua*, Lat.] The same with corniculate: used of plants, whose seed is contained in many distinct seed-vessels. *Baily.*

MULTI'SONOUS. *adj.* [*multisonus*, Lat.] Having many sounds. *Dict.*

MU'LTITUDE. *n. s.* [*multitude*, Fr. *multitudo*, Lat.]

1. The state of being many; the state of being more than one.

2. Number; many; more than one.

It is impossible that any *multitude* can be actually infinite, or so great that there cannot be a greater. *Hale.*

3. A great number; loosely and indefinitely.

It is a fault in a *multitude* of preachers, that they utterly neglect method in their harangues. *Watts.*

4. A crowd or throng; the vulgar.

He the vast hissing *multitude* admires. *Addison.*

MULTITU'DINOUS. *adj.* [from *multitude.*]

1. Having the appearance of a multitude.

Will all great Neptune's ocean wash this blood
Clean from my hand? No, this my hand will rather
Thy *multitudinous* sea incarnardine,
Making the green one red. *Shakespeare's Macbeth.*

2. Manifold.

At once pluck out
The *multitudinous* tongue, let them not lick
The sweet that is their poison. *Shakespeare.*

MULTI'VAGANT. } *adj.* [*multivagus*, Latin.] That wanders or
MULTI'VAGOUS. } strays much abroad. *Dict.*

MULTI'VIOUS. *adj.* [*multus* and *via*, Lat.] Having many ways; manifold. *Dict.*

MULTO'CULAR. *adj.* [*multus* and *oculus*, Latin.] Having more eyes than two.

Flies are *multocular*, having as many eyes as there are perforations in their corneæ. *Derham's Physico-Theology.*

MUM. *interjeƈt.* [Of this word I know not the original: it may be obſerved, that when it is pronounced it leaves the lips cloſed.] A word denoting prohibition to ſpeak, or reſolution not to ſpeak; ſilence; huſh.

Mum then, and no more proceed. *Shakeſp. Tempeſt.*
Well ſaid, maſter; *mum!* and gaze your fill. *Shakeſp.*
The citizens are *mum*, ſay not a word. *Shak. Rich.* III.
Intruſt it under ſolemn vows
Of *mum*, and ſilence, and the roſe. *Hudibras, p.* iii.

MUM. *n. ſ.* [*mumme*, German.] Ale brewed with wheat.

In Shenibank, upon the river Elbe, is a ſtorehouſe for the wheat of which *mum* is made at Brunſwick. *Mortimer.*

Sedulous and ſtout
With bowls of fat'ning *mum*. *Philips.*
The clam'rous crowd is huſh'd with mugs of *mum*,
Till all tun'd equal ſend a general hum. *Pope.*

To MU'MBLE. *v. n.* [*mompelen*, Dutch; *mutio*, Lat.]

1. To ſpeak inwardly; to grumble; to mutter; to ſpeak with imperfect ſound or articulation.

As one then in a dream, whoſe drier brain
Is toſt with troubled ſights, and fancies weake
He *mumbled* ſoft, but would not all his ſilence break.
Fairy Queen, b. i.

Peace, you *mumbling* fool;
Utter your gravity o'er a goſſip's bowl. *Shakeſpeare.*
A wrinkled hag, with age grown double,
Picking dry ſticks, and *mumbling* to herſelf. *Otway.*

2. To chew; to bite ſoftly; to eat with the lips cloſe.

The man, who laugh'd but once to ſee an aſs
Mumbling to make the groſs-grain'd thiſtles paſs,
Might laugh again to ſee a jury chaw
The prickles of unpalateable law. *Dryden.*

To MU'MBLE. *v. a.*

1. To utter with a low inarticulate voice.

Some carrytale, ſome pleaſeman, ſome ſlight zany,
Some *mumble*-news; told our intents before. *Shakeſpeare.*
Here ſtood he in the dark,
Mumbling of wicked charms, conj'ring the moon
To ſtand 's auſpicious miſtreſs. *Shakeſp. King Lear.*
He
With *mumbl'd* pray'rs attones the deity. *Dryden's Juv.*

2. To mouth gently.

Spaniels civilly delight
In *mumbling* of the game they dare not bite. *Pope.*

3. To ſlubber over; to ſuppreſs; to utter imperfectly.

The raiſing of my rabble is an exploit of conſequence; and not to be *mumbled* up in ſilence for all her pertneſs. *Dry.*

MU'MBLER. *n. ſ.* [from *mumble.*] One that ſpeaks inarticulately; a mutterer.

MU'MBLINGLY. *adv.* [from *mumbling.*] With inarticulate utterance.

To MUMM. *v. a.* [*mumme*, Daniſh.] To maſk; to frolick in diſguiſe.

The thriftleſs games
With *mumming* and with maſking all around. *Hubberd.*

MU'MMER. *n. ſ.* [*mumme*, Daniſh.] A maſker; one who performs frolicks in a perſonated dreſs.

If you chance to be pinch'd with the colick, you make faces like *mummers*. *Shakeſp. Coriolanus.*
Jugglers and dancers, anticks, *mummers*. *Milton.*
I began to ſmoke that they were a parcel of *mummers*. *Add.*
Peel'd, patch'd and pyebald, linſey-woolſey brothers;
Grave *mummers!* *Pope's Dunciad, b.* iii.

MU'MMERY. *n. ſ.* [*momerie*, French.] Maſking; frolick in maſks; foolery.

Here mirth's but *mummery*,
And ſorrows only real be. *Wotton.*
This open day-light doth not ſhew the maſques and *mummeries*, and triumphs of the world, half ſo ſtately as candle-light. *Bacon's Nat. Hiſt.* N°. 1.
Your fathers
Diſdain'd the *mummery* of foreign ſtrollers. *Fenton.*

MU'MMY. *n. ſ.* [*mumie*, Fr. *mumia*, Lat. derived by *Salmaſius* from *amomum*, by *Bochart* from the Arabick.]

1. A dead body preſerved by the Egyptian art of embalming.

We have two different ſubſtances preſerved for medicinal uſe under the name of *mummy:* one is the dried fleſh of human bodies embalmed with myrrh and ſpice; the other is the liquor running from ſuch *mummies* when newly prepared, or when affected by great heat, or by damps: this is ſometimes of a liquid, ſometimes of a ſolid form, as it is preſerved in vials well ſtopped, or ſuffered to dry and harden in the air: the firſt kind is brought to us in large pieces, of a lax and friable texture, light and ſpungy, of a blackiſh brown colour, and often black and clammy on the ſurface; it is of a ſtrong but not agreeable ſmell: the ſecond ſort, in its liquid ſtate, is a thick, opake, and viſcous fluid, of a blackiſh and a ſtrong, but not diſagreeable ſmell: in its indurated ſtate it is a dry, ſolid ſubſtance, of a fine ſhining black colour and cloſe texture, eaſily broken, and of a good ſmell: this ſort is extremely dear, and the firſt ſort ſo cheap, that as all kinds of *mummy* are brought from Egypt we are not to imagine it to be the ancient Egyptian *mummy*. What our druggiſts are ſupplied with is the fleſh of executed criminals, or of any other bodies the Jews can get, who fill them with the common bitumen ſo plentiful in that part of the world, and adding aloes, and ſome other cheap ingredients, ſend them to be baked in an oven till the juices are exhaled, and the embalming matter has penetrated ſo thoroughly that the fleſh will keep. *Mummy* has been eſteemed reſolvent and balſamick; and beſides it, the ſkull, and even the moſs growing on the ſkulls of human ſkeletons, have been celebrated for antiepileptick virtues; the fat alſo of the human body has been recommended in rheumatiſms, and every other part or humour have been in repute for the cure of ſome diſeaſe: at preſent we are wiſe enough to know, that the virtues aſcribed to the parts of the human body are all either imaginary, or ſuch as may be found in other animal ſubſtances: the *mummy* and the ſkull alone of all theſe horrid medicines retain their places in the ſhops. *Hill's Mat. Med.*

The ſilk
Was dy'd in *mummy*, which the ſkilful
Conſerv'd of maidens hearts. *Shakeſp. Othello.*

It is ſtrange how long carcaſes have continued uncorrupt, as appeareth in the *mummies* of Egypt, having laſted ſome of them three thouſand years. *Bacon's Nat. Hiſt.* N°. 771.

Sav'd by ſpice, like *mummies*, many a year,
Old bodies of philoſophy appear. *Dunciad, b.* i.

2. *Mummy* is uſed among gardeners for a ſort of wax uſed in the planting and grafting of trees. *Chambers.*

3. *To beat to a* MUMMY. To beat ſoundly. *Ainſ.*

To MUMP. *v. a.* [*mompelin*, Dutch.]

1. To nibble; to bite quick; to chew with a continued motion.

Let him not pry nor liſten,
Nor friſk about the houſe
Like a tame *mumping* ſquirrel with a bell on. *Otway.*

2. To talk low and quick.

3. [In cant language.] To go a begging. *Ainſ.*

MU'MPER. *n. ſ.* [In cant language.] A beggar.

MUMPS. *n. ſ.* [*mompelen*, Dutch.] Sullenneſs; ſilent anger. *Skinner.*

MUMPS. *n. ſ.* The ſquinancy. *Ainſ.*

To MUNCH. *v. a.* [*manger*, French.] To chew by great mouthfuls.

Say, ſweet love, what thou deſir'ſt to eat?
—Truly, a peck of provender; I could *munch* you good dry oats. *Shakeſpeare's Midſummer Night's Dream.*

To MUNCH. *v. n.* To chew eagerly by great mouthfuls.

It is the ſon of a mare that's broken looſe, and *munching* upon the melons. *Dryden's Don Sebaſtian.*

MU'NCHER. *n. ſ.* [from *munch.*] One that munches.

MUND. *n. ſ.*

Mund is peace, from which our lawyers call a breach of the peace, *mundbrech:* ſo Eadmund is happy peace; Æthelmund, noble peace; Ælmund, all peace; with which theſe are much of the ſame import: Irenæus, Heſychius, Lenis, Pacatus, Sedatus, Tranquillus, &c. *Gibſon's Camden.*

MUNDA'NE. *adj.* [*mundanus*, Lat.] Belonging to the world.

The platonical hypotheſis of a *mundane* ſoul will relieve us. *Glanville's Scep.*

The atoms which now conſtitute heaven and earth, being once ſeparate in the *mundane* ſpace, could never without God, by their mechanical affections, have convened into this preſent frame of things. *Bentley's Sermons.*

MUNDA'TION. *n. ſ.* [*mundus*, Lat.] The act of cleanſing.

MUNDA'TORY. *adj.* [from *mundus*, Lat.] Having the power to cleanſe.

MU'NDICK. *n. ſ.* A kind of marcaſite or ſemimetal found in tin mines.

When any metals were in conſiderable quantity, theſe bodies loſe the name of marcaſites, and are called ores: in Cornwal and the Weſt they call them *mundick*. *Woodward.*

Beſides ſtones, all the ſorts of *mundick* are naturally figured. *Grew's Coſmol. b.* i.

MUNDIFICA'TION. *n. ſ.* [*mundus* and *facio*, Latin.] Cleanſing any body, as from droſs, or matter of inferior account to what is to be cleanſed. *Quincy.*

MUNDI'FICATIVE. *adj.* [*mundus* and *facio*, Lat.] Cleanſing; having the power to cleanſe.

Gall is very *mundificative*, and was a proper medicine to clear the eyes of Tobit. *Brown's Vulgar Errours, b.* i.

We incarned with an addition to the fore-mentioned *mundicative*. *Wiſeman's Surgery.*

To MU'NDIFY. *v. a.* [*mundus* and *facio*, Lat.] To cleanſe; to make clean.

Simple wounds, ſuch as are *mundified* and kept clean, do not need any other hand but that of nature. *Brown.*

The ingredients actuate the ſpirits, abſorb the inteſtinal ſuperfluities, reclude oppilation, and *mundify* the blood. *Harvey on the Plague.*

MUNDI'VAGANT. *adj.* [*mundivagus*, Lat.] Wandering through the world. *Dict.*

MUNDU'NGUS. *n. s.* Stinking tobacco. *Bailey.*

MU'NERARY. *adj.* [from *munus*, Lat.] Having the nature of a gift.

MU'NGREL. *n. s.* [frequently written *mongrel*. See MONGREL.] Any thing generated between different kinds; any thing partaking of the qualities of different causes or parents.

Mastiff, greyhound, *mungrel* grim,
Hound or spaniel, brache or hym,
Or bobtail tike, or trundle tail. *Shakesp.*

MU'NGREL. *adj.* Generated between different natures; baseborn; degenerate.

Thou art nothing but the composition of a knave, beggar, coward, pander, and the son and heir of a *mungrel* bitch. *Shakesp. King Lear.*

My people are grown half wild, they would not precipitate themselves else into such a mixt *mungrel* war. *Howel.*

Mungrel curs bawl, snarle and snap, where the fox flies before them, and clap their tails between the legs when an adversary makes head against them. *L'Estrange.*

A foreign son is sought and a mix'd *mungrel* brood. *Dry.*

MUNI'CIPAL. *adj.* [*municipal*, Fr. *municipalis*, *municipium*, Lat.] Belonging to a corporation.

A counsellor, bred up in the knowledge of the *municipal* and statute laws, may honestly inform a just prince how far his prerogative extends. *Dryden.*

MUNI'FICENCE. *n. s.* [*munificence*, Fr. *munificentia*, Lat.] Liberality; the act of giving.

A state of poverty obscures all the virtues of liberality and *munificence*. *Addison's Spectator*, Nº 257.

2. In *Spenser* it is used, as it seems, for fortification or strength, from *munitiones facere*.

Their importune sway
This land invaded with like violence,
Until that Locrine for his realms defence,
Did head against them make, and strong *munificence*. *Fairy Queen, b.* ii.

MUNIFICENT. *adj.* [*munificus*, Lat.] Liberal; generous.

Is he not our most *munificent* benefactor, our wisest counsellor and most potent protector. *Atterbury.*

MUNIFICENTLY. *adv.* [from *munificent.*] Liberally; generously.

MU'NIMENT. *n. s.* [*munimentum*, Lat.]

1. Fortification; strong hold.
2. Support; defence.

The arm our soldier,
Or steed the leg, the tongue our trumpeter;
With other *muniments* and petty helps
In this our fabrick. *Shakesp. Coriolanus.*

To MUNI'TE. *v. a.* [*munio*, Lat.] To fortify; to strengthen. A word not in use.

Heat doth attenuate, and the more gross and tangible parts contract, both to avoid vacuum, and to *munite* themselves against the force of the fire. *Bacon's Nat. Hist.*

Men, in the procuring or *muniting* of religious unity, must not dissolve the laws of charity and human society. *Bacon.*

MUNI'TION. *n. s.* [*munition*, Fr. *munitio*, Lat.]

1. Fortification; strong hold.

Victors under-pin their acquests jure belli, that they might not be lost by the continuation of external forces of standing armies, castles, garrisons, *munitions*. *Hale.*

2. Ammunition; materials for war.

What penny hath Rome borne,
What men provided, what *munition* sent,
To underprop this action? *Shakesp. King John.*

The king of Tripolie in every hold
Shut up his men, *munition* and his treasure. *Fairfax.*

It is a little city, strong and well stored with *munition*. *Sandys's Journey.*

MU'NNION. *n. s.*

The upright posts, that divide the several lights in a window frame, are called *munnions*. *Moxon.*

MU'RAGE. *n. s.* [from *murus*, Lat.] Money paid to keep walls in repair.

MU'RAL. *adj.* [*muralis*, *urus*, Lat.] Pertaining to a wall.

And repair'd
Her *mural* breach, returning whence it rowl'd. *Milton.*

In the nectarine and the like delicate *mural* fruit, the later your pruning, the better. *Evelyn's Kalendar.*

A soldier would venture his life for a *mural* crown. *Addis.*

MU'RDER. *n. s.* [moꝛðoꝛ, moꝛben, Sax. *murdrum*, law Lat. the etymology requires that it should be written, as it anciently often was, *murther*; but of late the word itself has commonly, and its derivatives universally, been written with *d.*] The act of killing a man unlawfully; the act of killing criminally.

Kill men i' th' dark! where be these bloody thieves?
Ho *murder*! *murder*! *Shakesp. Othello.*

Now witchcraft celebrates
Pale Hecate's offerings; and wither'd *murder*,
With Tarquin's ravishing strides, towards his design
Moves like a ghost. *Shakesp. Macbeth.*

Blood hath been shed ere now, i' th' olden time,
Ere human statute purg'd the general weal;
Ay, and since too, *murders* have been perform'd
Too terrible for th' ear. *Shakesp. Macbeth.*

Slaughter grows *murder* when it goes too far,
And makes a massacre what was a war. *Dryden.*

The killing of their children had, in the account of God, the guilt of *murder*, as the offering them to idols had the guilt of idolatry. *Locke.*

To MU'RDER. *v. a.* [from the noun.]

1. To kill a man unlawfully.

If he dies, I *murder* him, not they. *Dryden.*

2. To destroy; to put an end to.

Can'st thou quake and change thy colour,
Murder thy breath in middle of a word,
And then again begin, and stop again. *Shakesp.*

Let the mutinous winds
Strike the proud cedars to the fiery sun;
Murd'ring impossibility, to make
What cannot be, slight work. *Shakesp. Coriolanus.*

MU'RDERER. *n. s.* [from *murder.*] One who has shed human blood unlawfully; one who has killed a man criminally.

Thou dost kill me with thy unkind falsehood, and it grieves me not to die; but it grieves me that thou art the *murderer*. *Sidney, b.* ii.

I am his host,
Who should against his *murd'rer* shut the door,
Not bear the knife myself. *Shakesp. Macbeth.*

Thou tell'st me there is *murder* in mine eyes;
'Tis pretty sure,
That eyes, that are the frail'st and softest things,
Who shut their coward gates on atomies,
Should be call'd tyrants, butchers, *murderers*. *Shak.*

The very horrour of the fact had stupified all curiosity, and so dispersed the multitude, that even the *murderer* himself might have escaped. *Wotton.*

Like some rich or mighty *murderer*,
Too great for prison, which he breaks with gold,
Who fresher for new mischiefs does appear,
And dares the world to tax him with the old. *Dryden.*

This stranger having had a brother killed by the conspirator, and having till now sought in vain for an opportunity of revenge, chanced to meet the *murderer* in the temple. *Addison's Guardian*, Nº 177.

With equal terrors, not with equal guilt,
The *murderer* dreams of all the blood he spilt. *Swift.*

MU'RDERESS. *n. s.* [from *murderer.*] A woman that commits murder.

When by thy scorn, O *murd'ress*! I am dead,
Then shall my ghost come to thy bed,
And thee feign'd vestal in worse arms shall see. *Donne.*

Diana's vengeance on the victor shown,
The *murd'ress* mother, and consuming son. *Dryden.*

Art thou the *murd'ress* then of wretched Laius. *Dryden.*

MU'RDERMENT. *n. s.* [from *murder.*] The act of killing unlawfully.

To her came message of the *murderment*. *Fairfax.*

MU'RDEROUS. *adj.* [from *murder.*] Bloody; guilty of murder; addicted to blood.

Upon thy eye-balls *murd'rous* tyranny
Sits in grim majesty to fright the world. *Shakesp.*

Oh *murd'rous* coxcomb! what should such a fool
Do with so good a wife? *Shakespeare's Othello.*

Enforc'd to fly
Thence into Egypt, till the *murd'rous* king
Were dead, who sought his life; and missing, fill'd
With infant blood the streets of Bethlehem. *Milton.*

If she has deform'd this earthly life
With *murd'rous* rapine and seditious strife;
In everlasting darkness must she lie. *Prior.*

MURE. *n. s.* [*mur*, Fr. *murus*, Lat.] A wall. Not in use.

The incessant care and labour of his mind
Hath wrought the *mure*, that should confine it in,
So thin, that life looks through and will break out. *Shak.*

To MURE. *v. a.* [*murer*, Fr. from *murus*, Lat.] To inclose in walls.

All the gates of the city were *mured* up, except such as were reserved to sally out at. *Knolles's Hist. of the Turks.*

MU'RENGER. *n. s.* [*murus*, Latin.] An overseer of a wall. *Ains.*

MURIA'TICK. *adj.* Partaking of the taste or nature of brine, ar any such like pickles, from muria, brine or pickle. *Quincy.*

If the scurvy be entirely *muriatick*, proceeding from a diet of salt flesh or fish, antiscorbutick vegetables may be given with success, but tempered with acids. *Arbuthnot.*

MURK. *n. s.* [*morck*, Danish, dark.] Darkness: want of light.

Ere twice in *murk* and occidental damp,
Moist Hesperus hath quench'd his sleepy lamp. *Shakesp.*

MU'RK. *n. s.* Husks of fruit. *Ains.*

MU'RKY. *adj.* [*morck*, Danish.] Dark; cloudy; wanting light.

The *murkieſt* den,
The moſt opportune place, the ſtrong'ſt ſuggeſtion
Shall never melt mine honour into luſt. *Shakeſp. Tempeſt.*

So ſcented the grim feature, and up-turn'd
His noſtrils wide into the *murky* air,
Sagacious of his quarry. *Milton's Par. Loſt.*

A *murky* ſtorm deep low'ring o'er our heads
Hung imminent, that with impervious gloom
Oppos'd itſelf to Cynthia's ſilver ray. *Addiſon.*

MU'RMUR. *n. ſ. murmur*, Lat. *murmure*, Fr.]

1. A low ſhrill noiſe.

Flame as it moveth within itſelf, or is blown by a bellows, giveth a *murmur* or interiour ſound. *Bacon's Nat. Hiſt.*

When the wing'd colonies firſt tempt the ſky,
Or ſetting, ſeize the ſweets the bloſſoms yield,
Then a low *murmur* runs along the field. *Pope.*

2. A complaint half ſuppreſſed; a complaint not openly uttered.

Some diſcontents there are; ſome idle *murmurs*;
How idle *murmurs*!
The doors are all ſhut up; the wealthier ſort,
With arms acroſs, and hats upon their eyes,
Walk to and fro before their ſilent ſhops. *Dryden.*

To MU'RMUR. *v. n.* [*murmuro*, Lat. *murmurer*, Fr.]

1. To give a low ſhrill ſound.

The *murmuring* ſurge,
That on th' unnumber'd idle pebbles chafes,
Can ſcarce be heard ſo high. *Shakeſp. King Lear.*

Amid an iſle around whoſe rocky ſhore
The foreſts *murmur*, and the ſurges roar,
A goddeſs guards in her enchanted dome. *Pope.*

The buſy bees with a ſoft *murmuring* ſtrain,
Invite to gentle ſleep the lab'ring ſwain. *Dryden.*

2. To grumble; to utter ſecret and ſullen diſcontent. With *at* before things, and *againſt* before perſons.

The good we have enjoy'd from heav'n's free will;
And ſhall we *murmur* to endure the ill? *Dryden.*

Murmur not *at* your ſickneſs, for thereby you will ſin againſt God's providence. *Wake's Prep. for Death.*

The good conſequences of this ſcheme, which will execute itſelf without *murmuring againſt* the government, are very viſible. *Swift.*

MU'RMURER. *n. ſ.* [from *murmur.*] One who repines; one who complains ſullenly; a grumbler; a repiner; a complainer.

Heav'n's peace be with him!
That's chriſtian care enough; for living *murmurers*
There's places of rebuke. *Shakeſp. Henry VIII.*

The *murmurer* is turned off to the company of thoſe doleful creatures, which were to inhabit the ruins of Babylon. *Government of the Tongue.*

Still might the diſcontented *murmurer* cry,
Ah hapleſs fate of man! ah wretch doom'd once to die. *Blackmore on the Creation.*

MU'RNIVAL. *n. ſ.* [*morneſle*, Fr. from *morner*, to ſtun.] Four cards of a ſort. *Skinner and Ainſworth.*

MU'RRAIN. *n. ſ.* [The etymology of this word is not clear; *mur* is an old world for a catarrh, which might well anſwer to the glanders; *muriana*, low Latin. *Skinner* derives it from *mori*, to die.] The plague in cattle.

Away ragg'd rams, care I what *murrain* kill. *Sidney.*

Some trials would be made of mixtures of water in ponds for cattle, to make them more milch, to fatten, or to keep them from *murrain.* *Bacon.*

A hallowed band
Cou'd tell what *murrains*, in what months begun. *Garth.*

MURRE. *n. ſ.* A kind of bird.

Among the firſt ſort we reckon coots, meawes, *murres*, creyſers and curlews. *Carew.*

MU'RREY. *adj.* [*morée*, Fr. *morello*, Italian; from *moro*, a moor.] Darkly red.

The leaves of ſome trees turn a little *murrey* or reddiſh. *Bacon's Natural Hiſtory.*

They employ it in certain proportions, to tinge their glaſs both with red colour, or with a purpliſh or *murrey.* *Boyle.*

Painted glaſs of a ſanguine red, will not aſcend in powder above a *murrey.* *Brown's Vulgar Errours.*

Cornelius jumps out, a ſtocking upon his head, and a waiſtcoat of *murrey*-coloured ſattin upon his body. *Arbuth.*

MU'RRION. *n. ſ.* [often written *morion.* See MORION. *Junius* derives it from *murus*, a wall.] A helmet; a caſque; armour for the head.

Their beef they often in their *murrions* ſtew'd,
And in their baſket-hilts their bev'rage brew'd. *King.*

MURTH *of Corn. n. ſ.* Plenty of grain. *Ainſ.*

MU'SCADEL. } *adj.* [*muſcat*, *muſcadel*, Fr. *moſcatello*, Italian;
MU'SCADINE. } either from the fragance reſembling the nutmeg, *nux moſcata*, or from *muſca*, a fly; flies being eager of thoſe grapes.] A kind of ſweet grape, ſweet wine and ſweet pear.

He quafft off the *muſcadel*,
And threw the ſops all in the ſexton's face. *Shakeſp.*

MU'SCLE. *n. ſ.* [*muſcle*, Fr. *muſculus*, Lat. muſcula, Sax.]

Muſcle is a bundle of thin and parallel plates of fleſhy threads or fibres, incloſed by one common membrane: all the fibres of the ſame plate are parallel to one another, and tied together at extremely little diſtances by ſhort and tranſverſe fibres: the fleſhy fibres are compoſed of other ſmaller fibres, incloſed likewiſe by a common membrane: each leſſer fibre conſiſts of very ſmall veſicles or bladders, into which we ſuppoſe the veins, arteries and nerves to open, for every muſcle receives branches of all thoſe veſſels, which muſt be diſtributed to every fibre: the two ends of each muſcle or the extremities of the fibres are, in the limbs of animals, faſtened to two bones, the one moveable, the other fixed; and therefore, when the muſcles contract, they draw the moveable bone according to the direction of their fibres. *Quincy.*

The inſtruments of motion are the *muſcles*, the fibres whereof, contracting themſelves, move the ſeveral parts of the body. *Locke.*

2. A bivalve ſhell-fiſh.

Of ſhell-fiſh, there are wrinkles, limpers, cockles and *muſcles.* *Carew's Survey of Cornwall.*

It is the obſervation of Ariſtotle, that oyſters and *muſcles* grow fuller in the waxing of the moon. *Hakewill.*

Two pair of ſmall *muſcle* ſhells was found in a limeſtone quarry. *Woodward on Foſſils.*

MUSCO'SITY. *n. ſ.* [*muſcoſus*, Lat.] Moſſineſs.

MU'SCULAR. *adj.* [from *muſculus*, Latin.] Performed by muſcles.

By the *muſcular* motion and perpetual flux of the liquids, a great part of the liquids are thrown out of the body. *Arb.*

MUSCULA'RITY. *n. ſ.* [from *muſcular.*] The ſtate of having muſcles.

The guts of a ſturgeon, taken out and cut to pieces, will ſtill move, which may depend upon their great thickneſs and *muſcularity.* *Grew's Muſæum.*

MU'SCULOUS. *adj.* [*muſculeux*, Fr. *muſculoſus*, Latin.]

1. Full of muſcles; brawny.

2. Pertaining to a muſcle.

The uvea has a *muſculous* power, and can dilate and contract that round hole, called the pupil of the eye, for the better moderating the tranſmiſſion of light. *More.*

MUSE. *n. ſ.* [from the verb.]

1. Deep thought; cloſe attention; abſence of mind; brown ſtudy.

The tidings ſtrange did him abaſhed make,
That ſtill he ſat long time aſtoniſhed
As in great *muſe*, ne word to creature ſpake. *Fa. Queen.*

He was fill'd
With admiration and deep *muſe*, to hear
Of things ſo high and ſtrange. *Milton.*

2. The power of poetry.

Begin my *muſe.* *Cowley.*

The *muſe*-inſpired train
Triumph, and raiſe their drooping heads again. *Waller.*

Lodona's fate, in long oblivion caſt,
The *muſe* ſhall ſing. *Pope.*

To MUSE. *v. n.* [*muſer*, Fr. *muyſen*, Dutch; *muſſo*, Latin.]

1. To ponder; to think cloſe; to ſtudy in ſilence.

If he ſpake courteouſly, he angled the people's hearts; if he were ſilent, he *muſed* upon ſome dangerous plot. *Sidney.*

St. Auguſtine, ſpeaking of devout men, noteth, how they daily frequented the church, how attentive ear they give unto the chapters read, how careful they were to remember the ſame, and to *muſe* thereupon by themſelves. *Hooker.*

Cæſar's father oft,
When he hath *muſ'd* of taking kingdoms in,
Beſtow'd his lips on that unworthy place,
As it rain'd kiſſes. *Shakeſp.*

My mouth ſhall ſpeak of wiſdom; and my heart *muſe* of underſtanding. *Pſalm* xlix. *v.* 3.

Her face upon a ſudden glittered, ſo that I was afraid of her, and *muſed* what it might be. 2 *Eſdras* x. 25.

All men *muſed* in their hearts of John, whether he were the Chriſt or not. *Luke* iii. 15.

On theſe he *muſ'd* within his thoughtful mind. *Dryden.*

We *muſe* ſo much on the one, that we are apt to overlook and forget the other. *Atterbury's Sermons.*

Man ſuperiour walks
Amid the glad creation, *muſing* praiſe,
And looking lively gratitude. *Thomſon's Spring.*

2. To be abſent of mind; to be attentive to ſomething not preſent; to be in a brown ſtudy.

Why haſt thou loſt the freſh blood in thy cheeks?
And given my treaſures and my rights of thee,
To thick-ey'd *muſing* and curs'd melancholy. *Shakeſpeare.*

You ſuddenly aroſe and walk'd about,
Muſing and ſighing with yours arms acroſs. *Shakeſpeare.*

The ſad king
Feels ſudden terror and cold ſhivering,
Liſts not to eat, ſtill *muſes*, ſleeps unſound. *Daniel.*

3. To

3. To wonder; to be amazed.

Muse not that I thus suddenly proceed;
For what I will, I will. *Shakesp.*

Do not *muse* at me,
I have a strange infirmity. *Shakesp. Macbeth.*

MU'SEFUL. *adj.* [from *muse.*] Deep thinking; silently thoughtful.

Full of *museful* mopings, which presage
The loss of reason, and conclude in rage. *Dryden.*

MU'SER. *n. s.* [from *muse.*] One who muses; one apt to be absent of mind.

MU'SET. *n. s.* [in hunting.] The place through which the hare goes to relief. *Bailey.*

MU'SEUM. *n. s.* [μυσεῖον.] A repository of learned curiosities.

MU'SHROOM. *n. s.* *mouscheron*, French.]

1. *Mushrooms* are by curious naturalists esteemed perfect plants, though their flowers and seeds have not as yet been discovered: the true champignon or *mushroom* appears at first of a roundish form like a button, the upper part of which, as also the stalk, is very white, but being opened, the under part is of a livid flesh colour, but the fleshy part, when broken, is very white; when they are suffered to remain undisturbed, they will grow to a large size, and explicate themselves almost to a flatness, and the red part underneath will change to a dark colour: in order to cultivate them, open the ground about the roots of the *mushrooms*, where you will find the earth very often full of small white knobs, which are the off-sets or young *mushrooms*; these should be carefully gathered, preserving them in lumps with the earth about them, and planted in hot beds. *Miller.*

2. An upstart; a wretch risen from the dunghill; a director of a company.

Mushrooms come up in a night, and yet they are unsown; and therefore such as are upstarts in state, they call in reproach *mushrooms*. *Bacon's Natural History.*

Tully, the humble *mushroom* scarcely known,
The lowly native of a country town. *Dryden.*

MU'SHROOMSTONE. *n. s.* [*mushroom* and *stone.*] A kind of fossil.

Fifteen *mushroomstones* of the same shape. *Woodward.*

MU'SICK. *n. s.* [μυσικὴ; *musique*, Fr.]

1. The science of harmonical sounds.

The man that hath no *musick* in himself,
Nor is not mov'd with concord of sweet sounds,
Is fit for treasons. *Shakesp. Merchant of Venice.*

Now look into the *musick*-master's gains,
Where noble youth at vast expence is taught,
But eloquence not valu'd at a groat. *Dryden's Juvenal.*

2. Instrumental or vocal harmony.

When she spake,
Sweet words, like droping honey, she did shed;
And 'twixt the pearls and rubies softly brake
A silver sound, that heavenly *musick* seem'd to make. *F. Qu.*

Such *musick*
Before was never made,
But when of old the sons of morning sung. *Milton.*

By *musick* minds an equal temper know,
Nor swell too high, nor sink too low;
Warriours she fires with animated sounds,
Pours balm into the bleeding lover's wounds. *Pope.*

We have dancing-masters and *musick*-masters. *Arb. and Pope.*

MU'SICAL. *adj.* [*musical*, Fr. from *musick.*]

1. Harmonious; melodious; sweet sounding.

The merry birds
Chanted above their chearful harmony,
And made emongst themselves a sweet consort,
That quicken'd the dull sp'rit with *musical* comfort *F. Qu.*

Sweet bird that shunn'st the noise of folly,
Most *musical*, most melancholly;
Thee chauntress oft the wood among,
I woo to hear thy even-song. *Milton.*

Neither is it enough to give his author's sense, in poetical expressions and in *musical* numbers. *Dryden.*

2. Belonging to musick.

Several *musical* instruments are to be seen in the hands of Apollo's muses, which might give great light to the dispute between the ancient and modern music. *Addison.*

MU'SICALLY. *adv.* [from *musical.*] Harmoniously; with sweet sound.

Valentine, *musically* coy,
Shun'd Phædra's arms. *Addison.*

MU'SICALLNESS. *n. s.* [from *musical.*] Harmony.

MU'SICIAN. *n. s.* [*musicus*, Lat. *musicien*, Fr.] One skilled in harmony; one who performs upon instruments of musick.

Though the *musicians* that shall play to you,
Hand in the air a thousand leagues from hence;
Yet strait they shall be here. *Shakesp. Henry IV.*

The nightingale, if she should sing by day,
When every goose is cackling, would be thought
No better a *musician* than the wren. *Shakesp.*

A painter may make a better face than ever was; but he must do it by a kind of felicity, as a *musician* that maketh an excellent air in musick, and not by rule. *Bacon's Essays.*

The praise of Bacchus then the sweet *musician* sung;
Of Bacchus ever fair and ever young. *Dryden.*

MUSK. *n. s.* [*muschio*, Italian; *musc*, Fr.]

Musk is a dry, light and friable substance of a dark blackish colour, with some tinge of a purplish or blood colour in it, feeling somewhat smooth or unctuous: its smell is highly perfumed, and too strong to be agreeable in any large quantity: its taste is bitterish: it is brought from the East Indies, mostly from the kingdom of Bantam, some from Tonquin and Cochin China: the animal which produces it is of a very singular kind, not agreeing with any established genus: it is of the size of a common goat but taller; its head resembles that of the greyhound, and its ears stand erect like those of the rabbit: its tail is also erect and short, its legs moderately long, and its hoofs deeply cloven: its hair is a dusky brown, variegated with a faint cast of red and white, every hair being partycoloured: the bag which contains the *musk*, is three inches long and two wide, and situated in the lower part of the creature's belly; it consists of a thin membrane covered thinly with hair, resembling a small purse, and when genuine, the scent is so strong as to offend the head greatly: toward the orifice of the bag there are several glands, which serve for the secretion of this precious perfume, for the sake of which the Indians kill the animal. *Hill.*

Some putrefactions and excrements yield excellent odours; as civet and *musk*. *Bacon's Natural History.*

MUSK. *n. s.* [*musca*, Lat.] Grape hyacinth or grape flower.

Musk hath a bulbous shoot; the leaves are long and narrow; the flower is hermaphroditical, consisting of one leaf, and shaped like a pitcher, and cut at the top into six segment, which are reflexed; the ovary becomes a triangular fruit, divided into three cells, which are full of round seeds. *Miller.*

MU'SKAPPLE. *n. s.* A kind of apple. *Ains.*

MU'SKCAT. *n. s.* [*musk* and *cat.*] The animal from which musk is got.

MU'SKCHERRY. *n. s.* A sort of cherry. *Ains.*

MU'SKET. *n. s.* [*mousquet*, Fr. *mosquetto*, Italian, a small hawk. Many of the fire-arms are named from animals.]

1. A soldier's handgun.

Thou
Wast shot at with fair eyes, to be the mark
Of smoky *muskets*. *Shakesp. All's well that ends well.*

Practise to make swifter motions than any you have out of your *muskets*. *Bacon.*

They charge their *muskets*, and with hot desire
Of full revenge, renew the fight with fire. *Waller.*

He perceived a body of their horse within *musket*-shot of him, and advancing upon him. *Clarendon.*

One was brought to us, shot with a *musket*-ball on the right side of his head. *Wiseman's Surgery.*

2. A male hawk of a small kind, the female of which is the sparrow hawk; so that eyas *musket* is a young unfledged male hawk of that kind. *Hanmer.*

Here comes little Robin.—
—How now my eyas *musket*, what news with you. *Shak.*

The *musket* and the coystrel were too weak,
Too fierce the falcon; but above the rest,
The noble buzzard ever pleas'd me best. *Dryden.*

MUSKETEE'R. *n. s.* [from *musket.*] A soldier whose weapon is his musket.

Notwithstanding they had lined some hedges with *musketeers*, they pursued them till they were dispersed. *Clarendon.*

MUSKETOO'N. *n. s.* [*mousqueton*, Fr.] A blunderbuss; a short gun of a large bore. *Dict.*

MU'SKINESS. *n. s.* [from *musk.*] The scent of musk.

MUSKME'LON. *n. s.* [*musk* and *melon.*] A fragrant melon.

The way of maturation of tobacco must be from the heat of the earth or sun; we see some leading of this in *muskmelons*, which are sown upon a hot bed dunged below, upon a bank turned upon the South sun. *Bacon.*

MU'SKPEAR. *n. s.* [*musk* and *pear.*] A fragrant pear.

MU'SKROSE. *n. s.* [*musk* and *rose.*] A rose so called, I suppose, from its fragrance.

In May and June come roses of all kinds, except the *musk*, which comes later. *Bacon's Essays.*

Thyrsis, whose artful strains have oft delay'd
The huddling brook to hear his madrigal,
And sweeten'd every *muskrose* of the dale. *Milton.*

The *muskrose* will, if a lusty plant, bear flowers in Autumn without cutting. *Boyle.*

MU'SKY. *adj.* [from *musk.*] Fragrant; sweet of scent.

There eternal summer dwells,
And West winds, with *musky* wing,
About the cedar'n allies fling
Nard and Cassia's balmy smells. *Milton.*

MU'SLIN. *n. s.* A fine stuff made of cotton.

By the use of certain attire made of cambrick or *muslin* upon her head, she attained to such an evil art in the motion of her eyes. *Tatler, Nº 110.*

In half-whipt *muslin* needles useless lie,
And shuttle-cocks across the counter fly. *Gay.*

Mu'srol. *n. s.* [*muserole*, French] The noseband of a horse's bridle. *Bailey.*

Muss. *n. s.* A scramble.

When I cry'd hoa!
Like boys unto a *muss*, kings would start forth,
And cry, your will? *Shakesp. Ant. and Cleopatra.*

Mussita'tion. *n. s.* [*mussito*, Lat.] Murmur; grumble.

Mu'ssulman. *n. s.* A Mahometan believer.

MUST. *verb imperfect.* [*mussen*, Dutch.] To be obliged. It is only used before a verb. *Must* is of all persons and tenses, and used of persons and things.

Do you confess the bond?
——I do.
——Then *must* the Jew be merciful.
——On what compulsion *must* I? tell me that. *Shakespeare.*

Must I needs bring thy son unto the land from whence thou camest? *Gen.* xxiv. 5.

Fade, flowers, fade, nature will have it so;
'Tis but what we *must* in our Autumn do. *Waller.*

Because the same self-existent being necessarily is what he is, 'tis evident that what he may be, or hath the power of being, he *must* be. *Grew.*

Every father and brother of the convent has a voice in the election, which *must* be confirmed by the pope. *Addison.*

MUST. *n. s.* [*mustum*, Latin.] New wine; new wort.

If in the *must* of wine, or wort of beer, before it be tunned, the burrage stay a small time, and be often changed, it makes a sovereign drink for melancholy. *Bacon's Natural History.*

As a swarm of flies in vintage time,
About the wine-press where sweet *must* is pour'd,
Beat off, returns as oft with humming sound. *Milton.*

The wime itself was suiting to the rest,
Still working in the *must*, and lately press'd. *Dryden.*

A frugal man that with sufficient *must*
His casks replenish'd yearly; he no more
Desir'd, nor wanted. *Phillips.*

Liquors, in the act of fermentation, as *must* and new ale, produce spasms in the stomach. *Arbuthnot on Aliments.*

To Must. *v. a.* [*mws*, Welsh, stinking; *mos*, Dutch, mouldiness; or perhaps from *moist.*] To mould; to make mouldy.

Others are made of stone and lime; but they are subject to give and be moist, which will *must* corn. *Mortimer.*

To Must. *v. n.* To grow mouldy.

Musta'ches. *n. s.* [*mustaches*, French.] Whiskers; hair on the upper lip.

This was the manner of the Spaniards, to cut off their beards, save only their *mustaches*, which they wear long. *Spens.*

Mu'stard. *n. s.* [*mwstard*, Welsh; *moustard*, Fr.] A plant.

The flower consists of four leaves, which are placed in form of a crest, out of whose flower-cup rises the pointal, which afterward becomes a fruit or pod, divided into two cells by an intermediate partition, to which the valves adhere on both sides, and are filled with roundish seeds: these pods generally end in a fungous horn, containing the like seeds. To these marks must be added, an acrid burning taste, peculiar to mustard. *Miller.*

The pancakes were naught, and the *mustard* was good. *Shak.*

Sauce like himself, offensive to its foes,
The roguish *mustard*, dang'rous to the nose. *King.*

Mustard, taken in great quantities, would quickly bring the blood into an alkaline state, and destroy the animal. *Arbuthnot.*

'Tis your's to shake the soul,
With thunder rumbling from the *mustard* bowl. *Pope.*

Stick your candle in a bottle, a coffee cup, or a *mustard* pot. *Swift.*

Common *mustard* seed is attenuant and resolvent: it warms the stomach, and excites appetite; but its principal medicinal use is external in sinapisms. *Hill's Mat. Med.*

To Mu'ster. *v. n.* To assemble in order to form an army.

Why does my blood thus *muster* to my heart,
So dispossessing all my other parts
Of necessary fitness? *Shakesp. Meas. for Measure.*

They reach the destin'd place;
And *muster* there, and round the centre swarm,
And draw together. *Blackmore's Creation.*

To MU'STER. *v. a.* [*mousteren*, Dutch.]

1. To review forces.

The captain, half of whose soldiers are dead, and the other quarter never *mustered* nor seen, demands payment of his whole account. *Spenser on Ireland.*

The principal scribe of the host *mustered* the people. 2 *Kings.*

Old Anchises
Review'd his *muster'd* race, and took the tale. *Dryden.*

A man might have three hundred and eighteen men in his family, without being heir to Adam, and might *muster* them up, and lead them out against the Indians. *Locke.*

2. To bring together.

Had we no quarrel to Rome, but that
Thou art thence banish'd, we would *muster* all
From twelve to seventy. *Shakesp. Coriolanus.*

I'll *muster* up my friends, and meet your grace. *Shakesp.*

I could *muster* up, as well as you,
My giants and my witches too. *Donne.*

A daw tricked himself up with all the gay feathers he could *muster.* *L'Estrange.*

All the wise sayings and advices which philosophers could *muster* up to this purpose, have proved ineffectual to the common people. *Tillotson.*

Having *mustered* up all the forces he could think of, the clouds above, and the deeps below: these, says he, are all the stores we have for water; and Moses directs us to no other for the causes of the deluge. *Woodward's Natural History.*

Mu'ster. *n. s.* [from the verb.]

1. A review of a body of forces.

All the names
Of thy confederates too, be no less great
In hell than here: that when we would repeat
Our strengths in *muster*, we may name you all. *Ben. Johns.*

2. A register of forces mustered.

Ye publish the *musters* of your own bands, and proclaim them to amount to thousands. *Hooker.*

Deception takes wrong measures, and makes false *musters*, which sounds a retreat instead of a charge, and a charge instead of a retreat. *South's Sermons.*

3. A collection: as, a *muster* of peacocks. *Ainsworth.*

4. *To pass* Muster. To be allowed.

Such excuses will not *pass muster* with God, who will allow no man's idleness to be the measure of possible or impossible. *South's Sermons.*

Double dealers may *pass muster* for a while; but all parties wash their hands of them in the conclusion. *L'Estrange.*

Mu'sterbook. *n. s.* [*muster* and *book.*] A book in which the forces are registered.

Shadow will serve for Summer: prick him; for we have a number of shadows to fill up the *musterbook.* *Shakesp. H.* IV.

Mu'stermaster. *n. s.* [*muster* and *master.*] One who superintends the muster to prevent frauds.

A noble gentleman, then *mustermaster*, was appointed embassador unto the Turkish emperor. *Knolles's History.*

Mustermasters carry the best and ablest men in their pockets. *Raleigh's Essays.*

Mu'ster-roll. *n. s.* [*muster* and *roll.*] A register of forces.

How many insignificant combatants are there in the Christian camp, that only lend their names to fill up the *muster-roll*, but never dream of going upon service? *Decay of Piety.*

One tragick sentence, if I dare deride,
Which Betterton's grave action dignify'd;
Or well-mouth'd Booth with emphasis proclaims,
Though but perhaps a *muster-roll* of names. *Pope.*

Mu'stily. *adv.* [from *musty.*] Mouldily.

Mu'stiness. *n. s.* [from *musty.*] Mould; damp foulness.

Keep them dry and free from *mustiness.* *Evelyn's Kalendar.*

Mu'sty. *adj.* [from *must.*]

1. Mouldy; spoiled with damp; moist and fetid.

Was't thou fain, poor father,
To hovel thee with swine and rogues forlorn,
In short and *musty* straw. *Shakesp. King Lear.*

Pistachoes, so they be good and not *musty*, made into a milk, are an excellent nourisher. *Bacon's Natural History.*

2. Stale; spoiled with age.

While the grass grows—the proverb is somewhat *musty.* *Sh.*

Let those that go by water to Gravesend prefer lying upon the boards, than on *musty* infectious straw. *Harvey.*

3. Vapid with fetidness.

Let not, like Nævius, every error pass;
The *musty* wine, foul cloth, or greasy glass. *Pope.*

4. Dull; heavy; wanting activity; wanting practice in the occurrences of life.

Xantippe, being married to a bookish man who has no knowledge of the world, is forced to take his affairs into her own hands, and to spirit him up now and then, that he may not grow *musty* and unfit for conversation. *Addis. Spectator.*

Mutabi'lity. *n. s.* [*mutabilité*, Fr. *mutabilis*, Latin.]

1. Changeableness; not continuance in the same state.

The *mutability* of that end, for which they are made, maketh them also changeable. *Hooker.*

My fancy was the air, most free,
And full of *mutability*,
Big with chimeras. *Suckling.*

Plato confesses that the heavens and the frame of the world are corporeal, and therefore subject to *mutability.* *Stillingfleet.*

2. Inconstancy; change of mind.

Ambitions, covetings, change of prides, disdain,
Nice longings, slanders, *mutability.* *Shakesp. Cymbeline.*

Mu'table. *adj.* [*mutabilis*, Latin.]

1. Subject to change; alterable.

Of things of the most accidental and *mutable* nature, accidental in their production, and *mutable* in their continuance, yet God's prescience is as certain in him as the memory is or can be in us. *South's Sermons.*

2. Inconstant; unsettled.

For the *mutable* rank-scented many,
Let them regard me, as I do not flatter. *Shakesp. Coriolanus.*

I saw thee *mutable*
Of fancy, fear'd lest one day thou would'st leave me. *Milt.*

MU'TABLENESS. *n. s.* [from *mutable.*] Changeableness; uncertainty; instability.

MUTA'TION. *n. s.* [*mutation*, French; *mutatio*, Lat.] Change; alteration.

His honour
Was nothing but *mutation*, ay, and that
From one bad thing to worse. *Shakespeare's Cymbeline.*

The vicissitude or *mutations* in the superior globe are no fit matter for this present argument. *Bacon's Essays.*

To make plants grow out of the sun or open air is a great *mutation* in nature, and may induce a change in the seed. *Bacon.*

MUTE. *adj.* [*muet*, French; *mutus*, Latin.]

1. Silent; not vocal; not having the use of voice.

Why did he reason in my soul implant,
And speech, th' effect of reason? To the *mute*
My speech is lost; my reason to the brute. *Dryden.*

Mute solemn sorrow, free from female noise,
Such as the majesty of grief destroys. *Dryden.*

2. Having nothing to say.

Say she be *mute*, and will not speak a word,
Then I'll commend her volubility. *Shakespeare.*

All sat *mute*,
Pondering the danger with deep thoughts. *Milton.*

All the heav'nly choir stood *mute*,
And silence was in heav'n. *Milt. Paradise Lost, b.* iii.

The whole perplex'd ignoble crowd,
Mute to my questions, in my praises loud,
Echo'd the word. *Prior.*

MUTE. *n. s.*

1. One that has no power of speech.

Either our history shall with full mouth
Speak freely of our acts; or else our grave,
Like Turkish *mute*, shall have a tongueless mouth. *Shakes.*

Your *mute* I'll be;
When my tongue blabs, then let mine eyes not see. *Shakes.*

He that never hears a word spoken, no wonder if he remain speechless; as one must do, who from an infant should be bred up amongst *mute*, and have no teaching. *Holder.*

Let the figures, to which art cannot give a voice, imitate the *mutes* in their actions. *Dryden's Dufresnoy.*

2. A letter which without a vowel can make no sound.

Grammarians note the easy pronunciation of a *mute* before a liquid, which doth not therefore necessarily make the preceding vowel long. *Holder's Elements of Speech.*

To MUTE. *v. n.* [*mutir*, French.] To dung as birds.

Mine eyes being open, the sparrows *muted* warm dung into mine eyes. *Tob.* ii. 10.

I could not fright the crows,
Or the least bird from *muting* on my head. *Ben. Johnson.*

The bird not able to digest the fruit, from her inconverted *muting* ariseth this plant. *Brown's Vulgar Errours.*

MU'TELY. *adv.* [from *mute*] Silently; not vocally.

Driving dumb silence from the portal door,
Where he had *mutely* sat two hours before. *Milton.*

To MU'TILATE. *v. a.* [*mutiler*, Fr. *mutilo*, Latin.] To deprive of some essential part.

Such fearing to concede a monstrosity, or *mutilate* the integrity of Adam, preventively conceive the creation of thirteen ribs. *Brown's Vulgar Errours.*

Sylburgius justly complains that the place is *mutilated. Still.*

Among the *mutilated* poets of antiquity there is none whose fragments are so beautiful as those of Sappho. *Addison.*

Aristotle's works were corrupted, from Strabo's account of their having been *mutilated* and consumed with moisture. *Baker.*

MUTILA'TION. *n. s.* [*mutilation*, Fr. *mutilatio*, from *mutilo*, Lat.] Deprivation of a limb, or any essential part.

The subject had been oppressed by fines, imprisonments, *mutilations*, pillories, and banishments. *Clarendon.*

Mutilations are not transmitted from father to son, the blind begetting such as can see: cripples, mutilate in their own persons, do come out perfect in their generations. *Brown.*

MU'TINE. *n. s.* [*mutin*, French.] A mutineer; a mover of insurrection. Not in use.

In my heart there was a kind of fighting,
That would not let me sleep; methought I lay
Worse than the *mutines* in the bilboes. *Shakesp. Hamlet.*

Like the *mutines* of Jerusalem,
Be friends a while. *Shakespeare's King John.*

MUTINE'ER. *n. s.* [from *mutin*, French.] A mover of sedition; an opposer of lawful authority.

The war of the duke of Urbin, head of the Spanish *mutineers*, was unjust. *Bacon's War with Spain.*

Set wide the mufti's garden-gate;
For there our *mutineers* appoint to meet. *Dryden.*

They have cashiered several of their followers as *mutineers*, who have contradicted them in political conversations. *Addis.*

MU'TINOUS. *adj.* [*mutiné*, French.] Seditious; busy in insurrection; turbulent.

It tauntingly replied
To th' discontented members, th' *mutinous* parts,
That envied his receipt. *Shakesp. Coriolanus.*

The laws of England should be administered, and the *mutinous* severely suppressed. *Hayward.*

Lend me your guards, that if persuasion fail,
Force may against the *mutinous* prevail. *Waller.*

My ears are deaf with this impatient crowd;
Their wants are now grown *mutinous* and loud. *Dryden.*

MU'TINOUSLY. *adv.* [from *mutinous.*] Seditiously; turbulently.

A woman, a young woman, a fair woman, was to govern a people in nature *mutinously* proud, and always before used to hard governours. *Sidney.*

Men imprudently often, seditiously and *mutinously* sometimes, employ their zeal for persons. *Spratt's Sermons.*

MU'TINOUSNESS. *n. s.* [from *mutinous.*] Seditiousness; turbulence.

To MU'TINY. *v. n.* [*mutiner*, French.] To rise against authority; to make insurrection; to move sedition.

The spirit of my father begins to *mutiny* against this servitude. *Shakespeare's As you like it.*

The people *mutiny*, the fort is mine,
And all the soldiers to my will incline. *Waller.*

When Cæsar's army *mutinied*, and grew troublesome, no argument could appease them. *South's Sermons.*

MU'TINY. *n. s.* [from the verb.] Insurrection; sedition.

The king fled to a strong castle, where he was gathering forces to suppress this *mutiny*. *Sidney.*

I' th' war,
Their *mutinies* and revolts, wherein they shew'd
Most valour, spoke not for them. *Shakesp. Coriolanus.*

In most strange postures
We've seen him set himself.
—There is a *mutiny* in's mind. *Shakes. Henry* VIII.

Less than if this frame
Of heav'n were falling, and these elements
In *mutiny* had from her axle torn
The stedfast earth. *Milton's Parad. Lost, b.* ii.

Soldiers grow pernicious to their master who becomes their servant, and is in danger of their *mutinies*, as much as any government of seditious. *Temple.*

To MU'TTER. *v. n.* [*mutire*, *mussare*, Latin.] To grumble; to murmur.

What would you ask me, that I would deny,
Or stand so *mutt'ring* on? *Shakespeare's Othello.*

How! what does his cashier'd worship *mutter*? *Shakes.*

Sky lowr'd, and *mutt'ring* thunder some sad drops
Wept, at completing of the mortal sin
Original! *Milton's Par. Lost, b.* ix.

They may freely trespass, and do as they please; no man dare accuse them, no, not so much as *mutter* against them. *Burton on Melancholy.*

Bold Britons, at a brave bear-garden fray,
Are rous'd; and clatt'ring sticks cry, play, play, play:
Mean time your filthy foreigner will stare,
And *mutter* to himself, ha, *gens barbare!*
And it is well he *mutters*, well for him;
Our butchers else would tear him limb from limb. *Dryden.*

When the tongue of a beautiful female was cut out, it could not forbear *muttering*. *Addison's Spectator.*

To MU'TTER. *v. a.* To utter with imperfect articulation; to grumble forth.

Amongst the soldiers this is *muttered*,
That here you maintain sev'ral factions. *Shakes. Hen.* VI.

A kind of men, so loose of soul,
That in their sleep will *mutter* their affairs. *Shakes. Othello.*

Your lips have spoken lies, your tongue hath *muttered* perverseness. *Is.* lix. 2.

A hateful prattling tongue,
That blows up jealousies, and heightens fears,
By *muttering* pois'nous whispers in mens ears. *Creech.*

MU'TTER. *n. s.* [from the verb.] Murmur; obscure utterance.

Without his rod revers'd,
And backward *mutters* of dissevering power,
We cannot free the lady. *Milton.*

MU'TTERER. *n. s.* [from *mutter.*] Grumbler; murmurer.

MU'TTERINGLY. *adv.* [from *muttering.*] With a low voice; without distinct articulation.

MU'TTON. *n. s.* [*mouton*, French.]

1. The flesh of sheep dressed for food.

The fat of roasted *mutton* or beef, falling on the birds, will baste them. *Swift's Directions to the Cook.*

2. A sheep: now only in ludicrous language.

Here's too small a pasture for such store of *muttons*. *Shak.*

The flesh of *muttons* is better tasted where the sheep feed upon wild thyme and wholesome herbs. *Bacon's Nat. Hist.*

Within a few days were brought out of the country two thousand *muttons*. *Hayward's Edw.* VI.

MUTTONFI'ST.

Mutтonfi'st. *n. s.* [*mutton* and *fist.*] A hand large and red.

Will he who saw the soldiers *muttonfist*,
And saw thee maul'd appear within the list
To witness truth. *Dryden's Juvenal, sat.* 16.

MU'TUAL. *adj.* [*mutuel*, French; *mutuus*, Lat.] Reciprocal; each acting in return or correspondence to the other.

Note a wild and wanton herd,
Fetching mad bounds, bellowing and neighing loud,
If they perchance but hear a trumpet sound,
You shall perceive them make a *mutual* stand,
By the sweet power of musick. *Shakesp. Merch. of Venice.*

What should most excite a *mutual* flame,
Your rural cares and pleasures are the same. *Pope.*

Mu'tually. *adv.* [from *mutual.*] Reciprocally; in return.

He never bore
Like labour with the rest; where th' other instruments
Did see, and hear, devise, instruct, walk, feel,
And *mutually* participate. *Shakespeare's Coriolanus.*

Dear love I bear to fair Anne Page,
Who *mutually* hath answer'd my affection. *Shakespeare.*

The tongue and pen *mutually* assist one another, writing what we speak, and speaking what we write. *Holder.*

Pellucid substances act upon the rays of light at a distance, in refracting, reflecting and inflecting them, and the rays *mutually* agitate the parts of those substances at a distance for heating them. *Newton's Opticks.*

They *mutually* teach, and are taught, that lesson of vain confidence and security. *Atterbury's Sermons.*

May I the sacred pleasures know
Of strictest amity, nor ever want
A friend with whom I *mutually* may share
Gladness and anguish. *Philips.*

Mutua'lity. *n. s.* [from *mutual.*] Reciprocation.

Villanous thoughts, Roderigo! when these *mutualities* so marshal the way, hard at hand comes the incorporate conclusion. *Shakespeare's Othello.*

Mu'zzle. *n. s.* [*museau*, French.]

1. The mouth of any thing; the mouth of a man in contempt.

But ever and anon turning her *muzzle* toward me, she threw such a prospect upon me, as might well have given a surfeit to any weak lover's stomach. *Sidney, b.* ii.

Huygens has proved, that a bullet continuing in the velocity with which it leaves the *muzzle* of the cannon, would require twenty-five years to pass from us to the sun. *Cheyne.*

If the poker be out of the way, or broken, stir the fire with the tongs; if the tongs be not at hand, use the *muzzle* of the bellows. *Swift's Rules to Servants.*

2. A fastening for the mouth, which hinders to bite.

The fifth Harry from curbed licence plucks
The *muzzle* of restraint; and the wild dog
Shall flesh his tooth on ev'ry innocent. *Shakesp. Henry* IV.

Greyhounds, snowy fair,
And tall as stags, ran loose, and cours'd around his chair;
With golden *muzzles* all their mouths were bound. *Dryden.*

To Mu'zzle. *v. n.* To bring the mouth near.

The bear *muzzles*, and smells to him, puts his nose to his mouth and to his ears, and at last leaves him. *L'Estrange.*

To Mu'zzle. *v. a.*

1. To bind the mouth.

This butcher's cur is venom mouth'd, and I
Have not the pow'r to *muzzle* him; therefore best
Not wake him in his slumber. *Shakesp. Henry* VIII.

My dagger *muzzled*,
Lest it should bite its master, and so prove,
As ornaments oft do, too dangerous. *Shak. Winter's Tale.*

The bear, the boar, and every savage name,
Wild in effect, though in appearance tame,
Lay waste thy woods, destroy thy blissful bow'r,
And *muzzled* though they seem, the mutes devour. *Dryden.*

Through the town with slow and solemn air,
Led by the nostril, walks the *muzzled* bear. *Gay's Past.*

2. To fondle with the mouth close. A low word.

The nurse was then *muzzling* and coaxing of the child. *L'Estrange's Fables.*

My. pronoun possessive. [See Mine.] Belonging to me. *My* is used before a substantive, and *mine* anciently and properly before a vowel. *My* is now commonly used indifferently before both. *My* is used when the substantive follows, and *mine* when it goes before: as, *this is* my *book*; *this book is* mine.

Her feet she in *my* neck doth place. *Spenser.*

I conclude *my* reply with the words of a Christian poet. *Bramhall.*

If *my* soul had free election
To dispose of her affection. *Waller.*

I shall present *my* reader with a journal. *Addison.*

My'nchen. *n. s.* [mynchen, Saxon.] A nun. *Dict.*

My'ography. *n. s.* [μυογραφία.] A description of the muscles.

My'ology. *n. s.* [*myologie*, French.] The description and doctrine of the muscles.

To instance in all the particulars, were to write a whole system of *myology*. *Cheyne's Phil. Principles.*

My'opy. *n. s.* Shortness of sight.

My'riad. *n. s.* [μυρίας.]

1. The number of ten thousand.

2. Proverbially any great number.

Assemble thou,
Of all those *myriads*, which we lead, the chief. *Milton.*

Are there legions of devils who are continually designing and working our ruin? there are also *myriads* of good angels who are more cheerful and officious to do us good. *Tillotson.*

Safe sits the goddess in her dark retreat;
Around her, *myriads* of ideas wait,
And endless shapes. *Prior.*

My'rmidon. *n. s.* [μυρμηδών.] Any rude ruffian; so named from the soldiers of Achilles.

The mass of the people will not endure to be governed by Clodius and Curio, at the head of their *myrmidons*, though these be ever so numerous, and composed of their own representatives. *Swift.*

Myro'balan. *n. s.* [*myrobalanus*, Latin.] A fruit.

The *myrobalans* are a dried fruit, of which we have five kinds: they are fleshy, generally with a stone and kernel, having the pulpy part more or less of an austere acrid taste: they are the production of five different trees growing in the East Indies, where they are eaten preserved: they serve also for making and for dressing leather: they have been long in great esteem for their quality of opening the bowels in a gentle manner, and afterwards strengthening them by their astringency; but the present practice rejects them all. *Hill.*

The *myrobalan* hath parts of contrary natures; for it is sweet, and yet astringent. *Bacon's Nat. Hist.* N°. 644.

Myro'polist. *n. s.* [μῦρον and πωλέω.] One who sells unguents.

Myrrh. *n. s.* [*myrrha*, Latin; *myrrhe*, Fr.] A gum.

Myrrh is a vegetable product of the gum resin kind, sent to us in loose granules from the size of a pepper corn to that of a walnut, of a reddish brown colour, with more or less of an admixture of yellow: its taste is bitter and acrid, with a peculiar aromatick flavour, but very nauseous: its smell is strong, but not disagreeable: it is brought from Ethiopia, but the tree which produces it is wholly unknown. Our *myrrh* is the very drug known by the ancients under the same name: internally applied it is a powerful resolvent, and externally applied it is discutient and vulnerary. *Hill's M. Med.*

The *myrrhe* sweet bleeding in the bitter wound. *Spenser.*

I dropt in a little honey of roses, with a few drops of tincture of *myrrh*. *Wiseman's Surgery.*

My'rrhine. *adj.* [*myrrhynus*, Latin.] Made of the myrrhine stone.

How they quaff in gold,
Crystal and *myrrhine* cups imboss'd with gems
And studs of pearl. *Milton's Par. Reg. b.* iv.

My'rtiform. *n. s.* [*myrtus* and *form.*] Having the shape of myrtle.

My'rtle. *n. s.* [*myrtus*, Latin; *myrte*, Fr.] A fragrant tree sacred to Venus.

The flower of the *myrtle* consists of several leaves disposed in a circular order, which expand in form of a rose; upon the top of the foot-stalk is the ovary, which has a short starlike cup, divided at the top into five parts, and expanded; the ovary becomes an oblong umbilicated fruit, divided into three cells, which are full of kidney-shaped seeds. *Miller.*

There will I make thee beds of roses
With a thousand fragrant posies;
A cap of flowers, and a girdle
Imbroider'd all with leaves of *myrtle*. *Shakespeare.*

I was of late as petty to his ends,
As is the morn dew on the *myrtle* leaf
To his grand sea. *Shakesp. Antony and Cleopatra.*

Democritus would have Concord like a fair virgin, holding in one hand a pomegranate, in the other a bundle of *myrtle*; for such is the nature of these trees, that if they be planted though a good space one from the other, they will meet, and with twining one embrace the other. *Peacham.*

Nor can the muse the gallant Sidney pass
The plume of war! with early lawrels crown'd,
The lover's *myrtle* and the poet's bay. *Thomson's Summer.*

Myse'lf. *n. s.* [*my* and *self.*]

1. An emphatical word added to *I*: as, *I* myself *do it*; that is, not I by proxy; not another.

As his host,
I should against his murth'rer shut the door,
Not bear the knife *myself*. *Shakespeare's Macbeth.*

2. The reciprocal of *I.* in the oblique case.

They have missed another pain, against which I should have been at a loss to defend *myself*. *Swift's Examiner.*

Mystago'gue. *n. s.* [μυσαγωγὸς; *mystagogus*, Latin.] One who interprets divine mysteries; also one who keeps church relicks, and shews them to strangers. *Bailey.*

Myste'riarch. *n. s.* [μυςήριον and ἀρχὴ.] One presiding over mysteries.

MYSTE'RIOUS. *adj.* [*myſterieux*, French, from *myſtery.*]

1. Inacceſſible to the underſtanding; awfully obſcure.

God at laſt
To Satan, firſt in ſin, his doom apply'd,
Though in *myſterious* terms. *Milton's Par. Loſt. b.* x.
Then the true Son of knowledge firſt appear'd,
And the old dark *myſterious* clouds were clear'd. *Denham.*

2. Artfully perplexed.

Thoſe princes who were moſt diſtinguiſhed for their *myſterious* ſkill in government, found, by the event, that they had ill conſulted their own quiet, or the happineſs of their people. *Swift's Thoughts on the State of Affairs.*

MYSTE'RIOUSLY. *adv.* [from *myſterious.*]

1. In a manner above underſtanding.
2. Obſcurely; enigmatically.

Our duty of preparation contained in this one word, try or examine, being after the manner of myſteries, *myſteriouſly* and ſecretly deſcribed, there is reaſon to believe that there is in it very much duty. *Taylor's Worthy Communicant.*

Each ſtair *myſteriouſly* was meant. *Milton.*

MYSTE'RIOUSNESS. *n. ſ.* [from *myſterious.*]

1. Holy obſcurity.

My purpoſe is, to gather together into an union all thoſe ſeveral portions of truth, and differing apprehenſions of *myſteriouſneſs.* *Taylor's Worthy Communicant.*

2. Artful difficulty or perplexity.

To MY'STERIZE. *v. a.* [from *myſtery.*] To explain as enigmas.

Myſterizing their enſigns, they make the particular ones of the twelve tribes accommodable unto the twelve ſigns of the zodiack. *Brown's Vulgar Errours, b.* v.

MY'STERY. *n. ſ.* [μυςήριον; *myſtere*, Fr.]

1. Something above human intelligence; ſomething awfully obſcure.

They can judge as fitly of his worth,
As I can of thoſe *myſteries* which heav'n
Will not have earth to know. *Shakeſpeare's Coriolanus.*

Upon holy days, let the matter of your meditations be according to the *myſtery* of the day; and to your ordinary devotions of every day, add the prayer which is fitted to the *myſtery.* *Taylor.*

If God ſhould pleaſe to reveal unto us this great *myſtery* of the trinity, or ſome other *myſteries* in our holy religion, we ſhould not be ableto underſtand them, unleſs he would beſtow on us ſome new faculties of the mind. *Swift's Serm.*

2. An enigma; any thing artfully made difficult.

To thy great comfort in this *myſtery* of ill opinions, here's the twin brother of thy letter. *Shak. Mer. Wives of Windſor.*

Important truths ſtill let your fables hold,
And moral *myſteries* with art unfold. *Granville.*

3. A trade; a calling: in this ſenſe it ſhould, according to *Warburton*, be written *miſtery*, from *meſtiero*, French, a trade.

And that which is the nobleſt *myſterie*,
Brings to reproach and common infamy. *Hubberd's Tale.*

Inſtruction, manners, *myſteries* and trades,
Degrees, obſervances, cuſtoms and laws,
Decline to your confounding contraries. *Shakeſpeare.*

MY'STICAL. }
MY'STICK. } *adj.* [*myſticus*, Latin.]

1. Sacredly obſcure.

Let God himſelf that made me, let not man that knows not himſelf, be my inſtructor concerning the *myſtical* way to heaven. *Hooker, b.* i.

From ſalvation all fleſh being excluded this way, God hath revealed a way *myſtical* and ſupernatural. *Hooker, b.* i.

2. Involving ſome ſecret meaning; emblematical.

Ye five other wand'ring fires! that move
In *myſtick* dance not without ſong, reſound
His praiſe, who out of darkneſs call'd up light. *Milton.*

It is Chriſt's body in the ſacrament and out of it; but in the ſacrament not the natural truth, but the ſpiritual and *myſtical.* *Taylor's Worthy Communicant.*

It is plain from the Apocalypſe, that *myſtical* Babylon is to be conſumed by fire. *Burnet's Theory of the Earth.*

3. Obſcure; ſecret.

Leſt new fears diſturb the happy ſtate,
Know, I have ſearch'd the *myſtick* rolls of fate. *Dryden.*

MY'STICALLY. *adv.* [from *myſtical.*] In a manner, or by an act, implying ſome ſecret meaning.

Theſe two in thy ſacred boſom hold,
Till *myſtically* join'd but one they be. *Donne.*

MY'STICALNESS. *n. ſ.* [from *myſtical.*] Involution of ſome ſecret meaning.

MYTHOLO'GICAL. *adj.* [from *mythology.*] Relating to the explication of fabulous hiſtory.

The original of the conceit was probably hieroglyphical, which after became *mythological*, and by tradition ſtole into a total verity, which was but partially true in its covert ſenſe and morality. *Brown's Vulgar Errours.*

MYTHOLO'GICALLY. *adv.* [from *mythological.*] In a manner ſuitable to the ſyſtem of fables.

MYTHO'LOGIST. *n. ſ.* [from *mythology.*] A relator or expoſitor of the ancient fables of the heathens.

The grammarians and *mythologiſts* ſeem to be altogether unacquainted with his writings. *Creech.*

It was a celebrated problem among ancient *mythologiſts*, What was the ſtrongeſt thing, what the wiſeſt, and what the greateſt? *Norris's Miſcel.*

To MYTHO'LOGIZE. *v. n.* [from *mythology.*] To relate or explain the fabulous hiſtory of the heathens.

MYTHO'LOGY. *n. ſ.* [μῦθος and λόγος; *mythologie*, French.] Syſtem of fables; explication of the fabulous hiſtory of the gods of the heathen world.

The modeſty of *mythology* deſerves to be commended: the ſcenes there are laid at a diſtance; it is once upon a time, in the days of yore, and in the land of Utopia. *Bentley.*

N.

N, A semivowel, has in English an invariable sound; as, *no*, *name*, *net*; it is sometimes after *m* almost lost; as, *condemn*, *contemn*.

To NAB. *v. a.* [*nappa*, Swedish.] To catch unexpectedly; to seize without warning. A word seldom used but in low language.

NADIR. *n. s.* [Arabick.] The point under foot directly opposite to the zenith.

As far as four bright signs comprize,
The distant zenith from the *nadir* lies. *Creech.*

NAFF. *n. s.* A kind of tufted sea-bird.

NAG. *n. s.* [*nagge*, Dutch.]

1. A small horse. A horse in familiar language.

A hungry lion would fain have been dealing with good horse-flesh; but the *nag* would be too fleet. *L'Estrange.*

Thy *nags*, the leanest things alive,
So very hard thou lov'st to drive. *Prior.*

2. A paramour; in contempt.

Your ribauld *nag* of Egypt
Hoists sails, and flies. *Shakespeare's Ant. and Cleopatra.*

NAIL. *n. s.* [nœgl, Saxon; *nagel*, German.]

1. The hard crust or horny substance at the ends of the fingers and toes.

My *nails* can reach unto thine eyes. *Shakespeare.*

The meanest sculptor in th' Æmilian square,
Can imitate in brass, the *nails* and hair;
Expert in trifles. *Dryden.*

The *nails* of our fingers give strength to those parts in the various functions they are put to; and defend the numerous nerves and tendons that are under them. *Ray.*

2. The talons of birds and beasts.

3. A spike of metal by which things are fastened together.

As one *nail* by strength drives out another;
So the remembrance of my former love
Is by a newer object soon forgotten. *Shakespeare.*

For the body of the ships, no nation doth equal England, nor for the oaken timber to build them; and we need not borrow iron for spikes or *nails*, to fasten them together. *Bacon's Advice to Villiers.*

The load-stone mines in the shore of India, are so placed in abundance and vigor, that it proves an adventure of hazard to pass those coasts in a ship with iron *nails*. *Brown's Vulgar Errours, b.* ii. *c.* 3.

A beechen pail
Hung by the handle, on a driven *nail*. *Dryden.*

An equivocal word used for the *nail* of the hand or foot, and for an iron *nail* to fasten any thing. *Watts.*

4. A Stud; a boss.

5. A kind of measure; two inches and a quarter.

6. On the *nail*. Readily; immediately; without delay. I suppose from a counter studded with nails.

We want our money on the *nail*,
The banker's ruin'd if he pays. *Swift's Poems.*

To NAIL. *v. a.* [from the noun.]

1. To fasten with nails.

To the cross he *nails* thy enemies,
The law that is against thee, and the sins
Of all mankind, with him are crucify'd. *Milton's P. Lost.*

He clasp'd his hand upon the wounded part.
The second shaft came swift and unespy'd,
And pierc'd his hand, and *nail'd* it to his side. *Dryden.*

2. To stud with nails.

In golden armour glorious to behold,
The rivets of your arms were *nail'd* with gold. *Dryden.*

NAILER. *n. s.* [from *nail.*] One whose trade is to forge nails; a nail-maker.

NA'KED. *adj.* [nacod, Saxon.]

1. Wanting cloaths; uncovered; bare.

A philosopher being asked in what a wise man differed from a fool? answered, send them both *naked* to those who know them not, and you shall perceive. *Bacon, Apophth.* 242.

He pitying how they stood
Before him *naked* to the air, that now
Must suffer change;
As father of his family, he clad
Their nakedness with skins of beasts. *Milton, P. Lost.*

Ungrateful men,
Behold my bosom *naked* to your swords,
And let the man that's injur'd strike the blow. *Addison.*

2. Unarmed; defenceless; unprovided.

Had I but serv'd my God with half the zeal
I serv'd my king, he would not in mine age
Have left me *naked* to mine enemies. *Shakes. Henry* VIII.

3. Plain; evident; not hidden.

The truth appears so *naked* on my side,
That any purblind eye may find it out. *Shakes. Hen.* VI.

4. Mere; bare; wanting the necessary additions; simple; abstracted.

Not that God doth require nothing unto happiness at the hands of men, saving only a *naked* belief, for hope and charity we may not exclude; but that without belief all other things are as nothing, and it is the ground of those other divine virtues. *Hooker, b.* i. *p.* 37.

NA'KEDLY. *adv.*

1. Without covering.

2. Simply; merely; barely; in the abstract.

Though several single letters *nakedly* considered, are found to be articulations only of spirit or breath, and not of breath vocalized; yet there is that property in all letters of aptness, to be conjoined in syllables. *Holder.*

3. Discoverably; evidently.

So blinds the sharpest counsels of the wise
This overshadowing Providence on high,
And dazzleth all their clearest sighted eyes,
That they see not how *nakedly* they lie. *Daniel Civil War.*

NA'KEDNESS. *n. s.* [from *naked.*]

1. Nudity; want of covering.

My face I'll grime with filth;
And with presented *nakedness* out-face
The winds and persecutions of the sky. *Sha. K. Lear.*

Nor he their outward only, with the skins
Of beasts; but inward *nakedness*, much more
Opprobrious! with his robe of righteousness
Arraying, cover'd from his father's sight. *Milton.*

I entreat my gentle readers to sew on their tuckers again, and not to imitate the *nakedness*, but the innocence of their mother Eve. *Addison's Guard.* Nº. 100.

Thou to be strong must put off every dress,
Thy only armour is thy *nakedness*. *Prior.*

2. Want of provision for defence.

Spies, to see the *nakedness* of the land are come. *Gen.* xlii. 9.

3. Plainness; evidence; want of concealment.

Why seek'st thou to cover with excuse
That which appears in proper *nakedness*? *Shakes.*

NALL. *n. s.* An awl, such as collar-makers use. *Tusser.*

Whole bridle and saddle, whitleather and *nall*,
With collars and harness. *Tusser's Husb.*

NAME. *n. s.* [*nama*, Saxon; *naem*, Dutch; *anam*, Erse.]

1. The discriminative appellation of an individual.

What is thy *name*?
Thou'lt be afraid to hear it.
No: though thou call'st thyself a hotter *name*
Than any is in hell.
My *name's* Macbeth. *Shakespeare's Macbeth.*

He called their *names* after the *names* his father had called them. *Gen.* xxvi. 18.

I know thee by *name*. *Ex.* xxxiii. 17.

2. The term by which any kind or species is distinguished.

What's in a *name*? That which we call a rose,
By any other *name* would smell as sweet. *Shakes.*

If every particular idea that we take in, should have a distinct *name*, *names* must be endless. *Locke.*

3. Person.

They list with women each degen'rate *name*,
Who dares not hazard life for future fame. *Dryden.*

4. Reputation; character.

The king's army was the last enemy the west had been acquainted with, and had left no good *name* behind. *Clarendon, b.* viii.

5. Renown; fame; celebrity; eminence; praise; remembrance; memory; distinction; honour.

What men of *name* resort to him?
Sir Walter Herbert, a renowned soldier;
And Rice ap Thomas with a valiant crew,
And many others of great *name* and worth. *Shakes.*

Visit eminent persons of great *name* abroad; to tell how the life agreeth with the fame. *Bacon's Essays*, Nº. 19.

Here rest thy bones in rich Hesperia's plains,
Thy *name*, 'tis all a ghost can have, remains. *Dryden.*

A hundred knights
Approv'd in fight, and men of mighty *name*. *Dryden.*

These shall be towns of mighty fame,
Tho' now they lie obscure, and lands without a *name*. *Dryden, Æn.* vi.

Bartolus is of great *name*; whose authority is as much valued amongst the modern lawyers, as Papinian's was among the ancients. *Baker's Reflect. on Learning.*

6. Power delegated; imputed character.

In the *name* of the people,
And in the power of us the tribunes, we
Banish him. *Shakespeare's Coriolanus.*

7. Fictitious imputation.

When Ulysses with fallacious arts,
Had forg'd a treason in my patron's *name*,
My kinsman fell. *Dryden, Æn.*

8. Appearance; not reality; assumed character.

I'll to him again, in the *name* of Brook;
He'll tell me all his purpose. *Sha. Mer. W. of Windsor.*

There is a friend which is only a friend in *name*. *Ecclus.* xxxvii.

9. An opprobrious appellation.

Bids her confess; calls her ten thousand *names*;
In vain she kneels. *Granvil's Poems.*

Like the watermen of Thames
I row by, and call them *names*. *Swift's Miscel.*

To Name. *v. a.* [from the noun.]

1. To discriminate by a particular appellation.

I mention here a son of the king's whom Florizel
I now *name* to you; and with speed so pace
To speak of Perdita. *Shakespeare's Win. Tale.*

Thou hast had seven husbands, neither wast thou *named* after any of them. *Tob.* iii. 8.

His name was called Jesus, which was so *named* of the angel before he was conceived. *Luke* ii. 21.

2. To mention by name.

Accustom not thy mouth to swearing: neither use thyself to the *naming* of the Holy One. *Ecclus.* xxiii. 9.

3. To specify; to nominate.

Did my father's godson seek your life?
He whom my father *nam'd?* your Edgar. *Shakespeare.*

Bring me him up whom I shall *name*. 1 *Sam.* xxviii. 8.

Let any one *name* that proposition, whose terms or ideas were either of them innate. *Locke.*

4. To utter; to mention.

Let my name be *named* on them. *Gen.* xlviii. 16.

Na'meless. *adj.* [from *name*.]

1. Not distinguished by any discriminative appellation.

On the cold earth lies th' unregarded king,
A headless carcass, and a *nameless* thing. *Denham.*

The milky way,
Fram'd of many *nameless* stars. *Waller.*

Thy reliques, Rowe, to this fair shrine we trust,
And sacred, place by Dryden's awful dust;
Beneath a rude and *nameless* stone he lies,
To which thy tomb shall guide enquiring eyes. *Pope.*

2. One of which the name is not known or mentioned.

Little credit is due to accusations of this kind, when they come from suspected, that is, from *nameless* pens. *Atterbury's Sermons.*

Na'mely. *adv.* [from *name*.] Particularly; specially; to mention by *name*.

It can be to nature no injury, that of her we say the same which diligent beholders of her works have observed; *namely*, that she provideth for all living creatures nourishment which may suffice. *Hooker, b.* iii. *s.* 4.

Which of these sorrows is he subject to?
To none of these, except it be the last;
Namely, some love that drew him oft from home. *Sha.*

The council making remonstrances unto queen Elizabeth, of the continual conspiracies against her life; and *namely*, that a man was lately taken, who stood ready in a very dangerous and suspicious manner to do the deed; advised her to go less abroad weakly attended. But the queen answered, that she had rather be dead, than put in custody. *Bacon, Apophth.* 14.

For the excellency of the soul, *namely*, its power of divining in dreams; that several such divinations have been made, none can question. *Addison's Spectator.*

Solomon's choice does not only instruct us in that point of history, but furnishes out a very fine moral to us; *namely*, that he who applies his heart to wisdom, does at the same time take the most proper method for gaining long life, riches, and reputation. *Addison's Guardian.*

Na'mer. *n. s.* [*name*.] One who calls or knows any by name.

Na'mesake. *n. s.* One that has the same name with another.

Nor does the dog fish at sea, much more make out the dog of land, than that his cognominal, or *namesake* in the heavens. *Brown's Vulgar Errours, b.* iii.

One author is a mole to another: it is impossible for them to discover beauties; they have eyes only for blemishes: they can indeed see the light, as is said of their *namesakes*; but immediately shut their eyes. *Addison's Spectator.*

NAP. *n. s.* [hnæppan, Saxon, to sleep.]

1. Slumber; a short sleep.

Mopsa sat swallowing of sleep with open mouth making such a noise, as no body could lay the stealing of a *nap* to her charge. *Sidney, b.* ii.

Let your bounty
Take a *nap*, and I will awake it anon. *Shakespeare.*

The sun had long since in the lap
Of Thetis, taken out his *nap*. *Hudibras, p.* ii.

So long as I'm at the forge you are still taking your *nap*. *L'Estrange, Fab.*

2. [hnoppa, Saxon.] Down; villous substance.

Amongst those leaves she made a butterfly
With excellent device and wondrous flight;
The velvet *nap*, which on his wings doth lie,
The silken down, with which his back is dight. *Spenser.*

Jack Cade the clothier, means to dress the Commonwealth, and set a new *nap* upon it. *Shakes.*

Plants, though they have no prickles, have a kind of downy or velvet rind upon their leaves; which down or *nap* cometh of a subtil spirit, in a soft or fat substance. *Bacon.*

Ah! where must needy poet seek for aid
When dust and rain at once his coat invade;
His only coat! where dust confus'd with rain
Roughens the *nap*, and leaves a mingled stain. *Swift.*

To Napp. *v. a.* [hnæppan, Saxon.] To sleep; to be drowsy or secure.

They took him *napping* in his bed. *Hudibras, p.* i.

A wolf took a dog *napping* at his master's door. *L'Estran.*

What is seriously related by Helmont, that foul linen, stopt in a vessel that hath wheat in it, will in twenty-one days time turn the wheat into mice; without conjuring, one may guess to have been the philosophy and information of some housewife, who had not so carefully covered her wheat, but that the mice could come at it, and were there taken *napping*, just when they had made an end of their good chear. *Bentley's Sermons.*

Na'ptaking. *n. s.* [*nap* and *take*.] Surprize; seizure on a sudden; unexpected onset, like that made on men asleep.

Naptakings, assaults, spoilings, and firings, have in our forefather's days, between us and France, been very common. *Carew.*

NAPE. *n. s.* [Of uncertain etymology. *Skinner* imagines it to come from *nap*, the hair that grows on it; *Junius*, with his usual Greek sagacity, from νάπη, *a hill*; perhaps from the same root with *knob*.] The joint of the neck behind.

Turn your eyes towards the *napes* of your necks, and make but an interiour survey of your good selves. *Shakes.*

Domitian dreamed, the night before he was slain, that a golden head was growing out of the *nape* of his neck. *Bacon.*

Na'pery. *n. s.* [*naperia*, Italian.] Table-linen. *Dict.*

Na'phew. *n. s.* [*napus*, Lat.] An herb.

Na'phtha. *n. s.* [*naphtha*, Latin.]

Naphtha is a very pure, clear, and thin mineral fluid, of a very pale yellow, with a cast of brown in it. It is soft and oily to the touch, of a sharp and unpleasing taste, and of a brisk and penetrating smell; of the bituminous kind. It is extremely ready to take fire, and in places where it is frequent, it exhales a vapour that takes fire at the approach of any flame, and burns to a great distance, sometimes spreading in an instant over half a mile or more of ground, and continuing alight a great while. It is found floating on the waters of springs. It is principally used externally in paralytick cases, and in pains of the limbs. *Hill's Mat. Med.*

Strabo represents it as a liquation of bitumen. It swims on the top of the water of wells and springs. That found about Babylon is in some springs whitish, tho' it be generally black, and differs little from Petroleum. *Woodward.*

Na'ppiness. *n. s.* [*nappy*.] The quality of having a nap.

Na'pkin. *n. s.* [from *nap*; which etymology is oddly favoured by *Virgil*, *Tonsisque ferunt mantilia villis*; *naperia*, Italian.]

1. Cloaths used at table to wipe the hands.

By art were weaved *napkins*, shirts, and coats, inconsumptible by fire. *Brown's Vulgar Errours.*

The same matter was woven into a *napkin* at Louvain, which was cleansed by being burnt in the fire. *Wilkins.*

Napkins, Heliogabalus had of cloth of gold, but they were most commonly of linnen, or soft wool. *Arbuthnot.*

2. A

2. A hankerchief. Obsolete. This sense is retained in Scotland.

I am glad I have found this *napkin*;
This was her first remembrance from the moor. *Shakesp.*

NA'PLESS. *adj.* [from *nap.*] Wanting nap; threadbare.

Were he to stand for consul, ne'er would he
Appear in th' market place, nor on him put
The *napless* vesture of humility. *Shakesp. Coriolanus.*

NA'PPY. *adj.* [from *nap.* Mr. *Lye* derives it from *nappe*, Saxon, a cup.] Frothy; spumy; from *nap*; whence apples and ale are called lamb's wooll.

When I my thresher heard,
With *nappy* beer I to the barn repair'd. *Gay's Past.*

NARCI'SSUS. *n. s.* [Latin; *narcisse*, Fr.] A daffodil.

Nor *Narcissus* fair
As o'er the fabled mountain hanging still. *Thomson.*

NARCO'TICK. *adj.* [ναρκόω; *narcotique*, Fr.] Producing torpor, or stupefaction.

Narcotick includes all that part of the materia medica, which any way produces sleep, whether called by this name, or hypnoticks, or opiates. *Quincy.*

The ancients esteemed it *narcotick* or stupefactive, and it is to be found in the list of poisons by *Dioscorides*. *Brown's Vulgar Errours, b.* vi.

NARD. *n. s.* [*nardus*, Lat. νάρδος, Gr.]

1. Spikenard; a kind of ointment.

2. An odorous shrub.

Smelt o'the bud o'the briar,
Or the *nard* in the fire. *Ben. Johnson's Underwoods.*

He now is come
Into the blissful field, thro' groves of myrrh,
And flow'ring odours, cassia, *nard* and balm. *Milton.*

NARE. *n. s.* [*naris*, Latin.] A nostril not used, except as in the following passage, in affectation.

There is a Machiavelian plot,
Though every *nare* olfact it not. *Hudibras, p.* i. *cant.* 1.

NA'RWHALE. *n. s.* A species of whale.

Those long horns preserved as precious beauties, are but the teeth of *narwhales*. *Brown's Vulg. Err. b.* iii.

NA'RRABLE. *adj.* [from *narro.*] Capable to be told or related.

NA'RRATE. *v. a.* [*narro*, Latin.] To relate; to tell; a word only used in Scotland.

NARRA'TION. *n. s.* [*narratio*, Latin; *narration*, Fr.] Account; relation; history.

He did doubt of the truth of that *narration*. *Abbot.*

They that desire to look into the *narrations* of the story, for the variety of the matter we have been careful might have profit. 2 *Mac.* ii. 24.

Homer introduces the best instructions, in the midst of the plainest *narrations*. *Notes on the Odyssy.*

NA'RRATIVE. *adj.* [*narratif-ve*, Fr. from *narro*, Lat.]

1. Relating; giving an account.

The words of all judicial acts are written narratively, unless it be in sentences dispositive and enacting; therefore credit ought to be given to these acts, though the words be *narrative*. *Ayliffe's Parergon.*

2. Storytelling; apt to relate things past.

Age, as *Davenant* says, is always *narrative*. *Dryden.*

The poor, the rich, the valiant and the sage,
And boasting youth, and *narrative* old age. *Pope.*

NA'RRATIVE. *n. s.* A relation; an account; a story.

In the instructions I here give to others, concerning what they should do, take a *narrative* of what you have done. *South's Sermons.*

Cynthio was much taken with my *narrative*. *Tatler*, N°. 58.

NA'RRATIVELY. *adv.* [from *narrative.*] By way of relation.

The words of all judicial acts are written *narratively*, unless it be in sentences wherein dispositive and enacting terms are made use of. *Ayliffe's Parergon.*

NARRA'TOR. *n. s.* [*narrateur*, French; from *narro*, Latin.] A teller; a relater.

Consider whether the *narrator* be honest and faithful, as well as skilful; whether he hath no peculiar gain or profit by believing or reporting it. *Watts's Logick.*

To NA'RRIFY. *v. a.* [from *narro*, Latin.] To relate; to give account of; not in use.

I ever *narrify'd* my friends,
Of whom he is chief, with all the size that verity
Would without lapsing suffer. *Shakespeare.*

NA'RROW. *adj.* [neaꞃu, Saxon, from nyꞃ, near.]

1. Not broad or wide, having but a small distance from side to side.

Edward from Belgia,
Hath pass'd in safety thro' the *narrow* seas. *Shakespeare.*

The Angel stood in a *narrow* place, where was no way to turn either to the right hand or to the left. *Numb.* ii. 26.

In a *narrow*-bottom'd ditch cattle cannot turn themselves. *Mortimer's Husbandry.*

2. Small; of no great extent.

From this *narrow* time of gestation may ensue a smallness in the exclusion; but this inferreth no informity. *Brown.*

3. Covetous; avaritious.

To *narrow* breasts he comes all wrapt in gain,
To swelling hearts he shines in honour's fire. *Sidney.*

4. Contracted; of confined sentiments; ungenerous.

Nothing more shakes any society than mean divisions between the several orders of its members, and their *narrow*-hearted repining at each other's gain. *Sprat's Serm.*

The greatest understanding is *narrow*. How much of God and nature is there, whereof we never had any idea? *Grew, Cosmol. b.* ii. *c.* 8.

The hopes of receiving good from those whom we gratify, would produce but a very *narrow* and stinted charity. *Smallridge's Sermons.*

A salamander grows familiar with a stranger at first sight, and is not so *narrow*-spirited as to observe, whether the person she talks to, be in breeches or in petticoats. *Addison.*

It is with *narrow*-soul'd people as with *narrow*-neck'd bottles; the less they have in them the more noise they make in pouring it out. *Swift's Miscellanies.*

5. Near; within a small distance.

Then Mnestheus to the head his arrow drove,
But made a glancing shot, and miss'd the dove;
Yet miss'd so *narrow*, that he cut the cord
Which fasten'd by the foot the flitting bird. *Dryden.*

6. Close; vigilant; attentive.

The orb he roam'd
With *narrow* search; and with inspection deep
Consider'd ev'ry creature, which of all
Most opportune might serve his wiles. *Milt. Par. Lost.*

Many malicious spies are searching into the actions of a great man, who is not always the best prepared for so *narrow* an inspection. *Addison's Spectator*, N°. 265.

To NA'RROW. *v. a.* [from the adjective.]

1. To diminish with respect to breadth or wideness.

In the wall he made *narrowed* rests, that the beams should not be fastened in the walls of the house. 1 *Kings* vi. 6.

By reason of the great Continent of Brasilia, the needle deflecteth toward the land twelve degrees; but at the Straits of Magellan, where the land is *narrowed*, and the sea on the other side, it varieth about five or six. *Brown's V. Err.*

A government, which by alienating the affections, losing the opinions, and crossing the interests of the people, leaves out of its compass the greatest part of their consent, may justly be said, in the same degrees it loses ground, to *narrow* its bottom. *Temple's Miscel.*

2. To contract; to impair in dignity of extent or influence.

One science is incomparably above all the rest, where it is not by corruption *narrowed* into a trade, for mean or ill ends, and secular interests; I mean, theology, which contains the knowledge of God and his creatures. *Locke's Works.*

3. To contract in sentiment or capacity of knowledge.

Desuetude does contract and *narrow* our faculties, so that we can apprehend only those things in which we are conversant. *Government of the Tongue.*

How hard it is to get the mind, *narrowed* by a scanty collection of common ideas, to enlarge itself to a more copious stock. *Locke's Works.*

Lo! ev'ry finish'd son returns to thee!
Bounded by nature, *narrow'd* still by art,
A trifling head, and a contracted heart. *Pope's Dunc. b.* iv.

4. To confine; to limit.

By admitting too many things at once into one question, the mind is dazzled and bewildered; whereas by limiting and *narrowing* the question, you take a fuller survey of the whole. *Watts's Logick.*

Our knowledge is much more *narrow'd*, if we confine ourselves to our own solitary reasonings, without much reading. *Watts.*

5. [In farriery.] A horse is said to *narrow*, when he does not take ground enough, and does not bear far enough out to the one hand or to the other. *Farr. Dict.*

NA'RROWLY. *adv.* [from *narrow.*]

1. With little breadth or wideness; with small distance between the sides.

2. Contractedly; without extent.

The church of England is not so *narrowly* calculated, that it cannot fall in with any regular species of government. *Swift's Sentim. of the Church of England.*

3. Closely; vigilantly; attentively.

My fellow-schoolmaster
Doth watch Bianca's steps so *narrowly*. *Shakespeare.*

If it be *narrowly* considered, this colour will be reprehended or encountered, by imputing to all excellencies in compositions a kind of poverty. *Bacon.*

For a considerable treasure hid in my vineyard, search *narrowly* when I am gone. *L'Estrange.*

A man's reputation draws eyes upon him that will *narrowly* inspect every part of him. *Addison.*

4. Nearly; within a little.

Some private vessels took one of the Aquapulca ships, and very *narrowly* missed of the other. *Swift.*

5. Avaritiously; sparingly.

NA'RROWNESS. *n. s.* [from *narrow.*]

1. Want of breadth or wideneſs.

In our Gothic cathedrals, the *narrowneſs* of the arch makes it riſe in height, or run out in length. *Addiſon on Italy.*

2. Want of extent; want of comprehenſion.

That prince, who ſhould be ſo wiſe and godlike, as by eſtabliſhed laws of liberty to ſecure protection and encouragement to the honeſt induſtry of mankind, againſt the oppreſſion of power, and *narrowneſs* of party, will quickly be too hard for his neighbours. *Locke's Works.*

3. Confined ſtate; contractedneſs.

The moſt learned and ingenious ſociety in Europe, confeſs the *narrowneſs* of human attainments. *Glanv. Scept.*

Cheap vulgar arts, whoſe *narrowneſs* affords
No flight for thoughts, but poorly ſticks at words. *Denham.*

The latin, a moſt ſevere and compendious language, often expreſſes that in one word, which either the barbarity or the *narrowneſs* of modern tongues cannot ſupply in more. *Dryden.*

4. Meanneſs; poverty.

If God will fit thee for this paſſage, by taking off thy load, and emptying thy bags, and ſo ſuit the *narrowneſs* of thy fortune to the narrowneſs of the way thou art to paſs, is there any thing but mercy in all this? *South's Sermons.*

5. Want of capacity.

Another diſpoſition in men, which makes them improper for philoſophical contemplations, is not ſo much from the *narrowneſs* of their ſpirit and underſtanding, as becauſethey will not take time to extend them. *Burn. Theo. of the Earth.*

NAS. [from *ne has*, or *has not.*]

For pity'd is miſhap that *nas* remedy,
But ſcorn'd been deeds of fond foolery. *Spenſer.*

NA'SAL. *adj.* [*naſus*, Latin.] Belonging to the noſe.

To pronounce the *naſals*, and ſome of the vowels ſpiritally, the throat is brought to labour, and it makes a guttural pronunciation. *Holder's Elements of Speech.*

When the diſcharge leſſens, paſs a ſmall probe through the *naſal* duct into the noſe every time it is dreſt, in order to dilate it a little. *Sharp's Surgery.*

NA'SICORNOUS. *adj.* [*naſus* and *cornu.*] Having the horn on the noſe.

Some unicorns are among inſects; as thoſe four kinds of *naſicornous* beetles deſcribed by Muffetus. *Brown's V. Err.*

NA'STY. *adj.* [*naſt*, *nat*, German, wet.]

1. Dirty; filthy; ſordid; nauſeous; polluted.

Sir Thomas More, in his anſwer to Luther, has thrown out the greateſt heap of *naſty* language that perhaps ever was put together. *Atterbury.*

A nice man, is a man of *naſty* ideas. *Swift.*

2. Obſcene; leud.

NA'STILY. *adv.* [from *naſty.*]

1. Dirtily; filthily; nauſeouſly.

The moſt pernicious infection next the plague, is the ſmell of the jail, when priſoners have been long and cloſe and *naſtily* kept. *Bacon's Natural Hiſtory.*

2. Obſcenely; groſly.

NA'STINESS. *n. s.* [from *naſty.*]

1. Dirt; filth.

This cauſed the ſeditious to remain within their ſtation, which by reaſon of the *naſtineſs* of the beaſtly multitude, might more fitly be termed a kennel than a camp. *Hayward.*

Haughty and huge, as high Dutch bride,
Such *naſtineſs* and ſo much pride
Are oddly join'd by fate, *Swift.*

2. Obſcenity; groſsneſs of ideas.

Their *naſtineſs*, their dull obſcene talk and ribauldry, cannot but be very nauſeous and offenſive to any who does not baulk his own reaſon, out of love to their vice. *South.*

A divine might have employed his pains to better purpoſe, than in the *naſtineſs* of Plautus and Ariſtophanes. *Dry.*

NA'TAL. *adj.* [*natal*, Fr. *natalis*, Latin.] Native; relating to nativity.

Since the time of Henry III. princes children took names from their *natal* places, as Edward of Carnarvon, Thomas of Brotherton. *Camden.*

Propitious ſtar! whoſe ſacred pow'r
Preſided o'er the monarch's *natal* hour,
Thy radiant voyages for ever run. *Prior.*

NATA'TION. *n. s.* [*natatio*, Latin.] The act of ſwimming.

In progreſſive motion, the arms and legs move ſucceſſively, but in *natation* both together. *Brown's Vulgar Errours.*

NA'THLESS. *ad.* [*na*, that is, *not the leſs*, Saxon.] Nevertheleſs; formed thus, *natheleſs*, *nath'leſs*. Obſolete.

Nath'leſs, my brother ſince we paſſed are
Unto this point, we will appeaſe our jar. *Spenſer.*

The torrid clime
Smote on him ſore beſides, vaulted with fire.
Nathleſs he ſo endur'd, 'till on the beach
Of that inflmed ſea he ſtood, and call'd
His legions. *Milton's Paradiſe Loſt.*

NA'THMORE. *adv.* [*na the more.*] Never the more.

Yet *nathmore* by his bold hearty ſpeech,
Could his blood-frozen heart embolden'd be. *Spenſer.*

NA'TION. *n. s.* [*nation*, Fr. *natio*, Latin.] A people diſtinguiſhed from another people; generally by their language, original, or government.

If Edward III. had proſpered in his French wars, and peopled with Engliſh the towns which he won, as he began at Calais driving out the French, his ſucceſſors holding the ſame courſe, would have filled all France with our *nation*. *Ral.*

A *nation* properly ſignifies a great number of families derived from the ſame blood, born in the ſame country, and living under the ſame government. *Temple.*

NA'TIONAL. *adj.* [*national*, Fr. from *nation.*]

1. Publick; general; not private; not particular.

They in their earthly Canaan plac'd,
Long time ſhall dwell and proſper: but when ſins
National interrupt their public peace. *Milton's P. Loſt.*

Such a *national* devotion inſpires men with ſentiments of religious gratitude, and ſwells their hearts with joy and exultation. *Addiſon's Freeholder*, Nº. 49.

The aſtoniſhing victories our armies have been crowned with, were in ſome meaſure the bleſſings returned upon that *national* charity which has been ſo conſpicuous. *Addiſon.*

God, in the execution of his judgments, never viſits a people with public and general calamities, but where their ſins are public and *national* too. *Rogers's Sermons.*

2. Bigotted to one's own country.

NA'TIONALLY. *adv.* [from *national.*] With regard to the nation.

The term adulterous chiefly relates to the Jews, who being *nationally* eſpouſed to God by covenant, every ſin of theirs was in a peculiar manner ſpiritual adultery. *South.*

NA'TIONALNESS. *n. s.* [from *national.*] Reference to the people in general.

NA'TIVE. *adj.* [*nativus*, Latin; *natif-ve*, Fr.] Produced by nature; natural, not artificial.

She more ſweet than any bird on bough,
Would oftentimes amongſt them bear a part,
And ſtrive to paſs, as ſhe could well enough,
Their *native* muſick by her ſkilful art. *Fairy Q. b.* ii.

This doctrine doth not enter by the ear,
But of itſelf is *native* in the breaſt. *Davies.*

2. Natural; ſuch as is according to nature.

The members retired to their homes, reaſſume the *native* ſedateneſs of their temper. *Swift.*

3. Conferred by birth.

But ours is a privilege ancient and *native*,
Hangs not on an ordinance, or power legiſlative;
And firſt, 'tis to ſpeak whatever we pleaſe. *Denham.*

4. Relating to the birth; pertaining to the time or place of birth.

If theſe men have defeated the law, and outrun *native* puniſhment; though they can outſtrip men they have no wings to fly from God. *Shakeſpeare's Henry* V.

Many of our bodies ſhall, no doubt,
Find *native* graves. *Shakeſ. Hen.* V.

5. Original; natural.

Have I now ſeen death? is this the way
I muſt return to *native* duſt? O ſight
Of terror, foul, and ugly to behold. *Milt. Par. Loſt.*

NA'TIVE. *n. s.*

1. One born in any place; original inhabitant.

Th' accuſation,
All cauſe unborn, could never be the *native*
Of our ſo frank donation. *Shakeſpeare's Coriolanus.*

Make no extirpation of the *natives*, under pretence of planting religion, God ſurely will no way be pleaſed with ſuch ſacrifices. *Bacon's Advice to Villiers.*

Tully, the humble muſhroom ſcarcely known,
The lowly *native* of a country town. *Dryden's Juv.*

There ſtood a monument to Tacitus the hiſtorian, to the emperors Tacitus and Florianus, all *natives* of the place. *Addiſon on Italy.*

2. Offspring.

NA'TIVENESS. *n. s.* [from *native.*] State of being produced by nature.

NA'TIVITY. *n. s.* [*nativité*, French.]

1. Birth; iſſue into life.

Concluding ever with a thankſgiving for the *nativity* of our Saviour, in whoſe birth the births of all are only bleſſed. *Bacon.*

2. Time, place, or manner of birth.

My huſband, and my children both,
And you the calenders of their *nativity*,
Go to a goſſip's feaſt. *Shakeſ. Com. of Errors.*

They ſay there is divinity in odd numbers, either in *nativity*, chance, or death. *Shakeſ. Merr. W. of Win.*

When I vow, I weep; and vows ſo born,
In their *nativity* all truth appears. *Shakeſ. Mid. N. Dream.*

Thy birth and thy *nativity* is of Canaan. *Ezek.* xvi. 3.

3. State or place of being produced.

Theſe, in their dark *nativity*, the deep
Shall yield us, pregnant with infernal flame. *Milton.*

NA'TURAL. *adj.* [*naturel*, French, from *nature.*]

1. Pro-

1. Produced or effected by nature.

There is no *natural* motion of any particular heavy body, which is perpetual, yet it is possible from them to contrive such an artificial revolution as shall constantly be the cause of itself. *Wilkins's Dedalus.*

2. Illegitimate.

This would turn the vein of that we call *natural*, to that of legal propagation; which has ever been encouraged as the other has been disfavoured by all institutions. *Temple.*

3. Bestowed by nature.

If there be any difference in *natural* parts, it should seem that the advantage lies on the side of children born from noble and wealthy parents. *Swift.*

4. Not forced; not farfetched; dictated by nature.

I will now deliver a few of the properest and *naturallest* considerations that belong to this piece. *Wotton's Arch.*

5. Consonant to natural notions.

Such unnatural connections become, by custom, as *natural* to the mind as sun and light: fire and warmth go together, and so seem to carry with them as *natural* an evidence as self-evident truths themselves. *Locke.*

6. Tender; affectionate by nature.

To leave his wife, to leave his babes,
He wants the *nat'ral* touch. *Shakespeare's Macbeth.*

7. Unaffected; according to truth and reality.

What can be more *natural* than the circumstances in the behaviour of those women who had lost their husbands on this fatal day. *Addison.*

8. Opposed to violent; as, a *natural* death.

NA'TURAL. *n. s.* [from *nature.*]

1. An idiot; one whom nature debars from understanding; a fool.

That a monster should be such a *natural.* *Shakespeare.*

Take the thoughts of one out of that narrow compass he has been all his life confined to, you will find him no more capable of reasoning than a perfect *natural.* *Locke.*

2. Native; original inhabitant.

The inhabitants and *naturals* of the place, should be in a state of freemen. *Abbot's Description of the World.*

Oppression, in many places, wears the robes of justice, which domineering over the *naturals* may not spare strangers, and strangers will not endure it. *Raleigh's Essays.*

3. Gift of nature; nature; quality.

The wretcheder are the contemners of all helps; such as presuming on their own *naturals*, deride diligence, and mock at terms when they understand not things. *Ben. Johnson.*

To consider them in their pure *naturals*, the earl's intellectual faculties were his stronger part, and the duke, his practical. *Wotton.*

NA'TURALIST. *n. s.* [from *natural.*] A student in physicks, or natural philosophy.

Admirable artifice! wherewith Galen, tho' a mere *naturalist*, was so taken, that he could not but adjudge the honour of a hymn to the wise creator. *More.*

It is not credible, that the *naturalist* could be deceived in his account of a place that lay in the neighbourhood of Rome. *Addison on Italy.*

NATURALIZA'TION. *n. s.* [from *naturalize.*] The act of investing aliens with the privileges of native subjects.

The Spartans were nice in point of *naturalization*; whereby, while they kept their compass, they stood firm; but when they did spread, they became a windfal. *Bacon's Ess.*

Encouragement may be given to any merchants that shall come over and turn a certain stock of their own, as *naturalization*, and freedom from customs the two first years. *Temple.*

Enemies, by taking advantage of the general *naturalization* act, invited over foreigners of all religions. *Swift.*

To NA'TURALIZE. *v. a.* [from *natural.*]

1. To adopt into a community; to invest with the privileges of native subjects.

The great lords informed the king, that the Irish might not be *naturalized* without damage to themselves or the crown. *Davies on Ireland.*

2. To make natural; to make easy like things natural.

He rises fresh to his hammer and anvil; custom has *naturalized* his labour to him. *South's Sermons.*

NA'TURALLY. *adv.* [from *natural.*]

1. According to the power or impulses of unassisted nature.

Our sovereign good is desired *naturally*; God, the author of that natural desire, hath appointed natural means whereby to fulfil it; but man having utterly disabled his nature unto these means, hath had other revealed, and hath received from heaven a law to teach him, how that which is desired *naturally*, must now supernaturally be attained. *Hooker.*

If sense be not certain in the reports it makes of things to the mind, there can be *naturally* no such thing as certainty or knowledge. *South's Sermons.*

2. According to nature; without affectation.

That part
Was aptly fitted, and *naturally* perform'd. *Shakespeare.*

This answers fitly and *naturally* to the place of the abyss before the deluge, inclos'd within the vault of the earth. *Burnet's Theory of the Earth.*

The thoughts are to be measured only by their propriety; that is, as they flow more or less *naturally* from the persons and occasions. *Dryden.*

3. Spontaneously.

NA'TURALNESS. *n. s.* [from *natural.*]

1. The state of being given or produced by nature.

The *naturalness* of a desire, is the cause that the satisfaction of it is pleasure, and pleasure importunes the will; and that which importunes the will, puts a difficulty on the will refusing or forbearing it. *South's Sermons.*

2. Conformity to truth and reality; not affectation.

He must understand what is contained in the temperament of the eyes, in the *naturalness* of the eyebrows. *Dryden.*

Horace speaks of these parts in an ode that may be reckoned among the finest for the *naturalness* of the thought, and the beauty of the expression. *Addison.*

NA'TURE. *n. s.* [*natura*, Latin; *nature*, French.]

1. An imaginary being supposed to preside over the material and animal world.

Thou, *nature*, art my goddess; to thy law
My services are bound. *Shakespeare's K. Lear.*

When it was said to Anaxagoras, the Athenians have condemned you to die; he said again, and *nature* them. *Bacon.*

Let the postilion *nature* mount, and let
The coachman art be set. *Cowley.*

Heav'n bestows
At home all riches that wise *nature* needs. *Cowley.*

Simple *nature* to his hope has giv'n,
Beyond the cloud-topt hill an humbler heav'n. *Pope.*

2. The native state or properties of any thing, by which it is discriminated from others.

Between the animal and rational province, some animals have a dark resemblance of the influxes of reason: so between the corporeal and intellectual world, there is man participating much of both *natures.* *Hale's Orig. of Mankind.*

3. The constitution of an animated body.

Nature, as it grows again tow'rd earth,
Is fashion'd for the journey, dull and heavy. *Shakes.*

We're not ourselves,
When *nature*, being opprest, commands the mind
To suffer with the body. *Shakespeare's King Lear.*

4. Disposition of mind; temper.

Nothing could have subdu'd *nature*
To such a lowness but his unkind daughters. *Shakes.*

A credulous father, and a brother noble,
Whose *nature* is so far from doing harms,
That he suspects none; on whose foolish honesty
My practices ride easy. *Shakespeare's King Lear.*

5. The regular course of things.

My end
Was wrought by *nature*, not by vile offence. *Shakes.*

6. The compass of natural existence.

If their dam may be judge, the young apes are the most beautiful things in *nature.* *Glanv.*

7. Natural affection, or reverence; native sensations.

Have we not seen
The murd'ring son ascend his parent's bed,
Thro' violated *nature* force his way,
And stain the sacred womb where once he lay? *Pope.*

8. The state or operation of the material world.

He binding *nature* fast in fate,
Left conscience free and will. *Pope.*

9. Sort; species.

A dispute of this *nature* caused mischief in abundance betwixt a king and an archbishop. *Dryden.*

10. Sentiments or images adapted to nature, or conformable to truth and reality.

Only *nature* can please those tastes which are unprejudiced and refined. *Addison.*

Nature and Homer were he found the same. *Pope.*

11. Physics; the science which teaches the qualities of things.

Nature and *nature's* laws lay hid in night,
God said, let Newton be, and all was light. *Pope.*

NATU'RITY. *n. s.* [from *nature.*] The state of being produced by nature. A word not used.

This cannot be allowed, except we impute that unto the first cause which we impose not on the second; or what we deny unto nature we impute unto *naturity.* *Browne's V. Err.*

NA'VAL. *adj.* [*naval*, Fr. *navalis*, Latin.]

1. Consisting of ships.

Encamping on the main,
Our *naval* army had besieged Spain;
They that the whole world's monarchy design'd,
Are to their ports by our bold fleet confin'd. *Waller.*

As our high vessels pass their watry way,
Let all the *naval* world due homage pay. *Prior.*

2. Belonging to ships.

Masters of such numbers of strong and valiant men, as well

well as of all the *naval* ftores that furnifh the world. *Temple.*

NAVE. *n. f.* [naf, Saxon.]

1. The middle part of the wheel in which the axle moves.

Out, out, thou ftrumpet fortune! all you gods
In general fynod take away her pow'r;
Break all the fpokes and fellies from her wheel,
And bowl the round *nave* down the hill of heav'n,
As low as to the fiends. *Shakefpeare's Hamlet.*

In the wheels of waggons the hollows of the *naves*, by their fwift rotations on the ends of the axle-trees, produce a heat fometimes fo intenfe as to fet them on fire. *Ray.*

2. [From *navis*, *nave*, old Fr.] The middle part of the church diftinct from the aifles or wings.

It comprehends the *nave* or body of the church, together with the chancel. *Ayliffe's Par.*

NA'VEL. *n. f.* [napela, navela, Saxon.]

1. The point in the middle of the belly, by which embryos communicate with the parent.

The ufe of the *navel* is to continue the infant unto the mother, and by the veffels thereof to convey its aliments. *Brown's Vulgar Errours, b.* v.

As children, while within the womb they live,
Feed by the *navel*: here they feed not fo. *Davies.*

There is a fuperintending Providence, that fome animals will hunt for the teat before they are quite gotten out of the fecundines and parted from the *navelftring.* *Derham.*

2. The middle; the interiour part.

Being preft to the war,
Even when the *navel* of the ftate was touch'd,
They would not thread the gates. *Shakef. Cor.*

Within the *navel* of this hideous wood,
Immur'd in cyprefs fhades, a forcerer dwells. *Milton.*

NA'VELGALL. *n. f.*

Navelgall is a bruife on the top of the chine of the back, behind the faddle, right againft the *navel*, occafioned either by the faddle being fplit behind, or the ftuffing being wanting, or by the crupper buckle fitting down in that place, or fome hard weight or knobs lying directly behind the faddle.

NA'VELWORT. *n. f.*

It hath the appearance of houfebeck; from which it differs only in having an oblong tubulous flower of one leaf, divided at the top into five parts. This plant is ufed in medicine, and grows wild upon old walls. *Miller.*

NA'VEW. *n. f.* [*napus*, Lat. *navet*, *naveau*, Fr.]

It agrees in moft refpects with the turnep; but has a leffer root, and fomewhat warmer in tafte. The fpecies are three. In the ifle of Ely the third fpecies, which is wild, is very much cultivated, it being the cole feed from which they draw the oil. *Miller.*

NAUGHT. *adj.* [nahτ, naphihτ, Saxon; that is, *ne aught*, not any thing.] Bad; corrupt; worthlefs.

With them that are able to put a difference between things *naught* and things indifferent in the church of Rome, we are yet at controverfy about the manner of removing that which is *naught.* *Hooker, b.* iv.

Thy fifter's *naught*: Oh Regan! fhe hath tied
Sharp-tooth'd unkindnefs like a vulture here. *Shakef.*

NAUGHT. *n. f.* Nothing. This is commonly, though improperly, written *nought.* See AUGHT and OUGHT.

Be you contented
To have a fon fet your decrees at *naught*,
To pluck down juftice from your awful bench. *Shak.*

NA'UGHTILY. *adv.* [from *naughty.*] Wickedly; corruptly.

NA'UGHTINESS. *n. f.* [from *naughty.*] Wickednefs; badnefs. Slight wickednefs or parvefcuity, as of children.

No remembrance of *naughtinefs* delights but mine own; and methinks the accufing his traps might in fome manner excufe my fault, which certainly I loth to do. *Sidney, b.* ii.

NA'UGHTY. *adj.* [See NAUGHT.]

1. Bad; wicked; corrupt.

A prince of great courage and beauty, but foftered up in blood by his *naughty* father. *Sidney, b.* ii.

Thefe *naughty* times
Put bars between the owners and their rights. *Shakef.*

How far that little candle throws his beams!
So fhines a good deed in a *naughty* world. *Shakef.*

2. It is now feldom ufed but in ludicrous cenfure.

If gentle flumbers on thy temples creep,
But *naughty* man, thou doft not mean to fleep,
Betake thee to thy bed. *Dryden.*

NAVI'CULAR. *adj.* [*navicularis*, Lat. *naviculaire*, Fr.] In anatomy, the third bone in each foot that lies between the aftragalus and offa cuneiformia. *Dict.*

NA'VIGABLE. *adj.* [*navigable*, Fr. *navigabilis*, Latin.] Capable of being paffed by fhips or boats.

The firft-peopled cities were all founded upon thefe *navigable* rivers, or their branches, by which the one might give fuccour to the other. *Raleigh's Hift. of the World.*

Almighty Jove furveys
Earth, air, and fhores, and *navigable* feas. *Dryden.*

NA'VIGABLENESS. *n. f.* [from *navigable.*] Capacity to be paffed in veffels.

To NA'VIGATE. *v. n.* [*navigo*, Lat. *naviger*, Fr.] To fail; to pafs by water.

The Phœnicians *navigated* to the extremities of the weftern ocean. *Arbuthnot on Coins.*

To NA'VIGATE. *v. a.* To pafs by fhips or boats.

Drufus, the father of the emperor Claudius, was the firft who *navigated* the northern ocean. *Arbuthnot on Coins.*

NAVIGA'TION. *n. f.* [*navigation*, Fr. from *navigate.*]

1. The act or practice of paffing by water.

Our fhipping for number, ftrength, mariners, pilots, and all things that appertain to *navigation*, is as great as ever. *Bacon.*

The loadftone is that great help to *navigation.* *More.*

Rude as their fhips, was *navigation* then,
No ufeful compafs or meridian known;
Coafting, they kept the land within their ken,
And knew no north but when the poleftar fhone. *Dryden.*

When Pliny names the Pœni as inventors of *navigation*, it muft be underftood of the Phœnicians, from whom the Carthaginians are defcended. *Arbuthnot on Coins.*

2. Veffels of *navigation.*

Tho' you untie the winds, and let them fight
Againft the churches, tho' the yefty waves
Confound and fwallow *navigation* up. *Shakef. Mac.*

NAVIGA'TOR. *n. f.* [*navigateur*, Fr. from *navigate.*] Sailor; feaman; traveller by water.

By the founding of *navigators*, that fea is not three hundred and fixty foot deep. *Brerewo.*

The rules of *navigators* muft often fail. *Brown's V. Err.*

The contrivance may feem difficult, becaufe thefe fubmarine *navigators* will want winds, tides, and the fight of the heavens. *Wilkin's Math. Magic.*

This terreftrial globe, which before was only a globe in fpeculation, has fince been furrounded by the boldnefs of many *navigators.* *Temple.*

NAU'LAGE. *n. f.* [*naulum*, Lat.] The freight of paffengers in a fhip.

NAU'MACHY. *n. f.* [*naumachie*, Fr. *naumachia*, Latin.] A mock fea fight.

To NAU'SEATE. *v. n.* [from *naufen*, Latin.] To grow fqueamifh; to turn away with difguft.

Don't over-fatigue the fpirits, left the mind be feized with a laffitude, and *naufeate*, and grow tired of a particular fubject before you have finifhed it. *Watts's Improv. of the Mind.*

To NAU'SEATE. *v. a.*

1. To loath; to reject with difguft.

While we fingle out feveral difhes, and reject others, the felection feems arbitrary; for many are cryed up in one age, which are decryed and *naufeated* in another. *Brown's V. Err.*

Old age, with filent pace, comes creeping on,
Naufeates the praife, which in her youth fhe won,
And hates the mufe by which fhe was undone. *Dryden.*

Thofe heads, as ftomachs, are not fure the beft,
Which *naufeate* all, and nothing can digeft. *Pope.*

2. To ftrike with difguft.

He let go his hold and turned from her, as if he were *naufeated*, then gave her a lafh with his tail. *Swift.*

NAU'SEOUS. *adj.* [from *naufea*, Latin; *naufeé*, Fr.] Loathfome; difguftful; regarded with abhorrence.

Thofe trifles wherein children take delight,
Grow *naufeous* to the young man's appetite.
And from thofe gaieties our youth requires
To exercife their minds, our age retires. *Denham.*

Food of a wholefom juice is pleafant to the tafte and agreeable to the ftomach, 'till hunger and thirft be well appeafed, and then it begins to be lefs pleafant, and at laft even *naufeous* and loathfome. *Ray.*

Old thread-bare phrafes will often make you go out of your way to find and apply them, and are *naufeous* to rational hearers. *Swift.*

NAU'SEOUSLY. *adv.* [from *naufeous.*] Loathfomely; difguftfully.

This, though cunningly concealed, as well knowing how *naufeoufly* that drug would go down in a lawful monarchy, which was prefcribed for a rebellious commonwealth, yet they always kept in referve. *Dryden.*

Their fatire's praife;
So *naufeoufly* and fo unlike they paint. *Garth's Difp.*

NAU'SEOUSNESS. *n. f.* [from *naufeous.*] Loathfomenefs; quality of raifing difguft.

The *naufeoufnefs* of fuch company difgufts a reafonable man, when he fees he can hardly approach greatnefs but as a moated caftle; he muft firft pafs through the mud and filth with which it is encompaffed. *Dryden's Aurengzebe.*

NAU'TICAL. } *adj.* [*nauticus*, Latin.] Pertaining to failors.
NAU'TICK. }

He elegantly fhewed by whom he was drawn, which depainted the *nautical* compafs with *aut magnes, aut magna.* *Cam.*

NAU'TILUS. *n. f.* [Latin; *nautile*, Fr.] A fhell fifh furnifhed with fomething analogous to oars and a fail.

Learn of the little *nautilus* to sail,
Spread the thin oar and catch the driving gale. *Pope.*

NA'VY. *n. s.* [from *navis*, Lat.] An assembly of ships, commonly ships of war; a fleet.

On the western coast rideth a puissant *navy*. *Sha. Rich.* III.

Levy money, and return the same to the treasurer of the *navy* for his majesty's use. *Clarendon.*

The narrow seas can scarce their *navy* bear,
Or crowded vessels can their soldiers hold. *Dryden.*

NAY. *adv.* [*na*, Saxon, or *ne aye.*]

1. No; an adverb of negation.

Disputes in wrangling spend the day,
Whilst one says only yea, and t'other *nay*. *Denham.*

2. Not only so but more. A word of amplification.

A good man always profits by his endeavour, yea, when he is absent; *nay*, when dead, by his example and memory; so good authors in their stile. *Ben. Johnson's Discov.*

This is then the allay of Ovid's writings, which is sufficiently recompensed by his other excellencies; *nay*, this very fault is not without its beauties; for the most severe censor cannot but be pleased. *Dryden.*

If a son should strike his father, not only the criminal but his whole family would be rooted out, *nay*, the inhabitants of the place where he lived, would be put to the sword, *nay*, the place itself would be razed. *Addis. Spect.* Nº. 189.

3. Word of refusal.

They have beaten us openly uncondemned, being Romans, and have cast us into prison; and now do they thrust us out privily? *nay* verily; but let them come themselves and fetch us out. *Acts* xvi. 37.

The fox made several excuses, but the stork would not be said *nay*; so that at last he promised him to come. *L'Estrange, Fable* 31.

He that will not when he may,
When he would he shall have *nay*. *Prov.*

NA'YWORD. *n. s.* [*nay* and *word.*]

1. The side of denial; the saying nay.

You would believe my saying,
Howe'er you lean to th' *nayword*. *Shak. Win. Tale.*

2. A proverbial reproach; a bye word.

If I do not gull him into a *nayword*, and make him a common recreation, do not think I have wit enough to lie straight in my bed. *Shakespeare's Twelfth Night.*

3. A watchword. Not in use.

I have spoke with her; and we have a *nayword* how to know one another. I come to her in white, and cry mum; she cries budget; and by that we know one another. *Sha.*

NE. *adv.* [Saxon. This particle was formerly of very frequent use, both singly and by contraction in compound words; as, *nill* for *ne will* or *will not*; *nas* for *ne has* or *has not*; *nis* for *ne is* or *is not.*] Neither; and not.

His warlike shield all cover'd closely was,
Ne might of mortal eye be ever seen,
Not made of steel, nor of enduring brass. *Fairy Qu.*

NEAF. *n. s.* [*nefi*, Islandick.] A fist. It is retained in Scotland; and in the plural *neaves*.

Give me thy *neaf*, Monsieur Mustardseed. *Shakespeare.*

To NEAL. *v. a.* [onœlan, Saxon; to kindle.] To temper by a gradual and regulated heat.

The workmen let it cool by degrees in such relentings of fire, as they call their *nealing* heats; lest it should shiver in pieces by a violent succeeding of air in the room of fire. *Digby on Bodies.*

This did happen for want of the glasses being gradually cooled or *nealed*. *Boyle.*

If you file, engrave, or punch upon your steel, *neal* it first, because it will make it softer, and consequently work easier. The common way is to give it a blood-red heat in the fire, then let it cool of itself. *Moxon's Mech. Exer.*

To NEAL. *v. n.* To be tempered in fire.

Reduction is chiefly effected by fire, wherein if they stand and *neal*, the imperfect metals vapour away. *Bacon.*

NEAP. *adj.* [neplob, Saxon; næpug, poor.] Low; decrescent. Used only of the tide, and therefore sometimes used substantively.

The mother of waters, the great deep, hath lost nothing of her ancient bounds. Her motion of ebbing and flowing, of high springs and dead *neaps*, are as constant as the changes of the moon. *Hakewill on Providence.*

How doth the sea constantly observe its ebbs and flows, its springs and *neap*-tides, and still retain its saltness, so convenient for the maintenance of its inhabitants. *Ray.*

NEAR. *prep.* [nep, Saxon; *naer*, Dutch and Scottish.] At no great distance from; close to; nigh.

I have heard thee say,
No grief did ever come so *near* thy heart,
As when thy lady and thy true love died. *Shakespeare.*

Thou thought'st to help me, and such thanks I give,
As one *near* death to those that wish him live. *Shakes.*

With blood the dear alliance shall be bought,
And both the people *near* destruction brought. *Dryden.*

To the warlike steed thy studies bend,
Near Pisa's flood the rapid wheels to guide. *Dryden's Virg.*

This child was very *near* being excluded out of the species of man, barely by his shape. *Locke.*

NEAR. *adv.*

1. Almost.

2. At hand; not far off. Unless it be rather in this sense an adjective.

Thou art *near* in their mouth, and far from their reins. *Jer.* xii. 2.

He serv'd great Hector, and was ever *near*,
Not with his trumpet only, but his spear. *Dryden's Æn.*

3. Within a little.

Self-pleasing and humourous minds are so sensible of every restraint, as they will go *near* to think their girdles and garters to be bonds and shackles. *Bacon's Essays*, Nº. 8.

This eagle shall go *near*, one time or other, to take you for a hare. *L'Estrange, Fable* 107.

He that paid a bushel of wheat per acre, would pay now about twenty-five pounds per annum; which would be *near* about the yearly value of the land. *Locke.*

The Castilian would rather have died in slavery himself, than paid such a sum as he found would go *near* to ruin him. *Addison's Spectator.*

NEAR. *adj.*

1. Not distant. [Sometimes it is doubtful whether *near* be an adjective or adverb.]

This city is *near* to flee unto. *Gen.* xix. 20.

The will, free from the determination of such desires, is left to the pursuit of *nearer* satisfactions. *Locke.*

After he has continued his doubling in his thoughts, and enlarged his idea as much as he pleases, he is not one jot *nearer* the end of such addition than at first setting out. *Locke.*

2. Advanced towards the end of an enterprise or disquisition.

Unless they add somewhat else to define more certainly what ceremonies shall stand for best, in such sort that all churches in the world shall know them to be the best, and so know them that there may not remain any question about this point; we are not a whit the *nearer* for that they have hitherto said. *Hooker, b.* iv. *s.* 13.

3. Close; not rambling; observant of stile or manner of the thing copied.

Hannibal Caro's, in the Italian, is the *nearest*, the most poetical, and the most sonorous of any translation of the Æneid. Yet though he takes the advantage of blank verse, he commonly allows two lines for one in Virgil, and does not always hit his sense. *Dryden.*

4. Closely related.

If one shall approach to any that is *near* of kin to him. *Lev.* xviii. 6.

5. Intimate; familiar; admitted to confidence.

If I had a suit to master Shallow, I would humour his men with the imputation of being *near* their master. *Shak.*

6. Touching; pressing; affecting; dear.

Ev'ry minute of his being thrusts
Against my *near'st* of life. *Shakespeare's Macbeth.*

He could never judge that it was better to be deceived than not, in a matter of so great and *near* concernment. *Locke.*

7. Parsimonious, inclining to covetousness; as, a *near* man.

NEAR hand. Closely; without acting or waiting at a distance.

The entring *near* hand into the manner of performance of that which is under deliberation, hath overturned the opinion of the possibility or impossibility. *Bacon's Holy War.*

NEA'RLY. *adv.* [from *near.*]

1. At no great distance; not remotely.

Many are the enemies of the priesthood: they are diligent to observe whatever may *nearly* or remotely blemish it. *Atterbury.*

2. Closely; pressingly.

Nearly it now concerns us, to be sure
Of our omnipotence. *Milton's Paradise Lost, b.* v.

It concerneth them *nearly*, to preserve that government which they had trusted with their money. *Swift's Miscel.*

3. In a niggardly manner.

NEA'RNESS. *n. s.* [from *near.*]

1. Closeness; not remoteness; approach.

God, by reason of *nearness*, forbad them to be like the Canaanites or Egyptian. *Hooker, b.* iv. *s.* 6.

Fine and delicate sculptures be helped with *nearness*, and gross with distance; which was well seen in the controversy between Phidias and Alcmenes about the statue of Venus. *Wotton's Architecture.*

Those blessed spirits that are in such a *nearness* to God, may well be all fire and love, but you at such a distance cannot find the effects of it. *Duppa.*

The best rule is to be guided by the *nearness*, or distance at which the repetitions are placed in the original. *Pope.*

2. Alliance of blood or affection.

Whether there be any secret passages of sympathy between persons of near blood; as, parents, children, brothers and sisters. There be many reports in history, that upon the death of persons of such *nearness*, men have had an inward feeling of it. *Bacon's Natural History.*

3. Tendency to avarice; caution of expence.

It shews in the king a *nearness*, but yet with a kind of justness. So these little grains of gold and silver, helped not a little to make up the great heap. *Bacon's Hen. VII.*

NEAT. *n. s.* [neat nyten, Saxon; *naut*, Islandick and Scot.]

1. Black cattle; oxen. It is commonly used collectively.

The steer, the heifer, and the calf,
Are all call'd *neat*. *Shakespeare's Win. Tale.*

A present for any emperor that ever trod on *neats* leather. *Shakespeare's Tempest.*

Smoak preserveth flesh; as we see in bacon, *neats* tongues, and martlemas beef. *Bacon's Natural History.*

His droves of asses, camels, herds of *neat*,
And flocks of sheep, grew shortly twice as great. *Sandy.*

What care of *neat*, or sheep is to be had,
I sing, Mecænas. *May's Virgil's Georgics.*

Some kick'd until they can feel, whether
A shoe be Spanish or *neats* leather. *Hudidras, p.* i.

As great a drover, and as great
A critick too, in hog or *neat*. *Hud. p.* i. *cant.* 2.

Set it in rich mould, with *neats* dung and lime mingled. *Mortimer's Art of Husbandry.*

2. A cow or ox.

Who both by his calf and his lamb will be known,
May well kill a *neat* and a sheep of his own. *Tuss. Husb.*

Go and get me some repast.—
What say you to a *neat's* foot?
'Tis passing good; I prythee, let me have it. *Shakes.*

NEAT. *adj.* [*net*, French; *nitidus*, Latin.]

1. Elegant, but without dignity.

The thoughts are plain, yet admit a little quickness and passion; the expression humble, yet as pure as the language will afford; *neat*, but not florid; easy, and yet lively. *Pope.*

2. Cleanly.

Herbs and other country messes,
Which the *neat*-handed Phyllis dresses. *Milt. Poems.*

3. Pure; unadulterated; unmingled; in the cant of trade.

Tuns of sweet old wines, along the wall;
Neat and divine drink, kept to chear withal
Ulysses' old heart. *Chapman's Odyssey, b.* ii.

NE'ATHERD. *n. s.* [neaѕхyꞃb, Saxon.] A cowkeeper; one who has the care of black cattle. Βȣ́κολος, bubulcus.

There *netherd* with cur and his horn,
Be a fence to the meadow and corn. *Tuss. Husb.*

The swains and tardy *neatherds* came, and last
Menalcas, wet with beating winter mast. *Dryden.*

NEA'TLY. *adj.* [from *neat*.]

1. Elegantly, but without dignity; sprucely.

I will never trust a man again for keeping his sword clean; nor believe he can have every thing in him, by wearing his apparel *neatly*. *Shakespeare's All's well that ends well.*

To love an altar built,
Of twelve vast French romances *neatly* gilt. *Pope.*

2. Cleanlily.

NEA'TNESS. *n. s.* [from *neat*.]

1. Spruceness; elegance without dignity.

Pelagius carped at the curious *neatness* of men's apparel. *Hooker, b.* v. *s.* 29.

2. Cleanliness.

NEB. *n. s.* [nebbe, Saxon.]

1. Nose; beak; mouth. Retained in the north.

How she holds up the *neb!* the bill to him,
And arms her with the boldness of a wife. *Shakes.*

Take a glass with a belly and a long *neb*. *Bacon.*

2. [In Scotland.] The bill of a bird. See NIB.

NE'BULA. n. s. [Lat.] It is applied to appearances, like a cloud in the human body; as also to films upon the eyes.

NE'BULOUS. *adj.* [*nebulosus*, Latin.] Misty; cloudy.

NE'CESSARIES. *n. s.* [from *necessary*.] Things not only convenient but needful; things not to be left out of daily use. *Quibus doleat natura negatis.*

The supernatural *necessaries* are, the preventing, assisting, and renewing grace of God, which we suppose God ready to annex to the revelation of his will, in the hearts of all that with obedient humble spirits receive and sincerely embrace it. *Hammond's Fundamentals.*

The right a son has, to be maintained and provided with the *necessaries* and conveniencies of life, out of his father's stock, gives him a right to succeed to his father's property for his own good. *Locke.*

NE'CESSARILY. *adv.* [from *necessary*.]

1. Indispensably.

I would know by some special instance, what one article of Christian faith, or what duty required *necessarily* unto all mens salvation there is, which the very reading of the word of God is not apt to notify. *Hooker, b.* v. *s.* 22.

2. By inevitable consequence.

They who recall the church unto that which was at the first, must *necessarily* set bounds and limits unto their speeches. *Hooker, b.* iv. *s.* 2.

They subjected God to the fatal chain of causes, whereas they should have resolved the necessity of all inferiour events into the free determination of God himself; who executes *necessarily*, that which he first proposed freely. *South's Serm.*

NE'CESSARINESS. *n. s.* [from *necessary*.] The state of being necessary.

NE'CESSARY. *adj.* [*necessarius*, Latin.]

1. Needful; indispensably requisite.

All greatness is in virtue understood;
'Tis only *necessary* to be good. *Dryden's Aureng.*

A certain kind of temper is *necessary* to the pleasure and quiet of our minds, consequently to our happiness; and that is holiness and goodness. *Tillotson.*

The Dutch would go on to challenge the military government and the revenues, and reckon them among what shall be thought *necessary* for their barrier. *Swift's Miscel.*

2. Not free; fatal; impelled by fate.

3. Conclusive; decisive by inevitable consequence.

No man can shew by any *necessary* argument, that it is naturally impossible that all the relations concerning America should be false. *Tillotson's Preface.*

To NECE'SSITATE. *v. a.* [from *necessitas*, Latin.] To make necessary; not to leave free; to exempt from choice.

Hast thou proudly ascribed the good thou hast done to thy own strength, or imputed thy sins and follies to the *necessitating* and inevitable decrees of God. *Duppa's Rules for Devo.*

The marquis of Newcastle being pressed on both sides, was *necessitated* to draw all his army into York. *Clarend.*

Man seduc'd,
And flatter'd out of all, believing lies
Against his maker: no decree of mine
Concurring to *necessitate* his fall. *Milton's Par. Lost.*

Our voluntary service he requires,
Not our *necessitated*. *Milton's Paradise Lost, b.* v.

Neither the Divine Providence, or his determinations, persuasions, or inflexions of the understanding or will of rational creatures doth deceive the understanding, or pervert the will, or *necessitate* or incline either to any moral evil. *Hale's Origin of Mankind.*

The politician never thought that he might fall dangerously sick, and that sickness *necessitate* his removal from the court. *South's Serm.*

Th' eternal, when he did the world create
And other agents did *necessitate*;
So what he order'd they by nature do;
Thus light things mount, and heavy downward go,
Man only boasts an arbitrary state. *Dryden.*

The perfections of any person may create our veneration; his power, our fear; and his authority arising thence, a servile and *necessitated* obedience; but love can be produced only by kindness. *Rogers.*

NECESSITA'TION. *n. s.* [from *necessitate*.] The act of making necessary; fatal compulsion.

This necessity, grounded upon the *necessitation* of a man's will without his will, is so far from lessening those difficulties which flow from the fatal destiny of the Stoicks, that it increaseth them. *Bramhall against Hobbs.*

Where the law makes a certain heir, there is a *necessitation* to one; where the law doth not name a certain heir, there is no *necessitation* to one, and there they have power or liberty to choose. *Bramhall against Hobbs.*

NECE'SSITIED. *adj.* [from *necessity*.] In a state of want. Not used.

This ring was mine, and when I gave it Helen,
I bad her, if her fortunes ever stood
Necessitied to help, that by this token
I would relieve her. *Shakespeare's All's well that ends well.*

NECE'SSITOUS. *adj.* [from *necessity*.] Pressed with poverty.

They who were envied, found no satisfaction in what they were envied for, being poor and *necessitous*. *Clarend.*

There are multitudes of *necessitous* heirs and penurious parents, parsons in pinching circumstances, with numerous families of children. *Arbuthnot.*

NECE'SSITOUSNESS. *n. s.* [from *necessitous*.] Poverty; want; need.

Universal peace is demonstration of universal plenty, for where there is want and *necessitousness*, there will be quarrelling. *Burnet's Theory of the Earth.*

NECE'SSITUDE. *n. s.* [*necessitudo*, Latin.]

1. Want; need.

The mutual *necessitudes* of human nature necessarily maintain mutual offices between them. *Hale's Orig. of Man.*

2. Friendship.

NECE'SSITY. *n. s.* [*necessitas*, Latin.]

1. Cogency; compulsion; fatality.

Necessity and chance
Approach not me; and what I will is fate. *Milton.*

2. State of being necessary; indispensableness.

Urge the *necessity*, and state of times. *Shakes. Rich.* II.

Racine

Racine used the chorus in his Esther, but not that he found any *necessity* of it: it was only to give the ladies an occasion of entertaining the king with vocal musick. *Dryden's Dufresnoy.*

We see the *necessity* of an augmentation, to bring the enemy to reason. *Addison.*

3. Want; need; poverty.

The art of our *necessities* is strange,
That can make vile things precious. *Shakes. K. Lear.*

The cause of all the distractions in his court or army, proceeded from the extreme poverty, and *necessity* his majesty was in. *Clarendon, b. viii.*

We are first to consult our own *necessities*, but then the *necessities* of our neighbours have a christian right to a part of what we have to spare. *L'Estrange, Fable 217.*

4. Things necessary for human life.

These should be hours for *necessities*,
Not for delights; times to repair our nature
With comforting repose, and not for us
To waste these times. *Shakespeare's Henry VIII.*

5. Cogency of argument; inevitable consequence.

There never was a man of solid understanding, whose apprehensions are sober, and by a pensive inspection advised, but that he hath found by an irresistible *necessity*, one true God and everlasting being. *Raleigh's History.*

Good nature or beneficence and candour, is the product of right reason, which of *necessity* will give allowance to the failings of others. *Dryden.*

NECK. *n. s.* [hneca, Saxon; *neck*, Dutch.]

1. The part between the head and body.

He'll beat Bufidius' head below his knee,
And tread upon his *neck*. *Shakespeare's Coriolanus.*

The length of the face twice exceedeth that of the *neck*. *Brown's Vulgar Errours.*

She clapp'd her leathern wing against your tow'rs,
And thrust out her long *neck*, ev'n to your doors. *Dryd.*

I look on the tucker to be the ornament and defence of the female *neck*. *Addison's Guardian, N°. 109.*

2. A long narrow part.

The access of the town was only by a *neck* of land, between the sea on the one part, and the harbour water on the other. *Bacon.*

Thou walk'st as on a narrow mountain's *neck*,
A dreadful height, with scanty room to tread. *Dryden.*

3. *On the* neck; immediately after; from one following another closely.

He depos'd the king,
And, on the *neck* of that, task'd the whole state. *Shakes.*

Instantly on the *neck* of this came news, that Ferdinando and Isabella, had concluded a peace. *Bacon.*

4. To break the neck of an affair; to hinder any thing being done; or, to do more than half.

NE'CKBEEF. *n. s.* [*neck* and *beef.*] The coarse flesh of the *neck* of cattle, sold to the poor at a very cheap rate.

They'll sell (as cheap as *neckbeef*) for counters at cards. *Swift.*

NE'CKCLOATH. *n. s.* [*neck* and *cloath.*] That which men wear on their neck.

Will she with huswife's hand provide thy meat,
And ev'ry sunday morn thy *neckcloath* plait? *Gay.*

NE'CKERCHIEF. } *n. s.* A gorget; handkerchief for a woman's
NE'CKATEE. } neck.

NE'CKLACE. *n. s.* [*neck* and *lace.*] An ornamental string of beads or precious stones, worn by women on their neck.

Ladies, as well then as now, wore estates in their ears. Both men and women wore torques, chains, or *necklaces* of silver and gold set with precious stones. *Arbuthnot on Coins.*

Or lose her heart, or *necklace*, at a ball. *Pope.*

NE'CKWEED. *n. s.* [*neck* and *weed.*] Hemp.

NE'CROMANCER. *n. s.* [νεκρὸς and μάντις.] One who by charms can converse with the ghosts of the dead; a conjurer; an inchanter.

I am employed like the general who was forced to kill his enemies twice over, whom a *necromancer* had raised to life. *Swift's Miscellanies.*

NE'CROMANCY. *n. s.* [νεκρὸς and μάντις; *necromance*, Fr.]

1. The art of revealing future events, by communication with the dead.

The resurrection of Samuel is nothing but delusion in the practice of *necromancy* and popular conception of ghosts. *Brown's Vulgar Errours, b. i.*

2. Enchantment; conjuration.

He did it partly by *necromancy*, wherein he was much skilled. *Abbot's Description of the World.*

This palace standeth in the air,
By *necromancy* placed there,
That it no tempests needs to fear. *Drayt. Nym.*

NE'CTARED. *adj.* [from *nectar.*] Tinged with nectar; mingled with nectar; abounding with nectar.

He gave her to his daughters to imbathe
In *nectar'd* lavers strew'd with asphodil. *Milton.*

How charming is divine philosophy!
Not harsh and crabbed, as dull fools suppose,
But musical as is Apollo's lute,
And a perpetual feast of *nectar'd* sweets,
Where no crude surfeit reigns. *Milton's Poems.*

He with the Nais wont to dwell,
Leaving the *nectar'd* feasts of Jove. *Fenton.*

NECTA'REOUS. *adj.* [*nectareus*, Latin.] Resembling nectar; sweet as nectar.

Annual for me, the grape, the rose renew,
The juice *nectareous* and the balmy dew. *Pope.*

NE'CTARINE. *adj.* [from *nectar.*] Sweet as nectar.

To their supper-fruits they fell;
Nectarine fruits. *Milt. Par. Lost.*

NE'CTARINE. *n. s.* [*nectarine*, French.] A fruit of the plum kind.

This fruit differs from a peach in having a smooth rind and the flesh firmer. *Miller.*

The only *nectarines* are the murry and the French; of the last there are two sorts, one, which is the best, very round, and the other something long; of the murry there are several sorts. *Temple.*

NEED. *n. s.* [neoꝺ, Saxon; *nood*, Dutch.]

1. Exigency; pressing difficulty; necessity.

The very stream of his life, and the business he hath helmed, must, upon a warranted *need*, give him a better proclamation. *Shakespeare's Measure for Measure.*

That spirit that first rush'd on thee,
In the camp of Dan,
Be efficacious in thee now at *need*. *Milton's Agonistes.*

In thy native innocence proceed,
And summon all thy reason at thy *need*. *Dryden.*

2. Want; distressful poverty.

Famine is in thy cheeks;
Need and oppression stare within thine eyes,
Contempt and beggary hang upon thy back. *Shakes.*

Defer not to give to him that is in *need*. *Ecclus. iv. 3.*

The distant heard, by fame, her pious deeds;
And laid her up for their extreamest *needs*;
A future cordial for a fainting mind. *Dryden.*

God sometimes calls upon thee to relieve the *needs* of thy brother, sometimes the necessities of thy country, and sometimes the urgent wants of thy prince. *South's Sermons.*

3. Want; lack of any thing for use.

God grant we never may have *need* of you. *Shakes.*

God who sees all things intuitively, neither stands in *need* of logic, nor uses it. *Baker.*

To NEED. *v. a.* [from the noun.] To want; to lack; to be in want of; to require.

Basest beggars
Are in the poorest thing superfluous;
Allow not nature more than nature *needs*,
Man's life is cheap as beasts. *Shakespeare's K. Lear.*

The whole *need* not a physician, but the sick. *Matt* ix. 12.

Thou thy regal sceptre shalt lay by,
For regal sceptre then no more shall *need*. *Milt. P. Lost.*

To ask whether the will has freedom? is to ask, whether one power has another? A question too absurd to *need* an answer. *Locke.*

To NEED. *v. n.*

1. To be wanted; to be necessary.

More ample spirit than hitherto was wont,
Here *needs* me rie whiles the famous ancestors
Of my most dreadful sovereign I recount. *Spenser.*

When we have done it, we have done all that is in our power, and all that *needs*. *Locke.*

2. To have necessity of any thing; to be in want of any thing.

We have instances of perception whilst we are asleep: but how incoherent and how little conformable to the perfection of a rational being, those who are acquainted with dreams *need* not be told. *Locke.*

He that would discourse of things, as they agreed in the complex idea of extension and solidity, *needed* but use the word body. *Locke.*

NEEDER. *n. s.* [from *need.*] One that wants any thing.

If the time thrust forth
A cause for thy repeal, we shall not send
O'er the vast world, to seek a single man;
And lose advantage, which doth ever cool
In th' absence of the *needer*. *Shakespeare's Coriolanus.*

NEEDFUL. *adj.* [*need* and *full.*] Necessary; indispensably requisite.

Give us all things that be *needful*, both for our souls and bodies. *Common Prayer.*

Do you consent we shall acquaint him with it,
As *needful* in our loves, fitting our duty? *Sha. Ham.*

All things *needful* for defence abound,
Mnestheus, and brave Seresthus walk the round. *Dryden.*

To my present purpose it is not *needful* to use arguments, to evince the world to be finite. *Locke.*

A lonely desart and an empty land,

Shall scarce afford, for *needful* hours of rest,
A single house to their benighted guest. *Addison on Italy.*

NEE'DFULLY. *adv.* [from *needful.*] Necessarily.

They who
Dare for these poems, yet both ask and read,
And like them too; must *needfully*, tho' few,
Be of the best. *Ben. Johnson.*

NEE'DFULNESS. *n. s.* [from *needful.*] Necessity.

NEE'DILY. *adv.* [from *needy.*] In poverty; poorly.

NEEDINESS. *n. s.* [from *needy.*] Want; poverty.

Whereas men have many reasons to persuade; to use them all at once, weakneth them. For it argueth a *neediness* in every of the reasons, as if one did not trust to any of them, but fled from one to another. *Bacon.*

NEE'DLE. *n. s.* [næbl, Saxon.]

1. A small instrument pointed at one end to pierce cloath, and perforated at the other to receive the thread, used in sewing.

For him you waste in tears your widow'd hours,
For him your curious *needle* paints the flowers. *Dryden.*

2. The small steel bar which in the mariners compass stands regularly north and south.

The use of the loadstone, and the mariners *needle* was not then known. *Burnet's Theory of the Earth.*

NEE'DLE-FISH. *n. s.* [*needle* and *fish.*] A kind of sea-fish.

One rhomboidal bony scale of the *needle-fish. Woodward.*

NEE'DLEFUL. *n. s.* [*needle* and *full.*] As much thread as is generally put at one time in the needle.

NEE'DLER. } *n. s.* [from *needle.*] He who makes
NEE'DLEMAKER. } needles.

NEE'DLEWORK. *n. s.* [*needle* and *work.*]

1. The business of a sempstress.
2. Embroidery by the needle.

In *needleworks* and embroideries, it is more pleasing to have a lively work upon a lightsome ground, than a dark and melancholy work upon a lightsome ground. *Bacon.*

In a curious brede of *needlework*, one colour falls away by such just degrees, and another rises so insensibly, that we see the variety without being able to distinguish the total vanishing of the one from the first appearance of the other. *Addison's Ess. on the Georgicks.*

NEE'DLESLY. *adv.* [from *needless.*] Unnecessarily; without need.

We render languages more difficult to be learnt, and *needlesly* advance orthography into a troublesome art. *Holder.*

NEE'DLESSNESS. *n. s.* [from *needless.*] Unnecessariness.

To explain any of St. Paul's Epistles, after so great a train of expositors, might seem censurable for its *needlessness*, did not the daily examples of pious and learned men justify it. *Locke's Ess. on St. Paul's Epistles.*

NEE'DLESS. *adj.* [from *need.*]

1. Unnecessary; not requisite.

Their exception against casiness, as if that did nourish ignorance, proceedeth altogether of a *needless* jealousy. *Hook.*

This sudden stab of rancour I misdoubt;
Pray God, I say, I prove a *needless* coward. *Sha. R. III.*

Would not these be great and *needless* abatements of their happiness, if it were confined within the compass of this life only? *Atterbury.*

2. Not wanting; out of use.

For his weeping in the *needless* stream,
Poor dear, quoth he, thou mak'st a testament,
As worldings do, giving thy sum of more
To that which had too much. *Sha. As you Like it.*

NEE'DMENT. *n. s.* [from *need.*] Something necessary.

Behind
His scrip did hang, in which his *needments* he did bind.
Fairy Queen, b. i. *cant.* 6.

NEEDS. *adv.* [nebeꝛ, Saxon, unwilling.] Necessarily; by compulsion; indispensably.

The general and perpetual voice of men is as the sentence of God himself; for that which all men have at all times learned, nature herself must *needs* have taught. *Hooker.*

God must *needs* have done the thing which they imagine was to be done. *Hooker, b.* iii.

I must *needs* after him, madam, with my letter. *Sha.*

Another being elected and his ambassadors returned, he would *needs* know the cause of his repulse in that competition. *Davies on Ireland.*

I perceive
Thy mortal sight to fail: objects divine
Must *needs* impair, and weary human sense. *Milt. P. Lost.*

To say the principles of nature must *needs* be such as our philosophy makes them, is to set bounds to omnipotence. *Glanville, Sceps. c.* 25.

I have affairs below,
Which I must *needs* dispatch before I go. *Dryden.*

NEEDY. *adj.* [from *need.*] Poor; necessitous; distressed by poverty.

Their gates to all were open evermore,
And one sat waiting ever them before,
To call in comers by, that *needy* were and poor. *Fa. Q.*
— In his *needy* shop a tortoise hung,
An alligator stuff'd, and other skins
Of ill-shap'd fishes. *Shakespeare's Romeo and Juliet.*

The poor and *needy* praise thy name. *Ps.* lxxiv. 21.

We bring into the world a poor *needy* uncertain life, short at the longest, and unquiet at the best. *Temple.*

Nuptials of form, of int'rest, or of state,
Those seeds of pride are fruitful in debate:
Let happy men for gen'rous love declare,
And chuse the *needy* virgin, chaste and fair. *Granv.*

To relieve the *needy*, and comfort the afflicted, are duties that fall in our way every day. *Addison's Spect.* N°. 93.

NE'ER. [for *never.*]

It appears I am no horse,
That I can argue and discourse;
Have but two legs, and *ne'er* a tail. *Hudibras.*

To NEESE. *v. n.* [*nyse*, Danish; *niesen*, Dutch.] To sneese; to discharge flatulencies by the nose. Retained in Scotland.

He went up and stretched himself upon him; and the child *neesed* seven times, and opened his eyes. 2 *Kings* iv. 35.

By his *neesings* a light doth shine, and his eyes are like the eye-lids of the morning. *Job* xli. 18.

NEF. n. s. [old French, from *nave.*] The body of a church.

The church of St. Justina, designed by Palladio, is the most handsome, luminous, disencumbered building in Italy. The long *nef* consists of a row of five cupola's, the cross one has on each side a single cupola deeper than the others. *Addison's Remarks on Italy.*

NEFA'RIOUS. *adj.* [*nefarius*, Latin.] Wicked; abominable.

The most *nefarious* bastards, are they whom the law stiles incestuous bastards, which are begotten between ascendants and descendants, and between collateral, as far as the divine prohibition extends. *Ayliffe's Parergon.*

NEGA'TION. *n. s.* [*negatio*, Lat. *negation*, Fr.]

1. Denial; the contrary to affirmation.

Chance properly signifies, that all events called casual, among inanimate bodies, are mechanically and naturally produced according to the determinate figures, textures, and motions of those bodies, with this only *negation*, that those inanimate bodies are not conscious of their own operations. *Bentley.*

Our assertions and *negations* should be yea and nay, for whatsoever is more than these is sin. *Rogers, Serm.* 9.

2. Description by negative.

Negation is the absence of that which does not naturally belong to the thing we are speaking of, or which has no right, obligation, or necessity to be present with it; as when we say a stone is inanimate, or blind, or deaf. *Watts's Logick.*

NE'GATIVE. *adj.* [*negatif*, Fr. *negativus*, Latin.]

1. Denying; contrary to affirmative.
2. Implying only the absence of something.

There is another way of denying Christ with our mouths which is *negative*, when we do not acknowledge and confess him. *South's Sermons.*

Consider the necessary connection that is between the *negative* and positive part of our duty. *Tillotson, Serm.* 1.

3. Having the power to withhold, though not to compel.

Denying me any power of a *negative* voice as king, they are not ashamed to seek to deprive me of the liberty of using my reason with a good conscience. *King Charles.*

NE'GATIVE. *n. s.*

1. A proposition by which something is denied.

Of *negatives* we have far the least certainty; and they are usually hardest, and many times impossible to be proved. *Tillotson, Serm.* 1.

2. A particle of denial; as, *not.*

A purer substance is defin'd,
But by an heap of *negatives* combin'd;
Ask what a spirit is, you'll hear them cry,
It hath no matter, no mortality. *Cleaveland's Poems.*

NE'GATIVELY. *adv.* [from *negative.*]

1. With denial; in the form of denial; not affirmatively.

When I asked him whether he had not drunk at all? he answered *negatively.* *Boyle.*

2. In form of speech implying the absence of something.

The fathers draw arguments from the Scripture *negatively* in reproof of that which is evil; Scriptures teach it not, avoid it therefore. *Hooker, b.* ii.

I shall shew what this image of God in man is, *negatively*, by shewing wherein it does not consist; and positively, by shewing wherein it does. *South's Serm.*

To NE'GLECT. *v. a.* [*neglectus*, Latin.]

1. To omit by carelessness.

If he *neglect* to hear them, tell it unto the church. *Mat.* xviii. 17.

2. To treat with scornful heedlessness.
3. To postpone.

I have been long a sleeper; but I trust
My absence doth *neglect* no great design,
Which by my presence might have been concluded. *Sha.*

NE'GLECT. *n. s.* [*neglectus*, Latin.]

1. Instance of inattention.
2. Careless treatment; scornful inattention.

3 I have

I have perceived a moſt faint *neglect* of late, which I have rather blamed as my own jealous curioſity, than as a very pretence or purpoſe of unkindneſs. *Shakeſ. King Lear.*

3. Negligence; frequency of neglect.

Age breeds *neglect* in all, and actions
Remote in time, like objects
Remote in place, are not beheld at half their greatneſs. *Denham.*

4. State of being unregarded.

Reſcue my poor remains from vile *neglect*,
With virgin honours let my herſe be deck't,
And decent emblem. *Prior.*

NEGLE'CTER. *n. ſ.* [from *neglect.*] One who neglects.

GLE'CTFUL. *adj.* [*neglect* and *full.*]

NE Heedleſs; careleſs; inattentive.

Moral ideas not offering themſelves to the ſenſes, but being to be framed to the underſtanding, people are *neglectful* of a faculty they are apt to think wants nothing. *Locke.*

Though the Romans had no great genius for trade, yet they were not entirely *neglectful* of it. *Arbuth. on Coins.*

2. Treating with indifference.

If the father careſs them when they do well, ſhew a cold and *neglectful* countenance to them upon doing ill, it will make them ſenſible of the difference. *Locke on Education.*

NEGLE'CTION. *n. ſ.* [from *neglect.*] The ſtate of being negligent.

NEGLE'CTFULLY. *adv.* [from *neglectful.*] With heedleſs inattention; careleſs indifference.

Sleeping *neglection* doth betray to loſs
The conqueſts of our ſcarce cold conqueror. *Shakeſ.*

NEGLE'CTIVE. *adj.* [from *neglect.*] Inattentive to, or regardleſs of.

I wanted not probabilities ſufficient to raiſe jealouſies in any king's heart, not wholly ſtupid, and *neglective* of the publick peace. *King Charles.*

NE'GLIGENCE. *n. ſ.* [*negligence*, Fr. *negligentia*, Latin.]

1. Habit of omitting by heedleſſneſs, or of acting careleſly.
2. Inſtance of neglect.

She let it drop by *negligence*,
And, to th'advantage, I being here, took't up. *Shakeſ.*

NE'GLIGENT. *adj.* [*negligent*, Fr. *negligens*, Latin.]

1. Careleſs; heedleſs; habitually inattentive.

My ſons, be not now *negligent*; for the Lord hath choſen you to ſtand before him. 2 *Chron.* xxix. 11.

2. Careleſs of any particular.

We have been *negligent* in not hearing his voice. *Bar.* i. 19.

3. Scornfully regardleſs.

Let ſtubborn pride poſſeſs thee long,
And be thou *negligent* of fame;
With ev'ry muſe to grace thy ſong,
May'ſt thou deſpiſe a poet's name. *Swift's Miſcel.*

NE'GLIGENTLY. *adv.* [from *negligent.*]

1. Careleſly; heedleſly; without exactneſs.

Inſects have voluntary motion, and therefore imagination; and whereas ſome of the ancients have ſaid that their motion is indeterminate, and their imagination indefinite, it is *negligently* obſerved; for ants go right forwards to their hills, and bees know the way to their hives. *Bacon's Nat. Hiſt.*

Of all our elder plays,
This and Philaſter have the loudeſt fame;
Great are their faults, and glorious is their flame.
In both our Engliſh genius is expreſt,
Lofty and bold, but *negligently* dreſt. *Waller.*

In comely figure rang'd my jewels ſhone,
Or *negligently* plac'd for thee alone. *Prior.*

2. With ſcornful inattention.

To **NEGO'TIATE.** *v. n.* [*negocier*, French; from *negotium*, Latin.] To have intercourſe of buſineſs; to traffick; to treat.

Have you any commiſſion from your lord to *negotiate* with my face? *Shakeſpeare's Twelfth Night.*

She was a buſy *negotiating* woman, and in her withdrawing chamber had the fortunate conſpiracy for the king againſt king Richard been hatched. *Bacon's Hen.* VII.

It is a common error in *negotiating*; whereas men have many reaſons to perſuade, they ſtrive to uſe them all at once, which weakeneth them. *Bacon.*

A ſteward to embezzle thoſe goods he undertakes to manage; an embaſſador to betray his prince for whom he ſhould *negotiate*; are crimes that double their malignity from the quality of the actors. *Decay of Piety.*

I can diſcover none of theſe frequent intercourſes and negotiations, unleſs that Luther *negotiated* with a black boar. *Atterbury.*

NEGOTIA'TION. *n. ſ.* [*negociation*, Fr. from *negotiate.*] Treaty of buſineſs.

Oil is ſlow, ſmooth, and ſolid; ſo are Spaniards obſerved to be in their motion: Though it be a queſtion yet unreſolved, whether their affected gravity and ſlowneſs in their *negotiations* have tended more to their prejudice or advantage. *How.*

NEGOTIA'TOR. *n. ſ.* [*negociateur*, Fr. from *negotiate.*] One employed to treat with others.

Thoſe who have defended the proceedings of our *negotiators* at Gertruydenburg, dwell much upon their zeal in endeavouring to work the French up to their demands; but ſay nothing to juſtify thoſe demands. *Swift.*

NEGO'TIATING. *adj.* [from *negotiate.*] Employed in negotiation.

NE'GRO. *n. ſ.* [Spaniſh; *negre*, Fr.] A blackmoore.

Negroes tranſplanted into cold and flegmatic habitations, continue their hue in themſelves and their generations. *Brown.*

NEIF. *n. ſ.* [*nefi*, Iſlandick; *neef*, Scottiſh.] Fiſt.

Sweet knight, I kiſs thy *neif.* *Shakeſ. Hen.* IV. *p.* ii.

To **NEIGH.** *v. n.* [hnægan, Saxon; *negen*, Dutch.] To utter the voice of a horſe or mare.

Note a wild and wanton herd,
Or race of youthful and unhandled colts,
Fetching mad bounds, bellowing and *neighing* loud. *Sha.*

They were as fed horſes, every one *neighed.* *Jer.* v. 8.

Run up the ridges of the rocks amain;
And with ſhrill *neighings* fill the neighbouring plain. *Dry.*

The gen'rous horſe, that nobly wild,
Neighs on the hills, and dares the angry lion. *Smith.*

NEIGH. *n. ſ.* [from the verb.] The voice of an horſe.

It is the prince of palfreys; his *neigh* is like the bidding of a monarch, and his countenance enforces homage. *Sha.*

NEI'GHBOUR. *n. ſ.* [nehgebur, Saxon.]

1. One who lives near to another.

He ſent ſuch an addition of foot, as he could draw out of Oxford and the *neighbour* garriſons. *Clarendon.*

2. One who lives in familiarity with another; a word of civility.

Maſters, my good friends, mine honeſt *neighbours*,
Will you undo yourſelves? *Shakeſpeare's Macbeth.*

3. Any thing next or near.

This man ſhall ſet me packing;
I'll lug the guts into the *neighbour* room. *Shakeſpeare.*

4. Intimate; confidant.

The deep revolving witty Buckingham
No more ſhall be the *neighbour* to my counſels. *Shakeſ.*

5. [In divinity.] One partaking of the ſame nature, and therefore entitled to good offices.

The Goſpel allows no ſuch term as a ſtranger; makes every man my *neighbour.* *Sprat's Sermons.*

To **NEI'GHBOUR.** *v. a.* [from the noun.]

1. To adjoin to; to confine on.

The ſtrawberry grows underneath the nettle,
And wholſome berries thrive and ripen beſt,
Neighbour'd by fruit of baſer quality. *Shakeſ. Hen.* V.

Give me thy hand,
Be pilot to me, and thy places ſhall
Still *neighbour* mine. *Shakeſpeare's Winter's Tale.*

Theſe grow on the leiſurely aſcending hills that *neighbour* the ſhore. *Sandy's Journey.*

Things nigh equivalent and *neighbouring* value,
By lot are parted. *Anon.*

2. To acquaint with; to make near to.

That being of ſo young days brought up with him,
And ſince ſo *neighbour'd* to his youth and 'haviour. *Sha.*

NEI'GHBOURHOOD. *n. ſ.* [from *neighbour.*]

1. Place adjoining.

I could not bear
To leave thee in the *neighbourhood* of death,
But flew in all the haſte of love to find thee. *Add. Cato.*

2. State of being near each other.

Conſider ſeveral ſtates in a *neighbourhood*; in order to preſerve peace between theſe ſtates, it is neceſſary they ſhould be formed into a balance. *Swift.*

3. Thoſe that live within reach of communication.

NEI'GHBOURLY. *adj.* [from *neighbour.*] Becoming a neighbour; kind; civil.

The Scottiſh lord, hath a *neighbourly* charity in him; for he borrowed a box of the ear of the Engliſhman, and ſwore he would pay when he was able. *Shakeſ. Merch. of Ven.*

He ſteals away my cuſtomers; twelve he has under bonds never to return; judge you if this be *neighbourly* dealing. *Arbuthnot's Hiſt. of J. Bull.*

NEI'GHBOURLY. *adv.* [from *neighbour.*] With ſocial civility.

NEI'THER. *conjunct.* [naþðeр, Saxon, *ne either.*]

1. Not either. A particle uſed in the firſt branch of a negative ſentence, and anſwered by *nor.*

Fight *neither* with ſmall *nor* great, ſave only with the king. 1 *Kings* xxii. 31.

2. It is ſometimes the ſecond branch of a negative or prohibition to any ſentence.

Ye ſhall *not* eat of it, *neither* ſhall ye touch it. *Gen.* iii. 3.

3. Sometimes at the end of a ſentence it follows as a negative; and often, though not very grammatically, yet emphatically, after another negative.

If it be thought that it is the greatneſs of diſtance, whereby the ſound cannot be heard; we ſee that lightnings and coruſcations, near at hand, yield no ſound *neither.* *Bacon.*

Men come not to the knowledge of which are thought innate, 'till they come to the uſe of reaſon, nor then *neither.* *Locke.*

NEI'THER. *pronoun.* Not either; nor one nor other.

He *neither* loves,
Nor either cares for him. *Shakespeare's Ant. and Cleo.*

Which of them shall I take?
Both, one, or *neither?* *neither* can be enjoy'd
If both remain alive. *Shakespeare's K. Lear.*

Suffice it that he's dead; all wrongs die with him:
Thus I absolve myself, and excuse him,
Who sav'd my life and honour, but praise *neither.* *Dryd.*

Experience makes us sensible of both, though our narrow understandings can comprehend *neither.* *Locke.*

They lived with the friendship and equality of brethren, *neither* lord, *neither* slave to his brother; but independent of each other. *Locke.*

NEO'PHYTE. *n. s.* [*neophyte*, Fr. νέος and φύω.] One regenerated; a convert.

NEOTE'RICK. *adj.* [*neotericus*, Latin.] Modern; novel; late.

We are not to be guided either by the misreports of some ancients, or the capricio's of one or two *neotericks.* *Grew.*

NEP. *n. s.* [*nepeta*, Lat.] An herb.

NE'PENTHE. *n. s.* [νὴ and πένθος.] A drug that drives away all pains.

There where no passion, pride, or shame transport,
Lull'd with the sweet *nepenthe* of a court;
There where no fathers, brothers, friends disgrace,
Once break their rest nor stir them from their place. *Pope.*

NE'PHEW. *n. s.* [*nepos*, Latin; *neveu*, French.]

1. The son of a brother or sister.

Immortal offspring of my brother Jove;
My brightest *nephew* and whom best I love. *Dryden.*

I ask, whether in the inheriting of this paternal power, the grandson by a daughter, hath a right before a *nephew* by a brother? *Locke.*

2. The grandson. Out of use.

With what intent they were first published, those words of the *nephew* of Jesus do plainly enough signify, after that my grand-father Jesus had given himself to the reading of the law and the prophets, and other books of our fathers, and had gotten therein sufficient judgment, he proposed also to write something pertaining to learning and wisdom. *Hooker, b. v. s. 21.*

Her sire at length is kind,
Prepares his empire for his daughter's ease,
And for his hatching *nephews* smooths the seas. *Dryden.*

3. Descendant, however distant. Out of use.

All the sons of these five brethren reign'd
By due success, and all their *nephews* late,
Even thrice eleven descents the crown retain'd. *Fairy Q.*

NEPHRI'TICK. *adj.* [νεφριτικός; *nephretique*, Fr.]

1. Belonging to the organs of urine.
2. Troubled with the stone.

The diet of *nephritic* persons ought to be such as is opposite to the alkalescent nature of the salts in their blood. *Arbuthnot on Aliments.*

3. Good against the stone.

The *nephritic* stone is commonly of an uniform dusky green; but some samples I have seen of it that are variegated with white, black, and sometimes yellow. *Woodw. Mett. Foss.*

NE'POTISM. *n. s.* [*nepotisme*, French; *nepos*, Latin.] Fondness for nephews.

To this humour of *nepotism* Rome owes its present splendor; for it would have been impossible to have furnished out so many glorious palaces with such a profusion of pictures and statues, had not the riches of the people fallen into different families. *Addison on Italy.*

NERVE. *n. s.* [*nervus*, Latin; *nerf*, Fr.] The organs of sensation passing from the brain to all parts of the body.

The *nerves* do ordinarily accompany the arteries through all the body; they have also blood-vessels, as the other parts of the body. Wherever any *nerve* sends out a branch, or receives one from another, or where two *nerves* join together, there is generally a ganglio or plexus. *Quincy.*

What man dare, I dare:
Approach thou like the rugged Russian bear;
Take any shape but that, and my firm *nerves*
Shall never tremble. *Shakespeare's Macbeth.*

2. It is used by the poets for sinew or tendon.

Strong Tharysmed discharged a speeding blow
Full on his neck, and cut the *nerves* in two. *Pope's Odyss.*

NE'RVELESS. *adj.* [from *nerve.*] Without strength.

There sunk Thalia, *nerveless*, faint and dead,
Had not her sister Satire held her head. *Dunciad, b. iv.*

NE'RVOUS. *adj.* [*nervosus*, Latin.] Well strung; strong; vigorous.

What *nervous* arms he boasts, how firm his tread,
His limbs how turn'd. *Pope's Odyssey, b. viii.*

2. Relating to the nerves; having the seat in the nerves.
3. [In medical cant.] Having weak or diseased nerves.

Poor, weak, *nervous* creatures. *Cheney.*

NE'RVY. *adj.* [from *nerve.*] Strong; vigorous. Not in use.

Death, that dark spirit, in his *nervy* arm doth lie,
Which being advanc'd, declines, and then men die. *Sha.*

NESCIENCE. *n. s.* [from *nescio*, Latin.] Ignorance; the state of not knowing.

Many of the most accomplished wits of all ages, have resolved their knowledge into Socrates his sum total, and after all their pains in quest of science, have sat down in a professed *nescience.* *Glanv. Sceps. c. ii.*

NESH. *adj.* [neſc, Saxon.] Soft; tender; easily hurt. *Skin.*

NESS.

1. A termination added to an adjective to change it into a substantive, denoting *state* or *quality*; as, *poisonous*, *poisonousness*; *turbid*, *turbidness*; *lovely*, *loveliness*; from niſſe, Saxon.
2. The termination of many names of places where there is a headland or promontory; from neſe, Saxon; a *nose of land*, or headland; as INVERNESS.

NEST. *n. s.* [neſt, Saxon.]

1. The bed formed by the bird for incubation and feeding her young.

If a bird's *nest* chance to be before thee in the way, thou shalt not take the dam with the young. *Deut. xxii. 6.*

2. Any place where animals are produced.

Redi found that all kinds of putrefaction did only afford a *nest* and aliment for the eggs and young of those insects he admitted. *Bentley.*

3. An abode; place of residence; a receptacle. Generally in a bad sense: as, a nest of rogues and thieves.

Come from that *nest*
Of death, contagion, and unnatural sleep. *Shakes.*

4. A warm close habitation, generally in contempt.

Some of our ministers having livings offered unto them, will neither, for zeal of religion, nor winning souls to God, be drawn forth from their warm *nests.* *Spenser.*

5. Boxes or drawers; little pockets or conveniences.

To NEST. *v. n.* [from the noun.] To build nests.

The cedar stretched his branches as far as the mountains of the moon, and the king of birds *nested* within his leaves. *Howel's Vocal Forest.*

NE'STEGG. *n. s.* [*nest* and *egg.*] An egg left in the nest to keep the hen from forsaking it.

Books and money laid for shew,
Like *nesteggs*, to make clients lay. *Hudibras.*

To NE'STLE. *v. n.* [from *nest.*] To settle; to harbour; to lie close and snug, as a bird in her nest.

Their purpose was, to fortify in some strong place of the wild country, and there *nestle* 'till greater succours came. *Bacon's War with Spain.*

A cock got into a stable was *nestling* in the straw among the horses. *L'Estrange.*

The king's fisher wonts commonly by the waterside, and *nestles* in hollow banks. *L'Estrange.*

Flutt'ring there they *nestle* near the throne,
And lodge in habitations not their own. *Dryden.*

The floor is strowed with several plants, amongst which the snails *nestle* all the winter. *Addison on Italy.*

Mark where the shy directors creep,
Nor to the shore approach too nigh;
The monsters *nestle* in the deep,
To seize you in your passing by. *Swift's Miscel.*

To NESTLE. *v. a.*

1. To house, as in a nest.

Poor heart!
That labour'st yet to *nestle* thee,
Thou think'st by hov'ring here to get a part,
In a forbidden or forbidding tree. *Donne.*

Cupid found a downy bed,
And *nestl'd* in his little head. *Prior.*

2. To cherish, as a bird her young.

This Ithacus, so highly is endear'd
To this Minerva, that her hand is ever in his deeds:
She, like his mother, *nestles* him. *Chapman's Iliads.*

NE'STLING. *n. s.* [from *nestle.*] A bird just taken out of the nest.

NET. *n. s.* [*nati*, Gothick; neτ, Saxon.] A texture woven with large interstices or meshes, used commonly as a snare for animals.

Poor bird! thoud'st never fear the *net*, nor lime,
The pitfall nor the gin. *Shakespeare's Macbeth.*

He made *nets* of chequer-work for the chapiters, upon the top of the pillars. *1 Kings vii. 17.*

Impatience intangles us like the fluttering of a bird in a *net*, but cannot at all ease our trouble. *Taylor's Holy Living.*

The vegetative tribes,
Wrapt in a filmy *net*, and clad with leaves. *Thomson.*

NETHER. *adj.* [neoðer, Saxon; *neder*, Dutch. It has the form of a comparative, but is never used in expressed, but only in implied comparison; for we see the *nether* part, but never say this part is *nether* than that, nor is any positive in use, though it seems comprised in the word *beneath.* *Nether* is not now much in use.]

1. Lower; not upper.

No man shall take the *nether* or the upper millstone to pledge; for he taketh a man's life to pledge. *Deut.* xxiv. 6.

In his picture are two principal errors, the one in the complexion and hair, the other in the mouth, which commonly they draw with a full and *nether* great lip. *Peacham.*

This odious offspring,
Thine own begotten, breaking violent way
Tore through my entrails; that with fear and pain
Distorted, all my *nether* shape thus grew
Transform'd. *Milton's Paradise Lost, b.* ii.

The upper part thereof was whey,
The *nether*, orange mix'd with grey. *Hudibras, p.* i.

A beauteous maid above, but magic arts,
With barking dogs deform'd her *nether* parts. *Roscommon.*

As if great Atlas from his height
Shou'd sink beneath his heav'nly weight,
And with a mighty flaw, the flaming wall
Shou'd gape immense, and rushing down o'erwhelm this *nether* ball. *Dryden.*

Two poles turn round the globe;
The first sublime in heaven, the last is whirl'd
Below the regions of the *nether* world. *Dryden.*

2. Being in a lower place.

This shews you are above,
You justices, that these our *nether* crimes,
So speedily can venge. *Shakespeare's King Lear.*

Numberless were those bad angels, seen
Hov'ring on wing under the cope of hell,
'Twixt upper, *nether*, and surrounding fires. *Milton.*

3. Infernal; belonging to the regions below.

No less desire
To found this *nether* empire, which might rise,
In emulation, opposite to heav'n. *Milton's Par. Lost.*

The gods with hate beheld the *nether* sky,
The ghosts repine. *Dryden's Æn.*

NE'THERMOST. *n. s.* [*super.* of *nether.*] Lowest.

Great is thy mercy toward me, and thou hast delivered my soul from the *nethermost* hell. *Psalm* lxxxvi. 13.

Undaunted to meet there whatever pow'r,
Or spirit, of the *nethermost* abyss
Might in that noise reside. *Milton's Paradise Lost, b.* ii.

All that can be said of a liar lodged in the very *nethermost* hell, is this, that if the vengeance of God could prepare any place worse than hell for sinners, hell itself would be too good for him. *South's Sermons.*

Heraclitus tells us, that the eclipse of the sun was after the manner of a boat, when the concave, as to our sight, appears uppermost, and the convex *nethermost*. *Keil aga. Bur.*

NE'TTING. *n. s.* A reticulated piece of work.

NE'TTLE. *n. s.* [netel, Saxon.] A stinging herb well known.

It hath an apetalous flower, consisting of many stamina included in an empalement; but these are barren; for the embryos are produced either on different plants, or on different parts of the same plant, without any visible flower, which becomes a bivalve seed-vessel, sometimes gathered into round heads, and at other times small and hairy, inclosing several seeds. *Miller.*

The strawberry grows underneath the *nettle*,
And wholsom berries thrive and ripen best,
Neighbour'd by fruit of baser quality. *Shakes. Hen.* V.

Some so like to thorns and *nettles* live,
That none for them can, when they perish, grieve. *Waller.*

To NE'TTLE. *v. a.* [from the noun.] To sting; to irritate; to provoke.

The princes were so *nettled* at the scandal of this affront, that every man took it to himself. *L'Estrange.*

Although at every part of the Apostles discourse some of them might be uneasy and *nettled*, yet a moderate silence and attention was still observed. *Bentley.*

NE'TWORK. *n. s.* [*net* and *work.*] Any thing reticulated or decussated, at equal distances, with interstices between the intersections.

Nor any skill'd in workmanship emboss'd;
Nor any skill'd in loops of fing'ring fine;
Might in their diverse cunning ever dare,
With this so curious *network* to compare. *Spenser.*

A large cavity in the sinciput was filled with ribbons, lace, and embroidery, wrought together in a curious piece of *network*. *Addison's Spectator.*

NE'VER. *adv.* [*ne ever*, næfre, Saxon; *ne* æfre, *not ever.*]

1. At no time.

2. It is used in a form of speech handed down by the best writers, but lately accused, I think, with justice, of solecism; as, *he is mistaken though never so wise.* It is now maintained, that propriety requires it to be expressed thus, *he is mistaken though* ever *so wise*; that is, *he is mistaken* how *wise* soever *he be.* The common mode can only be defended by supplying a very harsh and unprecedented ellipsis; *he is mistaken though so wise*, as *never was any:* such however is the common use of the word among the best authors.

By its own force destroy'd, fruition ceas'd,
And always weary'd, I was *never* pleas'd. *Prior.*

Never any thing was so unbred as that odious man. *Congreve's Way of the World.*

Be it *never* so true which we teach the world to believe, yet if once their affections begin to be alienated, a small thing persuadeth them to change their opinions. *Hooker.*

Ask me *never* so much dowry and gift, and I will give according as ye shall say. *Gen.* xxxiv. 12.

In a living creature, though *never* so great, the sense and the affects of any one part of the body, instantly make a transcursion throughout the whole body. *Bacon's Nat. Hist.*

They destroyed all, were it *never* so pleasant, within a mile of the town. *Knolles's Hist. of the Turks.*

He that shuts his eyes against a small light, would not be brought to see that which he had no mind to see, let it be placed in *never* so clear a light, and *never* so near him. *Atterbury's Sermons.*

That prince whom you espouse, although *never* so vigorously, is the principal in war, you but a second. *Swift.*

3. In no degree.

Whosoever has a faithful friend to guide him, may carry his eyes in another man's head, and yet see *never* the worse. *South's Sermons.*

4. It seems in some phrases to have the sense of an adjective. Not any.

He answered him to *never* a word, insomuch that the governour marvelled. *Matt.* xxvii. 14.

5. It is much used in composition; as, *never*-ending, having no end; of which some examples are subjoined.

Nature assureth us by *never*-failing experience, and reason by infallible demonstration, that our times upon the earth have neither certainty nor durability. *Raleigh.*

Ye myrtles brown, with ivy *never* sear,
I come to pluck your berries harsh and crude. *Milton.*

Your *never*-failing sword made war to cease,
And now you heal us with the acts of peace. *Waller.*

So corn in fields, and in the garden flow'rs,
Revive and raise themselves with mod'rate show'rs;
But over-charg'd with *never*-ceasing rain,
Become too moist. *Waller.*

Our heroes of the former days,
Deserv'd and gain'd their *never*-fading bays. *Roscommon.*

Not Thracian Orpheus should transcend my lays,
Nor Linus crown'd with *never*-fading bays. *Dryden.*

Leucippus, with his *never*-erring dart. *Dryd. Ovid.*

Farewel, ye *never*-opening gates. *Dryden.*

He to quench his drought so much inclin'd,
May snowy fields and nitrous pastures find;
Meet stores of cold so greedily pursu'd,
And be refresh'd with *never*-wasting food. *Blackmore.*

Norton hung down his *never*-blushing head,
And all was hush'd, as folly's self lay dead. *Pope's Dunc.*

What the weak head with strongest bias rules,
Is pride, the *never*-failing vice of fools. *Pope.*

Thy busy *never*-meaning face,
Thy screw'd up front, thy state grimace. *Swift.*

NE'VERTHELESS. *adv.* [*never the less.*] Notwithstanding that.

They plead that even such ceremonies of the church of Rome as contain in them nothing which is not of itself agreeable to the word of God, ought *nevertheless* to be abolished. *Hooker, b.* iv.

Many of our men were gone to land, and our ships ready to depart; *nevertheless* the admiral, with such ships only as could suddenly be put in readiness, made forth towards them. *Bacon.*

Creation must needs infer providence; and God's making the world, irrefragably proves that he governs it too; or that a being of a dependent nature remains *nevertheless* independent upon him in that respect. *South's Sermons.*

NEU'ROLOGY. *n. s.* [νεῦρον and λόγος.] A description of the nerves.

NEU'ROTOMY. *n. s.* [νεῦρον and τέμνω.] The anatomy of the nerves.

NEU'TER. *adj.* [*neuter*, Latin; *neutre*, Fr.]

1. Indifferent; not engaged on either side.

The general division of the British nation is into whigs and tories; there being very few, if any, who stand *neuter* in the dispute, without ranging themselves under one of these denominations. *Addison's Freeholder*, N°. 54.

2. [In grammar.] A noun that implies no sex.

The adjectives are *neuter*, and animal must be understood to make it grammar. *Dryden.*

A verb *neuter* is that which signifies neither action nor passion, but some state or condition of being; as, *sedeo*, I sit. *Clarke's Latin Grammar.*

NEU'TER. *n. s.* One indifferent and unengaged.

The learned heathens may be looked upon as *neuters* in the matter, when all these prophecies were new to them, and their education had left the interpretation of them indifferent. *Addison on the Christian Religion.*

NEU'TRAL. *adj.* [*neutral*, French.]

1. Indifferent; not acting; not engaged on either side.

Who can be wise, amaz'd, temp'rate and furious,
Loyal and *neutral*, in a moment? No man. *Shakespeare.*

He no sooner heard that king Henry was settled by his victory, but forthwith he sent ambassadors unto him, to pray that he would stand *neutral*. *Bacon's Hen.* VII.

The allies may be supplied for money, from Denmark and other *neutral* states. *Addison on the War.*

2. Indifferent; neither good nor bad.

Some things good, and some things ill do seem,
And *neutral* some, in her fantastic eye. *Davies.*

3. Neither acid nor alkaline.

Salts which are neither acid nor alkaline, are called *neutral*. *Arbuthnot.*

NEU'TRAL. *n. s.* One who does not act nor engage on either side.

The treacherous who have misled others, and the *neutrals* and the false-hearted friends and followers, who have started aside like a broken bow, are to be noted. *Bacon.*

NEUTRA'LITY. *n. s.* [*neutralité*, French.]

1. A state of indifference; of neither friendship nor hostility.

Men who possess a state of *neutrality* in times of publick danger, desert the common interest of their fellow-subjects. *Addison.*

The king, late griefs revolving in his mind,
These reasons for *neutrality* assign'd. *Garth's Ovid.*

All pretences to *neutrality* are justly exploded, only intending the safety and ease of a few individuals, while the publick is embroiled. This was the opinion and practice of the latter Cato. *Swift.*

2. A state between good and evil.

There is no health: physicians say, that we
At best enjoy but a *neutrality*. *Donne.*

NEU'TRALLY. *adv.* [from *neutral.*] Indifferently; on neither part.

NEW. *adj.* [*newyd*, Welsh; neop, Saxon; *neuf*, Fr.]

1. Not old; fresh; lately produced, made or had; novel. It is used of things: as, *young* of persons.

What's the *newest* grief? ———
—That of an hour's age doth hiss the speaker;
Each minute teems a *new* one. *Shakespeare's Macbeth.*

Do not all men complain how little we know, and how much is still unknown? And can we ever know more, unless something *new* be discovered? *Burnet.*

2. Modern; of the present time.

Whoever converses much among old books, will be something hard to please among *new*. *Temple's Miscellanies.*

3. Not antiquated; having the effect of novelty.

There names inscrib'd unnumber'd ages past,
From time's first birth, with time itself shall last;
These ever *new*, nor subject to decays,
pread and grow brighter with the length of days. *Pope.*

4. Not habituated; not familiar.

Such assemblies, though had for religion's sake, may serve the turn of heretics, and such as privily will instil their poison into *new* minds. *Hooker, b.* v.

Seiz'd with wonder and delight,
Gaz'd all around me, *new* to the transporting sight. *Dryd.*

Twelve mules, a strong laborious race,
New to the plough, unpractis'd in the trace. *Pope.*

5. Renovated; repaired, so as to recover the first state.

Men after long emaciating diets, wax plump, fat, and almost *new*. *Bacon's Natural History.*

6. Fresh after any thing.

Nor dare we trust so soft a messenger,
New from her sickness to that northern air. *Dryden.*

7. Not of ancient extraction.

A superior capacity for business, and a more extensive knowledge, are steps by which a *new* man often mounts to favour, and outshines the rest of his contemporaries. *Addis.*

NEW. *adv.* This is, I think, only used in composition for *newly*, which the following examples may explain.

As soon as she had written them, a new swarm of thoughts stinging her mind, she was ready with her foot to give the *new*-born letters both to death and burial. *Sidney, b.* ii.

God hath not then left this to chuse that, neither would reject that to chuse this, were it not for some *new*-grown occasion, making that which hath been better worse. *Hooker.*

So dreadfully he towards him did pass,
Forelifting up aloft his speckled breast,
And often bounding on the bruised grass,
As for great joyance of his *new*-come guest. *Fairy Q.*

Who are the violets now
That strow the green lap of the *new*-come spring. *Shakes.*

Your master's lines
Are full of *new*-found oaths; which he will break
As easily as I do tear this paper. *Shakespeare.*

Will you with those infirmities she owes,
Unfriended, *new*-adopted to our hate,
Dower'd with our curse, and stranger'd with our oath,
Take her or leave her? *Shakespeare's King Lear.*

Left by a multitude
The *new*-heal'd wound of malice should break out. *Shak.*

Bow, stubborn knees; and heart with strings of steel
Be soft as sinews of the *new*-born babe. *Shakes. Ham.*

Now hath my soul brought forth her prodigy,
And I a gasping, *new*-deliver'd mother,
Have woe to woe, sorrow to sorrow join'd. *Sha. R.* II.

I am in parliament pledge for his truth,
And lasting fealty to the *new*-made king. *Sha. R.* II.

He saw heav'n blossom with a *new*-born light,
On which, as on a glorious stranger gaz'd
The golden eyes of night; whose beams made bright
The way to Beth'lem, and as boldly blaz'd;
Nor ask'd leave of the sun, by day as night. *Crashaw.*

I've seen the morning's lovely ray
Hover o'er the *new*-born day;
With rosy wings so richly bright,
As if he scorn'd to think of night,
When a ruddy storm, whose scoul
Made heaven's radiant face look foul,
Call'd for an untimely night
To blot the newly blossom'd light. *Crashaw.*

Some tree, whose broad smooth leaves together sow'd,
And girded on our loins, may cover round
Those middle parts; that this *new*-comer shame,
There sit not, and reproach us as unclean. *Milt. P. Lost.*

Their father's state,
And *new*-entrusted sceptre. *Milton's Poems.*

The *new*-created world, which fame in heav'n
Long had foretold. *Milton's Paradise Lost.*

His evil
Thou usest, and from thence createst more good,
Witness this *new*-made world, another heav'n. *Milton.*

All clad in liveliest colours, fresh and fair
As the bright flowers that crown'd their brighter hair;
All in that *new*-blown age which does inspire
Warmth in themselves, in their beholders fire. *Cowley.*

While from above adorn'd with radiant light,
A *new*-born sun surpris'd the dazzled sight. *Roscommon.*

If it could, yet that it should always run them into such a machine as is already extant, and not often into some *new*-fashioned one, such as was never seen before, no reason can be assigned or imagined. *Ray on the Creation.*

This English edition is not so properly a translation, as a new composition, there being several additional chapters in it, and several *new*-moulded. *Burnet's Theory of the Earth.*

New-found lands accrue to the prince whose subject makes the first discovery. *Burnet's Theory of the Earth.*

Let this be nature's frailty, or her fate,
Or Isgrim's counsel, her *new*-chosen mate. *Dryden.*

When the flood in its own depths was drown'd,
It left behind it false and slipp'ry ground;
And the more solemn pomp was still deferr'd,
'Till *new*-born nature in fresh looks appear'd. *Dryden.*

Shewn all at once you dazzled so our eyes,
As *new*-born Pallas did the Gods surprise;
When springing forth from Jove's *new*-closing wound,
She struck the warlike spear into the ground. *Dryden.*

A bird *new*-made, about the banks she plies,
Not far from shore, and short excursions tries. *Dryden.*

Our house has sent to-day
T' insure our *new*-built vessel, call'd a play. *Dryden.*

'Twas easy now to guess from whence arose,
Her *new*-made union with her ancient foes. *Dryden.*

Then curds and cream,
And *new*-laid eggs, which Baucis' busy care
Turn'd by a gentle fire, and roasted rare. *Dryd. Boccace.*

When pleading Matho, born abroad for air,
With his fat paunch fills his *new*-fashioned chair. *Dryd.*

A *new*-form'd faction does your power oppose,
The fight's confus'd, and all who met were foes. *Dryden.*

If thou ken'st from far
Among the Pleiads a *new*-kindled star;
If any sparkles than the rest more bright,
'Tis she that shines in that propitious light. *Dryden.*

If we consider *new*-born children, we shall have little reason to think that they bring many ideas into the world with them. *Locke.*

Drummers with vellom-thunder shake the pile,
To greet the *new*-made bride. *Gay's Trivia.*

Ah Blouzelind! I love thee more by half,
Than does their fawns, or cows the *new*-fall'n calf. *Gay's Pastorals.*

The proctor exhibits his proxy from the dean and chapter, and presents the *new*-elected bishop to the vicar-general. *Ayliffe's Parergon*

The *new*-fallen young here bleating for their dams,
The larger here, and there the lesser lambs. *Pope.*

A *new*-married man and an ass, are bride-led; an old-married man and a pack-horse, sadd-led. *Arbuth. and Pope.*

Learn

Learn all the *new*-fashion words and oaths. *Swift.*

NEWFA'NGLED. *adj.* [*new* and *fangle.*] Formed with vain or foolish love of novelty.

At Christmas I no more desire a rose,
Than wish a snow in May's *newfangled* shows;
But like of each thing, that in season grows. *Shakes.*

Those charities are not *neufangled* devices of yesterday, but are most of them as old as the reformation. *Atterbury.*

NEWFA'NGLEDNESS. } *n. s.* [from *newfangled.*] Vain and NEWFAN'GLENESS. } foolish love of novelty.

So to *newfanglenefs* both of manner, apparel, and each thing else, by the custom of self-guilty evil, glad to change though often for a worse. *Sidney, b.* ii.

Yet he them in *newfanglenefs* did pass. *Hubberd's Tale.*

The women would be loth to come behind the fashion in *newfangledness* of the manner, if not in costliness of the matter. *Carew.*

NE'WEL. *n. s.*

1. The compass round which the staircase is carried.

Let the stairs to the upper rooms be upon a fair open *newel*, and finely railed in. *Bacon, Essay* 46.

2. *Newel*; novelty. *Spenser.*

NE'WING. *n. s.* [from *new.*] Yest or barm. *Ains.*

NE'WLY. *adv.* [from *new.*] Freshly; lately.

Such is the power of that sweet passion,
That it all sordid baseness doth repel,
And the refined mind doth *newly* fashion
Into a fairer form. *Spenser's Hymn on Love.*

Her breath indeed those hands have *newly* stopp'd. *Sha.*

They *newly* learned by the king's example, that attainders do not interrupt the conveying of title to the crown. *Bacon.*

Her lips were red, and one was thin,
Compar'd to that was next her chin;
Some bee had stung it *newly*. *Suckling.*
Then rubb'd it o'er with *newly* gather'd mint. *Dryd.*

NE'WNESS. *n. s.* [from *new.*] Freshness; lateness; novelty; recentness; state of being new.

His device was to come without any device, all in white like a new knight, but so new as his *newness* shamed most of the others long exercise. *Sidney, b.* ii.

Away, my friends, new flight;
And happy *newness* that intends old right. *Shakespeare.*

Words borrowed of antiquity do lend majesty to stile, they have the authority of years, and out of their intermission do win to themselves a kind of grace-like *newness*. *B. John.*

Their stories, if they had been preserved, and what else was then performed in that *newness* of the world, there could nothing of more delight have been left to posterity. *Raleigh's Hist. of the World.*

In these disturbances,
And *newness* of a wav'ring government,
T' avenge them of their former grievances. *Dan. C. War.*

Newness in great matters, was a worthy entertainment for a searching mind; it was an high taste, fit for the relish. *South's Sermons.*

There are some *newnesses* of English, translated from the beauties of modern tongues, as well as from the elegances of the latin; and here and there some old words are sprinkled, which for their significance and sound, deserved not to be antiquated. *Dryden's Don Sebastian.*

When Horace writ his satyrs, the monarchy of his Cæsar was in its *newness*, and the government but just made easy to his conquered people. *Dryden's Juvenal.*

NEWS. *n. s.* without the singular, [from *new*, *nouvelles*, Fr.]

1. Fresh account of any thing; something not heard before.

As he was ready to be greatly advanced for some noble pieces of service which he did, he heard *news* of me. *Sidney.*

When Rhea heard these *news*, she fled from her husband to her brother Saturn. *Raleigh's Hist. of the World.*

Evil *news* rides fast, while good *news* baits. *Milt. Agonist.*

With such amazement as weak mothers use,
And frantick gesture, he receives the *news*. *Waller.*

Now the books, and now the bells,
And now our act the preacher tells,
To edify the people;
All our divinity is *news*,
And we have made of equal use
The pulpit and the steeple. *Denham.*

The amazing *news* of Charles at once was spread,
At once the general voice declared
Our gracious prince was dead. *Dryden.*

It is no *news* for the weak and poor to be a prey to the strong and rich. *L'Estrange.*

They have *news*-gatherers and intelligencers distributed into their several walks, who bring in their respective quotas, and make them acquainted with the discourse of the whole kingdom. *Spectator*, N°. 439.

2. Papers which give an account of the transactions of the present times.

Their papers, filled with a different party spirit, divide the people into different sentiments, who generally consider rather the principles than the truth of the *news*-writer. *Addis.*

Advertise both in every *news*-paper; and let it not be your fault or mine, if our country-men will not take warning. ——*Swift's Drapiers Letters.*

Wood is generally his own *news*-writer. I cannot but observe from that paragraph, that this public enemy treats this kingdom with contempt. *Swift's Drapiers Letters.*

Pamphlets and *news*-papers have been full of me. *Pope.*

NE'WS-MONGER. *n. s.* [*news* and *monger.*] One that deals in news; one whose employment it is to hear and to tell news.

Many tales devis'd,
Which oft the ear of greatness needs must hear,
By smiling pick-thanks and base *news-mongers*. *Shakes.*

This was come as a judgment upon him for laying aside his father's will, and turning stock-jobber, *news-monger*, and busy body, meddling with other peoples affairs. *Arbuthnot.*

NEWT. *n. s.* [eꝼeꞇe, Saxon. *Newt* is supposed by *Skinner* to be contracted from *an evet.*] Eft; small lizard: they are supposed to be appropriated some to the land, and some to the water.

Oh thou! whose self-same mettle,
Whereof thy proud child, arrogant man, is puft,
Engenders the black toad, and adder blue,
The gilded *newt*, and eyeless venom'd worm. *Shakes.*

Newts and blind worms do no wrong;
Come not near our fairy queen. *Sha. M. Night's Dream.*

Such humidity is observed in *newts* and water-lizards, especially if their skins be perforated or pricked. *Brown's V. Err.*

NEW-YEAR'S-GIFT. *n. s.* [*new*, *year*, and *gift.*] Present made on the first day of the year.

If I be served such a trick, I'll have my brains taken out and buttered, and give them to a dog for a *new-year's-gift*. *Shakespeare's Merry Wives of Windsor.*

When he sat on the throne distributing *new-year's-gifts*, he had his altar of incense by him, that before they received gifts they might cast a little incense into the fire; which all good christians refused to do. *Stillingfleet.*

NEXT. *adj.* [nexꞇ, Saxon, by a colloquial change from neȝhꞅꞇ or nyhꞅꞇ, the superlative of neh or nyh; *neest*, Scottish.]

1. Nearest in place; immediately succeeding in order.

Want supplieth itself of what is *next*, and many times the *next* way. *Bacon, Essay* 14.

The queen already sat
High on a golden bed; her princely guest
Was *next* her side, in order sat the rest. *Dryd. Virg. Æn.*

The *next* in place and punishment were they,
Who prodigally throw their souls away. *Dryden, Æn.* vi.

2. Nearest in any gradation.

If the king himself had stayed at London, or, which had been the *next* best, kept his court at York, and sent the army on their proper errand, his enemies had been speedily subdued. *Clarendon.*

O fortunate young man! at least your lays
Are *next* to his, and claim the second praise. *Dryden.*

Finite and infinite, being by the mind looked on as modifications of expansion and duration, the *next* thing to be considered, is, how the mind comes by them. *Locke.*

That's a difficulty *next* to impossible. *Rowe.*

NEXT. *adv.* At the time or turn immediately succeeding.

Th' unwary nymph
Desir'd of Jove, when *next* he sought her bed,
To grant a certain gift. *Addison's Ovid Metam. b.* iii.

NI'AS. *n. s.* [*niais*, French.] Simple, silly, and foolish.

A *nias* hawk is one taken newly from the nest, and not able to help itself; and hence nisey, a silly person. *Bailey.*

NIB. *n. s.* [neb, Saxon, the face; *nebbe*, Dutch, the bill.]

1. The bill or beck of a bird. See NEB.

2. The point of any thing, generally of a pen.

A tree called the bejuco, which twines about other trees, with its end hanging downwards, travellers cut the *nib* off it, and presently a spout of water runs out from it as clear as crystal. *Derham.*

NI'BBED. *adj.* [from *nib.*] Having a nib.

To NIBBLE. *v. a.* [from *nib*, the beak or mouth.]

1. To bite by little at a time; to eat slowly.

Thy turfy mountains, where live *nibbling* sheep,
And flat meads thatch'd with stover them to keep. *Sha.*

It is the rose that bleeds, when he
Nibbles his nice phlebotomy. *Cleaveland's Poems.*

Had not he better have born wats *nibbling* of his plants and roots now, than the huntsman's eating of him out of house and home. *L'Estrange, Fable* 387.

Many there are who *nibble* without leave;
But none, who are not born to taste, survive. *Granvil.*

2. To bite as a fish does the bait.

The roving trout
Greedily sucks in the twining bait,
And tugs and *nibbles* at the fallacious meat. *Gay.*

To NI'BBLE. *v. n.*

1. To bite at.

As pidgeons bill, so wedlock would be *nibbling*. *Shakes.*

They

They gape at rich revenues which you hold,
And fain would *nibble* at your grandame gold. *Dryden.*

But if you would be *nibbling*, here is a hand to ſtay your ſtomach. *Dryden's Don Sebaſtian.*

Plunging himſelf in mud, and then lifting up his head a little, he caſts out the ſaid ſtring; which the little fiſhes taking for a worm, and *nibbling* at it, he immediately plucks them both in together. *Grew's Muſæum.*

2. To carp at; to find fault with.

Inſtead of returning a full anſwer to my book, he manifeſtly falls a *nibbling* at one ſingle paſſage in it. *Tillot. Pref.*

NIBBLER. *n. ſ.* [from *nibble.*] One that bites by little at a time.

NICE. *adj.* [neʒe, Saxon, ſoft.]

1. Accurate in judgment to minute exactneſs; ſuperfluouſly exact. It is often uſed to expreſs a culpable delicacy.

Such a man was Argalus, as hardly the *niceſt* eye can find a ſpot in. *Sidney.*

He that ſtands upon a ſlipp'ry place,
Makes *nice* of no vile hold to ſtay him up. *Sha. K. John.*

Nor be ſo *nice* in taſte myſelf to know,
If what I ſwallow be a thruſh or no. *Dryd. Perſius.*

Thus critics, of leſs judgment than caprice,
Curious, not knowing, not exact, but *nice*,
Form ſhort ideas, and offend in arts,
As moſt in manners, by a love to parts. *Pope on Crit.*

Our author, happy in a judge ſo *nice*,
Produc'd his play, and begg'd the knight's advice. *Pope.*

2. Delicate; ſcrupulouſly and minutely cautious.

The letter was not *nice*, but full of charge
Of dear import. *Shakeſ. Romeo and Juliet.*

Dear love! continue *nice* and chaſte;
For if you yield, you do me wrong;
Let duller wits to love's end haſte,
I have enough to woo thee long. *Donne.*

Of honour men at firſt like women *nice*,
Raiſe maiden ſcruples at unpractis'd vice. *E. Hallifax.*

Having been compiled by Gratian, in an ignorant age, we ought not to be too *nice* in examining it. *Baker*

3. Faſtidious; ſqueamiſh.

God hath here
Varied his bounty ſo with new delights,
As may compare with heaven; and to taſte,
Think not I ſhall be *nice*. *Milt. Par. Loſt.*

4. Eaſily injured; delicate.

With how much eaſe is a young muſe betray'd?
How *nice* the reputation of the maid? *Roſcommon.*

5. Formed with minute exactneſs.

Indulge me but in love, my other paſſions
Shall riſe and fall by virtue's *niceſt* rules. *Addiſon's Cato.*

6. Requiring ſcrupulous exactneſs.

Suppoſing an injury done, it is a *nice* point to proportion the reparation to the degree of the indignity. *L'Eſtrange.*

My progreſs in making this *nice* and troubleſome experiment, I have ſet down more at large. *Newton's Opt.*

7. Refined.

A *nice* and ſubtile happineſs I ſee
Thou to thyſelf propoſeſt, in the choice
Of thy aſſociates, Adam; and wilt taſte
No pleaſure, tho' in pleaſure ſolitary. *Milt. P. Loſt.*

8. Having lucky hits. This ſignification is not in uſe.

When my hours
Were *nice* and lucky, men did ranſom lives
Of me for jeſts. *Shakeſ. Ant. and Cleopatra.*

NI'CELY. *adv.* [from *nice.*]

1. Accurately; minutely; ſcrupulouſly.

Theſe kind of knaves in this plainneſs
Harbour more craft, and more corrupter ends,
Than twenty ſilky ducking obſervants
That ſtretch their duties *nicely*. *Shakeſpeare's K. Lear.*

What mean thoſe ladies which, as tho'
They were to take a clock to pieces, go
So *nicely* about the bride? *Donne.*

He ought to ſtudy the grammar of his own tongue, that he may underſtand his own country-ſpeech *nicely*, and ſpeak it properly. *Locke.*

The next thing of which the doſes ought to be *nicely* determined, are opiates. *Arbuthnot on Coins.*

At *nicely* carving ſhew thy wit;
But ne'er preſume to eat a bit. *Swift's Miſcell.*

2. Delicately.

The inconveniences attending the beſt of governments, we quickly feel, and are *nicely* ſenſible of the ſhare that we bear in them. *Atterbury.*

NI'CENESS. *n. ſ.* [from *nice.*]

1. Accuracy; minute exactneſs.

Where's now that labour'd *niceneſs* in thy dreſs,
And all thoſe arts that did the ſpark expreſs. *Dryden.*

2. Superfluous delicacy or exactneſs.

A ſtrange *niceneſs* were it in me to refrain that from the ears of a perſon repreſenting ſo much worthineſs, which I am glad even to rocks and woods to utter. *Sidney.*

Unlike the *niceneſs* of our modern dames,
Affected nymphs, with new affected names. *Dryden.*

Nor place them where
Roaſt crabs offend the *niceneſs* of their noſe. *Dryden.*

NI'CETY. *n. ſ.* [from *nice.*]

1. Minute accuracy of thought.

Nor was this *nicety* of his judgment confined only to literature, but was the ſame in all other parts of art. *Prior.*

2. Accurate performance.

As for the workmanſhip of the old Roman pillars, the ancients have not kept to the *nicety* of proportion and the rules of art ſo much as the moderns. *Addiſon on Italy.*

3. Faſtidious delicacy; ſqueamiſhneſs.

He them with ſpeeches meet
Does fair intreat; no courting *nicety*,
But ſimple true, and eke unfeigned ſweet. *Fairy Q.*

So love doth loath diſdainful *nicety*. *Spenſer.*

4. Minute obſervation; punctilious diſcrimination; ſubtilty.

If reputation attend theſe conqueſts, which depend on the fineneſs and *niceties* of words, it is no wonder if the wit of men ſo employed, ſhould perplex and ſublitize the ſignification of ſounds. *Locke.*

His concluſions are not built upon any *niceties*, or ſolitary and uncommon appearances, but on the moſt ſimple and obvious circumſtances of theſe terreſtrial bodies. *Woodw.*

5. Delicate management; cautious treatment.

Love ſuch *nicety* requires,
One blaſt will put out all his fires. *Swift's Poems.*

6. Effeminate ſoftneſs.

7. Niceties, in the plural, is generally applied to dainties or delicacies in eating.

NICHAR. *n. ſ.*

The characters are: it hath a polypetalous or a monopetalous flower, cut very deeply into ſeveral ſegments, but is almoſt of an anomalous figure; from whoſe calyx ariſes the pointal, which afterwards becomes a pod, beſet all over with prickles, in which are contained one or two round hard ſeeds. *Miller.*

NICHE. *n. ſ.* [French.] A hollow in which a ſtatue may be placed.

Niches, containing figures of white ſtone or marble, ſhould not be coloured in their concavity too black. *Wotton.*

They not from temples, nor from gods refrain,
But the poor lares from the *niches* ſeize,
If they be little images that pleaſe. *Dryden.*

On the ſouth a long majeſtic race
Of Ægypt's prieſts, the gilded *niches* grace. *Pope.*

The heirs to titles and large eſtates are well enough qualified to read pamphlets againſt religion and high-flying; whereby they fill their *niches*, and carry themſelves through the world with that dignity which beſt becomes a ſenator and a ſquire. *Swift's Miſcellanies.*

NICK. *n. ſ.* [*nicke*, Teutonick, the twinkling of an eye.]

1. Exact point of time at which there is neceſſity or convenience.

That great inſtrument of ſtate had foreknowledge of it, but ſuffered the fatal thread to be ſpun out to that length for ſome politick reſpects, and then to cut it off in the very *nick*. *Howel's Vocal Foreſt.*

What in our watches that in us is found,
So to the height and *nick* we up be wound,
No matter by what hand or trick. *Suckling.*

That trick,
Had it come in the *nick*,
Had touch'd us to the quick. *Denham.*

Though dame fortune ſeem to ſmile,
And leer upon him for a while;
She'll after ſhew him in the *nick*
Of all his glories a dog trick. *Hudibras, p. i. cant. 3.*

And ſome with ſymbols, ſigns, and tricks,
Engraved in planetary *nicks*,
With their own influences will fetch them
Down from their orbs, arreſt and catch them. *Hud.*

This *nick* of time is the critical occaſion for the gaining of a point. *L'Eſtrange.*

2. A notch cut in any thing. [Corrupted from *nock* or *notch.*]

3. A ſcore; a reckoning.

Launce his man told me, he lov'd her art of all *nick*. *Shak.*

4. A winning throw. [*niche*, Fr. a ludicrous trick.]

Come, ſeven's the main,
Cries Ganymede; the uſual trick
Seven, ſlur a ſix, eleven a *nick*. *Prior.*

To NICK. *v. a.* [from the noun.]

1. To hit; to touch luckily; to perform by ſome ſlight artifice uſed at the lucky moment.

Is not the winding up of witneſs
A *nicking* more than half the buſ'neſs? *Hudibras, p. ii.*

The juſt ſeaſon of doing things muſt be *nick'd*, and all accidents improved. *L'Eſtrange, Fable 38.*

Take away paſſion while it is predominant and afloat, and juſt in the critical height of it, *nick* it with ſome lucky or unlucky word, and you may certainly over-rule it. *South.*

2. To cut in nicks or notches.

His beard they have ſing'd off with brands of fire;
And ever as it blaz'd they threw on him
Great pails of puddled mire to quench the hair.
My maſter preaches patience, and the while
His man with ſciſſars *nicks* him like a fool. *Shakeſpeare.*

Breaks watchmen's heads, and chairmen's glaſſes,
And thence proceeds to *nicking* ſaſhes. *Prior.*

3. To ſuit, as tallies cut in nicks.

Words *nicking* and reſembling one another, are applicable to different ſignifications. *Camden's Remains.*

4. To defeat or cozen, as at dice; to diſappoint by ſome trick or unexpected turn.

Why ſhould he follow you?
The itch of his affection ſhould not then
Have *nick'd* his captainſhip, at ſuch a point. *Shakeſpeare.*

NICKNA'ME. *n. ſ.* [*nom de nique*, French.] A name given in ſcoff or contempt; a term of deriſion; an opprobious or contemptuous appellation.

The time was when men were had in price for learning; now letters only make men vile. He is upbraidingly called a poet, as if it were a contemptible *nickname*. *Ben. Johnſon.*

My mortal enemy hath not only falſely ſurmiſed me to be a feigned perſon, giving me *nicknames*, but alſo hath offered large ſums of money to corrupt the princes with whom I have been retained. *Bacon's Hen.* VII.

So long as her tongue was at liberty, there was not a word to be got from her, but the ſame *nickname* in deriſion. *L'Eſtrange.*

To NICKNA'ME. *v. a.* To call by an opprobrious appellation.

You *nickname* virtue vice;
For virtue's office never breaks men's troth. *Shakeſ.*

Leſs ſeem theſe facts which treaſons *nickname* force,
Than ſuch a fear'd ability for more. *Denham.*

To NI'CTATE. *v. a.* [*nicto*, Latin.] To wink.

There are ſeveral parts peculiar to brutes, which are wanting in man; as the ſeventh or ſuſpenſory muſcle of the eye, the *nictating* membrane, and the ſtrong aponeuroſes on the ſides of the neck. *Ray.*

NIDE. *n. ſ.* [*nidus*, Lat.] A brood: as, a nide of pheaſants.

NIDGET. *n. ſ.* [corrupted from *nithing* or *niding*. The opprobrious term with which the man was anciently branded who refuſed to come to the royal ſtandard in times of exigency.] A coward; a daſtard.

There was one true Engliſh word of greater force than them all, now out of all uſe; it ſignifieth no more than abject, baſeminded, falſe-hearted, coward, or *nidget*. *Camden.*

NIDIFICA'TION. *n. ſ.* [*nidificatio*, Latin.] The act of building neſts.

That place, and that method of *nidification*, doth abundantly anſwer the creature's occaſions. *Derham.*

NI'DING. *adj.* [from nið, Saxon, vileneſs.]

Niding, an old Engliſh word ſignifying abject, baſe-minded, falſe-hearted, coward, or nidget. *Carew.*

NIDO'ROUS. *adj.* [*nidoreux*, from *nidor.*] Reſembling the ſmell or taſte of roaſted fat.

Incenſe and *nidorous* ſmells, ſuch as of ſacrifices, were thought to intoxicate the brain, and to diſpoſe men to devotion; which they may do by a kind of contriſtation of the ſpirits, and partly alſo by heating and exalting them. *Bac.*

The ſigns of the functions of the ſtomach being depraved, are eructatious either with the taſte of the aliment, acid, *nidoroſe*, or fœtid, reſembling the taſte of rotten eggs. *Arbuthnot on Aliments.*

NI'DOROSITY. *n. ſ.* [from *nidorous.*] Eructation with the taſte of undigeſted roaſt-meat.

The cure of this *nidoroſity* is, by vomiting and purging. *Floyer on the Humours.*

NIDULA'TION. *n. ſ.* [*nidulor*, Latin.] The time of remaining in the neſt.

The ground of this popular practice might be the common opinion concerning the virtue prognoſtic of theſe birds, the natural regard they have unto the winds, and they unto them again, more eſpecially remarkable in the time of their *nidulation*, and bringing forth their young. *Brown's V. Err.*

NIECE. *n. ſ.* [*niece*, *niepce*, French; *neptis*, Latin.] The daughter of a brother or ſiſter.

My *niece* Plantagenet,
Led in the hand of her kind aunt of Gloſter. *Sha. R.* III.

While he thus his *niece* beſtows,
About our iſle he builds a wall. *Waller.*

NI'GGARD. *n. ſ.* [*ninggr*, Iſlandick.] A miſer; a curmudgeon; a ſordid, avaricious, parcimonious fellow.

If thou do, then let thy bed be turned from fine gravel to weeds or mud. If thou do, let ſome unjuſt *niggards* make weres to ſpoil thy beauty. *Sidney, b.* ii.

Be not a *niggard* of your ſpeech. *Shakeſ. Macbeth.*

Serve him as a grudging maſter,
As a penurious *niggard* of his wealth. *Milton's Poems.*

Be *niggards* of advice on no pretence;
For the worſt avarice is that of ſenſe. *Pope on Crit.*

NI'GGARD. *adj.*

1. Sordid; avaricious; parcimonious.

One ſhe found
With all the gifts of bounteous nature crown'd,
Of gentle blood; but one whoſe *niggard* fate
Had ſet him far below her high eſtate. *Dryden.*

2. Sparing; wary.

Moſt free of queſtion, but to our demands
Niggard in his reply. *Shakeſpeare's Hamlet.*

To NI'GGARD. *v. a.* [from the noun.] To ſtint.

The deep of night is crept upon our talk,
And nature muſt obey neceſſity;
Which we will *niggard* with a little reſt. *Shakeſpeare.*

NI'GGARDISH. *adj.* [from *niggard.*] Having ſome diſpoſition to avarice.

NI'GGARDLINESS. *n. ſ.* [from *niggardly.*] Avarice; ſordid parcimony.

Niggardlineſs is not good huſbandry, nor generoſity, profuſion. *Addiſon's Spectator*, Nº. 443.

NI'GGARDLY. *adj.* [from *niggard.*]

1. Avaricious; ſordidly parcimonious.

Where the owner of the houſe will be bountiful, it is not for the ſteward to be *niggardly*. *Hall.*

Love is like a penurious god, very *niggardly* of his opportunities: he muſt be watched like a hard-hearted treaſurer. *Dryden's Spaniſh Friar.*

Why are we ſo *niggardly* to ſtop at one fifth? Why do we not raiſe it one full moiety, and thereby double our money? *Locke.*

Providence not *niggardly* but wiſe,
Here laviſhly beſtows, and there denies,
That by each other's virtues we may riſe. *Granvil.*

Tiberius was noted for his *niggardly* temper; he uſed only to give to his attendants their diet. *Arbuthnot on Coins.*

2. Sparing; wary.

I know your mind, and I will ſatisfy it; neither will I do it like a *niggardly* anſwerer, going no farther than the bounds of the queſtion. *Sidney.*

NI'GGARDLY. *adv.* Sparingly; parcimoniouſly.

I have long loved her, followed her, ingroſs'd opportunities to meet her; feed every ſlight occaſion that could but *niggardly* give me ſight of her. *Shakeſ. M. W. of Windſor.*

NI'GGARDNESS. *n. ſ.* [from *niggard.*] Avarice; ſordid parcimony.

All preparations, both for food and lodging, ſuch as would make one deteſt *niggardneſs*, it is ſo ſluttiſh a vice. *Sidney.*

NIGH. *prep.* [nyꝫ, Saxon.] At no great diſtance from.

They ſhone
Stars diſtant, but *nigh* hand ſeem'd other worlds. *Milton.*

Nigh this receſs, with terror they ſurvey,
Where death maintains his dread tyrannic ſway. *Garth.*

NIGH. *adv.*

1. Not at a great diſtance.

The day of the Lord cometh, for it is *nigh* at hand. *Jo.* ii. 1.

He was ſick *nigh* unto death. *Phil.* ii. 27.

2. To a place near.

He drew *nigh*, and to me held,
Ev'n to my mouth, of that ſame fruit held part
Which he had pluck'd. *Milton's Paradiſe Loſt, b.* v.

I will defer that anxious thought,
And death, by fear, ſhall not be *nigher* brought. *Dryd.*

NIGH. *adj.*

1. Near; not diſtant; not remote.

The loud tumult ſhews the battle *nigh*. *Prior.*

2. Allied cloſely by blood.

He committed the protection of his ſon Aſanes to two of his *nigh* kinſmen and aſſured friends. *Knolles.*

His uncle or uncle's ſon, or any that is *nigh* of kin unto him of his family, may redeem him. *Lev.* xxv. 49.

His ſiſter a virgin, that is *nigh* unto him. *Lev.* xxi. 3.

To NIGH. *v. n.* [from the particle.] To approach; to advance; to draw near.

Now day is done, and night is *nighing* faſt. *Hubberd.*

NI'GHLY. *adv.* [from *nigh* the adjective.] Nearly; within a little.

A man born blind, now adult, was taught by his touch to diſtinguiſh between a cube and a ſphere of the ſame metal, and *nighly* of the ſame bigneſs. *Locke.*

NI'GHNESS. *n. ſ.* [from *nigh.*] Nearneſs; proximity.

NIGHT. *n. ſ.* [*nauts*, Gothick; nıht, Saxon; *nuit*, Fr.]

1. The time of darkneſs; the time from ſun-ſet to ſun-riſe.

The duke of Cornwall, and Regan his dutcheſs, will be here this *night*. *Shakeſpeare's K. Lear.*

In the morning he ſhall devour the prey, and at *night* divide the ſpoil. *Gen.* xlix. 27.

Pharaoh roſe up in the *night*. *Exodus* xii. 30.

They did eat and drink, and tarried all *night*. *Gen.* xxiv. 54.

Let them ſleep, let them ſleep on,
'Till this ſtormy *night* be gone,
And th' eternal morrow dawn,
Then the curtains will be drawn;
And they waken with that light,
Whoſe day ſhall never ſleep in *night*. *Craſhaw.*

Dire

Dire Tiſiphone there keeps the ward,
Girt in her ſanguine gown by *night* and day,
Obſervant of the ſouls that paſs the downward way. *Dryd.*

2. It is much uſed in compoſition.

TO-NIGHT. *adverbially.* In this night; at this night.

There came men in hither *to-night* of the children of Iſrael, to ſearch out the country. *Joſ.* ii. 2.

NIGHTBRA'WLER. *n. ſ.* [*night* and *brawler.*] One who raiſes diſturbances in the night.

You unlace your reputation,
And ſpend your rich opinion for the name
Of a *night-brawler.* *Shakeſ. Othello.*

NIGHTCAP. *n. ſ.* [*night* and *cap.*] A cap worn in bed, or in undreſs.

The rabblement houted, and clapt their chopt hands, and threw up their ſweaty *night-caps.* *Shakeſ. Jul. Cæſar.*

Great mountains have a perception of the diſpoſition of the air to tempeſts ſooner than the vallies below; and therefore they ſay in Wales, when certain hills have their *night-caps* on, they mean miſchief. *Bacon's Nat. Hiſtory.*

How did the humbled ſwain deteſt
His prickly beard, and hairy breaſt!
His *night-cap* border'd round with lace,
Could give no ſoftneſs to his face. *Swift's Poems.*

NIGHTCROW. *n. ſ.* [*night* and *crow.*] A bird that cries in the night.

The owl ſhriek'd at thy birth, an evil ſign;
The *night-crow* cry'd, a boding luckleſs time. *Shakeſ.*

NI'GHTDEW. *n. ſ.* [*night* and *dew.*] Dew that wets the ground in the night.

All things are huſh'd, as nature's ſelf lay dead,
The mountains ſeem to nod their drowſy head;
The little birds in dreams their ſongs repeat,
And ſleeping flowers beneath the *night-dew* ſweat;
E'en luſt and envy ſleep. *Dryden's Ind. Emperor.*

NI'GHTDOG. *n. ſ.* [*night* and *dog.*] A dog that hunts in the night. Uſed by deer-ſtealers.

When *night-dogs* run, all ſorts of deer are chaſed. *Sha.*

NI'GHTDRESS. *n. ſ.* [*night* and *dreſs.*] The dreſs worn at night.

The fair ones feel ſuch maladies as theſe,
When each new *night-dreſs* gives a new diſeaſe. *Pope.*

NI'GHTED. *adj.* [from *night.*] Darkened; clouded; black.

It was great ign'rance, Gloſter's eyes being out,
To let him live: Edmund, I think, is gone;
In pity of his miſery to diſpatch
His *nighted* life. *Shakeſpeare's King Lear.*
Good Hamlet, caſt thy *nighted* colour off,
And let thine eye look like a friend on Denmark. *Sha.*

NI'GHTFARING. *n. ſ.* [*night* and *fare.*] Travelling in the night.

Will-a-Wiſp miſleads *night-faring* clowns,
O'er hills, and ſinking bogs, and pathleſs downs. *Gay.*

NI'GHTFIRE. *n. ſ.* [*night* and *fire.*] Ignis fatuus; Will-a-Wiſp.

Fooliſh *night-fires*, womens and childrens wiſhes,
Chaſes in arras, gilded emptineſs:
Theſe are the pleaſures here. *Herbert.*

NI'GHTFLY. *n. ſ.* [*night* and *fly.*] Moth that flies in the night.

Why rather, ſleep, lieſt thou in ſmoaky cribs,
And huſh't with buzzing *night-flies* to thy ſlumber;
Than in the perfum'd chambers of the great,
And lull'd with ſounds of ſweeteſt melody? *Shakeſpeare.*

NI'GHTFOUNDERED. *n. ſ.* [from *night* and *founder.*] Loſt or diſtreſſed in the night.

Either ſome one like us *night-foundered* here,
Or elſe ſome neighbour woodman, or at worſt,
Some roving robber calling to his fellows. *Milton.*

NI'GHTGOWN. *n. ſ.* [*night* and *gown.*] A looſe gown uſed for an undreſs.

Since his majeſty went into the field,
I have ſeen her riſe from her bed, throw
Her *night-gown* upon her. *Shakeſpeare's Macbeth.*

They have put me in a ſilk *night-gown*, and a gaudy fool's cap. *Addiſon's Guardian*, Nº. 113.

No meagre muſe-rid mope, aduſt and thin,
In a dun *night-gown* of his own looſe ſkin. *Pope's Dunc.*

NI'GHTHAG. *n. ſ.* [*night* and *hag.*] Witch ſuppoſed to wander in the night.

Nor uglier follows the *night-hag*, when called
In ſecret, riding through the air ſhe comes
Lur'd with the ſmell of infant-blood, to dance
With Lapland witches. *Milton's Paradiſe Loſt*, *b.* ii.

NI'GHTINGALE. *n. ſ.* [from *night* and *galan*, Saxon, to ſing; *galm*, Teutonick, is a ſound or echo.]

1. A ſmall bird that ſings in the night with remarkable melody; Philomel.

I think,
The *nightingale*, if ſhe ſhould ſing by day,
When every gooſe is cackling, would be thought
No better a muſician than the wren. *Shakeſpeare.*

Although the wezon, throtle, and tongue, be the inſtruments of voice, and by their agitations concur in thoſe delightful modulations, yet cannot we aſſign the cauſe unto any particular formation; and I perceive the *nightingale* hath ſome diſadvantage in the tongue. *Brown's V. Err.*

Thus the wiſe *nightingale* that leaves her home,
Purſuing conſtantly the chearful ſpring,
To foreign groves does her old muſick bring. *Waller.*

2. A word of endearment.

My *nightingale!*
We'll beat them to their beds. *Shak. Ant. and Cleopatra.*

N'IGHTLY. *adv.* [from *night.*]

1. By night.

Thee, Sion! and the flow'ry brooks beneath,
That waſh thy hallow'd feet, and warbling flow,
Nightly I viſit. *Milton's Paradiſe Loſt*, *b.* iii.
Soon as the evening ſhades prevail,
The moon takes up the wondrous tale,
And *nightly* to the liſtning earth
Repeats the ſtory of her birth. *Addiſon's Spectator.*

2. Every night.

Let all things ſuffer,
Ere we will eat our meal in fear, and ſleep
In the affliction of thoſe terrible dreams
That ſhake us *nightly.* *Shakeſpeare's Macbeth.*

NI'GHTLY. *adj.* [from *night.*] Done by night; acting by night; happening by night.

May the ſtars and ſhining moon attend
Your *nightly* ſports, as you vouchſafe to tell
What nymphs they were who mortal forms excel. *Dryd.*
Soon as the flocks ſhook off the *nightly* dews,
Two ſwains, whom love kept wakeful and the muſe,
Pour'd o'er the whit'ning vale their fleecy care. *Pope.*

NI'GHTMAN. *n. ſ.* [*night* and *man.*] One who carries away ordure in the night.

NI'GHTMARE. *n. ſ.* [*night*, and according to *Temple*, *mara*, a ſpirit that, in the heathen mythology, was related to torment or ſuffocate ſleepers.] A morbid oppreſſion in the night, reſembling the preſſure of weight upon the breaſt.

Saint Withold footed thrice the would,
He met the *nightmare*, and her name he told;
Bid her alight, and her troth plight. *Shakeſ. K. Lear.*

The forerunners of an apoplexy are, dulneſs, drowſineſs, vertigoes, tremblings, oppreſſions in ſleep, and *night-mares.* *Arbuthnot on Aliments.*

NI'GHTPIECE. *n. ſ.* [*night* and *piece.*] A picture ſo coloured as to be ſuppoſed ſeen by candle light; not by the light of the day.

He hung a great part of the wall with *night-pieces*, that ſeemed to ſhow themſelves by the candles which were lighted up; and were ſo inflamed by the ſun-ſhine which fell upon them, that I could ſcarce forbear crying out fire. *Addiſon.*

NI'GHTRAIL. *n. ſ.* [*night* and reȝl, Saxon, a gown or robe.] A looſe cover thrown over the dreſs at night.

An antiquary will ſcorn to mention a pinner or *night-rail*; but will talk as gravely as a father of the church on the vitta and peplus. *Addiſon on ancient Medals.*

NI'GHTRAVEN. *n. ſ.* [*night* and *raven.*] A bird ſuppoſed of ill omen, that cries loud in the night.

The ill-fac't owl, death's dreadful meſſenger,
The hoarſe *night-raven*, trump of doleful drere. *Spenſer.*
I pray his bad voice bode no miſchief:
I had as lief have heard the *night-raven*,
Come what plague would have come after it. *Shakeſ.*

NIGHTROBBER. *n. ſ.* [*night* and *robber.*] One who ſteals in the dark.

Highways ſhould be fenced on both ſides, whereby thieves and *night-robbers* might be more eaſily purſued and encountered. *Spenſer's Ireland.*

NI'GHTRULE. *n. ſ.* [*night* and *rule.*] A tumult in the night.

How now, mad ſprite,
What *night-rule* now about this haunted grove? *Shakeſ.*

NI'GHTSHADE. *n. ſ.* [niht ſcada, Saxon.]

1. A plant of two kinds, common and deadly night-ſhade.

The flower conſiſts of one leaf, which is divided into five parts, and expands in form of a ſtar: from the flower-cup riſes the pointal, which afterward becomes a round, oval, ſoft, ſucculent fruit, containing many flat ſeeds in each. The ſpecies are nine. This the phyſicians have directed to be uſed in medicine, under the title of *ſolanum hortenſe.* *Miller.*

2. Deadly.

Deadly *night-ſhade* (belladona) a [illegible] plant. The flower is bell-ſhaped, of one leaf, divi[illegible]ded into five acute ſegments at the top, and ſucceede[illegible] by a globular ſoft fruit, divided into two cells whi[illegible]ch contain the ſeeds. It is a very ſtrong poiſon. *Miller.*

NI'GHT[illegible]SHINING. *n. ſ.* [*night* and *ſhine.*] Shewing brightneſs in the night.

None of these *noctilucæ*, or *night-shining* bodies, have been observed in any of the antient sepulchres. *Wilkin's Dædalus.*

NI'GHTSHRIEK. *n. s.* [*night* and *shriek.*] A cry in the night.

I have almost forgot the taste of fears:
The time has been, my senses would have cool'd
To hear a *night-shriek*; and my fell of hair
Would at a dismal treatise rouse and stir,
As life were in't. *Shakespeare's Macbeth.*

NI'GHTTRIPPING. *n. s.* [*night* and *trip.*] Going lightly in the night.

Could it be prov'd,
That some *night-tripping* fairy had exchang'd
In cradle cloaths, our children where they lay,
Then would I have his Harry, and he mine. *Shakes.*

NI'GHTWALK. *n. s.* [*night* and *walk.*] Walk in the night.

If in his *night-walk* he met with irregular scholars, he took their names, and a promise to appear, unsent for, next morning. *Walton's Life of Sanderson.*

NI'GHTWALKER. *n. s.* [*night* and *walk.*] One who roves in the night upon ill designs.

Men that hunt so, be either privy stealers, or *night-walkers.* *Ascham's Schoolmaster.*

NI'GHTWARBLING. [*night* and *warble.*] Singing in the night.

Now is the pleasant time,
The cool, the silent, save where silence yields
To the *night-warbling* bird. *Milton's Par. Lost, b.* v.

NI'GHTWARD. *adj.* [*night* and *ward.*] Approaching towards night.

Their *night-ward* studies, wherewith they close the day's work. *Milton on Education.*

NI'GHTWATCH. *n. s.* [*night* and *watch.*] A period of the night as distinguished by change of the watch.

I remember thee upon my bed, and meditate on thee in the *night-watches.* *Psalms* lxiii. 6.

NIGRE'SCENT. *adj.* [*nigrescens,* Latin.] Growing black; approaching to blackness.

NIGRIFICA'TION. *n. s.* [*niger* and *facio.*] The act of making black.

NIHI'LITY. *n. s.* [*nihilité,* Fr. *nihilum,* Latin.] Nothingness; the state of being nothing.

Not being is considered as excluding all substance, and then all modes are also necessarily excluded; and this we call pure *nihility,* or mere nothing. *Watts's Logick.*

To NILL. *v. a.* [from *ne will,* nillan, Saxon.] Not to will; to refuse; to reject.

Certes, said he, I *nill* thine offer'd grace,
Ne to be made so happy do intend,
Another bliss before mine eyes I place,
Another happiness, another end. *Spenser's Fairy Q.*
In all affections she concurreth still;
If now, with man and wife to will and *nill*
The self-same things, a note of concord be,
I know no couple better can agree. *Ben. Johnson.*

NILL. *n. s.* The shining sparks of brass in trying and melting the ore.

To NIM. *v. a.* [*nemen,* Dutch, to take.] To take. In cant, to steal.

They'll question Mars, and by his look
Detect who 'twas that *nimm'd* a cloak. *Hudibras, p.* i.

They could not keep themselves honest of their fingers, but would be *nimming* something or other for the love of thieving. *L'Estrange, Fable* 241.

NI'MBLE. *adj.* [from *nim,* or numan, Saxon, tractable.] Quick; active; ready; speedy; lively; expeditious.

They being *nimbler*-jointed than the rest,
And more industrious, gathered more store. *Spenser.*
You *nimble* lightnings, dart your blinding flames
Into her scornful eyes. *Shakespeare's K. Lear.*
You have dancing shoes
With *nimble* soles. *Shakespeare's Romeo and Juliet.*
His off'ring soon propitious fire from heaven,
Consum'd with *nimble* glance and grateful steam;
The others not, for his was not sincere. *Milt. P. Lost.*
Thro' the mid seas the *nimble* pinnace sails,
Aloof from Crete before the northern gales. *Pope.*

NI'MBLENESS. *n. s.* [from *nimble.*] Quickness; activity; speed; agility; readiness; dexterity; celerity; expedition; swiftness.

The hounds were straight uncoupled, and ere long the stag thought it better to trust to the *nimbleness* of his feet, than to the slender fortification of his lodging. *Sidney.*

Himself shewing at one instant both steadiness and *nimbleness.* *Sidney, b.* ii.

All things are therefore partakers of God; they are his offspring, his influence is in them, and the personal wisdom of God is for that very cause said to excel in *nimbleness* or agility, to pierce into all intellectual, pure and subtile spirits, to go through all, and to reach unto every thing which is. *Hooker, b.* v. *s.* 5.

We, lying still,
Are full of rest, defence and *nimbleness.* *Shakes.*

Ovid ranged over all Parnassus with great *nimbleness* and agility; but as he did not much care for the toil requisite to climb the upper part of the hill, he was generally roving about the bottom. *Addison's Guardian,* №. 115.

NI'MBLEWITTED. *adj.* [*nimble* and *wit.*] Quick; eager to speak.

Sir Nicholas Bacon, when a certain *nimble-witted* counsellor at the bar, who was forward to speak, did interrupt him often, said unto him, There is a great difference betwixt you and me; a pain to me to speak, and a pain to you to hold your peace. *Bacon, Apophth.* 124.

NI'MBLY. *adv.* [from *nimble.*] Quickly; speedily; actively.

He capers *nimbly* in a lady's chamber,
To the lascivious playing of a lute. *Sha. Rich.* III.
The air
Nimbly and sweetly recommends itself. *Shakesp.*
Most legs can *nimbly* run, tho' some be lame. *Davies.*

The liquor we poured from the crystals, and set it in a digesting furnace to evaporate more *nimbly.* *Boyle.*

NI'MBLESS. *n. s.* Nimbleness. *Spenser.*

NI'MIETY. *n. s.* [*nimietas,* school Latin.] The state of being too much.

NI'MMER. *n. s.* [from *nim.*] A thief; a pilferer.

NI'NCOMPOOP. *n. s.* [A corruption of the Latin *non compos.*] A fool; a trifler.

An old ninnyhammer, a dotard, a *nincompoop,* is the best language she can afford me. *Addison.*

NINE. *n. s.* [*niun,* Gothick; nigon, Saxon.] One more than eight; one less than ten.

The weyward sisters,
Thus do go about, about,
Thrice to thine and thrice to mine,
And thrice again, to make up *nine.* *Shakes. Macbeth.*

A thousand scruples may startle at first, and yet in conclusion prove but a *nine*-days wonder. *L'Estrange.*

The faults are *nine* in ten owing to affectation, and not to the want of understanding. *Swift's Miscell.*

NI'NEFOLD. *n. s.* [*nine* and *fold.*] Nine times; any thing nine times repeated.

This huge convex of fire,
Outrageous to devour, immures us round *ninefold.* *Milt.*

NI'NEPENCE. *n. s.* [*nine* and *pence.*] A silver coin valued at nine-pence.

Three silver pennies, and a *nine-pence* bent. *Gay's Past.*

NI'NEPINS. *n. s.* [*nine* and *pin.*] A play where nine pieces of wood are set up on the ground to be thrown down by a bowl.

A painter made blossoms upon the trees in December, and school-boys playing at *nine-pins* upon the ice in July. *Peacham on Drawing.*

For as when merchants break, o'erthrown
Like *nine-pins,* they strike others down. *Hud. p.* ii.

NI'NESCORE. *adj.* [*nine* and *score.*] Nine times twenty.

Eugenius has two hundred pounds a year; but never values himself above *nine-score,* as not thinking he has a right to the tenth part, which he always appropriates to charitable uses. *Addison's Spectator,* №. 177.

NI'NETEEN. *adj.* [nigontyne, Saxon.] Nine and ten; one less than twenty.

Nineteen in twenty of perplexing words might be changed into easy ones, such as occur to ordinary men. *Swift.*

NI'NETEENTH. *adj.* [nigonteoða, Saxon.] The ordinal of nineteen; the ninth after the tenth.

In the *nineteenth* year of king Nebuchadnezzer king of Babylon, came Nebuzaradan. 2 *Kings* xxv. 8.

NI'NETY. *adj.* [hundnigontig, Saxon.] Nine times ten.

Enos lived *ninety* years and begat Cainan. *Gen.* v. 9.

NINTH. *adj.* [negoða, Saxon.] That which precedes the tenth; the first after the eighth; the ordinal of nine.

Upon a strict observation of many, I have not found any that see the *ninth* day. *Brown's Vulgar Errours.*

NI'NTIETH. *adj.* [hundnigonteogoða, Saxon.] The ordinal of ninety; the tenth nine times told.

NI'NNY. *n. s.* [*ninno,* a child, Spanish.] A fool; a simpleton.

What a pied *ninny's* this? *Shakespeare's Tempest.*
The dean was so shabby, and look'd like a *ninny,*
That the captain suppos'd he was curate. *Swift.*

NI'NNYHAMMER. *n. s.* [from *ninny.*] A simpleton.

Another vents her passion in scurrilous terms; an old *ninny-hammer,* a dotard, a nincompoop, is the best language she can afford me. *Addison's Guardian,* №. 109.

Have you no more manners than to rail at Hocus, that has saved that clod-pated, numskull'd, *ninny-hammer* of yours from ruin, and all his family. *Arbuth. John Bull.*

To NIP. *v. a.* [*nijpen,* Dutch.]

1. To pinch off with the nails; to bite with the teeth.

In oranges and lemons, the *nipping* of their rind giveth out their smell more. *Bacon's Nat. Hist.* №. 388.

2. To cut off by any slight means.

The small shoots that extract the sap of the most leading branches, must be *nipt* off. *Mortimer's Husb.*

3. To blast; to destroy before full growth.

This is the state of man; to-day he puts forth

The

The tender leaves of hopes, to-morrow blossoms,
And bears his blushing honours thick upon him;
The third day comes a frost, a killing frost;
And when he thinks, good easy man, full surely
His greatness is a ripening, *nips* his root;
And then he falls as I do. *Shakespeare's Henry* VIII.

A flower doth spread and dye,
Thou would'st extend me to some good,
Before I were by frost's extremity *nipt* in the bud. *Herb.*

His delivery now proves
Abortive, as the first-born bloom of spring,
Nipt with the lagging rear of winter's frost. *Milton.*

Had he not been *nipped* in the bud, he might have made a formidable figure in his own works among posterity. *Add.*

From such encouragement it is easy to guess to what perfection I might have brought this great work, had it not been *nipt* in the bud. *Arbuthnot's John Bull.*

4. To pinch as frost.

The air bites shrewdly, it is very cold. —
—It is a *nipping* and an eager air. *Shakes. Hamlet.*

When isicles hang by the wall,
And Dick the shepherd blows his nail;
When blood is *nipt*, and ways be foul,
Then nighty sings the staring owl. *Sha. Love's L. Lost.*

5. To vex; to bite.

And sharp remorse his heart did prick and *nip*,
That drops of blood thence like a well did play. *Fairy Q.*

6. To satirise; to ridicule; to taunt sarcastically.

But the right gentle mind would bite his lip
To hear the javel so good men to *nip*. *Hubberd's Tale.*

Quick wits commonly be in desire new-fangled; in purpose unconstant; bold with any person; busy in every matter; soothing such as be present, *nipping* any that is absent. *Ascham's Schoolmaster.*

NIP. *n. s.* [from the verb.]

1. A pinch with the nails or teeh.

I am sharply taunted, yea, sometimes with pinches, *nips*, and bobs. *Ascham's Schoolmaster.*

2. A small cut.

What this a sleeve? 'tis like a demicannon;
What up and down carv'd like an apple-tart?
Here's snip, and *nip*, and cut, and slish, and slash,
Like to a censer in a barber's shop. *Shakespeare.*

3. A blast.

So hasty fruits and too ambitious flow'rs,
Scorning the midwifry of rip'ning show'rs,
In spight of frosts, spring from th' unwilling earth,
But find a *nip* untimely as their birth. *Stepney.*

4. A taunt; a sarcasm.

NI'PPER. *n. s.* [from *nip.*] A satirist. Out of use.

Ready backbiters, sore *nippers*, and spiteful reporters privily of good men. *Ascham.*

NI'PPERS. *n. s.* [from *nip.*] Small pincers.

NI'PPINGLY. *adv.* [from *nip.*] With bitter sarcasm.

NI'PPLE. *n. s.* [nypele, Saxon.]

1. The teat; the dug; that which the sucking young take into their mouths.

Tho' tender 'tis to love the babe that milks me.—
I would, while it was smiling in my face,
Have pluckt my *nipple* from his boneless gums. *Shakesp.*

In creatures that nourish their young with milk, are adapted the *nipples* of the breast to the mouth and organs of suction. *Ray on the Creation.*

2. The orifice at which any animal liquor is separated.

In most other birds there is only one gland, in which are divers little cells ending in two or three larger cells, lying under the *nipple* of the oil bag. *Derham's Physico Theol.*

NI'PPLEWORT. *n. s.* [Lampsana.] A very common weed.

NISI PRIUS. *n. s.*

[In law.] A judicial writ, which lieth in case where the inquest is panelled, and returned before the justices of the bank; the one party or the other making petition to have this writ for the ease of the country. It is directed to the sheriff, commanding that he cause the men impanelled to come before the justices in the same county, for the determining of the cause there, except it be so difficult that it need great deliberation: in which case, it is sent again to the bank. It is so called from the first words of the writ *nisi apud talem locum prius venerint*; whereby it appeareth, that justices of assizes and justices of *nisi prius*, differ. So that justices of *nisi prius*, must be one of them before whom the cause is depending in the bench, with some other good men of the county associated to him. *Cowel.*

NIT. *n. s.* [hnitu, Saxon.] The egg of a louse, or small animal.

The whame, or burrel-fly, is vexatious to horses in summer, not by stinging them, but only by their bombylious noise, or tickling them in sticking their *nits*, or eggs, on the hair. *Derham's Physico Theol.*

NI'TENCY. *n. s.* [*nitentia*, Latin.]

1. Lustre; clear brightness.

2. [From the Latin, *nitor.*] Endeavour; spring to expand itself.

The atoms of fire accelerate the motion of these particles; from which acceleration their spring, or endeavour outward will be augmented; that is, those zones will have a strong *nitency* to fly wider open. *Boyle.*

NI'THING. *n. s.* A coward, dastard, poltroon.

NI'TID. *adj.* [*nitidus*, Latin.] Bright; shining; lustrous.

We restore old pieces of dirty gold to a clean and *nitid* yellow, by putting them into fire and aqua fortis, which take off the adventitious filth. *Boyle on Colours.*

NI'TRE. *n. s.* [*nitre*, Fr. *nitrum*, Latin.]

The salt which we know at this time, under the name of *nitre* or salt-petre, is a crystalline pellucid, but somewhat whitish substance, of an acrid and bitterish taste, impressing a peculiar sense of coldness upon the tongue. This salt, though it affords, by means of fire, an acid spirit capable of dissolving almost every thing, yet manifests no sign of its containing any acid at all in its crude state. *Nitre* is of the number of those salts which are naturally blended in imperceptible particles in earths, stones, and other fossile substances, as the particles of metals are in their ores: it is sometimes however found pure, in form of an efflorescence, either on its ores or on the surface of old walls; these efflorescences dissolved in proper water, shooting into regular and proper crystals of *nitre*. That this salt should be found on the surface of walls is not wonderful, since it is found only on or near the surface of the earth where it is produced. The earth from which *nitre* is made, both in Persia and the East-Indies, is a kind of yellowish marl found in the bare cliffs of the sides of hills exposed to the northern and eastern winds, and never in any other situation. From this marl the salt is separated by water; but the crystals into which it shoots, as we receive them from the East-Indies, are small, imperfect, and impure. Earths of whatever kind, moistened by the dung and excrement of animals, frequently afford *nitre* in large quantities. The earths at the bottom of pigeon-houses, and those of stables and cow-houses, all afford *nitre*, on being thrown into water and boiled. In France, where very little *nitre* is imported, they make it from the rubbish of old mortar and plaister of buildings; and the mortar of old walls with us, if moistened with urine and exposed to the air in a proper situation that is open to the north east, and covered over to defend it from wet, never fails to afford *nitre* in a few weeks, and that in proportion of one tenth of the weight of the ingredients. There is no question but a manufactory of *nitre* might be established in England to as much advantage as that of France. The place where the materials are exposed, is to be carefully examined. It must be moderate as to the great points of moisture and dryness; if there be too much moisture the *nitre* which is already formed will be washed away, and without some moisture the salts will hardly be ever formed. Heat and coldness, unless excessive, can be of no consequence. It is on account of the requisiteness of so certain a degree of moisture to the materials from which *nitre* is obtained, that the north east winds are of so much use in the production of it. In spring and autumn, which are the seasons when this salt is principally made, these two winds are neither too moist nor too dry, especially in the night; the south and west winds are destructive, because they bring storms and showers. In medicine, *nitre* is cooling and diuretick, and good in burning fevers. The natrum or *nitre* of the ancients, is a genuine, native, and pure salt, extremely different from our *nitre*, and from all other native salts; being a fixed alkali plainly of the nature of those made by fire from vegetables, yet being capable of a regular crystallization, which those salts are not. It is found on or very near the surface of the earth, in thin flat cakes, spungy, light, and friable; and when pure, of a pale brownish white colour. It is of an acrid taste, like pot-ashes. About Smyrna and Ephesus, and through a great part of Asia Minor, this salt is extremely frequent on the surface of the earth, and also in Sindy, a province of the inner Asia, where they sweep it up and call it soap-earth, using a solution or lye of it in washing. The natrum or *nitre* of the ancients, has been by some supposed to be a lost substance, and by others to be the same with our *nitre* or salt-petre; but both these opinions are erroneous, this salt being the true natrum of the ancients, answering perfectly to its description, and having all its uses and virtues. In scripture we find that the salt called *nitre* would ferment with vinegar, and had an abstersive quality, properties which perfectly agree with this salt but not with salt-petre, as do many different qualities ascribed to it by the ancients. *Hill on Foss.*

Some tumultuous cloud,
Instinct with fire and *nitre*, hurried him. *Milton.*

Some steep their seed, and some in cauldrons boil,
With vigorous *nitre* and with lees of oil. *Dryden.*

NI'TROUS. *adj.* [*nitreux*, Fr. from *nitre.*] Impregnated with nitre; consisting of nitre.

Earth and water, mingled by the heat of the sun, gather a *nitrous* fatness more than either of them have severally. *Bacon's Natural History.*

The northern air being more fully charged with those particles supposed *nitrous*, which are the aliment of fire, is fittest to maintain the vital heat in that activity which is sufficient to move such an unweildy bulk with due celerity. *Ray.*

He to quench his drought so much inclin'd,
May snowy fields and *nitrous* pastures find,
Meet stores of cold so greedily pursu'd,
And be refresh'd with never-wasting food. *Blackmore.*

NI'TRY. *adj.* [from *nitre.*] Nitrous.

Winter my theme confines; whose *nitry* wind
Shall crust the slabby mire, and kennels bind. *Gay.*

NI'TTILY. *adv.* [from *nitty.*] Lousily.

One Bell was put to death at Tyburn for moving a new rebellion; he was a man *nittily* needy, and therefore adventrous. *Hayward.*

NI'TTY. *adj.* [from *nit.*] Abounding with the eggs of lice.

NI'VAL. *adj.* [*nivalis*, Latin.] Abounding with snow. *Dict.*

NI'VEOUS. *adj.* [*niveus*, Latin.] Snowy; resembling snow.

Cinabar becomes red by the acid exhalation of sulphur, which otherways presents a pure and *niveous* white. *Brown.*

NI'ZY. *n. s.* A dunce; a simpleton. A low word.

NO. *adv.* [na, Saxon.]

1. The word of refusal.

Our courteous Antony,
Whom ne'er the word of *no*, woman heard speak,
Being barber'd ten times o'er, goes to the feast. *Shakes.*

Henceforth my wooing mind shall be exprest,
In russet yeas and honest kersy *noes.* *Sha. L. Labours Lost.*

If you will not consider these things now, the time will shortly come when you shall consider them whether you will or *no.* *Calamy's Serm.*

2. The word of denial opposite to concession or affirmation.

I think it would not sort amiss, to handle the question, whether a war for the propagation of the Christian faith, without another cause of hostility, be lawful or *no*, and in what cases? *Bacon.*

3. It sometimes confirms a foregoing negative.

My name's Macbeth: —
—The Devil himself could not pronounce a title
More hateful to mine ear. —
—*No*, nor more fearful. *Shakespeare's Macbeth.*

Never more
This hand shall combat on the crooked shore:
No; let the Grecian pow'rs opprest in fight,
Unpity'd perish in their tyrant's sight. *Dryd. Homer.*

4. It sometimes strengthens a following negative; *no not*, not even.

No not the bow which so adorns the skies,
So glorious is, or boasts so many dies. *Waller.*

No. *adj.*

1. Not any; none.

Let their be *no* strife between me and thee. *Gen.* xiii. 8.

Woman and fool are two hard things to hit,
For true *no* meaning puzzles more than wit. *Pope.*

2. It seems an adjective in these phrases, no longer, no more, no where.

When we saw that they were *no* where, we came to Samuel. 1 *Sam.* x. 14.

In vain I reach my feeble hands to join
In sweet embraces; ah! *no* longer thine. *Dryden.*

3. *No one*; none; not any one.

No one who doeth good to those only from whom he expects to receive good, can ever be fully satisfied of his own sincerity. *Smalridge's Serm.*

To NOBI'LITATE. *v. a.* [*nobilito*, Latin.] To ennoble; to make noble.

NOBI'LITY. *n. s.* [*nobilitas*, Latin.]

1. Antiquity of family joined with splendour.

When I took up Boccace unawares, I fell on the same argument of preferring virtue to *nobility* of blood, and titles, in the story of Sigismunda. *Dryden, Fab. Pref.*

Long galleries of ancestors,
Challenge, nor wonder, or esteem from me,
" Virtue alone is true *nobility.*" *Dryden.*

2. Rank or dignity of several degrees, conferred by sovereigns. *Nobility* in England is extended to five ranks; duke, marquis, earl, viscount, baron.

3. The persons of high rank; the persons who are exalted above the commons.

It is a purpos'd thing,
To curb the will of the *nobility.* *Shakes. Coriolanus.*

4. Dignity; grandeur; greatness.

Though she hated Ampialus, yet the *nobility* of her courage prevailed over it; and she desired he might be pardoned that youthful errour; considering the reputation he had to be the best knight in the world; so as hereafter he governed himself, as one remembering his fault. *Sidney*, *b.* ii.

But ah, my muse, I would thou hadst facility
To work my goddess so by thy invention,
On me to cast those eyes where shine *nobility.* *Sidney.*

Base men, being in love, have then a *nobility* in their natures more than is native to them. *Shakespeare's Othello.*

They thought it great their sov'reign to controul,
And nam'd their pride, *nobility* of soul. *Dryden.*

NO'BLE. *adj.* [*noble*, Fr. *nobilis*, Latin.]

1. Of an ancient and splendid family.

2. Exalted to a rank above commonalty.

From virtue first began,
The diff'rence that distinguish'd man from man:
He claim'd no title from descent of blood,
But that which made him *noble*, made him good. *Dryd.*

3. Great; worthy; illustrious.

Thus this man died, leaving his death for an example of a *noble* courage, and a memorial of virtue. 2 *Mac.* vi. 31.

To vice industrious, but to *nobler* deeds
Tim'rous. *Milton.*

A *noble* stroke he lifted high,
Which hung not, but with tempest fell. *Milt.*

Those two great things that so engross the desires and designs of both the *nobler* and ignobler sort of mankind, are to be found in religion; namely, wisdom and pleasure. *South.*

4. Exalted; elevated; sublime.

My share in pale Pyrene I resign,
And claim no part in all the mighty nine:
Statues, with winding ivy crown'd belong
To *nobler* poets, for a *nobler* song. *Dryd.*

5. Magnificent; stately: as, a *noble* parade.

6. Free; generous; liberal.

7. Principal; capital: as, the heart is one of the *noble* parts of the body.

NO'BLE. *n. s.*

1. One of high rank.

Upon the *nobles* of the children of Israel he laid not his hand. *Ex.* xxiv. 11.

How many *nobles* then should hold their places,
That must strike sail to spirits of vile sort! *Shakesp.*

What the *nobles* once said in parliament, Nolumus leges Angliæ mutari, is imprinted in the hearts of all the people. *Bacon.*

The *nobles* amongst the Romans took special care in their last wills, that they might have a lamp in their monuments. *Wilkin's Math. Magic.*

See all our *nobles* begging to be slaves,
See all our fools aspiring to be knaves. *Pope, Dial.* i.

It may be the disposition of young *nobles*, that they expect the accomplishments of a good education without the least expence of time or study. *Swift's Modern Education.*

The second natural division of power, is of such men who have acquired large possessions, and consequently dependencies; or descend from ancestors who have left them great inheritances, together with an hereditary authority: these easily unite in thoughts and opinions. Thus commences a great council or senate of *nobles*, for the weighty affairs of the nation. *Swift.*

2. A coin rated at six shillings and eight-pence; the sum of six and eight-pence.

Shortly after he coined *nobles*, of noble, fair, and fine gold. *Camden's Remains.*

Many fair promotions
Are daily given, to enoble those
That scarce, some two days since, were worth a *noble. Sha.*

Upon every writ procured for debt or damage, amounting to forty pounds or more, a *noble*, that is six shillings and eight-pence, is, and usually hath been paid to fine. *Bacon.*

NO'BLE *liverwort.* [Hepatica.] A plant.

The characters are: the root is fibrose and perennial: the leaf consists of three lobes on a pedicle, which arises from the root; as does the pedicle of the flower, which is naked and single: the cup of the flower is, for the most part, composed of one leaf sometimes cut into three or four deep divisions: the flower consists of many leaves, which expand in form of a rose: the fruit is globular, consisting of one single cell curvated. *Miller.*

NO'BLEMAN. *n. s.* [*noble* and *man.*] One who is ennobled.

If I blush,
It is to see a *nobleman* want manners. *Shakes. Hen.* VIII.

The *nobleman* is he, whose noble mind
Is fill'd with inborn worth. *Dryden's Wife of Bath.*

NO'BLENESS. *n. s.* [from *noble.*]

1. Greatness; worth; dignity; magnanimity.

The *nobleness* of life
Is to do this; when such a mutual pair,
And such a twain can do't. *Shakes. Ant. and Cleopatra.*

Any thing
That my ability may undergo,
And *nobleness* impose. *Shakespeare's Winter's Tale.*

True *nobleness* would
Learn him forbearance from so foul a wrong. *Shakesp.*

He that does as well in private between God and his own soul, as in public, hath given himself a good testimony that his purposes are full of honesty, *nobleness*, and integrity. *Taylor's Holy Living.*

Greatneſs of mind, and *nobleneſs*, their ſeat
Build in her loveliest. *Milton's Par. Loſt.*

There is not only a congruity herein between the *nobleneſs* of the faculty and the object, but alſo the faculty is enriched and advanced by the worth of the object. *Hale.*

You have not only been careful of my fortune, which was the effect of your *nobleneſs*, but you have been ſolicitous of my reputation, which is that of your kindneſs. *Dryden.*

2. Splendour of deſcent; luſtre of pedigree.

No'bless. *n. ſ.* [*nobleſſe*, French.]

1. Nobility. This word is not now uſed in any ſenſe.

Fair branch of *nobleſs*, flower of chivalry,
That with your worth the world amazed make. *Fairy Q.*

2. Dignity; greatneſs.

Thou whoſe *nobleſs* keeps one ſtature ſtill,
And one true poſture, tho' beſieg'd with ill. *Ben. Johnſon.*

3. Noblemen collectively.

Let us haſte to hear it,
And call the *nobleſs* to the audience. *Shakeſp. Ham.*

I know no reaſon we ſhould give that advantage to the commonalty of England to be foremoſt in brave actions, which the *nobleſs* of France would never ſuffer in their peaſants. *Dryden's Pref. to Ann. Mirab.*

No'bly. *adv.* [from *noble.*]

1. Of ancient and ſplendid extraction.

Only a ſecond laurel did adorn
His Collegue Catulus, tho' *nobly* born;
He ſhar'd the pride of the triumphal bay,
But Marius won the glory of the day. *Dryden.*

2. Greatly; illuſtriouſly; magnanimouſly.

Did he not ſtraight the two delinquents tear,
That were the ſlaves of drink and thralls of ſleep?
Was not that *nobly* done? *Shakeſpeare's Macbeth.*

This fate he could have 'ſcap'd, but would not loſe
Honour for life; but rather *nobly* choſe
Death from their fears, than ſafety from his own. *Denham.*

3. Grandly; ſplendidly.

There could not have been a more magnificent deſign than that of Trajan's pillar. Where could an emperor's aſhes have been ſo *nobly* lodged, as in the midſt of his metropolis, and on the top of ſo exalted a monument. *Addiſon on Italy.*

No'body. *n. ſ.* [*no* and *body.*] No one; not any one.

This is the tune of our catch plaid by the picture of *nobody.* *Shakeſpeare's Tempeſt.*

It fell to ſecretary Coke's turn, for whom *nobody* cared, to be made the ſacrifice; and he was put out of his office. *Clarendon, b.* ii.

If in company you offer ſomething for a jeſt, and *nobody* ſeconds you on your own laughter, you may condemn their taſte, and appeal to better judgments; but in the mean time you make a very indifferent figure. *Swift's Miſcel.*

No'cent. *adj.* [*nocens*, Latin.]

1. Guilty; criminal.

The earl of Devonſhire being intereſted in the blood of York, that was rather feared than *nocent*; yet as one, that might be the object of others plots, remained priſoner in the Tower during the king's life. *Bacon's Henry* VII.

2. Hurtful; miſchievous.

His head, well-ſtor'd with ſubtile wiles:
Not yet in horrid ſhade, or diſmal den,
Nor *nocent* yet; but on the graſſy herb,
Fearleſs unfear'd he ſlept. *Milton's Paradiſe Loſt, b.* ix.

The warm limbec draws
Salubrious waters from the *nocent* brood. *Philips.*

They meditate whether the virtues of the one will exalt or diminiſh the force of the other, or correct any of its *nocent* qualities. *Watts's Improvement of the Mind.*

Nock. *n. ſ.* [*nocchia*, Italian.]

1. A ſlit; a nick; a notch.

2. The fundament. *Les feſſes.*

When the date of *nock* was out,
Off dropt the ſympathetick ſnout. *Hudibras.*

Nocta'mbulo. *n. ſ.* [*nox* and *ambulo*, Latin.] One who walks in his ſleep.

Reſpiration being carried on in ſleep, is no argument againſt its being voluntary. What ſhall we ſay of *noctambulo's?* There are voluntary motions carried on without thought, to avoid pain. *Arbuthnot on Air.*

Nocti'dial. *adj.* [*noctis* and *dies.*] Compriſing a night and a day.

The *noctidial* day, the lunar periodic month, and the ſolar year, are natural and univerſal; but incommenſurate each to another, and difficult to be reconciled. *Holder.*

Nocti'ferous. *adj.* [*nox* and *fero.*] Bringing night. *Dict.*

Nocti'vagant. *adj.* [*noctivagus*, Latin.] Wandering in the night. *Dict.*

No'ctuary. *n. ſ.* [from *noctis*, Latin.] An account of what paſſes by night.

I have got a parcel of viſions and other miſcellanies in my *noctuary*, which I ſhall ſend you to enrich your paper. *Addiſon's Spectator*, Nº. 586.

No'cturn. *n. ſ.* [*nocturne*, Fr. *nocturnus*, Latin.] An office of devotion performed in the night.

The reliques being conveniently placed before the church-door, the vigils are to be celebrated that night before them, and the *nocturn* and the mattins for the honour of the ſaints whoſe the reliques are. *Stillingfleet.*

NOCTU'RNAL. *adj.* [*nocturnus*, Latin.] Nightly.

From gilded roofs depending lamps diſplay
Nocturnal beams, that emulate the day. *Dryden.*

I beg leave to make you a preſent of a dream, which may ſerve to lull your readers 'till ſuch time as you yourſelf ſhall gratify the public with any of your *nocturnal* diſcoveries. *Add.*

Noctu'rnal. *n. ſ.* An inſtrument by which obſervations are made in the night.

That projection of the ſtars which includes all the ſtars in our horizon, and therefore reaches to the thirty-eight degree and a half of ſouthern latitude, though its centre is the north pole, gives us a better view of the heavenly bodies as they appear every night to us; and it may ſerve for a *nocturnal*, and ſhew the true hour of the night. *Watts.*

To NOD. *v. n.* [Of uncertain derivation: νεύω, Gr. *nuto*, Lat. *amneidio*, Welſh.]

1. To decline the head with a quick motion.

Let every feeble rumour ſhake your hearts;
Your enemies with *nodding* of their plumes,
Fan you into deſpair. *Shakeſpeare's Coriolanus.*

Cleopatra hath *nodded* him to her. *Shakeſ. A. and Cleop.*

On the faith of Jove rely,
When *nodding* to thy ſuit he bows the ſky. *Dryden.*

2. To pay a ſlight bow.

Caſſius muſt bend his body,
If Cæſar careleſly but *nod* on him. *Shakeſ. Jul. Cæſar.*

3. To bend downwards with quick motion.

When a pine is hewn on the plains,
And the laſt mortal ſtroke alone remains,
Lab'ring in pangs of death, and threatning all,
This way and that ſhe *nods*, conſidering where to fall. *Dryden's Ovid, b.* x.

He climbs the mountain rocks,
Fir'd by the *nodding* verdure of its brow. *Thomſ. Spring.*

4. To be drowſy.

Your two predeceſſors were famous for their dreams and viſions, and contrary to all other authors, never pleaſed their readers more than when they were *nodding.* *Add. Guard.*

Nod. *n. ſ.* [from the verb.]

1. A quick declination of the head.

Children being to be reſtrained by the parents only in vicious things; a look or *nod* only ought to correct them when they do amiſs. *Locke on Education.*

A mighty king I am, an earthly God;
Nations obey my word, and wait my *nod*:
And life or death depend on my decree. *Prior.*

2. A quick declination.

Like a drunken ſailor on a maſt,
Ready with every *nod* to tumble down
Into the fatal bowels of the deep. *Shakeſp. R.* III.

3. The motion of the head in drowſineſs.

Every drowſy *nod* ſhakes their doctrine who teach, that the ſoul is always thinking. *Locke.*

4. A ſlight obeiſance.

Will he give you the *nod?* *Sha. Troil. and Creſſida.*

Since the wiſdom of their choice is rather to have my cap than my heart, I will practiſe the inſinuating *nod*, and be off to them moſt counterfeitly. *Shakeſpeare's Coriolanus.*

Noda'tion. *n. ſ.* [from *nodo.*] The ſtate of being knotted, or act of making knots.

No'dder. *n. ſ.* [from *nod.*] One who makes nods.

A ſet of *nodders*, winkers, and whiſperers, whoſe buſineſs is to ſtrangle all other offspring of wit in their birth. *Pope.*

No'ddle. *n. ſ.* [hnol, Saxon.] A head; in contempt.

Her care ſhall be
To comb your *noddle* with a three-legg'd ſtool. *Shakeſ.*

Let our wines without mixture, or ſtain, be all fine,
Or call up the maſter and break his dull *noddle.* *B. John.*

My head's not made of braſs,
As friar Bacon's *noddle* was. *Hudibras, p.* ii. *cant.* I.

He would not have it ſaid before the people, that images are to be worſhipped with Latria, but rather the contrary, becauſe the diſtinctions neceſſary to defend it are too ſubtile for their *noddles.* *Stillingfleet.*

Come, maſter, I have a project in my *noddle*, that ſhall bring my miſtreſs to you back again, with as good will as ever ſhe went from you. *L'Eſtrange.*

Why ſhouldſt thou try to hide thyſelf in youth?
Impartial Proſerpine beholds the truth;
And laughing at ſo fond and vain a taſk,
Will ſtrip thy hoary *noddle* of its maſk. *Addiſon.*

Thou that art ever half the city's grace,
And add'ſt to ſolemn *noddles*, ſolemn pace. *Fenton.*

No'ddy. *n. ſ.* [from *naudin*, French.] A ſimpleton; an idiot.

The whole race of bawling, fluttering *noddies*, by what title soever dignified, are a-kin to the ass in this fable. *L'Estrange, Fable* 150.

Node. *n. s.* [*nodus*, Latin.]

1. A knot; a knob.
2. A swelling on the bone.

If *nodes* be the cause of the pain, foment with spirit of wine wherein opium and saffron have been dissolved. *Wiseman's Surgery.*

3. Intersection.

All these variations are finished in nineteen years, nearly agreeing with the course of the *nodes*; i. e. the points in the ecliptic where the moon crosseth that circle as she passeth to her northern or southern latitude; which *nodes* are called the head and tail of the dragon. *Holder.*

Nodo'sity. *n. s.* [from *nodosus*, Latin.] Complication; knot.

These the midwife cutteth off, contriving them into a knot close unto the body of the infant; from whence ensueth that tortuosity, or complicated *nodosity* we call the navel. *Brown's Vulgar Errours, b.* v.

No'dous. *adj.* [*nodosus*, Latin.] Knotty; full of knots.

This is seldom affected with the gout, and when that becometh *nodous*, men continue not long after. *Brown's V. Err.*

No'dule. *n. s.* [*nodulus*, Latin.] A small lump.

Those minerals in the strata, are either found in grains, or else they are amassed into balls, lumps, or *nodules*: which *nodules* are either of an irregular figure, or of a figure somewhat more regular. *Woodward's Nat. Hist.*

No'ggen. *adj.* Hard; rough; harsh.

He put on a hard, coarse, *noggen* shirt of pendrel. *Escape of King Charles.*

No'ggin. *n. s.* [*nossel*, German.] A small mug.

All this while Frog laughed in his sleeve, gave the esquire the other *noggin* of brandy, and clapped him on the back. *Arbuthnot's Hist. of J. Bull.*

Noi'ance. *n. s.* [See Annoiance.] Mischief; inconvenience.

To borrow to-day, and to-morrow to mis,
For lender and borrower *noiance* it is. *Tuss. Husb.*

The single and peculiar life is bound,
With all the strength and armour of the mind,
To keep itself from *noiance*. *Shakespeare's Hamlet.*

To Noie. *v. a.* To annoy. An old word disused.

Let servant be ready with mattock in hand,
To stub out the bushes that *noieth* the land. *Tuss. Husb.*

Noi'er. *n. s.* [from *noie.*] One who annoys. An old word in disuse.

The north is a *noier* to grass of all suits,
The east a destroyer to herbs and all fruits. *Tuss. Husb.*

Noi'ous. *adj.* [*noioso*, Italian.] Hurtful; mischievous; troublesome; inconvenient. Obsolete.

Being bred in a hot country, they found much hair on their faces to be *noious* unto them. *Spenser.*

The false Duessa leaving *noious* night,
Return'd to stately palace of dame Pride. *Fairy Q.*

But neither darkness foul, nor filthy bands,
Nor *noious* smell his purpose could withhold. *Fairy Q.*

NOISE. *n. s.* [*noise*, French.]

1. Any kind of sound.

Noises, as of waters falling down, sounded about them, and sad visions appeared unto them. *Wisd.* xvii. 4.

Whether it were a whistling sound, or a melodious *noise* of birds among the spreading branches, these things made them swoon. *Wisd.* xvii. 18.

Great motions in nature pass without sound or *noise*. The heavens turn about in a most rapid motion, without *noise* to us perceived; though in some dreams they have been said to make an excellent musick. *Bacon's Nat. Hist.*

Fear
Shakes your hearts, while thro' the isle they hear
A lasting *noise*, as horrid and as loud
As thunder makes, before it breaks the cloud. *Waller.*

2. Outcry; clamour; boasting or importunate talk.

What *noise* have we had about transplantation of diseases, and transfusion of blood. *Baker on Learning.*

3. Occasion of talk.

Socrates lived in Athens during the great plague, which has made so much *noise* through all ages, and never caught the least infection. *Addison's Spectator*, N°. 195.

To Noise. *v. n.* [from the noun.] To sound loud.

Harm
Those terrors, which thou speak'st of, did me none;
Tho' *noising* loud and threatning nigh. *Milt. P. Reg.*

To Noise. *v. a.* To spread by rumour, or report.

All these sayings were *noised* abroad throughout all the hill country. *Luke* i. 65.

I shall not need to relate the affluence of young nobles from hence into Spain, after the voice of our prince's being there had been quickly *noised*. *Wotton.*

They might buz and whisper it one to another; and tacitly withdrawing from the presence of the apostle, they then lift up their voices and *noised* it about the city. *Bentley.*

Noi'seful. *adj.* [*noise* and *full.*] Loud; clamourous.

That eunuch, guardian of rich Holland's trade,
Whose *noiseful* valour does no foe invade,
And weak assistance will his friends destroy. *Dryden.*

Noi'seless. *adj.* [from *noise.*] Silent; without sound.

On our quick'st decrees,
Th' inaudible and *noiseless* foot of time
Steals, ere we can effect them. *Shakespeare.*

So *noiseless* would I live, such death to find,
Like timely fruit, not shaken by the wind,
But ripely dropping from the sapless bough. *Dryden.*

Noi'siness. *n. s.* [from *noisy.*] Loudness of sound; importunity of clamour.

Noi'semaker. *n. s.* [*noise* and *maker.*] Clamourer.

The issue of all this noise is, the making of the *noisemakers* still more ridiculous. *L'Estrange.*

NOI'SOME. *adj.* [*noioso*, Italian.]

1. Noxous; mischievous; unwholesome.

In case it may be proved, that among the number of rites and orders common unto both, there are particulars, the use whereof is utterly unlawful in regard of some special bad and *noisome* quality; there is no doubt but we ought to relinquish such rites and orders, what freedom soever we have to retain the other still. *Hooker, b.* iv.

All my plants I save from nightly ill
Of *noisome* winds, and blasting vapours chill. *Milton.*

Gravisca *noisome* from the neighb'ring fen,
And his own Cære sent three hundred men. *Dryden.*

The *noisome* pest'lence, that in open war
Terrible, marches thro' the mid-day air,
And scatters death. *Prior.*

2. Offensive; disgusting.

The seeing these effects, will be
Both *noisome* and infectious. *Shakes. Cymbeline.*

The brake and the cockle are *noisome* too much. *Tuss.*

Foul words are but foul wind, and foul wind is but foul breath, and foul breath is *noisome*. *Shakespeare's M. Ad. Ab.*

The filthiness of his smell was *noisome* to all his army. 2 *Mac.* ix. 9.

An error in the judgment, is like an impostem in the head, which is always *noisome*, and frequently mortal. *South.*

Noi'somely. *adv.* [from *noisome.*] With a fœtid stench; with an infectious steam.

Noi'someness. *n. s.* [from *noisome.*] Aptness to disgust; offensiveness.

If he must needs be seen, with all his filth and *noisomness* about him, he promises himself however, that it will be some allay to his reproach, to be but one of many to march in a troop. *South's Serm.*

Noi'sy. *adj.* [from *noise.*]

1. Sounding loud.
2. Clamorous; turbulent.

O leave the *noisy* town, O come and see
Our country cotts, and live content with me! *Dryden.*

To *noisy* fools a grave attention lend. *Smith.*

Although he employs his talents wholly in his closet, he is sure to raise the hatred of the *noisy* crowd. *Swift.*

Noll. *n. s.* [ƿnol, Saxon.] A head; a noddle.

An ass's *noll* I fixed on his head. *Shakespeare.*

NO'LI me tangere. [Latin.]

1. Kind of cancerous swelling, exasperated by applications.
2. A plant.

Noli me tangere may be planted among your flowers, for the rarity of it. *Mortimer's Husb.*

Noli'tion. *n. s.* [*nolitio*, Latin.] Unwillingness; opposed to volition.

The proper acts of the will are, volition, *nolition*, choice, resolution, and command, in relation to subordinate faculties. *Hale's Origin of Mankind.*

No'mancy. *n. s.* [*nomance*, *nomancie*, Fr. *nomen*, Latin; and μαντεία, Greek.] The art of divining the fates of persons by the letters that form their names. *Dict.*

No'mbles. *n. s.* The entrails of a deer.

NOMENCLA'TOR. *n. s.* [Lat. *nomenclateur*, Fr.] One who calls things or persons by their proper names.

There were a set of men in old Rome called *nomenclators*; that is, men who could call every man by his name. *Addison's Guardian*, N°. 107.

Are envy, pride, avarice, and ambition, such ill *nomenclators* that they cannot furnish appellations for their owners? *Swift.*

Nomencla'ture. *n. s.* [*nomenclature*, Fr. *nomenclatura*, Lat.]

1. The act of naming.

To say where notions cannot fitly be reconciled, that there wanteth a term or *nomenclature* for it, is but a shift of ignorance. *Bacon's Nat. Hist.*

2. A vocabulary; a dictionary.

The watry plantations fall not under that *nomenclature* of Adam, which unto terrestrious animals assigned a name appropriate unto their natures. *Brown's V. Err.*

No'minal. *adj.* [*nominalis*, Latin.] Refering to names rather than to things; not real; titular.

Profound in all the *nominal*,
And real ways beyond them all. *Hudibras, p. i.*

The *nominal* essence of gold is that complex idea the word gold stands for; as a body yellow, of a certain weight, malleable, fusible and fixed. But the real essence is the constitution of the insensible parts of that body on which those qualities depend. *Locke.*

Were these people as anxious for the doctrines essential to the church of England, as they are for the *nominal* distinction of adhering to its interests. *Addison.*

NO'MINALLY. *adv.* [from *nominal.*] By name; with regard to a name; titularly.

To NO'MINATE. *v. a.* [*nomino*, Latin.]

1. To name; to mention by name.

Suddenly to *nominate* them all,
It is impossible. *Shakes. Henry VI. p. iii.*

One lady, I may civilly spare to *nominate*, for her sex's sake, whom he termed the spider of the court. *Wotton.*

2. To entitle.

Aread, old father, why of late
Didst thou behight me born of English blood,
Whom all a fairy's son doen *nominate*. *Fairy Q.*

3. To set down; to appoint by name.

If you repay me not on such a day, let the forfeit
Be *nominated* for an equal pound
Of your fair flesh to be cut off. *Shakespeare.*

Never having intended, never designed any heir in that sense, we cannot expect he should *nominate* or appoint any person to it. *Locke.*

NOMINA'TION. *n. s.* [*nomination*, Fr. from *nominate.*]

1. The act mentioning by name.

The forty-one immediate electors of the duke, must be all of several families, and of them twenty-five at least concur to this *nomination*. *Wotton's D. of Venice.*

2. The power of appointing.

The *nomination* of persons to places, being so principal and inseparable a flower of his crown, he would reserve to himself. *Clarendon.*

In England the king has the *nomination* of an archbishop; and after such *nomination*, he sends a congé d'elire to the dean and chapter, to elect the person thus elected by him. *Ayliffe's Parergon.*

NO'MINATIVE. [in grammar, *nominatif*, Fr.] The case that primarily designates the name of any thing, and is called right, in opposition to the other cases called oblique.

NON. *v. a.* [Latin.] Not. It is never used separately, but sometimes prefixed to words with a negative power.

Since you to *non*-regardance cast my faith,
And I partly know the instrument
That screws me from my true place in your favour;
Live you the marble-breasted tyrant still. *Shakes.*

A mere inclination to matters of duty, men reckon a willing of that thing; when they are justly charged with an actual *non*-performance of what the law requires? *South.*

For an account at large of bishop Sanderson's last judgment concerning God's concurrence, or *non*-concurrence with the actions of men, and the positive entity of sins of commission, I refer you to his letters. *Pierce.*

The third sort of agreement or disagreement in our ideas, which the perception of the mind is employed about, is coexistence, or *non*-existence in the same subject. *Locke.*

It is not a *non*-act, which introduces a custom, a custom being a common usage. *Ayliffe's Parergon.*

In the imperial chamber this answer is not admitted, viz. I do not believe it as the matter is alledged. And the reason of this *non*-admission is, because of its great uncertainty. *Ayliffe's Parergon.*

An apparitor came to the church, and informed the parson, that he must pay the tenths to such a man; and the bishop certified the ecclesiastical court under his seal on the *non*-payment of them, that he refused to pay them. *Ayliffe.*

The *non*-appearance of persons to support the united sense of both houses of parliament, can never be construed as a general diffidence of being able to support the charge against the patent and patentee. *Swift.*

This may be accounted for by the turbulence of passions upon the various and surprising turns of good and evil fortune, in a long evening at play; the mind being wholly taken up, and the consequence of *non*-attention so fatal. *Swift.*

NO'NAGE. *n. s.* [*non* and *age.*] Minority; time of life before legal maturity.

In him there is a hope of government;
Which in his *nonage*, counsel under him,
And in his full and ripen'd years, himself
Shall govern well. *Shakespeare's Richard III.*

Be love but there, let poor six years
Be pos'd with the maturest fears
Man trembles at, we straight shall find
Love knows no *nonage* nor the mind. *Crashaw.*

We have a mistaken apprehension of antiquity, calling that so which in truth is the world's *nonage*. *Glanville.*

Those charters were not avoidable for the king's *nonage*; and if there could have been any such pretence, that alone would not avoid them. *Hale.*

After Chaucer there was a Spenser, a Harrington, a Fairfax, before Waller and Denham were in being; and our numbers were in their *nonage* 'till these last appeared. *Dryd.*

In their tender *nonage*, while they spread
Their springing leaves, and lift their infant head,
Indulge their childhood, and the nursling spare. *Dryden.*

NONCE. *n. s.* [The original of this word is uncertain; *Skinner* imagines it to come from *own* or *once*; or from *nutz*, German, *need* or *use*: *Junius* derives it less probably from *noiance*, to do *for the nonce*; being, according to him, to do it *merely for mischief.*] Purpose; intent; design. Not now in use.

I saw a wolf
Nursing two whelps; I saw her little ones
In wanton dalliance the teat to crave,
While she her neck wreath'd from them for the *nonce*. *Spen.*

They used at first to fume the fish in a house built for the *nonce*. *Carew.*

When in your motion you are hot,
And that he calls for drink, I'll have prepar'd him
A chalice for the *nonce*. *Shakes. Hamlet.*

Such a light and metall'd dance,
Saw you never;
And they lead men for the *nonce*,
That turn round like grindle-stones. *Ben. Johnson.*

A voider for the *nonce*,
I wrong the devil should I pick their bones. *Cleaveland.*

Coming ten times for the *nonce*,
I never yet could see it flow but once. *Cotton.*

NONCONFO'RMITY. *n. s.* [*non* and *conformity.*]

1. Refusal of compliance.

The will of our maker, whether discovered by reason or revelation, carries the highest authority with it; a conformity or *nonconformity* to it, determines their actions to be morally good or evil. *Watts's Logick.*

2. Refusal to join in the established religion.

Since the liturgy, rites, and ceremonies of our church, are so much struck at, and all upon a plea of conscience, it will concern us to examine the force of this plea, which our adversaries are still setting up as the grand pillar and butteress of *nonconformity*. *South's Sermons.*

The lady will plead the toleration which allows her *nonconformity* in this particular. *Addison's Spectator.*

NONCONFO'RMIST. *n. s.* [*non* and *conformist.*] One who refuses to join in the established worship.

On his death-bed he declared himself a *non-conformist*, and had a fanatic preacher to be his spiritual guide. *Swift.*

NONE. *adj.* [ne one, nan, ne ane, Saxon.]

1. Not one.

Ye shall flee when *none* pursueth you. *Lev.* xxvi. 17.

That fowl which is *none* of the lightest, can easily move itself up and down in the air without stirring its wings. *Wilk.*

Another, which is *none* of the least advantages of hope is, its great efficacy in preserving us from setting too high a value on present enjoyments. *Addison's Spectator.*

2. Not any.

Six days shall ye gather it, but on the sabbath there shall be *none*. *Exodus* xvi. 26.

Thy life shall hang in doubt, and shalt have *none* assurance of this life. *Deutr.* xxii. 66.

Before the deluge, the air was calm; *none* of those tumultuary motions of vapours, which the mountains and winds cause in ours. *Burnet's Theory of the Earth.*

The most glaring and notorious passages, are *none* of the finest. *Fenton on the Classicks.*

3. Not other.

This is *none* other but the house of God, and the gate of heaven. *Gen.* xxviii. 17.

4. *None of* sometimes signifies only emphatically *not.*

My people would not hearken to my voice: and Israel would *none of* me. *Ps.* lxxxi. 11.

NONE'NTITY. *n. s.* [*non* and *entity.*]

1. Nonexistence.

When they say nothing from nothing, they must understand it as excluding all causes. In which sense it is most evidently true; being equivalent to this proposition, that nothing can make itself, or, nothing cannot bring its no-self out of *nonentity* into something. *Bentley's Serm.*

2. A thing not existing.

There was no such thing as rendering evil for evil, when evil was truly a *nonentity*, and no where to be found. *South.*

We have heard, and think it pity that your inquisitive genius should not be better employed, than in looking after that theological *nonentity*. *Arbut. and Pope's Mart. Scrib.*

NONEXI'STENCE. *n. s.* [*non* and *existence.*] Inexistence; state of not existing.

A method of many writers, which depreciates the esteem of miracles is, to salve not only real verities, but also *nonexistences*. *Brown's Vulgar Errours, b.* iv.

NONJU'RING.

NONJU'RING. *adj.* [*non* and *juro*, Latin.] Belonging to those who will not swear allegiance to the Hanoverian family.

This objection was offered me by a very pious, learned, and worthy gentleman of the *nonjuring* party. *Swift.*

NONJU'ROR. *n. s.* [from *non* and *juror.*] One who conceiving James II. unjustly deposed, refuses to swear allegiance to those who have succeeded him.

NONNA'TURALS. *n. s.* [*non naturalia.*]

Physicians reckon these to be six, viz. air, meat and drink, sleep and watching, motion and rest, retention and excretion, and the passions of the mind.

The six *nonnaturals* are such as neither naturally constitutive, nor merely destructive, do preserve or destroy according unto circumstance. *Brown's V. Err.*

NONPARE'IL. *n. s.* [*non* and *pareil*, French.]

1. Excellence unequalled.

My lord and master loves you: O such love
Could be but recompens'd tho' you were crown'd
The *nonpareil* of beauty. *Shakes. Twelfth Night.*

2. A kind of apple.

3. Printers letter of a small size, on which small Bibles and Common Prayers are printed.

NO'NPLUS. *n. s.* [*non* and *plus*, Latin.] Puzzle; inability to say or do more. A low word.

Let it seem never so strange and impossible, the *nonplus* of my reason will yield a fairer opportunity to my faith. *South.*

One or two rules, on which their conclusions depend, in most men have governed all their thoughts: take these from them and they are at a loss, and their understanding is perfectly at a *nonplus.* *Locke.*

Such an artist did not begin the matter at a venture, and when put to a *nonplus*, pause and hesitate which way he should proceed; but he had first in his comprehensive intellect a compleat idea of the whole organical body. *Bentley.*

To NO'NPLUS. *v. a.* [from the noun.] To confound; to puzzle; to put to a stand; to stop.

Nor is the composition of our own bodies the only wonder; we are as much *nonplust* by the most contemptible worm and plant. *Glanv. Scept. c.* vii.

His parts were so accomplisht,
That right or wrong he ne'er was *nonplust.* *Hudibras.*

That sin that is a pitch beyond all those, must needs be such an one as must *nonplus* the devil himself to proceed farther. *South.*

What, you are confounded, and stand mute?
Somewhat *nonplust* to hear you deny your name. *Dryden.*

Tom has been eloquent for half an hour together, when he has been *nonplused* by Mr. Dry's desiring him to tell what it was that he endeavoured to prove. *Spect.* 471.

NONRE'SIDENCE. *n. s.* [*non* and *residence.*] Failure of residence.

If the character of persons chosen into the church had been regarded, there would be fewer complaints of *nonresidence.* *Swift.*

NONRE'SIDENT. *n. s.* [*non* and *resident.*] One who neglects to live at the proper place.

As to nonresidence, there are not ten clergymen in the kingdom who can be termed *nonresidents.* *Swift.*

NONRESI'STANCE. *n. s.* [*non* and *resistance.*] The principle of not opposing the king; ready obedience to a superior.

NO'NSENSE. *n. s.* [*non* and *sense.*]

1. Unmeaning or ungrammatical language.

'Till understood, all tales,
Like *nonsense*, are not true nor false. *Hud. p.* iii.

Many copies dispersed gathering new faults, I saw more *nonsense* than I could have crammed into it. *Dryden.*

This *nonsense* got into all the following editions by a mistake of the stage editors. *Pope's Notes on Shakesp.*

2. Trifles; things of no importance.

What's the world to him,
'Tis *nonsense* all. *Thomson.*

NONSE'NSICAL. *adj.* [from *nonsense.*] Unmeaning; foolish.

They had produced many other inept combinations, or aggregate forms of particular things, and *nonsensical* systems of the whole. *Ray on the Creation.*

NONSE'NSICALNESS. *n. s.* [from *nonsensical.*] Ungrammatical jargon; foolish absurdity.

NONSO'LVENT. *n. s.* [*non* and *solvent.*] One who cannot pay his debts.

NONSOLU'TION. *n. s.* [*non* and *solution.*] Failure of solution.

Athenæus instances ænigmatical propositions, and the forfeitures and rewards upon their solution and *nonsolution.* *Broome.*

NONSPA'RING. *adj.* [*non* and *sparing.*] Merciless; all-destroying.

Is't I expose
Those tender limbs of thine to the event
Of the *nonsparing* war. *Shakes. All's well that Ends well.*

To NONSUI'T. *v. a.* [*non* and *suit.*] To deprive of the benefit of a legal process for some failure in the management.

The addresses of both houses of parliament, the council, and the declarations of most counties and corporations, are laid aside as of no weight, and the whole kingdom of Ireland *nonsuited*, in default of appearance. *Swift.*

NOO'DLE. *n. s.* [from *noddle* or *noddy.*] A fool; a simpleton.

NOOK. *n. s.* [from *een hoeck*, German.] A corner; a covert made by an angle or intersection.

Safely in harbour
Is the king's ship, in the deep *nook*, where once
Thou call'dst me up. *Shakespeare's Tempest.*

Buy a foggy and a dirty farm
In that *nook* shotten isle of Albion. *Shakes. Hen.* V.

The savages were driven out of the great Ards, into a little *nook* of land near the river of Strangford; where they now possess a little territory. *Davies.*

Unsphere
The spirit of Plato to unfold,
What worlds or what vast regions hold
Th' immortal mind that hath forsook
Her mansion in this fleshly *nook.* *Milton's Poems.*

Ithuriel and Zephon,
Search thro' this garden, leave unsearch'd no *nook.* *Milt.*

A third form'd within the ground
A various mold; and from the boiling cells,
By strange conveyance, fill'd each hollow *nook.* *Milton.*

NOON. *n. s.* [non, Saxon; *nawn*, Welsh; *none*, Erse; supposed to be derived from *nona*, Latin, the *ninth hour*, at which their *cœna* or chief meal was eaten; whence the other nations called the time of their *dinner* or chief meal, though earlier in the day, by the same name.]

1. The middle hour of the day; twelve; the time when the sun is in the meridian.

Fetch forth the stocks, there shall he sit 'till *noon.*—
'Till *noon!* 'till night, my lord, *Shakes. K. Lear.*

The day already half his race had run,
And summon'd him to due repast at *noon.* *Dryden.*

If I turn my eyes at *noon* towards the sun, I cannot avoid the ideas which the light or sun produces in me. *Locke.*

2. It is taken for midnight.

Full before him at the *noon* of night,
He saw a quire of ladies. *Dryden.*

NOO'NDAY. *n. s.* [*noon* and *day.*] Midday.

The bird of night did sit,
Ev'n at *noonday*, upon the market-place,
Houting and shrieking. *Shak. Jul. Cæsar.*

The dimness of our intellectual eyes, Aristotle fitly compares to those of an owl at *noonday.* *Boyle.*

NOO'NDAY. *adj.* Meridional.

The scorching sun was mounted high,
In all its lustre to the *noonday* sky. *Addison's Ovid.*

NOO'NING. *n. s.* [from *noon.*] Repose at noon.

NOO'NTIDE. *n. s.* [*noon* and *tide.*] Midday; time of noon.

Sorrow breaks seasons and reposing hours,
Makes the night morning, and the *noontide* night. *Sha.*

NOO'NTIDE. *adj.* Meridional.

Phaeton hath tumbled from his car,
And made an evening at the *noontide* prick. *Shakespeare.*

All things in best order to invite
Noontide repast, or afternoon's repose. *Milt. Par. Lost.*

We expect the morning red in vain;
'Tis hid in vapours, or obscur'd in rain.
The *noontide* yellow we in vain require;
'Tis black in storm, or red in light'ning fire. *Prior.*

NOOSE. *n. s.* [*nosada*, entangled; a word found in the glosses of *Lipsius.* Mr. *Lye.*] A running knot which the more it is drawn binds the closer.

Can'st thou with a weak angle strike the whale?
Catch with a hook, or with a *noose* inthral? *Sandys.*

Where the hangman does dispose,
To special friend the knot of *noose.* *Hud. p.* i.

They run their necks into a *noose*,
They'd break 'em after, to break loose. *Hud. p.* iii.

Falsely he falls into some dangerous *noose*,
And then as meanly labours to get loose. *Dryden.*

A rope and a *noose* are no jesting matters. *J. Bull.*

To NOOSE. *v. a.* [from the noun.] To tie in a noose; to catch; to entrap.

The sin is woven with threads of different sizes, the least of them strong enough to *noose* and entrap us. *Gov. Tongue.*

NOPE. *n. s.* A kind of bird called a bullfinch or redtail.

NOR. *conjunct.* [*ne or.*]

1. A particle marking the second or subsequent branch of a negative proposition; correlative to neither or not.

I neither love, *nor* fear thee. *Shakespeare.*
Neither love will twine, *nor* hay. *Marvel.*

2. Two negatives are sometimes joined, but ill.

Mine eyes,
Which I have darted at thee, hurt thee not;
Nor, I am sure there is no force in eyes
That can do hurt. *Shakespeare's As you like it.*

3. Neither is sometimes included in nor, but not elegantly.

Pow'r, disgrace, *nor* death could ought divert
Thy glorious tongue thus to reveal thy heart. *Daniel.*

Simois *nor* Xanthus shall be wanting there;
A new Achilles shall in arms appear. *Dryden.*

4. Nor is sometimes used in the first branch for neither.

Idle nymph, I pray thee, be
Modest, and not follow me,
I *nor* love myself, *nor* thee. *Ben. Johnson.*

Nor did they not perceive their evil plight,
Or the fierce pains not feel *Milton.*
But how perplex, alas! is human fate?
I whom *nor* avarice, *nor* pleaſures move;
Yet muſt myſelf be made a ſlave to love. *Walſh.*

NORTH. *n. ſ.* [noꝛð, Saxon.] The point oppoſite to the ſun in the meridian.

More unconſtant than the wind; who wooes
Ev'n now the frozen boſom of the *north*;
And being anger'd puffs away from thence,
Turning his face to the dew dropping ſouth. *Shakeſ.*
The tyrannous breathing of the *north*,
Shakes all our buds from blowing. *Shakeſ. Cymb.*
Fierce Boreas iſſues forth
T' invade th' frozen waggon of the *north*. *Dryd.*

NORTH. *adj.* Northern; being in the north.

This ſhall be your *north* border from the great ſea to mount Hor. *Num.* xxxiv. 7.

NORTHEA'ST. *n. ſ.* [*noordeaſt*, Dutch.] The point between the north and eaſt.

The inferiour ſea towards the ſoutheaſt, the Ionian towards the ſouth, and the Adriatick on the *northeaſt* ſide, were commanded by three different nations. *Arbuthnot.*

NO'RTHERLY. *adj.* [from *north*.] Being towards the north.

The *northerly* and ſoutherly winds, commonly eſteemed the cauſes of cold and warm weather, are really the effects of the cold or warmth of the atmoſphere. *Derham.*

NO'RTHERN. *adj.* [from *north*.] Being in the north.

Proud *northern* lord, Clifford of Cumberland. *Shakeſ.*

If we erect a red-hot wire until it cool, and then hang it up with wax and untwiſted ſilk, where the lower end which cooled next the earth doth reſt, that is the *northern* point. *Brown's Vulgar Errours.*

NORTHSTA'R. *n. ſ.* [*north* and *ſtar*.] The poleſtar; the lodeſtar.

If her breath were as terrible as her terminations, there were no living near her, ſhe would infect to the *northſtar*. *Shakeſpeare's M. Ad. Ab.*

NO'RTHWARD. *adj.* [*north* and peaꞃd, Saxon.] Being towards the north.

NO'RTHWARD. } *adv.* [*north* and peaꞃd, Saxon.] Towards
NO'RTHWARDS. } the north.

Miſlike me not for my complexion,
The ſhadow'd livery of the burniſh'd ſun.
Bring me the faireſt creature *northward* born,
Where Phœbus' fire ſcarce thaws the icicles,
And prove whoſe blood is reddeſt. *Shakeſpeare.*

Going *northward* aloof, as long as they had any doubt of being purſued, at laſt they croſſed the ocean to Spain. *Bacon.*

Northward beyond the mountains we will go,
Where rocks lie cover'd with eternal ſnow. *Dryden.*

A cloſe priſoner in a room, twenty foot ſquare, being at the north ſide of his chamber, is at liberty to walk twenty foot ſouthward, not walk twenty foot *northward*. *Locke.*

NORTHWE'ST. *n. ſ.* [*north* and *weſt*.] The point between the north and weſt.

The bathing places that they may remain under the ſun until evening, he expoſeth unto the ſummer ſetting, that is *northweſt*. *Brown's Vulgar Errours, b.* vi.

NORTHWI'ND. *n. ſ.* [*north* and *wind*.] The wind that blows from the north.

The clouds were fled,
Driven by a keen *northwind*. *Milton.*
When the fierce *northwind*, with his airy forces
Rears up the Baltick to a foaming fury. *Watts.*

NOSE. *n. ſ.* [nœꞅe, noꞅa, Saxon.]

1. The prominence on the face, which is the organ of ſcent and the emunctory of the brain.

Down with the *noſe*,
Take the bridge quite away
Of him that, his particular to forefend,
Smells from the gen'ral weal. *Shakeſ. Timon of Athens.*
Noſe of Turks and Tartars lips. *Shakeſ. Macbeth.*
Our decrees,
Dead to infliction, to themſelves are dead;
And liberty plucks juſtice by the *noſe*. *Sha. M. of Ven.*

There can be no reaſon given why a viſage ſomewhat longer, or a *noſe* flatter, could not have conſiſted with ſuch a ſoul. *Locke.*

Poetry takes me up ſo entirely, that I ſcarce ſee what paſſes under my *noſe*. *Pope's Letters.*

2. The end of any thing.

The lungs are as bellows, the aſpera arteria is the *noſe* of the bellows, or as a channel in the ſound board of an organ. *Holder's Elements of Speech.*

3. Scent; ſagacity.

We are not offended with a dog for a better *noſe* than his maſter. *Collier on Envy.*

4. *To lead by the* NOSE. To drag by force: as, a bear by his ring. To lead blindly.

Tho' authority be a ſtubborn bear,
Yet he is oft led by the *noſe* with gold. *Sha. W. Tale.*

In ſuits which a man doth not underſtand, it is good to refer them to ſome friend, but let him chuſe well his referendaries, elſe he may be led by the *noſe*. *Bacon.*

That ſome occult deſign doth lie
In bloody cynarctomachy,
Is plain enough to him that knows,
How ſaints lead brothers by the *noſe*. *Hudibras, p.* i.

This is the method of all popular ſhams, when the multitude are to be led by the *noſes* into a fool's paradiſe. *L'Eſt.*

5. *To thruſt one's* NOSE *into* the affairs of others. To be meddling with other people's matters; to be a buſy body.

6. *To put one's* NOSE *out of* joint. To put one out in the affections of another.

To NOSE. *v. a.* [from the noun.]

1. To ſcent; to ſmell.

Noſe him as you go up the ſtairs. *Shakeſ. Hamlet.*

2. To face; to oppoſe.

To NOSE. *v. n.* To look big; to bluſter.

Adult'rous Anthony
Gives his potent regiment to a trull
That *noſes* it againſt us. *Shakeſ. Ant. and Cleopatra.*

NOSE'BLEED. *n. ſ.* [*noſe* and *bleed*.] A kind of herb.

NO'SEGAY. *n. ſ.* [*noſe* and *gay*.] A poſie; a bunch of flowers.

She hath made me four and twenty *noſegays* for the ſhearers. *Shakeſpeare's Winter's Tale.*

Ariel ſought
The cloſe receſſes of the virgin's thought;
As on the *noſegay* in her breaſt reclin'd,
He watch'd th' ideas riſing in her mind. *Pope.*

Get you gone in the country to dreſs up *noſegays* for a holyday. *Arbuthnot's Hiſt. of J. Bull.*

NO'SELESS. *adj.* [from *noſe*.] Wanting a noſe; deprived of the noſe.

Mangled Myrmidons,
Noſeleſs, and handleſs, hackt and chipt, come to him. *Sha.*

NOSE'SMART. *n. ſ.* [*noſe* and *ſmart*.] The herb creſſes.

NO'SLE. *n. ſ.* [from *noſe*.] The extremity of a thing: as, the *noſle* of a pair of bellows.

NO'SOLOGY. *n. ſ.* [νόσος and λόγος.] Doctrine of diſeaſes.

NOSOPOE'TICK. *adj.* [νόσος and ποιέω.] Producing diſeaſes.

The qualities of the air are *noſopoetick*; that is, have a pow'r of producing diſeaſes. *Arbuthnot on Air.*

NO'STRIL. *n. ſ.* [*noſe* and ðyꞃl, a hole, Saxon.] The cavity in the noſe.

Turn then my freſheſt reputation to
A favour that may ſtrike the dulleſt *noſtril*. *Shakeſp.*

Stinks which the *noſtrils* ſtraight abhor, are not the moſt pernicious. *Bacon's Nat. Hiſt.*

He form'd thee, Adam, and in thy *noſtrils* breath'd
The breath of life. *Milton's P. Loſt, b.* vii.

The ſecondary action ſubſiſteth not alone, but in concomitancy with the other; ſo the *noſtrils* are uſeful both for reſpiration and ſmelling, but the principal uſe is ſmelling. *Brown's Vulgar Errours, b.* iii.

Theſe ripe fruits recreate the *noſtrils* with their aromatick ſcent. *More's Divine Dialogues.*

NO'STRUM. *n. ſ.* [Latin.] A medicine not yet made publick, but remaining in ſome ſingle hand.

Very extraordinary, and one of his *noſtrums*, let it be writ upon his monument, *Hic jacet auctor hujus argumenti*; for no body ever uſed it before. *Stillingfleet.*

What drop or *noſtrum* can this plague remove? *Pope.*

NOT. *adv.* [ne auꞅꞇ, Saxon; *niet*, Dutch.]

1. The particle of negation, or refuſal.

If thou be the world's great parent,
How falls it then that with thy furious fervour
Thou doſt afflict as well the *not* deſerver,
As him that doth thy lovely heſts deſpiſe? *Spenſer.*
His countenance likes me *not*. *Shakeſp. K. Lear.*

The man held his peace, to wit whether the Lord had made his journey proſperous or *not*. *Gen.* xxiv. 21.

Let each man do as to his fancy ſeems;
I wait, *not* I, 'till you have better dreams. *Dryden.*

This objection hinders *not* but that the heroic action enterpriſed for the Chriſtian cauſe, and executed happily, may be as well executed now as it was of old. *Dryden.*

Grammar being to teach men *not* to ſpeak, but to ſpeak correctly: where rhetoric is *not* neceſſary, grammar may be ſpared. *Locke on Education.*

This day, be bread and peace my lot;
All elſe beneath the ſun
Thou know'ſt if beſt beſtow'd or *not*,
And let thy will be done. *Pope's Univerſal Prayer.*

2. It denotes ceſſation or extinction. No more.

Thine eyes are upon me, and I am *not*. *Job* vii. 8.

NO'TABLE. *adj.* [*notable*, Fr. *notabilis*, Latin.] Remarkable; memorable; obſervable.

The ſucceſs of thoſe wars was too *notable* to be unknown to your ears; which, it ſeems, all worthy fame hath glory to come unto. *Sidney, b.* ii.

The ſame is notified in the *notable* places of the dioceſs. *Whitgifte.*

In the parliament at Kilkenny, many *notable* laws were enacted, which ſhew, for the law doth beſt diſcover enormities, how much the Engliſh colonies were corrupted. *Davies on Ireland.*

Two young men appeared *notable* in ſtrength, excellent in beauty, and comely in apparel. *2 Mac.* iii. 26.

They bore two or three charges from the horſe with *notable* courage, and without being broken. *Clarendon.*

Both armies lay ſtill without any *notable* action, for the ſpace of ten days. *Clarendon, b.* viii.

Varro's aviary is ſtill ſo famous, that it is reckoned for one of thoſe *notables* which men of foreign nations record. *Addiſon.*

Cæſar, whoſe great ſagacity and conduct put his ſucceſs as much out of the power of chance as human reaſon could well do, yet upon occaſion of a *notable* experiment, that had like to have loſt him his whole army at Dyrrachium, tells us the power of it in his commentaries. *South's Serm.*

It is impoſſible but a man muſt have firſt paſſed this *notable* ſtage, and got his conſcience thoroughly debauched and hardened, before he can arrive to the height of ſin. *South.*

2. Careful; buſtling, in contempt and irony.

This abſolute monarch was as *notable* a guardian of the fortunes, as of the lives of his ſubjects. When any man grew rich, to keep him from being dangerous to the ſtate, he ſent for all his goods. *Addiſon's Freeholder,* Nº. 10.

No'TABLENESS. *n. ſ.* [from *notable.*] Appearance of buſineſs; importance. In contempt.

No'TABLY. *adv.* [from *notable.*]

1. Memorably; remarkably.

This we ſee *notably* proved, in that the oft polling of hedges conduces much to their laſting. *Bacon's Nat. Hiſt.*

2. With conſequence; with ſhew of importance; ironically.

Mention the king of Spain or Poland, and he talks very *notably*; but if you go out of the gazette, you drop him. *Addiſon's Spectator,* Nº. 105.

No'TARIAL. *adj.* [from *notary.*] Taken by a notary.

It may be called an authentick writing, though not a publick inſtrument, through want of a *notarial* evidence. *Alyliffe.*

No'TARY. *n. ſ.* [*notaire,* Fr. from *notarius,* Latin.] An officer whoſe buſineſs it is to take notes of any thing which may concern the publick.

There is a declaration made to have that very book, and no other ſet abroad, wherein their preſent authoriſed *notaries* do write thoſe things fully and only, which being written and there read, are by their own open teſtimony acknowledged to be their own. *Hooker.*

Go with me to a *notary,* ſeal me there
Your bond. *Shakeſ. M. of Venice.*

One of thoſe with him, being a *notary,* made an entry of this act. *Bacon's New Atlantis.*

So I but your recorder am in this,
Or mouth and ſpeaker of the univerſe,
A miniſterial *notary*; for 'tis
Not I, but you and fame that make this verſe. *Donne.*

They have in each province, intendants and *notaries. Temp.*

Nota'tion. *n. ſ.* [*notatio,* Latin.]

1. The act or practice of recording any thing by marks: as, by figures or letters.

Notation teaches how to deſcribe any number by certain notes and characters, and to declare the value thereof being ſo deſcribed, and that is by degrees and periods. *Cocker.*

2. Meaning; ſignification.

A foundation being primarily of uſe in architecture, hath no other literal *notation* but what belongs to it in relation to a building. *Hammond.*

Conſcience, according to the very *notation* of the word, imports a double knowledge; one of a divine law, and the other of a man's own action; and ſo is properly the application of a general law, to a particular inſtance of practice. *South's Sermons.*

NOTCH. *n. ſ.* [*nocchia,* Italian.] A nick; a hollow cut in any thing.

The convex work is compoſed of black and citrin pieces in the margin, of a pyramidal figure appoſitely ſet, and with tranſverſe *notches.* *Grew's Muſæum.*

From his rug the ſkew'r he takes,
And on the ſtick ten equal *notches* makes:
There take my tally of ten thouſand pound *Swift.*

He ſhew'd a comma ne'er could claim
A place in any Britiſh name;
Yet making here a perfect botch,
Thruſts your poor vowel from his *notch.* *Swift.*

To Notch. *v. a.* [from the noun.] To cut in ſmall hollows.

He was too hard for him directly: before Corioli, he ſcotcht him and *notcht* him like a carbonado. *Shakeſ.*

The convex work is compoſed of black and citrin pieces, cancellated and tranſverſely *notched.* *Grew's Muſæum.*

From him whoſe quills ſtand quiver'd at his ear,
To him who *notches* ſticks at Weſtminſter. *Pope.*

Notchwee'd. *n. ſ.* [*notch* and *weed.*] An herb called orach.

Note. [for *ne mote.*] May not.

Ne let him then admire,
But yield his ſenſe to be too blunt and baſe,
That *note* without an hound fine footing trace. *Fairy Q.*

NOTE. *n. ſ.* [*nota,* Lat. *notte,* Fr.]

1. Mark; token.

Whoſoever appertain to the viſible body of the church, they have alſo the *notes* of external profeſſion whereby the world knoweth what they are. *Hooker, b.* iii.

2. Notice; heed.

Give order to my ſervants that they take
No *note* at all of our being abſent hence. *Shakeſp.*

I will beſtow ſome precepts on this virgin,
Worthy the *note.* *Shakeſp. All's well that ends well.*

3. Reputation; conſequence.

Divers men of *note* have been brought over into England. *Abbot's Deſcription of the World.*

Andronicus and Junia are of *note* among the apoſtles. *Rom.* xvi. 7.

As for metals, authors of good *note* aſſure us, that even they have been obſerved to grow. *Boyle.*

4. Reproach; ſtigma.

The more to aggravate the *note,*
With a foul traytor's name ſtuff I thy throat. *Shakeſp.*

5. Account; information; intelligence.

She that from Naples
Can have no *note*; unleſs the ſun were poſt,
The man i'th' moon's too ſlow. *Shakeſp. Tempeſt.*

In ſuits of favour, the firſt coming ought to take little place; ſo far forth conſideration may be had of his truſt, that if intelligence of the matter could not otherwiſe have been had but by him, advantage be not taken of the *note,* but the party left to his other means, and in ſome ſort recompenſed for his diſcovery. *Bacon, Eſſay* 49.

6. Tune; voice.

Theſe are the *notes* wherewith are drawn from the hearts of the multitude ſo many ſighs; with theſe tunes their minds are exaſperated againſt the lawful guides and governors of their ſouls. *Hooker, b.* iv.

The wakeful bird tunes her nocturnal *note.* *Milton.*

I now muſt change thoſe *notes* to tragick. *Milton.*

You that can tune your ſounding ſtrings ſo well,
Of ladies beauties and of love to tell;
Once change your *note,* and let your lute report
The juſteſt grief that ever touch'd the court. *Waller.*

One common *note* on either lyre did ſtrike,
And knaves and fools we both abhorr'd alike. *Dryden.*

7. Single ſound in muſick.

From harmony, from heavenly harmony!
This univerſal frame began:
From harmony to harmony,
Thro' all the compaſs of the *notes* it ran,
The diapaſon cloſing full in man. *Dryden.*

8. State of being obſerved.

Small matters come with great commendation, becauſe they are continually in uſe and in *note*; whereas the occaſion of any great virtue cometh but on feſtivals. *Bacon.*

9. Short hint; ſmall paper.

He will'd me
In heedfull'ſt reſervation to beſtow them,
As *notes* whoſe faculties incluſive were,
More than they were in note. *Shakeſpeare.*

In the body's priſon ſo ſhe lies,
As through the body's windows ſhe muſt look,
Her divers pow'rs of ſenſe to exerciſe,
By gath'ring *notes* out of the world's great book. *Davies.*

10. Abbreviation; ſymbol.

Contract it into a narrow compaſs by ſhort *notes* and abbreviations. *Baker on Learning.*

11. A ſmall letter.

A hollow cane within her hand ſhe brought,
But in the concave had incloſ'd a *note.* *Dryden.*

12. Written paper.

I cannot get over the prejudice of taking ſome little offence at the clergy, for perpetually reading their ſermons; perhaps my frequent hearing of foreigners, who never make uſe of *notes,* may have added to my diſguſt. *Swift.*

13. A paper given in confeſſion of a debt.

His *note* will go farther than my bond. *John Bull.*

14. Explanatory annotation.

The beſt writers have been perplexed with *notes,* and obſcured with illuſtrations. *Felton on the Claſſicks.*

No'tebook. *n. ſ.* [*note* and *book.*] A book in which notes and memorandums are ſet down.

Caſſius all his faults obſerv'd;
Set in a *notebook,* learn'd, and conn'd by rote,
To caſt into my teeth. *Shakeſp. J. Cæſar.*

To Note. *v. a.* [*noto,* Latin; *noter,* French.]

1. To

1. To obſerve; to remark; to heed; to attend; to take notice of.

The fool hath much pined away.
No more of that, I have *noted* it well. *Shakeſ. K. Lear.*

If much you *note* him,
You ſhall offend him. *Shakeſpeare's Macbeth.*

I began to *note*
The ſtormy Hyades, the rainy goat. *Addiſ. Ovid.*

Wandring from clime to clime, obſervant ſtray'd,
Their manners *noted*, and their ſtates ſurvey'd. *Pope.*

2. To deliver; to ſet down.

Saint Auguſtin ſpeaking of devout men, *noteth* how they daily frequented the church, how attentive ear they gave unto the leſſons and chapters read. *Hooker, b.* v.

Note it in a book, that it may be for ever and ever. *Iſ.* xxx. 8.

3. To charge with a crime.

Sine veſte Dianam, agrees better with Livia, who had the fame of chaſtity, than with either of the Julia's, who were both *noted* of incontinency. *Dryden.*

4. [In muſick.] To ſet down the notes of a tune.

NO'TED. *part. adj.* [from *note.*] Remarkable; eminent; celebrated.

A *noted* chymiſt procured a privilege, that none but he ſhould vend a ſpirit. *Boyle.*

Juſtinian's laws, if we may believe a *noted* author, have not the force of laws in France or Holland. *Baker.*

NO'TER. *n. ſ.* [from *note.*] He who takes notice.

NO'THING. *n. ſ.* [*no* and *thing*; *nathing*, Scottiſh.]

1. Negation of being; nonentity; univerſal negation; oppoſed to ſomething.

It is moſt certain, that there never could be *nothing*. For, if there could have been an inſtant, wherein there was *nothing*, then either *nothing* made ſomething, or ſomething made itſelf; and ſo was, and acted, before it was. But if there never could be *nothing*; then there is, and was, a being of neceſſity, without any beginning. *Grew's Coſ.*

We do not create the world from *nothing* and by *nothing*; we aſſert an eternal God to have been the efficient cauſe of it. *Bentley's Serm.*

This *nothing* is taken either in a vulgar or philoſophical ſenſe; ſo we ſay there is *nothing* in the cup in a vulgar ſenſe, when we mean there is no liquor in it; but we cannot ſay there is *nothing* in the cup, in a ſtrict philoſophical ſenſe, while there is air in it. *Watts's Logick.*

2. Nonexiſtence.

Mighty ſtates characterleſs are grated
To duſty *nothing*. *Shakeſ. Troilus and Creſſida.*

3. Not any thing; no particular thing.

There ſhall *nothing* die. *Ex.* ix. 4.

Yet had his aſpect *nothing* of ſevere,
But ſuch a face as promis'd him ſincere. *Dryden.*

Philoſophy wholly ſpeculative, is barren and produces *nothing* but vain ideas. *Dryden's Don Sebaſtian.*

Nothing at all was done, while any thing remained undone. *Addiſon on the War.*

4. No other thing.

Nothing but a ſteady reſolution brought to practice; God's grace uſed, his commandments obeyed, and his pardon begged; *nothing* but this will intitle you to God's acceptance. *Wakes's Prep. for Death.*

Words are made to declare ſomething; where they are, by thoſe who pretend to inſtruct, otherwiſe uſed, they conceal indeed ſomething; but that which they conceal, is *nothing* but the ignorance, error, or ſophiſtry of the talker, for there is, in truth, *nothing* elſe under them. *Locke.*

5. No quantity or degree.

The report which the troops of horſe make, would add *nothing* of courage to their fellows. *Clarendon.*

6. No importance; no uſe; no value.

The outward ſhew of churches, draws the rude people to the reverencing and frequenting thereof, whatever ſome of our late too nice fools ſay, there is *nothing* in the ſeemly form of the church. *Spenſer's Ireland.*

Behold, ye are of *nothing*, and your work of naught. *Iſaiah* xli. 24.

7. No poſſeſſion or fortune.

A moſt homely ſhepherd; a man that from very *nothing* is grown into an unſpeakable eſtate. *Shak. W. Tale.*

8 No difficulty; no trouble.

We are induſtrious to preſerve our bodies from ſlavery, but we make *nothing* of ſuffering our ſouls to be ſlaves to our luſts. *Ray on the Creation.*

9. A thing of no proportion.

The charge of making the ground, and otherwiſe is great, but *nothing* to the profit. *Bacon's Nat. Hiſt.*

10. Trifle; ſomething of no conſideration or importance.

I had rather have one ſcratch my head i'th' ſun,
When the alarum were ſtruck, than idly ſit
To hear my *nothings* monſter'd. *Shakeſpeare's Cor.*

My dear *nothings*, take your leave,
No longer muſt you me deceive,
'Tis *nothing*, ſays the fool; but ſays the friend,
This *nothing*, Sir, will bring you to your end.
Do I not ſee your dropſy-belly ſwell? *Dryden.*

That period includes more than a hundred ſentences that might be writ to expreſs multiplication of *nothings*, and all the fatiguing perpetual buſineſs of having no buſineſs to do. *Pope's Letters.*

11. Nothing has a kind of adverbial ſignification. In no degree; not at all.

Who will make me a liar, and make my ſpeech *nothing* worth? *Job* xxiv. 25.

Auria *nothing* diſmayed with the greatneſs of the Turks' fleet, ſtill kept on his courſe. *Knolles's Hiſt. of the Turks.*

But Adam with ſuch counſel *nothing* ſway'd. *Milton.*

NO'THINGNESS. *n. ſ.* [from *nothing.*]

1. Nihility; nonexiſtence.

His art did expreſs
A quinteſſence even from *nothingneſs*,
From dull privations, and lean emptineſs. *Donne.*

2. Nothing; thing of no value.

I a *nothingneſs* in deed and name,
Did ſcorn to hurt his forfeit carcaſe. *Hudibras, p.* i.

NO'TICE. *n. ſ.* [*notice*, French; *notitia*, Latin.]

1. Remark; heed; obſervation; regard.

The thing to be regarded in taking *notice* of a child's miſcarriage is, what root it ſprings from. *Locke.*

This is done with little *notice*: very quick the actions of the mind are performed. *Locke.*

How ready is envy to mingle with the *notices* which we take of other perſons! *Watts.*

2. Information; intelligence given or received.

I have given him *notice*, that the duke of Cornwal and his dutcheſs will be here. *Shakeſpeare's K. Lear.*

NOTIFICA'TIONS. *n. ſ.* [*notification*, F. from *notify.*] Act of making known; repreſentation by marks or ſymbols.

Four or five torches elevated or depreſſed out of their order, either in breadth or longways, may, by agreement, give great variety of *notifications*. *Holder's Elements of Speech.*

To NO'TIFY. *v. a.* [*notifier*, Fr. *notifico*, Latin.] To declare; to make known; to publiſh.

There are other kind of laws, which *notify* the will of God. *Hooker, b.* ii. *ſ.* 2.

The ſame is *notified* in the notableſt places of the whole dioceſs. *Whitgifte.*

Good and evil operate upon the mind of man, by thoſe reſpective appellations by which they are *notified* and conveyed to the mind. *South's Serm.*

This ſolar month is by civil ſanction *notified* in authentic calendars the chief meaſure of the year: a kind of ſtandard by which we meaſure time. *Holder.*

NO'TION. *n. ſ.* [*notion*, Fr. *notio*, Latin.]

1. Thought; repreſentation of any thing formed by the mind; idea; image; conception.

Many actions are puniſhed by law, that are acts of ingratitude; but this is merely accidental to them, as they are ſuch acts; for if they were puniſhed properly under that *notion*, and upon that account, the puniſhment would equally reach all actions of the ſame kind. *South's Serm.*

The fiction of ſome beings which are not in nature; ſecond *notions*, as the logicians call them, has been founded on the conjunction of two natures, which have a real ſeparate being. *Dryden's State of Innocence.*

What hath been generally agreed on, I content myſelf to aſſume under the *notion* of principles, in order to what I have farther to write. *Newt. Opt.*

There is nothing made a more common ſubject of diſcourſe than nature and it's laws; and yet few agree in their *notions* about theſe words. *Cheyne's Phil. Prin.*

That *notion* of hunger, cold, ſound, colour, thought, wiſh, or fear, which is in the mind, is called the idea of hunger, cold, ſound, wiſh, &c. *Watts's Logick.*

2. Sentiment; opinion.

God hath bid dwell far off all anxious cares,
And not moleſt us; unleſs we ourſelves
Seek them with wand'ring thoughts and *notions* vain. *Milt.*

It would be incredible to a man who has never been in France, ſhould one relate the extravagant *notion* they entertain of themſelves, and the mean opinion they have of their neighbours. *Addiſon's Freeholder*, N°. 30.

Senſual wits they were, who, it is probable, took pleaſure in ridiculing the *notion* of a life to come. *Atterbury.*

3. Senſe; underſtanding; intellectual power. This ſenſe is frequent in Shakeſpeare, but not in uſe.

His *notion* weakens, his diſcernings
Are lethargy'd *Shakeſpeare's K. Lear.*

So told, as earthly *notion* can receive. *Milt. P. Loſt.*

NO'TIONAL. *adj.* [from *notion.*]

1. Imaginary; ideal; intellectual; ſubſiſting only in idea; viſionary; fantaſtical.

The general and indefinite contemplations and notions, of the elements and their conjugations, of the influences of heaven,

heaven, are to be set aside, being but *notional* and ill-limited; and definite axioms are to be drawn out of measured instances. *Bacon's Natural History*, N°. 835.

Happiness, object of that waking dream
Which we call life, mistaking; fugitive theme
Of my pursuing verse, ideal shade,
Notional good, by fancy only made. *Prior.*

We must be wary, lest we ascribe any real subsistence or personality to this nature or chance; for it is merely a *notional* and imaginary thing; an abstract universal, which is properly nothing; a conception of our own making, occasioned by our reflecting upon the settled course of things; denoting only thus much, that all those bodies move and act according to their essential properties, without any consciousness or intention of so doing. *Bentley's Serm.*

2. Dealing in ideas, not realities.

The most forward *notional* dictators sit down in a contented ignorance. *Glanv. Sceps. c.* xx.

Notiona'lity. *n. s.* [from *notional.*] Empty, ungrounded opinion. A word not in use.

I aimed at the advance of science, by discrediting empty and talkative *notionality*. *Glanv. to Albius.*

No'tionally. *adv.* [from *notional.*] In idea; mentally; in our conception, though not in reality.

The whole rational nature of man consists of two faculties, understanding and will, whether really or *notionally* distinct, I shall not dispute. *Norris's Miscel.*

Notori'ety. *n. s.* [*notorieté*, Fr. from *notorious.*] Publick knowledge; publick exposure.

We see what a multitude of pagan testimonies may be produced for all those remarkable passages: and indeed of several, that more than answer your expectation, as they were not subjects in their own nature so exposed to publick *notoriety*. *Addison on Christ. Relig.*

NOTO'RIOUS. *adj.* [*notorius*, Lat. *notoire*, Fr.] Publickly known; evident to the world; apparent; not hidden. It is commonly used of things known to their disadvantage; whence by those who do not know the true signification of the word, an atrocious crime is called a *notorious* crime, whether publick or secret.

What need you make such ado in cloaking a matter too *notorious*. *Whitgifte.*

The goodness of your intercepted packets
You writ to the pope against the king; your goodness,
Since you provoke me, shall be most *notorious*. *Shakes.*

I shall have law in Ephesus,
To your *notorious* shame. *Shakes. Com. Err.*

In the time of king Edward III. the impediments of the conquest of Ireland are *notorious*. *Davies.*

What *notorious* vice is there that doth not blemish a man's reputation? *Tillotson.*

The inhabitants of Naples have been always very *notorious* for leading a life of laziness and pleasure, which arises partly out of the plenty of their country, and partly out of the temper of their climate. *Addison on Italy.*

The bishops have procured some small advancement of rents; although it be *notorious* that they do not receive the third penny of the real value. *Swift's Miscell.*

Noto'riously. *adv.* [from *notorious.*] Publickly; evidently; openly.

The exposing himself *notoriously*, did sometimes change the fortune of the day. *Clarendon, b.* viii.

This is *notoriously* discoverable in some differences of brake or fern. *Brown's Vulgar Errours, b.* ii.

Ovid tells us, that the cause was *notoriously* known at Rome, though it be left so obscure to after ages. *Dryden.*

Should the genius of a nation be more fixed in government, than in morals, learning, and complexion; which do all *notoriously* vary in every age. *Swift.*

Noto'riousness. *n. s.* [from *notorious.*] Publick fame; notoriety.

To Nott. *v. a.* To shear. *Ains.*

No'twheat. *n. s.* [*not* and *wheat.*]

Of wheat there are two sorts; French, which is bearded, and requireth the best soil, and *notwheat*, so termed because it is unbearded, being contented with a meaner earth. *Carew.*

Notwithsta'nding. *conj.* [This word, though in conformity to other writers called here a conjunction, is properly a participal adjective, as it is compounded of *not* and *withstanding*, and answers exactly to the Latin *non obstante*; it is most properly and analogically used in the ablative case absolute with a noun; as, *he is rich notwithstanding his loss*; it is not so proper to say, *he is rich notwithstanding he has lost much*; yet this mode of writing is too frequent, *Addison* has used it: but when a sentence follows, it is more grammatical to insert *that*; as, *he is rich notwithstanding that he has lost much.* When *notwithstanding* is used absolutely, the expression is elliptical, *this* or *that* being understood, as in the following passages of *Hooker.*]

1. Without hindrance or obstruction from.

Those on whom Christ bestowed miraculous cures, were so transported that their gratitude made them, *notwithstanding* his prohibition, proclaim the wonders he had done for them. *Decay of Piety.*

2. Although. This use is not proper.

A person languishing under an ill habit of body, may lose several ounces of blood, *notwithstanding* it will weaken him for a time, in order to put a new ferment into the remaining mass, and draw into it fresh supplies. *Addison.*

3. Nevertheless; however.

They which honour the law as an image of the wisdom of God himself, are *notwithstanding* to know that the same had an end in Christ. *Hooker, b.* iv.

The knowledge is small, which we have on earth concerning things that are done in heaven: *notwithstanding* this much we know even of saints in heaven, that they pray. *Hooker, b.* v. *s.* 23.

He hath a tear for pity, and a hand
Open as day, for melting charity:
Yet *notwithstanding*, being incens'd, he's flint;
As humourous as winter. *Shakes. Henry* IV.

NO'TUS. n. s. [Latin.] The southwind.

With adverse blast upturns them from the south,
Notus and Afer black, with thund'rous clouds
From Sierra Liona. *Milton's Par. Lost, b.* x.

Nova'tion. *n. s.* [*novatio*, Latin.] The introduction of something new.

NOVA'TOR. n. s. [Latin.] The introducer of something new.

NO'VEL. *adj.* [*novellus*, Latin; *nouvelle*, French.]

1. New; not ancient; not used of old; unusual.

The Presbyterians are exacters of submission to their *novel* injunctions, before they are stamped with the authority of laws. *King Charles.*

It is no *novel* usurpation, but though void of other title, has the prescription of many ages. *Decay of Piety.*

2. [In the civil law.] Appendant to the code, and of later enaction.

By the *novel* constitutions, burial may not be denied to any one. *Ayliffe's Parergon.*

No'vel. *n. s.* [*nouvelle*, French.]

1. A small tale, generally of love.

Nothing of a foreign nature; like the trifling *novels* which Ariosto inserted in his poems. *Dryden.*

Her mangl'd fame in barb'rous pastime lost,
The coxcomb's *novel* and the drunkard's toast. *Prior.*

2. A law annexed to the code.

By the civil law, no one was to be ordained a presbyter till he was thirty-five years of age: though by a later *novel* it was sufficient, if he was above thirty. *Ayliffe's Par.*

No'velist. *n. s.* [from *novel.*]

1. Innovator; assertor of novelty.

Telesius, who hath renewed the philosophy of Parmenides, is the best of *novelists*. *Bacon's Nat. Hist.* N°. 69.

Aristotle rose,
Who nature's secrets to the world did teach,
Yet that great soul our *novelists* impeach. *Denham.*

The fooleries of some affected *novelist* have discredited new discoveries. *Glanv. Sceps.*

2. A writer of novels.

No'velty. *n. s.* [*nouveauté*, French.] Newness; state of being unknown to former times.

They which do nothing but that which men of account did before them, are, although they do amiss, yet the less faulty, because they are not the authors of harm: and doing well, their actions are freed from prejudice or *novelty*. *Hooker, b.* v. *s.* 7.

Novelty is only in request; and it is dangerous to be aged in any kind of course. *Shakes. Measure for Measure.*

As religion entertains our speculations with great objects, so it entertains them with new; and *novelty* is the great parent of pleasure; upon which account it is that men are so much pleased with variety. *South's Sermons.*

NOVE'MBER. n. s. [Latin.] The eleventh month of the year, or the ninth reckoned from March, which was, when the Romans named the months, accounted the first.

November is drawn in a garment of changeable green, and black upon his head. *Peacham on Drawing.*

No'venary. *n. s.* [*novenarius*, Latin.] Number of nine; nine collectively.

Ptolomy by parts and numbers implieth climacterical years; that is, septenaries and *novenaries*. *Brown's V. Err.*

Looking upon them as in their original differences and combinations, and as selected out of a natural stock of nine quaternions, or four *novenaries*, their nature and differences lie most obvious to be understood. *Holder.*

Nove'rcal. *adj.* [*nivercalis*, from *noverca*, Latin.] Having the manner of a stepmother; beseeming a stepmother.

When the whole tribe of birds by incubation, produce their young, it is a wonderful deviation, that some few families should do it in a more *novercal* way. *Derham.*

Nought. *n. s.* [ne auht, not any thing, Saxon; as therefore we write *aught* not *ought* for *any thing*, we should, according to analogy, write *naught* not *nought*, for *nothing*; but a custom has irreversibly prevailed of using *naught* for *bad*, and *nought* for *nothing*.]

1. Not any thing; nothing.

In young Rinaldo fierce desires he spy'd,
And noble heart, of rest impatient,
To wealth or sovereign power he *nought* apply'd. *Fairfax.*

Who cannot see this palpable device?
Yet who so bold, but says he sees it not?
Bad is the world, and it will come to *nought*,
When such ill dealings must be seen in thought. *Shakes.*

Such smiling rogues as these sooth ev'ry passion;
Renege, affirm, and turn their halcyon beaks
With ev'ry gale and vary of their masters,
As knowing *nought*, like dogs, but following. *Shakes.*

Ye are of nothing, and your werk of *nought*. *Is.* xli. 24.

Be frustrate all ye stratagems of hell,
And devilish machinations come to *nought*. *Par. Reg.*

2. To set at *nought*; not to value; to slight; to scorn; to disregard.

Ye have set at *nought* all my counsel, and would none of my reproof. *Prov.* i. 25.

NO'VICE. *n. s.* [*novice*, French; *novitius*, Latin.]

1. One not acquainted with any thing; a fresh-man; one in the rudiments of any knowledge.

Triple-twin'd whore! 'tis thou
Hast sold me to this *novice*. *Shakesp. Ant. and Cleopat.*

Brave plantagenet,
That princely *novice* was struck dead by thee. *Shakesp.*

Bring me to the sight of Isabella,
A *novice* of this place. *Shakes. Measure for Meas.*

You are *novices*; 'tis a world to see
How tame, when men and women are alone,
A meacock wretch can make the curstest shrew. *Shakes.*

We have *novices* and apprentices, that the succession of the former employed men do not fail. *Bacon.*

If any unexperienced young *novice* happens into the fatal neighbourhood of such pests, presently they are plying his full purse and his empty pate. *South's Sermons.*

I am young, a *novice* in the trade,
The fool of love, unpractis'd to persuade;
And want the soothing arts that catch the fair,
But caught myself lie struggling in the snare.
And she I love, or laughs at all my pain,
Or knows her worth too well, and pays me with disdain. *Dry.*

In these experiments I have set down such circumstances by which either the phenomenon might be rendered more conspicuous, or a *novice* might more easily try them, or by which I did try them only. *Newt. Opt.*

2. One who has entered a religious house, but not yet taken the vow.

NO'VITIATE. *n. s.* [*noviciat*, French.]

1. The state of a novice; the time in which the rudiments are learned.

This is so great a masterpiece in sin, that he must have passed his tyrocinium or *novitiate* in sinning, before he come to this, be he never so quick a proficient. *South's Sermons.*

2. The time spent in a religious house, by way of trial, before the vow is taken.

NO'VITY. *n. s.* [*novitas*, Latin.] Newness; novelty.

Some conceive she might not yet be certain, that only man was privileged with speech, and being in the *novity* of the creation and unexperience of all things, might not be affrighted to hear a serpent speak. *Brown's V. Err.*

NOUL. The crown of the head. See NOLL. *Spenser.*

NOULD. Ne would; would not. *Spenser.*

NOUN. *n. s.* [*nom*, French; *nomen*, Latin.] The name of any thing in grammar.

A *noun* is the name of a thing, whether substance, mode or relation, which in speech is used to signify the same when there is occasion to affirm or deny any thing about it, or to express any relation it has in discourse to any other thing. *Clarke's Lat. Grammar.*

Thou hast men about thee, that usually talk of a *noun* and a verb, and such abominable words as no christian ear can endure to hear. *Shakespeare's Henry* VI.

The boy, who scarce has paid his entrance down,
To his proud pedant, or declin'd a *noun*. *Dryden.*

To NOU'RISH. *v. a.* [*nourrir*, French; *nutrio*, Latin.]

1. To encrease or support by food, or aliment of any kind.

He planteth an ash, and the rain doth *nourish* it. *Is.* xliv. 14.

Thro' her *nourish'd* powers enlarg'd by thee,
She springs aloft. *Thomson's Summer.*

2. To support; to maintain.

Whilst I in Ireland *nourish* a mighty band,
I will stir up in England some black storm. *Shakespeare.*

Pharaoh's daughter took him up, and *nourished* him for her own son. *Acts* vii. 21.

3. To encourage; to foment.

What madness was it with such proofs to *nourish* their contentions, when there were such effectual means to end all controversy? *Hooker, b.* ii. *s.* 7.

In soothing them, we *nourish* 'gainst our senate
The cockle of rebellion. *Shakes.*

Gorgias hired soldiers, and *nourished* war continually with the Jews. 2 *Mac.* x. 14.

4. To train, or educate.

Thou shalt be a good minister of Jesus Christ, *nourished* up in the words of faith. 1 *Tim.* iv. 6.

I travel not, neither do I *nourish* up young men, nor bring up virgins. *Is.* xxiii. 4.

5. To promote growth or strength, as food.

In vegetables there is one part more nourishing than another; as grains and roots *nourish* more than their leaves. *Bacon's Nat. Hist.* N°. 45.

To NOU'RISH. *v. n.* To gain nourishment. Unusual.

Fruit trees grow full of moss, which is caused partly by the coldness of the ground, whereby the parts *nourish* less. *Bacon's Natural History*, N°. 544.

NOU'RISHABLE. *adj.* [from *nourish*.] Susceptive of nourishment.

The chyle is mixed herewith, partly for its better conversion into blood, and partly for its more ready adhesion to all the *nourishable* parts. *Grew's Cosmol. b.* i. *c.* 5.

NOU'RISHER. *n. s.* [from *nourish*.] The person or thing that nourishes.

Sleep, chief *nourisher* in life's feast. *Shakespeare.*

A restorer of thy life, and a *nourisher* of thine old age. *Ruth* iv. 15.

Milk warm from the cow is a great *nourisher*, and a good remedy in consumptions. *Bacon's Nat. History.*

Bran and swine's dung laid up together to rot, is a very great *nourisher* and comforter to a fruit tree. *Bacon.*

Please to taste
These bounties, which our *nourisher* hath caus'd
The earth to yield. *Milton's Paradise Lost, b.* v.

NOU'RISHMENT. *n. s.* [*nourissement*, French.]

1. That which is given or received, in order to the support or encrease of growth or strength; food; sustenance; nutriment.

When the *nourishment* grows unfit to be assimilated, or the central heat grows too feeble to assimilate it, the motion ends in confusion, putrefaction, and death. *Newt. Opt.*

2. Nutrition; support of strength.

By temperance taught,
In what thou eat'st and drink'st; seeking from thence
Due *nourishment*, no gluttonous delight. *Milt. Par. Lost.*

3. Sustentation; supply of things needful.

He instructeth them, that as in the one place they use to refresh their bodies, so they may in the other learn to seek the *nourishment* of their souls. *Hooker, b.* v.

NO'URSLING. *n. s.* The nurse; the nursling. *Spenser.*

NOU'RITURE. *n. s.* [*nourriture*, French: this was afterwards contracted to *nurture*.] Education; institution.

Thither the great magician Merlin came,
As was his use, oftimes to visit me;
For he had charge my discipline to frame,
And tutors *nouriture* to oversee. *Fairy Queen, b.* i.

To NOU'SEL. *v. a.* [The same I believe with nuzzel, and both, in their original import, corrupted from *nursle*.] To nurse up.

Bald friars and knavish shavelings sought to *nousel* the common people in ignorance, lest being once acquainted with the truth of things, they would in time smell out the untruth of their packed pelf and masspenny religion. *Spens.*

To NOU'SEL. *v. a.* [*nuzzle*, *noozle*, *noose*.] To entrap; ensnare; as in a noose or trap. They nuzzle hogs to prevent their digging.

NOW. *adv.* [*nu*, Sax. *nun*, Germ.]

1. At this time; at the time present.

Thy servants trade hath been about cattle, from our youth even until *now*. *Gen.* xlvi. 34.

The Lord shall raise him up a king over Israel that day: but what? even*now*. 1 *Kings* xiv. 14.

Refer all the actions of this short and dying life to that state which will shortly begin, but never have an end; and this will approve itself to be wisdom at last, whatever the world judge of it *now*. *Tillotson.*

Now that languages abound with words standing for such combinations, an usual way of getting these complex ideas, is by the explication of those terms that stand for them. *Locke.*

2. A little while ago.

Now the blood of twenty thousand men
Did triumph in my face, and they are fled. *Shakes.*

How frail our passions!
They that but *now* for honour and for plate,
Made the sea blush, with blood resign their hate. *Waller.*

3. At one time or respect; at another time.

Now high, *now* low, *now* master up, *now* miss. *Pope.*

4. It is sometimes a particle of connection, like the French *or*, and Latin *autem*; as, if this be true, he is guilty; *now* this is true, therefore he is guilty.

Now whatsoever he did or suffered, the end thereof was to

to open the doors of the kingdom of heaven, which our iniquities had shut up. *Hooker, b. v. ſ.* 44.

He ſeeks their hate with greater devotion than they can render it him. *Now* to affect the malice of the people, is as bad as that which he diſlikes, to flatter them. *Shakeſ.*

Then cried they all again, ſaying, not this man but Barabbas; *now* Barabbas was a robber. *St. John.*

Now by theſe numbers he implieth climacterical years. *Bro.*

Pheaſants which are granivorous birds, the young live moſtly upon ants eggs. *Now* birds, being of a hot nature, are very voracious, therefore there had need be an infinite number of inſects produced for their ſuſtenance. *Ray.*

The other great and undoing miſchief which befals men, is by their being miſrepreſented. *Now* by calling evil good, a man is miſrepreſented to others in the way of ſlander and detraction. *South's Sermons.*

Helim bethought himſelf, that the firſt day of the full moon of the month Tizpa, was near at hand. *Now* it is a received tradition among the Perſians, that the ſouls of the royal family, who are in a ſtate of bliſs, do, on the firſt full moon after their deceaſe, paſs through the eaſtern gate of the black palace. *Addiſon's Guardian.*

The praiſe of doing well
Is to the ear, as ointment to the ſmell.
Now if ſome flies, perchance, however ſmall
Into the alabaſter urn ſhould fall,
The odours die. *Prior.*

The only motives that can be imagined of obedience to laws, are either the value and certainty of rewards, or an apprehenſion of juſtice and ſeverity. *Now* neither of theſe, excluſive of the other, is the true principle of our obedience to God. *Rogers, Serm.* 1.

A human body a forming in ſuch a fluid in any imaginable poſture, will never be reconcilable to this hydroſtatical law. There will be always ſomething lighter beneath, and ſomething heavier above. *Now* what can make the heavier particles of bone aſcend above the lighter ones of fleſh, or depreſs theſe below thoſe, againſt the tendency of their own nature. *Bentley's Sermons.*

5. After this; ſince things are ſo, in familiar ſpeech.

How ſhall any man diſtinguiſh *now* betwixt a paraſite and a man of honour, where hypocriſy and intereſt look ſo like duty and affection? *L'Eſtrange.*

6. Now and then; at one time and another uncertainly. This word means, with regard to time, what is meant by *here and there*, with reſpect to place.

Now and then they ground themſelves on human authority, even when they moſt pretend divine. *Hooker, b.* ii. *ſ.* 7.

Now and *then* ſomething of extraordinary, that is any thing of your production, is requiſite to refreſh your character. *Dryden.*

A moſt effectual argument againſt ſpontaneous generation is, that there are no new ſpecies produced, which would *now* and *then* happen, were there any ſuch thing. *Ray.*

He who reſolves to walk by the goſpel rule of forbearing all revenge, will have opportunities every *now* and then to exerciſe his forgiving temper. *Atterbury.*

They *now* and *then* appear in the offices of religion, and avoid ſome ſcandalous enormities. *Rogers, Serm.* 13.

Now. *n. ſ.* Preſent moment.

Nothing is there to come, and nothing paſt,
But an eternal *now* does ever laſt. *Cowley.*
She vaniſh'd, we can ſcarcely ſay ſhe dy'd,
For but a *now* did heav'n and earth divide:
This moment perfect health, the next was death. *Dryden.*
Not leſs ev'n in this deſpicable *now*,
Than when my name fill'd Africk with affrights. *Dryden.*

Nowadays. *adv.* [This word, though common and uſed by the beſt writers, is perhaps barbarous.] In the preſent age.

Not ſo great as it was wont of yore,
It's *nowadays*, ne half ſo ſtraight and ſore. *Hubberd.*
Reaſon and love keep little company together *nowadays.*
Shakeſpeare's Midſummer's N. Dream.

It was a veſtal and a virgin fire, and differed as much from that which paſſes by this name *nowadays*, as the vital heat from the burning of a fever. *South's Sermons.*

Such are thoſe principles, which by reaſon of the bold cavils of perverſe and unreaſonable men, we are *nowadays* put to defend. *Tillotſon, Serm.* 1.

What men of ſpirit *nowadays*,
Come to give ſober judgment of new plays. *Garrick's Ep.*

No'wed. *adj.* [*noué*, French.] Knotted; inwreathed.

Reuben is conceived to bear three barres waved, Judah a lion rampant, Dan a ſerpent *nowed.* *Brown's V. Err.*

Nowes. *n. ſ.* [from *nou*, old French.] The marriage knot. Out of uſe.

Thou ſhalt look round about and ſee
Thouſands of crown'd ſouls throng to be
Themſelves thy crown, ſons of thy *nowes*;
The virgin births with which thy ſpouſe
Made fruitful thy fair ſoul. *Craſhaw.*

No'where. *adv.* [*no* and *where.*] Not in any place.

Some men, of whom we think very reverendly, have in their books and writings *nowhere* mentioned or taught that ſuch things ſhould be in the church. *Hooker, b.* ii.

True pleaſure and perfect freedom are *nowhere* to be found but in the practice of virtue. *Tillotſon, Serm.* 28.

No'wise. *n. ſ.* [*no* and *wiſe*: this is commonly ſpoken and written by ignorant barbarians, *noways.*] Not in any manner or degree.

A power of natural gravitation, without contact or impulſe, can in *nowiſe* be attributed to mere matter. *Bentley.*

NO'XIOUS. *adj.* [*noxius*, Latin.]

1. Hurtful; harmful; baneful; miſchievous; deſtructive; pernicious; unwholſome.

Preparation and correction, is not only by addition of other bodies, but ſeparation of *noxious* parts from their own. *Brown's Vulgar Errours, b.* iv.

Kill *noxious* creatures, where 'tis ſin to ſave,
This only juſt prerogative we have. *Dryden.*
See pale Orion ſheds unwholſome dews,
Ariſe, the pines a *noxious* ſhade diffuſe;
Sharp Boreas blows, and nature feels decay,
Time conquers all, and we muſt time obey. *Pope.*

Too frequent an appearance in places of much reſort, is *noxious* to ſpiritual promotions. *Swift's Miſcell.*

2. Guilty; criminal.

Thoſe who are *noxious* in the eye of the law, are juſtly puniſhed by them to whom the execution of the law is committed. *Bramhall againſt Hobbs.*

No'xiousness. *n. ſ.* [from *noxious.*] Hurtfulneſs; inſalubrity.

The writers of politicks have warned us of the *noxiouſneſs* of this doctrine to all civil governments, which the chriſtian religion is very far from diſturbing. *Hammond.*

No'xiously. *adv.* [from *noxious.*] Hurtfully; pernicioully.

No'zle. *n. ſ.* [from *noſe.*] The noſe; the ſnout; the end.

It is nothing but a paultry old ſconce, with the *nozle* broke off. *Arbuthnot and Pope's Mart. Scrib.*

To Nu'bble. *v. a.* To bruiſe with handy cuffs. *Ainſ.*

Nu'biferous. *adj.* [*nubifer*, Latin.] Bringing clouds. *Dict.*

To Nu'bilate. *v. a.* [*nubilo*, Latin.] To cloud. *Dict.*

Nu'bile. *adj.* [*nubile*, Fr. *nubilis*, Latin.] Marriageable; fit for marriage.

The cowſlip ſmiles, in brighter yellow dreſt,
Than that which veils the *nubile* virgin's breaſt. *Prior.*

Nu'ciferous. *adj.* [*nuces* and *fero*, Latin.] Nutbearing. *Dict.*

NU'CLEUS. *n. ſ.* [Latin.] A kernel; any thing about which matter is gathered or conglobated.

The cruſts are each in all parts nearly of the ſame thickneſs, their figure ſuited to the *nucleus*, and the outer ſurface of the ſtone exactly of the ſame form with that of the *nucleus.* *Woodward on Foſſils.*

Nu'dation. *n. ſ.* [*nudation nudo*, Latin.] The act of making bare or naked.

Nu'dity. *n. ſ.* [*nudité*, Fr. *nudus*, Latin.] Naked parts.

There are no ſuch licences permitted in poetry any more than in painting, to deſign and colour obſcene *nudities.* *Dryd.*

Nu'el. See Newel.

Nuga'city. *n. ſ.* [*nugacis*, Latin.] Futility; trifling talk or behaviour.

Nuga'tion. *n. ſ.* [*nugor*, Latin.] The act or practice of trifling.

The received opinion, that putrefaction is cauſed either by cold, or peregrine and preternatural heat, is but *nugation.* *Bacon's Natural Hiſtory.*

Nu'gatory. *adj.* [*nugatorius*, Latin.] Trifling; futile; inſignificant.

Some great men of the laſt age, before the mechanical philoſophy was revived, were too much addicted to this *nugatory* art: when occult quality, and ſympathy and antipathy were admitted for ſatisfactory explications of things. *Bentley.*

Nui'sance. *n. ſ.* [*nuiſance*, French.]

1. Something noxious or offenſive.

This is the liar's lot, he is accounted a peſt and a *nuiſance*; a perſon marked out for infamy and ſcorn. *South's Serm.*

A wiſe man who does not aſſiſt with his counſels, a rich man with his charity, and a poor man with his labour, are perfect *nuiſances* in a commonwealth. *Swift's Miſcell.*

2. [In law.] Something that incommodes the neighbourhood.

To Null. *v. a.* [*nullus*, Latin.] To annul; to annihilate; to deprive of efficacy or exiſtence.

Thy fair enchanted cup, and warbling charms,
No more on me have power, their force is *null'd.* *Milt.*

Reaſon hath the power of *nulling* or governing all other operations of bodies. *Grew's Coſmol. b.* ii.

Null. *adj.* [*nullus*, Latin.] Void; of no force; ineffectual.

With what impatience muſt the muſe behold
The wife, by her procuring huſband ſold?
For tho' the law makes *null* th' adulterer's deed
Of lands to her, the cuckold may ſucceed. *Dryden.*

The pope's confirmation of the church lands to thoſe who hold them by king Henry's donation, was *null* and fraudulent. *Swift's Miſcell.*

Null. *n. s.* Something of no power, or no meaning. Marks in ciphered writing which stand for nothing, and are inserted only to puzzle, are called *nulls*.

If part of the people be somewhat in the election, you cannot make them *nulls* or ciphers in the privation or translation. *Bacon's War with Spain.*

Nullibi'ety. *n. s.* [from *nullibi*, Latin.] The state of being nowhere.

To Nu'llify. *v. a.* [from *nullus*, Latin.] To annul; to make void.

Nu'llity. *n. s.* [*nullité*, French.]

1. Want of force or efficacy.

It can be no part of my business to overthrow this distinction, and to shew the *nullity* of it; which has been solidly done by most of our polemick writers. *South's Sermons.*

The jurisdiction is opened by the party, in default of justice from the ordinary, as by appeals or *nullities*. *Ayliffe.*

2. Want of existence.

A hard body struck against another hard body, will yield an exteriour sound, in so much as if the percussion be over soft, it may induce a *nullity* of sound; but never an interiour sound. *Bacon's Nat. Hist.*

NUMB. *adj.* [benumen, benumeb, Saxon.]

1. Torpid; deprived in a great measure of the power of motion and sensation; chill; motionless.

Like a stony statue, cold and *numb*. *Shakespeare.*

Leaning long upon any part maketh it *numb* and asleep; for that the compression of the part suffereth not the spirits to have free access; and therefore when we come out of it, we feel a stinging or pricking, which is the re-entrance of the spirits. *Bacon's Nat. Hist.*

2. Producing chillness; benumbing.

When we both lay in the field,
Frozen almost to death, how he did lap me
Ev'n in his garments, and did give himself
All thin and naked to the *numb* cold night. *Shakes.*

To Numb. *v. a.* To make torpid; to make dull of motion or sensation; to deaden; to stupify.

Bedlam beggars, with roaring voices
Strike in their *numb'd* and mortify'd bare arms,
Pins, wooden pricks, nails, sprigs of rosemary;
And with this horrible object, from low farms,
Inforce their charity. *Shakes. K. Lear.*

She can unlock
The clasping charm, and thaw the *numbing* spell. *Milt.*

Plough naked, swain, and naked sow the land,
For lazy winter *numbs* the lab'ring hand. *Dryden.*

Nought shall avail
The pleasing song, or well repeated tale,
When the quick spirits their warm march forbear,
And *numbing* coldness has unbrac'd the ear. *Prior.*

The fool *numbs* me like the torpor. *Bolingb. to Swift.*

Nu'mbedness. *n. s.* [from *numbed.*] Torpor; interruption of sensation.

If the nerve be quite divided, the pain is little, only a kind of stupor or *numbedness*. *Wiseman's Surgery.*

To NU'MBER. *v. a.* [*nombrer*, French; *numero*, Latin.]

1. To count; to tell; to reckon how many.

If a man can *number* the dust of the earth, then shall thy seed also be *numbered*. *Gen.* xiii. 16.

Number them by their armies. *Numbers* i. 3.

I will *number* you to the sword. *Is.* lxv. 12.

The gold, the vest, the tripods *number'd* o'er,
All these he found. *Pope's Odyssey, b.* 13.

2. To reckon as one of the same kind.

He was *numbered* with the transgressors, and bare the sin of many. *Is.* liii. 12.

Nu'mber. *n. s.* [*nombre*, French; *numerus*, Latin.]

1. The species of quantity by which it is computed how many.

Hye thee, from this slaughter-house,
Lest thou increase the *number* of the dead. *Sha. Rich.* III.

The silver, the gold, and the vessels, were weighed by *number* and by weight. *Ezra* viii. 34.

Thou shalt take a few in *number*, and bind them in thy skirts. *Ezek.* v. 3.

There is but one gate for strangers to enter at, that it may be known what *numbers* of them are in the town. *Addison.*

2. Any particular aggregate of units, as *even* or *odd*.

This is the third time; I hope good luck lies in odd *numbers*: they say there is divinity in odd *numbers*, either in nativity, chance, or death. *Shakesp. M. W. of Wind.*

3. Many; more than one.

Much of that we are to speak may seem to a *number* perhaps tedious, perhaps obscure, dark, and intricate. *Hooker.*

Water lilly hath a root in the ground; and so have a *number* of other herbs that grow in ponds. *Bacon.*

Ladies are always of great use to the party they espouse, and never fail to win over *numbers*. *Addison.*

4. Multitude that may be counted.

Of him came nations and tribes out of *number*. 2 *Esd.* iii. 7.

Loud as from numbers without *number*. *Milton.*

5. Comparative multitude.

Number itself importeth not much in armies, where the people are of weak courage: for, as Virgil says, it never troubles a wolf how many the sheep be. *Bacon.*

6. Aggregated multitude.

If you will, some few of you shall see the place; and then you may send for your sick, and the rest of your *number*, which ye will bring on land. *Bacon's N. Atlantis.*

7. Harmony; proportions calculated by *number*.

They, as they move
Their starry dance in *numbers* that compute
Days, months, and years, tow'rds his all-chearing lamp,
Turn swift. *Milton.*

8. Verses; poetry.

Should the muses bid my *numbers* roll
Strong as their charms. *Pope.*

9. [In grammar.]

In the noun is the variation or change of termination to signify a *number* more than one. When men first invented names, their application was to single things; but soon finding it necessary to speak of several things of the same kind together, they found it likewise necessary to vary or alter the noun. *Clark's Lat. Grammar.*

How many *numbers* is in nouns? —
— Two. *Shakesp. Merry W. of Windsor.*

Nu'mberer. *n. s.* [from *number.*] He who numbers.

Nu'mberless. *adj.* [from *number.*] Innumerable; more than can be reckoned.

I forgive all;
There cannot be those *numberless* offences
'Gainst me. *Shakespeare.*

About his chariot *numberless* were pour'd
Cherub and seraph. *Milton's Paradise Lost.*

Deserts so great,
Though *numberless*, I never shall forget. *Denham.*

The soul converses with *numberless* beings of her own creation. *Addison's Spectator*, Nº. 488.

Travels he then a hundred leagues,
And suffers *numberless* fatigues. *Swift's Miscell.*

Nu'mbles. *n. s.* [*nombles*, Fr.] The entrails of a deer. *Bailey.*

Nu'mbness. *n. s.* [from *numb.*] Torpor; interruption of action or sensation; deadness; stupefaction.

Stir, nay, come away;
Bequeath to death your *numbness*; for from him
Dear life redeems you. *Shakes. Winter's Tale.*

'Till length of years
And sedentary *numbness* craze my limbs
To a contemptible old age obscure. *Milt. Agon.*

Cold *numbness* strait bereaves
Her corps of sense, and th' air her soul receives. *Denham.*

Silence is worse than the fiercest and loudest accusations; since it may proceed from a kind of *numbness* or stupidity of conscience, and an absolute dominion obtained by sin over the soul, so that it shall not so much as dare to complain, or make a stir. *South's Sermons.*

Nu'merable. *adj.* [*numerabilis*, Latin.] Capable to be numbered.

Nu'meral. *adj.* [*numeral*, Fr. from *numerus*, Latin.] Relating to number; consisting of number.

Some who cannot retain the several combinations of numbers in their distinct orders, and the dependance of so long a train of *numeral* progressions, are not able all their life time regularly to go over any moderate series of numbers. *Locke.*

Nu'merally. *adv.* [from *numeral.*] According to number.

The blasts and undulary breaths thereof, maintain no certainty in their course; nor are they *numerally* fear'd by navigators. *Brown's Vulgar Errours, b.* vii.

Nu'merary. *adj.* [*numerus*, Lat.] Any thing belonging to a certain number.

A supernumerary canon, when he obtains a prebend, becomes a *numerary* canon. *Ayliffe's Parergon.*

Numera'tion. *n. s.* [*numeration*, Fr. *numeratio*, Latin.]

1. The art of numbering.

Numeration is but still the adding of one unite more, and giving to the whole a new name or sign, whereby to know it from those before and after. *Locke.*

2. Number contained.

In the legs or organs of progression in animals, we may observe an equality of length, and parity of *numeration*. *Brown.*

3. The rule of arithmetick which teaches the notation of numbers, and method of reading numbers regularly noted.

NUMERA'TOR. n. s. [Latin.]

1. He that numbers.

2. [*Numerateur*, Fr.] That number which serves as the common measure to others.

Nume'rical. *adj.* [from *numerus*, Latin.]

1. Numeral; denoting number; pertaining to numbers.

The *numerical* characters are helps to the memory, to record and retain the several ideas about which the demonstration is made. *Locke.*

2. The same not only in kind or species, but number.

Contemplate upon his astonishing works, particularly in the resurrection and reparation of the same *numerical* body, by a re-union of all the scattered parts. *South.*

NUME'RICALLY. *adv.* [from *numerical.*] Respecting sameness in number.

I must think it improbable, that the sulphur of antimony would be but *numerically* different from the distilled butter or oil of roses. *Boyle.*

NU'MERIST. *n. s.* [from *numerus*, Latin.] One that deals in numbers.

We cannot assign a respective fatality unto each which is concordant unto the doctrine of the *numerists.* *Brown.*

NUMERO'SITY. *n. s.* [from *numerosus*, Latin.]

1. Number; the state of being numerous.

Of assertion if *numerosity* of asserters were a sufficient demonstration, we might sit down herein as an unquestionable truth. *Brown's V. Errours.*

2. Harmony; numerous flow.

N'UMEROUS. *adj.* [*numerosus*, Latin.]

1. Containing many; consisting of many; not few; many.

Queen Elizabeth was not so much observed for having a *numerous*, as a wise council. *Bacon.*

We reach our foes,
Who now appear so *numerous* and bold. *Waller.*

2. Harmonious; consisting of parts rightly numbered; melodious; musical.

Thy heart, no ruder than the rugged stone,
I might, like Orpheus, with my *num'rous* moan
Melt to compassion. *Waller.*

His verses are so *numerous*, so various, and so harmonious, that only Virgil, whom he professedly imitated, has surpassed him. *Dryden.*

NU'MEROUSNESS. *n. s.* [from *numerous.*]

1. The quality of being numerous.

2. Harmony; musicalness.

That which will distinguish his style is, the *numerousness* of his verse. There is nothing so delicately turned in all the Roman language. *Dryden.*

NU'MMARY. *adj.* [from *nummus*, Latin.] Relating to money.

The money drachma in process of time decreased; but all the while the ponderal drachma continued the same, just as our ponderal libra remains as it was, though the *nummary* hath much decreased. *Arbuthnot on Coins.*

NU'MMULAR. *adj.* [*nummularius*, Latin.] Relating to money. *Dict.*

NU'MSKULL. *n. s.* [Probably from *numb*, dull, torpid, insensible, and *skull.*]

1. A dullard; a dunce; a dolt; a blockhead.

Or toes and fingers, in this case,
Of *Numskulls* self should take the place. *Prior.*

2. The head. In burlesque.

They have talked like *numskulls.* *Arb. and Pope.*

NU'MSKULLED. *adj.* [from *numskull.*] Dull; stupid; doltish.

Hocus has saved that clod-pated, *numskulled*, ninnyhammer of yours from ruin, and all his family. *J. Bull.*

NUN. *n. s.* A woman dedicated to the severer duties of religion, secluded in a cloister from the world, and debarred by a vow from the converse of men.

My daughters
Shall be praying *nuns*, not weeping queens. *Shakesp.*

The most blooming toast in the island might have been a *nun.* *Addison's Freeholder*, N°. 4.

Ev'ry shepherd was undone,
To see her cloister'd like a *nun.* *Swift's Miscell.*

NUN. *n. s.* A kind of bird. *Ainsworth.*

NU'NCIATURE. *n. s.* [from *nuncio*, Latin.] The office of a nuncio.

NU'NCIO. n. s. [Italian, from *nuncio*, Latin.]

1. A messenger; one that brings tidings.

She will attend it better in thy youth
Than in a *nuncio* of more grave aspect. *Shakespeare.*

They honoured the *nuncios* of the spring; and we find the Rhodians had a solemn song to welcome in the swallow. *Bro.*

2. A kind of spiritual envoy from the pope.

This man was honoured with the character of *nuncio* to the Venetians. *Atterbury.*

NU'NCHION. *n. s.* A piece of victuals eaten between meals.

Laying by their swords and trunchions,
They took their breakfasts or their *nunchions.* *Hud.*

NUNCUPA'TIVE. } *adj.* [*nuncupatus*, Lat. *nuncupatif*, Fr.]
NUNCUPA'TORY. } Publickly or solemnly declaratory; verbally pronounced.

NU'NDINAL. } *adj.* [*nundinal*, Fr. from *nundinæ*, Lat.] Be-
NU'NDINARY. } longing to fairs. *Dict.*

NU'NNERY. *n. s.* [from *nun.*] A house of nuns; of women under a vow of chastity, dedicated to the severer duties of religion.

I put your sister into a *nunnery*, with a strict command not to see you, for fear you should have wrought upon her to have taken the habit. *Dryden's Spanish Friar.*

NU'PTIAL. *adj.* [*nuptial*, French; *nuptialis*, Latin.] Pertaining to marriage; constituting marriage; used or done in marriage.

Confirm that amity
With *nuptial* knot, if thou vouchsafe to grant
Bona to England's king. *Shakesp.*

Because propagation of families proceedeth from the *nuptial* copulation, I desired to know of him what laws and customs they had concerning marriage. *Bacon.*

Then all in heat
They light the *nuptial* torch. *Milton's Paradise Lost.*

Whoever will partake of God's secrets, must first pare off whatsoever is amiss, and not eat of this sacrifice with a defiled head, nor come to this feast without a *nuptial* garment. *Taylor.*

Fir'd with her love, and with ambition led,
The neighb'ring princes court her *nuptial* bed. *Dryden.*

Let our eternal peace be seal'd by this,
With the first ardour of a *nuptial* kiss. *Dryd. Aurengzebe.*

NU'PTIALS. *n. s.* like the Latin without singular. [*nuptiæ*, Lat.] Marriage.

This is the triumph of the nuptial day,
My better *nuptials*, which in spite of fate,
For ever join me to my dear Morat. *Dryd. Aurengz.*

2. It is in Shakespeare singular, but contrarily to use.

Lift up your countenance, as 'twere the day
Of celebration of that *nuptial*, which
We two have sworn shall come. *Shakes. W. Tale.*

NURSE. *n. s.* [*nourrice*, French.]

1. A woman that has the care of another's child.

Unnatural curiosity has taught all women, but the beggar, to find out *nurses*, which necessity only ought to commend. *Raleigh's History of the World.*

2. A woman that has care of a sick person.

Never master had,
A page so kind, so duteous, diligent,
So feat, so *nurse*-like. *Shakesp. Cymbeline.*

One Mrs. Quickly, which is in the manner of his *nurse*, or his dry *nurse* or his cook. *Shakes. M. W. of Wind.*

3. One who breeds, educates, or protects.

Rome, the *nurse* of judgment,
Invited by your noble self, hath sent
One general tongue unto us. *Shakes. Henry* VIII.

We must lose
The country, our dear *nurse*, or else thy person,
Our comfort in the country. *Shakesp. Coriolanus.*

4. An old woman in contempt.

Can tales more senseless, ludicrous, and vain,
By winter-fires old *nurses* entertain? *Blackmore.*

5. The state of being nursed.

Can wedlock know so great a curse,
As putting husbands out to *nurse*? *Cleaveland.*

6. In composition, any thing that supplies food.

Put into your breeding pond three melters for one spawner; but if into a *nurse* pond or feeding pond, then no care is to be taken. *Walton's Angler.*

To NURSE. *v. a.* [from the noun, or by contraction from *nourish*; *nourrir*, Fr.]

1. To bring up a child not one's own.

Shall I call a nurse of the Hebrew women, that she may *nurse* the child? *Ex.* ii. 7.

2. To bring up any thing young.

I was *nursed* in swaddling cloaths with cares. *Wisd.* vii. 7.

Him in Egerian groves Aricia bore,
And *nurs'd* his youth along the marshy shore. *Dryden.*

3. To feed; to keep; to maintain.

Thy daughters shall be *nursed* at thy side. *Is.* lx. 4.

The Niseans in their dark abode,
Nurs'd secretly with milk the thriving God. *Addison.*

4. To tend the sick.

5. To pamper; to foment; to encourage; to soften; to cherish.

And what is strength, but an effect of youth, which if time *nurse*, how can it ever cease? *Davies.*

By what fate has vice so thriven amongst us, and by what hands been *nurs'd* up into so uncontrouled a dominion? *Locke on Education.*

Our monarchs were acknowledged here,
That they their churches *nursing* fathers were. *Denham.*

NU'RSER. *n. s.* [from *nurse.*]

1. One that nurses.

See where he lies, inhersed in the arms
Of the most bloody *nurser* of his harms. *Shakesp.*

2. A promoter; a fomenter.

NU'RSERY. *n. s.* [from *nurse.*]

1. The act or office of nursing.

I lov'd her most, and thought to set my rest
On her kind *nursery.* *Shakespeare's K. Lear.*

2. That which is the object of a nurse's care.

She went forth among her fruits and flow'rs,
To visit how they prosper'd, bud and bloom
Her *nursery*: they at her coming sprung,
And touch'd by her fair tendance gladlier grew. *Milton.*

3. A plantation of young trees to be transplanted to other grounds.

Your *nursery* of stocks ought to be in a more barren ground than the ground is whereunto you remove them. *Bacon.*

My

My paper is a kind of *nursery* for authors, and some who have made a good figure here, will hereafter flourish under their own names. *Addison's Guard.*

4. Place where young children are nursed and brought up.

I' th' swathing cloaths, the other from their *nursery*
Were stol'n. *Shakespeare's Cymbeline.*

You see before you the spectacle of a Plantagenet, who hath been carried from the *nursery* to the sanctuary, from the sanctuary to the direful prison, from the prison to the hand of the cruel tormentor, and from that hand to the wide wilderness; for so the world hath been to me. *Bacon.*

Forthwith the devil did appear,
Not in the shape in which he plies
At miss's elbow when she lies;
Or stands before the *nurs'ry* doors,
To take the naughty boy that roars. *Prior.*

They have public *nurseries*, where all parents are obliged to send their infants to be educated. *Gull. Trav.*

5. The place or state where any thing is fostered or brought up, from a *nursery* of children, or whence any thing is to be removed from a *nursery* of trees.

This keeping of cows is of itself a very idle life, and a fit *nursery* for a thief. *Spenser on Ireland.*

To see fair Padua, *nursery* of arts,
I am arriv'd from fruitful Lombardy. *Shakespeare.*

A luxurious court is the *nursery* of diseases; it breeds them, it encourages, nourishes, and entertains them. *L'Estrange.*

A *nursery* erects its head,
Where queens are form'd and future heroes bred;
Where unfledg'd actors learn to laugh and cry. *Dryden.*

NU'RSLING. *n. s.* [from *nurse.*] One nursed up; a fondling.

Then was she held in sovereign dignity,
And made the *nursling* of nobility. *Spenser.*

I was his *nursling* once, and choice delight,
His destin'd from the womb. *Milt. Agonistes.*

In their tender nonage, while they spread
Their springing leaves and lift their infant head,
Indulge their childhood, and the *nursling* spare. *Dryden.*

NU'RTURE. *n. s.* [contracted from *nourriture*, French.]

1. Food; diet.

For this did th' angel twice descend?
Ordain'd thy *nurture* holy, as of a plant
Select and sacred. *Milton's Agonistes.*

2. Education; institution. Little used.

She should take order for bringing up of wards in good *nurture*, not suffer them to come into bad hands. *Spenser.*

The thorny point
Of bare distress, hath ta'en from me the shew
Of smooth civility; yet am I inland bred,
And know some *nurture.* *Shakes. As you like it.*

To NU'RTURE. *v. a.* [from the noun.]

1. To educate; to train; to bring up.

Thou broughtest it up with thy righteousness, and *nurturedst* it in thy law, and reformedst it with thy judgment. *2 Esdr.* viii. 12.

He was *nurtured* where he had been born in his first rudiments, till the years of ten. *Wotton.*

When an insolent despiser of discipline, *nurtured* into impudence, shall appear before a church governour, severity and resolution are that governour's virtues. *South.*

2. To *nurture up*; to bring by care and food to maturity.

They suppose mother earth to be a great animal, and to have *nurtured up* her young offspring with a conscious tenderness. *Bentley's Serm.*

To NU'STLE. *v. a.* To fondle; to cherish. Corrupted from *nursle.* *Ains.*

NUT. *n. s.* [hnut, Saxon; *noot*, Dutch; *noix*, Fr.]

1. The fruit of certain trees; it consists of a kernel covered by a hard shell. If the shell and kernel are in the center of a pulpy fruit, they then make not a nut but a stone.

One chanc'd to find a *nut*
In the end of which a hole was cut,
Which lay upon a hazel-root,
There scatter'd by a squirrel;
Which out the kernel gotten had;
When quoth this Fay, dear queen be glad,
Let Oberon be ne'er so mad,
I'll set you safe from peril. *Drayt. Nymphid.*

Nuts are hard of digestion, yet possess some good medicinal qualities. *Arbuthnot ou Aliments.*

2. A small body with teeth, which correspond with the teeth of wheels.

The force of this faculty may be more conveniently used by the multiplication of several wheels, together with *nuts* belonging unto each, that are used for the roasting of meat. *Wilkin's Mathem. Magick.*

Clocks and jacks, though the screws and teeth of the wheels and *nuts* be never so smooth, yet if they be not oiled, will hardly move. *Ray on the Creation.*

NU'TBROWN. *adj.* [*nut* and *brown.*] Brown like a nut kept long.

Young and old come forth to play,
Till the live-long daylight fail,
Then to the spicy *nutbrown* ale. *Milton's Poems.*

When this *nutbrown* sword was out,
With stomach huge he laid about. *Hudibras, p.* i.

Two milk-white kids run frisking by her side,
For which the *nutbrown* lass, Erithacis,
Full often offer'd many a savoury kiss. *Dryden.*

King Hardicnute, midst Danes and Saxons stout,
Carous'd in *nutbrown* ale, and din'd on grout. *King.*

NU'TCRACKERS. *n. s.* [*nut* and *crack.*] An instrument used to enclose nuts and break them by pressure.

He cast every human feature out of his countenance, and became a pair of *nutcrackers.* *Addison's Spectator.*

NU'TGALL. *n. s.* [*nut* and *gall.*] Excrescence of an oak.

In vegetable excretions, maggots terminate in flies of constant shapes, as in the *nutgalls* of the outlandish oak. *Brown.*

NU'THATCH.
NU'TJOBBER. } *n. s.* A bird. *Ains.*
NU'TPECKER.

NU'THOOK. *n. s.* [*nut* and *hook.*] A stick with a hook at the end to pull down boughs that the nuts may be gathered.

Nuthook, Nuthook, you lie. *Shakesp. Henry* IV.

NU'TMEG. *n. s.* [*nut* and *muguet*, French.]

The *nutmeg* is a kernel of a large fruit not unlike the peach, and separated from that and from its investient coat, the mace before it is sent over to us; except that the whole fruit is sometimes sent over in preserve, by way of sweet-meat or as a curiosity. The *nutmeg* is of a roundish or oval figure, of a compact or firm texture, and its surface furrowed: it is of an extremely agreeable smell and an aromatick taste. There are two kinds of *nutmeg*; the male which is long and cylindrical, but it has less of the fine aromatick flavour than the female, which is of the shape of an olive. The Dutch import the *nutmegs* and mace from the East-Indies, and supply all Europe with them. The tree which produces them is not unlike our pear-tree in its manner of growth: its leaves, whether green or dried, have, when bruised, a very fragrant smell; and the trunk or branches, cut or broken off, yield a red liquor like blood. This tree is carefully cultivated. But that which produces the male *nutmeg* grows wild in the mountainous parts of the Moluccas. *Nutmeg* is much used in our foods, and is of excellent virtues as a medicine. *Hill.*

The second a dry and flosculous coat, commonly called mace; the fourth a kernel included in the shell, which lieth under the mace, is the same we call *nutmeg.* *Brown's V. Err.*

I to my pleasant gardens went,
Where *nutmegs* breathe a fragrant scent. *Sandys.*

NU'TSHELL. *n. s.* [*nut* and *shell.*] The hard substance that incloses the kernel of the nut.

I could be bounded in a *nutshell*, and count myself a king of infinite space. *Shakespeare's Hamlet.*

A fox had me by the back, and a thousand pound to a *nutshell*, I had never got off again. *L'Estrange.*

It seems as easy to me, to have the idea of space empty of body, as to think of the hollow of a *nutshell* without a kernel. *Locke.*

NU'TTREE. *n. s.* [*nut* and *tree.*] A tree that bears nuts; ahazle.

Of trees you shall have the *nuttree* and the oak. *Peacham.*

Like beating *nuttrees*, makes a larger crop. *Dryden.*

NUTRICA'TION. *n. s.* [*nutricatio*, Lat.] Manner of feeding or being fed.

Besides the teeth, the tongue of this animal is a second argument to overthrow this airy *nutrication.* *Brown.*

NU'TRIMENT. *n. s.* [*nutrimentum*, Latin.] That which feeds or nourishes; food; aliment.

This slave
Has my lord's meat in him,
Why should it thrive and turn to *nutriment?* *Shakesp.*

The stomach returns what it has received, in strength and *nutriment*, diffused into all the parts of the body. *South.*

Does not the body thrive and grow,
By food of twenty years ago?
And is not virtue in mankind,
The *nutriment* that feeds the mind? *Swift's Miscell.*

NUTRIME'NTAL. *adj.* [from *nutriment.*] Having the qualities of food; alimental.

By virtue of this oil vegetables are *nutrimental*, for this oil is extracted by animal digestion as an emulsion. *Arb.*

NUTRI'TION. *n. s.* [from *nutritio*, *nutrio*, Lat. *nutrition*, Fr.] The act or quality of nourishing, supporting strength, or encreasing growth.

New parts are added to our substance to supply our continual decayings; nor can we give a certain account how the aliment is so prepared for *nutrition*, or by what mechanism it is so regularly distributed. *Glanv. Sceps. c.* iii.

The obstruction of the glands of the mesentery is a great impediment to *nutrition*; for the lymph in those glands is a necessary constituent of the aliment before it mixeth with the blood. *Arbuthnot on Aliments.*

Fix'd like a plant on his peculiar spot,
To draw *nutrition*, propagate, and rot. *Pope.*

NUTRI'TIOUS. *adj.* [from *nutrio*, Latin.] Having the quality of nourishing.

O may'st thou often see
Thy furrows whiten'd by the woolly rain
Nutritious! secret nitre lurks within. *Philips.*

The heat equal to incubation is only *nutritious*; and the *nutritious* juice itself resembles the white of an egg in all its qualities. *Arbuthnot on Aliments.*

NU'TRITIVE. *adj.* [from *nutrio*, Latin.] Nourishing; nutrimental; alimental.

NU'TRITURE. *n. s.* [from *nutrio*, Latin.] The power of nourishing.

Never make a meal of flesh alone, have some other meat with it of less *nutriture*. *Harvey on Consump.*

To NU'ZZLE. *v. a.* [This word, in its original signification, seems corrupted from *nursle*; but when its original meaning was forgotten, writers supposed it to come from *nozzle* or *nose*, and in that sense used it.]

1. To nurse; to foster.

Old men long *nuzzled* in corruption, scorning them that would seek reformation. *Sidney.*

2. To go with the nose down like a hog.

He charged through an army of lawyers, sometimes with sword in hand, at other times *nuzzling* like an eel in the mud. *Arbuthnot's John Bull.*

Sir Roger shook his ears, and *nuzzled* along, well satisfied that he was doing a charitable work. *Arb. J. Bull.*

The blessed benefit, not there confin'd,
Drops to the third, who *nuzzles* close behind. *Pope.*

NYMPH. *n. s.* [νύμφη; *nympha*, Lat.]

1. A goddess of the woods, meadows, or waters.

And as the moisture which the thirsty earth
Sucks from the sea, to fill her empty veins,
From out her womb at last doth take a birth,
And runs a *nymph* along the grassy plains. *Davies.*

2. A lady. In poetry.

This resolve no mortal dame,
None but those eyes cou'd have o'erthrown;
The *nymph* I dare not, need not name. *Waller.*

NYS. [A corruption of *ne is.*] None is; not is. Obsolete.

Thou findest fault, where *nys* to be found,
And buildest strong work upon a weak ground. *Spenser.*

O.

O Has in English a long found; as, *drone*, *groan*, *ſtone*, *alone*, *cloke*, *broke*, *coal*, *droll*; or ſhort, *got*, *knot*, *ſhot*, *prong*, *long*. It is uſually denoted long by a ſervile *a* ſubjoined; as, *moan*, or by *e* at the end of the ſyllable; as, *bone:* when theſe vowels are not appended, it is generally ſhort, except before *ll*; as, *droll*, *ſcroll*, and even then ſometimes ſhort; as, *loll*.

1. O is uſed as an interjection of wiſhing or exclamation.

O that we, who have reſiſted all the deſigns of his love, would now try to defeat that of his anger! *Decay of Piety.*

O! were he preſent, that his eyes and hands
Might ſee, and urge, the death which he commands. *Dryd.*

2. O is uſed with no great elegance by *Shakeſpeare* for a circle or oval.

Can this cockpit hold
The vaſty field of France? or may we cram
Within this wooden *O*, the very caſks
That did affright the air at Agincourt? *Shakeſp.*

OAF. *n. ſ.* [This word is variouſly written; *auff*, *ofe*, and *oph*; it ſeems a corruption of *ouph*, a demon or fairy, in German *alf*, from which *elf:* and means properly the ſame with *changeling*; a fooliſh child left by malevolent *ouphs* or *fairies*, in the place of one more witty, which they ſteal away.]

1. A changeling; a fooliſh child left by the fairies.

Theſe, when a child haps to be got,
Which after proves an idiot,
When folk perceives it thriveth not,
The fault therein to ſmother:
Some ſilly doating brainleſs calf,
That underſtands things by the half,
Says that the fairy left this *oaf*,
And took away the other. *Drayt. Nymphid.*

2. A dolt; a blockhead; an idiot.

OA'FISH. *adj.* [from *oaf*.] Stupid; dull; doltiſh.

OA'FISHNESS. *n. ſ.* [from *oafiſh*.] Stupidity; dullneſs.

OAK. *n. ſ.* [ac, æc, Saxon; which, ſays *Skinner*, to ſhew how eaſy it is to play the fool, under a ſhew of literature and deep reſearches, I will, for the diverſion of my reader, derive from οἶκος, a houſe; the oak being the beſt timber for building. *Skinner* ſeems to have had *Junius* in his thoughts, who on this very word has ſhewn his uſual fondneſs for Greek etymology, by a derivation more ridiculous than that by which *Skinner* has ridiculed him. *Ac* or *oak*, ſays the grave critick, ſignified among the Saxons, like *robur* among the Latins, not only an *oak* but *ſtrength*, and may be well enough derived, *non incommode deduci poteſt*, from ἀλκὴ, ſtrength; by taking the three firſt letters and then ſinking the λ, as is not uncommon.]

The *oak*-tree hath male flowers, or katkins, which conſiſt of a great number of ſmall ſlender threads. The embryos, which produced at remote diſtances from theſe on the ſame tree, do afterwards become acorns, which are produced in hard ſcaly cups: the leaves are ſinuated. The ſpecies are five. *Miller.*

He return'd with his brows bound with *oak*. *Shakeſp.*

He lay along
Under an *oak*, whoſe antique root peeps out
Upon the brook that brawls along this wood. *Shakeſp.*

No tree beareth ſo many baſtard fruits as the *oak:* for beſides the acorns, it beareth galls, *oak* apples, *oak* nuts, which are inflammable, and *oak* berries, ſticking cloſe to the body of the tree without ſtalk. *Bacon's Nat. Hiſtory.*

The monarch *oak*, the patriarch of the trees,
Shoots riſing up and ſpreads by ſlow degrees:
Three centuries he grows, and three he ſtays
Supreme in ſtate; and in three more decays. *Dry.*

An *oak* growing from a plant to a great tree, and then lopped, is ſtill the ſame *oak*. *Locke.*

A light earthy, ſtony, and ſparry matter, incruſted and affixed to *oak* leaves. *Woodward on Foſſ.*

In the days of Homer every grove, river, fountain, and *oak* tree, were thought to have their peculiar deities. *Odyſſ.*

Let India boaſt her plants, nor envy we
The weeping amber and the balmy tree,
While by our *oaks* the precious loads are born,
And realms commanded which thoſe trees adorn. *Pope.*

OAK. [*Evergreen.*]

The leaves are, for the moſt part, indented, or ſinuated, and in ſome the edges of the leaves are prickly, and are evergreen: it hath amentaceous flowers, which are produced at remote diſtances from the fruit on the ſame tree: the fruit is an acorn like the common *oak*. The wood of this tree is accounted very good for many ſorts of tools and utenſils; and affords the moſt durable charcoal in the world. *Miller.*

OAKA'PPLE. *n. ſ.* [*oak* and *apple*.] A kind of ſpongy excreſcence on the oak.

Another kind of excreſcence is an exudation of plants joined with putrefaction, as in *oakapples*, which are found chiefly upon the leaves of oaks. *Bacon's Nat. Hiſt.*

OA'KEN. *adj.* [from *oak*.] Made of oak; gathered from oak.

No nation doth equal England for *oaken* timber wherewith to build ſhips. *Bacon's Advice to Villiers.*

By lot from Jove I am the pow'r
Of this fair wood, and live in *oaken* bow'r. *Milton.*

Clad in white velvet all their troop they led,
With each an *oaken* chaplet on his head. *Dryden.*

An *oaken* garland to be worn on feſtivals, was the recompenſe of one who had covered a citizen in battle. *Addiſon.*

He ſnatched a good tough *oaken* cudgel, and began to brandiſh it. *Arbuthnot's J. Bull.*

OA'KENPIN. *n. ſ.* An apple.

Oakenpin, ſo called from its hardneſs, is a laſting fruit, yields excellent liquor, and is near the nature of the Weſtbury apple, though not in form. *Mortimer.*

OA'KUM. *n. ſ.* [A word probably formed by ſome corruption.] Cords untwiſted and reduced to hemp, with which, mingled with pitch, leaks are ſtopped.

They make their *oakum*, wherewith they chalk the ſeams of the ſhips, of old ſeer and weather beaten ropes, when they are over ſpent and grown ſo rotten as they ſerve for no other uſe but to make rotten *oakum*, which moulders and waſhes away with every ſea as the ſhips labour and are toſſed. *Ral.*

Some drive old *oakum* thro' each ſeam and rift;
Their left hand does the calking-iron guide;
The rattling mallet with the right they lift. *Dryden.*

OAR. *n. ſ.* [ape, Saxon; perhaps by alluſion to the common expreſſion of plowing the water, from the ſame root with *ear*, to plow, *aro*, Lat.] A long pole with a broad end, by which veſſels are driven in the water, the reſiſtance made by water to the oar puſhing on the veſſel.

Th' *oars* were ſilver,
Which to the tune of flutes kept ſtroke, and made
The water which they beat, to follow faſter,
As amorous of their ſtrokes. *Shakeſp. Jul. Cæſar.*

So tow'rds a ſhip the *oar-finn'd* gallies ply,
Which wanting ſea to ride, or wind to fly,
Stands but to fall reveng'd. *Denham's Poems.*

In ſhipping ſuch as this, the Iriſh kern
And untaught Indian, on the ſtream did glide,
E'er ſharp-keel'd boats to ſtem the flood did learn,
Or fin-like *oars* did ſpread from either ſide. *Dryden.*

Its progreſſive motion may be effected by the help of ſeveral *oars*, which in the outward ends of them ſhall be like the fins of a fiſh to contract and dilate. *Wilkins.*

To OAR. *v. n.* [from the noun.] To row.

He more undaunted on the ruin rode,
And *oar'd* with labouring arms along the flood. *Pope.*

To OAR. *v. a.* To impel by rowing.

His bold head
'Bove the contentious waves he kept, and *oar'd*
Himſelf with his good arms in luſty ſtrokes
To th' ſhore. *Shakeſpeare's Tempeſt.*

Oa'ry. *adj.* [from *oar.*] Having the form or uſe of oars.
His hair transforms to down, his fingers meet,
In ſkinny films, and ſhape his *oary* feet. *Addiſon.*
The ſwan with arched neck,
Between her white wings mantling, proudly rows
Her ſtate with *oary* feet. *Milton.*

Oast. *n. ſ.* A kiln. Not in uſe.
Empty the binn into a hog-bag, and carry them immediately to the *oaſt* or kiln, to be dried. *Mortimer.*

Oatca'ke. *n. ſ.* [*oat* and *cake.*] Cake made of the meal of oats.
Take a blue ſtone they make haver or *oatcakes* upon, and lay it upon the croſs bars of iron. *Peacham.*

Oa'ten. *adj.* [from *oat.*] Made of oats; bearing oats.
When ſhepherds pipe on *oaten* ſtraws,
And merry larks are ploughmens clocks. *Shakeſp.*

OATH. *n. ſ.* [*aith*, Gothick; að, Saxon. The diſtance between the noun *oath*, and the verb *ſwear*, is very obſervable, as it may ſhew that our oldeſt dialect is formed from different languages.] An affirmation, negation, or promiſe, corroborated by the atteſtation of the Divine Being.
Read over Julia's heart, thy firſt beſt love,
For whoſe dear ſake thou then did'ſt rend thy faith
Into a thouſand *oaths*; and all thoſe *oaths*
Deſcended into perjury to love me. *Shakeſpeare.*
He that ſtrikes the firſt ſtroke, I'll run him up to the hilts as I am a ſoldier.
—An *oath* of mickle might; and fury ſhall abate. *Sha.*
We have conſultations, which inventions ſhall be publiſhed, which not: and take an *oath* of ſecrecy for the concealing of thoſe which we think fit to keep ſecret. *Bacon.*
Thoſe called to any office of truſt, are bound by an *oath* to the faithful diſcharge of it: but an *oath* is an appeal to God, and therefore can have no influence, except upon thoſe who believe that he is. *Swift.*

Oa'thable. *adj.* [from *oath.* A word not uſed.] Capable of having an oath adminiſtered.
You're not *oathable*,
Altho' I know you'll ſwear
Into ſtrong ſhudders th' immortal gods. *Shakeſpeare.*

Oathbrea'king. *n. ſ.* [*oath* and *break.*] Perjury; the violation of an oath.
His *oathbreaking* he mended thus,
By now forſwearing that he is forſworn. *Shak. Hen.* IV.

Oa'tmalt. *n. ſ.* [*oat* and *malt.*] Malt made of oats.
In Kent they brew with one half *oatmalt*, and the other half barleymalt. *Mortimer's Huſb.*

Oa'tmeal. *n. ſ.* [*oat* and *meal.*] Flower made by grinding oats.
Oatmeal and butter, outwardly applied, dry the ſcab on the head. *Arbuthnot on Aliment.*
Our neighbours tell me oft, in joking talk,
Of aſhes, leather, *oatmeal*, bran, and chalk. *Gay.*

Oa'tmeal. *n. ſ.* An herb. *Ainſworth.*

Oats. *n. ſ.* [aten, Saxon.] A grain, which in England is generally given to horſes, but in Scotland ſupports the people.
It is of the graſs leaved tribe; the flowers have no petals, and are diſpoſed in a looſe panicle: the grain is eatable. The meal makes tolerable good bread. *Miller.*
The *oats* have eaten the horſes. *Shakeſpeare.*
It is bare mechaniſm, no otherwiſe produced than the turning of a wild *oatbeard*, by the inſinuation of the particles of moiſture. *Locke.*
For your lean cattle, fodder them with barley ſtraw firſt, and the *oat* ſtraw laſt. *Mortimer's Huſbandry.*
His horſe's allowance of *oats* and beans, was greater than the journey required. *Swift.*

Oa'tthistle. *n. ſ.* [*oat* and *thiſtle.*] An herb. *Ainſ.*

Obambula'tion. *n. ſ.* [*obambulatio*, from *obambulo*, Latin.] The act of walking about. *Dict.*

To Obdu'ce. *v. a.* [*obduco*, Latin.] To draw over as a covering.
No animal exhibits its face in the native colour of its ſkin but man; all others are covered with feathers, hair, or a cortex that is *obduced* over the cutis. *Hale.*

Obduc'tion. *n. ſ.* [from *obductio*, *obduco*, Latin.] The act of covering, or laying a cover.

Obdu'racy. *n. ſ.* [from *obdurate.*] Inflexible wickedneſs; impenitence; hardneſs of heart.
Thou think'ſt me as far in the Devil's book, as thou and Falſtaff, for *obduracy* and perſiſtency. *Shakeſpeare's Henry* IV.
God may, by a mighty grace, hinder the abſolute completion of ſin in final *obduracy*. *South's Serm.*

OBDU'RATE. *adj.* [*obduratus*, Latin.]
1. Hard of heart; inflexibly obſtinate in ill; hardned; impenitent.
Oh! let me teach thee for thy father's ſake,
That gave thee life, when well he might have ſlain thee;
Be not *obdurate*, open thy deaf ears. *Shakeſpeare.*
If when you make your pray'rs,
God ſhould be ſo *obdurate* as yourſelves,
How would it fare with your departed ſouls? *Shakeſp.*
Women are ſoft, mild, pitiful, and flexible;
Thou ſtern, *obdurate*, flinty, rough, remorſeleſs. *Shakeſp.*
To convince the proud what ſigns avail,
Or wonders move th' *obdurate* to relent;
They harden'd more, by what might more reclaim. *Milt.*
Obdurate as you are, oh! hear at leaſt
My dying prayers, and grant my laſt requeſt. *Dryden.*
2. Hardned; firm; ſtubborn.
Sometimes the very cuſtom of evil makes the heart *obdurate* againſt whatſoever inſtructions to the contrary. *Hooker.*
A pleaſing ſorcery could charm
Pain for a while, or anguiſh, and excite
Fallacious hope, or arm th' *obdurate* breaſt
With ſtubborn patience, as with triple ſteel. *Milton.*
No ſuch thought ever ſtrikes his marble, *obdurate* heart, but it preſently flies off and rebounds from it. It is impoſſible for a man to be thorough-paced in ingratitude, till he has ſhook off all fetters of pity and compaſſion. *South.*
3. Harſh; rugged.
They joined the moſt *obdurate* conſonants without one intervening vowel. *Swift.*

Obdu'rately. *adv.* [from *obdurate.*] Stubbornly; inflexibly; impenitently.

Obdu'rateness. *n. ſ.* [from *obdurate.*] Stubbornneſs; inflexibility; impenitence.

Obdura'tion. *n. ſ.* [from *obdurate.*] Hardneſs of heart; ſtubbornneſs.
What occaſion it had given them to think, to their greater *obduration* in evil, that through a froward and wanton deſire of innovation, we did conſtrainedly thoſe things, for which conſcience was pretended? *Hooker, b.* iv.

Obdu'red. *adj.* [*obduratus*, Latin.] Hardned; inflexible; impenitent.
This ſaw his hapleſs foes, but ſtood *obdur'd*,
And to rebellious fight rallied their pow'rs
Inſenſate. *Milton's Paradiſe Loſt, b.* vi.

Obe'dience. *n. ſ.* [*obedience*, Fr. *obedientia*, Latin.] Obſequiouſneſs; ſubmiſſion to authority; compliance with command or prohibition.
If you violently proceed againſt him, it would ſhake in pieces the heart of his *obedience*. *Shakeſpeare's K. Lear.*
Thy huſband
Craves no other tribute at thy hands,
But love, fair looks, and true *obedience*. *Shakeſp.*
His ſervants ye are, to whom ye obey, whether of ſin unto death, or of *obedience* unto righteouſneſs. *Rom.* vi. 16.
It was both a ſtrange commiſſion, and a ſtrange *obedience* to a commiſſion, for men ſo furiouſly aſſailed, to hold their hands. *Bacon's War with Spain.*
Nor can this be,
But by fulfilling that which thou didſt want,
Obedience to the law of God, impos'd
On penalty of death. *Milton's Paradiſe Loſt, b.* xii.

OBE'DIENT. *adj.* [*obediens*, Latin.] Submiſſive to authority; compliant with command or prohibition; obſequious.
To this end did I write, that I might know the proof of you, whether ye be *obedient* in all things. 2 *Cor.* ii. 9.
To this her mother's plot
She, ſeemingly *obedient*, likewiſe hath
Made promiſe. *Shakeſp. M. W. of Wind.*
He humbled himſelf, and became *obedient* unto death. *Phil.* ii. 8.
Religion hath a good influence upon the people, to make them *obedient* to government, and peaceable one towards another. *Tillotſon, Serm.* 3.
The chief his orders gives; th' *obedient* band,
With due obſervance, wait the chief's command. *Pope.*

Obe'diential. *adj.* [*obedientiel*, Fr. from *obedient.*] According to the rule of obedience.
Faith is ſuch as God will accept of, when it affords fiducial reliance on the promiſes, and *obediential* ſubmiſſion to the command. *Hammond.*
Faith is then perfect, when it produces in us a fiduciary aſſent to whatever the goſpel has revealed, and an *obediential* ſubmiſſion to the commands. *Wake's Prep. for Death.*

Obe'diently. *adv.* [from *obedient.*] With obedience.
We ſhould behave ourſelves reverently and *obediently* towards the Divine Majeſty, and juſtly and charitably towards men. *Tillotſon.*

Obe'isance. *n. ſ.* [*obeiſance*, Fr. This word is formed by corruption from *abaiſance*, an act of reverence.] A bow; a courteſy; an act of reverence made by inclination of the body or knee.
Bartholomew my page,
See dreſt in all ſuits like a lady;
Then call him Madam, do him all *obeiſance*. *Shakeſpeare.*
Bathſheba bowed and did *obeiſance* unto the king. 1 *K.* i. 16.

The lords and ladies paid
Their homage, with a low *obeiſance* made;
And ſeem'd to venerate the ſacred ſhade. *Dryden.*

O'BELISK. *n. ſ.* [*obeliſcus*, Latin.]

1. A magnificent high piece of ſolid marble, or other fine ſtone, having uſually four faces, and leſſening upwards by degrees, till it ends in a point like a pyramid. *Harris.*

Between the ſtatues *obeliſks* were plac'd,
And the learn'd walls with hieroglyphicks grac'd. *Pope.*

2. A mark of cenſure in the margin of a book, in the form of a dagger [†].

He publiſhed the tranſlation of the Septuagint, having compared it with the Hebrew, and noted by aſteriſks what was defective, and by *obeliſks* what redundant. *Grew.*

OBEQUITA'TION. *n. ſ.* [from *obequito*, Latin.] The act of riding about.

OBERRA'TION. *n. ſ.* [from *oberro*, Latin.] The act of wandering about.

OBE'SE. *adj.* [*obeſus*, Latin.] Fat; loaden with fleſh.

OBE'SENESS. } *n. ſ.* [from *obeſe.*] Morbid fatneſs; incumbrance of fleſh.
OBE'SITY. }

On theſe many diſeaſes depend; as on the ſtraitneſs of the cheſt, a phthiſis; on the largeneſs of the veins, an atrophy; on their ſmallneſs, *obeſity*. *Grew's Coſmol. b.* ii.

To OBE'Y. *v. a.* [*obeïr*, French; *obedio*, Latin.]

1. To pay ſubmiſſion to; to comply with, from reverence to authority.

The will of heav'n
Be done in this and all things! I *obey*. *Shakeſ. Hen.* VIII.

I am aſham'd, that women are ſo ſimple
To ſeek for rule, ſupremacy, and ſway,
When they are bound to ſerve, love, and *obey*. *Shakeſp.*

Let not ſin reign in your mortal body, that ye ſhould *obey* it in the luſts thereof. *Rom.* vi. 12.

Was ſhe thy God, that her thou didſt *obey*,
Before his voice? *Milton's Paradiſe Loſt, b.* x.

Africk and India ſhall his pow'r *obey*,
He ſhall extend his propagated ſway
Beyond the ſolar year, without the ſtarry way. *Dryden.*

2. It had formerly ſometimes *to* before the perſon obeyed, which *Addiſon* has mentioned as one of *Milton's* latiniſms; but it is frequent in old writers; when we borrowed the French word we borrowed the ſyntax, *obeir au roi.*

He commanded the trumpets to ſound; *to* which the two brave knights *obeying*, they performed their courſes, breaking their ſtaves. *Sidney.*

The flit bark, *obeying to* her mind,
Forth launched quickly, as ſhe did deſire. *Fairy Q.*

His ſervants ye are, *to* whom ye *obey*. *Rom.* vi. 16.

Nor did they not perceive the evil plight
In which they were, or the fierce pains not feel,
Yet *to* their general's voice they ſoon *obey'd*. *Milton.*

O'BJECT. *n. ſ.* [*objet*, Fr. *objectum*, Latin.]

1. That about which any power or faculty is employed.

Pardon
The flat unrais'd ſpirit, that hath dar'd,
On this unworthy ſcaffold to bring forth
So great an *object*. *Shakeſpeare's Henry* V.

They are her fartheſt reaching inſtrument,
Yet they no beams unto their *objects* ſend;
But all the rays are from their *objects* ſent,
And in the eyes with pointed angles end. *Davies.*

The *object* of true faith is, either God himſelf, or the word of God: God who is believed in, and the word of God as the rule of faith, or matter to be believed. *Hamm.*

Thoſe things in ourſelves, are the only proper *objects* of our zeal, which, in others, are the unqueſtionable ſubjects of our praiſes. *Sprat's Serm.*

Truth is the *object* of our underſtanding, as good is of the will. *Dryden's Dufreſnoy.*

2. Something preſented to the ſenſes to raiſe any affection or emotion in the mind.

Diſhonour not your eye
By throwing it on any other *object*. *Shakeſp.*

Why elſe this double *object* in our ſight,
Of flight purſu'd in the air, and o'er the ground. *Milton.*

This paſſenger felt ſome degree of concern, at the ſight of ſo moving an *object*, and therefore withdrew. *Atterbury.*

3. [In grammar.] Any thing influenced by ſomewhat elſe.

The accuſative after a verb tranſitive, or a ſentence in room thereof, is called, by grammarians, the *object* of the verb. *Clarke's Latin Grammar.*

OBJE'CTGLASS. *n. ſ.* Glaſs remoteſt from the eye.

An *objectglaſs* of a teleſcope I once mended, by grinding it on pitch with putty, and leaning eaſily on it in the grinding, leſt the putty ſhould ſcratch it. *Newt. Opt.*

To O'BJECT. *v. a.* [*objecter*, Fr. *objicio*, *objectum*, Latin.]

1. To oppoſe; to preſent in oppoſition.

Flowers growing ſcattered in divers beds, will ſhew more ſo as that they be *object* to view at once. *Bacon.*

Pallas to their eyes
The miſt *objected*, and condens'd the ſkies. *Pope.*

2. To propoſe as a charge criminal; or a reaſon adverſe: with *to* or *againſt.*

Were it not ſome kind of blemiſh to be like unto Infidels and Heathens, it would not ſo uſually be *objected*; men would not think it any advantage in the cauſe of religion to be able therewith juſtly to charge their adverſaries. *Hooker.*

The book requireth due examination, and giveth liberty to *object* any crime againſt any ſuch as are to be ordered. *Whitgifte.*

Men in all deliberations find eaſe to be of the negative ſide, and affect a credit to *object* and foretel difficulties: for when propoſitions are denied, there is an end of them; but if they be allowed, it requireth a new work; which falſe point of wiſdom is the bane of buſineſs. *Bacon.*

This the adverſaries of faith have too much reaſon to *object againſt* too many of its profeſſors; but *againſt* the faith itſelf nothing at all. *Sprat's Serm.*

It was *objected againſt* a late painter, that he drew many graceful pictures, but few of them were like. *Dryden.*

Others *object* the poverty of the nation, and difficulties in furniſhing greater ſupplies. *Addiſon's State of the War.*

There was but this ſingle fault that Eraſmus, though an enemy, could *object to* him. *Atterbury.*

OBJE'CTION. *n. ſ.* [*objection*, Fr. *objectio*, Latin.]

1. The act of preſenting any thing in oppoſition.

2. Criminal charge.

Speak on, Sir,
I dare your worſt *objections*. *Shakeſp. Henry* VIII.

3. Adverſe argument.

There is ever between all eſtates a ſecret war. I know well this ſpeech is the *objection* and not the deciſion; and that it is after refuted. *Bacon's War with Spain.*

Whoſoever makes ſuch *objections* againſt an hypotheſis, hath a right to be heard, let his temper and genius be what it will. *Burnet's Theory of the Earth.*

4. Fault found.

I have ſhewn your verſes to ſome, who have made that *objection* to them. *Walſh's Let.*

O'BJECTIVE. *adj.* [*objectif*, Fr. *objectus*, Latin.]

1. Belonging to the object; contained in the object.

Certainty, according to the ſchools, is diſtinguiſhed into *objective* and ſubjective. *Objective* certainty is when the propoſition is certainly true in itſelf; and ſubjective, when we are certain of the truth of it. The one is in things, the other in our minds. *Watts's Logick.*

2. Made an object; propoſed as an object.

If this one ſmall piece of nature ſtill affords new matter for our diſcovery, when ſhould we be able to ſearch out the vaſt treaſuries of *objective* knowledge that lies within the compaſs of the univerſe? *Hale's Origin of Man.*

O'BJECTIVELY. *adv.* [from *objective.*]

1. In manner of an object.

This may fitly be called a determinate idea, when, ſuch as it is at any time *objectively* in the mind, it is annexed, and without variation determined to an articulate ſound, which is to be ſteadily the ſign of that very ſame object of the mind. *Locke's Epiſtle to the Reader.*

2. In a ſtate of oppoſition.

The baſiliſk ſhould be deſtroyed, in regard he firſt receiveth the rays of his antipathy and venomous emiſſion, which *objectively* move his ſenſe. *Brown's V. Err.*

O'BJECTIVENESS. *n. ſ.* [from *objective.*] The ſtate of being an object.

Is there ſuch a motion or *objectiveneſs* of external bodies, which produceth light? The faculty of light is fitted to receive that impreſſion or *objectiveneſs*, and that *objectiveneſs* fitted to that faculty. *Hale's Origin of Mankind.*

OBJE'CTOR. *n. ſ.* [from *object.*] One who offers objections; one who raiſes difficulties.

But theſe *objectors* muſt the cauſe upbraid,
That has not mortal man, immortal made. *Blackm.*

Let the *objectors* conſider, that theſe irregularities muſt have come from the laws of mechaniſm. *Bentley's Serm.*

OBIT. [a corruption of *obiit*, or *obivit.*] Funeral obſequies. *Ainſ.*

To OBJU'RGATE. *v. a.* [*objurgo*, Latin.] To chide; to reprove.

OBJURGA'TION. *n. ſ.* [*objurgatio*, Lat.] Reproof; reprehenſion.

If there be no true liberty, but all things come to paſs by inevitable neceſſity, then what are all interrogations and *objurgations*, and reprehenſions and expoſtulations? *Bramh.*

OBJU'RGATORY. *adj.* [*objurgatorius*, Latin.] Reprehenſory; culpatory; chiding.

OBLA'TE. *adj.* [*oblatus*, Latin.] Flatted at the poles. Uſed of a ſpheroid.

By gravitation bodies on this globe will preſs towards its center, though not exactly thither, by reaſon of the *oblate* ſpheroidical

ſpheroidical figure of the earth, ariſing from its diurnal rotation about its axis. *Cheyne's Phil. Prin.*

OBLA'TION. *n. ſ.* [*oblation*, Fr. *oblatus*, Latin.] An offering; a ſacrifice; any thing offered as an act of worſhip or reverence.

With that ſhe looked upon the picture before her, and ſtraight ſighed, and ſtraight tears followed, as if the idol of duty ought to be honoured with ſuch *oblations*. *Sidney.*

Many conceive in this *oblation*, not a natural but a civil kind of death, and a ſeparation from the world. *Brown.*

The will gives worth to the *oblation*, as to God's acceptance, ſets the pooreſt giver upon the ſame level with the richeſt. *South's Sermons.*

I wiſh
The kind *oblation* of a falling tear. *Dryden.*

Behold the coward, and the brave,
All make *oblations* at this ſhrine. *Swift's Poems.*

OBLECTA'TION. *n. ſ.* [*oblectatio*, Lat.] Delight; pleaſure.

To O'BLIGATE. *v. a.* [*obligo*, Latin.] To bind by contract or duty.

OBLIGA'TION. *n. ſ.* [*obligatio*, from *obligo*, Lat. *obligation*, Fr.]

1. The binding power of any oath, vow, duty; contract.

Your father loſt a father;
That father his; and the ſurvivor bound
In filial *obligation*, for ſome term,
To do obſequious ſorrow. *Shakeſpeare's Hamlet.*

There was no means for him as a chriſtian, to ſatisfy all *obligations* both to God and man, but to offer himſelf for a mediator of an accord and peace. *Bacon's Henry VII.*

The better to ſatisfy this double *obligation*, you have early cultivated the genius you have to arms. *Dryden.*

No ties can bind, that from conſtraint ariſe,
Where either's forc'd, all *obligation* dies. *Granvile.*

2. An act which binds any man to ſome performance.

The heir of an obliged perſon is not bound to make reſtitution, if the *obligation* paſſed only by a perſonal act; but if it paſſed from his perſon to his eſtate, then the eſtate paſſes with all its burthen. *Taylor's Rule of Living Holy.*

3. Favour by which one is bound to gratitude.

Where is the *obligation* of any man's making me a preſent of what he does not care for himſelf? *L'Eſtrange.*

So quick a ſenſe did the Iſraelites entertain of the merits of Gideon, and the *obligation* he had laid upon them, that they tender him the regal and hereditary government of that people. *South's Sermons.*

O'BLIGATORY. *adj.* [*obligatione*, Fr. from *obligate.*] Impoſing an obligation; binding; coercive; with *to* or *on.*

And concerning the lawfulneſs, not only permiſſively, but whether it be not *obligatory to* Chriſtian princes and ſtates. *Bac.*

As long as the law is *obligatory*, ſo long our obedience is due. *Taylor's Rule of Living Holy.*

A people long uſed to hardſhips, look upon themſelves as creatures at mercy, and that all impoſitions laid on them by a ſtronger hand, are legal and *obligatory*. *Swift.*

If this patent is *obligatory on* them, it is contrary to acts of parliament, and therefore void. *Swift.*

To OBLI'GE. *v. a.* [*obliger*, Fr. *obligo*, Latin.]

1. To bind; to impoſe obligation; to compel to ſomething.

Religion *obliges* men to the practice of thoſe virtues which conduce to the preſervation of our health. *Tillotſon.*

The law muſt *oblige* in all precepts, or in none. If it *oblige* in all, all are to be obeyed; if it *oblige* in none, it has no longer the authority of a law. *Rogers, Serm.* 15.

2. To indebt; to lay obligations of gratitude.

He that depends upon another, muſt
Oblige his honour with a boundleſs truſt. *Waller.*

Since love *obliges* not, I from this hour
Aſſume the right of man's deſpotic power. *Dryden.*

Vain wretched creature, how art thou miſled,
To think thy wit theſe godlike notions bred!
Theſe truths are not the product of thy mind,
But dropt from heav'n, and of a nobler kind:
Reveal'd religion firſt inform'd thy ſight,
And reaſon ſaw not, till faith ſprung the light.
Thus man by his own ſtrength to heaven wou'd ſoar,
And wou'd not be *oblig'd* to God for more. *Dryden.*

When int'reſt calls off all her ſneaking train,
When all th' *oblig'd* deſert, and all the vain,
She waits or to the ſcaffold or the cell. *Pope.*

To thoſe hills we are *obliged* for all our metals, and with them for all the conveniencies and comforts of life. *Bentley.*

3. To pleaſe; to gratify.

A great man gets more by *obliging* his inferiour, than by diſdaining him; as a man has a greater advantage by ſowing and dreſſing his ground, than he can have by trampling upon it. *South's Sermons.*

Some natures are ſo ſour and ſo ungrateful, that they are never to be *obliged*. *L'Eſtrange.*

Happy the people, who preſerve their honour
By the ſame duties that *oblige* their prince! *Add. Cato.*

OBLI'GEE. *n. ſ.* [from *oblige.*] The perſon bound by a legal or written contract.

OBLI'GEMENT. *n. ſ.* [*obligement*, French.] Obligation.

I will not reſiſt, whatever it is, either of divine or human *obligement*, that you lay upon me. *Milton's Education.*

Let this fair princeſs but one minute ſtay,
A look from her will your *obligements* pay. *Dryden.*

OBLI'GER. *n. ſ.* He who binds by contract.

OBLI'GING. *part. adj.* [*obligeant*, Fr. from *oblige.*] Civil; complaiſant; reſpectful; engaging.

Nothing could be more *obliging* and reſpectful than the lion's letter was, in appearance; but there was death in the true intent. *L'Eſtrange, Fab.* 54.

Monſeigneur Strozzi has many curioſities, and is very *obliging* to a ſtranger who deſires the ſight of them. *Addiſon.*

Obliging creatures! make me ſee
All that diſgrac'd my betters, met in me. *Pope.*

So *obliging* that he ne'er *oblig'd*. *Pope.*

OBLI'GINGLY. *adv.* [from *obliging.*] Civilly; complaiſantly.

Eugenius informs me very *obligingly*, that he never thought he ſhould have diſliked any paſſage in my paper. *Addiſon.*

I ſee her taſte each nauſeous draught,
And ſo *obligingly* am caught;
I bleſs the hand from whence they came,
Nor dare diſtort my face for ſhame. *Swift's Miſcell.*

OBLI'GINGNESS. *n. ſ.* [from *obliging.*]

1. Obligation; force.

They look into them not to weigh the *obligingneſs*, but to quarrel the difficulty of the injunctions: not to direct practice, but excuſe prevarications. *Decay of Piety.*

2. Civility; complaiſance.

OBLIQUA'TION. *n. ſ.* [*obliquatio*, from *obliquo*, Latin.] Declination from perpendicularity; obliquity.

The change made by the *obliquation* of the eyes, is leaſt in colours of the denſeſt than in thin ſubſtances. *Newt. Opt.*

OBLI'QUE. *adj.* [*oblique*, Fr. *obliquus*, Latin.]

1. Not direct; not perpendicular; not parallel.

One by his view
Mought deem him born with ill-diſpos'd ſkies,
When *oblique* Saturn ſat in the houſe of th' agonies. *Fairy Q.*

If ſound be ſtopped and repercuſſed, it cometh about on the other ſide in an *oblique* line. *Bacon's Nat. Hiſt.*

May they not pity us, condemn'd to bear
The various heav'n of an *obliquer* ſphere;
While by fix'd laws, and with a juſt return,
They feel twelve hours that ſhade, for twelve that burn. *Prior.*

Bavaria's ſtars muſt be accus'd which ſhone
That fatal day the mighty work was done,
With rays *oblique* upon the gallic ſun. *Prior.*

It has a direction *oblique* to that of the former motion. *Cheyne's Phil. Prin.*

Criticks form a general character from the obſervation of particular errors, taken in their own *oblique* or imperfect views; which is as unjuſt, as to make a judgment of the beauty of a man's body, from the ſhade it caſts in ſuch and ſuch a poſition. *Notes on the Odyſſey.*

2. Not direct. Uſed of ſenſe.

Has he given the lie
In circle, or *oblique*, or ſemicircle,
Or direct parallel; you muſt challenge him. *Shakeſp.*

3. [In grammar.] Any caſe in nouns except the nominative.

OBLI'QUELY. *adv.* [from *oblique.*]

1. Not directly; not perpendicularly.

Of meridian altitude, it hath but twenty-three degrees, ſo that it plays but *obliquely* upon us, and as the ſun doth about the twenty-third of January. *Brown's Vulgar Err.*

Declining from the noon of day,
The ſun *obliquely* ſhoots his burning ray. *Po. Ra. Locke.*

2. Not in the immediate or direct meaning.

His diſcourſe tends *obliquely* to the detracting from others, or the extolling of himſelf. *Addiſon's Spectator*, Nº. 255.

OBLI'QUENESS. } *n. ſ.* [*olbiquité*, Fr. from *oblique.*]
OBLI'QUITY.

1. Deviation from phyſicial rectitude; deviation from paralleliſm or perpendicularity.

Which elſe to ſeveral ſpheres thou muſt aſcribe,
Mov'd contrary with thwart *obliquities*. *Milt. P. Loſt.*

2. Deviation from moral rectitude.

There is in rectitude, beauty; as contrariwiſe in *obliquity*, deformity. *Hooker, b.* i. *ſ.* 8.

Count Rhodophill cut out for government and high affairs, and balancing all matters in the ſcales of his high underſtanding, hath rectified all *obliquities*. *Howel's Vocal For.*

For a rational creature to conform himſelf to the will of God in all things, carries in it a rational rectitude or goodneſs; and to diſobey or oppoſe his will in any thing, imports a moral *obliquity*. *South's Sermons.*

To OBLI'TERATE. *v. a.* [*oblitero*, *ob* and *litera*, Latin.]

1. To efface any thing written.

2. To wear out; to deſtroy; to efface.

Wars and deſolations *obliterate* many ancient monuments. *Hale's Origin of Mankind.*

Let men conſider themſelves as enſnared in that unhappy contract,

contract, which has rendered them part of the Devil's possession, and contrive how they may *obliterate* that reproach, and disentangle their mortgaged souls. *Decay of Piety.*

These simple ideas, the understanding can no more refuse to have, or alter, or blot them out, than a mirrour can refuse, alter, or *obliterate* the images, which the objects set before it produce. *Locke.*

OBLITERA'TION. *n. s.* [*obliteratio*, Latin.] Effacement; extinction.

Considering the casualties of wars, transmigrations, especially that of the general flood, there might probably be an *obliteration* of all those monuments of antiquity that ages precedent at some time have yielded. *Hale's Origin of Mankind.*

OBLI'VION. *n. s.* [*oblivio*, Latin.]

1. Forgetfulness; cessation of remembrance.

Water-drops have worn the stones of Troy,
And blind *oblivion* swallow'd cities up,
And mighty states characterless are grated
To dusty nothing. *Shakesp. Troil. and Cressida.*

Thou shouldst have heard many things of worthy memory, which now shall die in *oblivion*, and thou return unexperienced to thy grave. *Shakesp. Taming of the Shrew.*

Knowledge is made by *oblivion*, and to purchase a clear and warrantable body of truth, we must forget and part with much we know. *Brown's Vulgar Err. Pref.*

Can they imagine, that God has therefore forgot their sins, because they are not willing to remember them? Or will they measure his pardon by their own *oblivion*. *South.*

Among our crimes *oblivion* may be set;
But 'tis our king's perfection to forget. *Dryden.*

2. Amnesty; general pardon of crimes in a state.

By the act of *oblivion*, all offences against the crown, and all particular trespasses between subject and subject, were pardoned, remitted, and utterly extinguished. *Davies.*

OBLI'VIOUS. *adj.* [*obliviosus*, Latin.] Causing forgetfulness.

Raze out the written troubles of the brain,
And with some sweet *oblivious* antidote
Cleanse the stuff'd bosom. *Shakespeare's Macbeth.*

The British souls
Exult to see the crouding ghosts descend
Unnumber'd; well aveng'd, they quit the cares
Of mortal life, and drink th' *oblivious* lake. *Philips.*

Oh born to see what none can see awake!
Behold the wonders of th' *oblivious* lake. *Pope's Dunc.*

OBLO'NG. *adj.* [*oblong*, Fr. *oblongus*, Latin.] Longer than broad; the same with a rectangle parallelogram, whose sides are unequal. *Harr.*

The best figure of a garden I esteem an *oblong* upon a descent. *Temple's Miscell.*

Every particle, supposing them globular or not very *oblong*, would be above nine million times their own length from any other particle. *Bentley's Sermons.*

OBLO'NGLY. *adv.* [from *oblong*.] In an oblong direction.

The surface of the temperate climates is larger than it would have been, had the globe of our earth or of the planets, been either spherical, or *oblongly* spheroidical. *Cheyne.*

OBLO'NGNESS. *n. s.* [from *oblong*.] The state of being oblong.

O'BLOQUY. *n. s.* [*obloquor*, Lat.]

1. Censorious speech; blame; slander; reproach.

Reasonable moderation hath freed us from being deservedly subject unto that bitter kind of *obloquy*, whereby as the church of Rome doth, under the colour of love towards those things which be harmless, maintain extremely most hurtful corruptions; so we peradventure might be upbraided, that under colour of hatred towards those things that are corrupt, we are on the other side as extreme, even against most harmless ordinances. *Hooker, b. iv. s. 14.*

Here new aspersions, with new *obloquies*,
Are laid on old deserts. *Daniel's Civil War.*

Canst thou with impious *obloquy* condemn
The just decree of God, pronounc'd and sworn? *Milton.*

Shall names that made your city the glory of the earth, be mentioned with *obloquy* and detraction? *Addison.*

Every age might perhaps produce one or two true genius, if they were not sunk under the censure and *obloquy* of plodding, servile, imitating pedants. *Swift.*

2. Cause of reproach; disgrace. Not proper.

My chastity's the jewel of our house,
Bequeathed down from many ancestors;
Which were the greatest *obloquy* i'th' world
In me to lose. *Shakespeare's All's well that ends well.*

OBMUTE'SCENCE. *n. s.* [from *obmutesco*, Latin.] Loss of speech.

A vehement fear often produceth *obmutescence*. *Brown.*

OBNO'XIOUS. *n. s.* [*obnoxius*, Latin.]

1. Subject.

I propound a character of justice in a middle form, between the speculative discourses of philosophers, and the writings of lawyers, which are tied and *obnoxious* to their particular laws. *Bacon's Holy War.*

2. Liable to punishment.

All are *obnoxious*; and this faulty land,
Like fainting Hester, does before you stand,
Watching your sceptre. *Waller.*

We know ourselves *obnoxious* to God's severe justice, and that he is a God of mercy and hateth sin; and therefore that we might not have the least suspicion of his unwillingness to forgive, he hath sent his only begotten son into the world, by his dismal sufferings and cursed death, to expiate our offences. *Calamy's Sermons.*

Thy name, O Varus, if the kinder pow'rs
Preserve our plains, and shield the Mantuan tow'rs,
Obnoxious by Cremona's neighb'ring crime,
The wings of swans, and stronger pinion'd rhyme
Shall raise aloft. *Dryd.*

3. Liable; exposed.

Long hostility had made their friendship weak in itself, and more *obnoxious* to jealousies and distrusts. *Hayward.*

But what will not ambition and revenge
Descend to? who aspires, must down as low
As high he soar'd; *obnoxious* first or last,
To basest things. *Milton's Paradise Lost.*

Beasts lie down,
To dews *obnoxious* on the grassy floor. *Dryden.*

OBNO'XIOUSNESS. *n. s.* [from *obnoxious*.] Subjection; liableness to punishment.

OBNO'XIOUSLY. *adv.* [from *obnoxious*.] In a state of subjection; in the state of one liable to punishment.

To O'BNUBILATE. *v. a.* [*obnubilo*, Latin.] To cloud; to obscure.

O'BOLE. *n. s.* [*obolus*, Lat.] In pharmacy, twelve grains. *Ains.*

OBRE'PTION. *n. s.* [*obreptio*, Latin.] The act of creeping on.

To OBRO'GATE. *v. a.* [*obrogo*, Lat.] To proclaim a contrary law for the dissolution of the former. *Dict.*

OBSCE'NE. *adj.* [*obscene*, Fr. *obscœnus*, Latin.]

1. Immodest; not agreeable to chastity of mind; causing lewd ideas.

Chemos th' *obscene* dread of Moab's sons. *Milton.*

Words that were once chaste, by frequent use grow *obscene* and uncleanly. *Watts's Logick.*

2. Offensive; disgusting.

A girdle foul with grease binds his *obscene* attire. *Dryden.*

Home as they went, the sad discourse renew'd,
Of the relentless dame to death pursu'd,
And of the sight *obscene* so lately view'd. *Dryden.*

3. Inauspicious; ill omined.

Care shuns thy walks, as at the chearful light
The groaning ghosts, and birds *obscene* take flight. *Dryd.*

It is the sun's fate like your's, to be displeasing to owls and *obscene* animals, who cannot bear his lustre. *Pope's Lett.*

OBSCE'NELY. *adj.* [from *obscene*.] In an impure and unchaste manner.

OBSCE'NENESS. } *n. s.* [*obscenité*, Fr. from *obscene*.] Impurity of
OBSCE'NITY. } thought or language; unchastity; lewdness.

Mr. Cowley asserts plainly, that *obscenity* has no place in wit. *Dryden.*

Those fables were tempered with the Italian severity, and free from any note of infamy or *obsceneness*. *Dryden.*

Thou art wickedly devout,
In Tiber ducking thrice by break of day,
To wash th' *obscenities* of night away. *Dryden.*

No pardon vile *obscenity* should find,
Tho' wit and art conspire to move your mind. *Pope.*

OBSCURA'TION. *n. s.* [*obscuratio*, Lat.]

1. The act of darkening.

As to the sun and moon, their *obscuration* or change of colour happens commonly before the eruption of a fiery mountain. *Burnet.*

2. A state of being darkened.

OBSCU'RE. *adj.* [*obscur*, Fr. *obscurus*, Latin.]

1. Dark; unenlightened; gloomy, hindring sight.

Whoso curseth his father or mother, his lamp shall be put out in *obscure* darkness. *Prov. xx. 20.*

Who shall tempt with wand'ring feet
The dark unbottom'd infinite abyss,
And thro' the palpable *obscure* find out
His uncouth way? *Milton's Paradise Lost.*

2. Living in the dark.

The *obscure* bird clamour'd the live-long night. *Shakesp.*

3. Not easily intelligible; abstruse; difficult.

I explain some of the most *obscure* passages, and those which are most necessary to be understood, and this according to the manner wherein he used to express himself. *Dryd.*

4. Not noted; not observable.

He says, that he is an *obscure* person; one, I suppose, that is in the dark. *Atterbury.*

To OBSCU'RE. *v. a.* [*obscuro*, Latin.]

1. To darken; to make dark.

Sudden the thunder blackens all the skies,
And the winds whistle, and the surges roll
Mountains on mountains, and *obscure* the pole. *Pope.*

2. To make less visible.

They are all couched in a pit hard by Herne's oak, with *obscured* lights; which at the very instant of Falstaff's and our meeting, they will at once display to the night. *Shakes.*

What must I hold a candle to my shames?
They in themselves, good sooth, are too, too light.
Why, 'tis an office of discovery, love,
And I should be *obscur'd.* *Shakes. M. of Venice.*

Thinking by this retirement to *obscure* himself from God, he infringed the omnisciency and essential ubiquity of his maker. *Brown's Vulgar Errours.*

3. To make less intelligible.

By private consent it hath been used in dangerous times to *obscure* writing, and make it hard to be read by others not acquainted with the intrigue. *Holder.*

There is scarce any duty which has been so *obscured* by the writings of learned men, as this. *Wake.*

4. To make less glorious, beautiful, or illustrious.

Think'st thou, vain spirit, thy glories are the same,
And seest not sin *obscures* thy godlike frame?
I know thee now by thy ungrateful pride,
That shows me what thy faded looks did hide. *Dryden.*

OBSCU'RELY. *adv.* [from *obscure.*]

1. Not brightly; not luminously.
2. Out of sight; privately; without notice; not conspicuously.

Such was the rise of this prodigious fire,
Which in mean buildings first *obscurely* bred,
From thence did soon to open streets aspire. *Dryden.*

There live retir'd,
Content thyself to be *obscurely* good. *Addison's Cato.*

Let him go, pursued by silent wrath,
Meet unexpected daggers in his way,
And in some distant land *obscurely* die. *Irene.*

3. Not clearly; not plainly.

OBSCU'RENESS. }
OBSCU'RITY. } *n. s.* [*obscuritas*, Lat. *obscurité*, Fr.]

1. Darkness; want of light.

Lo! a day of darkness and *obscurity*, tribulation and anguish, upon the earth. *Esther* xi. 8.

Should Cynthia quit thee, Venus, and each star,
It would not form one thought dark as mine are:
I could lend them *obscureness* now, and say,
Out of myself there should be no more day. *Donne.*

2. Unnoticed state; privacy.

You are not for *obscurity* design'd,
But, like the sun, must cheer all human kind. *Dryd.*

3. Darkness of meaning.

Not to mention that *obscureness* that attends prophetic raptures, there are divers things knowable by the bare light of nature, which yet are so uneasy to be satisfactorily understood by our imperfect intellects, that let them be delivered in the clearest expressions, the notions themselves will yet appear obscure. *Boyle on Colours.*

That this part of sacred scripture had difficulties in it: many causes of *obscurity* did readily occur to me. *Locke.*

What lies beyond our positive idea towards infinity, lies in *obscurity*, and has the undeterminate confusion of a negative idea, wherein I know I do not comprehend all I would, it being too large for a finite capacity. *Locke.*

OBSECRA'TION. *n. s.* [*obsecratio*, from *obsecro*, Lat.] Intreaty; supplication.

That these were comprehended under the sacra, is manifest from the old form of *obsecration.* *Stillingfleet.*

OBSE'QUIES. *n. s.* [*obseques*, French. I know not whether this word be not anciently mistaken for *exequies*, *exequiæ*, Latin: this word, however, is apparently derived from *obsequium.*]

1. Funeral rites; funeral solemnities.

There was Dorilaus valiantly requiting his friends help, in a great battle deprived of life, his *obsequies* being not more solemnized by the tears of his partakers, than the blood of his enemies. *Sidney, b.* ii.

Fair Juliet, that with angels dost remain,
Accept this latest favour at my hand;
That living honour'd thee, and being dead,
With fun'ral *obsequies* adorn thy tomb. *Shakesp.*

These tears are my sweet Rutland's *obsequies.* *Shakesp.*

I spare the widows tears, their woful cries,
And howling at their husbands *obsequies*;
How Theseus at these fun'rals did assist,
And with what gifts the mourning dames dismist. *Dryden.*

His body shall be royally interr'd,
I will, myself,
Be the chief mourner at his *obsequies.* *Dryden.*

Alas! poor Poll, my Indian talker dies,
Go birds and celebrate his *obsequies.* *Creech.*

2. It is found in the singular, perhaps more properly.

Or tune a song of victory to me,
Or to thyself, sing thine own *obsequy.* *Crashaw.*

Him I'll solemnly attend,
With silent *obsequy* and funeral train,
Home to his father's house. *Milton's Agonistes.*

OBSE'QUIOUS. *adj.* [from *obsequium*, Latin.]

1. Obedient; compliant; not resisting.

Adore not so the rising son, that you forget the father, who raised you to this height; nor be you so *obsequious* to the father, that you give just cause to the son to suspect that you neglect him. *Bacon's Advice to Villiers.*

At his command th' up-rooted hills retir'd
Each to his place; they heard his voice, and went
Obsequious. *Milton's Paradise Lost.*

I follow'd her; she what was honour knew,
And with *obsequious* majesty, approv'd
My pleaded reason. *Milton's Paradise Lost, b.* viii.

A genial cherishing heat acts so upon the fit and *obsequious* matter, as to organize and fashion it according to the exigencies of its own nature. *Boyle.*

His servants weeping,
Obsequious to his orders, bear him hither. *Add. Cato.*

The vote of an assembly, which we cannot reconcile to public good, has been conceived in a private brain, afterwards supported by an *obsequious* party. *Swift.*

2. In *Shakespeare* it seems to signify, funereal; such as the rites of funerals require.

Your father lost a father;
That father his; and the surviver bound
In filial obligation, for some term,
To do *obsequious* sorrow. *Shakesp. Hamlet.*

OBSE'QUIOUSLY. *adv.* [from *obsequious.*]

1. Obediently; with compliance.

They rise, and with respectful awe,
At the word giv'n, *obsequiously* withdraw. *Dryden.*

We cannot reasonably expect, that any one should readily and *obsequiously* quit his own opinion, and embrace ours with a blind resignation. *Locke.*

2. In *Shakespeare* it signifies, with funeral rites; with reverence for the dead.

I a while *obsequiously* lament
The untimely fall of virtuous Lancaster. *Shakesp. R.* III.

OBSE'QUIOUSNESS. *n. s.* [from *obsequious.*] Obedience; compliance.

They apply themselves both to his interest and humour, with all the arts of flattery and *obsequiousness*, the surest and the readiest ways to advance a man. *South's Sermons.*

OBSE'RVABLE. *adj.* [from *observo*, Lat.] Remarkable; eminent; such as may deserve notice.

They do bury their dead with *observable* ceremonies. *Abbot.*

These proprieties affixed unto bodies from considerations deduced from east, west, or those *observable* points of the sphere, will not be justified from such foundations. *Brown*

I took a just account of every *observable* circumstance of the earth, stone, metal, or other matter, from the surface quite down to the bottom of the pit, and entered it carefully into a journal. *Woodward's Nat. Hist.*

The great and more *observable* occasions of exercising our courage, occur but seldom. *Rogers.*

OBSE'RVABLY. *adv.* [from *observable.*] In a manner worthy of note.

It is prodigious to have thunder in a clear sky, as is *observably* recorded in some histories. *Brown's Vulgar Err.*

OBSE'RVANCE. *n. s.* [*observance*, Fr. *observo*, Latin.]

1. Respect; ceremonial reverence.

In the wood, a league without the town,
Where I did meet thee once with Helena,
To do *observance* on the morn of May. *Shakespeare.*

Arcite left his bed, resolv'd to pay
Observance to the month of merry May. *Dryden.*

2. Religious rite.

Some represent to themselves the whole of religion as consisting in a few easy *observances*, and never lay the least restraint on the business or diversions of this life. *Rogers.*

3. Attentive practice.

Use all th' *observance* of civility,
Like one well studied in a sad ostent
To please his grandam. *Shakesp. M. of Venice.*

If the divine laws were proposed to our *observance*, with no other motive than the advantages attending it, they would be little more than an advice. *Rogers, Sermon* 1.

4. Rule of practice.

There are other strict *observances*;
As, not to see a woman. *Shakesp. L. Labours Lost.*

5. Careful obedience.

We must attend our creator in all those ordinances which he has prescribed to the *observance* of his church. *Rogers.*

6. Observation; attention.

There can be no observation or experience of greater certainty, as to the increase of mankind, than the strict and vigilant *observance* of the calculations and registers of the bills of births and deaths. *Hale's Origin of Mankind.*

7. Obedient regard.

Having had such experience of his fidelity and *observance* abroad, he found himself engaged in honour to support him. *Wotton.*

Love rigid honesty
And strict *observance* of impartial laws. *Roscommon.*

Obse'rvant. *adj.* [*observans*, Latin.]

1. Attentive; diligent; watchful.

These writers, which gave themselves to follow and imitate others, were *observant* sectators of those masters they admired. *Raleigh's History of the World.*

Wandring from clime to clime *observant* stray'd,
Their manners noted, and their states survey'd. *Pope.*

2. Obedient; respectful.

We are told how *observant* Alexander was of his master Aristotle. *Digby on the Soul, Dedicat.*

3. Respectfully attentive.

She now *observant* of the parting ray,
Eyes the calm sun-set of thy various day. *Pope.*

4. Meanly dutiful; submissive.

How could the most base men attain to honour but by such an *observant* slavish course. *Raleigh.*

Obse'rvant. *n. s.* [This word has the accent on the first syllable in *Shakespeare.*] A slavish attendant. Not in use.

These kind of knaves in this plainness,
Harbour more craft, and more corrupter ends,
Than twenty silky ducking *observants*
That stretch their duties nicely. *Shakesp. K. Lear.*

Observa'tion. *n. s.* [*observatio*, from *observo*, Lat. *observation*, Fr.]

1. The act of observing, noting, or remarking.

These cannot be infused by *observation*, because they are the rules by which men take their first apprehensions and *observations* of things; as the being of the rule must be before its application to the thing directed by it. *South's Serm.*

The rules of our practice are taken from the conduct of such persons as fall within our *observation*. *Rogers.*

2. Notion gained by observing; note; remark; animadversion.

In matters of human prudence, we shall find the greatest advantage by making wise *observations* on our conduct, and of the events attending it. *Watts's Logick.*

Observa'tor. *n. s.* [*observateur*, Fr. from *observo*, Lat.] One that observes; a remarker.

The *observator* of the bills of mortality, hath given us the best account of the number that late plagues have swept away. *Hale's Origin of Mankind.*

She may be handsome, yet be chaste, you say,—
Good *observator*, not so fast away. *Dryden.*

Obse'rvatory. *n. s.* [*observatoire*, French.] A place built for astronomical observations.

Another was found near the *observatory* in Greenwich Park. *Woodward on Fossils.*

To OBSE'RVE. *v. a.* [*observer*, Fr. *observo*, Latin.]

1. To watch; to regard attentively.

Remember, that as thine eye *observes* others, so art thou *observed* by angels and by men. *Taylor.*

2. To find by attention; to note.

If our idea of infinity be got from the power we *observe* in ourselves, of repeating without end our own ideas, it may be demanded why we do not attribute infinity to other ideas, as well as these of space and duration. *Locke.*

One may *observe* them discourse and reason pretty well, of several other things, before they can tell twenty. *Locke.*

3. To regard or keep religiously.

A night to be much *observed* unto the Lord, for bringing them out of Egypt. *Ex.* xii. 42.

4. To obey; to follow.

To Obse'rve. *v. n.*

1. To be attentive.

Observing men may form many judgments by the rules of similitude and proportion, where causes and effects are not entirely the same. *Watts's Logick.*

2. To make a remark.

Wherever I have found her notes to be wholly another's, which is the case in some hundreds, I have barely quoted the true proprietor, without *observing* upon it. *Pope's Lett.*

O'bserver. *n. s.* [from *observe.*]

1. One who looks vigilantly on persons and things; close remaker.

He reads much;
He is a great *observer*; and he looks
Quite thro' the deeds of men. *Shakesp. Jul. Cæsar.*

Angelo,
There is a kind of character in thy life,
That to th' *observer* doth thy history
Fully unfold. *Shakespeare's Measure for Measure.*

Careful *observers* may foretel the hour,
By sure prognostics when to dread a show'r. *Swift.*

2. One who looks on; the beholder.

If a slow pac'd star had stol'n away,
From the *observer*'s marking, he might stay
Three hundred years to see't again. *Donne.*

Company, he thinks, lessens the shame of vice, by sharing it; and therefore, if he cannot wholly avoid the eye of the *observer*, he hopes to distract it at least by a multiplicity of objects. *South's Sermons.*

3. One who keeps any law or custom or practice.

Many nations are superstitious, and diligent *observers* of old customs, which they receive by continual tradition from their parents, by recording of their bards and chronicles. *Spenser on Ireland.*

The king after the victory, as one that had been bred under a devout mother, and was in his nature a great *observer* of religious forms, caused Te Deum to be solemnly sung in the presence of the whole army upon the place. *Bacon.*

He was so strict an *observer* of his word, that no consideration whatever could make him break it. *Prior.*

Himself often read useful discourses to his servants on the Lord's day, of which he was always a very strict and solemn *observer*. *Atterbury's Serm.*

Obse'rvingly. *adv.* [from *observing.*] Attentively; carefully.

There is some soul of goodness in things evil,
Would men *observingly* distil it out. *Shakesp. Henry* V.

Obse'ssion. *n. s.* [*obsessio*, Latin.]

1. The act of besiging.

2. The first attack of Satan, antecedent to possession.

Obsi'dional. *adj.* [*obsidionalis*, Lat.] Belonging to a siege. *Dict.*

OBSOLE'TE. *adj.* [*obsoletus*, Lat.] Worn out of use; disused; unfashionable.

Obsolete words may be laudably revived, when either they are more sounding, or more significant than those in practice. *Dryden's Juvenal Ded.*

What if there be an old dormant statute or two against him, are they not now *obsolete?* *Swift.*

Obsole'teness. *n. s.* [from *obsolete.*] State of being worn out of use; unfashionableness.

Obsta'cle. *n. s.* [*obstacle*, Fr. *obstaculum*, Lat.] Something opposed; hindrance; obstruction.

Conscience is a blushing shame-fac'd spirit,
That mutinies in a man's bosom: it fills
One full of *obstacles*. *Shakespeare's Rich.* III.

If all *obstacles* were cut away,
And that my path were even to the crown,
As the ripe reverence and due of birth. *Shakes. R.* III.

Disparity in age seems a greater *obstacle* to an intimate friendship than inequality of fortune. For the humours, business, and diversions, of young and old, are generally very different. *Collier on Friendship.*

Some conjectures about the formation of sand-stone, the origin of mountains and islands, I am obliged to look into that they may not remain as *obstacles* to the less skilful. *Woodw. Nat. Hist.*

What more natural and usual *obstacle* to those who take voyages, than winds and storms. *Pope.*

Obstetrica'tion. *n. s.* [from *obstetricor*, Lat.] The office of a midwife.

Obste'trick. *adj.* [from *obstetrix*, Lat.] Midwifish; befitting a midwife; doing the midwife's office.

There all the learn'd shall at the labour stand,
And Douglas lend his soft *obstetrick* hand. *Dunciad, b.* iv.

O'bstinacy. *n. s.* [*obstination*, Fr. *obstinatio*, Lat. from *obstinate.*] Stubbornness; contumacy; pertinacy; persistency.

Chusing rather to use all extremities, which might drive men to desperate *obstinacy*, than to apply moderate remedies. *King Charles.*

Most writers use their words loosely and uncertainly, and do not make plain and clear deductions of words one from another, which were not difficult to do, did they not find it convenient to shelter their ignorance, or *obstinacy*, under the obscurity of their terms. *Locke.*

What crops of wit and honesty appear,
From spleen, from *obstinacy*, hate or fear. *Pope's Ess.*

O'BSTINATE. *adj.* [*obstinatus*, Lat.] Stubborn; contumacious; fixed in resolution. Absolutely used, it has an ill sense; but relatively, it is neutral.

The queen is *obstinate*,
Stubborn to justice, apt t' accuse it, and
Disdainful to be try'd by't. *Shakesp. Henry* VIII.

Yield,
Except you mean with *obstinate* repulse,
To slay your sov'reign. *Shakesp.*

I have known great cures done by *obstinate* resolutions of drinking no wine. *Temple.*

Her father did not fail to find
In all she spoke, the greatness of her mind;
Yet thought she was not *obstinate* to die,
Nor deem'd the death she promis'd was so nigh. *Dryden.*

Look on Simo's mate;
No ass so meek, no ass so *obstinate*. *Pope's Ep.* ii.

O'bstinately. *adv.* [from *obstinate.*] Stubbornly; inflexibly; with unshaken determination.

Pembroke abhorred the war as *obstinately*, as he loved hunting and hawking. *Clarendon, b.* ii.

A Greek made himself their prey,
T' impose on their belief, and Troy betray;
Fix'd on his aim, and *obstinately* bent
To die undaunted, or to circumvent. *Dryden.*

OBT

Inflexible to ill, and *obstinately* just. *Addison.*
My spouse maintains her royal trust,
Tho' tempted chaste, and *obstinately* just. *Pope.*

O'BSTINATENESS. *n. s.* [from *obstinate.*] Stubbornness.

OBSTIPA'TION. *n. s.* [from *obstipo*, Lat.] The act of stopping up any passage.

OBSTRE'PEROUS. *adj.* [*obstreperus*, Lat.] Loud; clamorous; noisy; turbulent; vociferous.

These *obstreperous* scepticks are the bane of divinity, who are so full of the spirit of contradiction, that they raise daily new disputes. *Howel's Vocal Forest.*

These *obstreperous* villains shout, and know not for what they make a noise. *Dryden.*

The players do not only connive at his *obstreperous* approbation, but repair at their own cost whatever damages he makes. *Addison's Spectator*, N°. 235.

OBSTRE'PEROUSLY. *adv.* [from *obstreperous.*] Loudly; clamorously; noisily.

OBSTRE'PEROUSNESS. *n. s.* [from *obstreperous.*] Loudness; clamour; noise; turbulence.

OBSTRI'CTION. *n. s.* [from *obstrictus*, Latin.] Obligation; bond.

He hath full right t' exempt
Whom so it pleases him by choice,
From national *obstriction*. *Milton's Agonistes.*

To OBSTRU'CT. *v. a.* [*obstruo*, Lat.]

1. To hinder; to be in the way of; to block up; to bar.

He them beholding, soon
Comes down to see their city, ere the tow'r
Obstruct Heav'n-tow'rs. *Milton's Paradise Lost.*

Fat people are most subject to weakness in fevers, because the fat, melted by the feverish heat, *obstructs* the small canals. *Arbuthnot on Aliments.*

2. To oppose; to retard.

OBSTRU'CTER. *n. s.* [from *obstruct.*] One that hinders or opposes.

OBSTRU'CTION. *n. s.* [*obstructio*, Lat. *obstruction*, Fr. from *obstruct.*]

1. Hindrance; difficulty.

Sure God by these discoveries did design,
That his clear light thro' all the world should shine;
But the *obstruction* from that discord springs,
The prince of darkness makes 'twixt Christian kings. *Denh.*

2. Obstacle; impediment; that which hinders.

All *obstructions* in parliament, that is, all freedom in differing in votes, and debating matters with reason and candour, must be taken away. *King Charles.*

In his winter quarters the king expected to meet with all the *obstructions* and difficulties his enraged enemies could lay in his way. *Clarendon, b.* viii.

Whenever a popular assembly free from *obstructions*, and already possessed of more power than an equal balance will allow, shall continue to think that they have not enough, I cannot see how the same causes can produce different effects among us, from what they did in Greece and Rome. *Swift.*

3. [In physick.]

The blocking up of any canal in the human body, so as to prevent the flowing of any fluid through it, on account of the increased bulk of that fluid, in proportion to the diameter of the vessel. *Quincy.*

4. In *Shakespeare* it once signifies something heaped together.

Aye but to die, and go we know not where;
To lie in cold *obstruction*, and to rot;
This sensible warm motion to become
A kneaded clod. *Shakespeare's Measure for Measure.*

OBSTRU'CTIVE. *adj.* [*obstructif*, Fr. from *obstruct.*] Hindering; causing impediment.

Having thus separated this doctrine of God's predetermining all events from three other things confounded with it, it will now be discernible how noxious and *obstructive* this doctrine is to the superstructing all good life. *Hammond.*

OBSTRU'CTIVE. *n. s.* Impediment; obstacle.

The second *obstructive* is that of the fiduciary, that faith is the only instrument of his justification, and excludes good works from contributing any thing toward it. *Hammond.*

O'BSTRUENT. *adj.* [*obstruens*, Lat.] Hindering; blocking up.

OBSTUPEFA'CTION. *n. s.* [*obstupefacio*, Latin.] The act of inducing stupidity, or interruption of the mental powers.

OBSTUPEFA'CTIVE. *adj.* [from *obstupefacio*, Lat.] Obstructing the mental powers; stupifying.

The force of it is *obstupefactive*, and no other. *Abbot.*

To OBTA'IN. *v. a.* [*obtenir*, Fr. *obtineo*, Latin.]

1. To gain; to acquire; to procure.

May be that I may *obtain* children by her. *Gen.* xvi. 2.

We have *obtained* an inheritance. *Eph.* i. 11.

Whatever once is denied them, they are certainly not to *obtain* by crying. *Locke's Education.*

The juices of the leaves are *obtained* by expression, which is the nutritious juice rendered somewhat more oleaginous. *Arbuthnot on Aliments.*

2. To impetrate; to gain by the concession or excited kindness of another.

In such our prayers cannot serve us as means to *obtain* the thing we desire. *Hooker, b.* v. *s.* 48.

By his own blood he entered in once into the holy place, having *obtained* eternal redemption for us. *Heb.* ix. 12.

If they could not be *obtained* of the proud and crafty tyrant, then to conclude peace with him upon any conditions. *Knolles's History of the Turks.*

Some pray for riches, riches they *obtain*;
But watch'd by robbers for their wealth are slain. *Dryden.*

The conclusion of the story I forbore, because I could not *obtain* from myself to shew Absalom unfortunate. *Dryden.*

To OBTAI'N. *v. n.*

1. To continue in use.

The Theodosian Code, several hundred years after Justinian's time, did *obtain* in the western parts of Europe. *Bak.*

2. To be established.

Our impious use no longer shall *obtain*,
Brothers no more, by brothers, shall be slain. *Dryden.*

The situation of the sun and earth, which the theorist supposes, is so far from being preferable to this which at present *obtains*, that this hath infinitely the advantage of it. *Woodw.*

The general laws of fluidity, elasticity, and gravity, *obtain* in animal and inanimate tubes. *Cheyne's Phil. Prin.*

3. To prevail; to succeed.

There is due from the judge to the advocate, some commendation where causes are fair pleaded; especially towards the side which *obtaineth* not. *Bacon.*

OBTA'INABLE. *adj.* [from *obtain.*] To be procured.

Spirits which come over in distillations, miscible with water, and wholly combustible, are *obtainable* from plants by previous fermentation. *Arbuthnot on Aliments.*

OBTA'INER. *n. s.* [from *obtain.*] He who obtains.

To OBTE'MPERATE. *v. a.* [*obtemperer*, Fr. *obtempero*, Lat.] To obey. *Dict.*

To OBTE'ND. *v. a.* [*obtendo*, Lat.]

1. To oppose; to hold out in opposition.

2. To pretend; to offer as the reason of any thing.

Thou dost with lies the throne invade,
Obtending Heav'n for whate'er ills befal. *Dryden.*

OBTENEBRA'TION. *n. s.* [*ob* and *tenebræ*, Latin.] Darkness; the state of being darkened; the act of darkening; cloudiness.

In every megrim or vertigo, there is an *obtenebration* joined with a semblance of turning round. *Bacon's Nat. Hist.*

OBTE'NSION. *n. s.* [from *obtend.*] The act of obtending.

To OBTE'ST. *v. a.* [*obtestor*, Latin.] To beseech; to supplicate.

Suppliants demand
A truce, with olive branches in their hand;
Obtest his clemency, and from the plain
Beg leave to draw the bodies of their slain. *Dryden.*

OBTESTA'TION. *n. s.* [*obtestatio*, Lat. from *obtest.*] Supplication; entreaty.

OBTRECTA'TION. *n. s.* [*obtrectio*, Lat.] Slander; detraction; calumny.

To OBTRU'DE. *v. a.* [*obtrudo*, Latin.] To thrust into any place or state by force or imposture; to offer with unreasonable importunity.

It is their torment, that the thing they shun doth follow them, truth, as it were, even *obtruding* itself into their knowledge, and not permitting them to be so ignorant as they would be. *Hooker, b.* v. *s.* 2.

There may be as great a vanity in retiring and withdrawing men's conceits from the world, as in *obtruding* them. *Bac.*

Some things are easily granted; the rest ought not to be *obtruded* upon me with the point of the sword. *King Charles.*

Who can abide, that against their own doctors six whole books should, by their fatherhoods of Trent, be under pain of a curse, imperiously *obtruded* upon God and his church? *Hall.*

Why shouldst thou then *obtrude* this diligence
In vain, where no acceptance it can find? *Milton.*

Whatever was not by them thought necessary, must not by us be *obtruded* on, or forced into that catalogue. *Hamm.*

A cause of common error is the credulity of men; that is, an easy assent to what is *obtruded*, or believing at first ear what is delivered by others. *Brown's V. Err.*

The objects of our senses *obtrude* their particular ideas upon our minds, whether we will or no; and the operations of our minds will not let us be without some obscure notions of them. *Locke.*

Whether thy great forefathers came
From realms that bear Vesputio's name;
For so conjectures would *obtrude*,
And from thy painted skin conclude. *Swift.*

OBTRU'DER. *n. s.* [from *obtrude.*] One that obtrudes.

They will do justice to the inventors or publishers of the true experiments, as well as upon the *obtruders* of false ones. *Boyle.*

Obtru'sion. *n. s.* [from *obtrusus*, Latin.] The act of obtruding.

No man can think it other than the badge and method of slavery, by savage rudeness and importunate *obtrusions* of violence, to have the mist of his errour and passion dispelled. *King Charles.*

Obtru'sive. *adj.* [from *obtrude.*] Inclined to force one's self or any thing else, upon others.

Not obvious, not *obstrusive*, but retir'd
The more desirable. *Milton's Paradise Lost, b.* viii.

To **Obtu'nd.** *v. a.* [*obtundo*, Latin.] To blunt; to dull; to quell; to deaden.

Avicen countermands letting blood in cholerick bodies, because he esteems the blood a bridle of gall, *obtunding* its acrimony and fierceness. *Harvey on Consump.*

Obtura'tion. *n. s.* [from *obturatus*, Lat.] The act of stopping up any thing with something smeared over it.

Obtu'sangular. *adj.* [from *obtuse* and *angle.*] Having angles larger than right angles.

OBTU'SE. *adj.* [*obtusus*, Latin.]

1. Not pointed; not acute.
2. Not quick; dull; stupid.

Thy senses then
Obtuse, all taste of pleasures must forego. *Milt. P. Lost.*

3. Not shrill; obscure: as, an *obtuse* sound.

Obtu'sely. *adv.* [from *obtuse.*]

1. Without a point.
2. Dully; stupidly.

Obtu'seness. *n. s.* [from *obtuse.*] Bluntness; dulness.

Obtu'sion. *n. s.* [from *obtuse.*]

1. The act of dulling.
2. The state of being dulled.

Obtusion of the senses, internal and external. *Harvey.*

Obve'ntion. *n. s.* [*obvenio*, Latin.] Something happening not constantly and regularly, but uncertainly; incidental advantage.

When the country grows more rich and better inhabited, the tythes and other *obventions*, will also be more augmented and better valued. *Spenser on Ireland.*

To **Obve'rt.** *v. a.* [*obverto*, Lat.] To turn towards.

The laborant with an iron rod stirred the kindled part of the nitre, that the fire might be more diffused, and more parts might be *obverted* to the air. *Boyle.*

A man can from no place behold, but there will be amongst innumerable superficieculæ, that look some one way, and some another, enough of them *obverted* to his eye to afford a confused idea of light. *Boyle on Colours.*

An erect cone placed in an horizontal plane, at a great distance from the eye, we judge to be nothing but a flat circle, if its base be *obverted* towards us. *Watts's Logick.*

To **O'bviate.** *v. a.* [from *obvius*, Lat. *obvier*, Fr.] To meet in the way; to prevent.

To lay down every thing in its full light, so as to *obviate* all exceptions, and remove every difficulty, would carry me out too far. *Woodward's Nat. Hist.*

O'BVIOUS. *adj.* [*obvius*, Latin.]

1. Meeting any thing; opposed in front to any thing.

To the evil turn
My *obvious* breast; arming to overcome
By suffering, and earn rest from labour won. *Milton.*

2. Open; exposed.

Whether such room in nature unpossest
Only to shine, yet scarce to contribute
Each orb a glimpse of light, convey'd so far
Down to this habitable, which returns
Light back to them, is *obvious* to dispute. *Milton.*

3. Easily discovered; plain; evident; easily found.

Why was the sight
To such a tender ball as th' eye confin'd,
So *obvious* and so easy to be quench'd? *Milton.*

Entertain'd with solitude,
Where *obvious* duty ere while appear'd unsought. *Milt.*

They are such lights as are only *obvious* to every man of sense, who loves poetry and understands it. *Dryden.*

I am apt to think many words difficult or obscure, which are *obvious* to scholars. *Swift.*

These sentiments, whether they be impressed on the soul, or arise as *obvious* reflections of our reason, I call natural, because they have been found in all ages. *Rogers.*

All the great lines of our duty are clear and *obvious*; the extent of it understood, the obligation acknowledged, and the wisdom of complying with it freely confessed. *Rogers.*

O'bviously. *adv.* [from *obvious.*] Evidently; apparently.

All purely identical propositions *obviously* and at first blush, contain no instruction. *Locke.*

O'bviousness. *n. s.* [from *obvious.*] State of being evident or apparent.

Slight experiments are more easily and cheaply tried; I thought their easiness or *obviousness* fitter to recommend than depreciate them. *Boyle.*

To **Obu'mbrate.** *v. a.* [*obumbro*, Lat.] To shade; to cloud.

The rays of royal majesty reverberated so strongly upon Villerio, dispelled all those clouds which did hang over and *obumbrate* him. *Howel's Vocal Forest.*

Obumbra'tion. *n. s.* [from *obumbro*, Latin.] The act of darkening or clouding.

OCCA'SION. *n. s.* [*occasion*, Fr. *occasio*, Lat.]

1. Occurrence; casualty; incident.

The laws of Christ we find rather mentioned by *occasion* in the writings of the Apostles, than any solemn thing directly written to comprehend them in legal sort. *Hooker.*

2. Opportunity; convenience.

Unweeting, and unware of such mishap,
She brought to mischief through *occasion*,
Where this same wicked villain did me light upon. *Fa. Q.*

That woman that cannot make her fault her husband's *occasion*, let her never nurse her child herself, for she will breed it like a fool. *Shakesp. As you like it.*

Because of the money returned in our sacks are we brought in, that he may seek *occasion*, fall upon us, and take us for bondmen. *Gen.* xliii. 18.

Use not liberty for an *occasion*. *Gal.* v. 13.

Let me not let pass
Occasion which now smiles. *Milt. Par. Lost, b.* ix.

I'll take th' *occasion* which he gives to bring
Him to his death. *Waller.*

With a mind as great as theirs he came
To find at home *occasion* for his fame,
Where dark confusions did the nations hide. *Waller.*

From this admonition they took only *occasion* to redouble their fault, and to sleep again. *South.*

This one has *occasion* of observing more than once in several fragments of antiquity, that are still to be seen in Rome. *Addison on Italy.*

3. Accidental cause.

Have you ever heard what was the *occasion* and first beginning of this custom? *Spenser on Ireland.*

The fair for whom they strove,
Nor thought, when she beheld the fight from far,
Her beauty was th' *occasion* of the war. *Dryden.*

4. Reason not cogent, but opportune.

Your own business calls on you,
And you embrace th' *occasion* to depart. *Shakespeare.*

Concerning ideas lodged in the memory, and upon *occasion* revived by the mind, it takes notice of them as of a former impression. *Locke.*

5. Incidental need; casual exigence.

Never master had
A page so kind, so duteous, diligent,
So tender over his *occasions*. *Shakespeare's Cymbeline.*

Antony will use his affection where it is:
He married but his *occasion* here. *Shakes. Ant. and Cleop.*

My *occasions* have found time to use them toward a supply of money. *Shakesp. Timon of Athens.*

They who are desirous of a name in painting, should read with diligence, and make their observations of such things as they find for their purpose, and of which they may have *occasion*. *Dryden's Dufresnoy.*

Syllogism is made use of on *occasion* to discover a fallacy hid in a rhetorical flourish. *Locke.*

The ancient canons were very well fitted for the *occasions* of the church in its purer ages. *Baker on Learning.*

God hath put us into an imperfect state, where we have perpetual *occasion* of each other's assistance. *Swift.*

A prudent chief not always must display
His pow'rs in equal ranks, and fair array,
But with th' *occasion* and the place comply,
Conceal his force, nay, seem sometimes to fly. *Pope.*

To **Occa'sion.** *v. a.* [*occasionner*, Fr. from the noun.]

1. To cause casually.

Who can find it reasonable that the soul should, in its retirement, during sleep, never light on any of those ideas it borrowed not from sensation, preserve the memory of no ideas but such, which being *occasioned* from the body, must needs be less natural to a spirit? *Locke.*

The good Psalmist condemns the foolish thoughts, which a reflection on the prosperous state of his affairs had sometimes *occasioned* in him. *Atterbury.*

2. To cause; to produce.

I doubt not, whether the great encrease of that disease may not have been *occasioned* by the custom of much wine introduced into our common tables. *Temple.*

By its styptic quality it affects the nerves, very often *occasioning* tremors. *Arbuthnot on Aliments.*

3. To influence.

If we enquire what it is that *occasions* men to make several combinations of simple ideas into distinct modes, and neglect others which have as much an aptness to be combined, we shall find the reason to be the end of language. *Locke.*

Occa'sional. *adj.* [*occasionel*, Fr. from *occasion.*]

1. Incidental; casual.

Thus much is sufficient out of scripture, to verify our explication

plication of the deluge, according to the Mosaical history of the flood, and according to many *occasional* reflections dispersed in other places of scripture concerning it. *Burnet.*

2. Producing by accident.

The ground or *occasional* original hereof, was the amazement and sudden silence the unexpected appearance of wolves does often put upon travellers. *Brown's Vulgar Errours.*

3. Produced by occasion or incidental exigence.

Those letters were not writ to all;
Nor first intended but *occasional*,
Their absent sermons. *Dryd. Hind. and Panth.*

OCCA'SIONALLY. *adv.* [from *occasional.*] According to incidental exigence; incidentally.

Authority and reason on her wait,
As one intended first, not after made
Occasionally. *Milton's Paradise Lost, b.* viii.

I have endeavoured to interweave with the assertions some of the proofs whereon they depend, and *occasionally* scatter several of the more important observations throughout the work. *Woodw. Nat. Hist.*

OCCA'SIONER. *n. s.* [from *occasion.*] One that causes, or promotes by design or accident.

She with true lamentations made known to the world, that her new greatness did no way comfort her in respect of her brother's loss, whom she studied all means possible to revenge upon every one of the *occasioners.* *Sidney, b.* ii.

Some men will load me as if I were a wilful and resolved *occasioner* of my own and my subjects miseries. *K. Charles.*

In case a man dig a pit and leave it open, whereby it happeneth his neighbour's beast to fall thereinto and perish, the owner of the pit is to make it good, in as much as he was the *occasioner* of that loss to his neighbour. *Sanderson.*

OCCECA'TION. *n. s.* [*occæcatio*, from *occæco*, Latin.] The act of blinding or making blind.

Those places speak of obduration and *occecation*, so as if the blindness that is in the minds, and hardness that is in the hearts of wicked men, were from God. *Sanderson.*

O'CCIDENT. *n. s.* [from *occidens*, Latin.] The west.

The envious clouds are bent
To dim his glory, and to stain the tract
Of his bright passage to the *occident.* *Shakes. R.* II.

OCCIDE'NTAL. *adj.* [*occidentalis*, Latin.] Western.

Ere twice in murk and *occidental* damp,
Moist Hesperus hath quench'd his sleepy lamp. *Shakesp.*

If she had not been drained, she might have tiled her palaces with *occidental* gold and silver. *Howel.*

East and west have been the obvious conceptions of philosophers, magnifying the condition of India above the setting and *occidental* climates. *Brown's Vulgar Err.*

OCCI'DUOUS. *adj.* [*occidens*, Latin.] Western.

OCCI'PITAL. *adj.* [*occipitalis*, Latin.] Placed in the hinder part of the head.

O'CCIPUT. *n. s.* [Latin.] The hinder part of the head.

His broad-brim'd hat
Hangs o'er his *occiput* most quaintly,
To make the knave appear more saintly. *Butler.*

OCCI'SION. *n. s.* [from *occisio*, Latin.] The act of killing.

To OCCLU'DE. *v. a.* [*occludo*, Latin.] To shut up.

They take it up, and roll it upon the earths, whereby *occluding* the pores they conserve the natural humidity, and so prevent corruption. *Brown.*

OCCLU'SE. *adj.* [*occlusus*, Latin.] Shut up; closed.

The appulse is either plenary and *occluse*, so as to preclude all passages of breath or voice through the mouth; or else partial and pervious, so as to give them some passages out of the mouth. *Holder's Elements of Speech.*

OCCLU'SION. *n. s.* [from *occlusio*, Latin.] The act of shutting up.

OCCU'LT. *adj.* [*occulte*, Fr. *occultus*, Lat.] Secret; hidden; unknown; undiscoverable.

If his *occult* guilt
Do not itself unkennel in one speech,
It is a damned ghost that we have seen. *Shakesp. Ham.*

An artist will play a lesson on an instrument without minding a stroke; and our tongues will run divisions in a tune not missing a note, even when our thoughts are totally engaged elsewhere: which effects are to be attributed to some secret act of the soul, which to us is utterly *occult*, and without the ken of our intellects. *Glanv. Sceps. c.* iv.

These instincts we call *occult* qualities; which is all one with saying that we do not understand how they work. *L'Est.*

These are manifest qualities, and their causes only are *occult.* And the Aristotelians gave the name of *occult* qualities not to manifest qualities, but to such qualities only as they supposed to lie hid in bodies, and to be the unknown causes of manifest effects. *Newt. Opt.*

OCCULTA'TION. *n. s.* [*occultatio*, Latin.]

In astronomy, is the time that a star or planet is hid from our sight, when eclipsed by interposition of the body of the moon, or some other planet between it and us. *Harris.*

OCCU'LTNESS. *n. s.* [from *occult.*] Secretness; state of being hid.

O'CCUPANCY. *n. s.* [from *occupans*, Latin.] The act of taking possession.

Of moveables, some are things natural; others, things artificial. Property in the first is gained by *occupancy*, in the latter by improvement. *Warburton on Literary Property.*

O'CCUPANT. *n. s.* [*occupans*, Latin.] He that takes possession of any thing.

Of beasts and birds the property passeth with the possession, and goeth to the *occupant*; but of civil people not so. *Bacon.*

To O'CCUPATE. *v. a.* [*occupo*, Latin.] To possess; to hold; to take up.

Drunken men are taken with a plain destitution in voluntary motion; for that the spirits of the wine oppress the spirits animal, and *occupate* part of the place where they are, and so make them weak to move. *Bacon's Nat. History.*

OCCUPA'TION. *n. s.* [from *occupation*, Fr. *occupatio*, Lat.]

1. The act of taking possession.

Spain hath enlarged the bounds of its crown within this last sixscore years, much more than the Ottomans: I speak not of matches or unions, but of arms, *occupations*, invasions. *Bacon.*

2. Employment; business.

Such were the distresses of the then infant world; so incessant their *occupations* about provision for food, that there was little leisure to commit any thing to writing. *Woodw.*

In your most busy *occupations*, when you are never so much taken up with other affairs, yet now and then send up an ejaculation to the God of your salvation. *Wake.*

3. Trade; calling; vocation.

The red pestilence strike all trades in Rome,
And *occupations* perish. *Shakespeare's Coriolanus.*

He was of the same craft with them, and wrought, for by their *occupation* they were tent-makers. *Acts* xviii. 3.

O'CCUPIER. *n. s.* [from *occupy.*]

1. A possessor; one who takes into his possession.

If the title of *occupiers* be good in a land unpeopled, why should it be bad accounted in a country peopled over thinly? *Raleigh's Essays.*

2. One who follows any employment.

Thy merchandise and the *occupiers* of thy merchandise, shall fall into the midst of the seas. *Ezek.* xxvii. 27.

To O'CCUPY. *v. a.* [*occuper*, Fr. *occupo*, Latin.]

1. To possess; to keep; to take up.

How shall he that *occupieth* the room of the unlearned say amen at thy giving of thanks, seeing he understandeth not what thou sayest? 1 *Cor.* xiv. 16.

Powder being suddenly fired altogether, upon this high rarefaction, requireth a greater space than before its body *occupied.* *Brown's Vulgar Err. b.* ii.

He must assert, that there were infinite generations before that first deluge; and then the earth could not receive them, but the infinite bodies of men must *occupy* an infinite space. *Bentley's Sermons.*

2. To busy; to employ.

They *occupied* themselves about the sabbath, yielding exceeding praise to the Lord. 2 *Mac.* viii. 27.

How can he get wisdom that driveth oxen and is *occupied* in their labours, and whose talk is of bullocks? *Ecc.* xxxviii. 25.

He that giveth his mind to the law of the most high, and is *occupied* in the meditation thereof, will seek out the wisdom of all the ancient, and be *occupied* in prophesies. *Ecclus* xxxix. 1.

3. To follow as business.

They *occupy* their business in deep waters. *Comm. Prayer.*

Mariners were in thee to *occupy* thy merchandise. *Ez.* xxvii. 9.

4. To use; to expend.

All the gold *occupied* for the work, was twenty and nine talents. *Exodus* xxxviii. 24.

To OCCU'PY. *v. n.* To follow business.

He called his ten servants, and delivered them ten pounds, and said unto them, *occupy* till I come. *Luke* xix. 13.

To OCCU'R. *v. n.* [*occurro*, Latin.]

1. To be presented to the memory or attention.

There doth not *occur* to me any use of this experiment for profit. *Bacon's Nat. Hist.*

The mind should be always ready to turn itself to the variety of objects that *occur*, and allow them as much consideration as shall be thought fit. *Locke.*

The far greater part of the examples that *occur* to us, are so many encouragements to vice and disobedience. *Rogers.*

2. To appear here and there.

In scripture, though the word heir *occur*, yet there is no such thing as heir in our author's sense. *Locke.*

3. To clash; to strike against; to meet.

All bodies have a determinate motion according to the degrees of their external impulse, their inward principle of gravitation, and the resistance of the bodies they *occur* with. *Bentley's Sermons.*

4. To obviate; to make opposition to. A latinism.

Before I begin that I must *occur* to one specious objection against this proposition. *Bentley's Serm.*

OCCU'RRENCE. *n. s.* [*occurrence*, Fr. from *occur*: this was perhaps originally *occurrentus*.]

1. Incident; accidental event.

In education most time is to be bestowed on that which is of the greatest consequence in the ordinary course and *occurrences* of that life the young man is designed for. *Locke.*

2. Occasional presentation.

Voyages detain the mind by the perpetual *occurrence* and expectation of something new. *Watts.*

OCCU'RRENT. *n. s.* [*occurrent*, Fr. *occurrens*, Lat.] Incident; any thing that happens.

Contentions were as yet never able to prevent two evils, the one a mutual exchange of unseemly and unjust disgraces, the other a common hazard of both, to be made a prey by such as study how to work upon all *occurrents*, with most advantage in private. *Hooker's Dedicat.*

He did himself certify all the news and *occurrents* in every particular, from Calice, to the mayor and aldermen of London. *Bacon's Henry* VII.

OCCU'RSION. *n. s.* [*occursum*, Latin.] Clash; mutual blow.

In the resolution of bodies by fire, some of the dissipated parts may, by their various *occursion* occasioned by the heat, stick closely. *Boyle.*

Now should those active particles, ever and anon justled by the *occursion* of other bodies, so orderly keep their cells without alteration of site. *Glanv. Sceps.*

O'CEAN. *n. s.* [*ocean*, Fr. *oceanus*, Latin.]

1. The main; the great sea.

The golden sun salutes the morn,
And, having gilt the *ocean* with his beams,
Gallops the zodiack. *Shakesp. Tit. and Andronicus.*
Will all great Neptune's *ocean* wash this blood
Clean from my hand? *Shakesp. Macbeth.*

2. Any immense expanse.

Time, in general, is to duration, as place to expansion. They are so much of those boundless *oceans* of eternity and immensity, as is set out and distinguished from the rest, to denote the position of finite real beings, in those uniform, infinite *oceans* of duration and space. *Locke.*

O'CEAN. *adj.* [This is not usual, though conformable to the original import of the word.] Pertaining to the main or great sea.

In bulk as huge as that sea-beast
Leviathan, which God of all his works
Created hugest that swim th' *ocean* stream. *Milt. P. Lost.*
Bounds were set
To darkness, such as bound the *ocean* wave. *Milton.*

OCEA'NICK. *n. s.* [from *ocean.*] Pertaining to the ocean. *Dict.*

OCE'LLATED. *adj.* [*ocellatus*, Latin.] Resembling the eye.

The white butterfly lays its offspring on cabbage leaves; a very beautiful reddish *ocellated* one. *Derham's Physico-Theol.*

O'CHRE. *n. s.* [*ochre*, *ocre*, Fr. ὤχρα.]

The earths distinguished by the name of *ochres* are those which have rough or naturally dusty surfaces, are but slightly coherent in their texture, and are composed of fine and soft argillaceous particles, and are readily diffusible in water. They are of various colours; such as red, yellow, blue, green, black. The yellow sort are called *ochres* of iron, and the blue *ochres* of copper. *Hill's Mat. Med.*

O'CHREOUS. *adj.* [from *ochre.*] Consisting of ochre.

In the interstices of the flakes is a grey, chalky, or *ochreous* matter. *Woodward on Fossils.*

O'CHREY. *adj.* [from *ochre.*] Partaking of ochre.

This is conveyed about by the water; as we find in earthy, *ochrey*, and other loose matter. *Woodw. on Foss.*

O'CHIMY. *n. s.* [formed by corruption from *alchimy.*] A mixed base metal.

O'CTAGON. *n. s.* [ὀκτὼ and γωνία.] In geometry, a figure consisting of eight sides and angles; and this, when all the sides and angles are equal, is called a regular *octagon*, which may be inscribed in a circle. *Harris.*

OCTA'GONAL. *adj.* [from *octagon.*] Having eight angles and sides.

OCTA'NGULAR. *adj.* [*octo* and *angulus*, Lat.] Having eight angles. *Dict.*

OCTA'NGULARNESS. *n. s.* [from *octangular.*] The quality of having eight angles. *Dict.*

OCTA'NT. } *adj.* In astrology, is, when a planet is in such
OCTI'LE. } an aspect or position with respect to another, that their places are only distant an eighth part of a circle or forty-five degrees. *Dict.*

OCTA'VE. *n. s.* [*octave*, Fr. *octavus*, Lat.]

1. The eighth day after some peculiar festival.
2. [In musick.] An eighth or an interval of eight sounds.
3. Eight days together after a festival. *Ains.*

OCTA'VO. [Lat.] A book is said to be in *octavo* when a sheet is folded into eight leaves. *Dict.*

They now accompany the second edition of the original experiments, which were printed first in English in *octavo*. *Boyle.*

OCTE'NNIAL. *adj.* [from *octennium*, Lat.]

1. Happening every eighth year.
2. Lasting eight years.

OCTO'BER. *n. s.* [*October*, Lat. *octobre*, Fr.] The tenth month of the year, or the eighth numbered from March.

October is drawn in a garment of yellow and carnation; upon his head a garland of oak leaves, in his right hand the sign scorpio, in his left a basket of servises. *Peacham.*

OCTOE'DRICAL. *adj.* Having eight sides. *Dict.*

OCTO'GENARY. *adj.* [*octogeni*, Lat.] Of eighty years of age. *Dict.*

O'CTONARY. *adj.* [*octonarius*, Lat.] Belonging to the number eight. *Dict.*

OCTONO'CULAR. *adj.* [*octo* and *occulus.*] Having eight eyes.

Most animals are binocular; spiders for the most part *octonocular*, and some senocular. *Derham's Physico-Theol.*

OCTOPE'TALOUS. *adj.* [ὀκτὼ and πέταλον, Gr.] Having eight flower leaves. *Dict.*

O'CTOSTYLE. *n. s.* [ὀκτὼ and στύλος, Gr.] In the ancient architecture, is the face of a building or ordonnance containing eight columns. *Harris.*

OCTUPLE. *adj.* [*octuplus*, Lat.] Eight fold. *Dict.*

O'CULAR. *adj.* [*oculaire*, Fr. from *oculus*, Lat.] Depending on the eye; known by the eye.

Prove my love a whore,
Be sure of it: give me the *ocular* proof,
Or thou hadst better have been born a dog. *Shakespeare.*

He that would not believe the menace of God at first, it may be doubted whether before an *ocular* example he believed the curse at first. *Brown's V. Err.*

O'CULARLY. *adv.* [from *ocular.*] To the observation of the eye.

The same is *ocularly* confirmed by Vives upon Austin. *Bro.*

O'CULATE. *adj.* [*oculatus*, Latin.] Having eyes; knowing by the eye.

O'CULIST. *n. s.* [from *oculus*, Latin.] One who professes to cure distempers of the eyes.

If there be a speck in the eye, we take them off; but he were a strange *oculist* who would pull out the eye. *Bacon.*

I am no *oculist*, and if I should go to help one eye and put out the other, we should have but an untoward business of it. *L'Estrange.*

O'CULUS *beli.* [Latin.]

The *oculus beli* of the modern jewellers, and probably of Pliny, is only an accidental variety of the agat kind; having a grey horny ground, with circular delineations, and a spot in the middle of them something resembling the sight of the eye; whence the stone had its name. *Woodw.*

ODD. *adj.* [*udda*, Swedish.]

1. Not even; not divisible into equal numbers.

This is the third time; I hope
Good luck lies in *odd* numbers. *Shakespeare.*

What verity there is in that numeral conceit, in the lateral division of man by even and *odd*; ascribing the *odd* unto the right side, and the even unto the left; and so by parity, or imparity of letters in mens names, to determine misfortunes. *Brown's Vulgar Errours, b.* iv.

2. More than a round number; indefinitely exceeding any number specified.

The account of the profits of Ulster, from the fifth year of Edward IIId. until the eighth, do amount but to nine hundred and *odd* pounds. *Davies on Ireland.*

Sixteen hundred and *odd* years after the earth was made, it was destroyed in a deluge of water. *Burnet's Theory.*

The year, without regard to days, ends with an *odd* day and *odd* hours, *odd* minutes and *odd* seconds of minutes; so that it cannot be measured by any even number of days, hours, or minutes. *Holder on Time.*

3. Particular; uncouth; extraordinary; not like others; not to be numbered among any class. In a sense of contempt or dislike.

Her madness hath the *oddest* frame of sense,
Such a dependency of thing on thing,
As e'er I heard in madness. *Shakes. Measure for Meas.*

Of thee, kind boy, I ask no red and white,
To make up my delight,
No *odd* becoming graces,
Black eyes, or little know not what's in faces. *Suckling.*

This blue colour being made by nothing else than by reflexion of a specular superficies, seems so *odd* a phenomenon and so difficult to be explained by the vulgar hypothesis of philosophers, that I could not but think it deserved to be taken notice of. *Newt. Opt.*

When I broke loose from writers who have employed their wit and parts in propagating of vice, I did not question but I should be treated as an *odd* kind of a fellow. *Spectator.*

No fool Pythagoras was thought;
He made his list'ning scholars stand,
Their mouth still cover'd with their hand:
Else, may be, some *odd* thinking youth,
Might have refus'd to let his ears
Attend the music of the spheres. *Prior.*

So

So proud I am no ſlave,
So impudent I own myſelf no knave,
So *odd*, my country's ruin makes me grave. *Pope.*

4. Not noted; not taken into the common account; unheeded.

I left him cooling of the air with ſighs,
In an *odd* angle of the iſle. *Shakeſp. Tempeſt.*

There are yet miſſing ſome few *odd* lads that you remember not. *Shakeſpeare's Tempeſt.*

5. Strange; unaccountable; fantaſtical.

How ſtrange or *odd* ſoe'er I bear myſelf,
As I, perchance, hereafter ſhall think meet,
To put an antick diſpoſition on. *Shakeſ. Hamlet.*

It is an *odd* way of uniting parties to deprive a majority of part of their ancient right, by conferring it on a faction, who had never any right at all. *Swift.*

Patients have ſometimes coveted *odd* things which have relieved them; as ſalt and vinegar. *Arbuthn. on Aliments.*

6. Uncommon; particular.

The *odd* man to perform all three perfectly is, Joannes Sturmius. *Aſcham's Schoolmaſter.*

7. Unlucky.

The truſt Othello puts him in,
On ſome *odd* time of his infirmity,
Will ſhake this iſland. *Shakeſp. Othello.*

8. Unlikely; in appearance improper.

Mr. Locke's Eſſay would be a very *odd* book for a man to make himſelf maſter of, who would get a reputation by critical writings. *Addiſon's Spectator*, N°. 291.

O'DDLY. *adv.* [from *odd.* This word and *oddneſs*, ſhould, I think, be written with one *d*; but the writers almoſt all combine againſt it.]

1. Not evenly.

2. Strangely; particularly; unaccountably; uncouthly.

How *oddly* will it ſound, that I,
Muſt aſk my child forgiveneſs. *Shakeſ. Tempeſt.*

One man is preſſed with poverty, and looks ſomewhat *oddly* upon it. *Collier on the Spleen.*

The dreams of ſleeping men are made up of the waking man's ideas, though for the moſt part *oddly* put together. *Locke.*

This child was near being excluded out of the ſpecies of man barely by his ſhape. It is certain a figure a little more *oddly* turned had caſt him, and he had been executed. *Locke.*

The real eſſence of ſubſtances we know not; and therefore are ſo undetermined in our nominal eſſences, which we make ourſelves, that if ſeveral men were to be aſked concerning ſome *oddly*-ſhaped fetus, whether it were a man or no? it is paſt doubt, one ſhould meet with different anſwers. *Locke.*

Her aukward love indeed was *oddly* fated;
She and her Polly were too near related. *Prior.*

As maſters in the clare obſcure,
With various light your eyes allure:
A flaming yellow here they ſpread;
Draw off in blue, or charge in red;
Yet from theſe colours *oddly* mix'd,
Your ſight upon the whole is fix'd. *Prior.*

They had ſeen a great black ſubſtance lying on the ground very *oddly*-ſhaped. *Gulliv. Trav.*

Foſſils are very *oddly* and elegantly ſhaped, according to the modification of their conſtituent ſalts, or the cavities they are formed in. *Bentley's Serm.*

O'DDNESS. *n. ſ.* [from *odd.*]

1. The ſtate of being not even.

2. Strangeneſs; particularity; uncouthneſs.

Coveting to recommend himſelf to poſterity, Cicero begged it as an alms of the hiſtorians, to remember his conſulſhip: and obſerve the *oddneſs* of the event; all their hiſtories are loſt, and the vanity of his requeſt ſtands recorded in his own writings. *Dryden's Aurengzebe, Pref.*

A knave is apprehenſive of being diſcovered; and this habitual concern puts an *oddneſs* into his looks. *Collier.*

My wife fell into a violent diſorder, and I was a little diſcompoſed at the *oddneſs* of the accident. *Swift.*

ODDS. *n. ſ.* [from *odd.*]

1. Inequality; exceſs of either compared with the other.

Between theſe two caſes there are great *odds.* *Hooker.*

The caſe is yet not like, but there appeareth great *odds* between them. *Spenſer on Ireland.*

I will lay the *odds* that ere this year expire,
We bear our civil ſwords and native fire,
As far as France. *Shakeſpeare's Henry* IV. *p.* ii.

Cromwel, with *odds* of number and of fate,
Remov'd this bulwark of the church and ſtate. *Waller.*

I chiefly who enjoy
So far the happier lot, enjoying thee
Pre-eminent by ſo much *odds.* *Milton's Paradiſe Loſt.*

Shall I give him to partake
Full happineſs with me? or rather not;
But keep the *odds* of knowledge in my pow'r
Without co-partner? *Milton's Paradiſe Loſt, b.* ix.

All theſe, thus unequally furniſhed with truth, and advanced in knowledge, I ſuppoſe of equal natural parts; all the *odds* between them has been the different ſcope that has been given to their underſtandings to range in. *Locke.*

Judging is balancing an account, and determining on which ſide the *odds* lie. *Locke.*

2. More than an even wager.

Since every man by nature is very prone to think the beſt of himſelf, and of his own condition; it is *odds* but he will find a ſhrewd temptation. *South's Serm.*

The preſbyterian party endeavoured one day to introduce a debate about repealing the teſt clauſe, when there appeared at leaſt four to one *odds* againſt them. *Swift.*

Some biſhop beſtows upon them ſome inconſiderable benefice, when 'tis *odds* they are already encumbered with a numerous family. *Swift's Miſcell.*

3. Advantage; ſuperiority.

And tho' the ſword, ſome underſtood,
In force had much the *odds* of wood,
'Twas nothing ſo; both ſides were balanc'd
So equal, none knew which was valiant'ſt. *Hudibras.*

4. Quarrel; debate; diſpute.

I can't ſpeak
Any beginning to this peeviſh *odds.* *Shakeſ. Othello.*

What is the night?
Almoſt at *odds* with the morning, which is which. *Shak.*

He flaſhes into one groſs crime or other,
That ſets us all at *odds.* *Shakeſp. King Lear.*

The fox, the ape, and the humble-bee,
Were ſtill at *odds*, being but three;
Until the gooſe came out of door,
And ſtaid the *odds* by adding four. *Sha. L. Lab. Loſt.*

Gods of whatſoe'er degree,
Reſume not what themſelves have given,
Or any brother God in heav'n;
Which keeps the peace among the Gods,
Or they muſt always be at *odds.* *Swift's Miſcell.*

ODE. *n. ſ.* [ᾠδὴ.] A poem written to be ſung to muſick; a lyrick poem; the ode is either of the greater or leſs kind. The leſs is characteriſed by ſweetneſs and eaſe; the greater by ſublimity, rapture, and quickneſs of tranſition.

A man haunts the foreſt that abuſes our young plants with carving Roſalind on their barks; hangs *odes* upon hawthorns, and elegies on brambles, all forſooth deifying the name of Roſalind. *Shakeſp. As you like it.*

O run, prevent them with thy humble *ode*,
And lay it lowly at his bleſſed feet. *Milt. Poems.*

What work among you ſcholar Gods!
Phœbus muſt write him am'rous *odes*;
And thou, poor couſin, muſt compoſe
His letters in ſubmiſſive proſe. *Prior.*

O'DIBLE. *adj.* [from *odi.*] Hateful. *Dict.*

O'DIOUS. *adj.* [*odieux*, Fr. *odioſus*, Latin.]

1. Hateful; deteſtable; abominable.

For ever all goodneſs will be moſt charming; for ever all wickedneſs will be moſt *odious.* *Sprat's Serm.*

Hatred is the paſſion of defence, and there is a kind of hoſtility included in its very eſſence. But then, if there could have been hatred in the world, when there was ſcarce any thing *odious*, it would have acted within the compaſs of its proper object. *South's Sermons.*

Let not the Trojans, with a feign'd pretence
Of proffer'd peace, delude the Latian prince:
Expel from Italy that *odious* name. *Dryden.*

She breathes the *odious* fume
Of nauſeous ſteams, and poiſons all the room. *Granv.*

2. Expoſed to hate.

Another means for raiſing money, was, by inquiring after offences of officers in great place, who as by unjuſt dealing they became moſt *odious*, ſo by juſtice in their puniſhments the prince acquired both love and applauſe. *Hayward.*

He had rendered himſelf *odious* to the parliament. *Clarend.*

3. Cauſing hate; invidious.

The ſeventh from thee,
The only righteous in a world perverſe,
And therefore hated, therefore ſo beſet
With foes, for daring ſingle to be juſt,
And utter *odious* truth, that God would come
To judge them with his ſaints. *Milton's Par. Loſt.*

O'DIOUSLY. *adv.* [from *odious.*]

1. Hatefully; abominably.

Had thy love, ſtill *odiouſly* pretended,
Been as it ought, ſincere, it would have taught thee
Far other reas'nings. *Milton's Agoniſtes.*

2. Invidiouſly; ſo as to cauſe hate.

Arbitrary power no ſober man can fear, either from the king's diſpoſition or his practice; or even where you would *odiouſly* lay it, from his miniſters. *Dryden.*

O'DIOUSNESS. *n. ſ.* [from *odious.*]

1. Hatefulneſs.

Have a true ſenſe of his ſin, of its *odiouſneſs*, and of its danger *Wake's Prep. for Death.*

2. The

2. The ſtate of being hated.

There was left of the blood royal, an aged gentleman of approved goodneſs, who had gotten nothing by his couſin's power but danger from him, and *odiouſneſs* for him. *Sidney.*

O'DIUM. *n. ſ.* [Latin.] Invidiouſneſs; quality of provoking hate.

The *odium* and offences which ſome men's rigour or remiſneſs had contracted upon my government, I was reſolved to have expiated. *King Charles.*

She threw the *odium* of the fact on me,
And publickly avowed her love to you. *Dryden.*

ODONTA'LGICK. *adj.* [ὀδὼν and ἄλγος.] Pertaining to the tooth-ach.

O'DORATE. *adj.* [*odoratus*, Latin.] Scented; having a ſtrong ſcent, whether fœtid or fragrant.

Smelling is with a communication of the breath, or vapour of the object *odorate.* *Bacon's Nat. Hiſt.*

ODORI'FEROUS. *adj.* [*odorifer*, Lat.] Giving ſcent; uſually, ſweet of ſcent; fragrant; perfumed.

A bottle of vinegar ſo buried, came forth more lively and *odoriferous*, ſmelling almoſt like a violet. *Bacon.*

Gentle gales
Fanning their *odoriferous* wings, diſpenſe
Native perfumes, and whiſper whence they ſtole
Theſe balmy ſpoils. *Milton's Par. Loſt, b.* iv.

Smelling bodies ſend forth effluvias of ſteams, without ſenſibly waſting. Thus a grain of muſk will ſend forth *odoriferous* particles for ſcores of years, without its being ſpent. *Locke.*

ODORI'FEROUSNESS. *n. ſ.* [from *odoriferous.*] Sweetneſs of ſcent; fragrance.

O'DOROUS. *adj.* [*odorus*, Lat.] Fragrant; perfumed; ſweet of ſcent.

Such fragrant flowers do give moſt *odorous* ſmell,
But her ſweet odour did them all excel. *Spenſer.*

Their private roofs on *od'rous* timber borne,
Such as might palaces for kings adorn. *Waller.*

We ſmell, becauſe parts of the *odorous* body touch the nerves of our noſtrils. *Cheyne's Phil. Prin.*

O'DOUR. *n. ſ.* [*odor*, Lat. *odeur*, Fr.]

1. Scent, whether good or bad.

Democritus, when he lay a dying, ſent for loaves of new bread, which having opened and poured a little wine into them, he kept himſelf alive with the *odour* till a certain feaſt was paſt. *Bacon.*

Infuſions in air, for ſo we may call *odours*, have the ſame diverſities with infuſions in water; in that the ſeveral *odours* which are in one flower or other body, iſſue at ſeveral times, ſome earlier, ſome later. *Bacon.*

They refer ſapor unto ſalt, and *odour* unto ſulphur; they vary much concerning colour. *Brown's Vulgar Errours.*

2. Fragrance; perfume; ſweet ſcent.

Me ſeem'd I ſmelt a garden of ſweet flow'rs,
That dainty *odours* from them threw around,
For damſels fit to deck their lover's bow'rs. *Spenſer.*

By her interceſſion with the king ſhe would lay a moſt ſeaſonable and popular obligation upon the whole nation, and leave a pleaſant *odour* of her grace and favour to the people behind her. *Clarend.*

The Levites burned the holy incenſe in ſuch quantities as refreſhed the whole multitude with its *odours*, and filled all the region about them with perfume. *Addiſon's Freehold.*

OE. This combination of vowels does not properly belong to our language, nor is ever found but in words derived from the Greek, and not yet wholly conformed to our manner of writing: *oe* has in ſuch words the ſound of *E.*

OECONO'MICKS. *n. ſ.* [οἰκονομικός, *œconomique*, Fr. from *oeconomy.* Both it and its derivatives are under *economy.*] Management of houſehold affairs.

A prince's leaving his buſineſs wholly to his miniſters, is as dangerous an errour in politicks, as a maſter's committing all to his ſervant, is in *oeconomicks.* *L'Eſtrange.*

OECU'MENICAL. *adj.* [οἰκουμενικὸς, from οἰκουμενη.] General; reſpecting the whole habitable world.

This Nicene council was not received as an *oecumenical* council in any of the eaſtern patriarchates, excepting only that of Conſtantinople. *Stillingfleet.*

OEDE'MA. *n. ſ.* [οἴδημα, from οἰδέω, to ſwell.] A tumour. It is now and commonly by ſurgeons confined to a white, ſoft, inſenſible tumour, proceeding from cold and aqueous humours, ſuch as happen to hydropick conſtitutions. *Quincy.*

OEDEMA'TICK. } *adj.* [from *oedema.*] Pertaining to an oedema.
OEDE'MATOUS. }

It is primarily generated out of the effuſion of melancholick blood, or ſecondarily out of the dregs and remainder of a phlegmonous or *oedematick* tumour. *Harvey on Conſump.*

The great diſcharge of matter, and the extremity of pain waſted her, *oedematous* ſwellings aroſe in her legs, and ſhe languiſhed and died. *Wiſeman's Surgery.*

OE'ILIAD. *n. ſ.* [from *oeil*, French.] Glance; wink; token of the eye.

She gave *oeiliads* and moſt ſpeaking looks
To noble Edmund. *Shakeſp. King Lear.*

O'ER. contracted from *over.* See OVER.

His tears defac'd the ſurface of the well,
With circle after circle as they fell,
And now the lovely face but half appears,
O'er run with wrinkles and defac'd with tears. *Addiſon.*

OE'SOPHAGUS. *n. ſ.* [from οἰσός, wicker, from ſome ſimilitude in the ſtructure of this part to the contexture of that; and φάγω to eat.] The gullet; a long, large, and round canal, that deſcends from the mouth, lying all along between the windpipe and the joints of the neck and back, to the fifth joint of the back, where it turns a little to the right, and gives way to the deſcending artery; and both run by one another, till at the ninth the *oeſophagus* turns again to the left, pierces the midriff, and is continued to the left orifice of the ſtomach. *Quincy.*

Wounds penetrating the *oeſophagus* and *aſpera arteria*, require to be ſtitched cloſe, eſpecially thoſe of the *oeſophagus*, where the ſuſtenance and ſaliva ſo continually preſſeth into it. *Wiſeman's Surgery.*

OF. *prep.* [oꝼ, Saxon.]

1. It is put before the ſubſtantive that follows another in conſtruction; as, *of theſe part were ſlain*; that is, *part of theſe.*

I cannot inſtantly raiſe up the groſs
Of full three thouſand ducats. *Shakeſpeare.*

He to his natural endowments *of* a large invention, a ripe judgment, and a ſtrong memory, has joined the knowledge *of* the liberal arts. *Dryden.*

All men naturally fly to God in extremity, and the moſt atheiſtical perſon in the world, when forſaken of all hopes *of* any other relief, is forced to acknowledge him. *Tillotſon.*

They will receive it at laſt with an ample accumulation *of* intereſt. *Smallridge's Serm.*

Since the rouſing *of* the mind with ſome degrees *of* vigour, does ſet it free from thoſe idle companions. *Locke.*

The value of land is raiſed only by a greater plenty *of* money. *Locke.*

2. It is put after comparative and ſuperlative adjectives.

The moſt renowned *of* all are thoſe to whom the name is given Philippinæ. *Abbot's Deſcript. of the World.*

We profeſs to be animated with the beſt hopes *of* any men in the world. *Tillotſon's Serm.*

At midnight, the moſt diſmal and unſeaſonable time *of* all other, then all thoſe virgins aroſe and trimmed their lamps. *Tillotſon, Serm.* 31.

We are not to deſcribe our ſhepherds as ſhepherds at this day really are, but as they may be conceived then to have been, when the beſt *of* men followed the employment. *Pope.*

Peace, *of* all worldly bleſſings, is the moſt valuable. *Small.*

3. From.

The captain of the Helots, with a blow whoſe violence grew *of* fury, not *of* ſtrength, or *of* ſtrength proceeding *of* fury, ſtruck Palladius upon the ſide of the head. *Sidney.*

One that I brought up *of* a puppey, one that
I ſav'd from drowning. *Shak. Two Gent. of Verona.*

He borrowed a box of the ear *of* the Engliſhman, and ſwore he would pay him again when he was able. *Shakeſ.*

It was called Corcyra *of* Corcyra, the daughter of Æſopus. *Sandy's Travels.*

4. Concerning; relating to.

The quarrel is not now *of* fame and tribute,
Or *of* wrongs done unto confederates,
But for your own republick. *Ben. Johnſon's Cat.*

This cannot be underſtood *of* the firſt diſpoſition of the waters, as they were before the flood. *Burnet.*

All have this ſenſe *of* war. *Smallridge's Serm.*

5. Out of.

Yet *of* this little he had ſome to ſpare,
To feed the famiſh'd and to clothe the bare. *Dryden.*

Look once again, and for thy huſband loſt,
Lo all that's left *of* him, thy huſband's ghoſt. *Dryden.*

6. Among.

He is the only perſon *of* all others for an epic poem. *Dryd.*

Of all our heroes thou canſt boaſt alone,
That Jove, whene'er he thunders, calls thee ſon. *Dryd.*

Neither can I call to mind any clergyman *of* my own acquaintance who is wholly exempt from this error. *Swift.*

7. By. This ſenſe was once very frequent, but is not now in uſe.

She dying
Shall be lamented, pitied, and excus'd
Of every bearer. *Shakeſpeare.*

Like heav'n in all, like earth in this alone,
That tho' great ſtates by her ſupport do ſtand,
Yet ſhe herſelf ſupported is *of* none,
But by the finger of the Almighty's hand. *Davies.*

I was friendly entertained *of* the Engliſh conſul. *Sandys.*

Leſt a more honourable man than thoſe be bidden *of* him. *N. Teſt.*

8. Accord-

8. According to.

The senate
And people of Rome, *of* their accustom'd greatness,
Will sharply and severely vindicate
Not only any fact, but any practice
'Gainst the state. *Ben. Johnson's Catiline.*

They do *of* right belong to you, being most of them first preached amongst you. *Tillotson's Ded.*

Tancred, whose delight
Was plac'd in his fair daughter's daily sight,
Of custom, when his state affairs were done,
Would pass his pleasing hours with her alone. *Dryden.*

9. Noting power, ability, choice, or spontaneity. With the reciprocal pronoun.

Some soils put forth odorate herbs *of* themselves; as wild thyme. *Bacon's Nat. Hist.*

Of himself man is confessedly unequal to his duty. *Steph.*

The Venice glasses would crack *of* themselves. *Boyle.*

Of himself is none,
But that eternal infinite and one,
Who never did begin, who ne'er can end;
On him all beings, as their source, depend. *Dryden.*

The thirsty cattel, *of* themselves obtain'd
From water, and their grassy fare disdain'd. *Dryden.*

To assert mankind to have been *of* himself, and without a cause, hath this invincible objection against it, that we plainly see every man to be from another. *Tillotson.*

No particle of matter, nor any combination of particles; that is, no bodies can either move *of* themselves, or *of* themselves alter the direction of their motion. *Cheyne.*

A free people met together, as soon as they fall into any acts of civil society, do *of* themselves divide into three powers. *Swift.*

It was civil in angel or elf,
For he ne'er could have filled it so well *of* himself. *Swift.*

10. Noting properties or qualities.

He was a man *of* a decayed fortune, and *of* no good education. *Clarend.*

The colour of a body may be changed by a liquor which of itself is *of* no colour, provided it be saline. *Boyle.*

The fresh eglantine exhal'd a breath,
Whose odours were *of* pow'r to raise from death. *Dryd.*

A man may suspend the act of his choice from being determined for or against the thing proposed, till he has examined whether it be really *of* a nature, in itself and consequences, to make him happy or no. *Locke.*

The value of land is raised, when remaining *of* the same fertility it comes to yield more rent. *Locke.*

11. Noting extraction.

Lunsford was a man *of* an ancient family in Sussex. *Clar.*

Mr. Rowe was born *of* an ancient family in Devonshire, that for many ages had made a handsome figure in their country. *Rowe's Life.*

12. Noting adherence, or belonging.

Tubal, a wealthy Hebrew *of* my tribe,
Will furnish me. *Shakes. Merch. of Venice.*

Pray that in towns and temples *of* our own,
The name of great Anchises may be known. *Dryden.*

13. Noting the matter of any thing.

The chariot was all *of* cedar, gilt and adorned with crystal, save that the fore end had pannels of saphires set in borders of gold, and the hinder end the like of emeralds of the Peru colour. *Bacon's New Atlantis.*

The common materials which the ancients made their ships *of*, were the wild ash, the evergreen oak, the beech, and the alder. *Arbuthnot on Coins.*

14. Noting the motive.

It was not *of* my own choice that I undertook this work. *Dryden's Dufresnoy.*

Our sov'reign Lord has ponder'd in his mind
The means to spare the blood of gentle kind;
And *of* his grace and inborn clemency,
He modifies his severe decree. *Dryden.*

15. Noting form or manner of existence.

As if our Lord, even of purpose to prevent this fancy of extemporal and voluntary prayers, had not left *of* his own framing, one which might both remain as a part of the church liturgy, and serve as a pattern whereby to frame all other prayers with efficacy, yet without superfluity of words. *Hooker, b. v. s. 2.*

16. Noting something that has some particular quality.

Mother, says the thrush, never had any such a friend as I have *of* this swallow. No, says she, nor ever mother such a fool as I have *of* this same thrush. *L'Estrange.*

17. Noting faculties of power granted.

If any man minister, let him do it as *of* the ability which God giveth. *1 Peter iv. 11.*

18. Noting preference, or postponence.

Your highness shall repose you at the Tower.
—I do not like the Tower *of* any place. *Shakesp.*

19. Noting change of one state to another.

O miserable *of* happy! is this the end
Of this new glorious world, and me so late
The glory of that glory, who now become
Accurs'd, *of* blessed? *Milton's Paradise Lost, b. x.*

20. Noting causality.

Good nature, by which I mean beneficence and candour, is the product of right reason; which *of* necessity will give allowance to the failures of others; by considering that there is nothing perfect in mankind. *Dryden.*

21. Noting proportion.

How many are there *of* an hundred, even amongst scholars themselves. *Locke.*

22. Noting kind or species.

To cultivate the advantages of success, is an affair *of* the cabinet; and the neglect of this success may be of the most fatal consequence to a nation. *Swift.*

23. It is put before an indefinite expression of time: as, of late, in late times.

Of late, divers learned men have adopted the three hypostatical principles. *Boyle on Colours.*

Off. *adv.* [*af*, Dutch.]

1. Of this adverb the chief use is to conjoin it with verbs: as, to *come off*; to *fly off*; to *take off*; which are found under the verbs.

2. It is generally opposed to *on*: as, to lay *on*; to take *off*. In this case it signifies, disunion; separation; breach of continuity.

Since the wisdom of their choice is rather to have my cap than my heart, I will practice the insinuating nod, and be *off* to them most counterfitly. *Shakesp. Coriolanus.*

Where are you, Sir John? come, *off* with your boots. *Sha.*

See
The lurking gold upon the fatal tree;
Then rend it *off*. *Dryden, Æn. vi.*

A piece of silver coined for a shilling, that has half the silver clipped *off*, is no more a shilling than a piece of wood, which was once a sealed yard, is still a yard, when one half of it is broke *off*. *Locke.*

3. It signifies distance.

West of this forest, scarcely *off* a mile,
In goodly form comes on the enemy. *Shakespeare.*

About thirty paces *off* were placed harquebusiers. *Knolles.*

4. In painting or statuary it signifies projection or relief.

'Tis a good piece;
This comes *off* well and excellent. *Shakespeare.*

5. It signifies evanescence; absence or departure.

Competitions intermit, and go *off* and on as it happens, upon this or that occasion. *L'Estrange.*

6. It signifies any kind of disappointment; defeat; interruption; adverse division: as, the affair is *off*; the match is *off*.

7. In favour.

The questions no way touch upon puritanism, either *off* or on. *Sanderson.*

8. From; not toward.

Philoclea, whose delight of hearing and seeing was before a stay from interrupting her, gave herself to be seen unto her with such a lightening of beauty upon Zelmane, that neither she could look on, nor would look *off*. *Sidney, b. ii.*

9. *Off* hand; not studied.

Several starts of fancy *off* hand look well enough. *L'Est.*

Off. *interject.* An expression of abhorrence, or command to depart.

Off, or I fly for ever from thy sight. *Smith's Phædr.*

Off. *prep.*

1. Not on.

I continued feeling again the same pain; and finding it grow violent I burnt it, and felt no more after the third time; was never *off* my legs, nor kept my chamber a day. *Temple.*

2. Distant from.

Cicero's Tusculum was at a place called Grotto Ferrate, about two miles *off* this town, though most of the modern writers have fixed it to Frescati. *Addison on Italy.*

Offal. *n. s.* [*off fall*, says *Skinner*, that which falls from the table: perhaps from *offa*, Latin.]

1. Waste meat; that which is not eaten at the table.

He let out the *offals* of his meat to interest, and kept a register of such debtors in his pocket-book. *Arbuthnot.*

2. Carrion; coarse flesh.

I should have fatted all the region kites
With this slave's *offal*. *Shakesp. Hamlet.*

Cram'd, and gorg'd, nigh burst,
With suck'd and glutted *offal*. *Milton's Par. Lost.*

3. Refuse; that which is thrown away as of no value.

To have right to deal in things sacred, was accounted an argument of a noble and illustrious descent; God would not accept the *offals* of other professions. *South.*

If a man bemoan his lot,
That after death his mouldring limbs shall rot,
A secret sting remains within his mind;
The fool is to his own cast *offals* kind. *Dryden.*

They commonly fat hogs with *offal* corns. *Mort.*

4. Any thing of no esteem.

What trash is Rome? what rubbish and what *offal*? *Sha.*

O'FFENCE. *n. s.* [*offense*, Fr. *offensa*, from *offendo*, Lat.]

1. Crime; act of wickedness.

Thither with speed their hasty course they ply'd,
Where Christ the Lord for our *offences* dy'd. *Fairfax.*

Thou hast stol'n that, which after some few hours
Were thine without *offence*. *Shakesp. Henry* IV.

2. A transgression.

If, by the law of nature, every man hath not a power to punish *offences* against it, I see not how the magistrates of any community can punish an alien of another country. *Locke.*

3. Injury.

I have given my opinion against the authority of two great men, but I hope without *offence* to their memories; for I loved them living, and reverence them dead. *Dryden.*

4. Displeasure given; cause of disgust; scandal.

Giving no *offence* in any thing, that the ministry be not blamed. 2 *Cor.* vi. 3.

He remembered the injury of the children of Bean, who had been a snare and an *offence* unto the people. 1 *Mac.* iv.

The pleasures of the touch are greater than those of the other senses; as in warming upon cold, or refrigeration upon heat: for as the pains of the touch are greater than the *offences* of other senses, so likewise are the pleasures. *Bacon.*

5. Anger; displeasure conceived.

Earnest in every present humour, and making himself brave in his liking, he was content to give them just cause of *offence* when they had power to make just revenge. *Sidney.*

6. Attack; act of the assailant.

Courtesy that seemed incorporated in his heart, would not be persuaded to offer any *offence*, but only to stand upon the best defensive guard. *Sidney.*

OFFE'NCEFUL. *adj.* [*offence* and *full.*] Injurious; giving displeasure.

It seems your most *offenceful* act
Was mutually committed. *Shakesp. Measure for Meas.*

OFFE'NCELESS. *adj.* [from *offence.*] Unoffending; innocent.

You are but now cast in his mood, a punishment more in policy than in malice; even so as one would beat his *offenceless* dog to affright an imperious lion. *Shakesp. Othello.*

To OFFE'ND. *v. a.* [*offendo*, Latin.]

1. To make angry.

If much you note him
You shall *offend* him, and extend his passion,
Feed and regard him not. *Shakesp. Macbeth.*

Three sorts of men my soul hateth, and I am greatly *offended* at their life. *Ecclus* xxv. 2.

The emperor himself came running to the place in his armour, severely reproving them of cowardice who had forsaken the place, and grievously *offended* with them who had kept such negligent watch. *Knolles's Hist. of the Turks.*

2. To assail; to attack.

He was fain to defend himself, and withal so to *offend* him, that by an unlucky blow the poor Philoxenus fell dead at his feet. *Sidney.*

3. To trangress; to violate.

4. To injure.

Cheaply you sin, and punish crimes with ease,
Not as th' *offended*, but th' offenders please. *Dryden.*

To OFFE'ND. *v. n.*

1. To be criminal; to trangress the law.

This man that of earthly matter maketh graven images, knoweth himself to *offend* above all others. *Wisd.* xiv. 13.

Whosoever shall keep the whole law, and yet *offend* in one point, he is guilty of all. *James* ii. 10.

2. To cause anger.

I shall *offend*, either to detain or give it. *Shakesp. Lear.*

3. To commit transgression.

Our language is extremely imperfect, and in many instances it *offends* against every part of grammar. *Swift.*

OFFE'NDER. *n. s.* [from *offend.*]

1. A criminal; one who has committed a crime; a transgressor; a guilty person.

All that watch for iniquity are cut off, that make a man an *offender* for a word. *Is.* xxix. 21.

So like a fly the poor *offender* dies;
But like the wasp, the rich escapes and flies. *Denham.*

How shall I lose the sin, yet keep the sense,
And love th' *offender*, yet detest th' offence? *Pope.*

The conscience of the *offender* shall be sharper than an avenger's sword. *Clarissa.*

2. One who has done an injury.

All vengeance comes too short,
Which can pursue th' *offender*. *Shakesp. King Lear.*

OFFE'NDRESS. *n. s.* [from *offender.*] A woman that offends.

Virginity murthers itself, and should be buried in highways out of all sanctified limit, as a desperate *offendress* against nature. *Shakesp. All's well that ends well.*

OFFE'NSIVE. *adj.* [*offensif*, Fr. from *offensus*, Lat.]

1. Causing anger; displeasing; disgusting.

Since no man can do ill with a good conscience, the consolation which we herein seem to find is but a meer deceitful pleasing of ourselves in error, which at the length must needs turn to our greater grief, if that which we do to please God most, be for the manifold defects thereof *offensive* unto him. *Hooker, b.* v. *s.* 4.

It shall suffice, to touch such customs of the Irish as seem *offensive* and repugnant to the good government of the realm. *Spenser on Ireland.*

2. Causing pain; injurious.

It is an excellent opener for the liver, but *offensive* to the stomach. *Bacon's Nat. Hist.*

Some particular acrimony in the stomach sometimes makes it *offensive*, and which custom at last will overcome. *Arbuth.*

3. Assailant; not defensive.

He recounted the benefits and favours that he had done him, in provoking a mighty and opulent king by an *offensive* war in his quarrel. *Bacon.*

We enquire concerning the advantages and disadvantages betwixt those military *offensive* engines used among the ancients, and those of these latter ages. *Wilkins.*

OFFE'NSIVELY. *adv.* [from *offensive.*]

1. Mischievously; injuriously.

In the least thing done *offensively* against the good of men, whose benefit we ought to seek for as our own, we plainly shew that we do not acknowledge God to be such as indeed he is. *Hooker, b.* v. *s.* 2.

2. So as to cause uneasiness or displeasure.

A lady had her sight disordered, so that the images in her hangings did appear to her, if the room were not extraordinarily darkened, embellished with several *offensively* vivid colours. *Boyle on Colours.*

3. By way of attack; not defensively.

OFFE'NSIVENESS. *n. s.* [from *offensive.*]

1. Injuriousness; mischief.

2. Cause of disgust.

The muscles of the body, being preserved sound and limber upon the bones, all the motions of the parts might be explicated with the greatest ease and without any *offensiveness*. *Grew's Musæum.*

To O'FFER. *v. a.* [*offero*, Lat. *offrir*, Fr.]

1. To present to any one; to exhibit any thing so as that it may be taken or received.

The heathen women under the Mogul, *offer* themselves to the flames at the death of their husbands. *Collier.*

Some ideas forwardly *offer* themselves to all mens understandings; some sort of truths result from any idea, as soon as the mind puts them into propositions. *Locke.*

Servants placing happiness in strong drink, make court to my young master, by *offering* him that which they love. *Locke.*

2. To sacrifice; to immolate; to present as an act of worship.

They *offered* unto the Lord of the spoil which they had brought, seven hundred oxen. 2 *Chron.* xv. 11.

He shall *offer* of it all the fat thereof. *Lev.* vii. 3.

An holy priesthood to *offer* up spiritual sacrifices. 1 *Pet.* ii. 5.

Whole herds of *offer'd* bulls about the fire,
And bristled boars and woolly sheep expire. *Dryden.*

When a man is called upon to *offer* up himself to his conscience, and to resign to justice and truth, he should be so far from avoiding the lists, that he should rather enter with inclination, and thank God for the honour. *Collier.*

3. To bid, as a price or reward.

Nor shouldst thou *offer* all thy little store,
Will rich Iolas yield, but *offer* more. *Dryden.*

4. To attempt; to commence.

Lysimachus armed about three thousand men, and began first to *offer* violence. 2 *Mac.* iv. 40.

5. To propose.

In all that great extent wherein the mind wanders in remote speculations, it stirs not one jot beyond those ideas which sense or reflection have *offered* for its contemplation. *Locke.*

Our author *offers* no reason. *Locke.*

To O'FFER. *v. n.*

1. To be present; to be at hand; to present itself.

No thought can imagine a greater heart to see and contemn danger, where danger would *offer* to make any wrongful threatning upon him. *Sidney, b.* ii.

Th' occasion *offers*, and the youth complies. *Dryden.*

2. To make an attempt.

We came close to the shore, and *offered* to land. *Bacon.*

One *offers*, and in *off'ring* makes a stay;
Another forward sets, and doth no more. *Dan. Civ. War.*

I would treat the pope and his cardinals roughly, if they *offered* to see my wife without my leave. *Dryden.*

3. With *at*.

I will not *offer at* that I cannot master. *Bacon.*

I hope they will take it well that I should *offer at* a new thing, and could forbear presuming to meddle where any of the learned pens have ever touched before. *Graunt.*

Write down and make signs to him to pronounce them, and guide him by shewing him by the motion of your own lips

lips to *offer at* one of those letters; which being the easiest, he will stumble upon one of them. *Holder.*

The masquerade succeeded so well with him, that he would be *offering at* the shepherd's voice and call too. *L'Estrange.*

It contains the grounds of his doctrine, and *offers at* somewhat towards the disproof of mine. *Atterbury.*

Without *offering at* any other remedy, we hastily engaged in a war, which hath cost us sixty millions. *Swift.*

O'FFER. *n. s.* [*offre*, Fr. from the verb.]

1. Proposal of advantage to another.

Some nymphs there are, too conscious of their face;
These swell their prospects, and exalt their pride,
When *offers* are disdain'd, and love deny'd. *Pope.*

2. First advance.

Force compels this *offer*,
And it proceeds from policy, not love. —
— Mowbray, you overween to take it so:
This *offer* comes from mercy, not from fear. *Shakesp.*
What wouldst beg, Laertes,
That shall not be my *offer*, not thy asking? *Shakesp.*

3. Proposal made.

Th' *offers* he doth make,
Were not for him to give, nor them to take. *Daniel.*

I enjoined all the ladies to tell the company, in case they had been in the siege and had the same *offer* made them as the good women of that place, what every one of them would have brought off with her, and have thought most worth the saving. *Addison's Spectator.*

It carries too great an imputation of ignorance, or folly, to quit and renounce former tenets upon the *offer* of an argument which cannot immediately be answered. *Locke.*

4. Price bid; act of bidding a price.

When stock is high, they come between,
Making by second hand their *offers*;
Then cunningly retire unseen,
With each a million in his coffers. *Swift.*

5. Attempt; endeavour.

Many motions, though they be unprofitable to expel that which hurteth, yet they are *offers* of nature, and cause motions by consent; as in groaning, or crying upon pain. *Bacon.*

It is in the power of every one to make some essay, some *offer* and attempt, so as to shew that the heart is not idle or insensible, but that it is full and big, and knows itself to be so, though it wants strength to bring forth. *South's Serm.*

One sees in it a kind of *offer* at modern architecture, but at the same time that the architect has shown his dislike of the gothic manner, one may see that they were not arrived at the knowledge of the true way. *Addison on Italy.*

6. Something given by way of acknowledgment.

Fair streams that do vouchsafe in your clearness to represent unto me my blubbered face, let the tribute *offer* of my tears procure your stay a while with me, that I may begin yet at last to find something that pities me. *Sidney, b.* ii.

O'FFERER. *n. s.* [from *offer*.]

1. One who makes an offer.

2. One who sacrifices, or dedicates in worship.

If the mind of the *offerer* be good, this is the only thing God respecteth. *Hooker, b.* v. *s.* 34.

When he commanded Abraham to sacrifice Isaac, the place of the offering was not left undetermined, and to the *offerer's* discretion. *South's Sermons.*

O'FFERING. *n. s.* [from *offer*.] A sacrifice; any thing immolated, or offered in worship.

Plucking the entrails of an *offering* forth,
They could not find a heart within the beast. *Shakesp.*
They are polluted *offerings*, more abhorr'd
Than spotted livers in the sacrifice. *Shakespeare.*

When thou shalt make his soul an *offering* for sin, he shall see his seed. *Is.* liii. 10.

The gloomy god
Stood mute with awe, to see the golden rod;
Admir'd the destin'd *off'ring* to his queen,
A venerable gift so rarely seen. *Dryden.*
What nations now to Juno's pow'r will pray,
Or *off'rings* on my slighted altars lay? *Dryd. Virg.*
I'll favour her,
That my awaken'd soul may take her flight,
Renew'd in all her strength, and fresh with life,
An *offering* fit for heaven. *Addison's Cato.*

OFFE'RTORY. *n. s.* [*offertoire*, Fr.] The thing offered; the act of offering.

He went into St. Paul's church, where he made *offertory* of his standards, and had orizons and Te Deum sung. *Bacon.*

OFFE'RTURE. *n. s.* [from *offer*.] Offer; proposal of kindness. A word not in use.

Thou hast prevented us with *offertures* of thy love, even when we were thine enemies. *King Charles.*

O'FFICE. *n. s.* [*office*, Fr. *officium*, Latin.]

1. A publick charge or employment.

You have contriv'd to take
From Rome all season'd *office*, and to wind
Yourself into a power tyrannical. *Shakesp. Coriolanus.*
Methought this staff, mine *office*-badge in court,
Was broke in twain. *Shakesp. Henry* VI. *p.* ii.
The insolence of *office*. *Shakespeare.*

2. Agency; peculiar use.

All things that you should use to do me wrong,
Deny their *office*. *Shakesp. King Lear.*

In this experiment the several intervals of the teeth of the comb do the *office* of so many prisms, every interval producing the phenomenon of one prism. *Newt. Opt.*

3. Business; particular employment.

The sun was sunk, and after him the star
Of Hesperus, whose *office* is to bring
Twilight upon the earth. *Milt. Par. Lost, b.* ix.

4. Act of good or ill voluntarily tendered.

Wolves and bears
Casting their savageness aside, have done
Like *offices* of pity. *Shakesp. Winter's Tale.*

Mrs. Ford, I see you are obsequious in your love, and I profess requital to a hair's breadth; not only in the simple *office* of love, but in all the accoustrement, complement, and ceremony of it. *Shakesp. Merry W. of Windsor.*

I would I could do a good *office* between you. *Shakesp.*

The wolf took this occasion to do the fox a good *office*. *L'Estrange.*

You who your pious *offices* employ
To save the reliques of abandon'd Troy. *Dryd. Virg.*

5. Act of worship.

This gate
Instructs you how t' adore the heavens, and bows you
To morning's holy *office*. *Shakesp. Cymbeline.*

6. Formulary of devotions.

Whosoever hath children or servants, let him take care that they say their prayers before they begin their work: the Lord's prayer, the ten commandments, and the creed, is a very good *office* for them, if they are not fitted for more regular *offices*. *Taylor's Devotion.*

7. Rooms in a house appropriated to particular business.

What do we but draw anew the model
In fewer *offices*? at least desist
To build at all. *Shakesp. Henry* IV. *p.* ii.

Let *offices* stand at distance, with some low galleries to pass from them to the palace itself. *Bacon.*

8. Place where business is transacted. [*Officina*, Lat.]

What shall good old York see there,
But empty lodgings and unfurnish'd walls,
Unpeopled *offices*, untroden stones? *Sha. Rich.* II.

Empson and Dudley, though they could not but hear of these scruples in the king's conscience, yet as if the king's soul and his money were in several *offices*, that the one was not to intermeddle with the other, went on with as great rage as ever. *Bacon's Henry* VII.

To O'FFICE. *v. a.* [from the noun.] To perform; to discharge; to do.

I will be gone, altho'
The air of Paradise did fan the house,
And angels *offic'd* all. *Sha. All's well that ends well.*

O'FFICER. *n. s.* [*officier*, French.]

1. A man employed by the publick.

'Tis an office of great worth,
And you an *officer* fit for the place. *Shakespeare.*
Submit you to the people's voices,
Allow their *officers*, and be content
To suffer lawful censure. *Shakesp. Coriolanus.*

The next morning there came to us the same *officer* that came to us at first to conduct us to the stranger's house. *Bac.*

If it should fall into the French hands, all the princes would return to be the several *officers* of his court. *Temple.*

As a magistrate or great *officer* he locks himself up from all approaches. *South's Sermons.*

Birds of prey are an emblem of rapacious *officers*. A superior power takes away by violence from them, that which by violence they took away from others. *L'Estrange.*

2. A commander in the army.

If he did not nimbly ply the spade,
His surly *officer* ne'er fail'd to crack
His knotty cudgel on his tougher back. *Dryden.*
I summon'd all my *officers* in haste,
All came resolv'd to die in my defence. *Dryden.*

The bad disposition he made in landing his men, shews him not only to be much inferiour to Pompey as a sea *officer*, but to have had little or no skill in that element. *Arb.*

3. One who has the power of apprehending criminals.

The thieves are possest with fear
So strongly, that they dare not meet each other;
Each takes his fellow for an *officer*. *Shakesp. Henry* IV.
We charge you
To go with us unto the *officers*. *Shakesp. Henry* VI.

O'FFICERED. *adj.* [from *officer*.] Commanded; supplied with commanders.

What could we expect from an army *officered* by Irish papists and outlaws. *Addison's Freeholder.*

OFFI'CIAL. *adj.* [*official*, Fr. from *office.*]

1. Conducive; appropriate with regard to their use.

In this animal are the guts, the stomach, and other parts *official* unto nutrition, which, were its aliment the empty reception of air, their provisions had been superfluous. *Brown.*

2. Pertaining to a publick charge.

The tribunes
Endue you with the people's voice. Remains
That in th' *official* marks invested, you
Anon do meet the senate. *Shakesp. Coriolanus.*

OFFI'CIAL. *n. s.*

Official is that person to whom the cognizance of causes is committed by such as have ecclesiastical jurisdiction. *Ayl.*

A poor man found a priest over familiar with his wife, and because he spake it abroad and could not prove it, the priest sued him before the bishop's *official* for defamation. *Camden.*

OFFI'CIALTY. *n. s.* [*officialité*, Fr. from *official.*] The charge or post of an official.

The office of an *officialty* to an archdeacon. *Ayliffe.*

To OFFI'CIATE. *v. a.* [from *office.*] To give, in consequence of office.

All her number'd stars that seem to rowl
Spaces incomprehensible, for such
Their distance argues, and their swift return
Diurnal, merely to *officiate* light
Round this opacous earth, this punctual spot. *Milton.*

To OFFI'CIATE. *v. n.*

1. To discharge an office, commonly in worship.

No minister *officiating* in the church, can with a good conscience omit any part of that which is commanded by the aforesaid law. *Sanderson.*

Who of the bishops or priests that *officiates* at the altar, in the places of their sepulchres, ever said we offer to thee Peter or Paul? *Stillingfleet.*

To prove curates no servants, is to rescue them from that contempt which they will certainly fall into under this notion; which considering the number of persons *officiating* this way, must be very prejudicial to religion. *Collier.*

2. To perform an office for another.

OFFICI'NAL. *adj.* [from *officina*, a shop.] Used in a shop, or belonging to it: thus *officinal* plants and drugs are those used in the shops.

OFFI'CIOUS. *adj.* [*officieux*, Fr. *officiosus*, Lat.]

1. Kind; doing good offices.

Yet, not to earth are those bright luminaries
Officious; but to thee, earth's habitant. *Milt. P. Lost.*

2. Importunely forward.

You are too *officious*
In her behalf that scorns your services. *Shakesp.*

At Taunton they killed in fury an *officious* and eager commissioner for the subsidy. *Bacon's Henry VII.*

Cato, perhaps
I'm too *officious*, but my forward cares
Would fain preserve a life of so much value. *Addison.*

OFFI'CIOUSLY. *adv.* [from *officious.*]

1. Importunately forward.

The most corrupt are most obsequious grown,
And those they scorn'd, *officiously* they own. *Dryden.*

Flatt'ring crouds *officiously* appear,
To give themselves, not you, an happy year. *Dryd.*

2. Kindly; with unasked kindness.

Let thy goats *officiously* be nurst,
And led to living streams to quench their thirst. *Dryd.*

OFFI'CIOUSNESS. *n. s.* [from *officious.*]

1. Forwardness of civility, or respect, or endeavour. Commonly in an ill sense.

I shew my *officiousness* by an offering, though I betray my poverty by the measure. *South's Serm.*

2. Service.

In whom is required understanding as in a man, courage and vivacity as in a lion, service and ministerial *officiousness* as in the ox, and expedition as in the eagle. *Brown's V. Err.*

O'FFING. *n. s.* [from *off.*] The act of steering to a distance from the land.

O'FFSET. *n. s.* [*off* and *set.*] Sprout; shoot of a plant.

They are multiplied not only by the seed, but many also by the root, producing *offsets* or creeping under ground. *Ray.*

Some plants are raised from any part of the root, others by *offsets*, and in others the branches set in the ground will take root. *Locke.*

OFFSCOU'RING. *n. s.* [*off* and *scour.*] Recrement; part rubbed away in cleaning any thing.

Thou hast made us as the *offscouring* and refuse in the midst of the people. *Lam.* iii. 45.

O'FFSPRING. *n. s.* [*off* and *spring.*]

1. Propagation; generation.

All things coveting to be like unto God in being ever, that which cannot hereunto attain personally, doth seem to continue itself by *offspring* and propagation. *Hooker.*

2. The thing propagated or generated; children; descendents.

When the fountain of mankind
Did draw corruption, and God's curse, by sin;
This was a charge, that all his heirs did bind,
And all his *offspring* grew corrupt therein. *Davies.*

To the Gods alone
Our future *offspring*, and our wives are known. *Dryd.*

His principal actor is the son of a goddess, not to mention the *offspring* of other deities. *Addison's Spectator.*

3. Production of any kind.

Tho' both fell before their hour,
Time on their *offspring* hath no pow'r;
Nor fire nor fate their bays shall blast,
Nor death's dark vail their days o'ercast. *Denham.*

To OFFU'SCATE. *v. a.* [*offusco*, Lat. *offusquer*, Fr.] To dim; to cloud; to darken.

OFFUSCA'TION. *n. s.* [from *offuscate.*] The act of darkening.

OFT. *adv.* [oft, Saxon.] Often; frequently; not rarely; not seldom.

In labours more abundant, in stripes above measure, in prisons more frequent, in deaths *oft.* 2 *Cor.* ii. 23.

It may be a true faith, for so much as it is; it is one part of true faith, which is *oft* mistaken for the whole. *Hamm.*

Favours to none, to all she smiles extends,
Oft she rejects, but never once offends. *Po. Ra. Locke.*

O'FTEN. *adv.* [from oft, Saxon; in the comparative, oftner; superlative, oftnest.] Oft; frequently; many times; not seldom.

The queen that bore thee,
Oftner upon her knees than on her feet,
Died ev'ry day she liv'd. *Shakesp. Macbeth.*

Use a little wine for thy stomach's sake, and thine *often* infirmities. 1 *Tim.* v. 23.

In journeying *often*, in perils in the wilderness. 2 *Cor.* ii. 26.

Who does not more admire Cicero as an author, than as a consul of Rome, and does not *oftner* talk of the celebrated writers of our own country in former ages, than of any among their contemporaries? *Addison's Freeholder.*

OFTENTI'MES. *adv.* [*often* and *times.* From the composition of this word it is reasonable to believe, that *oft* was once an adjective, of which *often* was the plural; which seems retained in the phrase *thine often infirmities.* See OFTEN.] Frequently; many times; often.

Is our faith in the blessed trinity a matter needless, to be so *oftentimes* mentioned and opened in the principal part of that duty which we owe to God, our public prayer? *Hooker.*

The difficulty was by what means they could ever arrive to places *oftentimes* so remote from the ocean. *Woodw.*

It is equally necessary that there should be a future state, to vindicate the justice of God, and solve the present irregularities of providence, whether the best men be *oftentimes* only, or always the most miserable. *Atterbury.*

OFTTI'MES. *adv.* [*oft* and *times.*] Frequently; often.

Ofttimes nothing profits more
Than self-esteem, grounded on just and right,
Well manag'd. *Milton's Paradise Lost, b.* viii.

Ofttimes before I hither did resort,
Charm'd with the conversation of a man
Who led a rural life. *Dryden and Lee.*

OGE'E. } *n. s.* Is a sort of moulding in architecture, consist-
OGIVE. } ing of a round and a hollow: it is almost in the form of an S, and is the same with what Vitruvius calls cima. Cima reversa, is an *ogee* with the hollow downwards. *Harris.*

To O'GLE. *v. a.* [*oogh*, an eye, Dutch.] To view with side glances, as in fondness; or with a design not to be heeded.

From their high scaffold with a trumpet cheek,
And *ogling* all their audience, then they speak. *Dryden.*

If the female tongue will be in motion, why should it not be set to go right? Could they talk of the different aspects and conjunctions of the planets, they need not be at the pains to comment upon *oglings* and clandestine marriages. *Addison's Guardian,* N°. 155.

Whom is he *ogling* yonder? himself in his looking-glass. *Martinus Scriblerius.*

O'GLER. *n. s.* [*oogheler*, Dutch.] A sly gazer; one who views by side glances.

Upon the disuse of the neck-piece, the whole tribe of *oglers* stared the fair sex in the neck rather than in the face. *Addison's Guardian,* N°. 100.

Jack was a prodigious *ogler*; he would ogle you the outside of his eye inward, and the white upward. *J. Bull.*

O'GLIO. *n. s.* [from *olla*, Spanish.] A dish made by mingling different kinds of meat; a medley; a hotchpotch.

These general motives of the common good, I will not so much as once offer up to your lordship, though they have still the upper end; yet, like great *oglio's*, they rather make a shew than provoke appetite. *Suckling.*

Where is there such an *oglio* or medley of various opinions in the world again, as those men entertain in their service, without any scruple as to the diversity of their sects and opinions? *King Charles.*

He

He that keeps an open house, should consider that there are *oglio's* of guests, as well as of dishes, and that the liberty of a common table is as good as a tacit invitation to all sorts of intruders. *L'Estrange.*

Oh. *interject.* An exclamation denoting pain, sorrow, or surprise.

He,
Like a full acorn'd boar, a churning on,
Cry'd, *oh!* and mounted. *Shakesp. Cymbeline.*

Oh me! all the horse have got over the river, what shall we do? *Walton's Angler.*

My eyes confess it,
My every action speaks my heart aloud;
But *oh*, the madness of my high attempt
Speaks louder yet! *Dryden's Spanish Friar.*

OIL. *n. s.* [œl, Saxon; *oleum*, Latin.]

1. The juice of olives expressed.

Bring pure *oil* olive beaten for the light. *Ex.* xxvii. 20.

2. Any fat, greasy, unctuous, thin matter.

In most birds there is only one gland; in which are divers cells, ending in two or three larger cells, lying under the nipple of the *oil* bag. *Derham's Physico-Theol.*

3. The juices of certain vegetables, expressed or drawn by the still without fermentation, or after the spirit.

Oil with chemists called sulphur, is the second of their hypostatical, and of the true five chymical principles. It is an inflammable, unctuous, subtile substance, which usually rises after the spirit. The chemists attribute to this principle all the diversity of colours, and all the beauty and deformity. It sweetens the acrimony of salts, and by stopping or filling up the pores of a mixt body, keeps it longer from corruption, where it abounds. There are two sorts of *oil* which seem to be mixt with spirit; for it can never be drawn pure, and which will swim upon water, such as *oil* of aniseed and lavender, which the chemists call essential, and is commonly drawn in a limbeck with store of water: and another kind which probably is mixt with salts; and these will sink in water, such as the *oil* of guiacum and cloves. *Harris.*

After this expressed *oil*, we made trial of a distilled one; and for that purpose made choice of the common *oil* or spirit. *Boyle.*

To **Oil.** *v. a.* [from the noun.] To smear or lubricate with oil.

The men fell a rubbing of armour, which a great while had lain *oiled.* *Wotton.*

Amber will attract straws thus *oiled*, it will convert the needles of dials, made either of brass or iron, although they be much *oiled*, for in those needles consisting free upon their center there can be no adhesion. *Brown's V. Err.*

Swift *oils* many a spring which Harley moves. *Swift.*

Oi'lcolour. *n. s.* [*oil* and *colour.*] Colour made by grinding coloured substances in oil.

Oilcolours, after they are brought to their due temper, may be preserved long in some degree of softness, kept all the while under water. *Boyle.*

Oi'liness. *n. s.* [from *oily.*] Unctuousness; greasiness; quality approaching to that of oil.

Basil hath fat and succulent leaves; which *oiliness*, if drawn forth by the sun, will make a very great change. *Bacon.*

Wine is inflammable, so as it hath a kind of *oiliness. Bac.*

Smoke from unctuous bodies and such whose *oiliness* is evident, he nameth nidor. *Brown's Vulgar Err.*

Chyle has the same principles as milk, viscidity from the caseous parts, an *oiliness* from the butyraceous parts, and an acidity from the tartareous. *Flyer.*

The flesh of animals which live upon other animals, is most antiacid; though offensive to the stomach sometimes by reason of their *oiliness.* *Arbuthnot on Aliments.*

Oi'lman. *n. s.* [*oil* and *man.*] One who trades in oils and pickles.

Oi'lshop. *n. s.* [*oil* and *shop.*] A shop where oils and pickles are sold.

Oi'ly. *adj.* [from *oil.*]

1. Consisting of oil; containing oil; having the qualities of oil.

The like cloud, if it were *oily* or fatty, will not discharge; not because it sticketh faster, but because air preyeth upon water and flame, and fire upon oil. *Bacon's Nat. Hist.*

Flame is grosser than gross fire, by reason of the mixture with it of that viscous *oily* matter, which, being drawn out of the wood and candle, serves for fewel. *Digby.*

Watry substances are more apt to putrify than *oily.* *Bacon.*

2. Fat; greasy.

This *oily* rascal is known as well as Paul's;
Go call him forth. *Shakesp. Henry* IV.

Oi'lygrain. *n. s.* A plant.

The flowers are produced from the wings of the leaves without any footstalk; the flower cup consists of one leaf, divided into five long slender segments; the flower is of one leaf, in shape like those of the fox-glove; the pointal, which rises in the middle of the flower, afterward becomes an oblong four cornered pod, divided into four distinct cells, which are replete with esculent seeds. *Miller.*

Oi'lypalm. *n. s.*

It grows in great plenty on the coast of Guiney, as also in Cape Verd island, where it grows as high as the main mast of a ship. But these trees have been transplanted to Jamaica and Barbados, in both which places they thrive very well. The inhabitants make an oil from the pulp of the fruit, and draw a wine from the body of the trees, which inebriates; and with the rind of these trees they make mats to lie on. *Miller.*

To **OINT.** *v. a.* [*oint*, French.] To anoint; to smear with something unctuous.

They *oint* their naked limbs with mother'd oil,
Or from the founts where living sulphurs boil,
They mix a med'cine to foment their limbs. *Dryden.*

Ismarus was not wanting to the war,
Directing *ointed* arrows from afar;
And death with poison arm'd. *Dryden's Æneis.*

Oi'ntment. *n. s.* [from *oint.*] Unguent; unctuous matter to smear any thing.

Life and long health that gracious *ointment* gave,
And deadly wounds could heal, and rear again
The senseless corpse appointed for the grave. *Fairy Q.*

O'ker. *n. s.* [See **Ochre.**] A colour.

And Klaius taking for his younglings cark,
Lest greedy eyes to them might challenge lay,
Busy with *oker* did their shoulders mark. *Sidney.*

Red *oker* is one of the most heavy colours; yellow *oker* is not so, because it is clearer. *Dryden's Dufresnoy.*

OLD. *adj.* [ealꝺ, Saxon; *alt*, German.]

1. Past the middle part of life; not young.

To *old* age since you your self aspire,
Let not *old* age disgrace my high desire. *Sidney.*
He wooes high and low, rich and poor, young and *old.*
Shakesp. Merry Wives of Wind.

2. Of long continuance; begun long ago.

When Gardiner was sent over as embassador into France, with great pomp, he said unto an *old* acquaintance of his that came to take his leave of him, Now I am in my *gloria patri.* Yea, said his friend, and I hope, *et nunc et semper.* Or, replied the bishop, if it please the king my master, *sicat erat in principio*, a poor scholar of Cambridge again. *Camden's Remains.*

3. Not new.

The vine beareth more grapes when it is young; but grapes that make better wine when it is *old*; for that the juice is better concocted. *Bacon's Nat. History.*

4. Ancient; not modern.

The Genoese are cunning, industrious, and inured to hardship; which was likewise the character of the *old* Ligurians. *Addison on Italy.*

5. Of any specified duration.

How *old* art thou? Not so young, Sir, to love a woman for singing; nor so *old* to doat on her for any thing. I have years on my back forty-eight. *Shakesp. King Lear.*

Plead you to me, fair dame, I know you not.
In Ephesus I am but two hours *old*,
As strange unto your town as to your talk. *Shakesp.*

Any man that shall live to see thirty persons descended of his body alive together, and all above three years *old*, makes this feast, which is done at the cost of the state. *Bacon.*

6. Subsisting before something else.

The Latian king, unless he shall submit,
Own his *old* promise, and his new forget,
Let him in arms the pow'r of Turnus prove. *Dryd.*

He must live in danger of his house falling about his ears, and will find it cheaper to build it again from the ground in a new form; which may not be so convenient as the *old.* *Swift's Proj. for the Advan. of Relig.*

7. Long practised.

Then said I unto her that was *old* in adulteries, will they now commit whoredoms with her? *Ezek.* xxiii. 43.

8. A word to signify in burlesque language, more than enough.

Here will be *old* Utis; it will be an excellent stratagem. *Shakespeare's Henry* IV. *p.* ii.

Here's a knocking indeed; if a man were porter of hell gate, he should have *old* turning the key. *Shakesp.*

9. *Of old*; long ago; from ancient times.

These things they cancel, as having been instituted in regard of occasions peculiar to the times *of old*, and as being now superfluous. *Hooker, b.* v. *s.* 35.

Whether such virtue spent *of old* now fail'd
More angels to create. *Milt. P. Lost, b.* ix.

A land there is, Hesperia nam'd *of old*,
The soil is fruitful, and the men are bold;
Now call'd Italia, from the leader's name. *Dryden.*

In days *of old* there liv'd of mighty fame,
A valiant prince, and Theseus was his name. *Dryd.*

Oldfa'shioned. *adj.* [*old* and *fashion.*] Formed according to obsolete custom.

Some are offended that I turned these tales into modern English;

English; because they look on Chaucer as a dry, *oldfashioned* wit, not worth reviving. *Dryden.*

He is one of those *oldfashioned* men of wit and pleasure, that shews his parts by raillery on marriage. *Addison.*

O'LDEN. *adj.* [from *old*; perhaps the Saxon plural.] Ancient This word is not now in use.

Blood hath been shed ere now, i'th' *olden* time,
Ere human statute purg'd the gen'ral weal. *Shakesp.*

O'LDNESS. *n. s.* [from *old.*] Old age; antiquity; not newness; quality of being old.

This policy and reverence of ages, makes the world bitter to the best of our times; keeps our fortunes from us till our *oldness* cannot relish them. *Shakesp. King Lear.*

OLEA'GINOUS. *adj.* [*oleaginus*, Lat. from *oleum*, *oleagineux*, Fr.] Oily; unctuous.

The sap when it first enters the root, is earthy, watery, poor, and scarce *oleaginous*. *Arbuthnot on Aliments.*

OLEA'GINOUSNESS. *n. s.* [from *oleaginous.*] Oilinefs.

In speaking of the *oleaginousness* of urinous spirits, I employ the word most rather than all. *Boyle.*

OLE'ANDER. *n. s.* [*oleandre*, Fr.] The plant rosebay.

OLE'ASTER. *n. s.* [Latin.] Wild olive; a species of olive. It is a native of Italy, but hardy, and will endure the cold of our climate, and grow to the height of sixteen or eighteen feet. It blooms in June, and perfumes the circumambient air to a great distance. Its leaves are silver-coloured. *Miller.*

OLE'OSE. *adj.* [*oleosus*, Lat.] Oily.

Rain water may be endued with some vegetating or prolifick virtue, derived from some saline or *oleose* particles it contains. *Ray on the Creation.*

In falcons is a small quantity of gall, the *oleous* parts of the chyle being spent most on the fat. *Floyer on the Humours.*

To OLFA'CT. *v. a.* [*olfactus*, Lat.] To smell. A burlesque word.

There is a machiavilian plot,
Tho' every nare *olfact* it not. *Hudibras, p.* i.

OLFA'CTORY. *adj.* [*olfactoire*, Fr. from *olfacio*, Lat.] Having the sense of smelling.

Effluvias, or invisible particles that come from bodies at a distance, immediately affect the *olfactory* nerves. *Locke.*

O'LID. }
O'LIDOUS. } *adj.* [*olidus*, Lat.] Stinking; fœtid.

The fixt salt would have been not unlike that of men's urine; of which *olid* and despicable liquor I chose to make an instance, because chemists are not wont to care for extracting the fixt salt of it. *Boyle.*

In a civet cat a different and offensive odour proceeds partly from its food, that being especially fish, whereof this humour may be a garous excretion and *olidous* separation. *Brown.*

OLIGA'RCHY. *n. s.* [ὀλιγαρχία.] A form of government which places the supreme power in a small number; aristocracy.

The worst kind of *oligarchy*, is, when men are governed indeed by a few, and yet are not taught to know what those few be, to whom they should obey. *Sidney, b.* ii.

We have no aristocracies but in contemplation, all *oligarchies*, wherein a few men domineer, do what they list. *Burt.*

After the expedition into Sicily, the Athenians chose four hundred men for administration of affairs, who became a body of tyrants, and were called an *oligarchy*, or tyranny of the few; under which hateful denomination they were soon after deposed. *Swift.*

O'LIO. *n. s.* [*olla*, Span.] A mixture; a medly. See OGLIO.

Ben Johnson, in his Sejanus and Cataline, has given us this *olio* of a play, this unnatural mixture of comedy and tragedy. *Dryd. on Dram. Poetry.*

I am in a very chaos to think I should so forget myself. But I have such an *olio* of affairs, I know not what to do. *Congreve's Way of the World.*

O'LITORY. *n. s.* [*olitor*, Latin.] Belonging to the kitchen gaden.

Gather your *olitory* seeds. *Evelyn's Kalendar.*

OLIVA'STER. *adj.* [*olivastre*, Fr.] Darkly brown; tawny.

The countries of the Abysenes, Barbary, and Peru, where they are tawny, *olivaster* and pale, are generally more sandy. *Bacon's Nat. History*, N°. 399.

O'LIVE. *n. s.* [*olive*, Fr. *olea*, Lat.] A plant producing oil; the emblem of peace.

The leaves are for the most part oblong and ever-green; the flower consists of one leaf, the lower part of which is hollowed, but the upper part is divided into four parts; the ovary, which is fixed in the center of the flower cup, becomes an oval, soft, pulpy fruit, abounding with a fat liquor inclosing an hard rough stone. *Miller.*

To thee, heav'ns, in thy nativity,
Adjudg'd an *olive* branch and laurel crown,
As likely to be blest in peace and war. *Sha. Hen.* VI.

In the purlews of this forest, stands
A sheepcote fenc'd about with *olive* trees. *Shakespeare.*

The seventh year thou shalt let it rest. In like manner thou shalt deal with thy vineyard and *olive* yard. *Ex.* xxiii. 11.

He led
Mutuscans from their *olive* bearing town,
And all th' Eretian pow'rs. *Dryden's Æn.* viii.

It is laid out into a grove, a vineyard, and an allotment for *olives* and herbs. *Notes on the Odyssey.*

O'MBRE. *n. s.* [*hombre*, Spanish.] A game of cards played by three.

He would willingly carry her to the play; but she had rather go to lady Centaure's and play at *ombre*. *Tatler.*

O'MEGA. *n. s.* [ὠμέγα.] The last letter of the alphabet, therefore taken in the Holy Scripture for the last.

I am alpha and *omega*, the beginning and the ending. *Rev.* i. 8.

O'MELET. *n. s.* [*omelette*, Fr.] A kind of pancake made with eggs.

O'MENED. *adj.* [from *omen.*] Containing prognosticks.

Fame may prove,
Or *omen'd* voice, the messenger of Jove,
Propitious to the search. *Pope's Odyssey, b.* i.

O'MEN. *n. s.* [*omen*, Latin.] A sign good or bad; a prognostick.

When young kings begin with scorn of justice,
They make an *omen* to their after reign. *Dryden.*

The speech had *omen* that the Trojan race
Should find repose, and this the time and place. *Dryden.*

Choose out other smiling hours,
Such as have lucky *omens* shed
O'er forming laws and empires rising. *Prior.*

OME'NTUM. *n. s.* [Latin.]

The cawl, called also reticulum, from its structure, resembling that of a net. When the peritonæum is cut, as usual, and the cavity of the abdomen laid open, the *omentum* or cawl presents itself first to view. This membrane, which is like a wide and empty bag, covers the greatest part of the guts. *Quincy.*

O'MER. *n. s.* A Hebrew measure about three pints and a half English. *Bailey.*

To O'MINATE. *v. a.* [*ominor*, Lat.] To foretoken; to shew prognosticks.

This *ominates* sadly, as to our divisions with the Romanists. *Decay of Piety.*

OMINA'TION. *n. s.* [from *ominor*, Lat.] Prognostick.

The falling of salt is an authentick presagement of ill luck, yet the same was not a general prognostick of future evil among the ancients; but a particular *omination* concerning the breach of friendship. *Brown's V. Err. b.* v.

O'MINOUS. *adj.* [from *omen.*]

1. Exhibiting bad tokens of futurity; foreshewing ill; inauspicious.

Let me be duke of Clarence;
For Glo'ster's dukedom is *ominous*. *Shakesp. Henry* VI.

Pomfret, thou bloody prison,
Fatal and *ominous* to noble peers. *Shakesp. Rich.* III.

These accidents the more rarely they happen, the more *ominous* are they esteemed, because they are never observed but when sad events do ensue. *Hayward.*

Roving the Celtic and Iberian fields,
He last betakes him to this *ominous* wood. *Mil. Poems.*

As in the heathen worship of God, a sacrifice without an heart was accounted *ominous*; so in the christian worship of him, an heart without a sacrifice is worthless. *South's Serm.*

Pardon a father's tears,
And give them to Charinus' memory;
May they not prove as *ominous* to thee. *Dryden.*

2. Exhibiting tokens good or ill.

Though he had a good *ominous* name to have made a peace, nothing followed. *Bacon's Henry* VII.

O'MINOUSLY. *adv.* [from *ominous.*] With good or bad omen.

OMI'NOUSNESS. *n. s.* [from *ominous.*] The quality of being ominous.

OMI'SSION. *n. s.* [*omissus*, Lat.]

1. Neglect to do something; forbearance of something to be done.

Would it not impose a total *omission* of physic. *Brown.*

If he has made no provision for this great change, the *omission* can never be repaired, the time never redeemed. *Roger's Serm.* 12.

2. Neglect of duty, opposed to commission or perpetration of crimes.

Omission to do what is necessary,
Seals a commission to a blank of danger. *Shakespeare.*

The most natural division of all offences, is into those of *omission* and those of commission. *Addison's Freeholder.*

To O'MIT. *v. a.* [*omitto*, Lat.]

1. To leave out; not to mention.

These personal comparisons I *omit*, because I would say nothing that may savour of a spirit of flattery. *Bacon.*

Great Cato there, for gravity renown'd,
Who can *omit* the Gracchi, who declare
The Scipio's worth? *Dryden, Æn.* vi.

2. To neglect to practise.

Her father *omitted* nothing in her education, that might make

make her the most accomplished woman of her age. *Addis.*

OMI'TTANCE. *n. s.* [from *omit.*] Forbearance.

He said, mine eyes were black, and my hair black;
And now I am remember'd, scorn'd at me!
I marvel why I answer'd not again;
But that's all one, *omittance* is no quittance. *Shakesp.*

OMNIFA'RIOUS. *adj.* [*omnifariam*, Lat.] Of all varieties or kinds.

These particles could never of themselves, by *omnifarious* kinds of motion, whether fortuitous or mechanical, have fallen into this visible system. *Bentley's Serm.*

But if thou *omnifarious* drinks wou'dst brew;
Besides the orchard, ev'ry hedge and bush
Affords assistance. *Philips.*

OMNI'FEROUS. *adj.* [*omnis* and *fero*, Lat.] All-bearing. *Dict.*

OMNI'FICK. *adj.* [*omnis* and *facio*, Lat.] All-creating.

Silence, ye troubled waves, and thou deep, peace!
Said then th' *omnific* word, your discord end. *Milton.*

OMNI'FORM. *adj.* [*omnis* and *forma*, Lat.] Having every shape. *Dict.*

OMNI'GENOUS. *adj.* [*omnigenus*, Lat.] Consisting of all kinds. *Dict.*

OMNI'POTENCE. } *n. s.* [*omnipotentia*, Lat.] Almighty power;
OMNI'POTENCY. } unlimited power.

Whatever fortune
Can give or take, love wants not, or despises;
Or by his own *omnipotence* supplies. *Denham.*

As the soul bears the image of the divine wisdom, so this part of the body represents the *omnipotency* of God, whilst it is able to perform such wonderful effects. *Wilkins.*

The greatest danger is from the greatest power, and that is *omnipotency.* *Tillotson, Serm.* 1.

Will *omnipotence* neglect to save,
The suffering virtue of the wise and brave. *Pope.*

OMNI'POTENT. *adj.* [*omnipotens*, Lat.] Almighty; powerful without limit.

You were also Jupiter, a swan, for the love of Leda: oh *omnipotent* love! how near the god drew to the complexion of a goose?. *Shakesp. Merry Wives of Wind.*

The perfect being must needs be *omnipotent*; both as self-existent and as immense: for he that is self-existent, having the power of being, hath the power of allbeing; equal to the cause of all being, which is to be *omnipotent.* *Grew's Cosmol. b.* i. *c.* 1.

OMNIPRE'SENCE. *n. s.* [*omnis* and *præsens*, Lat.] Ubiquity; unbounded presence.

He also went
Invisible, yet staid, such privilege
Hath *omnipresence.* *Milton's Par Lost, b.* vii.

Adam, thou know'st his *omnipresence* fills
Land, sea, and air. *Milton's Par. Lost. b.* ix.

The soul is evolved and present to every part: and if my soul can have its effectual energy upon my body with ease, with how much more facility can a being of immense existence and *omnipresence*, of infinite wisdom and power, govern a great but finite universe? *Hale.*

OMNIPRE'SENT. *adj.* [*omnis* and *præsens*, Latin.] Ubiquitary; present in every place.

Omniscient master, *omnipresent* king,
To thee, to thee, my last distress I bring. *Prior.*

OMNI'SCIENCE. } *n. s.* [*omnis* and *scientia*, Lat.] Boundless
OMNI'SCIENCY. } knowledge; infinite wisdom.

In all this misconstruction of my actions, as I have no judge but God above me, so I can have comfort to appeal to his *omniscience.* *King Charles.*

Thinking by this retirement to obscure himself from God, he infringed the *omnisciency* and essential ubiquity of his maker, who as he created all things, so is he beyond and in them all. *Brown's Vulgar Errours, b.* i.

An immense being does strangely fill the soul; and omnipotency, *omnisciency*, and infinite goodness, enlarge the spirit while it fixtly looks upon them. *Burnet.*

Since thou boast'st th' *omniscience* of a God,
Say in what cranny of Sebastian's soul,
Unknown to me, so loath'd a crime is lodg'd? *Dryden.*

OMNI'SCIENT. *adj.* [*omnis* and *scio*, Lat.] Infinitely wise; knowing without bounds; knowing every thing.

By no means trust to your own judgment alone; for no man is *omniscient.* *Bacon's Adv. to Villiers.*

What can 'scape the eye
Of God all-seeing, or deceive his heart
Omniscient? *Milton's Paradise Lost, b.* x.

Whatsoever is known, is some way present; and that which is present, cannot but be known by him who is *omniscient.* *South's Sermons.*

Omniscient master, omnipresent king,
To thee, to thee, my last distress I bring. *Prior.*

OMNI'SCIOUS. *adj.* [*omnis* and *scio*, Lat.] All-knowing.

I dare not pronounce him *omniscious*, that being an attribute individually proper to the Godhead, and incommunicable to any created substance. *Hakewill on Providence.*

OMNI'VOROUS. *adj.* [*omnis* and *voro*, Lat.] All-devouring. *Dict.*

OMO'PLATE. *n. s.* [ὦμος and πλατὺς.] The shoulder blade. *Dict.*

OMPHALO'PTICK. *n. s.* [ὀμφαλὸς and ὀπτικὸς.] An optic glass that is convex on both sides, commonly called a convex lens. *Dict.*

ON. *prep.* [*aen*, Dutch; *an*, German.]

1. It is put before the word, which signifies that which is under, that by which any thing is supported, which any thing covers, or where any thing is fixed.

He is not lolling *on* a lewd love bed,
But *on* his knees at meditation. *Shakesp. Rich.* III.

What news?—
—Richmond is *on* the seas.—
—There let him sink and be the seas *on* him. *Shakesp.*

Distracted terror knew not what was best;
On what determination to abide. *Daniel's Civ. War.*

How soon hath time, the suttle thief of youth,
Stol'n *on* his wing my three and twentieth year,
My hasting days fly on with full career. *Milton.*

As some to witness truth heav'n's call obey,
So some *on* earth must, to confirm it, stay. *Dryden.*

They stooping low,
Perch'd *on* the double tree. *Dryden's Æn.* vi.

2. It is put before any thing that is the subject of action.

Th' unhappy husband, husband now no more,
Did *on* his tuneful harp his loss deplore. *Dryden.*

3. Noting addition or accumulation.

Mischiefs *on* mischiefs, greater still and more,
The neighb'ring plain with arms is cover'd o'er. *Dryden.*

4. Noting a state of progression.

Ho Mæris! whither *on* thy way so fast?
This leads to town. *Dryden.*

5. It sometimes notes elevation.

Chuse next a province for thy vineyard's reign,
On hills above, or in the lowly plain. *Dryden.*

6. Noting approach or invasion.

Their navy ploughs the wat'ry main,
Yet soon expect it *on* your shores again. *Dryden.*

On me, *on* me let all thy fury fall,
Nor err from me, since I deserve it all. *Pope.*

7. Noting dependance or reliance.

On God's providence and *on* your bounty, all their present support and future hopes depend. *Smallridge.*

8. At, noting place.

On each side her,
Stood pretty dimpled boys, like smiling
Cupids. *Sha. Ant. and Cleo.*

9. It denotes the motive or occasion of any thing.

The same prevalence of genius, the world cannot pardon your concealing, *on* the same consideration; because we neither have a living Varus nor a Horace. *Dryden.*

The joy of a monarch for the news of a victory, must not be expressed like the ecstasy of a harlequin *on* the receipt of a letter from his mistress. *Dryden's Dufresnoy.*

The best way to be used by a father *on* any occasion, to reform any thing he wishes mended in his son. *Locke.*

We abstain *on* such solemn occasions from things lawful, out of indignation that we have often gratified ourselves in things unlawful. *Smallridge's Sermons.*

10. It denotes the time at which any thing happens: as, this happened *on* the first day. *On* is used, I think, only before day or hour.

11. It is put before the object of some passion.

Compassion *on* the king commands me stoop. *Shakesp.*

Cou'd tears recal him into wretched life,
Their sorrow hurts themselves; *on* him is lost. *Dryden.*

12. In forms of denunciation it is put before the thing threatned.

Hence *on* thy life; the captive maid is mine,
Whom not for price or pray'rs I will resign. *Dryden.*

13. Noting imprecation.

Sorrow *on* thee, and all the pack of you,
That triumph thus upon my misery! *Shakespeare.*

14. Noting invocation.

On thee, dear wife, in deserts all alone
He call'd. *Dryden's Virg. Georg.* iv.

15. Noting the state of any thing.

—The earth shook to see the heav'ns *on* fire,
And not in fear of your nativity. *Shakesp. Henry* IV.

The horses burnt as they stood fast tied in the stables, or by chance breaking loose ran up and down with their tails and mains *on* a light fire. *Knolles's Hist. of the Turks.*

His fancy grows in the progress, and becomes *on* fire like a chariot wheel by its own rapidity. *Pop. Pref. to Iliad.*

16. Noting stipulation or condition.

I can be satisfied *on* more easy terms. *Dryden.*

17. Noting distinction or opposition.

The Rhodians, *on* the other side, mindful of their former honour, valiantly repulsed the enemy. *Knolles.*

18. Before

18. Before *it*, by corruption, it ſtands for *of*.

This tempeſt,
Daſhing the garment of this peace, aboded
The ſudden breach *on't*. *Shakeſpeare's Henry* VIII.

A thriving gameſter has but a poor trade *on't*, who fills his pockets at the price of his reputation. *Locke's Educat.*

19. Noting the manner of an event.

Note,
How much her grace is alter'd *on* the ſudden? *Shakeſp.*

20. *On*, the ſame with *upon*. See Upon.

On. *adv.*

1. Forward; in ſucceſſion.

As he forbore one act, ſo he might have foreborn another, and after that another, and ſo *on*, till he had by degrees weakened, and at length mortified and extinguiſhed the habit itſelf. *South's Sermons.*

If the tenant fail the landlord, he muſt fail his creditor, and he his, and ſo *on*. *Locke.*

Theſe ſmaller particles are again compoſed of others much ſmaller, all which together are equal to all the pores or empty ſpaces between them; and ſo *on* perpetually till you come to ſolid particles, ſuch as have no pores. *Newt.*

2. Forward; in progreſſion.

On indeed they went; but oh! not far;
A fatal ſtop travers'd their head-long courſe. *Daniel.*

So ſaying, *on* he led his radiant files. *Milton.*

Hopping and flying, thus they led him *on*
To the ſlow lake. *Dryden.*

What kindled in the dark the vital flame,
And ere the heart was form'd, puſh'd *on* the red'ning ſtream. *Blackmore on Creation.*

Go to, I did not mean to chide you;
On with your tale. *Rowe's J. Shore.*

3. In continuance; without ceaſing.

Let them ſleep, let them ſleep *on*,
Till this ſtormy night be gone,
And th' eternal morrow dawn. *Craſhaw.*

Sing *on*, ſing *on*, for I can ne'er be cloy'd. *Dryden.*

You roam about, and never are at reſt;
By new deſires, that is, new torments ſtill poſſeſt:
As in a fev'riſh dream you ſtill drink *on*,
And wonder why your thirſt is never gone. *Dryden.*

The peaſants defy the ſun; they work *on* in the hotteſt part of the day without intermiſſion. *Locke's Educat.*

4. Not off.

5. Upon the body, as part of dreſs.

A long cloak he had *on*. *Sidney.*

Stiff in brocade, and pinch'd in ſtays,
Her patches, paint, and jewels *on*;
All day let envy view her face,
And Phyllis is but twenty-one. *Prior.*

6. It notes reſolution to advance.

Since 'tis decreed, and to this period lead
A thouſand ways, the nobleſt path we'll tread;
And bravely *on*, till they or we, or all,
A common ſacrifice to honour fall. *Denham.*

On. *interject.* A word of incitement or encouragement to attack; elliptically for *go on*.

Therefore *on*, or ſtrip your ſword ſtark-naked; for meddle you muſt. *Shakeſpeare's Tweſth Night.*

Cheerly *on*, couragious friends,
To reap the harveſt of perpetual peace,
By this one bloody trial of ſharp war. *Shakeſp. R.* III.

Once. *adv.* [from *one*.]

1. One time.

Trees that bear maſt, are fruitful but *once* in two years; the cauſe is, the expence of ſap. *Bacon.*

Forthwith from out the ark a raven flies,
And after him the ſurer meſſenger,
A dove, ſent forth *once* and again to ſpy
Green trees or ground. *Milton's Paradiſe Loſt, b.* ix.

You came out like ſome great monarch, to take a town but *once* a year, as it were for your diverſion, though you had no need to extend your territories. *Dryden.*

O virgin! daughter of eternal night,
Give me this *once* thy labour, to ſuſtain
My right, and execute my juſt diſdain. *Dryden.*

In your tuneful lays,
Once more reſound the great Apollo's praiſe. *Pope.*

2. A ſingle time.

Who this heir is, he does not *once* tell us. *Locke.*

3. The ſame time.

At *once* with him they roſe:
Their riſing all at *once* was as the ſound
Of thunder heard remote. *Milton's Par. Loſt, b.* ii.

Fir'd with this thought, at *once* he ſtrain'd the breaſt,
And on the lips a burning kiſs impreſs'd. *Dryden.*

Now that the fixed ſtars, by reaſon of their immenſe diſtance, appear like points, unleſs ſo far as their light is dilated by refraction may appear from hence, that when the moon paſſes over them and eclipſes them, their light vaniſhes, not gradually like that of the planets, but all at *once*. *Newt.*

4. At a point of time indiviſible.

Night came on, not by degrees prepared,
But all at *once*; at *once* the winds ariſe,
The thunders roll. *Dryden's Cimon and Iphig.*

5. One time, though no more.

Fuſcinus, thoſe ill deeds that ſully fame,
In blood *once* tainted, like a current run
From the lewd father to the lewder ſon. *Dryden.*

6. At the time immediate.

This hath all its force at *once*, upon the firſt impreſſion, and is ever afterwards in a declining ſtate. *Atterbury.*

7. Formerly; at a former time.

Thereon his arms and *once*-lov'd portrait lay,
Thither our fatal marriage-bed convey. *Denham.*

My ſoul had *once* ſome fooliſh fondneſs for thee,
But hence 'tis gone. *Addiſon.*

8. *Once* ſeems to be rather a noun than an adverb, when it has *at* before it, and when it is joined with an adjective: as, *this once*, *that once*.

One. *adj.* [an, œne, Saxon; *een*, Dutch; *ein*, German; ἓν, Greek.]

1. Leſs than two; ſingle; denoted by an unite.

The man he knew was one that willingly,
For *one* good look would hazard all. *Daniel.*

Pindarus the poet, and *one* of the wiſeſt, acknowledged alſo *one* God the moſt high, to be the father and creator of all things. *Raleigh.*

If *one* muſt be rejected, *one* ſucceed,
Make him my Lord, within whoſe faithful breaſt
Is fix'd my image, and who loves me beſt. *Dryden.*

Love him by parts in all your num'rous race,
And from thoſe parts form *one* collected grace;
Then when you have refin'd to that degree,
Imagine all in *one*, and think that *one* is he. *Dryden.*

2. Indefinitely; any.

We ſhall
Preſent our ſervices to a fine new prince,
One of theſe days. *Shakeſpeare.*

I took pains to make thee ſpeak, taught thee each hour
One thing or other. *Shakeſpeare's Tempeſt.*

When any *one* heareth the word of the kingdom, and underſtandeth it not, then cometh the wicked one and catcheth away that which was ſown in his heart. *Matt.* xiii. 19.

If any *one* prince made a felicity in this life, and left fair fame after death, without the love of his ſubjects, there were ſome colour to deſpiſe it. *Suckling.*

3. Different; diverſe; oppoſed to *another*.

What a precious comfort to have ſo many, like brothers, commanding *one* another's fortunes. *Shakeſpeare.*

It is *one* thing to draw outlines true, the features like, the proportions exact, the colouring tolerable, and another thing to make all theſe graceful. *Dryden.*

Suppoſe the common depth of the ſea, taking *one* place with another, to be about a quarter of a mile. *Burnet.*

It is *one* thing to think right, and another thing to know the right way to lay our thoughts before others with advantage and clearneſs. *Locke.*

My legs were cloſed together by ſo many wrappers *one* over another, that I looked like an Egyptian mummy. *Add.*

Two bones rubbed hard againſt *one* another, or with a file, produce a fetid ſmell. *Arbuthnot on Aliments.*

At *one* time they keep their patients ſo warm, as almoſt to ſtifle them, and all of a ſudden the cold regimen is in vogue. *Baker on Learning.*

4. One of two oppoſed to the *other*.

Aſk from the *one* ſide of heaven unto the other, whether there hath been any ſuch thing as this. *Deutr.* iv. 32.

Both the matter of the ſtone and marchaſite, had been at once fluid bodies, till *one* of them, probably the marchaſite, firſt growing hard, the other, as being yet of a more yielding conſiſtence, accommodated itſelf to the harder's figure. *Boyle.*

There can be no reaſon why we ſhould prefer any *one* action to another, but becauſe we have greater hopes of advantage from the *one* than from the other. *Smallridge.*

5. Particularly one.

One day when Phæbe fair,
With all her band was following th' chaſe,
This nymph quite tir'd with heat of ſcorching air,
Sat down to reſt. *Fairy Queen, b.* i.

6. Some future.

Heav'n waxeth old, and all the ſpheres above
Shall *one* day faint, and their ſwift motion ſtay;
And time itſelf, in time ſhall ceaſe to move,
But the ſoul ſurvives and lives for aye. *Davies.*

One. *n. ſ.* [There are many uſes of the word *one*, which ſerve to denominate it a ſubſtantive though ſome of them may ſeem rather to make it a pronoun relative, and ſome may perhaps

perhaps be considered as consistent with the nature of an adjective.]

1. A single person.

If *one* by *one* you wedded all the world,
She you kill'd would be unparallel'd. *Shakespeare.*

Although the beauties, riches, honours, sciences, virtues, and perfections of all men were in the present possession of *one*, yet somewhat beyond and above all this there would still be sought and earnestly thirsted for. *Hooker, b.* i.

From his lofty steed he flew,
And raising *one* by *one* the suppliant crew,
To comfort each. *Dryden's Knight's Tale.*

When join'd in *one*, the good, the fair, the great,
Descends to view the muse's humble seat. *Granvile.*

2. A single mass or aggregate.

It is *one* thing only as a heap is *one*. *Blackmore.*

3. The first hour.

Till 'tis *one* o'clock, our dance of custom
Let us not forget. *Shakesp. M. Wives of Wind.*

4. The same thing.

I marvel, why I answer'd not again;
But that's all *one*, omittance is no quittance. *Shakesp.*

To be in the understanding, and not to be understood, is all *one* as to say any thing is, and is not in the understanding. *Locke.*

5. A person.

A good acquaintance with method will greatly assist every *one* in ranging human affairs. *Watts's Logick.*

6. A person by way of eminence.

Ferdinand
My father, king of Spain, was reckon'd *one*,
The wisest prince that there had reign'd. *Shakesp.*

7. A distinct or particular person.

That man should be the teacher is no part of the matter; for birds will learn *one* of another. *Bacon's Nat. Hist.*

No nations are wholly aliens and strangers the *one* to the other. *Bacon's Holy War.*

One or other sees a little box which was carried away with her, and so discovers her to her friends. *Dryden.*

8. Persons united.

As I have made ye *one*, lords, *one* remain:
So I grow stronger, you more honour gain. *Shakes.*

9. Concord; agreement; one mind.

The king was well instructed how to carry himself between Ferdinando and Philip, resolving to keep them at *one* within themselves. *Bacon's Henry* VII.

He is not at *one* with himself what account to give of it. *Tillotson.*

10. [*On, l'on*, French. It is used sometimes a general or indefinite nominative for any man, any person. For *one* the English formerly used *men*; as, *they live obscurely* men *know not how, or die obscurely*, men *mark not when. Ascham.* For which it would now be said, *one knows not how, one knows not when*; or, *it is not known how.*] Any person; any man indefinitely.

It is not so worthy to be brought to heroical effects by fortune or necessity, like Ulysses and Æneas, as by *one's* own choice and working. *Sidney, b.* ii.

One may be little the wiser for reading this dialogue, since it neither sets forth what Erona is, nor what the cause should be which threatens her with death. *Sidney, b.* ii.

One would imagine these to be the expressions of a man blessed with ease, affluence and power; not of one who had been just stripped of all those advantages. *Atterbury.*

For provoking of urine, *one* should begin with the gentlest first. *Arbuthnot on Aliments.*

For some time *one* was not thought to understand Aristotle, unless he had read him with Averroe's comment. *Baker.*

11. A person of particular character.

Then must you speak
Of *one* that lov'd not wisely, but too well;
Of *one* not easily jealous; but being wrought
Perplex'd in the extreme. *Shakesp. Othello.*

With lives and fortunes trusting *one*
Who so discreetly us'd his own. *Waller.*

Edward I. was *one* that very well knew how to use a victory, as well as obtain it. *Hale.*

One who contemned divine and human laws. *Dryden.*

12. *One* has sometimes a plural, either when it stands for persons indefinitely; as, *the* great ones *of the world*: or when it relates to some thing going before, and is only the representative of the antecedent noun. This relative mode of speech, whether singular or plural, is in my ear not very elegant, yet is used by good authors.

Be not found here; hence with your little *ones*. *Shakesp.*

These successes are more glorious which bring benefit to the world, than such ruinous *ones* as are dyed in human blood. *Glanvile's Sceps. Pref.*

He that will overlook the true reason of a thing which is but *one*, may easily find many false *ones*, error being infinite. *Tillotson, Serm.* 1.

The following plain rules and directions, are not the less useful because they are plain *ones*. *Atterbury.*

There are many whose waking thoughts are wholly employed on their sleeping *ones*. *Addison's Spectator.*

Arbitrary power tends to make a man a bad sovereign, who might possibly have been a good *one*, had he been invested with an authority limited by law. *Addison's Freeholder.*

This evil fortune which attends extraordinary men, hath been imputed to divers causes that need not be set down, when so obvious an *one* occurs, that when a great genius appears the dunces are all in conspiracy against him. *Swift.*

ONE'EYED. *adj.* [*one* and *eye.*] Having only one eye.

A sign-post dauber wou'd disdain to paint
The *oneey'd* heroe on his elephant. *Dryden.*

The mighty family
Of *oneey'd* brothers hasten to the shore. *Addison.*

ONEIROCRI'TICAL. *adj.* [ὀνειροκριτικός, Gr. *onirocritique*, Fr. it should therefore according to analogy be written *onirocritical* and *onirocritick.*] Interpretative of dreams.

If a man has no mind to pass by abruptly from his imagined to his real circumstances, he may employ himself in that new kind of observation which my *oneirocritical* correspondent has directed him to make. *Addison's Spectator.*

ONEIROCRI'TICK. *n. s.* [ὀνειροκριτικὸς, Gr.] An interpreter of dreams.

Having surveyed all ranks and professions, I do not find in any quarter of the town an *oneirocritick*, or an interpreter of dreams. *Addison's Spectator*, N°. 505.

ONE'NESS. *n. s.* [from *one.*] Unity; the quality of being one.

Our God is one, or rather very *oneness* and mere unity, having nothing but itself in itself, and not consisting, as all things do besides God, of many things. *Hooker.*

The *oneness* of our Lord Jesus Christ, referring to the several hypostases, is the one eternal indivisible divine nature, and the eternity of the son's generation, and his co-eternity, and his consubstantiality with the father when he came down from Heaven and was incarnate. *Hammond.*

O'NERARY. *adj.* [*onerarius*, Lat. *oneraise*, Fr.] Fitted for carriage or burthens.

To O'NERATE. *v. a.* [*onero*, Lat.] To load; to burthen.

ONERA'TION. *n. s.* [from *onerate.*] The act of loading. *Dict.*

O'NEROUS. *adj.* [*onereux*, Fr. *onerosus*, Lat.] Burthensome; oppressive.

A banished person, that is absent out of necessity, retains all things *onerous* to himself, as a punishment for his crime. *Ayliffe's Parergon.*

ONION. *n. s.* [*oignon*, French.]

It hath an orbicular, coated, bulbous root; the leaves are hollow or pip; the stalk also hollow and swells out in the middle; the flowers consisting of six leaves are collected into a spherical head; the style of the flower becomes a roundish fruit divided into three cells, containing roundish seeds. *Mill.*

If the boy have not a woman's gift
To rain a shower of commanded tears,
An *onion* will do well. *Sha. Taming of the Shrew.*
I an ass, am *onion*-ey'd. *Sha. Ant. and Cleopatra.*

This is ev'ry cook's opinion,
No sav'ry dish without an *onion*:
But lest your kissing should be spoil'd,
Your *onions* must be throughly boil'd. *Swift.*

O'NLY. *adj.* [from *one*, *onely*, or *onelike.*]

1. Single; one and no more.

Of all whom fortune to my sword did bring,
This *only* man was worth the conquering. *Dryden.*

2. This and no other.

The logick now in use has long possessed the chair, as the *only*. art taught in the schools for the direction of the mind in the study of the sciences. *Locke.*

3. This above all other: as, he is the *only* man for musick.

O'NLY. *adv.*

1. Simply; singly; merely; barely.

I propose my thoughts *only* as conjectures. *Burnet.*

The posterity of the wicked inherit the fruit of their father's vices; and that not *only* by a just judgment, but from the natural course of things. *Tillotson, Serm.* 4.

All who deserve his love, he makes his own;
And to be lov'd himself, needs *only* to be known. *Dryd.*

Nor must this contrition be exercised by us, *only* for grosser evils; but when we live the best. *Wake.*

2. So and no otherwise.

Every imagination of the thoughts of his heart, was *only* evil continually. *Gen.* vi. 5.

3. Singly without more: as, *only begotten.*

O'NOMANCY. *n. s.* [ὄνομα and μαντεία.] Divination by a name.

Destinies were superstitiously, by *onomancy*, deciphered out of names, as though the names and natures of men were suitable, and fatal necessities concurred herein with voluntary motion. *Camden.*

ONOMA'NTICAL. *adj.* [ὄνομα and μάντις.] Predicting by names.

Theodatus, when curious to know the success of his wars against the Romans, an *onomantical* or name-wisard Jew, willed

willed him to ſhut up a number of ſwine and give ſome of them Roman names, others Gothiſh names with ſeveral marks, and there to leave them. *Camden.*

O'NSET. *n. ſ.* [*on* and *ſet.*]

1. Attack; ſtorm; aſſault; firſt brunt.

As well the ſoldier dieth, which ſtandeth ſtill, as he that gives the braveſt *onſet.* *Sidney, b.* ii.

All breathleſs, weary, faint,
Him ſpying, with freſh *onſet* he aſſail'd,
And kindling new his courage, ſeeming queint,
Struck him ſo hugely, that through great conſtraint
He made him ſtoop. *Fairy Queen, b.* ii.

The ſhout
Of battle now began, and ruſhing ſound
Of *onſet.* *Milton's Paradiſe Loſt, b.* vi.

Sometimes it gains a point; and preſently it finds itſelf baffled and beaten off; yet ſtill it renews the *onſet,* attacks the difficulty afreſh; plants this reaſoning and that argument, like ſo many intellectual batteries, till at length it forces a way into the obſtinate encloſed truth. *South.*

Without men and proviſions it is impoſſible to ſecure conqueſts that are made in the firſt *onſets* of an invaſion. *Addiſ.*

Obſerve
The firſt impetuous *onſets* of his grief;
Uſe every artifice to keep him ſtedfaſt. *Philips.*

2. Something added by way of ornamental appendage. This ſenſe, ſays *Nicholſon,* is ſtill retained in Northumberland, where *onſet* means a *tuft.*

I will with deeds requite thy gentleneſs;
And for an *onſet,* Titus, to advance
Thy name and honourable family,
Lavinia will I make my empreſs. *Shakeſp. Tit. And.*

To O'NSET. *v. a.* [from the noun.] To ſet upon; to begin.

This for a while was hotly *onſetted* and a reaſonable price offered, but ſoon cooled again. *Carew.*

O'NSLAUGHT. *n. ſ.* [*on* and *ſlay.* See SLAUGHTER.] Attack; ſtorm; onſet.

They made a halt
To view the ground, and where t'aſſault,
Then call'd a council, which was beſt,
By ſiege or *onſlaught* to inveſt
The enemy; and 'twas agreed
By ſtorm and *onſlaught* to proceed. *Hudibras, p.* i.

ONTO'LOGIST. *n. ſ.* [from *ontology.*] One who conſiders the affections of being in general; a metaphyſician.

ONTO'LOGY. *n. ſ.* [ὄντα and λόγος.] The ſcience of the affections of being in general; metaphyſicks.

The modes, accidents and relations that belong to various beings, are copiouſly treated of in metaphyſicks, or more properly *ontology.* *Watts's Logick.*

O'NWARD. *adv.* [onƿeaꞃꝺ, Saxon.]

1. Forward; progreſſively.

My lord,
When you went *onward* on this ended action,
I look'd upon her with a ſoldier's eye. *Shakeſpeare.*

Satan was now at hand, and from his ſeat
The monſter moving *onward* came as faſt,
With horrid ſtrides. *Milt. Par. Loſt, b.* ii.

Him thro' the ſpicy foreſt *onward* come
Adam diſcern'd, as in the door he ſat
Of his cool bow'r. *Milt. Paradiſe Loſt, b.* v.

Not one looks backward, *onward* ſtill he goes,
Yet ne'er looks forward farther than his noſe. *Pope.*

2. In a ſtate of advanced progreſſion.

Philoxenus came to ſee how *onward* the fruits were of his friends labour. *Sidney.*

You are already ſo far *onward* of your way, that you have forſaken the imitation of ordinary converſe. *Dryden.*

3. Somewhat farther.

A little *onward* lend thy guiding hand
To theſe dark ſteps, a little farther on. *Milton.*

O'NYCHA. *n. ſ.* It is found in two different ſenſes in ſcripture. — The odoriferous ſnail or ſhell, and the ſtone named onyx. The greateſt part of commentators explain it by the onyx or odoriferous ſhell, like that of the ſhell-fiſh called purpura. The onyx is fiſhed for in watry places of the Indies, where grows the ſpicanardi, which is the food of this fiſh and what makes its ſhell ſo aromatick. *Calmet.*

Take ſweet ſpices, *onycha,* and galbanum. *Ex.* xxx. 34.

O'NYX. *n. ſ.* [ὄνυξ.] The *onyx* is a ſemipellucid gem, of which there are ſeveral ſpecies, but the blueiſh white kind, with brown and white zones, is the true *onyx* legitima of the ancients. It is a very elegant and beautiful gem, and the regular arrangement and diſpoſition of its colours make amends for their want of ſhow. *Hill's Mat. Med.*

Nor are her rare endowments to be ſold,
For glittering ſand by Ophir ſhown,
The blue-ey'd ſaphir, or rich *onyx* ſtone. *Sandys.*

The *onyx* is an accidental variety of the agat kind: it is of a dark horny colour, in which is a plate of a bluiſh white, and ſometimes of red: when on one or both ſides the white, there happens to lie alſo a plate of a reddiſh or freſh colour, the jewellers call the ſtone a ſardonyx. *Woodward on Foſſ.*

OOZE. *n. ſ.* [either from *eaux,* waters, French; or pæꞅ, wetneſs, Saxon.]

1. Soft mud; mire at the bottom of water; ſlime.

My ſon i' th' *ooze* is bedded. *Shakeſp. Tempeſt.*

Some carried up into their grounds the *ooze* or ſalt water mud, and found good profit thereby. *Carew.*

Old father Thames rais'd up his rev'rend head,
Deep in his *ooze* he ſought his ſedgy bed,
And ſhrunk his waters back into his urn. *Dryden.*

2. Soft flow; ſpring. This ſeems to be the meaning in *Prior.*

From his firſt fountain and beginning *ooze,*
Down to the ſea each brook and torrent flows. *Prior.*

3. The liquor of a tanner's vat.

To OOZE. *v. n.* [from the noun.] To flow by ſtealth; to run gently; to drain away.

When the contracted limbs were cramp'd, even then
A wat'riſh humour ſwell'd and *ooz'd* agen. *Dryden.*

Where creeping waters *ooze,*
Where marſhes ſtagnate, and where rivers wind,
Cluſter the rolling fogs. *Thomſ. Autumn.*

The lilly drinks
The latent rill, ſcarce *oozing* thro' the graſs. *Thomſon.*

O'OZY. *adj.* [from *ooze.*] Miry; muddy; ſlimy.

From his *oozy* bed,
Old father Thames advanc'd his rev'rend head. *Pope.*

To OPA'CATE. *v. a.* [*opaco,* Lat.] To ſhade; to cloud; to darken; to obſcure.

The ſame corpuſcles upon the unſtopping of the glaſs, did *opacate* that part of the air they moved in. *Boyle.*

OPA'CITY. *n. ſ.* [*opacité,* Fr. *opacitas,* Lat.] Cloudineſs; want of tranſparency.

Can any thing eſcape the perſpicacity of thoſe eyes in whoſe opticks there is no *opacity?* *Brown.*

Had there not been any night, ſhadow or *opacity,* we ſhould never have had any determinate conceit of darkneſs. *Glanv.*

How much any body hath of colour, ſo much hath it of *opacity,* and by ſo much the more unfit is it to tranſmit the ſpecies. *Ray on the Creation.*

The leaſt parts of almoſt all natural bodies, are in ſome meaſure tranſparent; and the *opacity* of thoſe bodies ariſeth from the multitude of reflexions cauſed in their internal parts. *Newt. Opt.*

OPA'COUS. *adj.* [*opacus,* Latin.] Dark; obſcure; not tranſparent.

When he perceives that theſe *opacous* bodies do not hinder the eye from judging light to have an equal diffuſion through the whole place that it irradiates, he can have no difficulty to allow air, that is diaphanous, and more ſubtile far than they, and conſequently, diviſible into leſſer atoms; and having leſſer pores, gives leſs ſcope to our eyes to miſs light. *Digby.*

Upon the firm *opacous* globe
Of this round world, whoſe firſt convex divides
The luminous inferior orbs, incloſ'd
From chaos, and th' inroad of darkneſs old,
Satan alighted. *Milton's Paradiſe Loſt, b.* iii.

O'PAL. *n. ſ.* The *opal* is a very elegant and a very ſingular kind of ſtone, it hardly comes within the rank of the pellucid gems, being much more opake, and leſs hard. It is found always in the pebble ſhape of various ſizes, from the head of a pin to the bigneſs of a walnut. It is naturally bright, ſmooth and gloſſy, and ſhows all its beauty without the help of the lapidary: in colour it much reſembles the fineſt mother of pearl; its baſis ſeeming a bluiſh or greyiſh white, but with a property of reflecting all the colours of the rainbow, as turned differently to the light, among which the green and the blue are particularly beautiful, but the fiery red is the fineſt of all. This ſtone is found in the Eaſt-Indies, in Egypt, Perſia and Tartary, and in ſome parts of Europe, particularly in Bohemia; but the oriental is much the fineſt. *Hill's Mat. Med.*

Thy mind is a very *opal.* *Shakeſp. Twelfth Night.*

Th' empyreal heav'n, extended wide
In circuit, undetermin'd ſquare or round;
With *opal* tow'rs, and battlements adorn'd
Of living ſaphir. *Milton's Par. Loſt, b.* ii.

We have this ſtone from Germany, and is the ſame with the *opal* of the ancients. *Woodw. on Foſſ.*

OPA'QUE. *adj.* [*opacus,* Lat.]

They
Shot upward ſtill direct, whence no way round
Shadow from body *opaque* can fall. *Milt. Par. Loſt.*

Theſe diſappearing fixt ſtars were actually extinguiſhed and turned into more *opaque* and groſs planet-like bodies. *Cheyne's Phil. Prin.*

To OPE. }
To O'PEN. } *v. a.* [open, Saxon; *op,* Iſlandick, a hole. *Ope* is uſed only in poetry, when one ſyllable is more convenient than two.]

1. To uncloſe; to unlock; to put into ſuch a ſtate as that the inner parts may be ſeen or entered. The contrary to *ſhut.*

The

The world's mine oyster,
Which I with sword will *open*. *Shakesp. M. W. of Wind.*
Before you fight, *ope* this letter. *Shakesp. K. Lear.*
They consent to work us harm and woe,
To *ope* the gates, and so let in our foe. *Fairfax.*

If a man *open* a pit and not cover it, and an ox fall therein, the owner of the pit shall make it good. *Ex.* xxi. 23.

Let us pass through your land, and none shall do you any hurt; howbeit they would not *open* unto him. 1 *Mac.* v. 48.

Open thy mouth for the dumb in the cause of all such as are appointed to destruction. *Prov.* xxxi. 8.

Open to me the gates of righteousness. *Ps.* cxviii. 19.

Adam, now *ope* thine eyes; and first behold
Th' effects which thy original crime hath wrought
In some to spring from thee. *Milt. Par. Lost*, *b.* xi.

Our fleet Apollo sends,
Where Tuscan Tyber rolls with rapid force,
And where Numicus *opes* his holy source. *Dryden.*

When first you *ope* your doors, and passing by
The sad ill-omen'd object meets your eye. *Dryden.*

When the matter is made, the side must be *opened* to let it out. *Arbuthnot on Aliments.*

2. To show; to discover.

The English did adventure far for to *open* the north parts of America. *Abbot's Description of the World.*

3. To divide; to break.

The wall of the cathedral church was *opened* by an earthquake, and shut again by a second. *Addison on Italy.*

4. To explain; to disclose.

Some things wisdom *openeth* by the sacred books of scripture, some things by the glorious works of nature. *Hooker.*

Paul reasoned with them out of the scriptures, *opening* and alleging, that Christ must needs have suffered and risen again from the dead. *Acts* xvii. 3.

After the earl of Lincoln was slain, the king *opened* himself to some of his council, that he was sorry for the earl's death, because by him he might have known the bottom of his danger. *Bacon's Henry* VII.

Gramont governour of Bayonne, took an exquisite notice of their persons and behaviour, and *opened* himself to some of his train, that he thought them to be gentlemen of much more worth than their habits bewrayed. *Wotton.*

A friend who relates his success, talks himself into a new pleasure; and by *opening* his misfortunes, leaves part of them behind him. *Collier on Friendship.*

5. To begin.

You retained him only for the *opening* of your cause, and your main lawyer is yet behind. *Dryd. Ep. to the Whigs.*

Homer *opens* his poem with the utmost simplicity and modesty, he continually grows upon the reader. *Notes on Odyss.*

To Ope.
To O'pen. } *v. n.*

1. To unclose itself; not to remain shut; not to continue closed.

The hundred doors
Ope of themselves; a rushing whirlwind roars
Within the cave. *Dryden, Æn.* vi.

My old wounds are *open'd* at this view,
And in my murd'rer's presence bleed anew. *Dryden.*

Unnumber'd treasures *ope* at once,
From each she nicely culls with curious toil,
And decks the goddess. *Pope's Rape of the Lock.*

2. To bark. A term of hunting.

If I cry out thus upon no trail, never trust me when I *open* again. *Shakesp. Merry Wives of Windsor.*

The night restores our actions done by day;
As hounds in sleep will *open* for their prey. *Dryden.*

Cytheron loudly calls me to my way;
Thy hounds, Taygetus, *open* and pursue their prey. *Dryd.*

Hark! the dog *opens*, take thy certain aim;
The woodcock flutters. *Gay's Rural Sports.*

Ope.
O'pen. } *adj.* [*Ope* is scarcely used but by old authors, and by them in the primitive not figurative sense.]

1. Unclosed; not shut.

The gates are *ope*; now prove good seconds;
'Tis for the followers fortune widens them;
Not for the fliers. *Shakesp. Coriolanus.*

Most sacrilegious murther hath broke *ope*
The lord's anointed temple, and stole thence
The life o' th' building. *Shakesp. Macbeth.*

Then sent Sanballat his servant, with an *open* letter in his hand. *Neh.* vi. 5.

With the same key set *ope* the door
Wherewith you lock'd it fast before. *Cleaveland.*

Thro' the gate,
Wide *open* and unguarded, Satan pass'd. *Milt. P. Lost.*

They meet the chiefs returning from the fight,
And each with *open* arms embrac'd her chosen knight. *Dry.*

He, when Æneas on the plain appears,
Meets him with *open* arms and falling tears. *Dryden.*

The bounce broke *ope* the door. *Dryden.*

The door was *ope*, they blindly grope the way. *Dryden.*

2. Plain; apparent; evident.

They crucify to themselves the son of God afresh, and put him to an *open* shame. *Hebr.* vi. 6.

Th' under-work, transparent, shews too plain:
Where *open* acts accuse, th' excuse is vain. *Daniel.*

3. Not wearing disguise; clear; artless; sincere.

He was so secret therein, as not daring to be *open*, that to no creature he ever spake of it. *Sidney.*

Lord Cordes, the hotter he was against the English in time of war, had the more credit in a negotiation of peace; and besides was held a man *open* and of good faith. *Bacon.*

The French are always *open*, familiar, and talkative; the Italians stiff, ceremonious, and reserved. *Addison.*

This reserved mysterious way of acting towards persons, who in right of their posts expected a more *open* treatment, was imputed to some hidden design. *Swift.*

His generous, *open*, undesigning heart,
Has begg'd his rival to sollicit for him. *Addison's Cato.*

4. Not clouded; clear.

With dry eyes, and with an *open* look,
She met his glance midway. *Dryden's Boccace.*

Then shall thy Craggs
On the cast ore another Pollio shine;
With aspect *open* shall erect his head. *Pope.*

5. Not hidden; exposed to view.

In that little spot of ground that lies between those two great oceans of eternity, we are to exercise our thoughts, and lay *open* the treasures of the divine wisdom and goodness hid in this part of nature and providence. *Burnet.*

These innate notions should lie *open* fairly to every one's view. *Locke.*

Moral principles require reasoning and discourse to discover the certainty of their truths: they lie not *open* as natural characters engraven on the mind. *Locke.*

6. Not restrained; not denied.

If Demetrius and the craftsmen have a matter against any man, the law is *open* and there are deputies; let them implead one another. *Acts* xix. 38.

7. Not cloudy; not gloomy.

An *open* and warm winter portendeth a hot and dry summer. *Bacon's Nat. Hist.*

8. Uncovered.

Here is better than the *open* air. *Shakesp. K. Lear.*

And when at last in pity, you will die,
I'll watch your birth of immortality;
Then, turtle-like, I'll to my mate repair,
And teach you your first flight in *open* air. *Dryden.*

9. Exposed; without defence.

The service that I truly did his life,
Hath left me *open* to all injuries. *Shakesp. Henry* IV.

10. Attentive.

Thine eyes are *open* upon all the sons of men, to give every one according to his ways. *Jer.* xxxii. 19.

The eyes of the Lord are upon the righteous, and his ears are *open* unto their cry. *Ps.* xxxiv. 15.

O'pener. *n. s.* [from *open.*]

1. One that opens; one that unlocks; one that uncloses.

True *opener* of mine eyes,
Much better seems this vision, and more hope
Of peaceful days portends, than those two past. *Milt.*

2. Explainer; interpreter.

To us, th' imagin'd voice of heav'n itself;
The very *opener* and intelligencer
Between the grace, the sanctities of heav'n,
And our dull workings. *Shakesp. Henry* IV.

3. That which separates; disuniter.

There may be such *openers* of compound bodies, because there wanted not some experiments in which it appeared. *Boyle.*

Openey'ed. *adj.* [*open* and *eye.*] Vigilant; watchful.

While you here do snoring lie,
Openeyed conspiracy
His time doth take. *Shakespeare's Tempest.*

Openha'nded. *adj.* [*open* and *hand.*] Generous; liberal; munificent.

Good heav'n who renders mercy back for mercy,
With *openhanded* bounty shall repay you. *Rowe.*

Openhea'rted. *adj.* [*open* and *heart.*] Generous; candid; not meanly subtle.

I know him well; he's free and *openhearted*. *Dryden.*

Of an *openhearted* generous minister you are not to say that he was in an intrigue to betray his country; but in an intrigue with a lady. *Arbuthnot's J. Bull.*

Openhea'rtedness. *n. s.* [*open* and *heart.*] Liberality; munificence; generosity.

O'pening. *n. s.* [from *open.*]

1. Aperture; breach.

The fire thus up, makes its way through the cracks and *openings* of the earth. *Woodw. Nat. Hist.*

2. Discovery at a distance; faint knowledge; dawn.

God has been pleased to dissipate this confusion and chaos, and

and to give us some openings, some dawnings of liberty and settlement. *South's Sermons.*

The *opening* of your glory was like that of light; you shone to us from afar and disclosed your first beams on distant nations. *Dryden.*

O'PENLY. *adv.* [from *open.*]

1. Publickly; not secretly; in sight; not obscurely.

Their actions always spoken of with great honour, are now called *openly* into question. *Hooker, b.* v.

Prayers are faulty, not whensoever they be *openly* made, but when hypocrisy is the cause of open praying. *Hooker.*

Why should you have put me to deny
This claim which now you wear so *openly*. *Shakesp.*

I knew the time,
Now full, that I no more should live obscure,
But *openly* begin, as best becomes
The authority which I deriv'd from heav'n. *Par. Reg.*

How grosly and *openly* do many of us contradict the plain precepts of the gospel, by our ungodliness and worldly lusts. *Tillotson, Serm.* 5.

We express our thanks by *openly* owning our parentage, and paying our common devotions to God on this day's solemnity. *Atterbury's Sermons.*

2. Plainly; apparently; evidently; without disguise.

Darah
Too *openly* does love and hatred show:
A bounteous master, but a deadly foe. *Dryden.*

OPENMOU'THED. *adj.* [*open* and *mouth.*] Greedy; ravenous; clamorous; vociferous.

Up comes a lion *openmouthed* toward the ass. *L'Estrange.*

O'PENNESS. *n. s.* [from *open.*]

1. Plainness; clearness; freedom from obscurity or ambiguity.

Deliver with more *openness* your answers
To my demands. *Shakesp. Cymbeline.*

2. Plainness; freedom from disguise.

The noble *openness* and freedom of his reflexions, are expressed in lively colours. *Felton on the Classicks.*

These, letters all written in the *openness* of friendship, will prove what were my real sentiments. *Pope's Letters.*

O'PERA. *n. s.* [Italian.]

An *opera* is a poetical tale or fiction, represented by vocal and instrumental musick, adorned with scenes, machines, and dancing. *Dryden's Pref. to Albion.*

O'PERABLE. *adj.* [from *operor*, Latin.] To be done; practicable.

Being uncapable of *operable* circumstances, or rightly to judge the prudentiality of affairs, they only gaze upon the visible success, and thereafter condemn or cry up the whole progression. *Brown's Vulgar Errours, b.* i.

O'PERANT. *adj.* [*operant*, French.] Active; having power to produce any effect. A word not in use.

Earth, yield me roots!
Who seeks far better of thee, sauce his palate
With thy most *operant* poison! *Shakesp. Tim. of Athens.*

I must leave thee, love, and shortly too;
My *operant* powers their functions leave to do. *Shakesp.*

To O'PERATE. *v. n.* [*operor*, Latin; *operer*, French.] To act; to have agency; to produce effects.

The virtues of private persons *operate* but on a few; their sphere of action is narrow, and their influence is confined to it. *Atterbury's Sermons.*

Bodies produce ideas in us, manifestly by impulse, the only way which we can conceive bodies *operate* in. *Locke.*

It can *operate* on the guts and stomach, and thereby produce distinct ideas. *Locke.*

A plain convincing reason *operates* on the mind, both of a learned and ignorant hearer as long as they live. *Swift.*

Where causes *operate* freely, with a liberty of indifference to this or the contrary, the effect will be contingent, and the certain knowledge of it belongs only to God. *Watts.*

OPERA'TION. *n. s.* [*operatio*, Lat .*operation*, French.]

1. Agency; production of effects; influence.

There are in men *operations*, some natural, some rational, some supernatural, some politick, some finally ecclesiastical. *Hooker.*

By all the *operations* of the orbs,
From whom we do exist and cease to be,
Here I disclaim all my paternal care. *Shakesp. Lear.*

All *operations* by transmission of spirits and imagination, work at distance and not at touch. *Bacon's Nat. Hist.*

Waller's presence had an extraordinary *operation* to procure any thing desired. *Clarendon, b.* viii.

The tree whose *operation* brings
Knowledge of good and ill, shun to taste. *Milt. P. Lost.*

If the *operation* of these salts be in convenient glasses promoted by warmth, the ascending steams may easily be caught and reduced into a penetrant spirit. *Boyle.*

The pain and sickness caused by manna, are the effects of its *operation* on the stomach and guts by the seize, motion and figure of its insensible parts. *Locke.*

2. Action; effect.

Repentance and renovation consist not in the strife, wish, or purpose, but in the actual *operations* of good life. *Hamm.*

That false fruit
Far other *operation* first display'd,
Carnal desire inflaming. *Milton's Par. Lost, b.* ix.

Speculative painting, without the assistance of manual *operation*, can never attain to perfection, but slothfully languishes; for it was not with his tongue that Apelles performed his noble works. *Dryden's Dufresnoy.*

In this understanding piece of clock-work, his body as well as other senseless matter has colour, warmth and softness. But these qualities are not subsistent in those bodies, but are *operations* of fancy begotten in something else. *Bentley.*

3. [In chirurgery.] The part of the art of healing which depends on the use of instruments.

4. The motions or employments of an army.

O'PERATIVE. *adj.* [from *operate.*] Having the power of acting; having forcible agency.

To be over curious in searching how God's all-piercing and *operative* spirit distinguishing gave form to the matter of the universal, is a search like unto his, who not contented with a known ford, will presume to pass over the greatest rivers in all parts where he is ignorant of their depths. *Ral.*

Many of the nobility endeavoured to make themselves popular, by speaking in parliament against those things which were most grateful to his majesty; and he thought a little discountenance upon those persons would suppress that spirit within themselves, or make the poison of it less *operative* upon others. *Clarendon.*

In actions of religion we should be zealous, active and *operative*, so far as prudence will permit. *Taylor.*

This circumstance of the promise must give life to all the rest, and make them *operative* toward the producing of good life. *Decay of Piety.*

It holds in all *operative* principles, especially in morality; in which, not to proceed, is certainly to go backward. *South.*

The will is the conclusion of an *operative* syllogism. *Norr.*

OPERA'TOR. *n. s.* [*operateur*, Fr. from *operate.*] One that performs any act of the hand; one who produces any effect.

An imaginary *operator* opening the first with a great deal of nicety, upon a cursory view appeared like the head of another. *Addison's Spectator*, N°. 275.

To administer this dose, there cannot be fewer than fifty thousand *operators*, allowing one *operator* to every thirty. *Swift.*

OPERO'SE. *adj.* [*operosus*, Latin.] Laborious; full of trouble and tediousness.

Such an explication is purely imaginary, and also very *operose*, and would affect a great part of the universe; they would be as hard put to it to get rid of this water, when the deluge was to cease, as they were at first to procure it. *Burnet's Theory of the Earth.*

Written language, as it is more *operous*, so it is more digested, and is permanent. *Holder.*

OPHIO'PHAGOUS. *adj.* [ὄφις and φάγω.] Serpenteating. Not used.

All snakes are not of such poisonous qualities as common opinion presumeth; as is confirmable from *ophiophagous* nations, and such as feed upon serpents. *Brown's V. Err.*

OPHI'TES. *n. s.* A stone.

Ophites has a dusky greenish ground, with spots of a lighter green, oblong, and usually near square. *Woodw. on Foss.*

OPHTHA'LMICK. *adj.* [*ophthalmique*, Fr from ὀφθαλμος, Gr.] Relating to the eye.

O'PHTHALMY. *n. s.* [*ophthalmie*, Fr. from ὀφθαλμος, Gr.] A disease of the eyes, being an inflammation in the coats, proceeding from arterious blood gotten out of the vessels and collected into those parts. *Dict.*

The use of cool applications, externally, is most easy to the eye; but after-all, there will sometimes ensue a troublesome *ophthalmy*. *Sharp's Surgery.*

O'PIATE. *n. s.* A medicine that causes sleep.

They chose atheism as an *opiate*, to still those frightning apprehensions of hell, by inducing a dulness and lethargy of mind, rather than to make use of that native and salutary medicine, a hearty repentance. *Bentley's Serm.*

O'PIATE. *adj.* Soporiferous; somniferous; narcotick; causing sleep.

The particular ingredients of those magical ointments, are *opiate* and soporiferous. For anointing of the forehead and back bone, is used for procuring dead sleeps. *Bacon.*

All their shape
Spangled with eyes, more num'rous than those
Of Argus, and more wakeful than to drouze,
Charm'd with Arcadian pipe, the past'ral reed
Of Hermes, or his *opiate* rod. *Milton's Par. Lost.*

Lettuce, which has a milky juice with an anodyne or *opiate* quality resolvent of the bile, is proper for melancholy. *Arbuthnot on Aliments.*

O'PIFICE. *n. s.* [*opificium*, Lat.] Workmanship; handiwork. *Dict.*

O'PIFICER. *n. s.* [*opifex*, Lat.] One that performs any work; artist. A word not received.

An

There is an infinite diſtance betwixt the poor mortal artiſt, and the almighty *opificer*. *Bentley's Serm.*

OPI'NABLE. *adj.* [*opinor*, Lat.] Which may be thought. *Dict.*

OPINA'TION. *n. ſ.* [*opinor*, Lat.] Opinion; notion. *Dict.*

OPINA'TOR. *n. ſ.* [*opinor*, Lat.] One who holds an opinion.

Conſider againſt what kind of *opinators* the reaſon above given is levelled. *Hale's Origin of Mankind.*

To OPI'NE. *v. n.* [*opinor*, Latin.] To think; to judge; to be of opinion.

Fear is an ague, that forſakes
And haunts by fits thoſe whom it takes;
And they'll *opine* they feel the pain
And blows they felt to-day, again. *Hudibras, p.* i.

In matters of mere ſpeculation, it is not much material to the welfare of government, or of themſelves, whether they *opine* right or wrong, and whether they be philoſophers or no. *South's Serm.*

But I, who think more highly of our kind,
Opine, that nature, as in duty bound,
Deep hid the ſhining miſchief under ground. *Pope.*

OPI'NIATIVE. *adj.* [from *opinion.*]

1. Stiff in a preconceived notion.

2. Imagined; not proved.

It is the more difficult to find out truth, becauſe it is in ſuch inconſiderable proportions ſcattered in a maſs of *opiniative* uncertainties; like the ſilver in Hiero's crown of gold. *Glanv. Sceps. c.* 9.

OPINIA'TOR. *n. ſ.* [*opiniatre*, French.] One fond of his own notion; inflexible; adherent to his own opinion.

What will not *opiniators* and ſelf-believing men diſpute of and make doubt of? *Raleigh.*

Eſſex left lord Roberts governour; a man of a ſour and ſurly nature, a great *opiniator*, and one who muſt be overcome before he would believe that he could be ſo. *Clarend.*

For all his exact plot, down was he caſt from all his greatneſs, and forced to end his days in a mean condition; as it is pity but all ſuch politick *opiniators* ſhould. *South's Serm.*

OPINIA'TRE. *adj.* [French.] Obſtinate; ſtubborn.

Inſtead of an able man, you deſire to have him an inſignificant wrangler, *opiniatre* in diſcourſe, and priding himſelf in contradicting others. *Locke.*

OPINIA'TRETY. } *n. ſ.* [*opiniatretè*, French.] Obſtinacy; in-
OPI'NIATRY. } flexibility; determination of mind; ſtubbornneſs. This word, though it has been tried in different forms, is not yet received, nor is it wanted.

Leſt popular *opiniatry* ſhould ariſe, we will deliver the chief opinions. *Brown's Vulgar Errours, b.* vii.

The one ſets the thoughts upon wit and falſe colours, and not upon truth; the other teaches fallacy, wrangling and *opiniatry*. *Locke's Education.*

So much as we ourſelves conſider and comprehend of truth and reaſon, ſo much we poſſeſs of real and true knowledge. The floating of other men's opinions in our brains, make us not one jot the more knowing, though they happen to be true: what in them was ſcience, is in us but *opiniatrety*. *Locke.*

I can paſs by *opiniatry* and the buſy meddling of thoſe who thruſt themſelves into every thing. *Woodw. Letters.*

I was extremely concerned at his *opiniatrety* in leaving me; but he ſhall not get rid ſo. *Pope.*

OPI'NION. *n. ſ.* [*opinion*, Fr. *opinio*, Lat.]

1. Perſwaſion of the mind, without proof or certain knowledge.

Opinion is a light, vain, crude and imperfect thing, ſettled in the imagination, but never arriving at the underſtanding, there to obtain the tincture of reaſon. *Ben. Johnſon.*

Opinion is, when the aſſent of the underſtanding is ſo far gained by evidence of probability, that it rather inclines to one perſwaſion than to another, yet not altogether without a mixture of incertainty or doubting. *Hale.*

Stiff in *opinion*, ever in the wrong. *Dryden.*

Bleſt be the princes who have fought
For pompous names, or wide dominion,
Since by their error we are taught,
That happineſs is but *opinion*. *Prior.*

2. Sentiments; judgment; notion.

Can they make it out againſt the common ſenſe and *opinion* of all mankind, that there is no ſuch thing as a future ſtate of miſery for ſuch as have lived ill here. *South.*

Charity itſelf commands us, where we know no ill, to think well of all; but friendſhip, that always goes a pitch higher, gives a man a peculiar right and claim to the good *opinion* of his friend. *South's Sermons.*

We may allow this to be his *opinion* concerning heirs, that where there are divers children the eldeſt ſon has the right to be heir. *Locke.*

Philoſophers are of *opinion*, that infinite ſpace is poſſeſſed by God's infinite omnipreſence. *Locke.*

I ſhall conclude my paper with a ſtory out of Boccalini, which ſufficiently ſhews us the *opinion* that judicious author entertained of the ſort of critics I have been here mentioning. *Addiſon's Spectator*, N°. 291.

3. Favourable judgment.

In actions of arms ſmall matters are of great moment, eſpecially when they ſerve to raiſe an *opinion* of commanders. *Hayward.*

Howſoever I have no *opinion* of thoſe things; yet ſo much I conceive to be true, that ſtrong imagination hath more force upon things living, than things merely inanimate. *Bacon.*

To OPI'NION. *v. a.* [from the noun.] To opine; to think. A word out of uſe, and unworthy of revival.

The ſtoicks *opinioned* the ſouls of wiſe men dwell about the moon, and thoſe fools wandered about the earth: whereas the Epicureans held that death was nothing, nor after death. *Brown's V. Err.*

That the ſoul and the angels are devoid of quantity and dimenſion, is generally *opinioned*. *Glanv. Sceps. c.* xiii.

It is *opinioned*, that the earth reſts as the world's centre; while the heavens are the ſubject of the univerſal motions. *Glanv. Sceps. c.* xi.

OPI'NIONATIVE. *adj.* [from *opinion.*] Fond of preconceived notions; ſtubborn.

Striking at the root of pedantry and *opinionative* aſſurance, would be no hindrance to the world's improvement. *Glanv.*

One would rather chuſe a reader without art, than one ill inſtructed with learning, but *opinionative* and without judgment. *Burnet's Theory of the Earth.*

OPI'NIONATIVELY. *adv.* [from *opinionative.*] Stubbornly.

OPI'NIONATIVENESS. *n. ſ.* [from *opinionative.*] Obſtinacy.

OPI'NIONIST. *n. ſ.* [*opinioniſte*, Fr. from *opinion.*] One fond of his own notions.

Every conceited *opinioniſt* ſets up an infallible chair in his own brain. *Glanv. to Albius.*

OPI'PAROUS. *adj.* [*opiparus*, Lat.] Sumptuous. *Dict.*

OPITULA'TION. *n. ſ.* [*opitulatio*, Lat.] An aiding; a helping. *Dict.*

O'PIUM. *n. ſ.* A juice, partly of the reſinous, partly of the gummy kind. It is brought to us in flat cakes or maſſes, uſually of a roundiſh figure, very heavy and of a denſe texture, not perfectly dry: its colour is a dark browniſh yellow; its ſmell is very unpleaſant, of a dead faint kind; and its taſte very bitter and very acrid. It is brought from Natolia, from Egypt, and from the Eaſt-Indies, where it is produced from the white garden poppy; a plant of which every part is full of a milky juice, and with which the fields of Aſia-Minor are in many places ſown as ours are with corn. When the heads grow to maturity, but are yet ſoft, green and full of juice, inciſions are made in them, and from every one of theſe a few drops flow of a milky juice, which ſoon hardens into a ſolid conſiſtence. Theſe drops are gathered with great care, and the fineſt *opium* proceeds from the firſt inciſions. In the countries where *opium* is produced, multitudes are employed in preparing it with water, honey and ſpices, and working it up into cakes; but what we generally have is the mere crude juice, or at moſt worked up with water, or a ſmall quantity of honey ſufficient to bring it into form. The ancients were greatly divided about the virtues and uſe of *opium*; ſome calling it a poiſon, and others the greateſt of all medicines. At preſent it is in high eſteem, and externally applied it is emollient, relaxing and diſcutient, and greatly promotes ſuppuration. A moderate doſe of *opium* taken internally, is generally under a grain, yet cuſtom will make people bear a dram as a moderate doſe; but in that caſe nature is vitiated. Its firſt effect is the making the patient cheerful, as if he had drank moderately of wine; it removes melancholy, excites boldneſs, and diſſipates the dread of danger; and for this reaſon the Turks always take it when they are going to battle in a larger doſe than ordinary: it afterward quiets the ſpirits, eaſes pain, and diſpoſes to ſleep. After the effect of a doſe of *opium* is over, the pain generally returns in a more violent manner; the ſpirits, which had been elevated by it, become lower than before, and the pulſe languid. An immoderate doſe of *opium* brings on a ſort of drunkenneſs, cheerfulneſs and loud laughter, at firſt, and, after many terrible ſymptoms, death itſelf. Thoſe who have accuſtomed themſelves to an immoderate uſe of *opium*, are ſubject to relaxations and weakneſſes of all the parts of the body; they are apt to be faint, idle and thoughtleſs, and are generally in a ſtupid and uncomfortable ſtate, except juſt after they have taken a freſh doſe: they loſe their appetite, and in fine grow old before their time. *Hill.*

Sleep hath forſook and giv'n me o'er
To death's benumbing *opium* as my only cure. *Milton.*

The colour and taſte of *opium* are, as well as its ſoporific or anodyne virtues, mere powers depending on its primary qualities, whereby it is fitted to produce different operations on different parts of our bodies. *Locke*

O'PLE-TREE. *n. ſ.* [*ople* and *tree.*] A ſort of tree. *Ainſ.*

OPOBA'LSAMUM. *n. ſ.* [Latin.] Balm of Gilead.

OPO'PONAX. *n. ſ.* [Latin.] A gum reſin of a tolerably firm texture, in ſmall looſe granules, and ſometimes in large maſſes, which are impure. It is of a ſtrong diſagreeable ſmell, and an acrid and extremely bitter taſte. It is brought to us from the

the East, and was well known to the Greeks; but we are entirely ignorant of the plant which produces this drug. It is attenuating and discutient, and gently purgative. *Hill.*

O'PPIDAN. *n. s.* [*oppidanus*, Lat.] A townsman; an inhabitant of a town.

To OPPI'GNERATE. *v. a.* [*oppignero*, Lat.] To pledge; to pawn.

The duke of Guise Henry was the greatest usurer in France, for that he had turned all his estate into obligations; meaning that he had sold and *oppignorated* all his patrimony, to give large donatives to other men. *Bacon.*

Ferdinando merchanded at this time with France, for the restoring Roussillion and Perpignan, *oppignorated* to them. *Bacon's Henry VII.*

To O'PPILATE. *v. a.* [*oppilo*, Lat. *oppiler*, Fr.] To heap up obstruction.

OPPILA'TION. *n. s.* [*oppilation*, Fr. from *oppilate.*] Obstruction; matter heaped together.

The ingredients prescribed in their substance actuate the spirits, reclude *oppilations*, and mundify the blood. *Harvey.*

O'PPILATIVE. *adj.* [*oppilative*, Fr.] Obstructive.

OPPLE'TED. *adj.* [*oppletus*, Lat.] Filled; crouded.

OPPO'NENT. *adj.* [*opponens*, Lat.] Opposite; adverse.

Ere the foundations of this earth were laid,
It was *opponent* to our search ordain'd,
That joy, still sought, should never be attain'd. *Prior.*

OPPO'NENT. *n. s.* [*opponens*, Lat.]

1. Antagonist; adversary.

2. One who begins the dispute by raising objections to a tenet.

Inasmuch as ye go about to destroy a thing which is in force, and to draw in that which hath not as yet been received, to impose on us that which we think not ourselves bound unto; that therefore ye are not to claim in any conference other than the plaintiffs or *opponents* part. *Hooker.*

How becomingly does Philopolis exercise his office, and seasonably commit the *opponent* with the respondent, like a long practised moderator. *More.*

OPPORTU'NE. *adj.* [*opportune*, Fr. *opportunus*, Latin.] Seasonable; convenient; fit; timely; well-timed; proper.

There was nothing to be added to this great king's felicity, being at the top of all worldly bliss, and the perpetual constancy of his prosperous successes, but an *opportune* death to withdraw him from any future blow of fortune. *Bacon.*

Will lift us up in spite of fate,
Nearer our ancient seat; perhaps in view
Of those bright confines, whence with neighb'ring arms
And *opportune* excursion, we may chance
Re-enter heav'n. *Milton's Paradise Lost, b.* ii.

Consider'd every creature, which of all
Most *opportune* might serve his wiles; and found
The serpent subtlest beast of all the field. *Milton.*

OPPORTU'NELY. *adv.* [from *opportune.*] Seasonably; conveniently; with opportunity either of time or place.

He was resolved to chuse a war rather than to have Bretagne carried by France, being situate so *opportunely* to annoy England either for coast or trade. *Bacon's Henry VII.*

Against these there is a proper objection, that they offend uniformity; whereof I am therefore *opportunely* induced to say somewhat. *Wotton's Architecture.*

This experiment does *opportunely* supply the deficiency. *Boyle.*

OPPORTU'NITY. *n. s.* [*opportunité*, Fr. *opportunitas*, Lat.] Fit fit place; time; convenience; suitableness of circumstances to any end.

A wise man will make more *opportunities* than he finds. Mens behaviour should be like their apparel, not too straight but free for exercise. *Bacon, Essay* 53.

Opportunity, like a sudden gust,
Hath swell'd my calmer thoughts into a tempest.
Accursed *opportunity!*
That work'st our thoughts into desires, desires
To resolutions; those being ripe and quicken'd,
Thou giv'st them birth, and bring'st them forth to action. *Denham.*

Tho' their advice be good, their counsel wise,
Yet length still loses *opportunities*. *Denham.*

Neglect no *opportunity* of doing good, nor check thy desire of doing it, by a vain fear of what may happen. *Atterb.*

All poets have taken an *opportunity* to give long descriptions of the night. *Broome's Notes on the Odyssey.*

To OPPO'SE. *v. a.* [*opposer*, French; *oppono*, Latin.]

1. To act against; to be adverse; to hinder; to resist.

There's no bottom, none
In my voluptuousness: and my desire
All continent impediments would o'erbear,
That did *oppose* my will. *Shakespeare's Macbeth.*

2. To put in opposition; to offer as an antagonist or rival.

If all men are not naturally equal, I am sure all slaves are; and then I may, without presumption, *oppose* my single opinion to his. *Locke.*

3. To place as an obstacle.

Since he stands obdurate,
And that no lawful means can carry me
Out of his envy's reach, I do *oppose*
My patience to his fury. *Shakesp. Merch. of Venice.*

I thro' the seas pursu'd their exil'd race,
Engag'd the heav'ns, *oppos'd* the stormy main;
But billows roar'd and tempests rag'd in vain. *Dryden.*

4. To place in front.

Her grace sat down
In a rich chair of state; *opposing* freely
The beauty of her person to the people. *Shakespeare.*

To OPPO'SE. *v. n.*

1. To act adversely.

A servant, thrill'd with remorse,
Oppos'd against the act, bending his sword
To his great master. *Shakesp. King Lear.*

He practised to dispatch such of the nobility as were like to *oppose* against his mischievous drift, and in such sort to encumber and weaken the rest, that they should be no impediments to him. *Hayward.*

2. To object in a disputation; to have the part of raising difficulties against a tenet supposed to be right.

OPPO'SELESS. *adj.* [from *oppose.*] Irresistible; not to be opposed.

I could bear it longer, and not fall
To quarrel with your great *opposeless* wills. *Shakespeare.*

OPPO'SER. *n. s.* [from *oppose.*] One that opposes; antagonist; enemy; rival.

Now the fair goddess fortune
Fall deep in love with thee, and her great charms
Misguide thy *opposers* swords: bold gentleman!
Prosperity be thy page. *Shakesp. Coriolanus.*

Brave wits that have made essays worthy of immortality; yet by reason of envious and more popular *opposers*, have submitted to fate, and are almost lost in oblivion. *Glanv.*

I do not see how the ministers could have continued in their stations, if their *opposers* had agreed about the methods by which they should be ruined. *Swift.*

A hardy modern chief,
A bold *opposer* of divine belief. *Blackmore.*

O'PPOSITE. *adj.* [*opposite*, Fr. *oppositus*, Lat.]

1. Placed in front; facing each other.

To th' other five,
Their planetary motions and aspects,
In sextile, square, trine and *opposite*,
Of noxious efficacy. *Milton's Paradise Lost, b.* x.

2. Adverse; repugnant.

Nothing of a foreign nature, like the trifling novels, by which the reader is misled into another sort of pleasure, *opposite* to that which is designed in an epick poem. *Dryd.*

This is a prospect very uneasy to the lusts and passions, and *opposite* to the strongest desires of flesh and blood. *Roger.*

3. Contrary.

In this fallen state of man religion begins with repentance and conversion, the two *opposite* terms of which are God and sin. *Tillotson, Serm.* 1.

Particles of speech have divers, and sometimes almost *opposite* significations. *Locke.*

O'PPOSITE. *n. s.* Adversary; opponent; antagonist; enemy.

To the best and wisest, while they live, the world is continually a froward *opposite*, a curious observer of their defects and imperfections; their virtues it afterwards as much admireth. *Hooker, b.* v. *s.* 7.

He is the most skilful, bloody, and fatal *opposite* that you could have found in Illyria. *Shakesp. Twelfth Night.*

The knight whom fate or happy chance
Shall grace his arms so far in equal fight,
From out the bars to force his *opposite*,
The prize of valour and of love shall gain. *Dryden.*

O'PPOSITELY. *adv.* [from *opposite.*]

1. In such a situation as to face each other.

The lesser pair are joined edge to edge, but not *oppositely* with their points downward, but upward. *Grew's Mus.*

2. Adversely.

I oft have seen, when corn was ripe to mow,
And now in dry, and brittle straw did grow,
Winds from all quarters *oppositely* blow. *May's Virgil.*

O'PPOSITENESS. *n. s.* [from *opposite.*] The state of being opposite.

OPPOSI'TION. *n. s.* [*opposition*, Fr. *oppositio*, Lat.]

1. Situation so as to front something opposed.

2. Hostile resistance.

He
Cry'd oh! and mounted; found no *opposition*
From what he look'd for should oppose. *Shakespeare.*

Virtue which breaks thro' all *opposition*,
And all temptation can remove,
Most shines, and most is acceptable above. *Milton.*

He considers Lausus rescuing his father at the hazard of his own life, as an image of himself when he took Anchises on his shoulders, and bore him safe thro' the rage of the fire and the *opposition* of his enemies. *Dryden's Dufresnoy.*

3. Contrariety of affection.

They who never tried the experiment of a holy life, measure

sure the laws of God not by their intrinsical goodness, but by the reluctancy and *opposition* which they find in their own hearts. *Tillotson, Serm.* 6.

4. Contrariety of interest; contrariety of measures.

5. Contrariety of meaning; diversity of meaning.

The parts of every true *opposition* do alway both concern the same subject, and have reference to the same thing, sith otherwise they are but in shew opposite, and not in truth. *Hooker, b.* v. *s.* 48.

Reason can never permit the mind to reject a greater evidence, to embrace what is less evident, nor allow it to entertain probability in *opposition* to knowledge and certainty. *Locke.*

To OPPRESS. *v. a.* [*oppressus*, Lat.]

1. To crush by hardship or unreasonable severity.

Israel and Judah were *oppressed* together, and all that took them captives held them fast, they refused to let them go. *Jer.* l. 33.

Alas! a mortal most *opprest* of those
Whom fate has loaded with a weight of woes. *Pope.*

2. To overpower; to subdue.

We're not ourselves,
When nature, being *opprest*, commands the mind
To suffer with the body. *Shakesp. King Lear.*

In blazing height of noon,
The sun *oppress'd*, is plung'd in thickest gloom. *Thoms.*

OPPRE'SSION. *n. s.* [*oppression*, Fr. from *oppress.*]

1. The act of oppressing; cruelty; severity.

2. The state of being oppressed; misery.

Famine is in thy cheeks;
Need and *oppression* stare within thine eyes,
Contempt and beggary hang upon thy back. *Shakesp.*

Cæsar himself has work, and our *oppression*
Exceeds what we expected. *Shakes. Ant. and Cleop.*

3. Hardship; calamity.

We are all subject to the same accidents; and when we see any under particular *oppression*, we should look upon it as the common lot of human nature. *Addis. Spectator.*

4. Dullness of spirits; lassitude of body.

Drousiness, *oppression*, heaviness, and lassitude, are signs of a too plentiful meal. *Arbuthnot on Aliment.*

OPPRE'SSIVE. *adj.* [from *oppress.*]

1. Cruel; inhuman; unjustly exactious or severe.

2. Heavy; overwhelming.

Alicia, reach thy friendly arm,
And help me to support that feeble frame,
That nodding totters with *oppressive* woe,
And sinks beneath its load. *Rowe's Jane Shore.*

OPPRE'SSOR. *n. s.* [*oppresseur*, Fr. from *oppress.*] One who harrasses others with unreasonable or unjust severity.

I from *oppressors* did the poor defend,
The fatherless, and such as had no friend. *Sandys.*

The cries of orphans, and th' *oppressor's* rage,
Had reach'd the stars. *Dryden.*

Power when employed to relieve the oppressed, and to punish the *oppressor*, becomes a great blessing. *Swift.*

OPPRO'BRIOUS. *adj.* [from *opprobrium*, Lat.] Reproachful; disgraceful; causing infamy; scurrilous.

Himself pronounceth them blessed, that should for his name sake be subject to all kinds of ignominy and *opprobrious* malediction. *Hooker, b.* v. *s.* 48.

I will not here defile
My unstain'd verse with his *opprobrious* name. *Daniel.*

Solomon he led by fraud to build
His temple right against the temple of God,
On the *opprobrious* hill. *Milton's Paradise Lost, b.* i.

They see themselves unjustly aspersed, and vindicate themselves in terms no less *opprobrious* than those by which they are attacked. *Addison's Freeholder*, Nº. 137.

OPPRO'BRIOUSLY. *ad.* [from *opprobrious.*] Reproachfully; scurrilously.

Think you, this little prating York
Was not incensed by his subtle mother,
To taunt and scorn you thus *opprobriously*. *Shakesp. R.* III.

OPPRO'BRIOUSNESS. *n. s.* [from *opprobrious.*] Reproachfulness; scurrility.

To OPPU'GN. *v. a.* [*oppugno*, Lat.] To oppose; to attack; to resist.

For the ecclesiastical laws of this land we are led by a great reason to observe, and ye be by no necessity bound to *oppugn* them. *Hooker's Pref.*

They said the manner of their impeachment they could not but conceive did *oppugn* the rights of parliament. *Clar.*

If nothing can *oppugn* his love,
And virtue invious ways can prove,
What cannot he confide to do
That brings both love and virtue too? *Hud. p.* i.

The ingredients reclude oppilations, mundify the blood, and *oppugn* putrefaction. *Harvey.*

OPPU'GNANCY. *n. s.* [from *oppugn.*] Opposition.

Take but degree away, untune that string,
And hark what discord follows, each thing meets
In meer *oppugnancy*. *Shakespeare's. Troil. and Cress.*

OPPU'GNER. *n. s.* [from *oppugn.*] One who opposes or attacks.

The modern and degenerate Jews be, upon the score of being the great patrons of man's free will, not causelesly esteemed the great *oppugners* of God's free grace. *Boyle.*

OPSI'MATHY. *n. s.* [ὀψιμαθία.] Late education; late erudition.

OPSONA'TION. *n. s.* [*opsonatio*, Latin.] Catering; a buying provisions. *Dict.*

O'PTABLE. *adj.* [*optabilis*, Lat.] Desirable; to be wished.

O'PTATIVE. *adj.* [*optativus*, Lat.] Expressive of desire. [In grammar.]

The verb undergoes in Greek a different formation to signify wishing, which is called the *optative* mood. *Clarke.*

O'PTICAL. *n. s.* [ὀπτικός.] Relating to the science of optics.

It seems not agreeable to what anatomists and *optical* writers deliver, touching the relation of the two eyes to each other. *Boyle.*

O'PTICIAN. *n. s.* [from *optick.*] One skilled in opticks.

O'PTICK. *adj.* [ὀπτικος; *optique*, Fr.]

1. Visual; producing vision; subservient to vision.

May not the harmony and discord of colours arise from the proportions of the vibrations propagated through the fibres of the *optic* nerves into the brain, as the harmony and discord of sounds arise from the proportions of the vibrations of the air? *Newt. Opt.*

2. Relating to the science of vision.

Where our master handleth the contractions of pillars, we have an *optic* rule, that the higher they are the less should be always their diminution aloft, because the eye itself doth naturally contract all objects, according to the distance. *Wotton's Architecture.*

O'PTICK. *n. s.* An instrument of sight; an organ of sight.

Can any thing escape the perspicacity of those eyes which were before light, and in whose *opticks* there is no opacity. *Brown.*

Our corporeal eyes we find
Dazzle the *opticks* of our mind. *Denham.*

You may neglect, or quench, or hate the flame,
Whose smoke too long obscur'd your rising name,
And quickly cold indiff'rence will ensue,
When you love's joys thro' honour's *optick* view. *Prior.*

Why has not man a microscopick eye?
For this plain reason, man is not a fly.
Say what the use, were finer *opticks* giv'n,
T'inspect a mite, not comprehend the heav'n. *Pope.*

O'PTICK. *n. s.* [ὀπτικὴ.] The science of the nature and laws of vision.

No spherical body of what bigness soever illuminates the whole sphere of another, although it illuminate something more than half of a lesser, according unto the doctrine of *opticks*. *Brown's Vulgar Err. b.* vi.

Those who desire satisfaction in the appearance, must go to the admirable treatise of *opticks* by Sir Isaac Newton. *Cheyne's Phil. Prin.*

O'PTIMACY. *n. s.* [*optimates*, Lat.] Nobility; body of nobles.

In this high court of parliament there is a rare co-ordination of power, a wholesome mixture betwixt monarchy, *optimacy*, and democracy. *Howel.*

OPTI'MITY. *n. s.* [from *optimus.*] The state of being best.

O'PTION. *n. s.* [*optio*, Lat.] Choice; election.

Transplantation must proceed from the *option* of the people, else it sounds like an exile; so the colonies must be raised by the leave of the king and not by his command. *Bacon.*

Which of these two rewards we will receive, he hath left to our *option*. *Smallridge's Serm.*

O'PULENCE. } *n. s.* [*opulence*, Fr. *opulentia*, Latin.] Wealth;
O'PULENCY. } riches; affluence.

It must be a discovery of the infinite flatteries that follow youth and *opulency*. *Shakesp. Tim. of Athens.*

After eight years spent in outward *opulency* and inward murmur, that it was not greater; after vast sums of money and great wealth gotten, he died unlamented. *Clarendon.*

He had been a person not only of great *opulence*, but authority. *Atterbury.*

There in full *opulence* a banker dwelt,
Who all the joys and pangs of riches felt;
His side board glitter'd with imagin'd plate,
And his proud fancy held a vast estate. *Swift.*

O'PULENT. *adj.* [*opulent*, Fr. *opulentus*, Lat.] Rich; wealthy; affluent.

He made him his ally, and provoked a mighty and *opulent* king by an offensive war in his quarrel. *Bacon.*

To begin with the supposed policy of gratifying only the rich and *opulent*. Does our wise man think that the grandee whom he courts does not see through all the little plots of his courtship. *South's Sermons.*

O'PULENTLY. *adv.* [from *opulent.*] Richly; with splendor.

OR. *conjunct.* [oðeꞃ, Saxon.]

1. A disjunctive particle, marking distribution, and sometimes opposition.

Inquire what the antients thought concerning this world, whether it was to perish *or* no; whether to be destroyed

ſtroyed *or* to ſtand eternally? *Burnet.*

He my muſe's homage ſhou'd receive,
If I cou'd write *or* Holles cou'd forgive. *Garth.*

Every thing that can be divided by the mind into two *or* more ideas, is called complex. *Watts's Logick.*

2. It correſponds to *either*; he muſt *either* fall *or* fly.

3. *Or* is ſometimes redundant; but is then more properly omitted.

How great ſoever the ſins of any unreformed perſon are, Chriſt died for him becauſe he died for all; only he muſt reform and forſake his ſins, *or* elſe he ſhall never receive benefit of his death. *Hammond's Fund.*

4. [oꞃ, or æꞃe, Saxon.] Before; *or ever*, is *before ever*.

Or we go to the declaration of this pſalm, it ſhall be convenient to ſhew who did write this pſalm. *Fiſher.*

The dead man's knell
Is there ſcarce aſk'd for whom, and good men's lives
Expire before the flowers in their caps,
Dying *or ere* they ſicken. *Shakeſp. Macbeth.*

Learn before thou ſpeak, and uſe phyſick *or ever* thou be ſick. *Ecclus* xviii. 19.

OR. n. ſ. [French.] Gold.

The ſhow'ry arch
With liſted colours gay, *or*, azure, gules,
Delights and puzzles the beholders eyes. *Philips.*

O'RACH. *n. ſ.* The flower is without leaves, but conſiſts of many ſtamina ariſing from a five leav'd empalement; the pointal becomes a flat orbicular ſeed, encloſed in the empalement, which becomes a foliaceous capſule, including two ſorts of ſeeds. There are thirteen ſpecies; of which the firſt called garden *orach*, was cultivated as a culinary herb, and uſed as ſpinach, though it is not generally liked by the Engliſh, but ſtill eſteemed by the French. It was formerly uſed in medicine. *Miller.*

O'RACLE. *n. ſ.* [*oracle*, Fr. *oraculum*, Lat.]

1. Something delivered by ſupernatural wiſdom.

The main principle whereupon our belief of all things therein contained dependeth, is, that the ſcriptures are the *oracles* of God himſelf. *Hooker, b.* iii. *ſ.* 8.

2. The place where, or perſon of whom the determinations of heaven are enquired.

Why, by the verities on thee made good,
May they not be my *oracles* as well,
And ſet me up in hope? *Shakeſp. Macbeth.*

God hath now ſent his living *oracle*
Into the world to teach his final will,
And ſends his ſpirit of truth henceforth to dwell
In pious hearts, an inward *oracle*,
To all truth requiſite for men to know. *Par. Reg.*

3. Any perſon or place where certain deciſions are obtained.

There mighty nations ſhall enquire their doom,
The world's great *oracle* in times to come. *Pope.*

4 One famed for wiſdom; one whoſe determinations are not to be diſputed.

To O'RACLE. *v. n.* [from the noun.] To utter oracles. A word not received.

No more ſhalt thou by *oracling* abuſe
The gentiles. *Paradiſe Regained, b.* i.

ORA'CULAR. } *adj.* [from *oracle.*] Uttering oracles; reſembling oracles.
ORA'CULOUS. }

Thy counſel would be as the oracle of
Urim and thummim, thoſe *oraculous* gems
On Aaron's breaſt, or tongue of ſeers old
Infallible. *Milton's Paradiſe Reg. b.* iii.

Here Charles contrives the ord'ring of his ſtates,
Here he reſolves his neighb'ring princes fates;
What nation ſhall have peace, where war be made,
Determin'd is in this *orac'lous* ſhade. *Walker.*

Though their general acknowledgments of the weakneſs of human underſtanding look like cold and ſceptical diſcouragements; yet the particular expreſſions of their ſentiments are as *oraculous* as if they were omniſcient. *Glanv Sceps.*

They have ſomething venerable and *oracular*, in that unadorned gravity and ſhortneſs in the expreſſion. *Pop. Pref.*

Th' *orac'lous* ſeer frequents the Pharian coaſt,
Proteus a name tremendous o'er the main. *Pope.*

ORA'CULOUSLY. *adv.* [from *oraculous.*] In manner of an oracle.

The teſtimony of antiquity, and ſuch as paſs *oraculouſly* amongſt us, were not always ſo exact as to examine the doctrine they delivered. *Brown's Vulgar Err. b.* i.

Hence riſe the branching beech and vocal oak,
Where Jove of old *oraculouſly* ſpoke. *Dryden.*

ORA'CULOUSNESS. *n. ſ.* [from *oracular.*] The ſtate of being oracular.

O'RAISON. *n. ſ.* [*oraiſon*, Fr. *oratio*, Lat.] Prayer; verbal ſupplication; or oral worſhip: more frequently written *oriſon.*

Stay, let's hear the *oraiſons* he makes. *Shakeſpeare.*

Buſineſs might ſhorten, not diſturb her pray'r;
Heav'n had the beſt, if not the greater ſhare:
An active life, long *oraiſons* forbids,
Yet ſtill ſhe pray'd, for ſtill ſhe pray'd by deeds. *Dryden.*

O'RAL. *adj.* [*oral*, Fr. *os*, *orris*, Latin.] Delivered by mouth; not written.

Oral diſcourſe, whoſe tranſient faults dying with the ſound that gives them life, and ſo not ſubject to a ſtrict review, more eaſily eſcapes obſervation. *Locke's Educat.*

St. John was appealed to as the living *oracle* of the church; and as his *oral* teſtimony laſted the firſt century, many have obſerved, that by a particular providence ſeveral of our Saviour's diſciples, and of the early converts, lived to a very great age, that they might perſonally convey the truth of the goſpel to thoſe times which were very remote. *Addiſon.*

O'RALLY. *adv.* [from *oral.*] By mouth; without writing.

Oral tradition were incompetent without written monuments to derive to us the original laws of a kingdom, becauſe they are complex, not *orally* traducible to ſo great a diſtance of ages. *Hale's Comm. Laws of Eng.*

O'RANGE. *n. ſ.* [*orange*, Fr. *aurentia*, Latin.] The leaves have two lobes or appendages at their baſe like ears, and cut in form of a heart; the fruit is round and depreſſed, and of a yellow colour when ripe, in which it differs from the citron and lemon. The ſpecies are eight. *Miller.*

I will diſcharge it in your ſtraw-colour'd beard, your *orange* tawny beard. *Shakeſp. Midſ. Night's Dream.*

The notary came aboard, holding in his hand a fruit like an *orange*, but of colour between *orange* tawny and ſcarlet, which caſt a moſt excellent odour, and is uſed for a preſervative againſt infection. *Bacon's New Atlantis.*

Fine *oranges*, ſauce for your veal,
Are charming when ſqueez'd in a pot of brown ale. *Swift.*

The ideas of *orange* colour and azure, produced in the mind by the ſame infuſion of lignum nephriticum, are no leſs diſtinct ideas than thoſe of the ſame colours taken from two different bodies. *Locke.*

O'RANGERY. *n. ſ.* [*orangerie*, Fr.] Plantation of oranges.

A kitchen garden is a more pleaſant ſight than the fineſt *orangery*, or artificial green houſe. *Spectator*, N°. 477.

O'RANGEMUSK. *n. ſ.* See PEAR, of which it is a ſpecies.

O'RANGEWIFE. *n. ſ.* [*orange* and *wife.*] A woman who ſells oranges.

You wear out a good wholeſome forenoon in hearing a cauſe between an *orangewife* and a foſſet ſeller. *Shakeſ.*

ORA'TION. *n. ſ.* [*oration*, Fr. *oratio*, Lat.] A ſpeech made according to the laws of rhetorick; a harangue; a declamation.

There ſhall I try,
In my *oration*, how the people take
The cruel iſſue of theſe bloody men. *Shakeſp. Jul. Cæſ.*

This gives life and ſpirit to every thing that is ſpoken, awakens the dulleſt ſpirits, and adds a ſingular grace and excellency both to the perſon and his *oration.* *Watts.*

ORATO'RICAL. *adj.* [from *oratour.*] Rhetorical; befitting an oratour.

Where he ſpeaks in an *oratorical*, affecting, or perſuaſive way, let this be explained by other places where he treats of the ſame theme in a doctrinal way. *Watts.*

O'RATOUR. *n. ſ.* [*orateur*, Fr. *orator*, Lat.]

1. A publick ſpeaker; a man of eloquence.

Poor queen and ſon! your labour is but loſt;
For Warwick is a ſubtle *orator.* *Shakeſp. Henry* VI.

As when of old ſome *orator* renown'd,
In Athens or free Rome, where eloquence
Flouriſh'd, ſince mute! to ſome great cauſe addreſs'd,
Stood in himſelf collected; while each part,
Motion, each act, won audience. *Milton's Par. Loſt.*

The conſtant deſign of both theſe *orators* in all their ſpeeches, was to drive ſome one particular point. *Swift.*

I have liſtened to an *orator* of this ſpecies, without being able to underſtand one ſingle ſentence. *Swift.*

Both *orators* ſo much renown'd,
In their own depths of eloquence were drown'd. *Dryden.*

2. A petitioner. This ſenſe is uſed in addreſſes to chancery.

O'RATORY. *n. ſ.* [*oratoria*, *ars*, Lat.]

1. Eloquence; rhetorical ſkill.

Each paſture ſtored with ſheep feeding with ſober ſecurity, while the pretty lambs with bleating *oratory* craved the dams comfort. *Sidney.*

When a world of men
Could not prevail with all their *oratory*,
Yet hath a woman's kindneſs over-rul'd. *Shakeſpeare.*

When my *oratory* grew tow'rd end,
I bid them that did love their country's good,
Cry, God ſave Richard. *Shakeſp. Rich.* III.

Sighs now breath'd
Unutterable, which the ſpirit of pray'r
Inſpir'd, and wing'd for heav'n with ſpeedier flight
Than loudeſt *oratory.* *Milton's Paradiſe Loſt, b.* xi.

By this kind of *oratory* and profeſſing to decline their own inclinations and wiſhes, purely for peace and unity, they prevailed over thoſe who were ſtill ſurpriſed. *Clarend.*

The former who had to deal with a people of much more politeneſs, learning, and wit, laid the greateſt weight of his *oratory* upon the ſtrength of his arguments. *Swift.*

Come

Come harmless characters, that no one hit,
Come Henley's *oratory*, Osborn's wit. *Pope.*

2. Exercise of eloquence.

The Romans had seised upon the fleet of the Antiates, among which there were six armed with rostra, with which the consul Menenius adorned the publick place of *oratory*. *Arb.*

3. [*Oratoire*, French.]

Oratory signifies a private place, which is deputed and allotted for prayer alone, and not for the general celebration of divine service. *Ayliffe's Parergon.*

They began to erect to themselves *oratories* not in any sumptuous or stately manner, which neither was possible by reason of the poor estate of the church, and had been perilous in regard of the world's envy towards them. *Hooker.*

Do not omit thy prayers for want of a good *oratory* or place to pray in; nor thy duty for want of temporal encouragements. *Taylor's Guide to Devotion.*

ORB. *n. s.* [*orbe*, Fr. *orbis*, Latin.]

1. Sphere; orbicular body; circular body.

A mighty collection of water inclosed in the bowels of the earth, constitutes an huge *orb* in the interior or central parts; upon the surface of which *orb* of water the terrestrial strata are expanded. *Woodw. Nat. Hist.*

The with a storm of darts to distance drive
The Trojan chief; who held at bay from far,
On his Vulcanian *orb* sustain'd the war. *Dryden.*

2. Mundane sphere; celestial body; light of heaven.

nI the floor of heav'n
There's not the smallest *orb* which thou behold'st,
But in his motion like an angel sings,
Still quiring to the young-ey'd cherubims. *Shakesp.*

3. Wheel; any rolling body.

The *orbs*
Of his fierce chariot roll'd as with the sound
Of torrent floods. *Milton's Paradise Lost, b.* vi.

4. Circle; line drawn round.

5. Circle described by any of the mundane spheres.

Astronomers, to solve the phenomena, framed to their conceit eccentricks and epicycles, and a wonderful engine of *orbs*, though no such things were. *Bacon.*

With smiling aspect you serenely move,
In your fifth *orb*, and rule the realm of love. *Dryden.*

6. Period; revolution of time.

Self-begot, self-rais'd,
By our own quick'ning pow'r, when fatal course
Had circled his full *orb*, the birth mature
Of this our native heav'n. *Milt. Par. Lost, b.* v.

7. Sphere of action.

Will you again unknit
This churlish knot of all abhorred war,
And move in that obedient *orb* again,
Where you did give a fair and nat'ral light. *Shakesp.*

8. It is applied by *Milton* to the eye, as being luminous and spherical.

A drop serene hath quench'd their *orbs*,
Or dim suffusion veil'd. *Milton.*

ORBA'TION. *n. s.* [*orbatus*, Lat.] Privation of parents or children.

O'RBED. *adj.* [from *orb*.]

1. Round; circular; orbicular.

All those sayings will I overswear,
And all those swearings keep as true in soul,
As doth that *orbed* continent the fire,
That severs day from night. *Shakesp. Twelfth Night.*

2. Formed into a circle.

Truth and justice then
Will down return to men,
Orb'd in a rainbow, and like glories wearing. *Milton.*

3. Rounded.

A golden axle did the work uphold,
Gold was the beam, the wheels were *orb'd* with gold. *Addis.*

ORBI'CULAR. *adj.* [*orbiculaire*, Fr. *orbiculatus*, Lat.]

1. Spherical.

He shall monarchy with thee divide
Of all things, parted by th' empyreal bounds,
His quadrature from thy *orbicular* world. *Milton.*

2. Circular.

The form of their bottom is not the same; for whereas before it was of an *orbicular* make, they now look as if they were pressed. *Addison's Guardian*, N°. 114.

By a circle I understand not here a perfect geometrical circle, but an *orbicular* figure, whose length is equal to its breadth, and which as to sense may seem circular. *Newt.*

ORBI'CULARLY. *adj.* [from *orbicular*.] Spherically; circularly.

ORBI'CULARNESS. *n. s.* [from *orbicular*.] The state of being orbicular.

ORBI'CULATED. *adj.* [*orbiculatus*, Latin.] Moulded into an orb.

O'RBIT. *n. s.* [*orbite*, Fr. *orbita*, Latin.] The line described by the revolution of a planet.

Suppose more suns in proper *orbits* roll'd,
Dissolv'd the snows and chac'd the polar cold. *Blackm.*

Suppose the earth placed nearer to the sun, and revolve for instance in the *orb it* of Mercury; there the whole ocean would even boil with extremity of heat, and be all exhaled into vapours; all plants and animals would be scorched. *Bent.*

ORBITY. *n. s.* [*orbus*, Latin.] Loss, or want of parents or children.

ORC. *n. s.* [*orca*, Lat. ὄρυγα.] A sort of sea-fish. *Ains.*

An island salt and bare,
The haunt of seals and *orcs*, and sea-maws clang. *Milt.*

O'RCHAL. *n. s.* A stone from which a blue colour is made. *Ains.*

O'RCHANET. *n. s.* An herb. *Ains.*

O'RCHARD. *n. s.* [either *hortyard* or *wortyard*, says *Skinner*; oꞃꞇᵹeaꞃꝺ, Saxon. *Junius*.] A garden of fruit-trees.

Planting of *orchards* is very profitable, as well as pleasurable. *Bacon's Advice to Villiers.*

They overcome their riches, not by making
Baths, *orchards*, fish pools. *Ben. Johnson.*

Her private *orchards* wall'd on ev'ry side,
To lawless Sylvans all access deny'd. *Pope.*

O'RCHESTRE. *n. s.* [French. ὀρχήστρα.] The place where the musicians are set at a publick show.

ORD. *n. s.* An edge or sharpness; as in *ordhelm*, *ordbright*, &c. and in the Islandish tongue, *ord* signifies a spear or dart. *Gib.*

Ord, in old English, signified *beginning*; whence probably the proverbial phrase *odds* [*ords*] *and ends*, for scraps or remnants.

To O'RDAIN. *v. a.* [*ordino*, Lat. *ordonner*, Fr.]

1. To appoint; to decree.

Know the cause why musick was *ordain'd*;
Was it not to refresh the mind of man
After his studies, or his usual pain? *Shakespeare.*

Jeroboam *ordained* a feast. 1 *Kings* xii. 32.

He hath also prepared for him the instruments of death; he *ordaineth* his arrows against the persecutors. *Ps.* vii. 13.

As many as were *ordained* to eternal life, believed. *Acts* xiii. 48.

He commanded us to testify that it is he which was *ordained* of God to be the judge of quick and dead. *Acts* x. 42.

The fatal tent,
The scene of death, and place *ordain'd* for punishment. *Dryd.*

To souls oppress'd and dumb with grief,
The Gods *ordain* this kind relief,
That musick should in sounds convey
What dying lovers dare not say. *Waller.*

My reason bends to what thy eyes *ordain*;
For I was born to love, and thou to reign. *Prior.*

2. To establish; to settle; to institute.

Mulmutius
Ordain'd our laws, whose use the sword of Cæsar
Hath too much mangled. *Shakesp. Cymbeline.*

I will *ordain* a place for Israel. 1 *Chron.* xvii. 9.

God from Sinai descending, will himself
In thunder, lightning, and loud trumpets sound,
Ordain them laws. *Milton's Par. Lost, b.* xii.

For thee I have *ordain'd* it, and
Have suffer'd, that the glory may be thine
Of ending this great war; since none but thou
Can end it. *Milton's Par. Lost, b.* vi.

Some laws *ordain*, and some attend the choice
Of holy senates, and elect by voice. *Dryden.*

3. To set in an office.

All signified unto you by a man, who is *ordained* over the affairs, shall be utterly destroyed. *Esther*, xiii. 6.

4. To invest with ministerial function, or sacerdotal power.

Meletius was *ordained* by Arian bishops, and yet his ordination was never questioned. *Stillingfleet.*

O'RDAINER. *n. s.* [from *ordain*.] He who ordains.

O'RDEAL. *n. s.* [oꞃꝺal, Sax. *ordalium*, low Lat. *ordalie*, Fr.] A trial by fire or water, by which the person accused appealed to heaven, by walking blindfold over hot bars of iron; or being thrown, I suppose, into the water; whence the vulgar trial of witches.

Their *ordeal* laws they used in doubtful cases, when clear proofs wanted. *Hakewill on Providence.*

In the time of king John, the purgation per ignem et aquam, or the trial by *ordeal* continued; but it ended with this king. *Hale.*

O'RDER. *n. s.* [*ordo*, Lat. *ordre*, Fr.]

1. Method; regular disposition.

To know the true state of Solomon's house, I will keep this *order*; I will set forth the end of our foundation, the instruments for our works, the several employments assigned, and the ordinances we observe. *Bacon's New Atlantis.*

As St. Paul was full of the doctrine of the gospel; so it lay all clear and in *order*, open to his view. *Locke.*

2. Established process.

The moderator, when either of the disputants breaks the rules, may interpose to keep them to *order*. *Watts.*

3. Proper state.

Any of the faculties wanting, or out of *order*, produce suitable defects in mens understandings. *Locke.*

4. Regularity; settled mode.

This order with her sorrow she accords,
Which orderless all form of *order* brake. *Daniel.*

5. Mandate;

5. Mandate; precept; command.

Give *order* to my servants, that they take
No note of our being absent. *Shakesp. Mer. of Ven.*

If the lords of the council issued out any *order* against them, or if the king sent a proclamation for their repair to their houses, presently some nobleman deputed by the tables published a protestation against those *orders* and proclamations. *Clarendon.*

Upon this new fright, an *order* was made by both houses for disarming all the papists in England; upon which, and the like *orders*, though seldom any thing was after done, yet it served to keep up the apprehensions in the people, of dangers and designs, and to disincline them from any reverence or affection to the queen. *Clarendon.*

I have received an *order* under your hand for a thousand pounds in words at length. *Tatler*, N°. 60.

6. Rule; regulation.

The church hath authority to establish that for an *order* at one time, which at another time it may abolish, and in both do well. *Hooker*, *b.* v. *s.* 8.

7. Regular government.

The night, their number, and the sudden act
Would dash all *order*, and protect their fact. *Daniel.*

8. A society of dignified persons distinguished by marks of honour.

Elves,
The several chairs of *order* look you scour,
With juice of balm and ev'ry precious flow'r. *Shakesp.*

Princes many times make themselves desires, and set their hearts upon toys; sometimes upon a building; sometimes upon erecting of an *order*. *Bacon.*

She left immortal trophies of her fame,
And to the noblest *order* gave the name. *Dryden.*
By shining marks, distinguish'd they appear,
And various *orders* various ensigns bear. *Granville.*

9. A rank, or class.

The king commanded the high priest and the priests of the second *order*, to bring forth out of the temple all the vessels. 2 *Kings* xxiii. 4.

Th' Almighty seeing,
From his transcendent seat the saints among,
To those bright *orders* utter'd thus his voice. *Milton.*

10. A religious fraternity.

Find a bare foot brother out,
One of our *order* to associate me,
Here visiting the sick. *Shakesp. Rom. and Juliet.*

11. [In the plural.] Hierarchical state.

If the faults of men in *orders* are only to be judged among themselves, they are all in some sort parties. *Dryden.*

Having in his youth made a good progress in learning, that he might dedicate himself more intirely to religion he entered into holy *orders*, and in a few years became renowned for his sanctity of life. *Addison's Spectator*, N°. 164.

12. Means to an end.

Virgins must remember, that the virginity of the body is only excellent in *order* to the purity of the soul; for in the same degree that virgins live more spiritually than other persons, in the same degree is their virginity a more excellent state. *Taylor's Rule of Living Holy.*

We should behave reverently towards the Divine Majesty, and justly towards men; and in *order* to the better discharge of these duties, we should govern ourselves in the use of sensual delights, with temperance. *Tillotson, Serm.* 6.

The best knowledge is that which is of greatest use in *order* to our eternal happiness. *Tillotson, Serm.* 1.

What we see is in *order* only to what we do not see; and both these states must be joined together. *Atterbury.*

One man pursues power in *order* to wealth, and another wealth in *order* to power, which last is the safer way, and generally followed. *Swift's Exam.* N°. 27.

13. Measures; care.

It were meet you should take some *order* for the soldiers, which are now first to be discharged and disposed of some way; which may otherwise grow to as great inconvenience as all this that you have quit us from. *Spenser on Ireland.*

Provide me soldiers,
Whilst I take *order* for mine own affairs. *Shakesp.*

The money promised unto the king, he took no *order* for, albeit Sostratus required it. 2 *Mac.* iv. 27.

If any of the family be distressed, *order* is taken for their relief and competent means to live. *Bacon.*

14. [In architecture.] A system of the several members, ornaments, and proportions of columns and pilasters; or it is a regular arrangement of the projecting parts of a building, especially those of a column; so as to form one beautiful whole: or *order* is a certain rule for the proportions of columns, and for the figures which some of the parts ought to have, on the account of the proportions that are given them. There are five *orders* of columns; three of which are Greek, *viz.* the doric, ionic, and corinthian; and two Italian, *viz.* the tuscan and composite. The whole is composed of two parts at least, the column and the entablature, and of four parts at the most; where there is a pedestal under the columns, and one acroter or little pedestal on the top of the entablature. The column has three parts; the base, the shaft, and the capital; which parts are all different in the several *orders*.

In the tuscan *order*, any height being given, divide it into ten parts and three quarters, called diameters, by diameters is meant the thickness of the shaft at the bottom, the pedestal having two; the column with base and capital, seven; and the entablature one and three quarters.

In the doric *order*, the whole height being given, is divided into twelve diameters or parts, and one third; the pedestal having two and one third, the column eight, and the entablature two.

In the ionic *order*, the whole height is dividedinto thirteen diameters and a half, the pedestal having two and two thirds, the column nine, and the entablature one and four fifths. In the corinthian *order*, the whole height is divided into fourteen diameters and a half, the pedestal having three, the column nine and a half, and the entablature two.

In the composite *order*, the whole height is divided into fifteen diameters and one third; the pedestal having three and one third, the column ten, and the entablature two.

In a colonnade or range of pillars, the intercolumination or space between columns in the tuscan *order*, is four diameters. In the doric *order*, two and three quarters; in the ionic *order*, two and a quarter; in the corinthian *order*, two; and in the composite *order*, one and a half. *Builder's Dict.*

To O'RDER. *v. a.* [from the noun.]

1. To regulate; to adjust; to manage; to conduct.

To him that *ordereth* his conversation aright, will I shew the salvation of God. *Ps.* l. 23.

As the sun when it ariseth in the heaven, so is the beauty of a good wife in the *ordering* of her house. *Ecclus* xxvi. 16.

Thou hast *ordered* all in measure, number, and weight. *Wisd.* xi. 20.

Bias being asked how a man should *order* his life? answered, as if a man should live long, or die quickly. *Bacon.*

2. To manage; to procure.

The kitchin clerk that hight digestion,
Did *order* all the cates in seemly wise. *Fairy Queen.*

3. To methodise; to dispose fitly.

These were the *orderings* of them in their service, to come into the house of the Lord. 1 *Chron.* xxiv. 19.

4. To direct; to command.

5. To ordain to sacerdotal function.

The book requireth due examination, and giveth liberty to object any crime against such as are to be *ordered*. *Whitgift.*

O'RDERER. *n. s.* [from *order*.] One that orders, methodises, or regulates.

That there should be a great disposer and *orderer* of all things, a wise rewarder and punisher of good and evil, hath appeared so equitable to men, that they have concluded it necessary. *Suckling.*

O'RDERLESS. *adj.* [from *order*.] Disorderly; out of rule.

All form is formless, order *orderless*,
Save what is opposite to England's love. *Shakespeare.*

O'RDERLINESS. *n. s.* [from *orderly*.] Regularity; methodicalness.

O'RDERLY. *adj.* [from *order*.]

1. Methodical; regular.

The book requireth but *orderly* reading. *Hooker.*

2. Not tumultuous; well regulated.

Balfour, by an *orderly* and well-governed march, passed in the king's quarters without any considerable loss, to a place of safety. *Clarendon*, *b.* viii.

3. According with established method.

As for the orders established, sith the law of nature, of God and man, do all favourthat which is in being, till *orderly* judgment of decision be given against it, it is but justice to exact obedience of you. *Hooker's Pref.*

A clergy reformed from popery in such a manner, as happily to preserve the mean between the two extremes, in doctrine, worship, and government, perfected this reformation by quiet and *orderly* methods, free from those confusions and tumults that elsewhere attended it. *Atterbury.*

O'RDERLY. *adv.* [from *order*.] Methodically; according to order; regularly; according to rule.

All parts of knowledge have been thought by wise men to be then most *orderly* delivered and proceeded in, when they are drawn to their first original. *Hooker*, *b.* i.

Ask him his name, and *orderly* proceed
To swear him. *Shakesp. Rich.* III.

Make it *orderly* and well,
According to the fashion of the time. *Shakespeare.*

It is walled with brick and stone, intermixed *orderly*. *Sandys.*

How should those active particles, ever and anon justled by the occursion of other bodies, whereof there is an infinite store, so *orderly* keep their cells without any alteration of site. *Glanville.*

In the body, when the principal parts, the heart and liver, do their offices, and all the inferior smaller vessels act *orderly* and duly, there arises a sweet enjoyment upon the whole, which we call health. *South's Serm.*

O'RDINABLE. *adj.* [*ordino*, Lat.] Such as may be appointed.

All the ways of œconomy God hath used toward a rational creature, to reduce mankind to that course of living which is most perfectly agreeable to our nature, and by the mercy of God *ordinable* to eternal bliss. *Hamm.*

O'RDINAL. *adj.* [*ordinal*, Fr. *ordinalis*, Lat.] Noting order: as, second, third.

The moon's age is thus found, add to the epact the day of the month and the *ordinal* number of that month from March inclusive, because the epact begins at March, and the sum of those, casting away thirty or twenty-nine, as often as it ariseth, is the age of the moon. *Holder.*

O'RDINAL. *n. s.* [*ordinal*, Fr. *ordinale*, Latin.] A ritual; a book containing orders. *Ainf.*

O'RDINANCE. *n. s.* [*ordonnance*, French.]

1. Law; rule; prescript.

It seemeth hard to plant any sound *ordinance*, or reduce them to a civil government; since all their ill customs are permitted unto them. *Spenser on Ireland.*

Let Richard and Elizabeth,
The true succeeders of each royal house,
By God's fair *ordinance* conjoin together! *Shakesp.*

2. Observance commanded.

One *ordinance* ought not to exclude the other, much less to disparage the other, and least of all to undervalue that which is the most eminent. *Taylor.*

3. Appointment.

Things created to shew bare heads,
When one but of my *ordinance* stood up,
To speak of peace or war. *Shakesp. Coriolanus.*

4. A cannon. It is now generally written for distinction *ordnance*; its derivation is not certain.

Caves and womby vaultages of France,
Shall chide your trespass and return your mock,
In second accent to his *ordinance.* *Shakesp. Hen. V.*

O'RDINARILY. *adv.* [from *ordinary.*]

1. According to established rules; according to settled method.

We are not to look that the church should change her publick laws and ordinances, made according to that which is judged *ordinarily*, and commonly fittest for the whole, although it chance that for some particular men the same be found inconvenient. *Hooker, b.* iv. *s.* 12.

Springs and rivers do not derive the water which they *ordinarily* refund, from rain. *Woodward's Nat. Hist.*

2. Commonly; usually.

The instances of human ignorance were not only clear ones, but such as are not so *ordinarily* suspected. *Glanv.*

Prayer ought to be more than *ordinarily* fervent and vigorous before the sacrament. *South's Sermons.*

O'RDINARY. *adj.* [*ordinarius*, Latin.]

1. Established; methodical; regular.

Though in arbitrary governments there may be a body of laws observed in the *ordinary* forms of justice, they are not sufficient to secure any rights to the people; because they may be dispensed with. *Addison's Freeholder.*

The standing *ordinary* means of conviction failing to influence them, it is not to be expected that any extraordinary means should be able to do it. *Atterbury.*

2. Common; usual.

Yet did she only utter her doubt to her daughters, thinking, since the worst was past, she would attend a further occasion, least over much haste might seem to proceed of the *ordinary* mislike between sisters in law. *Sidney.*

It is sufficient that Moses have the *ordinary* credit of an historian given him. *Tillotson, Serm.* 1.

This designation of the person our author is more than *ordinary* obliged to take care of, because he hath made the conveyance, as well as the power itself, sacred. *Locke.*

There is nothing more *ordinary* than children's receiving into their minds propositions from their parents; which being fastened by degrees, are at last, whether true or false, riveted there. *Locke.*

Method is not less requisite in *ordinary* conversation, than in writing. *Addison's Spectator*, N°. 476.

3. Mean; of low rank.

These are the paths wherein ye have walked, that are of the *ordinary* sort of men; these are the very steps ye have trodden, and the manifest degrees whereby ye are of your guides and directors trained up in that school. *Hooker.*

Men of common capacity, and but *ordinary* judgment, are not able to discern what things are fittest for each kind and state of regiment. *Hooker, b.* i. *s.* 10.

Every *ordinary* reader, upon the publishing of a new poem, has will and ill-nature enough to turn several passages of it into ridicule, and very often in the right place. *Addison.*

My speculations, when sold single, are delights for the rich and wealthy; after some time they come to the market in great quantities, and are every *ordinary* man's money. *Addison's Spectator*, N°. 488.

You will wonder how such an *ordinary* fellow as Wood, could get his majesty's broad seal. *Swift.*

4. Ugly; not handsome: as she is an *ordinary* woman.

O'RDINARY. *n. s.*

1. Established judge of ecclesiastical causes.

The evil will
Of all their parishioners they had constrain'd,
Who to the *ordinary* of them complain'd. *Hubberd.*

If fault be in these things any where justly found, law hath refered the whole disposition and redress thereof to the *ordinary* of the place. *Hooker, b.* v. *s.* 12.

2. Settled establishment.

Spain had no other wars save those which were grown into an *ordinary*; now they have coupled therewith the extraordinary of the Valtoline and Palatinate. *Bacon.*

3. Actual and constant office.

Villiers had an intimation of the king's pleasure to be his cup-bearer at large; and the summer following he was admitted in *ordinary.* *Wott.*

4. Regular price of a meal.

Our courteous Antony,
Being barber'd ten times o'er, goes to the feast;
And for his *ordinary* pays his heart
For what his eyes eat only. *Shakesp. Ant. and Cleopat.*

5. A place of eating established at a certain price.

They reckon all their errors for accomplishments; and all the odd words they have picked up in a coffee-house, or a gaming *ordinary*, are produced as flowers of style. *Swift.*

To O'RDINATE. *v. a.* [*ordinatus*, Latin.]

1. To appoint.

Finding how the certain right did stand,
With full consent this man did *ordinate*
The heir apparent to the crown and land. *Daniel.*

O'RDINATE. *adj.* [*ordinatus*, Lat.] Regular; methodical.

Ordinate figures are such as have all their sides, and all their angles equal. *Ray on the Creation.*

ORDINA'TION. *n. s.* [*ordinatio*, Lat. from *ordinate.*]

1. Established order or tendency.

Virtue and vice have a natural *ordination* to the happiness and misery of life respectively. *Norris.*

2. The act of investing any man with sacerdotal power.

Though ordained by Arian bishops, his *ordination* was never questioned. *Stillingfleet.*

St. Paul looks upon Titus as advanced to the dignity of a prime ruler of the church, and entrusted with a large diocese under the immediate government of their respective elders; and those deriving authority from his *ordination.* *South.*

O'RDNANCE. *n. s.* [This was anciently written more frequently *ordinance*; but *ordnance* is used for distinction.] Cannon; great guns.

Have I not heard great *ordnance* in the field?
And heav'n's artillery thunder in the skies? *Shakesp.*

When a ship feels or rolls in foul weather, the breaking loose of *ordnance* is a thing very dangerous. *Raleigh.*

There are examples now of wounded persons that have roared for anguish and torment at the discharge of *ordnance*, though at a very great distance. *Bentley's Serm.*

ORDO'NNANCE. *n. s.* [French.] Disposition of figures in a picture.

O'RDURE. *n. s.* [*ordure*, French; from *sordes*, Lat. *Skinner.*] Dung; filth.

Gard'ners with *ordure* hide those roots
That shall first spring and be most delicate. *Shakesp.*

Working upon human *ordure*, and by long preparation rendering it odoriferous, he terms it *zibetta occidentalis.* *Brown.*

We added fat pollutions of our own,
T' encrease the steaming *ordures* of the stage. *Dryden.*

Renew'd by *ordure*'s sympathetick force,
As oil'd with magic juices for the course,
Vig'rous he rises. *Pope.*

ORE. *n. s.* [oȝe, or oȝa, Saxon; *oor*, Dutch, a mine.]

1. Metal unrefined; metal yet in its mineral state.

Round about him lay on every side,
Great heaps of gold that never would be spent;
Of which some were rude *ore* not purify'd
Of Mulciber's devouring element. *Fairy Queen.*

They would have brought them the gold *ore* aboard their ships. *Raleigh's Apology.*

A hill not far,
Shone with a glossy scurf, undoubted sign
That in his womb was hid metallic *ore*,
The work of sulphur. *Milton's Paradise Lost, b.* i.

Who have labour'd more
To search the treasures of the Roman store,
Or dig in Grecian mines for purer *ore*? *Roscommon.*

We walk in dreams on fairy land,
Where golden *ore* lies mixt with common sand. *Dryden.*

Those who unripe veins in mines explore,
On the rich bed again the warm turf lay,
'Till time digests the yet imperfect *ore*,
And know it will be gold another day. *Dryden.*

Thoſe profounder regions they explore,
Where metals ripen in vaſt cakes of *ore*. *Garth.*

2. Metal.

The liquid *ore* he drain'd
Firſt his own tools; then what might elſe be wrought,
Fuſile, or grav'n in metal. *Milt. Par. Loſt, b.* xi.

O'REWEED. } O'REWOOD. } *n. ſ.* A weed either growing upon the rocks under high water mark, or broken from the bottom of the ſea by rough weather, and caſt upon the next by the wind and flood. *Carew's Survey of Cornwall.*

O'RGAL. *n. ſ.* Lees of wine. *Ainſ.*

O'RGAN. *n. ſ.* [*organe*, Fr. ὄργανον.]

1. Natural inſtrument; as the tongue is the organ of ſpeech, the lungs of reſpiration.

When he ſhall hear ſhe died upon his words,
The ever lovely *organ* of her life
Shall come apparell'd in more precious habit,
Than when ſhe liv'd indeed. *Shakeſpeare.*

For a mean and *organ*, by which this operative virtue might be continued, God appointed the light to be united, and gave it alſo motion and heat. *Raleigh.*

The aptneſs of birds is not ſo much in the conformity of the *organs* of ſpeech, as in their attention. *Bacon.*

Wit and will
Can judge and chuſe, without the body's aid;
Tho' on ſuch objects they are working ſtill,
As thro' the body's *organs* are convey'd. *Davies.*

2. An inſtrument of muſick conſiſting of pipes filled with wind and of ſtops, touched by the hand. [*Orgue*, Fr.]

A hand of a vaſt extenſion, and a prodigious number of fingers playing upon all the *organ* pipes in the world, and making every one ſound a particular note. *Keil.*

While in more lengthen'd notes and ſlow,
The deep, majeſtick, ſolemn *organs* blow. *Pope.*

ORGA'NICAL. } ORGA'NICK. } *adj.* [*organique*, Fr. *organicus*, Lat.]

1. Conſiſting of various parts co-operating with each other.

He rounds the air, and breaks the hymnick notes
In birds, heav'n's choriſters, *organick* throats;
Which, if they did not die, might ſeem to be
A tenth rank in the heavenly hierarchy. *Donne.*

He with ſerpent tongue
Organick, or impulſe of vocal air,
His fraudulent temptation thus began. *Milt. P. Loſt.*

The *organical* ſtructure of human bodies, whereby they live and move and are vitally informed by the ſoul, is the workmanſhip of a moſt wiſe, powerful, and beneficent being. *Bentley's Sermons.*

2. Inſtrumental; acting as inſtruments of nature or art, to a certain end.

Read with them thoſe *organick* arts which enable men to diſcourſe and write perſpicuouſly, elegantly, and according to the fitteſt ſtyle of lofty, mean, or lowly. *Milton.*

3. Reſpecting organs.

She could not produce a monſter of any thing that hath more vital and *organical* parts than a rock of marble. *Ray.*

They who want the ſenſe of diſcipline, or hearing, are alſo by conſequence deprived of ſpeech, not by any immediate, *organical* indiſpoſition, but for want of diſcipline. *Holder's Elements of Speech.*

ORGA'NICALLY. *adv.* [from *organical.*] By means of organs or inſtruments; by organical diſpoſition of parts.

All ſtones, metals, and minerals, are real vegetables; that is, grow *organically* from proper ſeeds, as well as plants. *Locke on Nat. Philoſophy.*

ORGA'NICALNESS. *n. ſ.* [from *organical.*] State of being organical.

O'RGANISM. *n. ſ.* [from *organ.*] Organical ſtructure.

How admirable is the natural ſtructure or *organiſm* of bodies. *Grew's Coſmol. b.* i. *c.* 4.

O'RGANIST. *n. ſ.* [*organiſte*, Fr. from *organ.*] One who plays on the organ.

He is an *organiſt*, and ſerves that office in a publick choir. *Boyle on Colours.*

ORGANIZA'TION. *n. ſ.* [from *organize.*] Conſtruction in which the parts are ſo diſpoſed as to be ſubſervient to each other.

Every man's ſenſes differ as much from others in their figure, colour, ſite, and infinite other peculiarities in the *organization*, as any one man's can from itſelf, through divers accidental variations. *Glanv. Scepſ. c.* xxvi.

That being then one plant, which has ſuch an *organization* of parts in one coherent body, partaking of one common life, it continues to be the ſame plant, though that life be communicated to new particles of matter, in a like continued *organization*. *Locke.*

To O'RGANIZE. *v. a.* [*organiſer*, Fr. from *organ.*] To conſtruct ſo as that one part co-operates with another; to form organically.

As the ſoul doth *organize* the body, and give unto every member thereof that ſubſtance, quantity, and ſhape, which nature ſeeth moſt expedient, ſo the inward grace of ſacraments may teach what ſerveth beſt for their outward form. *Hooker, b.* v. *ſ.* 58.

A genial and cheriſhing heat ſo acts upon the fit and obſequious matter, wherein it was harboured, as to *organize* and faſhion that diſpoſed matter according to the exigencies of its own nature. *Boyle.*

Thoſe nobler faculties in the mind, matter *organized* could never produce. *Ray on the Creation.*

The identity of the ſame man conſiſts in a participation of the ſame continued life, by conſtantly fleeting particles in ſucceſſion vitally united to the ſame *organized* body. *Locke.*

O'RGANLOFT. *n. ſ.* [*organ* and *loft.*] The loft where the organs ſtand.

Five young ladies of no ſmall fame for their great ſeverity of manners, would go no where with their lovers but to an *organloft* in a church, where they had a cold treat and ſome few opera ſongs. *Tatler*, Nº. 61.

O'RGANPIPE. *n. ſ.* [*organ* and *pipe.*] The pipe of a muſical organ.

The thunder,
That deep and dreadful *organpipe* pronounc'd
The name of Proſper. *Shakeſpeare's Tempeſt.*

O'RGANY. *n. ſ.* [*origanum*, Lat.] An herb. *Ainſ.*

ORGA'SM. *n. ſ.* [*orgaſme*, Fr. ὀργασμός.] Sudden vehemence.

By means of the curious lodgment and inoſculation of the auditory nerves, the *orgaſms* of the ſpirits ſhould be allayed, and perturbations of the mind quieted. *Derham's Phyſico-Theol.*

O'RGEIS. *n. ſ.* A ſea-fiſh, called likewiſe *organling*. Both ſeem a corruption of the orkenyling, as being taken on the Orkeny coaſt. *Ainſ.*

ORGI'LLOUS. *adj.* [*orgueilleux*, French.] Proud; haughty.

From iſles of Greece
The princes *orgillous*, their high blood chafed,
Have to the port of Athens ſent their ſhips. *Shakeſp.*

O'RGIES. *n. ſ.* [*orgies*, Fr. *orgia*, Lat.] Mad rites of Bacchus; frantick revels.

Theſe are nights
Solemn to the ſhining rites,
Of the fairy prince and knights,
While the moon their *orgies* lights. *Ben. Johnſon.*

She feign'd nocturnal *orgies*; left my bed,
And, mix'd with Trojan dames, the dances led. *Dryd.*

O'RICHALCH. *n. ſ.* [*orichalcum*, Lat.] Braſs.

Not Bilbo ſteel, nor braſs from Corinth fet,
Nor coſtly *orichalch* from ſtrange Phœnice,
But ſuch as could both Phœbus' arrows ward,
And th' hailing darts of heav'n beating hard. *Spenſer.*

O'RIENT. *adj.* [*oriens*, Latin.]

1. Riſing as the ſun.

Moon that now meet'ſt the *orient* ſun, now fly'ſt
With the fix'd ſtars. *Milton's Par. Loſt, b.* v.

When fair morn *orient* in heav'n appear'd. *Milton.*

2. Eaſtern; oriental.

3. Bright; ſhining; glittering; gaudy; ſparkling.

The liquid drops of tears that you have ſhed,
Shall come again transform'd to *orient* pearl;
Advantaging their loan with intereſt,
Oftentimes double gain of happineſs. *Shakeſp.*

There do breed yearly an innumerable company of gnats, whoſe property is to fly unto the eye of the lion, as being a bright and *orient* thing. *Abbot on the World.*

We have ſpoken of the cauſe of *orient* colours in birds; which is by the fineneſs of the ſtrainer. *Bacon's Nat. Hiſt.*

Morning light
More *orient* in yon weſtern cloud, that draws
O'er the blue firmament a radiant white. *Milton.*

In thick ſhelter of black ſhades imbowr'd,
He offers to each weary traveller
His *orient* liquor in a cryſtal glaſs,
To quench the drouth of Phœbus. *Milton.*

The chiefs about their necks the ſcutcheons wore,
With *orient* pearls and jewels powder'd o'er. *Dryden.*

O'RIENT. *n. ſ.* [*orient*, Fr.] The eaſt; the part where the ſun firſt appears.

ORIE'NTAL. *adj.* [*oriental*, French.] Eaſtern; placed in the eaſt; proceeding from the eaſt.

Your ſhips went as well to the pillars of Hercules, as to Pequin upon the *oriental* ſeas, as far as to the borders of the eaſt Tartary. *Bacon's New Atlantis.*

Some aſcribing hereto the generation of gold, conceive the bodies of this ſituation to receive ſome appropriate influence from the ſun's aſcendent, and *oriental* radiations. *Brown's Vulgar Err. b.* vi.

ORIE'NTAL. *n. ſ.* An inhabitant of the eaſtern parts of the world.

They have been of that great uſe to following ages, as to be imitated by the Arabians and other *orientals*. *Grew.*

ORIE'NTALISM. *n. ſ.* [from *oriental.*] An idiom of the eaſtern languages; an eaſtern mode of ſpeech.

ORIE'NTALITY. *n. s.* [from *oriental.*] State of being oriental.
His revolution being regular, it hath no power nor efficacy peculiar from its *orientality*, but equally disperseth his beams. *Brown's V. Err. b.* vi.

O'RIFICE. *n. s.* [*orifice*, Fr. *orificium*, Lat.] Any opening or perforation.
The prince of Orange, in his first hurt by the Spanish boy, could find no means to stanch the blood, but was fain to have the *orifice* of the wound stopped by men's thumbs, succeeding one another for the space of two days. *Bacon.*

Their mouths
With hideous *orifice* gap'd on us wide,
Portending hollow truce. *Milton's Par. Lost, b.* vi.

Ætna was bored through the top with a monstruous *orifice*. *Addison's Guardian*, Nº. 103.
Blood-letting, Hippocrates saith, should be done with broad lancets or swords, in order to make a large *orifice* by stabbing or pertusion. *Arbuthnot on Coins.*

O'RIFLAMB. *n. s.* [probably a corruption of *auriflamma*, Lat. or *flamme d'or*, Fr. in like manner as *orpiment* is corrupted.] A golden standard. *Ains.*

O'RIGAN. *n. s.* [*origan*, Fr. *origanum*, Lat.] Wild marjorum.
I saw her in her proper hue,
Bathing herself in *origan* and thyme. *Fairy Queen.*

O'RIGIN. }
ORI'GINAL. } *n. s.* [*origine*, Fr. *origo*, Lat.]

1. Beginning; first existence.
The sacred historian only treats of the *origins* of terrestrial animals. *Bentley's Sermons.*

2. Fountain; source; that which gives beginning or existence.
Nature which contemns its *origin*,
Cannot be border'd certain in itself. *Shakesp. King Lear.*

If any station upon earth be honourable, theirs was; and their posterity therefore have no reason to blush at the memory of such an *original*. *Atterbury.*

Original of beings! pow'r divine!
Since that I live and that I think, is thine. *Prior.*

These great orbs,
Primitive founts, and *origins* of light. *Prior.*

3. First copy; archetype; that from which any thing is transcribed or translated. In this sense *origin* is not used.
Compare this translation with the *original*, and the three first stanzas are rendered almost word for word, and not only with the same elegance, but with the same turn of expression. *Addison's Spectator*, Nº. 229.
External material things, as the objects of sensation; and the operations of our minds within, as the objects of reflection; are the only *originals* from whence all our ideas take their beginnings. *Locke.*

4. Derivation; descent.
They, like the seed from which they sprung, accurst
Against the gods immortal hatred nurst;
An impious, arrogant, and cruel brood,
Expressing their *original* from blood. *Dryden.*

ORI'GINAL. *adj.* [*originel*, Fr. *originalis*, Latin.] Primitive; pristine; first.
The *original* question was, whether God by this law hath forbidden the giving any worship to himself by an image? *Stillingfleet on Idolatry.*
Had Adam obeyed God, his *original* perfection, the knowledge and ability God at first gave him, would still have continued. *Wake's Prep. for Death.*

You still, fair mother, in your offspring trace
The stock of beauty destin'd for the race;
Kind nature, forming them the pattern took,
From heav'n's first work, and Eve's *original* look. *Prior.*

ORI'GINALLY. *adv.* [from *original.*]

1. Primarily; with regard to the first cause.
A very great difference between a king that holdeth his crown by a willing act of estates, and one that holdeth it *originally* by the law of nature and descent of blood. *Bacon.*
A present blessing upon our fasts, is neither *originally* due from God's justice, nor becomes due to us from his veracity. *Smallridge's Sermons.*

2. At first.
The metallic and mineral matter, found in the perpendicular intervals of the strata, was *originally*, and at the time of the deluge, lodged in the bodies of those strata. *Woodw.*

3. As the first author.
For what *originally* others writ,
May be so well disguis'd and so improv'd,
That with some justice it may pass for yours. *Roscomm.*

ORI'GINALNESS. *n. s.* [from *original.*] The quality or state of being original.

ORI'GINARY. *adj.* [*originaire*, Fr. from *origin.*]

1. Productive; causing existence.
The production of animals in the *originary* way, requires a certain degree of warmth, which proceeds from the sun's influence. *Cheyne's Phil. Prin.*

2. Primitive; that which was the first state.
Remember I am built of clay, and must
Resolve to my *originary* dust. *Sandy's Par. on Job.*

To ORI'GINATE. *v. a.* [from *origin.*] To bring into existence.

ORIGINA'TION. *n. s.* [*originatio*, Lat. from *originate.*] The act of bringing into existence; first production.
The tradition of the *origination* of mankind seems to be universal; but the particular methods of that *origination* excogitated by the heathen, were particular. *Hale.*
This eruca is propagated by animal parents, to wit, butterflies, after the common *origination* of all caterpillars. *Ray.*
Descartes first introduced the fancy of making a world, and deducing the *origination* of the universe from mechanical principles. *Keil.*

O'RISONS. *n. s.* [*oraison*, French: this word is variously accented; *Shakespeare* has the accent both on the first and second syllables; *Milton* and *Crashaw* on the first, others on the second.] A prayer; a supplication.

Nymph, in thy *orisons*
Be all thy sins remember'd. *Shakesp. Hamlet.*

Alas! your too much love and care of me,
Are heavy *orisons* 'gainst this poor wretch. *Shakesp.*

He went into St. Paul's church, where he had *orisons* and Te Deum sung. *Bacon's Henry* VII.

My wakeful lay shall knock
At th' oriental gates, and duly mock
The early larks shrill *orisons*, to be
An anthem at the day's nativity. *Crashaw.*

His daily *orisons* attract our ears. *Sandys on Job.*

Lowly they bow'd, adoring, and began
Their *orisons*, each morning duly paid. *Milton.*

So went he on with his *orisons*,
Which, if you mark them well, were wise ones. *Cotton.*

Here at dead of night
The hermit oft, mid his *orisons*, hears
Aghast the voice of time disparting tow'rs. *Dyer.*

O'RLOP. *n. s.* [*overloop*, Dutch.] The middle deck. *Skinn.*
A small ship of the king's called the Pensie, was assailed by the Lyon, a principal ship of Scotland; wherein the Pensie so applyed her shot, that the Lyon's *oreloop* was broken, her sails and tackling torn; and lastly, she was boarded and taken. *Hayward.*

O'RNAMENT. *n. s.* [*ornamentum*, Lat. *ornement*, Fr.]

1. Embellishment; decoration.
So may the outward shows be least themselves;
The world is still deceiv'd with *ornament*. *Shakesp.*

The Tuscan chief, to me has sent
Their crown, and ev'ry regal *ornament*. *Dryden.*

No circumstances of life can place a man so far below the notice of the world, but that his virtues or vices will render him, in some degree, an *ornament* or disgrace to his profession. *Rogers, Serm.* 9.

2. Honour; that which confers dignity.
The persons of different qualities in both sexes, are indeed allowed their different *ornaments*; but these are by no means costly, being rather designed as marks of distinction than to make a figure. *Addison on Italy.*

ORNAME'NTAL. *adj.* [from *ornament.*] Serving to decoration; giving embellishment.
Some think it most *ornamental* to wear their bracelets on their wrists, others about their ancles. *Brown.*
If the kind be capable of more perfection, though rather in the *ornamental* parts of it, than the essential, what rules of morality or respect have I broken, in naming the defects that they may hereafter be amended? *Dryden.*
Even the Heathens have esteemed this variety not only *ornamental* to the earth, but a proof of the wisdom of the creator. *Woodw. Nat. Hist.*
If no advancement of knowledge can be had from universities, the time there spent is lost; every *ornamental* part of education is better taught elsewhere. *Swift on Religion.*

ORNAME'NTALLY. *adv.* [from *ornamental.*] In such a manner as may confer embellishment.

ORNA'MENTED. *adj.* [from *ornament.*] Embellished; bedecked.

O'RNATE. *adj.* [*ornatus*, Lat.] Bedecked; decorated; fine.
What thing of sea or land,
Female of sex it seems,
That so bedeck'd, *ornate* and gay,
Comes this way sailing. *Milton's Agonistes.*

O'RNATENESS. *n. s.* [from *ornate.*] Finery; state of being embellished.

ORNA'TURE. *n. s.* [*ornatus*, Lat.] Decoration. *Ains.*

ORNI'SCOPIST. *n. s.* [ὄρνις and σκοπέω.] One who examines the flight of birds in order to foretel futurity.

ORNI'THOLOGY. *n. s.* [ὄρνις and λόγος.] A discourse on birds.

O'RPHAN. *n. s.* [ὀρφανός; *orphelin*, Fr.] A child who has lost father or mother, or both.

Poor *orphan* in the wide world scattered,
As budding branch rent from the native tree,
And thrown forth until it be withered:
Such is the state of man. *Fairy Queen, b.* ii.

Who can be bound by any solemn vow
To reave the *orphan* of his patrimony,

To wring the widow from her custom'd right,
And have no other reason for his wrong,
But that he was bound by a solemn oath? *Shakesp.*

Sad widows, by thee rifled, weep in vain,
And ruin'd *orphans* of thy rapes complain. *Sandys.*

The sea with spoils his angry bullets strow,
Widows and *orphans* making as they go. *Waller.*

Pity, with a parent's mind,
This helpless *orphan* whom thou leav'st behind. *Dryden.*

O'RPHAN. *adj.* [*orphelin*, Fr.] Bereft of parents.

This king left *orphan* both of father and mother, found his estate, when he came to age, so disjointed even in the noblest and strongest limbs of government, that the name of a king was grown odious. *Sidney, b.* ii.

O'RPHANAGE. } *n. s.* [*orphelinage*, Fr. from *orphan.*] State
O'RPHANISM. } of an orphan.

ORPI'MENT. *n. s.* [*auripigmentum*, Lat. *orpiment*, *orpin*, Fr.]

True and genuine *orpiment* is a foliaceous fossil, sometimes found in masses of two or three inches diameter, and one inch in thickness; but it is oftener met with in smaller congeries of flakes from an eighth of an inch to a third in diameter, lodged in zarnich. See ZARNICH. It is of a fine and pure texture, remarkably heavy, and its colour is a bright and beautiful yellow, like that of gold. It is not hard but very tough, easily bending without breaking: some have declared *orpiment* to be only muscovy talk, stained by accident. But talk is always elastick, but *orpiment* not so; talk also remains unaltered in the strongest fire, whereas *orpiment* melts readily, and as readily burns away. *Orpiment* has been supposed to contain gold, and is found in mines of gold, silver, and copper, and sometimes in the strata of marl. It is frequent in the East-Indies and the Turkish dominions, the finest coming from Smyrna. We have it also in Germany and Saxony. The ancients were well acquainted with this drug, which they called arsenicon; and though they were utterly unacquainted with the poisonous substance called arsenick, yet *orpiment* has been by some very unjustly deemed a poison; but it appears to be an innocent medicine which the ancients prescribed internally. The painters are very fond of it as a gold colour. *Hill's Mat. Med.*

For the golden colour, it may be made by some small mixture of *orpiment*, such as they use to brass in the yellow alchymy; it will easily recover that which the iron loseth. *Bacon.*

ORPHANOTROPHY. *n. s.* [ὀρφανὸς and τροφή.] An hospital for orphans.

O'RPINE. *n. s.* [*orpin*, Fr.] Liverer or rose root, *anacampseros*, *Telephum*, or *Rhodia radis*. A plant. It hath a rose shaped flower, consisting of several leaves placed orbicularly; out of whose many-leaved empalement rises the pointal, which afterward becomes a three-cornered fruit, consisting of one cell, which is filled with roundish seeds: the leaves are placed alternately on the branches. It is a low plant, whose branches trail on the ground; the leaves are small and roundish, of a glaucous colour, and of a pretty thick consistence. The flowers are small, and of a whitish green colour. *Miller.*

Cool violets and *orpine* growing still,
Embathed balm and cheerful galingale. *Spenser.*

O'RRERY. *n. s.* An instrument which by many complicated movements represents the revolutions of the heavenly bodies. It was first made by Mr. Rowley, a mathematician born at Litchfield, and so named from his patron the earl of Orrery: by one or other of this family almost every art has been encouraged or improved.

O'RRIS. *n. s.* [*oris*, Latin.] A plant and flower.

It hath no leaves to the flower, but consists of many stamina arising from a five-leaved empalement. The pointal becomes the seed, which is flat and orbicular, and inclosed in the empalement, which becomes a foliaceous capsule, in which are included two sorts of seeds. *Miller.*

The nature of the *orris* root is almost singular; for roots that are in any degree sweet, it is but the same sweetness with the wood or leaf; but the *orris* is not sweet in the leaf; neither is the flower any thing so sweet as the root. *Bacon.*

O'RRIS. *n. s.* [old Fr.] A sort of gold or silver lace.

ORTS. *n. s.* seldom with a singular. [This word is derived by *Skinner* from *ort*, German, the *fourth part of any thing*; by Mr. *Lye* more reasonably from *orda*, Irish, a fragment. In Anglo Saxon, *ord* signifies the beginning; whence in some provinces *odds* and *ends*; for *ords* and *ends* signify remnants, scattered pieces, refuse; from *ord* thus used probably came *ort.*] Refuse; things left or thrown away.

He must be taught, and train'd, and bid go forth;
A barren-spirited fellow, one that feeds
On abject *orts* and imitations. *Shakesp. Jul. Cæs.*

The fractions of her faith, *orts* of her love,
The fragments, scraps, the bits, and greasy reliques
Of her o'er eaten faith, are bound to Diomede. *Shakesp.*

Much good do't you then;
Brave plush and velvet men,
Can feed on *orts* and safe in your stage-cloths,
Dare quit, upon your oaths,
The stagers, and the stage-wrights too. *Ben. Johnson.*

O'RTHODOX. *adj.* [ὀρθὸς and δοκέω; *orthodox*, Fr.] Sound in opinion and doctrine; not heretical.

Be you persuaded and settled in the true protestant religion professed by the church of England; which is as sound and *orthodox* in the doctrine thereof, as any Christian church in the world. *Bacon.*

Eternal bliss is not immediately superstructed on the most *orthodox* beliefs; but as our Saviour saith, if ye know these things, happy are ye if ye do them; the doing must be first superstructed on the knowing or believing, before any happiness can be built on it. *Hammond.*

O'RTHODOXLY. *adv.* [from *orthodox.*] With soundness of opinion.

The doctrine of the church of England, expressed in the thirty-nine articles, is so soundly and so *orthodoxly* settled, as cannot be questioned without extreme danger to the honour of our religion. *Bacon.*

O'RTHODOXY. *n. s.* [ὀρθοδοξία; *orthodoxie*, Fr. from *orthodox.*] Soundness in opinion and doctrine.

I do not attempt explaining the mysteries of the christian religion, since Providence intended there should be mysteries, it cannot be agreeable to piety, *orthodoxy*, or good sense, to go about it. *Swift.*

O'RTHODROMICKS. *n. s.* [from ὀρθὸς and δρόμος.] The art of sailing in the ark of some great circle, which is the shortest or straightest distance between any two points on the surface of the globe. *Harris.*

O'RTHODROMY. *n. s.* [ὀρθὸς and δρόμος; *orthodromie*, Fr.] Sailing in a straight course.

O'RTHOGON. *n. s.* [ὀρθὸς and γωνία.] A rectangled figure.

The square will make you ready for all manner of compartments; your cylinder for vaulted turrets and round buildings; your *orthogon* and pyramid, for sharp steeples. *Peach.*

O'RTHOGONAL. *adj.* [*orthogonel*, Fr. from *orthogon.*] Rectangular.

O'RTHOGRAPHER. *n. s.* [ὀρθὸς and γράφω.] One who spells according to the rules of grammar.

He was wont to speak plain, like an honest man and a soldier; and now he is turn'd *orthographer*, his words are just so many strange dishes. *Shakespeare.*

ORTHOGRA'PHICAL. *n. s.* [from *orthography.*]

1. Rightly spelled.
2. Relating to the spelling.

I received from him the following letter, which, after having rectified some little *orthographical* mistakes, I shall make a present of to the public. *Addison's Spectator.*

3. Delineated according to the elevation, not the ground-plot.

In the *orthographical* schemes there should be a true delineation and the just dimensions of each face, and of what belongs to it. *Mortimer's Husb.*

ORTHOGRA'PHICALLY. *adv.* [from *orthographical.*]

1. According to the rules of spelling.
2. According to the elevation.

ORTHO'GRAPHY. *n. s.* [ὀρθὸς and γράφω; *orthographie*, Fr.]

1. The part of grammar which teaches how words should be spelled.

This would render languages much more easy to be learned, as to reading and pronouncing, and especially as to the writing them, which now as they stand we find to be troublesome, and it is no small part of grammar which treats of *orthography* and right pronunciation. *Holder.*

2. The art or practice of spelling.

In London they clip their words after one manner about the court, another in the city, and a third in the suburbs; all which reduced to writing, would entirely confound *orthography*. *Swift.*

3. The elevation of a building delineated.

You have the *orthography* or upright of this ground-plat, and the explanation thereof with a scale of feet and inches. *Moxon's Mech. Exer.*

ORTHO'PNOEA. *n. s.* [ὀρθόπνοια; *orthopnée*, Fr.] A disorder of the lungs, in which respiration can be performed only in an upright posture.

His disease was an asthma oft turning to an *orthopnœa*; the cause a translation of tartarous humours from his joints to his lungs. *Harvey on Consumptions.*

O'RTIVE. *adj.* [*ortive*, Fr. *ortivus*, Lat.] Relating to the rising of any planet or star.

O'RTOLAN. *n. s.* [French.] A small bird accounted very delicious.

Nor *ortolans* nor godwits. *Cowley.*

O'RVAL. *n. s.* [*orvale*, Fr. *orvala*, Lat.] The herb clary. *Dict.*

ORVIE'TAN. *n. s.* [*orvietano*, Italian; so called from a mountebank at Orvieto in Italy.] An antidote or counter poison; a medicinal composition or electuary, good against poison. *Bailey.*

OSCHEO'CELE. *n. s.* [ὄσχεον and κήλη.] A kind of hernia when the intestines break into the scrotum. *Dict.*

OSCILLA'TION. *n. s.* [*oscillum*, Latin.] The act of moving backward and forward like a pendulum.

OSCI'LLATORY. *adj.* [*oscillum*, Lat.] Moving backwards and forwards like a pendulum.

The

The actions upon the solids are stimulating or increasing their vibrations, or *oscillatory* motions. *Arbuthnot.*

OSCI'TANCY. *n. s.* [*oscitantia*, Lat.]

1. The act of yawning.
2. Unusual sleepiness; carelessness.

If persons of so circumspect a piety, have been thus overtaken, what security can there be for our wreckless *oscitancy?* *Government of the Tongue.*

It might proceed from the *oscitancy* of transcribers, who, to dispatch their work the sooner, used to write all numbers in cyphers. *Addison's Spectator*, N°. 470.

OSCI'TANT. *adj.* [*oscitans*, Latin.]

1. Yawning; unusually sleepy.
2. Sleepy; sluggish.

Our *oscitant* lazy piety gave vacancy for them, and they will now lend none back again for more active duty. *Decay of Piety.*

OSCITA'TION. *n. s.* [*oscito*, Lat.] The act of yawning.

I shall defer considering this subject till I come to my treatise of *oscitation*, laughter, and ridicule. *Tatler*, N°. 63.

O'SIER. *n. s.* [*osier*, French.] A tree of the willow kind, growing by the water, of which the twigs are used for basket-work.

The rank of *osiers*, by the murmuring stream,
Left on your right hand, brings you to the place. *Shak.*
Ere the sun advance his burning eye,
I must fill up this *osier* cage of ours
With baleful weeds and precious juiced flowers. *Shakesp.*
Bring them for food sweet boughs and *osiers* cut,
Nor all the winter long thy hay rick shut. *May's Virg.*
Like her no nymph can willing *osiers* bend,
In basket-works, which painted streaks commend. *Dryd.*
Along the marshes spread,
We made the *osier* fringed bank our bed. *Po. Odyss.*

O'SMUND. *n. s.* A plant. It is sometimes used in medicine. It grows upon bogs in divers parts of England. *Miller.*

O'SPRAY. *n. s.* [corrupted from *ossifraga*, Latin.] The sea-eagle, of which it is reported, that when he hovers in the air, all the fish in the water turn up their bellies, and lie still for him to seize which he pleases. *Hanmer.*

I think he'll be to Rome
As is the *ospray* to the fish who takes it,
By sovereignty of nature. *Shakesp. Coriolanus.*

Among the fowls shall not be eaten, the eagle, the ossifrage, and the *ospray.* *Numbers* xi. 13.

O'SSELET. *n. s.* [French.] A little hard substance arising on the inside of a horse's knee, among the small bones; it grows out of a gummy substance which fastens those bones together. *Farrier's Dict.*

O'SSICLE. *n. s.* [*ossiculum*, Latin.] A small bone.

There are three very little bones in the ear, upon whose right constitution depends the due tension of the tympanum; and if the action of one little muscle, which serves to draw one of these *ossicles*, fixt to the tympanum, be lost or abated, the tension of that membrane ceasing, sound is hindred from coming into the ear. *Holder on Speech.*

O'SSIFICK. *adj.* [*ossa* and *facio*, Lat.] Having the power of making bones, or changing carneous or membranous to bony substance.

If the caries be superficial, and the bone firm, you may by medicaments consume the moisture in the caries, dry the bone, and dispose it, by virtue of its *ossifick* faculty, to thrust out a callus, and make separation of its caries. *Wiseman.*

OSSIFICA'TION. *n. s.* [from *ossify.*] Change of carneous, membranous, or cartilaginous, into bony substance.

Ossifications or indurations of the artery, appear so constantly in the beginnings of aneurisms, that it is not easy to judge whether they are the cause or the effect of them. *Sharp.*

OSSI'FRAGE. *n. s.* [*ossifraga*, Lat. *ossifrague*, Fr.] A kind of eagle, whose flesh is forbid under the name of gryphon. The *ossifraga* or *ospray*, is thus called, because it breaks the bones of animals in order to come at the marrow. It is said to dig up bodies in church-yards, and eat what it finds in the bones, which has been the occasion that the Latins called it *avis bustaria.* *Calmet.*

Among the fowls shall not be eaten the eagle and the *ossifrage*, and the ospray. *Numb.* xi. 13.

To O'SSIFY. *v. a.* [*ossa* and *facio.*] To change to bone.

The dilated aorta every where in the neighbourhood of the cyst is generally *ossifyed.* *Sharp's Surgery.*

OSSI'VOROUS. *adj.* [*ossa* and *voro.*] Devouring bones.

The bore of the gullet is not in all creatures alike answerable to the body or stomach: as in the fox, which feeds on bones, and swallows whole, or with little chewing; and next in a dog and other *ossivorous* quadrupeds, it is very large. *Derham's Physico-Theol.*

O'SSUARY. *n. s.* [*ossuarium*, Lat.] A charnel house; a place where the bones of dead people are kept. *Dict.*

OST. }
OUST. } *n. s.* A vessel upon which hops or malt are dried. *Dict.*

OSTE'NSIVE. *adj.* [*ostentif*, Fr. *ostendo*, Lat.] Showing; betokening.

O'STENT. *n. s.* [*ostentum*, Latin.]

1. Appearance; air; manner; mien.

Use all th' observance of civility,
Like one well studied in a sad *ostent*,
To please his grandam. *Shakesp. Merch. of Ven.*

2. Show; token. These senses are peculiar to *Shakespeare.*

Be merry, and employ your chiefest thoughts
To courtship, and such fair *ostents* of love
As shall conveniently become you there. *Shakesp.*

3. A portent; a prodigy; any thing ominous.

Latinus, frighted with this dire *ostent*,
For counsel to his father Faunus went;
And sought the shades renown'd for prophecy,
Which near Albunia's sulph'rous fountain lie. *Dryden.*

OSTENTA'TION. *n. s.* [*ostentation*, Fr. *ostentatio*, Lat.]

1. Outward show; appearance.

If these shows be not outward, which of you
But is four Volscians? —
— March on my fellows;
Make good this *ostentation*, and you shall
Divide in all with us. *Shakesp. Coriolanus.*
You are come
A market-maid to Rome, and have prevented
The *ostentation* of our love. *Shakespeare.*

2. Ambitious display; boast; vain show. This is the usual sense.

If all these secret springs of detraction fail, yet a vain *ostentation* of wit sets a man on attacking an established name, and sacrificing it to the mirth and laughter of those about him. *Addison's Spectator*, N°. 256.

He knew that good and bountiful minds were sometimes inclined to *ostentation*, and ready to cover it with pretence of inciting others by their example, and therefore checks this vanity: Take heed, says he, that you do not your alms before men, to be seen. *Atterbury.*

3. A show; a spectacle. Not in use.

The king would have me present the princess with some delightful *ostentation*, show, pageant, antick, or firework. *Shakespeare's Love's Lab. Lost.*

OSTENTA'TIOUS. *adj.* [*ostento*, Latin.] Boastful; vain; fond of show; fond to expose to view.

Your modesty is so far from being *ostentatious* of the good you do, that it blushes even to have it known; and therefore I must leave you to the satisfaction of your own conscience, which, though a silent panegyrick, is yet the best. *Dryden.*

They let Ulysses into his disposition, and he seems to be ignorant, credulous, and *ostentatious.* *Broome on the Odyss.*

OSTENTA'TIOUSLY. *adv.* [from *ostentatious.*] Vainly; boastfully.

OSTENTA'TIOUSNESS. *n. s.* [from *ostentatious.*] Vanity; boastfulness.

OSTENTA'TOUR. *n. s.* [*ostentateur*, Fr. *ostento*, Lat.] A boaster; a vain setter to show.

OSTEO'COLLA. *n. s.* [ὀστέον and κολλάω; *osteocolle*, Fr.] *Osteocolla* is frequent in Germany, and has long been famous for bringing on a callus in fractured bones; but the present practice with us takes no notice of it. *Hill's Mat. Med.*

Osteocolla is a spar, generally coarse, concreted with earthy or stony matter, precipitated by water, and incrusted upon sticks, stones, and other like bodies. *Woodward.*

OSTEO'COPE. *n. s.* [ὀστέον and κόπτω; *osteocope*, Fr.] Pains in the bones, or rather in the nerves and membranes that encompass them. *Dict.*

OSTE'OLOGY. *n. s.* [ὀστέον and λέγω; *osteologie*, Fr.] A description of the bones.

Richard Farloe, well known for his acuteness in dissection of dead bodies, and his great skill in *osteology*, has now laid by that practice. *Tatler*, N°. 62.

OSTI'ARY. *n. s.* [*ostium*, Lat.] The opening at which a river disembogues itself.

It is generally received, that the Nilus hath seven *ostiaries*, that is, by seven channels disburtheneth itself unto the sea. *Brown's Vulgar Errours, b.* vi.

O'STLER. *n. s.* [*hostelier*, French.] The man who takes care of horses at an inn.

The smith, the *ostler*, and the boot-catcher, ought to partake. *Swift's Direct. to the Groom.*

O'STLERY. *n. s.* [*hostelerie*, French.] The place belonging to the ostler.

O'STRACISM. *n. s.* [ὀστρακισμός; *ostracisme*, Fr.] A manner of passing sentence, in which the note of acquital or condemnation was marked upon a shell which the voter threw into a vessel. Banishment; publick censure.

Virtue in courtiers hearts
Suffers an *ostracism*, and departs;
Profit, ease, fitness, plenty, bid it go,
But whither, only knowing you, I know. *Donne.*

Publick envy is as an *ostracism*, that eclipseth men when they grow too great; and therefore it is a bridle to keep them within bounds. *Bacon's Essays*, N°. 9.

Hyperbolus by suffering did traduce
The *ostracism*, and sham'd it out of use. *Cleaveland.*

This

This man, upon a slight and false accusation of favouring arbitrary power, was banished by *ostracism*; which in English would signify, that they voted he should be removed from their presence and council for ever. *Swift.*

OSTRA'CITES. *n. s.* *Ostracites* expresses the common oyster in its fossil state, under whatever circumstances it has been petrified. *Hill's Mat. Med.*

O'STRICH. *n. s.* [*autruche*, Fr. *struthio*, Lat.] *Ostrich* is ranged among birds. It is very large, its wings very short, and the neck about four or five spans. The feathers of its wings are in great esteem, and are used as an ornament for hats, beds, canopies: they are stained of several colours, and made into pretty tufts. They are hunted by way of course, for they never fly; but use their wings to assist them in running more swiftly. The *ostrich* swallows bits of iron or brass, in the same manner as other birds will swallow small stones or gravel, to assist in digesting or comminuting their food. It lays its eggs upon the ground, hides them under the sand, and the sun hatches them. *Calmet.*

I'll make thee eat iron like an *ostrich*, and swallow my sword like a great pin, ere thou and I part. *Shakesp.*

Gavest thou the goodly wings unto the peacock? or wings and feathers unto the *ostrich*. *Job* xxxix. 13.

The Scots errant fight, and fight to eat,
Their *ostrich* stomachs make their swords their meat. *Cleav.*

Modern *ostriches* are dwindled to meer larks, in comparison with those of the ancients. *Arbuthnot.*

OTACOU'STICK. *n. s.* [ὦτα and ἀκέω; *otacoustique*, Fr.] An instrument to facilitate hearing.

In a hare, which is very quick of hearing, it is supplied with a bony tube; which, as a natural *otacoustick*, is so directed backward, as to receive the smallest and most distant sound that comes behind her. *Grew's Cosmol. b.* i.

O'THER. *pron.* [oðeɲ, Sax. *autre*, Fr.]

1. Not the same; not this; different.

Of good actions some are better than *other* some. *Hooker.*

Will it not be received
That they have don't,
Who dares receive it *other*? *Shakesp. K. Lear.*

He that will not give just occasion to think, that all government in the world is the product only of force and violence, and that men live together by no *other* rules but that of beasts, where the strongest carries; and so lay a foundation for perpetual disorder and mischief, tumult, sedition and rebellion; things that the followers of that hypothesis so loudly cry out against, must of necessity find out another state of government. *Locke.*

No leases shall ever be made *other* than leases for years not exceeding thirty-one, in possession, and not in reversion or remainder. *Swift.*

2. Not I, or he, but some one else.

Were I king,
I should cut off the nobles for their lands;
Desire his jewels and this *other*'s house. *Shakesp.*

Physicians are some of them so conformable to the humour of the patient, as they press not the true cure of the disease; and some *other* are so regular in proceeding according to art, as they respect not the condition of the patient. *Bacon, Essay* 31.

The dismayed matrons and maidens, some in their houses, *other* some in the churches with floods of tears and lamentable cries, poured forth their prayers to the Almighty, craving his help in that their hard distress. *Knolles.*

The king had all he crav'd, or could compel,
And all was done—let *others* judge how well. *Daniel.*

3. Not the one, not this, but the contrary.

There is that controling worth in goodness, that the will cannot but like and desire it; and on the *other* side, that odious deformity in vice, that it never offers itself to the affections of mankind, but under the disguise of the *other*. *South.*

4. Correlative to *each*.

In lowliness of mind let each esteem *other* better than themselves. *Phil.* ii. 3.

Scotland and thou did each in *other* live,
Nor would'st thou her, nor could she thee survive. *Dryd.*

5. Something besides.

The learning of Latin being nothing but the learning of words, join as much *other* real knowledge with it as you can. *Locke on Education, s.* 169.

6. The next.

Thy air,
Thou *other* gold bound brow, is like the first;
A third is like the former. *Shakesp. Macbeth.*

7. The third past.

Bind my hair up: as 'twas yesterday:
No, nor the t' *other* day. *Ben. Johnson.*

8. It is sometimes put elliptically for *other thing*; something different.

I can expect no *other* from those that judge by single sights and rash measures, than to be thought fond or insolent. *Glanv.*

O'THERGATES. *adv* [*other* and *gate*, for way.] In another manner.

If sir Toby had not been in drink, he would have tickled you *othergates* than he did. *Shakesp. Twelfth Night.*

O'THERGUISE. *adj.* [*other* and *guise*. This is often mistaken, and sometimes written *otherguess*.] Of another kind.

O'THERWHERE. *adv.* [*other* and *where*.] In other places.

As Jews they had access to the temple and synagogues, but as Christians they were of necessity forced *otherwhere* to assemble themselves. *Hooker, b.* v. *s.* 11.

His godlike acts, and his temptations fierce,
And former sufferings, *otherwhere* are found. *Milton.*

O'THERWHILE. *adv.* [*other* and *while*.] At other times.

O'THERWISE. *adv.* [*other* and *wise*.]

1. In an indifferent manner.

They only plead, that whatsoever God revealeth, as necessary for all Christian men to do and believe, the same we ought to embrace, whether we have received it by writing or *otherwise*, which no man denieth. *Hooker, b.* i.

The whole church hath not tied the parts unto one and the same thing, they being therein left each to their own choice, may either do as others do, or else *otherwise*, without any breach of duty at all. *Hooker, b.* iv. *s.* 13.

In these good things, what all others should practise, we should scarce know to practise *otherwise*. *Sprat.*

Thy father was a worthy prince,
And merited, alas! a better fate;
But heaven thought *otherwise*. *Addison's Cato.*

2. By other causes.

Sir John Norris failed in the attempts of Lisborn, and returned with the loss, by sickness and *otherwise*, of eight thousand men. *Raleigh.*

3. In other respects.

It is said truly, that the best men *otherwise*, are not always the best in regard of society. *Hooker, b.* i.

Men seldom consider God any *otherwise* than in relation to themselves, and therefore want some extraordinary benefits to excite their attention and engage their love. *Roger.*

O'TTER. *n. s.* [oteɲ, Saxon.] An amphibious animal that preys upon fish.

The toes of the *otter*'s hinder feet, for the better swimming, are joined together with a membrane, as in the bevir; from which he differs principally in his teeth, which are canin; and in his tail, which is felin, or a long taper: so that he may not be unfitly called *putoreus aquaticus*, or the water pole-cat. He makes himself burrows on the water side, as a bevir; is sometimes tamed and taught, by nimbly surrounding the fishes to drive them into the net. *Grew.*

At the lower end of the hall is a large *otter*'s skin stuffed with hay. *Addison's Spectator*, Nº. 115.

Would you preserve a num'rous finny race?
Let your fierce dogs the rav'nous *otter* chase;
Th' amphibious monster ranges all the shores,
Darts thro' the waves, and ev'ry haunt explores. *Gay.*

O'VAL. *adj.* [*ovale*, Fr. *ovum*, an egg.] Oblong; resembling the longitudinal section of an egg.

The mouth is low and narrow, but, after having entered pretty far in the grotto, opens itself on both sides in an *oval* figure of an hundred yards. *Addison on Italy.*

Mercurius, nearest to the central sun,
Does in an *oval* orbit, circling run;
But rarely is the object of our sight,
In solar glory sunk. *Blackmore on Creat. b.* ii.

O'VAL. *n. s.*

A synonimous word, or a mere negation of the contrary; a translation of the word into another tongue, or a grammatical explication of it, is sometimes sufficient; as a triangle is that which has three angles, or an *oval* is that which has the shape of an egg. *Watts's Logick.*

OVA'RIOUS. *adj.* [from *ovum*.] Consisting of eggs.

He to the rocks
Dire clinging gathers his *ovarious* food. *Thomson.*

O'VARY. *n. s.* [*ovaire*, Fr. *ovarium*, Latin.] The part of the body in which impregnation is performed.

The *ovary* or part where the white involveth it, is in the second region of the matrix, which is somewhat long and inverted. *Brown's V. Err. b.* iii.

OVA'TION. *n. s.* [*ovation*, Fr. *ovatio*, Lat.] A lesser triumph among the Romans allowed to those commanders who had won a victory without much blood shed, or defeated some less formidable enemy. *Dict.*

O'UBAT. }
OU'BUST. } *n. s.* A sort of caterpillar; an insect. *Dict.*

OUCH. *n. s.* An ornament of gold or jewels.

Ouches or spangs, as they are of no great cost, so they are of most glory. *Bacon, Essay* 38.

OUCH of a boar. The blow given by a boar's tusk. *Ainsw.*

O'VEN. *n. s.* [oɲen, Saxon.] An arched cavity heated with fire to bake bread.

He loudly bray'd, that like was never heard,
And from his wide devouring *oven* sent
A flake of fire, that flashing in his beard,
Him all amaz'd. *Fairy Queen.*

Here's yet in the word hereafter, the kneading, the making of of the cake, the heat of the *oven*, and the baking. *Shakesp.*

Bats have been found in *ovens* and other hollow close places, mattted one upon another; and therefore it is likely that they sleep in the winter, and eat nothing. *Bacon.*

O'VER hath a double signification in the names of places, according to the different situations of them. If the place be upon or near a river, it comes from the Saxon ofer, a brink or bank: but if there is in the neighbourhood another of the same name, distinguished by the addition of nether, then *over* is from the Gothick *ufar*, above. *Gibson's Camden.*

O'VER. *prep.* [*ufar*, Gothick; ofer, Saxon.]

1. Above; with respect to excellence or dignity.

How happy some, *o'er* other some can be!
Thro' Athens I am thought as fair as she. *Shakesp.*

Young Pallas shone conspicuous *o'er* the rest;
Gilded his arms, embroider'd was his vest. *Dryden.*

High, *over* all, was your great conduct shown,
You sought our safety, but forgot your own. *Dryden.*

The commentary which attends this poem, will have one advantage *over* most commentaries, that it is not made upon conjectures. *Advert. to Pope's Dunciad.*

And it will afford field enough for a divine to enlarge on, by shewing the advantages which the Christian world has *over* the Heathen. *Swift.*

2. Above, with regard to rule or authority.

The church has *over* her bishops, able to silence the factious, no less by their preaching than by their authority. *South.*

Captain, yourself are the fittest to live and reign not *over*, but next and immediately under the people. *Dryden.*

3. Above in place.

He was more than *over* shoes in love. *Shakesp.*
The street should see as she walkt *over* head. *Shakesp.*

Thrice happy is that humble pair,
Beneath the level of all care;
Over whose heads those arrows fly,
Of sad distrust and jealousy. *Waller.*

4. Across: as, *he leaped* over *the brook.*

Certain lakes and pits, such as that of Avennes poison birds which fly *over* them. *Bacon's Nat. Hist.*

The geese fly *o'er* the barn, the bees in arms
Drive headlong from their waxen cells in swarms. *Dryd.*

5. Through.

All the world *over*, those that received not the commands of Chirst and his doctrines of purity and perseverance, were signally destroyed. *Hammond.*

6. Upon.

Wise governours have as great a watch *over* fames, as they have of the actions and designs. *Bacon.*

Angelic quires
Sung heav'nly anthems of his victory
O'er temptation and the tempter proud. *Milton.*

7. Before. This is only used in *over* night.

On their intended journey to proceed,
And *o'er* night whatso thereto did need. *Hubberd.*

O'VER. *adv.*

1. Above the top.

Give, and it shall be given unto you; good measure, pressed down and shaken together and running *over*, shall men give. *Luke* vi. 38.

2. More than a quantity assigned.

Even here likewise the laws of nature and reason be of necessary use; yet somewhat *over* and besides them is necessary, namely human and positive law. *Hooker, b.* i.

And when they had mete it, he that gathered much had nothing *over*, and he that gathered little had no lack. *Ex.* xvi. 18.

The ordinary soldiers having all their pay, and a month's pay *over*, were sent into their countries. *Hayward.*

The eastern people determined their digit by the breadth of barley corns, six making a digit, and twenty-four a hand's breadth: a small matter *over* or under. *Arbuthnot.*

3. From side to side.

The fan of an Indian king, made of the feathers of a peacock's tail, composed into a round form, bound altogether with a circular rim, above a foot *over*. *Grew.*

4. From one to another.

This golden cluster the herald delivereth to the Tirsan, who delivereth it *over* to that son that he had formerly chosen. *Bacon's New Atlantis.*

5. From a country beyond the sea.

It hath a white berry, but is not brought *over* with the coral. *Bacon's Nat. History.*

They brought new customs and new vices *o'er*;
Taught us more arts than honest men require. *Philips.*

6. On the surface.

The first came out red all *over*, like an hairy garment. *Gen.* xxv. 25.

7. Past. This is rather the sense of an adjective.

Soliman pausing a little upon the matter, the heat of his fury being something *over*, suffered himself to be intreated. *Knolles's Hist. of the Turks.*

Meditate upon the effects of anger; and the best time to do this, is to look back upon anger when the fit is *over*. *Bacon.*

What the garden choicest bears
To sit and taste, till this meridian heat
Be *over*, and the sun more cool decline. *Milton.*

The act of stealing was soon *over*, and cannot be undone, and for it the sinner is only answerable to God or his vicegerent. *Taylor's Rule of Living Holy.*

He will, as soon as his first surprize is *over*, justly begin to wonder how such a favour came to be bestowed on him. *Atterbury's Sermons.*

There youths and nymphs in consort gay,
Shall hail the rising, close the parting day;
With me, alas! with me those joys are *o'er*,
For me the vernal garlands bloom no more. *Pope.*

8. Throughout; completely.

Well,
Have you read *o'er* the letters I sent you? *Shakesp.*

Let them argue *over* all the topicks of divine goodness and human weakness, yet how trifling must be their plea! *South's Sermons.*

9. With repetition; another time.

He *o'er* and *o'er* divides him,
'Twixt his unkindness and his kindness. *Shakespeare.*

Sitting or standing still confin'd to roar,
In the same verse, the same rules *o'er* and *o'er*. *Dryden.*

Longing they look, and gaping at the sight,
Devour her *o'er* and *o'er* with vast delight. *Dryden.*

Thou, my Hector, art thyself alone,
My parents, brothers, and my lord in one:
O kill not all my kindred *o'er* again,
Nor tempt the dangers of the dusty plain;
But in this tow'r, for our defence, remain. *Dryden.*

Whenever children forget, or do an action aukwardly, make them do it *over* and *over* again, till they are perfect. *Locke on Education.*

If this miracle of Christ's rising from the dead, be not sufficient to convince a resolved libertine, neither would the rising of one now from the dead be sufficient for that purpose; since it would only be the doing that *over* again which hath been done already. *Atterbury.*

The most learned will never find occasion to act *over* again what is fabled of Alexander the Great, that when he had conquered the eastern world, he wept for want of more worlds to conquer. *Watts.*

10. Extraordinary; in a great degree.

The word symbol should not seem to be *over* difficult. *Baker.*

11. OVER *and above.* Besides; beyond what was first supposed or immediately intended.

Moses took the redemption money of them that were *over and above*. *Numb.* iii. 49.

He gathered a great mass of treasure, and gained *over and above* the good will and esteem of all people wherever he came. *L'Estrange.*

12. OVER *against.* Opposite; regarding in front.

In Ticinum is a church with windows only from above. It reporteth the voice thirteen times, if you stand by the close end of the wall, *over against* the door. *Bacon.*

I visit his picture, and place myself *over against* it whole hours together. *Addison's Spectator*, N°. 241.

Over against this church stands a large hospital, erected by a shoemaker. *Addison on Italy.*

13. In composition it has a great variety of significations; it is arbitrarily prefixed to nouns, adjectives, or other parts of speech in a sense equivalent to more than enough; too much.

Devilish Macbeth,
By many of these trains hath sought to win me
Into his pow'r: and modest wisdom plucks me
From *over-credulous* haste. *Shakesp. Macbeth.*

St. Hierom reporteth, that he saw a satyr; but the truth hereof I will not rashly impugn, or *over-boldly* affirm. *Peach.*

These *over-busy* spirits, whose labour is their only reward, hunt a shadow and chase the wind. *Decay of Piety.*

If the ferment of the breast be vigorous, an *over-fermentation* in the part, produceth a phlegmon. *Wiseman.*

A gangrene doth arise in phlegmons, through the unseasonable application of *over-cold* medicaments. *Wiseman.*

Poets, like lovers, should be bold and dare,
They spoil their business with an *over-care*:
And he who servilely creeps after sense,
Is safe, but ne'er will reach an excellence. *Dryden.*

Wretched man! *o'erfeeds*
His cramm'd desires, with more than nature needs. *Dryd.*

Bending o'er the cup, the tears she shed,
Seem'd by the posture to discharge her head,
O'er-fill'd before. *Dryden's Boccace.*

Crude humour or phlegm, are produced by *over-digestion*. *Floyer.*

As they are likely to *over-flourish* their own case, so their flattery is hardest to be discovered: for who would imagine that

that himself was guilty of putting tricks upon himself? *Collier.*

He has afforded us only the twilight of probability; suitable to that state of mediocrity he has placed us in here; wherein to check our *over-confidence* and presumption, we might, by every day's experience, be made sensible of our shortsightedness. *Locke.*

This part of grammar has been much neglected, as some others *over-diligently* cultivated. It is easy for men to write one after another, of cases and genders. *Locke.*

It is an ill way of establishing this truth, and silencing atheists, to take some men's having that idea of God in their minds, for the only proof of a deity; and out of an *over-fondness* of that darling invention, cashier all other arguments. *Locke.*

A grown person surfeiting with honey, no sooner hears the name of it, but his fancy immediately carries sickness and qualms to his stomach: had this happened to him by an *over-dose* of honey, when a child, all the same effects would have followed, but the cause would have been mistaken, and the antipathy counted natural. *Locke.*

He *over-acted* his part; his passions, when once let loose, were too impetuous to be managed. *Atterbury.*

Take care you *over-burn* not the turf; it is only to be burnt so as may make it break. *Mortimer.*

Don't *over-fatigue* the spirits, lest the mind be seized with a lassitude, and thereby nauseate and grow tir'd of a particular subject. *Watts.*

The memory of the learner should not be too much crowded with a tumultuous heap of ideas, one idea effaces another. An *over-greedy* grasp does not retain the largest handful. *Watts.*

To O'VER-ABOUND. *v. n.* [*over* and *abound.*] To abound more than enough.

Both imbibe
Fitting congenial juice, so rich the soil,
So much does fructuous moisture *o'er-abound.* *Philips.*

The learned, never *over-abounding* in transitory coin, should not be discontented. *Pope's Letters.*

To O'VER-ACT. *v. a.* [*over* and *act.*] To act more than enough.

You *over-act*, when you should underdo:
A little call yourself again, and think. *Ben. Johnson.*

Princes courts may *over-act* their reverence, and make themselves laughed at for their foolishness and extravagant relative worship. *Stillingfleet.*

Good men often blemish the reputation of their piety, by *over-acting* some things in religion; by an indiscreet zeal about things wherein religion is not concerned. *Tillotson.*

To O'VER-ARCH. *v. a.* [*over* and *reach.*] To cover as with an arch.

Where high Ithaca o'erlooks the floods,
Brown with *o'er-arching* shades and pendent woods. *Pope.*

To O'VER-AWE. *v. a.* [*over* and *awe.*] To keep in awe by superiour influence.

The king was present in person to overlook the magistrates, and to *over-awe* these subjects with the terror of his sword. *Spenser on Ireland.*

Her graceful innocence, her every air
Of gesture, or least action, *over-aw'd*
His malice. *Milton's Par. Lost, b.* ix.

I could be content to be your chief tormentor, ever paying you mock reverence, and sounding in your ears, the empty title which inspired you with presumption, and *over-awed* my daughter to comply. *Addison's Guardian.*

A thousand fears
Still *over-awe* when she appears. *Granvile's Poems.*

To O'VER-BALANCE. *v. a.* To weigh down; to preponderate.

Not doubting but by the weight of reason I should conterpoise the *over-balancings* of any factions. *King Charles.*

The hundred thousand pounds per annum, wherein we *over-balance* them in trade, must be paid us in money. *Locke.*

When these important considerations are set before a rational being, acknowledging the truth of every article, should a bare single possibility be of weight enough to *over-balance* them. *Rogers, Serm.* xii.

O'VER-BALANCE. *n. s.* [*over* and *balance.*] Something more than equivalent.

Our exported commodities would, by the return, encrease the treasure of this kingdom above what it can ever be by other means, than a mighty *over-balance* of our exported to our imported commodities. *Temple.*

The mind should be kept in a perfect indifference, not inclining to either side, any further than the *over-balance* of probability gives it the turn of assent and belief. *Locke.*

O'VER-BATTLE. *adj.* [Of this word I know not the derivation; *batten* is to grow fat, and to *battle*, is at Oxford to feed on trust.] Too fruitful; exuberant.

In the church of God sometimes it cometh to pass, as in *over-battle* grounds; the fertile disposition whereof is good, yet because it exceedeth due proportion, it bringeth abundantly through too much rankness, things less profitable, whereby that which principally it should yield, being either prevented in place or defrauded of nourishment, faileth. *Hooker.*

To O'VER-BEAR. *v. a.* [*over* and *bear.*] To repress; to subdue; to whelm; to bear down.

What more savage than man, if he see himself able by fraud to over-reach, or by power to *over-bear* the laws. *Hook.*

My desire
All continent impediment would *over-bear*,
That did oppose my will. *Shakesp. Macbeth.*

The ocean o'er-peering of his list,
Eats not the flats with more impetuous haste
Than young Laertes, in a riotous head
O'er-bears your officers. *Shakespeare.*

Our counsel, it pleas'd your highness
To *over-bear.* *Shakesp. King John.*

Glo'ster, thou shalt well perceive,
That nor in birth or for authority,
The bishop will be *over-borne* by thee. *Shakesp.*

The Turkish commanders, with all their forces, assailed the city, thrusting their men into the breaches by heaps, as if they would, with very multitude, have discouraged or *over-born* the Christians. *Knolles.*

The point of reputation, when news first came of the battle lost, did *over-bear* the reason of war. *Bacon.*

Yet fortune, valour, all is *over-born*,
By numbers; as the long resisting bank
By the impetuous torrent. *Denham.*

A body may as well be *over-born* by the violence of a shallow, rapid stream, as swallowed up in the gulph of smooth water. *L'Estrange.*

Crowding on the last the first impel;
Till *over-born* with weight the Cyprians fell. *Dryden.*

The judgment, if swayed by the *over-bearing* of passion, and stored with lubricous opinions instead of clearly conceived truths, will be erroneous. *Glanv. Sceps. c.* 27.

Take care that the memory of the learner be not too much crowded with a tumultuous heap, or *over-bearing* multitude of documents at one time. *Watts.*

The horror or loathsomness of an object may *over-bear* the pleasure which results from its greatness, novelty, or beauty. *Addison's Spectator.*

To O'VER-BID. *v. a.* [*over* and *bid.*] To offer more than equivalent.

You have *o'er-bid* all my past sufferings,
And all my future too. *Dryd. Span. Friar.*

To O'VER-BLOW. *v. n.* [*over* and *blow.*] To be past its violence.

To O'VER-BLOW. *v. a.* [*over* and *blow.*] To drive away as clouds before the wind.

Led with delight, they thus beguile the way,
Until the blustring storm is *over-blown.* *Fairy Queen.*

All those tempests being *over-blown*, there long after arose a new storm which over-run all Spain. *Spenser.*

This ague fit of fear is *over-blown*,
An easy task it is to win our own. *Shakesp. Rich.* II.

Some angel that beholds her there,
Instruct us to record what she was here;
And when this cloud of sorrow's *o'er-blown*,
Thro' the wide world we'll make her graces known. *Waller.*

Seiz'd with secret joy,
When storms are *over-blown.* *Dryden's Virg.*

O'VER-BOARD. *adv.* [*over* and *board.* See BOARD.] Off the ship; out of the ship.

The great assembly met again; and now he that was the cause of the tempest being thrown *over-board*, there were hopes a calm should ensue. *Howel.*

A merchant having a vessel richly fraught at sea in a storm, there is but one certain way to save it, which is, by throwing its rich lading *over-board.* *South's Serm.*

The trembling dotard, to the deck he drew,
And hoisted up and *over-board* he threw;
This done, he seised the helm. *Dryden.*

He obtained liberty to give them only one song before he leaped *over-board*, which he did, and then plunged into the sea. *L'Estrange.*

Though great ships were commonly bad sea-boats, they had a superiour force in a sea engagement: the shock of them being sometimes so violent, that it would throw the crew on the upper deck of lesser ships *over-board.* *Arbuthnot.*

To O'VER-BULK. *v. a.* [*over* and *bulk.*] To oppress by bulk.

The feeding pride,
In rank Achilles, must or now be cropt,
Or shedding, breed a nursery of like evils,
To *over-bulk* us all. *Shakesp. Troil. and Cressida.*

To O'VER-BURDEN. *v. a.* [*over* and *burthen.*] To load with too great weight.

If she were not cloyed with his company, and that she thought not the earth *over-burthened* with him, she would cool his fiery grief. *Sidney, b.* ii.

To O'VER-BUY. *v. a.* [*over* and *buy.*] To buy too dear.

He, when want requires, is only wise,
Who slights not foreign aids, nor *over-buys*;
But on our native strength, in time of need, relies. *Dryd.*

To O'VER-CARRY. *v. a.* [*over* and *carry.*] To hurry too far; to be urged to any thing violent or dangerous.

He was the king's uncle, but yet of no capacity to succeed; by reason whereof his natural affection and duty was less easy to be *over-carried* by ambition. *Hayward.*

To O'VER-CAST. *v. a. pret. over-cast.* [*over* and *cast.*]

1. To cloud; to darken; to cover with gloom.

As they past,
The day with clouds was sudden *over-cast.* *Fairy Queen.*
Hie, Robin, *over-cast* the night;
The starry welkin cover thou anon,
With drooping fogs, as black as Acheron. *Shakesp.*

Our days of age are sad and *over-cast*, in which we find that of all our vain passions and affections past, the sorrow only abideth. *Raleigh's Hist. of the World.*

I of fumes and humid vapours made,
No cloud in so serene a mansion find,
To *over-cast* her ever-shining mind. *Waller.*
Those clouds that *over-cast* our morn shall fly,
Dispell'd to farthest corners of the sky. *Dryden.*
The dawn is *over-cast*, the morning lours,
And heavily in clouds brings on the day. *Addison.*

2. To cover. This sense is hardly retained but by needle-women, who call that which is incircled with a thread, *over-cast.*

When malice would work that which is evil, and in working avoid the suspicion of an evil intent, the colour wherewith it *over-casteth* itself is always a fair and plausible pretence of seeking to further that which is good. *Hooker.*

Their arms abroad with gray moss *over-cast*,
And their green leaves trembling with every blast. *Spenser.*

3. To rate too high in computation.

The king in his accompt of peace and calms, did much *over-cast* his fortunes, which proved full of broken seas, tides, and tempests. *Bacon's Henry VII.*

To O'VER-CHARGE. *v. a.* [*over* and *charge.*]

1. To oppress; to cloy; to surcharge.

On air we feed in every instant, and on meats but at times; and yet the heavy load of abundance, wherewith we oppress and *over-charge* nature, maketh her to sink unawares in the mid-way. *Raleigh's Hist. of the World.*

A man may as well expect to grow stronger by always eating, as wiser by always reading. Too much *over-charges* nature, and turns more into disease than nourishment. *Collier.*

2. To load; to crowd too much.

Our language is *over-charged* with consonants. *Pope.*

3. To burthen.

He whispers to his pillow,
The secrets of his *over-charged* soul. *Shakesp.*

4. To rate too high.

Here's Glo'ster, a foe to citizens,
O'er-charging your free purses with large fines. *Shakesp.*

5. To fill too full.

Her heart is but *o'er-charg'd*; she will recover. *Shakesp.*

The fumes of passion do as really intoxicate, and confound the judging and discerning faculty, as the fumes of drink discompose and stupify the brain of a man *over-charged* with it. *South's Sermons.*

If they would make distinct abstract ideas of all the varieties in human actions, the number must be infinite, and the memory *over-charged* to little purpose. *Locke.*

The action of the Iliad and Æneid in themselves exceeding short, are so beautifully extended by the invention of episodes, that they make up an agreeable story sufficient to employ the memory without *over-charging* it. *Addison's Spectator.*

6. To load with too great a charge.

They were
As canons *over-charg'd* with double cracks. *Shakesp.*
Who in deep mines, for hidden knowledge toils,
Like guns *o'er-charg'd*, breaks, misses, or recoils. *Denham.*

To O'VER-CLOUD. *v. a.* [*over* and *cloud.*] To cover with clouds.

The silver empress of the night
O'er-clouded, glimmers in a fainter light. *Tickel.*

To O'VER-CLOY. *v. a.* [*over* and *cloy.*] To fill beyond satiety.

A scum of Britons and base lackey peasants,
Whom their *o'er-cloyed* country vomits forth
To desperate adventures and destruction. *Shakesp.*

To O'VERCOME. *v. a.* pret. *I overcame*; part. pass. *overcome*; anciently *overcomen*, as in *Spenser.* [*overcomen*, Dutch.]

1. To subdue; to conquer; to vanquish.

They *overcommen*, were deprived
Of their proud beauty, and the one moiety
Transformed to fish, for their bold surquedry. *Spenser.*
This wretched woman, *overcome*
Of anguish rather than of crime hath been. *Spenser.*

Of whom a man is *overcome*, of the same is he brought in bondage. 2 *Pet.* ii. 19.

Fire by thicker air *o'ercome*,
And downward forc'd in earth's capacious womb,
Alters its particles; is fire no more. *Prior.*

2. To over-flow; to surcharge.

Th' unfallow'd glebe
Yearly *o'ercomes* the granaries with stores. *Philips.*

3. To come over or upon; to invade suddenly. Not in use.

Can't such things be,
And *overcome* us like a summer's cloud,
Without our special wonder? *Shakesp. Macbeth.*

To O'VERCOME. *v. n.* To gain the superiority.

That thou mightest be justified in thy sayings, and mightest *overcome* when thou art judged. *Rom.* iii. 4.

O'VERCOMER. *n. s.* [from the verb.] He who overcomes.

To O'VER-COUNT. *v. a.* [*over* and *count.*] To rate above the true value.

Thou know'st how much
We do *o'er-count* thee. *Shakesp. Ant. and Cleop.*

To O'VER-COVER. *v. a.* [*over* and *cover.*] To cover compleatly.

Shut me nightly in a charnel house,
O'er-cover'd quite with dead mens rattling bones,
With reeky shanks and yellow chapless skulls. *Shakesp.*

To O'VER-CROW. *v. a.* [*over* and *crow.*] To crow as in triumph.

A base varlet, that being but of late grown out of the dunghil, beginneth now to *over-crow* so high mountains, and make himself the great protector of all out-laws. *Spenser.*

To O'VERDO. *v. a.* [*over* and *do.*] To do more than enough.

Any thing so *over-done* is from the purpose of playing; whose end is to hold the mirrour up to nature. *Shakesp.*

Nature so intent upon finishing her work, much oftner *over-does* than under-does. You shall hear of twenty animals with two heads, for one that hath none. *Grew.*

When the meat is *over-done*, lay the fault upon your lady who hurried you. *Swift.*

To O'VER-DRESS. *v. a.* [*over* and *dress.*] To adorn lavishly.

In all, let nature never be forgot;
But treat the goddess like a modest fair,
Nor *over-dress*, nor leave her wholly bare. *Pope.*

To O'VER-DRIVE. *v. a.* [*over* and *drive.*] To drive too hard, or beyond strength.

The flocks and herds with young, if men should *over-drive* one day, all will die. *Gen.* xxxiii. 13.

To O'VER-EYE. *v. a.* [*over* and *eye.*]

1. To superintend.

2. To observe; to remark.

I am doubtful of your modesties,
Lest *over eying* of his odd behaviour,
You break into some merry passion. *Shakesp.*

To OVER-EMPTY. *v. a.* [*over* and *empty.*] To make too empty.

The women would be loth to come behind the fashion in new-fangledness of the manner, if not in costliness of the matter, which might *over-empty* their husbands purses. *Carew.*

OVERFAL. *n. s.* [*over* and *fall.*] Cataract.

Tostatus addeth, that those which dwell near those falls of water, are deaf from their infancy, like those that dwell near the *overfals* of Nilus. *Raleigh's Hist. of the World.*

To OVER-FLOAT. *v. n.* [*over* and *float.*] To swim; to float.

The town is fill'd with slaughter, and *o'er-floats*
With a red deluge, their increasing moats. *Dryden.*

To OVER-FLOW. *v. n.* [*over* and *flow.*]

1. To be fuller than the brim can hold.

While our strong walls secure us from the foe,
E'er yet with blood our ditches *over-flow.* *Dryden.*

Had I the same consciousness that I saw Noah's flood, as that I saw the *over-flowing* of the Thames last winter, I could not doubt, that I who saw the Thames *over-flowed*, and viewed the flood at the general deluge, was the same self. *Locke.*

2. To exuberate.

A very ungrateful return to the author of all we enjoy, but such as an *over-flowing* plenty too much inclines men to make. *Rogers, Sermon* 2.

To O'VER-FLOW. *v. a.*

1. To fill beyond the brim.

Suppose thyself in as great a sadness as ever did load thy spirit, wouldst thou not bear it chearfully if thou wert sure that some excellent fortune would relieve and recompense thee so as to *over-flow* all thy hopes. *Taylor.*

New milk that all the winter never fails,
And all the summer *over-flows* the pails. *Dryden.*

2. To deluge; to drown; to over-run; to over-power.

The Scythians, at such time as the northern nations *overflowed* all Christendom, came down to the sea-coast. *Spenser.*

Clanius *over-flow'd* th' unhappy coast. *Dryden.*

Do not the Nile and the Niger make yearly inundations in our days, as they have formerly done? and are not the countries

countries so *over-flown*, still situate between the tropicks? *Bentley's Sermons.*

Sixteen hundred and odd years after the earth was made, it was *over-flowed* and destroyed in a deluge of water, that overspread the face of the whole earth, from pole to pole, and from east to west. *Burnet.*

Thus oft by mariners are shewn,
Earl Godwin's castles *over-flown*. *Swift.*

O'VER-FLOW. *n. s.* [*over* and *flow.*] Inundation; more than fulness; such a quantity as runs over; exuberance.

Did he break out into tears?—
In great measure—
—A kind *over-flow* of kindness. *Shakespeare.*

Where there are great *over-flows* in fens, the drowning of them in winter maketh the summer following more fruitful; for that it keepeth the ground warm. *Bacon's Nat. Hist.*

It requires pains to find the coherence of abstruse writings: so that it is not to be wondered, that St. Paul's epistles have, with many, passed rather for disjointed pious discourses, full of warmth and zeal and *over-flows* of light, rather than for calm, strong, coherent reasonings all through. *Locke's Ess. on St. Paul's Epist.*

After every *over-flow* of the Nile, there was not always a mensuration. *Arbuthnot on Coins.*

If this softens not the expression, it may be ascribed to an *over-flow* of gratitude in the general disposition of Ulysses. *Broome's Notes on the Odyssey.*

O'VER-FLOWING. *n. s.* [from *over-flow.*] Exuberance; copiousness.

When men are young, they might vent the *over-flowings* of their fancy that way. *Denham's Dedicat.*

When the *over-flowings* of ungodliness make us afraid, the ministers of religion cannot better discharge their duty of opposing it. *Rogers, Serm. 17.*

O'VER-FLOWINGLY. *adv.* [from *over-flowing.*] Exuberantly; in great abundance. A word not elegant nor in use.

Nor was it his indigence that forced him to make the world; but his goodness pressed him to impart the goods which he so *over-flowingly* abounds with. *Boyle.*

To O'VER-FLY. *v. a.* [*over* and *fly.*] To cross by flight.

A sailing kite
Can scarce *o'er-fly* them in a day and night. *Dryden.*

O'VER-FORWARDNESS. *n. s.* [*over* and *forwardness.*] Too great quickness; too great readiness.

By an *over-forwardness* in courts to give countenance to frivolous exceptions, though they make nothing to the true merit of the cause, it often happens that causes are not determined according to their merits. *Hale.*

To O'VER-FREIGHT. *v. a.* pret. *over-freighted*; part. *over-fraught.* [*over* and *freight.*] To load too heavily; to fill with too great quantity.

A boat *over-freighted* with people, in rowing down the river, was, by the extreme weather, sunk. *Carew.*

Grief, that does not speak,
Whispers the *o'er-fraught* heart and bids it break. *Shakesp.*

Sorrow has so *o'er-fraught*
This sinking barque, I shall not live to shew
How I abhor my first rash crime. *Denham.*

To O'VER-GET. *v. a.* [*over* and *get.*] To reach; to come up with.

With six hours hard riding, through so wild places, as it was rather the cunning of my horse sometimes, than of myself, so rightly to hit the way, I *over-got* them a little before night. *Sidney, b. ii.*

To O'VER-GLANCE. *v. a.* [*over* and *glance.*] To look hastily over.

I have, but with a cursory eye,
O'er-glanc'd the articles. *Shakesp. Hen. V.*

O'VER-GO. *v. a.* [*over* and *go.*] To surpass; to excel.

Thinking it beyond the degree of humanity to have a wit so far *over-going* his age, and such dreadful terror proceed from so excellent beauty. *Sidney.*

Great nature hath laid down at last,
That mighty birth wherewith so long she went,
And *over-went* the times of ages past,
Here to lye in upon our soft content. *Daniel.*

To O'VER-GORGE. *v. a.* [*over* and *gorge.*] To gorge too much.

Art thou grown great,
And, like ambitious Sylla, *over-gorg'd.* *Shakesp.*

O'VER-GREAT. *adj.* [*over* and *great.*] Too great.

Though putting the mind unprepared upon an unusual stress ought to be avoided; yet this must not run it, by an *over-great* shyness of difficulties, into a lazy sauntring about obvious things. *Locke.*

To O'VERGROW. *v. a.* [*over* and *grow.*]

1. To cover with growth.

Roof and floor, and walls were all of gold,
But *over-grown* with dust and old decay,
And hid in darkness that none could behold
The hue thereof. *Fairy Queen, b. ii.*

The woods and desart caves,
With wild thyme and the gadding vine *o'er-grown*,
And all their echo's mourn. *Milton.*

2. To rise above.

If the binds be very strong and much *over-grown* the poles, some advise to strike off their heads with a long switch. *Mort.*

To O'VER-GROW. *v. n.* To grow beyond the fit or natural size.

One part of his army, with incredible labour, cut a way thorough the thick and *over-grown* woods, and so came to Solyman. *Knolles's Hist. of the Turks.*

A huge *over-grown* ox was grazing in a meadow. *L'Est.*

Him for a happy man I own,
Whose fortune is not *over-grown.* *Swift.*

O'VER-GROWTH. *n. s.* [*over* and *growth.*] Exuberant growth.

The *over-growth* of some complexion,
Oft breaking down the pales and forts of reason. *Shakesp.*

The fortune in being the first in an invention, doth cause sometimes a wonderful *over-growth* in riches. *Bacon.*

Suspected to a sequent king, who seeks
To stop their *over-growth*, as in-mate guests
Too numerous. *Milton's Paradise Lost, b. xii.*

To O'VER-HALE. *v. a.* [*over* and *hale.*]

1. To spread over.

The welked Phœbus gan availe
His weary wain, and now the frosty night
Her mantle black thro' heaven gan *over-hale.* *Spens.*

2. To examine over again: as, he *over-haled* my account.

To O'VER-HANG. *v. a.* [*over* and *hang.*] To jut over; to impend over.

Lend the eye a terrible aspect,
Let the brow overwhelm it,
As fearfully as doth a galled rock
O'er-hang and jutty his confounded base. *Shakesp.*

Hide me ye forests, in your closest bow'rs,
Where flows the murm'ring brook, inviting dreams,
Where bord'ring hazle *over-hangs* the streams. *Gay.*

If you drink tea upon a promontory that *over-hangs* the sea, it is preferable to an assembly. *Pope.*

To O'VER-HANG. *v. n.* To jut over.

The rest was craggy cliff, that *over-hung*
Still as it rose, impossible to climb. *Milt. P. Lost.*

To O'VER-HARDEN. *v. a.* [*over* and *harden.*] To make too hard.

By laying it in the air, it has acquired such a hardness, that it was brittle like *over-hardened* steel. *Boyle.*

O'VER-HEAD. *adv.* [*over* and *head.*] Aloft; in the zenith; above; in the cieling.

Over-head the moon
Sits arbitress, and nearer to the earth
Wheels her pale course. *Milton's Par. Lost, b. i.*

The four stars *over-head*, represent the four children. *Addis.*

To O'VER-HEAR. *v. a.* [*over* and *hear.*] To hear those who do not mean to be heard.

I am invisible,
And I will *over-hear* their conference. *Shakespeare.*

They had a full sight of the Infanta at a mask dancing, having *over-heard* two gentlemen who were tending towards that sight, after whom they pressed. *Wotton.*

That such an enemy we have who seeks
Our ruin, both by thee inform'd I learn,
And from the parting angel *over-heard.* *Milton.*

They were so loud in their discourse, that a black-berry from the next hedge *over-heard* them. *L'Estrange.*

The nurse,
Though not the words, the murmurs *over-heard.* *Dryden.*

The witness *over-hearing* the word pillory repeated, slunk away privately. *Addison.*

To O'VER-HEAT. *v. a.* [*over* and *heat.*] To heat too much.

Pleas'd with the form and coolness of the place,
And *over-heated* by the morning chace. *Addison.*

It must be done upon the receipt of the wound, before the patient's spirits be *over-heated* with pain or fever. *Wiseman.*

To O'VER-HEND. *v. a.* [*over* and *hend.*] To overtake; to reach.

Als his fair Leman flying through a brook,
He *over-hent* nought moved with her piteous look. *Spens.*

To O'VER-JOY. *v. a.* [*over* and *joy.*] To transport; to ravish.

He that puts his confidence in God only, is neither *over-joyed* in any great good things of this life, nor sorrowful for a little thing. *Taylor's Guide to Devotion.*

The bishop, partly astonished and partly *over-joyed* with these speeches, was struck into a sad silence for a time. *Hayw.*

This love-sick virgin, *over-joy'd* to find
The boy alone; still follow'd him behind. *Addison.*

O'VER-JOY. *n. s.* Transport; ecstasy.

The mutual conf'rence that my mind hath had,
Makes me the bolder to salute my king
With ruder terms; such as my wit affords,
And *over-joy* of heart doth minister. *Shakesp. Hen. VI.*

To O'VER-RIPEN. *v. a.* [*over* and *ripen.*] To make too ripe.

Why

Why droops my lord, like *over-ripen'd* corn,
Hanging the head with Ceres' plenteous load? *Shakesp.*

To OVERLA'BOUR. *v. a.* [*over* and *labour.*] To take too much pains on any thing; to harrass with toil.

She without noise will over-see
His children and his family;
And order all things till he come,
Sweaty and *over-labour'd* home. *Dryden.*

To OVERLA'DE. *v. a.* [*over* and *lade.*] To over-burthen.

Thus to throng and *over-lade* a soul
With love, and then to have a room for fear,
That shall all that controul,
What is it but to rear
Our passions and our hopes on high,
That thence they may descry
The noblest way how to despair and die? *Suckling.*

OVERLA'RGE. *adj.* [*over* and *large.*] Larger than enough.

Our attainments cannot be *over-large*, and yet we manage a narrow fortune very unthriftily. *Collier.*

OVERLA'SHINGLY. *n. s.* [*over* and *lash.*] With exaggeration. A mean word, now obsolete.

Although I be far from their opinion who write too *overlashingly*, that the Arabian tongue is in use in two third parts of the inhabited world, yet I find that it extendeth where the religion of Mahomet is professed. *Brerewood.*

To OVERLA'Y. *v. a.* [*over* and *lay.*]

1. To oppress by too much weight or power.

Some commons are barren, the nature is such,
And some *over-layeth* the commons too much. *Tuss.*

Not only that mercy which keepeth from being *over-laid* and opprest, but mercy which saveth from being touched with grievous miseries. *Hooker, b.* v. *s.* 48.

When any country is *over-laid* by the multitude which live upon it, there is a natural necessity compelling it to disburthen itself and lay the load upon others. *Raleigh.*

We praise the things we hear with much more willingness than those we see; because we envy the present, and reverence the past; thinking ourselves instructed by the one, and *over-laid* by the other. *Ben. Johnson.*

Good laws had been antiquated by the course of time, or *over-laid* by the corruption of manners. *King Charles.*

Our sins have *over-laid* our hopes. *King Charles.*

The strong Emetrius came in Arcite's aid,
And Palamon with odds was *over-laid.* *Dryden.*

2. To smother with too much or too close covering.

Nor then destroys it with too fond a stay,
Like mothers, which their infants *over-lay.* *Milton.*

3. To smother; to crush; to overwhelm.

Ships burnt in fight, or forc'd on rocky shores,
The new-born babes by nurses *over-laid.* *Dryden.*

They quickly stifled and *over-laid* those infant principles, of piety and virtue, sown by God in their hearts; so that they brought a voluntary darkness and stupidity upon their minds. *South's Sermons.*

The gods have made your noble mind for me,
And her insipid soul for Ptolemy:
A heavy lump of earth without desire,
A heap of ashes that *o'er-lays* your fire. *Dryden.*

The stars, no longer *over-laid* with weight,
Exert their heads from underneath the mass,
And upward shoot. *Dryden.*

Season the passions of a child with devotion, which seldom dies; though it may seem extinguished for a while, it breaks out as soon as misfortunes have brought the man to himself. The fire may be covered and *over-laid*, but cannot be entirely quenched and smothered. *Addison's Spectator*, N°. 201.

In preaching, no men succeed better than those who trust to the fund of their own reason, advanced but not *over-laid* by commerce with books. *Swift.*

4. To cloud; to over-cast.

Phœbus' golden face it did attaint,
As when a cloud his beams doth *over-lay.* *Fairy Queen.*

5. To cover superficially.

The *over-laying* of their chapiters was of silver, and all the pillars were filleted with silver. *Ex.* xxxviii. 17.

By his prescript a sanctuary is fram'd
Of cedar, *over-laid* with gold. *Milt. Par. Lost.*

6. To join by something laid over.

Thou us impower'd
To fortify thus far, and *over-lay*,
With this portentous bridge, the dark abyss. *Milton.*

To OVERLE'AP. *v. a.* [*over* and *leap.*] To pass by a jump.

A step
On which I must fall down or else *o'er-leap*,
For in my way it lies. *Shakesp. Macbeth.*

In vain did nature's wise command
Divide the waters from the land;
If daring ships and men prophane,
Th' eternal fences *over-leap*,
And pass at will the boundless deep. *Dryden.*

OVERLEATHER. *n. s.* [*over* and *leather.*] The part of the shoe that covers the foot.

I have sometimes more feet than shoes; or such shoes as my toes look through the *over-leather.* *Shakesp.*

OVERLI'GHT. *n. s.* [*over* and *light.*] Too strong light.

An *over-light* maketh the eyes dark; insomuch as perpetual looking against the sun would cause blindness. *Bacon.*

To OVERLI'VE. *v. a.* [*over* and *live.*] To live longer than another; to survive; to out-live.

Musidorus, who shewed a mind not to *over-live* Pyrocles, prevailed. *Sidney, b.* ii.

He concludes in hearty prayers,
That your attempts may *over-live* the hazard
And fearful meeting of their opposite. *Shakesp.*

They *over-lived* that envy, and had their pardons afterwards. *Hayward.*

To OVERLI'VE. *v. n.* To live too long.

Why do I *over-live?*
Why am I mock'd with death, and lengthen'd out
To deathless pain? *Milton's Par. Lost, b.* x.

OVERLI'VER. *n. s.* [from *over-live.*] Survivor; that which lives longest.

A peace was concluded, to continue for both the kings lives, and the *over-liver* of them. *Bacon's Hen.* VII.

To OVERLO'AD. *v. a.* [*over* and *load.*] To burthen with too much.

The memory of youth is charged and *over-loaded*, and all they learn is meer jargon. *Felton.*

O'VERLONG. *adj.* [*over* and *long.*] Too long.

I have transgressed the laws of oratory, in making my periods and parentheses *over-long.* *Boyle.*

To OVERLO'OK. *v. a.* [*over* and *look.*]

1. To view from a higher place.

The pile *o'er-look'd* the town, and drew the sight,
Surpris'd at once with rev'rence and delight. *Dryden.*

I will do it with the same respect to him, as if he were alive, and *over-looking* my paper while I write. *Dryden.*

2. To view fully; to peruse.

Wou'd I had *o'er-look'd* the letter. *Shakespeare.*

3. To superintend; to over-see.

He was present in person to *over-look* the magistrates, and to over-awe those subjects with the terror of his sword. *Spens.*

In the greater out parishes many of the poor parishioners through neglect do perish, for want of some heedful eye to *over-look* them. *Graunt.*

4. To review.

The time and care that are required,
To *over-look* and file, and polish well,
Fright poets from that necessary toil. *Roscommon.*

5. To pass by indulgently.

This part of good-nature which consists in the pardoning and *over-looking* of faults, is to be exercised only in doing ourselves justice in the ordinary commerce of life. *Addison.*

In vain do we hope that God will *over-look* such high contradiction of sinners, and pardon offences committed against the plain convictions of conscience. *Rogers.*

6. To neglect; to slight.

Of the two relations, Christ *over-looked* the meaner, and entitled and denominated them solely from the more honourable. *South's Sermons.*

To *over-look* the entertainment before him, and languish for that which lies out of the way, is sickly and servile. *Collier.*

The suffrage of our poet laureat should not be *over-looked.* *Addison's Spectator*, N°. 488.

Religious fear, when produced by just apprehensions of a divine power, naturally *over-looks* all human greatness that stands in competition with it, and extinguishes every other terror. *Addison's Guardian*, N°. 117.

The happiest of mankind, *over-looking* those solid blessings which they already have, set their hearts upon somewhat they want. *Atterbury's Sermons.*

They *over-look* truth in the judgments they pass on adversity and prosperity. The temptations that attend the former they can easily see, and dread at a distance; but they have no apprehensions of the dangerous consequences of the latter. *Atterbury's Sermons.*

O'VERLOOKER. *n. s.* [*over* and *look.*]

The original word signifies an *over-looker*, or one who stands higher than his fellows and *over-looks* them. *Watts.*

O'VERLOOP. *n. s.* The same with *orlop.*

In extremity we carry our ordnance better than we were wont, because our nether *over-loops* are raised commonly from the water; to wit, between the lower part of the port and the sea. *Raleigh.*

OVERMA'STED. *adj.* [*over* and *mast.*] Having too much mast.

Cloanthus better mann'd, pursu'd him fast,
But his *o'er-masted* gally check'd his haste. *Dryden.*

To OVERMA'STER. *v. a.* [*over* and *master.*] To subdue; to govern.

For your desire to know what is between us,
O'er-master it as you may. *Shakespeare's Hamlet.*

So

So sleeps a pilot, whose poor bark is prest
With many a merciless *o'er-mast'ring* wave. *Crashaw.*

Over-mastered with a score of drunkards, the only soldiery left about them, or else to comply with all rapines and violences. *Milton on Education.*

To OVERMA'TCH. *v. a.* [*over* and *match.*] To be too powerful; to conquer; to oppress by superior force.

I have seen a swan
With bootless labour swim against the tide,
And spend her strength with *over-matching* waves. *Shakesp.*

Sir William Lucy, with me
Set from our *o'er-match'd* forces forth for aid. *Shakesp.*

Assist, lest I who erst
Thought none my equal, now be *over-match'd*. *Par. Reg.*

How great soever our curiosity be, our excess is greater, and does not only *over-match*, but supplant it. *Dec. of Piety.*

He from that length of time dire omens drew,
Of English *over-match'd*, and Dutch too strong,
Who never fought three days but to pursue. *Dryden.*

It moves our wonder, that a foreign guest
Should *over-match* the most, and match the best. *Dryden.*

OVERMA'TCH. *n. s.* [*over* and *match.*] One of superior powers; one not to be overcome.

Spain is no *over-match* for England, by that which leadeth all men; that is, experience and reason. *Bacon.*

Eve was his *over-match*, who self-deceiv'd
And rash, before-hand had no better weigh'd
The strength he was to cope with or his own. *Milton.*

In a little time there will scarce be a woman of quality in Great-Britain, who would not be an *over-match* for an Irish priest. *Addison's Freeholder*, N°. 89.

OVER-ME'ASURE. *n. s.* [*over* and *measure.*] Something given over the due measure.

To OVER-MI'X. *v. a.* [*over* and *mix.*] To mix with too much.

Those things these parts o'er-rule, no joys shall know,
Or little pleasure *over-mixt* with woe. *Creech.*

OVERMO'ST. *adj.* [*over* and *most.*] Highest; over the rest in authority. *Ainsw.*

OVERMU'CH. *adj.* [*over* and *much.*] Too much; more than enough.

It was the custom of those former ages, in their *over-much* gratitude, to advance the first authors of any useful discovery among the number of their gods. *Wilkins.*

An *over-much* use of salt, besides that it occasions thirst and *over-much* drinking, has other ill effects. *Locke.*

OVERMU'CH. *adv.* In too great a degree.

The fault which we find in them is, that they *over-much* abridge the church of her power in these things. Whereupon they re-charge us, as if in these things we gave the church a liberty which hath no limits or bounds. *Hooker.*

Perhaps
I also erred, in *over-much* admiring
What seem'd in thee so perfect, that I thought
No evil durst attempt thee. *Milton's Par. Lost, b.* ix.

Deject not then so *over-much* thyself,
Who hast of sorrow thy full load besides. *Milton.*

OVERMU'CH. *n. s.* More than enough.

By attributing *over-much* to things
Less excellent, as thou thyself perceiv'st. *Milton.*

With respect to the blessings the world enjoys, even good men may ascribe *over-much* to themselves. *Grew.*

OVERMU'CHNESS. *n. s.* [from *over-much.*] Exuberance; superabundance.

There are words that do as much raise a stile, as others can depress it; superlation and *over-muchness* amplifies. It may be above faith, but not above a mean. *Ben. Johnson.*

OVERNI'GHT. *n. s.* [*over* and *night.* This seems to be used by *Shakespeare* as a noun, but by *Addison* more properly, as I have before placed it, as a noun with a preposition.] Night before bed-time.

If I had given you this at *over-night*,
She might have been o'erta'en. *Shakespeare.*

Will confesses, that for half his life his head ached every morning with reading men *over-night*. *Addison.*

To OVERNA'ME. *v. a.* [*over* and *name.*] To name in a series.

Over-name them; and as thou namest them I will describe them. *Shakesp. Merch. of Venice.*

To OVERO'FFICE. *v. a.* [*over* and *office.*] To lord by virtue of an office.

This might be the fate of a politician which this ass *over-offices*. *Shakesp. Hamlet.*

OVEROFFI'CIOUS. *adj.* [*over* and *officious.*] Too busy; too importunate.

This is an *over-officious* truth, and is always at a man's heels; so that if he looks about him, he must take notice of it. *Collier on Human Reason.*

To OVERPA'SS. *v. a.* [*over* and *pass.*]

1. To cross.

I stood on a wide river's bank,
Which I must needs *o'er-pass*,
When on a sudden Torrismond appear'd,
Gave me his hand, and led me lightly o'er. *Dryden.*

What have my Scyllas and my Syrtes done,
When these they *o'er-pass*, and those they shun? *Dryden.*

2. To over-look; to pass with disregard.

The complaint about psalms and hymns might as well be *over-past* without any answer, as it is without any cause brought forth. *Hooker, b.* v. *s.* 37.

Remember that Pellean conqueror,
A youth, how all the beauties of the east
He slightly view'd, and slightly *over-pass'd*. *Milton.*

3. To omit in a reckoning.

Arithmetical progression demonstrates how fast mankind would increase, *over-passing* as miraculous, though indeed natural, that example of the Israelites who were multiplied in two hundred and fifteen years, from seventy to sixty thousand able men. *Raleigh.*

4. To omit; not to receive.

If the grace of him which saveth *over-pass* some, so that the prayer of the church for them be not received, this we may leave to the hidden judgments of righteousness. *Hooker.*

OVERPA'ST. *part. adj.* [from *over-pass.*] Gone; past.

What canst thou swear by now?—
—By time to come,—
That thou hast wronged in the time *o'er-past*. *Shakesp.*

To OVERPA'Y. *v. a.* [*over* and *pay.*] To reward beyond the price.

Take this purse of gold,
And let me buy your friendly help thus far,
Which I will *over-pay*, and pay again,
When I have found it. *Shakespeare.*

You have yourself, your kindness *over-paid*,
He ceases to oblige who can upbraid. *Dryden.*

Wilt thou with pleasure hear thy lover's strains,
And with one heav'nly smile *o'er-pay* his pains. *Prior.*

To OVERPE'RCH. *n. s.* [*over* and *perch.*] To fly over.

With love's light wings did I *o'er-perch* these walls,
For stony limits cannot hold love out. *Shakesp.*

To OVERPE'ER. *v. a.* [*over* and *peer.*] To over-look; to hover above. It is now out of use.

The ocean *over-peering* of his list,
Eats not the flats with more impetuous haste,
Than young Laertes, in a riotous head,
O'er-bears your officers. *Shakesp. Hamlet.*

Your Argosies with portly sail,
Do *over-peer* the petty traffickers,
That curt'sy to them, do them reverence. *Shakesp.*

Mountainous error wou'd be too highly heapt,
For truth to *o'er-peer*. *Shakesp. Coriolanus.*

Thus yields the cedar to the ax's edge,
Whose top branch *o'er-peer'd* Jove's spreading tree,
And kept low shrubs from winter's pow'rful wind. *Shakesp.*

They are invincible by reason of the *over-peering* mountains that back the one, and slender fortifications of the other to land-ward. *Sandys's Journey.*

O'VERPLUS. *n. s.* [*over* and *plus.*] Surplus; what remains more than sufficient.

Some other sinners there are, from which that *overplus* of strength in persuasion doth arise. *Hooker's Pref.*

A great deal too much of it was made, and the *overplus* remained still in the mortar. *L'Estrange.*

It would look like a fable to report, that this gentleman gives away all which is the *overplus* of a great fortune. *Addis.*

To O'VERPLY. *v. a.* [*over* and *ply.*] To employ too laboriously.

What supports me, dost thou ask?
The conscience, friend, t' have lost them *over-ply'd*,
In liberty's defence. *Milton's Poems.*

To OVERPO'ISE. *v. a.* [*over* and *poise.*] To outweigh.

Whether cripples who have lost their thighs will float; their lungs being able to waft up their bodies, which are in others *over-poised* by the hinder legs; we have not made experiment. *Brown's Vulgar Err. b.* iv.

The scale
O'er-pois'd by darkness, lets the night prevail;
And day, that lengthen'd in the summer's height,
Shortens till winter, and is lost in night. *Creech.*

OVERPO'ISE. *n. s.* [from the verb.] Preponderant weight.

Horace, in his first and second book of odes, was still rising, but came not to his meridian till the third. After which his judgment was an *over-poise* to his imagination. He grew too cautious to be bold enough, for he descended in his fourth by slow degrees. *Dryden.*

Some *over-poise* of sway, by turns they share,
In peace the people, and the prince in war. *Dryden.*

To OVERPO'WER. *v. a.* [*over* and *power.*] To be predominant over; to oppress by superiority.

Now in danger try'd, now known in arms
Not to be *over-power'd*. *Milt. Par. Lost.*

As much light *over-powers* the eye, so they who have weak eyes, when the ground is covered with snow, are wont to complain of too much light. *Boyle.*

Reason allows none to be confident, but him only who

governs the world, who knows all things, and can do all things; and therefore can neither be surprised nor *over-powered*. *South's Sermons.*

After the death of Crassus, Pompey found himself out-witted by Cæsar; he broke with him, *over-powered* him in the senate, and caused many unjust decrees to pass against him. *Dryden's Dedicat. to Æneid.*

Inspiration is, when such an *over-powering* impression of any proposition is made upon the mind by God himself, that gives a convincing and indubitable evidence of the truth and divinity of it. *Watts's Logick.*

The historian makes these mountains the standards of the rise of the water; which they could never have been, had they not been standing, when it did so rise and *over-power* the earth. *Woodw. Nat. Hist.*

To Overpre'ss. *v. a.* [*over* and *press.*] To bear upon with irresistible force; to overwhelm; to crush.

Having an excellent horse under him, when he was *over-pressed* by some, he avoided them. *Sidney.*

Michael's arm main promontories flung,
And *over-press'd* whole legions weak with sin. *Roscomm.*

When a prince enters on a war, he ought maturely to consider whether his coffers be full, his people rich by a long peace and free trade, not *over-pressed* with many burthensome taxes. *Swift.*

To Overpri'ze. *v. a.* [*over* and *prize.*] To value at too high price.

Parents *over-prize* their children, while they behold them through the vapours of affection. *Wotton.*

Overra'nk. *n. s.* [*over* and *rank.*] Too rank.

It produces *over-rank* binds. *Mortimer's Husbandry.*

Overra'te. *v. a.* [*over* and *rate.*] To rate at too much.

While vain shows and scenes you *over-rate*,
'Tis to be fear'd, ———
That as a fire the former house o'erthrew,
Machines and tempests will destroy the new. *Dryden.*

To avoid the temptations of poverty, it concerns us not to *over-rate* the conveniencies of our station, and in estimating the proportion fit for us, to fix it rather too low than too high; for our desires will be proportioned to our wants, real or imaginary, and our temptations to our desires. *Rogers.*

To Overre'ach. *v. a.* [*over* and *reach.*]

1. To rise above.

The mountains of Olympus, Atho and Atlas, *over-reach* and surmount all winds and clouds. *Raleigh.*

Sixteen hundred years after the earth was made, it was overflowed in a deluge of water in such excess, that the floods *over-reached* the tops of the highest mountains. *Burnet.*

2. To deceive; to go beyond; to circumvent. A sagacious man is said to have a long *reach*.

What more cruel than man, if he see himself able by fraud to *over-reach*, or by power to over-bear the laws whereunto he should be subject. *Hooker, b. v. s. 2.*

I have laid my brain in the sun and dried it, that it wants matter to prevent so gross *over-reaching*. *Shakesp.*

Shame to be overcome, or *over-reach'd*,
Would utmost vigour raise, and rais'd unite. *Milton.*

A man who had been matchless held
In cunning, *over-reach'd* where least he thought,
To save his credit, and for very spight
Still will be tempting him who foils him still. *Milton.*

There is no pleasanter encounter than a trial of skill betwixt sharpers to *over-reach* one another. *L'Estrange.*

Forbidding oppression, defrauding and *over-reaching* one another, perfidiousness and treachery. *Tillotson.*

Such a principle is ambition, or a desire of fame, by which many vicious men are *over-reached*, and engaged contrary to their natural inclinations in a glorious and laudable course of action. *Addison's Spectator*, N°. 255.

John had got an impression that Lewis was so deadly cunning a man, that he was afraid to venture himself alone with him; at last he took heart of grace; let him come up, quoth he, it is but sticking to my point, and he can never *over-reach* me. *History of J. Bull.*

To Overre'ach. *v. n.* A horse is said to *over-reach*, when he brings his hinder feet too far forwards, and strikes his toes against his fore shoes. *Farr. Dict.*

Overre'acher. *n. s.* [from *over-reach.*] A cheat; a deceiver.

To Overre'ad. *v. a.* [*over* and *read.*] To peruse.

The contents of this is the return of the duke; you shall anon *over-read* it at your pleasure. *Shakespeare.*

To O'ver-red. *v. a.* [*over* and *red.*] To smear with red.

Prick thy face and *over-red* thy fear,
Thou lilly liver'd boy. *Shakesp. Macbeth.*

To O'verroast. *v. a.* [*over* and *roast.*] To roast too much.

'Twas burnt and dried away,
And better 'twere, that both of us did fast,
Since of ourselves, ourselves are cholerick,
Than feed it with such *over-roasted* flesh. *Shakesp.*

To Overru'le. *v. a.* [*over* and *rule.*]

1. To influence with predominant power; to be superior in authority.

Which humour perceiving to *over-rule* me, I strave against it. *Sidney.*

That which the church by her ecclesiastical authority shall probably think and desire to be true or good, must in congruity of reason *over-rule* all other inferior arguments whatsoever. *Hooker, b. v. s. 8.*

Except our own private, and but probable resolutions, be by the law of publick determinations *over-ruled*, we take away all possibility of sociable life in the world. *Hooker.*

What if they be such as will be *over-ruled* with some one, whom they dare not displease. *Whitgifte.*

So much his passion and animosity *over-ruled* his conscience. *Clarendon, b. viii.*

A wise man shall *over-rule* his stars, and have a greater influence upon his own content, than all the constellations and planets of the firmament. *Taylor.*

He is acted by a passion which absolutely *over-rules* him; and so can no more recover himself, than a bowl rolling down an hill stop itself in the midst of its career. *South.*

'Tis temerity for men to venture their lives upon unequal encounters; unless where they are obliged by an *over-ruling* impulse of conscience and duty. *L'Estrange.*

A man may, by the influence of an *over-ruling* planet, be inclined to lust, and yet by the force of reason overcome that bad influence. *Swift.*

2. To govern with high authority; to superintend.

Wherefore does he not now come forth and openly *over-rule*, as in other matters he is accustomed? *Hayward.*

3. To supersede: as in law to *over-rule* a plea is to reject it as incompetent.

Thirty acres make a farthing land, nine farthings a Cornish acre, and four Cornish acres a knights fee. But this rule is *over-ruled* to a greater or lesser quantity, according to the fruitfulness or barrenness of the soil. *Carew.*

To Overru'n. *v. a.* [*over* and *run.*]

1. To harrass by incursions; to ravage; to rove over in a hostile manner.

Those barbarous nations that *over-ran* the world, possessed those dominions, whereof they are now so called. *Spenser.*

Till the tears she shed,
Like envious floods *o'er-ran* her lovely face,
She was the fairest creature in the world. *Shakesp.*

They err, who count it glorious to subdue
By conquest far and wide, to *over-run*
Large countries, and in field great battles win,
Great cities by assault. *Milton's Paradise Lost.*

The nine
Their fainting foes to shameful flight compell'd,
And with resistless force *o'er-run* the field. *Dryden.*

Gustavus Adolphus could not enter this part of the empire after having *over-run* most of the rest. *Addison.*

A commonwealth may be *over-run* by a powerful neighbour, which may produce bad consequences upon your trade and liberty. *Swift's Miscell.*

2. To out-run.

Pyrocles being come to sixteen, *over-run* his age in growth, strength, and all things following it, that not Musidorus could perform any action on horse or foot more strongly, or deliver that strength more nimbly, or become the delivery more gracefully, or employ all more virtuously. *Sidney, b. ii.*

We may out-run
By violent swiftness, that which we run at,
And lose by *over-running*. *Shakesp. Henry VIII.*

Ahimaz ran by the way of the plain, and *over-ran* Cushi. *2 Sam. xviii. 23.*

Galilæus noteth, that if an open trough, wherein water is, be driven faster than the water can follow, the water gathereth upon an heap towards the hinder end, where the motion began; which he supposeth, holding confidently the motion of the earth to be the cause of the ebbing and flowing of the ocean; because the earth *over-runneth* the water. *Bacon's Nat. History.*

3. To overspread; to cover all over.

With an *over-running* flood he will make an utter end of the place. *Nah. i. 8.*

This disposition of the elements and the parts of the earth, shews us the footsteps of some kind of ruin which happened in such a way, that at the same time a general flood of waters would necessarily *over-run* the whole earth. *Burnet's Theory of the Earth.*

4. To mischief by great numbers; to pester.

To flatter foolish men into a hope of life where there is none, is much the same with betraying people into an opinion, that they are in a virtuous and happy state, when they are *over-run* with passion and drowned in their lusts. *L'Estrange.*

Were it not for the incessant labours of this industrious animal, Egypt would be *over-run* with crocodiles. *Addison.*

Such provision made, that a country should not want springs as as were convenient for it; nor be *over-run* with them, and afford little or nothing else; but a supply every where suitable to the necessities of each climate and region of the globe. *Woodw. Nat. Hist.*

5. To injure by treading down.

His tears defac'd the surface of the well,
And now the lovely face but half appears,
O'er-run with wrinkles and deform'd with tears. *Addison.*

6. Among printers, to be obliged to change the disposition of the lines and words in correcting, by reason of the insertions.

To OVERRU'N. *v. n.* To overflow; to be more than full.

Though you have left me,
Yet still my soul *o'er-runs* with fondness towards you. *Smith.*

Cattle in inclosures shall always have fresh pasture, that now is all trampled and *over-run*. *Spenser.*

To OVERSE'E. *v. a.* [*over* and *see.*]

1. To superintend; to overlook.

He had charge my discipline to frame,
And tutors nourture to *oversee*. *Fairy Queen.*

She without noise will *oversee*
His children and his family. *Dryden.*

2. To overlook; to pass by unheeded; to omit.

I who resolve to *oversee*
No lucky opportunity,
Will go to council to advise
Which way t' encounter, or surprise. *Hud. p.* iii.

OVERSE'EN. *part.* [from *oversee.*] Mistaken; deceived.

A common received error is never utterly overthrown, till such times as we go from signs unto causes, and shew some manifest root or fountain thereof common unto all, whereby it may clearly appear how it hath come to pass that so many have been *overseen*. *Hooker, b.* i. *s.* 8.

They rather observed what he had done, and suffered for the king and for his country, without farther enquiring what he had omitted to do, or been *overseen* in doing. *Clarend.*

OVERSE'ER. *n. s.* [from *oversee.*]

1. One who overlooks; a superintendent.

There are in the world certain voluntary *overseers* of all books, whose censure, in this respect, would fall sharp on us. *Hooker, b.* v. *s.* 31.

Jehiel and Azariah were *overseers* under Cononiah. 2 *Chron.* xxxi. 13.

To entertain a guest, with what a care
Wou'd he his houshold ornaments prepare;
Harrass his servants, and as *o'erseer* stand,
To keep them working with a threat'ning wand.
Clean all my plate, he cries. *Dryden.*

2. An officer who has the care of the parochial provision for the poor.

The church-wardens and *overseers* of the poor might find it possible to discharge their duties, whereas now in the greater out-parishes many of the poorer parishioners, through neglect, do perish for want of some heedful eye to overlook them. *Graunt's Bills of Mort.*

To OVERSE'T. *v. a.* [*over* and *set.*]

1. To turn the bottom upwards; to throw off the basis.

The tempests met,
The sailors master'd, and the ship *o'er-set*. *Dryden.*

It is forced through the hiatus's at the bottom of the sea with such vehemence, that it puts the sea into the most horrible perturbation, even when there is not the least breath of wind; *over-setting* ships in the harbours, and sinking them. *Woodw. Nat. Hist.*

Would the confederacy exert itself, as much to annoy the enemy, as they do for their defence, we might bear them down with the weight of our armies, and *over-set* the whole power of France. *Addison on the War.*

2. To throw out of regularity.

His action against Catiline ruined the consul, when it saved the city; for it so swelled his soul, that ever afterwards it was apt to be *over-set* with vanity. *Dryden.*

To OVERSE'T. *v. n.* To fall off the basis.

Part of the weight will be under the axle-tree, which will so far counterpoise what is above it, that it will very much prevent the *over-setting*. *Mortimer's Husb.*

To OVERSHA'DE. *v. a.* [*over* and *shade.*] To cover with any thing that causes darkness.

Black night *o'er-shade* thy day, and death thy life. *Shakesp.*

Dark cloudy death *o'er-shades* his beams of life,
And he nor sees, nor hears us. *Shakesp.*

No great and mighty subject might eclipse or *over-shade* the imperial power. *Bacon.*

If a wood of leaves *o'er-shade* the tree,
In vain the hind shall vex the threshing floor,
For empty chaff and straw will be thy store. *Dryden.*

Should we mix our friendly talk,
O'er-shaded in that fav'rite walk;
Both pleas'd with all we thought we wanted. *Prior.*

To OVERSHA'DOW. *v. a.* [*over* and *shadow.*]

1. To throw a shadow over any thing.

Weeds choak and *over-shadow* the corn, and bear it down, or starve and deprive it of nourishment. *Bacon.*

Death,
Let the damps of thy dull breath
Over-shadow even the shade,
And make darkness self afraid. *Crashaw.*

Darkness must *over-shadow* all his bounds,
Palpable darkness, and blot out three days. *Milton.*

2. To shelter; to protect; to cover with superiour influence.

My *over-shadowing* spirit and might, with thee
I send along: ride forth and bid the deep
Within appointed bounds. *Milton's Par. Lost.*

On her should come
The holy ghost, and the power of the highest
O'er shadow her. *Paradise Regain'd, b.* i.

To OVERSHO'OT. *v. n.* [*over* and *shoot.*] To fly beyond the mark.

Often it drops, or *over-shoots* by the disproportions of distance or application. *Collier on Human Reason.*

To OVERSHOO'T. *v. a.*

1. To shoot beyond the mark.

Every inordinate appetite defeats its own satisfaction, by *over-shooting* the mark it aims at. *Tillotson.*

2. [With the reciprocal pronoun.] To venture too far; to assert too much.

Leave it to themselves to consider, whether they have in this point or not *over-shot themselves*; which God doth know is quickly done, even when our meaning is most sincere. *Hooker, b.* ii. *s.* 8.

In finding fault with the laws I doubt me, you shall much *over-shoot yourself*, and make me the more dislike your other dislikes of that government. *Spenser on Ireland.*

For any thing that I can learn of them, you have *over-shot yourself* in reckoning. *Whitgifte.*

O'VERSIGHT. *n. s.* [from *over* and *sight.*]

1. Superintendence.

They gave the money, being told unto them that had the *over-sight* of the house. 2 *Kings* xii. 11.

Feed the flock of God, taking the *over-sight* thereof, not by constraint, but willingly. 1 *Pet.* v. 2.

2. Mistake; error.

Amongst so many huge volumes, as the infinite pains of St. Augustine have brought forth, what one hath gotten greater love, commendation, and honour, than the book wherein he carefully owns his *over-sights* and sincerely condemneth them. *Hooker's Pref.*

His son mark'd this *over-sight*,
And then mistook reverse of wrong for right. *Pope.*

To OVERSI'ZE. *v. a.* [*over* and *size.*]

1. To surpass in bulk.

Those bred in a mountainous country, *over-size* those that dwell on low levels. *Sandys Journey.*

2. [*over* and *size*, a compost with which masons cover walls.] To plaster over.

He thus *o'er-siz'd* with coagulate gore,
Old grandsire Priam seeks. *Shakesp. Hamlet.*

To OVERSKI'P. *v. a.* [*over* and *skip.*]

1. To pass by leaping.

Presume not ye that are sheep, to make yourselves guides of them that should guide you; neither seek ye to *over-skip* the fold, which they about you have pitched. *Hooker.*

2. To pass over.

Mark if to get them she *o'er-skip* the rest,
Mark if she read them twice, or kiss the name. *Donne.*

3. To escape.

When that hour *o'er-skips* me in the day,
Wherein I sigh not, Julia, for thy sake;
The next ensuing hour some foul mischance
Torment me. *Shakesp. Two Gent. of Verona.*

Who alone suffers, suffers most i' th' mind;
But then the mind much suff'rance does *o'er-skip*,
When grief hath mates and bearing fellowship. *Shakesp.*

To OVERSLE'EP. *v. a.* [*over* and *sleep.*] To sleep too long.

To OVERSLI'P. *v. a.* [*over* and *slip.*] To pass undone, unnoticed, or unused; to neglect.

The carelessness of the justices in imposing this rate, or the negligence of the constables in collecting it, or the backwardness of the inhabitants in paying the same, *over-slipped* the time. *Carew's Survey of Cornwall.*

It were injurious to *over-slip* a noble act in the duke during this employment, which I must celebrate above all his expences. *Wotton.*

To OVERSNO'W. *v. a.* [*over* and *snow.*] To cover with snow.

These I wielded while my bloom was warm,
Ere age unstrung my nerves, or time *o'er-snow'd* my head. *Dryden's Æneis.*

OVERSO'LD. *part.* [from *oversel.*] Sold at too high a price.

Life with ease I can disclaim,
And think it *over-sold* to purchase fame. *Dryden.*

OVERSO'ON. *adv.* [*over* and *soon.*] Too soon.

The lad may prove well enough, if he *over-soon* think not too well of himself, and will bear away that he heareth of his elders. *Sidney, b.* ii.

OVERSPE'NT. *part.* [*over* and *ſpend.*] Wearied; harraſſed; foreſpent. The verb *overſpend* is not uſed.

Theſtylis, wild thyme, and garlick beats,
For harveſt-hinds, *o'erſpent* with toil and heats. *Dryden.*

To OVERSPREA'D. *v. a.* [*over* and *ſpread.*] To cover over; to fill; to ſcatter over.

Whether they were Spaniards, Gauls, Africans, Gothes, or ſome other which did *overſpread* all chriſtendom, it is impoſſible to affirm. *Spenſer.*

Of the three ſons of Noah was the whole earth *overſpread.* *Gen.* ix. 19.

Darkneſs Europe's face did *overſpread*,
From lazy cells, where ſuperſtition bred. *Denham.*

Not a deluge that only over-run ſome particular region; but that *overſpread* the face of the whole earth from pole to pole, and from eaſt to weſt. *Burnet.*

To OVERSTA'ND. *v. a.* [*over* and *ſtand.*] To ſtand too much upon conditions.

Her's they ſhall be, ſince you refuſe the price;
What madman would *o'erſtand* his market twice. *Dryd.*

To OVERSTA'RE. *v. a.* [*over* and *ſtare.*] To ſtare wildly.

Some warlike ſign muſt be uſed; either a ſlovenly buſkin, or an *overſtaring* frounced head. *Aſcham.*

To OVERSTO'CK. *v. a.* [*over* and *ſtock.*] To fill too full; to croud.

If raillery had entered the old Roman coins, we ſhould have been *overſtocked* with medals of this nature. *Addiſon.*

Some biſhop, not *overſtocked* with relations, or attached to favourites, beſtows ſome inconſiderable benefice. *Swift.*

Since we are ſo bent upon enlarging our flocks, it may be worth enquiring what we ſhall do with our wool, in caſe Barnſtaple ſhould be ever *overſtocked.* *Swift.*

To OVERSTO'RE. *v. a.* [*over* and *ſtore.*] To ſtore with too much.

Fiſhes are more numerous than beaſts or birds, as appears by their numerous ſpawn; and if all theſe ſhould come to maturity, even the ocean itſelf would have been long ſince *overſtored* with fiſh. *Hale's Origin of Mankind.*

To OVERSTRAI'N. *v. n.* [*over* and *ſtrain.*] To make too violent efforts.

Craſſus loſt himſelf, his equipage, and his army, by *overſtraining* for the Parthian gold. *Collier.*

He wiſhed all painters would imprint this leſſon deeply in their memory, that with *overſtraining* and earneſtneſs of finiſhing their pieces, they often did them more harm than good. *Dryden's Dufreſnoy.*

To OVERSTRAI'N. *v. a.* To ſtretch too far.

Confeſſors were apt to *overſtrain* their privileges, in which St. Cyprian made a notable ſtand againſt them. *Ayliffe.*

To OVERSWA'Y. *v. a.* [*over* and *ſway.*] To over-rule; to bear down.

When they are the major part of a general aſſembly, then their voices being more in number, muſt *overſway* their judgments who are fewer. *Hooker.*

Great command *o'erſways* our order. *Shakeſp.*

To OVERSWE'LL. *v. a.* [*over* and *ſwell.*] To riſe above.

Fill, Lucius, 'till the wine *o'erſwell* the cup;
I cannot drink too much of Brutus' love. *Shakeſp.*

When his banks the prince of rivers, Po,
Doth *overſwell*, he breaks with hideous fall. *Fairfax.*

O'VERT. *adj.* [*ouvert*, Fr.] Open; publick; apparent.

To vouch this, is no proof,
Without more certain and more *overt* teſt,
Than theſe thin habits and poor likelihoods. *Shakeſp.*

Overt and apparent virtues bring forth praiſe; but there be ſecret and hidden virtues that bring forth fortune; certain deliveries of a man's ſelf. *Bacon.*

My repulſe at Hull, was the firſt *overt* eſſay to be made how patiently I could bear the loſs of my kingdoms. *K. Charles.*

The deſign of their deſtruction may have been projected in the dark; but when all was ripe, their enemies proceeded to ſo many *overt* acts in the face of the nation, that it was obvious to the meaneſt. *Swift.*

Whereas human laws can reach no farther than to reſtrain the *overt* action, religion extends to the ſecret motions of the ſoul. *Rogers, Serm.* 17.

O'VERTLY. *adv.* [from the adjective.] Openly.

To OVERTA'KE. *v. a.* [*over* and *take.*]

1. To catch any thing by purſuit; to come up to ſomething going before.

We durſt not continue longer ſo near her confines, leſt her plagues might ſuddenly *overtake* us before we did ceaſe to be partakers with her ſins. *Hooker.*

If I had given you this at over-night,
She might have been *o'ertaken*; and yet ſhe writes
Purſuit would be but vain. *Shakeſpeare.*

I ſhall ſee
The winged vengeance *overtake* ſuch children. *Shakeſp.*

The enemy ſaid, I will purſue, I will *overtake*, I will divide the ſpoil. *Ex.* xv. 9.

My ſoul, more earneſtly releas'd,
Will out-ſtrip hers, as bullets flown before
A later bullet may *o'ertake*, the powder being more. *Donne.*

To thy wiſhes move a ſpeedy pace,
Or death will ſoon *o'ertake* thee in the chace. *Dryden.*

How muſt he tremble for fear vengeance ſhould *overtake* him, before he has made his peace with God? *Rogers.*

2. To take by ſurprize.

If a man be *overtaken* in a fault, ye which are ſpiritual reſtore ſuch an one in the ſpirit of meekneſs. *Gal.* vi. 1.

To OVERTA'SK. *v. a.* [*over* and *taſk.*] To burthen with too heavy duties or injunctions.

That office is performed by the parts with difficulty, becauſe they were *overtaſked.* *Harvey on Conſumptions.*

To OVERTA'X. *v. a.* [*over* and *tax.*] To tax too heavily.

To OVERTHRO'W. *v. a.* [*over* and *throw*; *preter. overthrew*; *part. overthrown.*]

1. To turn upſide down.

Pittacus was a wiſe and valiant man, but his wife *overthrew* the table when he had invited his friends. *Taylor.*

2. To throw down; to ruin; to demoliſh.

When the walls of Thebes he *overthrew*,
His fatal hand my royal father ſlew. *Dryden.*

3. To defeat; to conquer; to vanquiſh.

Our endeavour is not ſo much to *overthrow* them with whom we contend, as to yield them juſt and reaſonable cauſes. *Hooker, b.* v. *ſ.* 1.

To Sujah next, your conquering army drew,
Him they ſurpris'd, and eaſily *o'erthrew.* *Dryden.*

4. To deſtroy; to miſchief; to bring to nothing.

She found means to have us accuſed to the king, as though we went about ſome practiſe to *overthrow* him in his own eſtate. *Sidney, b.* ii.

Here's Glo'ſter
O'er-charging your free purſes with large fines,
That ſeeks to *overthrow* religion. *Shakeſp. Hen.* VI.

Thou walkeſt in peril of thy *overthrowing.* *Ecc.* xiii. 13.

God *overthroweth* the wicked for their wickedneſs. *Prov.* xxi. 12.

OVERTHRO'W. *n. ſ.* [from the verb.]

1. The ſtate of being turned upſide down.

2. Ruin; deſtruction.

Of thoſe chriſtian oratories, the *overthrow* and ruin is deſired, not by infidels, pagans, or Turks, but by a ſpecial refined ſect of chriſtian believers. *Hooker, b.* v. *ſ.* 17.

They return again into Florida, to the murther and *overthrow* of their own countrymen. *Abbot.*

I ſerve my mortal foe,
The man who caus'd my country's *overthrow.* *Dryden.*

3. Defeat; diſcomfiture.

From without came to mine eyes the blow,
Whereto mine inward thoughts did faintly yield;
Both theſe conſpir'd poor reaſon's *overthrow*;
Falſe in myſelf, thus have I loſt the field. *Sidney.*

Quiet ſoul, depart;
For I have ſeen our enemies *overthrow.* *Shakeſp.*

From theſe divers Scots feared more harm by victory than they found among their enemies by their *overthrow.* *Hayw.*

Poor Hannibal is maul'd,
The theme is giv'n, and ſtrait the council's call'd,
Whether he ſhould to Rome directly go,
To reap the fruit of the dire *overthrow.* *Dryden*

4. Degradation.

His *overthrow* heap'd happineſs upon him;
For then, and not 'till then he felt himſelf,
And found the bleſſedneſs of being little. *Shakeſp.*

OVERTHRO'WER. *n. ſ.* [from *overthrow.*] He who overthrows.

OVERTHWA'RT. *adj.* [*over* and *thwart.*]

1. Oppoſite; being over againſt.

We whiſper, for fear our *overthwart* neighbours
Should hear us, and betray us to the government. *Dryd.*

2. Croſſing any thing perpendicularly.

3. Perverſe; adverſe; contradictious.

Two or three acts diſpoſed them to croſs and oppoſe any propoſition; and that *overthwart* humour was diſcovered to rule in the breaſts of many. *Clarendon.*

OVERTHWA'RTLY. *adv.* [from *overthwart.*]

1. Acroſs; tranſverſely.

The brawn of the thigh ſhall appear, by drawing ſmall hair ſtrokes from the hip to the knee, ſhadowed again *overthwartly.* *Peacham on Drawing.*

2. Pervicaciouſly; perverſely.

OVERTHWA'RTNESS. *n. ſ.* [from *overthwart.*] Pervicacity; perverſeneſs.

OVERTOO'K. *pret.* and *part. paſſ.* of *overtake.*

To OVERTO'P. *v. a.* [*over* and *top.*]

1. To riſe above; to raiſe the head above.

Pile your duſt upon the quick and dead,
T' *o'ertop* old Pelion or the ſkyiſh head
Of blue Olympus. *Shakeſp. Hamlet.*

In the dance the graceful goddeſs leads
The quire of nymphs, and *overtops* their heads. *Dryd.*

2. To excel; to ſurpaſs.

Who ever yet
Have ſtood to charity, and diſplay'd th' effects

Of difpofition gentle and of wifdom,
O'ertopping woman's power. *Shakefp. Hen.* VIII.

As far as the foul *o'ertops* the body, fo far its pains, or rather mournful fenfations, exceed thofe of the carcafe. *Harv.*

3. To obfcure; to make of lefs importance by fuperiour excellence.

Whereas he had been heretofore an arbiter of Europe, he fhould now grow lefs, and be *over-topped* by fo great a conjunction. *Bacon's Henry* VII.

One whom you love,
Had champion kill'd, or trophy won,
Rather than thus be *overtopt*,
Wou'd you not wifh his laurels cropt? *Swift.*

To OVERTRI'P. *v. a.* [*over* and *trip.*] To trip over; to walk lightly over.

In fuch a night,
Did Thifbe fearfully *o'ertrip* the dew,
And faw the lion's fhadow ere himfelf,
And ran difmay'd away. *Shakefp. Merch. of Venice.*

O'VERTURE. *n. f.* [*ouverture*, French.]

1. Opening; difclofure; difcovery.

I wifh
You had only in your filent judgment try'd it,
Without more *overture*. *Shakefp. Win. Tale.*

2. Propofal; fomething offered to confideration.

Mac Murugh moved Henry to invade Ireland, and made an *overture* unto him for obtaining of the fovereign lordfhip thereof. *Davies on Ireland.*

All thefe fair *overtures*, made by men well efteemed for honeft dealing, could not take place. *Hayward.*

We with open breaft
Stand ready to receive them, if they like
Our *overture*, and turn not back perverfe. *Milton.*

The earl of Pembroke, who abhorred the war, promoted all *overtures* towards accommodation with great importunity. *Clarendon.*

If a convenient fupply offers itfelf to be feifed by force or gained by fraud, human nature perfuades us to hearken to the inviting *overture*. *Rogers, Serm.* 2.

Suppofe five hundred men propofing, debating, and voting, according to their own little or much reafon, abundance of indigefted and abortive, many pernicious and foolifh *overtures* would arife. *Swift.*

To OVERTU'RN. *v. a.* [*over* and *turn.*]

1. To throw down; to topple down; to fubvert; to ruin.

He is wife in heart and mighty in ftrength—which removeth the mountains, and *overturneth* them in his anger. *Job* ix. 5.

Thefe will fometimes *overturn*, and fometimes fwallow up towns, and make a general confufion in nature. *Burnet.*

This he obviates, by faying we fee all the ideas in God; which is an anfwer to this objection, but fuch an one as *overturns* his whole hypothefis, and renders it ufelefs and as unintelligible, as any of thofe he has laid afide. *Locke.*

If we will not encourage publick works of beneficence, till we are fecure that no ftorm fhall *overturn* what we help to build; there is no room left for charity. *Atterbury.*

A monument of deathlefs fame,
A woman's hand *o'erturns*. *Rowe.*

2. To over-power; to conquer.

Pain exceffive *overturns* all patience. *Milton.*

OVERTU'RNER. *n. f.* [from *overturn.*] Subverter.

I have brought before you a robber of the publick treafure, an *overturner* of law and juftice, and the deftruction of the Sicilian province. *Swift.*

To OVERVA'LUE. *v. a.* [*over* and *value.*] To rate at too high a price.

We have juft caufe to ftand in fome fear, leaft by thus *overvaluing* their fermons they make the price and eftimation of fcripture, otherwife notified, to fall. *Hooker.*

To OVERVEI'L. *v. a.* [*over* and *veil.*] To cover.

The day begins to break, and night is fled;
Whofe pitchy mantle *overveil'd* the earth. *Shakefp.*

To OVERVO'TE. *v. a.* [*over* and *vote.*] To conquer by plurality of votes.

The lords and commons might be content to be *overvoted* by the major part of both houfes, when they had ufed each their own freedom. *King Charles.*

To OVERWA'TCH. *v. n.* [*over* and *watch.*] To fubdue with long want of reft.

Morpheus is difpatch'd;
Which done, the lazy monarch *overwatch'd*,
Down from his propping elbow drops his head,
Diffolv'd in fleep, and fhrinks within his bed. *Dryden.*

OVERWA'TCHED. *adj.* Tired with too much watching.

While the dog hunted in the river, he had withdrawn himfelf to pacify with fleep his *over-watched* eyes. *Sidney.*

OVERWEA'K. *adj.* [*over* and *weak.*] Too weak; too feeble.

Paternal perfuafions, after mankind began to forget the original giver of life, became in all *overweak* to refift the firft inclination of evil; or after, when it became habitual, to conftrain it. *Raleigh's Hift. of the World.*

To OVERWEA'RY. *adj.* [*over* and *weary.*] To fubdue with fatigue.

Might not Palinurus fall afleep and drop into the fea, having been *over-wearied* with watching. *Dryden.*

To OVERWEA'THER. *v. a.* [*over* and *weather.*] To batter by violence of weather.

How like a younker or a prodigal,
The fkarfed bark puts from her native bay,
Hugg'd and embraced by the ftrumpet wind!
How like the prodigal doth fhe return,
With *over-weather'd* ribs and ragged fails,
Lean, rent, and beggar'd by the ftrumpet wind. *Shakefp.*

To OVERWEE'N. *v. n.* [*over* and *ween.*] To think too highly; to think with arrogance.

To reach beyond the truth of any thing in thought; efpecially in the opinion of a man's felf. *Hanmer.*

Oft have I feen a hot *o'erweening* cur,
Run back and bite, becaufe he was with-held. *Shakefp.*

My mafter hath fent for me, to whofe feeling forrows I might be fome allay, or I *o'erween* to think fo. *Shakefp.*

Lafh hence thefe *overweening* rags of France,
Thefe famifh'd beggars, weary of their lives. *Shakefp.*

My eye's too quick, my heart *o'erweens* too much,
Unlefs my hand and ftrength could equal them. *Shakefp.*

Take heed of *overweening*, and compare
Thy peacock's feet with thy gay peacock's train;
Study the beft and higheft things that are,
But of thyfelf an humble thought retain. *Davies.*

They that *overween*,
And at thy growing virtues fret their fpleen,
No anger find in thee. *Milton.*

He might have learnt
Lefs *overweening*, fince he fail'd in Job,
Whofe conftant perfeverance overcame
Whate'er his cruel malice could invent. *Par. Reg.*

No man is fo bold, rafh, and *overweening* of his own works, as an ill painter and a bad poet. *Dryden.*

Enthufiafm, though founded neither on reafon nor revelation, but rifing from the conceits of a warmed or *overweening* brain, works more powerfully on the perfuafions and actions of men, than either or both together. *Locke.*

Men of fair minds and not given up to the *overweening* of felf-flattery, are frequently guilty of it: and, in many cafes, one with amazement hears the arguings, and is aftonifhed at the obftinacy of a worthy man who yields not to the evidence of reafon. *Locke.*

Now enters *overweening* pride,
And fcandal ever gaping wide. *Swift.*

OVERWEE'NINGLY. *adv.* [from *overween.*] With too much arrogance; with too high an opinion.

To OVERWEI'GH. *v. a.* [*over* and *weigh.*] To preponderate.

Sharp and fubtile difcourfes of wit, procure many times very great applaufe, but being laid in the balance with that which the habit of found experience delivereth, they are *overweighed*. *Hooker, b.* v. *f.* 7.

My unfoil'd name, the aufterenefs of my life,
Will fo your accufation *overweigh*,
That you fhall ftifle in your own report. *Shakefp.*

OVERWEI'GHT. *n. f.* [*over* and *weight.*] Preponderance.

Sinking into water is but an *overweight* of the body, in refpect of the water. *Bacon's Nat. Hift.*

To OVERWHE'LM. *v. a.* [*over* and *whelm.*]

1. To crufh underneath fomething violent and weighty.

What age is this, where honeft men,
Plac'd at the helm,
A fea of fome foul mouth or pen,
Shall *overwhelm*? *Ben. Johnfon.*

Back do I tofs thefe treafons to thy head,
With the hell hated lie *o'erwhelm* thy heart. *Shakefp.*

How trifling an apprehenfion is the fhame of being laughed at by fools, when compared with that everlafting fhame and aftonifhment which fhall *overwhelm* the finner, when he fhall appear before the tribunal of Chrift. *Rogers.*

Blind they rejoice, though now even now they fall;
Death haftes amain; one hour *o'erwhelms* them all. *Pope.*

2. To overlook gloomily.

Let the brow *o'erwhelm* it,
As fearfully as doth a galled rock
O'erhang and jutty his confounded bafe. *Shakefpeare.*

An apothecary late I noted,
In tatter'd weeds with *overwhelming* brows,
Culling of fimples. *Shakefp. Rom. and Juliet.*

OVERWHE'LMINGLY. *adv.* [from *overwhelming.*] In fuch a manner as to overwhelm.

Men fhould not tolerate themfelves one minute in any known fin, nor impertinently betray their fouls to ruin for that which they call light and trivial; which is fo indeed in refpect respect of the acquest, but *overwhelmingly* ponderous in regard of the pernicious consequents. *Decay of Piety.*

OVERWI'SE. *v. a.* [*over* and *wise.*] Wise to affectation.

Make not thyself *overwise.* *Eccl.* vii. 16.

OVERWROU'GHT. *part.* [*over* and *wrought.*]

1. Laboured too much.

Apelles said of Protogenes, that he knew not when to give over. A work may be *overwrought,* as well as underwrought: too much labour often takes away the spirit, by adding to the polishing; so that there remains nothing but a dull correctness, a piece without any considerable faults, but with few beauties. *Dryden's Dufresnoy.*

2. Worked all over.

Of Gothic structure was the northern side,
O'erwrought with ornaments of barbarous pride. *Pope.*

3. It has in *Shakespeare* a sense which I know not well how to reconcile to the original meaning of the word, and therefore conclude it misprinted for *overraught*; that is, *overreached* or cheated.

By some device or other,
The villain is *o'erwrought* of all my money:
They say this town is full of cozenage. *Shakesp.*

OVERWO'RN. *part.* [*over* and *worn.*]

1. Worn out; subdued by toil.

With watching *overworn,* with cares opprest,
Unhappy I had laid me down to rest. *Dryden.*

2. Spoiled by time.

The jealous *o'erworn* widow and herself,
Are mighty gossips in this monarchy. *Shakesp.*

OVERYEA'RED. *adj.* [*over* and *year.*] Too old.

Among them dwelt
A maid, whose fruit was ripe, not *overyeared.* *Fairfax.*

OVERZEA'LOUS. *adj.* [*over* and *zealous.*] Too zealous.

It is not of such weighty necessity to determine one way or the other, as some *overzealous* for or against the immateriality of the soul, have been forward to make the world believe. *Locke.*

OUGHT. *n. s.* [aphit, that is, *a whit,* Saxon. This word is therefore more properly written *aught.* See AUGHT.] Any thing; not nothing.

For *ought* that I can understand, there is no part but the bare English pale, in which the Irish have not the greatest footing. *Spenser on Ireland.*

He asked him if he saw *ought.* *Mark* viii. 23.

To do *ought* good never will be our task;
But ever to do ill our sole delight. *Milton's Par. Lost.*

Universal Lord! be bounteous still
To give us only good; and if the night
Have gather'd *ought* of evil, or conceal'd,
Disperse it, as now light dispels the dark. *Milton.*

OUGHT. *verb imperfect.* [This word the etymologists make the preterite of *owe,* but it has often a present signification.]

1. [Preterite of owe.] Owed; was bound to pay; have been indebted.

Apprehending the occasion, I will add a continuance to that happy motion, and besides give you some tribute of the love and duty I long have *ought* you. *Spelman.*

This blood which men by treason sought,
That followed, sir, which to myself I *ought.* *Dryden.*

2. To be obliged by duty.

Judges *ought* to remember, that their office is to interpret law, and not to make or give law. *Bacon.*

Morals criticks *ought* to show. *Pope.*

She acts just as she *ought,*
But never, never reach'd one generous thought. *Pope.*

3. To be fit; to be necessary.

If grammar *ought* to be taught, it must be to one that can speak the language already. *Locke.*

OVIFO'RM. *adj.* [*ovum* and *forma,* Lat.] Having the shape of an egg.

This notion of the mundane egg, or that the world was *oviform,* hath been the sense and language of all antiquity. *Burn.*

O'VIPAROUS. *adj.* [*ovum* and *pario,* Latin.] Bringing forth eggs; not viviparous.

That fishes and birds should be *oviparous,* is a plain sign of providence. *More's Ant. against Atheism.*

Birds and *oviparous* creatures have eggs enough at first conceived in them to serve them for many years laying. *Ray.*

OUNCE. *n. s.* [*once,* Fr. *uncia,* Latin.] A name of weight of different value in different denominations of weight. In troy weight, an *ounce* is twenty penny-weight; a penny-weight, twenty-four grains.

The blood he hath lost,
Which I dare vouch is more than that he hath
By many an *ounce,* he dropt it for his country. *Shakesp.*

A sponge dry weigheth one *ounce* twenty-six grains; the same sponge being wet, weigheth fourteen *ounces* six drams and three quarters. *Bacon.*

OUNCE. *n. s.* [*once,* French; *onza,* Spanish.] A lynx; a panther.

The *ounce,*
The libbard, and the tiger, as the mole
Rising, the crumbled earth above them threw
In hillocks. *Milton's Par. Lost, b.* vii.

OUPHE. *n. s.* [*auff,* Teutonick.] A fairy; a goblin.

Nan Page and my little son, we'll dress
Like urchins, *ouphes,* and fairies, green and white. *Shak.*

OU'PHEN. *n. s.* [from *ouph.*] Elfish.

Fairies, black, gray, green, and white,
Ye moon shine revellers and shades of night,
You *ouphen* heirs of fixed destiny,
Attend your office. *Shakespeare.*

OUR. *pron. poss.* [upe, Saxon.]

1. Pertaining to us; belonging to us.

You shall
Lead *our* first battle, brave Macduff, and we
Shall take upon us what else remains. *Shakespeare.*

Our wit is given almighty God to know,
Our will is given to love him being known;
But God could not be known to us below,
But by his works which through the sense are shown.
So in *our* little world this soul of ours
Being only one, and to one body ty'd,
Doth use on divers objects divers powers,
And so are her effects diversify'd. *Davies.*

2. When the substantive goes before, it is written *ours.*

Edmund, whose virtue in this instance,
So much commands itself, you shall be *ours.* *Shakesp.*

Thou that hast fashion'd twice this soul of *ours,*
So that she is by double title thine, *Davies.*

Be *ours,* who e'er thou art,
Forget the Greeks. *Denham.*

Taxallan, shook by Montezuma's powers,
Has, to resist his forces, call'd in *ours.* *Dryden.*

Reading furnishes the mind only with materials of knowledge, it is thinking makes what we read *ours*: it is not enough to cram ourselves with a great load of collections, unless we chew them over again, they will not give us strength. *Locke.*

Their organs are better disposed than *ours,* for receiving grateful impressions from sensible objects. *Atterbury.*

OURSE'LVES. *reciprocal pronoun.* [the plural of myself.]

1. We; not others.

We *ourselves* might distinctly number in words a great deal farther than we usually do, would we find out but some fit denominations to signify them by. *Locke.*

2. Us; not others, in the oblique cases.

Safe in *ourselves,* while on *ourselves* we stand,
The sea is ours, and that defends the land. *Dryden.*

OURSELF is used in the regal stile.

To make society
The sweeter welcome, we will keep *ourself*
Till supper-time alone. *Shakesp. Macbeth.*

We *ourself* will follow
In the main battle. *Shakespeare.*

Not so much as a treaty can be obtained, unless we would denude *ourself* of all force to defend us. *Clarendon.*

OUSE. *n. s.* Tanners bark. *Ainsworth.*

OU'SEL. *n. s.* [oyle, Saxon.] A blackbird.

The merry lark her mattins sings aloft,
The thrush replies, the mavis descant plays,
The *ousel* shrills, the ruddock warbles soft;
So goodly all agree, with sweet consent,
To this day's merriment. *Spenser.*

The *ousel* cock so black of hue,
With orange tawney bill. *Shakespeare.*

Thrushes and *ousels,* or blackbirds, were commonly sold for three pence a-piece. *Hakewill on Providence.*

To OUST. *v. a.* [*ouster, ôter,* French.] To vacate; to take away.

Multiplication of actions upon the case were rare formerly, and thereby wager of law *ousted,* which discouraged many suits. *Hale.*

OUT. *adv.* [ut, Saxon; *uyt,* Dutch.]

1. Not within.

The gown with stiff embroid'ry shining,
Looks charming with a slighter lining;
The *out,* if Indian figures stain,
The inside must be rich and plain. *Prior.*

2. It is generally opposed to *in.*

That blind rascally boy, that abuses every one's eyes because his own are *out,* let him be judge how deep I am in love. *Shakesp.*

3. In a state of disclosure.

Fruits and grains are half a year in concocting; whereas leaves are *out* and perfect in a month. *Bacon.*

4. Not in confinement or concealment.

Nature her custom holds,
Let shame say what it will; when these are gone,
The woman will be *out.* *Shakespeare.*

5. From the place or house.
Out with the dog, says one; what cur is that? says another: whip him *out*, says the third. *Shakesp.*
6. From the inner part.
This is the place where the priests shall boil the trespass offering; that they bear it not *out* into the utter court, to sanctify the people. *Ezek.* xlvi. 20.
7. Not at home.
8. In a state of extinction.
It was great ign'rance, Gloster's eyes being *out*,
To let him live; where he arrives he moves
All hearts. *Shakesp. King Lear.*
This candle burns not clear; 'tis I must snuff it,
Then *out* it goes. *Shakesp. Henry* VIII.
Bid thy ceremony give thee cure!
Thinkst thou the firy fever will go *out*
With titles blown from adulation. *Shakesp. Hen.* V.
Her candle goeth not *out* by night. *Prov.* xxxi. 18.
9. In a state of being exhausted.
When the butt is *out* we will drink water, not a drop before; bear up and board them. *Shakesp. Tempest.*
Large coals are properest for dressing meat; and when they are *out*, if you happen to miscarry in any dish, lay the fault upon want of coals. *Swift.*
10. Not in an affair.
So we'll live and hear poor rogues
Talk of court news, and we'll talk with them too,
Who loses, and who wins; who's in, who's *out*. *Shak.*
The knave will stick by thee: he will not *out*, he is true bred. *Shakesp. Henry* IV. *p.* ii.
I am not so as I should be;
But I'll ne'er *out*. *Shakesp. Ant. and Cleop.*
11. To the end.
Hear me *out*;
He reap'd no fruit of conquest, but these blessings. *Dryd.*
You have still your happiness in doubt,
Or else 'tis past, and you have dream'd it *out*. *Dryden.*
The tale is long, nor have I heard it *out*;
Thy father knows it all. *Addison's Cato.*
12. Loudly; without restraint.
At all I laugh, he laughs no doubt;
The only difference is, I dare laugh *out*. *Pope.*
13. Not in the hands of the owner.
If the laying of taxes upon commodities does affect the land that is *out* at rack rent, it is plain it does equally affect all the other land in England too. *Locke.*
Those lands were *out* upon leases of four years, after the expiration of which term the tenants were obliged to renew. *Arbuthnot on Coins.*
14. In an errour.
You are mightily *out* to take this for a token of esteem, which is no other than a note of infamy. *L'Estrange.*
As he that hath been often told his fault,
And still persists, is as impertinent,
As a musician that will always play,
And yet is always *out* at the same note. *Roscommon.*
According to Hobbes's comparison of reasoning with casting up accounts, whoever finds a mistake in the sum total, must allow himself *out*, though after repeated trials he may not see in which article he has misreckoned. *Swift.*
15. At a loss; in a puzzle.
Like a dull actor now:
I have forgot my part, and I am *out*,
Even to a full disgrace. *Shakesp. Coriolanus.*
This youth was such a mercurial, as the like hath seldom been known; and could make his own part, if at any time he chanced to be *out*. *Bacon's Hen.* VII.
16. With torn cloaths.
Evidences swore;
Who hither coming *out* at heels and knees,
For this had titles. *Dryden.*
17. Away; at a loss.
I never was *out* at a mad frolick, though this is the maddest I ever undertook. *Dryden.*
Let all persons avoid niceness in their clothing or diet, because they dress and comb *out* all their opportunities of morning devotion, and sleep *out* the care for their souls. *Taylor.*
18. It is used emphatically before *alas.*
Out, alas! no sea, I find,
Is troubled like a lover's mind. *Suckling.*
19. It is added emphatically to verbs of discovery.
If ye will not do so, be sure your sin will find you *out*. *Num.* xxxii. 23.

OUT. *interject.* An expression of abhorrence or expulsion.
Out upon this half-fac'd fellowship. *Shakesp.*
Out on thee, rude man! thou dost shame thy mother. *Sha.*
Out Varlet from my sight. *Shakesp. K. Lear.*
Out, you mad headed ape! a weazel hath not such a deal of spleen. *Shakesp. Hen.* IV.
Out of my door, you witch! you hag!
Out, out, out. *Shakesp. M. W. of Wind.*
Out, out, hyena; these are thy wonted arts,
To break all faith. *Milton's Agonistes.*
Out upon it, I have lov'd
Three whole days together;
And am like to love three more,
If it prove fair weather. *Suckling.*

OUT *of. prep.* [*Of* seems to be the preposition, and *out* only to modify the sense of *of.*]
1. From; noting produce.
So many Neroes and Caligulas,
Out of these crooked shores must daily raise. *Spens.*
Those bards coming many hundred years after, could not know what was done in former ages, nor deliver certainty of any thing, but what they feigned *out of* their own unlearned heads. *Spenser on Ireland.*
Alders and ashes have been seen to grow out of steeples; but they manifestly grow *out of* clefts. *Bacon.*
He is softer than Ovid; he touches the passions more delicately, and performs all this *out of* his own fund, without diving into the sciences for a supply. *Dryden.*
2. Not in; noting exclusion or dismission.
The sacred nymph
Was *out of* Dian's favour, as it then befel. *Fa. Queen.*
Guiltiness
Will speak, though tongues were *out of* use. *Shakesp.*
The cavern's mouth alone was hard to find,
Because the path disus'd was *out of* mind. *Dryden.*
My retreat the best companions grace,
Chiefs *out of* war, and statesmen *out of* place. *Pope.*
Does he fancy we can sit,
To hear his *out of* fashion wit?
But he takes up with younger folks,
Who, for his wine, will bear his jokes. *Swift.*
They are *out of* their element, and logic is none of their talent. *Baker on Learning.*
3. No longer in.
Enjoy the present smiling hour;
And put it *out of* fortune's pow'r. *Dryden.*
4. Not in; noting unfitness.
He is witty *out of* season; leaving the imitation of nature, and the cooler dictates of his judgment. *Dryden.*
Thou'lt say my passion's *out of* season,
That Cato's great example and misfortunes
Should both conspire to drive it from my thoughts. *Addis.*
5. Not within; relating to a house.
Court holy water in a dry house, is better than the rain waters *out of* door. *Shakesp. King Lear.*
6. From; noting extraction.
Juices of fruits are watry and oily: among the watry are all the fruits *out of* which drink is expressed; as the grape, the apple, the pear, and cherry. *Bacon.*
7. From; noting copy.
St. Paul quotes one of their poets for this saying, notwithstanding T. G's censure of them *out of* Horace. *Stilling.*
8. From; noting rescue.
Christianity recovered the law of nature *out of* all those errors with which it was overgrown in the times of paganism. *Addison's Freeholder.*
9. Not in; noting exorbitance or irregularity.
Why publish it at this juncture; and so, *out of* all method, apart and before the work. *Swift.*
Using old thread-bare phrases, will often make you go *out of* your way to find and apply them. *Swift.*
10. From one thing to something different.
He that looks on the eternal things that are not seen, will, through those opticks, exactly discern the vanity of all that is visible; will be neither frighted nor flattered *out of* his duty. *Decay of Piety.*
Words are able to persuade men *out of* what they find and feel, and to reverse the very impressions of sense. *South.*
11. To a different state from; in a different state, noting disorder.
That noble and most sovereign reason,
Like sweet bells jangl'd *out of* tune and harsh;
That unmatch'd form and feature of blown youth,
Blasted with extasy. *Shakesp. Hamlet.*
When the mouth is *out of* taste, it maketh things taste sometimes salt, chiefly bitter, and sometimes loathsome, but never sweet. *Bacon.*
By the same fatal blow, the earth fell *out of* that regular form wherein it was produced at first, into all these irregularities in its present form. *Burnet on the Earth.*
They all at once employ their thronging darts,
But *out* of order thrown, in air they join,
And multitude makes frustrate the design. *Dryden.*
12. Not according to.
That there be an equality, so that no man acts or speaks *out of* character. *Pope's View of Ep. Poem.*
13. To a different state from; noting separation.
Whosoever doth measure by number, must needs be greatly *out of* love with a thing that hath so many faults; whosoever

by weight cannot chuse but esteem very highly of that wherein the wit of so scrupulous adversaries hath not hitherto observed any defect, which themselves can seriously think to be of moment. *Hooker, b.* v. *s.* 27.

If ridicule were employed to laugh men *out of* vice and folly, it might be of some use; but it is made use of to laugh men *out of* virtue and good sense, by attacking every thing solemn and serious. *Addison's Spectator.*

14. Beyond.

Amongst those things which have been received with great reason, ought that to be reckoned which the antient practise of the church hath continued *out of* mind. *Hooker, b.* v. *s.* 9.

What, *out of* hearing gone? no sound, no word?
Alack, where are you? *Shakespeare.*

I have been an unlawful bawd, time *out* of mind. *Shak.*

Few had the least suspicion of their intentions, till they were both *out of* distance to have their conversion attempted. *Clarendon, b.* viii.

With a longer peace, the power of France with so great revenues, and such application, will not encrease every year *out of* proportion to what ours will do. *Temple.*

He shall only be prisoner at the soldiers quarters; and when I am *out of* reach, he shall be released. *Dryden.*

We see people lulled asleep with solid and elaborate discourses of piety, who would be transported *out of* themselves by the bellowings of enthusiasm. *Addison.*

Milton's story was transacted in regions that lie *out of* the reach of the sun and the sphere of the day. *Addison.*

Women weep and tremble at the sight of a moving preacher, though he is placed quite *out of* their hearing. *Addison.*

15. Deviating from: Noting irregularity.

Heaven defend but still I should stand so,
So long as *out of* limit, and true rule,
You stand against anointed majesty! *Shakesp.*

The supream being has made the best arguments for his own existence, in the formation of the heavens and the earth, and which a man of sense cannot forbear attending to, who is *out of* the noise of human affairs. *Addison.*

16. Past; without; noting something worn out or exhausted.

I am *out of* breath:
—How art thou *out of* breath, when thou hast breath?
To say to me that thou art *out of* breath? *Shakesp.*

Out of hope to do any good, he directed his course to Corone. *Knolles.*

He found himself left far behind,
Both *out of* heart and *out of* wind. *Hudibras.*

I published some fables, which are *out of* print. *Arbuth.*

17. By means of.

Out of that will I cause those of Cyprus to mutiny. *Shak.*

18. In consequence of; noting the motive or reason.

She is persuaded I will marry her, *out of* her own love and flattery, not *out of* my promise. *Shakesp. Othello.*

The pope, *out of* the care of an universal father, had in the conclave divers consultations about an holy war against the Turk. *Bacon's Hen.* VII.

Not *out of* cunning, but a train
Of atoms justling in his brain,
As learn'd philosophers give out. *Hudibras, p.* ii.

Cromwell accused the earl of Manchester, of having betrayed the parliament *out of* cowardice. *Clarendon.*

Those that have recourse to a new creation of waters, are such as do it *out of* laziness and ignorance, or such as do it *out of* necessity. *Burnet's Theory of the Earth.*

Distinguish betwixt those that take state upon them, purely *out of* pride and humour, and those that do the same in compliance with the necessity of their affairs. *L'Estrange.*

Make them conformable to laws, not only for wrath and *out of* fear of the magistrate's power, which is but a weak principle of obedience; but *out of* conscience, which is a firm and lasting principle. *Tillotson.*

What they do not grant *out of* the generosity of their nature, they may grant *out of* mere impatience. *Smallridge.*

Our successes have been the consequences of a necessary war; in which we engaged, not *out of* ambition, but for the defence of all that was dear to us. *Atterbury.*

19. *Out of hand*; immediately; as that is easily used which is ready in the hand.

He bade to open wide his brazen gate,
Which long time had been shut, and *out of hand*,
Proclaimed joy and peace through all his state. *Fa. Queen.*

No more ado,
But gather we our forces *out of hand*,
And set upon our boasting enemy. *Shakesp.*

To OUT. *v. a.* To expel; to deprive.

The members of both houses who withdrew, were counted deserters, and *outed* of their places in parliament. *K. Charles.*

So many of their orders, as were *outed* from their fat possessions, would endeavour a re-entrance against those whom they account hereticks. *Dryden.*

OUT, in composition, generally signifies something beyond or more than another.

Out-fawn as much, and *out*-comply,
And seem as scrupulously just,
To bait the hooks for greater trust. *Hud. p.* ii. *can.* 3.

To OUTA'CT. *v. a.* [*out* and *act.*] To do beyond.

He has made me heir to treasures,
Would make me *out-act* a real widow's whining. *Otway.*

To OUTBA'LANCE. *v. a.* [*out* and *balance.*] To over-weigh; to preponderate.

Let dull Ajax bear away my right,
When all his days *outbalance* this one night. *Dryden.*

To OUTBA'R. *v. a.* [*out* and *bar.*] To shut out by fortification.

These to *outbar* with painful pionings,
From sea to sea he heap'd a mighty mound. *Fa. Queen.*

To OUTBI'D. *v. a.* [*out* and *bid.*] To over-power by bidding a higher price.

If in thy heart
New love created be by other men,
Which have their stocks entire, and can in tears,
In sighs, in oaths, in letters *outbid* me,
This new love may beget new fears. *Donne.*

For Indian spices, for Peruvian gold,
Prevent the greedy, and *outbid* the bold. *Pope.*

OUTBI'DDER. *n. s.* [*out* and *bid.*] One that out-bids.

OUTBLO'WED. *adj.* [*out* and *blow.*] Inflated; swollen with wind.

At their roots grew floating palaces,
Whose *outblow'd* bellies cut the yielding seas. *Dryden.*

OU'TBORN. *adj.* [*out* and *born.*] Foreign; not native.

OU'TBOUND. *adj.* [*out* and *bound.*] Destinated to a distant voyage.

Triumphant flames upon the water float,
And *outbound* ships at home their voyage end. *Dryden.*

To OUTBRA'VE. *v. a.* [*out* and *brave.*] To bear down and disgrace by more daring, insolent, or splendid appearance.

We see the danger, and by fits take up some faint resolution to *outbrave* and break through it. *L'Estrange.*

I would out-stare the sternest eyes that look,
Outbrave the heart most daring on the earth,
To win thee, lady. *Shakespeare.*

Here Sodom's tow'rs raise their proud tops on high,
The tow'rs, as well as men, *out-brave* the sky. *Cowley.*

To OUTBRA'ZEN. *v. a.* [*out* and *brazen.*] To bear down with impudence.

OU'TBREAK. *n. s.* [*out* and *break.*] That which breaks forth; eruption.

Breathe his faults so quaintly,
That they may seem the taints of liberty,
The flash and *outbreak* of a fiery mind. *Shakesp.*

To OUTREA'THE. *v. a.* [*out* and *breath.*]

1. To weary by having better breath.

Mine eyes saw him
Rendering faint quittance, wearied and *outbreath'd*,
To Henry Monmouth. *Shakespeare.*

2. To expire.

That sign of last *outbreathed* life did seem. *Spenser.*

OUTCA'ST. *part.* [*out* and *cast.* It may be observed, that both the participle and the noun are indifferently accented on either syllable. It seems most analogous to accent the participle on the last, and the noun on the first.]

1. Thrown into the air as refuse, as unworthy of notice.

Abandon soon, I read, the caitive spoil
Of that same *outcast* carcass. *Fairy Queen, b.* ii. *c.* 8.

2. Banished; expelled.

Behold, instead
Of us *outcast* exil'd, his new delight
Mankind created. *Milton's Paradise Lost, b.* iv.

OUTCA'ST. *n. s.* Exile; one rejected; one expelled.

Let's be no stoicks, nor no stocks,
Or so devote to Aristotle,
As Ovid, be an *outcast* quite abjur'd. *Shakesp.*

O blood-bespotted Neapolitan,
Outcast of Naples, England's bloody scourge! *Shakesp.*

For me, *outcast* of human race,
Love's anger only waits, and dire disgrace. *Prior.*

He dies sad *outcast* of each church and state! *Pope.*

To OUTCRA'FT. *v. a.* [*out* and *craft.*] To excel in cunning.

Italy hath *outcrafted* him,
And he's at some hard point. *Shakesp. Cymbeline.*

O'UTCRY. *n. s.* [*out* and *cry.*]

1. Cry of vehemence; cry of distress; clamour.

These *outcries* the magistrates there shun, since they are readily hearkened unto here. *Spenser on Ireland.*

So strange thy *outcry*, and thy words so strange
Thou interposest, that my sudden hand
Prevented, spares. *Milt. Par. Lost, b.* ii.

I make my way
Where noises, tumults, *outcries*, and alarms
I heard. *Denham.*

2. Clamour of detestation.

There is not any one vice, incident to the mind of man, against which the world has raised such a loud and universal *outcry*, as against ingratitude. *South's Serm.*

3. A publick sale; an auction. *Ainſ.*

OUTDA'RE. *v. a.* [*out* and *dare.*] To venture beyond.

Myſelf, my brother, and his ſon,
That brought you home, and boldly did *outdare*
The dangers of the time. *Shakeſpeare.*

To OUTDA'TE. *v. a.* [*out* and *date.*] To antiquate.

Works and deeds of the law, in thoſe places, ſignify legal obedience, or circumciſion, and the like judaical *outdated* ceremonies; faith, the evangelical grace of giving up the whole heart to Chriſt, without any ſuch judaical obſervances. *Hamm.*

To OUTDO'. *v. a.* [*out* and *do.*] To excel; to ſurpaſs; to perform beyond another.

He hath in this action *outdone* his former deeds doubly. *Shak.*

What brave commander is not proud to ſee
Thy brave Melantius in his gallantry?
Our greateſt ladies love to ſee their ſcorn
Outdone by thine, in what themſelves have worn. *Waller.*

Heav'nly love ſhall *outdo* helliſh hate,
Giving to death, and dying to redeem,
So dearly to redeem what helliſh hate
So eaſily deſtroy'd. *Milton.*

Here let theſe who boaſt in mortal things,
Learn how their greateſt monuments of fame,
And ſtrength, and art, are eaſily *outdone*
By ſpirits reprobate. *Milton.*

An impoſtor *outdoes* the original. *L'Eſtrange.*

Now all the gods reward and bleſs my ſon;
Thou haſt this day thy father's youth *outdone.* *Dryden.*

I muſt confeſs the encounter of that day
Warm'd me indeed, but quite another way;
Not with the fire of youth, but generous rage,
To ſee the glories of my youthful age
So far *outdone.* *Dryden.*

The boy's mother deſpiſed for not having read a ſyſtem of logick, *outdoes* him in it. *Locke.*

I grieve to be *outdone* by Gay,
In my own humourous biting way. *Swift.*

To OUTDWE'L. *v. a.* [*out* and *dwell.*] To ſtay beyond.

He *outdwels* his hour,
For lovers ever run before the clock. *Shakeſp.*

OU'TER. *adj.* [from *out.*] That which is without; oppoſed to *inner.*

The kidney is a conglomerated gland only in the *outer* part: for the inner part, whereof the papillæ are compoſed, is muſcular. *Grew's Coſmol. b.* i. *c.* 5.

OU'TERLY. *adv.* [from *outer.*] Towards the outſide.

In the lower jaw, two tuſks like thoſe of a boar, ſtanding *outerly*, an inch behind the cutters. *Grew's Muſæum.*

OU'TERMOST. *adj.* [ſuperlative, from *outer.*] Remoteſt from the midſt.

Try if three bells were made one within another, and air betwixt each; and the *outermoſt* bell were chimed with a hammer, how the ſound would differ from a ſingle bell. *Bacon.*

The *outermoſt* corpuſcles of a white body, have their various little ſurfaces of a ſpecular nature. *Boyle.*

To OUTFA'CE. *v. a.* [*out* and *face.*]

1. To brave; to bear down by ſhew of magnanimity; to bear down with impudence.

We ſhall have old ſwearing
That they did give the rings away to men;
But we'll *outface* them and out-ſwear them too. *Shakeſp.*

Doſt thou come hither
To *outface* me with leaping in her grave?
Be buried quick with her, and ſo will I. *Shakeſp.*

Be fire with fire;
Threaten the threatner; and *outface* the brow
Of bragging horror. *Shakeſp. King John.*

They bewrayed ſome knowledge of their perſons, but were *outfaced.* *Wotton.*

2. To ſtare down.

We behold the ſun and enjoy his light, as long as we look towards it circumſpectly: we warm ourſelves ſafely while we ſtand near the fire; but if we ſeek to *outface* the one, to enter into the other, we forthwith become blind or burnt. *Ral.*

To OUTFA'WN. *v. a.* [*out* and *fawn.*] To excel in fawning.

In affairs of leſs import,
That neither do us good nor hurt,
And they receive as little by,
Outfawn as much and out-comply. *Hudibras.*

To OUTFLY'. *v. a.* [*out* and *fly.*] To leave behind in flight.

His evaſion wing'd thus ſwift with ſcorn,
Cannot *outfly* our apprehenſions. *Shakeſpeare.*

Horoſcop's great ſoul,
Rais'd on the pinions of the bounding wind,
Outflew the rack, and left the hours behind. *Garth.*

OUTFO'RM. *n. ſ.* [*out* and *form.*] External appearance.

Cupid, who took vain delight
In meer *outforms*, until he loſt his ſight,
Hath chang'd his ſoul, and made his object you. *B. Johnſ.*

To OUTFRO'WN. *v. a.* [*out* and *frown.*] To frown down; to over-bear by frowns.

For thee, oppreſſed king, am I caſt down,
Myſelf could elſe *outfrown* falſe fortune's frown. *Shakeſ.*

OU'TGATE. *n. ſ.* [*out* and *gate.*] Outlet; paſſage outwards.

Thoſe places are ſo fit for trade, having moſt convenient *out-gates* by divers ways to the ſea, and in-gates to the richeſt parts of the land, that they would ſoon be enriched. *Spenſ.*

To OUTGI'VE. *v. a.* [*out* and *give.*] To ſurpaſs in giving.

The bounteous play'r *outgave* the pinching lord. *Dryden.*

To OUTGO. *v. a.* pret. *outwent*; part. *outgone.* [*out* and *go.*]

1. To ſurpaſs; to excel.

For frank, well ordered and continual hoſpitality, he *outwent* all ſhew of competence. *Carew.*

While you practiſed the rudiments of war, you *out-went* all other captains; and have ſince found none but yourſelf alone to ſurpaſs. *Dryden.*

Where they apply themſelves, none of their neighbours *out-go* them. *Locke on Education.*

2. To go beyond; to leave behind in going.

Many ran afoot thither out of all cities, and *out-went* them, and came unto him. *Mark* vi. 33.

3. To circumvent; to overreach.

Molleſſon
Thought us to have *out-gone*
With a quaint invention. *Denham.*

To OUTGRO'W. *v. a.* [*out* and *grow.*] To ſurpaſs in growth; to grow too great or too old for any thing.

Much their work *outgrew*,
The hands diſpatch of two, gard'ning ſo wide. *Milton.*

When ſome virtue much *outgrows* the reſt,
It ſhoots too faſt and high. *Dryden.*

This eſſay wears a dreſs that poſſibly is not ſo ſuitable to the graver geniuſes, who have *outgrown* all gaieties of ſtile and youthful reliſhes. *Glanv. Scepſ. Pref.*

The lawyer, the tradeſman, the mechanic, have found ſo many arts to deceive, that they far *outgrow* the common prudence of mankind. *Swift.*

OU'TGUARD *n. ſ.* [*out* and *guard.*] One poſted at a diſtance from the main body, as a defence.

As ſoon as any foreign object preſſes upon the ſenſe, thoſe ſpirits which are poſted upon the *out-guards*, immediately ſcowre off to the brain. *South.*

You beat the *outguards* of my maſter's hoſt. *Dryden.*

Theſe *out-guards* of the mind are ſent abroad,
And ſtill patrolling beat the neighb'ring road,
Or to the parts remote obedient fly
Keep poſts advanc'd, and on the frontier lye. *Blackmore.*

OUTJE'ST. *v. a.* [*out* and *jeſt.*] To over-power by jeſting.

The fool labours to *outjeſt*
His heart ſtruck injuries. *Shakeſp. K. Lear.*

To OUTKNA'VE. *v. a.* [*out* and *knave.*] To ſurpaſs in knavery.

The world calls it out-witting a man, when he's only *outknaved.* *L'Eſtrange.*

OUTLA'NDISH. *adj.* [*out* and *land.*] Not native; foreign.

Yourſelf tranſplant
A while from hence: perchance *outlandiſh* ground
Bears no more wit than ours; but yet more ſcant
Are thoſe diverſions there which here abound. *Donne.*

Tedious waſte of time to ſit and hear
So many hollow compliments and lies,
Outlandiſh flatteries. *Milt. Par. Reg. b.* iv.

Upon the approach of the king's troops under General Wills, who was uſed to the *outlandiſh* way of making war, we put in practice paſſive obedience. *Addiſon.*

To OUTLA'ST. *v. a.* [*out* and *laſt.*] To ſurpaſs in duration.

Good houſewives, to make their candles burn the longer, lay them in bran, which makes them harder; inſomuch as they will *out-laſt* other candles of the ſame ſtuff, half in half. *Bacon's Nat. Hiſt.* N°. 371.

Summer's chief honour, if thou hadſt *outlaſted*,
Bleak winter's force that made thy bloſſoms dry. *Milt.*

The preſent age hath attempted perpetual motions, whoſe revolutions might *outlaſt* the exemplary mobility, and out-meaſure time itſelf. *Brown's V. Err.*

What may be hop'd,
When not from Helicon's imagin'd ſpring,
But ſacred writ, we borrow what we ſing?
This with the fabrick of the world begun,
Elder than light, and ſhall *outlaſt* the ſun. *Waller.*

OUTLAW. *n. ſ.* [utlaga, Saxon.] One excluded from the benefit of the law. A blunderer; a robber; a bandit.

An *outlaw* in a caſtle keeps. *Shakeſp. Hen.* VI.

Gathering unto him all the ſcatterlings and *outlaws* out of the woods and mountains, he marched forth into the Engliſh pale. *Spenſer on Ireland.*

As long as they were out of the protection of the law; ſo as every Engliſhman might kill them, how ſhould they be other than *outlaws* and enemies to the crown of England? *Davies on Ireland.*

You may as well ſpread out the unſun'd heaps
Of miſers treaſure by an *outlaw's* den,

And tell me it is safe, as bid me hope
Danger will let a helpless maiden pass. *Milton.*

A drunkard is *outlawed* from all worthy and creditable converse: men abhor, loath, and despise him. *South.*

To Ou'tlaw. *v. a.* To deprive of the benefits and protection of the law.

I had a son
Now *outlaw'd* from my blood; he sought my life. *Shak.*
He that is drunken,
Is *outlaw'd* by himself: all kind of ill
Did with his liquor slide into his veins. *Herbert.*

Like as there are particular persons *outlawed* and proscribed by civil laws, so are there nations that are *outlawed* and proscribed by the law of nature and nations. *Bacon.*

All those spiritual aids are withdrawn, which should assist him to good, or fortify him against ill; and like an *out-lawed* person he is exposed to all that will assault him. *Decay of Piety.*

Ou'tlawry. [from *outlaw.*] A decree by which any man is cut off from the community, and deprived of the protection of the law.

By proscription and bills of *outlawry*,
Octavius, Antony, and Lepidus,
Have put to death an hundred senators. *Shakesp.*

Divers were returned knights and burgesses for the parliament; many of which had been by Richard III. attainted by *outlawries.* *Bacon's Henry* VII.

To Outlea'p. *v. a.* [*out* and *leap.*] To pass by leaping; to start beyond.

Outlea'p. *n. s.* [from the verb.] Sally; flight; escape.

Since youth must have some liberty, some *outleaps*, they might be under the eye of a father, and then no very great harm can come of it. *Locke on Education.*

Ou'tlet. *n. s.* [*out* and *let.*] Passage outwards; discharge outwards; egress; passage of egress.

Colonies and foreign plantations, are very necessary, as *outlets* to a populous nation. *Bacon.*

The enemy was deprived of that useful *out-let.* *Clarend.*

So 'scapes th' insulting fire his narrow jail,
And makes small *outlets* into open air. *Dryden.*

Have a care that these members be neither the inlets nor *outlets* of any vices; that they neither give admission to the temptation, nor be expressive of the conception of them. *Ray.*

Ou'tline. *n. s.* [*out* and *line.*] Contour; line by which any figure is defined; extremity.

Painters, by their *outlines*, colours, lights, and shadows, represent the same in their pictures. *Dryden.*

To Outli've. *v. a.* [*out* and *live.*] To live beyond; to survive.

Will these mossed trees,
That have *outliv'd* the eagle, page thy keels,
And skip when thou point'st out. *Shakesp.*
Die two months ago, and not forgotten,
Yet then there is hopes a great man's memory
May *outlive* his life half a year. *Shakesp. Hamlet.*
He that *outlives* this day, and comes safe home,
Will stand a tiptoe when this day is nam'd. *Shakesp.*

His courage was so signal that day, that too much could not be expected from it, if he had *outlived* it. *Clarend.*

Thou must *outlive*
Thy youth, thy strength, thy beauty, which will change
To wither'd, weak, and gray. *Milt. Par. Lost.*
Time, which made them their fame *outlive*,
To Cowley scarce did ripeness give. *Denham.*

The soldier grows less apprehensive, by computing upon the disproportion of those that *outlive* a battle, to those that fall in it. *L'Estrange.*

Since we have lost
Freedom, wealth, honour, which we value most,
I wish they would our lives a period give;
They live too long who happiness *outlive.* *Dryden.*

It is of great consequence where noble families are gone to decay; because their titles *outlive* their estates. *Swift.*

Pray *outlive* me, and then die as soon as you please. *Swift.*

Outli'ver. *n. s.* [*out* and *live.*] A surviver.

To Outloo'k. *v. a.* [*out* and *look.*] To face down; to browbeat.

I cull'd these fiery spirits from the world,
To *outlook* conquest, and to win renown,
Ev'n in the jaws of danger and of death. *Shakesp.*

To Outlu'stre. *v. a.* [*out* and *lustre.*] To excel in brightness.

She went before others I have seen, as that diamond of yours *outlustres* many I have beheld. *Shakesp. Cymbeline.*

Ou'tlying. part. *adj.* [*out* and *lie.*] Not in the common course of order. Removed from something else.

The last survey I proposed of the four *out-lying* empires, was that of the Arabians. *Temple.*

We have taken all the *out-lying* parts of the Spanish monarchy, and made impressions upon the very heart of it. *Addis.*

To Outmea'sure. *v. a.* [*out* and *measure.*] To exceed in measure.

The present age hath attempted perpetual motions and engines, and those revolutions might out-last the exemplary mobility, and *out-measure* time itself. *Brown's V. Err.*

To Outnu'mber. *v. a.* [*out* and *number.*] To exceed in number.

The ladies came in so great a body to the opera, that they *outnumbered* the enemy. *Addison's Spectator.*

To Outma'rch. *v. a.* [*out* and *march.*] To leave behind in the march.

The horse *out-marched* the foot, which, by reason of the heat, was not able to use great expedition. *Clarend.*

Ou'tmost. *adj.* [*out* and *most.*] Remotest from the middle.

Chaos retir'd,
As from her *outmost* works a broken foe. *Milton.*

If any man suppose that it is not reflected by the air, but by the *outmost* superficial parts of the glass, there is still the same difficulty. *Newt. Opt.*

The generality of men are readier to fetch a reason from the immense distance of the starry heavens, and the *outmost* walls of the world. *Bentley's Sermons.*

Outpa'rish. *n. s.* [*out* and *parish.*] Parish not lying within the walls.

In the greater *outparishes* many of the poorer parishioners, through neglect, do perish for want of some heedful eye to overlook them. *Graunt's Mort.*

Outpa'rt. *n. s.* [*out* and *part.*] Part remote from the center or main body.

He is appointed to supply the bishop's jurisdiction and other judicial offices in the *outparts* of his diocese. *Ayliffe.*

To Outpa'ce. *v. a.* [*out* and *pace.*] To outgo; to leave behind.

Arion's speed
Could not *outpace* thee; or the horse Laomedon did breed. *Chapman's Iliads.*

To Outpou'r. *v. a.* [*out* and *power.*] To emit; to send forth in a strain.

He looked and saw what number, numberless
The city gates *outpour'd*; light arm'd troops
In coats of mail and military pride. *Milt. Par. Reg.*

To Outpri'ze. *v. a.* [*out* and *prize.*] To exceed in the value set upon it.

Either your unparagon'd mistress is dead, or
She's *outprized* by a trifle. *Shakesp. Cymbeline.*

To Ou'trage. *v. a.* [*outrager*, Fr.] To injure violently or contumeliously; to insult roughly and tumultuously; to endangering life.

Ah heavens! that do this hideous act behold,
And heavenly virgin thus *outraged* see;
How can the vengeance just so long withhold! *Fa. Queen.*

The news put divers young bloods into such a fury, as the English embassadors were not without peril to be *outraged.* *Bacon's Henry* VII.

Base and insolent minds *outrage* men, when they have hopes of doing it without a return. *Atterbury.*

This interview *outrages* all decency; she forgets her modesty, and betrays her virtue, by giving too long an audience. *Pope's Odyssey, b.* vi.

To Ou'trage. *v. n.* To commit exorbitancies.

Three or four great ones in court will *outrage* in apparel, huge hose, monstrous hats, and garish colours. *Ascham.*

Ou'trage. *n. s.* [*outrage*, Fr.]

1. Open violence; tumultuous mischief.

He wrought great *outrages*, wasting all the country where he went. *Spenser on Ireland.*

He doth himself in secret shrowd,
To fly the vengeance for his *outrage* due. *Fa. Queen.*
In that beastly fury
He has been known to commit *outrage*,
And cherish factions. *Shakesp. Timon of Athens.*
Uncharitably with me have you dealt,
And shamefully my hopes by you are butcher'd;
My charity is *outrage.* *Shakesp. Rich.* III.

2. This word seems to be used by *Philips* for mere commotion, without any ill import, contrary to the universal use of writers.

See with what *outrage* from the frosty north,
The early valiant Swede draws forth his wings
In battailous array. *Philips.*

OUTRA'GIOUS. *adj.* [*outrageux*, French. It should, I think, be written *outrageous*; but the custom seems otherwise.]

1. Violent; furious; raging; exorbitant; tumultuous; turbulent.

Under him they committed divers the most *outragious* villanies, that a base multitude can imagine. *Sidney.*

As she went her tongue did walk,
In foul reproach and terms of vile despight,
Provoking him by her *outragious* talk,
To heap more vengeance on that wretched wight. *F. Qu.*
They view'd the vast immeasurable abyss,
Outragious as a sea, dark, wasteful, wild. *Milton.*
When he knew his rival freed and gone,
He swells with wrath; he makes *outragious* moan:
He frets, he fumes, he stares, he stamps the ground;
The hollow tow'r with clamours rings around. *Dryden.*

2. Excessive;

2. Excessive; passing reason or decency.

My characters of Antony and Cleopatra, though they are favourable to them, have nothing of *outragious* panegyrick. *Dryden's Dufresnoy.*

3. Enormous; atrocious.

Think not, although in writing I prefer'd
The manner of thy vile *outragious* crimes,
That therefore I have forg'd. *Shakesp. Hen.* VI.

OUTRA'GIOUSLY. *adv.* [from *outrageous.*] Violently; tumultuously; furiously.

That people will have colour of employment given them, by which they will poll and spoil so *outragiously*, as the very enemy cannot do worse. *Spenser on Ireland.*

Let lust burn never so *outragiously* for the present, yet age will in time chill those heats. *South's Sermons.*

OUTRA'GIOUSNESS. *n. s.* [from *outragious.*] With fury; with violence.

Virgil, more discreet than Homer, has contented himself with the partiality of his deities, without bringing them to the *outragiousness* of blows. *Dryden.*

To OUTREA'CH. *v. a.* [*out* and *reach.*] To go beyond.

This usage is derived from so many descents of ages, that the cause and author *outreach* remembrance. *Carew.*

Our forefathers could never dream so high a crime as parricide, whereas this *outreaches* that fact, and exceeds the regular distinctions of murder. *Brown.*

To OUTRI'DE. *v. a.* [*out* and *ride.*] To pass by riding.

This advantage age from youth hath won,
As not to be *outridden*, though out-run. *Dryden.*

OUTRI'GHT. *adv.* [*out* and *right.*]

1. Immediately; without delay.

When these wretches had the rope about their necks, the first was to be pardoned, the last hanged *outright*. *J. Bull.*

2. Completely.

By degrees accomplish'd in the beast,
He neigh'd *outright*, and all the steed exprest. *Addison.*

To OUTROA'R. *v. a.* [*out* and *roar.*] To exceed in roaring.

O that I were
Upon the hill of Basan, to *outroar*
The horned herd! *Shakesp. Ant. and Cleop.*

OUTRO'DE. *n. s.* [*out* and *rode.*] Excursion.

He set horsemen and footmen, to the end that issuing out, they might make *outrodes* upon the ways of Judea. 1 *Mac.* xv. 41.

To OUTROO'T. *v. a.* [*out* and *root.*] To extirpate; to eradicate.

Pernicious discord seems
Outrooted from our more than iron age;
Since none, not ev'n our kings, approach their temples
With any mark of war's destructive rage,
But sacrifice unarm'd. *Rowe's Amb. Step-Mother.*

To OUTRU'N. *v. a.* [*out* and *run.*]

1. To leave behind in running.

By giving th' house of Lancaster leave to breathe,
It will *outrun* you, father, in the end. *Shakesp.*

The expedition of my violent love
Outruns the pauser reason. *Shakesp. Macbeth.*

We may *outrun*,
By violent swiftness, that which we run at. *Shakesp.*

When things are come to the execution, there is no secrecy comparable to celerity, like the motion of a bullet in the air, which flieth so swift as it *outruns* the eye. *Bacon.*

This advantage age from youth hath won,
As not to be out-riden, though *outrun*. *Dryden.*

2. To exceed.

We *outrun* the present income, as not doubting to reimburse ourselves out of the profits of some future project. *Addis.*

To OUTSAI'L. *v. a.* [*out* and *sail.*] To leave behind in sailing.

The word signifies a ship that *outsails* other ships. *Broome.*

To OUTSCO'RN. *v. a.* [*out* and *scorn.*] To bear down or confront by contempt; to despise; not to mind.

He strives in his little world of man t' *outscorn*
The to and fro conflicting wind and rain. *Shakesp.*

To OUTSE'L. *v. a.* [*out* and *sell.*]

1. To exceed in the price for which a thing is sold; to sell at a higher rate than another.

It would soon improve to such a height, as to *outsel* our neighbours, and thereby advance the proportion of our exported commodities. *Temple.*

2. To gain an higher price.

Her pretty action did *outsel* her gift,
And yet enrich'd it too. *Shakesp. Cymbeline.*

To OUTSHI'NE. *v. a.* [*out* and *shine.*]

1. To emit lustre.

Witness my son, now in the shade of death;
Whose bright *outshining* beams thy cloudy wrath
Hath in eternal darkness folded up. *Shakesp. R.* III.

2. To excel in lustre.

By Shakespeare's, Johnson's, Fletcher's lines,
Our stage's lustre Rome's *outshines*. *Denham.*

Beauty and greatness are so eminently joined in your royal highness, that it were not easy for any but a poet to determine which of them *outshines* the other. *Dryden.*

Homer does not only *outshine* all other poets in the variety, but also in the novelty of his characters. *Addison.*

We should see such as would *outshine* the rebellious part of their fellow-subjects, as much in their gallantry as in their cause. *Addison's Freeholder,* Nº. 24.

Such accounts are a tribute due to the memory of those only, who have *outshone* the rest of the world by their rank as well as their virtues. *Atterbury's Sermons.*

Happy you!
Whose charms as far all other nymphs *outshine*,
As others gardens are excell'd by thine. *Pope.*

To OUTSHOO'T. *v. a.* [*out* and *shoot.*]

1. To exceed in shooting.

The forward youth
Will learn to *outshoot* you in your proper bow. *Dryden.*

2. To shoot beyond.

Men are resolved never to *outshoot* their forefathers mark; but write one after another, and so the dance goes round in a circle. *Norris.*

OUTSI'DE. *n. s.* [*out* and *side.*]

1. Superficies; surface; external part.

What pity that so exquisite an *outside* of a head should not have one grain of sense in it. *L'Estrange.*

The leathern *outside*, boist'rous as it was,
Gave way and bent. *Dryden.*

2. Extreme part; part remote from the middle.

Hold an arrow in a flame for the space of ten pulses, and when it cometh forth, those parts which were on the *outsides* of the flame are blacked and turned into a coal. *Bacon.*

3. Superficial appearance.

You shall find his vanities forespent
Were but the *outside* of the Roman Brutus,
Covering discretion with a coat of folly. *Shakespeare.*

The ornaments of conversation, and the *outside* of fashionable manners, will come in their due time. *Locke.*

Created beings see nothing but our *outside*, and can therefore only frame a judgment of us from our exterior actions. *Addison's Spectator,* Nº. 257.

4. The utmost. A barbarous use.

Two hundred load upon an acre, they reckon the *outside* of what is to be laid. *Mortimer's Husbandry.*

5. Person; external man.

Fortune forbid, my *outside* have not charm'd her! *Shak.*

Your *outside* promiseth as much as can be expected from a gentleman. *Bacon.*

What admir'st thou, what transports thee so?
An *outside?* fair, no doubt, and worthy well
Thy cherishing and thy love. *Milton's Par. Lost, b.* viii.

6. Outer side; part not inclosed.

I threw open the door of my chamber, and found my family standing on the *outside*. *Spect.* Nº. 577

To OUTSI'T. *v. a.* [*out* and *sit.*] To sit beyond the time of any thing.

He that prolongs his meals and sacrifices his time, as well as his other conveniences, to his luxury, how quickly does he *outsit* his pleasure? *South.*

To OUTSLEE'P. *v. a.* [*out* and *sleep.*] To sleep beyond.

Lovers, to bed; 'tis almost fairy time:
I fear we shall *outsleep* the coming morn. *Shakesp.*

To OUTSPEA'K. *v. a.* [*out* and *speak.*] To speak something beyond; to exceed.

Rich stuffs and ornaments of houshold
I find at such proud rate, that it *outspeaks*
Possession of a subject. *Shakesp. Hen.* VIII.

To OUTSPO'RT. *v. a.* [*out* and *sport.*] To sport beyond.

Let's teach ourselves that honourable stop,
Not to *outsport* discretion. *Shakesp. Othello.*

To OUTSPREA'D. *v. a.* [*out* and *spread.*] To extend; to diffuse.

With sails *outspread* we fly. *Pope.*

To OUTSTA'ND. *v. a.* [*out* and *stand.*]

1. To support; to resist.

Each could demolish the other's work with ease enough, but not a man of them tolerably defend his own; which was sure never to *outstand* the first attack that was made. *Woodw.*

2. To stand beyond the proper time.

I have *outstood* my time, which is material
To th' tender of our present. *Shakesp. Cymbeline.*

To OUTSTA'ND. *v. n.* To protuberate from the main body.

To OUTSTA'RE. *v. a.* [*out* and *stare.*] To face down; to brow-beat; to outface with effrontery.

I would *outstare* the sternest eyes that look,
To win thee, lady. *Shakesp. Merch. of Venice.*

These curtain'd windows, this self-prison'd eye,
Outstares the lids of large-lookt tyranny. *Crashaw.*

OUTSTREE'T. *n. s.* [*out* and *street.*] Street in the extremities of a town.

To OUTSTRE'TCH. *v. a.* [*out* and *stretch.*] To extend; to spread out.

Make him stand upon the mole-hill,
That caught at mountains with *out-stretched* arms. *Shakesp.*

Out-ſtretch'd he lay, on the cold ground, and oft
Curs'd his creation. *Milton's Par. Loſt, b.* x.
A mountain, at whoſe verdant feet
A ſpacious plain, *out-ſtretch'd* in circuit wide
Lay pleaſant. *Milt. Par. Reg. b.* iii.
Does Theſeus burn?
And muſt not ſhe with *out-ſtretch'd* arms receive him?
And with an equal ardour meet his vows? *Smith.*

To OU'TSTRIP. *v. a.* [This word *Skinner* derives from *out* and *ſpritzen*, to *ſpout*, German. I know not whether it might not have been originally *out-trip*, the *ſ* being afterward inſerted.] To outgo; to leave behind.

If thou wilt *out-ſtrip* death, go croſs the ſeas,
And live with Richmond from the reach of hell. *Shak.*
Do not ſmile at me, that I boaſt her off;
For thou ſhalt find, ſhe will *out-ſtrip* all praiſe,
And make it halt behind her. *Shakeſp. Tempeſt.*
Thou both their graces in thyſelf haſt more
Out-ſtript, than they did all that went before. *B. Johnſon.*
My ſoul, more earneſtly releas'd,
Will *out-ſtrip* hers; as bullets flown before
A latter bullet may o'ertake, the powder being more. *Donne.*

A fox may be out-witted, and a hare *out-ſtript*. *L'Eſtran.*

He got the ſtart of them in point of obedience, and thereby *out-ſtript* them at length in point of knowledge. *South.*

With ſuch array Harpalice beſtrode
Her Thracian courſer, and *out-ſtrip'd* the rapid flood. *Dryd.*

To OU'T-SWEETEN. *v. a.* [*out* and *ſweeten.*] To excel in ſweetneſs.

The leaf of eglantine, which not to ſlander,
Out-ſweeten'd not thy breath. *Shakeſp. Cymbeline.*

To OUTSWEA'R. *v. a.* [*out* and *ſwear.*] To over-power by ſwearing.

We ſhall have old ſwearing,
But we'll out-face them, and *out-ſwear* them too. *Shakeſp.*

To OUT-TO'NGUE. *v. a.* [*out* and *tongue.*] To bear down by noiſe.

Let him do his ſpite:
My ſervices which I have done the ſignory,
Shall *out-tongue* his complaints. *Shakeſp. Othello.*

To OUTTA'LK. *v. a.* [*out* and *talk.*] To over-power by talk.

This gentleman will *out-talk* us all. *Shakeſpeare.*

To OUT-VA'LUE. *v. a.* [*out* and *value.*] To tranſcend in price.

He gives us in this life an earneſt of expected joys, that *out-values* and tranſcends all thoſe momentary pleaſures it requires us to forſake. *Boyle.*

To OUTVE'NOM. *v. a.* [*out* and *venom.*] To exceed in poiſon.

'Tis ſlander;
Whoſe edge is ſharper than the ſword, whoſe tongue
Out-venoms all the worms of Nile. *Shakeſp. Cymbeline.*

To OUTVI'E. *v. a.* [*out* and *vie.*] To exceed; to ſurpaſs.

For folded flocks, on fruitful plains,
Fair Britain all the world *outvies*. *Dryden.*

The farmers uſed to make gratias to the Engliſh merchants, endeavouring ſometimes to *out-vie* one another in ſuch indulgencies. *Addiſon.*

One of theſe petty ſovereigns will be ſtill endeavouring to equal the pomp of greater princes, as well as to *out-vie* thoſe of his own rank. *Addiſon.*

To OUT-VI'LLAIN. *v. a.* [*out* and *villain.*] To exceed in villainy.

He hath *out-villain'd* villainy ſo far, that the rarity redeems him. *Shakeſp. All's well that ends well.*

To OUTVOI'CE. *v. a.* [*out* and *voice.*] To out-roar; to exceed in clamour.

The Engliſh beach
Pales in the flood with men, with wives and boys,
Whoſe ſhouts and claps *out-voice* the deep-mouth'd ſea. *Sha.*

To OUTVO'TE. *v. a.* [*out* and *vote.*] To conquer by plurality of ſuffrages.

They were *out-voted* by other ſects of philoſophers, neither for fame, nor number leſs than themſelves. *South.*

To OUTWA'LK. [*out* and *walk.*] To leave one in walking.

OUTWA'LL. *n. ſ.* [*out* and *wall.*]
1. Outward part of a building.
2. Superficial appearance.

For confirmation that I am much more
Than my *out-wall*, open this purſe and take
What it contains. *Shakeſp. K. Lear.*

OU'TWARD. *adj.* [uτpeaɲδ, Saxon.]
1. External: oppoſed to inward.

If theſe ſhews be not *outward*, which of you
But is four Volſcians? *Shakeſp. Coriolanus.*
Oh what may man within him hide,
Though angel on the *outward* ſide! *Shakeſp.*
He took a low'ring leave; but who can tell
What *outward* hate might inward love conceal? *Dryden.*

2. Extrinſick; adventitious.

Princes have their titles for their glories,
An *outward* honour, for an inward toil. *Shakeſp.*
Part in peace, and having mourn'd your ſin
For *outward* Eden loſt, find paradiſe within. *Dryden.*

3. Foreign, not inteſtine.

It was intended to raiſe an *outward* war to join with ſome ſedition within doors. *Hayward.*

4. Tending to the out-parts.

The fire will force its *outward* way,
Or, in the priſon pent, conſume the prey. *Dryden.*

5. [In theology.] Carnal; corporeal; not ſpiritual.

When the ſoul being inwardly moved to lift itſelf up by prayer, the *outward* man is ſurprized in ſome other poſture; God will rather look to the inward motions of the mind, than to the outward form of the body. *Duppa.*

OU'TWARD. *n. ſ.* External form.

I do not think
So fair an *outward*, and ſuch ſtuff within,
Endows a man but him. *Shakeſp. Cymbeline.*

OU'TWARD. *adv.*
1. To foreign parts. As a ſhip *outward* bound.
2. To the outer parts.

OU'TWARDLY. *adv.* [from *outward.*]
1. Externally: oppoſed to inwardly

That which inwardly each man ſhould be, the church *outwardly* ought to teſtify. *Hooker, b.* v. *ſ.* 6.
Griev'd with diſgrace, remaining in their fears:
However ſeeming *outwardly* content,
Yet th' inward touch their wounded honour bears. *Daniel.*

2. In appearance not ſincerely.

Many wicked men are often touched with ſome inward reverence for that goodneſs which they cannot be perſuaded to practiſe; nay, which they *outwardly* ſeem to deſpiſe. *Sprat.*

OU'TWARDS. *adv.* Towards the out-parts.

Do not black bodies conceive heat more eaſily from light than thoſe of other colours do, by reaſon that the light falling on them is not reflected *outwards*, but enters the bodies, and is often reflected and refracted within them until it be ſtifled and loſt? *Newton's Opticks.*

To OUTWEA'R. *v. a.* [*out* and *wear.*] To paſs tediouſly.

By the ſtream, if I the night *out-wear*,
Thus ſpent already how ſhall nature bear
The dews deſcending and nocturnal air. *Pope.*

To OUTWEE'D. *v. a.* [*out* and *weed.*] To extirpate as a weed.

Wrath is a fire, and jealouſy a weed;
The ſparks ſoon quench, the ſpringing weed *out-weed*, *Spenſ.*

To OUTWEI'GH. *v. a.* [*out* and *weigh.*]
1. To exceed in gravity.

Theſe inſtruments require ſo much ſtrength for the ſupporting of the weight to be moved, as may be equal unto it, beſides that other ſuper-added power whereby it is *out-weighed* and moved. *Wilkins's Math. Mag.*

2. To preponderate; to excel in value or influence.

If any think brave death *out-weighs* bad life,
Let him expreſs his diſpoſition. *Shakeſp. Coriolanus.*
All your care is for your prince I ſee,
Your truth to him *out-weighs* your love to me. *Dryden.*

Whenever he finds the hardſhip of his ſlavery *out-weigh* the value of his life, it is in his power, by reſiſting the will of his maſter, to draw on himſelf the death he deſires. *Locke.*

The marriage of the clergy is attended with the poverty of ſome of them, which is balanced and *out-weighed* by many ſingle advantages. *Atterbury.*

To OUTWE'LL. *v. a.* [*out* and *well.*] To pour out.

As when old father Nilus 'gins to ſwell,
With timely pride about the Ægyptian vale,
His fattie waves do fertile ſlime *out-well*,
And overflow each plain and lowly dale. *Fa. Queen.*

To OU'TWIT. *v. a.* [*out* and *wit.*] To cheat; to overcome by ſtratagem.

A fox may be *out-witted*, and a hare out-ſtript. *L'Eſt.*

The truer hearted any man is, the more liable he is to be impoſed on; and then the world calls it *out-witting* a man, when he is only out-knaved. *L'Eſtrange.*

Nothing is more equal in juſtice, and indeed more natural in the direct conſequence of effects and cauſes, than for men wickedly wiſe to *out-wit* themſelves; and for ſuch as wreſtle with providence, to trip up their own heels. *South.*

After the death of Craſſus, Pompey found himſelf *out-witted* by Cæſar and broke with him. *Dryden.*

OU'TWORK. *n. ſ.* [*out* and *work.*] The parts of a fortification next the enemy.

Take care of our *out-work*, the navy royal, which are the walls of the kingdom; and every great ſhip is an impregnable fort; and our many ſafe and commodious ports as the redoubts to ſecure them. *Bacon.*

Death hath taken in the *out-works*,
And now aſſails the fort; I feel, I feel him
Gnawing my heart-ſtrings. *Denham.*

OUTWO'RN. *part.* [from *out-wear.*] Conſumed or deſtroyed by uſe.

Better at home lie bed-rid, idle,
Inglorious, unemploy'd, with age *out-worn*. *Milton.*

To OUTWRE'ST. *v. a.* [*out* and *wrest.*] To extort by violence.

The growing anguish
Rankled so sore and fester'd inwardly,
Till that the truth thereof I did *out-wrest.* *Fa. Queen.*

OUTWROU'GHT. *part.* [*out* and *wrought.*] Out-done; exceeded in efficacy.

In your violent acts,
The fall of torrents and the noise of tempests,
The boyling of Carybdis, the sea's wildness,
The eating force of flames, and wings of winds,
Be all *out-wrought* by your transcendent furies. *B. Johns.*

To OUTWO'RTH. *v. a.* [*out* and *worth.*] To excel in value.

A beggar's book
Out-worths a noble's blood. *Shakesp. Hen.* VIII.

To OWE. *v. a.* [*eg aa*, I *owe*, or I *ought*, Islandick.]

1. To be obliged to pay; to be indebted.

I *owe* you much, and, like a witless youth,
That which I *owe* is lost. *Shakesp. Merch. of Ven.*
Let none seek needless causes to approve
The faith they *owe.* *Milt. Par. Lost*, *b.* ix.
All your parts of pious duty done,
You *owe* your Ormond nothing but a son. *Dryden.*
Thou hast deserv'd more love than I can show,
But 'tis thy fate to give, and mine to *owe.* *Dryden.*

If, upon the general balance of trade, English merchants *owe* to foreigners one hundred thousand pounds, if commodities do not, our money must go out to pay it. *Locke.*

2. To be obliged to ascribe; to be obliged for.

By me upheld, that he may know how frail
His fall'n condition is, and to me *owe*
All his deliv'rance, and to none but me. *Milton.*

3. To have from any thing as the consequence of a cause.

O deem thy fall not *ow'd* to man's decree,
Jove hated Greece, and punish'd Greece in thee. *Pope.*

4. To possess; to be the right owner of. For *owe*, which is, in this sense, obsolete, we now use *own.*

Thou dost here usurp
The name thou *ow'st* not, and hast put thyself
Upon this island as a spy. *Shakesp. Tempest.*
Fate, shew thy force; ourselves we do not *owe*;
What is decreed must be; and be this so. *Shakesp.*
Not poppy nor mandragora,
Nor all the drowsy sirups of the world,
Shall ever med'cine thee to that sweet sleep
Which thou *owed'st* yesterday. *Shakesp. Othello.*
If any happy eye
This roving wanton shall descry,
Let the finder surely know
Mine is the wag; 'tis I that *owe*
The winged wand'rer. *Crashaw.*

5. A practice has long prevailed among writers, to use *owing*, the active participle of *owe*, in a passive sense, for *owed* or *due.* Of this impropriety *Bolinbroke* was aware, and, having no quick sense of the force of English words, has used *due*, in the sense of consequence or imputation, which by other writers is only used of *debt.* We say, the money is *due* to me; *Bolinbroke* says, the effect is *due* to the cause.

6. Consequential.

This was *owing* to an indifference to the pleasures of life, and an aversion to the pomps of it. *Atterbury.*

7. Due as a debt.

You are both too bold;
I'll teach you all what's *owing* to your queen. *Dryden.*

The debt, *owing* from one country to the other, cannot be paid without real effects sent thither to that value. *Locke.*

8. Imputable to, as an agent.

If we estimate things, what in them is *owing* to nature, and what to labour, we shall find in most of them $\frac{99}{100}$ to be on the account of labour. *Locke.*

The custom of particular impeachments was not limited any more than that of struggles between nobles and commons, the ruin of Greece was *owing* to the former, as that of Rome was to the latter. *Swift.*

OWL. } *n. s.* [ule, Saxon; *hulotte*, French and Scottish.] A
O'WLET. } bird that flies about in the night and catches mice.

Adder's fork, and blind worm's sting,
Lizard's leg, and *owlet's* wing
For a charm. *Shakesp. Macbeth.*
Return to her!
No! rather I abjure all roofs, and chuse
To be a comrade with the wolf and *owl.* *Shakesp.*
'Twas when the dog-star's unpropitious ray
Smote ev'ry brain, and wither'd every bay;
Sick was the sun, the *owl* forsook his bow'r. *Dunciad.*

O'WLER. *n. s.* One who carries contraband goods. Perhaps from the necessity of carrying on an illicit trade by night.

By running goods, these graceless *owlers* gain. *Swift.*

We understand by some *owlers*, old people die in France. *Tatler*, N°. 56.

OWN. *n. s.* [agen, Saxon; *eygen*, Dutch.]

1. This is a word of no other use than as it is added to the possessive pronouns, my, thy, his, our, your, their. It seems to be a substantive; as, *my own*, *my peculiar*: but is, in reality, the participle passive of the verb *owe*, in the participle *owen* or *own*: *my own*; the thing *owned* by, or belonging to me.

Inachus in his cave alone,
Wept not another's losses, but his *own.* *Dryden.*

2. It is added generally by way of emphasis or corroboration.

I yet never was forsworn,
Scarcely have coveted what was my *own.* *Shakesp.*

Every nation made gods of their *own*, and put them in high places. 2 *Kings* xvii. 29.

For my *own* share one beauty I design,
Engage your honours that she shall be mine. *Dryden.*

It is conceit rather than understanding, if it must be under the restraint of receiving and holding opinions by the authority of any thing but their *own* perceived evidence. *Locke.*

Will she thy linen wash, or hosen darn,
And knit thee gloves made of her *own* spun yarn. *Gay.*
Passion and pride were to her soul unknown,
Convinc'd that virtue only is our *own.* *Pope.*

3. Sometimes it is added to note opposition or contradistinction; domestick; not foreign; mine, his, or yours; not another's.

These toils abroad, these tumults with his *own*,
Fell in the revolution of one year. *Daniel.*

There's nothing sillier than a crafty knave out-witted, and beaten at his *own* play. *L'Estrange.*

To OWN. *v. a.* [from the noun.]

1. To acknowledge; to avow for one's own.

When you come, find me out,
And *own* me for your son. *Dryden's Cleomenes.*

2. To possess; to claim; to hold by right.

Tell me, ye Trojans, for that name you *own*;
Nor is your course upon our coasts unknown. *Dryden.*
Others on earth o'er human race preside,
Of these the chief, the care of nations *own*,
And guard with arms divine the British throne *Pope.*

3. To avow.

I'll venture out alone,
Since you, fair princess, my protection *own.* *Dryden.*

4. To confess; not to deny.

Make this truth so evident, that those who are unwilling to *own* it may yet be ashamed to deny it. *Tillotson.*

Others will *own* their weakness of understanding. *Locke.*

OW'NERSHIP. *n. s.* [from *owner.*] Property; rightful possession.

In a real action, the proximate cause is the property or *ownership* of the thing in controversy. *Ayliffe's Par.*

O'WNER. *n. s.* [from *own.*] One to whom any thing belongs; master; rightful possessor.

A bark
Stays but till her *owner* comes aboard. *Shakesp.*
Is it not enough to break into my garden,
Climbing my walls in spight of me the *owner*,
But thou wilt brave me. *Shakesp.*

Here shew favour, because it happeneth that the *owner* hath incurred the forfeiture of eight years profit of his lands, before he cometh to the knowledge of the process against him. *Bacon.*

They intend advantage of my labours,
With no small profit daily to my *owners.* *Milton.*
These wait the *owners* last despair,
And what's permitted to the flames invade. *Dryden.*

A freehold, though but in ice and snow, will make the *owner* pleased in the possession, and stout in the defence of it. *Addison's Freeholder*, N°. 1.

That small muscle draws the nose upwards, when it expresses the contempt which the *owner* of it has upon seeing any thing he does not like. *Addison's Spectator.*

Victory hath not made us insolent, nor have we taken advantage to gain any thing beyond the honour of restoring every one's right to their just *owners.* *Atterbury.*

What is this wit, which must our cares employ?
The *owner's* wife, that other men enjoy. *Pope.*

OWRE. *n. s.* [*urus jubatus*, Lat.] A beast. *Ainsworth.*

OX. *n. s.* plur. OXEN. [oxa, Saxon; *oxe*, Danish.]

1. The general name for black cattle.

The black *ox* hath not trod on his foot. *Camden.*
Sheep run not half so tim'rous from the wolf,
Or horse or *oxen* from the leopard,
As you fly from your oft-subdued slaves. *Shakesp.*

I saw the river Clitumnus, celebrated by the poets for making cattle white that drink of it. The inhabitants of that country have still the same opinion, and have a great many *oxen* of a whitish colour to confirm them in it. *Addis.*

2. A castrated bull.

The horns of *oxen* and cows are larger than the bulls; which is caused by abundance of moisture. *Bacon.*

Although there be naturally more males than females, yet artificially, that is, by making geldings, *oxen* and weahers, there are fewer. *Graunt.*

The field is spacious I design to sow,
With *oxen* far unfit to draw the plough. *Dryden.*

The

The frowning bull
And *ox* half-rais'd. *Thomson's Summer.*

OXBA'NE. *n. s.* A plant. *Ainsworth.*

O'XEYE. *n. s.* [*Buphthalmus.*] The whole face of the plant is like tansy; the flowers are radiated, and the most part produced simply; the flowers of the disk are separated with an imbricated little leaf. *Miller.*

OXG'ANG *of Land.* *n. s.* Twenty acres. *Ainsworth.*

OXHE'AL. *n. s.* A plant. *Ainsworth.*

O'XFLY. *n. s.* [*ox* and *fly.*] A fly of a particular kind.

OXLI'P. *n. s.* The same with *cowslip*; a vernal flower.

A bank whereon the wild thyme blows,
Where *oxlip* and the nodding violet grows. *Shakesp.*

OXSTA'LL. *n. s.* [*ox* and *stall.*] A stand for oxen.

O'XTONGUE. *n. s.* A plant. *Ainsworth.*

O'XYCRATE. *n. s.* [οξύκρατον, *oxycrat*, Fr. οξὺς and κεράω.] A mixture of water and vinegar.

Apply a mixture of the same powder, with a compress prest out of *oxycrate*, and a suitable bandage. *Wiseman.*

O'XYMEL. *n. s.* [ὀξύμελι, οξὺς, and μελι.] A mixture of vinegar and honey.

In fevers, the aliments prescribed by Hippocrates, were ptisans and decoctions of some vegetables, with *oxymel* or the mixture of honey and vinegar. *Arbuthnot.*

OXYMO'RON. *n. s.* [οξύμωρον.] A rhetorical figure, in which an epithet of a quite contrary signification is added to any word. *Dict.*

OXY'RRHODINE. *n. s.* [οξυῤῥόδινον, ὀξὺς and ῥόδον.] A mixture of two parts of oil of roses with one of vinegar of roses.

The spirits, opiates, and cool things, readily compose *oxyrrhodines.* *Floyer on the Humours.*

O'YER. *n. s.* [*oyer*, old French, to hear.] A court of *oyer* and terminer, is a judicature where causes are *heard* and determined.

OYE'S. *n. s.* [*oyez*, *hear ye*, French.] Is the introduction to any proclamation or advertisement given by the publick criers both in England and Scotland. It is thrice repeated.

Fairies, black, grey, green, and white,
Attend your office and your quality.
Crier hobgoblin make the fairy *O yes.* *Shakesp.*

O yes! if any happy eye
This roving wanton shall descry;
Let the finder surely know
Mine is the wag. *Crashaw.*

OY'LETHOLE. *n. s.* See OYLET. [It may be written *oylet*, from *oeillet*, French; but *eylet* seems better.]

Distinguish'd slashes deck the great,
As each excels in birth or state;
His *oyletholes* are more and ampler,
The king's own body was a samplar. *Prior.*

O'YSTER. *n. s.* [*oester*, Dutch; *huitre*, Fr.] A bivalve testaceous fish.

I will not lend thee a penny—
—Why then the world's mine *oyster* which
I with sword will open. *Shakesp. Merr. W. of Wind.*

Rich honesty dwells like your miser, sir, in a poor house; as your pearl in your foul *oyster.* *Shakesp.*

Another mass held a kind of *oyster* shell, and other bivalves. *Woodward on Fossils.*

There may be as many ranks of beings in the invisible world superior to us, as we are superior to all the ranks of being in this visible world; though we descend below the *oyster* to the least animated atoms discovered by microscopes. *Watts's Improv. of the Mind.*

Where *oyster* tubs in rows
Are rang'd beside the posts, there stay thy haste. *Gay.*

O'YSTERWENCH. } *n. s.* [*oyster* and *wench*, or *woman.*] A
O'YSTERWOMAN. } woman whose business is to sell oysters. Proverbially. A low woman.

Off goes his bonnet to an *oysterwench.* *Shakesp.*

The *oysterwomen* lock'd their fish up,
And trudg'd away to cry no bishop. *Hudibras.*

OZÆ'NA. *n. s.* [ὄζαινα, from ὄζω; *ozene*, Fr.] An ulcer in the inside of the nostrils that gives an ill stench. *Quincy.*

P.

P Is a labial consonant, formed by a slight compression of the anterior part of the lips; as, *pull*, *pelt*. It is confounded by the Germans and Welsh with *b*: it has an uniform sound: it is sometimes mute before *t*; as, *accompt*, *receipt*; but the mute *p* is in modern orthography commonly omitted.

PA'BULAR. *adj.* [*pabulun*, Lat.] Affording aliment or provender.

PABULA'TION. *n. s.* [*pabulum*, Lat.] The act of feeding or procuring provender.

PA'BULOUS. *adj.* [*pabulum*, Lat.] Alimental; affording aliment.

We doubt the air is the *pabulous* supply of fire, much less that flame is properly air kindled. *Brown's Vulgar Err.*

PACE. *n. s.* [*pas*, French.]

1. Step; single movement in walking.

Behind her death,
Close following *pace* for *pace*, not mounted yet
On his pale horse. *Milton's Paradise Lost*, *b.* x.

2. Gait; manner of walk.

He himself went but a kind of languishing *pace*, with his eyes sometimes cast up to heaven, as though his fancies strove to mount higher. *Sidney.*

He saw Menalcas come with heavy *pace*;
Wet were his eyes, and chearless was his face. *Addison.*

3. Degree of celerity. To *keep pace*, is not to be left behind.

To-morrow, and to-morrow, and to-morrow,
Creeps in this petty *pace* from day to-day,
To the last syllable of recorded time;
And all our yesterdays have lighted fools
The way to dusky death. *Shakesp. Macbeth.*

Bring me word
How the world goes, that to the *pace* of it
I may spur on my journey. *Shakesp. Coriolanus.*

His teachers were fain to restrain his forwardness; that his brothers, under the same training, might hold *pace* with him. *Wotton's Buckingham.*

The beggar sings ev'n when he sees the place,
Beset with thieves, and never mends his *pace*. *Dryden.*

Just as much
He mended *pace* upon the touch. *Hudibras*, *p.* i.

Marcia could answer thee in sighs, keep *pace*
With all thy woes, and count out tear for tear. *Addison.*

Hudibras applied his spur to one side of his horse, as not doubting but the other would keep *pace* with it. *Addison.*

4. Step; gradation of business. A gallicism.

The first *pace* necessary for his majesty to make, is to fall into confidence with Spain. *Temple.*

5. A measure of five feet. The quantity supposed to be measured by the foot from the place where it is taken up to that where it is set down.

Measuring land by walking over it, they styled a double step; i. e. the space from the elevation of one foot, to the same foot set down again, mediated by a step of the other foot; a *pace* equal to five foot; a thousand of which *paces* made a mile. *Holder on Time.*

The violence of tempests never moves the sea above six *paces* deep. *Wilkin's Math. Magic.*

6. A particular movement which horses are taught, though some have it naturally, made by lifting the legs on the same side together.

They rode, but authors having not
Determin'd whether *pace* or trot;
That's to say, whether tollutation,
As they do term it, or succussation. *Hudibras.*

To PACE. *v. n.* [from the noun.]

1. To move on slowly.

He soft arrived on the grassie plain,
And fairly *paced* forth with easy pain. *Hubberd.*

As we *pac'd* along
Upon the giddy footing of the hatches,
Methought, that Gloster stumbl'd. *Shakesp. R.* III.

I beheld
Crispinus, both in birth and manners vile,
Pacing in pomp with cloak of Tyrian dye,
Chang'd oft a day. *Dryden's Juvenal.*

The moon rose in the clearest sky I ever saw, by whose solemn light I *paced* on slowly without interruption. *Pope.*

The nymph, obedient to divine command,
To seek Ulysses, *pac'd* along the sand. *Pope.*

2. To move.

Remember well, with speed so *pace*,
To speak of Perdita. *Shakesp. Winter's Tale.*

3. [Used of horses.] To move by raising the legs on the same side together.

To PACE. *v. a.*

1. To measure by steps.

Where is the horse that doth untread again
His tedious measures with th' unbated fire,
That he did *pace* them first. *Shakesp. Merch. of Ven.*

2. To direct to go.

If you can, *pace* your wisdom
In that good path that I would wish it go,
And you shall have your bosom on this wretch. *Shakesp.*

PA'CED. *adj.* [from *pace.*] Having a particular gait.

Revenge is sure, though sometimes slowly *pac'd*;
Awake, awake, or sleeping sleep thy last. *Dryden.*

PA'CER. *n. s.* [from *pace.*] He that paces.

PACIFICA'TION. *n. s.* [*pacification*, Fr. from *pacify.*]

1. The act of making peace.

He sent forthwith to the French king his chaplain, chusing him because he was a churchman, as best sorting with an ambassy of *pacification*. *Bacon's Hen.* VII.

David, by an happy and seasonable *pacification*, was took off from acting that bloody tragedy. *South.*

2. The act of appeasing or pacifying.

A world was to be saved by a *pacification* of wrath, through the dignity of that sacrifice which should be offered. *Hooker.*

PACIFICA'TOR. *n. s.* [*pacificateur*, Fr. from *pacify.*] Peace-maker.

He set and kept on foot a continual treaty of peace; besides he had in consideration the bearing the blessed person of a *pacificator*. *Bacon's Henry* VII.

PA'CIFICATORY. *adj.* [from *pacificator.*] Tending to make peace.

PACI'FICK. *adj.* [*pacifique*, Fr. *pacificus*, Lat.] Peace-making; mild; gentle; appeasing.

God now in his gracious *pacifick* manner comes to treat with them. *Hammond's Fundamentals.*

Returning, in his bill
An olive leaf he brings, *pacifick* sign! *Milton.*

PACI'FIER. *n. s.* [from *pacify.*] One who pacifies.

To PA'CIFY. *v. a.* [*pacifier*, Fr. *pacifio*, Lat.] To appease; to still resentment; to quiet an angry person; to compose any desire.

While the dog hunted in the river, he had withdrawn to *pacify* with sleep his over-watched eyes. *Sidney*, *b.* ii.

Menelaus promised Ptolemy money, if he would *pacify* the king. 2 *Mac.* iv. 45.

The most high is not *pacified* for sin by the multitude of sacrifices. *Ecclus* xxxiv. 19.

Although in his journey he heard news of the victory, yet he went on as far as York, to *pacify* and settle those countries. *Bacon's Henry* VII.

O villain! to have wit at will upon all other occasions, and not one diverting syllable now at a pinch to *pacify* our mistress. *L'Estrange.*

Nor William's pow'r, nor Mary's charms
Could or repel, or *pacify* his arms. *Prior.*

PACK. *n. s.* [*pack*, Dutch.]

1. A large bundle of any thing tied up for carriage.

Themistocles said to the king of Persia, that speech was like cloth of Arras, opened and put abroad, whereby the imagery appears in figures; whereas in thoughts they lie but as in *packs*. *Bacon, Essays* 28.

Had sly Ulysses at the sack
Of Troy, brought thee his pedlar's *pack*. *Cleaveland.*

Our knight did bear no less a *pack*
Of his own buttocks on his back. *Hudibras*, *p.* i.

2. A burden;

2. A burden; a load.

I rather chose
To cross my friend in his intended drift,
Than, by concealing it, heap on your head
A *pack* of sorrows. *Shakesp. Merch. of Ven.*

But when they took notice how stupid a beast it was, they loaded it with *packs* and burdens, and set boys upon the back of it. *L'Estrange.*

3. A due number of cards.

Women to cards may be compar'd, we play
A round or two, when us'd we throw away,
Take a fresh *pack*. *Granville.*

It is wonderful to see persons of sense passing away a dozen hours together in shuffling and dividing a *pack* of cards. *Addis.*

4. A number of hounds hunting together.

Two ghosts join their *packs* to hunt her o'er the plain. *Dryd.*

The fury fires the *pack*; they snuff, they vent,
And feed their hungry nostrils with the scent. *Dryden.*

The savage soul of game is up at once,
The *pack* full-opening various. *Thomson's Summer.*

5. A number of people confederated in any bad design or practice.

You panderly rascals! there's a knot, a gang, a *pack*, a conspiracy, against me. *Shakesp. Mer. W. of Wind.*

Never such a *pack* of knaves and villains, as they who now governed in the parliament. *Clarendon.*

Bickerstaff is more a man of honour, than to be an accomplice with a *pack* of rascals that walk the streets on nights. *Swift.*

6. Any great number, as to quantity and pressure: as a *pack* or world of troubles. *Ainsworth.*

To Pack. *v. a.* [*packen*, Dutch.]

1. To bind up for carriage.

A poor merchant driven on unknown land,
That had by chance *pack'd* up his choicest treasure
In one dear casket, and sav'd only that. *Otway.*

Resolv'd for sea, the slaves thy baggage *pack*,
Each saddled with his burden on his back. *Dryden.*

What we looked upon as brains, were an heap of strange materials, *packed* up with wonderful art in the skull. *Addison.*

2. To send in a hurry.

He cannot live, I hope, and must not die,
Till George be *pack'd* with post horse up to heav'n. *Shakesp.*

3. To sort the cards so as that the game shall be iniquitously secured. It is applied to any iniquitous procurement of collusion.

Enos has
Packt cards with Cæsar, and false play'd. *Shakesp.*

There be that can *pack* cards and yet cannot play well; so there are some that are good in canvasses and factions, that are otherwise weak men. *Bacon's Essays*, Nº. 23.

The judge shall jobb, the bishop bite the town,
And mighty dukes *pack* cards for half a crown. *Pope.*

4. To unite picked persons in some bad design.

When they have *pack'd* a parliament,
Will once more try th' expedient:
Who can already muster friends,
To serve for members to our ends. *Hudibras.*

Brutes, called men, in full cry *pack'd* by the court or country, run down in the house of commons, a deserted horned beast of the court. *Wycherly.*

So many greater fools than they,
Will *pack* a crowded audience the third day. *Southern.*

The expected council was dwindling into a conventicle; a *pack'd* assembly of Italian bishops, not a free convention of fathers from all quarters. *Atterbury.*

To Pack. *v. n.*

1. To tie up goods.

The marigold, whose courtier's face
Ecchoes the sun, and doth unlace
Her at his rise, at his full stop
Packs and shuts up her gaudy shop. *Cleaveland.*

2. To go off in a hurry; to remove in haste.

New farmer thinketh each hour a day,
Until the old farmer be *packing* away. *Tuss. Husb.*

Rogues, hence, avaunt!
Seek shelter, *pack*. *Shakesp. M. W. of Wind.*

The wind no sooner came good, but away *pack* the gallies with all the haste they could. *Carew.*

A thief kindled his torch at Jupiter's altar, and then robbed the temple: as he was *packing* away with his sacrilegious burden, a voice pursued him. *L'Estrange.*

If they had been an hundred more, they had been all sent *packing* with the same answer. *Stillingfleet.*

Pack hence, and from the cover'd benches rise,
This is no place for you. *Dryden.*

Poor Stella must *pack* off to town,
From purling streams and fountains bubbling,
To Liffy's stinking tide at Dublin. *Swift.*

3. To concert bad measures; to confederate in ill; to practise unlawful confederacy or collusion.

That this so profitable a merchandize, riseth not to a proportionable enhauncement with other less beneficial commodities, they impute partly to the eastern buyers *packing*, partly to the owners not venting the same. *Carew.*

Go *pack* with him. *Shakesp. Titus Andronicus.*

Pa'ckcloath. *n. s.* [*pack* and *cloath.*] A cloath in which goods are tied up.

Pa'cker. *n. s.* [from *pack.*] One who binds up bales for carriage.

Pa'cket. *n. s.* [*pacquet*, French.] A small pack; a mail of letters.

In the dark
Grop'd I to find out them,
Finger'd their *packet*, and in fine withdrew. *Shakesp.*

There passed continually *packets* and dispatches between the two kings. *Bacon's Henry* VII.

Upon your late command
To guard the passages, and search all *packets*,
This to the prince was intercepted. *Denham.*

People will wonder how the news could come, especially if the wind be fair when the *packet* goes over. *Swift.*

To Pa'cket. *v. a.* [from the noun.] To bind up in parcels.

My resolution is to send you all your letters, well sealed and *packeted*. *Swift.*

Pa'ckhorse. *n. s.* [*pack* and *horse.*] A horse of burden; a horse employed in carrying goods.

Ere you were queen, ay, or your husband king,
I was a *packhorse* in his great affairs. *Shakesp.*

It is not to be expected that a man, who drudges on in a laborious trade, should be more knowing in the variety of things done in the world, than a *packhorse* who is driven constantly forwards and backwards to market, should be skilled in the geography of the country. *Locke.*

Pa'cksaddle. *n. s.* [*pack* and *saddle.*] A saddle on which burdens are laid.

Your beards deserve not so honourable a grave as to stuff a butcher's cushion, or to be entombed in an asses *packsaddle*. *Shakespeare's Coriolanus.*

That brave prancing courser, hath been so broken and brought low by her, that he will patiently take the bit and bear a *packsaddle* or panniers. *Howel's Vocal Forest.*

The bunch on a camel's back may be instead of a *packsaddle* to receive the burthen. *More's Antidote against Atheism.*

Pa'ckthread. *n. s.* [*pack* and *thread.*] Strong thread used in tying up parcels.

About his shelves
Remnants of *packthread*, and old cakes of roses
Were thinly scatter'd. *Shakesp. Rom. and Juliet.*

Girding of the body of the tree about with *packthread*, restraineth the sap. *Bacon's Nat. Hist.* Nº. 419.

I can compare such productions to nothing but rich pieces of patchwork, sewed together with *packthread*. *Felton.*

His horse is vicious, for which reason I tie him close to his manger with a *packthread*. *Addison's Spectator.*

The cable was about as thick as *packthread*. *Swift.*

Pa'ckwax. *n. s.*

Several parts peculiar to brutes, are wanting in man; as the strong aponeuroses on the sides of the neck, called *packwax*. *Ray on the Creation.*

Pact. *n. s.* [*pact*, Fr. *pactum*, Latin.] A contract; a bargain; a covenant.

The queen, contrary to her *pact* and agreement concerning the marriage of her daughter, delivered her daughters out of sanctuary unto king Richard. *Bacon.*

Pa'ction. *n. s.* [*paction*, Fr. *pactio*, Latin.] A bargain; a covenant.

The French king sent for Matthew earl of Levenox, encouraging him to remove the earl of Arraine from the regency of Scotland, and reverse such *pactions* as he had made. *Hayward.*

There never could be any room for contracts or *pactions*, between the supreme being and his intelligent creatures. *Cheyne.*

Pacti'tious. *n. s.* [*pactio*, Lat.] Settled by covenant.

PAD. *n. s.* [from paab, Sax. whence likewise path, or paaδ.]

1. The road; a foot path.

We have seen this to be the discipline of the state, as well as of the *pad*. *L'Estrange.*

The squire of the *pad* and the knight of the post,
Find their pains no more baulk'd, and their hopes no more crost. *Prior.*

2. An easy paced horse.

Let him walk a foot with his *pad* in his hand; but let not them be accounted no poets who mount and shew their horsemanship. *Dryden's Ded. to Juvenal.*

A grey *pad* is kept in the stable with great care, out of regard to his past services. *Addison.*

I would have set you on an easier *pad*, and relieved the wandering knight with a night's lodging. *Pope's Letters.*

3. A robber that infests the roads on foot.

4. A low soft saddle: properly a saddle or bolster stuffed with straw. [*Pajado*, Spanish, of *paja*, straw.

Tremellius was called ſcropha or ſow, becauſe he hid his neighbour's ſow under a *pad*, and commanded his wiſe to lie thereon; he ſware that he had no ſow but the great ſow that lay there, pointing to the *pad* and the ſow his wife. *Camden.*

We ſhall not need to ſay what lack
Of leather was upon his back;
For that was hidden under *pad*. *Hudibras, p.* i.

To PAD. *v. n.* [from the noun.]
1. To travel gently.
2. To rob on foot.
3. To beat a way ſmooth and level.

PA'DAR. *n. ſ.* Grouts; coarſe flower.

In the bolting and ſifting of near fourteen years of ſuch power and favour, all that came out could not be expected to be pure and fine meal, but muſt have amongſt it *padar* and bran in this lower age of human fragility. *Wotton.*

PA'DDER. *n. ſ.* [from *pad.*] A robber; a foot highwayman.

Spurr'd as jockies uſe, to break,
Or *padders* to ſecure a neck. *Hud. p.* iii. *cant.* 1.

Worſe than all the clatt'ring tiles, and worſe
Than thouſand *padders*, is the poet's curſe;
Rogues that in dog days cannot rhime forbear;
But without mercy read, to make you hear. *Dryden.*

If he advanced himſelf by a voluntary engaging in unjuſt quarrels, he has no better pretence to honour than what a reſolute and ſucceſsful *padder* may challenge. *Collier.*

To PA'DDLE. *v. n.* [*patouiller*, Fr.]
1. To row; to beat water as with oars.

As the men were *paddling* for their lives. *L'Eſtrange.*
Paddling ducks the ſtanding lake deſire. *Gay.*

2. To play in the water.

The brain has a very unpromiſing aſpect for thinking: it looks like an odd ſort of bog for fancy to *paddle* in. *Collier.*

A wolf lapping at the head of a fountain, ſpyed a lamb *paddling* a good way off. *L'Eſtrange.*

3. To finger.

Paddling palms, and pinching fingers,
And making practis'd ſmiles,
As in a looking-glaſs. *Shakeſp. Winter's Tale.*

PA'DDLE. *n. ſ.* [*pattal*, Welſh.]
1. An oar, particularly that which is uſed by a ſingle rower in a boat.
2. Any thing broad like the end of an oar.

Have a *paddle* upon thy weapon. *Deut.* xxiii. 13.

PA'DDLER. *n. ſ.* [from *paddle.*] One who paddles. *Ainſ.*

PA'DDOCK. *n. ſ.* [paba, Saxon; *padde*, Dutch.] A great frog or toad.

Where I was wont to ſeek the honey bee,
Working her former rooms in waxen frame;
The griſly toad ſtool grown there mought I ſee,
And loathing *paddocks* lording on the ſame. *Spenſer.*

The *paddock*, or frog *paddock*, breeds on the land, is bony and big, eſpecially the ſhe. *Walton.*

The water ſnake whom fiſh and *paddocks* fed,
With ſtaring ſcales lies poiſon'd. *Dryden.*

PA'DDOCK. *n. ſ.* [corrupted from *parrack.*] A ſmall incloſure for deer.

PADELI'ON. *n. ſ.* [*pas de lion*, Fr. *pes leonis*, Lat.] An herb. *Ain.*

PA'DLOCK. *n. ſ.* [*padde*, Dutch.] A lock hung on a ſtaple to hold on a link.

Let all her ways be unconfin'd;
And clap your *padlock* on her mind. *Prior.*

To PA'DLOCK. *v. a.* [from the noun.] To faſten with a padlock.

Some illiterate people have *padlock'd* all thoſe pens that were to celebrate their heroes, by ſilencing grub-ſtreet. *J. Bull.*

PA'DOWPIPE. *n. ſ.* An herb. *Ainſworth.*

PÆ'AN. *n. ſ.* [from the ſongs ſung at feſtivals to Apollo, beginning *Io pæan.*] A ſong of triumph.

O may I live to hail the glorious day,
And ſing loud *pæans* thro' the crouded way. *Roſcomm.*

See from each clime the learn'd their incenſe bring:
Hear, in all tongues conſenting *pæans* ring. *Pope.*

PA'GAN. *n. ſ.* [paʒanıſc, Saxon; *paganus*, Latin; from *pagus*, a village; the villages continuing heathen after the cities were chriſtian.] A Heathen; one not a Chriſtian.

PA'GAN. *adj.* Heatheniſh.

Their cloaths are after ſuch a *pagan* cut too,
That ſure they have worn out Chriſtendom. *Shakeſp.*

The ſecret ceremonies I conceal,
Uncouth, perhaps unlawful, to reveal;
But ſuch they were as *Pagan* uſe requir'd. *Dryden.*

PA'GANISM. *n. ſ.* [*paganiſm*, Fr. from *pagan.*] Heatheniſm.

The name of popery is more odious than very *paganiſm* amongſt divers of the more ſimple ſort. *Hooker, b.* iv.

Our labarum, in a ſtate of *paganiſm* you have on a coin of Tiberius. It ſtands between two other enſigns. *Addiſ.*

PAGE. *n. ſ.* [*page*, French.]
1. One ſide of the leaf of a book.

If a man could have opened one of the *pages* of the divine counſel, and ſeen the event of Joſeph's being ſold to the merchants, he might have dried up the young man's tears. *Taylor's Rule of Living Holy.*

Thy name to Phœbus and the muſes known,
Shall in the front of ev'ry *page* be ſhown. *Dryden.*

A printer divides a book into ſheets, the ſheets into *pages*, the *pages* into lines, and the lines into letters. *Watts.*

2. [*page*, Fr.] A young boy attending on a great perſon.

The fair goddeſs Fortune,
Fall deep in love with thee, and her great charms
Miſguide thy oppoſers ſwords!
Proſperity be thy *page!* *Shakeſp. Coriolanus.*

Pages following him,
Even at the heels in golden multitudes. *Shakeſp.*

He had two *pages* of honour, on either hand one. *Bacon.*

Where is this mankind now? who lives to age
Fit to be made Methuſalem his *page*. *Donne.*

This day thou ſhalt my rural *pages* ſee,
For I have dreſs'd them both to wait on thee. *Dryden.*

Philip of Macedon had a *page* attending in his chamber, to tell him every morning, Remember, O king, that thou art mortal. *Wake's Prep. for Death.*

To PAGE. *v. a.* [from the noun.]
1. To mark the pages of a book.
2. To attend as a page.

Will theſe moſs'd trees
That have out-liv'd the eagle, *page* thy heels
And ſkip when thou point'ſt out? *Shakeſp.*

PA'GEANT. *n. ſ.* [Of this word the etymologiſts give no ſatisfactory account. It may perhaps be *payen geant, a pagan giant*, a repreſentation of triumph uſed at return from holy wars; as we have yet the Saracen's head.]
1. A ſtatue in a ſhow.
2. Any ſhow; a ſpectacle of entertainment.

When all our *pageants* of delight were plaid,
Our youth got me to play the woman's part,
And I was trim'd in madam Julia's gown. *Shakeſp.*

I'll play my part in fortune's *pageant*. *Shakeſp.*

This wide and univerſal theatre,
Preſents more woful *pageants* than the ſcene
Wherein we play. *Shakeſp. As you like it.*

The poets contrived the following *pageant* or machine for the pope's entertainment; a huge floating mountain that was ſplit in the top in imitation of Parnaſſus. *Addiſon.*

PA'GEANT. *adj.* Showy; pompous; oſtentatious; ſuperficial.

Were ſhe ambitious, ſhe'd diſdain to own
The *pageant* pomp of ſuch a ſervile throne. *Dryden.*

To PA'GEANT. *v. a.* [from the noun.] To exhibit in ſhow; to repreſent.

With ridiculous and aukward action,
Which, ſlanderer, he imitation calls,
He *pageants* us. *Shakeſp. Troil. and Creſſida.*

PA'GEANTRY. *n. ſ.* [from *pageant.*] Pomp; ſhow.

All theſe inconveniences are conſequent to this dogmatizing, ſuppoſing men in the right; but if they be in the wrong, what a ridiculous *pageantry* is it to ſee ſuch a philoſophical gravity ſet man out a ſoleciſm. *Governm. of the Tongue.*

Such *pageantry* be to the people ſhown;
There boaſt thy horſe's trappings and thy own. *Dryden.*

PA'GINAL. *n. ſ.* [*pagina*, Latin.] Conſiſting of pages.

An expreſſion proper into the *paginal* books of our times, but not ſo agreeable unto volumes or rolling books, in uſe among the Jews. *Brown's Vulgar Errours.*

PA'GOD. *n. ſ.* [probably na Indian word.]
1. An Indian idol.

They worſhip idols called *pagods*, after ſuch a terrible repreſentation as we make of devils. *Stillingfleet.*

2. The temple of the idol.

See thronging millions to the *pagod* run,
And offer country, parent, wife, or ſon. *Pope.*

PAID. *adj.* the preterite and participle paſſive of pay.

This puniſhment purſues the unhappy maid,
And thus the purple hair is dearly *paid*. *Dryden.*

PAI'GLES. *n. ſ.* Flowers; alſo called cowſlips. *Dict.*

PAIL. *n. ſ.* [*paila*, Spaniſh.] A wooden veſſel in which milk or water is commonly carried.

In the country when their wool is new ſhorn, they ſet *pails* of water by in the ſame room, to increaſe the weight. *Bacon's Nat. Hiſt.* Nº. 78.

New milk that all the winter never fails,
And all the ſummer overflows the *pails*. *Dryden.*

PAI'LFUL. *n. ſ.* [*pail* and *full.*] The quantity that a pail will hold.

Yond ſame cloud cannot chuſe but fall by *pailfuls*. *Shak.*

PAILMA'IL. *n. ſ.* [This is commonly written *pellmell*; nor do I know which of the too is right.] Violent; boiſterous.

A ſtroke with a *pailmail* beetle upon a bowl, makes it fly from it. *Digby on the Soul.*

PAIN. *n. ſ.* [*peine*, Fr. *pin*, Sax. *pœna*, Lat.]
1. Puniſhment denounced.

There the princeſſes determining to bathe themſelves, thought it was ſo priviledged a place, upon *pain* of death, as no body durſt preſume to come thither. *Sidney, b.* ii.

On *pain* of death no perſon being ſo bold,
Or daring hardy, as to touch the liſt. *Shakeſp. Rich.* III.

Interpoſe,

Interpose, on *pain* of my displeasure,
Betwixt your swords. *Dryden's Don Sebastian.*

None shall presume to fly under *pain* of death, with wings of any other man's making. *Addison's Guardian.*

2. Penalty; punishment.

Because Eusebius hath yet said nothing, we will by way of mulct or *pain*, lay it upon him. *Bacon.*

3. Sensation of uneasiness.

As the *pains* of the touch are greater than the offences of the other senses; so likewise are the pleasures. *Bacon.*

Pain is perfect misery, the worst
Of evils; and excessive, overturns
All patience. *Milton's Par. Lost, b.* vi.

He would believe, but yet is still in *pain*,
Presses the pulse, and feels the leaping vein. *Dryden.*

4. [In the plural.] Labour; work; toil.

Many have taken the *pains* to go out of Europe to reside as friars in America. *Abbot's Descrip. of the World.*

One laboureth and taketh *pains*, and maketh haste, and is so much the more behind. *Ecclus* xi. 11.

The *pains* they had taken, was very great. *Clarend.*

If philosophy be uncertain, the former will conclude it vain; and the latter may be in danger of pronouncing the same on their *pains*, who seek it, if after all their labour they must reap the wind, mere opinion and conjecture. *Glanv.*

She needs no weary steps ascend,
All seems before her feet to bend;
And here, as she was born she lies,
High without taking *pains* to rise. *Waller.*

The deaf person must be discreetly treated, and by pleasant usage wrought upon, to take some *pains* at it, watching your seasons and taking great care, that he may not hate his task, but do it chearfully. *Holder.*

If health be such a blessing, it may be worth the *pains* to discover the regions where it grows, and the springs that feed it. *Temple.*

They called him a thousand fools for his *pains*. *L'Estran.*

Some natures the more *pains* a man takes to reclaim them, the worse they are. *L'Estrange, Fab.* 242.

Her nimble feet refuse
Their wonted speed, and she took *pains* to lose. *Dryden.*

The fame with *pains* we gain, but lose with ease,
Sure some to vex, but never all to please. *Pope.*

A reasonable clergyman, if he will be at the *pains*, can make the most ignorant man comprehend what is his duty, and convince him that he ought to perform it. *Swift.*

5. Labour; task. The singular, is, in this sense, obsolete.

He soft arrived on the grassy plain,
And fairly paced forth with easy *pain*. *Hubberd.*

Tone *paine* in a cottage doth take,
When t'other trim bowers do make. *Tusser's Husb.*

When of the dew, which th' eye and ear do take,
From flow'rs abroad and bring into the brain,
She doth within both wax and honey make:
This work is hers, this is her proper *pain*. *Davies.*

When a lion shakes his dreadful mane,
And angry grows, if he that first took *pain*
To tame his youth, approach the haughty beast,
He bends to him, but frights away the rest. *Waller.*

6. Uneasiness of mind.

It bid her feel
No future *pain* for me; but instant wed
A lover more proportion'd to her bed. *Prior.*

7. The throws of child-birth.

She bowed herself and travailed; for her *pains* came upon her. 1 *Sam.* iv. 19.

To Pain. *v. a.* [from the noun.]

1. To afflict; to torment; to make uneasy.

I am *pained* at my very heart, because thou hast heard, O my soul, the sound of the trumpet. *Jer.* iv. 19.

She drops a doubtful word that *pains* his mind,
And leaves a rankling jealousy behind. *Dryden.*

Excess of cold as well as heat, *pains* us, because it is equally destructive to that temper which is necessary to the preservation of life. *Locke.*

Pleasure arose in those very parts of his leg, that just before had been so much *pained* by the fetter. *Addison.*

2. [With the reciprocal pronoun.] To labour.

Though the lord of the liberty do *pain himself* to yield equal justice unto all, yet can there not but great abuses lurk in so absolute a privilege. *Spenser on Ireland.*

He *pained himself* to raise his note. *Dryden.*

Pa'inful. *adj.* [*pain* and *full.*]

1. Full of pain; miserable; beset with affliction.

Is there yet no other way, besides
These *painful* passages, how we may come
To death. *Milton's Par. Lost, b.* xi.

2. Giving pain; afflictive.

Evils have been more *painful* to us in the prospect, than by their actual pressure. *Addison's Spectator.*

I am sick of this bad world!
The day light and the sun grow *painful* to me. *Addison.*

Long abstinence may be *painful* to acid constitutions, by the uneasy sensation it creates in the stomach. *Arbuthnot.*

3. Difficult; requiring labour.

The *painful* service,
The extreme dangers, and the drops of blood
Shed for my thankless country, are requited
But with that surname. *Shakesp. Coriolanus.*

When I thought to know this, it was too *painful* for me. *Psalm* lxxiii. 16.

Surat he took, and thence preventing fame,
By quick and *painful* marches hither came. *Dryden.*

Ev'n I, tho' slow to touch the *painful* string,
Awake from slumber, and attempt to sing. *Smith.*

4. Industrious; laborious.

To dress the vines new labour is requir'd,
Nor must the *painful* husbandman be tir'd. *Dryden.*

Great abilities when employed as God directs, do but make the owners of them greater and more *painful* servants to their neighbours: however, they are real blessings when in the hands of good men. *Swift.*

Painfu'lly. *adv.* [from *painful.*]

1. With great pain or affliction.

2. Laboriously; diligently.

Such as sit in ease at home, raise a benefit out of their hunger and thirst, that serve their prince and country *painfully* abroad. *Raleigh's Essays.*

Robin red-breast *painfully*
Did cover them with leaves. *Children in the Wood.*

Painfu'lness. *n. s.* [from *painful.*]

1. Affliction; sorrow; grief.

With diamond in window-glass she graved,
Erona die, and end this ugly *painfulness*. *Sidney.*

No custom can make the *painfulness* of a debauch easy, or pleasing to a man; since nothing can be pleasant that is unnatural. *South's Sermons.*

2. Industry; laboriousness.

Painfulness, by feeble means shall be able to gain that which in the plenty of more forcible instruments, is through sloth and negligence lost. *Hooker, b.* v. *s.* 22.

Pai'nim. *n. s.* (*payen*, French.] Pagan; infidel.

The cross hath been a very ancient bearing, even before the birth of our Saviour, among the *Painims* themselves. *Peacham on Blazoning.*

Such dire atchievements sings the bard that tells
Of palfrey'd dames, bold knights, and magic spells;
Where whole brigades one champion's arms o'erthrow,
Slay *Painims* vile that force the fair. *Tickel.*

Pai'nim. *adj.* Pagan; infidel.

Champions bold,
Defy'd the best of *Painim* chivalry,
To mortal combat, or carriere with lance. *Milton.*

The Solymean sultan he o'erthrew,
His moony troops returning bravely smear'd
With *Painim* blood effus'd. *Philips.*

Pai'nless. *adj.* [from *pain.*] Without pain; without trouble.

The deaths thou show'st are forc'd;
Is there no smooth descent? no *painless* way
Of kindly mixing with our native clay? *Dryden.*

Painsta'ker. *n. s.* [*pains* and *take.*] Labourer; laborious person.

O Thomas, Thomas, hazard not thy life,
I'll prove a true *painstaker* day and night;
I'll spin and card, and keep our children tight. *Gay.*

Painsta'king. *adj.* [*pains* and *take.*] Laborious; industrious.

To PAINT. *v. a.* [*peindre*, French.]

1. To represent by delineation and colours.

Live to be the shew and gaze o'th' time,
We'll have thee as our rarer monsters are,
Painted upon a pole. *Shakesp. Macbeth.*

2. To cover with colours representative of something.

Who fears a sentence or an old man's saw,
Shall by a *painted* cloth be kept in awe. *Shakesp.*

3. To represent by colours, appearances, or images.

Till we from an author's words *paint* his very thoughts in our minds, we do not understand him. *Locke.*

4. To describe; to represent.

The lady is disloyal. ——
— Disloyal? —
— The word is too good to *paint* out her wickedness. *Sha.*

5. To colour; to diversify.

Such is his will that *paints*
The earth with colours fresh,
The darkest skies with store
Of starry lights. *Spenser.*

6. To deck with artificial colours.

Hath not old custom made this life more sweet
Than that of *painted* pomp? are not these woods
More free from peril than the court? *Shakesp.*

Jezebeel *painted* her face and tired her head. 2 *King* ix. 30.

To Paint. *v. n.* To lay colours on the face.

Such a sin to *paint*, *Pope.*

PAINT. *n. s.* [from the verb.]

1. Colours representative of any thing.

Poets are limners
To copy out ideas in the mind,
Words are the *paint* by which their thoughts are shown,
And nature is their object to be drawn. *Granville.*

The church of the annunciation looks beautiful in the inside, all but one corner of it being covered with statues, gilding, and *paint*. *Addison on Italy.*

Her charms in breathing *paint* engage,
Her modest cheek shall warm a future age. *Pope.*

2. Colours laid on the face.

Together lay her pray'r book and her *paint*. *Anon.*

PAI'NTER. *n. s.* [*peintre*, Fr. from *paint*.] One who professes the art of representing objects by colours.

In the placing let some care be taken how the *painter* did stand in the working. *Wotton's Architecture.*

Beauty is only that which makes all things as they are in their proper and perfect nature; which the best *painters* always chuse by contemplating the forms of each. *Dryden.*

PAI'NTING. *n. s.* [from *paint*.]

1. The art of representing objects by delineation and colours.

If *painting* be acknowledged for an art, it follows that no arts are without their precepts. *Dryden.*

'Tis in life as 'tis in *painting*,
Much may be right, yet much be wanting. *Prior.*

2. Picture; the painted resemblance.

This is the very *painting* of your fear;
This is the air-drawn dagger which you said,
Led you to Duncan. *Shakesp. Macbeth.*

Painting is welcome;
The *painting* is almost the natural man:
For since dishonour trafficks with man's nature,
He is but outside: pencil'd figures are
Ev'n such as they give out. *Shakesp. Timon of Athens.*

3. Colours laid on.

If any such be here
That love this *painting*, wherein you see me smear'd,
Let him express his disposition, *Shakesp. Coriolanus.*

PAI'NTURE. *n. s.* [*peinture*, French.] The art of painting. A French word.

To the next realm she stretch'd her sway,
For *painture* near adjoining lay,
A plenteous province. *Dryden.*

The show'ry arch
With lifted colours gay, or, azure, gules,
Delights and puzzles the beholders eye,
That views the watry brede with thousand shews
Of *painture* vary'd. *Philips.*

PAIR. *n. s.* [*paire*, Fr. *par*, Latin.]

1. Two things suiting one another, as a pair of gloves.

2. A man and wife.

O when meet now,
Such *pairs* in love and mutual honour join'd? *Milton.*

Baucis and Philemon there
Had liv'd long marry'd and a happy *pair*;
Now old in love. *Dryden.*

3. Two of a sort; a couple; a brace.

All his lovely looks, his pleasing fires,
All his sweet motions, all his taking smiles,
He does into one *pair* of eyes convey. *Suckling.*

The many *pairs* of nerves branching themselves to all the parts of the body, are wonderful to behold. *Ray.*

To PAIR. *v. n.* [from the noun.]

1. To be joined in pairs; to couple.

Our dance, I pray;
Your hand, my Perdita; so turtles *pair*. *Shakesp.*

2. To suit; to fit as a counterpart.

Had our prince seen the hour, he had *pair'd*
Well with this lord; there was not a full month
Between their births. *Shakesp. Winter's Tale.*

Ethelinda!
My heart was made to fit and *pair* with thine,
Simple and plain, and fraught with artless tenderness. *Rowe.*

To PAIR. *v. a.*

1. To join in couples.

Minds are so hardly match'd, that ev'n the first,
Tho' *pair'd* by heav'n, in Paradise were curs'd. *Dryden.*

2. To unite as correspondent or opposite.

Turtles and doves with diff'ring hues unite,
And glossy jet is *pair'd* with shining white. *Pope.*

PA'LACE. *n. s.* [*palais*, Fr. *palatium*, Lat.] A royal house; an house eminently splendid.

You forgot,
We with colours spread,
March'd thro' the city to the *palace* gates. *Shakespeare.*

Palaces and pyramids do slope
Their heads to their foundations. *Shakesp. Macbeth.*

The *palace* yard is fill'd with floating tides,
And the last comers bear the former to the sides. *Dryden.*

Palaces and fanes, and villas rise, *Anon.*
The suns bright *palace* on high columns rais'd,
With burning gold and flaming jewels blaz'd. *Addison.*
And gardens smile around. *Thomson's Summer.*

The old man early rose, walk'd forth and sate
On polish'd stone before his *palace* gate. *Pope.*

PALA'CIOUS. *adj.* [from *palace*.] Royal; noble; magnificent.

London encreases daily, turning of great *palacious* houses into small tenements. *Graunt's Bills of Mort.*

PALA'NQUIN. *n. s.* Is a kind of covered carriage used in the eastern countries that is supported on the shoulders of slaves, and wherein persons of distinction are carried.

PA'LATABLE. *adj.* [from *palate*.] Gustful; pleasing to the taste.

There is nothing so difficult as the art of making advice agreeable. How many devices have been made use of to render this bitter potion *palatable*. *Addison.*

They by th' alluring odour drawn in haste,
Fly to the dulcet cates, and crowding sip
Their *palatable* bane. *Philips.*

PA'LATE. *n. s.* [*palatum*, Latin.]

1. The instrument of taste.

Let their beds
Be made as soft as yours, and let their *palates*
Be season'd with such viands. *Shakesp. Merch. of Ven.*

These ivory feet were carved into the shape of lions; without these their greatest dainties could not relish to their *palates*. *Hakewill on Providence.*

Light and colours come in only by the eyes; all kind of sounds only by the ears; the several tastes and smells by the nose and *palate*. *Locke.*

By nerves about our *palate* plac'd,
She likewise judges of the taste:
Else, dismal thought! our warlike men
Might drink thick port for fine champagne. *Prior.*

The vulgar boil, the learned roast an egg;
Hard task to hit the *palate* of such guests. *Pope.*

2. Mental relish; intellectual taste.

It may be the *palate* of the soul is indisposed by listlessness or sorrow. *Taylor.*

The men of nice *palates* could not relish Aristotle, as drest up by the schoolmen. *Baker on Learning.*

PA'LATICK. *adj.* [from *palate*.] Belonging to the palate; a roof of the mouth.

The three labials, P. B. M. are parallel to the three gingival T. D. N. and to the three *palatic* K. G. L. *Holder.*

PA'LATINE. *n. s.* [*palatin*, Fr. from *palatinus* of *palatium*, Lat.] One invested with regal rights and prerogatives.

Many of those lords, to whom our kings had granted those petty kingdoms, did exercise *jura regalia*, insomuch as there were no less than eight counties *palatines* in Ireland at one time. *Davies on Ireland.*

These absolute *palatines* made barons and knights, did exercise high justice in all points within their territories. *Davies.*

PA'LATINE. *adj.* Possessing royal privileges.

PALE. *adj.* [*pale*, Fr. *pallidus*, Lat.]

1. Not ruddy; not fresh of colour; wan; white of look.

Look I so *pale*, lord Dorset, as the rest?
Ay, my good Lord; and no man in the presence;
But his red colour hath forsook his cheeks. *Shakesp.*

Was the hope drunk
Wherein you drest yourself; hath it slept since?
And wakes it now to look so green and *pale*. *Shakesp.*

Tell *pale*-hearted fear, it lies;
And sleep in spite of thunder. *Shakesp. Macbeth.*

2. Not high coloured; approaching to colourless transparency.

When the urine turns *pale*, the patient is in danger. *Arbuth.*

3. Not bright; not shining; faint of lustre; dim.

The night, methinks, is but the day-light sick,
It looks a little *paler*. *Shakesp. Merch. of Venice.*

To PALE. *v. a.* [from the adjective.] To make pale.

The glow worm shews the matin to be near,
And 'gins to *pale* his uneffectual fire. *Shakesp. Hamlet.*

To teach it good and ill, disgrace or fame,
Pale it with rage, or redden it with shame. *Prior.*

PALE. *n. s.* [*palus*, Latin.]

1. Narrow piece of wood joined above and below to a rail, to inclose grounds.

Get up o'th' rail, I'll peck you o'er the *pales* else. *Shak.*

As their example still prevails,
She tempts the stream, or leaps the *pales*. *Prior.*

Deer creep through when a *pale* tumbles down. *Mortimer.*

2. Any inclosure.

A ceremony, which was then judged very convenient for the whole church even by the whole, those few excepted, which brake out of the common *pale*. *Hooker, b. iv. s. 13.*

Let my due feet never fail
To walk the studious cloister's *pale*,
And love the high embowed roof. *Milton.*

He hath proposed a standing revelation, so well confirmed by miracles, that it should be needless to recur to them for the conviction of any man born within the *pale* of christianity. *Atterbury's Sermons.*

Confine the thoughts to exercise the breath;
And keep them in the *pale* of words till death. *Dunciad.*

3. Any district or territory.

There is no part but the bare English *pale*, in which the Irish have not the greatest footing. *Spenser.*

The lords justices put arms into the hands of divers noblemen of that religion, within the *pale*. *Clarendon.*

4. The *pale* is the third and middle part of the scutcheon, being derived from the chief to the base, or nether part of the scutcheon, with two lines. *Peacham.*

To PALE. *v. a.* [from the noun.]

1. To inclose with pales.

The diameter of the hill of twenty foot, may be *paled* in with twenty deals of a foot broad. *Mort. Husb.*

2. To inclose; to encompass.

Whate'er the ocean *pales*, or sky inclips,
Is thine. *Shakesp. Ant. and Cleopat.*

The English beach
Pales in the flood with men, with wives and boys. *Shak.*

Will you *pale* your head in Henry's glory,
And rob his temples of the diadem,
Now in his life? *Shakesp. Henry IV.*

PA'LEEYED. *adj.* [*pale* and *eye*.] Having eyes dimmed.

No nightly trance, or breathed spell,
Inspires the *paleey'd* priest from the prophetic cell. *Milton.*

Shrines, where their vigils *paleey'd* virgins keep,
And pitying saints, whose statues learn to weep. *Pope.*

PALEFA'CED. *adj.* [*pale* and *face*.] Having the face wan.

Why have they dar'd to march
So many miles upon her peaceful bosom,
Frighting her *palefac'd* villages with war. *Shakesp.*

Let *palefac'd* fear keep with the mean born man,
And find no harbour in a royal heart. *Shakesp.*

PA'LELY. *adv.* [from *pale*.] Wanly; not freshly; not ruddily.

PA'LENESS. *n. s.* [from *pale*.]

1. Wanness; want of colour; want of freshness; sickly whiteness of look.

Her blood durst not yet come to her face, to take away the name of *paleness* from her most pure whiteness. *Sidney.*

The blood the virgin's cheek forsook,
A livid *paleness* spreads o'er all her look. *Po. Ra. Lock.*

2. Want of colour; want of lustre.

The *paleness* of this flow'r
Bewray'd the faintness of my master's heart. *Shakesp.*

PA'LENDAR. *n. s.* A kind of coasting vessel.

Solyman sent over light horsemen in great *palendars*, which running all along the sea coast, carried the people and the cattle. *Knolles's Hist. of the Turks.*

PA'LEOUS. *n. s.* [*palea*, Latin.] Husky; chaffy.

This attraction have we tried in straws and *paleous* bodies. *Brown's Vulgar Errours.*

PA'LETTE. *n. s.* [*palette*, French.] A light board on which a painter holds his colours when he paints.

Let the ground of the picture be of such a mixture, as there may be something in it of every colour that composes your work, as it were the contents of your *palette*. *Dryden.*

Ere yet thy pencil tries her nicer toils,
Or on thy *palette* lie the blended oils,
Thy careless chalk has half atchiev'd thy art,
And her just image makes Cleôra start. *Tickell.*

When sage Minerva rose,
From her sweet lips smooth elocution flows,
Her skilful hand an iv'ry *pallette* grac'd,
Where shining colours were in order plac'd. *Gay.*

PA'LFREY. *n. s.* [*palefroy*, French.] A small horse fit for ladies: it is always distinguished in the old books from a war horse.

Her wanton *palfrey* all was overspread
With tinsel trappings, woven like a wave. *Fa. Queen.*

The damsel is mounted on a white *palfrey*, as an emblem of her innocence. *Addison's Spectator*, N°. 99.

The smiths and armorers on *palfreys* ride, *Dryden.*

PA'LFREYED. *adj.* [from *palfrey*.] Riding on a palfrey.

Such dire atchivements sings the bard that tells,
Of *palfrey'd* dames, bold knights, and magick spells;
Where whole brigades one champion's arms o'erthrow,
And cleave a giant at a random blow. *Tickell.*

PALIFICA'TION. *n. s.* [*palus*, Latin.] The act or practice of making ground firm with piles.

I have said nothing of *palification* or piling of the groundplot commanded by Vitruvius, when we build upon a moist soil. *Wotton.*

PA'LINDROME. *n. s.* [παλινδρομία, πάλιν and δρομέω.] A word or sentence which is the same read backward or forwards: as, *madam*; or this sentence, *Subi dura a rudibus.*

PA'LINODE. }
PA'LINODY. } *n. s.* [παλινῳδία.] A recantation.

I, of thy excellence, have oft been told;
But now my ravisht eyes thy face behold:
Who therefore in this weeping *palinod*
Abhor myself, that have displeas'd my God,
In dust and ashes mourn. *Sandys's Paraph. on Job.*

PALISA'DE. }
PALISA'DO. } *n. s.* [*palisade*, Fr. *palisado*, Span. from *palus*, Lat.] Pales set by way of inclosure or defence.

The Trojans round the place a rampire cast,
And *palisades* about the trenches plac'd. *Dryden.*

The wood is useful for *pallisadoes* for fortifications, being very hard and durable. *Mortimer's Husbandry.*

The city is surrounded with a strong wall, and that wall guarded with *palisades*. *Broome's Notes on the Odyssey.*

To PALISA'DE. *v. a.* [from the noun.] To inclose with palisades.

PA'LISH. *adj.* [from *pale*.] Somewhat pale.

Spirit of nitre makes with copper a *palish* blue; spirit of urine a deep blue. *Arbuthnot on Air.*

PALL. *n. s.* [*pallium*, Latin.]

1. A cloak or mantle of state.

With princely pace,
As fair Aurora in her purple *pall*,
Out of the East the dawning day doth call;
So forth she comes. *Fairy Queen, b. i. cant. 4.*

Let gorgeous tragedy
In scepter'd *pall* come sweeping by. *Milton.*

2. The mantle of an archbishop.

An archbishop ought to be consecrated and anointed, and after consecration he shall have the *pall* sent him. *Ayliffe.*

3. The covering thrown over the dead.

The right side of the *pall* old Egeus kept,
And on the left the royal Theseus wept. *Dryden.*

To PALL. *v. a.* [from the noun.] To cloak; to invest.

Come thick night
And *pall* thee in the dunnest smoak of hell,
That my keen knife see not the wound it makes. *Shakesp.*

To PALL. *v. n.* [Of this word the etymologists give no reasonable account: perhaps it is only a corruption of *pale*, and was applied originally to colours.] To grow vapid; to become insipid.

Empty one bottle into another swiftly, lest the drink *pall. Bac.*

Beauty soon grows familiar to the lover,
Fades in the eye, and *palls* upon the sense. *Addison.*

To PALL. *v. a.*

1. To make insipid or vapid.

Reason and reflection, representing perpetually to the mind the meanness of all sensual gratifications, blunt the edge of his keenest desires, and *pall* all his enjoyments. *Atterbury.*

Wit, like wine, from happier climates brought,
Dash'd by these rogues, turns English common draught,
They *pall* Moliere's and Lopez' sprightly strain. *Swift.*

2. To impair spriteliness; to dispirit.

A miracle
Their joy with unexpected sorrow *pall'd*. *Dryden.*

Ungrateful man,
Base, barbarous man, the more we raise our love
The more we *pall*, and cool, and kill his ardour. *Dryden.*

3. To weaken; to impair.

For this,
I'll never follow thy *pall'd* fortunes more. *Shakesp.*

4. To cloy.

Palled appetite is humorous, and must be gratified with sauces rather than food. *Tatler*, N°. 54.

PA'LLET. *n. s.* [*paillet*, in *Chaucer*, which was probably the French word from *paille*, straw, and secondarily, a bed.]

1. A small bed; a mean bed.

Why rather, sleep, liest thou in smoaky cribs,
Upon uneasy *pallets* stretching thee,
And husht with buzzing night flies to thy slumber;
Than in the perfum'd chambers of the great,
Under the canopies of costly state,
And lull'd with sounds of sweetest melody? *Shakesp.*

His secretary was laid in a *pallet* near him for ventilation of his thoughts. *Wotton's Buckingham.*

If your stray attendance be yet lodg'd,
Or shroud within these limits, I shall know
Ere morrow wake, or the low-roosted lark
From her thatch't *pallet* rouse. *Milton.*

2. [*palette*, French.] A small measure, formerly used by chirurgeons.

A surgeon drew from a patient in four days, twenty-seven *pallets*, every pallet containing three ounces. *Hakewill.*

PALLMA'LL. *n. s.* [*pila* and *malleus*, Lat. *pale maille*, French] A play in which the ball is struck with a mallet through an iron ring.

PA'LLIAMENT. *n. s.* [*pallium*, Lat.] A dress; a robe.

The people of Rome,
Send thee by me their tribune,
This *palliament* of white and spotless hue. *Shakesp.*

PA'LLIARDISE. *n. s.* [*pailliardise*, Fr.] Fornication; whoring. Obsolete.

To PA'LLIATE. *v. a.* [*pallio*, Lat. from *pallium*, a cloak; *pallier*, French.]

1. To cover with excuse.

They never hide or *palliate* their vices, but expose them freely to view. *Swift's Advan. of Religion.*

2. To extenuate; to soften by favourable representations.

The fault is to extenuate, *palliate*, and indulge. *Dryden.*

3. To cure imperfectly or temporarily, not radically; to ease, not cure.

PALLIA'TION. *n. s.* [*palliation*, Fr. from *palliate.*]

1. Extenuation; alleviation; favourable representation.

I saw clearly through all the pious disguises and soft *palliations* of some men. *King Charles.*

Such bitter invectives against other mens faults, and indulgence or *palliation* of their own, shews their zeal lies in their spleen. *Government of the Tongue.*

2. Imperfect or temporary, not radical cure; mitigation, not cure.

If the just cure of a disease be full of peril, let the physician resort to *palliation*. *Bacon's Nat. Hist.*

PALLIATIVE. *adj.* [*palliatif*, Fr. from *palliate.*]

1. Extenuating; favourably representative.

2. Mitigating, not removing; temporarily or partially, not radically curative.

Consumption pulmonary seldom admits of any other than a *palliative* cure, and is generally incurable when hereditary. *Arbuthnot on Diet.*

PA'LLIATIVE. *n. s.* [from *palliate.*] Something mitigating; something alleviating.

It were more safe to trust to the general aversion of our people against this coin, than apply those *palliatives* which weak, perfidious, or abject politicians administer. *Swift.*

PA'LLID. *adj.* [*pallidus*, Latin.] Pale; not high-coloured; not bright: *pallid* is seldom used of the face.

Of every sort, which in that meadow grew,
They gather'd some; the violet *pallid* blue. *Spenser.*
When from the *pallid* sky the sun descends. *Thomson.*

PALM. *n. s.* [*palma*, Latin; *palmier*, Fr.]

1. A tree of great variety of species; of which the branches were worn in token of victory.

The *palm*-tree hath a single imbranched stalk; the leaves are disposed in a circular form on the top, which, when they wither or fall off, are succeeded by new ones out of the middle of those which remain; among which sheaths or plain twigs break forth, opening from the bottom to the top, very full of flowers and clusters of embryos. There are twenty-one species of this tree, of which the most remarkable are, the greater *palm* or date-tree. The dwarf *palm* grows in Spain, Portugal, and Italy, from whence the leaves are sent hither and made into flag-brooms. The oily *palm* is a native of Guinea and Cape Verd island, but has been transplanted to Jamaica and Barbadoes. It grows as high as the main mast of a ship. *Miller.*

Get the start of the majestick world,
And bear the *palm* alone. *Shakesp. Jul. Cæsar.*
Go forth into the mount and fetch *palm*-branches. *Neh.* viii. 15.

Nothing better proveth the excellency of this soil, than the abundant growing of the *palm*-trees without labour of man. This tree alone giveth unto man whatsoever his life beggeth at nature's hand. *Raleigh.*

Above others who carry away the *palm* for excellence, is Maurice Landgrave of Hess. *Peacham of Musick.*

Fruits of *palm*-tree, pleasantest to thirst
And hunger both. *Milton's Par. Lost.*
Thou youngest virgin, daughter of the skies,
Whose *palms* new pluck'd from Paradise,
With spreading branches more sublimely rise. *Dryden.*

2. Victory; triumph. [*palme*, Fr.]

Namur subdu'd is England's *palm* alone;
The rest besieg'd; but we constrain'd the town. *Dryden.*

3. The hand spread out; the inner part of the hand. [*palma*, Lat.]

By this virgin *palm* now kissing thine,
I will be thine. *Shakespeare.*

Drinks of extreme thin parts fretting, put upon the back of your hand, will, with a little stay, pass through to the *palm*, and yet taste mild to the mouth. *Bacon.*

Seeking my success in love to know,
I try'd th' infallible prophetick way,
A poppy-leaf upon my *palm* to lay. *Dryden.*

4. A hand, or measure of length, comprising three inches. [*palme*, Fr.]

The length of a foot is a sixth part of the stature; a span one eighth of it; a *palm* or hand's breadth one twenty-fourth; a thumb's breadth or inch one seventy-second; a forefinger's breadth one ninety-sixth. *Holder on Time.*

Henry VIII. of England, Francis I. of France, and Charles V. emperor, were so provident, as scarce a *palm* of ground could be gotten by either, but that the other two would set the balance of Europe upright again. *Bacon.*

The same hand into a fist may close,
Which instantly a *palm* expanded shows. *Denham.*

To PALM. *v. a.* [from the noun.]

1. To conceal in the palm of the hand, as jugglers.

Palming is held foul play amongst gamesters. *Dryden.*
They *palm'd* the trick that lost the game. *Prior.*

2. To impose by fraud.

If not by scriptures, how can we be sure,
Reply'd the panther, what traditions pure?
For you may *palm* upon us new for old. *Dryden.*

Moll White has made the country ring with several imaginary exploits *palmed* upon her. *Addison's Spectator.*

3. To handle.

Frank carves very ill, yet will *palm* all the meat. *Prior.*

4. To stroak with the hand. *Ainsworth.*

PA'LMER. *n. s.* [from *palm.*] A pilgrim: they who returned from the holy land carried branches of palm.

My sceptre, for a *palmer's* walking staff. *Shakesp.*
Behold yon isle, by *palmers*, pilgrims trod,
Men bearded, bald, cowl'd, uncowl'd, shod, unshod. *Pope.*

PA'LMER. *n. s.* A crown encircling a deer's head.

PA'LMERWORM. *n. s.* [*palmer* and *worm.*] A worm covered with hair, supposed to be so called because he wanders over all plants.

A flesh fly, and one of those hairy worms that resemble caterpillars and are called *palmerworms*, being conveyed into one of our small receivers, the bee and the fly lay with their bellies upward, and the worm seemed suddenly struck dead. *Boyle.*

PALME'TTO. *n. s.* A species of the palm-tree: It grows in the West-Indies to be a very large tree; with the leaves the inhabitants thatch their houses. These leaves, before they are expanded, are cut and brought into England to make womens plaited hats; and the berries of these trees were formerly much used for buttons.

Broad o'er my head the verdant cedars wave,
And high *palmettos* lift their graceful shade. *Thomson.*

PALMI'FEROUS. *adj.* [*palma* and *fero*, Lat.] Bearing palms. *Dict.*

PA'LMIPEDE. *adj.* [*palma* and *pes*, Lat.] Webfooted; having the toes joined by a membrane.

It is described like fissipedes, whereas it is a *palmipede* or fin-footed like swans. *Brown's Vulgar Err. b.* v.

Water-fowl which are *palmipede*, are whole footed, have very long necks, and yet but short legs, as swans. *Ray.*

PA'LMISTER. *n. s.* [from *palma.*] One who deals in palmistry. *Dict.*

PA'LMISTRY. *n. s.* [*palma*, Latin.]

1. The cheat of foretelling fortune by the lines of the palm.

We shall not query what truth there is in *palmistry*, or divination, from those lines of our hands of high denomination. *Brown's Vulgar Errours, b.* v.

Here while his canting drone-pipe scan'd,
The mystick figures of her hand,
He tipples *palmistry*, and dines
On all her fortune-telling lines. *Cleaveland.*
With the fond maids in *palmistry* he deals;
They tell the secret first which he reveals. *Prior.*

2. *Addison* uses it for the action of the hand.

Going to relieve a common beggar, he found his pocket was picked; that being a kind of *palmistry* at which this vermin are very dextrous. *Addison's Spectator.*

PA'LMY. *adj.* [from *palm.*] Bearing palms.

In the most high and *palmy* state of Rome,
A little ere the mightiest Julius fell,
The graves stood tenantless. *Shakesp. Hamlet.*
She pass'd the region which Panchea join'd,
And flying, left the *palmy* plains behind. *Dryden.*

PALPABI'LITY. *n. s.* [from *palpable.*] Quality of being perceivable to the touch.

He first found out *palpability* of colours; and by the delicacy of his touch, could distinguish the different vibrations of the heterogeneous rays of light. *Mart. Scriblerius.*

PA'LPABLE. *n. s.* [*palpable*, Fr. *palpor*, Latin.]

1. Perceptible by the touch.

Art thou but
A dagger of the mind, a false creation?
I see thee yet in form as *palpable*,
As this which now I draw. *Shakesp. Macbeth.*
Darkness must overshadow all his bounds,
Palpable darkness! and blot out three days. *Milton.*

2. Gross; coarse; easily detected.

That grosser kind of heathenish idolatry, whereby they worshipped the very works of their own hands, was an absurdity to reason so *palpable*, that the prophet David, comparing idols and idolaters together, maketh almost no odds between them. *Hooker, b.* i. *s.* 8.

They grant we err not in *palpable* manner, we are not openly and notoriously impious. *Hooker, b.* v. *s.* 27.

He must not think to shelter himself from so *palpable* an absurdity, by this impertinent distinction. *Tillotson.*

Having no surer guide, it was no wonder that they fell into gross and *palpable* mistakes. *Woodward's Nat. History.*

3. Plain; easily perceptible.

That they all have so testified, I see not how we should possibly wish a proof more *palpable*, than this manifestly received and every where continued custom of reading them publickly. *Hooker, b.* v. *s.* 22.

Since there is so much dissimilitude between cause and effect in the more *palpable* phænomena, we can expect no less between them and their invisible efficients. *Glanville.*

PALPA'BLENESS. *n. s.* [from *palpable.*] Quality of being palpable; plainness; grossness.

PA'LPABLY. *adv.* [from *palpable.*]

1. In such a manner as to be perceived by the touch.
2. Grossly; plainly.

Clodius was acquitted by a corrupt jury, that had *palpably* taken shares of money, before they gave up their verdict, they prayed of the senate a guard, that they might do their consciences justice. *Bacon.*

PALPA'TION. *n. s.* [*palpatio*, *palpor*, Lat.] The act of feeling.

To PA'LPITATE. *v. a.* [*palpito*, Latin; *palpiter*, Fr.] To beat as the heart; to flutter; to go *pit a pat*.

PALPITA'TION. *n. s.* [*palpitation*, Fr. from *palpitate.*] Beating or panting; that alteration in the pulse of the heart, upon frights or any other causes, which makes it felt: for a natural uniform pulse goes on without distinction.

The heart strikes five hundred sort of pulses in an hour; and hunted into such continual *palpitations*, through anxiety and distraction, that fain would it break. *Harvey.*

I knew the good company too well to feel any *palpitations* at their approach. *Tatler*, N°. 86.

Anxiety and *palpitations* of the heart, are a sign of weak fibres. *Arbuthnot on Aliments.*

Her bosom heaves
With *palpitations* wild. *Thomson's Spring.*

PA'LSGRAVE. *n. s.* [*paltsgraff*, German.] A count or earl who has the overseeing of a prince's palace. *Dict.*

PA'LSICAL. *adj.* [from *palsy.*] Afflicted with the palsy; paralytick.

PA'LSIED. *adj.* [from *palsy.*] Diseased with a palsy.

Pall'd, thy blazed youth
Becomes assuaged, and doth beg the alms
Of *palsied* eld. *Shakesp. Measure for Measure.*

Though she breaths in a few pious peaceful souls, like a *palsied* person, she scarce moves a limb. *Decay of Piety.*

Let not old age long stretch his *palsy'd* hand,
Those who give late are importun'd each day. *Gay.*

PA'LSY. *n. s.* [*paralysis*, Lat. thence *paralysy*, *parasy*, *palasy*, *palsy.*] A privation of motion or sense of feeling, or both, proceeding from some cause below the cerebellum, joined with a coldness, softness, flaccidity, and at last wasting of the parts. If this privation be in all the parts below the head, except the thorax and heart, it is called a paraplegia; if in one side only, a hemiplegia; if in some parts only of one side, a paralysis. There is a three fold division of a *palsy*; the first is a privation of motion, sensation remaining. Secondly, a privation of sensation, motion remaining. And lastly, a privation of both together. *Quincy.*

The *palsy*, and not fear, provokes me. *Shakesp.*

A *palsy* may as well shake an oak, as shake the delight of conscience. *South's Sermons.*

To PA'LTER. *v. n.* [from *paltron*, *Skinner.*] To shift; to dodge; to play tricks.

I must
To the young man send humble treaties,
And *palter* in the shift of lowness. *Shakespeare.*

Be these juggling fiends no more believ'd,
That *palter* with us in a double sense;
That keep the word of promise to our ear,
And break it to our hope. *Shakesp. Macbeth.*

Romans, that have spoke the word,
And will not *palter?* *Shakesp. Jul. Cæsar.*

To PA'LTER. *v. a.* To squander: as, he palters his fortune. *Ainsworth.*

PA'LTERER. *n. s.* [from *palter.*] An unsincere dealer; a shifter.

PA'LTRINESS. *n. s.* [from *paltry.*] The state of being paltry.

PA'LTRY. *adj.* [*poltron*, French; a scoundrel; *paltrocca*, a low whore, Italian.] Sorry; worthless; despicable; contemptible; mean.

Then turn your forces from this *paltry* siege,
And stir them up against a mightier task. *Shakesp.*

A very dishonest *paltry* boy, as appears in leaving his friend here in necessity, and denying him. *Shakesp.*

Whose compost is *paltry* and carried too late,
Such husbandry useth that many do hate. *Tuss. Husb.*

For knights are bound to feel no blows,
From *paltry* and unequal foes. *Hudibras. p. iii.*

It is an ill habit to squander away our wishes upon *paltry* fooleries. *L'Estrange, Fab.* 140.

When such *paltry* slaves presume
To mix in treason, if the plot succeeds,
They're thrown neglected by; but if it fails,
They're sure to die like dogs. *Addison's Cato.*

PA'LY. *adj.* [from *pale.*] Pale. Used only in poetry.

Fain would I go to chafe his *paly* lips,
With twenty thousand kisses. *Shakesp. Hen.* VI.

From camp to camp,
Fire answers fire, and through their *paly* flames
Each battle sees the others umber'd face. *Shakesp.*

The roses in thy lips and cheeks shall fade
To *paly* ashes. *Shakesp. Romeo and Juliet.*

A dim gleam the *paly* lanthorn throws
O'er the mid pavement. *Gay.*

PAM. *n. s.* [probably from *palm*, victory; as *trump* from *triumph.*] The knave of clubs.

Ev'n mighty *pam* that kings and queens o'erthrew,
And mow'd down armies in the fights of lu. *Pope.*

To PA'MPER. *v. a.* [*pamberare*, Italian.] To glut; to fill with food; to saginate; to feed luxuriously.

It was even as two physicians should take one sick body in hand, of which the former would minister all things meet to purge and keep under the body, the other to *pamper* and strengthen it suddenly again; whereof what is to be looked for but a most dangerous relapse? *Spenser.*

You are more intemperate in your blood
Than Venus, or those *pamperd* animals
That rage in savage sensuality. *Shakesp.*

They are contented as well with mean food, as those that with the rarities of the earth do *pamper* their voracities. *Sandys.*

Praise swelled thee to a proportion ready to burst, it brought thee to feed upon the air, and to starve thy soul, only to *pamper* thy imagination. *South's Sermons.*

With food
Distend his chine and *pamper* him for sport. *Dryden.*

His lordship lolls within at ease,
Pamp'ring his paunch with foreign rarities. *Dryden.*

To *pamper'd* insolence devoted fall,
Prime of the flock and choicest of the stall. *Pope.*

PA'MPHLET. *n. s.* [*par un filet*, Fr. Whence this word is written anciently, and by *Caxton paunflet.*] A small book, properly a book sold unbound, and only stitched.

Com'st thou with deep premeditated lines,
With written *pamphlets* studiously devis'd? *Shakesp.*

I put forth a slight *pamphlet* about the elements of architecture. *Wotton.*

He could not, without some tax upon himself and his ministers for the not executing the laws, look upon the bold licence of some in printing *pamphlets*. *Clarendon.*

As when some writer in a publick cause,
His pen, to save a sinking nation draws,
While all is calm, his arguments prevail,
'Till pow'r discharging all her stormy bags,
Flutters the feeble *pamphlet* into rags. *Swift.*

To PA'MPHLET. *v. n.* [from the noun.] To write small books.

I put pen to paper, and something I have done, though in a poor *pamphleting* way. *Howel's Pre-eminence of Parliament.*

PAMPHLETEE'R. *n. s.* [from *pamphlet.*] A scribbler of small books.

The squibs are those who in the common phrase are called libellers, lampooners, and *pamphleteers*. *Tatler.*

With great injustice I have been pelted by *pamphleteers*. *Swift.*

To PAN. *v. a.* An old word denoting to close or join together. *Ainsworth.*

PAN. *n. s.* [*ponne*, Saxon.]

1. A vessel broad and shallow, in which provisions are dressed or kept.

This were but to leap out of the *pan* into the fire. *Spenser.*

The pliant brass is laid
On anvils, and of heads and limbs are made,
Pans, cans. *Dryden.*

2. The part of the lock of the gun that holds the powder.

Our attempts to fire the gun-powder in the *pan* of the pistol, succeeded not. *Boyle.*

3. Any thing hollow: as, the brain *pan*.

PANACE'A. *n. s.* [*panacée*, Fr. πανάκεια, from πᾶν ἄκος.] An universal medicine.

PANACE'A. *n. s.* An herb. *Ainsworth.*

PA'NCAKE. *n. s.* [*pan* and *cake.*] Thin pudding baked in the frying-pan.

A certain knight swore by his honour they were good *pancakes*, and swore by his honour the mustard was naught. *Shak.*

The flour makes a very good *pancake*, mixed with a little wheat flour. *Mortimer's Husbandry.*

PANA'DO. *n. s.* [from *panis*, thread.] Food made by boiling bread in water.

Their diet ought to be very sparing; gruels, *panados*, and chicken broth. *Wiseman's Surgery.*

PANCRA'TICAL. *adj.* [πᾶν and κρατὸς.] Excelling in all the gymnastick exercises.

He was the most *pancratical* man of Greece, and, as Galen reporteth, able to persist erect upon an oily plank, and not to be removed by the force of three men. *Brown.*

PA'NCREAS. *n. s.* [πᾶν and κρέας.] The *pancreas* or sweet bread, is a gland of the conglomerate sort, situated between the bottom of the stomach and the vertebræ of the loins: it lies across the abdomen, reaching from the liver to the spleen, and is strongly tied to the peritonæum, from which it receives its common membranes. It weighs commonly four or five ounces. It is about six fingers breadth long, two broad, and one thick. Its substance is a little soft and supple. *Quincy.*

PAN-

PANCREA'TICK. *adj.* [from *pancreas.*] Contained in the pancreas.

In man and viviparous quadrupeds, the food moiſtened with the ſaliva is firſt chewed, then ſwallowed into the ſtomach, and ſo evacuated into the inteſtines, where being mixed with the choler and *pancreatick* juice, it is further ſubtilized, and eaſily finds its way in at the ſtreight orifices of the lacteous veins. *Ray on the Creation.*

The bile is ſo acrid, that nature has furniſhed the *pancreatic* juice to temper its bitterneſs. *Arbuthnot.*

PA'NCY. } *n. ſ.* [corrupted, I ſuppoſe, from *panacey, panacea.*]
PA'NSY. } A flower: a kind of violet.

The daughters of the flood have ſearch'd the mead
For violets pale, and cropp'd the poppy's head;
Pancies to pleaſe the ſight, and caſſia ſweet to ſmell. *Dryd.*

The real eſſence of gold is as impoſſible for us to know, as for a blind man to tell in what flower the colour of a *panſy* is, or is not to be found, whilſt he has no idea of the colour of a *panſy.* *Locke.*

PA'NDECT. *n. ſ.* [*pandecta*, Latin.]

1. A treatiſe that comprehends the whole of any ſcience.

It were to be wiſhed, that the commons would form a *pandect* of their power and privileges, to be confirmed by the entire legiſlative authority. *Swift.*

2. The digeſt of the civil law.

PANDE'MICK. *adj.* [πᾶς and δῆμος.] Incident to a whole people.

Thoſe inſtances bring a conſumption, under the notion of a *pandemick* or endemick, or rather vernacular diſeaſe to England. *Harvey on Conſumptions.*

PA'NDER. *n. ſ.* [This word is derived from *Pandarus*, the pimp in the ſtory of *Troilus* and *Creſſida*; it was therefore originally written *pandar*, till its etymology was forgotten.] A pimp; a male bawd; a procurer.

Let him with his cap in hand,
Like a baſe *pander*, hold the chamber door
Whilſt by a ſlave
His faireſt daughter is contaminated. *Shakeſp. Hen.* V.

If thou fear to ſtrike, and to make me certain it is done, thou art the *pander* to her diſhonour, and equally to me diſloyal. *Shakeſp. Cymbeline.*

If ever you prove falſe to one another, ſince I have taken ſuch pains to bring you together, let all pitiful goers-between be call'd *panders* after my name. *Shakeſp. Troil and Creſſida.*

Camillo was his help in this, his *pander*,
There is a plot againſt my life. *Shakeſp. Wint. Tale.*

The ſons of happy Punks, the *pander's* heir,
Are privileged
To clap the firſt, and rule the theatre. *Dryden.*

Thou haſt confeſs'd thyſelf the conſcious *pandar*
Of that pretended paſſion;
A ſingle witneſs infamouſly known,
Againſt two perſons of unqueſtion'd fame. *Dryden.*

My obedient honeſty was made
The *pander* to thy luſt and black ambition. *Rowe.*

To PA'NDER. *v. a.* [from the noun.] To pimp; to be ſubſervient to luſt or paſſion.

Proclaim no ſhame,
When the compulſive ardour gives the charge,
Since firſt itſelf as actively doth burn,
And reaſon *panders* will. *Shakeſp. Hamlet.*

PA'NDERLY. *adj.* [from *pander.*] Pimping; pimplike.

Oh you *panderly* raſcals! there's a conſpiracy againſt me. *Shakeſp. Merry Wives of Windſor.*

PANDICULA'TION. *n. ſ.* [*pandiculans*, Lat.] The reſtleſsneſs, ſtretching, and uneaſineſs that uſually accompany the cold fits of an intermitting fever.

Windy ſpirits, for want of a due volatilization, produce in the nerves a *pandiculation*, or oſcitation, or ſtupor, or cramp in the muſcles. *Floyer on the Humours.*

PANE. *n. ſ.* [*paneau*, French.]

1. A ſquare of glaſs.

The letters appear'd reverſe thro' the *pane*,
But in Stella's bright eyes they were plac'd right again. *Sw.*

The face of Eleanor owes more to that ſingle *pane* than to all the glaſſes ſhe ever conſulted. *Pope's Letters.*

2. A piece mixed in variegated works with other pieces.

Him all repute
For his device in handſoming a ſuit,
To judge of lace, pink, *panes*, print, and plait,
Of all the court to have the beſt conceit. *Donne.*

PANEGY'RICK. *n. ſ.* [*panegyrique*, Fr. πανήγυρις.] An elogy; an encomiaſtick piece.

The Athenians met at the ſepulchres of thoſe who were ſlain at Marathon, and there made *panegyricks* upon them. *Stillingfleet.*

That which is a ſatyr to other men muſt be a *panegyrick* to your lordſhip. *Dryden.*

As he continues the exerciſes of theſe eminent virtues, he may be one of the greateſt men that our age has bred; and leave materials for a *panegyrick*, not unworthy the pen of ſome future Pliny. *Prior.*

PANEGY'RIST. *n. ſ.* [from *panegyrick*; *panegyriſte*, Fr.] One that writes praiſe; encomiaſt.

Add theſe few lines out of a far more ancient *panegyriſt* in the time of Conſtantine the great. *Camden.*

PA'NEL. *n. ſ.* [*panellum*, law Latin; *paneau*, French.]

1. A ſquare, or piece of any matter inſerted between other bodies.

The chariot was all of cedar, ſave that the fore end had *panels* of ſapphires, ſet in borders of gold. *Bacon.*

Maximilian, his whole hiſtory is digeſted into twenty-four ſquare *panels* of ſculpture in bas relief. *Addiſon's Italy.*

This fellow will join you together as they join wainſcot; then one of you will prove a ſhrunk *panel*, and, like green timber, warp. *Shakeſpeare's As you like it.*

A bungler thus, who ſcarce the nail can hit,
With driving wrong will make the *panel* ſplit. *Swift.*
He gave the *panel* to the maid. *Prior.*

2. [Panel, *panellum*, Lat. of the French, *panne*, id eſt, *pellis* or *paneau*, a piece or pane in Engliſh.] A ſchedule or roll, containing the names of ſuch jurors, as the ſheriff provides to paſs upon a trial. And empannelling a jury, is nothing but the entering them into the ſheriff's roll or book. *Cowel.*

Then twelve of ſuch as are indifferent, and are returned upon the principal *panel*, or the tales, are ſworn to try the ſame, according to evidence. *Hale's Hiſt. of England.*

PANG. *n. ſ.* [either from *pain*, or *bang*, Dutch, uneaſy.] Extreme pain; ſudden paroxiſm of torment.

Say, that ſome lady
Hath for your love as great a *pang* of heart,
As you have for Olivia. *Shakeſpear's Twelfth Night.*
See how the *pangs* of death do make him grin! *Shak.*

Suff'rance made
Almoſt each *pang* a death. *Shakeſp. Hen.* VIII.

Earth trembl'd from her entrails, as again
In *pangs*; and nature gave a ſecond groan. *Milt. Par. Loſt.*

Juno pitying her diſaſtrous fate,
Sends Iris down, her *pangs* to mitigate. *Denham.*

My ſon advance
Still in new impudence, new ignorance.
Succeſs let others teach, learn thou from me
Pangs without birth, and fruitleſs induſtry. *Dryden.*

I will give way
To all the *pangs* and fury of deſpair. *Addiſon.*

I ſaw the hoary traitor
Grin in the *pangs* of death, and bite the ground. *Addiſon.*

Ah! come not, write not, think not once of me,
Nor ſhare one *pang* of all I felt for thee. *Pope.*

To PANG. *v. a.* [from the noun.] To torment cruelly.

If fortune divorce
It from the bearer; 'tis a ſuff'rance *panging*,
As ſoul and bodies parting. *Shakeſp.*

I grieve myſelf
To think, when thou ſhalt be diſedg'd by her,
Whom now thou tir'ſt on, how thy memory
Will then be *pang'd* by me. *Shakeſpeare.*

PA'NICK. *adj.* [from *pan*, groundleſs fears being ſuppoſed to be ſent by Pan.] Violent without cauſe.

The ſudden ſtir and *panical* fear, when chantecleer was carried away by reynard. *Camden's Remains.*

Which many reſpect to be but a *panick* terror, and men do fear, they juſtly know not what. *Brown's Vulgar Errors.*

I left the city in a *panic* fright;
Lions they are in council, lambs in fight. *Dryden.*

PA'NNADE. *n. ſ.* The curvet of a horſe. *Ainſworth.*

PA'NNEL. *n. ſ.* [*panneel*, Dutch; *paneau*, French.] A kind of ruſtick ſaddle.

A *pannel* and wanty, pack-ſaddle and ped,
With line to fetch litter, and halters for hed. *Tuſſer.*

His ſtrutting ribs on both ſides ſhow'd,
Like furrows he himſelf had plow'd;
For underneath the ſkirt of *pannel*,
'Twixt every two there was a channel. *Hudibras.*

PA'NNEL. *n. ſ.* The ſtomach of a hawk. *Ainſworth.*

PA'NNICLE. } *n. ſ.* A plant.
PA'NNICK. }

The *pannicle* is a plant of the millet kind, differing from that, by the diſpoſition of the flowers and ſeeds, which, of this, grow in a cloſe thick ſpike: It is ſowed in ſeveral parts of Europe, in the fields, as corn for the ſuſtenance of the inhabitants; it is frequently uſed in particular places of Germany to make bread. *Miller.*

September is drawn with a chearful countenance; in his left hand a handful of millet, oats, and *pannicle*. *Peacham.*

Panick affords a ſoft demulcent nouriſhment. *Arbuth.*

PANNI'ER. *n. ſ.* [*panier*, French.] A baſket; a wicker veſſel, in which fruit, or other things, are carried on a horſe.

The worthleſs brute
Turns a mill, or drags a loaded life,
Beneath two *panniers*, and a baker's wife. *Dryden.*

We have reſolved to take away their whole club in a pair of *panniers*, and impriſon them in a cupboard. *Addiſon.*

In

Pano'ply. *n. s.* [πανοπλία.] Complete armour.

In arms they stood
Of golden *panoply*, refulgent host!
Soon banded. *Milton's Paradise Lost.*

We had need to take the christian *panoply*, to put on the whole armour of God. *Ray on the Creation.*

To PANT. *v. n.* [*panteler*, old French.]

1. To palpitate; to beat as the heart in sudden terror, or after hard labour.

Yet might her piteous heart be seen to *pant* and quake. *Fairy Queen.*

Below the bottom of the great abyss,
There where one centre reconciles all things,
The world's profound heart *pants*. *Crashaw.*

If I am to lose by sight the soft *pantings*, which I have always felt, when I heard your voice, pull out these eyes before they lead me to be ungrateful. *Tatler.*

2. To have the breast heaving, as for want of breath.

Pluto *pants* for breath from out his cell,
And opens wide the grinning jaws of hell. *Dryden.*

3. To play with intermission.

The whisp'ring breeze
Pants on the leaves, and dies upon the trees. *Pope.*

4. To long; to wish earnestly.

They *pant* after the dust of the earth, on the head of the poor. *Amos* ii. 7.

Who *pants* for glory, finds but short repose,
A breath revives him, and a breath o'erthrows. *Pope.*

Pant. *n. s.* [from the verb.] Palpitation; motion of the heart.

Leap thou, attire and all,
Through proof of harness, to my heart, and there
Ride on the *pants* triumphing. *Shakespeare.*

Pa'ntaloon. *n. s.* [*pantalon*, French.] A man's garment anciently worn, in which the breeches and stockings were all of a piece. *Hanmer.*

The sixth age shifts
Into the lean and slipper'd *pantaloon*,
With spectacles on nose, and pouch on side. *Shakes.*

The French we conquer'd once,
Now give us laws for *pantaloons*,
The length of breeches and the gathers. *Hudibras.*

Pantess. *n. s.* The difficulty of breathing in a hawk. *Ains.*

Panthe'on. *n. s.* [πάνθειον.] A temple of all the gods.

Pa'nther. *n. s.* [πανθήρ, *panthera*, Lat. *panthere*, Fr.] A spotted wild beast; a lynx; a pard.

An it please your majesty,
To hunt the *panther* and the hart with me,
With horn and hound. *Shakespeare.*

Pan, or the universal, is painted with a goat's face, about his shoulders a *panther's* skin. *Peacham.*

The *panther's* speckled hide,
Flow'd o'er his armour with an easy pride. *Pope.*

Pa'ntile. *n. s.* A gutter tile.

Pa'ntingly. *adv.* [from *panting*.] With palpitation.

She heav'd the name of father
Pantingly forth, as if it prest her heart. *Shakespeare.*

Pa'ntler. *n. s.* [*panetier*, French.] The officer in a great family, who keeps the bread. *Hanmer.*

When my old wife liv'd,
She was both *pantler*, butler, cook. *Shakespeare.*

He would have made a good *pantler*, he would have chipped bread well. *Shakespear's Henry* IV.

Pa'ntofle. *n. s.* [*pantoufle*, French; *pantofula*, Italian.] A slipper.

Melpomene has on her feet, her high cothurn or tragick *pantofles* of red velvet and gold, beset with pearls. *Peacham.*

Pa'ntomime. *n. s.* [πᾶς and μῖμος; *pantomime*, Fr.]

1. One who has the power of universal mimickry; one who expresses his meaning by mute action; a buffoon.

Not that I think those *pantomimes*,
Who vary action with the times,
Are less ingenious in their art,
Than those who duly act one part. *Hudibras.*

2. A scene; a tale exhibited only in gesture and dumb-shew.

He put off the representation of *pantomimes* till late hours, on market-days. *Arbuthnot.*

Exulting folly hail'd the joyful day,
And *pantomime* and song confirm'd her sway. *Anon.*

Pa'nton. *n. s.* A shoe contrived to recover a narrow and hoof-bound heel. *Farrier's Dict.*

Pa'ntry. *n. s.* [*paneterie*, Fr. *panarinm*, Lat.] The room in which provisions are reposited.

The Italian artizans distribute the kitchin, *pantry*, bakehouse under ground. *Wotton's Architect.*

What work would they make in the *pantry* and the larder. *L' Estrange.*

He shuts himself up in the *pantry* with an old gipsy, once in a twelvemonth. *Addison's Spect.*

Pap. *n. s.* [*papa*, Italian; *pappe*, Dutch; *papilla*, Latin.]

1. The nipple; the dug sucked.

Some were so from their source endu'd,
By great dame nature, from whose fruitful *pap*,
Their well-heads spring. *Fairy Queen.*

Out sword, and wound
The *pap* of Pyramus.
Ay, that left *pap*, where heart doth hop;
Thus die I. *Shakespear's Midsummer Night's Dream.*

An infant making to the *paps* would press,
And meets instead of milk, a falling tear. *Dryden.*

In weaning young creatures, the best way is never to let them suck the *paps*. *Ray on the Creation.*

That Timothy Trim, and Jack were the same person, was proved particularly by a mole under the left *pap*. *Arbuth.*

2. Food made for infants, with bread boiled in water.

Sleep then a little, *pap* content is making. *Sidney.*

The noble soul by age grows lustier;
We must not starve, nor hope to pamper her
With woman's milk and *pap* unto the end. *Donne.*

Let the powder, after it has done boiling, be well beaten up with fair water to the consistence of thin *pap*. *Boyle.*

3. The pulp of fruit. *Ains.*

Pa'pa. *n. s.* [παππᾶς; *papa*, Lat.] A fond name for father, used in many languages.

Where there are little masters and misses in a house, bribe them, that they may not tell tales to *papa* and mamma. *Swift.*

Papa'cy. *n. s.* [*papat*, *papauté*, Fr. from *papa*, the pope.] popedom; office and dignity of bishops of Rome.

Now there is ascended to the *papacy* a personage, that though he loves the chair of the *papacy* well, yet he loveth the carpet above the chair. *Bacon.*

Pa'pal. *adj.* [*papal*, French.] Popish; belonging to the pope; annexed to the bishoprick of Rome.

The pope released Philip from the oath, by which he was bound to maintain the privileges of the Netherlands; this *papal* indulgence hath been the cause of so many hundred thousands slain. *Raleigh.*

Pa'paw. *n. s.* [*papaya*, low Lat. *papaya*, *papayer*, Fr.]

The *papaw* hath a simple stalk; the flowers are male and female in different plants: the male flowers, which are barren, are tubulous, consisting of one leaf, and expand in form of a star: the female flowers consist of several leaves, which expand in form of a rose, out of whose flower-cup rises the pointal, which afterwards becomes fleshy fruit, shaped like a cucumber or melon. *Miller.*

The fair *papaw*,
Now but a seed, preventing nature's law,
In half the circle of the hasty year,
Projects a shade, and lovely fruits does wear. *Waller.*

Papa'verous. *adj.* [*papavereus*, from *papaver*, Lat. a poppy.] Resembling poppies.

Mandrakes afford a *papaverous* and unpleasant odour, whether in the leaf or apple. *Brown's Vulgar Errors.*

PA'PER. *n. s.* [*papier*, French; *papyrus*, Latin.]

1. Substance on which men write and print; made by macerating linen rags in water, and then spreading them in thin sheets.

I have seen her unlock her closet, take forth *paper*. *Shake.*

2. Piece of paper.

'Tis as impossible to draw regular characters on a trembling mind, as on a shaking *paper*. *Locke on Education.*

3. Single sheet printed, or written. It is used particularly of essays or journals, or any thing printed on a sheet. [*Feuille volante.*]

What see you in those *papers*, that you lose
So much complexion? look ye how they change!
Their cheeks are *paper*. *Shakespear's Hen.* V.

Nothing is of more credit or request, than a petulant *paper*, or scoffing verses. *Ben Johnson.*

They brought a *paper* to me to be sign'd. *Dryden.*
Do the prints and *papers* lie? *Swift.*

Pa'per. *adj.* Any thing slight or thin.

There is but a thin *paper* wall between great discoveries and a perfect ignorance of them. *Burnet.*

To Pa'per. *v. a.* [from the noun.]. To register.

He makes up the file
Of all the gentry: and his own letter
Must fetch in him he *papers*. *Shakespear's Hen.* VIII.

Pa'permaker. *n. s.* [*paper* and *make*.] One who makes paper.

Pa'permill. *n. s.* [*paper* and *mill*.] A mill in which rags are ground for paper.

Thou hast caused printing to be used; and contrary to the king, and his dignity, thou hast built a *paper-mill*. *Shakesp.*

Pape'scent. *adj.* Containing pap; inclinable to pap.

Demulcent, and of easy digestion, moistening and resolvent of the bile, are vegetable sopes; as honey, and the juices of ripe fruits, some of the cooling, lactescent, *papescent* plants; as cichory and lettuce. *Arbuthnot on Aliments.*

PAPI'LIO. *n. s.* [Lat. *papillon*, Fr.] A butterfly; a moth of various colours.

Conjecture cannot estimate all the kinds of *papilios*, natives of this island, to fall short of three hundred. *Ray.*

Papiliona'ceous. *adj.* [from *papilio*, Latin.]

The flowers of some plants are called *papilionaceous* by botanists, which represent something of the figure of a butterfly, with its wings displayed: and here the petala, or flower leaves, are always of a diform figure: they are four in number, but joined together at the extremities; one of these is usually larger than the rest, and is erected in the middle of the flower, and

and by ſome called vexillum: the plants, that have this flower, are of the leguminous kind; as peaſe, vetches, &c. *Quincy.*

PA'PILLARY. } *adj.* [from *papilla.*] Having emulgent veſſels,
PA'PILLOUS. } or reſemblances of paps.

Malpighi concludes, becauſe the outward cover of the tongue is perforated, under which lie *papillary* parts, that in theſe the taſte lieth. *Derham's Phyſico-Theology.*

The *papillous* inward coat of the inteſtines is extremely ſenſible. *Arbuthnot on Aliments.*

PAPI'ST. *n. ſ.* [*papiſte*, Fr. *papiſta*, Latin.] One that adheres to the communion of the pope and church of Rome.

The principal clergymen had frequent conferences with the prince, to perſuade him to change his religion, and become a *papiſt.* *Clarendon.*

PAPI'STICAL. *adj.* [from *papiſt.*] Popiſh; adherent to popery.

There are ſome *papiſtical* practitioners among you. *Whitg.*

PAPI'STRY. *n. ſ.* [from *papiſt.*] Popery; the doctrine of the Romiſh church.

Papiſtry, as a ſtanding pool, covered and overflowed all England. *Aſcham's Shcoolmaſter.*

A great number of pariſhes in England conſiſt of rude and ignorant men, drowned in *papiſtry.* *Whitgifte.*

PA'PPOUS. *adj.* [*papposus*, low Latin.] Having that ſoft light down, growing out of the ſeeds of ſome plants; ſuch as thiſtles, dandelyon, hawk-weeds, which buoys them up ſo in the air, that they can be blown any where about with the wind: and, therefore, this diſtinguiſhes one kind of plants, which is called pappoſa, or papposi flores. *Quincy.*

Another thing argumentative of providence is, that *pappous* plumage growing upon the tops of ſome ſeeds, whereby they are wafted with the wind, and by that means diſſeminated far and wide. *Ray on the Cneation.*

Dandelion, and moſt of the *pappous* kind, have long numerous feathers, by which they are wafted every way. *Derh.*

PA'PPY. *adj.* [from *pap.*] Soft; ſucculent; eaſily divided.

Theſe were converted into fens, where the ground, being ſpungy, ſucked up the water, and the looſen'd earth ſwell'd into a ſoft and *pappy* ſubſtance. *Burnet.*

Its tender and *pappy* fleſh cannot, at once, be fitted to be nouriſhed by ſolid diet. *Ray on the Creation.*

PAR. n. ſ. [Latin.] State of equality; equivalence; equal value. This word is not elegantly uſed, except as a term of traffick.

To eſtimate the *par*, it is neceſſary to know how much ſilver is in the coins of the two countries, by which you charge the bill of exchange. *Locke.*

My friend is the ſecond after the treaſurer; the reſt of the great officers are much upon a *par.* *Gulliver's Travels.*

PARA'BLE. *adj.* [*parabilis*, Latin.] Eaſily procured. Not in uſe.

They were not well wiſhers unto *parable* phyſic, or remedies eaſily acquired, who derived medicines from the phœnix. *Brown's Vulgar Errours.*

PA'RABLE. *n. ſ.* [παραβολὴ; *parabole*, Fr.] A ſimilitude; a relation under which ſomething elſe is figured.

Balaam took up his *parable*, and ſaid. *Numbers*, xxiii. 7.
He ſpake many things in *parables.* *Matt.* xiii. 3.

What is thy fulſome *parable* to me?
My body is from all diſeaſes free. *Dryden.*

PA'RABOLA. n. ſ. [Latin.]

The *parabola* is a conick ſection, ariſing from a cone's being cut by a plane parallel to one of its ſides, or parallel to a plane that touches one ſide of the cone. *Harris.*

Had the velocities of the ſeveral planets been greater or leſs than they are now, at the ſame diſtances from the ſun, they would not have revolved in concentrick circles as they do, but have moved in hyperbola's or *parabola's*, or in ellipſes, very excentrick. *Bentley's Sermons.*

PARABO'LICAL. } *adj.* [*parabolique*, Fr. from *parable.*]
PARABO'LICK. }

1. Expreſſed by parable or ſimilitude.

Such from the text deſcry the *parabolical* expoſition of Cajetan. *Brown's Vulgar Errours.*

The whole ſcheme of theſe words is figurative, as being a *parabolical* deſcription of God's vouchſafing to the world the invaluable bleſſing of the goſpel, by the ſimilitude of a king. *South's Sermons.*

2. Having the nature or form of a parabola. [from *parabola.*]

The pellucid coat of the eye doth not lie in the ſame ſuperficies with the white of the eye, but riſeth up a hillock above its convexity, and is of an hyperbolical or *parabolical* figure. *Ray on the Creation.*

The incident ray will deſcribe, in the refracting medium, the *parabolick* curve. *Cheyne's Phil. Prin.*

PA'RABOLICALLY. *adv.* [from *parabolical.*]

1. By way of parable or ſimilitude.

Theſe words, notwithſtanding *parabolically* intended, admit no literal inference. *Brown's Vulgar Errours.*

2. In the form of a parabola.

PARA'BOLISM. *n. ſ.* In algebra, the diviſion of the terms of an equation, by a known quantity that is involved or multiplied in the firſt term. *Dict.*

PARA'BOLOID. *n. ſ.* [παραβολὴ and εἶδος.] A paraboliform curve in geometry, whoſe ordinates are ſuppoſed to be in ſuptriplicate, ſubquadruplicate, &c. ratio of their reſpective abſciſſæ: There is another ſpecies; for if you ſuppoſe the parameter, multiplied into the ſquare of the abſciſſa, to be equal to the cube of the ordinate; then the curve is called a ſemicubical *paraboloid.* *Harris.*

PARACENTE'SIS. *n. ſ.* [παρακέντησις, παρακεντέω, to pierce. *paracenteſe*, Fr.] That operation, whereby any of the venters are perforated to let out any matter; as tapping in a tympany. *Quincy.*

PARACE'NTRICAL. } *adj.* [παρὰ and κέντρον.] Deviating from
PARACE'NTRICK. } circularity.

Since the planets move in the elliptick orbits, in one of whoſe foci the ſun is, and, by a radius from the ſun, deſcribe equal areas in equal times, we muſt find out a law for the *paracentrical* motion, that may make the orbits elliptic. *Cheyne.*

PARA'DE. *n. ſ.* [*parade*, Fr.]

1. Shew; oſtentation.

He is not led forth as to a review, but as to a battle; nor adorned for *parade*, but execution. *Granville.*

The rites perform'd, the parſon paid,
In ſtate returned the grand *parade.* *Swift.*
Be rich; but of your wealth make no *parade*,
At leaſt, before your maſter's debts are paid. *Swift.*

2. Military order.

The cherubim ſtood arm'd
To their night-watches in warlike *parade.* *Milton.*

3. Place where troops draw up to do duty and mount guard.

4. Guard; poſture of defence.

Accuſtom him to make judgment of men by their inſide, which often ſhews itſelf in little things, when they are not in *parade*, and upon their guard. *Locke on Education.*

PA'RADIGM. *n. ſ.* [παράδειγμα.] Example.

PARADISI'ACAL. *adj.* [from *paradiſe.*] Suiting paradiſe; making paradiſe.

The antients expreſs the ſituation of *paradiſiacal* earth in reference to the ſea. *Burnet's Theory of the Earth.*

Such a mediocrity of heat would be ſo far from exalting the earth to a more happy and *paradiſiacal* ſtate, that it would turn it to a barren wilderneſs. *Woodw. Nat. Hiſt.*

The ſummer is a kind of heaven, when we wander in a *paradiſiacal* ſcene, among groves and gardens; but, at this ſeaſon, we are like our poor firſt parents, turned out of that agreeable, though ſolitary life, and forced to look about for more people to help to bear our labours, to get into warmer houſes, and hive together in cities. *Pope.*

PA'RADISE. *n. ſ.* [παράδεισος; *paradiſe*, Fr.]

1. The bliſsful regions, in which the firſt pair was placed.

Longer in that *paradiſe* to dwell,
The law I gave to nature him forbids. *Milton.*

2. Any place of felicity.

What fool is not ſo wiſe,
To loſe an oath to win a *paradiſe.* *Shakeſpeare.*
Conſideration, like an angel, came,
And whipt th' offending Adam out of him;
Leaving his body as a *paradiſe*,
T' invelope and contain celeſtial ſpirits. *Shakeſpeare.*
If ye ſhould lead her into a fool's *paradiſe*,
It were very groſs behaviour. *Shakeſp. Romeo and Juliet.*
Why, nature, bower the ſpirit of a fiend
In mortal *paradiſe* of ſuch ſweet fleſh. *Shakeſpeare.*
The earth
Shall all be *paradiſe*, far happier place,
Than this of Eden, and far happier days. *Milton.*

PA'RADOX. *n. ſ.* [*paradoxe*, Fr. παράδοξος.] A tenet contrary to received opinion; an aſſertion contrary to appearance; a poſition in appearance abſurd.

A gloſſe there is to colour that *paradox*, and make it appear in ſhew not to be altogether unreaſonable. *Hooker.*

You undergo too ſtrict a *paradox*,
Striving to make an ugly deed look fair. *Shakeſp.*

In their love of God, men can never be too affectionate: it is as true, though it may ſeem a *paradox*, that in their hatred of ſin, men may be ſometimes too paſſionate. *Sprat.*

PARADO'XICAL. *adj.* [from *paradox.*]

1. Having the nature of a paradox.

What hath been every where opinioned by all men, is more than *paradoxical* to diſpute. *Brown's Vulgar Errours.*

Strange it is, how the curioſity of men, that have been active in the inſtruction of beaſts, among thoſe many *paradoxical* and unheard-of imitations, ſhould not attempt to make one ſpeak. *Brown's Vulgar Errours.*

Theſe will ſeem ſtrange and *paradoxical* to one that takes a proſpect of the world. *Norris.*

2. Inclined to new tenets, or notions contrary to received opinions.

PARADO'XICALLY. *adv.* [from *paradox.*] In a paradoxical manner; in a manner contrary to received opinions.

If their vanity of appearing ſingular puts them upon advancing paradoxes, and proving them as *paradoxically*, they are uſually laught at. *Collier on Pride.*

PARADOXI'CALNESS. *n. s.* [from *paradox.*] State of being paradoxical.

PARADOXO'LOGY. *n. s.* [from *paradox.*] The use of paradoxes.
Perpend the difficulty, which obscurity, or unavoidable *paradoxology*, must put upon the attempter. *Brown.*

PARAGO'GE. *n. s.* [παραγωγὴ; *paragoge*, Fr.] A figure whereby a letter or syllable is added at the end of a word, without adding any thing to the sense of it. *Dict.*

PA'RAGON. *n. s.* [*paragon*, from *parage*, equality, old French; *paragone*, Italian.]

1. A model; a pattern; something supremely excellent.
An angel! or, if not,
An earthly *paragon*. *Shakespeare.*
Tunis was never grac'd before with such a *paragon* to their queen. *Shakesp. Tempest.*

2. Companion; fellow.
Alone he rode without his *paragon*. *Spenser.*

To PA'RAGON. *v. a.* [*parangonner*, French.]

1. To compare.
The picture of Pamela, in little form, he wore in a tablet, purposing to *paragon* the little one with Artesia's length, not doubting but even, in that little quantity, the excellency of that would shine through the weakness of the other. *Sidney.*
I will give thee bloody teeth,
If thou with Cæsar *paragon* again
My man of men. *Shakespeare.*
Proud seat
Of Lucifer, so by allusion call'd
Of that bright star to Satan *paragon'd*. *Milt. Par. Lost.*

2. To equal.
He hath atchiev'd a maid
That *paragons* description and wild fame;
One that excels the quirks of blazoning pens. *Shakesp.*
We will wear our mortal state with her,
Catharine our queen, before the primest creature
That's *paragon'd* i' th' world. *Shakes. Hen.* VIII.

PA'RAGRAPH. *n. s.* [*paragraphe*, Fr. παράγραφη.] A distinct part of a discourse.
Of his last *paragraph*, I have transcribed the most important parts. *Swift.*

PARAGRA'PHICALLY. *adv.* [from *paragraph.*] By paragraphs; with distinct breaks or divisions.

PARALLA'CTICAL. } *adj.* [from *parallax.*] Pertaining to a
PARALLA'CTICK. } parallax.

PA'RALLAX. *n. s.* [παράλλαξις.] The distance between the true and apparent place of the sun, or any star viewed from the surface of the earth.
By what strange *parallax* or optick skill
Of vision multiply'd *Milton's Paradise Regained.*
Light moves from the sun to us in about seven or eight minutes time, which distance is about 70,000,000 English miles, supposing the horizontal *parallax* of the sun to be about twelve seconds. *Newton's Optics.*

PA'RALLEL. *adj.* [παράλληλος; *parallele*, Fr.]

1. Extended in the same direction, and preserving always the same distance.
Distorting the order and theory of causes perpendicular to their effects, he draws them aside unto things whereto they run *parallel*, and their proper motions would never meet together. *Brown's Vulgar Errours.*

2. Having the same tendency.
When honour runs *parallel* with the laws of God and our country, it cannot be too much cherished; but when the dictates of honour are contrary to those of religion and equity, they are the great depravations of human nature. *Addison.*

3. Continuing the resemblance through many particulars; equal; like.
The foundation principle of peripateticism is exactly *parallel* to an acknowledged nothing. *Glanville.*
I shall observe something *parallel* to the wooing and wedding suit in the behaviour of persons of figure. *Addison.*
Compare the words and phrases in one place of an author, with the same in other places of the same author, which are generally called *parallel* places. *Watts.*

PA'RALLEL. *n. s.* [from the adjective.]

1. Lines continuing their course, and still remaining at the same distance from each other.
Who made the spider *parallels* design,
Sure as De Moivre, without rule or line? *Pope.*

2. Lines on the globe marking the latitude.

3. Direction conformable to that of another line.
Dissentions, like small streams, are first begun,
Scarce seen they rise but gather as they run;
So lines, that from their *parallel* decline,
More they proceed, the more they still disjoin. *Garth.*

4. Resemblance; conformity continued through many particulars; likeness.
Such a resemblance of all parts,
Life, death, age, fortune, nature, arts;
She lights her torch at theirs to tell,
And shew the world this *parallel*. *Denham.*
'Twixt earthly females and the moon,
All *parallels* exactly run. *Swift's Miscel.*

5. Comparison made.
The *parallel* holds in the gainlesness, as well as laboriousness of the work. *Decay of Piety.*
A reader cannot be more rationally entertained, than by comparing and drawing a *parallel* between his own private character, and that of other persons. *Addison.*

6. Any thing resembling another.
Thou ungrateful brute, if thou wouldst find thy *parallel*, go to hell, which is both the region and the emblem of ingratitude. *South's Sermons.*
For works like these, let deathless journals tell,
None but thyself can be thy *parallel*. *Pope.*

To PA'RALLEL. *v. a.* [from the noun.]

1. To place, so as always to keep the same direction with another line.
The Azores having a middle situation between these continents and that vast tract of America, the needle seemeth equally distracted by both, and diverting unto neither, doth *parallel* and place itself upon the true meridian. *Brown.*

2. To keep in the same direction; to level.
His life is *parallel'd*
Ev'n with the stroke and line of his great justice. *Shakesp.*

3. To correspond to.
That he stretched out the north over the empty places, seems to *parallel* the expression of David, he stretched out the earth upon the waters. *Burnet.*

4. To be equal to; to resemble through many particulars.
In the fire, the destruction was so swift, sudden, vast and miserable, as nothing can *parallel* in story. *Dryden.*

5. To compare.
I *parallel'd* more than once, our idea of substance, with the Indian philosopher's he-knew-not-what, which supported the tortoise. *Locke.*

PARALLE'LISM. *n. s.* [*parallelisme*, Fr. from *parallel.*] State of being parallel.
The *parallelism* and due proportionated inclination of the axis of the earth. *More's Divine Dialogues.*
Speaking of the *parallelism* of the axis of the earth, I demand, whether it be better to have the axis of the earth steady and perpetually *parallel* to itself, or to have it carelessly tumble this way and that way. *Ray on the Creation.*

PARALLE'LOGRAM. *n. s.* [παράλληλος and γράμμα; *parallelograme*, Fr.] In geometry, a right lined quadrilateral figure, whose opposite sides are parallel and equal. *Harris.*
The experiment we made in a loadstone of a *parallelogram*, or long figure, wherein only inverting the extremes, as it came out of the fire, we altered the poles. *Brown.*
We may have a clear idea of the area of a *parallogram*, without knowing what relation it bears to the area of a triangle. *Watts's Logick.*

PARALLELOGRA'MICAL. *adj.* [from *parallelogram.*] Having the properties of a parallelogram.

PARALLELO'PIPED. *n. s.* [from *parallelopipede*, Fr.] A solid figure contained under six parallelograms, the opposites of which are equal and parallel; or it is a prism, whose base is a parallelogram: it is always triple to a pyramid of the same base and height. *Harris.*
Two prisms alike in shape I tied so, that their axes and opposite sides being parallel, they composed a *parallelopiped*. *Newton's Optics.*
Crystals that hold lead are yellowish, and of a cubic or *parallelopiped* figure. *Woodward.*

PA'RALOGISM. *n. s.* [παραλόγισμος; *paralogisme*, Fr.] A false argument.
That because they have not a bladder of gall, like those we observe in others, they have no gall at all, is a *paralogism* not admittible, a fallacy that dwells not in a cloud, and needs not the sun to scatter it. *Brown's Vulgar Errours.*
Modern writers, making the drachma less than the denarius, others equal, have been deceived by a double *paralogism*, in standing too nicely upou the bare words of the ancients, without examining the things. *Arbuthnot.*
If a syllogism agree with the rules given for the construction of it, it is called a true argument: if it disagree with these rules, it is a *paralogism*, or false argument. *Watts.*

PA'RALOGY. *n. s.* False reasoning.
That Methuselah was the longest liver of all the posterity of Adam, we quietly believe; but that he must needs be so, is perhaps below *parology* to deny. *Brown.*

PA'RALYSIS. [παράλυσις; *paralysie*, Fr.] A palsy.

PARALY'TICAL. } *adj.* [from *paralysis*; *paralytique*, Fr.] Pal-
PARALY'TICK. } sied; inclined to palsy.
Nought shall it profit, that the charming fair,
Angelic, softest work of heav'n, draws near
To the cold shaking *paralytick* hand,
Senseless of beauty. *Prior.*
If a nerve be cut, or streightly bound, that goes to any muscle, that muscle shall immediately lose its motion; which is the case of *paralyticks*. *Derham.*
The difficulties of breathing and swallowing, without any tumour after long diseases, proceed commonly from a resolution or *paralytical* disposition of the parts. *Arbuthnot.*

PARAMETER.

PARA'METER. *n. s.* The latus rectum of a parabola, is a third proportional to the abscissa and any ordinate; so that the square of the ordinate is always equal to the rectangle under the *parameter* and abscissa: but, in the ellipsis and hyperbola, it has a different proportion. *Harris.*

PARAMO'UNT. *adj.* [*per* and *mount.*]

1. Superiour; having the highest jurisdiction; as lord *paramount*, the chief of the seigniory.

Leagues within the state are ever pernicious to monarchies; for they raise an obligation, *paramount* to obligation of sovereignty, and make the king, tanquam unus ex nobis. *Bacon.*

The dogmatist's opinioned assurance is *paramount* to argument, *Glanville.*

If all power be derived from Adam, by divine institution, this is a right antecedent and *paramount* to all government; and therefore the positive laws of men cannot determine that which is itself the foundation of all law. *Locke.*

Mankind, seeing the apostles possessed of a power plainly *paramount* to the powers of all the known beings, whether angels or dæmons, could not question their being inspired by God. *West on the Resurrection.*

2. Eminent; of the highest order.

John a Chamber was hanged upon a gibbet raised a stage higher in the midst of a square gallows, as a traitor *paramount*; and a number of his chief accomplices were hanged upon the lower story round him. *Bacon.*

PA'RAMOUNT. *n. s.* The chief.

In order came the grand infernal peers,
'Midst came their mighty *paramount*. *Milton's P. L.*

PA'RAMOUR. *n. s.* [*par* and *amour*, Fr.]

1. A lover or woer.

Upon the floor
A lovely bevy of fair ladies sat,
Courted of many a jolly *paramour*,
The which them did in modestwise amate,
And each one sought his lady to aggrate. *Fa. Queen.*

No season then for her
To wanton with the sun her lusty *paramour*. *Milt.*

2. A mistress. It is obsolete in both senses, though not inelegant or unmusical.

Shall I believe
That unsubstantial death is amorous,
And that the lean abhorred monster keeps
Thee here in dark to be his *paramour*. *Shakespeare.*

PA'RANYMPH. *n. s.* [παρὰ and νυμφὴ; *paranymphe*, Fr.]

1. A brideman; one who leads the bride to her marriage.

The Timnian bride
Had not so soon prefer'd
Thy *paranymph*, worthless to thee compar'd,
Successor in thy bed. *Milton's Agonistes.*

2. One who countenances or supports another.

Sin hath got a *paranymph* and a sollicitor, a warrant and an advocate. *Taylor's Worthy Communicant.*

PARA'PEGM. *n. s.* [παραπήγμα, παραπήγνυμι.] A brazen table fixed to a pillar, on which laws and proclamations were anciently engraved: also a table set up publickly, containing an account of the rising and setting of the stars, eclipses of the sun and moon, the seasons of the year, &c. whence astrologers give this name to the tables, on which they draw figures according to their art. *Philips.*

Our forefathers, observing the course of the sun, and marking certain mutations to happen in his progress through the zodiac, set them down in their *parapegms*, or astronomical canons. *Brown's Vulgar Errours.*

PA'RAPET. *n. s.* [*parapet*, Fr. *parapetto*, Italian.] A wall breast high.

There was a wall or *parapet* of teeth set in our mouth to restrain the petulancy of our words. *Ben Johnson.*

PARAPHIMO'SIS. *n. s.* [παραφίμωσις; *paraphimose*, Fr.] A disease when the præputium cannot be drawn over the glans.

PARAPHERNA'LIA. *n. s.* [Lat. *paraphernaux*, Fr.] Goods in the wife's disposal.

PA'RAPHRASE. *n. s.* [παράφρασις; *paraphrase*, Fr.] A loose interpretation; an explanation in many words.

All the laws of nations were but a *paraphrase* upon this standing rectitude of nature, that was ready to enlarge itself into suitable determinations, upon all emergent objects and occasions. *South's Sermons.*

In *paraphrase*, or translation with latitude, the author's words are not so strictly followed as his sense, and that too amplified, but not altered: such is Mr. Waller's translation of Virgil's fourth Æneid. *Dryden.*

To PA'RAPHRASE. *v. a.* [*paraphraser*, Fr. παραφράζω.] To interpret with laxity of expression; to translate loosely.

We are put to construe and *paraphrase* our own words, to free ourselves from the ignorance and malice of our adversaries. *Stillingfleet's Def. of Dis. on Romish Idolatry.*

What needs he *paraphrase* on what we mean,
We were at worst but wanton; he's obscene. *Dryden.*

Where translation is impracticable, they may *paraphrase*.— But it is intolerable, that under a pretence of *paraphrasing* and translating, a way should be suffered of treating authors to a manifest disadvantage. *Felton on the Classicks.*

PA'RAPHRAST. *n. s.* [*paraphraste*, Fr. παραφραστής.] A lax interpreter; one who explains in many words.

The fittest for publick audience are such, as following a middle course between the rigor of literal translators and the liberty of *paraphrasts*, do, with great shortness and plainess, deliver the meaning. *Hooker.*

The chaldean *paraphrast* renders Gerah by Meath. *Arbuth.*

PARAPHRA'STICAL. } *ajd.* [from *paraphrase.*] Lax in inter-
PARAPHRA'STIC. } pretation; not literal; not verbal.

PARAPHRENI'TIS. *n. s.* [παρὰ and φρενίτις; *paraphrenesie*, Fr.]

Paraphrenitis is an inflammation of the diaphragm. The symptoms are a violent fever, a most exquisite pain increased upon inspiration, by which it is distinguished from a pleurisy, in which the greatest pain is in expiration. *Arbuth.*

PA'RASANG. *n. s.* [*parasanga*, low Latin.] A Persian measure of length.

Since the mind is not able to frame an idea of any space without parts, instead thereof it makes use of the common measures, which, by familiar use, in each country, have imprinted themselves on the memory; as inches and feet, or cubits and *parasangs*. *Locke.*

PA'RASITE. *n. s.* [*parasite*, Fr. *parasita*, Latin.] One that frequents rich tables, and earns his welcome by flattery.

He is a flatterer,
A *parasite*, a keeper back of death,
Who gently would dissolve the bands of life,
Which false hopes linger. *Shakespeare.*

Most smiling, smooth, detested *parasites*,
Courteous destroyers, affable wolves, meek bears,
You fools of fortune. *Shakespeare.*

Come, you *parasite*, answer me
Directly to this question. *Shakespeare.*

Diogenes, when mice came about him, as he was eating, said, I see, that even Diogenes nourisheth *parasites*. *Bacon.*

Thou, with trembling fear,
Or like a fawning *parasite*, obeyed;
Then to thyself ascrib'st the truth foretold. *Milton.*

The people sweat not for their king's delight,
T' enrich a pimp, or raise a *parasite*. *Dryden.*

PARASI'TICAL. } *adj.* [*parasitique*, Fr. from *parasite.*] Flat-
PARASI'TICK. } tering; wheedling.

The bishop received small thanks for his *parasitick* presentation. *Hakewill on Providence.*

Some *parasitick* preachers have dared to call those martyrs, who died fighting against me. *King Charles.*

PA'RASOL. *n. s.* A small sort of canopy or umbrello carried over the head, to shelter from rain and the heat of the sun. *Dict.*

PARASYNA'XIS. *n. s.* In the civil law, a conventicle or unlawful meeting. *Dict.*

To PA'RBOIL. *v. a.* [*parbouiller*, French.] To half boil; to boil in part.

Parboil two large capons upon a soft fire, by the space of an hour, till, in effect, all the blood be gone. *Bacon.*

From the sea into the ship we turn,
Like *parboil'd* wretches, on the coals to burn. *Donne.*

Like the scum, starved men did draw,
From *parboil'd* shoes and boots. *Donne.*

To PARBREAK. *v. n.* [*brecker*, Dutch.] To vomit.

PA'RBREAK. *n. s.* [from the verb.] Vomit.

Her filthy *parbreak* all the place defiled has. *Fa. Queen.*

PA'RCEL. *n. s. parcelle*, French; *particula*, Latin.]

1. A small bundle.

2. A part of the whole taken separately.

Women, Silvius, had they mark'd him
In *parcels*, as I did, would have gone near
To fall in love with him. *Shakespeare.*

I drew from her a prayer of earnest heart,
That I would all my pilgrimage dilate;
Whereof by *parcels* she had something heard,
But not distinctively. *Shakespear's Othello.*

An inventory thus importing,
The several *parcels* of his plate, his treasure,
Rich stuffs and ornaments of houshold. *Shakespeare.*

I have known pensions given to particular persons, any one of which, if divided into smaller *parcels*, and distributed to those, who distinguish themselves by wit or learning, would answer the end. *Swift.*

The same experiments succeed on two *parcels* of the white of an egg, only it grows somewhat thicker upon mixing with an acid. *Arbuthnot on Aliments.*

3. A quantity or mass.

What can be rationally conceived in so transparent a substance as water for the production of these colours, besides the various sizes of its fluid and globular *parcels*. *Newton.*

4. A number of persons, in contempt.

This youthful *parcel*
Of noble batchelors stand at my bestowing. *Shakesp.*

5. Any

5. Any number or quantity in contempt.

They came to this conclusion; that, unless they could, by a *parcel* of fair words and pretences, engage them into a confederacy, there was no good to be done. *L'Estrange.*

To PARCEL. *v. a.* [from the noun.]

1. To divide into portions.

If they allot and *parcel* out several perfections to several deities, do they not, by this, assert contradictions, making deity only to such a measure perfect; whereas a deity implies perfection beyond all measure. *South's Sermons.*

Those ghostly kings would *parcel* out my pow'r,
And all the fatness of my land devour. *Dryden.*

2. To make up into a mass.

What a wounding shame,
That mine own servant should
Parcel the sum of my disgraces by
Addition of his envy! *Shakesp.*

PARCENER. *n. s.* [In common law.] When one dies possessed of an estate, and having issue only daughters, or his sisters be his heirs; so that the lands descend to those daughters or sisters: these are called *parceners*, and are but as one heir. *Dict.*

PARCE'NERY. *n. s.* [from *parsonier*, French.] A holding or occupying of land by more persons pro indiviso, or by joint tenants, otherwise called coparceners: for if they refuse to divide their common inheritance, and chuse rather to hold it jointly, they are said to hold in parcinarie. *Cowel.*

To PARCH. *v. a.* [from περικαίειν, says Junius; from *percoquo*, says Skinner; neither of them seem satisfied with their conjecture: perhaps from *perustus*, burnt, to *perust*, to *parch*; perhaps from *parchment*, the effect of fire upon parchment being almost proverbial.] To burn slightly and superficially; to scorch; to dry up.

Hath thy fiery heart so *parcht* thine entrails,
That not a tear can fall. *Shakesp.*

Did he so often lodge in open field
In winter's cold, and summer's *parching* heat,
To conquer France. *Shakesp. Henry IV.*

Torrid heat,
And vapours as the Libyan air adust,
Began to *parch* that temperate clime. *Milt. Par. Lost.*

I'm stupify'd with sorrow, past relief
Of tears; *parch'd* up and wither'd with my grief. *Dryd.*

Without this circular motion of our earth, one hemisphere would be condemned to perpetual cold and darkness, the other continually roasted and *parched* by the sun beams. *Ray.*

The Syrian star
With his sultry breath infects the sky;
The ground below is *parch'd*, the heav'ns above us fry. *Dryden's Horace.*

Full fifty years
I have endur'd the biting winter's blast,
And the severer heats of *parching* summer. *Rowe.*

He is like a man distressed with thirst in the *parched* places of the wilderness, he searches every pit, but finds no water. *Rogers's Sermons.*

To PARCH. *v. n.* To be scorched.

We were better *parch* in Africk sun,
Than in the pride and salt scorn of his eyes. *Shakesp.*

If to prevent the acrospiring, it be thrown thin, many corns will dry and *parch* into barley. *Mort. Husb.*

PARCHMENT. *n. s.* [*parchemin*, French; *pergamena*, Latin.] Skins dressed for the writer. Among traders, the skins of sheep are called parchment, those of calves vellum.

Is not this a lamentable thing, that the skin of an innocent lamb should be made *parchment*; that *parchment*, being scribbled o'er, should undo a man? *Shakesp. Hen. VI.*

In the coffin, that had the books, they were found as fresh as if newly written, being written in *parchment*, and covered with watch candles of wax. *Bacon.*

Like flying shades before the clouds we shew,
We shrink like *parchment* in consuming flame. *Dryden.*

PARCHMENT-MAKER. *n. s.* [*parchment* and *maker*.] He who dresses parchment.

PARD. } *n. s.* *pardus*, *pardalis*, Latin.] The leopard;
PA'RDALE. } in poetry, any of the spotted beasts.

The *pardale* swift, and the tyger cruel. *Fa. Queen.*

As fox to lambs, as wolf to heifer's calf;
As *pard* to the hind, or step-dame to her son. *Shakesp.*

Ten brace of greyhounds, snowy fair,
And tall as stags, ran loose, and cours'd around his chair,
A match for *pards* in flight, in grappling for the bear. *Dryd.*

To PA'RDON. *v. a.* [*pardonner*, French.]

1. To excuse an offender.

When I beheld you in Cilicia,
An enemy to Rome, I *pardon'd* you. *Dryden.*

2. To forgive a crime.

3. To remit a penalty.

That thou may'st see the diff'rence of our spirit,
I *pardon* thee thy life before thou ask it. *Shakespeare.*

4. Pardon me, is a word of civil denial, or slight apology.

Sir, *pardon* me, it is a letter from my brother. *Shakesp.*

PA'RDON. *n. s.* [*pardon*, Fr. from the verb.]

1. Forgiveness of an offender.

2. Forgiveness of a crime; indulgence.

He that pleaseth great men, shall get *pardon* for iniquity. *Ecclus* xx. 27.

A slight pamphlet, about the elements of architecture, hath been entertained with some *pardon* among my friends. *Wotton.*

3. Remission of penalty.

4. Forgiveness received.

A man may be safe as to his condition, but, in the mean time, dark and doubtful as to his apprehensions; secure in his *pardon*, but miserable in the ignorance of it; and so passing all his days in the disconsolate, uneasy vicissitudes of hopes and fears, at length go out of the world, not knowing whither he goes. *South's Sermons.*

5. Warrant of forgiveness, or exemption from punishment.

The battle done, and they within our power,
Shall never see his *pardon*. *Shakespeare's K. Lear.*

PA'RDONABLE. *adj.* [*prrdonable*, Fr. from *pardon*.] Venial; excusable.

That which we do being evil, is notwithstanding by so much more *pardonable*, by how much the exigences of so doing, or the difficulty of doing otherwise is greater, unless this necessity or difficulty have originally risen from ourselves. *Hooker.*

A blind man sitting in the chimney corner is *pardonable* enough, but sitting at the helm, he is intolerable. *South.*

What English readers, unacquainted with Greek or Latin, will believe me, when we confess we derive all that is *pardonable* in us from ancient fountains. *Dryden.*

PA'RDONABLENESS. *n. s.* [from *pardonable*.] Venialness: susceptibility of pardon.

Saint John's word is, all sin is trangression of the law; Saint Paul's, the wages of sin is death: put these two together, and this conceit of the natural *pardonableness* of sin vanishes away. *Hall.*

PA'RDONABLY. *adv.* [from *pardonable*.] Venially; excusably.

I may judge when I write more or less *pardonably*. *Dryd.*

PA'RDONER. *n. s.* [from *pardon*.]

1. One who forgives another.

This is his pardon, purchas'd by such sin,
For which the *pardoner* himself is in. *Shakesp.*

2. Fellows that carried about the pope's indulgencies, and sold them to such as would buy them, against whom *Luther* incensed the people of Germany. *Cowel.*

To PARE. *v. a.* [This word is reasonably deduced by *Skinner* from the French phrase, *parer les ongles*, to dress the horses hoofs when they are shaved by the farrier: thus we first said, *pare* your nails; and from thence transfered the word to general use.] To cut off extremities or the surface; to cut away by little and little; to diminish.

The creed of Athanasius, and that sacred hymn of glory, than which nothing doth sound more heavenly in the ears of faithful men, are now reckoned as superfluities, which we must in any case *pare* away, lest we cloy God with too much service. *Hooker.*

I have not alone
Imploy'd you where high profits might come home;
But *par'd* my present havings to bestow
My bounties upon you. *Shakespeare's Henry VIII.*

I am a man, whom fortune hath cruelly scratch'd.
—'Tis too late to *pare* her nails now. *Shakesp.*

The lion, mov'd with pity, did endure
To have his princely paws all *par'd* away. *Shakesp.*

The king began to *pare* a little the privilege of clergy, ordaining that clerks convict, should be burned in the hand. *Bacon's Henry VII.*

Pick out of tales the mirth, but not the sin.
He *pares* his apple, that will cleanly feed. *Herbert.*

Whoever will partake of God's secrets, must first look into his own, he must *pare* off whatsoever is amiss, and not without holiness approach to the holiest of all holies. *Taylor.*

All the mountains were *pared* off the earth, and the surface of it lay even, or in an equal convexity every where with the surface of the sea. *Burnet.*

The most poetical parts, which are description and images, were to be *pared* away, when the body was swollen into too large a bulk for the representation of the stage. *Dryden.*

The sword, as it was justly drawn by us, so can it scarce safely be sheathed, 'till the power of the great troubler of our peace be so far *pared* and reduced, as that we may be under no apprehensions. *Atterbury.*

'Twere well if she would *pare* her nails. *Pope.*

PAREGO'RICK. *adj.* [παρηγορικός.] Having the power in medicine to comfort, mollify and assuage. *Dict.*

PARE'NCHYMA. *n. s.* [παρέγχυμα.] A spongy or porous substance; in physick, a part through which the blood is strained for its better fermentation and perfection. *Dict.*

PARENCHY'MATOUS. } *adj.* [from *parenchyma*.] Relating to
PARENCHY'MOUS. } the parenchyma; spongy.

Ten thousand seeds of the plant, hart's-tongue, hardly make the bulk of a pepper corn. Now the covers and true body of each seed, the *parenchymatous* and ligneous parts of both moderately multiplied, afford an hundred thousand millions of formed atoms in the space of a pepper corn. *Grew.*

Thoſe parts, formerly reckoned *parenchymatous*, are now found to be bundleof exceedingly ſmall threads. *Cheyne.*

PARE'NESIS. *n. ſ.* [παραίνεσις.] Perſuaſion. *Dict.*

PA'RENT. *n. ſ.* [*parent*, Fr. *parens*, Latin.] A father or mother.

All true virtues are to honour true religion as their *parent*, and all well-ordered commonweales to love her as their chiefeſt ſtay. *Hooker.*

As a publick *parent* of the ſtate,
My juſtice, and thy crime, requires thy fate. *Dryden.*
In vain on the diſſembl'd mother's tongue
Had cunning art, and ſly perſuaſion hung;
And real care in vain and native love
In the true *parent's* panting breaſt had ſtrove. *Prior.*

PA'RENTAGE. *n. ſ.* [*parentage*, Fr. from *parent.*] Extraction; birth; condition with reſpect to the rank of parents.

A gentleman of noble *parentage*,
Of fair demeaſns, youthful and nobly allied. *Shakeſp.*
Though men eſteem thee low of *parentage*,
Thy father is th' eternal king. *Milt. Par. Reg.*
To his levee go,
And from himſelf your *parentage* may know. *Dryden.*

We find him, not only boaſting of his *parentage*, as an Iſraelite at large, but particularizing his deſcent from Benjamin. *Atterbury's Sermons.*

PARE'NTAL. *adj.* [from *parent.*] Becoming parents; pertaining to parents.

It overthrows the careful courſe and *parental* proviſion of nature, whereby the young ones newly excluded, are ſuſtained by the dam. *Brown's Vulgar Errours.*

Theſe eggs hatched by the warmth of the ſun into little worms, feed without any need of *parental* care. *Derham.*

Young ladies, on whom *parental* controul ſits heavily, give a man of intrigue room to think, that they want to be parents. *Clariſſa.*

PARENTA'TION. *n. ſ.* [from *parento*, Latin.] Something done or ſaid in honour of the dead.

PARE'NTHESIS. *n. ſ.* [*parentheſe*, Fr. παρα, ἐν and τίθημι.] A ſentence ſo included in another ſentence, as that it may be taken out, without injuring the ſenſe of that which incloſes it: being commonly marked thus, ( ).

In vain is my perſon excepted by a *parentheſis* of words, when ſo many hands are armed againſt me with ſwords. *King Charles.*

In his Indian relations, are contained ſtrange and incredible accounts; he is ſeldom mentioned, without a derogatory *parentheſis* in any author. *Brown's Vulgar Errours.*

Thou ſhalt be ſeen,
Tho' with ſome ſhort *parentheſis* between,
High on the throne of wit. *Dryden.*

Don't ſuffer every occaſional thought to carry you away into a long *parentheſis*, and thus ſtretch out your diſcourſe, and divert you from the point in hand. *Watts's Logick.*

PARENTHE'TICAL. *adj.* [from *parentheſis.*] Pertaining to a parentheſis.

PA'RER. *n. ſ.* [from *pare.*] An inſtrument to cut away the ſurface.

A hone and a *parer*, like ſole of a boot,
To pare away graſſe, and to raiſe up the root. *Tuſſer.*

PA'RERGY. *n. ſ.* [παρα and ἔργον.] Something unimportant; ſomething done by the by.

The ſcripture being ſerious, and commonly omitting ſuch *parergies*, it will be unreaſonable to condemn all laughter. *Brown's Vulgar Errours.*

PA'RGET. *n. ſ.* Plaſter laid upon roofs of rooms.

Gold was the *parget*, and the cieling bright
Did ſhine all ſcaly with great plates of gold;
The floor with jaſp and emerald was dight. *Spenſer.*

Of Engliſh talc, the coarſer ſort is called plaſter or *parget*; the finer, ſpaad. *Woodward.*

To PA'RGET. *v. a.* [from the noun.] To plaſter; to cover with plaſter.

There are not more arts of diſguiſing our corporeal blemiſhes than our moral; and yet, whilſt we thus paint and *parget* our own deformities, we cannot allow any the leaſt imperfection of another's to remain undetected. *Government of the Tongue.*

PA'RGETER. *n. ſ.* [from *parget.*] A plaſterer.

PARHE'LION. *n. ſ.* [παρα and ἥλιος.] A mock ſun.

To neglect that ſupreme reſplendency, that ſhines in God, for thoſe dim repreſentations of it, that we ſo doat on in the creature, is as abſurd, as it were for a Perſian to offer his ſacrifice to a *parhelion*, inſtead of adoring the ſun. *Boyle.*

PARI'ETAL. *adj.* [from *paries*, Latin.] Conſtituting the ſides or walls.

The lower part of the *parietal* and upper part of the temporal bones were fractured. *Sharp's Surgery.*

PARI'ETARY. *n. ſ.* [*parietaire*, Fr. *paries*, Lat.] An herb. *Ainſ.*

PA'RING. *n. ſ.* [from *pare.*] That which is pared off any thing, the rind.

Virginity breeds mites, much like a cheeſe; and conſumes itſelf to the very *paring*. *Shakeſpeare.*

To his gueſt, tho' no way ſparing,
He eat himſelf the rind and *paring*. *Pope.*

In May, after rain, pare off the ſurface of the earth, and with the *parings* raiſe your hills high, and enlarge their breadth. *Mortimer's Huſbandry.*

PARIS. *n. ſ.* An herb. *Ainſworth.*

PA'RISH. *n. ſ.* [*parochia*, low Lat. *parroiſſe*, Fr. of the Greek παροικία, *i. e. accolarum conventus, accolatus, ſacra vicinia.*] The particular charge of a ſecular prieſt. Every church is either cathedral, conventual, or parochial: cathedral is that, where there is a biſhop ſeated, ſo called a cathedra: conventual conſiſts of regular clerks, profeſſing ſome order of religion, or of a dean and chapter, or other college of ſpiritual men: parochial is that which is inſtituted for ſaying divine ſervice, and adminiſtring the holy ſacraments to the people, dwelling within a certain compaſs of ground near unto it. Our realm was firſt divided into pariſhes by Honorius, archbiſhop of Canterbury, in the year of our Lord 636. *Cowel.*

Dametas came piping and dancing, the merrieſt man in a *pariſh*. *Sidney.*

The tythes, his *pariſh* freely paid, he took;
But never ſu'd, or curs'd with bell or book. *Dryd.*

PA'RISH. *adj.*

1. Belonging to the pariſh; having the care of the pariſh.

A *pariſh* prieſt was of the pilgrim train,
An awful, reverend and religious man. *Dryden.*
Not *pariſh* clerk, who calls the pſalm ſo clear. *Gay.*

The office of the church is performed by the *pariſh* prieſt, at the time of his interment. *Ayliffe.*

A man, after his natural death, was not capable of the leaſt *pariſh* office. *Arbuthnot and Pope's Mart. Scrib.*

2. Maintained by the pariſh.

The ghoſt and the *pariſh* girl are entire new characters. *Gay.*

PARI'SHIONER. *n. ſ.* [*parroiſſien*, Fr. from *pariſh.*] One that belongs to the pariſh.

I praiſe the Lord for you, and ſo may my *pariſhioners*; for their ſons are well tutor'd by you. *Shakeſpeare.*

Hail biſhop Valentine, whoſe day this is,
All the air is thy dioceſe;
And all the chirping choriſters,
And other birds are thy *pariſhioners*. *Donne.*

In the greater out-pariſhes, many of the *pariſhioners*, thro' neglect, do periſh. *Graunt.*

I have depoſited thirty marks, to be diſtributed among the poor *pariſhioners*. *Addiſon's Spectator.*

PA'RITOR. *n. ſ.* [for *apparitor.*] A beadle; a ſummoner of the courts of civil law.

You ſhall be ſummon'd by an hoſt of *paritours*; you ſhall be ſentenced in the ſpiritual court. *Dryden.*

PA'RITY. *n. ſ.* [*parité*, Fr. *paritas*, Lat.] Equality; reſemblance.

We may here juſtly tax the diſhoneſty and ſhamefulneſs of the mouths, who have upbraided us with the opinion of a certain ſtoical *parity* of ſins. *Hall.*

That Chriſt or his apoſtles ever commanded to ſet up ſuch a *parity* of preſbyters, and in ſuch a way as thoſe Scots endeavour, I think is not very diſputable. *K. Charles.*

Survey the total ſet of animals, and we may, in their legs or organs of progreſſion, obſerve an equality of length and *parity* of numeration; that is, not any to have an odd leg, or the movers of one ſide not exactly anſwered by the other. *Brown's Vulgar Errours.*

Thoſe accidental occurences, which excited Socrates to the diſcovery of ſuch an invention, might fall in with that man that is of a perfect *parity* with Socrates. *Hale.*

Their agreement, in eſſential characters, makes rather an identity than a *parity*. *Glanville.*

Women could not live in that *parity* and equality of expence with their huſbands, as now they do. *Graunt.*

By an exact *parity* of reaſon, we may argue, if a man has no ſenſe of thoſe kindneſſes that paſs upon him, from one like himſelf, whom he ſees and knows, how much leſs ſhall his heart be affected with the grateful ſenſe of his favours, whom he converſes with only by imperfect ſpeculations, by the diſcourſes of reaſon, or the diſcoveries of faith. *South's Sermons.*

By *parity* of reaſon, we muſt expect a peace ſo much worſe about two years hence. *Swift's Miſcellanies.*

PARK. *n. ſ.* [peappuc, Sax. *parc*, Fr.] A piece of ground incloſed and ſtored with wild beaſts of chaſe, which a man may have by preſcription or the king's grant. Manwood, in his foreſt-laws, defines it thus: a park is a place for privilege for wild beaſts of venery, and alſo for other wild beaſts, that are beaſts of the foreſt and of the chaſe: and thoſe wild beaſts are to have a firm peace and protection there, ſo that no man may hurt or chaſe them within the park, without licenſe of the owner: a park is of another nature, than either a chaſe or a warren; for a park muſt be incloſed, and may not lie open; if it does, it is a good cauſe of ſeizure into the king's hands: and the owner cannot have action againſt ſuch as hunt in his park, if it lies open. *Cowel.*

We have *parks* and incloſures of all ſorts of beaſts and birds, which we uſe not only for view or rareneſs, but likewiſe for diſſections and trials. *Bacon.*

To PARK.

To PARK. *v. a.* [from the noun.] To inclose as in a park.
How are we *park'd*, and bounded in a pale?
A little herd of England's tim'rous deer,
Maz'd with a yelping kennel of French curs. *Shakesp.*

PA'RKER. *n. s.* [from *park.*] A park-keeper. *Ainsworth.*

PA'RKLEAVES. *n. s.* An herb. *Ainsworth.*

PARLE. *n. s.* [from *parler*, French.] Conversation; talk; oral treaty; oral discussion of any thing.
Of all the gentlemen,
That every day with *parle* encounter me,
In thy opinion, which is worthiest love. *Shakesp.*
Our trumpet call'd you to this general *parle.* *Shakesp.*
The bishop, by a *parle*, is, with a show
Of combination, cunningly betray'd. *Daniel.*
Why meet we thus like wrangling advocates,
To urge the justice of our cause with words?
I hate this *parle*; 'tis tame: if we must meet,
Give me my arms. *Rowe's Ambitious Step-mother.*

To PA'RLEY. *v. n.* [from *parler*, French.] To treat by word of mouth; to talk; to discuss any thing orally. It is much used in war, for a meeting of enemies to talk.
A Turk desired the captain to send some, with whom they might more conveniently *parley.* *Knolles's Hist. of the Turks.*
He *parleys* with her a while, as imagining she would advise him to proceed. *Broome.*

PA'RLEY. *n. s.* [from the verb.] Oral treaty; talk; conference; discussion by word of mouth.
Seek rather by *parley*, to recover them than by the sword. *Sid.*
Well, by my will, we shall admit no *parley*:
A rotten case abides no handling. *Shakesp.*
In such a *parley* should I answer thee. *Shakesp.*
Summon a *parley*, we will talk with him. *Shakesp.*
Let us resolve never to have any *parley* with our lusts, but to make some considerable progress in our repentance. *Calamy.*
No gentle means could be essay'd;
'Twas beyond *parley* when the siege was laid. *Dryden.*
Force, never yet a generous heart did gain;
We yield on *parley*, but are storm'd in vain. *Dryden.*
Yet when some better fated youth
Shall with his am'rous *parley* move thee,
Reflect one moment on his truth,
Who dying thus, persists to love thee. *Prior.*

PA'RLIAMENT. *n. s.* [*parliamentum*, low Lat. *parlement*, Fr.] In England, is the assembly of the king and three estates of the realm; namely, the lords spiritual, the lords temporal, and commons, for the debating of matters touching the common wealth, especially the making and correcting of laws; which assembly or court is, of all others, the highest, and of greatest authority. *Cowel.*
The king is fled to London,
To call a present court of *parliament.* *Shakesp.*
Far be the thought of this from Henry's heart,
To make a shambles of the *parliament* house. *Shakesp.*
The true use of *parliaments* is very excellent; and be often called, and continued as long as is necessary. *Bacon.*
I thought the right way of *parliaments*, the most safe for my crown, as best pleasing to my people. *King Charles.*
These are mob readers: if Virgil and Martial stood for *parliament*-men, we know who would carry it. *Dryden.*

PARLIAME'NTARY. *adj.* [from *parliament.*] Enacted by parliament; suiting the parliament; pertaining to parliament.
To the three first titles of the two houses, or lines, and conquest, were added two more; the authorities *parliamentary* and papal. *Bacon.*
Many things, that obtain as common law, had their original by *parliamentary* acts or constitutions, made in writings by the king, lords, and commons. *Hale.*
Credit to run ten millions in debt, without *parliamentary* security; I think to be dangerous and illegal. *Swift.*

PA'RLOUR. *n. s.* [*parloir*, French; *parlatorio*, Italian.]
1. A room in monasteries, where the religious meet and converse.
2. A room in houses on the first floor, elegantly furnished for reception or entertainment.
Can we judge it a thing seemly, for a man to go about the building of an house to the God of heaven, with no other appearance than if his end were to rear up a kitchen or a *parlour* for his own use. *Hooker.*
Back again fair Alma led them right,
And soon into a goodly *parlour* brought. *Fa. Queen.*
It would be infinitely more shameful, in the dress of the kitchen, to receive the entertainments of the *parlour.* *South.*
Roof and sides were like a *parlour* made,
A soft recess, and a cool summer shade. *Dryden.*

PA'RLOUS. *adj.* [This might seem to come from *parler*, Fr. to speak; but *Junius* derives it, I think, rightly, from *perilous*, in which sense it answers to the Latin *improbus.*] Keen; sprightly; waggish.
Midas durst communicate
To none but to his wife his ears of state;
One must be trusted, and he though her fit,
As passing prudent, and a *parlous* wit. *Dryden.*

PA'RLOUSNESS. *n. s.* [from *parlous.*] Quickness; keeness of temper.

PAR

PARMA-CITTY. *n. s.* Corruptedly for sperma ceti. *Ains.*

PA'RNEL. *n. s.* [the diminutive of *petronella.*] A punk; a slut. Obsolete. *Skinner.*

PARO'CHIAL. *adj.* [*parochialis*, from *parochia*, low Lat.] Belonging to a parish.
The married state of *parochial* pastors hath given them the opportunity of setting a more exact and universal pattern of holy living, to the people committed to their charge. *Atterbury.*

PA'RODY. *n. s.* [*parodie*, Fr. παρωδία.] A kind of writing, in which the words of an author or his thoughts are taken, and by a slight change adapted to some new purpose.
The imitations of the ancients are added together with some of the *parodies* and allusions to the most excellent of the moderns. *Pope's Dunciad.*

To PA'RODY. *v. a.* [*parodier*, Fr. from *parody.*] To copy by way of parody.
I have translated, or rather *parodied*, a poem of Horace, in which I introduce you advising me. *Pope.*

PARO'NYMOUS. *adj.* [παρώνυμος.] Resembling another word.
Shew your critical learning in the etymology of terms, the synonimous and the *paronymous* or kindred names. *Watts.*

PA'ROLE. *n. s.* [*parole*, French.] Word given as an assurance; promise given by a prisoner not to go away.
Love's votaries enthral each others soul,
'Till both of them live but upon *parole.* *Cleaveland.*
Be very tender of your honour, and not fall in love; because I have a scruple, whether you can keep your *parole*, if you become a prisoner to the ladies. *Swift.*

PARONOMA'SIA. *n. s.* [παρωνομασία.] A rhetorical figure, in which, by the change of a letter or syllable, several things are alluded to. It is called, in Latin, *agnominatio.* *Dict.*

PA'ROQUET. *n. s.* [*parroquet* or *perroquet*, French.] A small species of parrot.
The great, red and blue, are parrots; the middlemost, called popinjays; and the lesser, *parroquets*: in all above twenty sorts. *Grew.*
I would not give my *paroquet*
For all the doves that ever flew. *Prior.*

PARONNY'CHIA. *n. s.* [παρωνυχία; *paronychie*, Fr.] A preternatural swelling or sore under the root of the nail in one's finger; a felon; a whitlow. *Dict.*

PARO'TID. *adj.* [*parotide*, Fr. παρωτὶς, παρα and ὦτα.] Salivary; so named because near the ears.
Beasts and birds, having one common use of spittle, are furnished with the *parotid* glands, which help to supply the mouth with it. *Grew.*

PA'ROTIS. *n. s.* [παρωτὶς.] A tumour in the glandules behind and about the ears, generally called the emunctories of the brain; though, indeed, they are the external fountains of the saliva of the mouth. *Wiseman.*

PA'ROXYSM. [παροξυσμος; *paroxysme*, Fr.] A fit; periodical exacerbation of a disease.
I fancied to myself a kind of ease, in the change of the *paroxysm.* *Dryden.*
Amorous girls, through the fury of an hysteric *paroxysm*, are cast into a trance for an hour. *Harvey.*
The greater distance of time there is between the *paroxysms*, the fever is less dangerous, but more obstinate. *Arbuthnot.*

PA'RRICIDE. *n. s.* [*parricide*, Fr. *parricida*, Latin.]
1. One who destroys his father.
I told him the revenging gods
'Gainst *parricides* did all the thunder bend,
Spoke with how manifold and strong a bond
The child was bound to th' father. *Shakesp.*
2. One who destroys or invades any to whom he owes particular reverence; as his country or patron.
3. [*Parricide*, Fr. *parricidium*, Lat.] The murder of a father; murder of one to whom reverence is due.
Although he were a prince in military virtue approved, and likewise a good law-maker; yet his cruelties and *parricides* weighed down his virtues. *Bacon.*
Morat was always bloody, now he's base;
And has so far in usurpation gone,
He will by *parricide* secure the throne. *Dryden.*

PARRICI'DAL. } PARRICI'DIOUS. } *adj.* [from *parricida*, Latin.] Relating to parricide; committing parricide.
He is now paid in his own way, the *parricidious* animal, and punishment of murtherers is upon him, *Brown.*

PA'RROT. *n. s.* [*perroquet*, French.] A particoloured bird of the species of the hooked bill, remarkable for the exact imitation of the human voice.
Some will ever more peep thro' their eyes,
And laugh like *parrots* at a bag-piper. *Shakesp.*
Who taught the *parrot* human notes to try?
Twas witty want, fierce hunger to appease. *Dryden.*
The great, red and blue, *parrot*: of these, the middlemost are called popinjays; and the lesser, parroquets: in all above twenty sorts. *Grew.*

To PA'RRY. *v. n.* [*parer*, French.] To put by thrusts; to fence.
A man of courage, who cannot fence, and will put all upon one thrust, and not stand *parrying*, has the odds against a moderate fencer. *Locke.*

I could

I could
By dint of logick ſtrike thee mute,
With learned ſkill, now puſh, now *parry*,
From Darii to Bocardo vary. *Prior.*

To Parse. *v. a.* [from *pars*, Latin.] To reſolve a ſentence into the elements or parts of ſpeech. It is a word only uſed in grammar ſchools.

Let him conſtrue the letter into Engliſh, and *parſe* it over perfectly. *Aſcham's Schoolmaſter.*

Let ſcholars reduce the words to their original, to the firſt caſe of nouns, or firſt tenſe of verbs, and give an account of their formations and changes, their ſyntax and dependencies, which is called *parſing*. *Watts's Improv. of the Mind.*

Parsimo'nious. *adj.* [from *parſimony*.] Covetous; frugal; ſparing. It is ſometimes of a good, ſometimes of a bad ſenſe.

A prodigal king is nearer a tyrant, than a *parſimonious*; for ſtore at home draweth not his contemplations abroad, but want ſupplieth itſelf of what is next. *Bacon.*

Extraordinary funds for one campaign may ſpare us the expence of many years, whereas a long *parſimonious* war will drain us of more men and money. *Addiſon.*

Parſimonious age and rigid wiſdom. *Rowe.*

Parsimo'niously. *adv.* [from *parſimonious*.] Covetouſly; frugally; ſparingly.

Our anceſtors acted *parſimoniouſly*, becauſe they only ſpent their own treaſure for the good of their poſterity; whereas we ſquandered away the treaſures of our poſterity. *Swift.*

Parsimo'niousness. *n. ſ.* [from *parſimonious*.] A diſpoſition to ſpare and ſave.

PARSI'MONY. *n. ſ.* [*parſimonia*, Latin.] Frugality; covetouſneſs; niggardlineſs; ſaving temper.

The ways to enrich, are many: *parſimony* is one of the beſt, and yet is not innocent; for it withholdeth men from works of liberality. *Bacon.*

Theſe people, by their extreme *parſimony*, ſoon grow into wealth from the ſmalleſt begininings. *Swift.*

Pa'rsley. *n. ſ.* [*perſil*, Fr. *apium*, Lat. *perſli*, Welſh.] The leaves are divided into wings, growing upon a branched rib, and for the moſt part cut into ſmall ſegments: the petals of the flowers are whole and equal, each flower being ſucceeded by two gibbous channelled ſeeds. *Miller.*

A wench married in the afternoon, as ſhe went to the garden for *parſley* to ſtuff a rabbit. *Shakeſp.*

Green beds of *parſley* near the river grow. *Dryden.*

Sempronia dug Titus out of the *parſley*-bed, as they uſe to tell children, and thereby became his mother. *Locke.*

Pa'rsnep. *n. ſ.* [*paſtinaca*, Latin.] A plant with roſe and umbellated flowers, conſiſting of many petals or leaves placed orbicularly, and reſting on the empalement, which turns to a fruit compoſed of two ſeeds, which are oval, and generally caſting off their cover; to which you may add, that the leaves are winged and large. *Miller.*

November is drawn in a garment of changeable green, and black bunches of *parſneps* and turneps in his right hand. *Peacham on Blazoning.*

PA'RSON. *n. ſ.* [Derived either from *perſona*, becauſe the *parſon* omnium *perſonam* in eccleſia ſuſtinet; or from *parocheanus*, the pariſh prieſt.]

1. The prieſt of a pariſh; one that has a parochial charge or cure of ſouls.

Abbot was preferred by king James to the biſhoprick of Coventry and Litchfield, before he had been *parſon*, vicar or curate of any pariſh church. *Clarendon.*

2. A clergyman.

Sometimes comes ſhe with a tithe pig's tail,
Tickling the *parſon* as he lies a ſleep;
Then dreams he of another benefice. *Shakeſp.*

3. It is applied to the teachers of the preſbyterians.

Pa'rsonage. *n. ſ.* [from *parſon*.] The benefice of a pariſh.

I have given him the *parſonage* of the pariſh. *Addiſon.*

PART. *n. ſ.* [*pars*, Latin.]

1. Something leſs than the whole; a portion; a quantity taken from a larger quantity.

Helen's cheeks, but not her heart,
Atalanta's better *part*. *Shakeſp.*

The people ſtood at the nether *part* of the mount. *Exodus* xix. 17.

This law wanted not *parts* of prudent and deep foreſight, for it took away occaſion to pry into the kings title. *Bacon.*

The citizens were for the moſt *part* ſlain or taken. *Knolles.*

Henry had divided
The perſon of himſelf into four *parts*. *Daniel.*

Theſe conclude that to happen often, which happeneth but ſometimes, that never, which happeneth but ſeldom; and that always, which happeneth for the moſt *part*. *Brown.*

Beſides his abilities as a ſoldier, which were eminent, he had very great parts of breeding, being a very great ſcholar in the political *parts* of learning. *Clarendon.*

When your judgement ſhall grow ſtronger, it will be neceſſary to examine, *part* by *part*, thoſe works, which have given reputation to the maſters. *Dryden.*

Of heavenly *part*, and *part* of earthly blood;
A mortal woman mixing with a god. *Dryden.*

Our ideas of extenſion and number, do they not contain a ſecret relation of the *parts*? *Locke.*

2. Member.

He fully poſſeſſed the revelation he had received from God: all the *parts* were formed, in his mind, into one harmonious body. *Locke.*

3. That which, in diviſion, falls to each.

Go not without thy wife, but let me bear
My *part* of danger, with an equal ſhare. *Dryden.*
Had I been won, I had deſerv'd your blame,
But ſure my *part* was nothing but the ſhame. *Dryden.*

4. Share; concern.

Foraſmuch as the children are partakers of fleſh and blood, he alſo took *part* of the ſame. *Hebrews* ii. 14.

Sheba ſaid, we have no *part* in David, neither have we inheritance in the ſon of Jeſſe. 2 *Samuel* xx. 1.

The ungodly made a covenant with death, becauſe they are worthy to take *part* with it. *Wiſdom* i. 16.

Agamemnon provokes Apollo, whom he was willing to appeaſe afterwards at the coſt of Achilles, who had no *part* in his fault. *Pope.*

5. Side; party.

Michael Caſſio,
When I have ſpoken of you diſpraiſingly,
Hath ta'en your *part*. *Shakeſp.*

And that he might on many props repoſe,
He ſtrengths his own, and who his *part* did take. *Daniel.*

Let not thy divine heart
Forethink me any ill,
Deſtiny may take thy *part*,
And may thy tears fulfill. *Donne.*

Some other pow'r
Might have aſpir'd, and me tho' mean
Drawn to his *part*. *Milton.*

Call up their eyes, and fix them on your example; that ſo natural ambition might take *part* with reaſon and their intereſt to encourage imitation. *Glanville.*

A brand preſerv'd to warm ſome prince's heart,
And make whole kingdoms take her brother's *part* *Waller.*

The arm thus waits upon the heart,
So quick to take the bully's *part*;
That one, tho' warm, decides more ſlow,
Than t' other executes the blow. *Prior.*

6. Something relating or belonging.

For Zelmane's *part*, ſhe would have been glad of the fall, which made her bear the ſweet burden of Philoclea, but that ſhe feared ſhe might receive ſome hurt. *Sidney.*

For my *part*, I would entertain the legend of my love, with quiet hours. *Shakeſp. Henry* IV.

For your *part*, it not appears to me,
That you ſhould have an inch of any ground
To build a grief upon. *Shakeſp. Henry* IV.

For my *part*, I have no ſervile end in my labour, which may reſtrain or embaſe the freedom of my poor judgment. *Wotton.*

For my *part*, I think there is nothing ſo ſecret, that ſhall not be brought to light, within the compaſs of the world. *Burnet's Theory of the Earth.*

7. Particular office or character.

The pneumatical part, which is in all tangible bodies, and hath ſome affinity with the air, performeth the *parts* of the air: as, when you knock upon an empty barrel, the ſound is, in part, created by the air on the outſide, and, in part, by the air in the inſide. *Bacon's Nat. Hiſt.*

Accuſe not nature, ſhe hath done her *part*;
Do thou but thine. *Milt. Par. Loſt.*

8. Character appropriated in a play.

That *part*
Was aptly fitted, and naturally performed. *Shakeſp.*

Have you the lion's *part* written? give it me, for I am ſlow of ſtudy. *Shakeſp. Midſum. Night's Dream.*

God is the maſter of the ſcenes: we muſt not chuſe which *part* we ſhall act; it concerns us only to be careful, that we do it well. *Taylor's Holy Living.*

9. Buſineſs; duty.

Let them be ſo furniſhed and inſtructed for the military *part*, as they may defend themſelves. *Bacon.*

10. Action; conduct.

Find him, my lord,
And chide him hither ſtraight; this *part* of his
Conjoins with my diſeaſe. *Shakeſp.*

11. Relation reciprocal.

Inquire not whether the ſacraments confer grace by their own excellency, becauſe they, who affirm they do, require ſo much duty on our *parts*, as they alſo do, who attribute the effect to our moral diſpoſition. *Taylor.*

The ſcripture tells us the terms of this covenant on God's *part* and ours; namely, that he will be our God, and we ſhall be his people. *Tillotſon's Sermons.*

It

It might be deem'd, on our historian's *part*,
Or too much negligence, or want of art,
If he forgot the vast magnificence
Of royal Theseus. *Dryden.*

12. In good part; in ill part; as well done; as ill done.

God accepteth it in good *part*, at the hands of faithful men. *Hooker.*

13. [In the plural.] Qualities; powers; faculties; or accomplishments.

Who is courteous, noble, liberal, but he that hath the example before his eyes of Amphialus; where are all heroical *parts*, but in Amphialus? *Sidney.*

Such licentious *parts* tend, for the most part, to the hurt of the English, or maintenance of their own lewd liberty. *Spenser on Ireland.*

I conjure thee, by all the *parts* of man,
Which honour does acknowledge. *Shakesp.*

Solomon was a prince adorned with such *parts* of mind, and exalted by such a concurrence of all prosperous events to make him magnificent. *South's Sermons.*

The Indian princes discover fine *parts* and excellent endowments, without improvement. *Felton on the Classicks.*

14. [In the plural.] Quarters; regions; districts.

Although no man was, in our *parts*, spoken of, but he, for his manhood; yet, as though therein he excelled himself, he was called the courteous Amphialus. *Sidney.*

When he had gone over those *parts*, he came into Greece. *Acts* xx. 2.

All *parts* resound with tumults, plaints, and fears,
And griesly death, in sundry shapes, appears. *Dryden.*

PART. *adv.* Partly; in some measure.

For the fair kindness you have shew'd me,
And *part* being prompted, by your present trouble,
I'll lend you something. *Shakespeare's Twelfth Night.*

To PART. *v. a.*

1. To divide; to share; to distribute.

All that believed, sold their goods, and *parted* them to all men, as every man had need. *Acts* ii. 45.

Jove himself no less content wou'd be
To *part* his throne, and share his heav'n with thee. *Pope.*

2. To separate; to disunite.

A chariot of fire *parted* them both asunder, and Elijah went up into heaven. 2 *Kings* ii. 11.

Nought but death shall *part* thee and me. *Ruth* i. 17.

All the world,
As 'twere the bus'ness of mankind to *part* us,
Is arm'd against my love, *Dryden.*

3. To break into pieces.

Part it in pieces, and pour oil thereon. *Leviticus* ii. 6.

4. To keep asunder.

In the narrow seas, that *part*
The French and English, there miscarried
A vessel of our country. *Shakesp.*

5. To separate combatants.

Who said
King John did fly, an hour or two before
The stumbling night did *part* our weary powers. *Shakesp.*

Jove did both hosts survey,
And, when he pleas'd to thunder, *part* the fray. *Waller.*

6. To secern.

The liver minds his own affair,
And *parts* and strains the vital juices. *Prior.*

To PART. *v. n.*

1. To be separated.

Powerful hands will not *part*
Easily from possession won with arms. *Milt. Par. Reg.*

'Twas for him much easier to subdue
Those foes he fought with, than to *part* from you. *Dryd.*

2. To quit each other.

He wrung Bassanio's hand, and so they *parted.* *Shakesp.*

This was the design of a people, that were at liberty to *part* asunder, but desired to keep in one body. *Locke.*

What! *part*, for ever *part?* unkind Ismena;
Oh! can you think, that death is half so dreadful,
As it would be to live without thee. *Smith.*

If it pleases God to restore me to my health, I shall make a third journey; if not, we must *part*, as all human creatures have *parted.* *Swift.*

3. To take farewel.

Ere I could
Give him that *parting* kiss, which I had set
Betwixt two charming words, comes in my father. *Shakesp.*

Nuptial bow'r! by me adorn'd, from thee
How shall I *part*, and whither wander. *Milton.*

Upon his removal, they *parted* from him with tears in their eyes. *Swift.*

4. To have share.

As his part is, that goeth down to the battle, so shall his part be, that tarrieth by the stuff; they shall *part* alike. *Isaiah* xxx. 24.

5. [*Partir*, Fr.] To go away; to set out.

So *parted* they; the angel up to heaven
From the thick shade, and Adam to his bow'r. *Milton.*

Thy father
Embrac'd me, *parting* for the Etrurian land. *Dryden.*

6. *To* PART *with.* To quit; to resign; to lose; to be separated from.

For her sake, I do rear up her boy;
And for her sake, I will not *part* with him. *Shakesp.*

An affectionate wife, when in fear of *parting* with her beloved husband, heartily desired of God his life or society, upon any conditions that were not sinful. *Taylor.*

Celia, for thy sake, I *part*
With all that grew so near my heart;
And that I may successful prove,
Transform myself to what you love. *Waller.*

Thou marble hew'st, ere long to *part* with breath,
And houses rear'st, unmindful of thy death. *Sandys.*

Lixiviate salts, though, by piercing the bodies of vegetables, they dispose them to *part* readily with their tincture; yet some tinctures they do not only draw out, but likewise alter. *Boyle.*

The ideas of hunger and warmth are some of the first that children have, and which they scarce ever *part* with. *Locke.*

What a despicable figure must mock-patriots make, who venture to be hang'd for the ruin of those civil rights, which their ancestors, rather than *part* with, chose to be cut to pieces in the field of battle? *Addison's Freeholder.*

The good things of this world so delight in, as remember, that we are to *part* with them, to exchange them for more durable enjoyments. *Atterbury's Sermons.*

As for riches and power, our Saviour plainly determines, that the best way to make them blessings, is to *part* with them. *Swift's Miscellanies.*

PA'RTABLE. *adj.* [from *part.*] Divisible; such as may be parted.

His hot love was *partable* among three other of his mistresses. *Camden's Remains.*

PA'RTAGE. *n. s.* [*partage*, Fr.] Division; act of sharing or parting. A word merely French.

Men have agreed to a disproportionate and unequal possession of the earth, having found out a way, how a man may fairly possess more land, than he himself can use the product of, by receiving, in exchange, for the overplus, gold and silver: this *partage* of things, in an equality of private possessions, men have made practicable out of the bounds of society, without compact, only by putting a value on gold and silver, and tacitely agreeing in the use of money. *Locke.*

To PA'RTAKE. *v. n.* Preterite, *I partook:* participle passive, *partaken.* [*part* and *take.*]

1. To have share of any thing; to take share with.

Partake and use my kingdom as your own,
And shall be yours while I command the crown. *Dryden.*

How far brutes *partake* in this faculty, is not easy to determine. *Locke.*

2. To participate; to have something of the property, nature, claim, or right.

The attorney of the dutchy of Lancaster *partakes* partly of a judge, and partly of an attorney-general. *Bacon.*

3. To be admitted to; not to be excluded.

You may *partake* of any thing we say;
We speak no treason. *Shakesp. Rich.* III.

4. Sometimes with *in* before the thing partaken of.

I took occasion to conjecture, how far brutes *partook* with men, *in* any of the intellectual faculties. *Locke.*

Truth and falshood have no other trial, but reason and proof, which they made use of to make themselves knowing, and so must others too, that will *partake in* their knowledge. *Locke.*

5. To combine; to enter into some design. An unusual sense.

As it prevents factions and *partakings*, so it keeps the rule and administration of the laws uniform. *Hale.*

To PARTA'KE. *v. a.*

1. To share; to have part in.

By and by, thy bosom shall *partake*
The secrets of my heart. *Shakesp.*

At season fit,
Let her with thee *partake*, what thou hast heard. *Milton.*

My royal father lives,
Let ev'ry one *partake* the general joy. *Dryden.*

2. To admit to part; to extend participation. Obsolete.

My friend, hight Philemon, I did *partake*
Of all my love, and all my privity,
Who greatly joyous seemed for my sake. *Fa. Queen.*

Your exultation *partake* to every one. *Shakesp.*

PARTA'KER. *n. s.* [from *partake.*]

1. A partner in possessions; a sharer of any thing; an associate with.

They whom earnest lets hinder from being *partakers* of the whole, have yet, through length of divine service, opportunity for access unto some reasonable part thereof. *Hooker.*

Didst thou
Make us *partakers* of a little gain;
That now our loss might be ten times as much. *Shakesp.*
With such she must return at setting light,
Tho' not *partaker*, witness of their night. *Prior.*

His bitterest enemies were *partakers* of his kindness, and he still continued to entreat them to accept of life from him, and, with tears of compassion, bewailed their infidelity. *Calamy's Sermons.*

2. Sometimes with *in* before the thing partaken.
Wish me *partaker in* thy happiness,
When thou do'st meet good hap. *Shakesp.*

If we had been in the days of our fathers, we would not have been *partakers* with them *in* the blood of the prophets. *Matthew* xxiii. 30.

3. Accomplice; associate.

Thou consentedst, and hast been *partaker* with adulterers. *Psalm* l. 18.

He took upon him the person of the duke of York, and drew with him complices and *partakers*. *Bacon.*

PA'RTER. *n. s.* [from *part.*] One that parts or separates.

The chief *parter* of the fray was night, which, with her black arms, pulled their malicious sights one from the other. *Sidney.*

PA'RTERRE. *n. s.* [*parterre*, Fr.] A level division of ground, that, for the most part, faces the south and best front of an house, and is generally furnished with greens, flowers, &c. *Miller.*

There are as many kinds of gardening, as of poetry; your makers of *parterres* and flower gardens are epigramatists and sonneteers. *Spectator*, N° 477.

The vast *parterres* a thousand hands shall make;
Lo! Cobham comes, and floats them with a lake. *Pope.*

PA'RTIAL. *adj.* [*partial*, French.]

1. Inclined antecedently to favour one party in a cause, or one side of the question more than the other.

Ye have not kept my ways, but have been *partial* in the law. *Mal.* ii. 9.

2. Inclined to favour without reason.

Self-love will make men *partial* to themselves and friends, and ill nature, passion, and revenge will carry them too far in punishing others; and hence, God hath appointed governments to restrain the partiality and violence of men. *Locke.*

Authors are *partial* to their wit, 'tis true,
But are not criticks to their judgment too. *Pope.*

In these, one may be sincerer to a reasonable friend, than to a fond and *partial* parent. *Pope.*

3. Affecting only one part; subsisting only in a part; not general; not universal; not total.

If we compare these *partial* dissolutions of the earth with an universal dissolution, we may as easily conceive an universal deluge from an universal dissolution, as a *partial* deluge from a *partial*. *Burnet's Theory of the Earth.*

That which weakens religion, will at length destroy it; for the weakening of a thing is only a *partial* destruction of it. *South's Sermons.*

All discord, harmony, not understood;
All *partial* evil, universal good. *Pope.*

PARTIA'LITY. *n. s.* [*partialité*, Fr. from *partial.*] Unequal state of the judgment and favour of one above the other, without just reason.

Then would the Irish party cry out *partiality*, and complain he is not used as a subject, he is not suffered to have the free benefit of the law. *Spenser on Ireland,*

Partiality is properly the understanding's judging according to the inclination of the will and affections, and not according to the exact truth of things, or the merits of the cause. *South.*

As there is a *partiality* to opinions, which is apt to mislead the understanding; so there is also a *partiality* to studies, which is prejudicial to knowledge. *Locke.*

To PARTIALI'ZE. *v. a.* [*partialiser*, Fr. from *partial.*] To make partial. A word, perhaps, peculiar to *Shakespeare*, and not unworthy of general use.

Such neighbour-nearness to our sacred blood
Should nothing privilege him, nor *partialize*
Th' unstooping firmness of my upright soul. *Shakesp.*

PA'RTIALLY. *adv.* [from *partial.*]

1. With unjust favour or dislike.

2. In part; not totally.

That stole into a total verity, which was but *partially* true in its covert sense. *Brown's Vulgar Errours.*

The message he brought, opened a clear prospect of eternal salvation, which had been but obscurely and *partially* figured in the shadows of the law. *Rogers's Sermons.*

PARTIBI'LITY. *n. s.* [from *partible.*] Divisibility; separability.

PA'RTIBLE. *adj.* [from *part.*] Divisible; separable.

Make the moulds *partible*, glued or cemented together, that you may open them, when you take out the fruit. *Bacon.*

The same body, in one circumstance, is more weighty, and, in another, is more *partible*. *Digby on the Soul.*

PARTI'CIPABLE. *adj.* [from *participate.*] Such as may be shared or partaken.

Plato, by his ideas, means only the divine essence with this connotation, as it is variously imitable or *participable* by created beings. *Norris's Miscellanies.*

PARTI'CIPANT. *adj.* [*participant*, Fr. from *participate.*] Sharing; having share or part.

During the parliament, he published his proclamation, offering pardon to all such as had taken arms, or been *participant* of any attempts against him; so as they submitted themselves. *Bacon.*

The prince saw he should confer with one *participant* of more than monkish speculations. *Wotton.*

If any part of my body be so mortified, as it becomes like a rotten branch of a tree, it putrefies, and is not *participant* of influence derived from my soul, because it is now no longer in it to quicken it. *Hale.*

To PARTI'CIPATE. *v. n.* [*participo*, Lat. *participer*, Fr.]

1. To partake; to have share.

Th' other instruments
Did see, and hear, devise, instruct, walk, feel;
And mutually *participate*. *Shakesp.*

2. With *of*.

An aged citizen brought forth all his provisions, and said, that as he did communicate unto them his store, so would he *participate of* their wants. *Hayward.*

3. With *in*.

His delivery, and thy joy thereon,
In both which we, as next, *participate*. *Milton.*

4. To have part of more things than one.

Few creatures *participate* of the nature of plants and metals both. *Bacon.*

God, when heav'n and earth he did create,
Form'd man, who should of both *participate*. *Denham.*

Those bodies, which are under a light, which is extended and distributed equally through all, should *participate* of each others colours. *Dryden.*

5. To have part of something common with another.

The species of audibles seem to *participate* more with local motion, like percussions made upon the air. *Bacon.*

To PARTI'CIPATE. *v. a.* To partake; to receive part of; to share.

As Christ's incarnation and passion can be available to no man's good, which is not made partaker of Christ, neither can we *participate* him without his presence. *Hooker.*

The French seldom atchieved any honourable acts without Scottish hands, who therefore are to *participate* the glory with them. *Camden's Remains.*

Fellowship,
Such as I seek, fit to *participate*
All rational delight; wherein the brute
Cannot be human consort. *Milt. Par. Lost.*

PARTICIPA'TION. *n. s.* [*participation*, Fr. from *participate.*]

1. The state of sharing something in common.

Civil society doth more content the nature of man, than any private kind of solitary living; because, in society, this good of mutual *participation* is so much larger. *Hooker.*

Their spirits are so married in conjunction, with the *participation* of society, that they flock together in consent, like so many wild geese. *Shakesp. Henry* IV.

A joint coronation of himself and his queen might give any countenance of *participation* of title. *Bacon.*

2. The act or state of partaking or having part of something.

All things seek the highest, and covet more or less the *participation* of God himself. *Hooker.*

Those deities are so by *participation*, and subordinate to the supreme. *Stillingfleet.*

What an honour, that God should admit us into such a blessed *participation* of himself? *Atterbury.*

Convince them, that brutes have the least *participation* of thought, and they retract. *Bentley's Sermons.*

Your genius should mount above that mist, in which its *participation* and neighbourhood with earth long involved it. *Pope.*

3. Distribution; division into shares.

It sufficeth not, that the country hath wherewith to sustain even more than to live upon it, if means be wanting whereby to drive convenient *participation* of the general store into a great number of well-deservers. *Raleigh.*

PARTICI'PIAL. *adj.* [*participialis*, Lat.] Having the nature of a participle.

PARTICI'PIALLY. *adv.* [from *participle.*] In the sense or manner of a participle.

PA'RTICIPLE. *n. s.* [*participium*, Lat.]

1. A word partaking at once the qualities of a noun and verb.

A *participle* as is a particular sort of adjective, formed from a verb, and together with its signification of action, passion, or some other manner of existence, signifyingthe time thereof. *Clarke's Latin Grammar.*

2. Any thing that participates of different things.

The *participles* or confiners between plants and living creatures, are such as are fixed, though they have a motion in their parts: such as, oysters and cockles. *Bacon.*

PA'RTICLE. *n. s.* [*particule*, Fr. *particula*, Lat.]

1. Any small portion of a greater substance.

From any of the other unreasonable demands, the houses had not given their commissioners authority in the least *particle* to recede. *Clarendon.*

There is not one grain in the universe, either too much or too little, nothing to be added, nothing to be spared; nor so much as any one *particle* of it, that mankind may not be either the better or the worse for, according as 'tis applied. *L'Estr.*

With *particles* of heav'nly fire,
The God of nature did his soul inspire. *Dryden.*

Curious wits,
With rapture, with astonishment reflect,
On the small size of atoms, which unite
To make the smallest *particle* of light. *Blackmore.*

It is not impossible, but that microscopes may, at length, be improved to the discovery of the *particles* of bodies, on which their colours depend. *Newton's Opticks.*

Blest with more *particles* of heav'nly flame. *Granville.*

2. A word unvaried by inflexion.

'Till Arianism had made it a matter of great sharpness and subtility of wit to be a sound believing christian, men were not curious what syllables or *particles* of speech they used. *Hooker, b.* v.

The Latin varies the signification of verbs and nouns, not as the modern languages, by *particles* prefixed, but by changing the last syllables. *Locke on Education.*

Particles are the words, whereby the mind signifies what connection it gives to the several affirmations and negations, that it unites in one continued reasoning or narration. *Locke.*

In the Hebrew tongue, there is a *particle*, consisting but of one single letter, of which there are reckoned up above fifty several significations. *Locke.*

PARTI'CULAR. *adj.* [*particulier*, French.]

1. Relating to single persons; not general.

He, as well with general orations, as *particular* dealing with men of most credit, made them see how necessary it was. *Sidney.*

As well for *particular* application to special occasions, as also in other manifold respects, infinite treasures of wisdom are abundantly to be found in the holy scripture. *Hooker.*

2. Individual; one distinct from others.

Wheresoever one plant draweth such a *particular* juice out of the earth, as it qualifieth the earth, so as that juice, which remaineth, is fit for the other plant; there the neighbourhood doth good. *Bacon.*

This is true of actions considered in their general nature or kind, but not considered in their *particular* individual instances. *South's Sermons.*

Artists, who propose only the imitation of such a *particular* person, without election of ideas, have often been reproached for that omission. *Dryden.*

3. Noting properties or things peculiar.

Of this prince there is little *particular* memory; only that he was very studious and learned. *Bacon.*

4. Attentive to things single and distinct.

I have been *particular* in examining the reason of children's inheriting the property of their fathers, because it will give us farther light in the inheritance of power. *Locke.*

5. Single; not general.

Rather performing his general commandment, which had ever been, to embrace virtue, than any new *particular*, sprung out of passion, and contrary to the former. *Sidney.*

6. Odd; having something that eminently distinguishes him from others. This is commonly used in a sense of contempt.

PARTI'CULAR. *n. s.*

1. A single instance; a single point.

I must reserve some *particulars*, which it is not lawful for me to reveal. *Bacon.*

Those notions are universal, and what is universal must needs proceed from some universal constant principle; the same in all *particulars*, which can be nothing else but human nature. *South's Sermons.*

Having the idea of an elephant or an angle in my mind, the first and natural enquiry is, whether such a thing does exist? and this knowledge is only of *particulars*. *Locke.*

And if we will take them, as they were directed, in *particular* to her, or in her, as their representative, to all other women, they will, at most, concern the female sex only, and import no more but that subjection, they should ordinarily be in, to their husbands. *Locke.*

The master could hardly sit on his horse for laughing, all the while he was giving me the *particulars* of this story. *Addis.*

Vespasian he resembled in many *particulars*. *Swift.*

2. Individual; private person.

It is the greatest interest of *particulars*, to advance the good of the community. *L'Estrange.*

3. Private interest.

Our wisdom must be such, as doth not propose to itself τὸ ἴδιον our own *particular*, the partial and immoderate desire whereof poisoneth wheresoever it taketh place; but the scope and mark, which we are to aim at, is the publick and common good. *Hooker.*

They apply their minds even with hearty affection and zeal, at the least, unto those branches of publick prayer, wherein their own *particular* is moved. *Hooker, b.* 5.

His general lov'd him
In a most dear *particular*. *Shakesp.*

4. Private character; single self; state of an individual.

For his *particular*, I'll receive him gladly;
But not one follower. *Shakespeare's K. Lear.*

5. A minute detail of things singly enumerated.

The reader has a *particular* of the books, wherein this law was written. *Ayliffe's Parergon.*

6. Distinct not general recital.

Invention is called a muse, authors ascribe to each of them, in *particular*, the sciences which they have invented. *Dryden.*

PARTI'CULARITY. *n. s.* [*particularité*, Fr. from *particular.*]

1. Distinct notice or enumeration; not general assertion.

So did the boldness of their affirmation accompany the greatness of what they did affirm, even descending to *particularities*, what kingdoms he should overcome. *Sidney.*

2. Singleness; individuality.

Knowledge imprinted in the minds of all men, whereby both general principles for directing of human actions are comprehended, and conclusions derived from them, upon which conclusions groweth, in *particularity*, the choice of good and evil. *Hooker, b.* ii.

3. Petty account; private incident.

To see the titles that were most agreeable to such an emperor, the flatteries that he lay most open to, with the like *particularities* only to be met with on medals, are certainly not a little pleasing. *Addison.*

4. Something belonging to single persons.

Let the general trumpet blow his blast,
Particularities and petty sounds
To cease. *Shakesp. Henry* VI.

5. Something peculiar.

I saw an old heathen altar, with this *particularity*, that it was hollowed like a dish at one end; but not the end on which the sacrifice was laid. *Addison's Remarks on Italy.*

He applied himself to the coquette's heart; there occurred many *particularities* in this dissection. *Addison.*

To PARTI'CULARIZE. *v. a.* [*particulariser*, Fr. from *particular.*] To mention distinctly; to detail; to shew minutely.

The leanness that afflicts us, is an inventory to *particularize* their abundance. *Shakesp. Coriolanus.*

He not only boasts of his parentage as an Israelite, but *particularizes* his descent from Benjamin. *Atterbury's Sermons.*

PARTI'CULARLY. *v. a.* [from *particular.*]

1. Distinctly; singly; not universally.

Providence, that universally casts its eye over all the creation, is yet pleased more *particularly* to fasten it upon some. *South's Sermons.*

2. In an extraordinary degree.

This exact propriety of Virgil, I *particularly* regarded as a great part of his character. *Dryden.*

With the flower and the leaf I was so *particularly* pleased, both for the invention and the moral, that I commend it to the reader. *Dryden.*

To PARTI'CULATE. *v. a.* [from *particular.*] To make mention singly. Obsolete.

I may not *particulate* of Alexander Hales, the irrefragable doctor. *Camden's Remains.*

PA'RTISAN. *n. s.* [*pertisan*, French.]

1. A kind of pike or halberd.

Let us
Find out the prettiest dazied plot we can,
And make him with our pikes and *partisans*
A grave. *Shakespeare's Hamlet.*
Shall I strike at it with my *partisan*. *Shakesp. Hamlet.*

2. [From *parti*, French.] An adherent to a faction.

Some of these *partisans* concluded, the government had hired men to be bound and pinnioned. *Addison.*

I would be glad any *partisan* would help me to a tolerable reason, that, because Clodius and Curio agree with me in a few singular notions, I must blindly follow them in all. *Swift.*

3. The commander of a party.

4. A commander's leading staff. *Ainsworth.*

PARTI'TION. *n. s.* [*partition*, Fr. *partitio*, Latin.]

1. The act of dividing; a state of being divided.

We grew together,
Like to a double cherry, seeming parted,
But yet an union in *partition*. *Shakesp.*

2. Division; separation; distinction.

We have, in this respect, our churches divided by certain *partition*, although not so many in number as theirs. *Hooker.*

Can we not
Partition make with spectacles so precious
'Twixt fair and foul? *Shakespeare's Cymbeline.*

We shall be winnow'd with so rough a wind,
That ev'n our corn shall seem as light as chaff,
And good from bad find no *partition*. *Shakesp.*

The day, month and year, measured by them, are used as standard measures, as likely others arbitrarily deduced from them by *partition* or collection. *Holder on Time.*

3. Part divided from the rest; separate part.

Lodg'd in a small *partition*; and the rest
Ordain'd for uses to his Lord best known. *Milton.*

4. That by which different parts are separated.

It doth not follow, that God, without respect, doth teach us to erect between us and them a *partition* wall of difference, in such things indifferent as have hitherto been disputed of. *Hooker, b. iv. s.* 6.

Make *partitions* of wood in a hogshead, with holes in them, and mark the difference of their sound from that of an hogshead without such *partitions*. *Bacon.*

Partition firm and sure,
The waters underneath from those above
Dividing. *Milton's Paradise Lost.*

Enclosures our factions have made in the church, become a great *partition* wall to keep others out of it. *Decay of Piety.*

At one end of it, is a great *partition*, designed for an opera. *Addison.*

The *partition* between good and evil is broken down; and where one sin has entered, legions will force their way. *Rogers's Sermons.*

5. Part where separation is made.

The mound was newly made, no sight could pass
Betwixt the nice *partitions* of the grass,
The well-united sods so closely lay. *Dryden.*

To Parti'tion. *v. a.* To divide into distinct parts.

These sides are uniform without, though severally *partitioned* within. *Bacon.*

Pa'rtlet. *n. s.* A name given to a hen; the original signification being a ruff or band, or covering for the neck. *Hanmer.*

Thou dotard, thou art woman tir'd; unroosted
By thy dame *partlet* here. *Shakesp.*

Tir'd with pinn'd ruffs, and fans, and *partlet* strips. *Hall.*

Dame *partlet* was the sovereign of his heart;
He feather'd her. *Dryden's Fables.*

Pa'rtly. *adv.* [from *part.*] In some measure; in some degree; in part.

That part, which, since the coming of Christ, *partly* hath embraced, and *partly* shall hereafter embrace the christian religion, we term, as by a more proper name, the church of Christ. *Hooker, b.* iii. *s.* 1.

The inhabitants of Naples have been always very notorious for leading a life of laziness and pleasure, which I take to arise out of the wonderful plenty of their country, that does not make labour so necessary to them, and *partly* out of the temper of their climate, that relaxes the fibres of their bodies, and disposes the people to such an idle indolent humour. *Addison's Remarks on Italy.*

Pa'rtner. *n. s.* [from *part.*]

1. Partaker; sharer; one who has part in any thing; associate.

My noble *partner*,
You greet with present grace,
That he seems rapt withal. *Shakesp. Macbeth.*

Noble *partners*
Touch you the sowrest points with sweetest terms. *Shakesp.*

Those of the race of Sem were no *partners* in the unbelieving work of the tower. *Raleigh's History.*

To undergo
Myself the total crime; or to accuse
My other self, the *partner* of my life. *Milton.*

Sapor, king of Persia, had an heaven of glass, which, proudly sitting in his estate, he trod upon, calling himself brother to the sun and moon, and *partner* with the stars. *Peacham of Geometry.*

The soul continues in her action, till her *partner* is again qualified to bear her company. *Addison.*

2. One who dances with another.

Lead in your ladies every one; sweet *partner*,
I must not yet forsake you. *Shakespeare's Henry* VIII.

To Pa'rtner. *v. a.* [from the noun.] To join; to associate with a partner.

A lady who
So fair, and fasten'd to an empery,
Would make the great'st king double: to be *partner'd*
With tomboys, hir'd with self-exhibition,
Which your own coffers yield. *Shakesp.*

Pa'rtnership. *n. s.* [from *partner.*]

1. Joint interest or property.

He does possession keep,
And is too wise to hazard *partnership*. *Dryden.*

2. The union of two or more in the same trade.

'Tis a necessary rule in alliances, *partnerships* and all manner of civil dealings, to have a strict regard to the disposition of those we have to do withal. *L'Estrange.*

Pa'rtook. Preterite of *partake.*

Pa'rtridge. *n. s.* [*perdrix*, Fr. *pertris*, Welsh; *perdix*, Lat.] A bird of game.

The king is come out to seek a flea, as when one doth hunt a *partridge* in the mountains. 1 *Sam.* xxvi. 20.

Partu'rient. *adj.* [*parturiens*, Lat.] About to bring forth.

Parturi'tion. *n. s.* [from *parturio*, Latin.] The state of being about to bring forth.

Conformation of parts is required, not only unto the previous conditions of birth, but also unto the *parturition* or very birth. *Brown's Vulgar Errours.*

Pa'rty. *n. s.* [*partie*, French.]

1. A number of persons confederated by similiarity of designs or opinions in opposition to others; a faction.

When any of these combatants strips his terms of ambiguity, I shall think him a champion for truth, and not the slave of vain glory or a *party*. *Locke.*

This account of *party* patches will appear improbable to those, who live at a distance from the fashionable world. *Addis.*

Party writers are so sensible of the secret virtue of an *innuendo*, that they never mention the q—n at length. *Spectat.*

This *party* rage in women only serves to aggravate animosities that reign among them. *Addis. Spect.* Nº 81.

As he never leads the conversation into the violence and rage of *party* disputes, I listened to him with pleasure. *Tatler.*

Division between those of the same *party*, exposes them to their enemies. *Pope.*

The most violent *party* men are such, as, in the conduct of their lives, have discovered least sense of religion or morality. *Swift.*

2. One of two litigants.

When you are hearing a matter between *party* and *party*, if pinched with the cholick, you make faces like mummers, and dismiss the controversy more entangled by your hearing: all the peace you make in their cause, is calling both *parties* knaves. *Shakesp.*

The cause of both *parties* shall come before the judges. *Exodus* xxii. 9.

If a bishop be a *party* to a suit, and excommunicates his adversary; such excommunication shall not bar his adversary from his action. *Ayliffe's Parergon.*

3. One concerned in any affair.

The child was prisoner to the womb, and is
Free'd and enfranchis'd; not a *party* to
The anger of the king, nor guilty of
The trespass of the queen. *Shakesp.*

I do suspect this trash
To be a *party* in this injury. *Shakesp.*

4. Side; persons engaged against each other.

Our Foes compell'd by need, have peace embrac'd:
The peace, both *parties* want, is like to last. *Dryden.*

5. Cause; side.

Ægle came in, to make their *party* good. *Dryden.*

6. A select assembly.

Let me extol a cat, on oysters fed,
I'll have a *party* at the Bedford-head. *Pope.*

If the clergy would a little study the arts of conversation, they might be welcome at every *party*, where there was the least regard for politeness or good sense. *Swift.*

7. Particular person; a person distinct from, or opposed to, another.

As she paced on, she was stopped with a number of trees, so thickly placed together, that she was afraid she should, with rushing through, stop the speech of the lamentable *party*, which she was so desirous to understand. *Sidney.*

The minister of justice may, for publick example, virtuously will the execution of that *party*, whose pardon another, for consanguinity's sake, as virtuously may desire. *Hooker.*

If the jury found, that the *party* slain was of English race, it had been adjudged felony. *Davies on Ireland.*

How shall this be compast? canst thou bring me to the *party*? *Shakespear's Tempest.*

The smoke received into the nostrils, causes the *party* to lie as if he were drunk. *Abbot's Descript. of the World.*

The imagination of the *party* to be cured, is not needful to concur; for it may be done without the knowledge of the *party* wounded. *Bacon's Natural History.*

He that confesses his sin, and prays for pardon, hath punished his fault: and then there is nothing left to be done by the offended *party*, but to return to charity. *Taylor.*

Though there is a real difference between one man and another, yet the *party*, who has the advantage, usually magnifies the inequality. *Collier on Pride.*

8. A detachment of soldiers: as, he commanded that *party* sent thither.

Party-coloured. *adj.* [*party* and *coloured.*] Having diversity of colours.

The fulsome ewes,
Then conceiving, did, in yeaning time,
Fall *party-colour'd* lambs. *Shakesp. Merch. of Venice.*

The leopard was valuing himself upon the lustre of his *party-coloured* skin. *L'Estrange.*

From one father both,
Both girt with gold, and clad in *party-colour'd* cloth. *Dryd.*

Constrain'd him in a bird, and made him fly
With *party-colour'd* plumes a chattering pie. *Dryden.*

I looked with as much pleasure upon the little *party-coloured* assembly, as upon a bed of tulips. *Addison's Spect.*

Nor is it hard to beautify each month
With files of *party-colour'd* fruits. *Phillips.*

Four knaves in garb succinct, a trusty band,
And *party-coloured* troops, a shining train,
Draw forth to combat on the velvet plain. *Pope.*

Party-ju'ry. *n. s.* [in law.] A jury in some trials half foreigners and half natives.

Pa'rty-man. *n. s.* [*party* and *man.*] A factious person; an abettor of a party.

Party-wall. *n. s.* [*party* and *wall.*] Wall that separates one house from the next.

'Tis an ill custom among bricklayers to work up a whole story of the *party-walls*, before they work up the fronts. *Moxon's Mechanical Exercises.*

PA'RVIS. *n. s.* [Fr.] A church or church porch: applied to the mootings or law-disputes among young students in the inns of courts, and also to that disputation at Oxford, called *disputatio in parvis.* *Bailey.*

Pa'rvitude. *n. s.* [from *parvus*, Latin.] Littleness; minuteness.

The little ones of *parvitude* cannot reach to the same floor with them. *Glanville.*

Pa'rvity. *n. s.* [from *parvus*, Lat.] Littleness; minuteness.

What are these for fineness and *parvity*, to those minute animalcula discovered in pepper-water. *Ray.*

PAS. *n. s.* [French.] Precedence; right of going foremost.

In her poor circumstances, she still preserv'd the mien of a gentlewoman; when she came into any full assembly, she would not yield the *pas* to the best of them. *Arbuthnot.*

Pa'schal. *adj.* [*pascal*, French; *paschalis*, Latin.]

1. Relating to the passover.
2. Relating to Easter.

Pash. *n. s.* [*paz*, Spanish.] A kiss. *Hanmer.*

Thou want'st a rough *pash*, and the shoots that I have,
To be full like me. *Shakesp. Winter's Tale.*

To Pash. *v. a.* [*perssen*, Dutch.] To strike; to crush.

With my armed fist
I'll *pash* him o'er the face. *Shakespeare.*

Thy cunning engines have with labour rais'd
My heavy anger, like a mighty weight,
To fall and *pash* thee dead. *Dryden.*

Pasque-flower. *n. s.* [*pulsatilla*, Latin.]

The flower consists of several leaves, which are placed in a circular order, and expand in form of a rose; out of the middle of which rises a pointal, beset, for the most part, with chives, which afterward becomes a fruit, in which the seeds are gathered, as it were in a little head, each ending in a small hair: to which must be added some little leaves, encompassing the pedicle below the flower; as the anemone, from which the *pasque-flower* differs in the seed, ending in a tail. *Miller.*

Pa'squil. }
Pa'squin. } *n. s.* [from *pasquino*, a statue at Rome, to which they affix any lampoon or paper of satirical observation.] A lampoon.
Pa'squinade. }

He never valued any *pasquils* that were dropped up and down, to think them worthy of his revenge. *Howel.*

The *pasquils*, lampoons, and libels, we meet with now-a-days, are a sort of playing with the four and twenty letters, without sense, truth, or wit. *Tatler*, Nº 92.

To Pass. *v. n.* [*passer*, French; *passus*, a step, Latin.]

1. To go; to move from one place to another; to be progressive.

Tell him his long trouble is *passing*
Out of this world. *Shakesp. Henry* VIII.

If I have found favour in thy sight, *pass* not away from thy servant. *Genesis.*

While my glory *passeth* by, I will put thee in a clift of the rock, and will cover thee, while I *pass* by. *Exodus* xxxiii. 22.

Thus will I cut off him that *passeth* out, and him that returneth. *Ezekiel* xxxv. 7

They took the fords of Jordan, and suffered not a man to *pass* over. *Judges* iii. 28.

This heap and this pillar be witness, that I will not *pass* over to thee, and that thou shall not *pass* over it and this pillar unto me for harm. *Genesis* xxxi. 52.

An idea of motion not *passing* on, is not better than idea of motion at rest. *Locke.*

Heedless of those cares, with anguish stung,
He felt their fleeces as they *pass'd* along. *Pope.*

If the cause be visible, we stop at the instrument, and seldom *pass* on to him that directed it. *Wake's Prep. for Death.*

2. To go; to make way.

Her face, her hands were torn
With *passing* through the brakes. *Dryden.*

3. To make transition from one thing to another.

Others dissatisfied with what they have, and not trusting to those innocent ways of getting more, fall to others, and *pass* from just to unjust. *Temple's Miscellanies.*

4. To vanish; to be lost.

Trust not too much to that enchanting face;
Beauty's a charm, but soon the charm will *pass.* *Dryden.*

5. To be spent; to go away.

The time, when the thing existed, is the idea of that space of duration, which *passed* between some fixed period and the being of that thing. *Locke.*

We see, that one who fixes his thoughts very intently on one thing, so as to take but little notice of the succession of ideas that *pass* in his mind, whilst he is taken up with that earnest contemplation, lets slip out of his account a good part of that duration, and thinks that time shorter than it is. *Locke.*

6. To be at an end; to be over.

Their officious haste,
Who would before have born him to the sky,
Like eager Romans, ere all rites were *past*,
Did let too soon the sacred eagle fly. *Dryden.*

7. To die; to pass from the present life to another state.

The pangs of death do make him grin;
Disturb him not, let him *pass* peaceably. *Shakesp.*

8. To be changed by regular gradation.

Inflammations are translated from other parts to the lungs; a pleurisy easily *passeth* into a peripneumony. *Arbuthnot.*

9. To go beyond bounds. Obsolete.

Why this *passes*, Mr. Ford:—you are not to go loose any longer, you must be pinnioned. *Shakesp.*

10. To be in any state.

I will cause you to *pass* under the rod, and I will bring you into the bond of the covenant. *Ezekiel* xx. 37.

11. To be enacted.

Many of the nobility spoke in parliament against those things, which were most grateful to his majesty, and which still *passed*, notwithstanding their contradiction. *Clarendon.*

Neither of these bills have yet *passed* the house of commons, and some think they may be rejected. *Swift.*

This pernicious project, if *passed* into a law, would have been of the worst consequence. *Swift.*

12. To be effected; to exist. Unless this may be thought a noun with the articles suppressed, and be explained thus: it came to the *pass* that.

I have heard it enquired, how it might be brought to *pass* that the church should every where have able preachers to instruct the people. *Hooker, b.* v. *s.* 3.

When the case required dissimulation, if they used it, it came to *pass* that the former opinion of their good faith made them almost invisible. *Bacon's Essays.*

13. To gain reception; to become current: as, this money will not *pass.*

That trick, said she, will not *pass* twice. *Hudibras.*

Their excellencies will not *pass* for such in the opinion of the learned, but only as things which have less of error in them. *Dryden.*

False eloquence *passeth* only where true is not understood, and no body will commend bad writers, that is acquainted with good. *Felton on the Classicks.*

The grossest suppositions *pass* upon them, that the wild Irish were taken in toyls; but that, in some time, they would grow tame. *Swift.*

14. To be practised artfully or successfully.

This practice hath most shrewdly *past* upon thee;
But when we know the grounds and authors of it,
Thou shalt be both the plaintiff and the judge. *Shakesp.*

Though frauds may *pass* upon men, they are as open as the light to him that searches the heart. *L'Estrange.*

15. To be regarded as good or ill.

He rejected the authority of councils, and so do all the reformed; so that this won't *pass* for a fault in him, 'till 'tis proved one in us. *Atterbury.*

16. To occur; to be transacted.

If we would judge of the nature of spirits, we must have recourse to our own consciousness of what *passes* within our own mind. *Watts's Logick.*

17. To be done.

Zeal may be let loose in matters of direct duty, as in prayers, provided that no indirect act *pass* upon them to defile them. *Taylor's Rule of Living Holy.*

18. To heed; to regard.

As for these silken-coated slaves, I *pass* not;
It is to you, good people, that I speak,
O'er whom, in time to come, I hope to reign. *Shakesp.*

19. To determine finally; to judge capitally.

Though well we may not *pass* upon his life,
Without the form of justice; yet our pow'r
Shall do a court'sy to our wrath. *Shakesp.*

20. To be supremely excellent.

21. To thrust; to make a push in fencing.

To see thee fight, to see thee *pass* thy puncto. *Shakesp.*

Both advance
Against each other, and with sword and lance
They lash, they foin, they *pass*, they strive to bore
Their corslets. *Dryden.*

22. To omit.

Full piteous seems young Alma's case,
As in a luckless gamester's place,
She would not play, yet must not *pass*. *Prior.*

23. To go through the alimentary duct.

Substances hard cannot be dissolved, but they will *pass*; but such, whose tenacity exceeds the powers of digestion, will neither *pass*, nor be converted into aliment. *Arbuthnot.*

24. To be in a tolerable state.

A middling sort of man was left well enough to *pass* by his father, but could never think he had enough, so long as any had more *L'Estrange.*

25. *To* PASS *away*. To be lost; to glide off.

Defining the soul to be a substance that always thinks, can serve but to make many men suspect, that they have no souls at all, since they find a good part of their lives *pass away* without thinking. *Locke.*

26. *To* PASS *away*. To vanish.

To PASS. *v. a.*

1. To go beyond.

As it is advantageable to a physician to be called to the cure of a declining disease; so it is for a commander to suppress a sedition, which has *passed* the height: for in both the noxious humour doth first weaken, and afterwards waste to nothing. *Hayward.*

2. To go through: as, the horse *passed* the river.

3. To spend; to live through.

Were I not assured he was removed to advantage, I should *pass* my time extremely ill without him. *Collier.*

You know in what deluding joys we *past*
The night that was by heav'n decreed our last. *Dryden.*

We have examples of such, as *pass* most of their nights without dreaming. *Locke.*

The people, free from cares, serene, and gay,
Pass all their mild untroubled hours away. *Addison.*

In the midst of the service, a lady, who had *passed* the winter at London with her husband, entered the congregation. *Addison's Spectator*, Nº 129.

4. To impart to any thing the power of moving.

Dr. Thurston thinks the principal use of inspiration to be, to move, or *pass* the blood, from the right to the left ventricle of the heart. *Derham's Physico-Theology.*

5. To carry hastily.

I had only time to *pass* my eye over the medals, which are in great number. *Addison's Remarks on Italy.*

6. To transfer to another proprietor.

He that will *pass* his land,
As I have mine, may set his hand
And heart unto this deed, when he hath read;
And make the purchase spread. *Herbert.*

7. To strain; to percolate.

They speak of severing wine from water, *passing* it through ivy wood. *Bacon's Natural History.*

8. To vent; to let out.

How many thousands take upon them to *pass* their censures on the personal actions of others, and pronounce boldly on the affairs of the publick. *Watts.*

They will commend the work in general, but *pass* so many sly remarks upon it afterwards, as shall destroy all their cold praises. *Watts's Improvement of the Mind.*

9. To utter ceremoniously.

Many of the lords and some of the commons *passed* some compliments to the two lords. *Clarendon.*

10. To utter solemnly.

He *past* his promise, and was as good as his word. *L'Estrange.*

11. To transmit.

Waller *passed* over five thousand horse and foot by Newbridge. *Clarendon, b.* viii.

12. To put an end to.

This night
We'll *pass* the business privately and well. *Shakespeare.*

13. To surpass; to excel.

She more sweet than any bird on bough
Would oftentimes emongst them bear a part,
And strive to *pass*, as she could well enough,
Their native music by her skilful art. *Fairy Queen.*

Whom do'st thou *pass* in beauty? *Ezekiel* xxxii. 19.

Martial, thou gav'st far nobler epigrams
To thy Domitian, than I can my James;
But in my royal subject I *pass* thee,
Thou flattered'st thine, mine cannot flatter'd be. *B. Johns.*

The ancestor and all his heirs,
Though they in number *pass* the stars of heav'n,
Are still but one. *Davies.*

14. To omit; to neglect.

If you fondly *pass* our proffer'd offer,
'Tis not the rounder of your old fac'd walls
Can hide you. *Shakespeare's King John.*

Let me o'erleap that custom; for I cannot
Put on the gown, stand naked, and entreat them;
Please you that I may *pass* this doing. *Shakespeare.*

I *pass* the wars, that spotted linx's make
With their fierce rivals. *Dryden.*

I *pass* their warlike pomp, their proud array. *Dryden.*

15. To transcend; to transgress.

They did *pass* those bounds, and did return since that time. *Burnet's Theory of the Earth.*

16. To admit; to allow.

The money of every one that *passeth* the account, let the priests take. *2 Kings* xii. 4.

I'll *pass* them all upon account,
As if your nat'ral self had don't. *Hudibras.*

17. To enact a law.

How does that man know, but the decree may be already *passed* against him, and his allowance of mercy spent. *South.*

Among the laws that *pass'd*, it was decreed,
That conquer'd Thebes from bondage should be freed. *Dryden's Knight's Tale.*

Could the same parliament which addressed with so much zeal and earnestness against this evil, *pass* it into a law? *Swift.*

His majesty's ministers proposed the good of the nation, when they advised the *passing* this patent. *Swift.*

18. To impose fraudulently.

Th' indulgent mother did her care employ,
And *pass'd* it on her husband for a boy. *Dryden.*

19. To practice artfully; to make succeed.

Time lays open frauds, and after that discovery there is no *passing* the same trick upon the mice. *L'Estrange.*

20. To send from one place to another: as, *pass* that beggar to his own parish.

21. *To* PASS *away*. To spend; to waste.

The father waketh for the daughter, lest she *pass away* the flower of her age. *Ecclus.* xlii. 9.

22. *To* PASS *by*. To excuse; to forgive.

However God may *pass by* single sinners in this world; yet when a nation combines against him, the wicked shall not go unpunished. *Tillotson's Sermons.*

23. *To* PASS *by*. To neglect; to disregard.

How far ought this enterprize to wait upon these other matters, to be mingled with them, or to *pass by* them, and give law to them, as inferior unto itself? *Bacon.*

It conduces much to our content, if we *pass by* those things which happen to our trouble, and consider that which is prosperous; that, by the representation of the better, the worse may be blotted out. *Taylor's Holy Living.*

Certain passages of scripture we cannot, without injury to truth, *pass by* here in silence. *Burnet's Theory of the Earth.*

24. *To* PASS *over*. To omit; to let go unregarded.

Better to *pass* him o'er, than to relate
The cause I have your mighty sire to hate. *Dryden.*

It does not belong to this place to have that point debated, nor will it hinder our pursuit to *pass* it *over* in silence. *Watts.*

The poet *passes* it *over* as hastily as he can, as if he were afraid of staying in the cave. *Dryden.*

The queen asked him, who he was; but he *passes over* this without any reply, and reserves the greatest part of his story to a time of more leisure. *Broome.*

PASS. *n. s.* [from the verb.]

1. A narrow entrance; an avenue.

The straight *pass* was damm'd
With dead men. *Shakespear's Cymbeline.*

It would be easy to defend the *passes* into the whole country, that the king's army should never be able to enter. *Clar.*

Truth is a strong hold, fortified by God and nature, and diligence is properly the understanding's laying siege to it; so that it must be perpetually observing all the avenues and *passes* to it, and accordingly making its approaches. *South.*

2. Passage; road.

The Tyrians had no *pass* to the Red Sea, but through the territory of Solomon, and by his sufferance. *Raleigh.*

Pity tempts the *pass*;
But the tough metal of my heart resists. *Dryden.*

3. A permission to go or come any where.

They shall protect all that come in, and send them to the lord deputy, with their safe conduct or *pass*, to be at his disposition. *Spenser on Ireland.*

We bid this be done,
When evil deeds have their permissive *pass*,
And not the punishment. *Shakespeare.*

Give quiet *pass*
Through your dominions for this enterprize. *Shakespeare.*

A gentleman had a *pass* to go beyond the seas. *Claren.*

If they should send for a *pass* to France, the ceremony in asking and granting it would be liable to the same objections of delay. *Clarendon.*

4. An order by which vagrants or impotent persons are sent to their place of abode.

5. Push; thrust in fencing.

'Tis dangerous when the baser nature comes
Between the *pass* and fell incensed points
Of mighty opposites. *Shakesp. Hamlet.*

The king hath laid, that in a dozen *passes* between you and him, he shall not exceed you three hits. *Shakespeare.*

With seeming innocence the crowd beguil'd;
But made the desperate *passes*, when he smil'd. *Dryden.*

6. State; condition.

To what a *pass* are our minds brought, that, from the right line of virtue, are wryed to these crooked shifts? *Sidney.*

After King Henry united the roses, they laboured to reduce both English and Irish, which work, to what *pass* and perfection it was brought, in queen Elizabeth's reign, hath been declared. *Davies's State of Ireland.*

I could see plate, hangings and paintings about my house till you had the ordering of me, but I am now brought to such *pass*, that I can see nothing at all. *L'Estrange.*

Matters have been brought to this *pass*, that if one among a man's sons had any blemish, he laid him aside for the ministry, and such an one was presently approved. *South.*

PA'SSABLE. *adj.* [*passible*, Fr. from *pass*.]

1. Possible to be passed or travelled through or over.

Antiochus departed in all haste, weening in his pride to make the land navigable, and the sea *passable* by foot. *2 Mac.*

2. Supportable; tolerable; allowable.

His body is a *passable* carkass, if he be not hurt. It is a thoroughfare for steel. *Shakespeare's Cymbeline.*

They are crafty and of a *passable* reach of understanding. *Howel.*

In counterfeits, it is with men as with false money; one piece is more or less *passable* than another. *L'Estrange.*

Lay by Virgil, my version will appear a *passable* beauty when the original muse is absent. *Dryden.*

White and red well mingled on the face, make what was before but *passable*, appear beautiful. *Dryden.*

3. Capable of admission or reception.

These stage advocates are not only without truth, but without colour: could they have made the slander *passable*, we should have heard farther. *Collier.*

4. Popular; well received. This is a sense less usual.

Where there is no eminent odds in sufficiency, it is better to take with the more *passable*, than with the more able. *Bac.*

A man of the one faction, which is most *passable* with the other, commonly giveth best way. *Bacon's Essays.*

PASSA'DO. n. s. [Italian.] A push; a thrust.

A duellist, a gentleman of the very first house; ah! the immortal *passado*. *Shakespeare's Romeo and Juliet.*

PA'SSAGE. *n. s.* [*passage*, French.]

1. Act of passing; travel; course; journey.

The story of such a *passage* was true, and Jason with the rest went indeed to rob Colchos, to which they might arrive by boat. *Raleigh's History of the World.*

So shalt thou best prepar'd endure
Thy mortal *passage* when it comes. *Milton.*

Live like those who look upon themselves as being only on their *passage* through this state, but as belonging to that which is to come. *Atterbury's Sermons.*

Though the *passage* be troublesome, yet it is secure, and shall in a little time bring us ease and peace at the last. *Wake.*

2. Road; way.

Human actions are so uncertain, as that seemeth the best course, which hath most *passages* out of it. *Bacon.*

The land enterprize of Panama was grounded upon a false account, that the *passages* towards it were no better fortified than Drake had left them. *Bacon.*

Is there yet no other way besides
These painful *passages*, how we may come
To death, and mix with our connatural dust? *Milton.*

Against which open'd from beneath
A *passage* down to th' earth, a *passage* wide. *Milton.*

When the *passage* is open, land will be turned most to great cattle; when shut, to sheep. *Temple.*

The Persian army had advanced into the straight *passages* of Cilicia, by which means Alexander with his small army was able to fight and conquer them. *South's Seromns.*

The *passage* made by many a winding way,
Reach'd e'en the room, in which the tyrant lay. *Dryden.*

He plies him with redoubled strokes;
Wheels as he wheels; and with his pointed dart
Explores the nearest *passage* to his heart. *Dryden.*

I wished for the wings of an eagle, to fly away to those happy seats; but the genius told me there was no *passage* to them, except through the gates of death. *Addison.*

I have often stopped all the *passages* to prevent the ants going to their own nest. *Addison's Guardian*, N° 157.

When the gravel is separated from the kidney, oily substances relax the *passages*. *Arbuthnot on Diet.*

3. Entrance or exit; liberty to pass.

What, are my doors oppos'd against my *passage*? *Shak.*

4. The state of decay. Not in use.

Would some part of my young years
Might but redeem the *passage* of your age! *Shakesp.*

5. Intellectual admittance; mental acceptance.

I would render this treatise intelligible to every rational man, however little versed in scholastick learning, among whom I expect it will have a fairer *passage* than among those deeply imbued with other principles. *Digby.*

6. Occurrence; hap.

It is no act of common *passage*, but
A strain of rareness. *Shakespeare.*

7. Unsettled state; aptness by condition or nature to change the place of abode.

Most traders in Ireland are but factors; the cause must be rather an ill opinion of security than of gain: the last intices the poorer traders, young beginners, or those of *passage*; but without the first, the rich will never settle in the country. *Temple's Miscellanies.*

In man the judgment shoots at flying game;
A bird of *passage!* lost as soon as found;
Now in the moon perhaps, now under ground. *Pope.*

8. Incident; transaction.

This business as it is a very high *passage* of state, so it is worthy of serious consideration. *Hayward.*

Thou do'st in thy *passages* of life
Make me believe that thou art only mark'd
For the hot vengeance of heav'n. *Shakesp. Henry IV.*

9. Management: conduct.

Upon consideration of the conduct and *passage* of affairs in former times, the state of England ought to be cleared of an imputation cast upon it. *Davies on Ireland.*

10. Part of a book; single place in a writing. *Endroit*, Fr.

A critic who has no taste nor learning, seldom ventures to praise any *passage* in an author who has not been before received by the publick. *Addison's Spectator*, N° 291.

As to the cantos, all the *passages* are as fabulous as the vision at the beginning. *Pope.*

PA'SSED. Preterite and participle of *pass*.

Why sayest thou my way is hid from the Lord, and my judgment is *passed* over from my God? *Isaiah* xl. 27.

He affirmed, that no good law *passed* since king William's accession, except the act for preserving the game. *Addison.*

The description of a life, *passed* away in vanity and among the shadows of pomp, may be soon finely drawn in the same place. *Addison's Spectator*, N° 210.

PA'SSENGER. *n. s.* [*passager*, French.]

1. A traveller; one who is upon the road; a wayfarer.

All the way, the wanton damsel found
New mirth, her *passenger* to entertain. *Fairy Queen.*

What hollowing, and what stir is this?
These are my mates that make their wills their law,
Have some unhappy *passenger* in chase. *Shakespeare.*

The nodding horror of whose shady brows
Threats the forlorn and wand'ring *passenger*. *Milton.*

Apelles, when he had finished any work, exposed it to the sight of all *passengers*, and concealed himself to hear the censure of his faults. *Dryden's Dufresnoy.*

2. One who hires in any vehicle the liberty of travelling.

The diligent pilot in a dangerous tempest doth attend the unskilful words of a *passenger*. *Sidney.*

PASSENGER *falcon. n. s.* A kind of migratory hawk. *Ains.*

P'ASSER. *n. s.* [from *pass*.] One who passes; one that is upon the road.

Under you ride the home and foreign shipping in so near a distance, that, without troubling the *passer* or borrowing Stentor's voice, you may confer with any in the town. *Carew.*

Have we so soon forgot,
When, like a matron, butcher'd by her sons,
And cast beside some common way a spectacle
Of horror and affright to *passers* by,
Our groaning country bled at every vein. *Rowe.*

PASSIBI'LITY. *n. s.* [*passibilité*, Fr. from *passible*.] Quality of receiving impressions from external agents.

The last doubt, touching the *passibility* of the matter of the heavens, is drawn from the eclipses of the sun and moon. *Hakewill on Providence.*

PA'SSIBLE. *adj.* [*passible*, Fr. *passibilis*, Lat.] Susceptive of impressions from external agents.

Theodoret disputeth with great earnestness, that God cannot be said to suffer; but he thereby meaneth Christ's divine nature against Apollinarius, which held even deity itself *passible*. *Hooker, b.* v. 53.

PA'SSIBLENESS. *n. s.* [from *passible*.] Quality of receiving impressions from external agents.

It drew after it the heresy of the *passibleness* of the deity, because the deity of Christ was become, in their conceits, the same nature with the humanity that was passible. *Brerewood on Languages.*

PASSING. *participial adj.* [from *pass*.]

1. Supreme; surpassing others; eminent.

No strength of arms shall win this noble fort,
Or shake this puissant wall, such *passing* might
Have spells and charms, if they be said aright. *Fairfax.*

Sir Hudibras his *passing* worth,
The manner how he sallied forth. *Hudibras.*

2. It is used adverbially to enforce the meaning of another word. Exceeding.

Oberon is *passing* fell and wroth. *Shakespeare.*

Many

Many in each region *passing* fair
As the noon sky; more like to goddesses
Than mortal creatures. *Milton's Paradise Lost.*

She was not only *passing* fair,
But was withal discreet and debonair. *Dryden.*

While thus we stood as in a stound,
Full soon by bonfire and by bell,
We learnt our liege was *passing* well. *Gay.*

PA'SSINGBELL. *n. s.* [*passing* and *bell.*] The bell which rings at the hour of departure, to obtain prayers for the passing soul: it is often used for the bell, which rings immediately after death.

Those loving papers,
Thicken on you now, as pray'rs ascend
To heaven in troops at a good man's *passingbell.* *Donne.*

A talk of tumult, and a breath
Would serve him as his *passingbell* to death. *Daniel.*

Before the *passingbell* begun,
The news through half the town has run. *Swift.*

PA'SSION. *n. s.* [*passion*, French; *passio*, Latin.]

1. Any effect caused by external agency.

The differences of mouldable and not mouldable, scissible and not scissible, and many other *passions* of matter are plebeian notions, applied to the instruments men ordinarily practise. *Bacon.*

A body at rest affords us no idea of any active power to move, and when, set in motion, it is rather a *passion* than an action in it. *Locke.*

2. Violent commotion of the mind.

All the other *passions* fleet to air,
As doubtful thoughts and rash embrac'd despair. *Shakesp.*

Thee every thing becomes, to chide, to laugh,
To weep: whose every *passion* fully strives
To make itself in thee fair and admired. *Shakespeare.*

Vex'd I am
Of late, with *passions* of some difference. *Shakespeare.*

I am doubtful, lest
You break into some merry *passion*,
And so offend him:
If you should smile, he grows impatient. *Shakesp.*

In loving thou do'st well, in *passion* not;
Wherein true love consists not. *Milton's Par. Lost.*

Cruel his eye, but cast
Signs of remorse and *passion*, to behold
The fellows of his crime condemn'd
For ever now to have their lot in pain. *Milton's Par. Lost.*

Passion's too fierce to be in fetters bound,
And nature flies him like enchanted ground. *Dryden.*

All the art of rhetorick, besides order and perspicuity, only moves the *passions*, and thereby misleads the judgment. *Locke.*

3. Anger.

The word *passion* signifies the receiving any action in a large philosophical sense; in a more limited philosophical sense, it signifies any of the affections of human nature; as love, fear, joy, sorrow: but the common people confine it only to anger. *Watts.*

4. Zeal; ardour.

Where statesmen are ruled by faction and interest, they can have no *passion* for the glory of their country, nor any concern for the figure it will make. *Addison on Medals.*

5. Love.

For your love,
You kill'd her father: you confess'd you drew
A mighty argument to prove your *passion* for the daughter.
Dryden and Lee's Oedipus.

He, to grate me more,
Publickly own'd his *passion* for Amestris. *Rowe.*

Survey yourself, and then forgive your slave,
Think what a *passion* such a form must have. *Granvil.*

6. Eargerness.

Abate a little of that violent *passion* for fine cloaths, so predominant in your sex. *Swift.*

7. Emphatically. The last suffering of the redeemer of the world.

He shewed himself alive after his *passion*, by many infallible proofs. *Acts* i. 3.

To PA'SSION. *v. n.* [*passionner*, Fr. from the noun.] To be extremely agitated; to express great commotion of mind. Obsolete.

'Twas Ariadne *passioning*
For Theseus' perjury and unjust flight. *Shakespeare.*

PASSION-FLOWER. *n. s.* [*granadilla*, Latin.]

Passion-flower hath a double calyx, the first consisting of three leaves, the other of five, which expand in form of a star: the flowers consist of five leaves each, and are of a rosaceous form: in the centre of the flower arises the pointal, with a crown fringed at the bottom, but furnished with a tender embryo at the top, on which stand three clubs, under which are the stamina, with rough obtuse apices, which always incline downward; the embryo turns to an oval or globular fruit, fleshy, and consisting of one cell, which is full of seeds adhering to the sides, and covered with a sort of hood or veil. *Miller.*

PA'SSION-WEEK. *n. s.* The week immediately preceding Easter, named in commemoration of our Saviour's crucifixion.

PA'SSIONATE. *adj.* [*passionné*, French.]

1. Moved by passion; causing or expressing great commotion of mind.

My whole endeavour is to resolve the conscience, and to shew what, in this controversy, the heart is to think, if it will follow the light of sound and sincere judgment, without either cloud of prejudice or mist of *passionate* affection. *Hooker.*

Thucydides observes, that men are much more *passionate* for injustice than for violence; because the one coming as from an equal seems rapine; when the other proceeding from one stronger is but the effect of necessity. *Clarendon.*

Good angels looked upon this ship of Noah's with a *passionate* concern for its safety. *Burnet.*

Men, upon the near approach of death, have been rouzed up into such a lively sense of their guilt, such a *passionate* degree of concern and remorse, that, if ten thousand ghosts had appeared to them, they scarce could have had a fuller conviction of their danger. *Atterbury's Sermons.*

2. Easily moved to anger.

Homer's Achilles is haughty and *passionate*, impatient of any restraint by laws, and arrogant in arms. *Prior.*

To PA'SSSIONATE. *v. a.* [from *passion.*] An old word. Obsolete.

1. To affect with passion.

Great pleasure mix'd with pitiful regard,
That godly king and queen did *passionate*,
Whilst they his pitiful adventures heard,
That oft they did lament his luckless state. *Fairy Queen.*

2. To express passionately.

Thy neice and I want hands,
And cannot *passionate* our tenfold grief
With folded arms. *Shakespeare's Titus Andronicus.*

PA'SSIONATELY. *adv.* [from *passionate.*]

1. With passion; with desire, love or hatred; with great commotion of mind.

Whoever *passionately* covets any thing he has not, has lost his hold. *L'Estrange.*

If sorrow expresses itself never so loudly and *passionately*, and discharge itself in never so many tears, yet it will no more purge a man's heart, than the washing of his hands can cleanse the rottenness of his bones. *South's Sermons.*

I made Melesinda, in opposition to Nourmahal, a woman *passionately* loving of her husband, patient of injuries and contempt, and constant in her kindness. *Dryden.*

2. Angrily.

They lay the blame on the poor little ones, sometimes *passionately* enough, to divert it from themselves. *Locke.*

PA'SSIONATENESS. *n. s.* [from *passionate.*]

1. State of being subject to passion.
2. Vehemence of mind.

To love with some *passionateness* the person you would marry, is not only allowable but expedient. *Boyle.*

PA'SSIVE. *adj.* [*passif*, French; *passivus*, Latin.]

1. Receiving impression from some external agent.

High above the ground
Their march was, and the *passive* air upbore
Their nimble tread. *Milton's Paradise Lost.*

The active informations of the intellect, filling the *passive* reception of the will, like form closing with matter, grew actuate into a third and distinct perfection of practice. *South.*

As the mind is wholly *passive* in the reception of all its simple ideas, so it exerts several acts of its own, whereby, out of its simple ideas, the other is formed. *Locke.*

The *vis inertiæ* is a *passive* principle by which bodies persist in their motion or rest, receive motion in proportion to the force impressing it, and resist as much as they are resisted: by this principle alone, there never could have been any motion in the world. *Newton's Opticks.*

2. Unresisting; not opposing.

Not those alone, who *passive* own her laws,
But who, weak rebels, more advance her cause. *Dunciad.*

3. Suffering; not acting.

4. [In grammar.]

A verb *passive* is that which signifies passion or the effect of action: as, *doceor*, I am taught. *Clarke's Lat. Gram.*

PA'SSIVELY. *adv.* [from *passive.*] With a passive nature.

Though some are *passively* inclin'd,
The greater part degenerate from their kind. *Dryden.*

PA'SSIVENESS. *n. s.* [from *passive.*]

1. Quality of receiving impression from external agents.
2. Passibility; power of suffering.

We shall lose our *passiveness* with our being, and be as incapable of suffering as heaven can make us. *Decay of Piety.*

PASSI'VITY. *n. s.* [from *passive.*] Passiveness. An innovated word.

There being no mean between penetrability and impenetrability, between *passivity* and activity, these being contrary and opposite, the infinite rarefaction of the one quality is the position of its contrary. *Cheyne's Philosophical Principles.*

PA'SSOVER.

Pa'ssover. *n. s.* [*pass* and *over*.]

1. A feast instituted among the Jews in memory of the time when God, smiting the first-born of the Egyptians, *passed over* the habitations of the Hebrews.

The Jews *passover* was at hand, and Jesus went up. *Jo.* ii. 13.

The Lord's *passover*, commonly called Easter, was ordered by the common law to be celebrated every year on a Sunday. *Ayliffe's Parergon.*

2. The sacrifice killed.

Take a lamb, and kill the *passover*. *Exodus* xii. 21.

Pa'ssport. *n. s.* [*passport*, Fr.] Permission of egress.

Under that pretext, fain she would have given a secret *passport* to her affection. *Sidney.*

Giving his reason *passport* for to pass
Whither it would, so it would let him die. *Sidney.*

Let him depart; his *passport* shall be made,
And crowns for convoy put into his purse. *Shakespeare.*

Having used extreme caution in granting *passports* to Ireland, he conceived that paper not to have been delivered. *Clar.*

The gospel has then only a free admission into the assent of the understanding, when it brings a *passport* from a rightly disposed will, as being the faculty of dominion, that commands all, that shuts out, and lets in, what objects it pleases. *South's Sermons.*

Admitted in the shining throng,
He shows the *passport* which he brought along;
His *passport* is his innocence and grace,
Well known to all the natives of the place. *Dryden.*

At our meeting in another world;
For thou hast drunk thy *passport* out of this. *Dryden.*

Past. *participial adj.* [from *pass*.]

1. Not present; not to come.

Past, and to come, seem best; things present worst. *Shak.*

For several months *past*, papers have been written upon the best publick principle, the love of our country. *Swift.*

This not alone has shone on ages *past*,
But lights the present, and shall warm the last. *Pope.*

2. Spent; gone through; undergone.

A life of glorious labours *past*. *Pope.*

Past. *n. s.* Elliptically used for past time.

The *past* is all by death possest,
And frugal fate that guards the rest,
By giving bids us live to-day. *Fenton.*

Past. *preposition.*

1. Beyond in time.

Sarah was delivered of a child, when she was *past* age. *Hebrews* xi. 11.

2. No longer capable of.

Fervent prayers he made, when he was esteemed *past* sense, and so spent his last breath in committing his soul unto the Almighty. *Hayward.*

3. Beyond; out of reach of.

We must not
Prostitute our *past* cure malady
To empiricks. *Shakespear's All's well that ends well.*

What's gone, and what's *past* help,
Should be *past* grief. *Shakesp. Winter's Tale.*

Many men have not yet sinned themselves *past* all sense or feeling, but have some regrets; and when their spirits are at any time disturbed with the sense of their guilt, they are for a little time more watchful over their ways; but they are soon disheartened. *Calamy's Sermons.*

Love, when once *past* government, is consequently *past* shame. *L'Estrange.*

Her life she might have had; but the despair
Of saving his, had put it *past* her care. *Dryden.*

I'm stupify'd with sorrow, *past* relief
Of tears. *Dryden.*

That the bare receiving a sum should sink a man into a servile state, is *past* my comprehension. *Collier on Pride.*

That he means paternal power, is *past* doubt from the inference he makes. *Locke.*

4. Beyond; further than.

We will go by the king's high way, until we be *past* thy borders. *Numbers* xxi. 22.

5. Above; more than.

The northern Irish Scots have bows not *past* three quarters of a yard long, with a string of wreathed hemp and their arrows not much above an ell. *Spenser on Ireland.*

The same inundation was not deep, not *past* forty foot from the ground. *Bacon.*

PASTE. *n. s.* [*paste*, French.]

1. Any thing mixed up so as to be viscous and tenacious: such as flour and water for bread or pies; or various kinds of earth mingled for the potter.

Except you could bray Christendom in a mortar, and mould it into a new *paste*, there is no possibility of an holy war. *Bacon's Holy War.*

With particles of heav'nly fire
The God of nature did his soul inspire;
Which wise Prometheus temper'd into *paste*,
And, mixt with living streams, the godlike image cast. *Dryd.*

When the gods moulded up the *paste* of man,
Some of their dough was left upon their hands. *Dryden.*

He has the whitest hand that ever you saw, and raises *paste* better than any woman. *Addison's Spectator*, N° 482.

2. Flour and water boiled together so as to make a cement.

3. Artificial mixture, in imitation of precious stones.

To Paste. *v. a.* [*paster*, Fr. from the noun.] To fasten with paste.

By *pasting* the vowels and consonants on the sides of dice, his eldest son played himself into spelling. *Locke.*

Young creatures have learned their letters and syllables, by having them *pasted* upon little flat tablets. *Watts.*

Pa'steboard. *n s.* [*paste* and *board*.] Masses made anciently by pasting one paper on another: now made sometimes by macerating paper and casting it in moulds, sometimes by pounding old cordage, and casting it in forms.

Tintoret made chambers of board and *pasteboard*, proportioned to his models, with doors and windows, through which he distributed, on his figures, artificial lights. *Dryden.*

I would not make myself merry even with a piece of *pasteboard*, that is invested with a publick character. *Addison.*

Pa'steboard. *adj.* Made of pasteboard.

Put silkworms on whited brown paper into a *pasteboard* box. *Mortimer's Husbandry.*

Pa'stel. *n. s.* An herb. *Ainsworth.*

Pa'stern. *n. s.* [*pasturon*, French.]

1. The knee of an horse.

I will not change my horse with any that treads on four *pasterns*. *Shakespear's Henry* V.

The colt that for a stallion is design'd,
Upright he walks on *pasterns* firm and straight,
His motions easy, prancing in his gait. *Dryden.*

Being heavy, he should not tread stiff, but have a *pastern* made him, to break the force of his weight: by this his body hangs on the hoof, as a coach doth by the leathers. *Grew.*

2. The legs of an human creature in contempt.

So straight she walk'd, and on her *pasterns* high:
If seeing her behind, he lik'd her pace,
Now turning short, he better lik'd her face. *Dryden.*

Pa'stil. *n. s.* [*pastillus*, Lat. *pastille*, Fr.] A roll of paste.

To draw with dry colours, make long *pastils*, by grinding red led with strong wort, and so roll them up like pencils, drying them in the sun. *Peacham on Drawing.*

Pa'stime. *n. s.* [*pass* and *time*.] Sport; amusement; diversion.

It was more requisite for Zelmane's hurt to rest, than sit up at those *pastimes*; but she, that felt no wound but one, earnestly desired to have the pastorals. *Sidney, b.* i.

I'll be as patient as a gentle stream,
And make a *pastime* of each weary step,
'Till the last step has brought me to my love. *Shakesp.*

Pastime passing excellent,
If husbanded with modesty. *Shakespeare.*

With these
Find *pastime*, and bear rule; thy realm is large. *Milton.*

A man, much addicted to luxury, recreation and *pastime* should never pretend to devote himself entirely to the sciences, unless his soul be so refined, that he can taste these entertainments eminently in his closet. *Watts.*

Pa'stor. *n. s.* [*pastor*, Latin; *pasteur*, old French.]

1. A shepherd.

Receive this present by the muses made,
The pipe on which the Ascræan *pastor* play'd. *Dryden.*

The *pastor* shears their hoary beards,
And eases of their hair the loaden herds. *Dryden.*

2. A clergyman who has the care of a flock; one who has souls to feed with sound doctrine.

The *pastor* maketh suits of the people, and they with one voice testify a general assent thereunto, or he joyfully beginneth, and they with like alacrity follow, dividing between them the sentences wherewith they strive, which shall much shew his own, and stir up others zeal to the glory of God. *Hooker, b.* v. *s.* 39.

The first branch of the great work belonging to a *pastor* of the church, was to teach. *South's Sermons.*

A breach in the general form of worship was reckoned too unpopular to be attempted, neither was the expedient then found out of maintaining separate *pastors* out of private purses. *Swift.*

Pa'storal. *adj.* [*pastoralis*, Latin; *pastoral*, French.]

1. Rural; rustick; beseeming shepherds; imitating shepherds.

In those *pastoral* pastimes, a great many days were sent to follow their flying predecessors. *Sidney.*

2. Relating to the care of souls.

Their lord and master taught concerning the *pastoral* care he had over his own flock. *Hooker, b.* v. *s.* 19.

The bishop of Salisbury recommended the tenth satire of Juvenal, in his *pastoral* letter, to the serious perusal of the divines of his diocese. *Dryden.*

Pa'storal. *n. s.* A poem in which any action or passion is represented by its effects upon a country life; or according to the common practice in which speakers take upon them the character of shepherds; an idyl; a bucolick.

Paſtoral is an imitation of the action of a ſhepherd, the form of this imitation is dramatick or narrative, or mixed of both, the fable ſimple, the manners not too polite nor too ruſtick. *Pope.*

The beſt actors in the world, for tragedy, comedy, hiſtory, *paſtoral.* *Shakeſp. Hamlet.*

There ought to be the ſame difference between *paſtorals* and elegies, as between the life of the country and the court; the latter ſhould be ſmooth, clean, tender and paſſionate: the thoughts may be bold, more gay, and more elevated than in *paſtoral.* *Walſh.*

PA'STRY. *n. ſ.* [*paſtiſſerie*, Fr. from *paſte.*]

1. The act of making pies.

Let never freſh machines your *paſtry* try;
Unleſs grandees or magiſtrates are by,
Then you may put a dwarf into a pye. *King.*

2. Pies or baked paſte.

Remember
The ſeed cake, the *paſtries* and the furmenty pot. *Tuſſer.*
They call for dates and quinces in the *paſtry.* *Shakeſp.*
Beaſts of chaſe, or fowls of game,
In *paſtry* built, or from the ſpit, or boil'd,
Gris amber ſteam'd. *Milton's Paradiſe Regain'd.*

3. The place where paſtry is made.

PA'STRY-COOK. *n. ſ.* [*paſtry* and *cook.*] One whoſe trade is to make and ſell things baked in paſte.

I wiſh you knew what my huſband has paid to the *paſtry-cooks* and confectioners. *Arbuthnot.*

PA'STURABLE. *adj.* [from *paſture.*] Fit for paſture.

PA'STURAGE. *n. ſ.* [*paſturage*, French.]

1. The buſineſs of feeding cattle.

I wiſh there were ſome ordinances, that whoſoever keepeth twenty kine, ſhould keep a plough going; for otherwiſe all men would fall to *paſturage*, and none to huſbandry. *Spenſer on Ireland.*

2. Lands grazed by cattle.

France has a ſheep by her to ſhew, that the riches of the country conſiſted chiefly in flocks and *paſturage.* *Addiſon.*

3. The uſe of paſture.

Cattle fatted by good *paſturage*, after violent motion, die ſuddenly. *Arbuthnot on Aliments.*

PA'STURE. *n. ſ.* [*paſture*, French.]

1. Food; the act of feeding.

Unto the conſervation is required a ſolid *paſture*, and a food congenerous unto nature. *Brown's Vulgar Errours.*

2. Ground on which cattle feed.

A careleſs herd,
Full of the *paſture*, jumps along by him,
And never ſtays. *Shakeſpeare's As you like it.*

When there was not room for their herds to feed together, they, by conſent, ſeparated and enlarged their *paſture* where it beſt liked them. *Locke.*

The new tribes look abroad
On nature's common, far as they can ſee
Or wing, their range and *paſture.* *Thomſon's Spring.*

3. Human culture; education.

From the firſt *paſtures* of our infant age,
To elder cares and man's ſeverer page
We laſh the pupil. *Dryden.*

To PA'STURE. *v. a.* [from the noun.] To place in a paſture.

To PA'STURE. *v. n.* [from the noun] To graze on the ground.

The cattle in the fields and meadows green
Thoſe rare and ſolitary; theſe in flocks
Paſturing at once, and in broad herds upſprung. *Milton.*

PA'STY. *n. ſ.* [*paſte*, French.] A pye of cruſt raiſed without a diſh.

Of the paſte a coffin will I rear,
And make two *paſties* of your ſhameful heads. *Shakeſp.*

I will confeſs what I know; if ye pinch me like a *paſty*, I can ſay no more. *Shakeſpeare.*

If you'd fright an alderman and mayor,
Within a *paſty* lodge a living hare. *King.*

A man of ſober life,
Not quite a madman, though a *paſty* fell,
And much too wiſe to walk into a well. *Pope.*

PAT. *adj.* [from *pas*, Dutch, *Skinner.*] Fit; convenient; exactly ſuitable either as to time or place. This is a low word, and ſhould not be uſed but in burleſque writings.

Pat pat; and here's a marvellous convenient place for our rehearſal. *Shakeſpear's Midſummer Night's Dream.*

Now I might do it *pat*, now he is praying. *Shakeſp.*

They never ſaw two things ſo *pat*,
In all reſpects, as this and that. *Hudibras, p.* ii.

Zuinglius dreamed of a text, which he found very *pat* to his doctrine of the Euchariſt. *Atterbury.*

He was ſurely put to't at the end of a verſe,
Becauſe he could find no word to come *pat* in. *Swift.*

PAT. *n. ſ.* [*patte*, Fr. is a foot, and thence *pat* may be a blow with the foot.]

1. A light quick blow; a tap.

The leaſt noiſe is enough to diſturb the operation of his brain; the *pat* of a ſhuttle-cock, or the creaking of a jack will do. *Collier on human Reaſon.*

2. Small lump of matter beat into ſhape with the hand.

To PAT. *v. a.* [from the noun.] To ſtrike lightly; to tap.

Children prove, whether they can rub upon the breaſt with one hand, and *pat* upon the forehead with another, and ſtraightways they *pat* with both. *Bacon's Nat. Hiſt.*

Gay *pats* my ſhoulder, and you vaniſh quite. *Pope.*

PA'TACHE. *n. ſ.* A ſmall ſhip. *Ainſworth.*

PA'TACOON. *n. ſ.* A Spaniſh coin worth four ſhillings and eight pence Engliſh. *Ainſworth.*

To PATCH. *v. n.* [*pudtzer*, Daniſh; *pezzare*, Italian.]

1. To cover with a piece ſewed on.

They would think themſelves miſerable in a *patched* coat, and yet their minds appear in a pie-bald livery of coarſe patches and borrowed ſhreds. *Locke.*

2. To decorate the face with ſmall ſpots of black ſilk.

In the middle boxes, were ſeveral ladies who *patched* both ſides of their faces. *Addiſon's Spectator*, Nº 81.

We begg'd her but to *patch* her face,
She never hit one proper place. *Swift.*

3. To mend clumſily; to mend ſo as that the original ſtrength or beauty is loſt.

Any thing mended, is but *patch'd.* *Shakeſp.*

Phyſick can but mend our crazy ſtate,
Patch an old building, not a new create. *Dryden.*

Broken limbs, common prudence ſends us to the ſurgeons to piece and *patch up.* *L'Eſtrange.*

4. To make up of ſhreds or different pieces. Sometimes with *up* emphatical.

If we ſeek to judge of thoſe times, which the ſcriptures ſet us down without error, by the reigns of the Aſſyrian princes, we ſhall but *patch up* the ſtory at adventure, and leave it in confuſion. *Raleigh's Hiſtory of the World.*

His glorious end was a *patch'd* work of fate,
Ill ſorted with a ſoft effeminate life. *Dryden.*

There is that viſible ſymmetry in a human body, as gives an intrinſick evidence, that it was not formed ſucceſſively and *patched up* by piece-meal. *Bentley's Sermons.*

Enlarging an author's ſenſe, and building fancies of our own upon his foundation, we may call paraphraſing; but more properly changing, adding, *patching*, piecing. *Felton.*

PATCH. *n. ſ.* [*pezzo*, Italian.]

1. A piece ſewed on to cover a hole.

Patches ſet upon a little breach,
Diſcredit more in hiding of the flaw,
Than did the flaw before it was ſo patch'd. *Shakeſp.*

If the ſhoe be ript, or *patches* put;
He's wounded! ſee the plaiſter on his foot. *Dryden.*

They ſuffer their minds to appear in a pie-bald livery of coarſe *patches* and borrowed ſhreds, ſuch as the common opinion of thoſe they converſe with clothe them in. *Locke.*

2. A piece inſerted in moſaick or variegated work.

3. A ſmall ſpot of black ſilk put on the face.

How! providence! and yet a Scottiſh crew!
Then madam nature wears black *patches* too. *Cleaveland.*

If to every common funeral,
By your eyes martyr'd, ſuch grace were allow'd,
Your face wou'd wear not *patches*, but a cloud. *Suckling.*

They were patched differently, and caſt hoſtile glances upon one another, and their *patches* were placed in different ſituations as party-ſignals to diſtinguiſh friends from foes. *Addiſ.*

This the morning omens ſeem'd to tell;
Thrice from my trembling hand the *patch*-box fell. *Pope.*

4. A ſmall particle; a parcel of land.

We go to gain a little *patch* of ground,
That hath in it no profit but the name. *Shakeſp.*

5. A paltry fellow. Obſolete.

What a py'd ninny's this? thou ſcurvy *patch!* *Shakeſp.*

PA'TCHER. *n. ſ.* [from *patch.*] One that patches; a botcher.

PA'TCHERY. *n. ſ.* [from *patch.*] Botchery; bungling work. Forgery. A word not in uſe.

You hear him cogg, ſee him diſſemble,
Know his groſs *patchery*, love him, and feed him,
Yet remain aſſur'd that he's a made-up villain. *Shakeſp.*

PA'TCHWORK. *n. ſ.* [*patch* and *work.*] Work made by ſewing ſmall pieces of different colours interchangeably together.

When my cloaths were finiſhed, they looked like the *patchwork*, only mine were all of a colour. *Gulliver's Travels.*

Whoever only reads to tranſcribe ſhining remarks, without entering into the genius and ſpirit of the author, will be apt to be miſled out of the regular way of thinking; and all the product of all this will be found a manifeſt incoherent piece of *patchwork.* *Swift.*

Foreign her air, her robe's diſcordant pride
In *patchwork* flut'ring. *Dunciad.*

PATE. *n. ſ.* [This is derived by *Skinner* from *tête*, Fr.] The head. Now commonly uſed in contempt or ridicule, but antiently in ſerious language.

Senſeleſs man, that himſelf doth hate,
To love another,
Here take thy lover's token on thy *pate.* *Fairy Queen.*

Behold the deſpaire,
By cuſtome and covetous *pates*,
By gaps and opening of gates. *Tuſſer.*

He is a traitor, let him to the tower,
And crop away that factious *pate* of his. *Shakeſp.*

Steal by line and level is an excellent paſs of *pate*. *Shakeſp.*

That ſly devil,
That broker that ſtill breaks the *pate* of faith,
That daily breakvow. *Shakeſp.*

I had broke thy *pate*,
And aſk'd thee mercy for't. *Shakeſp.*

Who dares
Say this man is a flatterer. The learned *pate*
Ducks to the golden fool. *Shakeſp.*

Thank your gentler fate,
That, for a bruis'd or broken *pate*,
Has freed you from thoſe knobs that grow
Much harder on the married brow. *Hudibras.*

If only ſcorn attends men for aſſerting the church's dignity, many will rather chuſe to neglect their duty, than to get a broken *pate* in the church's ſervice. *South's Sermons.*

If any young novice happens into the neighbourhood of flatterers, preſently they are plying his full purſe and empty *pate* with addreſſes ſuitable to his vanity. *South.*

PA'TED. *adj.* [from *pate.*] Having a pate. It is uſed only in compoſition: as, long-*pated* or cunning; ſhallow-*pated* or fooliſh.

PATE'FACTION. *n. ſ.* [*patefactio*, Latin.] Act or ſtate of opening. *Ainſworth.*

PA'TEN. *n. ſ.* [*patina*, Latin.] A plate. Not in uſe.

The floor of heav'n
Is thick inlaid with *patens* of bright gold;
There's not the ſmalleſt orb which thou behold'ſt,
But in his motion like an angel ſings. *Shakeſp.*

PA'TENT. *adj.* [*patens*, Latin; *patent*, French.]

1. Open to the peruſal of all: as, letters *patent*.
2. Something appropriated by letters patent.

Madder is eſteemed a commodity that will turn to good profit; ſo that, in king Charles the firſt's time, it was made a *patent* commodity. *Mortimer's Huſbandry.*

PA'TENT. *n. ſ.* A writ conferring ſome excluſive right or privilege.

If you are ſo fond over her iniquity, give her *patent* to offend; for if it touch not you, it comes near no body. *Shakeſpeare.*

So will I grow, ſo live, ſo die,
Ere I will yield my virgin *patent* up
Unto his lordſhip. *Shakeſpeare's Midſum. Night's Dream.*

We are cenſured as obſtinate, in not complying with a royal *patent*. *Swift.*

PATENTEE'. *n. ſ.* [from *patent.*] One who has a patent.

If his tenant and *patentee* diſpoſe of his gift, without his kingly conſent, the lands ſhall revert to the king. *Bacon.*

In the patent granted to lord Dartmouth, the ſecurities obliged the *patentee* to receive his money back upon every demand. *Swift.*

PATER-NOSTER. n. ſ. [Lat.] The Lord's prayer.

No penny no *pater-noſter*. *Camden's Remains.*

PATE'RNAL. *adj.* [*paternus*, Lat. *paternel*, Fr.]

1. Fatherly; having the relation of a father; pertaining to a father.

I diſclaim all my *paternal* care,
Propinquity and property of blood,
And as a ſtranger to my heart and me
Hold thee. *Shakeſpeare's King Lear.*

Admonitions fraternal or *paternal* of his fellow chriſtians or governors of the church. *Hammond.*

They ſpend their days in joy unblam'd; and dwell
Long time in peace, by families and tribes,
Under *paternal* rule. *Milton's Paradiſe Loſt.*

2. Hereditary; received in ſucceſſion from one's father.

Men plough with oxen of their own
Their ſmall *paternal* field of corn. *Dryden.*

He held his *paternal* eſtate from the bounty of the conqueror. *Dryden.*

Retreat betimes
To thy *paternal* ſeat, the Sabine field,
Where the great Cato toil'd with his own hands. *Addiſon.*

PATE'RNITY. *n. ſ.* [from *paternus*, Lat. *paternité*, Fr.] Fatherſhip; the relation of a father.

The world, while it had ſcarcity of people, underwent no other dominion than *paternity* and elderſhip. *Raleigh.*

A young heir, kept ſhort by his father, might be known by his countenance; in this caſe, the *paternity* and filiation leave very ſenſible impreſſions. *Arbuthnot.*

PATH. *n. ſ.* [pað, Saxon.] Way; road; track. In converſation it is uſed of a narrow way to be paſſed on foot; but in ſolemn language means any paſſage.

For darkneſs, where is the place thereof? that thou ſhouldſt know the *paths* to the houſe thereof. *Job* xxxviii. 20.

On the glad earth the golden age renew,
And thy great father's *path* to heav'n purſue. *Dryden.*

The dewy *paths* of meadows we will tread,
For crowns and chaplets. *Dryden's Theocritus.*

There is but one road by which to climb up, and they have a very ſevere law againſt any that enters the town by another *path*, leſt any new one ſhould be worn on the mountain. *Addiſon's Remarks on Italy.*

PATHE'TICAL. } PATHE'TICK. } [παθητικὸς; *pathetique*, Fr.] Affecting the paſſions; paſſionate; moving.

His page that handful of wit;
'Tis a moſt *pathetical* neat. *Shakeſp.*

How *pathetick* is that expoſtulation of Job, when, for the trial of his patience, he was made to look upon himſelf in this deplorable condition. *Spectator*, Nº 571.

Tully conſidered the diſpoſitions of a ſincere and leſs mercurial nation, by dwelling on the *pathetick* part. *Swift.*

While thus *pathetick* to the prince he ſpoke,
From the brave youth the ſtreaming paſſion broke. *Pope.*

PATHE'TICALLY. *adv.* [from *pathetical.*] In ſuch a manner as may ſtrike the paſſions.

Theſe reaſons, ſo *pathetically* urged and ſo admirably raiſed by the proſopopoia of nature, ſpeaking to her children with ſo much authority, deſerve the pains I have taken. *Dryden.*

PATHE'TICALNESS. *n. ſ.* [from *pathetical.*] Quality of being pathetick; quality of moving the paſſion.

PA'THLESS. *adj.* [from *path.*] Untrodden; not marked with paths.

Aſk thou the citizens of *pathleſs* woods;
What cut the air with wings, what ſwim in floods. *Sandys.*

Like one that had been led aſtray
Through the heav'ns wide *pathleſs* way. *Milton.*

In fortune's empire blindly thus we go,
And wander after *pathleſs* deſtiny,
Whoſe dark reſorts ſince prudence cannot know;
In vain it would provide. *Dryden.*

Through miſts obſcure, ſhe wings her tedious way,
Now wanders dazzl'd with too bright a day;
And from the ſummit of a *pathleſs* coaſt
Sees infinite, and in that ſight is loſt. *Prior.*

PA'THOGNOMONICK. *adj.* [παθογνωμονικὸς, πάθος and γινώσκω.] Such ſigns of a diſeaſe as are inſeparable, deſigning the eſſence or real nature of the diſeaſe; not ſymptomatick. *Quincy.*

He has the true *pathognomonick* ſign of love, jealouſy; for no body will ſuffer his miſtreſs to be treated ſo. *Arbuthnot.*

PA'THOLOGICAL. *adj.* [*pathologique*, Fr. from *pathology.*] Relating to the tokens or diſcoverable effects of a diſtemper.

PA'THOLOGIST. *n. ſ.* [πάθος and λέγω.] One who treats of pathology.

PA'THOLOGY. *n. ſ.* [πάθος and λέγω; *pathologie*, Fr.] That part of medicine which relates to the diſtemper, with their differences, cauſes and effects incident to the human body. *Quincy.*

PA'THWAY. *n. ſ.* [*path* and *way.*] A road; ſtrictly a narrow way to be paſſed on foot.

Alas, that love, whoſe view is muffl'd ſtill,
Should without eyes ſee *pathways* to his ill. *Shakeſp.*

In the way of righteouſneſs is life, and in the *pathway* thereof there is no death. *Proverbs* xii. 28.

When in the middle *pathway* baſks the ſnake;
O lead me, guard me from the ſultry hours. *Gay.*

PA'TIBLE. *adj.* [from *patior*, Lat.] Sufferable; tolerable. *Dict.*

PA'TIBULARY. *adj.* [*patibulaire*, Fr. from *patibulum*, Latin.] Belonging to the gallows. *Dict.*

PA'TIENCE. *n. ſ.* [*patience*, French; *patientia*, Latin.]

1. The power of ſuffering; indurance; the power of expecting long without rage or diſcontent; the power of ſupporting faults or injuries without revenge; long ſuffering.

The king becoming graces,
Devotion, *patience*, courage, fortitude;
I have no reliſh of them. *Shakeſp. Macbeth.*

Neceſſary *patience* in ſeeking the Lord, is better than he that leadeth his life without a guide. *Eccluſ.* xx. 32.

Have *patience* with me, and I will pay thee all. *Matthew.*

Chriſtian fortitude and *patience* have their opportunity in times of affliction and perſecution. *Sprat's Sermons.*

Frequent debauch to habitude prevails,
Patience of toil and love of virtue fails. *Prior.*

2. Sufferance; permiſſion.

By their *patience*, be it ſpoken, the apoſtles preached as well when they wrote, as when they ſpake the goſpel. *Hooker.*

3. An herb. A ſpecies of dock.

Patience, an herb, makes a good boiled ſallad. *Mortimer.*

PA'TIENT. *adj.* [*patient*, Fr. *patiens*, Latin.]

1. Having the quality of enduring.

Wheat, which is the beſt ſort of grain, of which the pureſt bread is made, is *patient* of heat and cold. *Ray.*

2. Calm under pain or affliction.

Be *patient*, and I will ſtay. *Shakeſp. Henry* VI.

Griev'd, but unmov'd, and *patient* of your ſcorn,
I die. *Dryden's Theocritus.*

3. Not revengeful againſt injuries.
4. Not eaſily provoked.

Warn them that are unruly, ſupport the weak, be *patient* toward all men. 1 *Theſſalonians* v. 14.

5. Not

Not hasty; not viciously eager or impetuous.

Too industrious to be great,
Nor *patient* to expect the turns of fate,
They open'd camps deform'd by civil fight. *Prior.*

PA'TIENT. *n. s.* [*patient*, Fr.]

1. That which receives impressions from external agents.

Malice is a passion so impetuous and precipitate, that it often involves the agent and the *patient*. *Gov. of the Tongue.*

To proper *patients* he kind agents brings,
In various leagues binds disagreeing things. *Creech.*

Action and passion are modes which belong to substances: when a smith with a hammer strikes a piece of iron, the hammer and the smith are both agents or subjects of action; the one supreme, and the other subordinate: the iron is the *patient* or the subject of passion, in a philosophical sense, because it receives the operation of the agent. *Watts's Logick.*

2. A person diseased. It is commonly used of the relation between the sick and the physician.

You deal with me like a physician, that seeing his *patient* in a pestilent fever, should chide instead of administring help, and bid him be sick no more. *Sidney.*

Through ignorance of the disease, through unreasonableness of the time, instead of good he worketh hurt, and out of one evil throweth the *patient* into many miseries. *Spenser.*

A physician uses various methods for the recovery of sick persons; and though all of them are disagreeable, his *patients* are never angry. *Addison.*

3. It is sometimes, but rarely used absolutely for a sick person.

Nor will the raging fever's fire abate
With golden canopies or beds of state;
But the poor *patient* will as soon be sound
On the hard matress or the mother ground. *Dryden.*

To PA'TIENT. *v. a.* [*patienter*, Fr.] To compose one's self; to behave with patience. Obsolete.

Patient yourself, madam, and pardon me. *Shakesp.*

PA'TIENTLY. *adv.* [from *patient*.]

1. Without rage under pain or affliction.

Lament not, Eve, but *patiently* resign
What justly thou hast lost. *Milton's Paradise Lost.*

Ned is in the gout,
Lies rack'd with pain, and you without,
How *patiently* you hear him groan!
How glad the case is not your own. *Swift.*

2. Without vicious impetuosity.

That which they grant, we gladly accept at their hands, and wish that *patiently* they would examine how little cause they have to deny that which as yet they grant not. *Hooker.*

Could men but once be persuaded *patiently* to attend to the dictates of their own minds, religion would gain more proselytes. *Calamy's Sermons.*

PA'TINE. *n. s.* [*patina*, Lat.] The cover of a chalice. *Ainf.*

PA'TLY. *adv.* [from *pat*.] Commodiously; fitly.

PA'TRIARCH. *n. s.* [*patriarche*, Fr. *patriarcha*, Latin.]

1. One who governs by paternal right; the father and ruler of a family.

So spake the *patriarch* of mankind; but Eve
Persisted, yet submiss. *Milton's Paradise Lost.*

The monarch oak, the *patriarch* of the trees,
Shoots rising up, and spreads by slow degrees,
Three centuries he grows, and three he stays
Supreme in state; and in three more decays. *Dryden.*

2. A bishop superior to archbishops.

The *patriarchs* for an hundred years had been of one house, to the prejudice of the church, and there yet remained one bishop of the same kindred. *Raleigh.*

Where secular primates were heretofore given, the ecclesiastical laws have ordered *patriarchs* and ecclesiastical primates to be placed. *Ayliffe's Parergon.*

PATRIA'RCHAL. *adj.* [*patriarchal*, Fr. from *patriarch*.]

1. Belonging to patriarchs; such as was possessed or enjoyed by patriarchs.

Such drowsy sedentary souls have they,
Who would to *patriarchal* years live on,
Fix'd to hereditary clay,
And know no climate but their own. *Norris.*

Nimrod enjoyed this *patriarchal* power; but he against right enlarged his empire, by seizing violently on the rights of other lords. *Locke.*

2. Belonging to hierarchical patriarchs.

Archbishops or metropolitans in France are immediately subject to the pope's jurisdiction; and, in other places, they are immediately subject to the *patriarchal* sees. *Ayliffe.*

PA'TRIARCHATE. } *n. s.* [*patriarchat*, Fr. from *patriarch*.] A
PA'TRIARCHSHIP. } bishoprick superior to archbishopricks.

Prelacies may be termed the greater benefices; as that of the pontificate, a *patriarchship* and archbishoprick. *Ayliffe.*

PATRIA'RCHY. *n. s.* Jurisdiction of a patriarch; patriarchate.

Calabria pertained to the *patriarch* of Constantinople, as appeareth in the novel of Leo Sophus, touching the precedence of metropolitans belonging to that *patriarchy*. *Brerewood.*

PA'TRICIAN. *adj.* [*patricien*, Fr. *patricius*, Lat.] Senatorial; noble; not plebeian.

I see
Th' insulting tyrant prancing o'er the field,
His horse's hoofs wet with *patrician* blood! *Addison.*

PATRI'CIAN. *n. s.* A nobleman.

Noble *patricians*, patrons of my right,
Defend the justice of my cause with arms. *Shakesp.*

You'll find Gracchus, from *patrician* grown
A fencer and the scandal of the town. *Dryden.*

Your daughters are all married to wealthy *patricians*. *Swift.*

PATRIMO'NIAL. *adj.* [*patrimonial*, Fr. from *patrimony*.] Possessed by inheritance.

The expence of the duke of Ormond's own great *patrimonial* estate, that came over at that time, is of no small consideration in the stock of this kingdom. *Temple.*

Their *patrimonial* sloth the Spaniards keep,
And Philip first taught Philip how to sleep. *Dryden.*

PA'TRIMONY. *n. s.* [*patrimonium*, Latin; *patrimoine*, Fr.] An estate possessed by inheritance.

Inclosures they would not forbid, for that had been to forbid the improvement of the *patrimony* of the kingdom. *Bacon.*

So might the heir, whose father hath, in play,
Wasted a thousand pounds of ancient rent,
By painful earning of one groat a day,
Hope to restore the *patrimony* spent. *Davies.*

In me all
Posterity stands curs'd! fair *patrimony*
That I must leave ye, sons. *Milton's Par. Lost.*

For his redemption, all my *patrimony*
I am ready to forego and quit. *Milton's Agonistes.*

Their ships like wasted *patrimonies* shew;
Where the thin scatt'ring trees admit the light,
And shun each other's shadows as they grow. *Dryden.*

The shepherd last appears,
And with him all his *patrimony* bears;
His house and houshold gods, his trade of war,
His bow and quiver, and his trusty cur. *Dryden.*

PA'TRIOT. *n. s.* One whose ruling passion is the love of his country.

Patriots who for sacred freedom stood. *Tickel.*

The firm *patriot* there,
Who made the welfare of mankind his care,
Shall know he conquer'd. *Addison's Cato.*

Here tears shall flow from a more gen'rous cause,
Such tears as *patriots* shed for dying laws. *Pope.*

PA'TRIOTISM. *n. s.* [from *patriot*.] Love of one's country; zeal for one's country.

To PATRO'CINATE. *v. a.* [*patrocinor*, Latin; *patrociner*, old French.] To patronise; to protect; to defend. *Dict.*

PA'TROL. *n. s.* [*patrouille*, *patouille*, old French.]

1. The act of going the rounds in a garrison to observe that orders are kept.

2. Those that go the rounds.

O thou! by whose almighty nod the scale
Of empire rises, or alternate falls,
Send forth the saving virtues round the land
In bright *patrol*. *Thomson's Summer.*

To PA'TROL. *v. n.* [*patrouiller*, Fr.] To go the rounds in a camp or garison.

These out guards of the mind are sent abroad
And still *patrolling* beat the neighb'ring road,
Or to the parts remote obedient fly,
Keep posts advanc'd, and on the frontier lie. *Blackmore.*

PA'TRON. *n. s.* [*patron*, Fr. *patronus*, Latin.]

1. One who countenances, supports or protects. Commonly a wretch who supports with insolence, and is paid with flattery.

I'll plead for you, as for my *patron*. *Shakesp.*

Ne'er let me pass in silence Dorset's name;
Ne'er cease to mention the continu'd debt,
Which the great *patron* only would forget. *Prior.*

2. A guardian saint.

Thou amongst those saints, whom thou do'st see,
Shall be a saint, and thine own nation's friend
And *patron*. *Fairy Queen, b.* i.

St. Michael is mentioned as the *patron* of the Jews, and is now taken by the Christians, as the protector general of our religion. *Dryden.*

3. Advocate; defender; vindicator.

We are no *patrons* of those things; the best defence whereof is speedy redress and amendment. *Hooker, b.* ii. *s.* 1.

Whether the minds of men have naturally imprinted on them the ideas of extension and number, I leave to those who are the *patrons* of innate principles. *Locke.*

4. One who has donation of ecclesiastical preferment.

PA'TRONAGE. *n. s.* [from *patron*.]

1. Support; protection.

Lady, most worthy of all duty, how falls it out, that you, in whom all virtue shines, will take the *patronage* of fortune, the only rebellious handmaid against virtue. *Sidney.*

Here's *patronage*, and here our art descries,
What breaks its bonds, what draws the closer ties,
Shows what rewards our services may gain,
And how too often we may court in vain. *Creech.*

2. Guardianship

2. Guardianship of saints.

From certain passages of the poets, several ships made choice of some god or other for their guardians, as among the Roman Catholicks every vessel is recommended to the *patronage* of some particular saint. *Addison.*

3. Donation of a benefice; right of conferring a benefice.

To PA'TRONAGE. *v. a.* [from the noun.] To patronise; to protect. A bad word.

Dar'st thou maintain the former words thou spak'st?
Yes, sir, as well as you dare *patronage*
The envious barking of your saucy tongue. *Shakesp.*
An out-law in a castle keeps,
And uses it to *patronage* his theft. *Shakesp.*

PATRO'NAL. *adj.* [from *patronus*, Lat.] Protecting; supporting; guarding; defending; doing the office of a patron.

The name of the city being discovered unto their enemies, their penates and *patronal* gods might be called forth by charms. *Brown's Vulgar Errours.*

PA'TRONESS. *n. s.* [feminine of *patron*; *patrona*, Lat.]

1. A female that defends, countenances or supports.

Of close escapes the aged *patroness*,
Blacker than earst, her sable mantle spred,
When with two trusty maids in great distress,
Both from mine uncle and my realm I fled. *Fairfax.*

All things should be guided by her direction, as the sovereign *patroness* and protectress of the enterprise. *Bacon.*

Befriend me night, best *patroness* of grief,
Over the pole thy thickest mantle throw. *Milton.*

He petitioned his *patroness*, who gave him for answer, that providence had assigned every bird its proportion. *L'Estrange.*

It was taken into the protection of my *patronesses* at court. *Swift.*

2. A female guardian saint.

To PA'TRONISE. *v. a.* [from *patron.*] To protect; to support; to defend; to countenance.

Churchmen are to be had in due respect for their work sake, and protected from scorn; but if a clergyman be loose and scandalous, he must not be *patronised* nor winked at. *Bac.*

All tenderness of conscience against good laws, is hypocrisy, and *patronised* by none but men of design, who look upon it as the fittest engine to get into power. *South's Sermons.*

I have been esteemed and *patronised* by the grandfather, the father and the son. *Dryden.*

PATRONY'MICK. *n. s.* [πατρωνυμικὸς, *patronymique*, Fr.] Name expressing the name of the father or ancestor: as, *Tydides*, the son of Tydeus.

It ought to be rendered the son, Tectonides being a *patronymick.* *Broome.*

PA'TTEN *of a pillar. n. s.* Its base. *Ainsworth.*

PA'TTENMAKER. *n. s.* [*patten* and *maker.*] He that makes pattens.

PA'TTEN. *n. s.* [*patin*, Fr.] A shoe of wood with an iron ring, worn under the common shoe by women to keep them from the dirt.

Their shoes and *pattens* are snouted and piked more than a finger long, crooking upwards, which they call crackowes, which were fastened to the knees with chains of gold and silver. *Camden's Remains.*

Good housewives
Underneath th' umbrella's oily shed,
Safe through the wet on clinking *pattens* tread. *Gay.*

To PA'TTER. *v. n.* [from *patte*, Fr. the foot.] To make a noise like the quick steps of many feet.

Patt'ring hail comes pouring on the main,
When Jupiter descends in harden'd rain. *Dryden.*
The stealing shower is scarce to *patter* heard
By such as wander through the forest walks. *Thomson.*

PA'TTERN. *n. s.* [*patron*, Fr. *patroon*, Dutch.]

1. The original proposed to imitation; the archetype; that which is to be copied; an exemplar.

As though your desire were, that the churches of old should be *patterns* for us to follow, and even glasses wherein we might see the practice of that which by you is gathered out of scripture. *Hooker.*

I will be the *pattern* of all patience;
I will say nothing. *Shakesp. King Lear.*
A *pattern* to all princes living with her,
And all that shall succeed. *Shakesp. Henry VIII.*

The example and *pattern* of the church of Rome. *Claren.*

Lose not the honour you have early won,
But stand the blameless *pattern* of a son. *Dryden.*

Measure the excellency of a virtuous mind; not as it is the copy, but the *pattern* of regal power. *Grew.*

This *pattern* should be our guide, in our present state of pilgrimage. *Atterbury's Sermons.*

Christianity commands us to act after a nobler *pattern*, than the virtues even of the most perfect men. *Rogers.*

Take *pattern* by our sister star,
Delude at once and bless our sight;
When you are seen, be seen from far,
And chiefly chuse to shine by night. *Swift.*

2. A specimen; a part shown as a sample of the rest.

A gentleman sends to my shop for a *pattern* of stuff; if he like it, he compares the *pattern* with the whole piece, and probably we bargain. *Swift.*

3. An instance; an example.

What God did command touching Canaan, the same concerneth not us otherwise than only as a fearful *pattern* of his just displeasure against sinful nations. *Hooker, b. v. s. 17.*

4. Any thing cut out in paper to direct the cutting of cloth.

To PA'TTERN. *v. a.* [*patronner*, Fr. from the noun.]

1. To make in imitation of something; to copy.

Ay, such a place there is, where we did hunt,
Pattern'd by that the poet here describes. *Shakesp.*

2. To serve as an example to be followed. Neither sense is now much in use.

When I that censure him do so offend,
Let mine own judgment *pattern* out my death,
And nothing come in partial. *Shakesp.*

PA'VAN. } PA'VIN. } *n. s.* A kind of light tripping dance. *Ains.*

PAU'CILOQUY. *n. s.* [*pauciloquium*, Lat.] Sparing and rare speech. *Dict.*

PAU'CITY. [*paucitas*, from *paucus*, Latin.]

1. Fewness; smallness of number.

The multitude of parishes, and *paucity* of schools. *Hooker.*

In such slender corpuscles as those of colour, may easily be conceived a greater *paucity* of protuberant corpuscles. *Boyle.*

Socrates well understood what he said touching the rarity and *paucity* of friends. *L'Estrange.*

2. Smallness of quantity.

This *paucity* of blood is agreeable to many other animals: as, lizzards, frogs and other fishes. *Brown's Vulgar Errours.*

To PAVE. *v. a.* [*pavio*, Lat. *paver*, Fr.]

1. To lay with brick or stone; to floor with stone.

Should she kneel down,
Her brother's ghost his *paved* bed would break,
And take her hence in horrour. *Shakesp.*

Let not the court be *paved*, for that striketh up a great heat in summer, and much cold in winter. *Bacon.*

From this chymic flame
I see a city of more precious mold,
With silver *pav'd*, and all divine with gold. *Dryden.*

The streets are *paved* with brick or freestone. *Addison.*

2. To make a passage easy.

It might open and *pave* a prepared way to his own title. *Bac.*

PA'VEMENT. *n. s.* [*pavimentum*, Lat.] Stones or bricks laid on the ground; stone floor.

The marble *pavement* closes, he is enter'd
Into his radiant roof. *Shakesp. Cymbeline.*
A broad and ample road, whose dust is gold,
And *pavement* stars seen in the galaxy. *Milton.*
The long laborious *pavement* here he treads,
That to proud Rome th' admiring nations leads. *Addison.*

The foundation of Roman ways was made of rough stone joined together with cement; upon this was laid another layer, consisting of small stones and cement, to plane the inequalities of the lower stratum in which the stones of the upper *pavement* were fixed: for there can be no very durable *pavement*, but a double one. *Arbuthnot on Coins.*

PA'VER. } PA'VIER. } *n. s.* [from *pave.*] One who lays with stones.

For thee the sturdy *paver* thumps the ground,
Whilst ev'ry stroke his lab'ring lungs resound. *Gay.*

PAVI'LION. *n. s.* [*pavillon*, French.] A tent; a temporary or moveable house.

Flowers being under the trees, the trees were to them a *pavillion*, and the flowers to the trees a mosaical floor. *Sidney.*

She did lie
In her *pavilion*, cloth of gold, of tissue. *Shakesp.*
He, only he, heaven's blew *pavilion* spreads,
And on the ocean's dancing billows treads. *Sandy.*

It was usual for the enemy, when there was a king in the field, to demand by a trumpet in what part of the camp he resided, that they might avoid firing upon the royal *pavilion.* *Addison's Freeholder*, Nº 23

The glowing fury springs,
Once more invades the guilty dome, and shrouds
Its bright *pavilions* in a veil of clouds. *Pope.*

To PAVI'LION. *v. a.* [from the noun.]

1. To furnish with tents.

Jacob in Mahanaim saw
The field *pavilion'd* with his guardians bright. *Milton.*

2. To be sheltered by a tent.

With his batt'ning flocks the careful swain
Abides *pavilion'd* on the grassy plain.

PAUNCH. *n. s.* [*panse*, French; *pança*, Spanish; *pantex*, Latin.] The belly; the region of the guts.

Demades, the orator, was talkative, and would eat hard; Antipater would say of him, that he was like a sacrifice, that nothing was left of it but the tongue and the *paunch.* *Bacon.*

Pleading Matho born abroad for air,
With his fat *paunch* fills his new-faſhion'd chair. *Dryden.*

To PAUNCH. *v. a.* [from the noun.] To pierce or rip the belly; to exenterate; to take out the paunch; to eviſcerate.

With a log
Batter his ſkull, or *paunch* him with a ſtake. *Shakeſp.*
Chiron attack'd Talthibius with ſuch might,
One paſs had *paunch'd* the huge hydropick knight. *Garth.*

PAU'PER. *n. ſ.* [Latin.] A poor perſon; one who receives alms.

PAUSE. *n. ſ.* [*pauſe*, Fr. *pauſa*, low Latin; παύω.]

1. A ſtop; a place or time of intermiſſion.

Neither could we ever come to any *pauſe*, whereon to reſt our aſſurance this way. *Hooker, b.* ii. *ſ.* 4.

Comes a fellow crying out for help,
And Caſſio following with determin'd ſword,
To execute upon him; this gentleman
Steps in to Caſſio, and intreats his *pauſe*. *Shakeſp.*

Some *pauſe* and reſpite only I require,
Till with my tears I ſhall have quench'd my fire. *Denham.*

The puniſhment muſt always be rigorouſly exacted, and the blows by *pauſes* laid on till they reach the mind, and you perceive the ſigns of a true ſorrow. *Locke.*

Whilſt thoſe exalted to primeval light,
Only perceive ſome little *pauſe* of joys
In thoſe great moments, when their god employs
Their miniſtry. *Prior.*

What *pauſe* from woe, what hopes of comfort bring
The names of wiſe or great. *Prior.*

Our diſcourſe is not kept up in converſation, but falls into more *pauſes* and intervals than in our neighbouring countries. *Addiſon's Spectator*, Nº 133.

2. Suſpenſe; doubt.

Like a man to double buſineſs bound,
I ſtand in *pauſe* where I ſhall firſt begin,
And both neglect. *Shakeſp. Hamlet.*

3. Break; paragraph; apparent ſeparation of the parts of a diſcourſe.

He writes with warmth, which uſually neglects method, and thoſe partitions and *pauſes* which men, educated in the ſchools, obſerve. *Locke.*

4. Place of ſuſpending the voice marked in writing.

5. A ſtop or intermiſſion in muſick.

To PAUSE. *v. n.*

1. To wait; to ſtop; not to proceed; to forbear for a time.

Tarry; *pauſe* a day or two,
Before you hazard: for in chuſing wrong
I loſe your company; therefore forbear a while. *Shakeſp.*
Give me leave to read philoſophy.
And, while I *pauſe*, ſerve in your harmony: *Shakeſp.*
Pauſing a while, thus to herſelf ſhe mus'd. *Milton.*

2. To deliberate.

Bear Worceſter to death, and Vernon too.
Other offenders we will *pauſe* upon. *Shakeſp. Henry* IV.

Solyman *pauſing* a little upon the matter, the heat of his fury being over, ſuffered himſelf to be intreated. *Knolles.*

3. To be intermitted.

What awe did the ſlow ſolemn knell inſpire,
The pealing organ, and the *pauſing* choir,
And the laſt words, that duſt to duſt convey'd! *Tickell.*

PAUSER. *n. ſ.* [from *pauſe*.] He who pauſes; he who deliberates.

The expedition of my violent love
Outruns the *pauſer*, reaſon. *Shakeſpeare's Macbeth.*

PAW. *n. ſ.* [*pawen*, Welſh.]

1. The foot of a beaſt of prey.

One choſe his ground,
Whence ruſhing he might ſureſt ſeize them both
Grip'd in each *paw*. *Milton's Paradiſe Loſt.*

The bee and ſerpent know their ſtings, and the bear the uſe of his *paws*. *More's Antidote againſt Atheiſm.*

If lions had been brought up to painting, where you have one lion under the feet of a man, you ſhould have had twenty men under the *paw* of a lion. *L'Eſtrange.*

Each claims poſſeſſion,
Both their *paws* are faſtened on the prey. *Dryden.*

2. Hand. In contempt.

Be civil to the wretch imploring,
And lay your *paws* upon him without roaring. *Dryden.*

To PAW. *v. n.* [from the noun.] To draw the fore foot along the ground.

The fiery courſer, when he hears from far,
The ſprightly trumpets and the ſhouts of war,
Pricks up his ears, and trembling with delight
Shifts place, and *paws*, and hopes the promis'd fight. *Dryden.*

Th' impatient courſer pants in every vein,
And *pawing*, ſeems to beat the diſtant plain,
Hills, vales, and floods appear already croſs'd,
And ere he ſtarts, a thouſand ſteps are loſt. *Pope.*

Once, a fiery horſe, *pawing* with his hoof, ſtruck a hole in my handkerchief. *Swift.*

9

To PAW. *v. a.*

1. To ſtrike with a draught of the fore foot.

His hot courſer *paw'd* th' Hungarian plain,
And adverſe legions ſtood the ſhock in vain. *Tickell.*

2. To handle roughly.

3. To fawn; to flatter. *Ainſworth.*

PAWN. *n. ſ.* [*pand*, Dutch; *pan*, French.] Something given to pledge as a ſecurity for money borrowed or promiſe made.

Her oath for love, her honour's *pawn*. *Shakeſp.*

As for mortgaging and pawning, men will not take *pawns* without uſe; or they will look for the forfeiture. *Bacon.*

He retains much of his primitive eſteem, that abroad his very word will countervail the bond or *pawn* of another. *Howel.*

Here's the very heart, and ſoul, and life-blood of Gomez; *pawns* in abundance, 'till the next bribe helps their huſbands to redeem them. *Dryden's Spaniſh Fryar.*

2. The ſtate of being pledged.

Sweet wife, my honour is at *pawn*,
And, but my going, nothing can redeem it. *Shakeſp.*
Redeem from broking *pawn* the blemiſh'd crown,
Wipe off the duſt that hides our ſceptre's gilt. *Shakeſp.*

3. A common man at cheſs. *Ainſworth.*

PA'WED. *adj.* [from *paw*.]

1. Having paws.

2. Broad footed. *Ainſworth.*

To PAWN. *v. a.* [from the noun.] To pledge; to give in pledge. It is now ſeldom uſed but of pledges given for money.

I hold it cowardiſe
To reſt miſtruſtful, where a noble heart
Hath *pawn'd* an open hand in ſign of love. *Shakeſp.*

Let's lead him on with a fine baited delay, 'till he hath *pawn'd* his horſes. *Shakeſpeare's Merry Wives of Windſor.*

Pawn me to this your honour, ſhe is his. *Shakeſp.*

I dare *pawn* down my life for him, that he hath writ this to feel my affection to your honour. *Shakeſpeare.*

Will you thus break your faith?——
I *pawn'd* you none:
I promis'd you redreſs. *Shakeſp. Henry* IV.

I'll *pawn* the little blood which I have left,
To ſave the innocent. *Shakeſp. Winter's Tale.*

If any thought annoys the gallant youth,
'Tis dear remembrance of that fatal glance,
For which he lately *pawn'd* his heart. *Waller.*

She who before had mortgag'd her eſtate,
And *pawn'd* the laſt remaining piece of plate. *Dryden.*

One part of the nation is *pawned* to the other, with hardly a poſſibility of being ever redeemed. *Swift.*

PA'WNBROKER. *n. ſ.* [*pawn* and *broker*.] One who lends money upon pledge.

The uſurers or money-changers were a ſort of a ſcandalous employment at Rome; thoſe money-ſcriveners ſeem to have been little better than our *pawnbrokers*. *Arbuthnot.*

To PAY. *v. a.* [*paier*, Fr. *apagar*, Spaniſh; *pacare*, Lat.]

1. To diſcharge a debt.

You have done enough, and have perform'd
A ſaint-like ſorrow; and indeed *paid* down
More penitence, than done treſpaſs. *Shakeſp.*

Your ſon has *paid* a ſoldier's debt;
He only liv'd but till he was a man. *Shakeſp.*

She does what ſhe will, ſay what ſhe will, take all, *pay* all. *Shakeſp. Merry Wives of Windſor.*

The king and prince
Then *paid* their off'rings in a ſacred grove
To Hercules. *Dryden.*

An hundred talents of ſilver did the children of Ammon *pay*. 2 *Chronicles* xxvii. 5.

I have peace offerings with me; this day have I *paid* my vows. *Proverbs* vii. 14.

Have patience, and I will *pay* thee all. *Matthew* viii. 26.

The wicked borroweth, and *payeth* not again. *Pſ.* xxxvii. 21.

2. To diſmiſs one to whom any thing is due with his money.

3. To attone; to make amends by ſuffering; with *for* before the cauſe of payment.

If this prove true, they'll *pay for't*. *Shakeſp.*

Bold Prometheus, whoſe untam'd deſire
Rival'd the ſun with his own heav'nly fire,
Now doom'd the Scythian vulture's endleſs prey,
Severely *pays for* animating clay. *Roſcommon.*

Men of parts, who were to act according to the reſult of their debates, and often *pay for* their miſtakes with their heads, found thoſe ſcholaſtick forms of little uſe to diſcover truth. *Locke.*

4. To beat.

I follow'd me cloſe, and, with a thought, ſeven of the eleven I *paid*. *Shakeſp. Henry* IV.

Forty things more,
For which, or pay me quickly, or I'll *pay* you. *B. Johnſ.*

5. To reward; to recompenſe.

She I love, or laughs at all my pain,
Or knows her worth too well; and *pays* me with diſdain. *Dryden's Knight's Tale.*

6. To give

6. To give the equivalent for any thing bought.

Riches are got by conſuming leſs of foreign commodities, than what by commodities or labour is *paid* for. *Locke.*

PAY. *n. ſ.* [from the verb.] Wages; hire; money given in return for ſervice.

Come on, brave ſoldiers, doubt not of the day;
And, that once gotten, doubt not of large *pay*. *Shakeſp.*

The ſoldier is willing to be converted, for there is neither *pay* nor plunder to be got. *L'Eſtrange.*

Money, inſtead of coming over for the *pay* of the army, has been tranſmitted thither for the *pay* of thoſe forces called from thence. *Temple.*

Here only merit conſtant *pay* receives,
Is bleſt in what it takes, and what it gives. *Pope.*

PA'YABLE. *adj.* [*paiable*, Fr. from *pay.*]

1. Due; to be paid.

The marriage-money, the princeſs brought, was *payable* ten days after the ſolemnization. *Bacon's Henry* VII.

The farmer rates or compounds the ſums of money *payable* to her majeſty, for the alienation of lands, made without or by licence. *Bacon.*

2. Such as there is power to pay.

To repay by a return equivalent, is not in every one's power; but thanks are a tribute *payable* by the pooreſt. *South.*

PA'YDAY. *n. ſ.* [*pay* and *day.*] Day on which debts are to be diſcharged or wages paid.

Labourers pay away all their wages, and live upon truſt till next *payday*. *Locke.*

PA'YER. *n. ſ.* [*paieur*, Fr. from *pay.*] One that pays.

PA'YMASTER. *n. ſ.* [*pay* and *maſter.*] One who is to pay; one from whom wages or reward is received.

Howſoever they may bear ſail for a time, yet are they ſo ſure *paymaſters* in the end, that few have held out their lives ſafely. *Hayward.*

If we deſire that God ſhould approve us, it is a ſign we do his work, and expect him our *paymaſter*. *Taylor.*

PA'YMENT. *n. ſ.* [from *pay.*]

1. The act of paying.

2. The diſcharge of debt or promiſe.

Thy huſband commits his body
To painful labour both by ſea and land,
And craves no other tribute at thy hands
But love, fair looks, and true obedience;
Too little *payment* for ſo great a debt. *Shakeſp.*

Perſons of eminent virtue, when advanced, are leſs envied, for their fortune ſeemeth but due unto them; and no man envieth the *payment* of a debt. *Bacon.*

3. A reward.

Give her an hundred marks.
—An hundred marks! by this light I'll ha' more.
An ordinary groom is for ſuch *payment*. *Shakeſp.*

The wages that ſin bargains with the ſinner, are life, pleaſure and profit; but the wages it pays him with, are death, torment and deſtruction: he that would underſtand the falſehood and deceit of ſin thoroughly, muſt compare its promiſes and its *payments* together. *South's Sermons.*

4. Chaſtiſement; ſound beating. *Ainſworth.*

To PAYSE. *v. n.* [Uſed by *Spenſer* for *poiſe.*] To balance.

Ne was it iſland then, ne was it *pays'd*
Amid the ocean waves,
But was all deſolate. *Fairy Queen.*

PA'YSER. *n. ſ.* [for *poiſer.*] One that weighs.

To mange this coinage, porters bear the tin, *poizers* weigh it, a ſteward, comptroller and receiver keep the account. *Carew.*

PEA. *n. ſ.* [*piſum*, Latin; piſa, Saxon; *pois*, French.]

A *pea* hath a papilionaceous flower, and out of his empalement riſes the pointal, which becomes a long pod full of roundiſh ſeeds; the ſtalks are fiſtulous and weak, and ſeem to perforate the leaves by which they are embraced; the other leaves grow by pairs along the midrib, ending in a tendril.

1. The ſpecies are fixteen: the greater garden pea, with white flowers and fruit. 2. Hotſpur pea. 3. Dwarf pea. 4. French dwarf pea. 5. Pea with an eſculent huſk. 6. Sickle pea. 7. Common white pea. 8. Green rouncival pea. 9. Grey pea. 10. Maple rouncival pea. 11. Roſe pea. 12. Spaniſh moretto pea. 13. Marrowfat or Dutch admiral pea. 14. Union pea. 15. Sea pea. 16. Pig pea. *Miller.*

PEACE. *n. ſ.* [*paix*, French; *pax*, Latin.]

1. Reſpite from war.

The Dane and Swede rouz'd up to fierce alarms,
Bleſs the wiſe conduct of her pious arms;
Soon as her fleets appear, their terrours ceaſe,
And all the northern world lies huſh'd in *peace*. *Addiſon.*

No joys to him pacifick ſcepters yield,
War ſounds the trump, he ruſhes to the field,
Peace courts his hand, but ſpreads her charms in vain. *Anon.*

2. Quiet from ſuits or diſturbances.

The king gave judgment againſt Warren, and commanded that Sherborn ſhould hold his land in *peace*. *Davies.*

3. Reſt from any commotion.

4. Stilneſs from riots or tumults.

Keep *peace* upon your lives; he dies that ſtrikes again. *Sha.*

All aſſembled here in arms againſt God's *peace* and the king's, we charge you to repair to your dwelling places. *Shak.*

Shallow, you have yourſelf been a great fighter, though now a man of *peace*. *Shakeſp. Merry Wives of Windſor.*

5. Reconciliation of differences.

Let him make *peace* with me. *Iſaiah* xxvii. 5.

6. A ſtate not hoſtile.

If I have rewarded evil unto him that was at *peace* with me, let the enemy perſecute my ſoul. *Pſalm* vii. 4.

There be two falſe *peaces* or unities: the one grounded upon an implicit ignorance. *Bacon.*

7. Reſt; quiet; content; freedom from terrour; heavenly reſt.

Well, *peace* be with him that hath made us heavy!
—*Peace* be with us, leſt we be heavier! *Shakeſpeare.*

Peace be unto thee, fear not, thou ſhalt not die. *Judg.* vi. 23.

The God of hope fill you with all joy and *peace* in believing, that ye may abound in hope. *Romans* xv. 13.

Religion directs us rather to ſecure inward *peace* than outward eaſe, to be more careful to avoid everlaſting torment than light afflictions. *Tillotſon's Sermons.*

8. Silence; ſuppreſſion of the thoughts.

'Twill out;—I *peace!*
No, I will ſpeak as liberal as the air. *Shakeſpeare.*

In an examination, a freed ſervant, who had much power with Claudius, very ſaucily had almoſt all the words; and amongſt other things, he aſked in ſcorn one of the examinates, who was a freed ſervant of Scribonianus; I pray, Sir, if Scribonianus had been emperor, what would you have done? he anſwered, I would have ſtood behind his chair and held my *peace*. *Bacon.*

She ſaid; and held her *peace*: Æneas went
Sad from the cave. *Dryden.*

PEACE. *interjection.* A word commanding ſilence.

Peace! fear, thou comeſt too late, when already the arm is taken. *Sidney*, *b.* ii.

Hark! *peace!*
It was the owl that ſhriek'd, the fatal bellman,
Which gives the ſtern'ſt good night. *Shakeſp.*

Peace, good reader do not weep;
Peace, the lovers are aſleep;
They, ſweet turtles, folded lie,
In the laſt knot that love could tie.
Let them ſleep, let them ſleep on,
'Till this ſtormy night be gone;
And th' eternal morrow dawn,
Then the curtains will be drawn,
And they waken with that light,
Whoſe day ſhall never ſleep in night. *Craſhaw.*

But *peace*, I muſt not quarrel with the will
Of higheſt diſpenſation. *Milton's Agoniſtes.*

Silence, ye troubled waves, and, thou deep, *peace!*
Said then th' omnific word. *Milton.*

I prythee *peace!*
Perhaps ſhe thinks they are too near of blood. *Dryden.*

PEA'CE-OFFERING. *n. ſ.* [*peace* and *offer.*] Among the Jews, a ſacrifice or gift offered to God for attonement and reconciliation for a crime or offence.

A ſacrifice of *peace-offering* offer without blemiſh. *Lev.* iii. 1.

PEA'CEABLE. *adj.* [from *peace.*]

1. Free from war; free from tumult.

The moſt *peaceable* way for you, if you do take a thief, is to let him ſhew himſelf, and ſteal out of your company. *Shak.*

The reformation of England was introduced in a *peaceable* manner, by the ſupreme power in parliament. *Swift.*

2. Quiet; undiſturbed.

The laws were firſt intended for the reformation of abuſes and *peaceable* continuance of the ſubject. *Spenſer.*

Lie, Philo, untouch'd on my *peaceable* ſhelf,
Nor take it amiſs, that ſo little I heed thee;
I've no envy to thee, and ſome love to myſelf,
Then why ſhould I anſwer; ſince firſt I muſt read thee. *Pri.*

3. Not violent; not bloody.

The Chaldæans flattered both Cæſar and Pompey with long lives and a happy and *peaceable* death; both which fell out extremely contrary. *Hale's Origin of Mankind.*

4. Not quarrelſome; not turbulent.

Theſe men are *peaceable*, therefore let them dwell in the land and trade. *Geneſis* xxxiv. 21.

PEA'CEABLENESS. *n. ſ.* [from *peaceable.*] Quietneſs; diſpoſition to peace.

Plant in us all thoſe precious fruits of piety, juſtice, and charity, and *peaceableneſs*, and bowels of mercy toward all others. *Hammond's Fundamentals.*

PEA'CEABLY. *adv.* [from *peaceable.*]

1. Without war; without tumult.

To his crown, ſhe him reſtor'd,
In which he dy'd, made ripe for death by eld,
And after will'd it ſhould to her remain,
Who *peaceably* the ſame long time did weld. *Fa. Queen.*

The balance of power was provided for, elſe Piſiſtratus could never have governed ſo *peaceably*, without changing any of Solon's laws. *Swift.*

2. Without disturbance.

The pangs of death do make him grin;
Disturb him not, let him pass *peaceably*. *Shakesp.*

PEA'CEFUL. *adj.* [*peace* and *full*.]

1. Quiet; not in war.

That rouz'd the Tyrrhene realm with loud alarms,
And *peaceful* Italy involv'd in arms. *Dryden.*

2. Pacifick; mild.

As one disarm'd, his anger all he lost;
And thus with *peaceful* words uprais'd her soon. *Milton.*

The *peaceful* power that governs love repairs,
To feast upon soft vows and silent pray'rs. *Dryden.*

3. Undisturbed; still; secure.

Succeeding monarchs heard the subjects cries,
Nor saw displeas'd the *peaceful* cottage rise. *Pope.*

PEA'CEFULLY. *adv.* [from *peaceful*.]

1. Quietly; without disturbance.

Our lov'd earth; where *peacefully* we slept,
And far from heav'n quiet possession kept. *Dryden.*

2. Mildly; gently.

PEA'CEFULNESS. *n. s.* [from *peaceful*.] Quiet; freedom from disturbance.

PEA'CEMAKER, *n. s.* [*peace* and *maker*.] One who reconciles differences.

Peace, good queen;
And whet not on these too too furious peers,
For blessed are the *peacemakers*. *Shakesp.*

Think us,
Those we profess, *peacemakers*, friends and servants. *Shak.*

PEACEPA'RTED. *adj.* [*peace* and *parted*.] Dismissed from the world in peace.

We should prophane the service of the dead
To sing a requiem, and such rest to her
As to *peaceparted* souls. *Shakesp. Hamlet.*

PEACH. *n. s.* [*pesche*, Fr. *malum persicum*, Lat.]

A *peach* hath long narrow leaves; the flower consists of several leaves, which are placed in a circular order, and expand in form of a rose; the pointal, which rises from the center of the flower cup, becomes a roundish fleshy fruit, having a longitudinal furrow inclosing a rough rugged stone. *Miller.*

September is drawn with a chearful countenance: in his left hand a handful of millet, withal carrying a cornucopia of ripe *peaches*, pears and pomegranates. *Peacham.*

The sunny wall,
Presents the downy *peach*. *Thomson's Autumn.*

To PEACH. *v. n.* [Corrupted from *impeach*.] To accuse of some crime.

If you talk of *peaching*, I'll *peach* first, and see whose oath will be believed; I'll trounce you. *Dryden*

PEACH-COLOURED. *adj.* [*peach* and *colour*.] Of a colour like a peach.

One Mr. Caper comes, at the suit of Mr. Threepile the mercer, for some four suits of *peach-coloured* sattin, which now peaches him a beggar. *Shakesp. Measure for Measure.*

PEA'CHICK. *n. s.* [*pea* and *chick*.] The chicken of a peacock.

Does the sniveling *peachick* think to make a cuckold of me. *Southern.*

PEA'COCK. *n. s.* [papa, Saxon, *pavo*, Lat.] Of this word the etymology is not known: perhaps it is *peak* cock, from the tuft of feathers on its head; the peak of women being an ancient ornament: if it be not rather a corruption of *beaucoq*, Fr. from the more striking lustre of its spangled train.] A fowl eminent for the beauty of his feathers, and particularly of his tail.

Let frantick Talbot triumph for a while;
And, like a *peacock*, sweep along his tail. *Shakesp.*

The birds that are hardest to be drawn, are the tame birds; as cock, turky-cock and *peacock*. *Peacham.*

The *peacock*, not at thy command, assumes
His glorious train; nor estrich her rare plumes. *Sandys.*

The *peacock's* plumes thy tackle must not fail,
Nor the dear purchase of the sable's tail. *Gay.*

PEA'HEN. *n. s.* [*pea* and *hen*; *pava*, Lat.] The female of the peacock.

PEAK. *n. s.* [peac, Saxon; *pique*, *pic*, French.]

1. The top of a hill or eminence.

Thy sister seek,
Or on Meander's bank or Latmus' *peak*. *Prior.*

2. Any thing acuminated.

3. The rising forepart of a head-dress.

To PEAK. *v. n.* [*pequeno*, Spanish, *little*, perhaps *lean*: but I believe this word has some other derivation: we say a withered man has a sharp face; Falstaff dying, is said to have *a nose as sharp as a pen*: from this observation, a sickly man is said to *peak* or grow acuminated.

1. To look sickly.

Weary se'nnights, nine times nine,
Shall he dwindle, *peak* and pine. *Shakesp. Macbeth.*

2. To make a mean figure; to sneak.

I, a dull and muddy mettled rascal, *peak*,
Like John a dreams, unpregnant of my cause, *Shakesp.*

The *peaking* cornuto her husband, dwelling in a continual larum of jealousy, comes me in the instant of our encounter. *Shakesp.*

PEAL. *n. s.* [Perhaps from *pello*, *pellere tympana*.]

1. A succession of loud sounds: as, of bells, thunder, cannon, loud instruments.

They were saluted by the way, with a fair *peal* of artillery from the tower. *Hayward.*

The breach of faith cannot be so highly expressed, as in that it shall be the last *peal* to call the judgments of God upon men. *Bacon's Essays.*

Woods of oranges will smell into the sea perhaps twenty miles; but what is that, since a *peal* of ordnance will do as much, which moveth in a small compass? *Bacon.*

A *peal* shall rouse their sleep;
Then all thy saints assembled, thou shalt judge
Bad men and angels. *Milt. Par. Reg.*

I myself,
Vanquish'd with a *peal* of words, O weakness!
Gave up my fort of silence to a woman. *Milton.*

From the Moors camp the noise grows louder still;
Peals of shouts that rend the heav'n's, *Dryden.*

Oh! for a *peal* of thunder that would make
Earth, sea and air, and heaven and Cato tremble! *Addis.*

2. It is once used by *Shakespeare* for a low dull noise, but improperly.

Ere to black Hecat's summons
The shard-born beetle with his drowsy hums,
Hath rung night's yawning *peal*, there shall be done
A deed of dreadful note. *Shakesp. Macbeth.*

To PEAL. *v. n.* [from the noun.] To play solemnly and loud.

Let the *pealing* organ blow,
To the full-voic'd quire below,
In service high and anthems clear,
As may with sweetness through mine ear,
Dissolve me into extasies,
And bring all heav'n before my eyes. *Milton.*

The *pealing* organ, and the pausing choir;
And the last words, that dust to dust convey'd. *Tickell.*

To PEAL. *v. a.*

1. To assail with noise.

Nor was his ear less *peal'd*
With noises loud and ruinous, than when Bellona storms,
With all her batt'ring engines bent to rase
Some capital city. *Milton's Paradise Lost.*

2. To stir with some agitation: as, to *peal* the pot, is when it boils to stir the liquor therein with a ladle. *Ains.*

PEAR. *n. s.* [*poire*, French; *pyrum*, Latin.]

The flower consists of several leaves, placed in a circular order, and expand in form of a rose, whose flower cup becomes a fleshy fruit, which is more produced toward the footstalk than the apple, but is hollowed like a navel at the extreme part; the cells, in which the seeds are lodged, are separated by soft membranes, and the seeds are oblong. The species are eighty-four: 1. Little musk *pear*, commonly called the supreme. 2. The Chio *pear*, commonly called the little bastard musk *pear*. 3. The hasting *pear*, commonly called the green chissel. 4. The red muscadelle, it is also called the fairest. 5. The little muscat. 6. The jargonelle. 7. The Windsor *pear*. 8. The orange musk. 9. Great blanket. 10. The little blanket *pear*. 11. Long stalked blanket *pear*. 12. The skinless *pear*. 13. The musk robin *pear*. 14. The musk drone *pear*. 15. The green orange *pear*. 16. Cassolette. 17. The Magdalene *pear*. 18. The great onion *pear*. 19. The August muscat. 20. The rose *pear*. 21. The perfumed *pear*. 22. The summer bon chrêtien, or good christian. 23. Salviati. 24. Rose water *pear*. 25. The choaky *pear*. 26. The russelet *pear*. 27. The prince's *pear*. 28. The great mouth water *pear*. 29. Summer burgamot. 30. The Autumn burgamot. 31. The Swiss burgamot. 32. The red butter *pear*. 33. The dean's *pear*. 34. The long green *pear*; it is called the Autumn month water *pear*. 35. The white and grey monsieur John. 36. The flowered muscat. 37. The vine *pear*. 38. Rousseline *pear*. 39. The knave's *pear*. 40. The green sugar *pear*. 41. The marquis's *pear*. 42. The burnt cat; it is also called the virgin of Xantonee. 43. Le Besidery; it is so called from Heri, which is a forest in Bretagne between Bennes and Nantes, where this *pear* was found. 44. The crasane, or burgamot crasane; it is also called the flat butter *pear*. 45. The lansac, or dauphin *pear*. 46. The dry martin. 47. The villain of Anjou; it is also called the tulip *pear* and the great orange. 48. The large stalked *pear*. 49. The Amadot *pear*. 50. Little lard *pear*. 51. The good Lewis *pear*. 52. The colmar *pear*; it is also called the manna *pear* and the late burgamot. 53. The winter long green *pear*, or the landry wilding. 54. La virgoule, or la virgoleuse. 55. Poire d'Ambrette; this is so called from its musky flavour, which resembles the smell of the sweet sultan flower, which is called Ambrette in France. 56. The winter thorn *pear*. 57. The St. Germain *pear*, or the unknown of la Fare; it being first discovered upon the banks of a river called by that name in the parish of St. Germain. 58. The St. Augustine. 59. The Spanish bon chrêtien. 60. The pound *pear*. 61. The wilding

wilding of Caſſoy, a foreſt in Brittany, where it was diſcovered. 62. The lord Martin *pear*. 63. The winter citron *pear*; it is alſo called the muſk orange *pear* in ſome places. 64. The winter roſſelet. 65. The gate *pear*: this was diſcovered in the province of Poictou, where it was much eſteemed. 66. Bergamotte Bugi; it is alſo called the Eaſter burgamot. 67. The winter bonchrêtien *pear*. 68. Catillac or cadillac. 69. La paſtourelle. 70. The double flowering *pear*. 71. St. Martial; it is alſo called the angelic *pear*. 72. The wilding of Chaumontelle. 73. Carmelite. 74. The union *pear*. 75. The aurate. 76. The fine preſent; it is alſo called St. Sampſon. 77. Le rouſſelet de reims. 78. The ſummer thorn *pear*. 79. The egg *pear*; ſo called from the figure of its fruit, which is ſhaped like an egg. 80. The orange tulip *pear*. 81. La manſuette. 82. The German muſcat. 83. The Holland burgamot. 84. The *pear* of Naples. *Miller.*

They would whip me with their fine wits, till I were as creſt-faln as a dried *pear*. *Shakeſpeare's Merch. of Venice.*

Auguſt ſhall bear the form of a young man, of a choleric aſpect, upon his arm a baſket of *pears*, plums and apples. *Peac.*

The juicy *pear*
Lies in a ſoft profuſion ſcatter'd round. *Thomſon.*

PEARL. *n. ſ.* [*perle*, Fr. *perla*, Spaniſh; ſuppoſed by *Salmaſius* to come from *ſpherula*, Latin.]

Pearls, though eſteemed of the number of gems by our jewellers, are but a diſtemper in the creature that produces them: the fiſh in which *pearls* are moſt frequently found is the Eaſt Indian berbes or *pearl* oyſter: others are found to produce *pearls*; as the common oyſter, the muſcle, and various other kinds; but the Indian *pearls* are ſuperior to all: ſome *pearls* have been known of the ſize of a pigeon's egg; as they increaſe in ſize, they are leſs frequent and more valued: the true ſhape of the *pearl* is a perfect round; but ſome of a conſiderable ſize are of the ſhape of a pear, and ſerve for ear-rings: their colour ought to be a pure, clear and brilliant white, and they bring their natural poliſh with them, to which art can never attain: it is reported, that *pearls* naturally of a yellowiſh caſt, never alter, that this tinge never grows deeper, and that the luſtre of the *pearl* never fades, which is therefore juſtly preferred by the Orientals to ſuch as are purely white: from the name unio given to the *pearl*, ſome have been led to believe, that there was only one found in each ſhell; this is indeed uſually the caſe in oyſters and muſcles; but in the oriental *pearl* ſhell ſix or eight are frequent, and ſometimes twenty or more. *Hill.*

A *pearl*-julep was made of a diſtilled milk. *Wiſeman.*

Flow'rs purfled, blue and white,
Like ſaphire, *pearl*, in rich embroidery
Buckled below fair knighthood's bending knee. *Shakeſp.*

Cataracts *pearl*-coloured, and thoſe of the colour of burniſhed iron, are eſteemed proper to endure the needle. *Sharp.*

PEARL. *n. ſ.* [*albugo*, Lat.] A white ſpeck or film growing on the eye. *Ainſworth.*

PEARLED. *adj.* [from *pearl.*] Adorned or ſet with pearls.

The water nymphs
Held up their *pearled* wriſts, and took her in,
Bearing her ſtraight to aged Nereus' hall. *Milton.*

PEA'RLEYED. *adj.* [*pearl* and *eye.*] Having a ſpeck in the eye.

PEA'RLGRASS.
PEA'RPLANT. } *n ſ.* Plants. *Ainſworth.*
PEA'RLWORT.

PEA'RLY. *adj.* [from *pearl.*]

1. Abounding with pearls; containing pearls.

Some in their *pearly* ſhells at eaſe, attend
Moiſt nutriment. *Milton's Paradiſe Loſt.*

Another was inveſted with a *pearly* ſhell, having the ſutures finely diſplayed upon its ſurface. *Woodward.*

2. Reſembling pearls.

Which when ſhe heard, full *pearly* floods
I in her eyes might view. *Drayton.*

'Tis ſweet the bluſhing morn to view,
And plains adorn'd with *pearly* dew, *Dryden.*

For what the day devours, the nightly dew
Shall to the morn in *pearly* drops renew. *Dryden.*

PEARMAI'N. *n. ſ.* An apple.

Pearmain is an excellent and well known fruit. *Mortimer.*

PEA'RTREE. *n. ſ.* [*pear* and *tree.*] The tree that bears pears.

The *peartree* criticks will have to borrow his name of πῦρ, fire. *Bacon.*

PEA'SANT. *n. ſ.* [*paiſant*, Fr.] A hind; one whoſe buſineſs is rural labour.

He holdeth himſelf a gentleman, and ſcorneth to work, which, he ſaith, is the life of a *peaſant* or churl. *Spenſer.*

Our ſuperfluous lacqueys and our *peaſants*,
Who in unneceſſary action ſwarm
About our ſquares of battle. *Shakeſp.*

I had rather coin my heart, than wring
From the hard hands of *peaſants* their vile traſh. *Shakeſp.*

'Tis difficult for us, who are bred up with the ſame infirmities about us with which we were born, to raiſe our thoughts and imaginations to thoſe intellectual perfections that attended our nature in the time of innocence, as it is for a *peaſant* bred up in the obſcurities of a cottage, to fancy in his mind the unſeen ſplendours of a court. *South's Sermons.*

The citizens would bring two thouſand men, with which they could make head againſt twelve thouſand *peaſants*. *Addiſon.*

PEA'SANTRY. *n. ſ.* Peaſants; ruſticks; country people.

How many then ſhould cover, that ſtand bare!
How much low *peaſantry* would then be gleaned
From the true ſeed of honour? how much honour
Pickt from the chaff? *Shakeſp. Merch. of Venice.*

The *peaſantry* in France under a much heavier preſſure of want and poverty than the day-labourers of England of the reformed religion, underſtood it much better than thoſe of a higher condition among us. *Locke.*

PEA'SCOD.
PEA'SHELL. } *n. ſ.* [*pea*, *cod* and *ſhell.*] The huſk that contains peas.

Thou art a ſheal'd *peaſcod*. *Shakeſp. King Lear.*

I ſaw a green caterpillar as big as a ſmall *peaſcod*. *Walton.*

As *peaſcods* once I pluck'd, I chanc'd to ſee
One that was cloſely fill'd with three times three.
I o'er the door the ſpell in ſecret laid. *Gay.*

PEASE. *n. ſ.* [*Pea*, when it is mentioned as a ſingle body, makes *peas*; but when ſpoken of collectively, as food or a ſpecies, it is called *peaſe*, anciently *peaſon*; pıſa, Saxon; *pois*, French; *piſo*, Italian; *piſum*, Latin.] Food of peaſe.

Sowe *peaſon* and beans in the wane of the moon;
Who ſoweth them ſooner, he ſoweth too ſoone. *Tuſſer.*

Peaſe, deprived of any aromatic parts, are mild and demulcent; but, being full of aerial particles, are flatulent. *Arb.*

PEAT. *n. ſ.* A ſpecies of turf uſed for fire.

Turf and *peat*, and cowſheards are cheap fuels and laſt long. *Bacon's Natural Hiſtory.*

Carew, in his ſurvey of Cornwall, mentions nuts found in *peat*-earth two miles Eaſt of St. Michael's mount. *Woodw.*

PEAT. *n ſ.* [from *petit*, Fr.] A little fondling; a darling; a dear play thing. It is now commonly called *pet*.

A pretty *peat*! it is beſt put finger in the eye,
An ſhe knew why. *Shakeſp. Taming of the Shrew.*

A citizen and his wife
Both riding on one horſe, upon the way
I overtook; the wench a pretty *peat*. *Donne.*

PE'BBLE.
PE'BBLESTONE. } *n. ſ.* [pæbolſtana, Saxon.] A ſtone diſtinct from flints, being not in layers, but in one homogeneous maſs, though ſometimes of many colours. Popularly a ſmall ſtone.

Through the midſt of it ran a ſweet brook, which did both hold the eye open with her azure ſtreams, and yet ſeek to cloſe the eye with the purling noiſe it made upon the *pebbleſtones* it ran over. *Sidney, b.* i.

The biſhop and the duke of Gloſter's men,
Forbidden late to carry any weapon,
Have fill'd their pockets full of *pebbleſtones*. *Shakeſp.*

Suddenly a file of boys deliver'd ſuch a ſhower of *pebbles* looſe ſhot, that I was fain to draw mine honour in. *Shakeſp.*

You may ſee *pebbles* gathered together, and a cruſt of cement between them, as hard as the *pebbles*. *Bacon.*

Collecting toys,
As children gath'ring *pebbles* on the ſhore. *Milton.*

Providence permitted not the ſtrength of the earth to ſpend itſelf in baſe gravel and *pebbles* inſtead of quarries of ſtones. *More's Antidote againſt Atheiſm.*

Winds murmur'd through the leaves your long delay;
And fountains o'er the *pebbles* chid your ſtay. *Dryden.*

Another body, that hath only the reſemblance of an ordinary *pebble*, ſhall yield a metallic and valuable matter. *Woodw.*

PEBBLE-CRYSTAL. *n. ſ.*

The cryſtal, in form of nodules, is found lodged in the earthy ſtrata left in a train by the water departing at the concluſion of the deluge: this ſort, called by the lapidaries *pebble-cryſtal*, is in ſhape irregular. *Woodward.*

PE'BBLED. *adj.* [from *pebble.*] Sprinkled or abounding with pebbles.

This bank fair ſpreading in a *pebbled* ſhore. *Thomſon.*

PEBBLY. *adj.* [from *pebble.*] Full of pebbles.

Strow'd bibulous above I ſee the ſands,
The *pebbly* gravel next. *Thomſon.*

PECCABI'LITY. *n. ſ.* [from *peccable.*] State of being ſubject to ſin.

Where the common *peccability* of mankind is urged to induce commiſeration towards the offenders; if this be of force in ſin, where the concurrence of the will renders the perſon more inexcuſable, it will ſurely hold much more in bare error which is purely involuntary. *Decay of Piety.*

PE'CCABLE. *adj.* [from *pecco*, Lat.] Incident to ſin.

PECCADI'LLO. [Spaniſh; *peccadille*, French.] A petty fault; a ſlight crime; a venial offence.

He means thoſe little vices, which we call follies and the defects of the human underſtanding, or at moſt the *peccadillos* of life, rather than the tragical vices to which men are hurried by their unruly paſſions. *Dryden.*

'Tis low ebb with his accuſers, when ſuch *peccadilos* as theſe are put in to ſwell the charge. *Atterbury.*

PE'CCANCY. *n. ſ.* [from *peccant.*] Bad quality.

Apply refrigerants without any preceding evacuation, becauſe the diſeaſe took its original merely from the diſaffection of the part, and not from the *peccancy* of the humours. *Wiſem.*

PE'CCANT. *adj.* [*peccant*, Fr. *peccans*, Latin.]

1. Guilty; criminal.

From them I will not hide
My judgments, how with mankind I proceed;
As how with *peccant* angels late they ſaw. *Milton.*

That ſuch a *peccant* creature ſhould diſapprove and repent of every violation of the rules of juſt and honeſt, this right reaſon could not but infer. *South's Sermons.*

2. Ill diſpoſed; corrupt; bad; offenſive to the body; injurious to health. It is chiefly uſed in medical writers.

With laxatives preſerve your body ſound,
And purge the *peccant* humours that abound. *Dryden.*

Such as have the bile *peccant* or deficient are relieved by bitters, which are a ſort of ſubſidiary gall. *Arbuthnot.*

3. Wrong; bad; deficient; unformal.

Nor is the party cited bound to appear, if the citation be *peccant* in form or matter. *Ayliffe's Parergon.*

PECK. *n. ſ.* [from pocca, or perhaps from ꝼat, a veſſel. *Skinner.*

1. The fourth part of a buſhel.

Burn our veſſels, like a new
Seal'd *peck* or buſhel, for being true. *Hudibras.*

To every hill of aſhes, ſome put a *peck* of unſlacked lime, which they cover with the aſhes till rain ſlacks the lime, and then they ſpread them. *Mortimer's Huſbandry.*

He drove about his turnips in a cart;
And from the ſame machine ſold *pecks* of peaſe. *King.*

2. Proverbially. [In low language.] A great deal.

Her finger was ſo ſmall, the ring
Would not ſtay on which they did bring;
It was too wide a *peck*;
It look'd like the great collar juſt
About our young colt's neck. *Suckling.*

To PECK. *v. a.* [*becquer*, French; *picken*, Dutch.]

1. To ſtrike with the beak as a bird.

2. To pick up food with the beak.

She was his only joy, and he her pride,
She, when he walk'd, went *pecking* by his ſide. *Dryden.*

Can any thing be more ſurpriſing, than to conſider Cicero obſerving, with a religious attention, after what manner the chickens *pecked* the grains of corn thrown them. *Addiſon.*

3. To ſtrike with any pointed inſtrument.

With a pick-ax of iron about ſixteen inches long, ſharpened at the one end to *peck*, and flat headed at the other to drive little iron wedges to cleave rocks. *Carew's Survey of Cornwall.*

4. To ſtrike; to make blows.

Two contrary factions, both inveterate enemies of our church, which they are perpetually *pecking* and ſtriking at with the ſame malice. *South's Sermons.*

They will make head againſt a common enemy, whereas mankind lie *pecking* at one another, till they are torn to pieces. *L'Eſtrange.*

5. The following paſſage is perhaps more properly written to *peck*, to *throw*.

Get up o' th' rail, I'll *peck* you o'er the pales elſe. *Shakeſp.*

PE'CKER. *n. ſ.* [from *peck.*]

1. One that pecks.

2. A kind of bird: as, the wood-*pecker*.

The titmouſe and the *peckers* hungry brood,
And Progne with her boſom ſtain'd in blood. *Dryden.*

PECKLED. *adj.* [corrupted from *ſpeckled.*] Spotted; varied with ſpots.

Some are *peckled*, ſome greeniſh. *Walton's Angler.*

PECTI'NAL. *n. ſ.* [from *pecten*, Lat. a comb.]

There are other fiſhes whoſe eyes regard the heavens, as plain and cartilaginous fiſhes, as *pectinals*, or ſuch as have their bones made laterally like a comb. *Brown.*

PE'CTINATED. *adj.* [from *pecten.*] Put one within another alternately. This ſeems to be the meaning.

To ſit croſs leg'd or with our fingers *pectinated*, is accounted bad. *Brown's Vulgar Errours.*

PECTINA'TION. *n. ſ.* The ſtate of being pectinated.

The complication or *pectination* of the fingers was an hieroglyphic of impediment. *Brown's Vulgar Errours.*

PE'CTORAL. *adj.* [from *pectoralis*, Latin.] Belonging to the breaſt.

Being troubled with a cough, *pectorals* were preſcribed, and he was thereby relieved. *Wiſeman.*

PE'CTORAL. *n. ſ.* [*pectorale*, Lat. *pectoral*, Fr.] A breaſt plate.

PECU'LATE. } *n. ſ.* [*peculatus*, Latin; *peculat*, Fr..] Robbery
PECU'LATION. } of the publick; theft of publick money.

PECU'LATOR. [Latin.] Robber of the publick.

PECU'LIAR. *adj.* [*peculiaris*, from *peculium*, Lat. *pecule*, Fr.]

1. Appropriate; belonging to any one with excluſion of others.

I agree with Sir William Temple, that the word humour is *peculiar* to our Engliſh tongue; but not that the thing itſelf is *peculiar* to the Engliſh, becauſe the contrary may be found in many Spaniſh, Italian and French productions. *Swift.*

2. Not common to other things.

The only ſacred hymns they are that chriſtianity hath *peculiar* unto itſelf, the other being ſongs too of praiſe and of thankſgiving, but ſongs wherewith as we ſerve God, ſo the Jews likewiſe. *Hooker, b. v. ſ. 39.*

Space and duration being ideas that have ſomething very abſtruſe and *peculiar* in their nature, the comparing them one with another may be of uſe for their illuſtration. *Locke.*

3. Particular; ſingle. To join *moſt* with *peculiar*, though found in *Dryden*, is improper.

One *peculiar* nation to ſelect
From all the reſt, of whom to be invok'd. *Milton.*

I neither fear, nor will provoke the war;
My fate is Juno's moſt *peculiar* care. *Dryden.*

PECULIAR. *n. ſ.*

1. The property; the excluſive property.

By tincture or reflection, they augment
Their ſmall *peculiar*. *Milt. Par. Loſt.*

Revenge is ſo abſolutely the *peculiar* of heaven, that no conſideration whatever can empower even the beſt men to aſſume the execution of it. *South's Sermons.*

2. Something abſcinded from the ordinary juriſdiction.

Certain *peculiars* there are, ſome appertaining to the dignities of the cathedral church at Exon. *Carew.*

PECULIA'RITY. *n ſ.* [from *peculiar.*] Particularity; ſomething found only in one.

If an author poſſeſſed any diſtinguiſhing marks of ſtyle or *peculiarity* of thinking, there would remain in his leaſt ſucceſsful writings ſome few tokens whereby to diſcover him. *Swift.*

PECU'LIARLY. *adv.* [from *peculiar.*]

1. Particularly; ſingly.

That is *peculiarly* the effect of the ſun's variation. *Woodw.*

2. In a manner not common to others.

PECU'NIARY. *adj.* [*pecuniarius*, from *pecunia*, Lat. *pecuniaire*, Fr.]

1. Relating to money.

Their impoſtures delude not only unto *pecuniary* defraudations, but the irreparable deceit of death. *Brown.*

2. Conſiſting of money.

Pain of infamy is a ſeverer puniſhment upon ingenuous natures than a *pecuniary* mulct. *Bacon.*

The injured perſon might take a *pecuniary* mulct by way of attonement. *Broome.*

PED. *n. ſ.*

1. A ſmall packſaddle. A *ped* is much ſhorter than a pannel, and is raiſed before and behind, and ſerves for ſmall burdens.

A pannel and wanty, packſaddle and *ped*. *Tuſſer.*

2. A baſket; a hamper.

A haſk is a wicker *ped*, wherein they uſe to carry fiſh. *Spenſ.*

PEDAGO'GICAL. *adj.* [from *pedagogue.*] Suiting or belonging to a ſchoolmaſter.

PE'DAGOGUE. *n. ſ.* [*pedagogus*, Lat. παιδαγωγὸς, παὶς and ἄγω.] One who teaches boys; a ſchoolmaſter; a pedant.

Few *pedagogues* but curſe the barren chair,
Like him who hang'd himſelf for mere deſpair
And poverty. *Dryden.*

To PE'DAGOGUE. *v. a.* [παιδαγωγέω, from the noun.] To teach with ſuperciliouſneſs.

This may confine their younger ſtiles,
Whom Dryden *pedagogues* at Will's;
But never cou'd be meant to tie
Authentic wits, like you and I. *Prior.*

PE'DAGOGY. *n. ſ.* [παιδαγωγία.] The maſterſhip; diſcipline.

In time the reaſon of men ripening to ſuch a pitch, as to be above the *pedagogy* of Moſes's rod and the diſcipline of types, God thought fit to diſplay the ſubſtance without the ſhadow. *South's Sermons.*

PE'DAL. *adj.* [*pedalis*, Lat.] Belonging to a foot. *Dict.*

PE'DALS. *n. ſ.* [*pedalis*, Lat. *pedales*, Fr.] The large pipes of an organ: ſo called becauſe played upon and ſtopt with the foot. *Dict.*

PEDA'NEOUS. *adj.* [*pedaneus*, Lat.] Going on foot. *Dict.*

PE'DANT. *n. ſ.* [*pedant*, French.]

1. A ſchoolmaſter.

A *pedant* that keeps a ſchool i' th' church. *Shakeſp.*

The boy who ſcarce has paid his entrance down
To his proud *pedant*, or declin'd a noun. *Dryden.*

2. A man vain of low knowledge; a man awkwardly oſtentatious of his literature.

The *pedant* can hear nothing but in favour of the conceits he is amorous of. *Glanville.*

The preface has ſo much of the *pedant*, and ſo little of the converſation of men in it, that I ſhall paſs it over. *Addiſon.*

In learning let a nymph delight,
The *pedant* gets a miſtreſs by't. *Swift.*

PEDA'NTIC. } *adj.* [*pedanteſque*, Fr. from *pedant.*] Awk-
PEDA'NTICAL. } wardly oſtentatious of learning.

Mr. Cheeke had eloquence in the Latin and Greek tongues; but for other ſufficiencies *pedantick* enough. *Hayward.*

When we ſee any thing in an old ſatyriſt, that looks forced and *pedantick*, we ought to conſider how it appeared in the time the poet writ. *Addiſon.*

The obſcurity is brought over them by ignorance and age, made yet more obſcure by their *pedantical* elucidators. *Felton.*

A ſpirit

A ſpirit of contradiction is ſo *pedantic* and hateful, that a man ſhould watch againſt every inſtance of it. *Watts.*

We now believe the Copernican ſyſtem; yet we ſhall ſtill uſe the popular terms of ſun-riſe and ſun-ſet, and not introduce a new *pedantick* deſcription of them from the motion of the earth. *Bentley's Sermons.*

PEDA'NTICALLY. *adv.* [from *pedantical.*] With awkward oſtentation of literature.

The earl of Roſcommon has excellently rendered it; too faithfully is, indeed, *pedantically*; 'tis a faith like that, which proceeds from ſuperſtition. *Dryden.*

PE'DANTRY. *n. ſ.* [*pedanterie*, Fr.] Awkward oſtentation of needleſs learning.

'Tis a practice that ſavours much of *pedantry*, a reſerve of puerility we have not ſhaken off from ſchool. *Brown.*

Horace has enticed me into this *pedantry* of quotation. *Cowl.*

Make us believe it, if you can: it is in Latin, if I may be allowed the *pedantry* of a quotation, *non perſuadebis, etimaſi perſuaſeris.* *Addiſon's Freeholder.*

From the univerſities the young nobility are ſent for fear of contracting any airs of *pedantry* by a college education. *Swift.*

To PE'DDLE. *v. n.* To be buſy about trifles. *Ainſ.* It is commonly written *piddle*: as, what *piddling* work is here.

PEDERE'RO. *n. ſ.* [*pedrero*, Spaniſh, from *piedra*, a ſtone with which they charged it.] A ſmall cannon managed by a ſwivel. It is frequently written *paterero.*

PE'DESTAL. *n. ſ.* [*piedſtal*, Fr.] The lower member of a pillar; the baſis of a ſtatue.

The poet bawls
And ſhakes the ſtatues and the *pedeſtals.* *Dryden.*

In the centre of it was a grim idol; the forepart of the *pedeſtal* was curiouſly emboſſed with a triumph. *Addiſon.*

So ſtiff, ſo mute! ſome ſtatue you would ſwear
Stept from its *pedeſtal* to take the air. *Pope.*

PEDE'STRIOUS. *adj.* [*pedeſtris*, Latin.] Not winged; going on foot.

Men conceive they never lie down, and enjoy not the poſition of reſt, ordained unto all *pedeſtrious* animals. *Brown.*

PE'DICLE. *n. ſ.* [from *pedis*, Lat. *pedicule*, Fr.] The footſtalk, that by which a leaf or fruit is fixed to the tree.

The cauſe of the holding green, is the cloſe and compact ſubſtance of their leaves and *pedicles.* *Bacon.*

PEDI'CULAR. *adj.* [*pedicularis*, Lat. *pediculaire*, Fr.] Having the phthyriaſis or louſy diſtemper. *Ainſworth.*

PE'DIGREE. *n. ſ.* [*pere* and *degré*, *Skinner.*] Genealogy; lineage; account of deſcent.

I am no herald to enquire of men's *pedegrees*, it ſufficeth me if I know their virtues. *Sidney.*

You tell a *pedigree*
Of threeſcore and two years, a ſilly time. *Shakeſpeare.*

Alterations of firnames, which in former ages have been very common, have obſcured the truth of our *pedigrees*, that it will be no little hard labour to deduce many of them. *Cam.*

To the old heroes hence was giv'n
A *pedigree* which reach'd to heav'n. *Waller.*

The Jews preſerved the *pedigrees* of their ſeveral tribes, with a more ſcrupulous exactneſs than any other nation. *Atter.*

PE'DIMENT. *n. ſ.* [*pedis*, Lat.] In architecture, an ornament that crowns the ordonances, finiſhes the fronts of buildings, and ſerves as a decoration over gates, windows and niches: it is ordinarily of a triangular form, but ſometimes makes the arch of a circle. *Dict.*

PE'DLER. *n. ſ.* [a *petty dealer*; a contraction produced by frequent uſe.] One who travels the country with ſmall commodities.

All as a poor *pedler* he did wend,
Bearing a truſſe of trifles at his backe;
As bells and babies and glaſſes in his packe. *Spenſer.*

If you did but hear the *pedler* at the door, you would never dance again after a tabor and pipe *Shakeſpeare.*

He is wit's *pedler*, and retails his wares
At wakes and waſſals, meetings, markets, fairs. *Shakeſp.*

Had ſly Ulyſſes at the ſack
Of Troy brought thee his *pedler*'s pack. *Cleaveland.*

A narrow education may beget among ſome of the clergy in poſſeſſion ſuch contempt for all innovators, as merchants have for *pedlers.* *Swift.*

Atlas was ſo exceeding ſtrong,
He bore the ſkies upon his back,
Juſt as a *pedler* does his pack. *Swift.*

PE'DLERY. *adj.* [from *pedler.*] Wares ſold by pedlers.

The ſufferings of thoſe of my rank are trifles in compariſon of what all thoſe who travel with fiſh, poultry, *pedlery* ware to ſell. *Swift.*

PE'DDLING. *adj.* Petty dealing; ſuch as pedlers have.

So ſlight a pleaſure I may part with, and find no miſs; this *peddling* profit I may reſign, and 'twill be no breach in my eſtate. *Decay of Piety.*

PE'DOBAPTISM. *n. ſ.* [παιδὸς and βάπτισμα.] Infant baptiſm. *Dict.*

PE'DOBAPTIST. *n. ſ.* [παιδὸς and βαπτιστής.] One that holds or practiſes infant baptiſm.

To PEEL. *v. a.* [*peler*, Fr. from *pellis.*]

1. To decorticate; to flay.

The ſkilful ſhepherd *peel'd* me certain wands,
And ſtuck them up before the fulſome ewes. *Shakeſp.*

2. [From *piller*, to rob.] To plunder. According to analogy this ſhould be written *pill.*

Who once juſt and temp'rate conquer'd well,
But govern ill the nations under yoke,
Peeling their provinces, exhauſted all
But luſt and rapine. *Milton's Paradiſe Regained.*

Lord-like at eaſe, with arbitary pow'r,
To *peel* the chiefs, the people to devour;
Theſe, traitor, are thy talents. *Dryden.*

PEEL. *n. ſ.* [*pellis*, Latin; *pelure*, French.] The ſkin or thin rind of any thing.

PEEL. *n. ſ.* [*paelle*, Fr.] A broad thin board with a long handle, uſed by bakers to put their bread in and out of the oven.

PEELER. *n. ſ.* [from *peel.*]

1. One who ſtrips or flays.

2. A robber; a plunderer.

Yet otes with her ſucking a *peeler* is found,
Both ill to the maiſter and worſe to ſome ground. *Tuſſer.*

As 'tis a *peeler* of land, ſow it upon lands that are rank. *Mortimer's Huſbandry.*

To PEEP. *v. n.* [This word has no etymology, except that of *Skinner*, who derives it from *opheſſen*, Dutch, *to lift up*; and of *Caſaubon*, who derives it from ὀπιπευτὴς, a *ſpy*; perhaps it may come from *pip*, *pipio*, Latin, *to cry as young birds*: when the chickens firſt broke the ſhell and cried, they were ſaid to begin to *pip* or *peep*; and the word that expreſſed the act of crying, was by miſtake applied to the act of appearing that was at the ſame time: this is offered till ſomething better may be found.]

1. To make the firſt appearance.

She her gay painted plumes diſordered,
Seeing at laſt herſelf from danger rid,
Peeps forth and ſoon renews her native pride. *Fa. Queen.*

Your youth
And the true blood, which *peeps* forth fairly through it,
Do plainly give you out an unſtain'd ſhepherd. *Shakeſp.*

England and France might through their amity,
Breed him ſome prejudice; for from this league,
Peep'd harms that menac'd him. *Shakeſp. Henry VIII.*

I can ſee his pride
Peep through each part of him. *Shakeſp. Henry VIII.*

The tim'rous maiden-bloſſoms on each bough
Peept forth from their firſt bluſhes; ſo that now
A thouſand ruddy hopes ſmil'd in each bud,
And flatter'd every greedy eye that ſtood. *Craſhaw.*

With words not hers, and more than human ſound,
She makes th' obedient ghoſts *peep* trembling through the ground. *Roſcommon.*

Earth, but not at once, her viſage rears,
And *peeps* upon the ſeas from upper grounds. *Dryden.*

Fair as the face of nature did appear,
When flowers firſt *peep'd*, and trees did bloſſoms bear,
And winter had not yet deform'd th' inverted year. *Dryd.*

Printing and letters had juſt *peeped* abroad in the world; and the reſtorers of learning wrote very eagerly againſt one another. *Atterbury.*

Though but the very white end of the ſprout *peep* out in the outward part of the couch, break it open, you will find the ſprout of a greater largeneſs. *Mortimer's Huſbandry.*

So pleas'd at firſt the tow'ring Alps we try,
And the firſt clouds and mountains ſeem the laſt;
But thoſe attain'd, we tremble to ſurvey
The growing labours of the lengthen'd way;
Th' increaſing proſpect tires our wand'ring eyes,
Hills *peep* o'er hills, and Alps on Alps ariſe. *Pope.*

Moſt ſouls but *peep* out once an age,
Dull ſullen pris'ners in the body's cage. *Pope.*

2. To look ſlily, cloſely or curiouſly; to look through any crevice.

Who is the ſame, which at my window *peeps.* *Spenſer.*

Come thick night!
That my keen knife ſee not the wound it makes;
Nor heav'n *peep* through the blanket of the dark,
To cry hold. *Shakeſp. Macbeth.*

Nature hath fram'd ſtrange fellows in her time;
Some that will evermore *peep* through their eyes,
And laugh like parrots at a bag-piper. *Shakeſp.*

A fool will *peep* in at the door. *Eccluſ.* xxi. 23.

The trembling leaves through which he play'd,
Dappling the walk with light and ſhade,
Like lattice-windows give the ſpy
Room but to *peep* with half an eye. *Cleaveland.*

All doors are ſhut, no ſervant *peeps* abroad,
While others outward went on quick diſpatch. *Dryden.*

The

The daring flames *peept* in, and saw from far
The awful beauties of the sacred quire;
But since it was prophan'd by civil war,
Heav'n thought it fit to have it purg'd by fire. *Dryden.*

From each tree
The feather'd people look down to *peep* on me. *Dryden.*

Those remote and vast bodies were formed not merely to be *peept* at through an optick glass. *Bentley's Sermons.*

O my muse, just distance keep;
Thou art a maid, and must not *peep*. *Prior.*

In vain his little children *peeping* out
Into the mingling storm, demand their fire. *Thomson.*

PEEP. *n. s.*

1. First appearance: as, at the *peep* and first break of day.

2. A sly look.

Would not one think, the almanackmaker was crept out of his grave to take t'other *peep* at the stars. *Swift.*

PEE'PER. *n. s.* Young chickens just breaking the shell.

Dishes I chuse, though little, yet genteel;
Snails the first course, and *peepers* crown the meal. *Bramst.*

PEE'PHOLE. } *n. s.* [*peep* and *hole.*] Hole through which
PEE'PINGHOLE. } one may look without being discovered.

By the *peepholes* in his crest,
Is it not virtually confest,
That there his eyes took distant aim. *Prior.*

The fox spied him through a *peepinghole* he had found out to see what news. *L'Estrange.*

PEER. *n. s.* [*pair*, French.]

1. Equal; one of the same rank.

His *peers* upon this evidence
Have found him guilty of high treason. *Shakesp.*

Amongst a man's *peers*, a man shall be sure of familiarity; and therefore it is good a little to keep state. *Bacon.*

Oh! what is man, great maker of mankind!
That thou to him so great respect do'st bear!
That thou adorn'st him with so bright a mind,
Mak'st him a king, and ev'n an angel's *peer*. *Davies.*

2. One equal in excellence or endowments.

In song he never had his *peer*,
From sweet Cecilia down to chanticleer. *Dryden.*

3. Companion: fellow.

He all his *peers* in beauty did surpass. *Fairy Queen.*

If you did move to-night,
In the dances, with what spight
Of your *peers* you were beheld,
That at every motion swell'd. *Benj. Johnson.*

Who bear the bows were knights in Arthur's reign,
Twelve they, and twelve the *peers* of Charlemagne. *Dryd.*

4. A nobleman: of nobility we have five degrees, who are all nevertheless called *peers*, because their essential privileges are the same.

I see thee compast with thy kingdom's *peers*,
That speak my salutation in their minds:
Hail king of Scotland! *Shakesp. Macbeth.*

King Henry's *peers* and chief nobility
Destroy'd themselves, and lost the realm of France. *Shakes.*

Be just in all you say, and all you do;
Whatever be your birth, you're sure to be
A *peer* of the first magnitude to me. *Dryden.*

To PEER. *v. n.* [By contraction from *appear.*]

1. To come just in sight.

As the sun breaks through the darkest clouds,
So honour *peereth* in the meanest habit. *Shakesp.*

Yet a many of your horsemen *peer*,
And gallop o'er the field. *Shakespear's Henry V.*

Ev'n through the hollow eyes of death
I spy life *peering* *Shakesp.*

See how his gorget *peers* above his gown,
To tell the people in what danger he was. *Ben. Johnson.*

Hell itself will pass away,
And leave her dolorous mansion to the *peering* day. *Milt.*

2. To look narrowly; to peep.

Now for a clod-like hare in form they *peer*,
Now bolt and cudgel squirrels leap do move,
Now the ambitious lark with mirrour clear
They catch, while he, fool! to himself makes love. *Sidn.*

Peering in maps for ports, and peers, and roads,
And every object that might make me fear
Misfortune to my ventures. *Shakesp. Merch. of Venice.*

PEE'RAGE. *n. s.* [*pairie*, Fr. from *peer.*]

1. The dignity of a peer.

His friendships he to few confin'd;
No fools of rank or mongrel breed,
Who fain would pass for Lords indeed;
Where titles give no right or power,
And *peerage* is a wither'd flower. *Swift.*

2. The body of peers.

Not only the penal laws are in force against papists, and their number is contemptible, but also the *peerage* and commons are excluded from parliament. *Dryden.*

PEE'RDOM. *n. s.* [from *peer.*] Peerage. *Ainsworth.*

PEE'RESS. *n. s.* [female of *peer.*] The lady of a peer; a woman ennobled.

Statesman and patriot ply alike the stocks;
Peeress and butler share alike the box. *Pope.*

PEE'RLESS. *adj.* [from *peer.*] Unequalled; having no peer.

I bind,
On pain of punishment, the world to weet,
We stand up *peerless*. *Shakesp.*

You,
So perfect, and so *peerless*, are created
Of every creature's best. *Shakespeare's Tempest.*

Her *peerless* feature, joined with her birth,
Approves her fit for none, but for a king. *Shakesp.*

Hesperus, that led
The starry host, rode brightest; till the moon,
Rising in clouded majest, yat length,
Apparent queen, unveil'd her *peerless* light. *Milton.*

Such music worthiest were to blaze
The *peerless* light of her immortal praise,
Whole lustre leads us. *Milton.*

Her dress, her shape, her matchless grace,
Were all observ'd, as well as heav'nly face;
With such a *peerless* majesty she stands,
As in that day she took the crown. *Dryden.*

PEE'RLESSNESS. *n. s.* [from *peerless.*] Universal superiority.

PEE'VISH. *adj.* [This word *Junius*, with more reason than he commonly discovers, supposes to be formed by corruption from *perverse*; *Skinner* rather derives it from *beeish*, as we say *waspish.*] Petulant; waspish; easily offended; irritable; irascible; soon angry; perverse; morose; querulous; full of expressions of discontent; hard to please.

For what can breed more *peevish* incongruities,
Than man to yield to female lamentations. *Sidney.*

She is *peevish*, sullen, froward,
Proud, disobedient, stubborn, lacking duty. *Shakesp.*

If thou hast the metal of a king,
Being wrong'd as we are by this *peevish* town,
Turn thou the mouth of thy artillery,
As we will ours, against these saucy walls. *Shakesp.*

I will not presume
To send such *peevish* tokens to a king. *Shakesp.*

Those deserve to be doubly laugh'd at, that are *peevish* and angry for nothing to no purpose. *L'Estrange.*

Neither will it be satire or *peevish* invective to affirm, that infidelity and vice are not much diminished. *Swift.*

PEE'VISHLY. *adv.* [from *peevish.*] Angrily; querulously; morosely.

He was so *peevishly* opiniative and proud, that he would neither ask nor hear the advice of any. *Hayward.*

PEE'VISHNESS. *n. s.* [from *peevish.*] Irascibility; querulousness; fretfulness; perverseness.

Some miscarriages in government might escape through the *peevishness* of others, envying the publick should be managed without them. *King Charles.*

It will be an unpardonable, as well as childish *peevishness*, if we undervalue the advantages of our knowledge, and neglect to improve it. *Locke.*

You may find
Nothing but acid left behind:
From passion you may then be freed,
When *peevishness* and spleen succeed. *Swift.*

PEG. *n. s.* [*pegghe*, Teutonick.]

1. A piece of wood driven into a hole, which does the office of an iron nail.

Solid bodies foreshew rain; as boxes and *pegs* of wood, when they draw and wind hard. *Bacon.*

The teeth are about thirty in each jaw; all of them claviculares or *peg* teeth, not much unlike the tusks of a mastiff. *Grew's Musæum.*

If he pretends to be cholerick, we shall treat him like his little friend Dicky, and hang him upon a *peg* till he comes to himself. *Addison's Guardian*, Nº 108.

The *pegs* and nails in a great building, though they are but little valued in themselves, are absolutely necessary to keep the whole frame together. *Addison's Spectator.*

A finer petticoat can neither make you richer, more virtuous or wise, than if it hung upon a *peg*. *Swift.*

2. The pins of an instrument in which the strings are strained.

You are well tun'd now; but I'll let down
The *pegs* that make this musick. *Shakesp. Othello.*

3. *To take a* PEG *lower*; to depress; to sink: perhaps from relaxing the cords of musical instruments.

Remember how in arms and politicks,
We still have worsted all your holy tricks,
Trepann'd your party with intrigue,
And took your grandees down a *peg*. *Hudibras.*

4. The nickname of Margaret.

To PEG. *v. a.* To fasten with a peg.

I will rend an oak,
And *peg* thee in his knotty entrails, 'till
Thou'st howl'd away twelve winters. *Shakesp. Tempest.*

Taking the shoots of the past spring, and *pegging* them down in very rich earth, by that time twelvemonth they will be ready to remove. *Evelyn's Kalendar.*

PELF. *n. s.* [In low Latin, *pelfra*, not known whence derived; *peuffe*, in Norman, is *frippery*.] Money; riches.

The thought of this doth pass all worldly *pelf*. *Sidney.*

Hardy elf,
Thou darest view my direful countenance,
I read thee rash and heedless of thyself,
To trouble my still seat and heaps of precious *pelf*. *Fairy Queen.*

Immortal gods, I crave no *pelf*;
I pray for no man but myself. *Shakespeare.*

He call'd his money in;
But the prevailing love of *pelf*
Soon split him on the former shelf:
He put it out again. *Dryden's Horace.*

To the poor if he refus'd his *pelf*,
He us'd them full as kindly as himself. *Swift.*

PE'LICAN. *n. s.* [*pelicanus*, low Lat. *pellican*, Fr.]

There are two sorts of *pelicans*; one lives upon the water and feeds upon fish; the other keeps in deserts, and feeds upon serpents and other reptiles: the *pelican* has a peculiar tenderness for its young; it generally places its nest upon a craggy rock: the *pelican* is supposed to admit its young to suck blood from its breast. *Calmet.*

Should discarded fathers
Have this little mercy on their flesh;
'Twas this flesh begot those *pelican* daughters. *Shakesp.*

The *pelican* hath a beak broad and flat, like the slice of apothecaries. *Hakewill on Providence.*

PE'LLET. *n. s.* [from *pila*, Lat. *pelote*, Fr.]

1. A little ball.

That which is sold to the merchants, is made into little *pellets*, and sealed. *Sandys.*

I dressed with little *pellets* of lint. *Wiseman's Surgery.*

2. A bullet; a ball.

The force of gunpowder hath been ascribed to rarefaction of the earthy substance into flame, and so followeth a dilatation; and therefore, lest two bodies should be in one place, there must needs also follow an expulsion of the *pellet* or blowing up of the mine: but these are ignorant speculations; for flame, if there were nothing else, will be suffocated with any hard body, such as a *pellet* is, or the barrel of a gun; so as the hard body would kill the flame. *Bacon.*

A cube or *pellet* of yellow wax as much as half the spirit of wine, burnt only eighty-seven pulses. *Bacon.*

How shall they reach us in the air with those *pellets* they can hardly roll upon the ground. *L'Estrange.*

In a shooting trunk, the longer it is to a certain limit, the more forcibly the air passes and drives the *pellet*. *Ray.*

PE'LLETED. *adj.* [from *pellet*.] Consisting of bullets.

My brave Egyptians all,
By the discandying of this *pelleted* storm,
Lie graveless. *Shakespeare.*

PE'LLICLE. *n. s.* [*pellicula*, Lat.]

1. A thin skin.

After the discharge of the fluid, the *pellicle* must be broke. *Sharp's Surgery.*

2. It is often used for the film which gathers upon liquors impregnated with salts or other substances, and evaporated by heat.

PE'LLITORY. *n. s.* [*parietaria*, Lat.] An herb.

The *pellitory* hath an apetalous flower, whose flower cup is divided into four parts, which is sometimes bell-shaped like a funnel, with four stamina or threads surrounding the pointal, which becomes for the most part an oblong seed, surrounded by the flower cup; to which may be added, the flowers are produced from the wings of the leaves. *Miller.*

PE'LLMELL. *n. s.* [*pesle mesle*, Fr.] Confusedly; tumultuously; one among another.

When we have dash'd them to the ground,
Then defie each other; and *pell mell*
Make work upon ourselves. *Shakespeare's King John.*

Never yet did insurrection want
Such moody beggars, starving for a time
Of *pellmell* havock and confusion. *Henry IV.*

He knew when to fall on *pellmell*,
To fall back and retreat as well. *Hudibras.*

PELLS. *n. s.* [*pellis*, Lat.]

Clerk of the *pells*, an officer belonging to the exchequer, who enters every teller's bill into a parchment roll called *pellis acceptorum*, the roll of receipts; and also makes another roll called *pellis exituum*, a roll of the disbursements. *Bailey.*

PELLU'CID. *adj.* [*pellucidus*, Lat.] Clear; transparent; not opake; not dark.

The colours are owing to the intermixture of foreign matter with the proper matter of the stone: this is the case of agates and other coloured stones, the colours of several whereof may be extracted, and the bodies rendered as *pellucid* as crystal, without sensibly damaging the texture. *Woodward.*

If water be made warm in any *pellucid* vessel emptied of air, the water in the vacuum will bubble and boil as vehemently as it would in the open air in a vessel set upon the fire, till it conceives a much greater heat. *Newton's Opticks.*

PELLU'CIDITY. } *n. s.* [from *pellucid*.] Transparency; clear-
PELLU'CIDNESS. } ness; not opacity.

The air is a clear and pellucid menstruum, in which the insensible particles of dissolved matter float, without troubling the *pellucidity* of the air; when on a sudden by a precipitation they gather into visible misty drops that make clouds. *Locke.*

We consider their *pellucidness* and the vast quantity of light, that passes through them without reflection. *Keil.*

PELT. *n. s.* [from *pellis*, Lat.]

1. Skin; hide.

The camels hair is taken for the skin or *pelt* with the hair upon it. *Brown's Vulgar Errours.*

A scabby tetter on their *pelts* will stick,
When the raw rain has pierc'd them to the quick. *Dryden.*

2. The quarry of a hawk all torn. *Ainsworth.*

PELT-MONGER. *n. s.* [*pellio*, Lat. *pelt* and *monger*.] A dealer in raw hides.

To PELT. *v. a.* [*poltern*, German, *Skinner*; contracted from *pellet*, Mr. *Lye*.] It is generally used of something thrown, rather with teazing frequency than destructive violence.

1. To strike with something thrown.

Poor naked wretches wheresoe'er you are
That bide the *pelting* of this pitiless storm!
How shall your houseless heads and unfed sides,
Your loop'd and window'd raggedness defend you. *Shakesp.*

Do but stand upon the foaming shore,
The chiding billows seem to *pelt* the clouds. *Shakesp.*

No zealous brother there would want a stone
To maul us cardinals, and *pelt* pope Joan. *Dryden.*

Obscure persons have insulted men of great worth, and *pelted* them from coverts with little objections. *Atterbury.*

The whole empire could hardly subdue me, and I might easily with stones *pelt* the metropolis to pieces. *Gulliver.*

2. To throw; to cast.

My Phillis me with *pelted* apples plies,
Then tripping to the woods the wanton hies. *Dryden.*

PE'LTING. *adj.* This word in *Shakespeare* signifies, I know not why, mean; paltry; pitiful.

Could great men thunder, Jove could ne'er be quiet;
For every *pelting* petty officer
Would use his heav'n for thunder. *Shakespeare.*

Fogs falling in the land,
Have every *pelting* river made so proud,
That they have overborn their continents. *Shakesp.*

They from sheepcotes and poor *pelting* villages
Enforce their charity. *Shakesp.*

A tenement or *pelting* farm. *Shakesp.*

PE'LVIS. *n. s.* [Latin.] The lower part of the belly.

PEN. *n. s.* [*penna*, Latin.]

1. An instrument of writing.

Never durst poet touch a *pen* to write,
Until his ink were temper'd with love's sighs. *Shakesp.*

Eternal deities!
Who write whatever time shall bring to pass,
With *pens* of Adamant on plates of brass. *Dryden.*

He takes the papers, lays them down again;
And, with unwilling fingers, tries the *pen*. *Dryden.*

I can, by designing the letters, tell what new idea it shall exhibit the next moment, barely by drawing my *pen* over it, which will neither appear, if my hands stand still; or though I move my *pen*, if my eyes be shut. *Locke.*

2. Feather.

The *pens* that did his pinnions bind,
Were like main-yards with flying canvas lin'd. *Fairy Queen.*

3. Wing; though even here it may mean *feather*.

Feather'd soon and fledg'd,
They summ'd their *pens*; and soaring th' air sublime,
With clang despis'd the ground. *Milton's Paradise Lost.*

4. [From pennan, Saxon.] A small inclosure; a coop.

My father stole two geese out of a *pen*. *Shakesp.*

The cook was ordered to dress capons for supper, and take the best in the *pen*. *L'Estrange.*

She in *pens* his flocks will fold. *Dryden's Horace.*

Ducks in thy ponds, and chickens in thy *pens*,
And be thy turkeys num'rous as thy hens. *King.*

The gather'd flocks
Are in the wattled *pen* innumerous press'd,
Head above head. *Thomson's Summer.*

To PEN. *v. a.* [pennan and pinban, Saxon.]

1. To coop; to shut up; to incage; to imprison in a narrow place.

Away with her,
And *pen* her up. *Shakesp. Cymbeline.*

My heavy son
Private in his chamber *pens* himself. *Shakesp.*

The plaister alone would *pen* the humour already contained in the part, and forbid new humour. *Bacon.*

As when a prowling wolf,
Whom hunger drives to seek new haunt for prey,
Watching where shepherds *pen* their flocks at eve

In hurdled cotes, amid the field secure
Leaps o'er the fence with ease into the fold. *Milton.*

The glass, wherein it is *penned* up, hinders it to deliver itself by an expansion of its parts. *Boyle.*

The prevention of mischief is prescribed by the Jewish custom; they *pen* up their daughters, and permit them to be acquainted with none. *Harvey on Consumptions.*

Ah! that your bus'ness had been mine,
To *pen* the sheep. *Dryden.*

2. [From the noun.] To write. It probably meant at first only the manual exercise of the pen, or mechanical part of writing; but it has been long used with relation to the stile or composition.

For prey these shepherds two he took,
Whose metal stiff he knew he could not bend
With hearsay pictures, or a window look,
With one good dance or letter finely *penn'd*. *Sidney.*

I would be loth to cast away my speech; for, besides that it is excellently well *penn'd*, I have taken great pains to con it. *Shakespeare's Twelfth Night.*

Read this challenge, mark but the *penning* of it. *Shakesp.*

A sentence spoken by him in English, and *penned* out of his mouth by four good secretaries, for trial of our orthography, was set down by them. *Camden's Remains.*

He frequented sermons, and *penned* notes with his own hand. *Hayward on Edward VI.*

The digesting my thoughts into order, and the setting them down in writing was necessary; for without such strict examination, as the *penning* them affords, they would have been disjointed and roving ones. *Digby on the Soul.*

Almost condemn'd, he mov'd the judges thus:
Hear, but instead of me, my Oedipus;
The judges hearing with applause, at th' end
Freed him, and said, no fool such lines had *penn'd*. *Denh.*

Gentlemen should extempore, or after a little meditation, speak to some subject without *penning* of any thing. *Locke.*

Should I publish the praises that are so well *penn'd*, they would do honour to the persons who write them. *Addison.*

Twenty fools I never saw
Come with petitions fairly *penn'd*,
Desiring I should stand their friend. *Swift.*

PE'NAL. *adj.* [*penal*, Fr. from *pœna*, Lat.]

1. Denouncing punishment; enacting punishment.

Gratitude plants such generosity in the heart of man, as shall more effectually incline him to what is brave and becoming than the terror of any *penal* law. *South.*

2. Used for the purposes of punishment; vindictive.

Adamantive chains and *penal* fire. *Milton.*

PE'NALTY. }
PENA'LITY. } *n. s.* [from *penalité*, old French.]

1. Punishment; censure; judicial infliction.

Many of the ancients denied the Antipodes, and some unto the *penality* of contrary affirmations; but the experience of navigations, can now assert them beyond all dubitation. *Brown.*

Political power is a right of making laws with *penalties* of death, and consequently all less *penalties*, for preserving property, and employing the force of the community in the execution of laws. *Locke.*

Beneath her footstool, science groans in chains,
And wit dreads exile, *penalties* and pains. *Dunciad.*

2. Forfeiture upon non-performance.

Lend this money, not as to thy friend,
But lend it rather to thine enemy,
Who, if he break, thou may'st with better face
Exact the *penalty*. *Shakesp. Merch. of Venice.*

PE'NNANCE. *n. s.* [*penence*, old French; for *penitence*.] Infliction either publick or private, suffered as an expression of repentance for sin.

And bitter *pennance*, with an iron whip,
Was wont him once to disciple every day. *Fairy Queen.*

Mew her up,
And make her bear the *pennance* of her tongue. *Shakesp.*

No penitentiary, though he had enjoined him never so straight *pennance* to expiate his first offence, would have counselled him to have given over the pursuit of his right. *Bacon.*

The scourge
Inexorable, and the torturing hour
Calls us to *pennance*. *Milton's Paradise Lost.*

A Lorain surgeon, who whipped the naked part with a great rod of nettles till all over blistered, persuaded him to perform this *pennance* in a sharp fit he had. *Temple.*

PENCE. *n. s.* The plural of *penny*; formed from *pennies*, by a contraction usual in the rapidity of colloquial speech.

The same servant found one of his fellow servants, which owed him an hundred *pence*, and took him by the throat. *Mat.*

PE'NCIL. *n. s.* [*penicillum*, Latin.]

1. A small brush of hair which painters dip in their colours.

Pencils can by one slight touch restore
Smiles to that changed face, that wept before. *Dryden.*

For thee the groves green liv'ries wear,
For thee the graces lead the dancing hours,
And nature's ready *pencil* paints the flow'rs. *Dryden.*

A sort of pictures there is, wherein the colours, as laid by the *pencil* on the table, mark out very odd figures. *Locke.*

The faithful *pencil* has design'd
Some bright idea of the master's mind,
Where a new world leaps out at his command,
And ready nature waits upon his hand. *Pope.*

One dips the *pencil*, t' other strings the lyre. *Pope.*

2. A black lead pen, with which cut to a point they write without ink.

Mark with a pen or *pencil* the most considerable things in the books you desire to remember. *Watts.*

3. Any instrument of writing without ink.

To PE'NCIL. *v. n.* [from the noun.] To paint.

Painting is almost the natural man;
For since dishonour trafficks with man's nature,
He is but outside: *pencil'd* figures are
Ev'n such as they give out. *Shakespeare's Timon of Athens.*

PE'NDANT. *n. s.* [*pendant*, French.]

1. A jewel hanging in the ear.

The spirits
Some thrid the mazy ringlets of her hair,
Some hang upon the *pendents* of her ear. *Pope.*

2. Any thing hanging by way of ornament.

Unripe fruit, whose verdant stalks do cleave
Close to the tree, which grieves no less to leave
The smiling *pendant* which adorns her so,
And until Autumn, on the bough should grow. *Waller.*

3. A pendulum. Obsolete.

To make the same *pendant* go twice as fast as it did, or make every undulation of it in half the time it did, make the line, at which it hangs, double in geometrical proportion to the line at which it hanged before. *Digby on the Soul.*

4. A small flag in ships.

PE'NDENCE. *n. s.* [from *pendeo*, Lat.] Slopeness; inclination.

The Italians give the cover a graceful *pendence* or slopeness, dividing the whole breadth into nine parts, whereof two shall serve for the elevation of the highest top or ridge from the lowest. *Wotton's Architecture.*

PE'NDENCY. *n. s.* [from *pendeo*, Lat.] Suspense; delay of decision.

The judge shall pronounce in the principal cause, nor can the appellant allege *pendency* of suit. *Ayliffe.*

PE'NDENT. *adj.* [*pendens*, Latin; some write *pendant*, from the French.]

1. Hanging.

Quaint in green she shall be loose enrob'd
With ribbans *pendent*, flaring 'bout her head. *Shakesp.*

I sometimes mournful verse indite, and sing
Of desperate lady near a purling stream,
Or lover *pendent* on a willow tree. *Phillips.*

2. Jutting over.

A *pendent* rock,
A forked mountain, or blue promontory
With trees upon't, that nod unto the world,
And mock our eyes with air. *Shakesp.*

3. Supported above the ground.

They brought, by wond'rous art
Pontifical, a ridge of *pendent* rock
Over the vex'd abyss. *Milton's Paradise Lost.*

PE'NDING. *n. s.* [*pendente lite.*] Depending; remaining yet undecided.

A person *pending* suit with the diocesan, shall be defended in the possession. *Ayliffe.*

PENDULO'SITY. }
PE'NDULOUSNESS. } *n. s.* [from *pendulous.*] The state of hanging; suspension.

His slender legs he encreased by riding, that is, the humours descended upon their *pendulosity*, having no support or suppedaneous stability. *Brown's Vulgar Errours.*

PE'NDULOUS. *adj.* [*pendulus*, Lat.] Hanging; not supported below.

All the plagues, that in the *pendulous* air
Hang fated o'er men's faults, light on thy daughters. *Shak.*

Bellerophon's horse, fram'd of iron, and placed between two loadstones with wings expanded, hung *pendulous* in the air. *Brown's Vulgar Errours.*

The grinders are furnished with three roots, and in the upper jaw often four, because these are *pendulous*. *Ray.*

PE'NDULUM. *n. s.* [*pendulus*, Lat. *pendule*, Fr.] Any weight hung so as that it may easily swing backwards and forwards, of which the great law is, that its oscillations are always performed in equal time.

Upon the bench I will so handle 'em,
That the vibration of this *pendulum*
Shall make all taylors yards of one
Unanimous opinion. *Hudibras.*

PE'NETRABLE. *adj.* [*penetrable*, Fr. *penetrabilis*, Latin.]

1. Such as may be pierced; such as may admit the entrance of another body.

Let him try thy dart,
And pierce his only *penetrable* part. *Dryden.*

2. Susceptive of moral or intellectual impression.

I am not made of stone,
But *penetrable* to your kind entreaties. *Shakesp.*

Peace,

Peace,
And let we wring your heart, for so I shall,
If it be made of *penetrable* stuff. *Shakesp. Hamlet.*

PENETRABI'LITY. *n. s.* [from *penetrable.*] Susceptibility of impression from another body.

There being no mean between *penetrability* and impenetrability, passivity and activity, they being contrary; therefore the infinite rarefaction of the one quality is the position of its contrary. *Cheyne's Philosophical Principles.*

PE'NETRAIL. *n. s.* [*penetralia*, Latin.] Interiour parts. Not in use.

The heart resists purulent fumes, into whose *penetrails* to insinuate some time must be allowed. *Harvey.*

PE'NETRANCY. *n. s.* [from *penetrant.*] Power of entering or piercing.

The subtlitiy, activity and *penetrancy* of its effluvia no obstacle can stop or repel, but they will make their way through all bodies. *Ray on the Creation.*

PE'NETRANT. *adj.* [*penetrant*, Fr.] Having the power to pierce or enter; sharp; subtile.

If the operation of these salts be in convenient glasses promoted by warmth, the ascending steams may easily be caught and reduced into a *penetrant* spirit. *Boyle.*

The food, mingled with some dissolvent juices, is evacuated into the intestines, where it is further subtilized and rendered so fluid and *penetrant*, that the finer part finds its way in at the streight orifices of the lacteous veins. *Ray.*

To PE'NETRATE. *v. a. penetro*, Lat. *penetrer*, Fr.]

1. To pierce; to enter beyond the surface; to make way into a body.

Marrow is, of all other oily substances, the most *penetrating*. *Arbuthnot on Aliments.*

2. To affect the mind.

3. To reach the meaning.

To PE'NETRATE. *v. n.* To make way.

There shall we clearly see the uses of these things, which here were too subtile for us to *penetrate*. *Ray.*

If we reached no farther than metaphor, we rather fancy than know, and are not yet *penetrated* into the inside and reality of the thing. *Locke.*

PENETRA'TION. *n. s.* [*penetration*, Fr. from *penetrate.*]

1. The act of entering into any body.

It warms
The universe, and to each inward part
With gentle *penetration* though unseen
Shoots invisible virtue even to the deep. *Milton's Par. Lost.*

2. Mental entrance into any thing abstruse.

A *penetration* into the abstruse difficulties and depths of modern algebra and fluxions, is not worth the labour of those who design either of the three learned professions. *Watts.*

3. Acuteness; sagacity.

The proudest admirer of his own parts might consult with others, though of inferior capacity and *penetration*. *Watts.*

PE'NETRATIVE. *adj.* [from *penetrate.*]

1. Piercing; sharp; subtile.

Let not air be too gross, nor too *penetrative*, nor subject to any foggy noisomeness from fens. *Wotton.*

2. Acute; sagacious; discerning.

O thou, whose *penetrative* wisdom found
The south sea rocks and shelves, where thousands drown'd.
Swift's Miscellanies.

3. Having the power to impress the mind.

Would'st thou see
Thy master thus with pleacht arms, bending down
His corrigible neck, his face subdu'd
To *penetrative* shame. *Shakespeare.*

PE'NETRATIVENESS. *n. s.* [from *penetrative.*] The quality of being penetrative.

PE'NGUIN. *n. s.* [*anser magellanicus*, Latin.]

1. A bird. This bird was found with this name, as is supposed, by the first discoverers of America; and *penguin* signifying in Welsh a white head, and the head of this fowl being white, it has been imagined, that America was peopled from Wales; whence *Hudibras*:

British Indians nam'd from *penguins*.

Grew gives another account of the name, deriving it from *pinguis*, Lat. *fat*; but is, I believe, mistaken.

The *penguin* is so called from his extraordinary fatness: for though he be no higher than a large goose, yet he weighs sometimes sixteen pounds: his wings are extreme short and little, altogether unuseful for flight, but by the help whereof he swims very swiftly. *Grew's Musæum.*

2. A fruit.

The *penguin* is very common in the West Indies, where the juice of its fruit is often put into punch, being of a sharp acid flavour: there is also a wine made of the juice of this fruit, but it will not keep good long. *Miller.*

PENI'NSULA. *n. s.* [Lat. *pene insula*; *peninsule*, Fr.] A piece of land almost surrounded by the sea, but joined by a narrow neck to the main.

Aside of Milbrook lieth the *peninsula* of Inswork, on whose neckland standeth an ancient house. *Carew.*

PENI'NSULATED. *adj.* [from *peninsula.*] Almost surrounded by water.

PE'NITENCE. *n. s.* [*penitence*, Fr. *pœnitentia*, Lat.] Repentance; sorrow for crimes; contrition for sin, with amendments of life or change of the affections.

Death is deferr'd, and *penitence* has room
To mitigate, if not reverse the doom. *Dryden.*
May *penitence* fly round thy mournful bed,
And wing thy latest prayer to pitying heav'n. *Irene.*

PE'NITENT. *adj.* [*penitent*, Fr. *pœnitens*, Lat.] Repentant; contrite for sin; sorrowful for past transgressions, and resolutely amending life.

Much it joys me
To see you become so *penitent*. *Shakespeare.*
Give me
The *penitent* instrument to pick that bolt. *Shakespeare.*
Nor in the land of their captivity
Humbled themselves, or *penitent* besought
The God of their forefathers. *Milton's Par. Regain'd.*
Provoking God to raise them enemies;
From whom as oft he saves them *penitent*. *Milton.*
The proud he tam'd, the *penitent* he cheer'd,
Nor to rebuke the rich offender fear'd.
His preaching much, but more his practice wrought
A living sermon of the truths he taught. *Dryden.*

PE'NITENT. *n. s.*

1. One sorrowful for sin.

Concealed treasures shall be brought into use by the industry of converted *penitents*, whose carcases the impartial laws shall dedicate to the worms of the earth. *Bacon.*

The repentance, which is formed by a grateful sense of the divine goodness towards him, is resolved on while all the appetites are in their strength: the *penitent* conquers the temptations of sin in their full force. *Rogers's Sermons.*

2. One under censures of the church, but admitted to pennance.

The counterfeit Dionysius describes the practice of the church, that the catechumens and *penitents* were admitted to the lessons and psalms, and then excluded. *Stillingfleet.*

3. One under the direction of a confessor.

PENITE'NTIAL. *adj.* [from *penitence.*] Expressing penitence; enjoined as pennance.

I have done pennance for contemning love,
Whose high imperious thoughts have punish'd me
With bitter fasts and *penitential* groans. *Shakespeare.*

Is it not strange, that a rational man should adore leeks and garlick, and shed *penitential* tears at the smell of a deified onion? *South's Sermons.*

PENITE'NTIAL. *n. s.* [*penitenciel*, Fr. *pœnitentiale*, low Latin.] A book directing the degrees of pennance.

The *penitentials* or book of pennance contained such matters as related to the imposing of pennance, and the reconciliation of the person that suffered pennance. *Ayliffe.*

PENITE'NTIARY. *n. s.* [*penitencier*, Fr. *pœnitentiarius*, low Latin.]

1. One who prescribes the rules and measures of pennance.

Upon the loss of Urbin, the duke's undoubted right, no *penitentiary*, though he had enjoined him never so straight pennance to expiate his first offence, would have counselled him to have given over pursuit of his right, which he prosperously re-obtained. *Bacon.*

The great *penitentiary* with his counsellors prescribes the measure of pennance. *Ayliffe's Parergon.*

2. A penitent; one who does pennance.

A prison restrained John Northampton's liberty, who, for abusing the same in his unruly mayoralty of London, was condemned hither as a perpetual *penitentiary*. *Carew.*

To maintain a painful fight against the law of sin, is the work of the *penitentiary*. *Hammond.*

3. The place where pennance is enjoined. *Ainsworth.*

PE'NITENTLY. *adv.* [from *penitent.*] With repentance; with sorrow for sin; with contrition.

PENKNIFE. *n. s.* [*pen* and *knife.*] A knife used to cut pens.

Some schoolmen, fitter to guide *penknives* than swords, precisely stand upon it. *Bacon.*

PE'NMAN. *n. s.* [*pen* and *man.*]

1. One who professes the act of writing.

2. An author; a writer.

The four evangelists, within fifty years after our Saviour's death, consigned to writing that history, which had been published only by the apostles and disciples: the further consideration of these holy *penmen* will fall under another part of this discourse. *Addison on the Christian Religion.*

The descriptions which the evangelists give, shew that both our blessed Lord and the holy *penmen* of his story were deeply affected. *Atterbury.*

PE'NNACHED. *adj.* [*pennaché*, Fr.] Is only applied to flowers when the ground of the natural colour of their leaves is radiated and diversified neatly without any confusion. *Trevoux.*

Carefully protect from violent rain your *pennached* tulips, covering them with matrasses. *Evelyn.*

PE'NNANT. *n. s.* [*pennon*, Fr.]
1. A small flag, ensign or colours.
2. A tackle for hoisting things on board. *Ainsworth.*

PE'NNATED. *adj.* [*pennatus*, Latin.]
1. Winged.
2. *Pennated*, amongst botanists, are those leaves of plants as grow directly one against another on the same rib or stalk; as those of ash and walnut-tree. *Quincy.*

PE'NNER. *n. s.* [from *pen.*]
1. A writer.
2. A pencase. *Ains.* So it is called in Scotland.

PENNI'LESS. *adj.* [from *penny.*] Moneyless: poor; wanting money.

PE'NNON. *n. s.* [*pennon*, Fr.] A small flag or colour.

Her yellow locks crisped like golden wire,
About her shoulders weren loosely shed,
And when the wind amongst them did inspire,
They waved like a *pennon* wide dispred. *Fairy Queen.*

Harry sweeps through our land
With *pennons* painted in the blood of Harfleur. *Shakesp.*

High on his pointed lance his *pennon* bore,
His Cretan fight, the conquer'd Minotaur. *Dryden.*

PE'NNY. *n. s.* plural *pence.* [penig, Saxon.]
1. A small coin, of which twelve make a shilling: a penny is the radical denomination from which English coin is numbered, the copper halfpence and farthings being only *nummorum famuli*, a subordinate species of coin.

She sighs and shakes her empty shoes in vain,
No silver *penny* to reward her pain. *Dryden.*

One frugal on his birth-day fears to dine,
Does at a *penny's* cost in herbs repine. *Dryden.*

2. Proverbially. A small sum.

You shall hear
The legions, now in Gallia, sooner landed
In our not fearing Britain, than have tidings
Of any *penny* tribute paid. *Shakespear's Cymbeline.*

We will not lend thee a *penny*. *Shakespeare.*

Because there is a latitude of gain in buying and selling, take not the utmost *penny* that is lawful, for although it be lawful, yet it is not safe. *Taylor's Living Holy.*

3. Money in general.

Pepper and Sabean incense take;
And with post-haste thy running markets make;
Be sure to turn the *penny*. *Dryden.*

It may be a contrivance of some printer, who hath a mind to make a *penny*. *Swift's Miscellanies.*

PE'NNYROYAL, or *pudding grass.* *n. s.* [*pulegium*, Lat.]
Pennyroyal hath a labiated flower consisting of one leaf, whose upper lip or crest is entire, but the lower lip or beard is divided into three parts; out of the flower cup rises the pointal attended by four embryos, which afterwards become so many seeds: to which may be added, that the flowers grow in short thick whorles. *Miller.*

PE'NNYWEIGHT. *n. s.* [*penny* and *weight.*] A weight containing twenty-four grains troy weight.

The Sevil piece of Eight is 1 ¼ *pennyweight* in the pound worse than the English standard, weighs fourteen *pennyweight*, contains thirteen *pennyweight*, twenty-one grains and fifteen mites, of which there are twenty in the grain of sterling silver, and is in value forty-three English pence and eleven hundredths of a penny. *Arbuthnot on Coins.*

PE'NNYWISE. *adj.* [*penny* and *wise.*] One who saves small sums at the hazard of larger; one who is a niggard on improper occasions.

Be not *pennywise*; riches have wings and fly away of themselves. *Bacon.*

PENNYWORTH. *n. s.* [*penny* and *worth.*]
1. As much as is bought for a penny.
2. Any purchase; any thing bought or sold for money.

As for corn it is nothing natural, save only for barley and oats, and some places for rye; and therefore the larger *pennyworths* may be allowed to them. *Spenser on Ireland.*

Pirates may make cheap *penn'worths* of their pillage,
And purchase friends. *Shakespeare's Henry* VI.

You know I say nothing to him, for he hath neither Latin, French nor Italian, and you may come into court, and swear that I have a poor *pennyworth* of the English. *Shakespeare.*

Lucian affirms, that the souls of usurers after their death are translated into the bodies of asses, and there remain certain days for poor men to take their *pennyworths* out of their bones and sides by cudgel and spur. *Peacham.*

Though in purchases of church lands men have usually the cheapest *pennyworths*, yet they have not always the best bargains. *South's Sermons.*

3. Something advantageously bought; a purchase got for less than it is worth.

For fame he pray'd, but let the event declare
He had no mighty *penn'worth* of his pray'r. *Dryden.*

4. A small quantity.

My friendship I distribute in *pennyworths* to those about me and who displease me least. *Swift.*

8

PENSILE. *adj.* [*pensilis*, Latin.]
1. Hanging; suspended.

There are two trepidations; the one manifest and local, as of the bell when it is *pensile*; the other, secret of the minute parts.

This ethereal space,
Yielding to earth and sea the middle place,
Anxious I ask you, how the *pensile* ball
Should never strive to rise, nor never fear to fall. *Prior.*

2. Supported above the ground.

The marble brought, erects the spacious dome,
Or forms the pillars long-extended rows,
On which the planted grove and *pensile* garden grows. *Prior.*

PE'NSILENESS. *n. s.* [from *pensile.*] The state of hanging.

PENSION. *n. s.* [*pension*, Fr.] An allowance made to any one without an equivalent. In England it is generally understood to mean pay given to a state hireling for treason to his country.

A charity bestowed on the education of her young subjects has more merit than a thousand *pensions* to those of a higher fortune. *Addison's Guardian*, N° 105.

He has liv'd with the great without flattery, and been a friend to men in power without *pensions*. *Pope.*

To PE'NSION. *v. a.* [from the noun.] To support by an arbitrary allowance.

One might expect to see medals of France in the highest perfection, when there is a society *pensioned* and set apart for the designing of them. *Addison on Ancient Medals.*

The hero William and the martyr Charles,
One knighted Blackmore, and one *pension'd* Quarles. *Pope.*

PE'NSIONARY. *adj.* [*pensionnaire*, French.] Maintained by pensions.

Scorn his houshold policies,
His silly plots and *pensionary* spies. *Donne.*

They were devoted by *pensionary* obligations to the olive. *Howel's Vocal Forest.*

PE'NSIONER. *n. s.* [from *pension.*]
1. One who is supported by an allowance paid at the will of another; a dependant.

Prices of things necessary for sustentation, grew excessive to the hurt of *pensioners*, soldiers, and all hired servants. *Camd.*

Hovering dreams,
The fickle *pensioners* of Morpheus' train. *Milton.*

The rector is maintained by the perquisites of the curate's office, and therefore is a kind of *pensioner* to him. *Collier.*

2. A slave of state hired by a stipend to obey his master.

In Britain's senate he a seat obtains,
And one more *pensioner* St. Stephen gains. *Pope.*

PE'NSIVE. *adj.* [*pensif*, French; *pensivo*, Italian.]
1. Sorrowfully thoughtful; sorrowful; mournfully serious; melancholy.

Think it still a good work, which they in their *pensive* care for the well bestowing of time account waste. *Hooker.*

Are you at leisure, holy father,—
—My leisure serves me, *pensive* daughter, now. *Shakesp.*

Anxious cares the *pensive* nymph opprest,
And secret passions labour'd in her breast. *Pope.*

2. It is generally and properly used of persons; but *Prior* has applied it to things.

We at the sad approach of death shall know
The truth, which from these *pensive* numbers flow,
That we pursue false joy, and suffer real woe. *Prior.*

PE'NSIVELY. *adv.* [from *pensive.*] With melancholy; sorrowfully; with gloomy seriousness.

So fair a lady did I spy,
On herbs and flowers she walked *pensively*
Mild, but yet love she proudly did forsake. *Spenser.*

PE'NSIVENESS. *n. s.* [from *pensive.*] Melancholy; sorrowfulness; gloomy seriousness.

Concerning the blessings of God, whether they tend unto this life or the life to come, there is great cause why we should delight more in giving thanks than in making requests for them, inasmuch as the one hath *pensiveness* and fear, the other always joy annexed. *Hooker*, *b.* v. *s.* 43.

Would'st thou unlock the door
To cold despairs and gnawing *pensiveness*. *Herbert.*

PENT. part. pass. of *pen.* Shut up.

Cut my lace asunder,
That my *pent* heart may have some scope to beat. *Shakesp.*

The son of Clarence have I *pent* up close. *Shakespeare.*

Pent to linger
But with a grain a day, I would not buy
Their mercy. *Shakespeare's Coriolanus.*

Their armour help'd their harm, crush'd in, and bruis'd
Into their substance *pent*. *Milton.*

The soul pure fire, like ours, of equal force;
But *pent* in flesh, must issue by discourse. *Dryden.*

Pent up in Utica he vainly forms
A poor epitome of Roman greatness. *Addison's Cato.*

PENTACA'PSULAR. *adj.* [πέντε and *capsular.*] Having five cavities.

PE'NTACHORD. *adj.* [πέντε and χορδὴ.] An instrument with five strings.

PE'NTAEDROUS.

PENTAE'DROUS. *adj.* [πέντε and ἕδρα.] Having five sides.

The *pentaedrous* columnar coralloid bodies are composed of plates set lengthways, and passing from the surface to the axis. *Woodward on Fossils.*

PENTAGON. *n. s.* [*pentagon*, Fr. πέντε and γωνία.] A figure with five angles.

I know of that famous piece at Capralora, cast by Baroccio into the form of a *pentagon* with a circle inscribed. *Wotton.*

PENTA'GONAL. *adj.* [from *pentagon.*] Quinquangular; having five angles.

The body being cut transversely, its surface appears like a net made up of *pentagonal* mashes, with a *pentagonal* star in each mash. *Woodward on Fossils.*

PENTA'METER. *n. s.* [*pentametre*, Fr. *pentametrum*, Lat.] A Latin verse of five feet.

Mr. Distich may possibly play some *pentameters* upon us, but he shall be answered in Alexandrines. *Addison.*

PENTA'NGULAR. *adj.* [πέντε and *angular.*] Five cornered.

His thick and bony scales stand in rows, so as to make the flesh almost *pentangular*. *Grew.*

PENTAPE'TALOUS. *adj.* [πέντε and *petala*, Lat.] Having five petals.

PE'NTASPAST. *adj.* [*pentaspaste*, Fr. πέντε and σπάω.] An engine with five pullies. *Dict.*

PENTA'STICK. *n. s.* [πέντε and στίχος.] A composition consisting of five verses.

PE'NTASTYLE. *n. s.* [πέντε and στῦλος.] In architecture, a work in which are five rows of columns. *Dict.*

PE'NTATEUCH. *n. s.* [πέντε and τεῦχος; *pentateuque*, Fr.] The five books of Moses.

The author in the ensuing part of the *pentateuch* makes not unfrequent mention of the angels. *Bentley.*

PE'NTECOST. *n. s.* [πεντηκοστή; *pentacoste*, Fr.] A feast among the Jews.

Pentecost signifies the fiftieth, because this feast was celebrated the fiftieth day after the sixteenth of Nisan, which was the second day of the feast of the passover: the Hebrews call it the feast of weeks, because it was kept seven weeks after the passover: they then offered the first fruits of the wheat harvest, which then was completed: it was instituted to oblige the Israelites to repair to the temple, there to acknowledge the Lord's dominion, and also to render thanks to God for the law he had given them from mount Sinai, on the fiftieth day after their coming out of Egypt. *Calmet.*

'Tis since the nuptial of Lucentio,
Come *pentecost* as quickly as it will
Some five and twenty years. *Shakespeare's Romeo and Juliet.*

PENTECO'STAL. *adj.* [from *pentecost.*] Belonging to Whitsuntide.

I have composed sundry collects, made up out of the church collects with some little variation; as the collects adventual, quadragesimal, paschal or *pentecostal*. *Sanderson.*

PE'NTHOUSE. *n. s.* [*pent*, from *pente*, Fr. and *house.*] A shed hanging out aslope from the main wall.

This is the *penthouse* under which Lorenzo desir'd us to make a stand. *Shakespeare's Merchant of Venice.*

Sleep shall neither night nor day
Hang upon his *penthouse* lid. *Shakespeare.*

The Turks lurking under their *penthouse*, laboured with mattocks to dig up the foundation of the wall. *Knolles.*

A blow was received by riding under a *penthouse*. *Wiseman.*

Those defensive engines, made by the Romans into the form of *penthouses* to cover the assailants from the weapons of the besieged, would he presently batter in pieces with stones and blocks. *Wilkins.*

My *penthouse* eye-brows and my shaggy beard
Offend your sight; but these are manly signs. *Dryden.*

The chill rain
Drops from some *penthouse* on her wretched head. *Rowe.*

PE'NTICE. *n. s.* [*appentir*, French; *pendice*, Italian. It is commonly supposed a corruption of *penthouse*; but perhaps *pentice* is the true word.] A sloping roof.

Climes that fear the falling and lying of much snow, ought to provide more inclining *pentices*. *Wotton.*

PE'NTILE. *n. s.* [*pent* and *tile.*] A tile formed to cover the sloping part of the roof.

Pentiles are thirteen inches long, with a button to hang on the laths; they are hollow and circular. *Moxon.*

PENT *up. part. adj.* [*pent*, from *pen* and *up.*] Shut up.

Close *pentup* guilts
Rive your concealing continents. *Shakesp. K. Lear.*

PENULTIMA. n. s. [Latin.] The last syllable but one.

PENU'MBRA. *n. s.* [*pene* and *umbra*, Latin.] An imperfect shadow.

The breadth of this image answered to the sun's diameter, and was about two inches and the eighth part of an inch, including the *penumbra*. *Newton.*

PENU'RIOUS. *adj.* [from *penuria*, Latin.]

1. Niggardly; sparing; not liberal; sordidly mean.

What more can our *penurious* reason grant
To the large whale or castled elephant, *Prior.*

2. Scant; not plentiful.

Some *penurious* spring by chance appear'd
Scanty of water. *Addison.*

PENU'RIOUSLY. *adv.* [from *penurious.*] Sparingly; not plentifully.

PENU'RIOUSNESS. *n. s.* [from *penurious.*] Niggardliness; parsimony.

If we consider the infinite industry and *penuriousness* of that people, it is no wonder that, notwithstanding they furnish as great taxes as their neighbours, they make a better figure. *Addison on the State of the War.*

PE'NURY. *n. s.* [*penuria*, Lat.] Poverty; indigence.

The *penury* of the ecclesiastical estate. *Hooker.*

Who can perfectly declare
The wondrous cradle of thy infancy?
When thy great mother Venus first thee bare,
Begot of plenty and of *penury*. *Spenser.*

Sometimes am I king;
Then treason makes me wish myself a beggar;
And so I am: then crushing *penury*
Persuades me, I was better when a king;
Then I am king'd again. *Shakesp. Richard III.*

All innocent they were exposed to hardship and *penury*, which, without you, they could never have escaped. *Sprat.*

Let them not still be obstinately blind,
Still to divert the good design'd,
Or with malignant *penury*
To starve the royal virtues of his mind. *Dryden.*

May they not justly to our climes upbraid
Shortness of night, and *penury* of shade. *Prior.*

PE'ONY. *n. s.* [*pæonia*, Latin.]

The *peony* hath a flower composed of several leaves, which are placed orbicularly, and expand in form of a rose, out of whose empalement rises the pointal, which afterwards becomes a fruit, in which several little horns bent downwards are gathered, as it were, into a little head covered with down opening lengthways, containing many globular seeds. *Miller.*

A physician had often tried the *peony* root unseasonably gathered without success; but having gathered it when the decreasing moon passes under Aries and tied the slit root about the necks of his patients, he had freed more than one from epileptical fits. *Boyle.*

PE'OPLE. *n. s.* [*peuple*, Fr. *populus*, Lat.]

1. A nation; these who compose a community.

Prophesy again before many *peoples* and nations and tongues. *Revelations* x. 11.

Ants are a *people* not strong, yet they prepare their meat in summer. *Proverbs* xxx. 25.

What is the city but the *people*?
True the *people* are the city. *Shakesp. Coriolanus.*

2. The vulgar.

The knowing artist may
Judge better than the *people*, but a play
Made for delight,
If you approve it not, has no excuse. *Waller.*

3. The commonalty; not the princes or nobles.

4. Persons of a particular class.

If a man temper his actions to content every combination of *people*, the musick will be the fuller. *Bacon.*

A small red flower in the stubble fields country *people* call the wincopipe. *Bacon.*

5. Men, or persons in general. In this sense, the word *people* is used indefinitely, like *on* in French.

The frogs petitioning for a king, bids *people* have a care of struggling with heaven. *L'Estrange.*

People were tempted to lend by great premiums and large interest. *Swift's Miscellanies.*

Watery liquor will keep an animal from starving by diluting the fluids; for *people* have lived twenty-four days upon nothing but water. *Arbuthnot on Aliments.*

People in adversity should preserve laudable customs. *Clarissa.*

To PEO'PLE. *v. a.* [*peupler*, French.] To stock with inhabitants.

Suppose that Brute, or whosoever else that first *peopled* this island, had arrived upon Thames, and called the island after his name Britannia. *Raleigh's History of the World.*

He would not be alone, who all things can;
But *peopled* Heav'n with angels, earth with man. *Dryden.*

Beauty a monarch is,
Which kingly power magnificently proves
By crouds of slaves, and *peopled* empire loves. *Dryden.*

A *peopl'd* city made a desert place. *Dryden.*

Imperious death directs his ebon lance;
Peoples great Henry's tombs, and leads up Holben's dance. *Prior.*

PE'PASTICKS. *n. s.* [πεπαίνω.] Medicines which are good to help the rawness of the stomach and digest crudities. *Dict.*

PE'PPER. *n. s.* [*piper*, Lat. *poivre*, Fr.]

We have three kinds of *pepper*; the black, the white, and the long, which are three different fruits produced by three distinct plants: black *pepper* is a dried fruit of the size of a vetch and roundish, but rather of a deep brown than a black colour:

colour: with this we are supplied by the Dutch from their East Indian settlements in Java, Malabar and Sumatra, and the plant has the same heat and fiery taste that we find in the *pepper*: white *pepper* is commonly factitious, and prepared from the black by taking off the outer bark, but there is a rarer sort, which is a genuine fruit naturally white: long *pepper* is a fruit gathered while unripe and dried, of an inch or an inch and half in length, and of the thickness of a large goose quill: it much resembles the catkins of some of our trees, and contains several seeds singly in small membranaceous cells, and these seeds are of an acrid, hot and bitterish taste: the whole fruit is of a brownish grey colour and cylindrick in its figure. *Hill.*

Scatter o'er the blooms the pungent dust
Of *pepper*, fatal to the frosty tribe. *Thomson's Spring.*

To Pe'pper. *v. a.* [from the noun.]

1. To sprinkle with pepper.
2. To beat; to mangle with shot or blows.

I have *peppered* two of them; two I have paid, two rogues in buckram suits. *Shakesp. Henry* IV.

Pe'pperbox. *n. s.* [*pepper* and *box.*] A box for holding pepper.

I will not take the leacher; he cannot creep into a halfpenny purse nor into a *pepperbox*. *Shakesp.*

Pe'ppercorn. *n. s.* [*pepper* and *corn.*] Any thing of inconsiderable value.

Our performances, though dues, are like those *peppercorns* which freeholders pay their landlord to acknowledge that they hold all from him. *Boyle.*

Folks from mud-wall'd tenement
Bring landlords *peppercorn* for rent. *Prior.*

Pe'ppermint. *n. s.* [*pepper* and *mint.*] Mint eminently hot.

Pe'pperwort. *n. s.* [*pepper* and *wort.*] A plant.

Pepperwort hath a flower consisting of four leaves, which are placed in form of a cross, from whose cup arises the pistillum, which afterward becomes a spear-shaped fruit, which is divided in the middle by a partition into two cells, which contain many oblong seeds. *Miller.*

Pe'ptick. *adj.* [πεπ]ικός.] What helps digestion. *Ainsf.*

Pera'cute. *n. s.* [*peracutus*, Lat.] Very sharp; very violent.

Malign, continual *peracute* fevers, after most dangerous attacks, suddenly remit of the ardent heat. *Harvey.*

Peradve'nture. *adv.* [*par adventure*, Fr.]

1. Perhaps; may be; by chance.

That wherein they might not be like unto either, was such *peradventure* as had been no whit less unlawful. *Hooker.*

As you return, visit my house; let our old acquaintance be renew'd; *peradventure* I will with you to court. *Shakes.*

What *peradventure* may appear very full to me, may appear very crude and maimed to a stranger. *Digby.*

2. Doubt; question. It is sometimes used as a noun, but not gracefully nor properly.

Though men's persons ought not to be hated, yet without all *peradventure* their practices justly may. *South.*

To PERA'GRATE. *v. a.* [*peragro*, Lat.] To wander over; to ramble through. *Dict.*

Peragra'tion. *n. s.* [from *peragrate.*] The act of passing through any state or space.

A month of *peragration* is the time of the moon's revolution from any part of the zodiac unto the same again, and this containeth but twenty-seven days and eight hours. *Brown.*

The moon has two accounts which are her months or years of revolution; one her periodic month, or month of *peragration*, which chiefly respects her own proper motion or place in the zodiack, by which she like the sun performs her revolution round the zodiack from any one point to the same again. *Holder on Time.*

To PERA'MBULATE. *v. a.* [*perambulo*, Lat.]

1. To walk through.
2. To survey, by passing through.

Persons the lord deputy should nominate to view and *perambulate* Irish territories, and thereupon to divide and limit the same. *Davies on Ireland.*

Perambula'tion. *n. s.* [from *perambulate.*]

1. The act of passing through or wandering over.

The duke looked still for the coming back of the Armada, even when they were wandering and making their *perambulation* of the northern seas. *Bacon.*

2. A travelling survey.

France is a square of five hundred and fifty miles traverse, thronging with such multitudes, that the general calcul, made in the last *perambulation* exceeded eighteen millions. *Howel.*

Pe'rcase, *adv.* [*par* and *case.*] Perchance; perhaps. Not used.

A virtuous man will be virtuous in solitudine, and not only in theatro, though *percase* it will be more strong by glory and fame, as an heat which is doubled by reflexion. *Bacon.*

Pe'rceant. *adj.* [*perçant*, Fr.] Piercing; penetrating.

Wond'rous quick and *perceant* was his spright
As eagle's eyes, that can behold the sun. *Fairy Queen.*

Percei'vable. *adj.* [from *perceive.*] Perceptible; such as falls under perception.

The body, though it really moves, yet not changing *perceivable* distance with some other bodies, as fast as the ideas of our own minds will follow one another, seems to stand still; as the hands of clocks. *Locke.*

That which we perceive when we see figure, as *perceivable* by sight, is nothing but the termination of colour. *Locke.*

Percei'vably. *adv.* [from *perceivable.*] In such a manner as may be be observed or known.

To PERCEI'VE. *v. a.* [*percipio*, Lat.]

1. To discover by some sensible effects.

Consider,
When you above *perceive* me like a crow,
That it is place which lessens and sets off. *Shakesp.*

2. To know; to observe.

Jesus *perceived* in his spirit, that they so reasoned within themselves. *Mark* ii. 8.

His sons come to honour, and he knoweth it not; and they are brought low, but he *perceiveth* it not. *Job* xiv. 21.

'Till we ourselves see it with our own eyes, and *perceive* it by our own understandings, we are still in the dark. *Locke.*

How do they come to know that themselves think, when they themselves do not *perceive* it. *Locke.*

3. To be affected by.

The upper regions of the air *perceive* the collection of the matter of tempests before the air here below. *Bacon.*

Perceptibi'lity. *n. s.* [from *perceptible.*]

1. The state of being an object of the senses or mind; the state of being perceptible.
2. Perception; the power of perceiving.

The illumination is not so bright and fulgent, as to obscure or extinguish all *perceptibility* of the reason. *More.*

PERCE'PTIBLE. *adj.* [*perceptible*, Fr. *perceptus.* Lat.] Such as may be known or observed.

No sound is produced but with a *perceptible* blast of the air, and with some resistance of the air strucken. *Bacon.*

When I think, remember or abstract; these intrinsick operations of my mind are not *perceptible* by my sight, hearing, taste, smell or feeling. *Hale's Origin of Mankind.*

It perceives them immediately, as being immediately objected to and *perceptible* to the sense; as I perceive the sun by my sight. *Hale's Origin of Mankind.*

In the anatomy of the mind, as in that of the body, more good will accrue to mankind by attending to the large, open and *perceptible* parts, than by studying too much finer nerves. *Pope's Essay on Man.*

Perce'ptibly. *adv.* [from *perceptible.*] In such a manner as may be perceived.

The woman decays *perceptibly* every week. *Pope.*

Perce'ption. *n. s.* [*perception*, Fr. *perceptio*, Lat.]

1. The power of perceiving; knowledge; consciousness.

Matter hath no life nor *perception*, and is not conscious of its own existence. *Bentley's Sermons.*

Perception is that act of the mind, or rather a passion or impression, whereby the mind becomes conscious of any thing; as when I feel hunger, thirst, cold or heat. *Watts.*

2. The act of perceiving; observation.
3. Notion; idea.

By the inventors, and their followers that would seem not to come too short of the *perceptions* of the leaders, they are magnified. *Hale's Origin of Mankind.*

4. The state of being affected by something.

Great mountains have a *perception* of the disposition of the air to tempests sooner than the vallies below; and therefore they say in Wales, when certain hills have their night caps on, they mean mischief. *Bacon.*

This experiment discovereth *perception* in plants to move towards that which should comfort them, though at a distance. *Bacon's Natural History.*

PERCE'PTIVE. *adj.* [*perceptus*, Lat.] Having the power of perceiving.

There is a difficulty that pincheth: the soul is awake and sollicited by external motions, for some of them reach the *perceptive* region in the most silent repose and obscurity of night: what is it then that prevents our sensations? *Glanvil.*

Whatever the least real point of the essence of the *perceptive* part of the soul does perceive, every real point of the *perceptive* must perceive at once. *More's Divine Dialogues.*

Percepti'vity. *n. s.* [from *perceptive.*] The power of perception or thinking. *Locke.*

Perch. *n. s.* [*perca*, Lat. *perche*, Fr.]

The *perch* is one of the fishes of prey, that, like the pike and trout, carries his teeth in his mouth, he dare venture to kill and destroy several other kinds of fish: he has a hooked or hog back, which is armed with stiff bristles, and all his skin armed with thick hard scales, and hath two fins on his back: he spawns but once a year, and is held very nutritive. *Walton's Angler.*

Perch. *n. s.* [*pertica*, Lat. *perche*, Fr.]

1. A measure of five yards and a half; a pole.
2. [*perche*, Fr.] Something on which birds roost or sit.

For the narrow *perch* I cannot ride. *Dryden.*

To Perch. *v. n.* [*percher*, Fr. from the noun.] To sit or roost as a bird.

He *percheth* on some branch thereby,
To weather him and his moist wings to dry. *Spenser.*

The

The world is grown so bad,
That wrens make prey, where eagles dare not *perch*. *Shak.*
The morning muses *perch* like birds, and sing
Among his branches. *Crashaw.*

Let owls keep close within the tree, and not *perch* upon the upper boughs. *South's Sermons.*

They wing'd their flight aloft, then stooping low,
Perch'd on the double tree, that bears the golden bough. *Dry.*

Glory like the trembling eagle stood
Perch'd on my beaver: in the Granic flood,
When fortune's self my standard trembling bore,
And the pale fates stood frighted on the shore. *Lee.*

Hosts of birds that wing the liquid air,
Perch'd in the boughs, had nightly lodging there. *Dryden.*

To Perch. *v. a.* To place on a perch.

It would be notoriously perceptible, if you could *perch* yourself as a bird on the top of some high steeple. *More.*

As evening dragon came,
Assailant on the *perched* roosts,
And nests in order rang'd
Of some villatic fowl. *Milton's Agonistes.*

Percha'nce. *adv.* [*per* and *chance.*] Perhaps; peradventure.

How long within this wood intend you stay?—
—*Perchance* till after Theseus' wedding day. *Shakesp.*

Finding him by nature little studious, she chuse rather to endue him with ornaments of youth; as dancing and fencing, not without aim then *perchance* at a courtier's life. *Wotton.*

Only Smithfield ballad *perchance* to embalm the memory of the other. *L'Estrange.*

Pe'rchers. *n. s.* Paris candles used in England in ancient times; also the larger sort of wax candles, which were usually set upon the altar. *Bailey.*

Perci'pient. *adj.* [*percipiens*, Lat.] Perceiving; having the power of perception.

No article of religion hath credibility enough for them; and yet these cautious and quicksighted gentlemen can wink and swallow down this sottish opinion about *percipient* atoms. *Bentley's Sermons.*

Sensation and perception are not inherent in matter as such; for if it were so, every stock or stone would be a *percipient* and rational creature. *Bentley's Sermons.*

Pe'rcipient. *n. s.* One that has the power of perceiving.

The soul is the sole *percipient*, which hath animadversion and sense properly so called, and the body is only the receiver of corporeal impressions. *Glanville's Scept.*

Nothing in the extended *percipient* perceives the whole, but only part. *More's Divine Dialogues.*

Perclose. *n. s.* [*per* and *close.*] Conclusion; last part.

By the *perclose* of the same verse, vagabond is understood for such an one as travelleth in fear of revengement. *Raleigh.*

To Pe'rcolate. *v. a.* [*percolo*, Lat.] To strain.

The evidences of fact are *percolated* through a vast period of ages. *Hale's Origin of Mankind.*

Percola'tion. *n. s.* [from *percolate.*] The act of straining; purification or separation by straining.

Experiments touching the straining and passing of bodies one through another, they call *percolation*. *Bacon.*

Water passing through the veins of the earth is rendered fresh and potable, which it cannot be by any *percolations* we can make, but the saline particles will pass through a tenfold filtre. *Ray on the Creation.*

To Percu'ss. *v. a.* [*percussus*, Lat.] To strike.

Flame *percussed* by air giveth a noise; as in blowing of the fire by bellows; and so likewise flame *percussing* the air strongly *Bacon's Natural History.*

Percu'ssion. *n. s.* [*percussio*, Lat. *percussion*, Fr.]

1. The act of striking; stroke.

With thy grim looks, and
The thunder-like *percussion* of thy sounds,
Thou mad'st thine enemies shake. *Shakesp.*

The *percussion* of the greater quantity of air is produced by the greatness of the body percussing. *Bacon.*

Some note, that the times when the stroke or *percussion* of an envious eye doth most hurt are, when the party envied is beheld in glory. *Bacon's Essays.*

The vibrations or tremors excited in the air by *percussion*, continue a little time to move from the place of *percussion* in concentric spheres to great distances. *Newton's Opticks.*

Marbles taught him *percussion* and the laws of motion, and tops the centrifugal motion. *Pope and Arbuthnot's Scriblerus.*

2. Effect of sound in the ear.

In double rhymes the *percussion* is stronger. *Rymer.*

Percu'tient. *n. s.* [*percutiens*, Latin.] Striking; having the power to strike.

Inequality of sounds is accidental, either from the roughness or obliquity of the passage, or from the doubling of the *percutient*. *Bacon.*

Perdi'tion. *n. s.* [*perditio*, Lat. *perdition*, Fr.]

1. Destruction; ruin; death.

Upon tidings now arrived, importing the meer *perdition* of the Turkish fleet, every man puts himself in triumph. *Shakesp.*

We took ourselves for free men, seeing there was no danger of our utter *perdition*, and lived most joyfully; going abroad, and seeing what was to be seen. *Bacon.*

Quick let us part! *Perdition*'s in thy presence,
And horror dwells about thee! *Addison's Cato.*

2. Loss.

There's no soul lost,
Nay not so much *perdition* as an hair
Betid to any creature in the vessel
Thou saw'st sink. *Shakesp. Tempest.*

3. Eternal death.

As life and death, mercy and wrath, are matters of knowledge, all men's salvation and some men's endless *perdition* are things so opposite, that whoever doth affirm the one, must necessarily deny the other. *Hooker, b. v. s. 49.*

Men once fallen away from undoubted truth, do after wander for ever more in vices unknown, and daily travel towards their eternal *perdition*. *Raleigh's History of the World.*

Pe'rdue. *adv.* [This word, which among us is adverbially taken, comes from the French *perdue*, or forlorn hope: as *perdue* or advanced centinel..] Close; in ambush.

Few minutes he had lain *perdue*,
To guard his desp'rate avenue. *Hudibras.*

Pe'rdulous. *adj.* [from *perdo*, Lat.] Lost; thrown away.

There may be some wandering *perdulous* wishes of known impossibilities; as a man who hath committed an offence, may wish he had not committed it: but to chuse efficaciously and impossibly, is as impossible as an impossibility. *Bramhall.*

Pe'rdurable. *adj.* [*perdurable*, Fr. *perduro*, Lat.] Lasting; long continued. A word not in use, nor accented according to analogy.

Confess me knit to thy deserving with
Cables of *perdurable* toughness. *Shakesp. Othello.*
O *perdurable* shame; let's stab ourselves. *Shakesp.*

Pe'rdurably. *adv.* [from *perdurable.*] Lastingly.

Why would he for the momentary trick,
Be *perdurably* fin'd? *Shakesp. Measure for Measure.*

Perdura'tion. *n. s.* [*perduro*, Lat.] Long continuance. *Ainsw.*

Pe'regal. *adj.* [French.] Equal. Obsolete.

Whilom thou wast *peregal* to the best,
And wont to make the jolly shepherds glad;
With piping and dancing, did pass the rest. *Spenser.*

To Pe'regrinate. *v. n.* [*peregrinus*, Lat.] To travel; to live in foreign countries. *Dict.*

Peregrina'tion. *n. s.* [from *peregrinus*, Lat.] Travel; abode in foreign countries.

It was agreed between them, what account he should give of his *peregrination* abroad. *Bacon's Henry VII.*

That we do not contend to have the earth pass for a paradise, we reckon it only as the land of our *peregrination*, and aspire after a better country. *Bentley's Sermons.*

Pe'regrine. *adj.* [*peregrin*, old Fr. *peregrinus*, Lat.] Foreign; not native; not domestick.

The received opinion, that putrefaction is caused by cold or *peregrine* and preternatural heat, is but nugation. *Bacon.*

To Pere'mpt. *v. a.* [*peremptus*, Lat.] To kill; to crush. A law term.

Nor is it any objection, that the cause of appeal is *perempted* by the desertion of an appeal; because the office of the judge continues after such instance is *perempted*. *Ayliffe.*

Pe'remption. *n. s.* [*peremptio*, Lat. *peremption*, Fr.] Crush; extinction. Law term.

This *peremption* of instance was introduced in favour of the publick, lest suits should otherwise be rendered perpetual. *Ayliffe's Parergon.*

Pere'mptorily. *adv.* [from *peremptory.*] Absolutely; positively; so as to cut off all farther debate.

Norfolk denies them *peremptorily*. *Daniel.*

Not to speak *peremptorily* or conclusively, touching the point of possibility, till they have heard me deduce the means of the execution. *Bacon's Holy War.*

Some organs are so *peremptorily* necessary, that the extinguishment of the spirits doth speedily follow, but yet so as there is an interim. *Bacon's Natural History.*

In all conferences it was insisted *peremptorily*, that the king must yield to what power was required. *Clarendon.*

Some talk of letters before the deluge; but that is a matter of mere conjecture, and nothing can be *peremptorily* determined either the one way or the other. *Woodward.*

Never judge *peremptorily* on first appearances. *Clarissa.*

Pere'mptoriness. *n. s.* [from *peremptory.*] Positiveness; absolute decision; dogmatism.

Peremptoriness is of two sorts; the one a magisterialness in matters of opinion; the other a positiveness in relating matters of fact. *Government of the Tongue.*

Self-conceit and *peremptoriness* in a man's own opinion are not commonly reputed vices. *Tillotson's Sermons.*

Pe'remptory. *adj.* [*peremptorius*, low Lat. *peremptoire*, Fr. from *peremptus*, killed.] Dogmatical; absolute; such as destroys all further expostulation.

As touching the apostle, wherein he was so resolute and *peremptory*, our Lord Jesus Christ made manifest unto him, even

even by intuitive revelation, wherein there was no poſſibility of errour. *Hooker.*

He may have fifty-ſix exceptions *peremptory* againſt the jurors, of which he ſhall ſhew no cauſe. *Spenſer.*

To-morrow be in readineſs to go;
Excuſe it not for I am *peremptory.* *Shakeſpeare.*
Not death himſelf
In mortal fury is half ſo *peremptory,*
As we to keep this city. *Shakeſpear's King John.*

Though the text and the doctrine run *peremptory* and abſolute, whoſoever denies Chriſt, ſhall aſſuredly be denied by him; yet ſtill there is a tacit condition, unleſs repentance intervene. *South's Sermons.*

The more modeſt confeſs, that learning was to give us a fuller diſcovery of our ignorance, and to keep us from being *peremptory* and dogmatical in our determinations. *Collier.*

He would never talk in ſuch a *peremptory* and diſcouraging manner, were he not aſſured that he was able to ſubdue the moſt powerful oppoſition againſt the doctrine which he taught. *Addiſon on the Chriſtian Religion.*

PERE'NNIAL. *adj.* [*perennis*, Latin.]
1. Laſting through the year.

If the quantity were preciſely the ſame in theſe *perennial* fountains, the difficulty would be greater. *Cheyne.*

2. Perpetual; unceaſing.

The matter wherewith theſe *perennial* clouds are raiſed, is the ſea that ſurrounds them. *Harvey.*

PERE'NNITY. *n. ſ.* [from *perennitas*, Lat.] Equality of laſting through all ſeaſons; perpetuity.

That ſprings have their origin from the ſea, and not from rains and vapours, I conclude from the *perennity* of divers ſprings. *Derham's Phyſico-Theology.*

PE'RFECT. *adj.* [*perfectus*, Lat. *parfait*, Fr.]
1. Complete; conſummate; finiſhed; neither defective nor redundant.

We count thoſe things *perfect*, which want nothing requiſite for the end, whereto they were inſtituted. *Hooker.*

2. Fully informed; fully ſkilful.

Within a ken our army lies;
Our men more *perfect* in the uſe of arms,
Our armour all as ſtrong, our cauſe the beſt;
Then reaſon wills our hearts ſhould be as good. *Shakeſp.*
Fair dame! I am not to you known,
Though in your ſtate of honour I am *perfect.* *Shakeſpeare.*

I do not take myſelf to be ſo *perfect* in the privileges of Bohemia, as to handle that part; and will not offer at that I cannot maſter. *Bacon.*

3. Pure; blameleſs; clear; immaculate. This is a ſenſe chiefly theological.

My parts, my title, and my *perfect* ſoul
Shall manifeſt me rightly. *Shakeſp. Othello.*

Thou ſhalt be *perfect* with the Lord thy God. *Deutr.* xviii.

4. Safe; Out of danger.

Thou art *perfect* then, our ſhip hath touch'd upon
The deſerts of Bohemia. *Shakeſpeare's Winter's Tale.*

To PE'RFECT. *v. a.* [*perfectus*, from *perficio*, Latin; *parfaire*, French.]
1. To finiſh; to complete; to conſummate; to bring to its due ſtate.

If we love one another, God dwelleth in us, and his love is *perfected* in us. 1 *John* iv. 12.

Beauty now muſt *perfect* my renown;
With that I govern'd him that rules this iſle. *Waller.*

In ſubſtances reſt not in the ordinary complex idea commonly received, but enquire into the nature and properties of the things themſelves, and thereby *perfect* our ideas of their diſtinct ſpecies. *Locke.*

Endeavour not to ſettle too many habits at once, leſt by variety you confound them, and ſo *perfect* none. *Locke.*

What toil did honeſt Curio take
To get one medal wanting yet,
And *perfect* all his Roman ſet? *Prior.*

2. To make ſkilful; to inſtruct fully.

Her cauſe and yours
I'll *perfect* him withal, and he ſhall bring you
Before the duke. *Shakeſpear's Meaſure for Meaſure.*

PE'RFECTER. [from *perfect.*] One that makes perfect.

This practice was altered; they offered not to Mercury, but to Jupiter the *perfecter.* *Pope's Odyſſey.*

PERFE'CTION. *n. ſ.* [*perfectio*, Lat. *perfection*, Fr.]
1. The ſtate of being perfect.

Man doth ſeek a triple *perfection*; firſt a ſenſual, conſiſting in thoſe things which very life itſelf requireth, either as neceſſary ſupplements or as ornaments thereof; then an intellectual, conſiſting in thoſe things which none underneath man is capable of; laſtly, a ſpiritual and divine, conſiſting in thoſe things whereunto we tend by ſupernatural means here, but cannot here attain. *Hooker, b.* i.

It is a judgment maim'd and moſt imperfect,
That will confeſs *perfection* ſo could err
Againſt all rules of nature. *Shakeſp. Othello.*

True virtue being united to the heavenly grace of faith makes up the higheſt *perfection.* *Milton on Education.*

No human underſtanding being abſolutely ſecured from miſtake by the *perfection* of its own nature, it follows that no man can be infallible but by ſupernatural aſſiſtance. *Tillotſ.*

Many things impoſſible to thought,
Have been by need to full *perfection* brought. *Dryden.*

2. Something that concurs to produce ſupreme excellence.

What tongue can her *perfections* tell,
In whoſe each part all pens may dwell? *Sidney.*
You knot of mouth-friends; ſmoke and lukewarm water
Is your *perfection.* *Shakeſp. Timon of Athens.*

An heroick poem requires, as its laſt *perfection*, the accompliſhment of ſome extraordinary undertaking, which requires more of the active virtue than the ſuffering. *Dryden.*

3. Attribute of God.

If God be infinitely holy, juſt and good, he muſt take delight in thoſe creatures that reſemble him moſt in theſe *perfections.* *Atterbury's Sermons.*

To PERFE'CTIONATE. *v. a.* [*perfectionner*, Fr. from *perfection.*] To make perfect; to advance to perfection. This is a word propoſed by *Dryden*, but not received nor worthy of reception.

Painters and ſculptors, chuſing the moſt elegant natural beauties, *perfectionate* the idea, and advance their art above nature itſelf in her individual productions; the utmoſt maſtery of human performance. *Dryden.*

He has founded an academy for the progreſs and *perfectionating* of painting. *Dryden.*

PERFE'CTIVE. *adj.* [from *perfect.*] Conducing to bring to perfection.

Praiſe and adoration are actions *perfective* of our ſouls. *More.*

Eternal life ſhall not conſiſt in endleſs love; the other faculties ſhall be employed in actions ſuitable to, and *perfective* of their natures. *Ray on the Creation.*

PERFE'CTIVELY. *adv.* [from *perfective.*] In ſuch a manner as brings to perfection.

As virtue is ſeated fundamentally in the intellect, ſo *perfectively* in the fancy; ſo that virtue is the force of reaſon in the conduct of our actions and paſſions to a good end. *Grew.*

PE'RFECTLY. *adv.* [from *perfect.*]
1. In the higheſt degree of excellence.
2. Totally; completely.

Chawing little ſponges dipt in oil, when *perfectly* under water, he could longer ſupport the want of reſpiration. *Boyle.*

Words recal to our thoughts thoſe ideas only which they have been wont to be ſigns of, but cannot introduce any *perfectly* new and unknown ſimple ideas. *Locke.*

3. Exactly; accurately.

We know bodies and their properties moſt *perfectly.* *Locke.*

PE'RFECTNESS. *n. ſ.* [from *perfect.*]
1. Completeneſs.
2. Goodneſs; virtue. A ſcriptural word.

Put on charity, which is the bond of *perfectneſs.* *Col.* iii. 14.

3. Skill.

Is this your *perfectneſs?* *Shakeſp.*

PERFI'DIOUS. *adj.* [*perfidus*, Lat. *perfide*, Fr.] Treacherous; falſe to truſt; guilty of violated faith.

Tell me, *perfidious*, was it fit
To make my cream a perquiſite,
And ſteal to mend your wages. *Widow and Cat.*

PERFI'DIOUSLY. *adv.* [from *perfidious.*] Treacherouſly; by breach of faith.

Perfidiouſly
He has betray'd your buſineſs, and given up
For certain drops of ſalt, your city Rome. *Shakeſp.*
They eat *perfidiouſly* their words. *Hudibras.*

Can he not deliver us poſſeſſion of ſuch places as would put him in a worſe condition, whenever he ſhould *perfidiouſly* renew the war? *Swift's Miſcellanies.*

PERFI'DIOUSNESS. *n. ſ.* [from *perfidious.*] The quality of being perfidious.

Some things have a natural deformity in them; as perjury, *perfidiouſneſs* and ingratitude. *Tillotſon's Sermons.*

PE'RFIDY. *n. ſ.* [*perfidia*, Lat. *perfidie*, Fr.] Treachery; want of faith; breach of faith.

PE'RFLABLE. *adj.* [from *perflo*, Lat.] Having the wind driven through.

To PERFLATE. *v. a.* [*perflo*, Lat.] To blow through.

If Eaſtern winds did *perflate* our climates more frequently, they would clarify and refreſh our air. *Harvey.*

The firſt conſideration in building of cities, is to make them open, airy and well *perflated.* *Arbuthnot on Air.*

PERFLA'TION. *n. ſ.* [from *perflate.*] The act of blowing through.

Miners, by *perflations* with large bellows, give motion to the air, which ventilates and cools the mines. *Woodward.*

To PE'RFORATE. *v. a.* [*perforo*, Lat.] To pierce with a tool; to bore.

Draw the bough of a low fruit tree newly budded without twiſting, into an earthern pot *perforate* at the bottom, and then cover the pot with earth, it will yield a very large fruit. *Bacon's Natural Hiſtory.*

A *perforated* bladder does not ſwell. *Boyle.*

The labour'd chyle pervades the pores,
In all the arterial *perforated* ſhores. *Blackmore.*

The aperture was limited by an opaque circle placed between the eye-glaſs and the eye, and *perforated* in the middle with a little round hole for the rays to paſs through to the eye. *Newton's Opticks.*

Worms *perforate* the guts. *Arbuthnot on Diet.*

PERFORA'TION. *n. ſ.* [from *perforate.*]

1. The act of piercing or boring.

The likelieſt way is the *perforation* of the body of the tree in ſeveral places one above another, and the filling of the holes. *Bacon.*

The induſtrious *perforation* of the tendons of the ſecond joints of fingers and toes, and the drawing the tendons of the third joints through them. *More's Divine Dialogues.*

2. Hole; place bored.

That the nipples ſhould be made ſpongy, and with ſuch *perforations* as to admit paſſage to the milk, are arguments of providence. *Ray on the Creation.*

PERFORA'TOR. *n. ſ.* [from *perforate.*] The inſtrument of boring.

The patient placed in a convenient chair, dipping the trocar in oil, ſtab it ſuddenly through the teguments, and withdrawing the *perforator*, leave the waters to empty by the canula. *Sharp's Surgery.*

PERFO'RCE. *adv.* [*per* and *force.*] By violence; violently.

Guyon to him leaping, ſtaid
His hand, that trembled as one terrifyd;
And though himſelf were at the ſight diſmayd,
Yet him *perforce* reſtrain'd. *Fairy Queen.*

Jealous Oberon would have the child,
But ſhe *perforce* withholds the loved boy. *Shakeſp.*

She amaz'd, her cheeks
All trembling and ariſing, full of ſpots,
And pale with death at hand, *perforce* ſhe breaks
Into the inmoſt rooms. *Peacham on Poetry.*

To PERFO'RM. *v. a.* [*performare*, Italian.] To execute; to do; to diſcharge; to atchieve an undertaking; to accompliſh.

All three ſet among the foremoſt ranks of fame for great minds to attempt, and great force to *perform* what they did attempt. *Sidney, b.* ii.

Haſt thou, ſpirit,
Perform'd to point the tempeſt that I bad thee? *Shakeſp.*

What cannot you and I *perform* upon
Th' unguarded Duncan? *Shakeſp. Macbeth.*

I will cry unto God that *performeth* all things for me. *Pſalms* lvii. 2.

Let all things be *performed* after the law of God diligently. 1 *Eſdras* viii. 21.

Thou, my love,
Perform his fun'rals with paternal care. *Dryden.*

You *perform* her office in the ſphere,
Born of her blood, and make a new Platonick year. *Dryd.*

To PERFO'RM. *v. n.* To ſucceed in an attempt.

When a poet has *performed* admirably in ſeveral illuſtrious places, we ſometimes alſo admire his very errors. *Watts.*

PERFO'RMABLE. *adj.* [from *perform.*] Practicable; ſuch as may be done.

Men forget the relations of hiſtory, affirming that elephants have no joints, whereas their actions are not *performable* without them. *Brown's Vulgar Errours.*

PERFO'RMANCE. *n. ſ.* [from *perform.*]

1. Completion of ſomething deſigned; execution of ſomething promiſed.

His promiſes were, as he then was, mighty;
But his *performance*, as he now is, nothing. *Shakeſp.*

Promiſing is the very air o' th' time; it opens the eyes of expectation: *performance* is ever the duller for his act, and but in the plainer kind of people, the deed is quite out of uſe. *Shakeſp. Timon of Athens.*

Perform the doing of it; that as there was a readineſs to will, ſo there may be a *performance.* 2 *Cor.* viii. 11.

The only means to make him ſucceſsful in the *performance* of theſe great works, was to be above contempt. *South.*

2. Compoſition; work.

In the good poems of other men, I can only be ſure, that 'tis the hand of a good maſter; but in your *performances* 'tis ſcarcely poſſible for me to be deceived. *Dryden.*

Few of our comic *performances* give good examples. *Clariſ.*

3. Action; ſomething done.

In this ſlumbry agitation, beſides her walking and other actual *performances*, what have you heard her ſay? *Shakeſp.*

PERFO'RMER. *n. ſ.* [from *perform.*]

1. One that performs any thing.

The merit of ſervice is ſeldom attributed to the true and exact *performer.* *Shakeſp.*

2. It is generally applied to one that makes a publick exhibition of his ſkill.

To PERFRI'CATE. *v. n.* [*perfrico*, Lat.] To rub over. *Dict.*

PERFU'MATORY. *adj.* [from *perfume.*] That which perfumes.

PERFU'ME. *n. ſ.* [*parfume*, Fr.]

1. Strong odour of ſweetneſs uſed to give ſcents to other things.

Pomanders and knots of powders for drying rheums are not ſo ſtrong as *perfumes*; you may have them continually in your hand, whereas *perfumes* you can take but at times. *Bacon.*

Perfumes, though groſs bodies that may be ſenſibly waſted, yet fill the air, ſo that we can put our noſe in no part of the room where a *perfume* is burned, but we ſmell it. *Digby.*

2. Sweet odour; fragrance.

No rich *perfumes* refreſh the fruitful field,
Nor fragrant herbs their native incenſe yield. *Pope.*

To PERFU'ME. *v. a.* [from the noun.] To ſcent; to impregnate with ſweet ſcent.

Your papers
Let me have them very well *perfum'd*,
For ſhe is ſweeter than perfume itſelf
To whom they go. *Shakeſpeare's Taming of the Shrew.*

Why rather, ſleep, lieſt thou in ſmoky cribs,
And huſht with buzzing night-flies to thy ſlumber,
Than in the *perfum'd* chambers of the great,
Under the canopies of coſtly ſtate,
And lull'd with ſounds of ſweeteſt melody? *Shakeſp.*

Then will I raiſe aloft the milk-white roſe,
With whoſe ſweet ſmell the air ſhall be *perfum'd.* *Shakeſp.*

The diſtilled water of wild poppy, mingled at half with roſe water, take with ſome mixture of a few cloves in a *perfuming* pan. *Bacon's Natural Hiſtory.*

Smells adhere to hard bodies; as in *perfuming* of gloves, which ſheweth them corporeal. *Bacon's Nat. Hiſt.*

The pains ſhe takes are vainly meant,
To hide her amorous heart,
'Tis like *perfuming* an ill ſcent,
The ſmell's too ſtrong for art. *Granville.*

See ſpicy clouds from lowly Sharon riſe,
And Carmel's flow'ry top *perfumes* the ſkies! *Pope.*

PERFU'MER. *n. ſ.* [from *perfume.*] One whoſe trade is to ſell things made to gratify the ſcent.

A moſs the *perfumers* have out of apple trees, that hath an excellent ſcent. *Bacon's Natural Hiſtory.*

Firſt iſſued from *perfumers* ſhops
A croud of faſhionable fops. *Swift.*

PERFU'NCTORILY. *adv.* [*perfunctoriè*, Lat.] Careleſly; negligently.

His majeſty caſting his eye *perfunctorily* upon it, and believing it had been drawn by mature advice, no ſooner received it, than he delivered it to the lord-keeper. *Clarendon.*

Whereas all logic is reducible to the four principal operations of the mind, the two firſt of theſe have been handled by Ariſtotle very *perfunctorily*; of the fourth he has ſaid nothing at all. *Baker's Reflection on Learning.*

PERFU'NCTORY. *adj.* [*perfunctoriè*, Lat.] Slight; careleſs; negligent.

A tranſient and *perfunctory* examination of things leads men into conſiderable miſtakes, which a more correct and rigorous ſcrutiny would have detected. *Woodward.*

To PERFU'SE. *v. a.* [*perfuſus*, Lat.] To tincture; to overſpread.

Theſe dregs immediately *perfuſe* the blood with melancholy, and cauſe obſtructions. *Harvey on Conſumptions.*

PERHA'PS. *adv.* [*per* and *hap.*] Peradventure; it may be.

Perhaps the good old man that kiſs'd his ſon,
And left a bleſſing on his head,
His arms about him ſpread,
Hopes yet to ſee him ere his glaſs be run. *Flatman.*

Somewhat excellent may be invented, *perhaps* more excellent than the firſt deſign, though Virgil muſt be ſtill excepted, when that *perhaps* takes place. *Dryden.*

His thoughts inſpir'd his tongue,
And all his ſoul receiv'd a real love.
Perhaps new graces darted from her eyes,
Perhaps ſoft pity charm'd his yielding ſoul,
Perhaps her love, *perhaps* her kingdom charm'd him. *Smith.*

PE'RIAPT. *n. ſ.* [περιάπτω.] Amulet; charm worn as preſervatives againſt diſeaſes or miſchief. *Hanmer.*

The regent conquers, and the Frenchmen fly:
Now help, ye charming ſpells and *periapts.* *Shakeſpeare.*

PERI'CARDIUM. *n. ſ.* [περὶ and καρδία; *pericarde*, Fr.]

The *pericardium* is a thin membrane of a conick figure that reſembles a purſe, and contains the heart in its cavity: its baſis is pierced in five places, for the paſſage of the veſſels which enter and come out of the heart: the uſe of the *pericardium* is to contain a ſmall quantity of clear water, which is ſeparated by ſmall glands in it, that the ſurface of the heart may not grow dry by its continual motion. *Quincy.*

PERICA'RPIUM. *n. ſ.* [*pericarpe*, Fr.] In botany, a pelli[...] or thin membrane encompaſſing the fruit or grain of a plan[t], that part of a fruit that envelops the ſeed.

Beſides this uſe of the pulp or *pericarpium* for the gua[rd of] the ſeed, it ſerves alſo for the ſuſtenance of animals.

PERICLITA'TION. *n. ſ.* [from *periclitor*, Lat. *pericliter*, Fr.]

1. The ſtate of being in danger.

2. Trial; experiment.

PERICRA'NIUM. *n. s.* [from περὶ and *cranium*; *pericrane*, Fr.]

The *pericranium* is the membrane that covers the skull: it is a very thin and nervous membrane of an exquisite sense, such as covers immediately not only the cranium, but all the bones of the body, except the teeth; for which reason it is also called the periosteum. *Quincy.*

Having divided the *pericranium*, I saw a fissure running the whole length of the wound. *Wiseman's Surgery.*

PERI'CULOUS. *adj.* [*periculosus*, Lat.] Dangerous; jeopardous; hazardous. A word not in use.

As the moon every seventh day arriveth unto a contrary sign, so Saturn, which remaineth about as many years in one sign, and holdeth the same consideration in years as the moon in days, doth cause these *periculous* periods. *Brown.*

PERIE'RGY. *n. s.* [περὶ and ἔργον.] Needless caution in an operation; unnecessary diligence.

PERIGE'E. } *n. s.* [περὶ and γῆ; *perigée*, Fr.] Is a point in
PERIGE'UM. } the heavens, wherein a planet is said to be in its nearest distance possible from the earth. *Harris.*

By the proportion of its motion, it was at the creation, at the beginning of Aries, and the *perigeum* or nearest point in Libra. *Brown's Vulgar Errours.*

PERIHE'LIUM. *n. s.* [περὶ and ἥλιος; *perihelie*, Fr.] Is that point of a planet's orbit, wherein it is nearest the sun. *Harris.*

Sir Isaac Newton has made it probable, that the comet, which appeared in 1680, by approaching to the sun in its *perihelium*, acquired such a degree of heat, as to be 50000 years a cooling. *Cheyne's Philosophical Principles.*

PE'RIL. *n. s.* [*peril*, Fr. *perikel*, Dutch; *periculum*, Lat.]

1. Danger; hazard; jeopardy.

Dear Pyrocles, be liberal unto me of those things, which have made you indeed precious to the world, and now doubt not to tell of your *perils*. *Sidney, b.* ii.

How many *perils* do infold
The righteous man to make him daily fall. *Fairy Queen.*

In the act what *perils* shall we find,
If either place, or time, or other course,
Cause us to alter th' order now assign'd. *Daniel.*

The love and pious duty which you pay,
Have pass'd the *perils* of so hard a way. *Dryden.*

Strong, healthy and young people are more in *peril* by pestilential fevers, than the weak and old. *Arbuthnot.*

2. Denunciation; danger denounced.

I told her,
On your displeasure's *peril*,
She should not visit you. *Shakesp. Winter's Tale.*

PE'RILOUS. *adj.* [*perileux*, Fr. from *peril.*]

1. Dangerous; hazardous; full of danger.

Alterations in the service of God, for that they impair the credit of religion, are therefore *perilous* in common-weals, which have no continuance longer than religion hath all reverence done unto it. *Hooker, b.* v. *s.* 2.

Her guard is chastity,
She that has that is clad in compleat steel,
And like a quiver'd nymph with arrows keen
May trace huge forests and unharbour'd heaths,
Infamous hills and sandy *perilous* wilds. *Milton.*

Dictate propitious to my duteous ear,
What arts can captivate the changeful seer:
For *perilous* th' assay, unheard the toil
T' elude the prescience of a God by guile. *Pope.*

Into the *perilous* flood
Bear fearless. *Thomson.*

2. It is used by way of emphasis, or ludicrous exaggeration of any thing bad.

Thus was th' accomplish'd squire endu'd
With gifts and knowledge *per'lous* shrewd. *Hudibras.*

3. Smart; witty. In this sense it is, I think, only applied to children, and probably obtained its signification from the notion, that children eminent for wit, do not live; a witty boy was therefore a *perilous* boy, or a boy in danger. It is vulgarly *parlous*.

'Tis a *per'lous* boy,
Bold, quick, ingenious, forward, capable;
He's all the mother's from the top to toe. *Shakesp.*

PE'RILOUSLY. *adv.* [from *perilous.*] Dangerously.

PE'RILOUSNESS. *n. s.* [from *perilous.*] Dangerousness.

PERI'METER. *n. s.* [περὶ and μετρέω; *perimetre*, Fr.] The compass or sum of all the sides which bound any figure of what kind soever, whether rectilinear or mixed.

By compressing the glasses still more, the diameter of this ring would increase, and the breadth of its orbit or *perimeter* decrease, until another new colour emerged in the centre of the last. *Newton's Opticks.*

PE'RIOD. *n. s.* [*periode*, Fr. περίοδος.]

1. A circuit.

2. Time in which any thing is performed, so as to begin again in the same manner.

Tell these, that the sun is fixed in the centre, that the earth with all the planets roll round the sun in their several *periods*: they cannot admit a syllable of this new doctrine. *Watts.*

3. A stated number of years; a round of time, at the end of which the things comprised within the calculation shall return to the state in which they were at beginning.

A cycle or *period* is an account of years that has a beginning and end too, and then begins again as often as it ends. *Holder on Time.*

We stile a lesser space a cycle, and a greater by the name of *period*; and you may not improperly call the beginning of a large *period* the epocha thereof. *Holder on Time.*

4. The end or conclusion.

If my death might make this island happy,
And prove the *period* of their tyranny,
I would expend it with all willingness;
But mine is made the prologue to their play. *Shakesp.*

There is nothing so secret that shall not be brought to light within the compass of our world; whatsoever concerns this sublunary world in the whole extent of its duration, from the chaos to the last *period*. *Burnet's Theory of the Earth.*

What anxious moments pass between
The birth of plots and their last fatal *periods*.
Oh! 'tis a dreadful interval of time. *Addison.*

5. The state at which any thing terminates.

Beauty's empires, like to greater states,
Have certain *periods* set, and hidden fates. *Suckling.*

Light-conserving stones must be set in the sun before they retain light, and the light will appear greater or lesser, until they come to their utmost *period*. *Digby.*

6. Length of duration.

Some experiment would be made how by art to make plants more lasting than their ordinary *period*; as to make a stalk of wheat last a whole year. *Bacon's Natural History.*

7. A complete sentence from one full stop to another.

Periods are beautiful, when they are not too long: for so they have their strength too as in a pike or javelin. *B. Johns.*

Is this the confidence you gave me,
Lean on it safely, not a *period*
Shall be unsaid for me. *Milton.*

Syllogism is made use of to discover a fallacy, cunningly wrapt up in a smooth *period*. *Locke.*

For the assistance of weak memories, the first words of every *period* in every page may be written in distinct colours. *Watts's Improvement of the Mind.*

From the tongue
Th' unfinish'd *period* falls. *Thomson's Spring.*

To PE'RIOD. *v. a.* [from the noun.] To put an end to. A bad word.

Your letter he desires
To those have shut him up, which failing to him,
Periods his comfort. *Shakesp. Timon of Athens.*

PERIO'DICK. } *adj.* [*periodique*, Fr. from *period.*]
PERIO'DICAL. }

1. Circular; making a circuit; making a revolution.

Was the earth's *periodick* motion always in the same plane with that of the diurnal, we should miss of those kindly increases of day and night. *Derham.*

Four moons perpetually roll round the planet Jupiter, and are carried along with him in his *periodical* circuit round the sun. *Watts's Improvement of the Mind.*

2. Happening by revolution at some stated time.

Astrological undertakers would raise men out of some slimy soil, impregnated with the influence of the stars upon some remarkable and *periodical* conjunctions. *Bentley.*

3. Regular; performing some action at stated times.

The confusion of mountains and hollows furnished me with a probable reason for those *periodical* fountains in Switzerland, which flow only at such particular hours of the day. *Addison.*

4. Relating to periods or revolutions.

It is implicitly denied by Aristotle in his politicks, in that discourse against Plato, who measured the vicissitude and mutation of states by a *periodical* fatality of number. *Brown.*

PERIO'DICALLY. *adv.* [from *periodical.*] At stated periods.

The three tides ought to be understood of the space of the night and day, and then there will be a regular flux and reflux thrice in that time every eight hours *periodically*. *Broome.*

PERI'OSTEUM. *n. s.* [περὶ and ὀςέον; *perioste*, Fr.]

All the bones are covered with a very sensible membrane, called the *periosteum*. *Cheyne's Philosophical Principles.*

PERI'PHERY. *n. s.* [περὶ and φέρω; *peripherie*, Fr.] Circumference.

Neither is this sole vital faculty sufficient to exterminate noxious humours to the *periphery* or outward parts. *Harvey.*

To PERI'PHRASE. *v. a.* [*periphraser*, Fr.] To express one word by many; to express by circumlocution.

PERI'PHRASIS. *n. s.* [περίφρασις; *periphrase*, Fr.]. Circumlocution; use of many words to express the sense of one: as, for *death*, we may say, *the loss of life*.

They make the gates of Thebes and the mouths of this river a constant *periphrasis* for this number seven. *Brown.*

She contains all bliss,
And makes the world but her *periphrasis*. *Cleaveland.*

They shew their learning uselesly, and make a long *periphrasis* on every word of the book they explain. *Watts.*

The *periphrases* and circumlocutions, by which Homer expresses the single act of dying, have supplied succeeding poets with all their manners of phrasing it. *Pope*

PERIPHRA'STICAL. *adj.* [from *periphrasis.*] Circumlocutory; expressing the sense of one word in many.

PERIPNEU'MONY. } *n. s.* [περὶ and πνεύμων; *peripneumonie,* PERIPNEUMO'NIA. } Fr.] An inflammation of the lungs.

Lungs oft imbibing phlegmatick and melancholick humours, are now and then deprehended schirrous, by dissipation of the subtiler parts, and lapidification of the grosser that remain, or may be left indurated, through the gross reliques of *peripneumonia* or inflammation of the lungs. *Harvey.*

A *peripneumony* is the last fatal symptom of every disease; for no body dies without a stagnation of the blood in the lungs, which is the total extinction of breath. *Arbuthnot.*

To PE'RISH. *v. n.* [*perir,* Fr. *pereo,* Lat.]

1. To die; to be destroyed; to be lost; to come to nothing.

I burn, I pine, I *perish,*
If I atchieve not this young modest girl. *Shakesp.*

If I have seen any *perish* for want of cloathing, then let mine arm fall from my shoulder-blade. *Job* xxxi. 29.

He keepeth back his soul from the pit, and his life from *perishing* by the sword. *Job* xxxiii. 18.

They *perish* quickly from off the good land. *Deut.* xi. 18.

I *perish* with hunger. *Luke* xv. 17.

The sick, when their case comes to be thought desperate, are carried out and laid on the earth to *perish* without assistance or pity. *Locke.*

Characters drawn on dust, that the first breath of wind effaces, are altogether as useful as the thoughts of a soul that *perish* in thinking. *Locke.*

Exposing their children, and leaving them in the fields to *perish* by want, has been the practice. *Locke.*

Still when the lust of tyrant pow'r succeeds,
Some Athens *perishes,* or some Tully bleeds. *Pope.*

In the Iliad, the anger of Achilles had caused the death of so many Grecians; and in the Odyssey, the subjects *perished* through their own fault. *Pope.*

2. To be in a perpetual state of decay.

Duration, and time which is a part of it, is the idea we have of *perishing* distance, of which no two parts exist together, but follow in succession; as expansion is the idea of lasting distance, all whose parts exist together. *Locke.*

3. To be lost eternally.

These, as natural brute beasts made to be destroyed, speak evil of the things they understand not, and shall utterly *perish.* 2 *Peter* ii. 12.

O suffer me not to *perish* in my sins, Lord carest thou not that I *perish,* who wilt that all should be saved, and that none should *perish.* *Moreton's Daily Exercise.*

To PE'RISH. *v. a.* To destroy; to decay. Not in use.

The splitting rocks cow'r'd in the sinking sands,
And would not dash me with their ragged sides;
Because thy flinty heart, more hard than they,
Might in thy palace *perish* Margaret. *Shakesp. Henry* VI.

Rise, prepar'd in black, to mourn thy *perish'd* lord. *Dryden.*

He was so reserved, that he would impart his secrets to nobody; whereupon this closeness did a little *perish* his understandings. *Collier on Friendship.*

Familiar now with grief your ears refrain,
And in the publick woe forget your own,
You weep not for a *perish'd* lord alone. *Pope.*

PE'RISHABLE. *adj.* [from *perish.*] Liable to perish; subject to decay; of short duration.

We derogate from his eternal power to ascribe to them the same dominion over our immortal souls, which they have over all bodily substances and *perishable* natures. *Raleigh.*

To these purposes nothing can so much contribute as medals of undoubted authority not *perishable* by time, nor confined to any certain place. *Addison.*

It is princes greatest present felicity to reign in their subjects hearts; but these are too *perishable* to preserve their memories, which can only be done by the pens of faithful historians. *Swift.*

Human nature could not sustain the reflection of having all its schemes and expectations to determine with this frail and *perishable* composition of flesh and blood. *Rogers.*

Thrice has he seen the *perishable* kind
Of men decay. *Pope's Odyssey.*

PE'RISHABLENESS. *n. s.* [from *perishable.*] Liableness to be destroyed; liableness to decay.

Suppose an island separate from all commerce, but having nothing because of its commoness and *perishableness,* fit to supply the place of money; what reason could any have to enlarge his possessions beyond the use of his family. *Locke.*

PERISTA'LTICK. *adj.* [περιςέλλω; *peristaltique,* Fr.]

Peristaltick motion is that vermicular motion of the guts, which is made by the contraction of the spiral fibres, whereby the excrements are pressed downwards and voided. *Quincy.*

The *peristaltick* motion of the guts, and the continual expression of the fluids, will not suffer the least matter to be applied to one point the least instant. *Arbuthnot.*

PERISTE'RION. *n. s.* The herb vervain. *Dict.*

PERISTY'LE. *n. s.* [*peristile,* Fr.] A circular range of pillars.

The Villa Gordiana had a *peristyle* of two hundred pillars. *Arbuthnot on Coins.*

PE'RISYSTOLE. *n. s.* [περὶ and ςυςολή.] The pause or interval betwixt the two motions of the heart or pulse; namely, that of the systole or contraction of the heart, and that of diastole or dilatation. *Dict.*

PERITONE'UM. *n. s.* [περιτόναιον; *peritoine,* Fr.] This lies immediately under the muscles of the lower belly, and is a thin and soft membrane, which encloses all the bowels contained in the lower belly, covering all the inside of its cavity. *Dict.*

Wounds penetrating into the belly, are such as reach no farther inward than to the *peritoneum.* *Wiseman.*

PE'RJURE. *n. s.* [*perjurus,* Lat.] A perjured or forsworn person. A word not in use.

Hide thee, thou bloody hand,
Thou *perjure,* thou simular of virtue,
Thou art incestuous. *Shakesp. King Lear.*

To PE'RJURE. *v. a.* [*perjuro,* Lat.] To forswear; to taint with perjury. It is used with the reciprocal pronoun.

Who should be trusted now, when the right hand
Is *perjur'd* to the bosom. *Shakesp.*

The law is not made for a righteous man, but for the lawless and disobedient, for *perjured* persons. 1 *Tim.* i. 10.

PE'RJURER. *n. s.* [from *perjure.*] One that swears falsely.

The common oath of the Scythians was by the sword and fire; for that they accounted those two special divine powers, which should work vengeance on the *perjurers.* *Spenser.*

PERJU'RY. *n. s.* [*perjurium,* Lat.] False oath.

My great father-in-law, renowned Warwick,
Cried aloud —— What scourge for *perjury*
Can this dark monarchy afford false Clarence,
And so he vanish'd. *Shakesp. Richard* III.

PE'RIWIG. *n. s.* [*perruque,* Fr.] Adscititious hair; hair not natural, worn by way of ornament or concealment of baldness.

Her hair is auburn, mine is perfect yellow;
If that be all the difference in his love,
I'll get me such a colour'd *periwig.* *Shakesp.*

It offends me to hear a robusteous *periwig*-pated fellow tear a passion to tatters, to split the ears of the groundlings. *Shakespeare.*

The sun's
Dishevel'd beams and scatter'd fires
Serve but for ladies *periwigs* and tires
In lovers sonnets. *Donne.*

Madam time, be ever bald,
I'll not thy *periwig* be call'd. *Cleaveland.*

For vailing of their visages his highness and the marquis bought each a *periwig,* somewhat to overshadow their foreheads. *Wotton.*

They used false hair or *periwigs.* *Arbuthnot on Coins.*

From her own head Megara takes
A *periwig* of twisted snakes,
Which in the nicest fashion curl'd,
Like toupets. *Swift's Miscellanies.*

To PE'RIWIG. *v. a.* [from the noun.] To dress in false hair.

Now when the winter's keener breath began
To crystallize the Baltick ocean,
To glaze the lakes, to bridle up the floods,
And *periwig* with snow the bald-pate woods. *Sylvester.*

Near the door an entrance gapes,
Crouded round with antick shapes,
Discord *periwig'd* with snakes,
See the dreadful strides she takes. *Swift's Miscellanies.*

PE'RIWINKLE. *n. s.*

1. A small shell fish; a kind of fish snail.

Thetis is represented by a lady of a brownish complexion, her hair disheveled about her shoulders, upon her head a coronet of *periwinkle* and escalop shells. *Peacham.*

2. A plant.

The *periwinkle* hath a flower cup, consisting of one leaf, that is divided into five long narrow segments: the flower also consists of one leaf, which expands in form of a salver, and is cut into five broad segments: the pointal, which arises from the center of the flower cup, becomes a fruit composed of two husks or pods, which contain oblong, cylindrical, furrowed seeds; to which may be added, that this plant shoots out many long creeping branches that strike out roots at their joints. *Miller.*

There are in use, for the prevention of the cramp, bands of green *periwinkle* tied about the calf of the leg. *Bacon.*

The common simples with us are comfry, bugle, ladies mantle, and *periwinkle.* *Wiseman's Surgery.*

To Perk. *v. n.* [from *perch*, *Skinner.*] To hold up the head with an affected briskness.

If you think it a disgrace,
That Edward's miss thus *perks* it in your face,
To see a piece of failing flesh and blood,
Let the modest matrons of the town
Come here in crouds, and stare the strumpet down. *Pope.*

To Perk. *v. a.* To dress; to prank.

'Tis better to be lowly born,
And range with humble livers in content,
Than to be *perk'd* up in a glist'ring grief,
And wear a golden sorrow. *Shakesp. Henry* VIII.

Perk. *adj.* Pert; brisk; airy. Obsolete.

My ragged ronts
Wont in the wind, and wag their wriggle tails,
Peark as a peacock, but nought avails. *Spenser.*

Pe'rlous. *adj.* [from *perilous.*] Dangerous; full of hazard.

A *perlous* passage lies,
Where many maremaids haunt, making false melodies. *Spenser's Fairy Queen.*

Late he far'd
In Phædria's fleet bark over the *perlous* shard. *Fa. Queen.*

Pe'rmagy. *n. s.* A little Turkish boot. *Dict.*

Pe'rmanence. } *n. s.* [from *permanent.*] Duration; consistency; continuance in the same state; lastingness.
Pe'rmanency. }

Salt, they say, is the basis of solidity and *permanency* in compound bodies, without which the other four elements might be variously blended together, but would remain incompacted. *Boyle.*

Shall I dispute whether there be any such material being that hath such a *permanence* or fixedness in being. *Hale.*

From the *permanency* and immutability of nature hitherto, they argued its *permanency* and immutability for the future. *Burnet's Theory of the Earth.*

Such a punctum to our conceptions is almost equivalent to *permanency* and rest. *Bentley.*

PE'RMANENT. *adj.* [*permanent*, Fr. *permanens*, Lat.] Durable; not decaying; unchanged.

If the authority of the maker do prove unchangeableness in the laws which God hath made, then must all laws which he hath made be necessarily forever *permanent*, though they be but of circumstance only. *Hooker. b.* iii. *s.* 10.

That eternal duration should be at once, is utterly unconceivable, and that one *permanent* instant should be commensurate or rather equal to all successions of ages. *More.*

Pure and unchang'd, and needing no defence
From sins, as did my frailer innocence;
Their joy sincere, and with no more sorrow mixt,
Eternity stands *permanent* and fixt. *Dryden.*

Pe'rmanently. *adv.* [from *permanent.*] Durably; lastingly.

It does, like a compact or consistent body, deny to mingle *permanently* with the contiguous liquor. *Boyle.*

Perma'nsion. *n. s.* [from *permaneo*, Lat.] Continuance.

Although we allow that hares may exchange their sex sometimes, yet not in that vicissitude it is presumed; from female unto male, and from male to female again, and so in a circle without a *permansion* in either. *Brown's Vulgar Errours.*

Pe'rmeable. *adj.* [from *permeo*, Lat.] Such as may be passed through.

The pores of a bladder are not easily *permeable* by air. *Boyle.*

To PE'RMEATE. *v. a.* [*permeo*, Lat.] To pass through.

This heat evaporates and elevates the water of the abyss, pervading not only the fissures, but the very bodies of the strata, *permeating* the interstices of the sand or other matter whereof they consist. *Woodward's Natural History.*

Pe'rmeant. *adj.* [*permeans*, Lat.] Passing through.

It entereth not the veins, but taketh leave of the *permeant* parts at the mouths of the meseraicks. *Brown.*

Permea'tion. *n. s.* [from *permeate.*] The act of passing through.

Permi'scible. *adj.* [from *permisceo*, Lat.] Such as may be mingled.

Permi'ssible. *adj.* [*permissus*, Lat.] What may be permitted.

Permi'ssion. *n. s.* [*permission*, Fr. *permissus*, Lat.] Allowance; grant of liberty.

With thy *permission* then, and thus forewarn'd,
The willinger I go. *Milton.*

You have given me your *permission* for this address, and encouraged me by your perusal and approbation. *Dryden.*

PERMI'SSIVE. *adj.* [from *permitto*, Latin.]

1. Granting liberty, not favour; not hindering, though not approving.

We bid this be done,
When evil deeds have their *permissive* pass,
And not the punishment. *Shakesp. Measure for Measure.*

Hypocrisy, the only evil that walks
Invisible, except to God alone
By his *permissive* will, through heav'n and earth. *Milton.*

2. Granted; suffered without hindrance; not authorised or favoured.

If this doth authorise usury, which before was but *permissive*, it is better to mitigate usury by declaration, than to suffer it to rage by connivance. *Bacon's Essays.*

Thus I embolden'd spake, and freedom us'd
Permissive, and acceptance found. *Milton's Par. Lost.*

Clad
With what *permissive* glory since his fall
Was left him, or false glitter. *Milton's Par. Lost.*

Permi'ssively. *adv.* [from *permissive.*] By bare allowance; without hindrance.

As to a war for the propagation of the christian faith, I would be glad to hear spoken concerning the lawfulness, not only *permissively*, but whether it be not obligatory to christian princes to design it. *Bacon's Holy War.*

Permi'stion. *n. s.* [*permistus*, Lat.] The act of mixing.

To PE'RMIT. *v. a.* [*permitto*, Lat. *permettre*, Fr.]

1. To allow without command.

What things God doth neither command nor forbid, the same he *permitteth* with approbation either to be done or left undone. *Hooker, b.* ii. *s.* 4.

2. To suffer, without authorising or approving.

3. To allow; to suffer.

Women keep silence in the churches; for it is not *permitted* unto them to speak. 1 *Corinthians* xiv. 34.

Ye gliding ghosts, *permit* me to relate
The mystick wonders of your silent state. *Dryden.*

Age oppresses us by the same degrees that it instructs us, and *permits* not that our mortal members, which are frozen with our years, should retain the vigour of our youth. *Dryden.*

We should not *permit* an allowed, possible, great and weighty good to slip out of our thoughts, without leaving any relish, any desire of itself there. *Locke.*

After men have acquired as much as the laws *permit* them, they have nothing to do but to take care of the publick. *Swift.*

4. To give up; to resign.

Nor love thy life, nor hate; but what thou liv'st,
Live well; how long, how short, *permit* to heav'n. *Milton.*

If the course of truth be *permitted* unto itself, it cannot escape many errours. *Brown's Vulgar Errours.*

To the gods *permit* the rest. *Dryden.*

Whate'r can urge ambitious youth to fight,
She pompously displays before their sight;
Laws, empire, all *permitted* to the sword. *Dryden.*

Let us not aggravate our sorrows,
But to the gods *permit* th' event of things. *Addison's Cato.*

Permi't. *n. s.* A written permission from an officer for transporting of goods from place to place, showing the duty on them to have been paid.

Permi'ttance. *n. s.* [from *permit.*] Allowance; forbearance of opposition; permission. A bad word.

When this system of air comes, by divine *permittance*, to be corrupted by poisonous acrimonious steams, what havock is made in all living creatures? *Derham's Physico-Theology.*

Permi'xtion. *n. s.* [from *permistus*, Lat.] The act of mingling; the state of being mingled.

They fell into the opposite extremity of one nature in Christ, the divine and human natures in Christ, in their conceits, by *permixtion* and confusion of substances, and of properties growing into one upon their adunation. *Brerewood.*

Permu'tation. *n. s.* [*permutation*, Fr. *permutatio*, Lat.] Exchange of one for another.

A *permutation* of number is frequent in languages. *Bentley.*

Gold and silver, by their rarity, are wonderfully fitted for this use of *permutation* for all sorts of commodities. *Ray.*

To Permu'te. *v. a.* [*permuto*, Lat. *permuter*, Fr.] To exchange.

Permu'ter. *n. s.* [*permutant*, Fr. from *permute.*] An exchanger; he who permutes.

PERNI'CIOUS. *adj.* [*perniciosus*, Lat. *pernicieux*, Fr.]

1. Mischievous in the highest degree; destructive.

To remove all out of the church, whereat they shew themselves to be sorrowful, would be, as we are persuaded, hurtful, if not *pernicious* thereunto. *Hooker, b.* iv. *s.* 10.

I call you servile ministers,
That have with two *pernicious* daughters join'd
Your high engender'd battles, 'gainst a head
So old and white as this. *Shakesp. King Lear.*

Let this *pernicious* hour
Stand ay accursed in the kalendar! *Shakesp.*

2. [*Pernix*, Latin.] Quick. An use which I have found only in *Milton*, and which, as it produces an ambiguity, ought not to be imitated.

Part incentive reed
Provide, *pernicious* with one touch to fire. *Milton.*

Perni'ciously. *adv.* [from *pernicious.*] Destructively; mischievously; ruinously.

Some wilful wits wilfully against their own knowledge, *perniciously* against their own conscience, have openly taught. *Ascham's Schoolmaster.*

All the commons
Hate him *perniciously*, and wish him
Ten fathom deep. *Shakesp. Henry* VIII.

Perni'ciousness. *n. s.* [from *pernicious.*] The quality of being pernicious.

PERNI'CITY. *n. s.* [from *pernix.*] Swiftness; celerity.

Others armed with hard shells, others with prickles, the rest that have no such armature endued with great swiftness or *pernicity.* *Ray on the Creation.*

PERORA'TION. *n. s.* [*peroratio*, Lat.] The conclusion of an oration.

What means this passionate discourse?
This *peroratian* with such circumstances? *Shakesp.*
True woman to the last—my *peroration*
I come to speak in spite of suffocation. *Smart.*

To PERPE'ND. *v. a.* [*perpendo*, Lat.] To weigh in the mind; to consider attentively.

Thus it remains and the remainder thus;
Perpend. *Shakespeare's Hamlet.*
Perpend, my princess, and give ear. *Shakesp.*

Consider the different conceits of men, and duly *perpend* the imperfection of their discoveries. *Brown.*

PERPE'NDER. *n. s.* [*perpigne*, Fr.] A coping stone.

PE'RPENDICLE. *n. s.* [*perpendicule*, Fr. *perpendiculum*, Lat.] Any thing hanging down by a strait line. *Dict.*

PERPENDI'CULAR. *adj.* [*perpendiculaire*, Fr. *perpendicularis*, Latin.]

1. Crossing any other line at right angles. Of two lines, if one be perpendicular, the other is perpendicular too.

If in a line oblique their atoms rove,
Or in a *perpendicular* they move;
If some advance not slower in their race,
And some more swift, how could they be entangl'd.
Blackmore.

The angle of incidence, is that angle, which the line, described by the incident ray, contains with the *perpendicular* to the reflecting or refracting surface at the point of incidence. *Newton's Opticks.*

2. Cutting the horizon at right angles.

Some define the *perpendicular* altitude of the highest mountains to be four miles. *Brown's Vulgar Errours.*

PERPENDI'CULAR. *n. s.* A line crossing the horizon at right angles.

Though the quantity of water thus rising and falling be nearly constant as to the whole, yet it varies in the several parts of the globe; by reason that the vapours float in the atmosphere, and are not restored down again in a *perpendicular* upon the same precise tract of land. *Woodward.*

PERPENDI'CULARLY. *adv.* [from *perpendicular.*]

1. In such a manner as to cut another line at right angles.
2. In the direction of a strait line up and down.

Ten masts attacht make not the altitude reach,
Which thou hast *perpendicularly* fall'n. *Shakesp.*

Irons refrigerated North and South, not only acquire a directive faculty, but if cooled upright and *perpendicularly*, they will also obtain the same. *Brown's Vulgar Errours.*

Shoot up an arrow *perpendicularly* from the earth, the arrow will return to your foot again. *More.*

All weights naturally move *perpendicularly* downward. *Ray.*

PERPENDICULA'RITY. *n. s.* [from *perpendicular.*] The state of being perpendicular.

The meeting of two lines is the primary essential mode or difference of an angle; the *perpendicularity* of these lines is the difference of a right angle. *Watts's Logick.*

PERPE'NSION. *n. s.* [from *perpend.*] Consideration. Not in use.

Unto reasonable *perpensions* it hath no place in some sciences. *Brown's Vulgar Errours.*

To PE'RPETRATE. *v. a.* [*perpetro*, Lat. *perpetrer*, Fr.]

1. To commit; to act. Always in an ill sense.

Hear of such a crime
As tragick poets, since the birth of time,
Ne'er feign'd a thronging audience to amaze;
But true and *perpetrated* in our days. *Tate's Juvenal.*

My tender infants or my careful sire,
These they returning will to death require,
Will *perpetrate* on them the first design,
And take the forfeit of their heads for mine. *Dryden.*

The forest, which in after-times,
Fierce Romulus, for *perpetrated* crimes,
A sacred refuge made. *Dryden.*

2. It is used by *Butler* in a neutral sense, in compliance with his verse, but not properly.

Success, the mark no mortal wit,
Or surest hand can always hit;
For whatsoe'er we *perpetrate*,
We do but row, we're steer'd by fate. *Hudibras.*

PERPETRA'TION. *n. s.* [from *perpetrate.*]

1. The act of committing a crime.

A desperate discontented assassinate would, after the *perpetration*, have honested a meer private revenge. *Wotton.*

A woman, who lends an ear to a seducer, may be insensibly drawn into the *perpetration* of the most violent acts. *Clarissa.*

2. A bad action.

The strokes of divine vengeance, or of men's own consciences, always attend injurious *perpetrations.* *King Charles.*

PERPE'TUAL. *adj.* [*perpetuel*, Fr. *perpetuus*, Latin.]

1. Never ceasing; eternal with respect to futurity.

Mine is a love, which must *perpetual* be,
If you can be so just as I am true. *Dryden.*

2. Continual; uninterrupted; perennial.

Within those banks rivers now
Stream, and *perpetual* draw their humid train. *Milton.*

By the muscular motion and *perpetual* flux of the liquids, a great part of them is thrown out of the body. *Arbuthnot.*

3. Perpetual screw. A screw which acts against the teeth of a wheel, and continues its action without end.

A *perpetual* screw hath the motion of a wheel and the force of a screw, being both infinite. *Wilkin's Math. Magick.*

PERPE'TUALLY. *adv.* [from *perpetual.*] Constantly; continually; incessantly.

This verse is every where sounding the very thing in your ears; yet the numbers are *perpetually* varied, so that the same sounds are never repeated twice. *Dryden.*

In passing from them to great distances, doth it not grow denser and denser *perpetually*; and thereby cause the gravity of those great bodies towards one another. *Newton's Opticks.*

The bible and common prayer book in the vulgar tongue, being *perpetually* read in churches, have proved a kind of standard for language, especially to the common people. *Swift.*

To PERPE'TUATE. *v. a.* [*perpetuer*, Fr. *perpetuo*, Lat.]

1. To make perpetual; to preserve from extinction; to eternize.

Medals, that are at present only mere curiosities, may be of use in the ordinary commerce of life, and at the same time *perpetuate* the glories of her majesty's reign. *Addison.*

Man cannot devise any other method so likely to preserve and *perpetuate* the knowledge and belief of a revelation, so necessary to mankind. *Forbes.*

2. To continue without cessation or intermission.

What is it, but a continued *perpetuated* voice from heaven, resounding for ever in our ears? to give men no rest in their sins, no quiet from Christ's importunity, 'till they awake from their lethargick sleep and arise from so mortiferous a state, and permit him to give them life. *Hammond.*

PERPETUA'TION. *n. s.* [from *perpetuate.*] The act of making perpetual; incessant continuance.

Nourishing hair upon the moles of the face, is the *perpetuation* of a very ancient custom. *Brown's Vulgar Errours.*

PERPE'TUITY. *n. s.* [*perpetuité*, Fr. *perpetuitas*, Lat.]

1. Duration to all futurity.

For men to alter those laws, which God for *perpetuity* hath established, were presumption most intolerable. *Hooker.*

Yet am I better
Than one that's sick o' th' gout, since he had rather
Groan so in *perpetuity*, than be cur'd
By the sure physician, death. *Shakesp. Cymbeline.*

Time as long again
Would be fill'd up with our thanks;
And yet we should, for *perpetuity*,
Go hence in debt. *Shakespeare's Winter's Tale.*

Nothing wanted to his noble and heroical intentions, but only to give *perpetuity* to that which was in his time so happily established. *Bacon.*

2. Exemption from intermission or cessation.

A cycle or period begins again as often as it ends, and so obtains a *perpetuity.* *Holder.*

3. Something of which there is no end.

A mess of pottage for a birth-right, a present repast for a *perpetuity.* *South's Sermons.*

The ennobling property of the pleasure, that accrues to a man from religion, is, that he that has the property, may be also sure of the *perpetuity.* *South's Sermons.*

The laws of God as well as of the land
Abhor a *perpetuity* should stand;
Estates have wings, and hang in fortune's power. *Pope.*

To PERPLE'X. *v. a.* [*perplexus*, Latin.]

1. To disturb with doubtful notions; to entangle; to make anxious; to teaze with suspense or ambiguity; to distract; to embarrass; to puzzle.

Being greatly *perplexed* in his mind, he determined to go into Persia. *1 Mac.* iii. 31.

Themselves with doubts they day and night *perplex.* *Denh.*

He *perplexes* the minds of the fair sex with nice speculations of philosophy, when he should engage their hearts. *Dryden.*

We can distinguish no general truths, or at least shall be apt to *perplex* the mind. *Locke.*

2. To make intricate; to involve; to complicate.

Their way
Lies through the *perplex'd* paths of this drear wood. *Milt.*
We both are involv'd
In the same intricate *perplext* distress. *Addison's Cato.*

What was thought obscure, *perplexed*, and too hard for our weak parts, will lie open to the understanding in a fair view. *Locke.*

3. To plague; to torment; to vex. A sense not proper.

Chloe's the wonder of her sex,
'Tis well her heart is tender,
How might such killing eyes *perplex*,
With virtue to defend her. *Granville.*

PERPLE'X. *adj.* [*perplex*, Lat. *perplexus*, Lat.] Intricate; difficult. *Perplexed* is the word in use.

How the soul directs the spirits for the motion of the body, according to the several animal exigents, is *perplex* in the theory. *Glanville's Scept.*

PERPLE'XEDLY. *adv.* [from *perplexed.*] Intricately; with involution.

PERPLE'XEDNESS. *n. s.* [from *perplexed.*]

1. Embarassment; anxiety.
2. Intricacy; involution; difficulty.

Obscurity and *perplexedness* have been cast upon St. Paul's Epistles from without. *Locke.*

PERPLE'XITY. *n. s.* [*perplexité*, Fr.]

1. Anxiety; distraction of mind.

The fear of him ever since hath put me into such *perplexity*, as now you found me. *Sidney, b.* ii.

Perplexity not suffering them to be idle, they think and do, as it were, in a phrensy. *Hooker, b.* v, *s.* 3.

The royal virgin, which beheld from far,
In pensive plight and sad *perplexity*,
The whole atchievement of this doubtful war,
Came running fast to greet his victory. *Fairy Queen.*

2. Entanglement; intricacy.

Let him look for the labyrinth; for I cannot discern any, unless in the *perplexity* of his own thoughts. *Stillingfleet.*

PERPOTA'TION. *n. s.* [*per* and *poto*, Latin.] The act of drinking largely.

PE'RQUISITE. *n. s.* [*perquisitus*, Lat.] Something gained by a place or office over and above the settled wages.

Tell me, perfidious, was it fit
To make my cream a *perquisite*,
And steal to mend your wages. *Widow and Cat.*

To an honest mind, the best *perquisites* of a place are the advantages it gives a man of doing good. *Addison.*

To what your lawful *perquisites* amount. *Swift.*

PERQUISI'TION. *n. s.* [*perquisitus*, Lat.] An accurate enquiry; a thorough search. *Ainsworth.*

PE'RRY. *n. s.* [*poire*, Fr. from *poire.*] Cyder made of pears.

Perry is the next liquor in esteem after cyder, in the ordering of which, let not your pears be over ripe before you grind them; and with some sorts of pears, the mixing of a few crabs in the grinding is of great advantage, making *perry* equal to the redstreak cyder. *Mortimer.*

To PE'RSECUTE. *v. a.* [*persecuter*, Fr. *persecutus*, Lat.]

1. To harrass with penalties; to persue with malignity. It is generally used of penalties inflicted for opinions.

I *persecuted* this way unto the death. *Acts* xxii. 4.

2. To persue with repeated acts of vengeance or enmity.

They might have fallen down, being *persecuted* of vengeance, and scattered abroad. *Wisdom* xi. 20.

Relate,
For what offence the queen of heav'n began
To *persecute* so brave, so just a man! *Dryden.*

3. To importune much: as, he *persecutes* me with daily solicitations.

PERSECU'TION. *n. s.* [*persecution*, Fr. *persecutio*, Lat. from *persecute.*]

1. The act or practice of persecuting.

The Jews raised *persecution* against Paul and Barnabas, and expelled them. *Acts* xiii. 50.

Heavy *persecution* shall arise
On all, who in the worship persevere
Of spirit and truth. *Milton.*

The deaths and sufferings of the primitive christians had a great share in the conversion of those learned Pagans, who lived in the ages of *persecution*. *Addison.*

2. The state of being persecuted.

Our necks are under *persecution*; we labour and have no rest. *Lam.* v. 5.

Christian fortitude and patience had their opportunity in times of affliction and *persecution*. *Sprat's Sermons.*

PE'RSECUTOR. *n. s.* [*persecuteur*, Fr. from *persecute.*] One who harrasses others with continued malignity.

What man can do against them, not afraid,
Though to the death; against such cruelties
With inward consolations recompens'd;
And oft supported so, as shall amaze
Their proudest *persecutors*. *Milton's Paradise Lost.*

Henry rejected the pope's supremacy, but retained every corruption besides, and became a cruel *persecutor*. *Swift.*

PERSEVE'RANCE. *n. s.* [*perseverance*, Fr. *perseverantia*, Lat. This word was once improperly acccented on the second syllable.] Persistence in any design or attempt; steadiness in pursuits; constancy in progress. It is applied alike to good and ill.

The king becoming graces,
Bounty, *persev'rance*, mercy, lowliness;
I have no relish of them. *Shakesp. Macbeth.*

Perseverance keeps honour bright:
To have done, is to hang quite out of fashion,
Like rusty mail in monumental mockery. *Shakespeare.*

They hate repentance more than *perseverance* in a fault. *King Charles.*

Wait the seasons of providence with patience and *perseverance* in the duties of our calling, what difficulties soever we may encounter. *L'Estrange.*

Patience and *perseverance* overcome the greatest difficulties. *Clarissa.*

And *perseverance* with his batter'd shield. *Brooke.*

PERSEVE'RANT. *adj.* [*perseverant*, Fr. *perseverans*, Lat.] Persisting; constant. *Ainsworth.*

To PERSEVE'RE. *v. n.* [*persevero*, Lat. *perseverer*, Fr. This word was anciently accented less properly on the second syllable.] To persist in an attempt; not to give over; not to quit the design.

But my rude musick, which was wont to please
Some dainty ears, cannot with any skill
The dreadful tempest of her wrath appease,
Nor move the dolphin from her stubborn will;
But in her pride she doth *persevere* still. *Spenser.*

Thrice happy, if they know
Their happiness, and *persevere* upright! *Milton.*

Thus beginning, thus we *persevere*;
Our passions yet continue what they were. *Dryden.*

To *persevere* in any evil course, makes you unhappy in this life, and will certainly throw you into everlasting torments in the next. *Wake's Preparation for Death.*

PERSEVE'RINGLY. *adv.* [from *persevere.*] With perseverance.

To PERSI'ST. *v. n.* [*persisto*, Lat. *persister*, Fr.] To persevere; to continue firm; not to give over.

Nothing can make a man happy, but that which shall last as long as he lasts; for an immortal soul shall *persist* in being not only when profit, pleasure and honour, but when time itself shall cease. *South's Sermons.*

If they *persist* in pointing their batteries against particular persons, no laws of war forbid the making reprisals. *Addison.*

PERSI'STANCE. } *n. s.* [from *persist.* *Persistence* seems more
PERSI'STENCY. } proper.]

1. The state of persisting; steadiness; constancy; perseverance in good or bad.

The love of God better can consist with the indeliberate commissions of many sins, than with an allowed *persistance* in any one. *Government of the Tongue.*

2. Obstinacy; obduracy; contumacy.

Thou think'st me as far in the devil's book, as thou and Falstaff, for obduracy and *persistency*. *Shakesp.*

PERSI'STIVE. *adj.* [from *persist.*] Steady; not receding from a purpose; persevering.

The protractive tryals of great Jove,
To find *persistive* constancy in men. *Shakesp.*

PE'RSON. *n. s.* [*personne*, Fr. *persona*, Lat.]

1. Individual or particular man or woman.

A *person* is a thinking intelligent being, that has reason and reflection, and can consider itself as itself, the same thinking thing, in different times and places. *Locke.*

2. Man or woman considered as opposed to things, or distinct from them.

A zeal for *persons* is far more easy to be perverted, than a zeal for things. *Sprat's Sermons.*

To that we owe the safety of our *persons* and the propriety of our possessions. *Atterbury's Sermons.*

3. Human Being; considered with respect to mere corporal existence.

'Tis in her heart alone that you must reign;
You'll find her *person* difficult to gain. *Dryden.*

4. Man or woman considered as present, acting or suffering.

If I am traduc'd by tongues which neither know
My faculties nor *person*;
'Tis but the fate of place, and the rough brake
That virtue must go through. *Shakesp. Henry* VIII.

The rebels maintained the fight for a small time, and for their *persons* shewed no want of courage. *Bacon.*

5. A general loose term for a human being; one; a man.

Be a *person*'s attainments ever so great, he should always remember, that he is God's creature. *Clarissa.*

6. One's self; not a representative.

When I purposed to make a war by my lieutenant, I made declaration thereof to you by my chancellor; but now that I mean to make a war upon France in *person*, I will declare it to you myself. *Bacon's Henry* VII.

The king in *person* visits all around,
Comforts the sick, congratulates the sound,
And holds for thrice three days a royal feast. *Dryden.*

7. Exteriour appearance.

For her own *person*,
It beggar'd all description. *Shakesp.*

8. Man or woman represented in a fictitious dialogue.

All things are lawful unto me, saith the apostle, speaking, as it seemeth, in the *person* of the christian gentile for the maintenance of liberty in things indifferent. *Hooker.*

These tables Cicero pronounced under the *person* of Crassus, were of more use and authority than all the books of the philosophers. *Baker's Reflections on Learning.*

9. Character.

From his first appearance upon the stage, in his new *person* of a sycophant or jugler, instead of his former *person* of a prince,

prince, he was exposed to the derision of the courtiers and the common people, who flocked about him, that one might know where the owl was, by the flight of birds. *Bacon.*

He hath put on the *person* not of a robber and a murtherer, but of a traitor to the state. *Hayward.*

10. Character of office.

I then did use the *person* of your father;
The image of his power lay then in me:
And in th' administration of his law,
While I was busy for the commonwealth,
Your highness pleased to forget my place. *Shakesp.*

How different is the same man from himself, as he sustains the *person* of a magistrate and that of a friend. *South.*

11. [In grammar.] The quality of the noun that modifies the verb.

Dorus the more blushed at her smiling, and she the more smiled at his blushing; because he had, with the remembrance of that plight he was in, forgot in speaking of himself the third *person.* *Sidney.*

If speaking of himself in the first *person* singular has so various meanings, his use of the first *person* plural is with greater latitude. *Locke.*

PE'RSONABLE. *adj.* [from *person.*]

1. Handsome; graceful; of good appearance.

Were it true that her son Ninias had such a stature, as that Simiramis, who was very *personable*, could be taken for him; yet it is unlikely that she could have held the empire forty-two years after by any such subtilty. *Raleigh.*

2. [In law.] One that may maintain any plea in a judicial court. *Ainsworth.*

PERSO'NAGE. *n. s.* [*personage*, Fr.]

1. A considerable person; man or woman of eminence.

It was a new sight fortune had prepared to those woods, to see these great *personages* thus run one after the other. *Sidney.*

It is not easy to research the actions of eminent *personages*, how much they have blemished by the envy of others, and what was corrupted by their own felicity. *Wotton.*

2. Exteriour appearance; air; stature.

She hath made compare
Between our statures, she hath urg'd his height;
And with her *personage*, her tall *personage*,
She hath prevail'd with him. *Shakespeare.*

The lord Sudley was fierce in courage, courtly in fashion, in *personage* stately, in voice magnificent, but somewhat empty of matter. *Hayward.*

3. Character assumed.

The great diversion is masking: the Venetians, naturally grave, love to give into the follies of such seasons, when disguised in a false *personage.* *Addison's Remarks on Italy.*

4. Character represented.

Some persons must be found out, already known by history, whom we may make the actors and *personages* of this fable. *Broome's View of Epic Poems.*

PE'RSONAL. *adj.* [*personel*, Fr. *personalis*, Lat.]

1. Belonging to men or women, not to things; not real.

Every man so termed by way of *personal* difference only. *Hooker, b. v. s. 13.*

2. Affecting individuals or particular people; peculiar; proper to him or her; relating to one's private actions or character.

For my part,
I know no *personal* cause to spurn at him;
But for the general. *Shakesp. Julius Cæsar.*

It could not mean, that Cain as elder had a natural dominion over Abel, for the words are conditional; if thou doest well, and so *personal* to Cain. *Locke.*

Publick reproofs of sin are general, though by this they lose a great deal of their effect; but in private conversations the application may be more *personal*, and the proofs when so directed come home. *Rogers.*

3. Present; not acting by representative.

The fav'rites that the absent king
In deputation left,
When he was *personal* in the Irish war. *Shakesp.*

4. Exteriour; corporal.

This heroick constancy determined him to desire in marriage a princess, whose *personal* charms were now become the least part of her character. *Addison.*

5. [In law.] Something moveable; something appendant to the person, as money; not real, as land.

This sin of kind not *personal*
But real and hereditary was. *Davies.*

6. [In grammar.] A personal verb is that which has all the regular modification of the three persons; opposed to impersonal that has only the third.

PERSONALITY. *n. s.* [from *personal.*] The existence or individuality of any one.

Person belongs only to intelligent agents, capable of a law, and happiness and misery: this *personality* extends itself beyond present existence to what is past, only by consciousness, whereby it imputes to itself past actions, just upon the same ground that it does the present. *Locke.*

PERSO'NALLY. *adv.* [from *personal.*]

1. In person; in presence; not by representative.

Approbation not only they give, who *personally* declare their assent by voice, sign or act, but also when others do it in their names. *Hooker, b. i. s. 10.*

I could not *personally* deliver to her
What you commanded me, but by her woman
I sent your message. *Shakesp. Henry VIII.*

There are many reasons, why matters of such a wonderful nature should not be taken notice of by those Pagan writers, who lived before our Saviour's disciples had *personally* appeared among them. *Addison.*

2. With respect to an individual; particularly.

She bore a mortal hatred to the house of Lancaster, and *personally* to the king. *Bacon's Henry VII.*

3. With regard to numerical existence.

The converted man is *personally* the same he was before, and is neither born nor created a-new in a proper literal sense. *Rogers's Sermons.*

To PE'RSONATE. *v. a.* [from *persona*, Latin.]

1. To represent by a fictitious or assumed character, so as to pass for the person represented.

This lad was not to *personate* one, that had been long before taken out of his cradle, but a youth that had been brought up in a court, where infinite eyes had been upon him. *Bacon's Henry VII.*

2. To represent by action or appearance; to act.

Herself a while she lays aside, and makes
Ready to *personate* a mortal part. *Crashaw.*

3. To pretend hypocritically, with the reciprocal pronoun.

It has been the constant practice of the Jesuits to send over emissaries, with instructions to *personate* themselves members of the several sects amongst us. *Swift.*

4. To counterfeit; to feign. Little in use.

Piety is opposed to that *personated* devotion, under which any kind of impiety is disguised. *Hammond's Fundamentals.*

Thus have I played with the dogmatist in a *personated* scepticism. *Glanvill's Sceps.*

5. To resemble.

The lofty cedar *personates* thee. *Shakesp. Cymbeline.*

6. To make a representative of, as in picture. Out of use.

Whose eyes are on this sovereign lady fixt,
One do I *personate* of Timon's frame,
Whom fortune with her iv'ry hand wafts to her. *Shakesp.*

7. To describe. Out of use.

I am thinking, what I shall say; it must be a *personating* of himself; a satyr against the softness of prosperity. *Shakesp.*

I will drop in his way some obscure epistles
Of love, wherein, by the colour of his beard, the
Shape of his leg, the manner of his gait, the
Expressure of his eye, forehead and complexion,
He shall find himself most feelingly *personated. Shakespeare.*

PERSONA'TION. *n. s.* [from *personate.*] Counterfeiting of another person.

This being one of the strangest examples of a *personation* that ever was, it deserveth to be discovered and related at the full. *Bacon's Henry VII.*

PERSONIFICA'TION. *n. s.* [from *personify.*] Prosopopœia; the change of things to persons: as,

Confusion heard his voice. *Milton.*

To PE'RSONIFY. *v. a.* [from *person.*] To change from a thing to a person.

PE'RSPECTIVE. *n. s.* [*perspectif*, Fr. *perspicio*, Lat.]

1. A glass through which things are viewed.

If it tend to danger, they turn about the *perspective*, and shew it so little, that he can scarce discern it. *Denham.*

It may import us in this calm, to hearken to the storms raising abroad; and by the best *perspectives*, to discover from what coast they break. *Temple.*

You hold the glass, but turn the *perspective*,
And farther off the lessen'd object drive. *Dryden.*
Faith for reason's glimmering light shall give
Her immortal *perspective.* *Prior.*

2. The science by which things are ranged in picture, according to their appearance in their real situation.

Medals have represented their buildings according to the rules of *perspective.* *Addison on Ancient Medals.*

3. View; visto.

Lofty trees, with sacred shades,
And *perspectives* of pleasant glades,
Where nymphs of brightest form appear. *Dryden.*

PE'RSPECTIVE. *adj.* Relating to the science of vision; optick; optical.

We have *perspective* houses, where we make demonstrations of all lights and radiations; and out of things uncoloured and transparent, we can represent unto you all several colours. *Bacon.*

PERSPICA'CIOUS. *adj.* [*perspicax*, Lat.] Quicksighted; sharp of sight.

It is as nice and tender in feeling, as it can be *perspicacious* and quick in seeing. *South's Sermons.*

PERSPICA'CIOUSNESS. *n. s.* [from *perspicacious.*] Quickness of sight.

PERSPICA'CITY. *n. s.* [*perspicacité*, Fr.] Quickness of sight.

He that laid the foundations of the earth cannot be excluded the secrecy of the mountains; nor can there any thing escape the *perspicacity* of those eyes, which were before light, and in whose opticks there is no opacity. *Brown.*

PERSPI'CIENCE. *n. s.* [*perspiciens*, Lat.] The act of looking sharply. *Dict.*

PE'RSPICIL. *n. s.* [*perspicillum*, Lat.] A glass through which things are viewed; an optick glass.

Let truth be
Ne'er so far distant, yet chronology,
Sharp-sighted as the eagle's eye, that can
Out-stare the broad-beam'd day's meridian,
Will have a *perspicil* to find her out,
And through the night of error and dark doubt,
Discern the dawn of truth's eternal ray,
As when the rosy morn buds into day. *Crashaw.*

The *perspicil*, as well as the needle, hath enlarged the habitable world. *Glanvill's Sceps.*

PERSPICU'ITY. *n. s.* [*perspicuité*, Fr. from *perspicuous.*]

1. Clearness to the mind; easiness to be understood; freedom from obscurity or ambiguity.

The verses containing precepts, have not so much need of ornament as of *perspicuity*. *Dryden.*

Perspicuity consists in the using of proper terms for the thoughts, which a man would have pass from his own mind into that of another's. *Locke's Thoughts on Reading.*

2. Transparency; translucency; diaphaneity.

As for diaphaneity and *perspicuity* it enjoyeth that most eminently, as having its earthy and salinous parts so exactly resolved, that its body is left imporous. *Brown.*

PERSPI'CUOUS. *adj.* [*perspicuus*, Latin.]

1. Transparent; clear; such as may be seen through; diaphanous; translucent; not opake.

As contrary causes produce the like effects, so even the same proceed from black and white; for the clear and *perspicuous* body effecteth white, and that white a black. *Peacham.*

2. Clear to the understanding; not obscure; not ambiguous.

The purpose is *perspicuous* even as substance,
Whose grossness little characters sum up. *Shakesp.*

All this is so *perspicuous*, so undeniable, that I need not be over industrious in the proof of it. *Sprat's Sermons.*

PERSPI'CUOUSLY. *adv.* [from *perspicuous.*] Clearly; not obscurely.

The case is no sooner made than resolved; if it be made not enwrapped, but plainly and *perspicuously*. *Bacon.*

PERSPI'CUOUSNESS. *n. s.* [from *perspicuous.*] Clearness; freedom from obscurity.

PERSPI'RABLE. *adj.* [from *perspire.*]

1. Such as may be emitted by the cuticular pores.

That this attraction is performed by effluviums, is plain and granted by most; for electricks will not commonly attract, unless they attract or become *perspirable*. *Brown.*

In an animal under a course of hard labour, aliment too vaporous or *perspirable* will subject it to too strong a perspiration, debility and sudden death. *Arbuthnot on Aliments.*

2. Perspiring; emitting perspiration. Not proper.

Hair cometh not upon the palms of the hands or soles of the feet, which are parts more *perspirable*: and children are not hairy, for that their skins are most *perspirable*. *Bacon.*

PERSPIRA'TION. *n. s.* [from *perspire.*] Excretion by the cuticular pores.

Insensible *perspiration* is the last and most perfect action of animal digestion. *Arbuthnot on Aliments.*

PERSPI'RATIVE. *adj.* [from *perspire.*] Performing the act of perspiration.

To PERSPI'RE. *v. n.* [*perspiro*, Lat.]

1. To perform excretion by the cuticular pores

2. To be excreted by the skin.

Water, milk, whey taken without much exercise, so as to make them *perspire*, relax the belly. *Arbuthnot.*

To PERSTRI'NGE. *v. a.* [*perstringo*, Lat.] To graze upon; to glance upon. *Dict.*

PERSUA'DABLE. *adj.* [from *persuade.*] Such as may be persuaded.

To PERSUA'DE. *v. a.* [*persuadeo*, Lat. *persuader*, Fr.]

1. To bring to any particular opinion.

Let every man be fully *persuaded* in his own mind. *Romans.*

We are *persuaded* better things of you, and things that accompany salvation. *Hebrews* vi. 9.

Joy over them that are *persuaded* to salvation. 2 *Esdras* vii.

Let a man be ever so well *persuaded* of the advantages of virtue, yet, till he hungers and thirsts after righteousness, his will will not be determined to any action in pursuit of this confessed great good. *Locke.*

Men should seriously *persuade* themselves, that they have here no abiding place, but are only in their passage to the heavenly Jerusalem. *Wake's Preparation for Death.*

2. To influence by argument or expostulation. *Persuasion* seems rather applicable to the passions, and *argument* to the reason; but this is not always observed.

Philoclea's beauty not only *persuaded*, but so *persuaded* as all hearts must yield: Pamela's beauty used violence, and such as no heart could resist. *Sidney.*

They that were with Simon, being led with covetousness, were *persuaded* for money. 2 *Mac.* x. 20.

To sit cross-leg'd, or with our fingers pectinated, is accounted bad, and friends will *persuade* us from it. *Brown.*

I should be glad, if I could *persuade* him to write such another critick on any thing of mine; for when he condemns any of my poems, he makes the world have a better opinion of them. *Dryden.*

3. To inculcate by argument or expostulation.

To children, afraid of vain images, we *persuade* confidence by making them handle and look nearer such things. *Taylor.*

4. To treat by persuasion. A mode of speech not in use.

Twenty merchants have all *persuaded* with him;
But none can drive him from the envious plea
Of forfeiture. *Shakespeare.*

PERSUA'DER. *n. s.* [from *persuade.*] One who influences by persuasion; an importunate adviser.

The earl, speaking in that imperious language wherein the king had written, did not irritate the people, but make them conceive by the haughtiness of delivery of the king's errand, that himself was the author or principal *persuader* of that counsel. *Bacon's Henry* VII.

He soon is mov'd
By such *persuaders* as are held upright. *Daniel's Civil War.*

Hunger and thirst at once,
Pow'rful *persuaders!* quicken'd at the scent
Of that alluring fruit, urg'd me so keen. *Milton.*

PERSUA'SIBLE. *adj.* [*persuasibilis*, Lat. *persuasible*, Fr. from *persuadeo*, Latin.] To be influenced by persuasion.

It makes us apprehend our own interest in that obedience, makes us tractable and *persuasible*, contrary to that brutish stubborness of the horse and mule, which the Psalmist reproaches. *Government of the Tongue.*

PERSUA'SIBLENESS. *n. s.* [from *persuasible.*] The quality of being flexible by persuasion.

PERSUA'SION. *n. s.* [*persuasion*, Fr. from *persuasus*, Lat.]

1. The act of persuading; the act of influencing by expostulation; the act of gaining or attempting the passions.

If 't prove thy fortune, Polydore, to conquer,
For thou hast all the arts of fine *persuasion*,
Trust me, and let me know thy love's success. *Otway.*

2. The state of being persuaded; opinion.

The most certain token of evident goodness is, if the general *persuasion* of all men does so account it. *Hooker.*

You are a great deal abus'd in too bold a *persuasion*. *Shakespeare.*

When we have no other certainty of being in the right, but our own *persuasions* that we are so; this may often be but making one error the gage for another. *Gov. of the Tongue.*

The obedient and the men of practice shall ride upon those clouds, and triumph over their present imperfections; till *persuasion* pass into knowledge, and knowledge advance into assurance, and all come at length to be compleated in the beatifick vision. *South's Sermons.*

PERSUA'SIVE. *adj.* [*persuasif*, Fr. from *persuade.*] Having the power of persuading; having influence on the passions.

In prayer, we do not so much respect what precepts art delivereth, touching the method of *persuasive* utterance in the presence of great men, as what doth most avail to our own edification in piety and godly zeal. *Hooker.*

Let Martius resume his farther discourse, as well for the *persuasive* as for the consult, touching the means that may conduce unto the enterprize. *Bacon.*

Notwithstanding the weight and fitness of the arguments to persuade, and the light of man's intellect to meet this *persuasive* evidence with a suitable assent, no assent followed, nor were men thereby actually persuaded. *South's Sermons.*

PERSUA'SIVELY. *adv.* [from *persuasive.*] In such a manner as to persuade.

The serpent with me
Persuasively hath so prevail'd, that I
Have also tasted. *Milton.*

Many who live upon their estates cannot so much as tell a story, much less speak clearly and *persuasively* in any business. *Locke on Education.*

PERSUA'SIVENESS. *n. s.* [from *persuasive.*] Influence on the passions.

An opinion of the successfulness of the work being as necessary to found a purpose of undertaking it, as either the authority of commands, or the *persuasiveness* of promises, or pungency of menaces can be. *Hammond's Fundamentals.*

PERSUA'SORY. *adj.* [*persuasorius*, Lat. from *persuade.*] Having the power to persuade.

Neither is this *persuasory*. *Brown.*

PERT.

PERT *adj.* [*pert*, Welsh; *pert*, Dutch; *appert*, French.]

1. Lively; brisk; smart.

Awake the *pert* and nimble spirit of mirth;
Turn melancholy forth to funerals. *Shakesp.*

On the tawny sands and shelves,
Trip the *pert* fairies and the dapper elves. *Milton.*

2. Saucy; petulant; with bold and garrulous loquacity.

All servants might challenge the same liberty, and grow *pert* upon their masters; and when this sauciness became universal, what less mischief could be expected than an old Scythian rebellion? *Collier on Pride.*

A lady bids me in a very *pert* manner mind my own affairs, and not pretend to meddle with their linnen. *Addison.*

Vanessa
Scarce list'ned to their idle chat,
Further than sometimes by a frown,
When they grew *pert*, to pull them down. *Swift.*

To PERTA'IN. *v. n.* [*pertineo*, Lat.] To belong; to relate.

As men hate those that affect that honour by ambition, which *pertaineth* not to them, so are they much more odious, who through fear betray the glory which they have. *Hayward.*

A cheveron or rafter of an house, a very honourable bearing, is never seen in the coat of a king, because it *pertaineth* to a mechanical profession. *Peacham.*

PERTEREBRA'TION. *n. s.* [*per* and *terebratio*, Lat.] The act of boring through. *Ainsworth.*

PERTINA'CIOUS. *adj.* [from *pertinax.*]

1. Obstinate; stubborn; perversely resolute.

One of the dissenters appeared to Dr. Sanderson to be so bold, so troublesome and illogical in the dispute, as forced him to say, that he had never met with a man of more *pertinacious* confidence and less abilities. *Walton.*

2. Resolute; constant; steady.

Diligence is a steady, constant and *pertinacious* study, that naturally leads the soul into the knowledge of that, which at first seemed locked up from it. *South's Sermons.*

PERTINA'CIOUSLY. *adv.* [from *pertinacious.*] Obstinately; stubbornly.

They deny that freedom to me, which they *pertinaciously* challenge to themselves. *King Charles.*

Metals *pertinaciously* resist all transmutation; and though one would think they were turned into a different substance, yet they do but as it were lurk under a vizard. *Ray.*

Others have sought to ease themselves of all the evil of affliction by disputing subtilly against it, and *pertinaciously* maintaining, that afflictions are no real evils, but only in imagination. *Tillotson's Sermons.*

PERTINA'CITY. } *n. s.* [*pertinacia*, Lat. from *pertinacious.*]
PERTINA'CIOUSNESS. }

1. Obstinacy; stubbornness.

In this reply, was included a very gross mistake, and if with *pertinacity* maintained, a capital errour. *Brown.*

2. Resolution; constancy.

PE'RTINACY. *n. s.* [from *pertinax.*]

1. Obstinacy; stubbornness; persistency.

Their *pertinacy* is such, that when you drive them out of one form, they assume another. *Duppa.*

It holds forth the *pertinacy* of ill fortune, in pursuing people into their graves. *L'Estrange.*

2. Resolution; steadiness; constancy.

St. Gorgonia prayed with passion and *pertinacy*, till she obtained relief. *Taylor.*

They with a *pertinacy* unmatch'd,
For new recruits of danger watch'd. *Hudibras.*

PE'RTINENCE. } *n. s.* [from *pertineo*, Lat.] Justness of relation to the matter in hand; propriety to the purpose; appositeness.
PE'RTINENCY. }

I have shewn the fitness and *pertinency* of the apostle's discourse to the persons he addressed to, whereby it appeareth that he was no babbler, and did not talk at random. *Bentley.*

PE'RTINENT. *adj.* [*pertinens*, Lat. *pertinent*, Fr.]

1. Related to the matter in hand; just to the purpose; not useless to the end proposed; apposite; not foreign from the thing intended.

My caution was more *pertinent*
Than the rebuke you give it. *Shakesp. Coriolanus.*

I set down, out of experience in business, and conversation in books, what I thought *pertinent* to this business. *Bacon.*

Here I shall seem a little to digress, but you will by and by find it *pertinent*. *Bacon.*

If he could find *pertinent* treatises of it in books, that would reach all the particulars of a man's behaviour; his own ill-fashioned example would spoil all. *Locke.*

2. Relating; regarding; concerning. In this sense the word now used is *pertaining*.

Men shall have just cause, when any thing *pertinent* unto faith and religion is doubted of, the more willingly to incline their minds towards that which the sentence of so grave, wise and learned in that faculty shall judge most sound. *Hooker.*

PE'RTINENTLY. *adv.* [from *pertinent.*]. Appositely; to the purpose.

Be modest and reserved in the presence of thy betters, speaking little, answering *pertinently*, not interposing without leave or reason. *Taylor's Rule of Living Holy.*

PE'RTINENTNESS. *n. s.* [from *pertinent.*] Appositeness. *Dict.*

PERTI'NGENT. *adj.* [*pertingens*, Lat.] Reaching to; touching. *Dict.*

PE'RTLY. *adv.* [from *pert.*]

1. Briskly; smartly.

I find no other difference betwixt the common town-wits and the downright country fools, than that the first are *pertly* in the wrong, with a little more gaiety; and the last neither in the right nor the wrong. *Pope.*

2. Saucily; petulantly.

Yonder walls, that *pertly* front your town,
Yond towers, whose wanton tops do buss the clouds,
Must kiss their own feet. *Shakespeare.*

When you *pertly* raise your snout,
Fleer, and gibe, and laugh, and flout;
This, among Hibernian asses,
For sheer wit, and humour passes. *Swift.*

PE'RTNESS. *n. s.* [from *pert.*]

1. Brisk folly; sauciness; petulance.

Dulness delighted ey'd the lively dunce,
Remembring she herself was *pertness* once. *Dunciad.*

2. Petty liveliness; spriteliness without force, dignity or solidity.

There is in Shaftsbury's works a lively *pertness* and a parade of literature; but it is hard that we should be bound to admire the reveries. *Watts's Improvement of the Mind.*

PERTRA'NSIENT. *adj.* [*pertransiens*, Lat.] Passing over. *Dict.*

To PERTU'RB. } *v. a.* [*perturbo*, Latin.]
To PERTU'RBATE. }

1. To disquiet; to disturb; to deprive of tranquility.

Rest, rest, *perturbed* spirit. *Shakesp.*

His wasting flesh with anguish burns,
And his *perturbed* soul within him mourns. *Sandys.*

2. To disorder; to confuse; to put out of regularity.

They are content to suffer the penalties annexed, rather than *perturb* the publick peace. *King Charles.*

The inservient and brutal faculties controul'd the suggestions of truth; pleasure and profit overswaying the instructions of honesty, and sensuality *perturbing* the reasonable commands of virtue. *Brown's Vulgar Errours.*

The accession or secession of bodies from the earth's surface *perturb* not the equilibration of either hemisphere. *Brown.*

PERTURBA'TION. *n. s.* [*perturbatio*, Lat. *perturbation*, Fr.]

1. Disquiet of mind; deprivation of tranquillity.

Love was not in their looks, either to God,
Nor to each other; but apparent guilt,
And shame, and *perturbation*, and despair. *Milton.*

The soul as it is more immediately and strongly affected by this part, so doth it manifest all its passions and *perturbations* by it. *Ray on the Creation.*

2. Restlessness of passions.

Natures, that have much heat, and great and violent desires and *perturbations*, are not ripe for action, till they have passed the meridian of their years. *Bacon's Essays.*

3. Disturbance; disorder; confusion; commotion.

Although the long dissentions of the two houses had had lucid intervals, yet they did ever hang over the kingdom, ready to break forth into new *perturbations* and calamities. *Bacon.*

4. Cause of disquiet.

O polish'd *perturbation!* golden care!
That keep'st the ports of slumber open wide
To many a watchful night: sleep with it now,
Yet not so sound, and half so deeply sweet,
As he, whose brow with homely biggen bound,
Sleeps out the watch of night. *Shakesp. Henry IV.*

5. Commotion of passions.

Restore yourselves unto your temper, fathers;
And, without *perturbation*, hear me speak. *Ben. Johnson.*

PERTURBA'TOUR. *n. s.* [*perturbator*, Lat. *perturbateur*, Fr.] Raiser of commotions.

PERTU'SED. *adj.* [*pertusus*, Lat.] Bored; punched; pierced with holes. *Dict.*

PERTU'SION. *n. s.* [from *pertusus*, Latin.]

1. The act of piercing or punching.

The manner of opening a vein in Hippocrates's time, was by stabbing or *pertusion*, as it is performed in horses. *Arbuth.*

2. Hole made by punching or piercing.

An empty pot without earth in it, may be put over a fruit the better, if some few *pertusions* be made in the pot. *Bacon.*

To PERVA'DE. *v. a.* [*pervado*, Lat.]

1. To pass through an aperture; to permeate.

The labour'd chyle *pervades* the pores
In all the arterial perforated shores. *Blackmore.*

Paper dipped in water or oil, the oculus mundi stone steeped in water, linen-cloth oiled or varnished, and many other substances soaked in such liquors as will intimately *pervade* their little pores, become by that means more transparent than otherwise. *Newton's Opticks.*

2. To paſs through the whole extenſion.

Matter, once bereaved of motion, cannot of itſelf acquire it again, nor till it be ſtruck by ſome other body from without, or be intrinſically moved by an immaterial ſelf-active ſubſtance, that can penetrate and *pervade* it. *Bentley.*

What but God?
Pervades, adjuſts and agitates the whole. *Thomſon.*

PERVA'SION. *n. ſ.* [from *pervade.*] The act of pervading or paſſing through.

If fuſion be made rather by the ingreſs and tranſcurſions of the atoms of fire, than by the bare propagation of that motion, with which fire beats upon the outſide of the veſſels, that contain the matter to be melted; both thoſe kinds of fluidity, aſcribed to ſaltpetre, will appear to be cauſed by the *pervaſion* of a foreign body. *Boyle.*

PE'RVERSE. *adj.* [*pervers*, Fr. *perverſus*, Lat.]

1. Diſtorted from the right.

And nature breeds
Perverſe, all monſtrous, all prodigious things. *Milton.*

2. Obſtinate in the wrong; ſtubborn; untractable.

Then for the teſtimony of truth haſt born
Univerſal reproach; far worſe to bear
Than violence; for this was all thy care
To ſtand approv'd in ſight of God, though worlds
Judg'd thee *perverſe*. *Milton's Paradiſe Loſt.*

To ſo *perverſe* a ſex all grace is vain,
It gives them courage to offend again. *Dryden.*

3. Petulant; vexatious.

Oh gentle Romeo,
If thou doſt love, pronounce it faithfully,
Or if you think I am too quickly won,
I'll frown and be *perverſe*, and ſay thee nay,
So thou wilt wooe: but elſe not for the world. *Shakeſp.*

PERVE'RSELY. *adv.* [from *perverſe.*] With intent to vex; peeviſhly; vexatiouſly; ſpitefully; croſsly; with petty malignity.

Men *perverſely* take up picques and diſpleaſures at others, and then every opinion of the diſliked perſon muſt partake of his fate. *Decay of Piety.*

Men that do not *perverſely* uſe their words, or on purpoſe ſet themſelves to cavil, ſeldom miſtake the ſignification of the names of ſimple ideas. *Locke.*

A patriot is a dangerous poſt,
When wanted by his country moſt,
Perverſely comes in evil times,
Where virtues are imputed crimes. *Swift.*

PERVE'RSENESS. *n. ſ.* [from *perverſe.*]

1. Petulance; peeviſhneſs; ſpiteful croſſneſs.

A wholeſome tongue is a tree of life; *perverſeneſs* therein is a breach in the ſpirit. *Proverbs* xv. 4.

Virtue hath ſome *perverſeneſs*; for ſhe will
Neither believe her good, nor others ill. *Donne.*

He whom he wiſhes moſt, ſhall ſeldom gain
Through her *perverſeneſs*; but ſhall ſee her gain'd
By a far worſe. *Milton's Paradiſe Loſt.*

The *perverſeneſs* of my fate is ſuch,
That he's not mine, becauſe he's mine too much. *Dryden.*

When a friend in kindneſs tries
To ſhew you where your error lies,
Conviction does but more incenſe;
Perverſeneſs is your whole defence. *Swift.*

2. Perverſion; corruption. Not in uſe.

Neither can this be meant of evil governours or tyrants; for they are often eſtabliſhed as lawful potentates; but of ſome *perverſeneſs* and defection in the very nation itſelf. *Bacon.*

PERVE'RSION. *n. ſ.* [*perverſion*, Fr. from *perverſe.*] The act of perverting; change to ſomething worſe.

Women to govern men, ſlaves freemen, are much in the ſame degree; all being total violations and *perverſions* of the laws of nature and nations. *Bacon.*

He ſuppoſes that whole reverend body are ſo far from diſliking popery, that the hopes of enjoying the abby lands would be an effectual incitement to their *perverſion*. *Swift.*

PERVE'RSITY. *n. ſ.* [*perverſité*, Fr. from *perverſe.*] Perverſeneſs; croſſneſs.

What ſtrange *perverſity* is this of man!
When 'twas a crime to taſte th' inlightning tree,
He could not then his hand refrain. *Norris.*

To PERVE'RT. *v. a.* [*perverto*, Lat. *pervertir*, Fr.]

1. To diſtort from the true end or purpoſe.

Inſtead of good they may work ill, and *pervert* juſtice to extreme injuſtice. *Spenſer's State of Ireland.*

If thou ſeeſt the oppreſſion of the poor, and violent *perverting* of juſtice in a province, marvel not. *Ecclus.* v. 8.

If then his providence
Out of our evil ſeek to bring forth good,
Our labour muſt be to *pervert* that end,
And out of good ſtill to find means of evil. *Milton.*

He has *perverted* my meaning by his gloſſes; and interpreted my words into blaſphemy, of which they were not guilty. *Dryden.*

Porphyry has wrote a volume to explain this cave of the nymphs with more piety than judgment; and another perſon has *perverted* it into obſcenity; and both allegorically. *Broome.*

2. To corrupt; to turn from the right; oppoſed to convert, which is to turn from the wrong to the right.

The heinous and deſpiteful act
Of Satan, done in Paradiſe, and how
He in the ſerpent had *perverted* Eve,
Her huſband ſhe, to taſte the fatal fruit,
Was known in heav'n. *Milton's Paradiſe Loſt.*

PERVE'RTER. *n. ſ.* [from *pervert.*]

1. One that changes any thing from good to bad; a corrupter.

Where a child finds his own parents his *perverters*, he cannot be ſo properly born, as damned into the world. *South.*

2. One who diſtorts any thing from the right purpoſe.

He that reads a prohibition in a divine law, had need be well ſatisfied about the ſenſe he gives it, leſt he incur the wrath of God, and be found a *perverter* of his law. *Stillingfl.*

PERVE'RTIBLE. *adj.* [from *pervert.*] That may be eaſily perverted. *Ainſworth.*

PERVICA'CIOUS. *adj.* [*pervicax*, Lat.] Spitefully obſtinate; peeviſhly contumacious.

May private devotions be efficacious upon the mind of one of the moſt *pervicacious* young creatures! *Clariſſa.*

PERVICA'CIOUSLY. *adv.* [from *pervicacious.*] With ſpiteful obſtinacy.

PERVICA'CIOUSNESS. }
PERVICA'CITY. } *n. ſ.* [*pervicacia*, Lat. from *pervicacious.*] Spiteful obſtinacy.
PERVI'CACY. }

PE'RVIOUS. *adj.* [*pervius*, Latin.]

1. Admitting paſſage; capable of being permeated.

The Egyptians uſed to ſay, that unknown darkneſs is the firſt principle of the world; by darkneſs they mean God, whoſe ſecrets are *pervious* to no eye. *Taylor.*

Leda's twins
Conſpicuous both, and both in act to throw
Their trembling lances brandiſh'd at the foe,
Nor had they miſs'd; but he to thickets fled,
Conceal'd from aiming ſpears, not *pervious* to the ſteed. *Dryden.*

Thoſe lodged in other earth, more lax and *pervious*, decayed in tract of time, and rotted at length. *Woodward.*

2. Pervading; permeating. This ſenſe is not proper.

What is this little, agile, *pervious* fire,
This flutt'ring motion which we call the mind? *Prior.*

PE'RVIOUSNESS. *n. ſ.* [from *pervious.*] Quality of admitting a paſſage.

The *perviouſneſs* of our receiver to a body much more ſubtile than air, proceeded partly from the looſer texture of that glaſs the receiver was made of, and partly from the enormous heat, which opened the pores of the glaſs. *Boyle.*

There will be found another difference beſides that of *perviouſneſs*. *Holder's Elements of Speech.*

PERU'KE. *n. ſ.* [*peruque*, Fr.] A cap of falſe hair; a periwig.

I put him on a linen cap, and his *peruke* over that. *Wiſeman.*

To PERU'KE. *v. a.* [from the noun.] To dreſs in adſcititious hair.

PERU'KEMAKER. *n. ſ.* [*peruke* and *maker.*] A maker of perukes; a wigmaker.

PERU'SAL. [from *peruſe.*] The act of reading.

As pieces of miniature muſt be allowed a cloſer inſpection, ſo this treatiſe requires application in the *peruſal*. *Woodward.*

If upon a new *peruſal* you think it is written in the very ſpirit of the ancients, it deſerves your care, and is capable of being improved. *Atterbury.*

To PERU'SE. *v. a.* [*per* and *uſe.*]

1. To read.

Peruſe this writing here, and thou ſhalt know
The treaſon. *Shakeſp. Richard* II.

The petitions being thus prepared, do you conſtantly ſet apart an hour in a day to *peruſe* thoſe petitions. *Bacon.*

Carefully obſerve, whether he taſtes the diſtinguiſhing perfections or the ſpecifick qualities of the author whom he *peruſes*. *Addiſon's Spectator*, № 409.

2. To obſerve; to examine.

I hear the enemy;
Out ſome light horſemen, and *peruſe* their wings. *Shakeſ.*

I've *perus'd* her well;
Beauty and honour in her are ſo mingled,
That they have caught the king. *Shakeſpeare.*

Myſelf I then *perus'd*, and limb by limb
Survey'd. *Milton's Paradiſe Loſt.*

PERU'SER. *n. ſ.* [from *peruſe.*] A reader; examiner.

The difficulties and heſitations of every one will be according to the capacity of each *peruſer*, and as his penetration into nature is greater or leſs. *Woodward.*

PESA'DE. *n. ſ.*

Peſade is a motion a horſe makes in raiſing or lifting up his forequarters, keeping his hind legs upon the ground without ſtirring. *Farrier's Dict.*

PE'SSARY. *n. s.* [*pessarie*, Fr.] Is an oblong form of medicine, made to thrust up into the uterus upon some extraordinary occasions.

Of cantharides he prescribes five in a *pessary*, cutting off their heads and feet, mixt with myrrh. *Arbuthnot.*

PEST. *n. s.* [*peste*, Fr. *pestis*, Lat.]

1. Plague; pestilence.

Let fierce Achilles
The god propitiate, and the *pest* assuage. *Pope.*

2. Any thing mischievous or destructive.

The *pest* a virgin's face and bosom bears,
High on her crown a rising snake appears,
Guards her black front, and hisses in her hairs. *Pope.*

At her words the hellish *pest*
Forbore. *Milton's Paradise Lost.*

Of all virtues justice is the best;
Valour without it is a common *pest*. *Waller.*

To PE'STER. *v. a.* [*pester*, Fr.]

1. To disturb; to perplex; to harass; to turmoil.

Who then shall blame
His *pester'd* senses to recoil and start,
When all that is within him does condemn
Itself for being there. *Shakespeare's Macbeth.*

He hath not fail'd to *pester* us with message,
Importing the surrender of those lands. *Shakespeare.*

We are *pestered* with mice and rats, and to this end the cat is very serviceable. *More's Antidote against Atheism.*

They did so much *pester* the church and grossly delude the people, that contradictions themselves asserted by Rabbies were equally revered by them as the infallible will of God. *South's Sermons.*

A multitude of scribblers daily *pester* the world with their insufferable stuff. *Dryden.*

At home he was pursu'd with noise;
Abroad was *pester'd* by the boys. *Swift.*

2. To encumber.

Fitches and pease
For *pest'ring* too much on a hovel they lay. *Tusser.*

Confin'd and *pester'd* in this pinfold here,
Strive to keep up a frail and feverish being. *Milton.*

PE'STERER. *n. s.* [from *pester*.] One that pesters or disturbs.

PE'STEROUS. *adj.* [from *pester*.] Encumbering; cumbersome.

In the statute against vagabonds note the dislike the parliament had of goaling them, as that which was chargeable, *pesterous*, and of no open example. *Bacon's Henry* VII.

PE'STHOUSE. *n. s.* [from *pest* and *house*.] An hospital for persons infected with the plague.

PESTI'FEROUS. *adj.* [from *pestifer*, Lat.]

1. Destructive; mischievous.

Such is thy audacious wickedness,
Thy leud, *pestif'rous* and dissentious pranks,
The very infants prattle of thy pride. *Shakesp.*

You, that have discover'd secrets, and made such *pestiferous* reports of men nobly held, must die. *Shakesp.*

2. Pestilential; malignant; infectious.

It is easy to conceive how the steams of *pestiferous* bodies taint the air, while they are alive and hot. *Arbuthnot.*

PE'STILENCE. *n. s.* [*pestilence*, Fr. *pestilentia*, Lat.] Plague; pest; contagious distemper.

The red *pestilence* strike all trades in Rome,
And occupations perish. *Shakesp.*

When my eyes beheld Olivia first,
Methought she purg'd the air of *pestilence*. *Shakesp.*

PE'STILENT. *adj.* [*pestilent*, Fr. *pestilens*, Lat.]

1. Producing plagues; malignant.

Great ringing of bells in populous cities dissipated *pestilent* air, which may be from the concussion of the air, and not from the sound. *Bacon's Natural History.*

To those people that dwell under or near the equator, a perpetual spring would be a most *pestilent* and insupportable summer. *Bentley's Sermons.*

2. Mischievous; destructive.

There is nothing more contagious and *pestilent* than some kinds of harmony; than some nothing more strong and potent unto good. *Hooker, b.* v. *s.* 38.

Hoary moulded bread the soldiers thrusting upon their spears railed against king Ferdinand, who with such corrupt and *pestilent* bread would feed them. *Knolles.*

Which president, of *pestilent* import,
Against thee, Henry, had been brought. *Daniel.*

The world abounds with *pestilent* books, written against this doctrine. *Swift's Miscellanies.*

3. In ludicrous language, it is used to exaggerate the meaning of another word.

One *pestilent* fine,
His beard no bigger though than thine,
Walked on before the rest. *Suckling.*

PESTILE'NTIAL. *adj.* [*pestilenciel*, Fr. *pestilens*, Lat.]

1. Partaking of the nature of pestilence; producing pestilence; infectious; contagious.

These with the air passing into the lungs, infect the mass of blood, and lay the foundation of *pestilential* fevers. *Woodw.*

Fire involv'd
In *pestilential* vapours, stench and smoak. *Addison.*

2. Mischievous; destructive; pernicious.

If government depends upon religion, then this shews the *pestilential* design of those that attempt to disjoin the civil and ecclesiastical interests. *South's Sermons.*

PE'STILENTLY. *adv.* [from *pestilent*.] Mischievously; destructively.

PESTILLA'TION. *n. s.* [*pistillum*, Lat.] The act of pounding or breaking in a mortar.

The best diamonds are comminuble, and so far from breaking hammers, that they submit unto *pestillation*, and resist not any ordinary pestle. *Brown's Vulgar Errours.*

PE'STLE. *n. s.* [*pistillum*, Lat.] An instrument with which any thing is broken in a mortar.

What real alteration can the beating of the *pestle* make in any body, but of the texture of it. *Locke.*

Upon our vegetable food the teeth and jaws act as the *pestle* and mortar *Arbuthnot on Aliments.*

PESTLE *of Pork*. *n. s.* A gammon of bacon. *Ains.*

PET. *n. s.* [This word is of doubtful etymology; from *despit*, Fr. or *impetus*, Lat. perhaps it may be derived some way from *petit*, as it implies only a little fume or fret.]

1. A slight passion; a slight fit of anger.

If all the world
Should in a *pet* of temperance feed on pulse,
Drink the clear stream, and nothing wear but freeze,
Th' all-giver would be unthankt, would be unprais'd. *Milton.*

If we cannot obtain every vain thing we ask, our next business is to take *pet* at the refusal. *L'Estrange.*

Life, given for noble purposes, must not be thrown up in a *pet*, nor whined away in love. *Collier.*

They cause the proud their visits to delay,
And send the godly in a *pet* to pray. *Pope.*

2. A lamb taken into the house, and brought up by hand. A cade lamb. [Probably from *petit*, little.] *Hanmer.*

PE'TAL. *n. s.* [*petalum*, Latin.]

Petal is a term in botany, signifying those fine coloured leaves that compose the flowers of all plants: whence plants are distinguished into monopetalous, whose flower is one continued leaf; tripetalous, pentapetalous and polypetalous, when they consist of three, five or many leaves. *Quincy.*

PETA'LOUS. *adj.* [from *petal*.] Having petals.

PE'TAR. }
PE'TARD. } *n. s.* [*petard*, Fr. *petardo*, Italian.]

A *petard* is an engine of metal, almost in the shape of an hat, about seven inches deep, and about five inches over at the mouth: when charged with fine powder well beaten, it is covered with a madrier or plank, bound down fast with ropes, running through handles, which are round the rim near the mouth of it: this *petard* is applied to gates or barriers of such places as are designed to be surprized, to blow them up: they are also used in countermines to break through into the enemies galleries. *Military Dict.*

'Tis the sport to have the engineer
Hoist with his own *petar*. *Shakespeare's Hamlet.*

Find all his having and his holding,
Reduc'd t' eternal noise and scolding;
The conjugal *petard* that tears
Down all portcullices of ears. *Hudibras.*

PETE'CHIAL. *adj.* [from *petechiæ*, Lat.] Pestilentially spotted.

In London are many fevers with buboes and carbuncles, and many *petechial* or spotted fevers. *Arbuthnot.*

PE'TER-WORT. *n. s.* This plant differs from St. John's-wort, only in having a pyramidal seed-vessel, divided into five cells. *Miller.*

PETIT. *adj.* [French.] Small; inconsiderable.

By what small *petit* hints does the mind recover a vanishing notion? *South's Sermons.*

PETI'TION. *n. s.* [*petitio*, Latin.]

1. Request; intreaty; supplication; prayer.

We must propose unto all men certain *petitions* incident and very material in causes of this nature. *Hooker.*

My next poor *petition*
Is, that his noble grace would have some pity
Upon my wretched women. *Shakesp.*

Let my life be given at my *petition*, and my people at my request. *Esther* vii. 3.

Thou didst choose this house to be called by thy name, and to be a house of prayer and *petition* for thy people. 1 *Mac.* vii.

2. Single branch or article of a prayer.

Then pray'd that she might still possess his heart,
And no pretending rival share a part;
This last *petition* heard of all her pray'r. *Dryden.*

To PETI'TION. *v. a.* [from the noun.] To solicite; to supplicate.

You have *petition'd* all the gods
For my prosperity. *Shakesp. Coriolanus.*

The mother *petitioned* her goddess to bestow upon them the greatest gift that could be given. *Addison.*

PETI'TIONARILY. *adv.* [from *petitionary.*] By way of begging the question.

This doth but *petitionarily* infer a dextrality in the heavens, and we may as reasonably conclude a right and left laterality in the ark of Noah. *Brown.*

PETI'TIONARY. *n. s.* [from *petition.*]

1. Supplicatory; coming with petitions.

Pardon thy *petitionary* countrymen. *Shakesp.*

It is our base *petitionary* breath
That blows 'em to this greatness. *Ben. Johnson.*

2. Containing petitions or requests.

Petitionary prayer belongeth only to such as are in themselves impotent, and stand in need of relief from others. *Hooker.*

I return only yes or no to questionary and *petitionary* epistles of half a yard long. *Swift.*

PETI'TIONER. *n. s.* [from *petition.*] One who offers a petition.

When you have received the petitions, and it will please the *petitioners* well to deliver them into your own hand, let your secretary first read them, and draw lines under the material parts. *Bacon.*

What pleasure can it be to be encumbered with dependences, thronged and surrounded with *petitioners?* *South.*

Their prayers are to the reproach of the *petitioners*, and to the confusion of vain desires. *L'Estrange.*

His woes broke out, and begg'd relief
With tears, the dumb *petitioners* of grief. *Dryden.*

The Roman matrons presented a petition to the fathers; this raised so much raillery upon the *petitioners*, that the ladies never after offered to direct the lawgivers of their country. *Addison.*

PETI'TORY. *adj.* [*petitorius*, Lat. *petitoire*, Fr.] Petitioning; claiming the property of any thing. *Ains.*

PE'TRE. *n. s.* [from *petra*, a stone.] Nitre; salt petre. See NITRE.

Powder made of impure and greasy *petre*, hath but a weak emission, and gives but a faint report. *Brown.*

The vessel was first well nealed to prevent cracking, and covered to prevent the falling in of any thing, that might unseasonably kindle the *petre*. *Boyle.*

Nitre, while it is in its native state, is called *petre*-salt, when refined salt-*petre*. *Woodward.*

PETRE'SCENT. *adj.* [*petrescens*, Lat.] Growing stone; becoming stone.

A cave, from whose arched roof there dropped down a *petrescent* liquor, which oftentimes before it could fall to the ground congealed. *Boyle.*

PETRIFA'CTION. *n. s.* [from *petrifio*, Lat.]

1. The act of turning to stone; the state of being turned to stone.

Its concretive spirit has the seeds of *petrifaction* and gorgon within itself. *Brown.*

2. That which is made stone.

Look over the variety of beautiful shells, *petrifactions*, ores, minerals, stones, and other natural curiosities. *Cheyne.*

PETRI'FACTIVE. [from *petrifacio*, Lat.] Having the power to form stone.

There are many to be found, which are but the lapidescences and *petrifactive* mutation of bodies. *Brown.*

PETRIFI'CATION. *n. s.* [*petrification*, Fr. from *petrify.*] A body formed by changing other matter to stone.

In these strange *petrifications*, the hardening of the bodies seems to be effected principally, if not only, as in the induration of the fluid substances of an egg into a chick, by altering the disposition of their parts. *Boyle.*

PETRI'FICK. *adj.* [*petrificus*, Lat.] Having the power to change to stone.

The aggregated soil
Death with his mace *petrifick*, cold and dry,
As with a trident, smote. *Milton's Paradise Lost.*

To PE'TRIFY. *v. a.* [*petrifier*, Fr. *petra* and *fio*, Lat.] To change to stone.

Schism is markt out by the apostle to the Hebrews, as a kind of *petrifying* crime, which induces induration. *Decay of Piety.*

Though their souls be not yet wholly *petrified*, yet every act of sin makes gradual approaches to it. *Decay of Piety.*

A few resemble *petrified* wood. *Woodward.*

Full in the midst of Euclid dip at once,
And *petrify* a genius to a dunce. *Pope.*

To PE'TRIFY. *v. n.* To become stone.

Like Niobe we marble grow,
And *petrify* with grief. *Dryden.*

PETRO'L. / PETRO'LEUM. } *n. s.* [*petrole*, Fr.]

Petrol or *petroleum* is a liquid bitumen, black, floating on the water of springs. *Woodward.*

PE'TRONEL. *n. s.* [*petrinal*, Fr.] A pistol; a small gun used by a horseman.

And he with *petronel* upheav'd,
Instead of shield the blow receiv'd,
The gun recoil'd as well it might. *Hudibras.*

PE'TTICOAT. *n. s. petit* and *coat.*] The lower part of a woman's dress.

What trade art thou, Fuble?—a woman's taylor, sir.—Wilt thou make as many holes in an enemy's battle, as thou hast done in a woman's *petticoat?* *Shakespeare.*

Her feet beneath her *petticoat*,
Like little mice, stole in and out,
As if they fear'd the light. *Suckling.*

It is a great compliment to the sex, that the virtues are generally shewn in *petticoats*. *Addison.*

To fifty chosen sylphs, of special note,
We trust th' important charge, the *petticoat*;
Oft have we known that sevenfold fence to fail,
Though stiff with hoops, and arm'd with ribs of whale. *Pope's Rape of the Lock.*

PETTIFO'GGER. *n. s.* [corrupted from *pettivoguer*; *petit* and *voguer*, Fr.] A petty small-rate lawyer.

The worst conditioned and least cliented *petivoguers* get, under the sweet bait of revenge, more plentiful prosecution of actions. *Carew's Survey of Cornwall.*

Your *pettifoggers* damn their souls
To share with knaves in cheating fools. *Hudibras.*

Consider, my dear, how indecent it is to abandon your shop and follow *pettifoggers*; there is hardly a plea between two country esquires about a barren acre, but you draw yourself in as bail, surety or solicitor. *Arbuthnot's Hist. of J. Bull.*

Physicians are apt to despise empiricks, lawyers, *pettifoggers*, merchants and pedlars. *Swift.*

PE'TTINESS. *n. s.* [from *petty.*] Smallness; littleness; inconsiderableness; unimportance.

The losses we have borne, the subjects we
Have lost, and the disgrace we have digested;
To answer which, his *pettiness* would bow under. *Shakesp.*

PE'TTISH. *adj.* [from *pet.*] Fretful; peevish.

Nor doth their childhood prove their innocence;
They're froward, *pettish*, and unus'd to smile. *Creech.*

PETTI'SHNESS. *n. s.* [from *pettish.*] Fretfulness; peevishness.

Like children, when we lose our favourite plaything, we throw away the rest in a fit of *pettishness*. *Collier.*

PETTI'TOES. *n. s.* [*petty* and *toe.*]

1. The feet of a sucking pig.

2. Feet in contempt.

My good clown grew so in love with the wenches song, that he would not stir his *pettitoes*, till he had both tune and words. *Shakespeare's Winter's Tale.*

PE'TTO. [Italian.] The breast; figurative by privacy.

PE'TTY. *adj.* [*petit*, Fr.] Small; inconsiderable; inferiour; little.

When he had no power;
But was a *petty* servant to the state,
He was your enemy. *Shakespeare's Coriolanus.*

It is a common experience, that dogs know the dog-killer; when, as in time of infection, some *petty* fellow is sent out to kill the dogs. *Bacon's Nat. Hist.*

It importeth not much, some *petty* alteration or difference it may make. *Bacon.*

Will God incense his ire
For such a *petty* trespass. *Milton.*

From thence a thousand lesser poets sprung,
Like *petty* princes from the fall of Rome. *Denham.*

They believe one only chief and great God, which hath been from all eternity; who when he proposed to make the world, made first other gods of a principal order; and after, the sun, moon and stars, as *petty* gods. *Stillinfleet.*

By all I have read of *petty* commonwealths, as well as the great ones, it seems to me, that a free people do of themselves divide into three powers. *Swift.*

Bolonia water'd by the *petty* Rhine. *Addison.*

Can there an example be given, in the whole course of this war, where we have treated the *pettiest* prince, with whom we have had to deal, in so contemptuous a manner. *Swift's Miscellanies.*

PE'TTCOY. *n. s.* An herb. *Ainsworth.*

PE'TULANCE. / PE'TULANCY. } *n. s.* [*petulance*, Fr. *petulantia*, Lat.] Sauciness; peevishness; wantonness.

It was excellently said of that philosopher, that there was a wall or parapet of teeth set in our mouth, to restrain the *petulancy* of our words. *Ben. Johnson.*

Such was others *petulancy*, that they joyed to see their betters shamefully outraged and abused. *King Charles.*

Wise men knew that which looked like pride in some, and like *petulance* in others, would, by experience in affairs and conversation amongst men, be in time wrought off. *Clarendon.*

However their numbers, as well as their insolence and perverseness increased, many instances of *petulancy* and scurrility are to be seen in their pamphlets. *Swift.*

There appears in our age a pride and *petulancy* in youth, zealous to cast off the sentiments of their fathers and teachers. *Watts's Logick.*

PE'TULANT. *adj.* [*petulans*, Lat. *petulant*, Fr.]

1. Saucy; perverse.

If the opponent sees victory to incline to his side, let him shew the force of his argument, without too importunate and *petulant* demands of an answer. *Watts.*

2. Wanton.

2. Wanton.

The tongue of a man is so *petulant*, and his thoughts so variable, that one should not lay too great stress upon any present speeches and opinions. *Spectator*, N° 439.

PETU'LANTLY. *adv.* [from *petulant.*] With petulance: with saucy pertness.

PEW. *n. s.* [*puye*, Dutch.] A seat inclosed in a church.

When Sir Thomas More was lord chancellor, he did use, at mass, to sit in the chancel, and his lady in a *pew*. *Bacon.*

Should our sex take it into their heads to wear trunk breeches at church, a man and his wife would fill a whole *pew*. *Addison.*

PE'WET. *n. s.* [*piewit*, Dutch.]

1. A water fowl.

We reckon the dip-chick, so named of his diving and littleness, puffins, *pewets*, meawes. *Carew.*

2. The lapwing. *Ains.*

PE'WTER. *n. s.* [*peauter*, Dutch.] A compound of metals; an artificial metal.

Coarse *pewter* is made of fine tin and lead. *Bacon.*

The *pewter*, into which no water could enter, became more white, and liker to silver, and less flexible. *Bacon.*

Pewter dishes, with water in them, will not melt easily, but without it they will; nay, butter or oil, in themselves inflammable, yet, by their moisture, will do the like. *Bacon.*

2. The plates and dishes in a house.

The eye of the mistress was wont to make her *pewter* shine. *Addison.*

PEW'TERER. *n. s.* [from *pewter.*] A smith who works in pewter.

He shall charge you and discharge you with the motion of a *pewterer's* hammer. *Shakespear's Henry* IV.

We caused a skilful *pewterer* to close the vessel in our presence with soder exquisitely. *Boyle.*

PHÆNOMENON. *n. s.* This has sometimes *phænomena* in the plural. [φαίνομενον.] An appearance in the works of nature.

The paper was black, and the colours intense and thick, that the *phænomenon* might be conspicuous. *Newton.*

These are curiosities of little or no moment to the understanding the *phænomenon* of nature. *Newton.*

PHAGEDE'NA. *n. s.* [φαγέδαινα; from φάγω, *edo*, to eat.] An ulcer, where the sharpness of the humours eats away the flesh.

PHAGEDE'NICK. } PHAGEDE'NOUS. } *adj.* [*phagedenique*, Fr.] Eating; corroding.

Phagedenick medicines, are those which eat away fungous or proud flesh.

A bubo, according to its malignancy, either proves easily curable, or terminates in a *phagedenous* ulcer with jagged lips. *Wiseman's Surgery.*

When they are very putrid and corrosive, which circumstances give them the name of foul *phagedenick* ulcers, some spirits of wine should be added to the fomentation. *Sharp.*

PHA'LANX. *n. s.* [*phalanx*, Lat. *phalange*, Fr.] A troop of men closely embodied.

Far otherwise th' inviolable saints,
In cubic *phalanx* firm, advanc'd entire
Invulnerable, impenetrably arm'd. *Milton's Par. Lost.*

Who bid the stork, Columbus-like explore
Heav'ns not his own, and worlds unknown before?
Who calls the council, states the certain day?
Who forms the *phalanx*, and who points the way? *Pope.*

The Grecian *phalanx*, moveless as a tow'r,
On all sides batter'd, yet resists his pow'r. *Pope.*

PHANTA'SM. } PHANTA'SMA. } *n. s.* [φάντασμα, φαντασία; *phantasme*, *phantasie*, Fr.] Vain and airy appearance; something appearing only to imagination.

All the interim is
Like a *phantasma* or a hideous dream. *Shakespeare.*

This armado is a Spaniard that keeps here in court
A *phantasm*, a monarcho, and one that makes sport
To the prince and his book-mates. *Shakespeare.*

They believe, and they believe amiss, because they be but *phantasms* or apparitions. *Raleigh's Hist. of the World.*

If the great ones were in forwardness, the people were in fury, entertaining this airy body or *phantasm* with incredible affection; partly out of their great devotion to the house of York, partly out of proud humour. *Bacon's Henry* VII.

Why,
In this infernal vale first met, thou call'st
Me father, and that *phanta'm* call'st my son. *Milton.*

Assaying, by his devilish art, to reach
The organs of her fancy, and with them forge
Illusions, as he list, *phantasms* and dreams. *Milton.*

PHANTA'STICAL. } PHANTA'STICK. } See FANTASTICAL.

PHA'NTOM. *n. s.* [*phantome*, French.]

1. A spectre; an apparition.

If he cannot help believing, that such things he saw and heard, he may still have room to believe that, what this airy *phantom* said is not absolutely to be relied on. *Atterbury.*

A constant vapour o'er the palace flies;
Strange *phantoms* rising as the mists arise;
Dreadful as hermit's dreams in haunted shades,
Or bright, as visions of expiring maids. *Pope.*

2. A fancied vision.

Restless and impatient to try every scheme and overture of present happiness, he hunts a *phantom* he can never overtake. *Roger's Sermons.*

As Pallas will'd, along the sable skies,
To calm the queen, the *phantom* sister flies. *Pope.*

PHARISA'ICAL. *adj.* [from *pharisee.*] Ritual; externally religious, from the sect of the Pharisees, whose religion consisted almost wholly in ceremonies.

The causes of superstition are pleasing and sensual rites, excess of outward and *pharisaical* holiness, over-great reverence of traditions, which cannot but load the church. *Bacon.*

Suffer us not to be deluded with *pharisaical* washings instead of christian reformings. *King Charles.*

PHARMACE'UTICAL. } PHARMACE'UTICK. } *adj.* [φαρμακευτικὸς, from φαρμακεύω.] Relating to the knowledge or art of pharmacy, or preparation of medicines.

PHARMACO'LOGIST. *n. s.* [φάρμακον and λέγω.] One who writes upon drugs.

The osteocolla is recommended by the common *pharmacologists* as an absorbent and conglutinator of broken bones. *Woodward on Fossils.*

PHARMACO'LOGY. *n. s.* [φάρμακον and λέγω.] The knowledge of drugs and medicines.

PHARMACOPOEI'A. *n. s.* [φαρμακον and ποιέω; *pharmacopée*, Fr.] A dispensatory; a book containing rules for the composition of medicines.

PHARMACO'POLIST. *n. s.* [φάρμακον and πωλέω; *pharmacepole*, Fr.] An apothecary; one who sells medicines.

PHA'RMACY. *n. s.* [from φαρμακον, a medicine; *pharmacie*, Fr.] The art or practice of preparing medicines; the trade of an apothecary.

Each dose the goddess weighs with watchful eye,
So nice her art in impious *pharmacy*. *Garth.*

PHA'ROS. } PHARE. } *n. s.* [from *pharos* in Egypt.] A light-house; a lantern from the shore to direct sailors.

He augmented and repaired the port of Ostia, built a *pharos* or light-house. *Arbuthnot on Coins.*

PHARYNGO'TOMY. *n. s.* [φάρυγξ and τέμνω.] The act of making an incision into the wind-pipe, used when some tumour in the throat hinders respiration.

PHA'SELS. *n. s.* [*phaseoli*, Lat.] French beans. *Ains.*

PHA'SIS. *n. s.* In the plural *phases*. [φάσις; *phase*, Fr.] Appearance exhibited by any body; as the changes of the moon.

All the hypotheses yet contrived, were built upon too narrow an inspection of the *phases* of the universe. *Glanvill.*

He o'er the seas shall love, or fame pursue;
And other months, another *phasis* view;
Fixt to the rudder, he shall boldly steer,
And pass those rocks which Tiphys us'd to fear. *Creech.*

PHASM. *n. s.* [φάσμα.] Appearance; phantom; fancied apparition.

Thence proceed many aereal fictions and *phasms*, and chymæras created by the vanity of our own hearts or seduction of evil spirits, and not planted in them by God. *Hammond.*

PHE'ASANT. *n. s.* [*faisan*, Fr. *phasianus*, from *Phasis*, the river of Cholchos.] A kind of wild cock.

The hardest to draw are tame birds; as the cock, peacock and *pheasant*. *Peacham on Drawing.*

Preach as I please, I doubt our curious men
Will chuse a *pheasant* still before a hen. *Pope.*

PHEER. *n. s.* A companion. See FEER. *Spenser.*

To PHEESE. *v. a.* [perhaps to *feaze.*] To comb; to fleece; to curry.

An he be proud with me, I'll *pheese* his pride. *Shakesp.*

PHENI'COPTER. *n. s.* [φοινικόπτερος; *phœnicopterus*, Lat.] A kind of bird, which is thus described by *Martial:*

Dat mihi penna rubens nomen sed lingua gulosis
Nostra sapit; quid si garrula lingua foret?

He blended together the livers of guiltheads, the brains of pheasants and peacocks, tongues of *phenicopters*, and the melts of lampres. *Hakewill on Providence.*

PHE'NIX. *n. s.* [φοίνιξ; *phœnix*, Lat.] The bird which is supposed to exist single, and to rise again from its own ashes.

There is one tree, the *phenix* throne; one *phenix*
At this hour reigning there. *Shakesp. Tempest.*

To all the fowls he seems a *phenix*. *Milton.*

Having the idea of a *phenix* in my mind, the first enquiry is, whether such a thing does exist? *Locke.*

PHENO'MENON. *n. s.* [φαινομενον; *phenomene*, Fr. it is therefore often written *phænomenon*; but being naturalised, it has changed the *æ*, which is not in the English language, to *e.*]

1. Appearance; visible quality.

Short-sighted minds are unfit to make philosophers, whose business it is to describe in comprehensive theories, the *phenomena* of the world and their causes. *Burnet.*

The most considerable *phenomenon*, belonging to terrestrial bodies, is gravitation, whereby all bodies in the vicinity of the earth press towards its centre. *Bentley's Sermons.*

2. Any thing that strikes by any new appearance.

PHI'AL. *n. ſ.* [*phiala*, Lat. *phiôle*, Fr.] A ſmall bottle.

Upon my ſecure hour thy uncle ſtole
With juice of curſed hebenon in a *phial*. *Shakeſp.*

He proves his explications by experiments made with a *phial* full of water, and with globes of glaſs filled with water. *Newton's Opticks.*

PHILA'NTHROPY. *n. ſ.* [φιλέω and ἄνθρωπος.] Love of mankind; good nature.

Such a tranſient temporary good nature is not that *philanthropy*, that love of mankind, which deſerves the title of a moral virtue. *Addiſon's Spectator*, Nº 177.

PHILI'PPICK. *adj.* [from the invectives of Demoſthenes againſt Philip of Macedon.] Any invective declamation.

PHILO'LOGER. *n. ſ.* [φιλόλογος.] One whoſe chief ſtudy is language; a grammarian; a critick.

Philologers and critical diſcourſers, who look beyond the ſhell and obvious exteriors of things, will not be angry with our narrower explorations. *Brown.*

You expect, that I ſhould diſcourſe of this matter like a naturaliſt, not a *philologer*. *Boyle.*

The beſt *philologers* ſay, that the original word does not only ſignify domeſtick, as oppoſed to foreign, but alſo private, as oppoſed to common. *Sprat's Sermons.*

PHILO'LOGICAL. *adj.* [from *philology*.] Critical; grammatical.

Studies, called *philological*, are hiſtory, language, grammar, rhetorick, poeſy and criticiſm. *Watts.*

He who pretends to the learned profeſſions, if he doth not ariſe to be a critick himſelf in *philological* matters, ſhould frequently converſe with dictionaries, paraphraſts, commentators or other criticks, which may relieve any difficulties. *Watts.*

PHILO'LOGIST. *n. ſ.* [φιλόλογος.] A critick; a grammarian.

PHILO'LOGY. *n. ſ.* [φιλολογία; *philologie*, Fr.] Criticiſm; grammatical learning.

Temper all diſcourſes of *philology* with interſperſions of morality. *Walker.*

PHI'LOMEL. } *n. ſ.* [from *Philomela*, changed into a bird.]
PHILOME'LA. } The nightingale.

Time drives the flocks from field to fold,
When rivers rage, and rocks grow cold,
And *philomel* becometh dumb. *Shakeſp.*
Hears the hawk, when *philomela* ſings? *Pope.*
Liſtening *philomela* deigns
To let them joy. *Thomſon.*

PHI'LOMOT. *adj.* [corrupted from *feuille morte*, a dead leaf.] Coloured like a dead leaf.

One of them was blue, another yellow, and another *philomot*, the fourth was of a pink colour, and the fifth of a pale green. *Addiſon's Spectator*, Nº 265.

PHILO'SOPHEME. *n. ſ.* [φιλοσόφημα.] Principle of reaſoning; theorem. An unuſual word.

You will learn how to addreſs yourſelf to children for their benefit, and derive ſome uſeful *philoſophemes* for your own entertainment. *Watts.*

PHILO'SOPHER. *n. ſ.* [*philoſophus*, Lat. *philoſophe*, Fr.] A man deep in knowledge, either moral or natural.

Many ſound in belief have been alſo great *philoſophers*. *Hooker's Eccleſiaſtical Polity.*

That ſtone
Philoſophers in vain ſo long have ſought. *Milton.*

Adam, in the ſtate of innocence, came into the world a *philoſopher*, which ſufficiently appeared by his writing the natures of things upon their names; he could view eſſences in themſelves, and read forms without the comment of their reſpective properties. *South's Sermons.*

They all our fam'd *philoſophers* defie,
And would our faith by force of reaſon try. *Dryden.*

If the *philoſophers* by fire had been ſo wary in their obſervations and ſincere in their reports, as thoſe, who call themſelves *philoſophers*, ought to have been, our acquaintance with the bodies here about us had been yet much greater. *Locke.*

PHILOSOPHERS *ſtone. n. ſ.* A ſtone dreamed of by alchemiſts, which, by its touch, converts baſe metals into gold.

PHILOSO'PHICK. } *adj.* [*philoſophique*, Fr. from *philoſophy*.]
PHILOSO'PHICAL. }

1. Belonging to philoſophy; ſuitable to a philoſopher; formed by philoſophy.

Others in virtue plac'd felicity:
The ſtoic laſt in *philoſophick* pride
By him call'd virtue; and his virtuous man,
Wiſe, perfect in himſelf, and all poſſeſſing. *Milton.*
How could our chymick friends go on
To find the *philoſophick* ſtone. *Prior.*

When the ſafety of the publick is endangered, the appearance of a *philoſophical* or affected indolence muſt ariſe either from ſtupidity or perfidiouſneſs. *Addiſon's Freeholder.*

2. Skilled in philoſophy.

We have our *philoſophical* perſons to make modern and familiar, things ſupernatural and cauſeleſs. *Shakeſp.*

Acquaintance with God is not a ſpeculative knowledge, built on abſtracted reaſonings about his nature and eſſence, ſuch as *philoſophical* minds often buſy themſelves in, without reaping from thence any advantage towards regulating their paſſions, but practical knowledge. *Atterbury's Sermons.*

3. Frugal; abſtemious.

This is what nature's wants may well ſuffice:
But ſince among mankind ſo few there are,
Who will conform to *philoſophick* fare,
I'll mingle ſomething of our times to pleaſe. *Dryden.*

PHILOSO'PHICALLY. *adv.* [from *philoſophical*.] In a philoſophical manner; rationally; wiſely.

The law of commonweales that cut off the right hand of malefactors, if *philoſophically* executed, is impartial; otherwiſe the amputation not equally puniſheth all. *Brown.*

No man has ever treated the paſſion of love with ſo much delicacy of thought and of expreſſion, or ſearched into the nature of it more *philoſophically* than Ovid. *Dryden.*

If natural laws were once ſettled, they are never to be reverſed; to violate and infringe them, is the ſame as what we call miracle, and doth not ſound very *philoſophically* out of the mouth of an atheiſt. *Bentley's Sermons.*

To PHILO'SOPHIZE. *v. a.* [from *philoſophy*.] To play the philoſopher; to reaſon like a philoſopher; to moralize; to enquire into the cauſes of effects.

Qualities, that were occult to Ariſtotle, muſt be ſo to us; and we muſt not *philoſophize* beyond ſympathy and antipathy. *Glanvill's Scept.*

The wax *philoſophized* upon the matter, and finding out at laſt that it was burning, made the brick ſo hard, caſt itſelf into the fire. *L'Eſtrange.*

Two doctors of the ſchools were *philoſophizing* upon the advantages of mankind above all other creatures. *L'Eſtrange.*

Some of our *philoſophizing* divines have too much exalted the faculties of our ſouls, when they have maintained, that by their force mankind has been able to find out God. *Dryd.*

PHI'LOSOPHY. *n. ſ.* [*philoſophie*, Fr. *philoſophia*, Latin.]

1. Knowledge natural or moral.

I had never read, heard nor ſeen any thing, I had never any taſte of *philoſophy* nor inward feeling in myſelf, which for a while I did not call to my ſuccour. *Sidney.*

Hang up *philoſophy*;
Unleſs *philoſophy* can make a Juliet,
Diſplant a town, reverſe a prince's doom,
It helps not. *Shakeſp.*

The progreſs you have made in *philoſophy*, hath enabled you to benefit yourſelf with what I have written. *Digby.*

2. Hypotheſis or ſyſtem upon which natural effects are explained.

We ſhall in vain interpret their words by the notions of our *philoſophy*, and the doctrines in our ſchools. *Locke.*

3. Reaſoning; argumentation.

Of good and evil much they argu'd then
Vain wiſdom all and falſe *philoſophy*. *Milton.*

His deciſions are the judgment of his paſſions and not of his reaſon, the *philoſophy* of the ſinner and not of the man. *Rogers's Sermons.*

4. The courſe of ſciences read in the ſchools.

PHI'LTER. *n. ſ.* [φίλτρον; *philtre*, Fr.] Something to cauſe love.

The melting kiſs that ſips
The jellied *philtre* of her lips. *Cleaveland.*
This cup a cure for both our ills has brought,
You need not fear a *philter* in the draught. *Dryden.*

A *philter* that has neither drug nor enchantment in it, love if you would raiſe love. *Addiſon's Freeholder*, Nº 38.

To PHI'LTER. *v. a.* [from the noun.] To charm to love.

Let not thoſe that have repudiated the more inviting ſins, ſhew themſelves *philtred* and bewitched by this. *Gov. of Tong.*

PHIZ. *n. ſ.* [This word is formed by a ridiculous contraction from *phyſiognomy*, and ſhould thereſore, if it be written at all, be written *phyz*.] The face, in a ſenſe of contempt.

His air was too proud, and his features amiſs,
As if being a traitor had alter'd his *phiz*. *Stepney.*

PHLEBO'TOMIST. *n. ſ.* [*phlebotomiſte*, Fr. from φλέψ and τέμνω.] One that opens a vein; a bloodletter.

To PHLEBO'TOMIZE. *v. a.* [*phlebotomiſer*, Fr. from *phlebotomy*.] To let blood.

The frail bodies of men muſt have an evacuation for their humours, and be *phlebotomized*. *How. Tears.*

PHLEBO'TOMY. *n. ſ.* [φλεβοτομία, φλέψ, φλεβὸς, vena, and τέμνω; *phlebotomie*, Fr.] Bloodletting; the act or practice of opening a vein for medical intentions.

Although in indiſpoſitions of the liver or ſpleen, conſiderations are made in *phlebotomy* to their ſituation, yet, when the heart is affected, it is thought as effectual to bleed on the right as the left. *Brown's Vulgar Errours.*

Pains for the ſpending of the ſpirits, come neareſt to the copious and ſwift loſs of ſpirits by *phlebotomy*. *Harvey.*

PHLEGM. *n. ſ.* [φλέγμα; *phlegme*, Fr.]

1. The watry humour of the body, which, when it predominates, is ſuppoſed to produce ſluggiſhneſs or dulneſs.

Make the proper uſe of each extreme,
And write with fury, but correct with *phlegm*. *Roſcommon.*
He who ſupreme in judgment, as in wit,
Might boldly cenſure, as he boldly writ,
Yet judg'd with coolneſs, though he ſung with fire;

Our critics take a contrary extreme,
They judge with fury, but they write with *phle'm*. *Pope.*
Let melancholy rule supreme,
Choler preside, or blood or *phlegm*. *Swift.*

2. Water.

A linen cloth, dipped in common spirit of wine, is not burnt by the flame, because the *phlegm* of the liquor defends the cloth. *Boyle.*

PHLE'GMAGOGUES. *n. s.* [φλέγμα and ἄγω; *phlegmagogue*, Fr.] A purge of the milder sort, supposed to evacuate phlegm and leave the other humours.

The pituitous temper of the stomachick ferment must be corrected, and *phlegmagogues* must evacuate it. *Floyer.*

PHLEGMA'TICK. *adj.* [φλεγματικος; *phlegmatique*, Fr. from *phlegm.*]

1. Abounding in phlegm.

A neat's foot,
I fear, is too *phlegmatick* a meat. *Shakesp.*

The putrid vapours, though exciting a fever, do colliquate the *phlegmatick* humours of the body. *Harvey.*

Chewing and smoaking of tobacco is only proper for *phlegmatick* people. *Arbuthnot on Aliments.*

2. Generating phlegm.

Negroes, transplanted into cold and *phlegmatick* habitations, continue their hue in themselves and generations. *Brown.*

3. Watry.

Spirit of wine is inflammable by means of its oily parts, and being distilled often from salt of tartar, grows by every distillation more and more aqueous and *phlegmatick*. *Newton.*

4. Dull; cold; frigid.

As the inhabitants are of a heavy *phlegmatick* temper, if any leading member has more fire than comes to his share, it is quickly tempered by the coldness of the rest. *Addison.*

Who but a husband ever could persuade
His heart to leave the bosom of thy love,
For any *phlegmatick* design of state. *Southern.*

PHLE'GMON. *n. s.* [φλεγμονὴ.] An inflammation; a burning tumour.

Phlegmon or inflammation is the first degeneration from good blood, and nearest of kin to it. *Wiseman.*

PHLE'GMONOUS. *adj.* [from *phlegmon.*] Inflammatory; burning.

It is generated secondarly out of the dregs and remainder of a *phlegmonous* or œdematick tumour. *Harvey.*

PHLEME. *n. s.* [from *phlæbotomus*, Lat.] A fleam, so it is commonly written; an instrument which is placed on the vein and driven into it with a blow; particularly in bleeding of horses.

PHLOGI'STON. *n. s.* [φλογιστὸς, from φλέγω.]

1. A chemical liquor extremely inflammable.
2. The inflammable part of any body.

PHO'NICKS. *n. s.* [from φωνὴ.] The doctrine of sounds.

PHONOCA'MPTICK. *adj.* [φωνὴ and κάμπτω.] Having the power to inflect or turn the sound, and by that to alter it.

The magnifying the sound by the polyphonisms or repercussions of the rocks, and other *phonocamptick* objects. *Derham.*

PHO'SPHOR. / PHO'SHORUS. } *n. s.* [*phosphorus*, Lat.]

1. The morning star.

Why sit we sad when *phosphor* shines so clear, *Pope.*

2. A chemical substance which, exposed to the air, takes fire.

Of lambent flame you have whole sheets in a handful of *phosphor*. *Addison.*

Liquid and solid *phosphorus* show their flames more conspicuously, when exposed to the air. *Cheyne.*

PHRASE. *n. s.* [φράσις.]

1. An idiom; a mode of speech peculiar to a language.
2. An expression; a mode of speech.

Now mince the sin,
And mollify damnation with a *phrase*:
Say you consented not to Sancho's death,
But barely not forbad it. *Dryden.*

To fear the Lord, and depart from evil, are *phrases* which the scripture useth to express the sum of religion. *Tillotson.*

3. Stile; expression.

Thou speak'st
In better *phrase* and matter than thou didst. *Shakesp.*

To PHRASE. *v. a.* [from the noun.] To stile; to call; to term.

These suns,
For so they *phrase* them, by their heralds challenged
The noble spirits to arms. *Shakesp. Henry* VIII.

PHRASEO'LOGY. *n. s.* [φράσις and λέγω.]

1. Stile; diction.

The scholars of Ireland seem not to have the least conception of a stile, but run on in a flat *phraseology*, often mingled with barbarous terms. *Swift's Miscellanies.*

2. A phrase book. *Ainsw.*

PHRENI'TIS. *n. s.* [φρενῖτις.] Madness; inflammation of the brain.

It is allowed to prevent a *phrenitis*. *Wiseman's Surgery.*

PHRENE'TICK. / PHRE'NTICK. } *adj.* [φρενητικὸς; *phrenitique*, Fr.] Mad; inflamed in the brain; frantick.

Phreneticks imagine they see that without, which their imagination is affected with within. *Harvey.*

What œstrum, what *phrenetick* mood,
Makes you thus lavish of your blood. *Hudibras.*

The world was little better than a common fold of *phrenticks* and bedlams. *Woodward's Natural History.*

PHRE'NSY. *n. s.* [from φρενῖτις; *phrenesie*, Fr. whence, by contraction, *phrensy.*] Madness; franticness. This is too often written *frenzy*. See FRENZY.

Many never think on God, but in extremity of fear, and then perplexity not suffering them to be idle, they think and do as it were in a *phrensy*. *Hooker, b. v. s. 3.*

Demoniack *phrensy*, mooping melancholy. *Milton.*

Would they only please themselves in the delusion, the *phrensy* were more innocent; but lunaticks will needs be kings. *Decay of Piety.*

Phrensy or inflammation of the brain, profuse hemorrhages from the nose resolve, and copious bleeding in the temporal arteries. *Arbuthnot on Aliments.*

PHTHISI'CAL. *adj.* [φθισικὸς; *phtysique*, Fr. from *phthisick.*] Wasting.

Collection of purulent matter in the capacity of the breast, if not suddenly cured, doth undoubtedly impell the patient into a *phthisical* consumption. *Harvey on Consumptions.*

PHTHI'SICK. *n. s.* [φθίσις; *phtysie*, Fr.] A consumption.

His disease was a *phthisick* or asthma oft incurring to an orthopnea. *Harvey on Consumptions.*

PHTHI'SIS. *n. s.* [φθίσις.] A consumption.

If the lungs be wounded deep, though they escape the first nine days, yet they terminate in a *phthisis* or fistula. *Wiseman.*

PHILA'CTERY. *n. s.* [φυλακτήριον; *phylactere*, Fr.] A bandage on which was inscribed some memorable sentence.

The *philacteries* on their wrists and foreheads were looked on as spells, which would yield them impunity for their disobedience. *Hammond.*

Golden sayings
On large *phylacteries* expressive writ,
Were to the foreheads of the Rabbins ty'd. *Prior.*

PHY'SICAL. *adj.* [*physique*, Fr. from *physick.*]

1. Relating to nature or to natural philosophy; not moral.

The *physical* notion of necessity, that without which the work cannot possibly be done; it cannot be affirmed of all the articles of the creed, that they are thus necessary. *Hamm.*

To reflect on those innumerable secrets of nature and *physical* philosophy, which Homer wrought in his allegories, what a new scene of wonder may this afford us! *Pope.*

Charity in its origin is a *physical* and necessary consequence of the principle of re-union. *Cheyne's Philosophical Principles.*

2. Pertaining to the science of healing.
3. Medicinal; helpful to health.

Is Brutus sick? and is it *physical*
To walk unbraced, and suck up the humours
Of the dank morning. *Shakesp. Julius Cæsar.*

The blood, I drop, is rather *physical*
Than dangerous to me. *Shakesp. Coriolanus.*

4. Resembling physick.

PHY'SICALLY. *adv.* [from *physical.*] According to nature; by natural operation; in the way or sense of natural philosophy; not morally.

Time measuring out their motion, informs us of the periods and terms of their duration, rather than effecteth or *physically* produceth the same. *Brown's Vulgar Errours.*

The outward act of worship may be considered *physically* and abstractly from any law, and so it depends upon the nature of the intention, and morally, as good or evil: and so it receives its denomination from the law. *Stillingfleet.*

Though the act of the will commanding, and the act of any other faculty, executing that which is so commanded, be *physically* and in the precise nature of things distinct, yet morally as they proced from one entire, free, moral agent, may pass for one and the same action. *South's Sermons.*

I do not say, that the nature of light consists in small round globules, for I am not now treating *physically* of light or colours. *Locke.*

PHYSI'CIAN. *n. s.* [*physicien*, Fr. from *physick.*] One who professes the art of healing.

Trust not the *physician*,
His antidotes are poison, and he slays
More than you rob. *Shakesp. Timon of Athens.*

Some *physicians* are so conformable to the humour of the patient, as they press not the true cure of the disease, and others are so regular, as they respect not sufficiently the condition of the patient. *Bacon's Essays.*

His gratulatory verse to king Henry, is not more witty than the epigram upon the name of Nicolaus an ignorant *physician*, who had been the death of thousands. *Peacham of Poetry.*

Taught by thy art divine, the sage *physician*
Eludes the urn; and chains, or exiles death. *Prior.*

PHY'SICK. *n. s.* [φυσικὴ, which, originally signifying natural philosophy, has been transferred in many modern languages to medicine.] The science of healing.

Were

Were it my business to understand *physick*, would not the safer way be to consult nature herself in the history of diseases and their cures, than espouse the principles of the dogmatists, methodists or chymists. *Locke.*

2. Medicines; remedies.

In itself we desire health, *physick* only for health's sake. *Hooker, b. v. s.* 48.

Use *physick* or ever thou be sick. *Ecclus.* xviii. 19.

Prayer is the best *physick* for many melancholy diseases. *Peacham.*

He 'scapes the best, who nature to repair
Draws *physick* from the fields in draughts of vital air. *Dryd.*

3. [In common phrase.] A purge.

The people use *physick* to purge themselves of humours. *Abbot's Description of the World.*

To PHY'SICK. *v. a.* [from the noun.] To purge; to treat with physick; to cure.

The labour we delight in, *physicks* pain. *Shakesp.*

It is a gallant child; one that indeed *physicks* the subject, makes old hearts fresh. *Shakesp. Winter's Tale.*

Give him allowance as the worthier man;
For that will *physick* the great myrmidon
Who broils in loud applause. *Shakesp.*

In virtue and in health we love to be instructed, as well as *physicked* with pleasure. *L'Estrange.*

PHYSICO'THEOLOGY. *n. s.* [from *physico* and *theology*.] Divinity enforced or illustrated by natural philosophy.

PHYSIO'GNOMER. } *n. s. physionomiste*, Fr. [from *physiognomy*.]
PHYSIO'GNOMIST. } One who judges of the temper or future fortune by the features of the face.

Digonius, when he should have been put to death by the Turk, a *physiognomer* wished he might not die, because he would sow much dissention among the Christians. *Peacham.*

Apelles made his pictures so very like, that a *physiognomist* and fortune-teller, foretold by looking on them the time of their deaths, whom those pictures represented. *Dryden.*

Let the *physiognomists* examine his features. *Arb. and Pope.*

PHYSIOGNO'MICK. } *adj.* [Φυσιογνωμονικὸς; from *physiog-*
PHYSIOGNO'MONICK. } *nomy*.] Drawn from the contemplation of the face; conversant in contemplation of the face.

PHYSIO'GNOMY. *n. s.* [for *physiognomony*; φυσιογνωμονία; *physionomie*, Fr.]

1. The act of discovering the temper, and foreknowing the fortune by the features of the face.

In all *physiognomy*, the lineaments of the body will discover those natural inclinations of the mind which dissimulation will conceal, or discipline will suppress. *Bacon's Nat. Hist.*

2. The face; the cast of the look.

The astrologer, who spells the stars,
Mistakes his globes and in her brighter eye
Interprets heaven's *physiognomy*. *Cleaveland.*

They'll find i'th' *physiognomies*
O' th' planets all men's destinies. *Hudibras.*

The end of portraits consists in expressing the true temper of those persons which it represents, and to make known their *physiognomy*. *Dryden's Dufresnoy.*

The distinguishing characters of the face, and the lineaments of the body, grow more plain and visible with time and age; but the peculiar *physiognomy* of the mind is most discernible in children. *Locke.*

PHYSIO'LOGICAL. *adj.* [from *physiology*.] Relating to the doctrine of the natural constitution of things.

Some of them seem rather metaphysical than *physiological* notions. *Boyle.*

PHYSIO'LOGIST. *n. s.* [from *physiology*.] One versed in physiology; a writer of natural philosophy.

PHYSIO'LOGY. *n. s.* [φύσις and λέγω; *physiologie*, Fr.] The doctrine of the constitution of the works of nature.

Disputing *physiology* is of no accommodation to your designs. *Glanvill's Scept.*

Philosophers adapted their description of the deity to the vulgar, otherwise the conceptions of mankind could not be accounted for from their *physiology*. *Bentley's Sermons.*

PHYSY. *n. s.* [I suppose the same with *fusee*.] See FUSEE.

Some watches are made with four wheels, some have strings and *physies*, and others none. *Locke.*

PHYTI'VOROUS. *adj.* [φυτὸν and *voro*, Lat.] That eats grass or any vegetable.

Hairy animals with only two large foreteeth, are all *phytivorous*, and called the hare-kind. *Ray.*

PHYTO'GRAPHY. *n. s.* [φυτὸν and γράφω.] A description of plants.

PHYTOLOGY. *n. s.* [φυτὸν and γράφω.] The doctrine of plants; botanical discourse.

PI'ACLE. *n. s.* [*piaculum*, Lat.] An enormous crime. A word not used.

To tear the paps that gave them suck, can there be a greater *piacle* against nature, can there be a more execrable and horrid thing? *Howel's England's Tears.*

PIA'CULAR. } *adj.* [*piacularis*, from *piaculum*, Lat.]
PIA'CULOUS. }

1. Expiatory; having the power to attone.

2. Such as requires expiation.

It was *piaculous* unto the Romans to pare their nails upon the nundinæ, observed every ninth day. *Brown.*

3. Criminal; atrociously bad.

While we think it so *piaculous* to go beyond the ancients, we must necessarily come short of genuine antiquity and truth. *Glanvill's Scept.*

PIA-MATER. n. s. [Lat.] A thin and delicate membrane, which lies under the dura mater, and covers immediately the substance of the brain.

PI'ANET. *n. s.*

1. A bird; the lesser wood-pecker. *Bailey.*

2. The magpie. This name is retained in Scotland.

PIA'STER. *n. s.* [*piastra*, Italian.] An Italian coin, about five shillings sterling in value. *Dict.*

PIAZZA. n. s. [Italian.] A walk under a roof supported by pillars.

He stood under the *piazza*. *Arb. and Pope's Scriblerus.*

PICA. *n. s.* Among printers, a particular size of their types or letters. This dictionary is in small *pica*.

PICARO'ON. *n. s.* [from *picare*, Italian.] A robber; a plunderer.

Corsica and Majorca in all wars have been the nests of *picaroons*. *Temple's Miscellanies.*

PI'CCAGE. *n. s.* [*piccagium*, low Lat.] Money paid at fairs for breaking ground for booths. *Ains.*

To PICK. *v. a.* [*picken*, Dutch.]

1. To cull; to chuse; to select; to glean; to gather here and there.

This fellow *picks* up wit as pigeons peas. *Shakesp.*

He hath *pick'd* out an act,
Under whose heavy sense your brother's life
Falls into forfeit. *Shakesp. Measure for Measure.*

Trust me, sweet,
Out of this silence yet I *pick'd* a welcome:
And in the modesty of fearful duty
I read as much, as from the rattling tongue
Of saucy and audacious eloquence. *Shakesp.*

Contempt putteth an edge upon anger more than the hurt itself; and when men are ingenious in *picking* out circumstances of contempt, they do kindle their anger much. *Bacon.*

The want of many things fed him with hope, that he should out of these his enemies distresses *pick* some fit occasion of advantage. *Knolles's History of the Turks.*

They must *pick* me out with shackles tir'd,
To make them sport with blind activity. *Milton.*

What made thee *pick* and chuse her out,
T' employ their sorceries about? *Hudibras.*

How many examples have we seen of men that have been *picked* up and relieved out of starving necessities, afterwards conspire against their patrons. *L'Estrange.*

If he would compound for half, it should go hard but he'd make a shift to *pick* it up. *L'Estrange.*

A painter would not be much commended, who should *pick* out this cavern from the whole Æneids; he had better leave them in their obscurity. *Dryden.*

Imitate the bees, who *pick* from every flower that which they find most proper to make honey. *Dryden.*

He that is nourished by the acorns he *picked* up under an oak in the wood, has certainly appropriated them to himself. *Locke.*

He asked his friends about him, where they had *picked* up such a blockhead. *Addison's Spectator*, Nº 167.

The will may *pick* and chuse among these objects, but it cannot create any to work on. *Cheyne's Philosophical Principles.*

Deep through a miry lane she *pick'd* her way,
Above her ankle rose the chalky clay. *Gay.*

Thus much he may be able to *pick* out, and willing to transfer into his new history; but the rest of your character will probably be dropped, on account of the antiquated stile they are delivered in. *Swift.*

Heav'n, when it strives to polish all it can
Its last, best work, but forms a softer man,
Picks from each sex, to make the fav'rite blest, *Pope.*

2. To take up; to gather; to find industriously.

You owe me money, Sir John, and now you *pick* a quarrel to beguile me of it. *Shakesp. Henry* IV.

It was believed, that Perkin's escape was not without the king's privity, who had him all the time of his flight in a line; and that the king did this, to *pick* a quarrel to put him to death. *Bacon's Henry* VII.

They are as peevish company to themselves as to their neighbours; for there's not one circumstance in nature, but they shall find matters to *pick* a quarrel at. *L'Estrange.*

Pick the very refuse of those harvest fields. *Thomson.*

3. To separate from any thing useless or noxious, by gleaning out either part; to clean by picking away filth.

For private friends: his answer was,
He could not stay to *pick* them in a pile
Of musty chaff. *Shakesp. Coriolanus.*

It hath been noted by the ancients, that it is dangerous to *pick* one's ears whilst he yawneth; for that in yawning, the minor parchment of the ear is extended by the drawing of the breath. *Bacon's Natural History.*

He

He *picks* and culls his thoughts for conversation, by suppressing some, and communicating others. *Addison.*

You are not to wash your hands, till you have *picked* your sallad. *Swift.*

4. To clean, by gathering off gradually any thing adhering.

Hope is a pleasant premeditation of enjoyment; as when a dog expects, till his master has done *picking* a bone. *More.*

5. [*Piquer*, Fr.] To pierce; to strike with a sharp instrument.

Pick an apple with a pin full of holes not deep, and smear it with spirits, to see if the virtual heat of the strong waters will not mature it. *Bacon.*

In the face, a small wart or fiery pustule, being healed by scratching or *picking* with nails, will terminate corrosive. *Wiseman's Surgery.*

6. To strike with bill or beak; to peck.

The eye that mocketh at his father, the ravens of the valley shall *pick* out. *Proverbs* xxx. 17.

7. [*Picare*, Italian.] To rob.

The other night I fell asleep here, and had my pocket *pickt*; this house is turn'd bawdy-house, they *pick* pockets. *Shakesp.*

They have a design upon your pocket, and the word conscience is used only as an instrument to *pick* it. *South.*

8. To open a lock by a pointed instrument.

Did you ever find
That any art could *pick* the lock, or power
Could force it open. *Denham.*

9. *To* PICK *a hole in one's coat.* A proverbial expression for one finding fault with another.

To PICK. *v. n.*

1. To eat slowly and by small morsels.

Why stand'st thou *picking?* is thy palate sore,
That bete and radishes will make thee roar. *Dryden.*

2. To do any thing nicely and leisurely.

He was too warm on *picking* work to dwell,
But faggoted his notions as they fell,
And if they rhym'd and rattl'd, all was well. *Dryden.*

PICK. *n. s.* A sharp-pointed iron tool.

What the miners call chert and whern, the stone-cutters nicomia, is so hard, that the *picks* will not touch it; it will not split but irregularly. *Woodward on Fossils.*

PI'CKAPACK. *adv.* [from *pack*, by a reduplication very common in our language.] In manner of a pack.

In a hurry she whips up her darling under her arms, and carries the other a *pickapack* upon her shoulders. *L'Estr.*

PI'CKAXE. *n. s.* [*pick* and *axe.*] An axe not made to cut but pierce; an axe with a sharp point.

Their tools are a *pickaxe* of iron, seventeen inches long, sharpened at the one end to peck, and flat-headed at the other to drive iron wedges. *Carew's Survey of Cornwall.*

I'll hide my master from the flies, as deep
As these poor *pickaxes* can dig. *Shakesp. Cymbeline.*

As when bands
Of pioneers, with spade and *pickaxe* arm'd,
Forerun the royal camp, to trench a field. *Milton.*

PI'CKBACK. *adj.* [corrupted perhaps from *pickpack.*] On the back.

As our modern wits behold,
Mounted a *pickback* on the old,
Much farther off. *Hudibras.*

PI'CKED. *adj.* [*pique*, Fr.] Sharp; smart.

Let the stake be made *picked* at the top, that the jay may not settle on it. *Mortimer's Husbandry.*

To PI'CKEER. *v. a.* [*piccare*, Italian.]

1. To pirate; to pillage; to rob.

2. To make a flying skirmish. *Ainsworth.*

No sooner could a hint appear,
But up he started to *pickeer*,
And made the stoutest yield to mercy,
When he engag'd in controversy. *Hudibras.*

PI'CKER. *n. s.* [from *pick.*]

1. One who picks or culls.

The *pickers* pick the hops into the hair-cloth. *Mortimer.*

2. A pickax; an instrument to pick with.

With an iron *picker* clear all the earth out of the hills. *Mortimer's Husbandry.*

PICKE'REL. *n. s.* [from *pike.*] A small pike.

PICKEREL-WEED. *n. s.* [from *pike.*] A water plant, from which pikes are fabled to be generated.

The luce or pike is the tyrant of the fresh waters; they are bred, some by generation, and some not; as of a weed called *pickerel-weed*, unless Gosner be mistaken. *Walton.*

PI'CKLE. *n. s.* [*pekel*, Dutch.]

1. Any kind of salt liquor, in which flesh or other substance is preserved.

Thou shalt be whipt with wire, and stew'd in brine,
Smarting in lingring *pickle.* *Shakespeare.*

Some fish are gutted, split and kept in *pickle*; as whiting and mackerel. *Carew's Survey of Cornwall.*

He instructs his friends that dine with him in the best *pickle* for a walnut. *Addison's Spectator*, N° 482.

A third sort of antiscorbuticks are called astringent; as capers, and most of the common *pickles* prepared with vinegar. *Arbuthnot on Aliments.*

2. Thing kept in pickle.

3. Condition; state. A word of contempt and ridicule.

How cam'st thou in this *pickle?* *Shakespeare.*

A physician undertakes a woman with sore eyes; his way was to dawb 'em with ointments, and while she was in that *pickle*, carry off a spoon. *L'Estrange.*

Poor Umbra, left in this abandon'd *pickle*,
E'en sits him down. *Swift's Miscellanies.*

PI'CKLE or *pightel. n. s.* A small parcel of land inclosed with a hedge, which in some countries is called a *pingle.* *Phillips.*

To PI'CKLE. *v. a.* [from the noun.]

1. To preserve in pickle.

Autumnal cornels next in order serv'd,
In lees of wine well *pickl'd* and preserv'd. *Dryden.*

They shall have all, rather than make a war,
The Straits, the Guiney-trade, the herrings too;
Nay, to keep friendship, they shall *pickle* you. *Dryden.*

2. To season or imbue highly with any thing bad: as, a *pickled* rogue, or one consummately villainous.

PI'CKLEHERRING. *n. s.* [*pickle* and *herring.*] A jack-pudding; a merry-andrew; a zany; a buffoon.

Another branch of pretenders to this art, without horse or *pickleherring*, lie snug in a garret. *Spectator*, N° 572.

The *pickleherring* found the way to shake him, for upon his whistling a country jig, this unlucky wag danced to it with such a variety of grimaces, that the countryman could not forbear smiling, and lost the prize. *Addis. Spect.*

PI'CKLOCK. *n. s.* [*pick* and *lock.*]

1. An instrument by which locks are opened without the key.

We take him to be a thief too, Sir; for we have found upon him, Sir, a strange *picklock.* *Shakespeare.*

Scipio, having such a *picklock*, would spend so many years in battering the gates of Carthage. *Brown.*

It corrupts faith and justice, and is the very *picklock* that opens the way into all cabinets. *L'Estrange.*

Thou raisedst thy voice to describe the powerful Betty or the artful *picklock*, or Vulcan sweating at his forge, and stamping the queen's image on viler metals. *Arbuthnot.*

2. The person who picks locks.

PI'CKPOCKET. } *n. s.* [*pick* and *pocket.*] A thief who steals,
PI'CKPURSE. } by putting his hand privately into the pocket or purse.

I think he is not a *pickpurse* nor a horsestealer *Shakespeare.*

It is reasonable, when Esquire South is losing his money to sharpers and *pickpockets*, I should lay out the fruits of my honest industry in a law suit. *Arbuthnot's Hist. of J. Bull.*

Pickpockets and highwaymen observe strict justice among themselves. *Bentley's Sermons.*

His fellow *pickpurse*, watching for a job,
Fancies his fingers in the cully's fob. *Swift.*

A *pickpurse* at the bar or bench. *Swift.*

If a court or country's made a job,
Go drench a *pickpocket*, and join the mob. *Pope.*

PICKTOO'TH. *n. s.* [*pick* and *tooth.*] An instrument by which the teeth are cleaned.

If a gentleman leaves a *picktooth* case on the table after dinner, look upon it as part of your vails. *Swift.*

PICKTHA'NK. *n. s.* [*pick* and *thank.*] An officious fellow, who does what he is not desired; a whispering parasite.

With pleasing tales his lord's vain ears he fed,
A flatterer, a *pickthank*, and a lyer. *Fairfax.*

Many tales devis'd,
Oft the ear of greatness needs must hear,
By smiling *pickthanks* and base newsmongers. *Shakesp.*

The business of a *pickthank* is the basest of offices. *L'Estrange.*

If he be great and powerful, spies and *pickthanks* generally provoke him to persecute and tyrannize over the innocent and the just. *South's Sermons.*

PICT. *n. s.* [*pictus*, Lat.] A painted person.

Your neighbours would not look on you as men,
But think the nations all turn'd *picts* again. *Lee.*

PICTO'RIAL. *adj.* [from *pictor*, Lat.] Produced by a painter. A word not adopted by other writers, but elegant and useful.

Sea horses are but grotesco delineations, which fill up empty spaces in maps, as many *pictorial* inventions, not any physical shapes. *Brown's Vulgar Errours.*

PI'CTURE. *n. s.* [*pictura*, Latin.]

1. A resemblance of persons or things in colours.

Madam, if that your heart be so obdurate,
Vouchsafe me yet your *picture* for my love,
The *picture* that is hanging in your chamber. *Shakesp.*

Pictures and shapes are but secondary objects, and please or displease but in memory. *Bacon's Natural History.*

Devouring what he saw so well design'd,
He with an empty *picture* fed his mind. *Dryden.*

As soon as he begins to spell, as many *pictures* of animals should be got him as can be found with the printed names to them. *Locke.*

2. The science of painting.

3. The works of painters.

Quintilian, when he saw any well-expressed image of grief, either in *picture* or sculpture, would usually weep. *Wott.*

If nothing will satisfy him, but having it under my hand, that I had no design to ruin the company of *picture*-drawers, I do hereby give it him. *Stillingfleet.*

4. Any resemblance or representation.

Vouchsafe this *picture* of thy soul to see;
'Tis so far good, as it resembles thee. *Dryden.*

It suffices to the unity of any idea, that it be considered as one representation or *picture*, though made up of ever so many particulars. *Locke.*

To PICTURE. *v. a.* [from the noun.]

1. To paint; to represent by painting.

I have not seen him so *pictur'd. Shakespeare's Cymbeline.*

He who caused the spring to be *pictured*, added this rhyme for an exposition. *Carew's Survey of Cornwall.*

It is not allowable, what is observable of Raphael Urban; wherein Mary Magdalen is *pictured* before our Saviour washing his feet on her knees, which will not consist with the strict letter of the text. *Brown's Vulgar Errours.*

Love is like the painter, who, being to draw the picture of a friend having a blemish in one eye, would *picture* only the other side of his face. *South's Sermons.*

2. To represent.

All filled with these rueful spectacles of so many wretched carcasses starving, that even I, that do but hear it from you, and do *picture* it in my mind, do greatly pity it. *Spenser.*

Fond man,
See here thy *pictur'd* life. *Thomson's Winter.*

To PIDDLE. *v. n.* [This word is obscure in its etymology; *Skinner* derives it from *picciolo*, Italian; or *petit*, Fr. little; Mr. *Lye* thinks the diminutive of the Welsh *breyta*, to eat; perhaps it comes from *peddle*, for *Skinner* gives for its primitive signification, to deal in little things.]

1. To pick at table; to feed squeamishly, and without appetite.

From stomach sharp, and hearty feeding,
To *piddle* like a lady breeding. *Swift's Miscellanies.*

2. To trifle; to attend to small parts rather than to the main. *Ains.*

PI'DDLER. *n. s.* [from *piddle.*] One that eats squeamishly, and without appetite.

PIE. *n. s.* [This word is derived by *Skinner* from *biezan*, to build, that is to build of paste; by *Junius* derived by contraction from *pasty*; if pasties, doubled together without walls, were the first pies, the derivation is easy from *pie*, a foot; as in some provinces, an apple pasty is still called an apple foot.]

1. Any crust baked with something in it.

No man's *pie* is freed
From his ambitious finger. *Shakesp. Henry* VIII.

Mincing of meat in *pies* saveth the grinding of the teeth, and therefore more nourishing to them that have weak teeth. *Bacon's Natural History.*

He is the very Withers of the city; they have bought more editions of his works, than would serve to lay under all their *pies* at a lord mayor's Christmas. *Dryden.*

Chuse your materials right;
From thence of course the figure will arise,
And elegance adorn the surface of your *pies.* *King.*
Eat beef or *pie*-crust, if you'd serious be. *King.*

2. [*Pica*, Lat.] A magpie; a particoloured bird.

The *pie* will discharge thee for pulling the rest. *Tusser.*

The raven croak'd hoarse on the chimney's top,
And chattering *pies* in dismal discords sung. *Shakesp.*

Who taught the parrot human notes to try,
Or with a voice endu'd the chatt'ring *pie*?
'Twas witty want. *Dryden.*

3. The old popish service book, so called, as is supposed, from the different colour of the text and rubrick.

4. Cock and *pie* was a slight expression in *Shakespeare's* time, of which I know not the meaning.

Mr. Slender, come; we stay for you.—
—I'll eat nothing, I thank you, Sir.—
—By cock and *pie*, you shall not chuse, Sir; come, come. *Shakesp. Merry Wives of Windsor.*

PIE'BALD. *adj.* [from *pie.*] Of various colours; diversified in colour.

It was a particoloured dress,
Of patch'd and *piebald* languages. *Hudibras.*

They would think themselves miserable in a patched coat, and yet contentedly suffer their minds to appear abroad in a *piebald* livery of coarse patches and borrowed shreds. *Locke.*

They are pleased to hear of a *piebald* horse that is strayed out of a field near Islington, as of a whole troop that has been engaged in any foreign adventure. *Spectator*, N° 452.

Peel'd, patch'd, and *piebald*, linsey-woolsey brothers,
Grave mummers! sleeveless some, and shirtless others. *Pope.*

PIECE. *n. s.* [*piece*, Fr.]

1. A patch. *Ainsworth.*

2. A part of a whole; a fragment.

Bring it out *piece* by *piece.* *Ezekiel* xxiv. 26.

The chief captain, fearing lest Paul should have been pulled in *pieces* of them, commanded to take him by force. *Acts.*

These lesser rocks or great bulky stones, that lie scattered in the sea or upon the land, are they not manifest fragments and *pieces* of these greater masses. *Burnet.*

A man that is in Rome can scarce see an object, that does not call to mind a *piece* of a Latin poet or historian. *Addison.*

2. A part.

It is accounted a *piece* of excellent knowledge, to know the laws of the land. *Tillotson.*

3. A picture.

If unnatural, the finest colours are but dawbing, and the *piece* is a beautiful monster at the best. *Dryden.*

Each heav'nly *piece* unweary'd we compare,
Match Raphael's grace with thy lov'd Guido's air. *Pope.*

4. A composition; performance.

He wrote several *pieces*, which he did not assume the honour of. *Addison.*

5. A single great gun.

A *piece* of ord'nance 'gainst it I have plac'd. *Shakespeare.*

Many of the ships have brass *pieces*, whereas every *piece* at least requires four gunners to attend it. *Raleigh's Essays.*

Pyrrhus, with continual battery of great *pieces*, did batter the mount. *Knolles's History of the Turks.*

6. A hand gun.

When he cometh to experience of service abroad, or is put to a *piece* or a pike, he maketh as worthy a soldier as any nation he meeteth with. *Spenser.*

The ball goes on in the direction of the stick, or of the body of the *piece* out of which it is shot. *Cheyne.*

7. A coin; a single piece of money.

When once the poet's honour ceases,
From reason far his transports rove;
And Boileau, for eight hundred *pieces*,
Makes Louis take the wall of Jove. *Prior.*

7. In ridicule and contempt: as, a *piece* of a lawyer or smatterer.

8. *A*-PIECE. To each.

I demand, concerning all those creatures that have eyes and ears, whether they might not have had only one eye and one ear *a-piece.* *More's Antidote against Atheism.*

9. *Of a* PIECE *with.* Like; of the same sort; united; the same with the rest.

Truth and fiction are so aptly mix'd,
That all seems uniform and *of a piece.* *Roscommon.*

When Jupiter granted petitions, a cockle made request, that his house and his body might be all *of a piece.* *L'Estr.*

My own is *of a piece with* his, and were he living, they are such as he would have written. *Dryden.*

I appeal to my enemies, if I or any other man could have invented one which had been more *of a piece*, and more depending on the serious part of the design. *Dryden.*

Too justly vanish'd from an age like this;
Now she is gone, the world is *of a piece.* *Dryden.*

Nothing but madness can please madmen, and a poet must be *of a piece* with the spectators, to gain a reputation. *Dryden.*

To PIECE. *v. a.* [from the noun.]

1. To enlarge by the addition of a piece.

I speak too long, but 'tis to *piece* the time,
To draw it out in length, *Shakesp. Merch. of Venice.*

If aught within that little seeming substance,
Or all of it with our displeasure *piec'd*,
And nothing more may fitly like your grace,
She is yours. *Shakesp. King Lear.*

Plant it with women as well as men, that it may spread into generations, and not be *pieced* from without. *Bacon.*

2. To join; to unite.

3. *To* PIECE *out.* To encrease by addition.

He *pieces out* his wife's inclination; he gives her folly motion and advantage. *Shakesp. Merry Wives of Windsor.*

Whether the *piecing out* of an old man's life is worth the pains, I cannot tell. *Temple.*

To PIECE. *v. n.* [from the noun.] To join; to coalesce; to be compacted.

Let him, that was the cause of this, have power
To take off so much grief from you, as he
Will *piece* up in himself. *Shakesp.*

The cunning priest chose Plantagenet to be the subject his pupil should personate; because he was more in the present speech of the people, and it *pieced* better and followed more close upon the bruit of Plantagenet's escape. *Bacon.*

PIE'CER. *n. s.* [from *piece.*] One that pieces.

PIE'CELESS. *adj.* [from *piece.*] Whole; compact; not made of separate pieces.

In those poor types of God, round circles; so
Religion's types the *pieceless* centers flow,
And are in all the lines which all ways go. *Donne.*

PIE'CEMEAL. *adv.* [pice and mel; a word in Saxon of the same import.] In pieces; in fragments.

Why did I not his carcass *piecemeal* tear,
And cast it in the sea. *Denham.*

I'll be torn *piecemeal* by a horse,
E'er I'll take you for better or worse. *Hudibras.*

Neither was the body then subject to distempers, to die by *piecemeal*, and languish under coughs or consumptions. *South.*

Stage editors printed from the common *piecemeal* written parts in the playhouse. *Pope.*

Piecemeal they win this acre first, then that;
Glean on and gather up the whole estate. *Pope.*

PIE'CEMEAL. *adj.* Single; separate; divided.

Other blasphemies level; some at one attribute, some at another: but this by a more compendious impiety, shoots at his very being, and as if it scorned these *piecemeal* guilts, sets up a single monster big enough to devour them all. *Gov. of the Tong.*

PIE'D. *adj.* [from *pie.*] Variegated; particoloured.

They desire to take such as have their feathers of *pied*, orient and various colours. *Abbot's Descript. of the World.*

All the yeanlings, which were streak'd and *pied*,
Should fall as Jacob's hire. *Shakesp. Merch. of Venice.*

Pied cattle are spotted in their tongues. *Bacon.*

The seat, the soft wool of the bee,
The cover, gallantly to see,
The wing of a *pied* butterfly,
I trow 'twas simple trimming. *Drayton.*

Meadows trim with daisies *pied*,
Shallow brooks and rivers wide. *Milton.*

PIE'DNESS. *n. s.* [from *pied.*] Variegation; diversity of colour.

There is an art, which in their *piedness* shares
With great creating nature. *Shakesp. Winter's Tale.*

PIE'LED. *adj.* Perhaps for *peeled*, or bald; or *piled*, or having short hair.

Piel'd priest, dost thou command me be shut out?
I do. *Shakesp. Henry* VI.

PI'EPOWDER *court. n. s.* [from *pied*, foot, and *pouldre*, dusty.] A court held in fairs for redress of all disorders committed therein.

PIER. *n. s.* [*pierre*, Fr.] The columns on which the arch of a bridge is raised.

Oak, cedar and chesnut are the best builders, for *piers* sometimes wet, sometimes dry, take elm. *Bacon.*

The English took the galley, and drew it to shore, and used the stones to reinforce the *pier*. *Hayward.*

The bridge, consisting of four arches, is of the length of six hundred and twenty-two English feet and an half: the dimensions of the arches are as follows, in English measure; the height of the first arch one hundred and nine feet, the distance between the *piers* seventy-two feet and an half; in the second arch, the distance of the *piers* is one hundred and thirty feet; in the third, the distance is one hundred and nine feet; in the fourth, the distance is one hundred and thirty-eight feet. *Arbuthnot on Coins.*

To PIERCE. *v. a.* [*percer*, Fr.]

1. To penetrate; to enter; to force.

Steed threatens steed in high and boastful neighs,
Piercing the night's dull ear. *Shakesp. Henry* V.

The love of money is the root of all evil; which while some coveted after, they have *pierced* themselves through with many sorrows. 1 *Tim.* vi. 10.

With this fatal sword, on which I dy'd,
I *pierce* her open'd back or tender side. *Dryden.*

The glorious temple shall arise,
And with new lustre *pierce* the neighb'ring skies. *Prior.*

2. To touch the passions: to affect.

Did your letters *pierce* the queen;
She read them in my presence,
And now and then an ample tear trill'd down. *Shakesp.*

To PIERCE. *v. n.*

1. To make way by force.

Her sighs will make a batt'ry in his breast;
Her tears will *pierce* into a marble heart. *Shakesp.*

There is that speaketh like the *piercings* of a sword; but the tongue of the wise is health. *Proverbs* xii. 18.

Short arrows, called sprights, without any other heads, save wood sharpened, were discharged out of muskets, and would *pierce* through the sides of ships, where a bullet would not *pierce*. *Bacon's Natural History.*

2. To strike; to move; to affect.

Say, she be mute, and will not speak a word;
Then I'll commend her volubility;
And say she uttereth *piercing* eloquence. *Shakesp.*

3. To enter; to dive.

She would not *pierce* further into his meaning, than himself should declare, so would she interpret all his doings to be accomplished in goodness. *Sidney, b.* ii.

All men knew Nathaniel to be an Israelite; but our Saviour *piercing* deeper, giveth further testimony of him than men could have done. *Hooker, b.* iii. *s.* 1.

4. To affect severely.

They provide more *piercing* statutes daily to chain up the poor. *Shakesp.*

PIER'CER. *n. s.* [from *pierce.*]

1. An instrument that bores or penetrates.

Cart, ladder and wimble, with *perser* and pod. *Tusser.*

2. The part with which insects perforate bodies.

The hollow instrument, terebra, we may english *piercer*, wherewith many flies are provided, proceeding from the womb, with which they perforate the tegument of leaves, and through the hollow of it inject their eggs into the holes they have made. *Ray on the Creation.*

3. One who perforates.

PIE'RCINGLY. *adv.* [from *pierce.*] Sharply.

PIE'RCINGNESS. *n. s.* [from *piercing.*] Power of piercing.

We contemplate the vast reach and compass of our understanding, the prodigious quickness and *piercingness* of its thought. *Derham's Physico-Theology.*

PI'ETY. *n. s.* [*pietas*, Lat. *pieté*, Fr.]

1. Discharge of duty to God.

What *piety*, pity, fortitude did Æneas possess beyond his companions? *Peacham on Poetry.*

'Till future infancy, baptiz'd by thee,
Grow ripe in years, and old in *piety*. *Prior.*

There be who faith prefer and *piety* to God. *Milton.*

2. Duty to parents or those in superiour relation.

PIG. *n. s.* [*bigge*, Dutch.]

1. A young sow or boar.

Some men there are, love not a gaping *pig*,
Some that are mad, if they behold a cat. *Shakespeare.*

Alba, from the white sow nam'd,
That for her thirty sucking *pigs* was fam'd. *Dryden.*

The flesh-meats of an easy digestion, are *pig*, lamb, rabbit and chicken. *Floyer on the Humours.*

2. An oblong mass of lead or unforged iron.

A nodding beam or *pig* of lead,
May hurt the very ablest head. *Pope.*

To PIG. *v. a.* [from the noun.] To farrow; to bring pigs.

PI'GEON. *n. s.* [*pigeon*, Fr.] A fowl bred in cots or a small house: in some places called dovecote.

This fellow picks up wit as *pigeons* peas. *Shakesp.*

A turtle, dove and a young *pigeon*. *Gen.* xv. 9.

Perceiving that the *pigeon* had lost a piece of her tail, through the next opening of the rocks rowing with all their might, they passed safe, only the end of their poop was bruised. *Raleigh.*

Fix'd in the mast, the feather'd weapon stands,
The fearful *pigeon* flutters in her bands. *Dryden.*

See the cupola of St. Paul's covered with both sexes, like the outside of a *pigeon*-house. *Addison's Guardian.*

This building was design'd a model,
Or of a *pigeon*-house or oven,
To bake one loaf, or keep one dove in. *Swift.*

PI'GEONFOOT. *n. s.* An herb. *Ainsworth.*

PI'GEONLIVERED. *adj.* [*pigeon* and *liver.*] Mild; soft; gentle.

I am *pigeonliver'd*, and lack gall
To make oppression bitter. *Shakesp. Hamlet.*

PI'GGIN. *n. s.* In the northern provinces, a small vessel.

PIGHT. old preter. and part. pass. of *pitch.*] Pitched; placed; fixed; determined.

An hideous rock is *pight*,
Of mighty Magnes stone, whose craggy clift,
Depending from on high, dreadful to sight,
Over the waves his rugged arms doth lift. *Spenser.*

The body big and mightily *pight*,
Thoroughly rooted and wondrous height,
Whilom had been the king of the field,
And mockle mast to the husband did yield. *Spenser.*

Then brought she me into this desart vast,
And by my wretched lover's side me *pight*. *Fa. Queen.*

Stay yet, you vile abominable tents,
Thus proudly *pight* upon our Phrygian plains. *Shakesp.*

When I dissuaded him from his intent,
I found him *pight* to do it. *Shakesp.*

PI'GMENT. *n. s.* [*pigmentum*, Lat.] Paint; colour to be laid on any body.

Consider about the opacity of the corpuscles of black *pigments*, and the comparative diaphaneity of white bodies. *Boyle.*

PI'GMY. *n. s.* [*pigmée*, Fr. *pigmæus*, Lat.] A small nation, fabled to be devoured by the cranes; thence any thing mean or inconsiderable.

When cranes invade, his little sword and shield
The *pigmy* takes. *Dryden's Juvenal.*

The criticks of a more exalted taste, may discover such beauties in the antient poetry, as may escape the comprehension of us *pigmies* of a more limited genius. *Garth.*

But that it wanted room,
It might have been a *pigmy*'s tomb. *Swift.*

PIGNORA'TION. *n. s.* [*pignera*, Lat.] The act of pledging.

PI'GNUT. *n. s.* [*pig* and *nut.*] An earth nut.

I with my long nails will dig thee *pignuts*. *Shakesp.*

PI'GSNEY. *n. s.* [piga, Sax. a girl.] A word of endearment to a girl. It is used by *Butler* for the eye of a woman, I believe, improperly.

Shine upon me but benignly
With that one, and that other *pigsney*. *Hudibras.*

PIGWI'DGEON. *n. s.* This word is used by *Drayton* as the name of a fairy, and is a kind of cant word for any thing petty or small.

Where's the Stoick can his wrath appease,
To see his country sick of Pym's disease;
By Scotch invasion to be made a prey
To such *pigwidgeon* myrmidons as they? *Cleaveland.*

PIKE. *n. s.* [*picque*, Fr. his snout being sharp. *Skinner* and *Junius.*]

1. The luce or *pike* is the tyrant of the fresh waters: they are bred some by generation, and some not; as namely of a weed called pickerel-weed, unless Gesner be much mistaken; for he says, this weed and other glutinous matter, with the help of the sun's heat in some particular months, and in some ponds apted for it by nature, do become *pikes*: doubtless divers *pikes* are bred after this manner, or are brought into some ponds some other ways, that is past man's finding out: Sir Francis Bacon observes the *pike* to be the longest lived of any fresh water fish, and yet he computes it to be not usually above forty years; and others think it to be not above ten years: he is a solitary, melancholy and bold fish; he breeds but once a year, and his time of breeding, or spawning is usually about the end of February, or somewhat later, in March, as the weather proves colder or warmer: and his manner of breeding is thus; a he and a she *pike* will usually go together out of a river into some ditch or creek, and there the spawner casts her eggs, and the melter hovers over her all the time she is casting her spawn, but touches her not. *Walton's Angler.*

In a pond into which were put several fish and two *pikes*, upon drawing it some years afterwards there were left no fish, but the *pikes* grown to a prodigious size, having devoured the other fish and their numerous spawn. *Hale.*

The *pike* the tyrant of the floods. *Pope.*

2. [*Pique*, Fr.] A long lance used by the foot soldiers, to keep off the horse, to which bayonets have succeeded.

Beat you the drum that it speak mournfully,
Trail your steel *pikes*. *Shakesp. Coriolanus.*

Let us revenge this with our *pikes*, ere we become rakes; for I speak this in hunger for bread, not for revenge. *Shakesp.*

He wanted *pikes* to set before his archers. *Shakesp.*

They closed, and locked shoulder to shoulder, their *pikes* they strained in both hands and therewith their buckler in the left, the one end of the *pike* against the right foot, the other breast-high against the enemy. *Hayward.*

A lance he bore with iron *pike*;
Th' one half would thrust, the other strike. *Hudibras.*

3. A fork used in husbandry.

A rake for to rake up the fitches that lie,
A *pike* to pike them up handsome to drie. *Tusser.*

4. Among turners, two iron sprigs between, which any thing to be turned is fastened.

Hard wood, prepared for the lathe with rasping, they pitch between the *pikes*. *Moxon.*

PI'KED. *adj.* [*piqué*, Fr.] Sharp; accuminated; ending in a point. In *Shakespeare*, it is used of a man with a pointed beard.

Why then I suck my teeth, and catechise
My *piked* man of countries. *Shakesp. King John.*

PI'KEMAN. *n. s.* [*pike* and *man.*] A soldier armed with a pike.

Three great squadrons of *pikemen* were placed against the enemy. *Knolles's History of the Turks.*

PI'KESTAFF. *n. s.* [*pike* and *staff.*] The wooden frame of a pike.

To me it is as plain as a *pikestaff*, from what mixture it is, that this daughter silently lowers, t'other steals a kind look. *Tatler*, N° 75.

PILA'STER. *n. s.* [*pilastre*, Fr. *pilastro*, Italian.] A square column sometimes insulated, but oftner set within a wall, and only shewing a fourth or a fifth part of its thickness. *Dict.*

Pilasters must not be too tall and slender, lest they resemble pillars; nor too dwarfish and gross, lest they imitate the piles or piers of bridges. *Wotton.*

Bailt like a temple, where *pilasters* round
Were set. *Milton.*

The curtain rises, and a new frontispiece is seen, joined to the great *pilasters* each side of the stage. *Dryden.*

Clap four slices of *pilaster* on't,
That laid with bits of rustic makes a front. *Pope.*

PI'LCHER. *n. s.* [*Warburton* says we should read *pilche*, which signifies a cloke or coat of skins, meaning the scabbard: this is confirmed by *Junius*, who renders *pilly*, a garment of skins; pylece, Sax. *pellice*, Fr. *pelliccia*, Italian; *pellis*, Lat.]

1. A furred gown or case; any thing lined with fur. *Hanmer.*

Pluck your sword out of his *pilcher* by the ears. *Shakesp.*

2. A fish like a herring.

PILE. *n. s.* [*pile*, Fr. *pyle*, Dutch.]

1. A strong piece of wood driven into the ground to make firm a foundation.

The bridge the Turks before broke, by plucking up of certain *piles*, and taking away of the planks. *Knolles.*

If the ground be hollow or weak, he strengthens it by driving in *piles*. *Moxon.*

The foundation of the church of Harlem is supported by wooden *piles*, as the houses in Amsterdam are. *Locke.*

2. A heap; an accumulation.

That is the way to lay the city flat,
And bury all which yet distinctly ranges
In heaps and *piles* of ruin. *Shakesp.*

What *piles* of wealth hath he accumulated
To his own portion! what expence by th' honr
Seems to flow from him! how i' th' name of thrift,
Does he rake this together. *Shakesp.*

By the water passing through the stone to its perpendicular intervals, was brought thither all the metallic matter now lodged therein, as well as that which lies only in an undigested and confused *pile*. *Woodward.*

3. Any thing heaped together to be burned.

I'll bear your logs the while; pray give me it,
I'll carry't to the *pile*. *Shakesp. Tempest.*

Woe to the bloody city, I will even make the *pile* for fire great. *Ezekiel* xxiv. 9.

In Alexander's time, the Indian philosophers, when weary of living, lay down upon their funeral *pile* without any visible concern. *Collier on the Value of Life.*

The wife, and counsellor or priest,
Prepare and light his fun'ral fire,
And cheerful on the *pile* expire. *Prior.*

4. An edifice; a building.

Th' ascending *pile* stood fix'd her stately height. *Milt.*

Not to look back so far, to whom this isle
Owes the first glory of so brave a *pile*. *Denham.*

The *pile* o'erlook'd the town, and drew the sight. *Dryd.*

Fancy brings the vanish'd *piles* to view,
And builds imaginary Rome anew. *Pope's Miscellanies.*

No longer shall forsaken Thames
Lament his old Whitehall in flames;
A *pile* shall from its ashes rise,
Fit to invade or prop the skies. *Swift's Miscellanies.*

5. A hair. [*pilus*, Lat.]

Yonder's my lord, with a patch of velvet on's face; his left cheek is a cheek of two *pile* and a half, but his right cheek is worn bare. *Shakesp. All's well that ends well.*

6. Hairy surface; nap.

Many other sorts of stones are regularly figured; the amianthus of parallel threads, as in the *pile* of velvet. *Grew.*

7. [*Pilum*, Lat.] The head of an arrow.

His spear a bent,
The *pile* was of a horse fly's tongue,
Whose sharpness nought revers'd. *Drayton's Nymph.*

8. [*Pile*, Fr. *pila*, Italian.] One side of a coin; the reverse of cross.

Other men have been, and are of the same opinion, a man may more justifiably throw up cross and *pile* for his opinions, than take them up so. *Locke.*

9. [In the plural, *piles.*] The hæmorrhoids.

Wherever there is any uneasiness, solicit the humours towards that part, to procure the *piles*, which seldom miss to relieve the head. *Arbuthnot.*

To PILE. *v. a.*

1. To heap; to coacervate.

The fabrick of his folly, whose foundation
Is *pil'd* upon his faith, and will continue
The standing of his body. *Shakesp. Winter's Tale.*

Let them pull all about my ears,
Pile ten hills on the Tarpeian rock,
That the precipitation might downstretch
Below the beam of sight, yet will I still
Be thus. *Shakesp.*

Against beleagur'd heav'n the giants move;
Hills *pil'd* on hills, on mountains mountains lie,
To make their mad approaches to the sky. *Dryden.*

Men *pil'd* on men, with active leaps arise,
And build the breathing fabrick to the skies. *Addison.*

In all that heap of quotations which he has *piled* up, nothing is aimed at. *Atterbury.*

All these together are the foundation of all those heaps of comments, which are *piled* so high upon authors, that it is difficult sometimes to clear the text from the rubbish. *Felton.*

2. To fill with something heaped.

Attabaliba had a great house *piled* upon the sides with great wedges of gold. *Abbot's Descript. of the World.*

PI'LEATED. *adj.* [*pileus*, Lat.] In the form of a cover or hat.

A *pileated* echinus taken up with different shells of several kinds. *Woodward on Fossils.*

PI'LER. *n. s.* [from *pile.*] He who accumulates.

To PI'LFER. *v. a.* [*piller*, Fr.] To steal; to gain by petty robbery.

They not only steal from each other, but *pilfer* away all things that they can from such strangers as do land. *Abbot.*

He would not *pilfer* the victory; and the defeat was easy. *Bacon's Essays.*

Leaders, at an army's head,
Hemm'd round with glories, *pilfer* cloth or bread,
As meanly plunder, as they bravely fought. *Pope.*

To PI'LFER. *v. n.* To practise petty theft.

Your purpos'd low correction
Is such as basest and the meanest wretches,
For *pilf'rings* and most common trespasses,
Are punish'd with. *Shakesp. King Lear.*

They of those marches
Shall be a wall sufficient to defend
Our inland from the *pilfering* borderers. *Shakesp.*

I came

I came not here on such a trivial toy,
As a stray'd ewe, or to pursue the stealth
Of *pilfering* wolf. *Milton.*

When these plagiaries come to be stript of their *pilfered* ornaments, there's the daw of the fable. *L'Estrange.*

Ev'ry string is told,
For fear some *pilf'ring* hand should make too bold. *Dryden.*

PI'LFERER. *n. s.* [from *pilfer.*] One who steals petty things.

Hast thou suffered at any time by vagabonds and *pilferers*? Promote those charities which remove such pests of society into prisons and workhouses. *Atterbury's Sermons.*

PI'LFERINGLY. *adv.* With petty larceny; filchingly.

PI'LFERY. *n. s.* [from *pilfer.*] Petty theft.

A wolf charges a fox with a piece of *pilfery*; the fox denies, and the ape tries the cause. *L'Estrange.*

PI'LGRIM. *n. s.* [*pelgrim*, Dutch; *pelerin*, Fr. *pelegrino*, Italian; *peregrinus*, Lat.] A traveller; a wanderer; particularly one who travels on a religious account.

Two *pilgrims*, which have wandered some miles together, have a hearts-grief when they are near to part. *Drummond.*

Granting they could not tell Abraham's footstep from an ordinary *pilgrim's*; yet they should know some difference between the foot of a man and the face of Venus. *Stillingfleet.*

Like *pilgrims* to th' appointed place we tend;
The world's an inn, and death the journey's end. *Dryden.*

To PI'LGRIM. *v. n.* [from the noun.] To wander; to ramble.

The ambulo hath no certain home or diet, but *pilgrims* up and down every where, feeding upon all sorts of plants. *Grew.*

PI'LGRIMAGE. *n. s.* [*pelerinage*, Fr.]

1. A long journey; travel; more usually a journey on account of devotion.

We are like two men
That vow a long and weary *pilgrimage*. *Shakesp.*

In prison thou hast spent a *pilgrimage*,
And, like a hermit, overpast thy days. *Shakesp.*

Most miserable hour, that time ere saw
In lasting labour of his *pilgrimage*. *Shakesp. Henry VI.*

Painting is a long *pilgrimage*; if we do not actually begin the journey, and travel at a round rate, we shall never arrive at the end of it. *Dryden's Dufresnoy.*

2. *Shakespeare* used it for time irksomely spent, improperly.

PILL. *n. s.* [*pilula*, Lat. *pillule*, French.] Medicine made into a small ball or mass.

In the taking of a potion or *pills*, the head and the neck shake. *Bacon's Natural History.*

When I was sick, you gave me bitter *pills*. *Shakespeare.*

The oraculous doctor's mystick bills,
Certain hard words made into *pills*. *Crashaw.*

To PILL. *v. a.* [*piller*, Fr.]

1. To rob; to plunder.

So did he good to none, to many ill;
So did he all the kingdom rob and *pill*. *Hubberd.*

The commons hath he *pill'd* with grievous taxes,
And lost their hearts. *Shakesp. Richard II.*

Large-handed robbers your grave masters are,
And *pill* by law. *Shakesp. Timon of Athens.*

You wrangling pirates, that fall out
In sharing that which you have *pill'd* from me. *Shakesp.*

Suppose *pilling* and polling officers, as busy upon the people, as those flies were upon the fox. *L'Estrange.*

He who *pill'd* his province 'scapes the laws,
And keeps his money, though he lost his cause. *Dryden.*

2. For *peel*; to strip off the bark.

Jacob took him rods of green poplar, and *pilled* white streaks in them. *Genesis* xxx. 37.

To PILL. *v. n.* To be stript away; to come off in flakes or scoriæ. This should be *peel*; which see.

The whiteness *pilled* away from his eyes. *Tob.* xi. 13.

PILLAGE. *n. s.* [*pillage*, Fr.]

1. Plunder; something got by plundering or pilling.

Others, like soldiers,
Make boot upon the summer's velvet buds;
Which *pillage* they with merry march bring home. *Shak.*

2. The act of plundering.

Thy sons make *pillage* of her chastity. *Shakesp.*

To PI'LLAGE. *v. a.* [from the noun.] To plunder; to spoil.

The consul Mummius, after having beaten their army, took, *pillaged* and burnt their city. *Arbuthnot on Coins.*

PI'LLAGER. *n. s.* [from *pillage.*] A plunderer; a spoiler.

PI'LLAR. *n. s.* [*pilier*, Fr. *pilar*, Spanish; *pilastro*, Italian; *piler*, Welsh and Armorick.]

1. A column.

Pillars or columns, I could distinguish into simple and compounded. *Wotton's Architecture.*

The palace built by Picus vast and proud,
Supported by a hundred *pillars* stood. *Dryden.*

2. A supporter; a maintainer.

Give them leave to fly, that will not stay;
And call them *pillars* that will stand to us. *Shakesp.*

Note, and you shall see in him
The triple *pillar* of the world transform'd
Into a strumpet's stool. *Shakesp. Ant. and Cleopatra.*

I charge you by the law,
Whereof you are a well deserving *pillar*,
Proceed to judgment. *Shakesp. Merch. of Venice.*

PI'LLARED. *adj.* [from *pillar.*]

1. Supported by columns.

A *pillar'd* shade
High overarch'd, and echoing walks between. *Milton.*

If this fail,
The *pillar'd* firmament is rottenness,
And earth's base built on stubble. *Milton.*

2. Having the form of a column.

Th' infuriate hill shoots forth the *pillar'd* flame. *Thoms.*

PI'LLION. *n. s.* [from *pillow.*]

1. A soft saddle set behind a horseman for a woman to sit on.

The housse and *pillion* both were gone;
Phyllis, it seems, was fled with John. *Swift.*

2. A pad; a pannel; a low saddle.

I thought that the manner had been Irish, as also the furniture of his horse, his shank *pillion* without stirrups. *Spenser*

3. The pad of the saddle that touches the horse.

PI'LLORY. *n. s.* [*pillori*, Fr. *pillorium*, low Latin.] A frame erected on a pillar, and made with holes and folding boards, through which the heads and hands of criminals are put.

I have stood on the *pillory* for the geese he hath killed. *Shakespeare.*

As thick as eggs at Ward in *pillory*. *Pope.*

The jeers of a theatre, the *pillory* and the whipping-post are very near a-kin. *Watts's Improvement of the Mind.*

To PI'LLORY. *v. a.* [*pillorier*, Fr. from the noun.] To punish with the pillory.

To be burnt in the hand or *pillored*, is a more lasting reproach than to be scourged or confin'd. *Gov. of the Tongue.*

PI'LLOW. *n. s.* [pyle, Saxon; *pulewe*, Dutch.] A bag of down or feathers laid under the head to sleep on.

Pluck stout men's *pillows* from below their heads. *Shakespeare.*

One turf shall serve as *pillow* for us both,
One heart, one bed, two bosoms, and one troth. *Shakesp.*

A merchant died that was very far in debt, his goods and houshold stuff were set forth to sale; a stranger would needs buy a *pillow* there, saying, this *pillow* sure is good to sleep on, since he could sleep on it that owed so many debts. *Bacon.*

Thy melted maid,
Corrupted by thy lover's gold,
His letter at thy *pillow* laid. *Donne.*

Their feathers serve to stuff our beds and *pillows*, yielding us soft and warm lodging. *Ray on the Creation.*

To PI'LLOW. *v. a.* To rest any thing on a pillow.

When the sun in bed,
Curtain'd with cloudy red,
Pillows his chin upon an orient wave;
The flocking shadows pale
Troop to th' infernal jail. *Milton.*

PI'LLOWBEER. } *n. s.* The cover of a pillow.
PI'LLOWCASE. }

When you put a clean *pillowcase* on your lady's pillow, fasten it well with pins. *Swift.*

PILO'SITY. *n. s.* [from *pilosus*, Lat.] Hairiness.

At the years of puberty, all effects of heat do then come on, as *pilosity*, more roughness in the skin. *Bacon.*

PI'LOT. *n. s.* [*pilote*, Fr. *piloot*, Dutch.] He whose office is to steer the ship.

When her keel ploughs hell,
And deck knocks heaven; then to manage her,
Becomes the name and office of a *pilot*. *Ben. Johnson.*

To death I with such joy resort,
As seamen from a tempest to their port;
Yet to that port ourselves we must not force,
Before our *pilot*, nature, steers our course. *Denham.*

What port can such a *pilot* find,
Who in the night of fate must blindly steer? *Dryden.*

The Roman fleet, although built by shipwrights, and conducted by *pilots* without experience, defeated that of the Carthaginians. *Arbuthnot on Coins.*

To PI'LOT. *v. a.* [from the noun.] To steer; to direct in the course.

PI'LOTAGE. *n. s.* [*pilotage*, French, from *pilot.*]

1. Pilot's skill; knowledge of coasts.

We must for ever abandon the Indies, and lose all our knowledge and *pilotage* of that part of the world. *Raleigh.*

2. A pilot's hire. *Ainf.*

PI'LSER. *n. s.* The moth or fly that runs into a candle flame. *Ainf.*

PIME'NTA. *n. s.* [*piment*, French.] A kind of spice.

Pimenta, from its round figure, and the place whence it is brought, has been called Jamaica pepper, and from its mixt flavour of the several aromaticks, it has obtained the name of all-spice: it is a fruit gathered before it is ripe, and dried for medicinal and culinary use, of the size of a small pea, with a brown and rough surface, and it resembles that of cloves more than any other single spice. *Hill's Materia Medica.*

PIMP. *n. s.* [*pinge*, Fr. *Skinner.*] One who provides gratifications for the lust of others; a procurer; a pander.

I'm courted by all
As principal *pimp* to the mighty king Harry. *Addison.*

Lords keep a *pimp* to bring a wench;
So men of wit are but a kind
Of panders to a vicious mind;
Who proper objects must provide
To gratify their lust of pride. *Swift.*

To PIMP. *v. a.* [from the noun.] To provide gratifications for the lust of others; to pander; to procure.

But he's possest with a thousand imps,
To work whose ends his madness *pimps.* *Swift.*

Yet bards like these aspir'd to lasting praise,
And proudly hop'd to *pimp* in future days. *Anonymous.*

PI'MPERNEL. *n. s.* [*pimpernella*, Latin; *pimprenelle*, French.] A plant.

The flower of the *pimpernel* consists of one leaf shaped like a wheel and cut into several segments; the pointal, which rises out of the empalement, is fixed like a nail in the middle of the flower, and afterwards becomes a roundish fruit, which, when ripe, opens transversely into two parts, one incumbent on the other, inclosing many angular seeds, which adhere to the placenta. *Miller.*

PI'MPING. *adj.* [*pimple mensch*, a weak man, Dutch.] Little; petty: as, a *pimping* thing. *Skinner.*

PI'MPLE. *n. s.* [*pompette*, Fr.] A small red pustule.

If Rosalinda is unfortunate in her mole, Nigranilla is as unhappy in a *pimple.* *Addison's Spect.*

If e'er thy gnome could spoil a grace,
Or raise a *pimple* on a beauteous face. *Pope.*

PI'MPLED. *adj.* [from *pimple.*] Having red pustules; full of pimples: as, his face is *pimpled.*

PIN. *n. s.* [*espingle*, Fr. *spina*, *spinula*, Lat. *spilla*, Italian; rather from *pennum*, low Latin. *Isidore.*]

1. A short wire with a sharp point and round head, used by women to fasten their cloaths.

I'll make thee eat iron like an ostridge, and swallow my sword like a great *pin*, ere thou and I part. *Shakesp.*

Whatever spirit, careless of his charge,
His post neglects, or leaves the fair at large,
Shall feel sharp vengeance soon o'ertake his sins,
Be stopt in vials, or transfixt with *pins.* *Pope.*

2. Any thing inconsiderable or of little value.

Soon after comes the cruel Saracen,
In woven mail all armed warily,
And sternly looks at him, who not a *pin*
Does care for look of living creature's eye. *Fairy Queen.*

His fetch is to flatter to get what he can;
His purpose once gotten, a *pin* for thee than. *Tusser.*

Tut, a *pin*; this shall be answer'd. *Shakespeare.*

'Tis foolish to appeal to witness for proof, when 'tis not a *pin* matter whether the fact be true or false. *L'Estrange.*

3. Any thing driven to hold parts together; a peg; a bolt.

With *pins* of adamant
And chains, they made all fast. *Milton's Par. Lost.*

4. Any slender thing fixed in another body.

Bedlam beggars with roaring voices,
Sticks in their numb'd and mortified bare arms,
Pins, wooden pricks, nails, sprigs of rosemary. *Shakesp.*

These bullets shall rest on the *pins*; and there must be other *pins* to keep them. *Wilkins.*

5. That which locks the wheel to the axle; a linch pin.

6. The central part.

Romeo is dead, the very *pin* of his heart cleft with the blind hautboy's butshaft. *Shakesp. Romeo and Juliet.*

7. The pegs by which musicians intend or relax their strings.

8. A note; a strain. In low language.

A fir tree, in a vain spiteful humour, was mightily upon the *pin* of commending itself, and despising the bramble. *L'Est.*

As the woman was upon the peevish *pin*, a poor body comes, while the froward fit was upon her, to beg. *L'Estr.*

9. A horny induration of the membranes of the eye. *Hanmer.* *Skinner* seems likewise to say the same. I should rather think it an inflammation, which causes a pain like that of a pointed body piercing the eye.

Wish all eyes
Blind with the *pin* and web. *Shakespeare.*

10. A cylindrical roller made of wood.

They drew his brownbread face on pretty gins,
And made him stalk upon two rolling *pins.* *Corbet.*

11. A noxious humour in a hawk's foot. *Ains.*

To PIN. *v. a.* [from the noun.]

1. To fasten with pins.

If a word or two more are added upon the chief offenders, 'tis only a paper *pinn'd* upon the breast. *Pope.*

Not Cynthia when her manteau's *pinn'd* awry,
E'er felt such rage. *Pope.*

2. To fasten; to make fast.

Our gates,
Which yet seem shut, we have but *pinn'd* with rushes;
They'll open of themselves. *Shakesp. Macbeth.*

3. To join; to fix.

She lifted the princess from the earth, and so locks her in embracing, as if she would *pin* her to her heart. *Shakesp.*

If removing my consideration from the impression of the cubes to the cubes themselves, I shall *pin* this one notion upon every one of them, and accordingly conceive it to be really in them; it will fall out, that I allow existence to other entities, which never had any. *Digby of Bodies.*

I've learn'd how far I'm to believe
Your *pinning* oaths upon your sleeve. *Hudibras.*

They help to cozen themselves, by chusing to *pin* their faith on such expositors as explain the sacred scripture, in favour of those opinions that they beforehand have voted orthodox. *Locke.*

It cannot be imagined, that so able a man should take so much pains to *pin* so closely on his friend a story which, if he himself thought incredible, he could not but also think ridiculous. *Locke.*

4. [Pinban, Sax.] To shut up; to inclose; to confine: as, in pinfold.

If all this be willingly granted by us, which are accused to *pin* the word of God in so narrow room, let the cause of the accused be referred to the accuser's conscience. *Hooker.*

PI'NCASE. *n. s.* [*pin* and *case.*] A pincushion. *Ains.*

PI'NCERS. *n. s.* [*pincette*, Fr.]

1. An instrument by which nails are drawn, or any thing is griped, which requires to be held hard.

As superfluous flesh did rot,
Amendment ready still at hand did wait,
To pluck it out with *pincers* fiery hot,
That soon in him was left no one corrupt jot. *Fa. Queen.*

2. The claw of an animal.

Every ant brings a small particle of that earth in her *pincers*, and lays it by the hole. *Addison's Guardian.*

To PINCH. *v. a.* [*pincer*, Fr.]

1. To squeeze between the fingers, or with the teeth.

When the doctor spies his vantage ripe,
To *pinch* her by the hand,
The maid hath given consent to go with him. *Shakesp.*

2. To hold hard with an instrument.

3. To squeeze the flesh till it is pained or livid.

Thou shalt be *pinch'd*
As thick as honey-combs, each pinch more stinging
Than bees that made them. *Shakespeare's Tempest.*

He would *pinch* the children in the dark so hard, that he left the print in black and blue. *Arbuthnot's Hist. of J. Bull.*

4. To press between hard bodies.

5. To gall; to fret.

As they *pinch* one another by the disposition, he cries out, no more. *Shakesp. Antony and Cleopatra.*

6. To gripe; to oppress; to straiten.

Want of room upon the earth *pinching* a whole nation, begets the remediless war, vexing only some number of particulars, it draws on the arbitrary. *Raleigh's Essays.*

She *pinch'd* her belly with her daughter's too,
To bring the year about with much ado. *Dryden.*

Nic. Frog would *pinch* his belly to save his pocket. *Arb.*

7. To distress; to pain.

Avoid the *pinching* cold and scorching heat. *Milton.*

Afford them shelter from the wintry winds.
As the sharp year *pinches.* *Thomson's Autumn.*

8. To press; to drive to difficulties.

The beaver, when he finds himself hard *pinch'd*, bites 'em off, and by leaving them to his pursuers, saves himself. *L'Estrange.*

When the respondent is *pinched* with a strong objection, and is at a loss for an answer, the moderator suggests some answer to the objection of the opponent. *Watts.*

9. To try throughly; to force out what is contained within.

This is the way to *pinch* the question; therefore, let what will come of it, I will stand the test of your method. *Collier.*

To PINCH. *v. n.*

1. To act with force, so as to be felt; to bear hard upon; to be puzzling.

A difficulty *pincheth*, nor will it easily be resolved. *Glanv.*

But thou
Know'st with an equal hand to hold the scale,
See'st where the reasons *pinch*, and where they fail. *Dryd.*

2. To spare; to be frugal.

There is that waxeth rich by his wariness and *pinching.* *Ecclus.* xi. 18.

The poor that scarce have wherewithal to eat,
Will *pinch* and make the singing boy a treat. *Dryden.*

The bounteous player outgave the *pinching* lord. *Dryden.*

PINCH. *n. s.* [*pinçon*, French, from the verb.]

1. A painful squeeze with the fingers.

If any straggler from his rank be found,
A *pinch* must for the mortal sin compound. *Dryden.*

2. A gripe; a pain given.

There cannot be a *pinch* in death
More sharp than this is. *Shakesp. Cymbeline.*

3. Oppression;

3. Oppreſſion; diſtreſs inflicted.

Return to her: no, rather I chuſe
To be a comrad with the wolf and owl,
Neceſſity's ſharp *pinch*. *Shakeſp. King Lear.*

A farmer was put to ſuch a *pinch* in a hard winter, that he was forced to feed his family upon the main ſtock. *L'Eſtr.*

4. Difficulty; time of diſtreſs.

A good ſure friend is a better help at a *pinch*, than all the ſtratagems of a man's own wit. *Bacon.*

The devil helps his ſervants for a ſeaſon; but when they come once to a *pinch*, he leaves 'em in the lurch. *L'Eſtrange.*

The commentators never fail him at a *pinch*, and muſt excuſe him. *Dryden.*

They at a *pinch* can bribe a vote. *Swift's Miſcellanies.*

PI'NCHFIST. } *n. ſ.* [*pinch*, *fiſt*, and *penny.*] A miſer. *Ainſ.*
PI'NCHPENNY. }

PI'NCUSHION. *n. ſ.* [*pin* and *cuſhion.*] A ſmall bag ſtuffed with bran or wool on which pins are ſtuck.

She would ruin me in ſilks, were not the quantity, that goes to a large *pincuſhion*, ſufficient to make her a gown and petticoat. *Addiſon's Guardian*, Nº 271.

Thou art a retailer of phraſes, and doſt deal in remnants of remnants, like a maker of *pincuſhions*. *Congreve.*

PI'NDUST. *n. ſ.* [*pin* and *duſt.*] Small particles of metal made by cutting pins.

The little parts of *pinduſt*, when mingled with ſand, cannot, by their mingling, make it lighter. *Digby.*

PINE. *n. ſ.* [*pinus*, Lat. *pin*, French.]

The *pine*-tree hath amentaceous flowers or katkins, which are produced, at remote diſtances from the fruit, on the ſame tree; the ſeeds are produced in ſquamous cones: to which ſhould be added, that the leaves are longer than thoſe of a fir-tree, and are produced by pairs out of each ſheath. *Miller.*

You may as well forbid the mountain *pines*
To wag their high tops, and to make a noiſe,
When they are fretted with the guſts of heaven. *Shakeſp.*

Thus droops this lofty *pine*, and hangs his ſprayes;
Thus Eleanor's pride dies in her younger days. *Shakeſp.*

Go forth unto the mount, and fetch *pine*-branches. *Nehem.*

To PINE. *v. a.* [pinan, Sax. *pijnen*, Dutch.]

1. To languiſh; to wear away with any kind of miſery.

My hungry eyes through greedy covetiſe,
With no contentment can themſelves ſuffice;
But having, *pine*, and having not, complain. *Spenſer.*

I burn, I *pine*, I periſh,
If I atchieve not this young modeſt girl. *Shakeſp.*

Since my young lady's going into France, the fool hath much *pined* away. *Shakeſp. King Lear.*

See, ſee the *pining* malady of France,
Behold the moſt unnat'ral wounds,
Which thou thyſelf haſt giv'n her woful breaſt. *Shakeſp.*

Ye ſhall not mourn, but *pine* away for your iniquities. *Ezekiel* xxiv. 23.

The wicked with anxiety of mind
Shall *pine* away; in ſighs conſume their breath. *Sandys.*

To me who with eternal famine *pine*,
Alike is hell, or paradiſe, or heav'n. *Milton's Par. Loſt.*

Farewell the year, which threaten'd ſo
The faireſt light the world can ſhow;
Welcome the new, whoſe ev'ry day,
Reſtoring what was ſnatch'd away
By *pining* ſickneſs from the fair,
That matchleſs beauty does repair. *Waller.*

This night ſhall ſee the gaudy wreath decline,
The roſes wither, and the lilies *pine*. *Tickell.*

2. To languiſh with deſire.

We may again
Free from our feaſts and banquets bloody knives,
Do faithful homage and receive free honours:
All which we *pine* for. *Shakeſp. Macbeth.*

We ſtood amaz'd to ſee your miſtreſs mourn,
Unknowing that ſhe *pin'd* for your return. *Dryden.*

Your new commander need not *pine* for action. *Philips.*

To PINE. *v. a.*

1. To wear out; to make to languiſh.

Part us; I towards the north,
Where ſhivering cold and ſickneſs *pines* the clime. *Shakeſp.*

Beroe *pin'd* with pain,
Her age and anguiſh from theſe rites detain. *Dryden.*

Thus tender Spencer liv'd, with mean repaſt
Content, depreſs'd with penury, and *pin'd*
In foreign realm: yet not debas'd his verſe. *Philips.*

2. To grieve for; to bemoan in ſilence.

Abaſh'd the devil ſtood,
Virtue in her ſhape how lovely, ſaw; and *pin'd*
His loſs. *Milton's Paradiſe Loſt, b.* iv.

PI'NEAPPLE. *n. ſ.*

The *pineapple* hath a flower conſiſting of one leaf, divided into three parts, and is funnel-ſhaped: the embryos are produced in the tubercles: theſe become a fleſhy fruit full of juice: the ſeeds, which are lodged in the tubercles, are very ſmall and almoſt kidney-ſhaped. *Miller.*

Try if any words can give the taſte of a *pineapple*, and make one have the true idea of its reliſh. *Locke.*

If a child were kept where he never ſaw but black and white, he would have no more ideas of ſcarlet, than he that never taſted a *pineapple*, has of that particular reliſh. *Locke.*

PI'NEAL. *adj.* [*pineale*, Fr.] Reſembling a pineapple. An epithet given by *Des Cartes* from the form, to the gland which he imagined the ſeat of the ſoul.

Courtiers and ſpaniels exactly reſemble one another in the *pineal* gland. *Arbuthnot and Pope.*

PI'NFEATHERED. *adj.* [*pin* and *feather.*] Not fledged; having the feathers yet only beginning to ſhoot.

We ſee ſome raw *pinfeather'd* thing
Attempt to mount, and fights and heroes ſing;
Who for falſe quantities was whipt at ſchool. *Dryden.*

PI'NFOLD. *n. ſ.* [pinban, Sax. to ſhut up, and *fold.*] A place in which beaſts are confined.

The Iriſh never come to thoſe raths but armed; which the Engliſh nothing ſuſpecting, are taken at an advantage, like ſheep in the *pinfold*. *Spenſer on Ireland.*

I care not for thee.—
—If I had thee in Lipſbury *pinfold*, I would make thee care for me. *Shakeſp. King Lear.*

Confin'd and peſter'd in this *pinfold* here,
Strive to keep up a frail and feveriſh being. *Milton.*

Oaths were not purpos'd more than law
To keep the good and juſt in awe,
But to confine the bad and ſinful,
Like moral cattle in a *pinfold*. *Hudibras.*

PI'NGLE. *n. ſ.* A ſmall cloſe; an incloſure. *Ainſ.*

PI'NMONEY. *n. ſ.* [*pin* and *money.*] Money allowed to a wife for her private expences without account.

The woman muſt find out ſomething elſe to mortgage, when her *pinmoney* is gone. *Addiſon's Guardian.*

PI'NGUID. *adj.* [*pinguis*, Lat.] Fat; unctuous. Little uſed.

Some clays are more *pinguid*, and other more ſlippery; yet all of them are very tenacious of water on the ſurface. *Mortimer's Huſbandry.*

PI'NHOLE. *n. ſ.* [*pin* and *hole.*] A ſmall hole, ſuch as is made by the perforation of a pin.

The breaſt at firſt broke in a ſmall *pinhole*. *Wiſeman.*

PI'NION. *n. ſ.* [*pignon*, Fr.

1. The joint of the wing remoteſt from the body.

2. *Shakeſpeare* ſeems to uſe it for a feather or quill of the wing.

He is pluckt, when hither
He ſends ſo poor a *pinion* of his wing. *Shakeſp.*

3. Wing.

How oft do they with golden *pinions* cleave
The flitting ſkies, like flying purſuivant. *Fairy Queen.*

The God, who mounts the winged winds,
Faſt to his feet the golden *pinions* binds,
That high through fields of air his flight ſuſtain. *Pope.*

Though fear ſhould lend him *pinions* like the wind,
Yet ſwifter fate will ſeize him from behind. *Swift.*

4. The tooth of a ſmaller wheel, anſwering to that of a larger.

5. Fetters for the hands. *Ainſ.*

To PI'NION. *v. a.* [from the noun.]

1. To bind the wings.

Whereas they have ſacrificed to themſelves, they become themſelves ſacrifices to the inconſtancy of fortune, whoſe wings they thought by their ſelf-wiſdom to have *pinioned*. *Bacon's Eſſays*, Nº 24.

2. To confine by binding the wings.

3. To bind the arm to the body.

A ſecond ſpear ſent with equal force,
His right arm pierc'd, and holding on, bereſt
His uſe of both, and *pinion'd* down his left. *Dryden.*

4. To confine by binding the elbows to the ſides.

Swarming at his back the country cry'd,
And ſeiz'd and *pinion'd* brought to court the knight. *Dryden.*

5. To ſhackle; to bind.

Know, that I will not wait *pinion'd* at your maſter's court; rather make my country's high pyramids my gibbet, and hang me up in chains. *Shakeſp. Antony and Cleopatra.*

You are not to go looſe any longer, you muſt be *pinion'd*. *Shakeſp. Merry Wives of Windſor.*

O looſe this frame, this knot of man untie!
That my free ſoul may uſe her wing,
Which now is *pinion'd* with mortality,
As an entangled, hamper'd thing. *Herbert.*

In vain from chains and fetters free,
The great man boaſts of liberty;
He's *pinion'd* up by formal rules of ſtate. *Norris.*

6. To bind to.

A heavy lord ſhall hang at ev'ry wit;
And while on fame's triumphant car they ride,
Some ſlave of mine be *pinion'd* to their ſide. *Dunciad.*

PINK. *n. s.* [*pince*, Fr. from *pink*, Dutch, an eye; whence the French word *œillet.*]

1. A small fragrant flower of the gilliflower kind.

In May and June come *pinks* of all sorts; especially the blush *pink*. *Bacon's Essays.*

2. An eye; commonly a small eye: as, *pink*-eyed.

Come, thou monarch of the vine,
Plumpy Bacchus, with *pink* eyne,
In thy vats our cares be drown'd. *Shakespeare.*

3. Any thing supremely excellent. I know not whether from the flower or the eye, or a corruption of *pinacle*.

I am the very *pink* of courtesy. *Shakesp. Rom. and Jul.*

4. A colour used by painters.

Pink is very susceptible of the other colours by the mixture; if you mix brown-red with it, you will make it a very earthy colour. *Dryden's Dufresnoy.*

5. [*Pinque*, Fr.] A kind of heavy narrow-sterned ship.

This *pink* is one of Cupid's carriers;
Give fire, she is my prize. *Shakesp. Merry Wives of Winds.*

6. A fish; the minow. *Ainsworth.*

To PINK. *v. a.* [from *pink*, Dutch, an eye.] To work in oylet holes; to pierce in small holes.

A haberdasher's wife of small wit rail'd upon me, till her *pink'd* porringer fell off her head. *Shakesp. Henry* VIII.

The sea-hedgehog is enclosed in a round shell, handsomely wrought and *pink'd*. *Carew's Survey of Cornwall.*

Happy the climate, where the beau
Wears the same suit for use and show;
And at a small expence your wife,
If once well *pink'd*, is cloath'd for life. *Prior.*

To PINK. *v. n.* [*pincken*, Dutch; from the noun.] To wink with the eyes.

A hungry fox lay winking and *pinking*, as if he had sore eyes. *L'Estrange's Fables.*

PI'NMAKER. *n. s.* [*pin* and *make*.] He who makes pins.

PI'NNACE. *n. s.* [*pinasse*, Fr. *pinnacia*, Italian; *pinaça*, Span.] A boat belonging to a ship of war. It seems formerly to have signified rather a small sloop or bark attending a larger ship.

Whilst our *pinnace* anchors in the downs,
Here shall they make their ransom on the sand. *Shakesp.*

For fear of the Turks great fleet, he came by night in a small *pinnace* to the Rhodes. *Knolles's Hist. of the Turks.*

I sent a *pinnace* or post of advice, to make a discovery of the coast, before I adventured my greater ship. *Spelman.*

Thus to ballast love,
I saw I had love's *pinnace* overfraught. *Donne.*

I discharged a bark, taken by one of my *pinnaces*, coming from cape Blanch. *Raleigh's Apology.*

A *pinnace* anchors in a craggy bay. *Milton.*

Swift as a swallow sweeps the liquid way,
The winged *pinnace* shot along the sea. *Pope.*

PI'NNACLE. *n. s.* [*pinnacle*, Fr. *pinna*, Lat.]

1. A turret or elevation above the rest of the building.

My letting some men go up to the *pinnacle* of the temple, was a temptation to them to cast me down headlong. *K. Char.*

He who desires only heaven, laughs at that enchantment, which engages men to climb a tottering *pinnacle*, where the standing is uneasy, and the fall deadly. *Decay of Piety.*

He took up ship-money where Noy left it, and, being a judge, carried it up to that *pinnacle*, from whence he almost broke his neck. *Clarendon.*

Some metropolis
With glist'ring spires and *pinnacles* adorn'd. *Milton.*

2. A high spiring point.

The slipp'ry tops of human state,
The gilded *pinnacles* of fate. *Cowley.*

PI'NNER. *n. s.* [from *pinna* or *pinion*.]

1. The lappet of a head which flies loose.

Her goodly countenance I've seen,
Set off with kerchief starch'd, and *pinners* clean. *Gay.*

An antiquary will scorn to mention a *pinner* or a night-rail, but will talk on the vitta. *Addison on Ancient Medals.*

2. A pinmaker. *Ainsworth.*

PI'NNOCK. *n. s.* The tom-tit. *Ainsworth.*

PINT. *n. s.* [pinꞇ, Sax. *pinte*, Fr. *pinta*, low Lat.] Half a quart; in medicine, twelve ounces; a liquid measure.

Well, you'll not believe me generous, till I crack half a *pint* with you at my own charges. *Dryden.*

PI'NULES. *n. s.* In astronomy, the sights of an astrolabe. *Dict.*

PIO'NEER. *n. s.* [*pionier*, from *pion*, obsolete Fr. *pion*, according to *Scaliger*, comes from *peo* for *pedito*, a foot soldier, who was formerly employed in digging for the army. A *pioneer* is in Dutch, *spagenier*, from *spage*, a spade; whence *Junius* imagines that the French borrowed *pagenier*, which was afterwards called *pioneer*.] One whose business is to level the road, throw up works, or sink mines in military operations.

Well said, old mole, can'st work i' th' ground so fast?
A worthy *pioneer*? *Shakespeare's Hamlet.*

Three try new experiments, such as themselves think good; these we call *pioneers* or miners. *Bacon.*

His *pioneers*
Even the paths, and make the highways plain. *Fairfax.*

Of labouring *pioneers*
A multitude with spades and axes arm'd,
To lay hills plain, fell woods or vallies fill. *Milton.*

The Romans, after the death of Tiberius, sent thither an army of *pioneers* to demolish the buildings, and deface the beauties of the island. *Addison's Remarks on Italy.*

PI'ONING. *n. s.* Works of pioneers. *Spenser.*

PI'ONY. *n. s.* [*pæonia*, Lat.] A large flower. See PEONY.

PI'OUS. *adj.* [*pius*, Lat. *pieux*, Fr.]

1. Careful of the duties owed by created beings to God; godly; religious; such as is due to sacred things.

Pious awe that fear'd to have offended. *Milton.*

2. Careful of the duties of near relation.

As he is not called a just father, that educates his children well, but *pious*; so that prince, who defends and well rules his people, is religious. *Taylor's Rule of Living Holy.*

Where was the martial brother's *pious* care?
Condemn'd perhaps some foreign shore to tread. *Pope.*

3. Practised under the appearance of religion.

I shall never gratify spightfulness with any sinister thoughts of all whom *pious* frauds have seduced. *King Charles.*

PI'OUSLY. *adv.* [from *pious*.] In a pious manner; religiously; with regard; such as is due to sacred things.

The prime act and evidence of the christian hope is, to set industriously and *piously* to the performance of that condition, on which the promise is made. *Hammond.*

See lion-hearted Richard, with his force
Drawn from the North, to Jury's hallow'd plains;
Piously valiant. *Philips.*

This martial present *piously* design'd,
The loyal city give their best-lov'd king. *Dryden.*

Let freedom never perish in your hands!
But *piously* transmit it to your children. *Addison's Cato.*

PIP. *n. s.* [*pippe*, Dutch; *pepie*, Fr. deduced by *Skinner* from *pituita*; but probably coming from *pipio* or *pipilo*, on account of the complaining cry.]

1. A defluxion with which fowls are troubled; a horny pellicle that grows on the tip of their tongues.

When murrain reigns in hogs or sheep,
And chickens languish of the *pip*. *Hudibras.*

A spiteful vexatious gipsy died of the *pip*. *L'Estrange.*

2. A spot on the cards. I know not from what original, unless from *pict*, painting; in the country, the pictured or court cards are called *picts*.

When our women fill their imaginations with *pips* and counters, I cannot wonder at a new-born child, that was marked with the five of clubs. *Addison's Guardian.*

To PIP. *v. a.* [*pipio*, Lat.] To chirp or cry as a bird.

It is no unfrequent thing to hear the chick *pip* and cry in the egg, before the shell be broken. *Boyle.*

PIPE. *n. s.* [*pib*, Welsh; pıpe, Saxon.]

1. Any long hollow body; a tube.

The veins unfill'd, our blood is cold, and then
We powt upon the morning, are unapt
To give or to forgive; but when we've stuff'd
These *pipes*, and these conveyances of blood
With wine and feeding, we have suppler souls. *Shakesp.*

The part of the *pipe*, which was lowermost, will become higher; so that water ascends by descending. *Wilkins.*

It has many springs breaking out of the sides of the hills, and vast quantities of wood to make *pipes* of. *Addison.*

An animal, the nearer it is to its original, the more *pipes* it hath, and as it advanceth in age, still fewer. *Arbuthnot.*

2. A tube of clay through which the fume of tobacco is drawn into the mouth.

Try the taking of fumes by *pipes*, as in tobacco and other things, to dry and comfort. *Bacon's Natural History.*

His ancient *pipe* in sable dy'd,
And half unsmoak'd lay by his side. *Swift.*

My husband's a sot,
With his *pipe* and his pot. *Swift.*

3. An instrument of hand musick.

I have known, when there was no musick with him but the drum and the fife, and now had he rather hear the taber and the *pipe*. *Shakesp.*

The solemn *pipe* and dulcimer. *Milton.*

The shrill sound of a small rural *pipe*,
Was entertainment for the infant stage. *Roscommon.*

There is no reason, why the sound of a *pipe* should leave traces in their brains. *Locke.*

4. The organs of voice and respiration; as, the wind-*pipe*.

The exercise of singing openeth the breast and *pipes*. *Peac.*

5. The key of the voice.

My throat of war be turn'd,
Which quired with my drum, into a *pipe*
Small as an eunuch. *Shakesp. Coriolanus.*

6. An office of the exchequer.

That office of her majesty's exchequer, we, by a metaphor, call the *pipe*, because the whole receipt is finally conveyed into it by the means of divers small *pipes* or quills, as water into a cistern. *Bacon.*

7. [*Peep*, Dutch; *pipe*, Fr.] A liquid measure containing two hogsheads.

I think I shall drink in *pipe* wine with Falstaff; I'll make him dance. *Shakesp. Merry Wives of Windsor.*

To PIPE. *v. n.* [from the noun.]

1. To play on the pipe.

Merry Michael the Cornish poet *piped* thus upon his oaten pipe for merry England. *Camden's Remains.*

We have *piped* unto you, and you have not danced. *Mat.*

In singing, as in *piping*, you excel. *Dryden.*

Gaming goats, and fleecy flocks,
And lowing herds, and *piping* swains,
Come dancing to me. *Swift.*

2. To have a shrill sound.

His big manly voice,
Turning again toward childish treble, *pipes*
And whistles in his sound. *Shakesp. As You like it.*

PI'PER. *n. s.* [from *pipe.*] One who plays on the pipe.

Pipers and trumpeters shall be heard no more in thee. *Rev.*

PI'PETREE. *n. s.* The lilac tree.

PI'PING. *adj.* [from *pipe.* This word is only used in low language.]

1. Weak; feeble; sickly: from the weak voice of the sick.

I, in this weak *piping* time of peace,
Have no delight to pass away the time,
Unless to spy my shadow in the sun. *Shakesp.*

2. Hot; boiling: from the sound of any thing that boils.

PI'PKIN. *n. s.* [diminutive of *pipe*, a large vessel.] A small earthern boiler.

A *pipkin* there like Homer's tripod walks. *Pope.*

Some officer might give consent
To a large cover'd *pipkin* in his tent. *King.*

PI'PPIN. *n. s.* [*puppynghe*, Dutch. *Skinner.*] A sharp apple.

Pippins take their name from the small spots or pips that usually appear on the sides of them: some are called stone *pippins* from their obduratenefs; some Kentish *pippins*, because they agree well with that soil; others French *pippins*, having their original from France, which is the best bearer of any of these *pippins*; the Holland *pippin* and the russet *pippin*, from its russet hue; but such as are distinguished by the names of grey and white *pippins* are of equal goodness: they are generally a very pleasant fruit and of good juice, but slender bearers. *Mortimer's Husbandry.*

You shall see mine orchard, where, in an arbour, we will eat a last year's *pippin* of my own graffing. *Shakesp.*

At supper entertain yourself with a *pippin* roasted. *Harvey.*

The story of the *pippin*-woman, I look upon as fabulous. *Addison's Spectator*, Nº 247.

His foaming tusks let some large *pippin* grace,
Or midst those thund'ring spears an orange place. *King.*

This *pippin* shall another trial make;
See from the core two kernels brown I take. *Gay.*

PI'QUANT. *adj.* [*piquant*, French.]

1. Pricking; piercing; stimulating.

There are vast mountains of a transparent rock extremely solid, and as *piquant* to the tongue as salt. *Addison on Italy.*

2. Sharp; tart; pungent; severe.

Some think their wits asleep, except they dart out somewhat that is *piquant*, and to the quick: that is a vein that would be bridled; and men ought to find the difference between saltness and bitterness. *Bacon's Essays.*

Men make their railleries as *piquant* as they can to wound the deeper. *Government of the Tongue.*

PI'QUANCY. *n. s.* [from *piquant.*] Sharpness; tartness.

PI'QUANTLY. *adv.* [from *piquant.*] Sharply; tartly.

A small mistake may leave upon the mind the lasting memory of having been *piquantly*, though wittily taunted. *Locke.*

PIQUE. *n. s.* [*pique*, French.]

1. An ill will; an offence taken; petty malevolence.

He had never any the least *pique*, difference or jealousy with the king his father. *Bacon's Henry* VIII.

Men take up *piques* and displeasures at others, and then every opinion of the disliked person must partake of his fate. *Decay of Piety.*

Out of a personal *pique* to those in service, he stands as a looker-on, when the government is attacked. *Addison.*

2. A strong passion.

Though he have the *pique*, and long,
'Tis still for something in the wrong;
As women long, when they're with child,
For things extravagant and wild. *Hudibras, p.* iii.

3. Point; nicety; punctilio.

Add long prescription of establish'd laws,
And *pique* of honour to maintain a cause,
And shame of change. *Dryden.*

To PIQUE. *v. a.* [*piquer*, Fr.]

1. To touch with envy or virulency; to put into fret.

Piqu'd by Protogenes's fame,
From Co to Rhodes Apelles came
To see a rival and a friend,
Prepar'd to censure or commend. *Prior.*

The lady was *piqued* by her indifference, and began to mention going away. *Female Quixote.*

2. To offend; to irritate.

Why *pique* all mortals, that affect a name?
A fool to pleasure, yet a slave to fame! *Pope.*

3. [With the reciprocal pronoun.] To value; to fix reputation as on a point. [*se piquer*, French.]

Children, having made it easy to part with what they have, may *pique themselves* in being kind. *Locke.*

Men apply themselves to two or three foreign, dead, and which are called the learned, languages; and *pique themselves* upon their skill in them. *Locke on Education.*

To PIQUEE'R. See PICKEER.

PIQUEE'RER. *n. s.* A robber; a plunderer. Rather *pickeerer.*

When the guardian professed to engage in faction, the word was given, that the guardian would soon be seconded by some other *piqueerers* from the same camp. *Swift.*

PIQUE'T. *n. s.* [*picquet*, Fr.] A game at cards.

She commonly went up at ten,
Unless *piquet* was in the way. *Prior.*

Instead of entertaining themselves at ombre or *piquet*, they would wrestle and pitch the bar. *Spectator.*

PI'RACY. *n. s.* [πειρατεία; *piratica*, Lat. *piraterie*, Fr. from *pirate.*] The act or practice of robbing on the sea.

Our gallants, in their fresh gale of fortune, began to skum the seas with their *piracies.* *Carew's Survey of Cornwall.*

Now shall the ocean, as thy Thames, be free,
From both those fates of storms and *piracy.* *Waller.*

Fame swifter than your winged navy flies,
Sounding your name, and telling dreadful news
To all that *piracy* and rapine use. *Waller.*

His pretence for making war upon his neighbours was their *piracies*; though he practised the same trade. *Arbuthnot.*

PIRATE. *n. s.* [πειρατής; *pirata*, Lat. *pirate*, Fr.]

1. A sea-robber.

Wrangling *pirates* that fall out
In sharing that which you have pill'd from me. *Shakesp.*

Pirates all nations are to prosecute, not so much in the right of their own fears, as upon the band of human society. *Bacon.*

Relate, if business or the thirst of gain
Engage your journey o'er the pathless main,
Where savage *pirates* seek through seas unknown
The lives of others, vent'rous of their own. *Pope.*

2. Any robber; particularly a bookseller who seizes the copies of other men.

To PI'RATE. *v. n.* [from the noun.] To rob by sea.

When they were a little got out of their former condition, they robbed at land and *pirated* by sea. *Arbuthnot.*

Nabis possessed himself of the coast near to Sparta, and there *pirated* outrageously upon all the Peloponnesian trade. *Arbuthnot on Coins.*

To PI'RATE. *v. a.* [*pirater*, Fr.] To take by robbery.

They publickly advertised, they would *pirate* his edition. *Pope.*

PIRA'TICAL. *adj.* [*piraticus*, Lat. from *pirate.*] Predatory; robbing; consisting in robbery.

Having gotten together ships and barks, fell to a kind of *piratical* trade, robbing, spoiling and taking prisoners the ships of all nations. *Bacon's Henry* VII.

The errors of the press were multiplied by *piratical* printers; to not one of whom I ever gave any other encouragement, than that of not prosecuting them. *Pope.*

PISCA'TION. *n. s.* [*piscatio*, Lat.] The act or practice of fishing.

There are extant four books of cynegeticks, or venation; five of halieuticks, or *piscation*, commented by Ritterhusius. *Brown's Vulgar Errours.*

PI'SCARY. *n. s.* A privilege of fishing. *Dict.*

PI'SCATORY. *adj.* [*piscatorius*, Lat.] Relating to fishes.

On this monument is represented, in bas-relief, Neptune among the satyrs, to shew that this poet was the inventor of *piscatory* eclogues. *Addison's Remarks on Italy.*

PISCI'VOROUS. *adj.* [*piscis* and *voro.*] Fisheating; living on fish.

In birds that are not carnivorous, the meat is swallowed into the crop or into a kind of antestomach, observed in *piscivorous* birds, where it is moistened and mollified by some proper juice. *Ray on the Creation.*

PISH. *interj.* A contemptuous exclamation. This is sometimes spoken and written *pshaw.* I know not their etymology, and imagine them formed by chance.

There was never yet philosopher
That could endure the toothach patiently;
However they have writ,
And made a *pish* at chance or sufferance. *Shakesp.*

She frowned and cried *pish*, when I said a thing that I stole. *Spectator*, Nº 268.

To PISH. *v. n.* [from the interjection.] To express contempt.

He turn'd over your Homer, shook his head, and *pish'd* at every line of it. *Pope.*

PISMIRE. *n. s.* [myɼa, Sax. *pismiere*, Dutch.] An ant; an emmet.

His cloaths, as atoms might prevail,
Might fit a *pismire* or a whale. *Prior.*

Prejudicial to fruit are *pismires*, caterpillars and mice. *Mort.*

To PISS. *v. n.* [*pisser*, Fr. *pissen*, Dutch.] To make water.

I charge the *pissing* conduit run nothing but claret. *Shakesp.*

One ass *pisses*, the rest *piss* for company. *L'Estrange.*

Once possess'd of what with care you save,
The wanton boys would *piss* upon your grave. *Dryden.*

PISS. *n. s.* [from the verb.] Urine; animal water.

My spleen is at the little rogues, it would vex one more to be knock'd on the head with a *piss*-pot than a thunder bolt. *Pope to Swift.*

PI'SSABED. *n. s.* A yellow flower growing in the grass.

PI'SSBURNT. *adj.* Stained with urine.

PISTA'CHIO. *n. s.* [*pistache*, Fr. *pistacchi*, Italian; *pistachia*, Latin.]

The *pistachio* is a dry fruit of an oblong figure, pointed at both ends about half an inch in length, and a third of an inch in thickness: it has a double shell, the exteriour one membranaceous and thin, and the inner hard, tough and woody: the kernel is of a green colour and a soft and unctuous substance, much like the pulp of an almond, of a pleasant taste: *pistachios* were known to the ancients, and the Arabians call them *pestuch* and *festuch*, and we sometimes *fistich* nuts. *Hill.*

Pistachios, so they be good, and not musty, joined with almonds, are an excellent nourisher. *Bacon's Nat. Hist.*

PISTE. *n. s.* [French.] The track or tread a horseman makes upon the ground he goes over.

PISTI'LLATION. *n. s.* [*pistillum*, Lat.] The act of pounding in a mortar.

The best diamonds we have are comminuible, and so far from breaking hammers, that they submit unto *pistillation*, and resist not an ordinary pestle. *Brown's Vulgar Errours.*

PI'STOL. *n. s.* [*pistole*, *pistolet*, Fr.] A small handgun.

Three watch the door with *pistols*, that none should issue out. *Shakespeare's Merry Wives of Windsor.*

The whole body of the horse passed within *pistol*-shot of the cottage. *Clarendon, b.* viii.

Quicksilver discharged from a *pistol* will hardly pierce through a parchment. *Brown's Vulgar Errours.*

A woman had a tubercle in the great canthus of the eye, of the bigness of a *pistol*-bullet. *Wiseman's Surgery.*

To PI'STOL. *v. a.* [*pistoler*, Fr.] To shoot with a pistol.

PI'STOLE. *n. s.* [*pistole*, Fr.] A coin of many countries and many degrees of value.

I shall disburden him of many hundred *pistoles*, to make him lighter for the journey. *Dryden's Spanish Fryar.*

PISTO'LET. *n. s.* [diminutive of *pistol.*] A little pistol.

Those unlickt bear-whelps, unfil'd *pistolets*
That, more than cannon-shot, avails or lets. *Donne.*

PI'STON. *n. s.* [*piston*, Fr.] The movable part in several machines; as in pumps and syringes, whereby the suction or attraction is caused; am embolus.

PIT. *n. s.* [pɪt, Saxon.]

1. A hole in the ground.

Get you gone,
And from the *pit* of Acheron
Meet me i' th' morning. *Shakesp. Macbeth.*

Tumble me into some loathsome *pit*,
Where never man's eye may behold my body. *Shakesp.*

Our enemies have beat us to the *pit*;
It is more worthy to leap in ourselves,
Than tarry 'till they push us. *Shakesp. Julius Cæsar.*

Pits upon the sea-shore turn into fresh water, by percolation of the salt through the sand; but in some places of Africa, the water in such *pits* will become brackish again. *Bacon.*

2. Abyss; profundity.

Into what *pit* thou seest
From what height fallen. *Milton.*

3. The grave.

O Lord, think no scorn of me, lest I become like them that go down into the *pit*. *Psalm* xxviii. 1.

4. The area on which cocks fight; whence the phrase, to fly the *pit*.

Make him glad, at least, to quit
His victory, and fly the *pit*. *Hudibras.*

They managed the dispute as fiercely, as two game-cocks in the *pit*. *Locke on Education.*

5. The middle part of the theatre.

Let Cully, Cockwood, Fopling charm the *pit*,
And in their folly shew the writers wit. *Dryden.*

Now luck for us, and a kind hearty *pit*;
For he who pleases, never fails of wit. *Dryden.*

6. [*Pis*, *peis*, old Fr. from *pectus*, Lat.] Any hollow of the body: as, the *pit* of the stomach; the arm *pit*.

7. A dint made by the finger.

To PIT. *v. a.* To sink in hollows.

An anasarca, a species of dropsy, is characterised by the shining and softness of the skin, which gives way to the least impression, and remains *pitted* for some time. *Sharp.*

PITAPAT. *n. s.* [probably from *pas a pas*, or *patte patte*, Fr.]

1. A flutter; a palpitation.

A lion meets him, and the fox's heart went *pitapat.* *L'Estr.*

2. A light quick step.

Now I hear the *pitapat* of a pretty foot through the dark alley: no, 'tis the son of a mare that's broken loose, and munching upon the melons. *Dryden's Don Sebastian.*

PITCH. *n. s.* [pɪc, Sax. *pix*, Lat.] The resin of the pine extracted by fire and inspissated.

They that touch *pitch* will be defiled. *Proverbs.*

Of air and water mixed together, and consumed with fire, is made a black colour; as in charcoal, oil, *pitch* and links. *Peacham on Drawing.*

A vessel smear'd round with *pitch.* *Milton.*

2. [From *picts*, Fr. *Skinner.*] Any degree of elevation or height.

Lovely concord and most sacred peace
Doth nourish virtue, and fast friendship breeds,
Weak she makes strong, and strong things does increase,
Till it the *pitch* of highest praise exceeds. *Fairy Queen.*

How high a *pitch* his resolution soars. *Shakesp.*

Arm thy heart, and fill thy thoughts
To mount aloft with thy imperial mistress,
And mount her *pitch.* *Shakespeare's Titus Andronicus.*

Between two hawks, which flies the higher *pitch*,
I have, perhaps, some shallow judgment. *Shakesp.*

Down they fell,
Driv'n headlong from the *pitch* of heav'n, down
Into this deep. *Milton's Par. Lost, b.* ii.

Cannons shoot the higher *pitches*,
The lower we let down their breeches. *Hudibras.*

Alcibiades was one of the best orators of his age, notwithstanding he lived at a time when learning was at the highest *pitch.* *Addison's Whig Examiner.*

3. Highest rise.

A beauty waining, and distressed widow,
Seduc'd the *pitch* and height of all his thoughts
To base declension and loath'd bigamy. *Shakesp.*

4. State with respect to lowness or height.

From this high *pitch* let us descend
A lower flight; and speak of things at hand. *Milton.*

By how much from the top of wond'rous glory,
Strongest of mortal men,
To lowest *pitch* of abject fortune thou art fall'n. *Milton.*

5. Size; stature.

That infernal monster having cast
His weary foe into the living well,
'Gan high advance his broad discoloured breast
Above his wonted *pitch.* *Fairy Queen.*

Were the whole frame here,
It is of such a spacious lofty *pitch*,
Your roof were not sufficient to contain it. *Shakesp.*

It turn'd itself to Ralpho's shape;
So like in person, garb and *pitch*,
'Twas hard t' interpret which was which. *Hudibras.*

6. Degree; rate.

To overcome in battle, and subdue
Nations, and bring home spoils, with infinite
Manslaughter, shall be held the highest *pitch*
Of human glory. *Milton's Par. Lost, b.* xi.

Our resident Tom
From Venice is come,
And hath left the statesman behind him,
Talks at the same *pitch*,
Is as wise, is as rich,
And just where you left him, you find him. *Denham.*

Princes that fear'd him, grieve; concern'd to see
No *pitch* of glory from the grave is free. *Waller.*

Evangelical innocence, such as the gospel accepts, though mingled with several infirmities and defects, yet amounts to such a *pitch* of righteousness, as we call sincerity. *South.*

When the sun's heat is thus far advanced, 'tis but just come up to the *pitch* of another set of vegetables, and but great enough to excite the terrestial particles, which are more ponderous. *Woodward's Natural History.*

To PITCH. *v. a.* [*appicciare*, Italian.]

1. To fix; to plant.

On Dardan plains the Greeks do *pitch*
Their brave pavilions. *Shakespeare's Troilus and Cressida.*

Sharp stakes, pluckt out of hedges,
They *pitched* in the ground. *Shakesp. Henry* VI.

He counselled him how to hunt his game,
What dart to cast, what net, what toile to *pitch.* *Fairfax.*

David prepared a place for the ark of God, and *pitched* for it a tent. 1 *Chron.* xv. 1.

Mahometes *pitched* his tents in a little meadow. *Knolles.*

When the victor
Had conquered Thebes, he *pitched* upon the plain
His mighty camp. *Dryden's Knight's Tale.*

To Chassis' pleasing plains he took his way,
There *pitch'd* his tents, and there resolv'd to stay. *Dryden.*

The trenches first they pass'd, then took their way
Where their proud foes in *pitch'd* pavilions lay. *Dryden.*

2. To

2. To order regularly.

In ſetting down the form of common prayer, there was no need to mention the learning of a fit, or the unfitneſs of an ignorant miniſter, more than that he, which deſcribeth the manner how to *pitch* a field, ſhould ſpeak of moderation and ſobriety in diet. *Hooker, b.* v. *ſ.* 31.

One *pitched* battle would determine the fate of the Spaniſh continent. *Addiſon on the State of the War.*

3. To throw headlong; to caſt forward.

They'll not *pitch* me i' th' mire,
Unleſs he bid 'em. *Shakeſp. Tempeſt.*

They would wreſtle, and *pitch* the bar for a whole afternoon. *Spectator*, N° 434.

4. To ſmear with PITCH. [*pico*, Lat. from the noun.]

The ark *pitch* within and without. *Geneſis* vi. 14.

The Trojans mount their ſhips, born on the waves,
And the *pitch'd* veſſels glide with eaſy force. *Dryden.*

Some *pitch* the ends of the timber in the walls, to preſerve them from the mortar. *Moxon's Mechanical Exerciſe.*

I *pitched* over the convex very thinly, by dropping melted pitch upon it, and warming it to keep the pitch ſoft, whilſt I ground it with the concave copper wetted to make it ſpread evenly all over the convex. *Newton's Opticks.*

5. To darken.

The air hath ſtarv'd the roſes in her cheeks,
And *pitch'd* the lily tincture of her face. *Shakeſp.*

Damon
Roſe early from his bed; but ſoon he found
The welkin *pitch'd* with ſullen cloud. *Addiſon.*

6. To pave. *Ainſworth.*

To PITCH. *v. n.*

1. To light; to drop.

When the ſwarm is ſettled, take a branch of the tree whereon they *pitch*, and wipe the hive clean. *Mortimer.*

2. To fall headlong.

The courſer o'er the pommel caſt the knight;
Forward he flew, and *pitching* on his head,
He quiver'd with his feet, and lay for dead. *Dryden.*

3. To fix choice.

We think 'tis no great matter which,
They're all alike, yet we ſhall *pitch*
On one that fits our purpoſe. *Hudibras.*

A free agent will *pitch* upon ſuch a part in his choice, with knowledge certain. *More's Divine Dialogues.*

The ſubject I have *pitched* upon may ſeem improper. *South.*

I *pitched* upon this conſideration that parents owe their children, not only material ſubſiſtence, but much more ſpiritual contribution to their mind. *Digby on the Soul.*

The covetous man was a good while at a ſtand; but he came however by degrees to *pitch* upon one thing after another. *L'Eſtrange's Fables.*

Pitch upon the beſt courſe of life, and cuſtom will render it the moſt eaſy. *Tillotſon's Sermons.*

I tranſlated Chaucer, and amongſt the reſt *pitched* on the wife of Bath's tale. *Dryden's Fables.*

4. To fix a tent or temporary habitation.

They *pitched* by Emmaus in the plain. 1 *Mac.* iii. 40.

PI'TCHER. *n. ſ.* [*picher*, French.]

1. An earthen veſſel; a water pot.

With ſuddain fear her *pitcher* down ſhe threw
And fled away. *Fairy Queen, b.* i.

Pitchers have ears, and I have many ſervants;
Beſides old Gremio is hearkening. *Shakeſp.*

Pyreicus was only famous for counterfeiting all baſe things; as earthen *pitchers* and a ſcullery. *Peacham on Drawing.*

Hylas may drop his *pitcher*, none will cry,
Not if he drown himſelf. *Dryden.*

2. An inſtrument to pierce the ground in which any thing is to be fixed.

To the hills poles muſt be ſet deep in the ground, with a ſquare iron *pitcher* or crow. *Mortimer's Huſbandry.*

PI'TCHFORK. *n. ſ.* [*pitch* and *fork.*] A fork with which corn is thrown upon the waggon.

An old lord in Leiceſterſhire amuſed himſelf with mending *pitchforks* and ſpades for his tenants gratis. *Swift.*

PI'TCHINESS. *n. ſ.* [from *pitchy.*] Blackneſs; darkneſs.

PI'TCHY. *adj.* [from *pitch.*]

1. Smeared with pitch.

The planks, their *pitchy* cov'rings waſh'd away,
Now yield; and now a yawning breach diſplay. *Dryden.*

2. Having the qualities of pitch.

Native petroleum, found floating upon ſome ſprings, is no other than this very *pitchy* ſubſtance, drawn forth of the ſtrata by the water. *Woodward on Foſſils.*

3. Black; dark; diſmal.

Night is fled,
Whoſe *pitchy* mantle over-veil'd the earth. *Shakeſp.*

I will ſort a *pitchy* day for thee. *Shakeſp. Henry* VI.

Pitchy and dark the night ſometimes appears,
Friend to our woe, and parent of our fears;
Our joy and wonder ſometimes ſhe excites,
With ſtars unnumber'd. *Prior.*

PI'TCOAL. *n. ſ.* [*pit* and *coal.*] Foſſile coal.

The beſt fuel is peat, the next charcoal made of *pitcoal* or cinders. *Mortimer's Huſbandry.*

PI'T-MAN. *n. ſ.* [*pit* and *man.*] He that in ſawing timber works below in the pit.

With the pitſaw they enter the one end of the ſtuff, the topman at the top, and the *pitman* under him: the topman obſerving to guide the ſaw exactly, and the *pitman* drawing it with all his ſtrength perpendicularly down. *Moxon.*

PI'T-SAW. *n. ſ.* [*pit* and *ſaw.*] The large ſaw uſed by two men, of whom one is in the pit.

The *pitſaw* is not only uſed by thoſe workmen that ſaw timber and boards, but is alſo for ſmall matters uſed by joiners. *Moxon's Mechanical Exerciſes.*

PI'TEOUS. *adj.* [from *pity.*]

1. Sorrowful; mournful; exciting pity.

When they heard that *piteous* ſtrained voice,
In haſte forſook their rural merriment. *Fairy Queen.*

The moſt arch deed of *piteous* maſſacre,
That ever yet this land was guilty of. *Shakeſp. Rich.* III.

Which when Deucalion with a *piteous* look
Beheld, he wept. *Dryden.*

2. Compaſſionate; tender.

If the ſeries of thy joys
Permit one thought leſs cheerful to ariſe,
Piteous transfer it to the mournful ſwain. *Prior.*

She gave him, *piteous* of his caſe,
A ſhaggy tap'ſtry. *Pope's Dunciad.*

3. Wretched; paltry; pitiful.

Piteous amends! unleſs
Be meant our grand foe. *Milton's Par. Loſt.*

PI'TEOUSLY. *adv.* [from *piteous.*] In a piteous manner.

I muſt talk of murthers, rapes and maſſacres,
Ruthful to hear, yet *piteouſly* perform'd. *Shakeſp.*

PI'TEOUSNESS. *n. ſ.* [from *piteous.*] Sorrowfulneſs; tenderneſs.

PI'TFALL. *n. ſ.* [*pit* and *fall.*] A pit dug and covered, into which a paſſenger falls unexpectedly.

Poor bird! thoud'ſt never fear the net nor lime,
The *pitfall* nor the gin. *Shakeſp. Macbeth.*

Thieves dig concealed *pitfalls* in his way. *Sandys.*

Theſe hidden *pitfalls* were ſet thick at the entrance of the bridge, ſo that throngs of people fell into them. *Addiſon.*

PITH. *n. ſ.* [*pitte*, Dutch.]

1. The marrow of the plant; the ſoft part in the midſt of the wood.

If a cion, fit to be ſet in the ground, hath the *pith* finely taken forth, and not altogether, but ſome of it left, it will bear a fruit with little or no core. *Bacon's Natural Hiſtory.*

Her ſolid bones convert to ſolid wood,
To *pith* her marrow, and to ſap her blood. *Dryden.*

2. Marrow.

As doth the *pith*, which left our bodies ſlack,
Strings faſt the little bones of neck and back;
So by the ſoul doth death ſtring heav'n and earth. *Donne.*

The vertebres are all perforated in the middle, with a large hole for the ſpinal marrow or *pith* to paſs along. *Ray.*

3. Strength; force.

Pith in Scotland is ſtill retained as denoting ſtrength, either corporeal or intellectual: as, that defies all your *pith*.

Leave your England,
Guarded with grandſires, babies and old women,
Or paſs'd, or not arriv'd to *pith* and puiſſance. *Shakeſp.*

Since theſe arms of mine had ſeven years *pith*. *Shakeſp.*

4. Energy; cogency; fulneſs of ſentiment; cloſeneſs and vigour of thought and ſtile.

5. Weight; moment; principal part.

That's my *pith* of buſineſs
'Twixt you and your poor brother. *Shakeſp.*

Enterprizes of great *pith* and moment,
With this regard their currents turn awry,
And loſe the name of action. *Shakeſp. Hamlet.*

6. The quinteſcence; the chief part.

The owner of a foul diſeaſe,
To keep it from divulging, lets it feed
Ev'n on the *pith* of life. *Shakeſp. Hamlet.*

PI'THILY. *adv.* [from *pithy.*] With ſtrength; with cogency; with force.

PI'THINESS. *n. ſ.* [from *pithy.*] Energy; ſtrength.

No leſs deſerveth his wittineſs in deviſing, his *pithineſs* in uttering, his complaint of love, ſo lovely. *Spenſer.*

PI'THLESS. *adj.* [from *pith.*]

1. Wanting pith.

Weak ſhoulders over-born with burthening grief
And *pithleſs* arms, like to a wither'd vine
That drops his ſapleſs branches to the ground. *Shakeſpeare.*

2. Wanting energy; wanting force.

PI'THY. *adj.* [from *pith.*]

1. Conſiſting of pith.

The *pithy* fibres brace and ſtitch together the ligneous in a plant. *Grew's Coſmol. b.* i.

The Herefordian plant that likes
T' approach the quince, and th' alder's *pithy* ſtem. *Philips.*

2. Strong; forcible; energetick.
Yet she with *pithy* words, and counsel sad,
Still strove their sudden rages to revoke;
That at the last, suppressing fury mad,
They gan abstain. *Fairy Queen, b.* ii.
I must begin with rudiments of art,
More pleasant, *pithy* and effectual,
Than hath been taught by any. *Shak. Taming of the Shrew.*
Many rare *pithy* saws concerning
The worth of astrologic learning. *Hudibras.*
This *pithy* speech prevail'd, and all agreed. *Dryden.*

In all these, Goodman Fact was very short, but *pithy*; for he was a plain home-spun man. *Addison.*

PI'TIABLE. *adj.* [*pitoyable*, Fr. from *pity*.] Deserving pity.

The *pitiable* persons relieved, are constantly under your eye. *Atterbury's Sermons.*

PI'TIFUL. *adj.* [*pity* and *full*]

1. Melancholy; moving compassion.

Some, who have not deserved judgment of death, have been for their goods sake caught up and carried straight to the bough; a thing indeed very *pitiful* and horrible. *Spenser.*

A sight most *pitiful* in the meanest wretch,
Past speaking of in a king. *Shakesp. King Lear.*
Strangely visited people,
All swoln and ulc'rous, *pitiful* to the eye;
The mere despair of surgery he cures. *Shakesp. Macbeth.*
Will he his *pitiful* complaints renew?
For freedom with afflicted language sue. *Sandys.*

The conveniency of this will appear, if we consider what a *pitiful* condition we had been in. *Ray on the Creation.*

2. Tender; compassionate.
Would my heart were flint, like Edward's,
Or Edward's soft and *pitiful*, like mine. *Shakesp.*
Be *pitiful* to my condemned sons,
Whose souls are not corrupted. *Shakesp.*

3. Paltry; contemptible; despicable.

That's villainous, and shews a most *pitiful* ambition in the fool that uses it. *Shakesp. Hamlet.*

One, in a wild pamphlet, besides other *pitiful* malignities, would scarce allow him to be a gentleman. *Wotton.*

The accusations against him contained much frivolous matter or *pitiful*. *Hayward.*

This is the doom of fallen man, to exhaust his time and impair his health, and perhaps to spin out his days and himself into one *pitiful* controverted conclusion. *South.*

Sin can please no longer, than for that *pitiful* space of time while it is committing; and surely the present pleasure of a sinful act is a poor countervail for the bitterness which begins where the action ends, and lasts for ever. *South's Sermons.*

If these *pitiful* shanks were answerable to this branching head, I should defy all my enemies. *L'Estrange's Fables.*

What entertainment can be raised from so *pitiful* a machine, where we see the success of the battle from the beginning. *Dryden's Dedication to Juvenal.*

PI'TIFULLY. *adv.* [from *pitiful*.]

1. Mournfully; in a manner that moves compassion.
He beat him most *pitifully*; nay,
He beat him most unpitifully. *Shakesp.*

Some of the philosophers doubt whether there were any such thing as sense of pain; and yet, when any great evil has been upon them, they would sigh and groan as *pitifully* as other men. *Tillotson's Sermons.*

2. Contemptibly; despicably.

Those men, who give themselves airs of bravery on reflecting upon the last scenes of others, may behave the most *pitifully* in their own. *Clarissa.*

PI'TIFULNESS. *n. s.* [from *pitiful*.]

1. Tenderness; mercy; compassion.

Basilius giving the infinite terms of praises to Zelmane's valour in conquering, and *pitifulness* in pardoning, commanded no more words to be made of it. *Sidney, b.* ii.

2. Despicableness; contemptibleness.

PI'TILESLY. *adv.* [from *pitiless*.] Without mercy.

PI'TILESNESS. *n. s.* Unmercifulness.

PI'TILESS. *adj.* [from *pity*.] Wanting pity; wanting compassion; merciless.

Fair be ye sure, but proud and *pitiless*,
As is a storm, that all things doth prostrate,
Finding a tree alone all comfortless,
Beats on it strongly, it to ruinate. *Spenser.*
Hadst thou in person ne'er offended me,
Even for his sake am I now *pitiless*. *Shakesp.*
My chance, I see,
Hath made ev'n pity, *pitiless* in thee. *Fairfax.*
Upon my livid lips bestow a kiss,
Nor fear your kisses can restore my breath;
Even you are not more *pitiless* than death. *Dryden.*

PI'TTANCE. *n. s.* [*pitance*, Fr. *pietantia*, Italian.]

1. An allowance of meat in a monastry.

2. A small portion.
Then at my lodging,
The worst is this, that at so slender warning
You're like to have a thin and slender *pittance*. *Shakesp.*

The ass saved a miserable *pittance* for himself. *L'Estrange.*

I have a small *pittance* left, with which I might retire. *Arb.*

Many of them lose the greatest part of the small *pittance* of learning they received at the university. *Swift's Miscellanies.*

PI'TUITE. *n. s.* [*pituite*, Fr. *pituita*, Lat.] Phlegm.

Serous defluxions and redundant *pituite* were the product of the winter, which made women subject to abortions. *Arb.*

PITU'ITOUS. *adj.* [*pituitosus*, Lat. *pituiteux*, Fr.] Consisting of phlegm.

It is thus with women, only that abound with *pituitous* and watery humours. *Brown's Vulgar Errours, b.* iv.

The forerunners of an apoplexy are weakness, wateriness and turgidity of the eyes, *pituitous* vomiting and laborious breathing. *Arbuthnot on Diet.*

PI'TY. *n. s.* [*pitie*, Fr. *pieta*, Italian.]

1. Compassion; sympathy with misery; tenderness for pain or uneasiness.

Thou hast scourged and taken *pity* on me. *Tob.* xi. 15.
Wan and meagre let it look,
With a *pity*-moving shape. *Waller.*

An ant dropt into the water; a woodpigeon took *pity* of her, and threw her a little bough. *L'Estrange.*

Lest the poor should seem to be wholly disregarded by their maker, he hath implanted in men a quick and tender sense of *pity* and compassion. *Calamy's Sermons.*

When Æneas is forced in his own defence to kill Lausus, the poet shows him compassionate; he has *pity* on his beauty and youth, and is loth to destroy such a masterpiece of nature. *Dryden's Dufresnoy.*

The mournful train
With groans and hands upheld, to move his mind,
Besought his *pity* to their helpless kind. *Dryden.*

2. A ground of *pity*; a subject of *pity* or of grief.

That he is old, the more is the *pity*, his white hairs do witness it. *Shakesp. Henry IV.*

Julius Cæsar writ a collection of apophthegms; it is *pity* his book is lost. *Bacon.*

'Tis great *pity* we do not yet see the history of Chasmir. *Temple.*

See, where she comes, with that high air and mien,
Which marks in bonds the greatness of a queen,
What *pity* 'tis. *Dryden.*
What *pity* 'tis you are not all divine. *Dryden.*
Who would not be that youth? what *pity* is it
That we can die but once to serve our country? *Addis.*

3. It has in this sense a plural. In low language.

Singleness of heart being a virtue so necessary, 'tis a thousand *pities* it should be discountenanced. *L'Estrange.*

To PI'TY. *v. a.* [*pitoyer*, Fr.] To compassionate misery; to regard with tenderness on account of unhappiness.

When I desired their leave, that I might *pity* him, they took from me the use of mine own house. *Shakesp.*

He made them to be *pitied* of all. *Psalm* cvi. 46.
You I could *pity* thus forlorn. *Milton.*
Compassionate my pains! she *pities* me!
To one that asks the warm return of love,
Compassion's cruelty, 'tis scorn, 'tis death. *Addison.*

To PI'TY. *v. n.* To be compassionate.

I will not *pity* nor spare, nor have mercy, but destroy them. *Jeremiah* xiii. 14.

PI'VOT. *n. s.* [*pivot*, Fr.] A pin on which any thing turns.

When a man dances on the rope, the body is a weight balanced on its feet, as upon two *pivots*. *Dryden's Dufresnoy.*

PIX. *n. s.* [*pixis*, Lat.] A little chest or box, in which the consecrated host is kept in Roman catholick countries. *Hanmer.*

He hath stolen a *pix*, and hanged must a' be. *Shakesp.*

PI'ZZLE. *n. s.* [quasi *pissle*. *Minshew*.]

The *pizzle* in animals is official to urine and generation. *Brown's Vulgar Errours, b.* iii.

PLA'CABLE. *adj.* [*placabilis*, Lat.] Willing or possible to be appeased.

Since I sought
By pray'r th' offended deity t' appease;
Methought I saw him *placable* and mild,
Bending his ear. *Milton's Paradise Lost, b.* xi.

Those implanted anticipations are, that there is a god, that he is *placable*, to be feared, honoured, loved, worshipped and obeyed. *Hale's Origin of Mankind.*

PLACABI'LITY. } *n. s.* [from *placable*.] Willingness to be
PLA'CABLENESS. } appeased; possibility to be appeased.

The various methods of propitiation and atonement shew the general consent of all nations in their opinion of the mercy and *placability* of the divine nature. *Anonymous.*

PLACA'RD. } *n. s.* [*plakaert*, Dutch; *placard*, Fr.] An edict;
PLACA'RT. } a declaration; a manifesto.

To PLA'CATE. *v. a.* [*placeo*, Lat.] To appease; to reconcile. This word is used in Scotland.

That the effect of an atonement and reconciliation was to give all mankind a right to approach and rely on the protection and beneficence of a *placated* deity, is not deducible from nature. *Forbes.*

PLACE. *n. s.* [*place*, Fr. *piazza*, Italian; from *platea*, Lat.]

1. Particular portion of space.

Search you out a *place* to pitch your tents. *Deut.* i. 33.

We accept it always and in all *places*. *Acts* xxiv. 3.

Here I could frequent
With worship, *place* by *place*, where he vouchsaf'd
Presence divine. *Milton's Paradise Lost, b.* xi.

I will teach him the names of the most celebrated persons, who frequent that *place*. *Addison's Guardian*, No 107.

2. Locality; ubiety; local relation.

Place is the relation of distance betwixt any thing, and any two or more points considered as keeping the same distance one with another; and so as at rest: it has sometimes a more confused sense, and stands for that space which any body takes up. *Locke.*

3. Local existence.

The earth and the heaven fled away, and there was found no *place* for them. *Revelations* xx. 11.

4. Space in general.

All bodies are confin'd within some place;
But she all *place* within herself confines. *Davies.*

5. Separate room.

In his brain
He hath strange *places* cram'd with observation. *Shakesp.*

6. A seat; residence; mansion.

The Romans shall take away both our *place* and nation. *Jo.*

Saul set him up a *place*, and is gone down to Gilgal. 1 *Sam.*

7. Passage in writing.

Hosea saith of the Jews, they have reigned, but not by me; which *place* proveth, that there are governments which God doth not avow. *Bacon's Holy War.*

I could not pass by this *place*, without giving this short explication. *Burnet's Theory of the Earth.*

8. Ordinal relation.

What scripture doth plainly deliver, to that the first *place* both of credit and obedience is due. *Hooker, b.* v. *s.* 8.

Let the eye be satisfied in the first *place*, even against all other reasons, and let the compass be rather in your eyes than in your hands. *Dryden's Dufresnoy.*

We shall extinguish this melancholy thought, of our being overlooked by our maker, if we consider, in the first *place*, that he is omnipresent; and, in the second, that he is omniscient. *Spectator*, No 565.

9. Existence; state of being; validity; state of actual operation.

I know him a notorious liar;
Think him a great way fool, solely a coward;
Yet these fix'd evils sit so fit in him,
That they take *place*, when virtue's steely bones
Look bleak in the cold wind. *Shakesp.*

These fair overtures, made by men well esteemed for honest dealing, could take no *place*. *Hayward.*

They are defects, not in the heart, but in the brain; for they take *place* in the stoutest natures. *Bacon.*

With faults confess'd commission'd her to go,
If pity yet had *place*, and reconcile her foe. *Dryden.*

Where arms take *place*, all other pleas are vain;
Love taught me force, and force shall love maintain. *Dryden.*

To the joy of mankind, the unhappy omen took not *place*. *Dryden's Dedication to his Fables.*

Somewhat may be invented, perhaps more excellent than the first design; though Virgil must be still excepted, when that perhaps takes not *place*. *Dryden's Preface to Ovid.*

Mixt government, partaking of the known forms received in the schools, is by no means of Gothick invention, but hath *place* in nature and reason. *Swift.*

It is stupidly foolish to venture our salvation upon an experiment, which we have all the reason imaginable to think God will not suffer to take *place*. *Atterbury's Sermons.*

10. Rank; order of priority.

The heavens themselves, the planets, and this center
Observe degree, priority and *place*. *Shakesp.*

11. Precedence; priority. This sense is commonly used in the phrase *take place*.

Do you think I'd walk in any plot,
Where Madam Sempronia should take *place* of me,
And Fulvia come i' the rear. *Benj. Johnson's Catiline.*

There would be left no measures of credible and incredible, if doubtful propositions take *place* before self-evident. *Locke.*

As a British freeholder, I should not scruple taking *place* of a French marquis. *Addison's Freeholder.*

12. Office; publick character or employment.

Do you your office, or give up your *place*,
And you shall well be spared. *Shakesp.*

If I'm traduc'd by tongues that neither know
My faculties nor person;
'Tis but the fate of *place*, and the rough brake
That virtue must go through. *Shakesp. Henry* VIII.

The horsemen came to Lodronius, as unto the most valiant captain, beseeching him, instead of their treacherous general, to take upon him the *place*. *Knolles's Hist. of the Turks.*

Is not the bishop's bill deny'd,
And we still threaten'd to be try'd?
You see the king embraces
Those counsels he approv'd before;
Nor doth he promise, which is more,
That we shall have their *places*. *Denham.*

Pensions in private were the senate's aim;
And patriots for a *place* abandon'd fame. *Garth.*

Some magistrates are contented, that their *places* should adorn them; and some study to adorn their *places*, and reflect back the lustre they receive from thence. *Atterbury.*

13. Room; way; space for appearing or acting given by cession; not opposition.

Avenge not yourselves, but rather give *place* unto wrath. *Romans* xii. 19.

He took a stride, and to his fellows cry'd,
Give *place*, and mark the diff'rence if you can,
Between a woman warrior and a man. *Dryden.*

Victorious York did first, with fam'd success,
To his known valour, make the Dutch give *place*. *Dryd.*

The rustick honours of the scythe and share,
Give *place* to swords and plumes the pride of war. *Dryd.*

14. Ground; room.

Ye seek to kill me, because my word hath no *place* in you. *Jo.* viii. 37.

There is no *place* of doubting, but that it was the very same. *Hammond's Fundamentals.*

To PLACE. *v. a.* [*placer*, Fr. from the noun.]

1. To put in any place, rank or condition.

Place such over them to be rulers. *Ex.* xviii. 21.

He *placed* forces in all the fenced cities. 2 *Chro.* xvii. 2.

Those accusations had been more reasonable, if *placed* on inferior persons. *Dryden's Aurengz.*

2. To fix; to settle; to establish.

God or nature has not any where *placed* any such jurisdiction in the first born. *Locke.*

3. To put out at interest.

'Twas his care
To *place* on good security his gold. *Pope.*

PLA'CER. *n. s.* [from *place.*] One that places.

Sovereign lord of creatures all,
Thou *placer* of plants, both humble and tall. *Spenser.*

PLA'CID. *adj.* [*placidus*, Latin.]

1. Gentle; quiet; not turbulent.

It conduceth unto long life and to the more *placid* motion of the spirits, that men's actions be free. *Bacon.*

2. Soft; kind; mild.

That *placid* aspect and meek regard,
Rather than aggravate my evil state,
Would stand between me and thy father's ire. *Milton.*

PLA'CIDLY. *adv.* [from *placid.*] Mildly; gently.

If into a phial, filled with good spirit of nitre, you cast a piece of iron, the liquor, whose parts moved uniformly and *placidly* before, by altering its motion, it begins to penetrate and scatter abroad particles of the iron. *Boyle.*

The water easily insinuates itself into, and *placidly* distends the tubes and vessels of vegetables. *Woodward.*

PLA'CIT. *n. s.* [*placitum*, Lat.] Decree; determination.

We spend time in defence of their *placits*, which might have been employed upon the universal author. *Glanvill.*

PLA'CKET, or *plaquet. n. s.* A petticoat.

You might have pinch'd a *plaquet*, it was senseless. *Shak.*

The bone-ach is the curse dependant on those that war for a *plaquet*. *Shakesp. Troilus and Cressida.*

PLA'GIARISM. *n. s.* [from *plagiary.*] Theft; literary adoption of the thoughts or works of another.

With great impropriety, as well as *plagiarism*, they have most injuriously been transferred into proverbial maxims. *Swi.*

PLA'GIARY. *n. s.* [from *plagium*, Lat.]

1. A thief in literature; one who steals the thoughts or writings of another.

The ensuing discourse, lest I chance to be traduced for a *plagiary* by him who has played the thief, was one of those that, by a worthy hand, were stolen from me. *South.*

Without invention, a painter is but a copier, and a poet but a *plagiary* of others; both are allowed sometimes to copy and translate. *Dryden's Dufresnoy.*

2. The crime of literary theft. Not used.

Plagiary had not its nativity with printing, but began when the paucity of books scarce wanted that invention. *Brown.*

PLAGUE. *n. s.* [*plaghe*, Dutch; *plage*, Teut. *plaga*, Latin; πληγή.]

1. Pestilence; a disease eminently contagious and destructive.

Thou art a bile,
A *plague*-sore or imboss'd carbuncle
In my corrupted blood. *Shakesp. King Lear.*

The general opinion is, that years hot and moist are most pestilent; yet many times there have been great *plagues* in dry years. *Bacon's Nat. Hist.*

Snakes, that use within thy house for shade,
Securely lurk, and, like a *plague*, invade
Thy cattle with venom. *May's Virgil's Georgicks.*

 All

All thoſe *plagues*, which earth and air had brooded,
Firſt on inferior creatures try'd their force,
And laſt they ſeized on man. *Lee and Dryden.*

2. State of miſery.

I am ſet in my *plague*, and my heavineſs is ever in my ſight. *Pſalm* xxxviii. 17.

3. Any thing troubleſome or vexatious.

'Tis the time's *plague*, when madmen lead the blind. *Sha.*

I am not mad, too well I feel
The diff'rent *plague* of each calamity. *Shakeſp. K. John.*

Good or bad company is the greateſt bleſſing or greateſt *plague* of life. *L'Eſtrange.*

Sometimes my *plague*, ſometimes my darling. *Prior.*

To PLAGUE. *v. a.* [from the noun.]

1. To infect with peſtilence.

2. To trouble; to teaze; to vex; to harraſs; to torment; to afflict; to diſtreſs; to torture; to embarraſs; to excruciate; to make uneaſy; to diſturb.

If her nature be ſo,
That ſhe will *plague* the man that loves her moſt,
And take delight to encreaſe a wretch's woe,
Then all her nature's goodly gifts are loſt. *Spenſer.*

Say my requeſt's unjuſt,
And ſpurn me back; but if it be not ſo,
Thou art not honeſt, and the gods will *plague* thee. *Shak.*

Thus were they *plagu'd*
And worn with famine. *Milton.*

People are ſtormed out of their reaſon, *plagued* into a compliance, and forced to yield in their own defence. *Collier.*

When a Neapolitan cavalier has nothing elſe to do, he gravely ſhuts himſelf up in his cloſet, and falls a tumbling over his papers, to ſee if he can ſtart a law ſuit, and *plague* any of his neighbours. *Addiſon's Remarks on Italy.*

PLA'GUILY. *adv.* [from *plaguy.*] Vexatiouſly; horribly. A low word.

This whiſpering bodes me no good; but he has me ſo *plaguily* under the laſh, I dare not interrupt him. *Dryden.*

You look'd ſcornful, and ſniſt at the dean;
But he durſt not ſo much as once open his lips,
And the doctor was *plaguily* down in the hips. *Swift.*

PLA'GUY. *adj.* [from *plague.*] Vexatious; troubleſome. A low word.

Of heats,
Add one more to the *plaguy* bill. *Donne.*

What perils do environ
The man that meddles with cold iron,
What *plaguy* miſchiefs and miſhaps
Do dog him ſtill with after-claps. *Hudibras.*

PLAICE. *n. ſ.* [*plate*, Dutch.] A flat fiſh.

Of flat fiſh there are ſoles, flowkes, dabs and *plaice*. *Carew.*

PLAID. *n. ſ.* A ſtriped or variegated cloth; an outer looſe weed worn much by the highlanders in Scotland: there is a particular kind worn too by the women; but both theſe modes ſeem now nearly extirpated among them; the one by act of parliament, and the other by adopting the Engliſh dreſſes of the ſex.

PLAIN. *adj.* [*planus*, Latin.]

1. Smooth; level; flat; free from protuberances or excreſcencies. In this ſenſe, eſpecially in philoſophical writings, it is frequently written *plane*: as, a *plane* ſuperficies.

It was his policy to leave no hold behind him; but to make all *plain* and waſte. *Spenſer.*

The South and South-Eaſt ſides are rocky and mountainous, but *plain* in the midſt. *Sandys's Journey.*

Thy vineyard muſt employ thy ſturdy ſteer
To turn the glebe; beſides thy daily pain
To break the clods, and make the ſurface *plain*. *Dryden.*

Hilly countries afford the moſt entertaining proſpects, though a man would chuſe to travel through a *plain* one. *Add.*

2. Void of ornament; ſimple.

A crown of ruddy gold inclos'd her brow,
Plain without pomp, and rich without a ſhow. *Dryden.*

3. Artleſs; not ſubtle; not ſpecious; not learned; ſimple.

In choice of inſtruments, it is better to chuſe men of a *plainer* ſort, that are like to do that that is committed to them, and to report faithfully the ſucceſs, than thoſe that are cunning to contrive ſomewhat to grace themſelves, and will help the matter in report. *Bacon's Eſſays.*

Of many *plain*, yet pious chriſtians, this cannot be affirmed. *Hammond's Fundamentals.*

The experiments alledged with ſo much confidence, and told by an author that writ like a *plain* man, and one whoſe profeſſion was to tell truth, helped me to reſolve upon making the trial. *Temple.*

My heart was made to fit and pair within,
Simple and *plain*, and fraught with artleſs tenderneſs. *Rowe.*

Our troops beat an army in *plain* fight and open field. *Felt.*

Muſt then at once, the character to ſave,
The *plain* rough hero turn a crafty knave? *Pope.*

4. Honeſtly rough; open; ſincere; not ſoft in language.

Give me leave to be *plain* with you, that yourſelf give no juſt cauſe of ſcandal. *Bacon.*

5. Mere; bare.

He that beguil'd you in a plain accent, was a *plain* knave, which, for my part, I will not be. *Shakeſp. King Lear.*

Some have at firſt for wits, then poets paſt,
Turn'd criticks next, and prov'd *plain* fools at laſt. *Pope.*

6. Evident; clear; diſcernible; not obſcure.

They wondered there ſhould appear any difficulty in any expreſſions, which to them ſeemed very clear and *plain*. *Clar.*

Expreſs thyſelf in *plain*, not doubtful words,
That ground for quarrels or diſputes affords. *Denham.*

I can make the difference more *plain*, by giving you my method of proceeding in my tranſlations; I conſidered the genius and diſtinguiſhing character of my author. *Dryden.*

'Tis *plain* in the hiſtory, that Eſau was never ſubject to Jacob. *Locke.*

That children have ſuch a right, is *plain* from the laws of God; that men are convinced, that children have ſuch a right, is evident from the law of the land. *Locke.*

It is *plain*, that theſe diſcourſes are calculated for none, but the faſhionable part of womankind. *Addiſon's Spectator.*

To ſpeak one thing mix'd dialects they join;
Divide the ſimple, and the *plain* define. *Prior.*

7. Not varied by much art.

A plaining ſong *plain*-ſinging voice requires,
For warbling notes from inward cheering flow. *Sidney.*

PLAIN. *adv.*

1. Not obſcurely.

2. Diſtinctly; articulately.

The ſtring of his tongue was looſed, and he ſpake *plain*. *Mar.* vii. 35.

3. Simply; with rough ſincerity.

Goodman Fact is allowed by every body to be a *plain*-ſpoken perſon, and a man of very few words; tropes and figures are his averſion. *Addiſon's Count Tariff.*

PLAIN. *n. ſ.* [*plaine*, Fr.] Level ground; open; flat; often, a field of battle.

In a *plain* in the land of Shinar they dwelt. *Gen.* xi. 2.

The Scots took the Engliſh for fooliſh birds fallen into their net, forſook their hill, and marched into the *plain* directly towards them. *Hayward.*

They erected their caſtles and habitations in the *plains* and open countries, where they found moſt fruitful lands, and turned the Iriſh into the woods and mountains. *Davies.*

Pour forth Britannia's legions on the *plain*. *Arbuthnot.*

While here the ocean gains,
In other parts it leaves wide ſandy *plains*. *Pope.*

The impetuous courſer pants in ev'ry vein,
And pawing ſeems to beat the diſtant *plain*. *Pope.*

To PLAIN. *v. a.* [from the noun.] To level; to make even.

Upon one wing, the artillery was drawn, every piece having his guard of pioners to *plain* the ways. *Hayward.*

To PLAIN. *v. n.* [*plaindre*, *je plains*, Fr.] To lament; to wail.

Long ſince my voice is hoarſe, and throat is ſore,
With cries to ſkies, and curſes to the ground;
But more I *plain*, I feel my woes the more. *Sidney.*

A *plaining* ſong plain-ſinging voice requires
For warbling notes from inward cheering flow. *Sidney.*

The fox, that firſt this cauſe of grief did find,
'Gan firſt thus *plain* his caſe with words unkind. *Hubberd.*

The inceſſant weeping of my wife,
And piteous *plainings* of the pretty babes,
Forc'd me to ſeek delays. *Shakeſp.*

He to himſelf thus *plain'd*. *Milton.*

PLAINDEA'LING. *adj.* [*plain* and *deal.*] Acting without art.

Though I cannot be ſaid to be a flattering honeſt man; it muſt not be denied, but I am a *plaindealing* villain. *Shakeſp.*

Bring a *plaindealing* innocence into a conſiſtency with neceſſary prudence. *L'Eſtrange.*

PLA'INDEALING. *n. ſ.* Management void of art.

I am no politician; and was ever thought to have too little wit, and too much *plaindealing* for a ſtateſman. *Denham.*

It looks as fate with nature's law may ſtrive
To ſhew *plaindealing* once an age would thrive. *Dryden.*

PLA'INLY. *adv.* [from *plain.*]

1. Levelly; flatly.

2. Not ſubtilly; not ſpeciouſly.

3. Without ornament.

4. Without gloſs; ſincerely.

You write to me with the freedom of a friend, ſetting down your thoughts as they occur, and dealing *plainly* with me in the matter. *Pope.*

5. In earneſt; fairly.

They charged the enemies horſe ſo gallantly, that they gave ground; and at laſt *plainly* run to a ſafe place. *Clarend.*

6. Evidently; clearly; not obſcurely.

St. Auguſtine acknowledgeth, that they are not only ſet down, but alſo *plainly* ſet down in ſcripture; ſo that he which heareth or readeth, may without difficulty underſtand. *Hooker.*

Coriolanus neither cares whether they love or hate him; and out of his careleſſneſs, let's them *plainly* ſee't. *Shakeſp.*

By that seed
Is meant thy great deliverer, who shall bruise
The serpent's head; whereof to thee anon
Plainlier shall be reveal'd. *Milton's Par. Lost, b.* xii.

We see *plainly* that we have the means, and that nothing but the application of them is wanting. *Addison.*

PLA'INNESS. *n. s.* [from *plain.*]

1. Levelness; flatness.

2. Want of ornament; want of show.

If some pride with want may be allowed,
We in our *plainness* may be justly proud,
Whate'er he's pleas'd to own, can need no show. *Dryden.*

As shades most sweetly recommend the light,
So modest *plainness* sets off sprightly wit. *Pope.*

3. Openness; rough sincerity.

Well, said Basilius, I have not chosen Dametas for his fighting nor for his discoursing, but for his *plainness* and honesty, and therein I know he will not deceive me. *Sidney.*

Your *plainness* and your shortness please me well. *Shakesp.*

Think'st thou, that duty shall have dread to speak,
When pow'r to flatt'ry bows; to *plainness* honour
Is bound, when majesty to folly falls. *Shakesp. K. Lear.*

Plainness and freedom, an epistolary stile required. *Wake.*

4. Artlessness; simplicity.

All laugh to find
Unthinking *plainness* so o'erspreads thy mind,
That thou could'st seriously persuade the crowd
To keep their oaths. *Dryden's Juvenal.*

PLAINT. *n. s.* [*plainte*, French.]

1. Lamentation; complaint; lament.

Then pour out *plaint*, and in one word say this;
Helpless his *plaint*, who spoils himself of bliss. *Sidney.*

Bootless are *plaints*, and cureless are my wounds. *Shak.*

From inward grief
His bursting passion into *plaints* thus pour'd. *Milton.*

2. Exprobration of injury.

There are three just grounds of war with Spain; one of *plaint*, two upon defence. *Bacon.*

3. Expression of sorrow.

How many childrens *plaints*, and mother's cries! *Daniel.*

Where though I mourn my matchless loss alone,
And none between my weakness judge and me;
Yet even these gentle walls allow my moan,
Whose doleful echoes to my *plaints* agree. *Wotton.*

Listening where the hapless pair
Sat in their sad discourse, and various *plaint*,
Thence gather'd his own doom. *Milton's Par. Lost.*

For her relief,
Vext with the long expressions of my grief,
Receive these *plaints*. *Waller.*

PLA'INTFUL. *adj.* [*plaint* and *full.*] Complaining; audibly sorrowful.

To what a sea of miseries my *plaintful* tongue doth lead me. *Sidney, b.* ii.

PLA'INTIFF. *n. s.* [*plaintif*, Fr.] He that commences a suit in law against another; opposed to the defendant.

The *plaintiff* proved the debt by three positive witnesses, and the defendant was cast in costs and damages. *L'Estrange.*

You and I shall talk in cold friendship at a bar before a judge, by way of *plaintiff* and defendant. *Dryden.*

In such a cause the *plaintiff* will be hiss'd,
My lord, the judges laugh, and you're dismiss'd. *Pope.*

PLA'INTIFF. *adj.* [*plaintif*, Fr.] Complaining. A word not in use.

His younger son on the polluted ground,
First fruit of death, lies *plaintiff* of a wound
Giv'n by a brother's hand. *Prior.*

PLA'INTIVE. *adj.* [*plaintif*, Fr.] Complaining; lamenting; expressive of sorrow.

His careful mother heard the *plaintive* sound,
Encompass'd with her sea-green sisters round. *Dryden.*

The goddess heard,
Rose like a morning mist, and thus begun
To sooth the sorrows of her *plaintive* son. *Dryden.*

Can nature's voice
Plaintive be drown'd, or lessen'd in the noise,
Though shouts as thunder loud afflict the air. *Prior.*

Leviathans in *plaintive* thunders cry. *Young.*

PLA'INWORK. *n. s.* [*plain* and *work.*] Needlework as distinguished from embroidery; the common practice of sewing or making linen garments.

She went to *plainwork*, and to purling brooks. *Pope.*

PLAIT. *n. s.* [corrupted from *plight* or *plyght*, from to *ply* or fold.] A fold; a double.

Should the voice directly strike the brain,
It would astonish and confuse it much;
Therefore these *plaits* and folds the sound restrain,
That it the organ may more gently touch. *Davies.*

Nor shall thy lower garments artful *plait*,
From thy fair side dependent to thy feet,
Arm their chaste beauties with a modest pride,
And double ev'ry charm they seek to hide. *Prior.*

'Tis very difficult to trace out the figure of a vest through all the *plaits* and foldings of the drapery. *Addison.*

To PLAIT. *v. a.* [from the noun.]

1. To fold; to double.

The busy sylphs surround their darling care,
Some fold the sleeve, while others *plait* the gown;
And Betty's prais'd for labours not her own. *Pope.*

Will she on sunday morn thy neckcloth *plait*. *Gay.*

2. To weave; to braid.

Let it not be that outward adorning of *plaiting* the hair. 1 *Peter* iii. 3.

What she demands, incessant I'll prepare;
I'll weave her garlands, and I'll *plait* her hair;
My busy diligence shall deck her board,
For there at least I may approach my lord. *Prior.*

3. To intangle; to involve.

Time shall unfold what *plaited* cunning hides,
Who covers faults at last with shame derides. *Shakespeare.*

PLAI'TER. *n. s.* [from *plait.*] He that plaits.

PLAN. *n. s.* [*plan*, French.]

1. A scheme; a form; a model.

Remember, O my friends, the laws, the rights,
The generous *plan* of power delivered down
From age to age to your renown'd forefathers. *Addis.*

2. A plot of any building or ichnography; form of any thing laid down on paper.

Artists and *plans* reliev'd my solemn hours;
I founded palaces, and planted bow'rs. *Prior.*

To PLAN. *v. a.* [from the noun.] To scheme; to form in design.

Vouchsafe the means of vengeance to debate,
And *plan* with all thy arts the scene of fate. *Pope.*

PLA'NARY. *adj.* Pertaining to a plane. *Dict.*

PLA'NCHED. *adj.* [from *planch.*] Made of boards.

He hath a garden circummur'd with brick,
Whose Western side is with a vineyard backt,
And to that vineyard is a *planched* gate,
That makes his opening with this bigger key. *Shakesp.*

PLA'NCHER. *n. s.* [*plancher*, French.] A board; a plank.

Oak, cedar and chesnut are the best builders; some are best for *planchers*, as deal; some for tables, cupboards and desks, as walnuts. *Bacon's Nat. History.*

PLA'NCHING. *n. s.* In carpentry, the laying the floors in a building. *Dict.*

PLANE. *n. s.* [*planus*, Latin. *Plain* is commonly used in popular language, and *plane* in geometry.]

1. A level surface.

Comets, as often as they are visible to us, move in *planes* inclined to the *plane* of the ecliptick in all kinds of angles. *Bent.*

Projectils would ever move on in the same right line, did not the air, their own gravity, or the ruggedness of the *plane*, on which they move, stop their motion. *Cheyne.*

2. [*Plane*, Fr.] An instrument by which the surface of boards is smoothed.

The iron is set to make an angle of forty-five degrees with the sole of the *plane*. *Moxon's Mechanical Exercises.*

To PLANE. *v. a.* [*planer*, Fr. from the noun.]

1. To level; to smooth from inequalities.

The foundation of the Roman causeway was made of rough stone, joined with a most firm cement; upon this was laid another layer of small stones and cement, to *plane* the inequalities of rough stone, in which the stones of the upper pavement were fixt. *Arbuthnot on Coins.*

2. To smooth with a plane.

These hard woods are more properly scraped than *planed*. *Moxon's Mechanical Exercises.*

PLANE-TREE. *n. s.* [*platanus*, Lat. *plane*, *platane*, Fr.]

The *plane-tree* hath an amentaceous flower, consisting of several slender stamina, which are all collected into spherical little balls and are barren; but the embryos of the fruit, which are produced on separate parts of the same trees, are turgid, and afterwards become large spherical balls, containing many oblong seeds intermixed with down: it is generally supposed, that the introduction of this tree into England is owing to the great lord chancellor Bacon. *Miller.*

The beech, the swimming alder and the *plane*. *Dryd.*

PLA'NET. *n. s.* [*planeta*, Lat. πλανάω; *planette*, Fr.]

Planets are the erratick or wandering stars, and which are not like the fixt ones always in the same position to one another: we now number the earth among the primary *planets*, because we know it moves round the sun, as Saturn, Jupiter, Mars, Venus and Mercury do, and that in a path or circle between Mars and Venus: and the moon is accounted among the secondary *planets* or satellites of the primary, since she moves round the earth: all the *planets* have, besides their motion round the sun, which makes their year, also a motion round their own axes, which makes their day; as the earth's revolving so makes our day and night: it is more than probable, that the diameters of all the *planets* are longer than their axes: we know 'tis so in our earth; and Flamsteed and Cassini found it to be so in Jupiter: Sir Isaac Newton asserts our earth's equatorial diameter to exceed the other about thirty-four

four miles; and indeed else the motion of the earth would make the sea rise so high at the equator, as to drown all the parts thereabouts. *Harris.*

Barbarous villains! hath this lovely face
Rul'd like a wand'ring *planet* over me,
And could it not inforce them to relent. *Shakesp.*

And *planets*, *planet*-struck, real eclipse
Then suffer'd. *Milton's Paradise Lost, b.* x.

There are seven *planets* or errant stars in the lower orbs of heaven. *Brown's Vulgar Errours, b.* iv.

PLA'NETARY. *adj.* [*planetaire*, Fr. from *planet.*]

1. Pertaining to the planets.

Their *planetary* motions and aspects. *Milton.*

To marble and to brass, such features give,
Describe the stars and *planetary* way,
And trace the footsteps of eternal day. *Granvill.*

2. Under the denomination of any particular planet.

Darkling they mourn their fate, whom Circe's power,
That watch'd the moon and *planetary* hour,
With words and wicked herbs, from human kind
Had alter'd. *Dryden.*

I was born in the *planetary* hour of Saturn, and, I think, I have a piece of that leaden planet in me; I am no way facetious. *Addison's Spectator,* N° 487.

3. Produced by the planets.

Here's gold, go on;
Be as a *planetary* plague, when Jove
Will o'er some high-vic'd city hang his poison
In the sick air. *Shakesp. Timon of Athens.*

We make guilty of our disasters the sun, the moon and stars, as if we were villains by an enforced obedience of *planetary* influence. *Shakespeare's King Lear.*

4. Having the nature of a planet; erratick.

We behold bright planetary Jove,
Sublime in air through his wide province move;
Four second *planets* his dominion own,
And round him turn, as round the earth the moon. *Blackm.*

PLANE'TICAL. *adj.* [from *planet.*] Pertaining to planets.

Add the two Egyptian days in every month, the interlunary and plenilunary exemptions, the eclypses of sun and moon, conjunctions and oppositions *planetical.* *Brown.*

PLANE'TSTRUCK. *adj.* [*planet* and *strike.*] Blasted; *sidere afflatus.*

Wonder not much if thus amaz'd I look,
Since I saw you, I have been *planetstruck*;
A beauty, and so rare, I did descry. *Suckling.*

PLANIFO'LIOUS. *adj.* [*planus* and *folium*, Lat.] Flowers are so called, when made up of plain leaves, set together in circular rows round the center, whose face is usually uneven, rough and jagged. *Dict.*

PLANIME'TRICAL. *adj.* [from *planimetry.*] Pertaining to the mensuration of plane surfaces.

PLANIM'ETRY. *n. s.* [*planus*, Lat. and μετρέω; *planimetrie*, Fr.] The mensuration of plane surfaces.

PLANIPE'TALOUS. *adj.* [*planus*, Lat. and πέταλον.] Flat-leaved, as when the small flowers are hollow only at the bottom, but flat upwards, as in dandelion and succory. *Dict.*

To PLA'NISH. *v. a.* [from *plane.*] To polish; to smooth. A word used by manufacturers.

PLA'NISPHERE. *n. s.* [*planus*, Lat. and *sphere.*] A sphere projected on a plane; a map of one or both hemispheres.

PLANK. *n. s.* [*planche*, Fr.] A thick strong board.

They gazed on their ships, seeing them so great, and consisting of divers *planks.* *Abbot's Descript. of the World.*

The doors of *plank* were; their close exquisite,
Kept with a double key. *Chapman's Odyssey.*

The smoothed *plank* new rub'd with balm. *Milton.*

Some Turkish bows are of that strength, as to pierce a *plank* of six inches. *Wilkins.*

Deep in their hulls our deadly bullets light,
And through the yielding *planks* a passage find. *Dryden.*

Be warn'd to shun the watry way,
For late I saw adrift disjointed *planks*,
And empty tombs erected on the banks. *Dryden.*

To PLANK. *v. a.* [from the noun.] To cover or lay with planks.

If you do but *plank* the ground over, it will breed saltpetre. *Bacon's Natural History.*

A steed of monstrous height appear'd;
The sides were *plank'd* with pine. *Dryden.*

PLANOCO'NICAL. *adj.* [*planus* and *conus.*] Level on one side and conical on others.

Some few are *planoconical*, whose superficies is in part level between both ends. *Grew's Musæum.*

PLA'NOCONVEX. *n. s.* [*planus* and *convexus.*] Flat on the one side and convex on the other.

It took two object-glasses, the one a *planoconvex* for a fourteen feet telescope, and the other a large double convex for one of about fifty feet. *Newton's Opticks.*

PLANT. *n. s.* [*plant*, Fr. *planta*, Latin.]

1. Any thing produced from seed; any vegetable production.

What comes under this denomination, *Ray* has distributed under twenty-seven genders or kinds: 1. The imperfect *plants*, which do either totally want both flower and seed, or else seem to do so. 2. *Plants* producing either no flower at all, or an imperfect one, whose seed is so small as not to be discernible by the naked eye. 3. Those whose seeds are not so small, as singly to be invisible, but yet have an imperfect or staminous flower; *i. e.* such a one, as is without the petala, having only the stamina and the perianthium. 4. Such as have a compound flower, and emit a kind of white juice or milk when their stalks are cut off or their branches broken off. 5. Such as have a compound flower of a discous figure, the seed pappous, or winged with downe, but emit no milk. 6. The herbæ capitatæ, or such whose flower is composed of many small, long, fistulous or hollow flowers gathered round together in a round button or head, which is usually covered with a squamous or scaly coat. 7. Such as have their leaves entire and undivided into jags. 8. The corymbiferous *plants*, which have a compound discous flower, but the seeds have no downe adhering to them. 9. *Plants* with a perfect flower, and having only one single seed belonging to each single flower. 10. Such as have rough, hairy or bristly seeds. 11. The umbelliferous *plants*, which have a pentapetalous flower, and belonging to each single flower are two seeds, lying naked and joining together; they are called umbelliferous, because the *plant*, with its branches and flowers, hath an head like a lady's umbrella: [1.] Such as have a broad flat seed almost of the figure of a leaf, which are encompassed round about with something like leaves. [2.] Such as have a longish seed, swelling out in the middle, and larger than the former. [3.] Such as have a shorter seed. [4.] Such as have a tuberose root. [5.] Such as have a wrinkled, channelated or striated seed. 12. The stellate *plants*, which are so called, because their leaves grow on their stalks at certain intervals or distances in the form of a radiant star: their flowers are really monopetalous, divided into four segments, which look like so many petala; and each flower is succeeded by two seeds at the bottom of it. 13. The asperifolia, or rough leaved *plants*: they have their leaves placed alternately, or in no certain order on their stalks; they have a monopetalous flower cut or divided into five partitions, and after every flower there succeed usually four seeds. 14. The suffrutices, or verticilate *plants*: their leaves grow by pairs on their stalks, one leaf right against another; their leaf is monopetalous, and usually in form of an helmet. 15. Such as have naked seeds, more than four, succeeding their flowers, which therefore they call polyspermæ plantæ semine nudo; by naked seeds, they mean such as are not included in any seed pod. 16. Bacciferous *plants*, or such as bear berries. 17. Multisiliquous, or corniculate *plants*, or such as have, after each flower, many distinct, long, slender, and many times crooked cases or siliquæ, in which their seed is contained, and which, when they are ripe, open themselves and let the seeds drop out. 18. Such as have a monopetalous flower, either uniform or difform, and after each flower a peculiar seed-case containing the seed, and this often divided into many distinct cells. 19. Such as have an uniform tetrapetalous flower, but bear these seeds in oblong siliquous cases. 20. Vasculiferous *plants*, with a tetrapetalous flower, but often anomalous. 21. Leguminous *plants*, or such as bear pulse, with a papilionaceous flower. 22. Vasculiferous *plants*, with a pentapetalous flower; these have, besides the common calix, a peculiar case containing their seed, and their flower consisting of five leaves. 23. *Plants* with a true bulbous root, which consists but of one round ball or head, out of whose lower part go many fibres to keep it firm in the earth: the *plants* of this kind come up but with one leaf; they have no foot stalk, and are long and slender: the seed vessels are divided into three partitions: their flower is sexapetalous. 24. Such as have their fruits approaching to a bulbous form: these emit, at first coming up, but one leaf, and in leaves, flowers and roots resemble the true bulbous *plant*. 25. Culmiferous *plants*, with a grassy leaf, are such as have a smooth hollow-jointed stalk, with one sharp-pointed leaf at each joint, encompassing the stalk, and set out without any foot stalk: their seed is contained within a chaffy husk. 26. *Plants* with a grassy leaf, but not culmiferous, with an imperfect or staminous flower. 27. *Plants* whose place of growth is uncertain and various, chiefly water *plants*.

Butchers and villains,
How sweet a *plant* have you untimely cropt. *Shakesp.*

Between the vegetable and sensitive province there are *plant*-animals and some kind of insects arising from vegetables, that seem to participate of both. *Hale's Origin of Mankind.*

The next species of life above the vegetable, is that of sense; wherewith some of those productions, which we call *plant*-animals, are endowed. *Grew's Cosmol.*

It continues to be the same *plant*, as long as it partakes of the same life, though that life be communicated to new particles of matter, vitally united to the living *plant*, in a like continued organization, conformable to that sort of *plants*. *Locke.*

Once

Once I was skill'd in ev'ry herb that grew,
And ev'ry *plant* that drinks the morning dew. *Pope.*

2. A sapling.

A man haunts the forest, that abuses our young *plants* with carving Rosalind on their barks. *Shakesp. As You like it.*

Take a *plant* of stubborn oak,
And labour him with many a stubborn stroke. *Dryden.*

3. [*Planta*, Lat.] The sole of the foot. *Ainsworth.*

To PLANT. *v. a.* [*planto*, Lat. *planter*, Fr.]

1. To put into the ground in order to grow; to set; to cultivate.

Plant not thee a grove of any trees near unto the altar of the Lord. *Deutr.* xvi. 21.

2. To procreate; to generate.

The honour'd gods the chairs of justice
Supply with worthy men, *plant* love amongst you. *Shak.*
It engenders choler, *planteth* anger;
And better 'twere, that both of us did fast,
Than feed it with such overroasted flesh. *Shakesp.*

3. To place; to fix.

The fool hath *planted* in his memory
An army of good words. *Shakesp. Merch. of Venice.*
In this hour,
I will advise you where to *plant* yourselves. *Shakesp.*
The mind through all her powers
Irradiate, there *plant* eyes. *Milton.*
When Turnus had assembled all his pow'rs,
His standard *planted* on Laurentum's tow'rs;
Trembling with rage, the Latian youth prepare
To join th' allies. *Dryden's Æneis.*

4. To settle; to establish: as, to *plant* a colony.

If you *plant* where savages are, do not only entertain them with trifles and jingles, but use them justly. *Bacon.*

Create, and therein *plant* a generation. *Milton.*

To the *planting* of it in a nation, the soil may be mellowed with the blood of the inhabitants; nay, the old extirpated, and the new colonies *planted*. *Decay of Piety.*

5. To fill or adorn with something planted: as, he *planted* the garden or the country.

To build, to *plant*, whatever you intend,
In all let nature never be forgot. *Pope.*

6. To direct properly: as, to *plant* a cannon.

PLA'NTAGE. *n. s.* [*plantago*, Lat.] An herb.

Truth, tir'd with iteration,
As true as steel, as *plantage* to the moon. *Shakesp.*

PLA'NTAIN. *n. s.* [*plantain*, Fr. *plantago*, Lat.]

1. An herb.

The toad, being overcharged with the poison of the spider, as is ordinarily believ'd, has recourse to the *plantain* leaf. *More's Antidote against Atheism.*

The most common simples are mugwort, *plantain* and horsetail. *Wiseman's Surgery.*

2. A tree in the West Indies, which bears an esculent fruit.

I long my careless limbs to lay
Under the *plantain*'s shade. *Waller.*

PLA'NTAL. *adj.* [from *plant*.] Pertaining to plants.

There's but little similitude betwixt a terreous humidity and *plantal* germinations. *Glanvill's Sceps.*

PLANTA'TION. *n. s.* [*plantatio*, from *planto*, Latin.]

1. The act or practice of planting.

2. The place planted.

As swine are to gardens and orderly *plantations*, so are tumults to parliaments. *King Charles.*

Some peasants
Of the same soil their nursery prepare,
With that of their *plantation*; lest the tree
Translated should not with the soil agree. *Dryden.*
Whose rising forests, not for pride or show,
But future buildings, future navies grow:
Let his *plantations* stretch from down to down,
First shade a country, and then raise a town. *Pope.*

Virgil, with great modesty in his looks, was seated by Calliope in the midst of a *plantation* of laurel. *Addison.*

3. A colony.

Planting of countries is like planting of woods; the principal thing, that hath been the destruction of most *plantations*, hath been the base and hasty drawing of profit in the first years; speedy profit is not to be neglected, as far as may stand with the good of the *plantation*. *Bacon's Essays.*

4. Introduction; establishment.

Episcopacy must be cast out of this church, after possession here, from the first *plantation* of christianity in this island. *King Charles.*

PLA'NTED. *adj.* [from *plant*.] This word seems in *Shakespeare* to signify, settled; well grounded.

Our court is haunted
With a refined traveller of Spain;
A man in all the world's new fashion *planted*,
That hath a mint of phrases in his brain. *Shakesp.*

PLA'NTER. *n. s.* [*planteur*, Fr. from *plant*.]

1. One who sows, sets or cultivates; cultivator.

There stood Sabinus, *planter* of the vines,
And studiously surveys his gen'rous wines. *Dryden.*
What do thy vines avail,
Or olives, when the cruel battle mows
The *planters*, with their harvest immature? *Philips.*
That product only which our passions bear,
Eludes the *planter's* miserable care. *Prior.*

2. One who cultivates ground in the West Indian colonies.

A *planter* in the West Indies might muster up, and lead all his family out against the Indians, without the absolute dominion of a monarch, descending to him from Adam. *Locke.*

He to Jamaica seems transported,
Alone, and by no *planter* courted. *Swift's Miscellanies.*

3. One who disseminates or introduces.

Had these writings differed from the sermons of the first *planters* of christianity in history or doctrine, they would have been rejected by those churches which they had formed. *Add.*

PLASH. *n. s.* [*plasche*, Dutch; *platz*, Danish.]

1. A small lake of water or puddle.

He leaves
A shallow *plash* to plunge him in the deep,
And with satiety seeks to quench his thirst. *Shakesp.*

Two frogs consulted, in the time of drought, when many *plashes*, that they had repaired to, were dry, what was to be done. *Bacon.*

I understand the aquatile or water frog, whereof in ditches and standing *plashes* we behold millions. *Brown.*

With filth the miscreant lies bewray'd,
Fall'n in the *plash* his wickedness had laid. *Pope.*

2. [From the verb to *plash*.] Branch partly cut off and bound to other branches.

In the plashing your quick, avoid laying of it too low and too thick, which makes the sap run all into the shoots, and leaves the *plashes* without nourishment. *Mortimer.*

To PLASH. *v. a.* [*plesser*, Fr.] To interweave branches.

Plant and *plash* quicksets. *Evelyn.*

PLA'SHY. *adj.* [from *plash*.] Watry; filled with puddles.

Near stood a mill in low and *plashy* ground. *Betterton.*

PLASM. *n. s.* [πλάσμα.] A mould; a matrix in which any thing is cast or formed.

The shells served as *plasms* or moulds to this sand, which, when consolidated, and afterwards freed from its investient shell, is of the same shape with the cavity of the shell. *Woodward's Natural History.*

PLA'STER. *n. s.* [*plastre*. Fr. from πλαζω.]

1. Substance made of water and some absorbent matter, such as chalk or lime well pulverised, with which walls are overlaid or figures cast.

In the same hour came forth fingers of a man's hand, and wrote upon the *plaster* of the wall. *Dan.* v. 5.

In the worst inn's worst room, with mat half-hung,
The floors of *plaster*, and the walls of dung. *Pope.*

Maps are hung up so high, to cover the naked *plaster* or wainscot. *Watts's Improvement of the Mind.*

2. [*Emplastrum*, Lat. in English, formerly *emplaster*.] A glutinous or adhesive salve.

Seeing the sore is whole, why retain we the *plaster*? *Hook.*

You rub the sore,
When you should bring the *plaster*. *Shakespeare.*

It not only moves the needle in powder, but likewise, if incorporated with *plasters*, as we have made trial. *Brown.*

Plasters, that had any effect, must be by dispersing or repelling the humours. *Temple's Miscellanies.*

To PLA'STER. *v. a.* [*plastrer*, Fr. from the noun.]

1. To overlay as with plaster.

Boils and plagues
Plaster you o'er, that one infect another
Against the wind a mile. *Shakesp. Coriolanus.*
The harlot's cheek beautied with *plast'ring* art. *Shakesp.*

A heart settled upon a thought of understanding, is as a fair *plastering* on the wall. *Ecclus.* xxii. 17.

With a cement of flour, whites of eggs and stone powdered, piscina mirabilis is said to have the walls *plastered*. *Bacon.*

Plaster the chinky hives with clay. *Dryden.*

The brain is grown more dry in its consistence, and receives not much more impression, than if you wrote with your finger on a *plaster'd* wall. *Watts's Improvement of the Mind.*

2. To cover with a medicated plaster.

PLA'STERER. *n. s.* [*plastrier*, Fr. from *plaster*.]

1. One whose trade is to overlay walls with plaster.

Thy father was a *plasterer*,
And thou thyself a shearman. *Shakespeare's Henry* VI.

2. One who forms figures in plaster.

The *plasterer* makes his figures by addition, and the carver by subtraction. *Wotton.*

PLA'STICK. *adj.* [πλαςικος.] Having the power to give form.

Benign creator! let thy *plastick* hand
Dispose its own effect. *Prior.*

There is not any thing strange in the production of the said formed metals, nor other *plastick* virtue concerned in shaping them into those figures, than merely the configuration of the particles. *Woodward's Natural History.*

PLA'STRON. *n. s.* [French.] A piece of leather stuffed, which fencers use, when they teach their scholars, in order to receive the pushes made at them. *Trevoux.*

Against the post their wicker shields they crush,
Flourish the sword, and at the *plastron* push. *Dryden.*

TO PLAT. *v. a.* [from *plait.*] To weave; to make by texture.

I have seen nests of an Indian bird curiously interwoven and *platted* together. *Ray on the Creation.*

I never found so much benefit from any expedient, as from a ring, in which my mistress's hair is *platted* in a kind of true lovers knot. *Addison's Spectator*, Nº 245.

PLAT. *n. s.* [more properly *plot*; plot, Sax.] A small piece of ground.

Such pleasure took the serpent to behold
This flow'ry *plat*, the sweet recess of Eve. *Milton.*

On a *plat* of rising ground,
I hear the far-off curfeu sound,
Over some wide-water'd shore,
Swinging slow with sullen roar. *Milton.*

It passes through banks of violets and *plats* of willow of its own producing. *Spectator.*

PLA'TANE. *n. s.* [*platane*, Fr. *platanus*, Lat.] The plane tree.

The *platane* round,
The carver holm, the mapple seldom inward sound. *Spens.*

I espy'd thee, fair and tall,
Under a *platane*. *Milton.*

PLATE. *n. s.* [*plate*, Dutch; *plaque*, Fr.]

1. A piece of metal beat out into breadth.

In his livery
Walk'd crowns and coronets, realms and islands were
As *plates* dropt from his pocket. *Shakesp.*

Make a *plate*, and burnish it as they do iron. *Bacon.*

A leaden bullet-shot from one of these guns, the space of twenty paces, will be beaten into a thin *plate*. *Wilkins.*

The censers of these wretches, who could derive no sanctity to them; yet in that they had been consecrated by the offering incense, were appointed to be beaten into broad *plates*, and fastened upon the altar. *South's Sermons.*

Eternal deities!
Who rule the world with absolute decrees,
And write whatever time shall bring to pass
With pens of adamant on *plates* of brass. *Dryden.*

2. Armour of plates.

With their force they pierc'd both *plate* and mail,
And made wide furrows in their fleshes frail. *Fa. Queen.*

3. [*Plata*, Spanish.] Wrought silver.

They eat on beds of silk and gold,
And leaving *plate*,
Do drink in stone of higher rate. *Benj. Johnson's Cataline.*

The Turks entered into the trenches so far, that they carried away the *plate*. *Knolles's Hist. of the Turks.*

They that but now for honour and for *plate*
Made the sea blush with blood, resign their hate. *Waller.*

At your desert bright pewter comes too late,
When your first course was all serv'd up in *plate*. *King.*

4. [*Plat*, Fr. *piatta*, Italian.] A small shallow vessel of metal on which meat is eaten.

Ascanius this observ'd, and, smiling, said,
See, we devour the *plates* on which we fed. *Dryden.*

TO PLATE. *v. a.* [from the noun.]

1. To cover with plates.

The doors are curiously cut through and *plated.* *Sandys.*

M. Lepidus's house had a marble door-case; afterwards they had gilded ones, or rather *plated* with gold. *Arbuthnot.*

2. To arm with plates.

Plate sin with gold,
And the strong lance of justice hurtless breaks. *Shakesp.*

Marshal, ask yonder knight in arms,
Why *plated* in habiliments of war? *Shakesp.*

His goodly eyes,
That o'er the files and musters of the war,
Have glow'd like *plated* Mars. *Shakesp.*

The bold Ascalonite
Fled from his lion ramp, old warriours turn'd
Their *plated* backs under his heel. *Milton.*

3. To beat into laminæ or plates.

If to fame alone thou dost pretend,
The miser will his empty palace lend,
Set wide his doors, adorn'd with *plated* brass. *Dryden.*

If a thinned or *plated* body, of an uneven thickness, which appears all over of one uniform colour, should be slit into threads of the same thickness with the *plate*; I see no reason why every thread should not keep its colour. *Newton.*

PLA'TEN. *n. s.* Among printers, the flat part of the press whereby the impression is made.

PLA'TFORM. *n. s.* [*plat*, flat, Fr. and *form.*]

1. The sketch of any thing horizontally delineated; the ichnography.

When the workmen began to lay the *platform* at Chalcedon, eagles conveyed their lines to the other side of the streight. *Sandys's Journey.*

2. A place laid out after any model.

No artful wildness to perplex the scene;
Grove nods at grove, each alley has a brother,
And half the *platform* just reflects the other. *Pope.*

3. A level place before a fortification.

Where was this?
—Upon the *platform* where we watch. *Shakesp.*

4. A scheme; a plan.

Their minds and affections were universally bent even against all the orders and laws wherein this church is founded, conformable to the *platform* of Geneva. *Hooker.*

I have made a *platform* of a princely garden by precept, partly by drawing not a model, but some general lines of it. *Bacon's Essays.*

They who take in the entire *platform*, and see the chain, which runs through the whole, and can bear in mind the observations and proofs, will discern how these propositions flow from them. *Woodward.*

PLA'TICK *aspect.* In astrology, is a ray cast from one planet to another, not exactly, but within the orbit of its own light. *Bailey.*

PLATO'ON. *n. s.* [a corruption of *peloton*, Fr.] A small square body of musketeers, drawn out of a batallion of foot, when they form the hollow square, to strengthen the angles: the grenadiers are generally thus posted; yet a party from any other division is called a *platoon*, when intending to far from the main body. *Military Dict.*

In comely wounds shall bleeding worthies stand,
Webb's firm *platoon*, and Lumly's faithful band. *Tickell.*

PLA'TTER. *n. s.* [from *plate.*] A large dish, generally of earth.

The servants wash the *platter*, scour the plate,
Then blow the fire. *Dryden's Juvenal.*

Satira is an adjective, to which lanx, a charger, or large *platter* is understood. *Dryden.*

PLAU'DIT. } *n. s.* [A word derived from the Latin, *plaudite*,
PLAU'DITE. } the demand of applause made by the player, when he left the stage.] Applause.

True wisdom must our actions so direct,
Not only the last *plaudit* to expect. *Denham.*

She would so shamefully fail in the last act, that instead of a *plaudite*, she would deserve to be hissed off the stage. *More.*

Some men find more melody in discord than in the angelick quires; yet even these can discern musick in a consort of *plaudites*, eulogies given themselves. *Decay of Piety.*

PLAUSIBI'LITY. *n. s.* [*plausibilité*, Fr. from *plausible.*] Speciousness; superficial appearance of right.

Two pamphlets, called the management of the war, are written with some *plausibility*, much artifice and direct falsehoods. *Swift.*

The last excuse for the slow steps made in disarming the adversaries of the crown, was allowed indeed to have more *plausibility*, but less truth, than any of the former. *Swift.*

PLAU'SIBLE. *adj.* [*plausible*, Fr. *plausibilis*, from *plaudo*, Lat.] Such as gains approbation; superficially pleasing or taking; specious; popular; right in appearance.

Go you to Angelo, answer his requiring with a *plausible* obedience, agree with his demands to the point. *Shakesp.*

Judges ought to be more reverend than *plausible*, and more advised than confident. *Bacon.*

They found out that *plausible* and popular pretext of raising an army to fetch in delinquents. *King Charles.*

These were all *plausible* and popular arguments, in which they, who most desired peace, would insist upon many condescensions. *Clarendon.*

No treachery so *plausible*, as that which is covered with the robe of a guide. *L'Estrange.*

The case is doubtful, and may be disputed with *plausible* arguments on either side. *South.*

PLAU'SIBLENESS. *n. s.* [from *plausible.*] Speciousness; show of right.

The *plausibleness* of arminianism, and the congruity it hath with the principles of corrupt nature. *Sanderson.*

The notion of man's free will, and the nature of sin bears along with it a commendable plainness and *plausibleness*. *More.*

PLAU'SIBLY. *adv.* [from *plausible.*]

1. With fair show; speciously.

They could talk *plausibly* about that they did not understand, but their learning lay chiefly in flourish. *Collier.*

Thou can'st *plausibly* dispute,
Supreme of seers, of angel, man and brute. *Prior.*

2. With applause. Not in use.

I hope they will *plausibly* receive our attempts, or candidly correct our misconjectures. *Brown's Vulgar Errours.*

PLAU'SIVE. *adj.* [from *plaudo*, Lat.]

1. Applauding.
2. Plausible. A word not in use.

His *plausive* words
He scatter'd not in ears; but grafted them
To grow there and to bear. *Shakesp.*

To PLAY. *v. n.* [plegan, Saxon.]

1. To ſport; to frolick; to do ſomething not as a taſk, but for a pleaſure.

On ſmooth the ſeal and bended dolphins *play*. *Milton.*

2. To toy; to act with levity.

Thou with eternal wiſdom did'ſt converſe,
Wiſdom thy ſiſter and with her didſt *play*. *Milton.*

3. To be diſmiſſed from work.

I'll bring my young man to ſchool; look where his maſter comes; 'tis a *playing* day I ſee. *Shakeſp. Mer. W. of Windſ.*

4. To trifle; to act wantonly and thoughtleſly.

Men are apt to *play* with their healths and their lives as they do with their cloaths. *Temple.*

5. To do ſomething fanciful.

How every fool can *play* upon the word! *Shakeſp.*

6. To practiſe ſarcaſtick merriment.

I would make uſe of it rather to *play* upon thoſe I deſpiſed, than to trifle with thoſe I loved. *Pope.*

7. To mock; to practiſe illuſion.

I ſaw him dead; art thou alive,
Or is it fancy *plays* upon our eye-ſight. *Shakeſpeare.*

8. To game; to contend at ſome game.

Charles, I will *play* no more to-night;
My mind's not on't, you are too hard for me.
—Sir, I did never win of you before. *Shakeſp.*

When lenity and cruelty *play* for kingdoms,
The gentler gameſter is the ſooneſt winner. *Shakeſp.*

O perdurable ſhame!
Are theſe the wretches that we *play'd* at dice for. *Shakeſp.*

The low rated Engliſh *play* at dice. *Shakeſp.*

The clergyman *played* at whiſt and ſwobbers. *Swift.*

9. To do any thing trickiſh or deceitful.

His mother *played* falſe with a ſmith. *Shakeſpeare.*

Cawdor, Glamis, all
The wizzard women promis'd; and, I fear,
Thou *play'dſt* moſt foully for't. *Shakeſp. Macbeth.*

Life is not long enough for a coquette to *play* all her tricks in. *Addiſon's Spectator*, Nº 89.

10. To touch a muſical inſtrument.

Ev'ry thing that heard him *play*,
Ev'n the billows of the ſea
Hung their heads, and then lay by,
In ſweet muſick is ſuch art,
Killing care, and grief of heart,
Fall aſleep, or nearing die. *Shakeſp. Henry* VIII.

Thou art as a very lovely ſong of one that hath a pleaſant voice, and can *play* well on an inſtrument. *Ezekiel.*

Tully ſays, there conſiſteth in the practice of ſinging and *playing* on inſtruments great knowledge, and the moſt excellent inſtruction, which rectifies and orders our manners, and allays the heat of anger. *Peacham of Muſick.*

Wherein doth our practice of ſinging and *playing* with inſtruments in our cathedral churches differ from the practice of David. *Peacham of Muſick.*

Clad like a country ſwain, he pip'd, he ſung,
And *playing* drove his jolly troop along. *Dryden.*

Take thy harp and melt thy maid;
Play, my friend! and charm the charmer. *Glanvill.*

He applied the pipe to his lips, and began to *play* upon it: the ſound of it was exceeding ſweet. *Addiſon's Spectator.*

11. To operate; to act. Uſed of any thing in motion.

John hath ſeiz'd Arthur, and it cannot be,
That whilſt warm life *plays* in that infant's veins,
The miſplac'd John ſhould entertain
One quiet breath of reſt. *Shakeſp. King John.*

My wife cried out fire, and you brought out your buckets, and called for engines to *play* againſt it. *Dryden.*

By conſtant laws, the food is concocted, the heart beats, the blood circulates, the lungs *play*. *Cheyne.*

12. To wanton; to move irregularly.

Citherea all in ſedges hid,
Which ſeem to move and wanton with her breath,
Ev'n as the waving ſedges *play* with wind. *Shakeſp.*

This with exhilarating vapour bland
About their ſpirits *play'd*, and inmoſt powers
Made err. *Milton.*

In the ſtreams that from the fountain *play*,
She waſh'd her face. *Dryden.*

The ſetting ſun
Plays on their ſhining arms and burniſh'd helmets,
And covers all the field with gleams of fire. *Addiſon.*

13. To perſonate a drama.

A lord will hear you *play* to-night;
But I am doubtful of your modeſties,
Leſt, over-eying of his odd behaviour,
For yet his honour never heard a play,
You break into ſome merry paſſion. *Shakeſpeare.*

Ev'n kings but *play*; and when their part is done,
Some other, worſe or better, mount the throne. *Dryden.*

14. To repreſent a character.

Courts are theatres, where ſome men *play*;
Princes, ſome ſlaves, and all end in one day. *Donne.*

15. To act in any certain character.

Thus we *play* the fool with the time, and the ſpirits of the wiſe ſit in the clouds and mock us. *Shakeſp.*

I did not think to ſhed a tear
In all my miſeries; but thou haſt forc'd me,
Out of thy honeſt truth to *play* the woman. *Shakeſp.*

She hath wrought folly to *play* the whore. *Deut.* xxii. 21.

Be of good courage, and let us *play* the men for our people. 2 *Samuel* x. 12.

Alphonſe, duke of Ferrara, delighted himſelf only in turning and *playing* the joiner. *Peacham of Muſick.*

'Tis poſſible theſe Turks may *play* the villains. *Denham.*

A man has no pleaſure in proving that he has *played* the fool. *Collier of Friendſhip.*

To PLAY. *v. a.*

1. To put in action or motion: as, he *played* his cannon.

2. To uſe an inſtrument of muſick.

He *plays* a tickling ſtraw within his noſe. *Gay.*

3. To act a mirthful character.

Nature here
Wanton'd as in her prime, and *play'd* at will
Her virgin fancies. *Milton.*

4. To exhibit dramatically.

Your honour's players hearing your amendment,
Are come to *play* a pleaſant comedy. *Shakeſp.*

5. To act; to perform.

Doubt would fain have *played* his part in her mind, and called in queſtion, how ſhe ſhould be aſſured that Zelmane was not Pyrocles. *Sidney, b.* ii.

PLAY. *n. ſ.*

1. Action not impoſed; not work; diſmiſſion from work.

2. Amuſement; ſport.

My dearling and my joy;
For love of me leave off this dreadful *play*. *Fa. Queen.*

Two gentle fawns at *play*. *Milton.*

3. A drama; a comedy or tragedy, or any thing in which characters are repreſented by dialogue and action.

Only they,
That come to hear a merry *play*,
Will be deceiv'd. *Shakeſp. Henry* VIII.

A *play* ought to be a juſt image of human nature, repreſenting its humours and the changes of fortune to which it is ſubject, for the delight and inſtruction of mankind. *Dryden.*

Viſits, *plays* and powder'd beaux. *Swift.*

4. Game; practice of gaming; conteſt at a game.

I will play no more, my mind's not on't;
I did never win of you,
Nor ſhall not when my fancy's on my *play*. *Shakeſp.*

5. Practice in any conteſt.

When they can make nothing elſe on't, they find it the beſt of their *play* to put it off with a jeſt. *L'Eſtrange.*

He was reſolved not to ſpeak diſtinctly, knowing his beſt *play* to be in the dark, and that all his ſafety lay in the confuſion of his talk. *Tillotſon.*

In arguing the opponent uſes comprehenſive and equivocal terms, to involve his adverſary in the doubtfulneſs of his expreſſion, and therefore the anſwer on his ſide makes it his *play* to diſtinguiſh as much as he can. *Locke.*

Bull's friends adviſed to gentler methods with the young lord; but John naturally lov'd rough *play*. *Arbuthnot.*

6. Action; employment; office.

The ſenſeleſs plea of right by providence
Can laſt no longer than the preſent ſway;
But juſtifies the next who comes in *play*. *Dryden.*

7. Practice; action; manner of acting.

Determinining, as after I knew, in ſecret manner, not to be far from the place where we appointed to meet, to prevent any foul *play* that might be offered unto me. *Sidney, b.* ii.

8. Act of touching an inſtrument.

9. Irregular and wanton motion.

10. A ſtate of agitation or ventilation.

Many have been ſav'd, and many may,
Who never heard this queſtion brought in *play*. *Dryden.*

11. Room for motion.

The joints are let exactly into one another, that they have no *play* between them, leſt they ſhake upwards or downwards. *Moxon's Mechanical Exerciſes.*

12. Liberty of acting; ſwing.

Should a writer give the full *play* to his mirth, without regard to decency, he might pleaſe readers; but muſt be a very ill man, if he could pleaſe himſelf. *Addiſon's Freeholder.*

PLA'YBOOK. *n. ſ.* [*play* and *book.*] Book of dramatick compoſitions.

Your's was a match of common good liking, without any mixture of that ridiculous paſſion, which has no being but in *playbooks* and romances. *Swift.*

PLA'YDAY. *n. ſ.* [*play* and *day.*] Day exempt from taſks or work.

I thought the life of every lady
Should be one continual *playday*;
Balls and maſquerades and ſhows. *Swift's Miſcellanies.*

PLA'YDEBT. *n. s.* [*play* and *debt.*] Debt contracted by gaming.

There are multitudes of leases upon single lives, and *playdebts* upon joint lives. *Arbuthnot.*

She has several *playdebts* on her hand, which must be discharged very suddenly. *Spectator*, Nº 295.

PLA'YER. *n. s.* [from *play.*]

1. One who plays.

2. An idler; a lazy person.

You're pictures out of doors,
Saints in your injuries, devils being offended,
Players in your housewifery. *Shakespeare's Othello.*

3. Actor of dramatick scenes.

Like *players* plac'd to fill a filthy stage,
Where change of thoughts one fool to other shews,
And all but jests, serve only sorrow's rage. *Sidney.*

Certain pantomimi will represent the voices of *players* of interludes so to life, as you would think they were those *players* themselves. *Bacon's Natural History.*

A *player*, if left of his auditory and their applause, would straight be out of heart. *Bacon.*

Thine be the laurel then, support the stage;
Which so declines, that shortly we may see
Players and plays reduc'd to second infancy. *Dryden.*

His muse had starv'd, had not a piece unread,
And by a *player* bought, supply'd her bread. *Dryden.*

4. A mimick.

Thus said the *player* god; and adding art
Of voice and gesture, so perform'd his part,
She thought, so like her love the shade appears,
That Ceyx spake the words. *Dryden.*

5. One who touches a musical instrument.

Command thy servants to seek out a man, who is a cunning *player* on the harp. 1 *Samuel* xvi. 16.

6. A gamester.

7. One who acts in play in any certain manner.

The snake bit him fast by the tongue, which therewith began so to rankle and swell, that, by the time he had knocked this foul *player* on the head, his mouth was scarce able to contain it. *Carew's Survey of Cornwall.*

PLA'YFELLOW. *n. s.* [*play* and *fellow.*] Companion in amusement.

Inconstant in his choice of his friends, or rather never having a friend but *playfellows*, of whom, when he was weary, he could no otherwise rid himself than by killing them. *Sidn.*

She seem'd still back unto the land to look,
And her *playfellows* aid to call, and fear
The dashing of the waves. *Spenser.*

Your precious self had not then cross'd the eyes
Of my young *playfellow.* *Shakesp. Winter's Tale.*

Mischance and sorrow go along with you!
Heart's discontent and sour affliction
Be *playfellows* to keep you company! *Shakesp.*

Sweet *playfellow*, pray thou for us,
And good luck grant thee thy Demetrius. *Shakesp.*

This was the play at which Nero stakedthree thousand two hundred and twenty-nine pounds three shillings and four pence upon every cast; where did he find *playfellows?* *Arbuthnot on Coins.*

PLA'YFUL. *adj.* [*play* and *full.*] Sportive; full of levity.

He is scandalized at youth for being lively, and at childhood for being *playful.* *Addison's Spectator*, Nº 494.

PLA'YGAME. *n. s.* [*play* and *game.*] Play of children.

That liberty alone gives the true relish to their ordinary *playgames.* *Locke.*

PLA'YHOUSE. *n. s.* [*play* and *house.*] House where dramatick performances are represented.

These are the youths that thunder at a *playhouse*, and fight for bitten apples. *Shakesp. Henry* VIII.

He hurries me from the *playhouse* and scenes there, to the bear-garden. *Stillingfleet.*

I am a sufficient theatre to myself of ridiculous actions, without expecting company either in a court or *playhouse. Dry.*

Shakespear, whom you and ev'ry *playhouse* bill
Stile the divine. *Pope's Epistles of Horace.*

PLA'YPLEASURE. *n. s.* [*play* and *pleasure.*] Idle amusement.

He taketh a kind of *playpleasure* in looking upon the fortunes of others. *Bacon's Essays.*

PLAYSOME. *adj.* [*play* and *some.*] Wanton; full of levity.

PLA'YSOMENESS. *n. s.* [from *playsome.*] Wantonness; levity.

PLA'YTHING. *n. s.* [*play* and *thing.*] Toy; thing to play with.

O Castalio! thou hast caught
My foolish heart; and like a tender child,
That trusts his *plaything* to another hand,
I fear its harm, and fain would have it back. *Otway.*

A child knows his nurse, and by degrees the *playthings* of a little more advanced age. *Locke.*

The servants should be hindered from making court to them, by giving them fruit and *playthings.* *Locke.*

O Richard,
Would fortune calm her present rage,
And give us *playthings* for our age. *Prior.*

Allow him but the *plaything* of a pen,
He ne'er rebels or plots. *Pope.*

PLA'YWRIGHT. *n. s.* [*play* and *wright.*] A maker of plays.

He ended much in the character he had liv'd in; and Horace's rule for a play may as well be applied to him as a *playwright.* *Pope.*

PLEA. *n. s.* [*plaid*, old French.]

1. The act or form of pleading.

2. Thing offered or demanded in pleading.

The magnificoes have all persuaded with him;
But none can drive him from the envious *plea*
Of forfeiture of justice and his bond. *Shakesp.*

3. Allegation.

They tow'rds the throne supreme,
Accountable, made haste, to make appear
With righteous *plea*, their utmost vigilance. *Milton.*

4. An apology; an excuse.

The fiend, with necessity,
The tyrant's *plea*, excus'd his devilish deeds. *Milton.*
Thou determin'st weakness for no *plea.* *Milton.*

When such occasions are,
No *plea* must serve; 'tis cruelty to spare. *Denham.*

Whoever argues in defence of absolute power in a single person, though he offers the old plausible *plea*, that, it is his opinion, which he cannot help, unless he be convinced, ought to be treated as the common enemy of mankind. *Swift.*

To **PLEACH.** *v. a.* [*plesser*, Fr.] To bend; to interweave. A word not in use.

Would'st thou be window'd in great Rome, and see
Thy master thus, with *pleacht* arms, bending down
His corrigible neck. *Shakespeare.*

Steal into the *pleached* bower,
Where honey-suckles ripen'd by the sun,
Forbid the sun to enter. *Shakesp.*

To **PLEAD.** *v. n.* [*plaider*, Fr.]

1. To argue before a court of justice.

To his accusations
He *pleaded* still not guilty; and alleg'd
Many sharp reasons. *Shakesp. Henry* VIII.

O that one might *plead* for a man with God, as a man *pleadeth* for his neighbour! *Job.* xvi. 21.

Of beauty sing;
Let others govern or defend the state,
Plead at the bar, or manage a debate. *Granvill.*

Lawyers and divines write down short notes, in order to preach or *plead.* *Watts's Improvement of the Mind.*

2. To speak in an argumentative or persuasive way for or against; to reason with another.

I am
To *plead* for that, which I would not obtain. *Shakesp.*

Who is he that will *plead* with me; for now if I hold my tongue, I shall give up the ghost. *Job.* xiii. 19.

If nature *plead* not in a parent's heart,
Pity my tears, and pity her desert. *Dryden.*

It must be no ordinary way of reasoning, in a man that is *pleading* for the natural power of kings, and against all compact, to bring for proof an example, where his own account founds all the right upon compact. *Locke.*

3. To be offered as a plea.

Since you can love, and yet your error see,
The same resistless power may *plead* for me,
With no less ardour I my claim pursue;
I love, and cannot yield her even to you. *Dryden.*

To **PLEAD.** *v. a.*

1. To defend; to discuss.

Will you, we shew our title to the crown?
If not, our swords shall *plead* it in the field. *Shakesp.*

2. To allege in pleading or argument.

Don Sebastian came forth to intreat, that they might part with their arms like soldiers; it was told him, that they could not justly *plead* law of nations, for that they were not lawful enemies. *Spenser on Ireland.*

If they will *plead* against me my reproach, know that God hath overthrown me. *Job* xix. 5.

3. To offer as an excuse.

I will neither *plead* my age nor sickness, in excuse of faults. *Dryden.*

PLEA'DABLE. *adj.* [from *plead.*] Capable to be alleged in plea.

I ought to be discharged from this information, because this privilege is *pleadable* at law. *Dryden.*

PLEA'DER. *n. s.* [*plaideur*, Fr. from *plead.*]

1. One who argues in a court of justice.

The brief with weighty crimes was charg'd,
On which the *pleader* much enlarg'd. *Swift's Miscel.*

2. One who speaks for or against.

If you
Would be your country's *pleader*, your good tongue
Might stop our countryman. *Shakesp. Coriolanus.*

So fair a *pleader* any cause may gain. *Dryden.*

PLEA'DING. *n. s.* [from *plead.*] Act or form of pleading.

I the heavenly folk should know
These *pleadings* in the court below. *Swift's Miscel.*

PLEA'ANCE. *n. s.* [*plaisance*, Fr.] Gaiety; pleasantry; merriment.

The lovely *pleasance* and the lofty pride
Cannot expressed be by any art. *Spenser.*
Her words she drowned with laughing vain,
And wanting grace in utt'ring of the same,
That turned all her *pleasance* to a scoffing game. *F. Queen.*

Oh that men should put an enemy into their mouths, to steal away their brains! that we should with joy, *pleasance*, revel and applause transform ourselves into beasts. *Shakesp.*

PLE'ASANT. *adj.* [*plaisant*, French.]

1. Delightful; giving delight.

The gods are just, and of our *pleasant* vices
Make instruments to scourge us. *Shakesp. King Lear.*
What most he should dislike, seems *pleasant* to him;
What like, offensive. *Shakesp. King Lear.*

How good and how *pleasant* it is for brethren to dwell in unity! *Psalms.*

Verdure clad
Her universal face with *pleasant* green. *Milton.*

2. Grateful to the senses.

Sweeter thy discourse is to my ear,
Than fruits of palm-tree *pleasantest* to thirst. *Milton.*

3. Good humoured; cheerful.

In all thy humours, whether grave or mellow,
Thou'rt such a touchy, testy, *pleasant* fellow. *Addison.*

4. Gay; lively; merry.

Let neither the power nor quality of the great, or the wit of the *pleasant* prevail with us to flatter the vices, or applaud the prophaneness of wicked men. *Rogers's Sermons.*

5. Trifling; adapted rather to mirth than use.

They, who would prove their idea of infinite to be positive, seem to do it by a *pleasant* argument, taken from the negation of an end, which being negative, the negation of it is positive. *Locke.*

PLEA'SANTLY. *adv.* [from *pleasant.*]

1. In such a manner as to give delight.
2. Gayly; merrily; in good humour.

King James was wont *pleasantly* to say, that the duke of Buckingham had given him a secretary, who could neither write nor read. *Clarendon.*

3. Lightly; ludicrously.

Eusthathius is of opinion, that Ulysses speaks *pleasantly* to Elpenor. *Broome.*

PLEA'SANTNESS. *n. s.* [from *pleasant.*]

1. Delightfulness; state of being pleasant.

Doth not the *pleasantness* of this place carry in itself sufficient reward. *Sidney.*

2. Gaiety; cheerfulness; merriment.

It was refreshing, but composed, like the *pleasantness* of youth tempered with the gravity of age. *South.*

He would fain put on some *pleasantness*, but was not able to conceal his vexation. *Tillotson.*

PLEA'SANTRY. *n. s.* [*plaisanterie*, Fr.]

1. Gaiety; merriment.

The harshness of reasoning is not a little softened and smoothed by the infusions of mirth and *pleasantry*. *Addison.*

Such kinds of *pleasantry* are disingenuous in criticism, the greatest masters appear serious and instructive. *Addison.*

2. Sprightly saying; lively talk.

The grave abound in *pleasantries*, the dull in repartees and points of wit. *Addison's Spectator*, Nº 487.

To PLEASE. *v. a.* [*placeo*, Lat. *plaire*, Fr.]

1. To delight; to gratify; to humour.

They *please* themselves in the children of strangers. *Is.* ii. 6.

Whether it were a whistling wind, or a *pleasing* fall of water running violently. *Wisdom* xvii. 18.

Thou can'st not be so *pleas'd* at liberty,
As I shall be to find thou dar'st be free. *Dryden.*
Leave such to trifle with more grace and ease,
Whom folly *pleases*, and whose follies *please*. *Pope.*

2. To satisfy; to content.

Doctor Pinch
Establish him in his true sense again,
And I will *please* you what you will demand. *Shakesp.*
What next I bring shall *please*
Thy wish exactly to thy heart's desire. *Milton*

3. To obtain favour from; to be pleased *with*, is to approve; to favour.

This is my beloved son, in whom I am well *pleased*. *Mat.*

I have seen thy face, and thou wast *pleased* with me. *Gen.*

Fickle their state whom God
Most favours: who can *please* him long? *Milton.*

4. *To be* PLEASED. To like. A word of ceremony.

Many of our most skilful painters were *pleased* to recommend this author to me, as one who perfectly understood the rules of painting. *Dryden's Dufresnoy.*

To PLEASE. *v. n.*

1. To give pleasure.

What *pleasing* seem'd, for her now *pleases* more. *Milton.*

I found something that was more *pleasing* in them, than my ordinary productions. *Dryden.*

2. To gain approbation.

Their wine-offerings shall not be *pleasing* unto him. *Hosea.*

3. To like; to chuse.

Spirits, freed from mortal laws, with ease
Assume what sexes and what shapes they *please*. *Pope.*

4. To condescend; to comply. A word of ceremony.

Please you, lords,
In sight of both our battles we may meet. *Shakesp.*

The first words that I learnt were, to express my desire, that he would *please* to give me my liberty. *Gulliver.*

PLEA'SER. *n. s.* [from *please.*] One that courts favour.

PLEA'SINGLY. *adv.* [from *pleasing.*] In such a manner as to give delight.

Pleasingly troublesome thought and remembrance have been to me since I left you. *Suckling.*

Thus to herself she *pleasingly* began. *Milton.*

The end of the artist is *pleasingly* to deceive the eye. *Dryd.*

He gains all points, who *pleasingly* confounds,
Surprizes, varies, and conceals the bounds. *Pope.*

PLEA'SINGNESS. *n. s.* [from *pleasing.*] Quality of giving delight.

PLEA'SEMAN. *n. s.* [*please* and *man.*] A pickthank; an officious fellow.

Some carry tale, some *pleaseman*, some slight zany,
That knows the trick to make my lady laugh,
Told our intents. *Shakesp. Love's Labour Lost.*

PLEA'SURABLE. *adj.* [from *pleasure.*] Delightful; full of pleasure.

Planting of orchards is very profitable, as well as *pleasurable*. *Bacon.*

It affords a *pleasurable* habitation in every part, and that is the line ecliptick. *Brown's Vulgar Errours.*

There are, that the compounded fluid drain
From different mixtures: so the blended streams,
Each mutually correcting each, create
A *pleasurable* medley. *Philips.*
Our ill-judging thought
Hardly enjoys the *pleasurable* taste. *Prior.*

PLEA'SURE. *n. s.* [*plaisir*, French.]

1. Delight; gratification of the mind or senses.

Pleasure, in general, is the consequent apprehension of a suitable object, suitably applied to a rightly disposed faculty. *South's Sermons.*

A cause of men's taking *pleasure* in the sins of others, is, that poor spiritedness that accompanies guilt. *South's Sermons.*

In hollow caves sweet echo quiet lies;
Her name with *pleasure* once she taught the shore,
Now Daphne's dead, and *pleasure* is no more. *Pope.*

2. Loose gratification.

Convey your *pleasures* in a spacious plenty,
And yet seem cold. *Shakesp.*

Behold yon dame does shake the head to hear of *pleasure's* name. *Shakesp. King Lear.*

Not sunk in carnal *pleasure*. *Milton.*

3. Approbation.

The Lord taketh *pleasure* in them that fear him. *Psalms.*

4. What the will dictates.

Use your *pleasure*; if your love do not persuade you to come, let not my letter. *Shakesp. Merch. of Venice.*

He will do his *pleasure* on Babylon. *Is.* xlviii.

5. Choice; arbitrary will.

We ascribe not only effects depending on the natural period of time unto arbitrary calculations, and such as vary at *pleasure*, but confirm our tenets by the uncertain account of others. *Brown's Vulgar Errours*, *b.* iv.

Half their fleet offends
His open side, and high above him shews;
Upon the rest at *pleasure* he descends,
And doubly harm'd, he double harm bestows. *Dryden.*
Raise tempests at your *pleasure*. *Dryden.*

We can at *pleasure* move several parts of our bodies. *Locke.*

All the land in their dominions being acquired by conquest, was disposed by them according to their *pleasure*. *Arbuthnot.*

To PLEA'SURE. *v. a.* [from the noun.] To please; to gratify. This word, though supported by good authority, is, I think, inelegant.

Things, thus set in order,
Shall further thy harvest, and *pleasure* thee best. *Tusser.*

I count it one of my greatest afflictions, that I cannot *pleasure* such an honourable gentleman. *Shakespeare.*

If what pleases him, shall *pleasure* you,
Fight closer, or good faith you'll catch a blow. *Shakesp.*

When the way of *pleasuring* and displeasuring lieth by the favourite, it is impossible any should be overgreat. *Bacon.*

Nothing is difficult to love; it will make a man cross his own inclinations to *pleasure* them whom he loves. *Tillotson.*

PLEA'SUREFUL. *adj.* [*pleasure* and *full.*] Pleasant; delightful. Obsolete.

This country, for the fruitfulness of the land and the conveniency of the sea, hath been reputed a very commodious and *pleasureful* country. *Abbot's Descript. of the World.*

Plebe'ian. *n. s.* [*plebeïen*, Fr. *plebeius*, Lat.] One of the lower people.

Let him
Hoist thee up to the shouting *plebeians*. *Shakespeare.*
You're *plebeians*, if they be senators. *Shakespeare.*

Upon the least intervals of peace, the quarrels between the nobles and the *plebeians* would revive. *Swift.*

Plebe'ian. *adj.*

1. Popular; consisting of mean persons.

As swine are to gardens, so are tumults to parliaments, and *plebeian* concourses to publick counsels. *King Charles.*

2. Belonging to the lower ranks.

He through the midst unmark'd,
In shew *plebeian* angel militant
Of lowest order. *Milton's Par. Lost, b.* x.

3. Vulgar; low; common.

To apply notions philosophical to *plebeian* terms; or to say, where the notions cannot fitly be reconciled, that there wanteth a term or nomenclature for it, as the ancients used, they be but shifts of ignorance. *Bacon's Nat. Hist.*

The differences of mouldable and not mouldable, scissible and not scissible are *plebeian* notions. *Bacon.*

Dishonour not the vengeance I design'd.
A queen! and own a base *plebeian* mind! *Dryden.*

Pledge. *n. s.* [*pleige*, Fr. *pieggio*, Italian.]

1. Any thing put to pawn.

2. A gage; any thing given by way of warrant or security; a pawn.

These men at the first were only pitied; the great humility, zeal and devotion, which appeared to be in them, was in all men's opinion a *pledge* of their harmless meaning. *Hooker.*

If none appear to prove upon thy person
Thy heinous, manifest and many treasons;
There is my *pledge*, I'll prove it on thy heart. *Shakespeare.*

That voice their liveliest *pledge*
Of hope in fears and dangers. *Milton.*

Money is necessary both for counters and for *pledges*, and carrying with it even reckoning and security. *Locke.*

Hymen shall be aton'd, shall join two hearts,
And Aribert shall be the *pledge* of peace. *Rowe.*

3. A surety; a bail; an hostage.

What purpose could there be of treason, when the Guianians offered to leave *pledges*, six for one. *Raleigh.*

Good sureties will we have for thy return,
And at thy *pledges* peril keep thy day. *Dryden.*

To Pledge. *v. a.* [*pleiger*, Fr. *pieggiare*, Italian.]

1. To put in pawn.

Asleep and naked as an Indian lay,
An honest factor stole a gem away;
He *pledg'd* it to the knight; the knight had wit,
So kept the diamond. *Pope.*

2. To give as warrant or security.

3. To secure by a pledge.

I accept her;
And here to *pledge* my vow, I give my hand. *Shakesp.*

4. To invite to drink, by accepting the cup or health after another.

The fellow, that
Parts bread with him, and *pledges*
The breath of him in a divided draught,
Is th' readiest man to kill him. *Shakesp. Timon of Athens.*

To you noble lord of Westmoreland.
—I *pledge* your grace. *Shakesp. Henry* IV.

That flexanimous orator began the king of Homebia's health; he presently *pledg'd* it. *Howel's Vocal Forest.*

Ple'dget. *n. s.* [*plagghe*, Dutch.] A small mass of lint.

I applied a *pledget* of basilicon. *Wiseman's Surgery.*

Ple'iads. } *n. s.* [*pleiades*, Lat. πλειάδες.] A northern con-
Ple'iades. } stellation.

The *pleiades* before him danc'd,
Shedding sweet influence. *Milton.*

Then sailors quarter'd heav'n, and found a name
For *pleiads*, hyads and the northern car. *Dryden.*

Ple'narily. *adv.* [from *plenary.*] Fully; completely.

The cause is made a plenary cause, and ought to be determined *plenarily*. *Ayliffe's Parergon.*

PLE'NARY. *adj.* [from *plenus*, Lat.] Full; complete.

I am far from denying that compliance on my part, for *plenary* consent it was not, to his destruction. *King Charles.*

The cause is made a *plenary* cause. *Ayliffe.*

A treatise on a subject should be *plenary* or full, so that nothing may be wanting, nothing which is proper omitted. *Watts.*

Ple'nary. *n. s.* Decisive procedure.

A bare institution without induction does not make a *plenary* against the king, where he has a title to present. *Ayliffe.*

Ple'nariness. *n. s.* [from *plenary.*] Fulness; completeness.

Ple'nilunary. *adj.* [from *plenilunium*, Lat.] Relating to the full moon.

If we add the two Egyptian days in every month, the interlunary and *plenilunary* exemptions, there would arise above an hundred more. *Brown's Vulgar Errours.*

Ple'nipotence. *n. s.* [from *plenus* and *potentia*, Lat. Fulness of power.

Ple'nipotent. *adj.* [*plenipotens*, Lat.] Invested with full power.

My substitutes I send you, and create
Plenipotent on earth, of matchless might
Issuing from me. *Milton's Par. Lost*, x.

Plenipote'ntiary. *n. s.* [*plenipotentiaire*, Fr.] A negotiator invested with full power.

They were only the *plenipotentiary* monks of the patriarchal monks. *Stillingfleet.*

Ple'nist. *n. s.* [from *plenus*, Lat.] One that holds all space to be full of matter.

Those spaces, which the vacuists would have empty, because devoid of air, the *plenists* do not prove replenished with subtle matter by any sensible effects. *Boyle.*

Ple'nitude. *n. s.* [*plenitudo*, from *plenus*, Lat. *plenitude*, Fr.]

1. Fulness; the contrary to vacuity.

If there were every where an absolute *plenitude* and density without any pores between the particles of bodies, all bodies of equal dimensions would contain an equal quantity of matter, and consequently be equally ponderous. *Bentley's Sermons.*

2. Repletion; animal fulness; plethory.

Relaxation from *plenitude* is cured by spare diet. *Arbuth.*

3. Exuberance; abundance.

The *plenitude* of the pope's power of dispensing was the main question. *Bacon's Henry* VII.

4. Completeness.

The *plenitude* of William's fame
Can no accumulated stores receive. *Prior.*

Ple'nteous. *adj.* [from *plenty.*]

1. Copious; exuberant; abundant.

Author of evil, unknown till thy revolt
Now *plenteous* these acts of hateful strife. *Milton.*

Two *plenteous* fountains the whole prospect crown'd;
This through the gardens leads its streams around. *Pope.*

2. Fruitful; fertile.

Take up the fifth part of the land in the seven *plenteous* years. *Genesis* xli. 34.

Lab'ring the soil and reaping *plenteous* crop. *Milton.*

Ple'nteously. *adv.* [from *plenteous.*] Copiously; abundantly; exuberantly.

Thy due from me is tears,
Which nature, love and filial tenderness
Shall, O dear father, pay thee *plenteously*. *Shakesp.*

God created the great whales and each
Soul living, each that crept, which *plenteously*
The waters generated. *Milton's Par. Lost, b.* vii.

God proves us in this life, that he may the more *plenteously* reward us in the next. *Wake's Preparation for Death.*

Ple'nteousness. *n. s.* [from *plenteous.*] Abundance; fertility.

The seven years of *plenteousness* in Egypt were ended. *Genesis.*

Ple'ntiful. *adj.* [*plenty* and *full.*] Copious; abundant; exuberant; fruitful.

To Amalthea he gave a country, bending like a horn; whence the tale of Amalthea's *plentiful* horn. *Raleigh.*

He that is *plentiful* in expences, will hardly be preserved from decay. *Bacon's Essays.*

If it be a long winter, it is commonly a more *plentiful* year. *Bacon's Nat. Hist.*

When they had a *plentiful* harvest, the farmer had hardly any corn. *L'Estrange.*

Alcibiades was a young man of noble birth, excellent education and a *plentiful* fortune. *Swift.*

Ple'ntifully. *adv.* [from *plentiful.*] Copiously; abundantly.

They were not multiplied before, but they were at that time *plentifully* encreased. *Brown's Vulgar Errours.*

Bern is *plentifully* furnished with water, there being a great multitude of fountains. *Addison's Remarks on Italy.*

Ple'ntifulness. *n. s.* [from *plentiful.*] The state of being plentiful; abundance; fertility.

PLE'NTY. *n. s.* [from *plenus*, full.]

1. Abundance; such a quantity as is more than enough.

Peace,
Dear nurse of arts, *plenties* and joyful birth. *Shakesp.*

What makes land, as well as other things, dear, is *plenty* of buyers, and but few sellers; and so *plenty* of sellers and few buyers makes land cheap *Locke.*

2. Fruitfulness; exuberance.

The teeming clouds
Descend in gladsome *plenty* o'er the world. *Thomson.*

3. It is used, I think, barbarously for *plentiful.*

To grass with thy calves,
Where water is *plenty*. *Tusser's Husbandry.*

If reasons were as *plenty* as black berries, I would give no man a reason on compulsion. *Shakesp. Henry* IV.

4. A state in which enough is had and enjoyed.

Ye shall eat in *plenty* and be satisfied, and praise the Lord. *Joel* ii. 26.

PLE'ONASM. *n. s.* [*pleonasme*, Fr. *pleonasmus*, Lat.] A figure of rhetorick, by which more words are used than are necessary.

PLESH. *n. s.* [A word used by *Spenser* instead of *plash*, for the convenience of rhyme.] A puddle; a boggy marsh.

Out of the wound the red blood flowed fresh,
That underneath his feet soon made a purple *plesh*. *Spenser.*

PLE'THORA. *n. s.* [from πληθωρα.] The state in which the vessels are fuller of humours than is agreeable to a natural state or health; arises either from a diminution of some natural evacuations, or from debauch and feeding higher or more in quantity than the ordinary powers of the viscera can digest: evacuations and exercise are its remedies.

The diseases of the fluids are a *plethora*, or too great abundance of laudable juices. *Arbuthnot on Aliments.*

PLETHORE'TICK. } PLETHO'RICK. } *adj.* [from *plethora.*] Having a full habit.

The fluids, as they consist of spirit, water, salts, oil and terrestrial parts, differ according to the redundance of the whole or of any of these; and therefore the *plethorick* are phlegmatick, oily, saline, earthy or dry. *Arbuthnot.*

PLE'THORY. *n. s.* [*plethore*, Fr. from πληθώρα.] Fulness of habit.

In too great repletion, the elastick force of the tube throws the fluid with too great a force, and subjects the animal to the diseases depending upon a *plethory*. *Arbuthnot.*

PLE'VIN. *n. s.* [*pleuvine*, Fr. *plevina*, law Lat.] In law, a warrant or assurance. See REPLEVIN. *Dict.*

PLEU'RISY. *n. s.* [πλευρῖτις; *pleuresie*, Fr. *pleuritis*, Lat.]

Pleurisy is an inflammation of the pleura, though it is hardly distinguishable from an inflammation of any other part of the breast, which are all from the same cause, a stagnated blood; and are to be remedied by evacuation, suppuration or expectoration, or all together. *Quincy.*

PLEURI'TICAL. } PLEU'RITICK. } *adj.* [from *pleurisy.*]

1. Diseased with a pleurisy.

The viscous matter, which lies like leather upon the extravasated blood of *pleuritick* people, may be dissolved by a due degree of heat. *Arbuthnot on Aliments.*

2. Denoting a pleurisy.

His blood was *pleuritical*, it had neither colour nor consistence. *Wiseman's Surgery.*

PLI'ABLE. *adj.* [*pliable*, from *plier*, Fr. to bend.]

1. Easy to be bent; flexible.

Though an act be never so sinful, they will strip it of its guilt, and make the very law so *pliable* and bending, that it shall be impossible to be broke. *South's Sermons.*

Whether the different motions of the animal spirits may have any effect on the mould of the face, when the lineaments are *pliable* and tender, I shall leave to the curious. *Add.*

2. Flexible of disposition; easy to be persuaded.

PLI'ABLENESS. *n. s.* [from *pliable.*]

1. Flexibility; easiness to be bent.
2. Flexibility of mind.

Compare the ingenuous *pliableness* to virtuous counsels in youth, as it comes fresh out of the hands of nature, with the confirmed obstinacy in most sorts of sin, that is to be found in an aged sinner. *South's Sermons.*

PLI'ANCY. *n. s.* [from *pliant.*] Easiness to be bent.

Had not exercise been necessary, nature would not have given such an activity to the limbs, and such a *pliancy* to every part, as produces those compressions and extensions necessary for the preservation of such a system. *Addison's Spectator.*

PLI'ANT. *adj.* [*pliant*, French.]

1. Bending; tough; flexile; flexible; lithe; limber.

An anatomist promised to dissect a woman's tongue, and examine whether the fibres may not be made up of a finer and more *pliant* thread. *Addison's Spectator*, Nº 247.

2. Easy to take a form.

Particles of heav'nly fire,
Or earth but new divided from the sky,
And *pliant* still retain'd th' etherial energy. *Dryden.*
As the wax melts that to the flame I hold,
Pliant and warm may still her heart remain,
Soft to the print, but ne'er turn hard again. *Granville.*

3. Easily complying.

In languages the tongue is more *pliant* to all sounds, the joints more supple to all feats of activity, in youth than afterwards. *Bacon's Essays.*

Those, who bore bulwarks on their backs,
Now practise ev'ry *pliant* gesture,
Op'ning their trunk for ev'ry tester. *Swift's Miscel.*

4. Easily persuaded.

The will was then ductile and *pliant* to right reason, it met the dictates of a clarified understanding halfway. *South.*

PLI'ANTNESS. *n. s.* [from *pliant.*] Flexibility; toughness.

Greatness of weight, closeness of parts, fixation, *pliantness* or softness. *Bacon's Nat. Hist.*

PLI'CATURE. } PLICA'TION. } *n. s.* [*plicatura*, from *plico*, Lat.] Fold; double. *Plication* is used somewhere in *Clarissa*.

PLI'ERS. *n. s.* [from *ply.*] An instrument by which any thing is laid hold on to bend it.

Pliers are of two sorts, flat-nosed and round-nosed; their office is to hold and fasten upon a small work, and to fit it in its place: the round-nosed *pliers* are used for turning or boring wire or small plate into a circular form. *Moxon.*

I made a detention by a small pair of *pliers*. *Wiseman.*

To PLIGHT. *v. a.* [*plichten*, Dutch.]

1. To pledge; to give as surety.

He *plighted* his right hand
Unto another love, and to another land. *Fairy Queen.*
Saint Withold
Met the night mare, and her name told,
Bid her alight, and her troth *plight*. *Shakesp. King Lear.*
I again in Henry's royal name,
Give thee her hand for sign of *plighted* faith. *Shakespeare.*
Here my inviolable faith I *plight*,
Lo, thou be my defence, I, thy delight. *Dryden.*
New loves you seek,
New vows to *plight*, and *plighted* vows to break. *Dryden.*
I'll never mix my *plighted* hands with thine,
While such a cloud of mischiefs hangs about us. *Addison.*

2. To braid; to weave. [from *plico*, Lat. whence to ply or bend, and *plight*, *pleight* or *plait*, a fold or flexure.]

Her head she fondly would aguise
With gaudie girlonds, or fresh flowrets dight
About her neck, or rings of rushes *plight*. *Fairy Queen.*
I took it for a fairy vision
Of some gay creatures of the element,
That in the colours of the rainbow live,
And play i' th' *plighted* clouds. *Milton.*

PLIGHT. *n. s.* [This word *Skinner* imagines to be derived from the Dutch, *plicht*, office or employment; but *Junius* observes, that plihτ, Saxon, signifies distress or pressing danger; whence, I suppose, *plight* was derived, it being generally used in a bad sense.]

1. Condition; state.

When as the careful dwarf had told,
And made ensample of their mournful sight
Unto his master, he no longer would
There dwell in peril of like painful *plight*. *Fa. Queen.*
I think myself in better *plight* for a lender than you are. *Shakespeare.*
Beseech your highness,
My women may be with me; for, you see,
My *plight* requires it. *Shakesp. Winter's Tale.*
They in lowliest *plight* repentant stood
Praying. *Milton's Par. Lost, b.* xi.
Thou must not here
Lie in this miserable loathsome *plight*. *Milton.*
Most perfect hero tried in heaviest *plight*
Of labours huge and hard. *Milton.*

2. Good case.

Who abuseth his cattle and starves them for meat,
By carting or plowing, his gaine is not great;
Where he that with labour can use them aright,
Hath gaine to his comfort, and cattel in *plight*. *Tusser.*

3. Pledge; gage. [from the verb.]

That lord, whose hand must take my *plight*, shall carry
Half my love with him, half my care and duty. *Shakesp.*

4. [From to *plight.*] A fold; a pucker; a double; a purfle; a plait.

Yclad, for fear of scorching air,
All in a silken camus, lilly white,
Purfled upon with many a folded *plight*. *Fairy Queen.*

PLINTH. *n. s.* [πλίνθος.] In architecture, is that square member which serves as a foundation to the base of a pillar; Vitruvius calls the upper part or abacus of the Tuscan pillar, a *plinth*, because it resembles a square tile: moreover, the same denomination is sometimes given to a thick wall, wherein there are two or three bricks advanced in form of a platband. *Harris.*

To PLOD. *v. n.* [*ploeghen*, Dutch. *Skinner.*]

1. To toil; to moil; to drudge; to travel.

A *plodding* diligence brings us sooner to our journey's end, than a fluttering way of advancing by starts. *L'Estrange.*

He knows better than any man, what is not to be written; and never hazards himself so far as to fall, but *plods* on deliberately, and, as a grave man ought, puts his staff before him. *Dryden's State of Innocence.*

Th' unletter'd christian, who believes in gross,
Plods on to heav'n, and ne'er is at a loss. *Dryden.*

2. To travel laboriously.

Rogues, *plod* away o' the hoof, seek shelter, pack. *Sha.*
If one of mean affairs
May *plod* it in a week, why may not I
Glide thither in a day. *Shakesp. Cymbeline.*
Hast thou not held my stirrup?
Bare-headed, *plodded* by my foot-cloth mule,
And thought thee happy when I shook my head? *Shakesp.*
Ambitious love hath so in me offended,
That barefoot *plod* I the cold ground upon,
With sainted vow my faults to have amended. *Shakesp.*

3. To ſtudy cloſely and dully.

Univerſal *plodding* priſons up
The nimble ſpirits in the arteries;
As motion and long-during action tires
The ſinewy vigour of the traveller. *Shakeſp.*

He *plods* to turn his am'rous ſuit
T' a plea in law, and proſecute. *Hudibras, p.* iii.

She reaſon'd without *plodding* long,
Nor ever gave her judgment wrong. *Swift's Miſcel.*

PLO'DDER. *n. ſ.* [from *plod.*] A dull heavy laborious man.

Study is like the heav'ns glorious ſun,
That will not be deep ſearch'd with ſaucy looks;
What have continual *plodders* ever won,
Save baſe authority from other's books? *Shakeſp.*

PLOT. *n. ſ.* [plot, Saxon. See PLAT.]

1. A ſmall extent of ground.

It was a choſen *plot* of fertile land,
Amongſt wide waves ſet like a little neſt,
As if it had by nature's cunning hand
Been choicely picked out from all the reſt. *Fairy Queen.*

Plant ye with alders or willowes a *plot*,
Where yeerely as needeth mo poles may be got. *Tuſſer.*

Many unfrequented *plots* there are,
Fitted by kind for rape and villainy. *Shakeſpeare.*

Were there but this ſingle *plot* to loſe,
This mould of Marcius, they to duſt would grind it,
And throw't againſt the wind. *Shakeſp.*

When we mean to build,
We firſt ſurvey the *plot*, then draw the model,
And when we ſee the figure of the houſe,
Then we muſt rate the coſt of the erection. *Shakeſp.*

Weeds grow not in the wild uncultivated waſte, but in garden *plots* under the negligent hand of a gardener. *Locke.*

2. A plantation laid out.

Some goddeſs inhabiteth this region, who is the ſoul of this ſoil; for neither is any leſs than a goddeſs, worthy to be ſhrined in ſuch a heap of pleaſures; nor any leſs than a goddeſs could have made it ſo perfect a *plot*. *Sidney.*

3. A form; a ſcheme; a plan.

The law of England never was properly applied unto the Iriſh nation, as by a purpoſed *plot* of government, but as they could inſinuate and ſteal themſelves under the ſame by their humble carriage. *Spenſer on Ireland.*

4. [Imagined by *Skinner* to be derived from *platform*, but evidently contracted from *complot*, Fr.] A conſpiracy; a ſecret deſign formed againſt another.

I have o'erheard a *plot* of death upon him. *Shakeſp.*

Eaſy ſeems the thing to every one,
That nought could croſs their *plot*, or them ſuppreſs. *Dan.*

5. An intrigue; an affair complicated, involved and embarraſſed; the ſtory of a play, compriſing an artful involution of affairs, unravelled at laſt by ſome unexpected means.

If the *plot* or intrigue muſt be natural, and ſuch as ſprings from the ſubject, then the winding up of the *plot* muſt be a probable conſequence of all that went before. *Pope.*

Nothing muſt be ſung between the acts,
But what ſome way conduces to the *plot*. *Roſcommon.*

Our author
Produc'd his play, and begg'd the knight's advice,
Made him obſerve the ſubject and the *plot*,
The manners, paſſions, unities, what not? *Pope.*

They deny the *plot* to be tragical, becauſe its cataſtrophe is a wedding, which hath ever been accounted comical. *Gay.*

6. Stratagem; ſecret combination to any ill end.

Fruſtrate all our *plots* and wiles. *Milton.*

7. Contrivance; deep reach of thought.

Who ſays he was not
A man of much *plot*,
May repent that falſe accuſation;
Having plotted and pen'd
Six plays to attend
The farce of his negociation. *Denham.*

To PLOT. *v. n.* [from the noun.]

1. To form ſchemes of miſchief againſt another, commonly againſt thoſe in authority.

The ſubtle traitor
This day had *plotted* in the council houſe
To murther me. *Shakeſpeare's Richard* III.

The wicked *plotteth* againſt the juſt. *Pſalm* xxxvii. 12.

He who envies now thy ſtate,
Who now is *plotting* how he may ſeduce
Thee from obedience. *Milton's Par. Loſt, b.* vi.

The wolf that round th' incloſure prowl'd
To leap the fence, now *plots* not on the fold. *Dryden.*

2. To contrive; to ſcheme.

The count tells the marquis of a flying noiſe, that the prince did *plot* to be ſecretly gone; to which the marquis anſwer'd, that though love had made his highneſs ſteal out of his own country, yet fear would never make him run out of Spain. *Wotton.*

To PLOT. *v. a.*

1. To plan; to contrive.

With ſhame and ſorrow fill'd:
Shame for his folly; ſorrow out of time
For *plotting* an unprofitable crime. *Dryden.*

2. To deſcribe according to ichnography.

This treatiſe *plotteth* down Cornwall, as it now ſtandeth, for the particulars. *Carew's Survey of Cornwall.*

PLO'TTER. *n. ſ.* [from *plot.*]

1. Conſpirator.

As for you, Colonel, we ſhall try who's the greater *plotter* of us two; I againſt the ſtate, or you againſt the petticoat. *Dryden's Spaniſh Fryar.*

2. Contriver.

An irreligious moor,
Chief architect and *plotter* of theſe woes. *Shakeſp.*

PLO'VER. *n. ſ.* [*pluvier*, Fr. *pluvialis*, Lat.] A lapwing. A bird.

Of wild birds, Cornwall hath quail, rail, patridge, pheaſant and *plover*. *Carew's Survey of Cornwall.*

Scarce
The bittern knows his time: or from the ſhore,
The *plovers* when to ſcatter o'er the heath
And ſing. *Thomſon's Spring.*

PLOUGH. *n. ſ.* [ploȝ, Saxon; *plog*, Daniſh; *ploegh*, Dutch.]

1. The inſtrument with which the furrows are cut in the ground to receive the ſeed.

Look how the purple flower, which the *plough*
Hath ſhorn in ſunder, languiſhing doth die. *Peacham.*

Some *ploughs* differ in the length and ſhape of their beams; ſome in the ſhare, others in the coulter and handles. *Mort.*

In ancient times the ſacred *plough* employ'd
The kings and awful fathers. *Thomſon.*

2. A kind of plane. *Ainſworth.*

To PLOUGH. *v. n.* To practiſe aration; to turn up the ground in order to ſow feed.

Rebellion, inſolence, ſedition
We ourſelves have *plough'd* for, ſow'd and ſcatter'd,
By mingling them with us. *Shakeſp. Coriolanus.*

Doth the ploughman *plough* all day to ſow? *Iſ.* xxviii. 24.

They only give the land one *ploughing*, and ſow white oats, and harrow them as they do black. *Mortimer.*

To PLOUGH. *v. a.*

1. To turn up with the plough.

Let the Volſcians
Plough Rome and harrow Italy. *Shakeſp. Coriolanus.*

Shou'd any ſlave, ſo lewd, belong to you?
No doubt you'd ſend the rogue, in fetters bound,
To work in bridewell, or to *plough* your ground. *Dryden.*

A man may *plough*, in ſtiff grounds the firſt time fallowed, an acre a day. *Mortimer.*

You find it *ploughed* into ridges and furrows. *Mortimer.*

2. To bring to view by the plough.

Another of a duſky colour, near black; there are of theſe frequently *ploughed* up in the fields of Weldon. *Woodward.*

3. To furrow; to divide.

When the prince her fun'ral rites had paid,
He *plough'd* the Tyrrhene ſeas with ſails diſplay'd. *Addiſ.*

With ſpeed we *plough* the watry way,
My power ſhall guard thee. *Pope's Odyſſey.*

4. To tear; to furrow.

Let
Patient Octavia *plough* thy viſage up
With her prepared nails. *Shakeſp. Ant. and Cleopatra.*

PLOU'GHBOY. *n. ſ.* [*plough* and *boy.*] A boy that follows the plough; a coarſe ignorant boy.

A *ploughboy*, that has never ſeen any thing but thatched houſes and his pariſh church, imagines that thatch belongs to the very nature of a houſe. *Watts's Logick.*

PLOU'GHER. *n. ſ.* [from *plough.*] One who ploughs or cultivates ground.

When the country ſhall be repleniſhed with corn, as it will, if well followed; for the country people themſelves are great *ploughers* and ſmall ſpenders of corn: then there ſhould be good ſtore of magazines erected. *Spenſer.*

PLOUGHLA'ND. *n. ſ.* [*plough* and *land.*] A farm for corn.

Who hath a *ploughland* caſts all his feed-corn there,
And yet allows his ground more corn ſhould bear. *Donne.*

In this book are entered the names of the manors or inhabited townſhips, the number of *ploughlands* that each contains, and the number of the inhabitants. *Hale.*

PLOU'GHMAN. *n. ſ.* [*plough* and *man.*]

1. One that attends or uſes the plough.

When ſhepherds pipe on oaten ſtraws,
And merry larks are *ploughmen's* clocks,
The cuckow then on ev'ry tree. *Shakeſpeare.*

God provides the good things of the world, to ſerve the needs of nature by the labours of the *ploughman*. *Taylor.*

The careful *ploughman* doubting ſtands. *Milton.*

Your reign no leſs aſſures the *ploughman*'s peace,
Than the warm ſun advances his increaſe. *Waller.*

The merchant gains by peace, and the ſoldiers by war, the ſhepherd by wet ſeaſons, and the *ploughmen* by dry. *Temple.*

Who can ceaſe t' admire
The *ploughman* conſul in his coarſe attire. *Dryden.*
One
My *ploughman*'s is, t'other my ſhepherd's ſon. *Dryden.*

2. A groſs ignorant ruſtick.

Her hand! to whoſe ſoft ſeizure
The cignet's down is harſh, and, ſpite of ſenſe,
Hard as the palm of *ploughman.* *Shakeſp.*

3. A ſtrong laborious man.

A weak ſtomach will turn rye bread into vinegar, and a *ploughman* will digeſt it. *Arbuthnot on Aliments.*

PLOU'GHMONDAY. *n. ſ.* The monday after twelfth-day.

Ploughmunday next after that the twelftide is paſt,
Bids out with the plough, the worſt huſband is laſt. *Tuſſer.*

PLOUGHSHA'RE. *n. ſ.* [*plough* and *ſhare.*] The part of the plough that is perpendicular to the coulter.

As the earth was turned up, the *ploughſhare* lighted upon a great ſtone; we pulled that up, and ſo found ſome pretty things. *Sidney, b.* ii.

The pretty innocent walks blindfold among burning *ploughſhares* without being ſcorched. *Addiſon's Spectator.*

To PLUCK. *v. a.* [ploccian, Sax. *plocken*, Dutch.]

1. To pull with nimbleneſs or force; to ſnatch; to pull; to draw; to force on or off; to force up or down; to act upon with violence. It is very generally and licentiouſly uſed, particularly by *Shakeſpeare.*

It ſeemed better unto that noble king to plant a peaceable government among them, than by violent means to *pluck* them under. *Spenſer on Ireland.*

You were crown'd before,
And that high royalty was ne'er *pluck'd* off. *Shakeſp.*
Pluck down my officers, break my decrees,
For now a time is come to mock at form. *Shakeſp.*
Can'ſt thou not
Pluck from the memory a rooted ſorrow,
And with ſome ſweet oblivious antidote
Cleanſe the ſtuff'd boſom. *Shakeſpeare's Macbeth.*

When yet he was but tender bodied, when youth with comelineſs *plucked* all gaze his way. *Shakeſp. Macbeth.*

I gave my love a ring;
He would not *pluck* it from his finger, for the wealth
That the world maſters. *Shakeſp. Merch. of Venice.*
If you do wrongfully ſeize Hereford's right,
You *pluck* a thouſand dangers on your head. *Shakeſp.*
Dive into the bottom of the deep,
Where fathom line could never touch the ground,
And *pluck* up drowned honour by the locks. *Shakeſp.*

I will *pluck* them up by the roots out of my land. 2 *Chron.*

Pluck away his crop with his feathers. *Lev.* i. 16.

A time to plant, and a time to *pluck* up that which is planted. *Eccluſ.* iii. 2.

They *pluck* off their ſkin from off them. *Mic.* iii. 2.

Diſpatch 'em quick, but firſt *pluck* out their tongues,
Leſt with their dying breath they ſow ſedition. *Addiſon.*
Beneath this ſhade the weary peaſant lies,
Plucks the broad leaf, and bids the breezes riſe. *Gay.*
From the back
Of herds and flocks, a thouſand tugging bills
Pluck hair and wool. *Thomſon's Spring.*

2. To ſtrip of feathers.

Since I *pluckt* geeſe, I knew not what it was to be beaten. *Shakeſpeare.*

I come to thee from plume *pluck'd* Richard. *Shakeſp.*

3. To pluck up a heart or ſpirit. A proverbial expreſſion for taking up or reſuming of courage.

He willed them to *pluck* up their hearts, and make all things ready for a new aſſault, wherein he expected they ſhould with couragious reſolution recompenſe their late cowardice. *Knolles's Hiſtory of the Turks.*

PLUCK. *n. ſ.* [from the verb.]

1. A pull; a draw; a ſingle act of plucking.

Birds kept coming and going all the day long; but ſo few at a time, that the man did not think them worth a *pluck.* *L'Eſtrange.*

Were the ends of the bones dry, they could not, without great difficulty, obey the *plucks* and attractions of the motory muſcles. *Ray on the Creation.*

2. [*Plughk*, Erſe. I know not whether derived from the Engliſh, rather than the Engliſh from the Erſe.] The heart, liver and lights of an animal.

PLU'CKER. *n. ſ.* [from *pluck.*] One that plucks.

Thou ſetter up and *plucker* down of kings! *Shakeſp.*

Pull it as ſoon as you ſee the ſeed begin to grow brown, at which time let the *pluckers* tie it up in handfuls. *Mortimer.*

PLUG. *n. ſ.* [*plugg*, Swediſh; *plugghe*, Dutch.] A ſtopple; any thing driven hard into another body.

Shutting the valve with the *plug*, draw down the ſucker to the bottom. *Boyle.*

The fighting with a man's own ſhadow, conſiſts in the brandiſhing of two ſticks graſped in each hand, and loaden with *plugs* of lead at either end: this opens the cheſt. *Addiſ.*

In bottling wine, fill your mouth full of corks, together with a large *plug* of tobacco. *Swift's Direct. to the Butler.*

To PLUG. *v. a.* [from the noun.] To ſtop with a plug.

A tent *plugging* up the orifice, would make the matter recur to the part diſpoſed to receive it. *Sharp's Surgery.*

PLUM. *n. ſ.* [plum, plumtreop, Sax. *blumme*, Daniſh. A cuſtom has prevailed of writing *plumb*, but improperly.

1. A fruit.

The flower conſiſts of five leaves, which are placed in a circular order, and expand in form of a roſe, from whoſe flower-cup riſes the pointal, which afterwards becomes an oval or globular fruit, having a ſoft fleſhy pulp, ſurrounding an hard oblong ſtone, for the moſt part pointed; to which ſhould be added, the footſtalks are long and ſlender, and have but a ſingle fruit upon each: the ſpecies are; 1. The jeanhâtive, or white primordian. 2. The early black damaſk, commonly called the Morocco *plum.* 3. The little black damaſk *plum.* 4. The great damaſk violet of Tours. 5. The Orleans *plum.* 6. The Fotheringham *plum.* 7. The Perdrigon *plum.* 8. The violet Perdrigon *plum.* 9. The white Perdrigon *plum.* 10. The red imperial *plum*, ſometimes called the red bonum magnum. 11. The white imperial bonum magnum; white Holland or Mogul *plum.* 12. The Cheſton *plum.* 13. The apricot *plum.* 14. The maître claude. 15. La roche-courbon, or diaper rouge; the red diaper *plum.* 16. Queen Claudia. 17. Myrobalan *plum.* 18. The green gage *plum.* 19. The cloth of gold *plum.* 20. St. Catharine *plum.* 21. The royal *plum.* 22. La mirabelle. 23. The Brignole *plum.* 24. The empreſs. 25. The monſieur *plum*: this is ſometimes called the Wentworth *plum*, both reſembling the bonum magnum. 26. The cherry *plum.* 27. The white pear *plum.* 28. The muſcle *plum.* 29. The St. Julian *plum.* 30. The black bullace-tree *plum.* 31. The white bullace-tree *plum.* 32. The black thorn or ſloe-tree *plum.* *Miller.*

Philoſophers in vain enquired, whether the ſummum bonum conſiſted in riches, bodily delights, virtue or contemplation: they might as reaſonably have diſputed, whether the beſt reliſh were in apples, *plums* or nuts. *Locke.*

2. Raiſin; grape dried in the ſun.

I will dance, and eat *plums* at your wedding. *Shakeſp.*

3. [In the cant of the city.] The ſum of one hundred thouſand pounds.

By the preſent edict, many a man in France will ſwell into a *plum*, who fell ſeveral thouſand pounds ſhort of it the day before. *Addiſon.*

The miſer muſt make up his *plum*,
And dares not touch the hoarded ſum. *Prior.*

By fair dealing John had acquired ſome *plums*, which he might have kept, had it not been for his law-ſuit. *Arbuth.*

Aſk you,
Why ſhe and Sapho raiſe that monſtrous ſum?
Alas! they fear a man will coſt a *plum.* *Pope.*

4. A kind of play, called how many *plums* for a penny. *Ainſ.*

PLU'MAGE. *n. ſ.* [*plumage*, Fr.] Feathers; ſuit of feathers.

The *plumage* of birds exceeds the piloſity of beaſts. *Bacon.*

Say, will the falcon, ſtooping from above,
Smit with her varying *plumage*, ſpare the dove. *Pope.*

PLUMB. *n. ſ.* [*plomb*, Fr. *plumbum*, Lat.] A plummet; a leaden weight let down at the end of a line.

If the *plumb* line hang juſt upon the perpendicular, when the level is ſet flat down upon the work, the work is level. *Moxon's Mechanical Exerciſes.*

PLUMB. *adv.* [from the noun.] Perpendicularly to the horizon.

If all theſe atoms ſhould deſcend *plumb* down with equal velocity, being all perfectly ſolid and imporous, and the vacuum not reſiſting their motion, they would never the one overtake the other. *Ray on the Creation.*

Is it not a ſad thing to fall thus *plumb* into the grave? well one minute and dead the next. *Collier.*

To PLUMB. *v. a.* [from the noun.]

1. To ſound; to ſearch by a line with a weight at its end.

The moſt experienced ſeamen *plumbed* the depth of the channel. *Swift's Gulliver.*

2. To regulate any work by the plummet.

PLU'MBER. *n. ſ.* [*plombier*, Fr.] One who works upon lead. Commonly written and pronounced *plummer.*

PLU'MBERY. *n. ſ.* [from *plumber.*] Works of lead; the manufactures of a plumber. Commonly ſpelt *plummery.*

PLU'MCAKE. *n. ſ.* [*plum* and *cake.*] Cake made with raiſins.

He cramm'd them till their guts did ake
With caudle, cuſtard and *plumcake.* *Hudibras.*

PLUME. *n. ſ.* [*plume*, Fr. *pluma*, Lat.]

1. Feather of birds.

Let frantick Talbot triumph for a while,
And, like a peacock, ſweep along his tail;
We'll pull his *plumes*, and take away his train. *Shakeſp.*
Wings he wore of many a colour'd *plume.* *Milton.*

They appear made up of little bladders, like thoſe in the *plume* or ſtalk of a quill. *Grew's Muſæum.*

2. Feather worn as an ornament.

Let every feeble rumour ſhake your hearts,
Your enemies with nodding of their *plumes*
Fan you into deſpair. *Shakeſp. Coriolanus.*

Eastern travellers know that oſtridges feathers are common, and the ordinary *plume* of Janizaries. *Brown.*

The fearful infant
Daunted to ſee a face with ſteel o'erſpread,
And his high *plume* that nodded o'er his head. *Dryden.*

3. Pride; towering mien.

Great duke of Lancaſter, I come to thee
From *plume* pluckt Richard, who with willing ſoul
Adopts thee heir. *Shakeſpeare's Richard* II.

4. Token of honour; prize of conteſt.

Ambitious to win from me ſome *plume*. *Milton.*

5. *Plume* is a term uſed by botaniſts for that part of the ſeed of a plant, which in its growth becomes the trunk: it is incloſed in two ſmall cavities, formed in the lobes for its reception, and is divided at its looſe end into divers pieces, all cloſely bound together like a bunch of feathers, whence it has this name. *Quincy.*

To PLUME. *v. a.* [from the noun.]

1. To pick and adjuſt feathers.

Swans muſt be kept in ſome encloſed pond, where they may have room to come aſhore and *plume* themſelves. *Mort.*

2. [*Plumer*, Fr.] To ſtrip of feathers.

Such animals, as feed upon fleſh, devour ſome part of the feathers of the birds they gorge themſelves with, becauſe they will not take the pains fully to *plume* them. *Ray.*

3. To ſtrip; to pill.

They ſtuck not to ſay, that the king cared not to *plume* the nobility and people to feather himſelf. *Bacon.*

4. To place as a plume.

His ſtature reach'd the ſky, and on his creſt
Sat horror *plum'd*. *Milton's Par. Loſt, b.* iv.

5. To adorn with plumes.

Farewel the *plumed* troops, and the big war,
That make ambition virtue. *Shakeſp. Othello.*

PLUMEA'LLUM. *n. ſ.* [*alumen plumoſum*, Lat.] A kind of aſbeſtus.

Plumeallum, formed into the likeneſs of a wick, will adminiſter to the flame, and yet not conſume. *Wilkins.*

PLUMI'GEROUS. *adj.* [*pluma* and *gero*, Lat.] Having feathers; feathered. *Dict.*

PLU'MIPEDE. *n. ſ.* [*pluma* and *pes*, Lat.] A fowl that has feathers on the foot. *Dict.*

PLU'MMET. *n. ſ.* [from *plumb.*]

1. A weight of lead hung at a ſtring, by which depths are ſounded, and perpendicularity is diſcerned.

Deeper than did ever *plummet* ſound,
I'll drown my book. *Shakeſp. Tempeſt.*

Fly envious time
Call on the lazy leaden-ſtepping hours,
Whoſe ſpeed is but the heavy *plummet*'s pace. *Milton.*

2. Any weight.

God ſees the body of fleſh which you bear about you, and the *plummets* which it hangs upon your ſoul, and therefore, when you cannot riſe high enough to him, he comes down to you. *Duppa's Rules for Devotion.*

The heavineſs of theſe bodies, being always in the aſcending ſide of the wheel, muſt be counterpoiſed by a *plummet* faſtened about the pulley on the axis: this *plummet* will deſcend according as the ſand doth make the ſeveral parts of the wheel lighter or heavier. *Wilkins.*

PLUMO'SITY. *n. ſ.* [from *plumous.*] The ſtate of having feathers.

PLU'MOUS. *adj.* [*plumeux*, Fr. *plumoſus*, Lat.] Feathery; reſembling feathers.

This has a like *plumous* body in the middle, but finer. *Woodward on Foſſils.*

PLUMP. *adj.* [Of this word the etymology is not known. *Skinner* derives it from *pommelé*, Fr. full like a ripe apple; it might be more eaſily deduced from *plum*, which yet ſeems very harſh. *Junius* omits it.] Somewhat fat; not lean; ſleek; full and ſmooth.

The heifer, that valued itſelf upon a ſmooth coat and a *plump* habit of body, was taken up for a ſacrifice; but the ox, that was deſpiſed for his raw bones, went on with his work ſtill. *L'Eſtrange.*

Plump gentleman,
Get out as faſt as e'er you can;
Or ceaſe to puſh, or to exclaim,
You make the very croud you blame. *Prior.*

The famiſh'd cow
Grows *plump* and round, and full of mettle. *Swift.*

PLUMP. *n. ſ.* [from the adjective.] A knot; a tuft; a cluſter; a number joined in one maſs.

England, Scotland, Ireland lie all in a *plump* together, not acceſſible but by ſea. *Bacon.*

Warwick having eſpied certain *plumps* of Scottiſh horſemen ranging the field, returned towards the arriere to prevent danger. *Hayward.*

We reſted under a *plump* of trees. *Sandys.*

Spread upon a lake, with upward eye
A *plump* of fowl behold their foe on high;
They cloſe their trembling troop, and all attend
On whom the ſowſing eagle will deſcend. *Dryden.*

To PLUMP. *v. a.* [from the adjective.] To fatten; to ſwell; to make large.

The particles of air expanding themſelves, *plump* out the ſides of the bladder, and keep them turgid. *Boyle.*

I'm as lean as carrion; but a wedding at our houſe will *plump* me up with good chear. *L'Eſtrange.*

Let them lie for the dew and rain to *plump* them. *Mort.*

To PLUMP. *v. n.* [from the adverb.]

2. [From the adjective.] To be ſwollen. *Ainſworth.*

1. To fall like a ſtone into the water. A word formed from the ſound.

PLUMP. *adv.* [Probably corrupted from *plumb*, or perhaps formed from the ſound of a ſtone falling on the water.] With a ſudden fall.

I would fain now ſee 'em rowl'd
Down a hill, or from a bridge
Head-long caſt, to break their ridge;
Or to ſome river take 'em
Plump, and ſee if that would wake 'em. *B. Johnſon.*

Fluttering his pennons vain *plump* down he drops. *Milt.*

PLU'MPER. *n. ſ.* [from *plump.*] Something worn in the mouth to ſwell out the cheeks.

She dext'rouſly her *plumpers* draws,
That ſerve to fill her hollow jaws. *Swift's Miſcel.*

PLU'MPNESS. *n. ſ.* [from *plump.*] Fulneſs; diſpoſition towards fulneſs.

Thoſe convex glaſſes ſupply the defect of *plumpneſs* in the eye, and by encreaſing the refraction make the rays converge ſooner, ſo as to convene at the bottom of the eye. *Newton.*

PLU'MPORRIDGE. *n. ſ.* [*plum* and *porridge.*] Porridge with plums.

A rigid diſſenter, who dined at his houſe on Chriſtmas-day, eat very plentifully of his *plumporridge*. *Addiſon.*

PLUMPUDDING. *n. ſ.* [*plum* and *pudding.*] Pudding made with plums.

PLU'MPY. *adj.* Plump; fat.

Come, thou monarch of the vine,
Plumpy Bacchus, with pink eyne,
In thy vats our cares be drown'd. *Shakeſp.*

PLU'MY. *adj.* [from *plume.*] Feathered; covered with feathers.

Satan fell, and ſtraight a fiery globe
Of angels on full ſail of wing flew nigh,
Who on their *plumy* vans receiv'd him ſoft
From his uneaſy ſtation, and upbore
As on a floating couch through the blithe air. *Milton.*

Appear'd his *plumy* creſt, beſmear'd with blood. *Addiſon.*

Sometimes they are like a quill, with the *plumy* part only upon one ſide. *Grew's Coſmol. b.* i.

To PLU'NDER. *v. a.* [*plunderen*, Dutch.]

1. To pillage; to rob in an hoſtile way.

Nebuchadnezzar *plunders* the temple of God, and we find the fatal doom that afterwards befel him. *South's Sermons.*

Ships the fruits of their exaction brought,
Which made in peace a treaſure richer far,
Than what is *plunder'd* in the rage of war. *Dryden.*

2. To rob as a thief.

Their country's wealth our mightier miſers drain,
Or croſs, to *plunder* provinces, the main. *Pope.*

PLU'NDER. *n. ſ.* [from the verb.] Pillage; ſpoils gotten in war.

Let looſe the murmuring army on their maſters,
To pay themſelves with *plunder*. *Otway.*

PLU'NDERER. *n. ſ.* [from *plunder.*]

1. Hoſtile pillager; ſpoiler.

2. A thief; a robber.

It was a famous ſaying of William Rufus, whoſoever ſpares perjured men, robbers, *plunderers* and traitors, deprives all good men of their peace and quietneſs. *Addiſon.*

We cannot future violence o'ercome,
Nor give the miſerable province eaſe,
Since what one *plund'rer* left, the next will ſeize. *Dryden.*

To PLUNGE. *v. a.* [*plonger*, Fr.]

1. To put ſuddenly under water, or under any thing ſuppoſed liquid.

Plunge us in the flames. *Milton.*

Headlong from hence to *plunge* herſelf ſhe ſprings,
But ſhoots along ſupported on her wings. *Dryden.*

2. To put into any ſtate ſuddenly.

I mean to *plunge* the boy in pleaſing ſleep,
And raviſh'd in Idalian bow'rs to keep. *Dryden.*

3. To hurry into any diſtreſs.

O conſcience! into what abyſs of fears
And horrors haſt thou driv'n me? out of which
I find no way; from deep to deeper *plung'd*. *Milton.*

Without a prudent determination in matters before us, we ſhall be *plunged* into perpetual errors. *Watts.*

4. To force in ſuddenly. This word, to what action ſoever it be applied, commonly expreſſes either violence and ſuddenneſs in the agent, or diſtreſs in the patient.

At this advanc'd, and ſudden as the word,
In proud Plexippus' boſom *plung'd* the ſword. *Dryden.*

Let them not be too haſty to *plunge* their enquiries at once into the depths of knowledge. *Watts.*

To PLUNGE. *v. n.*

1. To ſink ſuddenly into water; to dive.

Accoutred as I was, I *plunged* in. *Shakeſp. Julius Cæſar.*

His courſer *plung'd*,
And threw him off; the waves whelm'd over him,
And helpleſs in his heavy arms he drown'd. *Dryden.*

When thou, thy ſhip o'erwhelm'd with waves, ſhalt be
Forc'd to *plunge* naked in the raging ſea. *Dryden.*

When tortoiſes have been a long time upon the water, their ſhell being dried in the ſun, they are eaſily taken; by reaſon they cannot *plunge* into the water nimbly enough. *Ray.*

2. To fall or ruſh into any hazard or diſtreſs.

He could find no other way to conceal his adultery, but to *plunge* into the guilt of a murther. *Tillotſon.*

Bid me for honour *plunge* into a war
Then ſhalt thou ſee that Marcus is not ſlow. *Addiſon.*

Impotent of mind and uncontroul'd,
He *plung'd* into the gulph which heav'n foretold. *Pope.*

Plunge. *n. ſ.*

1. Act of putting or ſinking under water.
2. Difficulty; ſtrait; diſtreſs.

She was weary of her life, ſince ſhe was brought to that *plunge*; to conceal her huſband's murder, or accuſe her ſon. *Sidney, b.* ii.

People, when put to a *plunge*, cry out to heaven for help, without helping themſelves. *L'Eſtrange.*

Wilt thou behold me ſinking in my woes?
And wilt thou not reach out a friendly arm,
To raiſe me from amidſt this *plunge* of ſorrows? *Addiſon.*

He muſt be a good man; a quality which Cicero and Quinctilian are much at a *plunge* in aſſerting to the Greek and Roman orators. *Baker's Reflections on Learning.*

Plu'ngeon. *n. ſ.* [*mergus*, Lat.] A ſea bird. *Ainſ.*

Plu'nger. *n. ſ.* [from *plunge.*] One that plunges; a diver.

Plu'nket. *n. ſ.* A kind of blue colour. *Ainſworth.*

PLU'RAL. *adj.* [*pluralis*, Lat.]

1. Implying more than one.

Thou haſt no faith left now, unleſs thoud'ſt two;
Better have none
Than *plural* faith, which is too much by one. *Shakeſp.*

2. [In grammar.]

The Greek and Hebrew have two variations, one to ſignify the number two, and another to ſignify a number of more than two; under one variation the noun is ſaid to be of the dual number, and under the other of the *plural.* *Clarke.*

Plu'ralist. *n. ſ.* [*pluraliſte*, Fr. from *plural.*] One that holds more eccleſiaſtical benefices than one with cure of ſouls.

If the *pluraliſts* would do their beſt to ſuppreſs curates, their number might be ſo retrenched, that they would not be in the leaſt formidable. *Collier on Pride.*

Plura'lity. *n. ſ.* [*pluralitè*, Fr.]

1. The ſtate of being or having a greater number.

It is not *plurality* of parts without majority of parts, that maketh the total greater; yet it ſeemeth to the eye a ſhorter diſtance of way, if it be all dead and continued, than if it have trees, whereby the eye may divide it. *Bacon.*

2. A number more than one.

Thoſe hereticks had introduced a *plurality* of gods, and ſo made the profeſſion of the unity part of the ſymbolum, that ſhould diſcriminate the orthodox from them. *Hammond.*

They could forego *plurality* of wives, though that be the main impediment to the converſion of the Eaſt Indies. *Bentl.*

'Tis impoſſible to conceive how any language can want this variation of the noun, where the nature of its ſignification is ſuch as to admit of *plurality.* *Clarke's Lat. Grammar.*

3. More cures of ſouls than one.
4. The greater number; the majority.

Take the *plurality* of the world, and they are neither wiſe nor good. *L'Eſtrange's Fables.*

Plu'rally. *adv.* [from *plural.*] In a ſenſe implying more than one.

Plush. *n. ſ.* [*peluche*, Fr.] A kind of villous or ſhaggy cloth; ſhag.

The bottom of it was ſet againſt a lining of *pluſh*, and the ſound was quite deaded, and but mere breath. *Bacon.*

The colour of *pluſh* or velvet will appear varied, if you ſtroak part of it one way, and part of it another. *Boyle.*

I love to wear cloths that are fluſh,
Not prefacing old rags with *pluſh.* *Cleaveland.*

Plu'sher. *n. ſ.* A ſea fiſh.

The pilchard is devoured by a bigger kind of fiſh called a *pluſher.* ſomewhat like the dog-fiſh, who leapeth above water, and therethrough bewrayeth them to the balker. *Carew.*

Plu'vial. } *adj.* from *pluvia*, Latin.] Rainy; relating to
Plu'vious. } rain.

The fungous parcels about the wicks of candles only ſignifieth a moiſt and *pluvious* air about them. *Brown.*

Plu'vial. *n. ſ.* [*pluvial*, Fr.] A prieſt's cope. *Ainſ.*

To Ply. *v. a.* [*plien*, to work at any thing, old Dutch. *Junius* and *Skinner.*]

1. To work on any thing cloſely and importunately.

The ſavage raves, impatient of the wound,
The wound's great author cloſe at hand provokes
His rage, and *plies* him with redoubled ſtrokes. *Dryden.*

The hero from afar
Plies him with darts and ſtones; and diſtant war. *Dryden.*

2. To employ with diligence; to keep buſy; to ſet on work.

Her gentle wit ſhe *plies*
To teach them truth. *Fairy Queen.*

Keep houſe, and *ply* his book, welcome his friends,
Viſit his countrymen, and banquet them. *Shakeſp.*

They their legs *ply'd*, not ſtaying
Until they reach'd the fatal champain. *Hudibras.*

He who exerts all the faculties of his ſoul, and *plies* all means and opportunities in the ſearch of truth, may reſt upon the judgment of his conſcience ſo informed, as a warrantable guide. *South's Sermons.*

The weary Trojans *ply* their ſhatter'd oars
To neareſt land. *Dryden's Virgil.*

I have *plied* my needle theſe fifty years, and by my good will would never have it out of my hand. *Spectator.*

3. To practiſe diligently.

He ſternly bad him other buſineſs *ply.* *Spenſer.*

Then commune how they beſt may *ply*
Their growing work. *Milton.*

Their bloody taſk, unweary'd ſtill, they *ply.* *Waller.*

4. To ſolicit importunately.

He *plies* her hard, and much rain wears the marble. *Sha.*

He *plies* the duke at morning and at night,
And doth impeach the freedom of the ſtate,
If they deny him juſtice. *Shakeſp. Merch. of Venice.*

Whoſoever has any thing of David's piety will be perpetually *plying* the throne of grace with ſuch like acknowledgments: as, bleſſed be that providence, which delivered me from ſuch a lewd company. *South's Sermons.*

To Ply. *v. n.*

1. To work, or offer ſervice.

He was forced to *ply* in the ſtreets as a porter for his livelihood. *Addiſon's Spectator,* Nº 94.

2. To go in haſte.

Thither he *plies* undaunted. *Milton.*

3. To buſy one's ſelf.

A bird new-made about the banks ſhe *plies*,
Not far from ſhore, and ſhort excurſions tries. *Dryden.*

4. [*Plier*, Fr.] To bend.

The willow *plied* and gave way to the guſt, and ſtill recovered itſelf again, but the oak was ſtubborn, and choſe rather to break than bend. *L'Eſtrange.*

Ply. *n. ſ.* [from the verb.]

1. Bent; turn; form; caſt; biaſs.

The late learners cannot ſo well take the *ply*, except it be in ſome minds that have not ſuffered themſelves to fix, but have kept themſelves open and prepared to receive continual amendment. *Bacon's Eſſays.*

2. Plait; fold.

The rugæ or *plies* of the inward coat of the ſtomach detain the aliment in the ſtomach. *Arbuthnot on Aliments.*

Ply'ers. *n. ſ.* See Pliers.

Pneuma'tical. } *adj.* [πνευματικὸς, from πνεῦμα.]
Pneuma'tick. }

1. Moved by wind; relative to wind.

I fell upon the making of *pneumatical* trials, whereof I gave an account in a book about the air. *Boyle.*

That the air near the ſurface of the earth will expand itſelf, when the preſſure of the incumbent atmoſphere is taken off, may be ſeen in the experiments made by Boyle in his *pneumatick* engine. *Locke's Elements of Natural Philoſophy.*

The lemon uncorrupt with voyage long,
To vinous ſpirits added,
They with *pneumatick* engine ceaſeleſs draw. *Philips.*

2. Conſiſting of ſpirit or wind.

All ſolid bodies conſiſt of parts *pneumatical* and tangible; the *pneumatical* ſubſtance being in ſome bodies the native ſpirit of the body, and in ſome other, plain air that is gotten in. *Bacon's Natural Hiſtory.*

The race of all things here is, to extenuate and turn things to be more *pneumatical* and rare; and not to retrograde, from *pneumatical*, to that which is denſe. *Bacon's Nat. Hiſt.*

Pneuma'ticks. *n. ſ.* [*pneumatique*, Fr. πνεῦμα.]

1. A branch of mechanicks, which conſiders the doctrine of the air, or laws according to which that fluid is condenſed, rarified or gravitates. *Harris.*
2. In the ſchools, the doctrine of ſpiritual ſubſtances, as God, angels and the ſouls of men. *Dict.*

Pneumato'logy. *n. ſ.* [πνευματολογία.] The doctrine of ſpiritual exiſtence.

To POACH. *v. a.* [*oeufs pochez*, Fr.]

1. To boil ſlightly.

The yolks of eggs are ſo well prepared for nouriſhment, that, ſo they be *poached* or rare boiled, they need no other preparation. *Bacon's Natural Hiſtory.*

2. To begin without completing: from the practice of boiling eggs ſlightly. Not in uſe.

Of later times, they have rather *poached* and offered at a number of enterprizes, than maintained any conſtantly. *Bacon.*

3. [*Pocher*, Fr. to pierce.] To ſtab; to pierce.

The flowk, ſole and plaice follow the tide up into the freſh rivers, where, at low water, the country people *poach* them with an inſtrument ſomewhat like the ſalmon ſpear. *Car.*

4. [From

4. [From *poche*, a pocket.] To plunder by ſtealth.

So ſhameleſs, ſo abandoned are their ways,
They *poach* Parnaſſus, and lay claim for praiſe. *Garth.*

To POACH. *v. n.* [from *poche*, a bag, Fr.]

1. To ſteal game; to carry off game privately in a bag.

In the ſchools
They *poach* for ſenſe, and hunt for idle rules. *Oldham.*

2. To be damp. A cant word.

Chalky and clay lands burn in hot weather, chap in ſummer, and *poach* in winter. *Mortimer's Huſbandry.*

POA'CHARD. *n. ſ.* A kind of water fowl.

POA'CHER. *n. ſ.* [from *poach.*] One who ſteals game.

You old *poachers* have ſuch a way with you, that all at once the buſineſs is done. *More's Foundling.*

POA'CHINESS. *n. ſ.* [from *poachy.*] Marſhineſs; dampneſs. A cant word.

The vallies becauſe of the *poachineſs* they keep for graſs. *Mort.*

POA'CHY. *adj.* Damp; marſhy. A cant word.

What uplands you deſign for mowing, ſhut up the beginning of February; but marſh lands lay not up till April, except your marſhes be very *poachy.* *Mortimer's Huſbandry.*

POCK. *n. ſ.* [from *pox.*] A puſtule raiſed by the ſmallpox.

POCKET. *n. ſ.* [pocca, Saxon; *pochet*, Fr.] The ſmall bag inſerted into cloaths.

Here's a letter
Found in the *pocket* of the ſlain Roderigo. *Shakeſp.*

Whilſt one hand exalts the blow,
And on the earth extends the foe;
T' other would take it wond'rous ill,
If in your *pocket* he lay ſtill. *Prior.*

As he was ſeldom without medals in his *pocket*, he would often ſhew us the ſame face on an old coin, that we ſaw in the ſtatue. *Addiſon on Ancient Medals.*

To POC'KET. *v. a.* [*pocheter*, Fr. from the noun.]

1. To put in the pocket.

Bleſs'd paper-credit!
Gold, imp'd with this, can compaſs hardeſt things,
Can *pocket* ſtates, or fetch or carry kings. *Pope.*

2. *To* POCKET *up.* A proverbial form that denotes the doing or taking any thing clandeſtinely.

If thy pocket were enriched with any other injuries but theſe, I am a villain; and yet you will ſtand to it, you will not *pocket* up wrongs. *Shakeſp. Henry* IV.

He lays his claim
To half the profit, half the fame,
And helps to *pocket* up the game. *Prior.*

PO'CKETBOOK. *n. ſ.* [*pocket* and *book.*] A paper book carried in the pocket for haſty notes.

Licinius let out the offals of his meat to intereſt, and kept a regiſter of ſuch debtors in his *pocketbook.* *Arbuthnot.*

Note down the matters of doubt in ſome *pocketbook*, and take the firſt opportunity to get them reſolved. *Watts.*

PO'CKETGLASS. *n. ſ.* [*pocket* and *glaſs.*] Portable looking-glaſs.

Powder and *pocketglaſs*, and beaus. *Prior.*

And vanity with *pocketglaſs*,
And impudence with front of braſs. *Swift's Miſcel.*

PO'CKHOLE. *n. ſ.* [*pock* and *hole.*] Pit or ſcar made by the ſmallpox.

Are theſe but warts and *pockholes* in the face
O' th' earth? *Donne.*

PO'CKINESS. *n. ſ.* [from *pocky.*] The ſtate of being pocky.

PO'CKY. *n. ſ. adj.* [from *pox.*] Infected with the pox.

My father's love lies thus in my bones; I might have loved all the *pocky* whores in Perſia, and have felt it leſs in my bones. *Denham's Sophy.*

POCU'LENT. *adj.* [*poculum*, Lat.] Fit for drink.

Some of theſe herbs, which are not eſculent, are notwithſtanding *poculent*; as hops and broom. *Bacon.*

POD. *n. ſ.* [*bode, boede*, Dutch, a little houſe. *Skinner.*] The capſule of legumes; the caſe of ſeeds.

To raiſe tulips, ſave the ſeeds which are ripe, when the the *pods* begin to open at the top, which cut off with the ſtalks from the root, and keep the *pods* upright, that the ſeed do not fall out. *Mortimer's Huſbandry.*

PODA'GRICAL. *adj.* [ποδαγρικὸς, ποδάγρα; from *podraga*, Lat.]

1. Afflicted with the gout.

From a magnetical activity muſt be made out, that a loadſtone, held in the hand of one that is *podagrical*, doth either cure or give great eaſe in the gout. *Brown's Vulgar Errours.*

2. Gouty; relating to the gout.

PO'DDER. *n. ſ.* [from *pod.*] A gatherer of peaſecods, beans and other pulſe. *Dict.*

PODGE. *n. ſ.* a puddle; a plaſh. *Skinner.*

PO'EM. *n. ſ.* [*poema*, Lat. ποίημα.] The work of a poet; a metrical compoſition.

A *poem* is not alone any work, or compoſition of the poets in many or few verſes; but even one alone verſe ſometimes makes a perfect *poem.* *Benj. Johnſon.*

The lady Anne of Bretaigne, paſſing through the preſence of France, and eſpying Chartier, a famous poet, faſt aſleep, kiſſing him, ſaid, we muſt honour the mouth whence ſo many golden *poems* have proceeded. *Peacham on Poetry.*

To you the promis'd *poem* I will pay. *Dryden.*

PO'ESY. *n. ſ.* [*poeſie*, Fr. *poeſis*, Lat. ποίησις.]

1. The art of writing poems.

A poem is the work of the poet; *poeſy* is his ſkill or craft of making; the very fiction itſelf, the reaſon or form of the work. *Benj. Johnſon.*

How far have we
Prophan'd thy heav'nly gift of *poeſy?*
Made proſtitute and profligate the muſe,
Whoſe harmony was firſt ordain'd above
For tongues of angels. *Dryden.*

2. Poem; metrical compoſition; poetry.

Muſick and *poeſy* uſe to quicken you. *Shakeſp.*

There is an hymn, for they have excellent *poeſy*; the ſubject is always the praiſes of Adam, Noah and Abraham, concluding ever with a thankſgiving for the nativity of our Saviour. *Bacon's New Atlantas.*

They apprehend a veritable hiſtory in an emblem or piece of chriſtian *poeſy.* *Brown's Vulgar Errours.*

3. A ſhort conceit engraved on a ring or other thing.

A paltry ring, whoſe *poeſy* was,
For all the world like cutler's poetry
Upon a knife; love me, and leave me not. *Shakeſp.*

PO'ET. *n. ſ.* [*poete*, Fr. *poeta*, Lat. ποιητὴς.] An inventor; an author of fiction; a writer of poems; one who writes in meaſure.

The *poet*'s eye in a fine frenzy rowling,
Doth glance from heav'n to earth, from earth to heav'n;
And, as imagination bodies forth
The forms of things unknown, the *poet*'s pen
Turns them to ſhape, and gives to ev'ry thing
A local habitation and a name. *Shakeſp.*

Our *poet* ape, who would be thought the chief,
His works become the frippery of wit,
From brocage he is grown ſo bold a thief,
While we the robb'd deſpiſe, and pity it. *B. Johnſon.*

'Tis not vain or fabulous
What the ſage *poets* taught by the heav'nly muſe
Story'd of old in high immortal verſe,
Of dire chimeras and enchanted iſles. *Milton.*

A *poet* is a maker, as the word ſignifies; and he who cannot make, that is invent, hath his name for nothing. *Dryden.*

POETA'STER. *n. ſ.* [Latin.] A vile petty poet.

Let no *poetaſter* command or intreat
Another extempore verſes to make. *Benj. Johnſon.*

Begin not as th' old *poetaſter* did,
Troy's famous war, and Priam's fate I ſing. *Roſcommon.*

Horace hath expoſed thoſe trifling *poetaſters*, that ſpend themſelves in glaring deſcriptions, and ſewing here and there ſome cloth of gold on their ſackcloth. *Felton.*

PO'ETESS. *n. ſ.* [from *poet*; *pica poetria*, Lat.] A ſhe poet.

POE'TICAL. }
POE'TICK. } *adj.* [ποιητικός; *poetique*, Fr. *poeticus*, Lat.] Expreſſed in poetry; pertaining to poetry; ſuitable to poetry.

Would the gods had made you *poetical.*
—I do not know what *poetical* is.
—The trueſt poetry is moſt feigning. *Shakeſp.*

With courage guard, and beauty warm our age,
And lovers fill with like *poetick* rage. *Waller.*

The moral of that *poetical* fiction, that the uppermoſt link of all the ſeries of ſubordinate cauſes is faſtened to Jupiter's chair, ſignifies that almighty God governs and directs ſubordinate cauſes and effects. *Hale.*

Neither is it enough to give his author's ſenſe in good Engliſh, in *poetical* expreſſions and in muſical numbers. *Dryden.*

The muſe ſaw it upward riſe,
Though mark'd by none but quick *poetick* eyes. *Pope.*

I alone can inſpire the *poetical* crowd. *Swift.*

POE'TICALLY. *adv.* [from *poetical.*] With the qualities of poetry; by the fiction of poetry.

The criticks have concluded, that the manners of the heroes are *poetically* good, if of a piece. *Dryden.*

The many rocks, in the paſſage between Greece and the bottom of Pontus, are *poetically* converted into thoſe fiery bulls. *Raleigh.*

To POETI'ZE. *v. n.* [*poetiſer*, Fr. from *poet.*] To write like a poet.

I verſify the truth, not *poetize.* *Donne.*

Virgil, ſpeaking of Turnus and his great ſtrength, thus *poetizes.* *Hakewill.*

POE'TRESS. *n. ſ.* [from *poetris*, Lat. whence *poetridas picas* in *Perſius.*] A ſhe poet.

Moſt peerleſs *poetreſs*,
The true Pandora of all heavenly graces. *Spenſer.*

POE'TRY. *n. ſ.* [ποιητρια; from *poet.*]

1. Metrical compoſition; the art or practice of writing poems.

Strike the beſt invention dead,
Till baffled *poetry* hangs down the head. *Cleaveland.*

Although in *poetry* it be neceſſary that the unities of time, place and action ſhould be explained, there is ſtill ſomething that gives a greatneſs of mind to the reader, which few of the criticks have conſidered. *Addiſon's Spectator*, Nº 409.

2. Poems; poetical pieces.

She taketh moſt delight
In muſick, inſtruments and *poetry* *Shakeſp.*

POI'GNANCY. *n. s.* [from *poignant.*]

1. The power of stimulating the palate; sharpness.

I sat quietly down at my morsel, adding only a principle of hatred to all succeeding measures by way of sauce; and one point of conduct in the dutchess's life added much *poignancy* to it. *Swift.*

2. The power of irritation; asperity.

POI'GNANT. *adj.* [*poignant*, Fr.]

1. Sharp; stimulating the palate.

No *poignant* sauce she knew, nor costly treat,
Her hunger gave a relish to her meat. *Dryden.*

The studious man, whose will was never determined to *poignant* sauces and delicious wine, is, by hunger and thirst, determined to eating and drinking. *Locke.*

2. Severe; piercing; painful.

If God makes use of some *poignant* disgrace to let out the poisonous vapour, is not the mercy greater than the severity of the cure? *South's Sermons.*

Full three long hours his tender body did sustain
Most exquisite and *poignant* pain. *Norris's Miscel.*

3. Irritating; satirical; keen.

POINT. *n. s.* [*poinct*, *point*, French.]

1. The sharp end of any instrument.

The thorny *point*
Of bare distress hath ta'en from me the shew
Of smooth fidelity. *Shakesp. As You like it.*

That bright beam, whose *point* now rais'd,
Bore him slope downward. *Milton.*

A pyramid reversed may stand for a while upon its *point*, if balanced by admirable skill. *Temple's Miscellanies.*

Doubts if he wielded not a wooden spear
Without a *point*; he look'd, the *point* was there. *Dryden.*

2. A string with a tag.

If your son have not the day,
For a silken *point* I'll give my baronry. *Shakesp.*

He hath ribbands of all colours; *points* more than all the lawyers can learnedly handle. *Shakespeare.*

I am resolved on two *points*;
That if one break, the other will hold;
Or if both break, your gaskins fall. *Shakesp.*

King James was wont to say, that the duke of Buckingham had given him a groom of his bed-chamber, who could not truss his *points*. *Clarendon.*

3. Headland; promontory.

I don't see why Virgil has given the epithet of Alta to Prochita, which is much lower than Ischia, and all the *points* of land that lie within its neighbourhood. *Addison.*

4. A sting of an epigram; a sentence terminated with some remarkable turn of words or thought.

He taxes Lucan, who crouded sentences together, and was too full of *points*. *Dryden on Heroick Plays.*

Studious to please the genius of the times,
With periods, *points* and tropes he slurs his crimes;
He robb'd not, but he borrow'd from the poor. *Dryden.*

Times corrupt, and nature ill inclin'd,
Produc'd the *point* that left a sting behind. *Pope.*

5. An indivisible part of space.

We sometimes speak of space, or do suppose a *point* in it at such a distance from any part of the universe. *Locke.*

6. An indivisible part of time; a moment.

Then neither from eternity before,
Nor from the time, when time's first *point* begun,
Made he all souls. *Davies.*

7. A small space.

On one small *point* of land,
Weary'd, uncertain and amaz'd, we stand. *Prior.*

8. Punctilio; nicety.

Shalt thou dispute
With God the *points* of liberty, who made
Thee what thou art. *Milton's Par. Lost, b.* v.

9. Part required of time or space; critical moment; exact place.

How oft, when men are at the *point* of death,
Have they been merry? which their keepers call
A lightning before death. *Shakesp. Romeo and Juliet.*

Esau said, behold I am at the *point* to die; and what profit shall this birthright do? *Gen.* xxv. 32.

Democritus, spent with age, and just at the *point* of death, called for loaves of new bread, and with the steam under his nose, prolonged his life till a feast was past. *Temple.*

They follow nature in their desires, carrying them no farther than she directs, and leaving off at the *point*, at which excess would grow troublesome. *Atterbury's Sermons.*

10. Degree; state.

The highest *point* outward things can bring one unto, is the contentment of the mind, with which no estate is miserable. *Sidney, b.* i.

In a commonwealth, the wealth of the country is so equally distributed, that most of the community are at their ease, though few are placed in extraordinary *points* of splendor. *Addison on the State of the War.*

11. Note of distinction in writing; a stop.

12. A spot; a part of a surface divided by spots; division by marks, into which any thing is distinguished in a circle or other plane: as, at tables the ace or sise *point*.

13. One of the degrees into which the circumference of the horizon, and the mariner's compass is divided.

Carve out dials *point* by *point*,
Thereby to see the minutes how they run. *Shakesp.*

There arose strong winds from the South, with a *point* east, which carried us up. *Bacon's New Atlantis.*

A seaman, coming before the judges of the admiralty for admittance into an office of a ship, was by one of the judges much slighted; the judge telling him, that he believed he could not say the *points* of his compass. *Bacon.*

Vapours fir'd shew the mariner
From what *point* of his compass to beware
Impetuous winds. *Milton's Par. Lost, b.* iv.

If you tempt her, the wind of fortune
May come about, and take another *point*,
And blast your glories. *Denham.*

At certain periods stars resume their place,
From the same *point* of heav'n their course advance. *Dryd.*

14. Particular place to which any thing is directed.

East and West are but respective and mutable *points*, according unto different longitudes or distant parts of habitation. *Brown's Vulgar Errours.*

Let the part, which produces another part, be more strong than that which it produces; and let the whole be seen by one *point* of sight. *Dryden's Dufresnoy.*

The poet intended to set the character of Arete in a fair *point* of light. *Broome.*

15. Respect; regard.

A figure like your father,
Arm'd at all *points* exactly cap-a-pe,
Appears before them. *Shakespeare's Hamlet.*

A war upon the Turk is more worthy than upon any other Gentiles, in *point* of religion and in *point* of honour. *Bacon.*

He had a moment's right in *point* of time;
Had I seen first, then his had been the crime. *Dryden.*

With the history of Moses, no book in the world in *point* of antiquity can contend. *Tillotson's Sermons.*

Men would often see, what a small pittance of reason is mixed with those huffing opinions they are swelled with, with which they are so armed at all *points*, and with which they so confidently lay about them. *Locke.*

I have extracted out of that pamphlet a few of those notorious falsehoods, in *point* of fact and reasoning. *Swift.*

16. An aim; the act of aiming or striking.

What a *point* your falcon made,
And what a pitch she flew above the rest. *Shakesp.*

17. The particular thing required.

You gain your *point*, if your industrious art
Can make unusual words easy. *Roscommon.*

There is no creature so contemptible, but, by resolution, may gain his *point*. *L'Estrange.*

18. Particular; instance; example.

I'll hear him his confessions justify,
And *point* by *point* the treasons of his master
He shall again relate. *Shakespeare's Henry* VIII.

Thou shalt be as free
As mountain winds; but then exactly do
All *points* of my command. *Shakesp. Tempest.*

His majesty should make a peace, or turn the war directly upon such *points*, as may engage the nation in the support of it. *Temple.*

He warn'd in dreams, his murder did foretel,
From *point* to *point*, as after it befel. *Dryden.*

This letter is, in every *point*, an admirable pattern of the present polite way of writing. *Swift.*

19. A single position; a single assertion; a single part of a complicated question; a single part of any whole.

Another vows the same;
A third t' a *point* more near the matter draws. *Daniel.*

Strange *point* and new!
Doctrine which would know whence learn'd. *Milton.*

Stanilaus endeavours to establish the duodecuple proportion, by comparing scripture together with Josephus: but they will hardly prove his *point*. *Arbuthnot on Coins.*

There is no *point* wherein I have so much laboured, as that of improving and polishing all parts of conversation between persons of quality. *Swift.*

The gloss produceth instances that are neither pertinent, nor prove the *point*. *Baker's Reflections on Learning.*

20. A note; a tune.

You, my lord archbishop,
Whose white investments figure innocence,
Wherefore do you so ill translate yourself
Into the harsh and boist'rous tongue of war?
Turning your tongue divine
To a loud trumpet, and a *point* of war. *Shakesp.*

21. *Pointblank*; directly: as, an arrow is shot to the *pointblank* or white mark.

This boy will carry a letter twenty mile, as easy as a cannon will shoot *pointblank* twelve score. *Shakesp.*

The other level *pointblank* at the inventing of causes and axioms. *Bacon.*

Unless it be the cannon ball,
That shot i'th'air *pointblank* upright,
Was born to that prodigious height,
That learn'd philosophers maintain,
It ne'er came back. *Hudibras, p.* ii.

The faculties that were given us for the glory of our master, are turned *pointblank* against the intention of them. *L'Estr.*

Estius declares, that although all the schoolmen were for Latria to be given to the cross, yet that it is *pointblank* against the definition of the council of Nice. *Stillingfleet.*

23. *Point de vise*; exact or exactly in the point of view.

Every thing about you should demonstrate a careless desolation; but you are rather *point de vise* in your accoutrements, as loving yourself, than the lover of another. *Shakesp.*

I will baffle Sir Toby, I will wash off gross acquaintance, I will be *point de vise* the very man. *Shakesp.*

Men's behaviour should be like their apparel, not too straight or *point de vise*, but free for exercise. *Bacon.*

To Point. *v. a.* [from the noun.]

1. To sharpen; to forge or grind to a point.

The princes of Germany had but a dull fear of the greatness of Spain; now that fear is sharpened and *pointed*, by the Spaniards late enterprizes upon the Palatinate. *Bacon.*

Part-new grind the blunted ax, and *point* the dart. *Dryd.*

What help will all my heav'nly friends afford,
When to my breast I lift the *pointed* sword. *Dryden.*

The two pinnæ stand upon either side, like the wings in the petasus of a Mercury, but rise much higher, and are more *pointed*. *Addison on Italy.*

Some on *pointed* wood
Transfix'd the fragments, some prepar'd the food. *Pope.*

2. To direct towards an object, by way of forcing it on the notice.

Alas to make me
A fixed figure, for the hand of scorn
To *point* his slow unmeaning finger at. *Shakesp. Othello.*

Mount Hermon, yonder sea, each place behold
As I *point*. *Milton.*

3. To direct the eye or notice.

Whosoever should be guided through his battles by Minerva, and *pointed* to every scene of them, would see nothing but subjects of surprize. *Pope.*

4. To show as by directing the finger.

From the great sea, you shall *point* out for you mount Hor. *Numb.* xxxiv. 7.

It will become us, as rational creatures, to follow the direction of nature, where it seems to *point* us out the way. *Locke.*

I shall do justice to those who have distinguished themselves in learning, and *point* out their beauties. *Addison.*

Is not the elder
By nature *pointed* out for preference? *Rowe.*

5. [*Pointer*, Fr.] To direct towards a place: as, the cannon were *pointed* against the fort.

6. To distinguish by stops or points.

To Point. *v. n.*

1. To note with the finger; to force upon the notice, by directing the finger towards it. With *at* commonly, sometimes *to* before the thing indigitated.

Now must the world *point at* poor Catharine,
And say, lo! there is mad Petruchio's wife. *Shakesp.*

Sometimes we use one finger only, as in *pointing at* any thing. *Ray on the Creation.*

Who fortune's fault upon the poor can throw,
Point at the tatter'd coat and ragged shoe. *Dryden.*

Rouse up for shame! our brothers of Pharsalia
Point at their wounds, and cry aloud to battle. *Addison.*

2. To distinguish words or sentences by points.

Ford the Jews are of their method of *pointing*. *Forbes.*

3. To indicate as dogs do to sportsmen.

The subtle dog scow'rs with sagacious nose,
Now the warm scent assures the covey near,
He treads with caution, and he *points* with fear. *Gay.*

4. To show.

To *point* at what time the balance of power was most equally held between their lords and commons in Rome, would perhaps admit a controversy. *Swift.*

Pointed. *adj.* or *participle.* [from *point.*]

1. Sharp; having a a sharp point or pic.

Who now reads Cowley? if he pleases, yet
His moral pleases, not his *pointed* wit; *Pope.*

A *pointed* flinty rock, all bare and black,
Grew gibbous from behind. *Dryden.*

2. Epigrammatical; abounding in conceits.

Poi'ntedly. *adv.* [from *pointed.*] In a pointed manner.

The copiousness of his wit was such, that he often writ too *pointedly* for his subject. *Dryden.*

Poi'ntedness. *n. s.* [from *pointed.*]

1. Sharpness; pickedness with asperity.

The vicious language is vast and gaping, swelling and irregular; when it contends to be high, full of rock, mountain and *pointedness*. *Benj. Johnson's Discovery.*

2. Epigrammatical smartness.

Like Horace, you only expose the follies of men; and in this excel him, that you add *pointedness* of thought. *Dryden.*

Pointel. *n. s.* Any thing on a point.

These poises or *pointels* are, for the most part, little balls, set at the top of a slender stalk, which they can move every way at pleasure. *Derham's Physico-Theology.*

Pointer. *n. s.* [from *point.*]

1. Any thing that points.

I ought to tell him what are the wheels, springs, *pointer*, hammer and bell whereby a clock gives notice of the time. *Watts.*

2. A dog that points out the game to sportsmen.

The well taught *pointer* leads the way,
The scent grows warm; he stops, he springs his prey. *Gay.*

Poi'ntingstock. *n. s.* [*pointing* and *stock.*] Something made the object of ridicule.

I, his forlorn dutchess,
Was made a wonder and a *pointingstock*
To every idle rascal follower. *Shakesp. Henry* VI.

Poi'ntless. *adj.* [from *point.*] Blunt; not sharp; obtuse.

Lay that *pointless* clergy-weapon by,
And to the laws, your sword of justice, fly. *Dryden.*

POI'SON. *n. s.* [*poison*, Fr.] That which destroys or injures life by a small quantity, and by means not obvious to the senses; venom.

The tongue is an unruly evil, full of deadly *poison*. *Ja.*

Themselves were first to do the ill,
E'er they thereof the knowledge could attain;
Like him that knew not *poison*'s power to kill,
Until, by tasting it, himself was slain. *Davies.*

One gives another a cup of *poison*, but at the same time tells him it is a cordial, and so he drinks it off and dies. *South.*

To Poi'son. *v. a.* [from the noun.]

1. To infect with poison.

Envy is a lawless enemy, against whom *poisoned* arrows may be used. *Anonymous.*

2. To attack, injure or kill by poison given.

He was so discouraged, that he *poisoned* himself and died. 2 *Mac.* x. 13.

Drink with Walters, or with Chartres eat;
They'll never *poison* you, they'll only cheat. *Pope.*

3. To corrupt; to taint.

The other messenger,
Whose welcome I perceiv'd, had *poison'd* mine. *Shakesp.*

Hast thou not
With thy false arts *poison'd* his people's loyalty? *Rowe.*

Poi'son-tree. *n. s.* [*toxicodendron.*] A plant. The flower consists of five leaves, which are placed orbicularly, and expand in form of a rose, out of whose flower cup rises the pointal, which afterwards becomes a roundish, dry, and for the most part a furrowed fruit, in which is contained one compressed seed. *Miller.*

Poi'soner. *n. s.* [from *poison.*]

1. One who poisons.

I must be the *poisoner*
Of good Polixenes. *Shakesp.*

So many mischiefs were in one combin'd;
So much one single *pois'ner* cost mankind. *Dryden.*

2. A corrupter.

Wretches who live upon other men's sins, the common *poisoners* of youth, getting their very bread by the damnation of souls. *South's Sermons.*

Poi'sonous. *adj.* [from *poison.*] Venomous; having the qualities of poison.

Those cold ways,
That seem like prudent helps, are very *poisonous*,
Where the disease is violent. *Shakesp. Coriolanus.*

Not sirius shoots a fiercer flame,
When with his *pois'nous* breath he blasts the sky. *Dryden.*

A lake, that has no fresh water running into it, will, by heat and its stagnation, turn into a stinking rotten puddle, sending forth nauseous and *poisonous* steams. *Cheyne.*

Poi'sonously. *adv.* [from *poisonous.*] Venomously.

Men more easily pardon ill things done, than ill things said; such a peculiar rancour and venom do they leave behind in men's minds, and so much more *poisonously* and incurably does the serpent bite with his tongue than his teeth. *South's Sermons.*

Poi'sonousness. *n. s.* [from *poisonous.*] The quality of being poisonous; venomousness.

Poitrel. *n. s.* [*poictrel, poitrine*, Fr. *pettorale*, Italian; *pectorale*, Lat.]

1. Armour for the breast of a horse. *Skinner.*

2. A graving tool. *Ainsworth.*

Poize. *n. s.* [*poids*, French.]

1. Weight; force of any thing tending to the center.

He fell, as an huge rockie clift,
Whose false foundation, waves have wash'd away
With dreadful *poize*, is from the main land reft. *F. Queen.*

When I have suit,
It shall be full of *poize* and difficulty,
And fearful to be granted. *Shakesp. Othello.*

2. Balance;

2. Balance, equipoize; equilibrium.

To do't at peril of your soul,
Were equal *poize* of sin and charity. *Shakesp.*

Where an equal *poize* of hope and fear
Does arbitrate th' event, my nature is
That I incline to hope. *Milton.*

The particles that formed the earth, must convene from all quarters towards the middle, which would make the whole compound to rest in a *poize*. *Bentley's Sermons.*

'Tis odd to see fluctuation in opinion so earnestly charged upon Luther, by such as have lived half their days in a *poize* between two churches. *Atterbury.*

3. A regulating power.

Men of an unbounded imagination often want the *poize* of judgment. *Dryden.*

To POIZE. *v. a.* [*peser*, French.]

1. To balance; to hold or place in equiponderance.

How nice to couch? how all her speeches *poized* be:
A nymph thus turn'd, but mended in translation. *Sidney.*

As the sands
Of Barca or Cyrene's torrid soil,
Levy'd to side with warring winds, and *poize*
Their lighter wings. *Milton's Par. Lost, b.* ii.

Nor yet was earth suspended in the sky,
Nor *poiz'd* did on her own foundation lie. *Dryden.*

Our nation with united int'rest blest,
Not now content to *poize*, shall sway the rest. *Dryden.*

Where could they find another form'd so fit,
To *poize* with solid sense a sprightly wit! *Dryden.*

Th' all-perfect mind
That *poiz'd*, impels and rules the steady whole. *Thomson.*

2. To be equiponderant to.

If the balance of our lives had not one scale of reason to *poize* another of sensuality, the baseness of our natures would conduct us to preposterous conclusions. *Shakesp. Othello.*

3. To weigh.

We *poizing* us in her defective scale
Shall weigh thee to the beam. *Shakespeare.*

He cannot sincerely consider the strength, *poize* the weight and discern the evidence of the clearest argumentations, where they would conclude against his desires. *South's Sermons.*

4. To oppress with weight.

I'll strive, with troubl'd thoughts, to take a nap,
Lest leaden slumber *poize* me down to-morrow,
When I should mount with wings of victory. *Shakesp.*

POKE. *n. s.* [pocca, Sax. *poche*, Fr.] A pocket; a small bag.

I will not buy a pig in a *poke*. *Camden's Remains.*

She suddenly unties the *poke*,
Which out of it sent such a smoke,
As ready was them all to choke,
So grievous was the pother. *Drayton's Nymphid.*

My correspondent writes against master's gowns and *poke* sleeves. *Spectator*, N° 619.

To POKE. *v. a.* [*poka*, Swedish.] To feel in the dark; to search any thing with a long instrument.

If these presumed eyes be clipped off, they will make use of their protrusions or horns, and *poke* out their way as before. *Brown's Vulgar Errours, b.* iii.

PO'KER. *n. s.* [from *poke*.] The iron bar with which men stir the fire.

With *poker* fiery red
Crack the stones, and melt the lead. *Swift.*

If the *poker* be out of the way, stir the fire with the tongs. *Swift's Rules to Servants.*

PO'LAR. *adj.* [*polaire*, Fr. from *pole*.] Found near the pole; lying near the pole; issuing from the pole.

As when two *polar* winds, blowing adverse
Upon the Cronian sea, together drive
Mountains of ice. *Milton's Par. Lost, b.* x.

I doubt
If any suffer on the *polar* coast,
The rage of Arctos, and eternal frost. *Prior.*

POLA'RITY. *n. s.* [from *polar*.] Tendency to the pole.

This *polarity* from refrigeration, upon extremity and defect of a loadstone, might touch a needle any where. *Brown.*

PO'LARY. *adj.* [*polaris*, Lat.] Tending to the pole; having a direction toward the poles.

Irons, heated red hot, and cooled in the meridian from North to South, contract a *polary* power. *Brown.*

POLE. *n. s.* [*polus*, Lat. *pole*, Fr.]

1. The extremity of the axis of the earth; either of the points on which the world turns.

From the centre thrice to the utmost *pole*. *Milton.*

From *pole* to *pole*
The forky lightnings flash, the roaring thunders roll. *Dry.*

2. [Pole, Sax. *pal*, *pau*, Fr. *palo*, Italian and Spanish; *palus*, Lat.] A long staff.

A long *pole*, struck upon gravel in the bottom of the water, maketh a sound. *Bacon's Nat. History.*

If after some distinguish'd leap,
He drops his *pole*, and seems to slip;
Straight gath'ring all his active strength,
He rises higher. *Prior.*

He ordered to arm long *poles* with sharp hooks, wherewith they took hold of the tackling which held the mainyard to the mast, then rowing the ship, they cut the tackling, and brought the mainyard by the board. *Arbuthnot on Coins.*

3. A tall piece of timber erected.

Wither'd is the garland of the war,
The soldier's *pole* is fall'n. *Shakesp. Ant. and Cleop.*

Live to be the show and gaze o' th' time,
We'll have thee as our rarer monsters are
Painted upon a *pole*, and underwrit,
Here may you see the tyrant. *Shakesp.*

4. A measure of length containing five yards and a half.

This ordinance of tithing them by the *pole* is not only fit for the gentlemen, but also the noblemen. *Spenser.*

Every *pole* square of mud, twelve inches deep, is worth six pence a *pole* to fling out. *Mortimer's Husbandry.*

5. An instrument of measuring.

A peer of the realm and a counsellor of state are not to be measured by the common yard, but by the *pole* of special grace. *Bacon.*

To POLE. *v. a.* [from the noun.] To furnish with poles.

Begin not to *pole* your hops. *Mortimer's Husbandry.*

PO'LEAXE. *n. s.* [*pole* and *axe*.] An axe fixed to a long pole.

To beat religion into the brains with a *poleaxe*, is to offer victims of human blood. *Howel's England's Tears.*

One hung a *poleaxe* at his saddle bow,
And one a heavy mace to stun the foe. *Dryden.*

PO'LECAT. *n. s.* [*Pole* or *Polish* cat, because they abound in Poland.] The fitchew; a stinking animal.

Polecats? there are fairer things than *polecats*. *Shakesp.*

Out of my door, you witch! you hag, you *polecat!* out, out, out; I'll conjure you. *Shakesp. Merry Wives of Windsor.*

She, at a pin in the wall, hung like a *polecat* in a warren, to amuse them. *L'Estrange.*

How should he, harmless youth,
Who kill'd but *polecats*, learn to murder men. *Gay.*

PO'LEDAVIES. *n. s.* A sort of coarse cloth. *Ainsworth.*

POLE'MICAL. } *adj.* [πολεμικὸς.] Controversial; disputative.
POLE'MICK. }

I have had but little respite from these *polemical* exercises, and, notwithstanding all the rage and malice of the adversaries of our church, I sit down contented. *Stillingfleet.*

The nullity of this distinction has been solidly shewn by most of our *polemick* writers of the protestant church. *South.*

The best method to be used with these *polemical* ladies, is to shew them the ridiculous side of their cause. *Addison.*

POLE'MICK. *n. s.* Disputant; controvertist.

Each staunch *polemick* stubborn as a rock,
Came whip and spur. *Dunciad, b.* iv.

POLE'MOSCOPE. *n. s.* [πόλεμ☉ and σκοπέω.] In opticks, is a kind of crooked or oblique perspective glass, contrived for seeing objects that do not lie directly before the eye. *Dict.*

PO'LESTAR. *n. s.* [*pole* and *star*.]

1. A star near the pole, by which navigators compute their northern latitude; cynosure; lodestar.

If a pilot at sea cannot see the *polestar*, let him steer his course by such stars as best appear to him. *King Charles.*

I was sailing in a vast ocean without other help than the *polestar* of the ancients. *Dryden.*

2. Any guide or director.

PO'LEY-MOUNTAIN. *n. s.* [*polium*, Lat.] A plant.

The *poley-mountain* hath a labiated flower, consisting of one leaf, whose stamina supply the place of a crest; the beard is divided into five segments as the germander; out of the flower cup rises the pointal, attended, as it were, by four embryos, which afterward become so many seeds shut up in the flower cup: the flowers are collected into an head upon the top of the stalks and branches. *Miller.*

POLI'CE. *n. s.* [French.] The regulation and government of a city or country, so far as regards the inhabitants.

PO'LICED. *adj.* [from *police*.] Regulated; formed into a regular course of administration.

Where there is a kingdom altogether unable or indign to govern, it is a just cause of war for another nation, that is civil or *policed*, to subdue them. *Bacon's Holy War.*

PO'LICY. *n. s.* [πολιτεία; *politia*, Lat.]

1. The art of government, chiefly with respect to foreign powers.

2. Art; prudence; management of affairs; stratagem.

The *policy* of that purpose is made more in the marriage, than the love of the parties. *Shakesp. Ant. and Cleopatra.*

If it be honour in your wars to seem
The same you are not, which for your best ends
You call your *policy*; how is't less or worse,
But it shall hold companionship in peace
With honour as in war. *Shakesp. Coriolanus.*

If she be curst, it is for *policy*,
For she's not froward, but modest. *Shakesp.*

The best rule of *policy*, is to prefer the doing of justice before all enjoyments. *King Charles.*

The

The wisdom of this world is sometimes taken in scripture for *policy*, and consists in a certain dexterity of managing business for a man's secular advantage. *South's Sermons.*

3. [*Poliça*, Spanish.] A warrant for money in the publick funds.

To PO'LISH. *v. a.* [*polio*, Lat. *polir*, Fr.]

1. To smooth; to brighten by attrition; to gloss.

He setteth to finish his work, and *polisheth* it perfectly. *Eccl.*

Pygmalion, with fatal art,
Polish'd the form that stung his heart. *Granvil.*

2. To make elegant of manners.

Studious they appear
Of arts that *polish* life, inventors rare. *Milton.*
Bid soft science *polish* Britain's heroes. *Irene.*

To PO'LISH. *v. n.* To answer to the act of polishing; to receive a gloss.

It is reported by the ancients, that there was a kind of steel, which would *polish* almost as white and bright as silver. *Bacon.*

PO'LISH. *n. s.* [*poli*, *polissure*, Fr. from the verb.]

1. Artificial gloss; brightness given by attrition.

Not to mention what a huge column of granite cost in the quarry, only consider the great difficulty of hewing it into any form, and of giving it the due turn, proportion and *polish*. *Addison's Remarks on Italy.*

Another prism of clearer glass and better *polish* seemed free from veins. *Newton's Opticks.*

2. Elegance of manners.

What are these wond'rous civilising arts,
This Roman *polish*, and this smooth behaviour,
That render man thus tractable and tame? *Addison's Cato.*

PO'LISHABLE. *adj.* [from *polish.*] Capable of being polished.

PO'LISHER. *n. s.* [from *polish.*] The person or instrument that gives a gloss.

I consider an human soul without education, like marble in the quarry, which shews none of its inherent beauties, till the skill of the *polisher* fetches out the colours. *Addison.*

POLI'TE. *adj.* [*politus*, Latin.]

1. Glossy; smooth.

Some of them are diaphanous, shining and *polite*; others not *polite*, but as if powder'd over with fine iron dust. *Woodw.*

If any sort of rays, falling on the *polite* surface of any pellucid medium, be reflected back, the fits of easy reflexion, which they have at the point of reflexion, shall still continue to return. *Newton's Opticks.*

The edges of the sand holes, being worn away, there are left all over the glass a numberless company of very little convex *polite* risings like waves. *Newton's Opticks.*

2. Elegant of manners.

A nymph of quality admires our knight,
He marries, bows at court, and grows *polite*. *Pope.*

POLI'TELY. *adv.* [from *polite.*] With elegance of manners; genteely.

POLI'TENESS. *n. s.* [*politesse*, Fr. from *polite.*] Elegance of manners; gentility; good breeding.

I have seen the dullest men aiming at wit, and others, with as little pretensions, affecting *politeness* in manners and discourse. *Swift.*

POLI'TICAL. *adj.* [πολιτικός.]

1. Relating to politicks; relating to the administration of publick affairs.

More true *political* wisdom may be learned from this single book of proverbs, than from a thousand Machiavel. *Rogers.*

2. Cunning; skilful.

POLI'TICALLY. *adv.* [from *political.*]

1. With relation to publick administration.

2. Artfully; politickly.

The Turks *politically* mingled certain Janizaries, harquebusiers with their horsemen. *Knolles's History of the Turks.*

POLITICA'STER. *n. s.* A petty ignorant pretender to politicks:

There are quacks of all sorts; as bullies, pedants, hypocrites, empiricks, law-jobbers and *politicasters*. *L'Estrange.*

POLITI'CIAN. *n. s.* [*politicien*, Fr.]

1. One versed in the arts of government; one skilled in politicks.

Get thee glass eyes,
And, like a scurvy *politician*, seem
To see things thou dost not. *Shakesp. King Lear.*

And 't be any way, it must be with valour; for policy I hate: I had as lief be a Brownist as a *politician*. *Shakespeare.*

Although I may seem less a *politician* to men, yet I need no secret distinctions nor evasions before God. *King Charles.*

While emp'rick *politicians* use deceit,
Hide what they give, and cure but by a cheat,
You boldly show that skill, which they pretend,
And work by means as noble as your end. *Dryden.*

Coffee, which makes the *politician* wise,
And see through all things with his half-shut eyes,
Sent up in vapours to the baron's brain
New stratagems, the radiant lock to gain. *Pope.*

2. A man of artifice; one of deep contrivance.

Your ill-meaning *politician* lords,
Under pretence of bridal friends and guests,
Appointed to await me thirty spies. *Milton.*

If a man succeeds in any attempt, though undertook with never so much rashness, his success shall vouch him a *politician*, and good luck shall pass for deep contrivance; for give any one fortune, and he shall be thought a wise man. *South.*

PO'LITICK. *adj.* [πολιτικός.]

1. Political; civil. In this sense *political* is almost always used, except in the phrase *body politick.*

Virtuously and wisely acknowledging, that he with his people made all but one *politick* body, whereof himself was the head; even so cared for them as he would for his own limbs. *Sidney*, *b.* ii.

No civil or *politick* constitutions have been more celebrated than his by the best authors. *Temple.*

2. Prudent; versed in affairs.

This land was famously enrich'd
With *politick* grave counsel; then the king
Had virtuous uncles. *Shakesp. Richard III.*

3. Artful; cunning. In this sense *political* is not used.

I have trod a measure; I have flatter'd a lady; I have been *politick* with my friend, smooth with mine enemy. *Shakesp.*

Authority followeth old men, and favour youth; but for the moral part, perhaps youth will have the preheminence, as age hath for the *politick.* *Bacon.*

No less alike the *politick* and wise,
All sly slow things, with circumspective eyes;
Men in their loose unguarded hours they take. *Pope.*

PO'LITICKLY. *adv.* [from *politick.*] Artfully; cunningly.

Thus have I *politickly* begun my reign,
And 'tis my hope to end successfully. *Shakesp.*

'Tis *politickly* done,
To send me packing with an host of men. *Shakesp.*

The dutchess hath been most *politickly* employed in sharpening those arms with which she subdued you. *Pope.*

PO'LITICKS. *n. s.* [*politique*, Fr. πολιτική.] The science of government; the art or practice of administring publick affairs.

Be pleas'd your *politicks* to spare,
I'm old enough, and can myself take care. *Dryden.*

It would be an everlasting reproach to *politicks*, should such men overturn an establishment formed by the wisest laws, and supported by the ablest heads. *Addison.*

Of crooked counsels and dark *politicks*. *Pope.*

PO'LITURE. *n. s.* [*politure*, Fr.] The gloss given by the act of polishing.

PO'LITY. *n. s.* [πολιτεία.] A form of government; civil constitution.

Because the subject, which this position concerneth, is a form of church government or church *polity*, it behoveth us to consider the nature of the church, as is requisite for men's more clear and plain understanding, in what respect laws of *polity* or government are necessary thereunto. *Hooker.*

The *polity* of some of our neighbours hath not thought it beneath the publick care, to promote and reward the improvement of their own language. *Locke on Education.*

POLL. *n. s.* [*polle*, *pol*, Dutch, the top.]

1. The head.

Look if the withered elder hath not his *poll* claw'd like a parrot. *Shakesp. Henry IV. p.* ii.

2. A catalogue or list of persons; a register of heads.

Have you a catalogue
Of all the voices that we have procur'd,
Set down by th' *poll.* *Shakesp. Coriolanus.*

The muster file, rotten and sound, amounts not to fifteen thousand *poll.* *Shakespeare.*

3. A fish called generally a chub. A chevin.

To POLL. *v. a.* [from the noun.]

1. To lop the top of trees.

The oft cutting and *polling* of hedges conduces much to their lasting. *Bacon's Natural History.*

May thy woods oft *poll'd* yet ever wear
A green, and, when she list, a golden hair. *Donne.*

2. In this sense is used *polled* sheep.

Polled sheep, that is sheep without horns, are reckoned the best breeders, because the ewes yean the *polled* lamb with the least danger. *Mortimer's Husbandry.*

3 To pull off hair from the head; to clip short; to shear.

Neither shall they shave, only *poll* their heads. *Ezekiel.*

4. To mow; to crop.

He'll go and sowle the porter of Rome gates by th' ears: he will mow down all before him, and leave his passage *poll'd.* *Shakesp. Coriolanus.*

5. To plunder; to strip; to pill.

They will *poll* and spoil so outrageously, as the very enemy cannot do much worse. *Spenser on Ireland.*

Take and exact upon them the wild exactions, coignie, livery and sorehon, by which they *poll* and utterly undo the poor tenants. *Spenser on Ireland.*

He told the people, that subsidies were not to be granted nor levied for wars in Scotland; for that the law had provided another course by service of escuage, much less when war was made but a pretence to *poll* and pill the people. *Bacon.*

Neither

Neither can justice yield her fruit with sweetness, amongst the briars and brambles of catching and *polling* clerks and ministers. *Bacon.*

4. To take a list or register of persons.
5. To enter one's name in a list or register.

Who ever brought to his rich daughter's bed,
The man that *polled* but twelve pence for his head? *Dryd.*

6. To insert into a number as a voter.

In solemn conclave sit, devoid of thought,
And *poll* for points of faith his trusty vote. *Tickell.*

PO'LLARD. *n. s.* [from *poll.*]

1. A tree lopped.

Nothing procureth the lasting of trees so much as often cutting; and we see all overgrown trees are *pollards* or dottards, and not trees at their full height. *Bacon.*

2. A clipped coin.

The same king called in certain counterfeit pieces coined by the French, called *pollards*, crocars and rosaries. *Camden.*

3. The chub fish. *Ainsworth.*

PO'LLEN. *n. s.* A fine powder, commonly understood by the word farina; as also a sort of fine bran. *Bailey.*

PO'LLENGER. *n. s.* Brushwood. This seems to be the meaning of this obsolete word.

Lop for thy fewel old *pollenger* grown,
That hinder the corne or the grasse to be mown. *Tusser.*

PO'LLER. *n. s.* [from *poll.*]

1. Robber; pillager; plunderer.

The *poller* and exacter of fees justifies the resemblance of the courts of justice to the bush, whereunto while the sheep flies for defence, he loses part of the fleece. *Bacon's Essays.*

2. He who votes or polls.

PO'LLEVIL. *n. s.* [*poll* and *evil.*]

Pollevil is a large swelling, inflammation or imposthume in the horse's poll or nape of the neck, just between the ears towards the mane. *Farrier's Dict.*

PO'LLOCK. *n. s.* A kind of fish.

The coast is plentifully stored with shellfish, sea-hedgehogs, scallops; and flat, as round, pilcherd, herring and *pollock.* *Carew's Survey of Cornwall.*

To POLLU'TE. *v. a.* [*polluo*, Lat. *polluer*, Fr.]

1. To make unclean, in a religious sense; to defile.

Hot and peevish vows
Are *polluted* offerings, more abhorr'd
Than spotted livers in the sacrifice. *Shakesp.*

2. To taint with guilt.

She woos the gentle air,
To hide her guilty front with innocent snow,
And on her naked shame,
Pollute with sinful blame,
The saintly veil of maiden white to throw. *Milton.*

3. To corrupt by mixtures of ill.

Envy you my praise, and would destroy
With grief my pleasures, and *pollute* my joy? *Dryden.*

4. *Milton* uses this word in an uncommon construction.

Polluted from the end of his creation. *Milton.*

POLLU'TEDNESS. *n. s.* [from *pollute.*] Defilement; the state of being polluted.

POLLU'TER. *n. s.* [from *pollute.*] Defiler; corrupter.

Ev'n he, the king of men,
Fell at his threshold, and the spoil of Troy
The foul *polluters* of his bed enjoy. *Dryden's Æneis.*

POLLU'TION. *n. s.* [*pollution*, Fr. *pollutio*, Latin.]

1. The act of defiling.

The contrary to consecration is *pollution*, which happens in churches by homicide, and burying an excommunicated person in the church. *Ayliffe's Parergon.*

2. The state of being defiled; defilement.

Their strife *pollution* brings
Upon the temple. *Milton's Par Lost, b.* xii.

PO'LTRON. *n. s.* [*pollice truncato*, from the thumb cut off; it being once a practice of cowards to cut off their thumbs, that they might not be compelled to serve in war. *Saumaise. Menage* derives it from the Italian *poltro*, a bed; as cowards feign themselves sick a bed: others derive it from *poletro* or *poltro*, a young unbroken horse.] A coward; a nidgit; a scoundrel.

Patience is for *poltrons.* *Shakesp.*

They that are bruis'd with wood or fists,
And think one beating may for once
Suffice, are cowards and *poltrons.* *Hudibras, p.* ii.

For who but a *poltron* possess'd with fear,
Such haughty insolence can tamely bear. *Dryden.*

PO'LY. *n. s.* [*polium*, Lat.] An herb. *Ainsworth.*

PO'LY. [πολυ.] A prefix often found in the composition of words derived from the Greek, and intimating multitude: as, *polygon*, a figure of many angles; *polypus*, an animal with many feet.

POLY'ACOUSTICK. *adj.* [πολὺς and ἀκούω.] Any thing that multiplies or magnifies sounds. *Dict.*

POLY'ANTHOS. *n. s.* [πολὺς and ἄνθος.] A plant.

Great varieties of *polyanthos* are annually produced, and its flowers are so numerous on one stalk, and so beautifully striped, that they are not inferior to auriculas in beauty. *Miller.*

The daisy, primrose, violet darkly blue,
And *polyanthos* of unnumber'd dyes. *Thomson.*

POLYE'DRICAL. } *adj.* [from πολύεδρος; *polyedre*, Fr.] Ha-
POLYE'DROUS. } ving many sides.

The protuberant particles may be spherical, elliptical, cylindrical, *polyedrical*, and some very irregular; and according to the nature of these, and the situation of the lucid body, the light must be variously effected. *Boyle.*

A tubercle of a pale brown spar, had the exterior surface covered with small *polyedrous* crystals, pellucid, with a cast of yellow. *Woodward.*

POLY'GAMIST. *n. s.* [from *polygamy.*] One that holds the lawfulness of more wives than one at a time.

POLY'GAMY. *n. s.* [*polygamie*, Fr. πολυγαμία.] Plurality of wives.

Polygamy is the having more wives than one at once. *Locke.*

They allow no *polygamy*: they have ordained, that none do intermarry or contract, until a month be past from their first interview. *Bacon.*

Christian religion, prohibiting *polygamy*, is more agreeable to the law of nature, that is, the law of God, than mahometism that allows it; for one man, his having many wives by law, signifies nothing, unless there were many women to one man in nature also. *Graunt.*

PO'LYGLOT. *adj.* [πολύγλωττος; *polyglotte*, Fr.] Having many languages.

The *polyglot* or linguist is a learned man. *Howel.*

PO'LYGON. *n. s.* [*polygone*, Fr. πολὺς and γωνία.] A figure of many angles.

He began with a single line; he joined two lines in an angle, and he advanced to triangles and squares, *polygons* and circles. *Watts's Improvement of the Mind.*

PO'LYGONAL. *adj.* [from *polygon.*] Having many angles.

PO'LYGRAM. *n. s.* [πολὺς and γράμμα.] A figure consisting of a great number of lines. *Dict.*

POLY'GRAPHY. *n. s.* [πολὺς and γραφὴ; *polygraphie*, Fr.] The art of writing in several unusual manners or cyphers; as also decyphering the same. *Dict.*

POLY'LOGY. *n. s.* [πολὺς and λογὸς.] Talkativeness. *Dict.*

POLY'MATHY. *n. s.* [πολυς and μάνθανω.] The knowledge of many arts and sciences; also an acquaintance with many different subjects. *Dict.*

POLY'PHONISM. *n. s.* [πολὺς and φωνὴ.] Multiplicity of sound.

The passages relate to the diminishing the sound of his pistol, by the rarity of the air at that great ascent into the atmosphere, and the magnifying the sound by the *polyphonisms* or repercussions of the rocks and caverns. *Derham.*

POLYPE'TALOUS. *adj.* [πολὺς and πέταλον.] Having many petals.

POLY'PODY. *n. s.* [*polypodium*, Latin.] A plant.

Polypody is a capillary plant with oblong jagged leaves, having a middle rib, which joins them to the stalks running through each division. *Miller.*

Polypody is common on the banks of ditches where there are stumps of old trees, on walls, and by the sides of woods: *polypody* is attenuant and dissolvent. *Hill's Materia Medica.*

A kind of *polypody* groweth out of trees, though it windeth not. *Bacon's Natural History.*

PO'LYPOUS. *adj.* [from *polypus.*] Having the nature of a polypus; having many feet or roots.

If the vessels drive back the blood with too great a force upon the heart, it will produce *polypous* concretions in the ventricles of the heart, especially when its valves are apt to grow rigid. *Arbuthnot on Aliments.*

POLY'PUS. *n. s.* [πολύπυς; *polype*, Fr.]

1. *Polypus* signifies any thing in general with many roots or feet, as a swelling in the nostrils; but it is likewise applied to a tough concretion of grumous blood in the heart and arteries. *Quincy.*

The *polypus* of the nose is said to be an excrescence of flesh, spreading its branches amongst the laminæ of the os ethmoides, and through the whole cavity of one or both nostrils. *Sharp's Surgery.*

The juices of all austere vegetables, which coagulate the spittle, being mixed with the blood in the veins, form *polypusses* in the heart. *Arbuthnot on Aliments.*

2. A sea animal with many feet.

The *polypus*, from forth his cave
Torn with full force, reluctant beats the wave,
His ragged claws are stuck with stones. *Pope.*

PO'LYSCOPE. *n. s.* [πολὺς and σκοπέω.] A multiplying glass. *Dict.*

POLY'SPAST. *n. s.* [*polyspaste*, Fr.] A machine consisting of many pullies. *Dict.*

POLY'SPERMOUS. *adj.* [πολὺς and σπέρμα.] Those plants are thus called, which have more than four seeds succeeding each flower, and this without any certain order or number. *Qu.*

POLYSYLLA'BICAL. *adj.* [from *polysyllable.*] Having many syllables; pertaining to a polysyllable.

Polysyllabical echoes are such as repeat many syllables or words distinctly. *Dict.*

POLYSY'LLABLE. *n. ſ.* [πολὺς and συλλαβὴ; *polyſyllabe*, Fr.] A word of many ſyllables.

In a *polyſyllable* word conſider to which ſyllable the emphaſis is to be given, and in each ſyllable to which letter. *Holder.*

Your high nonſenſe bluſters and makes a noiſe; it ſtalks upon hard words, and rattles through *polyſyllables.* *Addiſon.*

POLY'SYNDETON. *n. ſ.* [πολυζύνδετον.] A figure of rhethorick by which the copulative is often repeated: as, I came, *and* ſaw *and* overcame.

POLY'THEISM. *n. ſ.* [πολὺς and θεὸς; *polytheïſme*, Fr.] The doctrine of plurality of gods.

The firſt author of *polytheiſm*, Orpheus, did plainly aſſert one ſupreme God. *Stillingfleet.*

POLY'THEIST. *n. ſ.* [πολὺς and θεὸς; *polythée*, Fr.] One that holds plurality of gods.

Some authors have falſely made the Turks, *polytheiſts.* *Duncomb's Life of Hughes.*

PO'MACE. *n. ſ.* [*pomaceum*, Lat.] The droſs of cyder preſſings. *Dict.*

POMA'CEOUS. *adj.* [from *pomum*, Latin.] Conſiſting of apples.

Autumn paints
Auſonian hills with grapes, whilſt Engliſh plains
Bluſh with *pomaceous* harveſts breathing ſweets. *Philips.*

PO'MADE. *n. ſ.* [*pomade*, Fr. *pomado*, Italian.] A fragrant ointment.

PO'MANDER. *n. ſ.* [*pomme d' ambre*, Fr.] A ſweet ball; a perfumed ball or powder.

I have ſold all my trumpery; not a counterfeit ſtone, not a ribbon, glaſs, *pomander* or browch to keep my pack from faſting. *Shakeſp.*

They have in phyſick uſe of *pomander* and knots of powders for drying of rheums, comforting of the heart and provoking of ſleep. *Bacon's Natural Hiſtory.*

POMA'TUM. *n. ſ.* [Latin.] An ointment.

I gave him a little *pomatum* to dreſs the ſcab. *Wiſeman.*

To POME. *v. n.* [*pommer*, Fr.] To grow to a round head like an apple. *Dict.*

POMECI'TRON. *n. ſ.* [*pome* and *citron.*] A citron apple. *Dict.*

POMEGRA'NATE. *n. ſ.* [*pomum granatum*, Lat.]

1. The tree.

The flower of the *pomegranate* conſiſts of many leaves placed in a circular order, which expand in form of a roſe, whoſe bell-ſhaped multifid flower cup afterward becomes a globular fruit, having a thick, ſmooth, brittle rind, and is divided into ſeveral cells, which contain oblong hardy ſeeds, ſurrounded with a ſoft pulp. *Miller.*

It was the nightingale, and not the lark,
That pierc'd the fearful hollow of thine ear;
Nightly ſhe ſings on yon *pomegranate* tree. *Shakeſp.*

2. The fruit.

In times paſt they dyed ſcarlet with the ſeed of a *pomegranate.* *Peacham on Drawing.*

Nor on its ſlender twigs
Low bending be the full *pomegranate* ſcorn'd. *Thomſon.*

PO'MEROY. } *n. ſ.* A ſort of apple. *Ainſworth.*
PO'MEROYAL. }

PO'MIFEROUS. *adj.* [*pomifer*, Lat.] A term applied to plants which have the largeſt fruit, and are covered with thick hard rind, by which they are diſtinguiſhed from the bacciferous, which have only a thin ſkin over the fruit.

All *pomiferous* herbs, pumpions, melons, gourds and cucumbers, unable to ſupport themſelves, are either endued with a faculty of twining about others, or with claſpers and tendrils whereby they catch hold of them. *Ray on the Creation.*

Other fruits contain a great deal of cooling viſcid juice, combined with a nitrous ſalt, ſuch are many of the low *pomiferous* kind, as cucumbers and pompions. *Arbuth. on Aliments.*

PO'MMEL. *n. ſ.* [*pomeau*, Fr. *pomo*, Italian; *appel van t' ſwaerd*, Dutch.]

1. A round ball or knob.

Like *pommels* round of marble clear,
Where azur'd veins well mixt appear. *Sidney, b.* ii.

Huram finiſhed the two pillars and the *pommels*, and the chapters which were on the top of the two pillars. 2 *Chron.*

2. The knob that balances the blade of the ſword.

His chief enemy offered to deliver the *pommel* of his ſword in token of yielding. *Sidney.*

3. The protuberant part of the ſaddle before.

The ſtarting ſteed was ſeiz'd with ſudden fright,
And bounding, o'er the *pommel* caſt the knight. *Dryden.*

To PO'MMEL. *v. a.* [This word ſeems to come from *pommeler*, Fr. to variegate.] To beat with any thing thick or bulky, to beat black and blue; to bruiſe; to punch.

POMP. *n. ſ.* [*pompa*, Latin.]

1. Splendour; pride.

Take phyſick, *pomp*,
Expoſe thyſelf to feel what wretches feel. *Shakeſp.*

2. A proceſſion of ſplendour and oſtentation.

The bright *pomp* aſcended jubilant. *Milton.*

All eyes you draw, and with the eyes the heart;
Of your own *pomp* yourſelf the greateſt part. *Dryden.*

Such a numerous and innocent multitude, cloathed in the charity of their benefactors, was a more beautiful expreſſion of joy and thankſgiving, than could have been exhibited by all the *pomps* of a Roman triumph. *Addiſon's Guardian.*

PO'MPHOLYX. *n. ſ.*

Pompholyx is a white, light and very friable ſubſtance, found in cruſts adhering to the domes of the furnaces and to the covers of the large crucibles, in which braſs is made either from a mixture of copper and lapis calaminaris, or of copper and zink. *Hill's Materia Medica.*

PO'MPION. *n. ſ.* [*pompon*, Fr.] A pumkin. A ſort of large fruit. *Dict.*

PO'MPIRE. *n. ſ.* [*pomum* and *pyrus*, Lat.] A ſort of pearmain. *Ain.*

PO'MPOUS. *adj.* [*pompeux*, Fr.] Splendid; magnificent; grand.

What flatt'ring ſcenes our wand'ring fancy wrought,
Rome's *pompous* glories riſing to our thought. *Pope.*

An inſcription in the ancient way, plain, *pompous*, yet modeſt, will be beſt. *Atterbury to Pope.*

PO'MPOUSLY. *adv.* [from *pompous.*] Magnificently; ſplendidly.

Whate'er can urge ambitious youth to fight,
She *pompouſly* diſplays before their ſight. *Dryden.*

PO'MPOUSNESS. *n. ſ.* [from *pompous.*] Magnificence; ſplendour; ſhowineſs; oſtentatiouſneſs.

The Engliſh and French raiſe their language with metaphors, or by the *pompouſneſs* of the whole phraſe wear off any littleneſs that appears in the particular parts. *Addiſon.*

POND. *n. ſ.* [ſuppoſed to be the ſame with *pound*; pinban, Sax. to ſhut up.] A ſmall pool or lake of water; a baſon; water not running or emitting any ſtream.

In the midſt of all the place was a fair *pond*, whoſe ſhaking cryſtal was a perfect mirror to all the other beauties, ſo that it bare ſhew of two gardens. *Sidney.*

Through bogs and mires, and oft through *pond* or pool,
There ſwallow'd up. *Milton's Par. Loſt, b.* ix.

Had marine bodies been found in only one place, it might have been ſuſpected, that the ſea was, what the Caſpian is, a great *pond* or lake, confined to one part. *Woodward.*

His building is a town,
His *pond* an ocean. *Pope.*

To POND. *v. a.* To ponder. A corrupt obſolete word.

O my liege lord, the god of my life,
Pleaſeth you *pond* your ſuppliant's plaint. *Spenſer.*

To PO'NDER. *v. a.* [*pondero*, Latin.] To weigh mentally; to conſider; to attend.

Mary kept all theſe things, and *ponder'd* them in her heart. *Luke* ii. 19.

Colours, popularities and circumſtances ſway the ordinary judgment, not fully *pondering* the matter. *Bacon.*

This *ponder*, that all nations of the earth
Shall in his ſeed be bleſſed. *Milton's Par. Loſt, b.* xii.

Intent he ſeem'd,
Pond'ring future things of wond'rous weight. *Dryden.*

To PO'NDER. *v. n.* To think; to muſe. With *on.* This is an improper uſe of the word.

This tempeſt will not give me leave to *ponder*
On things would hurt me more. *Shakeſp. King Lear.*

Whom, *pond'ring* thus *on* human miſeries,
When Venus ſaw, her heav'nly ſire beſpoke. *Dryden.*

PO'NDERAL. *adj.* [from *pondus*, Lat.] Eſtimated by weight; diſtinguiſhed from numeral.

Thus did the money drachma in proceſs of time decreaſe; but all the while we may ſuppoſe the *ponderal* drachma to have continued the ſame, juſt as it has happened to us, as well as our neighbours, whoſe *ponderal* libra remains as it was, though the nummary hath much decreaſed. *Arbuthnot.*

PO'NDERABLE. *adj.* [from *pondero*, Lat.] Capable to be weighed; menſurable by ſcales.

The bite of an aſp will kill within an hour, yet the impreſſion is ſcarce viſible, and the poiſon communicated not *ponderable.* *Brown's Vulgar Errours.*

PONDERA'TION. *n. ſ.* [from *pondero*, Latin.] The act of weighing.

While we perſpire, we abſorb the outward air, and the quantity of perſpired matter, found by *ponderation*, is only the difference between that and the air imbibed. *Arbuthnot.*

PO'NDERER. *n. ſ.* [from *ponder.*] He who ponders.

PONDERO'SITY. *n. ſ.* [from *ponderous.*] Weight; gravity; heavineſs.

Cryſtal will ſink in water, as carrying in its own bulk a greater *ponderoſity* than the ſpace in any water it doth occupy. *Brown's Vulgar Errours.*

Gold is remarkable for its admirable ductility and *ponderoſity*, wherein it excels all other bodies. *Ray.*

PO'NDEROUS. *adj.* [*ponderoſus*, from *pondus*, Lat.]

1. Heavy; weighty.

It is more difficult to make gold, which is the moſt *ponderous* and materiate amongſt metals, of other metals leſs *ponderous* and materiate, than, *via verſa*, to make ſilver of lead or quickſilver; both which are more *ponderous* than ſilver. *Bacon.*

His *pond'rous* ſhield behind him caſt. *Milton.*

Upon

Upon laying a weight in one of the scales, inscribed eternity, though I threw in that of time, prosperity, affliction, wealth and poverty, which seemed very *ponderous*, they were not able to stir the opposite balance. *Addison.*

Because all the parts of an undistributed fluid are of equal gravity, or gradually placed according to the difference of it, any concretion, that can be supposed to be naturally made in such a fluid, must be all over of a similar gravity, or have the more *ponderous* parts nearer to its basis. *Bentley's Sermons.*

2. Important; momentous.

If your more *ponderous* and settl'd project
May suffer alteration, I'll point you
Where you shall have receiving shall become you. *Shakesp.*

3. Forcible; strongly impulsive.

Imagination hath more force upon things living, than things inanimate; and upon light and subtile motions, than upon motions vehement or *ponderous*. *Bacon.*

Impatient of her load,
And lab'ring underneath the *pond'rous* god,
The more she strove to shake him from her breast,
With far superior force he press'd. *Dryden.*
Press'd with the *pond'rous* blow,
Down sinks the ship within th' abyss below. *Dryden.*

PO'NDEROUSLY. *adv.* [from *ponderous.*] With great weight.

PO'NDEROUSNESS. *n. s.* [from *ponderous.*] Heaviness; weight; gravity.

The oil and spirit place themselves under or above one another, according as their *ponderousness* makes them swim or sink. *Boyle.*

PO'NDWEED. *n. s.* A plant. *Ainsworth.*

PO'NENT. *adj.* [*ponente*, Italian.] Western.

Thwart of these, as fierce,
Forth rush the levant and the *ponent* winds
Eurus and Zephyr. *Milton's Par. Lost, b.* x.

PO'NIARD. *n. s.* [*poignard*, Fr. *pugio*, Lat.] A dagger; a short stabbing weapon.

She speaks *poniards*, and every word stabs. *Shakesp.*

Melpomene would be represented, in her right hand a naked *poniard*. *Peacham on Drawing.*

Poniards hand to hand
Be banish'd from the field, that none shall dare
With shortned sword to stab in closer war. *Dryden.*

To PO'NIARD. *v. a.* [*poignardier*, French.] To stab with a poniard.

PONK. *n. s.* [Of this word I know not the original.] A nocturnal spirit; a hag.

Ne let the *ponk*, nor other evil sprights,
Ne let mischievous witches. *Spenser.*

PO'NTAGE. *n. s.* [*pons*, *pontis*, bridge.] Duty paid for the reparation of bridges.

In right of the church, they were formerly by the common law discharged from *pontage* and murage. *Ayliffe.*

PO'NTIFF. *n. s.* [*pontife*, Fr. *pontifex*, Latin.]

1. A priest; a high priest.

Livy relates, that there were found two coffins, whereof the one contained the body of Numa, and the other, his books of ceremonies, and the discipline of the *pontiffs*. *Bacon.*

2. The pope.

PONTI'FICAL. *adj.* [*pontifical*, Fr. *pontificalis*, Lat.]

1. Belonging to an high priest.

2. Popish.

It were not amiss to answer by a herald the next *pontifical* attempt, rather sending defiance than publishing answers. *Ral.*

The *pontifical* authority is as much superior to the regal, as the sun is greater than the moon. *Baker.*

3. Splendid; magnificent.

Thus did I keep my person fresh and new,
My presence, like a robe *pontifical*,
Ne'er seen, but wonder'd at. *Shakesp. Henry* IV.

4. [From *pons* and *facio.*] Bridge-building. This sense is, I believe, peculiar to *Milton*, and perhaps was intended as an equivocal satire on popery.

Now had they brought the work by wond'rous art
Pontifical, a ridge of pendent rock
Over the vex'd abyss. *Milton's Par. Lost, b.* x.

PONTI'FICAL. *n. s.* [*pontificale*, Lat.] A book containing rites and ceremonies ecclesiastical.

What the Greek and Latin churches did, may be seen in *pontificals*, containing the forms for consecrations. *South.*

By the *pontifical*, no altar is to be consecrated without reliques. *Stillingfleet.*

PONTI'FICALLY. *adv.* [from *pontifical.*] In a pontifical manner.

PONTI'FICATE. *n. s.* [*pontificat*, Fr. *pontificatus*, Lat.] Papacy; popedom.

He turned hermit in the view of being advanced to the *pontificate*. *Addison.*

Painting, sculpture and architecture may all recover themselves under the present *pontificate*, if the wars of Italy will give them leave. *Addison's Remarks on Italy.*

PO'NTIFICE. *n. s.* [*pons* and *facio.*] Bridgework; edifice of a bridge.

He, at the brink of Chaos, near the foot
Of this new wond'rous *pontifice*, unhop'd
Met his offspring dear. *Milton's Par. Lost, b.* x.

PO'NTLEVIS. *n. s.* In horsemanship, is a disorderly resisting action of a horse in disobedience to his rider, in which he rears up several times running, and rises up so upon his hindlegs, that he is in danger of coming over. *Bailey.*

PO'NTON. *n. s.* [French.]

Ponton is a floating bridge or invention to pass over water: it is made of two great boats placed at some distance from one another, both planked over, as is the interval between them, with rails on their sides: the whole so strongly built as to carry over horse and cannon. *Military Dict.*

The black prince passed many a river without the help of *pontons*. *Spectator*, N° 165.

PO'NY. *n. s.* [I know not the original of this word.] A small horse.

POOL. *n. s.* [pul, Saxon; *poel*, Dutch.] A lake of standing water.

Moss, as it cometh of moisture, so the water must but slide, and not stand in a *pool*. *Bacon.*

Sea he had search'd, and land,
From Eden over Pontus, and the *pool*
Mæotis. *Milton's Par. Lost, b.* ix.

Love oft to virtuous acts inflames the mind,
Awakes the sleepy vigour of the soul,
And brushing o'er, adds vigour to the *pool*. *Dryden.*

The circling streams, once thought the *pools* of blood,
From dark oblivion Harvey's name shall save. *Dryden.*

After the deluge, we suppose the vallies and lower grounds, where the descent and derivation of the water was not so easy, to have been full of lakes and *pools*. *Burnet.*

POOP. *n. s.* [*pouppe*, Fr. *puppis*, Lat.] The hindmost part of the ship.

Some sat upon the top of the *poop* weeping and wailing, till the sea swallowed them. *Sidney, b.* ii.

The *poop* was beaten gold. *Shakesp. Ant. and Cleop.*

Perceiving that the pigeon had only lost a piece of her tail through the next opening of the rocks, they passed safe, only the end of their *poop* was bruised. *Raleigh.*

He was openly set upon the *poop* of the gally. *Knolles.*

With wind in *poop*, the vessel ploughs the sea,
And measures back with speed her former way. *Dryden.*

POOR. *adj.* [*pauvre*, Fr. *povre*, Spanish.]

1. Not rich; indigent; necessitous; oppressed with want.

Poor cuckoldly knave.—I wrong him to call him *poor*; they say he hath masses of money. *Shakespeare.*

Who builds a church to God, and not to fame,
Will never mark the marble with his name;
Go search it there, where to be born and die,
Of rich and *poor* makes all the history. *Pope.*

2. Trifling; narrow; of little dignity, force or value.

A conservatory of snow and ice used for delicacy to cool wine, is a *poor* and contemptible use, in respect of other uses that may be made of it. *Bacon's Natural History.*

How *poor* are the imitations of nature in common course of experiments, except they be led by great judgment. *Bacon.*

When he delights in sin, as he observes it in other men, he is wholly transformed from the creature God first made him; nay, has consumed those *poor* remainders of good that the sin of Adam left him. *South.*

That I have wronged no man, will be a *poor* plea or apology at the last day; for it is not for rapin, that men are formally impeached and finally condemned; but I was an hungry, and ye gave me no meat. *Calamy's Sermons.*

3. Paltry; mean; contemptible.

A *poor* number it was to conquer Ireland to the pope's use. *Bacon.*

And if that wisdom still wise ends propound,
Why made he man, of other creatures, king;
When, if he perish here, there is not found
In all the world so *poor* and vile a thing? *Davies.*

The marquis, making haste to Scarborough, embarked in a *poor* vessel. *Clarendon, b.* viii.

We have seen how *poor* and contemptible a force has been raised by those who appeared openly. *Addis. Freeholder.*

4. Unimportant.

To be without power or distinction, is not, in my *poor* opinion, a very amiable situation to a person of title. *Swift.*

5. Unhappy; uneasy.

Vext sailors curse the rain,
For which *poor* shepherds pray'd in vain. *Waller.*
Vain privilege, *poor* woman have a tongue;
Men can stand silent, and resolve on wrong. *Dryden.*

6. Mean; depressed; low; dejected.

A soothsayer made Antonius believe, that his genius, which otherwise was brave, was, in the presence of Octavianus, *poor* and cowardly. *Bacon.*

7. [A word of tenderness.] Dear.

Poor, little, pretty, flutt'ring thing,
Must we no longer live together?
And dost thou prune thy trembling wing,
To take thy flight thou know'st not whither? *Prior.*

8. [A word of slight contempt.] Wretched.

The *poor* monk never saw many of the decrees and councils he had occasion to use. *Baker's Reflect. on Learning.*

9. Not good; not fit for any purpose.

I have very *poor* and unhappy brains for drinking: I could wish courtesy would invent some other entertainment. *Shakesp.*

10. *The* POOR. [collectively.] Those who are in the lowest rank of the community; those who cannot subsist but by the charity of others; but it is sometimes used with laxity for any not rich.

From a confin'd well manag'd store,
You both employ and feed the *poor*. *Waller.*

Never any time since the reformation can shew so many *poor* amongst the widows and orphans of churchmen, as this particular time. *Sprat's Sermons.*

Has God cast thy lot amongst the *poor* of this world, by denying thee the plenties of this life, or by taking them away? this may be preventing mercy; for much mischief riches do to the sons of men. *South's Sermons.*

The *poor* dare nothing tell but flatt'ring news. *Dryden.*

11. Barren; dry: as, a *poor* soil.

12. Lean; starved; emaciated: as, a *poor* horse.

Where juice wanteth, the language is thin, flagging, *poor*, starved and scarce covering the bone. *Benj. Johnson.*

13. Without spirit; flaccid.

POO'RLY. *adv.* [from *poor.*]

1. Without wealth.

Those thieves spared his life, letting him go to learn to live *poorly*. *Sidney, b.* ii.

2. Not prosperously; with little success.

If you sow one ground with the same kind of grain, it will prosper but *poorly*. *Bacon.*

3. Meanly; without spirit.

Your constancy
Hath left you unattended: be not lost
So *poorly* in your thoughts. *Shakesp. Macbeth.*
Nor is their courage or their wealth so low,
That from his wars they *poorly* would retire. *Dryden.*

4. Without dignity.

You meaner beauties of the night,
That *poorly* satisfy our eyes,
More by your number than your light,
You common people of the skies;
What are you when the sun shall rise. *Wotton.*

POORJOHN. *n. s.* A sort of fish. *Ainsworth.*

POO'RNESS. *n. s.* [from *poor.*]

1. Poverty; indigence; want.

If a prince should complain of the *poorness* of his exchequer, would he be angry with his merchants, if they brought him a cargo of good bullion. *Burnet's Theory of the Earth.*

2. Meanness; lowness; want of dignity.

The Italian opera seldom sinks into a *poorness* of language, but, amidst all the meanness of the thoughts, has something beautiful and sonorous in the expression. *Addison.*

There is a kind of sluggish resignation, as well as *poorness* and degeneracy of spirit, in a state of slavery. *Addison.*

3. Sterility; barrenness.

The *poorness* of the herbs shews the *poorness* of the earth, especially if in colour more dark. *Bacon.*

Enquire the differences of metals which contain other metals, and how that agrees with the *poorness* or riches of the metals in themselves. *Bacon.*

POO'RSPIRITED. *adj.* [*poor* and *spirit.*] Mean; cowardly.

Mirvan! *poorspirited* wretch! thou hast deceiv'd me. *Den.*

POO'RSPIRITEDNESS. *n. s.* Meanness; cowardice.

A cause of men's taking pleasure in the sins of others, is, from that meanness and *poorspiritedness* that accompanies guilt. *South's Sermons.*

POP. *n. s.* [*poppysma*, Lat.] A small smart quick sound. It is formed from the sound.

I have several ladies, who could not give a *pop* loud enough to be heard at the farther end of the room, who can now discharge a fan, that it shall make a report like a pocket-pistol. *Addison's Spectator*, N° 102.

To POP. *v. n.* [from the noun.] To move or enter with a quick, sudden and unexpected motion.

He that kill'd my king,
Popt in between th' election and my hopes. *Shakesp.*

A boat was sunk and all the folk drowned, saving one only woman, that in her first *popping* up again, which most living things accustom, espied the boat risen likewise, and floating by her, got hold of the boat, and sat astride upon one of its sides. *Carew's Survey of Cornwall.*

I startled at his *popping* upon me unexpectedly. *Addison.*

As he scratched to fetch up thought,
Forth *popp'd* the sprite so thin. *Swift's Miscellanies.*

Others have a trick of *popping* up and down every moment, from their paper to the audience, like an idle school-boy. *Swift.*

To POP. *v. a.*

1. To put out or in suddenly, slily or unexpectedly.

That is my brother's plea,
The which if he can prove, he *pops* me out
At least from fair five hundred pound a year. *Shakesp.*

He *popped* a paper into his hand. *Milton.*

A fellow, finding somewhat prick him, *pops* his finger upon the place. *L'Estrange's Fables.*

The commonwealth *popped* up its head for the third time under Brutus and Cassius, and then sunk for ever. *Dryden.*

Did'st thou never *pop*
Thy head into a tinman's shop? *Prior.*

2. To shift.

If their curiosity leads them to ask what they should not know, it is better to tell them plainly, that it is a thing that belongs not to them to know, than to *pop* them off with a falshood. *Locke on Education.*

POPE. *n. s.* [*papa*, Lat. πάππας.]

1. The bishop of Rome.

I refuse you for my judge; and
Appeal unto the *pope* to be judg'd by him. *Shakesp.*

He was organist in the *pope*'s chapel at Rome. *Peacham.*

Christianity has been more oppressed by those that thus fought for it, than those that were in arms against it; upon this score, the *pope* has done her more harm than the Turk. *Decay of Piety.*

2. A small fish.

A *pope*, by some called a ruffe, is much like a pearch for shape, but will not grow bigger than a gudgeon: he is an excellent fish, of a pleasant taste, and spawns in April. *Walton's Angler.*

PO'PEDOM. [*pope* and *dom.*] Papacy; papal dignity.

That world of wealth I've drawn together
For mine own ends; indeed, to gain the *popedom*. *Shakesp.*

PO'PERY. *n. s.* [from *pope.*] The religion of the church of Rome.

Popery for corruptions in doctrine and discipline, I look upon to be the most absurd system of christianity. *Swift.*

PO'PESEYE. *n. s.* [*pope* and *eye.*] The gland surrounded with fat in the middle of the thigh: why so called I know not.

PO'PGUN. *n. s.* [*pop* and *gun.*] A gun with which children play, that only makes a noise.

Life is not weak enough to be destroyed by this *popgun* artillery of tea and coffee. *Cheyne.*

POPI'NJAY. [*papegay*, Dutch; *papagayo*, Spanish.]

1. A parrot.

Young *popinjays* learn quickly to speak. *Ascham.*

The great red and blue parrot; there are of these greater, the middlemost called *popinjays*, and the lesser called perroquets. *Grew's Musæum.*

2. A woodpecker. So it seems to be used here.

Terpsichore would be expressed, upon her head a coronet of those green feathers of the *popinjay*, in token of that victory which the muses got of the daughters of Pierius, who were turned into *popinjays* or woodpeckers. *Peacham.*

3. A trifling fop.

I, all smarting with my wounds, being gall'd
To be so pester'd by a *popinjay*,
Answer'd neglectingly, I know not what. *Shakesp.*

PO'PISH. *adj.* [from *pope.*] Taught by the pope; relating to popery; peculiar to popery.

In this sense as they affirm, so we deny, that whatsoever is *popish* we ought to abrogate. *Hooker.*

I know thou art religious,
With twenty *popish* tricks and ceremonies. *Shakesp.*

PO'PISHLY. *adv.* [from *popish.*] With tendency to popery; in a popish manner.

She baffled the many attempts of her enemies, and entirely broke the whole force of that party among her subjects, which was *popishly* affected. *Addison's Freeholder.*

A friend in Ireland, *popishly* speaking, I believe constantly well disposed towards me. *Pope to Swift.*

PO'PLAR. *n. s.* [*peuplier*, Fr. *populus*, Lat.] A tree.

The leaves of the *poplar* are broad, and for the most part angular: the male trees produce amentaceous flowers, which have many little leaves and apices, but are barren: the female trees produce membraneous pods, which open into two parts, containing many seeds, which have a large quantity of down adhering to them, and are collected into spikes. *Miller.*

Po is drawn with the face of an ox, with a garland of *poplar* upon his head. *Peacham on Drawing.*

All he describ'd was present to their eyes,
And as he rais'd his verse, the *poplars* seem'd to rise. *Rosc.*
So falls a *poplar*, that in watry ground
Rais'd high the head. *Pope's Iliad.*

PO'PPY. *n. s.* [popıȝ, Sax. *papaver*, Lat.] A plant.

The flower of the *poppy*, for the most part, consists of four leaves, placed orbicularly, and expanded in form of a rose, out of whose flower cup, consisting of two leaves, rises the pointal, which afterwards becomes a fruit or pod that is oval or oblong, and adorned with a little head, under which, in some species, is opened a series of holes quite round into the cavity of the fruit, which is defended lengthwise with various leaves or plates, to which a great number of very small seeds adhere: of these are eighteen species: some sort is cultivated for medicinal use; and some suppose it to be the plant whence opium is produced. *Miller.*

His

His temples last with *poppies* were o'erspread,
That nodding seem'd to consecrate his head. *Dryden.*

Dr. Lister has been guilty of mistake, in the reflections he makes on what he calls the sleeping Cupid with *poppy* in his hands. *Addison's Remarks on Italy.*

PO'PULACE. *n. s.* [*populace*, Fr. from *populus*, Lat.] The vulgar; the multitude.

Now swarms the *populace*, a countless throng,
Youth and hoar age tumultuous pour along. *Pope.*

The tribunes and people having subdued all competitors, began the last game of a prevalent *populace*, to chuse themselves a master. *Swift.*

PO'PULACY. *n. s.* [*populace*, Fr.] The common people; the multitude.

Under colours of piety ambitious policies march, not only with security, but applause as to the *populacy*. *King Charles.*

When he thinks one monarch's lust too mild a regiment, he can let in the whole *populacy* of sin upon the soul. *D. of Piety.*

PO'PULAR. *adj.* [*populaire*, Fr. *popularis*, Lat.]

1. Vulgar; plebeian.

I was sorry to hear with what partiality and *popular* heat elections were carried in many places. *King Charles.*

The emmet join'd in her *popular* tribes
Of commonalty. *Milton.*

So the *popular* vote inclines. *Milton.*

2. Suitable to the common people.

Homilies are plain and *popular* instructions. *Hooker.*

3. Beloved by the people; pleasing to the people.

It might have been more *popular* and plausible to vulgar ears, if this first discourse had been spent in extolling the force of laws. *Hooker, b.* i.

Such as were *popular*,
And well-deserving, were advanc'd by grace. *Daniel.*

The old general was set aside, and prince Rupert put into the command, which was no *popular* change. *Clarendon.*

4. Studious of the favour of the people.

A *popular* man is, in truth, no better than a prostitute to common fame and to the people. *Dryden.*

His virtues have undone his country;
Such *popular* humanity is treason. *Addison's Cato.*

5. Prevailing or raging among the populace: as, a *popular* distemper.

POPULA'RITY. *n. s.* [*popularitas*, Lat. *popularité*, Fr. from *popular.*]

1. Graciousness among the people; state of being favoured by the people.

The best temper of minds desireth good name and true honour; the lighter, *popularity* and applause; the more depraved, subjection and tyranny. *Bacon.*

Your mind has been above the wretched affectation of *popularity*. *Dryden.*

Admire we then,
Or *popularity*, or stars, or strings,
The mob's applauses, or the gifts of kings. *Pope.*

He could be at the head of no factions and cabals, nor attended by a hired rabble, which his flatterers might represent as *popularity*. *Swift.*

2. Representation suited to vulgar conception; what affects the vulgar.

The persuader's labour is to make things appear good or evil, which as it may be performed by solid reasons, so it may be represented also by colours, *popularities* and circumstances, which sway the ordinary judgment. *Bacon.*

PO'PULARLY. *adv.* [from *popular.*]

1. In a popular manner; so as to please the crowd.

The victor knight
Bareheaded, *popularly* low had bow'd,
And paid the salutations of the crowd. *Dryden.*

Influenc'd by the rabble's bloody will,
With thumbs bent back, they *popularly* kill. *Dryden.*

2. According to vulgar conception.

Nor can we excuse the duty of our knowledge, if we only bestow those commendatory conceits, which *popularly* set forth the eminency thereof. *Brown's Vulgar Errours.*

To PO'PULATE. *v. n.* [from *populus*, people.] To breed people.

When there be great shoals of people, which go on to *populate*, without foreseeing means of life and sustentation, it is of necessity, that once in an age they discharge a portion of their people upon other nations. *Bacon's Essays.*

POPULA'TION. *n. s.* [from *populate.*] The state of a country with respect to numbers of people.

The *population* of a kingdom, especially if it be not mown down by wars, does not exceed the stock of the kingdom, which should maintain them; neither is the *population* to be reckoned, only by number; for a smaller number, that spend more and earn less, do wear out an estate sooner than a greater number, that live lower, and gather more. *Bacon.*

POPULO'SITY. *n. s.* [from *populous.*] Populousness; multitude of people.

How it conduceth unto *populosity*, we shall make but little doubt; there are two main causes of numerosity in any species; a frequent and multiparous way of breeding. *Brown.*

PO'PULOUS. *adj.* [*populosus*, Lat.] Full of people; numerously inhabited.

A wilderness is *populous* enough,
So Suffolk had thy heav'nly company. *Shakesp.*

Far the greater part have kept
Their station; heav'n yet *populous*, retains
Number sufficient to possess her realms. *Milton.*

PO'PULOUSLY. *adv.* [from *populous.*] With much people.

PO'PULOUSNESS. *n. s.* [from *populous.*] The state of abounding with people.

This will be allowed by any that considers the vastness, the opulence, the *populousness* of this region, with the ease and facility wherewith 'tis governed. *Temple's Miscellanies.*

PO'RCELAIN. *n. s.* [*porcelaine*, Fr. said to be derived from *pour cent anneés*; because it was believed by Europeans, that the materials of *porcelain* was matured under ground one hundred years.]

1. China; china ware; fine dishes, of a middle nature between earth and glass, and therefore semi-pellucid.

We have burials in several earths, where we put divers cements, as the Chinese do their *porcelain*. *Bacon.*

We are not thoroughly resolved concerning *porcelain* or china dishes; that according to common belief, they are made of earth, which lieth in preparation about a hundred years under ground. *Brown's Vulgar Errours.*

The fine materials made it weak;
Porcelain, by being pure, is apt to break. *Dryden.*

These look like the workmanship of heav'n:
This is the *porcelain* clay of human kind,
And therefore cast into these noble molds. *Dryden.*

2. [*Portulaca*, Lat.] An herb. *Ainsworth.*

PORCH. *n. s.* [*porche*, Fr. *porticus*, Lat.]

1. A roof supported by pillars before a door; an entrance.

Ehud went forth through the *porch*, and shut the doors of the parlour. *Judges* iii. 23.

Not infants in the *porch* of life were free,
The sick, the old, that could but hope a day
Longer by nature's bounty, not let stay. *Benj. Johnson.*

2. A portico; a covered walk.

All this done,
Repair to Pompey's *porch*, where you shall find us. *Shakesp.*

PO'RCUPINE. *n. s.* [*porc espi* or *epic*, Fr. *porcospino*, Italian.]

The *porcupine*, when full grown, is as large as a moderate pig: the quills, with which its whole body is covered, are black on the shoulders, thighs, sides and belly; on the back, hips and loins they are variegated with white and pale brown: the neck is short and thick, the nose blunt, the nostrils very large in form of slits; the upper lip is slit or cleft as in the hare, and it has whiskers like a cat: the eyes are small, and the ears very like those of the human species: the legs are short, and on the hinder feet are five toes, but only four upon the fore feet, and its tail is four or five inches long, beset with spines in an annular series round it: there is no other difference between the *porcupine* of Malacca and that of Europe, but that the former grows to a larger size. *Hill.*

This stubborn Cade
Fought so long, till that his thighs with darts
Were almost like a sharp-quill'd *porcupine*. *Shakespeare.*

Long bearded comets stick
Like flaming *porcupines* to their left sides,
As they would shoot their quills into their hearts. *Dryden.*

By the black prince of Monomotapa's side were the glaring cat-a-mountain and the quill-darting *porcupine*. *Ar. and Po.*

PORE. *n. s.* [*pore*, Fr. πόρος.]

1. Spiracle of the skin; passage of perspiration.

Witches, carrying in the air, and transforming themselves into other bodies, by ointments and anointing themselves all over, may justly move a man to think, that these fables are the effects of imagination; for it is certain, that ointments do all, if laid on any thing thick, by stopping of the *pores*, shut in the vapours, and send them to the head extremely. *Bac.*

Why was the sight
To such a tender ball as th' eye confin'd?
So obvious and so easy to be quench'd,
And not, as feeling through all parts diffus'd,
That she might look at will through every *pore*. *Milton.*

2. Any narrow spiracle or passage.

Pores are small interstices between the particles of matter which constitute every body, or between certain aggregates or combinations of them. *Quincy.*

From veins of vallies milk and nectar broke,
And honey sweating through the *pores* of oak. *Dryden.*

To PORE. *v. n* [πόρος is the *optick nerve*; but I imagine *pore* to come by corruption from some English word.] To look with great intenseness and care; to examine with great attention.

All delights are vain; but that most vain,
Which with pain purchas'd, doth inherit pain;
As painfully to *pore* upon a book,
To seek the light of truth, while truth the while
Doth falsely blind the eyesight, *Shakesp.*

A book

A book was writ, called Tetrachordon,
The ſubject new: it walk'd the town a while,
Numb'ring good intellects; now ſeldom *por'd* on. *Milton.*

The eye grows weary, with *poring* perpetually on the ſame thing. *Dryden's Dufreſnoy.*

Let him with pedants hunt for praiſe in books,
Pore out his life amongſt the lazy gownmen,
Grow old and vainly proud in fancy'd knowledge. *Rowe.*

With ſharpen'd ſight pale antiquaries *pore*,
Th' inſcription value, but the ruſt adore. *Pope.*

He hath been *poring* ſo long upon Fox's Martyrs, that he imagines himſelf living in the reign of queen Mary. *Swift.*

The deſign is to avoid the imputation of pedantry, to ſhew that they underſtand men and manners, and have not been *poring* upon old unfaſhionable books. *Swift.*

Po'reblind. *adj.* [commonly ſpoken and written *purblind.*] Nearſighted; ſhortſighted.

Poreblind men ſee beſt in the dimmer light, and likewiſe have their ſight ſtronger near at hand, than thoſe that are not *poreblind*, and can read and write ſmaller letters; for that the ſpirits viſual in thoſe that are *poreblind* are thinner and rarer than in others, and therefore the greater light diſperſeth them. *Bacon's Natural Hiſtory.*

Po'riness. *n. ſ.* [from *pory.*] Fullneſs of pores.

I took off the dreſſings, and ſet the trepan above the fractured bone, conſidering the *porineſs* of the bone below. *Wiſem.*

Pori'stick *method. n. ſ.* [πορισικος.] In mathematicks, is that which determines when, by what means, and how many different ways a problem may be ſolved. *Dict.*

PORK. *n. ſ.* [*porc*, Fr. *porcus*, Lat.] Swines fleſh unſalted.

You are no good member of the commonwealth; for, in converting Jews to chriſtians, you raiſe the price of *pork*. *Shakeſpeare's Merchant of Venice.*

All fleſh full of nouriſhment, as beef and *pork*, increaſe the matter of *phlegm*. *Floyer on the Humours.*

Po'rker. *n. ſ.* [from *pork.*] A hog; a pig.

Strait to the lodgments of his herd he run,
Where the fat *porkers* ſlept beneath the ſun. *Pope.*

Po'rkeater. *n. ſ.* [*pork* and *eater.*] One who feeds on pork.

This making of chriſtians will raiſe the price of hogs; if we grow all to be *porkeaters*, we ſhall not ſhortly have a raſher on the coals for money. *Shakeſp. Merch. of Venice.*

Po'rket. [from *pork.*] A young hog.

A prieſt appears
And off'rings to the flaming altars bears;
A *porket*, and a lamb that never ſuffer'd ſhears. *Dryden.*

Po'rkling. *n. ſ.* [from *pork.*] A young pig.

A hovel
Will ſerve thee in winter, moreover than that,
To ſhut up thy *porklings*, thou meaneſt to fat. *Tuſſer.*

Poro'sity. *n. ſ.* [from *porous.*] Quality of having pores.

This is a good experiment for the diſcloſure of the nature of colours; which of them require a finer *poroſity*, and which a groſſer. *Bacon's Natural Hiſtory.*

Po'rous. *adj.* [*poreux*, Fr. from *pore.*] Having ſmall ſpiracles or paſſages.

The rapid current, which through veins
Of *porous* earth with kindly thirſt updrawn,
Roſe a freſh fountain, and with many a rill
Water'd the garden. *Milton's Par. Loſt, b.* iv.

Of light the greater part he took, and plac'd
In the ſun's orb, made *porous* to receive
And drink the liquid light; firm to retain
Her gather'd beams; great palace now of light. *Milton.*

Po'rousness. *n. ſ.* [from *porous.*] The quality of having pores.

They will forcibly get into the *porouſneſs* of it, and paſs between part and part, and ſeparate the parts of that thing one from another; as a knife doth a ſolid ſubſtance, by having its thinneſt parts preſſed into it. *Digby on Bodies.*

Porphyre. } *n. ſ.* [from πορφύρα; *porphyrites*, Lat. *porphyre*,
Po'rphyry. } Fr.] Marble of a particular kind.

I like beſt the *porphyry*, white or green marble, with a mullar or upper ſtone of the ſame. *Peacham on Drawing.*

Conſider the red and white colours in *porphyre*; hinder light but from ſtriking on it, its colours vaniſh, and produce no ſuch ideas in us; but upon the return of light, it produces theſe appearances again. *Locke.*

Po'rpoise. } *n. ſ.* [*porc poiſſon*, Fr.] The ſea-hog.
Po'rpus. }

Amphibious animals link the terreſtrial and aquatick together; ſeals live at land and at ſea, and *porpoiſes* have the warm blood and entrails of a hog. *Locke.*

Parch'd with unextinguiſh'd thirſt,
Small beer I guzzle till I burſt;
And then I drag a bloated corpus
Swell'd with a dropſy like a *porpus*. *Swift.*

Porraceous. *adj.* [*porraceus*, Lat. *porrace*, Fr.] Greeniſh.

If the leſſer inteſtines be wounded, he will be troubled with *porraceous* vomiting. *Wiſeman's Surgery.*

Po'rret. *n. ſ.* [*porrum*, Lat.] A ſcallion.

It is not an eaſy problem to reſolve why garlick, molys and *porrets* have white roots, deep green leaves and black ſeeds. *Brown's Vulgar Errours.*

Po'rridge. *n. ſ.* [more properly *porrage*; *porrata*, low Latin, from *porrum*, a leek.] Food made by boiling meat in water; broth.

I had as lief you ſhould tell me of a meſs of *porridge*. *Sha.*

Po'rridgepot. *n. ſ.* [*porridge* and *pot.*] The pot in which meat is boiled for a family.

Po'rringer. *n. ſ.* [from *porridge.*]

1. A veſſel in which broth is eaten.

A ſmall wax candle put in a ſocket of braſs, then ſet upright in a *porringer* full of ſpirit of wine, then ſet both the candle and ſpirit of wine on fire, and you ſhall ſee the flame of the candle become four times bigger than otherwiſe, and appear globular. *Bacon's Nat. Hiſt.*

A phyſician undertakes a woman with ſore eyes, who dawbs 'em quite up with ointment, and, while ſhe was in that pickle, carries off a *porringer*. *L'Eſtrange.*

The *porringers*, that in a row
Hung high, and made a glitt'ring ſhow,
Were now but leathern buckets rang'd. *Swift.*

2. It ſeems in *Shakeſpeare*'s time to have been a word of contempt for a headdreſs; of which perhaps the firſt of theſe paſſages may ſhow the reaſon.

Here is the cap your worſhip did beſpeak.
—Why this was moulded on a *porringer*. *Shakeſp.*

A haberdaſher's wife of ſmall wit rail'd upon me, till her pink'd *porringer* fell off her head. *Shakeſp. Henry* VIII.

Porre'ction. *n. ſ.* [*porrectio*, Latin.] The act of reaching forth.

Port. *n. ſ.* [*port*, Fr. *portus*, Latin.]

1. A harbour; a ſafe ſtation for ſhips.

Her ſmall gondelay her *port* did make,
And that gay pair iſſuing on the ſhore,
Diſburden'd her. *Fairy Queen, b.* ii.

I ſhould be ſtill
Peering in maps for *ports*, and ways and roads. *Shakeſp.*

The earl of Newcaſtle ſeized upon that town; when there was not one *port* town in England, that avowed their obedience to the king. *Clarendon, b.* viii.

A weather beaten veſſel holds
Gladly the *port*. *Milton.*

2. [*Porta*, Lat. popꞇe, Sax. *porte*, Fr.] A gate.

Shew all thy praiſes within the *ports* of the daughter of Sion. *Pſalm* ix. 14.

Deſcend, and open your uncharged *ports*. *Shakeſp.*

He I accuſe,
The city *ports* by this hath entered. *Shakeſp. Coriolanus.*

O poliſh'd perturbation! golden care!
That keep'ſt the *ports* of ſlumber open wide
To many a watchful night; ſleep with it now!
Yet not ſo ſound, and half ſo deeply ſweet,
As he, whoſe brow with homely biggen bound,
Snores out the watch of night. *Shakeſp. Henry* IV.

The mind of man hath two *ports*; the one always frequented by the entrance of manifold vanities; the other deſolate and overgrown with graſs, by which enter our charitable thoughts and divine contemplations. *Raleigh.*

From their ivory *port* the cherubim
Forth iſſu'd. *Milton.*

3. The aperture in a ſhip, at which the gun is put out.

At Portſmouth the Mary Roſe, by a little ſway of the ſhip in caſting about, her *ports* being within ſixteen inches of the water, was overſet and loſt. *Raleigh.*

The linſtocks touch, the pond'rous ball expires,
The vig'rous ſeaman every *port* hole plies,
And adds his heart to every gun he fires. *Dryden.*

4. [*Portée*, Fr.] Carriage; air; mien; manner; bearing; external appearance; demeanour.

In that proud *port*, which her ſo goodly graceth,
Whiles her fair face ſhe rears up to the ſky,
And to the ground her eyelids low embraceth,
Moſt goodly temperature ye may deſcry. *Spenſer.*

Think you much to pay two thouſand crowns,
And bear the name and *port* of gentleman? *Shakeſp.*

See Godfrey there in purple clad and gold,
His ſtately *port* and princely look behold. *Fairfax.*

Their *port* was more than human, as they ſtood;
I took it for a fairy viſion
Of ſome gay creatures of the element,
That in the colours of the rainbow live. *Milton.*

A proud man is ſo far from making himſelf great by his haughty and contemptuous *port*, that he is uſually puniſhed with neglect for it. *Collier on Pride.*

Now lay the line, and meaſure all thy court,
By inward virtue, not external *port*;
And find whom juſtly to prefer above
The man on whom my judgment plac'd my love. *Dryden.*

Thy plumy creſt
Nods horrible, with more terrific *port*
Thou walk'ſt, and ſeem'ſt already in the fight. *Philips.*

To Port.

To Port. *v. a.* [*porto*, Lat. *porter*, Fr.] To carry in form.
Th' angelick squadron bright
Turn'd fiery red, sharpning in mooned horns
Their phalanx, and began to hem him round
With *ported* spears. *Milton's Par. Lost*, *b.* iv.

Po'rtable. *adj.* [*portabilis*, Lat.]
1. Manageable by the hand.
2. Such as may be born along with one.
The pleasure of the religious man is an easy and *portable* pleasure, such an one as he carries about in his bosom, without alarming the eye or envy of the world. *South.*
3. Such as is transported or carried from one place to another.
Most other *portable* commodities decay quickly in their use; but money is by slower degrees removed from, or brought into the free commerce of any country, than the greatest part of other merchandize. *Locke.*
4. Sufferable; supportable.
How light and *portable* my pains seem now,
When that which makes me bend, makes the king bow.
Shakespeare's King Lear.
All these are *portable*
With other graces weigh'd. *Shakesp. Macbeth.*

Po'rtableness. *n. s.* [from *portable.*] The quality of being portable.

Po'rtage. *n. s.* [*portage*, Fr.]
1. The price of carriage.
2. [From *port.*] Porthole.
Lend the eye a terrible aspect;
Let it pry through the *portage* of the head,
Like the brass cannon. *Shakespeare's Henry* V.

Po'rtal. *n. s.* [*portail*, Fr. *portella*, Italian.] A gate; the arch under which the gate opens.
King Richard doth appear,
As doth the blushing discontented sun,
From out the fiery *portal* of the east. *Shakesp. Rich.* II.
Though I should run
To those disclosing *portals* of the sun;
And walk his way, until his horses steep
Their fiery locks in the Iberian deep. *Sandys.*
He through heav'n
That open'd wide her blazing *portals*, led
To God's eternal house direct the way. *Milton.*
The sick for air before the *portal* gasp. *Dryden.*
The *portal* consists of a composite order unknown to the ancients. *Addison's Remarks on Italy.*

Po'rtance. *n. s.* [from *porter*, Fr.] Air; mien; port; demeanour.
There stepped forth a goodly lady,
That seem'd to be a woman of great worth,
And by her stately *portance* born of heav'nly birth. *F. Qu.*
Your loves,
Thinking upon his services, took from you
The apprehension of his present *portance*,
Which gibingly, ungravely, he did fashion. *Shakesp.*

Porta'ss. *n. s.* [sometimes called *portuis*, and by Chaucer *porthose.*] A breviary; a prayer book.
In his hand his *portesse* still he bare,
That much was worn, but therein little red;
For of devotion he had little care. *Fairy Queen.*
An old priest always read in his *portass* mumpsimus domine for sumpsimus; whereof when he was admonished, he said that he now had used mumpsimus thirty years, and would not leave his old mumpsimus for their new sumpsimus. *Camden.*

Portcu'llis. } *n. s.* [*portecoulisse*, Fr. quasi *porta clausa.*] A
Po'rtcluse. } sort of machine like a harrow, hung over the gates of a city, to be let down to keep out an enemy.
Over it a fair *portcullis* hong,
Which to the gate directly did incline,
With comely compass and compacture strong,
Neither unseemly short, nor yet exceeding long. *F. Qu.*
The cannon against St. Stephen's gate executed so well, that the *portcullis* and gate were broken, and entry opened into the city. *Hayward.*
She the huge *portcullis* high up drew,
Which but herself, not all the Stygian pow'rs
Cou'd once have mov'd. *Milton.*
Pyrrhus comes, neither men nor walls
His force sustain, the torn *portcullis* falls. *Denham.*
The upper eyelid claps down, and is as good a fence as a *portcullis* against the importunity of the enemy. *More.*
The gates are opened, the *portcullis* drawn;
And deluges of armies from the town
Come pouring in. *Dryden.*

To Portcullis. *v. a.* [from the noun.] To bar; to shut up.
Within my mouth you have engaol'd my tongue,
Doubly *portcullis'd* with my teeth and lips. *Shakesp.*

Po'rted. *adj.* [*porter*, Fr.] Borne in a certain or regular order.
They hem him round with *ported* spears. *Milton.*

To PORTE'ND. *v. a.* [*portendo*, Lat.] To foretoken; to foreshow as omens.
As many as remained, he earnestly exhorteth to prevent *portended* calamities. *Hooker.*
Doth this churlish superscription
Portend some alteration in good will? *Shakesp.*
A moist and a cool summer *portendeth* a hard winter. *Bacon.*
True opener of mine eyes,
Much better seems this vision, and more hope
Of peaceful days *portends*, than those two past. *Milton.*
True poets are the guardians of a state,
And when they fail, *portend* approaching fate. *Roscommon.*
The ruin of the state in the destruction of the church, is not only *portended* as its sign, but also inferred from it as its cause. *South's Sermons.*

Porte'nsion. *n. s.* [from *portend.*] The act of foretokening.
Although the red comets do carry the *portensions* of Mars, the brightly white should be of the influence of Venus. *Brown.*

PORTE'NT. *n. s.* [*portentum*, Lat.] Omen of ill; prodigy foretokening misery.
O, what *portents* are these?
Some heavy business hath my lord in hand,
And I must know it. *Shakespeare's Henry* IV.
My loss by dire *portents* the god foretold;
Yon riven oak, the fairest of the green. *Dryden.*

Porte'ntous. *adj.* [*portentosus*, Lat. from *portent.*] Monstrous; prodigious; foretokening ill.
They are *portentous* things
Unto the climate, that they point at. *Shakesp.*
This *portentous* figure
Comes armed through our watch so like the king
That was. *Shakesp. Hamlet.*
Overlay
With this *portentous* bridge the dark abyss. *Milton.*
No beast of more *portentous* size
In the Hercinian forest lies. *Roscommon.*
Let us look upon them as so many prodigious exceptions from our common nature, as so many *portentous* animals, like the strange unnatural productions of Africa. *South.*
Every unwonted meteor is *portentous*, and some divine prognostick. *Glanvil.*
The petticoat will shrink at your first coming to town; at least a touch of your pen will make it contract itself, and by that means oblige several who are terrified or astonished at this *portentous* novelty. *Addison's Spectator*, Nº 127.

PO'RTER. *n. s.* [*portier*, Fr. from *porta*, Lat. a gate.]
1. One that has the charge of the gate.
Porter, remember what I give in charge,
And, when you've so done, bring the keys to me. *Shakesp.*
Arm all my houshold presently, and charge
The *porter* he let no man in till day. *Benj. Johnson.*
Nic. Frog demanded to be his *porter*, and his fishmonger, to keep the keys of his gates, and furnish the kitchen. *Arb.*
2. One who waits at the door to receive messages.
A fav'rite *porter* with his master vie,
Be brib'd as often, and as often lie. *Pope.*
3. [*Porteur*, Fr. from *porto*, Lat. to carry.] One who carries burthens for hire.
It is with kings sometimes as with *porters*, whose packs may jostle one against the other, yet remain good friends still. *Howel.*
By *porter*, who can tell, whether I mean a man who bears burthens, or a servant who waits at a gate? *Watts.*

Po'rterage. *n. s.* [from *porter.*] Money paid for carriage.

Po'rtesse. *n. s.* A breviary. See Portass.

Po'rtglave. *n. s.* [*porter* and *glaive*, Fr. and Erse.] A sword bearer. *Ainsworth.*

Po'rtgrave. } *n. s.* [*porta*, Lat. and *grave*, Teut. a keeper.]
Po'rtgreve. } The keeper of a gate. Obsolete.

Po'rtico. *n. s.* [*porticus*, Lat. *portico*, Italian; *portique*, Fr.] A covered walk; a piazza.
The rich their wealth bestow
On some expensive airy *portico*;
Where safe from showers they may be born in state,
And free from tempests for fair weather wait. *Dryden.*

PORTION. *n. s.* [*portion*, Fr. *portio*, Latin.]
1. A part.
These are parts of his ways, but how little a *portion* is heard of him? *Job* xxvi. 14.
Like favour find the Irish, with like fate
Advanc'd to be a *portion* of our state. *Waller.*
In battles won, fortune a part did claim,
And soldiers have their *portion* in the fame. *Waller.*
Those great *portions* or fragments fell into the abyss; some in one posture, and some in another. *Burnet.*
Pirithous no small *portion* of the war
Press'd on, and shook his lance. *Dryden.*
2. A part assigned; an allotment; a dividend.
Here their pris'n ordain'd and *portion* set. *Milton.*
Shou'd you no honey vow to taste,
But what the master-bees have plac'd
In compass of their cells, how small
A *portion* to your share would fall? *Waller.*

Of words they seldom know more than the grammatical construction, unless they are born with a poetical genius, which is a rare *portion* amongst them. *Dryden.*

As soon as any good appears to make a part of their *portion* of happiness, they begin to desire it. *Locke.*

When he considers the manifold temptations of poverty and riches, and how fatally it will affect his happiness to be overcome by them, he will join with Agur in petitioning God for the safer *portion* of a moderate convenience. *Rogers.*

One or two faults are easily to be remedied with a very small *portion* of abilities. *Swift.*

3. Part of an inheritance given to a child; a fortune.

Leave to thy children tumult, strife and war,
Portions of toil, and legacies of care. *Prior.*

4. A wife's fortune.

To Po'rtion. *v. a.* [from the noun.]

1. To divide; to parcel.

The gods who *portion* out
The lots of princes as of private men,
Have put a bar between his hopes and empire. *Rowe.*
Argos the seat of sovereign rule I chose,
Where my Ulysses and his race might reign,
And *portion* to his tribes the wide domain. *Pope.*

2. To endow with a fortune.

Him *portion'd* maids, apprentic'd orphans blest,
The young who labour, and the old who rest. *Pope.*

Po'rtioner. *n. s.* [from *portion.*] One that divides.

Po'rtliness. *n. s.* [from *portly.*] Dignity of mien; grandeur of demeanour.

Such pride is praise, such *portliness* is honour,
That boldness innocence bears in her eyes;
And her fair countenance like a goodly banner
Spreads in defiance of all enemies. *Spenser.*

When substantialness combineth with delightfulness, fulness with fineness, seemliness with *portliness*, and currantness with stayedness, how can the language sound other than most full of sweetness? *Camden's Remains.*

Po'rtly. *adj.* [from *port.*]

1. Grand of mien.

Rudely thou wrong'st my dear heart's desire,
In finding fault with her too *portly* pride. *Spenser.*
Your Argosies with *portly* sail,
Like signiors and rich burghers on the flood,
Or as it were the pageants of the sea,
Do overpeer the petty traffickers. *Shakesp.*
A *portly* prince, and goodly to the sight,
He seem'd a son of Anak for his height. *Dryden.*

2. Bulky; swelling.

A goodly, *portly* man and a corpulent; of a chearful look, a pleasing eye, and a most noble carriage. *Shakesp.*

Our house little deserves
The scourge of greatness to be used on it;
And that same greatness too, which our own hands
Have help'd to make so *portly*. *Shakesp. Henry* IV.

Po'rtman. *n. s.* [*port* and *man.*] An inhabitant or burgess, as those of the cinque ports. *Dict.*

Portma'nteau. *n. s.* [*portemanteau.* Fr.] A chest or bag in which cloaths are carried.

I desired him to carry one of my *portmanteaus*; but he laughed, and bid another do it. *Spectator.*

Po'rtoise. *n. s.* In sea language, a ship is said to ride a *portoise*, when she rides with her yards struck down to the deck. *Dict.*

Po'rtrait. *n. s.* [*pourtrait*, Fr.] A picture drawn after the life.

As this idea of perfection is of little use in *portraits*, or the resemblances of particular persons, so neither is it in the characters of comedy and tragedy, which are always to be drawn with some specks of frailty, such as they have been described in history. *Dryden's Dufresnoy.*

The figure of his body was strong, proportionable, beautiful; and were his picture well drawn, it must deserve the praise given to the *portraits* of Raphael. *Prior.*

To Po'rtrait. *v. a.* [*portraire*, Fr. from the noun.] To draw; to portray. It is perhaps ill copied, and should be written in the following examples *portray*.

In most exquisite pictures, they blaze and *portrait* not only the dainty lineaments or beauty, but also round about shadow the rude thickets and craggy cliffs. *Spenser.*

I *portrait* in Arthur before he was king, the image of a brave knight, perfected in the twelve private moral virtues. *Spenser.*

Po'rtraiture. *n. s.* [*portraiture*, Fr. from *portray.*] Picture; painted resemblance.

By the image of my cause I see
The *portraiture* of his. *Shakesp. Hamlet.*
Let some strange mysterious dream,
Wave at his wings in airy stream
Of lively *portraiture* display'd,
Softly on my eye-lids laid. *Milton.*

Herein was also the *portraiture* of a hart. *Brown.*

This is the *portraiture* of our earth, drawn without flattery. *Burnet's Theory of the Earth.*

Her wry-mouth'd *portraiture*
Display'd the fates her confessors endure. *Pope.*

He delineates and gives us the *portraiture* of a perfect orator. *Baker's Reflections on Learning.*

To PO'RTRAY. *v. a.* [*pourtraire*, Fr.]

1. To paint; to describe by picture.

The Earl of Warwick's ragged staff is yet to be seen *portrayed* in many places of their church steeple. *Carew.*

Take a tile, and so *portray* upon it the city Jerusalem. *Ez.*

Our Phenix queen was *portrayed* too bright,
Beauty alone could beauty take so right. *Dryden.*

2. To adorn with pictures.

Shields
Various, with boastful argument *portray'd.* *Milton.*

Po'rtress. *n. s.* [from *porter*] A female guardian of a gate. *Janitrix.*

The *portress* of hell-gate reply'd. *Milton's Par. Lost.*
The shoes put on, our faithful *portress*
Admits us in to storm the fortress;
While like a cat with walnuts shod,
Stumbling at ev'ry step she trod. *Swift's Miscel.*

Po'rwigle. *n. s.* A tadpole or young frog not yet fully shaped.

That black and round substance began to grow oval, after a while the head, the eyes, the tail to be discernible, and at last to become that which the ancients called gyrinus, we a *porwigle* or tadpole. *Brown's Vulgar Errours.*

Po'ry. *adj.* [*poreux*, Fr. from *pore.*] Full of pores.

To the court arriv'd th' admiring son
Beholds the vaulted roofs of *pory* stone. *Dryden.*

To POSE. *v. a.* [from *pose*, an old word signifying heaviness or stupefaction. ȝepose. *Skinner.*]

1. To puzzle; to gravel; to put to a stand or stop.

Learning was *pos'd*, *philosophy* was set,
Sophisters taken in a fisher's net. *Herbert.*
How God's eternal son should be man's brother,
Poseth his proudest intellectual power. *Crashaw.*

As an evidence of human infirmities, I shall give the following instances of our intellectual blindness, not that I design to *pose* them with those common enigma's of magnetism. *Glanvill's Sceps.*

Particularly in learning of languages, there is least occasion for *posing* of children. *Locke on Education.*

2. To appose; to interrogate.

She in the presence of others *posed* him and sifted him, thereby to try whether he were indeed the very duke of York or no. *Bacon's Henry* VII.

Po'ser. *n. s.* [from *pose.*] One that asketh questions to try capacities; an examiner.

He that questioneth much, shall learn much; but let his questions not be troublesome, for that is fit for a *poser*. *Bacon.*

Posi'ted. *adj.* [*positus*, Lat. It has the appearance of a participle preter, but it has no verb.] Placed; ranged.

That the principle that sets on work these organs is nothing else but the modification of matter, or the natural motion thereof thus, or thus *posited* or disposed, is most apparently false. *Hale's Origin of Mankind.*

Posi'tion. *n. s.* [*position*, Fr. *positio*, Latin.]

1. State of being placed; situation.

Iron having stood long in a window, being thence taken, and by the help of a cork balanced in water, where it may have a free mobility, will bewray a kind of inquietude till it attain the former *position*. *Wotton.*

They are the happiest regions for fruits, by the excellence of soil, the *position* of mountains, and the frequency of streams. *Temple.*

Since no one sees all, and we have different prospects of the same thing, according to our different *positions* to it, it is not incongruous to try whether another may not have notions that escaped him. *Locke.*

By varying the *position* of my eye, and moving it nearer to or farther from the direct beam of the sun's light, the colour of the sun's reflected light constantly varied upon the speculum as it did upon my eye. *Newton's Opticks.*

We have a different prospect of the same thing, according to the different *position* of our understandings toward it. *Watts.*

Place ourselves in such a *position* toward the object, or place the object in such a *position* toward our eye, as may give us the clearest representation of it; for a different *position* greatly alters the appearance of bodies. *Watts's Logick.*

2. Principle laid down.

Of any offence or sin therein committed against God, with what conscience can ye accuse us, when your own *positions* are, that the things we observe should every one of them be dearer unto us than ten thousand lives. *Hooker.*

Let not the proof of any *positions* depend on the *positions* that follow, but always on those which go before. *Watts.*

3. Advancement of any principle.

A fallacious illation is to conclude from the *position* of the antecedent unto the *position* of the consequent, or the remotion of the consequent to the remotion of the antecedent. *Bro.*

4. [In

4. [In grammar.] The state of a vowel placed before two consonants, as *pómpous*; or a double consonant, as *áxle*.

POSI'TIONAL. *adj.* [from *position.*] Respecting position.

The leaves of catapūtia or spurge plucked upwards or downwards, performing their operations by purge or vomit; as old wives still do preach, is a strange conceit, ascribing unto plants *positional* operations. *Brown's Vulgar Errours.*

PO'SITIVE. *adj.* [*positivus*, Lat. *positif*, Fr.]

1. Not negative; capable of being affirmed; real; absolute.

The power or blossom is a *positive* good, although the remove of it, to give place to the fruit, be a comparative good. *Bacon.*

Hardness carries somewhat more of *positive* in it than impenetrability, which is negative; and is perhaps more a consequence of solidity, than solidity itself. *Locke.*

Whatsoever doth or can exist, or be considered as one thing, is *positive*; and so not only simple ideas and substances, but modes also are *positive* beings, though the parts, of which they consist, are very often relative one to another. *Locke.*

2. Absolute; particular; direct; not implied.

As for *positive* words, that he would not bear arms against king Edward's son; though the words seem calm, yet it was a plain and direct over-ruling of the king's title. *Bacon.*

3. Dogmatical; ready to lay down notions with confidence; stubborn in opinion.

I am sometimes doubting, when I might be *positive*, and sometimes confident out of season. *Rymer.*

Some *positive* persisting fops we know,
That, if once wrong, will needs be always so;
But you, with pleasure own your errors past,
And make each day a critick on the last. *Pope.*

4. Settled by arbitrary appointment.

In laws, that which is natural, bindeth universally, that which is *positive*, not so. *Hooker.*

Although no laws but *positive* be mutable, yet all are not mutable which be *positive*; *positive* laws are either permanent or else changeable, according as the matter itself is, concerning which they were made. *Hooker.*

Laws are but *positive*; love's pow'r we see,
Is nature's sanction, and her first decree. *Dryden.*

5. Having the power to enact any law.

Not to consent to the enacting of such a law, which has no view besides the general good, unless another law shall at the same time pass, with no other view but that of advancing the power of one party alone; what is this but to claim a *positive* voice, as well as a negative. *Swift.*

6. Certain; assured. *Ainsworth.*

PO'SITIVELY. *adv.* [from *positive.*]

1. Absolutely; by way of direct position.

Give me some breath, some little pause,
Before I *positively* speak in this. *Shakesp. Rich.* III.

The good or evil, which is removed, may be esteemed good or evil comparatively, and not *positively* or simply. *Bacon.*

2. Not negatively.

It is impossible that any successive duration should be actually and *positively* infinite, or have infinite successions already gone and past. *Bentley's Sermons.*

3. Certainly; without dubitation.

It was absolutely certain, that this part was *positively* yours, and could not possibly be written by any other. *Dryden.*

4. Peremptorily; in strong terms.

I would ask any man, that has but once read the bible, whether the whole tenor of the divine law does not *positively* require humility and meekness to all men. *Sprat.*

PO'SITIVENESS. *n. s.* [from *positive.*]

1. Actualness; not mere negation.

The *positiveness* of sins of commission lies both in the habitude of the will and in the executed act too; whereas the *positiveness* of sins of omission is in the habitude of the will only. *Norris.*

2. Peremptoriness; confidence.

This peremptoriness is of two sorts; the one a magisterialness in matters of opinion and speculation, the other a *positiveness* in relating matters of fact; in the one we impose upon men's understandings, in the other on their faith. *Government of the Tongue.*

POSITI'VITY. *n. s.* [from *positive.*] Peremptoriness; confidence. A low word.

Courage and *positivity* are never more necessary than on such an occasion; but it is good to join some argument with them of real and convincing force, and let it be strongly pronounced too. *Watts's Improvement of the Mind.*

PO'SITURE. *n. s.* [*positura*, Lat.] The manner in which any thing is placed.

Supposing the *positure* of the party's hand who did throw the dice, and supposing all other things, which did concur to the production of that cast, to be the very same they were, there is no doubt but in this case the cast is necessary. *Bramh.*

PO'SNET. *n. s.* [from *bassinet*, Fr. *Skinner.*] A little bason; a porringer; a skillet.

To make proof of the incorporation of silver and tin in equal quantity, and also whether it yield no soiliness more than silver; and again whether it will endure the ordinary fire, which belongeth to chaffing-dishes, *posnets* and such other silver vessels. *Bacon.*

PO'SSE. *n. s.* [Latin.] An armed power; from *posse comitatus*, the power of the shires. A low word.

The *posse* comitatus, the power of the whole county, is legally committed unto him. *Bacon.*

As if the passion that rules, were the sheriff of the place, and came with all the *posse*, the understanding is seized. *Locke.*

To POSSE'SS. *v. a.* [*possessus*, Lat. *posseder*, Fr.]

1. To have as an owner; to be master of; to enjoy or occupy actually.

She will not let instructions enter
Where folly now *possesses*? *Shakesp. Cymbeline.*
Record a gift,
Here in the court, of all he dies *possess'd*,
Unto his son. *Shakespeare's Merchant of Venice.*

Sundry more gentlemen this little hundred *possesseth* and possessioneth. *Carew's Survey of Cornwall.*

2. To seize; to obtain.

The English marched towards the river Eske, intending to *possess* a hill called Under-Eske. *Hayward.*

3. To give possession or command of any thing; to make master of. It has *of* before that which is possessed; sometimes anciently *with*.

Is he yet *possest*,
How much you would?
—Ay, ay, three thousand ducats. *Shakesp.*
This man, whom hand to hand I slew in fight,
May be *possessed with* some store of crowns. *Shakesp.*

This *possesses* us *of* the most valuable blessing of human life, friendship. *Government of the Tongue.*

Seem I to thee sufficiently *possess'd*
Of happiness or not, who am alone
From all eternity? *Milton's Par. Lost, b.* viii.

I hope to *possess* chymists and corpuscularians *of* the advantages to each party, by confederacy between them. *Boyle.*

The intent of this fable is to *possess* us *of* a just sense of the vanity of these craving appetites. *L'Estrange.*

Whole houses, *of* their whole desires *possest*,
Are often ruin'd at their own request. *Dryden.*
Of fortune's favour long *possess'd*,
He was with one fair daughter only bless'd. *Dryden.*

We *possessed* ourselves *of* the kingdom of Naples, the dutchy of Milan and the avenue of France in Italy. *Addison.*

Endowed with the greatest perfections of nature, and *possessed of* all the advantages of external condition, Solomon could not find happiness. *Prior.*

4. To fill with something fixed.

It is of unspeakable advantage to *possess* our minds with an habitual good intention, and to aim all our thoughts, words and actions at some laudable end. *Addison.*

Those, under the great officers, know every little case that is before the great man, and if they are *possessed* with honest minds, will consider poverty as a recommendation. *Addis.*

5. To have power over, as an unclean spirit.

Beware what spirit rages in your breast;
For ten inspir'd, ten thousand are *possest*. *Roscommon.*
Inspir'd within, and yet *possess'd* without. *Cleaveland.*

I think, that the man is *possessed*. *Swift.*

6. To affect by intestine power.

He's *possest* with greatness,
And speaks not to himself, but with a pride
That quarrels at self-breath. *Shakesp. Troil. and Cres.*
Let not your ears despise my tongue,
Which shall *possess* them with the heaviest sound
That ever yet they heard. *Shakesp.*
Possest with rumours full of idle dreams,
Not knowing what they fear, but full of fear. *Shakesp.*
What fury, O son,
Possesses thee, to bend that mortal dart
Against thy father's head? *Milton's Par. Lost, b.* ii.
With the rage of all their race *possest*,
Stung to the soul the brothers start from rest. *Pope.*

POSSE'SSION. *n. s.* [*possession*, Fr. *possessio*, Lat.]

1. The state of owning or having in one's own hands or power; property.

He shall inherit her, and his generation shall hold her in *possession*. *Eccluf.* iv. 16.

In *possession* such, not only of right,
I call you. *Milton.*

2. The thing possessed.

Do nothing to lose the best *possession* of life, that of honour and truth. *Temple.*

A man has no right over another's life, by his having a property in land and *possessions*. *Locke.*

To POSSE'SSION. *v. a.* To invest with property. Obsolete.

Sundry more gentlemen this little hundred possesseth and *possessioneth*. *Carew.*

POSSE'SSIONER. *n. s.* [from *possession.*] Master; one that has the power or property of any thing.

They were people, whom having been of old freemen and *possessioners*, the Lacedemonians had conquered. *Sidney.*

Po'ssessive. *adj.* [*possessivus*, Lat.] Having possession.

Po'ssessory. *adj.* [*possessoire*, Fr. from *possess.*] Having possession.

This he detains from the ivy much against his will; for he should be the true *possessory* lord thereof. *Howel.*

Posse'ssour. *n. s.* [*possessor*, Lat. *possesseur*, Fr.] Owner; master; proprietor.

Thou profoundest hell
Receive thy new *possessor*. *Milton.*

A considerable difference lies between the honour of men for natural and acquired excellencies and divine graces, that those having more of human nature in them, the honour doth more directly redound to the *possessor* of them. *Stillingfleet.*

'Twas the interest of those, who thirsted after the possessions of the clergy, to represent the *possessors* in as vile colours as they could. *Atterbury's Sermons.*

Po'sset. *n. s.* [*posca*, Lat.] Milk curdled with wine or any acid.

We'll have a *posset* at the latter end of a seacoal fire. *Shak.*

In came the bridemaids with the *posset*,
The bridegroom eat in spight. *Suckling.*

I allowed him medicated broths, *posset* ale and pearl julep. *Wiseman's Surgery.*

A sparing diet did her health assure;
Or sick, a pepper *posset* was her cure. *Dryden.*

The cure of the stone consists in vomiting with *posset* drink, in which althea roots are boiled. *Floyer on the Humours.*

Increase the milk when it is diminished by the too great use of flesh meats, by gruels and *posset* drink. *Arbuthnot.*

To Po'sset. *v. a.* [from the noun.] To turn; to curdle: as milk with acids. Not used.

Swift as quicksilver it courses through
The nat'ral gates and allies of the body;
And, with a sudden vigour, it doth *posset*
And curd, like eager droppings into milk,
The thin and wholesome blood. *Shakesp. Hamlet.*

Possibi'lity. *n. s.* [*possiblilité*, Fr.] The power of being in any manner; the state of being possible.

There is no let, but that as often as those books are read, and need so requireth, the stile of their differences may expresly be mentioned to bar even all *possibility* of error. *Hooker.*

Brother, speak with *possibilities*,
And do not break into these woeful extremes. *Shakesp.*

Consider him antecedently to his creation, while he yet lay in the barren womb of nothing, and only in the number of *possibilities*; and consequently could have nothing to recommend him to Christ's affection. *South's Sermons.*

A bare *possibility*, that a thing may be or not be, is no just cause of doubting whether a thing be or not. *Tillotson.*

According to the multifariousness of this imitability, so are the *possibilities* of being. *Norris.*

Example not only teaches us our duty, but convinces us of the *possibility* of our imitation. *Rogers's Sermons.*

PO'SSIBLE. *adj.* [*possible*, Fr. *possibilis*, Lat.] Having the power to be or to be done; not contrary to the nature of things.

Admit all these impossibilities and great absurdities to be *possible* and convenient. *Whitgifte.*

With men this is impossible, but with God all things are *possible*. *Mat.* xix. 26.

All things are *possible* to him that believeth. *Mar.* ix. 23.

Firm we subsist, but *possible* to swerve. *Milton.*

It will scarce seem *possible*, that God should engrave principles in men's minds in words of uncertain signification. *Locke.*

Set a pleasure tempting, and the hand of the Almighty visibly prepared to take vengeance, and tell whether it be *possible* for people wantonly to offend against the law. *Locke.*

Po'ssibly. *adv.* [from *possible.*]

1. By any power really existing.

Within the compass of which laws, we do not only comprehend whatsoever may be easily known to belong to the duty of all men, but even whatsoever may *possibly* be known to be of that quality. *Hooker, b.* i. *s.* 8.

Can we *possibly* his love desert? *Milton.*

2. Perhaps; without absurdity.

Possibly he might be found in the hands of the earl of Essex, but he would be dead first. *Clarendon, b.* viii.

Arbitrary power tends to make a man a bad sovereign, who might *possibly* have been a good one, had he been invested with an authority circumscrib'd by laws. *Addison.*

POST. *n. s.* [*poste*, Fr. *equis positis cursor.*]

1. A hasty messenger; a courier who comes and goes at stated times; commonly a letter carrier.

In certain places there be always fresh *posts*, to carry that farther which is brought unto them by the other. *Abbot.*

Thee I'll rake up, the *post* unsanctified
Of murth'rous lechers. *Shakesp. King Lear.*

I fear my Julia would not deign my lines,
Receiving them by such a worthless *post*. *Shakesp.*

A cripple in the way out-travels a footman, or a *post* out of the way. *Benj. Johnson's Discov.*

I send you the fair copy of the poem on dulness, which I should not care to hazard by the common *post*. *Pope.*

2. Quick course or manner of travelling. This is the sense in which it is taken; but the expression seems elliptical *to ride* post, is *to ride as a* post, or *to ride in the manner of a* post; *courir en poste*; whence *Shakespeare, to ride in* post.

I brought my master news of Juliet's death,
And then *in post* he came from Mantua
To this same monument. *Shakesp. Romeo and Juliet.*

Sent from Media *post* to Egypt. *Milton.*

He who rides *post* through an unknown country, cannot distinguish the situation of places. *Dryden.*

3. [*Poste*, Fr. from *positus*, Lat.] Situation; seat.

The waters rise every where upon the surface of the earth; which new *post*, when they had once seized on, they would never quit. *Burnet's Theory of the Earth.*

4. Military station.

See before the gate what stalking ghost
Commands the guard, what sentries keep the *post*. *Dryd.*

As I watch'd the gates,
Lodg'd on my *post*, a herald is arriv'd
From Cæsar's camp. *Addison's Cato.*

Whatever spirit careless of his charge
His *post* neglects, or leaves the fair at large,
Shall feel sharp vengeance. *Pope.*

Each of the Grecian captains he represents conquering a single Trojan, while Diomed encounters two at once; and when they are engaged, each in his distinct *post*, he only is drawn fighting in every quarter. *Pope.*

5. Place; employment; office.

Every man has his *post* assigned to him, and in that station he is well, if he can but think himself so. *L'Estrange.*

False men are not to be taken into confidence, nor fearful men into a *post* that requires resolution. *L'Estrange.*

Without letters a man can never be qualified for any considerable *post* in the camp; for courage and corporal force, unless joined with conduct, the usual effects of contemplation, is no more fit to command than a tempest. *Collier.*

While you, my lord, the rural shades admire,
And from Britannia's publick *posts* retire,
Me into foreign realms my fate conveys. *Addison.*

Certain laws, by suff'rers thought unjust,
Deny'd all *posts* of profit or of trust. *Pope.*

Many thousands there are, who determine the justice or madness of national administrations, whom neither God nor men ever qualified for such a *post* of judgment. *Watts.*

6. [*Postis*, Lat.] A piece of timber set erect.

The blood they shall strike on the two side *posts* and upper *post* of the house. *Ex.* xii. 7.

Fir-trees, cypresses and cedars being, by a kind of natural rigour, inflexible downwards, are thereby fittest for *posts* or pillars. *Wotton's Architecture.*

Post is equivocal; it is a piece of timber, or a swift messenger. *Watts's Logick.*

To Post. *v. n.* [*poster*, Fr. from the noun.] To travel with speed.

I *posted* day and night to meet you. *Shakesp.*

Will you presently take horse with him,
And with all speed *post* with him tow'rds the North? *Shak.*

Post speedily to my lord, your husband,
Shew him this letter. *Shakespeare's King Lear.*

Most wicked speed, to *post*
With such dexterity to incestuous sheets. *Shakesp.*

Then this, then that man's aid, they crave, implore;
Post here for help, seek there their followers. *Daniel.*

The Turkish messenger presently took horse, which was there in readiness for him, and *posted* towards Constantinople with as much speed as he could. *Knolles.*

Themistocles made Xerxes *post* apace out of Greece, by giving out that the Grecians had a purpose to break his bridge of ships athwart the Hellespont. *Bacon's Essays.*

Wer't thou of the golden-winged host,
Who having clad thyself in human weed,
To earth from thy prefixed seat did'st *post*. *Milton.*

Thousands at his bidding speed,
And *post* o'er land and ocean without rest. *Milton.*

With songs and dance we celebrate the day;
At other times we reign by night alone,
And *posting* through the skies pursue the moon. *Dryden.*

No wonder that pastorals are fallen into disesteem; I see the reader already uneasy at this part of Virgil, counting the pages, and *posting* to the Æneis. *Walsh.*

This only object of my real care,
In some few *posting* fatal hours is hurl'd
From wealth, from pow'r, from love and from the world. *Prior.*

To Post. *v. a.*

1. To fix opprobriously on posts.

Many gentlemen, for their integrity in their votes, were, by *posting* their names, exposed to the popular calumny and fury. *King Charles.*

On pain of being *posted* to your sorrow,
Fail not, at four, to meet me. *Granville.*

2. To place;

2. [*Poster*, Fr.] To place; to station; to fix.

The conscious priest, who was suborn'd before,
Stood ready *posted* at the postern door. *Dryden.*

He that proceeds upon other principles in his enquiry into any sciences, puts himself on that side, and *posts* himself in a party, which he will not quit till he be beaten out. *Locke.*

When a man is *posted* in the station of a minister, he is sure, beside the natural fatigue of it, to incur the envy of some, and the displeasure of others. *Addison's Freeholder.*

3. To register methodically; to transcribe from one book into another. A term common among merchants.

You have not *posted* your books these ten years; how should a man of business keep his affairs even at this rate? *Arbuthnot.*

4. To delay. Obsolete.

I have not stopt mine ears to their demands,
Nor *posted* off their suits with slow delays;
Then why should they love Edward more than me. *Shakespeare.*

PO'STAGE. *n. s.* [from *post.*] Money paid for conveyance of a letter.

Fifty pounds for the *postage* of a letter! to send by the church, is the dearest road in Christendom. *Dryden.*

POSTBOY. *n. s.* [*post* and *boy.*] Courier; boy that rides post.

This genius came thither in the shape of a *postboy*, and cried out, that Mons was relieved. *Tatler.*

To PO'STDATE. *v. a.* [*post*, after, Lat. and *date.*] To date later than the real time.

POSTDILU'VIAN. *adj.* [*post* and *diluvium*, Lat.] Posteriour to the flood.

Take a view of the *postdiluvian* state of this our globe, how it hath stood for this last four thousand years. *Woodw.*

POSTDILU'VIAN. *n. s.* [*post* and *diluvium*, Lat.] One that lived since the flood.

The antidiluvians lived a thousand years; and as for the age of the *postdiluvians* for some centuries, the annals of Phœnicia, Egypt and China agree with the tenor of the sacred story. *Grew's Cosmol. b.* iv.

PO'STER. *n. s.* [from *post.*] A courier; one that travels hastily.

Weird sisters hand in hand,
Posters of the sea and land,
Thus do go about. *Shakesp. Macbeth.*

POSTE'RIOR. *adj.* [*posterior*, Lat. *posterieur*, Fr.]

1. Happening after; placed after; following.

Where the anterior body giveth way, as fast as the *posterior* cometh on, it maketh no noise, be the motion never so great. *Bacon.*

No care was taken to have this matter remedied by the explanatory articles, *posterior* to the report. *Addison.*

Hesiod was *posterior* to Homer. *Broome.*

This orderly disposition of things includes the ideas of prior, *posterior* and simultaneous. *Watts's Logick.*

2. Backward.

And now had fame's *posterior* trumpet blown,
And all the nations summon'd. *Dunciad, b.* iv.

POSTE'RIORS. *n. s.* [*posteriora*, Lat.] The hinder parts.

To raise one hundred and ten thousand pounds, is as vain as that of Rabelais, to squeeze out wind from the *posteriors* of a dead ass. *Swift.*

POSTE'RIORITY. *n. s.* [*posteriorité*, Fr. from *posterior.*] The state of being after; opposite to *priority.*

Although the condition of sex and *posteriority* of creation might extenuate the error of a woman, yet it was unexcusable in the man. *Brown's Vulgar Errours.*

There must be a *posteriority* in time of every compounded body, to these more simple bodies out of which it is constituted. *Hale's Origin of Mankind.*

POSTE'RITY. *n. s.* [*posterité*, Fr. *posteritas*, Lat.] Succeeding generations; descendants: opposed to ancestors.

It was said,
It should not stand in thy *posterity*;
But that myself should be the father
Of many kings. *Shakesp. Macbeth.*

Since arms avail not now that Henry's dead!
Posterity await for wretched years. *Shakesp. Henry* VI.

Posterity inform'd by thee might know. *Milton.*

Their names shall be transmitted to *posterity*, and spoken of through all future ages. *Smalridge's Sermons.*

To th' unhappy, that unjustly bleed,
Heav'n gives *posterity* t' avenge the deed. *Pope.*

PO'STERN. *n. s.* [*poterne*, Fr. *posterne*, Dutch; *janua postica*, Lat.] A small gate; a little door.

E're dawning light
Discover'd had the world to heaven wide,
He by a privy *postern* took his flight,
That of no envious eyes he mote be spy'd. *Fa. Queen.*

Go on, good Eglamour,
Out at the *postern* by the abby wall. *Shakespeare.*

By-broken bywayes did I inward pass,
And in that window made a *postern* wide. *Fairfax.*

These issued into the base court through a privy *postern*, and sharply visited the assailants with halberds. *Hayward.*

POS

Great Britain hath had by his majesty a strong addition; the *postern*, by which we were so often entered and surprised, is now made up. *Raleigh's Essays.*

The conscious priest, who was suborn'd before,
Stood ready posted at the *postern* door. *Dryden.*

If the nerves, which are the conduits to convey them from without to the audience in the brain, be so disordered, as not to perform their functions, they have no *postern* to be admitted by, no other ways to bring themselves into view. *Locke.*

A private *postern* opens to my gardens
Through which the beauteous captive might remove. *Rowe.*

POSTEXI'STENCE. *n. s.* [*post* and *existence.*] Future existence.

As Simonides has exposed the vicious part of women from the doctrine of pre-existence, some of the ancient philosophers have satyrized the vicious part of the human species from a notion of the soul's *postexistence.* *Addison's Spect.*

POSTHA'CKNEY. *n. s.* [*post* and *hackney.*] Hired posthorses.

Espying the French ambassador with the king's coach attending him, made them balk the beaten road and teach *posthackneys* to leap hedges. *Wotton.*

POSTHA'STE. *n. s.* [*post* and *haste.*] Haste like that of a courier.

This is
The source of this our watch, and the chief head
Of this *posthaste* and romage in the land. *Shakesp.*

The duke
Requires your haste, *posthaste* appearance,
Ev'n on the instant. *Shakesp. Othello.*

This man tells us, that the world waxes old, though not in *posthaste.* *Hakewill on Providence.*

PO'STHORSE. *n. s.* [*post* and *horse.*] A horse stationed for the use of couriers.

He lay under a tree, while his servants were getting fresh *posthorses* for him. *Sidney, b.* ii.

He cannot live, I hope; and must not die,
Till George be pack'd with *posthorse* up to heav'n. *Shakesp.*

Xaycus was forthwith beset on every side and taken prisoner, and by *posthorses* conveyed with all speed to Constantinople. *Knolles's History of the Turks.*

PO'STHOUSE. *n. s.* [*post* and *house.*] Post office; house where letters are taken and dispatched.

An officer at the *posthouse* in London places every letter he takes in, in the box belonging to the proper road. *Watts.*

PO'STHUMOUS. *adj.* [*posthumus*, Lat. *posthume*, Fr.] Done, had, or published after one's death.

In our present miserable and divided condition, how just soever a man's pretensions may be to a great or blameless reputation, he must, with regard to his *posthumous* character, content himself with such a consideration as induced the famous Sir Francis Bacon, after having bequeathed his soul to God, and his body to the earth, to leave his fame to foreign nations. *Addison's Freeholder*, Nº 35.

PO'STICK. *adj.* [*posticus*, Lat.] Backward.

The *postick* and backward position of the feminine parts in quadrupeds can hardly admit the substitution of masculine generation. *Brown's Vulgar Errours.*

PO'STIL. *n. s.* [*postille*, Fr. *postilla*, Lat.] Gloss; marginal notes.

To PO'STIL. *v. a.* [from the noun.] To gloss; to illustrate with marginal notes.

I have seen a book of account of Empson's, that had the king's hand almost to every leaf by way of signing, and was in some places *postilled* in the margin with the king's hand. *Bacon's Henry* VII.

POSTI'LLER. *n. s.* [from *postil.*] One who glosses or illustrates with marginal notes.

It hath been observed by many holy writers, commonly delivered by *postillers* and commentators. *Brown.*

Hence you phantastick *postillers* in song,
My text defeats your art, ties nature's tongue. *Cleaveland.*

POSTI'LION. *n. s.* [*postillon*, French.]

1. One who guides the first pair of a set of six horses in a coach.

A young batchelor of arts came to town recommended to a chaplain's place; but none being vacant, modestly accepted of that of a *postilion.* *Tatler*, Nº 52.

2. One who guides a post chaise.

POSTLIMI'NIOUS. *adj.* [*postliminium*, Lat.] Done or contrived subsequently.

The reason why men are so short and weak in governing, is, because most things fall out to them accidentally, and come not into any compliance with their pre-conceiv'd ends, but are forced to comply subsequently, and to strike in with things as they fall out, by *postliminious* after-applications of them to their purposes. *South's Sermons.*

POSTMA'STER. *n. s.* [*post* and *master.*] One who has charge of publick conveyance of letters.

I came yonder at Eaton to marry Mrs. Anne Page; and 'tis a *postmaster*'s boy. *Shakesp. Merry Wives of Windsor.*

Without this letter, as he believes that happy revolution had never been effected, he prays to be made *postmaster* general. *Spectator*, Nº 629.

Postma'ster-general. *n. s.* He who presides over the posts or letter carriers.

Postmeri'dian. *adj.* [*postmeridianus*, Lat.] Being in the afternoon.

Over hasty digestion is the inconvenience of *postmeridian* sleep. *Bacon's Nat. Hist.*

Po'stoffice. *n. s.* [*post* and *office*.] Office where letters are delivered to the post; a posthouse.

If you don't send to me now and then, the *postoffice* will think me of no consequence; for I have no correspondent but you. *Gay to Swift.*

If you are sent to the *postoffice* with a letter, put it in carefully. *Swift.*

To **Postpo'ne.** *v. a.* [*postpono*, Lat. *postposer*, Fr.]

1. To put off; to delay.

You wou'd *postpone* me to another reign,
Till when you are content to be unjust. *Dryden.*

The most trifling amusement is suffered to *postpone* the one thing necessary. *Rogers's Sermons.*

2. To set in value below something else.

All other considerations should give way, and be *postponed* to this. *Locke on Education.*

Po'stscript. *n. s.* [*post* and *scriptum*, Lat.] The paragraph added to the end of a letter.

I think he prefers the publick good to his private opinion; and therefore is willing his proposals should with freedom be examined: thus I understand his *postscript*. *Locke.*

One, when he wrote a letter, would put that which was most material in the *postscript*. *Bacon's Essays.*

The following letter I shall give my reader at length, without either preface or *postscript*. *Addison's Spectator.*

Your saying that I ought to have writ a *postscript* to Gay's, makes me not content to write less than a whole letter. *Pope.*

To **PO'STULATE.** *v. a.* [*postulo*, Lat. *postuler*, Fr.] To beg or assume without proof.

They most powerfully magnify God, who, not from *postulated* and precarious inferences, entreat a courteous assent, but from experiments and undeniable effects. *Brown.*

Po'stulate. *n. s.* [*postulatum*, Lat.] Position supposed or assumed without proof.

This we shall induce not from *postulates* and intreated maxims, but from undeniable principles. *Brown.*

Some have cast all their learning into the method of mathematicians, under theorems, problems and *postulates*. *Watts.*

Postula'tion. *n. s.* [*postulatio*, Lat. *postulation*, Fr. from *postulate*.] The act of supposing without proof; gratuitous assumption.

A second *postulation* to elicit my assent, is the veracity of him that reports it. *Hale's Origin of Mankind.*

Po'stulatory. *adj.* [from *postulate*.]

1. Assuming without proof.
2. Assumed without proof.

Whoever shall peruse the phytognomy of Porta, and strictly observe how vegetable realities are forced into animal representations, may perceive the semblance is but *postulatory*. *Bro.*

Po'sture. *n. s.* [*posture*, Fr. *positura*, Latin.]

1. Place; situation.

Although these studies are not so pleasing as contemplations physical or mathematical, yet they recompense with the excellency of their use in relation to man, and his noblest *posture* and station in this world, a state of regulated society. *Hale.*

According to the *posture* of our affairs in the last campaign, this prince could have turned the balance on either side. *Addis.*

2. Voluntary collocation of the parts of the body with respect to each other.

He starts,
Then lays his finger on his temple; strait
Springs out into fast gait; then stops again,
Strikes his breast hard, and then anon he casts
His eyes against the moon, in most strange *postures*. *Shak.*

Where there are affections of reverence, there will be *postures* of reverence. *South's Sermons.*

The *posture* of a poetick figure is the description of his heroes in the performance of such or such an action. *Dryden.*

In the meanest marble statue, one sees the faces, *postures*, airs and dress of those that lived so many ages before us. *Add.*

3. State; disposition.

The lord Hopton left Arundel-castle, before he had put it into the good *posture* he intended. *Clarendon, b.* viii.

I am at the same point and *posture* I was, when they forced me to leave Whitehall. *King Charles.*

In this abject *posture* have ye sworn
T' adore the conqueror. *Milton.*

The several *postures* of his devout soul in all conditions of life, are displayed with great simplicity. *Atterbury.*

To **Po'sture.** *v. a.* [from the noun.] To put in any particular place or disposition.

The gillfins are so *postured*, as to move from back to belly and e contra. *Grew.*

POSTULA'TUM. *n. s.* [Latin.] Position assumed without proof.

Calumnies often refuted, are the *postulatums* of scriblers, upon which they proceed as upon first principles. *Addison.*

Posturema'ster. *n. s.* [*posture* and *master*.] One who teaches or practises artificial contortions of the body.

When the students have accomplished themselves in this part, they are to be delivered into the hands of a kind of *posturemaster*. *Spectator*, N° 305.

Po'sy. *n. s.* [contracted from *poesy*.]

1. A motto on a ring.

A paltry ring,
That she did give me, whose *posy* was,
Like cutler's poetry;
Love me and leave me not. *Shakesp. Merch. of Venice.*

You have chosen a very short text to enlarge upon; I should as soon expect to see a critick on the *posy* of a ring, as on the inscription of a medal. *Addison.*

2. A bunch of flowers. Of unknown derivation.

With store of vermeil roses,
To deck their bridegroom's *posies*. *Spenser.*

We make a difference between suffering thistles to grow among us, and wearing them for *posies*. *Swift.*

Pot. *n. s.* [*pot*, Fr. in all the senses, and Dutch; *potte*, Islandick.]

1. A vessel in which meat is boiled on the fire.

Toad that under the cold stone
Swelter'd, venom sleeping got;
Boil thou first i'th' charmed *pot*. *Shakesp. Macbeth.*

Gigantick hinds, as soon as work was done,
To their huge *pots* of boiling pulse would run,
Fell to with eager joy. *Dryden.*

2. Vessel to hold liquids.

The woman left her water *pot*, and went her way. *John.*

3. Vessel made of earth.

Whenever potters meet with any chalk or marl mixed with their clay, though it will with the clay hold burning, yet whenever any water comes near any such *pots* after they are burnt, both the chalk and marl will slack and spoil their ware. *Mortimer's Husbandry.*

4. A small cup.

But that I think his father loves him not,
I'd have him poison'd with a *pot* of ale. *Shakesp.*

Suppose your eyes sent equal rays,
Upon two distant *pots* of ale,
Not knowing which was mild or stale. *Prior.*

A soldier drinks his *pot*, and then offers payment. *Swift.*

5. *To go to* Pot. To be destroyed or devoured. A low phrase.

The sheep went first to *pot*, the goats next, and after them the oxen, and all little enough to keep life together. *L'Est.*

John's ready money went into the lawyers pockets; then John began to borrow money upon the bank stock, now and then a farm went to *pot*. *Arbuthnot's Hist. of J. Bull.*

To **Pot.** *v. a.* [from the noun.]

1. To preserve seasoned in pots.

Potted fowl and fish come in so fast,
That ere the first is out, the second stinks,
And mouldy mother gathers on the brinks. *Dryden.*

2. To inclose in pots of earth.

Pot them in natural, not forced earth; a layer of rich mould beneath, and about this natural earth to nourish the fibres, but not so as to touch the bulbs. *Evelyn.*

Acorns, mast and other seeds may be kept well, by being barrelled or *potted* up with moist sand. *Mortimer.*

PO'TABLE. *adj.* [*potable*, Fr. *potabilis*, Lat.] Such as may be drank; drinkable.

Thou best of gold are worst of gold,
Other less fine in carrat, is more precious,
Preserving life in med'cine *potable*. *Shakespeare.*

Dig a pit upon the sea shore, somewhat above the high water mark, and sink it as deep as the low water mark; and as the tide cometh in, it will fill with water fresh and *potable*. *Bacon's Nat. Hist.*

Rivers run *potable* gold. *Milton's Par. Lost.*

The said *potable* gold should be endued with a capacity of being agglutinated and assimilated to the innate heat. *Harvey.*

Where solar beams
Parch thirsty human veins, the damask'd meads
Unforc'd display ten thousand painted flow'rs
Useful in *potables*. *Philips.*

Po'tableness. *n. s.* [from *potable*.] Drinkableness.

Po'tager. *n. s.* [from *pottage*.] A porringer.

An Indian dish or *potager*, made of the bark of a tree, with the sides and rim sewed together after the manner of twiggen-work. *Grew's Musæum.*

Pota'rgo. *n. s.* A West Indian pickle.

What lord of old would bid his cook prepare
Mangos, *potargo*, champignons, cavarre. *King.*

Po'tash. *n. s.* [*potasse*, Fr.]

Potash, in general, is an impure fixed alcaline salt, made by burning from vegetables: we have five kinds of this salt now in use; 1. The German *potash*, made from burnt wood, and commonly sold under the name of pearlashes. 2. The Spanish called barilla, made by burning a species of kali, a plant which the Spaniards sow in the fields as we do corn. 3. The home-made *potash*, made from fern and other useless plants,

plants, collected in large quantities and burnt. 4. The Swedish, and 5. Russian kinds, with a volatile acid matter combined with them; but the Russian is stronger than the Swedish, which is made of decayed wood only: *potash* is of great use to the manufacturers of soap and glass, to bleachers and to dyers; it is also an ingredient in some medicinal compositions, but the Russian *potash* is greatly preferable to all the other kinds. *Hill's Materia Medica.*

Cheshire rock-salt, with a little nitre, allum and *potash*, is the common flux used for the running of the plate-glass. *Woodward on Fossils.*

POTA'TION. *n. s.* [*potatio*, Lat.] Drinking bout; draught.

Roderigo,
Whom love hath turned almost the wrong side out
To Desdemona, hath to night carouz'd
Potations pottle deep. *Shakesp. Othello.*

If I had a thousand sons, the first human principle I would teach them, should be to forswear thin *potations*, and to addict themselves to sack. *Shakespeare's Henry* IV.

POTA'TO. *n. s.* [I suppose an American word.] An esculent root.

The red and white *potatoes* are the most common esculent roots now in use, and were originally brought from Virginia into Europe. *Miller.*

On choicest melons and sweet grapes they dine,
And with *potatoes* fat their wanton swine. *Waller.*

The families of farmers live in filth and nastiness upon butter-milk and *potatoes*. *Swift.*

Leek to the Welch, to Dutchmen butter's dear,
Of Irish swains *potatoe* is the chear;
Oats for their feasts the Scottish shepherds grind,
Sweet turnips are the food of Blouzelind;
While she loves turnips, butter I'll despise,
Nor leeks, nor oatmeal, nor *potatoe* prize. *Gay.*

POTBE'LLIED. *adj.* [*pot* and *belly.*] Having a swoln paunch.

POTBE'LLY. *n. s.* [*pot* and *belly.*] A swelling paunch.

He will find himself a forked shadling animal and a *potbelly*. *Arbuthnot and Pope.*

To POTCH. *v. a.* [*pocher*, Fr. to thrust out the eyes as with the thumb.]

1. To thrust; to push.

Where
I thought to crush him in an equal force,
True sword to sword; I'll *potch* at him some way,
Or wrath or craft may get him. *Shakesp. Coriolanus.*

2. [*Pocher*, Fr.] To poach; to boil slightly.

In great wounds, it is necessary to observe a spare diet, as panadoes or a *potched* egg; this much availing to prevent inflammation. *Wiseman's Surgery.*

PO'TCOMPANION. *n. s.* A fellow drinker; a good fellow at carousals.

PO'TENCY. *n. s.* [*potentia*, Lat.]

1. Power; influence.

Now arriving
At place of *potency* and sway o'th' state,
If he should still malignantly remain
Fast foe to the plebeians, your voices might
Be curses to yourselves. *Shakesp. Coriolanus.*

I would I had your *potency*. *Shakesp.*

Thou hast sought to make us break our vow,
To come betwixt our sentence and our power,
Which nor our nature nor our place can bear,
Our *potency* make good. *Shakespeare.*

By what name shall we call such an one, as exceedeth God in *potency*. *Raleigh's History of the World.*

2. Efficacy; strength.

Use can master the devil, or throw him out
With wond'rous *potency*. *Shakesp. Hamlet.*

PO'TENT. *adj.* [*potens*, Latin.]

1. Powerful; forcible; strong; efficacious.

There is nothing more contagious than some kinds of harmony; than some nothing more strong and *potent* unto good. *Hooker.*

Why stand these royal fronts amazed thus?
Cry havock, kings; back to the stained field,
You equal *potents*, fiery kindled spirits! *Shakesp.*

I do believe,
Induc'd by *potent* circumstances, that
You are mine enemy. *Shakesp. Henry* VIII.

Here's another
More *potent* than the first. *Shakespeare's Macbeth.*

One would wonder how, from so differing premisses, they should infer the same conclusion, were it not that the conspiration of interest were too *potent* for the diversity of judgment. *Decay of Piety.*

When by command
Moses once more his *potent* rod extends
Over the sea; the sea his rod obeys. *Milton.*

Verses are the *potent* charms we use,
Heroick thoughts and virtue to infuse. *Waller.*

The magistrate cannot urge obedience upon such *potent* grounds, as the minister can urge disobedience. *South.*

How the effluvia of a magnet can be so rare and subtile, as to pass through a plate of glass without any resistance or diminution of their force, and yet so *potent* as to turn a magnetick needle through the glass. *Newton's Opticks.*

The chemical preparations are more vigorous and *potent* in their effects than the galenical. *Baker.*

Cyclop, since human flesh has been thy feast,
Now drain this goblet *potent* to digest. *Pope.*

2. Having great authority or dominion: as, potent *monarchs*.

PO'TENTATE. *n. s.* [*potentat*, Fr.] Monarch; prince; sovereign.

This gentleman is come to me,
With commendations from great *potentates*. *Shakesp.*

Kings and mightiest *potentates* must die. *Shakesp.*

These defences are but compliments,
To dally with confining *potentates*. *Daniel.*

All obey'd the superior voice
Of their great *potentate*; for great indeed
His name, and high was his degree in heav'n. *Milton.*

Exalting him not only above earthly princes and *potentates*, but above the highest of the celestial hierarchy. *Boyle.*

Each *potentate*, as wary fear, or strength,
Or emulation urg'd, his neighbour's bounds
Invades. *Philips.*

POTE'NTIAL. *adj.* [*potenciel*, Fr. *potentialis*, Latin.]

1. Existing in possibility, not in act.

This *potential* and imaginary materia prima cannot exist without form. *Raleigh's Hist. of the World.*

2. Having the effect without the external actual property.

The magnifico is much belov'd,
And hath in his effect a voice *potential*,
As double as the duke's. *Shakesp. Othello.*

Ice doth not only submit unto actual heat, but indureth not the *potential* calidity of many waters. *Brown.*

3. Efficacious; powerful.

Thou must make a dullard of the world,
If they not thought the profits of my death
Were very pregnant and *potential* spurs
To make thee seek it. *Shakesp.*

4. In grammar, *potential* is a mood denoting the possibility of doing any action.

POTENTIA'LITY. *n. s.* [from *potential.*] Possibility; not actuality.

Manna represented to every man the taste himself did like, but it had in its own *potentiality* all those tastes and dispositions eminently. *Taylor's Worthy Communicant.*

God is an eternal substance and act, without *potentiality* and matter, the principle of motion, the cause of nature. *Still.*

The true notion of a soul's eternity is this, that the future moments of its duration can never be all past and present; but still there will be a futurity and *potentiality* of more for ever and ever. *Bentley's Sermons.*

POTE'NTIALLY. *adv.* [from *potential.*]

1. In power or possibility; not in act or positively.

This duration of human souls is only *potentially* infinite; for their eternity consists only in an endless capacity of continuance without ever ceasing to be in a boundless futurity, that can never be exhausted, or all of it be past or present; but their duration can never be positively and actually eternal, because it is most manifest, that no moment can ever be assigned, wherein it shall be true, that such a soul hath then actually sustained an infinite duration. *Bentley.*

2. In efficacy; not in actuality.

They should tell us, whether only that be taken out of scripture which is actually and particularly there set down, or else that also which the general principles and rules of scripture *potentially* contain. *Hooker, b.* iii.

Blackness is produced upon the blade of a knife that has cut sour apples, if the juice, though both actually and *potentially* cold, be not quickly wiped off. *Boyle on Colours.*

PO'TENTLY. *adv.* [from *potent.*] Powerfully; forcibly.

You're *potently* oppos'd; and with a malice
Of as great size. *Shakesp. Henry* VIII.

Metals are hardened by often heating and quenching; for cold worketh most *potently* upon heat precedent. *Bacon.*

Oil of vitriol, though a *potently* acid menstruum, will yet precipitate many bodies mineral, and others dissolved not only in aquafortis, but in spirit of vinegar. *Boyle.*

POTE'NTNESS. *n. s.* [from *potent.*] Powerfulness; might; power.

PO'TGUN. *n. s.* [by mistake or corruption used for *popgun.*] A gun which makes a small smart noise.

An author, thus who pants for fame,
Begins the world with fear and shame,
When first in print, you see him dread
Each *potgun* levell'd at his head. *Swift's Miscel.*

POTHA'NGER. *n. s.* [*pot* and *hanger.*] Hook or branch on which the pot is hung over the fire.

PO'THECARY. *n. s.* [contracted by pronunciation and poetical convenience from *apothecary*; from *apotheca*, Lat.] One who compounds and sells physick.

Modern *'pothecaries*, taught the art
By doctor's bills to play the doctor's part,
Bold in the practice of mistaken rules,
Prescribe, apply, and call their masters fools. *Pope.*

PO'THER. *n. s.* [This word is of double orthography and uncertain etymology: it is sometimes written *podder*, sometimes *pudder*, and is derived by *Junius* from *foudre*, thunder, Fr. by *Skinner* from *peuteren* or *peteren*, Dutch, to shake or dig; and more probably by a second thought from *poudre*, Fr. dust.]

1. Bustle; tumult; flutter.

Such a *pother*,
As if that whatsoever god, who leads him,
Were crept into his human pow'rs,
And gave him graceful posture. *Shakesp. Coriolanus.*

Some hold the one, and some the other,
But howsoe'er they make a *pother*. *Hudibras.*

What a *pother* has been here with Wood and his brass,
Who would modestly make a few halfpennies pass? *Swift.*

'Tis yet in vain to keep a *pother*
About one vice, and fall into the other. *Pope.*

I always speak well of thee,
Thou always speak'st ill of me;
Yet after all our noise and *pother*,
The world believes nor one nor t'other. *Guardian.*

2. Suffocating cloud.

He suddenly unties the poke,
Which from it sent out such a smoke,
As ready was them all to choke,
So grievous was the *pother*. *Drayton.*

To PO'THER. *v. a.* To make a blustering ineffectual effort.

He that loves reading and writing, yet finds certain seasons wherein those things have no relish, only *pothers* and wearies himself to no purpose. *Locke.*

PO'THERB. *n. s.* [*pot* and *herb*.] An herb fit for the pot.

Sir Tristram telling us tobacco was a *potherb*, bid the drawer bring in t'other halfpint. *Tatler*, Nº 57.

Egypt baser than the beasts they worship;
Below their *potherb* gods that grow in gardens. *Dryden.*

Of alimentary leaves, the olera or *potherbs* afford an excellent nourishment; amongst those are the cole or cabbage kind. *Arbuthnot.*

Leaves eaten raw are termed sallad; if boiled, they become *potherbs*: and some of those plants, which are *potherbs* in one family, are sallad in another. *Watts.*

PO'THOOK. *n. s.* [*pot* and *hook*.] Hooks to fasten pots or kettles with; also ill formed or scrawling letters or characters.

PO'TION. *n. s.* [*potion*, Fr. *potio*, Lat.] A draught; commonly a physical draught.

For tastes in the taking of a *potion* or pills, the head and neck shake. *Bacon's Nat. Hist.*

The earl was by nature of so indifferent a taste, that he would stop in the midst of any physical *potion*, and after he had licked his lips, would drink off the rest. *Wotton.*

Most do taste through fond intemperate thirst,
Soon as the *potion* works, their human countenance,
Th' express resemblance of the gods, is chang'd
Into some brutish form of wolf or bear. *Milton.*

PO'TLID. *n. s.* [*pot* and *lid*.] The cover of a pot.

The columella is a fine, thin, light, bony tube; the bottom of which spreads about, and gives it the resemblance of a wooden *potlid* in country houses. *Derham.*

POTSHE'RD. *n. s.* [*pot* and *shard*; from *schaerde*; properly *potshard*.] A fragment of a broken pot.

At this day at Gaza, they couch *potsherds* or vessels of earth in their walls to gather the wind from the top, and pass it in spouts into rooms. *Bacon's Nat. Hist.*

He on the ashes sits, his fate deplores;
And with a *potsherd* scrapes the swelling sores. *Sandys.*

Whence come broken *potsherds* tumbling down,
And leaky ware from garret windows thrown;
Well may they break our heads. *Dryden.*

PO'TTAGE. *n. s.* [*potage*, Fr. from *pot*.] Any thing boiled or decocted for food. See PORRIDGE.

Jacob sod *pottage*, and Esau came from the field faint. *Gen.*

PO'TTER. *n. s.* [*potier*, Fr. from *pot*.] A maker of earthen vessels.

My thoughts are whirled like a *potter's* wheel. *Shakesp.*

Some press the plants with sherds of *potters* clay. *Dryd.*

A *potter* will not have any chalk or marl mixed with the clay; for though it will hold burning, yet whenever any water comes near any such pots, it will slack and spoil the ware. *Mortimer's Husbandry.*

He like the *potter* in a mould has cast
The world's great frame. *Prior.*

POTTERN-ORE. *n. s.*

An ore, which for its aptness to vitrify, and serve the potters to glaze their earthen vessels, the miners call *pottern-ore*. *Boyle.*

PO'TTING. *n. s.* [from *pot*.] Drinking.

I learnt it in England, where they are most potent in *potting*. *Shakesp. Othello.*

PO'TTLE. *n. s.* [from *pot*.] Liquid measure containing four pints.

He drinks you with facility your Dane dead drunk, ere the next *pottle* can be filled. *Shakesp. Othello.*

Roderigo hath to might carous'd
Potations *pottle* deep. *Shakesp.*

The oracle of Apollo
Here speaks out of his *pottle*,
Or the Tripos his tower bottle. *Benj. Johnson.*

POTVA'LIANT. *adj.* [*pot* and *valiant*.] Heated with courage by strong drink.

POTU'LENT. *adj.* [*potulentus*, Lat.]

1. Pretty much in drink. *Dict.*

2. Fit to drink.

POUCH. *n. s.* [*poche*, Fr.]

1. A small bag; a pocket.

Tester I'll have in *pouch*, when thou shalt lack. *Shakesp.*

From a girdle about his waist, a bag or *pouch* divided into two cells. *Gulliver's Travels.*

The spot of the vessel, where the disease begins, gives way to the force of the blood pushing outwards, as to form a *pouch* or cyst. *Sharp's Surgery.*

2. Applied ludicrously to a big belly or paunch.

To POUCH. *v. a.*

1. To pocket.

In January husband that *poucheth* the grotes,
Will break up his lay, or be sowing of otes. *Tusser.*

2. To swallow.

The common heron hath long legs for wading, a long neck to reach prey, and a wide extensive throat to *pouch* it. *Derham's Physico-Theology.*

3. To pout; to hang down the lip. *Ainsworth.*

POU'CHMOUTHED. *adj.* [*pouch* and *mouthed*.] Blubberliped. *Ains.*

PO'VERTY. *n. s.* [*pauvreté*, Fr.]

1. Indigence; necessity; want of riches.

My men are the poorest,
But *poverty* could never draw them from me. *Shakesp.*

Such madness, as for fear of death to die,
Is to be poor for fear of *poverty*. *Denham.*

These by their strict examples taught,
How much more splendid virtue was than gold;
Yet scarce their swelling thirst of fame could hide,
And boasted *poverty* with too much pride. *Prior.*

There is such a state as absolute *poverty*, when a man is destitute not only of the conveniencies, but the simple necessaries of life, being disabled from acquiring them, and depending entirely on charity. *Rogers.*

2. Meanness; defect.

There is in all excellencies in compositions a kind of *poverty*, or a casualty or jeopardy. *Bacon.*

POU'LDAVIS. *n. s.* A sort of sail cloath. *Ainsworth.*

POULT. *n. s.* [*poulet*, Fr.] A young chicken.

One wou'd have all things little, hence has try'd
Turkey *poults*, fresh from th' egg, in batter fry'd. *King.*

POU'LTERER. *n. s.* [from *poult*.] One whose trade is to sell fowls ready for the cook.

If thou dost it half so gravely, so majestically, hang me up by the heels for a *poulterer*'s hare. *Shakesp.*

Several nasty trades, as butchers, *poulterers* and fishmongers, are great occasions of plagues. *Harvey.*

POU'LTICE. *n. s.* [*pulte*, Fr. *pultis*, Lat.] A cataplasm; a soft mollifying application.

Poultice relaxeth the pores, and maketh the humour apt to exhale. *Bacon's Nat. Hist.*

If your little finger be sore, and you think a *poultice* made of our vitals will give it ease, speak, and it shall be done. *Sw.*

To POU'LTICE. *v. a.* [from the noun.] To apply a poultice or cataplasm.

POU'LTIVE. *n. s.* [A word used by *Temple*.] A poultice.

Poultives allayed pains, but drew down the humours, making the passages wider, and apter to receive them. *Temple.*

POU'LTRY. *n. s.* [*poulet*, Fr. *pullities*, Lat.] Domestick fowls.

The cock knew the fox to be a common enemy of all *poultry*. *L'Estrange.*

What louder cries, when Ilium was in flames,
Than for the cock the widow'd *poultry* made. *Dryden.*

Soldiers robbed a farmer of his *poultry*, and made him wait at table, without giving him a morsel. *Swift.*

POUNCE. *n. s.* [*ponzone*, Italian. *Skinner*.]

1. The claw or talon of a bird of prey.

As haggard hawk, presuming to contend
With hardy fowl, about his able might,
His weary *pounces*, all in vain doth spend
To truss the prey too heavy for his flight. *Fa. Queen.*

The new-dissembl'd eagle, now endu'd
With beak and *pounces* Hercules pursu'd. *Dryden.*

'Twas a mean prey for a bird of his *pounces*. *Atterbury.*

2. The powder of gum sandarach, so called because it is thrown upon paper through a perforated box.

To POUNCE. *v. a.* [*pongonare*, Italian.]

1. To pierce; to perforate.

Barbarous people, that go naked, do not only paint, but *pounce* and raise their skin, that the painting may not be taken forth, and make it into works. *Bacon's Nat. Hist.*

2. To pour

2. To pour or sprinkle through small perforations.

It may be tried by incorporating copple-dust, by pouncing into the quicksilver. *Bacon.*

3. To seize with the pounces or talons.

POU'NCED. *adj.* [from *pounce.*] Furnished with claws or talons.

From a craggy cliff,
The royal eagle draws his vigorous young
Strong *pounc'd.* *Thomson's Spring.*

POU'NCETBOX. *n. s.* [*pounce* and *box.*] A small box perforated.

He was perfumed like a milliner,
And, 'twixt his finger and his thumb, he held
A *pouncetbox*, which ever and anon
He gave his nose. *Shakesp. Henry* IV.

POUND. *n. s.* [ponð, punð, Sax. from *pondo*, Lat.]

1. A certain weight, consisting in troy weight of twelve, in averdupois of sixteen ounces.

He that said, that he had rather have a grain of fortune than a *pound* of wisdom, as to the things of this life, spoke nothing but the voice of wisdom. *South's Sermons.*

A *pound* doth consist of ounces, drams, scruples. *Wilkins.*

Great Hannibal within the balance lay,
And tell how many *pounds* his ashes weigh. *Dryden*

2. The sum of twenty shillings.

That exchequer of medals in the cabinets of the great duke of Tuscany, is not worth so little as an hundred thousand *pound.* *Peacham of Antiquities.*

3. [From pinðan, Sax.] A pinfold; an inclosure; a prison in which beasts are inclosed.

I hurry,
Not thinking it is levee-day,
And find his honour in a *pound*,
Hemm'd by a triple circle round. *Swift's Miscel.*

To POUND. *v. a.* [punian, Sax. whence in many places they use the word *pun.*]

1. To beat; to grind with a pestle.

His mouth and nostrils pour'd a purple flood,
And *pounded* teeth came rushing with his blood. *Dryden.*

Would'st thou not rather chuse a small renown
To be the mayor of some poor paltry town,
To *pound* false weights and scanty measures break. *Dryden.*

Tir'd with the search, not finding what she seeks,
With cruel blows she *pounds* her blubber'd cheeks. *Dryden.*

Shou'd their axle break, its overthrow
Would crush, and *pound* to dust the crowd below;
Nor friends their friends, nor sires their sons could know. *Dryden's Juvenal.*

Opaque white powder of glass, seen through a microscope, exhibits fragments pellucid and colourless, as the whole appeared to the naked eye before it was *pounded.* *Bentley.*

She describes
How under ground the rude Riphean race
Mimick brisk cyder, with the brakes product wild
Sloes *pounded.* *Philips.*

Lifted pestles brandished in the air,
Loud stroaks with *pounding* spice the fabrick rend,
And aromatick clouds in spires ascend. *Garth.*

2. To shut up; to imprison, as in a pound.

We'll break our walls,
Rather than they shall *pound* us up. *Shakesp.*

I ordered John to let out the good man's sheep that were *pounded* by night. *Spectator,* Nº 243.

POU'NDAGE. *n. s.* [from *pound.*]

1. A certain sum deducted from a pound; a sum paid by the trader to the servant that pays the money, or to the person who procures him customers.

In *poundage* and drawbacks I lose half my rent. *Swift.*

2. Payment rated by the weight of the commodity.

Tonnage and *poundage*, and other duties upon merchandizes, were collected by order of the board. *Clarend.*

POU'NDER. *n. s.* [from *pound.*]

1. The name of a heavy large pear.

Alcinous' orchard various apples bears,
Unlike are bergamots and *pounder* pears. *Dryden.*

2. Any person or thing denominated from a certain number of pounds: as, *a ten* pounder; a gun that carries a bullet of ten *pounds* weight; or in ludicrous language a man with ten *pounds* a year; in like manner, a note or bill is called a twenty *pounder* or ten *pounder*, from the sum it bears.

None of these forty or fifty *pounders* may be suffered to marry, under the penalty of deprivation. *Swift.*

3. A pestle. *Ainsworth.*

POU'PETON. *n. s.* [*poupée*, Fr.] A puppet or little baby.

POU'PICTS. *n. s.* In cookery, a mess of victuals made of veal stakes and slices of bacon. *Bailey.*

To POUR. *v. a.* [supposed to be derived from the Welsh *bwrw.*]

1. To let some liquid out of a vessel, or into some place or receptacle.

If they will not believe those signs, take of the water of the river, and *pour* it upon the dry land. *Exodus* iv. 9.

He said, *pour* out for the people, and there was no harm in the pot. 2 *Kings* iv. 41.

He stretched out his hand to the cup, and *poured* of the blood of the grape, he *poured* out at the foot of the altar a sweet smelling savour into the most high. *Eccluf.* l. 15.

A Samaritan bound up his wounds, *pouring* in oil and wine, and brought him to an inn. *Luke* x. 34.

Your fury then boil'd upward to a fome;
But since this message came, you sink and settle,
As if cold water had been *pour'd* upon you. *Dryden.*

2. To emit; to give vent to; to send forth; to let out; to send in a continued course.

Hie thee hither,
That I may *pour* my spirits in thine ear,
And chastise with the valour of my tongue
All that impedes thee from the golden round. *Shakesp.*

London doth *pour* out her citizens;
The mayor and all his brethren in best sort,
With the plebeians swarming. *Shakesp. Henry* V.

As thick as hail
Came post on post; and every one did bear
Thy praises in his kingdom's great defence,
And *pour'd* them down before him. *Shakesp. Macbeth.*

The devotion of the heart is the tongue of the soul; actuated and heated with love, it *pours* itself forth in supplications and prayers. *Duppa's Rules for Devotion.*

If we had groats or sixpences current by law, that wanted one third of the silver by the standard, who can imagine, that our neighbours would not *pour* in quantities of such money upon us, to the great loss of the kingdom. *Locke.*

Is it for thee the linnet *pours* his throat?
Loves of his own and raptures swell the note. *Pope.*

To POUR. *v. n.*

1. To stream; to flow.

2. To rush tumultuously.

If the rude throng *pour* on with furious pace,
And hap to break thee from a friend's embrace,
Stop short. *Gay.*

All his fleecy flock
Before him march, and *pour* into the rock,
Not one or male or female stay'd behind. *Pope.*

A ghastly band of giants,
Pouring down the mountains, crowd the shore. *Pope.*

A gathering throng,
Youth and white age tumultuous *pour* along. *Pope.*

POU'RER. *n. s.* [from *pour.*] One that pours.

POUSSE. *n. s.* The old word for *pease.* *Spenser.*

But who shall judge the wager won or lost?
That shall yonder heard groom and none other,
Which over the *pousse* hitherward doth post. *Spenser.*

POUT. *n. s.*

1. A kind of fish; a cod-fish.

2. A kind of bird.

Of wild birds, Cornwall hath quail, wood-dove, heathcock and *pout.* *Carew's Survey of Cornwall.*

To POUT. *v. n.* [*bouter*, Fr.]

1. To look sullen by thrusting out the lips.

Like a misbehav'd and sullen wench,
Thou *pout'st* upon thy fortune and thy love. *Shakesp.*

He had not din'd;
The veins unfill'd, our blood is cold; and then
We *pout* upon the morning, are unapt
To give or to forgive. *Shakesp. Coriolanus.*

I would advise my gentle readers, as they consult the good of their faces, to forbear frowning upon loyalists, and *pouting* at the government. *Addison's Freeholder,* Nº 8.

The nurse remained *pouting*, nor would she touch a bit during the whole dinner. *Arbuthnot and Pope.*

2. To gape; to hang prominent.

The ends of the wound must come over one another, with a compress to press the lips equally down, which would otherwise become crude, and *pout* out with great lips. *Wiseman.*

Satyrus was made up betwixt man and goat, with a human head, hooked nose and *pouting* lips. *Dryden.*

PO'WDER. *n. s.* [*poudre*, Fr.]

1. Dust; any body comminuted.

The calf which they had made, he burnt in the fire, and ground it to *powder.* *Ex.* xxxii. 20.

2. Gunpowder.

The seditious being furnished with artillery, *powder* and shot, battered Bishopsgate. *Hayward.*

As to the taking of a town, there were few conquerors could signalize themselves that way, before the invention of *powder* and fortifications. *Addison.*

3. Sweet dust for the hair.

When th' hair is sweet through pride or lust,
The *powder* doth forget the dust. *Herbert.*

Our humbler province is to tend the fair,
To save the *powder* from too rude a gale. *Pope.*

To PO'WDER. *v. a.* [from the noun.]

1. To reduce to dust; to comminute; to pound small.

2. [*Poudrer*, Fr.] To sprinkle, as with dust.

Powder thy radiant hair,
Which if without such ashes thou would'st wear,
Thou who, to all which come to look upon,
Wert meant for Phœbus, would'st be Phaeton. *Donne.*
In the galaxy, that milky way
Which nightly, as a circling zone, thou see'st
Powder'd with stars. *Milton's Par. Lost, b.* vii.
The *powder'd* footman
Beneath his flapping hat secures his hair. *Gay.*

3. To salt; to sprinkle with salt.

If you imbowel me to day, I'll give you leave to *powder* me and eat me to-morrow. *Shakesp. Henry* IV.

Salting of oysters, and *powdering* of meat, keepeth them from putrefaction. *Bacon's Nat. Hist.*

My hair I never powder, but my chief
Invention is to get me *powder'd* beef. *Cleaveland.*

Immoderate feeding upon *powdered* beef, pickled meats, anchovy, and debauching with brandy do inflame and acuate the blood. *Harvey on Consumptions.*

To Po'wder. *v. n.* To come tumultuously and violently. A low corrupt word.

Whilst two companions were disputing it at sword's point, down comes a kite *powdering* upon them, and gobbets up both. *L'Estrange.*

Po'wderbox. *n. s.* [*powder* and *box.*] A box in which powder for the hair is kept.

There stands the toillette,
The patch, the *powderbox*, pulville, perfumes. *Gay.*

Po'wderhorn. *n. s.* [*powder* and *horn.*] A horn case in which powder is kept for guns.

You may stick your candle in a bottle or a *powderhorn*. *Sw.*

Po'wdermill. *n. s.* [*powder* and *mill.*] The mill in which the ingredients for gunpowder are ground and mingled.

Upon the blowing up of a *powdermill*, the windows of adjacent houses are bent and blown outwards, by the elastick force of the air within exerting itself. *Arbuthnot.*

Po'wder-room. *n. s.* [*powder* and *room.*] The part of a ship in which the gunpowder is kept.

The flame invades the *powderrooms*, and then
Their guns shoot bullets, and their vessels men. *Waller.*

Powder-chests. *n. s.* On board a ship, wooden triangular chests filled with gunpowder, pebble-stones and such like materials, set on fire when a ship is boarded by an enemy, which soon makes all clear before them. *Dict.*

Powdering-tub. *n. s.* [*powder* and *tub.*]

1. The vessel in which meat is salted.

When we view those large bodies of oxen, what can we better conceit them to be, than so many living and walking *powdering-tubs*, and that they have animam salis. *More.*

2. The place in which an infected lecher is physicked to preserve him from putrefaction.

To the spital go,
And from the *powd'ring-tub* of infamy
Fetch forth the lazar kite Doll Tearsheet. *Shakesp.*

Po'wdery. *adj.* [*poudreux*, Fr. from *powder.*] Dusty; friable.

A brown *powdery* spar, which holds iron, is found amongst the iron ore. *Woodward on Fossils.*

PO'WER. *n. s.* [*pouvoir*, Fr.]

1. Command; authority; dominion; influence.

If law, authority and *pow'r* deny not,
It will go hard with poor Anthonio. *Shakesp.*

No man could ever have a just *power* over the life of another, by right of property in land. *Locke.*

Power is no blessing in itself, but when it is employ'd to protect the innocent. *Swift.*

2. Influence; prevalence upon.

This man had *power* with him, to draw him forth to his death. *Bacon's Essays.*

Dejected! no, it never shall be said,
That fate had *power* upon a Spartan soul;
My mind on its own centre stands unmov'd
And stable, as the fabrick of the world. *Dryden.*

3. Ability; force; reach.

That which moveth God to work is goodness, and that which ordereth his work is wisdom, and that which perfecteth his work is *power*. *Hooker.*

I have suffer'd in your woe;
Nor shall be wanting ought within my *pow'r*,
For your relief in my refreshing bow'r. *Dryden.*

You are still living to enjoy the blessings of all the good you have performed, and many prayers that your *power* of doing generous actions may be as extended as your will. *Dry.*

It is not in the *power* of the most enlarged understanding, to invent one new simple idea in the mind, not taken in by the ways aforementioned. *Locke.*

'Tis not in the *power* of want or slavery to make them miserable. *Addison's Guardian.*

Though it be not in our *power* to make affliction no affliction; yet it is in our *power* to take off the edge of it, by a steady view of those divine joys prepared for us in another state. *Atterbury's Sermons.*

4. Strength; motive force.

Observing in ourselves, that we can at pleasure move several parts of our bodies, which were at rest; the effects also that natural bodies are able to produce in one another, occurring every moment to our senses, we both these ways get the idea of *power*. *Locke.*

5. The moving force of an engine.

By understanding the true difference betwixt the weight and the *power*, a man may add such a fitting supplement to the strength of the *power*, that it shall move any conceivable weight, though it should never so much exceed that force, which the *power* is naturally endowed with. *Wilkins.*

6. Animal strength; natural strength.

Care, not fear; or fear not for themselves altered something the countenances of the two lovers: but so as any man might perceive, was rather an assembling of *powers* than dismayedness of courage. *Sidney, b.* i.

He died of great years, but of strong health and *powers*. *Bacon's Henry* VII.

7. Faculty of the mind.

If ever
You meet in some fresh cheek the *power* of fancy,
Then you shall know the wounds invisible,
That love's keen arrows make. *Shakesp.*

I was in the thought, they were not fairies, and yet the guiltiness of my mind, the sudden surprize of my *powers* drove the grossness of the foppery into a received belief. *Shakesp.*

In our little world, this soul of ours
Being only one, and to one body ty'd,
Doth use, on divers objects, divers *powers*;
And so are her effects diversify'd. *Davies.*

Maintain the empire of the mind over the body, and keep the appetites of the one in due subjection to the reasoning *powers* of the other. *Atterbury's Sermons.*

The design of this science is to rescue our reasoning *powers* from their unhappy slavery and darkness. *Watts.*

8. Government; right of governing.

My labour
Honest and lawful, to deserve my food
Of those who have me in their civil *power*. *Milton.*

9. Sovereign; potentate.

'Tis surprising to consider with what heats these two *powers* have contested their title to the kingdom of Cyprus, that is in the hands of the Turk. *Addison's Remarks on Italy.*

10. One invested with dominion.

After the tribulation of those days shall the sun be darkened, and the *powers* of the heavens shall be shaken. *Mat.*

The fables turn'd some men to flow'rs,
And others did with brutish forms invest;
And did of others make celestial *pow'rs*,
Like angels, which still travel, yet still rest. *Davies.*
If there's a *pow'r* above us,
And that there is all nature cries aloud
Through all her works, he must delight in virtue. *Addis.*

11. Divinity.

Merciful *powers*!
Restrain in me the cursed thoughts, that nature
Gives way to in repose. *Shakespeare's Macbeth.*
Cast down thyself, and only strive to raise
The glory of thy maker's sacred name;
Use all thy pow'rs, that blessed *pow'r* to praise,
Which gives thee pow'r to be and use the same. *Davies.*
With indignation, thus he broke
His awful silence, and the *pow'rs* bespoke. *Dryden.*
Tell me,
What are the gods the better for this gold?
The wretch that offers from his wealthy store
These presents, bribes the *pow'rs* to give him more. *Dryd.*

12. Host; army; military force.

He, to work him the more mischief, sent over his brother Edward with a *power* of Scots and Redshanks into Ireland, where they got footing. *Spenser's State of Ireland.*

Never such a *power*,
For any foreign preparation,
Was levied in the body of a land. *Shakesp. K. John.*
Young Octavius and Mark Antony
Come down upon us with a mighty *power*,
Bending their expedition tow'rd Philippi. *Shakesp.*
Who leads his *power*?
Under whose government come they along? *Shakesp.*
My heart, dear Harry,
Threw many a northward look, to see his father
Bring up his *pow'rs*; but he did long in vain. *Shakesp.*

Gazellus, upon the coming of the bassa, valiantly issued forth with all his *power*, and gave him battle. *Knolles.*

13. A large quantity; a great number. In low language: as, *a power of good things.*

Po'werable. *adj.* [from *power.*] Capable of performing any thing.

That you may see how *powerable* time is in altering tongues, I will set down the Lord's prayer as it was translated in sundry ag . *Camden.*

Powe'rful.

Po'werful. *adj.* [*power* and *ful.*]
1. Inveſted with command or authority; potent.
2. Forcible; mighty.

> We have ſuſtain'd one day in doubtful fight,
> What heaven's lord hath *powerfulleſt* to ſend
> Againſt us from about his throne. *Milton's Par. Loſt.*

Henry II. endeavouring to eſtabliſh his grandfather's laws, met with *powerful* oppoſition from archbiſhop Becket. *Ayliffe.*

3. Efficacious.

Po'werfully. *adv.* [from *powerful.*] Potently; mightily; efficaciouſly; forcibly.

The ſun and other *powerfully* lucid bodies dazzle our eyes. *Boyle.*

By aſſuming a privilege belonging to riper years, to which a child muſt not aſpire, you do but add new force to your example, and recommend the action more *powerfully.* *Locke.*

Before the revelation of the goſpel, the wickedneſs and impenitency of the heathen world was a much more excuſable thing, becauſe they had but very obſcure apprehenſions of thoſe things which urge men moſt *powerfully* to forſake their ſins. *Tillotſon's Sermons.*

The grain-gold, upon all the golden coaſt of Guinea, is diſplayed by the rains falling there with incredible force, *powerfully* beating off the earth. *Woodward.*

Po'werfulness. *n. ſ.* [from *powerful.*] Power; efficacy; might.

So much he ſtands upon the *powerfulneſs* of chriſtian religion, that he makes it beyond all the rules of moral philoſophy, ſtrongly effectual to expel vice, and plant in men all kind of virtue. *Hakewill on Providence.*

Po'werless. *adj.* [from *power.*] Weak; impotent.

> I give you welcome with a *pow'rleſs* hand,
> But with a heart full of unſtained love. *Shakeſp.*

Pox. *n. ſ.* [properly *pocks*, which originally ſignified a ſmall bag or puſtule; of the ſame original, perhaps, with *powke* or *pouch.* We ſtill uſe *pock*, for a ſingle puſtule; poccay, Sax. *pocken*, Dutch.]
1. Puſtules; efflorеſcencies; exanthematous eruptions.
2. The venereal diſeaſe. This is the ſenſe when it has no epithet.

Though brought to their ends by ſome other apparent diſeaſe, yet the *pox* hath been judged the foundation. *Wiſeman.*

> Wilt thou ſtill ſparkle in the box,
> Sill ogle in the ring?
> Can'ſt thou forget thy age and *pox.* *Dorſet.*

Poy. *n. ſ.* [*appoyo*, Spaniſh; *appuy, poids*, Fr.] A ropedancer's pole.

To Poze. *v. a.* To puzzle. See Pose and Appose.

> And ſay you ſo? then I ſhall *poze* you quickly. *Shakeſp.*

Of human infirmities I ſhall give inſtances, not that I deſign to *poze* them with thoſe common enigmas of magnetiſm, fluxes and refluxes. *Glanvill's Sceps.*

Pra'cticable. *adj.* [*practicable*, Fr.]
1. Performable; feaſible; capable to be practiſed.

This falls out for want of examining what is *practicable* and what not, and for want again of meaſuring our force and capacity with our deſign. *L'Eſtrange.*

An heroick poem ſhould be more like a glaſs of nature, figuring a more *practicable* virtue to us, than was done by the ancients. *Dryden on Heroick Plays.*

This is a *practicable* degree of chriſtian magnanimity. *Att.*

Some phyſicians have thought, that if it were *practicable* to keep the humours of the body in an exact balance of each with its oppoſite, it might be immortal; but this is impoſſible in the practice. *Swift.*

2. Aſſailable; fit to be aſſailed.

Pra'cticableness. *n. ſ.* [from *practicable.*] Poſſibility to be performed.

Pra'cticably. *adv.* [from *practicable.*] In ſuch a manner as may be performed.

The meaneſt capacity, when he ſees a rule *practicably* applied before his eyes, can no longer be at a loſs how 'tis to be performed. *Rogers.*

Pra'ctical. *adj.* [*practicus*, Lat. *pratique*, Fr. from *practice.*] Relating to action; not merely ſpeculative.

The image of God was no leſs reſplendent in man's *practical* underſtanding; namely, that ſtorehouſe of the ſoul, in which are treaſured up the rules of action and the ſeeds of morality. *South's Sermons.*

Religion comprehends the knowledge of its principles, and a ſuitable life and practice; the firſt, being ſpeculative, may be called knowledge; and the latter, becauſe 'tis *practical*, wiſdom. *Tillotſon's Sermons.*

Pra'ctically. *adv.* [from *practical.*]
1. In relation to action.
2. By practice; in real fact.

I honour her, having *practically* found her among the better ſort of trees. *Howel's Vocal Foreſt.*

Pra'cticalness. *n. ſ.* [from *practical.*] The quality of being practical.

PRA'CTICE. *n. ſ.* [πρακτικὴ; *pratique*, Fr.]
1. The habit of doing any thing.
2. Uſe; cuſtomary uſe.

Obſolete words may be laudably revived, when they are more ſounding, or more ſignificant than thoſe in *practice.* *Dry.*

> Of ſuch a *practice* when Ulyſſes told;
> Shall we, cries one, permit
> This lewd romancer and his bant'ring wit. *Tate.*

3. Dexterity acquired by habit.

> I'll prove it on his body, if he dare,
> Deſpite his nice fence and his active *practice.* *Shakeſp.*

4. Actual performance, diſtinguiſhed from theory.

There are two functions of the ſoul, contemplation and *practice*, according to that general diviſion of objects, ſome of which only entertain our ſpeculations, others alſo employ our actions; ſo the underſtanding, with relation to theſe, is divided into ſpeculative and practick. *South.*

5. Method or art of doing any thing.
6. Medical treatment of diſeaſes.

This diſeaſe is beyond my *practice*; yet I have known thoſe which have walked in their ſleep, who have died holily in their beds. *Shakeſpeare's Macbeth.*

7. Exerciſe of any profeſſion.
8. [Pɲæꞇ, Saxon, is cunning, ſlineſs, and thence *prat*, in *Douglaſs*, is a trick or fraud; latter times forgetting the orginal of words, applied to *practice* the ſenſe of *prat.*] Wicked ſtratagem; bad artifice. A ſenſe not now in uſe.

He ſought to have that by *practice*, which he could not by prayer; and being allowed to viſit us, he uſed the opportunity of a fit time thus to deliver us. *Sidney, b.* ii.

Partly with ſuſpicion of *practice*, the king was ſuddenly turned. *Sidney, b.* ii.

> It is the ſhameful work of Hubert's hand,
> The *practice* and the purpoſe of the king. *Shakeſp.*
> Shall we thus permit
> A blaſting and a ſcandalous breath to fall
> On him ſo near us? this needs muſt be *practice*;
> Who knew of your intent and coming hither? *Shakeſp.*
> Wiſe ſtates prevent purpoſes
> Before they come to practice, and foul *practices*
> Before they grow to act. *Denham's Sophy.*

Pra'ctick. *adj.* [πρακτικὸς; *practicus*, Lat. *pratique*, Fr.]
1. Relating to action; not merely theoretical.

> When he ſpeaks,
> The air, a charter'd libertine, is ſtill;
> And the mute wonder lurketh in men's ears,
> To ſteal his ſweet and honied ſentences;
> So that the act and *practick* part of life
> Muſt be the miſtreſs to this theorick. *Shakeſp.*

Whilſt they contend for ſpeculative truth, they, by mutual calumnies, forfeit the *practick.* *Gov. of the Tongue.*

> True piety without ceſſation toſt
> By theories, the *practick* part is loſt. *Denham.*

2. In *Spenſer* it ſeems to ſignify, ſly; artful.

> She uſed hath the *practick* pain
> Of this falſe footman, cloaked with ſimpleneſs. *F. Queen.*
> Thereto his ſubtile engines he doth bend,
> His *practick* wit, and his fair filed tongue,
> With thouſand other ſleights. *Fairy Queen.*

To PRA'CTISE. *v. a.* [πρακτικὸς; *pratiquer*, Fr.]
1. To do habitually.

Incline not my heart to *practiſe* wicked works with men that work iniquity. *Pſalm* cxl 4.

2. To do; not merely to profeſs: as, *to* practiſe *law or phyſick.*
3. To uſe in order to habit and dexterity.

To Pra'ctise. *v. n.*
1. To have a habit of acting in any manner formed.

> Will truth return unto them that *practiſe* in her. *Ecclus.*
> They ſhall *practiſe* how to live ſecure. *Milton.*
> Oft have we wonder'd
> How ſuch a ruling ſp'rit you cou'd reſtrain,
> And *practiſe* firſt over yourſelf to reign. *Waller.*

2. To tranſact; to negotiate ſecretly.

> I've *practis'd* with him,
> And found a means to let the victor know,
> That Syphax and Sempronius are his friends. *Addiſon.*

3. To try artifices.

> Others by guilty artifice and arts,
> Of promis'd kindneſs *practiſe* on our hearts;
> With expectation blow the paſſion up,
> She fans the fire without one gale of hope. *Granvil.*

4. To uſe bad arts or ſtratagems.

> If you there
> Did *practiſe* on my ſtate, your being in Egypt
> Might be my queſtion. *Shakeſp. Ant. and Cleop.*

If thou do'ſt him any ſlight diſgrace, he will *practiſe* ... thee by poiſon. *Shakeſpeare's As You ...*

5. To uſe medical methods.

I never thought I ſhould try a new experiment, bein... inclined to *practiſe* upon others, and as little that others ... *practiſe* upon me. *Temple's M...*

6. To exerciſe any profeſſion.

Pra'ctisant. *n. ſ.* [from *practiſe.*] An agent.

> Here enter'd Pucelle and her *practiſants.* *Shakeſp.*

PRA'CTISER. *n. s.* [from *practise.*]

1. One that practises any thing; one that does any thing habitually.

We will, in the principles of the politician, shew how little efficacy they have to advance the *practiser* of them to the things they aspire to. *South's Sermons.*

2. One who prescribes medical treatment.

Sweet *practiser*, thy physick I will try,
That ministers thine own death if I die. *Shakespeare.*

I had reasoned myself into an opinion, that the use of physicians, unless in some acute disease, was a great venture, and that their greatest *practisers* practised least upon themselves. *Temple.*

PRACTI'TIONER. *n. s.* [from *practice.*]

1. He who is engaged in the actual exerciseof any art.

The author exhorts all gentlemen *practitioners* to exercise themselves in the translatory. *Arbuthnot.*

I do not know a more universal and unnecessary mistake among the clergy, but especially the younger *practitioners. Sw.*

2. One who uses any sly or dangerous arts.

There is some papistical *practitioners* among you. *Whitgifte.*

3. One who does any thing habitually.

He must be first an exercised, thorough-paced *practitioner* of these vices himself. *South's Sermons.*

PRÆCOGNITA. n. s. [Latin.] Things previously known in order to understanding something else; thus the structure of the human body is one of the *præcognita* of physick.

Either all knowledge does not depend on certain *præcognita* or general maxims, called principles, or else these are principles. *Locke.*

PRAGMA'TICK. } *adj.* [πραγματα; *pragmatique*, Fr.]
PRAGMA'TICAL. } Meddling; impertinently busy; assuming business without leave or invitation.

No sham so gross, but it will pass upon a weak man that is *pragmatical* and inquisitive. *L'Estrange.*

Common estimation puts an ill character upon *pragmatick* meddling people. *Government of the Tongue.*

He understands no more of his own affairs, than a child; he has got a sort of a *pragmatical* silly jade of a wife, that pretends to take him out of my hands. *Arbuthnot.*

The fellow grew so *pragmatical*, that he took upon him the government of my whole family. *Arbuthnot.*

Such a backwardness there was among good men to engage with an usurping people, and *pragmatical* ambitious orators. *Swift.*

They are *pragmatical* enough to stand on the watch tower, but who assigned them the post? *Swift.*

PRAGMA'TICALLY. *adv.* [from *pragmatical.*] Meddlingly; impertinently.

PRAGMA'TICALNESS. *n. s.* [from *pragmatical.*] The quality of intermeddling without right or call.

PRAISE. *n. s.* [*prijs*, Dutch.]

1. Renown; commendation; fame; honour; celebrity.

Best of fruits, whose taste has taught
The tongue, not made for speech, to speak thy *praise. Milt.*

Lucan, content with *praise*, may lie at ease
In costly grotts and marble palaces;
But to poor Bassus what avails a name,
To starve on compliments and empty fame. *Dryden*

2. Glorification; tribute of gratitude; laud.

He hath put a new song in my mouth, even *praise* unto our God. *Psalm* xl. 3.

To God glory and *praise*. *Milton.*

3. Ground or reason of praise.

Praiseworthy actions are by thee embrac'd;
And 'tis my *praise* to make thy praises last. *Dryden.*

To PRAISE. *v. a.* [*prijsen*, Dutch.]

1. To commend; to applaud; to celebrate.

Will God incense his ire
For such a petty trespass, and not *praise*
Rather your dauntless virtue. *Milton.*

We *praise* not Hector, though his name we know
Is great in arms; 'tis hard to *praise* a foe. *Dryden.*

2. To glorify in worship.

The shepherds returned, glorifying and *praising* God for all the things that they had heard and seen. *Luke* ii. 20.

One generation shall *praise* thy works to another, and declare thy mighty works. *Psalm* cxlv. 4.

Their touch'd their golden harps, and hymning *prais'd*
God and his works. *Milton.*

PRAI'SEFUL. *adj.* [*praise* and *full.*] Laudable; commendable. Not now in use.

Of whose high praise, and *praiseful* bliss,
Goodness the pen, heaven the paper is. *Sidney.*

He ordain'd a lady for his prise,
Generally *praiseful*, fair and young, and skill'd in housewiferies. *Chapman's Iliad.*

PRAI'SER. *n. s.* [from *praise.*] One who praises; an applauder; a commender.

We men and *praisers* of men should remember, that if we have such excellencies, it is reason to think them excellent creatures, of whom we are. *Sidney.*

Forgive me, if my verse but say you are
A Sidney: but in that extend as far
As loudest *praisers*. *B. Johnson's Epig.*

Turn to God, who knows I think this true,
And useth oft, when such a heart missays,
To make it good; for such a *praiser* prays. *Donne.*

PRAISEWO'RTHY. *adj.* [*praise* and *worthy.*] Commendable; deserving praise.

The Tritonian goddess having heard
Her blazed fame, which all the world had fill'd,
Came down to prove the truth, and due reward
For her *praiseworthy* workmanship to yield. *Spenser.*

Since men have left to do *praiseworthy* things,
Most think all praises flatteries; but truth brings
That sound, and that authority with her name,
As to be rais'd by her is only fame. *Ben. Johnson.*

Firmus, who seized upon Egypt, was so far *praiseworthy*, that he encouraged trade. *Arbuthnot on Coins.*

PRAME. *n. s.* A flat bottomed boat. *Bailey.*

To PRANCE *v. a.* [*pronken*, Dutch, to set one's self to shew.]

1. To spring and bound in high mettle.

Here's no fantastick mask, nor dance,
But of our kids that frisk and *prance*;
Nor wars are seen,
Unless upon the green,
Two harmless lambs are butting one the other. *Wotton.*

With mud fill'd high, the rumbling cart draws near,
Now rule thy *prancing* steeds, lac'd charioteer. *Gay.*

Far be the spirit of the chace from them,
To spring the fence, to rein the *prancing* steed. *Thomson.*

2. To ride gallantly and ostentatiously.

The horses hoofs were broken by means of the *prancings*, the *prancings* of their mighty ones. *Judges* v. 22.

I see
Th' insulting tyrant, *prancing* o'er the field,
Strow'd with Rome's citizens, and drench'd in slaughter,
His horses hoofs wet with patrician blood. *Addison.*

3. To move in a warlike or showy manner.

We should neither have meat to eat, nor manufacture to cloathe us, unless we could *prance* about in coats of mail, or eat brass. *Swift.*

To PRANK. *v. a.* [*pronken*, Dutch.] To decorate; to dress or adjust to ostentation.

Some *prank* their ruffs, and others timely dight
Their gay attire. *Fairy Queen.*

In wine and meats she flow'd above the bank,
And in excess exceeded her own might,
In sumptuous tire she joy'd herself to *prank*,
But of her love too lavish. *Fairy Queen.*

These are tribunes of the people,
The tongues o' th' common mouth: I despise them:
For they do *prank* them in authority
Against all noble sufferance. *Shakesp.*

Your high self,
The gracious mark o' th' land, you have obscur'd
With a swain's wearing; and me, poor lowly maid,
Most goddess-like *prank'd* up. *Shakesp. Winter's Tale.*

'Tis that miracle, and queen of gems,
That nature *pranks*, her mind attracts my soul. *Shakesp.*

I had not unlock'd my lips
In this unhallowed air, but that this jugler
Would think to charm my judgment as mine eyes,
Obtruding false rules, *prankt* in reason's garb. *Milton.*

PRANK. *n. s.* A frolick; a wild flight; a ludicrous trick; a wicked act.

Lay home to him;
Tell him, his *pranks* have been too broad to bear with. *Sha.*

Such is thy audacious wickedness,
Thy lewd, pestif'rous and dissentious *pranks*;
The very infants prattle of thy pride. *Shakesp.*

They caused the table to be covered and meat set on, which was no sooner set down, than in came the harpies, and played their accustomed *pranks*. *Raleigh.*

They put on their cloaths, and played all those *pranks* you have taken notice of. *Addison's Guardian.*

PRA'SON. *n. s.* [πρασον.] A leek: also a sea weed as green as a leek. *Bailey.*

To PRATE. *v. n.* [*praten*, Dutch.] To talk carelesly and without weight; to chatter; to tattle; to be loquacious; to prattle.

His knowledge or skill is in *prating* too much. *Tusser.*

Behold me, which owe
A moiety of the throne, here standing
To *prate* and talk for life and honour, 'fore
Who please to hear. *Shakesp. Winter's Tale.*

This starved justice hath *prated* to me of the wildness of his youth, and the feats he hath done about Turnbal-street; and every third word a lie. *Shakesp. Henry* IV. *p.* ii.

After Flammock and the blacksmith had, by joint and several *pratings*, found tokens of consent in the multitude, they offered themselves to lead them. *Bacon's Henry* VII.

Oh listen with attentive sight
To what my *prating* eyes indite! *Cleaveland.*

What nonsense would the fool thy master *prate*,
When thou, his knave, can'st talk at such a rate. *Dryden.*
She first did wit's prerogative remove,
And made a fool presume to *prate* of love. *Dryden.*
This is the way of the world; the deaf will *prate* of discords in musick. *Watts.*

PRATE. *n. s.* [from the verb.] Tattle; slight talk; unmeaning loquacity.
If I talk to him; with his innocent *prate*,
He will awake my mercy which lies dead. *Shakesp.*
Would her innocent *prate* could overcome me;
Oh! what a conflict do I feel. *Denham's Sophy.*

PRA'TER. *n. s.* [from *prate.*] An idle talker; a chatterer.
When expectation rages in my blood,
Is this a time, thou *prater*; hence be gone. *Southern.*

PRA'TINGLY. *adv.* [from *prate.*] With tittle tattle; with loquacity.

PRATTIQUE. *n. s.* [French; *prattica*, Italian.] A licence for the master of a ship to traffick in the ports of Italy upon a certificate, that the place, from whence he came, is not annoyed with any infectious disease. *Bailey.*

To PRATTLE. *v. n.* [diminutive of *prate.*] To talk lightly; to chatter; to be trivially loquacious.
But I *prattle*
Something too wildly, and my father's precepts
I therein do forget. *Shakespeare's Tempest.*
What the great ones do, the less will *prattle* of. *Shak.*
A French woman teaches an English girl to speak and read French, by only *prattling* to her. *Locke.*
There is not so much pleasure to have a child *prattle* agreeably, as to reason well. *Locke on Education.*
His tongue, his *prattling* tongue, had chang'd him quite
To sooty blackness, from the purest white. *Ad. Ovid.*
A little lively rustick, trained up in ignorance and prejudice, will *prattle* treason a whole evening. *Addison.*
I must *prattle* on,
And beg your pardon, yet this half hour. *Prior.*
Let cred'lous boys and *prattling* nurses tell,
How if the festival of Paul be clear,
Plenty from lib'ral horn shall strow the year. *Gay.*

PRA'TTLE. *n. s.* [from the verb.] Empty talk; trifling loquacity.
In a theatre the eyes of men,
After a well-grac'd actor leaves the stage,
Are idly bent on him that enters next,
Thinking his *prattle* to be tedious. *Shakesp. Rich.* II.
The bookish theorick,
Wherein the toged consuls can propose
As masterly as he; mere *prattle*, without practice,
Is all his soldiership. *Shakesp. Othello.*
The insignificant *prattle* and endless garrulity of the philosophy of the schools. *Glanv.*

PRA'TTLER. *n. s.* [from *prattle.*] A trifling talker; a chatterer.
Poor *prattler!* how thou talk'st? *Shakesp.*
Prattler, no more, I say;
My thoughts must work, but like a noiseless sphere,
Harmonious peace must rock them all the day;
No room for *prattlers* there. *Herbert.*

PRA'VITY. *n. s.* [*pravitas*, Lat.] Corruption; badness; malignity.
Doubt not but that sin
Will reign among them, as of thee begot;
And therefore was law given them, to evince
Their natural *pravity*. *Milton's Par. Lost, b.* xii.
More people go to the gibbet for want of timely correction, than upon any incurable *pravity* of nature. *L'Estrange.*
I will shew how the *pravity* of the will could influence the understanding to a disbelief of Christianity. *South.*

PRAWN. *n. s.* A small crustaceous fish, like a shrimp, but larger.
I had *prawns*, and borrowed a mess of vinegar. *Shakesp.*

To PRAY. *v. n.* [*prier*, Fr. *pregare*, Italian.]
1. To make petitions to heaven.
I will buy with you, sell will you; but I will not eat with you, drink with you, nor *pray* with you. *Shakespeare.*
Pray for this good man and his issue. *Shakesp.*
Ne'er throughout the year to church thou go'st,
Except it be to *pray* against thy foes. *Shakesp.*
I tell him, we shall stay here at the least a month; and he heartily *prays*, some occasion may detain us longer. *Shakesp.*
Is any sick? let him call for the elders of the church, and let them *pray* over him. *Jam.* v. 14.
Unskilful with what words to *pray*, let me
Interpret for him. *Milton.*
He that *prays*, despairs not; but sad is the condition of him that cannot *pray*; happy are they that can, and do, and love to do it. *Taylor's Guide to Devotion.*
Thou, Turnus, shalt attone it by thy fate,
And *pray* to heav'n for peace, but *pray* too late. *Dryden.*
He prais'd my courage, *pray'd* for my success;
He was so true a father of his country,
To thank me for defending ev'n his foes. *Dryden.*
Should you *pray* to God for a recovery, how rash would it be to accuse God of not hearing your prayers, because you found your disease still to continue. *Wake.*
2. To entreat; to ask submissively.
You shall find
A conqu'ror that will *pray* in aid for kindness,
Where he for grace is kneel'd to. *Shakespeare.*
Pray that in towns and temples of renown,
The name of great Anchises may be known. *Dryden.*
3. I PRAY; that is, *I* pray *you to tell me* is a slightly ceremonious form of introducing a question.
But I *pray*, in this mechanical formation, when the ferment was expanded to the extremities of the arteries, why did it not break through the receptacle? *Bentley's Sermons.*
4. Sometimes only *pray* elliptically.
Barnard in spirit, sense and truth abounds;
Pray then what wants he? fourscore thousand pounds. *Pope.*

To PRAY. *v. a.*
1. To supplicate; to implore; to address with submissive petitions.
How much more, if we *pray* him, will his ear
Be open, and his heart to pity incline? *Milton.*
2. To ask for as a supplicant.
He that will have the benefit of this act, must *pray* a prohibition before a sentence in the ecclesiastical court. *Ayliffe.*
3. To entreat in ceremony or form.
Pray my collegue Antonius I may speak with him;
And as you go, call on my brother Quintus,
And *pray* him with the tribunes to come to me. *B. Johns.*

PRA'YER. *n. s.* [*priere*, Fr.]
1. Petition to heaven.
They did say their *prayers*, and address'd them
Again to sleep. *Shakesp. Macbeth.*
O remember, God!
O hear her *prayer* for them as now for us. *Shakesp.*
Were he as famous and as bold in war,
As he is fam'd for mildness, peace and *prayer*. *Shakesp.*
My heart's desire and *prayer* to God for Israel is, that they might be saved. *Romans* x. 1.
Sighs now breath'd
Inutterable, which the spirit of *prayer*
Inspir'd. *Milton.*
No man can always have the same spiritual pleasure in his *prayers*; for the greatest saints have sometimes suffered the banishment of the heart, sometimes are fervent, sometimes they feel a barrenness of devotion; for this spirit comes and goes. *Taylor's Guide to Devotion.*
2. Entreaty; submissive importunity.
Prayer among men is supposed a means to change the person to whom we pray; but prayer to God doth not change him, but fits us to receive the things prayed for. *Stillingfleet.*

PRA'YERBOOK. *n. s.* [*prayer* and *book.*] Book of publick or private devotions.
Get a *prayerbook* in your hand,
And stand between two churchmen;
For on that ground I'll build a holy descant. *Shakesp.*
I know not the names or number of the family which now reigns, farther than the *prayerbook* informs me. *Swift.*

PRE. [*præ*, Lat.] A particle which, prefixed to words derived from the Latin, marks priority of time or rank.

To PREACH. *v. n.* [*prædico*, Lat. *prescher*, Fr.] To pronounce a publick discourse upon sacred subjects.
From that time Jesus began to *preach*. *Mat.* iv. 17.
Prophets *preach* of thee at Jerusalem. *Neh.* vi. 7.
Divinity would not pass the yard and loom, the forge or anvil, nor *preaching* be taken in as an easier supplementary trade, by those that disliked the pains of their own. *D. of Pie.*
As he was sent by his father, so were the apostles commissionated by him to *preach* to the gentile world. *D. of Piety.*
The shape of our cathedral is not proper for our *preaching* auditories, but rather the figure of an amphitheatre with galleries. *Graunt.*

To PREACH. *v. a.*
1. To proclaim or publish in religious orations.
The Jews of Thessalonica had knowledge, that the word of God was *preached* of Paul. *Acts.*
2. To inculcate publickly; to teach with earnestness.
There is not any thing publickly notified, but we may properly say it is *preached*. *Hooker.*
He oft to them *preach'd*
Conversion and repentance. *Milton.*
Can they *preach* up equality of birth,
And tell us how we all began from earth. *Dryden.*
Huge heaps of slain;
Among the rest, the rich Galesus lies,
A good old man while peace he *preach'd* in vain,
Amidst the madness of th' unruly train. *Dryden.*

PREACH. *n. s.* [*presche*, Fr. from the verb.] A discourse; a religious oration.
This oversight occasioned the French spitefully to term religion in that sort exercised, a mere *preach*. *Hooker.*

Prea'cher. *n. s.* [*prescheur*, Fr. from *preach.*]

1. One who discourses publickly upon religious subjects.

The Lord gave the word; great was the company of the *preachers.* *Psalm* lxviii. 11.

You may hear the sound of a *preacher's* voice, when you cannot distinguish what he saith. *Bacon.*

Here lies a truly honest man,
One of those few that in this town
Honour all *preachers*; hear their own. *Crashaw.*

2. One who inculcates any thing with earnestness and vehemence.

No *preacher* is listened to but time, which gives us the same train of thought, that elder people have tried in vain to put into our heads before. *Swift.*

Prea'chment. *n. s.* [from *preach.*] A sermon mentioned in contempt; a discourse affectedly solemn.

Was't you, that revell'd in our parliament,
And made a *preachment* of your high descent. *Shakesp.*

All this is but a *preachment* upon the text at last. *L'Estrange.*

PRE'AMBLE. *n. s.* [*preambule*, Fr.] Something previous; introduction; preface.

How were it possible that the church should any way else with such ease and certainty provide, that none of her children may, as Adam, dissemble that wretchedness, the penitent confession whereof is so necessary a *preamble*, especially to common prayer. *Hooker, b.* v.

Truth as in this we do not violate, so neither is the same gainsayed or crossed, no not in those very *preambles* placed before certain readings, wherein the steps of the Latin service book have been somewhat too nearly followed. *Hooker.*

Doors shut, visits forbidden, and divers contestations with the queen, all *preambles* of ruin, though now and then he did wring out some petty contentments. *Wotton.*

This *preamble* to that history was not improper for this relation. *Clarendon's Hist. of the Rebellion.*

With *preamble* sweet
Of charming symphony they introduce
Their sacred song, and waken raptures high. *Milton.*

I will not detain you with a long *preamble.* *Dryden.*

Prea'mbulary. } *adj.* [from *preamble.*] Previous. Not in
Prea'mbulous. } use.

He not only undermineth the base of religion, but destroyeth the principle *preambulous* unto all belief, and puts upon us the remotest error from truth. *Brown.*

Preapprehe'nsion. *n. s.* [*pre* and *apprehend.*] An opinion formed before examination.

A conceit not to be made out by ordinary eyes, but such as regarding the clouds, behold them in shapes conformable to *preapprehensions.* *Brown's Vulgar Errours.*

Prease. *n. s.* Press; crowd. *Spenser.* See **Press.**

A ship into the sacred seas,
New-built, now launch we; and from out our *prease*
Chuse two and fifty youths. *Chapman.*

Prea'sing. *part. adj.* Crowding. *Spenser.*

Pre'bend. *n. s.* [*præbenda*, low Latin; *prebende*, Fr.]

1. A stipend granted in cathedral churches.

His excellency gave the doctor a *prebend* in St. Patrick's cathedral. *Swift's Miscellanies.*

2. Sometimes, but improperly, a stipendiary of a cathedral; a prebendary.

Deans and canons, or *prebends* of cathedral churches, in their first institution, were of great use, to be of counsel with the bishop. *Bacon.*

Pre'bendary. *n. s.* [*præbendarius*, Lat.] A stipendiary of a cathedral.

To lords, to principals, to *prebendaries.* *Hubberd.*

I bequeath to the Reverend Mr. Grattan, *prebendary* of St. Audeon's, my gold bottle-screw. *Swift's Last Will.*

PRECA'RIOUS. *adj.* [*precarius*, Lat. *precaire*, Fr.] Dependent; uncertain, because depending on the will of another; held by courtesy; changeable or alienable at the pleasure of another. No word is more unskilfully used than this with its derivatives. It is used for *uncertain* in all its senses; but it only means uncertain, as dependent on others: thus there are authors who mention the *precariousness* of an *account*, of the *weather*, of a *die.*

What subjects will *precarious* kings regard,
A beggar speaks too softly to be heard. *Dryden.*

Those who live under an arbitrary tyrannick power, have no other law but the will of their prince, and consequently no privileges but what are *precarious.* *Addison.*

This little happiness is so very *precarious*, that it wholly depends on the will of others. *Addison's Spectator.*

He who rejoices in the strength and beauty of youth, should consider by how *precarious* a tenure he holds these advantages, that a thousand accidents may before the next dawn lay all these glories in the dust. *Rogers's Sermons.*

Preca'riously. *n. s.* [from *precarious.*] Uncertainly by dependence; dependently; at the pleasure of others.

Our scene *precariously* subsists too long
On French translation and Italian song:
Dare to have sense yourselves; assert the stage,
Be justly warm'd with your own native rage. *Pope.*

Preca'riousness. *n. s.* [from *precarious.*] Uncertainty; dependence on others. The following passage from a book, otherwise elegantly written, affords an example of the impropriety mentioned at the word *precarious.*

Most consumptive people die of the discharge they spit up, which, with the *precariousness* of the symptoms of an oppressed diaphragm from a mere lodgement of extravasated matter, render the operation but little adviseable. *Sharp's Surgery.*

Precau'tion. *n. s. precaution*, Fr. [from *præcautus*, Lat.] Preservative caution; preventive measures.

Unless our ministers have strong assurances of his falling in with the grand alliance, or not opposing it, they cannot be too circumspect and speedy in taking their *precautions* against any contrary resolution. *Addison on the State of the War.*

To **Precau'tion.** *v. a.* [*precautioner*, Fr. from the noun.] To warn beforehand.

By the disgraces, diseases and beggary of hopeful young men brought to ruin, he may be *precautioned.* *Locke.*

Preceda'neous. *adj.* [This word is, I believe, mistaken by the author for *præcidaneous*; *præcidaneus*, Lat. cut or slain before. Nor is it used here in its proper sense.] previous; antecedent.

That priority of particles of simple matter, influx of the heavens and preparation of matter might be antecedent and *precedaneous*, not only in order, but in time, to their ordinary productions. *Hale's Origin of Mankind.*

To **Prece'de.** *v. a.* [*præcedo*, Lat. *preceder*, Fr.]

1. To go before in order of time.

How are we happy, still in fear of harm;
But harm *precedes* not sin. *Milton.*

Arius and Pelagius durst provoke,
To what the centuries *preceding* spoke. *Dryden.*

The ruin of a state is generally *preceded* by an universal degeneracy of manners and contempt of religion. *Swift.*

2. To go before according to the adjustment of rank.

Prece'dence. } *n. s.* [from *præcedo*, Lat.]
Prece'dency. }

1. The act or state of going before; priority.
2. Something going before; something past.

I do not like but yet; it does allay
The good *precedence.* *Shakesp. Ant. and Cleop.*

It is an epilogue or discourse, to make plain
Some obscure *precedence* that hath tofore been sain. *Shakesp.*

3. Adjustment of place.

The constable and marshal had cognizance, touching the rights of place and *precedence.* *Hale.*

4. The foremost place in ceremony.

None sure will claim in hell
Precedence; none, whose portion is small
Of present pain, that with ambitious mind
Will covet more. *Milton's Par. Lost.*

The royal olive accompanied him with all his court, and always gave him the *precedency.* *Howel.*

That person hardly will be found,
With gracious form and equal virtue crown'd;
Yet if another could *precedence* claim,
My fixt desires could find no fairer aim. *Dryden.*

5. Superiority.

Books will furnish him, and give him light and *precedency* enough to go before a young follower. *Locke.*

Being distracted with different desires, the next inquiry will be, which of them has the *precedency*, in determining the will, to the next action. *Locke.*

Prece'dent. *adj.* [*precedent*, Fr. *præcedens*, Lat.] Former; going before.

Do it at once,
Or thy *precedent* services are all
But accidents unpurpos'd. *Shakesp. Ant. and Cleop.*

Our own *precedent* passions do instruct us.
What levity's in youth. *Shakesp. Timon of Athens.*

When you work by the imagination of another, it is necessary that he, by whom you work, have a *precedent* opinion of you, that you can do strange things. *Bacon.*

Hippocrates, in his prognosticks, doth make good observations of the diseases that ensue upon the nature of the *precedent* four seasons of the year. *Bacon.*

The world, or any part thereof, could not be *precedent* to the creation of man. *Hale's Origin of Mankind.*

Truths, absolutely necessary to salvation, are so clearly revealed, that we cannot err in them, unless we be notoriously wanting to ourselves; herein the fault of the judgment is resolved into a *precedent* default in the will. *South.*

Pre'cedent. *n. s.* [The adjective has the accent on the second syllable, the substantive on the first.] Any thing that is a rule or example to future times; any thing done before of the same kind.

Examples for cases can but direct as *precedents* only. *Hooker.*

Eleven hours I've spent to write it over,
The *precedent* was full as long a doing. *Shakespeare.*

A reason mighty, strong and effectual,
A pattern, *precedent* and lively warrant
For me, most wretched, to perform the like. *Shakesp.*

No pow'r in Venice
Can alter a decree established:
'Twill be recorded for a *precedent*;
And many an errour, by the same example,
Will rush into the state. *Shakesp. Merch. of Venice.*

God, in the administration of his justice, is not tied to *precedents*, and we cannot argue, that the providences of God towards other nations shall be conformable to his dealings with the people of Israel. *Tillotson's Sermons.*

Such *precedents* are numberless; we draw
Our right from custom; custom is a law. *Granville.*

PRECE'DENTLY. *adv.* [from *precedent*, adj.] Beforehand.

PRECE'NTOR. *n. s.* [*præcentor*, Lat. *precenteur*, Fr.] He that leads the choir.

Follow this *precentor* of ours, in blessing and magnifying that God of all grace, and never yielding to those enemies, which he died to give us power to resist and overcome. *Hamm.*

PRE'CEPT. *n. s.* [*precepte*, Fr. *præceptum*, Lat.] A rule authoritatively given; a mandate; a commandment; a direction.

The custom of lessons furnishes the very simplest and rudest sort with infallible axioms and *precepts* of sacred truth, delivered even in the very letter of the law of God. *Hooker.*

'Tis sufficient, that painting be acknowledged for an art; for it follows, that no arts are without their *precepts*. *Dryden.*

A *precept* or commandment consists in, and has respect to, some moral point of doctrine, *viz.* such as concerns our manners, and our inward and outward good behaviour. *Ayliffe.*

PRECE'PTIAL. *adj.* [from *precept.*] Consisting of precepts. A word not in use.

Men
Can counsel, and give comfort to that grief
Which they themselves not feel; but tasting it,
Their counsel turns to passion, which before
Would give *preceptial* medicine to rage;
Fetter strong madness in a silken thread,
Charm ach with air, and agony with words. *Shakesp.*

PRECE'PTIVE. *adj.* [*preceptivus*, Lat. from *precept.*] Containing precepts; giving precepts.

The ritual, the *preceptive*, the prophetick and all other parts of sacred writ, were most sedulously, most religiously guarded by them. *Government of the Tongue.*

As the *preceptive* part enjoins the most exact virtue, so is it most advantageously enforced by the promissory, which, in respect of the rewards, and the manner of proposing them, is adapted to the same end. *Decay of Piety.*

The lesson given us here, is *preceptive* to us not to do any thing but upon due consideration. *L'Estrange.*

PRECE'PTOR. *n. s.* [*præceptor*, Lat. *precepteur*, Fr.] A teacher; a tutor.

Passionate chiding carries rough language with it, and the names that parents and *preceptors* give children, they will not be ashamed to bestow on others. *Locke.*

It was to thee, great Stagyrite unknown,
And thy *preceptor* of divine renown. *Blackmore.*

PRECE'SSION. *n. s.* [from *præcedo*, *præcessus*, Lat.] The act of going before.

PRECI'NCT. *n. s.* [*præcinctus*, Latin.] Outward limit; boundary.

The main body of the sea being one, yet within divers *precincts*, hath divers names; so the catholick church is in like sort divided into a number of distinct societies. *Hooker.*

Through all restraint broke loose, he wings his way
Not far off heav'n, in the *precincts* of light,
Directly towards the new-created world. *Milton.*

PRECIO'SITY. *n. s.* [from *pretiosus*, Lat.]
1. Value; preciousness.
2. Any thing of high price.

The index or forefinger was too naked whereto to commit their *preciosities*, and hath the tuition of the thumb scarce unto the second joint. *Brown's Vulgar Errours.*

Barbarians seem to exceed them in the curiosity of their application of these *preciosities*. *More's Divine Dialogues.*

PRE'CIOUS. *adj.* [*precieux*, Fr. *pretiosus*, Lat.]
1. Valuable; being of great worth.

Many things, which are most *precious*, are neglected only because the value of them lieth hid. *Hooker.*

I cannot but remember such things were,
That were most *precious* to me. *Shakesp. Macbeth.*

Why in that rawness left you wife and children,
Those *precious* motives, those strong knots of love,
Without leave taking? *Shakesp. Macbeth.*

I never saw
Such *precious* deeds in one that promis'd nought
But begg'ry and poor luck. *Shakesp. Cymbeline.*

These virtues are the hidden beauties of a soul, which make it lovely and *precious* in his sight, from whom no secrets are concealed. *Addison's Spectator.*

2. Costly; of great price: as, *a* precious *stone.*

Let none admire
That riches grow in hell; that soil may best
Deserve the *precious* bane. *Milton.*

3. Worthless. An epithet of contempt or irony.

More of the same kind, concerning these *precious* saints amongst the Turks, may be seen in Pietro della valle. *Locke.*

PRE'CIOUSLY. *adv.* [from *precious.*]
1. Valuably; to a great price.
2. Contemptibly. In irony.

PRE'CIOUSNESS. *n. s.* [from *precious.*] Valuableness; worth; price.

Its *preciousness* equalled the price of pearls. *Wilkins.*

PRE'CIPICE. *n. s.* [*præcipitium*, Lat. *precipice*, Fr.] A headlong steep; a fall perpendicular without gradual declivity.

You take a *precipice* for no leap of danger,
And woo your own destruction. *Shakesp. Henry* VIII.

Where the water dasheth more against the bottom, there it moveth more swiftly and more in *precipice*; for in the breaking of the waves there is ever a *precipice*. *Bacon.*

I ere long that *precipice* must tread,
Whence none return, that leads unto the dead. *Sandys.*

No stupendous *precipice* denies
Access, no horrer turns away our eyes. *Denham.*

Swift down the *precipice* of time it goes,
And sinks in minutes, which in ages rose. *Dryden.*

His gen'rous mind the fair ideas drew
Of fame and honour, which in dangers lay;
Where wealth, like fruit, on *precipices* grew,
Not to be gather'd but by birds of prey. *Dryden.*

Drink as much as you can get; because a good coachman never drives so well as when he is drunk; and then shew your skill, by driving to an inch by a *precipice*. *Swift.*

PRECI'PITANCE. } *n. s.* [from *precipitant.*] Rash haste; head-
PRECI'PITANCY. } long hurry.

Thither they haste with glad *precipitance*. *Milton.*

'Tis not likely that one of a thousand such *precipitancies* should be crowned with so unexpected an issue. *Glanvill.*

As the chymist, by catching at it too soon, lost the philosophical elixir, so *precipitancy* of our understanding is an occasion of error. *Glanvill's Sceps.*

We apply present remedies according unto indications, respecting rather the acuteness of disease and *precipitancy* of occasion, than the rising or setting of stars. *Brown.*

Hurried on by the *precipitancy* of youth, I took this opportunity to send a letter to the secretary. *Gulliver's Travels.*

A rashness and *precipitance* of judgment, and hastiness to believe something on one side or the other, plunges us into many errors. *Watts's Logick.*

PRECI'PITANT. *adj.* [*præcipitans*, Lat.]
1. Falling or rushing headlong.

Without longer pause,
Downright into the world's first region throws
His flight *precipitant*. *Milton's Par. Lost, b.* iii.

The birds heedless while they strain
Their tuneful throats, the tow'ring heavy lead
O'ertakes their speed; they leave their little lives
Above the clouds, *precipitant* to earth. *Philips.*

2. Hasty; urged with violent haste.

Should he return, that troop so blithe and bold,
Precipitant in fear, would wing their flight,
And curse their cumbrous pride's unwieldy weight. *Pope.*

3. Rashly hurried.

The commotions in Ireland were so sudden and so violent, that it was hard to discern the rise, or apply a remedy to that *precipitant* rebellion. *King Charles.*

PRECI'PITANTLY. *adv.* [from *precipitant.*] In headlong haste; in a tumultuous hurry.

To PRECI'PITATE. *v. a.* [*præcipito*, Lat. *precipiter*, Fr. in all the senses.]
1. To throw headlong.

She had a king to her son in law, yet was, upon dark and unknown reasons, *precipitated* and banished the world into a nunnery. *Bacon's Henry* VII.

Ere vengeance
Precipitate thee with augmented pain. *Milton.*

They were wont, upon a superstition, to *precipitate* a man from some high cliff into the sea, tying about him with strings many great fowls. *Wilkins.*

The virgin from the ground
Upstarting fresh, already clos'd the wound,
Precipitates her flight. *Dryden.*

The goddess guides her son, and turns him from the light,
Herself involv'd in clouds, *precipitates* her flight. *Dryden.*

2. To hasten unexpectedly.

Short, intermittent and swift recurrent pains do *precipitate* patients into consumptions. *Harvey.*

3. To hurry blindly or rashly.

As for having them obnoxious to ruin, if they be of fearful natures, it may do well; but if they be stout and daring, it may *precipitate* their designs, and prove dangerous. *Bacon.*

Dear Erythræa, let not such blind fury
Precipitate your thoughts, nor set them working,
Till time shall lend them better means,
Than lost complaints. *Denham's Sophy.*

3. To throw to the bottom. *A* term of chymistry opposed to sublime.

Gold endures a vehement fire long without any change, and after it has been divided by corrosive liquors into invisible parts, yet may presently be *precipitated*, so as to appear again in its own form. *Grew's Cosmol.*

To Preci'pitate. *v. n.*

1. To fall headlong.

Had'st thou been aught but goss'mer feathers,
So many fathom down *precipitating*,
Thoud'st shiver like an egg. *Shakesp. King Lear.*

2. To fall to the bottom as a sediment.

By strong water every metal will *precipitate*. *Bacon.*

3. To hasten without just preparation.

Neither did the rebels spoil the country, neither on the other side did their forces encrease, which might hasten him to *precipitate* and assail them. *Bacon.*

Preci'pitate. *adj.* [from the verb.]

1. Steeply falling.

Barcephas saith, it was necessary this paradise should be set at such a height, because the four rivers, had they not fallen so *precipitate*, could not have had sufficient force to thrust themselves under the great ocean. *Raleigh.*

When the full stores their antient bounds disdain,
Precipitate the furious torrent flows;
In vain would speed avoid, or strength oppose. *Prior.*

2. Headlong; hasty; rashly hasty.

The archbishop, too *precipitate* in pressing the reception of that which he thought a reformation, paid dearly for it. *Clarendon.*

3. Hasty; violent.

Mr. Gay died of a mortification of the bowels; it was the most *precipitate* case I ever knew, having cut him off in three days. *Pope to Swift.*

Preci'pitate. *n. s.* A corrosive medicine made by precipitating mercury.

As the escar separated, I rubb'd the super-excrescence of flesh with the vitriol-stone, or sprinkled it with *precipitate*. *Wiseman's Surgery.*

Preci'pitately. *adv.* [from *precipitate.*]

1. Headlong; steeply down.

2. Hastily; in blind hurry.

It may happen to those who vent praise or censure too *precipitately*, as it did to an English poet, who celebrated a nobleman for erecting Dryden's monument, upon a promise which he forgot, till it was done by another. *Swift.*

Not so bold Arnall; with a weight of scull
Furious he sinks, *precipitately* dull. *Pope's Dunciad.*

Precipita'tion. *n. s.* [*precipitation*, Fr. from *precipitate.*]

1. The act of throwing headlong.

Let them pile ten hills on the Tarpeian rock,
That the *precipitation* might down-stretch
Below the beam of sight, yet will I still
Be this to them. *Shakesp. Coriolanus.*

2. Violent motion downward.

That could never happen from any other cause than the hurry, *precipitation* and rapid motion of the water, returning at the end of the deluge, towards the sea. *Woodward.*

3. Tumultuous hurry; blind haste.

Here is none of the hurry and *precipitation*, none of the blustering and violence, which must have attended those suppostitious changes. *Woodward's Nat. Hist.*

4. In chemistry, Subsidency: contrary to sublimation.

Separation is wrought by *precipitation* or sublimation; that is, a calling of the parts up or down, which is a kind of attraction. *Bacon.*

The *precipitation* of the vegetative matter, after the deluge, and the burying it in the strata underneath amongst the sand, was to retrench the luxury of the productions of the earth, which had been so ungratefully abused by its former inhabitants. *Woodward's Nat. Hist.*

Preci'pitous. *adj.* [*præcipites*, Lat.]

1. Headlong; steep.

Monarchy, together with me, could not but be dashed in pieces by such a *precipitous* fall as they intended. *K. Charles.*

2. Hasty; sudden.

Though the attempts of some have been *precipitous*, and their enquiries so audacious as to have lost themselves in attempts above humanity, yet have the enquiries of most defected by the way. *Brown's Vulgar Errours.*

How precious the time is, how *precipitous* the occasion, how many things to be done in their just season, after once a ground is in order. *Evelyn's Kalendar.*

3. Rash; heady.

Thus fram'd for ill, he loos'd our triple hold,
Advice unsafe, *precipitous* and bold. *Dryden.*

PRE'CISE. *adj.* [*precis*, Fr. *præcisus*, Lat.]

1. Exact; strict; nice; having strict and determinate limitations.

Means more durable to preserve the laws of God from oblivion and corruption grew in use, not without *precise* direction from God himself. *Hooker, b.* i.

You'll not bear a letter for me; you stand upon your honour; why, thou unconfinable baseness, it is as much as I can do to keep the term of mine honour *precise*. *Shakesp.*

The state hath given you licence to stay on land six weeks, and let it not trouble you if your occasions ask farther time; for the law in this point is not *precise*. *Bacon.*

Let us descend from this top
Of speculation; for the hour *precise*
Exacts our parting. *Milton's Par. Lost, b.* xiii.

In human actions there are no degrees and *precise* natural limits described, but a latitude is indulged. *Taylor.*

The reasonings must be *precise*, though the practice may admit of great latitude. *Arbuthnot on Aliments.*

The *precise* difference between a compound and collective idea is this, that a compound idea unites things of a different kind, but a collective, things of the same kind. *Watts.*

2. Formal; finical; solemnly and superstitiously exact.

The raillery of the wits in king Charles the Second's reign, upon every thing which they called *precise*, was carried to so great an extravagance, that it almost put all Christianity out of countenance. *Addison.*

Preci'sely. *adv.* [from *precise.*]

1. Exactly; nicely; accurately.

Doth it follow, that all things in the church, from the greatest to the least, are unholy, which the Lord hath not himself *precisely* instituted? *Hooker, b.* v.

When the Lord had once *precisely* set down a form of executing that wherein we are to serve him, the fault appeareth greater to do that which we are not, than not to do that which we are commanded. *Hooker, b.* ii.

He knows,
He cannot so *precisely* weed this land,
As his misdoubts present occasion,
His foes are so enrooted with his friends. *Shakesp.*

Where more of these orders than one shall be set in several stories, there must be an exquisite care to place the columns *precisely* one over another. *Wotton's Architecture.*

In his tract my wary feet have stept,
His undeclined ways *precisely* kept. *Sandys.*

The rule, to find the age of the moon, cannot shew *precisely* an exact account of the moon, because of the inequality of the motions of the sun and of the moon. *Holder.*

Measuring the diameter of the fifth dark circle, I found it the fifth part of an inch *precisely*. *Newton's Opticks.*

2. With superstitious formality; with too much scrupulosity; with troublesome ceremony.

Preci'seness. *n. s.* [from *precise.*] Exactness; rigid nicety.

I will distinguish the cases; though give me leave, in the handling of them, not to sever them with too much *preciseness*. *Bacon.*

When you have fixed proper hours for particular studies, keep to them, not with a superstitious *preciseness*, but with some good degrees of a regular constancy. *Watts.*

Preci'sian. *n. s.* [from *precise.*]

1. One who limits or restrains.

Though love use reason for his *precisian*, he admits him not for his counsellor. *Shakesp. Merry Wives of Windsor.*

2. One who is superstitiously rigorous.

A profane person calls a man of piety a *precisian*. *Watts.*

Preci'sion. *n. s.* [*precision*, Fr.] Exact limitation.

He that thinks of being in general, thinks never of any particular species of being; unless he can think of it with and without *precision* at the same time. *Locke.*

I have left out the utmost *precisions* of fractions in these computations as not necessary; these whole numbers shewing well enough the difference of the value of guineas. *Locke.*

I was unable to treat this part more in detail, without sacrificing perspicuity to ornament, without wandering from the *precision* or breaking the chain of reasoning. *Pope.*

Preci'sive. *adj.* [from *precisus*, Lat.] Exactly limiting, by cutting off all that is not absolutely relative to the present purpose.

Precisive abstraction is when we consider those things apart, which cannot really exist apart; as when we consider mode, without considering its substance or subject. *Watts.*

To Preclu'de. *v. a.* [*præcludo*, Lat.] To shut out or hinder by some anticipation.

This much will obviate and *preclude* the objections of our adversaries, that we do not determine the final cause of the systematical parts of the world, merely as they have respect to the exigences or conveniences of life. *Bentley.*

If you once allow them such an acceptation of chance, you have *precluded* yourself from any more reasoning against them. *Bentley's Sermons.*

I fear there will be no way left to tell you, that I entirely esteem you; none but that which no bills can *preclude*, and no king can prevent. *Pope.*

PRECO'CIOUS. *adj.* [*præcocis*, Lat. *precose*, Fr.] Ripe before the time.

Many *precocious* trees, and such as have their spring in the winter, may be found in most parts. *Brown.*

Preco'city. *n. s.* [from *precocious.*] Ripeness before the time.

Some impute the cause of his fall to a *precocity* of spirit and valour in him; and that therefore some infectious southern air did blast him. *Howel's Vocal Forest.*

To Preco'gitate. *v. a.* [*præcogito*, Lat.] To consider or scheme beforehand.

Precogni'tion. *n. s.* [*præ* and *cognitio*, Lat.] Previous knowledge; antecedent examination.

Preconcei't. *n. s.* [*præ* and *conceit.*] An opinion previously formed.

A thing in reason impossible, which notwithstanding through their misfashioned *preconceit*, appeared unto them no less certain than if nature had written it in the very foreheads of all the creatures. *Hooker.*

To Preconcei've. *v. a.* [*præ* and *conceive.*] To form an opinion beforehand; to imagine beforehand.

In a dead plain the way seemeth the longer, because the eye hath *preconceived* it shorter than the truth; and the frustrations of that maketh it seem so. *Bacon.*

Fondness of *preconceived* opinions is not like to render your reports suspect, nor for want of sagacity or care, defective. *Glanvill's Sceps.*

The reason why men are so weak in governing is, because most things fall out accidentally, and come not into any compliance with their *preconceived* ends, but they are forced to comply subsequently. *South's Sermons.*

Preconce'ption. *n. s.* [*præ* and *conception.*] Opinion previously formed.

Custom with most men prevails more than truth, according to the notions and *preconceptions*, which it hath formed in our minds, we shape the discourse of reason itself. *Hakewill.*

Preco'ntract. *n. s.* [*præ* and *contract.* This was formerly accented on the last syllable.] A contract previous to another.

He is your husband on a *precontract*;
To bring you thus together, 'tis no sin. *Shakesp.*

To Precontra'ct. *v. a.* [*præ* and *contract.*] To contract or bargain beforehand.

Some are such as a man cannot make his wife, though he himself be unmarried, because they are already *precontracted* to some other; or else are in too near a degree of affinity or consanguinity. *Ayliffe.*

Precu'rse. *n. s.* [from *præcurro*, Lat.] Forerunning.

The like *precurse* of fierce events,
As harbingers preceding still the fates,
And prologue to the omen coming on,
Have heaven and earth together demonstrated. *Shakespeare.*

Precu'rsor. *n. s.* [*præcursor*, Lat. *precurseur*, Fr.] Forerunner; harbinger.

Jove's lightnings, the *precursors*
Of dreadful thunder claps, more momentary
Were not. *Shakesp. Tempest.*

This contagion might have been presaged upon consideration of its *precursors*, *viz.* a rude winter, and a close, sulphurous and fiery air. *Harvey on the Plague.*

Thomas Burnet played the *precurser* to the coming of Homer in his Homerides. *Pope.*

Preda'ceous. *adj.* [from *præda*, Lat.] Living by prey.

As those are endowed with poison, because they are *predaceous*; so these need it not, because their food is near at hand, and may be obtained without contest. *Derham.*

Pre'dal. *adj.* [from *præda*, Lat.] Robbing; practising plunder. This word is not countenanced from analogy.

Sarmatia, laid by *predal* rapine low,
Mourn'd the hard yoke, and sought relief in vain. *Sa. Boyse.*

Pre'datory. *adj.* [*prædatorius*, Lat. from *præda*, Lat.]

1. Plundering; practising rapine.

The king called his parliament, where he exaggerated the malice and the cruel *predatory* war made by Scotland. *Bacon.*

2. Hungry; preying; rapacious; ravenous.

The evils that come of exercise are, that it maketh the spirits more hot and *predatory*. *Bacon.*

Predecea'sed. *adj.* [*præ* and *deceased.*] Dead before.

Will you mock at an ancient tradition, began upon an honourable respect, and worn as a memorable trophy of *predeceased* valour. *Shakesp. Henry V.*

Predece'ssor. *n. s.* [*predecesseur*, Fr. *præ* and *decedo*, Lat.]

1. One that was in any state or place before another.

In these pastoral pastimes, a great many days were spent to follow their flying *predecessors*. *Sidney.*

There is cause, why we should be slow and unwilling to change, without very urgent necessity, the ancient ordinances, rites and long approved customs of our venerable *predecessors*. *Hooker.*

If I seem partial to my *predecessor* in the laurel, the friends of antiquity are not few. *Dryden.*

The present pope, who is well acquainted with the secret history, and the weakness of his *predecessor*, seems resolved to bring the project to its perfection. *Addison.*

The more beauteous Cloe sat to thee,
Good Howard, emulous of Apelles' art;
But happy thou from Cupid's arrow free,
And flames that pierc'd thy *predecessor*'s heart. *Prior.*

2. Ancestors.

Predestina'rian. *n. s.* [from *predestinate.*] One that holds the doctrine of predestination.

Why does the *predestinarian* so adventurously climb into heaven, to ransack the celestial archives, read God's hidden decrees, when with less labour he may secure an authentick transcript within himself. *Decay of Piety.*

To PREDE'STINATE. *v. a.* [*predestiner*, Fr. *præ* and *destino*, Lat.] To appoint beforehand by irreversible decree.

Some gentleman or other shall scape a *predestinate* scratcht face. *Shakespeare.*

Whom he did foreknow, he also did *predestinate* to be conformed to the image of his son. *Romans* viii. 29.

Having *predestinated* us unto the adoption of children by Jesus Christ to himself. *Eph.* i. 5.

To Prede'stinate. *v. n.* To hold predestination. In ludicrous language.

His ruff crest he rears,
And pricks up his *predestinating* ears. *Dryden.*

Predestina'tion. *n. s.* [*predestination*, Fr. from *predestinate.*] Fatal decree; pre-ordination.

Predestination we can difference no otherwise from providence and prescience, than this, that prescience only foreseeth, providence foreseeth and careth for, and hath respect to all creatures, and *predestination* is only of men; and yet not of all to men belonging, but of their salvation properly in the common use of divines; or perdition, as some have used it. *Raleigh's Hist. of the World.*

Nor can they justly accuse
Their maker, or their making, or their fate;
As if *predestination* over-rul'd
Their will, dispos'd by absolute decree,
Or high fore-knowledge. *Milton's Par. Lost, b.* iii.

Predestina'tor. *n. s.* [from *predestinate.*] One that holds predestination or the prevalence of pre-established necessity.

Me, mine example let the Stoicks use,
Their sad and cruel doctrine to maintain;
Let all *predestinators* me produce,
Who struggle with eternal fate in vain. *Cowley.*

To Prede'stine. *v. a.* [*præ* and *destine.*] To decree beforehand.

Ye careful angels, whom eternal fate
Ordains on earth and human acts to wait,
Who turn with secret pow'r this restless ball,
And bid *predestin'd* empires rise and fall. *Prior.*

Predetermina'tion. *n. s.* [*predetermination*, Fr. *præ* and *determination.*] Determination made beforehand.

This *predetermination* of God's own will is so far from being the determining of ours, that it is distinctly the contrary; for supposing God to predetermine that I shall act freely; 'tis certain from thence, that my will is free in respect of God, and not predetermined. *Hammond's Fundamentals.*

To Predete'rmine. *v. a.* [*præ* and *determine.*] To doom or confine by previous decree.

We see in brutes certain sensible instincts antecedent to their imaginative faculty, whereby they are *predetermined* to the convenience of the sensible life. *Hale.*

Pre'dial. [*prædium*, Lat.] Consisting of farms.

By the civil law, their *predial* estates are liable to fiscal payments and taxes, as not being appropriated for the service of divine worship, but for profane uses. *Ayliffe.*

Pre'dicable. *adj.* [*predicable*, Fr. *prædicabilis*, Lat.] Such as may be affirmed of something.

Predi'cable. *n. s.* [*prædicabile*, Lat.] A logical term, denoting one of the five things which can be affirmed of any thing.

These they call the five *predicables*; because every thing that is affirmed concerning any being, must be the genus, species, difference, some property or accident. *Watts.*

PRE'DICAMENT. *n. s.* [*predicament*, Fr. *prædicamentum*, Lat.]

1. A class or arrangement of beings or substances ranked according to their natures: called also categorema or category. *Harris.*

If there were nothing but bodies to be ranked by them in the *predicament* of place, then that description would be allowed by them as sufficient. *Digby on Bodies.*

2. Class or kind described by any definitive marks.

The offender's life lies in the mercy
Of the duke only, 'gainst all other voice;
In which *predicament* I say thou stand'st. *Shakesp.*
I shew the line and the *predicament*,
Wherein you range under this subtle king. *Shakesp.*

Predicame'ntal. *adj.* [from *predicament.*] Relating to predicaments.

Pre'dicant. *n. s.* [*prædicans*, Lat.] One that affirms any thing.

To PRE'DICATE. *v. a.* [*prædico*, Lat.] To affirm any thing of another thing.

All propositions, wherein a part of the complex idea, which any term stands for, is *predicated* of that term, are only verbal; *v. g.* to say that gold is a metal. *Locke.*

To PRE'DICATE. *v. n.* To affirm or speak.

It were a presumption to think, that any thing in any created nature can bear any perfect resemblance of the incomprehensible perfection of the divine nature, very being itself not *predicating* univocally touching him and any created being. *Hale's Origin of Mankind.*

PRE'DICATE. *n. s.* [*prædicatum*, Lat.] That which is affirmed of the subject; as *man is rational.*

The *predicate* is that which is affirmed or denied of the subject. *Watts's Logick.*

PREDICA'TION. *n. s.* [*prædicatio*, Lat. from *predicate.*] Affirmation concerning any thing.

Let us reason from them as well as we can; they are only about identical *predications* and influence. *Locke.*

To PREDI'CT. *v. a.* [*prædictus*, Lat. *predire*, Fr.] To foretell; to foreshow.

He is always inveighing against such unequal distributions; nor does he ever cease to *predict* publick ruins, till his private are repaired. *Government of the Tongue.*

PREDI'CTION. *n. s.* [*prædictio*, Lat. *prediction*, Fr. from *predict.*] Prophesy; declaration of something future.

These *predictions*
Are to the world in general, as to Cæsar. *Shakesp.*

The *predictions* of cold and long winters, hot and dry summers, are good to be known. *Bacon's Nat. Hist.*

How soon hath thy *prediction*, seer blest!
Measur'd this transient world the race of time,
Till time stand fix'd. *Milton's Par. Lost, b.* xii.

In Christ they all meet with an invincible evidence, as if they were not *predictions*, but after-relations; and the penmen of them not prophets but evangelists. *South's Sermons.*

He, who prophesy'd the best,
Approves the judgment to the rest;
He'd rather choose, that I should die,
Than his *prediction* prove a lie. *Swift's Miscel.*

PREDI'CTOR. *n. s.* [from *predict.*] Foreteller.

Whether he has not been the cause of this poor man's death, as well as the *predictor*, may be disputed. *Swift.*

PREDIGE'STION. *n. s.* [*præ* and *digestion.*] Digestion too soon performed.

Predigestion, or hasty digestion, fills the body full of crudities and seeds of diseases. *Bacon's Essays.*

To PREDISPO'SE. *v. a.* [*præ* and *dispose.*] To adapt previously to any certain purpose.

Vegetable productions require heat of the sun, to *predispose* and excite the earth and the seeds. *Burnet.*

Unless nature be *predisposed* to friendship by its own propensity, no arts of obligation shall be able to abate the secret hatreds of some persons towards others. *South's Sermons.*

PREDISPOSI'TION. *n. s.* [*præ* and *disposition.*] Previous adaptation to any certain purpose.

It was conceived to proceed from a malignity in the constitution of the air, gathered by the *predispositions* of seasons. *Bacon's Henry* VII.

Tunes and airs have in themselves some affinity with the affections; so as it is no marvel if they alter the spirits, considering that tunes have a *predisposition* to the motion of the spirits. *Bacon's Nat. Hist.*

External accidents are often the occasional cause of the king's evil; but they suppose a *predisposition* of the body. *Wiseman's Surgery.*

PREDO'MINANCE. } *n. s.* [*præ* and *domina*, Lat.] Prevalence;
PREDO'MINANCY. } superiority; ascendency; superior influence.

We make guilty of our disasters, the sun, the moon and the stars, as if we were knaves, thieves and treacherous by spherical *predominance.* *Shakesp. King Lear.*

An inflammation consists only of a sanguineous affluxion, or else is denominable from other humours, according to the *predominancy* of melancholy, phlegm or choler. *Brown.*

In human bodies, there is an incessant warfare amongst the humours for *predominancy.* *Howel's Vocal Forest.*

The true cause of the Pharisees disbelief of Christ's doctrine, was the *predominance* of their covetousness and ambition over their will. *South's Sermons.*

The several rays therefore in that white light do retain their colorific qualities, by which those of any sort, whenever they become more copious than the rest, do, by their excess and *predominance*, cause their proper colour to appear. *Newton.*

PREDO'MINANT. *adj.* [*predominant*, Fr. *præ* and *dominor.*] Prevalent; supreme in influence; ascendent.

Miserable were the condition of that church, the weighty affairs whereof should be ordered by those deliberations, wherein such an humour as this were *predominant.* *Hooker.*

Foul subornation is *predominant*,
And equity exil'd your highness' land. *Shakesp.*

It is a planet, that will strike
Where 'tis *predominant*; and 'tis powerful. *Shakesp.*

Those helps were overweighed by divers things that made against him, and were *predominant* in the king's mind. *Bacon.*

Whether the sun, *predominant* in heav'n,
Rise on the earth; or earth rise on the sun. *Milton.*

I could shew you several pieces, where the beauties of this kind are so *predominant*, that you could never be able to read or understand them. *Swift.*

To PREDO'MINATE. *v. n.* [*predominer*, Fr. *præ* and *dominor*, Lat.] To prevail; to be ascendent; to be supreme in influence.

So much did love t' her executed lord
Predominate in this fair lady's heart. *Daniel.*

The gods formed womens souls out of these principles which compose several kinds of animals; and their good or bad disposition arises, according as such and such principles *predominate* in their constitutions. *Addison.*

The rays, reflected least obliquely, may *predominate* over the rest, so much as to cause a heap of such particles to appear very intensely of their colour. *Newton's Opticks.*

Where judgment is at a loss to determine the choice of a lady who has several lovers, fancy may the more allowably *predominate.* *Clarissa.*

To PRE'ELECT. *v. a.* [*præ* and *elect.*] To chuse by previous decree.

PRE'EMINENCE. *n. s.* [*preeminence*, Fr. *præ* and *eminence.* It is sometimes written, to avoid the junction of *ee*, *preheminence.*]

1. Superiority of excellence.

I plead for the *preeminence* of epick poetry. *Dryden.*

Let profit have the *preeminence* of honour in the end of poetry; pleasure, though but the second in degree, is the first in favour. *Dryden.*

The *preeminence* of christianity to any other religious scheme which preceded it, appears from this, that the most eminent among the Pagan philosophers disclaimed many of those superstitious follies which are condemned by revealed religion. *Addison.*

2. Precedence; priority of place.

His lance brought him captives to the triumph of Artesia's beauty, such, as though Artesia be amongst the fairest, yet in that company were to have the *preeminence.* *Sidney.*

He toucheth it as a special *preeminence* of Junias and Andronicus, that in christianity they were his ancients. *Hooker.*

I do invest you jointly with my power,
Preeminence, and all the large effects
That troop with majesty. *Shakesp. King Lear.*

The English desired no *preeminence*, but offered equality both in liberty and privilege, and in capacity of offices and employments. *Hayward.*

Am I distinguish'd from you but by toils,
Superior toils, and heavier weight of cares!
Painful *preeminence.* *Addison's Cato.*

3. Superiority of power or influence.

That which standeth on record, hath *preeminence* above that which passeth from hand to hand, and hath no pens but the tongues, no book but the ears of men. *Hooker.*

Beyond the equator, the Southern point of the needle is sovereign, and the North submits his *preeminence.* *Brown.*

PRE'EMINENT. *adj.* [*preeminent*, Fr. *præ* and *eminent.*] Excellent above others.

Tell how came I here? by some great maker
In goodness and in pow'r *preeminent.* *Milton.*

We claim a proper interest above others, in the *preeminent* rights of the houshold of faith. *Sprat's Sermons.*

PRE'EMPTION. *n. s.* [*præemptio*, Lat.] The right of purchasing before another.

Certain persons, in the reigns of king Edward VI. and queen Mary, sought to make use of this *preemption*, but crossed in the prosecution, or defeated in their expectation, gave it over. *Carew.*

To PREENGA'GE. *v. a.* [*præ* and *engage.*] To engage by precedent ties or contracts.

The world has the unhappy advantage of *preengaging* our passions, at a time when we have not reflection enough to look beyond the instrument to the hand whose direction it obeys. *Rogers's Sermons.*

To Cipseus by his friends his suit he mov'd,
But he was *preengag'd* by former ties. *Dryden.*
Not only made an instrument;
But *preengaged* without my own consent. *Dryden.*

PREENGA'GEMENT. *n. s.* [from *preengage.*] Precedent obligation.

My *preengagements* to other themes were not unknown to those for whom I was to write. *Boyle.*

The opinions, suited to their respective tempers, will make way to their assent, in spite of accidental *preengagements.* *Glanvill's Sceps.*

Men are apt to think, that those obediences they pay to God shall, like a *preengagement*, disannull all after-contracts made by guilt. *Decay of Piety.*

As far as opportunity and former *preengagements* will give leave. *Collier of Friendship.*

To Preen. *v. a.* [*priinen*, Dutch, to dress or prank up.] To trim the feathers of birds, to enable them to glide more easily through the air: for this use nature has furnished them with two peculiar glands, which secrete an unctuous matter into a perforated oil bag, out of which the bird, on occasion, draws it with its bill. *Bailey.*

To Preesta'blish. *v. a.* [*præ* and *establish.*] To settle beforehand.

Preesta'blishment. *n. s.* [from *preestablish.*] Settlement beforehand.

To Preexi'st. *v. a.* [*præ* and *existo*, Lat.] To exist beforehand.

If thy *preexisting* soul
Was form'd at first with myriads more,
It did through all the mighty poets roll. *Dryden.*

Preexi'stence. *n. s.* [*preexistence*, Fr. from *preexist.*] Existence beforehand; existence of the soul before its union with the body.

Wisdom declares her antiquity and *preexistence* to all the works of this earth. *Burnet's Theory of the Earth.*

As Simonides has exposed the vicious part of women, from the doctrine of *preexistence*; some of the ancient philosophers have satyrized the vicious part of the human species, from a notion of the soul's postexistence. *Addison.*

Pre'existent. *adj.* [*preexistent*, Fr. *præ* and *existent.*] Existent beforehand; preceding in existence.

Artificial things could not be from eternity, because they suppose man, by whose art they were made, *preexistent* to them; the workman must be before the work. *Burnet.*

Blind to former, as to future fate,
What mortal knows his *preexistent* state? *Pope.*

If this *preexistent* eternity is not compatible with a successive duration, then some being, though infinitely above our finite comprehensions, must have had an identical, invariable continuance from all eternity, which being is no other than God. *Bentley's Sermons.*

PRE'FACE. *n. s.* [*preface*, Fr. *præfatio*, Lat.] Something spoken introductory to the main design; introduction; something proemial.

This superficial tale
Is but a *preface* to her worthy praise. *Shakesp.*

Sir Thomas More betrayed his depth of judgment in state affairs in his Utopia, than which, in the opinion of Budæus in a *preface* before it, our age hath not seen a thing more deep. *Peacham of Poetry.*

Heav'n's high behest no *preface* needs;
Sufficient that thy pray'rs are heard, and death
Defeated of his seizure. *Milton's Par. Lost, b.* xi.

To Pre'face. *v. n.* [*prefari*, Lat.] To say something introductory.

Before I enter upon the particular parts of her character, it is necessary to *preface*, that she is the only child of a decrepid father. *Spectator*, Nº 449.

To Pre'face. *v. a.*

1. To introduce by something proemial.

Thou art rash,
And must be *prefac'd* into government. *Southern.*

2. To face; to cover. A ludicrous sense.

I love to wear cloaths that are flush,
Not *prefacing* old rags with plush. *Cleaveland.*

Pre'facer. *n. s.* [from *preface.*] The writer of a preface.

If there be not a tolerable line in all these six, the *prefacer* gave me no occasion to write better. *Dryden.*

Pre'fatory. *adj.* [from *preface.*] Introductory.

If this proposition, whosoever will be saved, be restrained only to those to whom it was intended, the christians, then the anathema reaches not the heathens, who had never heard of Christ: after all, I am far from blaming even that *prefatory* addition to the creed. *Dryden.*

Pre'fect. *n. s.* [*præfectus*, Lat.] Governor; commander.

He is much
The better soldier, having been a tribune,
Prefect, lieutenant, prætor in the war. *Benj. Johnson.*

It was the custom in the Roman empire, for the *prefects* and vice-roys of distant provinces to transmit a relation of every thing remarkable in their administration. *Addison.*

Prefe'cture. *n. s.* [*prefecture*, Fr. *præfectura*, Lat.] Command; office of government.

To PREFE'R. *v. a.* [*preferer*, Fr. *præfero*, Lat.]

1. To regard more than another.

With brotherly love, in honour *prefer* one another. *Ro.*

2. With *above* before the thing postponed.

If I do not remember thee, let my tongue cleave to the roof of my mouth; if I *prefer* not Jerusalem *above* my chief joy. *Psalm* cxxxvii. 6.

3. With *before.*

He that cometh after me, is *preferred before* me; for he was before me. *Jo.* i. 15.

It may worthily seem unto you a most shameful thing, to have *prefered* an infamous peace *before* a most just war. *Knolles.*

O spirit, that dost *prefer*
Before all temples th' upright heart. *Milton.*

4. With *to.*

Would he rather leave this frantick scene,
And trees and beasts *prefer to* courts and men. *Prior.*

5. To advance; to exalt; to raise.

By the recommendation of the earl of Dunbar, he was *prefer'd to* the bishoprick of Coventry and Litchfield. *Clarend.*

He spake, and *to* her hand *prefer'd* the bowl. *Pope.*

6. To offer solemnly; to propose publickly; to exhibit.

They flatly disavouch
To yield him more obedience or support;
And as t' a perjur'd duke of Lancaster,
Their cartel of defiance they *prefer.* *Daniel.*

I, when my soul began to faint,
My vows and prayers *to* thee *prefer'd*;
The lord my passionate complaint,
Even from his holy temple, heard. *Sandys.*

Prefer a bill against all kings and parliaments since the conquest; and if that won't do, challenge the crown and the two houses. *Collier on Duelling.*

Take care,
Lest thou *prefer* so rash a pray'r;
Nor vainly hope the queen of love
Will e'er thy fav'rite's charms improve. *Prior.*

Every person within the church or commonwealth may *prefer* an accusation, that the delinquent may suffer condign punishment. *Ayliffe's Parergon.*

Pre'ferable. *adj.* [*preferable*, Fr. from *prefer.*] Eligible before something else. With *to* commonly before the thing refused.

The stronger ties we have to an unalterable pursuit of happiness, which is greatest good, the more are we free from any necessary compliance with our desire, set upon any particular, and then appearing *preferable* good, till we have duly examined it. *Locke.*

Though it be incumbent on parents to provide for their children, yet this debt to their children does not quite cancel the score due to their parents; but only is made by nature *preferable* to it. *Locke.*

Almost every man in our nation is a politician, and hath a scheme of his own, which he thinks *preferable* to that of any other. *Addison's Freeholder.*

Even in such a state as this, the pleasures of virtue would be superior to those of vice, and justly *preferable.* *Atterb.*

Pre'ferableness. *adj.* [from *preferable.*] The state of being preferable.

Pre'ferably. *adv.* [from *preferable.*] In preference; in such a manner as to prefer one thing to another.

How came he to chuse a comick *preferably* to the tragick poets; or how comes he to chuse Plautus *preferably* to Terence. *Dennis.*

Pre'ference. *n. s.* [*preference*, Fr. from *prefer.*]

1. The act of prefering; estimation of one thing above another; election of one rather than another.

It gives as much due to good works, as is consistent with the grace of the gospel; it gives as much *preference* to divine grace, as is consistent with the precepts of the gospel. *Sprat.*

Leave the criticks on either side, to contend about the *preference* due to this or that sort of poetry. *Dryden.*

We find in ourselves a power to begin or forbear several actions of our minds and motions of our bodies, barely by a thought or *preference* of the mind, ordering the doing, or not doing such a particular action. *Locke.*

The several musical instruments in the hands of the Apollo's, Muses and Fauns, might give light to the dispute for *preference* between the ancient and modern musick. *Addison.*

A secret pleasure touch'd Athena's soul
To see the *pref'rence* due to sacred age
Regarded. *Pope's Odyssey.*

2. With *to* before the thing postponed.

This passes with his soft admirers, and gives him the *preference to* Virgil. *Dryden.*

It directs one, in *preference to*, or with neglect of the other, and thereby either the continuation or change becomes voluntary. *Locke.*

3. With *above.*

I shall give an account of some of those appropriate and discriminating notices wherein the human body differs, and hath *preference above* the most perfect brutal nature. *Hale.*

4. With *before.*

Herein is evident the visible discrimination between the human nature, and its *preference before* it. *Hale.*

5. With *over.*

The knowledge of things alone gives a value to our reasonings, and *preference* to one man's knowledge *over* another. *Locke.*

Prefe'rment. *n. s.* [from *prefer.*]

1. Advancement to a higher station.

I'll move the king
To any shape of thy *preferment*, such
As thou'lt desire. *Shakesp. Cymbeline.*

If you hear of that blind traitor,
Preferment falls on him that cuts him off. *Shakesp.*

 Princes

Princes must, by a vigorous exercise of that law, make it every man's interest and honour to cultivate religion and virtue, by rendering vice a disgrace, and the certain ruin to *preferment* or pretensions. *Swift.*

2. A place of honour or profit.

All *preferments* should be placed upon fit men. *L'Estrange.*

3. Preference; act of prefering. Not in use.

All which declare a natural *preferment* of the one unto the motion before the other. *Brown's Vulgar Errours.*

Prefe'rer. [from *prefer.*] One who prefers.

To PREFI'GURATE. *v. a.* [*præ* and *figuro*, Lat.] To shew by an antecedent representation.

Prefigura'tion. *n. s.* [from *prefigurate.*] Antecedent representation.

The same providence that hath wrought the one, will work the other; the former being pledges, as well as *prefigurations* of the latter. *Burnet's Theory of the Earth.*

The variety of prophesies and *prefigurations* had their punctual accomplishment in the author of this institution. *Norris.*

To Prefi'gure. *v. a.* [*præ* and *figuro*, Lat.] To exhibit by antecedent representation.

What the Old Testament hath, the very same the New containeth; but that which lieth there, as under a shadow, is here brought forth into the open sun; things there *prefigured*, are here performed. *Hooker.*

Such piety, so chaste use of God's day,
That what we turn to feast, she turn'd to pray,
And did *prefigure* here in devout taste,
The rest of her high sabbath, which shall last. *Donne.*

If shame superadded to loss, and both met together, as the sinners portion here, perfectly *prefiguring* the two saddest ingredients in hell, deprivation of the blissful vision, and confusion of face, cannot prove efficacious to the mortifying of vice, the church doth give over the patient *Hammond.*

To Prefi'ne. *v. a.* [*prefinir*, Fr. *præfinio*, Lat.] To limit beforehand.

He, in his immoderate desires, *prefined* unto himself three years, which the great monarchs of Rome could not perform in so many hundreds. *Knolles's Hist. of the Turks.*

To PREFI'X. *v. a.* [*præfigo*, Lat.]

1. To appoint beforehand.

At the *prefix'd* hour of her awaking,
Came I to take her from her kindred's vault. *Shakesp.*

A time *prefix*, and think of me at last! *Sandys.*

Its inundation constantly increaseth the seventh day of June; wherein a larger form of speech were safer, than that which punctually *prefixeth* a constant day. *Brown.*

Booth's forward valour only serv'd to show,
He durst that duty pay we all did owe:
Th' attempt was fair; but heav'ns *prefixed* hour
Not come. *Dryden.*

2. To settle; to establish.

Because I would *prefix* some certain boundary between them, the old statutes end with king Edward II. the new or later statutes begin with king Edward III. *Hale's Law of England.*

These boundaries of species are as men, and not as nature makes them, if there are in nature any such *prefixed* bounds. *Locke.*

3. To put before another thing: as, *he* prefixed *an advertisement to his book.*

Prefi'x. *n. s.* [*præfixum*, Lat.] Some particle put before a word, to vary its signification.

In the Hebrew language the noun has its *prefixa* and affixa, the former to signify some few relations, and the latter to denote the pronouns possessive and relative. *Clarke.*

It is a *prefix* of augmentation to many words in that language. *Brown's Vulgar Errours.*

Prefi'xion. *n. s.* [*prefixion*, Fr. from *prefix.*] The act of prefixing. *Dict.*

To Prefo'rm. *v. a.* [*præ* and *form.*] To form beforehand.

If you consider the true cause,
Why all these things change, from their ordinance,
Their natures and *preformed* faculties,
To monstrous quality; why you shall find,
That heav'n made them instruments of fear
Unto some monstrous state. *Shakesp. Julius Cæsar.*

Pre'gnancy. *n. s.* [from *pregnant.*]

1. The state of being with young.

The breast is encompassed with ribs, and the belly left free, for respiration; and in females, for that extraordinary extension in the time of their *pregnancy.* *Ray on the Creation.*

2. Fertility; fruitfulness; inventive power; acuteness.

Pregnancy is made a tapster, and hath his quick wit wasted in giving reckonings. *Shakespeare's Henry IV.*

This writer, out of the *pregnancy* of his invention, hath found out an old way of insinuating the grossest reflections under the appearance of admonitions. *Swift's Miscel.*

PRE'GNANT. *adj.* [*pregnant*, Fr. *prægnans*, Lat.]

1. Teeming; breeding.

Thou
Dove-like sat'st brooding on the vast abyss,
And mad'st it *pregnant.* *Milton.*

His town, as fame reports, was built of old
By Danae, *pregnant* with almighty gold. *Dryden.*

Through either ocean, foolish man!
That *pregnant* word sent forth again,
Might to a world extend each atom there,
For every drop call forth a sea, a heav'n for ev'ry star. *Pri.*

2. Fruitful; fertile; impregnating.

All these in their *pregnant* causes mixt: *Milton.*

Call the floods from high, to rush amain
With *pregnant* streams, to swell the teeming grain. *Dryden.*

3. Full of consequence.

These knew not the just motives and *pregnant* grounds, with which I thought myself furnished. *King Charles.*

An egregious and *pregnant* instance how far virtue surpasses ingenuity. *Woodward's Nat. Hist.*

O detestable, passive obedience! did I ever imagine I should become thy votary in so *pregnant* an instance. *Arb.*

4. Evident; plain; clear; full. An obsolete sense.

This granted, as it is a most *pregnant* and unforc'd position, who stands so eminent in the degree of this fortune as Cassio? a knave very voluble. *Shakesp. Othello.*

Were't not that we stand up against them all,
'Twere *pregnant*, they should square between themselves. *Shakesp. Antony and Cleopatra.*

5. Easy to produce any thing.

A most poor man made tame to fortune's blows,
Who by the art of known and feeling sorrows,
Am *pregnant* to good pity. *Shakesp. King Lear.*

6. Free; kind. Obsolete.

My matter hath no voice, but to your own most *pregnant* and vouchsafed ear. *Shakespeare.*

Pre'gnantly. *adv.* [from *pregnant.*]

1. Fruitfully.

2. Fully; plainly; clearly.

A thousand moral paintings I can shew,
That shall demonstrate these quick blows of fortune
More *pregnantly* than words. *Shakesp. Timon of Athens.*

The dignity of this office among the Jews, is so *pregnantly* set forth in holy writ, that it is unquestionable; kings and priests are mentioned together. *South's Sermons.*

Pregusta'tion. *n. s.* [*præ* and *gusto*, Lat.] The act of tasting before another.

To PREJU'DGE. *v. a.* [*prejuger*, Fr. *præ* and *judico*, Lat.] To determine any question beforehand; generally to condemn beforehand.

If he stood upon his own title of the house of Lancaster, he knew it was condemn'd in parliament, and *prejudged* in the common opinion of the realm, and that it tended to the disinherison of the line of York. *Bacon's Henry VII.*

The child was strong and able, though born in the eight month, which the physicians do *prejudge.* *Bacon.*

The committee of council hath *prejudged* the whole case, by calling the united sense of both houses of parliament an universal clamour. *Swift.*

Some action ought to be entered, lest a greater cause should be injured and *prejudged* thereby. *Ayliffe.*

To Preju'dicate. *v. a.* [*præ* and *judico*, Lat.] To determine beforehand to disadvantage.

Our dearest friend
Prejudicates the business, and would seem
To have us make denial. *Shakespeare.*

Are you, in favour of his person, bent
Thus to *prejudicate* the innocent? *Sandys.*

Preju'dicate. *adj.* [from the verb.]

1. Formed by prejudice; formed before examination.

This rule of casting away all our former *prejudicate* opinions, is not proposed to any of us to be practised at once as subjects or christians, but merely as philosophers. *Watts.*

2. Prejudiced; prepossessed.

Their works will be embraced by most that understand them, and their reasons enforce belief from *prejudicate* readers. *Brown's Vulgar Errours.*

Prejudica'tion. *n. s.* [from *prejudicate.*] The act of judging beforehand.

PRE'JUDICE. *n. s.* [*prejudice*, Fr. *prejudicium*, Lat.]

1. Prepossession; judgment formed beforehand without examination. It is used for prepossession in favour of any thing or against it. It is sometimes used with *to* before that which the *prejudice* is against, but not properly.

The king himself frequently considered more the person who spoke, as he was in his *prejudice*, than the counsel itself that was given. *Clarendon, b. viii.*

My comfort is, that their manifest *prejudice to* my cause will render their judgment of less authority. *Dryden.*

There is an unaccountable *prejudice to* projectors of all kinds, for which reason, when I talk of practising to fly, silly people think me an owl for my pains. *Addison.*

2. Mischief; detriment; hurt; injury. This sense is only accidental or consequential; *a bad thing* being called *a prejudice*, only because *prejudice* is commonly *a bad thing*, and is not derived from the original or etymology of the word: it were therefore better to use it less; perhaps *prejudice* ought never to be applied to any mischief, which does not imply some partiality or prepossession. In some of the following examples its impropriety will be discovered.

I have not spake one the least word,
That might be *prejudice* of her present state,
Or touch of her good person. *Shakesp. Henry* VIII.

England and France might, through their amity,
Breed him some *prejudice*; for from this league
Peep'd harms that menac'd him. *Shakesp. Henry* VIII.

Factions carried too high and too violently, is a sign of weakness in princes, and much to the *prejudice* of their authority and business. *Bacon.*

How plain this abuse is, and what *prejudice* it does to the understanding of the sacred scriptures. *Locke.*

A prince of this character will instruct us by his example, to fix the unsteadiness of our politicks; or by his conduct hinder it from doing us any *prejudice*. *Addison.*

To PREJUDI'CE. *v. a.* [from the noun.]

1. To prepossess with unexamined opinions; to fill with prejudices.

Half-pillars wanted their expected height,
And roofs imperfect *prejudic'd* the sight. *Prior.*

Suffer not any beloved study to *prejudice* your mind, so far as to despise all other learning. *Watts.*

No snares to captivate the mind he spreads,
Nor bribes your eyes to *prejudice* your heads. *Anonym.*

2. To obstruct or injure by prejudices previously raised.

Companies of learned men, be they never so great and reverend, are to yield unto reason; the weight whereof is no whit *prejudiced* by the simplicity of his person, which doth alledge it. *Hooker, b.* ii. *s.* 7.

Neither must his example, done without the book, *prejudice* that which is well appointed in the book. *Whitgifte.*

I am not to *prejudice* the cause of my fellow-poets, though I abandon my own defence. *Dryden.*

3. To injure; to hurt; to diminish; to impair; to be detrimental to. This sense, as in the noun, is often improperly extended to meanings that have no relation to the original sense; who can read with patience of an ingredient that *prejudices* a medicine?

The strength of that law is such, that no particular nation can lawfully *prejudice* the same by any their several laws and ordinances, more than a man by his private resolutions, the law of the whole commonwealth wherein he liveth. *Hooker.*

The Danube rescu'd, and the empire sav'd,
Say, is the majesty of verse retriev'd?
And would it *prejudice* thy softer vein,
To sing the princes, Louis and Eugene? *Prior.*

To this is added a vinous bitter, warmer in the composition of its ingredients than the watry infusion; and, as gentian and lemon-peel make a bitter of so grateful a flavour, the only care required in this composition was to chuse such an addition as might not *prejudice* it. *London Dispensatory.*

PREJUDI'CIAL. *adj.* [*prejudiciable*, Fr. from *prejudice.*]

1. Obstructive by means of opposite prepossessions.

2. Contrary; opposite.

What one syllable is there, in all this, *prejudicial* any way to that which we hold? *Hooker, b.* ii. *s.* 5.

3. Mischievous; hurtful; injurious; detrimental. This sense is improper. See PREJUDICE, noun and verb.

His going away the next morning with all his troops, was most *prejudicial* and most ruinous to the king's affairs. *Claren.*

One of the young ladies reads, while the others are at work; so that the learning of the family is not at all *prejudicial* to its manufactures. *Addison's Guardian.*

A state of great prosperity, as it exposes us to various temptations, so it is often *prejudicial* to us, in that it swells the mind with undue thoughts. *Atterbury's Sermons.*

PREJUDI'CIALNESS. *n. s.* [from *prejudicial.*] The state of being prejudicial; mischievousness.

PRE'LACY. *n. s.* [from *prelate.*]

1. The dignity or post of a prelate or ecclesiastick of the highest order.

Prelacies may be termed the greater benefices; as that of the pontificate, a patriarchship, an archbishoprick and bishoprick. *Ayliffe's Parergon.*

2. Episcopacy; the order of bishops.

The presbyter, puff'd up with spiritual pride,
Shall on the necks of the lewd nobles ride,
His brethren damn, the civil power defy,
And parcel out republick *prelacy*. *Dryden.*

How many are there, that call themselves protestants, who put *prelacy* and popery together as terms convertible. *Swift.*

3. Bishops. Collectively.

Divers of the reverend *prelacy*, and other most judicious men, have especially bestowed their pains about the matter of jurisdiction. *Hooker's Dedication.*

PRE'LATE. *n. s.* [*prelat*, Fr. *prælatus*, Lat.] An ecclesiastick of the highest order and dignity.

It beseemed not the person of so grave a *prelate*, to be either utterly without counsel, as the rest were, or in a common perplexity to shew himself alone secure. *Hooker.*

Hear him but reason in divinity,
And, all-admiring, with an inward wish
You would desire the king were made a *prelate*. *Shakesp.*

The archbishop of Vienna, a reverend *prelate*, said one day to king Lewis XI. of France; sir, your mortal enemy is dead, what time duke Charles of Burgundy was slain. *Bacon.*

Yet Munster's *prelate* ever be accurst,
In whom we seek the German faith in vain. *Dryden.*

PRELA'TICAL. *adj.* [from *prelate.*] Relating to prelate or prelacy. *Dict.*

PRELA'TION. *n. s.* [*prælatus*, Lat.] Preference; setting of one above the other.

In case the father left only daughters, they equally succeeded as in co-patnership, without any *prelation* or preference of the eldest daughter to a double portion. *Hale.*

PRE'LATURE. } *n. s.* [*prælatura*, Lat. *prelature*, Fr.] The
PRE'LATURESHIP. } state or dignity of a prelate. *Dict.*

PRELE'CTION. *n. s.* [*prælectio*, Lat.] Reading; lecture; discourse.

He that is desirous to prosecute these asystata of infinitude, let him resort to the *prelections* of Faber. *Hale.*

PRELIBA'TION. *n. s.* [from *prælibo*, Lat.] Taste beforehand; effusion previous to tasting.

The firm belief of this, in an innocent soul, is a high *prelibation* of those eternal joys. *More's Divine Dialogues.*

PRELI'MINARY. *adj.* [*preliminaire*, Fr. *præ limine*, Lat.] Previous; introductory; proemial.

My master needed not the assistance of that *preliminary* poet to prove his claim; his own majestick mien discovers him to be the king. *Dryden.*

PRELI'MINARY. *n. s.* Something previous; preparatory measures.

The third consists of the ceremonies of the oath on both sides, and the *preliminaries* to the combat. *Notes on Iliad.*

PRELU'DE. *n. s.* [*prelude*, Fr. *præludium*, Lat.]

1. Some short flight of musick played before a full concert.

2. Something introductory; something that only shews what is to follow.

To his infant arms oppose
His father's rebels and his brother's foes;
Those were the *preludes* of his fate,
That form'd his manhood, to subdue
The hydra of the many-headed hissing crew. *Dryden.*

The last Georgick was a good *prelude* to the Æneis, and very well shewed what the poet could do in the description of what was really great. *Addison.*

One concession to a man is but a *prelude* to another. *Clarissa.*

To PRELU'DE. *v. a.* [*preluder*, Fr. *præludo*, Lat.] To serve as an introduction; to be previous to.

Either songster holding out their throats,
And folding up their wings, renew'd their notes,
As if all day, *preluding* to the fight,
They only had rehears'd, to sing by night. *Dryden.*

PRELU'DIOUS. *adj.* [from *prelude.*] Previous; introductory.

That's but a *preludious* bliss,
Two souls pickeering in a kiss. *Cleaveland.*

PRELU'DIUM. n. s. [Latin.] Prelude.

This Menelaus knows, expos'd to share
With me the rough *preludium* of the war. *Dryden.*

PRELU'SIVE. *adj.* [from *prelude.*] Previous; introductory; proemial.

The clouds
Softly shaking on the dimpled pool
Prelusive drops, let all their moisture flow. *Thomson.*

PREMATU'RE. *adj.* [*prematuré*, Fr. *præmaturus*, Lat.] Ripe too soon; formed before the time; too early; too soon said, believed, or done; too hasty.

'Tis hard to imagine, what possible consideration should persuade him to repent, 'till he deposited that *premature* persuasion of his being in Christ. *Hammond's Fundamentals.*

PREMATU'RELY. *adj.* [from *premature.*] Too early; too soon; with too hasty ripeness.

PREMATU'RENESS. } *n. s.* [from *premature.*] Too great haste;
PREMATU'RITY. } unseasonable earliness.

To PREME'DITATE. *v. a.* [*præmeditor*, Lat. *premediter*, Fr.] To contrive or form beforehand; to conceive beforehand.

Where I have come, great clerks have purposed
To greet me with *premeditated* welcomes. *Shakesp.*
With words *premeditated* thus he said. *Dryden.*

To PREME'DITATE. *v. n.* To have formed in the mind by previous meditation; to think beforehand.

Of themselves they were rude, and knew not so much as how to *premeditate*; the spirit gave them speech and eloquent utterance. *Hooker's Ecclesiastical Polity.*

PREMEDITA'TION. *n. s.* [*præmeditatio*, Lat. *premeditation*, Fr. from *premeditate.*] Act of meditating beforehand.

Are all th' unlook'd-for issue of their bodies
To take their rooms ere I can place myself.
A cold *premeditation* for my purpose? *Shakesp.*

Hope is a pleasant *premeditation* of enjoyment, as when a dog expects, till his master has done picking of the bone. *More's Antidote against Atheism.*

Verse is not the effect of sudden thought; but this hinders not, that sudden thought may be represented in verse, since those thoughts must be higher than nature can raise without *premeditation*. *Dryden on Dramatick Poetry.*

PRE'MICES. *n. s.* [*primitiæ*, Lat. *premices*, Fr.] First fruits.

A charger, yearly filled with fruits, was offered to the gods at their festivals, as the *premices* or first gatherings. *Dry.*

PRE'MIER. *adj.* [French.] First; chief.

The Spaniard challengeth the *premier* place, in regard of his dominions. *Camden's Remains.*

Thus families like realms, with equal fate,
Are sunk by *premier* ministers of state. *Swift.*

To PREMI'SE. *v. a.* [*præmissus*, Lat.]

1. To explain previously; to lay down premises.

The apostle's discourse here is an answer upon a ground taken; he *premiseth*, and then infers. *Burnet.*

I *premise* these particulars, that the reader may know I enter upon it as a very ungrateful task. *Addison.*

2. To send before the time. Not in use.

O let the vile world end,
And the *premised* flames of the last day
Knit earth and heav'n together! *Shakesp. Henry* VI.

To PREME'RIT. *v. a.* [*præmereor*, Lat.] To deserve before.

They did not forgive Sir John Hotham, who had so much *premerited* of them. *King Charles.*

PRE'MISES. *n. s.* [*præmissa*, Lat. *premisses*, Fr.]

1. Propositions antecedently supposed or proved.

They infer upon the *premises*, that as great difference as commodiously may be, there should be in all outward ceremonies between the people of God, and them which are not his people. *Hooker, b.* iv. *s.* 7.

This is so regular an inference, that whilst the *premises* stand firm, it is impossible to shake the conclusion. *Decay of Piety.*

She study'd well the point, and found
Her foes conclusions were not sound,
From *premises* erroneous brought,
And therefore the deduction's nought. *Swift's Miscel.*

2. In low language, houses or lands: as, *I was upon the* premisses.

PRE'MISS. *n. s.* [*præmissum*, Lat.] Antecedent proposition. This word is rare in the singular.

They know the major or minor, which is implied, when you pronounce the other *premiss* and the conclusion. *Watts.*

PRE'MIUM. *n. s.* [*præmium*, Lat.] Something given to invite a loan or a bargain.

No body cares to make loans upon a new project; whereas men never fail to bring in their money upon a land-tax, when the *premium* or interest allowed them is suited to the hazard they run. *Addison's Freeholder*, N° 23.

People were tempted to lend, by great *premiums* and large interest; and it concerned them to preserve that government, which they had trusted with their money. *Swift's Miscel.*

To PREMO'NISH. *v a.* [*præmoneo*, Lat.] To warn or admonish beforehand.

PREMO'NISHMENT. *n. s.* [from *premonish.*] Previous information.

After these *premonishments*, I will come to the compartition itself. *Wotton's Architecture.*

PREMONI'TION. *n. s.* [from *premonish.*] Previous notice; previous intelligence.

What friendly *premonitions* have been spent
On your forbearance, and their vain event. *Chapman.*

How great the force of such an erroneous persuasion is, we may collect from our Saviour's *premonition* to his disciples, when he tells them, that those who killed them should think they did God service. *Decay of Piety.*

PREMO'NITORY. *n. s.* [from *præ* and *moneo*, Lat.] Previously advising.

To PREMO'NSTRATE. *v. a.* [*præ* and *monstro*, Lat.] To show beforehand.

PREMUNI'RE. *n. s.* [Latin.]

1. A writ in the common law, whereby a penalty is incurrable, as infringing some statute.

Premunire is now grown a good word in our English laws, by tract of time; and yet at first it was merely mistaken for a premonere. *Bramhall against Hobbs.*

Woolsey incurred a *premunire*, forfeited his honour, estate and life, which he ended in great calamity. *South.*

2. The penalty so incurred.

3. A difficulty; a distress. A low ungrammatical word.

PREMU'NITION. *n. s.* [from *præmunio*, Lat.] An anticipation of objection.

To PRENO'MINATE. *v. a.* [*prænomino*, Lat.] To forename.

He you would sound,
Having ever seen, in the *prenominate* crimes,
The youth, you breathe of, guilty. *Shakesp. Hamlet.*

PRENOMINA'TION. *n. s.* [*præ* and *nomino*, Lat.] The privilege of being named first.

The watry productions should have the *prenomination*; and they of the land rather derive their names, than nominate those of the sea. *Brown's Vulgar Errours.*

PRENO'TION. *n. s.* [*prenotion*, Fr. *præ* and *nosco*, Lat.] Foreknowledge; prescience.

The hedgehog's presension of winds is so exact, that it stoppeth the north or southern hole of its nest, according unto *prenotion* of these winds ensuing. *Brown.*

PRE'NTICE. *n. s.* [contracted, by colloquial licence, from *apprentice.*] One bound to a master, in order to instruction in a trade.

My accuser is my *prentice*, and when I did correct him for his fault, he did vow upon his knees he would be even with me. *Shakesp. Henry* VI.

PRE'NTICESHIP. *n. s.* [from *prentice.*] The servitude of an apprentice.

He serv'd a *prenticeship*, who sets up shop,
Ward try'd on puppies, and the poor his drop. *Pope.*

PRENU'NCIATION. *n. s.* [*prænuncio*, Lat.] The act of telling before. *Dict.*

PREO'CCUPANCY. *n. s.* [from *preoccupate.*] The act of taking possession before another.

To PREO'CCUPATE. *v. a.* [*preoccuper*, Fr. *præoccupo*, Lat.]

1. To anticipate.

Honour aspireth to death; grief flieth to it; and fear *preoccupieth* it. *Bacon.*

2. To prepossess; to fill with prejudices.

That the model be plain without colours, lest the eye *preoccupate* the judgment. *Wotton's Architecture.*

PREOCCUPA'TION. *n. s.* [*preoccupation*, Fr. from *preoccupate.*]

1. Anticipation.

2 Prepossession.

3. Anticipation of objection.

As if, by way of *preoccupation*, he should have said; well, here you see your commission, this is your duty, these are your discouragements; never seek for evasions from worldly afflictions; this is your reward, if you perform it; this is your doom, if you decline it. *South's Sermons.*

To PREO'CCUPY. *v. a.* To prepossess; to occupy by anticipation or prejudices.

I think it more respectful to the reader to leave something to reflections, than *preoccupy* his judgment. *Arbuthnot.*

To PRE'OMINATE. *v. a.* [*præ* and *ominor*, Lat.] To prognosticate; to gather from omens any future event.

Because many ravens were seen when Alexander entered Babylon, they were thought to *preominate* his death. *Brown.*

PRE'OPINION. *n. s.* [*præ* and *opinio*, Lat.] Opinion antecedently formed; prepossession.

Diet holds no solid rule of selection; some, in indistinct voracity, eating almost any; others, out of a timorous *preopinion*, refraining from very many things. *Brown.*

To PRE'ORDAIN. *v. a.* [*præ* and *ordain.*] To ordain beforehand.

Sin is the contrariety to the will of God, and if all things be *preordained* by God, and so demonstrated to be willed by him, it remains there is no such thing as sin. *Hammond.*

Few souls *preordain'd* by fate,
The race of gods have reach'd that envy'd state. *Roscom.*

PREO'RDINANCE. *n. s.* [*præ* and *ordinance.*] Antecedent decree; first decree. Not in use.

These lowly courtesies
Might stir the blood of ordinary men,
And turn *preordinance* and first decree
Into the law of children. *Shakesp. Julius Cæsar.*

PREORDINA'TION. *n. s.* [from *preordain.*] The act of preordaining.

PREPARA'TION. *n. s.* [*preparatio*, Lat. *preparation*, Fr. from *prepare.*]

1. The act of preparing or previously fitting any thing to any purpose.

Nothing hath proved more fatal to that due *preparation* for another life, than our unhappy mistake of the nature and end of this. *Wake's Preparation for Death.*

2. Previous measures.

I will shew what *preparations* there were in nature for this great dissolution, and after what manner it came to pass. *Burnet's Theory of the Earth.*

3. Ceremonious introduction.

I make bold to press, with so little *preparation*, upon you. —You're welcome. *Shakesp. Merry Wives of Windsor.*

4. The act of making or fitting by a regular process.

In the *preparations* of cookery, the most volatile parts of vegetables are destroyed. *Arbuthnot on Aliments.*

5. Any thing made by process of operation.

I wish the chymists had been more sparing, who magnify their *preparations*, inveigle the curiosity of many, and delude the security of most. *Brown's Vulgar Errours.*

6. Accomplishment; qualification. Out of use.

Sir John, you are a gentleman of excellent breeding, authentick in your place and person, generally allowed for your many warlike, courtlike and learned *preparations*. *Shakesp.*

PREPA'RATIVE. *adj.* [*preparatif*, Fr. from *prepare.*] Having the power of preparing or qualifying.

Would men have spent toilsome days and watchful nights in the laborious quest of knowledge *preparative* to this work. *South's Sermons.*

PREPA'RATIVE. *n. s.* [*preparatif*, Fr. from *prepare.*]
1. That which has the power of preparing or previously fitting.
They tell us the profit of reading is singular, in that it serveth for a *preparative* unto sermons. *Hooker.*
My book of advancement of learning may be some *preparative* or key for the better opening of the instauration. *Bacon.*
Resolvedness in sin can, with no reason, be imagined a *preparative* to remission. *Decay of Piety.*
2. That which is done in order to something else.
The miseries, which have ensued, may be yet, through thy mercy, *preparatives* to us of future blessings. *K. Charles.*
Such a temper is a contradiction to repentance, as being founded in the destruction of those qualities, which are the only dispositions and *preparatives* to it. *South's Sermons.*
What avails it to make all the necessary *preparatives* for our voyage, if we do not actually begin the journey. *Dryden.*
PREPA'RATIVELY. *adv.* [from *preparative.*] Previously; by way of preparation.
It is *preparatively* necessary to many useful things in this life, as to make a man a good physician. *Hale.*
PREPA'RATORY. *adj.* [*preparatoire*, Fr.]
1. Antecedently necessary.
The practice of all these is proper to our condition in this world, and *preparatory* to our happiness in the next. *Tillotson.*
2. Introductory; previous; antecedent.
Preparatory, limited and formal interrogatories in writing preclude this way of occasional interrogatories. *Hale.*
Rains were but *preparatory*, the violence of the deluge depended upon the disruption of the great abyss. *Burnet.*
To PREPA'RE. *v. a.* [*præparo*, Lat. *preparer*, Fr.]
1. To fit for any thing; to adjust to any use; to make ready for any purpose.
Patient Octavia, plough thy visage up
With her *prepared* nails. *Shakesp. Ant. and Cleop.*
Confound the peace establish'd, and *prepare*
Their souls to hatred, and their hands to war. *Dryden.*
Our souls, not yet *prepar'd* for upper light,
Till doomsday wander in the shades of night. *Dryden.*
The beams of light had been in vain display'd,
Had not the eye been fit for vision made;
In vain the author had the eye *prepar'd*
With so much skill, had not the light appear'd. *Blackmore.*
2. To qualify for any purpose.
Some preachers, being *prepared* only upon two or three points of doctrine, run the same round. *Addison.*
3. To make ready beforehand.
There he maketh the hungry to dwell, that they may *prepare* a city for habitation. *Psalm* cviii. 36.
Now *prepare* thee for another sight. *Milton.*
He took the golden compasses, *prepar'd*
In God's eternal store, to circumscribe
This universe. *Milton.*
4. To form; to make.
The woman fled into the wilderness, where she hath a place *prepared* of God to feed her. *Rev.* xii. 6.
He hath founded it upon the seas, and *prepared* it upon the floods. *Psalm* xxiv. 2.
5. To make by regular process: as, *he* prepared *a medicine.*
To PREPA'RE. *v. n.*
1. To take previous measures.
Efficacy is a power of speech, which represents to our minds the lively ideas of things so truly, as if we saw them with our eyes; as Dido *preparing* to kill herself. *Peacham.*
2. To make every thing ready; to put things in order.
Go in, sirrah, bid them *prepare* for dinner. *Shakesp.*
The long-suffering of God waited in the days of Noah, while the ark was a *preparing.* 1 *Peter* iii. 2.
3. To make one's self ready; to put himself in a state of expectation.
PREPA'RE. *n. s.* [from the verb.] Preparation; previous measures. Not in use.
In our behalf
Go levy men, and make *prepare* for war. *Shakesp.*
PREPA'REDLY. *adv.* [from *prepared.*] By proper precedent measures.
She *preparedly* may frame herself
To th' way she's forc'd to. *Shakesp. Ant. and Cleop.*
PREPA'REDNESS. *n. s.* [from *prepare.*] State or act of being prepared: as, *he's in a* preparedness *for his final exit.*
PREPA'RER. *n. s.* [from *prepare.*]
1. One that prepares; one that previously fits.
The bishop of Ely, the fittest *preparer* of her mind to receive such a doleful accident, came to visit her. *Wotton.*
2. That which fits for any thing.
Codded grains are an improver of land, and *preparer* of it for other crops. *Mortimer's Husbandry.*
PREPE'NSE. } *adj.* [*prepensus*, Lat.] Forethought; precon-
PREPE'NSED. } ceived; contrived beforehand: as, *malice* prepense.
To PREPO'NDER. *v. a.* [from *preponderate.*] To outweigh.
Though pillars by channelling be seemingly ingrossed to our sight, yet they are truly weakned; and therefore ought not to be the more slender, but the more corpulent, unless apparences *preponder* truths. *Wotton's Architecture.*

PREPO'NDERANCE. } *n. s.* [from *preponderate.*] The state of
PREPO'NDERANCY. } outweighing; superiority of weight.
As to addition of ponderosity in dead bodies, comparing them unto blocks, this occasional *preponderancy* is rather an appearance than reality. *Brown's Vulgar Errours.*
The mind should examine all the grounds of probability, and, upon a due balancing the whole, reject or receive proportionably to the *preponderancy* of the greater grounds of probability. *Locke.*
Little light boats were the ships which people used, to the sides whereof this fish remora fastening, might make it swag, as the least *preponderance* on either side will do, and so retard its course. *Grew's Musæum.*
To PREPO'NDERATE. *v. a.* [*præpondero*, Lat.]
1. To outweigh; to overpower by weight.
An inconsiderable weight, by distance from the centre of the balance, will *preponderate* greater magnitudes. *Glanvill.*
The triviallest thing, when a passion is cast into the scale with it, *preponderates* substantial blessings. *Gov. of the Tongue.*
2. To overpower by stronger influence.
To PREPO'NDERATE. *v. n.*
1. To exceed in weight.
He that would make the lighter scale *preponderate*, will not so soon do it, by adding increase of new weight to the emptier, as if he took out of the heavier, what he adds to the lighter. *Locke.*
Unless the very mathematical center of gravity of every system be placed and fixed in the very mathematical center of the attractive power of all the rest, they cannot be evenly attracted on all sides, but must *preponderate* some way or other. *Bentley's Sermons.*
2. To exceed in influence or power analogous to weight.
In matters of probability, we cannot be sure that we have all particulars before us, and that there is no evidence behind, which may outweigh all that at present seems to *preponderate* with us. *Locke.*
By putting every argument on one side and the other into the balance, we must form a judgment which side *preponderates.* *Watts.*
PREPONDERA'TION. *n. s.* [from *preponderate.*] The act or state of outweighing any thing.
In matters, which require present practice, we must content ourselves with a mere *preponderation* of probable reasons. *Watts's Logick.*
To PREPO'SE. *v. a.* [*preposer*, Fr. *præpono*, Lat.] To put before. *Dict.*
PREPOSI'TION. *n. s.* [*præposition*, Fr. *præpositio*, Lat.] In grammar, a particle governing a case.
A *preposition* signifies some relation, which the thing signified by the word following it, has to something going before in the discourse; as, Cesar came *to* Rome. *Clarke's Lat. Gram.*
PREPO'SITOR. *n. s.* [*præpositor*, Lat.] A scholar appointed by the master to overlook the rest.
To PREPOSSE'SS. *v. a.* [*præ* and *possess.*] To fill with an opinion unexamined; to prejudice.
She was *prepossessed* with the scandal of salivating. *Wisem.*
PREPOSSE'SSION. *n. s.* [from *prepossess.*]
1. Preoccupation; first possession.
God hath taken care to anticipate and prevent every man to give piety the *prepossession*, before other competitors should be able to pretend to him; and so to engage him in holiness first and then in bliss. *Hammond's Fundamentals.*
2. Prejudice; preconceived opinion.
Had the poor vulgar rout only, who were held under the prejudices and *prepossessions* of education, been abused into such idolatrous superstitions, it might have been pitied, but not so much wondered at. *South's Sermons.*
With thought, from *prepossession* free, reflect
On solar rays, as they the sight respect. *Blackmore.*
PREPO'STEROUS. *adj.* [*præposterus*, Lat.]
1. Having that first which ought to be last; wrong; absurd; perverted.
Put a case of a land of Amazons, where the whole government, publick and private, is in the hands of women: is not such a *preposterous* government against the first order of nature, for women to rule over men, and in itself void? *Bac.*
Death from a father's hand, from whom I first
Receiv'd a being! 'tis a *preposterous* gift,
An act at which inverted nature starts,
And blushes to behold herself so cruel. *Denham.*
Such is the world's *preposterous* fate;
Amongst all creatures, mortal hate
Love, though immortal, doth create. *Denham.*
By this distribution of matter, continual provision is every where made for the supply of bodies, quite contrary to the *preposterous* reasonings of those men, who expected so different a result. *Woodward's Nat Hist.*
The method I take may be censured as *preposterous*, because I thus treat last of the antediluvian earth, which was first in order of nature. *Woodward's Nat. Hist.*
2. Applied to persons: foolish; absurd.
Preposterous ass! that never read so far
To know the cause why musick was ordain'd. *Shakesp.*

Prepo'sterously. *adv.* [from *preposterous.*] In a wrong situation; absurdly.

Those things do best please me,
That befal *prepost'rously.* *Shakesp. Midſ. Night's Dream.*

Upon this supposition, one animal would have its lungs, where another hath its liver, and all the other members *preposterously* placed; there could not be a like configuration of parts in any two individuals. *Bentley's Sermons.*

Prepo'sterousness. *n. s.* [from *preposterous.*] Absurdity; wrong order or method.

Pre'potency. *n. s.* [*præpotentia*, Lat.] Superior power; predominance.

If there were a determinate *prepotency* in the right, and such as ariseth from a constant root in nature, we might expect the same in other animals. *Brown.*

Prepu'ce. *n. s.* [*prepuce*, Fr. *præputium*, Lat.] That which covers the glans; foreskin.

The *prepuce* was much inflamed and swelled. *Wiseman.*

To Pre'require. *v. a.* [*præ* and *require.*] To demand previously.

Some primary literal signification is *prerequired* to that other of figurative. *Hammond.*

Prere'quisite. *adj.* [*præ* and *requisite.*] Something previously necessary.

The conformation of parts is necessary, not only unto the *prerequisite* and previous conditions of birth, but also unto the parturition. *Brown's Vulgar Errours.*

Before the existence of compounded body, there must be a pre-existence of active principles, necessarily *prerequisite* to the mixing these particles of bodies. *Hale.*

Prero'gative. *n. s.* [*prerogative*, Fr. *prærogativa*, low Lat.] An exclusive or peculiar privilege.

My daughters and the fair Parthenia might far better put in their claim for that *prerogative.* *Sidney.*

Our *prerogative*
Calls not your counsels, but our natural goodness
Imparts this. *Shakesp.*

How could communities,
The primogeniture, and due of birth,
Prerogative of age, sceptres, and crowns,
But by degree, stand in authentick place? *Shakesp.*

The great Caliph hath an old *prerogative* in the choice and confirmation of the kings of Assyria. *Knolles.*

They are the best laws, by which the king hath the justest *prerogative*, and the people the best liberty. *Bacon.*

Had any of these second causes despoiled God of his *prerogative*, or had God himself constrained the mind and will of man to impious acts by any celestial inforcements? *Raleigh.*

They obtained another royal *prerogative* and power, to make war and peace at their pleasure. *Davies.*

The house of commons to these their *prerogatives* over the lords, sent an order to the lieutenant of the tower, that he should cause him to be executed that very day. *Clarendon.*

For freedom still maintain'd alive,
Freedom an English subjects' sole *prerogative*,
Accept our pious praise. *Dryden.*

All wish the dire *prerogative* to kill,
Ev'n they wou'd have the pow'r, who want the will. *Dryden.*

It seems to be the *prerogative* of human understanding, when it has distinguished any ideas, so as to perceive them to be different, to consider in what circumstances they are capable to be compared. *Locke.*

I will not consider only the *prerogatives* of man above other animals, but the endowments which nature hath conferred on his body in common with them. *Ray on the Creation.*

Prero'gatived. *adj.* [from *prerogative.*] Having an exclusive privilege; having prerogative.

'Tis the plague of great ones,
Prerogativ'd are they less than the base;
'Tis destiny unshunable. *Shakesp.*

Pres. *Pres*, *prest*, seem to be derived from the Saxon, preost, a priest; it being usual in after times to drop the letter *o* in like cases. *Gibson's Camden.*

PRESA'GE. *n. s.* [*presage*, Fr. *præsagium*, Lat.] Prognostick; presension of futurity.

Joy and shout *presage* of victory. *Milton.*

Dreams have generally been considered by authors only as revelations of what has already happened, or as *presages* of what is to happen. *Addison.*

To Presa'ge. *v. a.* [*presager*, Fr. *præsagio*, Latin.]

1. To forebode; to foreknow; to foretell; to prophesy.

Henry's late *presaging* prophesy
Did glad my heart with hope. *Shakesp. Henry* VI.

What pow'r of mind
Foreseeing, or *presaging* from the depth
Of knowledge past or present, could have fear'd
How such united force of gods, how such
As stood like these, could ever know repulse. *Milton.*

This contagion might have been *presaged* upon consideration of its precursors. *Harvey on Consumptions.*

Wish'd freedom, I *presage* you soon will find,
If heav'n be just, and if to virtue kind. *Dryden.*

2. Sometimes with *of* before the thing foretold.

That by certain signs we may *presage*
Of heats and rains, and wind's impetuous rage,
The sov'reign of the heav'ns has set on high
The moon to mark the changes of the sky. *Dryden.*

2. To foretoken; to foreshow.

If I may trust the flattering ruth of sleep,
My dreams *presage* some joyful news at hand. *Shakesp.*

Dreams advise some great good *presaging.* *Milton.*

That cloud, that hangs upon thy brow, *presages*
A greater storm than all the Turkish power
Can throw upon us. *Denham's Sophy.*

When others fell, this standing did *presage*
The crown shou'd triumph over pop'lar rage. *Waller.*

Presa'gement. *n. s.* [from *presage.*]

1. Forebodement; presension.

I have spent much enquiry, whether he had any ominous *presagement* before his end. *Wotton.*

2. Foretoken.

The falling of salt is an authentick *presagement* of ill luck, from whence nothwithstanding nothing can be naturally feared. *Brown's Vulgar Errours.*

PRE'SBYTER. *n. s.* [*presbyter*, Lat. πρεσβύτερος.]

1. A priest.

Presbyters absent through infirmity from their churches, might be said to preach by those deputies who in their stead did but read homilies. *Hooker, b.* v. *s.* 20.

2. A presbyterian.

And *presbyters* have their jackpuddings too. *Butler.*

Presbyte'rian. *adj.* [πρεσβύτερος.] Consisting of elders; a term for a modern form of ecclesiastical government.

Chiefly was urged the abolition of episcopal, and the establishing of *presbyterian* government. *King Charles.*

Presbyte'rian. *n. s.* [from *presbyter.*] An abettor of presbytery or calvinistical discipline.

One of the more rigid *presbyterians.* *Swift.*

Presby'tery. *n. s.* [from *presbyter.*] Body of elders, whether priests or laymen.

Those which stood for the *presbytery*, thought their cause had more sympathy with the discipline of Scotland than the hierarchy of England. *Bacon.*

Flea-bitten synod, an assembly brew'd
Of clerks and elders ana, like the rude
Chaos of *presbyt'ry*, where laymen guide
With the tame woolpack clergy by their side. *Cleaveland.*

Pre'science. *n. s.* [*prescience*, Fr. from *prescient.*] Foreknowledge; knowledge of future things.

They tax our policy, and call it cowardice,
Forestall our *prescience*, and esteem no act
But that of hand. *Shakesp. Troilus and Cressida.*

Prescience or foreknowledge, considered in order and nature, if we may speak of God after the manner of men, goeth before providence; for God foreknew all things before he had created them, or before they had being to be cared for; and *prescience* is no other than an infallible foreknowledge. *Ral.*

If certain *prescience* of uncertain events imply a contradiction, it seems it may be struck out of the omnisciency of God, and leave no blemish behind. *More.*

Of things of the most accidental and mutable nature, God's *prescience* is certain. *South.*

Freedom was first bestow'd on human race,
And *prescience* only held the second place. *Dryden.*

PRE'SCIENT. *adj.* [*præsciens*, Lat.] Foreknowing; prophetick.

Henry, upon the deliberation concerning the marriage of his eldest daughter into Scotland, had shewed himself sensible and almost *prescient* of this event. *Bacon.*

Who taught the nations of the field and wood?
Prescient, the tides or tempests to withstand. *Pope.*

Pre'scious. *adj.* [*præscius*, Lat.] Having foreknowledge.

Thrice happy thou, dear partner of my bed,
Whose holy soul the stroke of fortune fled;
Prescious of ills, and leaving me behind,
To drink the dregs of life. *Dryden's Æneis.*

To Presci'nd. *v. a.* [*præscindo*, Lat.] To cut off; to abstract.

A bare act of obliquity does not only *prescind* from, but positively deny such a special dependence. *Norris.*

Presci'ndent. *adj.* [*præscindens*, Lat.] Abstracting.

We may, for one single act, abstract from a reward, which nobody, who knows the *prescindent* faculties of the soul, can deny. *Cheyne's Philosophical Principles.*

To PRESCRI'BE. *v. a.* [*præscribo*, Lat.]

1. To set down authoritatively; to order; to direct.

Doth the strength of some negative arguments prove this kind of negative argument strong, by force whereof all things are denied, which scripture affirmeth not, or all things, which scripture *prescribeth* not, condemned. *Hooker.*

To the blanc moon her office they *prescrib'd.* *Milton.*

There's joy, when to wild will you laws *prescribe*,
When you bid fortune carry back her bribe. *Dryden.*

When parents loves are order'd by a son,
Let streams *prescribe* their fountains where to run. *Dryden.*

2. To direct

2. To direct medically.

The end of satire is the amendment of vices by correction; and he who writes honestly is no more an enemy to the offender, than the physician to the patient, when he *prescribes* harsh remedies. *Dryden.*

The extremest ways they first ordain,
Prescribing such intolerable pain,
As none but Cæsar could sustain. *Dryden.*

By a short account of the pressing obligations which lie on the magistrate, I shall not so much *prescribe* directions for the future, as praise what is past. *Atterbury.*

Should any man argue, that a physician understands his own art best; and therefore, although he should *prescribe* poison to all his patients, he cannot be justly punished, but is answerable only to God. *Swift.*

To PRESCRI'BE. *v. n.*

1. To influence by long custom.

A reserve of puerility we have not shaken off from school, where being seasoned with minor sentences, they *prescribe* upon our riper years, and never are worn out but with our memories. *Brown's Vulgar Errours.*

2. To influence arbitrarily.

The assuming an authority of dictating to others, and a forwardness to *prescribe* to their opinions, is a constant concomitant of this biass of our judgments. *Locke.*

3. [*Prescrire*, Fr.] To form a custom which has the force of law.

That obligation upon the lands did not *prescribe* or come into disuse, but by fifty consecutive years of exemption. *Arb.*

4. To write medical directions and forms of medicine.

Modern 'pothecaries, taught the art
By doctor's bills to play the doctor's part,
Bold in the practice of mistaken rules,
Prescribe, apply, and call their masters fools. *Pope.*

PRE'SCRIPT. *adj.* [*præscriptus*, Lat.] Directed; accurately laid down in a precept.

Those very laws so added, they themselves do not judge unlawful; as they plainly confess both in matter of *prescript* attire, and of rites appertaining to burial. *Hooker.*

PRE'SCRIPT. *n. s.* [*præscriptum*, Lat.] Direction; precept; model prescribed.

By his *prescript*, a sanctuary is fram'd
Of cedar, overlaid with gold. *Milton.*

PRESCRI'PTION. *n. s.* [*prescription*, Fr. *præscriptio*, Lat. from *præscribo*, Lat.]

1. Rules produced and authorised by long custom; custom continued till it has the force of law.

You tell a pedigree
Of threescore and two years, a silly time
To make *prescription* for a kingdom's worth. *Shakesp.*

Use such as have prevailed before in things you have employed them; for that breeds confidence, and they will strive to maintain their *prescription*. *Bacon's Essays.*

It will be found a work of no small difficulty, to dispossess a vice from that heart, where long possession begins to plead *prescription*. *South's Sermons.*

Our poet bade us hope this grace to find,
To whom by long *prescription* you are kind. *Dryden.*

The Lucquese plead *prescription*, for hunting in one of the duke's forests, that lies upon their frontiers. *Addison.*

2. Medical receipt.

My father left me some *prescriptions*
Of rare and prov'd effects; such as his reading
And manifest experience had collected
For general sov'reignty. *Shakesp.*

Approving of my obstinacy against all common *prescriptions*, he asked me, whether I had never heard the Indian way of curing the gout by moxa. *Temple.*

PRE'SEANCE. *n. s.* [*preseance*, Fr.] Priority of place in sitting.

The ghests, though rude in their other fashions, may, for their discreet judgment in precedence and *preseance*, read a lesson to our civilest gentry. *Carew's Survey of Cornwall.*

PRE'SENCE. *n. s.* [*presence*, Fr. *præsentia*, Lat.]

1. State of being present; contrary to absence.

To-night we hold a solemn supper,
And I'll request your *presence*. *Shakesp.*

The *presence* of a king engenders love
Amongst his subjects and his loyal friends,
As it disanimates his enemies. *Shakesp. Henry VI.*

2. Approach face to face to a great personage.

The shepherd Dorus answered with such a trembling voice and abashed countenance, and oftentimes so far from the matter, that it was some sport to the young ladies, thinking it want of education, which made him so discountenanced with unwonted *presence*. *Sidney, b. i.*

Men that very *presence* fear,
Which once they knew authority did bear! *Daniel.*

3. State of being in the view of a superior.

Thou know'st the law of arms is such,
That, whoso draws a sword in th' *presence* 't's death. *Sha.*

I know not by what power I am made bold,
In such a *presence* here, to plead my thoughts. *Shakesp.*

Wisdom thy sister, and with her did'st play
In *presence* of th' Almighty. *Milton.*

Perhaps I have not so well consulted the repute of my intellectuals, in bringing their imperfections into such discerning *presences*. *Glanvill's Sceps.*

Since clinging cares and trains of inbred fears,
Not aw'd by arms, but in the *presence* bold,
Without respect to purple or to gold. *Dryden.*

4. A number assembled before a great person.

Look I so pale.
—Ay; and no man in the *presence*,
But his red colour hath forsook his cheeks. *Shakesp.*

Odmar, of all this *presence* does contain,
Give her your wreath whom you esteem most fair. *Dryden.*

5. Port; air; mien; demeanour.

Virtue is best in a body that is comely, and that hath rather dignity of *presence*, than beauty of aspect. *Bacon.*

A graceful *presence* bespeaks acceptance, gives a force to language, and helps to convince by look and posture. *Collier.*

How great his *presence*, how erect his look,
How ev'ry grace, how all his virtuous mother
Shines in his face, and charms me from his eyes. *Smith.*

6. Room in which a prince shows himself to his court.

By them they pass, all gazing on them round,
And to the *presence* mount, whose glorious view
Their frail amazed senses did confound. *Fairy Queen.*

An't please your grace, the two great cardinals
Wait in the *presence*. *Shakesp. Henry VIII.*

The lady Anne of Bretagne, passing through the *presence* in the court of France, and espying Chartier, a famous poet, leaning upon his elbow fast asleep, openly kissing him, said, we must honour with our kiss, the mouth from whence so many sweet verses have proceeded. *Peacham.*

7. Readiness at need; quickness at expedients.

A good bodily strength is a felicity of nature, but nothing comparable to a large understanding and ready *presence* of mind. *L'Estrange.*

Errors, not to be recall'd, do find
Their best redress from *presence* of the mind,
Courage our greatest failings does supply. *Waller.*

8. The person of a superior.

To her the sov'reign *presence* thus reply'd. *Milton.*

PRESENCE-CHAMBER. } *n. s.* [*presence* and *chamber* or *room.*]
PRESENCE-ROOM. } The room in which a great person receives company.

If these nerves, which are the conduits to convey them from without to their audience in the brain, the mind's *presence-room*, are so disordered, as not to perform their functions, they have no postern to be admitted by. *Locke.*

Kneller, with silence and surprise,
We see Britannia's monarch rise,
And aw'd by thy delusive hand,
As in the *presence-chamber* stand. *Addison.*

PRESE'NSION. *n. s.* [*præsensio*, Lat.] Perception beforehand.

The hedgehog's *presension* of winds is exact. *Brown.*

PRE'SENT. *adj.* [*present*, Fr. *præsens*, Lat.]

1. Not absent; being face to face; being at hand.

But neither of these are any impediment, because the regent thereof is of an infinite immensity more than commensurate to the extent of the world, and such as is most intimately *present* with all the beings of the world. *Hale.*

Be not often *present* at feasts, not at all in dissolute company; pleasing objects steal away the heart. *Taylor.*

Much I have heard
Incredible to me, in this displeas'd,
That I was never *present* on the place
Of those encounters. *Milton's Agonistes.*

2. Not past; not future.

Thou future things can'st represent
As *present*. *Milton.*

The moments past, if thou art wise, retrieve
With pleasant mem'ry of the bliss they gave;
The *present* hours in pleasant mirth employ,
And bribe the future with the hopes of joy. *Prior.*

The *present* age hath not been less inquisitive than the former ages were. *Woodward's Nat. Hist.*

3. Ready at hand; quick in emergencies.

If a man write little, he had need have a great memory; if he confer little, he had need have a *present* wit; and if he read little, he had need have much cunning. *Bacon.*

'Tis a high point of philosophy and virtue for a man to be so *present* to himself, as to be always provided against all accidents. *L'Estrange.*

4. Favourably attentive; not neglectful; propitious.

Be *present* to her now, as then,
And let not proud and factious men
Against your wills oppose their mights. *Benj. Johnson.*

The golden goddess, *present* at the pray'r,
Well knew he meant th' inanimated fair,
And gave the sign of granting his desire. *Dryden.*

Nor could I hope in any place but there,
To find a god so *present* to my pray'r. *Dryden.*

5. Unforgotten; not neglectful.

The ample mind keeps the several objects all within sight, and *present* to the soul. *Watts.*

6. Not abstracted; not absent of mind; attentive.

The

The PRESENT. An elliptical expression for *the present time*; the time now existing.

When he saw descend
The son of God to judge them, terrify'd
He fled; not hoping to escape, but shun
The *present*; fearing guilty, what his wrath
Might suddenly inflict. *Milton.*

Men that set their hearts only upon the *present*, without looking forward into the end of things are struck at. *L'Estr.*

Who, since their own short understandings reach
No further than the *present*, think ev'n the wise,
Speak what they think, and tell tales of themselves. *Rowe.*

At PRESENT. [*à present*, Fr.] At the present time; now; elliptically, for *the present time*.

The state is *at present* very sensible of the decay in their trade. *Addison.*

PRE'SENT. *n. s.* [*present*, Fr. from the verb.]

1. A gift; a donative; something ceremoniously given.

Plain Clarence!
I will send thy soul to heav'n,
If heav'n will take the *present* at our hands. *Shakesp.*

His dog to-morrow, by his master's command, he must carry for a *present* to his lady. *Shakesp.*

He sent part of the rich spoil, with the admiral's ensign, as a *present* unto Solyman. *Knolles's Hist. of the Turks.*

Say heav'nly muse, shall not thy sacred vein
Afford a *present* to the infant God?
Hast thou no verse, no hymn, no solemn strain,
To welcome him to this his new abode? *Milton.*

They that are to love inclin'd,
Sway'd by chance, not choice or art
To the first that's fair or kind,
Make a *present* of their heart. *Waller.*

Somewhat is sure design'd by fraud or force;
Trust not their *presents*, nor admit the horse. *Dryden.*

2. A letter or mandate exhibited.

Be it known to all men by these *presents*. *Shakesp.*

To PRESE'NT. *v. a.* [*præsento*, low Lat. *presenter*, Fr. in all the senses.]

1. To place in the presence of a superior.

On to the sacred hill
They led him high applauded, and *present*
Before the seat supreme. *Milton's Par. Lost, b.* vi.

2. To exhibit to view or notice.

He knows not what he says; and vain is it,
That we *present* us to him. *Shakesp. King Lear.*

3. To offer; to exhibit.

Thou therefore now advise,
Or hear what to my mind first thoughts *present*. *Milton.*

Now ev'ry leaf, and ev'ry moving breath
Presents a foe, and ev'ry foe a death. *Denham.*

Lectorides's memory is ever ready to offer to his mind something out of other men's writings or conversations, and is *presenting* him with the thoughts of other persons perpetually. *Watts's Improvement of the Mind.*

4. To give formally and ceremoniously.

Folks in mudwall tenement,
Affording pepper-corn for rent,
Present a turkey or a hen
To those might better spare them ten. *Prior.*

5. To put into the hands of another.

So ladies in romance assist their knight,
Present the spear, and arm him for the fight. *Dryden.*

6. To favour with gifts. To *present*, in the sense of to *give*, has several structures: we say absolutely, *to* present *a man*, to give something to him. This is less in use. The common phrases are *to* present *a gift to a man*; or, *to* present *the man with a gift.*

Thou spendest thy time in waiting upon such a great one, and thy estate in *presenting* him; and, after all, hast no other reward, but sometimes to be smiled upon, and always to be smiled at. *South's Sermons.*

He now *presents*, as ancient ladies do,
That courted long, at length are forc'd to woo. *Dryden.*

Octavia *presented* the poet, for his admirable elegy on her son Marcellus. *Dryden.*

Should I *present* thee with rare figur'd plate,
O how thy rising heart would throb and beat. *Dryden.*

7. To prefer to ecclesiastical benefices.

That he put these bishops in the places of the deceased by his own authority, is notoriously false; for the duke of Saxony always *presented*. *Atterbury.*

8. To offer openly.

He was appointed admiral, and *presented* battle to the French navy, which they refused. *Hayward.*

9. To introduce by something exhibited to the view or notice. Not in use.

Tell on, quoth she, the woful tragedy,
The which these reliques sad *present* unto. *Spenser.*

10. To lay before a court of judicature, as an object of enquiry.

The grand juries were practised effectually with to *present* the said pamphlet, with all aggravating epithets. *Swift.*

PRESENTA'NEOUS. *adj.* [from *præsentaneus*, Lat.] Ready quick; immediate.

Some plagues partake of such malignity, that, like a *presentaneous* poison, they enecate in two hours. *Harve*

PRESE'NTABLE. *adj.* [from *present*.] What may be presente

Incumbents of churches *presentable* cannot, by their so act, grant their incumbencies to others; but may mak leases of the profits thereof. *Ayliffe's Parergo*

PRESENTA'TION. *n. s.* [*presentation*, Fr. from *present*.]

1. The act of presenting.

Prayers are sometimes a *presentation* of mere desires, as mean of procuring desired effects at the hands of God. *Hooke*

2. The act of offering any one to an ecclesiastical benefice.

He made effectual provision for recovery of advowsons ar *presentations* to churches. *Hal*

What, shall the curate controul me? have not I the *presentation?* *Ga*

3. Exhibition.

These *presentations* of fighting on the stage, are necessar to produce the effects of an heroick play. *Dryde*

4. This word is misprinted for *presension*.

Although in sundry animals, we deny not a kind of natur meteorology, or innate *presentation* both of wind and weathe yet that proceeding from sense, they cannot retain that ap prehension after death. *Brown's Vulgar Errour*

PRESE'NTATIVE. *adj.* [from *present*.] Such as that presenta tions may be made of it.

Mrs. Gulston possessed of the impropriate parsonage of Barc well, did procure from the king leave to annex the same t the vicarage, and to make it *presentative*, and gave them bot to St. John's College in Oxon. *Spelma*

PRESE'NTEE. *n. s.* [from *presenté*, Fr.] One presented to benefice.

Our laws make the ordinary a disturber, if he does n give institution upon the fitness of a person presented to hin or at least give notice to the patron of the disability of h *presentee*. *Ayliffe's Parergo*

PRESE'NTER. *n. s.* [from *present*.] One that presents.

The thing was acceptable, but not the *presenter*. *L'Est*

PRESE'NTIAL. *adj.* [from *present*.] Supposing actual presenc

By union, I do not understand that which is local or *presential*, because I consider God as omnipresent. *Norri*

PRESENTIA'LITY. *n. s.* [from *presential*.] State of bein present.

This eternal, indivisible act of his existence makes a futures actually present to him; and it is the *presentiality* the object, which founds the unerring certainty of his know ledge. *South's Sermon*

To PRESE'NTIATE. *v. a.* [from *present*.] To make present.

The fancy may be so strong, as to *presentiate* upon on theatre, all that ever it took notice of in times past: th power of fancy, in *presentiating* any one thing that is pas being no less wonderful, than having that power, it shoul also acquire the perfection to *presentiate* them all. *Grew*

PRESENTI'FICK. *adj.* [*præsens* and *facio*, Latin.] Makin present. Not in use.

PRESENTI'FICKLY. *adv.* [from *presentifick*.] In such a manne as to make present.

The whole evolution of times and ages, from everlasting t everlasting, is collectedly and *presentifickly* represented to Go at once, as if all things and actions were, at this very instan really present and existent before him. *Mor*

PRE'SENTLY. *adv.* [from *present*.]

1. At present; at this time; now.

The towns and forts you *presently* have, are still left unt you to be kept either with or without garrisons, so as yo alter not the laws of the country. *Sidne*

I hope we may presume, that a rare thing it is not in th church of God, even for that very word which is read to b *presently* their joy, and afterwards their study that hear it. *Hooker, b.* v. *s.* 2

To speak of it as requireth, would require very long di course; all I will *presently* say is this. *Hooker, b.* i. *s.* 1c

Covetous ambition, thinking all too little which *present* it hath, supposeth itself to stand in need of all which it hat not. *Raleigh's Essay*

2. Immediately; soon after.

Tell him, that no history can match his policies, and *presently* the sot shall measure himself by himself. *South*

PRESE'NTMENT. *n. s.* [from *present*.]

1. The act of presenting.

When comes your book forth?
Upon the heels of my *presentment*. *Shakesp*

2. Any thing presented or exhibited; representation.

Thus I hurl
My dazzling spells into the spungy air,
Of power to cheat the eye with blear illusion,
And give it false *presentments*, lest the place
And my quaint habits breed astonishment. *Milton*

3. In law, *presentment* is a mere denunciation of the jurors them selves or some other officer, as justice, constable, searcher, sur veyors, and, without any information, of an offence inquir able in the court to which it is presented. *Cowe*

Th

The grand juries were practised effectually with, to present the said pamphlet with all aggravating epithets, and their *presentments* published for several weeks in all the news-papers. *Swift to Pope.*

PRE'SENTNESS. *n. s.* [from *present.*] Presence of mind; quickness at emergencies.

Goring had a much better understanding, a much keener courage, and *presentness* of mind in danger. *Clarendon.*

PRESERVA'TION. *n. s.* [from *preserve.*] The act of preserving; care to preserve; act of keeping from destruction, decay, or any ill.

Nature does require
Her times of *preservation*, which, perforce,
I give my tendance to. *Shakesp. Henry* VIII.

The eyes of the Lord are upon them that love him, he is their mighty protection, a *preservation* from stumbling, and a help from falling. *Ecclus.* xxxiv. 16.

Ev'ry senseless thing, by nature's light,
Doth *preservation* seek, destruction shun. *Davies.*

Our allwise maker has put into man the uneasiness of hunger, thirst, and other natural desires, to determine their wills for the *preservation* of themselves, and the continuation of their species. *Locke.*

PRESE'RVATIVE. *n. s.* [*preservatif*, Fr. from *preserve.*] That which has the power of preserving; something preventive; something that confers security.

If we think that the church needeth not those ancient *preservatives*, which ages before us were glad to use, we deceive ourselves. *Hooker.*

It hath been anciently in use to wear tablets of arsenick, as *preservatives* against the plague; for that being poisons themselves, they draw the venom to them from the spirits. *Bacon's Nat. Hist.*

Were there truth herein, it were the best *preservative* for princes, and persons exalted unto such fears. *Brown.*

Bodies kept clean, which use *preservatives*, are likely to escape infection. *Harvey.*

The most effectual *preservative* of our virtue, is to avoid the conversation of wicked men. *Rogers.*

Molly is an Egyptian plant, and was really made use of as a *preservative* against enchantment. *Broome's Notes on Odys.*

To PRESE'RVE. *v. a.* [*præservo*, low Latin; *preserver*, Fr.]

1. To save; to defend from destruction or any evil; to keep.

The Lord shall deliver me from every evil work, and *preserve* me unto his heavenly kingdom. 2 *Tim.* iv. 18.

God sent me to *preserve* you a posterity, and save your lives. *Gen.* xlv. 7.

She shall lead me soberly in my doings, and *preserve* me in her power. *Wisdom* ix. 11.

He did too frequently gratify their unjustifiable designs, a guilt all men, who are obnoxious, are liable to, and can hardly *preserve* themselves from. *Clarendon.*

We can *preserve* unhurt our minds. *Milton.*

To be indifferent, which of two opinions is true, is the right temper of the mind, that *preserves* it from being imposed on, till it has done its best to find the truth. *Locke.*

Every petty prince in Germany must be intreated to *preserve* the queen of Great Britain upon her throne. *Swift.*

2. To season fruits and other vegetables with sugar and in other proper pickles: as, *to* preserve *plumbs, walnuts, and cucumbers.*

PRESE'RVE. *n. s.* [from the verb.] Fruit preserved whole in sugar.

All this is easily discerned in those fruits, which are brought in *preserves* unto us. *Brown.*

The fruit with the husk, when tender and young, makes a good *preserve*. *Mortimer.*

PRESE'RVER. *n. s.* [from *preserve.*]

1. One who preserves; one who keeps from ruin or mischief.

Sit, my *preserver*, by thy patient's side. *Shakesp.*

To be always thinking, perhaps, is the privilege of the infinite author and *preserver* of things, who never slumbers nor sleeps; but is not competent to any finite being. *Locke.*

Andrew Doria has a statue erected to him, with the glorious title of deliverer of the commonwealth; and one of his family another, that calls him its *preserver*. *Addison.*

2. He who makes preserves of fruit.

To PRESIDE. *v. n.* [from *præsideo*, Lat. *presider*, Fr.] To be set over; to have authority over.

Some o'er the publick magazines *preside*,
And some are sent new forage to provide. *Dryden.*

O'er the plans
Of thriving peace, thy thoughtful sires *preside*. *Thomson.*

PRE'SIDENCY. *n. s.* [*presidence*, Fr. from *president.*] Superintendence.

What account can be given of the growth of plants from mechanical principles, moved without the *presidency* and guidance of some superior agent. *Ray on the Creation.*

PRE'SIDENT. *n. s.* [*præsidens*, Lat. *president*, Fr.]

1. One placed with authority over others; one at the head of others.

As the *president* of my kingdom, will I
Appear there for a man. *Shakesp. Ant. and Cleop.*

The tutor sits in the chair as *president* or moderator, to see that the rules of disputation be observed. *Watts.*

2. Governour; prefect.

How might those captive Israelites, under the oversight and government of Assyrian *presidents*, be able to leave the places they were to inhabit. *Brerewood on Languages.*

3. A tutelary power.

This last complaint th' indulgent ears did pierce
Of just Apollo, *president* of verse. *Waller.*

PRE'SIDENTSHIP. *n. s.* [from *president.*] The office and place of president.

When things came to trial of practice, their pastors learning would be at all times of force to overpersuade simple men, who, knowing the time of their own *presidentship* to be but short, would always stand in fear of their ministers perpetual authority. *Hooker's Preface.*

PRESI'DIAL. *adj.* [*præsidium*, Lat.] Relating to a garrison.

To PRESS. *v. a.* [*presser*, Fr. *premo, pressus*, Lat.]

1. To squeeze; to crush.

The grapes I *pressed* into Pharaoh's cup. *Gen.* xl. 11.

Good measure *pressed* down, shaken together, and running over, shall men give into your bosom. *Luke* vi. 38.

From sweet kernels *press'd*,
She tempers dulcet creams. *Milton.*

I put pledgets of lint *pressed* out on the excoriation. *Wisem.*

Their morning milk the peasants *press* at night,
Their evening milk before the rising light. *Dryden.*

After *pressing* out of the colesced for oil in Lincolnshire, they burn the cakes to heat their ovens. *Mortimer.*

2. To distress; to crush with calamities.

Once or twice she heav'd the name of father
Pantingly forth, as if it *prest* her heart. *Shakesp.*

3. To constrain; to compel; to urge by necessity.

The experience of his goodness in her own deliverance, might cause her merciful disposition to take so much the more delight in saving others, whom the like necessity should *press*. *Hooker.*

The posts that rode upon mules and camels, went out, being hastened and *pressed* on by the king's commands. *Esther.*

I was *prest* by his majesty's commands, to assist at the treaty. *Temple's Miscel.*

He gapes; and straight
With hunger *prest*, devours the pleasing bait. *Dryden.*

He *pressed* a letter upon me, within this hour, to deliver to you. *Dryden's Spanish Fryar.*

4. To drive by violence.

Come with words as medical as true,
Honest as either, to purge him of that humour
That *presses* him from sleep. *Shakesp.*

5. To affect strongly.

Paul was *pressed* in spirit, and testified to the Jews that Jesus was Christ. *Acts* xviii. 5.

Wickedness condemned by her own witness, and *pressed* with conscience, forecasteth grievous things. *Wisdom* xvii. 11.

6. To enforce; to inculcate with argument or importunity.

Be sure to *press* upon him every motive. *Addison.*

I am the more bold to *press* it upon you, because these accomplishments sit more handsomely on persons of quality, than any other. *Felton on the Classicks.*

Those who negotiated, took care to make demands impossible to be complied with; and therefore might securely *press* every article, as if they were in earnest. *Swift.*

7. To urge; to bear strongly on.

Chymists I may *press* with arguments, drawn from some of the eminentest writers of their sect. *Boyle.*

8. To compress; to hug, as in embracing.

He *press'd* her matron lips
With kisses pure. *Milton.*

She took her son, and *press'd*
Th' illustrious infant to her fragrant breast. *Dryden.*

His easy heart receiv'd the guilty flame,
And from that time he *prest* her with his passion. *Smith.*

Leucothoe shook,
And *press'd* Palemon closer in her arms. *Pope.*

9. To act upon with weight.

The place thou *pressest* on thy mother earth,
Is all thy empire now: now it contains thee. *Dryden.*

10. To make earnest. *Prest* is here perhaps rather an adjective; *preste*, Fr. or from *pressè* or *empressè*, Fr.

Let them be *pressed*, and ready to give succours to their confederates, as it ever was with the Romans; for if the confederate had leagues defensive with divers other states, and implored their aids, the Romans would ever be the formost. *Bacon's Essays.*

Prest for their country's honour and their king's,
On their sharp beaks they whet their pointed stings. *Dryd.*

11. To force into military service. This is properly *impress*.

Do but say to me what I should do,
That in your knowledge may by me be done,
And I am *prest* into it. *Shakesp.*

For every man that Bolingbroke hath *press'd*
To lift sharp steel against our golden crown,
Heav'n for his Richard hath in store
A glorious angel. *Shakesp. Richard* II.

From London by the king was I *prest* forth. *Shakesp.*

They are enforced of very necessity to *press* the best and greatest part of their men out of the West countries, which is no small charge. *Raleigh.*

The endeavour to raise new men for the recruit of the army by *pressing*, found opposition in many places. *Clarendon.*

The peaceful peasant to the wars is *prest*,
The fields lie fallow in inglorious rest. *Dryden.*

Must grandson Filbert to the wars be *prest*. *Gay.*

You were *pressed* for the sea-service, and got off with much a-do. *Swift.*

To Press. *v. n.*

1. To act with compulsive violence; to urge; to distress.

If there be fair proofs on the one side, and none at all on the other, and if the most *pressing* difficulties be on that side, on which there are no proofs, this is sufficient to render one opinion very credible, and the other altogether incredible. *Tillotson's Sermons.*

A great many uneasinesses always solliciting the will, it is natural, that the greatest and most *pressing* should determine it to the next action. *Locke.*

2. To go forward with violence to any object.

I make bold to *press*
With so little preparation.
—You're welcome. *Shakesp.*

I *press* toward the mark for the prize. *Phil.* iii. 14.

The Turks gave a great shout, and *pressed* in on all sides, to have entered the breach. *Knolles.*

Thronging crowds *press* on you as you pass,
And with their eager joy make triumph slow. *Dryden.*

Th' insulting victor *presses* on the more,
And treads the steps the vanquish'd trod before. *Dryden.*

She is always drawn in a posture of walking, it being as natural for Hope to *press* forward to her proper objects, as for Fear to fly from them. *Addison on Ancient Medals.*

Let us not therefore faint, or be weary in our journey, much less turn back or sit down in despair; but *press* chearfully forward to the high mark of our calling. *Rogers.*

3. To make invasion; to encroach.

On superior powers
Were we to *press*, inferior might *on* ours. *Pope.*

4. To croud; to throng.

For he had healed many, insomuch that they *pressed* upon him for to touch him. *Mar.* iii. 10.

Counsel she may; and I will give thy ear
The knowledge first of what is fit to hear:
What I transact with others or alone,
Beware to learn; nor *press* too near the throne. *Dryden.*

5. To come unseasonably or importunately.

6. To urge with vehemence and importunity.

He *pressed* upon them greatly; and they turned in. *Gen.*

The less blood he drew, the more he took of treasure; and, as some construed it, he was the more sparing in the one, that he might be the more *pressing* in the other. *Bacon.*

So thick the shiv'ring army stands,
And *press* for passage with extended hands. *Dryden.*

7. To act upon or influence.

When arguments *press* equally in matters indifferent, the safest method is to give up ourselves to neither. *Addison.*

8. *To* Press *upon.* To invade; to push against.

Patroclus *presses upon* Hector too boldly, and by obliging him to fight, discovers it was not the true Achilles. *Pope.*

Press. *n. s.* [*pressoir*, Fr. from the verb.]

1. The instrument by which any thing is crushed or squeezed.

The *press* is full, the fats overflow. *Joel* iii. 13.

When one came to the *press* fats to draw out fifty vessels out of the *press*, there were but twenty. *Hag.* ii. 16.

The stomach and intestines are the *press*, and the lacteal vessels the strainers, to separate the pure emulsion from the fæces. *Arbuthnot.*

They kept their cloaths, when they were not worn, constantly in a *press*, to give them a lustre. *Arbuthnot.*

2. The instrument by which books are printed.

These letters are of the second edition; he will print them out of doubt, for he cares not what he puts into the *press*, when he would put us two in. *Shakesp.*

3. Croud; tumult; throng.

Paul and Barnabas, when infidels admiring their virtues, went about to sacrifice unto them, rent their garments in token of horror, and as frighted, ran crying through the *press* of the people, O men wherefore do ye these things. *Hooker.*

She held a great gold chain ylinked well,
Whose upper end to highest heaven was knit,
And lower part did reach to lowest hell,
And all that *press* did round about her swell,
To catchen hold of that long chain. *Fairy Queen.*

Who is it in the *press* that calls on me?
I hear a tongue, shriller than all the musick,
Cry, Cæsar. *Shakesp. Julius Cæsar.*

Death having prey'd upon the outward parts,
Leaves them insensible; his siege is now
Against the mind; the which he pricks and wounds
With many legions of strange fantasies;
Which in their throng, and *press* to that last hold,
Confound themselves. *Shakesp. King Lear*

Ambitious Turnus in the *press* appears,
And aggravating crimes augment their fears. *Dryde*

A new express all Agra does affright,
Darah and Aurengzebe are join'd in fight;
The *press* of people thickens to the court,
Th' impatient croud devouring the report. *Dryder*

Through the *press* enrag'd Thalestris flies,
And scatters deaths around from both her eyes. *Pop*

4. A kind of wooden case or frame for cloaths and other uses.

Creep into the kill hole.—Neither *press*, coffer, chest trunk; but he hath an abstract for the remembrance of suc places. *Shakesp. Merry Wives of Windsor*

5. A commission to force men into military service. For *impres*

If I be not ashamed of my soldiers, I am a sowc'd gurnet I have misus'd the king's *press* damnably. *Shakes*

Concerning the musters and *presses* for sufficient mariners serve in his majesty's ships, either the care is very little, the bribery very great. *Raleig*

Pre'ssbed. *n. s.* [*press* and *bed.*] Bed so formed, as to be shu up in a case.

Pre'sser. *n. s.* [from *press.*] One that presses or works at a pres

Of the stuffs I give the profits to dyers and *pressers*. *Swif*

Pre'ssgang. *n. s.* [*press* and *gang.*] A crew that strols abou the streets to force men into naval service.

Pre'ssingly. *adv.* [from *pressing.*] With force; closely.

The one contracts his words, speaking *pressingly* and short the other d lights in long-breathed accents. *Howe*

Pre'ssion. *n. s.* [from *press.*] The act of pressing.

If light consisted only in *pression*, propagated without actu motion, it would not be able to agitate and heat the bodies which refract and reflect it: if it consisted in motion, propa gated to all distances in an instant, it would require an infini force every moment, in every shining particle, to generat that motion: and if it consisted in *pression* or motion, propa gated either in an instant or in time, it would bend into th shadow. *Newton's Optick*

Pre'ssitant. *adj.* Gravitating; heavy. A word not in use.

Neither the celestial matter of the vortices, nor the air nor water are *pressitant* in their proper places. *Mor*

Pre'ssman. *n. s.* [*press* and *man.*]

1. One who forces another into service; one who forces awa

One only path to all; by which the *pressmen* came. *Cha*

2. One who makes the impression of print by the press: d stinct from the compositor, who ranges the types.

Pre'ssmoney. *n. s.* [*press* and *money.*] Money given to a sol dier when he is taken or forced into the service.

Here Peascod, take my pouch, 'tis all I own,
'Tis my *pressmoney*.—Can this silver fail? *Ga*

Pre'ssure. *n. s.* [from *press.*]

1. The act of pressing or crushing.

2. The state of being pressed or crushed.

3. Force acting against any thing; gravitation; pression.

The inequality of the *pressure* of parts appeareth in this that if you take a body of stone, and another of wood of th same magnitude and shape, and throw them with equal forc you cannot throw the wood so far as the stone. *Baco*

Although the glasses were a little convex, yet this transpa rent spot was of a considerable breadth, which breadth seeme principally to proceed from the yielding inwards of the par of the glasses, by reason of their mutual *pressure*. *Newto*

The blood flows through the vessels by the excess of th force of the heart above the incumbent *pressure*, which in f people is excessive. *Arbuthno*

4. Violence inflicted; oppression.

A wise father ingenuously confessed, that those, which per suaded *pressure* of consciences, were commonly intereste therein. *Bacon's Essay*

5. Affliction; grievance; distress.

Mine own and my people's *pressures* are grievous, an peace would be very pleasing. *King Charle*

The genuine price of lands in England would be twent years purchase, were it not for accidental *pressures* under whic it labours. *Child's Discourse of Trad*

To this consideration he retreats, in the midst of all h *pressures*, with comfort; in this thought, notwithstanding th sad afflictions with which he was overwhelmed, he mightil exults. *Atterbury's Sermon*

Excellent was the advice of Elephas to Job, in the mid of his great troubles and *pressures*, acquaint thyself now wit God, and be at peace. *Atterbur*

6. Impression; stamp; character made by impression.

From my memory
I'll wipe away all trivial fond records,
All saws of books, all forms, all *pressures* past,
That youth and observation copy'd there. *Shakesp*

Prest. *adj.* [*prest* or *prêt*, Fr.]

1. Ready; not dilatory. This is said to have been the origina sense of the word *prest men*; men, not forced into the servic as now we understand it, but men, for a certain sum re ceived, *prest* or ready to march at command.

Eac

Each mind is *prest*, and open every ear,
To hear new tidings, though they no way joy us. *Fairfax.*

Grittus desired nothing more than, at his first entrance, to have confirmed the opinion of his authority in the minds of the vulgar people, by the *prest* and ready attendance of the Vayuod. *Knolles's Hist. of the Turks.*

2. Neat; tight. In both senses the word is obsolete.

More wealth any where, to be breefe
More people, more handsome and *prest*
Where find ye? *Tusser's Husbandry.*

PREST. *n. s.* [*prest*, Fr.] A loan.

He required of the city a *prest* of six thousand marks; but, after many parlees, he could obtain but two thousand pounds. *Bacon's Henry* VII.

PRESTIGA'TION. *n. s.* [*prestigatio*, Lat.] A deceiving; a juggling; a playing legerdemain. *Dict.*

PRE'STIGES. *n. s.* [*prestigiæ*, Lat.] Illusions; impostures; juggling tricks. *Dict.*

PRE'STO. *n. s.* [*presto*, Italian.] Quick; at once. A word used by those that show legerdemain.

Presto! begone! 'tis here again;
There's ev'ry piece as big as ten. *Swift.*

PRESU'MABLY. *adv.* [from *presume.*] Without examination.

Authors *presumably* writing by common places, wherein, for many years, promiscuously amassing all that make for their subject, break forth at last into useless rhapsodies. *Brown.*

To PRESU'ME. *v. n.* [*presumer*, Fr. *præsumo*, Lat.]

1. To suppose; to believe previously without examination.

O much deceiv'd, much failing, hapless Eve!
Of thy *presum'd* return! event perverse! *Milton.*

Experience supplants the use of conjecture in the point; we do not only *presume* it may be so, but actually find it is so. *Government of the Tongue.*

2. To suppose; to affirm without immediate proof.

Although in the relation of Moses there be very few persons mentioned, yet are there many more to be *presumed.* *Brown.*

I *presume*,
That as my hand has open'd bounty to you,
My heart dropp'd love; my pow'r rain'd honour more
On you, than any. *Shakesp. Henry* VIII.

3. To venture without positive leave.

There was a matter we were no less desirous to know, than fearful to ask, lest we might *presume* too far. *Bacon.*

I to the heav'nly vision thus *presum'd.* *Milton.*

4. To form confident or arrogant opinions.

The life of Ovid being already written in our language, I will not *presume* so far upon myself, to think I can add any thing to Mr. Sandys his undertaking. *Dryden.*

This man *presumes* upon his parts, that they will not fail him at time of need, and so thinks it superfluous labour to make any provision beforehand. *Locke.*

5. To make confident or arrogant attempts.

In this we fail to perform the thing, which God seeth meet, convenient and good; in that we *presume* to see what is meet and convenient, better than God himself. *Hooker.*

God, to remove his ways from human sense,
Plac'd heav'n from earth so far, that earthly sight,
If it *presume*, might err in things too high,
And no advantage gain. *Milton's Par. Lost, b.* viii.

6. It has *on* or *upon* sometimes before the thing supposed, or causing presumption.

He, that would not deceive himself, ought to build his hypothesis on matter of fact, and not *presume on* matter of fact, because of his hypothesis. *Locke.*

Luther *presumes upon* the gift of continency. *Atterbury.*

7. It has *of* sometimes, but not properly.

Presuming of his force, with sparkling eyes,
Already he devours the promis'd prize. *Dryden.*

PRESU'MER. *n. s.* [from *presume.*] One that presupposes; an arrogant person.

Heavy with some high minds is an overweight of obligation; otherwise great deservers do grow intolerable *presumers.* *Wotton.*

PRESU'MPTION. *n. s.* [*præsumptus*, Lat. *presomption*, Fr.]

1. Supposition previously formed.

Thou hast shewed us how unsafe it is to offend thee, upon *presumptions* afterwards to please thee. *King Charles.*

Though men in general believed a future state, yet they had but confused *presumptions* of the nature and condition of it. *Rog.*

2. Confidence grounded on any thing presupposed.

A *presumption*, upon this aid, was the principal motive for the undertaking. *Clarendon, b.* viii.

Those at home held their immoderate engrossments of power by no other tenure, than their own *presumption* upon the necessity of affairs. *Swift's Miscellanies.*

3. An argument strong, but not demonstrative; a strong probability.

The error and unsufficience of their arguments doth make it, on the contrary side against them, a strong *presumption*, that God hath not moved their hearts to think such things, as he hath not enabled them to prove. *Hooker, b.* v. *s.* 10.

4. Arrogance; confidence blind and adventurous; presumptuousness.

Let my *presumption* not provoke thy wrath;
For I am sorry, that with reverence
I did not entertain thee as thou art. *Shakesp.*

It warns a warier carriage in the thing,
Lest blind *presumption* work their ruining. *Daniel.*

I had the *presumption* to dedicate to you a very unfinished piece. *Dryden.*

5. Unreasonable confidence of divine favour.

The awe of his majesty will keep us from *presumption*, and the promises of his mercy from despair. *Rogers.*

PRESU'MPTIVE. *adj.* [*presomptive*, Fr. from *presume.*]

1. Taken by previous supposition.

We commonly take shape and colour for so *presumptive* ideas of several species, that, in a good picture, we readily say this is a lion, and that a rose. *Locke.*

2. Supposed: as, *the* presumptive *heir:* opposed to the heir apparent.

3. Confident; arrogant; presumptuous.

There being two opinions repugnant to each other, it may not be *presumptive* or sceptical to doubt of both. *Brown.*

PRESU'MPTUOUS. *adj.* [*presumptueux*, *presomptueux*, Fr.]

1. Arrogant; confident; insolent.

Presumptuous priest, this place commands my patience. *Shakesp. Henry* VI.

I follow him not
With any token of *presumptuous* suit;
Nor would I have him, till I do deserve him. *Shakesp.*

The boldness of advocates prevail with judges; whereas they should imitate God, who represseth the *presumptuous*, and giveth grace to the modest. *Bacon's Essays.*

Their minds somewhat rais'd
By false *presumptuous* hope. *Milton.*

Some will not venture to look beyond received notions of the age, nor have so *presumptuous* a thought, as to be wiser than their neighbours. *Locke.*

2. Irreverent with respect to holy things.

Thus I *presumptuous*: and the vision bright,
As with a smile more brighten'd, thus reply'd. *Milton.*

The pow'rs incens'd
Punish'd his *presumptuous* pride,
That for his daring enterprize she dy'd. *Dryden.*

Can'st thou love
Presumptuous Crete, that boasts the tomb of Jove. *Pope.*

PRESU'MPTUOUSLY. *adv.* [from *presumptuous.*]

1. Arrogantly; irreverently.

Do you, who study nature's works, decide,
Whilst I the dark mysterious cause admire;
Nor, into what the gods conceal, *presumptuously* enquire. *Addison's Remarks on Italy.*

2. With vain and groundless confidence in divine favour.

I entreat your prayers, that God will keep me from all premature persuasion of my being in Christ, and not suffer me to go on *presumptuously* or desperately in any course *Hamm.*

PRESU'MPTUOUSNESS. *n. s.* [from *presumptuous.*] Quality of being presumptuous; confidence; irreverence.

PRESUPPO'SAL. *n. s.* [*præ* and *supposal.*] Supposal previously formed.

All things necessary to be known that we may be saved, but known with *presupposal* of knowledge concerning certain principles, whereof it receiveth us already persuaded. *Hooker.*

To PRESUPPO'SE. *v. a.* [*presupposer*, Fr. *præ* and *suppose.*] To suppose as previous.

In as much as righteous life *presupposeth* life, in as much as to live virtuously it is impossible except we live; therefore the first impediment, which naturally we endeavour to remove, is penury and want of things, without which we cannot live. *Hooker, b.* i. *s.* 10.

All kinds of knowlege have their certain bounds; each of them *presupposeth* many necessary things learned in other sciences, and known beforehand. *Hooker, b.* i.

PRESUPPOSI'TION. *n. s.* [*presupposition*, Fr. *præ* and *supposition.*] Supposition previously formed.

PRESURMI'SE. *n. s.* [*præ* and *surmise.*] Surmise previously formed.

It was your *presurmise*,
That, in the dole of blows, your son might drop. *Shakesp.*

PRETE'NCE. *n. s.* [*prætensus*, Lat.]

1. A false argument grounded upon fictitious postulates.

This *pretence* against religion will not only be baffled, but we shall gain a new argument to persuade men over. *Tillots.*

2. The act of showing or alleging what is not real.

With flying speed and seeming great *pretence*
Came running in a messenger. *Fairy Queen.*

So strong his appetite was to those executions he had been accustom'd to in Ireland, without any kind of commission or *pretence* of authority. *Clarendon.*

O worthy not of liberty alone,
Too mean *pretence*, but honour. *Miller.*

Let not the Trojans, with a feign'd *pretence*
Of proffer'd peace, delude the Latian prince. *Dryden.*

I should have dressed the whole with greater care; but I had little time, which I am sure you know to be more than *pretence.* *Wake's Preparation for Death.*

3. Assumption;

3. Assumption; claim to notice.

Despise not these few ensuing pages; for never was any thing of this *pretence* more ingenuously imparted. *Evelyn.*

4. Claim true or false.

Spirits in our just *pretences* arm'd
Fell with us. *Milton.*

Primogeniture cannot have any *pretence* to a right of solely inheriting property or power. *Locke.*

5. *Shakespeare* uses this word with more affinity to the original Latin, for something threatened, or held out to terrify.

I have conceived a most faint neglect of late, which I have rather blamed as my own jealous curiosity, than as a very *pretence* and purpose of unkindness. *Shakesp.*

In the great hand of God I stand, and thence
Against the undivulg'd *pretence* I fight
Of treas'nous malice. *Shakesp. Macbeth.*

He hath writ this to feel my affection for your honour, and to no other *pretence* of danger. *Shakesp. King Lear.*

To PRETE'ND. *v. a.* [*prætendo*, Lat. *pretendre*, Fr.]

1. To hold out; to stretch forward. This is mere Latinity, and not used.

Lucagus, to lash his horses, bends
Prone to the wheels, and his left foot *pretends*. *Dryden.*

2. To portend; to foreshow. Not in use.

All these movements seemed to be *pretended* by moving of the earth in Sussex. *Hayward.*

3. To make any appearance of having; to allege falsely.

This let him know,
Lest wilfully transgressing he *pretend*
Surprisal. *Milton.*

What reason then can any man *pretend* against religion, when it is so apparently for the benefit, not only of human society, but of every particular person. *Tillotson.*

4. To show hypocritically.

'Tis their interest to guard themselves from those riotous effects of *pretended* zeal, nor is it less their duty. *D. of Piety.*

5. To hold out as a delusive appearance; to exhibit as a cover of something hidden. This is rather Latin.

Warn all creatures from thee
Henceforth; lest that too heav'nly form, *pretended*
To hellish falshood, snare them. *Milton's Par. Lost.*

6. To claim. In this sense we rather say, *pretend to.*

Chiefs shall be grudg'd the part which they *pretend*. *Dry.*

Are they not rich? what more can they *pretend?* *Pope.*

To PRE'TEND. *v. n.*

1. To put in a claim truly or falsely. It is seldom used without shade of censure.

What peace can be, where both to one *pretend?*
But they more diligent, and we more strong. *Dryden.*

In those countries that *pretend* to freedom, princes are subject to those laws which their people have chosen. *Swift.*

2. To presume on ability to do any thing; to profess presumptuously.

Of the ground of redness in this sea are we not fully satisfied; for there is another red sea, whose name we *pretend* not to make out from these principles. *Brown.*

PRETE'NDER. *n. s.* [from *pretend.*] One who lays claim to any thing.

The prize was disputed only till you were seen; now all *pretenders* have withdrawn their claims. *Dryden.*

Whatever victories the several *pretenders* to the empire obtained over one another, they are recorded on coins without the least reflection. *Addison on Ancient Medals.*

The numerous *pretenders* to places would never have been kept in order, if expectation had been cut off. *Swift.*

To just contempt ye vain *pretenders* fall,
The people's fable and the scorn of all. *Pope.*

Pretenders to philosophy or good sense grow fond of this sort of learning. *Watts.*

PRETE'NDINGLY. *adv.* [from *pretending.*] Arrogantly; presumptuously.

I have a particular reason to look a little *pretendingly* at present. *Collier on Pride.*

PRETE'NSION. *n. s.* [*pretensio*, Lat. *pretention*, Fr.]

1. Claim true or false.

But if to unjust things thou dost pretend,
Ere they begin, let thy *pretensions* end. *Denham.*

Men indulge those opinions and practices, that favour their *pretensions.* *L'Estrange.*

The commons demand that the consulship should lie in common to the *pretensions* of any Roman. *Swift.*

2. Fictitious appearance. A Latin phrase or sense.

This was but an invention and *pretension* given out by the Spaniards. *Bacon.*

PRE'TER. *n. s.* [*præter*, Lat.] A particle, which prefixed to words of Latin original, signifies *beside.*

PRE'TERIMPERFECT. *adj.* In grammar, denotes the tense not perfectly past.

PRE'TERIT. *adj.* [*preterit*, Fr. *præteritus*, Lat.] Past.

PRETERI'TION. *n. s.* [*preterition*, Fr. from *preterit.*] The act of going past; the state of being past.

PRE'TERITNESS. *n. s.* [from *preterit.*] State of being past; not presence; not futurity.

We cannot conceive a *preteritness* still backwards in infinitum, that never was present, as we can an endless futurity, that never will be present; so that though one is potentially infinite, yet nevertheless the other is positively finite: and this reasoning doth not at all affect the eternal existence of the adorable divinity, in whose invariable nature there is no past nor future. *Bentley's Sermons.*

PRETERLA'PSED. *adj.* [*præterlapsus*, Lat.] Past and gone.

We look with a superstitious reverence upon the accounts of *preterlapsed* ages. *Glanvill's Sceps.*

Never was there so much of either, in any *preterlapsed* age, as in this. *Walker.*

PRETERLE'GAL. *adj.* [*preter* and *legal.*] Not agreeable to law.

I expected some evil customs *preterlegal*, and abuses personal, had been to be removed. *King Charles.*

PRETERMI'SSION. *n. s.* [*pretermission*, Fr. *prætermissio*, Lat.] The act of omitting.

To PRETERMI'T. *v. a.* [*prætermitto*, Lat.] To pass by.

The fees, that are termly given to these deputies, for recompence of their pains, I do purposely *pretermit*; because they be not certain. *Bacon.*

PRE'TERNATURAL. *adj.* [*præter* and *natural.*] Different from what is natural; irregular.

We will enquire into the cause of this vile and *preternatural* temper of mind, that should make a man please himself with that, which can no ways reach those faculties, which nature has made the proper seat of pleasure. *South's Sermons.*

That form, which the earth is under at present, is *preternatural*, like a statue made and broken again. *Burnet.*

PRE'TERNATURALLY. *adv.* [from *preternatural.*] In a manner different from the common order of nature.

Simple air, *preternaturally* attenuated by heat, will make itself room, and break and blow up all that which resisteth it. *Bacon's Nat. Hist.*

PRE'TERNATURALNESS. *n. s.* [from *preternatural.*] Manner different from the order of nature.

PRE'TERPERFECT. *adj.* [*præteritum perfectum*, Lat.] A grammatical term applied to the tense which denotes time absolutely past.

The same natural aversion to loquacity has of late made a considerable alteration in our language, by closing in one syllable the termination of our *preterperfect* tense, as drown'd, walk'd, for drowned, walked. *Addison's Spectator.*

PRE'TERPLUPERFECT. *adj.* [*præteritum plusquam perfectum*, Lat.] The grammatical epithet for the tense denoting time relatively past, or past before some other past time.

PRETE'XT. *n. s.* [*prætextus*, Lat. *pretexte*, Fr.] Pretence; false appearance; false allegation.

My *pretext* to strike at him admits
A good construction. *Shakesp. Coriolanus.*

Under this *pretext*, the means he sought
To ruin such whose might did much exceed
His pow'r to wrong. *Daniel's Civil War.*

As chymists gold from brass by fire would draw,
Pretexts are into treason forg'd by law. *Denham.*

I shall not say with how much, or how little *pretext* of reason they managed those disputes. *Decay of Piety.*

They suck the blood of those they depend upon, under a *pretext* of service and kindness. *L'Estrange.*

PRE'TOR. *n. s.* [*prætor*, Lat. *preteur*, Fr.] The Roman judge. It is now sometimes taken for a mayor.

Good Cinna, take this paper;
And look you lay it in the *pretor*'s chair. *Shakesp.*

Porphyrius, whom you Egypt's *pretor* made,
Is come from Alexandria to your aid. *Dryden.*

An advocate, pleading the cause of his client before one of the *pretors*, could only produce a single witness, in a point where the law required two. *Spectator*, N° 556.

PRETORIAN. *adj.* [*pretorianus*, Lat. *pretorien*, Fr.] Judicial; exercised by the pretor.

The chancery had the *pretorian* power for equity; the star-chamber had the censorian power for offences. *Bacon.*

PRE'TTILY. *adv.* [from *pretty.*] Neatly; elegantly; pleasingly without dignity or elevation.

How *prettily* the young swain seems to wash
The hand was fair before. *Shakesp. Winter's Tale.*

One saith *prettily*; in the quenching of the flame of a pestilent ague, nature is like people that come to quench the fire of a house; so busy, as one letteth another. *Bacon.*

Children, kept out of ill company, take a pride to behave themselves *prettily*, after the fashion of others. *Locke.*

PRE'TTINESS. *n. s.* [from *pretty.*] Beauty without dignity; neat elegance without elevation.

There is goodliness in the bodies of animals, as in the ox, greyhound and stag; or majesty and stateliness, as in the lion, horse, eagle and cock; grave awfulness, as in mastiffs; or elegancy and *prettiness*, as in lesser dogs and most sort of birds; all which are several modes of beauty. *More.*

Those drops of *prettiness*, scatteringly sprinkled amongst the creatures, were designed to defecate and exalt our conceptions, not to inveigle or detain our passions. *Boyle.*

PRETTY.

PRETTY. *adj.* [præt, finery, Sax. *pretto*, Italian; *prat*, *pratigh*, Dutch.]

1. Neat; elegant; pleasing without surprise or elevation.

Of these the idle Greeks have many *pretty* tales. *Raleigh.*

They found themselves involved in a train of mistakes, by taking up some *pretty* hypothesis in philosophy. *Watts.*

2. Beautiful without grandeur or dignity.

The *pretty* gentleman is the most complaisant creature in the world, and is always of my mind. *Spectator.*

3. It is used in a kind of diminutive contempt in poetry, and in conversation: as, *a* pretty *fellow indeed!*

A *pretty* task; and so I told the fool,
Who needs must undertake to please by rule. *Dryden.*
He'll make a *pretty* figure in a triumph,
And serve to trip before the victor's chariot. *Addison.*

4. Not very small. This is a very vulgar use.

A knight of Wales, with shipping and some *pretty* company, did go to discover those parts. *Abbot.*

Cut off the stalks of cucumbers, immediately after their bearing, close by the earth, and then cast a *pretty* quantity of earth upon the plant, and they will bear next year before the ordinary time. *Bacon's Nat. Hist.*

I would have a mount of some *pretty* height, leaving the wall of the enclosure breast high. *Bacon's Essays.*

Of this mixture we put a parcel into a crucible, and suffered it for a *pretty* while to continue red hot. *Boyle.*

A weazle a *pretty* way off stood leering at him. *L'Estr.*

PRE'TTY. *adv.* In some degree. This word is used before adverbs or adjectives to intend their signification: it is less than *very.*

The world begun to be *pretty* well stocked with people, and human industry drained those unhabitable places. *Burnet.*

I shall not enquire how far this lofty method may advance the reputation of learning; but I am *pretty* sure 'tis no great addition to theirs who use it. *Collier.*

A little voyage round the lake took up five days, though the wind was *pretty* fair for us all the while. *Addison.*

I have a fondness for a project, and a *pretty* tolerable genius that way myself. *Addison's Guardian,* Nº 107.

These colours were faint and dilute, unless the light was trajected obliquely; for by that means they became *pretty* vivid. *Newton's Opticks.*

This writer every where insinuates, and, in one place, *pretty* plainly professes himself a sincere christian. *Atterbury.*

The copper halfpence are coined by the publick, and every piece worth *pretty* near the value of the copper. *Swift.*

The first attempts of this kind were *pretty* modest. *Baker.*

To PRE'VAIL. *v. n.* [*prevaloir*, Fr. *prævalere*, Lat.]

1. To be in force; to have effect; to have power; to have influence.

This custom makes the short-sighted bigots, and the warier scepticks, as far as it *prevails.* *Locke.*

2. To overcome; to gain the superiority. With *on* or *upon*, sometimes *over* or *against.*

They that were your enemies, are his,
And have *prevail'd* as much *on* him as you. *Shakesp.*

Nor is it hard for thee to preserve me amidst the unjust hatred and jealousness of too many, which thou hast suffered to *prevail upon* me. *King Charles.*

I told you then he should *prevail*, and speed
On his bad errand. *Milton.*

The millenium *prevailed* long *against* the truth upon the strength of authority. *Decay of Piety.*

While Malbro's cannon thus *prevails* by land,
Britain's sea-chiefs by Anna's high command,
Resistless o'er the Thuscan billows ride. *Blackmore.*
Thus song could *prevail*
O'er death and o'er hell,
A conquest how hard and how glorious;
Though fate had fast bound her
With Styx nine times round her,
Yet musick and love were victorious. *Pope.*

This kingdom could never *prevail against* the united power of England. *Swift.*

3. To gain influence; to operate effectually.

4. To persuade or induce by entreaty. It has *with*, *upon* or *on* before the person persuaded.

With minds obdurate nothing *prevaileth*, as well they that preach, as they that read unto such, shall still have cause to complain with the prophets of old, who will give credit unto our teaching? *Hooker, b.* v. *s.* 22.

He was *prevailed with* to restrain the earl of Bristol upon his first arrival. *Clarendon.*

The serpent *with* me
Persuasively have so *prevail'd*, that I
Have also tasted. *Milton.*

They are more in danger to go out of the way, who are marching under the conduct of a guide, that it is an hundred to one will mislead them, than he that has not yet taken a step, and is likelier to be *prevailed on* to enquire after the right way. *Locke.*

There are four sorts of arguments that men, in their reasonings with others, make use of to *prevail on* them. *Locke.*

The gods pray
He would resume the conduct of the day,
Nor let the world be lost in endless night;
Prevail'd upon at last, again he took
The harness'd steeds, that still with horror shook. *Addis.*

Upon assurances of revolt, the queen was *prevailed with* to send her forces upon that expedition. *Swift.*

Prevail upon some judicious friend to be your constant hearer, and allow him the utmost freedom. *Swift.*

PREVAI'LING. *adj.* [from *prevail.*] Predominant; having most influence.

Probabilities, which cross men's appetites and *prevailing* passions, run the same fate: let never so much probability hang on one side of a covetous man's reasoning, and money on the other, it is easy to foresee which will outweigh. *Locke.*

Save the friendless infants from oppression;
Saints shall assist thee with *prevailing* prayers,
And warring angels combat on thy side. *Rowe.*

PREVAI'LMENT. *n. s.* [from *prevail.*] Prevalence.

Messengers
Of strong *prevailment* in unharden'd youth. *Shakesp.*

PRE'VALENCE. } *n. s.* [*prevalence*, Fr. *prævalentia*, low Lat.]
PRE'VALENCY. } Superiority; influence; predominance.

The duke better knew, what kind of arguments were of *prevalence* with him. *Clarendon.*

Others finding that, in former times, many churchmen were employed in the civil government, imputed their wanting of these ornaments their predecessors wore, to the power and *prevalency* of the lawyers. *Clarendon.*

Animals, whose forelegs supply the use of arms, hold, if not an equality in both, a *prevalency* oft times in the other. *Brown's Vulgar Errours.*

Why, fair one, would you not rely
On reason's force with beauty's join'd;
Could I their *prevalence* deny,
I must at once be deaf and blind. *Prior.*

Least of all does this precept imply, that we should comply with any thing that the *prevalence* of corrupt fashion has made reputable. *Rogers's Sermons.*

PRE'VALENT. *adj.* [*prævalens*, Lat.] Victorious; gaining superiority.

Brennus told the Roman ambassadors, that *prevalent* arms were as good as any title, and that valiant men might account to be their own as much as they could get. *Raleigh.*

On the foughten field,
Michael and his angels *prevalent* encamping. *Milton.*

The conduct of a peculiar providence made the instruments of that great design *prevalent* and victorious, and all those mountains of opposition to become plains. *South's Sermons.*

2. Predominant; powerful.

Eve! easily may faith admit, that all
The good which we enjoy, from heav'n descends;
But, that from us ought should ascend to heav'n,
So *prevalent*, as to concern the mind
Of God high-blest; or to incline his will;
Hard to belief may seem. *Milton's Par. Lost.*

This was the most received and *prevalent* opinion, when I first brought my collection up to London. *Woodward.*

PRE'VALENTLY. *adv.* [from *prevalent.*] Powerfully; forcibly.

The ev'ning-star so falls into the main,
To rise at morn more *prevalently* bright. *Prior.*

To PREVA'RICATE. *v. n.* [*prævaricor*, Lat. *prevariquer*, Fr.] To cavil; to quibble; to shuffle.

Laws are either disannulled or quite *prevaricated* through change and alteration of times, yet they are good in themselves. *Spenser.*

He *prevaricates* with his own understanding, and cannot seriously consider the strength, and discern the evidence of argumentations against his desires. *South.*

Whoever helped him to this citation, I desire he will never trust him more; for I would think better of himself, than that he would wilfully *prevaricate.* *Stillingfleet.*

PREVARICA'TION. *n. s.* [*prævaricatio*, Lat. *prevarication*, Fr. from *prevaricate.*] Shuffle; cavil.

Several Romans, taken prisoners by Hannibal, were released upon obliging themselves by an oath to return again to his camp: among these was one, who, thinking to elude the oath, went the same day back to the camp, on pretence of having forgot something; but this *prevarication* was so shocking to the Roman senate, that they ordered him to be delivered up to Hannibal. *Addison's Freeholder.*

PREVARICA'TOR. *n. s.* [*prævaricator*, Lat. *prevaricateur*, Fr. from *prevaricate.*] A caviller; a shuffler.

PREVE'NIENT. *adj.* [*præveniens*, Lat.] Preceding; going before; preventive.

From the mercy-seat above
Prevenient grace descending, had remov'd
The stony from their hearts, and made new flesh
Regenerate grow instead. *Milton's Par. Lost.*

To PREVE'NE. *v. a.* [*prævenio*, Lat.] To hinder.

If thy indulgent care
Had not *preven'd*, among unbody'd shades
I now had wander'd. *Philips.*

To PREVENT. *v. a.* [*prævenio*, Lat. *prevenir*, Fr.]

1. To go before as a guide; to go before, making the way easy.

Are we to forsake any true opinion, or to shun any requisite action, only because we have in the practice thereof been *prevented* by idolaters. *Hooker, b.* v. *s.* 12.

Prevent him with the blessings of goodness. *Psalm* xxi. 3.

Prevent us, O Lord, in all our doings with thy most gracious favour. *Common Prayer.*

Let thy grace, O Lord, always *prevent* and follow us. *Common Prayer.*

2. To go before; to be before; to anticipate.

Mine eyes *prevent* the night-watches, that I might be occupied in thy words. *Psalm* cxix. 4.

The same officer told us, he came to conduct us, and that he had *prevented* the hour, because we might have the whole day before us for our business. *Bacon.*

Nothing engendred doth *prevent* his meat:
Flies have their tables spread, ere they appear;
Some creatures have in winter what to eat;
Others do sleep. *Herbert's Temple of Sacred Poems.*

Soon shalt thou find, if thou but arm their hands,
Their ready guilt *preventing* thy commands;
Coud'st thou some great proportion'd mischief frame,
They'd prove the father from whose loins they came. *Pope.*

3. To preoccupy; to preengage; to attempt first.

Thou hast *prevented* us with offertures of love, even when we were thine enemies. *King Charles.*

4. To hinder; to obviate; to obstruct. This is now almost the only sense.

They *prevented* me in the day of my trouble; but the Lord was my upholder. *Psalm* xviii. 18.

I do find it cowardly and vile,
For fear of what might fall, so to *prevent*
The time of life. *Shakesp. Julius Cæsar.*

This your sincerest care could not *prevent*,
Foretold so lately what would come to pass. *Milton.*

Too great confidence in success is the likeliest to *prevent* it; because it hinders us from making the best use of the advantages which we enjoy. *Atterbury.*

To PRE'VENT. *v. n.* To come before the time. A latinism.

Strawberries watered with water, wherein hath been steeped sheep's dung, will *prevent* and come early. *Bacon's Nat. Hist.*

PREVE'NTER. *n. s.* [from *prevent.*]

1. One that goes before.

The archduke was the assailant, and the *preventer*, and had the fruit of his diligence and celerity. *Bacon.*

2. One that hinders; an hinderer; an obstructer.

PREVE'NTION. *n. s.* [*prevention*, Fr. from *preventum*, Lat.]

1. The act of going before.

The greater the distance, the greater the *prevention*; as in thunder, where the lightning precedeth the crack a good space. *Bacon.*

No odds appear'd
In might or swift *prevention.* *Milton.*

2. Preoccupation; anticipation.

Atchievements, plots, orders, *preventions*,
Success or loss. *Shakesp.*

3. Hinderance; obstruction.

Half way he met
His daring foe, at this *prevention* more
Incens'd. *Milton.*

Prevention of sin is one of the greatest mercies God can vouchsafe. *South's Sermons.*

4. Prejudice; prepossession. A French expression.

In reading what I have written, let them bring no particular gusto or any *prevention* of mind, and that whatsoever judgment they make, it may be purely their own. *Dryden.*

PREVE'NTIONAL. *adj.* [from *prevention.*] Tending to prevention. *Dict.*

PREVE'NTIVE. *adj.* [from *prevent.*]

1. Tending to hinder.

Wars *preventive* upon just fears are true defensives, as well as upon actual invasions. *Bacon.*

2. Preservative; hindering ill. It has *of* before the thing prevented.

Physick is curative or *preventive* of diseases; *preventive* is that which, by purging noxious humours, preventeth sickness. *Brown.*

Procuring a due degree of sweat and perspiration, is the best *preventive* of the gout. *Arbuthnot.*

PREVE'NTIVE. *n. s.* [from *prevent.*] A preservative; that which prevents; an antidote.

PREVE'NTIVELY. *adv.* [from *preventive.*] In such a manner as tends to prevention.

Such as fearing to concede a monstrosity, or mutilate the integrity of Adam, *preventively* conceive the creation of thirteen ribs. *Brown's Vulgar Errours.*

PRE'VIOUS. *adj.* [*prævius*, Lat.] Antecedent; going before; prior.

By this *previous* intimation we may gather some hopes, that the matter is not desperate. *Burnet's Theory of the Earth.*

Sound from the mountain, *previous* to the storm,
Rolls o'er the muttering Earth. *Thomson.*

PRE'VIOUSLY. *adv.* [from *previous.*] Beforehand; antecedently.

Darting their stings, they *previously* declare
Design'd revenge, and fierce intent of war. *Prior.*

It cannot be reconciled with perfect sincerity, as *previously* supposing some neglect of better information. *Fiddes.*

PRE'VIOUSNESS. *n. s.* [from *previous.*] Antecedence.

PREY. *n. s.* [*præda*, Lat.]

1. Something to be devoured; something to be seized; food gotten by violence; ravine; wealth gotten by violence; plunder.

A garrison supported itself, by the *prey* it took from the neighbourhood of Aylesbury. *Clarendon, b.* viii.

The whole included race his purpos'd *prey.* *Milton.*

She sees herself the monster's *prey*,
And feels her heart and intrails torn away. *Dryden.*

Pindar, that eagle, mounts the skies,
While virtue leads the noble way;
Too like a vulture Boileau flies,
Where sordid int'rest shews the *prey.* *Prior.*

2. Ravage; depredation.

Hog in sloth, fox in stealth, lion in *prey.* *Shakesp.*

3. Animal of *prey*, is an animal that lives on other animals.

There are men of *prey*, as well as beasts and birds of *prey*, that live upon, and delight in blood. *L'Estrange.*

To PREY. *v. n.* [*prædor*, Lat.]

1. To feed by violence. With *on* before the object.

A lioness
Lay couching head on ground, with cat-like watch,
When that the sleeping man should stir: for 'tis
The royal disposition of that beast
To *prey on* nothing that doth seem as dead. *Shakesp.*

Put your torches out;
The wolves have *prey'd*, and look the gentle day
Dapples the drowsy east. *Shakesp.*

Jove venom first infus'd in serpents fell,
Taught wolves to *prey*, and stormy seas to swell. *May.*

Their impious folly dar'd to *prey*
On herds devoted to the god of day. *Pope.*

2. To plunder; to rob.

They pray continually unto their saint the commonwealth, or rather not pray to her, but *prey* on her; for they ride up and down on her, and make her their boots. *Shakesp.*

3. To corrode; to waste.

Language is too faint to show
His rage of love; it *preys* upon his life;
He pines, he sickens, he despairs, he dies. *Addison.*

PRE'YER. *n. s.* [from *prey.*] Robber; devourer; plunderer.

PRI'APISM. *n. s.* [*priapismus*, Lat. *priapisme*, Fr.] A preternatural tension.

Lust causeth a flagrancy in the eyes and *priapism.* *Bacon.*

The person every night has a *priapism* in his sleep. *Floyer.*

PRICE. *n. s.* [*prix*, Fr. *pretium*, Lat.]

1. Equivalent paid for any thing.

I will buy it of thee at a *price*; neither will I offer burnt-offerings unto the Lord my God, of that which cost me nothing. 2 *Samuel* xxiv. 24.

From that which hath its *price* in composition, if you take away any thing, or any part do fail, all is disgrace. *Bacon.*

If fortune has a niggard been to thee,
Devote thyself to thrift, not luxury;
And wisely make that kind of food thy choice,
To which necessity confines thy *price.* *Dryden.*

2. Value; estimation; supposed excellence.

We stand in some jealousy, lest by thus overvaluing their sermons; they make the *price* and estimation of scripture, otherwise notified, to fall. *Hooker.*

Sugar hath put down the use of honey, inasmuch as we have lost those preparations of honey which the ancients had, when it was more in *price.* *Bacon.*

3. Rate at which any thing is sold.

Supposing the quantity of wheat, in respect to its vent be the same, that makes the change in the *price* of wheat. *Locke.*

4. Reward; thing purchased at any rate.

Sometimes virtue starves, while vice is fed;
What then? is the reward of virtue bread?
That, vice may merit; 'tis the *price* of toil;
The knave deserves it, when he tills the soil. *Pope.*

To PRICE. *v. a.* To pay for.

Some shall pay the price of others guilt;
And he the man that made sans foy to fall,
Shall with his own blood *price* that he hath spilt. *F. Queen.*

To PRICK. *v. a.* [prician, Saxon.]

1. To pierce with a small puncture.

Leave her to heav'n,
And to those thorns that in her bosom lodge,
To *prick* and sting her. *Shakesp. Hamlet.*

There shall be no more a *pricking* brier unto the house of Israel, nor any grieving thorn. *Ezekiel* xxviii. 24.

If she *pricked* her finger, Jack laid the pin in the way. *Arb.*

2. To form or erect with an acuminated point.

The poets make fame a monster; they say, look how many feathers she hath, so many eyes she hath underneath, so many tongues, so many voices, she *pricks* up so many ears. *Bacon's Essays.*

A hunted

A hunted panther casts about
Her glaring eyes, and *pricks* her list'ning ears to scout. *Dry.*
His rough crest he rears,
And *pricks* up his predestinating ears. *Dryden.*
The fiery courser, when he hears from far
The sprightly trumpets and the shouts of war,
Pricks up his ears. *Dryden's Virgil's Georg.*

A greyhound hath *pricked* ears, but those of a hound hang down; for that the former hunts with his ears, the latter only with his nose. *Grew.*

The tuneful noise the sprightly courser hears,
Paws the green turf, and *pricks* his trembling ears. *Gay.*
Keep close to ears, and those let asses *prick*;
'Tis nothing—nothing; if they bite and kick. *Pope.*

3. To fix by the point.

I caused the edges of two knives to be ground truly strait, and *pricking* their points into a board, so that their edges might look towards one another, and meeting near their points contain a rectilinear angle, I fastened their handles together with pitch, to make this angle invariable. *Newton.*

4. To hang on a point.

The cooks slice it into little gobbets, *prick* it on a prong of iron, and hang it in a furnace. *Sandys.*

5. To nominate by a puncture or mark.

Those many then shall die, their names are *prickt.* *Shakespeare.*

Some who are *pricked* for sheriffs, and are fit, set out of the bill. *Bacon.*

6. To spur; to goad; to impel; to incite.

When I call to mind your gracious favours,
My duty *pricks* me on to utter that,
Which else no worldly good should draw from me. *Shakesp.*
Well, 'tis no matter, honour *pricks* me on;
But how if honour *prick* me off, when
I come on. *Shakesp. Henry IV.*
His high courage *prick'd* him forth to wed. *Pope.*

7. To pain; to pierce with remorse.

When they heard this, they were *pricked* in their hearts, and said, men and brethren what shall we do? *Acts* ii. 37.

8. To make acid.

They their late attacks decline,
And turn as eager as *prick'd* wine. *Hudibras, p.* ii.

9. To mark a tune.

To Prick. *v. n.* [*prijken*, Dutch.]

1. To dress one's self for show.

2. To come upon the spur. This seems to be the sense in *Spenser.*

After that Varlet's flight, it was not long,
Ere on the plain fast *pricking* Guyon spied,
One in bright arms embattled full strong. *Fa. Queen.*
A gentle knight was *pricking* on the plain,
Yclad in mighty arms of silver shield. *Fa. Queen.*
They had not ridden far, when they might see
One *pricking* towards them with hasty heat. *Fa. Queen.*

The Scottish horsemen began to hover much upon the English army, and to come *pricking* about them, sometimes within length of their staves. *Hayward.*

Before each van
Prick forth the airy knights. *Milton.*
In this king Arthur's reign,
A lusty knight was *pricking* o'er the plain. *Dryden.*

Prick. *n. s.* [pꞃıcca, Saxon.]

1. A sharp slender instrument; any thing by which a puncture is made.

The country gives me proof
Of bedlam beggars, who, with roaring voices,
Strike in their numb'd and mortified bare arms
Pins, wooden *pricks*, nails, sprigs of rosemary. *Shakesp.*

It is hard for thee to kick against the *pricks.* *Acts* ix. 5.

If the English would not in peace govern them by the law, nor could in war root them out by the sword, must they not be *pricks* in their eyes, and thorns in their sides. *Davies.*

If God would have had men live like wild beasts, he would have armed them with horns, tusks, talons or *pricks.* *Bramh.*

2. A thorn in the mind; a teasing and tormenting thought; remorse of conscience.

My conscience first receiv'd a tenderness,
Scruple, and *prick*, on certain speeches utter'd
By th' bishop of Bayon. *Shakesp. Henry VIII.*

3. A spot or mark at which archers aim.

For long shooting, their shaft was a cloth yard, their *pricks* twenty-four score; for strength, they would pierce any ordinary armour. *Carew's Survey of Cornwall.*

4. A point; a fixed place.

Now gins this goodly frame of temperance
Fairly to rise, and her adorned head
To *prick* of highest praise forth to advance. *Spenser.*
Phaeton hath tumbled from his car,
And made an evening at the noon-tide *prick.* *Shakesp.*

5. A puncture.

No asps were discovered in the place of her death, only two small insensible *pricks* were found in her arm. *Brown.*

6. The print of a hare in the ground.

Pri'cker. *n. s.* [from *prick.*]

1. A sharp-pointed instrument.

Pricker is vulgarly called an awl; yet, for joiner's use, it hath most commonly a square blade. *Moxon's Mechan. Exer.*

2. A light horseman.

They had horsemen, *prickers* as they are termed, fitter to make excursions and to chace, than to sustain any strong charge. *Hayward.*

Pri'cket. *n. s.* [from *prick.*] A buck in his second year.

I've call'd the deer; the princess kill'd a *pricket.* *Shakesp.*

The buck is called the first year a fawn, the second year a *pricket.* *Manwood of the Laws of the Forest.*

Pri'ckle. *n. s.* [from *prick.*] Small sharp point, like that of a brier.

The *prickles* of trees are a kind of excrescence; the plants that have *prickles*, are black and white, those have it in the bough; the plants that have *prickles* in the leaf, are holly and juniper; nettles also have a small venomous *prickle.* *Bacon.*

An herb growing in the water, called lincostis, is full of *prickles*: this putteth forth another small herb out of the leaf, imputed to moisture gathered between the *prickles.* *Bacon.*

A fox catching hold of a bramble to break his fall, the *prickles* ran into his feet. *L'Estrange.*

The man who laugh'd but once to see an ass
Mumbling to make the cross-grain'd thistles pass,
Might laugh again, to see a jury chaw
The *prickles* of unpalatable law. *Dryden.*
The flower's divine, where'er it grows,
Neglect the *prickles*, and assume the rose. *Watts.*

Pri'ckliness. *n. s.* [from *prickly.*] Fullness of sharp points.

Pri'cklouse. *n. s.* [*prick* and *louse.*] A word of contempt for a taylor. A low word.

A taylor and his wife quarreling; the woman in contempt called her husband *pricklouse.* *L'Estrange.*

Pri'cksong. *n. s.* [*prick* and *song.*] Song set to musick.

He fights as you sing *pricksongs*, keeps time, distance and proportion. *Shakesp. Romeo and Juliet.*

Pri'ckly. *adj.* [from *prick.*] Full of sharp points.

Artichoaks will be less *prickly* and more tender, if the seeds have their tops grated off upon a stone. *Bacon.*

I no more
Shall see you browzing, on the mountain's brow,
The *prickly* shrubs. *Dryden.*
How did the humbled swain detest
His *prickly* beard, and hairy breast! *Swift's Miscel.*

Pri'ckmadam. *n. s.* A species of houseleek, which see.

Pri'ckpunch. *n. s.*

Prickpunch is a piece of tempered steel, with a round point at one end, to prick a round mark in cold iron. *Moxon.*

Prickwood. *n. s.* A tree. *Ainsworth.*

Pride. *n. s.* [pꞃyꞇe or pꞃyꝺ, Saxon.]

1. Inordinate and unreasonable self-esteem.

I can see his *pride*
Peep through each part of him. *Shakesp. Henry VIII.*
Pride hath no other glass
To shew itself, but *pride*; for supple knees
Feed arrogance, and are the proud man's fees. *Shakesp.*
He his wonted *pride* soon recollects. *Milton.*
Vain aims, inordinate desires
Blown up with high conceits engend'ring *pride.* *Milton.*

2. Insolence; rude treatment of others; insolent exultation.

That witch
Hath wrought this hellish mischief unawares;
That hardly we escap'd the *pride* of France. *Shakesp.*
They undergo
This annual humbling certain number'd days,
To dash their *pride* and joy for man seduc'd. *Milton.*
Wantonness and *pride*
Raise out of friendship, hostile deeds in peace. *Milton.*

3. Dignity of manner; loftiness of air.

4. Generous elation of heart.

The honest *pride* of conscious virtue. *Smith.*

5. Elevation; dignity.

A falcon, tow'ring in her *pride* of place,
Was by a mousing owl hawkt at and kill'd. *Shakesp.*

6. Ornament; show; decoration.

Whose lofty trees, yclad with summer's *pride*,
Did spread so broad, that heavens light did hide. *F. Qu.*
Smallest lineaments exact,
In all the liveries deck'd of summer's *pride.* *Milton.*
Be his this sword,
Whose ivory sheath, inwrought with curious *pride*,
Adds graceful terror to the wearer's side. *Pope.*

7. Splendour; ostentation.

In this array the war of either side,
Through Athens pass'd with military *pride.* *Dryden.*

8. The state of a female beast soliciting the male.

It is impossible you should see this,
Were they as salt as wolves in *pride.* *Shakesp.*

To Pride. *v. a.* [from the noun.] To make proud; to rate himself high. It is only used with the reciprocal pronoun.

He could have made the most deformed beggar as rich, as those who most *pride themselves* in their wealth. *Go. of the Ton.*

This little impudent hardware-man turns into ridicule the direful apprehensions of the whole kingdom, *priding himself* as the cause of them. *Swift's Miscel.*

PRIE. *n. s.* I suppose an old name of privet.

Lop popler and sallow, elme, maple and *prie*,
Wel saved from cattel, till summer to lie. *Tusser.*

PRIEF for *proof.* *Spenser.*

PRI'ER. *n. s.* [from *pry.*] One who enquires too narrowly.

PRIEST. *n. s.* [ꝑꞃeoꞅꞇ, Sax. *prestre*, Fr.]

1. One who officiates in sacred offices.

I'll to the vicar,
Bring you the maid, you shall not lack a *priest*. *Shakesp.*

The high *priest* shall not uncover his head. *Lev.* xxi. 10.

Our practice of singing differs from the practice of David, the *priests* and Levites. *Peacham.*

These pray'rs I thy *priest* before thee bring. *Milton.*

2. One of the second order in the hierarchy, above a deacon, below a bishop.

No neighbours, but a few poor simple clowns,
Honest and true, with a well-meaning *priest*. *Rowe.*

PRI'ESTCRAFT. *n. s.* [*priest* and *craft.*] Religious frauds; management of wicked priests to gain power.

Puzzle has half a dozen common-place topicks; though the debate be about Doway, his discourse runs upon bigotry and *priestcraft*. *Spectator.*

From *priestcraft* happily set free,
Lo! ev'ry finish'd son returns to thee. *Pope.*

PRIE'STESS. *n. s.* [from *priest.*] A woman who officiated in heathen rites.

Then too, our mighty sire, thou stood'st disarm'd,
When thy rapt soul the lovely *priestess* charm'd,
That Rome's high founder bore. *Addison.*

These two, being the sons of a lady who was *priestess* to Juno, drew their mother's chariot to the temple. *Spectator.*

She as *priestess* knows the rites,
Wherein the God of earth delights. *Swift's Miscel.*

Th' inferior *priestess*, at her altar's side,
Trembling, begins the sacred rites of pride. *Pope.*

PRIE'STHOOD. *n. s.* [from *priest.*]

1. The office and character of a priest.

Jeroboam is reproved, because he took the *priesthood* from the tribe of Levi. *Whitgifte.*

The *priesthood* hath in all nations, and all religions, been held highly venerable. *Atterbury's Sermons.*

2. The order of men set apart for holy offices.

Is your *priesthood* grown so peremptory? *Shakesp.*

He pretends, that I have fallen foul on *priesthood*. *Dryden.*

3. The second order of the hierarchy. See PRIEST.

PRIE'STLINESS. *n. s.* [from *priestly.*] The appearance or manner of a priest.

PRIE'STLY. *adj.* [from *priest.*] Becoming a priest; sacerdotal; belonging to a priest.

In the Jewish church, none that was blind or lame was capable of the *priestly* office. *South's Sermons.*

How can incest suit with holiness,
Or *priestly* orders with a princely state? *Dryden.*

PRIE'STRIDDEN. *adj.* [*priest* and *ridden.*] Managed or governed by priests.

Such a cant of high-church and persecution, and being *priestridden*. *Swift.*

To PRIEVE for *prove.* *Spenser.*

PRIG. *n. s.* [A cant word derived perhaps from *prick*, as he *pricks* up, he is *pert*; or from *prickeared*, an epithet of reproach bestowed upon the presbyterian teachers.] A pert, conceited, saucy, pragmatical, little fellow.

The little man concluded, with calling monsieur Mesnager an insignificant *prig*. *Spectator*, Nº 482.

There have I seen some active *prig*,
To shew his parts, bestride a twig. *Swift's Miscel.*

PRILL. *n. s.* A birt or turbot. *Ainsworth.*

PRIM. *adj.* [by contraction from *primitive.*] Formal; precise; affectedly nice.

A ball of new dropt horse's dung,
Mingling with apples in the throng,
Said to the pippin, plump and *prim*,
See, brother, how we apples swim. *Swift's Miscel.*

To PRIM. *v. a.* [from the adjective.] To deck up precisely; to form to an affected nicety.

PRI'MACY. *n. s.* [*primatie*, *primace*, Fr. *primatus*, Lat.] The chief ecclesiastical station.

When he had now the *primacy* in his own hand, he thought he should be to blame if he did not apply remedies. *Clarend.*

PRI'MAGE. *n. s.* The freight of a ship. *Ainsworth.*

PRI'MAL. *adj.* [*primus*, Lat.] First. A word not in use, but very commodious for poetry.

It hath been taught us from the *primal* state,
That he, which is, was wish'd, until he were. *Shakesp.*

Oh! my offence is rank, it smells to heav'n,
It hath the *primal*, eldest curse upon't. *Shakesp.*

PRI'MARILY. *adv.* [from *primary.*] Originally; in the first intention; in the first place.

In fevers, where the heart *primarily* suffereth, we apply medicines unto the wrists. *Brown's Vulgar Errours.*

These considerations so exactly suiting the parable of the wedding-supper to this spiritual banquet of the gospel, if it does not *primarily*, and in its first design, intend it; yet certainly it may, with greater advantage of resemblance, be applied to it, than to any other duty. *South's Sermons.*

PRI'MARINESS. *n. s.* [from *primary.*] The state of being first in act or intention.

That which is peculiar, must be taken from the *primariness* and secondariness of the perception. *Norris.*

PRI'MARY. *adj.* [*primarius*, Lat.]

1. First in intention.

The figurative notation of this word, and not the *primary* or literal, belongs to this place. *Hammond.*

2. Original; first.

Before that beginning, there was neither *primary* matter to be informed, nor form to inform, nor any being but the eternal. *Raleigh's History of the World.*

When the ruins both *primary* and secondary were settled, the waters of the abyss began to settle too. *Burnet.*

These I call original or *primary* qualities of body, which produce simple ideas in us, *viz.* solidity, extension, figure and motion. *Locke.*

3. First in dignity; chief; principal.

As the six *primary* planets revolve about him, so the secondary ones are moved about them in the same sesquialteral proportion of their periodical motions to their orbs. *Bentley.*

PRI'MATE. *n. s.* [*primat*, Fr. *primas*, Lat.] The chief ecclesiastick.

When the power of the church was first established, the archbishops of Canterbury and York had then no preheminence one over the other; the former being *primate* over the Southern, as the latter was over the Northern parts. *Ayliffe.*

The late and present *primate*, and the lord archbishop of Dublin hath left memorials of his bounty. *Swift.*

PRI'MATESHIP. *n. s.* [from *primate.*] The dignity or office of a primate.

PRIME. *n. s.* [*primus*, Lat.]

1. The first part of the day; the dawn; the morning.

His larum bell might loud and wide be heard
When cause requir'd, but never out of time,
Early and late it rung at evening and at *prime*. *Spenser.*

Sure pledge of day, that crown'st the smiling morn
With thy bright circlet, praise him in thy sphere
While day arises, that sweet hour of *prime*. *Milton.*

2. The beginning; the early days.

Quickly sundry arts mechanical were found out in the very *prime* of the world. *Hooker, b.* i. *s.*

Nature here wanton'd as in her *prime*. *Milton.*

3. The best part.

Give no more to ev'ry guest,
Than he's able to digest,
Give him always of the *prime*,
And but little at a time. *Swift.*

4. The spring of life; the height of health, strength or beauty.

Make haste, sweet love, whilst it is *prime*,
For none can call again the passed time. *Spenser.*

Will she yet debase her eyes on me,
That cropt the golden *prime* of this sweet prince,
And made her widow to a woful bed? *Shakesp. Rich. III.*

Youth, beauty, wisdom, courage, virtue, all
That happiness and *prime* can happy call. *Shakesp.*

Likeliest she seem'd to Ceres in her *prime*. *Milton.*

No poet ever sweetly sung,
Unless he were, like Phœbus, young;
Nor ever nymph inspir'd to rhyme,
Unless, like Venus, in her *prime*. *Swift.*

Short were her marriage joys; for in the *prime*
Of youth, her lord expir'd before his time. *Dryden.*

5. Spring.

Hope waits upon the flow'ry *prime*,
And summer, though it be less gay,
Yet is not look'd on as a time
Of declination or decay. *Waller.*

The poet and his theme in spite of time,
For ever young enjoys an endless *prime*. *Granville.*

6. The height of perfection.

The plants which now appear in the most different seasons would have been all in *prime*, and flourishing together at the same time. *Woodward.*

7. The first canonical hour. *Ainsworth.*

8. The first part; the beginning: as, *the* prime *of the moon.*

PRIME. *adj.* [*primus*, Lat.]

1. Early; blooming.

His starry helm unbuckl'd, shew'd him *prime*
In manhood, where youth ended. *Milton's Par. Lost.*

2. Principal; first rate.

Divers of *prime* quality, in several counties, were, for refusing to pay the same, committed to prison. *Clarendon.*

Nor can I think, that God will so destroy
We his *prime* creatures dignify'd so high. *Milton.*

Humility and resignation are our *prime* virtues. *Dryden.*

3. First

3. First; original.

We smother'd
The most replenished sweet work of nature,
That from the *prime* creation e'er she fram'd. *Shakesp.*

Moses being chosen by God to be the ruler of his people, will not prove that priesthood belonged to Adam's heir, or the *prime* fathers. *Locke.*

4. Excellent. It may, in this loose sense, perhaps admit, though scarcely with propriety, a superlative.

We are contented with
Catharine our queen, before the *primest* creature
That's paragon'd i' th' world. *Shakesp. Henry* VIII.

To PRIME. *v. a.* [from the noun.]

1. To put in the first powder; to put powder in the pan of a gun.

A pistol of about a foot in length, we *primed* with well-dried gunpowder. *Boyle.*

Prime all your firelocks, fasten well the stake. *Gay.*
His friendship was exactly tim'd,
He shot before your foes were *prim'd*. *Swift's Miscel.*

2. [*Primer*, Fr. to begin.] To lay the first colours on in painting. A Gallicism.

PRI'MELY. *adv.* [from *prime.*]

1. Originally; primarily; in the first place; in the first intention.

Words signify not immediately and *primely* things themselves, but the conceptions of the mind about them. *South*

2. Excellently; supremely well. A low sense.

PRI'MENESS. *n. s.* [from *prime.*]

1. The state of being first.
2. Excellence.

PRI'MER. *n. s.*

1. An office of the blessed Virgin.

Another prayer to her is not only in the manual, but in the *primer* or office of the blessed Virgin. *Stillingfleet.*

2. [*Primarius*, Lat.] A small prayer book in which children are taught to read, so named from the Romish book of devotions; an elementary book.

The Lord's prayer, the creed and ten commandments he should learn by heart, not by reading them himself in his *primer*, but by somebody's repeating them before he can read. *Locke on Education.*

PRIME'RO. *n. s.* [Spanish.] A game at cards.

I left him at *primero*
With the duke of Suffolk. *Shakesp. Henry* VIII.

PRIME'VAL. } *adj.* [*primævus*, Lat.] Original; such as was
PRIME'VOUS. } at first.

Immortal dove,
Thou with almighty energy did'st move
On the wild waves, incumbent did'st display
Thy genial wings, and hatch *primeval* day. *Blackmore.*

All the parts of this great fabrick change;
Quit their old stations and *primeval* frame,
And lose their shape, their essence, and their name. *Prior.*

PRIMI'TIAL. *adj.* [*primitius*, *primitiæ*, Lat.] Being of the first production. *Ainsworth.*

PRI'MITIVE. *adj.* [*primitif*, Fr. *primitivus*, Lat.]

1. Ancient; original; established from the beginning.

Their superstition pretends, they cannot do God greater service, than utterly to destroy the *primitive* apostolical government of the church by bishops. *King Charles.*

David reflects sometimes upon the present form of the world, and sometimes upon the *primitive* form of it. *Burnet.*

The doctrine of purgatory, by which they mean an estate of temporary punishments after this life, was not known in the *primitive* church, nor can be proved from scripture. *Tillots.*

2. Formal; affectedly solemn; imitating the supposed gravity of old times.

3. Original; primary; not derivative: as, in grammar, *a* primitive *verb.*

Our *primitive* great sire, to meet
His godlike guest, walks forth. *Milton.*

PRI'MITIVELY. *adv.* [from *primitive.*]

1. Originally; at first.

Solemnities and ceremonies, *primitively* enjoined, were afterward omitted, the occasion ceasing. *Brown.*

2. Primarily; not derivatively.

3. According to the original rule; according to ancient practice.

The purest and most *primitively* reformed church in the world was laid in the dust. *South's Sermons.*

PRI'MITIVENESS. *n. s.* [from *primitive.*] State of being original; antiquity; conformity to antiquity.

PRI'MNESS. *n. s.* [from *prim.*] Affected niceness or formality.

PRIMOGE'NIAL. *adj.* [*primigenius*, Lat. it should therefore have been written *primigenial.*] Firstborn; original; primary; constituent; elemental.

The *primogenial* light at first was diffused over the face of the unfashioned chaos. *Glanvill's Sceps.*

It is not easy to discern, among many differing substances obtained from the same matter, what *primogenial* and simple bodies convened together compose it. *Boyle.*

The first or *primogenial* earth, which rose out of the chaos, was not like the present earth. *Burnet's Theory of the Earth.*

PRIMOGE'NITURE. *n. s.* [*primogeniture*, Fr. from *primo genitus*, Lat.] Seniority; eldership; state of being firstborn.

Because the scripture affordeth the priority of order unto Sem, we cannot from hence infer his *primogeniture*. *Brown.*

The first provoker has, by his seniority and *primogeniture*, a double portion of the guilt. *Government of the Tongue.*

PRIMO'RDIAL. *adj.* [*primordial*, Fr. *primordium*, Lat.] Original; existing from the beginning.

Salts may be either transmuted or otherwise produced, and so may not be *primordial* and immutable beings. *Boyle.*

PRIMO'RDIAL. *n. s.* [from the adj.] Origin; first principle.

The *primordials* of the world are not mechanical, but spermatical and vital. *More's Divine Dialogues.*

PRIMO'RDIAN. *n. s.* See PLUM, of which it is a species.

PRIMO'RDIATE. *adj.* [from *primordium*, Lat.] Original; existing from the first.

Not every thing chymists will call salt, sulphur or spirit, that needs always be a *primordiate* and ingenerable body. *Boyle.*

PRI'MROSE. *n. s.* [*primula veris*, Lat.] A plant.

The flower of the *primrose* consists of one leaf, the lower part of which is tubulose, but the upper part expands itself flat in form of a salver, and is cut into several segments; from the flower-cup, which is fistulous, arises the pointal, which, when the flower is decayed, becomes an oblong fruit or husk, lying almost concealed in the flower-cup, and opens at the top, in which are contained many roundish seeds fastened to the placenta. *Miller.*

Pale *primroses*,
That die unmarried, ere they can behold
Bright Phœbus in his strength. *Shakesp. Winter's Tale.*
I would look pale as *primrose*. *Shakesp. Henry* VI.

There followeth, for the latter part of January, *primroses*, anemonies, the early tulip. *Bacon's Essays.*

2. *Primrose* is used by *Shakespeare* for gay or flowery.

I had thought to have let in some of all professions, that go the *primrose* way to the everlasting bonefire. *Shakesp.*

PRINCE. *n. s.* [*prince*, Fr. *princeps*, Lat.]

1. A sovereign; a chief ruler.

Cœlestial! whether among the thrones, or nam'd
Of them the highest; for such of shape may seem
Prince above *princes*. *Milton's Par. Lost, b.* xi.

Forces come to be used by good *princes*, only upon necessity of providing for their defence. *Temple.*

Esau founded a distinct people and government, and was himself a distinct *prince* over them. *Locke.*

The succession of crowns, in several countries, places it on different heads, and he comes, by succession, to be a *prince* in one place, who would be a subject in another. *Locke.*

Had we no histories of the Roman emperors, but on their money, we should take them for most virtuous *princes*. *Addison.*

Our tottering state still distracted stands,
While that *prince* threatens, and while this commands. *Pope.*

2. A sovereign of rank next to kings.

3. Ruler of whatever sex.

Queen Elizabeth, a *prince* admirable above her sex for her princely virtues. *Camden.*

God put it into the heart of one of our *princes*, towards the close of her reign, to give a check to that sacrilege. *Atter.*

4. The son of a king; in England only the eldest son; the kinsman of a sovereign.

A *prince* of great courage and beauty, but fostered up in blood by his naughty father. *Sidney, b.* ii.

Heav'n forbid, that such a scratch should drive
The *prince* of Wales from such a field as this. *Shakesp.*

5. The chief of any body of men.

To use the words of the *prince* of learning hereupon, only in shallow and small boats, they glide over the face of the Virgilian sea. *Peacham on Poetry.*

To PRINCE. *v. n.* To play the prince; to take state.

Nature prompts them,
In simple and low things, to *prince* it, much
Beyond the trick of others. *Shakesp. Cymbeline.*

PRI'NCEDOM. *n. s.* [from *prince.*] The rank, estate or power of the prince; sovereignty.

Next Archigald, who, for his proud disdain,
Deposed was from *princedom* sovereign. *Fairy Queen.*

Under thee, as head supreme
Thrones, *princedoms*, pow'rs, dominions, I reduce. *Milton.*

PRI'NCELIKE. *adj.* [*prince* and *like.*] Becoming a prince.

The wrongs he did me were nothing *princelike*. *Shakesp.*

PRI'NCELINESS. *n. s.* [from *princely.*] The state, manner or dignity of a prince.

PRI'NCELY. *adj.* [from *prince.*]

1. Having the appearance of one highborn.

In war, was never lion rag'd more fierce,
In peace, was never gentle lamb more mild,
Than was that young and *princely* gentleman. *Shakesp.*

2. Having the rank of princes.

Meaning only to do honour to their *princely* birth, they flew among them all. *Sidney, b.* ii.

Be opposite all planets of good luck
To my proceeding; if with pure heart's love,
I tender not thy beauteous *princely* daughter. *Shakesp.*

The

The *princely* hierarch left his pow'rs to seize
Possession of the garden. *Milton.*

I expressed her commands
To mighty lords and *princely* dames. *Waller.*

So fled the dame, and o'er the ocean bore
Her *princely* burthen to the Gallick shore. *Waller.*

3. Becoming a prince; royal; grand; august.

I, that but now refus'd most *princely* gifts,
Am bound to beg of my lord general. *Shakesp.*

Princely counsel in his face yet shone. *Milton.*

Born to command, your *princely* virtues slept
Like humble David's, while the flock he kept. *Waller.*

PRI'NCELY. *adv.* [from *prince.*] In a princelike manner.

PRINCES-FEATHER. *n. s.* The herb amaranth. *Ains.*

PRI'NCESS. *n. s.* [*princesse*, Fr.]

1. A sovereign lady; a woman having sovereign command.

Ask why God's anointed he revil'd;
A king and *princess* dead. *Dryden.*

Princess ador'd and lov'd, if verse can give
A deathless name, thine shall for ever live. *Granvil.*

Under so excellent a *princess* as the present queen, we suppose a family strictly regulated. *Swift.*

2. A sovereign lady of rank, next to that of a queen.

3. The daughter of a king.

Here the bracelet of the truest *princess*,
That ever swore her faith. *Shakesp. Cymbeline.*

4. The wife of a prince: as, *the* princess *of Wales.*

PRI'NCIPAL. *adj.* [*principal*, Fr. *principalis*, Lat.]

1. Princely. A sense found only in *Spenser*. A Latinism.

Suspicion of friend, nor fear of foe,
That hazarded his health, had he at all;
But walk'd at will, and wandred to and fro,
In the pride of his freedom *principal.* *Spenser.*

2. Chief; of the first rate; capital; essential; important; considerable.

This later is ordered, partly and as touching *principal* matters by none but precepts divine only; partly and as concerning things of inferior regard by ordinances, as well human as divine. *Hooker, b.* v. *s.* 4.

Can you remember any of the *principal* evils, that he laid to the charge of women. *Shakesp. As You like it.*

PRI'NCIPAL. *n. s.* [from the adj.]

1. A head; a chief; not a second.

Seconds in factions do many times, when the faction subdivideth, prove *principals.* *Bacon.*

2. One primarily or originally engaged; not an accessary or auxiliary.

We were not *principals*, but auxiliaries in the war. *Swift.*

In judgment, some persons are present as *principals*, and others only as accessaries. *Ayliffe's Parergon.*

3. A capital sum placed out at interest.

Thou wilt not only loose the forfeiture,
But touch'd with human gentleness and love,
Forgive a moiety of the *principal.* *Shakesp.*

Taxes must be continued, because we have no other means for paying off the *principal.* *Swift's Miscellanies.*

4. The president or governour.

PRINCIPA'LITY. *n. s.* [*principaulté*, Fr.]

1. Sovereignty; supreme power.

Divine lady, who have wrought such miracles in me, as to make a prince none of the basest, to think all *principalities* base, in respect of the sheephook. *Sidney, b.* ii.

Nothing was given to Henry, but the name of king; all other absolute power of *principality* he had. *Spenser.*

2. A prince; one invested with sovereignty.

Then speak the truth by her; if not divine,
Yet let her be a *principality*,
Sov'reign to all the creatures on the earth. *Shakesp.*

Nisroch of *principalities* the prime. *Milton.*

3. The country which gives title to a prince: as, *the* principality *of Wales.*

To the boy Cæsar send this grizled head,
And he will fill thy wishes to the brim
With *principalities.* *Shakesp. Ant. and Cleop.*

The little *principality* of Epire was invincible by the whole power of the Turks. *Temple's Miscellanies.*

4. Superiority; predominance.

In the chief work of elements, water hath the *principality* and excess over earth. *Digby on Bodies.*

If any mystery be effective of spiritual blessings, then this is much more, as having the prerogative and *principality* above every thing else. *Taylor's Worthy Communicant.*

PRI'NCIPALLY. *adv.* [from *principal.*] Chiefly; above all; above the rest.

If the minister of divine offices shall take upon him that holy calling for covetous or ambitious ends, or shall not design the glory of God *principally*, he polluteth his heart. *Tayl.*

They wholly mistake the nature of criticism, who think its business is *principally* to find fault. *Dryden.*

The resistance of water arises *principally* from the vis inertiæ of its matter, and by consequence, if the heavens were as dense as water, they would not have much less resistance than water. *Newton's Opticks.*

What I *principally* insist on, is due execution. *Swi*

PRI'NCIPALNESS. *n. s.* [from *principal.*] The state of bei[ng] principal or chief.

PRI'NCIPIATION. *n. s.* [from *principium*, Lat.] Analysis in[to] constituent or elemental parts. A word not received.

The separating of any metal into its original or elemen[t] we will call *principiation.* *Baco*

PRI'NCIPLE. *n. s.* [*principium*, Lat. *principe*, Fr.]

1. Element; constituent part; primordial substance.

Modern philosophers suppose matter to be one simple *pri[n]ciple*, or solid extension diversified by its various shapes. *Watt*

2. Original cause.

Some few, whose lamp shone brighter, have been led,
From cause to cause to nature's secret head,
And found that one first *principle* must be. *Dryde*

For the performance of this, a vital or directive *princip[le]* seemeth to be assistant to the corporeal. *Grew's Cosmo*

3. Being productive of other being; operative cause.

The soul of man is an active *principle*, and will be employed one way or other. *Tillotson's Sermon*

4. Fundamental truth; original postulate; first position fro[m] which others are deduced.

Touching the law of reason, there are in it some thing[s] which stand as *principles* universally agreed upon; and out [of] those *principles*, which are in themselves evident, the greate[st] moral duties we owe towards God or man, may, witho[ut] any great difficulty, be concluded. *Hooke*

All of them may be called *principles*, when compared wit[h] a thousand other judgments, which we form under the regu[]lation of these primary propositions. *Watts's Logic*

5. Ground of action; motive.

Farewel, young lords; these warlike *principles*
Do not throw from you. *Shakes*

As no *principle* of vanity led me first to write it, so muc[h] less does any such motive induce me now to publish it. *Wak*

There would be but small improvements in the worl[d] were there not some common *principle* of action, workin[g] equally with all men. *Addison's Spectator*, N° 25

6. Tenet on which morality is founded.

I'll try
If yet I can subdue those stubborn *principles*
Of faith, of honour. *Addison's Cat*

A feather shooting from another's head,
Extracts his brain, and *principle* is fled. *Pop*

To PRI'NCIPLE. *v. a.* [from the noun.]

1. To establish or fix in any tenet; to impress with any ten[et] good or ill.

Wisest and best men full oft beguil'd,
With goodness *principl'd* not to reject
The penitent, but ever to forgive,
Are drawn to wear out miserable days. *Milto*

It is the concern of his majesty, and the peace of his go[]vernment, that the youth be *principled* with a thorough pe[r]suasion of the justness of the old king's cause. *Sout*

There are so many young persons, upon the well and i[ll] *principling* of whom next under God, depends the happine[ss] or misery of this church and state. *South's Sermon*

Governors should be well *principled* and good-natured. *L'Es*

Men have been *principled* with an opinion, that they mu[st] not consult reason in things of religion. *Lock*

Let an enthusiast be *principled*, that he or his teacher is in[]spired, and you in vain bring the evidence of clear reason against his doctrine. *Lock*

He seems a settled and *principled* philosopher, thanking for[]tune for the tranquility he has by her aversion. *Pope to Swif*

2. To establish firmly in the mind.

The promiscuous reading of the bible is far from being o[f] any advantage to children, either for the perfecting their read[]ing, or *principling* their religion. *Lock*

PRI'NCOCK. } *n. s.* [from *prink* or *prim cock*; perhaps *præcox* o[r]
PRI'NCOX. } *præcoquum* ingenium, Lat.] A coxcomb; conceited person; a pert young rogue.

You are a saucy boy;
This trick may chance to scathe you I know what;
You must contrary me! you are a *princox*, go. *Shakes*

To PRINK. *v. n.* [*pronken*, Dutch.] To prank; to deck fo[r] show.

Hold a good wager she was every day longer *prinking* i[n] the glass than you was. *Art of Tormenting*

To PRINT. *v. a.* [*imprimer*, *empreint*, Fr.]

1. To mark by pressing any thing upon another.

On his fiery steed betimes he rode,
That scarcely *prints* the turf on which he trod. *Dryde*

2. To impress any thing, so as to leave its form.

3. To form by impression.

Your mother was most true to wedlock, prince,
For she did *print* your royal father off,
Conceiving you. *Shakesp. Winter's Tal*

Ye shall not make any cuttings in your flesh for the dead nor *print* any marks upon you. *Lev.* ix. 28

Perhaps some footsteps *printed* in the clay,
Will to my love direct your wand'ring way. *Roscommo*

His royal bounty brought its own reward;
And in their minds so deep did *print* the sense,
That if their ruins sadly they regard,
'Tis but with fear. *Dryden.*

4. To impress words or make books, not by the pen, but the press.

Thou hast caused *printing* to be used; and, contrary to the king, his crown and dignity, built a paper-mill. *Shakesp.*

This nonsense got in by a mistake of the stage editors, who *printed* from the piecemeal written parts. *Pope.*

Is it probable, that a promiscuous jumble of *printing* letter should often fall into a method, which should stamp on paper a coherent discourse. *Locke.*

As soon as he begins to spell, pictures of animals should be got him, with the *printed* names to them. *Locke.*

To Print. *v. n.* To publish a book.

From the moment he *prints*, he must expect to hear no more truth. *Pope.*

Print. *n. s.* [*empreinte*, Fr.]

1. Mark or form made by impression.

Some more time
Must wear the *print* of his remembrance out. *Shakesp.*
Abhorred slave,
Which any *print* of goodness wilt not take,
Being capable of all ill! *Shakesp. Tempest.*
Attend the foot,
That leaves the *print* of blood where'er it walks. *Shakesp.*
Up they tost the sand,
No wheel seen, nor wheels *print* was in the mould imprest
Behind them. *Chapman's Iliads.*
Our life so fast away doth slide,
As doth an hungry eagle through the wind;
Or as a ship transported with the tide,
Which in their passage leave no *print* behind. *Davies.*
My life is but a wind,
Which passeth by, and leaves no *print* behind. *Sandys.*
O'er the smooth enamell'd green,
Where no *print* of step hath been. *Milton.*
While the heav'n, by the sun's team untrod,
Hath took no *print* of the approaching light,
And all the spangled host keep watch. *Milton.*

Before the lion's den appeared the footsteps of many that had gone in, but no *prints* of any that ever came out. *South.*

Winds bear me to some barren island,
Where *print* of human feet was never seen. *Dryden.*
From hence Astrea took her flight, and here
The *prints* of her departing steps appear. *Dryden.*

If they be not sometimes renewed by repeated exercise of the senses or reflection, the *print* wears out. *Locke.*

2. That which being impressed leaves its form.

3. Pictures cut in wood or copper to be impressed on paper. It is usual to say wooden *prints* and copper plates.

4. Picture made by impression.

From my breast I cannot tear
The passion, which from thence did grow;
Nor yet out of my fancy rase
The *print* of that supposed face. *Waller.*

The *prints*, which we see of antiquities, may contribute to form our genius, and to give us great ideas. *Dryden.*

Words standing for things, should be expressed by little draughts and *prints* made of them. *Locke.*

5. The form, size, arrangement, or other qualities of the types used in printing books.

To refresh the former hint;
She read her maker in a fairer *print*. *Dryden.*

6. The state of being published by the printer.

I love a ballad in *print*, or a life. *Shakesp.*
It is so rare to see
Ought that belongs to young nobility
In *print*, that we must praise. *Suckling.*

His natural antipathy to a man, who endeavours to signalize his parts in the world, has hindered many persons from making their appearance in *print*. *Addison.*

I published some tables, which were out of *print*. *Arbuth.*

The rights of the christian church are scornfully trampled on in *print*. *Atterbury.*

7. Single sheet printed and sold.

The *prints*, about three days after, were filled with the same terms. *Addison.*

The publick had said before, that they were dull; and they were at great pains to purchase room in the *prints*, to testify under their hands the truth of it. *Pope.*

Inform us, will the emperor treat,
Or do the *prints* and papers lie? *Pope.*

8. Formal method.

Lay his head sometimes higher, sometimes lower, that he may not feel every little change, who is not designed to have his maid lay all things in *print*, and tuck him in warm. *Locke.*

Pri'nter. *n. s.* [from *print.*]

1. One that prints books.

I find, at reading all over, to deliver to the *printer*, in that which I ought to have done to comply with my design, I am fallen very short. *Digby.*

To buy books, only because they were published by an eminent *printer*, is much as if a man should buy cloaths that did not fit him, only because made by some famous taylor. *Pope.*

See, the *printer*'s boy below;
Ye hawkers all, your voices lift. *Swift.*

2. One that stains linen.

Pri'ntless. *adj.* [from *print.*] That which leaves no impression.

Ye elves,
And ye, that on the sands with *printless* foot
Do chase the ebbing Neptune. *Shakesp. Tempest.*
Whilst from off the waters fleet,
Thus I set my *printless* feet
O'er the cowslip's velvet head,
That bends not as I tread. *Milton.*

PRI'OR. *adj.* [*prior*, Lat.] Former; being before something else; antecedent; anterior.

Whenever tempted to do or approve any thing contrary to the duties we are enjoined, let us reflect that we have a *prior* and superior obligation to the commands of Christ. *Rogers.*

Pri'or. *n. s.* [*prieur*, Fr.]

1. The head of a convent of monks, inferior in dignity to an abbot.

Neither she, nor any other, besides the *prior* of the convent, knew any thing of his name. *Addison's Spectator.*

2. *Prior* is such a person, as, in some churches, presides over others in the same churches. *Ayliffe's Parergon.*

Pri'oress. *n. s.* [from *prior.*] A lady superior of a convent of nuns.

When you have vow'd, you must not speak with men,
But in the presence of the *prioress*. *Shakesp.*

The reeve, miller and cook are distinguished from each other, as much as the mincing lady *prioress* and the broad speaking wife of Bath. *Dryden.*

Prio'rity. *n. s.* [from *prior*, adj.]

1. The state of being first; precedence in time.

From son to son of the lady, as they should be in *priority* of birth. *Hayward.*

Men still affirm, that it killeth at a distance, that it poisoneth by the eye, and by *priority* of vision. *Brown*

This observation may assist, in determining the dispute concerning the *priority* of Homer and Hesiod. *Broome.*

Though he oft renew'd the fight,
And almost got *priority* of fight,
He ne'er could overcome her quite. *Swift.*

2. Precedence in place.

Follow, Cominius; we must follow you,
Right worthy your *priority*. *Shakesp.*

Pri'orship. *n. s.* [from *prior.*] The state or office of prior.

Pri'ory. *n. s.* [from *prior.*]

1. A convent, in dignity below an abbey.

Our abbies and our *priories* shall pay
This expedition's charge. *Shakesp. King John.*

2. *Priories* are the churches which are given to priors in titulum, or by way of title. *Ayliffe's Parergon.*

Pri'sage. *n. s.* [from *prise.*]

Prisage, now called butlerage, is a custom whereby the prince challenges out of every bark loaden with wine, containing less than forty tuns, two tuns of wine at his price. *Cowel.*

PRISM. *n. s.* [*prisme*, Fr. πρίσμα.]

A *prism* of glass is a glass bounded with two equal and parallel triangular ends, and three plain and well polished sides, which meet in three parallel lines, running from the three angles of one end, to the three angles of the other end. *Newton's Opticks.*

Here, aweful Newton, the dissolving clouds
Form fronting, on the sun, thy showery *prism*. *Thomson.*

Prisma'tick. *adj.* [*prismatique*, Fr. from *prism.*] Formed as a prism.

If the mass of the earth was cubick, *prismatick*, or any other angular figure, it would follow, that one, too vast a part, would be drowned, and another be dry. *Derham.*

False eloquence, like the *prismatick* glass,
Its gaudy colours spreads on ev'ry place;
The face of nature we no more survey,
All glares alike, without distinction gay. *Pope.*

Prisma'tically. *adv.* [from *prismatick.*] In the form of a prism.

Take notice of the pleasing variety of colours exhibited by the triangular glass, and demand what addition or decrement of either salt, sulphur or mercury befalls the glass, by being *prismatically* figured; and yet it is known, that without that shape, it would not afford those colours as it does. *Boyle.*

Prismo'id. *n. s.* [πρίσμα and εἶδος.] A body approaching to the form of a prism.

PRI'SON. *n. s.* [*prison*, Fr.] A strong hold in which persons are confined; a gaol.

He hath commission
To hang Cordelia in the *prison*. *Shakesp. King Lear.*

I thought

For those rebellious here their *pris'n* ordain'd. *Milton.*

I thought our utmost good
Was in one word of freedom understood,
The fatal blessing came; from *prison* free,
I starve abroad, and lose the sight of Emily. *Dryden.*

Unkind! can you, whom only I adore,
Set open to your slave the *prison* door. *Dryden.*

The tyrant Æolus,
With pow'r imperial, curbs the struggling winds,
And sounding tempests in dark *prisons* binds. *Dryden.*

He, that has his chains knocked off, and the *prison* doors set open to him, is presently at liberty. *Locke.*

To PRI'SON. *v. a.* [from the noun.]

1. To emprison; to shut up in hold; to restrain from liberty.
2. To captivate; to enchain.

Culling their potent herbs and baleful drugs,
They, as they sung, would take the *prison'd* soul,
And lap it in Elysium. *Milton.*

3. To confine.

Universal plodding *prisons* up
The nimble spirits in the arteries. *Shakesp.*

Then did the king enlarge
The spleen he *prison'd*. *Chapman's Iliads.*

PRI'SONBASE. *n. s.* A kind of rural play, commonly called *prisonbars.*

The spachies of the court play every friday at ciocho di canni, which is no other than *prisonbase* upon horseback, hiting one another with darts, as the others do with their hands. *Sandys's Travels.*

PRI'SONER. *n. s.* [*prisonnier*, Fr.]

1. One who is confined in hold.

Cesar's ill-erected tower,
To whose flint bosom my condemned lord
Is doomed a *prisoner.* *Shakesp. Rich.* II.

The most pernicious infection, next the plague, is the smell of the jail, when *prisoners* have been long and close, and nastily kept. *Bacon.*

He that is tied with one slender string, such as one resolute struggle would break, he is *prisoner* only to his own sloth, and who will pity his thraldom. *Decay of Piety.*

A *prisoner* is troubled, that he cannot go whither he would; and he that is at large is troubled, that he does not know whither to go. *L'Estrange.*

2. A captive; one taken by the enemy.

So oft as homeward I from her depart,
I go like one that having lost the field,
Is *prisoner* led away with heavy heart. *Spenser.*

There succeeded an absolute victory for the English, the taking of the Spanish general d'Ocampo *prisoner*, with the loss of few of the English. *Bacon.*

He yielded on my word,
And as my *pris'ner*, I restore his sword. *Dryden.*

3. One under an arrest.

Tribune, a guard to seize the empress straight,
Secure her person *pris'ner* to the state. *Dryden.*

PRI'SONHOUSE. *n. s.* Gaol; hold in which one is confined.

I am forbid to tell the secrets of my *prisonhouse.* *Shakesp.*

PRI'SONMENT. *n. s.* [from *prison.*] Confinement: emprisonment; captivity.

May be he will not touch young Arthur's life,
But hold himself safe in his *prisonment.* *Shakesp.*

PRI'STINE. *adj.* [*pristinus*, Lat.] First; ancient; original.

Now their *pristine* worth
The Britons recollect. *Philips.*

This light being trajected only through the parallel superficies of the two prisms, if it suffered any change by the refraction of one superficies, it lost that impression by the contrary refraction of the other superficies, and so, being restored to its *pristine* constitution, became of the same nature and condition as at first. *Newton's Opticks.*

PRI'THEE. A familiar corruption of *pray thee*, or *I pray thee*, which some of the tragick writers have injudiciously used.

Well, what was that scream for, I *prithee*? *L'Estrange.*

Alas! why com'st thou at this dreadful moment,
To shock the peace of my departing soul?
Away! I *prithee* leave me! *Rowe's Jane Shore.*

PRI'VACY. *n. s.* [from *private.*]

1. State of being secret; secrecy.
2. Retirement; retreat.

Clamours our *privacies* uneasy make,
Birds leave their nests disturb'd, and beasts their haunts forsake. *Dryden.*

3. [*Privauté*, Fr.] Privity; joint knowledge; great familiarity. *Privacy* in this sense is improper.

You see Frog is religiously true to his bargain, scorns to hearken to any composition without your *privacy.* *Arbuthnot.*

4. Taciturnity. *Ainsworth.*

PRIVA'DO. n. s. [Spanish.] A secret friend.

The lady Brampton, an English lady, embarked for Portugal at that time, with some *privado* of her own. *Bacon.*

PRI'VATE. *adj.* [*privatus*, Lat.]

1. Not open; secret.

You shall go with me;
I have some *private* schooling for you both. *Shakesp.*

Fancy retires
Into her *private* cell, when nature rests. *Milton.*

The harmless freedom, and the *private* friend. *Anon.*

2. Alone; not accompanied.
3. Being upon the same terms with the rest of the community; particular: opposed to publick.

When publick consent of the whole hath established any thing; every man's judgment, being thereunto compared, were not *private*, howsoever his calling be to some kind of publick charge; so that of peace and quietness there is not any way possible, unless the probable voice of every intire society or body politic overrule all *private* of like nature in the same body. *Hooker's Preface.*

He sues
To let him breathe between the heav'ns and earth,
A *private* man in Athens. *Shakesp. Ant. and Cleop.*

What infinite heartease must kings neglect,
That *private* men enjoy? and what have kings,
That *private* have not too, save ceremony? *Shakesp.*

Peter was but a *private* man, and not to be any way compared with the dukes of his house. *Peacham of Antiquities.*

The first principles of christian religion should not be farced with school points and *private* tenets. *Sanderson.*

Dare you,
A *private* man presume to love a queen. *Dryden.*

4. Particular; not relating to the publick.

My end being *private*, I have not expressed my conceptions in the language of the schools. *Digby.*

5. *In* PRIVATE. Secretly; not publickly; not openly.

In private grieve, but with a careless scorn;
In publick seem to triumph, not to mourn. *Granville.*

PRI'VATE. *n. s.* A secret message.

His *private* with me of the dauphin's love,
Is much more general than these lines import. *Shakesp.*

PRIVATEER. *n. s.* [from *private.*] A ship fitted out by private men to plunder enemies.

He is at no charge for a fleet, further than providing *privateers*, wherewith his subjects carry on a pyratical war at their own expence. *Swift's Miscellanies.*

To PRI'VATEER. *v. a.* [from the noun.] To fit out ships against enemies, at the charge of private persons.

PRI'VATELY. *adv.* [from *private.*] Secretly; not openly.

There, this night,
We'll pass the business *privately* and well. *Shakesp.*

And as he sat upon the mount of Olives, the disciples came unto him *privately.* *Mat.* xxiv. 3.

PRI'VATENESS. *n. s.* [from *private.*]

1. The state of a man in the same rank with the rest of the community.
2. Secrecy; privacy.

Ambassadors attending the court in great number, he did content with courtesy, reward and *privateness.* *Bacon.*

3. Obscurity; retirement.

He drew him into the fatal circle from a resolved *privateness*, where he bent his mind to a retired course. *Wotton.*

PRIVA'TION. *n. s.* [*privation*, Fr. *privatio*, Lat.]

1. Removal or destruction of any thing or quality.

For, what is this contagious sin of kind,
But a *privation* of that grace within. *Davies.*

So bounded are our natural desires,
That wanting all, and setting pain aside,
With bare *privation* sense is satisfy'd. *Dryden.*

After some account of good, evil will be known by consequence, as being only a *privation* or absence of good. *South.*

A *privation* is the absence of what does naturally belong to the thing, or which ought to be present with it; as when a man or horse is deaf or dead, or a physician or divine unlearned; these are *privations.* *Watts's Logick.*

2. The act of the mind by which, in considering a subject, we separate it from any thing appendant.
3. The act of degrading from rank or office.

If part of the people or estate be somewhat in the election, you cannot make them nulls or cyphers in the *privation* or translation. *Bacon.*

If the *privation* be good, it follows not the former condition was evil, but less good; for the flower or blossom is a positive good, although the remove of it, to give place to the fruit, be a comparative good. *Bacon.*

PRI'VATIVE. *adj.* [*privatif*, Fr. *privativus*, Lat.]

1. Causing privation of any thing.
2. Consisting in the absence of something; not positive. *Privative* is in things, what negative is in propositions.

The impression from *privative* to active, as from silence to noise, is a greater degree than from less noise to more. *Bacon.*

The very *privative* blessings, the blessings of immunity, safeguard, liberty and integrity, which we enjoy, deserve the thanksgiving of a whole life. *Taylor.*

PRIVA'TIVE. *n. s.* That of which the essence is the absence of something, as silence is only the absence of sound.

Harmonical sounds and discordant sounds are both active and positive, but blackness and darkness are indeed but *privatives*, and therefore have little or no activity; somewhat they do contristate, but very little. *Bacon's Nat. Hist.*

Pri'vatively. *adv.* [from *privative.*] By the absence of something necessary to be present; negatively.

The duty of the new covenant is set down, first *privatively*, not like that of Mosaical observances external, but positively, laws given into the minds and hearts. *Hammond.*

Pri'vativeness. *n. s.* [from *privative.*] Notation of absence of something that should be present.

Pri'vet. *n. s.* The leaves grow by pairs opposite to each other; the flower consists of one leaf, is tubulous, and divided at the top into five segments; the ovary in the center of the flower-cup becomes a globular soft fruit full of juice, in which are lodged four seeds. *Miller.*

Pri'vet. *n. s.* Evergreen. It is distinguished from the phillyrea by the leaves being placed alternately upon the branches, whereas those of the phillyrea are produced by pairs opposite to each other: it hath three seeds inclosed in each berry, whereas the phillyrea has but one. *Miller.*

Pri'vilege. *n. s.* [*privilege*, Fr. *privilegium*, Lat.]

1. Peculiar advantage.

Here's my sword,
Behold it is the *privilege* of mine honours,
My oath, and my profession. *Shakesp.*

He went
Invisible, yet stay'd, such *privilege*
Hath omnipresence. *Milton.*

He claims his *privilege*, and says 'tis fit,
Nothing should be the judge of wit, but wit. *Denham.*

Smiles, not allow'd to beasts, from reason move,
And are the *privilege* of human love. *Dryden.*

The *privilege* of birth-right was a double portion. *Locke.*

2. Immunity; publick right.

I beg the ancient *privilege* of Athens. *Shakesp.*

A soul that can securely death defy,
And counts it nature's *privilege* to die. *Dryden.*

To **Pri'vilege.** *v. a.* [from the noun.]

1. To invest with rights or immunities; to grant a privilege.

The great are *privileg'd* alone,
To punish all injustice but their own. *Dryden.*

He happier yet, who *privileg'd* by fate
To shorter labour, and a lighter weight,
Receiv'd but yesterday the gift of breath,
Ordain'd to-morrow to return to death. *Prior.*

2. To exempt from censure or danger.

The court is rather deemed as a *privileged* place of unbridled licentiousness, than as the abiding of him, who, as a father, should give a fatherly example. *Sidney, b.* ii.

He took this place for sanctuary,
And it shall *privilege* him from your hands. *Shakesp.*

This place
Doth *privilege* me, speak what reason will. *Daniel.*

3. To exempt from paying tax or impost.

Many things are by our laws *privileged* from tythes, which by the canon law are chargeable. *Hale.*

Pri'vily. *adv.* [from *privy.*] Secretly; privately.

They have the profits of their lands by pretence of conveyances thereof unto their privy friends, who *privily* send them the revenues. *Spenser's State of Ireland.*

Pri'vity. *n. s.* [*privauté*, Fr. from *privy.*]

1. Private communication.

I will unto you in *privity* discover the drift of my purpose; I mean thereby to settle an eternal peace in that country, and also to make it very profitable to her majesty. *Spenser.*

2. Consciousness; joint knowledge; private concurrence.

The authority of higher powers have force even in these things which are done without their *privity*, and are of mean reckoning. *Hooker, b.* i. *s.* 7.

Upon this French going out, took he upon him,
Without the *privity* o' th' king, t' appoint
Who should attend him? *Shakesp. Henry* VIII.

All the doors were laid open for his departure, not without the *privity* of the prince of Orange, concluding that the kingdom might better be settled in his absence. *Swift.*

3. [In the plural.] Secret parts.

Few of them have any thing to cover their *privities*. *Abbot.*

PRI'VY. *adj.* [*privé*, Fr.]

1. Private; not publick; assigned to secret uses.

The party, 'gainst the which he doth contrive,
Shall seize on half his goods; the other half
Comes to the *privy* coffer of the state. *Shakesp.*

2. Secret; clandestine.

He took advantage of the night for such *privy* attempts, insomuch that the bruit of his manliness was spread every where. 2 *Mac.* viii. 7.

3. Secret; not shown.

The sword of the great men that are slain entereth into their *privy* chamber. *Ezek.* xxi. 14.

4. Admitted to secrets of state.

The king has made him
One of the *privy* council. *Shakesp. Henry* VIII.

One, having let his beard grow from the martyrdom of king Charles I. till the restoration, desired to be made a *privy* counsellor. *Spectator,* № 629.

5. Conscious to any thing; admitted to participation of knowledge.

Sir Valentine
This night intends to steal away your daughter;
Myself am one made *privy* to the plot. *Shakesp.*

Many being *privy* to the fact,
How hard is it to keep it unbetray'd? *Daniel.*

He would rather lose half of his kingdom, than be *privy* to such a secret, which he commanded me never to mention. *Gulliver's Travels.*

Pri'vy. *n. s.* Place of retirement; necessary house.

Your fancy
Would still the same ideas give ye,
As when you spy'd her on the *privy*. *Swift.*

PRIZE. *n. s.* [*prix*, Fr.]

1. A reward gained by contest with competitors.

If ever he go alone, I'll never wrestle for *prize*. *Shakesp.*

I fought and conquer'd, yet have lost the *prize*. *Dryden.*

The raising such silly competitions among the ignorant, proposing *prizes* for such useless accomplishments, and inspiring them with such absurd ideas of superiority, has in it something immoral as well as ridiculous. *Addison.*

2. A reward gained by any performance.

True poets empty fame and praise despise,
Fame is the trumpet, but your smile the *prize*. *Dryden.*

3. [*Prise*, Fr.] Something taken by adventure; plunder.

The king of Scots she did send to France,
To fill king Edward's fame with prisoner kings,
And make his chronicle as rich with *prize*,
As is the ouzy bottom of the sea
With sunken wreck. *Shakesp. Henry* V.

He acquitted himself like a valiant, but not like an honest man; for he converted the *prizes* to his own use. *Arbuthnot.*

Then prostrate falls, and begs with ardent eyes
Soon to obtain and long possess the *prize*:
The pow'rs gave ear. *Pope.*

To **Prize.** *v. a.* [from *appraise*; *priser*, Fr. *appreciare*. Lat.]

1. To rate; to value at a certain price.

Life I *prize* not a straw; but for mine honour
Which I would free. *Shakesp.*

Cast it unto the potter; a goodly price that I was *prized* at of them. *Zech.* xi. 13.

2. To esteem; to value highly.

I go to free us both of pain;
I *priz'd* your person, but your crown disdain. *Dryden.*

Some the French writers, some our own despise;
The ancients only, or the moderns *prize*. *Pope.*

Pri'zer. *n. s.* [*priseur*, Fr. from *prize.*] He that values.

It holds its estimate and dignity,
As well wherein 'tis precious of itself,
As in the *prizer*. *Shakesp. Troilus and Cressida.*

Pri'zefighter. *n. s.* [*prize* and *fighter.*] One that fights publickly for a reward.

Martin and Crambe engaged like *prizefighters*. *Arb. and Po.*

In Fig the *prizefighter* by day delight. *Bramston.*

PRO. [Latin.] For; in defence of; *pro* and *con*, for *pro* and *contra*, for and against. Despicable cant.

Doctrinal points in controversy had been agitated in the pulpits, with more warmth than had used to be; and thence the animosity increased in books *pro* and *con*. *Clarendon.*

Matthew met Richard, when
Of many knotty points they spoke,
And *pro* and *con* by turns they took. *Prior.*

Probabi'lity. *n. s.* [*probabilitas*, Lat. *probabilité*, Fr. from *probable.*] Likelihood; appearance of truth; evidence arising from the preponderation of argument: it is less than moral certainty.

Probability is the appearance of the agreement or disagreement of two ideas, by the intervention of proofs, whose connection is not constant; but appears for the most part to be so. *Locke.*

As for *probabilities*, what thing was there ever set down so agreeable with sound reason, but some probable shew against it might be made? *Hooker's Preface.*

If a truth be certain, and thwart interest, it will quickly fetch it down to but a *probability*; nay, if it does not carry with it an impregnable evidence, it will go near to debase it to a downright falsity. *South's Sermons.*

Though moral certainty be sometimes taken for a high degree of *probability*, which can only produce a doubtful assent; yet it is also frequently used for a firm assent to a thing upon such grounds, as are fit fully to satisfy a prudent man. *Tillotson's Sermons.*

For a perpetual motion, magnetical virtues are not without some strong *probabilities* of proving effectual. *Wilkins.*

PRO'BABLE. *adj.* [*probable*, Fr. *probabilis*, Lat.] Likely; having more evidence than the contrary.

The publick approbation, given by the body of this whole church unto those things which are establ shed, doth make it but *probable* that they are good, and therefore unto a necessary proof that they are not good it must give place. *Hooker.*

That

That is accounted *probable*, which has better arguments producible for it, than can be brought against it. *South.*

They assented to things, that were neither evident nor certain, but only *probable*; for they conversed, they merchandized upon a *probable* persuasion of the honesty and truth of those whom they corresponded with. *South's Sermons.*

PRO'BABLY. *adv.* [from *probable.*] Likely; in likelihood.

Distinguish betwixt what may possibly, and what will *probably* be done. *L'Estrange's Fables.*

Our constitution in church or state could not *probably* have been long preserved, without such methods. *Swift.*

PRO'BAT. n. s. [Latin.] The proof of wills and testaments of persons deceased in the spiritual court, either in common form by the oath of the executor, or with witnesses. *Dict.*

PROBA'TION. *n. s.* [*probatio*, Lat. from *probo*, Lat. *probation*, Fr.]

1. Proof; evidence; testimony.

Of the truth herein,
This present object made *probation*. *Shakesp. Hamlet.*

He was lapt in a most curious mantle, which, for more *probation*, I can produce. *Shakesp. Cymbeline.*

2. The act of proving by ratiocination or testimony.

When these principles, what is, is, and it is impossible for the same thing to be, and not to be, are made use of in the *probation* of propositions, wherein are words standing for complex ideas, as man or horse, there they make men receive and retain falsehood for manifest truth. *Locke.*

3. [*Probation*, Fr.] Trial; examination.

In the practical part of knowledge, much will be left to experience and *probation*, whereunto indication cannot so fully reach. *Bacon's Nat. Hist.*

4. Trial before entrance into monastick life; noviciate.

I suffer many things as an author militant, whereof, in your days of *probation*, you have been a sharer. *Pope to Swift.*

PROBA'TIONARY. *adj.* [from *probation.*] Serving for trial.

PROBA'TIONER. *n. s.* [from *probation.*]

1. One who is upon trial.

Hear a mortal muse thy praise rehearse,
In no ignoble verse;
But such as thy own verse did practise here,
When thy first fruits of poesy were giv'n,
To make thyself a welcome inmate there;
While yet a young *probationer*,
And candidate of heav'n. *Dryden.*

Build a thousand churches, where these *probationers* may read their wall lectures. *Swift.*

2. A novice.

This root of bitterness was but a *probationer* in the soil; and though it set forth some offsets to preserve its kind, yet Satan was fain to cherish them. *Decay of Piety.*

PROBA'TIONERSHIP. *n. s.* [fom *probationer.*] State of being a probationer; noviciate.

He has afforded us only the twilight of probability, suitable to that state of mediocrity and *probationership*, he has been pleased to place us in here, wherein to check our over-confidence. *Locke.*

PRO'BATORY. *adj.* [from *probo*, Lat.] Serving for trial.

Job's afflictions were no vindicatory punishments, but *probatory* chastisements to make trial of his graces. *Bramhall.*

PROBATUM EST. A Latin expression added to the end of a receipt, signifying *it is tried* or *proved.*

Vain the concern that you express,
That uncall'd Alard will possess
Your house and coach both day and night,
And that Macbeth was haunted less
By Banquo's restless sprite:
Lend him but fifty louis d' or,
And you shall never see him more;
Take my advice *probatum est?*
Why do the gods indulge our store,
But to secure our rest. *Prior.*

PROBE. *n. s.* [from *probo*, Lat.] A slender wire by which surgeons search the depth of wounds.

I made search with a *probe.* *Wiseman's Surgery.*

PROBE-SCISSORS. *n. s.* [*probe* and *scissor.*] Scissors used to open wounds, of which the blade thrust into the orifice has a button at the end.

The sinus was snipt up with *probe-scissors.* *Wiseman.*

To PROBE. *v. a.* [*probo*, Lat.] To search; to try by an instrument.

Nothing can be more painful, than to *probe* and search a purulent old sore to the bottom. *South's Sermons.*

He'd raise a blush, where secret vice he found;
And tickle, while he gently *prob'd* the wound. *Dryden.*

PRO'BITY. *n. s.* [*probité.* Fr. *probitas*, Lat.] Honesty; sincerity; veracity.

The truth of our Lord's ascension, might be deduced from the *probity* of the apostles. *Fiddes's Sermons.*

So near approach we their celestial kind,
By justice, truth, and *probity* of mind. *Pope.*

PROBLEM. *n. s.* [*probleme*, Fr. πρόβλημα.] A question proposed.

The *problem* is, whether a man constantly and strongly believing, that such a thing shall be, it doth help any thing to the effecting of the thing. *Bacon's Nat. Hist.*

Although in general one understood colours, yet were it not an easy *problem* to resolve, why grass is green? *Brown.*

This *problem* let philosophers resolve,
What makes the globe from West to East revolve. *Blackm.*

PROBLEMA'TICAL. *adj.* [from *problem*; *problematique*, Fr.] Uncertain; unsettled; disputed; disputable.

I promised no better arguments than might be expected in a point *problematical.* *Boyle.*

Diligent enquiries into remote and *problematical* guilt, leave a gate wide open to the whole tribe of informers. *Swift.*

PROBLEMA'TICALLY. *adv.* [from *problematical.*] Uncertainly.

PROBO'SCIS. *n. s.* [*proboscis*, Lat.] A snout; the trunk of an elephant; but it is used also for the same part in every creature, that bears any resemblance thereunto.

The elephant wreath'd to make them sport
His lithe *proboscis.* *Milton.*

PROCA'CIOUS. *adj.* [*procax*, Lat.] Petulant; loose. *Dict.*

PROCA'CITY. *n. s.* [from *procacious.*] Petulance. *Dict.*

PROCATA'RCTICK. *adj.* [προκαταρκτικὸς.] Forerunning; antecedent. See PROCATARXIS.

James IV. of Scotland, falling away in his flesh, without the precedence of any *procatarctick* cause, was suddenly cured by decharming the witchcraft. *Harvey on Consumptions.*

The physician enquires into the *procatarctick* causes. *Harv.*

PROCATA'RXIS. *n. s.* [προκαταρξις.]

Procatarxis is the pre-existent cause of a disease, which cooperates with others that are subsequent, whether internal or external; as anger or heat of climate, which bring such an ill disposition of the juices, as occasion a fever: the ill disposition being the immediate cause, and the bad air the procatartick cause. *Quincy.*

PROCE'DURE. *n. s.* [*procedure*, Fr. from *proceed.*]

1. Manner of proceeding; management; conduct.

This is the true *procedure* of conscience, always supposing a law from God, before it lays obligation upon man. *South.*

2. Act of proceeding; progress; process; operation.

Although the distinction of these several *procedures* of the soul do not always appear distinct, especially in sudden actions, yet in actions of weight, all these have their distinct order and *procedure.* *Hale's Origin of Mankind.*

3. Produce; thing produced.

No known substance, but earth and the *procedures* of earth, as tile and stone, yieldeth any moss or herby substance. *Bacon.*

To PROCEE'D. *v. n.* [*procedo*, Lat. *proceder*, Fr.]

1. To pass from one thing or place to another.

Adam
Proceeded thus to ask his heav'nly guest. *Milton.*

Then to the prelude of a war *proceeds*;
His horns, yet sore, he tries against a tree. *Dryden.*

I shall *proceed* to more complex ideas. *Locke.*

2. To go forward; to tend to the end designed.

Temp'rately *proceed* to what you would
Thus violently redress. *Shakesp. Coriolanus.*

These things, when they *proceed* not, they go backward. *Benj. Johnson's Catiline.*

3. To come forth from a place or from a sender.

I *proceeded* forth and came from God; neither came I of myself, but he sent me. *Jo.* viii. 42.

4. To go or march in state.

He ask'd a clear stage for his muse to *proceed* in. *Anon.*

5. To issue; to arise; to be the effect of; to be produced from.

A dagger of the mind, a false creation,
Proceeding from the heat oppressed brain. *Shakesp. Macbeth.*

From me what *proceed*
But all corrupt, both mind and will both deprav'd. *Milt.*

All this *proceeded* not from any want of knowledge. *Dryd.*

6. To prosecute any design.

He that *proceeds* upon other principles, in his enquiry into any sciences, posts himself in a party. *Locke.*

Since husbandry is of large extent, the poet singles out such precepts to *proceed* on, as are capable of ornament. *Addis.*

7. To be transacted; to be carried on.

He will, after his sour fashion tell you,
What hath *proceeded* worthy note to-day. *Shakesp.*

8. To make progress; to advance.

Violence
Proceeded, and oppression and sword law
Through all the plain. *Milton.*

9. To carry on juridical process.

Proceed by process, lest parties break out,
And sack great Rome with Romans. *Shakesp.*

Instead of a ship, to levy upon his county such a sum of money for his majesty's use, with direction in what manner he should *proceed* against such as refused. *Clarendon.*

To judgment he *proceeded* on th' accus'd. *Milton.*

10. To transact; to act; to carry on any affair methodically.

From them I will not hide
My judgments, how with mankind I *proceed*;
As how with peccant angels late they saw. *Milton.*

How

How ſeverely with themſelves *proceed*,
The men who write ſuch verſe as who can read?
Their own ſtrict judges, not a word they ſpare,
That wants or force, or light, or weight, or care. *Pope.*

11. To take effect; to have its courſe.

This rule only *proceeds* and takes place, when a perſon cannot of common law condemn another by his ſentence. *Ayliffe.*

12. To be propagated; to come by generation.

From my loins thou ſhalt *proceed*. *Milton.*

13. To be produced by the original efficient cauſe.

O Adam, one Almighty is, from whom
All things *proceed*, and up to him return. *Milton.*

PRO'CEED. *n. ſ.* [from the verb.] Produce: as, *the* proceeds *of an eſtate. Clariſſa.* Not an imitable word, though much uſed in law writings.

PROCEE'DER. *n. ſ.* [from *proceed.*] One who goes forward; one who makes a progreſs.

He that ſeeketh victory over his nature, let him not ſet himſelf too great nor too ſmall taſks; for the firſt will make him dejected by often failing; and the ſecond will make him a ſmall *proceeder*, though by often prevailings. *Bacon.*

PROCEE'DING. *n. ſ.* [*procedé*, Fr. from *proceed.*]

1. Progreſs from one thing to another; ſeries of conduct; tranſaction.

I'll acquaint our duteous citizens,
With all your juſt *proceedings* in this caſe. *Shakeſp.*
My dear love
To your *proceedings* bids me tell you this. *Shakeſp.*

The underſtanding brought to knowledge by degrees, and, in ſuch a general *proceeding*, nothing is hard. *Locke.*

It is a very unuſual *proceeding*, and I would not have been guilty of it for the world. *Arbuthnot's Hiſt. of J. Bull*

From the earlieſt ages of chriſtianity, there never was a precedent of ſuch a *proceeding*. *Swift.*

2. Legal procedure: as, *ſuch are the* proceedings *at law*.

PROCE'LLOUS. *adj.* [*procelloſus*, Lat.] Tempeſtuous. *Dict.*

PROCE'PTION. *n. ſ.* Preoccupation; act of taking ſomething ſooner than another. A word not in uſe.

Having ſo little power to offend others, that I have none to preſerve what is mine own from their *proception*. *King Charles.*

PROCE'RITY. *n. ſ.* [from *procerus*, Lat.] Talneſs; height of ſtature.

We ſhall make attempts to lengthen out the humane figure, and reſtore it to its ancient *procerity*. *Addiſon.*

PRO'CESS. *n. ſ.* [*proces*, Fr. *proceſſus*, Latin.]

1. Tendency; progreſſive courſe.

That there is ſomewhat higher than either of theſe two, no other proof doth need, than the very *proceſs* of man's deſire, which being natural ſhould be fruſtrate, if there were not ſome farther thing wherein it might reſt at the length contented, which in the former it cannot do. *Hooker.*

2. Regular and gradual progreſs.

Commend me to your honourable wife;
Tell her the *proceſs* of Antonio's end;
Say how I lov'd you; ſpeak me fair in death. *Shakeſp.*

They declared unto him the whole *proceſs* of that war, and with what ſucceſs they had endured *Knolles.*

Immediate are the acts of God, more ſwift
Than time or motion; but to human ears
Cannot without *proceſs* of ſpeech be told. *Milton.*
Saturnian Juno
Attends the fatal *proceſs* of the war. *Dryden.*

In the parable of the waſteful ſteward, we have a lively image of the force and *proceſs* of this temptation. *Rogers.*

3. Courſe; continual flux or paſſage.

I have been your wife, in this obedience,
Upward of twenty years; if in the courſe
And *proceſs* of this time you can report,
And prove it too againſt mine honour aught,
Turn me away. *Shakeſp. Henry* VIII.
This neither empire riſe,
By policy and long *proceſs* of time. *Milton.*

Many acts of parliament have, in long *proceſs* of time, been loſt, and the things forgotten. *Hale's Law of England.*

4. Methodical management of any thing.

Experiments, familiar to chymiſts, are unknown to the learned, who never read chymical *proceſſes*. *Boyle.*

An age they live releas'd
From all the labour, *proceſs*, clamour, woe,
Which our ſad ſcenes of daily action know. *Prior.*

5. Courſe of law.

Proceed by *proceſs*,
Leſt parties, as he is belov'd, break out. *Shakeſp.*

All *proceſſes* eccleſiaſtical ſhould be made in the king's name, as in writs at the common law. *Hayward.*

The patricians they choſe for their patrons, to anſwer for their appearance, and defend them in any *proceſs*. *Swift.*

PROCE'SSION. *n. ſ.* [*proceſſion*, Fr. *proceſſio*, Lat.] A train marching in ceremonious ſolemnity.

If there be cauſe for the church to go forth in ſolemn *proceſſion*, his whole family have ſuch buſineſs come upon them, that no one can be ſpared. *Hooker.*

Him all his train
Follow'd in bright *proceſſion*. *Milton.*

'Tis the *proceſſion* of a funeral vow,
Which cruel laws to Indian wives allow. *Drydenn.*
The prieſts, Potitius at their head,
In ſkins of beaſts involv'd, the long *proceſſion* led. *Dryden.*

When this vaſt congregation was formed into a regular *proceſſion* to attend the ark of the covenant, the king marched at the head of his people, with hymns and dances. *Addiſon.*

It is to be hoped, that the perſons of wealth, who made their *proceſſion* through the members of theſe new erected ſeminaries, will contribute to their maintenance. *Addiſon.*

The Ethiopians held an annual ſacrifice of twelve days to the Gods; all that time they carried their images in *proceſſion*, and placed them at their feſtivals. *Broome.*

To PROCE'SSION. *v. n.* [from the noun.] To go in proceſſion. A low word.

PROCE'SSIONAL. *adj.* [from *proceſſion.*] Relating to proceſſion.

PROCE'SSIONARY. *adj.* [from *proceſſion.*] Conſiſting in proceſſion.

Rogations or litanies were then the very ſtrength and comfort of God's church; whereupon, in the year 506, it was by the council of Aurelia decreed, that the whole church ſhould beſtow yearly at the feaſt of pentecoſt, three days in that *proceſſionary* ſervice. *Hooker.*

PRO'CHRONISM. *n. ſ.* [προχρόνισμ@.] An error in chronology; a dating a thing before it happened. *Dict.*

PRO'CIDENCE. *n. ſ.* [*procidentia*, Lat.] Falling down; dependence below its natural place.

PRO'CINCT. *n. ſ.* [*procinctus*, Lat.] Complete preparation; preparation brought to the point of action.

When all the plain
Cover'd with thick imbattl'd ſquadrons bright,
Chariots, and flaming arms, and fiery ſteeds,
Reflecting blaze on blaze, firſt met his view,
War he perceiv'd, war in *procinct*. *Milton.*

To PROCLAI'M. *v. a.* [*proclamo*, Lat. *proclamer*, Fr.]

1. To promulgate or denounce by a ſolemn or legal publication.

When thou comeſt nigh unto a city to fight againſt it, *proclaim* peace unto it. *Deut.* xx. 10.

I *proclaim* a liberty for you, ſaith the Lord, to the ſword and to the peſtilence. *Jer.* xxxiv. 17.

Heralds
With trumpet's ſound, throughout the hoſt *proclaim*
A ſolemn council. *Milton.*
While in another's name you peace declare,
Princeſs, you in your own *proclaim* a war. *Dryden.*
She to the palace led her gueſt,
Then offer'd incenſe, and *proclaim'd* a feaſt. *Dryden.*

2. To tell openly.

Some profligate wretches, were the apprehenſions of puniſhments or ſhame taken away, would as openly *proclaim* their atheiſm, as their lives do. *Locke.*

While the deathleſs muſe
Shall ſing the juſt, ſhall o'er their head diffuſe
Perfumes with laviſh hand, ſhe ſhall *proclaim*
Thy crimes alone. *Prior.*

3. To outlaw by publick denunciation.

I heard myſelf *proclaimed*. *Shakeſp.*

PROCLAI'MER. *n. ſ.* [from *proclaim.*] One that publiſhes by authority.

The great *proclaimer*, with a voice
More awful than the ſound of trumpet, cry'd
Repentance, and heaven's kingdom nigh at hand
To all baptiz'd. *Milton's Paradiſe Regain'd.*

PROCLAMA'TION. *n. ſ.* [*proclamatio*, Lat. *proclamation*, Fr. from *proclaim.*]

1. Publication by authority.

2. A declaration of the king's will openly publiſhed among the people.

If the king ſent a *proclamation* for their repair to their houſes, ſome nobleman publiſhed a proteſtation againſt thoſe *proclamations*. *Clarendon.*

PROCLI'VITY. *n. ſ.* [*proclivitas*; *proclivis*, Lat.]

1. Tendency; natural inclination; propenſion; proneneſs.

The ſenſitive appetite may engender a *proclivity* to ſteal, but not a neceſſity to ſteal. *Bramhall againſt Hobbs.*

2. Readineſs; facility of attaining.

He had ſuch a dextrous *proclivity*, as his teachers were fain to reſtrain his forwardneſs, that his brothers might keep pace with him. *Wotton.*

PROCLI'VOUS. *adj.* [*proclivis*, Lat.] Inclined; tending by nature. *Dict.*

PROCO'NSUL. *n. ſ.* [Latin.] A Roman officer, who governed a province with conſular authority.

Every child knoweth how dear the works of Homer were to Alexander, Virgil to Auguſtus, Auſonius to Gratian, who made him *proconſul*, Chaucer to Richard II. and Gower to Henry IV. *Peacham.*

PROCO'NSULSHIP. *n. ſ.* [from *proconſul.*] The office of a proconſul.

To PROCRA'STINATE. *v. a.* [*procraſtinor*, Lat.] To defer; to delay; to put off from day to day.

Hopeleſs and helpleſs doth Ægeon wind,
But to *procraſtinate* his lifeleſs end. *Shakeſp.*

Let

Let men seriously and attentively listen to that voice within them, and they will certainly need no other medium to convince them, either of the error or danger of thus *procrastinating* their repentance. *Decay of Piety.*

To PROCRA'STINATE. *v. n.* To be dilatory.

I *procrastinate* more than I did twenty years ago, and have several things to finish, which I put off to twenty years hence. *Swift to Pope.*

PROCRASTINA'TION. *n. s.* [*procrastinatio*, Lat. from *procrastinate.*] Delay; dilatoriness.

How desperate the hazard of such *procrastination* is, hath been convincingly demonstrated by better pens. *D. of Piety.*

PROCRASTINA'TOR. *n. s.* [from *procrastinate.*] A dilatory person.

PRO'CREANT. *adj.* [*procreans*, Lat.] Productive; pregnant.

The temple haunting martlet, does approve
By his lov'd mansionry, that heaven's breath
Smells wooingly here: no jutting frieze,
But this bird
Hath made his pendant bed, and *procreant* cradle. *Shakesp.*

To PRO'CREATE. *v. a.* [*procreo*, Lat. *procreer*, Fr.] To generate; to produce.

Flies crushed and corrupted, when inclosed in such vessels, did never *procreate* a new fly. *Bentley.*

Since the earth retains her fruitful power,
To *procreate* plants the forest to restore;
Say, why to nobler animals alone
Should she be feeble, and unfruitful grown. *Blackmore.*

PROCREA'TION. *n. s.* [*procreation*, Fr. *procreatio*, Lat. from *procreate.*] Generation; production.

The enclosed warmth, which the earth hath in itself, stirred up by the heat of the sun, assisteth nature in the speedier *procreation* of those varieties, which the earth bringeth forth. *Raleigh's Hist. of the World.*

Neither her outside form'd so fair, nor ought
In *procreation* common to all kinds. *Milton's Par. Lost.*

Uncleanness is an unlawful gratification of the appetite of *procreation.* *South's Sermons.*

PRO'CREATIVE. *adj.* [from *procreate.*] Generative; productive.

The ordinary period of the human *procreative* faculty in males is sixty-five, in females forty-five. *Hale.*

PRO'CREATIVENESS. *n. s.* [from *procreative.*] Power of generation.

These seem to have the accurst privilege of propagating and not expiring, and have reconciled the *procreativeness* of corporeal, with the duration of incorporeal substances. *Decay of Piety.*

PROCREA'TOR. *n. s.* [from *procreate.*] Generator; begetter.

PROCTOR. *n. s.* [contracted from *procurator*, Lat.]

1. A manager of another man's affairs.

The most clamorous for this pretended reformation, are either atheists, or else *proctors* suborned by atheists. *Hooker.*

2. An attorney in the spiritual court.

I find him charging the inconveniencies in the payment of tythes upon the clergy and *proctors.* *Swift.*

3. The magistrate of the university.

To PRO'CTOR. *v. a.* [from the noun.] To manage. A cant word.

I cannot *proctor* mine own cause so well
To make it clear. *Shakesp. Ant. and Cleop.*

PRO'CTORSHIP. *n. s.* [from *proctor.*] Office or dignity of a proctor.

From a scholar he became a fellow, and the president of the college, after he had received all the graces and degrees, the *proctorship* and the doctorship. *Clarendon.*

PROCU'MBENT. *adj.* [*procumbens*, Latin.] Lying down; prone.

PROCU'RABLE. *adj.* [from *procure.*] To be procured; obtainable; acquirable.

Though it be a far more common and *procurable* liquor than the infusion of lignum nephriticum, it may yet be easily substituted in its room. *Boyle on Colours.*

PRO'CURACY. *n. s.* [from *procure.*] The management of any thing.

PROCURA'TION. *n. s.* [from *procure.*] The act of procuring.

Those, who formerly were doubtful in this matter, upon strict and repeated inspection of these bodies, and *procuration* of plain shells from this island, are now convinced, that these are the remains of sea-animals. *Woodward's Nat. Hist.*

PROCURA'TOR. *n. s.* [*procurateur*, Fr. from *procuro*, Lat.] Manager; one who transacts affairs for another.

I had in charge at my depart from France,
As *procurator* for your excellence,
To marry princess Marg'ret for your grace. *Shakesp.*

They confirm and seal
Their undertaking with their dearest blood,
As *procurators* for the commonweal. *Daniel.*

When the *procurators* of king Antigonus imposed a rate upon the sick people, that came to Edepsum to drink the waters which were lately sprung, and were very healthful, they instantly dried up. *Taylor's Rule of Living Holy.*

PROCURATO'RIAL. *adj.* [from *procurator.*] Made by a proctor.

All *procuratorial* exceptions ought to be made before contestation of suit, and not afterwards, as being dilatory exceptions, if a proctor was then made and constituted. *Ayliffe.*

PROCU'RATORY. *adj.* [from *procurator.*] Tending to procuration.

To PROCU'RE. *v. a.* [*procuro*, Lat. *procurer*, Fr.]

1. To manage; to transact for another.

2. To obtain; to acquire.

They shall fear and tremble, for all the prosperity that I *procure* unto it. *Jer.* xxxiii. 9.

Happy though but ill,
If we *procure* not to ourselves more woe. *Milton.*

We no other pains endure,
Than those that we ourselves *procure.* *Dryden.*

Then by thy toil *procur'd*, thou food shalt eat. *Dryden.*

3. To persuade; to prevail on.

Is it my lady mother?
What unaccustom'd cause *procures* her hither? *Shakesp.*

Whom nothing can *procure*,
When the wide world runs biass, from his will
To writhe his limbs, and share, not mend the ill. *Herbert.*

4. To contrive; to forward.

Proceed, Salinus, to *procure* my fall,
And by the doom of death end woes and all. *Shakesp.*

To PRO'CURE. *v. n.* To bawd; to pimp.

Our author calls colouring, lena sororis, in plain English, the bawd of her sister, the design or drawing: she cloaths, she dresses her up, she paints her, she makes her appear more lovely than naturally she is, she *procures* for the design, and makes lovers for her. *Dryden's Dufresnoy.*

With what impatience must the muse behold,
The wife by her *procuring* husband sold. *Dryden.*

PROCU'REMENT. *n. s.* The act of procuring.

They mourn your ruin as their proper fate,
Cursing the empress; for they think it done
By her *procurement.* *Dryden's Aurengz.*

PROCU'RER. *n. s.* [from *procure.*]

1. One that gains; obtainer.

Angling was after tedious study, a moderator of passions, and a *procurer* of contentedness. *Walton's Angler.*

2. Pimp; pandar.

Strumpets in their youth, turn *procurers* in their age. *South.*

PROCU'RESS. *n. s.* [from *procure.*] A bawd.

I saw the most artful *procuress* in town, seducing a young girl. *Spectator.*

PRODI'GAL. *adj.* [*prodigus*, Lat. *prodigue*, Fr.] Profuse; wasteful; expensive; lavish; not frugal; not parcimonious.

Least I should seem over *prodigal* in the praise of my countrymen, I will only present you with some few verses. *Camd.*

Be now as *prodigal* of all dear grace,
As nature was in making graces dear,
When she did starve the general world beside,
And prodigally gave them all to you. *Shakesp.*

My chief care
Is to come fairly off from the great debts,
Wherein my time, something too *prodigal*,
Hath left me gaged. *Shakesp. Merch. of Venice.*

Diogenes did beg more of a *prodigal* man than the rest; whereupon one said, see your baseness, that when you find a liberal mind, you will take most of him; no, said Diogenes, but I mean to beg of the rest again. *Bacon.*

As a hero, whom his baser foes
In troops surround; now these assails, now those,
Though *prodigal* of life, disdains to die
By common hands. *Denham.*

Here patriots live, who for their country's good,
In fighting fields were *prodigal* of blood. *Dryden.*

The *prodigal* of soul rush'd on the stroke
Of lifted weapons, and did wounds provoke. *Dryden.*

O! beware,
Great warrior, nor too *prodigal* of life,
Expose the British safety. *Philips.*

Some people are *prodigal* of their blood, and others so sparing, as if so much life and blood went together. *Baker.*

PRO'DIGAL. *n. s.* A waster; a spendthrift.

A beggar suddenly grown rich, becomes a *prodigal*; for to obscure his former obscurity, he puts on riot and excess. *Benj. Johnson's Discovery.*

Thou
Ow'st all thy losses to the fates; but I,
Like wasteful *prodigals*, have cast away
My happiness. *Denham's Sophy.*

Let the wasteful *prodigal* be slain. *Dryden.*

PRODIGA'LITY. *n. s.* [*prodigalité*, Fr. from *prodigal.*] Extravagance; profusion; waste; excessive liberality.

A sweeter and lovelier gentleman,
Fram'd in the *prodigality* of nature,
The spacious world cannot again afford. *Shakesp.*

He that decries covetousness, should not be held an adversary to him that opposeth *prodigality.* *Glanvil.*

It is not always so obvious to distinguish between an act of liberality and act of *prodigality*. *South's Sermons.*

The most severe censor cannot but be pleased with the *prodigality* of his wit, though at the same time he could have wished, that the master of it had been a better manager. *Dry.*

PRO'DIGALLY. *adv.* [from *prodigal.*] Profusely; wastefully; extravagantly.

We are not yet so wretched in our fortunes,
Nor in our wills so lost, as to abandon
A friendship *prodigally*, of that price
As is the senate and the people of Rome. *B. Johnson.*

I cannot well be thought so *prodigally* thirsty of my subjects blood, as to venture my own life. *King Charles.*

The next in place and punishment are they,
Who *prodigally* throw their souls away;
Fools, who repining at their wretched state,
And loathing anxious life, suborn'd their fate. *Dryden.*

Nature not bounteous now, but lavish grows,
Our paths with flow'rs she *prodigally* strows. *Dryden.*

PRODI'GIOUS. *adj* [*prodigiosus*, Lat. *prodigieux*, Fr.] Amazing; astonishing; such as may seem a prodigy; portentous; enormous; monstrous; amazingly great.

If e'er he have a child, abortive be it,
Prodigious and untimely brought to light. *Shakesp.*

An emission of immateriate virtues we are a little doubtful to propound, it being so *prodigious*; but that it is constantly avouched by many. *Bacon's Nat. Hist.*

It is *prodigious* to have thunder in a clear sky. *Brown.*

Then entring at the gate,
Conceal'd in clouds, *prodigious* to relate,
He mix'd, unmark'd, among the busy throng. *Dryden.*

The Rhone enters the lake, and brings along with it a *prodigious* quantity of water. *Addison's Remarks on Italy.*

It is a scandal to christianity, that in towns, where there is a *prodigious* increase in the number of houses and inhabitants, so little care should be taken for churches. *Swift.*

PRODI'GIOUSLY. *adv.* [from *prodigious.*]

1. Amazingly; astonishingly; portentously; enormously.

I do not mean absolutely according to philosophick exactness infinite, but only infinite or innumerable as to us, or their number *prodigiously* great. *Ray on the Creation.*

2. It is sometimes used as a familiar hyperbole.

I am *prodigiously* pleased with this joint volume. *Pope.*

PRODI'GIOUSNESS. *n. s.* [from *prodigious.*] Enormousness; portentousness; amazing qualities.

PRO'DIGY. *n. s.* [*prodige*, Fr. *prodigium*, Lat.]

1. Any thing out of the ordinary process of nature, from which omens are drawn; portent.

Be no more an exhal'd meteor,
A *prodigy* of fear, and a portent
Of broached mischief, to the unborn times. *Shakesp.*

The party opposite to our settlement, seem to be driven out of all human methods, and are reduced to the poor comfort of *prodigies* and old womens fables. *Addison.*

2. Monster.

Most of mankind, through their own sluggishness, become nature's *prodigies*, not her children. *Benj. Johnson.*

3. Any thing astonishing for good or bad.

They would seem *prodigies* of learning. *Spectator.*

PRODI'TION. *n. s.* [*proditio*, Lat.] Treason; treachery. *Ain.*

PRO'DITOR. *n. s.* [Latin.] A traytor. Not in use.

Piel'd priest, dost thou command me be shut out?
—I do, thou most usurping *proditor*. *Shakesp.*

PRODITO'RIOUS. *adj.* [from *proditor*, Lat.]

1. Trayterous; treacherous; perfidious.

Now *proditorious* wretch! what hast thou done,
To make this barb'rous base assassinate? *Daniel.*

2. Apt to make discoveries.

Solid and conclusive characters are emergent from the mind, and start out of children when themselves least think of it; for nature is *proditorious*. *Wotton on Education.*

To PRODU'CE. *v. a.* [*produco*, Lat. *produire*, Fr.]

1. To offer to the view or notice.

Produce your cause, saith the Lord; bring forth your strong reasons. *Isa.* xli. 21.

2. To exhibit to the publick.

Your parents did not *produce* you much into the world, whereby you avoided many wrong steps. *Swift.*

3. To bring as an evidence.

It seems not meet, nor wholesome to my place,
To be *produc'd* against the Moor. *Shakesp. Othello.*

4. To bear; to bring forth, as a vegetable.

This soil *produces* all sorts of palm-trees. *Sandys.*

5. To cause; to effect; to generate; to beget.

Somewhat is *produced* of nothing; for lyes are sufficient to breed opinion, and opinion brings on substance. *Bacon.*

They by imprudence mix'd
Produce prodigious births of body or mind. *Milton.*

Thou all this good of evil shalt *produce*. *Milton.*

Clouds may rain, and rain *produce*
Fruits in her soften'd soil. *Milton.*

Observing in ourselves, that we can at pleasure move several parts of our bodies; the effects also, that natural bodies are able to *produce* in one another, occuring every moment to our senses, we both these ways get the idea of power. *Locke.*

Hinder light but from striking on porphyre, and its colours vanish, it no longer *produces* any such ideas; upon the return of light, it *produces* these appearances again. *Locke.*

This wonder of the sculptor's hand
Produc'd, his art was at a stand. *Addison.*

PRO'DUCE. *n. s.* [from the verb. This noun, though accented on the last syllable by *Dryden*, is generally accented on the former.]

1. Product; that which any thing yields or brings.

You hoard not health for your own private use,
But on the publick spend the rich *produce*. *Dryden.*

2. Amount; profit; gain; emergent sum or quantity.

In Staffordshire, after their lands are marled, they sow it with barley, allowing three bushels to an acre. Its common *produce* is thirty bushels. *Mortimer's Husbandry.*

This tax has already been so often tried, that we know the exact *produce* of it. *Addison's Freeholder*, N° 20.

PRODU'CENT. *n. s.* [from *produce.*] One that exhibits; one that offers.

If an instrument be produced with a protestation in favour of the *producent*, and the adverse party does not contradict, it shall be construed to the advantage of the *producent*. *Ayliffe.*

PRODU'CER. *n. s.* [from *produce.*] One that generates or produces.

By examining how I, that could contribute nothing to mine own being, should be here, I came to ask the same question for my father, and so am led in a direct line to a first *producer* that must be more than man. *Suckling.*

Whenever want of money, or want of desire in the consumer, make the price low, that immediately reaches the first *producer*. *Locke.*

PRODU'CIBLE. *adj.* [from *produce.*]

1. Such as may be exhibited.

That is accounted probable, which has better arguments *producible* for it, than can be brought against it. *South.*

Many warm expressions of the fathers are *producible* in this case. *Decay of Piety.*

2. Such as may be generated or made.

The salts *producible*, are the alcalis or fixt salts, which seem to have an antipathy with acid ones. *Boyle.*

PRODU'CIBLENESS. *n. s.* [from *producible.*] The state of being producible.

To confirm our doctrine of the *producibleness* of salts, Helmont assures us, that by Paracelsus's sal circulatum solid bodies, particularly stones, may be transmuted into actual salt equiponderant. *Boyle.*

PRO'DUCT. *n. s.* [*productus*, Lat. *produit*, Fr.]

1. Something produced, as fruits, grain, metals.

The landholder, having nothing but what the *product* of his land will yield, must take the market-rate. *Locke.*

Our British *products* are of such kinds and quantities, as can turn the balance of trade to our advantage. *Addison.*

Range in the same quarter, the *products* of the same season. *Spectator.*

See thy bright altars
Heap'd with the *products* of Sabæan springs. *Pope.*

2. Work; composition.

Most of those books, which have obtained great reputation in the world, are the *products* of great and wise men. *Watts.*

3. Thing consequential; effect.

These are the *product*
Of those ill-mated marriages. *Milton's Par. Lost.*

PRODU'CTILE. *adj.* [from *produco*, Lat.] Which may be produced.

PRODU'CTION. *n. s.* [*production*, Fr. from *product.*]

1. The act of producing.

A painter should foresee the harmony of the lights and shadows, taking from each of them that which will most conduce to the *production* of a beautiful effect. *Dryden.*

2. The thing produced; fruit; product.

The best of queens and best of herbs we owe
To that bold nation, which the way did show
To the fair region, where the sun does rise,
Whose rich *productions* we so justly prize. *Waller.*

What would become of the scrofulous consumptive *production*, furnished by our men of wit and learning. *Swift.*

3. Composition.

We have had our names prefixed at length, to whole volumes of mean *productions*. *Swift.*

PRODU'CTIVE. *adj.* [from *produce.*] Having the power to produce; fertile; generative; efficient.

In thee
Not in themselves, all their known virtue appears
Productive as in herb and plant. *M*

This is turning nobility unto a principle of virtue, making it *productive* of merit, as it is understood to have been originally a reward of it. *Spectator*, N° 537.

Be thou my aid, my tuneful song inspire,
And kindle, with thy own *productive* fire. *Dryden.*

If the *productive* fat of the marl be spent, it is not capable of being mended with new. *Mortimer.*

Numbers of Scots are glad to exchange their barren hills for our fruitful vales so *productive* of that grain. *Swift.*

Hymen's flames like stars unite,
And burn for ever one;
Chaste as cold Cynthia's virgin light,
Productive as the sun. *Pope.*

Plutarch, in his life of Theseus, says, that that age was *productive* of men of prodigious stature. *Broome.*

PRO'EM. *n. s.* [προοίμιον; *procemium*, Lat. *proeme*, old Fr.] Preface; introduction.

So gloz'd the tempter, and his *proem* tun'd. *Milton.*

Thus much may serve by way of *proem*,
Proceed we therefore to our poem. *Swift's Miscel.*

Justinian has, in the *proem* to the digests, only prefixed the term of five years for studying the laws. *Ayliffe.*

PROFANA'TION. *n. s.* [*profanation*, Fr. from *profano*, Lat.]

1. The act of violating any thing sacred.

He knew how bold men are to take even from God himself; how hardly that house would be kept from impious *profanation* he knew. *Hooker, b.* v. *s.* 12.

What I am and what I would, are to your ears, divinity; to any others, *profanation.* *Shakesp. Twelfth Night.*

'Twere *profanation* of our joys,
To tell the laity our love. *Donne.*

All *profanation* and invasion of things sacred, is an offence against the eternal law of nature. *South.*

Others think I ought not to have translated Chaucer: they suppose a veneration due to his old language, and that it is little less than *profanation* and sacrilege to alter it. *Dryden.*

2. Irreverence to holy things or persons.

Great men may jest with saints, 'tis wit in them;
But, in the less, foul *profanation.* *Shakesp.*

PROFA'NE. *adj.* [*profane*, Fr. from *profanus*, Lat.]

1. Irreverent to sacred names or things.

Profane fellow!
Wert thou the son of Jupiter, and no more
But what thou art besides, thou wert too base
To be his groom. *Shakesp. Cymbeline.*

These have caused the weak to stumble, and the *profane* to blaspheme, offending the one, and hardening the other. *South.*

2. Not sacred; secular.

The universality of the deluge is attested by *profane* history; for the fame of it is gone through the earth, and there are records or traditions concerning it in all the parts of this and the new-found world. *Burnet's Theory of the Earth.*

3. Polluted; not pure.

Nothing is *profane* that serveth to holy things. *Raleigh.*

4. Not purified by holy rites.

Far hence be souls *profane*,
The Sibyl cry'd, and from the grove abstain. *Dryden.*

To PROFA'NE. *v. a.* [*profano*, Lat. *profaner*, Fr.]

1. To violate; to pollute.

He then, that is not furnish'd in this sort,
Doth but usurp the sacred name of knight,
Profaning this most honourable order. *Shakesp.*

Foretasted fruit
Profan'd first by the serpent, by him first
Made common and unhallow'd. *Milton.*

Pity the temple *profaned* of ungodly men. 2 *Mac.* viii. 2.

How far have we
Profan'd thy heav'nly gift of poesy?
Made prostitute and profligate the muse,
Debas'd. *Dryden.*

2. To put to wrong use.

I feel me much to blame.
So idly to *profane* the precious time. *Shakesp.*

PROFA'NELY. *adv.* [from *profane.*] With irreverence to sacred names or things.

I will hold my tongue no more, as touching their wickedness, which they *profanely* commit. 2 *Esdr.* xv. 8.

Let none of things serious, much less of divine,
When belly and head's full, *profanely* dispute. *B. Johns.*

That proud scholar, intending to erect altars to Virgil, speaks of Homer too *profanely.* *Broome's Notes on the Odyssey.*

PROFA'NER. *n. s.* [from *profane.*] Polluter; violater.

The argument which our Saviour useth against *profaners* of the temple, he taketh from the use whereunto it was with solemnity consecrated. *Hooker. b.* v. *s.* 12.

Rebellious subjects, enemies to peace,
Profaners of this neighbour stained steel. *Shakesp.*

There are a lighter ludicrous sort of *profaners*, who use the scripture to furnish out their jests. *Gov. of the Tongue.*

PROFA'NENESS. *n. s.* [from *profane.*] Irreverence of what is sacred.

Apollo, pardon
My great *profaneness* 'gainst thy oracle! *Shakesp.*

You can banish from thence scurrility and *profaneness*, and restrain the licentious insolence of poets and their actors. *Dry.*

Edicts against immorality and *profaneness*, laws against oaths and execrations, we trample upon. *Atterbury.*

PROFE'CTION. *n. s.* [*profectio*, Lat.] Advance; progression.

This, with *profection* of the horoscope unto the seventh house or opposite signs, every seventh year oppresseth living natures. *Brown's Vulgar Errours.*

To PROFE'SS. *v. a.* [*professer*, Fr. from *professus*, Lat.]

1. To declare himself in strong terms of any opinion or passion.

Would you have me speak after my custom,
As being a *profess'd* tyrant to their sex. *Shakesp.*

Pretending first
Wise to fly pain, *professing* next the spy. *Milton.*

A servant to thy sex, a slave to thee,
A foe *profest* to barren chastity. *Dryden's Knight's Tale.*

2. To make a show of any sentiments by loud declaration.

Love well your father;
To your *professing* bosoms I commit him. *Shakesp.*

3. To declare publickly one's skill in any art or science, so as to invite employment.

What, master, read you? first resolve me that.
—I read that I *profess* the art of love. *Shakesp.*

Without eyes thou shalt want light; *profess* not the knowledge therefore that thou hast not. *Ecclus* iii. 25.

To PROFE'SS. *v. n.*

1. To declare openly.

The day almost itself *professes* yours,
And little is to do. *Shakesp. Macbeth.*

They *profess*, that they know God, but in works they deny him. *Tit.* i. 16.

Profess unto the Lord, that I am come unto the country, which the Lord sware unto our fathers. *Deutr.* xxvi. 3.

2. To declare friendship. Not in use.

As he does conceive,
He is dishonour'd by a man, which ever
Profess'd to him; why, his revenges must
In that be made more bitter. *Shakesp.*

PROFE'SSEDLY. *adv.* [from *professed.*] According to open declaration made by himself.

I could not grant too much to men, that being *professedly* my subjects, pretended religious strictness. *King Charles.*

Virgil, whom he *professedly* imitated, has surpassed him among the Romans. *Dryden's Dedication to Juvenal.*

England I travelled over, *professedly* searching all places I passed along. *Woodward.*

PROFE'SSION. *n. s.* [*profession*, Fr. from *profess.*]

1. Calling; vocation; known employment.

I must tell you,
You tender more your person's honour, than
Your high *profession* spiritual. *Shakesp. Henry* VIII.

If we confound arts with the abuse of them, we shall condemn all honest trades; for there are that deceive in all *professions*, and bury in forgetfulness all knowledge. *Raleigh.*

Some of our *profession* keep wounds tented. *Wiseman.*

No other one race, not the sons of any one other *profession*, not perhaps altogether, are so much scattered amongst all *professions*, as the sons of clergymen. *Sprat's Sermons.*

This is a practice, in which multitudes, besides those of the learned *professions*, may be engaged. *Watts.*

2. Declaration.

A naked *profession* may have credit, where no other evidence can be given. *Glanvill's Sceps.*

Most profligately false, with the strongest *professions* of sincerity. *Swift.*

3. The act of declaring one's self of any party or opinion.

For by oil in their lamps, and the first lighting of them, which was common to them both, is meant that solemn *profession* of faith and repentance, which all christians make in baptism. *Tillotson's Sermons.*

When christianity came to be taken up, for the sake of those civil encouragements which attended their *profession*, the complaint was applicable to christians. *Swift.*

PROFE'SSIONAL. *adj.* [from *profession.*] Relating to a particular calling or profession.

Professional, as well as national, reflections are to be avoided. *Clarissa.*

PROFE'SSOR. *n. s.* [*professeur*, Fr. from *profess.*]

1. One who declares himself of any opinion or party.

When the holiness of the *professors* of religion is decayed you may doubt the springing up of a new sect. *Bacon's Essays.*

2. One who publickly practises or teaches an art.

Professors in most sciences, are generally the worst qualified to explain their meanings to those who are not of their tribes. *Swift.*

3. One who is visibly religious.

Ordinary illiterate people, who were *professors*, that shewed a concern for religion, seemed much conversant in St. Paul's Epistles. *Locke.*

PROFE'SSORSHIP. *n. s.* [from *professor.*] The station or office of a publick teacher.

Dr. Prideaux succeeded him in the *professorship*, being then elected bishop of Worcester, Sanderson succeeded him in the regius *professorship.* *Walton.*

To PROFFER.

To PRO'FFER. *v. a.* [*profero*, Lat. *proferer*, Fr.]

1. To propose; to offer.

To them that covet such eye-glutting gain,
Proffer thy gifts, and fitter servants entertain. *Fairy Queen.*

None, among the choice and prime
Of those heav'n-warring champions, could be found
So hardy as to *proffer*, or accept
Alone, the dreadful voyage. *Milton's Par. Lost.*

Does Cato send this answer back to Cæsar,
For all his generous cares and *proffer'd* friendship. *Addis.*

2. To attempt. *Ainsworth.*

PRO'FFER. *n. s.* [from the verb.]

1. Offer made; something proposed to acceptance.

Basilius, content to take that, since he could have no more, allowed her reasons, and took her *proffer* thankfully. *Sidney.*

Proffers, not took, reap thanks for their reward. *Shakesp.*

The king
Great *proffers* sends of pardon and of grace,
If they would yield, and quietness embrace. *Daniel.*

He made a *proffer* to lay down his commission of command in the army. *Clarendon.*

But these, nor all the *proffers* you can make,
Are worth the heifer which I set to stake. *Dryden.*

2. Essay; attempt.

It is done with time, and by little and little, and with many essays and *proffers*. *Bacon's Essays.*

PRO'FFERER. *n. s.* [from *proffer*.] He that offers.

Maids, in modesty, say no, to that
Which they would have the *proff'rer* construe ay. *Shakesp.*

He who always refuses, taxes the *profferer* with indiscretion, and declares his assistance needless. *Collier.*

PROFI'CIENCE. } *n. s.* [from *proficio*, Lat.] Profit; advancement in any thing; improvement gained.
PROFI'CIENCY. }

It is applied to intellectual acquisition.

Persons of riper years, who flocked into the church during the three first centuries, were obliged to pass through instructions, and give account of their *proficiency*. *Addison.*

Some reflecting with too much satisfaction on their own *proficiencies*, or presuming on their election by God, persuade themselves into a careless security. *Rogers's Sermons.*

PROFI'CIENT. *n. s.* [*proficiens*, Lat.] One who has made advances in any study or business.

I am so good a *proficient* in one quarter of an hour, that I can drink with any tinker in his own language. *Shakesp.*

I am disposed to receive further light in this matter, from those whom it will be no disparagement for much greater *proficients* than I to learn. *Boyle.*

Young deathlings were, by practice, made
Proficients in their father's trade. *Swift's Miscel.*

PROFI'CUOUS. *adj.* [*proficuus*, Lat.] Advantageous; useful.

It is very *proficuous*, to take a good large dose. *Harvey.*

To future times
Proficuous, such a race of men produce,
As in the cause of virtue firm, may fix
Her throne inviolate. *Philips.*

PROFI'LE. *n. s.* [*profile*, Fr.] The side face; half face.

The painter will not take that side of the face, which has some notorious blemish in it; but either draw it in *profile*, or else shadow the more imperfect side. *Dryden.*

Till the end of the third century, I have not seen a Roman emperor drawn with a full face: they always appear in *profile*, which gives us the view of a head very majestic. *Addison.*

PRO'FIT. *n. s.* [*profit*, Fr.]

1. Gain; pecuniary advantage.

Thou must know,
'Tis not my *profit* that does lead mine honour. *Shakesp.*

He thinks it highly just, that all rewards of trust, *profit*, or dignity should be given only to those, whose principles direct them to preserve the constitution. *Swift.*

2. Advantage: accession of good.

What *profit* is it for men now to live in heaviness, and after death to look for punishment? *2 Esdr.* vii. 47.

Wisdom that is hid, and treasure that is hoarded up, what *profit* is in them both? *Ecclus.* xx. 30.

Say not what *profit* is there of my service; and what good things shall I have hereafter. *Ecclus.* xi. 23.

The king did not love the barren wars with Scotland, though he made his *profit* of the noise of them. *Bacon.*

3. Improvement; advancement; proficiency.

To PRO'FIT. *v. a.* [*profiter*, Fr.]

1. To benefit; to advantage.

Whereto might the strength of their hands *profit* me. *Job.*

Let it *profit* thee to have heard,
By terrible example, the reward
Of disobedience. *Milton's Par. Lost*, b. vi.

2. To improve; to advance.

'Tis a great means of *profiting* yourself, to copy diligently excellent pieces and beautiful designs. *Dryden.*

To PRO'FIT. *v. n.*

1. To gain advantage.

The Romans, though possessed of their ports, did not *profit* much by trade. *Arbuthnot on Coins.*

2. To make improvement.

Meditate upon these things; give thyself wholly to them; that thy *profiting* may appear to all. *1 Tim.* iv. 15.

She has *profited* so well already by your counsel, that she can say her lesson. *Dryden's Spanish Fryar.*

3. To be of use or advantage.

Oft times nothing profits more,
Than self-esteem grounded on just and right. *Milton.*

What *profited* thy thoughts, and toils, and cares,
In vigour more confirm'd, and riper years? *Prior.*

PRO'FITABLE. *adj.* [*profitable*, Fr. from *profit*.]

1. Gainful; lucrative.

A pound of man's flesh, taken from a man,
Is not so estimable or *profitable*,
As flesh of muttons, beefs, or goats. *Shakesp.*

The planting of hop-yards, sowing of wheat and rapeseed, are found very *profitable* for the planters, in places apt for them, and consequently *profitable* for the kingdom. *Bacon.*

2. Useful; advantageous.

To wail friends lost
Is not by much so wholesome, *profitable*,
As to rejoice at friends but newly found. *Shakesp.*

Then Judas, thinking indeed that they would be *profitable* in many things, granted them peace. *2 Mac.* xii.

What was so *profitable* to the empire, became fatal to the emperor. *Arbuthnot on Coins.*

PRO'FITABLENESS. *n. s.* [from *profitable*.]

1. Gainfulness.

2. Usefulness; advantageousness.

We will now briefly take notice of the *profitableness* of plants for physick and food. *More's Antidote against Atheism.*

What shall be the just portion of those, whom neither the condescension or kindness, nor wounds and sufferings of the son of God could persuade, nor yet the excellency, easiness and *profitableness* of his commands invite? *Calamy's Sermons.*

PRO'FITABLY. *adv.* [from *profitable*.]

1. Gainfully.

2. Advantageously; usefully.

You have had many opportunities to settle this reflection, and have *profitably* employed them. *Wake.*

PRO'FITLESS. *adj.* [from *profit*.] Void of gain or advantage.

We must not think the Turk is so unskilful,
To leave that latest, which concerns him first;
Neglecting an attempt of ease and gain,
To wake and wage a danger *profitless*. *Shakesp.*

PRO'FLIGATE. *adj.* [*profligatus*, Lat.] Abandoned; lost to virtue and decency; shameless.

Time sensibly all things impairs;
Our fathers have been worse than theirs,
And we than ours; next age will see
A race more *profligate* than we, }
With all the pains we take, have skill enough to be. *Rosc.* }

How far have we
Prophan'd thy heav'nly gift of poesy?
Made prostitute and *profligate* the muse,
Debas'd to each obscene and impious use,
Whose harmony was first ordain'd above
For tongues of angels, and for hymns of love. *Dryden.*

Though Phalaris his brazen bull were there,
And he wou'd dictate what he'd have you swear,
Be not so *profligate*, but rather chuse
To guard your honour, and your life to lose. *Dryden.*

Melancholy objects and subjects will, at times, impress the most *profligate* spirits. *Clarissa.*

PRO'FLIGATE. *n. s.* An abandoned shameless wretch.

It is pleasant to see a notorious *profligate* seized with a concern for his religion, and converting his spleen into zeal. *Add.*

I have heard a *profligate* offer much stronger arguments against paying his debts, than ever he was known to do against christianity; because he happened to be closer pressed by the bailiff than the parson. *Swift's Miscellanies.*

How could such a *profligate* as Antony, or a boy of eighteen, like Octavius, ever dare to dream of giving the law to such an empire and people. *Swift.*

To PRO'FLIGATE. *v. a.* [*profligo*, Lat.] To drive away. A word borrowed from the Latin without alteration of the sense, but not used.

Lavatories, to wash the temples, hands, wrists, and jugulars, do potently *profligate* and keep off the venom. *Harv.*

PRO'FLIGATELY. *adv.* [from *proflitate*.] Shamelesly.

Most *profligately* false, with the strongest professions of sincerity. *Swift's Miscellanies.*

PRO'FLIGATENESS. *n. s.* [from *profligate*.] The quality of being profligate.

PRO'FLUENCE. *n. s.* [from *profluent*.] Progress; course.

In the *profluence* or proceedings of their fortunes, there was much difference between them. *Wotton.*

PRO'FLUENT. *adj.* [from *profluens*, Lat.] Flowing forward.

Teach all nations what of him they learn'd,
And his salvation; them who shall believe
Baptizing in the *profluent* stream, the sign
Of washing them from guilt of sin. *Milton.*

PROFO'UND. *adj.* [*profond*, Fr. *profundus*, Lat.]

1. Deep; descending far below the surface; low with respect to the neighbouring places.

All else deep snow and ice,
A gulf *profound*, as that Serbonian bog
Betwixt Damiata and mount Casius old. *Milton.*

He hath hither thrust me down
Into this gloom of Tartarus *profound*. *Milton.*

2. Intellectually deep; not obvious to the mind; not easily fathomed by the mind: as, *a* profound *treatise*.

3. Lowly; humble; submiss; submissive.

What words wilt thou use to move thy God to hear thee? what humble gestures? what *profound* reverence? *Duppa.*

4. Learned beyond the common reach; knowing to the bottom.

Not orators only with the people, but even the very *profoundest* disputers in all faculties, have hereby often, with the best learned, prevailed most. *Hooker, b.* ii. *s.* 7.

5. Deep in contrivance.

The revolters are *profound* to make slaughter, though I have been a rebuker of them. *Hosea* v. 2.

PROFO'UND. *n. s.*

1. The deep; the main; the sea.

God, in the fathomless *profound*,
Hath all his choice commanders drown'd. *Sandys.*

Now I die absent in the vast *profound*;
And me without myself the seas have drown'd. *Dryden.*

2. The abyss.

If some other place th' ethereal king
Possesses lately, thither to arrive,
I travel this *profound*. *Milton's Par. Lost, b.* ii.

To PROFO'UND. *v. n.* [from the noun.] To dive; to penetrate. A barbarous word.

We cannot *profound* into the hidden things of nature, nor see the first springs that set the rest a-going. *Glanvil.*

PROFO'UNDLY. *adj.* [from *profound*.]

1. Deeply; with deep concern.

Why sigh you so *profoundly*? *Shakesp.*

The virgin started at her father's name,
And sigh'd *profoundly*, conscious of the shame. *Dryden.*

2. With great degrees of knowledge; with deep insight.

Domenichino was *profoundly* skill'd in all the parts of painting, but wanting genius, he had less of nobleness. *Dryden.*

PROFO'UNDNESS. *n. s.* [from *profound*.]

1. Depth of place.

2. Depth of knowledge.

Their wits, which did every where else conquer hardness, were with *profoundness* here over-matched. *Hooker.*

PROFU'NDITY. *n. s.* [from *profound*.] Depth of place or knowledge.

The other turn'd
Round through the vast *profundity* obscure. *Milton.*

PROFU'SE. *adj.* [*profusus*, Lat.] Lavish; too liberal; prodigal; overabounding; exuberant.

On a green shady bank, *profuse* of flow'rs,
Pensive I sat. *Milton's Par. Lost, b.* viii.

Oh liberty, thou goddess heav'nly bright,
Profuse of bliss, and pregnant with delight. *Addison.*

One long dead has a due proportion of praise; in which, whilst he lived, his friends were too *profuse*, and his enemies too sparing. *Addison.*

PROFU'SELY. *adv.* [from *profuse*.]

1. Lavishly; prodigally.

2. With exuberance.

Then spring the living herbs *profusely* wild. *Thomson.*

PROFU'SENESS. *n. s.* [from *profuse*.] Lavishness; prodigality.

One of a mean fortune manages his store with extreme parsimony; but, with fear of running into *profuseness*, never arrives to the magnificence of living. *Dryden.*

Profuseness of doing good, a soul unsatisfied with all it has done, and an unextinguished desire of doing more. *Dryden.*

Hospitality sometimes degenerates into *profuseness*, and ends in madness and folly. *Atterbury's Sermons.*

PROFU'SION. *n. s.* [*profusio*, Lat. *profusion*, Fr. from *profuse*.]

1. Lavishness; prodigality; extravagance.

What meant thy pompous progress through the empire?
Thy vast *profusion* to the factious nobles. *Rowe.*

2. Lavish expence; superfluous effusion.

He was desirous to avoid not only *profusion*, but the least effusion of christian blood. *Hayward.*

The great *profusion* and expence
Of his revenues bred him much offence. *Daniel.*

3. Abundance; exuberant plenty.

Trade is fitted to the nature of our country, as it abounds with a great *profusion* of commodities of its own growth, very convenient for other countries. *Addison.*

The raptur'd eye,
The fair *profusion*, yellow Autumn spies. *Thomson.*

To PROG. *v. n.*

1. To rob; to steal.

2. To shift meanly for provisions. A low word.

She went out *progging* for provisions as before. *L'Estr.*

PROG. *n. s.* [from the verb.] Victuals; provision of any kind. A low word.

O nephew! your grief is but folly,
In town you may find better *prog*. *Swift's Miscel.*

Spouse tuckt up doth in pattens trudge it,
With handkerchief of *prog*, like trull with budget;
And eat by turns plumcake and judge it. *Congreve.*

PROGENERA'TION. *n. s.* [*progenero*, Lat.] The act of begetting; propagation.

PROGE'NITOR. *n. s.* [*progenitus*, Lat.] A forefather; an ancestor in a direct line.

Although these things be already past away by her *progenitors* former grants unto those lords, yet I could find a way to remedy a great part thereof. *Spenser's State of Ireland.*

Like true subjects, sons of your *progenitors*,
Go chearfully together. *Shakesp.*

All generations had hither come,
From all the ends of th' Earth, to celebrate
And reverence thee, their great *progenitor*. *Milton.*

Power by right of fatherhood is not possible in any one, otherwise than as Adam's heir, or as *progenitor* over his own descendants. *Locke.*

The principal actors in Milton's poem are not only our *progenitors*, but representatives. *Addison.*

PRO'GENY. *n. s.* [*progenie*, old Fr. *progenies*, Lat.] Offspring; race; generation.

The sons of God have God's own natural son as a second Adam from heaven, whose race and *progeny* they are by spiritual and heavenly birth. *Hooker, b.* v. *s.* 56.

Not me begotten of a shepherd swain,
But issu'd from the *progeny* of kings. *Shakesp.*

By promise he receives
Gift to his *progeny* of all that land. *Milton.*

The base degenerate iron offspring ends;
A golden *progeny* from heav'n descends. *Dryden.*

Thus shall we live in perfect bliss, and see
Deathless ourselves, our num'rous *progeny*. *Dryden.*

We are the more pleased to behold the throne surrounded by a numerous *progeny*, when we consider the virtues of those from whom they descend. *Addison's Freeholder.*

PROGNO'STICABLE. *adj.* [from *prognosticate*.] Such as may be foreknown or foretold.

The causes of this inundation cannot be regular, and therefore their effects not *prognosticable* like eclipses. *Brown.*

To PROGNO'STICATE. *v. a.* [from *prognostick*.] To foretell; to foreshow.

He had now outlived the day, which his tutor Sandford had *prognosticated* upon his nativity he would not outlive. *Clarend.*

Unskill'd in schemes by planets to foreshow,
I neither will, nor can *prognosticate*,
To the young gaping heir, his father's fate. *Dryden.*

PROGNOSTICA'TION. *n. s.* [from *prognosticate*.]

1. The act of foreknowing or foreshowing.

If an oily palm be not a fruitful *prognostication*, I cannot scratch mine ear. *Shakesp. Antony and Cleopatra.*

Raw as he is, and in the hottest day *prognostication* proclaims, shall he be set against a brick-wall, the sun looking with a southward eye upon him, where he is to behold him, with flies blown to death. *Shakesp. Winter's Tale.*

This theory of the earth begins to be a kind of prophecy or *prognostication* of things to come, as it hath been hitherto an history of things past. *Burnet's Theory of the Earth.*

2. Foretoken.

He bid him farewell, arming himself in a black armour, as a badge or *prognostication* of his mind. *Sidney.*

PROGNOSTICA'TOR. *n. s.* [from *prognosticate*.] Foreteller; foreknower.

That astrologer, who made his almanack give a tolerable account of the weather by a direct inversion of the common *prognosticators*, to let his belief run quite counter to reports. *Government of the Tongue.*

PROGNO'STICK. *adj.* [*prognostique*, Fr. προγνωστικός.] Foretokening disease or recovery; foreshowing: as, *a* prognostick *sign*.

PROGNO'STICK. *n. s.* [from the adj.]

1. The skill of foretelling diseases or the event of diseases.

Hippocrates's *prognostick* is generally true, that it is very hard to resolve a small apoplexy. *Arbuthnot.*

2. A prediction.

Though your *prognosticks* run too fast,
They must be verify'd at last. *Swift.*

3. A token forerunning.

Whatsoever you are or shall be, has been but an easy *prognostick* from what you were. *South.*

Careful observers
By sure *prognosticks* may foretell a show'r. *Swift.*

PRO'GRESS. *n. s.* [*progrès*, Fr. from *progressus*, Lat.]

1. Course; procession; passage.

I cannot, by the *progress* of the stars,
Give guess how near to-day. *Shakesp. Julius Cæsar.*

The morn begins
Her rosy *progress* smiling. *Milton.*

The Sylphs behold it kindling as it flies,
And pleas'd pursue its *progress* through the skies. *Pope.*

2. Advancement;

2. Advancement; motion forward.

Through all thy veins shall run
A cold and drowzy humour, which shall seize
Each vital spirit; for no pulse shall keep
His nat'ral *progress*, but surcease to beat. *Shakesp.*

This motion worketh in round at first, which way to deliver itself; and then worketh in *progress*, where it findeth the deliverance easiest. *Bacon's Nat. Hist.*

Out of Ethiopia beyond Egypt had been a strange *progress* for ten hundred thousand men. *Raleigh's Hist. of the World.*

Whosoever understands the *progress* and revolutions of nature, will see that neither the present form of the earth, nor its first form, were permanent and immutable. *Burnet.*

It is impossible the mind should ever be stopped in its *progress* in this space. *Locke.*

The bounds of all body we have no difficulty to arrive at; but when the mind is there, it finds nothing to hinder its *progress* into the endless expansion. *Locke.*

Perhaps I judge hastily, there being several, in whose writings I have made very little *progress*. *Swift's Miscel.*

3. Intellectual improvement; advancement in knowledge.

Solon the wise his *progress* never ceas'd,
But still his learning with his days increas'd. *Denham.*

It is strange, that men should not have made more *progress* in the knowledge of these things. *Burnet.*

Several defects in the understanding hinder it in its *progress* to knowledge. *Locke.*

Others despond at the first difficulty, and conclude, that making any *progress* in knowledge, farther than serves their ordinary business, is above their capacities. *Locke.*

4. Removal from one place to another.

From Egypt arts their *progress* made to Greece,
Wrapt in the fable of the golden fleece. *Denham.*

5. A journey of state; a circuit.

He gave order, that there should be nothing in his journey like unto a warlike march, but rather like unto the *progress* of a king in full peace. *Bacon.*

O may I live to hail the day,
When the glad nation shall survey
Their sov'reign, through his wide command,
Passing in *progress* o'er the land. *Addison.*

To Pro'gress. *v. n.* [*progredior*, Lat.] To move forward; to pass. Not used.

Let me wipe off this honourable dew,
That silverly doth *progress* on thy cheeks. *Shakesp.*

Progre'ssion. *n. s.* [*progression*, Fr. *progressio*, Lat.]

1. Process; regular and gradual advance.

The squares of the diameters of these rings, made by any prismatick colour, were in arithmetical *progression*. *Newton.*

2. Motion forward.

Those worthies, who endeavour the advancement of learning, are likely to find a clearer *progression*, when so many rubs are levelled. *Brown's Vulgar Errours.*

In philosophical enquiries, the order of nature should govern, which in all *progression* is to go from the place one is then in, to that which lies next to it. *Locke.*

3. Course; passage.

He hath fram'd a letter, which accidentally, or by the way of *progression*, hath miscarried. *Shakesp.*

4. Intellectual advance.

For the saving the long *progression* of the thoughts to first principles, the mind should provide several intermediate principles. *Locke.*

Progre'ssional. *adj.* [from *progression*.] Such as are in a state of encrease or advance.

They maintain their accomplished ends, and relapse not again unto their *progressional* imperfections. *Brown.*

Progre'ssive. *adj.* [*progressif*, Fr. from *progress*.] Going forward; advancing.

Princes, if they use ambitious men, should handle it so, as they be still *progressive*, and not retrograde. *Bacon.*

In *progressive* motion, the arms and legs move successively; but in natation, both together. *Brown's Vulgar Errours.*

The *progressive* motion of this animal is made not by walking, but by leaping. *Ray on the Creation.*

Their course
Progressive, retrograde, or standing still. *Milton.*

Ere the *progressive* course of restless age
Performs three thousand times its annual stage,
May not our pow'r and learning be supprest,
And arts and empire learn to travel west? *Prior.*

Progre'ssively. *adv.* [from *progressive*.] By gradual steps or regular course.

The reason why they fall in that order, from the greatest epacts *progressively* to the least, is, because the greatest epacts denote a greater distance of the moon before the sun, and consequently a nearer approach to her conjunction. *Holder.*

Progre'ssiveness. *n. s.* [from *progressive*.] The state of advancing.

To PROHI'BIT. *v. a.* [*prohibeo*, Lat. *prohiber*, Fr.]

1. To forbid; to interdict by authority.

She would not let them know of his close lying in that *prohibited* place, because they would be offended. *Sidney.*

The weightiest, which it did command them, are to us in the gospel *prohibited*. *Hooker, b.* iv. *s.* 11.

2. To debar; to hinder.

Gates of burning adamant
Bar'd over us, *prohibit* all egress. *Milton.*

Prohi'biter. *n. s.* [from *prohibit*.] Forbidder; interdicter.

Prohibi'tion. *n. s.* [*prohibition*, Fr. *prohibitio*, Lat. from *prohibit*.] Forbiddance; interdict; act of forbidding.

Might there not be some other mystery in this *prohibition*, than they think of? *Hooker, b.* iv. *s.* 6.

'Gainst self-slaughter
There is a *prohibition* so divine,
That cravens my weak hand. *Shakesp. Cymbeline.*

He bestowed the liberal choice of all things, with one only *prohibition*, to try his obedience. *Raleigh's Hist. of the World.*

Let us not think hard
One easy *prohibition*, who enjoy
Free leave so large to all things else. *Milton's Par. Lost.*

The law of God in the ten commandments consists mostly of *prohibitions*; thou shalt not do such a thing. *Tillotson.*

Prohi'bitory. *adj.* [from *prohibit*.] Implying prohibition; forbidding.

A prohibition will lie on this statute, notwithstanding the penalty annexed; because it has words *prohibitory*, as well as a penalty annexed. *Ayliffe's Parergon.*

To PROJE'CT. *v. a.* [*projicio*, *projectus*, Lat.]

1. To throw out; to cast forward.

Th' ascending villas
Project long shadows o'er the crystal tide. *Pope.*

2. To exhibit a form, as of the image thrown on a mirrour.

Diffusive of themselves where e'er they pass,
They make that warmth in others they expect;
Their valour works like bodies on a glass,
And does its image on their men *project*. *Dryden.*

If we had a plan of the naked lines of longitude and latitude, *projected* on the meridian, a learner might much more speedily advance himself in the knowledge of geography. *Watts's Improvement of the Mind.*

3. [*Projetter*, Fr.] To scheme; to form in the mind; to contrive.

It ceases to be counsel, to compel men to assent to whatever tumultuary patrons shall *project*. *King Charles.*

What fit we then *projecting* peace and war? *Milton.*

What desire, by which nature *projects* its own pleasure or preservation, can be gratified by another man's personal pursuit of his own vice? *South's Sermons.*

To Pro'ject. *v. n.* To jut out; to shoot forward; to shoot beyond something next it.

Pro'ject. *n. s.* [*projet*, Fr. from the verb.] Scheme; design; contrivance.

It is a discovering the longitude, and deserves a much higher name than that of a *project*. *Addison's Guardian.*

In the various *projects* of happiness, devised by human reason, there still appeared inconsistencies not to be reconciled. *Rogers's Sermons.*

Proje'ctile. *n. s.* [from the adj.] A body put in motion.

Projectils would for ever move on in the same right line, did not the air, their own gravity, or the ruggedness of the plane stop their motion. *Cheyne's Philos. Principles.*

Proje'ctile. *adj.* [*projectile*, Fr.] Impelled forward.

Good blood, and a due *projectile* motion or circulation are necessary to convert the aliment into laudable juices. *Arbuth.*

Proje'ction. *n. s.* [from *project*.]

1. The act of shooting forwards.

If the electrick be held unto the light, many particles thereof will be discharged from it, which motion is performed by the breath of the effluvium issuing with agility; for as the electrick cooleth, the *projection* of the atoms ceaseth. *Brown.*

2. [*Projection*, Fr.] Plan; delineation. See to PROJECT.

For the bulk of the learners of astronomy, that *projection* of the stars is best, which includes in it all the stars in our horizon, reaching to the 38½ degree of the southern latitude. *Watts's Improvement of the Mind.*

3. Scheme; plan of action.

4. [*Projection*, Fr.] In chemistry, an operation; crisis of an operation; moment of transmutation.

A little quantity of the medicine, in the *projection*, will turn a sea of the baser metal into gold by multiplying. *Bacon.*

Proje'ctor. *n. s.* [from *project*.]

1. One who forms schemes or designs.

The following comes from a *projector*, a correspondent as diverting as a traveller; his subject having the same grace of novelty to recommend it. *Addison.*

Among all the *projectors* in this attempt, none have met with so general a success, as they who apply themselves to soften the rigour of the precept. *Rogers's Sermons.*

2. One who forms wild impracticable schemes.

Chymists, and other *projectors*, propose to themselves things utterly impracticable. *L'Estrange.*

Astrologers that future fates foreshew,
Projectors, quacks, and lawyers not a few. *Pope.*

PROJE'CTURE. *n. s.* [*projecture*, Fr. *projectura*, Lat.] A jutting out.

To PROIN. *v. a.* [a corruption of *prune.*] To lop; to cut; to trim; to prune.

I sit and *proin* my wings
After flight, and put new stings
To my shafts. *Benj. Johnson.*

The country husbandman will not give the *proining* knife to a young plant, as not able to admit the scar. *B. Johnson.*

To PROLA'TE. *v. a.* [*prolatum*, Lat.] To pronounce; to utter.

The pressures of war have somewhat cowed their spirits, as may be gathered from the accent of their words, which they *prolate* in a whining querulous tone, as if still complaining and crest-fallen. *Howel.*

PROLA'TE. *adj.* [*prolatus*, Lat.] Oblate; flat.

As to the *prolate* spheroidical figure, though it be the necessary result of the earth's rotation about its own axe, yet it is also very convenient for us. *Cheyne's Phil. Prin.*

PROLA'TION. *n. s.* [*prolatus*, Lat.]

1. Pronunciation; utterance.

Parrots, having been used to be fed at the *prolation* of certain words, may afterwards pronounce the same. *Ray.*

2. Delay; act of deferring. *Ainsworth.*

PROLE'GOMENA. *n. s.* [προλεγόμενα; *prolegomenes*, Fr.] Previous discourse; introductory observations.

PROLE'PSIS. *n. s.* [πρόληψις; *prolepse*, Fr.] A form of rhetorick, in which objections are anticipated.

This was contained in my *prolepsis* or prevention of his answer. *Bramhall against Hobbs.*

PROLE'PTICAL. *adj.* [from *prolepsis.*] Previous; antecedent.

The *proleptical* notions of religion cannot be so well defended by the professed servants of the altar. *Glanvil.*

PROLE'PTICALLY. *adv.* [from *proleptical.*] By way of anticipation. *Clarissa.*

PROLETA'RIAN. *adj.* Mean; wretched; vile; vulgar.

Like speculators should foresee,
From pharos of authority,
Portended mischiefs farther than
Low *proletarian* tything-men. *Hudibras, p. i.*

PROLIFICA'TION. *n. s.* [*proles* and *facio*, Lat.] Generation of children.

Their fruits, proceeding from simpler roots, are not so distinguishable as the offspring of sensible creatures, and *prolifications* descending from double origins. *Brown.*

PROLI'FICK. } *adj.* [*prolifique*, Fr. *proles* and *facio.*] Fruitful; generative; pregnant; productive.
PROLI'FICAL. }

Main ocean flow'd; not idle, but with warm
Prolifick humour soft'ning all her globe,
Fermented the great mother to conceive,
Satiate with genial moisture. *Milton's Par. Lost.*

Every dispute in religion grew *prolifical*, and in ventilating one question, many new ones were started. *Decay of Piety.*

His vital pow'r air, earth and seas supplies,
And breeds whate'er is bred beneath the skies;
For every kind, by thy *prolifick* might,
Springs. *Dryden.*

All dogs are of one species, they mingling together in generation, and the breed of such mixtures being *prolifick.* *Ray.*

From the middle of the world,
The sun's *prolifick* rays are hurl'd;
'Tis from that seat he darts those beams,
Which quicken earth with genial flames. *Prior.*

PROLI'FICALLY. *adv.* [from *prolifick.*] Fruitfully; pregnantly.

PROLI'X. *adj.* [*prolixe*, Fr. *prolixus*, Latin.]

1. Long; tedious; not concise.

According to the caution we have been so *prolix* in giving, if we aim at right understanding the true nature of it, we must examine what apprehension mankind make of it. *Digby.*

Should I at large repeat
The bead-roll of her vicious tricks,
My poem would be too *prolix.* *Prior.*

2. Of long duration. This is a very rare sense.

If the appellant appoints a term too *prolix*, the judge may then assign a competent term. *Ayliffe's Parergon.*

PROLI'XIOUS. *adj.* [from *prolix.*] Dilatory; tedious. A word of *Shakespeare's* coining.

Lay by all nicety and *prolixious* blushes. *Shakesp.*

PROLI'XITY. *n. s.* [*prolixité*, Fr. from *prolix.*] Tediousness; tiresome length; want of brevity.

It is true, without any slips of *prolixity*, or crossing the plain highway of talk, that the good Anthonio hath lost a ship. *Shakesp. Merchant of Venice.*

In some other passages, I may have, to shun *prolixity*, unawares slipt into the contrary extreme. *Boyle.*

PROLI'XLY. *adv.* [from *prolix.*] At great length; tediously.

On these *prolixly* thankful she enlarg'd. *Dryden.*

PROLI'XNESS. *n. s.* [from *prolix.*] Tediousness.

PROLOCU'TOR. *n. s.* [Latin.] The foreman; the speaker of a convocation.

The convocation the queen prorogued, though at the expence of Dr. Atterbury's displeasure, who was design'd their *prolocutor.* *Swift.*

PROLOCU'TORSHIP. *n. s.* [from *prolocutor.*] The office or dignity of prolocutor.

PRO'LOGUE. *n. s.* [πρόλογος; *prologue*, Fr. *prologus*, Latin.]

1. Preface; introduction to any discourse or performance.

Come, sit, and a song.
—Shall we clap into 't roundly, without hawking, or spitting, or saying we are hoarse, which are the only *prologues* to a bad voice? *Shakesp. As You Like it.*

In her face excuse
Came *prologue*, and apology too prompt. *Milton.*

2. Something spoken before the entrance of the actors of a play.

If my death might make this island happy,
And prove the period of their tyranny,
I would expend it with all willingness;
But mine is made the *prologue* to their play. *Shakesp.*

The peaking cornuto comes in the instant, after we had spoke the *prologue* of our comedy. *Shakesp.*

To PRO'LOGUE. *v. a.* [from the noun.] To introduce with a formal preface.

He his special nothing ever *prologues.* *Shakesp.*

To PROLO'NG. *v. a.* [*prolonger*, Fr. *pro* and *longus*, Lat.]

1. To lengthen out; to continue; to draw out.

Henceforth I fly not death, nor would *prolong*
Life much. *Milton.*

Th' unhappy queen with talk *prolong'd* the night. *Dryd.*

2. To put off to a distant time.

To-morrow in my judgment is too sudden;
For I myself am not so well provided,
As else I would be were the day *prolong'd.* *Shakesp.*

PROLONGA'TION. *n. s.* [*prolongation*, Fr. from *prolong.*]

1. The act of lengthening.

Nourishment in living creatures is for the *prolongation* of life. *Bacon's Nat. Hist.*

2. Delay to a longer time.

This ambassage concerned only the *prolongation* of days for payment of monies. *Bacon's Henry VII.*

PROLU'SION. *n. s.* [*prolusio*, Lat.] Entertainments; performance of diversion.

It is memorable, which Famianus Strada, in the first book of his academical *prolusions*, relates of Suarez. *Hakewill.*

PRO'MINENT. *adj.* [*prominens*, Lat.] Standing out beyond the near parts; protuberant; extant.

Whales are described with two *prominent* spouts on their heads, whereas they have but one in the forehead terminating over the windpipe. *Brown's Vulgar Errours.*

She has her eyes so *prominent*, and placed so that she can see better behind her than before her. *More.*

Two goodly bowls of massy silver,
With figures *prominent* and richly wrought. *Dryden.*

Some have their eyes stand so *prominent* as the hare, that they can see as well behind as before them. *Ray.*

PRO'MINENCE. } *n. s.* [*prominentia*, Latin; from *prominent.*] Protuberance; extant part.
PRO'MINENCY. }

It shows the nose and eyebrows, with the *prominencies* and fallings in of the features. *Addison on Ancient Medals.*

PROMI'SCUOUS. *adj.* [*promiscuus*, Lat.] Mingled; confused; undistinguished.

Glory he requires, and glory he receives,
Promiscuous from all nations. *Milton's Par. Lost.*

Promiscuous love by marriage was restrain'd. *Roscom.*

In rush'd at once a rude *promiscuous* crowd;
The guards, and then each other overbear,
And in a moment throng the theatre. *Dryden.*

No man, that considers the *promiscuous* dispensations of God's providence in this world, can think it unreasonable to conclude, that after this life good men shall be rewarded, and sinners punished. *Tillotson's Sermons.*

The earth was formed out of that *promiscuous* mass of sand, earth, shells, subsiding from the water. *Woodward.*

Clubs, diamonds, hearts, in wild disorder seen,
With throngs *promiscuous* strow the level green. *Pope.*

A wild, where weeds and flow'rs *promiscuous* shoot. *Pope.*

PROMI'SCUOUSLY. *adv.* [from *promiscuous.*] With confused mixture; indiscriminately.

We beheld where once stood Ilium, called Troy *promiscuously* of Tros. *Sandys's Journey.*

That generation, as the sacred writer modestly expresses it, married and gave in marriage without discretion or decency, but *promiscuously*, and with no better a guide than the impulses of a brutal appetite. *Woodward.*

Here might you see
Barons and peasants on the embattled field,
In one huge heap, *promiscuously* amast. *Philips.*

Unaw'd by precepts human or divine,
Like birds and beasts *promiscuously* they join. *Pope.*

PRO'MISE. *n. s.* [*promissum*, Lat. *promise*, *promesse*, Fr.]

1. Declaration of some benefit to be confered.

I eat the air, *promise* cramm'd; you cannot feed capons so. *Sha.*

His *promises* were, as he then was, mighty;
But his performance, as he now is, nothing. *Shakesp.*

O Lord, let thy *promise* unto David be established. *1 Chron.*

Behold, she said, perform'd in ev'ry part
My *promise* made; and Vulcan's labour'd art. *Dryden.*

Let

Let any man consider, how many sorrows he would have escaped, had God called him to his rest, and then say, whether the *promise* to deliver the just from the evils to come, ought not to be made our daily prayer. *Wake.*

2. Performance of promise; grant of the thing promised.

Now are they ready, looking for a *promise* from thee. *Acts.*

3. Hopes; expectation.

Your young prince Mamillius is a gentleman of the greatest *promise*. *Shakesp. Winter's Tale.*

To PRO'MISE. *v. a.* [*promettre*, Fr. *promitto*, Lat.]

1. To make declaration of some benefit to be confered.

While they *promise* them liberty, they themselves are the servants of corruption. 2 *Peter* ii. 18.

I could not expect such an effect as I found, which seldom reaches to the degree that is *promised* by the prescribers of any remedies. *Temple's Miscel.*

To PRO'MISE. *v n.*

1. To assure one by a promise.

Promising is the very air o' th' time; it opens the eyes of expectation: performance is ever the duller for his act. *Shak.*

I dare *promise* for this play, that in the roughness of the numbers, which was so designed, you will see somewhat more masterly than any of my former tragedies. *Dryden.*

As he *promised* in the law, he will shortly have mercy, and gather us together. 2 *Mac.* ii. 18.

All the pleasure we can take, when we met these *promising* sparks, is in the disappointment. *Felton.*

She brib'd my stay, with more than human charms;
Nay *promis'd*, vainly *promis'd* to bestow
Immortal life. *Pope's Odyssey.*

2. It is used of assurance, even of ill.

Will not the ladies be afraid of the lion?
—I fear it, I *promise* you. *Shakesp.*

PRO'MISEBREACH. *n. s.* [*breach* and *promise.*] Violation of promise. Not in use.

Criminal in double violation
Of sacred chastity, and of *promisebreach*. *Shakesp.*

PRO'MISEBREAKER. *n. s.* [*promise* and *break.*] Violator of promises.

He's an hourly *promisebreaker*, the owner of no one good quality worthy your entertainment. *Shakesp.*

PRO'MISER. *n. s.* [from *promise.*] One who promises.

Who let this *promiser* in? did you, good Diligence?
Give him his bribe again. *Benj. Johnson.*

Fear's a large *promiser*; who subject live
To that base passion, know not what they give. *Dryden.*

PRO'MISSORY. *adj.* [*promissoris*, Lat.] Containing profession of some benefit to be confered.

As the preceptive part enjoins the most exact virtue, so is it most advantageously enforced by the *promissory*, which is most exquisitely adapted to the same end. *Decay of Piety.*

The *promissory* lyes of great men are known by shouldering, hugging, squeezing, smiling and bowing. *Arbuthnot.*

PRO'MISSORILY. *adv.* [from *promissory.*] By way of promise.

Nor was he obliged by oath to a strict observation of that which *promissorily* was unlawful. *Brown.*

PRO'MONT. } *n. s.* [*promontoire*, Fr. *promontorium*, Latin.
PRO'MONTORY. } *Promont* I have observed only in *Suckling.*]

A headland; a cape; high land jutting into the sea.

The land did shoot out with a great *promontory*. *Abbot.*

I have dogs
Will climb the highest *promontory* top. *Shakesp.*

Like one that stands upon a *promontory*,
And spies a far off shore where he would tread. *Shakesp.*

A forked mountain, or blue *promontory*,
With trees upon't, nod unto the world,
And mock our eyes with air. *Shakesp. Ant. and Cleop.*

The waving sea can with each flood
Bath some high *promont*. *Suckling.*

They, on their heads,
Main *promontories* flung, which in the air
Came shadowing, and oppress'd whole legions arm'd. *Milt.*

Every gust of rugged winds,
That blows from off each beaked *promontory*. *Milton.*

If you drink tea upon a *promontory* that overhangs the sea, it is preferable to an assembly. *Pope.*

To PROMO'TE. *v. a.* [*promoveo*, *promotus*, Lat.]

1. To forward; to advance.

Next to religion, let your care be to *promote* justice. *Bacon.*

Nothing lovelier can be found,
Than good works in her husband to *promote*. *Milton.*

He that talks deceitfully for truth, must hurt it more by his example, than he *promotes* it by his arguments. *Atterb.*

Frictions of the extreme parts *promote* the flux of the juices in the joints. *Arbuthnot.*

2 [*Promouvoir*, Fr.] To elevate; to exalt; to prefer.

I will *promote* thee unto very great honour. *Num.* xxii. 17.

Shall I leave my fatness wherewith they honour God and man, and go to be *promoted* over the trees. *Judges* ix. 9.

Did I sollicit thee
From darkness to *promote* me. *Milton.*

PROMO'TER. *n. s.* [*promoteur*, Fr. from *promote.*]

1. Advancer; forwarder; encourager.

Knowledge hath received little improvement from the endeavours of many pretending *promoters*. *Glanvil.*

Our Saviour makes this return, fit to be engraven in the hearts of all *promoters* of charity; verily, I say unto you, inasmuch as you have done it unto one of the least of these my brethren, ye have done it unto me. *Atterbury.*

2. Informer; makebate. An obsolete use.

His eies be *promoters*, some trespas to spie. *Tusser.*

Informers and *promoters* oppress and ruin the estates of many of his best subjects. *Drummond.*

PROMO'TION. *n. s.* [*promotion*, Fr. from *promote.*] Advancement; encouragement; exaltation to some new honour or rank; preferment.

Many fair *promotions*
Are daily given to enoble those,
That scarce, some two days since, were worth a noble. *Sha.*

The high *promotion* of his grace of Canterbury,
Who holds his state at door 'mongst pursuivants. *Shakesp.*

My rising is thy fall,
And my *promotion* will be thy destruction. *Milton.*

Thou youngest virgin-daughter of the skies,
Made in the last *promotion* of the blest;
Whose palms, new pluck'd from paradise,
In spreading branches more sublimely rise. *Dryden.*

To PRO'MOVE. *v. a.* [*promoveo*, Lat. *promouvoir*, Fr.] To forward; to advance; to promote. A word little used.

Never yet was honest man,
That ever drove the trade of love:
It is impossible, nor can
Integrity our ends *promove*. *Suckling.*

PROMPT. *adj.* [*prompt*, Fr. *promptus*, Lat.]

1. Quick; ready; acute; easy.

The reception of light into the body of the building was very *prompt*, both from without and from within. *Wotton.*

Very discerning and *prompt* in giving orders, as occasions required. *Clarendon.*

Prompt eloquence
Flow'd from their lips, in prose or numerous verse. *Milton.*

To the stern sanction of th' offended sky,
My *prompt* obedience bows. *Pope.*

2. Quick; petulant.

I was too hasty to condemn unheard;
And you, perhaps, too *prompt* in your replies. *Dryden.*

3. Ready without hesitation; wanting no new motive.

Tell him, I'm *prompt*
To lay my crown at's feet, and there to kneel. *Shakesp.*

The brazen age,
A warlike offspring, *prompt* to bloody rage. *Dryden.*

Still arose some rebel slave,
Prompter to sink the state, than he to save. *Prior.*

4. Ready; told down: as, prompt *payment.*

To PROMPT. *v. a.* [*prontare*, Italian.]

1. To assist by private instruction; to help at a loss.

Sitting in some place, where no man shall *prompt* him, let the child translate his lesson. *Ascham.*

You've put me now to such a part, which never
I shall discharge to th' life.
—Come, come, we'll *prompt* you. *Shakesp. Coriolanus.*

My voice shall sound as you do *prompt* mine ear,
And I will stoop and humble my intents
To your well practis'd wise directions. *Shakesp.*

None could hold the book so well to *prompt* and instruct this stage play, as she could. *Bacon's Henry* VII.

He needed not one to *prompt* him, because he could say the prayers by heart. *Stillingfleet.*

Every one some time or other dreams he is reading books, in which case the invention *prompts* so readily, that the mind is imposed on. *Addison.*

Grace shines around her with serenest beams,
And whisp'ring angels *prompt* her golden dreams. *Pope.*

2. To incite; to instigate.

The Volscians stand
Ready, when time shall *prompt* them, to make road
Upon's again. *Shakesp. Coriolanus.*

Speak not by th' matter
Which your heart *prompts* you to, but with such words
But rooted in your tongue. *Shakesp.*

If they *prompt* us to anger, their design makes use of it to a further end, that the mind, being thus disquieted, may not be easily composed to prayer. *Duppa.*

Rage *prompted* them at length and found them arms. *Milt.*

Kind occasion *prompts* their warm desires. *Pope.*

3. To remind.

The inconcealable imperfections of ourselves will hourly *prompt* us our corruption, and loudly tell us we are sons of earth. *Brown's Vulgar Errours.*

PRO'MPTER. *n. s.* [from *prompt.*]

1. One who helps a publick speaker, by suggesting the word to him when he falters.

Were it my cue to fight, I should have known it
Without a *prompter*. *Shakesp. Othello.*

In florid impotence he speaks,
And as the *prompter* breathes, the puppet squeaks. *Pope.*

2. An

2. An admonisher; a reminder.

We understand our duty without a teacher, and acquit ourselves as we ought to do without a *prompter*. *L'Estrange.*

PRO'MPTITUDE. *n. s.* [*promptitude*, Fr. from *promptus*, Lat.] Readiness; quickness.

PRO'MPTLY. *adv.* [from *prompt.*] Readily; quickly; expeditiously.

He that does his merchandise chearfully, *promptly* and readily, and the works of religion slowly, it is a sign that his heart is not right with God. *Taylor.*

PRO'MPTNESS. *n. s.* [from *prompt.*] Readiness; quickness; alacrity.

Had not this stop been given him by that accidental sickness, his great courage and *promptness* of mind would have carried him directly forward to the enemy, till he had met him in the open plains of Persia. *South's Sermons.*

Firm and rigid muscles, strong pulse, activity, and *promptness* in animal actions, are signs of strong fibres. *Arbuthnot.*

PRO'MPTURE. *n. s.* [from *prompt.*] Suggestion; motion given by another; instigation. A word not used.

Though he hath fallen by *prompture* of the blood;
Yet hath he in him such a mind of honour,
That had he twenty heads to tender down
On twenty bloody blocks, he'd yield them up. *Shakesp.*

PRO'MPTUARY. *n. s.* [*promptuaire*, Fr. *promptuarium*, Lat.] A storehouse; a repository; a magazine.

This stratum is still expanded at top, serving as the seminary or *promptuary*, that furnisheth forth matter for the formation of animal and vegetable bodies. *Woodward.*

To PROMU'LGATE. *v. a.* [*promulgo*, Lat.] To publish; to make known by open declaration.

Those albeit I know he nothing so much hateth as to *promulgate*, yet I hope that this will occasion him to put forth divers other goodly works. *Spenser.*

Those, to whom he entrusted the *promulgating* of the gospel, had far different instructions. *Decay of Piety.*

It is certain laws, by virtue of any sanction they receive from the *promulgated* will of the legislature, reach not a stranger, if by the law of nature every man hath not a power to punish offences against it. *Locke.*

PROMULGA'TION. *n. s.* [*promulgatio*, Lat. from *promulgate.*] Publication; open exhibition.

The stream and current of this rule hath gone as far, it hath continued as long as the very *promulgation* of the gospel. *Hooker, b.* v. *s.* 42.

The very *promulgation* of the punishment will be part of the punishment, and anticipate the execution. *South.*

PROMULGA'TOR. *n. s.* [from *promulgate.*] Publisher; open teacher.

How groundless a calumny this is, appears from the sanctity of the christian religion, which excludes fraud and falsehood; so also from the designments and aims of its first *promulgators*. *Decay of Piety.*

To PROMU'LGE. *v. a.* [from *promulgo*, Lat.] To promulgate; to publish; to teach openly.

The chief design of them is, to establish the truth of a new revelation in those countries, where it is first *promulged* and propagated. *Atterbury.*

PROMU'LGER. *n. s.* [rom *promulge.*] Publisher; promulgator.

The *promulgers* of our religion, Jesus Christ and his apostles, raised men and women from the dead, not once only, but often. *Atterbury.*

PRONA'TOR. *n. s.* In anatomy, a muscle of the radius, of which there are two, that help to turn the palm downwards. *Dict.*

PRONE. *adj.* [*pronus*, Latin.]

1. Bending downward; not erect.

There wanted yet a creature not *prone*,
And brute as other creatures, but indu'd
With sanctity of reason, might erect
His stature, and upright with front serene
Govern the rest. *Milton's Par. Lost, b.* vii.

2. Lying with the face downwards: contrary to supine.

Upon these three positions in man, wherein the spine can only be at right lines with the thigh, arise those postures, *prone*, supine and erect. *Brown's Vulgar Errours.*

3. Precipitous; headlong; going downwards.

Down thither *prone* in flight
He speeds, and through the vast ethereal sky
Sails between worlds. *Milton's Par. Lost, b.* v.

4. Declivous; sloping.

Since the floods demand,
For their descent, a *prone* and sinking land:
Does not this due declivity declare
A wise director's providential care? *Blackmore.*

5. Inclined; propense; disposed. It has commonly an ill sense.

The labour of doing good, with the pleasure arising from the contrary, doth make men for the most part slower to the one and *proner* to the other, than that duty, prescribed them by law, can prevail sufficiently with them. *Hooker.*

Those who are ready to confess him in judgment and profession, are very *prone* to deny him shamefully in their doings. *South's Sermons.*

If we are *prone* to sedition, and delight in change, there is no cure more proper than trade, which supplies business to the active, and wealth to the indigent. *Addison.*

Still *prone* to change, though still the slaves of state. *Pope.*

PRO'NENESS. *n. s.* [from *prone.*]

1. The state of bending downwards; not erectness.

If erectness be taken, as it is largely opposed unto *proneness*, or the posture of animals looking downwards, carrying their venters, or opposite part to the spine, directly towards the earth, it may admit of question. *Brown's Vulg. Errours.*

2. The state of lying with the face downwards; not supineness.

3. Descent; declivity.

4. Inclination; propension; disposition to ill.

The holy spirit saw that mankind is unto virtue hardly drawn, and that righteousness is the less accounted of, by reason of the *proneness* of our affections to that which delighteth. *Hooker, b.* v. *s.* 8.

The soul being first from nothing brought,
When God's grace fails her, doth to nothing fall;
And this declining *proneness* unto nought,
Is ev'n that sin that we are born withal. *Davies.*

He instituted this way of worship, because of the carnality of their hearts, and their *proneness* of the people to idolatry. *Tillotson's Sermons.*

The *proneness* of good men to commiserate want, in whatsoever shape it appears. *Atterbury's Sermons.*

How great is the *proneness* of our nature, to comply with this temptation. *Rogers's Sermons.*

PRONG. *n. s.* [*pranghen*, Dutch, to squeeze. *Minshew.*] A fork.

The cooks make no more ado, but slicing it into little gobbets, prick it on a *prong* of iron, and hang it in a furnace. *Sandys's Journey.*

Whacum his sea-coal *prong* threw by,
And basely turn'd his back to fly. *Hudibras.*

Be mindful,
With iron teeth of rakes and *prongs* to move
The crusted earth. *Dryden's Virg. Georg.*

PRO'NITY. *n. s.* [from *prone.*] Proneness. A word not used.

Of this mechanick *pronity*, I do not see any good tendency. *More's Divine Dialogues.*

PRONOU'N. *n. s.* [*pronom*, Fr. *pronomen*, Lat.]

I, thou, he; we, ye, they, are names given to persons, and used instead of their proper names, from whence they had the name of *pronouns*, as though they were not nouns themselves, but used instead of nouns. *Clarke's Lat. Gram.*

To PRONOU'NCE. *v. a.* [*prononcer*, Fr. *pronuncio*, Lat.]

1. To speak; to utter.

He *pronounced* all these words unto me with his mouth. *Jer.* xxxvi. 18.

2. To utter solemnly; to utter confidently.

She
So good a lady, that no tongue could ever
Pronounce dishonour of her. *Shakesp. Henry* VIII.

I have *pronounced* the word, saith the Lord. *Jer.* xxxiv. 5.

So was his will
Pronounc'd among the gods. *Milton.*

Sternly he *pronounc'd* the rigid interdiction. *Milton.*

The *pronouncing* of sentence of death is the office of inferior magistrates. *Locke.*

Absalom *pronounced* a sentence of death against his brother. *Locke.*

3. To form or articulate by the organs of speech.

Language of man *pronounc'd*
By tongue of brute, and human sense express'd. *Milton.*

Though diversity of tongues continue, this would render the *pronouncing* them easier. *Holder.*

4. To utter rhetorically.

To PRONOU'NCE. *v. n.* To speak with confidence or authority.

How confidently soever men *pronounce* of themselves, and believe that they are then most pious, when they are most eager and unquiet; yet 'tis sure this is far removed from the true genius of religion. *Decay of Piety.*

Every fool may believe, and *pronounce* confidently; but wise men will, in matters of discourse, conclude firmly, and in matters of fact, act surely. *South's Sermons.*

PRONOU'NCER. *n. s.* [from *pronounce.*] One who pronounces.

The *pronouncer* thereof shall be condemned in expences. *Ayliffe's Parergon.*

PRONUNCIA'TION. *n. s.* [*pronunciatio*, from *pronuncio*, Lat. *pronunciation*, Fr.] The act or mode of utterance.

The design of speaking being to communicate our thoughts by ready, easy and graceful *pronunciation*, all kind of letters have been searched out, that were serviceable for the purpose. *Holder.*

It were easy to produce thousands of his verses, which are lame for want of half a foot, sometimes a whole one, and which no *pronunciation* can make otherwise. *Dryden.*

PROOF. *n. s.* [from *prove.*]

1. Evidence; testimony; convincing token; convincing argument; means of conviction.

That they all have always so testified, I see not how we should possibly wish a *proof* more palpable than this. *Hooker.*

This has neither evidence of truth, nor *proof* sufficient to give it warrant. *Hooker.*

Though the manner of their trials should be altered, yet the *proof* of every thing must needs be by the testimony of such persons as the parties shall produce. *Spenser.*

That which I shall report will bear no credit,
Were not the *proof* so high. *Shakesp.*

One soul in both, whereof good *proof*
This day affords. *Milton.*

This, vers'd in death, th' infernal knight relates,
And then for *proof* fulfill'd their common fates. *Dryden.*

Those intervening ideas, which serve to shew the agreement of any two others, are called *proofs.* *Locke.*

2. Test; trial; experiment.

Retire or taste thy folly, and learn by *proof,*
Hell-born! not to contend with spirits of heav'n. *Milton.*

Sampson,
This day to Dagon is a solemn feast,
Thy strength they know surpassing human race,
And now some publick *proof* thereof require
To honour this great feast. *Milton's Agonistes.*

When the imagination hath contrived the frame of such an instrument, and conceives that the event must infallibly answer its hopes, yet then does it strangely deceive in the *proof.* *Wilkins's Math. Magick.*

Gave, while he taught, and edify'd the more,
Because he shew'd, by *proof,* 'twas easy to be poor. *Dryd.*

My paper gives a timorous writer an opportunity of putting his abilities to the *proof.* *Addison.*

Here for ever must I stay,
Sad *proof* how well a lover can obey. *Pope.*

3. Firm temper; impenetrability; the state of being wrought and hardened, till the expected strength is found by trial to be attained.

Add *proof* unto mine armour with thy prayers,
And with thy blessings steel my lance's point. *Shakesp.*

To me the cries of fighting fields are charms,
Keen be my sabre, and of *proof* my arms;
I ask no other blessing of my stars. *Dryden.*

With arms of *proof,* both for myself and thee,
Chuse thou the best. *Dryden.*

4. Armour hardened till it will abide a certain trial.

He Bellona's bridegroom, lapt in *proof,*
Confronted him. *Shakesp. Macbeth.*

5. In printing, the rough draught of a sheet when first pulled.

PROOF. *adj.* [This word, though used as an adjective, is only elliptically put for *of proof.*]

1. Impenetrable; able to resist.

Now put your shields before your hearts, and fight
With hearts more *proof* than shields. *Shakesp.*

Opportunity I here have had
To try thee, sift thee, and confess have found thee
Proof against all temptation, as a rock
Of adamant. *Milton's Par. Regain'd.*

He past expression lov'd,
Proof to disdain, and not to be remov'd. *Dryden.*

When the mind is throughly tinctured, the man will be *proof* against all oppositions. *Collier.*

Guiltless of hate, and *proof* against desire;
That all things weighs, and nothing can admire. *Dryden.*

When a capuchin, that was thought *proof* against bribes, had undertaken to carry on the work, he died a little after. *Addison.*

2. It has either *to* or *against* before the power to be resisted.

Imagin'd wise,
Constant, mature, *proof against* all assaults. *Milton.*

Deep in the snowy Alps, a lump of ice
By frost was harden'd to a mighty price;
Proof to the sun it now securely lies,
And the warm dog-star's hottest rage defies. *Addison.*

The God of day,
To make him *proof against* the burning ray,
His temples with celestial ointment wet. *Addison.*

PROO'FLESS. *adj.* [from *proof.*] Unproved; wanting evidence.

Some were so manifestly weak and *proofless,* that he must be a very courteous adversary, that can grant them. *Boyle.*

To PROP. *v. a.* [*proppen,* Dutch.]

1. To support by something placed under or against.

What we by day
Lop overgrown, or *prop,* or bind,
One night derides. *Milton.*

2. To support by standing under or against.

Like these earth unsupported keeps its place,
Though no fixt bottom *props* the weighty mass. *Creech.*

Eternal snows the growing mass supply,
Till the bright mountains *prop* th' incumbent sky;
As Atlas fix'd each hoary pile appears. *Pope.*

3. To sustain; to support.

The nearer I find myself verging to that period, which is to be labour and sorrow, the more I *prop* myself upon those few supports that are left me. *Pope.*

PROP. *n. s.* [*proppe,* Dutch.] A support; a stay; that on which any thing rests.

The boy was the very staff of my age, my very *prop.* *Sha.*

You take my house, when you do take the *prop*
That doth sustain my house; you take my life,
When you do take the means whereby I live. *Shakesp.*

Some plants creep along the ground, or wind about other trees or *props,* and cannot support themselves. *Bacon.*

That he might on many *props* repose,
He strengths his own, and who his part did take. *Daniel.*

Again, if by the body's *prop* we stand,
If on the body's life, her life depend,
As Meleager's on the fatal brand,
The body's good she only would intend. *Davies.*

Fairest unsupported flower
From her best *prop* so far. *Milton.*

The current of his vict'ries found no stop,
Till Cromwell came, his party's chiefest *prop.* *Waller.*

'Twas a considerable time before the great fragments that fell rested in a firm posture; for the *props* and stays, whereby they leaned one upon another, often failed. *Burnet.*

The *props* return
Into thy house, that bore the burden'd vines. *Dryden.*

PRO'PAGABLE. *adj.* [from *propagate.*] Such as may be spread; such as may be continued by succession.

Such creatures as are produced each by its peculiar seed, constitute a distinct *propagable* sort of creatures. *Boyle.*

To PRO'PAGATE. *v. a.* [*propago,* Latin.]

1. To continue or spread by generation or successive production.

All that I eat, or drink, or shall beget,
Is *propagated* curse! *Milton's Par. Lost, b.* x.

Is it an elder brother's duty so
To *propagate* his family and name;
You would not have yours die and buried with you? *Otway.*

From hills and dales the cheerful cries rebound;
For echo hunts along, and *propagates* the sound. *Dryden.*

2. To extend; to widen.

I have upon a high and pleasant hill
Feign'd fortune to be thron'd: the base o' th' mount
Is rank'd with all deserts, all kind of natures,
That labour on the bosom of this sphere
To *propagate* their states. *Shakesp. Timon of Athens.*

3. To carry on from place to place; to promote.

Some have thought the *propagating* of religion by arms not only lawful, but meritorious. *Decay of Piety.*

Who are those that truth must *propagate,*
Within the confines of my father's state. *Dryden.*

Those who seek truth only, and desire to *propagate* nothing else, freely expose their principles to the test. *Locke.*

Because dense bodies conserve their heat a long time, and the densest bodies conserve their heat the longest, the vibrations of their parts are of a lasting nature; and therefore may be *propagated* along solid fibres of uniform dense matter to a great distance, for conveying into the brain the impressions made upon all the organs of sense. *Newton.*

4. To encrease; to promote.

Griefs of mine own lie heavy in my breast,
Which thou wilt *propagate,* to have them prest
With more of thine. *Shakesp.*

Sooth'd with his future fame,
And pleas'd to hear his *propagated* name. *Dryden.*

5. To generate.

Superstitious notions, *propagated* in fancy, are hardly ever totally eradicated. *Clarissa.*

To PRO'PAGATE. *v. n.* To have offspring.

No need that thou
Should'st *propagate,* already infinite,
And through all numbers absolute, though one. *Milton.*

PROPAGA'TION. *n. s.* [*propagatio,* Lat. *propagation,* Fr. from *propagate.*] Continuance or diffusion by generation or successive production.

Men have souls rather by creation than *propagation.* *Hooker.*

There are other secondary ways of the *propagation* of it, as lying in the same bed. *Wiseman's Surgery.*

There is not in all nature any spontaneous generation, but all come by *propagation,* wherein chance hath not the least part. *Ray on the Creation.*

Old stakes of olive trees in plants revive;
But nobler vines by *propagation* thrive. *Dryden.*

PROPA'GATOR. *n. s.* [from *propagate.*]

1. One who continues by successive production.

2. A spreader; a promoter.

Socrates, the greatest *propagator* of morality, and a martyr for the unity of the Godhead, was so famous for this talent, that he gained the name of the Drole. *Addison.*

To PROPE'L. *v. a.* [*propello,* Lat.] To drive forward.

Avicen witnesses the blood to be frothy that is *propelled* out of a vein of the breast. *Harvey.*

This

This motion, in some human creatures, may be weak in respect to the viscidity of what is taken, so as not to be able to *propel* it. *Arbuthnot on Aliments.*

That overplus of motion would be too feeble and languid to *propel* so vast and ponderous a body, with that prodigious velocity. *Bentley's Sermons.*

To PROPE'ND. *v. n.* [*propendeo*, Lat. to hang forwards.] To incline to any part; to be disposed in favour of any thing.

My sprightly brethren, I *propend* to you,
In resolution to keep Helen still. *Shakesp.*

PROPE'NDENCY. *n. s.* [from *propend.*]

1. Inclination or tendency of desire to any thing.

2. [From *propendo*, Lat. to weigh.] Preconsideration; attentive deliberation; perpendency.

An act above the animal actings, which are transient, and admit not of that attention, and *propendency* of actions. *Hale.*

PROPE'NSE. *adj.* [*propensus*, Lat.] Inclined; disposed. It is used both of good and bad.

Women, *propense* and inclinable to holiness, be otherwise edified in good things, rather than carried away as captives. *Hooker's Preface.*

I have brought scandal
In feeble hearts, *propense* enough before
To waver, or fall off, and join with idols. *Milton.*

PROPE'NSION. } *n. s.* [*propension*, Fr. *propensio*, Lat. from
PROPE'NSITY. } *propense.*]

1. Inclination; disposition to any thing good or bad.

Some miscarriages might escape, rather through necessities of state, than any *propensity* of myself to injuriousness. *K. Char.*

So forcible are our *propensions* to mutiny, that we equally take occasions from benefits or injuries. *Gov. of the Tongue.*

Let there be but *propensity*, and bent of will to religion, and there will be sedulity and indefatigable industry. *South.*

It requires a critical nicety to find out the genius or the *propensions* of a child. *L'Estrange.*

The natural *propension*, and the inevitable occasions of complaint, accidents of fortune. *Temple.*

He assists us with a measure of grace, sufficient to overbalance the corrupt *propensity* of the will. *Rogers.*

2. Tendency.

Bodies, that of themselves have no *propensions* to any determinate place, do nevertheless move constantly and perpetually one way. *Digby.*

This great attrition must produce a great *propensity* to the putrescent alkaline condition of the fluids. *Arbuthnot.*

PRO'PER. *adj.* [*propre*, Fr. *proprius*, Latin.]

1. Peculiar; not belonging to more; not common.

As for the virtues that belong unto moral righteousness and honesty of life, we do not mention them, because they are not *proper* unto christian men as they are christian, but do concern them as they are men. *Hooker.*

Men of learning hold it for a slip in judgment, when offer is made to demonstrate that as *proper* to one thing, which reason findeth common unto many. *Hooker.*

No sense the precious joys conceives,
Which in her private contemplations be;
For then the ravish'd spirit the senses leaves,
Hath her own pow'rs, and *proper* actions free. *Davies.*

Of nought no creature ever formed ought,
For that is *proper* to th' Almighty's hand. *Davies.*

Dufresnoy's rules, concerning the posture of the figures, are almost wholly *proper* to painting, and admit not any comparison with poetry. *Dryden's Dufresnoy.*

Outward objects, that are extrinsecal to the mind, and its own operations, proceeding from powers intrinsecal and *proper* to itself, which become also objects of its contemplation, are the original of all knowledge. *Locke.*

2. Noting an individual.

A *proper* name may become common, when given to several beings of the same kind; as Cæsar. *Watts.*

3. One's own. It is joined with any of the possessives: as, *my* proper, *their* proper.

The bloody book of law
You shall yourself read in the bitter letter,
After your own sense; yea, though *our proper* son
Stood in your action. *Shakesp. Othello.*

Court the age
With somewhat of *your proper* rage. *Waller.*

If we might determine it, *our proper* conceptions would be all voted axioms. *Glanvil's Sceps.*

Now learn the diff'rence at *your proper* cost,
Betwixt true valour and an empty boast. *Dryden.*

4. Natural; original.

In our *proper* motion we ascend
Up to our native seat. *Milton.*

5. Fit; accommodated; adapted; suitable; qualified.

In Athens all was pleasure, mirth and play,
All *proper* to the spring, and sprightly May. *Dryden.*

He is the only *proper* person of all others for an Epic poem, who, to his natural endowments of a large invention, a ripe judgment, and a strong memory, has joined the knowledge of the liberal arts. *Dryden.*

In debility, from great loss of blood, wine and all aliment, that is easily assimilated or turned into blood, are *proper*: for blood is required to make blood. *Arbuthnot.*

6. Exact; accurate; just.

7. Not figurative.

Those parts of nature, into which the chaos was divided, they signified by dark names, which we have expressed in their plain and *proper* terms. *Burnet's Theory of the Earth.*

8. It seems in *Shakespeare* to signify, mere; pure.

See thyself, devil;
Proper deformity seems not in the fiend
So horrid as in woman. *Shakesp. King Lear.*

9. [*Propre*, Fr.] Elegant; pretty.

Moses was a *proper* child. *Heb.* xi. 23.

10. Tall; lusty; handsome with bulk.

At last she concluded with a sigh, thou wast the *properest* man in Italy. *Shakesp.*

A *proper* goodly fox was carrying to execution. *L'Estrange.*

PRO'PERLY. *adv.* [from *proper.*]

1. Fitly; suitably.

2. In a strict sense.

What dies but what has life
And sin? the body *properly* hath neither. *Milton.*

The miseries of life are not *properly* owing to the unequal distribution of things. *Swift.*

There is a sense in which the works of every man, good as well as bad, are *properly* his own. *Rogers.*

PRO'PERNESS. *n. s.* [from *proper.*]

1. The quality of being proper.

2. Tallness.

PRO'PERTY. *n. s.* [from *proper.*]

1. Peculiar quality.

What special *property* or quality is that, which being no where found but in sermons, maketh them effectual to save souls? *Hooker, b.* v. *s.* 22.

A secondary essential mode, is any attribute of a thing, which is not of primary consideration, and is called a *property.* *Watts.*

2. Quality; disposition.

'Tis conviction, not force, that must induce assent; and sure the logick of a conquering sword has no great *property* that way; silence it may, but convince it cannot. *D. of Pict.*

It is the *property* of an old sinner to find delight in reviewing his own villanies in others. *South's Sermons.*

3. Right of possession.

Some have been deceived into an opinion, that the inheritance of rule over men, and *property* in things, sprung from the same original, and were to descend by the same rules. *Locke.*

Property, whose original is from the right a man has to use any of the inferior creatures, for subsistence and comfort, is for the sole advantage of the proprietor, so that he may even destroy the thing that he has *property* in. *Locke.*

4. Possession held in one's own right.

For numerous blessings yearly show'r'd,
And *property* with plenty crown'd,
Accept our pious praise. *Dryden.*

5. The thing possessed.

'Tis a thing impossible
I should love thee but as a *property.* *Shakesp.*

No wonder such men are true to a government, where liberty runs so high, where *property* is so well secured. *Swift.*

6. Nearness or right. I know not which is the sense in the following lines.

Here I disclaim all my paternal care,
Propinquity, and *property* of blood,
And as a stranger to my heart and me,
Hold thee. *Shakesp. King Lear.*

7. Something useful; an appendage.

I will draw a bill of *properties*, such as our play wants. *Shakesp. Midsummer's Night's Dream.*

The purple garments raise the lawyer's fees,
High pomp and state are useful *properties.* *Dryden.*

Greenfield was the name of the *property* man in that time, who furnished implements for the actors. *Pope.*

8. *Property* for *propriety.* Any thing peculiarly adapted.

Our poets excel in grandity and gravity, smoothness and *property*, in quickness and briefness. *Camden.*

To PROPE'RTY. *v. a.* [from the noun.]

1. To invest with qualities.

His rear'd arm
Crested the world; his voice was *property'd*
As all the tuned spheres. *Shakesp. Ant. and Cleop.*

2. To seize or retain as something owned, or in which one has a right; to appropriate; to hold. This word is not now used in either meaning.

His large fortune
Subdues and *properties* to his love and tendance
All sorts of hearts. *Shakesp. Timon of Athens.*

They have here *propertied* me, keep me in darkness, and do all they can to face me out of my wits. *Shakesp.*

I am too highborn to be *propertied*,
To be a secondary at controul. *Shakesp. King John.*

Propha'sis. *n. s.* [πρόφασις.] In medicine, a foreknowledge of diseases.

Prophe'cy. *n. s.* [προφητεία; *prophetie*, Fr.] A declaration of something to come; prediction.

He hearkens after *prophecies* and dreams. *Shakesp.*

Poets may boast
Their work shall with the world remain;
Both bound together, live or die,
The verses and the *prophecy*. *Waller.*

Pro'phesier. *n. s.* [from *prophesy.*] One who prophesies.

To Pro'phesy. *v. a.*

1. To predict; to foretell; to prognosticate.

Miserable England,
I *prophesy* the fearful'st time to thee,
That ever wretched age hath look'd upon. *Shakesp.*

I hate him, for he doth not *prophesy* good, but evil. 1 *Kings.*

The Lord sent me to *prophesy*, against this house, all the words that ye have heard. *Jer.* xxvi. 12.

2. To foreshow.

Methought thy very gait did *prophesy*
A royal nobleness. *Shakesp. King Lear.*

To Pro'phesy. *v. n.*

1. To utter predictions.

Strange screams of death,
And *prophesying* with accents terrible
Of dire combustion. *Shakesp.*

Receiv'd by thee, I *prophesy*, my rhimes,
Mix'd with thy works, their life no bounds shall see. *Tick.*

2. To preach. A scriptural sense.

Prophesy unto the wind, *prophesy*, son of man. *Ezekiel.*

The elders of the Jews builded, and prospered through the *prophesying* of Haggai. *Esra* vi. 14.

PRO'PHET. *n. s.* [*prophete*, Fr. προφήτης.]

1. One who tells future events; a predicter; a foreteller.

Ev'ry flower
Did as a *prophet* weep what it foresaw,
In Hector's wrath. *Shakesp. Troilus and Cressida.*

Jesters oft prove *prophets*. *Shakesp. King Lear.*

O *prophet* of glad tidings! finisher
Of utmost hope! *Milton.*

He lov'd so fast,
As if he fear'd each day wou'd be her last;
Too true a *prophet* to foresee the fate,
That should so soon divide their happy state. *Dryden.*

God, when he makes the *prophet*, does not unmake the man. *Locke.*

2. One of the sacred writers empowered by God to foretell futurity.

His champions are the *prophets* and apostles. *Shakesp.*

Pro'phetess. *n. s.* [*prophetesse*, Fr. from *prophet.*] A woman that foretells future events.

He shall split thy very heart with sorrow,
And say poor Marg'ret was a *prophetess*. *Shakesp.*

That it is consonant to the word of God, so in singing to answer, the practice of Miriam the *prophetess*, when she answered the men in her song, will approve. *Peacham.*

If my love but once were crown'd
Fair *prophetess*, my grief would cease. *Prior.*

Prophe'tick. }
Prophe'tical. } *adj.* [*prophetique*, Fr. from *prophet.*]

1. Foreseeing or foretelling future events.

Say, why
Upon this blasted heath you stop our way,
With such *prophetick* greeting. *Shakesp. Macbeth.*

The counsel of a wise and then *prophetical* friend was forgotten. *Wotton.*

Some perfumes procure *prophetical* dreams. *Bacon.*

'Till old experience do attain
To something like *prophetick* strain. *Milton.*

Some famous *prophetick* pictures represent the fate of England by a mole, a creature blind and busy, smooth and deceitful, continually working under ground, but now and then to be discerned in the surface. *Stillingfleet.*

No arguments made a stronger impression on these Pagan converts, than the predictions relating to our Saviour in those old *prophetick* writings deposited among the hands of the greatest enemies to christianity, and owned by them to have been extant many ages before his appearance. *Addison.*

2. It has *of* before the thing foretold.

The more I know, the more my fears augment,
And fears are oft *prophetick of* th' event. *Dryden.*

Prophe'tically. *adv.* [from *prophetical.*] With knowledge of futurity; in manner of a prophecy.

He is so *prophetically* proud of an heroical cudgelling, that he raves in saying nothing. *Shakesp. Troilus and Cressida.*

This great success among Jews and Gentiles, part of it historically true at the compiling of these articles, and part of it *prophetically* true then, and fulfilled afterward, was a most effectual argument to give authority to this faith. *Hammond.*

She sigh'd, and thus *prophetically* spoke. *Dryden.*

To Pro'phetize. *v. n.* [*prophetiser*, Fr. from *prophet.*] To give predictions.

Nature else hath conference
With profound sleep, and so doth warning send
By *prophetizing* dreams. *Daniel's Civil War.*

Prophyla'ctick. *adj.* [προφυλακτικός, from προφυλάσσω.] Preventive; preservative.

Medicine is distributed into *prophylactick*, or the art of preserving health; and therapeutick, or the art of restoring health. *Watts's Logick.*

Propi'nquity. *n. s.* [*propinquitas*, Lat.]

1. Nearness; proximity; neighbourhood.

They draw the retina nearer to the crystalline humour, and by their relaxation suffer it to return to its natural distance according to the exigency of the object, in respect of distance or *propinquity*. *Ray on the Creation.*

2. Nearness of time.

Thereby was declared the *propinquity* of their desolations, and that their tranquillity was of no longer duration, than those soon decaying fruits of summer. *Brown.*

3. Kindred; nearness of blood.

Here I disclaim all my paternal care,
Propinquity, and property of blood,
And as a stranger to my heart and me
Hold thee. *Shakesp. King Lear.*

Propi'tiable. *adj* [from *propitiate.*] Such as may be induced to favour; such as may be made propitious.

To PROPI'TIATE. *v. a.* [*propitio*, Lat.] To induce to favour; to gain; to conciliate; to make propitious.

You, her priest, declare
What off'rings may *propitiate* the fair,
Rich orient pearl, bright stones that ne'er decay,
Or polish'd lines which longer last than they. *Waller.*

They believe the affairs of human life to be managed by certain spirits under him, whom they endeavour to *propitiate* by certain rites. *Stillingfleet.*

Vengeance shall pursue the inhuman coast,
'Till they *propitiate* thy offended ghost. *Dryden.*

Let fierce Achilles, dreadful in his rage,
The God *propitiate*, and the pest assuage. *Pope.*

Propitia'tion. *n. s.* [*propiciation*, Fr. from *propitiate.*]

1. The act of making propitious.

2. The attonement; the offering by which propitiousness is obtained.

He is the *propitiation* for the sins of the whole world. 1 *Jo.*

Propitia'tor. *n. s.* [from *propitiate.*] One that propitiates.

Propi'tiatory. *adj.* [*propiciatoire*, Fr. from *propitiate.*] Having the power to make propitious.

Is not this more than giving God thanks for their virtues, when a *propitiatory* sacrifice is offered for their honour? *Stilling.*

Propi'tious. *adj.* [*propitius*, Lat. *propice*, Fr.] Favourable; kind.

T' assuage the force of this new flame,
And make thee more *propitious* in my need,
I mean to sing the praises of thy name. *Spenser.*

Let not my words offend thee,
My maker, be *propitious* while I speak! *Milton.*

Indulgent God! *propitious* pow'r to Troy,
Swift to relieve, unwilling to destroy. *Dryden.*

Would but thy sister Marcia be *propitious*
To thy friend's vows. *Addison's Cato.*

Ere Phœbus rose, he had implor'd
Propitious heav'n. *Pope's Rape of the Lock.*

Propi'tiously. *adv.* [from *propitious.*] Favourably; kindly.

So when a muse *propitiously* invites,
Improve her favours, and indulge her flights. *Roscommon.*

Propi'tiousness. *n. s.* [from *propitious.*] Favourableness; kindness.

All these joined with the *propitiousness* of climate to that sort of tree and the length of age it shall stand and grow, may produce an oak. *Temple.*

Propla'sm. *n. s.* [πρὸ and πλάσμα.] Mould; matrix.

Those shells serving as *proplasms* or moulds to the matter which so filled them, limited and determined its dimensions and figure. *Woodward's Nat. Hist.*

Propla'stice. *n. s.* [προπλαστική.] The art of making moulds for casting.

Propo'nent. *n. s.* [from *proponens*, Lat.] One that makes a proposal.

For mysterious things of faith rely
On the *proponent*, heaven's authority. *Dryden.*

PROPO'RTION. *n. s.* [*proportion*, Fr. *proportio*, Lat.]

1. Comparative relation of one thing to another; ratio.

Let any man's wisdom determine by lessening the territory, and increasing the number of inhabitants, what *proportion* is requisite to the peopling of a region in such a manner, that the land shall be neither too narrow for those whom it feedeth, nor capable of a greater multitude. *Raleigh.*

By *proportion* to these rules, we may judge of the obligation that lies upon all sorts of injurious persons. *Taylor.*

Things nigh equivalent and neighb'ring value
By lot are parted; but high heav'n thy share,
In equal balance weigh'd 'gainst earth and hell,
Flings up the adverse scale, and shuns *proportion*. *Prior.*

2. Settled

2. Settled relation of comparative quantity; equal degree.

Greater visible good does not always raise men's desires, in *proportion* to the greatness it is acknowledged to have, though every little trouble sets us on work to get rid of it. *Locke.*

He must be little skilled in the world, who thinks that men's talking much or little shall hold *proportion* only to their knowledge. *Locke.*

Several nations are recovered out of their ignorance, in *proportion* as they converse more or less with those of the reformed churches. *Addison's Remarks on Italy.*

In *proportion* as this resolution grew, the terrors before us seemed to vanish. *Tatler*, Nº 81.

3. Harmonick degree.

His volant touch
Instinct through all *proportions*, low and high,
Fled, and pursu'd transverse the resonant fugue. *Milton.*

4. Symmetry; adaptation of one to another.

It must be mutual in *proportion* due
Giv'n and receiv'd. *Milton.*

No man of the present age is equal in the strength, *proportion* and knitting of his limbs to the Hercules of Farnese. *Dryden's Dufresnoy.*

The *proportions* are so well observed, that nothing appears to an advantage, or distinguishes itself above the rest. *Addis.*

Harmony, with ev'ry grace,
Plays in the fair *proportions* of her face. *Mrs. Carter.*

5. Form; size.

All things receiv'd, do such *proportion* take,
As those things have, wherein they are receiv'd;
So little glasses little faces make,
And narrow webs on narrow frames are weav'd. *Davies.*

To PROPO'RTION. *v. a.* [*proportionner*, Fr. from the noun.]

1. To adjust by comparative relation.

Measure is that which perfecteth all things, because every thing is for some end; neither can that thing be available to any end, which is not proportionable thereunto: and to *proportion* as well excesses as defects, are opposite. *Hooker.*

Till body up to spirit work, in bounds
Proportion'd to each kind. *Milton.*

In the loss of an object, we do not *proportion* our grief to the real value it bears, but to the value our fancies set upon it. *Addison's Spectator*, Nº 256.

2. To form symmetrically.

Nature had *proportioned* her without any fault, quickly to be discovered by the senses; yet altogether seemed not to make up that harmony that Cupid delights in. *Sidney.*

PROPO'RTIONABLE. *adj.* [from *proportion.*] Adjusted by comparative relation; such as is fit.

His commandments are not grievous, because he offers us an assistance *proportionable* to the difficulty. *Tillotson.*

It was enlivened with an hundred and twenty trumpets, assisted with a *proportionable* number of other instruments. *Add.*

PROPO'RTIONABLY. *adv.* [from *proportion.*] According to proportion; according to comparative relations.

The mind ought to examine all the grounds of probability, and upon a due balancing the whole, reject or receive it *proportionably* to the preponderancy of the greater grounds of probability, on one side or the other. *Locke.*

The parts of a great thing are great, and there are *proportionably* large estates in a large country. *Arbuthnot.*

Though religion be more eminently necessary to those in stations of authority, yet these qualities are *proportionably* conducive to publick happiness in every inferior relation. *Rogers.*

PROPO'RTIONAL. *adj.* [*proportionel*, Fr. from *proportion.*] Having a settled comparative relation; having a certain degree of any quality compared with something else.

As likely tasting to attain
Proportional ascent, which cannot be
But to be gods or angels. *Milton's Par. Lost.*

Four numbers are said to be *proportional*, when the first containeth, or is contained by the second, as often as the third containeth, or is contained by the fourth. *Cocker.*

If light be swifter in bodies than in vacuo in the proportion of the sines which measure the refraction of the bodies, the forces of the bodies to reflect and refract light, are very nearly *proportional* to the densities of the same bodies. *Newton.*

PROPORTIONA'LITY. *n. s.* [from *proportional.*] The quality of being proportional.

All sense, as grateful, dependeth upon the equality or the *proportionality* of the motion or impression made. *Grew.*

PROPO'RTIONALLY. *adv.* [from *proportional.*] In a stated degree.

If these circles, whilst their centres keep their distances and positions, could be made less in diameter, their interfering one with another, and by consequence the mixture of the heterogeneous rays would be *proportionally* diminished. *Newt.*

PROPO'RTIONATE. *adj.* [from *proportion.*] Adjusted to something else, according to a certain rate or comparative relation.

The connection between the end and any means is adequate, but between the end and means *proportionate*. *Grew.*

The use of spectacles, by an adequate connection of truths, gave men occasion to think of microscopes and telescopes; but the invention of burning glasses depended on a *proportionate*; for that figure, which contracts the species of any body, that is, the rays by which it is seen, will, in the same proportion, contract the heat wherewith the rays are accompanied. *Grew's Cosmol.*

In the state of nature, one man comes by no absolute power, to use a criminal according to the passion or heats of his own will; but only to retribute to him, so far as conscience dictates, what is *proportionate* to his transgression. *Locke.*

To PROPO'RTIONATE. *v. a.* [from *proportion.*] To adjust, according to settled rates, to something else.

The parallelism and due *proportionated* inclination of the axis of the earth. *More's Divine Dialogues.*

Since every single particle hath an innate gravitation toward all others, *proportionated* by matter and distance, it evidently appears, that the outward atoms of the chaos would necessarily tend inwards, and descend from all quarters towards the middle of the whole space. *Bentley's Sermons.*

PROPO'RTIONATENESS. *n. s.* [from *proportionate.*] The state of being by comparison adjusted.

By this congruity of those faculties to their proper objects, and by the fitness and *proportionateness* of these objective impressions upon their respective faculties, accommodated to their reception, the sensible nature hath so much of perception, as is necessary for its sensible being. *Hale.*

PROPO'SAL. *n. s.* [from *propose.*]

1. Scheme or design propounded to consideration or acceptance.

If our *proposals* once again were heard,
We should compel them to a quick result. *Milton.*

The work, you mention, will sufficiently recommend itself, when your name appears with the *proposals*. *Add. to Po.*

2. Offer to the mind.

Upon the *proposal* of an agreeable object, a man's choice will rather incline him to accept than refuse it. *South.*

This truth is not likely to be entertained readily upon the first *proposal*. *Atterbury.*

To PROPO'SE. *v. a.* [*proposer*, Fr. *propono*, Lat.] To offer to the consideration.

Raphael to Adam's doubt *propos'd*,
Benevolent and facil thus reply'd. *Milton.*

My design is to treat only of those, who have chiefly *proposed* to themselves the latter as the principal reward of their labours. *Tatler*, Nº 81.

In learning any thing, there should be as little as possible first *proposed* to the mind at once, and that being understood, proceed then to the next adjoining part. *Watts.*

To PROPO'SE. *v. n.* To lay schemes. Not in use.

Run thee into the parlour,
There shalt thou find my cousin Beatrice,
Proposing with the prince and Claudio. *Shakesp.*

PROPO'SER. *n. s.* [from *propose.*] One that offers any thing to consideration.

Faith is the assent to any proposition, not made out by the deductions of reason, but upon the credit of the *proposer*, as coming from God. *Locke.*

He provided a statute, that whoever proposed any alteration to be made, should do it with a rope about his neck; if the matter proposed were generally approved, then it should pass into a law; if it went in the negative, the *proposer* to be immediately hanged. *Swift.*

PROPOSI'TION. *n. s.* [*proposition*, Fr. *propositio*, Lat.]

1. A sentence in which any thing is affirmed or decreed.

Chrysippus, labouring how to reconcile these two *propositions*, that all things are done by fate, and yet that something is in our own power, cannot extricate himself. *Hammond.*

The compounding of the representation of things, with an affirmation or negation, makes a *proposition*. *Hale.*

2. Proposal; offer of terms.

The enemy sent *propositions*, such as upon delivery of a strong fortified town, after a handsome defence, are usually granted. *Clarendon.*

PROPOSI'TIONAL. *adj.* [from *proposition.*] Considered as a proposition.

If it has a singular subject in its *propositional* sense, it is always ranked with universals. *Watts's Logick.*

To PROPOU'ND. *v. a.* [*propono*, Lat.]

1. To offer to consideration; to propose.

The parli'ment, which now is held, decreed
Whatever pleas'd the king but to *propound*. *Daniel.*

To leave as little as I may unto fancy, which is wild and irregular, I will *propound* a rule. *Wotton.*

Dar'st thou to the son of God *propound*
To worship thee. *Milton.*

The greatest stranger must *propound* the argument. *More.*

The arguments, which christianity *propounds* to us, are reasonable encouragements to bear sufferings patiently. *Tillotson.*

2. To offer; to exhibit.

A spirit rais'd from depth of under-ground,
That shall make answer to such questions,
As by your grace shall be *propounded* him. *Shakesp.*

PROPOU'NDER. *n. s.* [from *propound.*] He that propounds; he that offers; proposer.

PROPRI'ETARY.

PROPRI'ETARY. *n. s.* [*proprietaire*, Fr. from *propriety.*] Possessor in his own right.

'Tis a great mistake to think ourselves stewards in some of God's gifts, and *proprietaries* in others: they are all equally to be employed, according to the designation of the donor. *Government of the Tongue.*

PROPRI'ETARY. *adj.* Belonging to a certain owner.

Though sheep, which are *proprietary*, are seldom marked, yet they are not apt to straggle. *Grew's Cosmol.*

PROPRI'ETOR. *n. s.* [from *proprius*, Lat.] A possessor in his own right.

Man, by being master of himself, and *proprietor* of his own person, and the actions or labour of it, had still in himself the great foundation of property. *Locke.*

Though they are scattered on the wings of the morning, and remain in the uttermost parts of the sea, even there shall his right hand fetch them out, and lead them home to their ancient *proprietor.* *Rogers.*

PROPRI'ETRESS. *n. s.* [from *proprietor.*] A female possessor in her own right; a mistress.

A big-bellied bitch borrowed another bitch's kennel to lay her burthen in; the *proprietress* demanded possession, but the other begged her excuse. *L'Estrange.*

PROPRI'ETY. *n. s.* [*proprieté*, Fr. *proprietas*, Lat.]

1. Peculiarity of possession; exclusive right.

You that have promis'd to yourselves *propriety* in love,
Know womens hearts like straws do move. *Suckling.*

Benefit of peace, and vacation for piety, render it necessary by laws to secure *propriety.* *Hammond.*

Hail wedded love! mysterious law, true source
Of human offspring, sole *propriety*
In Paradise! of all things common else. *Milton.*

They secure *propriety* and peace. *Dryden.*

To that we owe not only the safety of our persons and the *propriety* of our possessions, but our improvement in the several arts. *Atterbury.*

2. Accuracy; justness.

Common use, that is the rule of *propriety*, affords some aid to settle the signification of language. *Locke.*

PROPT, for *propped.* [from *prop.*] Sustained by some prop.

See in her cell sad Eloisa spread,
Propt in some tomb, a neighbour of the dead. *Pope.*

To PROPU'GN. *v. a.* [*propugno*, Lat.] To defend; to vindicate.

Thankfulness is our meet tribute to those sacred champions for *propugning* of our faith. *Hammond.*

PROPUGNA'TION. *n. s.* [*propugnatio*, from *propugno*, Latin.] Defence.

What *propugnation* is in one man's valour,
To stand the push and enmity of those
This quarrel would excite? *Shakesp. Troilus and Cressida.*

PROPU'GNER. *n. s.* [from *propugn.*] A defender.

So zealous *propugners* are they of their native creed, that they are importunately diligent to instruct men in it, and in all the little sophistries for defending it. *Gov. of the Tongue.*

PROPU'LSION. *n. s.* [*propulsus*, Lat.] The act of driving forward.

Joy worketh by *propulsion* of the moisture of the brain, when the spirits dilate and occupy more room. *Bacon.*

The evanescent solid and fluid will scarce differ, and the extremities of those small canals will by *propulsion* be carried off with the fluid continually. *Arbuthnot on Aliments.*

PRORE. *n. s.* [*prora*, Lat.] The prow; the forepart of the ship. A poetical word used for a rhyme.

There no vessel, with vermilion *prore*,
Or bark of traffick, glides from shore to shore. *Pope.*

PROROGA'TION. *n. s.* [*prorogatio*, from *prorogo*, Lat. *prorogation*, Fr.]

1. Continuance; state of lengthening out to a distant time; prolongation.

The fulness and effluence of man's enjoyments in the state of innocence, might seem to leave no place for hope, in respect of any farther addition, but only of the *prorogation* and future continuance of what already he possessed. *South.*

2. Interruption of the session of parliament by the regal authority.

It would seem extraordinary, if an inferior court should take a matter out of the hands of the high court of parliament, during a *prorogation.* *Swift.*

To PRORO'GUE. *v. a.* [*prorogo*, Lat. *proroger*, Fr.]

1. To protract; to prolong.

He *prorogued* his government, still threatning to dismiss himself from publick cares. *Dryden.*

2. To put off; to delay.

My life were better ended by their hate,
Than death *prorogued*, wanting of thy love. *Shakesp.*

3. To interrupt the session of parliament to a distant time.

By the king's authority alone, they are assembled, and by him alone are they *prorogued* and dissolved, but each house may adjourn itself. *Bacon.*

PRORU'PTION. *n. s.* [*proruptus*, from *prorumpo*, Lat.] The act of bursting out.

Others ground this disruption upon their continued or protracted time of delivery, whereat, excluding but one a day, the latter brood impatient by a forcible *proruption* anticipates their period of exclusion. *Brown's Vulgar Errours.*

PROSA'ICK. *adj.* [*prosaique*, Fr. *prosaicus*, from *prosa*, Lat.] Belonging to prose; resembling prose.

To PROSCRI'BE. *v. a.* [*proscribo*, Lat.]

1. To censure capitally; to doom to destruction.

Robert Vere, earl of Oxford, through the malice of the peers, was banished the realm, and *proscribed.* *Spenser.*

I hid for thee
Thy murder of thy brother, being so brib'd,
And writ him in the list of my *proscrib'd*
After thy fact. *Benj. Johnson.*

Follow'd and pointed at by fools and boys,
But dreaded and *proscrib'd* by men of sense. *Roscommon.*

Some utterly *proscribe* the name of chance, as a word of impious and profane signification; and indeed if taken by us in that sense, in which it was used by the heathen, so as to make any thing casual, in respect of God himself, their exception ought justly to be admitted. *South's Sermons.*

2. To interdict. Not in use.

He shall be found,
And taken or *proscrib'd* this happy ground. *Dryden.*

PROSCRI'BER. *n. s.* [from *proscribe.*] One that dooms to destruction.

The triumvir and *proscriber* had descended to us in a more hideous form, if the emperor had not taken care to make friends of Virgil and Horace. *Dryden.*

PROSCRI'PTION. *n. s.* [*proscriptio*, Lat.] Doom to death or confiscation.

You took his voice who should be prickt to die,
In our black sentence and *proscription.* *Shakesp.*

Sylla's old troops
Are needy and poor; and have but left t' expect
From Catiline new bills and new *proscriptions.* *B. Johns.*

For the title of *proscription* or forfeiture, the emperor hath been judge and party, and justiced himself. *Bacon.*

PROSE. *n. s.* [*prose*, Fr. *prosa*, Lat.] Language not restrained to harmonick sounds or set number of syllables; discourse not metrical.

Things unattempted yet in *prose* or rhime. *Milton.*

The reformation of *prose* was owing to Boccace, who is the standard of purity in the Italian tongue, though many of his phrases are become obsolete. *Dryden.*

A poet lets you into the knowledge of a device better than a *prose* writer; as his descriptions are often more diffuse. *Add.*

Prose men alone for private ends,
I thought, forsook their ancient friends. *Prior.*

I will be still your friend in *prose*:
Esteem and friendship to express,
Will not require poetick dress. *Swift.*

My head and heart thus flowing through my quill,
Verse man and *prose* man, term me which you will. *Pope.*

To PRO'SECUTE. *v. a.* [*prosequor*, *prosecutus*, Lat.]

1. To persue; to continue endeavours after any thing.

I am belov'd of beauteous Hermia,
Why should not I then *prosecute* my right? *Shakesp.*

I must not omit a father's timely care,
To *prosecute* the means of thy deliverance
By ransom. *Milton's Agonistes.*

He *prosecuted* this purpose with strength of argument and close reasoning, without incoherent sallies. *Locke.*

2. To continue; to carry on.

The same reasons, which induced you to entertain this war, will induce you also to *prosecute* the same. *Hayward.*

All resolute to *prosecute* their ire,
Seeking their own and country's cause to free. *Daniel.*

He infested Oxford, which gave them the more reason to *prosecute* the fortifications. *Clarendon.*

With louder cries
She *prosecutes* her griefs, and thus replies. *Dryden.*

3. To proceed in consideration or disquisition of any thing.

It were an infinite labour to *prosecute* those things, so far as they might be exemplified in religious and civil actions. *Hooker, b. iv. s. 1.*

4. To persue by law; to sue criminally.

5. To *prosecute* differs from to *persecute*: to *persecute* always implies some cruelty, malignity or injustice; to *prosecute*, is to proceed by legal measures, either with or without just cause.

PROSECU'TION. *n. s.* [from *prosecute.*]

1. Persuit; endeavour to carry on.

Many offer at the effects of friendship, but they do not last; they are promising in the beginning, but they fail, jade, and tire in the *prosecution.* *South.*

Their jealousy of the British power, as well as their *prosecutions* of commerce and pursuits of universal monarchy, will fix them in their aversions towards us. *Addison.*

2. Suit against a man in a criminal cause.

PRO'SECUTOR. *n. s.* [from *prosecute.*] One that carries on any thing; a persuer of any purpose; one who persues another by law in a criminal cause.

PRO'SELYTE. *n. s.* [προσήλυτ☉; *proselite*, Fr.] A convert; one brought over to a new opinion.

He that saw hell in's melancholy dream,
Scar'd from his sins, repented in a fright,
Had he view'd Scotland, had turn'd *proselyte*. *Cleaveland.*

Men become professors and combatants for those opinions they were never convinced of, nor *proselytes* to. *Locke.*

Where'er you tread,
Millions of *proselytes* behind are led,
Through crowds of new-made converts still you go. *Granv.*

What numbers of *proselytes* may we not expect. *Addison.*

To PRO'SELYTE. *v. a.* To convert. A bad word.

Men of this temper cut themselves off from the opportunities of *proselyting* others, by averting them from their company. *Government of the Tongue.*

PROSEMINA'TION. *n. s.* [*prosemino*, *proseminatus*, Lat.] Propagation by seed.

Touching the impossibility of the eternal succession of men, animals or vegetables by natural propagation or *prosemination*, the reasons thereof shall be delivered. *Hale.*

PROSO'DIAN. *n. s.* [from *prosody*.] One skilled in metre or prosody.

Some have been so bad *prosodians*, as from thence to derive malum, because that fruit was the first occasion of evil. *Brown.*

PRO'SODY. *n. s.* [*prosodie*, Fr. προσωδία.] The part of grammar which teaches the sound and quantity of syllables, and the measures of verse.

PROSOPOPOE'IA. *n. s.* [προσωποποιία; *prosopopée*, Fr.] Personification; figure by which things are made persons.

These reasons are pathetically urged, and admirably raised by the *prosopopœia* of nature speaking to her children. *Dryden.*

PRO'SPECT. *n. s.* [*prospectus*, Lat.]

1. View of something distant.

Eden and all the coast in *prospect* lay. *Milton.*

The Jews being under the œconomy of immediate revelation, might be supposed to have had a freer *prospect* into that heaven, whence their law descended. *Decay of Piety.*

It is better to marry than to burn, says St. Paul; a little burning felt pushes us more powerfully, than greater pleasures in *prospect* allure. *Locke.*

2. Place which affords an extended view.

Him God beholding from his *prospect* high,
Wherein past, present, future he beholds,
Thus spake. *Milton's Par. Lost, b.* iii.

3. Series of objects open to the eye.

There is a very noble *prospect* from this place: on the one side lies a vast extent of seas, that runs abroad further than the eye can reach: just opposite stands the green promontory of Surrentum, and on the other side the whole circuit of the bay of Naples. *Addison.*

4. Object of view.

Man to himself
Is a large *prospect*, rais'd above the level
Of his low creeping thoughts. *Denham.*

Present, sad *prospect!* can he ought descry,
But what affects his melancholy eye;
The beauties of the ancient fabrick lost
In chains of craggy hills, or lengths of dreary coast. *Prior.*

5. View into futurity: opposed to retrospect.

To be king,
Stands not within the *prospect* of belief,
No more than to be Cawdor. *Shakesp. Macbeth.*

To him, who hath a *prospect* of the different state of perfect happiness or misery, that attends all men after this life, the measures of good and evil are mightily changed. *Locke.*

If there be no *prospect* beyond the grave, the inference is right; let us eat and drink, for to-morrow we shall die. *Locke.*

Against himself his gratitude maintain'd,
By favours past, not future *prospects* gain'd. *Smith.*

6. Regard to something future.

Is he a prudent man, as to his temporal estate, that lays designs only for a day, without any *prospect* to, or provision for the remaining part of his life. *Tillotson.*

To PROSPE'CT. *v. a.* [*prospectus*, Lat.] To look forward. *Dict.*

PROSPE'CTIVE. *adj.* [from *prospect*.]

1. Viewing at a distance.
2. Acting with foresight.

The French king and king of Sweden are circumspect, industrious and *prospective* too in this affair. *Child.*

To PRO'SPER. *v. a.* [*prospero*, Lat.] To make happy; to favour.

Kind gods, forgive
Me that, and *prosper* him. *Shakesp. King Lear.*

All things concur to *prosper* our design;
All things to *prosper* any love but mine. *Dryden.*

To PRO'SPER. *v. n.* [*prosperer*, Fr.]

1. To be prosperous; to be successful.

My word shall not return void, but accomplish that which I please, and it shall *prosper* in the thing whereto I sent it. *Is.*

This man encreased by little and little, and things *prospered* with him more and more. 2 *Mac.* viii. 8.

Surer to *prosper*, than prosperity
Could have assur'd us. *Milton.*

2. To thrive; to come forward.

All things do *prosper* best, when they are advanced to the better; a nursery of stocks ought to be in a more barren ground, than that whereunto you remove them. *Bacon.*

The plants, which he had set, did thrive and *prosper*. *Cowley.*

She visits how they *prosper'd*, bud, and bloom. *Milton.*

PROSPE'RITY. *n. s.* [*prosperitas*, Lat. *prosperité*, Fr.] Success; attainment of wishes; good fortune.

Prosperity, in regard of our corrupt inclination to abuse the blessings of Almighty God, doth prove a thing dangerous to the souls of men. *Hooker, b.* v. *s.* 48.

God's justice reaps that glory in our calamities, which we robbed him of in our *prosperity*. *King Charles.*

PRO'SPEROUS. *adj.* [*prosperus*, Lat.] Successful; fortunate.

Your good advice, which still hath been both grave
And *prosperous*. *Shakesp. Macbeth.*

Either state to bear *prosperous* or adverse. *Milton.*

May he find
A happy passage, and a *prosp'rous* wind. *Denham.*

PRO'SPEROUSLY. *adv.* [from *prosperous*.] Successfully; fortunately.

Prosperously I have attempted, and
With bloody passage led your wars, even to
The gates of Rome. *Shakesp. Coriolanus.*

In 1596, was the second invasion upon the main territories of Spain, *prosperously* atchieved by Robert earl of Essex, in consort with the earl of Nottingham. *Bacon.*

Those, who are *prosperously* unjust, are intitled to panegyrick, but afflicted virtue is stabbed with reproaches. *Dryden.*

PRO'SPEROUSNESS. *n. s.* [from *prosperous*.] Prosperity.

PROSPI'CIENCE. *n. s.* [from *prospicio*, Lat.] The act of looking forward.

PROSTERNA'TION. *n. s.* [from *prosterno*, Lat.] Dejection; depression; state of being cast down; act of casting down. A word not to be adopted.

Pain interrupts the cure of ulcers, whence are stirred up a fever, watching, and *prosternation* of spirits. *Wiseman.*

PRO'STHESIS. *n. s.* [πρόσθεσις.] In surgery, that which fills up what is wanting, as when fistulous ulcers are filled up with flesh. *Dict.*

To PRO'STITUTE. *v. a.* [*prostituo*, Lat. *prostituer*, Fr.]

1. To sell to wickedness; to expose to crimes for a reward. It is commonly used of women sold to whoredom by others or themselves.

Do not *prostitute* thy daughter, to cause her to be a whore. *Lev.* xix. 29.

Marrying or *prostituting*,
Rape or adultery. *Milton's Par. Lost, b.* xi.

Who shall prevail with them to do that themselves which they beg of God, to spare his people and his heritage, to *prostitute* them no more to their own sinister designs. *D. of Pie.*

Affections, consecrated to children, husbands, and parents, are vilely *prostituted* and thrown away upon a hand at loo. *Add.*

2. To expose upon vile terms.

It were unfit, that so excellent and glorious a reward, as the gospel promises, should stoop down like fruit upon a full laden bough, to be plucked by every idle and wanton hand, that heaven should be *prostituted* to slothful men. *Tillotson.*

PRO'STITUTE. *adj.* [*prostitutus*, Lat.] Vicious for hire; sold to infamy or wickedness; sold to whoredom.

Their common loves, a lewd abandon'd pack,
By sloth corrupted, by disorder fed,
Made bold by want, and *prostitute* for bread. *Prior.*

PRO'STITUTE. *n. s.* [from the verb.]

1. A hireling; a mercenary; one who is set to sale.

At open fulsome bawdry they rejoice,
Base *prostitute!* thus dost thou gain thy bread. *Dryden.*

No hireling she, no *prostitute* to praise. *Pope.*

2. [*Prostibula*, Lat.] A publick strumpet.

From every point they come,
Then dread no dearth of *prostitutes* at Rome. *Dryden.*

PROSTITU'TION. *n. s.* [*prostitution*, Fr. from *prostitute*.]

1. The act of setting to sale; the state of being set to sale.
2. The life of a publick strumpet.

An infamous woman, having passed her youth in a most shameless state of *prostitution*, now gains her livelihood by seducing others. *Addison's Spectator.*

PROSTRA'TE. *adj.* [*prostratus*, Lat. The accent was formerly on the first syllable.]

1. Lying at length.

Once I saw with dread oppressed
Her whom I dread; so that with *prostrate* lying,
Her length the earth in love's chief cloathing dressed. *Sidn.*

He heard the western lords would undermine
His city's wall, and lay his tow'rs *prostrate*. *Fairfax.*

Before fair Britomart she fell *prostrate*. *Spenser.*

Groveling and *prostrate* on yon lake of fire. *Milton.*

2. Lying at mercy.

Look gracious on thy *prostrate* thrall. *Shakesp.*

3. Thrown down in humblest adoration.

The warning sound was no sooner heard, but the churches were filled, the pavements covered with bodies *prostrate*, and washed with tears of devout joy. *Hooker.*

To

Let us to the place
Repairing where he judg'd us, *proſtrate* fall
Before him reverent; and there confeſs
Humbly our faults, and pardon beg. *Milton.*
While *proſtrate* here in humble grief I lie,
Kind virtuous drops juſt gath'ring in my eye. *Pope.*

To PRO'STRATE. *v. a.* [*proſtratus*, Lat.]
1. To lay flat; to throw down.
In the ſtreets many they ſlew, and fired divers places, *proſtrating* two pariſhes almoſt entirely. *Hayward.*
A ſtorm that all things doth *proſtrate*,
Finding a tree alone all comfortleſs,
Beats on it ſtrongly, it to ruinate. *Spenſer.*
Stake and bind up your weakeſt plants againſt the winds, before they come too fiercely, and in a moment *proſtrate* a whole year's labour. *Evelyn's Kalendar.*
The drops falling thicker, faſter, and with greater force, beating down the fruit from the trees, *proſtrating* and laying corn growing in the fields. *Woodward's Nat. Hiſt.*
2. [*Se proſterner*, Fr.] To throw down in adoration.
Some have *proſtrated* themſelves an hundred times in the day, and as often in the night. *Duppa.*

PROSTRA'TION. *n. ſ.* [*proſternation*, Fr. from *proſtrate.*]
1. The act of falling down in adoration.
Nor is only a reſolved *proſtration* unto antiquity, a powerful enemy unto knowledge, but any confident adherence unto authority. *Brown's Vulgar Errours.*
The worſhip of the Gods had been kept up in temples, with altars, images, ſacrifices, hymns and *proſtrations*. *Stilling.*
The truths, they had ſubſcribed to in ſpeculation, they reverſed by a brutiſh ſenſeleſs devotion, managed with a greater *proſtration* of reaſon than of body. *South's Sermons.*
2. Dejection; depreſſion.
A ſudden *proſtration* of ſtrength or weakneſs attends this colick. *Arbuthnot.*

PROSTY'LE. *n. ſ.* [*proſtyle*, Fr. πρόςυλ☉.] A building that has only pillars in the front. *Dict.*

PROSY'LLOGISM. *n. ſ.* [*pro* and *ſyllogiſm.*]
A *proſyllogiſm* is when two or more ſyllogiſms are ſo connected together, that the concluſion of the former is the major or the minor of the following. *Watts.*

PROTA'SIS. *n. ſ.* [*protaſe*, Fr. πρότασις.]
1. A maxim or propoſition.
2. In the ancient drama, the firſt part of a comedy or tragedy that explains the argument of the piece. *Dict.*

PROTA'TICK. *n. ſ.* [*protatique*, Fr. προτατικός.]
There are *protatick* perſons in the ancients, whom they uſe in their plays to hear or give the relation. *Dryden.*

To PROTE'CT. *v. a.* [*protectus*, Lat. *proteger*, Fr.] To defend; to cover from evil; to ſhield.
The king
Had virtuous uncles to *protect* his grace. *Shakeſp.*
Leave not the faithful ſide,
That gave thee being, ſtill ſhades thee and *protects*. *Milt.*
Full in the midſt of his own ſtrength he ſtands,
Stretching his brawny arms and leafy hands,
His ſhade *protects* the plains. *Dryden's Virgil.*

PROTE'CTION. *n. ſ.* [*protection*, Fr. from *protect.*]
1. Defence; ſhelter from evil.
Drive tow'rd Dover, friend, where thou ſhalt meet
Both welcome and *protection*. *Shakeſp. King Lear.*
If the weak might find *protection* from the mighty, they could not with juſtice lament their condition. *Swift.*
2. A paſſport; exemption from being moleſted: as, *he had a* protection *during the rebellion*.

PROTE'CTIVE. *adj.* [from *protect.*] Defenſive; ſheltering.
The ſtately ſailing ſwan guards his oſier iſle,
Protective of his young. *Thomſon.*

PROTE'CTOR. *n. ſ.* [*protecteur*, Fr. from *protect.*]
1. Defender; ſhelterer; ſupporter; one who ſhields from evil or oppreſſion; guardian.
Hither th' oppreſſed ſhall henceforth reſort,
Juſtice to crave, and ſuccour at your court;
And then your highneſs, not for our's alone,
But for the world's *protector* ſhall be known. *Waller.*
The king of Spain, who is *protector* of the commonwealth, received information from the great duke. *Addiſon.*
2. An officer who had heretofore the care of the kingdom in the king's minority.
Is it concluded, he ſhall be *protector*?
—It is determin'd, not concluded yet. *Shakeſp.*

PROTE'CTRESS. *n. ſ.* [*protectrice*, Fr. from *protector.*] A woman that protects.
All things ſhould be guided by her direction, as the ſovereign patroneſs and *protectreſs* of the enterprize. *Bacon.*
Behold thoſe arts with a propitious eye,
That ſuppliant to their great *protectreſs* fly. *Addiſon.*

To PROTE'ND. *v. a.* [*protendo*, Lat.] To hold out; to ſtretch forth.
All ſtood with their *protended* ſpears prepar'd. *Dryden.*
With his *protended* lance he makes defence. *Dryden.*

PROTE'RVITY. *n. ſ.* [*protervitas*, Latin.] Peeviſhneſs; petulance.

To PROTE'ST. *v. n.* [*proteſtor*, Lat. *proteſter*, Fr.] To give a ſolemn declaration of opinion or reſolution.
Here's the twin brother of thy letter; but let thine inherit firſt, for, I *proteſt*, mine never ſhall. *Shakeſp.*
The peaking cornuto comes in the inſtant, after we had *proteſted* and ſpoke the prologue of our comedy. *Shakeſp.*
I have long lov'd her; and I *proteſt* to you, beſtowed much on her; followed her with a doating obſervance. *Shakeſp.*
He *proteſts* againſt your votes, and ſwears
He'll not be try'd by any but his peers. *Denham.*
The conſcience has power to diſapprove and to *proteſt* againſt the exorbitances of the paſſions. *South.*

To PROTE'ST. *v. a.*
1. To prove; to ſhow; to give evidence of. Not uſed.
Many unſought youths, that even now
Proteſt their firſt of manhood. *Shakeſp. Macbeth.*
2. To call as a witneſs.
Fiercely they oppos'd
My journey ſtrange, with clamorous uproar,
Proteſting fate ſupreme. *Milton.*

PROTE'ST. *n. ſ.* [from the verb.] A ſolemn declaration of opinion againſt ſomething.

PRO'TESTANT. *adj.* [from *proteſt.*] Belonging to proteſtants.
Since the ſpreading of the *proteſtant* religion, ſeveral nations are recovered out of their ignorance. *Addiſon.*

PRO'TESTANT. *n. ſ.* [*proteſtant*, Fr. from *proteſt.*] One of thoſe who adhere to them, who, at the beginning of the reformation, proteſted againſt the errours of the church of Rome.
This is the firſt example of any proteſtant ſubjects, that have taken up arms againſt their king a *proteſtant*. *K. Charles.*

PROTESTA'TION. *n. ſ.* [*proteſtation*, Fr. from *proteſt.*] A ſolemn declaration of reſolution, fact or opinion.
He maketh *proteſtation* to them of Corinth, that the goſpel did not by other means prevail with them, than with others the ſame goſpel taught by the reſt of the apoſtles. *Hooker.*
But to your *proteſtation*; let me hear
What you profeſs. *Shakeſp. Winter's Tale.*
If the lords of the council iſſued out any order againſt them, ſome nobleman publiſhed a *proteſtation* againſt it. *Claren.*
I ſmiled at the ſolemn *proteſtation* of the poet in the firſt page, that he believes neither in the fates or deſtinies. *Addiſ.*

PROTE'STER. *n. ſ.* [from *proteſt.*] One who proteſts; one who utters a ſolemn declaration.
Did I uſe
To ſtale with ordinary oaths my love
To every new *proteſter*? *Shakeſp. Julius Cæſar.*
What if he were one of the lateſt *proteſters* againſt popery? and but one among many, that ſet about the ſame work? *Att.*

PROTHO'NOTARY. *n. ſ.* [*pronotaire*, Fr. *protonotarius*, Lat.] The head regiſter.
Saligniacus, the pope's *prothonotary*, denies the Nubians profeſſing of obedience to the biſhop of Rome. *Brerewood.*

PROTHONO'TARISHIP. *n. ſ.* [from *prothonotary.*] The office or dignity of the principal regiſter.
He had the *prothonotariſhip* of the chancery. *Carew.*

PRO'TOCOL. *n. ſ.* [*protokol*, Dutch; *protocole*, Fr. πρωτόκολλον, from πρῶτ☉ and κόλλη.] The original copy of any writing.
An original is ſtiled the *protocol*, or ſcriptura matrix; and if the *protocol*, which is the root and foundation of the inſtrument, does not appear, the inſtrument is not valid. *Ayliffe.*

PROTOMA'RTYR. *n. ſ.* [πρῶτ☉ and μάρτυς.] The firſt martyr. A term applied to St. Stephen.

PRO'TOPLAST. *n. ſ.* [πρῶτ☉ and πλαςός.] Original; thing firſt formed as a copy to be followed afterwards.
The conſumption was the primitive diſeaſe, which put a period to our *protoplaſts*, Adam and Eve. *Harvey.*

PRO'TOTYPE. *n. ſ.* [*prototype*, Fr. πρωτότυπον.] The original of a copy; exemplar; archetype.
Man is the *prototype* of all exact ſymmetry. *Wotton.*
The image and *prototype* were two diſtinct things; and therefore what belonged to the exemplar could not be attributed to the image. *Stillingfleet.*

To PROTRA'CT. *v. a.* [*protractus*, Lat.] To draw out; to delay; to lengthen; to ſpin to length.
Where can they get victuals to ſupport ſuch a multitude, if we do but *protract* the war. *Knolles.*
He ſhrives this woman to her ſmock;
Elſe ne'er could he ſo long *protract* his ſpeech. *Shakeſp.*

PROTRA'CT. *n. ſ.* [from the verb.] Tedious continuance.
Since I did leave the preſence of my love,
Many long weary days I have out-worn,
And many nights, that ſlowly ſeem'd to move
Their ſad *protract* from evening until morn. *Spenſer.*

PROTRA'CTER. *n. ſ.* [from *protract.*]
1. One who draws out any thing to tedious length.
2. A mathematical inſtrument for taking and meaſuring angles.

PROTRA'CTION. *n. ſ.* [from *protract.*] The act of drawing to length.
Thoſe delays
And long *protraction*, which he muſt endure,
Betrays the opportunity. *Daniel.*
As to the fabulous *protractions* of the age of the world by the Egyptians, they are uncertain idle traditions. *Hale.*

PROTRA'CTIVE. *adj.* [from *protract.*] Dilatory; delaying; ſpinning to length.

Our works are nought elſe
But the *protractive* tryals of great Jove,
To find perſiſtive conſtancy in men. *Shakeſp.*
He ſuffer'd their *protractive* arts,
And ſtrove by mildneſs to reduce their hearts. *Dryden.*

PROTREPTICAL. *adj.* [προτρεπτικός.] Hortatory; ſuaſory.

The means uſed are partly didactical and *protreptical*; demonſtrating the truths of the goſpel, and then urging the profeſſors to be ſtedfaſt in the faith, and beware of infidelity. *Ward on Infidelity.*

To PROTRU'DE. *v. a.* [*protrudo*, Lat.] To thruſt forward.

When the ſtomach has performed its office upon the food, it *protrudes* it into the guts, by whoſe periſtaltick motion it is gently conveyed along. *Locke.*

They were not left, upon the ſea's being *protruded* forwards, and conſtrained to fall off from certain coaſts by the mud or earth, which is diſcharged into it by rivers. *Woodward.*

By ſlow degrees,
High as the hills *protrude* the ſwelling vales. *Thomſon.*
His left arm extended, and fore finger *protruded.* *Garlick.*

To PROTRU'DE. *v. n.* To thruſt itſelf forward.

If the ſpirits be not merely detain'd, but *protrude* a little, and that motion be confuſed, there followeth putrefaction. *Bacon's Nat. Hiſt.*

PROTRU'SION. *n. ſ.* [*protruſus*, Lat.] The act of thruſting forward; thruſt; puſh.

To conceive this in bodies inflexible, and without all *protruſion* of parts, were to expect a race from Hercules his pillars. *Brown's Vulgar Errours.*

One can have the idea of one body moved, whilſt others are at reſt; then the place, it deſerted, gives us the idea of pure ſpace without ſolidity, whereinto another body may enter, without either reſiſtance or *protruſion* of any thing. *Locke.*

PROTU'BERANCE. *n. ſ.* [*protubero*, Lat.] Something ſwelling above the reſt; prominence; tumour.

If the world were eternal, by the continual fall and wearing of waters, all the *protuberances* of the earth would infinite ages ſince have been levelled, and the ſuperficies of the earth rendered plain. *Hale's Origin of Mankind.*

Mountains ſeem but ſo many wens and unnatural *protuberances* upon the face of the earth. *More.*

PROTU'BERANT. *adj.* [from *protuberate.*] Swelling; prominent.

One man's eyes are more *protuberant* and ſwelling out, another's more ſunk and depreſſed. *Glanvil's Sceps.*

Though the eye ſeems round, in reality the iris is *protuberant* above the white, elſe the eye could not have admitted a whole hemiſphere at one view. *Ray.*

To PROTU'BERATE. *v. n.* [*protubero*, Lat.] To ſwell forward; to ſwell out beyond the parts adjacent.

If the navel *protuberates*, make a ſmall puncture with a lancet through the ſkin, and the waters will be voided without any danger of a hernia ſucceeding. *Sharp's Surgery.*

PROUD. *adj.* [prude or prut, Saxon.]

1. Too much pleaſed with himſelf.

The *proudeſt* admirer of his own parts might find it uſeful to conſult with others, though of inferior capacity. *Watts.*

2. Elated; valuing himſelf. With *of* before the object.

Fortune, that with malicious joy,
Does man her ſlave oppreſs,
Proud of her office to deſtroy,
Is ſeldom pleas'd to bleſs. *Dryden's Horace.*
In vain *of* pompous chaſtity you're *proud*,
Virtue's adultery of the tongue, when loud. *Dryden.*
High as the mother of the gods in place,
And *proud*, like her, *of* an immortal race. *Dryden.*

3. Arrogant; haughty; impatient.

The patient in ſpirit is better than the *proud* in ſpirit. *Eccluſ.*
A foe ſo *proud* will not the weaker ſeek. *Milton.*

4. Daring; preſumptuous.

By his underſtanding he ſmiteth through the *proud.* *Job.*
The blood foretold the giant's fall,
By this *proud* Palmer's hand. *Drayton.*
The *proud* attempt thou haſt repell'd. *Milton.*
Proud Sparta with their wheels reſounds. *Pope.*

5. Lofty of mien; grand of perſon.

He like a *proud* ſteed rein'd, went haughty on. *Milton.*

6. Grand; lofty; ſplendid; magnificent.

So much is true, that the ſaid country of Atlantis, as well as that of Peru, then called Coya, as that of Mexico, then named Tyrambel, were mighty and *proud* kingdoms in arms, ſhipping and riches. *Bacon's New Atlantis.*

City and *proud* ſeat. *Milton.*
Storms of ſtones from the *proud* temple's height
Pour down, and on our batter'd helms alight. *Dryden.*
The palace built by Picus vaſt and *proud*,
Supported by a hundred pillars. *Dryden.*

7. Oſtentatious; ſpecious; grand.

I better brook the loſs of brittle life,
Than thoſe *proud* titles thou haſt won of me. *Shakeſp.*

8. Salacious; eager for the male.

That camphire begets in men an impotency unto venery, obſervation will hardly confirm, and we have found it fail in cocks and hens, which was a more favourable tryal than that of Scaliger, when he gave it unto a bitch that was *proud.* *Bro.*

9. [Pryde, Sax. is ſwelling.] Fungous; exuberant.

When the veſſels are too lax, and do not ſufficiently reſiſt the influx of the liquid, that begets a fungus or *proud* fleſh. *Arbuthnot on Aliments.*

This eminence is compoſed of little points, called fungus or *proud* fleſh. *Sharp's Surgery.*

PROU'DLY. *adv.* [from *proud.*] Arrogantly; oſtentatiouſly; in a proud manner.

He bears himſelf more *proudly*
Even to my perſon, than I thought he would. *Shakeſp.*
The ſwan
Between her white wings mantling *proudly* rows. *Milton.*
Ancus follows with a fawning air;
But vain within, and *proudly* popular. *Dryden.*
Proudly he marches on, and void of fear;
Vain inſolence. *Addiſon.*

To PROVE. *v. a.* [*probo*, Lat. *prouver*, Fr.]

1. To evince; to ſhow by argument or teſtimony.

Let the trumpet ſound,
If none appear to *prove* upon thy perſon
Thy heinous, manifeſt, and many treaſons,
There is my pledge; I'll *prove* it on thy heart. *Shakeſp.*
So both their deeds compar'd this day ſhall *prove.* *Milt.*
Smile on me, and I will *prove*,
Wonder is ſhorter liv'd than love. *Waller.*

If it *prove* any thing, it can only *prove* againſt our author, that the aſſignment of dominion to the eldeſt is not by divine inſtitution. *Locke.*

In ſpite of Luther's declaration, he will *prove* the tenet upon him. *Atterbury.*

2. To try; to bring to the teſt.

Wilt thou thy idle rage by reaſon *prove?*
Or ſpeak thoſe thoughts, which have no power to move? *Sandys.*
Thy overpraiſing leaves in doubt
The virtue of that fruit, in thee firſt *prov'd.* *Milton.*

3. To experience.

Delay not the preſent, but
Filling the air with ſwords advanc'd, and darts,
We *prove* this very hour. *Shakeſp. Coriolanus.*
Could ſenſe make Marius ſit unbound, and *prove*
The cruel lancing of the knotty gout. *Davies.*
Well I deſerv'd Evadne's ſcorn to *prove*,
That to ambition ſacrific'd my love. *Waller.*
Let him in arms the pow'r of Turnus *prove*,
And learn to fear whom he diſdains to love. *Dryden.*

To PROVE. *v. n.*

1. To make tryal.

Children *prove*, whether they can rub upon the breaſt with one hand, and pat upon the forehead with another. *Bacon.*

The ſons prepare
Meeting like winds broke looſe upon the main,
To *prove* by arms whoſe fate it was to reign. *Dryden.*

2. To be found by experience.

Prove true, imagination; oh, *prove* true,
That I, dear brother, be now ta'en for you. *Shakeſp.*

All eſculent and garden herbs, ſet upon the tops of hills, will *prove* more medicinal, though leſs eſculent. *Bacon.*

3. To ſucceed.

If the experiment *proved* not, it might be pretended, that the beaſts were not killed in the due time. *Bacon.*

4. To be found in the event.

The fair bloſſom hangs the head
Sideways, as on a dying bed,
And thoſe pearls of dew ſhe wears,
Prove to be preſaging tears. *Milton.*
The beauties which adorn'd that age,
The ſhining ſubjects of his rage;
Hoping they ſhould immortal *prove*,
Rewarded with ſucceſs in love. *Waller.*

When the inflammation ends in a gangrene, the caſe *proves* mortal. *Arbuthnot.*

Property, you ſee it alter,
Or in a mortgage *prove* a lawyer's ſhare,
Or in a jointure vaniſh from the heir. *Pope.*

PRO'VEABLE. *adj.* [from *prove.*] That may be proved.

PROVE'DITOR. } *n. ſ.* [*proveditore*, Italian.] One who under-
PROVEDO'RE. } takes to procure ſupplies for an army.

The Jews, in thoſe ages, had the office of *provedore.* *Friend.*

PRO'VENDER. *n. ſ.* [*provande*, Dutch; *provende*, Fr.] Dry food for brutes; hay and corn.

Good *provender* labouring horſes would have. *Tuſſer.*
I do appoint him ſtore of *provender*;
It is a creature that I teach to fight. *Shakeſp.*
Many a duteous and knee-crooking knave
Wears out his time, much like his maſter's aſs,
For nought but *provender.* *Shakeſp. Othello.*

Whene'er

Whene'er he chanc'd his hands to lay
On magazines of corn or hay,
Gold ready coin'd appear'd, instead
Of paultry *provender* and bread. *Swift's Miscel.*

For a fortnight before you kill them, fed them with hay or other *provender*. *Mortimer.*

PRO'VERB. *n. s.* [*proverbe*, Fr. *proverbium*, Lat.]

1. A short sentence frequently repeated by the people; a saw; an adage.

The sum of his whole book of *proverbs* is an exhortation to the study of this practick wisdom. *Decay of Piety.*

It is in praise and commendation of men, as it is in gettings and gains; for the *proverb* is true, that light gains make heavy purses; for light gains come thick, whereas great come but now and then. *Bacon's Essays.*

The Italian *proverb* says of the Genoese, that they have a sea without fish, land without trees, and men without faith. *Addison.*

2. A word, name or observation commonly received or uttered.

Thou hast delivered us for a spoil, and a *proverb* of reproach. *Tob.* iii. 4.

To PRO'VERB. *v. a.* [from the noun.] Not a good word.

1. To mention in a proverb.

Am I not sung and *proverb'd* for a fool
In ev'ry street; do they not say, how well
Are come upon him his deserts? *Milton's Agonistes.*

2. To provide with a proverb.

Let wantons, light of heart,
Tickle the senseless rushes with their heels:
For I am *proverb'd* with a grandsire phrase;
I'll be a candle-holder and look on. *Shakesp.*

PROVE'RBIAL. *adj.* [*proverbial*, Fr. from *proverb.*]

1. Mentioned in a proverb.

In case of excesses, I take the German *proverbial* cure, by a hair of the same beast, to be the worst in the world; and the best, the monks diet, to eat till you are sick, and fast till you are well again. *Temple's Miscel.*

Despis'd and curs'd Leontius must descend
Through hissing ages, a *proverbial* coward. *Irene.*

2. Resembling a proverb; suitable to a proverb.

This river's head being unknown, and drawn to a *proverbial* obscurity, the opinion thereof became without bounds. *Brown's Vulgar Errours.*

3. Comprised in a proverb.

Moral sentences and *proverbial* speeches are numerous in this poet. *Pope.*

PROVE'RBIALLY. *adv.* [from *proverbial.*] In a proverb.

It is *proverbially* said, formicæ sua bilis inest, habet & musca splenem; whereas these parts anatomy hath not discovered in insects. *Brown's Vulgar Errours.*

To PROVI'DE. *v. a.* [*provideo*, Lat.]

1. To procure beforehand; to get ready; to prepare.

God will *provide* himself a lamb for a burnt-offering. *Gen.*

Provide out of all, able men that fear God. *Ex.* xviii. 21.

He happier seat *provides* for us. *Milton.*

2. To furnish; to supply. With *of* or *with* before the thing provided.

Part incentive reed
Provide, pernicious with one touch to fire. *Milton.*

To make experiments of gold, be *provided of* a conservatory of snow, a good large vault under ground, and a deep well. *Bacon's Nat. Hist.*

The king forthwith *provides* him *of* a guard,
A thousand archers daily to attend. *Daniel.*

If I have really drawn a portrait to the knees, let some better artist *provide* himself *of* a deeper canvas, and taking these hints, set the figure on its legs, and finish it. *Dryden.*

He went,
With large expence and *with* a pompous train
Provided, as to visit France or Spain. *Dryden.*

An earth well *provided of* all requisite things for an habitable world. *Burnet's Theory of the Earth.*

Rome, by the care of the magistrates, was well *provided with* corn. *Arbuthnot on Coins.*

When the monasteries were granted away, the parishes were left destitute, or very meanly *provided of* any maintenance for a pastor. *Swift's Miscel.*

They were of good birth, and such who, although inheriting good estates, yet happened to be well educated, and *provided with* learning. *Swift.*

3. To stipulate.

4. *To* PROVIDE *against*. To take measures for counteracting or escaping any ill.

Sagacity of brutes in defending themselves, *providing against* the inclemency of the weather, and care for their young. *Hale.*

Some men, instructed by the lab'ring ant,
Provide against th' extremities of want. *Dryden.*

Fraudulent practices were *provided against* by laws. *Arbuth.*

5. *To* PROVIDE *for*. To take care of beforehand.

States, which will continue, are above all things to uphold the reverend regard of religion, and to *provide for* the same by all means. *Hooker, b.* v. *s.* 2.

He hath intent, his wonted followers
Shall all be very well *provided for*. *Shakesp.*

A provident man *provides for* the future. *Raleigh.*

My arbitrary bounty's undeny'd;
I give reversions, and *for* heirs *provide*. *Garth.*

He will have many dependents, whose wants he cannot *provide for*. *Addison.*

PROVIDED *that*. [This has the form of an adverbial expression, and the French number *pourveu que* among their conjunctions; it is however the participle of the verb *provide*, used as the Latin, *audito hæc fieri.*] Upon these terms; this stipulation being made.

If I come off, she your jewel, this your jewel, and my gold are yours; *provided* I have your commendation for my more free entertainment. *Shakesp. Cymbeline.*

I take your offer, and will live with you;
Provided that you do no outrages. *Shakesp.*

Provided that he set up his resolution, not to let himself down below the dignity of a wise man. *L'Estrange.*

PRO'VIDENCE. *n. s.* [*providence*, Fr. *providentia*, Lat.]

1. Foresight; timely care; forecast; the act of providing.

The only people, which as by their justice and *providence* give neither cause nor hope to their neighbours to annoy them, so are they not stirred with false praise to trouble others quiet. *Sidney.*

Providence for war is the best prevention of it. *Bacon.*

An established character spreads the influence of such as move in a high sphere, on all around; it reaches farther than their own care and *providence* can do. *Atterbury.*

2. The care of God over created beings; divine superintendence.

This appointeth unto them their kinds of working, the disposition whereof, in the purity of God's own knowledge, is rightly termed *providence*. *Hooker.*

Is it not an evident sign of his wonderful *providence* over us, when that food of eternal life, upon the utter want whereof our endless destruction ensueth, is prepared and always set in such a readiness. *Hooker.*

Eternal *providence* exceeding thought,
Where none appears can make herself away. *Spenser.*

Providence is an intellectual knowledge, both foreseeing, caring for, and ordering all things, and doth not only behold all past, all present, and all to come; but is the cause of their so being, which prescience is not. *Raleigh.*

The world was all before them, where to chuse
Their place of rest, and *providence* their guide. *Milton.*

They could not move me from my settled faith in God and his *providence*. *More's Divine Dialogues.*

3. Prudence; frugality; reasonable and moderate care of expence.

By thrift my sinking fortune to repair,
Though late, yet is at last become my care;
My heart shall be my own, my vast expence
Reduc'd to bounds, by timely *providence*. *Dryden.*

PRO'VIDENT. *adj.* [*providens*, Lat.] Forecasting; cautious; prudent with respect to futurity.

I saw your brother
Most *provident* in peril, bind himself
To a strong mast that liv'd upon the sea. *Shakesp.*

We ourselves account such a man for *provident*, as remembering things past, and observing things present, can, by judgment, and comparing the one with the other, provide for the future. *Raleigh.*

First crept
The parsimonious emmet, *provident*
Of future. *Milton.*

Orange, with youth, experience has,
In action young, in council old;
Orange is what Augustus was,
Brave, wary, *provident* and bold. *Waller.*

A very prosperous people, flushed with great successes, are seldom so pious, so humble, so just, or so *provident*, as to perpetuate their happiness. *Atterbury.*

PROVIDE'NTIAL. *adj.* [from *providence.*] Effected by providence; referrible to providence.

What a confusion would it bring upon mankind, if those, unsatisfied with the *providential* distribution of heats and colds, might take the government into their own hands. *L'Estrange.*

The lilies grow, and the ravens are fed, according to the course of nature, and yet they are made arguments of providence, nor are these things less *providential*, because regular. *Burnet's Theory of the Earth.*

The scorched earth, were it not for this remarkably *providential* contrivance of things, would have been uninhabitable. *Woodward.*

This thin, this soft contexture of the air,
Shows the wise author's *providential* care. *Blackmore.*

PROVIDE'NTIALLY. *adv.* [from *providential.*] By the care of providence.

Every animal is *providentially* directed to the use of its proper weapons. *Ray on the Creation.*

It happened very *providentially* to the honour of the christian religion, that it did not take its rise in the dark illiterate ages of the world, but at a time when arts and sciences were at their height. *Addison.*

PRO'VIDENTLY. *adv.* [from *provident.*] With foresight; with wise precaution.

Nature having designed water-fowls to fly in the air, and live in the water, she *providently* makes their feathers of such a texture, that they do not admit the water. *Boyle.*

PROVI'DER. *n. s.* [from *provide.*] He who provides or procures.

Here's money for my meat,
I would have left it on the board, so soon
As I had made my meal, and parted thence
With prayers for the *provider.* *Shakesp.*

PRO'VINCE. *n. s.* [*province*, Fr. *provincia*, Latin.]

1. A conquered country; a country governed by a delegate.

Those *provinces* these arms of mine did conquer. *Shak.*

Greece, Italy and Sicily were divided into commonwealths, till swallowed up, and made *provinces* by Rome. *Temple.*

See them broke with toils, or sunk in ease,
Or infamous for plunder'd *provinces.* *Pope.*

2. The proper office or business of any one.

I am fit for honour's toughest task;
Nor ever yet found fooling was my *province.* *Otway.*
Nor can I alone sustain this day's *province.* *More.*
'Tis thine, whate'er is pleasant, good or fair;
All nature is thy *province*, life thy care. *Dryden.*
'Tis not the pretor's *province* to bestow
True freedom. *Dryden's Persius.*

The woman's *province* is to be careful in her œconomy, and chaste in her affection. *Tatler.*

3. A region; a tract.

Over many a tract
Of heav'n they march'd, and many a *province* wide. *Milt.*

Their understandings are cooped up in narrow bounds; so that they never look abroad into other *provinces* of the intellectual world. *Watts's Improvement of the Mind.*

PROVI'NCIAL. *adj.* [*provincial*, Fr. from *province.*]

1. Relating to a province.

The duke dare not more stretch
This finger of mine, than he dare rack his own;
His subject am I not, nor here *provincial.* *Shakesp.*

2. Appendant to the provincial country.

Some have delivered the polity of spirits, and left an account even to their *provincial* dominions. *Brown.*

3. Not of the mother country; rude; unpolished.

They build and treat with such magnificence,
That, like th' ambitious monarchs of the age,
They give the law to our *provincial* stage. *Dryden.*

A country 'squire having only the *provincial* accent upon his tongue, which is neither a fault, nor in his power to remedy, must marry a cast wench. *Swift.*

4. Belonging only to an archbishop's jurisdiction; not æcumenical.

A law made in a *provincial* synod, is properly termed a *provincial* constitution. *Ayliffe's Parergon.*

PROVI'NCIAL. *n. s.* [*provincial*, Fr. from *province.*] A spiritual governor.

Valignanus was *provincial* of the Jesuits in the Indies. *Still.*

To PROVI'NCIATE. *v. a.* [from *province.*] To turn to a province. A word not in use.

When there was a design to *provinciate* the whole kingdom, Druina, though offered a canton, would not accept of it. *Howel's Vocal Forest.*

To PROVI'NE. *v. n.* [*provigner*, Fr.] To lay a stock or branch of a vine in the ground to take root for more encrease.

PROVI'SION. *n. s.* [*provision*, Fr. *provisio*, Latin.]

1. The act of providing beforehand.

Kalander knew, that *provision* is the foundation of hospitality, and thrift the fewel of magnificence. *Sidney.*

2. Measures taken beforehand.

Five days we do allot thee for *provision*,
To shield thee from disasters of the world. *Shakesp.*

He preserved all points of humanity, in taking order and making *provision* for the relief of strangers distressed. *Bacon.*

The prudent part is to propose remedies for the present evils, and *provisions* against future events. *Temple.*

Religion lays the strictest obligations upon men, to make the best *provision* for their comfortable subsistence in this world, and their salvation in the next. *Tillotson.*

3. Accumulation of stores beforehand; stock collected.

Mendoza advertised, that he would valiantly defend the city, so long as he had any *provision* of victuals. *Knolles.*

In such abundance lies our choice,
As leaves a greater store of fruit untouch'd,
Still hanging incorruptible, till men
Grow up to their *provision.* *Milton.*

David, after he had made such vast *provision* of materials for the temple, yet because he had dipt his hands in blood, was not permitted to lay a stone in that sacred pile. *South.*

4. Victuals; food; provender.

He caused *provisions* to be brought in. *Clarendon.*
Provisions laid in large for man or beast. *Milton.*

5. Stipulation; terms settled.

This law was only to reform the degenerate English, but there was no care taken for the reformation of the mere Irish, no ordinance, no *provision* made for the abolishing of their barbarous customs. *Davies on Ireland.*

PROVI'SIONAL. *adj.* [*provisionel*, Fr. from *provision.*] Temporarily established; provided for present need.

The commenda semestris grew out of a natural equity, that, in the time of the patron's respite given him to present, the church should not be without a *provisional* pastor. *Ayliffe.*

PROVI'SIONALLY. *adv.* [from *provisional.*] By way of provision.

The abbot of St. Martin was born, was baptized, and declared a man *provisionally*, till time should shew what he would prove, nature had moulded him so untowardly. *Locke.*

PROVI'SO. *n. s.* [Latin: as, *proviso rem ita se habituram esse.*] Stipulation; caution; provisional condition.

This *proviso* is needful, that the sheriff may not have the like power of life as the marshal hath. *Spenser.*

Some will allow the church no further power, than only to exhort, and this but with a *proviso* too, that it extends not to such as think themselves too wise to be advised. *South.*

He doth deny his prisoners,
But with *proviso* and exception,
That we, at our own charge, shall ransom strait
His brother-in-law. *Shakesp. Henry* IV.

PROVOCA'TION. *n. s.* [*provocatio*, Lat. *provocation*, Fr.]

1. An act or cause by which anger is raised.

It is a fundamental law, in the Turkish empire, that they may, without any other *provocation*, make war upon Christendom for the propagation of their law. *Bacon.*

Tempt not my swelling rage
With black reproaches, scorn and *provocation.* *Smith.*

2. An appeal to a judge.

A *provocation* is every act, whereby the office of the judge or his assistance is asked; a *provocation* including both a judicial and an extrajudicial appeal. *Ayliffe.*

3. I know not whether, in the following passage, it be *appeal* or *incitement.*

The like effects may grow in all towards their pastor, and in their pastor towards every of them, between whom there daily and interchangeably pass in the hearing of God himself, and in the presence of his holy angels, so many heavenly acclamations, exultations, *provocations*, and petitions. *Hooker.*

PROVOCA'TIVE. *n. s.* [from *provoke.*] Any thing which revives a decayed or cloyed appetite.

There would be no variety of tastes to sollicit his palate, and occasion excess, nor any artificial *provocatives* to relieve satiety. *Addison.*

PRO'VOCATIVENESS. *n. s.* [from *provocative.*] The quality of being provocative.

To PROVO'KE. *v. a.* [*provoquer*, Fr. *provoco*, Latin.]

1. To rouse; to excite by something offensive; to awake.

Ye *provoke* me unto wrath, burning incense unto other Gods. *Jer.* xliv. 8.

Neither to *provoke* nor dread
New war *provok'd.* *Milton.*
To whet their courage, and their rage *provoke.* *Dryden.*
I neither fear, nor will *provoke* the war. *Dryden.*

2. To anger; to enrage; to offend; to incense.

Though often *provoked*, by the insolence of some of the bishops, to a dislike of their overmuch fervour, his integrity to the king was without blemish. *Clarendon.*

Such acts
Of contumacy will *provoke* the highest. *Milton.*

Agamemnon *provokes* Apollo against them, whom he was willing to appease afterwards. *Pope.*

3. To cause; to promote.

Drink is a great provoker; it *provokes* and unprovokes. *Sha.*

One Petro covered up his patient with warm cloaths, and when the fever began a little to decline, gave him cold water to drink till he *provoked* sweat. *Arbuthnot.*

4. To challenge.

He now *provokes* the sea-gods from the shore,
With envy Triton heard the martial sound,
And the bold champion for his challenge drown'd. *Dryden.*

5. To induce by motive; to move; to incite.

We may not be startled at the breaking of the exterior earth; for the face of nature hath *provoked* men to think of, and observe such a thing. *Burnet's Theory of the Earth.*

To PROVO'KE. *v. n.*

1. To appeal. A Latinism.

Arius and Pelagius durst *provoke*
To what the centuries preceding spoke. *Dryden.*

2. To produce anger.

It was not your brother's evil disposition made him seek his death, but a *provoking* merit. *Shakesp. King Lear.*

The Lord abhorred them, because of the *provoking* of his sons. *Deutr.* xxxii. 19.

If we consider man in such a loathsome and *provoking* condition, was it not love enough, that he was permitted to enjoy a being. *Taylor.*

PROVO'KER. *n. s.* [from *provoke.*]

1. One that raises anger.

As in all civil insurrections, the ringleader is looked on with a peculiar severity, so, in this case, the first *provoker* has double portion of the guilt. *Government of the Tongue.*

2. Cauſer; promoter.

Drink, Sir, is a great *provoker* of noſepainting, ſleep, and urine. *Shakeſp. Macbeth.*

Provo'kingly. *adv.* [from *provoking.*] In ſuch a manner as to raiſe anger.

When we ſee a man that yeſterday kept a humiliation, to-day invading the poſſeſſions of his brethren, we need no other proof how hypocritically and *provokingly* he confeſſed his pride. *Decay of Piety.*

PRO'VOST. *n. ſ.* [pꞃaꝼaꞅꞇ, Sax. *provoſt*, Fr. *provoſto*, Ital. *præpoſitus*, Lat.]

1. The chief of any body: as, *the* provoſt *of a college.*

2. The executioner of an army.

Kingſton, *provoſt* marſhal of the king's army, was deemed not only cruel but inhuman in his executions. *Hayward.*

Pro'vostship. *n. ſ.* [from *provoſt.*] The office of a provoſt.

C. Piſo firſt roſe, and afterwards was advanced to the *provoſtſhip* of Rome by Tiberius. *Hakewill.*

Prow. *n. ſ.* [*proue*, Fr. *proa*, Spaniſh; *prora*, Lat.] The head or forepart of a ſhip.

The ſea-victory of Veſpaſian was a lady holding a palm in her hand, at her foot the *prow* of a ſhip. *Peacham.*

Straight to the Dutch he turns his dreadful *prow*,
More fierce th' important quarrel to decide. *Dryden.*

Prow. *adj.* Valiant. *Spenſer.*

Prowess. *n. ſ.* [*prodezza*, Italian; *proueſſe*, Fr.] Bravery; valour; military gallantry.

Men of ſuch *prowefs*, as not to know fear in themſelves, and yet to teach it in others that ſhould deal with them; for they had often made their lives triumph over moſt terrible dangers, never diſmayed, and ever fortunate. *Sidney.*

I hope
That your wiſdom will direct my thought,
Or that your *prowefs* can me yield relief. *Fa. Queen.*
By heav'ns mere grace, not by our *prowefs* done. *F. Qu.*
Henry the fifth,
By his *prowefs* conquered all France. *Shakeſp.*
Nor ſhould thy *prowefs* want praiſe and eſteem,
But that 'tis ſhewn in treaſon. *Shakeſp. Henry VI.*
Thoſe are they
Firſt ſeen in acts of *prowefs* eminent,
And great exploits; but of true virtue void. *Milton.*
Theſe beyond compare of mortal *prowefs.* *Milton.*
Michael! of cœleſtial armies prince;
And thou in military *prowefs* next,
Gabriel! *Milton's Par. Loſt, b.* vi.
The vigour of this arm was never vain,
And that my wonted *prowefs* I retain,
Witneſs theſe heaps of ſlaughter on the plain. *Dryden.*

Theſe were the entertainments of the ſofter nations, that fell under the virtue and *prowefs* of the two laſt empires. *Temp.*

Pro'west. *adj.* [the ſuperlative formed from *prow*, adj.]

1. Braveſt; moſt valiant.

They be two of the *proweſt* knights on ground,
And oft approv'd in many a hard aſſay,
And eke of ſureſt ſteel, that may be found,
Do arm yourſelf againſt that day them to confound. *F. Q.*

2. Brave; valiant.

The faireſt of her ſex, Angelica,
His daughter, ſought by many *proweſt* knights. *Milton.*

To PROWL. *v. a.* [Of this word the etymology is doubtful: the old dictionaries write *prole*, which the dreamer *Caſaubon* derives from προαλής, ready, quick. *Skinner*, a far more judicious etymologiſt, deduces it from *proieler*, a diminutive formed by himſelf from *proier*, to prey, Fr. perhaps it may be formed, by accidental corruption, from *patrol.*] To rove over.

He *prowls* each place, ſtill in new colours deckt,
Sucking one's ill, another to infect. *Sidney.*

To Prowl. *v. n.* To wander for prey; to prey; to plunder.

The champion robbeth by night,
And *prowleth* and filcheth by daie. *Tuſſer.*

Nor do they bear ſo quietly the loſs of ſome parcels confiſcated abroad, as the great detriment which they ſuffer by ſome *prowling* vice-admiral or publick miniſter. *Raleigh.*

As when a *prowling* wolf,
Whom hunger drives to ſeek new haunt for prey. *Milton.*
Shall he, who looks erect on heav'n,
E'er ſtoop to mingle with the *prowling* herd,
And dip his tongue in gore. *Thomſon.*
And here the fell attorney *prowls* for prey. *Anon.*

Pro'wler. *n. ſ.* [from *prowl.*] One that roves about for prey.

On churchyards drear,
The diſappointed *prowlers* fall, and dig
The ſhrouded body from the grave. *Thomſon.*

PRO'XIMATE. *adj.* [*proximus*, Lat.] Next in the ſeries of ratiocination; near and immediate: oppoſed to remote and mediate.

Writing a theory of the deluge, we were to ſhew the *proximate* natural cauſes of it. *Burnet's Theory of the Earth.*

Subſtance is the remote genus of bird, becauſe it agrees not only to all kinds of animals, but alſo to things inanimate; but animal is the *proximate* or neareſt genus of bird, becauſe it agrees to feweſt other things. *Watts's Logick.*

Pro'ximately. *adv.* [from *proximate.*] Immediately; without intervention.

The conſideration of our mind, which is incorporeal, and the contemplation of our bodies, which have all the characters of excellent contrivance; theſe alone eaſily and *proximately* guide us to the wiſe author of all things. *Bentley.*

Proxime. *adj.* [*proximus*, Lat.] Next; immediate.

A ſyllogiſm is made up of three propoſitions, and theſe of three terms variouſly joined: the three terms are called the remote matter of a ſyllogiſm, the three propoſitions the *proxime* or immediate matter of it. *Watts's Logick.*

Proxi'mity. *n. ſ.* [*proximité*, Fr. *proximitas*, from *proximus*, Lat.] Nearneſs.

When kingdoms have cuſtomably been carried by right of ſucceſſion, according to *proximity* of blood, the violation of this courſe hath always been dangerous. *Hayward.*

If he plead *proximity* of blood,
That empty title is with eaſe withſtood. *Dryden.*

Add the convenience of the ſituation of the eye, in reſpect of its *proximity* to the brain, the ſeat of common ſenſe. *Ray.*

I can call to my aſſiſtance
Proximity, mark that! and diſtance. *Prior.*

Muſt we ſend to ſtab or poiſon all the popiſh princes, who have any pretended title to our crown by the *proximity* of blood? *Swift's Miſcellanies.*

Pro'xy. *n. ſ.* [By contraction from *procuracy.*]

1. The agency of another.

2. The ſubſtitution of another; the agency of a ſubſtitute; appearance of a repreſentative.

None acts a friend by a deputy, or can be familiar by *proxy.* *South's Sermons.*

Had Hyde thus ſat by *proxy* too,
As Venus once was ſaid to do,
The painter muſt have ſearch'd the ſkies,
To match the luſtre of her eyes. *Granvil.*

3. The perſon ſubſtituted or deputed.

A wiſe man will commit no buſineſs of importance to a *proxy*, where he may do it himſelf. *L'Eſtrange.*

Pruce. *n. ſ.* [*Pruce* is the old name for Pruſſia.] Pruſſian leather.

Some leathern bucklers uſe
Of folded hides, and others ſhields of *pruce.* *Dryden.*

Prude. *n. ſ.* [*prude*, Fr.] A woman over nice and ſcrupulous, and with falſe affectation.

The graver *prude* ſinks downward to a gnome,
In ſearch of miſchief, ſtill on earth to roam. *Pope.*
Not one careleſs thought intrudes,
Leſs modeſt than the ſpeech of *prudes.* *Swift.*

Pru'dence. *n. ſ.* [*prudence*, Fr. *prudentia*, Lat.] Wiſdom applied to practice.

Under *prudence* is comprehended, that diſcrete, apt, ſuiting, and diſpoſing as well of actions as words, in their due place, time and manner. *Peacham.*

Prudence is principally in reference to actions to be done, and due means, order, ſeaſon, and method of doing or not doing. *Hale.*

PRU'DENT. *adj.* [*prudent*, Fr. *prudens*, Lat.]

1. Practically wiſe.

The ſimple inherit folly, but the *prudent* are crowned with knowledge. *Prov.* xiv. 18.

I have ſeen a ſon of Jeſſe, that is a man of war, and *prudent* in matters. 1 *Sam.* xvi. 18.

The monarch prevented all reply,
Prudent, leſt others might offer. *Milton.*

2. Foreſeeing by natural inſtinct.

So ſteers the *prudent* crane
Her annual voyage. *Milton.*

Prude'ntial. *adj.* [from *prudent.*] Eligible on principles of prudence.

He acts upon the ſureſt and moſt *prudential* grounds, who, whether the principles, which he acts upon, prove true or falſe, yet ſecures a happy iſſue to his actions. *South.*

Motives are only *prudential*, and not demonſtrative. *Tillot.*

Theſe virtues, though of excellent uſe, ſome *prudential* rules it is neceſſary to take with them in practice. *Rogers.*

Prude'ntials. *n. ſ.* Maxims of prudence or practical wiſdom.

Many ſtanzas, in poetick meaſures, contain rules relating to common *prudentials*, as well as to religion. *Watts.*

Prudentia'lity. *n. ſ.* [from *prudential.*] Eligibility on principles of prudence.

Being incapable rightly to judge the *prudentiality* of affairs, they only gaze upon the viſible ſucceſs, and thereafter condemn or cry up the whole progreſſion. *Brown.*

Prude'ntially. *adv.* [from *prudential.*] According to the rules of prudence.

If he acts piouſly, ſoberly and temperately, he acts *prudentially* and ſafely. *South's Sermons.*

Pru'dently. *adv.* [from *prudent.*] Diſcretely; judiciouſly.

Theſe laws were ſo *prudently* framed, as they are found fit for all ſucceeding times. *Bacon's Henry* VII.

Such

Such deep deſigns of empire does he lay
O'er them, whoſe cauſe he ſeems to take in hand;
And *prudently* would make them lords at ſea,
To whom with eaſe he can give laws by land. *Dryden.*

PRU'DERY. *n. ſ.* [from *prude.*] Overmuch nicety in conduct.

PRU'DISH. *adj.* [from *prude.*] Affectedly grave.

I know you all expect, from ſeeing me,
Some formal lecture, ſpoke with *prudiſh* face. *Garrick.*

To PRUNE. *v. a.* [of unknown derivation.]

1. To lop; to diveſt trees of their ſuperfluities.

So lop'd and *pruned* trees do flouriſh fair. *Davies.*

Let us ever extol
His bounty, following our delightful taſk,
To *prune* thoſe growing plants, and tend theſe flow'rs. *Milt.*

What we by day
Lop overgrown, or *prune*, or prop, or bind,
One night with wanton growth derides,
Tending to wild. *Milton's Par. Loſt, b.* ix.

Horace will our ſuperfluous branches *prune*,
Give us new rules, and ſet our harp in tune. *Waller.*

You have no leſs right to correct me, than the ſame hand that raiſed a tree, has to *prune* it. *Pope.*

2. To clear from excreſcencies.

His royal bird
Prunes the immortal wing, and cloys his beak. *Shakeſp.*

Many birds *prune* their feathers; and crows ſeem to call upon rain, which is but the comfort they receive in the relenting of the air. *Bacon's Nat. Hiſt.*

The muſe, whoſe early voice you taught to ſing,
Preſcrib'd her heights, and *prun'd* her tender wing. *Pope.*

To PRUNE. *v. n.* To dreſs; to prink. A ludicrous word.

Every ſcribbling man
Grows a fop as faſt as e'er he can,
Prunes up, and aſks his oracle the glaſs,
If pink or purple beſt become his face. *Dryden.*

PRUNE. *n. ſ.* [*prune*, *pruneau*, Fr. *prunum*, Lat.] A dried plum.

In drying of pears and *prunes* in the oven, and removing of them, there is a like operation. *Bacon's Nat. Hiſt.*

PRU'NEL. *n. ſ.* An herb. *Ainſworth.*

PRUNE'LLO. *n. ſ.*

1. A kind of ſtuff of which the clergymen's gowns are made.

Worth makes the man, and want of it, the fellow;
The reſt is all but leather or *prunello.* *Pope.*

2. [*Prunelle*, Fr.] A kind of plum. *Ainſworth.*

PRU'NER. *n. ſ.* [from *prune.*] One that crops trees.

Leſt thy redundant juice
Should fading leaves, inſtead of fruits, produce,
The *pruner*'s hand with letting blood muſt quench
Thy heat, and thy exub'rant parts retrench. *Denham.*

PRUNI'FEROUS. *adj.* [*prunum* and *fero*, Lat.] Plum bearing.

PRU'NINGHOOK. } *n. ſ.* A hook or knife uſed in lopping
PRU'NINGKNIFE. } trees.

Let thy hand ſupply the *pruningknife*,
And crop luxuriant ſtragglers. *Dryden.*

No plough ſhall hurt the glebe, no *pruninghook* the vine. *Dryden's Virgil.*

The cyder land obſequious ſtill to thrones,
Her *pruninghooks* extended into ſwords. *Philips.*

PRU'RIENCE. } *n. ſ.* [from *prurio*, Lat.] An itching or a great
PRU'RIENCY. } deſire or appetite to any thing. *Swift.*

PRU'RIENT. *adj.* [*pruriens*, Lat.] Itching. *Ainſworth.*

PRURIGINOUS. *adj.* [*prurio*, Lat.] Tending to an itch.

To PRY. *v. n.* [of unknown derivation.] To peep narrowly; to inſpect officiouſly, curiouſly, or impertinently.

I can counterfeit the deep tragedian,
Speak, and look back, and *pry* on ev'ry ſide,
Intending deep ſuſpicion. *Shakeſp. Richard* III.

I *pry'd* me through the crevice of a wall,
When for his hand he had his two ſons heads. *Shakeſp.*

Watch thou, and wake when others be aſleep,
To *pry* into the ſecrets of the ſtate. *Skakeſp.*

We of th' offending ſide
Muſt keep aloof from ſtrict arbitrement;
And ſtop all ſight holes, every loop, from whence
The eye of reaſon may *pry* in upon us. *Shakeſp.*

He that *prieth* in at her windows, ſhall alſo hearken at her doors. *Eccluſ.* xiv. 23.

And *pry*
In every buſh and brake, where hap may find
The ſerpent ſleeping. *Milton.*

We have naturally a curioſity to be *prying* and ſearching into forbidden ſecrets. *L'Eſtrange.*

Search well
Each grove and thicket, *pry* in ev'ry ſhape,
Leſt hid in ſome th' arch hypocrite eſcape. *Dryden.*

I wak'd, and looking round the bow'r
Search'd ev'ry tree, and *pry'd* on ev'ry flow'r,
If any where by chance I might eſpy
The rural poet of the melody. *Dryden.*

Nor need we with a *prying* eye ſurvey
The diſtant ſkies, to find the milky way. *Creech.*

Actions are of ſo mixt a nature, that as men *pry* into them, or obſerve ſome parts more than others, they take different hints, and put contrary interpretations on them. *Addiſon.*

All theſe I frankly own without denying;
But where has this Praxiteles been *prying.* *Addiſon.*

PSALM. *n. ſ.* [*pſalme*, *pſeaume*, Fr. ψαλμός.] A holy ſong.

The choice and flower of all things profitable in other books, the *pſalms* do both more briefly contain and more movingly expreſs, by reaſon of that poetical form wherewith they are written. *Hooker, b.* v. *ſ.* 37.

Sternhold was made groom of the chamber, for turning certain of David's *pſalms* into verſe. *Peacham.*

Thoſe juſt ſpirits that wear victorious palms,
Hymns devote and holy *pſalms*
Singing continually. *Milton.*

In another *pſalm*, he ſpeaks of the wiſdom and power of God in the creation. *Burnet's Theory of the Earth.*

PSA'LMIST. *n. ſ.* [*pſalmiſte*, Fr. from *pſalm.*] Writer of holy ſongs.

How much more rational is this ſyſtem of the *pſalmiſt*, than the Pagans ſcheme in Virgil, where one deity is repreſented as raiſing a ſtorm, and another as laying it? *Addiſ.*

PSA'LMODY. *n. ſ.* [*pſalmodie*, Fr. ψαλμῳδία.] The act or practice of ſinging holy ſongs.

PSALMO'GRAPHY. *n. ſ.* [ψαλμὸς and γράφω.] The act of writing pſalms.

PSA'LTER. *n. ſ.* [*pſautier*, Fr. ψαλτήριον.] The volume of pſalms; a pſalmbook.

PSA'LTERY. *n. ſ.* A kind of harp beaten with ſticks.

The trumpets, ſacbuts, *pſalteries* and fifes
Make the ſun dance. *Shakeſp. Coriolanus.*

Praiſe with trumpets, pierce the ſkies,
Praiſe with harps and *pſalteries.* *Sandys's Paraph.*

The ſweet ſinger of Iſrael with his *pſaltery*, loudly reſounded the benefits of the almighty creator. *Peacham.*

Nought ſhall the *pſalt'ry* and the harp avail,
When the quick ſpirits their warm march forbear,
And numbing coldneſs has unbrac'd the ear. *Prior.*

PSEU'DO. *n. ſ.* [from ψεῦδος.] A prefix, which, being put before words, ſignifies falſe or counterfeit: as, *pſeudapoſtle*, a counterfeit apoſtle.

PSEU'DOGRAPHY. *n. ſ.* Falſe writing.

I will not purſue the many *pſeudographies* in uſe, but ſhew of how great concern the emphaſis were, if rightly uſed. *Hold.*

PSEU'DOLOGY. *n. ſ.* [ψευδολογία.] Falſehood of ſpeech.

It is not according to the ſound rules of *pſeudology*, to report of a pious prince, that he neglects his devotion, but you may report of a merciful prince, that he has pardoned a criminal who did not deſerve it. *Arbuthnot.*

PSHAW. *interj.* An expreſſion of contempt.

A peeviſh fellow has ſome reaſon for being out of humour, or has a natural incapacity for delight, and therefore diſturbs all with piſhes and *pſhaws.* *Spectator,* Nº 438.

PTI'SAN. *n. ſ.* [*ptiſanne*, Fr. πτισανή.] A medical drink made of barley decocted with raiſins and liquorice.

Thrice happy were thoſe golden days of old,
When dear as Burgundy the *ptiſans* ſold;
When patients choſe to die with better will,
Than breathe and pay the apothecary's bill. *Garth.*

In fevers the aliments preſcribed by Hippocrates, were *ptiſans* and cream of barley. *Arbuthnot.*

PTY'ALISM. *n. ſ.* [*ptyaliſme*, Fr. πτυελισμός.] Salivation; effuſion of ſpittle.

PTY'SMAGOGUE. *n. ſ.* [πτύσμα and ἄγω.] A medicine which diſcharges ſpittle. *Dict.*

PUBE'RTY. *n. ſ.* [*puberté*, Fr. *pubertas*, Lat.] The time of life in which the two ſexes begin firſt to be acquainted.

The cauſe of changing the voice at the years of *puberty* ſeemeth to be, for that when much of the moiſture of the body, which did before irrigate the parts, is drawn down to the ſpermatical veſſels, it leaveth the body more hot than it was, whence cometh the dilatation of the pipes. *Bacon.*

All the carnivorous animals would have multiplied exceedingly, before theſe children that eſcaped could come to the age of *puberty.* *Bentley's Sermons.*

PUBE'SCENCE. *n. ſ.* [from *pubeſco*, Lat.] The ſtate of arriving at puberty.

Solon divided it into ten ſeptenaries; in the firſt is dentition or falling of teeth, in the ſecond *pubeſcence.* *Brown.*

PUBE'SCENT. *adj.* [from *pubeſcens*, Lat.] Arriving at puberty.

That the women are menſtruent, and the men *pubeſcent* at the year of twice ſeven, is accounted a punctual truth. *Brown.*

PU'BLICAN. *n. ſ.* [from *publicus*, Lat.]

1. A toll gatherer.

As Jeſus ſat at meat, many *publicans* and ſinners came and ſat down with him. *Matth.* ix. 10.

2. A man that keeps a houſe of general entertainment. In low language.

PUBLICA'TION. *n. ſ.* [*publico*, Lat.]

1. The act of publiſhing; the act of notifying to the world; divulgation; proclamation.

For the inſtruction of all men to eternal life, it is neceſſary, that the ſacred and ſaving truth of God be openly publiſhed unto them, which open *publication* of heavenly myſteries is by an excellency termed preaching. *Hooker.*

2. Edition;

2. Edition; the act of giving a book to the publick.

An imperfect copy having been offered to a bookseller, you consented to the *publication* of one more correct. *Pope.*

The *publication* of these papers was not owing to our folly, but that of others. *Swift.*

PU'BLICK. *adj.* [*public, publique,* Fr. *publicus,* Lat.]

1. Belonging to a state or nation; not private.

By following the law of private reason, where the law of *publick* should take place, they breed disturbance. *Hooker.*

Of royal maids how wretched is the fate,
Born only to be victims of the state;
Our hopes, our wishes, all our passions try'd
For *publick* use, the slaves of others pride. *Granvil.*

Have we not able counsellors, hourly watching over the *publick* weal. *Swift.*

2. Open; notorious; generally known.

Joseph being a just man, and not willing to make her a *publick* example, was minded to put her away privily. *Matth.*

3. General; done by many.

A dismal universal hiss, the sound
Of *publick* scorn. *Milton.*

4. Regarding not private interest, but the good of the community.

They were *publick* hearted men, as they paid all taxes, so they gave up all their time to their country's service, without any reward. *Clarendon.*

All nations that grew great out of little or nothing, did so merely by the *publick* mindedness of particular persons. *South.*

A good magistrate must be endued with a *publick* spirit, that is with such an excellent temper, as sets him loose from all selfish views, and makes him endeavour towards promoting the common good. *Atterbury.*

5. Open for general entertainment.

The income of the commonwealth is raised on such as have money to spend at taverns and *publick* houses. *Addison.*

PU'BLICK. *n. s.* [from *publicus,* Lat. *le publique,* Fr.]

1. The general body of mankind, or of a state or nation; the people.

The *publick* is more disposed to censure than to praise. *Add.*

2. Open view; general notice.

Philosophy, though it likes not a gaudy dress, yet, when it appears in *publick,* must have so much complacency, as to be cloathed in the ordinary fashion. *Locke.*

In private grieve, but with a careless scorn;
In *publick* seem to triumph, not to mourn. *Granville.*

In *publick* 'tis they hide,
Where none distinguish. *Pope.*

PU'BLICKLY. *adv.* [from *publick.*]

1. In the name of the community.

This has been so sensibly known by trading nations, that great rewards are *publickly* offered for its supply. *Addison.*

2. Openly; without concealment.

Sometimes also it may be private, communicating to the judges some things not fit to be *publickly* delivered. *Bacon.*

PU'BLICKNESS. *n. s.* [from *publick.*]

1. State of belonging to the community.

The multitude of partners does detract nothing from each private share, nor does the *publickness* of it lessen propriety in it. *Boyle.*

2. Openness; state of being generally known or publick.

PU'BLICKSPIRITED. *adj.* [*publick* and *spirit.*] Having regard to the general advantage above private good.

'Tis enough to break the neck of all honest purposes, to kill all generous and *publickspirited* motions in the conception. *L'Estrange.*

These were the *publickspirited* men of their age, that is, patriots of their own interest. *Dryden.*

Another *publickspirited* project, which the common enemy could not foresee, might set king Charles on the throne. *Add.*

It was generous and *publickspirited* in you, to be of the kingdom's side in this dispute, by shewing, without reserve, your disapprobation of Wood's design. *Swift.*

To PU'BLISH, *v. a.* [*publier,* Fr. *publico,* Lat.]

1. To discover to mankind; to make generally and openly known; to proclaim; to divulge.

How will this grieve you,
When you shall come to clearer knowledge, that
You thus have *published* me. *Shakesp. Winter's Tale.*

His commission from God and his doctrine tend to the impressing the necessity of that reformation, which he came to *publish.* *Hammond's Fundamentals.*

Suppose he should relent,
And *publish* grace to all. *Milton.*

Th' unwearied sun, from day to day,
Does his Creator's pow'r display,
And *publishes* to every land
The work of an almighty hand. *Addison's Spectator.*

2. To put forth a book into the world.

If I had not unwarily too far engaged myself for the present *publishing* it, I should have kept it by me. *Digby.*

PU'BLISHER. *n. s.* [from *publish.*]

1. One who makes publick or generally known.

Love of you
Hath made me *publisher* of this pretence. *Shakesp.*

The holy lives, the exemplary sufferings of the *publishers* of this religion, and the surpassing excellence of that doctrine which they published. *Atterbury.*

2. One who puts out a book into the world.

A collection of poems appeared, in which the *publisher* has given me some things that did not belong to me. *Prior.*

PUCE'LAGE. *n. s.* [French.] A state of virginity. *Dict.*

PUCK. *n. s.* [perhaps the same with *pug.*] Some sprite among the fairies, common in romances.

O gentle *puck,* take this transformed scalp
From off the head of this Athenian swain. *Shakesp.*

Turn your cloaks,
Quoth he, for *puck* is busy in these oaks,
And this is fairy ground. *Corbet.*

PU'CKBALL or *puckfist. n. s.* [from *puck* the fairy, a fairy's ball.] A kind of mushroom full of dust. *Dict.*

To PU'CKER. *v. a.* [from *puck* the fairy; as *elflocks,* from *elves;* or from *powk,* a pocket or hollow.] To gather into corrugations; to contract into folds or plications.

I saw an hideous spectre; his eyes were sunk into his head, his face pale and withered, and his skin *puckered* up in wrinkles. *Spectator,* N° 192.

A ligature above the part wounded is pernicious, as it *puckers* up the intestines, and disorders its situation. *Sharp.*

PU'DDER. *n. s.* [This is commonly written *pother.* See POTHER. This is most probably derived by Mr. *Lye* from *fudur,* Islandick, a rapid motion.] A tumult; a turbulent and irregular bustle.

Let the great gods,
That keep this dreadful *pudder* o'er our heads,
Find out their enemies. *Shakesp. King Lear.*

What a *pudder* is made about essences, and how much is all knowledge pestered by the careless use of words? *Locke.*

To PU'DDER. *v. n.* [from the noun.] To make a tumult; to make a bustle.

Mathematicians, abstracting their thoughts from names, and setting before their minds the ideas themselves, have avoided a great part of that perplexity, *puddering* and confusion, which has so much hindered knowledge. *Locke.*

To PU'DDER. *v. a.* To perplex; to disturb; to confound.

He that will improve every matter of fact into a maxim, will abound in contrary observations, that can be of no other use but to perplex and *pudder* him. *Locke.*

PU'DDING. *n. s.* [*potten,* Welsh, an intestine; *boudin,* French; *puding,* Swedish.]

1. A kind of food very variously compounded, but generally made of meal, milk, and eggs.

Sallads, and eggs, and lighter fare
Tune the Italian spark's guitar;
And if I take Dan Congreve right,
Pudding and beef make Britons fight. *Prior.*

2. The gut of an animal.

He'll yield the crow a *pudding* one of these days; the king has kill'd his heart. *Shakesp. Henry V.*

As sure as his guts are made of *puddings.* *Shakesp.*

3. A bowel stuffed with certain mixtures of meal and other ingredients.

Mind neither good nor bad, nor right nor wrong,
But eat your *pudding,* slave, and hold your tongue. *Prior.*

PU'DDINGPIE. *n. s.* [*pudding* and *pie.*] A pudding with meat baked in it.

Some cry the covenant, instead
Of *puddingpies* and gingerbread. *Hudibras.*

PU'DDINGTIME. *n. s.* [*pudding* and *time.*]

1. The time of dinner; the time at which pudding, anciently the first dish, is set upon the table.

2. Nick of time; critical minute.

Mars that still protects the stout,
In *puddingtime* came to his aid. *Hudibras.*

PU'DDLE. *n. s.* [from *puteolus,* Lat. *Skinner;* from *poil,* dirt, old Bavarian, *Junius;* hence *pool.*] A small muddy lake; a dirty plash.

The Hebrews drink of the well-head, the Greeks of the stream, and the Latins of the *puddle.* *Hall.*

Thou did'st drink
The stale of horses, and the gilded *puddle*
Which beasts would cough at. *Shakesp. Ant. and Cleop.*

A physician cured madmen thus: they were tied to a stake, and then set in a *puddle,* 'till brought to their wits. *L'Estr.*

Treading where the treacherous *puddle* lay,
His heels flew up; and on the grassy floor
He fell, besmear'd with filth. *Dryden's Virgil.*

Happy was the man, who was sent on an errand to the most remote street, which he performed with the greatest alacrity, ran through every *puddle,* and took care to return covered with dirt. *Addison's Freeholder.*

To PUDDLE. *v. a.* [from the noun.] To muddy; to pollute with dirt; to mix dirt and water.

As if I saw my sun shine in a *puddled* water, I cried out of nothing but Mopsa. *Sidney.*

Some unhatch'd practice
Hath *puddled* his clear spirit; and, in such cases,
Men's natures wrangle with inferiour things,
Though great ones are their object. *Shakesp. Othello.*

His beard they sing'd off with brand of fire,
And ever as it blaz'd, they threw on him
Great pails of *puddled* mire to quench the hair. *Shakesp.*

The noblest blood of Africk
Runs in my veins, a purer stream than thine;
For, though derived from the same source, thy current
Is *puddl'd* and defil'd with tyranny. *Dryden.*

PU'DDLY. *adj.* [from *puddle.*] Muddy; dirty; miry.
Limy, or thick *puddly* water killeth them. *Carew.*

PU'DDOCK or *purrock. n. s.* [for *paddock* or *parrock.*] A provincial word for a small inclosure. *Dict.*

PU'DENCY. *n. s.* [*pudens*, Lat.] Modesty; shamefacedness.
A *pudency* so rosy, the sweet view on't
Might well have warm'd old Saturn. *Shakesp.*

PUDI'CITY. *n. s.* [*pudicité*, Fr. from *pudicitia*, Lat.] Modesty; chastity. *Dict.*

PUEFE'LLOW. *n. s.* A partner.

This carnal cur
Preys on the issue of his mother's body;
And makes her *puefellow* with others moan. *Shakesp.*

PUE'RILE. *adj.* [*puerile*, Fr. *puerilis*, Lat.] Childish; boyish.
I looked upon the mansion with a veneration mixt with a pleasure, that represented her to me in those *puerile* amusements. *Pope.*

PUERI'LITY. *n. s.* [*puerilité*, Fr. from *puerilitas*, Lat.] Childishness; boyishness.
A reserve of *puerility* not shaken off from school. *Brown.*
Some men imagining themselves possessed with a divine fury, often fall into toys and trifles, which are only *puerilities.* *Dryden's Dufresnoy.*

PU'ET. *n. s.* A kind of water fowl.
Among the first sort are coots, sanderlings and *pewets.* *Car.*
The fish have enemies enough; as otters, the cormorant and the *puet.* *Walton's Angler.*

PUFF. *n. s.* [*pof*, Dutch, a blast which swells the checks.]
1. A quick blast with the mouth.

In garret vile, he with a warming *puff*
Regales chill'd fingers. *Philips.*

2. A small blast of wind.
The Rosemary, in the days of Henry VII. with a sudden *puff* of wind stooped her side, and took in water at her ports in such abundance, as that she instantly sunk. *Raleigh.*

The naked breathless body lies,
To every *puff* of wind a slave,
At the beck of every wave,
That once perhaps was fair, rich, stout and wise. *Flatman.*

A *puff* of wind blows off cap and wig. *L'Estrange.*

There fierce winds o'er dusky vallies blow,
Whose every *puff* bears empty shades away. *Dryden.*

With one fierce *puff* he blows the leaves away,
Expos'd the self-discover'd infant lay. *Dryden.*

3. A mushroom. *Ainsworth.*
4. Any thing light and porous: as, puff *paste.*
5. Something to sprinkle powder on the hair. *Ainsworth.*

To PUFF. *v. n.* [*boffen*, Dutch.]
1. To swell the cheeks with wind.
2. To blow with a quick blast.

Wherefore do you follow her,
Like foggy South *puffing* with wind and rain. *Shakesp.*

Distinction with a broad and powerful fan,
Puffing at all, winnows the light away. *Shakesp.*

3. To blow with scornfulness.
Some *puff* at these instances, as being such as were under a different œconomy of religion, and consequently not directly pertinent to ours. *South's Sermons.*
It is really to defy heaven, to *puff* at damnation, and bid omnipotence do its worst. *South.*

4. To breathe thick and hard.

Seldshown flamins
Do press among the popular throngs, and *puff*
To win a vulgar station. *Shakesp. Coriolanus.*

The ass comes back again, *puffing* and blowing, from the chase. *L'Estrange.*

A true son of the church
Came *puffing* with his greasy bald-pate choir,
And fumbling o'er his beads. *Dryden.*

5. To do or move with hurry, tumour, or tumultuous agitation.

More unconstant than the wind, who woes
Ev'n now the frozen bosom of the North,
And, being anger'd, *puffs* away from thence,
Turning his face to the dew-dropping South. *Shakesp.*

Then came brave glory *puffing* by
In silks that whistled, who but he?
He scarce allow'd me half an eye. *Herbert.*

6. To swell with the wind.
A new coal is not to be cast on the nitre, till the detonation be quite ended; unless the *puffing* matter blow the coal out of the crucible. *Boyle.*

To PUFF. *v. a.*
1. To swell as with wind.

Let him fall by his own greatness,
And *puff* him up with glory, till it swell
And break him. *Denham's Sophy.*

Flattering of others, and boasting of ourselves, may be referred to lying; the one to please others, and *puff* them up with self-conceit; the other to gain more honour than is due to ourselves. *Ray on the Creation.*

2. To drive or agitate with blasts of wind.

I have seen the cannon,
When it has blown his ranks into the air,
And from his arm *pufft* his own brother. *Shakesp.*

Have I not heard the sea, *puff'd* up with winds,
Rage like an angry boar chafed with sweat? *Shakesp.*

Th' unerring sun by certain signs declares,
When the South projects a stormy day,
And when the clearing North will *puff* the clouds away. *Dryden's Virgil's Georgicks.*

Why must the winds all hold their tongue?
If they a little breath should raise,
Would that have spoil'd the poet's song,
Or *puff'd* away the monarch's praise? *Prior.*

I have been endeavouring very busily to raise a friendship, which the first breath of any ill-natured by-stander could *puff* away. *Pope.*

3. To drive with a blast of breath scornfully.

When she dances in the wind,
And shakes her wings, and will not stay,
I *puff* the prostitute away;
The little or the much she gave is quietly resign'd. *Dryd.*

4. To swell or blow up with praise.
The attendants of courts engage them in quarrels of jurisdiction, being truly parasiti curiæ, in *puffing* a court up beyond her bounds for their own advantage. *Bacon.*

5. To swell or elate with pride.

His looke like a coxcombe up *puffed* with pride. *Tusser.*

This army, led by a tender prince,
Whose spirit with divine ambition *pufft*,
Makes mouths at the invisible event. *Shakesp. Hamlet.*

Think not of men above that which is written, that no one of you be *puffed* up one against another. 1 *Cor.* iv. 6.

Your ancestors, who *puff* your mind with pride,
Did not your honour, but their own advance. *Dryden.*

Who stands safest; tell me, is it he
That spreads and swells in *puff'd* posterity? *Pope.*

The Phæacians were so *puffed* up with their constant felicity, that they thought nothing impossible. *Broome.*

PU'FFER. *n. s.* [from *puff.*] One that puffs.

PU'FFIN. *n. s.* [*puffino*, Italian.]
1. A water fowl.
Among the first sort, we reckon the dipchick, murrs, creysers, curlews and *puffins.* *Carew's Survey of Cornwall.*
2. A kind of fish.
3. A kind of fungus filled with dust.

PU'FFINGAPPLE. *n. s.* A sort of apple. *Ainsworth.*

PU'FFINGLY. *adv.* [from *puffing.*]
1. Tumidly; with swell.
2. With shortness of breath.

PU'FFY. *adj.* [from *puff.*]
1. Windy; flatulent.
Emphysema is a light *puffy* tumour, easily yielding to the pressure of your fingers, and ariseth again in the instant you take them off. *Wiseman's Surgery.*
2. Tumid; turgid.
An unjudicious poet, who aims at loftiness, runs easily into the swelling *puffy* stile, because it looks like greatness. *Dryden.*

PUG. *n. s.* [piȝa, Saxon, a girl. *Skinner.*] A kind name of a monkey, or any thing tenderly loved.
Upon setting him down, and calling him *pug*, I found him to be her favourite monkey. *Addison's Spectator.*

PU'GGERED. *adj.* [perhaps for *puckered.*] Crowded; complicated. I never found this word in any other passage.
Nor are we to cavil at the red *puggered* attire of the turkey, and the long excrescency that hangs down over his bill, when he swells with pride. *More's Antidote against Atheism.*

PUGH. *interj.* [corrupted from *puff*, or borrowed from the sound.] A word of contempt.

PU'GIL. *n. s.* [*pugille*, Fr.] What is taken up between the thumb and two first fingers. *Dict.*
Take violets, and infuse a good *pugil* of them in a quart of vinegar. *Bacon's Nat. Hist.*

PUGNA'CIOUS. *adj.* [*pugnax*, Lat.] Inclinable to fight; quarrelsome; fighting.

PUGNA'CITY. *n. s.* [from *pugnax*, Lat.] Quarrelsomeness; inclination to fight.

PU'ISNE. *adj.* [*puis nè*, French. It is commonly spoken and written *puny.* See PUNY.]
1. Young; younger; later in time.
When the place of a chief judge becomes vacant, a *puisne* judge, who hath approved himself deserving, should be preferred. *Bacon's Advice to Villiers.*

If he undergo any alteration, it muft be in time, or of a *puifne* date to eternity. *Hale's Origin of Mankind.*

2. Petty; inconfiderable; fmall.

A *puifne* tilter, that fpurs his horfe but one fide, breaks his ftaff like a noble goofe. *Shakefp. As You Like it.*

PUI'SSANCE. *n. f.* [*puiffance*, Fr.] Power; ftrength; force.

The chariots were drawn not by the ftrength of horfes, but by the *puiffance* of men. *Deftruction of Troy.*

Grandfires, babies and old women;
Or paft, or not arriv'd to, pith and *puiffance*. *Shakefp.*

Look with forehead bold and big enough
Upon the pow'r and *puiffance* of the king. *Shakefp.*

Our *puiffance* is our own; our own right hand
Shall teach us higheft deeds. *Milton.*

PUI'SSANT. *adj.* [*puiffant*, Fr.] Powerful; ftrong; forcible.

The queen is coming with a *puiffant* hoft. *Shakefp.*

Told the moft piteous tale of Lear
That ever ear receiv'd; which in recounting
His grief grew *puiffant*, and the ftrings of life
Began to crack. *Shakefp. King Lear.*

For piety renown'd and *puiffant* deeds. *Milton.*

The climate of Syria, the far diftance from the ftrength of Chriftendom, and the near neighbourhood of thofe that were moft *puiffant* among the Mahometans, caufed that famous enterprife, after a long continuance of terrible war, to be quite abandoned. *Raleigh's Effays.*

PUI'SSANTLY. *adv.* [from *puiffant.*] Powerfully; forcibly.

PUKE. *n. f.* [of uncertain derivation.] Vomit; medicine caufing vomit.

To PUKE. *v. n.* To fpew; to vomit.

The infant
Mewling and *puking* in the nurfe's arms. *Shakefp.*

PU'KER. *n. f.* [from *puke.*] Medicine caufing a vomit.

The *puker* rue,
The fweetner faffafras are added too. *Garth.*

PU'LCHRITUDE. *n. f.* [*pulchritudo*, Lat.] Beauty; grace; handfomenefs; quality oppofite to deformity.

Neither will it agree unto the beauty of animals, wherein there is an approved *pulchritude*. *Brown's Vulgar Errours.*

Pulchritude is conveyed by the outward fenfes unto the foul, but a more intellectual faculty is that which relifhes it. *More.*

By their virtuous behaviour they compenfate the hardnefs of their favour, and by the *pulchritude* of their fouls make up what is wanting in the beauty of their bodies. *South.*

That there is a great *pulchritude* and comelinefs of proportion in the leaves, flowers and fruits of plants, is attefted by the general verdict of mankind. *Ray on the Creation.*

To PULE. *v. n.* [*piauler*, Fr.]

1. To cry like a chicken.

Let the fongs be loud and cheerful, and not chirpings or *pulings*; let the mufick likewife be fharp and loud. *Bacon.*

2. To whine; to cry; to whimper.

To fpeak *puling* like a beggar at Hallomafs. *Shakefp.*

To have a wretched *puling* fool,
A whining mammet, in her fortune's tender,
To anfwer, I'll not wed. *Shakefp. Romeo and Juliet.*

Weak *puling* things unable to fuftain
Their fhare of labour, and their bread to gain. *Dryden.*

When ice covered the water, the child bathed his legs; and when he began this cuftom, was *puling* and tender. *Locke.*

This *puling* whining harlot rules his reafon,
And prompts his zeal for Edward's baftard brood. *Rowe.*

PU'LICK. *n. f.* An herb. *Ainfworth.*

PULI'COSE. *adj.* [*pulicofus*, *pulex*, Latin.] Abounding with fleas. *Dict.*

PU'LIOL. *n. f.* An herb. *Ainfworth.*

To PULL. *v. a.* [pullian, Saxon.]

1. To draw violently towards one.

What they feem to offer us with the one hand, the fame with the other they *pull* back. *Hooker.*

He put forth his hand, and *pulled* the dove in. *Gen.* viii. 9.

His hand which he put forth dried up, fo that he could not *pull* it in again. 1 *Kings* xiii. 4.

Pull them out like fheep for the flaughter, and prepare them for the day of flaughter. *Jer.* vii. 11.

They *pulled* away the fhoulder and ftopped their ears. *Zech.*

Ill fortune never crufhed that man, whom good fortune deceived not; I therefore have counfelled my friends to place all things fhe gave them fo, as fhe might take them from them, not *pull* them. *Benj. Johnfon's Difcovery.*

2. To draw forcibly.

He was not fo defirous of wars, as without juft caufe of his own to *pull* them upon him. *Hayward.*

A boy came in great hurry to *pull* off my boots. *Swift.*

3. To pluck; to gather.

When bounteous Autumn rears his head,
He joys to *pull* the ripen'd pear. *Dryden.*

Flax *pulled* in the bloom, will be whiter and ftronger than if let ftand till the feed is ripe. *Mortimer.*

4. To tear; to rend.

He hath turned afide my ways, and *pulled* me in pieces; he hath made me defolate. *Lam.* iii. 2.

Ye *pull* off the robe with the garment from them that pafs by fecurely. *Mic.* ii. 8.

I rent my cloaths, and *pulled* off the hair from off my head. 1 *Efdr.* viii. 71.

5. *To* PULL *down.* To fubvert; to demolifh.

Although it was judged in form of a ftatute, that he fhould be banifhed, and his whole eftate confifcated, and his houfes *pulled down*, yet his cafe even then had no great blot of ignominy. *Bacon.*

In political affairs, as well as mechanical, it is far eafier to *pull down* than build up; for that ftructure, which was above ten fummers a building, and that by no mean artifts, was deftroyed in a moment. *Howel's Vocal Foreft.*

When God is faid to build or *pull down*, 'tis not to be underftood of an houfe; God builds and unbuilds worlds. *Burn.*

6. *To* PULL *down.* To degrade.

He begs the gods to turn blind fortune's wheel,
To raife the wretched, and *pull down* the proud. *Rofcom.*

What title has this queen but lawlefs force?
And force muft *pull* her *down.* *Dryden.*

7. *To* PULL *up.* To extirpate; to eradicate.

What cenfure, doubting thus of innate principles, I may deferve from men, who will be apt to call it *pulling up* the old foundations of knowledge, I cannot tell; I perfuade myfelf, that the way I have purfued, being conformable to truth, lays thofe foundations furer. *Locke.*

PULL. *n. f.* [from the verb.] The act of pulling; pluck.

This wreftling *pull* between Corineus and Gogmagog is reported to have befallen at Dover. *Carew.*

Duke of Glo'fter, fcarce himfelf,
That bears fo fhrewd a maim; two *pulls* at once;
His lady banifh'd, and a limb lopt off. *Shakefp.*

I awaked with a violent *pull* upon the ring, which was faftened at the top of my box. *Gulliver's Travels.*

PU'LLER. *n. f.* [from *pull.*] One that pulls.

Shamelefs Warwick, peace?
Proud fetter up and *puller* down of kings. *Shakefp.*

PU'LLEN. *n. f.* [*pulain*, old Fr.] Poultry. *Bailey.*

PU'LLET. *n. f.* [*poulet*, Fr.] A young hen.

Brew me a pottle of fack finely.
—With eggs, Sir?
—Simple of itfelf; I'll no *pullet* fperm in my brewage. *Sha.*

I felt a hard tumour on the right fide, the bignefs of a *pullet*'s egg. *Wifeman's Surgery.*

They died not becaufe the *pullets* would not feed, but becaufe the devil forefaw their death, he contrived that abftinence in them. *Brown's Vulgar Errours.*

PU'LLEY. *n. f.* [*poulie*, Fr.] A fmall wheel turning on a pivot, with a furrow on its outfide in which a rope runs.

Nine hundred of the ftrongeft men were employed to draw up thefe cords by many *pulleys* faftened on the poles, and, in three hours, I was raifed and flung into the engine. *Gulliver.*

Here *pullies* make the pond'rous oak afcend. *Gay.*

To PULLU'LATE. *v. n.* [*pullulo*, Lat. *pulluler*, Fr.] To germinate; to bud.

PU'LMONARY. *adj.* [from *pulmo*, Lat.] Belonging to the lungs.

The force of the air upon the *pulmonary* artery is but fmall in refpect of that of the heart. *Arbuthnot.*

Cold air, by its immediate contact with the furface of the lungs, is capable of producing defluxions upon the lungs, ulcerations, and all forts of *pulmonick* confumptions. *Arbuthnot.*

PU'LMONARY. *n. f.* [*pulmonaire*, Fr.] The herb lungwort. *Ainf.*

PU'LMONICK. *adj.* [*pulmo*, Lat.] Belonging to the lungs.

An ulcer of the lungs may be a caufe of *pulmonick* confumption, or confumption of the lungs. *Harvey.*

PULP. *n. f.* [*pulpa*, Lat. *pulpe*, Fr.]

1. Any foft mafs.

The jaw bones have no marrow fevered, but a little *pulp* of marrow diffufed. *Bacon's Nat. Hift.*

2. The foft part of fruit; the part of fruit diftinct from the feeds and rind.

The favoury *pulp* they chew, and in the rind,
Still as they thirfted, fcoop the brimming ftream. *Milton.*

Befides this ufe of the *pulp* or pericarpium for the guard of the feed, it ferves alfo by a fecondary intention for the fuftenance of man and other animals. *Ray.*

The grub
Oft unobferv'd invades the vital core,
Pernicious tenant, and her fecret cave
Enlarges hourly, preying on the *pulp*
Ceafelefs. *Philips.*

PU'LPIT. *n. f.* [*pulpitum*, Lat. *pulpitre*, *pupitre*, Fr.]

1. A place raifed on high, where a fpeaker ftands.

Produce his body to the market-place,
And in the *pulpit*, as becomes a friend,
Speak in the order of his funeral. *Shakefp. Julius Cæfar.*

2. The higher defk in the church where the fermon is pronounced; diftinct from the lower defk where prayers are read.

We fee on our theatres, the examples of vice rewarded, yet it ought not to be an argument againft the art, any more than the impieties of the *pulpit* in the late rebellion. *Dryden.*

Sir Roger has given a handsome *pulpit* cloth, and railed in the communion table. *Addison's Spectator*, N° 112.

Bishops were not wont to preach out of the *pulpit*. *Ayliffe*.

Pulpits their sacred satyr learn'd to spare,
And vice admir'd to find a flatt'rer there. *Pope*.

PU'LPOUS. *adj.* [from *pulp.*] Soft.

The redstreak's *pulpous* fruit
With gold irradiate, and vermilion shines. *Philips*.

PU'LPOUSNESS. *n. s.* [from *pulpous.*] The quality of being pulpous.

PU'LPY. *adj.* [from *pulp.*] Soft; pappy.

In the walnut and plumbs is a thick *pulpy* covering, then a hard shell, within which is the seed. *Ray on the Creation*.

Putrefaction destroys the specifick difference of one vegetable from another, converting them into a *pulpy* substance of an animal nature. *Arbuthnot on Aliments*.

PULSA'TION. *n. s.* [*pulsation*, Fr. *pulsatio*, from *pulso*, Lat.] The act of beating or moving with quick strokes against any thing opposing.

This original of the left vein was thus contrived, to avoid the *pulsation* of the great artery. *Brown's Vulgar Errours*.

These commotions of the mind and body oppress the heart, whereby it is choaked and obstructed in its *pulsation*. *Harvey*.

PULSA'TOR. *n. s.* [from *pulso*, Lat.] A striker; a beater.

PULSE. *n. s.* [*pulsus*, Lat.]

1. The motion of an artery as the blood is driven through it by the heart, and as it is perceived by the touch.

Pulse is thus accounted for: when the left ventricle of the heart contracts, and throws its blood into the great artery, the blood in the artery is not only thrust forward towards the extremities, but the channel of the artery is likewise dilated; because fluids, when they are pressed, press again to all sides, and their pressure is always perpendicular to the sides of the containing vessels; but the coats of the artery, by any small impetus, may be distended: therefore, upon the contraction or systole of the heart, the blood from the left ventricle will not only press the blood in the artery forwards, but both together will distend the sides of the artery: when the impetus of the blood against the sides of the artery ceases; that is, when the left ventricle ceases to contract, then the spiral fibres of the artery, by their natural elasticity, return again to their former state, and contract the channel of the artery, till it is again dilated by the diastole of the heart: this diastole of the artery is called its *pulse*, and the time the spiral fibres are returning to their natural state, is the distance between two *pulses*: this *pulse* is in all the arteries of the body at the same time; for, while the blood is thrust out of the heart into the artery, the artery being full, the blood must move in all the arteries at the same time; and because the arteries are conical, and the blood moves from the basis of the cone to the apex, therefore the blood must strike against the sides of the vessels, and consequently every point of the artery must be dilated at the same time that the blood is thrown out of the left ventricle of the heart; and as soon as the elasticity of the spiral fibres can overcome the impetus of the blood, the arteries are again contracted: thus two causes operating alternately, the heart and fibres of the arteries, keep the blood in a continual motion: an high *pulse* is either vehement or strong, but if the dilatation of the artery does not rise to its usual height, it is called a low or weak *pulse*; but if between its dilatations there passes more time than usual, it is called a slow *pulse*: again, if the coats of an artery feel harder than usual from any cause whatsoever, it is called an hard *pulse*; but if by any contrary cause they are softer, then it is called a soft *pulse*. *Quincy*.

Think you, I bear the shears of destiny?
Have I commandment on the *pulse* of life? *Shakesp*.

The prosperity of the neighbour kingdoms is not inferior to that of this, which, according to the *pulse* of states, is a great diminution of their health. *Clarendon*.

My body is from all diseases free;
My temp'rate *pulse* does regularly beat. *Dryden*.

If one drop of blood remain in the heart at every *pulse*, those, in many *pulses*, will grow to a considerable mass. *Arb*.

2. Oscillation; vibration; alternate expansion and contraction; alternate approach and recession.

The vibrations or *pulses* of this medium, that they may cause the alternate fits of easy transmission and easy reflexion, must be swifter than light, and by consequence above seven hundred thousand times swifter than sounds. *Newton*.

3. *To feel one's* PULSE. To try or know one's mind artfully.

4. [From *pull.*] Leguminous plants.

With Elijah he partook,
Or as a guest with Daniel at his *pulse*. *Milton*.

Mortals, from your fellows blood abstain!
While corn and *pulse* by nature are bestow'd. *Dryden*.

Tares are as advantageous to land as other *pulses*. *Mort*.

To PULSE. *v. n.* [from the noun.] To beat as the pulse.

The heart, when separated wholly from the body in some animals, continues still to *pulse* for a considerable time. *Ray*.

PU'LSION. *n. s.* [from *pulsus*, Lat.] The act of driving or of forcing forward: in opposition to suction or traction.

Admit it might use the motion of *pulsion*, yet it could never that of attraction. *More's Divine Dialogues*.

By attraction we do not here understand what is improperly called so, in the operations of drawing, sucking and pumping, which is really *pulsion* and trusion. *Bentley*.

PU'LVERABLE. *adj.* [from *pulveris*, Lat.] Possible to be reduced to dust.

In making the first ink, I could by filtration separate a pretty store of a black *pulverable* substance that remained in the fire. *Boyle on Colours*.

PULVERIZA'TION. *n. s.* [from *pulverize.*] The act of powdering; reduction to dust or powder.

To PU'LVERIZE. *v. a.* [from *pulveris*, Lat. *pulveriser*, Fr.] To reduce to powder; to reduce to dust.

If the experiment be carefully made, the whole mixture will shoot into fine crystals, that seem to be of an uniform substance, and are consistent enough to be even brittle, and to endure to be *pulverized* and sifted. *Boyle*.

PU'LVERULENCE. *n. s.* [*pulverulentia*, Lat.] Dustiness; abundance of dust.

PU'LVIL. *n. s.* [*pulvillum*, Lat.] Sweet scents.

The toilette, nursery of charms,
Completely furnish'd with bright beauty's arms,
The patch, the powder-box, *pulvil*, perfumes. *Gay*.

To PU'LVIL. *v. a.* [from the noun.] To sprinkle with perfumes in powder.

Have you *pulvilled* the coachman and postilion, that they may not stink of the stable. *Congreve's Way of the World*.

PU'MICE. *n. s.* [*pumex*, *pumicis*, Lat.]

The *pumice* is evidently a slag or cinder of some fossil, originally bearing another form, and only reduced to this state by the violent action of fire: it is a lax and spungy matter full of little pores and cavities, found in masses of different sizes and shapes, of a pale, whitish, grey colour: the *pumice* is found in many parts of the world, but particularly about the burning mountains Etna, Vesuvius and Hecla: it is used as a dentifrice. *Hill's Materia Medica*.

So long I shot, that all was spent,
Though *pumice* stones I hastily hent,
And threw; but nought availed. *Spenser*.

Etna and Vesuvius, which consist upon sulphur, shoot forth smoke, ashes and *pumice*, but no water. *Bacon*.

Near the Lucrine lake,
Steams of sulphur raise a stifling heat,
And through the pores of the warm *pumice* sweat. *Addison*.

PU'MMEL. *n. s.* See POMMEL.

PUMP. *n. s.* *pompe*, Dutch and French.]

1. An engine by which water is drawn up from wells: its operation is performed by the pressure of the air.

A *pump* grown dry will yield no water, unless you pour a little water into it first. *More's Antidote against Atheism*.

In the framing that great ship built by Hiero, Athenæus mentions this instrument as being instead of a *pump*, by the help of which one man might easily drain out the water though very deep. *Wilkins's Dædalus*.

These *pumps* may be made single with a common *pump* handle, for one man to work them, or double for two. *Mortimer*.

2. A shoe with a thin sole and low heel.

Get good strings to your beards, new ribbons to your *pumps*. *Shakesp. Midsummer Night's Dream*.

Gabriel's *pumps* were all unpink'd i' th' heel. *Shakesp*.

Follow me this jest, now, till thou hast worn out thy *pump*, that when the single sole of it is worn, the jest may remain singular. *Shakesp. Romeo and Juliet*.

Thalia's ivy shews her prerogative over comical poesy; her mask, mantle and *pumps* are ornaments belonging to the stage. *Peacham*.

The water and sweat
Splish splash in their *pumps*. *Swift's Miscel*.

To PUMP. *v. n.* [*pompen*, Dutch.] To work a pump; to throw out water by a pump.

The folly of him, who *pumps* very laboriously in a ship, yet neglects to stop the leak. *Decay of Piety*.

To PUMP. *v. a.*

1. To raise or throw out by means of a pump.

2. To examine artfully by sly interrogatories, so as to draw out any secrets or concealments.

The one's the learned knight, seek out,
And *pump* them what they come about. *Hudibras*.

Ask him what passes
Amongst his brethren, he'll hide nothing from you;
But *pump* not me for politicks. *Otway's Venice Preserv'd*.

PUM'PER. *n. s.* [from *pump.*] The person or the instrument that pumps.

The flame lasted about two minutes, from the time the *pumper* began to draw out air. *Boyle*.

PU'MPION. *n. s.* A plant.

The flower of the *pumpion* consists of one leaf, which is bell-shaped, expanded at the top, and cut into several segments: of these flowers some are male, and some female, as in the cucumbers and melons: the female flowers grow upon the top of the embryo, which afterwards becomes an oblong or round fleshy fruit, having sometimes an hard, rugged and

uneven

uneven rind, with knobs and furrows, and is often divided into three parts, inclosing flat seeds that are edged or rimmed about as it were with a ring, and fixed to a spongy placenta. *Miller.*

We'll use this gross watry *pumpion*, and teach him to know turtles from jays. *Shakesp. Merry Wives of Windsor.*

PUN. *n. s.* [I know not whence this word is to be deduced: to *pun*, is to grind or beat with a *pestle*; can *pun* mean an empty sound, like that of a mortar beaten, as *clench*, the old word for *pun*, seems only a corruption of *clink*?] An equivocation; a quibble; an expression where a word has at once different meanings.

It is not the word, but the figure that appears on the medal: cuniculus may stand for a rabbit or a mine, but the picture of a rabbit is not the picture of a mine: a *pun* can be no more engraven, than it can be translated. *Addison.*

But fill their purse, our poet's work is done,
Alike to them by pathos, or by *pun*. *Pope.*

To PUN. *v. n.* [from the noun.] To quibble; to use the same word at once in different senses.

The hand and head were never lost, of those
Who dealt in doggrel, or who *punn'd* in prose. *Dryden.*

You would be a better man, if you could *pun* like Sir Tristram. *Tatler*, N° 57.

To PUNCH. *v. a.* [*poinçonner*, Fr.] To bore or perforate by driving a sharp instrument.

When I was mortal, my anointed body
By thee was *punched* full of deadly holes. *Shakesp.*

By reason of its constitution it continued open, as I have seen a hole *punched* in leather. *Wiseman's Surgery.*

Your work will sometimes require to have holes *punched* in it at the forge, you must then make a steel punch, and harden the point of it without tempering. *Moxon.*

The fly may, with the hollow and sharp tube of her womb, *punch* and perforate the skin of the eruca, and cast her eggs into her body. *Ray on the Creation.*

PUNCH. *n. s.* [from the verb.]

1. A pointed instrument, which, driven by a blow, perforates bodies.

The shank of a key the *punch* cannot strike, because the shank is not forged with substance sufficient; but the drill cuts a true round hole. *Moxon's Mechanical Exercises.*

2. [Cant word.] A liquour made by mixing spirit with water, sugar, and the juice of lemons.

The West India dry gripes are occasioned by lime juice in *punch*. *Arbuthnot on Aliments.*

No brute can endure the taste of strong liquor, and consequently it is against all the rules of hieroglyph to assign those animals as patrons of *punch*. *Swift.*

3. [*Punchinello*, Italian.] The buffoon or harlequin of the puppet-show.

Of rareeshows he sung and *punch*'s feats. *Gay.*

4. *Punch* is a horse that is well set and well knit, having a short back and thin shoulders, with a broad neck, and well lined with flesh. *Farrier's Dict.*

5. [*Pumilio obesus*, Lat.] In contempt or ridicule, a short fat fellow.

PU'NCHEON. *n. s.* [*poinçon*, Fr.]

1. An instrument driven so as to make a hole or impression.

He granted liberty of coining to certain cities and abbies, allowing them one staple and two *puncheons* at a rate. *Camd.*

2. A measure of liquids.

PU'NCHER. *n. s.* [from *punch*.] An instrument that makes an impression or hole.

In the upper jaw are five teeth before, not incisors or cutters, but thick *punchers*. *Grew's Musæum.*

PUNCTI'LIO. *n. s.* A small nicety of behaviour; a nice point of exactness.

Common people are much astonished, when they hear of those solemn contests which are made among the great, upon the *punctilios* of a publick ceremony. *Addison.*

Punctilio is out of doors, the moment a daughter clandestinely quits her father's house. *Clarissa.*

PUNCTI'LIOUS. *adj.* [from *punctilio*.] Nice; exact; punctual to superstition.

Some depend on a *punctilious* observance of divine laws, which they hope will attone for the habitual transgression of the rest. *Rogers's Sermons.*

PUNCTI'LIOUSNESS. *n. s.* [from *punctilious*.] Nicety; exactness of behaviour.

PU'NCTO. *n. s.* [*punto*, Spanish.]

1. Nice point of ceremony.

The final conquest of Granada from the Moors, king Ferdinando displayed in his letters, with all the particularities and religious *punctos* and ceremonies that were observed in the reception of that city and kingdom. *Bacon's Henry VII.*

2. The point in fencing.

Vat be all you come for?
— To see thee here, to see thee there, to see thee pass thy *puncto*. *Shakesp. Merry Wives of Windsor.*

PU'NCTUAL. *adj.* [*punctuel*, Fr.]

1. Comprised in a point; consisting in a point.

PUN

This earth a spot, a grain,
An atom with the firmament compar'd,
And all her number'd stars, that seem to rowl
Spaces incomprehensible; for such
Their distance argues, and their swift return
Diurnal, merely to officiate light
Round this opacous earth, this *punctual* spot. *Milton.*

2. Exact; nice; punctilious.

A gentleman *punctual* of his word, when he had heard that two had agreed upon a meeting, and the one neglected his hour, would say of him, he is a young man then. *Bacon.*

This mistake to avoid, we must observe the *punctual* differences of time, and so distinguish thereof, as not to confound or lose the one in the other. *Brown's Vulgar Errours.*

That the women are menstruent, and the men pubescent at the year of twice seven, is accounted a *punctual* truth. *Bro.*

He was *punctual* and just in all his dealings. *Atterbury.*

The correspondence of the death and sufferings of our lord is so *punctual* and exact, that they seem rather like a history of events past, than a prophecy of such as were to come. *Rogers.*

PUNCTU'ALITY. *n. s.* [from *punctual*.] Nicety; scrupulous exactness.

For the encouragement of those that hereafter should serve other princes with that *punctuality* as Sophronio had done, he commanded him to offer him a blank, wherein he might set down his own conditions. *Howel's Vocal Forest.*

Though some of these *punctualities* did not so much conduce to preserve the text, yet all of them shew, the infinite care which was taken, that there might be no mistake in a single letter. *Grew's Cosmol.*

PU'NCTUALLY. *adv.* [from *punctual*.] Nicely; exactly; scrupulously.

There were no use at all for war or law, if every man had prudence to conceive how much of right were due both to and from himself, and were withal so *punctually* just as to perform what he knew requisite, and to rest contented with his own. *Raleigh's Essays.*

Concerning the heavenly bodies, there is so much exactness in their motions, that they *punctually* come to the same periods to the hundredth part of a minute. *Ray on the Creation.*

I freely bring what Moses hath related to the test, comparing it with things as now they stand; and finding his account to be *punctually* true, I fairly declare what I find. *Woodward.*

PU'NCTUALNESS. *n. s.* [from *punctual*.] Exactness; nicety.

The most literal translation of the scriptures, in the most natural signification of the words, is generally the best; and the same *punctualness* which debaseth other writings, preserveth the spirit and majesty of the sacred text. *Felton.*

PUNCTUA'TION. *n. s.* [*punctum*, Lat.] The act or method of pointing.

It ought to do it willingly, without being forced to it by any change in the words or *punctuation*. *Addison.*

PU'NCTURE. *n. s.* [*punctus*, Lat.] A small prick; a hole made with a very sharp point.

With the loadstone of Laurentius Guascus, whatsoever needles or bodies were touched, the wounds and *punctures* made thereby were never felt. *Brown's Vulgar Errours.*

Nerves may be wounded by scission or *puncture*: the former way being cut through, they are irrecoverable; but when pricked by a sharp-pointed weapon, which kind of wound is called a *puncture*, they are much to be regarded. *Wiseman.*

To PU'NCTULATE. *v. n.* [*punctulum*, Lat.] To mark with small spots.

The studds have their surface *punctulated*, as if set all over with other studds infinitely lesser. *Woodward.*

PU'NDLE. *n. s.* [*mulier pumila & obesa*, Lat.] A short and fat woman. *Ainsworth.*

PU'NGAR. *n. s.* [*pagurus*, Lat.] A fish. *Ainsworth.*

PU'NGENCY. *n. s.* [from *pungent*.]

1. Power of pricking.

Any substance, which by its *pungency* can wound the worms, will kill them, as steel and hartshorn. *Arbuthnot.*

2. Heat on the tongue; acridness.

3. Power to pierce the mind.

An opinion of the successfulness of the work is as necessary to found a purpose of undertaking it, as the authority of commands, the persuasiveness of promises, *pungency* of menaces, or prospect of mischiefs upon neglect can be. *Hamm.*

4. Acrimoniousness; keeness.

When he hath considered the force and *pungency* of these expressions applied to the fathers of that Nicene synod by the Western bishops, he may abate his rage towards me. *Stillingfl.*

PU'NGENT. *adj.* [*pungens*, Lat.]

1. Pricking.

Just where the breath of life his nostrils drew,
A charge of snuff the wily virgin threw;
The gnomes direct to ev'ry atom just,
The *pungent* grains of titillating dust. *Pope's Ra. of the Lock.*

2. Sharp on the tongue; acrid.

Do not the sharp and *pungent* tastes of acids arise from the strong attraction, whereby the acid particles rush upon, and agitate the particles of the tongue. *Newton's Opticks.*

3. Piercing;

3. Piercing; sharp.

Thou can'st set him on the rack,
Inclose him in a wooden tow'r,
With *pungent* pains on ev'ry side;
So Regulus in torments dy'd. *Swift's Miscellanies.*

4. Acrimonious; biting.

It consists chiefly a sharp and *pungent* manner of speech; but partly in a facetious way of jesting. *Dryden.*

PU'NICE. *n. s.* A wallouse; a bugg. *Hudibras. Ainsworth.*

PUNI'CEOUS. *adj.* [*puniceus*, Lat.] Purple. *Dict.*

PU'NINESS. *n. s.* [from *puny.*] Pettiness; smallness.

To PU'NISH. *v. a.* [*punio*, Lat.]

1. To chastise; to afflict with penalties or death for some crime.

Your purpos'd low correction
Is such, as basest and the meanest wretches
Are *punished* with. *Shakesp. King Lear.*

If you will not hearken, I will *punish* you seven times more for your sins. *Lev.* xxvi. 18.

2. To revenge a fault with pain or death.

PU'NISHABLE. *adj.* [*punissable*, Fr. from *punish.*] Worthy of punishment; capable of punishment.

Theft is naturally *punishable*, but the kind of punishment is positive, and such lawful, as men shall think with discretion convenient to appoint. *Hooker, b.* iii. *s.* 9.

Sith creatures, which have no understanding, can shew no will; and where no will is, there is no sin; and only that which sinneth, is subject to punishment; which way should any such creature be *punishable* by the law of God? *Hooker.*

Their bribery is less *punishable*, when bribery opened the door by which they entred. *Taylor's Rule of Living Holy.*

PU'NISHABLENESS. *n. s.* [from *punishable.*] The quality of deserving or admitting punishment.

PU'NISHER. *n. s.* [from *punish.*] One who inflicts pains for a crime.

This knows my *punisher*; therefore as far
From granting me, as I from begging peace. *Milton.*

PU'NISHMENT. *n. s.* [*punissement*, Fr.] Any infliction imposed in vengeance of a crime.

The house of endless pain is built thereby,
In which ten thousand sorts of *punishments*
The cursed creatures do eternally torment. *Fa. Queen.*

Unless it were a bloody murtherer,
I never gave them condign *punishment.* *Shakesp.*

Thou, through the judgment of God, shalt receive just *punishment* for thy pride. 2 *Mac.* vii. 36.

Is not destruction to the wicked? and a strange *punishment* to the workers of iniquity? *Job* xxxi. 3.

Had I a hundred mouths, a hundred tongues,
I could not half those horrid crimes repeat,
Nor half the *punishments* those crimes have met. *Dryden.*

The rewards and *punishments* of another life, which the Almighty has established, as the enforcements of his law, are of weight enough to determine the choice, against whatever pleasure or pain this life can shew. *Locke.*

PUNI'TION. *n. s.* [*punition*, Fr. *punitio*, Lat.] Punishment. *Ains.*

PU'NITIVE. *adj.* [from *punio*, Lat.] Awarding or inflicting punishment.

Neither is the cylinder charged with sin, whether by God or men, nor any *punitive* law enacted by either against its rolling down the hill. *Hammond's Fundamentals.*

PU'NITORY. *adj.* [from *punio*, Lat.] Punishing; tending to punishment.

PUNK. *n. s.* A whore; a common prostitute; a strumpet.

She may be a *punk*; for many of them are neither maid, widow, nor wife. *Shakesp. Measure for Measure.*

And made them fight, like mad or drunk,
For dame religion as for *punk.* *Hudibras.*

Near these a nursery erects its head,
Where unfledg'd actors learn to laugh and cry,
Where infant *punks* their tender voices try. *Dryden.*

PU'NSTER. *n. s.* [from *pun.*] A quibbler; a low wit who endeavours at reputation by double meaning.

His mother was cousin to Mr. Swan, gamester and *punster* of London. *Arbuthnot and Pope.*

To PUNT. *v. n.* To play at basset and ombre.

One is for setting up an assembly for basset, where none shall be admitted to *punt*, that have not taken the oaths. *Add.*

When a duke to Jansen *punts* at White's,
Or city heir in mortgage melts away,
Satan himself feels far less joy than they. *Pope.*

PU'NY. *adj.* [*puis nè*, Fr.]

1. Young.

2. Inferior; petty; of an under rate.

Is not the king's name forty thousand names?
Arm, arm, my name; a *puny* subject strikes
At thy great glory. *Shakesp. Rich.* II.

Know me not,
Lest that thy wives with spits, and boys with stones,
In *puny* battle slay me. *Shakesp. Coriolanus.*

Drive
The *puny* habitants; or if not drive,
Seduce them to our party. *Milton.*

This friendship is of that strength, as to remain unshaken by such assaults, which yet are strong enough to shake down and annihilate the friendship of little *puny* minds. *South.*

Jove at their head ascending from the sea,
A shoal of *puny* pow'rs attend his way. *Dryden.*

PU'NY. *n. s.* A young unexperienced unseasoned wretch.

Tenderness of heart makes a man but a *puny* in this sin; it spoils the growth, and cramps the crowning exploits of this vice. *South's Sermons.*

To PUP. *v. n.* [from *puppy.*] To bring forth whelps: used of a bitch bringing young.

PU'PIL. *n. s.* [*pupilla*, Lat.]

1. The apple of the eye.

Looking in a glass, when you shut one eye, the *pupil* of the other, that is open, dilateth. *Bacon's Nat. Hist.*

Setting a candle before a child, bid him look upon it, and his *pupil* shall contract itself very much to exclude the light; as when after we have been some time in the dark, a bright light is suddenly brought in and set before us, till the *pupils* of our eyes have gradually contracted. *Ray on the Creation.*

The uvea has a musculous power, and can dilate and contract that round hole in it, called the *pupil* of the eye. *More.*

The rays, which enter the eye at several parts of the *pupil*, have several obliquities to the glasses. *Newton's Opticks.*

2. [*Pupille*, Fr. *pupillus*, Lat.] A scholar; one under the care of a tutor.

My master sues to her, and she hath taught her suitor,
He being her *pupil*, to become her tutor. *Shakesp.*

One of my father's servants,
With store of tears this treason 'gan unfold,
And said my guardian would his *pupil* kill. *Fairfax.*

If this arch-politician find in his *pupils* any remorse, any fear of God's future judgments, he persuades them that God hath so great need of men's souls, that he will accept them at any time, and upon any condition. *Raleigh.*

Tutors should behave reverently before their *pupils.* *L'Est.*

The great work of a governor is, to settle in his *pupil* good habits, and the principles of virtue and wisdom. *Locke.*

3. A ward; one under the care of his guardian.

Tell me, thou *pupil* to great Pericles,
What are the grounds
To undertake so young so vast a care? *Dryden.*

So some weak shoot, which else would poorly rise,
Jove's tree adopts, and lifts him to the skies;
Through the new *pupil* soft'ning juices flow,
Thrust forth the gems, and give the flow'rs to blow. *Tickel.*

PU'PILAGE. *n. s.* [from *pupil.*]

1. State of being a scholar.

The severity of the father's brow, whilst they are under the discipline of *pupilage*, should be relaxed as fast as their age, discretion, and good behaviour allow. *Locke.*

2. Wardship; minority.

Three sons he dying left, all under age,
By means whereof their uncle Vortigern
Usurp'd the crown, during their *pupilage*;
Which the infant's tutors gathering to fear,
Them closely into Armorick did bear. *Fairy Queen.*

PU'PILARY. *adj.* [*pupillaire*, Fr. *pupillaris*, Lat. from *pupil.*] Pertaining to a pupil or ward.

PU'PPET. *n. s.* [*poupée*, Fr. *pupus*, Lat.]

1. A small image moved by men in a mock drama; a wooden tragedian.

Once Zelmane could not stir; but that as if they had been *puppets*, whose motion stood only upon her pleasure, Basilius with serviceable steps, Gynecia with greedy eyes would follow her. *Sidney, b.* ii.

Divers of them did keep in their houses certain things made of cotton wool, in the manner of *puppets.* *Abbot.*

His last wife was a woman of breeding, good humour and complaisance; as for you, you look like a *puppet* moved by clock-work. *Arbuthnot's History of John Bull.*

As the pipes of some carv'd organ move,
The gilded *puppets* dance. *Pope.*

In florid impotence he speaks,
And, as the prompter breathes, the *puppet* squeaks. *Pope.*

2. A word of contempt.

Thou, an Egyptian *puppet*, shalt be shewn
In Rome as well as I. *Shakesp. Cymbeline.*

Oh excellent motion! oh exceeding *puppet*! *Shakesp.*

PU'PPETMAN. *n. s.* [*puppet* and *man.*] Master of a puppet-show.

Why is a handsome wife ador'd
By every coxcomb but her lord?
From yonder *puppetman* inquire,
Who wisely hides his wood and wire. *Swift.*

PU'PPETSHOW. *n. s.* [*puppet* and *show.*] A mock drama performed by wooden images moved by wire.

Tim. you have a taste I know,
And often see a *puppetshow.* *Swift.*

To induce him to be fond of learning, he would frequently carry him to the *puppetshow.* *Arbuthnot and Pope.*

A pre-

A president of the council will make no more impression upon my mind, than the sight of a *puppetshow*. *Pope.*

PU'PPY. *n. s.* [*poupée*, Fr.]

1. A whelp; progeny of a bitch.

He
Talks as familiarly of roaring lions,
As maids of thirteen do of *puppy* dogs. *Shakesp.*

The rogues slighted me into the river with as little remorse, as they would have drowned a bitch's blind *puppies*, fifteen i' th' litter. *Shakesp. Merry Wives of Windsor.*

The sow to the bitch says, your *puppies* are all blind. *L'Est.*

Nature does the *puppy*'s eyelid close,
Till the bright sun has nine times set and rose. *Gay.*

2. A name of contemptuous reproach to a man.

I shall laugh myself to death at this *puppy* headed monster; a most scurvy monster! *Shakesp. Tempest.*

Thus much I have added, because there are some *puppies* which have given it out. *Raleigh.*

I found my place taken up by an ill-bred aukward *puppy*, with a money bag under each arm. *Addison's Guardian.*

To PU'PPY. *v. n.* [from the noun.] To bring whelps.

PURBLI'ND. *adj.* [corrupted from *poreblind*, which is still used in Scotland; *pore* and *blind*.] Nearsighted; shortsighted.

Speak to my gossip Venus one fair word,
One nickname to her *purblind* son and heir. *Shakesp.*

The truth appears so naked on my side,
That any *purblind* eye may find it out. *Shakesp.*

'Tis known to several
Of head piece extraordinary; lower messes
Perchance, are to this business *purblind*. *Shakesp.*

Like to *purblind* moles, no greater light than that little which they shun. *Drummond.*

Darkness, that here surrounded our *purblind* understandings, will vanish at the dawning of eternal day. *Boyle.*

Dropt in blear thick-sighted eyes,
They'd make them see in darkest night,
Like owls, though *purblind* in the light. *Hudibras.*

Purblind man
Sees but a part o' th' chain, the nearest links;
His eyes not carrying to that equal beam,
That poises all above. *Dryden and Lee's Oedipus.*

PURBLI'NDNESS. *n. s.* [from *purblind.*] Shortness of sight.

PU'RCHASABLE. *adj.* [from *purchase.*] That may be purchased or bought.

Money being the counterbalance to all things *purchasable* by it, as much as you take off from the value of money, so much you add to the price of things exchanged for it. *Locke.*

To PU'RCHASE. *v. a.* [*pourchasser*, Fr.]

1. To buy for a price.

You have many a *purchas'd* slave,
Which like your asses, and your dogs and mules,
You use in abject and in slavish part. *Shakesp.*

His sons buried him in the cave, which Abraham *purchased* of the sons of Heth. *Gen.* xxv.

2. To obtain at any expence, as of labour or danger.

A world who would not *purchase* with a bruise. *Milton.*

3. To expiate or recompense by a fine or forfeit.

I will be deaf to pleading and excuses,
Nor tears nor prayers shall *purchase* out abuses;
Therefore use none. *Shakesp. Romeo and Juliet.*

PU'RCHASE. *n. s.* [*pourchas*, old Fr. from the verb.]

1. Any thing bought or obtained for a price.

He that procures his child a good mind, makes a better *purchase* for him, than if he laid out the money for an addition to his former acres. *Locke on Education.*

Our thriving dean has purchas'd land;
A *purchase* which will bring him clear
Above his rent four pounds a year. *Swift.*

2. Any thing of which possession is taken.

A beauty waining and distressed widow
Made prize and *purchase* of his wanton eye;
Seduc'd the pitch and height of all his thoughts
To base declension. *Shakesp.*

The fox repairs to the wolf's cell, and takes possession of his stores; but he had little joy of the *purchase*. *L'Estrange.*

PU'RCHASER. *n. s.* [from *purchase.*] A buyer; one that gains any thing for a price.

Upon one only alienation and change, the *purchaser* is to pass both licence, fine and recovery. *Bacon.*

So unhappy have been the *purchasers* of church lands, that, though in such purchases, men have usually the cheapest pennyworths, yet they have not always the best bargains. *South.*

Most of the old statues may be well supposed to have been cheaper to their first owners, than they are to a modern *purchaser*. *Addison's Remarks on Italy.*

PURE. *adj.* [*pur*, *pure*, Fr. *purus*, Lat.]

1. Not filthy; not sullied.

There is a generation that are *pure* in their own eyes, and yet is not washed from their filthiness. *Prov.* xxx. 12.

2. Clear; not dirty; not muddy.

Thou *purest* stone, whose pureness doth present
My purest mind. *Sidney, b.* ii.

3. Unmingled; not altered by mixtures; mere.

What philosophy shall comfort a villain, that is haled to the rack for murthering his prince? his cup is full of *pure* and unmingled sorrow, his body is rent with torment, his name with ignominy, his soul with shame and sorrow, which are to last eternally. *Taylor's Rule of Living Holy.*

Pure and mixt, when applied to bodies, are much a kin to simple and compound; so a guinea is *pure* gold, if it has in it no allay. *Watts's Logick.*

4. Not connected with any thing extrinsick: as, *pure* mathematicks.

Mathematicks in its latitude is divided into *pure* and mixed; and though the *pure* do handle only abstract quantity in the general, as geometry; yet that which is mixed doth consider the quantity of some particular determinate subject. *Wilkins.*

When a proposition expresses that the predicate is connected with the subject, it is called a *pure* proposition; as every true christian is an honest man. *Watts.*

5. Free; clear.

His mind of evil *pure*
Supports him, and intention free from fraud. *Philips.*

6. Free from guilt; guiltless; innocent.

Who can say, I have made my heart clean, I am *pure* from my sin? *Prov.* xx. 9.

O welcome *pure* ey'd faith,
And thou unblemish'd form of chastity. *Milton.*

No hand of strife is *pure*, but that which wins. *Daniel.*

7. Incorrupt; not vitiated by any bad practice or opinion.

Her guiltless glory just Britannia draws
From *pure* religion, and impartial laws. *Tickel.*

8. Not vitiated with corrupt modes of speech.

As oft as I read those comedies, so oft doth sound in mine ear the *pure* fine talk of Rome. *Ascham.*

9. Mere: as, *a* pure *villain*, *purus putus nebulo*, Lat.

The lord of the castle was a young man of spirit, but had lately out of *pure* weariness of the fatigue, and having spent most of his money, left the king. *Clarendon.*

There happened a bloody civil war among the hawks, when the peaceable pigeons, in *pure* pity and good nature, send their mediators to make them friends again. *L'Estrange's Fables.*

10. Chaste; modest. *Ainsworth.*

PU'RELY. *adv.* [from *pure.*]

1. In a pure manner; not dirtily; not with mixture.

I will *purely* purge away thy dross, and take away all thy tin. *Isaiah* i. 25.

2. Innocently; without guilt.

3. Merely.

The being able to raise an army, and conducting it to fight against the king, was *purely* due to him, and the effect of his power. *Clarendon, b.* viii.

Upon the particular observations on the metallick and mineral bodies, I have not founded any thing but what *purely* and immediately concerns the natural history of those bodies. *Woodward's Nat. Hist.*

I converse in full freedom with men of both parties; and if not in equal number, it is *purely* accidental, as having made acquaintance at court more under one ministry than another. *Swift.*

PU'RENESS. *n. s.* [from *pure.*]

1. Clearness; freedom from extraneous or foul admixtures.

They came to the river side, which of all the rivers of Greece had the prize for excellent *pureness* and sweetness, in so much as the very bathing in it was accounted exceeding healthful. *Sidney.*

No circumstances are like to contribute more to the advancement of learning, than exact temperance, great *pureness* of air, equality of climate, and long tranquility of government. *Temple.*

2. Simplicity; exemption from composition.

An essence eternal and spiritual, of absolute *pureness* and simplicity. *Raleigh.*

My love was such,
It could, though he supply'd no fuel, burn;
Rich in itself, like elemental fire,
Whose *pureness* does no aliment require. *Dryden.*

3. Innocence; freedom from guilt.

May we evermore serve thee in holiness and *pureness* of living. *Common Prayer.*

4. Freedom from vitious modes of speech.

In all this good propriety of words, and *pureness* of phrases in Terence, you must not follow him always in placing of them. *Ascham's Schoolmaster.*

PU'RFILE. *n. s.* [*pourfilée*, Fr.] A sort of ancient trimming for women's gowns, made of tinsel and thread; called also bobbin work. *Bailey.*

To PU'RFLE. *v. a.* [*pourfiler*, Fr. *profilare*, Italian.] To decorate with a wrought or flowered border; to border with embroidery; to embroider.

A goodly lady clad in scarlet red,
Purfled with gold and pearl of rich assay. *Fa. Queen.*

An

Emrold tuffs, flow'rs *purfled* blue and white,
Like saphire, pearl, in rich embroidery,
Buckled below fair knighthood's bending knee. *Shakesp.*

Iris there with humid bow,
Waters the odorous banks that blow
Flowers of more mingled hew,
Than her *purfled* scarff can shew. *Milton.*

In velvet white as snow the troop was gown'd,
Their hoods and sleeves the same, and *purfled* o'er
With diamonds. *Dryden.*

PU'RFLE. } *n. s.* [*pourfilée*, Fr. from the verb.] A border of
PU'RFLEW. } embroidery.

PURGA'TION. *n. s.* [*purgation*, Fr. *purgatio*, Lat.]

1. The act of cleansing or purifying from vitious mixtures.

We do not suppose the separation finished, before the *purgation* of the air began. *Burnet's Theory of the Earth.*

2. The act of cleansing the body by downward evacuation.

Let the physician apply himself more to *purgation* than to alteration, because the offence is in quantity. *Bacon.*

3. The act of clearing from imputation of guilt.

If any man doubt, let him put me to my *purgation*. *Shak.*

Proceed in justice, which shall have due course,
Even to the guilt or the *purgation*. *Shakesp.*

PU'RGATIVE. *adj.* [*purgatif*, Fr. *purgativus*, Lat.] Cathartick; having the power to cause evacuations downward.

Purging medicines have their *purgative* virtue in a fine spirit, they endure not boiling without loss of virtue. *Bacon.*

All that is fill'd, and all that which doth fill
All the round world, to man is but a pill;
In all it works not, but it is in all
Poisonous, or *purgative*, or cordial. *Donne.*

Lenient *purgatives* evacuate the humours. *Wiseman.*

PU'RGATORY. *n. s.* [*purgatoire*, Fr. *purgatorium*, Lat.] A place in which souls are supposed by the papists to be purged by fire from carnal impurities, before they are received into heaven.

Thou thy folk, through pains of *purgatory*,
Dost bear unto thy bliss. *Spenser's Hymn on Love.*

In this age, there may be as great instances produced of real charity, as when men thought to get souls out of *purgatory*. *Stillingfleet.*

To PURGE. *v. a.* [*purger*, Fr. *purgo*, Lat.]

1. To cleanse; to clear.

It will be like that labour of Hercules, in *purging* the stable of Augeas, to separate from superstitious observations any thing that is clean and pure natural. *Bacon.*

2. To clear from impurities.

To the English court assemble now
From ev'ry region apes of idleness;
Now neighbour confines *purge* you of your scum. *Shakesp.*

Air ventilates and cools the mines, and *purges* and frees them from mineral exhalations. *Woodward.*

3. To clear from guilt.

Blood hath been shed ere now, i' th' olden time
Ere human statute *purg'd* the gen'ral weal. *Shakesp.*

My soul is *purg'd* from grudging hate;
And with my hand I seal my true heart's love. *Shakesp.*

The blood of Christ shall *purge* our conscience from dead works to serve God. *Heb.* ix. 14.

Syphax, we'll join our cares to *purge* away
Our country's crimes, and clear her reputation. *Addison.*

4. To clear from imputation of guilt.

He, I accuse,
Intends t' appear before the people, hoping
To *purge* himself with words. *Shakesp. Coriolanus.*

Marquis Dorset was hasting towards him, to *purge* himself of some accusation. *Bacon's Henry* VII.

5. To sweep or put away impurities.

I will *purge* out from among you the rebels. *Ezek.* xx. 38.

Simplicity and integrity in the inward parts, may *purge* out every prejudice and passion. *Decay of Piety.*

6. To evacuate the body by stool.

Sir Philip Calthrop *purged* John Drakes, the shoemaker of Norwich, of the proud humour. *Camden's Remains.*

The frequent and wise use of emaciating diets, and of *purgings*, is a principal means of a prolongation of life. *Bacon.*

If he was not cured, he *purged* him with salt water. *Arbuthnot.*

7. To clarify; to defecate.

To PURGE. *v. n.* To have frequent stools.

PURGE. *n. s.* [from the verb.] A cathartick medicine; a medicine that evacuates the body by stool.

Meet we the med'cine of the sickly weal,
And with him pour we in our country's *purge*
Each drop of us. *Shakesp.*

Pills nor laxatives I like;
Of these his gain the sharp physician makes,
And often gives a *purge*, but seldom takes. *Dryden.*

He was no great friend to purging and clisters; he was for mixing aloes with all *purges*. *Arbuthnot.*

PU'RGER. *n. s.* [from *purge*.]

1 One who clears away any thing noxious.

This shall make
Our purpose necessary, and not envious;
We shall be call'd *purgers*, not murtherers. *Shakesp.*

2. Purge; cathartick.

It is of good use in physick, if you can retain the purging virtue, and take away the unpleasant taste of the *purger*. *Bac.*

PURIFICA'TION. *n. s.* [*purification*, Fr. *purificatio*, Lat.]

1. The act of making pure; act of cleansing from extraneous mixture.

I discerned a considerable difference in the operations of several kinds of saltpetre, even after *purification*. *Boyle.*

2. The act of cleansing from guilt.

The sacraments, in their own nature, are just such as they seem, water, and bread, and wine; but because they are made signs of a secret mystery, and water is the symbol of *purification* of the soul from sin, and bread and wine, of Christ's body and blood; therefore the symbols receive the names of what they sign. *Taylor's Worthy Communicant.*

3. A rite performed by the Hebrews after childbearing.

PU'RIFICATIVE. } *adj.* [from *purify*.] Having power or ten-
PU'RIFICATORY. } dency to make pure.

PU'RIFIER. *n. s.* [from *purify*.] Cleanser; refiner.

He shall sit as a refiner and *purifier* of silver. *Mal.* iii. 3.

To PURI'FY. *v. a.* [*purifier*, Fr. *purifico*, Lat.]

1. To make pure.

2. To free from any extraneous admixture.

If any bad blood should be left in the kingdom, an honourable foreign war will vent or *purify* it. *Bacon's Henry* VII.

The mass of the air was many thousand times greater than the water, and would in proportion require a greater time to be *purified*. *Burnet's Theory of the Earth.*

By chace our long-liv'd fathers earn'd their food,
Toil strung the nerves, and *purified* the blood. *Dryden.*

3. To make clear.

It ran upon so fine and delicate a ground, as one could not easily judge, whether the river did more wash the gravel, or the gravel did *purify* the river. *Sidney, b.* ii.

4. To free from guilt or corruption.

He gave himself for us, that he might redeem us from all iniquity, and *purify* unto himself a peculiar people. *Tit.* ii. 14.

If God gives grace, knowledge will not stay long behind; since it is the same spirit and principle that *purifies* the heart, and clarifies the understanding. *South's Sermons.*

5. To free from pollution, as by lustration.

There were set six water pots of stone, after the manner of the *purifying* of the Jews. *Jo.* ii. 6.

6. To clear from barbarisms or improprieties.

He saw the French tongue abundantly *purified*. *Sprat.*

To PURIFY. *v. n.* To grow pure.

We do not suppose the separation of these two liquors wholly finished, before the purgation of the air began, though let them begin to *purify* at the same time. *Burnet.*

PU'RIST. *n. s.* [*puriste*, Fr.] One superstitiously nice in the use of words.

PU'RITAN. *n. s.* [from *pure*.] A sectary pretending to eminent purity of religion.

The schism which the papists on the one hand, and the superstition which the *puritan* on the other, lay to our charge, are very justly chargeable upon themselves. *Sanderson.*

PURITA'NICAL. *adj.* [from *puritan*.] Relating to puritans.

Such guides set over the several congregations will misteach them, by instilling into them *puritanical* and superstitious principles, that they may the more securely exercise their presbyterian tyranny. *Walton.*

PU'RITANISM. *n. s.* [from *puritan*.] The notions of a puritan.

A serious and unpartial examination of the grounds, as well of popery as *puritanism*, according to that measure of understanding God hath afforded me. *Walton.*

PU'RITY. *n. s.* [*purité*, Fr. *puritas*, Lat.]

1. Cleanness; freedom from foulness or dirt.

Her urn
Pours streams select, and *purity* of waters. *Prior.*

From the body's *purity*, the mind
Receives a secret aid. *Thomson's Summer.*

2. Freedom from guilt; innocence.

Death sets us safely on shore in our long-expected Canaan, where there are no temptations, no danger of falling, but eternal *purity* and immortal joys secure our innocence and happiness for ever. *Wake's Preparation for Death.*

3. Chastity; freedom from contamination of sexes.

Could I come to her with any detection in my hand, I could drive her then from the ward of her *purity*, her reputation, and her marriage vow. *Shakesp. Merry Wives of Windsor.*

PURL. *n. s.* [this is justly supposed by *Minshew* to be contracted from *purfle*.]

1. An embroidered and puckered border.

Himself came in next after a triumphant chariot made of carnation velvet, enriched with *purl* and pearl. *Sidney.*

The jagging of pinks is like the inequality of oak leaves; but they seldom have any small *purls*. *Bacon.*

2. [I know not whence derived.] A kind of medicated malt liquor, in which wormwood and aromaticks are infused.

To Purl. *v. n.* [of this word it is doubtful what is the primitive signification; if it is refered originally to the appearance of a quick stream, which is always dimpled on the surface, it may come from *purl*, a *pucker* or *fringe*; but if, as the use of authors seem to show, it relates to the sound, it must be derived from *porla*, Swedish, to *murmur*, according to Mr. *Lye*.] To murmur; to flow with a gentle noise.

Tones are not so apt to procure sleep, as some other sounds; as the wind, the *purling* of water, and humming of bees. *Bacon's Nat. Hist.*

Instruments that have returns, as trumpets; or flexions, as cornets; or are drawn up, and put from, as sacbuts, have a *purling* sound; but the recorder or flute, that have none of these inequalities, give a clear sound. *Bacon.*

All fish from sea or shore,
Freshet, or *purling* brook, or shell or fin. *Milton.*

My flow'ry theme,
A painted mistress, or a *purling* stream. *Pope.*

Around th' adjoining brook, that *purls* along
The vocal grove, now fretting o'er a rock. *Thomson.*

To Purl. *v. a.* To decorate with fringe or embroidery.

When was old Sherewood's head more quaintly curl'd,
Or nature's cradle more enchas'd and *purl'd*. *B. Johnson.*

Pu'rlieu. *n. s.* The grounds on the borders of a forest; border; inclosure.

In the *purlieus* of this forest stands
A sheepcote, fenc'd about with olive trees. *Shakesp.*

Such civil matters fall within the *purlieus* of religion. *L'Est.*

To understand all the *purlieus* of this place, and to illustrate this subject, I must venture myself into the haunts of beauty and gallantry. *Spectator.*

He may be left to rot among thieves in some stinking jail, merely for mistaking the *purlieus* of the law. *Swift.*

A party next of glitt'ring dames,
Thrown round the *purlieus* of St. James,
Came early out. *Swift.*

Pu'rlins. *n. s.* In architecture, those pieces of timber that lie across the rafters on the inside, to keep them from sinking in the middle of their length. *Bailey.*

To PURLOIN. *v. a.* [this word is of doubtful etymology. *Skinner* deduces it from *pour* and *loin*, French; Mr. *Lye* from pujllouhnan, Saxon, to lie hid.] To steal; to take by theft.

He, that brave steed there finding ready dight,
Purloin'd both steed and spear, and ran away full light. *F. Q.*

The Arimaspian by stealth
Had, from his wakeful custody, *purloin'd*
The guarded gold. *Milton.*

They not content like felons to *purloin*,
Add treason to it, and debase the coin. *Denham.*

Some writers make all ladies *purloin'd*,
And knights pursuing like a whirlwind. *Hudibras.*

When did the muse from Fletcher scenes *purloin*,
As thou whole Eth'ridge dost transfuse to thine? *Dryden.*

Your butler *purloins* your liquor, and the brewer sells your hog-wash. *Arbuthnot's History of John Bull.*

Prometheus once this chain *purloin'd*,
Dissolv'd, and into money coin'd. *Swift.*

Purlo'iner. *n. s.* [from *purloin.*] A thief; one that steals clandestinely.

It may seem hard, to see publick *purloiners* sit upon the lives of the little ones, that go to the gallows. *L'Estrange.*

Pu'rparty. *n. s.* [*pour* and *parti*, Fr.] Share; part in division.

Each of the coparceners had an entire county allotted for her *purparty*. *Davies on Ireland.*

PU'RPLE. *adj.* [*pourpre*, Fr. *purpureus*, Lat.]

1. Red tinctured with blue.

The poop was beaten gold,
Purple the sails, and so perfumed, that
The winds were love-sick with e'm. *Shakesp.*

You violets, that first appear,
By your pure *purple* mantles known;
What are you when the rose is blown? *Wotton.*

A small oval plate, cut off a flinty pebble, and polished, is prettily variegated with a pale grey, blue, yellow, and *purple*. *Woodward on Fossils.*

2. In poetry, red.

I view a field of blood,
And Tyber rolling with a *purple* flood. *Dryden.*

Their mangled limbs
Crashing at once, death dyes the *purple* seas
With gore. *Thomson's Summer.*

To Pu'rple. *v. a.* [*purpuro*, Lat.] To make red; to colour with purple.

Whilst your *purpled* hands do reak and smoak,
Fulfil your pleasure. *Shakesp. Julius Cæsar.*

Cruel and suddain, hast thou since
Purpled thy nail in blood of innocence? *Donne.*

Though fall'n on evil days,
In darkness, and with dangers compass'd round,
And solitude! yet, not alone, while thou
Visit'st my slumbers nightly; or when morn
Purples the East. *Milton's Par. Lost, b.* xxx.

Throw hither all your quaint enamel'd eyes,
That on the green turf suck the honied show'rs,
And *purple* all the ground with vernal flow'rs. *Milton.*

Aurora had but newly chas'd the night,
And *purpled* o'er the sky with blushing light. *Dryden.*

Not with more glories in th' ethereal plain,
The sun first rises o'er the *purpled* main. *Pope.*

Reclining soft in blissful bow'rs,
Purpled sweet with springing flow'rs. *Fenton.*

Pu'rples. *n. s.* [without a singular.] Spots of a livid red, which break out in malignant fevers; a purple fever.

Pu'rplish. *adj.* [from *purple.*] Somewhat purple.

I could change the colour, and make it *purplish*. *Boyle.*

Pu'rport. *n. s.* [*pourporte*, Fr.] Design; tendency of a writing or discourse.

That Plato intended nothing less, is evident from the whole scope and *purport* of that dialogue. *Norris.*

To Pu'rport. *v. a.* [from the noun.] To intend; to tend to show.

There was an article against the reception of the rebels, *purporting*, that if any such rebel should be required of the prince confederate, that the prince confederate should command him to avoid the country. *Bacon's Henry* VII.

They in most grave and solemn wise unfolded
Matter, which little *purported*, but words
Rank'd in right learned phrase. *Rowe.*

PU'RPOSE. *n. s.* [*propos*, Fr. *propositum*, Lat.]

1. Intention; design.

He quit the house of *purpose*, that their punishment
Might have the freer course. *Shakesp. King Lear.*

Change this *purpose*,
Which being so horrible, so bloody, must
Lead on to some foul issue. *Shakesp.*

He with troops of horsemen beset the passages of *purpose*, that when the army should set forward, he might in the streights, fit for his *purpose*, set upon them. *Knolles.*

And I persuade me God hath not permitted
His strength again to grow, were not his *purpose*
To use him farther yet. *Milton's Agonistes.*

St. Austin hath laid down a rule to this very *purpose*. *Burn.*

They, who are desirous of a name in painting, should read and make observations of such things as they find for their *purpose*. *Dryden's Dufresnoy.*

He travelled the world, on *purpose* to converse with the most learned men. *Guardian*, Nº 165.

The common materials, which the ancients made their ships of, were the ornus or wild ash; the fir was likewise used for this *purpose*. *Arbuthnot.*

I do this, on *purpose* to give you a more sensible impression of the imperfection of your knowledge. *Watts.*

Where men err against this method, it is usually on *purpose*, and to shew their learning. *Swift.*

2. Effect; consequence.

To small *purpose* had the council of Jerusalem been assembled, if once their determination being set down, men might afterwards have defended their former opinions. *Hooker.*

The ground will be like a wood, which keepeth out the sun, and so continueth the wet, whereby it will never graze, to *purpose* that year. *Bacon's Nat. Hist.*

Their design is a war, whenever they can open it with a prospect of succeeding to *purpose*. *Temple.*

Such first principles will serve us to very little *purpose*, and we shall be as much at a loss with, as without them, if they may, by any human power, such as is the will of our teachers, or opinions of our companions, be altered or lost in us. *Locke.*

He that would relish success to *purpose*, should keep his passion cool, and his expectation low. *Collier on Desire.*

What the Romans have done is not worth notice, having had little occasion to make use of this art, and what they have of it to *purpose* being borrowed from Aristotle. *Baker.*

3. Instance; example.

'Tis common for double-dealers to be taken in their own snares, as for the *purpose* in the matter of power. *L'Est.*

To Pu'rpose. *v. a.* [from the noun.] To intend; to design; to resolve.

What he did *purpose*, it was the pleasure of God that Solomon his son should perform. *Hooker.*

It is a *purpos'd* thing, and grows by plot,
To curb the nobility. *Shakesp. Coriolanus.*

I am *purposed*, that my mouth shall not transgress. *Ps.* xvii.

This is the purpose that is *purposed* upon the whole earth. *Is.* xiv. 26.

Paul *purposed* in the spirit, to go to Jerusalem. *Acts* xix. 21.

The christian captains, *purposing* to retire home, placed on each side of the army four ranks of waggons. *Knolles.*

The whole included race his *purpos'd* prey. *Milton.*

Oaths were not *purpos'd* more than law,
To keep the good and just in awe,
But to confine the bad and sinful,
Like moral cattle in a pinfold. *Hudibras.*

Doubling my crime, I promise and deceive,
Purpose to slay, whilst swearing to forgive. *Prior.*

PU'RPOSELY. *adv.* [from *purpose.*] By design; by intention.

Being the instrument which God hath *purposely* framed, thereby to work the knowledge of salvation in the hearts of men, what cause is there wherefore it should not be acknowledged a most apt mean? *Hooker.*

I have *purposely* avoided to speak any thing concerning the treatment due to such persons. *Addison.*

In composing this discourse, I *purposely* declined all offensive and displeasing truths. *Atterbury.*

The vulgar thus through imitation err,
As oft the learned by being singular;
So much they scorn the crowd, that if the throng
By chance go right, they *purposely* go wrong. *Pope.*

PU'RPRISE. *n. s.* [*pourpris*, old Fr. *purprisum*, law Lat.] A close or inclosure; as also the whole compass of a manour.

The place of justice is hallowed; and therefore not only the bench, but the foot-pace and precincts, and *purprise* ought to be preserved without corruption. *Bacon's Essays.*

PURR. *n. s.* A sea lark. *Ainsworth.*

To PURR. *v. a.* To murmur as a cat or leopard in pleasure.

PURSE. *n. s.* [*bourse*, Fr. *pwrs*, Welsh.] A small bag in which money is contained.

She bears the *purse* too; she is a region in Guiana all gold and bounty. *Shakesp. Merry Wives of Windsor.*

Shall the son of England prove a thief,
And take *purses*? *Shakesp. Henry IV.*

He sent certain of the chief prisoners, richly apparalled with their *purses* full of money, into the city. *Knolles.*

I will give him the thousand pieces, and, to his great surprise, present him with another *purse* of the same value. *Add.*

To PURSE. *v. a.* [from the noun.]

1. To put into a purse.

I am spell-caught by Philidel,
And *purs'd* within a net. *Dryden.*

I *purs'd* it up, but little reck'ning made,
'Till now that this extremity compell'd,
I find it true. *Milton.*

1. To contract as a purse.

Thou cried'st,
And did'st contract and *purse* thy brow together,
As if thou then had'st shut up in thy brain
Some horrible conceit. *Shakesp. Othello.*

PU'RSENET. *n. s.* [*purse* and *net.*] A net of which the mouth is drawn together by a string.

Conies are taken by *pursenets* in their burrows. *Mortimer.*

PU'RSEPROUD. *adj.* [*purse* and *proud.*] Puffed up with money.

PU'RSER. *n. s.* [from *purse.*] The paymaster of a ship.

PU'RSINESS. } *n. s.* [from *pursy.*] Shortness of breath.
PU'RSIVENESS. }

PU'RSLAIN. *n. s.* [*portulaca*, Lat.] A plant.

The flower of *purslain* consists of many leaves, which expand in form of a rose, out of whose flower-cup, which consists of one leaf, arises the pointal, which, together with the flower-cup, becomes a fruit, for the most part oval, full of small seeds, and furnished with two shells or husks at top; of which the outer one, which was the part of the flower-cup that was split in two, opens first; and the inner one, which is the pointal inlarged, opens last, doubly and transversely, while the lower part of the flower-cup adheres to the footstalk. *Miller.*

The medicaments, proper to diminish the milk, are lettice, *purslain* and endive. *Wiseman's Surgery.*

PURSU'ABLE. *adj.* [from *pursue.*] What may be pursued.

PURSU'ANCE. *n. s.* [from *pursue.*] Prosecution; process.

PURSU'ANT. *adj.* [from *pursue.*] Done in consequence or prosecution of any thing.

To PURSU'E. *v. a.* [*poursuivre*, Fr.]

1. To chase; to follow in hostility.

Love like a shadow flies, when substance love *pursues*;
Pursuing that that flies, and flying what *pursues*. *Shakesp.*

When Abram heard that his brother was taken captive, he armed his trained servants, and *pursued*. *Gen.* xiv. 14.

To thy speed add wings,
Lest with a whip of scorpions I *pursue*
Thy lingering. *Milton.*

2. To prosecute; to continue.

As righteousness tendeth to life; so he that *pursueth* evil, *pursueth* it to his own death. *Prov.* xii. 19.

Insatiate to *pursue*
Vain war with heaven. *Milton.*

I will *pursue*
This ancient story, whether false or true. *Dryden.*

When men *pursue* their thoughts of space, they stop at the confines of body, as if space were there at an end. *Locke.*

3. To imitate; to follow as an example.

The fame of ancient matrons you *pursue*,
And stand a blameless pattern to the new. *Dryden.*

4. To endeavour to attain.

Let us not then *pursue*
Splendid vassalage. *Milton.*

We happiness *pursue*; we fly from pain;
Yet the pursuit, and yet the flight is vain. *Prior.*

To PURSU'E. *v. n.* To go on; to proceed.

I have, *pursues* Carneades, wondered chymists should not consider. *Boyle.*

PURSU'ER. *n. s.* [from *pursue.*] One who follows in hostility.

Fled with the rest,
And falling from a hill he was so bruis'd,
That the *pursuers* took him. *Shakesp. Henry IV.*

His swift *pursuers* from heav'n's gates discern
Th' advantage, and descending tread us down
Thus drooping. *Milton's Par. Lost, b.* i.

Like a declining statesman left forlorn
To his friends pity and *pursuers* scorn. *Denham.*

PURSU'IT. *n. s.* [*poursuite*, Fr.]

1. The act of following with hostile intention.

Arm, warriors, arm for fight! the foe at hand,
Whom fled we thought, will save us long *pursuit*. *Milton.*

2. Endeavour to attain.

This means they long propos'd, but little gain'd,
Yet after much *pursuit*, at length obtain'd. *Dryden.*

Its honours and vanities are continually passing before him, and inviting his *pursuit*. *Rogers.*

He has annexed a secret pleasure to the idea of any thing that is new or uncommon, that he might encourage us in the *pursuit* after knowledge, and engage us to search into the wonders of his creation. *Addison.*

The will, free from the determination of such desires, is left to the *pursuit* of nearer satisfactions, and to the removal of those uneasinesses it feels in its longings after them. *Locke.*

3. Prosecution.

He concluded with sighs and tears, to conjure them, that they would no more press him to give his consent to a thing so contrary to his reason, the execution whereof would break his heart, and that they would give over further *pursuit* of it. *Clarendon.*

PU'RSUIVANT. *n. s.* [*poursuivant*, Fr.] A state messenger; an attendant on the heralds.

How oft do they with golden pinions cleave
The flitting skies, like flying *pursuivant*. *Fairy Queen.*

Pursuivants he often for them sent. *Hubberd.*

These grey locks, the *pursuivants* of death,
Argue the end of Edmund Mortimer. *Shakesp.*

Send out a *pursuivant* at arms
To Stanley's regiment; bid him bring his power
Before sun-rising. *Shakesp. Richard III.*

For helmets, crests, mantles, and supporters, I leave the reader to Edmond Bolton, Gerard Leigh, John Ferne, and John Guillim Portismouth, *pursuivants* of arms, who have diligently laboured in armory. *Camden's Remains.*

The *pursuivants* came next,
And like the heralds each his scutheon bore. *Dryden.*

PU'RSY. *adj.* [*poussif*, Fr.] Shortbreathed and fat.

In the fatness of these *pursy* times,
Virtue itself of vice must pardon beg,
Yea courb and woo for leave to do it good. *Shakesp.*

Now breathless wrong
Shall sit and pant in your great chairs of ease,
And *pursy* insolence shall break his wind
With fear and horrid flight. *Shakesp. Timon of Athens.*

By these, the Medes
Perfume their breaths, and cure old *pursy* men. *Temple.*

An hostess dowager,
Grown fat and *pursy* by retail
Of pots of beer and bottl'd ale. *Hudibras, p.* iii.

PU'RTENANCE. *n. s.* [*appertenance*, Fr.] The pluck of an animal.

Roast the lamb with fire, his head with his legs and with the *purtenance* thereof. *Ex.* xii. 9.

The shaft against a rib did glance
And gall'd him in the *purtenance*. *Hudibras, p.* i.

To PU'RVEY. *v. a.* [*pourvoir*, Fr.]

1. To provide with conveniencies. This sense is now not in use.

Give no odds to your foes, but do *purvey*
Yourself of sword before that bloody day. *Fa. Queen.*

His house with all convenience was *purvey'd*,
The rest he found. *Dryden.*

2. To procure.

What though from outmost land and sea *purvey'd*
For him; each rarer tributary life
Bleeds not. *Thomson's Summer.*

To PU'RVEY. *v. n.* To buy in provisions.

I the praise
Yield thee, so well this day thou hast *purvey'd*. *Milton*

PURVE'YANCE. *n. s.* [from *purvey.*]

1. Provision.

Whence mounting up, they find *purveyance* meet
Of all, that royal princes court became. *Fa. Queen.*

2. Procurement of victuals.

Some lands be more changeable than others; as for their lying near to the borders, or because of great and continual *purveyances* that are made upon them. *Bacon.*

PURVE'YOR. *n. s.* [from *purvey.*]

1. One that provides victuals.

The *purveyors* or victuallers are much to be condemned, as not a little faulty in that behalf. *Raleigh.*

2. A procurer; a pimp.

These women are such cunning *purveyors!*
Mark where their appetites have once been pleased,
The same resemblance in a younger lover,
Lies brooding in their fancies the same pleasures. *Dryden.*

The stranger, ravish'd at his good fortune, is introduced to some imaginary title; for this *purveyor* has her representatives of some of the finest ladies. *Addison.*

PU'RVIEW. *n. s.* [*pourveu*, French.] Proviso; providing clause.

Though the petition expresses only treason and felony, yet the act is general against all appeals in parliament; and many times the *purview* of an act is larger than the preamble or the petition. *Hale's Common Law of England.*

PU'RULENCE. } *n. s.* [from *purulent.*] Generation of pus or
PU'RULENCY. } matter.

Consumptions are induced by *purulency* in any of the viscera. *Arbuthnot on Diet.*

PU'RULENT. *adj.* [*purulent*, Fr. *purulentus*, Lat.] Consisting of pus or the running of wounds.

A carcase of man is most infectious and odious to man, and *purulent* matter of wounds to found flesh. *Bacon.*

It spews a filthy froth
Of matter *purulent* and white,
Which happen'd on the skin to light,
And there corrupting on a wound,
Spreads leprosy. *Swift's Miscel.*

An acrimonious or *purulent* matter, stagnating in some organ, is more easily deposited upon the liver than any other part. *Arbuthnot on Aliments.*

PUS. *n. s.* [Latin.] The matter of a well digested sore.

Acrid substances break the vessels, and produce an ichor instead of laudable *pus.* *Arbuthnot.*

To PUSH. *v. a.* [*pousser*, Fr.]

1. To strike with a thrust.

If the ox *push* a man-servant, he shall be stoned. *Ex.* xxi.

2. To force or drive by impulse of any thing.

The youth *push* away my feet. *Job* xxx. 12.

3. To force not by a quick blow, but by continued violence.

Shew your mended faiths,
To *push* destruction and perpetual shame
Out of the weak door of our fainting land. *Shakesp.*

Through thee will we *push* down our enemies. *Ps.* xliv. 5.

Waters forcing way,
Sidelong had *push'd* a mountain from his seat,
Half sunk with all his pines. *Milton.*

The description of this terrible scene threw her into an hysterick fit, which might have proved dangerous, if Cornelius had not been *pushed* out of the room. *Arbuthnot and Pope.*

4. To press forward.

He forewarns his care
With rules to *push* his fortune or to bear. *Dryden.*

With such impudence did he *push* this matter, that when he heard the cries of above a million of people begging for their bread, he termed it the clamours of faction. *Addison.*

Arts and sciences, in one and the same century, have arrived at great perfection, and no wonder, since every age has a kind of universal genius, which inclines those that live in it to some particular studies, the work then being *pushed* on by many hands, must go forward. *Dryden.*

5. To urge; to drive.

Ambition *pushes* the soul to such actions, as are apt to procure honour to the actor. *Addison's Spectator.*

6. To enforce; to drive to a conclusion.

We are *pushed* for an answer, and are forced at last freely to confess, that the corruptions of the administration were intolerable. *Swift.*

7. To importune; to teaze.

To PUSH. *v. n.*

1. To make a thrust.

But issues, ere the fight, his dread command,
That none shall dare
With shortned sword to stab in closer war,
Nor *push* with biting point, but strike at length. *Dryden.*

A calf will so manage his head, as though he would *push* with his horns even before they shoot. *Ray.*

Lambs, though they never saw the actions of their species, *push* with their foreheads, before the budding of a horn. *Addison.*

2. To make an effort.

War seem'd asleep for nine long years; at length
Both sides resolv'd to *push*, we try'd our strength. *Dryden.*

3. To make an attack.

The king of the South shall *push* at him, and the king of the North shall come against him. *Dan.* xi. 40.

PUSH. *n. s.* [from the verb.]

1. Thrust; the act of striking with a pointed instrument.

Ne might his corse be harmed
With dint of sword or *push* of pointed spear. *Spenser.*

So great was the puissance of his *push*,
That from his sadle quite he did him bear. *Fa. Queen.*

They, like resolute men, stood in the face of the breach, receiving them with deadly shot and *push* of pike, in such furious manner, that the Turks began to retire. *Knolles.*

2. An impulse; force impressed.

Jove was not more
With infant nature, when his spacious hand
Had rounded this huge ball of earth and seas
To give it the first *push*, and see it roll
Along the vast abyss. *Addison's Guardian.*

3. Assault; attack.

He gave his countenance against his name,
To laugh with gybing boys, and stand the *push*
Of every beardless vain comparative. *Shakesp. Henry IV.*

When such a resistance is made, these bold talkers will draw in their horns, when their fierce and feeble *pushes* against truth are repelled with pushing and confidence. *Watts.*

4. A forcible struggle; a strong effort.

A sudden *push* gives them the overthrow;
Ride, ride, Messala. *Shakesp.*

Away he goes, makes his *push*, stands the shock of a battle, and compounds for leaving of a leg behind him. *L'Estrange.*

We have beaten the French from all their advanced posts, and driven them into their last entrenchments: one vigorous *push*, one general assault will force the enemy to cry out for quarter. *Addison.*

5. Exigence; trial.

We'll put the matter to the present *push.* *Shakesp.*

'Tis common to talk of dying for a friend; but when it comes to the *push*, 'tis no more than talk. *L'Estrange.*

The question we would put, is not whether the sacrament of the mass be as truly propitiatory, as those under the law? but whether it be as truly a sacrifice? if so, then it is a true proper sacrifice, and is not only commemorative or representative, as we are told at a *push.* *Atterbury.*

6. A sudden emergence.

There's time enough for that;
Lest they desire, upon this *push*, to trouble
Your joys with like relation. *Shakesp. Winter's Tale.*

7. [*Pustula*, Lat.] A pimple; an efflorescence; a wheal.

He that was praised to his hurt, should have a *push* rise upon his nose; as a blister will rise upon one's tongue, that tells a lye. *Bacon's Essays.*

PU'SHER. *n. s.* [from *push.*] He who pushes forward.

PU'SHING. *adj.* [from *push.*] Enterprising; vigorous.

PU'SHPIN. *n. s.* [*push* and *pin.*] A child's play, in which pins are pushed alternately.

Men, that have wandering thoughts at the voice of wisdom out of the mouth of a philosopher, deserve as well to be whipt, as boys for playing at *pushpin*, when they should be learning. *L'Estrange.*

PUSILLANI'MITY. *n. s.* [*pusillanimité*, Fr. *pusillus* and *animus*, Lat.] Cowardice; meanness of spirit.

The property of your excellent sherris is the warming of the blood, which, before cold and settled, left the liver white and pale, the badge of *pusillanimity* and cowardice. *Shakesp.*

The Chinese sail where they will; which sheweth, that their law of keeping out strangers is a law of *pusillanimity* and fear. *Bacon's New Atlantis.*

It is obvious, to distinguish between an act of courage and an act of rashness, an act of *pusillanimity* and an act of great modesty or humility. *South's Sermons.*

PUSILLA'NIMOUS. *adj.* [*pusillanime*, Fr. *pusillus* and *animus*, Lat.] Meanspirited; narrowminded; cowardly.

An argument fit for great princes, that neither by overmeasuring their forces, they lose themselves in vain enterprizes; nor, by undervaluing them, descend to fearful and *pusillanimous* counsels. *Bacon's Essays.*

He became *pusillanimous*, and was easily ruffled with every little passion within; supine, and as openly exposed to any temptation from without. *Woodward's Nat. Hist.*

What greater instance can there be of a weak *pusillanimous* temper, than for a man to pass his whole life in opposition to his own sentiments. *Spectator*, Nº 576.

PUSILLA'NIMOUSNESS. *n. s.* [from *pusillanimous.*] Meanness of spirit.

PUSS. *n. s.* [I know not whence derived; *pusio*, Lat. is a dwarf.]

1. The fondling name of a cat.

A young fellow, in love with a cat, made it his humble suit to Venus to turn *puss* into a woman. *L'Estrange.*

Let *puss* practise what nature teaches. *Watts.*

I will permit my son to play at apodidrascinda, which can be no other than our *puss* in a corner. *Arbuth. and Pope.*

2. The sportsman's term for a hare.

Poor honest *puss*,
It grieves my heart to see thee thus;
But hounds eat sheep as well as hares. *Gay.*

PU'STULE. *n. s.* [*pustule*, Fr. *pustula*, Lat.] A small swelling; a pimple; a push; an efflorescence.

The blood turning acrimonious, corrodes the vessels, producing hemorrhages, *pustules* red, black and gangrenous. *Arb.*

PU'STULOUS. *adj.* [from *pustule.*] Full of pustules; pimply.

To PUT. *v. a.* [of this word, so common in the English language, it is very difficult to find the etymology; *putter*, to plant, is Danish. *Junius.*]

1. To lay or reposite in any place.

God planted a garden, and there he *put* a man. *Gen.* ii. 8.

Speak unto him, and *put* words in his mouth. *Ex.* iv. 15.

If a man *put* in his beast, and feed in another man's field; of the best of his own shall he make restitution. *Ex.* xxii. 5.

In these he *put* two weights. *Milton.*

Feed land with beasts and horses, and after both *put* in sheep. *Mortimer's Husbandry.*

2. To place in any situation.

When he had *put* them all out, he entereth in. *Mar.* v. 40.

Four speedy cherubims
Put to their mouths the sounding alchimy. *Milton.*

Put all your other subjects together; they have not taken half the pains for your majesty's service that I have. *L'Estr.*

3. To place in any state or condition.

Before we will lay by our just born arms,
We'll *put* thee down, 'gainst whom these arms we bear,
Or add a royal number to the dead. *Shakesp.*

Put me in a surety with thee. *Job* xvii. 3.

The stones he *put* for his pillows. *Gen.* xxviii. 11.

He hath *put* my brethren far from me. *Job* xix. 13.

As we were *put* in trust with the gospel, even so we speak, not as pleasing men, but God. 1 *Thes.* ii. 4.

They shall ride upon horses, every one *put* in array like a man to the battle against thee. *Jer.* l. 42.

He *put* them into ward three days. *Gen.* xlii. 17.

She shall be his wife, he may not *put* her away. *Deut.* xxii.

Daniel said, *put* these two aside. *Sus.* v. 51.

Having lost two of their bravest commanders at sea, they durst not *put* it to a battle at sea, and set up their rest wholly upon the land enterprize. *Bacon.*

This question ask'd *puts* me in doubt. *Milton.*

So nature prompts; so soon we go astray,
When old experience *puts* us in the way. *Dryden.*

Men may *put* government into what hands they please. *Locke.*

He that has any doubt of his tenets, received without examination, ought to *put* himself wholly into this state of ignorance, and throwing wholly by all his former notions, examine them with a perfect indifference. *Locke.*

Declaring by word or action a sedate, settled design upon another man's life, *puts* him in a state of war with him. *Locke.*

As for the time of *putting* the rams to the ewes, you must consider at what time your grass will maintain them. *Mort.*

If without any provocation gentlemen will fall upon one, in an affair wherein his interest and reputation are embarked, they cannot complain of being *put* into the number of his enemies. *Pope.*

4. To repose.

How wilt thou *put* thy trust on Egypt for chariots. 2 *Kings.*

God was entreated of them, because they *put* their trust in him. 1 *Chr.* v. 20.

5. To trust; to give up.

Thou shalt *put* all in the hands of Aaron, and wave them for a wave-offering. *Ex.* xxix. 24.

6. To expose; to apply to any thing.

A sinew cracked seldom recovers its former strength, or the memory of it leaves a lasting caution in the man, not to *put* the part quickly again to robust employment. *Locke.*

7. To push into action.

Thank him who *puts* me loth to this revenge. *Milton.*

When men and women are mixed and well chosen, and *put* their best qualities forward, there may be any intercourse of civility and good will. *Swift.*

8. To apply.

Your goodliest young men and asses he will *put* them to his work. 1 *Sam.* viii. 16.

No man, having *put* his hand to the plough and looking back, is fit for the kingdom of God. *Luke* ix. 62.

Rejoice before the Lord in all that thou *puttest* thine hands unto. *Deut.* xii. 18.

Chymical operations are excellent tools in the hands of a natural philosopher, and are by him applicable to many nobler uses, than they are wont to be *put* to in laboratories. *Boyle.*

The avarice of their relations *put* them to painting, as more gainful than any other art. *Dryden's Dufresnoy.*

The great difference in the notions of mankind, is from the different use they *put* their faculties to. *Locke.*

I expect an offspring, docile and tractable in whatever we *put* them to. *Tatler*, N° 75.

9. To use any action by which the place or state of any thing is changed.

I do but keep the peace, *put* up thy sword. *Shakesp.*

Put up your sword; if this young gentleman
Have done offence, I take the fault on me. *Shakesp.*

He *put* his hand unto his neighbour's goods. *Ex.* xxii.

Whatsoever cannot be digested by the stomach, is by the stomach either *put* up by vomit, or *put* down to the guts. *Bacon.*

It *puts* a man from all employment, and makes a man's discourses tedious. *Taylor's Rule of Living Holy.*

A nimble fencer will *put* in a thrust so quick, that the foil will be in your bosom, when you thought it a yard off. *Digby.*

A man, not having the power of his own life, cannot *put* himself under the absolute arbitrary power of another to take it. *Locke.*

Instead of making apologies, I will send it with my hearty prayers, that those few directions I have here *put* together, may be truly useful to you. *Wake.*

He will know the truth of these maxims, upon the first occasion that shall make him *put* together those ideas, and observe whether they agree or disagree. *Locke.*

When you cannot get dinner ready, *put* the clock back. *Swift's Directions to the Cook.*

10. To cause; to produce.

There is great variety in men's understanding; and their natural constitutions *put* so wide a difference between some men, that industry would never be able to master. *Locke.*

11. To comprise; to consign to writing.

Cyrus made proclamation, and *put* it also in writing. 2 *Chr.*

12. To add.

Whatsoever God doeth, nothing can be *put* to it, nor any thing taken from it. *Eccl.* iii. 14.

13. To place in a reckoning.

If we will rightly estimate things, we shall find, that most of them are wholly to be *put* on the account of labour. *Locke.*

That such a temporary life, as we now have, is better than no being, is evident by the high value we *put* upon it ourselves. *Locke.*

14. To reduce to any state.

Marcellus and Flavius, for pulling scarfs off Cæsar's images, are *put* to silence. *Shakesp. Julius Cæsar.*

This dishonours you no more,
Than to take in a town with gentle words,
Which else would *put* you to your fortune. *Shakesp.*

And five of you shall chase an hundred, and an hundred of you shall *put* ten thousand to flight. *Lev.* xxvi. 8.

With well-doing, ye may *put* to silence foolish men. 1 *Pet.*

The Turks were in every place *put* to the worst, and lay by heaps slain. *Knolles's Hist. of the Turks.*

This scrupulous way would make us deny our senses; for there is scarcely any thing but *puts* our reason to a stand. *Coll.*

Some modern authors, observing what straits they have been *put to* to find out water enough for Noah's flood, say, Noah's flood was not universal, but a national inundation. *Burnet's Theory of the Earth.*

We see the miserable shifts some men are *put* to, when that, which was founded upon, and supported by idolatry, is become the sanctuary of atheism. *Bentley.*

15. To oblige; to urge.

Those that *put* their bodies to endure in health, may, in most sicknesses, be cured only with diet and tendering. *Bacon.*

The discourse I mentioned was written to a private friend, who *put* me upon that task. *Boyle.*

He *put* to proof his high supremacy. *Milton.*

When the wisest counsel of men have with the greatest prudence made laws, yet frequent emergencies happen which they did not foresee, and therefore they are *put* upon repeals and supplements of such their laws; but Almighty God, by one simple foresight, foresaw all events, and could therefore fit laws proportionate to the things he made. *Hale.*

We are *put* to prove things, which can hardly be made plainer. *Tillotson.*

Where the loss can be but temporal, every small probability of it need not *put* us so anxiously to prevent it. *South.*

They should seldom be *put* about doing those things, but when they have a mind. *Locke.*

16. To propose; to state.

A man of Tyre, skilful to work in gold and silver, to find out every device which shall be *put* to him. 2 *Chr.* ii. 24.

Put it thus—unfold to Staius straight,
What to Jove's ear thou didst impart of late:
He'll stare. *Dryden.*

The question originally *put* and disputed in publick schools was, whether, under any pretence whatsoever, it may be lawful to resist the supreme magistrate. *Swift.*

I only *put* the question, whether, in reason, it would not have been proper the kingdom should have received timely notice. *Swift.*

I *put* the case at the worst, by supposing what seldom happens, that a course of virtue makes us miserable in this life. *Spectator*, N° 576.

17. To form; to regulate.

18. To reach to another.

Wo unto him that giveth his neighbour drink, that *putteſt* thy bottle to him, and makeſt him drunken. *Hab.* ii. 15.

19. To bring into any ſtate of mind or temper.

Solyman, to *put* the Rhodians out of all ſuſpicion of invaſion, ſent thoſe ſoldiers he had levied in the countries neareſt unto Rhodes far away, and ſo upon the ſudden to ſet upon them. *Knolles's Hiſtory of the Turks.*

His highneſs *put* him in mind of the promiſe he had made the day before, which was ſo ſacred, that he hoped he would not violate it. *Clarendon.*

To *put* your ladyſhip in mind of the advantages you have in all theſe points, would look like a deſign to flatter you. *Temple.*

I broke all hoſpitable laws,
To bear you from your palace-yard by might,
And *put* your noble perſon in a fright. *Dryden.*

The leaſt harm that befalls children, *puts* them into complaints and bawling. *Locke on Education.*

20. To offer; to advance.

I am as much aſhamed to *put* a looſe indigeſted play upon the publick, as I ſhould be to offer braſs money in a payment. *Dryden.*

Wherever he *puts* a ſlight upon good works, 'tis as they ſtand diſtinct from faith. *Atterbury.*

21. To unite; to place as an ingredient.

He has right to *put* into his complex idea, ſignified by the word gold, thoſe qualities, which upon trial he has found united. *Locke.*

22. *To* PUT *by.* To turn off; to divert.

Watch and reſiſt the devil; his chief deſigns are to hinder thy deſire in good, to *put* thee *by* from thy ſpiritual employment. *Taylor.*

A fright hath *put by* an ague fit, and mitigated a fit of the gout. *Grew's Coſmol.*

23. *To* PUT *by.* To thruſt aſide.

Baſilius, in his old years, marrying a young and fair lady, had of her thoſe two daughters ſo famous in beauty, which *put by* their young couſin from that expectation. *Sidney.*

Was the crown offer'd him thrice?
—Ay, marry, was't, and he *put* it *by* thrice,
Every time gentler than other. *Shakeſp. Julius Cæſar.*

Jonathan had died for being ſo,
Had not juſt God *put by* th' unnatural blow. *Cowley.*

When I drove a thruſt, home as I could,
To reach his traitor heart, he *put* it *by*,
And cried, ſpare the ſtripling. *Dryden.*

24. *To* PUT *down.* To baffle; to repreſs; to cruſh.

How the ladies and I have *put* him *down!* *Shakeſp.*

25. *To* PUT *down.* To degrade.

The greedy thirſt of royal crown
Stirr'd Porrex up to *put* his brother *down.* *Fa. Queen.*

The king of Egypt *put* Jehoahaz *down* at Jeruſalem. 2 *Ch.*

26. *To* PUT *down.* To bring into diſuſe.

Sugar hath *put down* the uſe of honey; inaſmuch as we have loſt thoſe preparations of honey, which the ancients had. *Bacon.*

With copper collars and with brawny backs,
Quite to *put down* the faſhion of our blacks. *Dryden.*

27. *To* PUT *down.* To confute.

We two ſaw you four ſet on four; mark now how a plain tale ſhall *put* you *down.* *Shakeſp. Henry* IV.

28. *To* PUT *forth.* To propoſe.

Samſon ſaid, I will now *put forth* a riddle unto you. *Judg.*

29. *To* PUT *forth.* To extend.

He *put forth* his hand, and pulled her in. *Gen.* viii. 9.

30. *To* PUT *forth.* To emit, as a ſprouting plant.

An excellent obſervation of Ariſtotle, why ſome plants are of greater age than living creatures, for that they yearly *put forth* new leaves; whereas living creatures *put forth*, after their period of growth, nothing but hair and nails, which are excrements. *Bacon's Nat. Hiſt.*

He ſaid, let th' earth
Put forth the verdant graſs, herb yielding ſeed,
And fruit-tree yielding fruit. *Milton.*

31. *To* PUT *forth.* To exert.

I *put* not *forth* my goodneſs. *Milton.*

In honouring God, *put forth* all thy ſtrength. *Taylor.*

We ſhould *put forth* all our ſtrength, and, without having an eye to his preparations, make the greateſt puſh we are able. *Addiſon.*

32. *To* PUT *in.* To interpoſe.

Give me leave to *put in* a word to tell you, that I am glad you allow us different degrees of worth. *Collier.*

33. *To* PUT *in practice.* To uſe; to exerciſe.

Neither gods nor man will give conſent,
To *put in practice* your unjuſt intent. *Dryden.*

34. *To* PUT *off.* To diveſt; to lay aſide.

None of us *put off* our cloaths, ſaving that every one *put* them *off* for waſhing. *Nehem.* iv. 23.

Put off thy ſhoes from off thy feet. *Ex.* ii. 5.

Ambition, like a torrent, ne'er looks back;
And is a ſwelling, and the laſt affection
A high mind can *put off.* *Benj. Johnſon's Cataline.*

It is the new ſkin or ſhell that *putteth off* the old; ſo we ſee, that it is the young horn that *putteth off* the old; and in birds, the young feathers *put off* the old; and ſo birds caſt their beaks, the new beak *putting off* the old. *Bacon.*

Ye ſhall die perhaps, by *putting off*
Human, to put on gods; death to be wiſh'd. *Milton.*

I for his ſake will leave
Thy boſom, and this glory next to thee
Freely *put off*, and for him laſtly die. *Milton.*

Let not the work of to-day be *put off* till to-morrow; for the future is uncertain. *L'Eſtrange.*

When a man ſhall be juſt about to quit the ſtage of this world, to *put off* his mortality, and to deliver up his laſt accounts to God, his memory ſhall ſerve him for little elſe, but to terrify him with a frightful review of his paſt life. *South.*

Now the cheerful light her fears diſpell'd,
She with no winding turns the truth conceal'd,
But *put* the woman *off*, and ſtood reveal'd. *Dryden.*

My friend, fancying her to be an old woman of quality, *put off* his hat to her, when the perſon pulling off his maſk, appeared a ſmock-faced young fellow. *Addiſon.*

Homer ſays he *puts off* that air of grandeur which ſo properly belongs to his character, and debaſes himſelf into a droll. *Broom's Notes on the Odyſſey.*

35. *To* PUT *off.* To defeat or delay with ſome artifice or excuſe.

The gains of ordinary trades are honeſt; but thoſe of bargains are more doubtful, when men ſhould wait upon others neceſſity, broke by ſervants to draw them on, *put off* others cunningly that would be better chapmen. *Bacon.*

I hoped for a demonſtration, but Themiſtius hopes to *put* me *off* with an harangue. *Boyle.*

Some hard words the goat gave, but the fox *puts off* all with a jeſt. *L'Eſtrange.*

I do not intend to be thus *put off* with an old ſong. *More.*

Do men in good earneſt think that God will be *put off* ſo? Or that the law of God will be baffled with a lie cloathed in a ſcoff? *South.*

This is a very unreaſonable demand, and we might *put* him *off* with this anſwer, that there are ſeveral things which all men in their wits diſbelieve, and yet none but madmen will go about to diſprove. *Bentley.*

36. *To* PUT *off.* To delay; to defer; to procraſtinate.

So many accidents may deprive us of our lives, that we can never ſay, that he who neglects to ſecure his ſalvation today, may without danger *put* it *off* to to-morrow. *Wake.*

37. *To* PUT *off.* To paſs fallaciouſly.

He ſeems generally to prevail, perſuading them to a confidence in ſome partial works of obedience, or elſe to *put off* the care of their ſalvation to ſome future opportunities. *Rog.*

38. *To* PUT *off.* To diſcard.

Upon theſe taxations,
The clothiers all *put off*
The ſpinſters, carders, fullers, weavers. *Shakeſp.*

39. *To* PUT *off.* To recommend; to vend or obtrude.

The effects which paſs between the ſpirits and the tangible parts, are not at all handled, but *put off* by the names of virtues, natures, actions, and paſſions. *Bacon.*

It is very hard, that Mr. Steele ſhould take up the artificial reports of his own faction, and then *put* them *off* upon the world as additional fears of a popiſh ſucceſſor. *Swift.*

40. *To* PUT *on* or *upon.* To impute; to charge.

41. *To* PUT *on* or *upon.* To inveſt with, as cloaths or covering.

Strangely viſited people he cures,
Hanging a golden ſtamp about their necks,
Put on with holy pray'rs. *Shakeſp. Macbeth.*

Give even way unto my rough affairs;
Put not you *on* the viſage of the times,
And be like them to Percy troubleſome. *Shakeſp.*

So ſhall inferior eyes,
That borrow their behaviour from the great,
Grow great by your example, and *put on*
The dauntleſs ſpirit of reſolution. *Shakeſp. King John.*

Rebekah took goodly raiment, and *put* them *upon* Jacob. *Gen.* xxvii. 15.

If God be with me, and give me bread to eat, and raiment to *put on*, then ſhall the Lord be my God. *Gen.* xxviii. 20.

She has
Very good ſuits, and very rich; but then
She cannot *put* 'em *on*; ſhe knows not how
To wear a garment. *Benj. Johnſon's Ca[illegible]*

Taking his cap from his head, he ſaid, this cap w[illegible] hold two heads, and therefore it muſt be fitted to one[illegible] ſo *put* it *on* again. *Knolles's Hiſt. of the* [illegible]

Avarice *puts on* the canonical habit. *Decay of* [illegible]

Mercury had a mind to learn what credit he had in [the] world, and ſo *put on* the ſhape of a man. *L'Eſtrange.*

The little ones are taught to be proud of their cloaths, before they can *put* them *on*. *Locke.*

42. *To* PUT *on.* To forward; to promote; to incite.

I grow fearful,
By what yourſelf too late have ſpoke and done,
That you protect this courſe, and *put* it *on*
By your allowance. *Shakeſp. King Lear.*

Say, you ne'er had don't,
But by our *putting on.* *Shakeſp. Coriolanus.*

Others envy to the ſtate draws, and *puts on*
For contumelies receiv'd. *Benj. Johnſon's Catiline.*

This came handſomely to *put on* the peace, becauſe it was a fair example of a peace bought. *Bacon's Henry* VII.

As danger did approach, her ſpirits roſe,
And *putting on* the king diſmay'd her foes. *Halifax.*

43. *To* PUT *on* or *upon.* To impoſe; to inflict.

I have offended; that which thou *putteſt on* me, I will bear. 2 *Kings* xviii. 14.

He not only undermineth the baſe of religion, but *puts upon* us the remoteſt error from truth. *Brown.*

The ſtork found he was *put upon*, but ſet a good face however upon his entertainment. *L'Eſtrange.*

Fallacies we are apt to *put upon* ourſelves, by taking words for things. *Locke.*

Why are ſcripture maxims *put upon* us, without taking notice of ſcripture examples which lie croſs them. *Atterbury.*

44. *To* PUT *on.* To aſſume; to take.

The duke hath *put on* a religious life,
And thrown into neglect the pompous court. *Shakeſp.*

Wiſe men love you, in their own deſpight,
And, finding in their native wit no eaſe,
Are forc'd to *put* your folly *on* to pleaſe. *Dryden.*

There is no quality ſo contrary to any nature which one cannot affect, and *put on* upon occaſion, in order to ſerve an intereſt. *Swift.*

45. *To* PUT *over.* To refer.

For the certain knowledge of that truth,
I *put* you *o'er* to heav'n, and to my mother. *Shakeſp.*

46. *To* PUT *out.* To place at uſury.

Lord, who ſhall abide in thy tabernacle? he that *putteth* not *out* his money to uſury. *Pſ.* xv. 5.

To live retir'd upon his own,
He call'd his money in;
But the prevailing love of pelf,
Soon ſplit him on the former ſhelf,
He *put* it *out* again. *Dryden's Horace.*

Money at uſe, when returned into the hands of the owner, uſually lies dead there till he gets a new tenant for it, and can *put* it *out* again. *Locke.*

An old uſurer, charmed with the pleaſures of a country life, in order to make a purchaſe, called in all his money; but, in a very few days after, he *put* it *out* again. *Addiſon.*

One hundred pounds only, *put out* at intereſt at ten per cent. doth in ſeventy years encreaſe to above one hundred thouſand pounds. *Child.*

47. *To* PUT *out.* To extinguiſh.

The Philiſtines *put out* his eyes. *Judg.* xvii. 21.

Whereſover the wax floated, the flame forſook it, till at laſt it ſpread all over, and *put* the flame quite *out.* *Bacon.*

I muſt die
Betray'd, captiv'd, and both my eyes *put out.* *Milton.*

In places that abound with mines, when the ſky ſeemed clear, there would ſuddenly ariſe a certain ſteam, which they call a damp, ſo groſs and thick, that it would oftentimes *put out* their candles. *Boyle.*

This barbarous inſtance of a wild unreaſonable paſſion, quite *put out* thoſe little remains of affection ſhe ſtill had for her lord. *Addiſon's Spectator*, Nº 171.

48. *To* PUT *out.* To emit, as a plant.

Trees planted too deep in the ground, for love of approach to the ſun, forſake their firſt root, and *put out* another more towards the top of the earth. *Bacon's Nat. Hiſt.*

49. *To* PUT *out.* To extend; to protrude.

When ſhe travailed, the one *put out* his hand. *Gen.*

50. *To* PUT *out.* To expel; to drive from.

When they have overthrown him, and the wars are finiſhed, ſhall they themſelves be *put out?* *Spenſer.*

I am reſolved, that when I am *put out* of the ſtewardſhip, they may receive me into their houſes. *Luke* xvi. 4.

The nobility of Caſtile *put out* the king of Arragon, in favour of king Philip. *Bacon's Henry* VII.

51. *To* PUT *out.* To make publick.

You tell us, that you ſhall be forced to leave off your modeſty; you mean that little which is left; for it was worn to rags when you *put out* this medal. *Dryden.*

When I was at Venice, they were *putting out* curious ſtamps of the ſeveral edifices, moſt famous for their beauty or magnificence. *Addiſon.*

52. *To* PUT *out.* To diſconcert.

There is no affectation in paſſion; for that *putteth* a man *out* of his precepts, and in a new caſe there cuſtom leaveth him. *Bacon.*

53. *To* PUT *to.* To kill by; to puniſh by.

From Ireland am I come,
To ſignify that rebels there are up,
And *put* the Engliſhmen *unto* the ſword. *Shakeſp.*

There were no barks to throw the rebels into, and ſend them away by ſea, they were *put* all *to* the ſword. *Bacon.*

Such as were taken on either ſide, were *put to* the ſword or to the halter. *Clarendon.*

Soon as they had him at their mercy,
They *put* him *to* the cudgel fiercely. *Hudibras.*

54. *To* PUT *to it.* To diſtreſs; to perplex; to preſs hard.

What would'ſt thou write of me, if thou ſhould'ſt praiſe me.
— O gentle lady, do not *put* me *to't*,
For I am nothing if not critical. *Shakeſp. Othello.*

Lord Angelo dukes it well in his abſence;
He *puts* tranſgreſſion *to't.* *Shakeſp. Meaſ. for Meaſ.*

They have a leader,
Tullus Aufidius, that will *put* you *to't.* *Shakeſp.*

It is to be *put to* queſtion in general, whether it be lawful for chriſtian princes to make an invaſive war, ſimply for the propagation of the faith? *Bacon.*

I was not more concern'd in that debate
Of empire, when our univerſal ſtate
Was *put to* hazard, and the giant race
Our captive ſkies were ready to embrace. *Dryden.*

He took the opportunity of purſuing an argument, which had been before ſtarted, and *put* it *to* her in a ſyllogiſm. *Add.*

They were actually making parties to go up to the moon together, and were more *put to it* how to meet with accommodations by the way, than how to go thither. *Addiſon.*

The figures and letters were ſo mingled, that the coiner was hard *put to it* on what part of the money to beſtow the inſcription. *Addiſon on Ancient Medals.*

I ſhall be hard *put to it*, to bring myſelf off. *Addiſon.*

55. *To* PUT *to.* To aſſiſt with.

Zelmane would have *put to* her helping hand, but ſhe was taken a quivering. *Sidney.*

The carpenters being ſet to work, and every one *putting to* his helping hand, the bridge was repaired. *Knolles.*

56. *To* PUT *to death.* To kill.

It was ſpread abroad, that the king had a purpoſe to *put to death* Edward Plantagenet in the Tower. *Bacon.*

One Bell was *put to death* at Tyburn, for moving a new rebellion. *Hayward.*

Teuta *put to death* one of the Roman ambaſſadors; ſhe was obliged, by a ſucceſsful war, which the Romans made, to content to give up all the ſea coaſt. *Arbuthnot.*

57. *To* PUT *together.* To accumulate into one ſum or maſs.

This laſt age has made a greater progreſs, than all ages before *put together.* *Burnet's Theory of the Earth.*

58. *To* PUT *up.* To paſs unrevenged.

I will indeed no longer endure it; nor am I yet perſuaded to *put up* in peace what already I have fooliſhly ſuffered. *Shak.*

It is prudence, in many caſes, to *put up* the injuries of a weaker enemy, for fear of incurring the diſpleaſure of a ſtronger. *L'Eſtrange.*

How many indignities does he paſs by, and how many aſſaults does he *put up* at our hands, becauſe his love is invincible. *South.*

The Canaanitiſh woman muſt *put up* a refuſal, and the reproachful name of dog, commonly uſed by the Jews of the heathen. *Boyle.*

Nor *put up* blow, but that which laid
Right worſhipful on ſhoulder-blade. *Hudibras.*

Such national injuries are not to be *put up*, but when the offender is below reſentment. *Addiſon.*

59. *To* PUT *up.* To emit; to cauſe to germinate, as plants.

Hartſhorn ſhaven, or in ſmall pieces, mixed with dung, and watered, *putteth up* muſhrooms. *Bacon.*

60. *To* PUT *up.* To expoſe publickly: as, *theſe goods are* put up *to ſale.*

61. *To* PUT *up.* To ſtart.

In town, whilſt I am following one character, I am croſſed in my way by another, and *put up* ſuch a variety of odd creatures in both ſexes, that they foil the ſcent of one another, and puzzle the chace. *Addiſon's Spectator.*

62. *To* PUT *up.* To hoard.

Himſelf never *put up* any of the rent, but diſpoſed of it by the aſſiſtance of a reverend divine to augment the vicar's portion. *Spelman.*

63. *To* PUT *up.* To hide.

Why ſo earneſtly ſeek you to *put up* that letter. *Shakeſp.*

64. *To* PUT *upon.* To incite; to inſtigate.

The great preparation *put* the king *upon* the reſolution of having ſuch a body in his way. *Clarendon, b.* viii.

Thoſe who have lived wickedly before, muſt meet with a great deal more trouble, becauſe they are *put upon* changing the whole courſe of their life. *Tillotſon.*

This caution will *put* them *upon* conſidering, and teach them the neceſſity of examining more than they do. *Locke.*

It need not be any wonder, why I should employ myself upon that study, or *put* others *upon* it. *Walker.*

He replied, with some vehemence, that he would undertake to prove trade would be the ruin of the English nation; I would fain have *put* him *upon* it. *Addison.*

This *put* me *upon* observing the thickness of the glass, and considering whether the dimensions and proportions of the rings may be truly derived from it by computation. *Newton.*

It banishes from our thoughts a lively sense of religion, and *puts* us *upon* so eager a pursuit of the advantages of life, as to leave us no inclination to reflect on the great author of them. *Atterbury.*

These wretches *put* us *upon* all mischief, to feed their lusts and extravagancies. *Swift.*

65. *To* Put *upon.* To impose; to lay upon.

When in swinish sleep,
What cannot you and I perform upon
Th' unguarded Duncan? what not *put upon*
His spungy officers, who shall bear the guilt
Of our great quell? *Shakesp. Macbeth.*

66. *To* Put *upon trial.* To expose or summon to a solemn and judicial examination.

Christ will bring all to life, and then they shall be *put* every one *upon* his own *trial*, and receive judgment. *Locke.*

Jack had done more wisely, to have *put* himself *upon* the trial of his country, and made his defence in form. *Arbuth.*

To Put. *v. n.*

1. To go or move.

The wind cannot be perceived, until there be an eruption of a great quantity from under the water; whereas in the first *putting* up, it cooleth in little portions. *Bacon.*

2. To shoot or germinate.

In fibrous roots, the sap delighteth more in the earth, and therefore *putteth* downward. *Bacon's Nat. Hist.*

3. To steer a vessel.

An ordinary fleet could not hope to succeed against a place that has always a considerable number of men of war ready to *put* to sea. *Addison.*

His fury thus appeas'd, he *puts* to land;
The ghosts forsake their seats. *Dryden.*

4. *To* Put *forth.* To leave a port.

Order for sea is given;
They have *put forth* the haven. *Shakesp. Ant. and Cleop.*

5. *To* Put *forth.* To germinate; to bud; to shoot out.

No man is free,
But that his negligence, his folly, fear,
Amongst the infinite doings of the world,
Sometimes *puts forth*. *Shakesp. Winter's Tale.*

The fig-tree *putteth forth* her green figs. *Cant.* ii. 13.

Take earth from under walls where nettles *put forth* in abundance, without any string of the nettles, and pot that earth, and set in it stock gilliflowers. *Bacon's Nat. Hist.*

Hirsute roots, besides the *putting forth* upwards and downwards, *putteth forth* in round. *Bacon's Nat. Hist.*

6. *To* Put *in.* To enter a haven.

As Homer went, the ship *put in* at Samos, where he continued the whole winter, singing at the houses of great men, with a train of boys after him. *Pope.*

7. *To* Put *in for.* To claim; to stand candidate for. A metaphor, I suppose, from putting each man his lot into a box.

This is so grown a vice, that I know not whether it do not *put in for* the name of virtue. *Locke.*

8. *To* Put *in.* To offer a claim.

They shall stand for seed; they had gone down too, but that a wise burgher *put in* for them. *Shakesp.*

Although astrologers may here *put in*, and plead the secret influence of this star, yet Galen, in his comment, makes no such consideration. *Brown's Vulgar Errours.*

If a man should *put in* to be one of the knights of Malta, he might modestly enough prove his six descents against a less qualified competitor. *Collier.*

9. *To* Put *off.* To leave land.

As the hackney boat was *putting off*, a boy desiring to be taken in, was refused. *Addison.*

10. *To* Put *over.* To sail cross.

Sir Francis Drake came coasting along from Cartagena, a city of the main land to which he *put over*, and took it. *Abbot.*

11. *To* Put *to sea.* To set sail; to begin the course.

It is manifest, that the duke did his best to come down, and to *put to sea*. *Bacon.*

He warn'd him for his safety to provide;
Not *put to sea*, but safe on shore abide. *Dryden.*

They *put to sea* with a fleet of three hundred sail, of which they lost the half. *Arbuthnot.*

With fresh provision hence our fleet to store,
Consult our safety, and *put* off *to sea*. *Pope.*

12. *To* Put *up.* To offer one's self a candidate.

Upon the decease of a lion, the beasts met to chuse a king, when several *put up*. *L'Estrange.*

13. *To* Put *up.* To advance to; to bring one's self forward.

With this he *put up* to my lord,
The courtiers kept their distance due,
He twich'd his sleeve. *Swift.*

14. *To* Put *up with.* To suffer without resentment.

Put. *n. s.* [from the verb.]

1. An action of distress.

The stag's was a forc'd *put*, and a chance rather than a choice. *L'Estrange.*

2. A rustick; a clown.

Queer country *puts* extol queen Bess's reign,
And of lost hospitality complain. *Bramston.*

3. Put *off.* Excuse; shift.

The fox's *put off* is instructive towards the government of our lives, provided his fooling be made our earnest. *L'Estr.*

Pu'tage. *n. s.* [*putain*, Fr.] In law, prostitution on the woman's part.

Pu'tanism. *n. s.* [*putanisme*, Fr.] The manner of living, or trade of a prostitute. *Dict.*

Pu'tative. *adj.* [*putatif*, Fr. from *puto*, Lat.] Supposed; reputed.

If a wife commits adultery, she shall lose her dower, though she be only a *putative*, and not a true and real wife. *Ayliffe.*

PU'TID. *adj.* [*putidus*, Lat.] Mean; low; worthless.

He that follows nature is never out of his way; whereas all imitation is *putid* and servile. *L'Estrange.*

Pu'tidness. *n. s.* [from *putid.*] Meanness; vileness.

Pu'tlog. *n. s.*

Putlogs are pieces of timber or short poles, about seven foot long, to bear the boards they stand on to work, and to lay bricks and mortar upon. *Moxon's Mech. Exercises.*

Pu'tredinous. *adj.* [from *putredo*, Lat.] Stinking; rotten.

A *putredinous* ferment coagulates all humours, as milk with rennet is turned. *Floyer.*

Putrefa'ction. *n. s.* [*putrefaction*, Fr. *putris* and *facio*, Lat.] The state of growing rotten; the act of making rotten.

Putrefaction is a kind of fermentation, or intestine motion of bodies, which tends to the destruction of that form of their existence, which is said to be their natural state. *Quincy.*

If the spirit protrude a little, and that motion be inordinate, there followeth *putrefaction*, which ever dissolveth the consistence of the body into much inequality. *Bacon.*

Vegetable *putrefaction* is produced by throwing green vegetables in a heap in open warm air, and pressing them together, by which they acquire a putrid stercoraceous taste and odour. *Arbuthnot on Aliments.*

From swampy fens,
Where *putrefaction* into life ferments,
And breathes destructive myriads. *Thomson's Summer.*

Putrefa'ctive. *adj.* [from *putrefacio*, Lat.] Making rotten.

They make *putrefactive* generations, conformable unto seminal productions. *Brown's Vulgar Errours.*

If the bone be corrupted, the *putrefactive* smell will discover it. *Wiseman's Surgery.*

To Pu'trefy. *v. a.* [*putrifier*, Fr. *putrefacio*, Lat.] To make rotten; to corrupt with rottenness.

To keep them here,
They would but stink, and *putrefy* the air. *Shakesp.*

Many ill projects are undertaken, and private suits *putrefy* the publick good. *Bacon.*

The ulcer itself being *putrefied*, I scarified it and the parts about, so far as I thought necessary, permitting them to bleed freely, and thrust out the rotten flesh. *Wiseman.*

A wound was so *putrefied*, as to endanger the bone. *Temple.*

Such a constitution of the air, as would naturally *putrefy* raw flesh, must endanger by a mortification. *Arbuthnot.*

To Pu'trefy. *v. n.* To rot.

From the sole of the foot, even unto the head, there is no soundness in it, but wounds, and bruises, and *putrefying* sores. *Is.* i. 6.

All imperfect mixture is apt to *putrefy*, and watry substances are more apt to *putrefy* than oily. *Bacon's Nat. Hist.*

These hymns, though not revive, embalm and spice
The world, which else would *putrefy* with vice. *Donne.*

The pain proceeded from some acrimony in the serum, which, falling into this declining part, *putrefied*. *Wiseman.*

Putre'scence. *n. s.* [from *putresco*, Latin.] The state of rotting.

Now if any ground this effect from gall or choler, because being the fiery humour, it will readiest surmount the water, we may confess in the common *putrescence*, it may promote elevation. *Brown's Vulgar Errours.*

Putre'scent. *adj.* [*putrescens*, Lat.] Growing rotten.

Aliment is not only necessary for repairing the fluids and solids of an animal, but likewise to keep the fluids from the *putrescent* alkaline state, which they would acquire by constant motion. *Arbuthnot on Aliments.*

PU'TRID. *adj.* [*putride*, Fr. *putridus*, Lat.] Rotten; corrupt.

The wine to *putrid* blood converted flows. *Waller.*

If a nurse feed only on flesh, and drink water, her milk, instead of turning sour, will turn *putrid*, and smell like urine. *Arbuthnot on Aliments.*

Putrid fever is that kind of fever, in which the humours, or part of them, have so little circulatory motion, that they fall into an intestine one, and *putrefy*, which is commonly the case after great evacuations, great or excessive heat. *Quin.*

PU'TRIDNESS. *n. s.* [from *putrid.*] Rottenness.

Nidorous ructus depend on the fœtid spirituosity of the ferment, and the *putridness* of the meat. *Floyer on the Humours.*

PU'TTER. *n. s.* [from *put.*]

1. One who puts.

The most wretched sort of people are dreamers upon events and *putters* of cases. *L'Estrange.*

2. PUTTER *on.* Inciter; instigator.

My good lord cardinal, they vent reproaches
Most bitterly on you, as *putter on*
Of these exactions. *Shakesp. Henry* VIII.
You are abus'd, and by some *putter on*,
That will be damn'd for't. *Shakesp. Winter's Tale.*

PU'TTINGSTONE. *n. s.*

In some parts of Scotland, stones for the same purpose are laid at the gates of great houses, which they call *puttingstones*, for trials of strength. *Pope.*

PU'TTOCK. *n. s.* [derived, by *Minshew*, from *buteo*, Lat.] A buzzard.

Who finds the partridge in the *puttock's* nest,
But may imagine how the bird was dead. *Shakesp.*

The next are those, which are called birds of prey, as the eagle, hawk, *puttock*, and cormorant. *Peacham.*

PU'TTY. *n. s.*

1. A kind of powder on which glass is ground.

An object glass of a fourteen foot telescope, made by an artificer at London, I once mended considerably, by grinding it on pitch with *putty*, and leaning on it very easily in the grinding, lest the *putty* should scratch it. *Newton.*

2. A kind of cement used by glaziers.

To PU'ZZLE. *v. a.* [for *postle*, from *pose. Skinner.*]

1. To perplex; to confound; to embarrass; to entangle; to gravel; to put to a stand; to teaze.

Your presence needs must *puzzle* Antony. *Shakesp.*

I say there is no darkness but ignorance, in which thou art more *puzzled* than the Egyptians in their fog. *Shakesp.*

Both armies of the enemy would have been *puzzled* what to have done. *Clarendon, b.* viii.

A very shrewd disputant in those points is dexterous in *puzzling* others, if they be not thorough-paced speculators in those great theories. *More's Divine Dialogues.*

He is perpetually *puzzled* and perplexed amidst his own blunders, and mistakes the sense of those he would confute. *Addison.*

Persons, who labour under real evils, will not *puzzle* themselves with conjectural ones. *Clarissa.*

2. To make intricate; to entangle.

The ways of heaven are dark and intricate,
Puzzled in mazes, and perplex'd with error. *Addison.*

These, as my guide informed me, were men of subtle tempers, and *puzzled* politicks, who would supply the place of real wisdom with cunning and avarice. *Tatler*, Nº 81.

I did not indeed at first imagine there was in it such a jargon of ideas, such an inconsistency of notions, such a confusion of particles, that rather *puzzle* than connect the sense, which in some places he seems to have aimed at, as I found upon my nearer perusal of it. *Addison.*

To PU'ZZLE. *v. n.* To be bewildered in one's own notions; to be aukward.

The servant is a *puzzling* fool, that heeds nothing. *L'Estr.*

PU'ZZLE. *n. s.* [from the verb.] Embarasment; perplexity.

Men in great fortunes are strangers to themselves, and while they are in the *puzzle* of business, they have no time to tend their health either of body or mind. *Bacon's Essays.*

PU'ZZLER. *n. s.* [from *puzzle.*] He who puzzles.

PY'GARG. *n. s.* A bird. *Ainsworth.*

PY'GMEAN. *adj.* [from *pygmy.*] Belonging to a pygmy.

They, less than smallest dwarfs in narrow room,
Throng numberless like that *pygmean* race
Beyond the Indian mount. *Milton.*

PY'GMY. *n. s.* [*pygmée*, Fr. πυγμαῖος.] A dwarf; one of a nation fabled to be only three spans high, and after long wars to have been destroyed by cranes.

If they deny the present spontaneous production of larger plants, and confine the earth to as *pygmy* births in the vegetable kingdom, as they do in the other; yet surely in such a supposed universal decay of nature, even mankind itself that is now nourished, though not produced, by the earth, must have degenerated in stature and strength in every generation. *Bentley.*

PYLO'RUS. *n. s.* [πυλωρὸς.] The lower orifice of the stomach.

PY'POWDER. See PIEPOWDER.

PY'RAMID. *n. s.* [*pyramide*, Fr. πύραμις, from πῦρ, fire; because fire always ascends in the figure of a cone.] In geometry, is a solid figure, whose base is a polygon, and whose sides are plain triangles, their several points meeting in one. *Harris.*

Know, Sir, that I will not wait pinion'd at your master's court; rather make my country's high *pyramids* my gibbet, and hang me up in chains. *Shakesp. Ant. and Cleopatra.*

An hollow crystal *pyramid* he takes,
In firmamental waters dipt above,
Of it a broad extinguisher he makes,
And hoods the flames. *Dryden.*

Part of the ore is shot into quadrilateral *pyramids. Woodw.*

PYRA'MIDAL. }
PYRAMI'DICAL. } *adj.* [from *pyramid.*] Having the form of a pyramid.

Of which sort likewise are the gems or stones, that are here shot into cubes, into *pyramidal* forms, or into angular columns. *Woodward's Nat. Hist.*

The *pyramidical* idea of its flame, upon occasion of the candles, is what is in question. *Locke.*

PYRAMI'DICALLY. *adv.* [from *pyramidical.*] In form of a pyramid.

Olympus is the largest, and therefore he makes it the basis upon which Ossa stands, that being the next to Olympus in magnitude, and Pelion being the least, is placed above Ossa, and thus they rise *pyramidically. Broome's Notes on Odyssey.*

PY'RAMIS. *n. s.* A pyramid.

The form of a *pyramis* in flame, which we usually see, is merely by accident, and that the air about, by quenching the sides of the flame, crusheth it, and extenuateth it into that form, for of itself it would be round, and therefore smoke is in the figure of a *pyramis* reversed; for the air quencheth the flame, and receiveth the smoke. *Bacon's Nat. Hist.*

PYRE. *n. s.* [*pyra*, Lat.] A pile to be burnt.

When his brave son upon the fun'ral *pyre*
He saw extended, and his beard on fire. *Dryden.*
With tender billet-doux he lights the *pyre*,
And breathes three am'rous sighs to raise the fire. *Pope.*

PYRI'TES. *n. s.* [from πῦρ.] Firestone.

Pyrites contains sulphur, sometimes arsenick, always iron, and sometimes copper. *Woodward.*

PY'ROMANCY. *n. s.* [πυρομαντία.] Divination by fire.

Divination was invented by the Persians, and is seldom or never taken in a good sense: there are four kinds of divination, hydromancy, *pyromancy*, aeromancy, geomancy. *Ayliffe.*

PYROTE'CHNICAL. *adj.* [*pyrotechnique*, Fr. from *pyrotechnicks.*] Engaged or skilful in fireworks.

PYROTE'CHNICKS. *n. s.* [πῦρ and τεχνὴ.] The act of employing fire to use or pleasure; the act of fireworks.

PYROTE'CHNY. *n. s.* [*pyrotechnie*, Fr.] The art of managing fire.

Great discoveries have been made by the means of *pyrotechny* and chymistry, which in late ages have attained to a greater height than formerly. *Hale's Origin of Mankind.*

PY'RRHONISM. *n. s.* [from *Pyrrho*, the founder of the scepticks.] Scepticism; universal doubt.

PYX. *n. s.* [*pyxis*, Latin.] The box in which the Romanists keep the host.

9

Q.

Q, Is a consonant borrowed from the Latin or French, for which, though *q* is commonly placed in the Saxon alphabet, the Saxons generally used *cp*, *cw*; as *cpellan* or *cwellan*, to quell: *qu* is, in English, pronounced as by the Italians and Spaniards *cw*; as *quail*, *quench*, except *quoit*, which is spoken, according to the manner of the French, *coit*: the name of this letter is *cue*, from *queue*, French, tail; its form being that of an O with a tail.

QUAB. *n. s.* [derived, by *Skinner*, from *gobio*, the Latin name.] A sort of fish.

To QUACK. *v. n.* [*quacken*, Dutch, to cry as a goose.]

1. To cry like a duck. This word is often written *quaake*, to represent the sound better.

Wild-ducks *quack* where grasshoppers did sing. *King.*

2. To chatter boastingly; to brag loudly; to talk ostentatiously.

Believe mechanick virtuosi
Can raise them mountains in Potosi,
Seek out for plants with signatures,
To *quack* of universal cures. *Hudibras, p.* iii.

QUACK. *n. s.* [from the verb.]

1. A boastful pretender to arts which he does not understand.

The change, schools and pulpits are full of *quacks*, jugglers and plagiaries. *L'Estrange.*

Some *quacks* in the art of teaching, pretend to make young gentlemen masters of the languages, before they can be masters of common sense. *Felton on the Classicks.*

2. A vain boastful pretender to physick; one who proclaims his own medical abilities in publick places.

At the first appearance that a French *quack* made in Paris: a little boy walked before him, publishing with a shrill voice, "My father cures all sorts of distempers;" to which the doctor added in a grave manner, "The child says true." *Addison.*

3. An artful tricking practitioner in physick.

Despairing *quacks* with curses fled the place,
And vile attorneys, now an useless race. *Pope.*

QUA'CKERY. *n. s.* [from *quack*.] Mean or bad acts in physick.

QUA'CKSALVER. *n. s.* [*quack* and *salve*.] One who brags of medicines or salves; a medicaster; a charlatan.

Saltimbancoes, *quacksalvers* and charlatans deceive the vulgar in lower degrees; were Æsop alive, the piazza and the pont neuf could speak their fallacies. *Brown.*

Many poor country vicars, for want of other means, are driven to their shifts; to turn mountebanks, *quacksalvers* and empiricks. *Burton on Melancholy.*

QUADRA'GESIMAL. *adj.* [*quadragesimal*, Fr. *quadragesima*, Latin.] Lenten; belonging to Lent; used in Lent.

I have composed prayers out of the church collects, advental, *quadragesimal*, paschal, or pentecostal. *Sanderson.*

QUA'DRANGLE. *n. s.* [*quadratus* and *angulus*, Latin.] A square; a surface with four right angles.

My choler being overblown
With walking once about the *quadrangle*,
I come to talk. *Shakesp. Henry* VI.

The escurial hath a *quadrangle* for every month in the year. *Howel.*

QUADRA'NGULAR. *adj.* [from *quadrangle*.] Square; having four right angles.

Common salt shooteth into little crystals, coming near to a cube, sometimes into square plates, sometimes into short *quadrangular* prisms. *Grew's Cosmol.*

Each environed with a crust, conforming itself to the planes, is of a figure *quadrangular*. *Woodward.*

I was placed at a *quadrangular* table, opposite to the macebearer. *Spectator*, N° 617.

QUA'DRANT. *n. s.* [*quadrans*, Lat.]

1. The fourth part; the quarter.

In sixty-three years may be lost eighteen days, omitting the intercalation of one day every fourth year, allowed for this *quadrant* or six hours supernumerary. *Brown.*

2. The quarter of a circle.

The obliquity of the ecliptick to the equator, and from thence the diurnal differences of the sun's right ascensions, which finish their variations in each *quadrant* of the circle of the ecliptick, being joined to the former inequality, arising from the excentricity, makes these quarterly and seeming irregular inequalities of natural days. *Holder on Time.*

3. An instrument with which altitudes are taken.

Some had compasses, others *quadrants*. *Tatler*, N° 81.

Thin taper sticks must from one center part;
Let these into the *quadrant's* form divide. *Gay.*

QUADRA'NTAL. *adj.* [from *quadrant*.] Included in the fourth part of a circle.

To fill that space of dilating, proceed in strait lines, and dispose of those lines in a variety of parallels: and to do that in a *quadrantal* space, there appears but one way possible; to form all the interfections, which the branches make, with angles of forty-five degrees only. *Derham's Physico-Theol.*

QUA'DRATE. *adj.* [*quadratus*, Latin.]

1. Square; having four equal and parallel sides.

2. Divisible into four equal parts.

The number of ten hath been extolled, as containing even, odd, long and plain, *quadrate* and cubical numbers. *Brown.*

Some tell us, that the years Moses speaks of were somewhat above the monthly year, containing in them thirty-six days, which is a number *quadrate*. *Hakewill on Providence.*

3. [*Quadrans*, Lat.] Suited; applicable. This perhaps were more properly *quadrant*.

The word consumption, being applicable to a proper or improper consumption, requires a generical description, *quadrate* to both. *Harvey on Consumptions.*

QUA'DRATE. *n. s.*

1. A square; a surface with four equal and parallel sides.

And 'twixt them both a *quadrate* was the base,
Proportion'd equally by seven and nine;
Nine was the circle set in heaven's place,
All which compacted, made a goodly diapase. *Fa. Queen.*

Whether the exact *quadrate* or the long square be the better, is not well determined; I prefer the latter, provided the length do not exceed the latitude above one third part. *Wotton.*

The powers militant
That stood for heav'n, in mighty *quadrate* join'd
Of union irresistible, mov'd on
In silence their bright legions. *Milton.*

To our finite understanding a *quadrate*, whose diagonal is commensurate to one of the sides, is a plain contradiction. *More's Divine Dialogues.*

2. [*Quadrat*, Fr.] In astrology, an aspect of the heavenly bodies, wherein they are distant from each other ninety degrees, and the same with quartile. *Dict.*

To QUA'DRATE. *v. n.* [*quadro*, Lat. *quadrer*, Fr.] To suit; to be accommodated.

Aristotle's rules for Epick poetry, which he had drawn from his reflections upon Homer, cannot be supposed to *quadrate* exactly with the heroick poems, which have been made since his time; as it is plain, his rules would have been still more perfect, could he have perused the Æneid. *Addison.*

QUA'DRATICK. *adj.* Four square; belonging to a square. *Dict.*

QUADRATICK *equations*. In algebra, are such as retain, on the unknown side, the square of the root or the number sought: and are of two sorts; first, simple quadraticks, where the square of the unknown root is equal to the absolute number given; secondly, affected quadraticks, which are such as have, between the highest power of the unknown number and the absolute number given, some intermediate power of the unknown number. *Harris.*

QUADRA'TURE. *n. s.* [*quadrature*, Fr. *quadratura*, Latin.]

1. The act of squaring.

The speculations of algebra, the doctrine of infinites, and the *quadrature* of curves should not intrench upon our studies of morality. *Watts's Improvement of the Mind.*

2. The

2. The first and last quarter of the moon.

It is full moon, when the earth being between the sun and moon, we see all the enlightened part of the moon; new moon, when the moon being between us and the sun, its enlightened part is turned from us; and half moon, when the moon being in the *quadratures*, we see but half the enlightened part. *Locke.*

3. The state of being square; a quadrate; a square.

All things parted by th' empyreal bounds,
His *quadrature* from thy orbicular world. *Milton.*

QUADRE'NNIAL. *adj.* [*quadriennium*, from *quatuor* and *annus*, Latin.]

1. Comprising four years.
2. Happening once in four years.

QUA'DRIBLE. *adj.* [from *quadro*, Lat.] That may be squared.

Sir Isaac Newton discovered a way of attaining the quantity of all *quadrible* curves analytically, by his method of fluxions, some time before the year 1688. *Derham.*

QUADRI'FID. *adj.* [*quadrifidis*, Lat.] Cloven into four divisions.

QUADRILA'TERAL. *adj.* [*quadrilatere*, Fr. *quatuor* and *latus*, Lat.] Having four sides.

Tin incorporated with crystal, disposes it to shoot into a *quadrilateral* pyramid, sometimes placed on a *quadrilateral* base or column. *Woodward on Fossils.*

QUADRILA'TERALNESS. *n. s.* [from *quadrilateral.*] The property of having four right lined sides, forming as many right angles. *Dict.*

QUA'DRILLE. *n. s.* A game at cards. *Dict.*

QUA'DRIN. *n. s.* [*quadrinus*, Lat.] A mite; a small piece of money, in value about a farthing. *Bailey.*

QUA'DRINOMICAL. *adj.* [*quatuor* and *nomen*, Lat.] Consisting of four denominations. *Dict.*

QUA'DRIPARTITE. *adj.* [*quatuor* and *partitus*, Lat.] Havingfour parties; divided into four parts.

QUA'DRIPARTITELY. *adv.* [from *quadripartite.*] In a quadripartite distribution.

QUADRIPARTI'TION. *n. s.* A division by four, or the taking the fourth part of any quantity or number. *Dict.*

QUADRIPHY'LLOUS. *adj.* [*quatuor* and φύλλον.] Having four leaves.

QUADRIRE'ME. *n. s.* [*quadriremis*, Lat.] A galley with four banks of oars.

QUADRISY'LLABLE. *n. s.* [*quatuor* and *syllable.*] A word of four syllables.

QUADRIVA'LVES. *n. s.* [*quatuor* and *valvæ*, Lat.] Doors with four folds.

QUADRI'VIAL. *adj.* [*quadrivium*, Lat.] Having four ways meeting in a point.

QUADRU'PED. *n. s.* [*quadrupede*, Fr. *quadrupes*, Lat.] An animal that goes on four legs, as perhaps all beasts.

The different flexure and order of the joints is not disposed in the elephant, as in other *quadrupeds*. *Brown.*

The fang teeth, eye teeth, or dentes canini of some *quadruped*. *Woodward on Fossils.*

Most *quadrupedes*, that live upon herbs, have incisor teeth to pluck and divide them. *Arbuthnot.*

The king of brutes,
Of *quadrupeds* I only mean. *Swift.*

QUADRU'PED. *adj.* Having four feet.

The cockney, travelling into the country, is surprized at many actions of the *quadruped* and winged animals. *Watts.*

QUADRUPLE. *adj.* [*quadruple*, Fr. *quadruplus*, Lat.] Fourfold; four times told.

A law, that to bridle theft doth punish thieves with a *quadruple* restitution, hath an end which will continue as long as the world itself continueth. *Hooker.*

The lives of men on earth might have continued double, treble or *quadruple*, to any of the longest times of the first age. *Raleigh's History of the World.*

Fat refreshes the blood in the penury of aliment during the winter, and some animals have a *quadruple* caul. *Arbuthnot.*

To QUADRU'PLICATE *v. a.* [*quadrupler*, Fr. *quadruplico*, Lat.] To double twice; to make fourfold.

QUADRUPLICA'TION. *n. s.* [from *quadruplicate.*] The taking a thing four times.

QUADRU'PLY. *adv.* [from *quadruple.*] To a fourfold quantity.

If the person accused maketh his innocence appear, the accuser is put to death, and out of his goods the innocent person is *quadruply* recompensed. *Swift.*

QUÆRE. [Latin.] Enquire; seek; a word put when any thing is recommended to enquiry.

Quære, if 'tis steeped in the same liquor, it may not prevent the fly and grub. *Mortimer's Husbandry.*

To QUAFF. *v. a.* [of this word the derivation is uncertain: *Junius*, with his usual idleness of conjecture, derives it from the Greek, κυαφίζειν in the Eolick dialect used for κυαθίζειν. *Skinner* from *go off*, as *go off*, *guoff*, *quoff*, *quaff*. It comes from *coeffer*, Fr. to be drunk.] To drink; to swallow in large draughts.

He calls for wine; a health, quoth he, as if
H' ad been abroad carousing to his mates
After a storm, *quafft* off the muscadel,
And threw the sops all in the sexton's face. *Shakesp.*

I found the prince,
With such a deep demeanour in great sorrow,
That tyranny, which never *quafft* but blood,
Would, by beholding him, have wash'd his knife
With gentle eye drops. *Shakesp. Henry* IV. *p.* ii.

On flow'rs repos'd, and with rich flow'rets crown'd,
They eat, they drink, and in communion sweet
Quaff immortality and joy. *Milton's Par. Lost, b.* v.

To QUAFF. *v. n.* To drink luxuriously.

We may contrive this afternoon,
And *quaff* carouses to our mistress' health. *Shakesp.*

Belshazzer, *quaffing* in the sacred vessels of the temple, sees his fatal sentence writ by the fingers of God. *South.*

Twelve days the gods their solemn revels keep,
And *quaff* with blameless Ethiops in the deep. *Dryden.*

QUA'FFER. *n. s.* [from *quaff.*] He who quaffs.

To QUA'FFER. *v. n.* [a low word, I suppose, formed by chance.] To feel out. This seems to be the meaning.

Ducks, having larger nerves that come into their bills than geese, *quaffer* and grope out their meat the most. *Derham.*

QUA'GGY. *adj.* [from *quagmire.*] Boggy; soft; not solid. *Ainf.*
This word is somewhere too in *Clarissa.*

QUA'GMIRE. *n. s.* [that is, *quakemire.*] A shaking marsh; a bog that trembles under the feet.

The fen and *quagmire*, so marish by kind,
Are to be drained. *Tusser.*

Your hearts I'll stamp out with my horse's heels,
And make a *quagmire* of your mingled brains. *Shakesp.*

Poor Tom! whom the foul fiend hath through ford and whirlpool, o'er bog and *quagmire*. *Shakesp.*

The wet particles might have easily ever mingled with the dry, and so all had either been sea or *quagmire*. *More.*

The brain is of such a clammy consistence, that it can no more retain motion than a *quagmire*. *Glanvill's Sceps.*

QUAID. *part.* [of this participle I know not the verb, and believe it only put by *Spenser*, who often took great liberties, for *quailed*, for the poor convenience of his rhyme.] Crushed; dejected; depressed.

Therewith his sturdy courage soon was *quaid*,
And all his senses were with sudden dread dismaid. *F. Qu.*

QUAIL. *n. s.* [*quaglia*, Italian.] A bird of game.

His *quails* ever
Beat mine, in-hoop'd at odds. *Shakesp. Ant. and Cleop.*

Hen birds have a peculiar sort of voice, when they would call the male, which is so eminent in *quails*, that men, by counterfeiting this voice with a *quail* pipe, easily drew the cocks into their snares. *Ray on the Creation.*

A fresher gale
Sweeping with shadowy gust the field of corn,
While the *quail* clamours for his running mate. *Thomson.*

QUAILPIPE. *n. s.* [*quail* and *pipe.*] A pipe with which fowlers allure quails.

A dish of wild fowl furnished conversation, which concluded with a late invention for improving the *quailpipe*. *Addison's Spectator*, N° 108.

To QUAIL. *v. n.* [*quelen*, Dutch.] To languish; to sink into dejection; to lose spirit. *Spenser.*

He writes there is no *quailing* now;
Because the king is certainly possest
Of all our purposes. *Shakesp. Henry* IV. *p.* i.

This may plant courage in their *quailing* breasts,
For yet is hope of life and victory. *Shakesp.*

After Solyman had with all his power in vain besieged Rhodes, his haughty courage began to *quail*, so that he was upon point to have raised his siege. *Knolles.*

While rocks stand,
And rivers stir, thou can'st not shrink or *quail*;
Yea, when both rocks and all things shall disband,
Then shalt thou be my rock and tower. *Herbert.*

When Dido's ghost appear'd,
It made this hardy warriour *quail*. *Wandering Pr. of Troy.*

At this the errant's courage *quails*. *Cleaveland.*

To pass the *quailing* and withering of all things by the recess, and their reviving by the reaccess of the sun, the sap in trees precisely follows the motion of the sun. *Hakewill.*

To QUAIL. *v. a.* [cpellan, Saxon.] To crush; to quell; to depress; to sink; to overpower.

To drive him to despair, and quite to *quail*,
He shewed him painted in a table plain
The damned ghosts. *Fairy Queen, b.* i.

Three, with fi'ry courage, he assails;
Three, all as kings adorn'd in royal wise:
And each successive after other *quails*,
Still wond'ring whence so many kings should rise. *Daniel.*

QUAINT. *adj.* [*coint*, Fr. *comptus*, Lat.]

1. Nice; scrupulously, minutely, superfluously exact; having petty elegance.

Each ear sucks up the words a true love scattereth,
And plain speech oft, than *quaint* phrase framed is. *Sidney.*

You

You were glad to be employ'd,
To shew how *quaint* an orator you are. *Shakesp.*

He spends some pages about two similitudes; one of mine, and another *quainter* of his own. *Stillingfleet.*

2. Subtle; artful. Obsolete.

As clerkes been full subtle and *queint*. *Chaucer.*

3. Neat; pretty; exact.

But for a fine, *quaint*, graceful and excellent fashion, yours is worth ten on't. *Shakesp.*

Her mother hath intended,
That, *quaint* in green, she shall be loose enrob'd
With ribbands pendent, flaring 'bout her head. *Shakesp.*

I never saw a better fashion'd gown,
More *quaint*, more pleasing, nor more commendable. *Sha.*

4. Subtly excogitated; finespun.

I'll speak of frays,
Like a fine bragging youth, and tell *quaint* lies,
How honourable ladies sought my love,
Which I denying they fell sick and died. *Shakesp.*

He his fabrick of the heav'ns
Hath left to their disputes, perhaps to move
His laughter at their *quaint* opinions wide
Hereafter. *Milton's Par. Lost, b.* viii.

5. *Quaint* is, in *Spenser*, quailed; depressed. I believe by a very licentious irregularity.

With such fair slight him Guyon fail'd:
Till at the last, all breathless, weary and faint,
Him spying, with fresh onset he assail'd,
And kindling new his courage, seeming *quaint*,
Struck him so hugely, that through great constraint
He made him stoop. *Fairy Queen, b.* ii.

6. Affected; foppish. This is not the true idea of the word, which *Swift* seems not to have well understood.

To this we owe those monstrous productions, which under the name of trips, spies, amusements, and other conceited appellations, have overrun us; and I wish I could say, those *quaint* fopperies were wholly absent from graver subjects. *Sw.*

QUAI'NTLY. *adv.* [from *quaint.*]

1. Nicely; exactly; with petty elegance.

When was old Sherewood's hair more *quaintly* curl'd,
Or nature's cradle more enchas'd and purl'd. *B. Johnson.*

2. Artfully.

Breathe his faults so *quaintly*,
That they seem the taints of liberty,
The flash and outbreak of a fiery mind. *Shakesp.*

3. Ingeniously with success. This is not the true sense.

As my Buxoma
With gentle finger stroak'd her milky care,
I *quaintly* stole a kiss. *Gay.*

QUAI'NTNESS. *n. s.* [from *quaint.*] Nicety; petty elegance.

There is a certain majesty in simplicity, which is far above all the *quaintness* of wit. *Pope.*

To QUAKE. *v. n.* [cpacan, Saxon.]

1. To shake with cold or fear; to tremble.

Dorus threw Pamela behind a tree, where she stood *quaking* like the partridge on which the hawk is even ready to seize. *Sidney, b.* i.

If Cupid hath not spent all his quiver in Venice, thou wilt *quake* for this. *Shakespeare.*

Do such business as the better day
Would *quake* to look on. *Shakesp. Hamlet.*

Who honours not his father,
Henry the fifth, that made all France to *quake*,
Shake he his weapon at us, and pass by. *Shakesp.*

The mountains *quake* at him, and the hills melt, and the earth is burnt at his presence. *Nah.* i. 5.

Son of man eat thy bread with *quaking*, and drink thy water with trembling and carefulness. *Ezek.* xii. 18.

In fields they dare not fight where honour calls,
The very noise of war their souls does wound,
They *quake* but hearing their own trumpets sound. *Dryden.*

2. To shake; not to be solid or firm.

Next Smedley div'd; slow circles dimpled o'er
The *quaking* mud, that clos'd and op'd no more. *Pope.*

QUAKE. *n. s.* [from the verb.] A shudder; a tremulous agitation.

As the earth may sometimes shake,
For winds shut up will cause a *quake*;
So often jealousy and fear,
Stol'n to mine heart, cause tremblings there. *Suckling.*

QUAKING-GRASS. *n. s.* An herb. *Ainsworth.*

QUALIFICA'TION. *n. s.* [*qualification*, Fr. from *qualify.*]

1. That which makes any person or thing fit for any thing.

It is in the power of the prince to make piety and virtue become the fashion, if he would make them necessary *qualifications* for preferment. *Swift.*

2. Accomplishment.

Good *qualifications* of mind enable a magistrate to perform his duty, and tend to create a publick esteem of him. *Atter.*

3. Abatement; diminution.

Neither had the waters of the flood infused such an impurity, as thereby the natural and powerful operation of all plants, herbs and fruits upon the earth received a *qualification* and harmful change. *Raleigh's History of the World.*

To QUALIFY. *v. a.* [*qualifier*, Fr.]

1. To fit for any thing.

Place over them such governors, as may be *qualified* in such manner as may govern the place. *Bacon's Advice to Villiers.*

I bequeath to Mr. John Whiteway the sum of one hundred pounds, in order to *qualify* him for a surgeon. *Swift's Will.*

2. To furnish with qualifications; to accomplish.

That which ordinary men are fit for, I am *qualified* in; and the best of me is diligence. *Shakesp. King Lear.*

She is of good esteem,
Her dowry wealthy, and of worthy birth,
Beside so *qualified*, as may beseem
The spouse of any noble gentleman. *Shakesp.*

3. To make capable of any employment or privilege.

4. To abate; to soften; to diminish.

I have heard,
Your grace hath ta'en great pains to *qualify*
His rig'rous course. *Shakesp. Merchant of Venice.*

I do not seek to quench your love's hot fire,
But *qualify* the fire's extreme rage,
Lest it should burn above the bounds of reason. *Shakesp.*

I have drunk but one cup to-night, and that was craftily *qualified* too; and behold what innovation it makes here. *Sha.*

They would report that they had records for twenty thousand years, which must needs be a very great untruth, unless we will *qualify* it, expounding their years not of the revolution of the sun, but of the moon. *Abbot.*

It hath so pleased God to provide for all living creatures, wherewith he hath filled the world, that such inconveniences, as we contemplate afar off, are found, by trial and the witness of men's travels, to be so *qualified*, as there is no portion of the earth made in vain. *Raleigh's Hist. of the World.*

So happy 'tis you move in such a sphere,
As your high majesty with awful fear
In human breasts might *qualify* that fire,
Which kindled by those eyes had flamed higher. *Waller.*

Children should be early instructed in the true estimate of things, by opposing the good to the evil, and compensating or *qualifying* one thing with another. *L'Estrange.*

My proposition I have *qualified* with the word, often; thereby making allowance for those cases, wherein men of excellent minds may, by a long practice of virtue, have renered even the heights and rigours of it delightful. *Atterbury.*

5. To ease; to assuage.

He balms and herbs therto apply'd,
And evermore with mighty spells them charm'd,
That in short space he has them *qualify'd*,
And him restor'd to health, that would have dy'd. *Spenser.*

6. To modify; to regulate.

It hath no larinx or throttle to *qualify* the sound. *Brown.*

QUA'LITY. *n. s.* [*qualitas*, Lat. *qualité*, Fr.]

1. Nature relatively considered.

These, being of a far other nature and *quality*, are not so strictly or everlastingly commanded in scripture. *Hooker.*

Other creatures have not judgment to examine the *quality* of that which is done by them, and therefore in that they do, they neither can accuse nor approve themselves. *Hooker.*

Since the event of an action usually follows the nature or *quality* of it, and the *quality* follows the rule directing it, it concerns a man, in the framing of his actions, not to be deceived in the rule. *South.*

The power to produce any idea in our mind, I call *quality* of the subject, wherein that power is. *Locke.*

2. Property; accident.

In the division of the kingdom, it appears not which of the dukes he values most; for *qualities* are so weighed, that curiosity in neither can make choice of either's moiety. *Shak.*

No sensible *qualities*, as light and colour, heat and sound, can be subsistent in the bodies themselves absolutely considered, without a relation to our eyes and ears, and other organs of sense: these *qualities* are only the effects of our sensation, which arise from the different motions upon our nerves from objects without, according to their various modification and position. *Bentley.*

3. Particular efficacy.

O, mickle is the powerful grace, that lies
In plants, herbs, stones, and their true *qualities*. *Shakesp.*

4. Disposition; temper.

To-night we'll wander through the streets, and note
The *qualities* of people. *Shakesp. Ant. and Cleopatra.*

5. Virtue or vice.

One doubt remains, said I, the dames in green,
What were their *qualities*, and who their queen? *Dryden.*

6. Accomplishment; qualification.

He had those *qualities* of horsemanship, dancing and fencing, which accompany a good breeding. *Clarendon.*

7. Character.

The attorney of the dutchy of Lancaster partakes of both *qualities*, partly of a judge in that court, and partly of an attorney general. *Bacon's Advice to Villiers.*

We,

We, who are hearers, may be allowed some opportunities in the *quality* of standers-by. *Swift.*

8. Comparative or relative rank.

It is with the clergy, if their persons be respected, even as it is with other men; their *quality* many times far beneath that which the dignity of their place requireth. *Hooker.*

We lived most joyful, obtaining acquaintance with many of the city, not of the meanest *quality*. *Bacon.*

The masters of these horses may be admitted to dine with the lord lieutenant: this is to be done, what *quality* soever the persons are of. *Temple.*

9. Rank; superiority of birth or station.

Let him be so entertained, as suits with gentlemen of your knowing to a stranger of his *quality*. *Shakesp. Cymbeline.*

10. Persons of high rank. Collectively.

I shall appear at the masquerade dressed up in my feathers, that the *quality* may see how pretty they will look in their travelling habits. *Addison's Guardian*, Nº 112.

Of all the servile herd, the worst is he,
That in proud dullness joins with *quality*,
A constant critick at the great man's board,
To fetch and carry nonsense for my lord. *Pope.*

QUALM. *n. s.* [cpealm, Saxon, a sudden stroke of death.] A sudden fit of sickness; a sudden seizure of sickly languor.

Some sudden *qualm* hath struck me to the heart,
And dimm'd mine eyes, that I can read no further. *Shak.*

Some distill'd carduus benedictus, laid to your heart, is the only thing for a *qualm*. *Shakesp.*

Compar'd to these storms, death is but a *qualm*,
Hell somewhat lightsome, the Bermudas calm. *Donne.*

I find a cold *qualm* come over my heart, that I faint, I can speak no longer. *Howel.*

All maladies
Of ghastly spasm, or racking torture, *qualms*
Of heart-sick agony. *Milton's Par. Lost.*

For who, without a *qualm*, hath ever look'd
On holy garbage, though by Homer cook'd. *Roscommon.*

They have a sickly uneasiness upon them, shifting and changing from one error, and from one *qualm* to another, hankering after novelties. *L'Estrange's Fables.*

Thy mother well deserves that short delight,
The nauseous *qualms* of ten months and travail to requite. *Dryden's Virgil.*

When he hath stretched his vessels with wine to their utmost capacity, and is grown weary and sick, and feels those *qualms* and disturbances that usually attend such excesses, he resolves, that he will hereafter contain himself within the bounds of sobriety. *Calamy.*

The *qualms* or ruptures of your blood
Rise in proportion to your food. *Prior.*

QUA'LMISH. *adj.* [from *qualm.*] Seized with sickly languor.

I am *qualmish* at the smell of leek. *Shakesp.*

You drop into the place,
Careless and *qualmish* with a yawning face. *Dryden.*

QUA'NDARY. *n. s.* [*qu'en dirai je*, Fr. *Skinner.*] A doubt; a difficulty; an uncertainty. A low word.

QUA'NTITIVE. *adj.* [*quantitivus*, Lat.] Estimable according to quantity.

This explication of rarity and density, by the composition of substance with quantity, may peradventure give little satisfaction to such who are apt to conceive therein no other composition or resolution, but such as our senses shew us, in compounding and dividing bodies according to *quantitive* parts. *Digby on Bodies.*

QUA'NTITY. *n. s.* [*quantité*, Fr. *quantitas*, Lat.]

1. That property of any thing which may be encreased or diminished.

Quantity is what may be increased or diminished. *Cheyne.*

2. Any indeterminate weight or measure.

3. Bulk or weight.

Unskill'd in hellebore, if thou shou'dst try
To mix it, and mistake the *quantity*,
The rules of physick wou'd against thee cry. *Dryden.*

4. A portion; a part.

If I were saw'd into *quantities*, I should make four dozen of such bearded hermites staves as master Shallow. *Shakesp.*

5. A large portion.

The warm antiscorbutical plants, taken in *quantities*, will occasion stinking breath, and corrupt the blood. *Arbuthnot.*

6. The measure of time in pronouncing a syllable.

The easy pronunciation of a mute before a liquid does not necessarily make the preceding vowel, by position, long in *quantity*; as patrem. *Holder's Elements of Speech.*

QUA'NTUM. *n. s.* [Latin.] The quantity; the amount.

The *quantum* of presbyterian merit, during the reign of that ill-advised prince, will easily be computed. *Swift.*

QUA'RANTAIN. } *n. s.* [*quarantain*, Fr.] The space of forty
QUA'RANTINE. } days, being the time which a ship, suspected of infection, is obliged to forbear intercourse or commerce.

Pass your *quarantine* among some of the churches round this town, where you may learn to speak before you venture to expose your parts in a city congregation. *Swift.*

QUA'RREL. *n. s.* [*querelle*, Fr.]

1. A brawl; a petty fight; a scuffle.

If I can fasten but one cup upon him,
With that which he hath drank to-night already,
He'll be as full of *quarrel* and offence,
As my young mistress' dog. *Shakesp. Othello.*

2. A dispute; a contest.

The part, which in this present *quarrel* striveth against the current and stream of laws, was a long while nothing feared. *Hooker's Dedication.*

As if earth too narrow were for fate,
On open seas their *quarrels* they debate;
In hollow wood they floating armies bear,
And forc'd imprison'd winds to bring 'em near. *Dryden.*

3. A cause of debate.

I could not die any where so contented, as in the king's company; his cause being just, and his *quarrel* honourable. *Shakesp. Henry V.*

If not in service of our God we fought,
In meaner *quarrel* if this sword were shaken,
Well might thou gather in the gentle thought,
So fair a princess should not be forsaken. *Fairfax.*

4. Something that gives a right to mischief or reprisal.

He thought he had a good *quarrel* to attack him. *Holingsh.*

Wives are young men's mistresses, companions for middle age, and old men's nurses; so a man may have a *quarrel* to marry when he will. *Bacon's Essays.*

5. Objection; ill will.

Herodias had a *quarrel* against him, and would have killed him, but she could not. *Mar.* vi. 19.

We are apt to pick *quarrels* with the world for every little foolery. *L'Estrange.*

I have no *quarrel* to the practice; it may be a diverting way. *Felton on the Classicks.*

6. In *Shakespeare*, it seems to signify any one peevish or malicious.

Better
She ne'er had known pomp, though't be temporal;
Yet if that *quarrel*, fortune, do divorce
It from the bearer, 'tis a suff'rance panging
As soul and body's sev'ring. *Shakesp. Henry VIII.*

7. [From *quadreau*, Fr. *quadrella*, Italian.] An arrow with a square head.

It is reported by William Brito, that the arcubalista or arbalist was first shewed to the French by our king Richard I. who was shortly after slain by a *quarrel* thereof. *Camden.*

Twang'd the string, outflew the *quarrel* long. *Fairfax.*

To QUA'RREL. *v. n.* [*quereller*, Fr.]

1. To debate; to scuffle; to squabble.

I love the sport well, but I shall as soon *quarrel* at it as any man. *Shakesp.*

Your words have taken such pains, as if they labour'd
To bring manslaughter into form, set *quarrelling*
Upon the head of valour. *Shakesp. Timon of Athens.*

Wine drunken with excess, maketh bitterness of the mind, with brawling and *quarrelling*. *Eccluſ.* xxxi. 29.

Beasts called sociable, *quarrel* in hunger and lust; and the bull and ram appear then as much in fury and war, as the lion and the bear. *Temple's Miscellanies.*

2. To fall into variance.

Our discontented counties do revolt;
Our people *quarrel* with obedience. *Shakesp. King John.*

3. To fight; to combat.

When once the Persian king was put to flight,
The weary Macedons refus'd to fight;
Themselves their own mortality confess'd,
And left the son of Jove to *quarrel* for the rest. *Dryden.*

4. To find fault; to pick objections.

To admit the thing, and *quarrel* about the name, is to make ourselves ridiculous. *Bramhall against Hobbs.*

They find out miscarriages wherever they are, and forge them often where they are not; they *quarrel* first with the officers, and then with the prince and state. *Temple.*

In a poem elegantly writ,
I will not *quarrel* with a slight mistake. *Roscommon.*

I *quarrel* not with the word, because used by Ovid. *Dryd.*

QUA'RRELLER. *n. s.* [from *quarrel.*] He who quarrels.

QUA'RRELLOUS. *adj.* [*querelleux*, Fr.] Petulant; easily provoked to enmity; quarrelsome.

Ready in gybes, quick answered, saucy, and
As *quarrellous* as the weazel. *Shakesp. Cymbeline.*

QUA'RRELSOME. *adj.* [from *quarrel.*] Inclined to brawls; easily irritated; irascible; cholerick; petulant.

Cholerick and *quarrelsome* persons will engage one into their quarrels. *Bacon's Essays.*

There needs no more to the setting of the whole world in a flame, than a *quarrelsome* plaintiff and defendant. *L'Estr.*

QUA'RRELSOMELY. *adv.* [from *quarrelsome.*] In a quarrelsome manner; petulantly; cholerickly.

QUA'RRELSOMENESS. *n. f.* [from *quarrelfome.*] Cholerickness; petulance.

QUA'RRY. *n. f.* [*quarrè*, Fr.]

1. A fquare.

To take down a *quarry* of glafs to fcowre, fodder, band, and to fet it up again, is three halfpence a foot. *Mortimer.*

2. [*Quadreau*, Fr.] An arrow with a fquare head.

The fhafts and *quarries* from their engines fly
As thick as falling drops in April fhow'rs. *Fairfax.*

3. [From *querir*, to feek, Fr. *Skinner*; from *carry*, *Kennet.*] Game flown at by a hawk.

Your wife and babes
Savagely flaughter'd; to relate the manner,
Were on the *quarry* of thefe murder'd deer
To add the death of you. *Shakefp. Macbeth.*

She dwells among the rocks, on every fide
With broken mountains ftrongly fortify'd;
From thence whatever can be feen furveys,
And ftooping, on the flaughter'd *quarry* preys. *Sandys.*

So fcented the grim feature, and up turn'd
His noftrils wide into the murky air,
Sagacious of his *quarry.* *Milton.*

They their guns difcharge;
This heard fome fhips of ours, though out of view,
And fwift as eagles to the *quarry* flew. *Waller.*

An hollow cryftal pyramid he takes,
In firmamental waters dipt above,
Of it a broad extinguifher he makes,
And hoods the flames that to their *quarry* ftrove. *Dryden.*

No toil, no hardfhip can reftrain
Ambitious man inur'd to pain;
The more confin'd, the more he tries,
And at forbidden *quarry* flies. *Dryden's Horace.*

Ere now the god his arrows had not try'd,
But on the trembling deer or mountain goat,
At this new *quarry* he prepares to fhoot. *Dryden.*

Let reafon then at her own *quarry* fly,
But how can finite grafp infinity. *Dryden.*

4. [*Quarriere*, *quarrel*, Fr. from *carrig*, Irifh, a ftone, Mr. *Lye*; *craigg*, Erfe, a rock.] A ftone mine; a place where they dig ftones.

The fame is faid of ftone out of the *quarry*, to make it more durable. *Bacon's Nat. Hift.*

Pyramids and tow'rs
From diamond *quarries* hewn, and rocks of gold. *Milton.*

Here though grief my feeble hands up lock,
Yet on the foften'd *quarry* would I fcore
My plaining verfe as lively as before. *Milton.*

An hard and unrelenting fhe,
As the new-crufted Niobe;
Or, what doth more of ftatue carry,
A nun of the Platonick *quarry.* *Cleaveland.*

He like Amphion makes thofe *quarries* leap
Into fair figures from a confus'd heap. *Waller.*

Could neceffity infallibly produce *quarries* of ftone, which are the materials of all magnificent ftructures. *More.*

For them alone the heav'ns had kindly heat
In eaftern *quarries*, ripening precious dew. *Dryden.*

As long as the next coal-pit, *quarry* or chalk-pit will give abundant atteftation to what I write, to thefe I may very fafely appeal. *Woodward's Nat. Hift.*

To QUA'RRY. *v. n.* [from the noun.] To prey upon. A low word not in ufe.

With cares and horrors at his heart, like the vulture that is day and night *quarrying* upon Prometheus's liver. *L'Eftrange.*

QU'ARRYMAN. *n. f.* [*quarry* and *man.*] One who digs in a quarry.

One rhomboidal bony fcale of the needle-fifh, out of Stunsfield quarry, the *quarryman* affured me was flat, covered over with fcales, and three foot long. *Woodward.*

QUART. *n. f.* [*quart*, Fr.]

1. The fourth part; a quarter. Not in ufe.

Albanact had all the northern part,
Which of himfelf Albania he did call,
And Camber did poffefs the weftern *quart.* *Fairy Queen.*

2. The fourth part of a gallon.

When I have been dry, and bravely marching, it hath ferved me inftead of a *quart* pot to drink in. *Shakefp.*

You have made an order, that ale fhould be fold at three halfpence a *quart.* *Swift's Mifcellanies.*

3. [*Quarte*, Fr.] The veffel in which ftrong drink is commonly retailed.

You'd rail upon the hoftefs of the houfe,
And fay you would prefent her at the leet,
Becaufe fhe bought ftone jugs and no feal'd *quarts.* *Shakefp.*

QUA'RTAN. *n. f.* [*febris quartana*, Lat.] The fourth day ague.

It were an uncomfortable receipt for a *quartan* ague, to lay the fourth book of Homer's Iliads under one's head. *Brown.*

Call her the metaphyficks of her fex,
And fay fhe tortures wits, as *quartans* vex
Phyficians. *Cleaveland.*

Among thefe, *quartans* and tertians of a long continuance moft menace this fymptom. *Harvey on Confumptions.*

A look fo pale no *quartan* ever gave,
Thy dwindled legs feem crawling to the grave. *Dryden.*

QUARTA'TION. *n. f.* [from *quartus*, Lat.] A chymical operation.

In *quartation*, which refiners employ to purify gold, although three parts of filver be fo exquifitely mingled by fufion with a fourth part of gold, whence the operation is denominated, that the refulting mafs acquires feveral new qualities; yet, if you caft this mixture into aqua fortis, the filver will be diffolved in the menftruum, and the gold like a dark powder will fall to the bottom. *Boyle.*

QUA'RTER. *n. f.* [*quart*, *quartier*, Fr.]

1. A fourth part.

It is an accuftomed action with her, to feem thus wafhing her hands; I have known her continue in this a *quarter* of an hour. *Shakefp. Macbeth.*

Suppofe the common depth of the fea, taking one place with another, to be about a *quarter* of a mile. *Burnet.*

Obferve what ftars arife or difappear,
And the four *quarters* of the rolling year. *Dryden.*

Suppofing only three millions to be paid, 'tis evident that to do this out of commodities, they muft, to the confumer, be raifed a *quarter* in their price; fo that every thing, to him that ufes it, muft be a *quarter* dearer. *Locke.*

2. A region of the fkies, as referred to the feaman's card.

I'll give thee a wind.
—I myfelf have all the other,
And the very points they blow,
And all the *quarters* that they know
I' th' fhipman's card. *Shakefp. Macbeth.*

His praife, ye winds! that from four *quarters* blow,
Breathe foft or loud. *Milton's Par. Loft, b.* v.

When the winds in fouthern *quarters* rife,
Ships, from their anchors torn, become their fport,
And fudden tempefts rage within the port. *Addifon.*

3. A particular region of a town or country.

The like is to be faid of the populoufnefs of their coafts and *quarters* there. *Abbot's Defcription of the World.*

No leaven fhall be feen in thy *quarters.* *Exodus* xiii. 7.

The fons of the church being fo much difperfed, though without being driven, into all *quarters* of the land, there was fome extraordinary defign of divine wifdom in it. *Sprat.*

A bungling cobler, that was ready to ftarve at his own trade, changes his *quarter*, and fets up for a doctor. *L'Eftr.*

4. The place where foldiers are lodged or ftationed.

Where is lord Stanley quarter'd?
—Unlefs I have mifta'en his *quarters* much,
His regiment lies half a mile
South from the mighty power of the king. *Shakefp.*

The *quarters* of the fev'ral chiefs they fhow'd,
Here Phenix, here Achilles made abode. *Dryden.*

It was high time to fhift my *quarters.* *Spectator.*

5. Proper ftation.

They do beft, who, if they cannot but admit love, yet make it keep *quarter*, and fever it wholly from their ferious affairs. *Bacon's Effays.*

Swift to their feveral *quarters* hafted then
The cumbrous elements. *Milton.*

6. Remiffion of life; mercy granted by a conqueror.

He magnified his own clemency, now they were at his mercy, to offer them *quarter* for their lives, if they gave up the caftle. *Clarendon, b.* viii.

When the cocks and lambs lie at the mercy of cats and wolves, they muft never expect better *quarter.* *L'Eftrange.*

Difcover the opinion of your enemies, which is commonly the trueft; for they will give you no *quarter*, and allow nothing to complaifance. *Dryden.*

7. Treatment fhown by an enemy.

To the young if you give any tolerable *quarter*, you indulge them in their idlenefs, and ruin them. *Collier.*

Mr. Wharton, who detected fome hundreds of the bifhop's miftakes, meets with very ill *quarter* from his lordfhip. *Swift.*

8. Friendfhip; amity; concord. Not now in ufe.

Friends, all but now,
In *quarter*, and in terms like bride and groom
Diverting them for bed, and then, but now
Swords out, and tilting one at other's breafts. *Shakefp.*

9. A meafure of eight bufhels.

There may be kept in it fourteen thoufand *quarters* of corn, which is two thoufand *quarters* in each loft. *Mortimer.*

10. Falfe *quarter* is a cleft or chink in a *quarter* of a horfe's hoof from top to bottom; it generally happens on the infide of it, that being the weakeft and thinneft part.

To QUA'RTER. *v. a.* [from the noun.]

1. To divide into four parts.

A thought that *quarter'd*, hath but one part wifdom,
And ever three parts coward. *Shakefp. Hamlet.*

2. To divide; to break by force.

You tempt the fury of my three attendants,
Lean famine, *quartering* fteel, and climbing fire. *Shakefp.*

Mothers fhall but fmile, when they behold
Their infants *quarter'd* by the hands of war. *Shakefp.*

3. To divide

3. To divide into distinct regions.

Then sailors *quarter'd* heav'n, and found a name
For ev'ry fixt and ev'ry wand'ring star. *Dryden.*

4. To station or lodge soldiers.

When they hear the Roman horses neigh,
Behold their *quarter'd* fires,
They will waste their time upon our note,
To know from whence we are. *Shakesp. Cymbeline.*
Where is lord Stanley *quarter'd?*
—His regiment lies half a mile south. *Shakesp. Rich.* III.
They o'er the barren shore pursue their way,
Where *quarter'd* in their camp, the fierce Thessalians lay. *Dryden.*

You have *quartered* all the foul language upon me, that could be raked out of Billingsgate. *Spectator*, N° 595.

5. To lodge; to fix on a temporary dwelling.

They mean this night in Sardis to be *quarter'd. Shakesp.*

6. To diet.

He fed on vermin;
And when these fail'd, he'd suck his claws,
And *quarter* himself upon his paws. *Hudibras, p.* i.

7. To bear as an appendage to the hereditary arms.

The first ordinary and natural, being compounded of argent and azure, is the coat of Beauchamp of Hack in the county of Somerset, now *quartered* by the earl of Hertford. *Peacham on Blazoning.*

QUA'RTERAGE. *n. s.* [from *quarter.*] A quarterly allowance.

He us'd two equal ways of gaining,
By hindring justice or maintaining;
To many a whore gave privilege,
And whipp'd for want of *quarterage.* *Hudibras, p.* iii.

QUA'RTERDAY. *n. s.* [*quarter* and *day.*] One of the four days in the year, on which rent or interest is paid.

The usurer would be very well satisfied to have all the time annihilated, that lies between the present moment and next *quarterday.* *Addison's Spectator*, N° 93.

QUA'RTERDECK. *n. s.* [*quarter* and *deck.*] The short upper deck.

QUA'RTERLY. *adj.* [from *quarter.*] Containing a fourth part.

The moon makes four *quarterly* seasons within her little year or month of consecution. *Holder on Time.*

From the obliquity of the ecliptick to the equator arise the diurnal differences of the sun's right ascension, which finish their variations in each quadrant of the ecliptick, and this being added to the former inequality from eccentricity, makes these *quarterly* and seemingly irregular inequalities of natural days. *Bentley.*

QUA'RTERLY. *adv.* Once in a quarter of a year.

QUA'RTERMASTER. *n. s.* [*quarter* and *master.*] One who regulates the quarters of soldiers.

The *quartermaster* general was marking the ground for the encampment of the covering army. *Tatler*, N° 62.

QUA'RTERN. *n. s.* A gill or the fourth part of a pint.

QUA'RTERSTAFF. *n. s.* A staff of defence: so called, I believe, from the manner of using it; one hand being placed at the middle, and the other equally between the middle and the end.

His *quarterstaff*, which he could ne'er forsake,
Hung half before, and half behind his back. *Dryden.*

Immense riches he squandered away at *quarterstaff* and cudgel play, in which he challenged all the country. *Arbuth.*

QUA'RTILE. *n. s.* An aspect of the planets, when they are three signs or ninety degrees distant from each other, and is marked thus □. *Harris.*

Mars and Venus in a *quartile* move
My pangs of jealousy for Ariet's love. *Dryden.*

QUA'RTO. *n. s.* [*quartus*, Lat.] A book in which every sheet, being twice doubled, makes four leaves.

Our fathers had a just value for regularity and systems; then folio's and *quarto's* were the fashionable sizes, as volumes in octavo are now. *Watts.*

To QUASH. *v. a.* [*quassen*, Dutch; *squacciare*, Italian; *quasso*, Latin.]

1. To crush; to squeeze.

The whales
Against sharp rocks like reeling vessels *quash'd*,
Though huge as mountains, are in pieces dash'd. *Waller.*

2. To subdue suddenly.

'Twas not the spawn of such as these,
That dy'd with Punick blood the conquer'd seas,
And *quash'd* the stern Æacides. *Roscommon.*

Our she confederates keep pace with us in *quashing* the rebellion, which had begun to spread itself among part of the fair sex. *Addison's Freeholder*, N° 15.

3. [*Cassus*, Lat. *casser*, Fr.] To annul; to nullify; to make void: as, *the indictment was* quashed.

To QUASH. *v. n.* To be shaken with a noise.

A thin and fine membrane strait and closely adhering to keep it from *quashing* and shaking. *Ray on the Creation.*

The water in this dropsy, by a sudden jirk, may be heard to *quash.* *Sharp's Surgery.*

QUASH. *n. s.* A pompion. *Ainsworth.*

QUA'TERCOUSINS. As, *they are not* quater-cousins, as it is commonly spoken *cater-cousins, plus ne sont pas de quatre cousins*, they are not of the four first degrees of kindred, that is, they are not friends. *Skinner.*

QUATE'RNARY. *n. s.* [*quaternarius*, Lat.] The number four.

The objections against the *quaternary* of elements and ternary of principles, needed not to be opposed so much against the doctrines themselves. *Boyle.*

QUATE'RNION. *n. s.* [*quaternio*, Lat.] The number four.

Air and the elements! the eldest birth
Of nature's womb, that in *quaternion* run
Perpetual circle, multiform; and mix
And nourish all things; let your ceaseless change
Vary to our great maker still new praise. *Milton.*

I have not in this scheme of these nine *quaternions* of consonants, distinct known characters, whereby to express them, but must repeat the same. *Holder's Elements of Speech.*

QUATE'RNITY. *n. s.* [*quaternus*, Lat.] The number four.

The number of four stands much admired, not only in the *quaternity* of the elements, which are the principles of bodies, but in the letters of the name of God. *Brown.*

QUA'TRAIN. *n. s.* [*quatrain*, Fr.] A stanza of four lines rhyming alternately: as,

Say, Stella, what is love, whose fatal pow'r
Robs virtue of content, and youth of joy?
What nymph or goddess in a luckless hour
Disclos'd to light the mischief-making boy. *Mrs. Mulso.*

I have writ my poem in *quatrains* or stanza's of four in alternate rhyme, because I have ever judged them of greater dignity for the sound and number, than any other verse in use. *Dryden.*

To QUA'VER. *v. n.* [cpavan, Saxon.]

1. To shake the voice; to speak or sing with a tremulous voice.

Miso sitting on the ground with her knees up, and her hands upon her knees tuning her voice with many a *quavering* cough, thus discoursed. *Sidney, b.* ii.

The division and *quavering*, which please so much in musick, have an agreement with the glittering of light playing upon a wave. *Bacon's Nat. Hist.*

Now sportive youth
Carol incondite rhythms with suiting notes,
And *quaver* unharmonious. *Philips.*

We shall hear her *quavering* them half a minute after us, to some sprightly airs of the opera. *Addison.*

2. To tremble; to vibrate.

A membrane, stretched like the head of a drum, is to receive the impulse of the sound, and to vibrate or *quaver* according to its reciprocal motions. *Ray on the Creation.*

If the eye and the finger remain quiet, these colours vanish in a second minute of time, but if the finger be moved with a *quavering* motion, they appear again. *Newton's Opticks.*

QUAY. *n. s.* [*quai*, Fr.] A key; an artificial bank to the sea or river, on which goods are conveniently unladen.

QUEAN. *n. s.* [cpean, Saxon, a barren cow; þorcpen, in the laws of Canute, a strumpet.] A worthless woman, generally a strumpet.

As fit as the nail to his hole, or as a scolding *quean* to a wrangling knave. *Shakesp.*

This well they understand like cunning *queans*,
And hide their nastiness behind the scenes. *Dryden.*
Such is that sprinkling, which some careless *quean*
Flirts on you from her mop. *Swift.*

QUEA'SINESS. *n. s.* [from *queasy.*] The sickness of a nauseated stomach.

QUEA'SY. *adj.* [of uncertain etymology.]

1. Sick with nausea.

He, *queasy* with his insolence already,
Will their good thoughts call from him. *Shakesp.*
Whether a rotten state and hope of gain,
Or to disuse me from the *queasy* pain
Of being belov'd and loving,
Out-push me first. *Donne.*

2. Fastidious; squeamish.

I, with your two helps, will so practise on Benedict, that, in despight of his quick wit and his *queasy* stomach, he shall fall in love with Beatrice. *Shakesp.*

The humility of Gregory the great would not admit the stile of bishop, but the ambition of Boniface made no scruple thereof, nor have *queasy* resolutions been harboured in their successors ever since. *Brown's Vulgar Errours.*

Men's stomachs are generally so *queasy* in these cases, that it is not safe to overload them. *Government of the Tongue.*

Without question,
Their conscience was too *queasy* of digestion. *Dryden.*

3. Causing nauseousness.

I have one thing of a *queasy* question,
Which I must act. *Shakesp. King Lear.*

To QUECK. *v. n.* To shrink; to show pain; perhaps to complain.

The lads of Sparta were accustomed to be whipped at altars, without so much as *quecking.* *Bacon.*

QUEEN. *n. s.* [cpen, Saxon, a woman, a wife, the wife of a king.]

1. The wife of a king.

He was lapt
In a most curious mantle, wrought by the hand
Of his *queen* mother. *Shakesp. Cymbeline.*

2. A woman who is sovereign of a kingdom.

That *queen* Elizabeth lived sixty-nine, and reigned forty-five years, means no more than, that the duration of her existence was equal to sixty-nine, and the duration of her government to forty-five annual revolutions of the sun. *Locke.*

Have I a *queen*
Past by my fellow rulers of the world?
Have I refus'd their blood to mix with yours,
And raise new kings from so obscure a race? *Dryden.*

To QUEEN. *v. n.* To play the queen.

A threepence bow'd would hire me,
Old as I am, to *queen* it. *Shakesp. Henry* VIII.

Of your own state take care: this dream of mine,
Being now awake, I'll *queen* it no inch farther,
But milk my ewes and weep. *Shakesp. Winter's Tale.*

QUEEN-APPLE. *n. s.* A species of apple.

The *queen-apple* is of the summer kind, and a good cyder apple mixed with others. *Mortimer's Husbandry.*

Her cheeks with kindly claret spread,
Aurora like new out of bed,
Or like the fresh *queen-apple*'s side,
Blushing at sight of Phœbus' pride. *Sidney, b.* ii.

QUEE'NING. *n. s.* An apple.

The winter *queening* is good for the table. *Mortimer.*

QUEER. *adj.* [of this word the original is not known: a correspondent supposes a *queer* man to be one who has a *quære* to his name in a list.] Odd; strange; original; particular.

He never went to bed till two in the morning, because he would not be a *queer* fellow; and was every now and then knocked down by a constable, to signalize his vivacity. *Spect.*

QUEE'RLY. *adv.* [from *queer.*] Particularly; oddly.

QUEE'RNESS. *n. s.* [from *queer.*] Oddness; particularity.

QUE'EST. *n. s.* [from *questus*, Lat. *Skinner.*] A ringdove; a kind of wild pigeon.

To QUELL. *v. a.* [cpellan, Saxon.] To crush; to subdue; originally, to kill.

What avails
Valour or strength, though matchless, *quell'd* with pain,
Which all subdues, and makes remiss the hands
Of mightiest? *Milton's Par. Lost, b.* vi.

Compassion *quell'd*
His best of man, and gave him up to tears
A space; till firmer thoughts restrain'd excess. *Milton.*

This *quell'd* her pride, but other doubts remain'd,
That once disdaining, she might be disdain'd. *Dryden.*

He is the guardian of the publick quiet, appointed to restrain violence, to *quell* seditions and tumults, and to preserve that peace which preserves the world. *Atterbury.*

To QUELL. *v. n.* To die. *Spenser.*

QUELL. *n. s.* [from the verb.] Murder. Not in use.

What can not we put upon
His spungy followers, who shall bear the guilt
Of our great *quell.* *Shakesp. Macbeth.*

QUE'LLER. *n. s.* [from *quell.*] One that crushes or subdues.

Hail son of the most high,
Queller of Satan, on thy glorious work
Now enter. *Milton's Paradise Regain'd, b.* iv.

QUE'LQUECHOSE. [French.] A trifle; a kickshaw.

From country grass to comfitures of court,
Or city's *quelquechoses*, let not report
My mind transport. *Donne.*

To QUEME. *v. n.* [cpeman, Saxon.] To please. An old word. *Skinner.*

To QUENCH. *v. a.*

1. To extinguish fire.

Since stream, air, sand, mine eyes and ears conspire,
What hope to *quench*, where each thing blows the fire. *Sidn.*

No English soul
More stronger to direct you than yourself;
If with the sap of reason you would *quench*,
Or but allay, the fire of passion. *Shakesp. Henry* VIII.

This is the way to kindle, not to *quench.* *Shakesp.*

A little fire is quickly trodden out,
Which, being suffer'd, rivers cannot *quench.* *Shakesp.*

The fire had power in the water, forgetting his own virtue; and the water forgat his own *quenching* nature. *Wisd.* xix. 20.

Milk *quencheth* wild-fire better than water, because it entreth better. *Bacon's Nat. Hist.*

Subdu'd in fire the stubborn metal lies;
One draws and blows reciprocating air,
Others to *quench* the hissing mass prepare. *Dryden.*

You have already *quench'd* sedition's brand,
And zeal, which burnt it, only warms the land. *Dryden.*

When your work is forged, do not *quench* it in water to cool it, but throw it down upon the floor or hearth to cool of itself; for the *quenching* of it in water will harden it. *Moxon.*

2. To still any passion or commotion.

But if all aim but this be lev'll'd false,
The supposition of the lady's death
Will *quench* the wonder of her infamy. *Shakesp.*

3. To allay thirst.

Every draught to him, that has *quenched* his thirst, is but a further quenching of nature, a provision for rheum and diseases, a drowning of the spirits. *South.*

4. To destroy.

When death's form appears, she feareth not
An utter *quenching* or extinguishment;
She would be glad to meet with such a lot,
That so she might all future ill prevent. *Davies.*

Covered with skin and hair keeps it warm, being naturally very cold, and also to *quench* and dissipate the force of any stroke, and retund the edge of any weapon. *Ray.*

To QUENCH. *v. n.* To cool; to grow cool.

Dost thou think, in time
She will not *quench*, and let instructions enter
Where folly now possesses? *Shakesp. Cymbeline.*

QUE'NCHABLE. *adj.* [from *quench.*] That may be quenched.

QUE'NCHER. *n. s.* [from *quench.*] Extinguisher; one that quenches.

QUE'NCHLESS. *adj.* [from *quench.*] Unextinguishable.

Come, bloody Clifford, rough Northumberland,
I dare your *quenchless* fury to more rage. *Shakesp.*

The judge of torments, and the king of tears,
He fills a burnish'd throne of *quenchless* fire. *Crashaw.*

QUE'RELE. *n. s.* [*querela*, Lat. *querelle*, Fr.] A complaint to a court.

A circumduction obtains not in causes of appeal, but in causes of first instance and simple *querele* only. *Ayliffe.*

QUE'RENT. *n. s.* [*querens*, Latin.] The complainant; the plaintiff.

QUERIMO'NIOUS. *adj.* [*querimonia*, Latin.] Querulous; complaining.

QUERIMO'NIOUSLY. *adv.* [from *querimonious.*] Querulously; with complaint.

To thee, dear Thom, myself addressing,
Most *querimoniously* confessing. *Denham.*

QUERIMO'NIOUSNESS. *n. s.* [from *querimonious.*] Complaining temper.

QUE'RIST. *n. s.* [from *quæro*, Lat.] An enquirer; an asker of questions.

I shall propose some considerations to my gentle *querist.* *Spect.*

The juggling sea god, when by chance trepan'd
By some instructed *querist* sleeping on the strand,
Impatient of all answers, strait became
A stealing brook. *Swift's Miscellanies.*

QUERN. *n. s.* [cpeoɲn, Saxon.] A handmill.

Skim milk, and sometimes labour in the *quern*,
And bootless make the breathless huswife churn. *Shakesp.*

Some apple-colour'd corn
Ground in fair *querns*, and some did spindles turn. *Chapm.*

QUE'RPO. *n. s.* [corrupted from *cuerpo*, Spanish.] A dress close to the body; a waistcoat.

I would fain see him walk in *querpo*, like a cased rabbit, without his holy furr upon his back. *Dryden.*

QUE'RRY, for *equerry. n. s.* [*ecuyer*, Fr.] A groom belonging to a prince, or one conversant in the king's stables, and having the charge of his horses; also the stable of a prince. *Bailey.*

QUE'RULOUS. *adj.* [*querulus*, Latin.] Mourning; habitually complaining.

Although they were a people by nature hard-hearted, *querulous*, wrathful and impatient of rest and quietness, yet was there nothing of force to work the subversion of their state, till the time before-mentioned was expired. *Hooker.*

The pressures of war have cowed their spirits, as may be gathered from the very accent of their words, which they prolate in a whining kind of *querulous* tone, as if still complaining and crest-fallen. *Howel's Vocal Forest.*

Though you give no countenance to the complaints of the *querulous*, yet curb the insolence of the injurious. *Locke.*

QUE'RULOUSNESS. *n. s.* [from *querulous.*] Habit or quality of complaining mournfully.

QUE'RY. *n. s.* [from *quære*, Lat.] A question; an enquiry to be resolved.

I shall conclude, with proposing only some *queries*, in order to a farther search to be made by others. *Newton.*

This shews the folly of this *query*, that might always be demanded, that would impiously and absurdly attempt to tie the arm of omnipotence from doing any thing at all, because it can never do its utmost. *Bentley.*

To QUE'RY. *v. a.* [from the noun.] To ask questions.

Three Cambridge sophs
Each prompt to *query*, answer and debate. *Pope.*

QUEST. *n. s.* [*queste*, Fr.]

1. Search; act of seeking.

None but such as this bold ape unblest,
Can ever thrive in that unlucky *quest.* *Hubberd's Tale.*

If lusty love should go in *quest* of beauty,
Where should he find it fairer than in Blanch. *Shakesp.*

Fair

Fair silver buskin'd nymphs,
I know this *quest* of yours and free intent
Was all in honour and devotion meant,
To the great mistress of your princely shrine. *Milton.*
An aged man in rural weeds,
Following, as seem'd, the *quest* of some stray ewe. *Milton.*
One for all
Myself expose, with lonely steps to tread
Th' unfounded deep, and the void immense
To search with wand'ring *quest* a place foretold
Should be. *Milton's Paradise Lost, b.* ii.
Since first break of dawn, the fiend,
Mere serpent in appearance, forth was come,
And on his *quest*, where likeliest he might find
The only two of mankind. *Milton.*

'Twould be not strange, should we find Paradise at this day where Adam left it; and I the rather note this, because I see there are some so earnest in *quest* of it. *Woodward.*

There's not an African,
That traverses our vast Numidian desarts
In *quest* of prey, and lives upon his bow,
But better practises these boasted virtues. *Addison's Cato.*

We see them active and vigilant in *quest* of delight. *Spect.*

2. [For *inquest.*] An empanell'd jury.
What's my offence?
Where is the evidence, that doth accuse me?
What lawful *quest* have given their verdict up
Unto the frowning judge. *Shakesp. Richard* III.

3. Searchers. Collectively.
You have been hotly call'd for,
When, being not at your lodging to be found,
The senate sent above three several *quests*
To search you out. *Shakesp. Othello.*

4. Enquiry; examination.
O place and greatness! millions of false eyes
Are stuck upon thee; volumes of report
Run with these false and most contrarious *quests*
Upon thy doings. *Shakesp. Measure for Measure.*

5. Request; desire; solicitation.
Gad not abroad at every *quest* and call
Of an untrained hope or passion. *Herbert.*

To QUEST. *v. n.* [*quêter*, Fr. from the noun.] To go in search.

QUE'STANT. *n. s.* [from *quester*, Fr.] Seeker; endeavourer after.
See, that you come
Not to woo honour, but to wed it; when
The bravest *questant* shrinks, find what you seek,
That fame may cry you loud. *Shakesp.*

QUE'STION. *n. s.* [*question*, Fr. *quæstio*, Latin.]

1. Interrogatory; any thing enquired.
Because he that knoweth least is fittest to ask *questions*, it is more reason for the entertainment of the time, that ye ask me *questions*, than that I ask you. *Bacon.*

2. Enquiry; disquisition.
It is to be put to *question*, whether it be lawful for christian princes to make an invasive war simply for the propagation of the faith. *Bacon's Holy War.*

3. A dispute; a subject of debate.
There arose a *question* between some of John's disciples and the Jews about purifying. *Jo.* iii. 25.

4. Affair to be examined.
In points of honour to be try'd,
Suppose the *question* not your own. *Swift.*

5. Doubt; controversy; dispute.
This is not my writing,
Though I confess much like the character:
But out of *question* 'tis Maria's hand. *Shakesp.*

'Tis time for him to shew himself, when his very being is called in *question*, and to come and judge the world, when men begin to doubt whether he made it. *Tillotson.*

The doubt of their being native impressions on the mind, is stronger against these moral principles than the other; not that it brings their truth at all in *question*. *Locke.*

Our own earth would be barren and desolate, without the benign influence of the solar rays, which without *question* is true of all the other planets. *Bentley.*

6. Judicial trial.
But whosoever be found guilty, the communion book hath surely deserved least to be called in *question* for this fault. *Hooker, b.* v. *s.* 31.

7. Examination by torture.
Such a presumption is only sufficient to put the person to the rack or *question*, according to the civil law, and not bring him to condemnation. *Ayliffe's Parergon.*

8. State of being the subject of present enquiry.
If we being defendants do answer, that the ceremonies in *question* are godly, comely, decent, profitable for the church, their reply is childish and unorderly to say, that we demand the thing in *question*, and shew the poverty of our cause, the goodness whereof we are fain to beg that our adversaries would grant. *Hooker, b.* iv. *s.* 4.

If he had said, it would purchase six shillings and threepence weighty money, he had proved the matter in *question*. *Locke.*

Nor are these assertions that dropped from their pens by chance, but delivered by them in places where they profess to state the points in *question*. *Atterbury's Preface.*

9. Endeavour; search. Not in use.
As it more concerns the Turk than Rhodes,
So may he with more facile *question* bear it;
For that it stands not in such warlike brace,
But altogether lacks the abilities
That Rhodes is dress'd in. *Shakesp.*

To QUE'STION. *v. n.* [from the noun.]

1. To enquire.
Suddenly out of this delightful dream
The man awoke, and would have *question'd* more;
But he would not endure the woful theme. *Spenser.*

He that *questioneth* much shall learn much, and content much; but especially if he apply his questions to the skill of the persons whom he asketh. *Bacon's Essays.*

2. To debate by interrogatories.
I pray you think you *question* with a Jew;
You may as well use question with the wolf,
Why he hath made the ewe bleat for the lamb. *Shakesp.*

To QUE'STION. *v. a.* [*questionner*, Fr.]

1. To examine one by questions.
Question your royal thoughts, make the case yours;
Be now the father, and propose a son;
Hear your own dignity so much prophan'd;
And then imagine me taking your part,
And in your pow'r so silencing your son. *Shakesp.*
But hark you, Kate,
I must not have you henceforth *question* me,
Whither I go. *Shakesp. Henry* IV, *p.* i.

This construction is not so undubitably to be received, as not at all to be *questioned*. *Brown's Vulgar Errours.*

2. To doubt; to be uncertain of.
O impotent estate of human life!
Where fleeting joy does lasting doubt inspire,
And most we *question* what we most desire. *Prior.*

3. To have no confidence in; to mention as not to be trusted.
Be a design never so artificially laid, if it chances to be defeated by some cross accident, the man is then run down, his counsels derided, his prudence *questioned*, and his person despised. *South's Sermons.*

QUE'STIONABLE. *adj.* [from *question.*]

1. Doubtful; disputable.
Your accustomed clemency will take in good worth, the offer of these my simple labours, bestowed for the necessary justification of laws heretofore made *questionable*, because not perfectly understood. *Hooker's Dedication.*

That persons drowned float, the ninth day when their gall breaketh, is a *questionable* determination, both in the time and cause. *Brown's Vulgar Errours.*

It is *questionable*, whether the use of steel springs was known in those ancient times. *Wilkins's Math. Magick.*

It is *questionable*, whether Galen ever saw the dissection of a human body. *Baker's Reflections on Learning.*

2. Suspicious; liable to suspicion; liable to question.
Be thy advent wicked or charitable,
Thou com'st in such a *questionable* shape,
That I will speak to thee. *Shakesp. Hamlet.*

QUE'STIONARY. *adj.* [from *question.*] Enquiring; asking questions.
I grow laconick even beyond laconicism; for sometimes I return only yes or no to *questionary* epistles of half a yard long. *Pope to Swift.*

QUE'STIONABLENESS. *n. s.* [from *question.*] The quality of being questionable.

QUE'STIONER. *n. s.* [from *question.*] An enquirer.

QUE'STIONLESS. *adv.* [from *question.*] Certainly; without doubt.
Questionless hence it comes that many were mistaken. *Ral.*
Questionless duty moves not so much upon command as promise; now that which proposes the greatest and most suitable rewards to obedience, and the greatest punishments to disobedience, doubtless is the most likely to inforce the one and prevent the other. *South.*

QUE'STMAN. } *n. s.* [*quest*, *man*, and *monger.*] Starter of
QUE'STMONGER. } lawsuits or prosecutions.
Their principal working was upon penal laws, wherein they spared none, great nor small, but raked over all new and old statutes, having ever a rabble of promoters, *questmongers*, and leading jurors at their command. *Bacon.*

QUE'STRIST. [from *quest.*] Seeker; pursuer.
Six and thirty of his knights,
Hot *questrists* after him, met him at the gate,
Are gone with him tow'rd Dover. *Shakesp. King Lear.*

QUE'STUARY. *adj.* [from *quæstus*, Lat.] Studious of profit.
Although lapidaries and *questuary* enquirers affirm it, yet the writers of minerals conceive the stone of this name to be a mineral concretion, not to be found in animals. *Brown.*

QUIB. *n. ſ.* A ſarcaſm; a bitter taunt. *Ainſ.* The ſame perhaps with *quip.*

To QUI'BBLE. *v. n.* [from the noun.] To pun; to play on the ſound of words.

The firſt ſervice was neats tongues ſliced, which the philoſophers took occaſion to diſcourſe and *quibble* upon in a grave formal way. *L'Eſtrange.*

QUI'BBLE. *n. ſ.* [from *quidlibet*, Latin.] A low conceit depending on the ſound of words; a pun.

This may be of great uſe to immortalize puns and *quibbles*, and to let poſterity ſee their forefathers were blockheads. *Add.*

Quirks or *quibbles* have no place in the ſearch after truth. *Watts.*

QUI'BBLER. *n. ſ.* [from *quibble.*] A punſter.

QUICK. *adj.* [cpic, Saxon.]

1. Living; not dead.

They ſwallowed us up *quick*, when their wrath was kindled againſt us. *Pſalm* cxxiv. 3.

If there be *quick* raw fleſh in the riſings, it is an old leproſy. *Lev.* xiii. 10.

The *quick* and the dead. *Common Prayer.*

As the ſun makes; here noon, there day, there night
Melts wax, dries clay, makes flow'rs, ſome *quick*, ſome dead. *Davies.*

Thence ſhall come,
When this world's diſſolution ſhall be ripe,
With glory and pow'r to judge both *quick* and dead. *Milt.*

2. Swift; nimble; done with celerity.

Prayers whereunto devout minds have added a piercing kind of brevity, thereby the better to expreſs that *quick* and ſpeedy expedition, wherewith ardent affections, the very wings of prayer, are delighted to preſent our ſuits in heaven. *Hooker, b.* v. *ſ.* 33.

3. Speedy; free from delay.

Oft he to her his charge of *quick* return
Repeated. *Milton's Paradiſe Loſt, b.* ix.

4. Active; ſpritely; ready.

A man of great ſagacity in buſineſs, and he preſerved ſo great a vigour of mind even to his death, when near eighty, that ſome, who had known him in his younger years, did believe him to have much *quicker* parts in his age than before. *Clarendon.*

A man muſt have paſſed his noviciate in ſinning, before he comes to this, be he never ſo *quick* a proficient. *South.*

The animal, which is firſt produced of an egg, is a blind and dull worm; but that which hath its reſurrection thence, is a *quick* eyed, volatile and ſprightly fly. *Grew's Coſmol.*

QUICK. *adv.* Nimbly; ſpeedily; readily.

Ready in gybes, *quick* anſwer'd, ſaucy, and
As quarrellous as the weazel. *Shakeſp. Cymbeline.*

This ſhall your underſtanding clear
Thoſe things from me that you ſhall hear,
Conceiving much the *quicker*. *Drayton's Nymphid.*

They gave thoſe complex ideas, that the things they were continually to give and receive information about, might be the eaſier and *quicker* underſtood. *Locke.*

This is done with little notice, if we conſider how very *quick* the actions of the mind are performed, requiring not time, but many of them crowded into an inſtant. *Locke.*

QUICK. *n. ſ.*

1. A live animal.

Peeping cloſe into the thick,
Might ſee the moving of ſome *quick*,
Whoſe ſhape appeared not;
But were it fairy, fiend or ſnake,
My courage earned it to wake,
And manful thereat ſhot. *Spenſer.*

2. The living fleſh; ſenſible parts.

If Stanley held, that a ſon of king Edward had ſtill the better right, it was to teach all England to ſay as much; and therefore that ſpeech touched the *quick*. *Bacon.*

Seiz'd with ſudden ſmart,
Stung to the *quick*, he felt it at his heart. *Dryden.*

The thoughts of this diſgraceful compoſition ſo touches me to the *quick*, that I cannot ſleep. *Arbuthnot's Hiſt. of J. Bull.*

Scarifying gangrenes, by ſeveral inciſions down to the *quick*, is almoſt univerſal, and with reaſon, ſince it not only diſcharges a pernicious ichor, but makes way for topical applications. *Sharp's Surgery.*

3. Living plants.

For incloſing of land, the moſt uſual way is with a ditch and bank ſet with *quick*. *Mortimer's Huſbandry.*

QUI'CKBEAM, or *quickentree. n. ſ.*

Quickbeam or wild ſorb, by ſome called the Iriſh aſh, is a ſpecies of wild aſh, preceded by bloſſoms of an agreeable ſcent. *Mortimer's Huſbandry.*

To QUI'CKEN. *v. a.* [cpiccan, Saxon.]

1. To make alive.

All they that go down into the duſt, ſhall kneel before him; and no man hath *quickened* his own ſoul. *Pſalm* xxii. 30.

I will never forget thy commandments; for with them thou haſt *quickened* me. *Pſalm* cxix.

This my mean taſk would be
As heavy to me, as 'tis odious; but
The miſtreſs which I ſerve, *quickens* what's dead,
And makes my labours pleaſures. *Shakeſp. Tempeſt.*

To *quicken* with kiſſing; had my lips that power,
Thus would I wear them out. *Shakeſp. Ant. and Cleop.*

Fair ſoul, ſince to the faireſt body join'd
You give ſuch lively life, ſuch *quick'ning* pow'r,
And influence of ſuch celeſtial kind,
As keeps it ſtill in youth's immortal flower. *Davies.*

He throws
His influence round, and kindles as he goes;
Hence flocks and herds, and men, and beaſts and fowls
With breath are *quicken'd*, and attract their ſouls. *Dryden.*

2. To haſten; to accelerate.

You may ſooner by imagination *quicken* or ſlack a motion, than raiſe or ceaſe it; as it is eaſier to make a dog go ſlower, than to make him ſtand ſtill. *Bacon's Nat. Hiſt.*

Others were appointed to conſider of penal laws and proclamations in force, and to *quicken* the execution of the moſt principal. *Hayward.*

Though any commodity ſhould ſhift hands never ſo faſt, yet, if they did not ceaſe to be any longer traffick, this would not at all make or *quicken* their vent. *Locke.*

3. To ſharpen; to actuate; to excite.

Though my ſenſes were aſtoniſhed, my mind forced them to *quicken* themſelves; becauſe I had learnt of him, how little favour he is wont to ſhew in any matter of advantage. *Sidney.*

It was like a fruitful garden without an hedge, that *quickens* the appetite to enjoy ſo tempting a prize. *South.*

They endeavour by brandy to *quicken* their taſte already extinguiſhed. *Tatler*, Nº 57.

This review he makes uſe of, as an argument of great force to *quicken* them in the improvement of thoſe advantages to which the mercy of God had called them by the goſpel. *Rogers's Sermons.*

The deſire of fame hath been no inconſiderable motive to *quicken* you in the purſuit of thoſe actions, which will beſt deſerve it. *Swift.*

To QUI'CKEN. *v. n.*

1. To become alive: as, *a woman* quickens *with child.*

Theſe hairs, which thou doſt raviſh from my chin,
Will *quicken* and accuſe thee; I'm your hoſt;
With robbers hands, my hoſpitable favour
You ſhould not ruffle thus. *Shakeſp. King Lear.*

They rub out of it a red duſt, that converteth after a while into worms, which they kill with wine when they begin to *quicken*. *Sandys's Journey.*

The heart is the firſt part that *quickens*, and the laſt that dies. *Ray on the Creation.*

2. To move with activity.

Sees by degrees a purer bluſh ariſe,
And keener lightnings *quicken* in her eyes. *Pope.*

QUI'CKENER. *n. ſ.* [from *quicken.*]

1. One who makes alive.

2. That which accelerates; that which actuates.

Love and enmity, averſation and fear are notable whetters and *quickeners* of the ſpirit of life in all animals. *More.*

QUI'CKLIME. *n. ſ.* [*calx viva*, Lat. *quick* and *lime.*] Lime unquenched.

After burning the ſtone, when lime is in its perfect and unaltered ſtate, it is called *quicklime*. *Hill's Materia Medica.*

QUI'CKLY. *adv.* [from *quick.*] Nimbly; ſpeedily; actively.

Thou com'ſt to uſe thy tongue: thy ſtory *quickly*. *Shak.*

Pleaſure dwells no longer upon the appetite than the neceſſities of nature, which are *quickly* and eaſily provided for; and then all that follows is an oppreſſion. *South.*

QUI'CKNESS. *n. ſ.* [from *quick.*]

1. Speed; velocity; celerity.

What any invention hath in the ſtrength of its motion, is abated in the ſlowneſs of it; and what it hath in the extraordinary *quickneſs* of its motion, muſt be allowed for in the great ſtrength that is required unto it. *Wilkins.*

Joy, like a ray of the ſun, reflects with a greater ardour and *quickneſs*, when it rebounds upon a man from the breaſt of his friend. *South's Sermons.*

2. Activity; briſkneſs.

The beſt choice is of an old phyſician and a young lawyer; becauſe, where errors are fatal, ability of judgment and moderation are required; but where advantages may be wrought upon, diligence and *quickneſs* of wit. *Wotton.*

The *quickneſs* of the imagination is ſeen in the invention, the fertility in the fancy, and the accuracy in the expreſſion. *Dryden.*

3. Keen ſenſibility.

Would not *quickneſs* of ſenſation be an inconvenience to an animal, that muſt lie ſtill. *Locke.*

4. Sharpneſs; pungency.

Thy gen'rous fruits, though gather'd ere their prime,
Still ſhew'd a *quickneſs*; and maturing time
But mellows what we write to the dull ſweets of rhime. *Dryden.*

Ginger renders it brisk, and corrects its windiness, and juice of corinths whereof a few drops tinge and add a pleasant *quickness*. *Mortimer's Husbandry.*

QUI'CKSAND. *n. s.* [*quick* and *sand.*] Moving sand; unsolid ground.

What is Edward, but a ruthless sea?
What Clarence, but a *quicksand* of deceit? *Shakesp.*

Undergirding the ship, and fearing lest they should fall into the *quicksands*, they strake sail, and so were driven. *Acts* xxvii.

But when the vessel is on *quicksands* cast,
The flowing tide does more the sinking haste. *Dryden.*

Trajan, by the adoption of Nerva, stems the tide to her relief, and like another Neptune shoves her off the *quicksands*. *Addison on Ancient Medals.*

I have marked out several of the shoals and *quicksands* of life, in order to keep the unwary from running upon them. *Addison.*

To QUI'CKSET. *v. a.* [*quick* and *set.*] To plant with living plants.

In making or mending, as needeth thy ditch,
Get set to *quickset* it, learn cunningly which. *Tusser.*

A man may ditch and *quickset* three poles a day, where the ditch is three foot wide and two foot deep. *Mortimer.*

QUI'CKSET. *n. s.* [*quick* and *set.*] Living plant set to grow.

Plant *quicksets* and transplant fruit trees towards the decrease. *Evelyn's Kalendar.*

Nine in ten of the *quickset* hedges are ruined for want of skill. *Swift's Miscellanies.*

QUICKSI'GHTED. *adj.* [*quick* and *sight.*] Having a sharp sight.

No body will deem the *quickestsighted* amongst them to have very enlarged views in ethicks. *Locke.*

No article of religion hath credility enough for them; and yet these same cautious and *quicksighted* gentlemen can swallow down this sottish opinion about percipient atoms. *Bentley.*

QUI'CKSIGHTEDNESS. *n. s.* [from *quicksighted.*] Sharpness of sight.

The ignorance that is in us no more hinders the knowledge that is in others, than the blindness of a mole is an argument against the *quicksightedness* of an eagle. *Locke.*

QUI'CKSILVER. *n. s.* [*quick* and *silver*; *argentum vivum*, Lat.]

Quicksilver, called mercury by the chymists, is a naturally fluid mineral, and the heaviest of all known bodies next to gold, and is the more heavy and fluid, as it is more pure; its nature is so homogene and simple, that it is a question whether gold itself be more so: it penetrates the parts of all the other metals, renders them brittle, and in part dissolves them: it is wholly volatile in the fire, and may be driven up in vapour by a degree of heat very little greater than that of boiling water: it is the least tenacious of all bodies, and every smaller drop may be again divided by the lightest touch into a multitude of others, and is the most divisible of all bodies: mercury very readily mixes with gold, silver, lead and tin, by chymical operations, but not without difficulty with copper and iron; and it mixes easily with zink and bismuth among the semimetals: the specifick gravity of pure mercury is to water as 14020 to 1000, and as it is the heaviest of all fluids, it is also the coldest, and when heated the hottest: of the various ores, in which mercury is found, cinnabar is the richest and most valuable, which is extremely heavy, and of a bright and beautiful red colour: native cinnabar is principally found in the mines of Friuli, belonging to the Venetians, in Italy, and some others in Spain, Hungary, and the East Indies: *quicksilver* is also found sometimes in its pure and fluid state lodged in cavities of hard stones in the cinnabar mines, and the purer ores are chiefly composed of cinnabar in small quantities, mixed with various other substances: the ancients all esteemed *quicksilver* a poison, nor was it brought into internal use till about two hundred and twenty years ago, which was first occasioned by the shepherds, who ventured to give it their sheep to kill worms, and as they received no hurt by it, it was soon concluded, that men might take it safely: in time, the diggers in the mines, when they found it crude, swallowed it in vast quantities, in order to sell it privately, when they had voided it by stool: but too free a use of so powerful a medicine cannot be always without danger: the miners seldom follow their occupation above three or four years, and then die in a most miserable condition; and the artificers, who have much dealing in it, are generally seized with paralytick disorders: however, under proper regulation, it is a most excellent medicine. *Hill's Materia Medica.*

Mercury is very improperly called a metal, for though it has weight and similarity of parts, it is neither dissolvable by fire, malleable nor fixed: it seems to constitute a particular class of fossils, and is rather the mother or basis of all metals, than a metal itself: mercury is of considerable use in gilding, making looking-glasses, in refining gold, and various other mechanical operations besides medicine. *Chambers.*

Cinnabar maketh a beautiful purple like unto a red rose; the best was wont to be made in Libia of brimstone and *quicksilver* burnt. *Peacham on Drawing.*

QUI'CKSILVERED. *adj.* [from *quicksilver.*] Overlaid with quicksilver.

Metal is more difficult to polish than glass, and is afterwards very apt to be spoiled by tarnishing, and reflects not so much light as glass *quicksilvered* over does: I would propound to use instead of the metal a glass ground concave on the foreside, and as much convex on the backside, and *quicksilvered* over on the convex side. *Newton's Opticks.*

QUI'DAM. [Latin.] Somebody.

For envy of so many worthy *quidams*, which catch at the garland, which to you alone is due, you will be persuaded to pluck out of the hateful darkness those so many excellent poems of yours, which lie hid, and bring them forth to eternal light. *Spenser.*

QUI'DDANY. *n. s.* [*cydonium*, *cydoniatum*, Lat. *quidden*, German, a quince.] Marmalade; confection of quinces made with sugar.

QUI'DDIT. *n. s.* [corrupted from *quidlibet*, Lat. or from *que dit*, Fr.] A subtilty; an equivocation. A low word.

Why may not that be the skull of a lawyer? where be his *quiddits* now? his quillets? his cases? and his tricks? *Shak.*

QUI'DDITY. *n. s.* [*quidditas*, low Latin.]

1. Essence; that which is a proper answer to the question, *quid est?* a scholastick term.

He could reduce all things to acts,
And knew their natures and abstracts,
Where entity and *quiddity*,
The ghosts of defunct bodies fly. *Hudibras, p.* i.

2. A trifling nicety; a cavil; a captious question.

Misnomer in our laws, and other *quiddities*, I leave to the professors of law. *Camden's Remains.*

QUI'ESCENCE. *n. s.* [from *quiesco*, Lat.] Rest; repose.

Whether the earth move or rest, I undertake not to determine: my work is to prove, that the common inducement to the belief of its *quiescence*, the testimony of sense, is weak and frivolous. *Glanvill's Sceps.*

QUIE'SCENT. *adj.* [*quiescens*, Latin.] Resting; not being in motion; not movent; lying at repose.

Though the earth move, its motion must needs be as insensible as if it were *quiescent*. *Glanvill's Sceps.*

The right side, from whence the motion of the body beginneth, is the active or moving side; but the sinister is the weaker or more *quiescent* side. *Brown's Vulgar Errours.*

Sight takes in at a greater distance and more variety at once, comprehending also *quiescent* objects, which hearing does not. *Holder's Elements of Speech.*

If it be in some part movent, and in some part *quiescent*, it must needs be a curve line, and so no radius. *Grew.*

Pression or motion cannot be propagated in a fluid in right lines beyond an obstacle which stops part of the motion, but will bend and spread every way into the *quiescent* medium, which lies beyond the obstacle. *Newton's Opticks.*

QUI'ET. *adj.* [*quiet*, Fr. *quietus*, Latin.]

1. Still; free from disturbance.

Breaking off the end for want of breath,
And slyding soft, as down to sleep her laid,
She ended all her woe in *quiet* death. *Fa. Queen.*

This life is best,
If *quiet* life is best; sweeter to you,
That have a sharper known. *Shakesp. Cymbeline.*

2. Peaceable; not turbulent; not offensive; mild.

Let it be in the ornament of a meek and *quiet* spirit. 1 *Pet.*

3. Still; not in motion.

They laid wait for him, and were *quiet* all the night. *Judges* xvi. 2.

4. Smooth; not ruffled.

Happy is your grace,
That can translate the stubborness of fortune
Into so *quiet* and so sweet a style. *Shakesp.*

QUI'ET. *n. s.* [*quies*, Lat.] Rest; repose; tranquillity; freedom from disturbance; peace; security.

They came into Laish unto a people that were at *quiet* and secure. *Judges* xviii. 27.

There fix'd their arms, and there renew'd their name,
And there in *quiet* rules. *Dryden's Æneis.*

Indulgent *quiet*, pow'r serene,
Mother of joy and love. *Hughes.*

To QUI'ET. *v. a.* [from the noun.]

1. To calm; to lull; to pacify; to put to rest.

The lowest degree of faith, that can *quiet* the soul of man, is a firm conviction that God is placable. *Forbes.*

2. To still.

Putting together the ideas of moving or *quieting* corporeal motion, joined to substance, we have the idea of an immaterial spirit. *Locke.*

QUI'ETER. *n. s.* [from *quiet.*] The person or thing that quiets.

QUI'ETISM. *n. s.* [from *quiet.*]

What is called by the poets apathy or dispassion, by the scepticks indisturbance, by the Molinists *quietism*, by common men peace of conscience, seems all to mean but great tranquility of mind. *Temple.*

QUI'ETLY. *adv.* [from *quiet.*]

1. Calmly: without violent emotion.

Let no man for his own poverty become more oppreſſing in his bargain, but *quietly*, modeſtly and patiently recommend his eſtate to God, and leave the ſucceſs to him. *Taylor.*

2. Peaceably; without offence.

Although the rebels had behaved themſelves *quietly* and modeſtly by the way as they went; yet they doubted that would but make them more hungry to fall upon the ſpoil in the end. *Bacon's Henry* VII.

3. At reſt; without agitation.

QUI'ETNESS. *n. ſ.* [from *quiet.*]

1. Coolneſs of temper.

This cruel *quietneſs* neither returning to miſlike nor proceeding to favour; gracious, but gracious ſtill after one manner. *Sidney, b.* ii.

That which we move for our better inſtruction ſake, turneth into anger and choler in them; they grow altogether out of *quietneſs* with it; they anſwer fumingly. *Hooker.*

2. Peace; tranquillity.

Stop effuſion of our chriſtian blood,
And 'ſtabliſh *quietneſs* on ev'ry ſide. *Shakeſp. Henry* VI.

What miſeries have both nations avoided, and what *quietneſs* and ſecurity attained by their peaceable union? *Hayward.*

3. Stilneſs; calmneſs.

QUI'ETSOME. *adj.* [from *quiet.*] Calm; ſtill; undiſturbed. Not in uſe.

Let the night be calm and *quietſome*,
Without tempeſtuous ſtorms or ſad affray. *Spenſer.*

QUI'ETUDE. *n. ſ.* [*quietude*, Fr. from *quiet.*] Reſt; repoſe; tranquillity. Not in common uſe.

From the equal diſtribution of the phlegmatick humour, the proper allay of fervent blood, will flow a future *quietude* and ſerenitude in the affections. *Wotton on Education.*

QUILL. *n. ſ.*

1. The hard and ſtrong feather of the wing, of which pens are made.

Birds have three other hard ſubſtances proper to them; the bill, which is of a like matter with the teeth, the ſhell of the egg, and their *quills.* *Bacon's Nat. Hiſtory.*

2. The inſtrument of writing.

I will only touch the duke's own deportment in that iſland, the proper ſubject of my *quill.* *Wotton's Buckingham.*

Thoſe lives they fail'd to reſcue by their ſkill,
Their muſe would make immortal with her *quill.* *Garth.*
From him whoſe *quills* ſtand quiver'd at his ear,
To him that notches ſticks at Weſtminſter. *Pope.*

3. Prick or dart of a porcupine.

Near theſe was the black prince of Monomotapa, by whoſe ſide was ſeen the *quill* darting porcupine. *Arbuth. and Pope.*

4. Reed on which weavers wind their threads.

The preſumptuous damſel raſhly dar'd
The goddeſs' ſelf to challenge to the field,
And to compare with her in curious ſkill,
Of works with loom, with needle, and with *quill.* *Spenſer.*

5. The inſtrument with which muſicians ſtrike their ſtrings.

His flying fingers and harmonious *quill*
Strike ſev'n diſtinguiſh'd notes, and ſev'n at once they fill. *Dryden's Æneis.*

QUI'LLET. *n. ſ.* [*quidlibet*, Lat.] Subtilty; nicety; fraudulent diſtinction.

Why may not that be the ſkull of a lawyer? where be his quiddits now? his *quillets?* his caſes? and his tricks? *Shak.*

A great ſoul weighs in the ſcale of reaſon, what it is to judge of, rather than dwell with too ſcrupulous a diligence upon little *quillets* and niceties. *Digby.*

Ply her with love letters and billets,
And bait them well for quirks and *quillets.* *Hudibras.*

QUILT. *n. ſ.* [*couette*, Fr. *kulcht*, Dutch; *culcita, culcitra*, Lat.] A cover made by ſtitching one cloth over another with ſome ſoft ſubſtance between them.

Quilts of roſes and ſpices are nothing ſo helpful, as to take a cake of new bread, and bedew it with a little ſack. *Bacon.*

In both tables, the beds were covered with magnificent *quilts* amongſt the richer ſort. *Arbuthnot on Coins.*

She on the *quilt* ſinks with becoming woe,
Wrapt in a gown, for ſickneſs and for ſhow. *Pope.*

To QUILT. *v. a.* [from the noun.] To ſtitch one cloth upon another with ſomething ſoft between them.

The ſharp ſteel arriving forcibly
On his horſe neck before the *quilted* ſell,
Then from the head the body ſundred quite. *Fairy Queen.*

A bag *quilted* with bran is very good, but it drieth too much. *Bacon's Natural Hiſtory.*

Entellus for the ſtrife prepares,
Strip'd of his *quilted* coat, his body bares,
Compos'd of mighty bone. *Dryden's Æneis.*
A chair was ready,
So *quilted*, that he lay at eaſe reclin'd. *Dryden.*

Mayn't I *quilt* my rope? it galls my neck. *Arbuthnot.*

QUI'NARY. *adj.* [*quinarius*, Lat.] Conſiſting of five.

This *quinary* number of elements ought to have been reſtrained to the generality of animals and vegetables. *Boyle.*

QUINCE. *n. ſ.* [*coin*, Fr. *quidden*, German.]

1. The tree.

The *quince* tree is of a low ſtature; the branches are diffuſed and crooked; the flower and fruit is like that of the pear treee; but, however cultivated, the fruit is ſour and aſtringent, and is covered with a kind of down: of this the ſpecies are ſix. *Miller.*

2. The fruit.

They call for dates and *quinces* in the paſtry. *Shakeſp.*

A *quince*, in token of fruitfulneſs, by the laws of Solon, was given to the brides of Athens upon the day of their marriage. *Peacham on Drawing.*

To QUINCH. *v. n.* [this word ſeems to be the ſame with *queech, winch* and *queck.*] To ſtir; to flounce as in reſentment or pain.

Beſtow all my ſoldiers in ſuch ſort as I have, that no part of all that realm ſhall be able to dare to *quinch.* *Spenſer.*

QUINCU'NCIAL. *adj.* [from *quincunx.*] Having the form of a quincunx.

Of a pentagonal or *quincuncial* diſpoſition, Sir Thomas Brown produces ſeveral examples in his diſcourſe about the quincunx. *Ray on the Creation.*

QUI'NCUNX. *n. ſ.* [Latin.]

Quincunx order is a plantation of trees, diſpoſed originally in a ſquare, conſiſting of five trees, one at each corner, and a fifth in the middle, which diſpoſition, repeated again and again, forms a regular grove, wood or wilderneſs; and, when viewed by an angle of the ſquare or paralellogram, preſents equal or parallel alleys.

Brown produces ſeveral examples in his diſcourſe about the *quincunx.* *Ray on the Creation.*

He whoſe light'ning pierc'd th' Iberian lines,
Now forms my *quincunx*, and now ranks my vines. *Pope.*

QUINQUAGE'SIMA. [Latin.] Quinquageſima ſunday, ſo called becauſe it is the fiftieth day before Eaſter, reckoned by whole numbers; ſhrove ſunday. *Dict.*

QUINQUA'NGULAR. *adj.* [*quinque* and *angulus*, Lat.] Having five corners.

Each talus, environed with a cruſt, conforming itſelf to the ſides of the talus, is of a figure *quinquangular.* *Woodw.*

Exactly round, ordinately *quinquangular*, or having the ſides parallel. *More's Antidote againſt Atheiſm.*

QUINQUARTI'CULAR. *adj.* [*quinque* and *articulus*, Lat.] Conſiſting of five articles.

They have given an end to the *quinquarticular* controverſy, for none have ſince undertaken to ſay more. *Sanderſon.*

QUI'NQUEFID. *adj.* [*quinque* and *findo*, Lat.] Cloven in five.

QUINQUEFO'LIATED. *adj.* [*quinque* and *folium*, Lat.] Having five leaves.

QUINQUE'NNIAL. *adj.* [*quinquennis*, Lat.] Laſting five years; happening once in five years.

QUI'NSY. *n. ſ.* [corrupted from *ſquinancy.*] A tumid inflammation in the throat, which ſometimes produces ſuffocation.

The throttling *quinſey* 'tis my ſtar appoints,
And rheumatiſms I ſend to rack the joints. *Dryden.*

Great heat and cold, ſucceeding one another, occaſion pleuriſies and *quinſies.* *Arbuthnot on Air.*

QUINT. *n. ſ.* [*quint*, Fr.] A ſet of five.

For ſtate has made a *quint*
Of generals he's lifted in't. *Hudibras, p.* iii.

QUI'NTAIN. *n. ſ.* [*quintain*, Fr.] A poſt with a turning top. See QUINTIN.

My better parts
Are all thrown down; and that, which here ſtands up,
Is but a *quintain*, a mere lifeleſs block. *Shakeſp.*

QUINTE'SSENCE. *n. ſ.* [*quinta eſſentia*, Lat.]

1. A fifth being.

From their groſs matter ſhe abſtracts the forms,
And draws a kind of *quinteſſence* from things. *Davies.*
The ethereal *quinteſſence* of heav'n
Flew upward, ſpirited with various forms,
That rowl'd orbicular, and turn'd to ſtars. *Milton.*

They made fire, air, earth, and water, to be the four elements, of which all earthly things were compounded, and ſuppoſed the heavens to be a *quinteſſence* or fifth ſort of body diſtinct from all theſe. *Watts's Logick.*

2. An extract from any thing, containing all its virtues in a ſmall quantity.

To me what is this *quinteſſence* of duſt? man delights not me, nor woman neither. *Shakeſp. Hamlet.*

Who can in memory, or wit, or will,
Or air, or fire, or earth, or water find?
What alchymiſt can draw, with all his ſkill,
The *quinteſſence* of theſe out of the mind. *Davies.*
For I am a very dead thing,
In whom love wrought new alchymy,
For by his art he did expreſs
A *quinteſſence* even from nothingneſs,
From dull privations and lean emptineſs. *Donne.*

Paracelſus, by the help of an intenſe cold, teaches to ſeparate the *quinteſſence* of wine. *Boyle.*

Let there be light! ſaid God; and forthwith light
Ethereal, firſt of things, *quinteſſence* pure,
Sprung from the deep. *Milton's Paradiſe Loſt, b.* vii.

When the supreme faculties move regularly, the inferior passions and affections following, there arises a serenity and complacency upon the whole soul, infinitely beyond the greatest bodily pleasures, the highest *quintessence* and elixir of worldly delights. *South's Sermons.*

QUINTE'SSENTIAL. *adj.* [from *quintessence.*] Consisting of quintessence.

Venturous assertions as would have puzzled the authors to have made them good, specially considering that there is nothing contrary to the *quintessential* matter and circular figure of the heavens; so neither is there to the light thereof. *Hakew.*

QUI'NTIN. *n. s.* [I know not whence derived; *Minshew* deduces it from *quintus*, Lat. and calls it a game celebrated every fifth year; *palus quintanus*, Lat. *Ainsf. quintaine*, Fr.] An upright post, on the top of which a cross post turned upon a pin, at one end of the cross post was a broad board, and at the other a heavy sand bag; the play was to ride against the broad end with a lance, and pass by before the sand bag coming round, should strike the tilter on the back.

At *quintin* he,
In honour of his bridaltee,
Hath challeng'd either wide countee;
Come cut and long tail, for there be
Six batchelors as bold as he,
Adjuting to his company,
And each one hath his livery. *Benj. Johnson.*

QUINTU'PLE. *n. s.* [*quintuplus*, Lat.] Fivefold.

In the country, the greatest proportion of mortality, one hundred and fifty-six, is above *quintuple* unto twenty-eight the least. *Graunt's Bills of Mortality.*

QUIP. *n. s.* [derived, by the etymologists, from *whip.*] A sharp jest; a taunt; a sarcasm.

Notwithstanding all her sudden *quips*,
The least whereof would quell a lover's hope,
Yet, spaniel like, the more she spurns my love,
The more it grows, and fawneth on her still. *Shakesp.*

If I sent him word his beard was not well cut, he would send me word, he cut it to please himself: this is called the *quip* modest. *Shakesp. As You Like it.*

Nymph bring with thee
Jest and youthful jollity,
Quips, and cranks, and wanton wiles,
Nods, and becks, and wreathed smiles. *Milton.*

To QUIP. *v. a.* To rally with bitter sarcasms. *Ainsworth.*

QUIRE. *n. s.* [*choeur*, Fr. *choro*, Italian.]

1. A body of singers; a chorus.

The trees did bud and early blossoms bore,
And all the *quire* of birds did sweetly sing,
And told that garden's pleasures in their caroling. *Fa. Qu.*

Myself have lim'd a bush for her,
And plac'd a *quire* of such enticing birds,
That she will light to listen to their lays. *Shakesp.*

At thy nativity a glorious *quire*
Of angels in the fields of Bethlehem sung
To shepherds watching at their folds by night,
And told them the Messiah now was born. *Milton.*

I may worship thee
For ay, with temples vow'd and virgin *quires*. *Milton.*

As in beauty she surpass'd the *quire*,
So nobler than the rest was her attire. *Dryden.*

2. The part of the church where the service is sung.

I am all on fire,
Not all the buckets in a country *quire*
Shall quench my rage. *Cleaveland.*

Some run for buckets to the hallow'd *quire*,
Some cut the pipes, and some the engines play. *Dryden.*

The fox obscene to gaping tombs retires,
And wolves with howling fill the sacred *quires*. *Pope.*

3. [*Cahier*, Fr.] A bundle of paper consisting of twenty-four sheets.

To QUIRE. *v. n.* [from the noun.] To sing in concert.

There's not the smallest orb which thou behold'st,
But in his motion like an angel sings,
Still *quiring* to the young-ey'd cherubims. *Shakesp.*

My throat of war be turn'd
Which *quired* with my drum, into a pipe
Small as an eunuch, or the virgin's voice
That babies lulls asleep. *Shakesp. Coriolanus.*

QUI'RISTER. *n. s.* [from *quire.*] Chorister; one who sings in concert, generally in divine service.

The coy *quiristers*, that lodge within,
Are prodigal of harmony. *Thomson's Spring.*

QUIRK. *n. s.* [of this word I can find no rational derivation.]

1. Quick stroke; sharp fit.

I've felt so many *quirks* of joy and grief,
That the first face of neither on the start,
Can woman me unto't. *Shakesp.*

2. Smart taunt.

Some kind of men quarrel purposely on others to taste their valour; belike, this is a man of that *quirk*. *Shakesp.*

I may chance to have some odd *quirks* and remnants of wit broken on me. *Shakesp.*

Conceits, puns, *quirks* or quibbles, jests and repartees may agreeably entertain, but have no place in the search after truth. *Watts's Improvement of the Mind.*

3. Subtilty; nicety; artful distinction.

Most fortunately he hath atchiev'd a maid,
That paragons description and wild fame,
One that excels the *quirks* of blazoning pens. *Shakesp.*

Let a lawyer tell them he has spied some defect in an entail; how solicitous are they to repair that error, and leave nothing to the mercy of a law *quirk?* *Decay of Piety.*

Ply her with love letters and billets,
And bait them well for *quirks* and quillets. *Hudibras.*

There are a thousand *quirks* to avoid the stroke of the law. *L'Estrange's Fables.*

4. Loose light tune.

Now the chappel's silver bell you hear,
That summons you to all the pride of pray'r;
Light *quirks* of musick, broken and uneven. *Pope.*

To QUIT. *v. a.* part. pass. *quit*; pret. *I have quit* or *quitted.* [*quiter*, Fr. *quitare*, Italian; *quitar*, Spanish.]

1. To discharge an obligation; to make even.

We will be *quit* of thine oath, which thou hast made us to swear. *Jos.* ii. 20.

By this act, old tyrant,
I shall be *quit* with thee; while I was virtuous,
I was a stranger to thy blood, but now
Sure thou wilt love me for this horrid crime. *Denham.*

To John I ow'd great obligation;
But John, unhappily, thought fit
To publish it to all the nation;
Sure John and I are more than *quit*. *Prior.*

2. To set free.

Thou art *quit* from a thousand calamities; therefore let thy joy, which should be as great for thy freedom from them, as is thy sadness when thou feelest any of them, do the same cure upon thy discontent. *Taylor.*

Henceforth I fly not death, nor would prolong
Life much: bent rather how I may be *quit*
Fairest and easiest of this cumb'rous charge. *Milton.*

To *quit* you wholly of this fear, you have already looked death in the face; what have you found so terrible in it. *Wake.*

3. To carry through; to discharge; to perform.

Never worthy prince a day did *quit*
With greater hazard, and with more renown. *Daniel.*

4. To clear himself of an affair.

Samson hath *quit* himself
Like Samson, and heroickly hath finish'd
A life heroick, on his enemies
Fully reveng'd hath left them years of mourning. *Milton.*

5. To repay; to requite.

He fair the knight saluted, louting low,
Who fair him *quitted*, as that courteous was. *Fa. Queen.*

Enkindle all the sparks of nature,
To *quit* this horrid act. *Shakesp. King Lear.*

6. To vacate obligations.

For our reward,
All our debts are paid; dangers of law,
Actions, decrees, judgments against us *quitted*. *B. Johns.*

One step higher
Would set me highest, and in a moment *quit*
The debt immense of endless gratitude. *Milton.*

7. To pay any obligation; to clear a debt; to be tantamount.

They both did fail of their purpose, and got not so much as to *quit* their charges; because truth, which is the secret of the most high God, whose proper handy-work all things are, cannot be compassed with that wit and those senses which are our own. *Hooker, b.* i.

Far other plaints, tears and laments
The time, the place, and our estates require,
Think on thy sins, which man's old foe presents
Before that judge that *quits* each soul his hire. *Fairfax.*

Does not the air feed the flame? and does not the flame at the same time warm and enlighten the air? and does not the earth *quit* scores with all the elements in the noble fruits that issue from it. *South's Sermons.*

Still I shall hear, and never *quit* the score,
Stunn'd with hoarse Codrus' Theseid o'er and o'er. *Dryd.*

Iron works ought to be confined to certain places, where there is no conveyance for timber to places of vent, so as to *quit* the cost of the carriage. *Temple's Miscellanies.*

8. [Contracted from *acquit.*] To absolve; to acquit.

Nor further seek what their offences be,
Guiltless I *quit*, guilty I set them free. *Fairfax.*

9. To abandon; to forsake.

Their father,
Then old and fond of issue, took such sorrow,
That he *quit* being. *Shakesp. Cymbeline.*

Honours are promis'd
To all will *quit* 'em; and rewards propos'd
Even to slaves that can detect their courses. *Benj. Johnson.*

Such variety of arguments only distract the understanding, such a superficial way of examining is to *quit* truth for appearance, only to serve our vanity. *Locke.*

10. To resign; to give up.

The prince, renown'd in bounty as in arms,
With pity saw the ill-conceal'd distress,
Quitted his title to Campaspe's charms,
And gave the fair one to the friend's embrace. *Prior.*

QUI'TCHGRASS. *n. s.* [cpice, Saxon.] Dog grass.

They are the best corn to grow on grounds subject to *quitchgrass* or other weeds. *Mortimer's Husbandry.*

QUITE. *adv.* [this is derived, by the etymologists, from *quitte*, discharged, free, Fr. which however at first appearance unlikely is much favoured by the original use of the word, which was, in this combination, *quite* and *clean*; that is, *with a clean riddance*: its present signification was gradually introduced.] Completely; perfectly.

Those latter exclude not the former *quite* and clean as unnecessary. *Hooker, b.* i.

He hath sold us, and *quite* devoured our money. *Gen.* xxxi.

If some foreign ideas will offer themselves, reject them, and hinder them from running away with our thoughts *quite* from the subject in hand. *Locke.*

The same actions may be aimed at different ends, and arise from *quite* contrary principles. *Addison's Spectator.*

QUI'TRENT. *n. s.* [*quit* and *rent.*] Small rent reserved.

Such a tax would be insensible, and pass but as a small *quitrent*, which every one would be content to pay towards the guard of the seas. *Temple's Miscellanies.*

My old master, a little before his death, wished him joy of the estate which was falling to him, desiring him only to pay the gifts of charity he had left as *quitrents* upon the estate. *Addison's Spectator*, Nº 517.

QUITS. *interj.* [from *quit.*] An exclamation used when any thing is repayed and the parties become even.

QUI'TTANCE. *n. s.* [*quitance*, Fr.]

1. Discharge from a debt or obligation; an acquitance.

Now I am remembr'd, he scorn'd at me!
But that's all one; omittance is no *quittance*. *Shakesp.*

2. Recompence; return; repayment.

Mine eyes saw him in bloody state,
Rend'ring faint *quittance*, wearied and outbreath'd,
To Henry Monmouth. *Shakesp. Henry* IV. *p.* ii.

Plutus, the god of gold,
Is but his steward; no meed but he repays
Sevenfold above itself; no gift to him
But breeds the giver a return exceeding
All use of *quittance*. *Shakesp. Timon of Athens.*

We shall forget the office of our hand,
Sooner than *quittance* of desert and merit. *Shakesp.*

To QUI'TTANCE. *v. a.* [from the noun.] To repay; to recompense. A word not used.

Embrace me then this opportunity,
As fitting best to *quittance* their deceit. *Shakesp.*

QUI'TTER. *n. s.*

1. A deliverer. *Ainsworth.*

2. Scoria of tin. *Ainsworth.*

QUI'TTERBONE. *n. s.*

Quitterbone is a hard round swelling upon the coronet, between the heel and the quarter, and grows most commonly on the inside of the foot. *Farrier's Dict.*

QUI'VER. *n. s.* [this word seems to be corrupted from *couvrir*, Fr. or *cover.*] A case for arrows.

As Dianne hunted on a day,
She chanc'd to come where Cupid lay,
His *quiver* by his head,
One of his shafts she stole away,
And one of hers did close convey
Into the other's stead;
With that love wounded my love's heart,
But Dianne beasts with Cupid's dart. *Spenser.*

Diana's nymphs would be arrayed in white, their arms and shoulders naked, bows in their hands, and *quivers* by their sides. *Peacham on Drawing.*

Her sounding *quiver* on her shoulder ty'd,
One hand a dart, and one a bow supply'd. *Dryden.*

QUI'VER. *adj.* Nimble; active.

There was a little *quiver* fellow, and he would manage you his piece thus; and he would about and about. *Shakesp.*

To QUI'VER. *v. n.*

1. To quake; to play with a tremulous motion.

The birds chaunt melody on every bush,
The green leaves *quiver* with the cooling wind. *Shakesp.*

O'er the pommel cast the knight,
Forward he flew, and pitching on his head,
He *quiver'd* with his feet, and lay for dead. *Dryden.*

With what a spring his furious soul broke loose,
And left the limbs still *quivering* on the ground. *Addison.*

Eurydice with *quiv'ring* voice he mourn'd,
And Heber's banks Eurydice return'd. *Gay's Trivia.*

Dancing sun beams on the waters play'd,
And verdant alders form'd a *quiv'ring* shade.
The dying gales that pant upon the trees,
The lakes that *quiver* to the curling breeze. *Pope.*

2. To shiver; to shudder.

Zelmane would have put to her helping hand, but she was taken with such a *quivering*, that she thought it more wisdom to lean herself to a tree and look on. *Sidney, b.* ii.

QUI'VERED. *adj.* [from *quiver.*]

1. Furnished with a quiver.

'Tis chastity,
She that has that, is clad in compleat steel,
And like a *quiver'd* nymph with arrows keen,
May trace huge forests and unharbour'd heaths,
Infamous hills, and perilous sandy wilds. *Milton.*

2. Sheathed as in a quiver.

From him whose quills stand *quivered* at his ear,
To him who notches sticks at Westminster. *Pope.*

To QUOB. *v. n.* [a low word.] To move as the embrio does in the womb; to move as the heart does when throbbing.

QUO'DLIBET. n. s. [Latin.] A nice point; a subtilty.

He who reading on the heart,
When all his *quodlibets* of art
Could not expound its pulse and heat,
Swore, he had never felt it beat. *Prior.*

QUODLIBETA'RIAN. *n. s.* [*quodlibet*, Lat.] One who talks or disputes on any subject. *Dict.*

QUODLIBE'TICAL. *adj.* [*quodlibet*, Lat.] Not restrained to a particular subject: in the schools theses or problems, anciently proposed to be debated for curiosity or entertainment, were so called. *Dict.*

QUOIF. *n. s.* [*coëffe*, Fr.]

1. Any cap with which the head is covered. See COIF.

Hence thou sickly *quoif*,
Thou art a guard too wanton for the head,
Which princes, flesh'd with conquest, aim to hit. *Shakesp.*

2. The cap of a serjeant at law.

To QUOIF. *v. a.* [*coeffer*, Fr.] To cap; to dress with a head-dress.

She is always *quoiffed* with the head of an elephant, to show that this animal is the breed of that country. *Addison.*

QUOI'FFURE. *n. s.* [*coeffure*, Fr.] Head-dress.

The lady in the next medal is very particular in her *quoiffure*. *Addison on Ancient Medals.*

QUOIL. *n. s.* See COIL.

QUOIN. *n. s.* [*coin*, Fr.]

1. Corner.

A sudden tempest from the desert flew
With horrid wings, and thundered as it blew,
Then whirling round, the *quoins* together strook. *Sandys.*

Build brick houses with strong and firm *quoins* or columns at each end. *Mortimer's Husbandry.*

2. An instrument for raising warlike engines. *Ainsworth.*

QUOIT. *n. s.* [*coete*, Dutch.]

1. Something thrown to a great distance to a certain point.

He plays at *quoits* well. *Shakesp. Henry* IV.

When he played at *quoits*, he was allowed his breeches and stockings. *Arbuthnot and Pope.*

2. The discus of the ancients is sometimes called in English *quoit*, but improperly; the game of *quoits* is a game of skill; the discus was only a trial of strength, as among us to throw the hammer.

To QUOIT. *v. n.* [from the noun.] To throw quoits; to play at quoits. *Dryden* uses it to throw the discus. See the noun.

Noble youths for mastership should strive
To *quoit*, to run, and steeds and chariots drive. *Dryden.*

To QUOIT. *v. a.* To throw.

Quoit him down, Bardolph, like a shove-groat shilling. *Shak.*

QUO'NDAM. [Latin.] Having been formerly. A ludicrous word.

This is the *quondam* king, let's seize upon him. *Shakesp.*

What lands and lordships for their owner know
My *quondam* barber, but his worship now. *Dryden.*

QUOOK. *preterite of quake.* Obsolete.

Freely up those royal spoils he took,
Yet at the lion's skin he inly *quook*. *Spenser.*

QUO'RUM. n. s. [Latin.] A bench of justices; such a number of any officers as is sufficient to do business.

They were a parcel of mummers, and being himself one of the *quorum* in his own country, he wondered that none of the Middlesex justices took care to lay some of them by the heels. *Addison's Freeholder*, Nº 44.

QUO'TA. *n. s.* [*quotus*, Lat.] A share; a proportion as assigned to each.

Scarce one in this list but engages to supply a *quota* of brisk young fellows, equipt with hats and feathers. *Addison.*

QUOTA'TION. *n. s.* [from *quote.*]

1. The act of quoting; citation.

2. Passage adduced out of an authour as evidence or illustration.

He, that has but ever so little examined the citations of writers, cannot doubt how little credit the *quotations* deserve, where the originals are wanting. *Locke.*

He rang'd his tropes, and preach'd up patience,
Back'd his opinion with *quotations*. *Prior.*

To QUOTE. *v. a.* [*quoter*, Fr.] To cite an authour or passage of an authour; to adduce by way of authority or illustration the words of another.

The second chapter to the Romans is here *quoted* only to paint the margent. *Whitgifte.*

St. Paul *quotes* one of their poets for this saying. *Stillingfl.*

He changed his mind, say the papers, and *quote* for it Melchior Adams and Hospinian. *Atterbury.*

He *quoted* texts right upon our Saviour, though he expounded them wrong. *Atterbury.*

He will, in the middle of a session, *quote* passages out of Plato and Pindar. *Swift's Miscellanies.*

QUO'TER. *n. s.* [from *quote.*] Citer; he that quotes.

I proposed this passage entire, to take off the disguise which its *quoter* put upon it. *Atterbury.*

QUOTH. *verb. imperfect.* [this is only part of cpoðan, Saxon, retained in English, and is now only used in ludicrous language. It is used by *Sidney* irregularly in the second person.] *Quoth I*, say I or said I; *quoth he*, says he or said he.

Enjoying *quoth* you. *Sidney*, *b.* ii.

Shall we, *quoth* he, so basely brook
This paltry ass. *Hudibras.*

QUOTI'DIAN. *adj.* [*quotidien*, Fr. *quotidianus*, Latin.] Daily; happening every day.

Quotidian things, and equidistant hence
Shut in for man in one circumference. *Donne.*

Nor was this a short fit of shaking, as an ague, but a *quotidian* fever, always increasing to higher inflammation. *King Charles.*

QUOTI'DIAN. *n. s.* [*febris quotidiana*, Lat.] A quotidian fever; a fever which returns every day.

If I could meet that fancymonger, I would give him some good counsel; for he seems to have the *quotidian* of love. *Shakespeare.*

QUO'TIENT. *n. s.* [*quotient*, Fr. *quoties*, Latin.]

In arithmetick, *quotient* is the number produced by the division of the two given numbers the one by the other. *Cocker.*

To make all the steps belonging to the same pair of stairs of an equal height, they consider the height of the room in feet and inches, and multiply the feet by twelve, whose product, with the number of odd inches, gives the sum of the whole height in inches, which sum they divide by the number of steps they intend to have in that height, and the *quotient* shall be the number of inches and parts that each step shall be high. *Moxon's Mechanical Exercise.*

R.

R, Is called the canine letter, because it is uttered with some resemblance to the growl or snarl of a cur: it has one constant sound in English, such as it has in other languages; as *red, rose, more, muriatick*: in words derived from the Greek, it is followed by an *h, rhapsody*: *r* is never mute, unless the second *r* may be accounted mute, where two *rr* are used; as *myrrh*.

To RA'BATE. *v. n.* [*rabattre*, Fr.] In falconry, to recover a hawk to the fist again. *Ainsworth.*

To RA'BBET. *v. a.* [*rabatre, raboter*, Fr.] To pare down pieces of wood so as to fit one another.

The rabbet plane is to cut part of the upper edge of a board straight or square down, that the edge of another board, cut down in the same manner, may join into the square of the first; and this lapping over of two boards is called *rabbeting*. *Moxon's Mechanical Exercises.*

The window frame hath every one of its lights *rabbetted* on its outside about half an inch into the frame, and all these rabbets, but that on the ground-sell, are groved square. *Moxon's Mechanical Exercises.*

RA'BBET. *n. s.* [from the verb.] A joint made by paring two pieces so that they wrap over one another.

Having drove in the hooks, they set the *rabbets* of the door within the *rabbets* of the door-post. *Moxon's Mechan. Exer.*

RA'BBI. }
RA'BBIN. } *n. s.* A doctor among the Jews.

The Hebrew *rabbins* say, that nature hath given man, for the pronouncing of all letters, the lips, the teeth, the tongue, the palate and throat. *Camden's Remains.*

Be not ye called *rabbi*; for one is your master, even Christ, and all ye are brethren. *Mat.* xxiii. 8.

RA'BBIT. *n. s.* [*robbe, robbekin*, Dutch.] A furry animal that lives on plants, and burrows in the ground.

I knew a wench married, as she went to the garden for parsly to stuff a *rabbit*. *Shakesp. Taming of the Shrew.*

A company of scholars, going to catch conies, carried one with them which had not much wit, and gave in charge, that if he saw any, he should be silent for fear of scaring of them; but he no sooner espied a company of *rabbits*, but he cried aloud, *ecce multi cuniculi*; which he had no sooner said, but the conies ran to their burrows; and he being checked by them for it, answered, who would have thought that the *rabbits* understood Latin? *Bacon's Apophthegms.*

RA'BBLE. *n. s.* [*rabula*, Lat. *rabulari*, low Lat.] A tumultuous croud; an assembly of low people.

Countrymen, will ye relent, and yield to mercy,
Or let a *rabble* lead you to your deaths? *Shakesp.*
Go bring the *rabble* here to this place. *Shakesp.*

Of these his several ravishments, betrayings, and stealing away of men's wives, came in all those ancient fables, and all that *rabble* of Grecian forgeries. *Raleigh.*

The better sort abhors scurrility,
And often censures what the *rabble* like. *Roscommon.*

That profane, atheistical, epicurean *rabble*, whom the whole nation so rings of, are not the wisest men in the world. *South's Sermons.*

To gratify the barbarous audience, I gave them a short *rabble* scene, because the mob are represented by Plutarch and Polybius with the same character of baseness and cowardice. *Dryden's Preface to Cleomenes.*

In change of government,
The *rabble* rule their great oppressors fate,
Do sov'reign justice and revenge the state. *Dryden.*

His enemies have been only able to make ill impressions upon the low and ignorant *rabble*, and to put the dregs of the people in a ferment. *Addison's Freeholder*, N° 24.

RA'BBLEMENT. *n. s.* [from *rabble*.] Croud; tumultuous assembly of mean people.

A rude *rabblement*,
Whose like he never saw, he durst not bide,
But got his ready steed, and fast away 'gan ride. *Fa. Qu.*

The *rabblement* houted, clap'd their chopt hands, and uttered a deal of stinking breath. *Shakesp. Julius Cæsar.*

There will be always tyrants, murderers, thieves, traitors, and other of the same *rabblement*. *Camden's Remains.*

RA'BID. *adj.* [*rabidus*, Lat.] Fierce; furious; mad.

RA'BINET. *n. s.* A kind of smaller ordnance. *Ainsworth.*

RACE. *n. s.* [*race*, Fr. from *radice*, Lat.]

1. A family ascending.

2. Family descending.

He in a moment will create
Another world; out of man, a *race*
Of men innumerable, there to dwell. *Milton.*
Male he created thee, but thy consort
Female for *race*. *Milton.*
High as the mother of the gods in place,
And proud like her of an immortal *race*. *Dryden.*
Hence the long *race* of Alban fathers come. *Dryden.*

3. A generation; a collective family.

A *race* of youthful and unhandled colts,
Fetching mad bounds. *Shakesp. Merchant of Venice.*

4. A particular breed.

Instead
Of spirits malign, a better *race* to bring
Into their vacant room. *Milton.*

In the *races* of mankind and families of the world, there remains not to one above another the least pretence to have the right of inheritance. *Locke.*

5. RACE *of ginger*. [*rayz de gengibre*, Spanish.] A root or sprig of ginger.

6. A particular strength or taste of wine, applied by *Temple* to any extraordinary natural force of intellect.

Of gardens there may be forms wholly irregular, that may have more beauty than of others; but they must owe it to some extraordinary dispositions of nature in the seat, or some great *race* of fancy or judgment in contrivance. *Temple.*

7. [*Ras*, Islandick.] Contest in running.

To describe *races* and games
Or tilting furniture. *Milton.*

8. Course on the feet.

The flight of many birds is swifter than the *race* of any beasts. *Bacon.*

9. Progress; course.

It suddenly fell from an excess of favour, which many examples having taught them, never stopt his *race* till it came to a headlong overthrow. *Sidney.*

My *race* of glory run, and *race* of shame. *Milton.*
Their ministry perform'd, and *race* well run. *Milton.*
The great light of day yet wants to run
Much of his *race* though steep. *Milton.*
He safe return'd, the *race* of glory past,
New to his friends embrace. *Pope's Odyssey.*

10. Train; process.

An offensive war is made, which is unjust in the aggressor; the prosecution and *race* of the war carrieth the defendant to invade the ancient patrimony of the first aggressor, who is now turned defendant; shall he sit down, and not put himself in defence? *Bacon.*

The *race* of this war fell upon the loss of Urbin, which he re-obtained. *Bacon.*

RA'CEHORSE. *n. s.* [*race* and *horse*.] Horse bred to run for prizes

The reason Hudibras gives, why those, who can talk on trifles, speak with the greatest fluency, is, that the tongue is like a *racehorse*, which runs the faster the less weight it carries. *Addison.*

RACEMA'TION. *n. s.* [*racemus*, Lat.] Cluster, like that of grapes.

A cock will in one day fertilitate the whole *racemation* or cluster of eggs, which are not excluded in many weeks after. *Brown's Vulgar Errours.*

RACEMI'FEROUS. *adj.* [*racemus* and *fera*, Latin.] Bearing clusters.

RA'CER.

RA'CER. *n. ſ.* [from *race.*] Runner; one that contends in ſpeed.

His ſtumbling founder'd jade can trot as high
As any other pegaſus can fly;
So the dull eel moves nimbler in the mud,
Than all the ſwift-finn'd *racers* of the flood. *Dorſet.*

A poet's form ſhe plac'd before their eyes,
And bade the nimbleſt *racer* ſeize the prize. *Pope.*

RA'CINESS. *n. ſ.* [from *racy.*] The quality of being racy.

RACK. *n. ſ.* [*racke*, Dutch, from *racken*, to ſtretch.]

1. An engine to torture.

Vex not his ghoſt; O let him paſs! he hates him
That would, upon the *rack* of this rough world,
Stretch him out longer. *Shakeſp. King Lear.*

Did ever any man upon the *rack* afflict himſelf, becauſe he had received a croſs anſwer from his miſtreſs. *Taylor.*

Let them feel the whip, the ſword, the fire,
And in the tortures of the *rack* expire. *Addiſon.*

2. Torture; extreme pain.

A fit of the ſtone puts a king to the *rack*, and makes him as miſerable as it does the meaneſt ſubject. *Temple.*

A cool behaviour ſets him on the *rack*, and is interpreted as an inſtance of averſion or indifference. *Addiſon.*

3. Any inſtrument by which extenſion is performed.

Theſe bows, being ſomewhat like the long bows in uſe amongſt us, were bent only by a man's immediate ſtrength, without the help of any bender or *rack* that are uſed to others. *Wilkins's Mathematical Magick.*

4. A diſtaff; commonly a portable diſtaff, from which they ſpin by twirling a ball.

The ſiſters turn the wheel,
Empty the woolly *rack*, and fill the reel. *Dryden.*

5. [*Racke*, Dutch, a track.] The clouds as they are driven by the wind.

That, which is now a horſe, even with a thought
The *rack* diſlimns, and makes it indiſtinct
As water is in water. *Shakeſp. Antony and Cleopatra.*

The great globe itſelf,
Yea, all, which it inherit, ſhall diſſolve;
And, like this inſubſtantial pageant, faded,
Leave not a *rack* behind. *Shakeſp. Tempeſt.*

We often ſee againſt ſome ſtorm,
A ſilence in the heav'ns, the *rack* ſtand ſtill,
The bold winds ſpeechleſs, and the orb below
As huſh as death. *Shakeſp. Hamlet.*

The winds in the upper region, which move the clouds above, which we call the *rack*, and are not perceived below, paſs without noiſe. *Bacon's Natural Hiſtory.*

As wint'ry winds contending in the ſky,
With equal force of lungs their titles try;
They rage, they roar: the doubtful *rack* of heav'n
Stands without motion, and the tide undriv'n. *Dryden.*

6. [þnacca, the occiput, Saxon; *racca*, Iſlandick, hinges or joints.] A neck of mutton cut for the table.

7. A grate.

8. A wooden grate in which hay is placed for cattle.

Their bulls they ſend to paſtures far,
Or hills, or feed them at full *racks* within. *May's Virgil.*

The beſt way to feed cattle with it, is to put it in *racks*, becauſe of the great quantity they tread down. *Mortimer.*

He bid the nimble hours
Bring forth the ſteeds; the nimble hours obey:
From their full *racks* the gen'rous ſteeds retire. *Addiſon.*

9. Arrack; a ſpirituous liquor. See ARRACK.

To RACK. *v. n.* [from the noun.] To ſtream as clouds before the wind.

Three glorious ſuns, each one a perfect ſun,
Not ſeparated with the *racking* clouds,
But ſever'd in a pale clear-ſhining ſky. *Shakeſp.*

To RACK. *v. a.* [from the noun.]

1. To torment by the rack.

Hold, O dreadful Sir,
You will not *rack* an innocent old man. *Dryden and Lee.*

2. To torment; to harraſs.

Th' apoſtate angle, though in pain,
Vaunting aloud, but *rack'd* with deep deſpair. *Milton.*

3. To harraſs by exaction.

The landlords there ſhamefully *rack* their tenants, exacting of them, beſides his covenants, what he pleaſeth. *Spenſer.*

The commons haſt thou *rack'd*; the clergy's bags
Are lank and lean with thy extortions. *Shakeſp.*

He took poſſeſſion of his juſt eſtate,
Nor *rack'd* his tenants with increaſe of rent. *Dryden.*

4. To ſcrew; to force to performance.

They *racking* and ſtretching ſcripture further than by God was meant, are drawn into ſundry inconveniencies. *Hooker.*

The wiſeſt among the heathens *racked* their wits, and caſt about every way, managing every little argument to the utmoſt advantage. *Tillotſon's Sermons.*

5. To ſtretch; to extend.

Nor have I money nor commodity
To raiſe a preſent ſum;
Try what my credit can in Venice do,
That ſhall be *rack'd* even to the uttermoſt. *Shakeſp.*

6. To defecate; to draw off from the lees. I know not whence this word is derived in this ſenſe; *rein*, German, is clear, pure, whence our word to *rinſe*; this is perhaps of the ſame race.

It is common to draw wine or beer from the lees, which we call *racking*, whereby it will clarify much the ſooner. *Bacon.*

Some roll their caſk about the cellar to mix it with the lees, and, after a few days reſettlement, *rack* it off. *Mortim.*

RACK-RENT. *n. ſ.* [*rack* and *rent.*] Rent raiſed to the uttermoſt.

Have poor families been ruined by *rack-rents*, paid for the lands of the church? *Swift's Miſcellanies.*

RACK-RENTER. *n. ſ.* [*rack* and *renter.*] One who pays the uttermoſt rent.

Though this be a quarter of his yearly income, and the publick tax takes away one hundred; yet this influences not the yearly rent of the land, which the *rack-renter* or under-tenant pays. *Locke.*

RA'CKET. *n. ſ.* [of uncertain derivation; M. *Caſaubon* derives it, after his cuſtom, from ῥαχία, the daſh of fluctuation againſt the ſhore.]

1. An irregular clattering noiſe.

That the tennis court keeper knows better than I, it is a low ebb of linen with thee, when thou keepeſt not *racket* there. *Shakeſp. Henry IV. p. ii.*

2. A confuſed talk, in burleſque language.

Ambition hath removed her lodging, and lives the next door to faction, where they keep ſuch a *racket*, that the whole pariſh is diſturbed and every night in an uproar. *Swift.*

3. [*Raquette*, Fr.] The inſtrument with which players ſtrike the ball. Whence perhaps all the other ſenſes.

When we have matcht our *rackets* to theſe balls,
We will in France play a ſet,
Shall ſtrike his father's crown into the hazard. *Shakeſp.*

The body, into which impreſſion is made, either can yield backward or it cannot: if it can yield backward, then the impreſſion made is a motion; as we ſee a ſtroke with a *racket* upon a ball, makes it fly from it. *Digby on the Soul.*

He talks much of the motives to do and forbear, how they determine a reaſonable man, as if he were no more than a tennis-ball, to be toſſed to and fro by the *rackets* of the ſecond cauſes. *Bramhall againſt Hobbs.*

RA'CKING. *n. ſ.*

Racking pace of a horſe is the ſame as an amble, only that it is a ſwifter time and a ſhorter tread; and though it does not rid ſo much ground, yet it is ſomething eaſier. *Far. Dict.*

RA'CKOON. *n. ſ.*

The *rackoon* is a New England animal, like a badger, having a tail like a fox, being cloathed with a thick and deep furr: it ſleeps in the day time in a hollow tree, and goes out a-nights, when the moon ſhines, to feed on the ſea ſide, where it is hunted by dogs. *Bailey.*

RA'CY. *adj.* [perhaps from *rayz*, Spaniſh, a root.] Strong; flavorous; taſting of the ſoil.

Rich *racy* verſes in which we
The ſoil, from which they come, taſte, ſmell, and ſee. *Cowley.*

From his brain that Helicon diſtil,
Whoſe *racy* liquor did his offspring fill. *Denham.*

The cyder at firſt is very luſcious, but if ground more early, it is more *racy*. *Mortimer's Huſbandry.*

The hoſpitable ſage, in ſign
Of ſocial welcome, mix'd the *racy* wine,
Late from the mellowing caſk reſtor'd to light,
By ten long years refin'd, and roſy bright. *Pope.*

RAD. the old pret. of *read.* *Spenſer.*

RAD.

Rad, *red* and *rod*, differing only in dialect, ſignify counſel; as Conrad, powerful or ſkilful in counſel; Ethelred, a noble counſellor; Rodbert, eminent for counſel: Eubulus and Thraſybulus have almoſt the ſame ſenſe. *Gibſon.*

RA'DDOCK, or *ruddock.* *n. ſ.* A bird.

The *raddock* would,
With charitable bill, bring thee all this. *Shakeſp.*

RA'DIANCE. } *n. ſ.* [*radiare*, Lat.] Sparkling luſtre; glitter.
RA'DIANCY. }

By the ſacred *radiance* of the ſun,
By all the operations of the orbs,
Here I diſclaim all my paternal care. *Shakeſp. K. Lear.*

Whether there be not too high an apprehenſion above its natural *radiancy*, is not without juſt doubt; however it be granted a very ſplendid gum, and whoſe ſparkles may ſomewhat reſemble the glances of fire. *Brown's Vulgar Errours.*

The ſon
Girt with omnipotence, with *radiance* crown'd
Of majeſty divine. *Milton.*

A glory ſurpaſſing the ſun in its greateſt *radiancy*, which, though we cannot deſcribe, will bear ſome reſemblance. *Burnet's Theory of the Earth.*

The rapid *radiance* inſtantaneous ſtrikes
Th' illumin'd mountain. *Thomſon's Spring.*

RA'DIANT. *adj.* [*radians*, Lat.] Shining; brightly ſparkling; emitting rays.

There was a ſun of gold *radiant* upon the top, and before, a ſmall cherub of gold with wings diſplayed. *Bacon.*

Mark what *radiant* ſtate ſhe ſpreads,
In circle round her ſhining throne,
Shooting her beams like ſilver threads,
This, this is ſhe alone. *Milton's Arcades.*

Virtue could ſee to do what virtue would
By her own *radiant* light, though ſun and moon
Were in the flat ſea ſunk. *Milton.*

I ſee the warlike hoſt of heaven,
Radiant in glitt'ring arms and beamy pride,
Go forth to ſuccour truth below. *Milton.*

To RA'DIATE. *v. n.* [*radio*, Lat.] To emit rays; to ſhine; to ſparkle.

Though with wit and parts their poſſeſſors could never engage God to ſend forth his light and his truth; yet now that revelation hath diſcloſed them, and that he hath been pleaſed to make them *radiate* in his word, men may recollect thoſe ſcatter'd divine beams, and kindling with them the topicks proper to warm our affections, enflame holy zeal. *Boyle.*

Light *radiates* from luminous bodies directly to our eyes, and thus we ſee the ſun or a flame; or it is reflected from other bodies, and thus we ſee a man or a picture. *Locke.*

RA'DIATED. *adj.* [*radiatus*, Lat.] Adorned with rays.

The *radiated* head of the phœnix gives us the meaning of a paſſage in Auſonius. *Addiſon.*

RADIA'TION. *n. ſ.* [*radiatio*, Lat. *radiation*, Fr.]

1. Beamy luſtre; emiſſion of rays.

We have perſpective houſes, where we make demonſtrations of all lights and *radiations*, and of all colours. *Bacon.*

Should I ſay I liv'd darker than were true,
Your *radiation* can all clouds ſubdue,
But one; 'tis beſt light to contemplate you. *Donne.*

2. Emiſſion from a center every way.

Sound paralleleth in many things with the light, and *radiation* of things viſible. *Bacon's Natural Hiſtory.*

RA'DICAL. *adj.* [*radical*, Fr. from *radix*, Latin.]

1. Primitive; original.

The differences, which are ſecondary and proceed from theſe *radical* differences, are, plants are all figurate and determinate, which inanimate bodies are not. *Bacon.*

Such a *radical* truth, that God is, ſpringing up together with the eſſence of the ſoul, and previous to all other thoughts, is not pretended to by religion. *Bentley.*

2. Implanted by nature.

The emiſſion of the looſe and adventitious moiſture doth betray the *radical* moiſture, and carrieth it for company. *Bac.*

If the *radical* moiſture of gold were ſeparated, it might be contrived to burn without being conſumed. *Wilkins.*

The ſun beams render the humours hot, and dry up the *radical* moiſture. *Arbuthnot.*

3. Serving to origination.

RA'DICALITY. *n. ſ.* [from *radical*.] Origination.

There may be equivocal ſeeds and hermaphroditical principles, that contain the *radicality* and power of different forms; thus, in the ſeeds of wheat, there lieth obſcurely the ſeminality of darnel. *Brown's Vulgar Errours.*

RA'DICALLY. *adv.* [from *radical*.] Originally; primitively.

It is no eaſy matter to determine the point of death in inſects, who have not their vitalities *radically* confined unto one part. *Brown's Vulgar Errours.*

Theſe great orbs thus *radically* bright,
Primitive founts, and origins of light
Enliven worlds deny'd to human ſight. *Prior.*

RA'DICALNESS. *n. ſ.* [from *radical*.] The ſtate of being radical.

To RA'DICATE. *v. a.* [*radicatus*, from *radix*, Lat.] To root; to plant deeply and firmly.

Meditation will *radicate* theſe ſeeds, fix the tranſient gleam of light and warmth, confirm reſolutions of good, and give them a durable conſiſtence in the ſoul. *Hammond.*

Nor have we let fall our pen upon diſcouragement of unbelief, from *radicated* beliefs, and points of high preſcription. *Brown's Vulgar Errours.*

If the object ſtays not on the ſenſe, it makes not impreſſion enough to be remembered; but if it be repeated there, it leaves plenty enough of thoſe images behind it, to ſtrengthen the knowledge of the object: in which *radicated* knowledge, if the memory conſiſt, there would be no need of reſerving thoſe atoms in the brain. *Glanvill's Defence.*

RADICA'TION. *n. ſ.* [*radication*, Fr. from *radicate*.] The act of fixing deep.

They that were to plant a church, were to deal with men of various inclinations, and of different habits of ſin, and degrees of *radication* of thoſe habits; and to each of theſe ſome proper application was to be made to cure their ſouls. *Hammond's Fundamentals.*

RA'DICLE. *n. ſ.* [*radicule*, Fr. from *radix*, Lat.]

Radicle is that part of the ſeed of a plant, which, upon its vegetation, becomes its root. *Quincy.*

RA'DISH. *n. ſ.* [rædic, Sax. *radis*, *raifort*, Fr. *raphanus*, Lat.] A root.

The flower of the *radiſh* conſiſts of four leaves, which are placed in the form of a croſs; out of the flower cup riſes the pointal, which afterward turns to a pod in form of an horn, that is thick, ſpungy, and furniſhed with a double row of roundiſh ſeeds, which are ſeparated by a thin membrane: there are five ſpecies; of that which is commonly cultivated in the kitchen-gardens for its root, there are ſeveral varieties; as the ſmall topped, the deep-red, and the long topped ſtripped *radiſh*. *Miller.*

RA'DIUS. *n. ſ.* [Latin.]

1. The ſemi-diameter of a circle.

2. A bone of the fore-arm, which accompanies the ulna from the elbow to the wriſt.

To RAFF. *v. a.* To ſweep; to huddle; to take haſtily without diſtinction.

Their cauſes and effects I thus *raff* up together. *Carew.*

To RA'FFLE. *v. n.* [*raffler*, to ſnatch, Fr.] To caſt dice for a prize, for which every one lays down a ſtake.

Letters from Hampſtead give me an account, there is a late inſtitution there, under the name of a *raffling* ſhop *Tatler.*

RA'FFLE. *n. ſ.* [*rafle*, Fr. from the verb.] A ſpecies of game or lottery, in which many ſtake a ſmall part of the value of ſome ſingle thing, in conſideration of a chance to gain it.

The toy, brought to Rome in the third triumph of Pompey, being a pair of tables for gaming, made of two precious ſtones, three foot broad, and four foot long, would have made a fine *raffle*. *Arbuthnot on Coins.*

RAFT. *n. ſ.* [probably from *ratis*, Latin.] A frame or float made by laying pieces of timber croſs each other.

Where is that ſon
That floated with thee on the fatal *raft*. *Shakeſp.*

Fell the timber of yon lofty grove,
And form a *raft*, and build the riſing ſhip. *Pope.*

RAFT. part. paſſ. of *reave* or *raff*. *Spenſer.* Torn; rent.

RA'FTER. *n. ſ.* [ræfter, Sax. *rafter*, Dutch; corrupted, ſays *Junius*, from *roof tree*.] The ſecondary timbers of the houſe; the timbers which are let into the great beam.

The *rafters* of my body, bone,
Being ſtill with you, the muſcle, ſinew and vein,
Which tile this houſe, will come again. *Donne.*

Shepherd,
I truſt thy honeſt offer'd courteſy,
Which oft is ſooner found in lowly ſheds
With ſmoky *rafters*, than in tap'ſtry halls. *Milton.*

On them the Trojans caſt
Stones, *rafters*, pillars, beams. *Denham.*

From the Eaſt, a Belgian wind
His hoſtile breath through the dry *rafters* ſent;
The flames impell'd. *Dryden.*

The roof began to mount aloft,
Aloft roſe every beam and *rafter*,
The heavy wall climb'd ſlowly after. *Swift's Miſcel.*

RA'FTERED. *adj.* [from *rafter*.] Built with rafters.

No *raft'red* roofs with dance and tabor ſound,
No noon-tide bell invites the country round. *Pope.*

RAG. *n. ſ.* [hꞃacobe, torn, Saxon; ῥάκ☉.]

1. A piece of cloth torn from the reſt; a tatter.

Cowls, hoods and habits, with their wearers toſt,
And flutter'd into *rags*. *Milton.*

Rags are a great improvement of chalky lands. *Mortimer.*

2. Any thing rent and tattered; worn out cloaths.

Fathers that wear *rags*,
Do make their children blind;
But fathers that bear bags,
Shall ſee their children kind. *Shakeſp. King Lear.*

Worn like a cloth,
Gnawn into *rags* by the devouring moth. *Sandys.*

Content with poverty, my ſoul I arm;
And virtue, though in *rags*, will keep me warm. *Dryden.*

3. A fragment of dreſs.

He had firſt matter ſeen undreſt;
He took her naked all alone,
Before one *rag* of form was on. *Hudibras, p. i.*

RAGAMU'FFIN. *n. ſ.* [from *rag* and I know not what elſe.]

I have led my *ragamuffins* where they were pepper'd; there's not three of my hundred and fifty left alive; and they are for the town's end to beg during life. *Shakeſp. Henry IV.*

Shall we brook that paltry aſs
And feeble ſcoundrel, Hudibras,
With that more paltry *ragamuffin*,
Ralpho, vapouring and huffing. *Hudibras, p. i.*

Attended with a crew of *ragamuffins*, ſhe broke into his houſe, turned all things topſy-turvy, and then ſet it on fire. *Swift.*

RAGE. *n. ſ.* [*rage*, Fr.]

1. Violent anger; vehement fury.

This tiger-footed *rage*, when it ſhall find
The harm of unſkann'd ſwiftneſs, will, too late,
Tie leaden pounds to's heels. *Shakeſp. Coriolanus.*

Desire not
T' allay my *rages* and revenges with
Your colder reasons. *Shakesp.*
Argument more heroick than the *rage*
Of Turnus for Lavinia disespous'd. *Milton.*

3. Vehemence or exacerbation of any thing painful.

The party hurtr who hath been in great *rage* of pain, till the weapon was re anointed. *Bacon's Natural History.*

Torment and loud lament and furious *rage*. *Milton.*
The *rage* of thirst and hunger now supprest. *Pope.*

To RAGE. *v. n.* [from the noun.]

1. To be in fury; to be heated with excessive anger.

Wine is a mocker, strong drink is *raging*; and whosoever is deceived thereby, is not wise. *Prov.* xx. 1.

Why do the heathen *rage*. *Psalm* ii. 1.

At this he inly *rag'd*, and as they talk'd,
Smote him into the midriff. *Milton.*

2. To ravage; to exercise fury.

Heart-rending news,
That death should license have to *rage* among
The fair, the wise, the virtuous. *Waller.*

3. To act with mischievous impetuousity.

The chariots shall *rage* in the streets, they shall justle one against another, seem like torches, and run like the lightenings. *Nah.* ii. 4.

The madding wheels of brazen chariots *rag'd*. *Milton.*

After these waters had *raged* on the earth, they began to lessen and shrink, and the great fluctuations of this deep being quieted by degrees, the waters retired. *Burnet.*

RA'GEFUL. *adj.* [*rage* and *full.*] Furious; violent.

This courtesy was worse than a bastinado to Zelmane; so that again with *rageful* eyes she bad him defend himself; for no less than his life would answer it. *Sidney, b.* ii.

A popular orator may represent vices in so formidable appearances, and set out each virtue in so amiable a form, that the covetous person shall scatter most liberally his beloved idol, wealth, and the *rageful* person shall find a calm. *Hamm.*

RA'GGED. *adj.* [from *rag.*]

1. Rent into tatters.

How like a prodigal,
The skarfed bark puts from her native bay,
Hugg'd and embraced by the strumpet wind;
How like the prodigal doth she return
With over-weather'd ribs and *ragged* sails,
Lean, rent, and beggar'd by the strumpet wind. *Shakesp.*

As I go in this *ragged* tattered coat, I am hunted away from the old woman's door by every barking cur. *Arbuthnot.*

2. Uneven; consisting of parts almost disunited.

The earl of Warwick's *ragged* staff is yet to be seen pourtrayed in their church steeple. *Carew's Survey of Cornwall.*

That some whirlwind bear
Unto a *ragged*, fearful, hanging rock,
And throw it thence into the raging sea. *Shakesp.*

The moon appears, when looked upon with a good glass, rude and *ragged*. *Burnet's Theory of the Earth.*

3. Dressed in tatters.

Since noble arts in Rome have no support,
And *ragged* virtue not a friend at court. *Dryden.*

4. Rugged; not smooth.

The wolf would barter away a *ragged* coat and a rawboned carcase, for a smooth fat one. *L'Estrange.*

What shepherd owns those *ragged* sheep? *Dryden.*

RA'GGEDNESS. *n. s.* [from *ragged.*] State of being dressed in tatters.

Poor naked wretches, whereso'er you are,
That bide the pelting of this pitiless storm!
How shall your houseless heads and unfed sides,
Your loop'd and window'd *raggedness* defend you. *Shakesp.*

RA'GINGLY. *adv.* [from *raging.*] With vehement fury.

RA'GMAN. *n. s.* [*rag* and *man.*] One who deals in rags.

RAGOU'T. *n. s.* [French] Meat stewed and highly seasoned.

To the stage permit
Ragouts for Tereus or Thyestes drest,
'Tis task enough for thee t' expose a Roman feast. *Dryden.*

No fish they reckon comparable to a *ragout* of snails. *Add.*

When art and nature join, th' effect will be
Some nice *ragout*, or charming fricasy. *King's Cookery.*

RA'GWORT. *n. s.* [*rag* and *wort.*] A plant.

Ragwort hath a radiated flower, the tube of which is almost of a cylindrical figure, and the seeds are fastened to a down; the leaves are deeply laciniated or jagged. *Miller.*

RA'GSTONE. *n. s.* [*rag* and *stone.*]

1. A stone so named from its breaking in a ragged, uncertain, irregular manner. *Woodward on Fossils.*

2. The stone with which they smooth the edge of a tool new ground and left ragged.

RAIL. *n. s.* [*riegel*, German.]

1. A cross beam fixed at the ends in two upright posts.

If you make another square, and also a tennant on each untennanted end of the stiles, and another mortess on the top and bottom *rails*, you may put them together. *Moxon.*

2. A series of posts connected with beams, by which any thing is inclosed: a *pale* is a series of small upright posts rising above the cross beam, by which they are connected: a *rail* is a series of cross beams supported with posts, which do not rise much above it.

A man, upon a high place without *rails*, is ready to fall. *Bacon's Natural History.*

A large square table for the commissioners, one side being sufficient for those of either party, and a *rail* for others which went round. *Clarendon.*

3. A kind of bird.

Of wild birds Cornwall hath quail, *rail*, partridge and pheasant. *Carew's Survey of Cornwall.*

4. [ɲæʒle, Saxon.] A woman's upper garment. This is preserved only in the word *nightrail.*

To RAIL. *v. a.* [from the noun.]

1. To inclose with rails.

The hand is square, with four rounds at the corners; this should first have been planched over, and *railed* about with ballisters. *Carew's Survey of Cornwall.*

As the churchyard ought to be divided from other profane places, so it ought to be fenced in and *railed*. *Ayliffe.*

Sir Roger has given a handsome pulpit-cloth, and *railed* in the communion-table. *Addison's Spectator,* N° 112.

2. To range in a line.

They were brought to London all *railed* in ropes, like a team of horses in a cart, and were executed some of them at London and Wapping, and the rest at divers places upon the sea coast. *Bacon's Henry* VII.

To RAIL. *v. n.* [*railler*, Fr. *rallen*, Dutch.] To use insolent and reproachful language; to speak to, or to mention in opprobrious terms.

Your husband is in his old lunes again; he so *rails* against all married mankind, curses all Eve's daughters. *Shakesp.*

What a monstrous fellow art thou? thus to *rail* on one, that is neither known of thee, nor knows thee. *Shakesp.*

'Till thou can'st *rail* the seals from off my bond,
Thou but offend'st thy lungs to speak so loud. *Shakesp.*

He tript me behind; being down, insulted, *rail'd*,
And put upon him such a deal of man,
That worthied him. *Shakesp. King Lear.*

Of words cometh *railings* and evil surmisings. 1 *Tim.* vi.

Angels bring not *railing* accusation against them. 2 *Pet.* ii.

If any is angry, and *rails* at it, he may securely. *Locke.*

Thou art my blood, where Johnson has no part;
Where did his wit on learning fix a brand,
And *rail* at arts he did not understand? *Dryden.*

Lesbia for ever on me *rails*,
To talk of me she never fails. *Swift.*

RAI'LER. *n. s.* [from *rail.*] One who insults or defames by opprobious language.

If I build my felicity upon my reputation, I am as happy as long as the *railer* will give me leave. *South's Sermons.*

Let no presuming impious *railer* tax
Creative wisdom. *Thomson's Summer.*

RAI'LLERY. *n. s.* [*raillerie*, Fr.] Slight satire; satirical merriment.

Let *raillery* be without malice or heat. *Benj. Johnson.*

A quotation out of Hudibras shall make them treat with levity an obligation wherein their welfare is concerned as to this world and the next: *raillery* of this nature is enough to make the hearer tremble. *Addison's Freeholder,* N° 6.

Studies employed on low objects; the very naming of them is almost sufficient to turn them into *raillery*. *Addison on Ancient Medals.*

To these we are solicited by the arguments of the subtile, and the *railleries* of the prophane. *Rogers's Sermons.*

RAI'MENT. *n. s.* [for *arraiment*, from *array.*] Vesture; vestment; cloaths; dress; garment. A word now little used but in poetry.

His *raiments*, though mean, received handsomeness by the grace of the wearer. *Sidney.*

O Protheus, let this habit make thee blush!
Be thou asham'd, that I have took upon me
Such an immodest *raiment*. *Shakesp.*

Living, both food and *raiment* she supplies. *Dryden.*

To RAIN. *v. n.* [ɲenian, Saxon; *regenen*, Dutch.]

1. To fall in drops from the clouds.

Like a low-hung cloud, it *rains* so fast,
That all at once it falls. *Dryden's Knight's Tale.*

The wind is South-West, and the weather lowring, and like to *rain*. *Locke.*

2. To fall as rain.

The eye marvelleth at the whiteness thereof, and the heart is astonished at the *raining* of it. *Ecclus.* xliii. 18.

They sat them down to weep; nor only tears
Rain'd at their eyes, but high winds rose within. *Milton.*

3. *It* RAINS. The water falls from the clouds.

That which serves for gain,
And follows but for form,
Will pack when *it* begins to *rain*,
And leave thee in the storm. *Shakesp. King Lear.*

To RAIN. *v. a.* To pour down as rain.

It *rain'd* down fortune, show'ring on your head. *Shak.*

Rain ſacrificial whiſp'rings in his ear,
Make ſacred even his ſtirrop. *Shakeſp. Timon of Athens.*
Iſrael here had famiſh'd, had not God
Rain'd from heav'n manna. *Milton's Paradiſe Loſt, b.* ii.

RAIN. *n. ſ.* [ꞃen, Saxon.] The moiſture that falls from the clouds.

When ſhall we three meet again;
In thunder, lightning, or in *rain.* *Shakeſp.*

With ſtrange *rains*, hails, and ſhowers were they perſecuted. *Wiſdom* xvi. 16.

The loſt clouds pour
Into the ſea an uſeleſs ſhow'r,
And the vext ſailors curſe the *rain*,
For which poor farmers pray'd in vain. *Waller.*

Rain is water by the heat of the ſun divided into very ſmall parts aſcending in the air, till encountering the cold, it be condenſed into clouds, and deſcends in drops. *Ray.*

RAI'NBOW. *n. ſ.* [*rain* and *bow.*] The iris; the ſemicircle of various colours which appears in ſhowery weather.

Caſting of the water in a moſt cunning manner, makes a perfect *rainbow*, not more pleaſant to the eye than to the mind, ſo ſenſibly to ſee the proof of the heavenly iris. *Sidney.*

To add another hue unto the *rainbow.* *Shakeſp.*

The *rainbow* is drawn like a nymph with large wings diſpread in the form of a ſemicircle, the feathers of ſundry colours. *Peach.*

They could not be ignorant of the promiſe of God never to drown the world, and the *rainbow* before their eyes to put them in mind of it. *Brown's Vulgar Errours.*

This *rainbow* never appears but where it rains in the ſunſhine, and may be made artificially by ſpouting up water, which may break aloft, and ſcatter into drops, and fall down like rain; for the ſun, ſhining upon theſe drops, certainly cauſes the bow to appear to a ſpectator ſtanding in a true poſition to the rain and ſun: this bow is made by refraction of the ſun's light in drops of falling rain. *Newton's Opticks.*

The dome's high arch reflects the mingled blaze,
And forms a *rainbow* of alternate rays. *Pope.*

RAI'NDEER. [hꞃanaꞃ, Saxon; *rangifer*, Latin.] A deer with large horns, which, in the northern regions, draws ſledges through the ſnow.

RAI'NINESS. *n. ſ.* [from *rainy*.] The ſtate of being ſhowery.

RAIN-WATER. *n. ſ.* [*rain* and *water.*] Water not taken from ſprings, but falling from the clouds.

Court holy water in a dry houſe, is better than the *rainwater* out o' doors. *Shakeſp. King Lear.*

We took diſtilled *rain-water.* *Boyle.*

Rain-water is to be preferred before ſpring-water. *Mort.*

RAI'NY. *adj.* [from *rain.*] Showery; wet.

Our gayneſs and our gilt are all beſmirch'd,
With *rainy* marching in the painful field. *Shakeſp. Hen.* V.

A continual dropping in a very *rainy* day, and a contentious woman are alike. *Prov.* xxvii. 15.

To RAISE. *v. a.* [*reſa*, Swediſh; *reiſer*, Daniſh.]

1. To lift; to heave.

The elders went to *raiſe* him up from the earth. 2 *Sam.* xii.

Such a bulk as no twelve bards could *raiſe*
Twelve ſtarv'ling bards. *Pope.*

2. To ſet upright: as, *he* raiſed *a maſt.*

3. To erect; to build up.

Take his carcaſe down from the tree, caſt it at the entering of the gate, and *raiſe* thereon a heap of ſtones. *Joſ.* viii.

4. To exalt to a ſtate more great or illuſtrious.

Counſellors may manage affairs, which nevertheleſs are far from the ability to *raiſe* and amplify an eſtate. *Bacon.*

Thou ſo pleas'd,
Can'ſt *raiſe* thy creature to what height thou wilt
Of union. *Milton.*

5. To amplify; to enlarge.

That eyeleſs head of thine was firſt fram'd fleſh,
To *raiſe* my fortunes. *Shakeſp. King Lear.*

6. To increaſe in current value.

The plate-pieces of eight were *raiſed* three-pence in the piece. *Temple's Miſcellanies.*

7. To elevate; to exalt.

The Perſians gazing on the ſun,
Admir'd how high 'twas plac'd, how bright it ſhone;
But as his pow'r was known, their thoughts were *rais'd*,
And ſoon they worſhip'd, what at firſt they prais'd. *Prior.*

8. To advance; to promote; to prefer.

This gentleman came to be *raiſed* to great titles. *Clarend.*

9. To excite; to put in action.

He *raiſeth* the ſtormy wind. *Pſalm* cvii. 28.

He might taint
Th' animal ſpirits, that from pure blood ariſe,
Thence *raiſe* diſtemper'd thoughts. *Milton.*

Gods encountering gods, Jove encouraging them with his thunders, and Neptune *raiſing* his tempeſts. *Pope.*

10. To excite to war or tumult; to ſtir up.

He firſt *rais'd* head againſt uſurping Richard. *Shakeſp.*

They neither found me in the temple diſputing with any man, neither *raiſing* up the people. *Acts* xxiv. 12.

Æneas then employs his pains
In parts remote to *raiſe* the Tuſcan ſwains. *Dryden.*

11. To rouſe; to ſtir up.

They ſhall not awake, nor be *raiſed* out of their ſleep. *Job.*

12. To give beginning to: as, *he* raiſed *the family.*

13. To bring into being.

Marry her, and *raiſe* up ſeed. *Gen.* xxxviii. 8.

I *raiſed* up of your ſons for prophets. *Amos* ii. 11.

I will *raiſe* up for them a plant of renown, and they ſhall be no more conſumed with hunger. *Ezek.* xxxiv. 29.

I will *raiſe* up evil againſt thee. 2 *Samuel* xii. 11.

One hath ventur'd from the deep to *raiſe*
New troubles. *Milton.*

God vouchſafes to *raiſe* another world
From him. *Milton.*

14. To call into view from the ſtate of ſeparate ſpirits.

The ſpirits of the deceaſed, by certain ſpells and infernal ſacrifices, were *raiſed.* *Sandys's Journey.*

Theſe are ſpectres, the underſtanding *raiſes* to itſelf, to flatter its own lazineſs. *Locke.*

15. To bring from death to life.

He was delivered for our offences, and *raiſed* again for our juſtification. *Romans* iv. 25.

It is ſown in diſhonour, it is *raiſed* in glory; it is ſown in weakneſs, it is *raiſed* in power. 1 *Cor.* xv. 23.

16. To occaſion; to begin.

Raiſe not a falſe report. *Exodus* xxiii. 1.

The common ferryman of Egypt, that wafted over the dead bodies from Memphis, was made by the Greeks to be the ferryman of hell, and ſolemn ſtories *raiſed* after him. *Bro.*

Wantonneſs and pride
Raiſe out of friendſhip hoſtile deeds in peace. *Milton.*

17. To ſet up; to utter loudly.

All gaze, and all admire, and *raiſe* a ſhouting ſound. *Dry.*

Soon as the prince appears, they *raiſe* a cry. *Dryden.*

18. To collect; to obtain a certain ſum.

Britain, once deſpis'd, can *raiſe*
As ample ſums, as Rome in Cæſar's days. *Arbuthnot.*

I ſhould not thus be bound,
If I had means, and could but *raiſe* five pound. *Gay.*

19. To collect; to aſſemble; to levy.

He out of ſmalleſt things could without end
Have *rais'd* inceſſant armies. *Milton.*

20. To give riſe to.

Higher argument
Remains, ſufficient of itſelf to *raiſe*
That name, unleſs years damp my wing. *Milton.*

21. *To* RAISE *paſte.* To form paſte into pies without a diſh.

Miſs Liddy can dance a jig, and *raiſe paſte.* *Spectator.*

RAI'SER. *n. ſ.* [from *raiſe.*] He that raiſes.

Then ſhall ſtand up in his eſtate a *raiſer* of taxes. *Dan.* xi.

They that are the firſt *raiſers* of their houſes, are moſt indulgent towards their children. *Bacon.*

He that boaſts of his anceſtors, the founders and *raiſers* of a family, doth confeſs that he hath leſs virtue. *Taylor.*

Raiſer of human kind! by nature caſt,
Naked and helpleſs. *Thomſon's Autumn.*

RAI'SIN. *n. ſ.* [*racemus*, Lat. *raiſin*, Fr.]

Raiſins are the fruit of the vine ſuffered to remain on the tree till perfectly ripened, and then dried either by the ſun or the heat of an oven: grapes of every kind, preſerved in this manner, are called *raiſins*, but thoſe dried in the ſun are much ſweeter and pleaſanter than thoſe dried in ovens; they are called jar *raiſins*, from their being imported in earthen jars: the fineſt are the fruit of the vitis Damaſcena. *Hill's Materia Med.*

Dried grapes or *raiſins*, boiled in a convenient proportion of water, make a ſweet liquor, which, being betimes diſtilled, afford an oil and ſpirit much like the *raiſins* themſelves. *Boyle.*

RAKE. *n. ſ.* [*raſtrum*, Lat. ꞃace, Sax. *racche*, Dutch.]

1. An inſtrument with teeth, by which the ground is divided, or light bodies are gathered up.

At Midſummer down with the brembles and brakes,
And after abroad with thy forkes and thy *rakes.* *Tuſſer.*

O that thy bounteous deity wou'd pleaſe
To guide my *rake* upon the chinking ſound
Of ſome vaſt treaſure hidden under grouud. *Dryden.*

He examines his face in the ſtream, combs his ruful locks with a *rake.* *Garth.*

2. [*Racaille*, Fr. the low rabble; or *rekel*, Dutch, a worthleſs cur dog.] A looſe, diſorderly, vicious, wild, gay, thoughtleſs fellow; a man addicted to pleaſure.

The next came with her ſon, who was the greateſt *rake* in the place, but ſo much the mother's darling, that ſhe left her huſband for the ſake of this graceleſs youth. *Addiſon.*

Rakes hate ſober grave gentlewomen. *Arbuthnot.*

Men, ſome to bus'neſs, ſome to pleaſure take;
But ev'ry woman is at heart a *rake.* *Pope.*

The ſire ſaw ſmiling his own virtues wake;
The mother begg'd the bleſſing of a *rake.* *Pope.*

To RAKE. *v. a.* [from the noun.]

1. To gather with a rake.

Mow barlie, and *rake* it, and ſet it on cocks. *Tuſſer.*

Harrows iron teeth ſhall every where
Rake helmets up. *May's Virgil's Georgicks.*

If

If it be such a precious jewel as the world takes it for, yet they are forced to *rake* it out of dunghills; and accordingly the apostle gives it a value suitable to its extract. *South.*

2. To clear with a rake.

As they *rake* the green appearing ground,
The russet hay-cock rises. *Thomson.*

3. To draw together by violence.

An eager desire to *rake* together whatsoever might prejudice or any way hinder the credit of apocryphal books, hath caused the collector's pen so to run as it were on wheels, that the mind, which should guide it, had no leisure to think. *Hooker, b.* v. *s.* 20.

What piles of wealth hath he accumulated!
How, i' th' the name of thrift,
Does he *rake* this together. *Shakesp. Henry* VIII.

A sport more formidable
Had *rak'd* together village rabble. *Hudibras, p.* i.

Ill-gotten goods are squandered away with as little conscience as they were *raked* together. *L'Estrange.*

4. To scour; to search with eager and vehement diligence.

The statesman *rakes* the town to find a plot. *Swift.*

5. To heap together and cover.

Here i' th' sands
Thee I'll *rake* up, the post unsanctified
Of murth'rous lechers. *Shakesp. King Lear.*

The blazing wood may to the eye seem great,
But 'tis the fire *rak'd* up that has the heat,
And keeps it long. *Suckling.*

To RAKE. *v. n.*

1. To search; to grope. It has always an idea of coarseness or noisomness.

If you hide the crown
Ev'n in your hearts, there will he *rake* for it. *Shakesp.*
It is as offensive, as to *rake* into a dunghill. *South.*

Another finds the way to dye in grain;
Or for the golden ore in rivers *rakes*,
Then melts the mass. *Dryden's Persius.*

One is for *raking* in Chaucer for antiquated words, which are never to be reviv'd, but when found or significancy is wanting. *Dryden.*

After having made essays into it, as they do for coal in England, they *rake* into the most promising parts. *Addison.*

2. To pass with violence.

When Pas hand reached him to take,
The fox on knees and elbows tumbled down:
Pas could not stay, but over him did *rake*,
And crown'd the earth with his first touching crown. *Sidn.*

The Belgians tack upon our rear,
And *raking* chase-guns through our sterns they send. *Dryd.*

RA'KER. *n. s.* [from *rake.*] One that rakes.

RA'KEHEL. *n. s.* [of this word the etymology is doubtful: as it is now written, it is apparently derived from *rake* and *hell*, and may aptly represent a wretch whose life is passed in places of lewdness and wickedness: *Skinner* derives it from *racaille*, French, the rabble; *Junius*, from *rekel*, Dutch, a mongrel dog.] A wild, worthless, dissolute, debauched, sorry fellow.

Out of the frie of these *rakehell* horse-boys, growing up in knavery and villainy, are their kern supplied. *Spenser.*

The king, when he heard of Perkins's siege of Exeter, said in sport, that the king of *rakehells* was landed in the West, and that he hoped now to see him. *Bacon.*

A *rakehell* of the town, whose character is set off with excessive prodigality, prophaneness, intemperance and lust, is rewarded with a lady of great fortune to repair his own, which his vices had almost ruined. *Swift.*

RA'KEHELLY. *adv.* [from *rakehell.*] Wild; dissolute.

I scorn the *rakehelly* rout of our ragged rhimers, which without learning boast, without judgment jangle, and without reason rage and foam. *Spenser's Pastorals.*

No breaking of windows or glasses for spight,
And spoiling the goods for a *rakehelly* prank. *Benj. Johnson.*

RA'KISH. *adj.* [from *rake.*] Loose; lewd; dissolute.

There seldom can be peculiarity in the love of a *rakish* heart. *Clarissa.*

To RA'LLY. *v. a.* [*rallier*, Fr.]

1. To put disordered or dispersed forces into order.

With *rallied* arms to try what may be yet
Regain'd in heav'n. *Milton.*

Publick arguing serves to whet the wits of hereticks, and by shewing weak parts of their doctrines, prompts them to *rally* all their sophistry to fortify them with fallacy. *D. of Pie.*

Luther deters men from solitariness; but he does not mean from a sober solitude, that *rallies* our scattered strengths, and prepares us against any new encounters from without. *Atterb.*

2. [*Railler*, Fr.] To treat with slight contempt; to treat with satirical merriment.

Honeycomb has not lived a month, for these forty years, out of the smoke of London, and *rallies* me upon a country life. *Addison's Spectator.*

If after the reading of this letter, you find yourself in a humour rather to *rally* and ridicule, than to comfort me, I desire you would throw it into the fire. *Addison.*

Strephon had long confess'd his am'rous pain,
Which gay Corinna *rally'd* with disdain. *Gay.*

To RA'LLY. *v. n.*

1. To come together in a hurry.

If God should shew this perverse man a new heaven and a new earth, springing out of nothing, he might say, that innumerable parts of matter chanced just then to *rally* together, and to form themselves into this new world. *Tillotson.*

2. To come again into order.

The Grecians *rally*, and their pow'rs unite;
With fury charge us. *Dryden's Æneis.*

3. To exercise satirical merriment.

RAM. *n. s.* [ꞃam, Saxon; *ram*, Dutch.]

1. A male sheep; in some provinces, a tup.

The ewes, being rank, turned to the *rams*. *Shakesp.*
An old sheep-whistling rogue, a *ram* tender. *Shakesp.*

You may draw the bones of a *ram*'s head hung with strings of beads and ribbands. *Peacham on Drawing.*

A *ram* their off'ring, and a *ram* their meat. *Dryden.*

The *ram*, having pass'd the sea, serenely shines,
And leads the year. *Creech's Manilius.*

2. An instrument with an iron head to batter walls.

Antony,
Let not the piece of virtue, which is set
As the cement of our love,
To keep it builded, be the *ram* to batter
The fortress of it. *Shakesp. Antony and Cleopatra.*

Judas calling upon the Lord, who without any *rams* or engines of war did cast down Jericho, gave a fierce assault against the walls. 2 *Mac.* xii. 15.

To RAM. *v. a.* [from the noun.]

1. To drive with violence, as with a battering ram.

Ram thou thy faithful tidings in mine ears,
That long time have been barren. *Shakesp.*

Having no artillery nor engines, and finding that he could do no good by *ramming* with logs of timber, he set one of the gates on fire. *Bacon's Henry* VII.

The charge with bullet, or paper wet and hard stopped, or with powder alone *rammed* in hard, maketh no great difference in the loudness of the report. *Bacon's Nat. Hist.*

A mariner loading his gun, while he was *ramming* in a cartridge, the powder took fire. *Wiseman's Surgery.*

Here many poor people roll in vast balls of snow, which they *ram* together, and cover from the sun shine. *Addison.*

A ditch drawn between two parallel furrows, was filled with some sound materials, and *rammed* to make the foundation solid. *Arbuthnot on Coins.*

2. To fill with any thing driven hard together.

As when that devilish iron engine wrought
In deepest hell, and fram'd by furies skill,
With windy nitre and quick sulphur fraught,
And *ramm'd* with bullet round ordain'd to kill. *Fa. Queen.*

He that proves the king,
To him will we prove loyal; till that time,
Have we *ramm'd* up our gates against the world. *Shakesp.*

They mined the walls, laid the powder, and *rammed* the mouth, but the citizens made a countermine. *Hayward.*

This into hollow engines, long and round,
Thick *ramm'd*, at th' other bore with touch of fire
Dilated and infuriate, shall send forth
Such implements of mischief, as shall dash
To pieces. *Milton's Paradise Lost, b.* vi.

Leave a convenient space behind the wall to *ram* in clay. *Mortimer's Husbandry.*

To RA'MBLE. *v. n.* [*rammelen*, Dutch, to rove loosely in lust; *ramb*, Swedish, to rove.] To rove loosely and irregularly; to wander.

Shame contracts the spirits, fixes the *ramblings* of fancy, and gathers the man into himself. *South.*

He that is at liberty to *ramble* in perfect darkness, what is his liberty better than if driven up and down as a bubble by the wind. *Locke.*

Chapman has taken advantage of an immeasurable length of verse, notwithstanding which, there is scarce any paraphrase so loose and *rambling* as his. *Pope.*

Never ask leave to go abroad, for you will be thought an idle *rambling* fellow. *Swift's Directions to Footmen.*

O'er his ample sides the *rambling* sprays
Luxuriant shoot. *Thomson's Spring.*

RA'MBLE. *n. s.* [from the verb.] Wandering irregular excursion.

This conceit puts us upon the *ramble* up and down for relief, 'till very weariness brings us at last to ourselves. *L'Estr.*

Coming home after a short Christmas *ramble*, I found a letter upon my table. *Swift.*

She quits the narrow path of sense
For a dear *ramble* through impertinence. *Swift's Miscel.*

RA'MBLER. *n. s.* [from *ramble.*] Rover; wanderer.

Says the *rambler*, we must e'en beat it out. *L'Estrange.*

RA'MBOOZE. } *n. s.* A drink made of wine, ale, eggs and sugar
RA'MBUSE. } in the winter time; or of wine, milk, sugar and rosewater in the summer time. *Bailey.*

RA'MEKIN. } *n. s.* [*ramequins*, Fr.] In cookery, small slices
RA'MEQUINS. } of bread covered with a farce of cheese and eggs. *Bailey.*

RA'MENTS. *n. s.* [*ramenta*, Lat.] Scrapings; shavings. *Dict.*

RAMIFICA'TION. *n. s.* [*ramification*, Fr. from *ramus*, Latin.] Division or separation into branches; the act of branching out.

By continuation of profane histories or other monuments kept together, the genealogies and *ramifications* of some single families to a vast extension may be preserved. *Hale.*

As the blood and chyle pass together through the *ramifications* of the pulmonary artery, they will be still more perfectly mixed; but if a pipe is divided into branches, and these again subdivided, the red and white liquors, as they pass through the *ramifications*, will be more intimately mixed; the more *ramifications*, the mixture will be the more perfect. *Arb.*

To RA'MIFY. *v. a.* [*ramifier*, Fr. *ramus* and *facio*, Lat.] To separate into branches.

The mint, grown to have a pretty thick stalk, with the various and *ramified* roots, which it shot into the water, presented a spectacle not unpleasant to behold. *Boyle.*

To RA'MIFY. *v. n.* To be parted into branches.

Asparagus affects the urine with a fœtid smell, especially if cut when they are white; when they are older, and begin to *ramify*, they lose this quality. *Arbuthnot on Aliments.*

RA'MMER. *n. s.* [from *ram.*]

1. An instrument with which any thing is driven hard.

The master bricklayer must try the foundations with an iron crow and *rammer*, to see whether the foundations are sound. *Moxon's Mechanical Exercises.*

2. The stick with which the charge is forced into the gun.

A mariner loading a gun suddenly, while he was ramming in a cartridge, the powder took fire, and shot the *rammer* out of his hand. *Wiseman's Surgery.*

RA'MMISH. *adj.* [from *ram.*] Strong scented.

RA'MOUS. *adj.* [from *ramus*, Latin.] Branchy; consisting of branches.

Which vast contraction and expansion seems unintelligible, by feigning the particles of air to be springy and *ramous*, or rolled up like hoops, or by any other means than a repulsive power. *Newton's Opticks.*

A *ramous* efflorescence, of a fine white spar, found hanging from a crust of like spar, at the top of an old wrought cavern. *Woodward on Fossils.*

To RAMP. *v. n.* [*ramper*, French; *rampare*, Italian; *ræmpen*, Saxon.]

1. To leap with violence.

Foaming tarr, their bridles they would champ,
And trampling the fine element, would fiercely *ramp*. *F. Q.*
Out of the thickest wood
A *ramping* lyon rushed suddenly,
Hunting full greedy after savage blood. *Fairy Queen.*

They gape upon me with their mouths; as a *ramping* and roaring lion. *Psalm* xxii. 13.

Upon a bull, that deadly bellowed,
Two horrid lions *rampt*, and seiz'd, and tugg'd off. *Chapm.*
Sporting the lion *ramp'd*; and in his paw
Dandled the kid. *Milton.*

2. To climb as a plant.

Furnished with claspers and tendrils, they catch hold of them, and so *ramping* upon trees, they mount up to a great height. *Ray on the Creation.*

RAMP. *n. s.* [from the verb.] Leap; spring.

He is vaulting variable *ramps*,
In your despight, upon your purse. *Shakesp. Cymbeline.*
The bold Ascalonite
Fled from his lion *ramp*, old warriors turn'd
Their plated backs under his heel. *Milton's Agonistes.*

RAMPA'LLIAN. *n. s.* A mean wretch. Not in use.

Away you scullion, you *rampallian*, you fustilarian. *Shak.*

RAMPA'NCY. *n. s.* [from *rampant.*] Prevalence; exuberance.

As they are come to this height and *rampancy* of vice, from the countenance of their betters, so they have took some steps in the same, that the extravagances of the young carry with them the approbation of the old. *South.*

RA'MPANT. *adj.* [*rampant*, Fr. from *ramp.*]

1. Exuberant; overgrowing restraint.

The foundation of this behaviour towards persons set apart for the service of God, can be nothing else but atheism; the growing *rampant* sin of the times. *South.*

The seeds of death grow up, till, like *rampant* weeds, they choak the tender flower of life. *Clarissa.*

2. [In heraldry.]

Rampant is when the lion is reared up in the escutcheon, as it were ready to combate with his enemy. *Peacham.*

If a lion were the proper coat of Judah, yet were it not probable a lion *rampant*, but couchant or dormant. *Brown.*

The lion *rampant* shakes his brinded mane. *Milton.*

To RA'MPART. } *v. a.* [from the noun.] To fortify with
To RA'MPIRE. } ramparts. Not in use.

Set but thy foot
Against our *rampir'd* gates, and they shall ope. *Shakesp.*

The marquis directed part of his forces to *rampart* the gates and ruinous places of the walls. *Hayward.*

RA'MPART. } *n. s.* [*rempart*, Fr.
RA'MPIRE. }

1. The platform of the wall behind the parapet.

2. The wall round fortified places.

She felt it, when past preventing, like a river; no *rampires* being built against it, till already it have overflowed. *Sidney.*

Yo' have cut a way for virtue, which our great men
Held shut up, with all *ramparts*, for themselves. *B. Johns.*

He who endeavours to know his duty, and practises what he knows, has the equity of God to stand as a mighty wall or *rampart* between him and damnation for any infirmities. *South.*

The son of Thetis, *rampire* of our host,
Is worth our care to keep. *Dryden.*
The Trojans round the place a *rampire* cast,
And palisades about the trenches plac'd. *Dryden.*
No standards, from the hostile *ramparts* torn,
Can any future honours give
To the victorious monarch's name. *Prior.*

RA'MPIONS. *n. s.* [*rapunculus*, Lat.] A plant.

The flower of *rampions* consists of one leaf, in its form approaching to a bell-shape; but is so expanded and cut, that it almost represents the figure of a star: the pointal is commonly split into two horned divisions, and the flower-cup becomes a fruit, which is divided into three cells inclosing many small seeds. *Miller.*

Rampion is a plant, whose tender roots are eaten in the spring, like those of radishes. *Mortimer's Husbandry.*

RA'MSONS. *n. s.* An herb. *Ainsworth.*

RAN. *preterite* of *run.*

The dire example *ran* through all the field,
Till heaps of brothers were by brothers kill'd. *Addison.*

To RANCH. *v. a.* [corrupted from *wrench.*] To sprain; to injure with violent contortion. This is the proper sense, but, in *Dryden*, it seems to be to *tear.*

Against a stump his tusk the monster grinds,
And *ranch'd* his hips with one continu'd wound. *Dryden.*
Emeticks *ranch*, and keen cathartics scour. *Garth.*

RA'NCID. *adj.* [*rancidus*, Lat.] Strong scented.

The oil, with which fishes abound, often turns *rancid*, and lies heavy on the stomach, and affects the very sweat with a *rancid* smell. *Arbuthnot on Aliments.*

RA'NCIDNESS. } *n. s.* [from *rancid*; *rancor*, Lat.] Strong scent,
RANCI'DITY. } as of old oil.

RA'NCOROUS. *adj.* [from *rancour.*] Malignant; malicious; spiteful in the utmost degree.

So flam'd his eyen with rage and *rancorous* ire. *Fa. Qu.*
Because I cannot
Duck with French nods and apish courtesy,
I must be held a *rancorous* enemy. *Shakesp. Rich.* III.

The most powerful of these were Pharisees and Sadducees; of whose chief doctrines some notice is taken by the evangelists, as well as of their *rancorous* opposition to the gospel of Christ. *West on the Resurrection.*

RA'NCOUR. *n. s.* [*rancoeur*, old Fr.] Inveterate malignity; malice; stedfast implacability; standing hate.

His breast full of *rancor* like canker to freat. *Tusser.*
As two brave knights in bloody fight
With deadly *rancour* he enranged found. *Fairy Queen.*

All the way that they fled for very *rancour* and despite; in their return, they utterly consumed and wasted whatsoever they had before left unspoiled. *Spenser's State of Ireland.*

Rancour will out, proud prelate; in thy face
I see thy fury. *Shakesp. Henry* VI. *p.* ii.
It issues from the *rancour* of a villain,
A recreant and most degen'rate traitor. *Shakesp. Rich.* II.
For Banquo's issue, Duncan have I murther'd;
Put *rancour* in the vessel of my peace
Only for them. *Shakesp. Macbeth.*
Such ambush
Waited with hellish *rancour* imminent. *Milton.*

No authors draw upon themselves more displeasure, than those who deal in political matters, which is justly incurred, considering that spirit of *rancour* and virulence, with which works of this nature abound. *Addison's Freeholder*, Nº 40.

Presbyterians and their abettors, who can equally go to a church or conventicle, or such who bear a personal *rancour* towards the clergy. *Swift.*

RAND. *n. s.* [*rand*, Dutch.] Border; seam: as, *the* rand *of a woman's shoe.*

RA'NDOM. *n. s.* [*randon*, Fr.] Want of direction; want of rule or method; chance; hazard; roving motion.

Thy words at *random* argue thy inexperience. *Milton.*
He lies at *random* carelesly diffus'd,
With languish'd head unpropt,
As one past hope abandon'd. *Milton.*
Fond love his darts at *random* throws,
And nothing springs from what he sows. *Waller.*

The striker must be dense, and in its best velocity: the angle, which the missive is to mount by, if we will have it go to its furthest *random*, must be the half of a right one; and the figure of the missive must be such, as may give scope to the air to bear it. *Digby.*

In

In the days of old the birds lived at *random* in a lawless state of anarchy; but in time they moved for the setting up of a king. *L'Estrange's Fables.*

Who could govern the dependance of one event upon another, if that event happened at *random*, and was not cast into a certain relation to some foregoing purpose to direct. *South.*

'Tis one thing when a person of true merit is drawn as like as we can; and another, when we make a fine thing at *random*, and persuade the next vain creature that 'tis his own likeness. *Pope.*

RA'NDOM. *adj.* Done by chance; roving without direction.

Virtue borrow'd but the arms of chance,
And struck a *random* blow! 'twas fortune's work,
And fortune take the praise. *Dryden.*

RA'NFORCE. *n. s.* The ring of a gun next the touch-hole. *Bailey.*

RANG. *preterite* of *ring.*

Complaints were sent continually up to Rome, and *rang* all over the empire. *Grew's Cosmol.*

To RANGE. *v. a.* [*ranger*, Fr. *rhenge*, Welsh.]

1. To place in order; to put in ranks.

Maccabeus *ranged* his army by bands, and went against Timotheus. 2 *Mac.* xii. 20.

He saw not the marquis till the battle was *ranged. Clarend.*

Somewhat rais'd
By false presumptuous hope, the *ranged* pow'rs
Disband, and wand'ring each his several way
Pursues. *Milton.*

Men, from the qualities they find united in them, and wherein they observe several individuals to agree, *range* them into sorts for the convenience of comprehensive signs. *Locke.*

A certain form and order, in which we have long accustomed ourselves to *range* our ideas, may be best for us now, though not originally best in itself. *Watts.*

2. To rove over.

To the copse thy lesser spaniel take,
Teach him to *range* the ditch and force the brake. *Gay.*

To RANGE. *v. n.*

1. To rove at large.

Cæsar's spirit *ranging* for revenge,
With Ate by his side come hot from hell,
Shall in these confines, with a monarch's voice,
Cry havock, and let slip the dogs of war. *Shakesp.*

'Tis better to be lowly born,
And *range* with humble livers in content,
Than to be perk'd up in a glist'ring grief,
And wear a golden sorrow. *Shakesp. Henry* VIII.

I saw him in the battle *range* about;
And watch'd him, how he singled Clifford forth. *Shakesp.*

As a roaring lion and a *ranging* bear; so is a wicked ruler over the poor people. *Prov.* xxviii. 15.

Other animals unactive *range*,
And of their doings God takes no account. *Milton.*

Thanks to my stars, I have not *rang'd* about
The wilds of life, e're I could find a friend. *Addison.*

2. To be placed in order.

That is the way to lay the city flat,
To bring the roof to the foundation,
And bury all which yet distinctly *ranges*
In heaps of ruin. *Shakesp. Coriolanus.*

RANGE. *n. s.* [*rangée*, Fr. from the verb.]

1. A rank; any thing placed in a line.

You fled
From that great face of war, whose several *ranges*
Frighted each other. *Shakesp. Antony and Cleopatra.*

The light, which passed through its several interstices, painted so many *ranges* of colours, which were parallel and contiguous, and without any mixture of white. *Newton.*

From this walk you have a full view of a huge *range* of mountains, that lie in the country of the Grisons. *Addison.*

These *ranges* of barren mountains, by condensing the vapours and producing rains, fountains and rivers, give the very plains that fertility they boast of. *Bentley's Sermons.*

2. A class; an order.

The next *range* of beings above him are the immaterial intelligences, the next below him is the sensible nature. *Hale.*

3. Excursion; wandring.

He may take a *range* all the world over, and draw in all that wide circumference of sin and vice, and center it in his own breast. *South's Sermons.*

4. Room for excursion.

A man has not enough *range* of thought, to look out for any good which does not relate to his own interest. *Addison.*

5. Compass taken in by any thing excursive, extended, or ranked in order.

Far as creation's ample *range* extends,
The scale of sensual mental pow'rs ascends. *Pope.*

Judge we by nature? habit can efface;
Affections? they still take a wider *range*. *Pope.*

6. Step of a ladder.

The liturgy, practised in England, would kindle that jealousy, as the prologue to that design, and as the first *range* of that ladder, which should serve to mount over all their customs. *Clarendon.*

7. A kitchen grate.

Its door forth right to him did open,
Therein an hundred *ranges* weren pight,
And hundred furnaces all burning bright. *Fairy Queen.*

It was a vault ybuilt for great dispence,
With many *ranges* rear'd along the wall,
And one great chimney. *Fairy Queen.*

The buttery must be visible, and we need for our *ranges*, a more spacious and luminous kitchen. *Wotton's Architect.*

The implements of the kitchen are spits, *ranges*, cobirons and pots. *Bacon's Physical Remains.*

He was bid at his first coming to take off the *range*, and let down the cinders. *L'Estrange.*

RA'NGER. *n. s.* [from *range.*]

1. One that ranges; a rover; a robber.

They walk not widely, as they were woont,
For fear of *raungers* and the great hoont,
But privily prolling to and fro. *Spenser's Pastorals.*

Come, says the *ranger*, here's neither honour nor money to be got by staying. *L'Estrange.*

2. A dog that beats the ground.

Let your obsequious *ranger* search around,
Nor will the roving spy direct in vain,
But numerous coveys gratify thy pain. *Gay's Rural Sports.*

3. An officer who tends the game of a forest.

Their father Tyrrheus did his fodder bring,
Tyrrheus chief *ranger* to the Latian king. *Dryden.*

RANK. *adj.* [ranc, Saxon.]

1. High growing; strong; luxuriant.

Down with the grasse,
That groweth in shadow so *ranke* and so stout. *Tusser.*

Is not thilk same goteheard proud,
That sits in younder bank,
Whose straying heard themselfe shrowde
Emong the bushes *rank*. *Spenser.*

Who would be out, being before his beloved mistress? —That should you, if I were your mistress, or I should think my honesty *ranker* than my wit. *Shakesp.*

In which disguise,
While other jests are something *rank* on foot,
Her father hath commanded her to slip
Away with Slender. *Shakesp. Merry Wives of Windsor.*

Seven ears came up upon one stalk, *rank* and good. *Gen.*

They fancy that the difference lies in the manner of appulse, one being made by a fuller or *ranker* appulse than the other. *Holder's Elements of Speech.*

The most plentiful season, that gives birth to the finest flowers, produces also the *rankest* weeds. *Addison.*

2. Fruitful; bearing strong plants.

Seven thousand broad-tail'd sheep graz'd on his downs;
Three thousand camels his *rank* pastures fed. *Sandys.*

Where land is *rank*, 'tis not good to sow wheat after a fallow. *Mortimer's Husbandry.*

3. [*Rancidus*, Lat.] Strong scented; rancid.

Rank smelling rue, and cummin good for eyes. *Spenser.*

In their thick breaths,
Rank of gross diet, shall we be enclouded,
And forc'd to drink their vapour. *Shakesp. Cymbeline.*

The ewes, being *rank*,
In the end of Autumn turned to the rams. *Shakesp.*

The drying marshes such a stench convey,
Such the *rank* steams of reeking Albula. *Addison.*

Hircina, *rank* with sweat, presumes
To censure Phillis for perfumes. *Swift's Miscellanies.*

4. High tasted; strong in quality.

Such animals as feed upon flesh, because such kind of food is high and *rank*, qualify it; the one by swallowing the hair of the beasts they prey upon, the other by devouring some part of the feathers of the birds they gorge themselves with. *Ray on the Creation.*

Divers sea fowl taste *rank* of the fish on which they feed. *Boyle.*

5. Rampant; highgrown.

For you, most wicked Sir, whom to call brother
Would infect my mouth, I do forgive
Thy *rankest* faults. *Shakesp. Tempest.*

This Epiphanius cries out upon as *rank* idolatry, and the device of the devil, who always brought in idolatry under fair pretences. *Stillingfleet's Def. of Discourse on Roman Idol.*

'Tis pride, *rank* pride, and haughtiness of soul,
The Romans call it stoicism. *Addison's Cato.*

6. Gross; coarse.

My wife's a hobby-horse, deserves name
As *rank* as any flax-wench, that puts to
Before her troth-plight. *Shakesp. Winter's Tale.*

This power of the people in Athens, claimed as the undoubted privilege of an Athenian born, was the *rankest* encroachment and the grossest degeneracy from the form Solon left. *Swift.*

7. The iron of a plane is set *rank*, when its edge stands so flat below the sole of the plane, that in working it will take off a thick shaving. *Moxon's Mechanical Exercises.*

Rank. *n. ſ.* [*rang*, Fr.]

1. Line of men placed a-breaſt.

> Fierce fiery warriors fight upon the clouds,
> In *ranks*, and ſquadrons, and right form of war,
> Which drizzled blood upon the capitol. *Shakeſp.*
>
> I have ſeen the cannon,
> When it hath blown his *ranks* into the air. *Shakeſp.*
>
> Is't not pity,
> That we, the ſons and children of this iſle,
> Fill up her enemies *ranks?* *Shakeſp. King John.*
>
> If you have a ſtation in the file,
> And not in the worſt *rank* of manhood, ſay it. *Shakeſp.*

2. A row.

> Weſt of this place down in the neighbour bottom,
> The *rank* of oſiers, by the murmuring ſtream,
> Left on your right hand brings you to the place. *Shakeſp.*
>
> A ſylvan ſcene, and as the *ranks* aſcend
> Shade above ſhade, a woody theatre. *Milton.*
>
> If ſhe walk, in even *ranks* they ſtand,
> Like ſome well-marſhall'd and obſequious band. *Waller.*
>
> He cou'd through *ranks* of ruin go,
> With ſtorms above and rocks below. *Dryden's Horace.*

3. Range of ſubordination.

The wiſdom and goodneſs of the maker plainly appears in the parts of this ſtupendous fabrick, and the ſeveral degrees and *ranks* of creatures in it. *Locke.*

4. Claſs; order.

The enchanting power of proſperity over private perſons is remarkable in relation to great kingdoms, where all *ranks* and orders of men, being equally concerned in publick bleſſings, equally join in ſpreading the infection. *Atterbury.*

5. Degree of dignity.

> Her charms have made me man, her raviſh'd love
> In *rank* ſhall place me with the bleſs'd above. *Dryden.*
>
> Theſe all are virtues of a meaner *rank*,
> Perfections that are plac'd in bones and nerves. *Addiſon.*

Lepidus's houſe, which in his conſulate was the fineſt in Rome, within thirty-five years was not in the hundredth *rank*. *Arbuthnot on Coins.*

6. Dignity; high place: as, *he is a man of* rank.

To **Rank.** *v. a.* [*ranger*, Fr. from the noun.]

1. To place a-breaſt.

> In view ſtood *rank'd* of ſeraphim another row. *Milton.*

2. To range in any particular claſs.

> If ſour woe delights in fellowſhip,
> And needly will be *rank'd* with other griefs;
> Why follow'd not, when ſhe ſaid Tybalt's dead,
> Thy father or thy mother. *Shakeſp.*
>
> He was a man
> Of an unbounded ſtomach, ever *ranking*
> Himſelf with princes. *Shakeſp. Henry* VIII.

Hereſy is *ranked* with idolatry and witchcraft. *Decay of Piety.*

I have *ranked* this diverſion of chriſtian practice among the effects of our contentions. *Decay of Piety.*

Poets were *ranked* in the claſs of philoſophers, and the ancients made uſe of them as preceptors in muſick and morality. *Broome's Notes on the Odyſſey.*

3. To arrange methodically.

> Who now ſhall rear you to the ſun, or *rank*
> Your tribes. *Milton.*

Ranking all things under general and ſpecial heads, renders the nature or uſes of a thing more eaſy to be found out, when we ſeek in what rank of beings it lies. *Watts's Logick.*

To **Rank.** *v. n.* To be ranged; to be placed.

> Let that one article *rank* with the reſt;
> And thereupon give me your daughter. *Shakeſp.*
>
> From ſtraggling mountaineers, for publick good,
> To *rank* in tribes, and quit the ſavage wood. *Tate.*

To **Ra'nkle.** *v. n.* [from *rank.*] To feſter; to breed corruption; to be inflamed in body or mind.

> As when two boars with *rankling* malice met,
> Their gory ſides freſh bleeding fiercely fret. *Fa. Queen.*
>
> I little ſmart did feel;
> But ſoon it ſore increaſed,
> And now it *rankleth* more and more,
> And inwardly it feſtereth ſore. *Spenſer's Paſtorals.*
>
> The grief thereof him wondrous ſore diſeaſed,
> Ne might his *rankling* pain with patience be appeaſed. *Fairy Queen.*
>
> That freſh bleeding wound
> Whilome doth *rankle* in my riven breaſt. *Fairy Queen.*
>
> Beware of yonder dog;
> Look, when he fawns, he bites; and, when he bites,
> His venom tooth will *rankle* to the death. *Shakeſp.*
>
> The ſtorm of his own rage the fool confounds,
> And envy's *rankling* ſting th' imprudent wounds. *Sandys.*
>
> Thou ſhalt feel, enrag'd with inward pains,
> The hydra's venom *rankling* in thy veins. *Addiſon.*
>
> I have endur'd the rage of ſecret grief,
> A malady that burns and *rankles* inward. *Rowe.*
>
> On the *rankl'd* ſoul the fury falls. *Thomſon.*

Ra'nkly. *adv.* [from *rank.*] Coarſely; groſly.

> 'Tis given out, that, ſleeping in my garden,
> A ſerpent ſtung me: ſo the whole ear of Denmark
> Is, by a forged proceſs of my death,
> *Rankly* abus'd. *Shakeſp. Hamlet.*

Ra'nkness. *n. ſ.* [from *rank.*] Exuberance; ſuperfluity of growth.

It bringeth forth abundantly, through too much *rankneſs*, things leſs profitable, whereby that which principally it ſhould yield, being either prevented in place, or defrauded of nouriſhment, faileth. *Hooker, b.* v. *ſ.* iii.

Begin you to grow upon me; I will phyſick your *rankneſs*. *Shakeſp. As You Like it.*

> Among the crowd i' th' abbey, where a finger
> Could not be wedg'd in more; I am ſtifled
> With the mere *rankneſs* of their joy. *Shakeſp. Hen.* VIII.
>
> We'll like a bated and retired flood,
> Leaving our *rankneſs* and irregular courſe,
> Stoop low within thoſe bounds, we have o'erlook'd. *Shak.*
>
> The crane's pride is in the *rankneſs* of her wing. *L'Eſtr.*
>
> He the ſtubborn ſoil manur'd,
> With rules of huſbandry the *rankneſs* cur'd;
> Tam'd us to manners. *Dryden.*

Ra'nny. *n. ſ.* The ſhrewmouſe.

The mus araneus, the ſhrewmouſe or *ranny*. *Brown.*

To **Ra'nsack.** *v. a.* [ran, Saxon, and *ſaka*, Swediſh, to ſearch for or ſeize.]

1. To plunder; to pillage.

> A covetous ſpirit,
> Warily awaited day and night,
> From other covetous fiends it to defend,
> Who it to rob and *ranſack* did intend. *Fairy Queen.*
>
> Their vow is made to *ranſack* Troy. *Shakeſp.*
>
> Men by his ſuggeſtion taught,
> *Ranſack'd* the centre, and with impious hands
> Rifled the bowels of the earth. *Milton.*
>
> The *ranſack'd* city, taken by our toils,
> We left, and hither brought the golden ſpoils. *Dryden.*
>
> The ſpoils which they from *ranſack'd* houſes brought,
> And golden bowls from burning altars caught. *Dryden.*

2. To ſearch narrowly.

I *ranſack* the ſeveral caverns, and ſearch into the ſtorehouſes of water, to find out where that mighty maſs of water, which overflowed the earth, is beſtowed. *Woodward.*

3. To violate; to deflower.

> With greedy force he 'gan the fort aſſail,
> Whereof he weened poſſeſſed ſoon to be,
> And with rich ſpoil of *ranſacked* chaſtity. *Fairy Queen.*

Ra'nsome. *n. ſ.* [*rançon*, Fr.] Price paid for redemption from captivity or puniſhment.

By his captivity in Auſtria, and the heavy *ranſom* that he paid for his liberty, Richard was hindered to purſue the conqueſt of Ireland. *Davies on Ireland.*

> Ere the third dawning light
> Return, the ſtars of morn ſhall ſee him riſe,
> The *ranſom* paid, which man from death redeemes,
> His death for man. *Milton's Paradiſe Loſt, b.* xii.
>
> Has the prince loſt his army or his liberty?
> Tell me what province they demand for *ranſom*. *Denham.*
>
> This as a *ranſom* Albemarle did pay,
> For all the glories of ſo great a life. *Dryden.*

To adore that great myſtery of divine love, God's ſending his only ſon into this world to ſave ſinners, and to give his life a *ranſom* for them, would be noble exerciſe for the pens of the greateſt wits. *Tillotſon's Sermons.*

> Th' avenging pow'r
> Thus will perſiſt, relentleſs in his ire,
> Till the fair ſlave be render'd to her ſire,
> And *ranſom* free reſtor'd to his abode. *Dryden.*

To **Ra'nsome.** *v. a.* [*rançonner*, Fr.] To redeem from captivity or puniſhment.

> How is't with Titus Lartius?
> —Condemning ſome to death and ſome to exile,
> *Ranſoming* him, or pitying, threatning the other. *Shakeſp.*

I will *ranſom* them from the grave, and redeem them from death. *Hoſea* xiii. 14.

> He'll dying riſe, and riſing with him raiſe
> His brethren, *ranſom'd* with his own dear life. *Milton.*

Ra'nsomeless. *adj.* [from *ranſome.*] Free from ranſome.

> *Ranſomeleſs* here we ſet our priſoners free. *Shakeſp.*
>
> Deliver him
> Up to his pleaſure *ranſomeleſs* and free. *Shakeſp.*

To **Rant.** *v. n.* [*randen*, Dutch, to rave.] To rave in violent or high ſounding language without proportionable dignity of thought.

Look where my *ranting* hoſt of the garter comes; there is either liquor in his pate, or money in his purſe, when he looks ſo merrily. *Shakeſp. Merry Wives of Windſor.*

> Nay, an thou'lt mouth, I'll *rant* as well as thou. *Shak.*

They have attacked me; ſome with piteous moans, others grinning and only ſhewing their teeth, others *ranting* and hectoring, others ſcolding and reviling. *Stillingfleet.*

RANT. *n. ſ.* [from the verb.] High ſounding language unſupported by dignity of thought.

Dryden himſelf, to pleaſe a frantick age,
Was forc'd to let his judgment ſtoop to rage,
To a wild audience he conform'd his voice,
Comply'd to cuſtom, but not err'd through choice;
Deem then the people's, not the writer's ſin,
Almanſor's rage, and *rants* of Maximin. *Granville.*

This is a ſtoical *rant*, without any foundation in the nature of man or reaſon of things. *Atterbury's Preface.*

RA'NTER. *n. ſ.* [from *rant.*] A ranting fellow.

RA'NTIPOLE. *adj.* [this word is wantonly formed from *rant.*] Wild; roving; rakiſh. A low word.

What at years of diſcretion, and comport yourſelf at this *rantipole* rate! *Congreve's Way of the World.*

To RA'NTIPOLE. *v. n.* To run about wildly. It is a low word.

The eldeſt was a termagant imperious wench; ſhe uſed to *rantipole* about the houſe, pinch the children, kick the ſervants, and torture the cats and dogs. *Arbuthnot.*

RA'NULA. n. ſ. [Latin.]

Ranula is a ſoft ſwelling, poſſeſſing thoſe ſalivals under the tongue: it is made by congeſtion, and its progreſs filleth up the ſpace between the jaws, and maketh a tumour externally under the chin. *Wiſeman's Surgery.*

RANU'NCULUS. *n. ſ.* Crowfoot.

Ranunculuſes excel all flowers in the richneſs of their colours: of them there is a great variety. *Mortimer.*

To RAP. *v. n.* [hꞃæppan, Saxon.] To ſtrike with a quick ſmart blow.

Knock me at this gate
And *rap* me well, or I'll knock your knave's pate. *Shakeſp.*
With one great peal they *rap* the door,
Like footmen on a viſiting day. *Prior.*

He was provoked in the ſpirit of magiſtracy, upon diſcovering a judge, who *rapped* out a great oath at his footman. *Addiſon.*

To RAP. *v. a.* [from *rapio extra ſe*, Lat.]

1. To affect with rapture; to ſtrike with extaſy; to hurry out of himſelf.

Theſe are ſpeeches of men, not comforted with the hope of that they deſire, but *rapped* with admiration at the view of enjoyed bliſs. *Hooker.*

Beholding the face of God, in admiration of ſo great excellency, they all adore him; and being *rapt* with the love of his beauty, they cleave inſeparably for ever unto him. *Hook.*

What, thus *raps* you? are you well? *Shakeſp.*
The government I caſt upon my brother,
And to my ſtate grew ſtranger, being tranſported
And *rapt* in ſecret ſtudies. *Shakeſp.*
You're *rapt* in ſome work, ſome dedication
To the great lord. *Shakeſp. Timon of Athens.*
I'm *rapt* with joy to ſee my Marcia's tears. *Addiſ. Cato.*

It is impoſſible duly to conſider theſe things, without being *rapt* into admiration of the infinite wiſdom of the divine architect. *Cheyne's Philoſophical Principles.*

Rapt into future times, the bard begun,
A virgin ſhall conceive, a virgin bear a ſon! *Pope.*
Let heav'n ſeize it, all at once 'tis fir'd,
Not touch'd, but *rapt*; not waken'd, but inſpir'd. *Pope.*

2. To ſnatch away.

He leaves the welkin way moſt beaten plain,
And *rapt* with whirling wheels, inflames the ſkyen,
With fire not made to burn, but fairly for to ſhyne. *F. Q.*
Underneath a bright ſea flow'd
Of jaſper, or of liquid pearl, whereon
Who after came from earth, ſailing arriv'd
Wafted by angels, or flew o'er the lake
Rap'd in a chariot drawn by fiery ſteeds. *Milton.*
Standing on earth, not *rapt* above the pole. *Milton.*

To RAP *and rend.* [more properly *rap and ran*; hræpan, Saxon, to bind, and *rana*, Iſlandick, to plunder.] To ſeize by violence.

Their huſbands robb'd, and made hard ſhifts
T' adminiſter unto their gifts
All they could *rap and rend* and pilfer,
To ſcraps and ends of gold and ſilver. *Hudibras, p.* ii.

RAP. *n. ſ.* [from the verb.] A quick ſmart blow.

How comeſt thou to go with thy arm tied up? has old Lewis given thee a *rap* over thy fingers ends? *Arbuthnot.*

RAPA'CIOUS. *adj.* [*rapace*, Fr. *rapax*, Lat.] Given to plunder; ſeizing by violence.

Well may thy Lord, appeas'd,
Redeem thee quite from death's *rapacious* claim. *Milton.*
Shall this prize,
Soon heighten'd by the diamond's circling rays,
On that *rapacious* hand for ever blaze? *Pope.*

RAPA'CIOUSLY. *adv.* [from *rapacious.*] By rapine; by violent robbery.

RAPA'CIOUSNESS. *n. ſ.* [from *rapacious.*] The quality of being rapacious.

RAPA'CITY. *n. ſ.* [*rapacitas*, Lat. *rapacité*, Fr. from *rapax.*] Addictedneſs to plunder; exerciſe of plunder; ravenouſneſs.

Any of theſe, without regarding the pains of churchmen, grudge them thoſe ſmall remains of ancient piety, which the *rapacity* of ſome ages has ſcarce left to the church. *Sprat.*

RAPE. *n. ſ.* [*rapt*, Fr. *raptus*, Latin.]

1. Violent defloration of chaſtity.

You are both decypher'd
For villains mark'd with *rape*. *Shakeſp. Titus Andronicus.*
Rape call you it, to ſeize my own,
My true betrothed love. *Shakeſp. Titus Andronicus.*

The parliament conceived, that the obtaining of women by force into poſſeſſion, howſoever afterwards aſſent might follow by allurements, was but a *rape* drawn forth in length, becauſe the firſt force drew on all the reſt. *Bacon's Henry* VII.

Witneſs that night
In Gibeah, when the hoſpitable door
Expos'd a matron, to avoid worſe *rape*. *Milton.*
The haughty fair,
Who not the *rape* ev'n of a god could bear. *Dryden.*
Tell Thracian tyrant's alter'd ſhape,
And dire revenge of Philomela's *rape*. *Roſcommon.*

2. Privation; act of taking away.

Pear grew after pear,
Fig after fig came; time made never *rape*
Of any dainty there. *Chapman's Odyſſey.*

3. Something ſnatched away.

Sad widows by thee rifled, weep in vain,
And ruin'd orphans of thy *rapes* complain. *Sandys.*
Where now are all my hopes? oh never more
Shall they revive! nor death her *rapes* reſtore! *Sandys.*

4. The juice of grapes is drawn as well from the *rape*, or whole grapes pluck'd from the cluſter, and wine pour'd upon them in a veſſel, as from a vat, where they are bruiſed. *Ray.*

5. A plant, from the ſeed of which oil is expreſſed.

RA'PID. *adj.* [*rapide*, Fr. *rapidus*, Lat.] Quick; ſwift.

Part ſhun the goal with *rapid* wheels. *Milton.*
While you ſo ſmoothly turn and rowl our ſphere,
That *rapid* motion does but reſt appear. *Dryden.*

RAPI'DITY. *n. ſ.* [*rapidité*, Fr. *rapiditas*, from *rapidus*, Lat.] Celerity; velocity; ſwiftneſs.

Where the words are not monoſyllables, we make them ſo by our *rapidity* of pronunciation. *Addiſon's Spectator.*

RAPI'DLY. *adv.* [from *rapid.*] Swiftly; with quick motion.

RAPI'DNESS. *n. ſ.* [from *rapid.*] Celerity; ſwiftneſs.

RA'PIER. *n. ſ.* [*rapiere*, Fr. ſo called from the quickneſs of its motion.] A ſmall ſword uſed only in thruſting.

I will turn thy falſehood to thy heart,
Where it was forged, with my *rapier*'s point. *Shakeſp.*

A ſoldier of far inferior ſtrength may manage a *rapier* or fire-arms ſo expertly, as to be an overmatch for his adverſary. *Pope's Eſſay on Homer's Battles.*

RAPIER-FISH. *n. ſ.*

The *rapier-fiſh*, called xiphias, grows ſometimes to the length of five yards: the ſword, which grows level from the ſnout of the fiſh, is here about a yard long, at the baſis four inches over, two-edged, and pointed exactly like a *rapier*: he preys on fiſhes, having firſt ſtabbed them with this ſword. *Grew's Muſæum.*

RA'PINE. *n. ſ.* [*rapina*, Lat. *rapine*, Fr.]

1. The act of plundering.

If the poverty of Scotland might, yet the plenty of England cannot, excuſe the envy and *rapine* of the church's rights. *King Charles.*

The logick of a conquering ſword may ſilence, but convince it cannot; its efficacy rather breeds averſion and abhorrence of that religion, whoſe firſt addreſs is in blood and *rapine*. *Decay of Piety.*

2. Violence; force.

Her leaſt action overaw'd
His malice, and with *rapine* ſweet bereav'd
His fierceneſs of its fierce intent. *Milton.*

RA'PPER. *n. ſ.* [from *rap.*] One who ſtrikes.

RA'PPORT. *n. ſ.* [*rappat*, Fr.] Relation; reference; proportion. A word introduced by the innovator, *Temple*, but not copied by others.

'Tis obvious what *rapport* there is between the conceptions and languages in every country, and how great a difference this muſt make in the excellence of books. *Temple.*

To RAPT. *v. n.* [this word is uſed by *Chapman* for *rap* improperly, as appears from the participle, which from *rapt* would be not *rapt*, but *rapted.*] To raviſh; to put in ecſtaſy.

You may ſafe approve,
How ſtrong in inſtigation to their love
Their *rapting* tunes are. *Chapman's Odyſſey.*

RAPT. *n. ſ.* [from *rap.*] A trance; an ecſtaſy.

RA'PTURE. *n. ſ.*

1. Ecſtaſy; tranſport; violence of any pleaſing paſſion; enthuſiaſm; uncommon heat of imagination.

Muſick, when thus applied, raiſes in the mind of the hearer great conceptions; it ſtrengthens devotion, and advances praiſe into *rapture*. *Addiſon's Spectator*, Nº 406.

You grow correct, that once with *rapture* writ. *Pope.*

2. Rapidity;

2. Rapidity; haste.

The wat'ry throng,
Wave rowling after wave, where way they found,
If steep, with torrent *rapture*; if through plain
Soft-ebbing; nor withstood them rock or hill. *Milton.*

RA'PTURED. *adj.* [from *rapture.*] Ravished; transported. A bad word.

He drew
Such madning draughts of beauty to the soul,
As for a while cancell'd his *raptur'd* thought
With luxury too daring. *Thomson's Summer.*

RA'PTUROUS. *adj.* [from *rapture.*] Ecstatick; transporting.

Are the pleasures of it so inviting and *rapturous?* is a man bound to look out sharp to plague himself? *Collier.*

RARE. *adj.* [*rarus*, Lat. *rare*, Fr. in all the senses but the last.]

1. Scarce; uncommon.

Live to be the shew, and gaze o' th' time;
We'll have you, as our *rarer* monsters are,
Painted upon a pole. *Shakesp.*

2. Excellent; incomparable; valuable to a degree seldom found.

This jealousy
Is for a precious creature; as she's *rare*,
Must it be great; and as his person's mighty,
Must it be violent. *Shakesp. Winter's Tale.*

On which was wrought the gods and giants fight,
Rare work, all fill'd with terror and delight. *Cowley.*

Above the rest I judge one beauty *rare.* *Dryden.*

3. Thinly scattered.

The cattle in the fields and meadows green
Those *rare* and solitary, these in flocks
Pasturing at once, and in broad herds upsprung. *Milton.*

4. Thin; subtle; not dense.

They are of so tender and weak a nature, as they affect only such a *rare* and attenuate substance, as the spirit of living creatures. *Bacon's Natural History.*

So eagerly the fiend
O'er bog or steep, through strait, rough, dense, or *rare*,
With head, hands, wings, or feet, pursues his way. *Milt.*

The dense and bright light of the circle will obscure the *rare* and weak light of these dark colours round about it, and render them almost insensible. *Newton's Opticks.*

Bodies are much more *rare* and porous than is commonly believed: water is nineteen times lighter, and by consequence nineteen times *rarer* than gold, and gold is so *rare*, as very readily, and without the least opposition, to transmit the magnetick effluvia, and easily to admit quicksilver into its pores, and to let water pass through it. *Newton's Opticks.*

5. Raw; not fully subdued by the fire. This is often pronounced *rear.*

New-laid eggs, with Baucis' busy care,
Turn'd by a gentle fire, and roasted *rare.* *Dryden.*

RA'REESHOW. *n. s.* [this word is formed in imitation of the foreign way of pronouncing *rare show.*] A show carried in a box.

The fashions of the town affect us just like a *rareeshow*, we have the curiosity to peep at them, and nothing more. *Pope.*

Of *rareeshows* he sung, and Punch's feats. *Gay.*

RAREFA'CTION. *n. s.* [*rarefaction*, Fr. from *rarefy.*] Extension of the parts of a body, that makes it take up more room than it did before; contrary to condensation.

The water within being rarefied, and by *rarefaction* resolved into wind, will force up the smoak. *Wotton's Architecture.*

When exhalations, shut up in the caverns of the earth by *rarefaction* or compression, come to be straitened, they strive every way to set themselves at liberty. *Burnet.*

RARE'FIABLE. *adj.* [from *rarefy.*] Admitting rarefaction.

To RA'REFY. *v. a.* [*rarefier*, Fr. *rarus* and *facio*, Lat. *rarify* were more proper.] To make thin: contrary to condense.

To the hot equator crouding fast,
Where highly *rarefied* the yielding air
Admits their steam. *Thomson.*

To RA'REFY. *v. n.* To become thin.

Earth *rarefies* to dew; expanded more
The subtil dew in air begins to soar. *Dryden's Fables.*

RA'RELY. *adv.* [from *rare.*]

1. Seldom; not often; not frequently.

Rarely they rise by virtue's aid, who lie
Plung'd in the depth of helpless poverty. *Dryden's Juven.*

Vanessa in her bloom,
Advanc'd like Atalanta's star,
But *rarely* seen, and seen from far. *Swift's Miscellanies.*

2. Finely; nicely; accurately.

How *rarely* does it meet with this time's guise,
When man was will'd to love his enemies. *Shakesp.*

RA'RENESS. *n. s.* [from *rare.*]

1. Uncommonness; state of happening seldom; infrequency.

Tickling is most in the soles, arm-holes and sides: the cause is the thinness of the skin, joined with the *rareness* of being touched there; for tickling is a light motion of the spirits, which the thinness of the skin, the suddeness and *rareness* of touch doth further. *Bacon.*

For the *rareness* and rare effect of that petition, I'll insert it as presented. *Clarendon.*

Of my heart I now a present make;
Accept it as when early fruit we send,
And let the *rareness* the small gift commend. *Dryden.*

2. Value arising from scarcity.

Roses set in a pool, supported with some stay, is matter of *rareness* and pleasure, though of small use. *Bacon.*

To worthiest things,
Virtue, art, beauty, fortune, now I see
Rareness or use, not nature, value brings. *Donne.*

RA'RITY. *n. s.* [*rarité*, Fr. *raritas*, Lat.]

1. Uncommonness; infrequency.

So far from being fond of any one for its *rarity*, if I meet with any in a field which pleases me, I give it a place in my garden. *Spectator.*

2. A thing valued for its scarcity.

Sorrow would be a *rarity* most belov'd,
If all could so become it. *Shakesp. King Lear.*

It would be a *rarity* worth the seeing, could any one shew us such a thing as a perfectly reconciled enemy. *South.*

I saw three *rarities* of different kinds, which pleased me more than any other shows of the place. *Addison.*

3. Thinness; subtlety: the contrary to density.

Bodies, under the same outward bulk, have a greater thinness and expansion, or thickness and solidity, which terms, in English, do not signify fully those differences of quantity; therefore I will do it under the names of *rarity* and density. *Digby.*

This I do, not to draw any argument against them from the universal rest or accurately equal diffusion of matter, but only that I may better demonstrate the great *rarity* and tenuity of their imaginary chaos. *Bentley's Sermons.*

RA'SCAL. *n. s.* [rascal, Saxon, a lean beast.] A mean fellow; a scoundrel; a sorry wretch.

For the *rascal* commons, lest he cared. *Spenser.*

And when him list the *rascal* routs appal,
Men into stones therewith he could transmew. *Fa. Queen.*

When Marcus Brutus grows so covetous
To lock such *rascal* counters from his friends:
Be ready, gods, with all your thunder-bolts,
Dash him to pieces. *Shakesp. Julius Cæsar.*

The *rascal* people, thirsting after prey,
Join with the traitor. *Shakesp. Henry VI. p. ii.*

But for our gentlemen,
The mouse ne'er shun'd the cat, as they did budge
From *rascals* worse than they. *Shakesp.*

I am accurst to rob in that thief's company; the *rascal* hath remov'd my horse. *Shakesp. Henry IV. p. i.*

Scoundrels are insolent to their superiors; but it does not become a man of honour to contest with mean *rascals.* *L'Est.*

Did I not see you, *rascal*, did I not!
When you lay snug to snap young Damon's goat? *Dryden.*

I have sense, to serve my turn, in store,
And he's a *rascal* who pretends to more. *Dryden's Persius.*

The poor girl provoked told him he lyed like a *rascal.* *Sw.*

RASCA'LLION. *n. s.* [from *rascal.*] One of the lowest people.

That proud dame
Us'd him so like a base *rascallion*,
That old pig—what d'ye call him—malion,
That cut his mistress out of stone,
Had not so hard a hearted one. *Hudibras, p. i.*

RASCA'LITY. *n. s.* [from *rascal.*] The low mean people.

Pretended philosophers judge as ignorantly in their way, as the *rascality* in theirs. *Glanvill's Sceps.*

Jeroboam having procured his people gods, the next thing was to provide priests; hereupon, to the calves he adds a commission, for the approving, trying and admitting the *rascality* and lowest of the people to minister in that service. *South.*

RA'SCALLY. *adj.* [from *rascal.*] Mean; worthless.

Would'st thou not be glad to have the niggardly *rascally* sheep-biter come by some notable shame. *Shakesp.*

Our *rascally* porter is fallen fast asleep with the black cloth and sconces, or we might have been tacking up by this time. *Swift.*

To RASE. *v. a.* [this word is written *rase* or *raze*: I would write *rase*, when it signifies to strike slightly, *perstringere*; and *raze*, when it signifies to ruin, *delere*; *raser*, Fr. *rasus*, Lat.]

1. To skim; to strike on the surface.

He certifies your lordship, that this night
He dreamt the boar had *rased* off his helm. *Shakesp.*

Was he not in the nearest neighbourhood to death? and might not the bullet, that *rased* his cheek, have gone into his head. *South's Sermons.*

2. To overthrow; to destroy; to root up.

Her battering engines bent to *rase* some city. *Milton.*

3. To blot out by rasure; to erase.

Though of their names in heav'nly records now
Be no memorial, blotted out and *rased.* *Milton.*

RASH. *adj.* [*rasch*, Dutch.] Hasty; violent; precipitate; acting without caution or reflection.

This is to be bold without shame, *rash* without skill, full of words without wit. *Ascham's Schoolmaster.*

Blast

Blast her pride, O ye blest gods! so will you wish on me, when the *rash* mood is on me. *Shakesp.*

I have scarce leisure to salute you,
My matter is so *rash*. *Shakesp. Troilus and Cressida.*

Be not *rash* with thy mouth, and let not thine heart be hasty to utter any thing before God; for God is in heaven, and thou upon earth; therefore let thy words be few. *Ecclus.*

Her *rash* hand in evil hour,
Forth reaching to the fruit, she pluck'd, she eat. *Milton.*

RASH. *n. s.* [*rascia*, Italian.]

1. Sattin. *Minshew.*

2. [Corrupted probably from *rush.*] An efflorescence on the body; a breaking out.

RA'SHER. *n. s.* [*rasura lardi*, Lat.] A thin slice of bacon.

If we grow all to be pork eaters, we shall not shortly have a *rasher* on the coals for money. *Shakesp. Merch. of Venice.*

White and black was all her homely cheer,
And *rashers* of sing'd bacon on the coals. *Dryden.*
Quenches his thirst with ale in nut-brown bowls,
And takes the hasty *rasher* from the coals. *King.*

RA'SHLY. *adv.* [from *rash.*] Hastily; violently; without due consideration.

This expedition was by York and Talbot
Too *rashly* plotted. *Shakesp. Henry* VI. *p.* i.

Men are not *rashly* to take that for done, which is not done. *Bacon's Natural History.*

He that doth any thing *rashly*, must do it willingly; for he was free to deliberate or not. *L'Estrange's Fables.*

Declare the secret villain,
The wretch so meanly base to injure Phædra,
So *rashly* brave to dare the sword of Theseus. *Smith.*

RA'SHNESS. *n. s.* [from *rash.*] Foolish contempt of danger; inconsiderate heat of temper; precipitation; temerity.

Who seeth not what sentence it shall enforce us to give against all churches in the world; in as much as there is not one, but hath had many things established in it, which though the scripture did never command, yet for us to condemn were *rashness*. *Hooker, b.* iii. *s.* 6.

Nature to youth hot *rashness* doth dispence,
But with cold prudence age doth recompence. *Denham.*

In so speaking, we offend indeed against truth; yet we offend not properly by falshood, which is a speaking against our thoughts; but by *rashness*, which is an affirming or denying, before we have sufficiently informed ourselves. *South.*

The vain Morat by his own *rashness* wrought,
Too soon discover'd his ambitious thought,
Believ'd me his, because I spoke him fair. *Dryden.*

RASP. *n. s.* [*raspo*, Italian.] A delicious berry that grows on a species of the bramble; a raspberry.

Sorrel set amongst *rasps*, and the *rasps* will be the smaller. *Bacon's Natural History.*

Now will the corinths, now the *rasps* supply
Delicious draughts, when prest to wines. *Philips.*

To RASP. *v. a.* [*raspen*, Dutch; *rasper*, Fr. *raspare*, Italian.] To rub to powder with a very rough file.

Some authors have advised the *rasping* of these bones; but in this case it is needless. *Wiseman's Surgery.*

Having prepared hard woods and ivory for the lathe with *rasping*, they pitch it between the pikes. *Moxon.*

RASP. *n. s.* [from the verb.] A large rough file, commonly used to wear away wood.

Case-hardening is used by file-cutters, when they make coarse files, and generally most *rasps* have formerly been made of iron and case-hardened. *Moxon's Mechanical Exercises.*

RA'SPATORY. *n. s.* [*raspatoir*, Fr. from *rasp.*] A chirurgeon's rasp.

I put into his mouth a *raspatory*, and pulled away the corrupt flesh, and with cauteries burnt it to a crust. *Wiseman's Surgery.*

RA'SPBERRY, or *Rasberry. n. s.* A kind of berry.

Raspberries are of three sorts; the common wild one, the large red garden *raspberry*, which is one of the pleasantest of fruits, and the white, which is little inferior to the red. *Mortimer's Husbandry.*

RASPBERRY-BUSH. *n. s.* A species of bramble.

RA'SURE. *n. s.* [*rasura*, Lat.]

1. The act of scraping or shaving.

2. A mark in a writing where something has been rubbed out.

Such a writing ought to be free from any vituperation of *rasure*. *Ayliffe's Parergon.*

RAT. *n. s.* [*ratte*, Dutch; *rat*, Fr. *ratta*, Spanish.] An animal of the mouse kind that infests houses and ships.

Our natures do pursue,
Like *rats* that ravin down their proper bane. *Shakesp.*
Make you ready your stiff bats and clubs,
Rome and her *rats* are at the point of battle. *Shakesp.*

I have seen the time, with my long sword I would have made you four tall fellows skip like *rats*. *Shakesp.*

Thus horses will knable at walls, and *rats* will gnaw iron. *Brown's Vulgar Errours.*

If in despair he goes out of the way like a *rat* with a dose of arsenick, why he dies nobly. *Dennis.*

To smell a RAT. To be put on the watch by suspicion as the cat by the scent of a rat; to suspect danger.

Quoth Hudibras, I *smell a rat*,
Ralpho, thou dost prevaricate. *Hudibras, p.* i.

RA'TABLE. *adj.* [from *rate.*] Set at a certain value.

The Danes brought in a reckoning of money by ores, per oras; I collect out of the abby-book of Burton, that twenty oræ were *ratable* to two marks of silver. *Camden's Remains.*

RA'TABLY. *adv.* Proportionably.

Many times there is no proportion of shot and powder allowed *ratably* by that quantity of the great ordnance. *Raleigh.*

RATA'FIA. *n. s.* A fine liquor, prepared from the kernels of apricots and spirits. *Bailey.*

RATA'N. *n. s.* An Indian cane. *Dict.*

RATCH. } *n. s.* In clockwork, a sort of wheel, which serves
RASH. } to lift up the detents every hour, and thereby make the clock strike. *Bailey.*

RATE. *n. s.* [*ratus*, Lat. *rate*, old Fr.]

1. Price fixed on any thing.

How many things do we value, because they come at dear *rates* from Japan and China, which if they were our own manufacture, common to be had, and for a little money, would be neglected? *Locke.*

I'll not betray the glory of my name,
'Tis not for me, who have preserv'd a state,
To buy an empire at so base a *rate*. *Dryden.*

The price of land has never changed, in the several changes have been made in the *rate* of interest by law; nor now that the *rate* of interest is by law the same, is the price of land every where the same. *Locke.*

2. Allowance settled.

His allowance was a continual allowance, a daily *rate* for every day. 2 *Kings* xxv. 30.

They obliged themselves to remit after the *rate* of twelve hundred thousand pounds sterling per annum, divided into so many monthly payments. *Addison.*

3. Degree; comparative height or valour.

I am a spirit of no common *rate*;
The summer still doth tend upon my state. *Shakesp.*
I have disabled mine estate,
By shewing something a more swelling port,
Than my faint means would grant continuance;
Nor do I now make moan to be abridged
From such a noble *rate*. *Shakesp. Merchant of Venice.*

In this did his holiness and godliness appear above the *rate* and pitch of other mens, in that he was so infinitely merciful. *Calamy's Sermons.*

To which relation whatsoever is done agreeably, is morally and essentially good; and whatsoever is done otherwise, is at the same *rate* morally evil. *South.*

4. Quantity assignable.

In goodly form comes on the enemy;
And by the ground they hide, I judge their number
Upon or near the *rate* of thirty thousand. *Shakesp.*

5. That which sets value.

Heretofore the *rate* and standard of wit was very different from what it is now-a-days: no man was then accounted a wit for speaking such things, as deserved to have the tongue cut out. *South's Sermons.*

A virtuous heathen is, at this *rate*, as happy as a virtuous christian. *Atterbury.*

6. Manner of doing any thing; degree to which any thing is done.

Many of the horse could not march at that *rate*, nor come up soon enough. *Clarendon, b.* viii.

Tom hinting his dislike of some trifle his mistress had said, she asked him how he would talk to her after marriage, if he talked at this *rate* before? *Addison.*

7. Tax imposed by the parish.

They paid the church and parish *rate*,
And took, but read not the receipt. *Prior.*

To RATE. *v. a.* [from the noun.]

1. To value at a certain price.

I freely told you, all the wealth I had
Ran in my veins, I was a gentleman;
And yet, dear lady,
Rating myself as nothing, you shall see
How much I was a braggart. *Shakesp. Merch. of Venice.*

We may there be instructed, how to name and *rate* all goods, by those that will concentre into felicity. *Boyle.*

You seem not high enough your joys to *rate*,
You stand indebted a vast sum to fate,
And should large thanks for the great blessing pay. *Dryden.*

2. [*Reita*, Islandick.] To chide hastily and vehemently.

Go *rate* thy minions, proud insulting boy,
Becomes it thee to be thus bold in terms
Before thy sovereign. *Shakesp. Henry* VI. *p.* iii.

An old lord of the council *rated* me the other day in the street about you, Sir. *Shakesp. Henry* IV. *p.* i.

What is all that a man enjoys, from a year's converse, comparable to what he feels for one hour, when his conscience shall take him aside and *rate* him by himself. *South.*

If words are sometimes to be used, they ought to be grave, kind and sober, representing the ill or unbecomingness of the faults, rather than a hasty *rating* of the child for it. *Locke.*

RATH. *n. s.* A hill. I know not whence derived.

There is a great use among the Irish, to make great assemblies together upon a *rath* or hill, there to parly about matters and wrongs between townships or private persons. *Spenser on Ireland.*

RATH. *adv.* Early.

Thus is my summer worn away and wasted,
Thus is my harvest hasten'd all too *rathe*,
The ear, that budded fair, is burnt and blasted,
And all my hoped gain is turn'd to scathe. *Spenser.*
Strong Lagæan wines
Rath ripe and purple grapes there be. *May's Virgil.*
Rath ripe are some, and some of later kind,
Of golden some, and some of purple rind. *May's Virgil.*

RATH. *adj.* [ꞃaꝺ, Saxon, quickly.] Early; coming before the time.

Bring the *rath* primrose that forsaken dies,
The tufted crow-toe and pale jessamine. *Milton.*

RA'THER. *adv.* [this is a comparative from *rath*; ꞃaꝺ, Saxon, soon. Now out of use. One may still say, by the same form of speaking, *I will* sooner *do this than that*; that is, *I like better to do this.*]

1. More willingly; with better liking.

Almighty God desireth not the death of a sinner, but *rather* that he should turn from his wickedness and live. *Common Prayer.*

2. Preferably to the other; with better reason.

'Tis *rather* to be thought, that an heir had no such right by divine institution, than that God should give such a right, but yet leave it undeterminate who such heir is. *Locke.*

3. In a greater degree than otherwise.

He sought through the world, but sought in vain,
And no where finding, *rather* fear'd her slain. *Dryden.*

4. More properly.

This is an art,
Which does mend nature, change it *rather*, but
The art itself is nature. *Shakesp. Winter's Tale.*

5. Especially.

You are come to me in a happy time,
The *rather* for I have some sport in hand. *Shakesp.*

6. *To have* RATHER. [this is, I think, a barbarous expression of late intrusion into our language, for which it is better to say *will rather.*] To desire in preference.

'Tis with reluctancy he is provoked by our impenitence to apply the discipline of severity and correction; he *had rather* mankind should adore him as their patron and benefactor. *Rogers's Sermons.*

RATIFICA'TION. *n. s.* [*ratification*, Fr. from *ratify.*] The act of ratifying; confirmation.

RA'TIFIER. *n. s.* [from *ratify.*] The person or thing that ratifies.

They cry, "chuse we Laertes for our king:"
The *ratifiers* and props of every word,
Caps, hands and tongues applaud it to the clouds. *Shakesp.*

To RA'TIFY. *v. a.* [*ratum facio*, Latin.] To confirm; to settle.

The church being a body which dieth not, hath always power, as occasion requireth, no less to ordain that which never was, than to *ratify* what hath been before. *Hooker.*

By the help of these, with him above
To *ratify* the work, we may again
Give to our tables meat, sleep to our nights. *Shakesp.*

We have *ratified* unto them the borders of Judæa. 1 *Mac.*

God *ratified* their prayers by the judgment they brought down upon the head of him, whom they prayed against. *South.*

Tell me, my friend, from whence had'st thou the skill,
So nicely to distinguish good from ill?
And what thou art to follow, what to fly,
This to condemn, and that to *ratify?* *Dryden.*

RA'TIO. *n. s.* [Latin.] Proportion.

Whatever inclinations the rays have to the plane of incidence, the sine of the angle of incidence of every ray considered apart, shall have to the sine of the angle of refraction a constant *ratio.* *Cheyne's Philosophical Principles.*

To RATIO'CINATE. *v. n.* [*ratiocinor*, Lat.] To reason; to argue.

RATIOCINA'TION. *n. s.* [*ratiocinatio*, Lat.] The act of reasoning; the act of deducing consequences from premises.

In simple terms, expressing the open notions of things, which the second act of reason compoundeth into propositions, and the last into syllogisms and forms of *ratiocination.* *Brown.*

Can any kind of *ratiocination* allow Christ all the marks of the Messiah, and yet deny him to be the Messiah? *South.*

Such an inscription would be self-evident without any *ratiocination* or study, and could not fail constantly to exert its energy in their minds. *Bentley.*

RATIO'CINATIVE. *adj.* [from *ratiocinate.*] Argumentative; advancing by process of discourse.

Some consecutions are so intimately and evidently connexed to, or found in the premises, that the conclusion is attained quasi per saltum, and without any thing of *ratiocinative* process, even as the eye sees his object immediately, and without any previous discourse. *Hale's Origin of Mankind.*

RA'TIONAL. *adj.* [*rationalis*, Latin.]

1. Having the power of reasoning.

2. Agreeable to reason.

What higher in her society thou find'st
Attractive, humane, *rational*, love still. *Milton.*

When the conclusion is deduced from the unerring dictates of our faculties, we say the inference is *rational.* *Glanvill.*

If your arguments be *rational*, offer them in as moving a manner as the nature of the subject will admit; but beware of letting the pathetick part swallow up the *rational.* *Swift.*

3. Wise; judicious: as, *a* rational *man.*

RATIONA'LE. *n. s.* [from *ratio*, Lat.] A detail with reasons: as, *Dr. Sparrow's* Rationale *of the Common Prayer.*

RA'TIONALIST. *n. s.* [from *rational.*] One who proceeds in his disquisitions and practice wholly upon reason.

He often used this comparison; the empirical philosophers are like to pismires; they only lay up and use their store: the *rationalists* are like to spiders; they spin all out of their own bowels: but give me a philosopher, who, like the bee, hath a middle faculty, gathering from abroad, but digesting that which is gathered by his own virtue. *Bacon.*

RATIONA'LITY. *n. s.* [from *rational.*]

1. The power of reasoning.

When God has made *rationality* the common portion of mankind, how came it to be thy inclosure? *Gov. of the Tong.*

2. Reasonableness.

In human occurrences, there have been many well directed intentions, whose *rationalities* will never bear a rigid examination. *Brown's Vulgar Errours.*

RA'TIONALLY. *adv.* [from *rational.*] Reasonably; with reason.

Upon the proposal of an agreeable object, it may *rationally* be conjectured, that a man's choice will rather incline him to accept than to refuse it. *South.*

RATIO'NALNESS. *n. s.* [from *rational.*] The state of being rational.

RA'TSBANE. *n. s.* [*rat* and *bane.*] Poison for rats; arsenick.

Poor Tom! that hath laid knives under his pillow, and halters in his pew, set *ratsbane* by his porridge. *Shakesp.*

He would throw *ratsbane* up and down a house, where children might come at it. *L'Estrange.*

When murder's out, what vice can we advance?
Unless the new-found pois'ning trick of France;
And when their art of *ratsbane* we have got,
By way of thanks, we'll send 'em o'er our plot. *Dryden.*

I can hardly believe the relation of his being poisoned, but sack might do it, though *ratsbane* would not. *Swift to Pope.*

RA'TTEEN. *n. s.* A kind of stuff.

We'll rig in Meath-street Egypt's haughty queen,
And Anthony shall court her in *ratteen.* *Swift.*

To RA'TTLE. *v. n.* [*ratelen*, Dutch.]

1. To make a quick sharp noise with frequent repetitions and collisions of bodies not very sonorous: when bodies are sonorous, it is called *jingling.*

The quiver *rattleth* against him. *Job* xxxix. 23.

The noise of a whip, of the *rattling* of the wheels, of prancing horses, and of the jumping chariots. *Nah.* iii. 2.

They had, to affright the enemies horses, big rattles covered with parchment, and small stones within; but the *rattling* of shot might have done better service. *Hayward.*

He was too warm on picking work to dwell;
He fagoted his notions as they fell,
And if they rhym'd and *rattled* all was well. *Dryden.*

There she assembles all her blackest storms,
And the rude hail in *rattling* tempest forms. *Addison.*

2. To speak eagerly and noisily.

With jealous eyes at distance she had seen
Whisp'ring with Jove the silver-footed queen;
Then, impotent of tongue, her silence broke,
Thus turbulent in *rattling* tone she spoke. *Dryden.*

He is a man of pleasure, and a free-thinker; he is an assertor of liberty and property; he *rattles* it out against popery. *Swift.*

To RA'TTLE. *v. a.*

1. To move any thing so as to make a rattle or noise.

Her chains she *rattles*, and her whip she shakes. *Dryden.*

2. To stun with a noise; to drive with a noise.

Sound but another, and another shall,
As loud as thine, *rattle* the welkin's ear,
And mock the deep-mouth'd thunder. *Shakesp.*

He should be well enough able to scatter the Irish as a flight of birds, and *rattle* away this swarm of bees with their king. *Bacon's Henry* VII.

3. To

3. To scold; to rail at with clamour.

Hearing Æsop had been beforehand, he sent for him in a rage, and *rattled* him with a thousand traitors and villains for robbing his house. *L'Estrange.*

She that would sometimes *rattle* off her servants pretty sharply, now if she saw them drunk, never took any notice. *Arbuthnot's History of John Bull.*

RA'TTLE. *n. s.* [from the verb.]

1. A quick noise nimbly repeated.

I'll hold ten pound my dream is out;
I'd tell it you but for the *rattle*
Of those confounded drums. *Prior.*

2. Empty and loud talk.

All this ado about the golden age, is but an empty *rattle* and frivolous conceit. *Hakewill on Providence.*

3. An instrument, which agitated makes a clattering noise.

The *rattles* of Isis and the cymbals of Brasilea nearly enough resemble each other. *Raleigh's History of the World.*

They had, to affright the enemies horses, big *rattles* covered with parchment and small stones within. *Hayward.*

Opinions are the *rattles* of immature intellects, but the advanced reasons have outgrown them. *Glanvill's Sceps.*

They want no *rattles* for their froward mood,
Nor nurse to reconcile them to their food. *Dryden.*
Farewel then verse, and love, and ev'ry toy,
The rhymes and *rattles* of the man or boy;
What right, what true, what fit we justly call,
Let this be all my care; for this is all. *Pope.*

4. A plant.

RA'TTLEHEADED. *adj* [*rattle* and *head.*] Giddy; not steady.

RA'TTLESNAKE. *n. s.* A kind of serpent.

The *rattlesnake* is so called, from the rattle at the end of his tail. *Grew's Musæum.*

She loses her being at the very sight of him, and drops plump into his arms, like a charmed bird into the mouth of a *rattlesnake.* *Moore's Foundling.*

RATTLESNAKE *Root. n. s.*

Rattlesnake root, called also seneka, belongs to a plant, a native of Virginia; the Indians use it as a certain remedy against the bite of a rattlesnake: it has been recommended in all cases, in which the blood is known to be thick and sizy. *Hill.*

RA'TTOON. *n. s.* A West Indian fox, which has this peculiar property, that if any thing be offered to it that has lain in water, it will wipe and turn it about with its fore feet, before it will put it to its mouth. *Bailey.*

To RA'VAGE. *v. a.* [*ravager*, Fr.] To lay waste; to sack; to ransack; to spoil; to pillage; to plunder.

Already Cæsar
Has *ravaged* more than half the globe, and sees
Mankind grown thin by his destructive sword. *Addison.*
His blasts obey, and quit the howling hill,
The shatter'd forest, and the *ravag'd* vale. *Thomson.*

RA'VAGE. *n. s.* [*ravage*, Fr. from the verb.] Spoil; ruin; waste.

Some cruel pleasure will from thence arise,
To view the mighty *ravage* of your eyes. *Dryden.*
Would one think 'twere possible for love
To make such *ravage* in a noble soul. *Addison.*

Those savages were not then, what civilized mankind is now; but without mutual society, without arms of offence, without houses or fortifications, an obvious and exposed prey to the *ravage* of devouring beasts. *Bentley.*

RA'VAGER. *n. s.* [from *ravage.*] Plunderer; spoiler.

When that mighty empire was overthrown by the northern people, vast sums of money were buried to escape the plundering of the conquerors; and what remained was carried off by those *ravagers.* *Swift's Miscellanies.*

RAU'CITY, *n. s.* [*raucus*, Lat.] Hoarseness; loud rough noise.

Inequality not stayed upon, but passing, is rather an encrease of sweetness; as in the purling of a wreathed string, and in the *raucity* of a trumpet. *Bacon's Nat. Hist.*

To RAVE. *v. n.* [*reven*, Dutch; *rêver*, Fr.]

1. To be delirious; to talk irrationally.

Men who thus *rave*, we may conclude their brains are turned, and one may as well read lectures at Bedlam as treat with such. *Government of the Tongue.*

It soon infecteth the whole member, and is accompanied with watching and *raving.* *Wiseman's Surgery.*

Her grief has wrought her into frenzy,
The images her troubled fancy forms
Are incoherent, wild; her words disjointed:
Sometimes she *raves* for musick, light and air;
Nor air, nor light nor musick calm her pains. *Smith.*

2. To burst out into furious exclamations as if mad.

Shall these wild distempers of thy mind,
This tempest of thy tongue, thus *rave*, and find
No opposition? *Sandys's Paraphrase on Job.*

Our *ravings* and complaints are but like arrows shot up into the air, at no mark, and so to no purpose. *Temple.*

Wonder at my patience,
Have I not cause to *rave*, and beat my breast,
To rend my heart with grief, and run distracted. *Addison.*

Revenge, revenge, thus *raving* through the streets,
I'll cry for vengeance. *Southern's Spartan Dame.*
He swore he could not leave me,
With ten thousand *ravings.* *Rowe's Royal Convert.*

3. To be unreasonably fond. With *upon* before the object of fondness. A colloquial and improper sense.

Another partiality is a fantastical and wild attributing all knowledge to the ancients or the moderns: this *raving upon* antiquity, in matter of poetry, Horace has wittily exposed in one of his satires. *Locke.*

To RA'VEL. *v. a.* [*ravelen*, Dutch, to entangle.]

1. To entangle; to entwist one with another; to make intricate; to involve; to perplex.

As you unwind her love from him,
Lest it should *ravel*, and be good to none,
You must provide to bottom it on me. *Shakesp.*
If then such praise the Macedonian got,
For having rudely cut the Gordian knot;
What glory's due to him that cou'd divide
Such *ravel'd* int'rests, has the knot unty'd,
And without stroke so smooth a passage made,
Where craft and malice such obstructions laid. *Waller.*

2. To unweave; to unknit: as, *to* ravel *out a twist or piece of knit work.*

Let him for a pair of reechy kisses,
Or padling in your neck with his damn'd fingers,
Make you to *ravel* all this matter out. *Shakesp. Hamlet.*
Sleep that knits up the *ravel'd* sleeve of care. *Shakesp.*

3. To hurry over in confusion. This seems to be the meaning in *Digby.*

They but *ravel* it over loosely, and pitch upon disputing against particular conclusions, that at the first encounter of them single, seem harsh to them. *Digby.*

To RA'VEL. *v. n.*

1. To fall into perplexity or confusion.

Give the reins to wandering thought,
Regardless of his glory's diminution;
Till by their own perplexities involv'd,
They *ravel* more, still less resolv'd,
But never find self-satisfying solution. *Milton's Agonistes.*

2. To work in perplexity; to busy himself with intricacies.

It will be needless to *ravel* far into the records of elder times; every man's memory will suggest many pertinent instances. *Decay of Piety.*

The humour of *ravelling* into all these mystical or intangled matters, mingling with the interest and passions of princes and of parties, and thereby heightened and inflamed, produced infinite disputes. *Temple.*

RA'VELIN. *n. s.* [French.] In fortification, a work that consists of two faces, that make a salient angle, commonly called half moon by the soldiers: it is raised before the courtines or counterscarps. *Dict.*

RA'VEN. *n. s.* [hꝛæꝼn, Saxon.] A large black fowl.

The *raven* himself is hoarse
That crokes the fatal entrance of Duncan
Under my battlements. *Shakesp. Macbeth.*
Come thou day in night,
For thou wilt lie upon the wings of night,
Whiter than snow upon a *raven's* back. *Shakesp.*

I have seen a perfectly white *raven*, as to bill as well as feathers. *Boyle on Colours.*

He made the greedy *ravens* to be Elias' caterers, and bring him food. *King Charles.*

On sev'ral parts a sev'ral praise bestows,
The ruby lips, and well-proportion'd nose,
The snowy skin, the *raven* glossy hair,
The dimpled cheek. *Dryden's Cymon and Iphigenia.*
The *raven* once in snowy plumes was drest,
White as the whitest dove's unsully'd breast,
His tongue, his prating tongue had chang'd him quite
To sooty blackness from the purest white. *Addison.*

To RA'VEN. *v. a.* [ꝛæꝼian, Saxon, to rob.] To devour with great eagerness and rapacity.

Thriftless ambition! that will *raven* up
Thine own life's means. *Shakesp.*
Our natures do pursue,
Like rats that *raven* down their proper bane,
A thirsty evil; and when we drink we die. *Shakesp.*
The cloyed will
That satiate, yet unsatisfied desire, that tub
Both fill'd and running, *ravening* first the lamb,
Longs after for the garbage. *Shakesp. Cymbeline.*

There is a conspiracy of the prophets, like a roaring lion *ravening* the prey. *Ezek.* xxii. 25.

To RA'VEN. *v. n.* To prey with rapacity.

Benjamin shall *raven* as a wolf; in the morning he shall devour the prey, and at night he shall divide the spoil. *Gen.*

The Pharisees make clean the outside of the cup; but their inward part is full of *ravening* and wickedness. *Luke* xi.

They gaped upon me with their mouths, as a *ravening* and a roaring lion. *Psalm* xxii. 13.

The more they fed, they *raven'd* ſtill for more,
They drain'd from Dan, and left Beerſheba poor;
But when ſome lay-preferment fell by chance,
The Gourmands made it their inheritance. *Dryden.*

Convulſions rack man's nerves and cares his breaſt,
His flying life is chas'd by *rav'ning* pains
Through all his doubles in the winding veins. *Blackmore.*

RA'VENOUS. *adj.* [from *raven.*] Furiouſly voracious; hungry to rage.

Thy deſires
Are wolfiſh, bloody, ſtarv'd and *ravenous.* *Shakeſp.*

As when a flock
Of *ravenous* fowl, though many a league remote,
Againſt the day of battle, to a field
Where armies lie encamp'd come flying, lur'd
With ſcent of living carcaſſes. *Milton's Paradiſe Loſt.*

What! the kind Iſmena,
That nurs'd me, watch'd my ſickneſs! oh ſhe watch'd me,
As *rav'nous* vultures watch the dying lion. *Smith.*

RA'VENOUSLY. *adv.* [from *ravenous.*] With raging voracity.

RA'VENOUSNESS. *n. ſ.* [from *ravenous.*] Rage for prey; furious voracity.

The *ravenouſneſs* of a lion or bear are natural to them; yet their miſſion upon an extraordinary occaſion may be an actus imperatus of divine providence. *Hale.*

RAUGHT. the old pret. and part. paſſ. of *reach.* Snatched; reached; attained.

His tail was ſtretched out in wond'rous length,
That to the houſe of heavenly gods it *raught*,
And with extorted power and borrow'd ſtrength,
The ever-burning lamps from thence it brought. *Fa. Qu.*

And that as ſoon as riper years he *raught*,
He might, for memory of that day's ruth,
Be called Ruddyman. *Fairy Queen.*

In like delights of bloody game,
He trained was till riper years he *raught*,
And there abode whilſt any beaſt of name
Walk'd in that foreſt. *Fairy Queen.*

This ſtaff of honour *raught*, there let it ſtand,
Where beſt it fits to be, in Henry's hand. *Shakeſp.*

The hand of death has *raught* him. *Shakeſp.*

Grittus furiouſly running in upon Schenden, violently *raught* from his head his rich cap of ſables, and with his horſemen took him. *Knolles's Hiſtory of the Turks.*

RA'VIN. *n. ſ.* [from *raven*; this were better written *raven.*]

1. Prey; food gotten by violence.

The lion ſtrangled for his lioneſſes, and filled his holes with prey, and his dens with *ravin.* *Nah.* ii. 2.

To me, who with eternal famine pine,
Alike is hell, or paradiſe, or heav'n;
There beſt; where moſt with *ravin* I may meet. *Milton.*

2. Rapine; rapaciouſneſs.

They might not lie long in a condition expoſed to the *ravin* of any vermin that may find them, being unable to eſcape. *Ray on the Creation.*

RA'VINGLY. *adv.* [from *rave.*] With frenzy; with diſtraction.

In this depth of muſes and divers ſorts of diſcourſes, would ſhe *ravingly* have remained. *Sidney, b.* ii.

To RA'VISH. *v. a.* [*ravir*, Fr.]

1. To conſtuprate by force.

They *raviſhed* the women and maids. *Lam.* v. 11.

They cut thy ſiſter's tongue, and *raviſh'd* her. *Shakeſp.*

2. To take away by violence.

Theſe hairs, which thou doſt *raviſh* from my chin,
Will quicken and accuſe thee. *Shakeſp. King Lear.*

Their vow is made
To ranſack Troy, within whoſe ſtrong immures
The *raviſh'd* Helen ſleeps. *Shakeſp. Troilus and Creſſida.*

I owe myſelf the care,
My fame and injur'd honour to repair;
From thy own tent, proud man, in thy deſpite,
This hand ſhall *raviſh* thy pretended right. *Dryden.*

3. To delight to rapture; to tranſport.

Thou haſt *raviſhed* my heart. *Cant.* iv. ix.

Be thou *raviſhed* always with her love. *Prov.* v. 19.

RA'VISHER. *n. ſ.* [*raviſſeur*, Fr. from *raviſh.*]

1. He that embraces a woman by violence.

They are cruel and bloody, common *raviſhers* of women, and murtherers of children. *Spenſer's State of Ireland.*

A *raviſher* muſt repair the temporal detriment to the maid, and give her a dowry, or marry her if ſhe deſire it. *Taylor.*

Turn hence thoſe pointed glories of your eyes!
For if more charms beneath thoſe circles riſe,
So weak my virtue, they ſo ſtrong appear,
I ſhall turn *raviſher* to keep you here. *Dryden.*

2. One who takes any thing by violence.

Shall the *raviſher* diſplay your hair,
While the fops envy, and the ladies ſtare. *Pope.*

RAVI'SHMENT. *n. ſ.* [*raviſſement*, Fr. from *raviſh.*]

1. Violation; forcible conſtupration.

Of his ſeveral *raviſhments*, betrayings and ſtealing away of men's wives, came in all thoſe ancient fables of his transformations and all that rabble of Grecian forgeries. *Raleigh.*

Tell them ancient ſtories of the *raviſhment* of chaſte maidens. *Taylor's Rule of Living Holy.*

I told them I was one of their knight-errants that delivered them from *raviſhment.* *Dryden.*

2. Tranſport; rapture; ecſtaſy; pleaſing violence on the mind.

All things joy, with *raviſhment*
Attracted by thy beauty ſtill to gaze. *Milton.*

Thee all things gaze on,
With *raviſhment* beheld! *Milton's Par. Loſt, b.* ix.

Can any mortal mixture of earth's mould
Breathe ſuch divine enchanting *raviſhment.* *Milton.*

What a *raviſhment* was that, when having found out the way to meaſure Hiero's crown, he leaped out of the bath, and, as if he were ſuddenly poſſeſt, ran naked up and down. *Wilkins's Dædalus.*

RAW. *adj.* [hneap, Saxon; *raa*, Daniſh; *rouw*, Dutch.]

1. Not ſubdued by the fire.

Full of great lumps of fleſh, and gobbets *raw.* *Spenſer.*

2. Not covered with the ſkin.

All aloud the wind doth blow,
And coughing drowns the parſon's ſaw;
And birds ſit brooding in the ſnow,
And Marian's noſe looks red and *raw.* *Shakeſp.*

If there be quick *raw* fleſh in the riſings, it is an old leproſy. *Lev.* xiii. 10.

3. Sore.

This her knight was feeble and too faint,
And all his ſinews waxen weak and *raw*
Through long impriſonment. *Spenſer.*

4. Immature; unripe.

5. Unſeaſoned; unripe in ſkill.

Some people, very *raw* and ignorant, are very unworthily and unfitly nominated to places, when men of deſert are held back and unpreferred. *Raleigh's Eſſays.*

People, while young and *raw*, and ſoft-natured, are apt to think it an eaſy thing to gain love, and reckon their own friendſhip a ſure price of another man's; but when experience ſhall have once opened their eyes, they will find that a friend is the gift of God. *South.*

Sails were ſpread to ev'ry wind that blew,
Raw were the ſailors. and the depths were new. *Dryden.*

Well I knew
What perils youthful ardour would purſue,
Young as thou wert in dangers, *raw* to war. *Dryden.*

6. New. This ſeems to be the meaning.

I have in my mind
A thouſand *raw* tricks of theſe bragging jacks. *Shakeſp.*

7. Bleak; chill.

They carried always with them that weed, as their houſe, their bed and their garment; and coming laſtly into Ireland, they found there more ſpecial uſe thereof, by reaſon of the *raw* cold climate. *Spenſer's State of Ireland.*

Youthful ſtill in your doublet and hoſe, this *raw* rheumatick day. *Shakeſp. Merry Wives of Windſor.*

Once upon a *raw* and guſty day,
The troubled Tyber chafing with his ſhores. *Sh*

God help thee, ſhallow man; God make
Inciſion in thee, thou art *raw.* *Sh*

8. Not concocted,

Diſtilled waters will laſt longer than *raw* waters. *B*

RA'WBONED. *adj.* [*raw* and *bone.*] Having bones ſca[rcely] covered with fleſh.

Lean *rawbon'd* raſcals! who would e'er ſuppoſe
They had ſuch courage. *Shakeſp. Henry* VI. *p.*

The wolf was content to barter away a *rawboned* carc[aſe] for a ſmooth and fat one. *L'Eſtra[nge].*

RA'WHEAD. *n. ſ.* [*raw* and *head.*] The name of a ſp[ectre] mentioned to fright children.

Hence draw thy theme, and to the ſtage permit
Rawhead and bloody bones, and hands and feet,
Ragouſts for Tereus or Thyeſtes dreſt. *Dr*

Servants awe children, and keep them in ſubjection, [by] telling them of *rawhead* and bloodybones. *L*

RA'WLY. *adv.* [from *raw.*]

1. In a raw manner.

2. Unſkilfully.

3. Newly.

Some crying for a ſurgeon, ſome upon the debts they o[we], ſome upon their children *rawly* left. *Shakeſp. H*

RA'WNESS. *n. ſ.* [from *raw.*]

1. State of being raw.

Chalk helpeth concoction, ſo it be out of a deep well; for then it cureth the *rawneſs* of the water. *Bacon.*

2. Unſkilfulneſs.

Charles V. conſidering the *rawneſs* of his ſeamen, eſtabliſhed a pilot major for their examination. *Hakewill.*

3. Haſty manner. This ſeems to be the meaning in this obſcure paſſage.

Why in that *rawneſs* left he wife and children,
Without leave taking. *Shakeſp.*

Ray. *n. s.* [*raie, rayon*, Fr. *radius*, Lat.]

1. A beam of light.

These eyes that roll in vain
To find thy piercing *ray*, and find no dawn. *Milton.*

The least light, or part of light, which may be stopt alone, or do or suffer any thing alone, which the rest of the light doth not or suffers not, I call a *ray* of light. *Newton.*

2. Any lustre corporeal or intellectual.

The air sharpen'd his visual *ray*. *Milton.*

3. [*Raye*, Fr. *raia*, Lat.] A fish. *Ainsworth.*

4. [*Lolium*, Lat.] An herb. *Ainsworth.*

To **Ray.** *v. a.* [*rayer*, Fr. from the noun.] To streak; to mark in long lines. An old word.

Beside a bubbling fountain low she lay,
Which she increased with her bleeding heart,
And the clean waves with purple gore did *ray*. *Fa. Qu.*

His horse is *raied* with the yellows. *Shakesp.*

Was ever man so beaten? was ever men so *raied?* was ever man so weary? *Shakesp. Taming of the Shrew.*

Ray, for *array*. *Spenser.*

Raze. *n. s.* [*rayz*, a root, Spanish.] A root of ginger. This is commonly written *race*, but less properly.

I have a gammon of bacon and two *razes* of ginger to be delivered. *Shakesp. Henry IV. p. i.*

To **Raze.** *v. a.* [*raser*, Fr. *rasus*, Lat. See **Rase**.

1. To overthrow; to ruin; to subvert.

Will you suffer a temple, how poorly built soever, but yet a temple of your deity, to be *razed*. *Sidney, b. ii.*

He yoaketh your rebellious necks,
Razeth your cities, and subverts your towns. *Shakesp.*

It grieved the tyrant, that so base a town should so long hold out, so that he would threaten to *raze* it. *Knolles.*

Shed christian blood, and populous cities *raze*;
Because they're taught to use some diff'rent phrase. *Waller.*

We touch'd with joy
The royal hand that *raz'd* unhappy Troy. *Dryden.*

The place would be *razed* to the ground, and its foundations sown with salt. *Addison's Spectator*, Nº 189.

2. To efface.

Fatal this marriage; cancelling your fame,
Razing the characters of your renown. *Shakesp.*

Pluck from the memory a rooted sorrow,
Raze out the written troubles of the brain. *Shakesp.*

He in derision sets
Upon their tongues a various spirit, to *raze*
Quite out their native language; and instead,
To sow a jangling noise of words. *Milton's Par. Lost.*

3. To extirpate.

I'll find a day to massacre them all,
And *raze* their faction and their family. *Shakesp.*

Ra'zor. *n. s.* [*rasor*, Lat.] A knife with a thick blade and fine edge used in shaving.

Zeal, except ordered aright, useth the *razor* with such eagerness, that the life of religion is thereby hazarded. *Hooker.*

These words are *razors* to my wounded heart. *Shakesp.*

Those thy boist'rous locks, not by the sword
Of noble warrior, so to stain his honour,
But by the barber's *razor* best subdu'd. *Milton's Agonistes.*

All our lords are by his wealth outvy'd,
Whose *razor* on my callow beard was try'd. *Dryden.*

Razor makers generally clap a small bar of Venice steel between two small bars of Flemish steel, and weld them together, to strengthen the back of the *razor*. *Moxon.*

Ra'zourable. *adj.* [from *razor*.] Fit to be shaved. Not in use.

New-born chins be rough and *razourable*. *Shakesp.*

Ra'zorfish. *n. s.*

The sheath or *razorfish* resembleth in length and bigness a man's finger. *Carew's Survey of Cornwall.*

Ra'zure. *n. s.* [*rasure*, Fr. *rasura*, Latin.] Act of erasing.

Oh! your desert speaks loud;
It well deserves with characters of brass
A forted residence, 'gainst the tooth of time
And *razure* of oblivion. *Shakesp. Measure for Measure.*

Re. Is an inseparable particle used by the Latins, and from them borrowed by us to denote iteration or backward action: as, *return*, to come back; to *revive*, to live again; *repercussion*, the act of driving back.

Rea'ccess. *n. s.* [*re* and *access*.] Visit renewed.

Let pass the quailing and withering of all things by the recess, and their reviving by the *reaccess* of the sun. *Hakewill.*

To **Reach.** *v. a.* ancient preterite *raught*. [ɲæcan, Saxon.]

1. To touch with the hand extended.

What are riches, empire, pow'r,
But larger means to gratify the will;
The steps by which we climb to rise and *reach*
Our wish, and that obtained, down with a scaffolding
Of scepters, crowns and thrones: they've serv'd their end,
And there like lumber to be left and scorn'd. *Congreve.*

2. To arrive at; to attain any thing distant; to strike from a distance.

Round the tree
They longing stood, but could not *reach*. *Milton.*

O patron pow'r, thy present aid afford,
That I may *reach* the beast. *Dryden.*

The coast so long desir'd
Thy troops shall *reach*, but having *reach'd*, repent. *Dryden.*

What remains beyond this, we have no more a positive notion of, than a mariner has of the depth of the sea; where, having let down his sounding-line, he *reaches* no bottom. *Locke.*

It must fall perhaps before this letter *reaches* your hands. *Pope.*

3. To fetch from some place distant, and give.

He *reached* me a full cup. 2 *Esdr.* xiv. 39.

4. To bring forward from a distant place.

Reach hither thy finger, and behold my hands; and *reach* hither thy hand, and thrust it into my side. *John* xx. 27.

5. To hold out; to stretch forth.

These kinds of goodness are so nearly united to the things which desire them, that we scarcely perceive the appetite to stir in *reaching* forth her hand towards them. *Hooker.*

When thou sittest among many, *reach* not thine hand out first. *Eccluf.* xxxi. 18.

6. To attain; to gain; to obtain.

The best accounts of the appearances of nature, which human penetration can *reach*, comes short of its reality. *Cheyne.*

7. To transfer.

Through such hands
The knowledge of the gods is *reach'd* to man. *Rowe.*

8. To penetrate to.

Whatever alterations are made in the body, if they *reach* not the mind, there is no perception. *Locke.*

9. To be adequate to.

The law *reached* the intention of the promoters, and this act fixed the natural price of money. *Locke.*

If these examples of grown men *reach* not the case of children, let them examine. *Locke on Education.*

10. To extend to.

Thy desire leads to no excess that *reaches* blame. *Milton.*

Her imprecations *reach* not to the tomb,
They shut not out society in death. *Addison's Cato.*

11. To extend; to spread abroad.

Trees *reach'd* too far their pamper'd boughs. *Milton.*

To **Reach.** *v. n.*

1. To be extended.

We hold that the power which the church hath lawfully to make laws doth extend unto sundry things of ecclesiastical jurisdiction, and such other matters whereto their opinion is, that the church's authority and power doth not *reach*. *Hooker.*

The new world *reaches* quite cross the torrid zone in one tropick to the other. *Boyle.*

When men pursue their thoughts of space, they are apt to stop at the confines of body, as if space were there at an end too, and *reached* no farther. *Locke.*

If I do not ask any thing improper, let me be buried by Theodosius; my vow *reaches* no farther than the grave. *Add.*

The influence of the stars *reaches* to many events, which are not in the power of reason. *Swift.*

2. To be extended far.

Great men have *reaching* hands. *Shakesp. Henry VI.*

3. To penetrate.

He hath delivered them into your hand, and ye have slain them in a rage, that *reacheth* up into heaven. 2 *Chr.* xxviii.

We *reach* forward into futurity, and bring up to our thoughts objects hid in the remotest depths of time. *Addison.*

4. To make efforts to attain.

Could a sailor always supply new line, and find the plummet sink without stopping, he would be in the posture of the mind, *reaching* after a positive idea of infinity. *Locke.*

5. To take in the hand.

Lest he *reach* of the tree of life, and eat. *Milton.*

Reach. *n. s.* [from the verb.]

1. Act of reaching or bringing by extension of the hand.

2. Power of reaching or taking in the hand.

There may be in a man's *reach* a book containing pictures and discourses, capable to delight and instruct him, which yet he may never have the will to open. *Locke.*

3. Power of attainment or management.

In actions, within the *reach* of power in him, a man seems as free as it is possible for freedom to make him. *Locke.*

4. Power; limit of faculties.

Our sight may be considered as a more diffusive kind of touch, that brings into our *reach* some of the most remote parts of the universe. *Addison.*

Be sure yourself and your own *reach* to know,
How far your genius, taste and learning go. *Pope.*

5. Contrivance; artful scheme; deep thought.

Drawn by others, who had deeper *reaches* than themselves to matters which they least intended. *Hayward.*

Some, under types, have affected obscurity to amuse and make themselves admired for profound *reaches*. *Howel.*

6. A fetch; an artifice to attain some distant advantage.

The duke of Parma had particular *reaches* and ends of his own underhand, to cross the design. *Bacon.*

7. Tendency to distant consequences.

Strain not my speech
To grosser issues, nor to larger *reach*,
Than to suspicion. *Shakesp. Othello.*

8. Extent.

8. Extent.

The confines met of empyrean heav'n,
And of this world: and, on the left hand, hell
With long *reach* interpos'd, *Milton's Par. Loft, b.* x.

To REA'CT. *v. a.* [*re* and *act.*] To return the impulse or impression.

The lungs being the chief instrument of sanguification, and acting strongly upon the chyle to bring it to an animal fluid, must be *reacted* upon as strongly. *Arbuthnot.*

Cut off your hand, and you may do
With t' other hand the work of two;
Because the soul her power contracts,
And on the brother limb *reacts.* *Swift's Miscellanies.*

REA'CTION. *n. s.* [*reaction*, Fr. from *react.*] The reciprocation of any impulse or force impressed, made by the body on which such impression is made: *action* and *reaction* are equal.

Do not great bodies conserve their heat the longest, their parts heating one another; and may not great, dense and fixed bodies, when heated beyond a certain degree, emit light so copiously, as, by the emission and *reaction* of its light, and the reflexions and refractions of its rays within its pores, to grow still hotter till it comes to a certain period of heat, such as is that of the sun? *Newton's Opticks.*

Alimentary substances, of a mild nature, act with small force upon the solids, and as the action and *reaction* are equal, the smallest degree of force in the solids digests them. *Arb.*

READ. *n. s.* [ꞃæð, Saxon; *raed*, Dutch.]

1. Counsel.

The man is blest that hath not lent
To wicked *read* his ear. *Sternhold.*

2. Saying; saw. This word is in both senses obsolete.

This *reade* is rife that oftentime
Great cumbers fall unsoft,
In humble dales is footing fast,
The trade is not so tickle. *Spenser.*

To READ. *v. a.* pret. *read*, part. pass. *read.* [ꞃæð, Saxon.]

1. To peruse any thing written.

I have seen her take forth paper, write upon't, *read* it, and afterwards seal it. *Shakesp. Macbeth.*

The passage you must have *read*, though since slipt out of your memory. *Pope.*

If we have not leisure to *read* over the book itself regularly, then by the titles of chapters we may be directed to peruse several sections. *Watts's Improvement of the Mind.*

2. To discover by characters or marks.

An armed corse did lye,
In whose dead face he *read* great magnanimity. *Spenser.*

3. To learn by observation.

Those about her
From her shall *read* the perfect ways of honour. *Shakesp.*

4. To know fully.

O most delicate fiend!
Who is't can *read* a woman? *Shakesp. Cymbeline.*

To READ. *v. n.*

1. To perform the act of perusing writing.

It shall be with him, and he shall *read* therein, that he may learn to fear the Lord. *Deut.* xvii. 19.

2. To be studious in books.

'Tis sure that Fleury *reads.* *Taylor.*

3. To know by reading.

I have *read* of an eastern king, who put a judge to death for an iniquitous sentence. *Swift.*

READ. *particip. adj.* [from *read*; the verb *read* is pronounced *reed*; the preterite and participle *red.*] Skilful by reading.

Virgil's shepherds are too well *read* in the philosophy of Epicurus. *Dryden.*

We have a poet among us, of a genius as exalted as his stature, and who is very well *read* in Longinus his treatise concerning the sublime. *Addison's Guardian*, Nº 108.

REA'DING. *n. s.* [from *read.*]

1. Study in books; perusal of books.

Though *reading* and conversation may furnish us with many ideas of men and things, yet it is our own meditation must form our judgment. *Watts's Improvement of the Mind.*

Less *reading* than makes felons 'scape,
Less human genius than God gives an ape,
Can make a Cibber. *Pope.*

2. A lecture; a prelection.

3. Publick recital.

The Jews always had their weekly *readings* of the law. *Hooker, b.* v. *s.* 8.

Give attendance to *reading*, exhortation and doctrine. 1 *Tim.* iv. 13.

4. Variation of copies.

That learned prelate has restored some of the *readings* of the authors with great sagacity. *Arbuthnot on Coins.*

READE'PTION. *n. s.* [*re* and *adeptus*, Latin.] Recovery; act of regaining.

Will any say, that the *readeption* of Trevigi was matter of scruple? *Bacon.*

REA'DER. *n. s.* [from *read.*]

1. One that peruses any thing written.

As we must take the care that our words and sense be clear, so if the obscurity happen through the hearers or *readers* want of understanding, I am not to answer for them. *B. Johnson.*

2. One studious in books.

Basiris' altars and the dire decrees
Of hard Euresthеus, ev'ry *reader* sees. *Dryden.*

3. One whose office is to read prayers in churches.

He got into orders, and became a *reader* in a parish church at twenty pounds a year. *Swift.*

REA'DERSHIP. *n. s.* [from *reader.*] The office of reading prayers.

When they have taken a degree, they get into orders, and sollicit a *readership.* *Swift's Miscellanies.*

REA'DILY. *adv.* [from *ready.*] Expeditely; with little hinderance or delay.

My tongue obey'd, and *readily* could name
Whate'er I saw. *Milton.*

Those very things, which are declined as impossible, are *readily* practicable in a case of extreme necessity. *South.*

I *readily* grant, that one truth cannot contradict another. *Locke.*

Every one sometime or other dreams that he is reading papers, in which case the invention prompts so *readily*, that the mind is imposed upon. *Addison's Spectator*, Nº 487.

REA'DINESS. *n. s.* [from *ready.*]

1. Expeditenefs; promptitude.

He would not forget the *readiness* of their king, in aiding him when the duke of Bretagne failed him. *Bacon.*

He opens himself to the man of business with reluctancy, but offers himself to the visits of a friend with facility and all the meeting *readiness* of desire. *South.*

2. The state of being ready or fit for any thing.

Have you an army ready?
—The centurions and their charges already in the entertainment to be on foot at an hour's warning.
—I am joyful to hear of their *readiness.* *Shakesp.*

They remained near a month, that they might be in *readiness* to attend the motion of the army. *Clarendon.*

3. Facility; freedom from hinderance or obstruction.

Nature has provided for the *readiness* and easiness of speech. *Holder's Elements of Speech.*

4. State of being willing or prepared.

A pious and well-disposed mind, attended with a *readiness* to obey the known will of God, is the surest means to enlighten the understanding to a belief of christianity. *South.*

Their conviction grew so strong, that they embraced the same truths, and laid down their lives, or were always in a *readiness* to do it, rather than depart from them. *Addison.*

READMI'SSION. *n. s.* [*re* and *admission.*] The act of admitting again.

In an exhausted receiver, animals, that seem as they were dead, revive upon the *readmission* of fresh air. *Arbuthnot.*

To REA'DMIT. *v. a.* [*re* and *admit.*] To let in again.

These evils I deserve,
Yet despair not of his final pardon,
Whose ear is ever open, and his eye
Gracious to *readmit* the suppliant. *Milton's Agonistes.*

After twenty minutes I *readmitted* the air. *Derham.*

To READO'RN. *v. a.* [*re* and *adorn.*] To decorate again; to deck a-new.

The streams now change their languid blue,
Regain their glory, and their fame renew,
With scarlet honours *readorn* the tide. *Blackmore.*

REA'DY. *adj.* [ꞃæð, Saxon; *redo*, Swedish; hꞃaðe, nimble, Saxon.]

1. Prompt; not delayed.

These commodities yield the *readiest* money of any in this kingdom, because they never fail of a price abroad. *Temple.*

He overlook'd his hinds; their pay was just
And *ready*: for he scorn'd to go on trust. *Dryden.*

2. Fit for a purpose; not to seek.

All things are *ready*, if our minds be so.
—Perish the man whose mind is backward now! *Shakesp.*

Make you *ready* your stiff bats and clubs;
Rome and her rats are at the point of battle. *Shakesp.*

One hand the sword, and one the pen employs,
And in my lap the *ready* paper lies. *Dryden.*

The sacred priests with *ready* knives bereave
The beasts of life, and in full bowls receive
The streaming blood. *Dryden's Æneis.*

3. Prepared; accommodated to any design, so as that there can be no delay.

Trouble and anguish shall prevail against him, as a king *ready* to the battle. *Job* xv. 24.

Death *ready* stands to interpose his dart. *Milton.*

The word which I have giv'n, I'll not revoke;
If he be brave, he's *ready* for the stroke. *Dryden.*

The imagination is always restless, and the will, reason being laid aside, is *ready* for every extravagant project. *Locke.*

4. Willing; eager.

Men, when their actions succeed not as they would, are always *ready* to impute the blame thereof unto the heavens, so as to excuse their own follies. *Spenser's State of Ireland.*

5. Being

5. Being at the point; not distant; near; about to do or be.
He knoweth that the day of darkness is *ready* at hand. *Job.*
Satan *ready* now
To stoop with weary'd wings and willing feet
On this world. *Milton's Paradise Lost.*
6. Being at hand; next to hand.
A sapling pine he wrench'd from out the ground,
The *readiest* weapon that his fury found. *Dryden.*
7. Facil; easy; opportune; near.
Sometimes the *readiest* way, which a wise man hath to conquer, is to fly. *Hooker's Preface.*
The race elect,
Safe towards Canaan from the shore advance
Through the wild desert, not the *readiest* way. *Milton.*
Proud of their conquest, prouder of their prey,
They leave the camp, and take the *readiest* way. *Dryden.*
The *ready* way to be thought mad, is to contend that you are not so. *Spectator*, N° 577.
8. Quick; not done with hesitation.
A *ready* consent often subjects a woman to contempt. *Clarissa.*
9. Expedite; nimble; not embarrassed; not slow.
Those, who speak in publick, are much better accepted, when they can deliver their discourse by the help of a lively genius and a *ready* memory, than when they are forced to read all. *Watts's Improvement of the Mind.*
10. *To make* READY. To make preparations.
He will shew you a large upper room; there *make ready* for us. *Mar.* xiv. 15.

REA'DY. *adv.* Readily; so as not to need delay.
We will go *ready* armed before the children of Israel. *Num.*

REA'DY. *n. s.* Ready money. A low word.
Lord Strutt was not flush in *ready*, either to go to law, or clear old debts. *Arbuthnot's History of John Bull.*

REAFFI'RMANCE. *n. s.* [*re* and *affirmance.*] Second confirmation.
Causes of deprivation are a conviction before the ordinary of a wilful maintaining any doctrine contrary to the thirty-nine articles, or a persisting therein without revocation of his error, or a *reaffirmance* after such revocation. *Ayliffe.*

RE'AL. *adj.* [*reel*, Fr. *realis*, Latin.]
1. Relating to things not persons; not personal.
Many are perfect in men's humours, that are not greatly capable of the *real* part of business; which is the constitution of one that hath studied men more than books. *Bacon.*
2. Not fictitious; not imaginary; true; genuine.
We do but describe an imaginary world, that is but little a-kin to the *real* one. *Glanvill's Sceps.*
When I place an imaginary name at the head of a character, I examine every letter of it, that it may not bear any resemblance to one that is *real.* *Addison.*
3. In law, consisting of things immoveable, as land.
I am hastening to convert my small estate, that is personal, into *real.* *Child's Discourse of Trade.*

RE'ALGAR. *n. s.* A mineral.
Realgar or sandaracha is red arsenick. *Harris.*
Put *realgar* hot into the midst of the quicksilver, whereby it may be condensed as well from within as without. *Bacon.*

REA'LITY. *n. s.* [*realité*, Fr. from *real.*]
1. Truth; verity; what is, not what merely seems.
I would have them well versed in the Greek and Latin poets, without which a man fancies that he understands a critic, when in *reality* he does not comprehend his meaning. *Addison's Spectator*, N° 291.
The best accounts of the appearances of nature in any single instance human penetration can reach, comes infinitely short of its *reality* and internal constitution; for who can search out the Almighty's works to perfection? *Cheyne.*
2. Something intrinsically important; not merely matter of show.
Of that skill the more thou know'st,
The more she will acknowledge thee her head,
And to *realities* yield all her shows,
Made so adorn for thy delight the more. *Milton.*

To RE'ALIZE. *v. a.* [*realiser*, Fr. from *real.*]
1. To bring into being or act.
Thus we *realize* what Archimedes had only in hypothesis, weighing a single grain against the globe of earth. *Glanvill.*
As a Diocesan, you are like to exemplify and *realize* every word of this discourse. *South.*
2. To convert money into land.

RE'ALLY. *adv.* [from *real.*]
1. With actual existence.
There cannot be a more important case of conscience for men to be resolved in, than to know certainly how far God accepts the will for the deed, and how far he does not; and to be informed truly when men do *really* will a thing, and when they have *really* no power to do, what they have willed. *South.*
2. In truth; truly; not seemingly.
The understanding represents to the will things *really* evil, under the notion of good. *South.*
These orators inflame the people, whose anger is *really* but a short fit of madness. *Swift.*
3. It is a slight corroboration of an opinion.
Why *really* sixty-five is somewhat old. *Young.*

REALM. *n. s.* [*roiaulme*, French.]
1. A kingdom; a king's dominion.
Is there any part of that *realm*, or any nation therein, which have not yet been subdued to the crown of England. *Spenser.*
They had gather'd a wise council to them
Of ev'ry *realm*, that did debate this business. *Shakesp.*
A son whose worthy deeds
Raise him to be the second in that *realm.* *Milton.*
2. Kingly government. This sense is not frequent.
Learn each small people's genius, policies,
The ant's republick, and the *realm* of bees. *Pope.*

REA'LTY. *n. s.* [a word peculiar, I believe, to *Milton.*]
Realty means not in this place reality in opposition to show, but loyalty; for the Italian Dictionary explains the adjective *reale* by loyal. *Pearce on Milton.*
O heaven, that such resemblance of the highest
Should yet remain, where faith and *realty*
Remain not. *Milton's Paradise Lost*, *b.* vi.

REAM. *n. s.* [*rame*, Fr. *riem*, Dutch.] A bundle of paper containing twenty quires.
All vain petitions mounting to the sky,
With *reams* abundant this abode supply. *Pope.*

To REA'NIMATE. *v. a.* [*re* and *animo*, Lat.] To revive; to restore to life.
We are our *reanimated* ancestors, and antedate their resurrection. *Glanvill's Sceps.*
The young man left his own body breathless on the ground, while that of the doe was *reanimated.* *Spectator*, N° 578.

To REANNE'X. *v. a.* [*re* and *annex.*] To annex again.
King Charles was not a little inflamed with an ambition to repurchase and *reannex* that dutchy. *Bacon's Henry* VII.

To REAP. *v. a.* [ꞃepan, Saxon.]
1. To cut corn at harvest.
From Ireland come I with my strength,
And *reap* the harvest which that rascal sow'd. *Shakesp.*
When ye *reap* the harvest, thou shalt not wholly *reap* the corners of thy field. *Lev.* xix. 9.
The hire of the labourers, which have *reaped* down your fields, is kept back by fraud. *Ja.* v. 5.
Is it fitting in this very field,
Where I so oft have *reap'd*, so oft have till'd,
That I should die for a deserter? *Gay.*
2. To gather; to obtain.
They that love the religion which they profess, may have failed in choice, but yet they are sure to *reap* what benefit the same is able to afford. *Hooker.*
What sudden anger's this? how have I *reap'd* it? *Shak.*
This is a thing,
Which you might from relation likewise *reap*,
Being much spoke of. *Shakesp. Cymbeline.*
Our sins being ripe, there was no preventing of God's justice from *reaping* that glory in our calamities, which we robbed him of in our prosperity. *King Charles.*

To REAP. *v. n.* To harvest.
They that sow in tears, shall *reap* in joy. *Psalm* cxxvi. 5.

REA'PER. *n. s.* [from *reap.*] One that cuts corn at harvest.
Your ships are not well mann'd,
Your mariners are muliteers, people
Ingrost by swift impress. *Shakesp. Ant. and Cleop.*
From hungry *reapers* they their sheaves withhold. *Sand.*
Here Ceres' gifts in waving prospect stand,
And nodding tempt the joyful *reaper*'s hand. *Pope.*
A thousand forms he wears,
And first a *reaper* from the field appears,
Sweating he walks, while loads of golden grain
O'ercharge the shoulders of the seeming swain. *Pope.*

REA'PINGHOOK. *n. s.* [*reaping* and *hook.*] A hook used to cut corn in harvest.
Some are brib'd to vow it looks
Most plainly done by thieves with *reapinghooks.* *Dryden.*

REAR. *n. s.* [*arrieare*, French.]
1. The hinder troop of an army, or the hinder line of a fleet.
The *rear* admiral, an arch pirate, was afterwards slain with a great shot. *Knolles's History of the Turks.*
Argive chiefs
Fled from his well-known face, with wonted fear,
As when his thund'ring sword and pointed spear
Drove headlong to their ships, and glean'd the *rear.* *Dryd.*
Snowy headed winter leads,
Yellow autumn brings the *rear.* *Waller.*
2. The last class.
Coins I place in the *rear*, because made up of both the other. *Peacham.*

REAR. *adj.* [ꞃꞃepe, Saxon.]
1. Raw; half roasted; half sodden.
2. Early. A provincial word.
O'er yonder hill does scant the dawn appear,
Then why does Cuddy leave his cot so *rear*? *Gay.*

To Rear. *v. a.* [aꞃæꞃan, Saxon.]
1. To raiſe up.
All the people ſhouted with a loud voice, for the *rearing* up of the houſe of the Lord. *1 Eſdr.* v. 62.
Who now ſhall *rear* you to the ſun, or rank
Your tribes. *Milton.*
2. To lift up from a fall.
Down again ſhe fell unto the ground,
But he her quickly *rear'd* up again. *Fa. Queen, b.* i.
In adoration at his feet I fell
Submiſs: he *rear'd* me. *Milton.*
3. To move upwards.
Up to a hill anon his ſteps he *rear'd*,
From whoſe high top to ken the proſpect round. *Milton.*
4. To bring up to maturity.
No creature goeth to generate, whilſt the female is buſy in ſitting or *rearing* her young. *Bacon's Natural Hiſtory.*
They were a very hardy breed, and *reared* their young ones without any care. *Mortimer's Huſbandry.*
They flouriſh'd long in tender bliſs, and *rear'd*
A numerous offspring, lovely like themſelves. *Thomſon.*
5. To educate; to inſtruct.
He wants a father to protect his youth,
And *rear* him up to virtue. *Southern.*
They have in every town publick nurſeries, where all parents, except cottagers and labourers, are obliged to ſend their infants to be *reared* and educated. *Swift.*
6. To exalt; to elevate.
Charity decent, modeſt, eaſy, kind,
Softens the high, and *rears* the abject mind. *Prior.*
7. To rouſe; to ſtir up.
Into the naked woods he goes,
And ſeeks the tuſky boar to *rear*,
With well-mouth'd hounds and pointed ſpear. *Dryden.*

Rea'rward. *n. ſ.* [from *rear.*]
1. The laſt troop.
He from the beginning began to be in the *rearward*, and before they left fighting, was too far off. *Sidney.*
The ſtandard of Dan was the *rearward* of the camp. *Num.*
2. The end; the tail; a train behind.
Why follow'd not, when ſhe ſaid Tybalt's dead,
Thy father or thy mother?
But with a *rearward* following Tybalt's death,
Romeo is baniſhed. *Shakeſp. Romeo and Juliet.*
3. The latter part. In contempt.
He was ever in the *rearward* of the faſhion. *Shakeſp.*

Rea'rmouse. *n. ſ.* [more properly *reremouſe*; hꞃeꞃemuꞅ, Sax.] The leather-winged bat.
Some war with *rearmice* for their leathern wings
To make my ſmall elves coats. *Shakeſp.*
Of flying fiſhes, the wings are not feathers, but a thin kind of ſkin, like the wings of a bat or *rearmouſe.* *Abbot.*

To Reasce'nd. *v. n.* [*re* and *aſcend.*] To climb again.
When as the day the heaven doth adorn,
I wiſh that night the noyous day would end;
And when as night hath us of light forlorn,
I wiſh that day would ſhortly *reaſcend.* *Spenſer.*
Taught by the heav'nly muſe to venture down
The dark deſcent, and up to *reaſcend.* *Milton.*
Theſe puiſſant legions, whoſe exile
Hath empty'd heav'n, ſhall fail to *reaſcend*,
Self-rais'd, and repoſſeſs their native ſeat? *Milton.*

To Reasce'nd. *v. a.* To mount again.
When the god his fury had allay'd,
He mounts aloft, and *reaſcends* the ſkies. *Addiſon.*

REA'SON. *n. ſ.* [*raiſon*, Fr. *ratio*, Lat.]
1. The power by which man deduces one propoſition from another, or proceeds from premiſes to conſequences; the rational faculty.
Reaſon is the director of man's will, diſcovering in action what is good; for the laws of well-doing are the dictates of right *reaſon.* *Hooker, b.* i. *ſ.* 7.
Though brutiſh that conteſt and foul,
When *reaſon* hath to deal with force; yet ſo
Moſt reaſon is that *reaſon* overcome. *Milton.*
Dim, as the borrow'd beams of moon and ſtars
To lonely, weary, wand'ring travellers,
Is *reaſon* to the ſoul: and as on high,
Thoſe rowling fires diſcover but the ſky,
Not light us here; ſo *reaſon's* glimmering ray
Was lent, not to aſſure our doubtful way,
But guide us upward to a better day. *Dryden.*
It would be well, if people would not lay ſo much weight on their own *reaſon* in matters of religion, as to think every thing impoſſible and abſurd, which they cannot conceive: how often do we contradict the right rules of *reaſon* in the whole courſe of our lives? *reaſon* itſelf is true and juſt, but the *reaſon* of every particular man is weak and wavering, perpetually ſwayed and turn'd by his intereſts, his paſſions and his vices. *Swift's Miſcellanies.*
2. Cauſe; ground or principle.
Virtue and vice are not arbitrary things, but there is a natural and eternal *reaſon* for that goodneſs and virtue, and againſt vice and wickedneſs. *Tillotſon.*
3. Cauſe efficient.
Spain is thin ſown of people, partly by *reaſon* of the ſterility of the ſoil, and partly their natives are exhauſted by ſo many employments in ſuch vaſt territories as they poſſeſs. *Bac.*
The *reaſon* of the motion of the balance in a wheel watch, is by the motion of the next wheel. *Hale.*
By *reaſon* of the ſickneſs of a reverend prelate, I have been overruled to approach this place. *Sprat.*
I have not obſerved equality of numbers in my verſe; partly by *reaſon* of my haſte, but more eſpecially becauſe I would not have my ſenſe a ſlave to ſyllables. *Dryden.*
4. Final cauſe.
Reaſon, in the Engliſh language, ſometimes is taken for true and clear principles; ſometimes for clear and fair deductions; ſometimes for the cauſe, particularly the final cauſe: but here for a faculty in man. *Locke.*
5. Argument; ground of perſuaſion; motive.
I maſk the buſineſs from the common eye
For ſundry weighty *reaſons.* *Shakeſp. Macbeth.*
If it be natural, ought we not rather to conclude, that there is ſome ground and *reaſon* for theſe fears, and that nature hath not planted them in us to no purpoſe. *Tillotſon.*
6. Ratiocination; diſcurſive power.
When ſhe rates things, and moves from ground to ground,
The name of *reaſon* ſhe obtains by this;
But when by *reaſon* ſhe the truth hath found,
And ſtandeth fixt, ſhe underſtanding is. *Davies.*
7. Clearneſs of faculties.
Lovers and madmen have their ſeething brains,
Such ſhaping fantaſies that apprehend
More than cool *reaſon* ever comprehends. *Shakeſp.*
When valour preys on *reaſon*,
It eats the ſword it fights with. *Shakeſp. Ant. and Cleop.*
8. Right; juſtice.
I was promis'd on a time,
To have *reaſon* for my rhyme:
From that time unto this ſeaſon,
I receiv'd nor rhyme nor *reaſon.* *Spenſer.*
Are you in earneſt?
Ay, and reſolv'd withal
To do myſelf this *reaſon* and this right. *Shakeſp.*
The papiſts ought in *reaſon* to allow them all the excuſes they make uſe of for themſelves; ſuch as an invincible ignorance, oral tradition and authority. *Stillingfleet.*
Let it drink deep in thy moſt vital part;
Strike home, and do me *reaſon* in thy heart. *Dryden.*
9. Reaſonable claim; juſt practice.
God brings good out of evil; and therefore it were but *reaſon* we ſhould truſt God to govern his own world, and wait till the change cometh, or the reaſon be diſcovered. *Taylor.*
Conſcience, not acting by law, is a boundleſs preſumptuous thing; and, for any one by virtue thereof, to challenge himſelf a privilege of doing what he will, and of being unaccountable, is in all *reaſon* too much, either for man or angel. *South.*
A ſevere reflection Montaigne has made on princes, that we ought not in *reaſon* to have any expectatious of favour from them. *Dryden's Dedication to Aurengzebe.*
We have as great aſſurance that there is a God, as the nature of the thing to be proved is capable of, and as we could in *reaſon* expect to have. *Tillotſon's Preface.*
When any thing is proved by as good arguments as a thing of that kind is capable of, we ought not in *reaſon* to doubt of its exiſtence. *Tillotſon.*
10. Rationale; juſt account.
To render a *reaſon* of an effect or phenomenon, is to deduce it from ſomething elſe more known than itſelf. *Boyle.*
11. Moderation; moderate demands.
The moſt probable way of bringing France to *reaſon*, would be by the making an attempt upon the Spaniſh Weſt Indies, and by that means to cut off all communication with this great ſource of riches. *Addiſon.*

To Rea'son. *v. n.* [*raiſonner*, Fr.]
1. To argue rationally; to deduce conſequences juſtly from premiſes.
No man, in the ſtrength of the firſt grace, can merit the ſecond; for *reaſon* they do not, who think ſo; unleſs a beggar, by receiving one alms, can merit another. *South.*
Ideas, as ranked under names, are thoſe, that for the moſt part men *reaſon* of within themſelves, and always thoſe which they commune about with others. *Locke.*
Every man's *reaſoning* and knowledge is only about the ideas exiſting in his own mind; and our knowledge and *reaſoning* about other things is only as they correſpond with thoſe our particular ideas. *Locke.*
Love is not to be *reaſon'd* down, or loſt
In high ambition. *Addiſon.*
In the lonely grove,
'Twas there juſt and good he *reaſon'd* ſtrong,
Clear'd ſome great truth. *Tickell.*
2. To debate; to diſcourſe; to talk; to take or give an account. Not in uſe.
Reaſon with the fellow,
Before you puniſh him, where he heard this. *Shakeſp.*

I *reaſon'd* with a Frenchman yeſterday,
Who told me in the narrow ſeas,
There miſcarried a veſſel of our country. *Shakeſp.*

Stand ſtill, that I may *reaſon* with you of all the righteous acts of the Lord. *1 Sam.* xii. 7.

3. To raiſe diſquiſitions; to make enquiries.

Jeſus, perceiving their thoughts, ſaid, what *reaſon* ye in your hearts? *Luke* v. 22.

They *reaſon'd* high
Of providence, foreknowledge, will and fate. *Milton.*

Already by thy *reaſoning* this I gueſs,
Who art to lead thy offspring; and ſuppoſeſt,
That bodies bright and greater ſhould not ſerve
The leſs not bright. *Milton.*

Down reaſon then, at leaſt vain *reaſoning* down. *Milt.*

To REA'SON. *v. a.* To examine rationally. This is a French mode of ſpeech.

When they are clearly diſcovered, well digeſted, and well *reaſoned* in every part, there is beauty in ſuch a theory. *Burn.*

REA'SONABLE. *adj.* [*raiſon*, Fr.]

1. Having the faculty of reaſon; endued with reaſon.

She perceived her only ſon lay hurt, and that his hurt was ſo deadly, as that already his life had loſt uſe of the *reaſonable* and almoſt ſenſible part. *Sidney.*

2. Acting, ſpeaking or thinking rationally.

The parliament was diſſolved, and gentlemen furniſhed with ſuch forces, as were held ſufficient to hold in bridle either the malice or rage of *reaſonable* people. *Hayward.*

3. Juſt; rational; agreeable to reaſon.

A law may be *reaſonable* in itſelf, although a man does not allow it, or does not know the reaſon of the lawgivers. *Swift.*

4. Not immoderate.

Let all things be thought upon,
That may with *reaſonable* ſwiftneſs add
More feathers to our wings. *Shakeſp. Henry* V.

5. Tolerable; being in mediocrity.

I could with *reaſonable* good manner receive the ſalutation of her and of the princeſs Pamela, doing them yet no further reverence than one princeſs oweth to another. *Sidney.*

A good way diſtant from the nigra rupes, there are four ſeveral lands of *reaſonable* quantity. *Abbot's Deſcr. of the World.*

Notwithſtanding theſe defects, the Engliſh colonies maintained themſelves in a *reaſonable* good eſtate, as long as they retained their own ancient laws. *Davies on Ireland.*

REA'SONABLENESS. *n. ſ.* [from *reaſonable.*]

1. The faculty of reaſon.

2. Agreeableneſs to reaſon.

They thought the work would be better done, if thoſe, who had ſatisfied themſelves with the *reaſonableneſs* of what they wiſh, would undertake the converting and diſpoſing of other men. *Clarendon.*

The paſſive reaſon, which is more properly *reaſonableneſs*, is that order and congruity which is impreſſed upon the thing thus wrought; as in a watch, the whole frame and contexture of it carries a *reaſonableneſs* in it, the paſſive impreſſion of the reaſon or intellectual idea that was in the artiſt. *Hale.*

3. Moderation.

REA'SONABLY. *adv.* [from *reaſonable.*]

1 Agreeably to reaſon.

Chaucer makes Arcite violent in his love, and unjuſt in the purſuit of it; yet when he came to die, he made him think more *reaſonably.* *Dryden's Preface to Fables.*

2. Moderately; in a degree reaching to mediocrity.

Some man *reaſonably* ſtudied in the law, ſhould be perſuaded to go thither as chancellor. *Bacon's Advice to Villiers.*

If we can by induſtry make our deaf and dumb perſons *reaſonably* perfect in the language and pronunciation, he may be alſo capable of the ſame privilege of underſtanding by the eye what is ſpoken. *Holder's Elements of Speech.*

REA'SONER. *n. ſ.* [*raiſonneur*, Fr. from *reaſon.*] One who reaſons; an arguer.

Due reverence pay
To learn'd Epicurus; ſee the way
By which this *reas'ner* of ſo high renown
Moves through th' ecliptick road the rolling ſun. *Blackm.*

The terms are looſe and undefined; and what leſs becomes a fair *reaſoner*, he puts wrong and invidious names on every thing to colour a falſe way of arguing. *Addiſon.*

Thoſe *reaſoners*, who employ ſo much of their zeal for the upholding the balance of power in Chriſtendom, by their practices are endeavouring to deſtroy it at home. *Swift.*

REA'SONING. *n. ſ.* [from *reaſon.*] Argument.

Thoſe who would make uſe of ſolid arguments and ſtrong *reaſonings* to a reader of ſo delicate a turn, would be like that fooliſh people, who worſhiped a fly, and ſacrified an ox to it. *Addiſon's Freeholder*, N° 32.

REA'SONLESS. *adj.* [from *reaſon.*] Void of reaſon.

This proffer is abſurd and *reaſonleſs.* *Shakeſp. Hen.* VI.

Is it
Her true perfection, or my falſe tranſgreſſion,
That makes me *reaſonleſs* to reaſon thus? *Shakeſp.*

That they wholly direct the *reaſonleſs* mind, I am reſolved; for all thoſe which were created mortal, as birds and beaſts, are left to their natural appetites. *Raleigh's Hiſt. of the World.*

Theſe reaſons in love's law have paſt for good,
Though fond and *reaſonleſs* to ſome. *Milton's Agoniſtes.*

To REASSE'MBLE. *v. a.* [*re* and *aſſemble.*] To collect anew.

There *reaſſembling* our afflicted pow'rs,
Conſult how to offend our enemy. *Milton.*

To REASSE'RT, *v. a.* [*re* and *aſſert.*] To aſſert anew; to maintain after ſuſpenſion or ceſſation.

His ſteps I followed, his doctrine I *reaſſerted.* *Atterbury.*

Young Oreſtes grown
To manly years ſhould *reaſſert* the throne. *Pope.*

To REASSU'ME. *v. a.* [*reaſſumo*, Lat. *re* and *aſſume.*] To reſume; to take again.

To him the ſon return'd
Into his bliſsful boſom *reaſſum'd*,
In glory as of old. *Milton.*

Nor only on the Trojans fell this doom,
Their hearts at laſt the vanquiſh'd *reaſſume.* *Denham.*

For this he *reaſſumes* the nod,
While Semele commands the god. *Prior.*

After Henry VIII. had *reaſſumed* the ſupremacy, a ſtatute was made, by which all doctors of the civil law might be made chancellors. *Ayliffe's Parergon.*

To REASSU'RE. [*raſſurer*, Fr.] To free from fear; to reſtore from terrour.

They roſe with fear,
Till dauntleſs Pallas *reaſſur'd* the reſt. *Dryden.*

REATE. *n. ſ.* A kind of long ſmall graſs that grows in water, and complicates itſelf together.

Let them lie dry ſix months to kill the water-weeds; as water-lilies, candocks, *reate* and bulruſhes. *Walton.*

To REAVE. *v. a.* pret. *reft.* [ꞃæꝼian, Saxon; whence to *bereave.*]

1. To take away by ſtealth or violence. An obſolete word.

Diſmounting from his lofty ſteed,
He to him leapt, in mind to *reave* his life. *Spenſer.*

Some make his meaſhy bed, but *reave* his reſt. *Carew.*

Who can be bound by any ſolemn vow,
To do a murd'rous deed, to rob a man,
To force a ſpotleſs virgin's chaſtity,
To *reave* the orphan of his patrimony,
And have no other reaſon for his wrong,
But that he was bound by a ſolemn oath. *Shakeſp. Hen.* VI.

2. It was uſed as well in a good as bad ſenſe.

They ſought my troubled ſenſe how to deceave
With talk, that might unquiet fancies *reave.* *Hubberd.*

Each ſucceeding time addeth or *reaveth* goods and evils, according to the occaſions itſelf produceth. *Carew.*

To REBA'PTIZE. *v. a.* [*rebaptiſer*, Fr. *re* and *baptize.*] To baptize again.

Underſtanding that the rites of the church were obſerved, he approved of their baptiſm, and would not ſuffer them to be *rebaptized.* *Ayliffe's Parergon.*

REBAPTIZA'TION. *n. ſ.* [*rebaptiſation*, Fr. from *rebaptize.*] Renewal of baptiſm.

In maintainance of *rebaptization*, their arguments are built upon this, that hereticks are not any part of the church of Chriſt. *Hooker, b.* iii. *ſ.* 1.

To REBA'TE. *v. n.* [*rebattre*, Fr.] To blunt; to beat to obtuſeneſs; to deprive of keenneſs.

He doth *rebate* and blunt his natural edge
With profits of the mind, ſtudy and faſt. *Shakeſp.*

The icy goat, the crab which ſquare the ſcales;
With thoſe of aries trine conſent to hate
The ſcales of libra, and her rays *rebate.* *Creech.*

He modifies his firſt ſevere decree;
The keener edge of battle to *rebate*,
The troops for honour fighting, not for hate. *Dryden.*

My flagging ſoul flies under her own pitch,
My ſenſes too are dull and ſtupify'd,
Their edge *rebated.* *Dryden's Don Sebaſtian.*

Their innocence unfeign'd long joys afford
To the honeſt nuptial bed, and, in the wane
Of life, *rebate* the miſeries of age. *Philips.*

RE'BECK. *n. ſ.* [*rebec*, Fr. *ribecca*, Italian.] A three ſtringed fiddle.

When the merry bells ring round,
And the jocund *rebecks* ſound,
To many a youth and many a maid,
Dancing in the checker'd ſhade. *Milton.*

RE'BEL. *n. ſ.* [*rebelle*, Fr. *rebellis*, Lat.] One who oppoſes lawful authority.

The merciless Macdonel
Worthy to be a *rebel*; for to that
The multiplying villanies of nature
Do ſwarm upon him. *Shakeſp. Macbeth.*

The *rebels* there are up,
And put the Engliſhmen unto the ſword. *Shakeſp.*

Shall man from nature's ſanction ſtray,
A *rebel* to her rightful ſway. *Fenton.*

To REBE'L. *v. n.* [*rebello*, Lat.] To riſe in oppoſition againſt lawful authority.

Boys, immature in knowledge,
Pawn their experience to their preſent pleaſure,
And ſo *rebel* to judgment. *Shakeſp. Ant. and Cleopatra.*

If

If they perceive dissention in our looks,
How will their grudging stomachs be provok'd
To wilful disobedience, and *rebel?* *Shakesp. Henry* VI.
Such smiling rogues as these sooth every passion,
That in the nature of their lords *rebels*;
Bring oil to fire. *Shakesp. King Lear.*
There was a time, when all the body's members
Rebell'd against the belly. *Shakesp. Coriolanus.*
Arm'd with thy might, rid heav'n of these *rebell'd. Milt.*
How cou'd my hand *rebel* against my heart?
How cou'd your heart *rebel* against your reason? *Dryden.*

Part of the angels *rebelled* against God, and thereby lost their happy state. *Locke.*

REBE'LLER. *n. s.* [from *rebel.*] One that rebels. *Dict.*

REBE'LLION. *n. s.* [*rebellion*, Fr. *rebellio*, Lat. from *rebel.*] Insurrection against lawful authority.

He was victorious in *rebellions* and seditions of people. *Bac.*

Adam's sin, or the curse upon it, did not deprive him of his rule, but left the creatures to a *rebellion* or reluctation. *Bacon's Holy War.*

Raz'd by *rebellion* from the books of life. *Milton.*

REBE'LLIOUS. *adj.* [from *rebel.*] Opponent to lawful authority.

From the day that thou didst depart out of Egypt, until ye came unto this place, ye have been *rebellious* against the Lord. *Deutr.* ix. 7.

This our son is stubborn and *rebellious*, he will not obey our voice. *Deutr.* xxi. 20.

REBE'LLIOUSLY. *adv.* [from *rebellious.*] In opposition to lawful authority.

When one shewed him where a nobleman, that had *rebelliously* born arms against him, lay very honourably intombed, and advised the king to deface the monument; he said, no, no, but I would all the rest of mine enemies were as honourably intombed. *Camden's Remains.*

REBE'LLIOUSNESS. *n. s.* [from *rebellious.*] The quality of being rebellious.

To REBE'LLOW. *v. n.* [*re* and *bellow.*] To bellow in return; to echo back a loud noise.

He loudly bray'd with beastly yelling sound,
That all the fields *rebellowed* again. *Fairy Queen.*
The resisting air the thunder broke,
The cave *rebellow'd*, and the temple shook. *Dryden.*
From whence were heard, *rebellowing* to the main,
The roars of lions. *Dryden's Æneis.*

REBOA'TION. *n. s.* [*reboo*, Lat.] The return of a loud bellowing sound.

To REBOU'ND. *v. n.* [*rebondir*, Fr. *re* and *bound.*] To spring back; to be reverberated; to fly back, in consequence of motion impressed and resisted by a greater power.

Whether it were a roaring voice of most savage wild beasts, or a *rebounding* echo from the hollow mountains. *Wisd.* xvii.

It with *rebounding* surge the bars assail'd. *Milton.*

Life and death are in the power of the tongue, and that not only directly with regard to the good or ill we may do to others, but reflexively with regard to what may *rebound* to ourselves. *Government of the Tongue.*

Bodies which are absolutely hard, or so soft as to be void of elasticity, will not *rebound* from one another: impenetrability makes them only stop. *Newton's Opticks.*

She bounding from the shelfy shore,
Round the descending nymph the waves *rebounding* roar. *Po.*

To REBOU'ND. *v. a.* To reverberate; to beat back.

All our invectives, at their supposed errors, fall back with a *rebounded* force upon our own real ones. *Decay of Piety.*

Silenus sung, the vales his voice *rebound*,
And carry to the skies the sacred sound. *Dryden.*
Flow'rs, by the soft South West
Open'd, and gather'd by religious hands,
Rebound their sweets from th' odoriferous pavement. *Prior.*

REBOU'ND. *n. s.* [from the verb.] The act of flying back in consequence of motion resisted; resilition.

I do feel,
By the *rebound* of yours, a grief that shoots
My very heart. *Shakesp. Antony and Cleopatra.*

If you strike a ball sidelong, not full upon the surface, the *rebound* will be as much the contrary way; whether there be any such resilience in echoes may be tried. *Bacon.*

The weapon with unerring fury flew,
At his left shoulder aim'd: nor entrance found;
But back, as from a rock, with swift *rebound*,
Harmless return'd. *Dryden.*

REBU'FF. *n. s.* [*rebuffade*, Fr. *rebuffo*, Italian.] Repercussion; quick and sudden resistance.

By ill chance
The strong *rebuff* of some tumultuous cloud,
Instinct with fire and nitre, hurried him
As many miles aloft. *Milton's Paradise Lost, b.* ii.

To REBU'FF. *v. a.* [from the noun.] To beat back; to oppose with sudden violence.

To REBUI'LD. *v. a.* [*re* and *build.*] To reedify; ro restore from demolition; to repair.

The fines imposed there were the more questioned, and repined against, because they were assigned to the *rebuilding* and repairing of St. Paul's church. *Clarendon.*

Fine is the secret, delicate the art,
To raise the shades of heroes to our view,
Rebuild fall'n empires, and old time renew. *Tickell.*

REBU'KABLE. *adj.* [from *rebuke.*] Worthy of reprehension.

Rebukable
And worthy shameful check it were, to stand
On mere mechanick compliment. *Shakesp. Ant. and Cleop.*

To REBU'KE. *v. a.* [*reboucher*, Fr.] To chide; to reprehend; to repress by objurgation.

I am asham'd; does not the stone *rebuke* me,
For being more stone than it? *Shakesp. Winter's Tale.*

He was *rebuked* for his iniquity; the dumb ass, speaking with man's voice, forbad the madness of the prophet. 2 *Pet.*

My son, despise not thou the chastening of the Lord, nor faint when thou art *rebuked* of him. *Heb.* xii. 15.

The proud he tam'd, the penitent he cheer'd,
Nor to *rebuke* the rich offender fear'd. *Dryden.*

REBU'KE. *n. s.* [from the verb.]

1. Reprehension; chiding expression; objurgation.

Why bear you these *rebukes*, and answer not? *Shakesp.*
If he will not yield,
Rebuke and dread correction wait on us,
And they shall do their office. *Shakesp. Henry* IV.

The channels of waters were seen; at thy *rebuke*, O Lord, at the blast of the breath of thy nostrils. *Psalm* xviii. 15.

Thy *rebuke* hath broken my heart; I am full of heaviness. *Psalm* lxix. 21.

The *rebukes* and chiding to children, should be in grave and dispassionate words. *Locke.*

Shall Cibber's son, without *rebuke*,
Swear like a lord? *Pope.*
Should vice expect to 'scape *rebuke*,
Because its owner is a duke? *Swift's Miscellanies.*

2. In low language, it signifies any kind of check.

He gave him so terrible a *rebuke* upon the forehead with his heel, that he laid him at his length. *L'Estrange.*

REBU'KER. *n. s.* [from *rebuke.*] A chider; a reprehender.

The revolters are profound to make slaughter, though I have been a *rebuker* of them all. *Hosea* v. 2.

RE'BUS. *n. s.* [*rebus*, Latin.] A word represented by a picture.

Some citizens, wanting arms, have coined themselves certain devices alluding to their names, which we call *rebus*: Master Jugge the printer, in many of his books, took, to express his name, a nightingale sitting in a bush with a scrole in her mouth, wherein was written jugge, jugge, jugge. *Peac.*

To REBU'T. *v. n.* [*rebuter*, Fr.] To retire back. Obsolete.

Themselves too rudely rigorous,
Astonied with the stroke of their own hand,
Do back *rebut*, and each to other yielded land. *Fa. Queen.*

REBU'TTER. *n. s.* An answer to a rejoinder.

To RECA'LL. *v. a.* [*re* and *call.*] To call back; to call again; to revoke.

They who *recal* the church unto that which was at the first, must set bounds unto their speeches. *Hooker, b.* iv. *s.* 2.

If Henry were *recall'd* to life again,
These news would cause him once more yield the ghost. *Shakesp. Henry* VI. *p.* i.
Neglected long, she let the secret rest,
Till lov'd *recall'd* it to her lab'ring breast. *Dryden.*

It is strange the soul should never once *recal* over any of its pure native ideas, before it borrowed any thing from the body; never any other ideas, but what derive their original from that union. *Locke.*

To the churches, wherein they were ordained, they might of right be *recalled* as to their proper church, under pain of excommunication. *Ayliffe's Parergon.*

It is necessary to *recall* to the reader's mind, the desire Ulysses has to reach his own country. *Broome's Notes on Odyss.*

If princes, whose dominions lie contiguous, be forced to draw from those armies which act against France, we must hourly expect having those troops *recalled*, which they now leave with us in the midst of a siege. *Swift's Miscellanies.*

RECA'LL. *n. s.* [from the verb.] Revocation; act or power of calling back.

Other decrees
Against thee are gone forth, without *recall.* *Milton.*
'Tis done, and since 'tis done, 'tis past *recal*;
And since 'tis past *recal*, must be forgotten. *Dryden.*

To RECA'NT. *v. a.* [*recanto*, Lat.] To retract; to recall; to contradict what one has once said or done.

He shall do this, or else I do *recant*
The pardon that I late pronounced. *Shakesp. Mer. of Ven.*
Ease would *recant* vows made in pain. *Milton.*

If it be thought, that the praise of a translation consists in adding new beauties, I shall be willing to *recant.* *Dryden.*

That the legislature should have power to change the succession, whenever the necessities of the kingdom require, is so useful towards preserving our religion and liberty, that I know not how to *recant.* *Swift.*

Recanta'tion. *n. s.* [from *recant.*] Retractation; declaration contradictory to a former declaration.

She could not see means to join this *recantation* to the former vow. *Sidney, b.* ii.

The poor man was imprisoned for this discovery, and forced to make a publick *recantation*. *Stillingfleet.*

Reca'nter. *n. s.* [from *recant.*] One who recants.

The publick body, which doth seldom
Play the *recanter*, feeling in itself
A lack of Timon's aid, hath sense withal
Of its own fall, restraining aid to Timon. *Shakesp.*

To RECAPI'TULATE. *v. a.* [*recapituler*, Fr. *re* and *capitulum*, Lat.] To repeat again distinctly; to detail again.

Hylobares judiciously and resentingly *recapitulates* your main reasonings. *More's Divine Dialogues.*

I have been forced to *recapitulate* these things, because mankind is not more liable to deceit, than it is willing to continue in a pleasing error. *Dryden's Dufresnoy.*

Recapitula'tion. *n. s.* [from *recapitulate.*] Detail repeated; distinct repetition of the principal points.

He maketh a *recapitulation* of the christian churches; among the rest he addeth the isle of Eden by name. *Raleigh.*

Instead of raising any particular uses from the point that has been delivered, let us make a brief *recapitulation* of the whole. *South.*

Recapi'tulatory. *adj.* [from *recapitulate.*] Repeating again.

Recapitulatory exercises. *Garretson.*

To Reca'rry. *v. a.* [*re* and *carry.*] To carry back.

When the Turks besieged Malta or Rodes, pigeons carried and *recarried* letters. *Walton's Angler.*

To Rece'de. *v. n.* [*recedo*, Latin.]

1. To fall back; to retreat.

A deaf noise of sounds that never cease,
Confus'd and chiding, like the hollow roar
Of tides, *receding* from th' insulted shoar. *Dryden.*
Ye doubts and fears!
Scatter'd by winds *recede*, and wild in forests rove. *Prior.*

All bodies, moved circularly, have a perpetual endeavour to *recede* from the center, and every moment would fly out in right lines, if they were not violently restrained by contiguous matter. *Bentley.*

2. To desist.

I can be content to *recede* much from my own interests and personal rights. *King Charles.*

They hoped that their general assembly would be persuaded to depart from some of their demands; but that, for the present, they had not authority to *recede* from any proposition. *Clarendon, b.* viii.

Recei'pt. *n. s.* [*receptum*, Latin.]

1. The act of receiving.

Villain, thou did'st deny the gold's *receipt*,
And told me of a mistress. *Shakesp. Com. of Err.*

It must be done upon the *receit* of the wound, before the patient's spirits be overheated. *Wiseman's Surgery.*

The joy of a monarch for the news of a victory must not be expressed like the ecstasy of a harlequin, on the *receipt* of a letter from his mistress. *Dryden.*

2. The place of receiving.

Jesus saw Matthew sitting at the *receipt* of custom. *Matt.*

3. [*Recepte*, Fr.] A note given, by which money is acknowledged to have been received.

4. Reception; admission.

It is of things heavenly an universal declaration, working in them, whose hearts God inspireth with the due consideration thereof, an habit or disposition of mind, whereby they are made fit vessels, both for the *receipt* and delivery of whatsoever spiritual perfection. *Hooker, b.* v. *s.* 37.

5. Reception; welcome.

The same words in my lady Philoclea's mouth might have had a better grace, and perchance have found a gentler *receipt*. *Sidney.*

6. [From *recipe.*] Prescription of ingredients for any composition.

On's bed of death
Many *receipts* he gave me, chiefly one
Of his old experience th' only darling. *Shakesp.*

That Medea could make old men young again, was nothing else, but that, from knowledge of simples, she had a *receipt* to make white hair black. *Brown's Vulgar Errours.*

Wise leeches will not vain *receipts* obtrude,
While growing pains pronounce the humours crude. *Dryd.*
Some dryly plain, without invention's aid,
Write dull *receipts* how poems may be made. *Pope.*

Scribonius found the *receipt* in a letter wrote to Tiberius, and was never able to procure the *receipt* during the emperor's life. *Arbuthnot on Coins.*

Recei'vable. *adj.* [*recevable*, Fr. from *receive.*] Capable of being received. *Dict.*

To RECEIVE. *v. a.* [*recevoir*, Fr. *recipio*, Lat.]

1. To take or obtain any thing as due.

If by this crime he owes the law his life,
Why, let the war *receive* 't in valiant gore. *Shakesp.*

A certain nobleman went into a far country, to *receive* for himself a kingdom, and return. *Luke* xiv. 12.

2. To take or obtain from another.

Ye shall *receive* of me gifts. *Dan.* ii. 6.

Though I should *receive* a thousand shekels of silver in mine hand, yet would I not put forth mine hand against the king's son. 2 *Sam.* xviii. 12.

What? shall we *receive* good at the hands of God, and shall we not *receive* evil? *Job* ii. 10.

To them hast thou poured a drink-offering? should I *receive* comfort in these? *Is.* lvii. 6.

He that doeth wrong, shall *receive* for the wrong done; and there is no respect of persons. *Col.* iii. 25.

They lived with the friendship and equality of brethren; *received* no laws from one another, but lived separately. *Locke.*

3. To take any thing communicated.

Put all in writing that thou givest out, and *receivest* in. *Ecclus.* xlii. 7.

Draw general conclusions from every particular they meet with: these make little true benefit of history; nay, being of forward and active spirits, *receive* more harm by it. *Locke.*

The idea of solidity we *receive* by our touch. *Locke.*

The same inability will every one find, who shall go about to fashion in his understanding any simple idea, not *received* in by his senses or by reflection. *Locke.*

To conceive the ideas we *receive* from sensation, consider them, in reference to the different ways, whereby they make their approaches to our minds. *Locke.*

4. To embrace intellectually.

We have set it down as a law, to examine things to the bottom, and not to *receive* upon credit, or reject upon improbabilities. *Bacon's Natural History.*

In an equal indifferency for all truth; I mean the *receiving* it, in the love of it, as truth; and in the examination of our principles, and not *receiving* any for such, till we are fully convinced of their certainty, consists the freedom of the understanding. *Locke.*

5. To allow.

Long *received* custom forbidding them to do as they did, there was no excuse to justify their act; unless, in the scripture, they could shew some law, that did licence them thus to break a *received* custom. *Hooker, b.* ii. *s.* 5.

Will it not be *receiv'd*,
When we have mark'd with blood those sleepy two,
And us'd their very daggers; that they have don't?
—Who dares *receive* it other? *Shakesp. Macbeth.*

Lest any should think that any thing in this number eight creates the diapason; this computation of eight is rather a thing *received*, than any true computation. *Bacon.*

6. To admit.

When they came to Jerusalem, they were *received* of the church. *Acts* xv. 4.

Thou shalt guide me with thy counsel, and afterward *receive* me to glory. *Psalm* lxxiii. 24.

Let her be shut out from the camp seven days, and after that *received* in again. *Numb.* xii. 14.

Free converse with persons of different sects will enlarge our charity towards others, and incline us to *receive* them into all the degrees of unity and affection, which the word of God requires. *Watts's Improvement of the Mind.*

7. To take as into a vessel.

He was taken up, and a cloud *received* him out of their sight. *Acts* i. 9.

8. To take into a place or state.

After the Lord had spoken, he was *received* up into heaven, and sat on the right hand of God. *Mar.* xvi. 19.

9. To conceive in the mind; to take intellectually.

To one of your *receiving*,
Enough is shewn. *Shakesp.*

10. To entertain as a guest.

Abundance fit to honour, and *receive*
Our heav'nly stranger. *Milton.*

Recei'vedness. *n. s.* [from *received.*] General allowance.

Others will, upon account of the *receivedness* of the proposed opinion, think it rather worth to be examined, than acquiesced in. *Boyle.*

Recei'ver. *n. s.* [*receveur*, Fr. from *receive.*]

1. One to whom any thing is communicated by another.

All the learnings that his time could make him *receiver* of, he took as we do air. *Shakesp. Cymbeline.*

She from whose influence all impression came,
But by *receivers* impotencies lame. *Donne.*

2. One to whom any thing is given or paid.

There is a *receiver*, who alone handleth the monies. *Bacon.*

In all works of liberality, something more is to be considered, besides the occasion of the givers; and that is the occasion of the *receivers*. *Sprat.*

Gratitude is a virtue, disposing the mind to an inward sense, and an outward acknowledgement of a benefit received, together with a readiness to return the same, as the occasions of the doer shall require, and the abilities of the *receiver* extend to. *South.*

If

If one third of the money in trade were locked up, landholders muſt receive one third leſs for their goods; a leſs quantity of money by one third being to be diſtributed amongſt an equal number of *receivers*. *Locke.*

Wood's halfpence will be offered for ſix a penny, and the neceſſary *receivers* will be loſers of two thirds in their pay. *Sw.*

3. One who partakes of the bleſſed ſacrament.

The ſignification and ſenſe of the ſacrament diſpoſe the ſpirit of the *receiver* to admit the grace of the ſpirit of God there conſigned. *Taylor's Worthy Communicant.*

4. One who cooperates with a robber, by taking the goods which he ſteals.

This is a great cauſe of the maintenance of thieves, knowing their *receivers* always ready; for were there no *receivers*, there would be no thieves. *Spenſer's State of Ireland.*

5. The veſſel into which ſpirits are emitted from the ſtill.

These liquors, which the wide *receiver* fill,
Prepar'd with labour, and refin'd with ſkill,
Another courſe to diſtant parts begin. *Blackmore.*

Alkaline ſpirits run in veins down the ſides of the *receiver* in diſtillations, which will not take fire. *Arbuthnot.*

6. The veſſel of the air pump, out of which the air is drawn, and which therefore receives any body on which experiments are tried.

The air that in exhauſted *receivers* of air pumps is exhaled from minerals, is as true as to elaſticity and denſity or rarefaction, as that we reſpire in. *Bentley.*

To Recele'brate. *v. a.* [*re* and *celebrate.*] To celebrate anew.

French air and Engliſh verſe here wedded lie:
Who did this knot compoſe,
Again hath brought the lilly to the roſe;
And with their chained dance,
Recelebrates the joyful match. *Benj. Johnſon.*

Re'cency. *n. ſ.* [*recens*, Lat.] Newneſs; new ſtate.

A ſchirrhus in its *recency*, whilſt it is in its augment, requireth milder applications than the confirmed one. *Wiſeman.*

Rece'nsion. *n. ſ.* [*recenſio*, Lat.] Enumeration; review.

In this *recenſion* of monthly flowers, it is to be underſtood from its firſt appearing to its final withering. *Evelyn's Kalen.*

RE'CENT. *adj.* [*recens*, Latin.]

1. New; not of long exiſtence.

The ancients were of opinion, that thoſe parts, where Egypt now is, were formerly ſea, and that a conſiderable portion of that country was *recent*, and formed out of the mud diſcharged into the neighbouring ſea by the Nile. *Woodward.*

2. Late; not antique.

Among all the great and worthy perſons, whereof the memory remaineth, either ancient or *recent*, there is not one that hath been tranſported to the mad degree of love. *Bacon.*

3. Freſh; not long diſmiſſed from.

Ulyſſes moves,
Urg'd on by want, and *recent* from the ſtorms,
The brackiſh ouze his manly grace deforms. *Pope.*

Re'cently. *adv.* [from *recent.*] Newly; freſhly.

Thoſe tubes, which are moſt *recently* made of fluids, are moſt flexible and moſt eaſily lengthened. *Arbuthnot.*

Re'centness. *n. ſ.* [from *recent.*] Newneſs; freſhneſs.

This inference of the *recentneſs* of mankind from the *recentneſs* of theſe apotheoſes of gentile deities, ſeems too weak to bear up this ſuppoſition of the novitas humani generis. *Hale.*

Rece'ptacle. *n. ſ.* [*receptaculum*, Lat.] A veſſel or place into which any thing is received.

When the ſharpneſs of death was overcome, he then opened heaven, as well to believing gentiles as Jews: heaven till then was no *receptacle* to the ſouls of either. *Hooker.*

The county of Tipperary, the only county palatine in Ireland, is by abuſe of ſome bad ones made a *receptacle* to rob the reſt of the counties about it. *Spenſer's State of Ireland.*

As in a vault, an ancient *receptacle*,
Where for theſe many hundred years, the bones
Of all my buried anceſtors are packt. *Shakeſp.*

The eye of the ſoul, or *receptacle* of ſapience and divine knowledge. *Raleigh's Hiſtory of the World.*

Leſt paradiſe a *receptacle* prove
To ſpirits foul, and all my trees their prey. *Milton.*

Their intelligence, put in at the top of the horn, ſhall convey it into a little *receptacle* at the bottom. *Addiſon.*

Theſe are conveniencies to private perſons; inſtead of being *receptacles* for the truly poor, they tempt men to pretend poverty, in order to ſhare the advantages. *Atterbury.*

Though the ſupply from this great *receptacle* below be continual and alike to all the globe; yet when it arrives near the ſurface, where the heat is not ſo uniform, it is ſubject to viciſſitudes. *Woodward.*

Receptibi'lity. *n. ſ.* [*receptus*, Lat.] Poſſibility of receiving.

The peripatetick matter is a pure unactuated power; and this conceited vacuum a mere *receptibility*. *Glanvill.*

Re'ceptary. *n. ſ.* [*receptus*, Lat.] Thing received. Not in uſe.

They, which behold the preſent ſtate of things, cannot condemn our ſober enquiries in the doubtful appertenancies of arts and *receptaries* of philoſophy. *Brown.*

Rece'ption. *n. ſ.* [*receptus*, Latin.]

1. The act of receiving.

Both ſerve completely for the *reception* and communication of learned knowledge. *Holder's Elements of Speech.*

In this animal are found parts official unto nutrition, which were its aliment the empty *reception* of air, proviſions had been ſuperfluous. *Brown's Vulgar Errours.*

2. The ſtate of being received.

3. Admiſſion of any thing communicated.

Cauſes, according ſtill
To the *reception* of their matter, act;
Not to th' extent of their own ſphere. *Milton's Par. Loſt.*

In ſome animals, the avenues, provided by nature for the *reception* of ſenſations, are few, and the perception, they are received with, obſcure and dull. *Locke.*

4. Readmiſſion.

All hope is loſt
Of my *reception* into grace. *Milton's Par. Loſt.*

5. The act of containing.

I cannot ſurvey this world of fluid matter, without thinking on the hand that firſt poured it out, and made a proper channel for its *reception*. *Addiſon.*

6. Treatment at firſt coming; welcome; entertainment.

This ſucceſſion of ſo many powerful methods being farther preſcribed by God, have found ſo diſcouraging a *reception*, that nothing but the violence of ſtorming or battery can pretend to prove ſucceſsful. *Hammond's Fundamentals.*

Pretending to conſult
About the great *reception* of their king,
Thither to come. *Milton.*

7. Opinion generally admitted.

Philoſophers, who have quitted the popular doctrines of their countries, have fallen into as extravagant opinions, as even common *reception* countenanced. *Locke.*

8. Recovery.

He was right glad of the French king's *reception* of thoſe towns from Maximilian. *Bacon's Henry VII.*

Re'ceptive. *adj.* [*receptus*, Lat.] Having the quality of admitting what is communicated.

The ſoul being, as it is active, perfected by love of that infinite good, ſhall, as it is *receptive*, be alſo perfected with thoſe ſupernatural paſſions of joy, peace and delight. *Hooker.*

The pretended firſt matter is capable of all forms, and the imaginary ſpace is *receptive* of all bodies. *Glanvill.*

Re'ceptory. *adj.* [*receptus*, Lat.] Generally or popularly admitted.

Although therein be contained many excellent things, and verified upon his own experience, yet are there many alſo *receptory*, and will not endure the teſt. *Brown.*

Rece'ss. *n. ſ.* [*receſſus*, Latin.]

1. Retirement; retreat; withdrawing; ſeceſſion.

What tumults could not do, an army muſt; my *receſs* hath given them confidence that I may be conquered. *K. Charles.*

Fair Thames ſhe haunts, and ev'ry neighb'ring grove,
Sacred to ſoft *receſs* and gentle love. *Prior.*

2. Departure.

We come into the world, and know not how; we live in it in a ſelf-neſcience, and go hence again, and are as ignorant of our *receſs*. *Glanvill's Scepſ.*

3. Place of retirement; place of ſecrecy; private abode.

This happy place, our ſweet
Receſs, and only conſolation left. *Milton's Par. Loſt.*
The deep *receſſes* of the grove he gain'd. *Dryden.*

I wiſh that a crowd of bad writers do not ruſh into the quiet of your *receſſes*. *Dryden's Don Sebaſtian.*

4. [*Recez*, Fr.] Perhaps an abſtract of the proceedings of an imperial diet.

In the imperial chamber, the proctors have a florin taxed and allowed them for every ſubſtantial *receſs*. *Ayliffe.*

5. Departure into privacy.

The great ſeraphick lords and cherubim,
In cloſe *receſs*, and ſecret conclave ſat. *Milton.*

In the *receſs* of the jury, they are to conſider their evidence. *Hale.*

6. Remiſſion or ſuſpenſion of any procedure.

On both ſides they made rather a kind of *receſs*, than a breach of treaty, and concluded upon a truce. *Bacon.*

I conceived this parliament would find work, with convenient *receſſes*, for the firſt three years. *King Charles.*

7. Removal to diſtance.

Whatſoever ſign the ſun poſſeſſed, whoſe *receſs* or vicinity defineth the quarters of the year, thoſe of our ſeaſons were actually exiſtent. *Brown's Vulgar Errours.*

8. Privacy; ſecrecy of abode.

Good verſe, *receſs* and ſolitude requires;
And eaſe from cares, and undiſturb'd deſires. *Dryden.*

9. Secret part.

In their myſteries, and moſt ſecret *receſſes*, and adyta of their religion, their heathen prieſts betrayed and led their votaries into all the moſt horrid unnatural ſins. *Hammond.*

Every ſcholar ſhould acquaint himſelf with a ſuperficial ſcheme of all the ſciences, yet there is no neceſſity for every man of learning to enter into their difficulties and deep *receſſes*. *Watts's Improvement of the Mind.*

Rece'ssion. *n. s.* [*recessio*, Lat.] The act of retreating.

To Recha'nge. *v. a.* [*rechanger*, Fr. *re* and *change.*] To change again.

Those endued with foresight, work with facility; others are perpetually changing and *rechanging* their work. *Dryden.*

To Recha'rge. *v. a.* [*recharger*, Fr. *re* and *charge.*]

1. To accuse in return.

The fault, that we find with them, is, that they overmuch abridge the church of her power in these things: whereupon they *recharge* us, as if in these things we gave the church a liberty, which hath no limits or bounds. *Hooker.*

2. To attack anew.

They charge, *recharge*, and all along the sea
They drive, and squander the huge Belgian fleet. *Dryden.*

Rechea't. *n. s.* Among hunters, a lesson which the huntsman winds on the horn, when the hounds have lost their game, to call them back from pursuing a counterscent. *Bail.*

That a woman conceived me, I thank her; but that I will have a *recheat* winded in my forehead, or hang my bugle in an invisible baldrick, all women shall pardon me. *Shakesp.*

Recidiva'tion. *n. s.* [*recidivus*, Lat.] Backsliding; falling again.

Our renewed obedience is still most indispensably required, though mixed with much of weakness, frailties, *recidivations*, to make us capable of pardon. *Hammond's Pract. Cat.*

Recidi'vous. *adj.* [*recidivus*, Lat.] Subject to fall again.

Re'cipe. *n. s.* [*recipe*, Lat. the term used by physicians, when they direct ingredients.] A medical prescription.

I should enjoin you travel; for absence doth in a kind remove the cause, and answers the physicians first *recipe*, vomiting and purging; but this would be too harsh. *Suckling.*

Th' apothecary train is wholly blind,
From files a random *recipe* they take,
And many deaths of one prescription make. *Dryden.*

Recipient. *n. s.* [*recipiens*, Latin.]

1. The receiver; that to which any thing is communicated.

Though the images, or whatever else is the cause of sense, may be alike as from the object, yet may the representations be varied according to the nature of the *recipient*. *Glanvill.*

2. [*Recipient*, Fr.] The vessel into which spirits are driven by the still.

The form of sound words, dissolved by chymical preparation, ceases to be nutritive; and after all the labours of the alembeck, leaves in the *recipient* a fretting corrosive. *D. of Pie.*

RECI'PROCAL. *adj.* [*reciprocus*, Lat. *reciproque*, Fr.]

1. Acting in vicissitude; alternate.

Corruption is *reciprocal* to generation; and they two are as nature's two boundaries, and guides to life and death. *Bacon.*

What if that light,
To the terrestial moon be as a star,
Enlight'ning her by day, as she by night,
This earth? *reciprocal*, if land be there,
Fields and inhabitants. *Milton.*

2. Mutual; done by each to each.

Where there's no hope of a *reciprocal* aid, there can be no reason for the mutual obligation. *L'Estrange.*

In *reciprocal* duties, the failure on one side justifies not a failure on the other. *Clarissa.*

3. Mutually interchangeable.

These two rules will render a definition *reciprocal* with the thing defined; which, in the schools, signifies, that the definition may be used in the place of the thing defined. *Watts.*

4. In geometry, reciprocal proportion is, when, in four numbers, the fourth number is so much lesser than the second, as the third is greater than the first, and vice versa. *Harris.*

According to the laws of motion, if the bulk and activity of aliment and medicines are in *reciprocal* proportion, the effect will be the same. *Arbuthnot on Aliments.*

Reci'procally. *adv.* [from *reciprocal.*] Mutually; interchangeably.

His mind and place
Infecting one another *reciprocally*. *Shakesp. Henry VIII.*

Make the bodies appear enlightened by the shadows which bound the sight, which cause it to repose for some space of time; and *reciprocally* the shadows may be made sensible by enlightening your ground. *Dryden.*

If the distance be about the hundredth part of an inch, the water will rise to the height of about an inch; and if the distance be greater or less in any proportion, the height will be *reciprocally* proportional to the distance very nearly: for the attractive force of the glasses is the same, whether the distance between them be greater or less; and the weight of the water drawn up is the same, if the height of it be *reciprocally* proportional to the height of the glasses. *Newton's Opticks.*

Those two particles do *reciprocally* affect each other with the same force and vigour, as they would do at the same distance in any other situation. *Bentley.*

Reci'procalness. *n. s.* [from *reciprocal.*] Mutual return; alternateness.

The *reciprocalness* of the injury ought to allay the displeasure at it. *Decay of Piety.*

To Reci'procate. *v. n.* [*reciprocus*, Lat. *reciproquer*, Fr.] To act interchangeably; to alternate.

One brawny smith the puffing bellows plies,
And draws, and blows *reciprocating* air. *Dryden.*

From whence the quick *reciprocating* breath,
The lobe adhesive, and the sweat of death. *Sewel.*

Reciproca'tion. *n. s.* [*reciprocatio*, from *reciprocus*, Latin.] Alternation; action interchanged.

Bodies may be altered by heat, and yet no such *reciprocation* of rarefaction, condensation and separation. *Bacon.*

That Aristotle drowned himself in Euripus, as despairing to resolve the cause of its *reciprocation* or ebb and flow seven times a day, is generally believed. *Brown.*

Where the bottom of the sea is owze or sand, it is by the motion of the waters, so far as the *reciprocation* of the sea extends to the bottom, brought to a level. *Ray.*

The systole resembles the forcible bending of a spring, and the diastole its flying out again to its natural site: what is the principal efficient of this *reciprocation*? *Ray.*

Reci'sion. *n. s.* [*recisus*, Lat.] The act of cutting off.

Recital. *n. s.* [from *recite.*]

1. Repetition; rehearsal.

The last are repetitions and *recitals* of the first. *Denham.*

This often sets him on empty boasts, and betrays him into vain fantastick *recitals* of his own performances. *Addison.*

2. Enumeration.

To make the rough *recital* aptly chime,
Or bring the sum of Gallia's loss to rhime,
Is mighty hard. *Prior.*

Recita'tion. *n. s.* [from *recite.*] Repetition; rehearsal.

If menaces of scripture fall upon men's persons, if they are but the *recitations* and descriptions of God's decreed wrath, and those decrees and that wrath have no respect to the actual sins of men; why should terrors restrain me from sin, when present advantage invites me to it? *Hammond.*

He used philosophical arguments and *recitations*. *Temple.*

Re'citative. } *n. s.* [from *recite.*] A kind of tuneful pronunciation, more musical than common speech, and less than song; chaunt.
Recitati'vo. }

He introduced the examples of moral virtue, writ in verse, and performed in *recitative* musick. *Dryden.*

By singing peers upheld on either hand,
Then thus in quaint *recitativo* spoke. *Dunciad, b.* iv.

To RECI'TE. *v. a.* [*recito*, Lat. *reciter*, Fr.] To rehearse; to repeat; to enumerate; to tell over.

While Telephus's youthful charms,
His rosy neck, and winding arms,
With endless rapture you *recite*,
And in the tender name delight. *Addison.*

The thoughts of gods let Granville's verse *recite*,
And bring the scenes of op'ning fate to light. *Pope.*

If we will *recite* nine hours in ten,
You lose your patience. *Pope's Epistles of Horace.*

Reci'te. *n. s.* [*recit*, Fr. from the verb.] Recital. Not in use.

This added to all former *recites* or observations of long-liv'd races, makes it easy to conclude, that health and long life are the blessings of the poor as well as rich. *Temple.*

To RECK. *v. n* [ꞃecan, Saxon.] To care; to heed; to mind; to rate at much; to be in care. Out of use. *Reck* is still retained in Scotland.

Thou's but a lazy loorde,
And *recks* much of thy swinke,
That with fond terms and witless words,
To bleer mine eyes do'st think. *Spenser.*

Good or bad,
What do I *reck*, sith that he dy'd entire. *Fairy Queen.*

I *reck* as little what betideth me,
As much I wish all good befortune you. *Shakesp.*

Of night or loneliness it *recks* me not;
I fear the dread events that dog them both,
Lest some ill-greeting touch attempt the person
Of our unowned sister. *Milton.*

With that care lost
Went all his fear; of God, or hell or worse
He *reck'd* not. *Milton.*

To Reck. *v. a.* To heed; to care for.

This son of mine, not *recking* danger, and neglecting the present good way he was in of doing himself good, came hither to do this kind office to my unspeakable grief. *Sidney.*

If I do lose thee, I do lose a thing,
That none but fools would *reck*. *Shakesp.*

Do not you as ungracious parsons do,
Who shew the steep and thorny way to heav'n;
Yet like unthinking reckless libertines,
That in the soft path of dalliance treads,
Recks not his own rede. *Shakesp.*

Re'ckless. *adj.* [from *reck*; ꞃecceleaꞅ, Saxon] Careless; heedless; mindless; untouched. See RECK.

It made the king as *reckless*, as them diligent. *Sidney.*

I'll after, more to be reveng'd of Eglamour
Than for the love of *reckless* Silvia. *Shakesp.*

He apprehends death no more dreadfully, but as a drunken sleep; careless, *reckless*, and fearless of what's past, present or to come; insensible of mortality and desperately mortal. *Sha.*

Next this was drawn the *reckless* cities flame,
When a strange hell pour'd down from heaven there came. *Cowley.*

RE'CKLESSNESS. *n. s.* [from *reck.* This word in the seventeenth article is erroneously written *wretchlessness.*] Carelessness; negligence.

Over many good fortunes began to breed a proud *recklessness* in them. *Sidney.*

To RE'CKON. *v. a.* [recan, Saxon; *reckenen*, Dutch.]

1. To number; to count.

The priest shall *reckon* unto him the money according to the years that remain, and it shall be abated. *Lev.* xxvii. 18.

Numb'ring of his virtues praise,
Death lost the *reckoning* of his days. *Crashaw.*

When are questions belonging to all finite existences by us *reckoned* from some known parts of this sensible world, and from some certain epochs marked out by motions in it. *Locke.*

The freezing of water, or the blowing of a plant, returning at equidistant periods, would as well serve men to *reckon* their years by, as the motions of the sun. *Locke.*

I *reckoned* above two hundred and fifty on the outside of the church, though I only told three sides of it. *Addison.*

Would the Dutch be content with the military government and revenues, and *reckon* it among what shall be thought necessary for their barrier? *Swift's Miscellanies.*

A multitude of cities are *reckoned* up by the geographers, particularly by Ptolemy. *Arbuthnot on Coins.*

2. To esteem; to account.

Where we cannot be persuaded that the will of God is, we should far reject the authority of men, as to *reckon* it nothing. *Hooker.*

Varro's aviary is still so famous, that it is *reckoned* for one of those notables, which men of foreign nations record. *Wott.*

For him I *reckon* not in high estate;
But thee, whose strength, while virtue was her mate,
Might have subdu'd the earth. *Milton's Agonistes.*

People, young and raw, and soft-natured, are apt to think it an easy thing to gain love, and *reckon* their own friendship a sure price of another man's: but when experience shall have shewn them the hardness of most hearts, the hollowness of others and the baseness of all, they will find that a friend is the gift of God, and that he only, who made hearts, can unite them. *South's Sermons.*

3. To assign in an account.

To him that worketh is the reward not *reckoned* of grace, but of debt. *Romans* iv. 4.

To RE'CKON. *v. n.*

1. To compute; to calculate.

We may fairly *reckon*, that this first age of apostles, with that second generation of many who were their immediate converts, extended to the middle of the second century. *Add.*

2. To state an account.

We shall not spend a large expence of time,
Before we *reckon* with your several loves,
And make us even with you. *Shakesp.*

3. To charge to account.

I call posterity
Into the debt, and *reckon* on her head. *Benj. Johnson.*

4. To pay a penalty.

If they fail in their bounden duty, they shall *reckon* for it one day. *Sanderson's Judgment.*

5. To call to punishment.

God suffers the most grievous sins of particular persons to go unpunished in this world, because his justice will have another opportunity to meet and *reckon* with them. *Tillotson.*

6. [*Compter sur*, Fr.] To lay stress or dependance upon.

You *reckon* upon losing your friends kindness, when you have sufficiently convinced them, they can never hope for any of yours. *Temple's Miscellanies.*

RE'CKONER. *n. s.* [from *reckon.*] One who computes; one who calculates cost.

Reckoners without their host must reckon twice. *Camden.*

RE'CKONING. *n. s.* [from *reckon.*]

1. Computation; calculation.

2. Account of time.

Can'st thou their *reck'nings* keep? the time compute?
When their swoln bellies shall enlarge their fruit. *Sandys.*

3. Accounts of debtor and creditor.

They that know how their own *reck'ning* goes,
Account not what they have, but what they lose. *Daniel.*

It is with a man and his conscience, as with one man and another; even *reckoning* makes lasting friends; and the way to make *reckonings* even, is to make them often. *South.*

4. Money charged by an host.

His industry is up stairs and down; his eloquence the parcel of a *reckoning.* *Shakesp. Henry* IV.

When a man's verses cannot be understood, it strikes a man more dead than a great *reckoning* in a little room. *Shak.*

A coin would have a nobler use than to pay a *reckoning.* *Add.*

5. Account taken.

There was no *reckoning* made with them of the money delivered into their hand. *2 Kings.*

6. Esteem; account; estimation.

Beauty, though in as great excellency in yourself as in any, yet you make no further *reckoning* of it, than of an outward fading benefit nature bestowed. *Sidney.*

Were they all of as great account as the best among them, with us notwithstanding they ought not to be of such *reckoning*, that their opinion should cause the laws of the church to give place. *Hooker's Preface.*

To RECLAI'M. *v. a.* [*reclamo*, Latin.]

1. To reform; to correct.

He spared not the heads of any mischievous practices, but shewed sharp judgment on them for ensample sake, that all the meaner sort, which were infected with that evil, might, by terror thereof, be *reclaimed* and saved. *Spenser.*

This errour whosoever is able to *reclaim*, he shall save more in one summer, than Themison destroy'd in any autumn. *Brown's Vulgar Errours.*

Reclaim your wife from strolling up and down
To all assizes. *Dryden's Juvenal.*

'Tis the intention of providence, in all the various expressions of his goodness, to *reclaim* mankind, and to engage their obedience. *Rogers's Sermons.*

The penal laws in being against papists have been found ineffectual, and rather confirm than *reclaim* men from their errors. *Swift.*

2. [*Reclamer*, Fr.] To reduce to the state desired.

It was for him to hasten to let his people see, that he meant to govern by law, howsoever he came in by the sword; and fit also to *reclaim* them, to know him for their king, whom they had so lately talked of as an enemy. *Bacon.*

Much labour is requir'd in trees, to tame
Their wild disorder, and in ranks *reclaim.* *Dryden.*

Minds she the dangers of the Lycian coast?
Or is her tow'ring flight *reclaim'd*,
By seas from Icarus's downfal nam'd?
Vain is the call, and useless the advice. *Prior.*

3. To recall; to cry out against.

The head-strong horses hurried Octavius, the trembling charioteer, along, and were deaf to his *reclaiming* them. *Dryd.*

Oh tyrant love!
Wisdom and wit in vain *reclaim*,
And arts but soften us to feel thy flame. *Pope.*

4. To tame.

Upon his fist he bore
An eagle well *reclaim'd.* *Dryden's Knight's Tale.*

Are not hawks brought to the hand, and lions, tygers and bears *reclaimed* by good usage? *L'Estrange's Fables.*

To RECLI'NE. *v. a.* [*reclino*, Lat. *recliner*, Fr.] To lean back; to lean sidewise.

The mother
Reclin'd her dying head upon his breast. *Dryden.*

While thus she rested, on her arm *reclin'd*,
The purling streams that through the meadow stray'd,
In drowsy murmurs lull'd the gentle maid. *Addison.*

To RECLI'NE. *v. n.* To rest; to repose; to lean.

RECLI'NE. *adj.* [*reclinis*, Lat.] In a leaning posture.

They sat *recline*
On the soft downy bank, damask'd with flow'rs. *Milton.*

To RECLO'SE. *v. a.* [*re* and *close.*] To close again.

The silver ring she pull'd, the door *reclos'd*;
The bolt, obedient to the silken cord,
To the strong staples inmost depth restor'd,
Secur'd the valves. *Pope's Odyssey.*

To RECLU'DE. *v. a.* [*recludo*, Lat.] To open.

The ingredients absorb the intestinal superfluities, *reclude* oppilations, and mundify the blood. *Harvey.*

RECLU'SE. *adj.* [*reclus*, Fr. *reclusus*, Lat.] Shut up; retired.

This must be the inference of a mere contemplative; a *recluse* that converses only with his own meditations. *D. of P.*

The nymphs
Melissan, sacred and *recluse* to Ceres,
Pour streams select, and purity of waters. *Prior.*

I all the live long day
Consume in meditation deep, *recluse* from human converse. *Philips.*

RECOAGULA'TION. *n. s.* [*re* and *coagulation.*] Second coagulation.

This salt, dissolved in a convenient quantity of water, does upon its *recoagulation* dispose of the aqueous particles among its own saline ones, and shoot into crystals. *Boyle.*

RECO'GNISANCE. *n. s.* [*recognisance*, Fr.]

1. Acknowledgement of person or thing.

2. Badge.

Apparent it is, that all men are either christians or not; if by external profession they be christians, then are they of the visible church of Christ; and christians by external profession they are all, whose mark of *recognizance* hath in it those things mentioned, yet although they be impious idolators and wicked hereticks. *Hooker, b.* iii. *s.* 1.

She did gratify his amorous works
With that *recognizance* and pledge of love,
Which I first gave her; an handkerchief. *Shakesp.*

3. A

3. A bond of record testifying the recognisor to owe unto the recognisee a certain sum of money; and is acknowledged in some court of record: and those that are mere recognisances are not sealed but enrolled: It is also used for the verdict of the twelve men empannelled upon an assize. *Cowel.*

The English should not marry with any Irish, unless bound by *recognisance* with sureties, to continue loyal. *Davies.*

To RECOGNI'SE. *v. a.* [*recognosco*, Lat.]

1. To acknowledge; to recover and avow knowledge of any person or thing.

The British cannon formidably roars,
While starting from his oozy bed,
Th' asserted ocean rears his reverend head,
To view and *recognise* his ancient lord. *Dryden.*
Then first he *recognis'd* th' æthereal guest,
Wonder and joy alternate fire his breast. *Pope.*

2. To review; to reexamine.

However their causes speed in your tribunals, Christ will *recognise* them at a greater. *South.*

RECOGNISEE'. *n. s.* He in whose favour the bond is drawn.

RECO'GNISOR. *n. s.* He who gives the recognisance.

RECOGNI'TION. *n. s.* [*recognitio*, Latin.]

1. Review; renovation of knowledge.

The virtues of some being thought expedient to be annually had in remembrance, brought in a fourth kind of publick reading, whereby the lives of such saints had, at the time of their yearly memorials, solemn *recognition* in the church of God. *Hooker, b.* iii. *s.* 20.

2. Knowledge confessed.

Every species of fancy hath three modes; *recognition* of a thing, as present; memory of it, as past; and foresight of it, as to come. *Grew's Cosmol.*

3. Acknowledgment.

If the *recognition* or acknowledgment of a final concord, upon any writ of covenant finally, be taken by justice of assize, and the yearly value of those lands be declared by affidavit made before the same justice; then is the *recognition* and value signed with the hand-writing of that justice. *Bacon.*

To RECOI'L. *v. n.* [*reculer*, Fr.]

1. To rush back in consequence of resistance, which cannot be overcome by the force impressed.

The very thought of my revenges that way
Recoil upon me; in himself too mighty. *Shakesp.*
Revenge, at first though sweet,
Bitter ere long, back on itself *recoils.* *Milton.*
Amazement seiz'd
All th' host of heav'n, back they *recoil'd*, afraid
At first. *Milton's Paradise Lost, b.* ii.
Evil on itself shall back *recoil.* *Milton.*
Who in deep mines for hidden knowledge toils,
Like guns o'ercharg'd, breaks, misses or *recoils.* *Denham.*
My hand's so soft, his heart so hard,
The blow *recoils*, and hurts me while I strike! *Dryden.*

Whatever violence may be offered to nature, by endeavouring to reason men into a contrary persuasion, nature will still *recoil*, and at last return to itself. *Tillotson.*

2. To fall back.

Ye both forewearied be; therefore a while
I read you rest, and to your bowers *recoil.* *Fairy Queen.*
Ten paces huge
He back *recoil'd*; the tenth on bended knee,
His massy spear upstay'd. *Milton's Par. Lost, b.* vi.

3. To fail; to shrink.

A good and virtuous nature may *recoil*
In an imperial charge. *Shakesp. Macbeth.*

To RECOI'N. *v. a.* [*re* and *coin.*] To coin over again.

Among the Romans, to preserve great events upon their coins, when any particular piece of money grew very scarce, it was often *recoined* by a succeeding emperor. *Addison.*

RECOI'NAGE. *n. s.* [*re* and *coinage.*] The act of coining anew.

The mint gained upon the late statute, by the *recoinage* of groats and half-groats, now twelvepences and sixpences. *Bac.*

To RECOLLE'CT. *v. a.* [*recollectus*, Lat.]

1. To recover to memory.

It did relieve my passion much;
More than light airs and *recollected* terms
Of these most brisk and giddy paced times. *Shakesp.*

Recollect every day the things seen, heard, or read, which made any addition to your understanding. *Watts's Logick.*

2. To recover reason or resolution.

The Tyrian queen
Admir'd his fortunes, more admir'd the man;
Then *recollected* stood. *Dryden's Æneis.*

3. To gather what is scattered; to gather again.

Now that God hath made his light radiate in his word, men may *recollect* those scattered divine beams, and kindling with them the topicks proper to warm our affections, enflame holy zeal. *Boyle.*

RECOLLE'CTION. *n. s.* [from *recollect.*] Recovery of notion; revival in the memory.

Recollection is when an idea is sought after by the mind, and with pain and endeavour found, and brought again in view. *Locke.*

Let us take care that we sleep not without such a *recollection* of the actions of the day as may represent any thing that is remarkable, as matter of sorrow or thanksgiving. *Taylor.*

The last image of that troubled heap,
When sense subsides, and fancy sports in sleep,
Though past the *recollection* of the thought,
Becomes the stuff of which our dream is wrought. *Pope.*

To RECO'MFORT. *v. a.* [*re* and *comfort.*]

1. To comfort or console again.

What place is there left, we may hope our woes to *recomfort.* *Sidney, b.* i.
Ne'er through an arch so hurried the blown tides,
As the *recomforted* through th' gates. *Shakesp. Coriolanus.*
As one from sad dismay
Recomforted, and, after thoughts disturb'd,
Submitting to what seem'd remediless. *Milton.*

2. To give new strength.

In strawberries, it is usual to help the ground with muck; and likewise to *recomfort* it sometimes with muck put to the roots; but to water with muck water is not practised. *Bacon.*

To RECOMME'NCE. *v. a.* [*recommencer*, Fr. *re* and *commence.*]

To begin anew.

To RECOMME'ND. *v. a.* [*recommender*, Fr. *re* and *commend.*]

1. To praise to another.

2. To make acceptable.

Mecenas *recommended* Virgil and Horace to Augustus, whose praises helped to make him popular while alive, and after his death have made him precious to posterity. *Dryden.*

A decent boldness ever meets with friends,
Succeeds, and ev'n a stranger *recommends.* *Pope.*

3. To commit with prayers.

They had been *recommended* to the grace of God. *Acts* xiv.

RECOMME'NDABLE. *adj.* [*recommendable*, Fr. from *recommend.*] Worthy of recommendation or praise.

Though these pursuits should make out no pretence to advantage, yet, upon the account of honour, they are *recommendable.* *Glanvill's Preface to Sceps.*

RECOMMENDA'TION. *n. s.* [*recommendation*, Fr. from *recommend.*]

1. The act of recommending.

2. That which secures to one a kind reception from another.

Poplicola's doors were opened on the outside, to save the people even the common civility of asking entrance; where misfortune was a powerful *recommendation*; and where want itself was a powerful mediator. *Dryden.*

RECOMME'NDATORY. *adj.* [from *recommend.*] That which commends to another.

Verses *recommendatory* they have commanded me to prefix before my book. *Swift.*

RECOMME'NDER. *n. s.* [from *recommend.*] One who recommends.

St. Chrysostom, as great a lover and *recommender* of the solitary state as he was, declares it to be no proper school for those who are to be leaders of Christ's flock. *Atterbury.*

To RECOMMI'T. *v. a.* [*re* and *commit.*] To commit anew.

When they had bailed the twelve bishops, who were in the Tower, the house of commons expostulated with them, and caused them to be *recommitted.* *Clarendon.*

To RECOMPA'CT. [*re* and *compact.*] To join anew.

Repair
And *recompact* my scatter'd body. *Donne.*

To RECOMPE'NSE. *v. a.* [*recompenser*, Fr. *re* and *compenso*, Lat.]

1. To repay; to requite.

Continue faithful, and we will *recompense* you. 1 *Mac.* x.

Hear from heaven, and requite the wicked, by *recompensing* his way upon his own head. 2 *Chron.* vi. 23.

2. To give in requital.

Thou wast begot of them, and how canst thou *recompense* them the things they have done for thee! *Eccluf.* viii. 28.

Recompense to no man evil for evil. *Rom.* xii. 17.

3. To compensate; to make up by something equivalent.

French wheat, which is bearded, requireth the best soil, *recompensing* the same with a profitable plenty. *Carew.*

Solyman, willing them to be of good cheer, said, that he would in short time find occasion for them to *recompense* that disgrace, and again to shew their approved valour. *Knolles.*

He is long ripening, but then his maturity, and the complement thereof, *recompenseth* the slowness of his maturation. *Hale's Origin of Mankind.*

4. To redeem; to pay for.

If the man have no kinsman to *recompense* the trespass unto, let it be *recompensed* unto the Lord. *Num.* v. 8.

RE'COMPENSE. *n. s.* [*recompense*, Fr. from the verb.]

Thou'rt so far before,
That swiftest wing of *recompense* is slow
To overtake thee. *Shakesp.*

2. Equivalent; compensation.

Wise men thought the vast advantage from their learning and integrity an ample *recompense* for any inconvenience from their passion. *Clarendon.*

Your mother's wrongs a *recompense* shall meet,
I lay my sceptre at her daughter's feet. *Dryden.*

Recompi'lement. *n. s.* [*re* and *compilement.*] New compilement.

Although I had a purpose to make a particular digest or *recompilement* of the laws, I laid it aside. *Bacon.*

To **Recompo'se.** *v. a.* [*recomposer*, Fr. *re* and *compose.*]

1. To settle or quiet anew.

Elijah was so transported, that he could not receive answer from God, till by musick he was *recomposed.* *Taylor.*

2. To form or adjust anew.

We produced a lovely purple, which we can destroy or *recompose* at pleasure, by severing or reapproaching the edges of the two irises. *Boyle on Colours.*

Recomposi'tion. *n. s.* [*re* and *composition.*] Composition renewed.

To **RECONCI'LE.** *v. a.* [*reconcilier*, Fr. *reconcilio*, Lat.]

1. To make to like again.

This noble passion,
Child of integrity, hath from my soul
Wip'd the black scruples, *reconcil'd* my thoughts
To thy good truth and honour. *Shakesp.*

Submit to Cæsar;
And *reconcile* thy mighty soul to life. *Addison's Cato.*

2. To make to be liked again.

Many wise men, who knew the treasurer's talent in removing prejudice, and *reconciling* himself to wavering affections, believ'd the loss of the duke was unseasonable. *Claren.*

He that has accustomed himself to take up with what easily offers itself, has reason to fear he shall never *reconcile* himself to the fatigue of turning things in his mind, to discover their more retired secrets. *Locke.*

2. To make any thing consistent.

The great men among the ancients understood how to *reconcile* manual labour with affairs of state. *Locke.*

Questions of right and wrong
Which though our consciences have *reconciled*,
My learning cannot answer. *Southern's Spartan Dame.*

Some figures monstrous and mishap'd appear,
Consider'd singly, or beheld too near;
Which but proportion'd to their light or place,
Due distance *reconciles* to form and grace. *Pope.*

3. To restore to favour.

So thou shalt do for every one that erreth and is simple, so shall ye *reconcile* the house. *Ezek.* xlv. 20.

Let him live before thee *reconcil'd.* *Milton.*

Reconci'leable. *adj.* [*reconciliable*, Fr. from *reconcile.*]

1. Capable of renewed kindness.

2. Consistent; possible to be made consistent.

What we did was against the dictates of our own conscience; and consequently never makes that act *reconcileable* with a regenerate estate, which otherwise would not be so. *Hammond.*

The different accounts of the numbers of ships are *reconcileable*, by supposing that some spoke of the men of war only, and others added the transports. *Arbuthnot.*

The bones, to be the most convenient, ought to have been as light, as was *reconcileable* with sufficient strength. *Cheyne.*

Reconci'leableness. *n. s.* [from *reconcileable.*]

1. Consistence; possibility to be reconciled.

The cylinder is an inanimate lifeless trunk, which hath nothing of choice or will in it; and therefore cannot be a fit resemblance to shew the *reconcileableness* of fate with choice. *Hammond.*

Discerning how the several parts of scripture are fitted to several times, persons and occurrences, we shall discover not only a *reconcileableness*, but a friendship and perfect harmony betwixt texts, that here seem most at variance. *Boyle.*

2. Disposition to renew love.

Reconci'lement. *n. s.* [from *reconcile.*]

1. Reconciliation; renewal of kindness; favour restored.

No cloud
Of anger shall remain; but peace assur'd
And *reconcilement.* *Milton's Paradise Lost, b.* iii.

Creature so fair! his *reconcilement* seeking,
Whom she had displeas'd. *Milton's Paradise Lost, b.* x.

2. Friendship renewed.

Injury went beyond all degree of *reconcilement.* *Sidney.*

On one side great reserve, and very great resentment on the other, have enflamed animosities, so as to make all *reconcilement* impracticable. *Swift.*

Reconci'ler. *n. s.* [from *reconcile.*]

1. One who renews friendship between others.

2. One who discovers the consistence between propositions.

Part of the world know how to accommodate St. James and St. Paul, better than some late *reconcilers.* *Norris.*

Reconcilia'tion. *n. s.* [*reconciliatio*, from *re* and *concilio*, Lat. *reconciliation*, Fr.]

1. Renewal of friendship.

2. Agreement of things seemingly opposite; solution of seeming contrarieties.

These distinctions of the fear of God give us a clear and easy *reconciliation* of those seeming inconsistencies of scripture, with respect to this affection. *Rogers.*

3. Attonement; expiation.

He might be a merciful and faithful high priest to make *reconciliation* for sin. *Heb.* ii. 17.

To **Reconde'nse.** *v. a.* [*re* and *condense.*] To condense anew.

In the heads of stills and necks of eolipiles, such vapours quickly are by a very little cold *recondensed* into water. *Boyle.*

Reco'ndite. *adj.* [*reconditus*, Lat.] Secret; profound; abstruse.

A disagreement between thought and expression seldom happens, but among men of more *recondite* studies and deep learning. *Felton on the Classicks.*

To **Recondu'ct.** *v. a.* [*reconduit*, Fr. *reconductus*, Lat. *re* and *conduct.*] To conduct again.

Wander'st thou within this lucid orb,
And stray'd from those fair fields of light above,
Amid'st this new creation want'st a guide,
To *reconduct* thy steps? *Dryden's State of Innocence.*

To **Reconjoi'n.** *v. a.* [*re* and *conjoin.*] To join anew.

Some liquors, although colourless themselves, when elevated into exhalations, exhibit a conspicuous colour, which they lose again when *reconjoined* into a liquor. *Boyle.*

To **Reco'nquer.** *v. a.* [*reconquerir*, Fr. *re* and *conquer.*] To conquer again.

Chatterton undertook to *reconquer* Orier. *Davies.*

To **Reconve'ne.** *v. n.* [*re* and *convene.*] To assemble anew.

A worse accident fell out about the time of the two houses *reconvening*, which made a wonderful impression. *Clarendon.*

To **Reco'nsecrate.** *v. a.* [*re* and *consecrate.*] To consecrate anew.

If a church should be consumed by fire, it shall, in such a case, be *reconsecrated.* *Ayliffe's Parergon.*

To **Reconve'y.** *v. a* [*re* and *convey.*] To convey again.

As rivers lost in seas, some secret vein
Thence *reconveys*, there to be lost again. *Denham.*

To **RECO'RD.** *v. a.* [*recordor*, Lat. *recorder*, Fr.]

1. To register any thing so that its memory may not be lost.

I made him my book, where my soul *recorded*
The history of all my secret thoughts. *Shakesp.*

He shall *record* a gift
Here in the court, of all he dies possess'd,
Unto his son Lorenzo. *Shakesp.*

Those things that are *recorded* of him and his impiety, are written in the chronicles. 1 *Esdr.* i. 42.

I call heaven and earth to *record* this day against you, that I have set before you life and death. *Deutr.* xxx. 20.

They gave complex ideas names, that they might the more easily *record* and discourse of those things they were daily conversant in. *Locke.*

2. To celebrate; to cause to be remembered solemnly.

They long'd to see the day, to hear the lark,
Record her hymns, and chant her carrols blest. *Fairfax.*

So ev'n and morn *recorded* the third day. *Milton.*

Reco'rd. *n. s.* [*record*, Fr. from the verb. The accent of the noun is indifferently on either syllable; of the verb always on the last.] Register; authentick memorial.

Is it upon *record?* or else reported
Successively, from age to age? *Shakesp. Rich.* III.

It cannot be
The Volscians dare break with us.
—We have *record* that very well it can;
And three examples of the like have been. *Shakesp.*

The king made a *record* of these things, and Mardocheus wrote thereof. *Esth.* xii. 4.

An ark, and in the ark his testimony,
The *records* of his covenant. *Milton.*

Of such a goddess no time leaves *record*,
Who burn'd the temple where she was ador'd. *Dryden.*

If he affirms such a monarchy continued to the flood, I would know what *records* he has it from. *Locke.*

Though the attested copy of a *record* be good proof, yet the copy of a copy never so well attested will not be admitted as a proof in judicature. *Locke.*

Thy elder look, great Janus! cast
Into the long *records* of ages past;
Review the years in fairest action drest. *Prior.*

Recorda'tion. *n. s.* [*recordatio*, Lat.] Remembrance. Not in use.

I never shall have length of life enough,
To rain upon remembrance with mine eyes,
That it may grow and spout as high as heav'n
For *recordation* to my noble husband. *Shakesp. Henry* IV.

Make a *recordation* to my soul
Of every syllable that here was spoke. *Shakesp.*

A man of the primitive temper, when the church by lowliness did flourish in high examples, which I have inserted as a due *recordation* of his virtues, having been much obliged to him for many favours. *Wotton.*

Reco'rder. *n. s.* [from *record.*]

1. One whose business is to register any events.

I but your *recorder* am in this,
Or mouth and speaker of the universe,
A ministerial notary; for 'tis
Not I, but you and fame that make the verse. *Donne.*

2. The

2. The keeper of the rolls in a city.

I ask'd, what meant this wilful silence?
His answer was, the people were not us'd
To be spoke to except by the *recorder*. *Shakesp. Rich.* III.

The office of *recorder* to this city being vacant, five or six persons are solliciting to succeed him. *Swift.*

3. A kind of flute; a wind instrument.

The shepherds went among them, and sang an eclogue, while the other shepherds, pulling out *recorders*, which possest the place of pipes, accorded their musick to the others voice. *Sidney, b.* ii.

In a *recorder*, the three uppermost holes yield one tone, which is a note lower than the tone of the first three. *Bacon.*

The figures of *recorders*, and flutes and pipes are straight; but the *recorder* hath a less bore and a greater above and below. *Bacon's Natural History.*

To RECOU'CH. *v. n.* [*re* and *couch.*] To lie down again.

Thou mak'st the night to overvail the day;
Then lions whelps lie roaring for their prey,
And at thy powerful hand demand their food;
Who when at morn they all *recouch* again,
Then toiling man till eve pursues his pain. *Wotton.*

To RECO'VER. *v. a.* [*recouvrer*, Fr. *recupero*, Lat.]

1. To restore from sickness or disorder.

Every of us, each for his self, laboured how to *recover* him, while he rather daily sent us companions of our deceit, than ever return'd in any sound and faithful manner. *Sidney.*

Would my Lord were with the prophet; for he would *recover* him of his leprosy. 2 *Kings* v. 3.

The clouds dispell'd, the sky resum'd her light,
And nature stood *recover'd* of her fright. *Dryden.*

2. To repair.

Should we apply this precept only to those who are concerned to *recover* time they have lost, it would extend to the whole race of mankind. *Rogers.*

Even good men have many failings and lapses to lament and *recover*. *Rogers.*

3. To regain.

Stay a while; and we'll debate,
By what safe means the crown may be *recover'd*. *Shakesp.*

The spirit of the Lord is upon me, to preach the gospel to the poor, and *recovering* of sight to the blind. *Luke* iv. 18.

Once in forty years cometh a pope, that casteth his eye upon the kingdom of Naples, to *recover* it to the church. *Bac.*

These Italians, in despight of what could be done, *recovered* Tiliaventum. *Knolles's History of the Turks.*

I who e'er while the happy garden sung,
By one man's disobedience lost, now sing
Recover'd Paradise to all mankind,
By one man's firm obedience. *Milton's Paradise Regain'd.*

Any other person may join with him that is injured, and assist him in *recovering* from the offender so much, as may make satisfaction. *Locke.*

4. To release.

That they may *recover* themselves out of the snare of the devil, who are taken captive by him. 2 *Tim.* ii. 26.

5. To attain; to reach; to come up to.

The forest is not three leagues off;
If we *recover* that, we're sure enough. *Shakesp.*

To RECO'VER. *v. n.* To grow well from a disease.

Adam, by this from the cold sudden damp
Recovering, his scatter'd spirits return'd. *Milton.*

RECO'VERABLE. *adj.* [*recouvrable*, Fr. from *recover.*]

1. Possible to be restored from sickness.
2. Possible to be regained.

A prodigal's course
Is like the sun's, but not like his, *recoverable*, I fear. *Shak.*

They promised the good people ease in the matter of protections, by which the debts from parliament men and their followers were not *recoverable*. *Clarendon.*

RECO'VERY. *n. s.* [from *recover.*]

1. Restoration from sickness.

Your hopes are regular and reasonable, though in temporal affairs; such as are deliverance from enemies, and *recovery* from sickness. *Taylor's Rule of Living Holy.*

The sweat sometimes acid, is a sign of *recovery* after acute distempers. *Arbuthnot on Aliments.*

2. Power or act of regaining.

What should move me to undertake the *recovery* of this, being not ignorant of the impossibility? *Shakesp.*

These counties were the keys of Normandy:
But wherefore weeps Warwick?
For grief that they are past *recovery*. *Shakesp. Henry* VI.

Mario Sanudo lived about the fourteenth age, a man full of zeal for the *recovery* of the Holy Land. *Arbuthnot on Coins.*

3. The act of cutting off an entail.

The spirit of wantonness is sure scared out of him; if the devil have him not in fee simple, with fine and *recovery*. *Shak.*

To RECOU'NT. *v. a.* [*reconter*, Fr.] To relate in detail; to tell distinctly.

Bid him *recount* the fore-recited practices. *Shakesp.*

How I have thought of these times,
I shall *recount* hereafter. *Shakesp. Julius Cæsar.*

Plato in Timæo produces an Egyptian priest, who *recounted* to Solon out of the holy books of Egypt the story of the flood universal, which happened long before the Grecian inundation. *Raleigh's History of the World.*

The talk of worldly affairs hindreth much, although *recounted* with a fair intention: we speak willingly, but seldom return to silence. *Taylor's Guide to Devotion.*

Say, from these glorious seeds what harvest flows,
Recount our blessings, and compare our woes.

RECOU'NTMENT. *n. s.* [from *recount.*] Relation; recital.

When from the first to last, betwixt us two,
Tears our *recountments* had most finely bath'd;
As how I came into that desart place. *Shakesp.*

RECOU'RED, for RECOVERED. *Spenser.*

RECOU'RSE. *n. s.* [*recursus*, Lat. *recours*, Fr.]

1. Frequent passage. Obsolete.

Not Priamus and Hecuba on knees,
Their eyes o'ergalled with *recourse* of tears. *Shakesp.*

2. Return; new attack.

Preventive physick, by purging noxious humours and the causes of diseases, preventeth sickness in the healthy, or the *recourse* thereof in the valetudinary. *Brown's Vulg. Errours.*

3. [*Recours*, Fr.] Application as for help or protection. This is the common use.

Thus died this great peer, in a time of great *recourse* unto him and dependance upon him, the house and town full of servants and suiters. *Wotton's Buckingham.*

The council of Trent commends the making *recourse*, not only to the prayers of the saints, but to their aid and assistance. *Stillingfleet's Def. of Dis. on Roman Idol.*

Can any man think, that this privilege was at first conferred upon the church of Rome, and that christians in all ages had constant *recourse* to it for determining their differences; and yet that that very church should now be at a loss where to find it? *Tillotson.*

All other means have fail'd to wound her heart,
Our last *recourse* is therefore to our art. *Dryden.*

4. Access.

The doors be lockt,
That no man hath *recourse* to her by night. *Shakesp.*

RE'CREANT. *adj.* [*recriant*, Fr.]

1. Cowardly; meanspirited; subdued; crying out for mercy; recanting out of fear.

Let be that lady debonaire,
Thou *recreant* knight, and soon thyself prepare
To battle. *Fairy Queen, b.* ii.

Dost
Thou wear a lion's hide? doff it for shame,
And hang a calf's skin on those *recreant* limbs. *Shakesp.*

Here standeth Thomas Mowbray, duke of Norfolk,
On pain to be found false and *recreant*. *Shakesp.*

Thou
Must, as a foreign *recreant*, be led
With manacles along our street. *Shakesp.*

The knight, whom fate and happy chance shall grace
From out the bars to force his opposite,
Or kill, or make him *recreant* on the plain,
The prize of valour and of love shall gain. *Dryden.*

2. Apostate; false.

Who for so many benefits receiv'd,
Turn'd *recreant* to God, ingrate and false,
And so of all true good himself despoil'd. *Milton's Par. Reg.*

To RE'CREATE. *v. a.* [*recreo*, Lat *recreer*, Fr.]

1. To refresh after toil; to amuse or divert in weariness.

He hath left you all his walks,
And to your heirs for ever; common pleasures,
To walk abroad and *recreate* yourselves. *Shakesp.*

Necessity and the example of St. John, who *recreated* himself with sporting with a tame partridge, teach us, that it is lawful to relax our bow, but not suffer it to be unstrung. *Tayl.*

Painters, when they work on white grounds, place before them colours mixt with blue and green, to *recreate* their eyes, white wearying and paining the sight more than any. *Dryden.*

2. To delight; to gratify.

These ripe fruits *recreate* the nostrils with their aromatick scent. *More's Divine Dialogues.*

3. To relieve; to revive.

Take a walk to refresh yourself with the open air, which inspired fresh doth exceedingly *recreate* the lungs, heart and vital spirits. *Harvey on Consumptions.*

RECREA'TION. *n. s.* [from *recreate.*]

1. Relief after toil or pain; amusement in sorrow or distress.

The chief *recreation* she could find in her anguish, was sometime to visit that place, where first she was so happy as to see the cause of her unhap. *Sidney, b.* ii.

I'll visit
The chapel where they lie, and tears, shed there,
Shall be my *recreation*. *Shakesp. Winter's Tale.*

The great men among the antients understood how to reconcile manual labour with affairs of state; and thought it no lessening to their dignity to make the one the *recreation* to the other. *Locke on Education.*

2. Refreshment;

2. Refreshment; amusement; diversion.

You may have the *recreation* of surprizing those with admiration, who shall hear the deaf person pronounce whatsoever they shall desire, without your seeming to guide him. *Holder's Elements of Speech.*

Nor is that man less deceived, that thinks to maintain a constant tenure of pleasure, by a continual pursuit of sports and *recreations*: for all these things, as they refresh a man when weary, so they weary him when refreshed. *South.*

RE'CREATIVE. *adj.* [from *recreate.*] Refreshing; giving relief after labour or pain; amusing; diverting.

Let the musick be *recreative*, and with some strange changes. *Bacon.*

Let not your recreations be lavish spenders of your time; but chuse such as are healthful, *recreative* and apt to refresh you: but at no hand dwell upon them. *Taylor.*

The access these trifles gain to the closets of ladies, seem to promise such easy and *recreative* experiments, which require but little time or charge. *Boyle.*

RE'CREATIVENESS. *n. s.* [from *recreative.*] The quality of being recreative.

RE'CREMENT. *n. s.* [*recrementum*, Lat.] Dross; spume; superfluous or useless parts.

The vital fire in the heart requires an ambient body of a yielding nature, to receive the superfluous serosities and other *recrements* of the blood. *Boyle.*

RECREMENTAL. } RECREMENTI'TIOUS. } *adj.* [from *recrement.*] Drossy.

To RECRI'MINATE. *v. n.* [*recriminer*, Fr. *re* and *criminor*, Latin.] To return one accusation with another.

It is not my business to *recriminate*, hoping sufficiently to clear myself in this matter. *Stillingfleet.*

How shall such hypocrites reform the state,
On whom the brothels can *recriminate?* *Dryden.*

To RECRI'MINATE. *v. a.* To accuse in return. Unusual.

Did not Joseph lie under black infamy? he scorned so much as to clear himself, or to *recriminate* the strumpet. *South.*

RECRIMINA'TION. *n. s.* [*recrimination*, Fr. from *recriminate.*] Return of one accusation with another.

Publick defamation will seem disobliging enough to provoke a return, which again begets a rejoinder, and so the quarrel is carried on with mutual *recriminations. Gov. of Tong.*

RECRIMINA'TOR. *n. s.* [from *recriminate.*] He that returns one charge with another.

RECRUDE'SCENT. *adj.* [*recrudescens*, Lat.] Growing painful or violent again.

To RECRUI'T. *v. a.* [*recruter*, Fr.]

1. To repair any thing wasted by new supplies.

He was longer in *recruiting* his flesh than was usual; but by a milk diet he recovered it. *Wiseman's Surgery.*

Increase thy care to save the sinking kind;
With greens and flow'rs *recruit* their empty hives,
And seek fresh forage to sustain their lives. *Dryden.*

Her cheeks glow the brighter, *recruiting* their colour;
As flowers by sprinkling revive with fresh odour. *Granville.*

This sun is set; but see in bright array
What hosts of heavenly lights *recruit* the day!
Love in a shining galaxy appears
Triumphant still. *Granville.*

Seeing the variety of motion, which we find in the world is always decreasing, there is a necessity of conserving and *recruiting* it by active principles; such as are the cause of gravity, by which planets and comets keep their motions in their orbs, and bodies acquire great motion in falling. *Newt.*

2. To supply an army with new men.

He trusted the earl of Holland with the command of that army, with which he was to be *recruited* and assisted. *Clar.*

To RECRUI'T. *v. n.* To raise new soldiers.

The French have only Switzerland besides their own country to *recruit* in; and we know the difficulties they meet with in getting thence a single regiment. *Addison.*

RECRUI'T. *n. s.* [from the verb.]

1. Supply of any thing wasted.

Whatever nature has in worth deny'd,
She gives in large *recruits* of needful pride. *Pope.*

The endeavour to raise new men for the *recruit* of the army found opposition. *Clarendon.*

2. New soldiers.

The pow'rs of Troy
With fresh *recruits* their youthful chief sustain:
Not theirs a raw and unexperienc'd train,
But a firm body of embattel'd men. *Dryden.*

RECTA'NGLE. *n. s.* [*rectangle*, Fr. *rectangulus*, Latin.] A figure which has one angle or more of ninety degrees.

If all Athens should decree, that in *rectangle* triangles the square, which is made of the side that subtendeth the right angle, is equal to the squares which are made of the sides containing the right angle, geometricians would not receive satisfaction without demonstration. *Brown's Vulgar Errours.*

The mathematician considers the truth and properties belonging to a *rectangle*, only as it is in idea in his own mind. *Locke.*

RECTA'NGULAR. *adj.* [*rectangulaire*, Fr. *rectus* and *angulus*, Latin.] Right angled; having angles of ninety degrees.

Bricks moulded in their ordinary *rectangular* form, if they shall be laid one by another in a level row between any supporters sustaining the two ends, then all the pieces will necessarily sink. *Wotton's Architecture.*

RECTA'NGULARLY. *adv.* [from *rectangular.*] With right angles.

At the equator, the needle will stand *rectangularly*; but approaching northward toward the tropic, it will regard the stone obliquely. *Brown's Vulgar Errours.*

RE'CTIFIABLE. *adj.* [from *rectify.*] Capable to be set right.

The natural heat of the parts being insufficient for a perfect and thorough digestion, the errors of one concoction are not *rectifiable* by another. *Brown's Vulgar Errours.*

RECTIFICA'TION. *n. s.* [*rectification*, Fr. from *rectify.*]

1. The act of setting right what is wrong.

It behoved the deity to renew that revelation from time to time, and to rectify abuses with such authority for the renewal and *rectification*, as was sufficient evidence of the truth of what was revealed. *Forbes.*

2. In chymistry, *rectification* is drawing any thing over again by distillation, to make it yet higher or finer. *Quincy.*

At the first *rectification* of some spirit of salt in a retort, a single pound afforded no less than six ounces of phlegm. *Boyle.*

To RE'CTIFY. *v. a.* [*rectifier*, Fr. *rectus* and *facio*, Lat.]

1. To make right; to reform; to redress.

That wherein unsounder times have done amiss, the better ages ensuing must *rectify* as they may. *Hooker.*

It shall be bootless,
That longer you defer the court, as well
For your own quiet, as to *rectify*
What is unsettled in the king. *Shakesp. Henry VIII.*

Where a long course of piety has purged the heart, and *rectified* the will, knowledge will break in upon such a soul, like the sun shining in his full might. *South.*

The substance of this theory I mainly depend on, being willing to suppose that many particularities may be *rectified* upon farther thoughts. *Burnet.*

If those men of parts, who have been employed in vitiating the age, had endeavoured to *rectify* and amend it, they needed not have sacrificed their good sense to their fame. *Add.*

The false judgment he made of things are owned; and the methods pointed out by which he *rectified* them. *Atterbury.*

2. To exalt and improve by repeated distillation.

The skin hath been kept white and smooth for above fifteen years, by being included with *rectified* spirit of wine in a cylindrical glass. *Grew's Musæum.*

RECTILI'NEAR. } RECTILI'NEOUS. } *adj.* [*rectus* and *linea*, Lat.] Consisting of right lines.

There are only three *rectilineous* and ordinate figures, which can serve to this purpose; and inordinate or unlike ones must have been not only less elegant, but unequal. *Ray.*

This image was oblong and not oval, but terminated with two *rectilinear* and parallel sides and two semicircular ends. *Newton's Opticks.*

The rays of light, whether they be very small bodies projected, or only motion and force propagated, are moved in right lines; and whenever a ray of light is by any obstacle turned out of its *rectilinear* way, it will never return into the same *rectilinear* way, unless perhaps by very great accident. *Newton's Opticks.*

RECTI'TUDE. *n. s.* [*rectitude*, Fr. from *rectus*, Lat.]

1. Straitness; not curvity.

2. Rightness; uprightness; freedom from moral curvity or obliquity.

Faith and repentance, together with the *rectitude* of their present engagement would fully prepare them for a better life. *King Charles.*

Calm the disorders of thy mind, by reflecting on the wisdom, equity and absolute *rectitude* of all his proceedings. *Att.*

RE'CTOR. *n. s.* [*recteur*, Fr. *rector*, Latin.]

1. Ruler; lord; governour.

God is the supreme *rector* of the world, and of all those subordinate parts thereof. *Hale's Origin of Mankind.*

When a *rector* of an university of scholars is chosen by the corporation or university, the election ought to be confirmed by the superior of such university. *Ayliffe's Parergon.*

2. Parson of an unimpropriated parish.

RE'CTORSHIP. *n. s.* [*rectorat*, Fr. from *rector.*] The rank or office of rector.

Had your bodies
No heart among you? or had you tongues to cry
Against the *rectorship* of judgment. *Shakesp.*

RECTORY. *n. s.* [*rectorerie*, Fr. from *rector.*]

A *rectory* or parsonage is a spiritual living, composed of land, tithe and other oblations of the people, separate or dedicate to God in any congregation for the service of his church there, and for the maintenance of the governor or minister thereof, to whose charge the same is committed. *Spelman.*

RECUBA'TION. *n. s.* [*recubo*, Latin.] The act of lying or leaning.

Whereas our translation renders it fitting, it cannot have that illation, for the French and Italian translations express neither position of session or *recubation*. *Brown.*

RECU'LE, for RECOIL. [*reculer*, Fr.] *Spenser.*

RECU'MBENCY. *n. s.* [from *recumbent*.]

1. The posture of lying or leaning.

In that memorable shew of Germanicus, twelve elephants danced unto the sound of musick, and after laid them down in tricliniums, or places of festival *recumbency*. *Brown.*

2. Rest; repose.

When the mind has been once habituated to this lazy *recumbency* and satisfaction on the obvious surface of things, it is in danger to rest satisfied there. *Locke.*

RECU'MBENT. *adj.* [*recumbens*, Lat.] Lying; leaning.

The Roman *recumbent*, or more properly accumbent, posture in eating was introduced after the first Punick war. *Arb.*

To RECU'R. *v. n.* [*recurro*, Lat.]

1. To come back to the thought; to revive in the mind.

The idea, I have once had, will be unchangeably the same, as long as it *recurs* the same in my memory. *Locke.*

In this life, the thoughts of God and a future state often offer themselves to us; they often spring up in our minds, and when expelled, *recur* again. *Calamy.*

A line of the golden verses of the Pythagoreans *recurring* on the memory, hath often guarded youth from a temptation to vice. *Watts.*

When any word has been used to signify an idea, that old idea will *recur* in the mind when the word is heard. *Watts.*

2. [*Recourir*, Fr.] To have recourse to; to take refuge in.

If to avoid succession in eternal existence, they *recur* to the punctum stans of the schools, they will thereby very little help us to a more positive idea of infinite duration. *Locke.*

The second cause we know, but trouble not ourselves to *recur* to the first. *Wake's Preparation for Death.*

To RECU'RE. *v. a.* [*re* and *cure*.] To recover from sickness or labour.

Through wise handling and fair governance,
I him *recured* to a better will,
Purged from drugs of foul intemperance. *Fairy Queen.*
Phœbus pure
In western waves his weary wagon did *recure*. *Fa. Queen.*
With one look she doth my life dismay,
And with another doth it straight *recure*. *Spenser.*
The wanton boy was shortly well *recur'd*
Of that his malady. *Spenser.*
Thy death's wound
He who comes thy Saviour shall *recure*,
Not by destroying Satan, but his works
In thee and in thy seed. *Milton's Par. Lost, b.* xii.

RECU'RE. *n. s.* Recovery; remedy.

Whatsoever fell into the enemies hands, was lost without *recure*: the old men were slain, the young men led away into captivity. *Knolles's History of the Turks.*

RECU'RRENCE. } *n. s.* [from *recurrent*.] Return.
RECU'RRENCY. }

Although the opinion at present be well suppressed, yet, from some strings of tradition and fruitful *recurrence* of error, it may revive in the next generation. *Brown's Vulg. Errours.*

RECU'RRENT. *adj.* [*recurrent*, Fr. *recurrens*, Lat.] Returning from time to time.

Next to lingring durable pains, short intermittent or swift *recurrent* pains precipitate patients unto consumptions. *Harv.*

RECU'RSION. *n. s.* [*recursus*, Lat.] Return.

One of the assistants told the *recursions* of the other pendulum hanging in the free air. *Boyle.*

RECURVA'TION. } *n. s.* [*recurvo*, Lat.] Flexure backwards.
RECU'RVITY. }

Ascending first into a capsulary reception of the breast bone by a serpentine *recurvation*, it ascendeth again into the neck. *Brown's Vulgar Errours.*

RECU'RVOUS. *adj.* [*recurvus*, Lat.] Bent backward.

I have not observed tails in all; but in others I have observed long *recurvous* tails, longer than their bodies. *Derham.*

RECU'SANT. *n. s.* [*recusans*, Lat.] One that refuses any terms of communion or society.

They demand of the lords, that no *recusant* lord might have a vote in passing that act. *Clarendon.*

Were all corners ransacked, what a multitude of *recusants* should we find upon a far differing account from that of conscience! *Decay of Piety.*

To RECU'SE. *v. n.* [*recuser*, Fr. *recuso*, Lat.] To refuse. A juridicial word.

The humility, as well of understanding as manners of the fathers, will not let them be troubled, when they are *recused* as judges. *Digby.*

A judge may proceed notwithstanding my appeal, unless I *recuse* him as a suspected judge. *Ayliffe's Parergon.*

RED. *adj.* [from the old Saxon, ꝛed; *rhud*, Welsh. As the town of Hertford, Mr. *Camden*, in his Britannia, noteth, first was called, by the Saxons, Herudford, the rud ford, or the red ford or water; high Dutch, *rot*; from the Greek, ἐρυθρὸν; French, *rouge*; Italian, *rubro*; from the Latin, *ruber*. *Peacham.*] Of the colour of blood, of one of the primitive colours, which is subdivided into many; as scarlet, vermilion, crimson.

Look I so pale.
—Ay, and no man in the presence,
But his *red* colour hath forsook his cheeks. *Shakesp.*
Bring me the fairest creature northward born,
To prove whose blood is *reddest*. *Shakesp. Merch. of Ven.*

His eyes shall be *red* with wine, and his teeth white with milk *Gen.* xlix. 12.

Th' angelick squadron turn'd fiery *red*. *Milton.*

If *red* lead and white paper be placed in the *red* light of the coloured spectrum, made in a dark chamber by the refraction of a prism, the paper will appear more lucid than the *red* lead, and therefore reflects the *red* making rays more copiously than *red* lead doth. *Newton's Opticks.*

The sixth *red* was at first of a very fair and lively scarlet, and soon after of a brighter colour, being very pure and brisk, and the best of all the *reds*. *Newton's Opticks.*

Why heavenly truth,
And moderation fair, were the *red* marks
Of superstition's scourge. *Thomson's Winter.*

To REDA'RGUE. *v. a.* [*redarguo*, Lat.] To refute. Not in use.

The last wittily *redargues* the pretended finding of coin, graved with the image of Augustus Cæsar, in the American mines. *Hakewill on Providence.*

REDBERRIED *shrub cassia. n. s.* A plant. It is male and female in different plants: the male hath flowers consisting of many stamina or threads, without any petals; these are always steril: the female plants, which have no conspicuous power, produce spherical berries, in which are included nuts of the same form. *Miller.*

RE'DBREAST. *n. s.* A small bird, so named from the colour of its breast.

No burial this pretty babe
Of any man receives,
But robin *redbreast* painfully
Did cover him with leaves. *Children in the Wood.*
The *redbreast*, sacred to the houshold gods,
Pays to trusted man his annual visit. *Thomson.*

RE'DCOAT. *n. s.* A name of contempt for a soldier.

The fearful passenger, who travels late,
Shakes at the moon-shine shadow of a rush,
And sees a *redcoat* rise from ev'ry bush. *Dryden.*

To RE'DDEN. *v. a.* [from *red*.] To make red.

In a heav'n serene, refulgent arms appear
Red'ning the skies, and glitt'ring all around,
The temper'd metals clash. *Dryden's Æneis.*

To RE'DDEN. *v. n.* To grow red.

With shame they *redden'd*, and with spight grew pale. *Dryden's Juvenal.*

Turn upon the ladies in the pit,
And if they *redden*, you are sure 'tis wit. *Addison.*
The poor inhabitant beholds in vain
The *red'ning* orange and the swelling grain. *Addison.*
For me the balm shall bleed, and amber flow,
The coral *redden*, and the ruby glow. *Pope.*
Appius *reddens* at each word you speak,
And stares, tremendous, with a threat'ning eye,
Like some fierce tyrant in old tapestry. *Pope.*

RE'DDISH. [from *red*.] Somewhat red.

A bright spot, white and somewhat *reddish*. *Lev.*

RE'DDISHNESS. *n. s.* [from *reddish*.] Tendency to redness.

Two parts of copper and one of tin, by fusion brought into one mass, the whiteness of the tin is more conspicuous than the *reddishness* of the copper. *Boyle.*

REDDI'TION. *n. s.* [from *reddo*, Lat.] Restitution.

She is reduced to a perfect obedience, partly by voluntary *reddition* and desire of protection, and partly by conquest. *Howel's Vocal Forest.*

RE'DDITIVE. *adj.* [*redditivus*, Lat.] Answering to an interrogative. A term of grammar.

RE'DDLE. *n. s.* A sort of mineral.

Reddle is an earth of the metal kind, of a tolerably close and even texture: its surface is smooth and somewhat glossy, and it is soft and unctuous to the touch, staining the fingers very much: it is remarkably heavy, and its colour of a fine florid, though not very deep red: our American colonies abound with it; and in England we have the finest in the world: it has been used as an astringent. *Hill's Mat. Med.*

REDE. *n. s.* [ꝛæd, Saxon.] Counsel; advice. Not used.

Do not as some ungracious pastors do,
Shew me the steep and thorny way to heav'n;
Whilst he a puft and reckless libertine,
Himself the primrose path of dalliance treads,
And recks not his own *rede*. *Shakesp. Hamlet.*

REDE. *v. a.* [ꝛædan, Saxon.] To advise.

I *rede* thee hence to remove,
Lest thou the price of my displeasure prove. *Spenser.*

To REDEE'M. *v. a.* [*redimo*, Lat.]

1. To ransom; to relieve from any thing by paying a price.

The kinsman said, I cannot *redeem* it for myself, lest I mar mine inheritance. *Ruth* iv. 6.

2. To rescue; to recover.

If, when I am laid into the tomb,
I wake before the time that Romeo
Comes to *redeem* me, there's a fearful point. *Shakesp.*
Thy father
Levied an army, weening to *redeem*
And re-instal me in the diadem. *Shakesp. Henry* VI.
Th' almighty from the grave
Hath me *redeem'd*; he will the humble save. *Sandys.*
Redeem Israel, O God, out of all his troubles. *Ps.* xxv.
Redeem from this reproach my wand'ring ghost. *Dryden.*

3. To recompense; to compensate; to make amends for.

Waywardly proud; and therefore bold, because extremely faulty; and yet having no good thing to *redeem* these. *Sidney.*

This feather stirs, she lives; if it be so,
It is a chance which does *redeem* all sorrows
That ever I have felt. *Shakesp. King Lear.*

Having committed a fault, he became the more obsequious and pliant to *redeem* it. *Wotton.*

Think it not hard, if at so cheap a rate
You can secure the constancy of fate,
Whose kindness sent what does your malice seem
By lesser ills the greater to *redeem*. *Dryden.*

4. To pay an atonement.

Thou hast one daughter,
Who *redeems* nature from the general curse,
Which twain have brought her to. *Shakesp.*

5. To save the world from the curse of sin.

Which of you will be mortal to *redeem*
Man's mortal crime. *Milton.*

REDEE'MABLE. *n. s.* [from *redeem.*] Capable of redemption.

REDEE'MABLENESS. *n. s.* [from *redeemable.*] The state of being redeemable.

REDEE'MER. *n. s.* [from *redeem.*]

1. One who ransoms or redeems.

She inflamed him so,
That he would algates with Pyrocles fight,
And his *redeemer* challeng'd for his foe,
Because he had not well maintain'd his right. *Fa. Queen.*

2. The Saviour of the world.

I every day expect an embassage
From my *redeemer* to redeem me hence;
And now in peace my soul shall part to heav'n. *Shakesp.*
Man's friend, his mediator, his design'd
Both ransom and *redeemer* voluntary. *Milton's Par. Lost.*

When saw we thee any way distressed, and relieved thee? will be the question of those, to whom heaven itself will be at the last day awarded, as having ministred to their *redeemer*. *Boyle.*

To REDELI'VER. *v. a.* [*re* and *deliver.*] To deliver back.

I have remembrances of yours,
That I have longed long to *redeliver*. *Shakesp.*

Instruments judicially exhibited, are not of the acts of courts; and therefore may be *redelivered* on the demand of the person that exhibited them. *Ayliffe's Parergon.*

REDELI'VERY. *n. s.* [from *redeliver.*] The act of delivering back.

To REDEMA'ND. *v. a.* [*redemander*, Fr. *re* and *demand.*] To demand back.

Threescore attacked the place where they were kept in custody, and rescued them: the duke *redemands* his prisoners, but receiving only excuses, he resolved to do himself justice. *Addison's Remarks on Italy.*

REDE'MPTION. *n. s.* [*redemption*, Fr. *redemptio*, Lat.]

1. Ransome; release.

Utter darkness his place
Ordain'd without *redemption*, without end. *Milton.*

2. Purchase of God's favour by the death of Christ.

I charge you, as you hope to have *redemption*,
That you depart, and lay no hands on me. *Shakesp.*
The Saviour son be glorify'd,
Who for lost man's *redemption* dy'd. *Dryden.*

REDE'MPTORY. *adj.* [from *redemptus*, Lat.] Paid for ransome.

Omega sings the exequies,
And Hector's *redemptory* price. *Chapman's Iliads.*

RE'DHOT. *adj.* [*red* and *hot.*] Heated to redness.

Iron *redhot* burneth and consumeth not. *Bacon.*

Is not fire a body heated so hot as to emit light copiously? for what else is a *redhot* iron than fire? and what else is a burning coal than *redhot* wood? *Newton's Opticks.*

The *redhot* metal hisses in the lake. *Pope.*

REDI'NTEGRATE. *adj.* [*redintegratus*, Latin.] Restored; renewed; made new.

Charles VIII. received the kingdom of France in flourishing estate, being *redintegrate* in those principal members, which anciently had been portions of the crown, and were after dissevered: so as they remained only in homage, and not in sovereignty. *Bacon's Henry* VII.

REDINTEGRA'TION. *n. s.* [from *redintegrate.*]

1. Renovation; restoration.

They kept the feast indeed, but with the leven of malice, and absurdly commemorated the *redintegration* of his natural body, by mutilating and dividing his mystical. *Dec. of Piety.*

2. *Redintegration* chymists call the restoring any mixed body or matter, whose form has been destroyed, to its former nature and constitution. *Quincy.*

He but prescribes as a bare chymical purification of nitre, what I teach as a philosophical *redintegration* of it. *Boyle.*

RE'DLEAD. *n. s.* [*red* and *lead.*] Minium. See MINIUM.

To draw with dry colours, make long pastils, by grinding *redlead* with strong wort, and so roll them up into long rolls like pencils, drying them in the sun. *Peacham.*

RE'DNESS. *n. s.* [from *red.*] The quality of being red.

There was a pretty *redness* in his lips. *Shakesp.*

In the red sea, most apprehend a material *redness*, from whence they derive its common denomination. *Brown.*

The glowing *redness* of the berries vies with the verdure of their leaves. *Spectator*, N° 477.

RE'DOLENCE. } *n. s.* [from *redolent.*] Sweet scent.
RE'DOLENCY. }

We have all the *redolence* of the perfumes we burn upon his altars. *Boyle.*

Their flowers attract spiders with their *redolency*. *Mortim.*

RE'DOLENT. *adj.* [*redolens*, Lat.] Sweet of scent.

Thy love excels the joys of wine;
Thy odours, O how *redolent*! *Sandys's Paraphrase.*

To REDOU'BLE. *v. a.* [*redoubler*, Fr. *re* and *double.*]

1. To repeat often.

So ended she; and all the rest around
To her *redoubled* that her undersong. *Spenser.*
They were
As cannons overcharg'd with double cracks,
So they *redoubled* strokes upon the foe. *Shakesp. Macbeth.*

2. To encrease by addition of the same quantity over and over.

Mimas and Parnassus sweat,
And Ætna rages with *redoubled* heat. *Addison.*

To REDOU'BLE. *v. n.* To become twice as much.

If we consider, that our whole eternity is to take its colour from those hours which we here employ in virtue or vice, the argument *redoubles* upon us, for putting in practice this method of passing away our time. *Addison's Spectator.*

REDOU'BT. *n. s.* [*reduit*, *redoute*, Fr. *ridotta*, Italian.] The outwork of a fortification; a fortress.

Every great ship is as an impregnable fort, and our many safe and commodious ports are as *redoubts* to secure them. *Bacon.*

REDOU'BTABLE. *adj.* [*redoubtable*, Fr.] Formidable; terrible to foes.

The enterprising Mr. Lintot, the *redoubtable* rival of Mr. Tonson, overtook me. *Pope.*

REDOU'BTED. *adj.* [*redoubté*, Fr.] Dread; awful; formidable.

His kingdom's seat Cleopolis is red,
There to obtain some such *redoubted* knight,
That parents dear from tyrant's power deliver might. *F. Q.*
So far be mine, my most *redoubted* lord,
As my true service shall deserve your love. *Shakesp.*

To REDOU'ND. *v. n.* [*redundo*, Latin.]

1. To be sent back by reaction.

The evil, soon
Driv'n back, *redounded*, as a flood, on those
From whom it sprung. *Milton's Paradise Lost, b.* vii.
Nor hope to be myself less miserable
By what I seek, but others to make such
As I, though thereby worse to me *redound*. *Milton.*

2. To conduce in the consequence.

As the care of our national commerce *redounds* more to the riches and prosperity of the publick, than any other act of government, the state of it should be marked out in every particular reign with greater distinction. *Addison.*

He had drawn many observations together, which very much *redound* to the honour of this prince. *Addison.*

3. To fall in the consequence.

As both these monsters will devour great quantities of paper, there will no small use *redound* from them to that manufacture. *Addison's Guardian*, N° 114.

The honour done to our religion ultimately *redounds* to God the author of it. *Rogers's Sermons.*

To REDRE'SS. *v. a.* [*redresser*, Fr.]

1. To set right; to amend.

In yonder spring of roses,
Find what to *redress* till noon. *Milton.*

2. To relieve; to remedy; to ease. It is sometimes used of persons, but more properly of things.

She felt with me, what I felt of my captivity, and streight laboured to *redress* my pain, which was her pain. *Sidney.*

'Tis thine, O king! th' afflicted to *redress*. *Dryden.*

In countries of freedom, princes are bound to protect their subjects in liberty, property and religion, to receive their petitions, and *redress* their grievances. *Swift.*

REDRE'SS. *n. ſ.* [from the verb.]
1. Reformation; amendment.
To ſeek reformation of evil laws is commendable, but for us the more neceſſary is a ſpeedy *redreſs* of ourſelves. *Hooker.*
2. Relief; remedy.
No humble ſuitors preſs to ſpeak for right;
No, not a man comes for *redreſs* to thee. *Shakeſp.*
Such people, as break the law of nations, all nations are intereſted to ſuppreſs, conſidering that the particular ſtates, being the delinquents, can give no *redreſs*. *Bacon.*
Grief, finding no *redreſs*, ferment and rage,
Nor leſs than wounds immedicable,
Rankle, and feſter, and gangrene
To black mortification. *Milton.*
3. One who gives relief.
Fair majeſty, the refuge and *redreſs*
Of thoſe whom fate purſues, and wants oppreſs. *Dryden.*

REDRE'SSIVE. *adj.* [from *redreſs.*] Succouring; affording remedy. A word not authoriſed.
The generous band,
Who, touch'd with human woe, *redreſſive* ſearch'd
Into the horrors of the gloomy jail. *Thomſon.*

To REDSEA'R. *v. n.* [*red* and *ſear.*] A term of workmen.
If iron be too cold, it will not feel the weight of the hammer, when it will not batter under the hammer; and if it be too hot, it will *redſear*, that is, break or crack under the hammer. *Moxon's Mechanical Exerciſes.*

RE'DSHANK. *n. ſ.* [*red* and *ſhank.*]
1. This ſeems to be a contemptuous appellation for ſome of the people of Scotland.
He ſent over his brother Edward with a power of Scots and *redſhanks* unto Ireland, where they got footing. *Spenſer.*
2. A bird. *Ainſworth.*

RE'DSTREAK. *n. ſ.* [*red* and *ſtreak.*]
1. An apple.
The *redſtreak*, of all cyder fruit, hath obtained the preference, being but a kind of wilding, and though kept long, yet is never pleaſing to the palate; there are ſeveral ſorts of *redſtreak*: ſome ſorts of them have red veins running through the whole fruit, which is eſteemed to give the cyder the richeſt tincture. *Mortimer.*
2. Cyder preſſed from the redſtreak.
Redſtreak he quaffs beneath the Chianti vine,
Gives Tuſcan yearly for thy Scudmore's wine. *Smith.*

To REDU'CE. *v. a.* [*reduco*, Lat. *reduire*, Fr.]
1. To bring back. Obſolete.
Abate the edge of traitors, gracious lord!
That would *reduce* theſe bloody days again. *Shakeſp.*
2. To bring to the former ſtate.
It were but juſt
And equal to *reduce* me to my duſt,
Deſirous to reſign and render back
All I receiv'd. *Milton.*
3. To reform from any diſorder.
That temper in the archbiſhop, who licenſed their moſt pernicious writings, left his ſucceſſor a very difficult work to do, to reform and *reduce* a church into order, that had been ſo long neglected, and ſo ill filled. *Clarendon.*
4. To bring into any ſtate of diminution.
A diaphanous body, *reduced* to very minute parts, thereby acquires many little ſurfaces in a narrow compaſs. *Boyle.*
His ire will quite conſume us, and *reduce*
To nothing this eſſential. *Milton.*
The ordinary ſmalleſt meaſure is looked on as an unit in number, when the mind by diviſion would *reduce* them into leſs fractions. *Locke.*
5. To degrade; to impair in dignity.
There is nothing ſo bad, but a man may lay hold of ſomething about it, that will afford matter of excuſe; nor nothing ſo excellent, but a man may faſten upon ſomething belonging to it, whereby to *reduce* it. *Tillotſon.*
6. To bring into any ſtate of miſery or meanneſs.
The moſt prudent part was his moderation and indulgence, not *reducing* them to deſperation. *Arbuthnot on Coins.*
7. To ſubdue.
Under thee, as head ſupreme,
Thrones, princedoms, pow'rs, dominions I *reduce*. *Milton.*
8. To bring into any ſtate more within reach or power.
To have this project *reduced* to practice, there ſeems to want nothing.
9. To reclaim to order.
There left deſert utmoſt hell,
Reduc'd in careful watch round their metropolis. *Milton.*
10. To ſubject to a rule; to bring into a claſs.

REDU'CEMENT. *n. ſ.* [from *reduce.*] The act of bringing back, ſubduing, reforming or diminiſhing.
The navy received bleſſing from pope Sixtus, and was aſſigned as an apoſtolical miſſion for the *reducement* of this kingdom to the obedience of Rome. *Bacon.*

REDU'CER. *n. ſ.* [from *reduce.*] One that reduces.
They could not learn to digeſt, that the man, which they ſo long had uſed to maſk their own appetites, ſhould now be the *reducer* of them into order. *Sidney, b.* ii.

REDU'CIBLE. *adj.* [from *reduce.*] Poſſible to be reduced.
All law that a man is obliged by, is *reducible* to the law of nature, the poſitive law of God in his word, and the law of man enacted by the civil power. *South.*
Actions, that promote ſociety and mutual fellowſhip, ſeem *reducible* to a proneneſs to do good to others, and a ready ſenſe of any good done by others. *South.*
All the parts of painting are *reducible* into theſe mentioned by our author. *Dryden's Dufreſnoy.*
If minerals are not convertible into another ſpecies, though of the ſame genus, much leſs can they be ſurmiſed *reducible* into a ſpecies of another genus. *Harvey on Conſumptions.*
Our damps in England are *reducible* to the ſuffocating or the fulminating. *Woodward.*

REDU'CIBLENESS. *n. ſ.* [from *reducible.*] Quality of being reducible.
Spirit of wine, by its pungent taſte, and eſpecially by its *reducibleneſs*, according to Helmont, into alcali and water, ſeems to be as well of a ſaline as a ſulphureous nature. *Boyle.*

REDU'CTION. *n. ſ.* [*reduction*, Fr. from *reductus*, Lat.]
1. The act of reducing.
Some will have theſe years to be but months; but we have no certain evidence that they uſed to account a month a year; and if we had, yet that *reduction* will not ſerve. *Hale.*
2. In arithmetick, *reduction* brings two or more numbers of different denominations into one denomination. *Cocker.*

REDU'CTIVE. *adj.* [*reductif*, Fr. *reductus*, Latin.] Having the power of reducing.
Thus far concerning theſe *reductives* by inundations and conflagrations. *Hale's Origin of Mankind.*

REDU'CTIVELY. *adv.* [from *reductive.*] By reduction; by conſequence.
If they be our ſuperiors, then 'tis modeſty and reverence to all ſuch in general, at leaſt *reductively*. *Hammond.*
Other niceties, though they are not matter of conſcience, ſingly and apart, are yet ſo *reductively*; that is, though they are not ſo in the abſtract, they become ſo by affinity and connection. *L'Eſtrange's Fables.*

REDU'NDANCE. } *n. ſ.* [*redundantia*, Lat. from *redundant.*] Su-
REDU'NDANCY. } perfluity; ſuperabundance.
The cauſe of generation ſeemeth to be fulneſs; for generation is from *redundancy*: this fulneſs ariſeth from the nature of the creature, if it be hot, and moiſt and ſanguine; or from plenty of food. *Bacon.*
It is a quality, that confines a man wholly within himſelf, leaving him void of that principle, which alone ſhould diſpoſe him to communicate and impart thoſe *redundancies* of good, that he is poſſeſſed of. *South.*
I ſhall ſhow our poets *redundance* of wit, juſtneſs of compariſons, and elegance of deſcriptions. *Garth.*
Labour ferments the humours, caſts them into their proper channels, and throws off *redundancies*. *Addiſon.*

REDU'NDANT. *adj.* [*redundans*, Latin.]
1. Superabundant; exuberant; ſuperfluous.
His head,
With burniſh'd neck of verdant gold, erect
Amidſt his circling ſpires, that on the graſs
Floated *redundant*. *Milton's Par. Loſt, b.* ix.
Notwithſtanding the *redundant* oil in fiſhes, they do not encreaſe fat ſo much as fleſh. *Arbuthnot on Aliments.*
2. Uſing more words or images than are uſeful.
Where the author is *redundant*, mark thoſe paragraphs to be retrenched; when he trifles, abandon thoſe paſſages. *Watts.*

REDU'NDANTLY. *adv.* [from *redundant.*] Superfluouſly; ſuperabundantly.

To REDU'PLICATE. *v. a.* [*re* and *duplicate.*] To double.

REDUPLICA'TION. *n. ſ.* [from *reduplicate.*] The act of doubling.
This is evident, when the mark of excluſion is put; as when we ſpeak of a white thing, adding the *reduplication*, as white; which excludes all other conſiderations. *Digby.*

REDU'PLICATIVE. *adj.* [*reduplicatif*, Fr. from *reduplicate.*] Double.
Some logicians mention *reduplicative* propoſitions; as men, conſidered as men, are rational creatures; i. e. becauſe they are men. *Watts's Logick.*

RE'DWING. *n. ſ.* A bird. *Ainſworth.*

To REE. *v. a.* [I know not the etymology.] To riddle; to ſift.
After malt is well rubbed and winnowed, you muſt then *ree* it over in a ſieve. *Mortimer's Huſbandry.*

To REE'CHO. *v. n.* [*re* and *echo.*] To echo back.
Around we ſtand, a melancholy train,
And a loud groan *reechoes* from the main. *Pope.*

REE'CHY. *adj.* [from *reech*, corruptly formed from *reek.*] Smoky; ſooty; tanned.
Let him, for a pair of *reechy* kiſſes,
Make you to ravel all this matter out. *Shakeſp. Hamlet.*
The kitchen malkin pins
Her richeſt lockram 'bout her *reechy* neck. *Shakeſp.*

REED. *n. ſ.* [ꞃeoꝺ, Saxon; *ried*, German; *arundo*, Lat.]
1. An hollow knotted ſtalk, which grows in wet grounds.
A *reed* is diſtinguiſhed from the graſſes by its magnitude, and by its having a firm ſtem: the ſpecies are, the large manured

nured cane or *reed*, the sugar cane, the common *reed*, the variegated *reed*, the Bambu cane, and dark red *reed*. *Miller*.

This Derceta, the mother of Semiramis, was sometimes a recluse, and falling in love with a goodly young man, she was by him with child, which, for fear of extreme punishment, she conveyed away and caused the same to be hidden among the high *reeds* which grew on the banks of the lake. *Raleigh's History of the World*.

The knotty bulrush next in order stood,
And all within of *reeds* a trembling wood. *Dryden*.
Her lover Cimon lay concealed in the *reeds*. *Broome*.

2. A small pipe.

I'll speak between the change of man and boy
With a *reed* voice. *Shakesp*.
Arcadian pipe, the pastoral *reed*
Of Hermes. *Milton*.

3. An arrow.

When the Parthian turn'd his steed,
And from the hostile camp withdrew;
With cruel skill the backward *reed*
He sent; and as he fled, he slew. *Prior*.

REE'DED. *adj.* [from *reed*.] Covered with reeds.

Where houses be *reeded*,
Now pare off the moss, and go beat in the reed. *Tusser*.

REE'DEN. *adj.* [from *reed*.] Consisting of reeds.

Honey in the sickly hive infuse
Through *reeden* pipes. *Dryden's Virgil's Georgicks*.

To REE'DIFY. *v. a.* [*reedifier*, Fr. *re* and *edify*.] To rebuild; to build again.

The ruin'd walls he did *reedify*. *Fa. Queen*.
This monument five hundred years hath stood,
Which I have sumptuously *reedified*. *Shakesp*.
The Æolians, who repeopled, *reedified* Ilium. *Sandys*.
The house of God they first *reedify*. *Milton*.

REE'DLESS. *adj.* [from *reed*.] Being without reeds.

Youths tomb'd before their parents were,
Whom foul Cocytus' *reedless* banks enclose. *May*.

REE'DY. *adj.* [from *reed*.] Abounding with reeds.

The sportive flood in two divides,
And forms with erring streams the *reedy* isles. *Blackmore*.
Around th' adjoining brook,
Now fretting o'er a rock,
Now scarcely moving through a *reedy* pool. *Thomson*.

REEK. *n. s.* [ꞃec, Saxon: *reuke*, Dutch.]

1. Smoke; steam; vapour.

'Tis as hateful to me as the *reek* of a lime kiln. *Shakesp*.

2. [*Reke*, German, any thing piled up.] A pile of corn or hay.

Nor barns at home, nor *reeks* are rear'd abroad. *Dryden*.

The covered *reek*, much in use westward, must needs prove of great advantage in wet harvests. *Mortimer*.

To REEK. *v. n.* [ꞃecan, Saxon.]

1. To smoke; to steam; to emit vapour.

They redoubled strokes upon the foe,
Except they meant to bathe in *reeking* wounds,
Or memorise another Golgotha. *Shakesp. Macbeth*.
To the battle came he; where he did
Run *reeking* o'er the lives of men, as if
'Twere a perpetual spoil. *Shakesp. Coriolanus*.
You remember
How under my oppression I did *reek*,
When I first mov'd you. *Shakesp*.
Dying like men, though buried in your dunghills,
They shall be fam'd; for there the sun shall greet them,
And draw their honours *reeking* up to heav'n. *Shakesp*.
I found me laid
In balmy sweat; which with his beams the sun
Soon dry'd, and on the *reeking* moisture fed. *Milton*.
Love one descended from a race of tyrants,
Whose blood yet *reeks* on my avenging sword. *Smith*.

REE'KY. *adj.* [from *reek*.] Smoky; tanned; black.

Shut me in a charnel house,
O'ercover'd quite with dead men's rattling bones,
With *reeky* shanks and yellow chapless skulls. *Shakesp*.

REEL. *n. s.* [ꞃeol, Saxon.] A turning frame, upon which yarn is wound into skeins from the spindle.

To REEL. *v. a.* [from the noun.] To gather yarn off the spindle.

It may be useful for the *reeling* of yarn. *Wilkins*.

To REEL. *v. n.* [*rollen*, Dutch; *ragla*, Swedish.] To stagger; to incline in walking, first to one side and then to the other.

Him when his mistress proud perceiv'd to fall,
While yet his feeble feet for faintness *reel'd*,
She 'gan call, help Orgoglio! *Fairy Queen, b.* i.
What news in this our tott'ring state?
—It is a *reeling* world,
And I believe will never stand upright,
Till Richard wear the garland. *Shakesp. Rich.* III.
It is amiss to sit
And keep the turn of tipling with a slave,
To *reel* the streets at noon. *Shakesp. Ant. and Cleopatra*.
They *reel* to and fro, and stagger like a drunken man. *Ps*.
Grope in the dark, and to no seat confine
Their wandring feet; but *reel* as drunk with wine. *Sandys*.
He with heavy fumes opprest,
Reel'd from the palace, and retir'd to rest. *Pope*.
Should he hide his face,
Th' extinguish'd stars would loosening *reel*
Wide from their spheres. *Thomson*.

REELE'CTION. *n. s.* [*re* and *election*.] Repeated election.

Several acts have been made, and rendered ineffectual, by leaving the power of *reelection* open. *Swift*.

To REENA'CT. *v. a.* [*re* and *enact*.] To enact anew.

The construction of ships was forbidden to senators, by a law made by Claudius the tribune, and *reenacted* by the Julian law of concessions. *Arbuthnot on Coins*.

To REENFO'RCE. *v. a.* [*re* and *enforce*.] To strengthen with new assistance.

The French have *reenforc'd* their scatter'd men. *Shakesp*.

They used the stones to *reenforce* the pier. *Hayward*.

The presence of a friend raises fancy, and *reenforces* reason. *Collier*.

REENFO'RCEMENT. *n. s.* [*re* and *enforcement*.] Fresh assistance.

Alone he enter'd
The mortal gate o' th' city, which he painted
With shunless destiny; aidless came off,
And with a sudden *reenforcement* struck
Corioli like a planet. *Shakesp. Coriolanus*.

They require a special *reenforcement* of sound endoctrinating to set them right. *Milton*.

What *reenforcement* we may gain from hope, *Milton*.

The words are a reiteration or *reenforcement* of a corollary. *Ward*.

To REENJO'Y. *v. a.* [*re* and *enjoy*.] To enjoy anew or a second time.

The calmness of temper Achilles *reenjoyed*, is only an effect of the revenge which ought to have preceded. *Pope*.

To REE'NTER. *v. a.* [*re* and *enter*.] To enter again; to enter anew.

With opportune excursion, we may chance
Reenter heav'n. *Milton*.

The fiery sulphurous vapours seek the centre from whence they proceed; that is, *reenter* again. *Mortimer's Husbandry*.

To REENTHRO'NE. *v. a.* To replace in a throne.

He disposes in my hands the scheme
To *reenthrone* the king. *Southerne*.

REE'NTRANCE. *n. s.* [*re* and *entrance*.] The act of entring again.

Their repentance, although not their first entrance, is notwithstanding the first step of their *reentrance* into life. *Hooker*.

The pores of the brain, through the which the spirits before took their course, are more easily opened to the spirits which demand *reentrance*. *Glanvill's Sceps*.

REE'RMOUSE. *n. s.* [hꞃeꞃemuꞅ, Saxon.] A bat.

To REESTA'BLISH. *v. a.* [*re* and *establish*.] To establish anew.

To *reestablish* the right of lineal succession to paternal government, is to put a man in possession of that government, which his fathers did enjoy. *Locke*.

Peace, which hath for many years been banished the christian world, will be speedily *reestablished*. *Smalridge*.

REESTA'BLISHER. *n. s.* [from *reestablish*.] One that reestablishes.

REESTA'BLISHMENT. *n. s.* [from *reestablish*.] The act of reestablishing; the state of being reestablished; restauration.

The Jews made such a powerful effort for their *restablishment* under Barchocab, in the reign of Adrian, as shook the whole Roman empire. *Addison*.

REEVE. *n. s.* [ᵹeꞃeꝼa, Saxon.] A steward. Obsolete.

The *reeve*, miller and cook are distinguished. *Dryden*.

To REEXA'MINE. *v. a.* [*re* and *examine*.] To examine anew.

Spend the time in *reexamining* more duly your cause. *Hook*.

To REFE'CT. *v. a.* [*refectus*, Lat.] To refresh; to restore after hunger or fatigue. Not in use.

A man in the morning is lighter in the scale, because in sleep some pounds have perspired; and is also lighter unto himself, because he is *refected*. *Brown's Vulgar Errours*.

REFE'CTION. *n. s.* [*refection*, Fr. from *refectio*, Lat.] Refreshment after hunger or fatigue.

After a draught of wine, a man may seem lighter in himself from sudden *refection*, though he be heavier in the balance, from a ponderous addition. *Brown*.

Fasting is the diet of angels, the food and *refection* of souls, and the richest aliment of grace. *South*.

For sweet *refection* due,
The genial viands let my train renew. *Pope*.

REFE'CTORY. *n. s.* [*refectoire*, Fr. from *refect*.] Room of refreshment; eating room.

He cells and *refectories* did prepare,
And large provisions laid of winter fare. *Dryden*.

To REFE'L. *v. a.* [*refello*, Lat.] To refute; to repress.

Friends not to *refel* ye,
Or any way quell ye,
Ye aim at a mystery,
Worthy a history. *Benj. Johnson's Gypsies*.

It

It instructs the scholar in the various methods of discovering and *refelling* the subtil tricks of sophisters. *Watts.*

To REFE'R. *v. a.* [*refero*, Lat. *referer*, Fr.]

1. To dismiss for information or judgment.

Those causes the divine historian *refers* us to, and not to any productions out of nothing. *Burnet's Theory of the Earth.*

2. To betake for decision.

The heir of his kingdom hath *referred* herself unto a poor, but worthy gentleman. *Shakesp. Cymbeline.*

3. To reduce to, as to the ultimate end.

You profess and practise to *refer* all things to yourself. *Bac.*

4. To reduce, as to a class.

The salts, predominant in quick lime, we *refer* rather to lixiviate, than acid. *Boyle on Colours.*

To REFE'R. *v. n.* To respect; to have relation.

Of those places, that *refer* to the shutting and opening the abyss, I take notice of that in Job. *Burnet.*

REFEREE'. *n. s.* [from *refer.*] One to whom any thing is referred.

Referees and arbitrators seldom forget themselves. *L'Estr.*

RE'FERENCE. *n. s.* [from *refer.*]

1. Relation; respect; view towards; allusion to.

The knowledge of that which man is in *reference* unto himself and other things in relation unto man, I may term the mother of all those principles, which are decrees in that law of nature, whereby human actions are framed. *Hooker.*

Jupiter was the son of Æther and Dies; so called, because the one had *reference* to his celestial conditions, the other discovered his natural virtues. *Raleigh's History of the World.*

Christian religion commands sobriety, temperance and moderation, in *reference* to our appetites and passions. *Tillotson.*

2. Dismission to another tribunal.

It passed in England without the least *reference* hither. *Sw.*

REFERE'NDARY. *n. s.* [*referendus*, Lat.] One to whose decision any thing is referred.

In suits, it is good to *refer* to some friend of trust; but let him chuse well his *referendaries*. *Bacon's Essays.*

To REFERME'NT, *v. a.* [*re* and *ferment.*] To ferment anew.

Th' admitted nitre agitates the flood,
Revives its fire, and *referments* the blood. *Blackmore.*

REFE'RRIBLE. *adj.* [from *refer.*] Capable of being considered, as in relation to something else.

Unto God all parts of time are alike, unto whom none are *referrible*, and all things present, unto whom nothing is past or to come, but who is the same yesterday, to-day and to-morrow. *Brown's Vulgar Errours.*

To REFI'NE. *v. a.* [*raffiner*, Fr.]

1. To purify; to clear from dross and recrement.

I will *refine* them as silver is *refined*, and will try them as gold is tried. *Zech.* xiii. 9.

Weigh ev'ry word, and ev'ry thought *refine*. *Anon.*

The red Dutch currant yields a rich juice, to be diluted with a quantity of water boiled with *refined* sugar. *Mortimer.*

2. To make elegant; to polish; to make accurate.

Queen Elizabeth's time was a golden age for a world of *refined* wits, who honoured poesy with their pens. *Peacham.*

Love *refines* the thoughts, and hath his seat
In reason. *Milton.*

The same traditional sloth, which renders the bodies of children, born from wealthy parents, weak, may perhaps *refine* their spirits. *Swift.*

To REFI'NE. *v. n.*

1. To improve in point of accuracy or delicacy.

Chaucer *refined* on Boccace, and mended stories. *Dryden.*

Let a lord but own the happy lines;
How the wit brightens, how the sense *refines*! *Pope.*

2. To grow pure.

The pure limpid stream, when foul with stains,
Works itself clear, and as it runs *refines*. *Addison.*

3. To affect nicety.

He makes another paragraph about our *refining* in controversy, and coming nearer still to the church of Rome. *Atterbury.*

REFI'NEDLY. *adv.* [from *refine.*] With affected elegance.

Will any dog
Refinedly leave his bitches and his bones,
To turn a wheel? *Dryden.*

REFI'NEMENT. *n. s.* [from *refine.*]

1. The act of purifying, by clearing any thing from dross and recrementitious matter.

The more bodies are of kin to spirit in subtilty and *refinement*, the more diffusive are they. *Norris.*

2. Improvement in elegance or purity.

From the civil war to this time, I doubt whether the corruptions in our language have not equalled its *refinements*. *Sw.*

3. Artificial practice.

The rules religion prescribes are more successful in publick and private affairs, than the *refinements* of irregular cunning. *Rog.*

4. Affectation of elegant improvement.

The flirts about town had a design to leave us in the lurch, by some of their late *refinements*. *Addison's Guardian.*

REFI'NER. *n. s.* [from *refine.*]

1. Purifier; one who clears from dross or recrement.

The *refiners* of iron observe, that that iron stone is hardest to melt, which is fullest of metal; and that easiest, which hath most dross. *Bacon's Physical Remains.*

2. Improver in elegance.

As they have been the great *refiners* of our language, so it hath been my chief ambition to imitate them. *Swift.*

3. Inventor of superfluous subtilties.

No men see less of the truth of things, than these great *refiners* upon incidents, who are so wonderfully subtle, and over wise in their conceptions. *Addison's Spectator*, Nº 170.

Some *refiners* pretend to argue for the usefulness of parties in such a government as ours. *Swift.*

To REFI'T. *v. a.* [*refait*, Fr. *re* and *fit.*] To repair; to restore after damage.

He will not allow that there are any such signs of art in the make of the present globe, or that there was so great care taken in the *refitting* of it up again at the deluge. *Woodw.*

Permit our ships a shelter on your shoars,
Refitted from your woods with planks and oars. *Dryden.*

To REFLE'CT. *v. a.* [*reflechir*, Fr. *reflecto*, Lat.] To throw back.

We, his gather'd beams
Reflected, may with matter sere foment. *Milton.*

Bodies close together *reflect* their own colour. *Dryden.*

To REFLE'CT. *v. n.*

1. To throw back light.

In dead men's sculls, and in those holes,
Where eyes did once inhabit, there were crept,
As 'twere in scorn of eyes, *reflecting* gems. *Shakesp.*

2. To bend back.

Inanimate matter moves always in a straight line, and never *reflects* in an angle, nor bends in a circle, which is a continual reflection, unless either by some external impulse, or by an intrinsick principle of gravity. *Bentley's Sermons.*

3. To throw back the thoughts upon the past or on themselves.

The imagination casts thoughts in our way, and forces the understanding to *reflect* upon them. *Duppa.*

In every action *reflect* upon the end; and in your undertaking it, consider why you do it. *Taylor.*

Who saith, who could such ill events expect?
With shame on his own counsels doth *reflect*. *Denham.*

When men are grown up, and *reflect* on their own minds, they cannot find any thing more ancient there, than those opinions which were taught them before their memory began to keep a register of their actions. *Locke.*

It is hard, that any part of my land should be settled upon one who has used me so ill; and yet I could not see a sprig of any bough of this whole walk of trees, but I should *reflect* upon her and her severity. *Addison's Spectator.*

Let the king dismiss his woes,
Reflecting on her fair renown;
And take the cypress from his brows,
To put his wonted laurels on. *Prior.*

4. To consider attentively.

Into myself my reason's eye I turn'd;
And as I much *reflected*, much I mourn'd. *Prior.*

5. To throw reproach or censure.

Neither do I *reflect* in the least upon the memory of his late majesty, whom I entirely acquit of any imputation. *Sw.*

6. To bring reproach.

Errors of wives *reflect* on husbands still. *Dryden.*

REFLE'CTENT. *adj.* [*reflectens*, Lat.] Bending back; flying back.

The ray descendent, and the ray *reflectent*, flying with so great a speed, that the air between them cannot take a formal play any way, before the beams of the light be on both sides of it; it follows, that, according to the nature of humid things, it must first only swell. *Digby on the Soul.*

REFLE'CTION. *n. s.* [from *reflect*: thence I think *reflexion* less proper: *reflexion*, Fr. *reflexus*, Lat.]

1. The act of throwing back.

The eye sees not itself,
But by *reflection* from other things. *Shakesp. Julius Cæsar.*

If the sun's light consisted but of one sort of rays, there would be but one colour, and it would be impossible to produce any new by *reflections* or refractions. *Cheyne.*

2. The act of bending back.

Inanimate matter moves always in a straight line, nor ever reflects in an angle or circle, which is a continual *reflection*, unless by some external impulse. *Bentley's Sermons.*

3. That which is reflected.

She shines not upon fools, lest the *reflection* should hurt her. *Shakesp. Cymbeline.*

As the sun in water we can bear,
Yet not the sun, but his *reflection* there;
So let us view her here, in what she was,
And take her image in this watry glass. *Dryden.*

4. Thought thrown back upon the past.

The three first parts I dedicate to my old friends, to take off those melancholy *reflections*, which the sense of age, infirmity and death may give them. *Denham.*

This dreadful image so possess'd her mind,
She ceas'd all farther hope; and now began
To make *reflection* on th' unhappy man. *Dryden.*

Job's

Job's *reflections* on his once flourishing estate, did at the same time afflict and encourage him. *Atterbury.*

What wounding reproaches of soul must he feel, from the *reflections* on his own ingratitude. *Rogers's Sermons.*

5. The action of the mind upon itself.

Reflection is the perception of the operations of our own minds within us, as it is employed about the ideas it has got. *Locke.*

6. Attentive consideration.

This delight grows and improves under thought and *reflection*; and while it exercises, does also endear itself to the mind; at the same time employing and inflaming the meditations. *South's Sermons.*

7. Censure.

He dy'd; and oh! may no *reflection* shed
Its pois'nous venom on the royal dead. *Prior.*

REFLE'CTIVE. *adj.* [from *reflect.*]

1. Throwing back images.

When the weary king gave place to night,
His beams he to his royal brother lent,
And so shone still in his *reflective* light. *Dryden.*

In the *reflective* stream the sighing bride
Viewing her charms impair'd, abash'd shall hide
Her pensive head. *Prior.*

2. Considering things past; considering the operations of the mind.

Forc'd by *reflective* reason I confess,
That human science is uncertain guess. *Prior.*

REFLE'CTOR. *n. s.* [from *reflect.*] Considerer.

There is scarce any thing that nature has made, or that men do suffer, whence the devout *reflector* cannot take an occasion of an aspiring meditation. *Boyle on Colours.*

REFLE'X. *adj.* [*reflexus*, Lat.] Directed backward.

The motions of my mind are as obvious to the *reflex* act of the soul, or the turning of the intellectual eye inward upon its own actions, as the passions of my sense are obvious to my sense; I see the object, and I perceive that I see it. *Hale.*

The order and beauty of the inanimate parts of the world, the discernible ends of them do evince by a *reflex* argument, that it is the workmanship, not of blind mechanism or blinder chance, but of an intelligent and benign agent. *Bentley.*

REFLE'X. *n. s.* [*reflexus*, Lat.] Reflection.

There was no other way for angels to sin, but by *reflex* of their understandings upon themselves. *Hooker.*

I'll say yon gray is not the morning's eye,
'Tis but the pale *reflex* of Cynthia's brow. *Shakesp.*

REFLEXIBI'LITY. *n. s.* [from *reflexible.*] The quality of being reflexible.

Reflexibility of rays is their disposition to be reflected or turned back into the same medium from any other medium, upon whose surface they fall; and rays are more or less reflexible, which are turned back more or less easily. *Newton.*

REFLE'XIBLE. *adj.* [from *reflexus*, Lat.] Capable to be thrown back.

Sir Isaac Newton has demonstrated, by convincing experiments, that the light of the sun consists of rays differently refrangible and *reflexible*; and that those rays are differently *reflexible*, that are differently refrangible. *Cheyne.*

REFLE'XIVE. *adj.* [*reflexus*, Lat.] Having respect to something past.

That assurance *reflexive* cannot be a divine faith, but at the most an human, yet such as perhaps I may have no doubting mixed with. *Hammond's Practical Catechism.*

REFLE'XIVELY. *adv.* [from *reflexive.*] In a backward direction.

Solomon tells us life and death are in the power of the tongue, and that not only directly in regard of the good or ill we may do to others, but *reflexively* also, in respect of what may rebound to ourselves. *Government of the Tongue.*

REFLOA'T. *n. s.* [*re* and *float.*] Ebb; reflux.

The main float and *refloat* of the sea, is by consent of the universe, as part of the diurnal motion. *Bacon.*

To REFLOU'RISH. *v. a.* [*re* and *flourish.*] To flourish anew.

Virtue given for lost
Revives, *reflourishes*, then vigorous most,
When most unactive deem'd. *Milton's Agonistes.*

To REFLO'W. *v. n.* [*refluer*, Fr. *re* and *flow.*] To flow back.

REFLU'ENT. *adj.* [*refluens*, Lat.] Running back; flowing back.

The liver receives the *refluent* blood almost from all the parts of the abdomen. *Arbuthnot on Aliments.*

Tell, by what paths,
Back to the fountain's head the sea conveys
The *refluent* rivers, and the land repays. *Blackmore.*

REFLU'X. *n. s.* [*reflux*, Fr. *refluxus*, Lat.] Backward course of water.

Besides
Mine own that 'bide upon me, all from me
Shall with a fierce *reflux* on me redound. *Milton.*

The variety of the flux and *reflux* of Euripus, or whether the same do ebb and flow seven times a day, is incontravertible. *Brown's Vulgar Errours.*

REFOCILLA'TION. *n. s.* [*refocillo*, Lat.] Restoration of strength by refreshment.

To REFO'RM. *v. a.* [*reformo*, Lat. *reformer*, Fr.] To change from worse to better.

A sect in England, following the very same rule of policy, seeketh to *reform* even the French reformation, and purge out from thence also dregs of popery. *Hooker, b. iv. s. 8.*

Seat worthier of Gods, was built
With second thoughts, *reforming* what was old. *Milton.*

May no such storm
Fall on our times, where ruin must *reform*. *Denham.*

Now low'ring looks presage approaching storms,
And now prevailing love her face *reforms*. *Dryden.*

One cannot attempt the perfect *reforming* the languages of the world, without rendering himself ridiculous. *Locke.*

The example alone of a vicious prince will corrupt an age; but that of a good one will not *reform* it. *Swift.*

To REFO'RM. *v. n.* To make a change from worse to better.

Was his doctrine of the mass struck out in this conflict? or did it give him occasion of *reforming* in this point? *Atterbury.*

REFO'RM. *n. s.* [French.] Reformation.

REFORMA'TION. *n. s.* [*reformation*, Fr. from *reform.*]

1. Change from worse to better.

Never came *reformation* in a flood
With such a heady current, scow'ring faults;
Nor ever Hydra-headed wilfulness
So soon did lose his seat, as in this king. *Shakesp. Henry V.*

Satire lashes vice into *reformation*. *Dryden.*

The pagan converts mention this great *reformation* of those who had been the greatest sinners, with that sudden and surprising change, which the christian religion made in the lives of the most profligate. *Addison.*

2. The change of religion from the corruptions of popery to its primitive state.

The burden of the *reformation* lay on Luther's shoulders. *Atterbury.*

REFO'RMER. *n. s.* [from *reform.*]

1. One who makes a change for the better; an amender.

Publick *reformers* had need first practise that on their own hearts, which they purpose to try on others. *King Charles.*

The complaint is more general, than the endeavours to redress it: Abroad every man would be a *reformer*, how very few at home. *Sprat's Sermons.*

It was honour enough, to behold the English churches reformed; that is, delivered from the *reformers*. *South.*

2. Those who changed religion from popish corruptions and innovations.

Our first *reformers* were famous confessors and martyrs all over the world. *Bacon.*

To REFRA'CT. *v. a.* [*refractus*, Lat.] To break the natural course of rays.

If its angle of incidence be large, and the refractive power of the medium not very strong to throw it far from the perpendicular, it will be *refracted*. *Cheyne's Phil. Princ.*

Rays of light are urged by the *refracting* media. *Cheyne.*

Refracted from yon eastern cloud,
The grand ethereal bow shoots up. *Thomson.*

REFRA'CTION. *n. s.* [*refraction*, Fr.]

Refraction, in general, is the incurvation or change of determination in the body moved, which happens to it whilst it enters or penetrates any medium: in dioptricks, it is the variation of a ray of light from that right line, which it would have passed on in, had not the density of the medium turned it aside. *Harris.*

Refraction, out of the rarer medium into the denser, is made towards the perpendicular. *Newton's Opticks.*

REFRA'CTIVE. *adj.* [from *refract.*] Having the power of refraction.

Those superficies of transparent bodies reflect the greatest quantity of light, which have the greatest refracting power; that is, which intercede mediums that differ most in their *refractive* densities. *Newton's Opticks.*

RE'FRACTORINESS. *n. s.* [from *refractory.*] Sullen obstinacy.

I did never allow any man's *refractoriness* against the privileges and orders of the houses. *King Charles.*

Great complaint was made by the presbyterian gang, of my *refractoriness* to obey the parliament's order. *Saunderson.*

REFRA'CTORY. *adj.* [*refractaire*, Fr. *refractarius*, Lat. and so should be written *refractary*. It is now accented on the first syllable, but by *Shakespeare* on the second.] Obstinate; perverse; contumacious.

There is a law in each well-order'd nation,
To curb those raging appetites that are
Most disobedient and *refractory*. *Shakesp.*

A rough hewn seaman, being brought before a wise justice for some misdemeanor, was by him ordered to be sent away to prison, and was *refractory* after he heard his doom, insomuch as he would not stir a foot from the place where he stood; saying, it was better to stand where he was, than go to a worse place. *Bacon's Apophthegms.*

Vulgar compliance with any illegal and extravagant ways, like violent motions in nature, soon grows weary of itself, and ends in a *refractory* sullenness. *King Charles.*

Refractory mortal! if thou will not truſt thy friends, take what follows; know aſſuredly, before next full moon, that thou wilt be hung up in chains. *Arbuthnot's Hiſt. of J. Bull.*

Theſe atoms of theirs may have it in them, but they are *refractory* and ſullen; and therefore, like men of the ſame tempers, muſt be banged and buffeted into reaſon. *Bentley.*

Re'fragable. *adj.* [*refragabilis*, Lat.] Capable of confutation and conviction.

To Refrai'n. *v. a.* [*refrener*, Fr. *re* and *frænum*, Lat.] To hold back; to keep from action.

Hold not thy tongue, O God, keep not ſtill ſilence; *refrain* not thyſelf. *Pſalm* lxxxiii. 1.

My ſon, walk not thou in the way with them, *refrain* thy foot from their path. *Prov.* i. 15.

Nor from the holy one of heav'n
Refrain'd his tongue. *Milton.*

Neptune aton'd, his wrath ſhall now *refrain*,
Or thwart the ſynod of the gods in vain. *Pope.*

To Refrai'n. *v. n.* To forbear; to abſtain; to ſpare.

In what place, or upon what conſideration ſoever it be, they do it, were it in their own opinion of no force being done, they would undoubtedly *refrain* to do it. *Hooker.*

For my name's ſake will I defer mine anger, and *refrain* for thee, that I cut thee not off. *Iſ.* xlviii. 9.

That they fed not on fleſh, at leaſt the faithful party before the flood, may become more probable, becauſe they *refrained* therefrom ſome time after. *Brown's Vulg. Err.*

Refrangibi'lity. *n. ſ.* [from *refrangible*.]

Refrangibility of the rays of light, is their diſpoſition to be refracted or turned out of their way, in paſſing out of one tranſparent body or medium into another. *Newton.*

REFRA'NGIBLE. *adj.* [*re* and *frango*, Lat.]

As ſome rays are more *refrangible* than others; that is, are more turned out of their courſe, in paſſing from one medium to another; it follows, that after ſuch refraction, they will be ſeparated, and their diſtinct colour obſerved. *Locke.*

Refrena'tion. *n. ſ.* [*re* and *fræno*, Lat.] The act of reſtraining.

To REFRE'SH. *v. a.* [*refraiſcher*, Fr. *refrigero*, Lat.]

1. To recreate; to relieve after pain, fatigue or want.

Service ſhall with ſteeled ſinews toil;
And labour ſhall *refreſh* itſelf with hope. *Shakeſp.*

Muſick was ordain'd to *refreſh* the mind of man,
After his ſtudies or his uſual pain. *Shakeſp.*

He was in no danger to be overtaken; ſo that he was content to *refreſh* his men. *Clarendon, b.* viii.

His meals are coarſe and ſhort, his employment warrantable, his ſleep certain and *refreſhing*, neither interrupted with the laſhes of a guilty mind, nor the aches of a crazy body. *South.*

If you would have trees to thrive, take care that no plants be near them, which may deprive them of nouriſhment, or hinder *refreſhings* and helps that they might receive. *Mortim.*

2. To improve by new touches any thing impaired.

The reſt *refreſh* the ſcaly ſnakes, that fold
The ſhield of Pallas, and renew their gold. *Dryden.*

3. To refrigerate; to cool.

A dew coming after heat *refreſheth*. *Ecclus.* xliii. 22.

Refre'sher. *n. ſ.* [from *refreſh*.] That which refreſhes.

The kind *refreſher* of the ſummer heats. *Thomſon.*

Refre'shment. *n. ſ.* [from *refreſh*.]

1. Relief after pain, want or fatigue.

2. That which gives relief, as food, reſt.

He was full of agony and horrour upon the approach of a diſmal death, and ſo had moſt need of the *refreſhments* of ſociety, and the friendly aſſiſtances of his diſciples. *South.*

Such honeſt *refreſhments* and comforts of life, our chriſtian liberty has made it lawful for us to uſe. *Sprat.*

Refri'gerant. *adj.* [*refrigerant*, Fr. from *refrigerate*.] Cooling; mitigating heat.

In the cure of gangrenes, you muſt beware of dry heat, and reſort to things that are *refrigerant*, with an inward warmth and virtue of cheriſhing. *Bacon.*

If it ariſe from an external cauſe, apply *refrigerants*, without any preceding evacuation. *Wiſeman's Surgery.*

To REFRI'GERATE. *v. a.* [*refrigero*, *re* and *frigus*, Lat.] To cool.

The great breezes, which the motion of the air in great circles, ſuch as the girdle of the world, produceth, do *refrigerate*; and therefore in thoſe parts noon is nothing ſo hot, when the breezes are great, as about ten of the clock in the forenoon. *Bacon's Natural Hiſtory.*

Whether they be *refrigerated* inclinatorily or ſomewhat equinoxically, though in a leſſer degree, they diſcover ſome verticity. *Brown's Vulgar Errours.*

Refrigera'tion. *n. ſ.* [*refrigeratio*, Lat. *refrigeration*, Fr.] The act of cooling; the ſtate of being cooled.

Divers do ſtut; the cauſe may be the *refrigeration* of the tongue, whereby it is leſs apt to move. *Bacon.*

If the mere *refrigeration* of the air would fit it for breathing, this might be ſomewhat helped with bellows. *Wilkins.*

Refri'gerative. } *adj.* [*refrigeratif*, Fr. *refrigeratorius*, Lat.]
Refri'geratory. } Cooling; having the power to cool.

Refri'geratory. *n. ſ.*

1. That part of a diſtilling veſſel that is placed about the head of a ſtill, and filled with water to cool the condenſing vapours; but this is now generally done by a worm or ſpiral pipe, turning through a tub of cold water. *Quincy.*

2. Any thing internally cooling.

A delicate wine, and a durable *refrigeratory*. *Mortimer.*

REFRI'GERIUM. *n. ſ.* [Latin.] Cool refreſhment; refrigeration.

It muſt be acknowledged, the ancients have talked much of annual *refrigeriums*, reſpites or intervals of puniſhment to the damned; as particularly on the feſtivals. *South.*

Reft. *part. pret.* of *reave*.

1. Deprived; taken away.

Thus we well left, he better *reft*,
In heaven to take his place,
That by like life and death, at laſt,
We may obtain like grace. *Aſcham's Schoolmaſter.*

I, in a deſperate bay of death,
Like a poor bark, of ſails and tackling *reft*,
Ruſh all to pieces on thy rocky boſom. *Shakeſp.*

Another ſhip had ſeiz'd on us,
And would have *reft* the fiſhers of their prey. *Shakeſp.*

Our dying hero, from the continent
Raviſh'd whole towns, and forts from Spaniards *reft*,
As his laſt legacy to Britain left. *Waller.*

2. *Preterite* of *reave*. Took away.

So 'twixt them both, they not a lamkin left,
And when lambs fail'd, the old ſheeps lives they *reft*. *Spenſ.*

About his ſhoulders broad he threw
An hairy hide of ſome wild beaſt, whom he
In ſavage foreſt by adventure ſlew,
And *reft* the ſpoil his ornament to be. *Spenſer.*

RE'FUGE. *n. ſ.* [*refuge*, Fr. *refugium*, Lat.]

1. Shelter from any danger or diſtreſs; protection.

Rocks, dens and caves! but I in none of theſe
Find place or *refuge*. *Milton's Par. Loſt, b.* ix.

The young ones, ſuppoſed to break through the belly of the dam, will, upon any fright, for protection run into it; for then the old one receives them in at her mouth, which way, the fright being paſt, they will return again; which is a peculiar way of *refuge*. *Brown's Vulgar Errours.*

Thoſe, who take *refuge* in a multitude, have an Arian council to anſwer for. *Atterbury.*

2. That which gives ſhelter or protection.

The Lord will be a *refuge* for the oppreſſed; a *refuge* in times of trouble. *Pſalm* ix. 9.

They ſhall be your *refuge* from the avenger of blood. *Joſ.*

Fair majeſty, the *refuge* and redreſs
Of thoſe whom fate purſues. *Dryden.*

3. Expedient in diſtreſs.

This laſt old man,
Whom with a crack'd heart I have ſent to Rome,
Lov'd me above the meaſure of a father:
Their lateſt *refuge* was to ſend him. *Shakeſp. Coriolanus.*

4. Expedient in general.

Light muſt be ſupplied among graceful *refuges*, by terracing any ſtory in danger of darkneſs. *Wotton.*

To Re'fuge. *v. a.* [*refugier*, Fr. from the noun.] To ſhelter; to protect.

Silly beggars,
Who ſitting in the ſtocks, *refuge* their ſhame,
That many have, and others muſt, ſit there. *Shakeſp.*

Dreads the vengeance of her injur'd lord;
Ev'n by thoſe gods, who *refug'd* her, abhorr'd. *Dryden.*

Refugee'. *n. ſ.* [*refugié*, Fr.] One who flies to ſhelter or protection.

Poor *refugees*, at firſt they purchaſe here;
And ſoon as denizen'd, they domineer. *Dryden.*

This is become more neceſſary in ſome of their governments, ſince ſo many *refugees* ſettled among them. *Addiſon.*

Refu'lgence. *n. ſ.* [from *refulgent*.] Splendour; brightneſs.

REFU'LGENT. *adj.* [*refulgens*, Latin.] Bright; ſhining; glittering; ſplendid.

He neither might, nor wiſh'd to know
A more *refulgent* light. *Waller.*

So conſpicuous and *refulgent* a truth is that of God's being the author of man's felicity, that the diſpute is not ſo much concerning the thing, as concerning the manner of it. *Boyle.*

Agamemnon's train,
When his *refulgent* arms flaſh'd through the ſhady plain,
Fled from his well-known face. *Dryden's Æneis.*

To Refu'nd. *v. n.* [*refundo*, Lat.]

1. To pour back.

Were the humours of the eye tinctured with any colour, they would *refund* that colour upon the object, and ſo it would not be repreſented as in itſelf it is. *Ray.*

2. To repay what is received; to reſtore.

A governor, that had pilled the people, was, for receiving of bribes, ſentenced to *refund* what he had wrongfully taken. *L'Eſtrange.*

Such wise men as himself account all that is past, to be also gone; and know, that there can be no gain in *refunding*, nor any profit in paying debts. *South.*

How to Icarius, in the bridal hour,
Shall I, by waste undone, *refund* the dow'r. *Pope.*

3. *Swift* has somewhere the absurd phrase, *to* refund *himself*, for to *reimburse*.

Refu'sal. *n. s.* [from *refuse*.]

1. The act of refusing; denial of any thing demanded or solicited.

God has born with all his weak and obstinate *refusals* of grace, and has given him time day after day. *Rogers.*

2. The preemption; the right of having any thing before another; option.

When employments go a begging for want of hands, they shall be sure to have the *refusal*. *Swift.*

To REFU'SE. *v. a.* [*refuser*, Fr.]

1. To deny what is solicited or required.

If he should chuse the right casket, you should *refuse* to perform his father's will, if you should *refuse* to accept him. *Shakesp. Merchant of Venice.*

Common experience has justly a mighty influence on the minds of men, to make them give or *refuse* credit to any thing proposed. *Locke.*

Women are made as they themselves would choose;
Too proud to ask, too humble to *refuse*. *Garth.*

2. To reject; to dismiss without a grant.

I may neither chuse whom I would, nor *refuse* whom I dislike. *Shakesp. Merchant of Venice.*

To Refu'se. *v. n.* Not to accept.

Wonder not then what God for you saw good
If I *refuse* not, but convert, as you,
To proper substance. *Milton.*

Re'fuse. *adj.* [from the verb. The noun has its accent on the first syllable, the verb on the second.] Unworthy of reception; left when the rest is taken.

Every thing vile and *refuse* they destroyed. *Sam.* xv. 9.

Please to bestow on him the *refuse* letters; he hopes by printing them to get a plentiful provision. *Spectator.*

Re'fuse. *n. s.* That which remains disregarded when the rest is taken.

We dare not disgrace our worldly superiours with offering unto them such *refuse*, as we bring unto God himself. *Hook.*

Many kinds have much *refuse*, which countervails that which they have excellent. *Bacon.*

I know not whether it be more shame or wonder, to see that men can so put off ingenuity, as to descend to so base a vice; yet we daily see it done, and that not only by the scum and *refuse* of the people. *Government of the Tongue.*

Down with the falling stream the *refuse* run,
To raise with joyful news his drooping son. *Dryden.*

This humourist keeps more than he wants, and gives a vast *refuse* of his superfluities to purchase heaven. *Addison.*

Refu'ser. *n. s.* [from *refuse*.] He who refuses.

Some few others are the only *refusers* and condemners of this catholick practice. *Taylor.*

Refu'tal. *n. s.* [from *refute*.] Refutation. *Dict.*

Refuta'tion. *n. s.* [*refutatio*, Lat. *refutation*, Fr. from *refute*.] The act of refuting; the act of proving false or erroneous.

'Tis such miserable absurd stuff, that we will not honour it with especial *refutation*. *Bentley.*

To REFU'TE. *v. a.* [*refuto*, Lat. *refuter*, Fr.] To prove false or erroneous. Applied to persons or things.

Self-destruction sought, *refutes*
That excellence thought in thee. *Milton's Par. Lost.*

He knew that there were so many witnesses in these two miracles, that it was impossible to *refute* such multitudes. *Add.*

To Regai'n. *v. a.* [*regagner*, Fr. *re* and *gain*.] To recover; to gain anew.

Hopeful to *regain*
Thy love, from thee I will not hide
What thoughts in my unquiet breast are ris'n. *Milton.*

We've driven back
These heathen Saxons, and *regain'd* our earth,
As earth recovers from an ebbing tide. *Dryden.*

As soon as the mind *regains* the power to stop or continue any of these motions of the body or thoughts, we then consider the man as a free agent. *Locke.*

Re'gal. *adj.* [*regal*, Fr. *regalis*, Lat.] Royal; kingly.

Edward, duke of York,
Usurps the *regal* title and the seat
Of England's true anointed lawful heir. *Shakesp.*

Why am I sent for to a king,
Before I have shook off the *regal* thoughts
Wherewith I reign'd. *Shakesp. Richard* II.

With them comes a third of *regal* port,
But faded splendour wan, who by his gait
And fierce demeanour seems the prince of hell. *Milton.*

When was there ever a better prince on the throne than the present queen? I do not talk of her government, her love of the people, or qualities that are purely *regal*; but her piety, charity, temperance and conjugal love. *Swift.*

Re'gal. *n. s.* [*regale*, Fr.] A musical instrument.

The sounds, that produce tones, are ever from such bodies as are in their parts and ports equal; and such are in the nightingale pipes of *regals* or organs. *Bacon.*

REGA'LE. *n. s.* [Latin.] The prerogative of monarchy.

To REGA'LE. *v. a.* [*regaler*, Fr. *regalare*, Italian.] To refresh; to entertain; to gratify.

I with warming puff *regale* chill'd fingers. *Philips.*

Rega'lement. *n. s.* [*regalement*, Fr.] Refreshment; entertainment.

The muses still require
Humid *regalement*, nor will aught avail
Imploring Phœbus with unmoisten'd lips. *Philips.*

REGA'LIA. *n. s.* [Latin.] Ensigns of royalty.

Rega'lity. *n. s.* [*regalis*, Latin.] Royalty; sovereignty; kingship.

Behold the image of mortality,
And feeble nature cloth'd with fleshly 'tire,
When raging passion with fierce tyranny,
Robs reason of her due *regality*. *Fairy Queen.*

He neither could, nor would, yield to any diminution of the crown of France, in territory or *regality*. *Bacon.*

He came partly in by the sword, and had high courage in all points of *regality*. *Bacon's Henry* VII.

The majesty of England might hang like Mahomet's tomb by a magnetick charm, between the privileges of the two houses, in airy imagination of *regality*. *King Charles.*

To REGA'RD. *v. a.* [*regarder*, Fr.]

1. To value; to attend to as worthy of notice.

This aspect of mine,
The best *regarded* virgins of our clime
Have lov'd. *Shakesp. Merchant of Venice.*

He denies
To know their God, or message to *regard*. *Milton.*

2. To observe; to remark.

If much you note him,
You offend him; feed and *regard* him not. *Shakesp.*

3. To mind as an object of grief or terrour.

The king marvelled at the young man's courage, for that he nothing *regarded* the pains. 2 *Mac.* vii. 12.

4. To observe religiously.

He that *regardeth* the day, *regardeth* it unto the Lord; and he that *regardeth* not the day, to the Lord he doth not *regard* it. *Rom.* xiv. 6.

5. To pay attention to.

He that observeth the wind shall never sow, and he that *regardeth* the clouds shall never reap. *Proverbs.*

6. To respect; to have relation to.

7. To look towards.

It is a peninsula, which *regardeth* the mainland. *Sandys.*

Rega'rd. *n. s.* [*regard*, Fr. from the verb.]

1. Attention as to a matter of importance.

The nature of the sentence he is to pronounce, the rule of judgment by which he will proceed, requires that a particular *regard* be had to our observation of this precept. *Atterbury.*

2. Respect; reverence.

To him they had *regard*, because long he had bewitched them. *Acts* viii. 11.

With some *regard* to what is just and right,
They'll lead their lives. *Milton.*

3. Note; eminence.

Mac Ferlagh was a man of meanest *regard* amongst them, neither having wealth nor power. *Spenser on Ireland.*

4. Respect; account.

Change was thought necessary, in *regard* of the great hurt which the church did receive by a number of things then in use. *Hooker, b.* iv. *s.* 14.

5. Relation; reference.

How best we may
Compose our present evils, with *regard*
Of what we are and where. *Milton.*

Their business is to address all the ranks of mankind, and persuade them to pursue and persevere in virtue, with *regard* to themselves; in justice and goodness, with *regard* to their neighbours; and piety towards God. *Watts.*

6. [*Regard*, Fr.] Look; aspect directed to another.

Soft words to his fierce passion she assay'd;
But her with stern *regard* he thus repell'd. *Milton.*

He, surpriz'd with humble joy, survey'd
One sweet *regard*, shot by the royal maid. *Dryden.*

7. Prospect; object of sight. Not proper, nor in use.

Throw out our eyes for brave Othello,
Even till we make the main and th' aerial blue
An indistinct *regard*. *Shakesp. Othello.*

Rega'rdable. *adj.* [from *regard*.]

1. Observable.

I cannot discover this difference of the badger's legs, although the *regardable* side be defined, and the brevity by most imputed unto the left. *Brown's Vulgar Errours.*

2. Worthy of notice.

Tintogel, more famous for his antiquity, than *regardable* for his present estate, abutteth on the sea. *Carew.*

Rega'rder. *n. s.* [from *regard*.] One that regards.

Rega'rdful.

REGA'RDFUL. *adj.* [*regard* and *full.*] Attentive; taking notice of.

Bryan was so *regardful* of his charge, as he never disposed any matter, but first he acquainted the general. *Hayward.*

Let a man be very tender and *regardful* of every pious motion made by the spirit of God to his heart. *South.*

REGA'RDFULLY. *adv.* [from *regardful.*]

1. Attentively; heedfully.
2. Respectfully.

Is this th' Athenian minion, whom the world
Voic'd so *regardfully*. *Shakesp. Timon of Athens.*

REGA'RDLESS. *adj.* [from *regard.*] Heedless; negligent; inattentive.

He likest is to fall into mischance,
That is *regardless* of his governance. *Spenser.*

Regardless of the bliss wherein he sat,
Second to thee, offer'd himself to die
For man's offence. *Milton's Par. Lost, b.* iii.

We must learn to be deaf and *regardless* of other things, besides the present subject of our meditation. *Watts.*

REGA'RDLESLY. *adv.* [from *regardless.*] Without heed.

REGA'RDLESNESS. *n. s.* [from *regardless.*] Heedlessness; negligence; inattention.

REGE'NCY. *n. s.* [from *regent.*]

1. Authority; government.

As Christ took manhood, that by it he might be capable of death, whereunto he humbled himself; so because manhood is the proper subject of compassion and feeling pity, which maketh the scepter of Christ's *regency* even in the kingdom of heaven amiable. *Hooker, b.* v. *s.* 51.

Men have knowledge and strength to fit them for action: women affection, for their better compliance; and herewith beauty to compensate their subjection, by giving them an equivalent *regency* over men. *Grew.*

2. Vicarious government.

This great minister, finding the *regency* shaken by the faction of so many great ones within, and awed by the terror of the Spanish greatness without, durst begin a war. *Temple.*

3. The district governed by a vicegerent.

Regions they pass'd, the mighty *regencies*
Of seraphim. *Milton.*

4. Those to whom vicarious regality is intrusted.

To REGE'NERATE. *v. a.* [*regenero*, Lat.]

1. To reproduce; to produce anew.

Albeit the son of this earl of Desmond, who lost his head, were restored to the earldom; yet could not the king's grace *regenerate* obedience in that degenerate house, but it grew rather more wild. *Davies on Ireland.*

Through all the soil a genial ferment spreads,
Regenerates the plants, and new adorns the meads. *Blackmore.*

An alkali, poured to that which is mixed with an acid, raiseth an effervescence, at the cessation of which, the salts, of which the acid is composed, will be *regenerated.* *Arbuthnot.*

2. [*Regenerer*, Fr.] To make to be born anew; to renew by change of carnal nature to a christian life.

No sooner was a convert initiated, but by an easy figure he became a new man, and both acted and looked upon himself as one *regenerated* and born a second time into another state of existence. *Addison on the Christian Religion.*

REGE'NERATE. *adj.* [*regeneratus*, Lat.]

1. Reproduced.

Thou! the earthly author of my blood,
Whose youthful spirit, in me *regenerate*,
Doth with a twofold vigor lift me up
To reach at victory. *Shakesp. Richard* II.

2. Born anew by grace to a christian life.

For from the mercy-seat above,
Prevenient grace descending, had remov'd
The stony from their hearts, and made new flesh
Regenerate grow instead. *Milton.*

If you fulfil this resolution, though you fall sometimes by infirmity; nay, though you should fall into some greater act, even of deliberate sin, which you presently retract by confession and amendment, you are nevertheless in a *regenerate* estate, you live the life of a christian here, and shall inherit the reward that is promised to such in a glorious immortality hereafter. *Wake's Preparation for Death.*

REGENERA'TION. *n. s.* [*regeneration*, Fr.] New birth; birth by grace from carnal affections to a christian life.

He saved us by the washing of *regeneration*, and renewing of the Holy Ghost. *Tit.* iii. 5.

REGE'NERATENESS. *n. s.* [from *regenerate.*] The state of being regenerate.

RE'GENT. *adj.* [*regent*, Fr. *regens*, Lat.]

1. Governing; ruling.

The operations of human life flow not from the corporeal moles, but from some other active *regent* principle that resides in the body, or governs it, which we call the soul. *Hale.*

2. Exercising vicarious authority.

He together calls the *regent* pow'rs
Under him *regent*. *Milton's Par. Lost, b.* iii.

RE'GENT. *n. s.*

1. Governour; ruler.

Now for once beguil'd
Uriel, though *regent* of the sun, and held
The sharpest-sighted spirit of all in heav'n. *Milton.*

Neither of these are any impediment, because the *regent* thereof is of an infinite immensity. *Hale.*

But let a heifer with gilt horns be led
To Juno, *regent* of the marriage bed. *Dryden.*

2. One invested with vicarious royalty.

Lord *regent*, I do greet your excellence
With letters of commission from the king. *Shakesp.*

RE'GENTSHIP. *n. s.* [from *regent.*]

1. Power of governing.
2. Deputed authority.

If York have ill demean'd himself in France,
Then let him be deny'd the *regentship*. *Shakesp.*

REGERMINA'TION. *n. s.* [*re* and *germination.*] The act of sprouting again.

RE'GIBLE. *adj.* Governable. *Dict.*

RE'GICIDE. *n. s.* [*regicida*, Lat.]

1. Murderer of his king.

I through the mazes of the bloody field,
Hunted your sacred life; which that I miss'd
Was the propitious error of my fate,
Not of my soul; my soul's a *regicide*. *Dryden.*

2. [*Regicidium*, Lat.] Murder of his king.

Were it not for this amulet, how were it possible for any to think they may venture upon perjury, sacrilege, murder, *regicide*, without impeachment to their saintship. *D. of Piety.*

Did fate or we, when great Atrides dy'd,
Urge the bold traitor to the *regicide*. *Pope's Odyssey.*

RE'GIMEN. *n. s.* [Latin.] That care in diet and living, that is suitable to every particular course of medicine.

Yet should some neighbour feel a pain,
Just in the parts where I complain,
How many a message would he send?
What hearty prayers, that I should mend?
Enquire what *regimen* I kept,
What gave me ease, and how I slept. *Swift.*

RE'GIMENT. *n. s.* [*regement*, old Fr.]

1. Established government; polity. Not in use.

We all make complaint of the iniquity of our times, not unjustly, for the days are evil; but compare them with those times wherein there were no civil societies, with those times wherein there was as yet no manner of publick *regiment* established, and we have surely good cause to think, that God hath blessed us exceedingly. *Hooker, b.* i. *s.* 10.

The corruption of our nature being presupposed, we may not deny, but that the law of nature doth now require of necessity some kind of *regiment*. *Hooker, b.* i. *s.* 10.

2. Rule; authority. Not in use.

The *regiment* of the soul over the body, is the *regiment* of the more active part over the passive. *Hale.*

3. [*Regiment*, Fr.] A body of soldiers under one colonel.

Th' adulterous Antony turns you off,
And gives his potent *regiment* to a trull. *Shakesp.*

Higher to the plain we'll set forth,
In best appointment, all our *regiments*. *Shakesp.*

The elder did whole *regiments* afford,
The younger brought his conduct and his sword. *Waller.*

The standing *regiments*, the fort, the town,
All but this wicked sister are our own. *Waller.*

Now thy aid
Eugene, with *regiments* unequal prest,
Awaits. *Philips.*

REGIME'NTAL. *adj.* [from *regiment.*] Belonging to a regiment; military.

RE'GION. *n. s.* [*region*, Fr. *regio*, Lat.]

1. Tract of land; country; tract of space.

All the *regions*
Do seemingly revolt; and, who resist,
Are mock'd for valiant ignorance. *Shakesp.*

Her eyes in heav'n
Would through the airy *region* stream so bright,
That birds would sing, and think it were not night. *Shak.*

The upper *regions* of the air perceive the collection of the matter of tempests before the air below. *Bacon.*

They rag'd the goddess, and with fury fraught,
The restless *regions* of the storms she sought. *Dryden.*

2. Part of the body.

The bow is bent and drawn, make from the shaft.
—Let it fall rather, though the fork invade
The *region* of my heart. *Shakesp. King Lear.*

3. Place; rank.

The gentleman kept company with the wild prince and Poins: he is of too high a *region*; he knows too much. *Shak.*

RE'GISTER. *n. s.* [*registre*, Fr. *registrum*, Lat.] An account of any thing regularly kept.

Joy may you have, and everlasting fame,
Of late most hard atchievement by you done,
For which inrolled is your glorious name
In heavenly *registers* above the sun. *Fairy Queen.*

Sir

Sir John, as you have one eye upon my follies, as you hear them unfolded, turn another into the *register* of your own. *Sha.*

This island, as appeareth by faithful *registers* of those times, had ships of great content. *Bacon's New Atlantis.*

Of these experiments, our friend, pointing at the *register* of this dialogue, will perhaps give you a more particular account. *Boyle.*

For a conspiracy against the emperor Claudius, it was ordered that Scribonianus's name and consulate should be effaced out of all publick *registers* and inscriptions. *Addison.*

2. [*Registrarius*, law Lat.] The officer whose business is to write and keep the register.

To RE'GISTER. *v. a.* [*registrer*, Fr. from the noun.]

1. To record; to preserve from oblivion by authentick accounts.

The Roman emperors *registered* their most remarkable buildings, as well as actions. *Addison's Remarks on Italy.*

2. To enrol; to set down in a list.

Such follow him, as shall be *register'd*;
Part good, part bad: of bad the longer scrowl. *Milton.*

RE'GISTRY. *n. s.* [from *register*.]

1. The act of inserting in the register.

A little fee was to be paid for the *registry*. *Graunt.*

2. The place where the register is kept.

3. A series of facts recorded.

I wonder why a *registry* has not been kept in the college of physicians of things invented. *Temple.*

RE'GLEMENT. *n. s.* [French.] Regulation. Not used.

To speak of the reformation and *reglement* of usury, by the balance of commodities and discommodities thereof, two things are to be reconciled. *Bacon's Essays.*

RE'GLET. *n. s.* [*reglette*, from *regle*, Fr.] Ledge of wood exactly planed, by which printers separate their lines in pages widely printed.

RE'GNANT. *adj.* [French.] Reigning; predominant; prevalent; having power.

Princes are shy of their successors, and there may be reasonably supposed in queens *regnant* a little proportion of tenderness that way, more than in kings. *Wotton.*

The law was *regnant*, and confin'd his thought,
Hell was not conquer'd, when the poet wrote. *Waller.*
His guilt is clear, his proofs are pregnant,
A traytor to the vices *regnant*. *Swift's Miscellanies.*

To REGO'RGE. *v. a.* [*re* and *gorge*.]

1. To vomit up; to throw back.

It was scoffingly said, he had eaten the king's goose, and did then *regorge* the feathers. *Hayward.*

2. To swallow eagerly.

Drunk with wine,
And fat *regorg'd* of bulls and goats. *Milton's Agonistes.*

3. [*Regorger*, Fr.] To swallow back.

As tides at highest mark *regorge* the flood,
So fate, that could no more improve their joy,
Took a malicious pleasure to destroy. *Dryden.*

To REGRA'FT. *v. a.* [*regreffer*, Fr. *re* and *graft*.] To graft again.

Oft *regrafting* the same cions, may make fruit greater. *Bac.*

To REGRA'NT. *v. a.* [*re* and *grant*.] To grant back.

He, by letters patents, incorporated them by the name of the dean and chapter of Trinity-church in Norwich, and *regranted* their lands to them. *Ayliffe's Parergon.*

To REGRA'TE. *v. a.*

1. To offend; to shock.

The cloathing of the tortoise and viper rather *regrateth*, than pleaseth the eye. *Derham's Physico-Theology.*

2. [*Regratter*, Fr.] To engross; to forestal.

Neither should they buy any corn, unless it were to make malt thereof; for by such engrossing and *regrating*, the dearth, that commonly reigneth in England, hath been caused. *Spens.*

REGRA'TER. *n. s.* [*regrattier*, Fr. from *regrate*.] Forestaller; engrosser.

To REGREE'T. *v. a.* [*re* and *greet*.] To resalute; to greet a second time.

Hereford, on pain of death,
Till twice five summers have enrich'd our fields,
Shall not *regreet* our fair dominions,
But lead the stranger paths of banishment. *Shakesp.*

REGREE'T. *n. s.* [from the verb.] Return or exchange of salutation. Not in use.

And shall these hands, so newly join'd in love,
Unyoke this seizure, and this kind *regreet?*
Play fast and loose with faith? *Shakesp. King John.*

REGRE'SS. *n. s.* [*regrès*, Fr. *regressus*, Latin.] Passage back; power of passing back.

'Tis their natural place which they always tend to; and from which there is no progress nor *regress*. *Burnet.*

To REGRE'SS. *v. n.* [*regressus*, Lat.] To go back; to return; to pass back to the former state or place.

All being forced unto fluent consistences, naturally *regress* unto their former solidities. *Brown.*

REGRE'SSION. *n. s.* [*regressus*, Lat.] The act of returning or going back.

To desire there were no God, were plainly to unwish their own being, which must needs be annihilated in the subtraction of that essence, which substantially supporteth them, and restrains from *regression* into nothing. *Brown.*

REGRE'T. *n. s.* [*regret*, Fr. *regretto*, Italian. *Prior* has used it in the plural; but, I believe, without authority.]

1. Vexation at something past; bitterness of reflection.

I never bare any touch of conscience with greater *regret*. *King Charles.*

A passionate *regret* at sin, a grief and sadness at its memory, enters us into God's roll of mourners. *Decay of Piety.*

Though sin offers itself in never so pleasing a dress, yet the remorse and inward *regrets* of the soul, upon the commission of it, infinitely overbalance those faint gratifications it affords the senses. *South's Sermons.*

2. Grief; sorrow.

Never any prince expressed a more lively *regret* for the loss of a servant, than his majesty did for this great man; in all offices of grace towards his servants, and in a wonderful solicitous care for the payment of his debts. *Clarendon.*

That freedom, which all sorrows claim,
She does for thy content resign;
Her piety itself would blame,
If her *regrets* should waken thine. *Prior.*

3. Dislike; aversion. Not proper.

Is it a virtue to have some ineffective *regrets* to damnation, and such a virtue too, as shall serve to balance all our vices. *Decay of Piety.*

To REGRE'T. *v. a.* [*regretter*, Fr. from the noun.]

1. To repent; to grieve at.

I shall not *regret* the trouble my experiments cost me, if they be found serviceable to the purposes of respiration. *Boyle.*

Calmly he look'd on either life, and here
Saw nothing to *regret*, or there to fear;
From nature's temp'rate feast rose satisfy'd,
Thank'd heav'n that he had liv'd, and that he dy'd. *Pope.*

2. To be uneasy at. Not proper.

Those, the impiety of whose lives makes them *regret* a deity, and secretly wish there were none, will greedily listen to atheistical notions. *Glanville's Sceps.*

REGUE'RDON. *n. s.* [*re* and *guerdon*.] Reward; recompense.

Stoop, and set your knee against my foot;
And in *reguerdon* of that duty done,
I gird thee with the valiant sword of York. *Shakesp.*

To REGUE'RDON. *v. a.* [from the noun.] To reward. The verb and noun are both obsolete.

Long since we were resolved of your truth,
Your faithful service and your toil in war;
Yet never have you tasted your reward,
Or been *reguerdon'd* with so much as thanks. *Shakesp.*

RE'GULAR. *adj.* [*regulier*, Fr. *regularis*, Lat.]

1. Agreeable to rule; consistent with the mode prescribed.

The common cant of criticks is, that though the lines are good, it is not a *regular* piece. *Guardian.*

The ways of heav'n are dark and intricate,
Puzzled in mazes, and perplex'd with errors;
Our understanding traces them in vain,
Lost and bewilder'd in the fruitless search;
Nor sees with how much art the windings run,
Nor where the *regular* confusion ends. *Addison.*

So when we view some well-proportion'd dome,
No monstrous height or breadth or length appear;
The whole at once is bold and *regular*. *Pope.*

2. Governed by strict regulations.

So just thy skill, so *regular* my rage. *Pope.*

3. In geometry, *regular* body is a solid, whose surface is composed of *regular* and equal figures, and whose solid angles are all equal, and of which there are five sorts, viz. 1. A pyramid comprehended under four equal and equilateral triangles. 2. A cube, whose surface is composed of six equal squares. 3. That which is bounded by eight equal and equilateral triangles. 4. That which is contained under twelve equal and equilateral pentagons. 5. A body consisting of twenty equal and equilateral triangles: and mathematicians demonstrate, that there can be no more *regular* bodies than these five. *Muschenbr.*

There is no universal reason, not confined to human fancy, that a figure, called *regular*, which hath equal sides and angles, is more beautiful than any irregular one. *Bentley.*

4. Instituted or initiated according to established forms or discipline: as, *a* regular *doctor*; regular *troops*.

RE'GULAR. *n. s.* [*regulier*, Fr.]

In the Romish church, all persons are said to be *regulars*, that do profess and follow a certain rule of life, in Latin stiled *regula*; and do likewise observe the three approved vows of poverty, chastity and obedience. *Ayliffe's Parergon.*

REGULA'RITY. *n. s.* [*regularité*, Fr. from *regular*.]

1. Agreeableness to rule.

2. Method; certain order.

Regularity is certain, where it is not so apparent, as in all fluids; for *regularity* is a similitude continued. *Grew.*

He was a mighty lover of *regularity* and order; and managed all his affairs with the utmost exactness. *Atterbury.*

REGULARLY. *adv.* [from *regular*.] In a manner concordant to rule.

If those painters, who have left us such fair platforms, had rigorously observed it in their figures, they had indeed made things more *regularly* true, but withal very unpleasing. *Dryd.*

With one judicious stroke,
On the plain ground Apelles drew
A circle *regularly* true. *Prior.*
Strains that neither ebb nor flow,
Correctly cold and *regularly* low. *Pope.*

To REGULATE. *v. a.* [*regula*, Lat.]

1. To adjust by rule or method.

Nature, in the production of things, always designs them to partake of certain, *regulated*, established essences, which are to be the models of all things to be produced: this, in that crude sense, would need some better explication. *Locke.*

2. To direct.

Regulate the patient in his manner of living. *Wiseman.*

Ev'n goddesses are women; and no wife
Has pow'r to *regulate* her husband's life. *Dryden.*

REGULATION. *n. s.* [from *regulate*.]

1. The act of regulating.

Being but stupid matter, they cannot continue any regular and constant motion, without the guidance and *regulation* of some intelligent being. *Ray on the Creation.*

2. Method; the effect of regulation.

REGULATOR. *n. s.* [from *regulate*.]

1. One that regulates.

The regularity of corporeal principles sheweth them to come at first from a divine *regulator*. *Grew's Cosmol.*

2. That part of a machine which makes the motion equable.

REGULUS. n. s. [Lat. *regule*, Fr.]

Regulus is the finer and most weighty part of metals, which settles at the bottom upon melting. *Quincy.*

To REGURGITATE. *v. a.* [*re* and *gurges*, Lat. *regorger*, Fr.] To throw back; to pour back.

The inhabitants of the city remove themselves into the country so long, until, for want of recept and encouragement, it *regurgitates* and sends them back. *Graunt.*

Arguments of divine wisdom, in the frame of animate bodies, are the artificial position of many valves, all so situate, as to give a free passage to the blood in their due channels, but not permit them to *regurgitate* and disturb the great circulation. *Bentley.*

To REGURGITATE. *v. n.* To be poured back.

Nature was wont to evacuate its vicious blood out of these veins, which passage being stopt, it *regurgitates* upwards to the lungs. *Harvey on Consumptions.*

REGURGITATION. *n. s.* [from *regurgitate*.] Resorption; the act of swallowing back.

Regurgitation of matter is the constant symptom. *Sharp.*

To REHEAR. *v. a.* [*re* and *hear*.] To hear again.

My design is to give all persons a *rehearing*, who have suffered under any unjust sentence. *Addison's Examiner.*

REHEARSAL. *n. s.* [from *rehearse*.]

1. Repetition; recital.

Twice we appoint, that the words which the minister pronounceth, the whole congregation shall repeat after him; as first in the publick confession of sins, and again in *rehearsal* of our Lord's prayer after the blessed sacrament. *Hooker.*

What dream'd my lord? tell me, and I'll requite it
With sweet *rehearsal* of my morning's dream. *Shakesp.*

What respected their actions as a rule or admonition, applied to yours, is only a *rehearsal*, whose zeal in asserting the ministerial cause is so generally known. *South.*

2. The recital of any thing previous to publick exhibition.

The chief of Rome,
With gaping mouths to these *rehearsals* come. *Dryden.*

To REHEARSE. *v. a.* [from *rehear*. *Skinner*.]

1. To repeat; to recite.

Rehearse not unto another that which is told. *Ecclus.*

Of modest poets be thou just,
To silent shades repeat thy verse,
'Till fame and echo almost burst,
Yet hardly dare one line *rehearse*. *Swift.*

2. To relate; to tell.

Great master of the muse! inspir'd
The pedigree of nature to *rehearse*,
And sound the maker's work in equal verse. *Dryden.*

3. To recite previously to publick exhibition.

All Rome is pleased, when Statius will *rehearse*. *Dryden.*

To REJECT. *v. a.* [*rejicio*, *rejectus*, Lat.]

1. To dismiss without compliance with proposal or acceptance of offer.

Barbarossa was *rejected* into Syria, although he perceived that it tended to his disgrace. *Knolles's History of the Turks.*

2. To cast off; to make an abject.

Thou hast *rejected* the word of the Lord, and the Lord hath *rejected* thee from being king. *1 Sam.* xv. 26.

Give me wisdom, and *reject* me not from among thy children. *Wisd.* ix. 4.

He is despised and *rejected* of men, a man of sorrows. *Is.*

3. To refuse; not to accept.

Because thou hast *rejected* knowledge, I will *reject* thee, that thou shalt be no priest. *Hosea* iv. 6.

Whether it be a divine revelation or no, reason must judge, which can never permit the mind to *reject* a greater evidence, to embrace what is less evident. *Locke.*

4. To throw aside.

REJECTION. *n. s.* [*rejectio*, Lat.] The act of casting off or throwing aside.

The *rejection* I use of experiments, is infinite; but if an experiment be probable and of great use, I receive it. *Bacon.*

Medicines urinative do not work by *rejection* and indigestion, as solutive do. *Bacon.*

REIGLE. *n. s.* [*regle*, Fr.] A hollow cut to guide any thing.

A flood gate is drawn up and let down through the *reigles* in the side posts. *Carew's Survey of Cornwall.*

To REIGN. *v. n.* [*regno*, Lat. *regner*, Fr.]

1. To enjoy or exercise sovereign authority.

This, done by them, gave them such an authority, that though he *reigned*, they in effect ruled, most men honouring them, because they only deserved honour. *Sidney*, b. ii.

Tell me, shall Banquo's issue ever
Reign in this kingdom? *Shakesp. Macbeth.*

A king shall *reign* in righteousness, and princes rule in judgment. *Is.* xxxi. 1.

Did he not first sev'n years a life-time *reign*. *Cowley.*

This right arm shall fix
Her seat of empire; and your son shall *reign*. *A. Philips.*

2. To be predominant; to prevail.

Now did the sign *reign*, under which Perkin should appear. *Bacon.*

More are sick in the summer, and more die in the winter, except in pestilent diseases, which commonly *reign* in summer or autumn. *Bacon.*

Great secrecy *reigns* in their publick councils. *Addison.*

3. To obtain power or dominion.

That as sin *reigned* unto death, even so might grace *reign* through righteousness unto eternal life by Jesus Christ. *Romans.*

REIGN. *n. s.* [*regne*, Fr. *regnum*, Lat.]

1. Royal authority; sovereignty.

He who like a father held his *reign*,
So soon forgot, was just and wise in vain. *Pope.*

2. Time of a king's government.

Queer country puts extol queen Bess's *reign*,
And of lost hospitality complain. *Bramston.*
Russel's blood
Stain'd the sad annals of a giddy *reign*. *Thomson.*

3. Kingdom; dominions.

Saturn's sons receiv'd the threefold *reign*
Of heav'n, of ocean and deep hell beneath. *Prior.*
That wrath which hurl'd to Pluto's gloomy *reign*,
The souls of mighty chiefs untimely slain. *Pope.*

To REIMBODY. *v. n.* [*re* and *imbody*, which is more frequently, but not more properly, written *embody*.] To embody again.

Quicksilver, broken into little globes, the parts brought to touch immediately *reimbody*. *Boyle.*

To REIMBURSE. *v. a.* [*re*, *in* and *bourse*, Fr. a purse.] To repay; to repair loss or expence by an equivalent.

Hath he saved any kingdom at his own expence, to give him a title of *reimbursing* himself by the destruction of ours? *Swift's Miscellanies.*

REIMBURSEMENT. *n. s.* [from *reimburse*.] Reparation or repayment.

If any person has been at expence about the funeral of a scholar, he may retain his books for the *reimbursement*. *Ayliffe.*

To REIMPREGNATE. *v. a.* [*re* and *impregnate*.] To impregnate anew.

The vigor of the loadstone is destroyed by fire, nor will it be *reimpregnated* by any other magnet than the earth. *Brown.*

REIMPRESSION. *n. s.* [*re* and *impression*.] A second or repeated impression.

REIN. *n. s.* [*resnes*, Fr.]

1. The part of the bridle, which extends from the horse's head to the driver's or rider's hand.

Every horse bears his commanding *rein*,
And may direct his course as please himself. *Shakesp.*
Take you the *reins*, while I from cares remove,
And sleep within the chariot which I drove. *Dryden.*
With hasty hand the ruling *reins* he drew;
He lash'd the coursers, and the coursers flew. *Pope.*

2. Used as an instrument of government, or for government.

The hard *rein*, which both of them have borne
Against the old kind king. *Shakesp. King Lear.*

3. *To give the* REINS. To give license.

War to disorder'd rage let loose the *reins*. *Milton.*
When to his lust Ægisthus *gave the rein*,
Did fate or we th' adulterous act constrain. *Pope.*

To REIN. *v. a.* [from the noun.]

1. To govern by a bridle.

He, like a proud steed *rein'd*, went haughty on. *Milton.*
His son retain'd
His father's art, and warriour steeds he *rein'd*. *Dryden.*

2. To restrain; to control.

And where you find a maid,
That, ere she sleep, hath thrice her pray'rs said,
Rein up the organs of her fantasy;
Sleep she as sound as careless infancy. *Shakesp.*

Being once chaft, he cannot
Be *rein'd* again to temperance; then he speaks
What's in his heart. *Shakesp. Coriolanus.*

REINS. *n. s.* [*renes*, Lat. *rein*, Fr.] The kidneys; the lower part of the back.

Whom I shall see for myself, though my *reins* be consumed. *Job* xix. 27.

To REINSE'RT. *v. a.* [*re* and *insert.*] To insert a second time.

To REINSPI'RE. *v. a.* [*re* and *inspire.*] To inspire anew.

Time will run
On smoother, till Favonius *reinspire*
The frozen earth, and cloath in fresh attire
The lilly and rose. *Milton.*

The mangled dame lay breathless on the ground,
When on a sudden *reinspir'd* with breath,
Again she rose. *Dryden.*

To REINSTA'L. *v. a.* [*re* and *instal.*]

1. To seat again.

That alone can truly *reinstall* thee
In David's royal seat, his true successor. *Milton.*

2. To put again in possession. This example is not very proper.

Thy father
Levied an army, weening to redeem
And *reinstal* me in the diadem. *Shakesp. Henry* VI.

To REINSTA'TE. *v. a.* [*re* and *instate.*] To put again in possession.

David, after that signal victory, which had preserved his life, *reinstated* him in his throne, and restored him to the ark and sanctuary; yet suffered the loss of his rebellious son to overwhelm the sense of his deliverance. *Gov. of the Tongue.*

Modesty *reinstates* the widow in her virginity. *Addison.*

The *reinstating* of this hero in the peaceable possession of his kingdom, was acknowledged. *Pope.*

To REI'NTEGRATE. *v. a.* [*reintegrer*, Fr. *re* and *integer*, Lat. It should perhaps be written *redintegrate.*] To renew with regard to any state or quality; to repair; to restore.

This league drove out all the Spaniards out of Germany, and *reintegrated* that nation in their ancient liberty. *Bacon.*

The falling from a discord to a concord hath an agreement with the affections, which are *reintegrated* to the better after some dislikes. *Bacon's Natural History.*

To REINVE'ST. *v. a.* [*re* and *invest.*] To invest anew.

To REJOI'CE. *v. n.* [*rejouir*, Fr.] To be glad; to joy; to exult; to receive pleasure from something past.

This is the *rejoicing* city that dwelt carelesly, that said, there is none beside me. *Zeph.* ii. 15.

I will comfort them, and make them *rejoice* from their sorrow. *Jer.* xxxi. 13.

Let them be brought to confusion, that *rejoice* at mine hurt. *Psalm* xxxv. 26.

Jethro *rejoiced* for all the goodness which the Lord had done. *Exodus* xviii. 9.

They *rejoice* each with their kind. *Milton.*

To REJOI'CE. *v. a.* To exhilarate; to gladden; to make joyful; to glad.

Thy testimonies are the *rejoicings* of my heart. *Ps.* cxix.

Alone to thy renown 'tis giv'n,
Unbounded through all worlds to go;
While she great saint *rejoices* heav'n,
And thou sustain'st the orb below. *Prior.*

I should give Cain the honour of the invention; were he alive, it would *rejoice* his soul to see what mischief it had made. *Arbuthnot on Coins.*

REJOI'CER. *n. s.* [from *rejoice.*] One that rejoices.

Whatsoever faith entertains, produces love to God; but he that believes God to be cruel or a *rejoicer* in the unavoidable damnation of the greatest part of mankind, thinks evil thoughts concerning God. *Taylor's Rule of Living Holy.*

To REJOI'N. *v. a.* [*rejoindre*, Fr.]

1. To join again.

The grand signior conveyeth his gallies down to Grand Cairo, where they are taken in pieces, carried upon camels backs, and *rejoined* together at Sues. *Brown's Vulg. Err.*

2. To meet one again.

Thoughts, which at Hyde-park-corner I forgot,
Meet and *rejoin* me in the pensive grot. *Pope.*

To REJOI'N. *v. n.* To answer to an answer.

It will be replied, that he receives advantage by this lopping of his superfluous branches; but I *rejoin*, that a translator has no such right. *Dryden's Preface to Ovid.*

REJOI'NDER, *n. s.* [from *rejoin.*]

1. Reply to an answer.

The quality of the person makes me judge myself obliged to a *rejoinder*. *Glanvill to Albius.*

2. Reply; answer.

Injury of chance rudely beguiles our lips
Of all *rejoindure*. *Shakesp. Troilus and Cressida.*

REJO'LT. *n. s.* [*rejaillir*, Fr.] Shock; succussion.

The sinner, at his highest pitch of enjoyment, is not pleased with it so much, but he is afflicted more; and as long as these inward *rejolts* and recoilings of the mind continue, the sinner will find his accounts of pleasure very poor. *South.*

REIT. *n. s.* Sedge or sea weed. *Bailey.*

To REI'TERATE. *v. a.* [*re* and *itero*, Lat. *reiterer*, Fr.] To repeat again and again.

You never spoke what did become you less
Than this; which to *reiterate*, were sin. *Shakesp.*

With *reiterated* crimes he might
Heap on himself damnation. *Milton.*

Although Christ hath forbid us to use vain repetitions when we pray, yet he hath taught us, that to *reiterate* the same requests will not be vain. *Smalridge.*

REITERA'TION. *n. s.* [*reiteration*, Fr. from *reiterate.*] Repetition.

It is useful to have new experiments tried over again; such *reiterations* commonly exhibiting new phenomena. *Boyle.*

The words are a *reiteration* or reinforcement of an application, arising from the consideration of the excellency of Christ above Moses. *Ward of Infidelity.*

To REJU'DGE. *v. a.* [*re* and *judge.*] To reexamine; to review; to recal to a new trial.

The muse attends thee to the silent shade;
'Tis hers the brave man's latest steps to trace,
Rejudge his acts, and dignify disgrace. *Pope.*

To REKI'NDLE. *v. a.* [*re* and *kindle.*] To set on fire again.

These disappearing, fixed stars were actually extinguished, and would for ever continue so, if not *rekindled*, and new recruited with heat and light. *Cheyne's Phil. Principles.*

Rekindled at the royal charms,
Tumultuous love each beating bosom warms. *Pope.*

To RELA'PSE. *v. n.* [*relapsus*, Lat.]

1. To slip back; to slide or fall back.

2. To fall back into vice or errour.

The oftner he hath *relapsed*, the more significations he ought to give of the truth of his repentance. *Taylor.*

3. To fall back from a state of recovery to sickness.

He was not well cured, and would have *relapsed*. *Wisem.*

RELA'PSE. *n. s.* [from the verb.]

1. Fall into vice or errour once forsaken.

This would but lead me to a worse *relapse*
And heavier fall. *Milton.*

We see in too frequent instances the *relapses* of those, who, under the present smart, or the near apprehension of the divine pleasure, have resolved on a religious reformation. *Rog.*

2. Regression from a state of recovery to sickness.

It was even as two physicians should take one sick body in hand; of which, the former would purge and keep under the body, the other pamper and strengthen it suddenly; whereof what is to be looked for, but a most dangerous *relapse*. *Spens.*

3. Return to any state. The sense here is somewhat obscure.

Mark a bounding valour in our English;
That being dead like to the bullet's grazing,
Breaks out into a second course of mischief,
Killing in *relapse* of mortality. *Shakesp. Henry* V

To RELA'TE. *v. a.* [*relatus*, Lat.]

1. To tell; to recite.

Your wife and babes
Savagely slaughter'd; to *relate* the manner,
Were to add the death of you. *Shakesp. Macbeth*

Here I could frequent
With worship place by place, where he vouchsaf'd
Presence divine; and to my sons *relate*. *Milton.*

The drama represents to view, what the poem only does *relate*. *Dryden.*

A man were better *relate* himself to a statue, than suffer his thoughts to pass in smother. *Bacon.*

2. To ally by kindred.

Avails thee not,
To whom *related*, or by whom begot;
A heap of dust alone remains. *Pope.*

3. To bring back; to restore. A Latinism. *Spenser.*

To RELA'TE. *v. n.* To have reference; to have respect.

All negative or privative words *relate* to positive ideas, and signify their absence. *Locke.*

As other courts demanded the execution of persons dead in law, this gave the last orders *relating* to those dead in reason. *Tatler*, Nº 110.

RELA'TER. *n. s.* [from *relate.*] Teller; narrator.

We shall rather perform good offices unto truth, than any disservice unto their *relaters*. *Brown's Vulgar Errours.*

Her husband the *relater* she prefer'd
Before the angel. *Milton's Paradise Lost, b.* viii.

The best English historian, when his style grows antiquated, will be only considered as a tedious *relater* of facts. *Swift.*

RELA'TION. *n. s.* [*relation*, Fr. from *relate.*]

1. Manner of belonging to any person or thing.

Under this stone lies virtue, youth,
Unblemish'd probity and truth;
Just unto all *relations* known,
A worthy patriot, pious son. *Waller.*

So

So far as ſervice imports duty and ſubjection, all created beings bear the neceſſary *relation* of ſervants to God. *South.*

Our neceſſary *relations* to a family, oblige all to uſe their reaſoning powers upon a thouſand occaſions. *Watts.*

2. Reſpect; reference; regard.

I have been importuned to make ſome obſervations on this art, in *relation* to its agreement with poetry. *Dryden.*

Relation conſiſts in the conſideration and comparing one idea with another. *Locke.*

3. Connexion between one thing and another.

Augurs, that underſtand *relations*, have
By magpies, choughs and rooks brought forth
The ſecret'ſt man of blood. *Shakeſp. Macbeth.*

4. Kindred; alliance of kin.

Relations dear, and all the charities
Of fathers, ſon and brother firſt were known. *Milton.*
Be kindred and *relation* laid aſide,
And honour's cauſe by laws of honour try'd. *Dryden.*

Are we not to pity and ſupply the poor, though they have no *relation* to us? no *relation*? that cannot be: the goſpel ſtiles them all our brethren; nay, they have a nearer *relation* to us, our fellow-members; and both theſe from their *relation* to our Saviour himſelf, who calls them his brethren. *Sprat.*

5. Perſon related by birth or marriage; kinſman; kinſwoman.

A ſhe-couſin, of a good family and ſmall fortune, paſſed months among all her *relations*. *Swift.*

Dependants, friends, *relations*,
Savag'd by woe, forget the tender tie. *Thomſon.*

6. Narrative; tale; account; narration; recital of facts.

In an hiſtorical *relation*, we uſe terms that are moſt proper. *Burnet's Theory of the Earth.*

The author of a juſt fable, muſt pleaſe more than the writer of an hiſtorical *relation*. *Dennis's Letters.*

RE'LATIVE. *adj.* [*relativus*, Lat. *relatif*, Fr.]

1. Having relation; reſpecting.

Not only ſimple ideas and ſubſtances, but modes are poſitive beings; though the parts of which they conſiſt, are very often *relative* one to another. *Locke.*

2. Conſidered not abſolutely, but as belonging to, or reſpecting ſomething elſe.

The eccleſiaſtical, as well as the civil governour, has cauſe to purſue the ſame methods of confirming himſelf; the grounds of government being founded upon the ſame bottom of nature in both, though the circumſtances and *relative* conſiderations of the perſons may differ. *South.*

Every thing ſuſtains both an abſolute and a *relative* capacity: an abſolute, as it is ſuch a thing, endued with ſuch a nature; and a *relative*, as it is a part of the univerſe, and ſo ſtands in ſuch relation to the whole. *South.*

Wholeſome and unwholeſome are *relative*, not real qualities. *Arbuthnot on Aliments.*

3. Particular; poſitive; cloſe in connection. Not in uſe.

I'll have grounds
More *relative* than this. *Shakeſp. Macbeth.*

RE'LATIVE. *n. ſ.*

1. Relation; kinſman.

'Tis an evil dutifulneſs in friends and *relatives*, to ſuffer one to periſh without reproof. *Taylor.*

2. Pronoun anſwering to an antecedent.

Learn the right joining of ſubſtantives with adjectives, and the *relative* with the antecedent. *Aſcham's Schoolmaſter.*

3. Somewhat reſpecting ſomething elſe.

When the mind ſo conſiders one thing, that it ſets it by another, and carries its view from one to the other, this is relation and reſpect; and the denominations given to poſitive things, intimating that reſpect, are *relatives*. *Locke.*

RE'LATIVELY. *adv.* [from *relative*.] As it reſpects ſomething elſe; not abſolutely.

All thoſe things, that ſeem ſo foul and diſagreeable in nature, are not really ſo in themſelves, but only *relatively*. *More.*

Theſe being the greateſt good or the greateſt evil, either abſolutely ſo in themſelves, or *relatively* ſo to us; it is therefore good to be zealouſly affected for the one againſt the other. *Sprat.*

Conſider the abſolute affections of any being as it is in itſelf, before you conſider it *relatively*, or ſurvey the various relations in which it ſtands to other beings. *Watts.*

RE'LATIVENESS. *n. ſ.* [from *relative*.] The ſtate of having relation.

To RELA'X. *v. a.* [*relaxo*, Lat.]

1. To ſlacken; to make leſs tenſe.

The ſinews, when the ſouthern wind bloweth, are more *relax*. *Bacon's Natural Hiſtory.*

2. To remit; to make leſs ſevere or rigorous.

The ſtatute of mortmain was at ſeveral times *relaxed* by the legiſlature. *Swift.*

3. To make leſs attentive or laborious.

Nor praiſe *relax*, nor difficulty fright. *Vanity of Wiſhes.*

4. To eaſe; to divert.

5. To open; to looſe.

It ſerv'd not to *relax* their ſerried files. *Milton.*

To RELAX. *v. n.* To be mild; to be remiſs; to be not rigorous.

If in ſome regards ſhe choſe
To curb poor Paulo in too cloſe;
In others ſhe *relax'd* again,
And govern'd with a looſer rein. *Prior.*

RELAXA'TION. *n. ſ.* [*relaxation*, Fr. *relaxatio*, Lat.]

1. Diminution of tenſion; the act of looſening.

Cold ſweats are many times mortal; for that they come by a *relaxation* or forſaking of the ſpirits. *Bacon.*

Many, who live healthy in a dry air, fall into all the diſeaſes that depend upon *relaxation* in a moiſt one. *Arbuthnot.*

2. Ceſſation of reſtraint.

The ſea is not higher than the land, as ſome imagined the ſea ſtood upon heap higher than the ſhore; and at the deluge a *relaxation* being made, it overflow'd the land. *Burnet.*

3. Remiſſion; abatement of rigour.

They childiſhly granted, by common conſent of their whole ſenate, under their town ſeal, a *relaxation* to one Bertelier, whom the elderſhip had excommunicated. *Hooker.*

The *relaxation* of the ſtatute of mortmain, is one of the reaſons which gives the biſhop terrible apprehenſions of popery coming on us. *Swift.*

4. Remiſſion of attention or application.

As God has not ſo devoted our bodies to toil, but that he allows us ſome recreation: ſo doubtleſs he indulges the ſame *relaxation* to our minds. *Government of the Tongue.*

There would be no buſineſs in ſolitude, nor proper *relaxations* in buſineſs. *Addiſon's Freeholder.*

RELA'Y. *n. ſ.* [*relais*, Fr.] Horſes on the road to relieve others.

To RELEA'SE. *v. a.* [*relaſcher*, *relaxer*, Fr.]

1. To ſet free from confinement or ſervitude.

Pilate ſaid, whom will ye that I *releaſe* unto you? *Mat.*

You *releas'd* his courage, and ſet free
A valour fatal to the enemy. *Dryden.*

Why ſhould a reaſonable man put it into the power of fortune to make him miſerable, when his anceſtors have taken care to *releaſe* him from her? *Dryden.*

2. To ſet free from pain.

3. To free from obligation.

Too ſecure, becauſe from death *releas'd* ſome days. *Milt.*

4. To quit; to let go.

He had been baſe, had he *releas'd* his right,
For ſuch an empire nóne but kings ſhould fight. *Dryden.*

5. To relax; to ſlacken. Not in uſe.

It may not ſeem hard, if in caſes of neceſſity certain profitable ordinances ſometimes be *releaſed*, rather than all men always ſtrictly bound to the general rigor thereof. *Hooker.*

RELEA'SE. *n. ſ.* [*relaſche*, Fr. from the verb.]

1. Diſmiſſion from confinement, ſervitude or pain.

O fatal ſearch! in which the lab'ring mind,
Still preſs'd with weight of woe, ſtill hopes to find
A ſhadow of delight, a dream of peace,
From years of pain, one moment of *releaſe*. *Prior.*

2. Relaxation of a penalty.

3. Remiſſion of a claim.

The king made a great feaſt, and made a *releaſe* to the provinces, and gave gifts. *Eſth.* ii. 18.

The king would not have one penny abated, of what had been granted by parliament; becauſe it might encourage other countries to pray the like *releaſe* or mitigation. *Bacon.*

4. Acquittance from a debt ſigned by the creditor.

To RE'LEGATE. *v. a.* [*releguer*, Fr. *relego*, Lat.] To baniſh; to exile.

RELEGA'TION. *n. ſ.* [*relegation*, Fr. *relegatio*, Lat.] Exile; judicial baniſhment.

According to the civil law, the extraordinary puniſhment of adultery was deportation or *relegation*. *Ayliffe.*

To RELE'NT. *v. n.* [*ralentir*, Fr.]

1. To ſoften; to grow leſs rigid or hard; to give.

In ſome houſes, ſweetmeats will *relent* more than in others. *Bacon.*

In that ſoft ſeaſon, when deſcending ſhow'rs
Call forth the greens, and wake the riſing flow'rs;
When opening buds ſalute the welcome day,
And earth *relenting* feels the genial ray. *Pope.*

2. To melt; to grow moiſt.

Crows ſeem to call upon rain, which is but the comfort they ſeem to receive in the *relenting* of the air. *Bacon.*

Salt of tartar, brought to fuſion, and placed in a cellar, will, in a few minutes, begin to *relent*, and have its ſurface ſoftened by the imbibed moiſture of the air, wherein if it be left long, it will totally be diſſolved. *Boyle.*

All nature mourns, the ſkies *relent* in ſhow'rs,
Huſh'd are the birds, and clos'd the drooping flow'rs;
If Delia ſmile, the flow'rs begin to ſpring,
The ſkies to brighten, and the birds to ſing. *Pope.*

3. To grow leſs intenſe.

I have marked in you a *relenting* truly, and a ſlacking of the main career, you had ſo notably begun, and almoſt performed. *Sidney.*

The workmen let glaſs cool by degrees in ſuch *relentings* of fire, as they call their nealing heats, leſt it ſhould ſhiver in pieces by a violent ſucceeding of air. *Digby on Bodies.*

4. To

4. To soften in temper; to grow tender; to feel compassion.

Can you behold
My tears, and not once *relent*? *Shakesp. Henry* VI.

I'll not be made a soft and dull-ey'd fool,
To shake the head, *relent*, and sigh, and yield
To christian intercessors. *Shakesp. Merch. of Venice.*

Undoubtedly he will *relent*, and turn
From his displeasure. *Milton.*

He sung, and hell consented
To hear the poet's pray'r;
Stern Prosperine *relented*,
And gave him back the fair. *Pope.*

To RELE'NT. *v. a.*

1. To slacken; to remit. Obsolete.

Apace he shot, and yet he fled apace,
And oftentimes he would *relent* his pace,
That him his foe more fiercely should pursue. *Fa. Queen.*

2. To soften; to mollify. Obsolete.

Air hated earth, and water hated fire,
Till love *relented* their rebellious ire. *Spenser.*

RELE'NTLESS. *adj.* [from *relent.*]

1. Unpitying; unmoved by kindness or tenderness.

For this th' avenging pow'r employs his darts;
Thus will persist, *relentless* in his ire,
Till the fair slave be render'd to her sire. *Dryden.*

Why should the weeping hero now
Relentless to their wishes prove. *Prior.*

2. In *Milton*, it perhaps signifies unremitted; intensely fixed upon disquieting objects.

Only in destroying, I find ease
To my *relentless* thoughts. *Milton's Par. Lost.*

RE'LEVANT. *adj.* [French.] Relieving. *Dict.*

RELEVA'TION. *n. s.* [*relevatio*, Lat.] A raising or lifting up.

RELI'ANCE. *n. s.* [from *rely.*] Trust, dependance; confidence; repose of mind. With *on* before the object of trust.

His days and times are past,
And my *reliance on* his fracted dates
Has smit my credit. *Shakesp. Timon of Athens.*

That pellucid gelatinous substance, which he pitches upon with so great *reliance* and positiveness, is chiefly of animal constitution. *Woodward.*

He secured and encreased his prosperity, by an humble behaviour towards God, and a dutiful *reliance on* his providence. *Atterbury's Sermons.*

They afforded a sufficient conviction of this truth, and a firm *reliance on* the promises contained in it. *Rogers.*

Resignation in death, and *reliance on* the divine mercies, give comfort to the friends of the dying. *Clarissa.*

Misfortunes often reduce us to a better *reliance*, than that we have been accustomed to fix upon. *Clarissa.*

RE'LICK. *n. s.* [*reliquiæ*, Lat. *relique*, Fr.]

1. That which remains; that which is left after the loss or decay of the rest. It is generally used in the plural.

Up dreary dame of darkness queen,
Go gather up the *reliques* of thy race,
Or else go them avenge. *Fairy Queen, b.* i.

Shall we go see the *relicks* of this town. *Shakesp.*

The fragments, scraps, the bits and greasy *reliques*
Of her o'ereaten faith are bound to Diomede. *Shakesp.*

Nor death itself can wholly wash their stains,
But long contracted filth ev'n in the soul remains;
The *relicks* of inveterate vice they wear,
And spots of sin. *Dryden's Æneis.*

2. It is often taken for the body deserted by the soul.

What needs my Shakespeare for his honour'd bones,
The labour of an age in piled stones;
Or that his hallow'd *reliques* should be hid
Under a star-ypointed pyramid. *Milton.*

In peace, ye shades of our great grandsires, rest;
Eternal spring, and rising flow'rs adorn
The *relicks* of each venerable urn. *Dryden.*

Shall our *relicks* second birth receive?
Sleep we to wake, and only die to live? *Prior.*

Thy *relicks*, Rowe, to this fair shrine we trust.
And sacred place by Dryden's awful dust;
Beneath a rude and nameless stone he lies,
To which thy tomb shall guide enquiring eyes. *Pope.*

3 That which is kept in memory of another, with a kind of religious veneration.

Cowls flutter'd into rags, then *reliques* leaves
The sport of winds. *Milton.*

This church is very rich in *relicks*; among the rest, they show a fragment of Thomas á Becket, as indeed there are very few treasuries of *relicks* in Italy, that have not a tooth or a bone of this saint. *Addison's Remarks on Italy.*

RE'LICKLY. *adv.* [from *relick.*] In the manner of relicks.

Thrifty wench scrapes kitchen stuff,
And barreling the droppings and the snuff
Of wasting candles, which in thirty year
Relickly kept, perhaps buys wedding cheer. *Donne.*

RE'LICT. *n. s.* [*relicte*, old Fr. *relicta*, Lat.] A widow; a wife desolate by the death of her husband.

If the fathers and husbands were of the houshold of faith, then certainly their *relicts* and children cannot be strangers in this houshold. *Sprat's Sermons.*

Chaste *relict!*
Honour'd on earth, and worthy of the love
Of such a spouse, as now resides above. *Garth.*

RELIE'F. *n. s.* [*relief*, Fr.]

1. The prominence of a figure in stone or metal; the seeming prominence of a picture.

The figures of many ancient coins rise up in a much more beautiful *relief* than those on the modern; the face sinking by degrees in the several declensions of the empire, till about Constantine's time, it lies almost even with the surface of the medal. *Addison on Ancient Medals.*

Not with such majesty, such bold *relief*,
The forms august of kings, or conqu'ring chief,
E'er swell'd on marble, as in verse have shin'd,
In polish'd verse, the manners and the mind. *Pope.*

2. The recommendation of any thing, by the interposition of something different.

3. Alleviation of calamity; mitigation of pain or sorrow.

Thoughts in my unquiet breast are risen,
Tending to some *relief* of our extremes. *Milton.*

4. That which frees from pain or sorrow.

So should we make our death a glad *relief*
From future shame. *Dryden's Knight's Tale.*

Nor dar'd I to presume, that press'd with grief,
My flight should urge you to this dire *relief*;
Stay, stay your steps. *Dryden's Æneis.*

5. Dismission of a sentinel from his post.

For this *relief*, much thanks; 'tis bitter cold,
And I am sick at heart. *Shakesp. Hamlet.*

6. [*Relevium*, law Lat.] Legal remedy of wrongs.

RELIE'VABLE. *adj.* [from *relieve.*] Capable of relief.

Neither can they, as to reparation, hold plea of things, wherein the party is *relievable* by common law. *Hale.*

To RELIE'VE. [*relevo*, Lat. *relever*, Fr.]

1. To recommend by the interposition of something dissimilar.

As the great lamp of day,
Through diff'rent regions, does his course pursue,
And leaves one world but to revive a new;
While, by a pleasing change, the queen of night
Relieves his lustre with a milder light. *Stepney.*

Since the inculcating precept upon precept will prove tiresome, the poet must not encumber his poem with too much business; but sometimes *relieve* the subject with a moral reflection. *Addison's Essay on the Georgicks.*

2. To support; to assist.

Parallels, or like relations, alternately *relieve* each other; when neither will pass asunder, yet are they plausible together. *Brown's Vulgar Errours.*

3. To ease pain or sorrow.

4. To succour by assistance.

From thy growing store,
Now lend assistance, and *relieve* the poor;
A pittance of thy land will set him free. *Dryden.*

5. To set a sentinel at rest, by placing another on his post.

Honest soldier, who hath *relieved* you?
—Bernado has my place, give you good night. *Shakesp.*

Relieve the centries that have watch'd all night. *Dryden.*

6. To right by law.

RELIE'VER. *n. s.* [from *relieve.*] One that relieves.

He is the protector of his weakness, and the *reliever* of his wants. *Rogers's Sermons.*

RELIE'VO. *n. s.* [Italian.] The prominence of a figure or picture.

A convex mirrour makes the objects in the middle come out from the superficies: the painter must do so in respect of the lights and shadows of his figures, to give them more *relievo* and more strength. *Dryden's Dufresnoy.*

To RELI'GHT. *v. a.* [*re* and *light.*] To light anew.

His pow'r can heal me, and *relight* my eye. *Pope.*

RELI'GION. *n. s.* [*religion*, Fr. *religio*, Lat.]

1. Virtue, as founded upon reverence of God, and expectation of future rewards and punishments.

He that is void of fear, may soon be just,
And no *religion* binds men to be traitors. *Benj. Johnson.*

One spake much of right and wrong,
Of justice, of *religion*, truth and peace
And judgment from above. *Milton.*

If we consider it as directed against God, it is a breach of *religion*; if as to men, it is an offence against morality. *South.*

By her inform'd, we best *religion* learn,
Its glorious object by her aid discern. *Blackmore.*

Religion or virtue, in a large sense, includes duty to God and our neighbour; but in a proper sense, virtue signifies duty towards men, and *religion* duty to God. *Watts.*

2. A system of divine faith and worship as opposite to others.

The image of a brute, adorn'd
With gay *religions*, full of pomp and gold. *Milton.*

The christian *religion*, rightly understood, is the deepest and choicest piece of philosophy that is. *More.*

The doctrine of the gospel proposes to men such glorious rewards and such terrible punishments as no *religion* ever did, and gives us far greater assurance of their reality and certainty than ever the world had. *Tillotson.*

RELI'GIONIST. *n. s.* [from *religion.*] A bigot to any religious persuasion.

The lawfulness of taking oaths may be revealed to the quakers, who then will stand upon as good a foot for preferment as any other subject; under such a motly administration, what pullings and hawlings, what a zeal and biass there will be in each *religionist* to advance his own tribe, and depress the others. *Swift.*

RELI'GIOUS. *adj.* [*religieux*, Fr. *religiosus*, Lat.]

1. Pious; disposed to the duties of religion.

It is a matter of sound consequence, that all duties are by so much the better performed, by how much the men are more *religious*, from whose habilities the same proceed. *Hook.*

When holy and devout *religious* christians
Are at their beads, 'tis hard to draw them from thence;
So sweet is zealous contemplation! *Shakesp.*

Their lives
Religious titled them the sons of God. *Milton.*

2. Teaching religion.

He God doth late and early pray,
More of his grace than gifts to lend;
And entertains the harmless day
With a *religious* book or friend. *Wotton.*

3. Among the Romanists, bound by the vows of poverty, chastity and obedience.

Certain fryars and *religious* men were moved with some zeal, to draw the people to the christian faith. *Abbot.*

France has vast numbers of ecclesiasticks, secular and *religious.* *Addison's State of the War.*

What the protestants would call a fanatick, is in the Roman church a *religious* of such an order; as an English merchant in Lisbon, after some great disappointments in the world, resolved to turn capuchin. *Addison.*

4. Exact; strict.

RELI'GIOUSLY. *adv.* [from *religious.*]

1. Piously; with obedience to the dictates of religion.

2. According to the rites of religion.

These are their brethren, whom you Goths behold
Alive and dead, and for their brethren slain
Religiously they ask a sacrifice. *Shakesp. Titus Andron.*

3. Reverently; with veneration.

Dost thou in all thy addresses to him, come into his presence with reverence, kneeling and *religiously* bowing thyself before him. *Duppa's Rules to Devotion.*

4. Exactly; with strict observance.

The privileges, justly due to the members of the two houses and their attendants, are *religiously* to be maintained. *Bacon.*

RELI'GIOUSNESS. *n. s.* [from *religious.*] The quality or state of being religious.

To RELI'NQUISH. *v. a.* [*relinquo*, Lat.]

1. To forsake; to abandon; to leave; to desert.

The habitation there was utterly *relinquished.* *Abbot.*

The English colonies grew poor and weak, though the English lords grew rich and mighty; for they placed Irish tenants upon the lands *relinquished* by the English. *Davies.*

2. To quit; to release; to give up.

The ground of God's sole property in any thing is, the return of it made by man to God; by which act he *relinquishes* and delivers back to God all his right to the use of that thing, which before had been freely granted him by God. *South's Sermons.*

3. To forbear; to depart from.

In case it may be proved, that amongst the number of rites and orders common unto both, there are particulars, the use whereof is utterly unlawful, in regard of some special bad and noisom quality; there is no doubt but we ought to *relinquish* such rites and orders, what freedom soever we have to retain the other still. *Hooker, b.* iv. *s.* 11.

RELI'NQUISHMENT. *n. s.* [from *relinquish.*] The act of forsaking.

Government or ceremonies, or whatsoever it be, which is popish, away with it: this is the thing they require in us, the utter *relinquishment* of all things popish. *Hooker.*

That natural tenderness of conscience, which must first create in the soul a sense of sin, and from thence produce a sorrow for it, and at length cause a *relinquishment* of it, is took away by a customary repeated course of sinning. *South.*

RE'LISH. *n. s.* [from *relecher*, Fr. to lick again. *Minshew, Skinner.*]

1. Taste; the effect of any thing on the palate; it is commonly used of a pleasing taste.

Under sharp, sweet and sour, are abundance of immediate peculiar *relishes* or tastes, which experienced palates can easily discern. *Boyle on Colours.*

These two bodies, whose vapours are so pungent, spring from saltpetre, which betrays upon the tongue no heat nor corrosiveness, but coldness mixed with a somewhat languid *relish* retaining to bitterness. *Boyle.*

Much pleasure we have lost, while we abstain'd
From this delightful fruit, nor known till now
True *relish*, tasting. *Milton.*

Could we suppose their *relishes* as different there as here, yet the manna in heaven suits every palate. *Locke.*

Sweet, bitter, sour, harsh and salt are all the epithets we have to denominate that numberless variety of *relishes* to be found distinct in the different parts of the same plant. *Locke.*

2. Taste; small quantity just perceptible.

The king becoming graces;
As justice, verity, temp'rance, stableness,
Devotion, patience, courage, fortitude;
I have no *relish* of them. *Shakesp. Macbeth.*

3. Liking; delight in any thing.

We have such a *relish* for faction, as to have lost that of wit. *Addison's Freeholder.*

Good men after death are distributed among these several islands with pleasures of different kinds, suitable to the *relishes* and perfections of those settled in them. *Addison's Spectator.*

4. Sense; power of perceiving excellence; taste.

A man, who has any *relish* for fine writing, discovers new beauties, or receives stronger impressions from the masterly strokes of a great author every time he peruses him. *Addison.*

Some hidden seeds of goodness and knowledge give him a *relish* of such reflections, as improve the mind, and make the heart better. *Addison's Spectator*, N° 262.

The pleasure of the proprietor, to whom things become familiar, depends, in a great measure, upon the *relish* of the spectator. *Seed's Sermons.*

5. Delight given by any thing; the power by which pleasure is given.

Expectation whirls me round;
Th' imaginary *relish* is so sweet,
That it enchants my sense. *Shakesp. Troilus and Cressida.*

When liberty is gone,
Life grows insipid, and has lost its *relish.* *Addison's Cato.*

6. Cast; manner.

It preserves some *relish* of old writing. *Pope.*

To RE'LISH. *v. a.* [from the noun.]

1. To give a taste to any thing.

On smoaking lard they dine;
A sav'ry bit that serv'd to *relish* wine. *Dryden.*

2. To taste; to have a liking.

I love the people;
Though it do well, I do not *relish* well
Their loud applause. *Shakesp.*

How will dissenting brethren *relish* it?
What will malignants say? *Hudibras, p.* i.

Men of nice palates would not *relish* Aristotle, as drest up by the schoolmen. *Baker's Reflections on Learning.*

He knows how to prize his advantages, and *relish* the honours which he enjoys. *Atterbury.*

To RE'LISH. *v. n.*

1. To have a pleasing taste.

The ivory feet of tables were carved into the shape of lions, without which, their greatest dainties would not *relish* to their palates. *Hakewill on Providence.*

2. To give pleasure.

Had I been the finder-out of this secret, it would not have *relished* among my other discredits. *Shakesp. Winter's Tale.*

3. To have a flavour.

A theory, which how much soever it may *relish* of wit and invention, hath no foundation in nature. *Woodward.*

RELI'SHABLE. *adj.* [from *relish.*] Gustable; having a taste.

To RELI'VE. *v. n.* [*re* and *live.*] To revive; to live anew.

The thing on earth, which is of most avail,
Any virtue's branch and beauty's bud,
Reliven not for any good. *Spenser.*

To RELO'VE. *v. a.* [*re* and *love.*] To love in return.

To own for him so familiar and levelling an affection as love, much more to expect to be *reloved* by him, were not the least saucy presumption man could be guilty of, did not his own commandments make it a duty. *Boyle.*

RELU'CENT. *adj.* [*relucens*, Latin.] Shining; transparent; pellucid.

In brighter mazes, the *relucent* stream
Plays o'er the mead. *Thomson's Summer.*

To RELU'CT. *v. n.* [*reluctor*, Lat.] To struggle again.

We, with studied mixtures, force our *relucting* appetites, and with all the spells of epicurism, conjure them up, that we may lay them again. *Decay of Piety.*

RELU'CTANCE. } *n. s.* [*reluctor*, Latin.] Unwillingness; re-
RELU'CTANCY. } pugnance; struggle in opposition.

A little more weight, added to the lower of the marbles, is able to surmount their *reluctancy* to separation, notwithstanding the supposed danger of thereby introducing a vacuum. *Boyle.*

It favours
Reluctance against God, and his just yoke
Laid on our necks. *Milton.*

Bear witness, heav'n, with what *reluctancy*
Her hapless innocence I doom to die. *Dryden.*

Æneas,

Æneas, when forced in his own defence to kill Laufus, the poet fhows compaffionate, and tempering the feverity of his looks with a *reluctance* to the action; he has pity on his beauty and his youth; and is loth to deftroy fuch a mafter-piece of nature. *Dryden's Dufrefnoy.*

How few would be at the pains of acquiring fuch an habit, and of conquering all the *reluctancies* and difficulties that lay in the way towards virtue. *Atterbury.*

Many hard ftages of difcipline muft he pafs through, before he can fubdue the *reluctances* of his corruption. *Rogers.*

With great *reluctancy* man is perfuaded to acknowledge this neceffity. *Rogers's Sermons.*

RELU'CTANT. *adj.* [*reluctans*, Lat.] Unwilling; acting with repugnance.

Reluctant; but in vain! a greater pow'r
Now rul'd him. *Milton's Paradife Loft, b.* x.

Some refuge in the mufe's art I found;
Reluctant now I touch'd the trembling ftring
Bereft of him, who taught me how to fing. *Tickell.*

To RELU'CTATE. *v. n.* [*reluctor*, Lat.] To refift; to ftruggle againft.

In violation of God's patrimony, the firft facrilege is looked on with fome horrour, and men devife colours to delude their *reluctating* confciences; but when they have once made the breach, their fcrupulofity foon retires. *Decay of Piety.*

RELUCTA'TION. *n. f.* [*reluctor*, Latin.] Repugnance; refiftance.

The king prevailed with the prince, though not without fome *reluctation*. *Bacon's Henry* VII.

Adam's fin, or the curfe upon it, did not deprive him of his rule, but left the creatures to a rebellion or *reluctation*. *Bac.*

To RELU'ME. *v. a.* To light anew; to rekindle.

Relume her ancient light, nor kindle new. *Pope.*

To RELU'MINE. *v. a.* To light anew.

Once put out thy light;
I know not where is that Promethean heat,
That can thy light *relumine*. *Shakefp. Othello.*

To RELY'. *v. n.* [*re* and *lye.*] To lean upon with confidence; to put truft in; to reft upon; to depend upon.

Go in thy native innocence! *rely*
On what thou haft of virtue; fummon all!
For God tow'rds thee hath done his part, do thine. *Milton.*

Egypt does not on the clouds *rely*,
But to the Nile owes more than to the fky. *Waller.*

Thus Solon to Pififtratus reply'd,
Demanded, on what fuccour he *rely'd*,
When with fo few he boldly did engage;
He faid, he took his courage from his age. *Denham.*

Though reafon is not to be *relied* upon, as univerfally fufficient to direct us what to do; yet it is generally to be *relied* upon and obeyed, where it tells us what we are not to do. *South.*

Fear *relies* upon a natural love of ourfelves, and is complicated with a neceffary defire of our own prefervation. *Till.*

Such variety of arguments only diftract the underftanding that *relies* on them. *Locke.*

The pope was become a party in the caufe, and could not be *relied* upon for a decifion. *Atterbury.*

Do we find fo much religion in the age, as to *rely* on the general practice for the meafures of our duty? *Rogers.*

No prince can ever *rely* on the fidelity of that man, who is a rebel to his Creator. *Rogers.*

To REMAI'N. *v. n.* [*remaneo*, Lat.]

1. To be left out of a greater quantity or number.

That that *remains*, fhall be buried in death. *Job* xxvii. 15.

Bake that which ye will bake to-day; and that which *remaineth* over, lay up until the morning. *Ex.* xvi. 23.

2. To continue; to endure; to be left.

He for the time *remain'd* ftupidly good. *Milton.*

If what you have heard, fhall *remain* in you, ye fhall continue in the fon. 1 *Jo.* ii. 24.

3. To be left after any event.

Childlefs thou art, childlefs *remain*. *Milton.*

In the families of the world, there *remains* not to one above another the leaft pretence to inheritance. *Locke.*

4. Not to be loft.

Now fomewhat fing, whofe endlefs fouvenance
Among the fhepherds may for aye *remain*. *Spenfer.*

I was increafed more than all that were before me, alfo my wifdom *remained* with me. *Ecclef.* ii. 9.

5. To be left as not comprifed.

That a father may have fome power over his children, is eafily granted; but that an elder brother has fo over his brethren, *remains* to be proved. *Locke.*

To REMAI'N. *v. a.* To await; to be left to.

Such end had the kid; for he would weaned be
Of craft, coloured with fimplicity;
And fuch end, pardie, does all them *remain*
That of fuch falfers friendfhip fhall be fain. *Spenfer.*

With oaken ftaff
I'll raife fuch outcries on thy clatter'd iron,
Which long fhall not withhold me from thy head,
That in a little time, while breath *remains* thee,
Thou oft fhalt wi h thyfelf at Gath to boaft,
But never fhalt fee Gath. *Milton.*

If thence he 'fcape, what *remains* him lefs
Than unknown dangers. *Milton.*

The eafier conqueft now
Remains thee, aided by this hoft of friends,
Back on thy foes more glorious to return. *Milton.*

REMAIN. *n. f.* [from the verb.]

1. Relick; that which is left. Generally ufed in the plural.

I grieve with the old, for fo many additional inconveniencies, more than their fmall *remain* of life feemed deftined to undergo. *Pope.*

2. The body left by the foul.

But fowls obfcene difmember'd his *remains*,
And dogs had torn him. *Pope's Odyffey.*

Oh would'ft thou fing what heroes Windfor bore,
Or raife old warriors, whofe ador'd *remains*,
In weeping vaults, her hallow'd earth contains. *Pope.*

3. Abode; habitation. Not in ufe.

A moft miraculous work in this good king,
Which, often fince my here *remain* in England,
I've feen him do. *Shakefp. Macbeth.*

REMAI'NDER. *adj.* [from *remain.*] Remaining; refufe; left.

His brain
Is as dry as the *remainder* bifket
After a voyage. *Shakefp. As You Like it.*

We turn not back the filks upon the merchant,
When we have fpoil'd them; nor the *remainder* viands
We do not throw in unrefpective place,
Becaufe we now are full. *Shakefp. Troilus and Creffida.*

REMAI'NDER. *n. f.*

1. What is left.

The gods protect you,
And blefs the good *remainders* of the court! *Shakefp.*

A fine is levied to grant a reverfion or *remainder*, expectant upon a leafe that yieldeth no rent. *Bacon.*

Mahomet's crefcent by our feuds encreaft,
Blafted the learn'd *remainders* of the Eaft. *Denham.*

Could bare ingratitude have made any one fo diabolical, had not cruelty came in as a fecond to its affiftance, and cleared the villain's breaft of all *remainders* of humanity? *South.*

There are two reftraints which God hath put upon human nature, fhame and fear; fhame is the weaker, and hath place only in thofe in whom there are fome *remainders* of virtue. *Tillotfon.*

What madnefs moves you, matrons, to deftroy
The laft *remainders* of unhappy Troy? *Dryden.*

If he, to whom ten talents were committed, has fquandered away five, he is concerned to make a double improvement of the *remainder*. *Rogers.*

If thefe decoctions be repeated till the water comes off clear, the *remainder* yields no falt. *Arbuthnot.*

Of fix millions raifed every year for the fervice of the publick, one third is intercepted through the feveral fubordinations of artful men in office, before the *remainder* is applied to the proper ufe. *Swift.*

2. The body when the foul is departed; remains.

Shew us
The poor *remainder* of Andronicus. *Shakefp.*

To REMA'KE. *v. a.* [*re* and *make.*] To make anew.

That, which fhe owns above her, muft perfectly *remake* us after the image of our maker. *Glanvill's Apology.*

To REMA'ND. *v. a.* [*re* and *mando*, Lat.] To fend back; to call back.

The better fort quitted their freeholds and fled into England, and never returned, though many laws were made to *remand* them back. *Davies on Ireland.*

Philoxenus, for defpifing fome dull poetry of Dionyfius, was condemned to dig in the quarries; from whence being *remanded*, at his return Dionyfius produced fome other of his verfes, which as foon as Philoxenus had read, he made no reply, but, calling to the waiters, faid, carry me again to the quarries. *Government of the Tongue.*

RE'MANENT. *n. f.* [*remanens*, Lat. *remanant*, old Fr. It is now contracted to *remnant.*] The part remaining.

Her majefty bought of his executrix the *remanent* of the laft term of three years. *Bacon.*

REMA'RK. *n. f.* [*remarque*, Fr.] Obfervation; note; notice taken.

He cannot diftinguifh difficult and noble fpeculations from trifling and vulgar *remarks*. *Collier on Pride.*

To REMA'RK. *v. a.* [*remarquer*, Fr.]

1. To note; to obferve.

It is eafy to obferve what has been *remarked*, that the names of fimple ideas are the leaft liable to miftakes. *Locke.*

The pris'ner Samfon here I feek.
—His manacles *remark* him, there he fits. *Milton.*

2. To diftinguifh; to point out; to mark.

REMA'RKABLE. *adj.* [*remarkable*, Fr.] Obfervable; worthy of note.

So did Orpheus plainly teach, that the world had beginning in time, from the will of the moft high God, whofe *remarkable* words are thus converted. *Raleigh.*

 'Tis

'Tis *remarkable*, that they
Talk most, who have the least to say. *Prior.*

What we obtain by conversation soon vanishes, unless we note down what *remarkables* we have found. *Watts.*

REMA'RKABLENESS. *n. s.* [from *remarkable.*] Observableness; worthiness of observation.

They signify the *remarkableness* of this punishment of the Jews, as signal revenge from the crucified Christ. *Hammond.*

REMA'RKABLY. *adv.* [from *remarkable.*] Observably; in a manner worthy of observation.

Chiefly assur'd,
Remarkably so late, of thy so true,
So faithful love. *Milton.*

Such parts of these writings, as may be *remarkably* stupid, should become subjects of an occasional criticism. *Watts.*

REMA'RKER. *n. s.* [*remarkeur*, Fr.] Observer; one that remarks.

If the *remarker* would but once try to outshine the author by writing a better book on the same subject, he would soon be convinced of his own insufficiency. *Watts.*

REME'DIABLE. *adj.* [from *remedy.*] Capable of remedy.

REME'DIATE. *adj.* [from *remedy.*] Medicinal; affording a remedy. Not in use.

All you, unpublish'd virtues of the earth,
Spring with my tears; be aidant and *remediate*
In the good man's distress. *Shakesp. King Lear.*

REME'DILESS. *adj.* [from *remedy.*] Not admitting remedy; irreparable; cureless; incurable.

Sad Æsculapius
Imprison'd was in chains *remediless*. *Fairy Queen.*

The war, grounded upon this general *remediless* necessity, may be termed the general, the *remediless*, or the necessary war. *Raleigh's Essays.*

We, by rightful doom *remediless*,
Were lost in death, till he that dwelt above
High-thron'd in secret bliss, for us frail dust
Emptied his glory. *Milton.*

Flatter him it may, as those are good at flattering, who are good for nothing else; but in the mean time, the poor man is left under a *remediless* delusion. *South.*

REME'DILESSNESS. *n. s.* [from *remediless.*] Incurableness.

REME'DY. *n. s.* [*remedium*, Lat. *remede*, Fr.]

1. A medicine by which any ilness is cured.

The difference between poisons and *remedies* is easily known by their effects; and common reason soon distinguishes between virtue and vice. *Swift.*

2. Cure of any uneasiness.

Here hope began to dawn; resolv'd to try,
She fix'd on this her utmost *remedy*. *Dryden.*
O how short my interval of woe!
Our griefs how swift, our *remedies* how slow. *Prior.*

3. That which counteracts any evil.

What may be *remedy* or cure
To evils, which our own misdeeds have wrought. *Milton.*

Civil government is the proper *remedy* for the inconveniencies of the state of nature. *Locke.*

Attempts have been made for some *remedy* against this evil. *Swift.*

4. Reparation; means of repairing any hurt.

Things, without all *remedy*,
Should be without regard. *Shakesp. Macbeth.*

In the death of a man there is no *remedy*. *Wisd.* ii. 1.

To REME'DY. *v. a.* [*remedier*, Fr.]

1. To cure; to heal.

Sorry we are, that any good and godly mind should be grieved with that which is done; but to *remedy* their grief, lieth not so much in us as in themselves. *Hooker.*

2. To repair or remove mischief.

To REME'MBER. *v. a.* [*remembrer*, old Fr. *remembrare*, Ital.]

1. To bear in mind any thing; not to forget.

Remember not against us former iniquities. *Ps.* lxxix. 8.

2. To recollect; to call to mind.

He having once seen and *remembered* me, even from the beginning began to be in the rierward. *Sidney.*

We are said to *remember* any thing, when the idea of it arises in the mind with a consciousness that we have had this idea before. *Watts's Improvement of the Mind.*

3. To keep in mind; to have present to the attention.

Remember what I warn thee, shun to taste;
And shun the bitter consequence. *Milton.*

This is to be *remembered*, that it is not possible now to keep a young gentleman from vice by a total ignorance of it; unless you will all his life mew him up. *Locke.*

4. To bear in mind, with intent of reward or punishment.

Cry unto God; for you shall be *remembered* of him. *Bar.*

He brings them back,
Rememb'ring mercy and his covenant sworn. *Milton.*

5. To mention; not to omit.

A citation ought to be certain, in respect of the person cited; for, if such certainty be therein omitted, such citation is invalid, as in many cases hereafter to be *remembered*. *Ayliffe.*

6. To put in mind; to force to recollect; to remind.

His hand and leg commanding without threatning, and rather *remembering* than chastising. *Sidney.*

Joy, being altogether wanting,
It doth *remember* me the more of sorrow. *Shakesp.*

These petitions, and the answer of the common council of London, were ample materials for a conference with the lords, who might be thereby *remembered* of their duty. *Claren.*

REME'MBERER. *n. s.* [from *remember.*] One who remembers.

A brave master to servants, and a *rememberer* of the least good office; for his flock he transplanted most of them into plentiful soils. *Wotton.*

REME'MBRANCE. *n. s.* [*remembrance*, Fr.]

1. Retention in memory.

Though Cloten then but young, time has not wore him
From my *remembrance*. *Shakesp. Cymbeline.*

Thee I have heard relating what was done,
Ere my *remembrance*. *Milton.*

Had memory been lost with innocence,
We had not known the sentence nor th' offence;
'Twas his chief punishment to keep in store
The sad *remembrance* what he was before. *Denham.*

Sharp *remembrance* on the English part,
And shame of being match'd by such a foe,
Rouse conscious virtue up in every heart. *Dryden.*

This ever grateful in *remembrance* bear
To me thou ow'st, to me the vital air. *Pope's Odyssey.*

2. Recollection; revival of any idea.

I hate thy beams,
That bring to my *remembrance* from what state
I fell; how glorious once above thy sphere. *Milton.*

Remembrance is when the same idea recurs, without the operation of the like object on the external sensory. *Locke.*

3. Honourable memory. Out of use.

Rosemary and rue keep
Seeming and savour all the winter long,
Grace and *remembrance* be unto you both. *Shakesp.*

4. Transmission of a fact from one to another.

Titan,
Among the heavens, th' immortal fact display'd,
Lest the *remembrance* of his grief should fail,
And in the constellations wrote his tale. *Addison.*

5. Account preserved.

Those proceedings and *remembrances* are in the Tower, beginning with the twentieth year of Edward I. *Hale.*

6. Memorial.

But in *remembrance* of so brave a deed,
A tomb and funeral honours I decreed. *Dryden.*

7. A token by which any one is kept in the memory.

I have *remembrances* of yours,
That I have longed to redeliver. *Shakesp. Hamlet.*

Keep this *remembrance* for thy Julia's sake. *Shakesp.*

8. Notice of something absent.

Let your *remembrance* still apply to Banquo;
Present him eminence, both with eye and tongue. *Shakesp.*

REME'MBRANCER. *n. s.* [from *remembrance.*]

1. One that reminds; one that puts in mind.

Sweet *remembrancer!* *Shakesp. Macbeth.*

A sly knave, the agent for his master,
And the *remembrancer* of her, to hold
The hand fast to her lord. *Shakesp. Cymbeline.*

God is present in the consciences of good and bad; he is there a *remembrancer* to call our actions to mind, and a witness to bring them to judgment. *Taylor.*

Would I were in my grave;
For, living here, you're but my curs'd *remembrancers:*
I once was happy. *Otway's Venice Preserv'd.*

2. An officer of the exchequer.

All are digested into books, and sent to the *remembrancer* of the exchequer, that he make processes upon them. *Bacon.*

To REME'RCIE. *v. a.* [*remercier*, Fr.] To thank. Obsolete.

Off'ring his service and his dearest life
For her defence, against that earle to fight;
She him *remercied*, as the patron of her life. *Spenser.*

To RE'MIGRATE. *v. n.* [*remigro*, Lat.] To remove back again.

Some other ways he proposes to divest some bodies of their borrowed shapes, and make them *remigrate* to their first simplicity. *Boyle.*

REMIGRA'TION. *n. s.* [from *remigrate.*] Removal back again.

The Scots, transplanted hither, became acquainted with our customs, which, by occasional *remigrations*, became diffused in Scotland. *Hale.*

To REMI'ND. *v. a.* [*re* and *mind.*] To put in mind; to force to remember.

When age itself, which will not be defied, shall begin to arrest, seize and *remind* us of our mortality by pains and dulness of senses; yet then the pleasure of the mind shall be in its full vigour. *South's Sermons.*

The brazen figure of the consul, with the ring on his finger, *reminded* me of Juvenal's majoris pondera gemmæ. *Addison's Remarks on Italy.*

REMINI'SCENCE. *n. s.* [*reminiscens*, Latin.] Recollection; recovery of ideas.

I cast about for all circumstances that may revive my memory or *reminiscence*. *Hale's Origin of Mankind.*

For the other part of memory, called *reminiſcence*, which is the retrieving of a thing at preſent forgot, or but confuſedly remembered, by ſetting the mind to ranſack every little cell of the brain; while it is thus buſied, how accidentally does the thing ſought for offer itſelf to the mind? *South.*

REMINISCE'NTIAL. *adj.* [from *reminiſcence.*] Relating to reminiſcence.

Would truth diſpenſe, we could be content with Plato, that knowledge were but remembrance, that intellectual acquiſition were but *reminiſcential* evocation. *Brown.*

REMI'SS. *adj.* [*remis*, Fr. *remiſſus*, Lat.]

1. Not vigorous; ſlack.

The water deſerts the ſaid corpuſcles, unleſs it flow forth with a precipitate motion; for then it hurries them out along with it, till its motion becomes more languid and *remiſs.* *Woodward's Natural Hiſtory.*

2. Not careful; ſlothful.

Mad ire and wrathful fury makes me weep,
That thus we die, while *remiſs* traitors ſleep. *Shakeſp.*

If when by God's grace we have conquered the firſt difficulties of religion, we grow careleſs and *remiſs*, and neglect our guard, God's ſpirit will not always ſtrive with us. *Tillotſ.*

Your candour, in pardoning my errors, may make me more *remiſs* in correcting them. *Dryden.*

3. Not intenſe.

Theſe nervous, bold, thoſe languid and *remiſs*;
Here cold ſalutes, but there a lover's kiſs. *Roſcommon.*

REMI'SSIBLE. *adj.* [from *remit.*] Admitting forgiveneſs.

REMI'SSION. *n. ſ.* [*remiſſion*, Fr. *remiſſio*, Lat.]

1. Abatement; relaxation; moderation.

Error, miſclaim and forgetfulneſs do now and then become ſuitors for ſome *remiſſion* of extreme rigour. *Bacon.*

2. Ceſſation of intenſeneſs.

In September and October theſe diſeaſes do not abate and remit in proportion to the *remiſſion* of the ſun's heat. *Woodw.*

This difference of intention and *remiſſion* of the mind in thinking, every one has experimented in himſelf. *Locke.*

3. In phyſick, *remiſſion* is when a diſtemper abates, but does not go quite off before it returns again.

4. Releaſe.

Not only an expedition, but the *remiſſion* of a duty or tax, were tranſmitted to poſterity after this manner. *Addiſon.*

Another ground of the biſhop's fears is the *remiſſion* of the firſt fruits and tenths. *Swift.*

5. Forgiveneſs; pardon.

My pennance is to call Lucetta back,
And aſk *remiſſion* for my folly paſt. *Shakeſp.*

That plea
With God or man will gain thee no *remiſſion.* *Milton.*

Many believe the article of *remiſſion* of ſins, but they believe it without the condition of repentance or the fruits of holy life. *Taylor's Rule of Living Holy.*

REMI'SSLY. *adv.* [from *remiſs.*]

1. Careleſly; negligently; without cloſe attention.

How ſhould it then be in our power to do it coldy or *remiſly?* ſo that our deſire being natural, is alſo in that degree of earneſtneſs whereunto nothing can be added. *Hooker.*

2. Not vigorouſly; not with ardour or eagerneſs; ſlackly.

There was not an equal concurrence in the proſecution of this matter among the biſhops; ſome of them proceeding more *remiſsly* in it. *Clarendon.*

REMI'SSNESS. *n. ſ.* [from *remiſs.*] Careleſsneſs; negligence; coldneſs; want of ardour; inattention.

Future evils,
Or new, or by *remiſsneſs* new conceiv'd,
Are now to have no ſucceſſive degrees. *Shakeſp.*

No great offenders 'ſcape their dooms;
Small praiſe from lenity and *remiſsneſs* comes. *Denham.*

Jack, through the *remiſsneſs* of conſtables, has always found means to eſcape. *Arbuthnot's Hiſtory of John Bull.*

The great concern of God for our ſalvation, is ſo far from an argument of *remiſsneſs* in us, that it ought to excite our utmoſt care. *Rogers's Sermons.*

To REMI'T. *v. a.* [*remitto*, Lat.]

1. To relax; to make leſs intenſe.

So willingly doth God *remit* his ire. *Milton.*

Our ſupreme foe may much *remit*
His anger; and perhaps thus far remov'd,
Not mind us not offending, ſatisfy'd
With what is puniſh'd. *Milton.*

2. To forgive a puniſhment.

With ſuppliant pray'rs their pow'rs appeaſe;
The ſoft Napæan race will ſoon repent
Their anger, and *remit* the puniſhment. *Dryden.*

The magiſtrate can often, where the publick good demands not the execution of the law, *remit* the puniſhment of criminal offences by his own authority, but yet cannot *remit* the ſatisfaction due to any private man. *Locke.*

3. [*Remettre*, Fr.] To pardon a fault.

At my lovely Tamora's intreats,
I do *remit* theſe young men's heinous faults. *Shakeſp.*

Whoſe ſoever ſins ye *remit*, they are *remitted* unto them; and whoſe ſoever ſins ye retain, they are retained. *Jo.* xx. 23.

4. To give up; to reſign.

In grievous and inhuman crimes, offenders ſhould be *remitted* to their prince to be puniſhed in the place where they have offended. *Hayward.*

Th' Ægyptian crown I to your hands *remit*;
And, with it, take his heart who offers it. *Dryden.*

Heaven thinks fit
Thee to thy former fury to *remit.* *Dryden's Tyran. Love.*

5. [*Remettre*, Fr.] To defer; to refer.

The biſhop had certain proud inſtructions in the front, though there were a pliant clauſe at the foot, that *remitted* all to the biſhop's diſcretion. *Bacon's Henry* VII.

I *remit* me to themſelves, and challenge their natural ingenuity to ſay, whether they have not ſometimes ſuch ſhiverings within them. *Government of the Tongue.*

6. To put again in cuſtody.

This bold return with ſeeming patience heard,
The pris'ner was *remitted* to the guard. *Dryden.*

7. To ſend money to a diſtant place.

They obliged themſelves to *remit* after the rate of twelve hundred thouſand pounds ſterling per annum, divided into ſo many monthly payments. *Addiſon's Remarks on Italy.*

8. To reſtore. Not in uſe.

The archbiſhop was retained priſoner, but after a ſhort time *remitted* to his liberty. *Hayward.*

To REMI'T. *v. n.*

1. To ſlacken; to grow leſs intenſe.

When our paſſions *remit*, the vehemence of our ſpeech *remits* too. *Broome's Notes on the Odyſſey.*

2. To abate by growing leſs eager.

As, by degrees, they *remitted* of their induſtry, loathed their buſineſs, and gave way to their pleaſures, they let fall thoſe generous principles, which had raiſed them to worthy thoughts. *South's Sermons.*

3. In phyſick, to grow by intervals leſs violent, though not wholly intermitting.

REMI'TMENT. *n. ſ.* [from *remit.*] The act of remitting to cuſtody.

REMI'TTANCE. *n. ſ.* [from *remit.*]

1. The act of paying money at a diſtant place.

2. Sum ſent to a diſtant place.

A compact among private perſons furniſhed out the ſeveral *remittances.* *Addiſon's Remarks on Italy.*

REMI'TTER. *n. ſ.* [*remettre*, Fr.] In common law, a reſtitution of one that hath two titles to lands or tenements, and is ſeized of them by his latter title, unto his title that is more ancient, in caſe where the latter is defective. *Cowel.*

You ſaid, if I return'd next ſize in Lent,
I ſhould be in *remitter* of your grace;
In th' interim my letters ſhould take place
Of affidavits. *Donne.*

RE'MNANT. *n. ſ.* [corrupted from *remanent.*] Reſidue; that which is left; that which remains.

Poor key-cold figure of a holy king!
Thou bloodleſs *remnant* of that royal blood,
Be't lawful that I invocate thy ghoſt? *Shakeſp. Rich.* III.

Bear me hence
From forth the noiſe and rumour of the field,
Where I may think the *remnant* of my thoughts. *Shakeſp.*

About his ſhelves
Remnants of packthread and old cakes of roſes
Were thinly ſcatter'd. *Shakeſp. Romeo and Juliet.*

I was entreated to get them ſome reſpite and breathing by a ceſſation, without which they ſaw no probability to preſerve the *remnant* that had yet eſcaped. *King Charles.*

Their Andes are far higher than thoſe with us; whereby it ſeems that the *remnants* of the generation of men were in ſuch a deluge ſaved. *Bacon.*

The *remnant* of my tale is of a length
To tire your patience. *Dryden's Knight's Tale.*

A feeble army and an empty ſenate,
Remnants of mighty battles fought in vain. *Addiſon.*

See the poor *remnants* of theſe ſlighted hairs!
My hands ſhall rend what e'en thy rapine ſpares. *Pope.*

The frequent uſe of the latter was a *remnant* of popery, which never admitted ſcripture in the vulgar tongue. *Swift.*

RE'MNANT. *adj.* [corruptly formed from *remanent.*] Remaining; yet left.

It bid her feel
No future pain for me; but inſtant wed
A lover more proportion'd to her bed;
And quiet dedicate her *remnant* life
To the juſt duties of an humble wife. *Prior.*

REMO'LTEN. *part.* [from *remelt.*] Melted again.

It were good to try in glaſs works, whether the crude materials, mingled with glaſs already made and *remolten*, do not facilitate the making of glaſs with leſs heat. *Bacon.*

REMO'NSTRANCE. *n. ſ.* [*remonſtrance*, Fr. from *remonſtrate.*]
1. Show; diſcovery. Not in uſe.

You may marvel, why I would not rather
Make raſh *remonſtrance* of my hidden power,
Than let him be ſo loſt. *Shakeſp. Meaſ. for Meaſ.*

2. Strong repreſentation.

The ſame God, which revealeth it to them, would alſo give them power of confirming it unto others, either with miraculous operation, or with ſtrong and invincible *remonſtrance* of ſound reaſon. *Hooker, b. v. ſ. 10.*

A large family of daughters have drawn up a *remonſtrance*, in which they ſet forth, that their father, having refuſed to take in the Spectator, they offered to 'bate him the article of bread and butter in the tea-table. *Addiſon's Spectator.*

Importunate paſſions ſurround the man, and will not ſuffer him to attend to the *remonſtrances* of juſtice. *Rogers.*

To REMO'NSTRATE. *v. n.* [*remonſtro*, Lat. *remonſtrer*, Fr.] To make a ſtrong repreſentation; to ſhow reaſons on any ſide in ſtrong terms.

RE'MORA. *n. ſ.* [Latin.]
1. A let or obſtacle.
2. A fiſh or a kind of worm that ſticks to ſhips, and retards their paſſage through the water.

Of fiſhes you ſhall find in arms the whale, herring, roach and *remora*. *Peacham on Blazoning.*

The *remora* is about three quarters of a yard long; his body before three inches and a half over, thence tapering to the tail end; his mouth two inches and a half over; his chops ending angularly; the nether a little broader; and produced forward near an inch; his lips rough with a great number of little prickles. *Grew.*

To REMO'RATE. *v. a.* [*remoror*, Latin.] To hinder; to delay. *Dict.*

REMO'RSE. *n. ſ.* [*remorſus*, Lat.]
1. Pain of guilt.

Not that he believed they could be reſtrained from that impious act by any *remorſe* of conſcience, or that they had not wickedneſs enough to deſign and execute it. *Clarendon.*

2. Tenderneſs; pity; ſympathetick ſorrow.

Many little eſteem of their own lives, yet, for *remorſe* of their wives and children, would be withheld. *Spenſer.*

Shylock, thou lead'ſt this faſhion of thy malice
To the laſt hour of act; and then 'tis thought,
Thou'lt ſhew thy mercy and *remorſe* more ſtrange,
Than is thy ſtrange apparent cruelty. *Shakeſp. Mer. of Ven.*

The rogues ſlighted me into the river, with as little *remorſe* as they would have drowned a bitch's blind puppies. *Shakeſp.*

Curſe on th' unpard'ning prince, whom tears can draw
To no *remorſe*; who rules by lion's law. *Dryden.*

REMO'RSEFUL. *adj.* [*remorſe* and *full.*] Tender; compaſſionate.

O Eglamour, think not I flatter,
Valiant and wiſe, *remorſeful*, well accompliſh'd. *Shakeſp.*

Love, that comes too late,
Like a *remorſeful* pardon ſlowly carried,
To the great ſender turns a ſowre offence. *Shakeſp.*

The gaudy, blabbing, and *remorſeful* day
Is crept into the boſom of the ſea. *Shakeſp. Henry VI.*

REMO'RSELESS. *adj.* [from *remorſe.*] Unpitying; cruel; ſavage.

Where were the nymphs, when the *remorſeleſs* deep
Clos'd o'er the head of your lov'd Lycidas. *Milton.*

O the inexpreſſible horrour that will ſeize upon a ſinner, when he ſtands arraigned at the bar of divine juſtice! when he ſhall ſee his accuſer, his judge, the witneſſes, all his *remorſeleſs* adverſaries. *South's Sermons.*

REMO'TE. *adj.* [*remotus*, Lat.]
1. Diſtant; not immediate.

In this narrow ſcantling of capacity, it is not all *remote* and even apparent good that affects us. *Locke.*

2. Diſtant; not at hand.
3. Removed far off; placed not near.

Wherever the mind places itſelf by any thought, either amongſt, or *remote* from all bodies, it can, in this uniform idea of ſpace, no where find any bounds. *Locke.*

In quiet ſhades, content with rural ſports,
Give me a life, *remote* from guilty courts. *Granville.*

4. Foreign.
5. Diſtant; not cloſely connected.

An unadviſed tranſiliency from the effect to the *remoteſt* cauſe. *Glanvill.*

Syllogiſm ſerves not to furniſh the mind with intermediate ideas, that ſhew the connection of *remote* ones. *Locke.*

6. Alien; not agreeing.

All thoſe propoſitions, how *remote* ſoever from reaſon, are ſo ſacred, that men will ſooner part with their lives, than ſuffer themſelves to doubt of them. *Locke.*

7. Abſtracted.

REMO'TELY. *adv.* [from *remote.*] Not nearly; at a diſtance.

It is commonly opinioned, that the earth was thinly inhabited, at leaſt not *remotely* planted before the flood. *Brown.*

Two lines in Mezentius and Lauſus are indeed *remotely* allied to Virgil's ſenſe, but too like the tenderneſs of Ovid. *Dry.*

While the fainting Dutch *remotely* fire
In the firſt front amidſt a ſlaughter'd pile,
High on the mound he dy'd. *Smith.*

REMO'TENESS. *n. ſ.* [from *remote.*] State of being remote; diſtance; not nearneſs.

The joys of heaven are like the ſtars, which by reaſon of our *remoteneſs* appear extremely little. *Boyle.*

Titian employed brown and earthly colours upon the forepart, and has reſerved his greater light for *remoteneſſes* and the back part of his landſchapes. *Dryden.*

If the greateſt part of bodies eſcape our notice by their *remoteneſs*, others are no leſs concealed by their minuteneſs. *Locke.*

His obſcurities generally ariſe from the *remoteneſs* of the cuſtoms, perſons and things he alludes to. *Addiſon.*

REMO'TION. *n. ſ.* [from *remotus*, Lat.] The act of removing; the ſtate of being removed to diſtance.

All this ſafety were *remotion*, and thy defence abſence. *Sha.*

This act perſuades me,
'Tis the *remotion* of the duke and her. *Shakeſp.*

The conſequent ſtrictly taken, may be a fallacious illation, in reference to antecedency or conſequence; as to conclude from the poſition of the antecedent unto the poſition of the conſequent, or from the *remotion* of the conſequent to the *remotion* of the antecedent. *Brown's Vulgar Errours.*

REMO'VABLE. *adj.* [from *remove.*] Such as may be removed.

The Iriſh biſhops have their clergy in ſuch ſubjection, that they dare not complain of them; for knowing their own incapacity, and that they are therefore *removeable* at their biſhop's will, yield what pleaſeth him. *Spenſer.*

In ſuch a chapel, ſuch curate is *removeable* at the pleaſure of the rector of the mother church. *Ayliffe's Parergon.*

REMO'VAL. *n. ſ.* [from *remove.*]
1. The act of putting out of any place.

By which *removal* of one extremity with another, the world, ſeeking to procure a remedy, hath purchaſed a mere exchange of the evil before felt. *Hooker.*

2. The act of putting away.

The *removal* of ſuch a diſeaſe is not to be attempted by active remedies, no more than a thorn in the fleſh is to be taken away by violence. *Arbuthnot.*

3. Diſmiſſion from a poſt.

If the *removal* of theſe perſons from their poſts has produced ſuch popular commotions, the continuance of them might have produced ſomething more fatal. *Addiſon.*

Whether his *removal* was cauſed by his own fears or other men's artifices, ſuppoſing the throne to be vacant, the body of the people was left at liberty to chuſe what form of government they pleaſed. *Swift.*

4. The ſtate of being removed.

The ſitting ſtill of a paralytick, whilſt he prefers it to a *removal*, is voluntary. *Locke.*

To REMO'VE. *v. a.* [*removeo*, Lat. *remuer*, Fr.]
1. To put from its place; to take or put away.

Good God *remove*
The means that makes us ſtrangers! *Shakeſp. Macbeth.*

He *removeth* away the ſpeech of the truſty, and taketh away the underſtanding of the aged. *Job* xii. 20.

Remove thy ſtroke away from me; I am conſumed by the blow. *Pſalm* xxxix. 13.

So would he have *removed* thee out of the ſtraight into a broad place. *Job* xxxvi. 16.

He longer in this paradiſe to dwell
Permits not; to *remove* thee I am come,
And ſend thee from the garden forth to till
The ground. *Milton's Paradiſe Loſt, b.* xi.

Whether he will *remove* his contemplation from one idea to another, is many times in his choice. *Locke.*

You, who fill the bliſsful ſeats above!
Let kings no more with gentle mercy ſway,
But every monarch be the ſcourge of God,
If from your thoughts Ulyſſes you *remove*,
Who rul'd his ſubjects with a father's love. *Pope's Odyſſey.*

2. To place at a diſtance.

They are farther *removed* from a title to be innate, and the doubt of their being native impreſſions on the mind, is ſtronger againſt theſe moral principles than the other. *Locke.*

To REMO'VE. *v. n.*
1. To change place.
2. To go from one place to another.

A ſhort exile muſt for ſhow precede;
The term expir'd, from Candia they *remove*,
And happy each at home enjoys his love. *Dryden.*

How oft from pomp and ſtate did I *remove*
To feed deſpair. *Prior.*

REMO'VE. *n. ſ.* [from the verb.]
1. Change of place.
2. Suſceptibility of being removed. Not in uſe.

What is early received in any conſiderable ſtrength of impreſs, grows into our tender natures; and therefore is of difficult *remove*. *Glanvill's Sceps.*

3. Translation of one to the place of another.

Rosaline, this favour thou shalt wear;
Hold, take you this, my sweet, and give me thine,
So shall Biron take me for Rosaline:
And change your favours too; so shall your loves
Woo contrary deceiv'd by these *removes*. *Shakesp.*

4. State of being removed.

This place should be both school and university, not needing a *remove* to any other house of scholarship. *Milton.*

He that considers how little our constitution can bear a *remove* into parts of this air, not much higher than that we breathe in, will be satisfied, that the allwise architect has suited our organs, and the bodies that are to effect them, one to another. *Locke.*

5. Act of moving a chesman or draught.

6. Departure; act of going away.

So look'd Astrea, her *remove* design'd,
On those distressed friends she left behind. *Waller.*

7. The act of changing place.

Let him, upon his *removes* from one place to another, procure recommendation to some person of quality residing in the place whither he removeth. *Bacon's Essays.*

8. A stop in the scale of gradation.

In all the visible corporeal world, quite down from us, the descent is by easy steps, and a continued series of things, that in each *remove* differ very little one from the other. *Locke.*

A freeholder is but one *remove* from a legislator, and ought to stand up in the defence of those laws. *Addison.*

9. A small distance.

The fiercest contentions of men are between creatures equal in nature, and capable, by the greatest distinction of circumstances, of but a very small *remove* one from another. *Rogers.*

10. Act of putting a horse's shoes upon different feet.

His horse wanted two *removes*, your horse wanted nails. *Sw.*

REMO'VED. *particip. adj.* [from *remove.*] Remote; separate from others.

Your accent is something finer, than you could purchase in so *removed* a dwelling. *Shakesp. As You Like it.*

REMO'VEDNESS. *n. s.* [from *removed.*] The state of being removed; remoteness.

I have eyes under my service, which look upon his *removedness*. *Shakesp.*

REMO'VER. *n. s.* [from *remove.*] One that removes.

The misslayer of a merstone is to blame; but the unjust judge is the capital *remover* of landmarks, when he defineth amiss. *Bacon.*

Hasty fortune maketh an enterpriser and *remover*, but the exercised fortune maketh the able man. *Bacon.*

To REMOU'NT. *v. n.* [*remonter*, Fr.] To mount again.

Stout Cymon soon *remounts*, and cleft in two
His rival's head. *Dryden.*

The rest *remounts* with the ascending vapours, or is washed down into rivers, and transmitted into the sea. *Woodward.*

REMU'NERABLE. *adj.* [from *remunerate.*] Rewardable.

To REMU'NERATE. *v. a.* [*remunero*, Lat. *remunerer*, Fr] To reward; to repay; to requite; to recompense.

Is she not then beholden to the man,
That brought her for this high good turn so far?
Yes; and will nobly *remunerate*. *Shakesp. Titus Andron.*

Money the king thought not fit to demand, because he had received satisfaction in matters of so great importance; and because he could not *remunerate* them with any general pardon, being prevented therein by the coronation pardon. *Bacon.*

In another parable, he represents the great condescensions, wherewith the Lord shall *remunerate* the faithful servant. *Boyle.*

REMUNERA'TION. *n. s.* [*remuneration*, Fr. *remuneratio*, Lat.] Reward; requital; recompense; repayment.

Bear this significant to the country maid, Jaquenetta; there is *remuneration*; for the best ward of mine honour is rewarding my dependants. *Shakesp. Love's Labour Lost.*

He begets a security of himself, and a careless eye on the last *remunerations*. *Brown's Vulgar Errours.*

A collation is a donation of some vacant benefice in the church, especially when such donation is freely bestowed without any prospect of an evil *remuneration*. *Ayliffe.*

REMUNERA'TIVE. *adj.* [from *remunerate.*] Exercised in giving rewards.

The knowledge of particular actions seems requisite to the attainment of that great end of God, in the manifestation of his punitive and *remunerative* justice. *Boyle.*

To REMU'RMUR. *v. a.* [*re* and *murmur.*] To utter back in murmurs; to repeat in low hoarse sounds.

Her fate is whisper'd by the gentle breeze,
And told in sighs to all the trembling trees;
The trembling trees, in ev'ry plain and wood,
Her fate *remurmur* to the silver flood. *Pope.*

To REMU'RMUR. *v. n.* [*remurmuro*, Lat] To murmur back; to echo a low hoarse sound.

Her fellow nymphs the mountains tear
With loud laments, and break the yielding air;
The realms of Mars *remurmur'd* all around,
And echoes to th' Athenian shoars rebound. *Dryden.*

His untimely fate, th' Angitian woods
In sighs *remurmur'd* to the Fucine floods. *Dryden.*

RENA'RD. *n. s.* [*renard*, a fox, Fr.] The name of a fox in fable.

Before the break of day,
Renard through the hedge had made his way. *Dryden.*

RENA'SCENT. *adj.* [*renascens*, Lat.] Produced again; rising again into being.

RENA'SCIBLE. *adj.* [*renascor*, Lat.] Possible to be produced again.

To RENA'VIGATE. [*re* and *navigate.*] To sail again.

RENCOU'NTER. *n. s.* [*rencontre*, Fr.]

1. Clash; collision.

You may as well expect two bowls should grow sensible by rubbing, as that the *rencounter* of any bodies should awaken them into perception. *Collier.*

2. Personal opposition.

Virgil's friends thought fit to alter a line in Venus's speech, that has a relation to the *rencounter*. *Addison.*

So when the trumpet sounding gives the sign,
The justling chiefs in rude *rencounter* join:
So meet, and so renew the dextrous fight;
Their clattering arms with the fierce shock resound. *Gran.*

3. Loose or casual engagement.

The confederates should turn to their advantage their apparent odds in men and horse; and by that means out-number the enemy in all *rencounters* and engagements. *Addison.*

4. Sudden combat without premeditation.

To RENCOU'NTER. *v. n.*] *rencontrer*, Fr.]

1. To clash; to collide.
2. To meet an enemy unexpectedly.
3. To skirmish with another.
4. To fight hand to hand.

To REND. *v. a. pret. and pret. pass. rent.* [ꞃenꞇan, Saxon.] To tear with violence; to lacerate.

Will you hence
Before the tag return, whose rage doth *rend*
Like interrupted waters, and o'erbear
What they are used to bear. *Shakesp. Coriolanus.*

He *rent* a lion as he would have *rent* a kid, and he had nothing in his hand. *Jud.* xiv. 4.

I will not *rend* away all the kingdom, but give one tribe to thy son. 1 *Kings* xi. 13.

By the thund'rer's stroke it from th' root is *rent*,
So sure the blows, which from high heaven are sent. *Cowley.*

What you command me to relate,
Renews the sad remembrance of our fate,
An empire from its old foundations *rent*. *Dryden.*

Look round to see
The lurking gold upon the fatal tree;
Then *rend* it off. *Dryden's Æneis.*

Is it not as much reason to say, when any monarchy was shattered to pieces, and divided amongst revolted subjects, that God was careful to preserve monarchical power, by *rending* a settled empire into a multitude of little governments. *Locke.*

When its way th' impetuous passion found,
I *rend* my tresses, and my breast I wound. *Pope.*

From cloud to cloud the *rending* lightnings rage. *Thomson.*

RE'NDER. *n. s.* [from *rend.*] One that rends; a tearer.

To RE'NDER. *v. a.* [*rendre*, Fr.]

1. To return; to pay back.

What shall I *render* unto the Lord for all his benefits. *Ps.*

They that *render* evil for good are adversaries. *Ps.* xxxviii.

Will ye *render* me a recompense? *Joel* iii. 4.

Let him look into the future state of bliss or misery, and see there God, the righteous judge, ready to *render* every man according to his deeds. *Locke.*

2. To restore; to give back.

Hither the seas at stated times resort,
And shove the loaden vessels into port;
Then with a gentle ebb retire again,
And *render* back their cargo to the main. *Addison.*

3. To give upon demand.

The sluggard is wiser in his own conceit, than seven men that can *render* a reason. *Proverbs* xxvi. 16.

4. To invest with qualities; to make.

Because the nature of man carries him out to action, it is no wonder if the same nature *renders* him solicitous about the issue. *South's Sermons.*

Love
Can answer love, and *render* bliss secure. *Thomson.*

5. To represent; to exhibit.

I heard him speak of that same brother,
And he did *render* him the most unnatural
That liv'd 'mongst men. *Shakesp.*

6. To translate.

Render it in the English a circle; but 'tis more truly *rendered* a sphere. *Burnet's Theory of the Earth.*

He has a clearer idea of strigil and sistrum, a curry-comb and cymbal, which are the English names dictionaries *render* them by. *Locke.*

He

He uses only a prudent dissimulation; the word we may almost literally *render* master of a great presence of mind. *Broome's Notes on the Odyssey.*

7. To surrender; to yield; to give up.

I will call him to so strict account,
That he shall *render* every glory up,
Or I will tear the reck'ning from his heart. *Shakesp.*

My *rend'ring* my person to them, may engage their affections to me. *King Charles.*

One, with whom he used to advise, proposed to him to *render* himself upon conditions to the earl of Essex. *Clarendon.*

Would he *render* up Hermione,
And keep Astyanax, I should be blest! *A. Philips.*

8. To offer; to give to be used.

Logick *renders* its daily service to wisdom and virtue. *Watts.*

RE'NDER. *n. s.* [from the verb.] Surrender.

Newness
Of Cloten's death, we being not known, nor muster'd
Among the bands, may drive us to a *render.* *Shakesp.*

RENDE'ZVOUS. *n. s.* [*rendez vous*, Fr.]

1. Assembly; meeting appointed.

A commander of many ships should rather keep his fleet together, than have it severed far asunder; for the attendance of meeting them again at the next *rendezvous* would consume time and victual. *Raleigh's Apology.*

2. A sign that draws men together.

The philosophers-stone and a holy war are but the *rendezvous* of cracked brains, that wear their feather in their head instead of their hat. *Bacon.*

3. Place appointed for assembly.

The king appointed his whole army to be drawn together to a *rendezvous* at Marlborough. *Clarendon.*

This was the general *rendezvous* which they all got to, and, mingling more and more with that oily liquor, they sucked it all up. *Burnet's Theory of the Earth.*

To RENDE'ZVOUS. *v. n.* [from the noun.] To meet at a place appointed.

RENDI'TION. *n. s.* [from *render.*] Surrendering; the act of yielding.

RENEGA'DE. } RENEGA'DO. } *n. s.* [*renegado*, Spanish; *renegat*, Fr.]

1. One that apostatises from the faith; an apostate.

There lived a French *renegado* in the same place, where the Castilian and his wife were kept prisoners. *Addison.*

2. One who deserts to the enemy; a revolter.

Some straggling soldiers might prove *renegadoes*, but they would not revolt in troops. *Decay of Piety.*

If the Roman government subsisted now, they would have had *renegade* seamen and shipwrights enough. *Arbuthnot.*

To RENE'GE. *v. a.* [*renego*, Lat. *renier*, Fr.] To disown.

His captain's heart,
Which, in the scuffles of great fights, hath burst
The buckles on his breast, *reneges* all temper. *Shakesp.*

Such smiling rogues as these sooth every passion,
Renege, affirm, and turn their halcyon beaks
With every gale and vary of their masters. *Shakesp.*

The design of this war is to make me *renege* my conscience and thy truth. *King Charles.*

To RENE'W. *v. a.* [*re* and *new*; *renova*, Lat.]

1. To renovate; to restore the former state.

In such a night
Medea gather'd the enchanted herbs,
That did *renew* old Æson. *Shakesp. Merch. of Venice.*

It is impossible for those that were once enlightened—if they shall fall away to *renew* them again unto repentance. *Hebrews* vi. 6.

Let us go to Gilgal, and *renew* the kingdom there. 1 *Sam.*

Renew'd to life, that she might daily die,
I daily doom'd to follow. *Dryden's Theo. and Honor.*

2. To repeat; to put again in act.

Thy famous grandfather
Doth live again in thee; long may'st thou live,
To bear his image, and *renew* his glories! *Shakesp.*

The body percussed hath, by reason of the percussion, a trepidation wrought in the minute parts, and so *reneweth* the percussion of the air. *Bacon's Natural History.*

The bearded corn ensu'd
From earth unask'd, nor was that earth *renew'd.* *Dryden.*

3. To begin again.

The last great age, foretold by sacred rhymes,
Renews its finish'd course, Saturnian times
Rowl round again. *Dryden's Virgil's Pastorals.*

4. In theology, to make anew; to transform to new life.

Be ye transformed by the *renewing* of your mind, that ye may prove what is that perfect will of God. *Rom.* xii. 2.

RENE'WABLE. *adj.* [from *renew.*] Capable to be renewed.

The old custom upon many estates is to let for leases of lives, *renewable* at pleasure. *Swift's Miscellanies.*

RENE'WAL. *n. s.* [from *renew.*] The act of renewing; renovation.

It behoved the deity, persisting in the purpose of mercy to mankind, to renew that revelation from time to time, and to rectify abuses, with such authority for the *renewal* and rectification, as was sufficient evidence of the truth of what was revealed. *Forbes.*

RENI'TENCY. *n. s.* [from *renitent.*] That resistance in solid bodies, when they press upon, or are impelled one against another, or the resistance that a body makes on account of weight. *Quincy.*

RENI'TENT. *adj.* [*renitens*, Lat.] Acting against any impulse by elastick power.

By an inflation of the muscles, they become soft, and yet *renitent*, like so many pillows, dissipating the force of the pressure, and so taking away the sense of pain. *Ray.*

RE'NNET. *n. s.* See RUNNET.

A putredinous ferment coagulates all humours, as milk with *rennet* is turned. *Floyer on the Humours.*

RE'NNET. } RENE'TING. } *n. s.* [properly *reinette*, a little queen.] A kind of apple.

A golden *rennet* is a very pleasant and fair fruit, of a yellow flush, and the best of bearers for all sorts of soil; of which there are two sorts, the large sort and the small. *Mort.*

Ripe pulpy apples, as pippins and *rennetings*, are of a syrupy tenacious nature. *Mortimer's Husbandry.*

To RE'NOVATE. *v. a.* [*renovo*, Lat.] To renew; to restore to the first state.

All nature feels the *renovating* force
Of winter, only to the thoughtless eye
In ruin seen. *Thomson's Winter.*

RENOVA'TION. *n. s.* [*renovation*, Fr. *renovatio*, Lat.] Renewal; the act of renewing; the state of being renewed.

Sound continueth some small time, which is a *renovation*, and not a continuance; for the body percussed hath a trepidation wrought in the minute parts, and so reneweth the percussion of the air. *Bacon's Natural History.*

The kings entered into speech of renewing the treaty; the king saying, that though king Philip's person were the same, yet his fortunes were raised; in which case a *renovation* of treaty was used. *Bacon's Henry* VII.

To second life,
Wak'd in the *renovation* of the just,
Resigns him up, with heav'n and earth renew'd. *Milton.*

To RENOU'NCE. *v. a.* [*renoncer*, Fr. *renuncio*, Lat.]

1. To disown; to abnegate.

From Thebes my birth I own; and no disgrace
Can force me to *renounce* the honour of my race. *Dryden.*

2. To quit upon oath.

This world I do *renounce*; and in your sights
Shake patiently my great affliction off. *Shakesp. K. Lear.*

To RENOU'NCE. *v. n.* To declare renunciation. The following passage is a mere Gallicism: *renoncer a mon sang.*

On this firm principle I ever stood;
He of my sons, who fails to make it good,
By one rebellious act *renounces to* my blood. *Dryden.*

RENOU'NCEMENT. *n. s.* [from *renounce.*] Act of renouncing; renunciation.

I hold you as a thing enskied and sainted;
By your *renouncement*, an immortal spirit. *Shakesp.*

RENO'WN. *n. s.* [*renommée*, Fr.] Fame; celebrity; praise widely spread.

She
Is daughter to this famous duke of Milan,
Of whom so often I have heard *renown.* *Shakesp.*

'Tis of more *renown*
To make a river, than to build a town. *Waller.*

Nor envy we
Thy great *renown*, nor grudge thy victory. *Dryden.*

To RENO'WN. *v. a.* [*renommer*, Fr. from the noun.] To make famous.

Let us satisfy our eyes
With the memorials and the things of fame,
That do *renown* this city. *Shakesp. Twelfth Night.*

Soft elocution does thy style *renown*,
Gentle or sharp according to thy choice,
To laugh at follies, or to lash at vice. *Dryden.*

In solemn silence stand
Stern tyrants, whom their cruelties *renown*,
And emperors in Parian marble frown. *Addison.*

A bard, whom pilfer'd pastorals *renown*,
Just writes to make his barrenness appear. *Pope.*

RENO'WNED. *particip. adj.* [from *renown.*] Famous; celebrated; eminent; famed.

These were the *renowned* of the congregation, princes of the tribes, heads of thousands. *Num.* i. 16.

That thrice *renowned* and learned French king, finding Petrarch's tomb without any inscription, wrote one himself; saying, shame it was, that he who sung his mistress's praise seven years before her death, should twelve years want an epitaph. *Peacham on Poetry.*

The rest were long to tell, though far *renown'd.* *Milton.*

Of all the cities in Romanian lands,
The chief and most *renown'd* Ravenna stands,
Adorn'd in ancient times with arms and arts. *Dryden.*

Ilva,
An isle *renown'd* for steel and unexhausted mines. *Dryden.*

RENT. *n. s.* [from *rend.*] A break; a laceration.

Thou viper
Haſt cancell'd kindred, made a *rent* in nature,
And through her holy bowels gnaw'd thy way,
Through thy own blood to empire. *Dryden.*

He who ſees this vaſt *rent* in ſo high a rock, how the convex parts of one ſide exactly tally with the concave of the other, muſt be ſatisfied, that it was the effect of an earthquake. *Addiſon's Remarks on Italy.*

To RENT. *v. a.* [rather to *rend.*] To tear; to lacerate.

A time to *rent*, and a time to ſew. *Eccluſ.* iii. 7.

To RENT. *v. n.* [now written *rant.*] To roar; to bluſter: we ſtill ſay, *a* tearing *fellow*, for *a noiſy bully*.

He ventur'd to diſmiſs his fear,
That partings wont to *rent* and tear,
And give the deſperateſt attack
To danger ſtill behind its back. *Hudibras, p.* iii.

RENT. *n. ſ.* [*rente*, Fr.]

1. Revenue; annual payment.

Idol ceremony,
What are thy *rents?* what are thy comings in?
O ceremony ſhew me but thy worth! *Shakeſp. Hen.* V.

I bought an annual *rent* or two,
And live juſt as you ſee I do. *Pope's Epiſt. of Horace.*

2. Money paid for any thing held of another.

Such is the mould, that the bleſt tenant feeds
On precious fruits, and pays his *rent* in weeds. *Waller.*

Folks in mudwall tenement,
Preſent a peppercorn for *rent.* *Prior.*

To RENT. *v. a.* [*renter*, Fr.]

1. To hold by paying rent.

When a ſervant is called before his maſter, it is often to know, whether he paſſed by ſuch a ground, if the old man, who *rents* it, is in good health. *Addiſon's Spectator.*

2. To ſet to a tenant.

RE'NTABLE. *adj.* [from *rent.*] That may be rented.

RE'NTAL. *n. ſ.* [from *rent.*] Schedule or account of rents.

RE'NTER. *n. ſ.* [from *rent.*] He that holds by paying rent.

The eſtate will not be let for one penny more or leſs to the *renter*, amongſt whomſoever the rent he pays be divided. *Locke.*

RENVE'RSED. *adj.* [*renverſé*, Fr.] Overturned. *Spenſer.*

RENUNCIA'TION. *n. ſ.* [*renunciatio*, from *renuncio*, Lat.] The act of renouncing.

He that loves riches, can hardly believe the doctrine of poverty and *renunciation* of the world. *Taylor.*

To REORDAI'N. *v. a.* [*reordiner*, Fr. *re* and *ordain.*] To ordain again, on ſuppoſition of ſome defect in the commiſſion of miniſtry.

REORDINA'TION. *n. ſ.* [from *reordain.*] Repetition of ordination.

He proceeded in his miniſtry without expecting any new miſſion, and never thought himſelf obliged to a *reordination.* *Atterbury.*

To REPA'CIFY. *v. a.* [*re* and *pacify.*] To pacify again.

Henry, who next commands the ſtate,
Seeks to *repacify* the people's hate. *Daniel.*

REPAI'D. *part.* of *repay.*

To REPAI'R. *v. a.* [*reparo*, Lat. *reparer*, Fr.]

1. To reſtore after injury or dilapidation.

Let the prieſts *repair* the breaches of the houſe. 2 *Kings.*

The fines impoſed were the more repined againſt, becauſe they were aſſigned to the rebuilding and *repairing* of St. Paul's Church. *Clarendon.*

Heav'n ſoon *repair'd* her mural breach. *Milton.*

2. To amend any injury by an equivalent.

He juſtly hath driv'n out his rebel foes
To deepeſt hell; and to *repair* their loſs
Created this new happy race of men. *Milton's Par. Loſt.*

3. To fill up anew, by ſomething put in the place of what is loſt.

To be reveng'd,
And to *repair* his numbers thus impair'd. *Milton.*

REPAI'R. *n. ſ.* [from the verb.] Reparation; ſupply of loſs; reſtoration after dilapidation.

Before the curing of a ſtrong diſeaſe,
Ev'n in the inſtant of *repair* and health,
The fit is ſtrongeſt. *Shakeſp. King Lear.*

Temperance, in all methods of curing the gout, is a regular and ſimple diet, proportioning the daily *repairs* to the daily decays of our waſting bodies. *Temple's Miſcellanies.*

All automata need a frequent *repair* of new ſtrength, the cauſes whence their motion does proceed, being ſubject to fail. *Wilkins's Mathematical Magick.*

To REPAI'R. *v. n.* [*repairer*, Fr.] To go to; to betake himſelf.

May all to Athens back again *repair.* *Shakeſp.*

Depart from hence in peace,
Search the wide world, and where you pleaſe *repair. Dryd.*

'Tis fix'd; th' irrevocable doom of Jove:
Haſte then, Cyllenius, through the liquid air,
Go mount the winds, and to the ſhades *repair.* *Pope.*

REPAI'R. *n. ſ.* [*repaire*, Fr. from the verb.]

1. Reſort; abode.

So 'ſcapes th' inſulting fire his narrow jail,
And makes ſmall outlets into open air;
There the fierce winds his tender force aſſail,
And beat him downward to his firſt *repair.* *Dryden.*

2. Act of betaking himſelf any whither.

The king ſent a proclamation for their *repair* to their houſes, and for a preſervation of the peace. *Clarendon.*

REPAI'RER. *n. ſ.* [from *repair.*] Amender; reſtorer.

He that governs well, leads the blind, but he that teaches, gives him eyes; and it is a glorious thing to have been the *repairer* of a decayed intellect. *South's Sermons.*

O ſacred reſt!
O peace of mind! *repairer* of decay,
Whoſe balms renew the limbs to labours of the day. *Dryd.*

REPA'NDOUS. *adj.* [*repandus*, Lat.] Bent upwards.

Though they be drawn *repandous* or convexedly crooked in one piece, yet the dolphin that carrieth Arion is concavouſly inverted, and hath its ſpine depreſſed in another. *Brown.*

RE'PARABLE. *adj.* [*reparable*, Fr. *reparabilis*, Lat.] Capable of being amended, retrieved, or ſupplied by ſomething equivalent.

The parts in man's body eaſily *reparable*, as ſpirits, blood and fleſh, die in the embracement of the parts hardly *reparable*, as bones, nerves and membranes. *Bacon.*

When its ſpirit is drawn from wine, it will not, by the re-union of its conſtituent liquors, be reduced to its priſtine nature; becauſe the workmanſhip of nature, in the diſpoſition of the parts, was too elaborate to be imitable, or *reparable* by the bare appoſition of thoſe divided parts to each other. *Boyle.*

An adulterous perſon is tied to reſtitution of the injury, ſo far as it is *reparable*, and can be made to the wronged perſon; to make proviſion for the children begotten in unlawful embraces. *Taylor's Rule of Living Holy.*

RE'PARABLY. *adv.* [from *reparable.*] In a manner capable of remedy by reſtoration, amendment or ſupply.

RE'PARATION. *n. ſ.* [*reparation*, Fr. *reparatio*, from *reparo*, Lat.]

1. The act of repairing.

Antonius Philoſophus took care of the *reparation* of the highways. *Arbuthnot on Coins.*

2. Supply of what is waſted.

When the organs of ſenſe want their due repoſe and neceſſary *reparations*, the ſoul exerts herſelf in her ſeveral faculties. *Addiſon.*

In this moveable body, the fluid and ſolid parts muſt be conſumed; and both demand a conſtant *reparation. Arbuthnot.*

3. Recompenſe for any injury; amends.

The king ſhould be able, when he had cleared himſelf, to make him *reparation.* *Bacon.*

I am ſenſible of the ſcandal I have given by my looſe writings, and make what *reparation* I am able. *Dryden.*

REPA'RATIVE. *n. ſ.* [from *repair.*] Whatever makes amends for loſs or injury.

New preparatives were in hand, and partly *reparatives* of the former beaten at ſea. *Wotton's Buckingham.*

REPARTEE'. *n. ſ.* [*repartie*, Fr.] Smart reply.

The fools overflowed with ſmart *repartees*, and were only diſtinguiſhed from the intended wits, by being called coxcombs. *Dryden's Dufreſnoy.*

Sullen was Jupiter juſt now:
And Cupid was as bad as he;
Hear but the younſter's *repartee.* *Prior.*

To REPARTEE'. *v. n.* To make ſmart replies.

High flights ſhe had, and wit at will,
And ſo her tongue lay ſeldom ſtill;
For in all viſits who but ſhe,
To argue, or to *repartee?* *Prior.*

To REPA'SS. *v. a.* [*repaſſer*, Fr.] To paſs again; to paſs back.

Well we have paſs'd, and now *repaſs'd* the ſeas,
And brought deſir'd help. *Shakeſp. Henry* VI.

We ſhall find ſmall reaſon to think, that Abraham paſſed and *repaſſed* thoſe ways more often than he was enforced ſo to do, if we conſider that he had no other comforter in this weariſom journey, than the ſtrength of his faith in God. *Ral.*

If his ſoul hath wing'd the deſtin'd flight,
Homeward with pious ſpeed *repaſs* the main,
To the pale ſhade funereal rites ordain. *Pope's Odyſſey.*

To REPA'SS. *v. n.* To go back in a road.

Five girdles bind the ſkies, the torrid zone
Glows with the paſſing and *repaſſing* ſun. *Dryden.*

REPA'ST. *n. ſ.* [*repas*, Fr. *re* and *paſtus*, Lat.]

1. A meal; act of taking food.

From dance to ſweet *repaſt* they turn
Deſirous; all in circles as they ſtood,
Tables are ſet. *Milton's Paradiſe Loſt, b.* v.

What neat *repaſt* ſhall feaſt us, light and choice,
Of Attick taſte, with wine. *Milton.*

Sleep, that is thy beſt *repaſt*,
Yet of death it bears a taſte,
And both are the ſame thing at laſt. *Denham.*

The day
Had ſummon'd him to due *repaſt* at noon. *Dryden.*

Keep regular hours for *repast* and sleep. *Arbuthnot.*
2. Food; victuals.
Go, and get me some *repast*;
I care not what, so it be wholsome food. *Shakesp.*
To REPA'ST. *v. a.* [*repaistre*, Fr. from the noun.] To feed; to feast.
To his good friends I'll ope my arm,
And, like the kind life-rend'ring pelican,
Repast them with my blood. *Shakesp.*
REPA'STURE. *n. s.* [*re* and *pasture.*] Entertainment. Not in use.
He from forage will incline to play;
But if thou strive, poor soul, what art thou then?
Food for his rage, *repasture* for his den. *Shakesp.*
To REPA'Y. *v. a.* [*repayer*, Fr. *re* and *pay.*]
1. To pay back in return, in requital, or in revenge.
According to their deeds he will *repay* recompense to his enemies; to the islands he will *repay* recompense. *Is.* lix. 18.
The false honour, which he had so long enjoyed, was plentifully *repaid* in contempt. *Bacon.*
2. To recompense.
He clad
Their nakedness with skins of beasts; or slain,
Or as the snake with youthful coat *repaid.* *Milton.*
3. To requite either good or ill.
The poorest service is *repaid* with thanks. *Shakesp.*
Fav'ring heav'n *repaid* my glorious toils
With a sack'd palace and barbarick spoils. *Pope.*
I have fought well for Persia, and *repaid*
The benefit of birth with honest service. *Rowe.*
4. To reimburse with what is owed.
If you *repay* me not on such a day,
Such sums as are express'd in the condition,
Let the forfeit be an equal pound of your fair flesh. *Shak.*
REPA'YMENT. *n. s.* [from *repay.*]
1. The act of repaying.
2. The thing repaid.
The centesima usura it was not lawful to exceed; and what was paid over it, was reckoned as a *repayment* of part of the principal. *Arbuthnot on Coins.*
To REPEA'L. *v. a.* [*rappeller*, Fr.]
1. To recall. Out of use.
I will *repeal* thee, or be well assur'd,
Adventure to be banished myself. *Shakesp. Henry* VI.
I here forget all former griefs;
Cancel all grudge, *repeal* thee home again. *Shakesp.*
2. To abrogate; to revoke.
Laws, that have been approved, may be again *repealed*, and disputed against by the authors themselves. *Hooker's Pref.*
Adam soon *repeal'd*
The doubts that in his heart arose. *Milton's Par. Lost.*
Statutes are silently *repealed*, when the reason ceases for which they were enacted. *Dryden's Preface to Fables.*
REPEA'L. *n. s.* [from the verb.]
1. Recall from exile. Not in use.
If the time thrust forth
A cause for thy *repeal*, we shall not send
O'er the vast world to seek a single man. *Shakesp.*
2. Revocation; abrogation.
The king being advertised, that the over-large grants of lands and liberties made the lords so insolent, did absolutely resume all such grants; but the earl of Desmond above all found himself grieved with this resumption or *repeal* of liberties, and declared his dislike. *Davies on Ireland.*
If the presbyterians should obtain their ends, I could not be sorry to find them mistaken in the point which they have most at heart, by the *repeal* of the test; I mean the benefit of employments. *Swift's Presbyterian Plea.*
To REPEA'T. *v. a.* [*repeto*, Lat. *repeter*, Fr.]
1. To iterate; to use again; to do again.
These evils thou *repeat'st* upon thyself,
Have banish'd me from Scotland. *Shakesp. Macbeth.*
He, though his power
Creation could *repeat*, yet would be loth
Us to abolish. *Milton.*
Where sudden alterations are not necessary, the same effect may be obtained by the *repeated* force of diet with more safety to the body. *Arbuthnot on Aliments.*
2. To speak again.
The psalms, for the excellency of their use, deserve to be oftner *repeated*; but that their multitude permitteth not any oftner repetition. *Hooker.*
3. To try again.
Neglecting for Creüsa's life his own,
Repeats the danger of the burning town. *Waller.*
Beyond this place you can have no retreat,
Stay here, and I the danger will *repeat.* *Dryden.*
4. To recite; to rehearse.
Thou their natures know'st, and gav'st them names,
Needless to thee *repeated.* *Milton.*
He *repeated* some lines of Virgil, suitable to the occasion. *Waller's Life.*
REPEA'TEDLY. *adv.* [from *repeated.*] Over and over; more than once.
And are not these vices, which lead into damnation, *repeatedly*, and most forcibly cautioned against? *Stephens.*
REPEA'TER. *n. s.* [from *repeat.*]
1. One that repeats; one that recites.
2. A watch that strikes the hours at will by compression of a spring.
To REPE'L. *v. a.* [*repello*, Lat.]
1. To drive back any thing.
Neither doth Tertullian bewray this weakness in striking only, but also in *repelling* their strokes with whom he contendeth. *Hooker, b.* ii. *s.* 5.
With hills of slain on ev'ry side,
Hippomedon *repell'd* the hostile tide. *Pope.*
2. To drive back an assailant.
Stand fast; and all temptation to transgress *repel.* *Milt.*
Repel the Tuscan foes, their city seize,
Protect the Latians in luxurious ease. *Dryden's Æneis.*
Your foes are such, as they, not you, have made,
And virtue may *repel*, though not invade. *Dryden.*
To REPE'L. *v. n.*
1. To act with force contrary to force impressed.
From the same *repelling* power it seems to be, that flies walk upon the water without wetting their feet. *Newton.*
2. In physick, to *repel* in medicine, is to prevent such an afflux of a fluid to any particular part, as would raise it into a tumour. *Quincy.*
REPE'LLENT. *n. s.* [*repellens*, Lat.] An application that has a repelling power.
In the cure of an erysipelas, whilst the body abounds with bilious humours, there is no admitting of *repellents*, and by discutients you will encrease the heat. *Wiseman.*
REPE'LLER. *n. s.* [from *repel.*] One that repels.
To REPE'NT. *v. n.* [*repentir*, Fr.]
1. To think on any thing past with sorrow.
God led them not through the land of the Philistines, lest peradventure the people *repent*, when they see war and they return. *Exodus* xiii. 17.
Nor had I any reservations in my own soul, when I passed that bill; nor *repentings* after. *King Charles.*
Upon any deviation from virtue, every rational creature so deviating, should condemn, renounce, and be sorry for every such deviation; that is, *repent* of it. *South.*
First she relents
With pity, of that pity then *repents.* *Dryden.*
Still you may prove the terror of your foes;
Teach traitors to *repent* of faithless leagues. *A. Philips.*
2. To express sorrow for something past.
Poor Enobarbus did before thy face *repent.* *Shakesp.*
3. To have such sorrow for sin, as produces amendment of life.
Nineveh *repented* at the preaching of Jonas. *Matt.* xii. 41.
To REPE'NT. *v. a.*
1. To remember with sorrow.
If Desdemona will return me my jewels, I will give over my suit, and *repent* my unlawful solicitation. *Shakesp.*
2. To remember with pious sorrow.
Thou, like a contrite penitent
Charitably warn'd of thy sins, dost *repent*
These vanities and giddinesses, lo
I shut my chamber-door; come, let us go. *Donne.*
His late follies he would late *repent.* *Dryden.*
3. [*Se repentir*, Fr.] It is used with the reciprocal pronoun.
I *repent me*, that the duke is slain. *Shakesp. Rich.* III.
No man *repented him* of his wickedness; saying, what have I done? *Jeremiah* viii. 6.
Judas, when he saw that he was condemned, *repented himself.* *Matthew* xxvii. 3.
My father has *repented him* ere now,
Or will *repent him* when he finds me dead. *Dryden.*
Each age sinn'd on;
Till God arose, and great in anger said,
Lo! it *repenteth me*, that man was made. *Prior.*
REPE'NTANCE. *n. s.* [*repentance*, Fr. from *repent.*]
1. Sorrow for any thing past.
2. Sorrow for sin, such as produces newness of life; penitence.
Repentance so altereth a man through the mercy of God, be he never so defiled, that it maketh him pure. *Whitgifte.*
Who by *repentance* is not satisfied,
Is nor of heav'n nor earth; for these are pleased;
By penitence th' eternal's wrath's appeas'd. *Shakesp.*
Repentance is a change of mind, or a conversion from sin to God: not some one bare act of change, but a lasting durable state of new life, which is called regeneration. *Hammond.*
This is a confidence, of all the most irrational; for upon what ground can a man promise himself a future *repentance*, who cannot promise himself a futurity. *South.*
REPE'NTANT. *adj.* [*repentant*, Fr. from *repent.*]
1. Sorrowful for the past.
2. Sorrowful for sin.
Thus they, in lowliest plight, *repentant* stood. *Milton.*
3. Expressing sorrow for sin.
After I have interr'd this noble king,
And wet his grave with my *repentant* tears,
I will with all expedient duty see you. *Shakesp. Rich.* III.

2. To describe; to show in any particular character.

This bank is thought the greatest load on the Genoese, and the managers of it have been *represented* as a second kind of senate. *Addison's Remarks on Italy.*

3. To fill the place of another by a vicarious character; to personate: as, *the parliament* represents *the people.*

4. To exhibit to show.

One of his cardinals admonished him against that unskilful piece of ingenuity, by *representing* to him, that no reformation could be made, which would not notably diminish the rents of the church. *Decay of Piety.*

REPRESENTA'TION. *n. s.* [*representation*, Fr. from *represent.*]

1. Image; likeness.

If images are worshipped, it must be as gods, which Celsus denied, or as *representations* of God; which cannot be, because God is invisible and incorporeal. *Stillingfleet.*

2. Act of supporting a vicarious character.

3. Respectful declaration.

REPRESE'NTATIVE. *adj.* [*representatif*, Fr. from *represent.*]

1. Exhibiting a similitude.

They relieve themselves with this distinction, and yet own the legal sacrifices, though *representative*, to be proper and real. *Atterbury.*

2. Bearing the character or power of another.

This counsel of four hundred was chosen, one hundred out of each tribe, and seems to have been a body *representative* of the people; though the people collective reserved a share of power. *Swift.*

REPRESE'NTATIVE. *n. s.*

1. One exhibiting the likeness of another.

A statue of rumour whispering an idiot in the ear, who was the *representative* of credulity. *Addison's Freeholder.*

2. One exercising the vicarious power given by another.

I wish the welfare of my country; and my morals and politicks teach me to leave all that to be adjusted by our *representatives* above, and to divine providence. *Blount to Pope.*

3. That by which any thing is shown.

Difficulty must cumber this doctrine, which supposes that the perfections of God are the *representatives* to us, of whatever we perceive in the creatures. *Locke.*

REPRESE'NTER. *n. s.* [from *represent.*]

1. One who shows or exhibits.

Where the real works of nature, or veritable acts of story, are to be described, art, being but the imitator or secondary *representer*, must not vary from the verity. *Brown.*

2. One who bears a vicarious character; one who acts for another by deputation.

My muse officious ventures
On the nation's *representers.* *Swift.*

REPRESE'NTMENT. *n. s.* [from *represent.*] Image or idea proposed, as exhibiting the likeness of something.

When it is blessed, some believe it to be the natural body of Christ; others, the blessings of Christ, his passion in *representment*, and his grace in real exhibition. *Taylor.*

We have met with some, whose reals made good their *representments.* *Brown's Vulgar Errours.*

To REPRE'SS. *v. a.* [*repressus*, Lat. *reprimer*, Fr.]

1. To crush; to put down; to subdue.

Discontents and ill blood having used always to *repress* and appease in person, he was loth they should find him beyond sea. *Bacon's Henry VII.*

Some, taking dangers to be the only remedy against dangers, endeavoured to set up the sedition again, but they were speedily *repressed*, and thereby the sedition suppressed wholly. *Hayward.*

Such kings
Favour the innocent, *repress* the bold,
And, while they flourish, make an age of gold. *Waller.*

How can I
Repress the horror of my thoughts, which fly
The sad remembrance. *Denham.*

Thus long succeeding criticks justly reign'd,
Licence *repress'd*, and useful laws ordain'd:
Learning and Rome alike in empire grew. *Pope.*

Armies stretch, *repressing* here
The frantick Alexander of the North. *Thomson.*

2. To compress. Not proper.

REPRE'SS. *n. s.* [from the verb.] Repression; act of crushing. Not in use.

Loud outcries of injury, when they tend nothing to the *repress* of it, is a liberty rather assumed by rage and impatience, than authorised by justice. *Government of the Tongue.*

REPRE'SSION. *n. s.* [from *repress.*] Act of repressing.

No declaration from myself could take place, for the due *repression* of these tumults. *King Charles.*

REPRE'SSIVE. *adj.* [from *repress.*] Having power to repress; acting to repress.

To REPRIE'VE. *v. a.* [*reprendre*, *repris*, Fr.] To respite after sentence of death; to give a respite.

Company, though it may *reprieve* a man from his melancholy, yet cannot secure him from his conscience. *South.*

Having been condemned for his part in the late rebellion, his majesty had been pleased to *reprieve* him, with several of his friends, in order to give them their lives. *Addison.*

He *reprieves* the sinner from time to time, and continues and heaps on him the favours of his providence, in hopes that, by an act of clemency so undeserved, he may prevail on his gratitude and repentance. *Rogers's Sermons.*

REPRIE'VE. *n. s.* [from the verb.] Respite after sentence of death.

In his *reprieve* he may be so fitted,
That his soul sicken not. *Shakesp. Meas. for Meas.*

I hope it is some pardon or *reprieve*
For Claudio. *Shakesp. Measure for Measure.*

He cannot thrive,
Unless her prayers, whom heav'n delights to hear,
And loves to grant, *reprieve* from the wrath
Of greatest justice. *Shakesp. All's well that ends well.*

The morning Sir John Hotham was to die, a *reprieve* was sent to suspend the execution for three days. *Clarendon.*

All that I ask, is but a short *reprieve*,
Till I forget to love, and learn to grieve. *Denham.*

To REPRIMA'ND. *v. a.* [*reprimander*, Fr. *reprimo*, Lat.] To chide; to check; to reprehend; to reprove.

Germanicus was severely *reprimanded* by Tiberius, for travelling into Egypt without his permission. *Arbuthnot.*

REPRIMA'ND. *n. s.* [*reprimande*, *reprimende*, Fr. from the verb.] Reproof; reprehension.

He inquires how such an one's wife or son do, whom he does not see at church; which is understood as a secret *reprimand* to the person absent. *Addison's Spectator*, Nº 112.

To REPRI'NT. *v. a.* [*re* and *print.*]

1. To renew the impression of any thing.

The business of redemption is to rub over the defaced copy of creation, to *reprint* God's image upon the soul, and to set forth nature in a second and a fairer edition. *South.*

2. To print a new edition.

My bookseller is *reprinting* the essay on criticism. *Pope.*

REPRI'SAL. *n. s.* [*represalia*, low Lat. *represaille*, Fr.] Something seized by way of retaliation for robbery or injury.

The English had great advantage in value of *reprisals*, as being more strong and active at sea. *Hayward.*

Sense must sure thy safest plunder be,
Since no *reprisals* can be made on thee. *Pope.*

REPRI'SE. *n. s.* [*reprise*, Fr.] The act of taking something in retaliation of injury.

Your care about your banks infers a fear
Of threat'ning floods and inundations near;
If so, a just *reprise* would only be
Of what the land usurp'd upon the sea. *Dryden.*

To REPROA'CH. *v. a.* [*reprocher*, Fr.]

1. To censure in opprobrious terms, as a crime.

Mezentius, with his ardour warm'd
His fainting friends, *reproach'd* their shameful flight,
Repell'd the victors. *Dryden's Æneis.*

The French writers do not burden themselves too much with plot, which has been *reproached* to them as a fault. *Dry.*

2. To charge with a fault in severe language.

If ye be *reproached* for the name of Christ, happy are ye.
1 *Peter* iv. 14.

That shame
There sit not, and *reproach* us as unclean. *Milton.*

2. To upbraid in general.

These things are grievous; the upbraiding of house-room, and *reproaching* of the lender. *Ecclus.* xxix. 28.

The very regret of being surpassed in any valuable quality, by a person of the same abilities with ourselves, will *reproach* our own laziness, and even shame us into imitation. *Rogers.*

REPROA'CH. *n. s.* [*reproche*, Fr. from the verb.] Censure; infamy; shame.

With his *reproach* and odious menace,
The knight emboiling in his haughty heart,
Knit all his forces. *Fairy Queen.*

If black scandal or foul-fac'd *reproach*
Attend the sequel of your imposition,
Your mere enforcement shall acquittance me. *Shakesp.*

Thou, for the testimony of truth, hast borne
Universal *reproach.* *Milton.*

REPROA'CHABLE. *adj.* [*reproachable*, Fr.] Worthy of reproach.

REPROA'CHFUL. *adj.* [from *reproach.*]

1. Scurrilous; opprobrious.

O monstrous! what *reproachful* words are these. *Shakesp.*

I have sheath'd
My rapier in his bosom, and withal
Thrust these *reproachful* speeches down his throat. *Shakesp.*

An advocate may be punished for *reproachful* language, in respect of the parties in suit. *Ayliffe's Parergon.*

2. Shameful; infamous; vile.

To make religion a stratagem to undermine government, is contrary to this superstructure, most scandalous and *reproachful* to christianity. *Hammond's Fundamentals.*

Thy punishment
He shall endure, by coming in the flesh
To a *reproachful* life and cursed death. *Milton's Par. Lost.*

REPROA'CHFULLY. *adv.* [from *reproach.*]

1. Opprobriously; ignominiously; scurrilously.

Shall I then be us'd *reproachfully?* *Shakesp. Hen.* VI.

I will that the younger women marry, and give none occasion to the adversary to speak *reproachfully.* 1 *Tim.* v. 14.

2. Shamefully; infamously.

RE'PROBATE. *adj.* [*reprobus,* Lat.] Lost to virtue; lost to grace; abandoned.

They profess to know God, but in works deny him, being abominable, and to every good work *reprobate.* *Tit.* i. 16.

Strength and art are easily outdone
By spirits *reprobate.* *Milton.*

God forbid, that every single commission of a sin, though great for its kind, and withal acted against conscience, for its aggravation, should so far deprave the soul, and bring it to such a *reprobate* condition, as to take pleasure in other men's sins. *South's Sermons.*

RE'PROBATE. *n. s.* A man lost to virtue; a wretch abandoned to wickedness.

What if we omit
This *reprobate,* till he were well inclin'd. *Shakesp.*

I acknowledge myself for a *reprobate,* a villain, a traytor to the king, and the most unworthy man that ever lived. *Ral.*

All the saints have profited by tribulations; and they that could not bear temptations, became *reprobates.* *Taylor.*

To RE'PROBATE. *v. a.* [*reprobo,* Lat.]

1. To disallow; to reject.

Such an answer as this is *reprobated* and disallowed of in law; I do not believe it, unless the deed appears. *Ayliffe.*

2. To abandon to wickedness and eternal destruction.

What should make it necessary for him to repent and amend, who either without respect to any degree of amendment is supposed to be elected to eternal bliss, or without respect to sin, to be irreversibly *reprobated.* *Hammond.*

A *reprobated* hardness of heart does them the office of philosophy towards a contempt of death. *L'Estrange.*

3. To abandon to his sentence, without hope of pardon.

Drive him out
To *reprobated* exile round the world,
A caitive, vagabond, abhorr'd, accurs'd. *Southerne.*

RE'PROBATENESS. *n. s.* [from *reprobate.*] The state of being reprobate.

REPROBA'TION. *n. s.* [*reprobation,* Fr. from *reprobate.*]

1. The act of abandoning or state of being abandoned to eternal destruction.

This sight would make him do a desperate turn;
Yea curse his better angel from his side,
And fall to *reprobation.* *Shakesp. Othello.*

Though some words may be accommodated to God's predestination, yet it is the scope of that text to treat of the *reprobation* of any man to hell-fire. *Bramhall against Hobbs.*

God, upon a true repentance, is not so fatally tied to the spindle of absolute *reprobation,* as not to keep his promise, and seal merciful pardons. *Maine.*

2. A condemnatory sentence.

You are empower'd to give the final decision of wit, to put your stamp on all that ought to pass for current, and set a brand of *reprobation* on clipt poetry and false coin. *Dryden.*

To REPRODU'CE. *v. a.* [*re* and *produce*; *reproduire,* Fr.] To produce again; to produce anew.

If horse dung *reproduceth* oats, it will not be easily determined where the power of generation ceaseth. *Brown.*

Those colours are unchangeable, and whenever all those rays with those their colours are mixed again, they *reproduce* the same white light as before. *Newton's Opticks.*

REPRODU'CTION. *n. s.* [from *reproduce.*] The act of producing anew.

I am about to attempt a *reproduction* in vitriol, in which it seems not unlikely to be performable. *Boyle.*

REPROO'F. *n. s.* [from *reprove.*]

1. Blame to the face; reprehension.

Good Sir John, as you have one eye upon my follies, turn another into the register of your own, that I may pass with a *reproof* the easier. *Shakesp. Merry Wives of Windsor.*

Fear not the anger of the wise to raise;
Those best can bear *reproof,* who merit praise. *Pope.*

2. Censure; slander. Out of use.

Why, for thy sake, have I suffer'd *reproof?* shame hath covered my face. *Psalm* lxix. 7.

REPRO'VABLE. *adj.* [from *reprove.*] Culpable; blamable; worthy of reprehension.

If thou dost find thy faith as dead after the reception of the sacrament as before, it may be thy faith was not only little, but *reproveable.* *Taylor's Worthy Communicant.*

To REPRO'VE. *v. a.* [*reprouver,* Fr.]

1. To blame; to censure.

I will not *reprove* thee for thy sacrifices. *Psalm* l. 8.

2. To charge to the face with a fault; to check; to chide; to reprehend.

What if they can better be content with one that can wink at their faults, than with him that will *reprove* them. *Whitg.*

There is no slander in an allow'd fool, though he do nothing but rail; nor no railing in a known discreet man, though he do nothing but *reprove.* *Shakesp. Twelfth Night.*

What if thy son
Prove disobedient and *reprov'd,* retort,
Wherefore didst thou beget me? *Milton.*

If a great personage undertakes an action passionately, let it be acted with all the malice and impotency in the world, he shall have enough to flatter him, but not enough to *reprove* him. *Taylor's Rule of Living Holy.*

3. To refute; to disprove.

My lords,
Reprove my allegation if you can. *Shakesp. Henry* VI.

4. To blame for. With *of.*

To *reprove* one *of* laziness, they will say, dost thou make idle a coat? that is a coat for idleness. *Carew.*

REPRO'VER. *n. s.* [from *reprove.*] A reprehender; one that reproves.

Let the most potent sinner speak out, and tell us, whether he can command down the clamours and revilings of a guilty conscience, and impose silence upon that bold *reprover.* *South.*

This shall have from every one, even the *reprovers* of vice, the title of living well. *Locke on Education.*

To REPRU'NE. *v. a.* [*re* and *prune.*] To prune a second time.

Reprune apricots and peaches, saving as many of the young likeliest shoots as are well placed. *Evelyn's Kalendar.*

RE'PTILE. *adj.* [*reptile,* Lat.] Creeping upon many feet. In the following lines *reptile* is confounded with *serpent.*

Cleanse baits from filth, to give a tempting gloss,
Cherish the sully'd *reptile* race with moss. *Gay.*

REPTI'LE. *n. s.* An animal that creeps upon many feet.

Terrestial animals may be divided into quadrupeds or *reptiles,* which have many feet, and serpents which have no feet. *Locke's Elements of Natural Philosophy.*

Holy retreat! sithence no female hither,
Conscious of social love and nature's rites,
Must dare approach, from the inferior *reptile,*
To woman, form divine. *Prior.*

REPU'BLICAN. *adj.* [from *republick.*] Placing the government in the people.

REPU'BLICAN. *n. s.* [from *republick.*] One who thinks a commonwealth without monarchy the best government.

These people are more happy in imagination than the rest of their neighbours, because they think themselves so; though such a chimerical happiness is not peculiar to *republicans.* *Add.*

REPU'BLICK. *n. s.* [*respublica,* Lat. *republique,* Fr.] Commonwealth; state in which the power is lodged in more than one.

Those that by their deeds will make it known,
Whose dignity they do sustain;
And life, state, glory, all they gain,
Count the *republick's,* not their own. *Benj. Johnson.*

They are indebted many millions more than their whole *republick* is worth. *Addison's State of the War.*

REPU'DIABLE. *adj.* [from *repudiate.*] Fit to be rejected.

To REPU'DIATE. *v. a.* [*repudio,* Lat. *repudier,* Fr.] To divorce; to reject; to put away.

Here is a notorious instance of the folly of the atheists, that while they *repudiate* all title to the kingdom of heaven, merely for the present pleasure of body, and their boasted tranquillity of mind, besides the extreme madness in running such a desperate hazard after death, they unwittingly deprive themselves here of that very pleasure and tranquillity they seek for. *Bentley's Sermons.*

Let not those, that have *repudiated* the more inviting sins, show themselves philtred and bewitched by this. *G. of Tongue.*

REPUDIA'TION. *n. s.* [*repudiation,* Fr. from *repudiate.*] Divorce; rejection.

It was allowed by the Athenians, only in case of *repudiation* of a wife. *Arbuthnot on Coins.*

REPU'GNANCE. } *n. s.* [*repugnance,* Fr. from *repugnant.*]
REPU'GNANCY. }

1. Inconsistency; contrariety.

But where difference is without *repugnancy,* that which hath been can be no prejudice to that which is. *Hooker.*

It is no affront to omnipotence, if, by reason of the formal incapacity and *repugnancy* of the thing, we aver that the world could not have been made from all eternity. *Bentley.*

2. Reluctance; unwillingness; struggle of opposite passion.

Why do fond men expose themselves to battle,
And let the foes quietly cut their throats,
Without *repugnancy?* *Shakesp. Timon of Athens.*

Thus did the passions act without any of their present jars, combats or *repugnances,* all moving with the beauty of uniformity and the stilness of composure. *South's Sermons.*

That which causes us to lose most of our time, is the *repugnance* which we naturally have to labour. *Dryden.*

REPU'GNANT. *adj.* [*repugnant,* Fr. *repugnans,* Lat.]

1. Disobedient; not obsequious.

His antique sword,
Rebellious to his arm, lies where it falls,
Repugnant to command. *Shakesp. Hamlet.*

2. Contrary; opposite.

Why I reject the other conjectures is; because they have not due warrant from observation, but are clearly *repugnant* thereunto. *Woodward's Natural History.*

There is no malice in this burning coal;
The breath of heav'n hath blown its spirit out,
And strew'd *repentant* ashes on its head. *Shakesp. K. John.*
Relentless walls! whose darksome round contains
Repentant sighs and voluntary pains. *Pope.*

To REPEO'PLE. *v. a.* [*re* and *people*; *repeupler*, Fr.] To stock with people anew.

An occurrence of such remark, as the universal flood and the *repeopling* of the world, must be fresh in memory for about eight hundred years; especially considering, that the peopling of the world was gradual. *Hale's Origin of Mankind.*

To REPERCU'SS. *v. a.* [*repercutio*, *repercussus*, Lat.] To beat back; to drive back; to rebound. Not in use.

Air in ovens, though it doth boil and dilate itself, and is *repercussed*, yet it is without noise. *Bacon.*

REPERCU'SSION. *n. s.* [from *repercuss*; *repercussio*, Lat. *repercussion*, Fr.] The act of driving back; rebound.

In echoes, there is no new elision, but a *repercussion*. *Bacon.*
They various ways recoil, and swiftly flow
By mutual *repercussions* to and fro. *Blackmore.*

REPERCU'SSIVE. *adj.* [*repercussif*, Fr.]
1. Having the power of driving back or causing a rebound.
2. Repellent.

Blood is stanched by astringent and *repercussive* medicines. *Bacon's Natural History.*

Defluxions, if you apply a strong *repercussive* to the place affected, and do not take away the cause, will shift to another place. *Bacon.*

3. Driven back; rebounding. Not proper.

Amid Carnarvon's mountains rages loud
The *repercussive* roar: with mighty crush
Tumble the smitten cliffs. *Thomson.*

REPERTI'TIOUS. *adj.* [*repertus*, Fr.] Found; gained by finding. *Dict.*

REPE'RTORY. *n. s.* [*repertoire*, Fr. *repertorium*, Lat.] A treasury; a magazine; a book in which any thing is to be found.

REPETI'TION. *n. s.* [*repetition*, Fr. *repetitio*, Lat.]
1. Iteration of the same thing.

The frequent *repetition* of aliment is necessary for repairing the fluids and solids. *Arbuthnot on Aliments.*

2. Recital of the same words over again.

The psalms, for the excellency of their use, deserve to be oftener repeated; but that the multitude of them permitteth not any oftner *repetition*. *Hooker, b.* v. *s.* 30.

3. The act of reciting or rehearsing.

If you conquer Rome, the benefit,
Which you shall thereby reap, is such a name,
Whose *repetition* will be dogg'd with curses. *Shakesp.*

4. Recital from memory, as distinct from reading.

To REPI'NE. *v. n.* [*re* and *pine.*] To fret; to vex himself; to be discontented.

Of late,
When corn was given them gratis, you *repin'd*. *Shakesp.*

The fines imposed were the more *repined* against, because they were assigned to the rebuilding of St. Paul's church. *Clar.*

If you think how many diseases, and how much poverty there is in the world, you will fall down upon your knees, and instead of *repining* at one affliction, will admire so many blessings received at the hand of God. *Temple.*

The ghosts *repine* at violated night;
And curse th' invading sun, and sicken at the sight. *Dryd.*
Just in the gate
Dwell pale diseases and *repining* age. *Dryden.*

REPI'NER. *n. s.* [from *repine.*] One that frets or murmurs.

To REPLA'CE. *v. a.* [*replacer*, Fr. *re* and *place.*]
1. To put again in the former place.

The earl being apprehended, upon examination cleared himself so well, as he was *replaced* in his government. *Bacon.*

The bowls, remov'd for fear,
The youths *replac'd*; and soon restor'd the chear. *Dryden.*

2. To put in a new place.

His gods put themselves under his protection, to be *replaced* in their promised Italy. *Dryden's Ded. to Virgil.*

To REPLA'NT. *v. a.* [*replanter*, Fr. *re* and *plant.*] To plant anew.

Small trees being yet unripe, covered in autumn with dung until the spring, take up and *replant* in good ground. *Bacon.*

REPLANTA'TION. *n. s.* [from *replant.*] The act of planting again.

To REPLAI'T. *v. a.* [*re* and *plait.*] To fold one part often over another.

In Raphael's first works, are many small foldings often *replaited*, which look like so many whip-cords. *Dryden.*

To REPLE'NISH. *v. a.* [*repleo*, from *re* and *plenus*, Lat. *repleni*, old Fr.]
1. To stock; to fill.

Multiply and *replenish* the earth. *Gen.* i. 28.
The waters
With fish *replenish'd*, and the air with fowl. *Milton.*

2. To finish; to consummate; to complete. Not proper, nor in use.

We smother'd
The most *replenished* sweet work of nature,
That from the prime creation e'er she fram'd. *Shakesp.*

To REPLE'NISH. *v. n.* To be stocked. Not in use.

The humours in men's bodies encrease and decrease as the moon doth; and therefore purge some day after the full; for then the humours will not *replenish* so soon. *Bacon.*

REPLE'TE. *adj.* [*replet*, Fr. *repletus*, Lat.] Full; completely filled; filled to exuberance.

The world's large tongue
Proclaims you for a man *replete* with mocks;
Full of comparisons and wounding flouts. *Shakesp.*

This mordication, if in over high a degree, is little better than the corrosion of poison; as sometimes in antimony, if given to bodies not *replete* with humours; for where humours abound, the humours save the parts. *Bacon's Nat. Hist.*

His words, *replete* with guile,
Into her heart too easy entrance won. *Milton.*

In a dog, out of whose eye being wounded the aqueous humour did copiously flow, yet in six hours the bulb of the eye was again *replete* with its humour, without the application of any medicines. *Ray on the Creation.*

REPLE'TION. *n. s.* [*repletion*, Fr.] The state of being over-full.

The tree had too much *repletion*, and was oppressed with its own sap; for *repletion* is an enemy to generation. *Bacon.*

All dreams
Are from *repletion* and complexion bred;
From rising fumes of undigested food. *Dryden.*
Thirst and hunger may be satisfy'd;
But this *repletion* is to love deny'd. *Dryden.*

The action of the stomach is totally stopped by too great *repletion*. *Arbuthnot on Aliments.*

REPLE'VIABLE. *adj.* [*replegiabilis*, barbarous Latin.] What may be replevined.

To REPLE'VIN. } *v. a. Spenser.* [*replegio*, low Lat. of *re* and
To REPLE'VY. } *plevir* or *plegir*, Fr. to give a pledge.] To take back or set at liberty any thing seized upon security given.

That you're a beast, and turn'd to grass,
Is no strange news, nor ever was;
At least to me, who once, you know,
Did from the pound *replevin* you. *Hudibras, p.* iii.

REPLICA'TION. *n. s.* [*replico*, Lat.]
1. Rebound; repercussion. Not in use.

Tyber trembled underneath his banks,
To hear the *replication* of your sounds,
Made in his concave shores. *Shakesp. Julius Cæsar.*

2. Reply; answer.

To be demanded of a spunge, what *replication* should be made by the son of a king? *Shakesp. Hamlet.*

This is a *replication* to what Menelaus had before offered, concerning the transplantation of Ulysses to Sparta. *Broome.*

To REPLY'. *v. n.* [*repliquer*, Fr.] To answer; to make a return to an answer.

O man! who art thou that *repliest* against God? *Rom.* ix.

Would we ascend higher to the rest of these lewd persons, we should find what reason Castalio's painter had to *reply* upon the cardinal, who blamed him for putting a little too much colour into St. Peter and Paul's faces: that it was true in their life time they were pale mortified men, but that since they were grown ruddy, by blushing at the sins of their successors. *Atterbury's Sermons.*

His trembling tongue invok'd his bride;
With his last voice Eurydice he cry'd:
Eurydice the rocks and river-banks *reply'd*. *Dryden.*

To RE'PLY. *v. a.* To return for an answer.

Perplex'd
The tempter stood, nor had what to *reply*. *Milton.*

RE'PLY. *n. s.* [*replique*, Fr.] Answer; return to an answer.

But now return,
And with their faint *reply* this answer join. *Shakesp.*

If I sent him word, it was not well cut; he would send me word, he cut it to please himself: if again, it was not well cut, this is called the *reply* churlish. *Shakesp.*

One rises up to make *replies* to establish or confute what has been offered on each side of the question. *Watts.*

To whom with sighs, Ulysses gave *reply*;
Ah, why ill-suiting pastime must I try? *Pope.*

REPLY'ER. *n. s.* [from *reply.*] He that makes a return to an answer.

At an act of the commencement, the answerer gave for his question, that an aristocracy was better than a monarchy: the *replyer* did tax him, that, being a private bred man, he would give a question of state: the answerer said, that the *replyer* did much wrong the privilege of scholars, who would be much streightened if they should give questions of nothing, but such things wherein they are practised; and added we have heard yourself dispute of virtue, which no man will say you put much in practice. *Bacon's Apopthegms.*

To REPO'LISH. *v. a.* [*repolir*, Fr. *re* and *polish.*] To polish again.

A sundred clock is piecemeal laid
Not to be lost, but by the maker's hand
Repolish'd, without error then to stand. *Donne.*

To REPO'RT. *v. a.* [*rapporter*, Fr.]

1. To noiſe by popular rumour.

Is it upon record? or elſe *reported* ſucceſſively from age to age? *Shakeſp. Richard* III.

It is *reported*,
That good duke Humphry traiterouſly is murther'd. *Shak.*

Report, ſay they, and we will *report* it. *Jer.* xx. 10.

There is a king in Judah; and now ſhall it be *reported* to the king. *Neh.* vi. 7.

2. To give repute.

Timotheus was well *reported* of by the brethren. *Acts* xvi.

A widow well *reported* of for good works. 1 *Tim.* v. 10.

3. To give an account of.

4. To return; to rebound; to give back.

In Ticinum is a church with windows only from above, that *reporteth* the voice thirteen times, if you ſtand by the cloſe end wall over againſt the door. *Bacon.*

Repo'rt. *n. ſ.* [from the noun.]

1. Rumour; popular fame.

2. Repute; publick character.

My body's mark'd
With Roman ſwords; and my *report* was once
Firſt with the beſt of note. *Shakeſp. Cymbeline.*

In all approving ourſelves as the miniſters of God, by honour and diſhonour, by evil *report* and good *report*. 2 *Cor.* iv.

3. Account returned.

We command our ambaſſadors to make *report* unto you. 1 *Mac.* xii. 13.

Sea nymphs enter with the ſwelling tide;
From Thetis ſent as ſpies to make *report*,
And tell the wonders of her ſov'reign's court. *Waller.*

4. Account given by lawyers of caſes.

After a man has ſtudied the general principles of the law, reading the *reports* of adjudged caſes, will richly improve his mind. *Watts's Improvement of the Mind.*

5. Sound; loud noiſe; repercuſſion.

The ſtronger ſpecies drowneth the leſſer; the *report* of an ordnance, the voice. *Bacon's Natural Hiſtory.*

The laſhing billows make a long *report*,
And beat her ſides. *Dryden's Ceyx and Alcyo.*

Repo'rter. *n. ſ.* [from *report.*] Relater; one that gives an account.

There ſhe appear'd; or my *reporter* devis'd well for her. *Shakeſp. Antony and Cleopatra.*

Rumours were raiſed of great diſcord among the nobility; for this cauſe the lords aſſembled, gave order to apprehend the *reporters* of theſe ſurmiſes. *Hayward.*

If I had known a thing they concealed, I ſhould never be the *reporter* of it. *Pope.*

Repo'rtingly. *adv.* [from *reporting.*] By common fame.

Others ſay thou doſt deſerve; and I
Believe it better than *reportingly.* *Shakeſp.*

Repo'sal. *n. ſ.* [from *repoſe.*] The act of repoſing.

Doſt thou think,
If I would ſtand againſt thee, would the *repoſal*
Of any truſt, virtue, or worth in thee,
Make thy words faith'd. *Shakeſp. King Lear.*

To REPO'SE. *v. a.* [*repono*, Lat.]

1. To lay to reſt.

Rome's readieſt champions, *repoſe* you here,
Secure from worldly chances and miſhaps;
Here lurks no treaſon, here no envy ſwells. *Shakeſp.*

I will *repoſe* myſelf with her; to live with her hath no ſorrow, but mirth. *Wiſdom* viii. 16.

Have ye choſ'n this place,
After the toil of battle, to *repoſe*
Your wearied virtue. *Milton's Paradiſe Loſt, b.* i.

2. To place as in confidence or truſt.

I *repoſe* upon your management, what is deareſt to me, my fame. *Dryden's Preface to Ann. Mirab.*

That prince was conſcious of his own integrity in the ſervice of God, and relied on this as a ſure foundation for that truſt he *repoſed* in him, to deliver him out of all his diſtreſſes. *Rogers's Sermons.*

3. To lodge; to lay up.

Pebbles, *repoſed* in thoſe cliffs amongſt the earth, being not ſo diſſoluble and likewiſe more bulky, are left behind. *Woodward's Natural Hiſtory.*

To Repo'se. *v. n.* [*repoſer*, Fr.]

1. To ſleep; to be at reſt.

Within a thicket I *repos'd*; when round
I ruffl'd up fal'n leaves in heap; and found,
Let fall from heaven, a ſleep interminate. *Chapman.*

2. To reſt in confidence.

And, for the ways are dangerous to paſs,
I do deſire thy worthy company,
Upon whoſe faith and honour I *repoſe*. *Shakeſp.*

Repo'se. *n. ſ.* [*repos*, Fr.]

1. Sleep; reſt; quiet.

Merciful pow'rs!
Reſtrain in me the curſed thoughts, that nature
Gives way to in *repoſe*. *Shakeſp. Macbeth.*

Th' hour
Of night, and of all things now retir'd to reſt,
Mind us of like *repoſe*. *Milton's Paradiſe Loſt, b.* iv.

Thoughtful of thy gain, I all the livelong day
Conſume in meditation deep, recluſe
From human converſe; nor at ſhut of eve
Enjoy *repoſe*. *Philips.*

2. Cauſe of reſt.

After great lights muſt be great ſhadows, which we call *repoſes*; becauſe in reality the ſight would be tired, if attracted by a continuity of glittering objects. *Dryden's Dufreſnoy.*

Repo'sedness. *n. ſ.* [from *repoſed.*] State of being at reſt.

To REPO'SITE. *v. a.* [*repoſitus*, Lat.] To lay up; to lodge as in a place of ſafety.

Others *repoſite* their young in holes, and ſecure themſelves alſo therein, becauſe ſuch ſecurity is wanting, their lives being ſought. *Derham's Phyſico-Theology.*

Reposi'tion. *n. ſ.* [from *repoſite.*] The act of replacing.

Being ſatisfied in the *repoſition* of the bone, take care to keep it ſo by deligation. *Wiſeman's Surgery.*

Repo'sitory. *n. ſ.* [*repoſitoire*, Fr. *repoſitorium*, Lat.] A place where any thing is ſafely laid up.

The mind of man, not being capable of having many ideas under view at once, it was neceſſary to have a *repoſitory* to lay up thoſe ideas. *Locke.*

He can take a body to pieces, and diſpoſe of them, to us not without the appearance of irretrievable confuſion, but with reſpect to his own knowledge into the moſt regular and methodical *repoſitories*. *Rogers's Sermons.*

To Reposse'ss. *v. a.* [*re* and *poſſeſs.*] To poſſeſs again.

How comes it now, that almoſt all that realm is *repoſſeſſed* of them? *Spenſer's State of Ireland.*

Her ſuit is now to *repoſſeſs* thoſe lands,
Which we in juſtice cannot well deny. *Shakeſp.*

Nor ſhall my father *repoſſeſs* the land,
The father's fortune never to return. *Pope's Odyſſey.*

To REPREHE'ND. *v. a.* [*reprehendo*, Lat.]

1. To reprove; to chide.

All as before his ſight, whoſe preſence to offend with any the leaſt unſeemlineſs, we would be ſurely as loth as they, who moſt *reprehend* or deride that we do. *Hooker, b.* v. *ſ.* 29.

Pardon me for *reprehending* thee,
For thou haſt done a charitable deed. *Shakeſp.*

They, like dumb ſtatues ſtar'd;
Which, when I ſaw, I *reprehended* them;
And aſk'd the mayor, what meant this wilful ſilence? *Sha.*

2. To blame; to cenſure.

I nor adviſe, nor *reprehend* the choice
Of Marcley-hill. *Philips.*

Friends *reprehend* him, *reprehend* him there:
For what? for ſtealing Gaffer Gap's gray mare. *Gay.*

3. To detect of fallacy.

This colour will be *reprehended* or encountered, by imputing to all excellencies in compoſitions a kind of poverty. *Bacon.*

4. To charge with as a fault. With *of* before the crime.

Ariſtippus, being *reprehended of* luxury by one that was not rich, for that he gave ſix crowns for a ſmall fiſh, anſwered, why, what would you have given? the other ſaid, ſome twelve pence: Ariſtippus ſaid again, and ſix crowns is no more with me. *Bacon's Apopthegms.*

Reprehe'nder. *n. ſ.* [from *reprehend.*] Blamer; cenſurer.

Theſe fervent *reprehenders* of things, eſtabliſhed by publick authority, are always confident and bold-ſpirited men; but their confidence for the moſt part riſeth from too much credit given to their own wits, for which cauſe they are ſeldom free from errours. *Hooker's Dedication.*

REPREHE'NSIBLE. *adj.* [*reprehenſible*, Fr. *reprehenſus*, Lat.] Blameable; culpable; cenſurable.

Reprehe'nsibleness. *n. ſ.* [from *reprehenſible.*] Blameableneſs.

Reprehe'nsibly. *adv.* [from *reprehenſible.*] Blameably; culpably.

Reprehe'nsion. *n. ſ.* [*reprehenſio*, Latin.] Reproof; open blame.

To a heart fully reſolute counſel is tedious, but *reprehenſion* is loathſome. *Bacon.*

There is likewiſe due to the publick a civil *reprehenſion* of advocates, where there appeareth cunning counſel, groſs neglect, and ſlight information. *Bacon's Eſſays.*

The admonitions, fraternal or paternal of his fellow chriſtians, or the governors of the church, then more publick *reprehenſions* and increpations. *Hammond.*

What effect can that man hope from his moſt zealous *reprehenſions*, who lays himſelf open to recrimination. *Go. of T.*

Reprehe'nsive. *adj.* [from *reprehend.*] Given to reproof.

To REPRESE'NT. *v. a.* [*repræſento*, Lat. *repreſenter*, Fr.]

1. To exhibit, as if the thing exhibited were preſent.

Before him burn
Seven lamps, as in a zodiac *repreſenting*
The heav'nly fires. *Milton's Paradiſe Loſt, b.* xii.

REPU'GNANTLY. *adv.* [from *repugnant.*] Contradictorily.

They speak not *repugnantly* thereto. *Brown's Vulg. Err.*

To REPU'LLULATE. *v. n.* [*re* and *pullulo*, Lat. *repulluler*, Fr.] To bud again.

Though tares *repullulate*; there is wheat still left in the field. *Howel's Vocal Forest.*

REPU'LSE. *n. s.* [*repulse*, Fr. *repulsa*, Latin.] The condition of being driven off or put aside from any attempt.

My *repulse* at Hull seemed an act of so rude disloyalty, that my enemies had scarce confidence enough to abet it. *K. Cha.*

Nor much expect
A foe so proud will first the weaker seek;
So bent, the more shall shame him his *repulse*. *Milton.*

By fate repell'd, and with *repulses* tir'd. *Denham.*

To REPU'LSE. *v. a.* [*repulsus*, Lat.] To beat back; to drive off.

The christian defendants still *repulsed* them with greater courage than they were able to assail them. *Knolles.*

This fleet, attempting St. Minoes, were *repulsed*, and without glory or gain, returned into England. *Hayward.*

Man complete to have discover'd and *repuls'd*
Whatever wiles of foe or seeming friend. *Milton.*

REPU'LSION. *n. s.* [*repulsus*, Lat.] The act or power of driving off from itself.

Air has some degree of tenacity, whereby the parts attract one another; at the same time, by their elasticity, the particles of air have a power of *repulsion* or flying off from one another. *Arbuthnot.*

REPU'LSIVE. *adj.* [from *repulse.*] Driving off; having the power to beat back or drive off.

The parts of the salt or vitriol recede from one another, and endeavour to expand themselves, and get as far asunder as the quantity of water, in which they float, will allow; and does not this endeavour imply, that they have a *repulsive* force by which they fly from one another, or that they attract the water more strongly than one another? *Newton's Opticks.*

To REPU'RCHASE. *v. a.* [*re* and *purchase.*] To buy again.

Once more we sit on England's royal throne,
Repurchas'd with the blood of enemies;
What valiant foe-men, like to autumn's corn,
Have we mow'd down in top of all their pride? *Shakesp.*

If the son alien those lands, and *repurchase* them again in fee, the rules of descents are to be observed, as if he were the original purchaser. *Hale's Law of England.*

RE'PUTABLE. *adj.* [from *repute.*] Honourable; not infamous.

If ever any vice shall become *reputable*, and be gloried in as a mark of greatness, what can we then expect from the man of honour, but to signalize himself. *Rogers's Sermons.*

In the article of danger, it is as *reputable* to elude an enemy as defeat one. *Broome.*

RE'PUTABLY. *adv.* [from *reputable.*] Without discredit.

To many such worthy magistrates, who have thus *reputably* filled the chief seats of power in this great city, I am now addressing my discourse. *Atterbury's Sermons.*

REPUTA'TION. *n. s.* [*reputation*, Fr. from *repute.*] Credit; honour; character of good.

Reputation is an idle and most false imposition; oft got without merit, and lost without deserving: you have lost no *reputation* at all, unless you repute yourself such a loser. *Shak.*

Versoy, upon the lake of Geneva, has the *reputation* of being extremely poor and beggarly. *Addison.*

A third interprets motions, looks and eyes;
At ev'ry word a *reputation* dies. *Pope's Rape of the Lock.*

To REPU'TE. *v. a.* [*reputo*, Lat. *reputer*, Fr.] To hold; to account; to think.

The king was *reputed* a prince most prudent. *Shakesp.*

I do *repute* her grace
The rightful heir to England's royal seat. *Shakesp.*

I do know of those,
That therefore only are *reputed* wise,
For saying nothing. *Shakesp. Merchant of Venice.*

Men, such as chuse
Law practice for mere gain, boldly *repute*
Worse than embrothel'd strumpets prostitute. *Donne.*

If the grand vizier be so great, as he is *reputed*, in politicks he will never consent to an invasion of Hungary. *Temple.*

REPU'TE. *n. s.* [from the verb.]

1. Character; reputation.

2. Established opinion.

He who reigns
Monarch in heav'n, till then as one secure,
Sat on his throne, upheld by old *repute*. *Milton.*

REPU'TELESS. *adj.* [from *repute.*] Disreputable; disgraceful. A word not inelegant, but out of use.

Opinion, that did help me to the crown,
Had left me in *reputeless* banishment,
A fellow of no mark nor livelihood. *Shakesp. Hen. V.*

REQUE'ST. *n. s.* [*requeste*, Fr.]

1. Petition; entreaty.

But ask what you would have reform'd,
I will both hear and grant you your *requests*. *Shakesp.*

Haman stood up to make *request* for his life to Esther. *Esth.*

All thy *request* for man, accepted son!
Obtain; all thy *request* was my decree. *Milton's Par. Lost.*

Ask him to lend
To this, the last *request* that I shall send,
A gentle ear. *Denham.*

2. Demand; repute; credit; state of being desired.

Tullus Aufidius will appear well in these wars, his great opposer Coriolanus being now in no *request* of his country. *Shakesp. Coriolanus.*

Whilst this vanity of thinking, that men are obliged to write either systems or nothing, is in *request*, many excellent notions are suppressed. *Boyle.*

Knowledge and fame were in as great *request* as wealth among us now. *Temple.*

To REQUE'ST. *v. a.* [*requester*, Fr.] To ask; to solicite; to entreat.

To-night we hold a solemn supper, Sir,
And I'll *request* your presence. *Shakesp. Macbeth.*

It was to be *requested* of Almighty God by prayer, that those kings would seriously fulfil all that hope of peace. *Knolles.*

The virgin quire for her *request*,
The god that sits at marriage feast;
He at their invoking came,
But with a scarce well-lighted flame. *Milton.*

In things not unlawful, great persons cannot be properly said to *request*, because all things considered, they must not be denied. *South's Sermons.*

REQUE'STER. *n. s.* [from *request.*] Petitioner; soliciter.

To REQUI'CKEN. *v. a.* [*re* and *quicken.*] To reanimate.

By and by the din of war 'gan pierce
His ready sense, when straight his doubled spirit
Requicken'd what in flesh was fatigate,
And to the battle came he. *Shakesp. Coriolanus.*

RE'QUIEM. *n. s.* [Latin.]

1. A hymn in which they implore for the dead *requiem* or rest.

We should profane the service of the dead,
To sing a *requiem* and such peace to her,
As to peace-parted souls. *Shakesp.*

2. Rest; quiet; peace. Not in use.

The midwife kneel'd at my mother's throes,
With pain produc'd, and nurs'd for future woes;
Else had I an eternal *requiem* kept,
And in the arms of peace for ever slept. *Sandys.*

REQUI'RABLE. *adj.* [from *require.*] Fit to be required.

It contains the certain periods of times, and all circumstances *requirable* in a history to inform. *Hale.*

To REQUI'RE. *v. a.* [*requiro*, Lat. *requerir*, Fr.]

1. To demand; to ask a thing as of right.

Ye me *require*
A thing without the compass of my wit;
For both the lineage and the certain sire,
From which I sprung, are from me hidden yet. *Spenser.*

We do *require* them of you, so to use them,
As we shall find their merits. *Shakesp. King Lear.*

This, the very law of nature teacheth us to do, and this the law of God *requireth* also at our hands. *Spelman.*

This imply'd
Subjection, but *requir'd* with gentle sway. *Milton.*

Oft our alliance other lands desir'd,
And what we seek of you, of us *requir'd*. *Dryden.*

God, when he gave the world in common to all mankind, commanded men also to labour, and the penury of his condition *required* it. *Locke.*

2. To make necessary; to need.

The king's business *required* haste. 1 *Sam.* xxi. 8.

High from the ground the branches would *require*
Thy utmost reach. *Milton.*

But why, alas! do mortal men complain;
God gives us what he knows our wants *require*,
And better things than those which we desire. *Dryden.*

RE'QUISITE. *adj.* [*requisitus*, Lat.] Necessary; needful; required by the nature of things.

When God new modelled the world by the introduction of a new religion, and that in the room of one set up by himself, it was *requisite*, that he should recommend it to the reasons of men with the same authority and evidence that enforced the former. *South's Sermons.*

Cold calleth the spirits to succour, and therefore they cannot so well close and go together in the head, which is ever *requisite* to sleep. *Bacon's Natural History.*

Prepare your soul with all those necessary graces, that are more immediately *requisite* to this performance. *Wake.*

RE'QUISITE. *n. s.* Any thing necessary.

Res non parta labore, sed relicta, was thought by a poet to be one of the *requisites* to a happy life. *Dryden.*

For want of these *requisites*, most of our ingenious young men take up some cried up English poet, adore him, and imitate him, without knowing wherein he is defective. *Dryden.*

This God on his part has declared for the *requisites* on ours, what we must do to obtain these blessings, is the great business of us all to know. *Wake.*

Re'quisitely. *adv.* [from *requisite.*] Necessarily; in a requisite manner.

We discern how *requisitely* the several parts of scripture are fitted to several times, persons, and occurrences. *Boyle.*

Re'quisiteness. *n. s.* [from *requisite.*] Necessity; the state of being requisite.

Discerning how exquisitely the several parts of scripture are fitted to the several times, persons and occurrences intended, we shall discover not only the sense of the obscurer passages, but the *requisiteness* of their having been written so obscurely. *Boyle.*

Requi'tal. *n. s.* [from *requite.*]

1. Return for any good or bad office; retaliation.

Should we take the quarrel of sermons in hand, and revenge their cause by *requital*, thrusting prayer in a manner out of doors under colour of long preaching? *Hooker.*

Since you
Wear your gentle limbs in my affairs,
Be bold, you do so grow in my *requital*,
As nothing can unroot you. *Shak. All's well that ends well.*

We hear
Such goodness of your justice, that our soul
Cannot but yield you forth to publick thanks,
Forerunning your *requital.* *Shakesp. Meas. for Meas.*

I see you are obsequious in your love, and I profess *requital.* *Shakespeare.*

No merit their aversion can remove,
Nor ill *requital* can efface their love. *Waller.*

2. Reward; recompense.

He ask'd me for a song,
And in *requital* op'd his leathern scrip,
And shew'd me simples of a thousand names,
Telling their strange and vigorous faculties. *Milton.*

I have ta'en a cordial,
Sent by the king or Haly, in *requital*
Of all my miseries, to make me happy. *Denham.*

In all the light that the heavens bestow upon this lower world, though the lower world cannot equal their benefaction, yet with a kind of grateful return it reflects those rays, that it cannot recompense; so that there is some return however, though there can be no *requital.* *South's Sermons.*

To REQUI'TE. *v. a.* [*requiter*, Fr.] To repay; to retaliate good or ill; to recompense.

If he love me to madness, I shall never *requite* him. *Shak.*

He hath *requited* me evil for good. 1 *Sam.* xxv. 21.

Open not thine heart to every man, lest he *requite* thee with a shrewd turn. *Ecclus.* viii. 19.

When Joseph's brethren saw that their father was dead, they said, Joseph will *requite* us all the evil we did. *Genesis* l.

An avenger against his enemies, and one that shall *requite* kindness to his friends. *Ecclus.* xxx. 6.

Him within protect from harms;
He can *requite* thee, for he knows the charms
That call fame on such gentle acts as these. *Milton.*

Great idol of mankind, we neither claim
The praise of merit, nor aspire to fame!
'Tis all we beg thee to conceal from sight
Those acts of goodness which themselves *requite*:
O let us still the secret joy partake,
To follow virtue ev'n for virtue's sake. *Pope.*

Unhappy Wallace,
Great patriot heroe! ill *requited* chief! *Thomson.*

Re'remouse. *n. s.* [hꞃeꞃemuꞅ, Saxon.] A bat.

Re'reward. *n. s.* The rear or last troop.

Resa'le. *n. s.* [*re* and *sale.*] Sale at second hand.

Monopolies and coemption of wares for *resale*, where they are not restrained, are great means to enrich. *Bacon.*

To **Resalu'te.** *v. a.* [*resaluto*, Lat. *resaluer*, Fr.] To salute or greet anew.

We drew her up to land,
And trod ourselves the *resaluted* sand. *Chapman.*

To *resalute* the world with sacred light,
Leucothea wak'd. *Milton.*

To **Resai'l.** *v. a.* [*re* and *sail.*] To sail back.

From Pyle *resailing*, and the Spartan court,
Horrid to speak! in ambush is decreed *Pope's Odyssey.*

To **Resci'nd.** *v. a.* [*rescindo*, Lat. *rescinder*, Fr.] To cut off; to abrogate a law.

It is the imposing a sacramental obligation upon him, which being the condition, upon the performance whereof all the promises of endless bliss are made over, it is not possible to *rescind* or disclaim the standing obliged by it. *Hammond.*

I spake against the test, but was not heard;
These to *rescind*, and peerage to restore. *Dryden.*

Resci'ssion. *n. s.* [*rescission*, Fr. *rescissus*, Lat.] The act of cutting off; abrogation.

If any infer *rescission* of their estate to have been for idolatry, that the governments of all idolatrous nations should be also dissolved, it followeth not. *Bacon.*

Resci'ssory. *adj.* [*rescissoire*, Fr. *rescissus*, Lat.] Having the power to cut off.

To **Rescri'be.** *v. a.* [*rescribo*, Lat. *rescrire*, Fr.]

1. To write back.

Whenever a prince on his being consulted *rescribes* or writes back Toleramus, he dispenses with that act otherwise unlawful. *Ayliffe's Parergon.*

2. To write over again.

Calling for more paper to *rescribe* them, he shewed him the difference betwixt the ink-box and the sand-box. *Howel.*

Re'script. *n. s.* [*rescrit*, Fr. *rescriptum*, Lat.] Edict of an emperour.

One finding a great mass of money digged under ground, and being somewhat doubtful, signified it to the emperor, who made a *rescript* thus; Use it. *Bacon's Apophthegms.*

The popes, in such cases, where canons were silent, did, after the manner of the Roman emperors, write back their determinations, which were stiled *rescripts* or decretal epistles, having the force of laws. *Ayliffe's Parergon.*

To RE'SCUE. *v. a.* [*rescorre*, old Fr.] To set free from any violence, confinement, or danger.

Sir Scudamore, after long sorrow, in the end met with Britomartis, who succoured him and *reskewed* his love. *Spens.*

My uncles both are slain in *rescuing* me. *Shakesp.*

We're beset with thieves;
Rescue thy mistress, if thou be a man. *Shakesp.*

Dr. Bancroft understood the church excellently, and had almost *rescued* it out of the hands of the Calvinian party. *Clar.*

He that is so sure of his particular election, as to resolve he can never fall, if he commit those acts, against which scripture is plain, that they that do them shall not inherit eternal life, must necessarily resolve, that nothing but the removing his fundamental error can *rescue* him from the superstructive. *Hammond's Fundamentals.*

Who was that just man, whom had not heav'n
Rescu'd, had in his righteousness been lost? *Milton.*

Riches cannot *rescue* from the grave,
Which claims alike the monarch and the slave. *Dryden.*

Re'scue. *n. s.* [*rescousse*, *rescosse*, old Fr. *rescussus*, low Lat.] Deliverance from violence, danger, or confinement.

How comes it, you
Have holp to make this *rescue.* *Shakesp. Coriolanus.*

Re'scuer. *n. s.* [from *rescue.*] One that rescues.

Resea'rch. *n. s.* [*recherche*, Fr.] Enquiry; search.

By a skilful application of those notices, may be gained in such *researches* the accelerating and bettering of fruits, emptying mines and draining fens. *Glanvill's Sceps.*

I submit those mistakes, into which I may have fallen, to the better consideration of others, who shall have made *research* into this business with more felicity. *Holder.*

A felicity adapted to every rank, such as the *researches* of human wisdom sought for, but could not discover. *Rogers.*

To **Resea'rch.** *v. a.* [*rechercher*, Fr.] To examine; to enquire.

It is not easy to *research* with due distinction, in the actions of eminent personages, both how much may have been blemished by the envy of others, and what was corrupted by their own felicity. *Wotton's Buckingham.*

To **Resea't.** *v. a.* [*re* and *seat.*] To seat again.

When he's produc'd, will you *reseat* him
Upon his father's throne? *Dryden's Spanish Fryar.*

Resei'zer. *n. s.* One that seizes again.

Resei'zure. *n. s.* [*re* and *seizure.*] Repeated seizure; seizure a second time.

Here we have the charter of foundation; it is now the more easy to judge of the forfeiture or *reseizure*: deface the image, and you divest the right. *Bacon.*

Rese'mblance. *n. s.* [*resemblance*, Fr.] Likeness; similitude; representation.

These sensible things, which religion hath allowed, are *resemblances* formed according to things spiritual, whereunto they serve as a hand to lead, and a way to direct. *Hooker.*

Fairest *resemblance* of thy maker fair,
Thee all things living gaze on. *Milton.*

One main end of poetry and painting is to please; they bear a great *resemblance* to each other. *Dryden's Dufresnoy.*

The quality produced hath commonly no *resemblance* with the thing producing it; wherefore, we look on it as a bare effect of power. *Locke.*

They are but weak *resemblances* of our intentions, faint and imperfect copies that may acquaint us with the general design, but can never express the life of the original. *Addison.*

So chymists boast they have a pow'r,
From the dead ashes of a flow'r,
Some faint *resemblance* to produce,
But not the virtue. *Swift's Miscellanies.*

I cannot help remarking the *resemblance* betwixt him and our author in qualities, fame, and fortune. *Pope.*

To **Rese'mble.** *v. a.* [*resembler*, Fr.]

1. To compare; to represent as like something else.

Most safely may we *resemble* ourselves to God, in respect of that pure faculty, which is never separate from the love of God. *Raleigh's History of the World.*

The torrid parts of Africk are *resembled* to a libbard's skin, the distance of whose spots represent the disperseness of habitations. *Brerewood on Languages.*

2. To

2. To be like; to have likeneſs to.

If we ſee a man of virtues, mixed with infirmities, fall into misfortune, we are afraid that the like misfortunes may happen to ourſelves, who *reſemble* the character. *Addiſon.*

To RESE'ND. *v. a.* [*re* and *ſend.*] To ſend back; to ſend again. Not in uſe.

I ſent to her, by this ſame coxcomb,
Tokens and letters, which ſhe did *reſend.* *Shakeſp.*

To RESE'NT. *v. a.* [*reſſentir*, Fr.]

1. To take well or ill.

A ſerious conſideration of the mineral treaſures of his territories, and the practical diſcoveries of them by way of my philoſophical theory, he then ſo well *reſented*, that afterwards, upon a mature digeſtion of my whole deſign, he commanded me to let your lordſhips underſtand, how great an inclination he hath to further ſo hopeful a work. *Bacon.*

2. To take ill; to conſider as an injury or affront. This is now the moſt uſual ſenſe.

Thou with ſcorn
And anger would'ſt *reſent* the offer'd wrong. *Milton.*

RESE'NTER *n. ſ.* [from *reſent.*] One who feels injuries deeply.

The earl was the worſt philoſopher, being a great *reſenter*, and a weak diſſembler of the leaſt diſgrace. *Wotton.*

RESE'NTFUL. *adj.* [*reſent* and *full.*] Malignant; eaſily provoked to anger, and long retaining it.

RESE'NTINGLY. *adv.* [from *reſenting.*] With deep ſenſe; with ſtrong perception; with anger.

Hylobares judiciouſly and *reſentingly* recapitulates your main reaſonings. *More's Divine Dialogues.*

RESE'NTMENT. *n. ſ.* [*reſſentiment*, Fr.]

1. Strong perception of good or ill.

He retains vivid *reſentments* of the more ſolid morality. *More's Divine Dialogues.*

Some faces we admire and dote on; others, in our impartial apprehenſions, no leſs deſerving, we can behold without *reſentment*; yea, with an invincible diſregard. *Glanvill.*

What he hath of ſenſible evidence, the very grand work of his demonſtration, is but the knowledge of his own *reſentment*; but how the ſame things appear to others, they only know that are conſcious to them; and how they are in themſelves, only he that made them. *Glanvill's Scepſ.*

2. Deep ſenſe of injury.

Can heav'nly minds ſuch high *reſentment* ſhow,
Or exerciſe their ſpight in human woe? *Dryden.*

I cannot, without ſome envy, and a juſt *reſentment* againſt the oppoſite conduct of others, reflect upon that generoſity, wherewith the heads of a ſtruggling faction treat thoſe who will undertake to hold a pen in their defence. *Swift.*

RESERVA'TION. *n. ſ.* [*reſervation*, Fr.]

1. Reſerve; concealment of ſomething in the mind.

Nor had I any *reſervations* in my own ſoul, when I paſſed that bill, nor repentings after. *King Charles.*

We ſwear with Jeſuitical equivocations and mental *reſervations.* *Sanderſon againſt the Covenant.*

2. Something kept back; ſomething not given up.

Ourſelf by monthly courſe,
With *reſervation* of an hundred knights,
By you to be ſuſtain'd, ſhall our abode
Make with you by due turns. *Shakeſp. King Lear.*

This is academical *reſervation* in matters of eaſy truth, or rather ſceptical infidelity againſt the evidence of reaſon. *Bro.*

Theſe opinions Steele and his faction are endeavouring to propagate among the people concerning the preſent miniſtry; with what *reſervation* to the honour of the queen, I cannot determine. *Swift's Miſcellanies.*

3. Cuſtody; ſtate of being treaſured up.

He will'd me,
In heedful'ſt *reſervation*, to beſtow them
As notes, whoſe faculties incluſive were,
More than they of note. *Shakeſp.*

RESE'RVATORY. *n. ſ.* [*reſervoir*, Fr.] Place in which any thing is reſerved or kept.

How I got ſuch notice of that ſubterranean *reſervatory* as to make a computation of the water now concealed therein, peruſe the propoſitions concerning earthquakes. *Woodward.*

To RESE'RVE. *v. a.* [*reſerver*, Fr. *reſervo*, Lat.]

1. To keep in ſtore; to ſave to ſome other purpoſe.

I could add many probabilities of the names of places; but they ſhould be too long for this, and I *reſerve* them for another. *Spenſer's State of Ireland.*

Haſt thou ſeen the treaſures of the hail, which I have *reſerved* againſt the day of trouble? *Job* xxxviii. 23.

David houghed all the chariot horſes, but *reſerved* of them for an hundred chariots. 2 *Sam.* viii. 4.

Flowers
Reſerv'd from night, and kept for thee in ſtore. *Milton.*

2. To retain; to keep; to hold.

Reſerve thy ſtate, with better judgment check
This hideous raſhneſs. *Shakeſp.*

Will he *reſerve* his anger for ever? will he keep it to the end? *Jer.* iii. 5.

3. To lay up to a future time.

The Lord knoweth how to deliver the godly out of temptations, and to *reſerve* the unjuſt unto the day of judgment to be puniſhed. 2 *Peter* ii. 9.

The breach ſeems like the ſciſſures of an earthquake, and threatens to ſwallow all that attempt to cloſe it, and *reſerves* its cure only for omnipotence. *Decay of Piety.*

Conceal your eſteem and love in your own breaſt, and *reſerve* your kind looks and language for private hours. *Swift.*

RESE'RVE. *n. ſ.* [from the verb.]

1. Store kept untouched.

The aſſent may be withheld upon this ſuggeſtion, that I know not yet all that may be ſaid: and therefore, though I be beaten, it is not neceſſary I ſhould yield, not knowing what forces there are in *reſerve* behind. *Locke.*

2. Something kept for exigence.

The virgins, beſides the oil in their lamps, carried likewiſe a *reſerve* in ſome other veſſel for a continual ſupply. *Tillotſon.*

3. Something concealed in the mind.

However any one may concur in the general ſcheme, it is ſtill with certain *reſerves* and deviations, and with a ſalvo to his own private judgement. *Addiſon's Freeholder.*

4. Exception; prohibition.

Is knowledge ſo deſpis'd?
Or envy, or what *reſerve* forbids to taſte? *Milton.*

5. Exception in favour.

Each has ſome darling luſt, which pleads for a *reſerve*, and which they would fain reconcile to the expectations of religion. *Rogers's Sermons.*

6. Modeſty; caution in perſonal behaviour.

Ere guardian thought cou'd bring its ſcatter'd aid,
My ſoul ſurpriz'd, and from herſelf disjoin'd,
Left all *reſerve*, and all the ſex behind. *Prior.*

RESE'RVED. *adj.* [from *reſerve.*]

1. Modeſt; not looſely free.

To all obliging, yet *reſerv'd* to all,
None could himſelf the favour'd lover call. *Walſh.*

2. Sullen; not open; not frank.

Nothing *reſerv'd* or ſullen was to ſee,
But ſweet regards. *Dryden.*

RESE'RVEDLY. *adv.* [from *reſerved.*]

1. Not with frankneſs; not with openneſs; with reſerve.

I muſt give only ſhort hints, and write but obſcurely and *reſervedly*, until I have opportunity to expreſs my ſentiments with greater copiouſneſs and perſpicuity. *Woodward.*

2. Scrupulouſly; coldly.

He ſpeaks *reſerv'dly*, but he ſpeaks with force;
Nor can a word be chang'd but for a worſe. *Pope.*

RESE'RVEDNESS. *n. ſ.* [from *reſerved.*] Cloſeneſs; want of frankneſs; want of openneſs.

Obſerve their gravity
And their *reſervedneſs*, their many cautions
Fitting their perſons. *Benj. Johnſon's Cataline.*

By formality, I mean ſomething more than ceremony and complement, even a ſolemn *reſervedneſs*, which may well conſiſt with honeſty. *Wotton.*

There was great warineſs and *reſervedneſs*, and ſo great a jealouſy of each other, that they had no mind to give or receive viſits. *Clarendon, b.* viii.

Diſſimulation can but juſt guard a man within the compaſs of his own perſonal concerns, which yet may be more effectually done by that ſilence and *reſervedneſs*, that every man may innocently practiſe. *South's Sermons.*

RESE'RVER. *n. ſ.* [from *reſerve.*] One that reſerves.

RESERVOI'R. *n. ſ.* [*reſervoir*, Fr.] Place where any thing is kept in ſtore.

There is not a ſpring or fountain, but are well provided with huge ciſterns and *reſervoirs* of rain and ſnow-water. *Add.*

Who ſees pale Mammon pine amidſt his ſtore,
Sees but a backward ſteward for the poor;
This year a *reſervoir*, to keep and ſpare;
The next, a fountain ſpouting through his heir. *Pope.*

To RESE'TTLE. *v. a.* [*re* and *ſettle.*] To ſettle again.

Will the houſe of Auſtria yield the leaſt article, even of uſurped prerogative, to *reſettle* the minds of thoſe princes in the alliance, who are alarmed at the conſequences of the emperor's death. *Swift.*

RESE'TTLEMENT. *n. ſ.* [from *reſettle.*]

1. The act of ſettling again.

To the quieting of my paſſions, and the *reſettlement* of my diſcompoſed ſoul, I conſider that grief is the moſt abſurd of all the paſſions. *Norris's Miſcellanies.*

2. The ſtate of ſettling again.

Some roll their caſk to mix it with the lees, and, after a *reſettlement*, they rack it. *Mortimer's Huſbandry.*

RESI'ANCE. *n. ſ.* [from *reſiant.*] Reſidence; abode; dwelling. *Reſiance* and *reſiant* are now only uſed in law.

The king forthwith baniſhed all Flemings out of his kingdom, commanding his merchant adventurers, which had a *reſiance* in Antwerp, to return. *Bacon's Henry* VII.

RESI'ANT. *adj.* [*reſſeant*, Fr.] Reſident; preſent in a place.

Solyman was come as far as Sophia, where the Turks great lieutenant in Europe is always *reſiant*, before that the Hungarians were aware. *Knolles's Hiſtory of the Turks.*

The Allobroges here *reſiant* in Rome. *Benj. Johnſ.*

To RESI'DE. *v. n.* [*resideo*, Lat. *resider*, Fr.]

1. To have abode; to live; to dwell; to be present.

How can God with such *reside*? *Milton.*

In no fix'd place the happy souls *reside*;
In groves we live, and lie on mossy beds. *Dryden's Æneis.*

2. [*Resido*, Lat.] To sink; to subside; to fall to the bottom.

Oil of vitriol and petroleum, a drachm of each, turn into a mouldy substance; there *residing* in the bottom a fair cloud and a thick oil on the top. *Boyle.*

RE'SIDENCE. *n. s.* [*residence*, Fr.]

1. Act of dwelling in a place.

Something holy lodges in that breast,
And with these raptures moves the vocal air,
To testify his hidden *residence*. *Milton.*

There was a great familiarity between the confessor and duke William; for the confessor had often made considerable *residences* in Normandy. *Hale's Law of England.*

2. Place of abode; dwelling.

Within the infant rind of this small flower,
Poison hath *residence* and medicine power. *Shakesp.*

Understand the same
Of fish within their wat'ry *residence*. *Milton's Par. Lost.*

Caprea had been the retirement of Augustus for some time, and the *residence* of Tiberius for several years. *Addison.*

3. [From *resido*, Lat.] That which settles at the bottom of liquours.

Separation is wrought by weight, as in the ordinary *residence* or settlement of liquors. *Bacon.*

Our clearest waters, and such as seem simple unto sense, are much compounded unto reason, as may be observed in the evaporation of water, wherein, besides a terreous *residence*, some salt is also found. *Brown's Vulgar Errours.*

RE'SIDENT. *adj.* [*residens*, Lat. *resident*, Fr.] Dwelling or having abode in any place.

I am not concerned in this objection; not thinking it necessary, that Christ should be personally present or *resident* on earth in the millenium. *Burnet's Theory of the Earth.*

He is not said to be *resident* in a place, who comes thither with a purpose of retiring immediately; so also he is said to be absent, who is absent with his family. *Ayliffe's Parergon.*

RE'SIDENT. *n. s.* [from the adj.] An agent, minister, or officer residing in any distant place with the dignity of an ambassador.

The pope fears the English will suffer nothing like a *resident* or consul in his kingdoms. *Addison.*

RESIDE'NTIARY. *adj.* [from *resident.*] Holding residence.

Christ was the conductor of the Israelites into the land of Canaan, and their *residentiary* guardian. *More.*

RESI'DUAL. } *adj.* [from *residuum*, Lat.] Relating to the
RESI'DUARY. } residue; relating to the part remaining.

'Tis enough to lose the legacy, or the *residuary* advantage of the estate left him by the deceased. *Ayliffe.*

RE'SIDUE. *n. s.* [*residu*, Fr. *residuum*, Lat.] The remaining part; that which is left.

The causes are all such as expel the most volatile parts of the blood, and fix the *residue*. *Arbuthnot on Aliments.*

To RESIE'GE. *v. a.* [*re* and *siege*, Fr.] To seat again. Obsolete.

In wretched prison long he did remain,
Till they outreigned had their utmost date,
And then therein *reseiged* was again,
And ruled long with honourable state. *Fairy Queen, b.* ii.

To RESI'GN. *v. a.* [*resigner*, Fr. *resigno*, Lat.]

1. To give up a claim or possession.

Resign
Your crown and kingdom, indirectly held. *Shakesp.*

I'll to the king, and signify to him,
That thus I have *resign'd* to you my charge. *Shakesp.*

To her thou didst *resign* thy place. *Milton.*

Phœbus *resigns* his darts, and Jove
His thunder, to the god of love. *Denham.*

Ev'ry Ismena would *resign* her breast;
And ev'ry dear Hippolytus be blest. *Prior.*

2. To yield up.

Whoever shall *resign* their reasons, either from the root of deceit in themselves, or inability to resist such trivial ingannations from others, although their condition may place them above the multitude, yet are they still within the line of vulgarity. *Brown's Vulgar Errours.*

Desirous to *resign* and render back
All I receiv'd. *Milton.*

Those, who always *resign* their judgment to the last man they heard or read, truth never sinks into those men's minds; but, cameleon-like, they take the colour of what is laid before them, and as soon lose and *resign* it to the next that comes in their way. *Locke.*

3. To give up in confidence. With *up* emphatical.

What more reasonable, than that we should in all things *resign up* ourselves to the will of God. *Tillotson.*

4. To submit; particularly to submit to providence.

Happy the man, who studies nature's laws.
His mind possessing in a quiet state,
Fearless of fortune, and *resign'd* to fate. *Dryden.*

A firm, yet cautious, mind,
Sincere, though prudent; constant, yet *resign'd*. *Pope.*

5. To submit without resistance or murmur.

What thou art, *resign* to death. *Shakesp. Henry VI.*

RESIGNA'TION. *n. s.* [*resignation*, Fr.]

1. The act of resigning or giving up a claim or possession.

Do that office of thine own good will;
The *resignation* of thy state and crown. *Shakesp. Rich.* II.

He intended to procure a *resignation* of the rights of the king's majesty's sisters and others, entitled to the possession of the crown. *Hayward.*

2. Submission; unresisting acquiescence.

We cannot expect, that any one should readily quit his own opinion, and embrace ours, with a blind *resignation* to an authority, which the understanding acknowledges not. *Locke.*

There is a kind of sluggish *resignation*, as well as poorness and degeneracy of spirit, in a state of slavery, that very few will recover themselves out of it. *Addison.*

3. Submission without murmur to the will of God.

RESI'GNER. *n. s.* [from *resign.*] One that resigns.

RESI'GNMENT. *n. s.* [from *resign.*] Act of resigning.

RESI'LIENCE. } *n. s.* [from *resilio*, Lat.] The act of starting
RESI'LIENCY. } or leaping back.

If you strike a ball sidelong, the rebound will be as much the contrary way; whether there be any such *resilience* in echoes, that is, whether a man shall hear better if he stand aside the body repercussing, than if he stand where he speaketh, may be tried. *Bacon's Natural History.*

RESI'LIENT. *adj.* [*resiliens*, Lat.] Starting or springing back.

RESILI'TION. *n. s.* [*resilio*, Lat.] The act of springing back; resilience.

RE'SIN. *n. s.* [*resine*, Fr. *resina*, Lat.] The fat sulphurous parts of some vegetable, which is natural or procured by art, and will incorporate with oil or spirit, not an aqueous menstruum. *Quincy.*

RE'SINOUS. *adj.* [from *resin*; *resineux*, Fr.] Containing resin; consisting of resin.

Resinous gums, dissolved in spirit of wine, are let fall again, if the spirit be copiously diluted. *Boyle on Colours.*

RE'SINOUSNESS. *n. s.* [from *resinous.*] The quality of being resinous.

RESIPI'SCENCE. *n. s.* [*resipiscence*, Fr. *resipiscentia*, low Lat.] Wisdom after the fact; repentance.

To RESI'ST. *v. a.* [*resisto*, Lat. *resister*, Fr.]

1. To oppose; to act against.

All the regions
Do seemingly revolt; and, who *resist*,
Are mock'd for valiant ignorance,
And perish constant fools. *Shakesp. Coriolanus.*

Submit to God; *resist* the devil, and he will flee. *Ja.* iv.

2. To not admit impression or force.

Nor keen nor solid could *resist* that edge. *Milton.*

RESI'STANCE. } [*resistance*, Fr. This word, like many others,
RESI'STENCE. } is differently written, as it is supposed to have come from the Latin or the French.]

1. The act of resisting; opposition.

Demetrius, seeing that the land was quiet, and that no *resistance* was made against him, sent away all his forces. 1 *Mac.*

2. The quality of not yielding to force or external impression.

The *resistance* of bone to cold is greater than of flesh; for that the flesh shrinketh, but the bone *resisteth*, whereby the cold becometh more eager. *Bacon.*

Musick so softens and disarms the mind,
That not an arrow does *resistance* find. *Waller.*

The idea of solidity we receive by our touch, and it arises from the *resistance* which we find in body to the entrance of any other body into the place it possesses. *Locke.*

But that part of the *resistence*, which arises from the vis inertiæ, is proportional to the density of the matter, and cannot be diminished by dividing the matter into smaller parts, nor by any other means, than by decreasing the density of the medium. *Newton's Opticks.*

RESISTIBI'LITY. *n. s.* [from *resistible.*] Quality of resisting.

Whether the *resistibility* of Adam's reason did not equivalence the facility of Eve's seduction, we refer unto schoolmen. *Brown's Vulgar Errours.*

The name body, being the complex idea of extension and *resistibility*, together, in the same subject, these two ideas are not exactly one and the same. *Locke.*

RESI'STIBLE. *adj.* [from *resist.*] That may be resisted.

That is irresistible; this, though potent, yet is in its own nature *resistible* by the will of man; though it many times prevails by its efficacy. *Hale's Origin of Mankind.*

RESI'STLESS. *adj.* [from *resist.*] Irresistable; that cannot be opposed.

Our own eyes do every where behold the sudden and *resistless* assaults of death. *Raleigh's History of the World.*

All at once to force *resistless* way. *Milton.*

Since you can love, and yet your error see,
The same *resistless* power may plead for me. *Dryden.*

She chang'd her state;
Resistless in her love, as in her hate. *Dryden.*

Though thine eyes *resistless* glances dart,
A stronger charm is thine, a generous heart. *Logie.*

RESPE'CTIVE. *adj.* [from *respect.*]

1. Particular; relating to particular persons or things.

Moses mentions the immediate causes, and St. Peter the more remote and fundamental causes, that constitution of the heavens, and that constitution of the earth, in reference to their *respective* waters, which made that world obnoxious to a deluge. *Burnet's Theory of the Earth.*

When so many present themselves before their *respective* magistrates to take the oaths, it may not be improper to awaken a due sense of their engagements. *Addison.*

2. [*Respectif*, Fr.] Relative; not absolute.

The medium intended is not an absolute, but a *respective* medium: the proportion recommended to all is the same; but the things to be desired in this proportion will vary. *Rog.*

3. Worthy of reverence. Not in use.

What should it be, that he respects in her,
But I can make *respective* in myself. *Shakesp.*

4. Accurate; nice; careful; cautious. Obsolete.

Respective and wary men had rather seek quietly their own, and wish that the world may go well, so it be not long of them, than with pain and hazard make themselves advisers for the common good. *Hooker, b. v. f. 1.*

He was exceeding *respective* and precise. *Raleigh.*

RESPE'CTIVELY. *adv.* [from *respective.*]

1. Particularly; as each belongs to each.

The interruption of trade between the English and Flemish began to pinch the merchants of both nations, which moved them by all means to dispose their sovereigns *respectively* to open the intercourse again. *Bacon.*

The impressions from the objects of the senses do mingle *respectively* every one with his kind. *Bacon's Natural History.*

Good and evil are in morality, as the East and West are in the frame of the world, founded in and divided by that fixed and unalterable situation, which they have *respectively* in the whole body of the universe. *South's Sermons.*

The principles of those governments are *respectively* disclaimed and abhorred by all the men of sense and virtue in both parties. *Addison's Freeholder, N° 54.*

2. Relatively; not absolutely.

If there had been no other choice, but that Adam had been left to the universal, Moses would not then have said, eastward in Eden, seeing the world hath not East nor West, but *respectively.* *Raleigh's History of the World.*

3. Partially; with respect to private views. Obsolete.

Among the ministers themselves, one being so far in estimation above the rest, the voices of the rest were likely to be given for the most part *respectively* with a kind of secret dependency. *Hooker's Preface.*

4. With great reverence. Not in use.

Honest Flaminius, you are very *respectively* welcome. *Shak.*

RESPE'RSION. *n. s.* [*respersio*, Lat.] The act of sprinkling.

RESPIRA'TION. *n. s.* [*respiration*, Fr. *respiratio*, from *respiro*, Lat.]

1. The act of breathing.

Apollonius of Tyana affirmed, that the ebbing and flowing of the sea was the *respiration* of the world, drawing in water as breath, and putting it forth again. *Bacon.*

Syrups or other expectoratives do not advantage in coughs, by slipping down between the epiglottis; for, as I instanced before, that must necessarly occasion a greater cough and difficulty of *respiration.* *Harvey on Consumptions.*

The author of nature foreknew the necessity of rains and dews to the present structure of plants, and the uses of *respiration* to animals; and therefore created those correspondent properties in the atmosphere. *Bentley's Sermons.*

2. Relief from toil.

Till the day
Appear of *respiration* to the just,
And vengeance to the wicked. *Milton's Par. Lost, b. xii.*

To RESPI'RE. *v. n.* [*respiro*, Lat. *respirer*, Fr.]

1. To breathe.

The ladies gasp'd, and scarcely could *respire*;
The breath they drew, no longer air, but fire,
The fainty knights were scorch'd. *Dryden.*

2. To catch breath.

Till breathless both themselves aside retire,
Where foaming wrath, their cruel tusks they whet,
And trample th' earth the whiles they may *respire.* *F. Q.*
I, a pris'ner chain'd, scarce freely draw
The air imprison'd also, close and damp,
Unwholesome draught; but here I feel amends,
The breath of heav'n fresh blowing, pure, and sweet,
With day-spring born; here leave me to *respire.* *Milton.*

3. To rest; to take rest from toil.

Hark! he strikes the golden lyre;
And see! the tortur'd ghosts *respire*,
See shady forms advance! *Pope's St. Cecilia.*

RESPI'TE. *n. s.* [*respit*, Fr.]

1. Reprieve; suspension of a capital sentence.

I had hope to spend
Quiet, though sad, the *respite* of that day,
That must be mortal to us both. *Milton.*

Wisdom and eloquence in vain would plead
One moment's *respite* for the learned head;
Judges of writings and of men have dy'd. *Prior.*

2. Pause; interval.

The fox then counsel'd th' ape, for to require
Respite till morrow t' answer his desire. *Hubberd's Tale.*

This customary war, which troubleth all the world, giveth little *respite* or breathing time of peace, doth usually borrow pretence from the necessary, to make itself appear more honest. *Raleigh's Essays.*

Some pause and *respite* only I require,
Till with my tears I shall have quench'd my fire. *Denham.*

To RESPI'TE. *v. a.* [from the noun.]

1. To relieve by a pause.

In what bow'r or shade
Thou find'st him, from the heat of noon retir'd,
To *respite* his day-labour with repast,
Or with repose. *Milton's Paradise Lost, b. v.*

2. [*Respiter*, old Fr.] To suspend; to delay.

An act passed for the satisfaction of the officers of the king's army, by which they were promised payment, upon the publick faith, in November following; till which time they were to *respite* it, and be contented that the common soldiers and inferior officers should be satisfied upon their disbanding. *Clarendon.*

RESPLE'NDENCE } *n. s.* [from *resplendent.*] Lustre; bright-
RESPLE'NDENCY. } ness; splendour.

Son! thou in whom my glory I behold
In full *resplendence*, heir of all my might. *Milton.*

To neglect that supreme *resplendency*, that shines in God, for those dim representations of it in the creature, is as absurd as it were for a Persian to offer his sacrifice to a parhelion instead of adoring the sun. *Boyle.*

RESPLE'NDENT. *adj.* [*resplendens*, Lat.] Bright; shining; having a beautiful lustre.

Rich in commodities, beautiful in situation, *resplendent* in all glory. *Camden's Remains.*

There all within full rich array'd he found,
With royal arras and *resplendent* gold. *Fairy Queen.*

The ancient electrum had in it a fifth of silver to the gold, and made a compound metal, as fit for most uses as gold, and more *resplendent.* *Bacon's Natural History.*

Empress of this fair world, *resplendent* Eve! *Milton.*

Every body looks most splendid and luminous in the light of its own colour: cinnaber in the homogeneal light is most *resplendent*, in the green light it is manifestly less *resplendent*, in the blue light still less. *Newton's Opticks.*

Resplendent brass, and more *resplendent* dames. *Pope.*

RESPLE'NDENTLY. *adv.* [from *resplendent.*] With lustre; brightly; splendidly.

To RESPO'ND. *v. n.* [*respondeo*, Lat. *respondre*, Fr.]

1. To answer. Little used.

2. To correspond; to suit.

To ev'ry theme *responds* thy various lay;
Here rowls a torrent, there meanders play. *Broome.*

RESPO'NDENT. *n. s.* [*respondens*, Lat.]

1. An answerer in a suit.

In giving an answer, the *respondent* should be in court, and personally admonished by the judge to answer the judge's interrogation. *Ayliffe's Parergon.*

2. One whose province, in a set disputation, is to refute objections.

How becomingly does Philopolis exercise his office, and seasonably commit the opponent with the *respondent*, like a long practised moderator? *More's Divine Dialogues.*

The *respondent* may easily shew, that though wine may do all this, yet it may be finally hurtful to the soul and body of him. *Watts's Logick.*

RESPO'NSE. *n. s.* [*responsum*, Lat.]

1. An answer.

Mere natural piety has taught men to receive the *responses* of the gods with all possible veneration. *Gov. of the Tongue.*

The oracles, which had before flourished, began to droop, and from giving *responses* in verse, descended to prose, and within a while were utterly silenced. *Hammond.*

2. [*Respons*, Fr.] Answer made by the congregation, speaking alternately with the priest in publick worship.

To make his parishioners kneel and join in the *responses*, he gave every one of them a hassock and common prayer book. *Addison's Spectator, N° 112.*

3. Reply to an objection in a formal disputation.

Let the respondent not turn opponent; except in retorting the argument upon his adversary after a direct *response*; and even this is allowed only as a confirmation of his own *response.* *Watts's Improvement of the Mind.*

RESPO'NSIBLE. *adj.* [from *responsus*, Lat.]

1. Answerable; accountable.

He as much satisfies the itch of telling news; he as much persuades his hearers; and all this while he has his retreat secure, and stands not *responsible* for the truth of his relations. *Government of the Tongue.*

2. Capable

2. Capable of discharging an obligation.

The necessity of a proportion of money to trade depends on money as a pledge, which writing cannot supply the place of; since the bill, I receive from one man, will not be accepted as security by another, he not knowing that the bill is legal, or that the man bound is honest or *responsible*. *Locke.*

RESPO'NSIBLENESS. *n. s.* [from *responsible*.] State of being obliged or qualified to answer.

RESPO'NSION. *n. s.* [*responsio*, Lat.] The act of answering.

RESPO'NSIVE. *adj.* [*responsif*, Fr. from *responsus*, Lat.]

1. Answering; making answer.

A certificate is a *responsive* letter, or letter by way of answer. *Ayliffe's Parergon.*

2. Correspondent; suited to something else.

Sing of love and gay desire,
Responsive to the warbling lyre. *Fenton.*

Be there Demodocus the bard of fame,
Taught by the gods to please, when high he sings
The vocal lay *responsive* to the strings. *Pope's Odyssey.*

RESPO'NSORY. *adj.* [*responsorius*, Lat.] Containing answer.

REST. *n. s.* [ꞃeꞅꞇ, Saxon; *ruste*, Dutch.]

1. Sleep; repose.

All things retir'd to *rest*, mind us of like repose. *Milton.*
My tost limbs are wearied into *rest*. *Pope.*

2. The final sleep; the quietness of death.

Oft with holy hymns he charm'd their ears;
For David left him, when he went to *rest*,
His lyre. *Dryden's Parson.*

3. Stilness; cessation of motion.

Putrefaction asketh *rest*; for the subtle motion, which putrefaction requireth, is disturbed by any agitation. *Bacon.*

What cause mov'd the Creator, in his holy *rest*,
So late to build. *Milton.*

All things past are equally and perfectly at *rest*; and to this way of consideration of them are all one, whether they were before the world, or but yesterday. *Locke.*

4. Quiet; peace; cessation from disturbance.

Learn of me, for I am meek and lowly in heart; and ye shall find *rest* unto your souls. *Mat.* xi. 29.

He giveth you *rest* from all your enemies. *Deut.* xii. 10.

Though the righteous be prevented with death; yet shall he be in *rest*. *Wisd.* iv. 7.

'Scap'd from such storms of pow'r, holding it best
To be below herself to be at *rest*. *Daniel's Civil War.*

The root cut off, from whence these tumults rose,
He should have *rest*, the commonwealth repose. *Daniel.*

Thus fenc'd, but not at *rest* or ease of mind. *Milton.*

With what a load of vengeance am I prest,
Yet never, never, can I hope for *rest*;
For when my heavy burden I remove,
The weight falls down, and crushes her I love. *Dryden.*

Like the sun, it had light and agility; it knew no *rest* but in motion, no quiet but in activity. *South's Sermons.*

Where can a frail man hide him? in what arms
Shall a short life enjoy a little *rest*. *Fanshaw.*

Thither, where sinners may have *rest*, I go. *Pope.*
The grave, where ev'n the great find *rest*. *Pope.*

The midnight murderer
Invades the sacred hour of silent *rest*. *Anonym.*

5. Cessation from bodily labour.

There the weary be at *rest*. *Job* iii. 17.

6. Support; that on which any thing leans or rests.

Forth prick'd Clorinda from the throng,
And 'gainst Tancredie set her spear in *rest*. *Fairfax.*

A man may think, that a musket may be shot off as well upon the arm, as upon a *rest*; but when all is done, good counsel setteth business straight. *Bacon.*

Their vizors clos'd, their lances in the *rest*,
Or at the helmet pointed, or the crest;
They speed the race. *Dryden's Knight's Tale.*

Take the handle in your right hand, and clasping the blade of it in your left, lean it steady upon the *rest*, holding the edge a little aslant over the work, so as a corner of the thin side of the chissel may bear upon the *rest*, and the flat side of the chissel may make a small angle with the *rest*. *Moxon.*

7. Place of repose.

Sustain'd by him with comforts, till we end
In dust, our final *rest* and native home. *Milton.*

8. Final hope.

He sets up his *rest*, to do more exploits with his mace, than a maurice pike. *Shakesp. Com. of Err.*

Sea fights have been final to the war, but this is, when princes set up their *rest* upon the battle *Bacon.*

This answer would render their counsels of less reverence to the people, if, upon those reasons, they should recede from what they had, with that confidence and disdain of the house of peers, demanded of the king; they therefore resolved to set up their *rest* upon that stake, and to go through with it, or perish in the attempt. *Clarendon.*

9. [*Reste*, Fr. *quod restat*, Latin.] Remainder; what remains.

Religion gives part of its reward in hand, the present comfort of having done our duty; and for the *rest*, it offers us the best security that heaven can give. *Tillotson.*

The pow'r in glory shone,
By her bent bow and her keen arrows known
The *rest* a huntress. *Dryden's Knight's Tale.*

REST. *adj.* [*restes*, Fr. *quod restat*, Lat.] Others; those not included in any proposition.

By description of their qualities, many things may be learned concerning the *rest* of the inhabitants. *Abbot.*

They had no other consideration of the publick, than that no disturbance might interrupt their quiet in their own days; and that the *rest*, who had larger hearts and more publick spirits, would extend their labour, activity, and advice only to secure the empire at home by all peaceable arts. *Clarendon.*

Plato, and the *rest* of the philosophers, acknowledged the unity, power, wisdom, goodness, and providence of the supreme God. *Stillingfleet.*

Arm'd like the *rest*, the Trojan prince appears,
And by his pious labour urges theirs. *Dryden.*

Upon so equal terms did they all stand, that no one had a fairer pretence of right than the *rest*. *Woodward.*

To REST. *v. n.* [from the noun.]

1. To sleep; to be asleep; to slumber.

Fancy then retires
Into her private cell, when nature *rests*. *Milton.*

2. To sleep the final sleep; to die.

Ἱερὸν ὕπνον
Κοιμᾶται· θνήσκειν μὴ λέγε τὺς ἀγαθὺς.

Glad I'd lay me down,
As in my mother's lap; there I should *rest*
And sleep secure. *Milton.*

3. To be at quiet; to be at peace; to be without disturbance.

Thither let us tend
From off the tossing of these fiery waves,
There *rest*, if any rest can harbour there. *Milton.*

4. To be without motion; to be still.

Over the tent a cloud shall *rest* by day. *Milton.*

5. To be fixed in any state or opinion.

He will not *rest* content, though thou givest many gifts. *Prov.* vi. 35.

Every creature has a share in the common blessings of providence; and every creature should *rest* well satisfied with its proportion in them. *L'Estrange.*

After such a lord I *rest* secure,
Thou wilt no foreign reins or Trojan load endure. *Dryden.*

There yet survives the lawful heir
Of Sancho's blood, whom, when I shall produce,
I *rest* assur'd to see you pale with fear. *Dryden.*

6. To cease from labour.

Six days thou shalt do thy work, and on the seventh day thou shalt *rest*. *Exodus* xxiii. 12.

The ark went before, to search out a *resting* place for them. *Numb.* x. 33.

From work *resting* he bless'd the seventh day. *Milton.*

When you enter into the regions of death, you *rest* from all your labours and your fears. *Taylor's Rule of Living Holy.*

7. To be satisfied; to acquiesce.

To urge the foe to battle,
Prompted by blind revenge and wild despair,
Were to refuse th' awards of providence,
And not to *rest* in heaven's determination. *Addison.*

8. To lean; to be supported.

As the vex'd world, to find repose, at last
Itself into Augustus' arms did cast;
So England now doth, with like toil opprest,
Her weary head upon your bosom *rest*. *Waller.*

On him I *rested*,
And, not without consid'ring, fix'd my fate. *Dryden.*

Sometimes it *rests* upon testimony, when testimony of right has nothing to do; because it is easier to believe, than to be scientifically instructed. *Locke.*

The philosophical use of words conveys the precise notions of things, which the mind may *rest* upon, and be satisfied with, in its search after knowledge. *Locke.*

9. [*Resto*, Lat. *rester*, Fr.] To be left; to remain.

Fall'n he is; and now
What *rests*, but that the mortal sentence pass
On his transgression. *Milton's Par. Lost, b.* x.

There *resteth* the comparative; that is, its being granted, that it is either lawful or binding, yet whether other things be not prefered before it, as extirpation of heresies. *Bacon.*

To REST. *v. a.*

1. To lay to rest.

Your piety has paid
All needful rites, to *rest* my wand'ring shade. *Dryden.*

2. To place as on a support.

RESTA'GNANT. *adj.* [*restagnans*, Lat.] Remaining without flow or motion.

Upon the tops of high mountains, the air, which bears against the *restagnant* quicksilver, is less pressed by the less ponderous incumbent air. *Boyle.*

RESO'LVABLE. *adj.* [from *resolve.*]

1. That may be analysed or separated.

Pride is of such intimate connection with ingratitude, that the actions of ingratitude seem directly *resolvable* into pride, as the principal reason of them. *South.*

As the serum of the blood is *resolvable* by a small heat, a greater heat coagulates, so as to turn it horny like parchment. *Arbuthnot on Aliments.*

2. Capable of solution or of being made less obscure.

The effect is wonderful in all, and the causes best *resolvable* from observations made in the countries themselves, the parts through which they pass. *Brown's Vulgar Errours.*

RESO'LUBLE. *adj.* [*resoluble*, Fr. *re* and *solubilis*, Lat.] That may be melted or dissolved.

Three is not precisely the number of the distinct elements, whereinto mixt bodies are *resoluble* by fire. *Boyle.*

To RESO'LVE. *v. a.* [*resolvo*, Lat. *resoudre*, Fr.]

1. To inform; to free from a doubt or difficulty.

In all things then are our consciences best *resolved*, and in most agreeable sort unto God and nature *resolved*, when they are so far persuaded, as those grounds of persuasion will bear. *Hooker, b.* ii. *s.* 7.

Give me some breath,
Before I positively speak in this;
I will *resolve* your grace immediately. *Shakesp. Rich.* III.

I cannot brook delay, *resolve* me now;
And what your pleasure is, shall satisfy me. *Shakesp.*

Resolve me, strangers, whence and what you are? *Dryd.*

2. To solve; to clear.

Examine, sift, and *resolve* their alleged proofs, till you come to the very root whence they spring, and it shall clearly appear, that the most which can be infered upon such plenty of divine testimonies, is only this, that some things, which they maintain, do seem to have been out of scripture not absurdly gathered. *Hooker, b.* ii. *s.* 7.

I *resolve* the riddle of their loyalty, and give them opportunity to let the world see, they mean not what they do, but what they say. *King Charles.*

He always bent himself rather judiciously to *resolve*, than by doubts to perplex a business. *Hayward.*

The gravers, when they have attained to the knowledge of these reposes, will easily *resolve* those difficulties which perplex them. *Dryden's Dufresnoy.*

The man, who would *resolve* the work of fate,
May limit number. *Prior.*

Happiness, it was presently *resolved* by all, must be some one uniform end, proportioned to the capacities of human nature, attainable by every man, independent on fortune. *Rogers's Sermons*

3. To settle in an opinion.

Long since we were *resolved* of your truth,
Your faithful service, and your toil in war. *Shakesp.*

4. To fix in a determination.

Good proof
This day affords, declaring thee *resolv'd*
To undergo with me one guilt. *Milton.*

I run to meet th' alarms,
Resolv'd on death, *resolv'd* to die in arms. *Dryden.*

Resolv'd for sea, the slaves thy baggage pack;
Nothing retards thy voyage, unless
Thy other lord forbids voluptuousness. *Dryden's Persius.*

5. To fix in constancy; to confirm.

Quit presently the chapel, or *resolve* you
For more amazement:
I'll make the statue move. *Shakesp.*

6. To melt; to dissolve.

Resolving is bringing a fluid, which is new concreted, into the state of fluidity again. *Arbuthnot on Aliments.*

Vegetable salts *resolve* the coagulated humours of a human body, and attenuate, by stimulating the solids, and dissolving the fluids. *Arbuthnot on Aliments.*

7. To analise.

Into what can we *resolve* this strong inclination of mankind to this error? it is altogether unimaginable, but that the reason of so universal a consent should be constant. *Tillotson.*

Ye immortal souls, who once were men,
And now *resolv'd* to elements agen. *Dryden.*

The decretals turn upon this point, and *resolve* all into a monarchical power at Rome. *Baker's Reflections on Learning.*

To RESO'LVE. *v. n.*

1. To determine; to decree within one's self.

Confirm'd, then I *resolve*
Adam shall share with me. *Milton.*

Covetousness is like the sea, that receives the tribute of all rivers, though far unlike it in lending any back; therefore those, who have *resolved* upon the thriving sort of piety, have seldom embarked all their hopes in one bottom. *D. of Pi.*

2. To melt; to be dissolved.

Have I not hideous death within my view?
Retaining but a quantity of life,
Which bleeds away, ev'n as a form of wax
Resolveth from its figure 'gainst the fire. *Shakesp.*

No man condemn me, who has never felt
A woman's power, or try'd the force of love;
All tempers yield and soften in those fires,
Our honours, interests, *resolving* down,
Run in the gentle current of our joys. *Southern's Oroonoko.*

When the blood stagnates in any part, it first coagulates, then *resolves* and turns alkaline. *Arbuthnot on Aliments.*

3. To be settled in opinion.

Let men *resolve* of that as they please: this every intelligent being must grant, that there is something that is himself, that he would have happy. *Locke.*

RESO'LVE. *n. s.* [from the verb.] Resolution; fixed determination.

I'm glad, you thus continue your *resolve*,
To suck the sweets of sweet philosophy. *Shakesp.*

When he sees
Himself by dogs, and dogs by men pursu'd,
He straight revokes his bold *resolve*, and more
Repents his courage, than his fear before. *Denham.*

Cæsar's approach has summon'd us together,
And Rome attends her fate from our *resolves*. *Addis. Cato.*

RESO'LVEDLY. *adv.* [from *resolved.*] With firmness and constancy.

A man may be *resolvedly* patient unto death; so that it is not the mediocrity of resolution, which makes the virtue; nor the extremity, which makes the vice. *Grew's Cosmol.*

RESO'LVEDNESS. *n. s.* [from *resolved.*] Resolution; constancy; firmness.

This *resolvedness*, this high fortitude in sin, can with no reason be imagined a preparative to its remission. *D. of Piety.*

RESO'LVENT. *n. s.* [*resolvens*, Latin.] That which has the power of causing solution.

In the beginning of inflammation, they require repellents; and in the increase, somewhat of *resolvents* ought to be mixed. *Wiseman's Surgery.*

Lactescent plants, as lettuce and endive, contain a most wholesome juice, *resolvent* of the bile, anodyne and cooling. *Arbuthnot on Aliments.*

RESO'LVER. *n. s.* [from *resolve.*]

1. One that forms a firm resolution.

Thy resolutions were not before sincere; consequently God that saw that, cannot be thought to have justified that unsincere *resolver*, that dead faith. *Hammond's Pract. Catech.*

2. One that dissolves; one that separates parts.

It may be doubted, whether or no the fire be the genuine and universal *resolver* of mixed bodies. *Boyle.*

RE'SOLUTE. *adj.* [*resolu*, Fr.] Determined; fixed; constant; steady; firm.

Be bloody, bold, and *resolute*; laugh to scorn
The pow'r of man; for none of woman born
Shall harm Macbeth. *Shakesp. Macbeth.*

Edward is at hand
Ready to fight; therefore be *resolute*. *Shakesp. Hen.* VI.

RE'SOLUTELY. *adv.* [from *resolute.*] Determinately; firmly; constantly; steadily.

We *resolutely* must,
To the few virtues that we have, be just. *Roscommon.*

A man, who lives a virtuous life, despises the pleasures of sin, and notwithstanding all the allurements of sense persists *resolutely* in his course. *Tillotson's Sermons.*

Some of those facts he examines, some he *resolutely* denies; others he endeavours to extenuate, and the rest he distorts with unnatural turns. *Swift's Miscellenies.*

RE'SOLUTENESS. *n. s.* [from *resolute.*] Determinateness; state of being fixed in resolution.

All that my *resoluteness* to make use of my ears, not tongue, could do, was to make them acquiesce. *Boyle.*

RESOLU'TION. *n. s.* [*resolutio*, Lat. *resolution*, Fr.]

1. Act of clearing difficulties.

In matters of antiquity, if their originals escape due relation, they fall into great obscurities, and such as future ages seldom reduce into a *resolution*. *Brown's Vulgar Errours.*

The unravelling and *resolution* of the difficulties, that are met with in the execution of the design, are the end of an action. *Dryden's Oedipus.*

2. Analysis; act of separating any thing into constituent parts.

To the present impulses of sense, memory and instinct, all the sagacities of brutes may be reduced; though witty men, by analytical *resolution*, have chymically extracted an artificial logick out of all their actions. *Hale's Orig. of Mankind.*

3. Dissolution.

In the hot springs of extreme cold countries, the first heats are unsufferable, which proceed out of the *resolution* of humidity congealed. *Digby on Bodies.*

4. [From *resolute.*] Fixed determination; settled thought.

I' th' progress of this business,
Ere a determinate *resolution*,
The bishop did require a respite. *Shakesp. Henry* VIII.

O Lord, *resolutions* of future reforming do not always satisfy thy justice, nor prevent thy vengeance for former miscarriages. *King Charles.*

We spend our days in deliberating, and we end them without coming to any *resolution*. *L'Estrange.*

How

How much this is in every man's power, by making *resolutions* to himself, is easy to try. *Locke.*

The mode of the will, which answers to dubitation, may be called suspension; that which answers to invention, *resolution:* and that which, in the phantastick will, is obstinacy, is constancy in the intellectual. *Grew's Cosmol.*

5. Constancy; firmness; steadiness in good or bad.

The rest of the Helots, which were otherwise scattered, bent thitherward, with a new life of *resolution*; as if their captain had been a root, out of which their courage had sprung. *Sidney.*

I would unstate myself to be in a due *resolution.* *Shakesp.*

They, who governed the parliament, had the *resolution* to act those monstrous things. *Clarendon, b.* viii.

What reinforcement we may gain from hope,
If not what *resolution* from despair. *Milton.*

6. Determination of a cause in courts of justice.

Nor have we all the acts of parliament or of judicial *resolutions*, which might occasion such alterations. *Hale.*

Re'solutive. *adj.* [*resolutus*, Lat. *resolutif*, Fr.] Having the power to dissolve.

Re'sonance. *n. s.* [from *resono*, Lat.] Sound; resound.

An ancient musician informed me, that there were some famous lutes that attained not their full seasoning and best *resonance*, till they were about fourscore years old. *Boyle.*

Re'sonant. *adj.* [*resonnant*, Fr. *resonans*, Lat.] Resounding.

His volant touch
Fled and pursu'd transverse the *resonant* fugue. *Milton.*

To Reso'rt. *v. n.* [*ressortir*, Fr.]

1. To have recourse.

The king thought it time to *resort* to other counsels, and to provide force to chastise them, who had so much despised all his gentler remedies. *Clarendon, b.* ii.

2. To go publickly.

Thither shall all the valiant youth *resort*,
And from his memory inflame their breasts
To matchless valour. *Milton's Agonistes.*
Hither the heroes and the nymphs *resort.* *Pope.*

3. To repair to.

The sons of light
Hasted, *resorting* to the summons high. *Milton.*
To Argos' realms the victor god *resorts*,
And enters cold Crotopus' humble courts. *Pope.*

4. To fall back. In law.

The inheritance of the son never *resorted* to the mother or to any of her ancestors, but both were totally excluded from the succession. *Hale's Law of England.*

Reso'rt. *n. s.* [from the verb.]

1. Frequency; assembly; meeting.

Unknown, unquestion'd in that thick *resort.* *Dryden.*

2. Concourse; confluence.

The like places of *resort* are frequented by men out of place. *Swift's Miscellanies.*

3. Act of visiting.

Join with me to forbid him her *resort.* *Shakesp.*

4. [*Ressort*, Fr.] Movement; active power; spring.

Some know the *resorts* and falls of business, that cannot sink into the main of it. *Bacon's Essays.*

In fortune's empire blindly thus we go,
We wander after pathless destiny,
Whose dark *resorts* since prudence cannot know,
In vain it would provide for what shall be. *Dryden.*

To Resou'nd. *v. a.* [*resono*, Lat. *resonner*, Fr.]

1. To echo; to sound back; to celebrate by sound.

The sweet singer of Israel with his psaltery loudly *resounded* the innumerable benefits of the Almighty Creator. *Peacham.*

The sound of hymns, wherewith thy throne
Incompass'd shall *resound* thee ever blest. *Milton.*

2. To sound; to tell so as to be heard far.

The man, for wisdom's various arts renown'd,
Long exercis'd in woes, oh muse! *resound.* *Pope.*

3. To return sounds; to sound with any noise.

With other echo late I taught your shades,
To answer and *resound* far other song. *Milton.*

To Resou'nd. *v. n.* To be echoed back.

What *resounds* in fable or romance of Uther's sons. *Milt.*

What is common fame, which sounds from all quarters of the world, and *resounds* back to them again, but generally a loud, rattling, impudent lye? *South's Sermons.*

Resou'rce. *n. s.* [It is commonly written *ressource*, which see: *ressource*, Fr. *Skinner* derives it from *resoudre*, Fr. to spring up.] Some new or unexpected means that offer; resort; expedient.

Pallas view'd
His foes pursuing, and his friends pursu'd;
Us'd threatnings, mix'd with pray'ers, his last *resource*;
With these to move their minds, with those to fire their force. *Dryden.*

To Reso'w. *v. a.* [*re* and *sow.*] To sow anew.

Over wet at sowing time breedeth much dearth, insomuch as they are forced to *resow* summer corn.. *Bacon.*

To Respea'k. *v. n.* [*re* and *speak.*] To answer.

The great cannon to the clouds shall tell,
And the king's rowse the heav'n shall bruit again,
Respeaking earthly thunder. *Shakesp. Hamlet.*

To RESPE'CT. *v. a.* [*respectus*, Lat.]

1. To regard; to have regard to.

Claudio, I quake,
Lest thou should'st seven winters more *respect*
Than a perpetual honour. *Shakesp. Meas. for Meas.*

In orchards and gardens we do not so much *respect* beauty, as variety of ground for fruits, trees, and herbs. *Bacon.*

2. [*Respecter*, Fr.] To consider with a lower degree of reverence.

There is nothing more terrible to a guilty heart, than the eye of a *respected* friend. *Sidney.*

Whoever tastes, let him with grateful heart
Respect that ancient loyal house. *Philips.*

I always loved and *respected* Sir William. *Swift to Gay.*

3. To have relation to.

4. To look toward.

The needle doth vary, as it approacheth the pole; whereas, were there such direction from the rocks, upon a nearer approachment, it would more directly *respect* them. *Brown.*

Palladius adviseth, the front of his house should so *respect* the South, that in the first angle it receive the rising rays of the winter sun, and decline a little from the winter setting thereof. *Brown's Vulgar Errours.*

Respe'ct. *n. s.* [*respect*, Fr. *respectus*, Lat.]

1. Regard; attention.

You have too much *respect* upon the world;
They lose it, that do buy it with much care. *Shakesp.*

I love
My country's good with a *respect* more tender
Than mine own life. *Shakesp. Coriolanus.*

2. Reverence; honour.

You know me dutiful, therefore
Let me not shame *respect*; but give me leave
To take that course by your consent and voice. *Shakesp.*

Æneas must be drawn a suppliant to Dido, with *respect* in his gestures, and humility in his eyes. *Dryden's Dufresnoy.*

I found the king abandon'd to neglect;
Seen without awe, and serv'd without *respect.* *Prior.*

3. Awful kindness.

He, that will have his son have a *respect* for him, must have a great reverence for his son. *Locke.*

4. Goodwill.

Pembroke has got
A thousand pounds a year, for pure *respect*;
No other obligation?
That promises more thousands. *Shakesp. Henry* VIII.

The Lord had *respect* unto Abel and his offering. *Gen.* iv.

5. Partial regard.

It is not good to have *respect* of persons in judgment. *Prov.*

6. Reverend character.

Many of the best *respect* in Rome,
Groaning under this age's yoke,
Have wish'd, that noble Brutus had his eyes. *Shakesp.*

7. Manner of treating others.

You must use them with fit *respects*, according to the bonds of nature; but you are of kin to their persons, not errors. *Bacon.*

The duke's carriage was to the gentlemen of fair *respect*, and bountiful to the soldier, according to any special value which he spied in any. *Wotton's Buckingham.*

8. Consideration; motive.

Whatsoever secret *respects* were likely to move them, for contenting of their minds, Calvin returned. *Hooker.*

The love of him, and this *respect* beside;
For that my grandsire was an Englishman,
Awakes my conscience to confess all this. *Shakesp.*

Since that *respects* of fortune are his love,
I shall not be his wife. *Shakesp. King Lear.*

9. Relation; regard.

In *respect* of the suitors which attend you, do them what right in justice, and with as much speed as you may. *Bacon.*

I have represented to you the excellency of the christian religion, in *respect* of its clear discoveries of the nature of God, and in *respect* of the perfection of its laws. *Tillotson.*

Every thing which is imperfect, as the world must be acknowledged in many *respects*, had some cause which produced it. *Tillotson.*

They believed but one supreme deity, which, with *respect* to the various benefits men received from him, had several titles. *Tillotson.*

Respe'cter. *n. s.* [from *respect.*] One that has partial regard.

Neither is any condition more honourable in the sight of God than another; otherwise he would be a *respecter* of persons: for he hath proposed the same salvation to all. *Swift.*

Respe'ctful. *adj.* [*respect* and *full.*] Ceremonious; full of outward civility.

Will you be only, and for ever mine?
From this dear bosom shall I ne'er be torn?
Or you grow cold, *respectful*, or forsworn? *Prior.*

With humble joy, and with *respectful* fear,
The list'ning people shall his story hear. *Prior.*

Respe'ctfully. *adv.* [from *respectful.*] With some degree of reverence.

To your glad genius sacrifice this day,
Let common meats *respectfully* give way. *Dryden.*

Respe'ctive.

To RESTA'GNATE. *v. n.* [*re* and *ſtagnate.*] To ſtand without flow.

The blood returns thick, and is apt to *reſtagnate. Wiſeman.*

RESTAGNA'TION. *n. ſ.* [from *reſtagnate.*] The ſtate of ſtanding without flow, courſe, or motion.

RESTAURA'TION. *n. ſ.* [*reſtauro*, Lat.] The act of recovering to the former ſtate.

Adam is in us an original cauſe of our nature, and of that corruption of nature which cauſeth death; Chriſt as the cauſe original of *reſtauration* to life. *Hooker, b.* v. *ſ.* 56.

O my dear father! *reſtauration* hang
Thy medicine on my lips; and let this kiſs
Repair thoſe violent harms, that my two ſiſters
Have in thy reverence made. *Shakeſp. King Lear.*

Spermatical parts will not admit a regeneration, much leſs will they receive an integral *reſtauration. Brown.*

To RESTE'M. *v. a.* [*re* and *ſtem.*] To force back againſt the current.

How they *reſtem*
Their backward courſe, bearing with frank appearance
Toward Cyprus. *Shakeſp. Othello.*

RE'STFUL. *adj.* [*reſt* and *ful.*] Quiet; being at reſt.

Is not my arm of length,
That reacheth from the *reſtful* Engliſh court,
As far as Calais to my uncle's head. *Shakeſp. Rich.* III.

RESTHA'RROW. *n. ſ.* A plant.

Reſtharrow hath a papilionaceous flower, which is ſucceeded by a ſwelling pod, and which is ſometimes long, and at other times ſhort; is bivalve, and filled with kidney-ſhaped ſeeds. *Miller.*

RESTI'FF. *adj.* [*reſtif*, Fr. *reſtivo*, Ital.]

1. Unwilling to ſtir; reſolute againſt going forward; obſtinate; ſtubborn. It is originally uſed of an horſe, that, though not wearied, will not be driven forward.

All, who before him did aſcend the throne,
Labour'd to draw three *reſtive* nations on. *Roſcommon.*

This *reſtiff* ſtubborneſs is never to be excuſed under any pretence whatſoever. *L'Eſtrange.*

Some, with ſtudious care,
Their *reſtiff* ſteeds in ſandy plains prepare. *Dryden.*

The archangel, when diſcord was *reſtive*, and would not be drawn from her beloved monaſtery with fair words, drags her out with many ſtripes. *Dryden's Dedication to Juvenal.*

So James the drowſy genius wakes
Of Britain, long entranc'd in charms,
Reſtiff, and ſlumb'ring on its arms. *Dryden.*

The pamper'd colt will diſcipline diſdain,
Impatient of the laſh, and *reſtiff* to the rein. *Dryden.*

2. Being at reſt; being leſs in motion. Not uſed.

Palſies ofteneſt happen upon the left ſide; the moſt vigorous part protecting itſelf, and protruding the matter upon the weaker and *reſtive* ſide. *Brown's Vulgar Errours.*

RESTI'FNESS. *n. ſ.* [from *reſtiff.*] Obſtinate reluctance.

Overt virtues bring forth praiſe; but ſecret virtues bring forth fortune: certain deliveries of a man's ſelf, which the Spaniſh name deſemboltura, partly expreſſeth, where there be not ſtands nor *reſtiveneſs* in a man's nature; but the wheels of his mind keep way with the wheels of his fortune. *Bacon.*

That it gave occaſion to ſome men's further *reſtiveneſs*, is imputable to their own depraved tempers. *King Charles.*

RESTI'NCTION. *n. ſ.* [*reſtinctus*, Lat.] The act of extinguiſhing.

RESTITU'TION. *n. ſ.* [*reſtitutio*, Lat.]

1. The act of reſtoring what is loſt or taken away.

To ſubdue an uſurper, ſhould be no unjuſt enterpriſe or wrongful war, but a *reſtitution* of ancient rights unto the crown of England, from whence they were moſt unjuſtly expelled and long kept out. *Spenſer on Ireland.*

He would pawn his fortunes
To hopeleſs *reſtitution*, ſo he might
Be call'd your vanquiſher. *Shakeſp. Coriolanus.*

Now is Cupid a child of conſcience, he makes *reſtitution.* *Shakeſp. Merry Wives of Windſor.*

He *reſtitution* to the value makes;
Nor joy in his extorted treaſure takes. *Sandys.*

Whoſoever is an effective real cauſe of doing a neighbour wrong, by what inſtrument ſoever he does it, is bound to make *reſtitution. Taylor's Rule of Living Holy.*

In caſe our offence againſt God hath been complicated with injury to men, it is but reaſonable we ſhould make *reſtitution. Tillotſon's Sermons.*

A great man, who has never been known willingly to pay a juſt debt, ought not all of a ſudden to be introduced, making *reſtitution* of thouſands he has cheated: let it ſuffice to pay twenty pounds to a friend, who has loſt his note. *Arbuth.*

2. The act of recovering its former ſtate or poſture.

In the woody parts of plants, which are their bones, the principles are ſo compounded, as to make them flexible without joints, and alſo elaſtick; that ſo their roots may yield to ſtones, and their trunks to the wind, with a power of *reſtitution. Grew's Coſmol.*

RE'STLESS. *adj.* [from *reſt.*]

1. Being without ſleep.

Reſtleſs he paſs'd the remnants of the night,
Till the freſh air proclaim'd the morning nigh:
And burning ſhips, the martyrs of the fight,
With paler fires beheld the eaſtern ſky. *Dryden.*

2. Unquiet; without peace.

Eaſe to the body ſome, none to the mind
From *reſtleſs* thoughts, that like a deadly ſwarm
Of hornets arm'd, no ſooner found alone,
But ruſh upon me thronging, and preſent
Times paſt, what once I was, and what I'm now. *Milton.*

Could we not wake from that lethargick dream,
But to be *reſtleſs* in a worſe extreme. *Denham.*

We find our ſouls diſordered and *reſtleſs*, toſſed and diſquieted by paſſions, ever ſeeking happineſs in the enjoyments of this world, and ever miſſing what they ſeek. *Atterbury.*

What tongue can ſpeak the *reſtleſs* monarch's woes,
When God and Nathan were declar'd his foes. *Prior.*

3. Unconſtant; unſettled.

He was ſtout of courage, ſtrong of hand,
Bold was his heart, and *reſtleſs* was his ſpright. *Fairfax.*

He's proud, fantaſtick, apt to change,
Reſtleſs at home, and ever prone to range. *Dryden.*

4. Not ſtill; in continual motion.

How could nature on their orbs impoſe
Such *reſtleſs* revolution, day by day
Repeated. *Milton.*

RE'STLESLY. *adv.* [from *reſtleſs.*] Without reſt; unquietly.

When the mind caſts and turns itſelf *reſtleſly* from one thing to another, ſtrains this power of the ſoul to apprehend, that to judge, another to divide, a fourth to remember: thus tracing out the nice and ſcarce obſervable difference of ſome things, and the real agreement of others; at length it brings all the ends of a long hypotheſis together. *South.*

RE'STLESSNESS. *n. ſ.* [from *reſtleſs.*]

1. Want of ſleep.

Reſtleſneſs and intermiſſion from ſleep, grieved perſons are moleſted with, whereby the blood is dried. *Harvey.*

2. Want of reſt; unquietneſs.

Let him keep the reſt,
But keep them with repining *reſtleſneſs*!
Let him be rich and weary, that at leaſt,
If goodneſs lead him not, yet wearineſs
May toſs him to my breaſt. *Herbert.*

3. Motion; agitation.

The trembling *reſtleſneſs* of the needle, in any but the north point of the compaſs, manifeſts its inclination to the pole; which its wavering and its reſt bear equal witneſs to. *Boyle.*

RESTO'RABLE. *adj.* [from *reſtore.*] What may be reſtored.

By cutting turf without any regularity, great quantities of *reſtorable* land are made utterly deſperate. *Swift.*

RESTORA'TION. *n. ſ.* [from *reſtore*; *reſtauration*, Fr.] The act of replacing in a former ſtate. This is properly *reſtauration.*

Hail, royal Albion, hail to thee,
Thy longing people's expectation!
Sent from the gods to ſet us free
From bondage and from uſurpation:
Behold the different climes agree,
Rejoicing in thy *reſtoration. Dryden's Albion.*

The Athenians, now deprived of the only perſon that was able to recover their loſſes, repent of their raſhneſs, and endeavour in vain for his *reſtoration. Swift.*

2. Recovery.

The change is great in this *reſtoration* of the man, from a ſtate of ſpiritual darkneſs, to a capacity of perceiving divine truth. *Rogers.*

RESTO'RATIVE. *adj.* [from *reſtore.*] That which has the power to recruit life.

Their taſte no knowledge works at leaſt of evil;
But life preſerves, deſtroys life's enemy,
Hunger, with ſweet *reſtorative* delight. *Milton.*

RESTO'RATIVE. *n. ſ.* [from *reſtore.*] A medicine that has the power of recruiting life.

I will kiſs thy lips;
Haply ſome poiſon yet doth hang on them,
To make me die with a *reſtorative. Shakeſp. Rom. and Jul.*

God ſaw it neceſſary by ſuch mortifications to quench the boundleſs rage of an inſatiable intemperance, to make the weakneſs of the fleſh, the phyſick and *reſtorative* of the ſpirit. *South's Sermons.*

Aſſes milk is an excellent *reſtorative* in conſumptions. *Mort.*

He preſcribes an Engliſh gallon of aſſes milk, eſpecially as a *reſtorative. Arbuthnot.*

To RESTO'RE. *v. a.* [*reſtaurer*, Fr. *reſtauro*, Lat.]

1. To give back what has been loſt or taken away.

Reſtore the man his wife. *Gen.* xx. 7.

He ſhall *reſtore* in the principal, and add the fifth part more. *Lev.* vi. 5.

She lands him on his native ſhores,
And to his father's longing arms *reſtores. Dryden.*

2. To bring back.

The father baniſh'd virtue ſhall *reſtore*,
And crimes ſhall threat the guilty world no more. *Dryd.*

Thus

Thus pencils can, by one slight touch, *restore*
Smiles to that changed face, that wept before. *Dryden.*

3. To retrieve; to bring back from degeneration, declension, or ruin to its former state.

These artificial experiments are but so many essays, whereby men attempt to *restore* themselves from the first general curse inflicted upon their labours. *Wilkins's Mathem. Magick.*

In his odysses, Homer explains, that the hardest difficulties may be overcome by labour, and our fortune *restored* after the severest afflictions. *Prior.*

4. To recover passages in books from corruption.

RESTO'RER. *n. s.* [from *restore.*] One that restores.

Next to the son,
Destin'd *restorer* of mankind, by whom
New heav'n and earth shall to the ages rise. *Milton.*

I foretel you, as the *restorer* of poetry. *Dryden.*

Here are ten thousand persons reduced to the necessity of a low diet and moderate exercise, who are the only great *restorers* of our breed, without which, the nation would in an age become one great hospital. *Swift.*

To RESTRAI'N. *v. a.* [*restreindre*, Fr. *restringo*, Lat.]

1. To withold; to keep in.

If she *restrain'd* the riots of your followers,
'Tis to such wholsome end as clears her. *Shakesp.*

The gods will plague thee,
That thou *restrain'st* from me the duty, which
To a mother's part belongs. *Shakesp. Coriolanus.*

2. To repress; to keep in awe.

The law of nature would be in vain, if there were no body that, in the state of nature, had a power to execute that law, and thereby preserve the innocent and *restrain* offenders. *Locke.*

That all men may be *restrained* from doing hurt to one another, the execution of the law of nature is in that state put into every man's hand, whereby every one has a right to punish the transgressors to such a degree as may hinder its violation. *Locke.*

3. To suppress; to hinder; to repress.

A heavy summons lies like lead upon me,
Merciful pow'rs!
Restrain in me the cursed thoughts, that nature
Gives way to in repose. *Shakesp. Macbeth.*

Compassion gave him up to tears
A space, till firmer thoughts *restrain'd* excess. *Milton.*

4. To abridge.

Me of my lawful pleasure she *restrain'd*,
And pray'd me oft forbearance. *Shakesp. Cymbeline.*

Though they two were committed, at least *restrained* of their liberty, yet this discovered too much of the humour of the court. *Clarendon, b.* ii.

5. To hold in.

His horse, with a half checked bit, and a headstall of sheep's leather, which being *restrained* to keep him from stumbling, hath been often burst, and now repaired with knots. *Shakespeare.*

6. To limit; to confine.

We *restrain* it to those only duties, which all men, by force of natural wit, understand to be such duties as concern all men. *Hooker, b.* i. *s.* 8.

Upon what ground can a man promise himself a future repentance, who cannot promise himself a futurity? whose life depends upon his breath, and is so *restrained* to the present, that it cannot secure to itself the reversion of the very next minute. *South's Sermons.*

Not only a metaphysical or natural, but a moral universality also is to be *restrained* by a part of the predicate; as all the Italians are politicians; that is, those among the Italians, who are politicians, are subtle politicians; *i. e.* they are generally so. *Watts's Logick.*

RESTRAI'NABLE. *adj.* [from *restrain.*] Capable to be restrained.

Therein we must not deny a liberty; nor is the hand of the painter more *restrainable*, than the pen of the poet. *Bro.*

RESTRAI'NEDLY. *adv.* [from *restrained.*] With restraint; without latitude.

That Christ's dying for all is the express doctrine of the scripture, is manifested by the world, which is a word of the widest extent, and although it be sometimes used more *restrainedly*, yet never doth signify a far smaller disproportionable part of the world. *Hammond's Fundamentals.*

RESTRAI'NER. *n. s.* [from *restrain.*] One that restrains; one that witholds.

If nothing can relieve us, we must with patience submit unto that restraint, and expect the will of the *restrainer*. *Brown's Vulgar Errours.*

RESTRAI'NT. *n. s.* [from *restrain*; *restreint*, Fr.]

1. Abridgement of liberty.

She will well excuse,
Why at this time the doors are barr'd against you;
Depart in patience,
And about evening come yourself alone,
To know the reason of this strange *restraint*. *Shakesp.*

I request
Th' enfranchisement of Arthur, whose *restraint*
Doth move the murm'ring lips of discontent. *Shakesp.*

It is to no purpose to lay *restraints* or give privileges to men, in such general terms, as the particular persons concerned cannot be known by. *Locke.*

I think it a manifest disadvantage, and a great *restraint* upon us. *Felton on the Classicks.*

2. Prohibition.

What mov'd our parents to transgress his will
For one *restraint*, lords of the world besides? *Milton.*

3. Limitation; restriction.

If all were granted, yet it must be maintained within any bold *restraints*, far otherwise than it is received. *Brown.*

4. Repression; hindrance of will; act of withholding.

There is no *restraint* to the Lord to save, by many or by few. *1 Sam.* xiv. 6.

Thus it shall befal
Him who, to worth in women overtrusting,
Lets her will rule; *restraint* she will not brook. *Milton.*

Is there any thing, which reflects a greater lustre upon a man's person, than a severe temperance and a *restraint* of himself from vicious pleasures? *South.*

To RESTRI'CT. *v. a.* [*restrictus*, Lat.] To limit; to confine. A word scarce English.

In the enumeration of constitutions in this chapter, there is not one that can be limited and *restricted* by such a distinction, nor can perhaps the same person, in different circumstances, be properly confined to one or the other. *Arbuthnot.*

RESTRI'CTION. *n. s.* [*restriction*, Fr.] Confinement; limitation.

This is to have the same *restriction* with all other recreations, that it be made a divertisement not a trade. *Go. of Ton.*

Iron manufacture, of all others, ought the least to be encouraged in Ireland; or, if it be, it requires the most *restriction* to certain places. *Temple's Miscellanies.*

All duties are matter of conscience; with this *restriction*, that a superior obligation suspends the force of an inferior. *L'Estrange.*

Each other gift, which God on man bestows,
Its proper bounds and due *restriction* knows;
To one fix'd purpose dedicates its power. *Prior.*

Celsus's rule, with the proper *restrictions*, is good for people in health. *Arbuthnot.*

RESTRI'CTIVE. *adj.* [from *restrict.*]

1. Expressing limitation.

They, who would make the *restrictive* particle belong to the latter clause, and not to the first, do not attend to the reason. *Stillingfleet's Def. of Dis. on Roman Idols.*

2. [*Restrictif*, Fr.] Styptick; astringent.

I applied a plaister over it, made up with my common *restrictive* powder. *Wiseman's Surgery.*

RESTRI'CTIVELY. *adv.* [from *restrictive.*] With limitation.

All speech, tending to the glory of God or the good of man, is aright directed; which is not to be understood so *restrictively*, as if nothing but divinity, or the necessary concerns of human life, may lawfully be brought into discourse. *Government of the Tongue.*

To RESTRI'NGE. *v. a.* [*restringo*, Lat.] To limit; to confine.

RESTRI'NGENT. *n. s.* [*restringens*, Lat. *restringent*, Fr.] That which hath the power of restraining.

The two latter indicate phlebotomy for revulsion, *restringents* to stench, and incrassatives to thicken the blood. *Harv.*

RE'STY. *adj.* [*restiff*, Fr.] Obstinate in standing still. See RESTIFF.

Come, our stomachs
Will make what's homely savoury, weariness
Can snore upon the flint, when *resty* sloth
Finds the down pillow hard. *Shakesp. Cymbeline.*

Men of discretion, whom people in power may with little ceremony load as heavy as they please, find them neither *resty* nor vicious. *Swift.*

To RESUBLI'ME. *v. a.* [*re* and *sublime.*] To sublime another time.

When mercury sublimate is *resublimed* with fresh mercury, it becomes mercurius dulcis, which is a white tasteless earth scarce dissolvable in water, and mercurius dulcis *resublimed* with spirit of salt returns into mercury sublimate. *Newton.*

To RESU'LT. *v. n.* [*resulter*, Fr. *resulto*, Lat.]

1. To fly back.

With many a weary step, and many a groan,
Up the high hill he heaves a huge round stone;
The huge round stone, *resulting* with a bound,
Thunders impetuous down, and smoaks along the ground. *Pope's Odyssey.*

2. [*Resulter*, Fr.] To rise as a consequence; to be produced as the effect of causes jointly concurring.

Rue prospers much, if set by a fig tree; which is caused, not by reason of friendship, but by extraction of a contrary juice; the one drawing juice fit to *result* sweet, the other bitter. *Bacon's Natural History.*

Such huge extremes, when nature doth unite,
Wonder from thence *results*, from thence delight. *Denh.*

Upon the dissolution of the first earth, this very face of things would immediately *result*. *Burnet's Theory of the Earth.*

Pleasure and peace do naturally *result* from a holy and good life. *Tillotson's Sermons.*

The horror of an object may overbear the pleasure *resulting* from its greatness. *Addison.*

Their effects are often very disproportionable to the principles and parts that *result* from the analysis. *Baker.*

3. To arise as a conclusion from premises.

RESU'LT. *n. s.* [from the verb.]

1. Resilience; act of flying back.

Sound is produced between the string and the air, by the return or the *result* of the string, which was strained by the touch to his former place. *Bacon's Natural History.*

2. Consequence; effect produced by the concurrence of co-operating causes.

Did my judgment tell me, that the propositions sent to me were the *results* of the major part of their votes, I should then not suspect my own judgement for not speedily concurring with them. *King Charles.*

As in perfumes, compos'd with art and cost,
'Tis hard to say what scent is uppermost,
Nor this part musk or civet can we call,
Or amber, but a rich *result* of all:
So she was all a sweet, whose ev'ry part,
In due proportion mix'd, proclaim'd the maker's art. *Dry.*

Buying of land is the *result* of a full and satiated gain: men in trade seldom lay out money upon land, till their profit has brought in more than trade can employ. *Locke.*

3. Inference from premises.

These things are a *result* or judgment upon fact. *South.*

4. Resolve; decision. Improper.

Rude, passionate, and mistaken *results* have, at certain times, fallen from great assemblies. *Swift.*

RESU'LTANCE. *n. s.* [*resultance*, Fr.] The act of resulting.

RESU'MABLE. *adj.* [from *resume*.] What may be taken back.

This was but an indulgence, and therefore *resumable* by the victor, unless there intervened any capitulation to the contrary. *Hale.*

To RESU'ME. *v. a.* [*resumo*, Lat.]

1. To take back what has been given.

The sun, like this, from which our sight we have,
Gaz'd on too long, *resumes* the light he gave. *Denham.*

Sees not my love, how time *resumes*
The glory which he lent these flow'rs;
Though none shou'd taste of their perfumes,
Yet must they live but some few hours:
Time, what we forbear, devours. *Waller.*

2. To take back what has been taken away.

That opportunity,
Which then they had to take from's, to *resume*
We have again. *Shakesp. Cymbeline.*

3. To take again.

He'll enter into glory, and *resume* his seat. *Milton.*

At this, with look serene, he rais'd his head;
Reason *resum'd* her place, and passion fled. *Dryden.*

4. *Dryden* uses it with *again*, but improperly, unless the resumption be repeated.

To him our common grandsire of the main
Had giv'n to change his form, and chang'd, *resume again.* *Dryden.*

5. To begin again what was broken off: as, *to* resume *a discourse.*

RESU'MPTION. *n. s.* [*resomption*, Fr. *resumptus*, Lat.] The act of resuming.

And if there be any fault in the last, it is the *resumption* or the dwelling too long upon his arguments. *Denham.*

RESU'MPTIVE. *adj.* [*resumptus*, Lat.] Taking back.

RESUPINA'TION. *n. s.* [*resupino*, Lat.] The act of lying on the back.

To RESU'RVEY. *v. a.* [*re* and *survey.*] To review; to survey again.

I have, with cursory eye, o'erglanc'd the articles;
Appoint some of your council presently
To sit with us, once more with better heed
To *resurvey* them. *Shakesp. Henry* V.

RESURRE'CTION. *n. s.* [*resurrection*, Fr. *resurrectum*, Lat.] Revival from the dead; return from the grave.

The Sadduces were grieved, that they taught, and preached through Jesus the *resurrection* from the dead. *Acts* iv. 2.

Nor after *resurrection* shall he stay
Longer on earth, than certain times t' appear
To his disciples. *Milton.*

He triumphs in his agonies, whilst the soul springs forward to the great object which she has always had in view, and leaves the body with an expectation of being remitted to her in a glorious and joyful *resurrection.* *Addison's Spectator.*

Perhaps there was nothing ever done in all past ages, and which was not a publick fact, so well attested as the *resurrection* of Christ. *Watts.*

To RESU'SCITATE. *v. a.* [*resuscito*, Latin.] To stir up anew; to revive.

We have beasts and birds for dissections, though divers parts, which you account vital, be perished and taken forth, *resuscitating* of some that seem dead in appearance. *Bacon.*

RESUSCITA'TION. *n. s.* [from *resuscitate.*] The act of stirring up anew; the act of reviving, or state of being revived.

Your very obliging manner of enquiring after me, at your *resuscitation*, should have been sooner answered; I sincerely rejoice at your recovery. *Pope.*

To RETAI'L. *v. a.* [*retailler*, Fr.]

1. To divide into small parcels.

Bound with triumphant garlands will I come,
And lead thy daughter to a conqueror's bed;
To whom I will *retail* my conquest won,
And she shall be sole victress, Cæsar's Cæsar. *Shakesp.*

2. To sell in small quantities.

All encouragement should be given to artificers; and those, who make, should also vend and *retail* their commodities. *Locke.*

3. To sell at second hand.

The sage dame,
By names of toasts, *retails* each batter'd jade. *Pope.*

4. To tell in broken parts.

He is furnish'd with no certainties,
More than he haply may *retail* from me. *Shakesp.*

RETAI'L. *n. s.* [from the verb.] Sale by small quantities.

The author, to prevent such a monopoly of sense, is resolved to deal in it himself by *retail.* *Addison.*

We force a wretched trade by beating down the sale,
And selling basely by *retail.* *Swift's Miscellanies.*

RETAI'LER. *n. s.* [from *retail.*] One who sells by small quantities.

From these particulars we may guess at the rest, as *retailers* do of the whole piece, by taking a view of its ends. *Hakew.*

To RETAI'N. *v. a.* [*retineo*, Lat. *retenir*, Fr.]

1. To keep; not to lose.

Where is the patience now,
That you so oft have boasted to *retain.* *Shakesp. K. Lear.*

Though th' offending part felt mortal pain,
Th' immortal part its knowledge did *retain.* *Denham.*

The vigor of this arm was never vain;
And that my wonted prowess I *retain*,
Witness these heaps of slaughter. *Dryden.*

A tomb and fun'ral honours I decreed;
The place your armour and your name *retains.* *Dryden.*

Whatever ideas the mind can receive and contemplate without the help of the body, it is reasonable to conclude, it can *retain* without the help of the body too. *Locke.*

2. To keep; not to lay aside.

Let me *retain*
The name and all the addition to a king;
The sway, beloved sons, be yours. *Shakesp. King Lear.*

As they did not like to *retain* God in their knowledge, God gave them over to a reprobate mind. *Rom.* i. 22.

Although they *retain* the word mandrake in the text, yet they retract it in the margin. *Brown's Vulgar Errours.*

Be obedient and *retain*
Unalterably firm his love entire. *Milton.*

They, who have restored painting in Germany, not having seen any of those fair reliques of antiquity, have *retained* much of that barbarous method. *Dryden.*

3. To keep; not to dismiss.

Receive him that is mine own bowels; whom I would have *retained* with me. *Philem.* xii. 13.

Hollow rocks *retain* the sound of blust'ring winds. *Milt.*

4. To keep in pay; to hire.

A Benedictine convent has now *retained* the most learned father of their order to write in its defence. *Addison.*

To RETAI'N. *v. n.*

1. To belong to; to depend on.

These betray upon the tongue no heat nor corrosiveness, but coldness mixed with a somewhat languid relish *retaining* to bitterness. *Boyle.*

In animals many actions depend upon their living form, as well as that of mixtion, and though they wholly seem to *retain* to the body, depart upon disunion. *Brown.*

2. To keep; to continue. Not in use.

No more can impure man *retain* and move
In the pure region of that worthy love,
Than earthly substance can unforc'd aspire,
And leave his nature to converse with fire. *Donne.*

RETAI'NER. *n. s.* [from *retain.*]

1. An adherent; a dependant: a hanger-on.

You now are mounted,
Where pow'rs are your *retainers.* *Shakesp. Henry* VIII.

One darling inclination of mankind affects to be a *retainer* to religion; the spirit of opposition, that lived long before christianity, and can easily subsist without it. *Swift.*

2. In common law, *retainer* signifieth a servant not menial nor familiar, that is not dwelling in his house; but only using or bearing his name or livery. *Cowel.*

3. The act of keeping dependants, or being in dependance.

By another law, the king's officers and farmers were to forfeit their places and holds, in case of unlawful *retainer*, or partaking in unlawful assemblies. *Bacon's Henry* VII.

A combination of honeſt men would endeavour to extirpate all the profligate immoral *retainers* to each ſide, that have nothing to recommend them but an implicit ſubmiſſion to their leaders. *Addiſon's Spectator.*

To RETA'KE. *v. a.* [*re* and *take.*] To take again.

A day ſhould be appointed, when the remonſtrance ſhould be *retaken* into conſideration. *Clarendon.*

To RETA'LIATE. *v. a.* [*re* and *talio*, Lat.] To return by giving like for like; to repay; to requite.

It is very unlucky, to be obliged to *retaliate* the injuries of authors, whoſe works are ſo ſoon forgotten, that we are in danger of appearing the firſt aggreſſors. *Swift.*

If a firſt miniſter of ſtate had uſed me as you have done, *retaliating* would be thought a mark of courage. *Swift.*

RETALIA'TION. *n. ſ.* [from *retaliate.*] Requital; return of like for like.

They thought it no irreligion to proſecute the ſevereſt *retaliation* or revenge; ſo that at the ſame time their outward man might be a ſaint, and their inward man a devil. *South.*

God, graciouſly becoming our debtor, takes what is done to others as done to himſelf, and by promiſe obliges himſelf to full *retaliation.* *Calamy's Sermons.*

To RETA'RD. *v. a.* [*retardo*, Lat. *retarder*, Fr.]

1. To hinder; to obſtruct in ſwiftneſs of courſe.

How Iphitus with me, and Pelias
Slowly retire; the one *retarded* was
By feeble age, the other by a wound. *Denham.*

2. To delay; to put off.

Nor kings nor nations
One moment can *retard* th' appointed hour. *Dryden.*

It is as natural to delay a letter at ſuch a ſeaſon, as to *retard* a melancholy viſit to a perſon one cannot relieve. *Pope.*

To RETA'RD. *v. n.* To ſtay back.

Some years it hath alſo *retarded*, and come far later, than uſually it was expected. *Brown's Vulgar Errours.*

RETARDA'TION. *n. ſ.* [*retardation*, Fr. from *retard.*] Hindrance; the act of delaying.

Out of this a man may deviſe the means of altering the colour of birds, and the *retardation* of hoary hairs. *Bacon.*

RETA'RDER. *n. ſ.* [from *retard.*] Hinderer; obſtructer.

This diſputing way of enquiry, is ſo far from advancing ſcience, that it is no inconſiderable *retarder.* *Glanvill.*

To RETCH. *v. n.* [hræcan, Saxon.] To force up ſomething from the ſtomach.

RE'TCHLESS. *adj.* [ſometimes written *wretchleſs*, properly *reckleſs.* See RECKLESS.] Careleſs.

He ſtruggles into breath, and cries for aid;
Then helpleſs in his mother's lap is laid:
He creeps, he walks, and iſſuing into man,
Grudges their life, from whence his own began;
Retchleſs of laws, affects to rule alone. *Dryden.*

RETE'CTION. *n. ſ.* [*retectus*, Lat.] The act of diſcovering to the view.

This is rather a reſtoration of a body to its own colour, or a *retection* of its native colour, than a change. *Boyle.*

RETE'NTION. *n. ſ.* [*retention*, Fr. *retentio*, from *retentus*, Lat.]

1. The act of retaining.

No woman's heart
So big to hold ſo much; they lack *retention.* *Shakeſp.*

A froward *retention* of cuſtom is as turbulent a thing, as an innovation; and they, that reverence too much old things, are but a ſcorn to the new. *Bacon's Natural Hiſtory.*

2. *Retention* and retentive faculty is that ſtate of contraction in the ſolid parts, which makes them hold faſt their proper contents. *Quincy.*

3. Memory.

The backward learner makes amends another way, expiating his want of docility with a deeper and a more rooted *retention.* *South's Sermons.*

Retention is the keeping of thoſe ſimple ideas, which from ſenſation or reflection the mind hath received. *Locke.*

4. Limitation.

His life I gave him, and did thereto add
My love without *retention* or reſtraint;
All his. *Shakeſp. Twelfth Night.*

5. Cuſtody; confinement; reſtraint.

I ſent the old and miſerable king
To ſome *retention* and appointed guard. *Shakeſp. K. Lear.*

RETE'NTIVE. *adj.* [*retentus*, Lat. *retentif*, Fr.]

1. Having the power of retention.

It keepeth ſermons in memory, and doth in that reſpect, although not feed the ſoul of man, yet help the *retentive* force of that ſtomach of the mind. *Hooker.*

Have I been ever free, and muſt my houſe
Be my *retentive* enemy, my goal? *Shakeſp.*

From *retentive* cage
When ſullen Philomel eſcapes, her notes
She varies, and of paſt impriſonment
Sweetly complains. *Philips.*

In Tot'nam fields the brethren with amaze
Prick all their ears up, and forget to graze;
Long Chancery-lane *retentive* rolls the ſound,
And courts to courts return it round and round. *Pope.*

2. Having memory.

To remember a ſong or tune, our ſouls muſt be an harmony continually running over in a ſilent whiſper thoſe muſical accents, which our *retentive* faculty is preſerver of. *Glan.*

RETE'NTIVENESS. *n. ſ.* [from *retentive.*] Having the quality of retention.

RE'TICENCE. *n. ſ.* [*reticence*, Fr. *reticentia*, from *reticeo*, Lat.] Concealment by ſilence. *Dict.*

RE'TICLE. *n. ſ.* [*reticulum*, Lat.] A ſmall net. *Dict.*

RETI'CULAR. *adj.* [from *reticulum*, Lat.] Having the form of a ſmall net.

RETI'CULATED. *adj.* [*reticulatus*, Lat.] Made of network; formed with interſtitial vacuities.

The intervals of the cavities, riſing a little, make a pretty kind of *reticulated* work. *Woodward on Foſſils.*

RE'TIFORM. *adj.* [*retiformis*, Lat.] Having the form of a net.

The uveous coat and inſide of the choroides are blackened, that the rays may not be reflected backwards to confound the ſight; and if any be by the *retiform* coat reflected, they are ſoon choaked in the black inſide of the uvea. *Ray.*

RETI'NUE. *n. ſ.* [*retenue*, Fr.] A number attending upon a principal perſon; a train; a meiny.

Not only this your all licens'd fool,
But other of your inſolent *retinue*,
Do hourly carp and quarrel. *Shakeſp. King Lear.*

What followers, what *retinue* can'ſt thou gain,
Or at thy heels the dizzy multitude,
Longer than thou can'ſt feed them on thy coſt? *Milton.*

There appears
The long *retinue* of a proſperous reign,
A ſeries of ſucceſsful years. *Dryden.*

Neither pomp nor *retinue* ſhall be able to divert the great, nor ſhall the rich be relieved by the multitude of his treaſurers. *Rogers's Sermons.*

To RETI'RE. *v. n.* [*retirer*, Fr.]

1. To retreat; to withdraw; to go to a place of privacy.

The mind contracts herſelf, and ſhrinketh in,
And to herſelf ſhe gladly doth *retire.* *Davies.*

The leſs I may be bleſt with her company, the more I will *retire* to God and my own heart. *King Charles.*

Thou open'ſt wiſdom's way,
And giv'ſt acceſs, though ſecret ſhe *retire.* *Milton.*

The parliament diſſolved, and gentlemen charged to *retire* to their country habitations. *Hayward.*

2. To retreat from danger.

Set up the ſtandard towards Zion, *retire*, ſtay not. *Jer.*

Set Uriah in the fore front of the hotteſt battle, and *retire* ye from him, that he may die. *2 Sam.* xi. 15.

From each hand with ſpeed *retir'd*,
Where erſt was thickeſt th' angelick throng. *Milton.*

3. To go from a publick ſtation.

He, that had driven many out of their country, periſhed in a ſtrange land, *retiring* to the Lacedemonians. *2 Mac.* v.

4. To go off from company.

The old fellow ſkuttled out of the room, and *retired.* *Arb.*

To RETI'RE. *v. a.* To withdraw; to take away.

He brake up his court, and *retired* himſelf, his wife, and children into a foreſt thereby. *Sidney.*

They, full of rage, *retired* themſelves into this caſtle. *Sidn.*

He, our hope, might have *retir'd* his power,
And driven into deſpair an enemy's hate. *Shakeſp.*

Thence *retire* me to my Milan. *Shakeſp. Tempeſt.*

There may be as great a variety in *retiring* and withdrawing men's conceits in the world, as in obtruding them. *Bacon.*

As when the ſun is preſent all the year,
And never doth *retire* his golden ray,
Needs muſt the ſpring be everlaſting there,
And every ſeaſon like the month of May. *Davies.*

Theſe actions in her cloſet, all alone,
Retir'd within herſelf, ſhe doth fulfill. *Davies.*

After ſome ſlight ſkirmiſhes, he *retired* himſelf into the caſtle of Farnham. *Clarendon.*

Hydra-like, the fire
Lifts up his hundred heads to aim his way;
And ſcarce the wealthy can one half *retire*,
Before he ruſhes in to ſhare the prey. *Dryden.*

RETI'RE. *n. ſ.* [from the verb.]

1. Retreat; receſſion.

I heard his praiſes in purſuit,
But ne'er, till now, his ſcandal of *retire.* *Shakeſp.*

Thou haſt talk'd
Of ſallies and *retires*, of trenches, tents. *Shakeſp.*

The battle and the *retire* of the Engliſh ſuccours were the cauſes of the loſs of that dutchy. *Bacon's Henry* VII.

2. Retirement; place of privacy. Not in uſe.

Eve, who unſeen
Yet all had heard, with audible lament
Diſcover'd ſoon the place of her *retire.* *Milton.*

RETI'RED. *part. adj.* [from *retire.*] Secret; private.

Language moſt ſhews a man; ſpeak that I may ſee thee: it ſprings out of the moſt *retired* and inmoſt parts of us. *B. Johnſ.*

You find the mind in ſleep *retired* from the ſenſes, and out of theſe motions made on the organs of ſenſe. *Locke.*

Some, accustomed to *retired* speculations, run natural philosophy into metaphysical notions and the abstract generalities of logick. *Locke.*

He was admitted into the most secret and *retired* thoughts and counsels of his royal master king William. *Addison.*

RETI'REDNESS. *n. s.* [from *retired.*] Solitude; privacy; secrecy.

Like one, who in her third widowhood doth profess
Herself a nun, ty'd to *retiredness*,
So affects my muse now a chaste fallowness. *Donne.*

How could he have the leisure and *retiredness* of the cloister, to perform all those acts of devotion in, when the burthen of the reformation lay upon his shoulders? *Atterbury.*

RETI'REMENT. *n. s.* [from *retire.*]

1. Private abode; secret habitation.

My *retirement* there tempted me to divert those melancholy thoughts. *Denham's Dedication.*

Caprea had been the *retirement* of Augustus for some time, and the residence of Tiberius for many years. *Addison.*

2. Private way of life.

An elegant sufficiency, content,
Retirement, rural quiet, friendship, books,
Progressive virtue, and approving heaven. *Thomson.*

3. Act of withdrawing.

Short *retirement* urges sweet return. *Milton.*

In this *retirement* of the mind from the senses, it retains a yet more incoherent manner of thinking, which we call dreaming. *Locke.*

RETO'LD. part. pass. of *retell.* Related or told again.

Whatever Harry Percy then had said
At such a time, with all the rest *retold*,
May reasonably die. *Shakesp.*

Upon his dead corpse there was such misuse
By those Welchwomen done, as may not be
Without much shame *retold* or spoken of. *Shakesp.*

To RETO'RT. *v. a.* [*retortus*, Lat.]

1. To throw back.

His virtues, shining upon others,
Heat them, and they *retort* that heat again
To the first giver. *Shakesp. Troilus and Cressida.*

He pass'd through hostile scorn;
And with *retorted* scorn his back he turn'd. *Milton.*

2. To return any argument, censure, or incivility.

His proof will easily be *retorted*, and the contrary proved, by interrogating; shall the adulterer inherit the kingdom of God? if he shall, what need I, that am now exhorted to reform my life, reform it? if he shall not, then certainly I, that am such, am none of the elect; for all, that are elect, shall certainly inherit the kingdom of God. *Hammond.*

What if toy son
Prove disobedient, and reprov'd, *retort*,
Wherefore did'st thou beget me? *Milton.*

The respondent may shew, how the opponent's argument may be *retorted* against himself. *Watts.*

3. To curve back.

It would be tried how the voice will be carried in an horn, which is a line arched; or in a trumpet, which is a line *retorted*; or in some pipe that were sinuous. *Bacon.*

RETO'RT. *n. s.* [*retorte*, Fr. *retortum*, Lat.]

1. A censure or incivility returned.

I said his beard was not cut well, he was in the mind it was: this is called the *retort* courteous. *Shakesp.*

2. A chymical glass vessel with a bent neck to which the receiver is fitted.

Recent urine distilled yields a limpid water; and what remains at the bottom of the *retort*, is not acid nor alkaline. *Arb.*

RETO'RTER. *n. s.* [from *retort.*] One that retorts.

RETO'RTION. *n. s.* [from *retort.*] The act of retorting.

To RETO'SS. *v. a.* [*re* and *toss.*] To toss back.

Tost and *retost* the ball incessant flies. *Pope's Odyssey.*

To RETOU'CH. *v. a.* [*retoucher*, Fr.] To improve by new touches.

He furnished me with all the passages in Aristotle and Horace, used to explain the art of poetry by painting; which, if ever I *retouch* this essay, shall be inserted. *Dryden.*

Lintot, dull rogue! will think your price too much:
"Not, Sir, if you revise it and *retouch*." *Pope.*

To RETRA'CE. *v. a.* [*retracer*, Fr.] To trace back.

Then if the line of Turnus you *retrace*,
He springs from Inachus of Argive race. *Dryden.*

To RETRA'CT. *v. a.* [*retractus*, Lat. *retracter*, Fr.]

1. To recall; to recant.

Were I alone to pass the difficulties,
Paris should ne'er *retract* what he hath done,
Nor faint in the pursuit. *Shakesp. Troilus and Cressida.*

Although they retain the word mandrake in the text, they in effect *retract* it in the margine. *Brown's Vulg. Errours.*

If his subtilities could have satisfied me, I would as freely have *retracted* this charge of idolatry, as I ever made it. *Still.*

She will, and she will not, she grants, denies,
Consents, *retracts*, advances, and then flies. *Granville.*

2. To take back; to resume.

A great part of that time, which the inhabitants of the former earth had to spare, and whereof they made so ill use, was employed in making provisions for bread; and the excess of fertility, which contributed so much to their miscarriages, was *retracted* and cut off. *Woodward's Natural History.*

RETRACTA'TION. *n. s.* [*retractation*, Fr. *retractatio*, Lat.] Recantation; change of opinion.

These words are David's *retractation*, or laying down of a bloody and revengeful resolution. *South's Sermons.*

RETRA'CTION. *n. s.* [from *retract.*]

1. Act of withdrawing something advanced.

They make bold with the deity, when they make him do and undo, go forward and backwards by such countermarches and *retractions*, as we do not repute to the Almighty. *Woodw.*

2. Recantation; declaration of change of opinion.

There came into her head certain verses, which if she had had present commodity, she would have adjoined as a *retraction* to the other. *Sidney, b.* ii.

3. Act of withdrawing a claim.

Other men's insatiable desire of revenge hath wholly beguiled both church and state, of the benefit of all my either *retractions* or concessions. *King Charles.*

RETRAI'CT. *n. s. Spenser.* [*retraitte* Fr.]

1. Retreat. Obsolete.

The earl of Lincoln, deceived of the country's concourse unto him, and seeing the business past *retraict*, resolved to make on where the king was, and give him battle. *Bacon.*

2. [*Retrait*, Fr. *ritratto*, Italian.] A cast of the countenance. Obsolete.

Upon her eyelids many graces sat,
Under the shadow of her even brows,
Working bellgards and amorous *retraite*,
And every one her with a grace endows. *Fairy Queen.*

RETREA'T. *n. s.* [*retraitte*, Fr.]

1. Place of privacy; retirement.

He built his son a house of pleasure, and spared no cost to make a delicious *retreat*. *L'Estrange.*

2. Place of security.

This place our dungeon, not our safe *retreat*,
Beyond his potent arm. *Milton.*

That pleasing shade they sought, a soft *retreat*
From sudden April showers, a shelter from the heat. *Dry.*

There is no such way to give defence to absurd doctrines, as to guard them round with legions of obscure and undefined words; which yet make these *retreats* more like the dens of robbers, than the fortresses of fair warriors. *Locke.*

3. Act of retiring before a superiour force.

Honourable *retreats* are no ways inferior to brave charges; as having less of fortune, more of discipline, and as much of valour. *Bacon.*

To RETREA'T. *v. n.* [from the noun.]

1. To go to a private abode.

Others more mild
Retreated in a silent valley, sing
Their own heroick deeds. *Milton.*

2. To take shelter; to go to a place of security.

3. To retire from a superiour enemy.

4. To go out of the former place.

The rapid currents drive
Towards the *retreating* sea their furious tide. *Milton.*

My subject does not oblige me to look after the water, or point forth the place whereunto it is now *retreated*. *Woodw.*

Having taken her by the hand, he *retreated* with his eye fixed upon her. *Arbuthnot and Pope.*

RETREA'TED. *part. adj.* [from *retreat.*] Retired; gone to privacy.

To RETRE'NCH. *v. a.* [*retrancher*, Fr.]

1. To cut off; to pare away.

The pruner's hand must quench
Thy heat, and thy exub'rant parts *retrench*. *Denham.*

Nothing can be added to the wit of Ovid's Metamorphoses; but many things ought to have been *retrenched*. *Dryden.*

We ought to *retrench* those superfluous expences to qualify ourselves for the exercise of charity. *Atterbury.*

2. To confine. Improper.

In some reigns, they are for a power and obedience that is unlimited; and in others, are for *retrenching* within the narrowest bounds, the authority of the princes, and the allegiance of the subject. *Addison's Freeholder*, N° 6.

To RETRE'NCH. *v. n.* To live with less magnificence or expence.

Can I *retrench*? yes mighty well
Shrink back to my paternal cell,
A little house, with trees a-row,
And like its master, very low. *Pope's Epist. of Horace.*

RETRE'NCHMENT. *n. s.* [*retranchement*, Fr. from *retrench.*] The act of lopping away.

I had studied Virgil's design, his judicious management of the figures, the sober *retrenchments* of his sense, which always leaves somewhat to gratify our imagination, on which it may enlarge at pleasure. *Dryden's Dedication to Virgil.*

The want of vowels in our language has been the general complaint of our politest authors, who nevertheless have made these *retrenchments*, and consequently encreased our former scarcity. *Addison.*

I would rather be an advocate for the *retrenchment*, than the encrease of this charity. *Atterbury.*

To RE'TRIBUTE. *v. a.* [*retribuo*, Lat. *retribuer*, Fr.] To pay back; to make repayment of.

Both the will and power to serve him are his upon so many scores, that we are unable to *retribute*, unless we do restore; and all the duties we can pay our maker are less properly requitals than restitutions. *Boyle.*

In the state of nature, a man comes by no arbitrary power to use a criminal, but only to *retribute* to him, so far as calm reason and conscience dictate, what is proportionate to his transgression. *Locke.*

RETRIBU'TION. *n. s.* [*retribution*, Fr. from *retribute.*] Repayment; return accommodated to the action.

The king thought he had not remunerated his people sufficiently with good laws, which evermore was his *retribution* for treasure. *Bacon's Henry* VII.

All who have their reward on earth, the fruits
Of painful superstition, and blind zeal,
Nought seeking but the praise of men, here find
Fit *retribution*, empty as their deeds. *Milton's Par. Lost.*

In good offices and due *retributions*, we may not be pinching and niggardly: it argues an ignoble mind, where we have wronged to higgle and dodge in the amends. *Hall.*

There is no nation, though plunged into never such gross idolatry, but has some awful sense of a deity, and a persuasion of a state of *retribution* to men after this life. *South.*

It is a strong argument for a state of *retribution* hereafter, that in this world virtuous persons are very often unfortunate, and vicious persons prosperous. *Addison's Spectator.*

RETRI'BUTORY. } *adj.* [from *retribute.*] Repaying; making
RETRI'BUTIVE. } repayment.

Something strangely *retributive* is working. *Clarissa.*

RETRIE'VABLE. *adj.* [from *retrieve.*] That may be retrieved.

To RETRIE'VE. *v. a.* [*retrouver*, Fr.]

1. To recover; to restore.

By this conduct we may *retrieve* the publick credit of religion, reform the example of the age, and lessen the danger we complain of. *Rogers's Sermons.*

2. To repair.

O reason! once again to thee I call;
Accept my sorrow, and *retrieve* my fall. *Prior.*

3. To regain.

With late repentance now they would *retrieve*
The bodies they forsook, and wish to live. *Dryden.*

Philomela's liberty *retriev'd*,
Cheers her sad soul. *Philips.*

4. To recall; to bring back.

If one, like the old Latin poets, came among them, it would be a means to *retrieve* them from their cold trivial conceits, to an imitation of their predecessors. *Berkeley to Pope.*

RETROCE'SSION. *n. s.* [*retrocessum*, Lat.] The act of going back.

RETROCOPU'LATION. *n. s.* [*retro* and *copulation.*] Post-coition.

From the nature of this position, there ensueth a necessity of *retrocopulation.* *Brown's Vulgar Errours.*

RETROGRADA'TION. *n. s.* [*retrogradation*, Fr. from *retrograde.*] The act of going backward.

As for the revolutions, stations, and *retrogadations* of the planets, observed constantly in most certain periods of time, sufficiently demonstrates, that their motions are governed by counsel. *Ray on the Creation.*

RE'TROGRADE. *adj.* [*retrograde*, Fr. *retro* and *gradior*, Lat.]

1. Going backward.

Princes, if they use ambitious men, should handle it so, as they be still progressive, and not *retrograde.* *Bacon.*

2. Contrary; opposite.

Your intent
In going back to school to Wittenberg,
It is most *retrograde* to our desire. *Shakesp. Hamlet.*

3. In astronomy, planets are *retrograde*, when by their proper motion in the zodiack, they move backward, and contrary to the succession of the signs; as from the second degree of Aries to the first: but this retrogradation is only apparent and occasioned by the observer's eye being placed on the earth; for to an eye at the sun, the planet will appear always direct, and never either stationary or *retrograde.* *Harris.*

Their wand'ring course, now high, now low, then hid,
Progressive, *retrograde*, or standing still,
In six thou see'st. *Shakesp. Paradise Lost.*

Two geomantick figures were display'd;
One when direct, and one when *retrograde.* *Dryden.*

To RE'TROGRADE. *v. n.* [*retrograder*, Fr. *retro* and *gradior*, Lat.] To go backward.

The race and period of all things here is to turn things more pneumatical and rare, and not to *retrograde* from pneumatical to that which is dense. *Bacon.*

RETROGRE'SSION. *n. s.* [*retro* and *gressus*, Lat.] The act of going backwards.

The account, established upon the rise and descent of the stars, can be no reasonable rule unto distant nations, and by reason of their *retrogression*, but temporary unto any one. *Bro.*

RETROMI'NGENCY. *n. s.* [*retro* and *mingo*, Lat.] The quality of staling backwards.

The last foundation was *retromingency*, or pissing backwards; for men observing both sexes to urine backwards, or averfly between their legs, they might conceive there were feminine parts in both. *Brown's Vulgar Errours.*

RETROMI'NGENT. *adj.* [*retro* and *mingens*, Lat.] Staling backward.

By reason of the backward position of the feminine parts of quadrupeds, they can hardly admit the substitution of masculine generations, except it be in *retromingents.* *Brown.*

RE'TROSPECT. *n. s.* [*retro* and *specio*, Lat.] Look thrown upon things behind or things past.

As you arraign his majesty by *retrospect*, so you condemn his government by second sight. *Addison's Freeholder*, Nº 9.

RETROSPE'CTION. *n. s.* [from *retrospect.*] Act or faculty of looking backwards.

Can'st thou take delight in viewing
This poor isle's approaching ruin,
When thy *retrospection* vast
Sees the glorious ages past?
Happy nation were we blind,
Or had only eyes behind. *Swift.*

RETROSPE'CTIVE. *adj.* [from *retrospect.*] Looking backwards.

In vain the grave, with *retrospective* eye,
Would from the apparent what conclude the why. *Pope.*

To RETU'ND. *v. a.* [*retundo*, Lat.] To blunt; to turn.

Covered with skin and hair keeps it warm, being naturally a very cold part, and also to quench and dissipate the force of any stroke that shall be dealt it, and *retund* the edge of any weapon *Ray on the Creation.*

To RETU'RN. *v. n.* [*retourner*, Fr.]

1. To come to the same place.

Return, my son David, for I will do thee no harm. 1 *Sam.*
Whoso rolleth a stone, it will *return* upon him. *Prov.* xxvi.
Go, *return* on thy way to the wilderness. 1 *Kings* xix. 15.

2. To come back to the same state.

The waters *returned* from off the earth continually. *Gen.*
Judgment shall *return* unto righteousness. *Psalm* xciv. 15.
In *returning* and rest shall ye be saved. *Isaiah* xxx. 15.

On their embattel'd ranks the waves *return.* *Milton.*

If they *returned* out of bondage, it must be into a state of freedom. *Locke.*

3. To go back.

I am in blood
Stept in so far, that should I wade no more,
Returning were as tedious as go o'er. *Shakesp. Macbeth.*

Hezekiah sent to the king of Assyria, saying, I have offended, *return* from me. 2 *Kings* xviii. 14.

To *return* to the business in hand, the use of a little insight in those parts of knowledge, is to accustom our minds to all sorts of ideas. *Locke.*

4. To make answer.

The thing of courage,
As rouz'd with rage, with rage doth sympathize;
And with an accent tun'd in self same key,
Returns to chiding fortune. *Shakesp. Troil. and Cressida.*

He said; and thus the queen of heaven *return'd*;
Must I, oh Jove in bloody wars contend! *Pope.*

5. To come back; to come again; to revisit.

Thou to mankind
Be good, and friendly still, and oft *return.* *Milton.*

6. After a periodical revolution, to begin the same again.

With the year
Seasons *return*, but not to me *returns*
Day, or the sweet approach of ev'n or morn. *Milton.*

7. To retort; to recriminate.

If you are a malicious reader, you *return* upon me, that I affect to be thought more impartial than I am. *Dryden.*

To RETU'RN. *v. a.*

1. To repay; to give in requital.

Return him a trespass offering. 1 *Sam.* vi. 3.

Thy Lord shall *return* thy wickedness upon thine own head. 1 *Kings* ii. 44.

What peace can we *return*,
But to our power, hostility, and hate. *Milton.*

When answer none *return'd*, I set me down. *Milton.*

2. To give back.

What counsel give ye to *return* answer to this people. 2 *Chr.*

3. To send back.

Reject not then what offer'd means, who knows
But God hath set before us, to *return* thee
Home to thy country and his sacred house. *Milton's Agon.*

4. To give account of.

Probably one fourth part more died of the plague than are *returned.* *Graunt's Bills of Mortality.*

5. To transmit.

Instead of a ship, he should levy money, and *return* the same to the treasurer for his majesty's use. *Clarendon.*

RETU'RN. *n. s.* [from the verb.]

1. Act of coming back to the same place.

The king of France so suddenly gone back!
Something since his coming forth is thought of,
That his *return* was now most necessary. *Shakesp.*

When forc'd from hence to view our parts he mourns;
Takes little journies, and makes quick *returns.* *Dryden.*

2. Retrogression.

3. Act of coming back to the ſame ſtate.

At the *return* of the year, the king of Syria will come up. *1 Kings* xx. 22.

4. Revolution; viciſſitude.

Weapons hardly fall under rule; yet even they have *returns* and viciſſitudes; for ordnance was known in the city of the Oxidraces in India, and is what the Macedonians called thunder and lightning. *Bacon's Eſſays.*

5. Repayment of money laid out in commodities for ſale.

As for any merchandize you have bought, ye ſhall have your *return* in merchandize or gold. *Bacon.*

As to roots accelerated in their ripening, there is the high price that thoſe things bear, and the ſwiftneſs of their *returns*; for, in ſome grounds, a radiſh comes in a month, that in others will not come in two, and ſo make double *returns*. *Bacon.*

6. Profit; advantage.

The fruit, from many days of recreation, is very little; but from theſe few hours we ſpend in prayer, the *return* is great. *Taylor's Rule of Living Holy.*

7. Remittance; payment from a diſtant place.

Within theſe two months, I do expect *return*
Of thrice three times the value of this bond. *Shakeſp.*

Brokers cannot have leſs money by them, than one twentieth part of their yearly *returns*. *Locke.*

8. Repayment; retribution; requital.

You made my liberty your late requeſt,
Is no *return* due from a grateful breaſt?
I grow impatient, 'till I find ſome way,
Great offices, with greater to repay. *Dryden.*

Since theſe are ſome of the *returns* which we made to God after obtaining our ſucceſſes, can we reaſonably preſume, that we are in the favour of God? *Atterbury.*

Nothing better becomes a perſon in a publick character, than ſuch a publick ſpirit; nor is there any thing likely to procure him larger *returns* of eſteem. *Atterbury.*

Returns, like theſe, our miſtreſs bids us make,
When from a foreign prince a gift her Britons take. *Prior.*

Ungrateful lord!
Would'ſt thou invade my life, as a *return*
For proffer'd love? *Rowe.*

9. Act of reſtoring or giving back; reſtitution.

The other ground of God's ſole property in any thing, is the gift, or rather the *return* of it made by man to God. *South.*

10. Relapſe.

This is breaking into a conſtitution to ſerve a preſent expedient; the remedy of an empirick, to ſtifle the preſent pain, but with certain proſpect of ſudden *returns*. *Swift.*

11. [*Retour*, Fr.]

Either of the adjoining ſides of the front of an houſe, or ground-plot, is called a *return* ſide. *Moxon's Mech. Exerc.*

Both theſe ſides are not only *returns*, but parts of the front, and a ſtately tower in the midſt of the front. *Bacon.*

RETU'RNABLE. *adj.* Allowed to be reported back. A law term.

It may be decided in that court, where the verdict is *returnable*. *Hale.*

He ſhall have an attachment againſt the ſheriff, directed to the coroner, and *returnable* into the king's bench. *Ayliffe.*

RETU'RNER. *n. ſ.* [from *return*.] One who pays or remits money.

The chapmen, that give higheſt for this, can make moſt profit by it, and thoſe are the *returners* of our money. *Locke.*

REVE. *n. ſ.* The bailiff of a franchiſe or manour.

The *reve*, the miller, and the mincing lady prioreſs ſpeak in character. *Dryden.*

To **REVEA'L.** *v. a.* [*revelo*, Lat. *reveler*, Fr.]

1. To ſhow; to diſcover; to lay open; to diſcloſe a ſecret.

Be aſhamed: ſpeaking again that which thou haſt heard, and *revealing* of ſecrets. *Eccluſ.* xli. 23.

I will cure them, and *reveal* unto them the abundance of peace. *Jer.* xxxiii. 6.

Light was the wound, the prince's care unknown,
She might not, would not yet *reveal* her own. *Waller.*

The anſwer to one who aſked what time was, *ſi non rogas intelligo*; that is, the more I think of time, the leſs I underſtand it; might perſuade one, that time, which *reveals* all other things, is itſelf not to be diſcovered. *Locke.*

2. To impart from heaven.

The ſufferings of this life are not to be compared with the glory which ſhall be *revealed* in us. *Romans* viii. 18.

REVEA'LER. *n. ſ.* [from *reveal*.]

1. Diſcoverer; one that ſhows or makes known.

The habit of faith in divinity is an argument of things unſeen, as a ſtable aſſent unto things inevident, upon authority of the divine *revealer*. *Brown's Vulgar Errours.*

The lives of the *revealers* may be juſtly ſet over againſt the revelation, to find whether they agree. *Atterbury.*

2. One that diſcovers to view.

He brought a taper; the *revealer* light
Expos'd both crime and criminal to ſight. *Dryden.*

To **RE'VEL.** *v. n.* [*Skinner* derives it from *reveiller*, Fr. to awake; Mr. *Lye* from *raveelen*, Dutch, to rove looſely about, which is much countenanced by the old phraſe, *revel-rout*.]

1. To feaſt with looſe and clamorous merriment.

My honey love,
Will we return unto thy father's houſe,
And *revel* it as bravely as the beſt. *Shakeſp.*

We'll keep no great ado—a friend or two.
Tybalt being ſlain ſo late,
It may be thought we held him careleſsly,
Being our kinſman, if we *revel* much. *Shakeſp.*

Antony, that *revels* long o' nights,
Is up. *Shakeſp. Julius Cæſar.*

We ſhall have *revelling* to-night;
I will aſſume thy part in ſome diſguiſe. *Shakeſp.*

He can report you more odd tales
Of our outlaw Robin Hood,
That *revell'd* here in Sherewood,
Though he ne'er ſhot in his bow. *Benj. Johnſon.*

Were the doctrine new,
That the earth mov'd, this day would make it true;
For every part to dance and *revel* goes,
They tread the air, and fall not where they roſe. *Donne.*

Whene'er I *revel'd* in the women's bow'rs;
For firſt I ſought her but at looſer hours:
The apples ſhe had gather'd ſmelt moſt ſweet. *Prior.*

RE'VEL. *n. ſ.* [from the verb.] A feaſt with looſe and noiſy jollity.

Let them pinch th' unclean knight,
And aſk him, why, that hour of fairy *revel*,
In their ſo ſacred paths he dares to tread? *Shakeſp.*

They could do no leſs but, under your fair conduct,
Crave leave to view theſe ladies, and intreat
An hour of *revels* with them. *Shakeſp.*

To **REVE'L.** *v. a.* [*revello*, Lat.] To retract; to draw back.

Thoſe, who miſcarry, eſcape by their flood, *revelling* the humours from their lungs. *Harvey.*

REVEL-ROUT. *n. ſ.* A mob; an unlawful aſſembly of a rabble. *Ainſworth.*

For this his minion, the *revel-rout* is done.
—I have been told, that you
Are frequent in your viſitation to her. *Rowe's Jane Shore.*

REVELA'TION. *n. ſ.* [from *revelation*, Fr.] Diſcovery; communication; communication of ſacred and myſterious truths by a teacher from heaven.

When the divine *revelations* were committed to writing, the Jews were ſuch ſcrupulous reverers of them, that they numbered even the letters of the Old Teſtament. *D. of Pie.*

As the goſpel appears in reſpect of the law to be a clearer *revelation* of the myſtical part, ſo it is a far more benign diſpenſation of the practical part. *Sprat.*

RE'VELLER. *n. ſ.* [from *revel*.] One who feaſts with noiſy jollity.

Fairies black, grey, green and white,
You moonſhine *revellers* attend your office. *Shakeſp.*

Unwelcome *revellers*, whoſe lawleſs joy
Pains the ſage ear, and hurts the ſober eye. *Pope.*

RE'VELRY. *n. ſ.* [from *revel*.] Looſe jollity; feſtive mirth.

Forget this new-fall'n dignity,
And fall into our ruſtick *revelry*. *Shakeſp.*

There let Hymen oft appear
In ſaffron robe with taper clear,
And pomp, and feaſt, and *revelry*,
With maſk and antick pageantry. *Milton.*

To **REVE'NGE.** *v. a.* [*revencher*, *revancher*, Fr.]

1. To return an injury.

2. To vindicate by puniſhment of an enemy.

If our hard fortune no compaſſion draws,
The gods are juſt, and will *revenge* our cauſe. *Dryden.*

3. To wreak one's wrongs on him that inflicted them. With the reciprocal pronoun.

Come, Antony and young Octavius,
Revenge yourſelves alone on Caſſius. *Shakeſp. Jul. Cæſar.*

It is a quarrel moſt unnatural,
To be *reveng'd* on *him* that loveth thee. *Shakeſp. Rich.* III.

Northumberland ſlew thy father;
And thine, lord Clifford; and you vow'd revenge:
If I be not, heav'ns be *reveng'd* on *me!* *Shakeſp.*

Edom hath *revenged himſelf* upon Judah. *Ezek.* xxv. 12.

O Lord, viſit me, and *revenge me* of my perſecutors. *Jer.*

Who ſhall come to ſtand againſt thee, to be *revenged* for the unrighteous men? *Wiſdom* xii. 12.

Your fury of a wife,
Not yet content to be *reveng'd* on *you*,
Th' agents of your paſſion will purſue. *Dryden.*

REVE'NGE. *n. ſ.* [*revenche*, *revanche*, Fr.] Return of an injury.

Revenges burn in them: for their dear cauſes
Would, to the bleeding and the grim alarm,
Excite the mortified man. *Shakeſp. Macbeth.*

May we, with the witneſs of a good conſcience, purſue him with further *revenge*. *Shakeſp. Merry Wives of Windſor.*

I will make mine arrows drunk with blood; from the beginning of *revenges* upon the enemy. *Deutr.* xxxii. 42.

Peradventure he will be enticed, and we ſhall prevail againſt him, and take our *revenge* on him. *Jer.* xx. 10.

Deformed perſons are commonly even with nature; for as nature has done ill by them, ſo they do by nature; being void of natural affection, they have their *revenge* of nature. *Bacon.*

What will not ambition and *revenge* deſcend to. *Milton.*

The ſatyr in a rage
Forgets his bus'neſs is to laugh and bite,
And will of death and dire *revenges* write. *Dryden.*

Draco, the Athenian lawgiver, granted an impunity to any perſon that took *revenge* upon an adulterer. *Broome.*

REVE'NGEFUL. *adj.* [frem *revenge.*] Vindictive; full of revenge; full of vengeance.

May my hands
Never brandiſh more *revengeful* ſteel
Over the glittering helmet of my foe. *Shakeſp. Rich.* II.

If thy *revengeful* heart cannot forgive,
Lo! here I lend thee this ſharp-pointed ſword,
Which hide in this true breaſt. *Shakeſp. Richard* III.

Into my borders now Jarbas falls,
And my *revengeful* brother ſcales the walls. *Denham.*

Repenting England, this *revengeful* day,
To Philip's manes did an off'ring bring. *Dryden.*

REVE'NGEFULLY. *adv.* [from *revengeful.*] Vindictively.

He ſmil'd *revengefully*, and leap'd
Upon the floor; thence gazing at the ſkies,
His eye-balls fiery red, and glowing vengeance;
Gods I accuſe you not. *Dryden and Lee's Oedipus.*

REVE'NGER. *n. ſ.* [from *revenge.*]

1. One who revenges; one who wreaks his own or another's injuries.

May be, that better reaſon will aſſwage
The raſh *revenger*'s heat; words, well diſpos'd,
Have ſecret pow'r t' appeaſe enflamed rage. *Fairy Queen.*

I do not know,
Wherefore my father ſhould *revengers* want,
Having a ſon and friends. *Shakeſp. Ant. and Cleop.*

So ſhall the great *revenger* ruinate
Him and his iſſue, by a dreadful fate. *Sandys's Paraphraſe.*

Morocco's monarch
Had come in perſon, to have ſeen and known
The injur'd world's *revenger* and his own. *Waller.*

2. One who puniſhes crimes.

What government can be imagined, without judicial proceedings? and what methods of judicature, without a religious oath, which ſuppoſes an omniſcient being, as conſcious to its falſehood or truth, and a *revenger* of perjury. *Bentley.*

REVE'NGEMENT. *n. ſ.* [from *revenge.*] Vengeance; return of an injury.

It may dwell
In her ſon's fleſh to mind *revengement*,
And be for all chaſte dames an endleſs monument. *F. Q.*

By the percloſe of the ſame verſe, vagabond is underſtood for ſuch a one as travelleth in fear of *revengement*. *Raleigh.*

REVE'NGINGLY. *adv.* [from *revenging.*] With vengeance; vindictively.

I've bely'd a lady,
The princeſs of this country; and the air on't
Revengingly enfeebles me. *Shakeſp. Cymbeline.*

RE'VENUE. *n. ſ.* [*revenu*, Fr. Its accent is uncertain.] Income; annual profits received from lands or other funds.

They privily ſend over unto them the *revenues*, wherewith they are there maintained. *Spenſer's State of Ireland.*

She bears a duke's *revenues* on her back,
And in her heart ſcorns our poverty. *Shakeſp. Hen.* VI.

Only I retain
The name and all th' addition to a king;
The ſway, *revenue*, beloved ſons, be yours. *Shakeſp.*

Many offices are of ſo ſmall *revenue*, as not to furniſh a man with what is ſufficient for the ſupport of his life. *Temple.*

If the woman could have been contented with golden eggs, ſhe might have kept that *revenue* on ſtill. *L'Eſtrange.*

His vaſſals eaſy, and the owner bleſt,
They pay a trifle, and enjoy the reſt:
Not ſo a nation's *revenues* are paid;
The ſervant's faults are on the maſter laid. *Swift.*

To REVE'RB. *v. a.* [*reverbero*, Lat.] To ſtrike againſt; to reverberate. Not in uſe.

Reſerve thy ſtate, with better judgment check
This hideous raſhneſs:
The youngeſt daughter does not love thee leaſt;
Nor are thoſe empty hearted, whoſe loud ſound
Reverbs no hollowneſs. *Shakeſp. King Lear.*

REVE'RBERANT. *adj.* [*reverberans*, Lat.] Reſounding; beating back. The reading in the following paſſage ſhould be, I think, *reverberant.*

Hollow your name to the *reverberate* hills,
And make the babbling goſſip of the air
Cry out, Olivia! *Shakeſp. Twelfth Night.*

To REVE'RBERATE. *v. a.* [*reverbero*, Lat. *reverberer*, Fr.]

1. To beat back.

Start
An echo with the clamour of thy drum,
And ev'n at hand a drum is ready brac'd,
That ſhall *reverberate* all as well as thine. *Shakeſp. K. John.*

Nor doth he know them for aught,
Till he behold them formed in th' applauſe
Where they're extended; which, like an arch, *reverb'rates*
The ſound again. *Shakeſp.*

As the ſight of the eye is like a glaſs, ſo is the ear a ſinuous cave, with a hard bone, to ſtop and *reverberate* the ſound. *Bacon.*

As we, to improve the nobler kinds of fruits, are at the expence of walls to receive and *reverberate* the faint rays of the ſun, ſo we, by the help of a good ſoil, equal the production of warmer countries. *Swift.*

2. To heat in an intenſe furnace, where the flame is reverberated upon the matter to be melted or cleaned.

Crocus martis, that is ſteel corroded with vinegar or ſulphur, and after *reverberated* with fire, the loadſtone will not attract. *Brown's Vulgar Errours.*

To REVE'RBERATE. *v. n.*

1. To be driven back; to bound back.

The rays of royal majeſty *reverberated* ſo ſtrongly upon Villerio, that they diſpelled all clouds. *Howel.*

2. To reſound.

REVERBERA'TION. *n. ſ.* [*reverberation*, Fr. from *reverberate.*] The act of beating or driving back.

To the reflection of viſibles, ſmall glaſſes ſuffice; but to the *reverberation* of audibles, are required greater ſpaces. *Bac.*

The firſt repetitions follow very thick; for two parallel walls beat the ſound back on each other, like the ſeveral *reverberations* of the ſame image from two oppoſite looking-glaſſes. *Addiſon.*

REVE'RBERATORY. *adj.* [*reverberatoire*, Fr.] Returning; beating back.

Good lime may be made of all kinds of flints, but they are hard to burn, except in a *reverberatory* kiln. *Moxon.*

To REVE'RE. *v. a.* [*reverer*, Fr. *revereor*, Lat.] To reverence; to honour; to venerate; to regard with awe.

An emperor often ſtamp'd on his coins the face or ornaments of his collegue, and we may ſuppoſe Lucius Verus would omit no opportunity of doing honour to Marcus Aurelius, whom he rather *revered* as his father, than treated as his partner in the empire. *Addiſon's Remarks on Italy.*

Jove ſhall again *revere* your pow'r,
And riſe a ſwan, or fall a ſhow'r. *Prior.*

Taught 'em how clemency made pow'r *rever'd*,
And that the prince belov'd was truly fear'd. *Prior.*

In my conqueſt be thy might declar'd,
And for thy juſtice be thy name *rever'd.* *Prior.*

RE'VERENCE. *n. ſ.* [*reverence*, Fr. *reverentia*, Lat.]

1. Veneration; reſpect; awful regard.

God is greatly to be feared in the aſſembly of the ſaints; and to be had in *reverence* of all about him. *Pſ.* lxxxix. 7.

When quarrels and factions are carried openly, it is a ſign the *reverence* of government is loſt. *Bacon's Eſſays.*

Higher of the genial bed,
And with myſterious *reverence* I deem. *Milton.*

In your prayers, uſe reverent poſtures and the loweſt geſtures of humility, remembring that we ſpeak to God, in our *reverence* to whom we cannot exceed. *Taylor.*

A poet cannot have too great a *reverence* for readers. *Dryd.*

The fear, acceptable to God, is a filial fear; an awful *reverence* of the divine nature, proceeding from a juſt eſteem of his perfections, which produces in us an inclination to his ſervice, and an unwillingneſs to offend him. *Rogers.*

2. Act of obeiſance; bow; courteſy.

Now lies he there,
And none ſo poor to do him *reverence.* *Shakeſp. Jul. Cæſ.*

Mordecai bowed not, nor did him *reverence.* *Eſth.* iii. 2.

He led her eas'ly forth,
Where Godfrey ſat among his lords and peers,
She *rev'rence* did, then bluſh'd as one diſmay'd. *Fairfax.*

Had not men the hoary heads rever'd,
Or boys paid *reverence*, when a man appear'd,
Both muſt have dy'd. *Dryden's Juvenal.*

Upſtarts the bedlam,
And *reverence* made, accoſted thus the queen. *Dryden.*

The monarch
Commands into the court the beauteous Emily:
So call'd, ſhe came; the ſenate roſe and paid
Becoming *rev'rence* to the royal maid. *Dryden.*

3. Title of the clergy.

Many now in health
Shall drop their blood, in approbation
Of what your *reverence* ſhall incite us to. *Shakeſp. Hen.* V.

4. Poetical title of a father.

O my dear father! let this kiſs
Repair thoſe violent harms, that my two ſiſters
Have in thy *reverence* made. *Shakeſp. King Lear.*

To RE'VERENCE. *v. a.* [from the noun.] To regard with reverence; to regard with awful reſpect.

Thoſe that I *rev'rence*, thoſe I fear, the wiſe;
At fools I laugh, not fear them. *Shakeſp. Cymbeline.*

While they pervert pure nature's healthful rules
To loathſome ſickneſs, worthily ſince they
God's image did not *reverence* in themſelves. *Milton.*

He ſlew Aetion, but deſpoil'd him not;
Nor in his hate the funeral rites forgot;
Arm'd as he was, he ſent him whole below,
And *reverenc'd* thus the manes of his foe. *Dryden.*

As his goodneſs will forbid us to dread him as ſlaves, ſo his majeſty will command us to *reverence* him as ſons. *Rogers.*

REVERENCER. *n. ſ.* [from *reverence.*] One who regards with reverence.

The Athenians quite ſunk in their affairs, had little commerce with the reſt of Greece, and were become great *reverencers* of crowned heads. *Swift.*

RE'VEREND. *adj.* [*reverend*, Fr. *reverendus*, Lat.]

1. Venerable; deſerving reverence; expecting reſpect by his appearance.

Let his lack of years be no impediment, to let him lack a *reverend* eſtimation. *Shakeſp. Merchant of Venice.*

Reverend and gracious ſenators. *Shakeſp.*

Onias, who had been high prieſt, *reverend* in converſation, and gentle in condition, prayed for the Jews. 2 *Mac.* xv. 12.

Rev'rend old man! lo here confeſt he ſtands. *Pope.*

2. The honorary epithet of the clergy. We ſtile a clergyman, *reverend*; a biſhop, right *reverend*; an archbiſhop, moſt *reverend*.

A *reverend* ſire among them came,
Who preach'd converſion and repentance. *Milton.*

RE'VERENT. *adj.* [*reverens*, Lat.] Humble; expreſſing ſubmiſſion; teſtifying veneration.

They forthwith to the place
Repairing where he judg'd them, proſtrate fell
Before him *reverent*. *Milton's Paradiſe Loſt.*

Meet then the ſenior, far renown'd for ſenſe,
With *rev'rent* awe, but decent confidence. *Pope.*

REVERE'NTIAL. *adj.* [*reverentielle*, Fr. from *reverent.*] Expreſſing reverence; proceeding from awe and veneration.

That oaths made in *reverential* fear
Of love and his wrath may any forſwear. *Donne.*

The leaſt degree of contempt weakens religion; it properly conſiſting in a *reverential* eſteem of things ſacred. *South.*

The reaſon of the inſtitution being forgot, the after-ages perverted it, ſuppoſing only a *reverential* gratitude paid to the earth as the common parent. *Woodward's Nat. Hiſt.*

All look up, with *reverential* awe,
At crimes that 'ſcape, or triumph o'er the law. *Pope.*

REVERE'NTIALLY. *adv.* [from *reverential.*] With ſhow of reverence.

The Jews, *reverentially* declining the ſituation of their temple, place their beds from North to South. *Brown.*

RE'VERENTLY. *adv.* [from *reverent.*] Reſpectfully; with awe; with reverence.

Chide him for faults, and do it *reverently*. *Shakeſp.*

To neareſt ports their ſhatter'd ſhips repair,
Where by our dreadful cannon they lay aw'd;
So *reverently* men quit th' open air,
When thunder ſpeaks th' angry gods abroad. *Dryden.*

Then down with all thy boaſted volumes, down;
Only reſerve the ſacred one:
Low, *reverently* low,
Make thy ſtubborn knowledge bow:
To look to heav'n be blind to all below. *Prior.*

REVE'RER. *n. ſ.* [from *revere.*] One who venerates; one who reveres.

When the divine revelations were committed to writing, the Jews were ſuch ſcrupulous *reverers* of them, that it was the buſineſs of the Maſorites, to number not only the ſections and lines, but even the words and letters of the Old Teſtament. *Government of the Tongue.*

REVE'RSAL. *n. ſ.* [from *reverſe.*] Change of ſentence.

The king, in the *reverſal* of the attainders of his partakers, had his will. *Bacon's Henry* VII.

To REVE'RSE. *v. a.* [*reverſus*, Lat.]

1. To turn upſide down.

A pyramid *reverſed* may ſtand upon his point, if balanced by admirable ſkill. *Temple's Miſcellanies.*

2. To overturn; to ſubvert.

Theſe now controul a wretched people's fate,
Theſe can divide, and theſe *reverſe* the ſtate. *Pope.*

3. To turn back.

Michael's ſword ſtay'd not;
But with ſwift wheel *reverſe*, deep entring ſhar'd
Satan's right ſide. *Milton.*

4. To contradict; to repeal.

Better it was in the eye of his underſtanding, that ſometime an erroneous ſentence definitive ſhould prevail, till the ſame authority, perceiving ſuch overſight, might afterwards correct or *reverſe* it, than that ſtrifes ſhould have reſpite to grow, and not come ſpeedily unto ſome end. *Hooker's Pref.*

A decree was made, that they had forfeited their liberties; and albeit they made great moans, yet could they not procure this ſentence to be *reverſed*. *Hayward.*

Death, his doom which I
To mitigate thus plead, not to *reverſe*,
To better life ſhall yield him. *Milton's Par. Loſt.*

Though grace may have *reverſed* the condemning ſentence, and ſealed the ſinner's pardon before God, yet it may have left no tranſcript of that pardon in the ſinner's breaſt. *South.*

Thoſe ſeem to do beſt, who, taking uſeful hints from facts, carry them in their minds to be judged of, by what they ſhall find in hiſtory to confirm or *reverſe* theſe imperfect obſervations. *Locke.*

5. To turn to the contrary.

Theſe plain characters we rarely find,
Though ſtrong the bent, yet quick the turns of mind;
Or puzzling contraries confound the whole,
Or affectations quite *reverſe* the ſoul. *Pope.*

6. To put each in the place of the other.

With what tyranny cuſtom governs men; it makes that reputable in one age, which was a vice in another, and *reverſes* even the diſtinctions of good and evil. *Rogers.*

7. To recall; to renew. Obſolete.

Well knowing true all he did rehearſe,
And to his freſh remembrance did *reverſe*
The ugly view of his deformed crimes. *Fairy Queen.*

To REVE'RSE. *v. n.* [*revertere*, *reverſus*, Lat.] To return. *Spenſ.*

REVE'RSE. *n. ſ.* [from the verb.]

1. Change; viciſſitude.

The ſtrange *reverſe* of fate you ſee;
I pity'd you, now you may pity me. *Dryden's Aurengz.*

By a ſtrange *reverſe* of things, Juſtinian's law, which for many ages was neglected, does now obtain, and the Theodoſian code is in a manner antiquated. *Baker.*

2. A contrary; an oppoſite.

Count Tariff appeared the *reverſe* of Goodman fact. *Add.*

The performances, to which God has annexed the promiſes of eternity, are juſt the *reverſe* of all the purſuits of ſenſe. *Rog.*

3. [*Revers*, Fr.] The ſide of the coin on which the head is not impreſſed.

As the Romans ſet down the image and inſcription of the conſul, afterward of the emperor on the one ſide, ſo they changed the *reverſe* always upon new events. *Camden.*

Our guard upon the royal ſide;
On the *reverſe* our beauty's pride. *Waller.*

Several *reverſes* are owned to be the repreſentations of antique figures. *Addiſon on Ancient Medals.*

REVE'RSIBLE. *adj.* [*reverſible*, Fr. from *reverſe.*] Capable of being reverſed.

REVE'RSION. *n. ſ.* [*reverſion*, Fr. from *reverſe.*]

1. The ſtate of being to be poſſeſſed after the death of the preſent poſſeſſor.

As were our England in *reverſion* his,
And he our ſubjects next degree in hope. *Shakeſp. Rich.* II.

A life in *reverſion* is not half ſo valuable, as that which may at preſent be entered on. *Hammond's Fundamentals.*

2. Succeſſion; right of ſucceſſion.

He was very old, and had out-lived moſt of his friends; many perſons of quality being dead, who had, for recompence of ſervices, procured the *reverſion* of his office. *Claren.*

Upon what ground can a man promiſe himſelf a future repentance, who cannot promiſe himſelf a futurity? whoſe life depends upon his breath, and is ſo reſtrained to the preſent, that it cannot ſecure to itſelf the *reverſion* of the very next minute. *South's Sermons.*

So many candidates there ſtand for wit,
A place at court is ſcarce ſo hard to get:
In vain they croud each other at the door;
For e'en *reverſions* are all begg'd before. *Dryden.*

REVE'RSIONARY. *adj.* [from *reverſion.*] To be enjoyed in ſucceſſion.

There are multitudes of *reverſionary* patents and *reverſionary* promiſes of preferments. *Arbuthnot.*

To REVE'RT. *v. a.* [*reverto*, Lat.]

1. To change; to turn to the contrary.

Wretched her ſubjects, gloomy ſits the queen,
Till happy chance *revert* the cruel ſcene;
And apiſh folly, with her wild reſort
Of wit and jeſt, diſturbs the ſolemn court. *Prior.*

2. To reverberate.

The ſtream boils
Around the ſtone, or from the hollow'd bank
Reverted plays in undulating flow. *Thomſon.*

To REVE'RT. *v. n.* [*revertir*, old Fr.] To return; to fall back.

My arrows,
Too ſlightly timbred for ſo loud a wind,
Would have *reverted* to my bow again. *Shakeſp. Hamlet.*

If his tenant and patentee ſhall diſpoſe of his gift without his kingly aſſent, the lands ſhall *revert* to the king. *Bacon.*

REVE'RT. *n. ſ.* [from the verb.] Return; recurrence. A muſical term.

Hath not muſick her figures the ſame with rhetorick? what is a *revert* but her antiſtrophe? *Peacham of Muſick.*

REVE'RTIBLE. *adj.* [from *revert.*] Returnable.

REVE'RY. *n. ſ.* [*reſverie*, Fr.] Looſe muſing; irregular thought.

Revery is when ideas float in our mind, without any reflection or regard of the underſtanding. *Locke.*

If the minds of men were laid open, we ſhould ſee but little difference between that of the wiſe man and that of the fool; there are infinite *reveries* and numberleſs extravagancies paſs through both. *Addiſon.*

I am really ſo far gone, as to take pleaſure in *reveries* of this kind. *Pope.*

To Reve'st. *v. a.* [*reveſtir*, *revêtir*, Fr. *reveſtio*, Lat.]
1. To clothe again.

Her, nathleſs,
Th' enchanter finding fit for his intents,
Did thus *reveſt*, and deckt with due habiliments. *Spenſer.*
When thou of life reneweſt the ſeeds,
The withered fields *reveſt* their chearful weeds. *Wotton.*

2. To reinveſt; to veſt again in a poſſeſſion or office.

Reve'stiary. *n. ſ.* [*reveſtiaire*, Fr. from *reveſtio*, Lat.] Place where dreſſes are repoſited.

The effectual power of words the Pythagoreans extolled; the impious Jews aſcribed all miracles to a name, which was ingraved in the *reveſtiary* of the temple. *Camden's Remains.*

Revi'ction. *n. ſ.* [*revictum*, Lat.] Return to life.

If the Rabines prophecy ſucceed, we ſhall conclude the days of the phenix, not in its own, but in the laſt and general flames, without all hope of *reviction*. *Brown.*

To Revi'ctual. *v. a.* [*re* and *victual.*] To ſtock with victuals again.

It hath been objected, that I put into Ireland, and ſpent much time there, taking care to *revictual* myſelf and none of the reſt. *Raleigh's Apology.*

To REVIE'W. *v. a.* [*re* and *view.*]
1. To look back.

So ſwift he flies, that his *reviewing* eye
Has loſt the chaſers, and his ear the cry. *Denham.*

2. To ſee again.

I ſhall *review* Sicilia; for whoſe ſight
I have a woman's longing. *Shakeſp. Winter's Tale.*

3. To conſider over again; to retrace; to reexamine.

Segrais ſays, that the Æneis is an imperfect work, and that death prevented the divine poet from *reviewing* it; and, for that reaſon, he had condemned it to the fire. *Dryden.*

Shall I the long laborious ſcene *review*,
And open all the wounds of Greece anew. *Pope.*

4. To ſurvey; to overlook; to examine.

Revie'w. *n. ſ.* [*reveuë*, Fr. from the verb.] Survey; reexamination.

We make a general *review* of the whole work, and a general *review* of nature; that, by comparing them, their full correſpondency may appear. *Burnet's Theory of the Earth.*

The works of nature will bear a thouſand views and *reviews*; the more narrowly we look into them, the more occaſion we ſhall have to admire. *Atterbury's Sermons.*

To REVI'LE. *v. a.* [*re* and *vile.*] To reproach; to vilify; to treat with contumely.

Aſked for their paſs by every ſquib,
That liſt at will them to *revile* or ſnib. *Spenſer.*
I read in's looks
Matter againſt me; and his eye *revil'd*
Me as his abject object. *Shakeſp. Henry VIII.*

Fear not the reproach of men, neither be afraid of their *revilings*. *Iſaiah* li. 7.

She ſtill beareth him an invincible hatred, *revileth* him to his face, and raileth at him in all companies. *Swift.*

Revi'le. *n. ſ.* [from the verb.] Reproach; contumely; exprobration. Not uſed, but elegant.

I heard thee in the garden, and of thy voice
Afraid, being naked, hid myſelf,—to whom
The gracious judge, without *revile*, reply'd. *Milton.*

Revi'ler. *n. ſ.* [from *revile.*] One who reviles; one who treats another with contumelious terms.

The bitterest *revilers* are often half-witted people. *G. of T.*

Revi'lingly. *adv.* [from *revile.*] In an opprobrious manner; with contumely.

The love I bear to the civility of expreſſion will not ſuffer me to be *revilingly* broad. *Maine.*

Revi'sal. *n. ſ.* [from *reviſe.*] Review; reexamination.

The *reviſal* of theſe letters has been a kind of examination of conſcience to me; ſo fairly and faithfully have I ſet down in them the undiſguiſed ſtate of the mind. *Pope.*

To REVI'SE. *v. a.* [*reviſus*, Lat.] To review; to overlook.

Lintot will think your price too much;
Not, Sir, if you *reviſe* it, and retouch. *Pope.*

Revi'se. *n. ſ.* [from the verb.]
1. Review; reexamination.

The author is to be excuſed, who never, in regard to his eyes and other impediments, gives himſelf the trouble of corrections and *reviſes*. *Boyle.*

2. Among printers, a ſecond proof of a ſheet corrected.

Revi'ser. *n. ſ.* [*reviſeur*, Fr. from *reviſe.*] Examiner; ſuperintendant.

Revi'sion. *n. ſ.* [*reviſion*, Fr. from *reviſe.*] Review.

To Revi'sit. *v. a.* [*reviſiter*, Fr. *reviſo*, *reviſito*, Lat.] To viſit again.

Thee I *reviſit* ſafe,
And feel thy ſov'reign vital lamp; but thou
Reviſit'ſt not theſe eyes, that rowl in vain,
To find thy piercing ray, and find no dawn. *Milton.*
Let the pale ſire *reviſit* Thebes, and bear
Theſe pleaſing orders to the tyrant's ear. *Pope's Statius.*

Revi'val. *n. ſ.* [from *revive.*] Recall from a ſtate of languour, oblivion, or obſcurity.

To REVI'VE. *v. n.* [*revivre*, Fr. *revivo*, Lat.]
1. To return to life.

The Lord heard Elijah, and the ſoul of the child came unto him again, and he *revived*. 1 *Kings* xvii. 22.

So he dies;
But ſoon *revives*: death over him no power
Shall long uſurp. *Milton.*

2. To return to vigour or fame; to riſe from languour, oblivion, or obſcurity.

I *revive* at this laſt ſight, aſſur'd that man ſhall live. *Milt.*

To Revi've. *v. a.*
1. To bring to life again.

Spot more delicious, than thoſe gardens feign'd
Of *reviv'd* Adonis. *Milton.*

2. To raiſe from languour, inſenſibility, or oblivion.

Noiſe of arms, or view of martial guiſe,
Might not *revive* deſire of knightly exerciſe. *Fa. Queen.*

God lighten our eyes, and give us a little *reviving* in our bondage. *Ezra* ix. 8.

3. To renew; to recollect; to bring back to the memory.

The memory is the power to *revive* again in our minds thoſe ideas, which after imprinting have been laid aſide out of ſight. *Locke.*

The mind has a power in many caſes to *revive* perceptions, which it has once had. *Locke.*

4. To quicken; to rouſe.

I ſhould *revive* the ſoldiers hearts;
Becauſe I ever found them as myſelf. *Shakeſp.*
What firſt Æneas in this place beheld,
Reviv'd his courage, and his fear expell'd. *Dryden.*
Old Egeus only could *revive* his ſon,
Who various changes of the world had known. *Dryden.*

Revi'ver. *n. ſ.* [from *revive.*] That which invigorates or revives.

To REVIVI'FICATE. *v. a.* [*revivifier*, Fr. *re* and *vivifico*, Lat.] To recall to life.

Revivifica'tion. *n. ſ.* [from *revivificate.*] The act of recalling to life.

As long as an infant is in the womb of its parent, ſo long are theſe medicines of *revivification* in preparing. *Spectator.*

Revivi'scency. *n. ſ.* [*reviviſco*, *reviviſcentia*, Lat.] Renewal of life.

Scripture makes mention of a reſtitution and *reviviſcency* of all things at the end of the world. *Burnet.*

Reu'nion. *n. ſ.* [*reunion*, Fr. *re* and *union.*] Return to a ſtate of juncture, coheſion, or concord.

She, that ſhould all parts to *reunion* bow,
She that had all magnetick force alone,
To draw and faſten ſundred parts in one. *Donne.*

To Reuni'te. *v. a.* [*re* and *unite.*]
1. To join again; to make one whole a ſecond time; to join what is divided.

By this match the line of Charles the great
Was *reunited* to the crown of France. *Shakeſp. Henry V.*

2. To reconcile; to make thoſe at variance one.

To Reuni'te. *v. n.* To cohere again.

Re'vocable. *adj.* [*revocable*, Fr. *revoco*, *revocabilis*, Lat.]
1. That may be recalled.

Howſoever you ſhew bitterneſs, do not act any thing that is not *revocable*. *Bacon's Eſſays.*

2. That may be repealed.

Re'vocableness. *n. ſ.* [from *revocable.*] The quality of being revocable.

To Re'vocate. *v. a.* [*revoco*, Lat.] To recall; to call back.

His ſucceſſor, by order, nullifies
Many his patents, and did *revocate*
And re-aſſume his liberalities. *Daniel's Civil War.*

Revoca'tion. *n. ſ.* [*revocation*, Fr. *revocatio*, Lat.]
1. Act of recalling.

One, that ſaw the people bent for the *revocation* of Calvin, gave him notice of their affection. *Hooker.*

2. State of being recalled.

Elaiana's king commanded Chenandra to tell him that he had received advice of his *revocation*. *Howel's Vocal Foreſt.*

3. Repeal; reverſal.

If a grievance be inflicted on a perſon, he may appeal, it is not neceſſary to pray a *revocation* of ſuch a grievance. *Ayliffe.*

To REVO'KE. *v. a.* [*revoquer*, Fr. *revoco*, Lat.]
1. To repeal; to reverſe.

That ſociety hath before conſented, without *revoking* the ſame after. *Hooker, b.* i. *ſ.* 10.

When we abrogate a law as being ill made, the whole cauſe for which it was made ſtill remaining, do we not herein *revoke* our very own deed, and upbraid ourſelves with folly, yea all that were makers of it with overſight and error. *Hook.*

What reaſon is there, but that thoſe grants and privileges ſhould be *revoked*, or reduced to the firſt intention. *Spenſer.*

Without my Aurengzebe I cannot live;
Revoke his doom, or elſe my ſentence give. *Dryden.*

2. To check; to repreſs.

She ſtrove their ſudden rages to *revoke*,
That at the laſt ſuppreſſing fury mad,
They 'gan abſtain. *Fairy Queen, b.* ii.

3. To

3. To draw back.

Shame were to *revoke*
The forward footing for an hidden shade. *Fairy Queen.*

Seas are troubled, when they do *revoke*
Their flowing waves into themselves again. *Davies.*

REVO'KEMENT. *n. s.* [from *revoke.*] Revocation; repeal; recall. Little in use.

Let it be nois'd,
That through our intercession, this *revokement*
And pardon comes. *Shakesp. Henry* VIII.

To REVO'LT. *v. n.* [*revolter*, Fr. *revoltare*, Italian.]

1. To fall off from one to another. It denotes something of pravity or rebellion.

All will *revolt* from me, and turn to him. *Shakesp.*

Our discontented counties do *revolt*,
Our people quarrel with obedience. *Shakesp. K. John.*

Jason and his company *revolted* from the kingdom. 2 *Mac.*

This people hath a *revolting* and a rebellious heart; they are *revolted* and gone. *Jer.* v. 53.

2. To change. Not in use.

You are already love's firm votary,
And cannot soon *revolt* and change your mind. *Shakesp.*

REVO'LT. *n. s.* [*revolte*, Fr. from the verb.]

1. Desertion; change of sides.

He was greatly strengthened, and the enemy as much enfeebled by daily *revolts*. *Raleigh's History of the World.*

If all our levies are made in Scotland or Ireland, may not those two parts of the monarchy be too powerful for the rest, in case of a *revolt*. *Addison's State of the War.*

2. A revolter; one who changes sides. Not in use.

You ingrate *revolts*,
You bloody Nero's, ripping up the womb
Of your dear mother England. *Shakesp. King John.*

3. Gross departure from duty.

Your daughter hath made a gross *revolt*;
Tying her duty, beauty, wit, and fortunes
To an extravagant and wheeling stranger. *Shakesp.*

REVO'LTED. *part. adj.* [from *revolt.*] Having swerved from duty.

Thou single hast maintain'd
Against *revolted* multitudes the cause of truth. *Milton.*

REVO'LTER. *n. s.* [from *revolt.*] One who changes sides; a deserter; a renegade.

Fair honour that thou dost thy God, in trusting
He will accept thee to defend his cause,
A murderer, a *revolter*, and a robber. *Milton's Agonistes.*

He was not a *revolter* from the truth, which he had once embraced. *Atterbury's Sermons.*

Those, who are negligent or *revolters*, shall perish. *Swift.*

To REVO'LVE. *v. n.* [*revolvo*, Lat.]

1. To roll in a circle; to perform a revolution.

They do not *revolve* about any common center. *Cheyne.*

If the earth *revolve* thus, each house near the equator must move a thousand miles an hour. *Watts's Impr. of the Mind.*

Each *revolving* year,
The teeming ewes a triple offspring bear. *Pope.*

2. To fall in a regular course of changing possessors; to devolve.

On the desertion of an appeal, the jurisdiction does *ipso jure revolve* to the judge *a quo*. *Ayliffe's Parergon.*

To REVO'LVE. *v. a.* [*revolvo*, Lat.]

1. To roll any thing round.

Then in the East her turn she shines,
Revolv'd on heav'n's great axis. *Milton.*

2. To consider; to meditate on.

You may *revolve* what tales I told you
Of courts, of princes, of the tricks of war. *Shakesp.*

REVOLU'TION. *n. s.* [*revolution*, Fr. *revolutus*, Lat.]

1. Course of any thing which returns to the point at which it began to move.

On their orbs impose
Such restless *revolution*, day by day
Repeated. *Milton's Paradise Lost, b.* viii.

They will be taught by the diurnal *revolution* of the heavens. *Watts's Improvement of the Mind.*

2. Space measured by some revolution.

At certain *revolutions* are they brought,
And feel by turns the bitter change. *Milton.*

Meteors have no more time allowed them for their mounting, than the short *revolution* of a day. *Dryden.*

The Persian wept over his army, that within the *revolution* of a single age, not a man would be left alive. *Wake.*

3. Change in the state of a government or country. It is used among us κατ' ἐξοχὴν, for the change produced by the admission of king William and queen Mary.

4. Rotation in general; returning motion.

Fear
Comes thund'ring back with dreadful *revolution*
On my defenseless head. *Milton.*

To REVO'MIT. *v. a.* [*revomir*, Fr. *re* and *vomit.*] To vomit; to vomit again.

They might cast it up, and take more vomiting and *revomiting* what they drink. *Hakewill on Providence.*

REVU'LSION. *n. s.* [*revulsion*, Fr. *revulsus*, Lat.] The act of revolving or drawing humours from a remote part of the body.

Derivation differs from *revulsion* only in the measure of the distance, and the force of the medicines used: if we draw it to some very remote or contrary part, we call it *revulsion*; if only to some neighbouring place, and by gentle means, we call it derivation. *Wiseman of Tumours.*

There is a way of *revulsion* to let blood in an adverse part. *Bacon's Natural History.*

I had heard of some strange cures of frenzies, by casual applications of fire to the lower parts, which seems reasonable enough, by the violent *revulsion* it may make of humours from the head. *Temple's Miscellanies.*

To REWA'RD. *v. a.* [*re* and *award*, to give in return. *Skinner.*]

1. To give in return.

Thou hast *rewarded* me good, whereas I have *rewarded* thee evil. 1 *Sam.* xxiv. 17.

They *rewarded* me evil for good. *Psalm* xxxv. 12.

2. To repay; to recompense for something good.

To judge th' unfaithful dead, but to *reward*
His faithful, and receive them into bliss. *Milton.*

The supreme being *rewards* the just, and punishes the unjust. *Broome's Notes on the Odyssey.*

REWA'RD. *n. s.* [from the verb.]

1. Recompense given for good.

Rewards and punishments do always presuppose something willingly done well or ill; without which respect, though we may sometimes receive good, yet then it is only a benefit and not a *reward*. *Hooker, b.* i. *s.* 9.

They have a good *reward* for their labour. *Eccluf.* iv. 9.

To myself I owe this due regard,
Not to make love my gift, but my *reward*. *Dryden.*

Men have consented to the immortality of the soul and the recompenses of another world, promising to themselves some *rewards* of virtue after this life. *Tillotson.*

2. It is sometimes used with a mixture of irony, for punishment or recompense of evil.

REWA'RDABLE. *adj.* [from *reward.*] Worthy of reward.

Men's actions are judged, whether in their own nature *rewardable* or punishable. *Hooker, b.* i. *s.* 9.

The action that is but indifferent, and without reward, if done only upon our own choice, is an act of religion, and *rewardable* by God, if done in obedience to our superiors. *Taylor's Rule of Living Holy.*

REWA'RDER. *n. s.* [from *reward.*] One that rewards; one that recompenses.

A liberal *rewarder* of his friends. *Shakesp. Rich.* III.

As the supreme Being is the only proper judge of our perfections, so is he the only fit *rewarder* of them. *Addison.*

Ill judges, as well as *rewarders*, have popular assemblies been, of those who best deserved from them. *Swift.*

To REWO'RD. *v. a.* [*re* and *word.*] To repeat in the same words.

Bring me to the test,
And I the matter will *reword*; which madness
Would gambol from. *Shakesp. Hamlet.*

RHABA'RBARATE. *adj.* [from *rhabarbara*, Lat.] Impregnated or tinctured with rhubarb.

The salt humours must be evacuated by the sennate, *rhabarbarate*, and sweet manna purgers, with acids added, or the purging waters. *Floyer on the Humours.*

RHA'BDOMANCY. *n. s.* [ῥάβδος and μαντεία.] Divination by a wand.

Of peculiar *rhabdomancy* is that which is used in mineral discoveries, with a forked hazel, commonly called Moses's rod, which, freely held forth, will stir and play if any mine be under it. *Brown's Vulgar Errours.*

RHA'PSODIST. *n. s.* [from *rhapsody.*] One who writes without regular dependence of one part upon another.

Ask our *rhapsodist*, if you have nothing but the excellence and loveliness of virtue to preach, and no future rewards or punishments, how many vicious wretches will you ever reclaim. *Watts's Improvement of the Mind.*

RHA'PSODY. *n. s.* [ῥαψῳδία; ῥάπτω, to sew, and ᾠδὴ, a song.] Any number of parts joined together, without necessary dependence or natural connection.

Such a deed, as sweet religion makes
A *rhapsody* of words. *Shakesp. Hamlet.*

This confusion and *rhapsody* of difficulties was not to be supposed in each single sinner. *Hammond.*

He, that makes no reflexions on what he reads, only loads his mind with a *rhapsody* of tales fit for the entertainment of others. *Locke.*

The words slide over the ears, and vanish like a *rhapsody* of evening tales. *Watts's Improvement of the Mind.*

RHE'TORICK. *n. s.* [ῥητορικὴ; *rhetorique*, Fr.]

1. The act of speaking not merely with propriety, but with art and elegance.

We could not allow him an orator, who had the best thoughts, and who knew all the rules of *rhetorique*, if he had not acquired the art of using them. *Dryden's Dufresnoy.*

Of the passions, and how they are moved, Aristotle, in his second book of *rhetorick*, hath admirably discoursed in a little compass. *Locke's Thoughts on Reading.*

Grammar teacheth us to speak properly, *rhetorick* instructs to speak elegantly. *Baker's Reflections on Learning.*

2. The power of persuasion; oratory.

The heart's still *rhetorick*, disclos'd with eyes. *Shakesp.*

His sober lips then did he softly part,
Whence of pure *rhetorick* whole streams outflow. *Fairfax.*

Enjoy your dear wit and gay *rhetorick*,
That hath so well been taught her dazling fence. *Milton.*

RHETO'RICAL. *adj.* [*rhetoricus*, Lat. from *rhetorick.*] Pertaining to rhetorick; oratorial; figurative.

The apprehension is so deeply riveted into my mind, that *rhetorical* flourishes cannot at all loosen it. *More.*

Because Brutus and Cassius met a blackmore, and Pompey had on a dark garment at Pharsalia, these were presages of their overthrow, which notwithstanding are scarce *rhetorical* sequels; concluding metaphors from realities, and from conceptions metaphorical inferring realities again. *Brown.*

The subject moral, logical, or *rhetorical*, which does not come under our senses. *Watts's Improvement of the Mind.*

RHETO'RICALLY. *adv.* [from *rhetorical.*] Like an orator; figuratively; with intent to move the passions.

To RHETO'RICATE. *v. n.* [*rhetoricor*, low Lat. from *rhetorick.*] To play the orator; to attack the passions.

'Twill be much more seasonable to reform, than apologize or *rhetoricate*; not to suffer themselves to perish in the midst of such solicitations to be saved. *Decay of Piety.*

RHETORI'CIAN. *n. s.* [*rhetoricien*, Fr. *rhetor*, Lat.] One who teaches the science of rhetorick.

The ancient sophists and *rhetoricians*, which ever had young auditors, lived till they were an hundred years old. *Bacon.*

'Tis the business of *rhetoricians* to treat the characters of the passions. *Dryden's Dufresnoy.*

A man may be a very good *rhetorician*, and yet at the same time a mean orator. *Baker's Reflections on Learning.*

RHETORI'CIAN. *adj.* Suiting a master of rhetorick.

Boldly presum'd with *rhetorician* pride,
To hold of any question either side. *Blackmore.*

RHEUM. *n. s.* [ῥεῦμα; *rheume*, Fr.] A thin watery matter oozing through the glands, chiefly about the mouth. *Quincy.*

Trust not those cunning waters of his eyes;
For villainy is not without such a *rheum*;
And he long traded in it, makes it seem
Like rivers of remorse. *Shakesp.*

You did void your *rheum* upon my beard. *Shakesp.*

Why holds thine eye that lamentable *rheum*,
Like a proud river peering o'er his bounds. *Shakesp.*

Each changing season does its poison bring,
Rheums chill the winter, agues blast the spring. *Prior.*

RHEU'MATICK. *adj.* [ῥευματικός; from *rheum.*] Proceeding from rheum or a peccant watry humour.

The moon, the governess of floods,
Pale in her anger, washes all the air,
That *rheumatick* diseases do abound. *Shakesp.*

The blood taken away looked very sizy or *rheumatick. Floy.*

RHEU'MATISM. *n. s.* [ῥευματισμός; *rheumatisme*, Fr. *rheumatismus*, Lat.] A painful distemper supposed to proceed from acrid humours.

Rheumatism is a distemper affecting chiefly the membrana communis musculorum, which it makes rigid and unfit for motion; and it seems to be occasioned almost by the same causes, as the mucilaginous glands in the joints are rendered stiff and gritty in the gout. *Quincy.*

The throtling quinsey 'tis my star appoints,
And *rheumatisms* I send to rack the joints. *Dryden.*

RHEU'MY. *adj.* [from *rheum.*] Full of sharp moisture.

Is Brutus sick?
And will he steal out of his wholsome bed,
To dare the vile contagion of the night?
And tempt the *rheumy* and unpurged air,
To add unto his sickness. *Shakesp. Julius Cæsar.*

The South he loos'd, who night and horror brings,
And fogs are shaken from his flaggy wings:
From his divided beard two streams he pours;
His head and *rheumy* eyes distil in show'rs. *Dryden.*

RHINO'CEROS. *n. s.* [ῥὶν and κέρας; *rhinocerot*, Fr.] A vast beast in the East Indies armed with a horn in his front.

Approach thou like the rugged Russian bear,
The arm'd *rhinoceros*, or Hyrcanian tyger;
Take any shape but that, and my firm nerves
Shall never tremble. *Shakesp. Macbeth.*

If you draw your beast in an emblem, shew a landscape of the country natural to the beast; as to the *rhinoceros* an East Indian landscape, the crocodile, an Egyptian. *Peacham.*

RHOMB. *n. s.* [*rhombe*, Fr. *rhombus*, Lat. ῥόμβος.] In geometry, a parallelogram or quadrangular figure, having its four sides equal, and consisting of parallel lines, with two opposite angles acute, and two obtuse: it is formed by two equal and right cones joined together at their base. *Trevoux and Harris.*

Save the sun his labour, and that swift
Nocturnal and diurnal *rhomb* suppos'd
Invisible else above all stars, the wheel
Of day and night. *Milton.*

See how in warlike muster they appear,
In *rhombs* and wedges, and half moons and wings. *Milton.*

RHO'MBICK. *adj.* [from *rhomb.*] Shaped like a rhomb.

Many other sorts of stones are regularly figured; the asteria in form of a star, and they are of a *rhombick* figure. *Grew.*

RHO'MBOID. *n. s.* [ῥομβοειδὴς; *rhomboïde*, Fr.] A figure approaching to a rhomb.

Many other sorts of stones are regularly figured; and they are of a rhombick figure; talk, of such as are *rhomboid. Grew.*

RHOMBOI'DAL. *adj.* [from *rhomboid.*] Approaching in shape to a rhomb.

Another *rhomboidal* selenites of a compressed form, had many others infixed round the middle of it. *Woodward.*

RHU'BARB. *n. s.* [*rhabarbara*, Lat.] A medicinal root slightly purgative, referred by botanists to the dock.

What *rhubarb*, senna, or what purgative drug
Would scour these English hence. *Shakesp. Macbeth.*

Having fixed the fontanel, I purged him with an infusion of *rhubarb* in small ale. *Wiseman's Surgery.*

RHYME. *n. s.* [ῥυθμός; *rhythme*, Fr.]

1. A harmonical succession of sounds.

2. The consonance of verses; the correspondence of the last sound of one verse to the last sound or syllable of another.

The youth with songs and *rhimes*:
Some dance, some hale the rope. *Denham.*

For *rhyme* the rudder is of verses,
With which like ships they steer their courses. *Hudibras.*

Such was the news, indeed, but songs and *rhymes*
Prevail as much in these hard iron times;
As would a plump of trembling fowl, that rise
Against an eagle sousing from the skies. *Dryden.*

If Cupid throws a single dart,
We make him wound the lover's heart;
But if he takes his bow and quiver,
'Tis sure he must transfix the liver;
For *rhime* with reason may dispense,
And sound has right to govern sense. *Prior.*

3. Poetry; a poem.

All his manly power it did disperse,
As he were warmed with inchanted *rhimes*,
That oftentimes he quak'd. *Fairy Queen, b.* i.

Who would not sing for Lycidas? he knew
Himself to sing, and build the lofty *rhyme*. *Milton.*

Now sportive youth,
Carol incondite *rhythms* with suiting notes,
And quaver inharmonious. *Philips.*

RHYME or *reason.* Number or sense.

I was promis'd on a time,
To have *reason* for my *rhyme*;
But from that time unto this season,
I had neither *rhyme* nor *reason*. *Spenser.*

The guiltiness of my mind drove the grosness of the foppery into a received belief, in despight of the teeth of all *rhime* and *reason*, that they were fairies. *Shakesp.*

To RHYME. *v. n.*

1. To agree in sound.

He was too warm on picking work to dwell,
But fagotted his notions as they fell,
And, if they *rhim'd* and rattled, all was well. *Dryden.*

2. To make verses.

These fellows of infinite tongue, that can *rhime* themselves into ladies favours, they do always reason themselves out again. *Shakesp. Henry* V.

There march'd the bard and blockhead, side by side,
Who *rhym'd* for hire, and patroniz'd for pride. *Dunciad.*

RHY'MER. } *n. s.* [from *rhyme.*] One who makes rhymes;
RHY'MSTER. } a versifier; a poet in contempt.

Scall'd *rhimers* will ballad us out o' tune. *Shakesp.*

It was made penal to the English, to permit the Irish to graze upon their lands, to entertain any of their minstrels, *rhimers*, or news-tellers. *Davies on Ireland.*

Rhymer come on, and do the worst you can;
I fear not you, nor yet a better man. *Dryden.*

His rhime is constrained at an age, when the passion of love makes every man a *rhimer*, though not a poet. *Dryden.*

I speak of those who are only *rhimsters*. *Dennis.*

So modern *rhimers* wisely blast
The poetry of ages past,
And from its ruin build their own. *Shakesp.*

RHY'THMICAL. *adj.* [ῥυθμικὸς; *rythmique*, Fr. from *rhyme* or *rhythm.*] Harmonical; having proportion of one sound to another.

RIB. *n. s.* [ꞃibbe, Saxon.] A bone in the body.

1. Of these there are twenty-four in number, *viz.* twelve on each side the twelve vertebræ of the back; they are segments of a circle; they grow flat and broad, as they approach the sternum; but the nearer they are to the vertebræ, the rounder and thicker they are; at which end they have a round head, which, being covered with a cartilage, is received into the sinus in the bodies of the vertebræ: the *ribs*, thus articulated, make an acute angle with the lower vertebræ: the *ribs* have each a small canal or sinus, which runs along their under sides, in which lies a nerve, vein, and artery: their extremities, which are fastened to the sternum, are cartilaginous, and the cartilages make an obtuse angle with the bony part of the *ribs*; this angle respects the head: the cartilages are harder

harder in women than in men, that they may better bear the weight of their breaſts: the *ribs* are of two ſorts; the ſeven upper are called true *ribs*, becauſe their cartilaginous ends are received into the ſinus of the ſternum: the five lower are called falſe *ribs*, becauſe they are ſofter and ſhorter, of which only the firſt is joined to the extremity of the ſternum, the cartilaginous extremities of the reſt being tied to one another, and thereby leaving a greater ſpace for the dilatation of the ſtomach and intrails: the laſt of theſe ſhort *ribs* is ſhorter than all the reſt: it is not tied to them, but ſometimes to the muſculus obliquus deſcendens. *Quincy.*

Why do I yield to that ſuggeſtion?
Whoſe horrid image doth upfix my hair,
And make my ſeated heart knock at my *ribs*,
Againſt the uſe of nature! *Shakeſp. Macbeth.*

He open'd my left ſide, and took
From thence a *rib*, with cordial ſpirits warm
And life blood ſtreaming freſh. *Milton's Par. Loſt, b.* viii.

He, who firſt the paſſage try'd,
In harden'd oak his heart did hide,
And *ribs* of iron arm'd his ſide,
Who tempted firſt the briny flood. *Dryden's Horace.*

2. Any piece of timber or other matter which ſtrengthens the ſide.

I ſhould not ſee the ſandy hour glaſs run,
But I ſhould think of ſhallows and of flats;
And ſee my wealthy Andrew dock'd in ſand,
Vailing her high top lower than her *ribs*,
To kiſs her burial. *Shakeſp. Merchant of Venice.*

RI'BALD. *n. ſ.* [*ribauld*, Fr. *ribaldo*, Italian.] A looſe, rough, mean, brutal wretch.

That lewd *ribbald*, with vile luſt advanced,
Laid firſt his filthy hands on virgin clean,
To ſpoil her dainty corſe ſo fair and ſheen. *Fairy Queen.*

Your *ribauld* nag of Egypt,
The breeze upon her, like a cow in June,
Hoiſts ſails, and flies. *Shakeſp. Antony and Cleopatra.*

The buſy day,
Wak'd by the lark, has rous'd the *ribald* crows,
And dreaming night will hide our joys no longer. *Shakeſp.*

Ne'er one ſprig of laurel grac'd theſe *ribbalds*,
From ſlaſhing Bentley down to pidling Tibbalds. *Pope.*

RI'BALDRY. *n. ſ.* [from *ribald*; *ribaudie*, old Fr.] Mean, lewd, brutal language.

Mr. Cowley aſſerts, that obſcenity has no place in wit; Buckingham ſays, 'tis an ill ſort of wit, which has nothing more to ſupport it than bare-faced *ribaldry*. *Dryden.*

The *ribaldry* of the low characters is different; the reeve, miller, and cook are diſtinguiſhed from each other. *Dryden.*

In the ſame antique loom theſe ſcenes were wrought,
Embelliſh'd with good morals and juſt thought,
True nature in her nobleſt light you ſee,
E'er yet debauch'd by modern gallantry
To trifling jeſts and fulſom *ribaldry*. *Granville.*

If the outward profeſſion of religion were once in practice among men in office, the clergy would ſee their duty and intereſt in qualifying themſelves for lay-converſation, when once they were out of fear of being choaked by *ribaldry* or prophaneneſs. *Swift.*

RI'BAND. *n. ſ.* [*rubande*, *ruban*, Fr.] A filet of ſilk; a narrow web of ſilk, which is worn for ornament.

Quaint in green, ſhe ſhall be looſe enrob'd,
With *ribbands* pendent, flaring 'bout her head. *Shakeſp.*

A *ribband* did the braided treſſes bind,
The reſt was looſe. *Dryden's Knight's Tale.*

See! in the liſts they wait the trumpets ſound;
Some love device is wrought on ev'ry ſword,
And ev'ry *riband* bears ſome myſtick word. *Granville.*

RI'BBED. *adj.* [from *rib.*]

1. Furniſhed with ribs.

Was I by rocks engender'd? *rib'd* with ſteel?
Such tortures to reſiſt, or not to feel? *Sandys.*

Hung on each bough a ſingle leaf appears,
Which ſhrivell'd in its infancy remains,
Like a clos'd fan, nor ſtretches wide its veins,
But as the ſeaſons in their circle run,
Opes its *ribb'd* ſurface to the nearer ſun. *Gay.*

2. Incloſed as the body by ribs.

Remember
The nat'ral brav'ry of your iſle, which ſtands
As Neptune's park, *ribbed* and paled in,
With rocks unſcaleable, and roaring waters. *Shakeſp.*

RI'BBON. *n. ſ.* See RIBAND.

To RI'BROAST. *v. n.* [*rib* and *roaſt.*] To beat ſoundly. A burleſque word.

That done, he riſes, humbly bows,
And gives thanks for the princely blows;
Departs not meanly proud, and boaſting
Of his magnificent *ribroaſting*. *Butler.*

I have been pinched in fleſh, and well *ribroaſted* under my former maſters; but I'm in now for ſkin and all. *L'Eſtrange.*

RI'BWORT. *n. ſ.* A plant.

RIC. *n. ſ.* *Ric* denotes a powerful, rich, or valiant man; as in theſe verſes of Fortunatus:

Hilperice potens, ſi interpres barbarus adſit,
Adjutor fortis hoc quoque nomen habet.
Hil'pric Barbarians a ſtout helper term.

So Alfric is altogether ſtrong; Æthelric, nobly ſtrong or powerful: to the ſame ſenſe as Polycrates, Crato, Plutarchus, Opimius. *Gibſon's Camden.*

RICE. *n. ſ.* [*oryza*, Lat.] One of the eſculent grains: it hath its grains diſpoſed into a panicle, which are almoſt of an oval figure, and are covered with a thick huſk, ſomewhat like barley: this grain is greatly cultivated in moſt of the Eaſtern countries. *Miller.*

Rice is the food of two thirds of mankind; it is kindly to human conſtitutions, proper for the conſumptive, and thoſe ſubject to hæmorrhages. *Arbuthnot.*

If the ſnuff get out of the ſnuffers, it may fall into a diſh of *rice* milk. *Swift's Directions to the Butler.*

RICH. *adj.* [*riche*, Fr. *ricco*, Italian; rica, Saxon.]

1. Wealthy; abounding in wealth; abounding in money or poſſeſſions; opulent.

I am as *rich* in having ſuch a jewel,
As twenty ſeas, if all their ſand were pearl. *Shakeſp.*

The *rich* ſhall not give more, and the poor no leſs. *Exod.*

A thief bent to unhoard the caſh
Of ſome *rich* burgher. *Milton.*

Several nations of the Americans are *rich* in land, and poor in all the comforts of life. *Locke.*

He may look upon the *rich* as benefactors, who have beautified the proſpect all around him. *Seed.*

2. Valuable; eſtimable; precious; ſplendid; ſumptuous.

Earth, in her *rich* attire,
Conſummate lovely ſmil'd. *Milton.*

3. Having any ingredients or qualities in a great quantity or degree.

So we th' Arabian coaſt do know
At diſtance, when the ſpices blow,
By the *rich* odour taught to ſteer,
Though neither day nor ſtar appear. *Waller.*

If life be ſhort, it ſhall be glorious,
Each minute ſhall be *rich* in ſome great action. *Rowe.*

Sauces and *rich* ſpices are fetched from India. *Baker.*

4. Fertile; fruitful.

There are, who fondly ſtudious of increaſe,
Rich foreign mold on their ill-natur'd land
Induce. *Philips.*

RICHED. *adj.* [from *rich.*] enriched. Obſolete.

Of all theſe bounds,
With ſhadowy foreſts, and with champions *rich'd*,
With plenteous rivers and wide ſkirted meads,
We make thee lady. *Shakeſp. King Lear.*

RI'CHES. *n. ſ.* [*richeſſes*, Fr.]

1. Wealth; money or poſſeſſion.

The inſtrumentalneſs of *riches* to charity has rendered it neceſſary by laws to ſecure propriety. *Hammond.*

Chemiſts ſeek *riches* by tranſmutation and the great elixir. *Sprat.*

Riches do not conſiſt in having more gold and ſilver, but in having more in proportion than our neighbours, whereby we are enabled to procure to ourſelves a greater plenty of the conveniencies of life, than comes within their reach, who, ſharing the gold and ſilver of the world in a leſs proportion, want the means of plenty and power, and ſo are poorer. *Locke.*

What *riches* give us, let us firſt enquire,
Meat, fire, and cloaths; what more? meat, cloaths, and fire. *Pope.*

2. Splendid ſumptuous appearance.

The *riches* of heav'ns pavement, trodden gold. *Milton.*

RI'CHLY. *adv.* [from *rich.*]

1. With riches; wealthily; ſplendidly; magnificently.

In Belmont is a lady *richly* left,
And ſhe is fair, of wondrous virtues. *Shakeſp.*

Women *richly* gay in gems. *Milton.*

2. Plenteouſly.

In animals, ſome ſmells are found more *richly* than in plants. *Brown's Vulgar Errours.*

After a man has ſtudied the laws of England, the reading the reports of adjudged caſes will *richly* improve him. *Watts.*

3. Truly; abundantly. An ironical uſe.

There is ſuch licentiouſneſs among the baſeſt of the people, that one would not be ſorry to ſee them beſtowing upon one another a chaſtiſement, which they ſo *richly* deſerve. *Addiſon.*

RI'CHNESS. *n. ſ.* [from *rich.*]

1. Opulence; wealth.

Of virtue you have left proof to the world;
And virtue is grateful with beauty and *richneſs* adorn'd. *Sid.*

2. Finery; ſplendour.

3. Fertility; fecundity; fruitfulneſs.

This town is famous for the *richneſs* of the ſoil. *Addiſon.*

4. Abundance or perfection of any quality.

I amuſed myſelf with the *richneſs* and variety of colours in the weſtern parts of heaven. *Spectator.*

5. Pampering qualities.

The lively tincture of whoſe guſhing blood
Shou'd clearly prove the *richneſs* of his food. *Dryden.*

RICK. *n. ſ.* See REEK.

1. A pile of corn or hay regularly heaped up in the open field, and ſheltered from wet.

An inundation
O'erflowed a farmer's barn and ſtable;
Whole *ricks* of hay and ſtacks of corn
Were down the ſudden current born. *Swift.*

Mice and rats do great injuries in the field, houſes, barns, and corn *ricks*. *Mortimer's Huſbandry.*

2. A heap of corn or hay piled by the gatherer.

In the North they bind them up in ſmall bundles, and make ſmall *ricks* of them in the field. *Mortimer's Huſbandry.*

RI'CKETS. *n. ſ.* [*rachitis*, Lat. A name given to the diſtemper at its appearance by *Gliſſon.*]

The *rickets* is a diſtemper in children, from an unequal diſtribution of nouriſhment, whereby the joints grow knotty, and the limbs uneven: its cure is performed by evacuation and friction. *Quincy.*

In ſome years, liver-grown, ſpleen, and *rickets* are put altogether, by reaſon of their likeneſs. *Graunt's Bills of Mort.*

O were my pupil fairly knock'd o' th' head,
I ſhou'd poſſeſs th' eſtate, if he were dead;
He's ſo far gone with the *rickets* and th' evil,
That one ſmall doſe will ſend him to the devil. *Dryden.*

So when at ſchool we firſt declaim,
Old Buſby walks us in a theme,
Whoſe props ſupport our infant vein,
And help the *rickets* in the brain;
But when our ſouls their force dilate,
Our thoughts grow up to wit's eſtate. *Prior.*

RI'CKETY. *adj.* [from *rickets.*] Diſeaſed with the rickets.

In a young animal, when the ſolids are too lax, the caſe of *rickety* children, the diet ſhould be gently aſtringent. *Arb.*

RI'CKLUS. *n. ſ.* A plant. *Ainſworth.*

RI'CTURE. *n. ſ.* [*rictura*, Lat.] A gaping. *Dict.*

RID. pret. of *ride*.

To RID. *v. a.* [from hreddan, Saxon.]

1. To ſet free; to redeem.

It is he that delivereth me from my cruel enemies; thou ſhalt *rid* me from the wicked man. *Pſalm* xviii. 49.

Rid me, and deliver me out of great waters. *Pſalm* cxliv.

I will bring you out from under their burthens, and *rid* you out of their bondage. *Exodus* vi. 6.

2. To clear; to diſencumber.

They were not before ſo willing to be *rid* of their learned paſtor, as now importunate to obtain him again from them, who had given him entertainment. *Hooker.*

I muſt *rid* all the ſeas of pirates. *Shakeſp.*

We'll uſe his countenance; which being done,
Let her, who would be *rid* of him, deviſe
His ſpeedy taking off. *Shakeſp. King Lear.*

Upon the word, ſtept forth
Three of thy crew, to *rid* thee of that care. *B. Johnſon.*

I can put on
Thy terrors, as I put thy mildneſs on,
Image of thee in all things; and ſhall ſoon,
Arm'd with thy might, *rid* heav'n of theſe rebell'd. *Milton.*

Did ſaints for this bring in their plate;
For when they thought the cauſe had need on't,
Happy was he that could be *rid* on't. *Hudibras.*

The god uneaſy till he ſlept again,
Reſolv'd at once to *rid* himſelf of pain. *Dryden.*

At any rate we deſire to be *rid* of the preſent evil, which we are apt to think nothing abſent can equal. *Locke.*

The greater viſible good does not always raiſe men's deſire, in proportion to the greatneſs it appears to have; though every little trouble moves us, and ſets on work to get *rid* of it. *Locke.*

The ladies aſked, whether we believed that the men of any town would, at the ſame conjuncture, have loaden themſelves with their wives; or rather, whether they would not have been glad of ſuch an opportunity to get *rid* of them? *Addiſon.*

The father, ſeeing himſelf entirely *rid* of Theodoſius, was not very much concerned at the obſtinate refuſal of his daughter. *Addiſon's Spectator*, N° 164.

3. To diſpatch.

Having the beſt at Barnet field,
We'll thither ſtraight; for willingneſs *rids* away. *Shakeſp.*

4. To drive away; to preſs away; to deſtroy.

Ah deathſmen! you have *rid* this ſweet young prince. *Sha.*

RI'DDANCE. *n. ſ.* [from *rid.*]

1. Deliverance.

Deliverance from ſudden death, *riddance* from all adverſity, and the extent of ſaving mercy towards all men. *Hooker.*

2. Diſencumbrance; loſs of ſomething one is glad to loſe.

I have too griev'd a heart
To take a tedious leave: thus loſers part.
—A gentle *riddance*. *Shakeſp. Merchant of Venice.*

By this, the cock had a good *riddance* of his rival. *L'Eſtr.*

3. Act of clearing away any encumbrances.

Thoſe bloſſoms, and thoſe dropping gums,
That lie beſtrown, unſightly and unſmooth,
Aſk *riddance*, if we mean to tread with eaſe. *Milton.*

RI'DDEN. the participle of *ride*.

He could never have *ridden* out an eternal period, but it muſt be by a more powerful being than himſelf. *Hale.*

RI'DDLE. *n. ſ.* [rædelſ, Saxon, from ræde, counſel, perhaps a trial of wit.]

1. An enigma; a puzzling queſtion; a dark problem.

How did you dare
To trade and traffick with Macbeth,
In *riddles* and in charms of death. *Shakeſp. Macbeth.*

The Theban monſter, that propos'd
Her *riddle*, and him, who ſolv'd it not, devour'd;
That once found out and ſolv'd, for grief and ſpight
Caſt herſelf headlong from the Iſmenian ſteep. *Milton.*

Her mother was thinking of a *riddle*. *Dryden.*

2. Any thing puzzling.

'Twas a ſtrange *riddle* of a lady;
Not love, if any lov'd her: hey day!
So cowards never uſe their might,
But againſt ſuch as will not fight. *Hudibras.*

3. [hriddle, Saxon.] A coarſe or open ſieve.

Horſe-beans and tares, ſown together, are eaſily parted with a *riddle*. *Mortimer's Huſbandry.*

To RI'DDLE. *v. a.* [from the noun.]

1. To ſolve; to unriddle. There is ſomething of whimſical analogy between the two ſenſes of the word *riddle*: as, we ſay, *to* ſift *a queſtion:* but their derivations differ.

Riddle me this, and gueſs him if you can,
Who bears a nation in a ſingle man? *Dryden's Juvenal.*

2. To ſeparate by a coarſe ſieve.

The fineſt ſifted mould muſt be *riddled* in. *Mortimer.*

To RI'DDLE. *v. n.* [from the noun.] To ſpeak ambiguouſly or obſcurely.

Be plain, good ſon, and homely in thy drift;
Riddling confeſſion finds but *riddling* ſhrift. *Shakeſp.*

RI'DDLINGLY. *adv.* [from *riddle.*] In the manner of a riddle.

Though like the peſtilence and old-faſhion'd love,
Riddlingly it catch men, and doth remove
Never, till it be ſtarv'd out, yet their ſtate
Is poor. *Donne:*

To RIDE. *v. n.* preter. *rid* or *rode*; part. *rid* or *ridden.* [ridan, Saxon; *rijden*, Dutch.]

1. To travel on horſeback.

Brutus and Caſſius
Are *rid*, like madmen, through the gates of Rome. *Shak.*

Were you but *riding* forth to air yourſelf,
Such parting were too petty. *Shakeſp. Cymbeline.*

Am not I thine aſs, upon which thou haſt *ridden*? *Numb.*

So ſtands a foreſt tall of mountain oaks
Advanc'd to mighty growth; the traveller
Hears from the humble valley, where he *rides*,
The hollow murmurs of the winds that blow
Amidſt the boughs. *Addiſon's Remarks on Italy.*

Let your maſter *ride* on before, and do you gallop after him. *Swift's Directions to the Groom.*

2. To travel in a vehicle; to be borne, not to walk.

Infected be the air whereon they *ride*. *Shakeſp.*

Upon this chaos *rid* the diſtreſſed ark, that bore the ſmall remains of mankind. *Burnet's Theory of the Earth.*

3. To be ſupported in motion.

As venerable Neſtor, hatch'd in ſilver,
Should with a bond of air, ſtrong as the axle-tree,
On which heav'n *rides*, knit all the Grecian ears
To his experienc'd tongue. *Shakeſp. Troilus and Creſſida:*

4. To manage an horſe.

Skill to *ride* ſeems a ſcience,
Proper to gentle blood; ſome others feign,
To manage ſteeds, as did this vaunter; but in vain. *F. Q.*

The horſes I ſaw well choſen, *ridden*, and furniſhed. *Shak.*

Inſpir'd by love, whoſe buſineſs is to pleaſe,
He *rode*, he fenc'd, he mov'd with graceful eaſe. *Dryden.*

5. To be on the water.

On the Weſtern coaſt
Rideth a puiſſant army. *Shakeſp. Rich.* III.

The ſea was grown ſo rough, that the admiral was not able longer to *ride* it out with his gallies; but was enforced to ſlip his anchors, and run his gallies on ground. *Knolles.*

They were then in a place to be aided by their ſhips, which *rode* near in Edinburgh Frith. *Hayward.*

Waiting him his royal fleet did *ride*,
And willing winds to their low'r'd ſails deny'd. *Dryden.*

Men once walk'd where ſhips at anchor *ride*. *Dryden.*

Now on their coaſts our conquering navy *rides*,
Way-lays their merchants, and their land beſets. *Dryden.*

6. To be ſupported by ſomething ſubſervient.

A credulous father, and a brother noble,
Whoſe nature is ſo far from doing harms,
That he ſuſpects none; on whoſe fooliſh honeſty
My practices *ride* eaſy. *Shakeſp. King Lear.*

To RIDE. *v. a.* To manage inſolently at will.

Humility does not make us ſervile or inſenſible, nor oblige us to be *ridden* at the pleaſure of every coxcomb. *Collier.*

The nobility could no longer endure to be *ridden* by bakers, coblers and brewers. *Swift's Preſbyterian Plea.*

RI'DER. *n. ſ.* [from *ride.*]

1. One who is carried on a horſe or in a vehicle.

The ſtrong camel and the gen'rous horſe,
Reſtrain'd and aw'd by man's inferior force,
Do to the *rider*'s will their rage ſubmit,
And anſwer to the ſpur, and own the bit. *Prior.*

2. One who manages or breaks horſes.

His horſes are bred better; and to that end *riders* dearly hired. *Shakeſp. As You Like it.*

I would with jockies from Newmarket dine,
And to rough *riders* give my choiceſt wine. *Bramſton.*

3. An inſerted leaf.

RIDGE. *n. ſ.* [hꞃıʒʒ, Saxon; *rig*, Daniſh; *rugge*, Dutch, the back.]

1. The top of the back.

He thought it was no time to ſtay;
But in a trice advanc'd the knight
Upon the bare *ridge* bolt upright. *Hudibras.*

2. The rough top of any thing, reſembling the vertebræ of the back.

As when a vulture on Imaus bred,
Whoſe ſnowy *ridge* the roving Tartar bounds,
Diſlodges from a region ſcarce of prey. *Milton.*
His ſons
Shall dwell to Seir, on that long *ridge* of hills! *Milton.*

The higheſt *ridges* of thoſe mountains ſerve for the maintenance of cattle for the inhabitants of the vallies. *Ray.*

3. A ſteep protuberance.

Part riſe in cryſtal wall, or *ridge* direct,
For haſte. *Milton's Paradiſe Loſt, b.* vii.
About her coaſts unruly waters roar,
And, riſing on a *ridge*, inſult the ſhore. *Dryden.*

4. The ground thrown up by the plow.

Thou viſiteſt the earth; thou watereſt the *ridges* thereof abundantly; thou ſettleſt the furrows thereof. *Pſalm* lxv. 10.

The body is ſmooth on that end, and on this 'tis ſet with *ridges* round the point. *Woodward.*

Wheat muſt be ſowed above furrow fourteen days before Michaelmas, and laid up in round high warm *ridges*. *Mort.*

Land for graſs lay down when you ſow wheat or rye; but then your corn ſhould be ſowed on broad *ridges*. *Mortimer.*

5. The top of the roof riſing to an acute angle.

Ridge tiles or roof tiles, being in length thirteen inches, and made circular breadthways like an half cylinder, whoſe diameter is about ten inches or more, and about half an inch and half a quarter in thickneſs, are laid upon the upper part or *ridge* of the roof, and alſo on the hips. *Moxon.*

6. *Ridges* of a horſe's mouth are wrinkles or riſings of the fleſh in the roof of the mouth, running acroſs from one ſide of the jaw to the other like fleſhy *ridges*, with interjacent furrows or ſinking cavities. *Farrier's Dict.*

To RIDGE. *v. a.* [from the noun.] To form a ridge.

Thou from heav'n
Feign'dſt at thy birth was given thee in thy hair,
Where ſtrength can leaſt abide, though all thy hairs
Were briſtles rang'd like thoſe that *ridge* the back
Of chaf'd wild boars, or ruffl'd porcupines. *Milton.*

RI'DGLING. } *n. ſ.* [*ovis rejicula*, Lat. *Ainſ.*] A ram half
RI'DGIL. } caſtrated.

Tend my herd, and ſee them fed;
To morning paſtures, evening waters led:
And 'ware the Libyan *ridgil*'s butting head. *Dryden.*
Tend them well, and ſee them fed
In paſtures freſh, and to their watering led;
And 'ware the *ridgling* with his butting head. *Dryden.*

RI'DGY. *adj.* [from *ridge.*] Riſing in a ridge.

Far in the ſea againſt the foaming ſhore,
There ſtands a rock, the raging billows roar
Above his head in ſtorms; but when 'tis clear,
Uncurl their *ridgy* backs, and at his feet appear. *Dryden.*

RI'DICULE. *n. ſ.* [*ridicule*, Fr. *ridiculum*, Lat.] Wit of that ſpecies that provokes laughter.

Sacred to *ridicule* his whole life long,
And the ſad burthen of ſome merry ſong. *Pope.*
Touch'd and ſham'd by *ridicule* alone. *Pope.*
Thoſe, who aim at *ridicule*,
Should fix upon ſome certain rule,
Which fairly hints they are in jeſt. *Swift's Miſcellanies.*

To RI'DICULE. *v. a.* [from the noun.] To expoſe to laughter; to treat with contemptuous merriment.

I wiſh the vein of *ridiculing* all that is ſerious and good may have no worſe effect upon our ſtate, than knight errantry had on theirs. *Temple.*

He often took a pleaſure to appear ignorant, that he might the better turn to *ridicule* thoſe that valued themſelves on their books. *Addiſon on Medals.*

RIDI'CULOUS. *adj.* [*ridicule*, Fr. *ridiculus*, Lat.] Worthy of laughter; exciting contemptuous merriment.

Thus was the building left
Ridiculous; and the work confuſion nam'd. *Milton.*

It was not in Titus's power not to be derided; but it was in his power not to be *ridiculous*. *South.*

RIDI'CULOUSLY. *adv.* [from *ridiculous.*] In a manner worthy of laughter or contempt.

Epicurus's diſcourſe concerning the original of the world is ſo *ridiculouſly* merry, that the deſign of his philoſophy was pleaſure and not inſtruction. *South.*

RIDI'CULOUSNESS. *n. ſ.* [from *ridiculous.*] The quality of being ridiculous.

What ſport do Tertullian, Minucius and Arnobius make with the images conſecrated to divine worſhip? from the meanneſs of the matter they are made, the caſualties of fire, and rottenneſs they are ſubject to, on purpoſe to repreſent the *riditulouſneſs* of worſhipping ſuch things. *Stillingfleet.*

RI'DING. *particip. adj.* Employed to travel on any occaſion.

It is provided by another provincial conſtitution, that no ſuffragan biſhop ſhall have more than one *riding* apparitor, and that archdeacons ſhall not have ſo much as one *riding* apparitor, but only a foot meſſenger. *Ayliffe's Parergon.*

RI'DING. *n. ſ.* [from *ride.*] A diſtrict viſited by an officer.

RI'DINGCOAT. *n. ſ.* [*riding* and *coat.*] A coat made to keep out weather.

When you carry your maſter's *ridingcoat* in a journey, wrap your own in it. *Swift's Directions to the Groom.*

RI'DINGHOOD. *n. ſ.* [*riding* and *hood.*] A hood uſed by women, when they travel, to bear off the rain.

The palliolum was like our *ridinghoods*, and ſerved both for a tunick and a coat. *Arbuthnot on Coins.*

Good houſewives all the winter's rage deſpiſe,
Defended by the *ridinghood*'s diſguiſe. *Gay.*

RIE. *n. ſ.* An eſculent grain. The flowers have no leaves, but conſiſt of ſeveral ſtamina, produced from the flower-cup; theſe flowers are collected into a ſmall ſpike, and are diſpoſed almoſt ſingly: from the flower-cup ariſes the pointal, afterward an oblong ſlender ſeed incloſed in an huſk, which was before the flower-cup: this differs from wheat in having a flatter ſpike, the corn larger and more naked. *Miller.*

Auguſt ſhall bear the form of a young man of a fierce aſpect, upon his head a garland of wheat and *rie*. *Peacham.*

RIFE. *adj.* [ꞃẏꝼe, Saxon; *rijf*, Dutch.] Prevalent; prevailing; abounding. It is now only uſed of epidemical diſtempers.

While thoſe reſtleſs deſires, in great men *rife*,
To viſit ſo low folks did much diſdain,
This while, though poor, they in themſelves did reign. *Sid.*
Guyon cloſely did await
Avantage; whilſt his foe did rage moſt *rife*;
Sometimes athwart, ſometimes he ſtrook him ſtraight,
And falſed oft his blows. *Fairy Queen, b.* ii.

The plague was then *rife* in Hungary. *Knolles.*

Bleſſings then are plentiful and *rife*,
More plentiful than hope. *Herbert.*
Space may produce new worlds; whereof ſo *rife*
There went a fame in heav'n, that he ere long
Intended to create. *Milton's Paradiſe Loſt, b.* i.
This is the place,
Whence ev'n now the tumult of loud mirth
Was *rife*, and perfect in my liſt'ning ear. *Milton.*
That grounded maxim
So *rife* and celebrated in the mouths
Of wiſeſt men, that to the publick good
Private reſpects muſt yield. *Milton.*

Before the plague of London, inflammations of the lungs were *rife* and mortal. *Arbuthnot on Air.*

RI'FELY. *adv.* [from *rife.*] Prevalently; abundantly.

It was *rifely* reported, that the Turks were coming in a great fleet. *Knolles's Hiſtory of the Turks.*

RI'FENESS. *n. ſ.* [from *rife.*] Prevalence; abundance.

He aſcribes the great *rifeneſs* of carbuncles in the ſummer, to the great heats. *Arbuthnot on Air.*

To RI'FLE. *v. a.* [*riffer*, *rifler*, Fr. *rijfelen*, Dutch.] To rob; to pillage; to plunder.

Stand, Sir, and throw us what you have about you; if not, we'll make you, Sir, and *rifle* you. *Shakeſp.*

Men, by his ſuggeſtion taught,
Ranſack'd the centre, and with impious hands
Rifled the bowels of their mother earth
For treaſures better hid. *Milton's Paradiſe Loſt, b.* i.

You have *rifled* my maſter, who ſhall maintain me? *L'Eſt.*

A commander in the parliament's rebel army *rifled* and defaced the cathedral at Litchfield. *South.*

Mine is thy daughter, prieſt, and ſhall remain,
And pray'rs, and tears, and bribes ſhall plead in vain,
Till time ſhall *rifle* every youthful grace. *Pope.*

RI'FLER. *n. ſ.* [from *rifle.*] Robber; plunderer; pillager.

RIFT. *n. ſ.* [from *rive.*] A cleft; a breach; an opening.

He pluckt a bough, out of whoſe *rift* there come
Small drops of gory blood. *Fairy Queen, b.* i.
She did confine thee
Into a cloven pine, within which *rift*
Impriſon'd, thou didſt painfully remain. *Shakeſp.*

In St. James's fields is a conduit of brick, unto which joineth a low vault; at the end of that is a round houſe, with a ſmall ſlit or *rift*; and in the conduit a window: if you cry out in the *rift*, it makes a fearful roaring at the window. *Bac.*

They have an idle tradition, that a missel bird, feeding upon a seed she cannot digest, expelleth it whole; which, falling upon a bough of a tree that hath some *rift*, putteth forth the misseltoe. *Bacon.*

Either tropick
'Gan thunder, and both ends of heav'n; the clouds
From many a horrid *rift* abortive pour'd
Fierce rain, with lightning mixt. *Milton.*

Some pick out bullets from the vessels sides,
Some drive old oakum through each seam and *rift*. *Dryd.*

To RIFT. *v. a.* [from the noun.] To cleave; to split.

To the dread rattling thunder
Have I giv'n fire, and *rifted* Jove's stout oak
With his own bolt. *Shakesp. Tempest.*

At sight of him the people with a shout
Rifted the air. *Milton's Agonistes.*

On *rifted* rocks, the dragon's late abodes,
The green reed trembles. *Pope's Messiah.*

To RIFT. *v. n.*

1. To burst; to open.

I'd shriek, that even your ears
Should *rift* to hear me. *Shakesp. Winter's Tale.*

Some trees are best for ship-timber, as oaks that grow in moist grounds; for that maketh the timber tough, and not apt to *rift* with ordnance. *Bacon's Natural History.*

When ice is congealed in a cup, it will swell instead of contracting, and sometimes *rift*. *Bacon's Nat. Hist.*

2. [*Raver*, Danish.] To belch; to break wind.

RIG. *n. s.* *Rig*, ridge, seem to signify the top of a hill falling on each side; from the Saxon, hꞃiȝȝ; and the Islandick, *hriggur*, both signifying a back. *Gibson's Camden.*

To RIG. *v. a.* [from *rig* or *ridge*, the back.]

1. To dress; to accoutre. Cloaths are proverbially said to be for the back, and victuals for the belly.

Jack was *rigged* out in his gold and silver lace, with a feather in his cap; and a pretty figure he made in the world. *L'Estrange.*

2. To fit with tackling.

He, like a foolish pilot, hath shipwreck'd
My vessel gloriously *rigg'd*. *Milton's Agonistes.*

The sinner shall set forth like a ship launched into the wide sea, not only well built and *rigged*; but also carried on with full wind. *South's Sermons.*

He bids them *rig* the fleet. *Denham.*

He *rigged* out another small fleet, and the Achæans engaged him with theirs. *Arbuthnot on Coins.*

RIGADOO'N. *n. s.* [*rigadon*, French.] A dance.

RIGA'TION. *n. s.* [*rigatio*, Lat.] The act of watering. *Dict.*

RI'GGER. *n. s.* [from *rig*.] One that rigs or dresses.

RI'GGING. *n. s.* [from *rig*.] The sails or tackling of a ship.

To plow the deep,
To make fit *rigging*, or to build a ship. *Creech.*

His batter'd *rigging* their whole war receives;
All bare, like some old oak with tempests beat,
He stands, and sees below his scatter'd leaves. *Dryden.*

RI'GGISH. *adj.* [from *rig*, an old word for a whore.] Wanton; whorish.

Vilest things
Become themselves in her, that the holy priests
Bless her, when she is *riggish*. *Shakesp. Ant. and Cleop.*

To RI'GGLE. *v. a.* [properly to *wriggle*.] To move backward and forward, as shrinking from pain.

RIGHT. *adj.* [ꞃiȝꞇ, Saxon; *recht*, Dutch; *ritto*, Italian; *rectus*, Latin.]

1. Fit; proper; becoming; suitable; true; not erroneous; not wrong.

How forcible are *right* words! but what doth your arguing reprove? *Job* vi. 25.

The words of my mouth are plain to him that understandeth, and *right* to them that find knowledge. *Prov.* viii.

The Lord God led me in the *right* way. *Gen.* xxiv. 48.

There being no law of nature, nor positive law of God, that determines which is the *right* heir in all cases, the right of succession could not have been certainly determined. *Locke.*

If there be no prospect beyond the grave, the inference is certainly *right*, let us eat and drink, for to-morrow we die. *Locke.*

Our calendar wants to be reformed, and the equinox rightly computed; and being once reformed and set *right*, it may be kept so, by omitting the additional day at the end of every hundred and thirty-four years. *Holder on Time.*

A time there will be, when all these unequal distributions of good and evil shall be set *right*, and the wisdom of all his transactions made as clear as the noon-day. *Atterbury.*

2. Not mistaken; passing a true judgement; passing judgement according to the truth of things.

You are *right*, justice and you weigh this well;
Therefore still bear the balance and the sword. *Shakesp.*

3. Just; honest; equitable.

Their heart was not *right* with him, neither were they stedfast in his covenant. *Psalm* lxxviii. 37.

4. Happy; convenient.

The lady has been disappointed on the *right* side, and found nothing more disagreeable in the husband, than she discovered in the lover. *Addison's Spectator.*

5. Not left.

It is not with that certainty to be received, what is believed concerning the *right* and left hand, that men naturally make use of the *right*, and that the use of the other is a digression. *Brown's Vulgar Errours.*

The left foot naked, when they march to fight,
But in a bull's raw hide they sheathe the *right*. *Dryden.*

6. Strait; not crooked.

The idea of a *right* lined triangle necessarily carries with it an equality of its angles to two right ones. *Locke.*

7. Perpendicular.

RIGHT. *interject.* An expression of approbation.

Right, cries his lordship, for a rogue in need
To have a taste, is insolence indeed:
In me 'tis noble, suits my birth and state. *Pope.*

RIGHT. *adv.*

1. Properly; justly; exactly; according to truth.

Then shall the *right* aiming thunder-bolts go abroad, and from the clouds, as from a well-drawn bow, shall they fly to the mark. *Wisdom* v. 21.

With strict discipline instructed *right*,
Have learn'd to use your arms before you fight. *Roscommon.*

Take heed you steer your vessel *right*, my son,
This calm of heaven, this mermaid's melody,
Into an unseen whirlpool draws you fast,
And in a moment sinks you. *Dryden's Spanish Fryar.*

To understand political power *right*, and derive it from its original, we must consider what state all men are naturally in, and that is a state of perfect freedom to order their actions, and dispose of their possessions and persons. *Locke.*

2. In a direct line.

Let thine eyes look *right* on, and let thine eyelids look straight before thee. *Proverbs* iv. 25.

Ye shall be driven out *right* forth, and none shall gather up him that wandereth. *Jer.* xlix. 5.

The people passed over *right* against Jericho. *Jos.* iii. 16.

Insects have voluntary motion, and therefore imagination; for ants go *right* forwards to their hills, and bees know the way from a flowery heath to their hives. *Bacon.*

This way, *right* down to Paradise descend. *Milton.*

3. In a great degree; very. Now obsolete.

I gat me to my Lord *right* humbly. *Psalm* xxx. 8.

Right noble princes,
I'll acquaint our duteous citizens. *Shakesp. Rich.* III.

Pardon us the interruption
Of thy devotion and *right* christian zeal, *Shakesp.*

I cannot joy, until I be resolv'd
Where our *right* valiant is become. *Shakesp. Henry* VI.

God shall help her *right* early. *Psalm* xlvi. 5.

The senate will smart deep
For your upbraidings: I should be *right* sorry
To have the means so to be veng'd on you,
As I shall shortly on them. *Benj. Johnson.*

Right many a widow his keen blade,
And many fatherless, had made. *Hudibras, p.* i.

4. It is still used in titles: as, right *honourable*; right *reverend*.

I mention the *right* honourable Thomas Howard lord high marshal. *Peacham on Drawing.*

RIGHT. *n. s.*

1. Justice; not wrong.

Persons of noble blood are less envied in their rising; for it seemeth but *right* done to their birth. *Bacon.*

In the midst of your invectives, do the Turks this *right*, as to remember that they are no idolaters. *Bacon.*

One rising, eminent
In wise deport, spake much of *right* and wrong,
Of justice, of religion, truth, and peace,
And judgement from above. *Milton's Par. Lost.*

Long love to her has borne the faithful knight,
And well deserv'd, had fortune done him *right*. *Dryden.*

He, that would do *right* to religion, cannot take a more effectual course, than by reconciling it with the happiness of mankind. *Tillotson.*

2. Freedom from errour.

Seldom your opinions err;
Your eyes are always in the *right*. *Prior.*

3. Just claim.

The Roman citizens were, by the sword, taught to acknowledge the pope their lord, though they knew not by what *right*. *Raleigh's Essays.*

The proud tyrant would many times say, that whatsoever belonged unto the empire of Rome, was of *right* his, for as much as he was possessed of the imperial scepter, which his great grandfather Mahomet had by law of arms won from Constantine. *Knolles's History of the Turks.*

Subdue by force, all who refuse
Right reason for their law; and for their king
Messiah, who by *right* of merit reigns. *Milton.*

My

My *right* to it appears,
By long poſſeſſion of eight hundred years. *Dryden.*

Might and *right* are inſeparable in the opinion of the world. *L'Eſtrange's Fables.*

Deſcriptions, figures, and fables muſt be in all heroick poems; every poet hath as much *right* to them, as every man hath to air. *Dryden.*

Judah pronounced ſentence of death againſt Thamar: our author thinks it is very good proof, that becauſe he did it, therefore he had a *right* to do it. *Locke.*

Agrippa is generally ranged in ſets of medals among the the emperors; as ſome among the empreſſes have no other *right*. *Addiſon.*

4. That which juſtly belongs to one.

To thee doth the *right* of her appertain, ſeeing thou only art of her kindred. *Tob.* vi. 11.

The cuſtom of employing theſe great perſons in all great offices, paſſes for a *right*. *Temple.*

The pris'ner freed himſelf by nature's laws,
Born free, he ſought his *right*. *Dryden's Knight's Tale.*

5. Property; intereſt.

A ſubject in his prince may claim a *right*,
Nor ſuffer him with ſtrength impair'd to fight. *Dryden.*

6. Power; prerogative.

God hath a ſovereign *right* over us, as we are his creatures, and by virtue of this *right*, he might, without injuſtice, have impoſed difficult taſks: but in making laws, he hath not made uſe of this *right*. *Tillotſon.*

7. Immunity; privilege.

The citizens,
Let them but have their *rights*, are ever forward
In celebration of this day with ſhews. *Shakeſp.*

Their only thoughts and hope was to defend their own *rights* and liberties, due to them by the law. *Clarendon.*

8. The ſide not left.

On his *right*
The radiant image of his glory ſat,
His only ſon. *Milton.*

9. *To* Rights. In a direct line; ſtraight.

Theſe ſtrata failing, the whole tract ſinks down *to rights* into the abyſs, and is ſwallowed up by it. *Woodward.*

10. *To* Rights. Deliverance from errour.

Several have gone about to inform them, and ſet them *to rights*; but for want of that knowledge of the preſent ſyſtem of nature, have not given the ſatisfaction expected. *Woodw.*

To Right. *v. a.* To do juſtice to; to eſtabliſh in poſſeſſions juſtly claimed; to relieve from wrong.

How will this grieve you,
When you ſhall come to clearer knowledge, that
You thus have publiſh'd me? gentle my lord,
You ſcarce can *right* me throughly. *Shakeſp.*

If the injured perſon be not *righted*, every one of them is wholy guilty of the injuſtice, and bound to reſtitution. *Taylor.*

I cou'd not expedient ſee,
On this ſide death, to *right* our family. *Waller.*

Make my father known,
To *right* my honour, and redeem your own. *Dryden.*

RI'GHTEOUS. *adj.* [ꞃihꞇpiꞅe, Saxon; whence *rightwiſe* in old authours, and *rightwiſely* in biſhop *Fiſher*: ſo much are words corrupted by pronunciation.]

1. Juſt; honeſt; virtuous; uncorrupt.

That far be from thee, to ſlay the *righteous* with the wicked; and that the *righteous* ſhould be as the wicked. *Gen.*

2. Equitable.

Kill my rival too; for he no leſs
Deſerves; and I thy *righteous* doom will bleſs. *Dryden.*

Ri'ghteously. *adv.* [from *righteous.*] Honeſtly; virtuouſly.

Athens did *righteouſly* decide,
When Phocion and when Socrates were try'd;
As *righteouſly* they did thoſe dooms repent,
Still they were wiſe, whatever way they went. *Dryden.*

Ri'ghteousness. *n. ſ.* [from *righteous.*] Juſtice; honeſty; virtue; goodneſs.

The ſcripture, aſcribing to the perſons of men *righteouſneſs*, in regard of their manifold virtues, may not be conſtrued, as though it did thereby clear them from all faults. *Hooker.*

Here wretched Phlegias warns the world with cries,
Cou'd warning make the world more juſt or wiſe;
Learn *righteouſneſs*, and dread th' avenging deities. *Dry.*

RI'GHTFUL. *adj.* [*right* and *full.*]

1. Having the right; having the juſt claim.

As in this haughty great attempt,
They laboured to ſupplant the *rightful* heir;
I loſt my liberty, and they their lives. *Shakeſp. Hen.* VI.

Some will mourn in aſhes, ſome coal black,
For the depoſing of a *rightful* king. *Shakeſp. Rich.* II.

2. Honeſt; juſt.

Nor would, for gold or fee,
Be won, their *rightful* cauſes down to tread. *Fairy Queen.*

Gather all the ſmiling hours;
Such as with friendly care have guarded
Patriots and kings in *rightful* wars. *Prior.*

Ri'ghtfully. *adv.* [from *rightful.*] According to right; according to juſtice.

Henry, who claimed by ſucceſſion, was ſenſible that his title was not ſound, but was *rightfully* in Mortimer, who had married the heir of York. *Dryden's Preface to Fables.*

Right-hand. *n. ſ.* Not the left.

The rank of oſiers, by the murmuring ſtream,
Left on your *right-hand* brings you to the place. *Shakeſp.*

Ri'ghtfulness. *n. ſ.* [from *rightful.*] Moral rectitude.

But ſtill although we fail of perfect *rightfulneſs*,
Seek we to tame theſe ſuperfluities,
Nor wholly wink though void of pureſt ſightfulneſs. *Sid.*

Ri'ghtly. *adv.* [from *right.*]

1. According to truth; properly; ſuitably; not erroneouſly.

Each of his reign allotted, *rightlier* call'd
Pow'rs of fire, air, water, and earth beneath. *Milton.*

Deſcend from heav'n, Urania! by that name
If *rightly* thou art call'd. *Milton's Paradiſe Loſt, b.* vii.

For glory done
Of triumph, to be ſtyl'd great conquerors,
Patrons of mankind, gods, and ſons of gods;
Deſtroyers *rightlier* call'd, and plagues of men. *Milton.*

A man can never have ſo certain a knowledge, that a propoſition, which contradicts the clear principles of his own knowledge, was divinely revealed, or that he underſtands the words *rightly*, wherein it is delivered; as he has, that the contrary is true. *Locke.*

Is this a bridal or a friendly feaſt?
Or from their deeds I *rightlier* may divine,
Unſeemly flown with inſolence or wine. *Pope's Odyſſey.*

2. Honeſtly; uprightly.

Let not my jealouſies be your diſhonour;
You may be *rightly* juſt, whatever I ſhall think. *Shakeſp.*

3. Exactly.

Should I grant, thou didſt not *rightly* ſee;
Then thou wert firſt deceiv'd. *Dryden.*

4. Straitly; directly.

We wiſh one end; but differ in order and way, that leadeth *rightly* to that end. *Aſcham's Schoolmaſter.*

Ri'ghtness. *n. ſ.* [from *right.*]

1. Conformity to truth; exemption from being wrong; rectitude.

It is not neceſſary for a man to be aſſured of the *rightneſs* of his conſcience, by ſuch an infallible certainty of perſuaſion, as amounts to the clearneſs of a demonſtration; but it is ſufficient if he knows it upon grounds of ſuch a probability, as ſhall exclude all rational grounds of doubting. *South.*

Like brute beaſts we travel with the herd, and are never ſo ſolicitous for the *rightneſs* of the way, as for the number or figure of our company. *Rogers's Sermons.*

2. Straitneſs.

Sounds move ſtrongeſt in a right line, which nevertheleſs is not cauſed by the *rightneſs* of the line, but by the ſhortneſs of the diſtance. *Bacon's Natural Hiſtory.*

RI'GID. *adj.* [*rigide*, Fr. *rigidus*, Latin.]

1. Stiff; not to be bent; unpliant.

A body, that is hollow, may be demonſtrated to be more *rigid* and inflexible, than a ſolid one of the ſame ſubſtance and weight. *Ray on the Creation.*

2. Severe; inflexible.

His ſevere judgment giving law,
His modeſt fancy kept in awe;
As *rigid* huſbands jealous are,
When they believe their wives too fair. *Denham.*

3. Sharp; cruel. It is uſed ſomewhat harſh by *Philips.*

Queen of this univerſe! do not believe
Thoſe *rigid* threats of death; ye ſhall not die. *Milton.*

Creſſy plains
And Agincourt, deep ting'd with blood, confeſs
What the Silures vigour unwithſtood
Could do in *rigid* fight. *Philips.*

Ri'gidity. *n. ſ.* [*rigidité*, Fr. from *rigid.*]

1. Stiffneſs.

Rigidity is ſaid of the ſolids of the body, when, being ſtiff or impliable, they cannot readily perform their reſpective offices; but a fibre is ſaid to be rigid, when its parts ſo ſtrongly cohere together, as not to yield to that action of the fluids, which ought to overcome their reſiſtance in order to the preſervation of health: it is to be remedied by fomentations.

Rigidity of the organs is ſuch a ſtate as makes them reſiſt that expanſion, which is neceſſary to carry on the vital functions: *rigidity* of the veſſels and organs muſt neceſſarily follow from the *rigidity* of the fibres. *Arbuthnot on Aliments.*

2. Stiffneſs of appearance; want of eaſy or airy elegance.

This ſevere obſervation of nature, by the one in her commoneſt, and by the other in her abſoluteſt forms, muſt needs produce in both a kind of *rigidity*, and conſequently more naturalneſs than gracefulneſs. *Wotton's Architecture.*

Ri'gidly. *adv.* [from *rigid.*]

1. Stifly; unpliantly.
2. Severely; inflexibly.

Ri'gidness. *n. ſ.* [from *rigid.*] Severity; inflexibility.

RI'GLET. *n. s.* [*regulet*, Fr.] A flat thin square piece of wood.

Thus the pieces that are intended to make the frames for pictures, before they are molded, are called *riglets*. *Mox.*

RI'GOL. *n. s.* A circle. Used in *Shakespeare* for a diadem.

This sleep is found; this is a sleep,
That, from this golden *rigol*, hath divorc'd
So many English kings. *Shakesp. Henry* IV.

RI'GOUR. *n. s.* [*rigor*, Latin.]

1. Cold; stiffness.

The rest his look
Bound with Gorgonian *rigour*, not to move. *Milton.*

2. A convulsive shuddering with sense of cold.

A right regimen, during the *rigor* or cold fit in the beginning of a fever, is of great importance; a long continued *rigor* is a sign of a strong disease: during the *rigor*, the circulation is less quick, and the blood actually stagnates in the extremities, and, pressing upon the heart, may produce concretions; therefore a *rigor* increaseth an inflammation. *Arb.*

3. Severity; sternness; want of condescension to others.

Nature has got the victory over passion, all his *rigour* is turned to grief and pity. *Denham's Sophy.*

Rigour makes it difficult for sliding virtue to recover. *Claris.*

4. Severity of conduct.

Does not looseness of life, and a want of necessary sobriety in some, drive others into *rigors* that are unnecessary? *Sprat.*

This prince lived in this convent, with all the *rigor* and austerity of a capuchin. *Addison's Remarks on Italy.*

5. Strictness; unabated exactness.

It may not seem hard, if in cases of necessity certain profitable ordinances sometimes be released, rather than all men always strictly bound to the general *rigor* thereof. *Hooker.*

Heat and cold are not, according to philosophical *rigour*, the efficients; but are names expressing our passions. *Glanvill.*

The base degenerate age requires
Severity and justice in its *rigour*:
This awes an impious bold offending world. *Addison.*

6. Rage; cruelty; fury.

He at his foe with furious *rigour* smites,
That strongest oak might seem to overthrow;
The stroke upon his shield so heavy lights,
That to the ground it doubleth him full low. *Fairy Queen.*

Driven by the necessities of the times and the temper of the people, more than led by his own disposition to any height and *rigour* of actions. *King Charles.*

7. Hardness; not flexibility; solidity; not softness.

The stones the *rigor* of their kind expel,
And supple into softness as they fell. *Dryden.*

RI'GOROUS. *adj.* [from *rigour*.] Severe; allowing no abatement.

He shall be thrown down the Tarpeian rock
With *rigorous* hands; he hath resisted law,
And therefore law shall scorn him further trial,
Than the severity of publick power. *Shakesp. Coriolanus.*

Are these terms hard and *rigorous*, beyond our capacities to perform? *Rogers's Sermons.*

RI'GOROUSLY. *adv.* [from *rigorous*.] Severely; without tenderness or mitigation.

Lest they faint
At the sad sentence *rigorously* urg'd,
For I behold them soften'd, and with tears
Bewailing their excess, all terror hide. *Milton.*

The people would examine his works more *rigorously* than himself, and would not forgive the least mistake. *Dryden.*

RILL. *n. s.* [*rivulus*, Lat.] A small brook; a little streamlet.

May thy brimmed waves from this
Their full tribute never miss,
From a thousand petty *rills*,
That tumble down the snowy hills. *Milton.*

To RILL. *v. n.* [from the noun.] To run in small streams.

Io! Apollo, mighty king, let envy,
Ill-judging and verbose, from Lethe's lake,
Draw tuns unmeasurable; while thy favour
Administers to my ambitious thirst
The wholesome draught from Aganippe's spring
Genuine, and with soft murmurs gently *rilling*
Adown the mountains where thy daughters haunt. *Prior.*

RI'LLET. *n. s.* [corrupted from *rivulet*.] A small stream.

A creek of Ose, between two hills, delivering a little fresh *rillet* into the sea. *Carew's Survey of Cornwall.*

RIM. *n. s.* [ꞃima, Saxon.]

1. A border; a margin.

It keeps of the same thickness near its centre; while its figure is capable of variation towards the *rim*. *Grew.*

2. That which encircles something else.

We may not affirm, that ruptures are confinable unto one side, as the peritoneum or *rim* of the belly may be broke; or its perforations relaxed in either. *Brown's Vulgar Errours.*

The drum-maker uses it for *rimbs*. *Mortimer's Husbandry.*

RIME. *n. s.* [hꞃim, Saxon.]

1. Hoar frost.

Breathing upon a glass giveth a dew; and in *rime* frosts you shall find drops of dew upon the inside of glass windows. *Bacon's Natural History.*

In a hoar frost, a *rime*, is a multitude of quadrangular prisms piled without any order one over another. *Grew.*

2. [*Rima*, Lat.] A hole; a chink.

Though birds have no epiglottis, yet can they contract the *rime* or chink of their larinx, so as to prevent the admission of wet or dry indigested. *Brown's Vulgar Errours.*

To RIME. *v. n.* [from the noun.] To freeze with hoar frost.

To RI'MPLE. *v. a.* To pucker; to contract into corrugations. See CRUMPLE and RUMPLE.

The skin was tense, also *rimpled* and blistered. *Wiseman.*

RI'MY. *adj.* [from *rime*.] Steamy; foggy; misty.

The air is now cold, hot, dry, or moist; and then thin, thick, foggy, *rimy*, or poisonous. *Harvey.*

RIND. *n. s.* [ꞃinꝺ, Saxon; *rinde*, Dutch.] Bark; husk.

Therewith a piteous yelling voice was heard,
Crying, O spare with guilty hands to tear
My tender sides in this rough *rind* embar'd. *Fairy Queen.*

Within the infant *rind* of this small flower
Poison hath residence, and medicine power. *Shakesp.*

These plants are neither red nor polished, when drawn out of the water, till their *rind* have been taken off. *Boyle.*

Others whose fruit, burnish'd with golden *rind*,
Hung amiable. *Milton's Paradise Lost.*

Thou can'st not touch the freedom of this mind
With all thy charms, although this corporal *rind*
Thou hast immanacl'd. *Milton.*

This monument, thy maiden beauty's due,
High on a plane-tree shall be hung to view;
On the smooth *rind* the passenger shall see
Thy name engrav'd, and worship Helen's tree. *Dryden.*

To RIND. *v. n.* [from the noun.] To decorticate; to bark; to husk.

RING. *n. s.* [hꞃinᵹ, Saxon.]

1. A circle; an orbicular line.

In this habit
Met I my father with his bleeding *rings*,
Their precious gems new lost. *Shakesp.*

Bubbles of water, before they began to exhibit their colours to the naked eye, have appeared through a prism girded about with many parallel and horizontal *rings*. *Newton.*

2. A circle of gold or some other matter worn as an ornament.

A quarrel.
—About a hoop of gold, a paltry *ring*. *Shakesp.*

I have seen old Roman *rings* so very thick about, and with such large stones in them, that 'tis no wonder a fop should reckon them a little cumbersome in the summer. *Addison.*

3. A circle of metal to be held by.

The *rings* of iron, that on the doors were hung,
Sent out a jarring sound, and harshly rung. *Dryden.*

Some eagle got the *ring* of my box in his beak, with an intent to let it fall, and devour it. *Gulliver.*

4. A circular course.

Chaste Diana,
Goddess presiding o'er the rapid race,
Place me, O place me in the dusty *ring*,
Where youthful charioteers contend for glory. *Smith.*

5. A circle made by persons standing round.

Make a *ring* about the corps of Cæsar,
And let me shew you him, that made the will. *Shakesp.*

The Italians, perceiving themselves almost environed, cast themselves into a *ring*, and retired back into the city. *Hayw.*

Round my arbour a new *ring* they made,
And footed it about the secret shade. *Dryden.*

6. A number of bells harmonically tuned.

A squirrel spends his little rage,
In jumping round a rowling cage;
The cage as either side turn'd up,
Striking a *ring* of bells a-top. *Prior.*

7. The sound of bells or any other sonorous body.

Stop the holes of a hawk's bell, it will make no *ring*, but a flat noise or rattle. *Bacon.*

Hawks bells, that have holes, give a greater *ring*, than if the pellet did strike upon brass in the open air. *Bacon.*

Sullen Moloch fled,
Hath left in shadows dread
His burning idol all of blackest hue;
In vain with cymbals *ring*,
They call the grisly king. *Milton.*

8. A sound of any kind.

The king, full of confidence, as he had been victorious in battle, and had prevailed with his parliament, and had the *ring* of acclamations fresh in his ears, thought the rest of his reign should be but play. *Bacon's Henry* VII.

To RING. *v. a.* pret. and part. pass. *rung*. [hꞃinᵹan, Saxon.]

1. To strike bells or any other sonorous body, so as to make it sound.

I 'gin to be aweary of the sun;
Ring the alarum bell. *Shakesp. Macbeth.*

2. [From *ring*.] To encircle.

Talbot,
Who, *ring'd* about with bold adversity,
Cries out for noble York and Somerset. *Shakesp. Hen.* VI.

3. To

3. To fit with rings.

Death, death; oh amiable lovely death!
Thou odoriferous stench, sound rottenness,
Arise forth from thy couch of lasting night,
Thou hate and terrour to prosperity,
And I will kiss thy detestable bones,
And put my eye-balls in thy vaulty brows,
And *ring* these fingers with thy houshold worms. *Shakesp.*

4. To restrain a hog by a ring in his nose.

To RING. *v. n.*

1. To sound as a bell or sonorous metal.

Ring out ye crystal spheres,
And let your silver chime
Move in melodious time;
And let the base of heav'n's deep organ blow. *Milton.*

No funeral rites nor man in mournful weeds,
Nor mournful bell shall *ring* her burial. *Shakesp.*

Easy it might be to *ring* other changes upon the same bells. *Norris's Miscellanies.*

At Latagus a weighty stone he flung;
His face was flatted, and his helmet *rung*. *Dryden.*

2. To practise the art of making musick with bells.

Signs for communication may be contrived at pleasure: four bells admit twenty-four changes in *ringing*; each change may, by agreement, have a certain signification. *Holder.*

3. To sound; to resound.

Hercules, missing his page, called him by his name aloud, that all the shore *rang* of it. *Bacon.*

The particular *ringing* sound in gold, distinct from the sound of other bodies, has no particular name. *Locke.*

With sweeter notes each rising temple *rung*,
A Raphael painted! and a Vida sung!
Immortal Vida! *Pope.*

4. To utter as a bell.

Ere to black Hecat's summons
The shard-born beetle, with his drowsy hums,
Hath *rung* night's yawning peal, there shall be done
A deed of dreadful note. *Shakesp. Macbeth.*

5. To tinkle.

My ears still *ring* with noise; I'm vext to death:
Tongue-kill'd, and have not yet recover'd breath. *Dryden.*

6. To be filled with a bruit or report.

That profane, atheistical, epicurean rabble, whom the whole nation so *rings* of, are not indeed, what they vote themselves, the wisest men in the world. *South.*

RING-BONE. *n. s.*

Ring-bone is a hard callous substance growing in the hollow circle of the little pastern of a horse, just above the coronet: it sometimes goes quite round like a ring, and thence it is called the *ring-bone*. *Farrier's Dictionary.*

RI'NGDOVE. *n. s.* [*rhingelduyve*, German.]

Pigeons are of several sorts, wild and tame; as wood pigeons, dovecote pigeons, and *ringdoves*. *Mortimer.*

RI'NGER. *n. s.* [from *ring*.] He who rings.

RINGLEA'DER. *n. s.* [*ring* and *leader*.] The head of a riotous body.

He caused to be executed some of the *ringleaders* of the Cornish men, in sacrifice to the citizens. *Bacon's Henry* VII.

The nobility escaped; the poor people, who had been deluded by these *ringleaders*, were executed. *Addison.*

RI'NGLET. *n. s.* [*ring*, with a diminutive termination.]

1. A small ring.

Silver the lintals, deep projecting o'er;
And gold the *ringlets* that command the door. *Pope.*

2. A circle.

You demy puppets, that
By moon-shine do the green *ringlets* make,
Whereof the ewe not bites. *Shakesp. Tempest.*

Never met we,
Upon the beached margent of the sea,
To dance our *ringlets* to the whistling wind,
But with thy brawls thou hast disturb'd our sport. *Shakesp.*

3. A curl.

With *ringlets* quaint, and wanton windings wove. *Milt.*

Her golden tresses in wanton *ringlets* wav'd,
As the vine curls her tendrils. *Milton.*

These in two sable *ringlets* taught to break,
Once gave new beauties to the snowy neck. *Pope.*

RI'NGSTREAKED. *adj.* [*ring* and *streaked*.] Circularly streaked.

He removed the he goats that were *ringstreaked* and spotted, and all the she goats that were speckled. *Gen.* xxx. 35.

RI'NGTAIL. *n. s.* [*ring* and *tail*.] A kind of kite with a whitish tail. *Bailey.*

RI'NGWORM. *n. s.* [*ring* and *worm*.] A circular tetter.

It began with a serpigo, making many round spots, such as is generally called *ringworms*. *Wiseman's Surgery.*

To RINSE. *v. a.* [from *rein*, German, pure, clear.]

1. To wash; to cleanse by washing.

This last costly treaty
Swallow'd so much treasure, and like a glass
Did break i' th' *rinsing*. *Shakesp. Henry* VIII.

Whomsoever he toucheth, and hath not *rinsed* his hands in water, he shall be unclean. *Lev.* xv. 11.

2. To wash the soap out of cloaths.

They cannot boil, nor wash, nor *rinse*, they say,
With water sometimes ink and sometimes whey,
According as you meet with mud or clay. *King.*

RI'NSER. *n. s.* [from *rinse*.] One that washes or rinses; a washer.

RI'OT. *n. s.* [*riotte*, old Fr. *riotto*, Italian.]

1. Wild and loose festivity.

When his headstrong *riot* hath no curb,
When rage and hot blood are his counsellors,
When means and lavish manners meet together,
Oh! with what wings shall his affection fly
Tow'rd fronting peril and oppos'd decay. *Shakesp. Hen.* IV.

So senseless of expence,
That he will neither know how to maintain it,
Nor cease his flow of *riot*. *Shakesp. Timon of Athens.*

All now was turn'd to jollity and game,
To luxury and *riot*, feast and dance. *Milton.*

2. A sedition; an uproar.

Transform'd to serpents all, as accessories
To his bold *riot*. *Milton.*

3. *To run* RIOT. To move or act without controll or restraint.

One man's head *runs riot* upon hawks and dice. *L'Estr.*

You never can defend his breeding,
Who, in his satyre's *running riot*,
Could never leave the world in quiet. *Swift's Miscel.*

To RI'OT. *v. n.* [*riotter*, old Fr.]

1. To revel; to be dissipated in luxurious enjoyments.

Let us walk honestly as in the day; not in *rioting* and drunkenness. *Romans* xiii. 13.

Now he exacts of all, wastes in delight,
Riots in pleasure, and neglects the law. *Daniel.*

2. To luxuriate; to be tumultuous.

Thy life a long dead calm of fix'd repose;
No pulse that *riots*, and no blood that glows. *Pope.*

3. To banquet luxuriously.

4. To raise a sedition or uproar.

RI'OTER. *n. s.* [from *riot*.]

1. One who is dissipated in luxury.

2. One who raises an uproar or sedition.

RI'OTISE. *n. s.* [from *riot*.] Dissoluteness; luxury.

From every work he challenged essoin
For contemplation sake; yet otherwise
His life he led in lawless *riotise*. *Fairy Queen.*

RI'OTOUS. *adj.* [*riotteux*, Fr. from *riot*.]

1. Luxurious; wanton; licentiously festive.

What needs me tell their feast and goodly guise,
In which was nothing *riotous* nor vain. *Fairy Queen.*

When all our offices have been opprest
With *riotous* feeders,
I have retir'd me to a wasteful cock,
And set mine eyes at flow. *Shakesp. Timon of Athens.*

John came neither eating nor drinking, that is far from the diet of Jerusalem and other *riotous* places, but fared coarsely. *Brown's Vulgar Errours.*

With them no *riotous* pomp nor Asian train,
T' infect a navy with their gaudy fears;
But war severely like itself appears. *Dryden.*

2. Seditious; turbulent.

RI'OTOUSLY. *adv.* [from *riotous*.]

1. Luxuriously; with licentious luxury.

He that gathereth by defrauding his own soul, gathereth for others that shall spend his goods *riotously*. *Ecclus.* xiv. 4.

2. Seditiously; turbulently.

RI'OTOUSNESS. *n. s.* [from *riotous*.] The state of being riotous.

To RIP. *v. a.* [hrypan, Saxon.]

1. To tear; to lacerate; to cut asunder by a continued act of the knife.

You bloody Nero's, *ripping* up the womb
Of your dear mother England, blush for shame. *Shakesp.*

Wilt thou dash their children, and *rip* up their women with child? *2 Kings* viii. 12.

The beast prevents the blow,
And upward *rips* the groin of his audacious foe. *Dryden.*

The *ripping* chissel is a socket chissel, about an inch broad, and hath a blunt edge. *Moxon's Mechanical Exercises.*

2. To take away by laceration or cutting.

Macduff was from his mother's womb
Untimely *ripp'd*. *Shakesp. Macbeth.*

Esculapius, because *ripped* from his mother's womb, was feigned to be the son of Apollo. *Hayward.*

Rip this heart of mine
Out of my breast, and shew it for a coward's. *Otway.*

The conscious husband
Charges on her the guilt of their disease;
Affecting fury acts a madman's part,
He'll *rip* the fatal secret from her heart. *Granvill.*

3. To disclose; to search out; to tear up; to bring to view.

Let it be lawful for me to *rip* up to the very bottom, how and by whom your discipline was planted, at such time as this age we live in began to make first trial thereof. *Hooker.*

You *rip* up the original of Scotland. *Spenser on Ireland.*

This *ripping* of anceftors is very pleafing unto me, and indeed favoureth of fome reading. *Spenser on Ireland.*

They *ripped* up all that had been done from the beginning of the rebellion. *Clarendon, b.* viii.

The relations confidering that a trial would *rip* up old fores, and difcover things not fo much to the reputation of the deceafed, they dropt their defign. *Arbuthnot.*

RIPE. *adj.* [ɲipe, Saxon; *rijp*, Dutch.]

1. Brought to perfection in growth; mature.

Macbeth
Is *ripe* for fhaking, and the pow'rs above
Put on their inftruments. *Shakesp.*

The time was the time of the firft *ripe* grapes. *Numb.* xiii.

Their fruit is improfitable, not *ripe* to eat. *Wisd.* iv. 5.

So may'ft thou live, till, like *ripe* fruit, thou drop
Into thy mother's lap, or be with eafe
Gather'd, not harfhly pluck'd, for death mature. *Milton.*

2. Refembling the ripenefs of fruit.

Thofe happieft fmiles,
That play'd on her *ripe* lip, feem'd not to know
What guefts were in her eyes, which parted thence,
As pearls from diamonds dropt. *Shakesp.*

3. Complete; proper for ufe.

I by letters fhall direct your courfe,
When time is *ripe*. *Shakesp. Henry* IV.

4. Advanced to the perfection of any quality.

There was a pretty rednefs in his lips,
A little *riper* and more lufty red
Than that mix'd in his cheeks. *Shakesp.*

O early *ripe!* to thy abundant ftore,
What could advancing age have added more. *Dryden.*

5. Finifhed; confummate.

Beafts are in fenfible capacity as *ripe*, even as men themfelves, perhaps more *ripe*. *Hooker, b.* i. *f.* 6.

6. Brought to the point of taking effect; fully matured.

He thence fhall come,
When this world's diffolution fhall be *ripe*. *Milton.*

While things were juft *ripe* for a war, the cantons, their protectors, interpofed as umpires in the quarrel. *Addison.*

7. Fully qualified by gradual improvement.

Ripe for heav'n, when fate Æneas calls,
Then fhalt thou bear him up, fublime, to me. *Dryden.*

To RIPE. *v. n.* [from the adj.] To ripen; to grow ripe; to be matured.

From hour to hour we *ripe* and *ripe*,
And then from hour to hour we rot and rot. *Shakesp.*

Slubber not bufinefs for my fake, Baffanio;
But ftay the very *riping* of the time. *Shakesp.*

Though no ftone tell thee what I was, yet thou,
In my grave's infide, fee what thou art now;
Yet tho'rt not yet fo good, till us death lay
To *ripe* and mellow there, w' are ftubborn clay. *Donne.*

To RIPE. *v. a.* To mature; to make ripe.

He is retir'd, to *ripe* his growing fortunes,
To Scotland. *Shakesp.*

RI'PELY. *adv.* [from *ripe.*] Maturely; at the fit time.

It fits us therefore *ripely*;
Our chariots and our horfemen be in readinefs. *Shakesp.*

To RI'PEN. *v. n.* [from *ripe.*] To grow ripe.

This is the ftate of man; to-day he puts forth
The tender leaves of hopes, to-morrow bloffoms,
And bears his blufhing honours thick upon him;
The third day comes a froft, a killing froft;
And when he thinks, good eafy man, full furely
His greatnefs is a *ripening*, nips his root;
And then he falls as I do. *Shakesp. Henry* VIII.

Afore the four grape is *ripening* in the flower. *Is.* xviii. 5.

The pricking of a fruit, before it *ripeneth*, ripens the fruit more fuddenly. *Bacon's Natural History.*

Trees, that *ripen* lateft, bloffom fooneft; as peaches and cornelians; and it is a work of providence that they bloffom fo foon; for otherwife they could not have the fun long enough to *ripen*. *Bacon's Natural History.*

Melons on beds of ice are taught to bear,
And ftrangers to the fun yet *ripen* here. *Granville.*

To RI'PEN. *v. a.* To mature; to make ripe.

My father was no traitor;
And that I'll prove on better men than Somerfet,
Were growing time once *ripen'd* to my will. *Shakesp.*

When to *ripen'd* manhood he fhall grow,
The greedy failor fhall the feas forego. *Dryden.*

That I fettled
Your father in his throne, was for your fake,
I left th' acknowledgment for time to *ripen*. *Dryden.*

The genial fun
Has daily, fince his courfe begun,
Rejoiced the metal to refine,
And *ripen'd* the Peruvian mine. *Addison.*

Be this the caufe of more than mortal hate,
The reft fucceeding times fhall *ripen* into fate. *Pope.*

Here elements have loft their ufes;
Air *ripens* not, nor earth produces. *Swift.*

Before the *ripen'd* field the reapers ftand. *Thomson.*

RI'PENESS. *n. f.* [from *ripe.*]

1. The ftate of being ripe; maturity.

They have compared it to the *ripenefs* of fruits. *Wiseman.*

Little matter is depofited in the abfcefs, before it arrives towards its *ripenefs*. *Sharp's Surgery.*

2. Full growth.

Time, which made them their fame out-live,
To Cowley fcarce did *ripenefs* give. *Denham.*

3. Perfection; completion.

To this purpofe were thofe harmonious tunes of pfalms devifed for us, that they, which are either in years but young, or touching perfection of virtue as yet not grown to *ripenefs*, might, when they think they fing, learn. *Hooker.*

This royal infant promifes
Upon this land a thoufand thoufand bleffings,
Which time fhall bring to *ripenefs*. *Shakesp. Hen.* VIII.

I to manhood am arriv'd fo near,
And inward *ripenefs* doth much lefs appear,
That fome more timely happy fpirits indu'th. *Milton.*

4. Fitnefs; qualification.

Men muft endure
Their going hence, ev'n as their coming hither:
Ripenefs is all. *Shakesp. King Lear.*

RI'PPER. *n. f.* [from *rip.*] One who rips; one who tears; one who lacerates.

To RI'PPLE. *v. n.* To fret on the furface, as water fwifty running.

RI'PTOWELL. *n. f.* A gratuity, or reward given to tenants, after they had reaped their lord's corn. *Bailey.*

To RISE. *v. n.* pret. *rofe*; part. *rifen.* [ɲiʃan, Saxon; *reifen*, Dutch.]

1. To change a jacent or recumbent, to an erect pofture.

I have feen her *rife* from her bed, and throw her nightgown upon her. *Shakesp. Macbeth.*

2. To get up from reft.

Never a wife leads a better life than fhe does; do what fhe will; go to bed when fhe lift; *rife* when fhe lift. *Shakesp.*

As wild affes in the defert, go they forth to their work, *rifing* betimes for a prey. *Job* xxiv. 5.

That is to live,
To reft fecure, and not *rife* up to grieve. *Daniel's Civ. War.*

Thy manfion wants thee, Adam, *rife*. *Milton.*

3. To get up from a fall.

True in our fall,
Falfe in our promis'd *rifing*. *Milton's Par Lost, b.* ix.

4. To fpring; to grow up.

They imagine
For one forbidden tree a multitude,
Now *ris'n* to work them farther woe. *Milton.*

5. To gain elevation of rank or fortune.

Some *rife* by fin, and fome by virtue fall. *Shakespeare.*

If they *rife* not with their fervice, they will make their fervice fall with them. *Bacon.*

To *rife* i' th' world,
No wife man that's honeft fhould expect. *Otway.*

Thofe, that have been raifed by fome great minifter, trample upon the fteps by which they *rife*, to rival him. *South.*

6. To fwell.

If the bright fpot ftay in his place, it is a *rifing* of the burning. *Lev.* xiii. 21.

7. To afcend; to move upwards.

The fap in old trees is not fo frank as to *rife* all to the boughs, but tireth by the way, and putteth out mofs. *Bacon.*

If two plane polifh'd plates of a polifh'd looking-glafs be laid together, fo that their fides be parallel, and at a very fmall diftance from one another, and then their lower edges be dipped into water, the water will *rife* up between them. *New.*

8. To break out from below the horizon, as the fun.

He maketh the fun to *rife* on the evil and the good. *Matt.* v.

The fun *rofe* upon him. *Gen.* xxxii. 31.

He affirmeth, that Tunny is fat upon the *rifing* of the Pleiades, and departs upon Arcturus. *Brown's Vulg. Errours.*

Whether the fun
Rife on the earth, or earth *rife* on the fun. *Milton.*

9. To take beginning; to come into exiftence, or notice.

10. To begin to act.

High winds began to *rife*. *Milton.*

With Vulcan's rage the *rifing* winds confpire,
And near our palace rolls the flood of fire. *Dryden.*

11. To appear in view.

The poet muft lay out all his ftrength, that his words may be glowing, and that every thing he defcribes may immediately prefent itfelf, and *rife* up to the reader's view. *Addison.*

12. To change a ftation; to quit a fiege.

He, *rifing* with fmall honour from Gunza, and fearing the power of the chriftians, was gone. *Knolles.*

13. To be excited; to be produced.

Indeed you thank'd me; but a nobler gratitude
Rofe in her foul; for from that hour fhe lov'd me. *Otway.*

A thought *rofe* in me, which often perplexes men of contemplative natures. *Spectator*, N°. 565.

14. To break into military commotions; to make insurrections.
At our heels all hell should *rise*,
With blackest insurrection. *Milton.*
Numidia's spacious kingdom lies
Ready to *rise* at its young prince's call. *Addison's Cato.*
No more shall nation against nation *rise*,
Nor ardent warriors meet with hateful eyes. *Pope.*
15. To be roused; to be excited to action.
Who will *rise* up for me against evil-doers? or who will stand up for me against the workers of iniquity? *Ps.* xciv.
Gather together, come against, and *rise* up to the battle. *Jer.*
He shall *rise* up at the voice of the bird, and all the daughters of musick shall be brought low. *Eccl.* xii. 4.
16. To make hostile attack.
If any man hate his neighbour, lie in wait, and *rise* up against him, and smite him mortally, and fleeth into one of these cities, the elders of his city shall fetch him thence. *Deut.*
17. To grow more or greater in any respect.
A hideous gabble *rises* loud
Among the builders. *Milton.*
The great duke *rises* on them in his demands, and will not be satisfied with less than a hundred thousand crowns, and a solemn embassy to beg pardon. *Addison's Remarks on Italy.*
18. To increase in price.
Bullion is *risen* to six shillings and five pence the ounce; *i. e.* that an ounce of uncoined silver will exchange for an ounce and a quarter of coined silver. *Locke.*
19. To be improved.
From such an untainted couple, we can hope to have our family *rise* to its ancient splendour of face, air, countenance, and shape. *Tatler,* N° 75.
20. To elevate the stile.
Your author always will the best advise,
Fall when he falls, and when he *rises*, *rise*. *Roscommon.*
21. To be revived from death.
After I am *risen* again, I will go before you. *Mat.* xxvi.
The stars of morn shall see him *rise*
Out of his grave. *Milton.*
22. To come by chance.
As they 'gan his library to view,
And antique registers for to avise,
There chanced to the prince's hand to *rise*
An ancient book. *Fairy Queen, b.* ii.
23. To be elevated in situation.
He bar'd an ancient oak of all her boughs;
Then on a *rising* ground the trunk he plac'd,
Which with the spoils of his dead foe he grac'd. *Dryden.*
A house we saw upon a *rising*. *Addison.*
Ash, on banks or *rising* grounds near rivers, will thrive exceedingly. *Mortimer's Husbandry.*

Rise. *n. s.* [from the verb.]
1. The act of rising.
2. The act of mounting from the ground.
In leaping with weights, the arms are first cast backwards and then forwards, with so much the greater force; for the hands go backward before they take their *rise*. *Bacon.*
3. Eruption; ascent.
Upon the candle's going out, there is a sudden *rise* of water; for the flame filling no more place, the air and water succeed. *Bacon.*
The hill submits itself
In small descents, which do its height beguile;
And sometimes mounts, but so as billows play,
Whose *rise* not hinders, but makes short our way. *Dryden.*
4. Place that favours the act of mounting aloft.
Rais'd so high, from that convenient *rise*
She took her flight, and quickly reach'd the skies. *Creech.*
Since the arguments against them rise from common received opinions, it happens, in controversial discourses, as it does in the assaulting of towns, where, if the ground be but firm, whereon the batteries are erected, there is no farther inquiry of whom it is borrowed, so it affords but a fit *rise* for the present purpose. *Locke.*
5. Elevated place.
Such a *rise*, as doth at once invite
A pleasure, and a reverence from the sight. *Denham.*
6. Appearance of the sun in the East.
Phœbus! stay;
The world to which you fly so fast,
From us to them can pay your haste
With no such object, and salute your *rise*
With no such wonder, as De Mornay's eyes. *Waller.*
7. Encrease in any respect.
8. Encrease of price.
Upon a breach with Spain, must be considered the present state of the king's treasure, the *rise* or fall that may happen in his constant revenue by a Spanish war. *Temple.*
The bishops have had share in the gradual *rise* of lands. *Sw.*
9. Beginning; original.
It has its *rise* from the lazy admonitions of those who give rules, and propose examples, without joining practice with their instructions. *Locke on Education.*
His reputation quickly peopled it, and gave *rise* to the republick, which calls itself after his name. *Addison.*
10. Elevation; encrease of sound.
In the ordinary *rises* and falls of the voice, there fall out to be two beemolls between the unison and the diapason. *Bacon.*

Ri'ser. *n. s.* [from *rise.*] One that rises.
The isle Æεa, where the palace stands
Of th' early *riser*, with the rosy hands,
Active Aurora; where she loves to dance. *Chapman.*

Risibi'lity. *n. s.* [from *risible.*] The quality of laughing.
How comes lowness of stile to be so much the propriety of satyr, that without it a poet can be no more a satyrist, than without *risibility* he can be a man. *Dryden.*
Whatever the philosophers may talk of their *risibility*, neighing is a more noble expression than laughing. *Arbuth.*

RI'SIBLE. *adj.* [*risible*, Fr. *risibilis*, Lat.]
1. Having the faculty or power of laughing.
We are in a merry world, laughing is our business; as if because it has been made the definition of man, that he is *risible*, his manhood consisted in nothing else. *Gov. of Tongue.*
2. Ridiculous; exciting laughter.

Risk. *n. s.* [*risque*, Fr. *riesg*, Spanish.] Hazard; danger; chance of harm.
Some run the *risk* of an absolute ruin for the gaining of a present supply. *L'Estrange's Fables.*
When an insolent despiser of discipline, nurtured into contempt of all order by a long *risk* of licence, shall appear before a church governor, severity and resolution are that governor's virtues. *South's Sermons.*
By allowing himself in what is innocent, he would run the *risk* of being betrayed into what is not so. *Atterbury.*
An innocent man ought not to run an equal *risk* with a guilty one. *Clarissa.*

To Risk. *v. a.* [*risquer*, Fr.] To hazard; to put to chance; to endanger.
Who would hope new fame to raise,
Or *risk* his well established praise,
That, his high genius to approve,
Had drawn a George or carv'd a Jove. *Addison.*

Ri'sker. *n. s.* [from *risk.*] He who risks.
He thither came, t' observe and smoak
What courses other *riskers* took. *Butler.*

Riss. the obsolete preterite of *rise*.
Riss not the consular men and left their places,
So soon as thou sat'st down; and fled thy side. *Benj. Johns.*

RITE. *n. s.* [*rit*, Fr. *ritus*, Lat.] Solemn act of religion; external observance.
The ceremonies, we have taken from such as were before us, are not things that belong to this or that sect, but they are the ancient *rites* and customs of the church. *Hooker.*
It is by God consecrated into a sacrament, a holy *rite*, a means of conveying to the worthy receiver the benefits of the body and blood of Christ. *Hammond's Fundamentals.*
When the prince her fun'ral *rites* had paid,
He plow'd the Tyrrhene seas. *Dryden.*

Ri'tual. *adj.* [*rituel*, Fr.] Solemnly ceremonious; done according to some religious institution.
Instant I bade the priests prepare
The *ritual* sacrifice, and solemn pray'r. *Prior.*
If to tradition were added, certain constant *ritual* and emblematical observances, as the emblems were expressive, the memory of the thing recorded would remain. *Forbes.*

Ri'tual. *n. s.* [from the adj.] A book in which the rites and observances of religion are set down.
An heathen *ritual* could not instruct a man better than these several pieces of antiquity in the particular ceremonies, that attended different sacrifices. *Addison's Remarks on Italy.*

Ri'tualist. *n. s.* [from *ritual.*] One skilled in the ritual.

RI'VAGE. *n. s.* [French.] A bank; a coast. Not in use.
Think
You stand upon the *rivage*, and behold
A city on th' inconstant billows dancing;
For so appears this fleet. *Shakesp. Henry* V.

RI'VAL. *n. s.* [*rivalis*, Lat.]
1. One who is in pursuit of the same thing which another man pursues; a competitour.
Oh love! thou sternly dost thy pow'r maintain,
And wilt not bear a *rival* in thy reign;
Tyrants and thou all fellowship disdain. *Dryden.*
2. A competitour in love.
She saw her father was grown her adverse party, and yet her fortune such as she must favour her *rival*. *Sidney.*
France and Burgundy,
Great *rivals* in our younger daughter's love. *Shakesp.*
Your *rival*'s image in your worth I view;
And what I lov'd in him, esteem in you. *Granville.*

Ri'val. *adj.* Standing in competition; making the same claim; emulous.
Had I but the means
To hold a *rival* place with one of them,
I should be fortunate. *Shakesp. Merchant of Venice.*

Equal

Equal in years, and *rival* in renown
With Epaphus, the youthful Phaeton,
Like honour claims. *Dryden.*

You bark to be employ'd,
While Venus is by *rival* dogs enjoy'd. *Dryden.*

To RI'VAL. *v. a.* [from the noun.]

1. To ſtand in competition with another; to oppoſe.

Thoſe, that have been raiſed by the intereſt of ſome great miniſter, trample upon the ſteps by which they riſe, to *rival* him in his greatneſs, and at length ſtep into his place. *South.*

2. To emulate; to endeavour to equal or excel.

Ambitious fool! with horny hoofs to paſs
O'er hollow arches of reſounding braſs;
To *rival* thunder in its rapid courſe,
And imitate inimitable force. *Dryden's Æneis.*

To RI'VAL. *v. n.* To be competitours. Out of uſe.

Burgundy,
We firſt addreſs'd tow'rd you, who with this king
Have *rival'd* for our daughter. *Shakeſp. King Lear.*

RIVA'LITY. } *n. ſ.* [*rivalitas*, Lat. from *rival.*] Competition;
RI'VALRY. } emulation.

It is the privilege of poſterity to ſet matters right between thoſe antagoniſts, who, by their *rivalry* for greatneſs, divided a whole age. *Addiſon.*

RI'VALSHIP. *n. ſ.* [from *rival.*] The ſtate or character of a rival.

To RIVE. *v. a.* part. *riven.* [ꞃẏꝼꞇ, broken Saxon; *rijven*, Dutch; *river*, Fr. to drive.] To ſplit; to cleave; to divide by a blunt inſtrument; to force in diſruption.

At his haughty helmet
So hugely ſtruck, that it the ſteel did *rive*,
And cleft his head. *Fairy Queen, b.* i.

The varlet at his plaint was grieved ſore,
That his deep wounded heart in two did *rive*. *Fa. Queen.*

Through *riven* clouds and molten firmament,
The fierce three-forked engine making way,
Both lofty towers and higheſt trees hath rent. *Fa. Queen.*

O Cicero!
I have ſeen tempeſts, when the ſcolding winds
Have *riv'd* the knotty oaks; but ne'er till now
Did I go through a tempeſt dropping fire. *Shakeſp.*

As one he ſtood eſcap'd from cruel fight,
Sore toil'd, his *riven* arms to havock hewn. *Milton.*

The neighbouring foreſts, formerly ſhaken and *riven* with the thunder-bolts of war, did envy the ſweet peace of Druina. *Howel's Vocal Foreſt.*

Had I not been blind, I might have ſeen
Yon *riven* oak, the faireſt of the green. *Dryden.*

Let it come;
Let the fierce light'ning blaſt, the thunder *rive* me. *Rowe.*

To RIVE. *v. n.* To be ſplit; to be divided by violence.

Freeſtone *rives*, ſplits, and breaks in any direction. *Woodw.*

To RIVE. for *derive* or *direct.*

Ten thouſand French have ta'en the ſacrament,
To *rive* their dangerous artillery
Upon no chriſtian ſoul but Engliſh Talbot. *Shakeſp.*

To RI'VEL. *v. a.* [ȝeꞃiꝼleꝺ, Saxon, corrugated, rumpled.] To contract into wringles and corrugations.

Then droop'd the fading flow'rs, their beauty fled,
And cloſ'd their ſickly eyes and hung the head,
And *rivel'd* up with heat, lay dying in their bed. *Dryd.*

And ſince that plenteous autumn now is paſt,
Whoſe grapes and peaches have indulg'd your taſte,
Take in good part, from our poor poet's board,
Such *rivel'd* fruits as winter can afford. *Dryden.*

Alum ſtipticks, with contracting pow'r,
Shrink his thin eſſence like a *rivel'd* flow'r. *Pope.*

RI'VEN. part. of *rive.*

RI'VER. *n. ſ.* [*riviere*, Fr. *rivus*, Lat.] A land current of water bigger than a brook.

It is a moſt beautiful country, being ſtored throughout with many goodly *rivers*, repleniſhed with all ſorts of fiſh. *Spenſ.*

The firſt of theſe *rivers* has been celebrated by the Latin poets for the gentleneſs of its courſe, as the other for its rapidity. *Addiſon's Remarks on Italy.*

RIVER-DRAGON. *n. ſ.* A crocodile. A name given by *Milton* to the king of Egypt.

Thus with ten wounds
The *river-dragon* tam'd at length, ſubmits
To let his ſojourners depart. *Milton's Par. Loſt.*

RIVER-GOD. *n. ſ.* Tutelary deity of a river.

His wig hung as ſtrait as the hair of a *river-god* riſing from the water. *Arbuthnot and Pope.*

RIVER-HORSE. *n. ſ.* Hippopotamus.

Roſe,
As plants ambiguous between ſea and land,
The *river-horſe* and ſcaly crocodile. *Milton.*

RI'VET. *n. ſ.* [*river*, Fr. to break the point of a thing; to drive.] A faſtening pin clenched at both ends.

The armourers accompliſhing the knights,
With buſy hammers cloſing *rivets* up,
Give dreadful note of preparation. *Shakeſp. Henry* V.

Thy armour
I'll fruſh, and unlock the *rivets* all,
But I'll be maſter of it. *Shakeſp. Troilus and Creſſida.*

Though Valeria's fair, and though ſhe loves me too,
'Gainſt her my ſoul is arm'd on every part;
Yet there are ſecret *rivets* to my heart,
Where Berenice's charms have found the way,
Subtile as lightnings. *Dryden's Tyrannick Love.*

The verſe in faſhion is, when numbers flow
So ſmooth and equal, that no ſight can find
The *rivet*, where the poliſh'd piece was join'd. *Dryden.*

The *rivets* of thoſe wings inclos'd
Fit not each other. *Dryden's Don Sebaſtian.*

This inſtrument ſhould move eaſy upon the *rivet*. *Sharp.*

To RI'VET. *v. a.* [from the noun.]

1. To faſten with rivets.

This man
If all our fire were out, would fetch down new,
Out of the hand of Jove; and *rivet* him
To Caucaſus, ſhould he but frown. *Benj. Johnſon.*

In *rivetting*, the pin you *rivet* in ſhould ſtand upright to the plate you *rivet* it upon; for if it do not ſtand upright, you will be forced to ſet it upright, after it is *rivetted*. *Moxon.*

2. To faſten ſtrongly; to make immoveable.

You were to blame to part with
A thing ſtuck on with oaths upon your finger,
And *rivetted* with faith unto your fleſh. *Shakeſp.*

Why ſhould I write this down, that's *rivetted*,
Screw'd to my mem'ry? *Shakeſp. Cymbeline.*

What one party thought to *rivet* to a ſettledneſs by the ſtrength and influence of the Scots, that the other rejects. *King Charles.*

Till fortune's fruitleſs ſpite had made it known,
Her blows not ſhook but *rivetted* his throne. *Dryden.*

Thus hath God not only *rivetted* the notion of himſelf into our natures, but likewiſe made the belief of his being neceſſary to the peace of our minds and happineſs of ſociety. *Till.*

If the eye ſees thoſe things *rivetted*, which are looſe, where will you begin to rectify the miſtake. *Locke.*

Where we uſe words of a looſe and wandering ſignification, hence follows miſtake and error, which thoſe maxims, brought as proofs to eſtabliſh propoſitions, wherein the terms ſtand for undetermined ideas, do by their authority confirm and *rivet*. *Locke.*

Rivet and nail me where I ſtand, ye pow'rs. *Congreve.*

They provoke him to the rage
Of fangs and claws, and, ſtooping from your horſe,
Rivet the panting ſavage to the ground. *Addiſon's Cato.*

A ſimilitude of nature and manners, in ſuch a degree as we are capable of, muſt tie the holy knot, and *rivet* the friendſhip between us. *Atterbury.*

RI'VULET. *n. ſ.* [*rivulus*, Lat.] A ſmall river; a brook; a ſtreamlet.

By fountain or by ſhady *rivulet*,
He ſought them. *Milton.*

The veins, where innumerable little *rivulets* have their confluence into the common channel of the blood. *Bentley.*

I ſaw the *rivulet* of Salforata, formerly called Albula, and ſmelt the ſtench that ariſes from its water, which Martial mentions. *Addiſon's Remarks on Italy.*

RIXDO'LLAR. *n. ſ.* A German coin, worth about four ſhillings and ſix-pence ſterling. *Dict.*

ROACH. *n. ſ.* [from *rutilus*, Lat. redhaired.]

A *roach* is a fiſh of no great reputation for his dainty taſte: his ſpawn is accounted much better than any other part of him: he is accounted the water ſheep, for his ſimplicity and fooliſhneſs; and it is noted, that *roaches* recover ſtrength, and grow in a fortnight after ſpawning. *Walton's Angler.*

If a gudgeon meet a *roach*,
He dare not venture to approach;
Yet ſtill he leaps at flies. *Swift.*

ROAD. *n. ſ.* [*rade*, Fr.]

1. Large way; path.

Would you not think him a madman, who, whilſt he might eaſily ride on the beaten *road* way, ſhould trouble himſelf with breaking up of gaps? *Suckling.*

To God's eternal houſe direct the way,
A broad and ample *road*. *Milton.*

To be indifferent whether we embrace falſehood or truth, is the great *road* to error. *Locke.*

Could ſtupid atoms, with impetuous ſpeed,
By diff'rent *roads* and adverſe ways proceed,
That here they might rencounter, here unite. *Blackmore.*

There is but one *road* by which to climb up. *Addiſon.*

2. [*Rade*, Fr.] Ground where ſhips may anchor.

I ſhould be ſtill
Peering in maps for ports and *roads*;
And every object that might make me fear
Misfortune to my ventures. *Shakeſp. Merch. of Venice.*

About the iſland are many *roads*, but only one harbour. *Sandys's Journey.*

3. Inrode; incursion.

The Volscians stand
Ready, when time shall prompt them, to make *road*
Upon's again. *Shakesp. Coriolanus.*

Cason was desirous of the spoil, for that he was, by the former *road* into that country, become famous and rich. *Knolles's History of the Turks.*

The king of Scotland, seeing none came into Perkin, turned his enterprize into a *road*, and wasted Northumberland with fire and sword. *Bacon's Henry* VII.

4. Journey. The word seems, in this sense at least, to be derived from *rode*, the preterite of *ride*: as we say, *a short* ride; *an easy* ride.

With easy *roads* he came to Leicester,
And lodg'd in the abbey. *Shakesp. Henry* VIII.

He from the East his flaming *road* begins. *Milton.*

To ROAM. *v. n.* [*romigare*, Italian. See Room.] To wander without any certain purpose; to ramble; to rove; to play the vagrant.

Five summers have I spent in farthest Greece,
Roaming clean through the bounds of Asia. *Shakesp.*

Daphne *roaming* through a thorny wood. *Shakesp.*

The lonely fox *roams* far abroad,
On secret rapin bent, and midnight fraud. *Prior.*

What were unenlighten'd man,
A savage *roaming* through the woods, and wild
In quest of prey. *Thomson's Summer.*

To Roam. *v. a.* To range; to wander over.

Now fowls in their clay nests were couch'd,
And now wild beasts came forth the woods to *roam*. *Milton.*

Roa'mer. *n. s.* [from *roam.*] A rover; a rambler; a wanderer.

Roan. *adj.* [*rouen*, Fr.]

Roan horse is a horse of a bay, sorrel, or black colour, with grey or white spots interspersed very thick. *Farr. Dict.*

To Roar. *v. n.* [ꞃapan, Saxon.]

1. To cry as a lion or other wild beast.

Roaring bulls he would him make to tame. *Spenser.*

Warwick and Montague,
That in their chains fetter'd the kingly lion,
And made the forest tremble when they *roar'd*. *Shakesp.*

Have I not in my time heard lions *roar*? *Shakesp.*

The young lions *roared* upon him and yelled. *Jer.* ii. 15.

The death of Daphnis woods and hills deplore,
They cast the sound to Libya's desart shore;
The Libyan lions hear, and hearing *roar*. *Dryden.*

2. To cry in distress.

At his nurse's tears
He whin'd and *roar'd* away your victory,
That pages blush'd at him. *Shakesp. Coriolanus.*

Sole on the barren sands the suff'ring chief
Roar'd out for anguish, and indulg'd his grief. *Dryden.*

3. To sound as the wind or sea.

South, East, and West, with mix'd confusion *roar*,
And rowl the foaming billows to the shore. *Dryden.*

Loud as the wolves on Orcas' stormy steep,
Howl to the *roaring* of the northern deep. *Pope.*

4. To make a loud noise.

The brazen throat of war had ceas'd to *roar*. *Milton.*

Consider what fatigues I've known,
How oft I cross'd where carts and coaches *roar'd*. *Gay.*

Roar. *n. s.* [from the verb.]

1. The cry of the lion or other beast.
2. An outcry of distress.
3. A clamour of merriment.

Where be your gibes now? your gambols? your songs? your flashes of merriment, that were wont to set the table in a *roar*? *Shakesp. Hamlet.*

4. The sound of the wind or sea.
5. Any loud noise.

Deep throated engines belch'd, whose *roar*
Imbowel'd with outrageous noise the air. *Milton.*

Oft on a plat of rising ground,
I hear the far-off curfew sound,
Over some wide-water'd shoar,
Swinging slow with sullen *roar*. *Milton.*

When cannons did diffuse,
Preventing posts, the terror, and the news;
Our neighbour princes trembled at their *roar*. *Waller.*

The waters, list'ning to the trumpet's *roar*,
Obey the summons, and forsake the shore. *Dryden.*

Roa'ry. *adj.* [better *rory*; *rores*, Lat.] Dewy.

On Lebanon his foot he set,
And shook his wings with *roary* May dews wet. *Fairfax.*

To Roast. *v. a.* [*rostir*, *rotir*, Fr. *rosten*, German; ꝛeꞃoꞅꞇoꝺ, Saxon, roasted; from *rastrum*, Lat. a grate; to *roast*, being, in its original sense, to broil on a gridiron.]

1. To dress meat, by turning it round before the fire.

He *roasteth* not that which he took in hunting. *D. of Piety.*

Roasting and boiling are below the dignity of your office. *Swift's Directions to the Cook.*

2. To impart dry heat to flesh.

Here elements have lost their uses,
Air ripens not, nor earth produces;
Fire will not *roast*, nor water boil. *Swift's Miscellanies.*

3. To dress at the fire without water.

In eggs boiled and *roasted*, there is scarce difference to be discerned. *Bacon's Natural History.*

4. To heat any thing violently.

Roasted in wrath and fire,
He thus o'ersized with coagulate gore,
Old Priam seeks. *Shakespeare.*

Roast. for *roasted.*

He lost his *roast* beef stomach, not being able to touch a sirloin. *Addison's Spectator,* № 517.

And if Dan Congreve judges right,
Roast beef and ale make Britons fight. *Prior.*

It warns the cook-maid, not to burn
The *roast* meat, which it cannot turn. *Swift's Miscel.*

To rule the Roast. To govern; to manage; to preside. It was perhaps originally *roist*, which signified a tumult, to direct the populace.

The new-made duke, that *rules the roast*. *Shakesp.*

Where champions *ruleth the rost*,
There dailie disorder is most. *Tusser's Husbandry.*

Alma slap-dash, is all again
In ev'ry sinew, nerve, and vein;
Runs here and there, like Hamlet's ghost,
While every where she *rules the roast*. *Prior.*

Rob. *n. s.* [I believe Arabick.] Inspissated juices.

The infusion, being evaporated to a thicker consistence, passeth into a jelly, *rob*, extract, which contain all the virtues of the infusion. *Arbuthnot on Aliments.*

To ROB. *v. a.* [*rober*, old Fr. *robbare*, Italian.]

1. To deprive of any thing by unlawful force, or by secret theft; to plunder. To be *robbed*, according to the present use of the word, is to be injured by theft secret or violent; to *rob*, is to take away by unlawful violence; and to *steal*, is to take away privately.

Is't not enough to break into my garden,
And, like a thief, to come to *rob* my grounds,
But thou wilt brave me with these sawcy terms? *Shakesp.*

Our sins being ripe, there was no preventing of God's justice from reaping that glory in our calamities, which we *robbed* him of in our prosperity. *King Charles.*

I have not here designed to *rob* him of any part of that commendation, which he has so justly acquired from the whole author, whose fragments only fall to my portion. *Dry.*

The water nymphs lament their empty urns,
Bœotia, *robb'd* of silver Dirce, mourns. *Addison.*

2. To set free; to deprive of something bad. Ironical.

Our house is hell, and thou, a merry devil,
Did'st *rob* it of some taste of tediousness. *Shakesp.*

3. To take away unlawfully.

Better be disdained of all, than fashion a carriage to *rob* love from any. *Shakesp.*

Procure, that the nourishment may not be *robbed* and drawn away. *Bacon's Natural History.*

Nor will I take from any man his due;
But thus assuming all, he *robs* from you. *Dryden.*

Oh double sacrilege on things divine,
To *rob* the relick, and deface the shrine! *Dryden.*

Ro'bber. *n. s.* [from *rob.*] A thief; one that robs by force, or steals by secret means; a plunderer.

These hairs, which thou dost ravish from my chin,
Will quicken and accuse thee; I'm your host;
With *robbers* hands, my hospitable favour
You should not ruffle thus. *Shakesp. King Lear.*

Barabbas was a *robber*. *St. John.*

Had'st thou not committed
Notorious murder on those thirty men
At Ascalon; then, like a *robber*, strip'd'st them
Of their robes. *Milton's Agonistes.*

The *robber* must run, ride, and use all the desperate ways of escape; and probably, after all, his sin betrays him to the goal, and from thence advances him to the gibbet. *South.*

Bold Prometheus did aspire,
And stole from heav'n the seeds of fire;
A train of ills, a ghastly crew,
The *robber's* blazing track pursue. *Dryden's Horace.*

Ro'bbery. *n. s.* [*roberie*, old Fr. from *rob.*] Theft perpetrated by force or with privacy.

Thieves for their *robbery* have authority,
When judges steal themselves. *Shakesp. Meas. for Meas.*

A storm or *robbery*
Shook down my mellow hangings. *Shakesp. Cymbeline.*

I hate *robbery* for burnt-offering. *Isaiah* lxi. 8.

Some more effectual way might be found, for suppressing common thefts and *robberies*. *Temple.*

Robe. *n. s.* [*robbe*, Fr. *robba*, Italian; *rauba*, low Lat.] A gown of state; a dress of dignity.

Through tatter'd cloaths small vices do appear;
Robes and furr'd gowns hide all. *Shakesp. King Lear.*

My

My Nan ſhall be the queen of all fairies,
Finely attir'd in a *robe* of white. *Shakeſp.*

The laſt good king, whom willing Rome obey'd,
Was the poor offspring of a captive maid;
Yet he thoſe *robes* of empire juſtly bore,
Which Romulus, our ſacred founder, wore. *Dryden.*

How by the fineſt art the native *robe*
To weave. *Thomſon's Autumn.*

To ROBE. *v. a.* [from the noun.] To dreſs pompouſly; to inveſt.

What chriſtian ſoldier will not be touched with a religious emulation, to ſee an order of Jeſus do ſuch ſervice for enlarging the chriſtian borders; and an order of St. George only to *robe*, and feaſt, and perform rites and obſervances. *Bacon.*

There in long robes the royal magi ſtand;
The ſage Chaldæans *rob'd* in white appear'd,
And Brachmans. *Pope's Temple of Fame.*

Robed in looſe array ſhe came to bathe. *Thomſon.*

RO'BERT. *n. ſ.* An herb. *Ainſ.*

ROBE'RSMAN. } *n. ſ.* In the old ſtatutes, a ſort of bold and
ROBE'RTSMAN. } ſtout robbers or night thieves, ſaid to be ſo called from Robinhood, a famous robber.

RO'BIN. } *n. ſ.* [*rubecula*, Lat.] A bird ſo named
ROBIN-RED-BREAST. } from his red breaſt.

Up a grove did ſpring, green as in May,
When April had been moiſt; upon whoſe buſhes
The pretty *robins*, nightingales, and thruſhes
Warbled their notes. *Suckling.*

The *robin-red-breaſt*, till of late had reſt,
And children ſacred held a martin's neſt. *Pope.*

ROBO'REOUS. *adj.* [*robur*, Lat.] Made of oak. *Dict.*

ROBU'ST. } *adj.* [*robuſtus*, Lat. *robuſte*, Fr.]
ROBU'STIOUS. }

1. Strong; ſinewy; vigorous; forceful.

Theſe redundant locks,
Robuſtious to no purpoſe, cluſtring down,
Vain monument of ſtrength. *Milton's Agoniſtes.*

2. Boiſterous; violent; unwieldy.

The men ſympathize with the maſtiffs, in *robuſtious* and rough coming on. *Shakeſp. Henry V.*

It offends me to hear a *robuſtious* periwig-pated fellow tear a paſſion to tatters, to very rags, to ſplit the ears of the groundlings. *Shakeſp. Hamlet.*

While I was managing this young *robuſtious* fellow, that old ſpark, who was nothing but ſkin and bone, ſlipt through my fingers. *Dryden's Don Sebaſtian.*

Romp-loving miſs
Is haul'd about in gallantry *robuſt*. *Thomſon's Autumn.*

3. Requiring ſtrength.

The tenderneſs of a ſprain remains a good while after, and leaves a laſting caution in the man, not to put the part quickly again to any *robuſt* employment. *Locke.*

4. *Robuſtious* is now only uſed in low language, and in a ſenſe of contempt.

ROBU'STNESS. *n. ſ.* [from *robuſt.*] Strength; vigour.

Beef may confer a *robuſtneſs* on my ſon's limbs, but will hebetate his intellectuals. *Arbuthnot and Pope.*

ROCAMBO'LE. *n. ſ.* See GARLICK.

Rocambole is a ſort of wild garlick, otherwiſe called Spaniſh garlick; the ſeed is about the bigneſs of ordinary peaſe. *Mort.*

Garlick, *rocambole*, and onions abound with a pungent volatile ſalt. *Arbuthnot on Aliments.*

ROCHE-ALUM. *n. ſ.* [*roche*, Fr. a rock.] A purer kind of alum.

Roche-alum is alſo good. *Mortimer's Huſbandry.*

RO'CHET. *n. ſ.* [*rochet*, Fr. *rochetum*, from *roccus*, low Lat. a coat.]

1. A ſurplice; the white upper garment of the prieſt officiating.

What zealous phrenzy did the ſenate ſeize,
That tare the *rotchet* to ſuch rags as theſe? *Cleaveland.*

2. [*Rubellio*, Lat.] A fiſh. *Ainſ.*

ROCK. *n. ſ.* [*roc*, *roche*, Fr. *rocca*, Italian.]

1. A vaſt maſs of ſtone.

The ſplitting *rocks* cow'r'd in the ſinking ſands,
And would not daſh me with their ragged ſides. *Shakeſp.*

There be *rock* herbs; but thoſe are where there is ſome mould. *Bacon's Natural Hiſtory.*

Diſtilling ſome of the tincted liquor, all that came over was as limpid and colourleſs as *rock* water, and the liquour remaining in the veſſel deeply ceruleous. *Boyle.*

Theſe leſſer *rocks*, or great bulky ſtones, are they not manifeſt fragments? *Burnet's Theory of the Earth.*

Of amber a nodule, inveſted with a coat, called *rock* amber. *Woodward on Foſſils.*

Pigeons or doves are of ſeveral ſorts; as wood pigeons and *rock* pigeons. *Mortimer's Huſbandry.*

Ye darkſome pines, that o'er yon *rocks* reclin'd,
Wave high, and murmur to the hollow wind. *Pope.*

2. Protection; defence. A ſcriptural ſenſe.

Though the reeds of Egypt break under the hand of him that leans on them, yet the *rock* of Iſrael will be an everlaſting ſtay. *King Charles.*

3. [*Rock*, Daniſh; *rocca*, Italian; *rucca*, Spaniſh; *ſpinrock*, Dutch.] A diſtaff held in the hand, from which the wool was ſpun by twirling a ball below.

A learned and a manly ſoul
I purpos'd her; that ſhould with even powers,
The *rock*, the ſpindle, and the ſheers, controul
Of deſtiny, and ſpin her own free hours. *Benj. Johnſon.*

On the *rock* a ſcanty meaſure place
Of vital flax, and turn'd the wheel apace. *Dryden.*

To ROCK. *v. a.* [*rocquer*, Fr.]

1. To ſhake; to move backwards and forwards.

If, by a quicker *rocking* of the engine, the ſmoke were more ſwiftly ſhaken, it would, like water, vibrate to and fro. *Boyle.*

The wind was laid; the whiſp'ring ſound
Was dumb; a riſing earthquake *rock'd* the ground. *Dryden.*

A living tortoiſe, being turned upon its back, could help itſelf only by its neck and head, by puſhing againſt the ground to *rock* itſelf as in a cradle, to find out the ſide towards which the inequality of the ground might more eaſily permit to roll its ſhell. *Ray on the Creation.*

2. To move the cradle, in order to procure ſleep.

Come, take hand with me,
And *rock* the ground whereon theſe ſleepers be. *Shakeſp.*

Leaning her head upon my breaſt,
My panting heart *rock'd* her aſleep. *Suckling.*

My bloody reſolutions,
Like ſick and froward children,
Were *rock'd* aſleep by reaſon. *Denham.*

While his ſecret ſoul on Flanders preys,
He *rocks* the cradle of the babe of Spain. *Dryden.*

High in his hall, *rock'd* in a chair of ſtate,
The king with his tempeſtuous council ſate. *Dryden.*

3. To lull; to quiet.

Sleep *rock* thy brain,
And never come miſchance between us twain! *Shakeſp.*

To ROCK. *v. n.* To be violently agitated; to reel to and fro.

The *rocking* town
Supplants their footſteps; to and fro they reel
Aſtoniſh'd. *Philips.*

I like this *rocking* of the battlements. *Young's Revenge.*

ROCK-DOE. *n. ſ.* A ſpecies of deer.

The *rock-doe* breeds chiefly upon the Alps: a creature of admirable ſwiftneſs; and may probably be that mentioned in the book of Job: her horns grow ſometimes ſo far backward, as to reach over her buttocks. *Grew's Muſæum.*

ROCK-RUBY. *n. ſ.* A name given improperly by lapidaries and jewellers to the garnet, when it is of a very ſtrong, but not deep red, and has a fair caſt of the blue. *Hill on Foſſils.*

Rock-ruby is of a deep red, and the hardeſt of all the kinds. *Woodward on Foſſils.*

ROCK-SALT. *n. ſ.* Mineral ſalt.

Two pieces of tranſparent *rock-ſalt*; one white, the other red. *Woodward on Foſſils.*

RO'CKER. *n. ſ.* [from *rock.*] One who rocks the cradle.

His fellow, who the narrow bed had kept,
Was weary, and without a *rocker* ſlept. *Dryden.*

RO'CKET. *n. ſ.* [*rocchetto*, Italian.] An artificial firework, being a cylindrical caſe of paper filled with nitre, charcoal, and ſulphur, and which mounts in the air to a conſiderable height, and there burſts.

Every *rocket* ended in a conſtellation, ſtrowing the air with a ſhower of ſilver ſpangles. *Addiſon.*

When bonefires blaze, your vagrant works ſhall riſe
In *rockets*, till they reach the wond'ring ſkies. *Garth.*

RO'CKET. *n. ſ.* A plant.

The flower of the *rocket* conſiſts of four leaves expanded in form of a croſs; the pointal becomes a pod, divided into two cells by an intermediate partition, to which the valves adhere on both ſides: theſe cells are full of roundiſh ſeeds; to which may be added, the whole plant hath a peculiar fetid ſmell. *Miller.*

Rocket is one of the ſallet furniture. *Mortimer's Huſbandry.*

RO'CKLESS. *adj.* [from *rock.*] Being without rocks.

A cryſtal brook
Is weedleſs all above, and *rockleſs* all below. *Dryden.*

RO'CKROSE. *n. ſ.* [*rock* and *roſe.*] A plant.

RO'CKWORK. *n. ſ.* [*rock* and *work.*] Stones fixed in mortar, in imitation of the aſperities of rocks.

The garden is fenced on the lower end, by a natural mound of *rockwork.* *Addiſon.*

RO'CKY. *adj.* [from *rock.*]

1. Full of rocks.

Val de Compare preſenteth her *rocky* mountains. *Sandys.*

Make the bold prince
Through the cold North and *rocky* regions run. *Waller.*

The vallies he reſtrains
With *rocky* mountains. *Dryden.*

Nature lodges her treaſures in *rocky* ground. *Locke.*

2. Resembling a rock.

Such destruction to withstand, he oppos'd the *rocky* orb
Of tenfold adamant, his ample shield. *Milton.*

3. Hard; stony; obdurate.

I, like a poor bark, of sails and tackling reft,
Rush all to pieces on thy *rocky* bosom. *Shakesp. Rich.* III.

ROD. *n. s.* [*roede*, Dutch.]

1. A long twig.

Some chuse a hazel *rod* of the same year's shoot, and this they bind on to another straight stick of any wood, and walking softly over those places, where they suspect the bowels of the earth to be enriched with metals, the wand will, by bowing towards it, discover it. *Boyle.*

2. A kind of scepter.

Sh' had all the royal makings of a queen;
As holy oil, Edward confessor's crown,
The *rod* and bird of peace. *Shakesp. Henry* VIII.

3. Any thing long and slender.

The past'ral reed of Hermes, or his opiate *rod. Milton.*

Let the fisherman
Increase his tackle, and his *rod* retie. *Gay.*

Haste, ye Cyclops, with your forked *rods*,
This rebel love braves all the gods,
And every hour by love is made,
Some heaven-defying Encelade. *Granville.*

4. An instrument for measuring.

Decempeda was a measuring *rod* for taking the dimensions of buildings, and signified the same thing as pertica, taken as a measure of length. *Arbuthnot on Coins.*

5. An instrument of correction, made of twigs tied together.

If he be but once so taken idly roguing, he may punish him with stocks; but if he be found again so loitering, he may scourge him with whips or *rods*. *Spenser on Ireland.*

I am whipt and scourg'd with *rods*,
Nettled, and stung with pismires, when I hear
Of Bolingbroke. *Shakesp. Henry* IV.

In this condition the *rod* of God hath a voice to be heard, and he, whose office it is, ought now to expound to the sick man the particular meaning of the voice. *Hammond.*

Grant me and my people the benefit of thy chastisements; that thy *rod*, as well as thy staff, may comfort us. *K. Charles.*

They trembling learn to throw the fatal dart,
And under *rods* of rough centurions smart. *Dryden.*

As soon as that sentence is executed, these *rods*, these instruments of divine displeasure, are thrown into the fire. *Att.*

A wit's a feather, and a chief a *rod*;
An honest man's the noblest work of God. *Pope.*

RODE. pret. of *ride*.

He in paternal glory *rode*. *Milton.*

RODOMONTA'DE. *n. s.* [from a boastful boisterous hero of Ariosto, called *Rodomonte*; *rodomontade*, Fr.] An empty noisy bluster or boast; a rant.

He only serves to be sport for his company; for in these gamesome days men will give him hints, which may put him upon his *rodomontades*. *Government of the Tongue.*

The libertines of painting have no other model but a *rodomontade* genius, and very irregular, which violently hurries them away. *Dryden's Dufresnoy.*

He talks extravagantly in his passion, but if I would quote a hundred passages in Ben Johnson's Cethegus, I could shew that the *rodomontades* of Almanzor are neither so irrational nor impossible, for Cethegus threatens to destroy nature. *Dry.*

To RODOMONTA'DE. *v. n.* [from the noun.] To brag thrasonically; to boast like Rodomonte.

ROE. *n. s.* [ꞃa, ꞃa-ꝺeoꞃ, Saxon.]

1. A species of deer.

He would him make
The *roe* bucks in flight to overtake. *Fairy Queen.*

They were as swift as the *roes* upon the mountains. 1 *Chr.*

Procure me a Troglodyte footman, who can catch a *roe* at his full speed? *Arbuthnot and Pope.*

2. The female of the hart.

Thy greyhounds are fleeter than the *roe*. *Shakesp.*

Run like a *roe* or hart upon
The lofty hills of Bitheron. *Sandys's Paraphrase.*

ROE. *n. s.* [properly *roan* or *rone*; *rann*, Danish: *rogen*, German.] The eggs of fish.

Here comes Romeo
Without his *roe*, like a dried herring. *Shakesp.*

ROGA'TION. *n. s.* [*rogation*, Fr. from *rogo*, Lat.] Litany; supplication.

He perfecteth the *rogations* or litanies before in use, and addeth unto them that which the present necessity required. *Hook.*

Supplications, with this solemnity for appeasing of God's wrath, were of the Greek church termed litanies, and *rogations* of the Latin. *Taylor.*

ROGATION-WEEK. *n. s.* The week immediately preceeding Whitsunday; thus called from three fasts observed therein, the Monday, Tuesday, and Wednesday, called rogation days, because of the extraordinary prayers and processions then made for the fruits of the earth, or as a preparation for the devotion of holy Thursday. *Dict.*

ROGUE. *n. s.* [of uncertain etymology.]

1. A wandering beggar; a vagrant; a vagabond.

For fear lest we, like *rogues*, should be reputed,
And for ear-marked beasts abroad be bruited. *Hubberd.*

The sheriff and the marshal may do the more good, and more terrify the idle *rogue*. *Spenser on Ireland.*

The scum of people and wicked condemned men spoileth the plantation; for they will ever live like *rogues*, and not fall to work, but be lazy and do mischief. *Bacon's Essays.*

The troops are all scattered, and the commanders very poor *rogues*. *Shakesp. All's well that ends well.*

2. A knave; a dishonest fellow; a villain; a thief.

Thou kill'st me like a *rogue* and a villain. *Shakesp.*

A *rogue* upon the highway may have as strong an arm, and take off a man's head as cleverly as the executioner; but then there is a vast disparity, when one action is murther, and the other justice. *South.*

If he call *rogue* and rascal from the garret,
He means you no more mischief than a parrot. *Dryden.*

The *rogue* and fool by fits is fair and wise,
And ev'n the best, by fits, what they despise. *Pope.*

3. A name of slight tenderness and endearment.

Oh, what a *rogue* and pleasant slave am I! *Shakesp.*

I never knew a woman love man so.
—Alas, poor *rogue*, I think indeed she loves. *Shakesp.*

4. A wag.

To ROGUE. *v. n.* [from the noun.]

1. To wander; to play the vagabond.

If he be but once so taken idly *roguing*, he may punish him with the stocks. *Spenser on Ireland.*

He *rogued* away at last, and was lost. *Carew.*

2. To play knavish tricks.

RO'GUERY. *n. s.* [from *rogue*.]

1. The life of a vagabond.

To live in one land is captivity,
To run all countries a wild *roguery*. *Donne.*

2. Knavish tricks.

They will afterwards hardly be drawn to their wonted lewd life in thievery and *roguery*. *Spenser on Ireland.*

You rogue, here's lime in this sack too; there is nothing but *roguery* to be found in villainous man. *Shakesp.*

Like the devil did tempt and sway 'em
To *rogueries*, and then betray 'em. *Hudibras, p.* i.

The kid smelt out the *roguery*. *L'Estrange's Fables.*

'Tis no scandal grown,
For debt and *roguery* to quit the town. *Dryden.*

The *roguery* of alchymy,
And we, the bubbled fools,
Spend all our present stock in hopes of golden rules. *Swift.*

3. Waggery; arch tricks.

RO'GUESHIP. *n. s.* [from *rogue*.] The qualities or personage of a rogue.

Say, in what nasty cellar under ground,
Or what church porch, your *rogueship* may be found? *Dry.*

RO'GUISH. *adj.* [from *rogue*.]

1. Vagrant; vagabond.

Though the persons, by whom it is used, be of better note than the former *roguish* sort; yet the fault is no less worthy of a marshal. *Spenser.*

2. Knavish; fraudulent.

He gets a thousand thumps and kicks,
Yet cannot leave his *roguish* tricks. *Swift's Miscellanies.*

3. Waggish; wanton; slightly mischievous.

The most bewitching leer with her eyes, the most *roguish* cast; her cheeks are dimpled when she smiles, and her smiles would tempt an hermit. *Dryden's Spanish Fryar.*

I am pleased to see my tenants pass away a whole evening in playing their innocent tricks; our friend Wimble is as merry as any of them, and shews a thousand *roguish* tricks on these occasions. *Addison's Spectator*, No 269.

Timothy used to be playing *roguish* tricks; when his mistress's back was turned, he would loll out his tongue. *Arb.*

RO'GUISHLY. *adv.* [from *roguish*.] Like a rogue; knavishly; wantonly.

RO'GUISHNESS. *n. s.* [from *roguish*.] The qualities of a rogue.

RO'GUY. *adj.* [from *rogue*.] Knavish; wanton. A bad word.

A shepherd's boy had gotten a *roguy* trick of crying a wolf, and fooling the country with false alarms. *L'Estrange.*

To ROIST. } *v. n.* [of this word the most probable ety-
To ROI'STER. } mology is from *rister*, Islandick, a violent man.]

To behave turbulently; to act at discretion; to be at free quarter; to bluster.

I have a *roisting* challenge sent amongst
The dull and factious nobles of the Greeks,
Will strike amazement to their drowsy spirits. *Shakesp.*

Among a crew of *roist'ring* fellows,
He'd sit whole ev'nings at the alehouse. *Swift.*

ROI'STER, or *roisterer*. *n. s.* [from the verb.] A turbulent, brutal, lawless, blustering fellow.

To ROLL. *v. a.* [*rouler*, Fr. *rollen*, Dutch; from *rotulo*, of *roto*, Lat.]

1. To move any thing by volutation, or successive application of the different parts of the surface, to the ground.

Who shall *roll* us away the stone from the door of the sepulchre? *Mark* xvii. 3.

2. To move any thing round upon its axis.

Heav'n shone and *roll'd* her motions. *Milton.*

3. To move in a circle.

To dress, and troll the tongue, and *roll* the eye. *Milton.*

4. To produce a periodical revolution.

5. To wrap round upon itself.

6. To enwrap; to involve in bandage.

By this *roiling*, parts are kept from joining together. *Wisem.*

7. To form by rolling into round masses.

Grind red-lead, or any other colour with strong wort, and so *roll* them up into long rolls like pencils. *Peacham.*

The pin ought to be as thick as a *rolling* pin. *Wiseman.*

8. To pour in a stream or waves.

A small Euphrates through the piece is *roll'd*,
And little eagles wave their wings in gold. *Pope.*

To Roll. *v. n.*

1. To be moved by the successive application of all parts of the surface to the ground.

Our nation is too great to be ruined by any but itself; and if the number and weight of it *roll* one way upon the greatest changes that can happen, yet England will be safe. *Temple.*

Reports, like snow-balls, gather still the farther they *roll*. *Government of the Tongue.*

Fire must rend the sky,
And wheel on th' earth, devouring where it *rolls*. *Milton.*

A tortoise, by pushing against the ground only with its neck and head, rocks itself as in a cradle, to find out the side towards which the inequality of the ground might more easily permit it to *roll* its shell. *Ray on the Creation.*

2. To run on wheels.

He next essays to walk, but downward press'd,
On four feet imitates his brother beast;
By slow degrees he gathers from the ground
His legs, and to the *rolling* chair is bound. *Dryden.*

3. To perform a periodical revolution.

Thus the year *rolls* within itself again. *Dryden.*
When thirty *rolling* years have run their race. *Dryden.*

4. To move with appearance of circular direction.

Thou, light,
Revisit'st not these eyes, which *roll* in vain,
To find the piercing ray, and find no dawn. *Milton.*
A boar is chaf'd, his nostrils flames expire,
And his red eye-balls *roll* with living fire. *Dryden.*

5. To float in rough water.

Twice ten tempestuous nights I *roll'd*, resign'd
To roaring billows and the warring wind. *Pope.*

6. To move as waves or volumes of water.

Wave *rolling* after wave in torrent rapture. *Milton.*
Till the huge surge *roll'd* off, then backward sweep
The refluent tides, and plunge into the deep. *Pope.*
Tempt icy seas, where scarce the waters *roll*. *Pope.*
Storms beat, and *rolls* the main;
Oh beat those storms, and *roll* the seas in vain. *Pope.*

7. To fluctuate; to move tumultuously.

Here tell me, if thou dar'st, my conscious soul,
What diff'rent sorrows did within thee *roll*. *Prior.*
The thoughts, which *roll* within my ravish'd breast,
To me, no seer, th' inspiring gods suggest. *Pope.*
In her sad breast the prince's fortunes *roll*,
And hope and doubt alternate seize her soul. *Pope.*

8. To revolve on its axis.

He fashion'd those harmonious orbs, that *roll*
In restless gyres about the Artick pole. *Sandys's Paraph.*

9. To be moved tumultuously.

Down they fell
By thousands, angel on archangel *roll'd*. *Milton.*

Roll. *n. s.* [from the verb.]

1. The act of rolling; the state of being rolled.

2. The thing rolling.

Listening senates hang upon thy tongue,
Devolving through the maze of eloquence
A *roll* of periods, sweeter than her song. *Thomson.*

3. [*Rouleau*, Fr.] Mass made round.

Large *rolls* of fat about his shoulders clung,
And from his neck the double dewlap hung. *Addison.*

To keep ants from trees, encompass the stem four fingers breadth with a circle or *roll* of wool newly plucked. *Mort.*

4. Writing rolled upon itself.

His chamber all was hanged about with *rolls*
And old records, from antient times deriv'd. *Fa. Queen.*

5. A round body rolled along.

Where land is clotty, and a shower of rain comes that soaks through, use a *roll* to break the clots. *Mortimer.*

6. [*Rotulus*, Lat.] Publick writing.

Cromwell is made master
O' th' *rolls* and the king's secretary. *Shakesp. Henry* VIII.

Darius made a decree, and search was made in the house of the *rolls*, where the treasures were laid up. *Ezra* vi. 1.

The *rolls* of parliament, the entry of the petitions, answers, and transactions in parliament are extant. *Hale.*

7. A register; a catalogue.

Beasts only cannot discern beauty; and let them be in the *roll* of beasts, that do not honour it. *Sidney.*

The *roll* and list of that army doth remain. *Davies.*

Of that short *roll* of friends writ in my heart,
There's none, that sometimes greet us not. *Donne.*

These signs have mark'd me extraordinary,
And all the courses of my life do shew,
I am not in the *roll* of common men. *Shakesp. Henry* IV.

'Tis a mathematical demonstration, that these twenty-four letters admit of so many changes in their order, and make such a long *roll* of differently ranged alphabets, not two of which are alike; that they could not all be exhausted, though a million millions of writers should each write above a thousand alphabets a-day, for the space of a million millions of years. *Bentl.*

8. Chronicle.

Please thy pride, and search the herald's *roll*,
Where thou shalt find thy famous pedigree. *Dryden.*
Busy angels spread
The lasting *roll*, recording what we said. *Prior.*
The eye of time beholds no name
So blest as thine, in all the *rolls* of fame. *Pope.*

9. Warrant. Not in use.

We have, with special *roll*,
Elected him our absence to supply. *Shakesp. Meas. for Meas.*

10. [*Role*, Fr.] Part; office. Not in use.

In human society, every man has his *roll* and station assigned him. *L'Estrange.*

Ro'ller. *n. s.* [*rouleau*, Fr. from *roll*.]

1. Any thing turning on its own axis, as a heavy stone to level walks.

When a man tumbles a *roller* down a hill, the man is the violent enforcer of the first motion; but when it is once tumbling, the property of the thing itself continues it. *Hamm.*

The long slender worms, that breed between the skin and flesh in the isle of Ormuz and in India, are generally twisted out upon sticks or *rollers*. *Ray on the Creation.*

They make the string of the pole horizontal towards the lathe, conveying and guiding the string from the pole to the work, by throwing it over a *roller*. *Moxon's Mech. Exer.*

Lady Charlotte, like a stroller,
Sits mounted on the garden *roller*. *Swift's Miscellanies.*

2. Bandage; fillet.

Fasten not your *roller* by tying a knot, lest you hurt your patient. *Wiseman's Surgery.*

Bandage being chiefly to maintain the due situation of a dressing, surgeons always turn a *roller* with that view. *Sharp.*

Ro'llingpin. *n. s.* [*rolling* and *pin*.] A round piece of wood tapering at each end, with which paste is moulded.

The pin should be as thick as a *rollingpin*. *Wiseman.*

Rollypooly. *n. s.* A sort of game, in which, when a ball rolls into a certain place, it wins. A corruption of *roll ball into the pool*.

Let us begin some diversion; what d'ye think of *routypouly* or a country dance? *Arbuthnot's History of John Bull.*

Ro'mage. *n. s.* [*ramage*, Fr.] A tumult; a bustle; an active and tumultuous search for any thing.

This is the main motive
Of this post haste, and *romage* in the land. *Shakesp.*

ROMA'NCE. *n. s.* [*roman*, Fr. *romanza*, Italian.

1. A military fable of the middle ages; a tale of wild adventures in war and love.

What resounds
In fable or *romance* of Uther's son. *Milton.*
A brave *romance* who would exactly frame,
First brings his knight from some immortal dame. *Waller.*

Some *romances* entertain the genius; and strengthen it by the noble ideas which they give of things; but they corrupt the truth of history. *Dryden's Dufresnoy.*

2. A lie; a fiction. In common speech.

To Roma'nce. *v. n.* [from the noun.] To lie; to forge.

This is strange *romancing*. *Pamela.*

Roma'ncer. *n. s.* [from *romance*.] A lier; a forger of tales.

The allusion of the daw extends to all impostors, vain pretenders, and *romancers*. *L'Estrange.*

Shall we, cries one, permit
This leud *romancer*, and his bantering wit. *Tate's Juven.*

To Ro'manize. *v. a.* [from *roman*, Fr.] To latinize; to fill with modes of the Roman speech.

He did too much *romanize* our tongue, leaving the words, he translated, almost as much Latin as he found them. *Dryd.*

Roma'ntick. *adj.* [from *romance*.]

1. Resembling the tales of romances; wild.

Philosophers have maintained opinions, more absurd than any of the most fabulous poets or *romantick* writers. *Keil.*

Zeal for the good of one's country a party of men have represented, as chimerical and *romantick*. *Addison.*

2. Improbable; false.

3. Fanciful; full of wild scenery.

The dun umbrage, o'er the falling stream,
Romantick hangs. *Thomson's Spring.*

RO'MISH. *adj.* [from *Rome.*] Popish.

Bulls or letters of election only serve in the *Romish* countries. *Ayliffe's Parergon.*

ROMP. *n. s.*

1. A rude, awkward, boisterous, untaught girl.

She was in the due mean between one of your affected courtesying pieces of formality, and your *romps* that have no regard to the common rules of civility. *Arbuthnot.*

2. Rough rude play.

Romp loving miss
Is haul'd about in gallantry robust. *Thomson.*

To ROMP. *v. n.* To play rudely, noisily, and boisterously.

In the kitchen, as in your proper element, you can laugh, squall, and *romp* in full security. *Swift's Rules to Servants.*

A stool is the first weapon taken up in a general *romping* or skirmish. *Swift's Rules to Servants.*

Men presume greatly on the liberties taken in *romping.* *Clarissa.*

RO'NDEAU. *n. s.* A kind of ancient poetry, commonly consisting of thirteen verses; of which eight have one rhyme and five another: it is divided into three couplets, and at the end of the second and third, the beginning of the *rondeau* is repeated in an equivocal sense, if possible. *Trevoux.*

RONT. *n. s.* An animal stinted in the growth.

My ragged *ronts* all shiver and shake,
As done high towers in an earthquake;
They wont in the wind, wag their wriggle tails,
Peark as a peacock, but nought it avails. *Spenser.*

RO'NDLES. *n. s.* [from *round.*] A round mass.

Certain *rondles* given in arms, have their names according to their several colours. *Peacham on Blazoning.*

RO'NION. *n. s.* [I know not the etymology, nor certainly the meaning of this word.] A fat bulky woman.

Give me, quoth I,
Aroint the witch! the rump fed *ronyon* cries. *Shakesp.*

ROOD. *n. s.* [from *rod.*]

1. The fourth part of an acre in square measure.

I've often wish'd that I had clear,
For life, six hundred pounds a year,
A terras-walk, and half a *rood*
Of land, set out to plant a wood. *Swift.*

2. A pole; a measure of sixteen feet and a half in long measure.

Satan,
With head uplift 'bove the wave, his other parts
Prone on the flood, extended long and large,
Lay floating many a *rood.* *Milton.*

For stone fences in the North, they dig the stones for eighteen-pence a *rood,* and make the walls for the same price, reckoning twenty-one foot to the *rood* or pole. *Mortimer.*

3. [roode, Saxon.] The cross.

By the holy *rood,*
I do not like these several councils. *Shakesp.*

ROOF. *n. s.* [hrof, Saxon.]

1. The cover of a house.

Her shoulders be like two white doves,
Perching within square royal *rooves.* *Sidney.*

Return to her, and fifty men dismiss'd?
No, rather I abjure all *roofs,* and chuse
To wage against the enmity o' th' air. *Shakesp. K. Lear.*

2. The vault; the inside of the arch that covers a building.

From the magnanimity of the Jews, in causes of most extreme hazard, those strange and unwonted resolutions have grown, which, for all circumstances, no people under the *roof* of heaven did ever match. *Hooker.*

The dust
Should have ascended to the *roof* of heav'n,
Rais'd by your populous troops. *Shakesp. Ant. and Cleop.*

In thy fane, the dusty spoils among,
High on the burnish'd *roof,* my banner shall be hung. *Dryden.*

3. The palate; the upper part of the mouth.

Swearing till my very *roof* was dry
With oaths of love. *Shakesp. Merchant of Venice.*

My very lips might freeze to my teeth, my tongue to the *roof* of my mouth, ere I should come by a fire to thaw me. *Shakesp. Taming of the Shrew.*

The nobles held their peace, and their tongue cleaved to the *roof* of their mouth. *Job* xxix. 10.

Some fishes have rows of teeth in the *roofs* of their mouths; as pikes, salmons, and trouts. *Bacon's Natural History.*

To ROOF. *v. a.* [from the noun.]

1. To cover with a roof.

He enter'd soon the shade
High *roof't,* and walks beneath, and alleys brown. *Milton.*

Large foundations may be safely laid;
Or houses *roof'd,* if friendly planets aid. *Creech.*

I have not seen the remains of any Roman buildings, that have not been *roofed* with vaults or arches. *Addison.*

2. To inclose in a house.

Here had we now our country's honour *roof'd,*
Were the grac'd person of our Banquo present. *Shakesp.*

ROO'FY. *adj.* [from *roof.*] Having roofs.

Snakes,
Whether to *roofy* houses they repair,
Or sun themselves abroad in open air,
In all abodes of pestilential kind
To sheep. *Dryden's Georgicks.*

ROOK. *n. s.* [hroc, Saxon.]

1. A bird resembling a crow: it feeds not on carrion, but grain.

Augurs, that understood relations, have,
By magpies, and by choughs, and *rooks,* brought forth
The secret'st man of blood. *Shakesp. Macbeth.*

Huge flocks of rising *rooks* forsake their food,
And crying seek the shelter of the wood. *Dryden.*

The jay, the *rook,* the daw
Aid the full concert. *Thomson's Spring.*

2. [*Rocco,* Italian.] A mean man at chess.

So have I seen a king on chess,
His *rooks* and knights withdrawn,
His queen and bishops in distress,
Shifting about grow less and less,
With here and there a pawn. *Dryden's Songs.*

3. A cheat; a trickish rapacious fellow.

I am, like an old *rook,* who is ruined by gaming, forced to live on the good fortune of the pushing young men. *Wycherly.*

To ROOK. *v. n.* [from the noun.] To rob; to cheat.

They *rook'd* upon us with design,
To out-reform and undermine. *Hudibras, p.* iii.

How any one's being put into a mixed herd of unruly boys, and there learning to *rook* at span-farthing, fits him for conversation, I do not see. *Locke on Education.*

ROO'KERY. *n. s.* [from *rook.*] A nursery of rooks.

No lone house in Wales, with a mountain and a *rookery,* is more contemplative than this court. *Pope.*

ROO'KY. *adj.* [from *rook.*] Inhabited by rooks.

Light thickens, and the crow
Makes wing to th' *rooky* wood. *Shakesp. Macbeth.*

ROOM. *n. s.* [rum, Saxon; *rums,* Gothick.]

1. Space; extent of place.

With new wonder, now he views,
To all delight of human sense expos'd
In narrow *room,* nature's whole wealth. *Milton.*

2. Space or place unoccupied.

If you will have a young man to put his travels into a little *room,* and in short time gather much, this he must do. *Bac.*

The dry land is much too big for its inhabitants; and that before they shall want *room* by encreasing and multiplying, there may be new heavens and a new earth. *Bentley.*

3. Way unobstructed.

Make *room,* and let him stand before our face. *Shakesp.*

What train of servants, what extent of field,
Shall aid the birth, or give him *room* to build? *Creech.*

This paternal regal power, being by divine right, leaves no *room* for human prudence to place it any where. *Locke.*

4. Place of another; stead.

In evils, that cannot be removed without the manifest danger of greater to succeed in their *rooms,* wisdom of necessity must give place to necessity. *Hooker, b.* v. *s.* 9.

For better ends our kind redeemer dy'd,
Or the fallen angels *rooms* will be but ill supply'd. *Rosc.*

By contributing to the contentment of other men, and rendering them as happy as lies in our power, we do God's work, are in his place and *room.* *Calamy's Sermons.*

5. Unobstructed opportunity.

When this princess was in her father's court, she was so celebrated, that there was no prince in the empire, who had *room* for such an alliance, that was not ambitious of gaining her into his family. *Addison's Freeholder,* N° 2.

It puts us upon so eager a pursuit of the advantages of life, as leaves no *room* to reflect on the great author of them. *Att.*

Will you not look with pity on me?
Is there no hope? is there no *room* for pardon? *A. Philips.*

6. An apartment in a house; so much of a house as is inclosed within partitions.

I found the prince in the next *room,*
Washing with kindly tears his gentle cheeks. *Shakesp.*

If when she appears in th' *room,*
Thou dost not quake, and art struck dumb;
Know this,
Thou lov'st amiss;
And to love true,
Thou must begin again, and love anew. *Suckling.*

In a prince's court, the only question a man is to ask is, whether it be the custom of the court, or will of the prince, to be uncovered in some *rooms* and not in others. *Stillingfleet.*

It will afford me a few pleasant *rooms,* for such a friend as yourself. *Pope.*

ROO'MAGE. *n. s.* [from *room.*] Space; place.

Man, of all sensible creatures, has the fullest brain to his proportion, for the lodging of the intellective faculties: it must be a silent character of hope, when there is good store of *roomage* and receipt, where those powers are stowed. *Wotton.*

ROO'MINESS. *n. s.* [from *roomy.*] Space; quantity of extent.

Roo'my. *adj.* [from *room.*] Spacious; wide; large.
With *roomy* decks, her guns of mighty strength,
Deep in her draught, and warlike in her length. *Dryden.*
This sort of number is more *roomy*; the thought can turn itself with greater ease in a larger compass. *Dryden.*

Roost. *n. s.* [hꞃoꞅꞇ, Saxon.]
1. That on which a bird sits to sleep.
Sooner than the mattin-bell was rung,
He clap'd his wings upon his *roost*, and sung. *Dryden.*
2. The act of sleeping.
A fox spied out a cock at *roost* upon a tree. *L'Estrange.*
Large and strong muscles move the wings, and support the body at *roost*. *Derham's Physico-Theology.*

To Roost. *v. n.* [*roesten*, Dutch; of the same etymology with *rest.*]
1. To sleep as a bird.
The cock *roosted* at night upon the boughs. *L'Estrange.*
2. To lodge. In burlesque.

ROOT. *n. s.* [*rôt*, Swedish; *roed*, Danish.]
1. That part of the plant which rests in the ground, and supplies the stems with nourishment.
The layers will in a month strike *root*, being planted in a light loamy earth, mixed with excellent rotten soil, and sifted. *Evelyn's Kalendar.*
When you would have many new *roots* of fruit trees, take a low tree and bow it, and lay all his branches aflat upon the ground, and cast earth upon them, and every twig will take *root*. *Bacon's Natural History.*
A flow'r in meadow ground, amellus call'd;
And from one *root* the rising stem bestows
A wood of leaves. *Dryden's Virgil's Georgicks.*
In October, the hops will settle and strike *root* against spring. *Mortimer's Husbandry.*
2. The bottom; the lower part.
Deep to the *roots* of hell the gather'd breach
They fasten'd. *Milton.*
These subterraneous vaults would be found especially about the *roots* of the mountains. *Burnet's Theory of the Earth.*
3. A plant of which the root is esculent.
Those plants, whose *roots* are eaten, are carrots, turnips, and radishes. *Watts.*
4. The original; the first cause.
Why did my parents send me to the schools,
That I with knowledge might enrich my mind?
Since the desire to know first made men fools,
And did corrupt the *root* of all mankind. *Davies.*
Whence,
But from the author of all ill, could spring
So deep a malice, to confound the race
Of mankind in one *root*. *Milton's Paradise Lost, b.* ii.
The love of money is the *root* of all evil, is a truth universally agreed in. *Temple.*
5. The first ancestor.
It was said,
That myself should be the *root*, and father
Of many kings. *Shakesp. Macbeth.*
They were the *roots*, out of which sprang two distinct people, under two distinct governments. *Locke.*
6. Fixed residence.
That love took deepest *root*, which first did grow. *Dry.*
7. Impression; durable effect.
Having this way eased the church, as they thought of superfluity, they went on till they had plucked up even those things also, which had taken a great deal stronger and deeper *root*. *Hooker, b.* iv. *s.* 14.

To Root. *v. n.* [from the noun.]
1. To fix the root; to strike far into the earth.
Her fallow leas
The darnel, hemlock and rank fumitory
Doth *root* upon. *Shakesp. Henry* V.
Underneath the grove of sycamour,
That westward *rooteth*, did I see your son. *Shakesp.*
The multiplying brood of the ungodly shall not take deep *rooting* from bastard slips, nor lay any fast foundation. *Wisd.*
After a year's *rooting*, then shaking doth the tree good, by loosening of the earth. *Bacon.*
The coulter must be proportioned to the soil, because, in deep grounds, the weeds *root* the deeper. *Mortimer.*
2. To turn up earth.

To Root. *v. a.* [from the noun.]
1. To fix deep in the earth.
When ocean, air, and earth at once engage,
And *rooted* forests fly before their rage,
At once the clashing clouds to battle move. *Dryden.*
Where th' impetuous torrent rushing down
Huge craggy stones, and *rooted* trees had thrown,
They left their coursers. *Dryden's Æneis.*
2. To impress deeply.
The great important end that God designs it for, the government of mankind, sufficiently shews the necessity of its being *rooted* deeply in the heart, and put beyond the danger of being torn up by any ordinary violence. *South.*

They have so *rooted* themselves in the opinions of their party, that they cannot hear an objection with patience. *Watts.*
3. To turn up out of the ground; to radicate; to extirpate.
He's a rank weed,
And we must *root* him out. *Shakesp. Henry* VIII.
Soon shall we drive back Alcibiades,
Who, like a boar too savage, doth *root* up
His country's peace. *Shakesp. Timon of Athens.*
The Egyptians think it sin to *root* up or to bite
Their leeks or onions, which they serve with holy rite.
Raleigh's History of the World.
Root up wild olives from thy labour'd lands. *Dryden.*
The royal husbandman appear'd,
And plough'd, and sow'd, and till'd;
The thorns he *rooted* out, the rubbish clear'd,
And blest th' obedient field. *Dryden.*
4. To destroy; to banish.
Not to destroy, but *root* them out of heav'n. *Milton.*
In vain we plant, we build, our stores increase,
If conscience *roots* up all our inward peace. *Granville.*

Roo'ted. *adj.* [from *root.*] Fixed; deep; radical.
Pluck from the memory a *rooted* sorrow,
Raze out the written troubles of the brain. *Shakesp.*
The danger is great to them, who, on a weaker foundation, do yet stand firmly *rooted*, and grounded in the love of Christ. *Hammond's Fundamentals.*
You always joined a violent desire of perpetually changing places with a *rooted* laziness. *Swift to Gay.*

Roo'tedly. *adv.* [from *rooted.*] Deeply; strongly.
They all do hate him as *rootedly* as I. *Shakesp.*

Roo'ty. *adj.* [from *root.*] Full of roots. *Dict.*

ROPE. *n. s.* [ꞃap, Saxon; *reep*, *roop*, Dutch.]
1. A cord; a string; a halter.
Thou drunken slave, I sent thee for a *rope*,
And told thee to what purpose. *Shakesp. Com. of Err.*
An anchor, let down by a *rope*, maketh a sound; and yet the *rope* is no solid body, whereby the sound can ascend. *Bac.*
Who would not guess there might be hopes,
The fear of gallowses and *ropes*
Before their eyes, might reconcile
Their animosities a while. *Hudibras.*
I cannot but confess myself mightily surprized, that, in a book, which was to provide chains for all mankind, I should find nothing but a *rope* of sand. *Locke.*
Hang yourself up in a true *rope*, that there may appear no trick in it. *Arbuthnot's History of John Bull.*
2. Any row of things depending: as, *a* rope *of onions.*

To Rope. *v. n.* [from the noun.] To draw out into viscosities; to concrete into glutinous filaments.
Such bodies partly follow the touch of another body, and partly stick to themselves: and therefore *rope* and draw themselves in threads; as pitch, glue and birdlime. *Bacon.*
In this close vessel place the earth accurs'd,
But fill'd brimful with wholesome water first,
Then run it through, the drops will *rope* around. *Dryden.*

Ro'pedancer. *n. s.* [*rope* and *dancer.*] An artist who dances on a rope.
Salvian, amongst other publick shews, mentions the Petaminarii; probably derived from the Greek πετάσθαι, which signifies to fly, and may refer to such kind of *ropedancers*.
Wilkins's Mathemaitcal Magick.
Statius, posted on the highest of the two summits, the people regarded with the same terror, as they look upon a daring *ropedancer*, whom they expect to fall every moment.
Addison's Guardian.
Nic bounced up with a spring equal to that of one of your nimblest tumblers or *ropedancers*, and fell foul upon John Bull, to snatch the cudgel he had in his hand. *Arbuthnot.*

Ro'piness. *n. s.* [from *ropy.*] Viscosity; glutinousness.

Ro'pemaker, or *roper*. *n. s.* [*rope* and *maker.*] One who makes ropes to sell.
The *ropemaker* bear me witness,
That I was sent for nothing but a rope. *Shakespeare.*

Ro'pery. *n. s.* [from *rope.*] Rogue's tricks. See Ropetrick.
What saucy merchant was this, that was so full of his *ropery*. *Shakesp. Merchant of Venice.*

Ro'petrick. *n. s.* [*rope* and *trick.*] Probably rogue's tricks; tricks that deserve the halter.
She may perhaps call him half a score knaves, or so: an he begin once, he'll rail in his *ropetricks*. *Shakespeare.*

Ro'py. *adj.* [from *rope.*] Viscous; tenacious; glutinous.
Ask for what price thy venal tongue was sold;
Tough, wither'd truffles, *ropy* wine, a dish
Of shotten herrings, or stale stinking fish. *Dryden's Juv.*
Take care
Thy muddy bev'rage to serene, and drive
Precipitant the baser *ropy* lees. *Philips.*

RO'QUELAURE. *n. s.* [French.] A cloak for men.
Within the *roquelaure's* clasp thy hands are pent. *Gay.*

Rora'tion. *n. s.* [*roris*, Latin.] A falling of dew. *Dict.*

Ro'rid. *n. s.* [*roridus*, Lat.] Dewy.

A vehicle conveys it through less accessible cavities into the liver, from thence into the veins, and so in a *rorid* substance through the capillary cavities. *Brown's Vulgar Errours.*

Rori'ferous. *adj.* [*ros* and *fero*, Lat.] Producing dew. *Dict.*

Rori'fluent. *adj.* [*ros* and *fluo*, Lat.] Flowing with dew. *Dict.*

Ro'sary. *n. s.* [*rosarium*, Lat.] A bunch of beads, on which the Romanists number their prayers.

No *rosary* this votress needs,
Her very syllables are beads. *Cleaveland.*

Every day propound to yourself a *rosary* or a chaplet of good works, to present to God at night. *Taylor.*

Ro'scid. *adj.* [*roscidus*, Lat.] Dewy; abounding with dew; consisting of dew.

Wine is to be forborn in consumptions, for the spirits of wine prey upon the *roscid* juice of the body. *Bacon.*

The ends of rainbows fall more upon one kind of earth than upon another; for that earth is most *roscid*. *Bacon.*

ROSE. *n. s.* [*rose*, Fr. *rosa*, Lat.] A flower.

The flower of the *rose* is composed of several leaves, which are placed circularly, and expand in a beautiful order, whose leafy flower-cup afterward becomes a roundish or oblong fleshy fruit inclosing several angular hairy seeds; to which may be added, it is a weak pithy shrub, for the most part beset with prickles, and hath pinnated leaves: the species are, 1. The wild briar, dog *rose*, or hep-tree. 2. Wild briar or dog *rose*, with large prickly heps. 3. The greater English apple-bearing *rose*. 4. The dwarf wild Burnet-leaved *rose*. 5. The dwarf wild Burnet-leaved *rose*, with variegated leaves. 6. The striped Scotch *rose*. 7. The sweet briar or eglantine. 8. Sweet briar, with a double flower. All the other sorts of *roses* are originally of foreign growth, but are hardy enough to endure the cold of our climate in the open air, and produce beautiful and fragrant flowers. *Miller.*

Make use of thy salt hours, season the slaves
For tubs and baths, bring down the *rose* cheek'd youth
To th' tub fast and the diet. *Shakesp. Timon of Athens.*

Patience thou young and *rose* lipp'd cherubin. *Shakesp.*

Let us crown ourselves with *rose* buds, before they be withered. *Wisdom* ii. 8.

This way of procuring autumnal *roses* will, in most *rose* bushes, fail; but, in some good bearers, it will succeed. *Boyle.*

Here without thorn the *rose*. *Milton.*

For her th' unfading *rose* of Eden blooms. *Pope.*

To speak under the **Rose.** To speak any thing with safety, so as not afterwards to be discovered.

By desiring a secrecy to words *spoke under the rose*, we mean, in society and compotation, from the ancient custom in symposiack meetings, to wear chaplets of *roses* about their heads. *Brown's Vulgar Errours.*

Rose. pret. of *rise*.

Eve *rose* and went forth 'mong her flow'rs. *Milton.*

Ro'seate. *adj.* [*rosat*, Fr. from *rose*.]

1. Rosy; full of roses.

I come, ye ghosts! prepare your *roseate* bow'rs,
Celestial palms and ever blooming flow'rs. *Pope.*

2. Blooming, fragrant, purple, as a rose.

Ro'sed. *adj.* [from the noun.] crimsoned; flushed.

Can you blame her, being a maid ret *rosed* over with the virgin crimson of modesty, if she deny the appearance of a naked blind boy. *Shakesp. Henry* V.

Rose-mallow. *n. s.* Is in every respect larger than the common mallow; the leaves are rougher, and the plant grows almost shrubby. *Miller.*

Ro'semary. *n. s.* [*rosmarinus*, Lat.] Is a verticillate plant, with a labiated flower, consisting of one leaf, whose upper lip or crest is cut into two parts, and turns up backward with crooked stamina or chives; but the under lip or beard is divided into three parts, the middle segment being hollow like a spoon; out of the two or three-teethed flower-cup rises the pointal, attended, as it were, by four embryoes, which afterward turn to so many seeds that are roundish, and are inclosed in the flower-cup. *Miller.*

Bedlam beggars, with roaring voices,
Strike in their numb'd and mortify'd bare arms
Pins, wooden pricks, nails, sprigs of *rosemary*;
And with this horrible object, from low farms,
Inforce their charity. *Shakesp. King Lear.*

Around their cell
Set rows of *rosemary* with flowering stem. *Dryden.*

Rosemary is small, but a very odoriferous shrub; the principal use of it is to perfume chambers, and in decoctions for washing. *Mortimer's Husbandry.*

The neighbours
Follow'd with wistful look the damsel bier,
Sprigg'd *rosemary* the lads and lasses bore. *Gay.*

Rose-noble. *n. s.* An English gold coin, in value anciently sixteen shillings. *Dict.*

The succeeding kings coined *rose-nobles* and double *rose-nobles*, the great sovereigns with the same inscription, *Jesus autem transiens per medium eorum ibat.* *Camden's Remains.*

Ro'sewater. *n. s.* [*rose* and *water*.] Water distilled from roses.

Attend him with a silver bason
Full of *rosewater*. *Shakesp.*

His drink should be cooling; as fountain water with *rose-water* and sugar of roses. *Wiseman's Surgery.*

Ro'set. *n. s.* [from *rose*.] A red colour for painters.

Grind ceruss with a weak water of gum-lake, *roset*, and vermillion, which maketh it a fair carnation. *Peacham.*

Ro'sier. *n. s.* [*rosier*, Fr.] A rosebush.

Her yellow golden hair
Was trimly woven, and in tresses wrought,
Ne other tire she on her head did wear,
But crowned with a garland of sweet *rosier*. *Fairy Queen.*

RO'SIN. *n. s.* [properly *resin*; *resine*, Fr. *resina*, Lat.]

1. Inspissated turpentine; a juice of the pine.

The billows from the kindling prow retire,
Pitch, *rosin*, searwood on red wings aspire. *Garth.*

2. Any inspissated matter of vegetables that dissolves in spirit.

Tea contains little of a volatile spirit; its *rosin* or fixed oil, which is bitter and astringent, cannot be extracted but by rectified spirit. *Arbuthnot on Aliments.*

To Ro'sin. *v. a.* [from the noun.] To rub with rosin.

Bouzebeus who could sweetly sing,
Or with the *rosin'd* bow torment the string. *Gay.*

Ro'siny. *adj.* [from *rosin*.] Resembling rosin. The example should perhaps be *rosely*. See ROSSEL.

The best soil is that upon a sandy gravel or *rosiny* sand. *Temp.*

RO'SSEL. *n. s.*

A true *rossel* or light land, whether white or black, is what they are usually planted in. *Mortimer's Husbandry.*

Ro'sselly. *adj.* [from *rossel*.]

In Essex, moory land is thought to be the most proper: that which I have observed to be the best soil is a *rosselly* top, and a brick earthy bottom. *Mortimer's Husbandry.*

Ro'strated. *adj.* [*rostratus*, Lat.] Adorned with beaks of ships.

He brought to Italy an hundred and ten *rostrated* gallies of the fleet of Mithridates. *Arbuthnot.*

RO'STRUM. *n. s.* [Latin.]

1. The beak of a bird.
2. The beak of a ship.
3. The scaffold whence orators harangued.

Vespasian erected a column in Rome, upon whose top was the prow of a ship, in Latin *rostrum*, which gave name to the common pleading place in Rome, where orations were made, being built of the prows of those ships of Antium, which the Romans overthrew. *Peacham on Drawing.*

Myself shall mount the *rostrum* in his favour,
And strive to gain his pardon from the people. *Addison.*

4. The pipe which conveys the distilling liquor into its receiver in the common alembicks; also a crooked scissars, which the surgeons use in some cases for the dilatation of wounds. *Quin.*

Ro'sy. *adj.* [*roseus*, Lat.] Resembling a rose in bloom, beauty, colour, or fragrance.

When the *rosy* fing'red morning fair,
Weary of aged Tithon's saffron bed,
Had spred her purple robe through dewy air. *Fa. Queen.*

A smile that glow'd
Cœlestial *rosy* red, love's proper hue. *Milton.*

Fairest blossom! do not slight
That age, which you may know so soon;
The *rosy* morn resigns her light,
And milder glory to the noon. *Waller.*

The *rosy* finger'd morn appears,
And from her mantle shakes her tears,
In promise of a glorious day. *Dryden's Albion.*

As Thessalian steeds the race adorn,
So *rosy* colour'd Helen is the pride
Of Lacedemon, and of Greece beside. *Dryden.*

While blooming youth and gay delight
Sit on thy *rosy* cheeks confest,
Thou hast, my dear, undoubted right
To triumph o'er this destin'd breast. *Prior.*

To ROT. *v. n.* [ꞃoꞇan, Saxon; *rotten*, Dutch.] To putrify; to lose the cohesion of its parts.

A man may *rot* even here. *Shakesp.*

From hour to hour we ripe and ripe,
And then from hour to hour we *rot* and *rot*. *Shakesp.*

Being more nearly exposed to the air and weather, the bodies of the animals would suddenly corrupt and *rot*; the bones would likewise all *rot* in time, except those which were secured by the extraordinary strength of their parts. *Woodward.*

To Rot. *v. a.* To make putrid; to bring to corruption.

No wood shone that was cut down alive, but such as was *rotted* in stock and root while it grew. *Bacon.*

Frowning Auster seeks the southern sphere,
And *rots*, with endless rain, th' unwholsome year. *Dryden.*

Rot. *n. s.* [from the verb.]

1. A distemper among sheep, in which their lungs are wasted.

In an unlucky grange, the sheep died of the *rot*, the swine of the mange, and not a goose or duckling throve. *B. Johns.*

The cattle muſt of *rot* and murrain die. *Milton.*

The wool of Ireland ſuffers under no defect, the country being generally full ſtocked with ſheep, and the ſoil little ſubject to other *rots* than of hunger. *Temple.*

2. Putrefaction; putrid decay.

Brandy ſcarce prevents the ſudden *rot*
Of freezing noſe, and quick decaying feet. *Philips.*

RO'TARY. *adj.* [*rota*, Latin.] Whirling as a wheel. *Dict.*

RO'TATED. *adj.* [*rotatus*, Lat.] Whirled round.

ROTA'TION. *n. ſ.* [*rotation*, Fr. *rotatio*, Lat.] The act of whirling round like a wheel; the ſtate of being ſo whirled round; whirl.

Of this kind is ſome diſpoſition of bodies to *rotation* from Eaſt to Weſt; as the main float and refloat of the ſea, by conſent of the univerſe as part of the diurnal motion. *Bacon.*

By a kind of circulation or *rotation*, arts have their ſucceſſive invention, perfection, and traduction from one people to another. *Hale's Origin of Mankind.*

The axle-trees of chariots take fire by the rapid *rotation* of the wheels. *Newton's Opticks.*

In the paſſions wild *rotation* toſt,
Our ſpring of action to ourſelves is loſt. *Pope.*
In fond *rotation* ſpread the ſpotted wing,
And ſhiver every feather with deſire. *Thomſon.*

ROTA'TOR. *n. ſ.* [Latin.] That which gives a circular motion.

This articulation is ſtrengthened by ſtrong muſcles; on the inſide by the triceps and the four little *rotators*. *Wiſeman.*

ROTE. *n. ſ.* [ꞃoꞇ, Saxon, merry.]

1. [*Rote*, old Fr.] A harp; a lyre. Obſolete.

Wele couthe he ſing, and playen on a *rote*. *Chaucer.*
Worthy of great Phœbus' *rote*,
The triumphs of Phlegrean Jove he wrote,
That all the gods admir'd his lofty note. *Spenſer.*

2. [*Routine*, Fr.] Words uttered by mere memory without meaning; memory of words without comprehenſion of the ſenſe.

Firſt rehearſe this ſong by *rote*,
To each word a warbling note. *Shakeſp.*
Thy loved did read by *rote*, and could not ſpell. *Shakeſp.*

He rather ſaith it by *rote* to himſelf, than that he can throughly believe it. *Bacon's Eſſays.*

All which he underſtood by *rote*,
And as occaſion ſerv'd would quote. *Hudibras, p. i.*
Learn Ariſtotle's rules by *rote*,
And at all hazard's boldly quote. *Swift's Miſcel.*

To ROTE. *v. a.* [from the noun.] To fix in the memory, without informing the underſtanding.

Speak to the people
Words *roted* in your tongue; baſtards and ſyllables
Of no allowance to your boſom's truth. *Shakeſp.*

RO'TGUT. *n. ſ.* [*rot* and *gut*.] Bad beer.

They overwhelm their panch daily with a kind of flat *rotgut*, we with a bitter dreggiſh ſmall liquor. *Harvey.*

ROTHER-NAILS. *n. ſ.* [a corruption of *rudder*.] Among ſhipwrights, nails with very full heads uſed for faſtening the rudder irons of ſhips. *Bailey.*

RO'TTEN. *adj.* [from *rot*.]

1. Putrid; carious; putreſcent.

Truſt not to *rotten* planks. *Shakeſp. Ant. and Cleopatra.*
Proſperity begins to mellow,
And drop into the *rotten* mouth of death. *Shakeſp.*
O bliſs-breeding ſun, draw from the earth
Rotten humidity; below thy ſiſter's orb
Infect the air. *Shakeſp. Timon of Athens.*

There is by invitation or excitation; as when a *rotten* apple lieth cloſe to another apple that is found; or when dung, which is already putrefied, is added to other bodies. *Bacon.*

Who braſs as *rotten* wood; and ſteel no more
Regards than reeds. *Sandys's Paraphraſe.*

It groweth by a dead ſtub of a tree, and about the roots of *rotten* trees, and takes his juice from wood putrefied. *Bacon.*

They ſerewood from the *rotten* hedges took,
And ſeeds of latent fire from flints provoke. *Dryden.*

2. Not firm; not truſty.

Hence, *rotten* thing, or I ſhall ſhake thy bones
Out of thy garments. *Shakeſp. Coriolanus.*

3. Not ſound; not hard.

You common cry of curs whoſe breath I hate,
As reek o' th' *rotten* fens. *Shakeſp. Coriolanus.*

They were left moiled with dirt and mire, by reaſon of the deepneſs of the *rotten* way. *Knolles's Hiſtory of the Turks.*

RO'TTENNESS. *n. ſ.* [from *rotten*.] State of being rotten; carioufneſs; putrefaction.

Diſeas'd ventures,
That play with all infirmities for gold,
Which *rottenneſs* lends nature! *Shakeſp. Cymbeline.*

If the matter ſtink and be oily, it is a certain ſign of a *rottenneſs*. *Wiſeman's Surgery.*

ROTU'ND. *adj.* [*rotonde*, Fr. *rotundus*, Lat.] Round; circular; ſpherical.

The croſs figure of the chriſtian temples is more proper for ſpacious buildings than the *rotund* of the heathen; the eye is much better filled at firſt entering the *rotund*, but ſuch as are built in the form of a croſs gives us a greater variety. *Add.*

ROTU'NDIFOLIOUS. *adj.* [*rotundus* and *folium*, Lat.] Having round leaves.

ROTU'NDITY. *n. ſ.* [*rotunditas*, Lat. *rotondité*, Fr. from *rotund*.] Roundneſs; ſphericity; circularity.

Thou all-ſhaking thunder,
Strike flat the thick *rotundity* o' th' world. *Shakeſp.*

With the *rotundity* common to the atoms of all fluids, there is ſome difference in bulk, elſe all fluids would be alike in weight. *Grew.*

Rotundity is an emblem of eternity, that has neither beginning nor end. *Addiſon on Ancient Medals.*

Who would part with theſe ſolid bleſſings, for the little fantaſtical pleaſantneſs of a ſmooth convexity and *rotundity* of a globe. *Bentley's Sermons.*

ROTU'NDO. *n. ſ.* [*rotondo*, Italian.] A building formed round both in the inſide and outſide; ſuch as the pantheon at Rome. *Trev.*

To ROVE. *v. n.* [*roffver*, Daniſh, to range for plunder.] To ramble; to range; to wander.

Thou'ſt years upon thee, and thou art too full
Of the wars ſurfeits, to go *rove* with one
That's yet unbruis'd. *Shakeſp. Coriolanus.*
Faultleſs thou dropt from his unerring ſkill,
With the bare power to ſin, ſince free of will;
Yet charge not with thy guilt his bounteous love,
For who has power to walk, has power to *rove*. *Arbuth.*

If we indulge the frequent riſe and *roving* of paſſions, we thereby procure an unattentive habit. *Watts.*

I view'd th' effects of that diſaſtrous flame,
Which kindled by th' imperious queen of love,
Conſtrain'd me from my native realm to *rove*. *Pope.*

To ROVE. *v. a.* To wander over.

Roving the field, I chanc'd
A goodly tree far diſtant to behold,
Loaden with fruit of faireſt colours. *Milton's Par. Loſt.*
Cloacina as the town ſhe *rov'd*,
A mortal ſcavenger ſhe ſaw, ſhe lov'd. *Gay.*

RO'VER. *n. ſ.* [from *rove*.]

1. A wanderer; a ranger.
2. A fickle inconſtant man.
3. A robber; a pirate.

This is the caſe of *rovers* by land, as ſome cantons in Arabia. *Bacon's Holy War.*

4. *At* ROVERS. Without any particular aim.

Nature ſhoots not *at rovers*: even inanimates, though they know not their perfection, yet are they not carried on by a blind unguided impetus; but that, which directs them, knows it. *Glanvill's Sceps.*

Providence never ſhoots *at rovers*: there is an arrow that flies by night as well as by day, and God is the perſon that ſhoots it. *South's Sermons.*

Men of great reading ſhow their talents on the meaneſt ſubjects; this is a kind of ſhooting *at rovers*. *Addiſon.*

ROUGE. *n. ſ.* [*rouge*, Fr.] Red paint.

ROUGH. *adj.* [ꞃuh, ꞃuhᵹe, Saxon; *rouw*, Dutch.]

1. Not ſmooth; rugged; having inequalities on the ſurface.

The fiend
O'er bog or ſteep, through ſtrait, *rough*, denſe, or rare,
Purſues his way. *Milton.*

Were the mountains taken all away, the remaining parts would be more unequal than the *roughest* ſea; whereas the face of the earth ſhould reſemble that of the calmeſt ſea, if ſtill in the form of its firſt maſs. *Burnet's Theory of the Earth.*

2. Auſtere to the taſte: as, rough *wine*.
3. Harſh to the ear.

Moſt by the numbers judge a poet's ſong,
And ſmooth or *rough* with them is right or wrong. *Pope.*

4. Rugged of temper; inelegant of manners; not ſoft; coarſe; not civil; ſevere; not mild; rude.

A fiend, a fury, pitileſs and *rough*,
A wolf; nay worſe, a fellow all in buff. *Shakeſp.*
Strait with a band of ſoldiers tall and *rough*
On him he ſeizes. *Cowley's Davideis.*

5. Not gentle; not proceeding by eaſy operation.

He gave not the king time to proſecute that gracious method, but forced him to a quicker and *rougher* remedy. *Clar.*

Hippocrates ſeldom mentions the doſes of his medicines, which is ſomewhat ſurprizing, becauſe his purgatives are generally very *rough* and ſtrong. *Arbuthnot on Coins.*

6. Harſh to the mind; ſevere.

Kind words prevent a good deal of that perverſeneſs, which *rough* and imperious uſage often produces in generous minds. *Locke.*

7. Hard featured; not delicate.

A ropy chain of rheums, a viſage *rough*,
Deform'd, unfeatur'd, and a ſkin of buff. *Dryden.*

8. Not poliſhed; not finiſhed by art: as, *a* rough *diamond*.
9. Terrible; dreadful.

Before the cloudy van,
On the *rough* edge of battle ere it join'd,
Satan advanc'd. *Milton.*

10. Rugged;

10. Rugged; disordered in appearance; coarse.
Rough from the tossing surge Ulysses moves,
Urg'd on by want, and recent from the storms,
The brackish ooze his manly grace deforms. *Pope.*
11. Tempestuous; stormy; boisterous.
Come what come may,
Time and the hour run through the *roughest* day. *Shakesp.*

To Rou'ghcast. *v. a.* [*rough* and *cast.*]
1. To mould without nicety or elegance; to form with asperities and inequalities.
Nor bodily, nor ghostly negro could
Roughcast thy figure in a sadder mould. *Cleaveland.*
2. To form any thing in its first rudiments.
In merriment they were first practised, and this *roughcast* unhewn poetry was instead of stage plays for one hundred and twenty years. *Dryden's Dedication to Juvenal.*

Rou'ghcast. *n. s.* [*rough* and *cast.*]
1. A rude model; a form in its rudiments.
The whole piece seems rather a loose model and *roughcast* of what I design to do, than a compleat work. *Digby.*
2. A kind of plaister mixed with pebbles, or by some other cause very uneven on the surface.
Some man must present a wall; and let him have some plaster, lome, or *roughcast* about him to signify wall. *Shakesp.*

Rou'ghdraught. *n. s.* [*rough* and *draught.*] A draught in its rudiments.
My elder brothers came
Roughdraughts of nature, ill design'd and lame,
Blown off, like blossoms, never made to bear;
'Till I came finish'd, her last labour'd care. *Dryden.*

To Rou'ghdraw. *v. a.* [*rough* and *draw.*] To trace coarsely.
His victories we scarce could keep in view,
Or polish 'em so fast, as he *roughdrew*. *Dryden.*

To Rou'ghen. *v. a.* [from *rough.*] To make rough.
Such difference there is in tongues, that the same figure, which *roughens* one, gives majesty to another; and that was it which Virgil studied in his verses. *Dryden's Ded. to Æneis.*
Ah! where must needy poet seek for aid,
When dust and rain at once his coat invade!
His only coat; when dust confus'd with rain,
Roughens the nap, and leaves a mingled stain. *Swift.*

To Rou'ghen. *u. n.* To grow rough.
The broken landskip
Ascending *roughens* into rigid hills. *Thomson's Spring.*

To Roughhew'. *v. a.* [*rough* and *hew.*] To give to any thing the first appearance of form.
There's a divinity that shapes our ends,
Roughhew them how we will. *Shakesp. Hamlet.*
The whole world, without art and dress,
Would be but one great wilderness,
And mankind but a savage herd,
For all that nature has conferr'd:
This does but *roughhew* and design,
Leaves art to polish and refine. *Hudibras, p.* iii.

Rou'ghhewn. *particip. adj.*
1. Rugged; unpolished; uncivil; unrefined.
A *roughhewn* seaman, being brought before a justice for some misdemeanour, was by him ordered away to prison; and would not stir; saying, it was better to stand where he was, than go to a worse place. *Bacon's Apophthegms.*
2. Not yet nicely finished.
I hope to obtain a candid construction of this *roughhewn* ill-timber'd discourse. *Howel's Vocal Forest.*

Rou'ghly. *adv.* [from *rough.*]
1. With uneven surface; with asperities on the surface.
2. Harshly; uncivilly; rudely.
Ne Mammon would there let him long remain,
For terror of the torments manifold,
In which the damned souls he did behold,
But *roughly* him bespake. *Fairy Queen, b.* ii.
Rebuk'd, and *roughly* sent to prison,
Th' immediate heir of England! was this easy? *Shakesp.*
3. Severely; without tenderness.
Some friends of vice pretend,
That I the tricks of youth too *roughly* blame. *Dryden.*
4. Austerely to the taste.
5. Boisterously; tempestuously.
6. Harshly to the ear.

Rou'ghness. *n. s.* [from *rough.*]
1. Superficial asperity; unevenness of surface.
The little *roughnesses* or other inequalities of the leather against the cavity of the cylinder, now and then put a stop to the descent or ascent of the sucker. *Boyle.*
While the steep horrid *roughness* of the wood
Strives with the gentle calmness of the flood. *Denham.*
When the diamond is not only found, but the *roughness* smoothed, cut into a form, and set in gold, then we cannot but acknowledge, that it is the perfect work of art and nature. *Dryden.*
Such a persuasion as this well fixed, will smooth all the *roughness* of the way that leads to happiness, and render all the conflicts with our lusts pleasing. *Atterbury.*
2. Austereness to the taste.
Divers plants contain a grateful sharpness, as lemons; or an austere and inconcocted *roughness*, as sloes. *Brown.*
3. Taste of astringency.
A tobacco-pipe broke in my mouth, and the spitting out the pieces left such a delicious *roughness* on my tongue, that I champed up the remaining part. *Spectator.*
4. Harshness to the ear.
In the *roughness* of the numbers and cadences of this play, which was so designed, you will see somewhat more masterly than in any of my former tragedies. *Dryden.*
The Swedes, Danes, Germans, and Dutch attain to the pronunciation of our words with ease, because our syllables resemble theirs in *roughness* and frequency of consonants. *Sw.*
5. Ruggedness of temper; coarseness of manners; tendency to rudeness; coarseness of behaviour and address.
Roughness is a needless cause of discontent; severity breedeth fear; but *roughness* breedeth hate: even reproofs from authority ought to be grave and not taunting. *Bacon.*
When our minds eyes are disengag'd,
They quicken sloth, perplexities unty,
Make *roughness* smooth, and hardness mollify. *Denham.*
Roughness of temper is apt to discountenance the timorous or modest. *Addison.*
6. Absence of delicacy.
Should feasting and balls once get among the cantons, their military *roughness* would be quickly lost, their tempers would grow too soft for their climate. *Addison.*
7. Severity; violence of discipline.
8. Violence of operation in medicines.
9. Unpolished or unfinished state.
10. Inelegance of dress or appearance.
11. Tempestuousness; storminess.
12. Coarseness of features.

Rought. old pret. of *reach.* [commonly written by *Spenser raught.*] Reached.
The moon was a month old, when Adam was no more,
And *rought* not to five weeks, when he came to fivescore.
Shakesp. Love's Labour Lost.

To Rou'ghwork. *v. a.* [*rough* and *work.*] To work coarsely over without the least nicety.
Thus you must continue, till you have *roughwrought* all your work from end to end. *Moxon's Mech. Exercises.*

Rou'nceval. *n. s.* [from *Rouncesval*, a town at the foot of the Pirenees.] See Pea, of which it is a species.
Dig garden,
And set as a daintie thy *runcival* pease. *Tusser.*

ROUND. *adj.* [*rond*, French; *rondo*, Italian; *rund*, Dutch; *rotundus*, Latin.]
1. Cylindrical.
Hollow engines long and *round* thick ram'd. *Milton.*
2. Circular.
His pond'rous shield large and *round* behind him. *Milton.*
3. Spherical; orbicular.
The outside bare of this *round* world. *Milton.*
4. [*Rotundo ore*, Lat.] Smooth; without defect in sound.
In his satyrs Horace is quick, *round*, and pleasant, and as nothing so bitter, so not so good as Juvenal. *Peacham.*
5. Not broken.
Pliny put a *round* number near the truth, rather than a fraction. *Arbuthnot on Coins.*
6. Large; not inconsiderable.
Three thousand ducats! 'tis a good *round* sum. *Shakesp.*
They set a *round* price upon your head. *Addison.*
It is not easy to foresee what a *round* sum of money may do among a people, who have tamely suffered the *Franche compté* to be seized on. *Addison's Remarks on Italy.*
She called for a *round* sum out of the privy purse. *Hooke.*
7. Plain; clear; fair; candid; open.
Round dealing is the honour of man's nature; and a mixture of falshood is like allay in gold and silver, which may make the metal work the better, but it embaseth it. *Bacon.*
8. Quick; brisk.
Painting is a long pilgrimage; if we do not actually begin the journey, and travel at a *round* rate, we shall never arrive at the end of it. *Dryden's Dufresnoy.*
Sir Roger heard them upon a *round* trot; and after pausing, told them, that much might be said on both sides. *Addis.*
9. Plain; free without delicacy or reserve; almost rough.
Let his queen mother all alone intreat him,
To shew his griefs; let her be *round* with him. *Shakesp.*
The kings interposed in a *round* and princely manner; not only by way of request and persuasion, but also by way of protestation and menace. *Bacon.*

Round. *n. s.*
1. A circle; a sphere; an orb.
Hie thee hither,
That I may pour my spirits in thine ear,
And chastise with the valour of my tongue
All that impedes thee from the golden *round*,
Which fate and metaphysick aid doth seem
To have crown'd thee withal. *Shakesp. Macbeth.*

I'll charm the air to give a ſound,
While you perform your antick *round*. *Shakeſp. Macbeth.*
Three or four we'll dreſs like urchins,
With *rounds* of waxen tapers on their heads,
And rattles in their hands. *Shakeſp. Mer. Wives of Windſ.*
What is this,
That riſes like the iſſue of a king,
And wears upon his baby brow the *round*
And top of ſovereignty? *Shakeſp. Macbeth.*

Hirſute roots are a middle ſort, between the bulbous and fibrous; that, beſides the putting forth ſap upwards and downwards, putteth forth in *round*. *Bacon.*

What if the ſun
Be centre to the world; and other ſtars,
By his attractive virtue and their own
Incited, dance about him various *rounds*. *Milton.*
Knit your hands, and beat the ground
In a light fantaſtick *round*. *Milton.*
He did foretel and propheſy of him,
Who to his realms that azure *round* hath join'd. *Denham.*
They meet, they wheel, they throw their darts afar;
Then in a *round* the mingled bodies run,
Flying they follow, and purſuing ſhun. *Dryden.*
How ſhall I then begin, or where conclude,
To draw a fame ſo truly circular?
For, in a *round*, what order can be ſhew'd,
Where all the parts ſo equal perfect are? *Dryden.*

The mouth of Veſuvio has four hundred yards in diameter; for it ſeems a perfect *round*. *Addiſon.*

This image on the medal plac'd,
With its bright *round* of titles grac'd,
And ſtampt on Britiſh coins ſhall live. *Addiſon.*

2. Rundle; ſtep of a ladder.
When he once attains the upmoſt *round*,
He then unto the ladder turns his back,
Looks in the clouds, ſcorning the baſe degrees
By which he did aſcend. *Shakeſp. Julius Cæſar.*

Many are kick'd down ere they have climbed the two or three firſt *rounds* of the ladder. *Government of the Tongue.*

All the *rounds* like Jacob's ladder riſe;
The loweſt hid in earth, the topmoſt in the ſkies. *Dryden.*

This is the laſt ſtage of human perfection, the utmoſt *round* of the ladder whereby we aſcend to heaven. *Norris.*

3. The time in which any thing has paſſed through all hands, and comes back to the firſt: hence applied to a carouſal.
A gentle *round* fill'd to the brink,
To this and t' other friend I drink. *Suckling.*
Women to cards may be compar'd; we play
A *round* or two, when us'd, we throw away. *Granville.*
The feaſt was ſerv'd; the bowl was crown'd;
To the king's pleaſure went the mirthful *round*. *Prior.*

4. A revolution; a courſe ending at the point where it began.
We, that are of purer fire,
Imitate the ſtarry quire,
Who, in their mighty watchful ſpheres,
Lead in ſwift *rounds* the months and years. *Milton.*

If nothing will pleaſe people, unleſs they be greater than nature intended, what can they expect, but the aſs's *round* of vexatious changes. *L'Eſtrange.*

How then to drag a wretched life beneath
An endleſs *round* of ſtill returning woes,
And all the gnawing pangs of vain remorſe?
What torment's this? *Smith.*
Till by one countleſs ſum of woes oppreſt,
Hoary with cares, and ignorant of reſt,
We find the vital ſprings relax'd and worn;
Compell'd our common impotence to mourn,
Thus through the *round* of age, to childhood we return. *Prior.*

5. [*Ronde*, Fr.] A walk performed by a guard or officer, to ſurvey a certain diſtrict.

ROUND. *adv.*

1. Every way; on all ſides.
The terror of God was upon the cities *round* about. *Gen.*
All ſounds whatſoever move *round*; that is, on all ſides, upwards, downwards, forwards, and backwards. *Bacon.*
In darkneſs and with dangers compaſs'd *round*. *Milton.*

2. [*En rond, à la ronde*, Fr.] In a revolution.
At the beſt 'tis but cunning; and if he can in his own fancy raiſe that to the opinion of true wiſdom, he comes *round* to practiſe his deceits upon himſelf. *Gov. of the Tong.*
Some preachers, prepared only upon two or three points, run the ſame *round* from one end of the year to another. *Add.*

3. Circularly.
One foot he center'd, and the other turn'd
Round through the vaſt profundity obſcure. *Milton.*

4. Not in a direct line.
If merely to come in, Sir, they go out;
The way they take is ſtrangely *round* about. *Pope.*

ROUND. *prep.*

1. On every ſide of.
To officiate light *round* this opacous earth. *Milton.*

2. About; circularly about.
He led the hero *round*
The confines of the bleſt Elyſian ground. *Dryden.*

3. All over.
Round the world we roam,
Forc'd from our pleaſing fields and native home. *Dryden.*

To ROUND. *v. a.* [*rotundo*, Lat. from the noun.]

1. To ſurround; to encircle.
Would that th' incluſive verge
Of golden metal, that muſt *round* my brow,
Were redhot ſteel to ſear me to the brain. *Shakeſp.*
We are ſuch ſtuff
As dreams are made on, and our little life
Is *rounded* with a ſleep. *Shakeſp. Tempeſt.*
This diſtemper'd meſſenger of wet,
The many coloured Iris, *rounds* thine eyes. *Shakeſp.*
The vileſt cockle gaping on the coaſt,
That *rounds* the ample ſea. *Prior.*

2. To make ſpherical or circular.
Worms with many feet, which *round* themſelves into balls, are bred chiefly under logs of timber. *Bacon.*
When ſilver has been leſſened in any piece carrying the publick ſtamp, by clipping, waſhing, or *rounding*, the laws have declared it not to be lawful money. *Locke.*
With the cleaving-knife and mawl ſplit the ſtuff into a ſquare piece near the ſize, and with the draw-knife *round* off the edges to make it fit for the lathe. *Moxon.*
Can any one tell, how the ſun, planets, and ſatellites were *rounded* into their particular ſpheroidical orbs. *Cheyne.*

3. To raiſe to a relief.
The figures on our modern medals are raiſed and *rounded* to a very great perfection. *Addiſon on Ancient Medals.*

4. To move about any thing.
To thoſe beyond the polar circle, day
Had unbenighted ſhone, while the low ſun,
To recompenſe his diſtance, in your ſight
Had *rounded* ſtill th' horizon, and not known
Or Eaſt or Weſt. *Milton's Paradiſe Loſt, b.* x.

5. To mould into ſmoothneſs.
Theſe accompliſhments, applied in the pulpit, appear by a quaint, terſe, florid ſtile *rounded* into periods and cadencies, without propriety or meaning. *Swift's Miſcellanies.*

To ROUND. *v. n.*

1. To grow round in form.
The queen, your mother, *rounds* apace; we ſhall
Preſent our ſervices to a fine new prince. *Shakeſp.*

2. [*Runen*, German; whence *Chaucer* writes it better *roun.*] To whiſper.
Being come to the ſupping place, one of Kalander's ſervants *rounded* in his ear; at which he retired. *Sidney.*
France,
Whom zeal and charity brought to the field
As God's own ſoldier, *rounded* in the ear,
With that ſame purpoſe changes. *Shakeſp.*
They're here with me already; whiſpering, *rounding*,
Sicilia is a ſo forth; 'tis far gone. *Shakeſp.*
Cicero was at dinner, where an ancient lady ſaid ſhe was but forty: one that ſat by *rounded* him in the ear, ſhe is far more out of the queſtion: Cicero anſwered, I muſt believe her, for I heard her ſay ſo any time theſe ten years. *Bacon.*
The fox *rounds* the new elect in the ear, with a piece of ſecret ſervice that he could do him. *L'Eſtrange.*

3. To go rounds.
They keep watch, or nightly *rounding* walk. *Milton.*

ROU'NDABOUT. *adj.* [This word is uſed as an adjective, though it is only an adverb united to a ſubſtantive by a colloquial licenſe of language, which ought not to have been admitted into books.]

1. Ample; extenſive.
Thoſe ſincerely follow reaſon, but for want of having large, ſound, *roundabout* ſenſe, have not a full view of all that relates to the queſtion. *Locke on Underſtanding.*

2. Indirect; looſe.
Paraphraſe is a *roundabout* way of tranſlating, invented to help the barrenneſs, which tranſlators, overlooking in themſelves, have apprehended in our tongue. *Felton.*

ROU'NDEL.
ROU'NDELAY. } *n. ſ.*

1. [*Rondelet*, French.] A kind of ancient poetry, which commonly conſiſts of thirteen verſes, of which eight are of one kind of rhyme and five of another: it is divided into three couplets; and at the end of the ſecond and third, the beginning of the *roundel* is repeated in an equivocal ſenſe, if poſſible. *Trevoux.*
Siker, ſike a *roundle* never heard I none,
Little lacketh Perigot of the beſt,
And Willie is not greatly over-gone,
So weren his under-ſongs well addreſt. *Spenſer's Paſt.*
To hear thy rimes and *roundelays*,
Which thou wert wont in waſtful hills to ſing,
I more delight than lark in ſummer days,
Whoſe echo made the neighb'ring groves to ring. *Spenſer.*

Come now a *roundel* and a fairy song. *Shakesp.*

They list'ning heard him, while he search'd the grove,
And loudly sung his *roundelay* of love,
But on the sudden stop'd. *Dryden's Knight's Tale.*

2. [*Rondelle*, Fr.] A round form or figure.

The Spaniards, casting themselves into *roundels*, and their strongest ships walling in the rest, made a flying march to Calais. *Bacon.*

The muses and graces made festivals; the fawns, satyrs, and nymphs did dance their *roundelays*. *Howel.*

ROU'NDER. *n. s.* [from *round.*] Circumference; inclosure.

If you fondly pass our proffer'd offer,
'Tis not the *rounder* of your old fac'd walls
Can hide you from our messengers of war. *Shakesp.*

ROU'NDHEAD. *n. s.* [*round* and *head.*] A puritan, so named from the practice once prevalent among them of cropping their hair round.

Your petitioner always kept hospitality, and drank confusion to the *roundheads*. *Spectator*, Nº 629.

ROU'NDHOUSE. *n. s.* [*round* and *house.*] The constable's prison, in which disorderly persons, found in the street, are confined.

They march'd to some fam'd *roundhouse*. *Pope.*

ROU'NDISH. *adj.* [from *round.*] Somewhat round; approaching to roundness.

It is not every small crack that can make such a receiver, as is of a *roundish* figure, useless to our experiment. *Boyle.*

ROU'NDLY. *adv.* [from *round.*]

1. In a round form; in a round manner.

2. Openly; plainly; without reserve.

Injoin gainsayers, giving them *roundly* to understand, that where our duty is submission, weak oppositions betoken pride. *Hooker, b.* v. *s.* 8.

You'll prove a jolly surly groom,
That take it on you at the first so *roundly*. *Shakesp.*

Mr. de Mortier *roundly* said, that to cut off all contentions of words, he would propose two means for peace. *Hayward.*

From a world of phœnomena, there is a principle that acts out of wisdom and counsel, as was abundantly evidenced, and as *roundly* acknowledged. *More's Divine Dialogues.*

He affirms every thing *roundly*, without any art, rhetorick, or circumlocution. *Addison's Count Tariff.*

3. Briskly; with speed.

When the mind has brought itself to attention, it will be able to cope with difficulties, and master them, and then it may go on *roundly*. *Locke.*

4. Completely; to the purpose; vigorously; in earnest.

I was called any thing, and I would have done any thing, indeed too, and *roundly* too. *Shakesp. Henry* IV.

This lord justice caused the earl of Kildare to be arrested, and cancelled such charters as were lately resumed, and proceeded every way so *roundly* and severely, as the nobility did much distaste him. *Davies on Ireland.*

ROU'NDNESS. *n. s.* [from *round.*]

1. Circularity; sphericity; cylindrical form.

The same reason is of the *roundness* of the bubble; for the air within avoideth discontinuance, and therefore casteth itself into a round figure. *Bacon's Natural History.*

Bracelets of pearl gave *roundness* to her arm,
And ev'ry gem augmented ev'ry charm. *Prior.*

Roundness is the primary essential mode or difference of a bowl. *Watts's Logick.*

2. Smoothness.

The whole period and compass of this speech was delightsome for the *roundness*, and grave for the strangeness. *Spenser.*

3. Honesty; openness; vigorous measures.

To ROUSE. *v. a.* [of the same class of words with *raise* and *rise.*]

1. To wake from rest.

At once the crowd arose, confus'd and high;
For Mars was early up, and *rous'd* the sky. *Dryden.*

Rev'rent I touch thee! but with honest zeal,
To *rouse* the watchmen of the publick weal,
To virtue's work provoke the tardy hall;
And goad the prelate slumb'ring in his stall. *Pope.*

2. To excite to thought or action.

The Dane and Swede, *rouz'd* up by fierce alarms,
Bless the wise conduct of her pious arms;
Soon as her fleets appear, their terrors cease,
And all the northern world lies hush'd in peace. *Addison.*

I'll thunder in their ears their country's cause,
And try to *rouse* up all that's Roman in them. *Addis. Cato.*

The heat, with which Luther treated his adversaries, though strained too far, was extremely well fitted by the providence of God to *rouse* up a people, the most phlegmatick of any in Christendom. *Atterbury.*

They would be very much *roused* and awakened by such a sight; but they would not however be convinced. *Atterbury.*

3. To put into action.

As an eagle, seeing prey appear,
His airy plumes doth *rouse* full rudely dight;
So shaked he, that horror was to hear. *Fairy Queen.*

Blust'ring winds had *rous'd* the sea. *Milton.*

4. To drive a beast from his laire.

The blood more stirs,
To *rouze* a lion, or to start a hare. *Shakesp. Henry* IV.

He stooped down, he couched as a lion, and as an old lion; who shall *rouse* him up? *Genesis* xlix. 9.

Th' unexpected sound
Of dogs and men his wakeful ear does wound;
Rous'd with the noise, he scarce believes his ear,
Willing to think th' illusions of his fear
Had giv'n this false alarm. *Denham.*

Now Cancer glows with Phœbus' fiery car,
The youth rush eager to the sylvan war;
Swarm o'er the lawns, the forest-walks surround,
Rouse the fleet hart, and cheer the op'ning hound. *Pope.*

To ROUSE. *v. n.*

1. To awake from slumber.

Men, sleeping found by whom they dread,
Rouse and bestir themselves ere well awake. *Milton.*

Richard, who now was half asleep,
Rous'd; nor would longer silence keep. *Prior.*

Melancholy lifts her head;
Morpheus *rouses* from his bed. *Pope's St. Cecilia.*

2. To be excited to thought or action.

Good things of day begin to droop and drowze,
While night's black agents to their prey do *rowze*. *Shakesp.*

ROUSE. *n. s.* [*rusch*, German, half drunk.] A dose of liquor rather too large.

They have given me a *rouse* already.
—Not past a pint as I am a soldier. *Shakesp. Othello.*

No jocund health that Denmark drinks to-day,
But the great cannon to the clouds shall tell;
And the king's *rouse* shall bruit it back again,
Respeaking earthly thunder. *Shakesp.*

ROU'SER. *n. s.* [from *rouse.*] One who rouses.

ROUT. *n. s.* [*rot*, Dutch.]

1. A clamorous multitude; a rabble; a tumultuous croud.

Besides the endless *routs* of wretched thralls,
Which thither were assembled day by day
From all the world. *Fairy Queen, b.* i.

A *rout* of people there assembled were,
Of every sort and nation under sky,
Which with great uproar preased to draw near
To th' upper part. *Spenser.*

If that rebellion
Came like itself in base and abject *routs*,
Led on by bloody youth, goaded with rage,
And countenanced by boys and beggary,
You, reverend father, then had not been there. *Shakesp.*

Farmers were to forfeit their holds in case of unlawful retainer, or partaking in *routs* and unlawful assemblies. *Bacon.*

Such a tacit league is against such *routs* and shoals, as have utterly degenerated from the laws of nature. *Bacon.*

Nor do I name of men the common *rout*,
That wandring loose about,
Grow up and perish, as the summer fly. *Milton's Agonistes.*

The mad ungovernable *rout*,
Full of confusion and the fumes of wine,
Lov'd such variety and antick tricks. *Roscommon.*

Harley spies
The doctor fasten'd by the eyes
At Charing-cross among the *rout*,
Where painted monsters are hung out. *Swift.*

2. [*Route*, Fr.] Confusion of an army defeated or dispersed.

Thy army,
As if they could not stand when thou wer't down,
Dispers'd in *rout*, betook them all to fly. *Daniel.*

Their mightiest quell'd, the battle swerv'd,
With many an inrode gor'd; deformed *rout*
Enter'd, and foul disorder. *Milton's Par. Lost, b.* vi.

To ROUT. *v. a.* To dissipate and put into confusion by defeat.

The next way to end the wars with him, and to *rout* him quite, should be to keep him from invading of those countries adjoining. *Spenser on Ireland.*

That party of the king's horse, that charged the Scots, so totally *routed* and defeated their whole army, that they fled. *Clarendon, b.* viii.

To ROUT. *v. n.* To assemble in clamorous and tumultuous crouds.

The meaner sort *routed* together, and suddenly assailing the earl in his house, slew him. *Bacon's Henry* VII.

ROUTE. *n. s.* [*route*, Fr.] Road; way.

Wide through the fuzzy field their *route* they take,
Their bleeding bosoms force the thorny brake. *Gay.*

ROW. *n. s.* [*reih*, German.] A rank or file; a number of things ranged in a line.

Lips never part, but that they show
Of precious pearl the double *row*. *Sidney, b.* ii.

After them all dancing on a *row*,
The comely virgins came with garlands dight,
As fresh as flowres. *Fairy Queen, b.* i.

Where any *row*
Of fruit trees, overwoody, reach'd too far
Their pamper'd boughs, and needed hands to check
Fruitless embraces *Milton's Paradise Lost, b.* v.
A triple mounted *row* of pillars, laid
On wheels. *Milton's Paradise Lost, b.* vi.
Where the bright seraphim in burning *row*,
Their loud uplifted angel trumpets blow. *Milton.*
The victor honour'd with a nobler vest,
Where gold and purple strive in equal *rows.* *Dryden.*
Why round our coaches crowd the white-glov'd beaux,
Why bows the sidebox from its inmost *rows.* *Pope.*

To ROW. *v. n.* [ꞃopan, Saxon.] To impel a vessel in the water by oars.

He saw them toiling in *rowing*; for the wind was contrary. *Mark* vi. 48.

Some of these troughs or canoes were so great, that above twenty men have been found *rowing* in one. *Abbot.*

The bold Britons then securely *row'd*;
Charles and his virtue was their sacred load. *Waller.*

The watermen turned their barge, and *rowed* softly, that they might take the cool of the evening. *Dryden.*

The *rowing* crew,
To tempt a fare, clothe all their tilts in blue. *Gay.*

To Row. *v. a.* To drive or help forward by oars.

The swan *rows* her state with oary feet. *Milton.*

Ro'wel. *n. s.* [*rouelle*, Fr.]

1. The points of a spur turning on an axis.

He gave his able horse the head,
And, bending forward, struck his agile heels
Against the panting sides of his poor jade
Up to the *rowel* head. *Shakesp. Henry* IV. *p.* ii.
A rider like myself, who ne'er wore *rowel*
Nor iron on his heel. *Shakesp. Cymbeline.*

A mullet is the *rowel* of a spur, and hath never but five points; a star hath six. *Peacham on Blazoning.*

He spurr'd his fiery steed
With goring *rowels*, to provoke his speed. *Dryden.*

2. A seton; a roll of hair or silk put into a wound to hinder it from healing, and provoke a discharge.

To Ro'wel. *v. a.* To pierce through the skin, and keep the wound open by a rowel.

Rowel the horse in the chest. *Mortimer's Husbandry.*

Ro'wen. *n. s.*

Rowen is a field kept up till after Michaelmas, that the corn left on the ground may sprout into green. *Notes on Tusser.*

Then spare it for *rowen*, til Michel be past,
To lengthen thy dairie, no better thou hast. *Tusser.*

Turn your cows, that give milk, into your *rowens*, till snow comes. *Mortimer's Husbandry.*

Ro'wer. *n. s.* [from *row.*] One that manages an oar.

Four gallies first, which equal *rowers* bear,
Advancing in the watry lists, appear. *Dryden.*

The bishop of Salisbury ran down with the stream thirty miles in an hour, by the help of but one *rower.* *Addison.*

RO'YAL. *adj*, [*roial*, Fr.]

1. Kingly; belonging to a king; becoming a king; regal.

The *royal* stock of David. *Milton.*
Thrice happy they, who thus in woods and groves,
From courts retired, possess their peaceful loves:
Of *royal* maids how wretched is the fate! *Granville.*

2. Noble; illustrious.

What news from Venice?
How doth that *royal* merchant, good Antonio? *Shakesp.*

Ro'yalist. *n. s.* [from *royal.*] Adherent to a king.

Where Candish fought, the *royalists* prevail'd,
Neither his courage nor his judgment fail'd. *Waller.*

The old church of England *royalists*, another name for a man who prefers his conscience before his interests, are the most meritorious subjects in the world, as having passed all those terrible tests, which domineering malice could put them to, and carried their credit and their conscience clear. *South.*

To Ro'yalize. *v. a.* [from *royal.*] To make royal.

Ere you were queen, ay, or your husband king,
To *royalize* his blood, I spilt mine own. *Shakesp.*

Ro'yally. *adv.* [from *royal.*] In a kingly manner; regally; as becomes a king.

It shall be my care,
To have you *royally* appointed. *Shakesp. Wint. Tale.*
His body shall be *royally* interr'd,
And the last funeral pomps adorn his herse. *Dryden.*

Ro'yalty. *n. s.* [*roialté*, Fr.]

1. Kingship; character or office of a king.

Suppose, that you have seen
The well appointed king at Hampton peer,
Embark his *royalty.* *Shakesp. Henry* V.

Draw, you rascal; you come with letters against the king, and take vanity the puppet's part against the *royalty* of her father. *Shakesp. King Lear.*

He will lose his head, ere give consent,
His master's son, as worshipfully he terms it,
Shall lose the *royalty* of England's throne. *Shakesp.*

If they had held their *royalties* by this title, either there must have been but one sovereign, or else every father of a family had as good a claim to *royalty* as these. *Locke.*

2. State of a king.

I will, alas! be wretched to be great,
And sigh in *royalty*, and grieve in state. *Prior.*

3. Emblems of royalty.

Wherefore do I assume
These *royalties*, and not refuse to reign. *Milton.*

To Royne. *v. a.* [*rogner*, Fr.] To gnaw; to bite. *Spenser.*

Ro'ynish. *adj.* [*rogneux*, Fr. mangy, paltry.] Paltry; sorry; mean; rude.

The *roynish* clown, at whom so oft
Your grace was wont to laugh, is also missing. *Shakesp.*

To RUB. *v. a.* [*rhubio*, Welsh; *reiben*, German, to wipe.]

1. To clean or smooth any thing by passing something over it; to scour; to wipe; to perfricate.

2. To touch so as to have something of that which touches behind.

Their straw-built citadel new *rub'd* with balm. *Milton.*

In narrow clefts, in the monument that stands over him, catholicks *rub* their beads, and smell his bones, which they say have in them a natural perfume, though very like apoplectick balsom; and what would make one suspect, that they *rub* the marble with it, it is observed, that the scent is stronger in the morning than at night. *Addison's Remarks on Italy.*

3. To move one body upon another.

Look, how she *rubs* her hands.
—It is an accustomed action with her, to seem thus washing her hands. *Shakesp. Macbeth.*

The bare *rubbing* of two bodies violently produces heat, and often fire. *Locke.*

Two bones, *rubbed* hard against one another, produce a fetid smell. *Arbuthnot on Aliments.*

4. To obstruct by collision.

'Tis the duke's pleasure,
Whose disposition all the world well know,
Will not be *rubb'd* nor stop'd. *Shakesp. King Lear.*

5. To polish; to retouch.

The whole business of our redemption is, to *rub* over the defaced copy of the creation, to reprint God's image upon the soul. *South.*

6. To remove by friction.

A forcible object will *rub* out the freshest colours at a stroke, and paint others. *Collier of the Aspect.*

If their minds are well principled with inward civility, a great part of the roughness, which sticks to the outside for want of better teaching, time, and observation, will *rub* off; but if ill, all the rules in the world will not polish them. *Locke.*

7. To touch hard.

He, who before he was espied, was afraid, after being perceived, was ashamed, now being hardly *rubbed* upon, left both fear and shame, and was moved to anger. *Sidney.*

8. *To* Rub *down.* To clean or curry a horse.

When his fellow beasts are weary grown,
He'll play the groom, give oats, and *rub* 'em *down.* *Dryd.*

9. *To* Rub *up.* To excite; to awaken.

You will find me not to have *rubbed up* the memory of what some heretofore in the city did. *South.*

10. *To* Rub *up.* To polish; to retouch.

To Rub. *v. n.*

1. To fret; to make a friction.

This last allusion gaul'd the panther more,
Because indeed it *rubb'd* upon the sore;
Yet seem'd she not to winch, though shrewdly pain'd. *Dry.*

2. To get through difficulties.

Many a lawyer, when once hampered, *rub* off as well as they can. *L'Estrange.*

'Tis as much as one can do, to *rub* through the world, though perpetually a doing. *L'Estrange.*

Rub. *n. s.* [from the verb.]

1. Collision; hindrance; obstruction.

The breath of what I mean to speak
Shall blow each dust, each straw, each little *rub*
Out of the path, which shall directly lead
Thy foot to England's throne. *Shakesp. King John.*
Now every *rub* is smoothed in our way. *Shakesp.*
Those you make friends,
And give your hearts to, when they once perceive
The least *rub* in your fortunes, fall away. *Shakesp.*

Upon this *rub*, the English embassadors thought fit to demur, and sent to receive directions. *Hayward.*

He expounds the giddy wonder
Of my weary steps, and under
Spreads a path clear as the day,
Where no churlish *rub* says nay. *Crashaw.*
He that once sins, like him that slides on ice,
Goes swiftly down the slippery ways of vice;
Though conscience checks him, yet those *rubs* gone o'er,
He slides on smoothly, and looks back no more. *Dryden.*

An hereditary right is to be preferred before election; because the government is so disposed, that it almost executes itself: and upon the death of a prince, the administration goes on without any *rub* or interruption. *Swift.*

2. Frication;

2. Frication; act of rubbing.
3. Inequality of ground, that hinders the motion of a bowl.
We'll play at bowls.
—'Twill make me think the world is full of *rubs*,
And that my fortune runs against the bias. *Shakesp.*
4. Difficulty; cause of uneasiness.
To sleep; perchance to dream; ay, there's the *rub*. *Sha.*

RUB-STONE. *n. s.* [*rub* and *stone.*] A stone to scour or sharpen.
A cradle for barlie, with *rub-stone* and sand. *Tusser.*

RU'BBER. *n. s.* [from *rub.*]
1. One that rubs.
2. The instrument with which one rubs.
Servants blow the fire with puffing cheeks, and lay
The *rubbers*, and the bathing sheets display. *Dryden.*
Rub the dirty tables with the napkins, for it will save your wearing out the common *rubbers*. *Swift.*
3. A coarse file.
The rough or coarse file, if large, is called a *rubber*, and takes off the unevenness which the hammer made in the forging. *Moxon's Mechanical Exercises.*
4. A game; a contest; two games out of three.
The ass was to stand by, to see two boobies try their title to him by a *rubber* of cuffs. *L'Estrange.*
If butchers had but the manners to go to sharps, gentlemen would be contented with a *rubber* at cuffs. *Collier on Duelling.*
5. A whetstone. *Ains.*

RUBI'CAN. *adj.* [*rubican*, Fr.] *Rubican* colour of a horse is one that is bay, sorrel, or black, with a light, grey, or white upon the flanks, but so that this grey or white is not predominant there. *Far. Dict.*

RU'BBAGE. } *n. s.* [from *rub*; as perhaps meaning, at first,
RU'BBISH. } dust made by rubbing. *Rubbage* is not used.]
1. Ruins of building; fragments of matter used in building.
What trash is Rome?
What *rubbish*, and what offal? when it serves
For the base matter to illuminate
So vile a thing as Cæsar. *Shakesp. Julius Cæsar.*
Such conceits seem too fine among this *rubbage*. *Wotton.*
A fabrick, though high and beautiful, if founded on *rubbish*, is easily made the triumph of the winds. *Glanv. Sceps.*
When the foundation of a state is once loosened, the least commotion lays the whole in *rubbish*. *L'Estrange.*
Th' Almighty cast a pitying eye,
He saw the town's one half in *rubbish* lie. *Dryden.*
The enemy hath avoided a battle, and taken a surer way to consume us, by letting our courage evaporate against stones and *rubbish*. *Swift.*
2. Confusion; mingled mass.
That noble art of political lying ought not to lie any longer in *rubbish* and confusion. *Arbuthnot's History of John Bull.*
3. Any thing vile and worthless.

RUBBLE-STONE. *n. s.*
Rubble-stones owe their name to their being rubbed and worn by the water, at the latter end of the deluge, departing in hurry and with great precipitation. *Woodward.*

RU'BICUND. *adj.* [*rubiconde*, Fr. *rubicundus*, Lat.] Inclining to redness. *Dict.*

RU'BIED. *adj.* [from *ruby.*] Red as a ruby.
Thrice upon thy fingers tip,
Thrice upon thy *rubied* lip. *Milton.*
Angels food, and *rubied* nectar flows
In pearl, in diamond, and in massy gold. *Milton.*

RUBI'FICK. *adj.* [*ruber* and *facio*, Lat.] Making red.
While the several species of rays, as the *rubifick*, are by refraction separated one from another, they retain those motions proper to each. *Grew's Cosmol.*

To RU'BIFY. *v. a.* To make red.
This topically applied, becomes a phænigmus or *rubifying* medicine, and of such fiery parts as to conceive fire of themselves, and burn a house. *Brown's Vulgar Errours.*

RU'BIOUS. *adj.* [*rubeus*, Lat.] Ruddy; red. Not used.
Diana's lip
Is not more smooth and *rubious*. *Shakesp. Twelfth Night.*

RU'BRICATED. *adj.* [from *rubrica*, Lat.] Smeared with red.

RU'BRICK. *n. s.* [*rubrique*, Fr. *rubrica*, Lat.] Directions printed in books of law and in prayer books; so termed, because they were originally distinguished by being in red ink.
No date prefix'd,
Directs me in the starry *rubrick* set. *Milton's Par. Reg.*
They had their particular prayers according to the several days and months; and their tables or *rubricks* to instruct them. *Stillingfleet.*

RU'BRICK. *adj.* Red.
The light and rays, which appear red, or rather make objects appear so, I call *rubrick* or red-making. *Newton.*
What though my name stood *rubrick* on the walls *Pope.*

To RU'BRICK. *v. a.* [from the noun.] To adorn with red.

RU'BIFORM. *adj.* [*ruber*, Lat. and *form.*] Having the form of red.
Of those rays, which pass close by the snow, the *rubiform* will be the least refracted; and so come to the eye in the directest lines. *Newton's Opticks.*

RU'BY. *n. s.* [from *ruber*, Lat.]
1. A precious stone of a red colour, next in hardness and value to a diamond.
Up, up, fair bride! and call
Thy stars from out their several boxes, take
Thy *rubies*, pearls, and diamonds forth, and make
Thyself a constellation of them all. *Donne.*
Melpomene would be represented like a manly lady, upon her head a dressing of pearl, diamonds, and *rubies*. *Peacham.*
Crowns were on their royal scutcheons plac'd,
With saphires, diamonds, and with *rubies* grac'd. *Dryden.*
2. Redness.
You can behold such sights,
And keep the natural *ruby* of your cheeks,
When mine is blanch'd with fear. *Shakesp. Macbeth.*
3. Any thing red.
Desire of wine
Thou could'st repress, nor did the dancing *ruby*
Sparkling, out-pour'd, the flavour, or the smell,
Or taste, that cheers the hearts of gods and men,
Allure thee from the cool crystalline stream. *Milton.*
4. A blain; a blotch; a carbuncle. *Ains.*

RU'BY. *adj.* [from the noun] Of a red colour.
Wounds, like dumb mouths, do ope their *ruby* lips. *Shak.*
Diana's lip
Is not more smooth and *ruby* than thy small pipe
Is at the maiden's organ shrill and sound. *Shakesp.*

RUCTA'TION. *n. s.* [*ructo*, Lat.] A belching arising from wind and indigestion.

To RUD. *v. a.* [ꞃuðu, Saxon, redness.] To make red.
Her cheeks, like apples, which the sun had *rudded*. *Spens.*

RU'DDER. *n. s.* [*roeder*, Dutch.]
1. The instrument at the stern of a vessel, by which its course is governed.
My heart was to thy *rudder* ty'd by th' string,
And thou should'st towe me after. *Shakesp.*
They loosed the *rudder* bands, and hoised up the main-sail, and made toward shore. *Acts* xxvii. 40.
Those, that attribute unto the faculty any first or sole power, have therein no other understanding, than such a one hath, who, looking into the stern of a ship, and finding it guided by the helm and *rudder*, doth ascribe some absolute virtue to the piece of wood, without all consideration of the hand that guides it. *Raleigh's History of the World.*
Fishes first to shipping did impart;
Their tail the *rudder*, and their head the prow. *Dryden.*
Thou held'st the *rudder* with a steady hand,
Till safely on the shore the bark did land. *Dryden.*
2. Any thing that guides or governs the course.

RU'DDINESS. [from *ruddy.*] The quality of approaching to redness.
The *ruddiness* upon her lip is wet;
You'll mar it, if you kiss it. *Shakesp. Winter's Tale.*
If the flesh lose its *ruddiness*, and look pale and withered, you may suspect it corrupting. *Wiseman's Surgery.*

RU'DDLE. *n. s.* [*rudul*, Islandick.] Red earth.
Ruddle owes its colour to an admixture of iron; and as that is in greater or less proportion, it is of a greater or less specifick gravity, consistence, or hardness. *Woodward.*

RU'DDOCK. *n. s.* [*rubecula*, Lat.] A kind of bird.
Of singing birds, they have linnets, and *ruddocks*. *Carew.*

RU'DDY. *adj.* [ꞃuðu, Saxon.]
1. Approaching to redness; pale red.
We may see the old man in a morning,
Lusty as health, come *ruddy* to the field,
And there pursue the chase, as if he meant
To o'ertake time, and bring back youth again. *Otway.*
New leaves on ev'ry bough were seen;
Some *ruddy* colour'd, some of lighter green. *Dryden.*
Ten wildings have I gather'd for my dear;
How *ruddy* like your lips their streaks appear! *Dryden.*
Ceres, in her prime,
Seems fertile, and with *ruddiest* freight bedeckt. *Philips.*
2. Yellow. Used, if to be used at all, only in poetry.
A crown of *ruddy* gold inclos'd her brow,
Plain without pomp. *Dryden.*

RUDE. *adj.* [ꞃeðe, Saxon; *rudis*, Lat.]
1. Rough; savage; coarse of manners; uncivil; brutal.
Ruffian, let go that *rude* uncivil touch;
Thou friend of an ill fashion. *Shakesp.*
Vane's bold answers, termed *rude* and ruffian-like, furthered his condemnation. *Hayward.*
You can with single look inflame
The coldest breast, the *rudest* tame. *Waller.*
It has been so usual to write prefaces, that a man is thought *rude* to his reader, who does not give him some account beforehand. *Walsh.*
2. Violent; tumultuous; boisterous; turbulent.
Clouds push'd with winds *rude* in their shock. *Milton.*
The water appears white near the shore, and a ship; because the *rude* agitation breaks it into foam. *Boyle.*

3. Harsh; inclement.

Spring does to flow'ry meadows bring,
What the *rude* winter from them tore. *Waller.*

4. Ignorant; raw; untaught.

Though I be *rude* in speech, yet not in knowledge. 2 *Cor.*

He was yet but *rude* in the profession of arms, though greedy of honour. *Wotton's Buckingham.*

Such tools as art yet *rude* had form'd. *Milton.*

5. [*Rude*, Fr.] Rugged; uneven; shapeless.

It was the custom to worship *rude* and unpolished stones. *Stillingfleet.*

6. Artless; inelegant.

I would know what ancient ground of authority he hath for such a senseless fable; and if he have any of the *rude* Irish books. *Spenser.*

One example may serve, till you review the Æneis in the original, unblemished by my *rude* translation. *Dryden.*

7. Such as may be done with strength without art.

To his country farm the fool confin'd;
Rude work well suited with a rustick mind. *Dryden.*

RU'DELY. *adv.* [from *rude.*]

1. In a rude manner.

Whether to knock against the gates of Rome,
Or *rudely* visit them in parts remote,
To fright them ere destroy. *Shakesp. Coriolanus.*

2. Without exactness; without nicety; coarsely:

I that am not shap'd for sportive tricks,
I that am *rudely* stampt, and want love's majesty
To strut before a wanton ambling nymyh. *Shakesp.*

3. Unskilfully.

My muse, though *rudely*, has resign'd
Some faint resemblance of his godlike mind. *Dryden.*

4. Violently; boisterously.

With his truncheon he so *rudely* stroke
Cymocles twice, that twice him forced his foot revoke. *Spen.*

RU'DENESS. *n. s.* [*rudesse*, Fr. from *rude.*]

1. Coarseness of manners; incivility.

This *rudeness* is a sauce to his good wit,
Which gives men stomach to digest his words
With better appetite. *Shakesp. Julius Cæsar.*

The publick will in triumphs rudely share,
And kings the *rudeness* of their joy must bear. *Dryden.*

The *rudeness*, tyranny, the oppression, and ingratitude of the late favourites towards their mistress, were no longer to be born. *Swift's Miscellanies.*

2. Ignorance; unskilfulness.

What he did amiss, was rather through *rudeness* and want of judgment, than any malicious meaning. *Hayward.*

3. Artlessness; inelegance; coarseness.

Let be thy bitter scorn,
And leave the *rudeness* of that antique age
To them, that liv'd therein in state forlorn. *Fairy Queen.*

4. Violence; boisterousness.

The ram, that batters down the wall,
For the great swing and *rudeness* of his poize,
They place before his hand that made the engine. *Shakesp.*

5. Storminess; rigour.

You can hardly be too sparing of water to your housed plants; the not observing of this, destroys more plants than all the *rudenesses* of the season. *Evelyn's Kalendar.*

RU'DENTURE *n. s.* [French.] In architecture, the figure of a rope or staff, sometimes plain and sometimes carved, wherewith the flutings of columns are frequently filled up. *Bailey.*

RU'DERARY. *adj.* [*rudera*, Lat.] Belonging to rubbish. *Dict.*

RUDERA'TION. *n. s.* In architecture, the laying of a pavement with pebbles or little stones. *Bailey.*

RU'DESBY. *n. s.* [from *rude.*] An uncivil turbulent fellow. A low word, now little used.

I must be forced
To give my hand, opposed against my heart,
Unto a mad-brain *rudesby*, full of spleen. *Shakesp.*

Out of my sight, *rudesby* be gone. *Shakesp.*

RU'DIMENT. *n. s.* [*rudiment*, Fr. *rudimentum*, Lat.]

1. The first principles; the first elements of a science.

Such as were trained up in the *rudiments*, and were so made fit to be by baptism received into the church, the fathers usually term hearers. *Hooker.*

To learn the order of my fingering,
I must begin with *rudiments* of art. *Shakesp.*

Thou soon shalt quit
Those *rudiments*, and see before thine eyes
The monarchies of th' earth, their pomp, and state,
Sufficient introduction to inform
Thee, of thyself so apt, in regal arts. *Milton's Par. Reg.*

Could it be believed, that a child should be forced to learn the *rudiments* of a language, which he is never to use, and neglect the writing a good hand, and casting accounts. *Locke.*

2. The first part of education.

He was nurtured where he was born in his first *rudiments*, till the years of ten, and then taught the principles of musick. *Wotton's Life of Villiers.*

The skill and *rudiments* austere of war. *Philips.*

3. The first, inaccurate, unshapen beginning or original of any thing.

Moss is but the *rudiment* of a plant, and the mould of earth or bark. *Bacon's Natural History.*

The *rudiments* of nature are very unlike the grosser appearances. *Glanvill's Sceps.*

So looks our monarch on this early fight,
Th' essay and *rudiments* of great success,
Which all-maturing time must bring to light. *Dryden.*

Shall that man pretend to religious attainments, who is defective and short in moral? which are but the *rudiments*, the beginnings, and first draught of religion; as religion is the perfection, refinement, and sublimation of morality. *South.*

God beholds the first imperfect *rudiments* of virtue in the soul, and keeps a watchful eye over it, till it has received every grace it is capable of. *Addison's Spectator.*

The sappy boughs
Attire themselves with blooms, sweet *rudiments*
Of future harvest. *Philips.*

RUDIME'NTAL. *adj.* [from *rudiment.*] Initial; relating to first principles.

Your first *rudimental* essays in spectatorship were made in my shop, where you often practised for hours. *Spectator.*

To RUE. *v. a.* [ƿeoƿian, Saxon.] To grieve for; to regret; to lament.

Thou temptest me in vain;
To tempt the thing which daily yet I *rue*,
And the old cause of my continued pain,
With like attempts to like end to renew. *Fairy Queen.*

You'll *rue* the time,
That clogs me with this answer. *Shakesp.*

France, thou shalt *rue* this treason with thy tears,
If Talbot but survive. *Shakesp. Henry* VI.

There are two councils held;
And that may be determin'd at the one,
Which may make you and him to *rue* at th' other. *Shak.*

Oh! treacherous was that breast, to whom you
Did trust our counsels, and we both may *rue*,
Having his falshood found too late, 'twas he
That made me cast you guilty, and you me. *Donne.*

I *rue*
That error now, which is become my crime. *Milton.*

Against this, thy will
Chose freely what it now so justly *rues*. *Milton.*

RUE. *n. s.* [*rue*, Fr. *ruta*, Lat.] An herb called, herb of grace, because holy water was sprinkled with it.

The flower of *rue* for the most part consists of four hollow leaves, which are placed orbicularly, and expand in form of a rose; out of whose flower-cup rises the pointal, which afterward becomes a roundish fruit, which is generally four cornered, and composed of four cells fixed to an hard shell of small angular seeds. *Miller.*

What savor is better,
For places infected, than wormwood and *rue*. *Tusser.*

Here did she drop a tear; here, in this place,
I'll set a bank of *rue*, sour herb of grace;
Rue, even for Ruth, here shortly shall be seen,
In the remembrance of a weeping queen. *Shakesp. Rich.* II.

The weasel, to encounter the serpent, arms herself with eating of *rue*. *More's Antidote against Atheism.*

RUE'FUL. *adj.* [*rue* and *full.*] Mournful; woful; sorrowful.

When we have our armour buckled on,
The venom'd vengeance ride upon our swords,
Spur them to *rueful* work, rein them from ruth. *Shakesp.*

Cocytus, nam'd of lamentation loud,
Heard on the *rueful* stream. *Milton's Paradise Lost.*

He sigh'd, and cast a *rueful* eye;
Our pity kindles, and our passions die. *Dryden.*

RUE'FULLY. *adv.* [from *rueful.*] Mournfully; sorrowfully.

Why should an ape run away from a snail, and very *ruefully* and frightfully look back, as being afraid? *More.*

RUE'FULNESS. *n. s.* [from *rueful.*] Sorrowfulness; mournfulness.

RUE'LLE. *n. s.* [French.] A circle; an assembly at a private house.

The poet, who flourished in the scene, is condemned in the *ruelle.* *Dryden's Preface to Æneis.*

RUFF. *n. s.* A puckered linen ornament, formerly worn about the neck. See RUFFLE.

You a captain; for what? for tearing a whore's *ruff* in a bawdy house? *Shakesp. Henry* IV. *p.* ii.

We'll revel it,
With *ruffs*, and cuffs, and fardingals. *Shakesp.*

Like an uproar in the town,
Before them every thing went down,
Some tore a *ruff*, and some a gown. *Drayton.*

Sooner may a gulling weather spy,
By drawing forth heav'n's scheme tell certainly,
What fashion'd hats, or *ruffs*, or suits next year,
Our giddy-headed antick youth will wear. *Donne.*

The ladies freed the neck from those yokes, those linnen *ruffs* in which the simplicity of their grandmothers had enclosed it. *Addison's Guardian*, Nº 100.

I rear'd this flow'r,
Soft on the paper *ruff* its leaves I spread. *Pope.*

2. [From *rough* scales.] A small river fish.

A *ruff* or pope is much like the pearch for shape, and taken to be better, but will not grow bigger than a gudgeon: he is an excellent fish and of a pleasant taste. *Walton.*

3. A state of roughness. Obsolete.

As fields set all their bristles up; in such a *ruff* wert thou. *Chapman's Iliads.*

4. New state. This seems to be the meaning of this cant word.

How many princes that, in the *ruff* of all their glory, have been taken down from the head of a conquering army to the wheel of the victor's chariot. *L'Estrange.*

Ru'ffian. *n. s.* [*ruffiano*, Italian; *ruffien*, Fr. a bawd; *roffver*, Danish, to pillage; perhaps it may be best derived from *rough.*] A brutal, boisterous, mischievous fellow; a cut-throat; a robber; a murderer.

Ruffian, let go that rude uncivil touch,
Thou friend of an ill fashion! *Shakesp. Two Gent. of Ver.*

Have you a *ruffian* that will swear? drink? dance?
Revel the night? rob? murder? *Shakesp. Henry IV.*

Sir Ralph Vane's bold answers termed rude and *ruffian* like, falling into years apt to take offence, furthered his condemnation. *Hayward.*

The boasted ancestors of these great men,
Whose virtues you admire, were all such *ruffians*,
This dread of nations, this almighty Rome,
That comprehends in her wide empire's bounds
All under heaven, was founded on a rape. *Addison's Cato.*

Ru'ffian. *adj.* Brutal; savagely boisterous.

Experienc'd age
May timely intercept the *ruffian* rage,
Convene the tribes. *Pope's Odyssey.*

To Ru'ffian. *v. n.* [from the noun.] To rage; to raise tumults; to play the ruffian. Not in use.

A fuller blast ne'er shook our battlements;
If it hath *ruffian'd* so upon the sea,
What ribs of oak, when mountains melt on them,
Can hold the mortise. *Shakesp. Othello.*

To Ru'ffle. *v. a.* [*ruyffelen*, Dutch, to wrinkle.]

1. To disorder; to put out of form; to make less smooth.

Naughty lady,
These hairs, which thou dost ravish from my chin,
Will quicken and accuse thee; I'm your host;
With robbers hands, my hospitable favour
You should not *ruffle* thus. *Shakesp. King Lear.*

In changeable taffeties, differing colours emerge and vanish upon the *ruffling* of the same piece of silk. *Boyle.*

As you come here to *ruffle* vizard punk;
When sober rail, and roar when you are drunk. *Dryden.*

As she first began to rise,
She smooth'd the *ruffled* seas, and clear'd the skies. *Dryden.*

Bear me, some god! oh quickly bear me hence
To wholsome solitude, the nurse of sense;
Where contemplation prunes her *ruffled* wings,
And the free soul looks down to pity kings. *Pope.*

2. To discompose; to disturb; to put out of temper.

Were I Brutus,
And Brutus, Antony, there were an Antony
Would *ruffle* up your spirits, and put a tongue
In every wound of Cæsar, that should move
The stones of Rome to rise and mutiny. *Shakesp.*

We are transported by passions, and our minds *ruffled* by the disorders of the body; nor yet can we tell, how the soul should be affected by such kind of agitations. *Glanvill.*

3. To put out of order; to surprise.

The knight found out
Th' advantage of the ground, where best
He might the *ruffl'd* foe infest. *Hudibras, p.* i.

4. To throw disorderly together.

Within a thicket I repos'd, when round
I *ruffl'd* up fal'n leaves in heap, and found,
Let fall from heaven, a sleep interminate. *Chapman.*

5. To contract into plaits.

A small skirt of fine *ruffled* linnen, running along the upper part of the stays before, is called the modesty-piece. *Addison.*

To Ru'ffle. *v. n.*

1. To grow rough or turbulent.

The night comes on; and the high winds
Do sorely *ruffle*, for many miles about
There's scarce a bush. *Shakesp. King Lear.*

The rising winds a *ruffling* gale afford. *Dryden.*

2. To be in loose motion; to flutter.

The fiery courser, when he hears from far
The sprightly trumpets and the shouts of war,
On his right shoulder his thick mane reclin'd,
Ruffles at speed, and dances in the wind. *Dryden.*

3. To be rough; to jar; to be in contention. Out of use.

A valiant son-in-law thou shalt enjoy;
One fit to bandy with thy lawless sons,
To *ruffle* in the commonwealth of Rome. *Shakesp.*

They would *ruffle* with jurors, and inforce them to find as they would direct. *Bacon's Henry* VII.

Ru'ffle. *n. s.* [from the verb.]

1. Plaited linnen used as an ornament.

The tucker is a slip of fine linnen, run in a small kind of *ruffle* round the uppermost verge of the women's stays. *Addison.*

2. Disturbance; contention; tumult.

Conceive the mind's perception of some object, and the consequent *ruffle* or special commotion of the blood. *Watts.*

Ru'fterhood. *n. s.* In falconry, a hood to be worn by a hawk when she is first drawn. *Bailey.*

Rug. *n. s.* [*rugget*, rough, Swedish.]

1. A coarse, nappy, woollen cloath.

January must be expressed with a horrid and fearful aspect, clad in Irish *rug* or coarse freeze. *Peacham on Drawing.*

2. A coarse nappy coverlet used for mean beds.

A *rug* was o'er his shoulders thrown;
A *rug*; for night-gown he had none. *Swift's Miscel.*

3. A rough woolly dog.

Mungrels, spaniels, curs,
Shoughes, water *rugs*, and demy wolves are cleped
All by the name of dogs. *Shakesp. Macbeth.*

RU'GGED. *adj.* [*rugget*, Swedish.]

1. Rough; full of unevenness and asperity.

Nature, like a weak and weary traveller,
Tir'd with a tedious and *rugged* way. *Denham.*

Since the earth revolves not upon a material and *rugged*, but a geometrical plane, their proportions may be varied in innumerable degrees. *Bentley.*

2. Not neat; not regular.

His hair is sticking;
His well-proportion'd beard made rough and *rugged*,
Like to the summer's corn by tempest lodg'd. *Shakesp.*

3. Savage of temper; brutal; rough.

The greatest favours to such an one neither soften nor win upon him; they neither melt nor endear him, but leave him as hard, as *rugged*, and as unconcerned as ever. *South's Sermons.*

4. Stormy; rude; tumultuous; turbulent; tempestuous.

Now bind my brows with iron, and approach
The *rugged'st* hour that time and spite dare bring,
To frown upon th' enrag'd Northumberland. *Shakesp.*

5. Rough or harsh to the ear.

A monosyllable line turns verse to prose, and even that prose is *rugged* and unharmonious. *Dryden's Dedic. to Æneis.*

6. Sour; surly; discomposed.

Sleek o'er your *rugged* looks,
Be bright and jovial 'mong your guests to-night. *Shakesp.*

7. Violent; rude; boisterous.

Fierce Talgol, gath'ring might,
With *rugged* truncheon charg'd the knight. *Hudibras.*

8. Rough; shaggy.

Through forests wild,
To chase the lion, boar, or *rugged* bear. *Fairfax.*

Ru'ggedly. *adv.* [from *rugged.*] In a rugged manner.

Ru'ggedness. [from *rugged.*]

1. The state or quality of being rugged.

2. Roughness; asperity.

Hardness and *ruggedness* is unpleasant to the touch. *Bacon.*

Syrups immediately abate and demulce the hoarseness and violence of a cough, by mollifying the *ruggedness* of the intern tunick of the gullet. *Harvey.*

This softness of the foot, which yields and fits itself to the *ruggedness* and unevenness of the roads, does render it less capable of being worn. *Ray on the Creation.*

Ru'gin. *n. s.* A nappy cloth.

The lips grew so painful, that she could not endure the wiping the ichor from it with a soft *rugin* with her own hand. *Wiseman's Surgery.*

Ru'gine. *n. s.* [*rugine*, Fr.] A chirurgeon's rasp.

If new flesh should not generate, bore little orifices into the bone, or rasp it with the *rugine*. *Sharp.*

Rugo'se. *adj.* [*rugosus*, Lat.] Full of wrinkles.

It is a relaxation of the sphincter to such a degree, that the internal *rugose* coat of the intestine turneth out, and beareth down. *Wiseman's Surgery.*

RU'IN. *n. s.* [*ruine*, Fr. *ruina*, Lat.]

1. The fall or destruction of cities or edifices.

2. The remains of building demolished.

The Veian and the Gabian tow'rs shall fall,
And one promiscuous *ruin* cover all;
Nor, after length of years, a stone betray
The place where once the very *ruins* lay. *Addison.*

Judah shall fall, oppress'd by grief and shame,
And men shall from her *ruins* know her fame. *Prior.*

Such a fool was never found,
Who pull'd a palace to the ground,
Only to have the *ruins* made
Materials for a house decay'd. *Swift.*

3. Destruction; loss of happiness or fortune; overthrow.

He parted frowning from me, as if *ruin*
Leapt from his eyes. *Shakesp. Henry* VIII.

Those whom God to *ruin* has design'd,
He fits for fate, and first destroys their mind. *Dryden.*

4. Mischief; bane.

The errors of young men are the *ruin* of business. *Bacon.*

Havock, and spoil, and *ruin* are my gain. *Milton.*

To Ru'in. *v. a.* [*ruiner*, Fr. from the noun.]

1. To subvert; to demolish.

A nation loving gold must rule this place,
Our temples *ruin*, and our rites deface. *Dryden.*

2. To destroy; to deprive of felicity or fortune.

By thee rais'd I *ruin* all my foes. *Milton.*

Dispose all honours of the sword and gown,
Grace with a nod, and *ruin* with a frown. *Dryden.*

A confident dependence ill-grounded creates such a negligence, as will certainly *ruin* us in the end. *Wake.*

3. To impoverish.

She would *ruin* me in silks, were not the quantity that goes to a large pincushion sufficient to make her a gown and petticoat. *Addison.*

To Ru'in. *v. n.*

1. To fall in ruins.

Hell heard th' unsufferable noise, hell saw
Heav'n *ruining* from heav'n, and would have fled
Affrighted, but strict fate had fix'd too deep
Her dark foundations, and too fast had bound. *Milton.*

2. To run to ruin.

Though he his house of polish'd marble build,
Yet shall it *ruin* like the moth's frail cell,
Or sheds of reeds, which summer's heat repel. *Sandys.*

3. To be brought to poverty or misery.

If we are idle, and disturb the industrious in their business, we shall *ruin* the faster. *Locke.*

To Ru'inate. *v. a.* [from *ruin*. This word is now obsolete.]

1. To subvert; to demolish.

I will not *ruinate* my father's house,
Who gave his blood to lime the stones together,
And set up Lancaster. *Shakesp. Henry* VI. *p.* iii.

We'll order well the state,
That like events may ne'er it *ruinate*. *Shakesp.*

2. To bring to meanness or misery irrecoverable.

The Romans came to pull down kingdoms; Philip and Nabis were already *ruinated*, and now was his turn to be assailed. *Bacon's War with Spain.*

So shall the great revenger *ruinate*
Him and his issue by a dreadful fate. *Sandys.*

Ruina'tion. *n. s.* [from *ruinate*.] Subversion; demolition; overthrow. Obsolete.

Roman coins were overcovered in the ground, in the sudden *ruination* of towns by the Saxons. *Camden's Remains.*

Ru'inous. *adj.* [*ruinosus*, Lat. *ruineux*, Fr.]

1. Fallen to ruin; dilapidated; demolished.

It is less dangerous, when divers parts of a tower are decayed, and the foundation firm, than when the foundation is *ruinous*. *Hayward.*

2. Mischievous; pernicious; baneful; destructive.

The birds,
After a night of storm so *ruinous*,
Clear'd up their choicest notes in bush and spray,
To gratulate the sweet return of morn. *Milton's Par. Reg.*

Those successes are more glorious, which bring benefit to the world, than such *ruinous* ones, as are dyed in human blood. *Glanvill's Preface to Sceps.*

A stop might be put to that *ruinous* practise of gaming. *Sw.*

Ru'inously. *adv.* [from *ruinous*.]

1. In a ruinous manner.

2. Mischievously; destructively.

If real uneasinesses may be admitted to be as deterring as imaginary ones, his own decree will retort the most *ruinously* on himself. *Decay of Piety.*

RULE. *n. s.* [*regula*, Lat.]

1. Government; empire; sway; supreme command.

I am asham'd, that women
Should seek for *rule*, supremacy, or sway,
When they are bound to serve, love, and obey. *Shakesp.*

May he live
Ever belov'd, and loving may his *rule* be! *Shakesp.*

A wise servant shall have *rule* over a son that causeth shame. *Proverbs* xvii. 2.

There being no law of nature nor positive law of God, that determines which is the positive heir, the right of succession; and consequently of bearing *rule*, could not have been determined. *Locke.*

This makes them apprehensive of every tendency, to endanger that form of *rule* established by the law of their country. *Addison's Freeholder*, N° 52.

Instruct me whence this uproar;
And wherefore Vanoe, the sworn friend to Rome,
Should spurn against our *rule*, and stir
The tributary provinces to war. *A. Philips's Briton.*

Sev'n years the traytor rich Mycenæ sway'd,
And his stern *rule* the groaning land obey'd. *Pope.*

2. An instrument by which lines are drawn.

If your influence be quite dam'd up
With black usurping mists, some gentle taper,
Though a rush-candle from the wicker hole
Of some clay habitation, visit us
With thy long levell'd *rule* of streaming light. *Milton.*

A judicious artist will use his eye, but he will trust only to his *rule*. *South's Sermons.*

3. Canon; precept by which the thoughts or actions are directed.

Adam's sin did not deprive him of his *rule*, but left the creatures to a reluctation. *Bacon.*

This little treatise will furnish you with infallible *rules* of judging truly. *Dryden's Dufresnoy.*

Know'st with an equal hand to hold the scale;
See'st where the reasons pinch, and where they fail,
And where exceptions o'er the general *rule* prevail. *Dry.*

We profess to have embraced a religion, which contains the most exact *rules* for the government of our lives. *Tillots.*

We owe to christianity the discovery of the most certain and perfect *rule* of life. *Tillotson.*

4. Regularity; propriety of behaviour.

Some say he's mad; others, that lesser hate him,
Do call it valiant fury; but for certain,
He cannot buckle his distemper'd cause
Within the belt of *rule*. *Shakesp. Macbeth.*

To Rule. *v. a.* [from the noun.]

1. To govern; to controll; to manage with power and authority.

It is a purpos'd thing
To curb the will of the nobility;
Suffer't, and live with such as cannot *rule*,
Nor ever will be *rul'd*. *Shakesp. Coriolanus.*

Marg'ret shall now be queen, and *rule* the king;
But I will *rule* both her, the king, and realm. *Shakesp.*

A greater power now *rul'd* him. *Milton.*

Rome! 'tis thine alone with awful sway,
To *rule* mankind, and make the world obey,
Disposing peace and war thy own majestick way. *Dryd.*

2. To manage.

He sought to take unto him the *ruling* of the affairs. 1 *Mac.*

3. To settle as by a rule.

Had he done it with the pope's license, his adversaries must have been silent; for that's a *ruled* case with the schoolmen. *Atterbury.*

To Rule. *v. n.* To have power or command.

Judah yet *ruleth* with God, and is faithful with the saints. *Hosea* xi. 12.

Thrice happy men! whom God hath thus advanc'd!
Created in his image, there to dwell,
And worship him; and in reward to *rule*
Over his works. *Milton's Paradise Lost. b.* vii.

We subdue and *rule* over all other creatures; and use for our own behoof those qualities wherein they excel. *Ray.*

He can have no divine right to my obedience, who cannot shew his divine right to the power of *ruling* over me. *Locke.*

Ru'ler. *n. s.* [from *rule*.]

1. Governour; one that has the supreme command.

Soon *rulers* grow proud, and in their pride foolish. *Sidney.*

God, by his eternal providence, has ordained kings; and the law of nature, leaders and *rulers* over others. *Raleigh.*

The pompous mansion was design'd
To please the mighty *rulers* of mankind;
Inferior temples use on either hand. *Addison.*

2. An instrument, by the direction of which lines are drawn.

They know how to draw a straight line between two points by the side of a *ruler*. *Moxon's Mechanical Exercises.*

Rum. *n. s.*

1. A country parson. A cant word.

I'm grown a mere mopus; no company comes,
But a rabble of tenants and rusty dull *rums*. *Swift.*

2. A kind of spirits distilled from molosses.

To RU'MBLE. *v. n.* [*rommelen*, Dutch.] To make a hoarse low continued noise.

The trembling streams, which wont in channels clear
To *rumble* gently down with murmur soft,
And were by them right tuneful taught to bear
A base's part amongst their consorts oft,
Now forc'd to overflow with brackish tears,
With troublous noise did dull their dainty ears. *Spenser.*

Rumble thy belly full, spit fire, spout rain;
Nor rain, wind, thunder, fire are my daughters;
I tax not you, you elements with unkindness. *Shakesp.*

At the rushing of his chariots, and at the *rumbling* of his wheels, the fathers shall not look back to their children for feebleness. *Jeremiah* xlvii. 3.

Our courtier thinks that he's preferr'd, whom every man envies;
When love so *rumbles* in his pate, no sleep comes in his eyes. *Suckling.*

Apollo

Apollo ſtarts, and all Parnaſſus ſhakes
At the rude *rumbling* Baralipton makes. *Roſcommon.*
The fire ſhe fann'd, with greater fury burn'd,
Rumbling within. *Dryden.*
Th' included vapours, that in caverns dwell,
Lab'ring with colick pangs, and cloſe confin'd,
In vain ſought iſſue from the *rumbling* wind. *Dryden.*

On a ſudden there was heard a moſt dreadful *rumbling* noiſe within the entrails of the machine, after which the mountain burſt. *Addiſon.*

Several monarchs have acquainted me, how often they have been ſhook from their reſpective thrones, by the *rumbling* of a wheelbarrow. *Spectator*, Nº 597.

RU'MBLER. *n. ſ.* [from *rumble.*] The perſon or thing that rumbles.

RU'MINANT. *adj.* [*ruminant*, Fr. *ruminans*, Latin.] Having the property of chewing the cud.

Ruminant creatures have a power of directing this periſtaltick motion upwards and downwards. *Ray.*

The deſcription, given of the muſcular part of the gullet, is very exact in *ruminants*, but not in men. *Derham.*

To RU'MINATE. *v. n.* [*ruminer*, Fr. *rumino*, Lat.]

1. To chew the cud.

Others fill'd with paſture gazing ſat,
Or bedward *ruminating*. *Milton's Par. Loſt, b.* iv.

The neceſſity of ſpittle to diſſolve the aliment, appears from the contrivance of nature in making the ſalivary ducts of animals, which *ruminate* or chew the cud, extremely open. *Arbuthnot on Aliments.*

On graſſy banks herds *ruminating* lie. *Thomſon.*

2. To muſe; to think again and again.

Alone ſometimes ſhe walk'd in ſecret where,
To *ruminate* upon her diſcontent. *Fairfax, b.* iv.
Of ancient prudence here he *ruminates*,
Of riſing kingdoms, and of falling ſtates. *Waller.*

I am at a ſolitude, an houſe between Hampſtead and London, wherein Sir Charles Sedley died: this circumſtance ſets me a thinking and *ruminating* upon the employments in which men of wit exerciſe themſelves. *Steele to Pope.*

He practiſes a ſlow meditation, and *ruminates* on the ſubject; and perhaps in two nights and days rouſes thoſe ſeveral ideas which are neceſſary. *Watts's Improv. of the Mind.*

To RU'MINATE. *v. a.* [*rumino*, Lat.]

1. To chew over again.
2. To muſe on; to meditate over and over again.

'Tis a ſtudied, not a preſent thought,
By duty *ruminated*. *Shakeſp. Antony and Cleopatra.*
Knock at the ſtudy, where he keeps,
To *ruminate* ſtrange plots of dire revenge. *Shakeſp.*
The condemned Engliſh
Sit patiently, and inly *ruminate*
The morning's danger. *Shakeſp.*
Mad with deſire ſhe *ruminates* her ſin,
And wiſhes all her wiſhes o'er again;
Now ſhe deſpairs, and now reſolves to try;
Wou'd not, and wou'd again, ſhe knows not why. *Dry.*

RUMINA'TION. *n. ſ.* [*ruminatio*, Lat. from *ruminate.*]

1. The property or act of chewing the cud.

Rumination is given to animals, to enable them at once to lay up a great ſtore of food, and afterwards to chew it. *Arb.*

2. Meditation; reflection.

It is a melancholy of mine own, extracted from many objects, in which my often *rumination* wraps me in a moſt humorous ſadneſs. *Shakeſp. As You like it.*

Retiring, full of *rumination* ſad,
He mourns the weakneſs of theſe latter times. *Thomſon.*

To RU'MMAGE. *v. a.* [*ranmen*, German, to empty. *Skinner. rimari*, Lat.] To ſearch; to plunder; to evacuate.

Our greedy ſeamen *rummage* every hold,
Smile on the booty of each wealthier cheſt. *Dryden.*

To RU'MMAGE. *v. n.* To ſearch places.

A fox was *rummaging* among a great many carved figures, there was one very extraordinary piece. *L'Eſtrange.*

Some on antiquated authors pore;
Rummage for ſenſe. *Dryden's Perſius.*

I have often *rummaged* for old books in Little-Britain and Duck-lane. *Swift.*

RU'MMER. *n. ſ.* [*roemer*, Dutch.] A glaſs; a drinking cup.

Imperial Rhine beſtow'd the generous *rummer*. *Philips.*

RU'MOUR. *n. ſ.* [*rumeur*, Fr. *rumor*, Lat.] Flying or popular report; bruit; fame.

We hold *rumour* from what we fear. *Shakeſp.*
There ran a *rumour*
Of many worthy fellows that were out. *Shakeſp. Macbeth.*
Great is the *rumour* of this dreadful knight,
And his atchievements of no leſs account. *Shakeſp.*

This *rumour* of him went forth throughout all Judea. *Luke.*

Rumour next and chance
And tumult and confuſion all embroil'd. *Milton.*
She heard an ancient *rumour* fly,
That times to come ſhould ſee the Trojan race
Her Carthage ruin. *Dryden's Æneis.*

To RU'MOUR. *v. a.* [from the noun.] To report abroad; to bruit.

Cateſby, *rumour* it abroad,
That Anne my wife is ſick, and like to die. *Shakeſp.*
All abroad was *rumour'd*, that this day
Samſon ſhould be brought forth. *Milton's Agoniſtes.*
'Twas *rumour'd*,
My father 'ſcap'd from out the citadel. *Dryden.*

RU'MOURER. *n. ſ.* [from *rumour.*] Reporter; ſpreader of news.

A ſlave
Reports, the Volſcians, with two ſeveral powers,
Are entered into the Roman territories.
—Go ſee this *rumourer* whipt: it cannot be. *Shakeſp.*

RUMP. *n. ſ.* [*rumpff*, German.]

1. The end of the backbone.

At her *rump* ſhe growing had behind
A fox's tail. *Fairy Queen, b.* i.
If his holineſs would thump
His reverend bum 'gainſt horſe's *rump*,
He might b' equipt from his own ſtable. *Prior.*
Rumps of beef with virgin honey ſtrew'd. *King.*
Laſt trotted forth the gentle ſwine,
To eaſe her itch againſt the ſtump,
And diſmally was heard to whine,
All as ſhe ſcrubb'd her meazly *rump*. *Swift's Miſcel.*

2. The buttocks.

A ſailor's wife had cheſnuts in her lap,
And mouncht,—give me quoth I
Aroint the witch!—the *rump* fed ronyon cries. *Shakeſp.*
He charg'd him firſt to bind
Crowdero's hands on *rump* behind. *Hudibras, p.* i.

To RU'MPLE. *v. a.* [*rompelen*, Dutch.] To cruſh or contract into inequalities and corrugations; to cruſh together out of ſhape.

Each vital ſpeck, in which remains
Th' entire, but *rumpled* animal, contains
Organs perplex'd. *Blackmore on the Creation.*
I *rumpled* petticoats, or tumbled beds,
Or diſcompos'd the head-dreſs of a prude. *Pope.*

Never put on a clean apron, 'till you have made your lady's bed, for fear of *rumpling* your apron. *Swift.*

RU'MPLE. *n. ſ.* [hꝛympelle, Saxon.] Pucker; rude plait.

Fair Virginia would her fate beſtow
On Rutila, and change her faultleſs make
For the foul *rumple* of her camel-back. *Dryden.*

To RUN. *v. n.* pret. *ran.* [*rinnan*, Gothick; ꝛẏnnan, Saxon; *rennen*, Dutch.]

1. To move ſwiftly; to ply the legs in ſuch a manner, as that both feet are at every ſtep off the ground at the ſame time; to make haſte; to paſs with very quick pace.

Their feet *run* to evil, and make haſte to ſhed blood. *Prov.*

Laban *ran* out unto the man unto the well. *Gen.* xxiv. 29.

When ſhe knew Peter's voice, ſhe *ran* in, and told how Peter ſtood before the gate. *Acts* xii. 14.

Since death's near, and *runs* with ſo much force,
We muſt meet firſt, and intercept his courſe. *Dryden.*
He *ran* up the ridges of the rocks amain. *Dryden.*

Let a ſhoe-boy clean your ſhoes and *run* of errands. *Swift.*

2. To uſe the legs in motion.

Seldom there is need of this, till young children can *run* about. *Locke.*

3. To move in a hurry.

The prieſt and people *run* about,
And at the ports all thronging out,
As if their ſafety were to quit
Their mother. *Benj. Johnſon.*

4. To paſs on the ſurface, not through the air.

The Lord ſent thunder, and the fire *ran* along upon the ground. *Exodus* ix. 23.

5. To ruſh violently.

Let not thy voice be heard, leſt angry fellows *run* upon thee, and thou loſe thy life. *Judges* xviii. 25.

Now by the winds and raging waves I ſwear,
Your ſafety more than mine was thus my care;
Leſt of the guide bereft, the rudder loſt,
Your ſhip ſhou'd *run* againſt the rocky coaſt. *Dryden.*

They have avoided that rock, but *run* upon another no leſs dangerous. *Burnet's Theory of the Earth.*

I diſcover thoſe ſhoals of life which are concealed in order to keep the unwary from *running* upon them. *Addiſon.*

6. To take a courſe at ſea.

Running under the iſland Clauda, we had much work to come by the boat. *Acts* xxvii. 16.

7. To contend in a race.

A horſe-boy, being lighter than you, may be truſted to *run* races with leſs damage to the horſes. *Swift.*

8. To fly; not to ſtand. It is often followed by *away* in this ſenſe.

My conſcience will ſerve me to *run* from this Jew, my maſter. *Shakeſp. Merchant of Venice.*

The difference between the valour of the Irish rebels and the Spaniards was, that the one *ran away* before they were charged, and the other ſtreight after. *Bacon.*

I do not ſee a face
Worthy a man; that dares look up and ſtand
One thunder out; but downward all like beaſts
Running away at every flaſh. *Benj. Johnſon.*

The reſt diſpers'd *run*, ſome diſguis'd,
To unknown coaſts; ſome to the ſhores do fly. *Daniel.*

They, when they're out of hopes of flying,
Will *run away* from death by dying. *Hudibras.*

Your child ſhrieks, and *runs away* at a frog. *Locke.*

9. To ſtream; to flow.

My ſtatues,
Like a fountain, with a hundred ſpouts,
Did *run* pure blood. *Shakeſp. Julius Cæſar.*

I command, that the conduit *run* nothing but claret. *Shak.*

The precious ointment upon the head *ran* down upon Aaron's beard. *Pſalm* cxxxiii. 2.

In ſome houſes, wainſcots will ſweat, ſo that they will almoſt *run* with water. *Bacon's Natural Hiſtory.*

Rivers *run* potable gold. *Milton.*

Caicus roll'd a crimſon flood,
And Thebes *ran* red with her own natives blood. *Dryden.*

The greateſt veſſel, when full, if you pour in ſtill, it muſt *run* out ſome way, and the more it *runs* out at one ſide, the leſs it *runs* out at the other. *Temple.*

Innumerable iſlands were covered with flowers, and interwoven with ſhining ſeas that *ran* among them. *Addiſon.*

Her fields he cloath'd, and chear'd her blaſted face
With *running* fountains and with ſpringing graſs. *Addiſon.*

10. To be liquid; to be fluid.

In lead melted, when it beginneth to congeal, make a little hole, in which put quickſilver wrapped in a piece of linnen, and it will fix and *run* no more, and endure the hammer. *Bacon's Natural Hiſtory.*

Stiff with eternal ice, and hid in ſnow,
The mountain ſtands; nor can the riſing ſun
Unfix her froſts, and teach 'em how to *run*. *Addiſon.*

As wax diſſolves, as ice begins to *run*,
And trickle into drops before the ſun,
So melts the youth. *Addiſon's Ovid's Metam.*

11. To be fuſible; to melt.

Her form glides through me, and my heart gives way;
This iron heart, which no impreſſion took
From wars, melts down, and *runs*, if ſhe but look. *Dryden.*

Suſſex iron ores *run* freely in the fire. *Woodward.*

Your iron muſt not burn in the fire; that is, *run* or melt; for then it will be brittle. *Moxon's Mech. Exerc.*

12. To paſs; to proceed.

You, having *run* through ſo much publick buſineſs, have found out the ſecret ſo little known, that there is a time to give it over. *Temple's Miſcellanies.*

If there remains an eternity to us after the ſhort revolution of time, we ſo ſwiftly *run* over here, 'tis clear, that all the happineſs, that can be imagined in this fleeting ſtate, is not valuable in reſpect of the future. *Locke.*

13. To go away; to vaniſh.

As faſt as our time *runs*, we ſhould be very glad in moſt parts of our lives that it *ran* much faſter. *Addiſon.*

14. To have a legal courſe; to be practiſed.

Cuſtoms *run* only upon our goods imported or exported, and that but once for all; whereas intereſt *runs* as well upon our ſhips as goods, and muſt be yearly paid. *Child.*

15. To have a courſe in any direction.

A hound *runs* counter, and yet draws dry foot well. *Sha.*

Little is the wiſdom, where the flight
So *runs* againſt all reaſon. *Shakeſp. Macbeth.*

That puniſhment follows not in this life the breach of this rule, and conſequently has not the force of a law, in countries where the generally allowed practice *runs* counter to it, is evident. *Locke.*

Had the preſent war *run* againſt us, and all our attacks upon the enemy been vain, it might look like a degree of frenzy to be determined on ſo impracticable an undertaking. *Addiſ.*

16. To paſs in thought or ſpeech.

Cou'd you hear the annals of our fate;
Through ſuch a train of woes if I ſhould *run*,
The day wou'd ſooner than the tale be done. *Dryden.*

By reading, a man antedates his life; and this way of *running* up beyond one's nativity, is better than Plato's preexiſtence. *Collier.*

Virgil, in his firſt Georgick, has *run* into a ſet of precepts foreign to his ſubject. *Addiſon's Eſſay on the Georgicks.*

Raw and injudicious writers propoſe one thing for their ſubject, and *run* off to another. *Felton.*

17. To be mentioned curſorily or in few words.

The whole *runs* on ſhort, like articles in an account, whereas, if the ſubject were fully explained, each of them might take up half a page. *Arbuthnot on Coins.*

18. To have a continual tenour of any kind.

Diſcourſes *ran* thus among the cleareſt obſervers: it was ſaid, that the prince, without any imaginable ſtain of his religion, had, by the ſight of foreign courts, much corroborated his judgement. *Wotton's Buckingham.*

The king's ordinary ſtyle *runneth*, our ſovereign lord the king. *Saunderſon.*

19. To be buſied upon.

His griſly beard his penſive boſom ſought,
And all on Lauſus *ran* his reſtleſs thought. *Dryden.*

When we deſire any thing, our minds *run* wholly on the good circumſtances of it; when 'tis obtained, our minds *run* wholly on the bad ones. *Swift.*

20. To be popularly known.

Men gave them their own names, by which they *run* a great while in Rome. *Temple.*

21. To have reception, ſucceſs, or continuance.

22. To go on by ſucceſſion of parts.

She ſaw with joy the line immortal *run*,
Each ſire impreſt, and glaring in his ſon. *Pope.*

23. To proceed in a train of conduct.

If you ſuſpend your indignation againſt my brother, till you can derive from him better teſtimony of his intent, you ſhould *run* a certain courſe. *Shakeſp. King Lear.*

24. To paſs into ſome change.

Is it really deſirable, that there ſhould be ſuch a being in the world as takes care of the frame of it, that it do not *run* into confuſion, and ruin mankind? *Tillotſon.*

Wonder at my patience;
Have I not cauſe to rave, and beat my breaſt,
To rend my heart with grief, and *run* diſtracted. *Addiſon.*

25. To paſs.

We have many evils to prevent, and much danger to *run* through. *Taylor.*

26. To proceed in a certain order.

Day yet wants much of his race to *run*. *Milton.*

Thus in a circle *runs* the peaſant's pain,
And the year rolls within itſelf again. *Dryden.*

This church is very rich in relicks, which *run* up as high as Daniel and Abraham. *Addiſon's Remarks on Italy.*

Milk by boiling will change to yellow, and *run* through all the intermediate degrees, till it ſtops in an intenſe red. *Arb.*

27. To be in force.

The owner hath incurred the forfeiture of eight years profits of his lands, before he cometh to the knowledge of the proceſs that *runneth* againſt him. *Bacon.*

The time of inſtance ſhall not commence or *run* till after conteſtation of ſuit. *Ayliffe's Parergon.*

28. To be generally received.

Neither was he ignorant what report *ran* of himſelf, and how he had loſt the hearts of his ſubjects. *Knolles.*

29. To be carried on in any manner.

Conceſſions, that *run* as high as any, the moſt charitable proteſtants make. *Atterbury.*

In popiſh countries the power of the clergy *runs* higher, and excommunication is more formidable. *Ayliffe's Parergon.*

30. To have a track or courſe.

Searching the ulcer with my probe, the ſinus *run* up above the orifice. *Wiſeman's Surgery.*

One led me over thoſe parts of the mines, where metalline veins *run*. *Boyle.*

31. To paſs progreſſively.

The planets do not of themſelves move in curve lines, but are kept in them by ſome attractive force, which, if once ſuſpended, they would for ever *run* out in right lines. *Cheyne.*

32. To make a gradual progreſs.

The wing'd colonies
There ſettling, ſeize the ſweets the bloſſoms yield,
And a low murmur *runs* along the field. *Pope.*

33. To be predominant.

This *run* in the head of a late writer of natural hiſtory, who is not wont to have the moſt lucky hits in the conduct of his thoughts. *Woodward on Foſſils.*

34. To tend in growth.

A man's nature *runs* either to herbs or weeds; therefore let him ſeaſonably water the one, and deſtroy the other. *Bac.*

35. To grow exuberantly.

Joſeph is a fruitful bough, whoſe branches *run* over the wall. *Geneſis* xlix. 22.

Study your race, or the ſoil of your family will dwindle into cits or *run* into wits. *Tatler*, Nº 75.

If the richneſs of the ground cauſe turnips to *run* to leaves, treading down the leaves will help their rooting. *Mortimer.*

In ſome, who have *run* up to men without a liberal education, many great qualities are darkened. *Felton.*

Magnanimity may *run* up to profuſion or extravagance. *Pope.*

36. To excern pus or matter.

Whether his fleſh *run* with his iſſue, or be ſtopped, it is his uncleanneſs. *Leviticus* xiii. 3.

37. To become irregular; to change to ſomething wild.

Many have *run* out of their wits for women. 1 *Eſdr.* iv.

Our king return'd,
The muſe *ran* mad to ſee her exil'd lord;
On the crack'd ſtage the bedlam heroes roar'd. *Granville.*

38. To

38. To get by artifice or fraud.

Hath publick faith, like a young heir,
For this tak'n up all forts of ware,
And *run* int' ev'ry tradefman's book,
'Till both turn'd bankrupts. *Hudibras, p.* i.

Run in truft, and pay for it out of your wages. *Swift.*

39. To fall by hafte, paffion, or folly into fault or misfortune.

If thou rememb'reft not the flighteft folly,
That ever love did make thee *run* into;
Thou haft not lov'd. *Shakefp. As You Like it.*

Solyman himfelf, in punifhing the perjury of another, *ran* into wilful perjury himfelf, perverting the commendation of juftice, which he had fo much defired by his moft bloody and unjuft fentence. *Knolles's Hiftory of the Turks.*

From not ufing it right, come all thofe miftakes we *run* into in our endeavours after happinefs. *Locke.*

40. To fall; to pafs.

In the middle of a rainbow, the colours are fufficiently diftinguifhed; but near the borders they *run* into one another, fo that you hardly know how to limit the colours. *Watts.*

41. To have a general tendency.

Temperate climates *run* into moderate governments, and the extremes into defpotick power. *Swift.*

42. To proceed as on a ground or principle.

It is a confederating with him, to whom the facrifice is offered: for upon that the apoftle's argument *runs. Atterbury.*

43. To go on with violence.

Tarquin, *running* into all the methods of tyranny, after a cruel reign was expelled. *Swift.*

44. *To* Run *after.* To fearch for; to endeavour at, though out of the way.

The mind, upon the fuggeftion of any new notion, *runs after* fimilies, to make it the clearer to itfelf; which, though it may be ufeful in explaining our thoughts to others, is no right method to fettle true notions in ourfelves. *Locke.*

45. *To* Run *away with.* To hurry without confent.

Thoughts will not be directed what objects to purfue, but *run away with* a man in purfuit of thofe ideas they have in view. *Locke.*

46. *To* Run *in with.* To clofe; to comply.

Though Ramus *run in with* the firft reformers of learning, in his oppofition to Ariftotle; yet he has given us a plaufible fyftem. *Baker.*

47. *To* Run *on.* To be continued.

If, through our too much fecurity, the fame fhould *run on*, foon might we feel our eftate brought to thofe lamentable terms, whereof this hard and heavy fentence was by one of the ancients uttered. *Hooker.*

48. *To* Run *over.* To be fo full as to overflow.

He fills his famifh'd maw, his mouth *runs o'er*
With unchew'd morfels, while he churns the gore. *Dryd.*

49. To be fo much as to overflow.

Milk while it boils, or wine while it works, *run* over the veffels they are in, and poffefs more place than when they were cool. *Digby on Bodies.*

50. *To* Run *out.* To be at an end.

When a leafe had *run out*, he ftipulated with the tenant to refign up twenty acres, without leffening his rent, and no great abatement of the fine. *Swift.*

51. *To* Run *out.* To fpread exuberantly.

Infectile animals, for want of blood, *run* all *out* into legs. *Hammond.*

The zeal of love *runs out* into fuckers, like a fruitful tree. *Taylor's Rule of Living Holy.*

Some papers are written with regularity; others *run out* into the wildnefs of effays. *Spectator.*

52. *To* Run *out.* To expatiate.

Nor is it fufficient to *run out* into beautiful digreffions, unlefs they are fomething of a piece with the main defign of the Georgick. *Addifon's Effay on the Georgicks.*

On all occafions, fhe *run out* extravagantly in praife of Hocus. *Arbuthnot.*

They keep to their text, and *run out* upon the power of the pope, to the diminution of councils. *Baker.*

He fhews his judgment, in not letting his fancy *run out* into long defcriptions. *Broome's Notes on the Odyffey.*

53. *To* Run *out.* To be wafted or exhaufted.

He hath *run out* himfelf, and led forth
His defp'rate party with him; blown together
Aids of all kinds. *Benj. Johnfon's Catiline.*

Th' eftate *runs out*, and mortgages are made,
Their fortune ruin'd, and their fame betray'd. *Dryden.*

From growing riches with good cheer,
To *running out* by ftarving here. *Swift.*

So little gets for what fhe gives,
We really wonder how fhe lives!
And had her ftock been lefs, no doubt,
She muft have long ago *run out.* *Swift.*

To Run. *v. a.*

1. To pierce; to ftab.

Poor Romeo is already dead, *run* through the ear with a love fong. *Shakefp. Romeo and Juliet.*

Hipparchus, going to marry, confulted Philander upon the occafion; Philander reprefented his miftrefs in fuch ftrong colours, that the next morning he received a challenge, and before twelve he was *run* through the body. *Spectator.*

2. To force; to drive.

In nature, it is not convenient to confider every difference that is in things, and divide them into diftinct claffes: this will *run* us into particulars, and we fhall be able to eftablifh no general truth. *Locke.*

Though putting the mind unprepared upon an unufual ftrefs may difcourage it, yet this muft not *run* it, by an over-great fhynefs of difficulties, into a lazy fauntring about ordinary things. *Locke.*

3. To force into any way or form.

Some, ufed to mathematical figures, give a preference to the methods of that fcience in divinity or politick enquiries; others, accuftomed to retired fpeculations, *run* natural philofophy into metaphyfical notions. *Locke.*

What is raifed in the day, fettles in the night; and its cold *runs* the thin juices into thick fizy fubftances. *Cheyne.*

The daily complaifance of gentlemen *runs* them into variety of expreffions; whereas your fcholars are more clofe, and frugal of their words. *Felton on the Criticks.*

4. To drive with violence.

They *ran* the fhip aground. *Acts* xxvii. 41.

This proud Turk offered fcornfully to pafs by without vailing, which the Venetian captains not enduring, fet upon him with fuch fury, that the Turks were enforced to *run* both their gallies on fhore. *Knolles's Hiftory of the Turks.*

A talkative perfon *runs* himfelf upon great inconveniencies, by blabbing out his own or others fecrets. *Ray.*

5. To melt.

The pureft gold muft be *run* and wafhed. *Felton.*

6. To incur.

He *runneth* two dangers, that he fhall not be faithfully counfeled, and that he fhall have hurtful counfel given. *Bacon.*

The tale I tell is only of a cock,
Who had not *run* the hazard of his life,
Had he believ'd his dream, and not his wife. *Dryden.*

Confider the hazard I have *run* to fee you here. *Dryden.*

O that I could now prevail with any one to count up what he hath got by his moft beloved fins, what a dreadful danger he *runs.* *Calamy.*

I fhall *run* the danger of being fufpected to have forgot what I am about. *Locke.*

7. To venture; to hazard.

He would himfelf be in the Highlands to receive them, and *run* his fortune with them. *Clarendon.*

Take here her reliques and her gods, to *run*
With them thy fate, with them new walls expect. *Denh.*

A wretched exil'd crew
Refolv'd, and willing under my command,
To *run* all hazards both of fea and land. *Dryden.*

8. To import or export without duty.

Heavy impofitions leffen the import, and are a ftrong temptation of *running* goods. *Swift.*

9. To profecute in thought.

To *run* the world back to its firft original, and view nature in its cradle, to trace the outgoings of the ancient of days in the firft inftance of his creative power, is a refearch too great for mortal enquiry. *South.*

The world hath not ftood fo long, but we can ftill *run* it up to thofe artlefs ages, when mortals lived by plain nature. *Burnet's Theory of the Earth.*

I would gladly underftand the formation of a foul, and *run* it up to its *punctum faliens.* *Collier.*

I have chofen to prefent you with fome peculiar thoughts, rather than *run* a needlefs treatife upon the fubject at length. *Felton.*

10. To pufh.

Some Englifh fpeakers *run* their hands into their pockets, others look with great attention on a piece of blank paper. *Add.*

11. *To* Run *down.* To chafe to wearinefs.

They *ran down* a ftag, and the afs divided the prey very honeftly. *L'Eftrange's Fables.*

12. *To* Run *down.* To crufh; to overbear.

Though out-number'd, overthrown,
And by the fate of war *run down*,
Their duty never was defeated. *Hudibras, p.* iii.

Some corrupt affections in the foul urge him on with fuch impetuous fury, that, when we fee a man overborn and *run down* by them, we cannot but pity the perfon, while we abhor the crime. *South's Sermons.*

It is no fuch hard matter to convince or *run down* a drunkard, and to anfwer any pretences he can alledge for his fin. *South's Sermons.*

The common cry
Then *ran* you *down* for your rank loyalty. *Dryden.*

Religion is *run down* by the licenfe of thefe times. *Berkley.*

13. *To* Run *over.* To recount curforily.

I fhall *run* them *over* flightly, remarking chiefly what is obvious to the eye. *Ray.*

I fhall

I ſhall not *run over* all the particulars, that would ſhew what pains are uſed to corrupt children. *Locke.*

14. *To* RUN *over.* To conſider curſorily.

These four every man ſhould *run over*, before he cenſure the works he ſhall view. *Wotton's Architecture.*

If we *run over* the other nations of Europe, we ſhall only paſs through ſo many different ſcenes of poverty. *Addiſon.*

15. To run through.

Should a man *run* over the whole circle of earthly pleaſures, he would be forced to complain that pleaſure was not ſatisfaction. *South.*

RUN. *n. ſ.* [from the verb.]

1. Act of running.

The aſs ſets up a hideous bray, and fetches a *run* at them open-mouth. *L'Eſtrange's Fables.*

2. Courſe; motion.

Want of motion, whereby the *run* of humours is ſtayed, furthers putrefaction. *Bacon.*

3. Flow; cadence.

He no where uſes any ſoftneſs, or any *run* of verſes to pleaſe the ear. *Broome's Notes on the Odyſſey.*

4. Courſe; proceſs.

5. Way of management; uncontrolled courſe.

Talk of ſome other ſubject; the thoughts of it make me mad; our family muſt have their *run.* *Arbuthnot.*

6. Long reception; continued ſucceſs.

It is impoſſible for detached papers to have a general *run* or long continuance, if not diverſified with humour. *Addiſon.*

7. Modiſh clamour.

You cannot but have obſerved, what a violent *run* there is among too many weak people againſt univerſity education. *Sw.*

8. *At the long* RUN. In fine; in concluſion; at the end.

They produce ill-conditioned ulcers, for the moſt part mortal *in the long run* of the diſeaſe. *Wiſeman.*

Wickedneſs may proſper for a while, but *at the long run*, he that ſets all knaves at work, will pay them. *L'Eſtrange.*

Shuffling may ſerve for a time, but truth will moſt certainly carry it *at the long run.* *L'Eſtrange.*

Hath falſhood proved *at the long run* more for the advancement of his eſtate than truth? *Tillotſon.*

RU'NAGATE. *n. ſ.* [corrupted from *renegat*, Fr.] A fugitive; rebel; apoſtate.

The wretch compel'd, a *runagate* became,
And learn'd what ill a miſer ſtate doth breed. *Sidney.*

God bringeth the priſoners out of captivity; but letteth the *runagates* continue in ſcarceneſs. *Pſalm* lxviii. 6.

I dedicate myſelf to your ſweet pleaſure,
More noble than that *runagate* to your bed. *Shakeſp.*

As Cain, after he had ſlain Abel, had no certain abiding; ſo the Jews, after they had crucified the ſon of God, became *runagates.* *Raleigh's Hiſtory of the World.*

RU'NAWAY. *n. ſ.* [*run* and *away.*] One that flies from danger; a fugitive.

Come at once,
For the cloſe night doth play the *runaway*,
And we are ſtaid for. *Shakeſp.*

Thou *runaway*, thou coward, art thou fled?
Speak in ſome buſh; where doſt thou hide thy head? *Shak.*

RU'NDLE. *n. ſ.* [corrupted from *roundle*, of *round.*]

1. A round; a ſtep of a ladder.

The angels did not fly, but mounted the ladder by degrees; we are to conſider the ſeveral ſteps and *rundles* we are to aſcend by. *Duppa.*

2. A peritrochium; ſomething put round an axis.

The third mechanical faculty, ſtiled *axis in peritrochio*, conſiſts of an axis or cylinder, having a *rundle* about it, wherein are faſtened divers ſpokes, by which the whole may be turned round. *Wilkins's Mathematical Magick.*

RU'NDLET. *n. ſ.* [perhaps *runlet* or *roundlet.*] A ſmall barrel.

Set a *rundlet* of verjuice overagainſt the ſun in ſummer, to ſee whether it will ſweeten. *Bacon's Natural Hiſtory.*

RUNG. pret. and part. paſſ. of *ring.*

The heav'ns and all the conſtellations *rung.* *Milton.*

RU'NNEL. *n. ſ.* [from *run.*] A rivulet; a ſmall brook.

With murmur loud, down from the mountain's ſide,
A little *runnel* tumbled neere the place. *Fairfax.*

RU'NNER. *n. ſ.* [from *run.*]

1. One that runs.

2. A racer.

Fore-ſpent with toil, as *runners* with a race,
I lay me down a little while to breathe. *Shakeſp.*
Here thoſe that in the rapid courſe delight,
The rival *runners* without order ſtand. *Dryden.*

3. A meſſenger.

To Tonſon or Lintot his lodgings are better known than to the *runners* of the poſt-office. *Swift to Pope.*

4. A ſhooting ſprig.

In every root there will be one *runner*, which hath little buds on it, which may be cut into. *Mortimer.*

5. One of the ſtones of a mill.

The mill goes much heavier by the ſtone they call the *runner*, being ſo large. *Mortimer.*

6. A bird. *Ainſ.*

RU'NNET. *n. ſ.* [ᵹerunnen, Saxon, coagulated.] A liquor made by ſteeping the ſtomach of a calf in hot water, and uſed to coagulate milk for curds and cheeſe. It is ſometimes written *rennet.*

The milk of the fig hath the quality of *runnet* to gather cheeſe. *Bacon's Natural Hiſtory.*

It coagulates the blood, as *runnet* turns milk. *More.*

The milk in the ſtomach of calves, coagulated by the *runnet*, is rendered fluid by the gall in the duodenum. *Arb.*

RU'NNION. *n. ſ.* [*rognant*, Fr. ſcrubbing.] A paltry ſcurvy wretch.

You witch! you poulcat! you *runnion!* *Shakeſp.*

RUNT. *n. ſ.* [*runte*, in the Teutonick dialects, ſignifies a bull or cow, and is uſed in contempt by us for ſmall cattle; as *keſyl*, the Welſh term for a horſe, is uſed for a worthleſs horſe.] Any animal ſmall below the natural growth of the kind.

Reforming Tweed
Hath ſent us *runts* even of her church's breed. *Cleaveland.*

Of tame pigeons, are cropers, carriers, and *runts.* *Walton.*

This overgrown *runt* has ſtruck off his heels, lowered his foretop, and contracted his figure. *Addiſon.*

RU'PTION. *n. ſ.* [*ruptus*, Lat.] Breach; ſolution of continuity.

The plenitude of veſſels or plethora cauſes an extravaſation of blood, by *ruption* or apertion. *Wiſeman.*

RU'PTURE. *n. ſ.* [*rupture*, Fr. from *ruptus*, Lat.]

1. The act of breaking; ſtate of being broken; ſolution of continuity.

Th' egg,
Burſting with kindly *rupture*, forth diſclos'd
Their callow young. *Milton.*

A lute ſtring will bear a hundred weight without *rupture*, but at the ſame time cannot exert its elaſticity. *Arbuthnot.*

The diets of infants ought to be extremely thin, ſuch as lengthen the fibres without *rupture.* *Arbuthnot.*

2. A breach of peace; open hoſtility.

When the parties, that divide the commonwealth, come to a *rupture*, it ſeems every man's duty to chuſe a ſide. *Swift.*

3. Burſtenneſs; hernia; preternatural eruption of the gut.

The *rupture* of the groin or ſcrotum is the moſt common ſpecies of hernia. *Sharp's Surgery.*

To RU'PTURE. *v. a.* [from the noun.] To break; to burſt; to ſuffer diſruption.

The veſſels of the brain and membranes, if *ruptured*, abſorb the extravaſated blood. *Sharp's Surgery.*

RUPTUREWORT. *n. ſ.* [*herniaria*, Lat.] A plant.

The calyx of *rupturewort* is quadrifid, or, for the moſt part, quinquefid, and expanded in form of a ſtar, having five ſtamina in the centre: the fruit, which grows in the bottom of the flower, becomes a membranaceous, furrowed, round capſule, which is divided into eight cells, each of which contains one ſmall pointed ſeed. *Miller.*

RU'RAL. *adj.* [*rural*, Fr. *ruralis*, from *rura*, Lat.] Country; exiſting in the country, not in cities; ſuiting the country; reſembling the country.

Lady, reſerved to do paſtor company honour,
Joining your ſweet voice to the *rural* muſick of deſert. *Sid.*

Here is a *rural* fellow,
That will not be deny'd your highneſs' preſence;
He brings you figs. *Shakeſp. Cymbeline.*

We turn
To where the ſilver Thames firſt *rural* grows. *Thomſon.*

RURA'LITY. } *n. ſ.* [from *rural.*] The quality of being
RU'RALNESS. } rural. *Dict.*

RU'RICOLIST. *n. ſ.* [*ruricola*, Lat.] An inhabitant of the country. *Dict.*

RU'RIGENOUS. *adj.* [*rura* and *gigno*, Lat.] Born in the country. *Dict.*

RUSE. n. ſ. [French.] Cunning; artifice; little ſtratagem; trick; wile; fraud; deceit. A French word neither elegant nor neceſſary.

I might here add much concerning the wiles and *ruſes*, which theſe timid creatures uſe to ſave themſelves. *Ray.*

RUSH. *n. ſ.* [ꞃiꞅc, Saxon.]

1. A plant.

A *ruſh* hath a flower compoſed of many leaves, which are placed orbicularly, and expand in form of a roſe; from the centre of which riſes the pointal, which afterward becomes a fruit or huſk, which is generally three-cornered, opening into three parts, and full of roundiſh ſeeds: they are planted with great care on the banks of the ſea in Holland, in order to prevent the water from waſhing away the earth; for the roots of theſe *ruſhes* faſten themſelves very deep in the ground, and mat themſelves near the ſurface, ſo as to hold the earth cloſely together. *Miller.*

He taught me how to know a man in love; in which cage of *ruſhes* I am ſure you are not priſoner. *Shakeſp.*

Man but a *ruſh* againſt Othello's breaſt,
And he retires. *Shakeſp. Othello.*

Is ſupper ready, the houſe trimm'd, *ruſhes* ſtrew'd, cobwebs ſwept? *Shakeſp. Taming of the Shrew.*

Your farm requites your pains;
Though *ruſhes* overſpread the neighb'ring plains. *Dryden.*

2. Any

2. Any thing proverbially worthless.

Not a *rush* matter, whether apes go on four legs or two. *L'Estrange.*

What occasion hast thou to give up, John Bull's friendship is not worth a *rush*. *Arbuthnot's Hist. of John Bull.*

Rush-candle. *n. s.* [*rush* and *candle*.] A small blinking taper, made by stripping a rush, except one small stripe of the bark which holds the pith together, and dipping it in tallow.

Be it moon or sun, or what you please;
And if you please to call it a *rush-candle*,
Henceforth it shall be so for me. *Shakesp.*

If your influence be quite dam'd up
With black usurping mists, some gentle taper,
Though a *rush-candle* from the wicker hole
Of some clay habitation, visit us. *Milton.*

To Rush. *v. n.* [hreoran, Saxon.] To move with violence; to go on with tumultuous rapidity.

The liers in wait hasted and *rushed* upon Gibeah. *Judges.*

Gorgias removed out of the camp by night, to the end he might *rush* upon the camp of the Jews. 1 *Mac.* iv. 2.

Every one that was a warrior *rushed* out upon them. *Judith.*

Armies *rush* to battle in the clouds. *Milton.*

Why wilt thou *rush* to certain death, and rage
In rash attempts beyond thy tender age,
Betray'd by pious love? *Dryden's Virgil.*

Desperate should he *rush*, and lose his life,
With odds oppress'd. *Dryden's Æneis.*

They will always strive to be good christians, but never think it to be a part of religion, to *rush* into the office of princes or ministers. *Sprat.*

You say, the sea
Does with its waves fall backward to the West,
And, thence repell'd, advances to the East;
While this revolving motion does indure,
The deep must reel, and *rush* from shoar to shoar. *Blackm.*

With a *rushing* sound th' assembly bend
Diverse their steps. *Pope's Odyssey.*

Now sunk the sun from his aereal height,
And o'er the shaded billows *rush'd* the night. *Pope.*

At first an azure sheet it *rushes* broad,
Then whit'ning by degrees, as prone it falls,
Dash'd in a cloud of foam, it sends aloft
A hoary mist. *Thomson.*

Rush. *n. s.* [from the verb.] Violent course.

A gentleman of his train spurred up his horse, and with a violent *rush* severed him from the duke. *Wotton.*

Him while fresh and fragant time
Cherisht in his golden prime,
Ere Hebe's hand had overlaid
His smooth cheeks with a downy shade,
The *rush* of death's unruly wave
Swept him off into his grave. *Crashaw.*

Auster spy'd him,
Cruel Auster thither hy'd him,
And with the *rush* of one rude blast,
Sham'd not spitefully to cast
All his leaves so fresh, so sweet,
And laid them trembling at his feet. *Crashaw.*

Ru'shy. *adj.* [from *rush*.]

1. Abounding with rushes.

In *rushy* grounds, springs are found at the first spit. *Mort.*

The timid hare to some lone seat
Retir'd; the *rushy* fen or rugged furze. *Thomson.*

2. Made of rushes.

What knight like him could toss the *rushy* lance. *Tickel.*

Rusk. *n. s.* Hard bread for stores.

The lady sent me divers presents of fruits, sugar, and *rusk*. *Raleigh.*

Ru'sma. *n. s.* A brown and light iron substance, with half as much quicklime steeped in water, the Turkish women make their psilothron, to take off their hair. *Grew.*

Ru'sset. *adj.* [*rousset*, Fr. *russus*, Lat.]

1. Reddishly brown.

The morn, in *russet* mantle clad,
Walks o'er the dew of yon high eastward hill. *Shakesp.*

Our summer such a *russet* livery wears,
As in a garment often dy'd appears. *Dryden.*

2. *Newton* seems to use it for grey; but, if the etymology be regarded, improperly.

This white spot was immediately encompassed with a dark grey or *russet*, and that dark grey with the colours of the first iris. *Newton's Opticks.*

3. Coarse; homespun; rustick. It is much used in descriptions of the manners and dresses of the country, I suppose, because it was formerly the colour of rustick dress: in some places, the rusticks still die cloaths spun at home with bark, which must make them *russet*.

Taffata phrases, silken terms precise,
Figures pedantical: these summer flies
Have blown me full of maggot ostentation:
Henceforth my wooing mind shall be exprest
In *russet* yeas, and honest kersy noes. *Shakesp.*

Ru'sset. *n. s.* Country dress. See Russet, *adj.*

The Dorick dialect has a sweetness in its clownishness, like a fair shepherdess in her country *russet*. *Dryden.*

Ru'sset. } *n. s.* A name given to several sorts of pears or
Ru'sseting. } apples from their colour.

The *russet* pearmain is a very pleasant fruit, continuing long on the tree, and in the conservatory partakes both of the *russeting* and pearmain in colour and taste; the one side being generally *russet*, and the other streaked like a pearmain. *Mortimer.*

RUST. *n. s.* [rust, Saxon.]

1. The red desquamation of old iron.

This iron began at the length to gather *rust*. *Hooker.*

Rust eaten pikes and swords in time to come,
When crooked plows dig up earth's fertile womb,
The husbandman shall oft discover. *May's Georgicks.*

But Pallas came in shape of *rust*,
And 'twixt the spring and hammer thrust,
Her Gorgon shield, which made the cock
Stand stiff, as 'twere transform'd to stock. *Hudibras.*

My scymitar got some *rust* by the sea water. *Gulliver.*

2. The tarnished or corroded surface of any metal.

By dint of sword his crown he shall increase,
And scour his armour from the *rust* of peace. *Dryden.*

3. Loss of power by inactivity.

4. Matter bred by corruption or degeneration.

Let her see thy sacred truths cleared from all *rust* and dross of human mixtures. *King Charles.*

To Rust. *v. n.* [from the noun.]

1. To gather rust; to have the surface tarnished or corroded.

Her fallow leas,
The darnel, hemlock, and rank fumitory
Doth rest upon, while that the culter *rusts*,
That should deracinate such savagery. *Shakesp. Hen.* V.

Our armours now may *rust*, our idle scymiters
Hang by our sides for ornament, not use. *Dryden.*

2. To degenerate in idleness.

Must I *rust* in Egypt, never more
Appear in arms, and be the chief of Greece.

To Rust, *v. a.*

1. To make rusty.

Keep up your bright swords, for the dew will *rust* them. *Shakesp. Othello.*

2. To impair by time or inactivity.

RU'STICAL. *adj.* [*rusticus*, Lat. *rustique*, Fr.] Rough; savage; boisterous; brutal; rude.

On he brought me unto so bare a house, that it was the picture of miserable happiness and rich beggary, served only by a company of *rustical* villains, full of sweat and dust, not one of them other than a labourer. *Sidney.*

This is by a *rustical* severity to banish all urbanity, whose harmless and confined condition is consistent with religion. *Brown's Vulgar Errours.*

He confounds the singing and dancing of the satires with the *rustical* entertainment of the first Romans. *Dryden.*

Ru'stically. *adv.* [from *rustical*.] Savagely; rudely; inelegantly.

My brother Jaques he keeps at school,
And report speaks goldenly of his profit;
For my part he keeps me *rustically* at home. *Shakesp.*

Quintius here was born,
Whose shining plough-share was in furrows worn,
Met by his trembling wife, returning home,
And *rustically* joy'd, as chief of Rome. *Dryden.*

Ru'sticalness. *n. s.* [from *rustical*.] The quality of being rustical; rudeness; savageness.

To Ru'sticate. *v. n.* [*rusticor*, Latin.] To reside in the country.

My lady Scudamore, from having *rusticated* in your company too long, pretends to open her eyes for the sake of seeing the sun, and to sleep because it is night. *Pope.*

To Ru'ticate. *v. a.* To banish into the country.

I was deeply in love with a milliner, upon which I was sent away, or, in the university phrase, *rusticated* for ever. *Spect.*

Rusti'city. *n. s.* [*rusticité*, Fr. *rusticitas*, from *rusticus*, Lat.]

1. Qualities of one that lives in the country; simplicity; artlessness; rudeness; savageness.

There presented himself a tall, clownish, young man, who, falling before the queen of the fairies, desired that he might have the atchievement of any adventure, which, during the feast, might happen; that being granted, he rested him on the floor, unfit for a better place by his *rusticity*. *Spenser.*

The sweetness and *rusticity* of a pastoral cannot be so well exprest in any other tongue as in the Greek, when rightly mixt with the Dorick dialect. *Addison.*

This so general expence of their time would curtail the ordinary means of knowledge, as 'twould shorten the opportunities of vice; and so accordingly an universal *rusticity* presently took place, and stopped not till it had over-run the whole stock of mankind. *Woodward's Natural History.*

2. Rural appearance.

RU'STICK. *adj.* [*rusticus*, Lat.]

1. Rural; country.

By Lelius willing missing was the odds of the Iberian side, and continued so in the next by the excellent running of a knight, though fostered so by the muses, as many times the very *rustick* people left both their delights and profits to harken to his songs. *Sidney, b.* ii.

2. Rude; untaught; inelegant.

An ignorant clown cannot learn fine language or a courtly behaviour, when his *rustick* airs have grown up with him till the age of forty. *Watts's Logick.*

3. Brutal; savage.

My soul foreboded I should find the bow'r
Of some fell monster, fierce with barb'rous pow'r;
Some *rustick* wretch, who liv'd in heav'n's despight,
Contemning laws, and trampling on the right. *Pope.*

4. Artless; honest; simple.

5. Plain; unadorned.

An altar stood, *rustick*, of grassy ford. *Milton.*
With unguents smooth the polish'd marble shone,
Where ancient Neleus sat, a *rustick* throne. *Pope.*

RU'STICK. *n. s.* A clown; a swain; an inhabitant of the country.

As nothing is so rude and insolent as a wealthy *rustick*, all this his kindness is overlooked, and his person most unworthily railed at. *South.*

RU'STINESS. *n. s.* [from *rusty.*] The state of being rusty.

To RU'STLE. *v. n.* [hrirtlan, Saxon.] To make a low continued rattle; to make a quick succession of small noises.

Let not the creaking of shoes, nor the *rustling* of silks, betray thy poor heart to woman. *Shakesp. King Lear.*

He is coming; I hear the straw *rustle.* *Shakesp.*

This life
Is nobler than attending for a check;
Richer, than doing nothing for a bauble;
Prouder, than *rustling* in unpaid-for silk. *Shakesp.*
Thick swarm'd, both on the ground, and in the air
Brush'd with the hiss of *rustling* wings. *Milton.*
As when we see the winged winds engage,
Rustling from ev'ry quarter of the sky,
North, East, and West, in airy swiftness vy. *Granville.*
All begin the attack;
Fans clap, silks *rustle*, and tough whalebones crack. *Pope.*
Not less their number than the milk-white swans,
That o'er the winding of Cayster's springs,
Stretch their long necks, and clap their *rustling* wings. *Po.*

RU'STY. *adj.* [from *rust.*]

1. Covered with rust; infected with rust.

After a long calm of peace, he was left engaged in a war with a *rusty* sword and empty purse. *Howel.*

Part scour the *rusty* shields with seam, and part
New grind the blunted ax. *Dryden's Æneis.*

2. Impaired by inactivity.

Hector, in his dull and long continued truce,
Is *rusty* grown. *Shakesp. Troilus and Cressida.*

To RUT. *v. n.* [*ruit*, Fr.] To desire to come together. Used of deer.

RUT. *n. s.* [*rut*, Fr.]

1. Copulation of deer.

The time of going to *rut* of deer is in September; for that they need the whole summer's feed to make them fit for generation: and if rain come about the middle of September, they go to *rut* somewhat the sooner. *Bacon.*

The ground hereof was the observation of this part in deer after immoderate venery, and about the end of their *rut.* *Bro.*

2. [*Route*, Fr.] The track of a cart wheel. *Ains.*

RUTH. *n. s.* [from *rue.*] Mercy; pity; tenderness; sorrow for the misery of another.

The Britons, by Maximilian laid way
With wretched miseries and woful *ruth*,
Were to those Pagans made an open prey. *Fa. Queen.*
All *ruth*, compassion, mercy he forgot. *Fairfax.*
She fair, he full of bashfulness and truth
Lov'd much, hop'd little, and desired nought;
He durst not speak, by suit to purchase *ruth.* *Fairfax.*
The better part with Mary and with Ruth
Chosen thou hast; and they that overween,
And at thy growing virtues fret their spleen,
No anger find in thee, but pity and *ruth.* *Milton.*

RU'THFUL. *adj.* [*ruth* and *full.*] Rueful; woful; sorrowful.

The inhabitants seldom take a *ruthful* and reaving experience of those harms, which infectious diseases carry with them. *Carew'e Survey of Cornwall.*

RU'THFULLY. *adv.* [from *ruthful.*]

1. Wofully; sadly.

The flower of horse and foot, lost by the valour of the enemy, *ruthfully* perished. *Knolles's History of the Turks.*

2. Sorrowfully; mournfully.

Help me, ye baneful birds, whose shrieking sound
Is sign of dreary death, my deadly cries
Most *ruthfully* to tune. *Spenser's Pastorals.*

3. Wofully. In irony.

By this Minerva's friend bereft
Oileades of that rich bowl, and left his lips, nose, eyes
Ruthfully smear'd. *Chapman's Iliads.*

RU'THLESS. *adj.* [from *ruth.*] Cruel; pitiless; uncompassionate; barbarous.

What is Edward but a *ruthless* sea?
What Clarence but a quicksand of deceit? *Shakesp.*
The *ruthless* flint doth cut my tender feet;
And when I start, the cruel people laugh. *Shakesp.*
His archers circle me; my reins they wound,
And *ruthless* shed my gall upon the ground. *Sandys.*
Their rage the hostile powers restrain,
All but the *ruthless* monarch of the main. *Pope.*
To *ruthless* deeds, blind rage, and fell revenge,
Their fervid spirits fires. *Thomson's Summer.*

RU'THLESSNESS. *n. s.* [from *ruthless.*] Want of pity.

RU'THLESLY. *adv.* [from *ruthless.*] Without pity; cruelly; barbarously.

RU'TTIER. *n. s.* [*routiere*, Fr.] A direction of the road or course at sea.

RU'TTISH. *adj.* [from *rut.*] Wanton; libidinous; salacious; lustful; lecherous.

That is an advertisement to one Diana, to take heed of the allurement of count Rousillon, a foolish idle boy; but for all that very *ruttish.* *Shakesp. All's well that ends well.*

RYE. *n. s.* [ryʒe, Saxon.]

1. A coarse kind of bread corn.

Between the acres of the *rye*,
These pretty country folks would lye. *Shakesp.*

Rye is more acrid, laxative, and less nourishing than wheat. *Arbuthnot on Aliments.*

2. A disease in a hawk. *Ains.*

RYE'GRASS. *n. s.* A kind of strong grass.

Some sow *ryegrass* with the corn at Michaelmas. *Mortimer.*

S.

S.

S, Has in Engliſh the ſame hiſſing ſound as in other languages, and unhappily prevails in ſo many of our words that it produces in the ear of a foreigner a continued ſibilation.

In the beginning of words it has invariably its natural and genuine ſound: in the middle it is ſometimes uttered with a ſtronger appulſe of the tongue to the palate, like *z*; as *roſe*, *roſeate*, *roſy*, *oſier*, *noſel*, *reſident*, *buſy*, *buſineſs*. It ſometimes keeps its natural ſound; as *looſe*, *deſignation*; for which I know not whether any rules can be given.

In the end of monoſyllables it is ſometimes *s*, as in *this*; and ſometimes *z*, as in *as*, *has*; and generally where *es* ſtands in verbs for *eth*, as *gives*. It ſeems to be eſtabliſhed as a rule, that no noun ſingular ſhould end with *ſ* ſingle: therefore in words written with diphthongs, and naturally long, an *e* is neverthleſs added at the end, as *gooſe*, *houſe*; and where the ſyllable is ſhort the *ſ* is doubled, and was once *ſſe*, as *aſs*, anciently *aſſe*; *wilderneſs*, anciently *wilderneſſe*; *diſtreſs*, anciently *diſtreſſe*.

SABA'OTH. } *n. ſ.* [An Hebrew word ſignifying *reſt*; *ſabbat*,
SA'BBATH. } French; *ſabatum*, Latin.]

1. A day appointed by God among the Jews, and from them eſtabliſhed among Chriſtians for publick worſhip; the ſeventh day ſet apart from works of labour to be employed in piety.

Holy Lord God of *ſabaoth*. *Common Prayer.*

I purpoſe,
And by our holy *ſabbath* have I ſworn,
To have the due and forfeit of my bond. *Shakeſpeare.*

Glad we return'd up to the coaſts of light,
Ere *ſabbath* ev'ning. *Milton.*

Here ev'ry day was *ſabbath*: only free
From hours of pray'r, for hours of charity,
Such as the Jews from ſervile toil releaſt,
Where works of mercy were a part of reſt:
Such as bleſt angels exerciſe above,
Vary'd with ſacred hymns and acts of love;
Such *ſabbaths* as that one ſhe now enjoys,
Ev'n that perpetual one, which ſhe employs:
For ſuch viciſſitudes in heav'n there are,
In praiſe alternate, and alternate pray'r. *Dryden.*

2. Intermiſſion of pain or ſorrow; time of reſt.

Never any *ſabbath* of releaſe
Could free his travels and afflictions deep. *Daniel's C. War.*

Nor can his bleſſed ſoul look down from heav'n,
Or break th' eternal *ſabbath* of his reſt,
To ſee her miſeries on earth. *Dryden.*

Peaceful ſleep out the *ſabbath* of the tomb,
And wake to raptures in a life to come. *Pope.*

SA'BBATHBREAKER. *n. ſ.* [*ſabbath* and *break*.] Violator of the ſabbath by labour or wickedneſs.

The uſurer is the greateſt *ſabbathbreaker*, becauſe his plough goeth every Sunday. *Bacon's Eſſays.*

SABBA'TICAL. *adj.* [*ſabbaticus*, Lat. *ſabbatique*, Fr. from *ſabbath*.] Reſembling the ſabbath; enjoying or bringing intermiſſion of labour.

The appointment and obſervance of the *ſabbatical* year, and after the ſeventh *ſabbatical* year, a year of jubilee, is a circumſtance of great moment. *Forbes.*

SA'BBATISM. *n. ſ.* [from *ſabbatum*, Latin.] Obſervance of the ſabbath ſuperſtitiouſly rigid.

SA'BINE. *n. ſ.* [*ſabine*, Fr. *ſabina*, Latin.] A plant.

Sabine or ſavin will make fine hedges, and may be brought into any form by clipping, much beyond any of the ſorts of trees commonly made uſe of for that purpoſe. *Mortimer.*

SA'BLE. *n. ſ.* [*zibella*, Latin.] Fur.

Sable is worn of great perſonages, and brought out of Ruſſia, being the fur of a little beaſt of that name, eſteemed for the perfectneſs of the colour of the hairs, which are very black. Hence *ſable*, in heraldry, ſignifies the black colour in gentlemens arms. *Peacham on Blazoning.*

Furiouſly running in upon him, with tumultuous ſpeech, he violently raught from his head his rich cap of *ſables*. *Knolles.*

The peacocks plumes thy tackle muſt not fail,
Nor the dear purchaſe of the *ſable*'s tail. *Gay.*

SA'BLE. *adj.* [Fr.] Black. A word uſed by heralds and poets.

By this the drooping daylight 'gan to fade,
And yield his room to ſad ſucceeding night,
Who with her *ſable* mantle 'gan to ſhade
The face of earth, and ways of living wight. *Fairy Queen.*

With him inthron'd
Sat *ſable* veſted night, eldeſt of things,
The conſort of his reign. *Milton's Paradiſe Loſt.*

They ſoon begin that tragick play,
And with their ſmoaky cannons baniſh day:
Night, horrour, ſlaughter, with confuſion meet,
And in their *ſable* arms embrace the fleet. *Waller.*

Adoring firſt the genius of the place,
And night, and all the ſtars that gild her *ſable* throne. *Dryd.*

SA'BLIERE. *n. ſ.* [French.]

1. A ſandpit. *Bailey.*

2. [In carpentry.] A piece of timber as long, but not ſo thick, as a beam. *Bailey.*

SA'BRE. *n. ſ.* [*ſabre*, French; I ſuppoſe, of Turkiſh original.] A cymetar; a ſhort ſword with a convex edge; a faulchion.

To me the cries of fighting fields are charms;
Keen be my *ſabre*, and of proof my arms;
I aſk no other bleſſing of my ſtars,
No prize but fame, no miſtreſs but the wars. *Dryden.*

Seam'd o'er with wounds, which his own *ſabre* gave,
In the vile habit of a village ſlave,
The foe deceiv'd. *Pope's Odyſſey.*

SABULO'SITY. *n. ſ.* [from *ſabulous*.] Grittineſs; ſandineſs.

SA'BULOUS. *adj.* [*ſabulum*, Latin.] Gritty; ſandy.

SACCA'DE. *n. ſ.* [French.] A violent check the rider gives his horſe, by drawing both the reins very ſuddenly: a correction uſed when the horſe bears heavy on the hand. *Bailey.*

SA'CCHARINE. *adj.* [*ſaccharum*, Latin.] Having the taſte or any other of the chief qualities of ſugar.

Manna is an eſſential *ſaccharine* ſalt, ſweating from the leaves of moſt plants. *Arbuthnot on Aliments.*

SACERDO'TAL. *adj.* [*ſacerdotalis*, Latin.] Prieſtly; belonging to the prieſthood.

They have ſeveral offices and prayers, eſpecially for the dead, in which functions they uſe *ſacerdotal* garments. *Stillingfl.*

He fell violently upon me, without reſpect to my *ſacerdotal* orders. *Dryden's Spaniſh Fryar.*

If ample powers, granted by the rulers of this world, add dignity to the perſons intruſted with theſe powers, behold the importance and extent of the *ſacerdotal* commiſſion. *Atterbury.*

SA'CHEL. *n. ſ.* [*ſacculus*, Lat.] A ſmall ſack or bag.

SACK. *n. ſ.* [שַׂק Hebrew; σάκκος; *ſaccus*, Latin; ſæc, Sax. It is obſervable of this word, that it is found in all languages, and it is therefore conceived to be antediluvian.]

1. A bag; a pouch; commonly a large bag.

Our *ſacks* ſhall be a mean to ſack the city,
And we be lords and rulers over Roan. *Shak. Henry* VI.

Vaſtius cauſed the authors of that mutiny to be thruſt into *ſacks*, and in the ſight of the fleet caſt into the ſea. *Knolles.*

2. The meaſure of three buſhels.

3. A woman's looſe robe.

To SACK. *v. a.* [from the noun.]

1. To put in bags.

Now the great work is done, the corn is ground,
The griſt is *ſack'd*, and every ſack well bound. *Betterton.*

2. [From *ſacar*, Spaniſh.] To take by ſtorm; to pillage; to plunder.

Edward Bruce ſpoiled and burnt all the old Engliſh pale inhabitants, and *ſacked* and raſed all cities and corporate towns. *Spenſer on Ireland.*

I'll make thee ſtoop and bend thy knee,
Or *ſack* this country with a mutiny. *Shakeſp. Henry* VI.

What armies conquer'd, periſh'd with thy ſword?
What cities *ſack'd*? *Fairfax.*

Who ſees theſe diſmal heaps, but would demand
What barbarous invader *ſack'd* the land? *Denham.*

The pope himſelf was ever after unfortunate, Rome being twice taken and *ſacked* in his reign. *South's Sermons.*

The great magazine for all kinds of treaſure is the bed of the Tiber: when the Romans lay under the apprehenſions of ſeeing their city *ſacked* by a barbarous enemy, they would take care to bestow such of their riches this way as could best bear the water. *Addison.*

SACK. *n. s.* [from the verb.]

1. Storm of a town; pillage; plunder.

If Saturn's son bestows
The *sack* of Troy, which he by promise owes,
Then shall the conqu'ring Greeks thy loss restore. *Dryden.*

2. A kind of sweet wine, now brought chiefly from the Canaries. [*Sec*, French, of uncertain etymology; but derived by *Skinner*, after *Mandeslo*, from *Xeque*, a city of *Morocco*.]

Please you drink a cup of *sack*. *Shakespeare.*

The butler hath great advantage to allure the maids with a glass of *sack*. *Swift.*

SA'CKBUT. *n. s.* [*sacabuche*, Spanish; *sambuca*, Latin; *sambuque*, French.] A kind of pipe.

The trumpets, *sackbuts*, psalteries and fife,
Make the sun dance. *Shakesp. Coriolanus.*

SA'CKCLOATH. *n. s.* [*sack* and *cloath.*] Cloath of which sacks are made; coarse cloath sometimes worn in mortification.

A sort of coarse stuff made of goats hair, of a black or dark colour, worn by soldiers and mariners; and used as a habit among the Hebrews in times of mourning and distress. It was called *sackcloth*, either because sacks were made of this sort of stuff, or because haircloaths were straight and close like a sack. *Calmet.*

To augment her painful penance more,
Thrice every week in ashes she did sit,
And next her wrinkled skin rough *sackcloth* wore. *F. Queen.*

Thus with *sackcloath* I invest my woe,
And dust upon my clouded forehead throw. *Sandys.*

Being clad in *sackcloath*, he was to lie on the ground, and constantly day and night to implore God's mercy for the sin he had committed. *Ayliffe's Parergon.*

SA'CKER. *n. s.* [from *sack.*] One that takes a town.

SA'CKFUL. *n. s.* [*sack* and *full.*] Top full.

Wood goes about with *sackfuls* of dross, odiously misrepresenting his prince's countenance. *Swift.*

SA'CKPOSSET. *n. s.* [*sack* and *posset.*] A posset made of milk, sack, and some other ingredients.

Snuff the candles at supper on the table, because the burning snuff may fall into a dish of soup or *sackposset*. *Swift.*

SA'CRAMENT. *n. s.* [*sacrement*, Fr. *sacramentum*, Latin.]

1. An oath; any ceremony producing an obligation.

2. An outward and visible sign of an inward and spiritual grace.

As often as we mention a *sacrament*, it is improperly understood; for in the writings of the ancient fathers all articles which are peculiar to Christian faith, all duties of religion containing that which sense or natural reason cannot of itself discern, are most commonly named *sacraments*; our restraint of the word to some few principal divine ceremonies, importeth in every such ceremony two things, the substance of the ceremony itself, which is visible; and besides that, somewhat else more secret, in reference whereunto we conceive that ceremony to be a *sacrament*. *Hooker.*

3. The eucharist; the holy communion.

Ten thousand French have ta'en the *sacrament*
To rive their dangerous artillery
Upon no Christian soul but English Talbot. *Shakes. H. VI.*

As we have ta'en the *sacrament*,
We will unite the white rose with the red. *Shakesp. R. III.*

Before the famous battle of Cressy, he spent the greatest part of the night in prayer; and in the morning received the *sacrament*, with his son, and the chief of his officers. *Addison.*

SACRAME'NTAL. *adj.* [*sacramental*, Fr. from *sacrament.*] Constituting a sacrament; pertaining to a sacrament.

To make complete the outward substance of a sacrament, there is required an outward form, which form *sacramental* elements receive from *sacramental* words. *Hooker.*

The words of St. Paul are plain; and whatever interpretation can be put upon them, it can only vary the way of the *sacramental* efficacy, but it cannot evacuate the blessing. *Taylor.*

SACRAME'NTALLY. *adv.* [from *sacramental.*] After the manner of a sacrament.

My body is *sacramentally* contained in this sacrament of bread. *Hall.*

The law of circumcision was meant by God *sacramentally* to impress the duty of strict purity. *Hammond.*

SA'CRED. *adj.* [*sacre*, French; *sacer*, Latin.]

1. Devoted to religious uses; holy.

Gods love to haunt her *sacred* shades. *Milton.*

2. Dedicated; consecrate; consecrated.

This temple and his holy ark,
With all his *sacred* things. *Milton.*

O'er its eastern gate was rais'd above
A temple, *sacred* to the queen of love. *Dryden.*

3. Inviolable.

The honour's *sacred*, which he talks on now,
Supposing that I lackt it. *Shakesp. Ant. and Cleopatra.*

How hast thou yielded to transgress
The strict forbiddance? how to violate
The *sacred* fruit? *Milton.*

Secrets of marriage still are *sacred* held;
There sweet and bitter by the wise conceal'd. *Dryden.*

SA'CREDLY. *adv.* [from *sacred.*] Inviolably; religiously.

When God had manifested himself in the flesh, how *sacredly* did he preserve this privilege? *South's Sermons.*

SA'CREDNESS. *n. s.* [from *sacred.*] The state of being sacred; state of being consecrated to religious uses; holiness; sanctity.

In the sanctuary the cloud, and the oracular answers, were prerogatives peculiar to the *sacredness* of the place. *South.*

This insinuates the *sacredness* of power, let the administration of it be what it will. *L'Estrange.*

SACRI'FICK. *adj.* [*sacrificus*, Latin.] Employed in sacrifice.

SACRI'FICABLE. *adj.* [from *sacrificor*, Lat.] Capable of being offered in sacrifice.

Although Jephtha's vow run generally for the words, whatsoever shall come forth; yet might it be restrained in the sense, for whatsoever was *sacrificable*, and justly subject to lawful immolation, and so would not have sacrificed either horse or dog. *Brown's Vulgar Errours.*

SACRIFICA'TOR. *n. s.* [*sacrificateur*, Fr. from *sacrificor*, Latin.] Sacrificer; offerer of sacrifice.

Not only the subject of sacrifice is unquestionable, but also the *sacrificator*, which the picture makes to be Jephtha. *Brown.*

SA'CRIFICATORY. *adj.* [from *sacrificor*, Latin.] Offering sacrifice.

To SA'CRIFICE. *v. a.* [*sacrifier*, French; *sacrifico*, Latin.]

1. To offer to heaven; to immolate.

Alarbus' limbs are lopt,
And intrails feed the *sacrificing* fire. *Shakes. Titus Andron.*

This blood, like *sacrificing* Abel's, cries
To me for justice. *Shakes. Richard II.*

I *sacrifice* to the Lord all that openeth the matrix, being males. *Ex.* xiii. 15.

Men from the herd or flock
Of *sacrificing* bullock, lamb, or kid. *Milton.*

2. To destroy or give up for the sake of something else.

'Tis a sad contemplation, that we should *sacrifice* the peace of the church to a little vain curiosity. *Decay of Piety.*

The breach of this rule, To do as one would be done to, would be contrary to that interest men *sacrifice* to when they break it. *Locke.*

Syphax loves you, and would *sacrifice*
His life, nay more, his honour, in your service. *Addison.*

A great genius sometimes *sacrifices* sound to sense. *Broome.*

3. To destroy; to kill.

4. To devote with loss.

Condemn'd to *sacrifice* his childish years
To babbling ign'rance, and to empty fears. *Prior.*

To SA'CRIFICE. *v. n.* To make offerings; to offer sacrifice.

He that *sacrificeth* of things wrongfully gotten, his offering is ridiculous. *Ecclus.* xxxiv. 18.

Let us go to *sacrifice* to the Lord. *Ex.* iii. 18.

Some mischief is befallen
To that meek man who well had *sacrific'd*. *Milton.*

SA'CRIFICE. *n. s.* [*sacrifice*, French; *sacrificium*, Latin.]

1. The act of offering to heaven.

God will ordain religious rites
Of *sacrifice*. *Milton.*

2. The thing offered to heaven, or immolated.

Upon such *sacrifice*
The gods themselves throw incense. *Shak. King Lear.*

Go with me like good angels to my end,
And as the long divorce of steel falls on me,
Make of your prayers one sweet *sacrifice*,
And lift my soul to heav'n. *Shakespeare.*

Moloch besmear'd with blood
Of human *sacrifice*. *Milton.*

My life if thou preserv'st, my life
Thy *sacrifice* shall be;
And death, if death must be my doom,
Shall join my soul to thee. *Addison's Spectator.*

3. Any thing destroyed, or quitted for the sake of something else.

4. Any thing destroyed.

SA'CRIFICER. *n. s.* [from *sacrifice.*] One who offers sacrifice; one that immolates.

Let us be *sacrificers*, but not butchers. *Shakesp.*

When some brawny *sacrificer* knocks,
Before an altar led, an offer'd ox,
His eyeballs rooted out are thrown to ground. *Dryden.*

A priest pours wine between the horns of a bull: the priest is veiled after the manner of the old Roman *sacrificers*. *Addison.*

SACRIFI'CIAL. *adj.* [from *sacrifice.*] Performing sacrifice; included in sacrifice.

Rain *sacrificial* whisp'rings in his ear;
Make sacred even his stirrop. *Shakesp. Timon.*

Tertullian's observation upon these *sacrificial* rites, is pertinent to this rule. *Taylor's Worthy Communicant.*

SA'CRILEGE. *n. s.* [*sacrilege*, Fr. *sacrilegium*, Lat.] The crime of appropriating to himself what is devoted to religion; the crime of robbing heaven; the crime of violating or profaning things sacred.

By what eclipse shall that sun be defac'd,
What mine hath erst thrown down so fair a tower!
What *sacrilege* hath such a saint disgrac'd? *Sidney.*

Then 'gan a curſed hand the quiet womb
Of his great grandmother with ſteel to wound,
And the hid treaſures in her ſacred tomb
With *ſacrilege* to dig. *Fairy Queen.*

We need not go many ages back to ſee the vengeance of God upon ſome families, raiſed upon the ruins of churches, and enriched with the ſpoils of *ſacrilege*. *South's Sermons.*

SACRILE'GIOUS. *adj.* [*ſacrilegus*, Lat. from *ſacrilege*.] Violating things ſacred; polluted with the crime of ſacrilege.

To *ſacrilegious* perjury ſhould I be betrayed, I ſhould account it greater miſery. *King Charles.*

By vile hands to common uſe debas'd,
With *ſacrilegious* taunt, and impious jeſt. *Prior.*

Still green with bays each ancient altar ſtands,
Above the reach of *ſacrilegious* hands. *Pope.*

Blaſphemy is a malediction, and a *ſacrilegious* detraction from the Godhead. *Ayliffe's Parergon.*

SACRILE'GIOUSLY. *adv.* [from *ſacrilegious*.] With ſacrilege.

When theſe evils befell him, his conſcience tells him it was for moſt *ſacrilegiouſly* pillaging and invading God's houſe. *South's Sermons.*

SA'CRING. *part.* [This is a participle of the French *ſacrer*. The verb is not uſed in Engliſh.] Conſecrating.

I'll ſtartle you,
Worſe than the *ſacring* bell. *Shakeſp. Henry* VIII.

The *ſacring* of the kings of France is the ſign of their ſovereign prieſthood as well as kingdom, and in the right thereof they are capable of holding all vacant benefices. *Temple.*

SA'CRIST. } *n. ſ.* [*ſacriſtain*, French.] He that has the care
SA'CRISTAN. } of the utenſils or moveables of the church.

A *ſcriſt* or treaſurer are not dignitaries in the church of common right, but only by cuſtom. *Ayliffe's Parergon.*

SA'CRISTY. *n. ſ.* [*ſacriſtie*, French.] An apartment where the conſecrated veſſels or moveables of a church are repoſited.

Bold Amycus from the robb'd veſtry brings
A ſconce that hung on high,
With tapers fill'd, to light the *ſacriſty*. *Dryden.*

A third apartment ſhould be a kind of *ſacriſty* for altars, idols, and ſacrificing inſtruments. *Addiſon.*

SAD. *adj.* [Of this word, ſo frequent in the language, the etymology is not known. It is probably a contraction of *ſagged*, heavy, burthened, overwhelmed, from *To ſag*, to load.]

1. Sorrowful; full of grief.

Do you think I ſhall not love a *ſad* Pamela ſo well as a joyful? *Sidney.*

I now muſt change
Thoſe notes to tragick; *ſad* taſk! *Milton.*

Six brave companions from each ſhip we loſt:
With ſails outſpread we fly th' unequal ſtrife,
Sad for their loſs, but joyful of our life. *Pope's Odyſſey.*

2. Habitually melancholy; heavy; gloomy; not gay; not cheerful.

It miniſtreth unto men, and other creatures, all celeſtial influences: it diſſipateth thoſe *ſad* thoughts and ſorrows, which the darkneſs both begetteth and maintaineth. *Raleigh.*

See in her cell *ſad* Eloiſa ſpread,
Propp'd on ſome tomb, a neighbour of the dead. *Pope.*

3. Serious; not light; not volatile; grave.

He with utterance grave, and countenance *ſad*,
From point to point diſcours'd his voyage. *Spenſer.*

The lady Katharine, a *ſad* and religious woman, when Henry VIII's reſolution of a divorce from her was firſt made known, ſaid that ſhe had not offended; but it was a judgment of God, for that her former marriage was made in blood. *Bac.*

If it were an embaſſy of weight, choice was made of ſome *ſad* perſon of known judgment and experience, and not of a young man, not weighed in ſtate matters. *Bacon.*

A *ſad* wiſe valour is the brave complexion
That leads the van, and ſwallows up the cities:
The gigler is a milk-maid, whom inflection,
Or a fir'd beacon, frighteth from his ditties. *Herbert.*

4. Afflictive; calamitous.

5. Bad; inconvenient; vexatious. A word of burleſque complaint.

Theſe qualifications make him a *ſad* huſband. *Addiſon.*

6. Dark coloured.

Cryſtal, in its reduction into powder, hath a vale and ſhadow of blue; and in its coarſe pieces is of a *ſadder* hue than the powder of Venice glaſs. *Brown's Vulgar Errours.*

I met him accidentally in London in *ſad* coloured clothes, far from being coſtly. *Walton's Life of Bp. Sanderſon.*

Scarce any tinging ingredient is of ſo general uſe as woad, or glaſtum; for though of itſelf it dye but a blue, yet it is uſed to prepare cloth for green, and many of the *ſadder* colours, when the dyers make them laſt without fading. *Boyle.*

Woad or wade is uſed by the dyers to lay the foundation of all *ſad* colours. *Mortimer's Huſbandry.*

7. Heavy; weighty; ponderous.

With that his hand, more *ſad* than lump of lead,
Uplifting high, he weened with Morddure,
His own good ſword, Morddure, to cleave his head. *F. Q.*

8. Coheſive; not light; firm; cloſe.

Chalky lands are naturally cold and *ſad*, and therefore require warm applications, and light compoſt. *Mortimer.*

To SA'DDEN. *v. a.* [from *ſad*.]

1. To make ſad.

2. To make melancholy; to make gloomy.

Her gloomy preſence *ſaddens* all the ſcene,
Shades ev'ry flow'r, and darkens ev'ry green;
Deepens the murmurs of the falling floods,
And breathes a browner horror on the woods. *Pope.*

3. To make dark coloured.

4. To make heavy; to make coheſive.

Marl is binding, and *ſaddening* of land is the great prejudice it doth to clay lands. *Mortimer's Huſbandry.*

SA'DDLE. *n. ſ.* [ſadl, Saxon; *ſadel*, Dutch.] The ſeat which is put upon the horſe for the accommodation of the rider.

His horſe hipped with an old moth-eaten *ſaddle*, and the ſtirrups of no kindred. *Shakeſp. Taming of the Shrew.*

The law made for apparel, and riding in *ſaddles*, after the Engliſh faſhion, is penal only to Engliſhmen. *Davies.*

One hung a pole-ax at his *ſaddle* bow,
And one a heavy mace. *Dryden's Knight's Tale.*

'Tis good to provide ourſelves of the virtuoſo's *ſaddle*, which will be ſure to amble, when the world is upon the hardeſt trot. *Dryden.*

The vent'rous knight is from the *ſaddle* thrown;
But 'tis the fault of fortune, not his own. *Dryden.*

To SA'DDLE. *v. a.* [from the noun.]

1. To cover with a ſaddle.

I will *ſaddle* me an aſs, that I may ride thereon. 2 *Sa.* xix.

Rebels, by yielding, do like him, or worſe,
Who *ſaddled* his own back to ſhame his horſe. *Cleaveland.*

No man, ſure, e'er left his houſe,
And *ſaddl'd* Ball, with thoughts ſo wild,
To bring a midwife to his ſpouſe,
Before he knew ſhe was with child. *Prior.*

2. To load; to burthen.

Reſolv'd for ſea, the ſlaves thy baggage pack,
Each *ſaddl'd* with his burden on his back;
Nothing retards thy voyage. *Dryden.*

SA'DDLEBACKED. *adj.* [*ſaddle* and *back*.]

Horſes, *ſaddlebacked*, have their backs low, and a raiſed head and neck. *Farrier's Dict.*

SA'DDLEMAKER. } *n. ſ.* [from *ſaddle*.] One whoſe trade is to
SA'DDLER. } make ſaddles.

Sixpence that I had
To pay the *ſaddler* for my miſtreſs' crupper,
The *ſaddler* had it. *Shakeſp. Comedy of Errours.*

The utmoſt exactneſs in theſe belongs to farriers, *ſaddlers*, and ſmiths. *Digby.*

The ſmith and the *ſaddler*'s journeyman ought to partake of your maſter's generoſity. *Swift's Direct. to the Groom.*

SA'DLY. *adv.* [from *ſad*.]

1. Sorrowfully; mournfully.

My father is gone wild into his grave;
For in his tomb lie my affections;
And with his ſpirit *ſadly* I ſurvive,
To mock the expectations of the world. *Shak. Henry* IV.

He griev'd, he wept, the ſight an image brought
Of his own filial love; a *ſadly* pleaſing thought. *Dryden.*

He *ſadly* ſuffers in their grief,
Out-weeps an hermit, and out-prays a ſaint. *Dryden.*

Common dangers paſt, a *ſadly* pleaſing theme. *Dryden.*

2. Calamitouſly; miſerably.

We may at preſent eaſily ſee, and one day *ſadly* feel. *South.*

SA'DNESS. *n. ſ.* [from *ſad*.]

1. Sorrowfulneſs; mournfulneſs; dejection of mind.

The ſoul receives intelligence
By her near genius of the body's end,
And ſo imparts a *ſadneſs* to the ſenſe. *Daniel's Civil War.*

And let us not be wanting to ourſelves,
Leſt ſo ſevere and obſtinate a *ſadneſs*
Tempt a new vengeance. *Denham's Sophy.*

A paſſionate regret at ſin, a grief and *ſadneſs* of its memory, enter into God's roll of mourners. *Decay of Piety.*

If the ſubject be mournful, let every thing in it have a ſtroke of *ſadneſs*. *Dryden.*

2. Melancholy look.

Dim *ſadneſs* did not ſpare
Celeſtial viſages. *Milton.*

3. Seriouſneſs; ſedate gravity.

SAFE. *adj.* [*ſauf*, French; *ſalvus*, Latin.]

1. Free from danger.

Our ſeparated fortune
Shall keep us both the *ſafer*; where we are,
There's daggers in men's ſmiles. *Shakeſp. Macbeth.*

But Trivia kept in ſecret ſhades alone,
Her care, Hippolytus, to fate unknown;
And call'd him Virbius in th' Egerian grove,
Where then he liv'd obſcure, but *ſafe* from Jove. *Dryden.*

Beyond the beating surge his course he bore,
With longing eyes observing, to survey
Some smooth ascent, or *safe* sequester'd bay. *Pope.*

2. Free from hurt.

Put your head into the mouth of a wolf, and when you've brought it out *safe* and sound, talk of a reward. *L'Estrange.*

3. Conferring security.

To write the same things to you, to me is not grievous, but to you *safe*. *Phil.* iii. 1.

Ascend; I follow thee, *safe* guide, the path
Thou lead'st me. *Milton.*

4. No longer dangerous; reposited out of the power of doing harm.

Banquo's *safe*.
——Ay, my good lord; *safe* in a ditch: he lies
With twenty trenched gashes on his head,
The least a death to nature. *Shakesp. Macbeth.*

Our great forbidder *safe*, with all his spies
About him. *Milton.*

SAFE. *n. s.* [from the adjective.] A buttery; a pantry. *Ainsw.*

SA'FECONDUCT. *n. s.* [*sauf conduit*, French.]

1. Convoy; guard through an enemy's country.

A trumpet was sent to sir William Waller, to desire a *safe-conduct* for a gentleman. *Clarendon.*

2. Pass; warrant to pass.

SA'FEGUARD. *n. s.* [*safe* and *guard.*]

1. Defence; protection; security.

We serve the living God as near as our wits can reach to the knowledge thereof, even according to his own will; and do therefore trust, that his mercy shall be our *safeguard. Hooker.*

If you do fight in *safeguard* of your wives,
Your wives shall welcome home the conquerors. *Shakesp.*

The smallest worm will turn, if trod upon;
And doves will peck in *safeguard* of their brood. *Shakesp.*

Cæsar, where dangers threatened on the one side, and the opinion that there should be in him little *safeguard* for his friends on the other, chose rather to venture upon extremities, than to be thought a weak protector. *Raleigh.*

Great numbers, descended from them, have, by the blessing of God upon their industry, raised themselves so high in the world as to become, in times of difficulty, a protection and a *safeguard* to that altar, at which their ancestors ministred. *Atterbury's Sermons.*

Thy sword, the *safeguard* of thy brother's throne,
Is now become the bulwark of thy own. *Granville.*

2. Convoy; guard through any interdicted road, granted by the possessor.

3. Pass; warrant to pass.

On *safeguard* he came to me. *Shakespeare.*

A trumpet was sent to the earl of Essex for a *safeguard* or pass to two lords, to deliver a message from the king to the two houses. *Clarendon.*

To SA'FEGUARD. *v. n.* [from the noun.] To guard; to protect.

We have locks to *safeguard* necessaries,
And pretty traps to catch the petty thieves. *Shak. Hen.* V.

SA'FELY. *adv.* [from *safe.*]

1. In a safe manner; without danger.

Who is there that hath the leisure and means to collect all the proofs, concerning most of the opinions he has, so as *safely* to conclude that he hath a clear and full view? *Locke.*

All keep aloof, and *safely* shout around;
But none presumes to give a nearer wound. *Dryden.*

2. Without hurt.

God *safely* quit her of her burthen, and with gentle travel, to the gladding of your highness with an heir. *Shak. H.* VIII.

SA'FENESS. *n. s.* [from *safe.*] Exemption from danger.

If a man should forbear his food or his business, 'till he had certainty of the *safeness* of what he was going about, he must starve and die disputing. *South's Sermons.*

SA'FETY. *n. s.* [from *safe.*]

1. Freedom from danger.

To that dauntless temper of his mind,
He hath a wisdom that doth guide his valour
To act in *safety*. *Shakesp. Macbeth.*

If her acts have been directed well,
While with her friendly clay she deign'd to dwell,
Shall she with *safety* reach her pristine seat,
Find her rest endless, and her bliss complete? *Prior.*

2. Exemption from hurt.

3. Preservation from hurt.

Let not my jealousies be your dishonours,
But mine own *safeties*: you may be rightly just,
Whatever I shall think. *Shak. Macbeth.*

4. Custody; security from escape.

Imprison him;
Deliver him to *safety*, and return. *Shak. King John.*

SA'FFLOW. *n. s.* A plant.

An herb they call *safflow*, or bastard saffron, dyers use for scarlet. *Mortimer's Husbandry.*

SA'FFRON. *n. s.* [*safran*, French, from *saphar*, Arabick. It was yellow, according to *Davies* in his Welsh dictionary. *Crocus*, Latin.]

It hath a flower consisting of one leaf, which is shaped like a lily, fistulous underneath, the tube widening into six segments, and resting on the footstalk: the pointal rises out of the bottom of the flower, and is divided into three-headed or crested capillaments; but the empalement afterwards turns to an oblong triangular fruit, divided into three cells, full of roundish seeds. It hath a tuberose root, and long nervous grassy leaves, with a longitudinal furrow through the middle of each. There are Spring-flowering crocuses, and those which flower in Autumn. Their seeds are ripe about the latter end of April: the time of planting is in July. About the beginning of September they begin to spire, and sometime after appear the saffron flowers, which are gathered as well before as after they are full-blown; and the most proper time for this is early in the morning: the chives being all picked out of the flowers, the next labour about them is to dry them on the kiln: at first they give it a pretty strong heat. The charges and profits attending the culture of saffron, have been computed in the following manner: the rent of an acre of ground, and the expence of manuring it, is reckoned at twenty-three pounds: the value of twenty-six pounds of saffron, the computed produce of an acre in three years, is, at a mean, supposed to be thirty-nine pounds; and consequently the neat profits of an acre of ground, producing saffron, will in three years amount to sixteen pounds. *Miller.*

Grind your bole and chalk, and five or six shives of saffron. *Peacham.*

SA'FFRON *Bastard. n. s.* [*carthamus*, Latin.] A plant.

This plant agrees with the thistle in most of its characters; but the seeds of it are always destitute of down. It is very much cultivated in Germany for the dyers use, and is brought from thence into England. As it grows it spreads into many branches, each producing a flower at the top of the shoot, which, when fully blown, is cut or pulled off, and dried, and it is the part the dyers use. *Miller.*

SA'FFRON. *adj.* Yellow; having the colour of saffron.

Are these your customers?
Did this companion, with the *saffron* face,
Revel and feast it at my house to-day,
Whilst upon me the guilty doors were shut? *Shakespeare.*

Soon as the white and red mixt finger'd dame
Had guilt the mountains with her *saffron* flame,
I sent my men to Circe's house. *Chapman's Odyssey.*

Now when the rosy morn began to rise,
And wav'd her *saffron* streamer through the skies. *Dryden.*

To SAG. *v. n.* To hang heavy.

The mind I say by, and the heart I bear,
Shall never *sag* with doubt, nor shake with fear. *Shakesp.*

To SAG. *v. a.* To load; to burthen.

SAGA'CIOUS. *adj.* [*sagax*, Latin.]

1. Quick of scent.

So scented the grim feature, and up-turn'd
His nostrils wide into the murky air;
Sagacious of his quarry from so far. *Milton's Paradise Lost.*

With might and main they chas'd the murd'rous fox,
Nor wanted horns t' inspire *sagacious* hounds. *Dryden.*

2. Quick of thought; acute in making discoveries.

Only *sagacious* heads light on these observations, and reduce them into general propositions. *Locke.*

SAGA'CIOUSLY. *adv.* [from *sagacious.*]

1. With quick scent.

2. With acuteness of penetration.

SAGA'CIOUSNESS. *n. s.* [from *sagacious.*] The quality of being sagacious.

SAGA'CITY. *n. s.* [*sagacité*, French; *sagacitas*, Latin.]

1. Quickness of scent.

2. Acuteness of discovery.

It requires too great a *sagacity* for vulgar minds to draw the line nicely between virtue and vice. *South.*

Sagacity finds out the intermediate ideas, to discover what connection there is in each link of the chain, whereby the extremes are held together. *Locke.*

Many were eminent in former ages for their discovery of it; but though the knowledge they have left be worth our study, yet they left a great deal for the industry and *sagacity* of after-ages. *Locke.*

SA'GAMORE. *n. s.*

1. [Among the American Indians.] A king or supreme ruler. *Bailey.*

2. The juice of some unknown plant used in medicine.

SAGE. *n. s.* [*sauge*, French; *salvia*, Latin.] A plant of which the school of *Salernum* thought so highly, that they left this verse:

Cur moriatur homo cui salvia *crescit in horto.*

It hath a labiated flower, consisting of one leaf, whose upper lip is sometimes arched, and sometimes hooked; but the under lip or beard is divided into three parts, bunching out, and not hollowed at the clare: out of the flower-cup rises the pointal, attended, as it were, by four embryoes, which afterward become so many seeds, which are roundish, shut up in an husk, which before was the flower-cup: to which may be added, that the stamina do somewhat resemble the os hyoides. *Miller.*

By

By the colour, figure, taste, and smell, we have as clear ideas of *sage* and hemlock, as we have of a circle. *Locke.*

Marbled with *sage* the hard'ning cheese she press'd. *Gay.*

SAGE. *adj.* [*sage*, Fr. *saggio*, Ital.] Wise; grave; prudent.

Tired limbs to rest,
O matron *sage*, quoth she, I hither came. *Fairy Queen.*

Vane, young in years, but in *sage* councils old,
Than whom a better senator ne'er held
The helm of Rome. *Milton.*

Can you expect that she should be so *sage*
To rule her blood, and you not rule your rage. *Waller.*

SAGE. *n. s.* [from the adjective.] A philosopher; a man of gravity and wisdom.

Though you profess
Yourselves such *sages*; yet know I no less;
Nor am to you inferior. *Sandys.*

At his birth a star proclaims him come,
And guides the eastern *sages*, who enquire
His place, to offer incense, myrrh, and gold. *Milton.*

For so the holy *sages* once did sing,
That he our deadly forfeit should release,
And with his father work us a perpetual peace. *Milton.*

Groves, where immortal *sages* taught,
Where heav'nly visions Plato fir'd. *Pope.*

SA'GELY. *adv.* [from *sage*.] Wisely; prudently.

SA'GENESS. *n. s.* [from *sage*.] Gravity; prudence. *Ainsw.*

SAGI'TTAL. *adj.* [from *sagitta*, Lat. an arrow.]

1. Belonging to an arrow.
2. [In anatomy.] A suture so called from its resemblance to an arrow.

His wound was between the *sagittal* and coronal sutures to the bone. *Wiseman's Surgery.*

SAGI'TTARY. *n. s.* [*sagittarius*, Latin; *sagittaire*, French.] A centaur; an animal half man half horse, armed with a bow and quiver.

The dreadful *sagittary*
Appals our numbers. *Shakesp. Troil. and Cressida.*

SA'GO. *n. s.* A kind of eatable grain. *Bailey.*

SA'ICK. *n. s.* [*saica*, Italian; *saique*, Fr.] A Turkish vessel proper for the carriage of merchandise. *Bailey.*

SAID. *preterite* and *part. pass.* of *say*.

1. Aforesaid.

King John succeeded his *said* brother in the kingdom of England and dutchy of Normandy. *Hale.*

2. Declared; shewed.

SAIL. *n. s.* [ꞅeꝫl, Saxon; *seyhel*, *seyl*, Dutch.]

1. The expanded sheet which catches the wind, and carries on the vessel on the water.

He came too late; the ship was under *sail*. *Shakespeare.*

They loosed the rudder-bands, and hoised up the main *sail* to the wind. *Acts* xxvii. 40.

The galley born from view by rising gales,
She follow'd with her sight and flying *sails*. *Dryden.*

2. [In poetry.] Wings.

He cutting way
With his broad *sails*, about him soared round;
At last, low stooping with unwieldy sway,
Snatch'd up both horse and man. *Fairy Queen.*

3. A ship; a vessel.

A *sail* arriv'd
From Pompey's son, who through the realms of Spain
Calls out for vengeance on his father's death. *Addis. Cato.*

4. *Sail* is a collective word, noting the number of ships.

So by a roaring tempest on the flood,
A whole armado of collected *sail*
Is scatter'd. *Shakespeare.*

It is written of Edgar, that he increased the fleet he found two thousand six hundred *sail*. *Raleigh's Essays.*

A feigned tear destroys us, against whom
Tydides nor Achilles could prevail,
Nor ten years conflict, nor a thousand *sail*. *Denham.*

He had promised to his army, who were discouraged at the sight of Seleucus's fleet, consisting of an hundred *sail*, that at the end of the Summer they should see a fleet of his of five hundred *sail*. *Arbuthnot on Coins.*

5. *To strike* SAIL. To lower the sail.

Fearing lest they should fall into the quicksands, they *strake sail*, and so were driven. *Acts* xxvii. 17.

6. A proverbial phrase for abating of pomp or superiority.

Margaret
Must *strike* her *sail*, and learn a while to serve
Where kings command. *Shakes. Henry VI.*

To SAIL. *v. n.* [from the noun.]

1. To be moved by the wind with sails.

I shall not mention any thing of the *sailing* waggons. *Mort.*

2. To pass by sea.

When *sailing* was now dangerous, Paul admonished them. *Acts.*

3. To swim.

To which the stores of Crœsus, in the scale,
Would look like little dolphins, when they *sail*
In the vast shadow of the British whale. *Dryden.*

4. To pass smoothly along.

Speak again, bright angel! for thou art
As glorious to this sight, being o'er my head,
As is a winged messenger from heav'n,
When he bestrides the lazy pacing clouds,
And *sails* upon the bosom of the air. *Shak. Rom. and Jul.*

To SAIL. *v. a.*

1. To pass by means of sails.

A thousand ships were mann'd to *sail* the sea. *Dryden.*

View Alcinous' groves, from whence
Sailing the spaces of the boundless deep,
To Ariconium precious fruits arriv'd. *Phillips.*

2. To fly through.

Sublime she *sails*
Th' aerial space, and mounts the winged gales. *Pope.*

SAILER. } *n. s.* [*sailor* is more usual, *sailer* more analogical;
SAILOR. } from *sail*.] A seaman; one who practises or understands navigation.

They had many times men of other countries that were no *sailors*. *Bacon.*

Batter'd by his lee they lay;
The passing winds through their torn canvas play,
And flagging sails on heartless *sailors* fall. *Dryden.*

Young Pompey built a fleet of large ships, and had good *sailors*, commanded by experienced captains. *Arbuthnot.*

Full in the openings of the spacious main
It rides, and, lo, descends the *sailer* train. *Pope's Odyssey.*

SAILYA'RD. *n. s.* [*sail* and *yard*.] The pole on which the sail is extended.

With glance so swift the subtle lightning past,
As split the *sailyards*. *Dryden's Juvenal.*

SAIM. *n. s.* [*saime*, Italian.] Lard. It still denotes this in Scotland: as swine's *saim*.

SAIN.

Some obscure precedence, that hath tofore been *sain*. *Shak.*

SA'INFOIN. *n. s.* [*sainfoin*, Fr.] A kind of herb.

SAINT. *n. s.* [*saint*, French; *sanctus*, Latin.] A person eminent for piety and virtue.

To thee be worship and thy *saints* for aye. *Shakesp.*

She will not stay the siege of loving terms,
Nor ope her lap to *saint* seducing gold. *Shakespeare.*

Then thus I cloath my naked villainy
With old odd ends, stol'n forth of holy writ,
And seem a *saint*, when most I play the devil. *Shakespeare.*

Miracles are required of all who aspire to this dignity, because they say an hypocrite may imitate a *saint* in all other particulars. *Addison on Italy.*

By thy example kings are taught to sway,
Heroes to fight, and *saints* may learn to pray. *Granville.*

So unaffected, so compos'd a mind;
So firm, yet soft, so strong, yet so refin'd,
Heav'n, as its purest gold, by tortures try'd;
The *saint* sustain'd it, but the woman dy'd. *Pope.*

To SAINT. *v. a.* [from the noun.] To number among saints; to reckon among saints by a publick decree; to canonize.

Are not the principles of those wretches still owned, and their persons *sainted*, by a race of men of the same stamp? *South.*

Over against the church stands a large hospital, erected by a shoemaker, who has been beatified, though never *sainted*. *Add.*

Thy place is here, sad sister; come away:
Once, like thyself, I trembled, wept, and pray'd;
Love's victim then, though now a *sainted* maid. *Pope.*

To SAINT. *v. n.* To act with a shew of piety.

Whether the charmer sinner it or *saint* it,
If folly grows romantick, I must paint it. *Pope.*

SAI'NTED. *adj.* [from *saint*.]

1. Holy; pious; virtuous.

Thy royal father
Was a most *sainted* king: the queen that bore thee,
Oftner upon her knees than on her feet,
Died every day she liv'd. *Shakesp. Macbeth.*

2. Holy; sacred.

I hold you as a thing enskied and *sainted*,
By your renouncement an immortal spirit,
And to be talk'd with in sincerity
As with a saint. *Shakespeare.*

The crown virtue gives,
After this mortal change, to her true servants,
Amongst the enthron'd gods on *sainted* hills. *Milton.*

SAINT *John's Wort*. *n. s.* A plant.

This plant hath a fibrose root: the leaves grow opposite by pairs at the joints of the stalks: the flower-cup consists of one leaf, which is divided into five parts, and expanded: the flower consists of five leaves expanded like a rose, having many stamina in the centre surrounding a conical ovary, which becomes a three-cornered pointed fruit, and is divided into three cells, containing many small seeds. There are thirty species of this plant, of which the four first sorts grow wild, and the rest are exoticks. The first sort, called common *Saint John's wort*, is used in medicine. *Miller.*

SA'INTLIKE. *adj.* [*saint* and *like*.]

1. Suiting a saint; becoming a saint.

If still thou do'st retain
The same ill habits, the same follies too,
Gloss'd over only with a *saintlike* show,
Still thou art bound to vice. *Dryden's Pers.*

2. Resembling

2. Reſembling a ſaint.

The king, in whoſe time it paſſed, whom catholicks count a *ſaintlike* and immaculate prince, was taken away in the flower of his age. *Bacon.*

SA'INTLY. *adj.* [from *ſaint.*] Like a ſaint; becoming a ſaint.

I mention ſtill
Him whom thy wrongs, with *ſaintly* patience borne,
Made famous in a land and times obſcure. *Milt. Par. Loſt.*

SA'INTSHIP. *n. ſ.* [from *ſaint.*] The character or qualities of a ſaint.

He that thinks his *ſaintſhip* licenſes him to cenſures, is to be looked on not only as a rebel, but an uſurper. *Decay of Piety.*

This favours ſomething ranker than the tenents of the fifth monarchy, and of ſovereignty founded upon *ſaintſhip*. *South.*

The devil was piqu'd ſuch *ſaintſhip* to behold,
And long'd to tempt him. *Pope.*

SAKE. *n. ſ.* [ſac, Saxon; *ſaecke*, Dutch.]

1. Final cauſe; end; purpoſe.

Thou neither do'ſt perſuade me to ſeek wealth
For empire's *ſake*, nor empire to affect
For glory's *ſake*. *Milton's Paradiſe Loſt.*

The prophane perſon ſerves the devil for nought, and ſins only for ſin's *ſake*. *Tillotſon.*

Wyndham like a tyrant throws the dart,
And takes a cruel pleaſure in the ſmart;
Proud of the ravage that her beauties make,
Delights in wounds, and kills for killing's *ſake*. *Granville.*

2. Account; regard to any perſon or thing.

Would I were young for your *ſake*, miſtreſs Anne! *Shakeſp.*

The general ſo likes your muſick, that he deſires you, for love's *ſake*, to make no more noiſe with it. *Shakeſp. Othello.*

SA'KER. *n. ſ.* [*Saker* originally ſignifies an hawk, the pieces of artillery being often denominated from birds of prey.]

The cannon, blunderbuſs, and *ſaker*,
He was th' inventor of, and maker. *Hudibras.*

According to obſervations made with one of her majeſty's *ſakers*, and a very accurate pendulum-chronometer, a bullet, at its firſt diſcharge, flies five hundred and ten yards in five half ſeconds, which is a mile in a little above ſeventeen half ſeconds. *Derham's Phyſico-Theology.*

SA'KERET. *n. ſ.* [from *ſaker.*] The male of a ſaker-hawk. This kind of hawk is eſteemed next after the falcon and gyrfalcon, but differently to be managed. *Bailey.*

SAL. n. ſ. [Latin.] Salt. A word often uſed in pharmacy.

Salſo acids will help its paſſing off; as *ſal* prunel. *Floyer.*

Sal gem is ſo called from its breaking frequently into gemlike ſquares. It differs not in property from the common ſalt of the ſalt ſprings, or that of the ſea, when all are equally pure. *Woodward's Met. Foſſ.*

Sal Ammoniack is found ſtill in Ammonia, as mentioned by the ancients, and from whence it had its name. *Woodward.*

SALA'CIOUS. *adj.* [*ſalacis*, Lat. *ſalace*, Fr.] Luſtful; lecherous.

One more *ſalacious*, rich, and old,
Out-bids, and buys her. *Dryden's Juven. Sat.*

Feed him with herbs
Of generous warmth, and of *ſalacious* kind. *Dryd. Virg.*

Animals ſpleened, grow extremely *ſalacious*. *Arbuthnot.*

SALA'CIOUSLY. *adv.* [from *ſalacious.*] Lecherouſly; luſtfully.

SALA'CITY. *n. ſ.* [*ſalacitas*, Lat. from *ſalacious.*] Luſt; lechery.

Immoderate *ſalacity* and exceſs of venery is ſuppoſed to ſhorten the lives of cocks. *Brown's Vulg. Errours.*

A corroſive acrimony in the ſeminal lympha produces *ſalacity*. *Floyer on the Humours.*

SA'LAD. *n. ſ.* [*ſalade*, Fr. *ſalaet*, Germ.] Food of raw herbs.

I climbed into this garden to pick a *ſalad*, which is not amiſs to cool a man's ſtomach. *Shakeſp. Henry VI.*

My *ſallet* days,
When I was green in judgment, cold in blood. *Shakeſpeare.*

You have, to rectify your palate,
An olive, capers, or ſome better *ſalad*,
Uſh'ring the mutton. *Ben. Johnſon.*

Some coarſe cold *ſalad* is before thee ſet;
Fall on. *Dryden's Perſ. Sat.*

The happy old Coricyan's fruits and *ſalads*, on which he lived contented, were all of his own growth. *Dryden.*

Leaves, eaten raw, are termed *ſalad*: if boiled, they become potherbs; and ſome of thoſe plants which are potherbs in one family, are *ſallad* in another. *Watts.*

SALAMA'NDER. *n. ſ.* [*ſalamandre*, Fr. *ſalamandra*, Lat.] An animal ſuppoſed to live in the fire, and imagined to be very poiſonous. *Ambroſe Parey* has a picture of the ſalamander, with a receipt for her bite; but there is no ſuch creature, the name being now given to a poor harmleſs inſect.

The *ſalamander* liveth in the fire, and hath force alſo to extinguiſh it. *Bacon's Natural Hiſtory.*

According to this hypotheſis the whole lunar world is a torrid zone, and may be ſuppoſed uninhabitable, except they are *ſalamanders* which dwell therein. *Glanv. Sceps.*

Whereas it is commonly ſaid that a *ſalamander* extinguiſheth fire, we have found by experience, that on hot coals it dieth immediately. *Brown's Vulgar Errours.*

The artiſt was ſo encompaſſed with fire and ſmoke, that one would have thought nothing but a *ſalamander* could have been ſafe in ſuch a ſituation. *Addiſon's Guardian.*

SALAMA'NDER'S *Hair.* } *n. ſ.* A kind of aſbeſtos, or mineral
SALAMA'NDER'S *Wool.* } flax.

There may be ſuch candles as are made of *ſalamander's wool*, being a kind of mineral, which whiteneth in the burning, and conſumeth not. *Bacon.*

Of Engliſh talc, the coarſer ſort is called plaiſter or parget; the finer, ſpaad, earth flax, or *ſalamander's hair*. *Woodward.*

SALAMA'NDRINE. *adj.* [from *ſalamander.*] Reſembling a ſalamander.

Laying it into a pan of burning coals, we obſerved a certain *ſalamandrine* quality, that made it capable of living in the midſt of fire, without being conſumed or ſinged. *Spectator.*

SA'LARY. *n. ſ.* [*ſalaire*, Fr. *ſalarium*, Latin.]

1. Salarium, or *ſalary*, is derived from *ſal*. *Arbuthnot.*

2. Stated hire; annual or periodical payment.

This is hire and *ſalary*, not revenge. *Shak. Hamlet.*

Several perſons, out of a *ſalary* of five hundred pounds, have always lived at the rate of two thouſand. *Swift.*

SALE. *n. ſ.* [*ſaal*, Dutch.]

1. The act of ſelling.

2. Vent; power of ſelling; market.

Nothing doth more enrich any country than many towns; for the countrymen will be more induſtrious in tillage, and rearing of all huſbandry commodities, knowing that they ſhall have ready *ſale* for them at thoſe towns. *Spenſer.*

3. A publick and proclaimed expoſition of goods to the market; auction.

Thoſe that won the plate, and thoſe thus ſold, ought to be marked ſo as they may never return to the race, or to the *ſale*. *Temple.*

4. State of being venal; price.

The other is not a thing for *ſale*, and only the gift of the gods. *Shakeſp. Cymbeline.*

Others more moderate ſeeming, but their aim
Private reward; for which both God and ſtate
They'd ſet to *ſale*. *Milton's Agoniſtes.*

The more money a man ſpends, the more muſt he endeavour to increaſe his ſtock; which at laſt ſets the liberty of a commonwealth to *ſale*. *Addiſon.*

5. It ſeems in *Spenſer* to ſignify a wicker baſket; perhaps from *ſallow*, in which fiſh are caught.

To make baſkets of bulruſhes was my wont;
Who to entrap the fiſh in winding *ſale*
Was better ſeen? *Spenſer.*

SA'LEABLE. *adj.* [from *ſale.*] Vendible; fit for ſale; marketable.

I can impute this general enlargement of *ſaleable* things to no cauſe ſooner than the Corniſhman's want of vent and money. *Carew.*

This vent is made quicker or ſlower, as greater or leſs quantities of any *ſaleable* commodity are removed out of the courſe of trade. *Locke.*

SA'LEABLENESS. *n. ſ.* [from *ſaleable.*] The ſtate of being ſaleable.

SA'LEABLY. *adv.* [from *ſaleable.*] In a ſaleable manner.

SA'LEBROUS. *adj.* [*ſalebroſus*, Latin.] Rough; uneven; rugged.

SA'LESMAN. *n. ſ.* [*ſale* and *man.*] One who ſells cloaths ready made.

Poets make characters, as *ſaleſmen* cloaths;
We take no meaſure of your fops and beaus. *Swift.*

SA'LEWORK. *n. ſ.* [*ſale* and *work.*] Work for ſale; work careleſly done.

I ſee no more in you than in the ordinary
Of nature's *ſalework*. *Shakeſp. As you like it.*

SA'LIANT. adj. [French.] Denotes a lion in a leaping poſture, and ſtanding ſo that his right foot is in the dexter point, and his hinder left foot in the ſiniſter baſe point of the eſcutcheon, by which it is diſtinguiſhed from rampant. *Harris.*

SA'LIANT, in heraldry, is when the lion is ſporting himſelf. *Peacham.*

SA'LIENT. *adj.* [*ſaliens*, Latin.]

1. Leaping; bounding; moving by leaps.

The legs of both ſides moving together, as frogs, and *ſalient* animals, is properly called leaping. *Brown's Vulg. Err.*

2. Beating; panting.

A *ſalient* point ſo firſt is call'd the heart,
By turns dilated, and by turns compreſt,
Expels and entertains the purple gueſt. *Blackmore.*

3. Springing or ſhooting with a quick motion.

Who beſt can ſend on high
The *ſalient* ſpout, far ſtreaming to the ſky. *Pope.*

SA'LINE. } *adj.* [*ſalinus*, Latin.] Conſiſting of ſalt; con-
SA'LINOUS. } ſtituting ſalt.

We do not eaſily aſcribe their induration to cold; but rather unto *ſalinous* ſpirits and concretive juices. *Brown.*

This *ſaline* ſap of the veſſels, by being refuſed reception of the parts, declares itſelf in a more hoſtile manner, by drying the radical moiſture. *Harvey on Conſumptions.*

If a very small quantity of any salt or vitriol be dissolved in a great quantity of water, the particles of the salt or vitriol will not sink to the bottom, though they be heavier in specie than the water; but will evenly diffuse themselves into all the water, so as to make it as *saline* at the top as at the bottom. *Newton's Opt.*

As the substance of coagulations is not merely *saline*, nothing dissolves them but what penetrates and relaxes at the same time. *Arbuthnot on Aliments.*

SA'LIGOTS. *n. s.* A kind of thistle. *Ainsworth.*

SALI'VA. n. s. [Latin.] Every thing that is spit up; but it more strictly signifies that juice which is separated by the glands called salival. *Quincy.*

Not meeting with disturbance from the *saliva*, I the sooner extirpated them. *Wiseman's Surgery.*

SA'LIVAL. } SA'LIVARY. } *adj.* [from *saliva*, Latin.] Relating to spittle.

The woodpecker, and other birds that prey upon flies, which they catch with their tongue, in the room of the said glands have a couple of bags filled with a viscous humour, which, by small canals, like the *salival*, being brought into their mouths, they dip their tongues herein, and so with the help of this natural birdlime attack the prey. *Grew.*

The necessity of spittle to dissolve the aliment appears from the contrivance of nature in making the *salivary* ducts of animals which ruminate, extremely open: such animals as swallow their aliment without chewing, want *salivary* glands. *Arbuthnot on Aliments.*

To SA'LIVATE. *v. a.* [from *saliva*, Latin.] To purge by the salival glands.

She was prepossessed with the scandal of *salivating*, and went out of town. *Wiseman's Surgery.*

SALIVA'TION. *n. s.* [from *salivate.*] A method of cure much practised of late in venereal, scrophulous, and other obstinate causes, by promoting a secretion of spittle. *Quincy.*

Holding of ill-tasted things in the mouth will make a small *salivation.* *Grew's Cosmol.*

SALI'VOUS. *adj.* [from *saliva.*] Consisting of spittle; having the nature of spittle.

There happeneth an elongation of the uvula, through the abundance of *salivous* humour flowing upon it. *Wiseman.*

SA'LLET. } SA'LLETING. } *n. s.* [corrupted by pronunciation from *salad.*]

I tried upon *sallet* oil. *Boyle.*

Sow some early *salleting.* *Mortimer's Husbandry.*

SA'LLIANCE. *n. s.* [from *sally.*] The act of issuing forth; sally. A word not inelegant, but out of use.

Now mote I weet,
Sir Guyon, why with so fierce *salliance*
And fell intent, ye did at earst me meet. *Fairy Queen.*

SA'LLOW. *n. s.* [*salix*, Latin.] A tree of the genus of willow. See WILLOW.

Sallows and reeds on banks of rivers born,
Remain to cut to stay thy vines. *Dryden.*

SA'LLOW. *adj.* [*salo*, German, black; *sale*, French, foul.] Sickly; yellow.

What a deal of brine
Hath washt thy *sallow* cheeks for Rosaline? *Shakespeare.*

The scene of beauty and delight is chang'd:
No roses bloom upon my fading cheek,
Nor laughing graces wanton in my eyes;
But haggard grief, lean-looking *sallow* care,
And pining discontent, a rueful train,
Dwell on my brow, all hideous and forlorn. *Rowe.*

SA'LLOWNESS. *n. s.* [from *sallow.*] Yellowness; sickly paleness.

A fish-diet would give such a *sallowness* to the celebrated beauties of this island, as would scarce make them distinguishable from those of France. *Addison.*

SA'LLY. *n. s.* [*sallie*, French.]

1. Eruption; issue from a place besieged; quick egress.

The deputy sat down before the town for the space of three Winter months; during which time *sallies* were made by the Spaniards, but they were beaten in with loss. *Bacon.*

2. Range; excursion.

Every one shall know a country better, that makes often *sallies* into it, and traverses it up and down, than he that, like a mill-horse, goes still round in the same track. *Locke.*

3. Flight; volatile or sprightly exertion.

These passages were intended for *sallies* of wit; but whence comes all this rage of wit? *Stillingfleet.*

4. Escape; levity; extravagant flight; frolick; wild gaiety; exorbitance.

At his return all was clear, and this excursion was esteemed but a *sally* of youth. *Wotton.*

'Tis but a *sally* of youth. *Denham's Sophy.*

We have written some things which we may wish never to have thought on: some *sallies* of levity ought to be imputed to youth. *Swift.*

The episodical part, made up of the extravagant *sallies* of the prince of Wales and Falstaff's humour, is of his own invention. *Shakespeare Illustrated.*

To SA'LLY. *v. n.* [from the noun.] To make an eruption; to issue out.

The Turks *sallying* forth, received thereby great hurt. *Knoll.*

The noise of some tumultuous fight:
They break the truce, and *sally* out by night. *Dryden.*

The summons take of the same trumpet's call,
To *sally* from one port, or man one publick wall. *Tate.*

SA'LLYPORT. *n. s.* [*sally* and *port.*] Gate at which sallies are made.

My slippery soul had quit the fort,
But that she stopp'd the *sallyport.* *Cleaveland.*

Love to our citadel resorts
Through those deceitful *sallyports*;
Our sentinels betray our forts. *Denham.*

SA'LMAGUNDI. *n. s.* [It is said to be corrupted from *selon mon gout*, or *sale à mon goût.*] A mixture of chopped meat and pickled herrings with oil, vinegar, pepper, and onions.

SA'LMON. *n. s.* [*salmo*, Latin; *saûmon*, French.]

The salmon is accounted the king of fresh-water fish, and is bred in rivers relating to the sea, yet so far from it as admits no tincture of brackishness. He is said to breed or cast his spawn in most rivers in the month of August: some say that then they dig a hole in a safe place in the gravel, and there place their eggs or spawn, after the melter has done his natural office, and then cover it over with gravel and stones, and so leave it to their Creator's protection; who, by a gentle heat which he infuses into that cold element, makes it brood and beget life in the spawn, and to become samlets early in the Spring: having spent their appointed time, and done this natural duty in the fresh waters, they haste to the sea before Winter, both the melter and spawner. Sir Francis Bacon observes the age of a *salmon* exceeds not ten years: his growth is very sudden, so that after he is got into the sea he becomes from a samlet, not so big as a gudgeon, to be a salmon, in as short a time as a gosling becomes a goose. *Walton's Angler.*

They poke them with an instrument somewhat like the *salmon* spear. *Carew's Survey of Cornwal.*

They take *salmon* and trouts by groping and tickling them under the bellies in the pools, where they hover, and so throw them on land. *Carew.*

Of fishes, you find in arms the whale, dolphin, *salmon* and trout. *Peacham.*

SA'LMONTROUT. *n. s.* A trout that has some resemblance to a salmon; a samlet.

There is in many rivers that relate to the sea *salmontrouts* as much different from others, in shape and spots, as sheep differ in their shape and bigness. *Walton's Angler.*

SALPI'CON. *n. s.* [In cookery.] A kind of farce put into holes cut in legs of beef, veal, or mutton. *Bailey.*

SALSAMENTA'RIOUS. *adj.* [*salsamentarius*, Latin.] Belonging to salt things. *Dict.*

SA'LSIFY. *n. s.* [Latin.] A plant.

Salsify, or the common sort of goatsbeard, is of a very long oval figure, as if it were cods all over streaked, and engraven in the spaces between the streaks, which are sharp pointed towards the end. *Mortimer's Husbandry.*

SALSOA'CID. *adj.* [*salsus* and *acidus*, Latin.] Having a taste compounded of saltness and sourness.

The *salsoacids* help its passing off; as sal prunel. *Floyer.*

SALSU'GINOUS. *adj.* [*salsugo*, Latin.] Saltish; somewhat salt.

The distinction of salts, whereby they are discriminated into acid, volatile, or *salsuginous*, if I may so call the fugitive salts of animal substances, and fixed or alcalizate, may appear of much use in natural philosophy. *Boyle.*

SALT. *n. s.* [*salt*, Gothick; ꞅealꞇ, Saxon; *sal*, Latin; *sel*, French.]

1. *Salt* is a body whose two essential properties seem to be dissolubility in water, and a pungent sapor: it is an active incombustible substance: it gives all bodies consistence, and preserves them from corruption, and occasions all the variety of tastes. There are three kinds of salts, fixed, volatile, and essential: fixed salt is drawn by calcining the matter, then boiling the ashes in a good deal of water: after this the solution is filtrated, and all the moisture evaporated, when the salt remains in a dry form at the bottom: this is called a lixivious salt. Essential salt is that drawn chiefly from the parts of animals, and some putrified parts of vegetables: it rises easily, and is the most volatile of any. The essential salt is drawn from the juice of plants by crystalization. *Harris.*

Is not discourse, manhood, learning, gentleness, virtue and liberality, the spice and *salt* that seasons a man? *Shakesp.*

He perfidiously has given up,
For certain drops of *salt*, your city Rome,
To his wife and mother. *Shak. Coriolanus.*

Since *salts* differ much, some being fixt, some volatile, some acid, and some urinous, the two qualities wherein they agree are, that it is easily dissoluble in water, and affects the palate with a sapour, good or evil. *Boyle.*

A particle

A particle of *salt* may be compared to a chaos, being dense, hard, dry, and earthy in the centre, and rare, soft, and moist in the circumference. *Newton's Opt.*

Salts are bodies friable and brittle, in some degree pellucid, sharp or pungent to the taste, and dissoluble in water; but after that is evaporated, incorporating, crystalizing, and forming themselves into angular figures. *Woodward.*

2. Taste; smack

Though we are justices and doctors, and churchmen, Mr. Page, we have some *salt* of our youth in us; we are the sons of women. *Shakesp. Merry Wives of Windsor.*

3. Wit; merriment.

SALT. *adj.*

1. Having the taste of salt: as *salt* fish.

We were better parch in Africk sun,
Than in the pride and *salt* scorn of his eyes. *Shakesp.*
Thou old and true Menenius,
Thy tears are *salter* than a younger man's,
And venomous to thine eyes. *Shakes. Coriolanus.*

It hath been observed by the ancients, that *salt* water will dissolve salt put into it in less time than fresh water. *Bacon.*

2. Impregnated with salt.

Hang him, mechanical *salt* butter rogue: I will awe him with my cudgel. *Shakes. Merry Wives of Windsor.*

A leap into *salt* waters very often gives a new motion to the spirits, and a new turn to the blood. *Addison.*

3. Abounding with salt.

He shall inhabit the parched places in the wilderness in a *salt* land, and not inhabited. *Jer.* xvii. 6.

In Cheshire they improve their lands by letting out the water of the *salt* springs on them, always after rain. *Mortim.*

4. [*Salax*, Lat.] Lecherous; salacious.

Be a whore still:
Make use of thy *salt* hours, season the slaves
For tubs and baths; bring down the rose-cheek'd youth
To the tub-fast, and the diet. *Shakesp. Timon.*
All the charms of love,
Salt Cleopatra, soften thy wan lip! *Shakes. Ant. and Cleop.*
This new married man, approaching here,
Whose *salt* imagination yet hath wrong'd
Your well defended honour, you must pardon. *Shakesp.*

To SALT. *v. a.* [from the noun.] To season with salt.

If the offering was of flesh, it was *salted* thrice. *Brown.*

SA'LT-PAN. } *n. s.* [*salt* and *pan*, or *pit*.] Pit where salt is
SA'LT-PIT. } got.

Moab and Ammon shall be as the breeding of nettles, *salt-pits*, and a perpetual desolation. *Zeph.* ii. 9.

Cicero prettily calls them salinas *salt-pans*, that you may extract salt out of, and sprinkle where you please. *Bacon.*

The stratum lay at about twenty-five fathom, by the duke of Somerset's *salt-pans* near Whitehaven. *Woodward on Fossils.*

SA'LTANT. *adj.* [*saltans*, Latin.] Jumping; dancing.

SALTA'TION. *n. s.* [*saltatio*, Latin.]

1. The act of dancing or jumping.

The locusts being ordained for *saltation*, their hinder legs do far exceed the others. *Brown's Vulgar Errours.*

2. Beat; palpitation.

If the great artery be hurt, you will discover it by its *saltation* and florid colour. *Wiseman's Surgery.*

SA'LTCAT. *n. s.*

Many give a lump of salt, which they usually call a *saltcat*, made at the salterns, which makes the pigeons much affect the place. *Mortimer's Husbandry.*

SALTCE'LLAR. *n. s.* [*salt* and *cellar*.] Vessel of salt set on the table.

When any salt is spilt on the table-cloth, shake it out into the *saltcellar*. *Swift's Directions to the Butler.*

SA'LTER. *n. s.* [from *salt*.]

1. One who salts.

2. One who sells salt.

After these local names, the most have been derived from occupations; as smith, *salter*, armorer. *Camden's Remains.*

SA'LTERN. *n. s.* A saltwork.

A lump of salt, which they usually call a saltcat, made for that purpose at the *salterns*, makes the pigeons much affect the place. *Mortimer's Husbandry.*

SALTI'NBANCO. *n. s.* [*saltare in banco*, to climb on a bench, as a mountebank mounts a bank.] A quack or mountebank.

Saltinbancoes, quacksalvers, and charlatans deceive them: were Æsop alive, the Piazza and Pont-neuf could not speak their fallacies. *Brown's Vulgar Errours.*

He play'd the *saltinbanco*'s part,
Transform'd t' a Frenchman by my art. *Hudibras.*

SA'LTIER. *n. s.* [*saultiere*, French.]

A *saltier* is made in the form of a St. Andrew's cross, and by some is taken to be an engine to take wild beasts withal: in French it is called *un sautoir*: it is an honourable bearing. *Peacham on Blazoning.*

SALTISH. *adj.* [from *salt*] Somewhat salt.

Soils of a *saltish* nature improve sandy grounds. *Mortimer.*

SA'LTLESS. *adj.* [from *salt*.] Insipid; not tasting of salt.

SA'LTLY. *adv.* [from *salt*.] With taste of salt; in a salt manner.

SA'LTNESS. *n. s.* [from *salt*.] Taste of salt.

Salt water passing through earth, through ten vessels, one within another, hath not lost its *saltness*, so as to become potable; but drained through twenty, become fresh. *Bacon.*

Some think their wits have been asleep, except they dart out somewhat that is piquant and to the quick: men ought to find the difference between *saltness* and bitterness. *Bacon.*

SA'LTPETRE. *n. s.* [*sal petræ*, Latin; *sal petre*, Fr.] Nitre.

Nitre, or *saltpetre*, having a crude and windy spirit, by the heat of the fire suddenly dilateth. *Bacon.*

Nitre or *saltpetre*, in heaps of earth, has been extracted, if they be exposed to the air, so as to be kept from rain. *Locke.*

SALVABI'LITY. *n. s.* [from *salvable*.] Possibility of being received to everlasting life.

Why do we Christians so fiercely argue against the *salvability* of each other, as if it were our wish that all should be damned, but those of our particular sect. *Decay of Piety.*

SA'LVABLE. *adj.* [from *salvo*, Latin.] Possible to be saved.

Our wild fancies about God's decrees, have in event reprobated more than those decrees, and have bid fair to the damning of many whom those left *salvable*. *Decay of Piety.*

SA'LVAGE. *adj.* [*saulvage*, French; *selvaggio*, Italian, from *silva*, Latin.] Wild; rude; cruel. It is now spoken and written *savage*.

May the Essexian plains
Prove as a desert, and none there make stay
But *savage* beasts, or men as wild as they. *Waller.*
A *savage* race inur'd to blood. *Dryden.*

SALVA'TION. *n. s.* [from *salvo*, Latin.] Preservation from eternal death; reception to the happiness of heaven.

As life and death, mercy and wrath, are matters of meer understanding or knowledge, all mens *salvation*, and all mens endless perdition, are things so opposite, that whosoever doth affirm the one must necessarily deny the other. *Hooker.*

Him the most High,
Wrap'd in a balmy cloud with winged steeds,
Did, as thou saw'st, receive; to walk with God
High in *salvation*, and the climes of bliss,
Exempt from death. *Milton's Parad. Lost, b.* xi.

SA'LVATORY. *n. s.* [*salvatoire*, French.] A place where any thing is preserved.

I consider the admirable powers of sensation, phantasy, and memory, in what *salvatories* or repositories the species of things past are conserved. *Hale's Origin of Mankind.*

SALU'BRIOUS. *adj.* [*salubris*, Latin.] Wholsome; healthful; promoting health.

The warm limbeck draws
Salubrious waters from the nocent brood. *Phillips.*

Must we then resign our worthy pastor to the *salubrious* air of Kiltearn, rather than he should longer breathe in the grosser vapours of Inverness? *Macbean's Remonstrance.*

SALU'BRITY. *n. s.* [from *salubrious*.] Wholsomeness; healthfulness.

SALVE. *n. s.* [This word is originally and properly *salf*, which having *salves* in the plural, the singular in time was borrowed from it: sealf, Saxon, undoubtedly from *salvus*, Latin.] A glutinous matter applied to wounds and hurts; an emplaster.

Let us hence, my sov'reign, to provide
A *salve* for any sore that may betide. *Shak. Henry* VI.
Go study *salve* and treacle; ply
Your tenant's leg, or his sore eye. *Cleaveland.*
Sleep is pain's easiest *salve*, and doth fulfil
All offices of death, except to kill. *Donne.*
The royal sword thus drawn, has cur'd a wound,
For which no other *salve* could have been found. *Waller.*
Though most were sorely wounded, none were slain;
The surgeons soon despoil'd them of their arms,
And some with *salves* they cure. *Dryden.*

2. Help; remedy.

If they shall excommunicate me, hath the doctrine of meekness any *salve* for me then? *Hammond.*

To SALVE. *v. a.* [*salvo*, Latin; or from the noun.]

1. To cure with medicaments applied.

Many skilful leeches him abide,
To *salve* his hurts. *Fairy Queen.*

It should be to little purpose for them to *salve* the wound, by making protestations in disgrace of their own actions. *Hook.*

The which if I perform, and do survive,
I do beseech your majesty may *salve*
The long grown wounds of my intemperature. *Sh. H.* IV.

2. To help; to remedy.

Some seek to *salve* their blotted name
With others blot, 'till all do taste of shame. *Sidney.*

Our mother-tongue, which truly of itself is both full enough for prose, and stately enough for verse, hath long time been counted most bare and barren of both; which default, when as some endeavoured to *salve* and cure, they patched up the holes with rags from other languages. *Spenser.*

3. To help or save by a *salvo*, an excuse, or reservation.

Ignorant I am, not how this is *salved*: they do it but after the truth is made manifest. *Hooker.*

My

My more particular,
And that which most with you should *salve* my going,
Is Fulvia's death. *Shakesp. Ant. and Cleopatra.*

The schoolmen were like the astronomers, who, to *salve* phœnomena, framed to their conceit eccentricks and epicycles; so they, to *salve* the practice of the church, had devised a great number of strange positions. *Bacon.*

There must be another state to make up the inequalities of this, and *salve* all irregular appearances. *Atterbury.*

This conduct might give Horace the hint to say, that when Homer was at a loss to bring any difficult matter to an issue, he laid his hero asleep, and this *salved* all difficulty. *Broome.*

4. [From *salve*, Latin.] To salute. Obsolete.

That stranger knight in presence came,
And goodly *salved* them; who nought again
Him answered as courtesy became. *Fairy Queen.*

SA'LVER. *n. s.* [A vessel, I suppose, used at first to carry away or save what was left.] A plate on which any thing is presented.

He has printed them in such a portable volume, that many of them may be ranged together on a single plate; and is of opinion, that a *salver* of spectators would be as acceptable an entertainment for the ladies, as a *salver* of sweetmeats. *Addis.*

Between each act the trembling *salvers* ring,
From soup to sweet wine. *Pope.*

SA'LVO. *n. s.* [from *salvo jure*, Latin, a form used in granting any thing: as *salvo jure putei.*] An exception; a reservation; an excuse.

They admit many *salvoes*, cautions, and reservations, so as they cross not the chief design. *King Charles.*

It will be hard if he cannot bring himself off at last with some *salvo* or distinction, and be his own confessor. *L'Estr.*

If others of a more serious turn join with us deliberately in their religious professions of loyalty, with any private *salvoes* or evasions, they would do well to consider those maxims in which all casuists are agreed. *Addison.*

SA'LUTARINESS. *n. s.* [from *salutary.*] Wholsomeness; quality of contributing to health or safety.

SA'LUTARY. *adj.* [*salutaire*, Fr. *salutaris*, Latin.] Wholsome; healthful; safe; advantageous; contributing to health or safety.

The gardens, yards, and avenues are dry and clean; and so more *salutary* as more elegant. *Ray.*

It was want of faith in our Saviour's countrymen, which hindered him from shedding among them the *salutary* emanations of his divine virtue; and he did not many mighty works there, because of their unbelief. *Bentley.*

SALUTA'TION. *n. s.* [*salutation*, Fr. *salutatio*, Latin.] The act or stile of saluting; greeting.

The early village cock
Hath twice done *salutation* to the morn. *Shakesp. R.* III.

Thy kingdom's peers
Speak my *salutation* in their minds;
Whose voices I desire aloud with mine,
Hail, king of Scotland! *Shakesp. Macbeth.*

On her the angel hail
Bestow'd, the holy *salutation* used
To blest Mary. *Milton.*

In all publick meetings, or private addresses, use those forms of *salutation*, reverence and decency, usual amongst the most sober persons. *Taylor's Rule of living holy.*

Court and state he wisely shuns;
Nor brib'd, to servile *salutations* runs. *Dryden's Horace.*

To SALU'TE. *v. a.* [*saluto*, Latin; *saluer*, French.]

1. To greet; to hail.

The golden sun *salutes* the morn,
And, having gilt the ocean with his beams,
Gallops the zodiack in his glist'ring coach. *Shakes. Tit. And.*

One hour hence
Shall *salute* your grace of York as mother. *Shak. R.* III.

2. To please; to gratify.

Would I had no being,
If this *salute* my blood a jot: it faints me,
To think what follows. *Shakesp. Henry* VIII.

3. To kiss.

SALU'TE. *n. s.* [from the verb.]

1. Salutation; greeting.

The custom of praying for those that sneeze is more ancient than these opinions hereof: so that not any one disease has been the occasion of this *salute* and deprecation. *Brown.*

O, what avails me now that honour high
To have conceiv'd of God, or that *salute*,
Hail highly favour'd, among women blest! *Parad. Reg.*

Continual *salutes* and addresses entertaining him all the way, kept him from saving so great a life, but with one glance of his eye upon the paper, 'till he came to the fatal place where he was stabbed. *South's Sermons.*

I shall not trouble my reader with the first *salutes* of our three friends. *Addison.*

2. A kiss.

There cold *salutes*, but here a lover's kiss. *Roscommon.*

SALU'TER. *n. s.* [from *salute.*] He who salutes.

SALUTI'FEROUS. *adj.* [*salutifer*, Latin.] Healthy; bringing health.

The king commanded him to go to the south of France, believing that nothing would contribute more to the restoring of his former vigour than the gentle *salutiferous* air of Montpelier. *Dennis's Letters.*

SAME. *adj.* [*samo*, Gothick; *sammo*, Swedish.]

1. Not different; not another; identical; being of the like kind, sort, or degree.

Miso, as spitefully as her rotten voice could utter it, set forth the *same* sins of Amphialus. *Sidney.*

The tenor of man's woe
Holds on the *same*. *Milton.*

Th' etherial vigour is in all the *same*,
And ev'ry soul is fill'd with equal flame. *Dryden's Æn.*

If itself had been coloured, it would have transmitted all visible objects tinctured with the *same* colour; as we see whatever is beheld through a coloured glass, appears of the *same* colour with the glass. *Ray on the Creation.*

The merchant does not keep money by him; but if you consider what money must be lodged in the bankers hands, the case will be much the *same*. *Locke.*

The *same* plant produceth as great a variety of juices as there is in the *same* animal. *Arbuthnot on Aliments.*

2. That which was mentioned before.

Do but think how well the *same* he spends,
Who spends his blood his country to relieve. *Daniel.*

SA'MENESS. *n. s.* [from *same.*] Identity; the state of being not another; not different.

Difference of persuasion in matters of religion may easily fall out, where there is the *sameness* of duty, allegiance, and subjection. *King Charles.*

If all courts have a *sameness* in them, things may be as they were in my time, when all employments went to parliamentmens friends. *Swift.*

SA'MLET. *n. s.* [*salmonet*, or *salmonlet.*] A little salmon.

Sir Francis Bacon observes the age of a salmon exceeds not ten years, so his growth is very sudden: after he is got into the sea he becomes from a *samlet*, not so big as a gudgeon, to be a salmon, in as short a time as a gosling becomes a goose. *Walton's Angler.*

SA'MPHIRE. *n. s.* [*saint Pierre*, French; *rithmum*, Latin.] A plant preserved in pickle.

The leaves are thick, succulent, narrow, branchy, and trifid: the flowers grow in an umbel, each consisting of five leaves, which expand in form of a rose: the empalement of the flower becomes a fruit, consisting of two plain and gently streaked leaves. This plant grows in great plenty upon the rocks near the sea-shore, where it is washed by the salt water. It is greatly esteemed for pickling, and is sometimes used in medicine. *Miller.*

Half way down
Hangs one that gathers *samphire*: dreadful trade!
Methinks he seems no bigger than his head. *Shakesp.*

SA'MPLE. *n. s.* [from *example.*] A specimen; a part of the whole shown that judgment may be made of the whole.

He intreated them to tarry but two days, and he himself would bring them a *sample* of the oar. *Raleigh.*

I have not engaged myself to any: I am not loaded with a full cargo: 'tis sufficient if I bring a *sample* of some goods in this voyage. *Dryden.*

I design this but for a *sample* of what I hope more fully to discuss. *Woodward's Natural History.*

Determinations of justice were very summary and decisive, and generally put an end to the vexations of a law-suit by the ruin both of plaintiff and defendant: travellers have recorded some *samples* of this kind. *Addison.*

From most bodies
Some little bits ask leave to flow;
And, as through these canals they roll,
Bring up a *sample* of the whole. *Prior.*

To SA'MPLE. *v. a.* To show something similar. *Ainsworth.*

SA'MPLER. *n. s.* [*exemplar*, Latin; whence it is sometimes written *samplar.*] A pattern of work; a piece worked by young girls for improvement.

O love, why do'st thou in thy beautiful *sampler* set such a work for my desire to set out, which is impossible. *Sidney.*

Fair Philomela, she but lost her tongue,
And in a tedious *sampler* sew'd her mind. *Shak. Tit. Andr.*

We created with our needles both one flower,
Both on one *samplar*, sitting on one cushion;
Both warbling of one song, both in one key,
As if our hands, our sides, voices and minds
Had been incorp'rate. *Shakespeare.*

Coarse complexions,
And cheeks of sorry grain, will serve to ply
The *sampler*, and to teize the housewife's wool. *Milton.*

I saw her sober over a *sampler*, or gay over a jointed baby. *Pope.*

SA'NABLE. *adj.* [*sanabilis*, Latin.] Curable; susceptive of remedy; remediable.

SANA'TION. *n. s.* [*sanatio*, Latin.] The act of curing.

Consider

Consider well the member, and, if you have no probable hope of *sanation*, cut it off quickly. *Wiseman's Surgery.*

SA'NATIVE. *adj.* [from *sano.*] Powerful to cure; healing.

The vapour of coltsfoot hath a *sanative* virtue towards the lungs. *Bacon's Natural History.*

SA'NATIVENESS. *n. s.* [from *sanative.*] Power to cure.

SANCTIFICA'TION. *n. s.* [*sanctification*, Fr. from *sanctifico*, low Latin.]

1. The state of being freed, or act of freeing from the dominion of sin for the time to come.

The grace of his *sanctification* and life, which was first received in him, might pass from him to his whole race, as malediction came from Adam unto all mankind. *Hooker.*

2. The act of making holy; consecration.

The bishop kneels before the cross, and devoutly adores and kisses it: after this follows a long prayer for the *sanctification* of that new sign of the cross. *Stillingfleet.*

SA'NCTIFIER. *n. s.* [from *sanctify.*] He that sanctifies or makes holy.

To be the *sanctifier* of a people, and to be their God, is all one. *Derham's Physico-Theology.*

To SA'NCTIFY. *v. a.* [*sanctifier*, Fr. *sanctifico*, Latin.]

1. To free from the power of sin for the time to come.

For if the blood of bulls, sprinkling the unclean, *sanctifieth* to the purifying of the flesh, how much more shall the blood of Christ? *Heb.* ix. 13.

2. To make holy; to make a means of holiness.

The gospel, by not making many things unclean, as the law did, hath *sanctified* those things generally to all, which particularly each man to himself must *sanctify* by a reverend and holy use. *Hooker.*

Those judgments God hath been pleased to send upon me, are so much the more welcome, as a means which his mercy hath *sanctified* so to me as to make me repent of that unjust act. *King Charles.*

Those external things are neither parts of our devotion, or by any strength in themselves direct causes of it; but the grace of God is pleased to move us by ways suitable to our nature, and to *sanctify* these sensible helps to higher purposes. *South.*

What actions can express the intire purity of thought, which refines and *sanctifies* a virtuous man? *Addison.*

3. To make free from guilt.

The holy man, amaz'd at what he saw,
Made haste to *sanctify* the bliss by law. *Dryden.*

4. To secure from violation.

Truth guards the poet, *sanctifies* the line. *Pope.*

SANCTIMO'NIOUS. *adj.* [from *sanctimonia*, Latin.] Saintly; having the appearance of sanctity.

A *sanctimonious* pretence, under a pomp of form, without the grace of an inward integrity, will not serve the turn. *L'Est.*

SA'NCTIMONY. *n. s.* [*sanctimonia*, Latin.] Holiness; scrupulous austerity; appearance of holiness.

If *sanctimony*, and a frail vow between an errant Barbarian and a supersubtle Venetian, be not too hard for my wit, and all the tribe of hell, thou shalt enjoy her. *Shak. Othello.*

Her pretence is a pilgrimage to St. Jaques le Grand, which holy undertaking, with most austere *sanctimony*, she accomplish'd. *Shakespeare's All's well that ends well.*

There was great reason why all discreet princes should beware of yielding hasty belief to the robes of *sanctimony*. *Ral.*

SA'NCTION. *n. s.* [*sanction*, French; *sanctio*, Latin.]

1. The act of confirmation which gives to any thing its obligatory power; ratification.

I have kill'd a slave,
And of his blood caus'd to be mixt with wine:
Fill every man his bowl. There cannot be
A fitter drink to make this *sanction* in. *Ben. Johns. Catil.*

Against the publick *sanctions* of the peace,
With fates averse, the rout in arms resort,
To force their monarch. *Dryden's Æn.*

There needs no positive law or *sanction* of God to stamp an obliquity upon such a disobedience. *South.*

By the laws of men, enacted by civil power, gratitude is not enforced; that is, not enjoined by the *sanction* of penalties, to be inflicted upon the person that shall not be found grateful. *South's Sermons.*

The satisfactions of the Christian life, in its present practice and future hopes, are not the mere raptures of enthusiasm, as the strictest professors of reason have added the *sanction* of their testimony. *Watts.*

This word is often made the *sanction* of an oath: it is reckoned a great commendation to be a man of honour. *Swift.*

Wanting *sanction* and authority, it is only yet a private work. *Baker on Learning.*

2. A law; a decree ratified. Improper.

'Tis the first *sanction* nature gave to man,
Each other to assist in what they can. *Denham.*

SA'NCTITUDE. *n. s.* [from *sanctus*, Latin.] Holiness; goodness; saintliness.

In their looks divine
The image of their glorious Maker shone,
Truth, wisdom, *sanctitude*, serene and pure. *Milton.*

SA'NCTITY. *n. s.* [*sanctitas*, Latin.]

1. Holiness; the state of being holy.

At his touch,
Such *sanctity* hath heaven given his hand,
They presently amend. *Shakespeare.*

God attributes to place
No *sanctity*, if none be thither brought
By men who there frequent. *Milton.*

2. Goodness; the quality of being good; purity; godliness.

This youth
I reliev'd with such *sanctity* of love,
And to his image, which methought did promise
Most venerable worth, did I devotion. *Shakespeare.*

It was an observation of the ancient Romans, that their empire had not more increased by the strength of their arms than the *sanctity* of their manners. *Addison.*

3. Saint; holy being.

About him all the *sanctities* of heav'n
Stood thick as stars, and from his sight receiv'd
Beatitude past utt'rance. *Milton.*

To SA'NCTUARISE. *v. n.* [from *sanctuary.*] To shelter by means of sacred privileges.

No place indeed should murder *sanctuarise*. *Shakesp.*

SA'NCTUARY. *n. s.* [*sanctuaire*, Fr. *sanctuarium*, Latin.]

1. A holy place; holy ground. Properly the *penetralia*, or most retired and awful part of a temple.

Having waste ground enough,
Shall we desire to raze the *sanctuary*,
And pitch our evils there. *Shakespeare.*

They often plac'd
Within his *sanctuary* itself their shrines. *Milton.*

Let it not be imagined, that they contribute nothing to the happiness of the country who only serve God in the duties of a holy life, who attend his *sanctuary*, and daily address his goodness. *Rogers's Sermons.*

2. A place of protection; a sacred asylum: whence a *sanctuary man*, one who takes shelter in a holy place.

Come, my boy, we will to *sanctuary*. *Shakesp. R.* III.

I'll hence forthwith unto the *sanctuary*,
To save at least the heir of Edward's right. *Shak. H.* VI.

Oft have I heard of *sanctuary* men;
But *sanctuary* children, ne'er 'till now. *Shakes. R.* III.

He fled to Beverly, where he and divers of his company registered themselves *sanctuary* men. *Bacon's Henry* VII.

Howsoever the *sanctuary* man was protected from his creditors, yet his goods out of *sanctuary* should not. *Bacon's H.* VII.

This our high place, our *sanctuary*, our hill. *Milton.*

3. Shelter; protection.

What are the bulls to the frogs, or the lakes to the meadows? Very much, says the frog; for he that's worsted will be sure to take *sanctuary* in the fens. *L'Estrange.*

The admirable works of painting were made fuel for the fire; but some reliques of it took *sanctuary* under ground, and escaped the common destiny. *Dryden's Dufresnoy.*

SAND. *n. s.* [*sand*, Danish and Dutch.]

1. Particles of stone not conjoined, or stone broken to powder.

That finer matter called *sand*, is no other than very small pebbles. *Woodward.*

Here i' th' *sands*
Thee I'll rake up, the post unsanctified. *Shakes. K. Lear.*

Hark, the fatal followers do pursue!
The *sands* are number'd that make up my life:
Here must I stay, and here my life must end. *Shak. H.* VI.

Sand hath always its root in clay, and there be no veins of *sand* any great depth within the earth. *Bacon.*

Calling for more paper to rescribe, king Philip shewed him the difference betwixt the ink box and *sand* box. *Howel.*

If quicksilver be put into a convenient glass vessel, and that vessel exactly stopped, and kept for ten weeks in a *sand* furnace, whose heat may be constant, the corpuscles that constitute the quicksilver will, after innumerable revolutions, be so connected to one another, that they will appear in the form of a red powder. *Boyle.*

Engag'd with money bags, as bold
As men with *sand* bags did of old. *Hudibras.*

The force of water casts gold out from the bowels of mountains, and exposes it among the *sands* of rivers. *Dryden.*

Shells are found in the great *sand* pit at Woolwich. *Woodw.*

Celia and I, the other day,
Walk'd o'er the *sand* hills to the sea. *Prior.*

2. Barren country covered with sands.

Most of his army being slain, he, with a few of his friends, sought to save themselves by flight over the desert *sands*. *Knolles.*

Her sons spread
Beneath Gibraltar to the Lybian *sands*. *Milton.*

SA'NDAL. *n. s.* [*sandale*, Fr. *sandalium*, Latin.] A loose shoe.

Thus sung the uncouth swain to th' oaks and rills,
While the still morn went out with *sandals* grey. *Milton.*

From his robe
Flows light ineffable: his harp, his quiver,
And Lycian bow are gold: with golden *sandals*
His feet are shod. *Prior.*

The

The *sandals* of celestial mold,
Fledg'd with ambrosial plumes, and rich with gold,
Surround her feet. *Pope's Odyssey.*

SA'NDARAK. *n. s.* [*sandaraque*, French; *sandaraca*, Latin.]
1. A mineral of a bright right colour, not much unlike to red arsenick. *Bailey.*
2. A white gum oozing out of the juniper-tree. *Bailey.*

SA'NDBLIND. *adj.* [*sand* and *blind.*] Having a defect in the eyes, by which small particles appear to fly before them.

My true begotten father, being more than *sandblind*, high gravelblind, knows me not. *Shakesp. Merch. of Venice.*

SA'NDBOX *Tree. n. s.* [*hura*, Latin.] A plant.

It hath a funnel-shaped flower, consisting of one leaf, which is spread open at the brim, and slightly cut into twelve parts: at the bottom of the tube is placed the pointal, which afterward becomes a globular compressed fruit, which has twelve cells, in each of which is contained one roundish flat seed. The fruit of this plant, if suffered to remain on 'till they are fully ripe, burst in the heat of the day with a violent explosion, making a noise like the firing of a pistol, and hereby the seeds are thrown about to a considerable distance. These seeds, when green, vomit and purge, and are supposed to be somewhat a-kin to *nux vomica*. *Miller.*

SA'NDED. *adj.* [from *sand.*]
1. Covered with sand; barren.

In well *sanded* lands little or no snow lies. *Mortimer.*

The river pours along
Resistless, roaring dreadful down it comes;
Then o'er the *sanded* valley floating spreads. *Thomson.*

2. Marked with small spots; variegated with dusky specks.

My hounds are bred out of the Spartan kind,
So flew'd, so *sanded*, and their heads are hung
With ears that sweep away the morning dew;
Crook-knee'd and dewlap'd, like Thessalian bulls;
Slow in pursuit; but match'd in mouth like bells,
Each under each. *Shakespeare.*

SA'NDERLING. *n. s.* A bird.

Among the first sort we reckon coots, *sanderlings*, pewets, and mews. *Carew.*

SA'NDERS. *n. s.* [*santalum*, Latin.] A precious kind of Indian wood, of which there are three sorts, red, yellow, and green. *Bailey.*

Aromatize it with *sanders*. *Wiseman's Surgery.*

SA'NDEVER. *n. s.*

That which our English glassmen call *sandever*, and the French, of whom probably the name was borrowed, *suindever*, is that recrement that is made when the materials of glass, namely, sand and a fixt lixiviate alkali, having been first baked together, and kept long in fusion, the mixture casts up the superfluous salt, which the workmen afterwards take off with ladles, and lay by as little worth. *Boyle.*

SA'NDISH. *adj.* [from *sand.*] Approaching to the nature of sand; loose; not close; not compact.

Plant the tenuifolia's and ranunculus's in fresh *sandish* earth, taken from under the turf. *Evelyn's Kalendar.*

SA'NDSTONE. *n. s.* [*sand* and *stone.*] Stone of a loose and friable kind, that easily crumbles into sand.

Grains of gold in *sandstone*, grey, variegated with a faint green and blue, from the mine of Costa Rica, which is not reckoned rich; but every hundred weight yields about an ounce of gold. *Woodward.*

SA'NDY. *adj.* [from *sand.*]
1. Abounding with sand; full of sand.

I should not see the *sandy* hourglass run,
But I should think of shallows and of flats. *Shakespeare.*

Safer shall he be on the *sandy* plains,
Than where castles mounted stand. *Shakesp. H. VI.*

A region so desert, dry, and *sandy*, that travellers are fain to carry water on their camels. *Brown's Vulg. Errours.*

Rough unweildy earth, nor to the plough
Nor to the cattle kind, with *sandy* stones
And gravel o'er-abounding. *Phillips.*

O'er *sandy* wilds were yellow harvests spread. *Pope.*

2. Consisting of sand; unsolid.

Favour, so bottomed upon the *sandy* foundation of personal respects only, cannot be long lived. *Bacon to Villiers.*

SANE. *adj.* [*sanus*, Latin.] Sound; healthy. *Baynard* wrote a poem on preserving the body in a *sane* and sound state.

SANG. The preterite of *sing*.

Then *sang* Moses and Israel this song unto the Lord. *Ex.* xv.

Thee next they *sang*, of all creation first. *Milton.*

SANGUI'FEROUS. *adj.* [*sanguifer*, Latin.] Conveying blood.

The fifth conjugation of the nerves is branched to the muscles of the face, particularly the cheeks, whose *sanguiferous* vessels it twists about. *Derham's Physico-Theology.*

SANGUIFICA'TION. *n. s.* [*sanguification*, Fr. *sanguis* and *facio*, Lat.] The production of blood; the conversion of the chyle into blood.

Since the lungs are the chief instrument of *sanguification*, the animal that has that organ faulty can never have the vital juices, derived from the blood, in a good state. *Arbuthnot.*

Asthmatick persons have voracious appetites, and consequently, for want of a right *sanguification*, are leucophlegmatick. *Arbuthnot on Aliments.*

SA'NGUIFIER. *n. s.* [*sanguis* and *facio*, Latin.] Producer of blood.

Bitters, like choler, are the best *sanguifiers*, and also the best febrifuges. *Floyer on the Humours.*

To SA'NGUIFY. *v. n.* [*sanguis* and *facio*, Latin.] To produce blood.

At the same time I think, I command: in inferior faculties, I walk, see, hear, digest, *sanguify*, and carnify, by the power of an individual soul. *Hale.*

SA'NGUINARY. *adj.* [*sanguinarius*, Lat. *sanguinaire*, French; from *sanguis*, Latin.] Cruel; bloody; murtherous.

We may not propagate religion by wars, or by *sanguinary* persecutions to force consciences. *Bacon.*

The scene is now more *sanguinary*, and fuller of actors: never was such a confused mysterious civil war as this. *Howel.*

Passion transforms us into a kind of savages, and makes us brutal and *sanguinary*. *Broome's Notes on the Odyssey.*

SA'NGUINARY. *n. s.* [*sanguis*, Lat.] An herb. *Ainsworth.*

SA'NGUINE. *adj.* [*sanguin*, Fr. *sanguineus*, from *sanguis*, Lat.]
1. Red; having the colour of blood.

This fellow
Upbraided me about the rose I wear;
Saying, the *sanguine* colour of the leaves
Did represent my master's blushing cheeks. *Shak. H.* VI.

A stream of nect'rous humour issuing flow'd
Sanguine. *Milton.*

Dire Tisiphone there keeps the ward,
Girt in her *sanguine* gown. *Dryden.*

Her flag aloft, spread ruffling to the wind,
And *sanguine* streamers seem the flood to fire:
The weaver, charm'd with what his loom design'd,
Goes on to sea, and knows not to retire. *Dryden.*

2. Abounding with blood more than any other humour; cheerful.

The cholerick fell short of the longevity of the *sanguine*. *Bro.*

Though these faults differ in their complexions as *sanguine* from melancholy, yet they are frequently united. *Gov. of Tongue.*

3. Warm; ardent; confident.

A set of *sanguine* tempers ridicule, in the number of fopperies, all such apprehensions. *Swift.*

SA'NGUINE. *n. s.* [from *sanguis.*] Blood colour.

A griesly wound,
From which forth gush'd a stream of gore, blood thick,
That all her goodly garments stain'd around,
And in deep *sanguine* dy'd the grassy ground. *Fa. Queen.*

SA'NGUINENESS. } *n. s.* [from *sanguine.*] Ardour; heat of ex-
SA'NGUINITY. } pectation; confidence. *Sanguinity* is perhaps only used by *Swift*.

Rage, or phrensy it may be, in some perhaps natural courage, or *sanguineness* of temper in others; but true valour it is not, if it knows not as well to suffer as to do. That mind is truly great, and only that, which stands above the power of all extrinsick violence; which keeps itself a distinct principality, independent upon the outward man. *Decay of Piety.*

I very much distrust your *sanguinity*. *Swift.*

SANGUI'NEOUS. *adj.* [*sanguineus*, Latin; *sanguin*, French.]
1. Constituting blood.

This animal of Plato containeth not only *sanguineous* and reparable particles, but is made up of veins, nerves, and arteries. *Brown's Vulgar Errours.*

2. Abounding with blood.

A plethorick constitution, in which true blood abounds, is called *sanguineous*. *Arbuthnot.*

SA'NHEDRIM. *n. s.* [*synedrium*, Latin.] The chief council among the Jews, consisting of seventy elders, over whom the high priest presided.

SA'NICLE. *n. s.* [*sanicle*, Fr. *sanicula*, Latin.] A plant.

It is an umbelliferous plant, and its flower consists of five leaves, placed orbicularly; but bent back to the centre of the flower, and resting on the empalement, which becomes a fruit composed of two seeds, which are gibbous and prickly on one side, but plain on the other. *Miller.*

SA'NIES. *n. s.* [Latin.] Thin matter; serous excretion.

It began with a round crack in the skin, without other matter than a little *sanies*. *Wiseman's Surgery.*

SA'NIOUS. *adj.* [from *sanies.*] Running a thin serous matter, not a well digested pus.

Observing the ulcer *sanious*, I proposed digestion as the only way to remove the pain. *Wiseman.*

SA'NITY. *n. s.* [*sanitas*, Latin.] Soundness of mind.

How pregnant, sometimes, his replies are?
A happiness that often madness hits on,
Which *sanity* and reason could not be
So prosp'rously delivered of. *Shakesp. Hamlet.*

SANK. The preterite of *sink*.

As if the opening of her mouth to Zelmane had opened some great floodgate of sorrow, whereof her heart could not abide the violent issue, she *sank* to the ground. *Sidney.*

Our men followed them close, took two ships, and gave divers others of their ships their death's wounds, whereof soon after they *sank* and perished. *Bacon's War with Spain.*

SANS. *prep.* [French.] Without. Out of use.
Last scene of all,
That ends this strange eventful history,
Is second childishness and mere oblivion,
Sans teeth, *sans* eyes, *sans* taste, *sans* every thing. *Shakesp.*
For nature so preposterously to err,
Being not deficient, blind, or lame of sense,
Sans witchcraft could not. *Shakesp. Othello.*

SAP. *n. s.* [ſæpe, Saxon; *sap*, Dutch.] The vital juice of plants; the juice that circulates in trees and herbs.
Now sucking of the *sap* of herbs most sweet,
Or of the dew, which yet on them does lie,
Now in the same bathing his tender feet. *Spenser.*
Though now this grained face of mine be hid
In *sap* consuming Winter's drizzled snow,
And all the conduits of my blood froze up,
Yet hath my night of life some memory. *Shakespeare.*
Wound the bark of our fruit-trees,
Lest, being over-proud with *sap* and blood,
With too much riches it confound itself. *Shakesp. R.* II.
His presence had infus'd
Into the plant sciential *sap*. *Milton.*
The *sap* which at the root is bred
In trees, through all the boughs is spread. *Waller.*
Vegetables consist of the same parts with animal substances, spirit, water, salt, oil, earth; all which are contained in the *sap* they derive from the earth. *Arbuthnot.*

To SAP. *v. a.* [*sapper*, French; *zappare*, Italian.] To undermine; to subvert by digging; to mine.
Their dwellings were *sapp'd* by floods,
Their houses fell upon their houshold gods. *Dryden.*

To SAP. *v. n.* To proceed by mine; to proceed invisibly.
For the better security of the troops, both assaults are carried on by *sapping*. *Tatler.*
In vain may heroes fight, and patriots rave,
If secret gold *saps* on from knave to knave. *Pope.*

SA'PPHIRE. *n. s.* [*sapphirus*, Latin: so that it is improperly written *saphyre*.] A precious stone of a blue colour.
Saphire is of a bright blue colour. *Woodward.*
In enroll'd tuffs, flow'rs purfled, blue and white,
Like *saphire*, pearl, in rich embroidery. *Shakespeare.*
He tinctures rubies with their rosy hue,
And on the *saphire* spreads a heavenly blue. *Blackmore.*
That the *saphire* should grow foul, and lose its beauty, when worn by one that is lecherous, and many other fabulous stories of gems, are great arguments that their virtue is equivalent to their value. *Derham.*

SA'PPHIRINE. *adj.* [*sapphirinus*, Latin.] Made of sapphire; resembling sapphire.
She was too *saphirine* and clear for thee;
Clay, flint, and jet now thy fit dwellings be. *Donne.*
A few grains of shell silver, with a convenient proportion of powdered crystal glass, having been kept three hours in fusion, I found the coliquated mass, upon breaking the crucible, of a lovely *saphirine* blue. *Boyle.*

SA'PID. *adj.* [*sapidus*, Latin.] Tasteful; palatable; making a powerful stimulation upon the palate.
Thus camels, to make the water *sapid*, do raise the mud with their feet. *Brown's Vulgar Errours.*
The most oily parts are not separated by a slight decoction, 'till they are disentangled from the salts; for if what remains of the subject, after the infusion and decoction be continued to be boiled down with the addition of fresh water, a fat, *sapid*, odorous, viscous, inflammable, frothy water will constantly be found floating a-top of the boiling liquor. *Arbuthn.*

SAPI'DITY. } *n. s.* [from *sapid.*] Tastefulness; power of stimulating the palate.
SA'PIDNESS. }
As for their taste, if their nutriment be air, neither can it be an instrument thereof; for the body of that element is ingustible, and void of all *sapidity*. *Brown's Vulg. Errours.*
If *sapidness* belong not to the mercurial principle of vegetables and animals, it will scarce be discriminated from their phlegm. *Boyle.*

SA'PIENCE. *n. s.* [*sapience*, Fr. *sapientia*, Latin.] Wisdom; sageness; knowledge.
By *sapience*, I mean what the ancients did by philosophy; the habit or disposition of mind which importeth the love of wisdom. *Grew.*
Ne only they that dwell in lowly dust,
The sons of darkness and of ignorance;
But they whom thou, great Jove, by doom unjust,
Did'st to the top of honour earst advance:
They now, puft up with's deignful insolence,
Despise the brood of blessed *sapience*. *Spenser.*
King James, of immortal memory, among all the lovers and admirers of divine and human *sapience*, accomplished at Theobalds his own days on earth. *Wotton.*
Because enterprises guided by ill counsels have equal success to those by the best judgment conducted, therefore had violence the same external figure with *sapience*. *Raleigh.*
Sapience and love
Immense, and all his father in him shone. *Milton.*
O sov'reign, virtuous, precious of all trees
In Paradise! of operation blest
To *sapience*. *Milton.*
Many a wretch in Bedlam,
Though perhaps among the rout
He wildly flings his filth about,
Still has gratitude and *sapience*
To spare the folks that give him ha'pence. *Swift.*

SA'PIENT. *adj.* [*sapiens*, Latin.] Wise; sage.
There the *sapient* king held dalliance. *Milton.*

SA'PLESS. *adj.* [*saploos*, Dutch.]
1. Wanting sap; wanting vital juice.
Pithless arms, like to a wither'd vine,
That droops his *sapless* branches to the ground. *Shak. H.VI.*
The tree of knowledge, blasted by disputes,
Produces *sapless* leaves instead of fruits. *Denham.*
This single stick was full of sap; but now in vain does art tie that withered bundle of twigs to its *sapless* trunk. *Swift.*
2. Dry; old; husky.
If by this bribe, well plac'd, he would ensnare
Some *sapless* usurer that wants an heir. *Dryden's Juven.*

SA'PLING. *n. s.* [from *sap.*] A young tree; a young plant.
Look how I am bewitch'd; behold, mine arm
Is, like a blasted *sapling*, wither'd up. *Shakesp. R.* III.
Nurse the *saplings* tall, and curl the grove
With ringlets quaint. *Milton.*
A *sapling* pine he wrench'd from out the ground,
The readiest weapon that his fury found. *Dryden.*
What planter will attempt to yoke
A *sapling* with a falling oak? *Swift.*
Slouch turn'd his head, saw his wife's vig'rous hand
Wielding her oaken *sapling* of command. *King's Laura.*

SAPONA'CEOUS. } *adj.* [from *sapo*, Latin, soap.] Sopy; resembling soap; having the qualities of soap.
SA'PONARY. }
By digesting a solution of salt of tartar with oil of almonds, I could reduce them to a soft *saponary* substance. *Boyle.*
Any mixture of an oily substance with salt, may be called a soap: bodies of this nature are called *saponaceous*. *Arbuthnot.*

SA'POR. *n. s.* [Latin.] Taste; power of affecting or stimulating the palate.
There is some *sapor* in all aliments, as being to be distinguished and judged by the gust, which cannot be admitted in air. *Brown's Vulgar Errours.*
The shape of those little particles of matter which distinguish the various *sapors*, odours, and colours of bodies. *Watts.*

SAPORI'FICK. *adj.* [*saporifique*, Fr. *sapor* and *facio*, Latin.] Having the power to produce tastes.

SA'PPINESS. *n. s.* [from *sappy.*] The state or the quality of abounding in sap; succulence; juiciness.

SA'PPY. *adj.* [from *sap.*]
1. Abounding in sap; juicy; succulent.
The *sappy* parts, and next resembling juice,
Were turn'd to moisture for the body's use,
Supplying humours, blood, and nourishment. *Dryden.*
The *sappy* boughs
Attire themselves with blooms, sweet rudiments
Of future harvest. *Phillips.*
The green heat the ripe, and the ripe give fire to the green; to which the bigness of their leaves, and hardness of their stalks, which continue moist and *sappy* long, doth much contribute. *Mortimer.*
2. Young; not firm; weak.
This young prince was brought up among nurses, 'till he arrived to the age of six years: when he had passed this weak and *sappy* age, he was committed to Dr. Cox. *Hayward.*

SA'RABAND. *n. s.* [*sarabande*, Spanish; *sarabande*, French.] A Spanish dance.
The several modifications of this tune-playing quality in a fiddle, to play preludes, *sarabands*, jigs and gavots, are as much real qualities in the instrument as the thought is in the mind of the composer. *Arbuthn. and Pope's Mart. Scribl.*

SA'RCASM. *n. s.* [*sarcasme*, Fr. *sarcasmus*, Latin.] A keen reproach; a taunt; a gibe.
Sarcasms of wit are transmitted in story. *Gov. of the Tongue.*
Rejoice, O young man, says Solomon, in a severe *sarcasm*, in the days of thy youth, and walk in the ways of thy heart; but know that for these things God will bring thee into judgment. *Rogers's Sermons.*
When an angry master says to his servant it is bravely done, it is one way of giving a severe reproach; for the words are spoken by way of *sarcasm*, or irony. *Watts.*

SARCA'STICALLY. *adv.* [from *sarcastick.*] Tauntingly; severely.
He asked a lady playing with a lap-dog, whether the women of that country used to have any children or no; thereby *sarcastically* reproaching them for misplacing that affection upon brutes, which could only become a mother to her child. *South.*

SARCA'STICAL. } *adj.* [from *sarcasm.*] Keen; taunting; severe.
SARCA'STICK. }
What a fierce and *sarcastick* reprehension would this have drawn from the friendship of the world, and yet what a gentle one did it receive from Christ? *South.*

SA'RCENET.

Sa'rcenet. *n. ſ.* [Suppoſed by *Skinner* to be *ſericum ſaracenicum*, Latin.] Fine thin woven ſilk.

Why art thou then exaſperate, thou idle immaterial ſkein of ſley'd ſilk, thou green *ſarcenet* flap for a ſore eye, thou taſſel of a prodigal's purſe? *Shakeſp. Troilus and Creſſida.*

If they be covered, though but with linnen or *ſarcenet*, it intercepts the effluvium. *Brown's Vulgar Errours.*

These are they that cannot bear the heat
Of figur'd ſilks and under *ſarcenets* ſweat. *Dryd. Juven.*

She darts from *ſarcenet* ambuſh wily leers,
Twitches thy ſleeve, or with familiar airs
Her fan will pat the cheek; theſe ſnares diſdain. *Gay.*

To Sa'rcle. *v. a.* [*ſarcler*, French; *ſarculo*, Latin.] To weed corn. *Ainſworth.*

Sarcoce'le. *n. ſ.* [σὰρξ and κήλη; *ſarcocele*, Fr.] A fleſhy excreſcence of the teſticles, which ſometimes grow ſo large as to ſtretch the ſcrotum much beyond its natural ſize. *Quincy.*

Sarco'ma. *n. ſ.* [σάρκωμα.] A fleſhy excreſcence, or lump, growing in any part of the body, eſpecially the noſtrils. *Bailey.*

Sarco'phagous. *adj.* [σὰρξ and φάγω.] Fleſh-eating; feeding on fleſh.

Sarco'phagy. *n. ſ.* [σὰρξ and φάγω.] The practice of eating fleſh.

There was no *ſarcophagy* before the flood; and, without the eating of fleſh, our fathers preſerved themſelves unto longer lives than their poſterity. *Brown's Vulg. Errours.*

Sarco'tick. *n. ſ.* [from σὰρξ; *ſarcotique*, Fr.] Medicines which fill up ulcers with new fleſh; the ſame as incarnatives.

By this means the humour was moderately repreſſed, and breathed forth; the eſcar alſo ſeparated in the fontanel: after which the ulcer incarned with common *ſarcoticks*, and the ulcerations about it were cured by ointment of tuty, and ſuch like epuloticks. *Wiſeman on Inflammations.*

Sarcula'tion. *n. ſ.* [*ſarculus*, Latin.] The act of weeding; plucking up weeds. *Dict.*

Sa'rdel.
Sa'rdine *Stone.* } *n. ſ.* A ſort of precious ſtone.
Sa'rdius.

He that ſat was to look upon, like a jaſper and a *ſardine ſtone.* *Rev.* iv. 3.

Thou ſhalt ſet in it four rows of ſtones: the firſt row ſhall be a *ſardius.* *Ex.* xxviii. 17.

Sa'rdonyx. *n. ſ.* A precious ſtone.

The onyx is an accidental variety of the agat kind: 'tis of a dark horny colour, in which is a plate of a bluiſh white, and ſometimes of red: when on one or both ſides the white there happens to lie alſo a plate of a reddiſh colour, the jewellers call the ſtone a *ſardonyx.* *Woodward.*

Sark. *n. ſ.* [ſcyrk, Saxon.]

1. A ſhark or ſhirk. *Bailey.*
2. In Scotland it denotes a ſhirt.

Flaunting beaus gang with their breaſts open, and their *ſarks* over their waiſtcoats. *Arbuthn. Hiſt. of John Bull.*

Sarn. *n. ſ.* A Britiſh word for pavement, or ſtepping ſtones, ſtill uſed in the ſame ſenſe in Berkſhire and Hampſhire.

Sa'rplier. *n. ſ.* [*ſarpilliere*, French.] A piece of canvas for wrapping up wares; a packing cloth. *Bailey.*

Sa'rrasine. *n. ſ.* [In botany.] A kind of birthwort. *Bailey.*

Sa'rsa.
Sarsapare'lla. } *n. ſ.* Both a tree and a plant. *Ainſworth.*

Sarse. *n. ſ.* A ſort of fine lawn ſieve. *Bailey.*

To Sarse. *v. a.* [*ſaſſer*, French.] To ſift through a ſarſe or ſearſe. *Bailey.*

Sart. *n. ſ.* [In agriculture.] A piece of woodland turned into arable. *Bailey.*

Sash. *n. ſ.* [Of this word the etymologiſts give no account: I ſuppoſe it comes from *ſcache*, of *ſçavoir*, to know, a *ſaſh* worn being a mark of diſtinction; and a *ſaſh* window being made particularly for the ſake of ſeeing and being ſeen.]

1. A belt worn by way of diſtinction; a ſilken band worn by officers in the army.
2. A window ſo formed as to be let up and down by pullies.

She ventures now to lift the *ſaſh*;
The window is her proper ſphere. *Swift.*

As for the poem he writ on your *ſaſh*,
My ſiſter tranſcrib'd it laſt night. *Swift.*

She broke a pane in the *ſaſh* window that looked into the yard. *Swift.*

Sa'shoon. *n. ſ.* A kind of leather ſtuffing put into a boot for the wearer's eaſe. *Ainſworth.*

Sa'ssafras. *n. ſ.* A tree: one of the ſpecies of the cornelian cherry. The wood is medicinal.

Sat. The preterite of *ſit.*

The picture of fair Venus, that
For which, men ſay, the goddeſs *ſat*,
Was loſt, 'till Lely from your look
Again that glorious image took. *Waller.*

I anſwered not the rehearſal, becauſe I knew the author *ſat* to himſelf when he drew the picture, and was the very Bays of his own farce. *Dryden.*

SA'TAN. *n. ſ.* [שׂטן. *Satanas*, Latin.] The prince of hell; the devil; any wicked ſpirit.

I beheld *Satan* as lightning fall from heaven. *Lu.* x. 18.

They are much increaſed by the falſe ſuggeſtions of *Satan.* *Sanderſon's Judgment in one View.*

The deſpiteful act
Of *Satan* done in Paradiſe. *Milton.*

Sata'nical.
Sata'nick. } *adj.* [from *Satan.*] Deviliſh; infernal.

The faint *ſatanick* hoſt
Defenſive ſcarce. *Milton.*

Sa'tchel. *n. ſ.* [*ſeckel*, German; *ſacculus*, Latin.] A little bag: commonly a bag uſed by ſchoolboys to carry their books.

The whining ſchoolboy with his *ſatchel*,
And ſhining morning face, creeping like ſnail
Unwillingly to ſchool. *Shak. As you like it.*

Schoolboys lag with *ſatchels* in their hands. *Swift.*

To Sate. *v. a.* [*ſatio*, Latin.] To ſatiate; to glut; to pall; to feed beyond natural deſires.

Sated at length, ere long I might perceive
Strange alteration in me. *Milton's Paradiſe Loſt.*

How will their bodies ſtript
Enrich the victors, while the vultures *ſate*
Their maws with full repaſt. *Phillips.*

Thy uſeleſs ſtrength, miſtaken king, employ,
Sated with rage, and ignorant of joy. *Prior.*

Sate'llite. *n. ſ.* [*ſatelles*, Lat. *ſatellite*, Fr. This word is commonly pronounced in proſe with the *e* mute in the plural, as in the ſingular, and is therefore only of three ſyllables; but *Pope* has in the plural continued the Latin form, and aſſigned it four; I think, improperly.] A ſmall planet revolving round a larger.

Four moons move about Jupiter, and five about Saturn, called their *ſatellites.* *Locke.*

The ſmalleſt planets are ſituated neareſt the ſun and each other; whereas Jupiter and Saturn, that are vaſtly greater, and have many *ſatellites* about them, are wiſely removed to the extreme regions of the ſyſtem. *Bentley.*

Aſk of yonder argent fields above,
Why Jove's *ſatellites* are leſs than Jove? *Pope.*

Satelli'tious. *adj.* [from *ſatelles*, Lat.] Conſiſting of ſatellites.

Their ſolidity and opacity, and their *ſatellitious* attendance, their revolutions about the ſun, and their rotations about their axis, are exactly the ſame. *Cheyne's Phil. Princ.*

To SA'TIATE. *v. a.* [*ſatio*, Latin.]

1. To ſatisfy; to fill.

Thoſe ſmells are the moſt grateful where the degree of heat is ſmall, or the ſtrength of the ſmell allayed; for theſe rather woo the ſenſe than *ſatiate* it. *Bacon.*

Buying of land is the reſult of a full and *ſatiated* gain; and men in trade ſeldom think of laying out their money upon land, 'till their profit has brought them in more than their trade can well employ. *Locke.*

The looſen'd winds
Hurl'd high above the clouds; 'till all their force
Conſum'd, her rav'nous jaws th' earth *ſatiate* clos'd. *Phillips.*

2. To glut; to pall; to fill beyond natural deſire.

They *ſatiate* and ſoon fill,
Though pleaſant. *Milton.*

Whatever novelty preſents, children are preſently eager to have a taſte, and are as ſoon *ſatiated* with it. *Locke.*

He may be *ſatiated*, but not ſatiſfy'd. *Norris.*

3. To gratify deſire.

I may yet ſurvive the malice of my enemies, although they ſhould be *ſatiated* with my blood. *King Charles.*

4. To ſaturate; to impregnate with as much as can be contained or imbibed.

Why does not ſalt of tartar draw more water out of the air, than in a certain proportion to its quantity, but for want of an attractive force after it is *ſatiated* with water? *Newton.*

Sa'tiate. *adj.* [from the verb.] Glutted; full to ſatiety. When it has *with*, it ſeems a participle; when *of*, an adjective.

Our generals, retir'd to their eſtates,
In life's cool evening, *ſatiate of* applauſe,
Nor think of bleeding ev'n in Brunſwick's cauſe. *Pope.*

Now may'rs and ſhrieves all huſh'd and *ſatiate* lay,
Yet eat, in dreams, the cuſtard of the day. *Pope's Dunc.*

Sati'ety. *n. ſ.* [*ſatietas*, Latin; *ſatieté*, Fr.] Fulneſs beyond deſire or pleaſure; more than enough; weariſomeneſs of plenty; ſtate of being palled or glutted.

He leaves a ſhallow plaſh to plunge him in the deep,
And with *ſatiety* ſeeks to quench his thirſt. *Shakeſpeare.*

Nothing more jealous than a favourite, eſpecially towards the waining time and ſuſpect of *ſatiety.* *Wotton.*

In all pleaſures there is *ſatiety*; and after they be uſed, their verdure departeth. *Hakewill.*

They ſatiate and ſoon fill,
Though pleaſant; but thy words, with grace divine
Imbu'd, bring to their ſweetneſs no *ſatiety.* *Milton.*

No action, the uſefulneſs of which has made it the matter of duty, but a man may bear the continual purſuit of, without loathing or *ſatiety.* *South.*

The joy unequal'd, if its end it gain,
Without *ſatiety*, though e'er ſo bleſt,
And but more reliſh'd as the more diſtreſs'd. *Pope.*

Sa'tin. *n. ſ.* [*ſatin*, French; *drapo di ſetan*, Italian; *ſattin*, Dutch.] A ſoft cloſe and ſhining ſilk.

Such a glittering ſhew it bare, and ſo bravely it was held up from the head: upon her body ſhe wore a doublet of ſky-colour *ſatin*, covered with plates of gold, and as it were nailed with precious ſtones, that in it ſhe might ſeem armed. *Sidney.*

The ladies dreſs'd in rich ſymars were ſeen,
Of Florence *ſatin*, flower'd with white and green,
And for a ſhade betwixt the bloomy gridelin. *Dryden.*

Her petticoat, transform'd apace,
Became black *ſatin* flounc'd with lace. *Swift.*

Lay the child carefully in a caſe, covered with a mantle of blue *ſatin*. *Arbuthn. and Pope.*

SA'TIRE. *n. ſ.* [*ſatira*, anciently *ſatura*, Lat. not from *ſatyrus*, a ſatyr; *ſatire*, Fr.] A poem in which wickedneſs or folly is cenſured. Proper *ſatire* is diſtinguiſhed, by the generality of the reflections, from a *lampoon* which is aimed againſt a particular perſon; but they are too frequently confounded.

He dares to ſing thy praiſes in a clime
Where vice triumphs, and virtue is a crime;
Where ev'n to draw the picture of thy mind,
Is *ſatyr* on the moſt of human kind. *Dryden.*

SATI'RICAL. } *adj.* [*ſatiricus*, Latin; *ſatirique*, French; from
SATI'RICK. } *ſatire.*]

1. Belonging to ſatire; employed in writing of invective.

You muſt not think, that a *ſatyrick* ſtyle
Allows of ſcandalous and brutiſh words. *Roſcommon.*

What human kind deſires, and what they ſhun,
Rage, paſſions, pleaſures, impotence of will,
Shall this *ſatirical* collection fill. *Dryden's Juvenal.*

2. Cenſorious; ſevere in language.

Slanders, ſir; for the *ſatirical* ſlave ſays here, that old men have grey beards; that their faces are wrinkled. *Shak. Hamlet.*

He that hath a *ſatirical* vein, as he maketh others afraid of his wit, ſo he had need be afraid of others memory. *Bacon.*

On me when dunces are *ſatirick*,
I take it for a panegyrick. *Swift.*

SATI'RICALLY. *adv.* [from *ſatirical.*] With invective; with intention to cenſure or viliſy.

He applies them *ſatirically* to ſome cuſtoms, and kinds of philoſophy, which he arraigns. *Dryden.*

SA'TIRIST. *n. ſ.* [from *ſatire.*] One who writes ſatires.

Wycherly, in his writings, is the ſharpeſt *ſatyriſt* of his time; but, in his nature, he has all the ſoftneſs of the tendereſt diſpoſitions: in his writings he is ſevere, bold, undertaking; in his nature gentle, modeſt, inoffenſive. *Granville.*

All vain pretenders have been conſtantly the topicks of the moſt candid *ſatyriſts*, from the Codrus of Juvenal to the Damon of Boileau. *Letter to the Publiſher of the Dunciad.*

Yet ſoft his nature, though ſevere his lay;
His anger moral, and his wiſdom gay:
Bleſt *ſatyriſt!* who touch'd the mean ſo true,
As ſhow'd vice had his hate and pity too. *Pope.*

To SA'TIRIZE. *v. a.* [*ſatirizer*, Fr. from *ſatire.*] To cenſure as in a ſatire.

Covetouſneſs is deſcribed as a veil caſt over the true meaning of the poet, which was to *ſatirize* his prodigality and voluptuouſneſs. *Dryden.*

Should a writer ſingle out and point his raillery at particular perſons, or *ſatirize* the miſerable, he might be ſure of pleaſing a great part of his readers; but muſt be a very ill man if he could pleaſe himſelf. *Addiſon.*

I inſiſt that my lion's mouth be not defiled with ſcandal; for I would not make uſe of him to revile the human ſpecies, and *ſatirize* his betters. *Addiſon's Spectator.*

It is as hard to *ſatirize* well a man of diſtinguiſhed vices, as to praiſe well a man of diſtinguiſhed virtues. *Swift.*

SATISFA'CTION. *n. ſ.* [*ſatisfactio*, Latin; *ſatisfaction*, French.]

1. The act of pleaſing to the full.

The mind, having a power to ſuſpend the execution and *ſatisfaction* of any of its deſires, is at liberty to conſider the objects of them. *Locke.*

2. The ſtate of being pleaſed.

'Tis a wretched *ſatisfaction* a revengeful man takes, even in loſing his life, provided his enemy go for company. *L'Eſtr.*

There are very few diſcourſes ſo ſhort, clear, and conſiſtent, to which moſt men may not, with *ſatisfaction* enough to themſelves, raiſe a doubt. *Locke.*

3. Releaſe from ſuſpenſe, uncertainty, or uneaſineſs.

Wilt thou leave me ſo unſatisfied?
—What *ſatisfaction* can you have? *Shakeſpeare.*

4. Gratification; that which pleaſes.

Run over the circle of earthly pleaſures, and had not God ſecured a man a ſolid pleaſure from his own actions, he would be forced to complain that pleaſure was not *ſatisfaction.* *South.*

Of ev'ry nation each illuſtrious name,
Such toys as theſe have cheated into fame;
Exchanging ſolid quiet to obtain
The windy *ſatisfaction* of the brain. *Dryden's Juvenal.*

5. Amends; atonement for a crime; recompenſe for an injury.

Die he or juſtice muſt; unleſs for him
Some other able, and as willing, pay
The rigid *ſatisfaction*, death for death. *Milt. Par. Loſt.*

SATISFA'CTIVE. *adj.* [*ſatisfactus*, Lat.] Giving ſatisfaction.

By a final and *ſatisfactive* diſcernment of faith, we lay the laſt effects upon the firſt cauſe of all things. *Brown's Vulg. Err.*

SATISFA'CTORILY. *adj.* [from *ſatisfactory.*] To ſatisfaction.

Bellonius hath been more *ſatisfactorily* experimental, not only affirming that chameleons feed on flies, but upon exenteration he found theſe animals in their bellies. *Brown's V. Er.*

They ſtrain their memory to anſwer him *ſatisfactorily* unto all his demands. *Digby.*

SATISFA'CTORINESS. *n. ſ.* [from *ſatisfactory.*] Power of ſatiſfying; power of giving content.

The incompleatneſs of the ſeraphick lover's happineſs, in his fruitions, proceeds not from their want of *ſatisfactorineſs*, but his want of an intire poſſeſſion of them. *Boyle.*

SATISFA'CTORY. *adj.* [*ſatisfactoire*, Fr. *ſatisfactus*, Latin.]

1. Giving ſatisfaction; giving content.

An intelligent American would ſcarce take it for a *ſatisfactory* account, if, deſiring to learn our architecture, he ſhould be told that a pillar was a thing ſupported by a baſis. *Locke.*

2. Atoning; making amends.

A moſt wiſe and ſufficient means of redemption and ſalvation, by the *ſatisfactory* and meritorious death and obedience of the incarnate ſon of God, Jeſus Chriſt. *Sanderſon.*

To SA'TISFY. *v. a.* [*ſatisfaire*, Fr. *ſatisfacio*, Latin.]

1. To content; to pleaſe to ſuch a degree as that nothing more is deſired.

A good man ſhall be *ſatisfied* from himſelf. *Prov.* xiv. 14.

Will he ſatisfy his rigour,
Satisfy'd never? *Milton.*

2. To feed to the fill.

Who hath cauſed it to rain on the earth, to *ſatisfy* the deſolate and waſte ground, and to cauſe the bud of the tender tree to ſpring forth? *Job* xxxviii. 27.

I will purſue and divide the ſpoil: my luſt ſhall be *ſatisfied* upon them. *Ex.* xv. 9.

The righteous eateth to the *ſatisfying* of his ſoul. *Prov.* xiii.

3. To recompenſe; to pay to content.

He is well paid that is well *ſatisfied*;
And I, delivering you, am *ſatisfied*,
And therein do account myſelf well paid. *Shakeſpeare.*

4. To free from doubt, perplexity, or ſuſpenſe.

Of many things uſeful and curious you may *ſatisfy* yourſelves in Leonardo de Vinci. *Dryden.*

When come to the utmoſt extremity of body, what can there put a ſtop and *ſatisfy* the mind that it is at the end of ſpace, when it is *ſatisfied* that body itſelf can move into it? *Locke.*

This I would willingly be *ſatisfied* in, whether the ſoul, when it thinks thus, ſeparate from the body, acts leſs rationally than when conjointly with it? *Locke.*

5. To convince.

He declares himſelf *ſatisfied* to the contrary, in which he has given up the cauſe. *Dryden.*

The ſtanding evidences of the truth of the Goſpel, are in themſelves moſt firm, ſolid, and *ſatisfying.* *Atterbury.*

To SA'TISFY. *v. n.* To make payment.

By the quantity of ſilver they give or take, they eſtimate the value of other things, and *ſatisfy* for them: thus ſilver becomes the meaſure of commerce. *Locke.*

SA'TURABLE. *adj.* [from *ſaturate.*] Impregnable with any thing 'till it will receive no more.

Be the figures of the ſalts never ſo various, yet if the atoms of water were fluid, they would always ſo conform to thoſe figures as to fill up all vacuities; and conſequently the water would be *ſaturable* with the ſame quantity of any ſalt, which it is not. *Grew's Coſmol. Sac.*

SA'TURANT. *adj.* [from *ſaturans*, Lat.] Impregnating to the fill.

To SA'TURATE. *v. a.* [*ſaturo*, Latin.] To impregnate 'till no more can be received or imbibed.

Rain-water is plentifully *ſaturated* with terreſtrial matter, and more or leſs ſtored with it. *Woodward.*

His body has been fully *ſaturated* with the fluid of light, to be able to laſt ſo many years without any ſenſible diminution, though there are conſtant emanations thereof. *Cheyne.*

Still night ſucceeds
A ſoften'd ſhade, and *ſaturated* earth
Awaits the morning beam. *Thomſon.*

SA'TURDAY. *n. ſ.* [ſæterſdæg, or ſæternſdæg, Saxon, according to *Verſtegan*, from ſæter, a Saxon idol; more probably from *Saturn*, *dies Saturni.*] The laſt day of the week.

This matter I handled fully in laſt *Saturday's* Spectator. *Add.*

SATU'RITY. *n. ſ.* [*ſaturitas*, from *ſaturo*, Latin.] Fulneſs; the ſtate of being ſaturated; repletion.

SA'TURN. *n. ſ.* [*ſaturne*, French; *ſaturnus*, Latin.]

1. The remoteſt planet of the ſolar ſyſtem: ſuppoſed by aſtrologers to impreſs melancholy, dulneſs, or ſeverity of temper.

The ſmalleſt planets are placed neareſt the ſun and each other; whereas Jupiter and *Saturn*, that are vaſtly greater, are wiſely removed to the extreme regions. *Bentley.*

From the far bounds
Of utmoſt *Saturn*, wheeling wide his round. *Thomſon.*

2. [In

2. [In chimeſtry.] Lead.

SA'TURNINE. *adj.* [*ſaturninus*, Lat. *ſaturnien*, Fr. from *Saturn.*] Not light; not volatile; gloomy; grave; melancholy; ſevere of temper: ſuppoſed to be born under the dominion of Saturn.

I may caſt my readers under two diviſions, the mercurial and *ſaturnine*: the firſt are the gay part, the others are of a more ſober and ſolemn turn. *Addiſon.*

SATU'RNIAN. *adj.* [*ſaturnius*, Latin.] Happy; golden: uſed by poets for times of felicity, ſuch as are feigned to have been in the reign of *Saturn.*

Th' Auguſtus, born to bring *Saturnian* times. *Pope.*

SA'TYR. *n. ſ.* [*ſatyrus*, Latin.] A ſylvan god: ſuppoſed among the ancients to be rude and lecherous.

Satyrs, as Pliny teſtifies, were found in times paſt in the eaſtern mountains of India. *Peacham on Drawing.*

SA'TYRIASIS. *n. ſ.* [from *ſatyr.*]

If the chyle be very plentiful it breeds a *ſatyriaſis*, or an abundance of ſeminal lympha's. *Floyer on the Humours.*

SA'VAGE. *adj.* [*ſauvage*, French; *ſelvaggio*, Italian.]

1. Wild; uncultivated.

These godlike virtues wherefore do'ſt thou hide,
Affecting private life, or more obſcure
In *ſavage* wilderneſs? *Milton.*

Cornels, and *ſavage* berries of the wood,
And roots and herbs, have been my meagre food. *Dryden.*

2. Untamed; cruel.

Chain me to ſome ſteepy mountain's top,
Where roaring bears and *ſavage* lions roam. *Shakeſpeare.*

Tyrants no more their *ſavage* nature kept,
And foes to virtue wonder'd how they wept. *Pope.*

3. Uncivilized; barbarous; untaught.

Hence with your little ones:
To fright you thus, methinks, I am too *ſavage*;
To do worſe to you, were fell cruelty. *Shakeſ. Macbeth.*

Thus people lived altogether a *ſavage* life, 'till Saturn, arriving on thoſe coaſts, deviſed laws to govern them by. *Raleigh.*

The *ſavage* clamour drown'd
Both harp and voice. *Milton.*

A herd of wild beaſts on the mountains, or a *ſavage* drove of men in caves, might be ſo diſordered; but never a peculiar people. *Spratt's Sermons.*

SA'VAGE. *n. ſ.* [from the adjective.] A man untaught and uncivilized; a barbarian.

Long after theſe times were they but *ſavages*. *Raleigh.*

The ſeditious lived by rapine and ruin of all the country, omitting nothing of that which *ſavages*, enraged in the height of their unruly behaviour, do commit. *Hayward.*

To deprive us of metals is to make us mere *ſavages*; to change our corn for the old Arcadian diet, our houſes and cities for dens and caves, and our clothing for ſkins of beaſts: 'tis to bereave us of all arts and ſciences, nay, of revealed religion. *Bentley.*

To SA'VAGE. *v. a.* [from the noun.] To make barbarous, wild, or cruel. A word not well authoriſed.

Friends, relations, love himſelf,
Savag'd by woe, forget the tender tie. *Thomſon.*

SA'VAGELY. *adv.* [from *ſavage.*] Barbarouſly; cruelly.

Your caſtle is ſurpris'd, your wife and babes
Savagely ſlaughter'd. *Shakeſp. Macbeth.*

SA'VAGENESS. *n. ſ.* [from *ſavage.*] Barbarouſneſs; cruelty; wildneſs.

A *ſavageneſs* in unreclaimed blood
Of general aſſault. *Shakeſp. Hamlet.*

Wolves and bears, they ſay,
Caſting their *ſavageneſs* aſide, have done
Like offices of pity. *Shakeſ. Winter's Tale.*

The Cyclops were a people of Sicily, remarkable for *ſavageneſs* and cruelty. *Broome's Notes on the Odyſſey.*

SA'VAGERY. *n. ſ.* [from *ſavage.*]

1. Cruelty; barbarity.

This is the bloodieſt ſhame,
The wildeſt *ſavag'ry*, the vileſt ſtroke,
That ever wall-ey'd wrath, or ſtaring rage,
Preſented to the tears of ſoft remorſe. *Shak. King John.*

2. Wild growth.

Her fallow lees
The darnel, hemlock, and rank fumitory,
Doth root upon; while that the culter ruſts,
That ſhould deracinate ſuch *ſavagery*. *Shakeſp. H. V.*

SA'VANNA. *n. ſ.* [Spaniſh, according to *Bailey.*] An open meadow without wood; paſture ground in America.

He that rides poſt through a country may tell how, in general, the parts lie; here a moraſs, and there a river; woodland in one part, and *ſavanna's* in another. *Locke.*

Plains immenſe,
And vaſt *ſavanna's*, where the wand'ring eye,
Unfix'd, is in a verdant ocean loſt. *Thomſon's Summer.*

SAUCE. *n. ſ.* [*ſauce*, *ſaulſe*, French; *ſalſa*, Italian.]

1. Something eaten with food to improve its taſte.

The bitter *ſauce* of the ſport was, that we had our honours for ever loſt, partly by our own faults, but principally by his faulty uſing of our faults. *Sidney.*

To feed were beſt at home;
From thence the *ſauce* to meat is ceremony;
Meeting were bare without it. *Shakeſp. Macbeth.*

Epicurean cooks
Sharpen with cloyleſs *ſauce* his appetite. *Shakeſpeare.*

Such was the *ſauce* of Moab's noble feaſt,
'Till night far ſpent invites them to their reſt. *Cowley.*

He that ſpends his time in ſports, is like him whoſe meat is nothing but *ſauces*; they are healthleſs, chargeable, and uſeleſs. *Taylor.*

High *ſauces* and rich ſpices are fetched from the Indies. *Baker.*

2. *To ſerve one the ſame* SAUCE. A vulgar phraſe to retaliate one injury with another.

To SAUCE. *v. a.* [from the noun.]

1. To accompany meat with ſomething of higher reliſh.

2. To gratify with rich taſtes. Obſolete.

Earth yield me roots;
Who ſeeks for better of thee, *ſauce* his palate
With thy moſt operant poiſon. *Shakeſpeare.*

3. To intermix or accompany with any thing good, or, ironically, with any thing bad.

Then fell ſhe to *ſauce* her deſires with threatnings, ſo that we were in a great perplexity, reſtrained to ſo unworthy a bondage, and yet reſtrained by love, which I cannot tell how, in noble minds, by a certain duty, claims an anſwering. *Sidney.*

All the delights of love, wherein wanton youth walloweth, be but folly mixed with bitterneſs, and ſorrow *ſauced* with repentance. *Spenſer.*

Thou ſay'ſt his meat was *ſauc'd* with thy upbraidings;
Unquiet meals make ill digeſtions. *Shakeſpeare.*

SA'UCEBOX. *n. ſ.* [from *ſauce*, or rather from *ſaucy.*] An impertinent or petulant fellow.

The fooliſh old poet ſays, that the ſouls of ſome women are made of ſea-water: this has encouraged my *ſaucebox* to be witty upon me. *Addiſon's Spectator.*

SA'UCEPAN. *n. ſ.* [*ſauce* and *pan.*] A ſmall ſkillet with a long handle, in which ſauce or ſmall things are boiled.

Your maſter will not allow you a ſilver *ſaucepan*. *Swift.*

SAU'CER. *n. ſ.* [*ſauciere*, Fr. from *ſauce.*]

1. A ſmall pan or platter in which ſauce is ſet on the table.

Infuſe a pugil of new violets ſeven times, and it ſhall make the vinegar ſo freſh of the flower, as, if brought in a *ſaucer*, you ſhall ſmell it before it come at you. *Bacon.*

Some have miſtaken blocks and poſts
For ſpectres, apparitions, ghoſts,
With *ſaucer* eyes and horns. *Hudibras.*

2. A piece or platter of china, into which a tea-cup is ſet.

SA'UCILY. *adv.* [from *ſaucy.*] Impudently; impertinently; petulantly; in a ſaucy manner.

Though this knave came ſomewhat *ſaucily* into the world before he was ſent for, yet was his mother fair. *Shakeſp.*

A freed ſervant, who had much power with Claudius, very *ſaucily*, had almoſt all the words; and amongſt other things, he aſked in ſcorn one of the examinates, who was likewiſe a freed ſervant of Scribonianus, I pray, ſir, if Scribonianus had been emperor, what would you have done? He anſwered, I would have ſtood behind his chair, and held my peace. *Bacon.*

A trumpet behaved himſelf very *ſaucily*. *Addiſon.*

SAU'CINESS. *n. ſ.* [from *ſaucy.*] Impudence; petulance; impertinence; contempt of ſuperiours.

With how ſweet ſaws ſhe blam'd their *ſaucineſs*,
To feel the panting heart, which through her ſide
Did beat their hands. *Sidney.*

By his authority he remains here, which he thinks is a patent for his *ſaucineſs*. *Shakeſp. All's well that ends well.*

Being intercepted in your ſport,
Great reaſon that my noble lord be rated
For *ſaucineſs*. *Shak. Titus Andronicus.*

It is *ſaucineſs* in a creature, in this caſe, to reply. *Bramh.*

Imputing it to the natural *ſaucineſs* of a pedant, they made him eat his words. *L'Eſtrange.*

You *ſaucineſs*, mind your pruning-knife, or I may uſe it for you. *Dryden's Don Sebaſtian.*

This might make all other ſervants challenge the ſame liberty, and grow pert upon their maſters; and when this *ſaucineſs* became univerſal, what leſs miſchief could be expected than an old Scythian rebellion? *Collier on Pride.*

SAUCISSE. *n. ſ.* [French.] In gunnery, a long train of powder ſewed up in a roll of pitched cloth, about two inches diameter, in order to fire a bombcheſt. *Bailey.*

SAUCISSON. *n. ſ.* [French.] In military architecture, faggots or faſcines made of large boughs of trees bound together. They are commonly uſed to cover men, to make epaulments, traverſes, or breaſtworks in ditches full of water, to render the way firm for carriages. *Bailey.*

SAU'CY. *adj.* [I know not how this word can be eaſily deduced from *ſauce*: it may come more properly from *ſalſus*, Latin.] Pert; petulant; contemptuous of ſuperiours; inſolent; impudent; impertinent.

You are more *ſaucy* with lords than the heraldry of your birth and virtue gives you commiſſion. *Shakeſpeare.*

Study is like the heav'ns glorious sun,
That will not be deep search'd with *saucy* looks;
Small have continual plodders ever won,
Save base authority from others' books. *Shakespeare.*

And if thou hast the mettle of a king,
Being wrong'd as we are by this peevish town,
Turn thou the mouth of thy artillery,
As we will ours against these *saucy* walls. *Shakesp. K. John.*

Power's first pedigree from force derives,
And calls to mind the old prerogatives
Of free-born man; and with a *saucy* eye
Searches the heart and soul of majesty. *Denham's Sophy.*

I lose my patience, when with *saucy* pride
By untun'd ears I hear his numbers try'd. *Roscommon.*

No *saucy* citizen shall dare
To strike a soldier, nor, when struck, resent
The wrong. *Dryden's Juvenal.*

Homer, to express a man both timorous and *saucy*, makes use of a kind of point, namely, that he had the eyes of a dog, but the heart of a deer. *Addison's Spectator.*

To SAVE. *v. a.* [*sauver*, *saulver*, French; *salvo*, Latin.]

1. To preserve from danger or destruction.

Let me die ere men can say God *save* the queen. *Shakesp.*

One shall cry, yet cannot he answer, nor *save* him out of his trouble. *Is.* xlvi. 7.

A wond'rous ark,
To *save* himself and houshold from amidst
A world devote to universal wreck. *Milton.*

We may be confident whatever he does is intended for our good, and whatever we interpret otherwise we can get nothing by repining, nor *save* any thing by resisting. *Temple.*

The circling streams, once thought but pools of blood,
From dark oblivion Harvey's name shall *save*. *Dryden.*

2. To preserve finally from eternal death.

Whatsoever we read in Scripture concerning the endless love and *saving* mercy which God sheweth towards his church, the only proper subject thereof is this church. *Hooker.*

There are some that will be *saved*, and some that will be damned. *Shakespeare.*

We are not of them who draw back unto perdition; but of them that believe, to the *saving* of the soul. *Heb.* x. 39.

His merits *save* them. *Milton.*

He who feareth God, and worketh righteousness, and perseveres in the faith and duties of our religion, shall certainly be *saved*. *Rogers.*

3. Not to spend; to hinder from being spent.

With your cost you terminate the cause,
And *save* th' expence of long litigious laws,
Where suits are travers'd, and so little won,
That he who conquers is but last undone. *Dryden.*

4. To reserve or lay by.

He shall not feel quietness, he shall not *save* of that which he desired. *Job* xx. 20.

5. To spare; to excuse.

Will you not speak to *save* a lady's blush? *Dryden.*

Our author *saves* me the comparison with tragedy. *Dryd.*

These sinews are not so much unstrung,
To fail me when my master should be serv'd;
And when they are, then will I steal to death,
Silent and unobserv'd, to *save* his tears. *Dryd. Don Sebast.*

6. To salve; to reconcile.

How build, unbuild, contrive
To *save* appearances; how gird the sphere
With centrick and eccentrick. *Milton's Parad. Lost.*

7. To take or embrace opportunely, so as not to lose.

The same persons, who were chief confidents to Cromwell, foreseeing a restoration, seized the castles in Ireland, just *saving* the tide, and putting in a stock of merit sufficient. *Swift.*

To SAVE. *v. n.* To be cheap.

Brass ordnance *saveth* in the quantity of the material, and in the charge of mounting and carriage. *Bacon's Phys. Rem.*

SAVE. *adv.* [This word, adverbially used, is, like *except*, originally the imperative of the verb.] Except; not including.

But being all defeated, *save* a few,
Rather than fly, or be captiv'd, herself she slew. *Fa. Qu.*

All the conspirators, *save* only he,
Did that they did in envy of great Cæsar. *Shakesp.*

He never put down a near servant, *save* only Stanley, the lord chamberlain. *Bacon's Henry* VII.

How have I then with whom to hold converse,
Save with the creatures which I made? *Milton.*

SA'VEALL. *n. s.* [*save* and *all.*] A small pan inserted into a candlestick to save the ends of candles.

SA'VER. *n. s.* [from *save.*]

1. Preserver; rescuer.

They were manifoldly acknowledged the *savers* of that country. *Sidney.*

2. One who escapes loss, though without gain.

Laws of arms permit each injur'd man
To make himself a *saver* where he can. *Dryden.*

Who dares affirm this is no pious age,
When charity begins to tread the stage?
When actors, who at best are hardly *savers*,
Will give a night of benefit to weavers? *Swift.*

3. A good husband.

4. One who lays up and grows rich.

By nature far from profusion, and yet a greater sparer than a *saver*; for though he had such means to accumulate, yet his garrisons and his feastings soaked his exchequer. *Wotton.*

SA'VIN. *n. s.* [*sabina*, Latin; *savin*, *sabin*, Fr.] A tree.

It hath compact, rigid, and prickly ever-green leaves: the fruit is small, spherical, and warted; and the whole plant has a very rank strong smell. The species are three, and commonly cultivated for medicinal use. *Miller.*

SA'VING. *adj.* [from *save.*]

1. Frugal; parcimonious; not lavish.

She loved money; for she was *saving*, and applied her fortune to pay John's clamorous debts. *Arbuthn. Hist. of J. Bull.*

Be *saving* of your candle. *Swift.*

2. Not turning to loss, though not gainful.

Silvio, finding his application unsuccessful, was resolved to make a *saving* bargain; and since he could not get the widow's estate, to recover what he had laid out of his own. *Addison.*

SA'VING. *adv.* [This is nothing more than a participle of the verb *save* adverbially used.] With exception in favour of.

All this world's glory seemeth vain,
And all their shows but shadows, *saving* she. *Spenser.*

Such laws cannot be abrogated, *saving* only by whom they were made; because the intent of them being known unto none but the author, he alone can judge how long it is requisite they should endure. *Hooker.*

Saving the reverence due to so great a man, I doubt not but they did all creep out of their holes. *Ray on the Creation.*

SA'VING. *n. s.* [from *save.*]

1. Escape of expence; somewhat preserved from being spent.

It is a great *saving* in all such lights, if they can be made as fair and right as others, and yet last longer. *Bacon.*

By reducing interest to four *per cent.* there was a considerable *saving* to the nation; but this year they give six. *Addison.*

2. Exception in favour.

Contend not with those that are too strong for us, but still with a *saving* to honesty; for integrity must be supported against all violence. *L'Estrange.*

SA'VINGLY. *adv.* [from *saving.*] With parcimony.

SA'VINGNESS. *n. s.* [from *saving.*]

1. Parcimony; frugality.

2. Tendency to promote eternal salvation.

SA'VIOUR. *n. s.* [*sauveur*, Latin.] Redeemer; he that has saved mankind from eternal death.

So judg'd he man, both judge and *Saviour* sent. *Milton.*

However consonant to reason his precepts appeared, nothing could have tempted men to acknowledge him as their God and *Saviour*, but their being firmly persuaded of the miracles he wrought. *Addison.*

To SA'UNTER. *v. n.* [*aller à la sainte terre*, from idle people who roved about the country, and asked charity under pretence of going *à la sainte terre*, to the holy land; or *sans terre*, as having no settled home.] To wander about idly; to loiter; to linger.

The cormorant is still *sauntering* by the sea-side, to see if he can find any of his brass cast up. *L'Estrange.*

Tell me, why *saunt'ring* thus from place to place
I meet thee? *Dryden's Juvenal.*

Though putting the mind upon an unusual stress that may discourage, ought to be avoided; yet this must not run it into a lazy *sauntering* about ordinary things. *Locke.*

Yourself look after him, to cure his *sauntering* at his business. *Locke.*

If men were weaned from their *sauntering* humour, wherein they let a good part of their lives run uselesly away, they would acquire skill in hundreds of things. *Locke.*

So the young 'squire, when first he comes
From country school to Will's or Tom's,
Without one notion of his own,
He *saunters* wildly up and down. *Prior.*

The brainless stripling
Spells uncouth Latin, and pretends to Greek;
A *saunt'ring* tribe! such born to wide estates,
With yea and no in senates hold debates. *Tickel.*

Here *saunt'ring* 'prentices o'er Otway weep. *Gay.*

Led by my hand, he *saunter'd* Europe round,
And gather'd ev'ry vice. *Dunciad.*

SA'VORY. *n. s.* [*savorée*, French; *satureia*, Latin.] A plant.

It is of the verticillate kind, with a labiated flower, whose upper lip or crest is divided into two parts; but the lower lip or beard is divided into three parts, the middle part being crenated: these flowers are produced from the wings of the leaves in a loose order, and not in whorles or spikes, as are most of this tribe of plants. *Miller.*

SA'VOUR. *n. s.* [*saveur*, French.]

1. A scent; odour.

What *savour* is better, if physick be true,
For places infected, than wormwood and rue? *Tusser.*

Benzo calls its smell a tartarous and hellish *savour.* *Abbot.*

Turn then my freſheſt reputation to
A *ſavour* that may ſtrike the dulleſt noſtril? *Shakeſpeare.*

I ſmell ſweet *ſavours*, and I feel ſoft things. *Shakeſp.*

That Jews ſtink naturally, that is, that there is in their race an evil *ſavour*, is a received opinion we know not how to admit. *Brown's Vulgar Errours.*

Truffles, which have an excellent oil, and a volatile ſalt of a grateful *ſavour*, are heating. *Arbuthnot on Diet.*

2. Taſte; power of affecting the palate.

I taſte
The *ſavour* of death from all things. *Milton.*

A directer influence from the ſun gives fruit a better *ſavour* and a greater worth. *South.*

To SA'VOUR. *v. n.* [*ſavourer*, Fr. from the noun.]

1. To have any particular ſmell or taſte.

2. To betoken; to have an appearance or taſte of ſomething.

This ripping of anceſtors is very pleaſing, and *ſavoureth* of good conceit and ſome reading. *Spenſer on Ireland.*

The duke's anſwers to his appeachments are very diligently and civilly couched; and though his heart was big, yet they all *ſavour* of an humble ſpirit. *Wotton.*

If 'twere a ſecret that concern'd my life,
This boldneſs might become thee;
But ſuch unneceſſary rudeneſs *ſavours*
Of ſome deſign. *Denham's Sophy.*

I have rejected every thing that *ſavours* of party. *Addiſon.*

To SA'VOUR. *v. a.*

1. To like.

Wiſdom and goodneſs to the vile ſeem vile;
Filths *ſavour* but themſelves. *Shakeſpeare.*

2. To exhibit taſte of.

Thou *ſavoureſt* not the things that be of God. *Goſpel.*

That *ſavours* only of rancour and pride. *Milton.*

SA'VOURILY. *adv.* [from *ſavoury.*]

1. With guſt; with appetite.

The collation he fell to very *ſavourily*. *L'Eſtrange's Fables.*

This mufti is ſome Engliſh renegado, he talks ſo *ſavourily* of toaping. *Dryd. Don Sebaſtian.*

2. With a pleaſing reliſh.

There's a dearth of wit in this dull town,
When ſilly plays ſo *ſavourily* go down. *Dryden.*

SA'VOURINESS. *n. ſ.* [from *ſavoury.*]

1. Taſte pleaſing and picquant.

2. Pleaſing ſmell.

SA'VOURY. *adj.* [*ſavoureux*, Fr. from *ſavour.*]

1. Pleaſing to the ſmell.

The pleaſant *ſavoury* ſmell
So quicken'd appetite, that I
Could not but taſte! *Milton's Paradiſe Loſt.*

From the boughs a *ſavoury* odour blown,
Grateful to appetite! more pleas'd my ſenſe
Than ſmell of ſweeteſt fennel, or the teats
Of ewe, or goat, dropping with milk at ev'n. *Milton.*

2. Picquant to the taſte.

Savoury meat, ſuch as my father loveth. *Gen.*

The *ſavoury* pulp they chew. *Milton.*

SAVO'Y. *n. ſ.* [*braſſica ſubaudica*, Latin.] A ſort of colwort.

SA'USAGE. *n. ſ.* [*ſauciſſe*, French; *ſalſum*, Latin.] A roll or ball made commonly of pork or veal, and ſometimes of beef, minced very ſmall, with ſalt and ſpice; ſometimes it is ſtuffed into the guts of fowls, and ſometimes only rolled in flower.

SAW. The preterite of *ſee.*

I never *ſaw* 'till now
Sight more deteſtable. *Milton.*

SAW. *n. ſ.* [*ſawe*, Daniſh; ꞅaga, or ꞅige, Saxon; *ſcie*, Fr.]

1. A dentated inſtrument, by the attrition of which wood or metal is cut.

The teeth are filed to an angle, pointing towards the end of the *ſaw*, and not towards the handle of the *ſaw*, or ſtraight between the handle and end; becauſe the *ſaw* is deſigned to act only in its progreſs forwards, a man having in that more ſtrength than he can have in drawing back his *ſaw*, and therefore when he draws it back, he bears it lightly off the unſawn ſtuff, which enables him the longer to continue his ſeveral progreſſions of the *ſaw*. *Moxon's Mech. Exer.*

The roach is a leather-mouth'd fiſh, and has *ſaw* like teeth in his throat. *Walton's Angler.*

Then *ſaws* were tooth'd, and ſounding axes made. *Dryd.*

If they cannot cut,
His *ſaws* are toothleſs, and his hatchets lead. *Pope.*

2. [Saga, Sax. *ſaeghe*, Dut.] A ſaying; a ſentence; a proverb.

Good king, that muſt approve the common *ſaw*:
Thou out of heaven's benediction com'ſt
To the warm ſun! *Shakeſpeare's King Lear.*

From the table of my memory
I'll wipe away all *ſaws* of books. *Shakeſ. Hamlet.*

His weapons, holy *ſaws* of ſacred writ;
His ſtudy in his tilt-yard. *Shakeſ. Henry VI.*

Strict age and ſour ſeverity,
With their grave *ſaws* in ſlumber lie. *Milton.*

To SAW. part. *ſawed* and *ſawn.* [*ſcier*, French; from the noun.]
To cut timber or other matter with a ſaw.

They were ſtoned, they were *ſawn* aſunder. *Heb.* xi. 37.

A carpenter, after he hath *ſawn* down a tree, and wrought it handſomely, ſets it in a wall. *Wiſd.* xiii. 11.

It is an incaleſcency, from a ſwift motion, ſuch as that of running, threſhing, or *ſawing*. *Ray on the Creation.*

If I cut my finger, I ſhall as certainly feel pain as if my ſoul was co-extended with the limb, and had a piece of it *ſawn* through. *Collier.*

Maſter-workmen, when they direct any of their underlings to *ſaw* a piece of ſtuff, have ſeveral phraſes for the *ſawing* of it: they ſeldom ſay, *ſaw* the piece of ſtuff; but, draw the ſaw through it; give the piece of ſtuff a kerf. *Moxon.*

It is the carpenters work to hew the timber, *ſaw* it out, and frame it. *Mortimer.*

SA'WDUST. *n. ſ.* [*ſaw* and *duſt.*] Duſt made by the attrition of the ſaw.

If the membrane be fouled by the *ſawduſt* of the bone, wipe it off with a ſponge. *Wiſeman's Surgery.*

Rotten *ſawduſt*, mixed with earth, enriches it very much. *Mortimer's Husbandry.*

SA'WFISH. *n. ſ.* [*ſaw* and *fiſh.*] A ſort of fiſh. *Ainſw.*

SA'WPIT. *n. ſ.* [*ſaw* and *pit.*] Pit over which timber is laid to be ſawn by two men.

Let them from forth a *ſawpit* ruſh at once
With ſome diffuſed ſong. *Shakeſp. Merry Wives of Windſ.*

They colour it by laying it in a *ſawpit* that hath oak ſawduſt therein. *Mortimer's Husbandry.*

SAW-WORT. *n. ſ.* [*ſerratula*, Latin.] A plant.

It hath a floſculous flower, conſiſting of ſeveral florets divided into many parts, reſting on the embryo, and contained in a ſcaly empalement, like the greater centaury, from which this differs in having ſmaller heads, and from the knapweed in having the borders of the leaves cut into ſmall ſharp ſegments, reſembling the teeth of a ſaw. *Miller.*

SAW-WREST. *n. ſ.* [*ſaw* and *wreſt.*] A ſort of tool.

With the *ſaw-wreſt* they ſet the teeth of the ſaw; that is, they put one of the notches of the wreſt between the firſt two teeth on the blade of the ſaw, and then turn the handle horizontally a little about upon the notch towards the end of the ſaw; and that at once turns the firſt tooth ſomewhat towards you, and the ſecond tooth from you. *Moxon's Mech. Exer.*

SA'WER. } *n. ſ.* [*ſcieur*, French; from *ſaw.*] One whoſe trade
SA'WYER. } is to ſaw timber into boards or beams.

The pit-ſaw is uſed by joiners, when what they have to do may be as ſoon done at home as ſend it to the *ſawyers*. *Moxon.*

SA'XIFRAGE. *n. ſ.* [*ſaxifrage*, Fr. *ſaxifraga*, Lat.] A plant.

The flower conſiſts of ſeveral leaves placed orbicularly, which expand in form of a roſe, out of whoſe multifid flower-cup riſes the pointal, which commonly ends in two horns, and afterward turns, together with the flower-cup, into a roundiſh fruit, which has likewiſe two horns and two cells, which are full of ſmall ſeeds. *Miller.*

Saxifrage, quaſi ſaxum frangere, to break the ſtone, is applicable to any thing having this property; but is a term moſt commonly given to a plant, from an opinion of its medicinal virtues to this effect. *Quincy.*

SA'XIFRAGE *Meadow. n. ſ.* [*ſilanum*, Latin.] A plant.

It hath a roſe and umbellated flower, conſiſting of ſeveral leaves placed circularly, and reſting upon the empalement, which afterward becomes a fruit compoſed of two ſhort channelled ſeeds.

SA'XIFRAGOUS. *adj.* [*ſaxum* and *frago*, Latin.] Diſſolvent of the ſtone.

Becauſe goat's blood was found an excellent medicine for the ſtone, it might be conceived to be able to break a diamond; and ſo it came to be ordered that the goats ſhould be fed on *ſaxifragous* herbs, and ſuch as are conceived of power to break the ſtone. *Brown's Vulgar Errours.*

To SAY. *v. a.* preter. *ſaid.* [ꞅecgan, Saxon; *ſeggen*, Dutch.]

1. To ſpeak; to utter in words; to tell.

Say it out, Diggon, for whatever it hight;
For nought but well mought him betight,
He is ſo meek. *Spenſer.*

In this ſlumbry agitation what have you heard her *ſay*? *Shak.*

Speak unto Solomon; for he will not *ſay* thee nay. 1 *Kings.*

2. To allege.

After all can be *ſaid* againſt a thing, this will ſtill be true, that many things poſſibly are, which we know not of. *Tillotſ.*

In vain ſhall we attempt to juſtify ourſelves, as the rich young man in the goſpel did, by appealing to the great duties of the law; unleſs we can *ſay* ſomewhat more, even that we have been liberal in our diſtributions to the poor. *Atterbury.*

3. To tell in any manner.

With flying ſpeed, and ſeeming great pretence,
Came meſſenger with letters which his meſſage *ſaid*. *F. Qu.*

To SAY. *v. n.*

1. To ſpeak; to pronounce; to utter.

He *ſaid* moreover, I have ſomewhat to *ſay* unto thee; and ſhe *ſaid*, *ſay* on. 1 *Kings* ii. 14.

Say nothing to any man, but go thy way. *Mar.* i. 44.

To the others he *ſaid*, go ye after him. *Ezek.* ix. 5.

The council-table and ſtar-chamber hold, as Thucydides *ſaid* of the Athenians, for honourable that which pleaſed, and for juſt that which profited. *Clarendon.*

The

The lion here has taken his right meaſures, that is to *ſay*, he has made a true judgment. *L'Eſtrange.*

He has left his ſucceſſion as undetermined as if he had *ſaid* nothing about it. *Locke.*

This ought to weigh with thoſe whoſe reading is deſigned for much talk and little knowledge, and I have nothing to *ſay* to it. *Locke.*

Of ſome propoſitions it may be difficult to *ſay* whether they affirm or deny; as when we *ſay*, Plato was no fool. *Watts.*

2. In poetry, *ſay* is often uſed before a queſtion; tell.

Say firſt what cauſe
Mov'd our grand parents to fall off? *Milton.*

Say, Stella, feel you no content,
Reflecting on a life well-ſpent. *Swift.*

SAY. *n. ſ.* [from the verb.]

1. A ſpeech; what one has to ſay.

He no ſooner ſaid out his *ſay*, but up riſes a cunning ſnap. *L'Eſtrange.*

2. [For *eſſay.*] Sample.

Since thy outſide looks ſo fair and warlike,
And that thy tongue ſome '*ſay* of breeding breathes,
By rule of knighthood I diſdain. *Shakeſpeare.*

So good a *ſay* invites the eye,
A little downward to eſpy
The lively cluſters of her breaſts. *Sidney.*

3. Trial by a ſample.

This gentleman having brought that earth to the publick '*ſay* maſters, and upon their being unable to bring it to fuſion, or make it fly away, he had procured a little of it, and with a peculiar flux ſeparated a third part of pure gold. *Boyle.*

4. [*Soie*, French.] Silk. Obſolete.

5. A kind of woollen ſtuff.

SA'YING. *n. ſ.* [from *ſay.*] Expreſſion; words; opinion ſententiouſly delivered.

I thank thee, Brutus,
That thou haſt prov'd Lucilius' *ſaying* true. *Shakeſpeare.*

Moſes fled at this *ſaying*, and was a ſtranger in Median. *Acts.*

Many are the *ſayings* of the wiſe,
Extolling patience as the trueſt fortitude. *Milton.*

Others try to divert the troubles of other men by pretty and plauſible *ſayings*, ſuch as this, that if evils are long, they are but light. *Tillotſon's Sermons.*

We poetick folks, who muſt reſtrain
Our meaſur'd *ſayings* in an equal chain,
Have troubles utterly unknown to thoſe,
Who let their fancy looſe in rambling proſe. *Prior.*

The ſacred function can never be hurt by their *ſayings*, if not firſt reproached by our doings. *Atterbury.*

SCAB. *n. ſ.* [ſcæb, Saxon; *ſcabbia*, Italian; *ſchabbe*, Dutch; *ſcabies*, Latin.]

1. An incruſtation formed over a ſore by dried matter.

What's the matter, you diſſentious rogues,
That rubbing the poor itch of your opinion,
Make yourſelves *ſcabs?* *Shakeſp. Coriolanus.*

That free from gouts thou may'ſt preſerve thy care,
And clear from *ſcabs*, produc'd by freezing air. *Dryden.*

2. The itch or mange of horſes.

3. A paltry fellow, ſo named from the itch often incident to negligent poverty.

I would thou did'ſt itch from head to foot, and I had the ſcratching of thee, I would make thee the loathſom'ſt *ſcab* in Greece. *Shak. Troilus and Creſſida.*

Well ſaid, wart, thou art a good *ſcab:* there is a teſter for thee. *Shakeſp. Henry IV.*

One of the uſurers, a head man of the city, took it in dudgeon to be ranked, cheek by joul, with a *ſcab* of a currier. *L'Eſtrange.*

This vap'ring *ſcab* muſt needs deviſe
To ape the thunder of the ſkies. *Swift.*

SCA'BBARD. *n. ſ.* [*ſchap*, German. *Junius.*] The ſheath of a ſword.

Enter fortune's gate,
Nor in thy *ſcabbard* ſheath that famous blade,
'Till ſettled be thy kingdom and eſtate. *Fairfax.*

What eyes! how keen their glances! you do well to keep 'em veil'd: they are too ſharp to be truſted out o' th' *ſcabbard.* *Dryden's Spaniſh Fryar.*

SCA'BBED. *adj.* [from *ſcab.*]

1. Covered or diſeaſed with ſcabs.

The briar fruit makes thoſe that eat them *ſcabbed.* *Bacon.*

2. Paltry; ſorry.

To you ſuch *ſcabb'd* harſh fruit is giv'n, as raw
Young ſoldiers at their exerciſings gnaw. *Dryden.*

SCA'BBEDNESS. *n. ſ.* [from *ſcabbed.*] The ſtate of being ſcabbed.

SCA'BBINESS. *n. ſ.* [from *ſcabby.*] The quality of being ſcabby.

SCA'BBY. *adj.* [from *ſcab.*] Diſeaſed with ſcabs.

Her writhled ſkin, as rough as mapple rind,
So *ſcabby* was, that would have loath'd all womankind. *F. Q.*

A *ſcabby* tetter on their pelts will ſtick,
When the raw rain has pierc'd them to the quick. *Dryden.*

If the grazier ſhould bring me one wether, fat and well fleeced, and expect the ſame price for a whole hundred, without giving me ſecurity to reſtore my money for thoſe that were lean, ſhorn, or *ſcabby*, I would be none of his cuſtomer. *Swift.*

SCA'BIOUS. *adj.* [*ſcabioſus*, Latin.] Itchy; leprous.

In the Spring *ſcabious* eruptions upon the ſkin were epidemical, from the acidity of the blood. *Arbuthnot on Air.*

SCA'BIOUS. *n. ſ.* [*ſcabieuſe*, Fr. *ſcabioſa*, Latin.] A plant.

It hath a floſculous flower, conſiſting of many unequal florets, contained in a common empalement: ſome of theſe, which occupy the middle, are cut into four or five ſegments; the reſt, which are placed at the edge, are bilabiated: each of theſe ſits on the top of the embryo, which is crowned, and is contained in a proper empalement, which afterward becomes a capſule, either ſimple or funnel-ſhaped, pregnant with a ſeed crowned, which before was the embryo. *Miller.*

SCA'BROUS. *adj.* [*ſcabreux*, Fr. *ſcaber*, Latin.]

1. Rough; rugged; pointed on the ſurface.

Urine, black and bloody, is occaſioned by ſomething ſharp or *ſcabrous* wounding the ſmall blood-veſſels: if the ſtone is ſmooth and well bedded, this may not happen. *Arbuthnot.*

2. Harſh; unmuſical.

Lucretius is *ſcabrous* and rough in theſe: he ſeeks them, as ſome do Chauceriſms with us, which were better expunged. *Ben. Johnſon's Diſcoveries.*

SCA'BROUSNESS. *n. ſ.* [from *ſcabrous.*] Roughneſs; ruggedneſs.

SCA'BWORT. *n. ſ.* A plant. *Ainſworth.*

SCAD. *n. ſ.* A kind of fiſh. Probably the ſame with *ſhad.*

Of round fiſh there are ſprat, barn, ſmelts, and *ſcad.* *Carew.*

SCA'FFOLD. *n. ſ.* [*eſchafaut*, French; *ſchavot*, Dutch, from *ſchawen*, to ſhow.]

1. A temporary gallery or ſtage raiſed either for ſhows or ſpectators.

Pardon
The flat unraiſed ſpirit, that hath dar'd
On this unworthy *ſcaffold* to bring forth
So great an object. *Shakeſ. Henry V.*

The throng
On banks and *ſcaffolds* under ſky might ſtand. *Milton.*

2. The gallery raiſed for execution of great malefactors.

Fortune ſmiling at her fortune therein, that a *ſcaffold* of execution ſhould grow a *ſcaffold* of coronation. *Sidney.*

3. Frames of timber erected on the ſide of a building for the workmen.

Theſe outward beauties are but the props and *ſcaffolds*
On which we built our love, which, now made perfect,
Stands without thoſe ſupports. *Denham's Sophy.*

Sylla added three hundred commons to the ſenate; then aboliſhed the office of tribune, as being only a *ſcaffold* to tyranny, whereof he had no further uſe. *Swift.*

To SCA'FFOLD. *v. a.* [from the noun.] To furniſh with frames of timber.

SCA'FFOLDAGE. *n. ſ.* [from *ſcaffold.*] Gallery; hollow floor.

A ſtrutting player doth think it rich
To hear the wooden dialogue and ſound,
'Twixt his ſtretch'd footing and the *ſcaffoldage.* *Shakeſp.*

SCA'FFOLDING. *n. ſ.* [from *ſcaffold.*]

1. Temporary frames or ſtages.

What are riches, empire, power,
But ſteps by which we climb to riſe and reach
Our wiſh; and, that obtain'd, down with the *ſcaffolding*
Of ſceptres and of thrones. *Congreve.*

Sickneſs, contributing no leſs than old age to the ſhaking down this *ſcaffolding* of the body, may diſcover the inward ſtructure. *Pope.*

2. Building ſlightly erected.

Send forth your lab'ring thought;
Let it return with empty notions fraught,
Of airy columns every moment broke,
Of circling whirlpools, and of ſpheres of ſmoke:
Yet this ſolution but once more affords
New change of terms and *ſcaffolding* of words. *Prior.*

SCALA'DE. } *n. ſ.* [French; *ſcalada*, Spaniſh, from *ſcala*, Latin,
SCALA'DO. } a ladder.] A ſtorm given to a place by raiſing ladders againſt the walls.

What can be more ſtrange than that we ſhould within two months have won one town of importance by *ſcalado*, battered and aſſaulted another, and overthrown great forces in the field? *Bacon.*

Thou raiſedſt thy voice to record the ſtratagems, the arduous exploits, and the nocturnal *ſcalade* of needy heroes, the terror of your peaceful citizens. *Arbuthn. Hiſt. of J. Bull.*

SCA'LARY. *adj.* [from *ſcala*, Latin.] Proceeding by ſteps like thoſe of a ladder.

He made at nearer diſtances certain elevated places and *ſcalary* aſcents, that they might better aſcend or mount their horſes. *Brown's Vulgar Errours.*

To SCALD. *v. a.* [*ſcaldare*, Italian; *calidus*, Latin.] To burn with hot liquor.

I am *ſcalded* with my violent motion,
And ſpleen of ſpeed to ſee you. *Shak. King John.*

O majeſty!

O majesty!
When thou do'st pinch thy bearer, thou do'st sit
Like a rich armour worn in heat of day,
That *scalds* with safety. *Shakesp. Henry* IV.
Thou art a soul in bliss; but I am bound
Upon a wheel of fire, that mine own tears
Do *scald* like molten lead. *Shakesp. King Lear.*
Here the blue flames of *scalding* brimstone fall,
Involving swiftly in one ruin all. *Cowley.*
Scalding tears wore a channel where they fell. *Dryden.*
That I grieve, 'tis true;
But 'tis a grief of fury, not despair!
And if a manly drop or two fall down,
It *scalds* along my cheeks, like the greenwood,
That, sputt'ring in the flame, works outward into tears.
Dryden's Cleomenes.

It depends not on his will to persuade himself, that what actually *scalds* him, feels cold. *Locke.*

Has he any other wound about him, except the accidental *scaldings* of his wort? *Addison.*

Warm cataplasms discuss; but *scalding* hot may confirm the tumour: heat, in general, doth not resolve and attenuate the juices of a human body; for too great heat will produce concretions. *Arbuthnot on Aliments.*

The best thing we can do is to *scald* him;
For which operation there's nothing more proper
Than the liquor he deals in, his own melted copper. *Swift.*

2. A provincial phrase in husbandry.

In Oxfordshire the four land they fallow when the sun is pretty high, which they call a *scalding* fallow. *Mortimer.*

SCALD. *n. s.* [from the verb.] Scurff on the head.
Her head, altogether bald,
Was overgrown with scurff and filthy *scald.* *Spenser.*

SCALD. *adj.* Paltry; sorry.
Saucy lictors
Will catch at us like strumpets, and *scald* rhymers
Ballad us out o' tune. *Shakespeare.*

SCA'LDHEAD. *n. s.* [*skalladur*, bald, Islandick. *Hickes.*] A loathsome disease; a kind of local leprosy in which the head is covered with a continuous scab.

The serum is corrupted by the infection of the touch of a salt humour, to which the scab, pox, and *scaldhead* are referable. *Floyer.*

SCALE. *n. s.* [ſcale, Saxon; *schael*, Dutch; *skal*, Islandick.]

1. A balance; a vessel suspended by a beam against another vessel.

If thou tak'st more
Or less than just a pound, if the *scale* turn
But in the estimation of a hair,
Thou diest. *Shak. Merchant of Venice.*
Your vows to her and me, put in two *scales*,
Will even weigh, and both as light as tales. *Shakespeare.*

Here's an equivocator, that could swear, in both the *scales*, against either *scale*; who committed treason enough for God's sake, yet could not equivocate to heaven. *Shakesp. Macbeth.*

Long time in even *scale*
The battle hung. *Milton's Parad. Lost*, *b.* vi.
The world's *scales* are even; what the main
In one place gets, another quits again. *Cleaveland.*
The *scales* are turn'd, her kindness weighs no more
Now than my vows. *Waller.*
In full assemblies let the crowd prevail;
I weigh no merit by the common *scale*,
The conscience is the test. *Dryden.*

If we consider the dignity of an intelligent being, and put that in the *scales* against brute inanimate matter, we may affirm, without overvaluing human nature, that the soul of one virtuous and religious man is of greater worth and excellency than the sun and his planets. *Bentley's Sermons.*

2. The sign Libra in the Zodiack.

Juno pours out the urn, and Vulcan claims
The *scales*, as the just product of his flames. *Creech.*

3. [*Escaille*, French; *squama*, Latin.] The small shells or crusts which lying one over another make the coats of fishes.

He puts him on a coat of mail,
Which was made of a fish's *scale.* *Drayton.*
Standing aloof, with lead they bruise the *scales*,
And tear the flesh of the incensed whales. *Waller.*

4. Any thing exfoliated or desquamated; a thin lamina.

Take jet and the *scales* of iron, and with a wet feather, when the smith hath taken an heat, take up the *scales* that fly from the iron, and those *scales* you shall grind upon your painter's stone. *Peacham.*

When a *scale* of bone is taken out of a wound, burning retards the separation. *Sharp's Surgery.*

5. [*Scala*, a ladder, Latin.] Ladder; means of ascent.

Love refines
The thoughts, and heart enlarges; hath his seat
In reason, and is judicious; is the *scale*
By which to heav'nly love thou may'st ascend. *Milton.*

On the bendings of these mountains the marks of several ancient *scales* of stairs may be seen, by which they used to ascend them. *Addison on Italy.*

6. The act of storming by ladders.

Others to a city strong
Lay siege, encamp'd; by batt'ry, *scale*, and mine
Assaulting. *Milt. Parad. Lost.*

7. Regular gradation; a regular series rising like a ladder.

Well hast thou the *scale* of nature set,
From centre to circumference; whereon
In contemplation of created things,
By steps we may ascend to God. *Milt. Par. Lost.*

The *scale* of the creatures is a matter of high speculation. *Grew.*

The higher nature still advances, and preserves his superiority in the *scale* of being. *Addison.*

All the integral parts of nature have a beautiful analogy to one another, and to their mighty original, whose images are more or less expressive, according to their several gradations in the *scale* of beings. *Cheyne's Phil. Princ.*

We believe an invisible world, and a *scale* of spiritual beings all nobler than ourselves. *Bentley's Sermons.*

Far as creation's ample range extends,
The *scale* of sensual mental pow'rs ascends. *Pope.*
In contemplation's *scale* I'll soar,
And be enraptur'd more and more;
Whilst thus new matter of surprise
In each gradation shall arise. *Macbean.*

8. A figure subdivided by lines like the steps of a ladder, which is used to measure proportions between pictures and the thing represented.

The map of London was set out in the year 1658 by Mr. Newcourt, drawn by a *scale* of yards. *Graunt.*

9. The series of harmonick or musical proportions.

The bent of his thoughts and reasonings run up and down this *scale*, that no people can be happy but under good governments. *Temple.*

10. Any thing marked at equal distances.

They take the flow o' th' Nile
By certain *scale* i' th' pyramid: they know
By th' height, the lowness, or the mean, if dearth
Or foizon follow. *Shak. Ant. and Cleopatra.*

To SCALE. *v. a.* [*scalare*, Italian.]

1. To climb as by ladders.

Often have I *scal'd* the craggy oak,
All to dislodge the raven of her nest:
How have I wearied, with many a stroke,
The stately walnut-tree, the while the rest
Under the tree fell all for nuts at strife! *Spenser.*

Upon the ceasing of the great artillery they assailed the breach, and others with their scaling ladders *scaled* the walls. *Knolles's History of the Turks.*

The way seems difficult, and steep, to *scale*
With upright wing against a higher foe. *Milton.*
Heav'n with these engines had been *scal'd*,
When mountains heap'd on mountains fail'd. *Waller.*
When the bold Typhæus *scal'd* the sky,
And forc'd great Jove from his own heav'n to fly,
The lesser gods all suffer'd. *Dryden.*

2. To measure or compare; to weigh.

You have found,
Scaling his present bearing with his past,
That he's your fixed enemy. *Shak. Coriolanus.*

3. [From *scale* of a fish.] To take off a thin lamina.

Raphael was sent to *scale* away the whiteness of Tobit's eyes. *Tob*, iii. 17.

4. To pare off a surface.

If all the mountains were *scaled*, and the earth made even, the waters would not overflow its smooth surface. *Burnet.*

To SCALE. *v. n.* To peel off in thin particles.

Those that cast their shell are the lobster and crab: the old skins are found, but the old shells never; so as it is like they *scale* off, and crumble away by degrees. *Bacon.*

SCA'LED. *adj.* [from *scale.*] Squamous; having scales like fishes.

Half my Egypt was submerg'd, and made
A cistern for *scal'd* snakes. *Shakesp. Ant. and Cleopat.*

SCALE'NE. *n. s.* [French; *scalenum*, Latin.] In geometry, a triangle that has its three sides unequal to each other. *Bailey.*

SCA'LINESS. *n. s.* [from *scaly.*] The state of being scaly.

SCALL. *n. s.* [*skalladur*, bald, Islandick. See SCALDHEAD.] Leprosy; morbid baldness.

It is a dry *scall*, a leprosy upon the head. *Lev.* xiii. 30.

SCA'LLION. *n. s.* [*scaloyna*, Italian; *ascalonia*, Latin.] A kind of onion.

SCA'LLOP. *n. s.* [*escallop*, French.] A fish with a hollow pectinated shell.

So th' emperour Caligula,
That triumph'd o'er the British sea,
Engag'd his legions in fierce bustles
With periwincles, prawns, and muscles;
And led his troops with furious gallops,
To charge whole regiments of *scallops.* *Hudibras.*

The

The sand is in Scilly glistering, which may be occasioned from freestone mingled with white *scallop* shells. *Mortimer.*

To SCA'LLOP. *v. a.* To mark on the edge with segments of circles.

SCALP. *n. s.* [*schelpe*, Dutch, a shell; *scalpo*, Italian.]

1. The scull; the cranium; the bone that incloses the brain.

High brandishing his bright dew-burning blade,
Upon his crested *scalp* so sore did smite,
That to the scull a yawning wound it made. *Fairy Queen.*

O gentle Puck, take this transformed *scalp*
From off the head of this Athenian swain,
That he awaking, when the others do,
May all to Athens back again repair. *Shakespeare.*

White beards have arm'd their thin and hairless *scalps*
Against thy majesty. *Shakesp. Richard* II.

The hairy *scalps*
Are whirl'd aloof, while numerous trunks bestrow
Th' ensanguin'd field. *Phillips.*

If the fracture be not complicated with a wound of the *scalp*, or the wound is too small to admit of the operation, the fracture must be laid bare by taking away a large piece of the *scalp*. *Sharp's Surgery.*

2. The integuments of the head.

To SCALP. *v. a.* [from the noun.] To deprive the scull of its integuments.

We seldom inquire for a fracture of the scull by *scalping*, but that the scalp itself is contused. *Sharp.*

SCA'LPEL. *n. s.* [Fr. *scalpellum*, Latin.] An instrument used to scrape a bone by chirurgeons.

SCA'LY. *adj.* [from *scale.*] Covered with scales.

The river horse and *scaly* crocodile. *Milton.*

His awful summons they so soon obey;
So hear the *scaly* herd when Proteus blows,
And so to pasture follow through the sea. *Dryden.*

A *scaly* fish with a forked tail. *Woodward.*

To SCA'MBLE. *v. n.* [This word, which is scarcely in use, has much exercised the etymological sagacity of *Meric Casaubon*; but, as is usual, to no purpose.]

1. To be turbulent and rapacious; to scramble; to get by struggling with others.

Have fresh chaff in the bin,
And somewhat to *scamble* for hog and for hen. *Tusser.*

Scambling, out-facing, fashion-mong'ring boys,
That lie, and cog, and flout, deprave and slander. *Shakesp.*

That self bill is urg'd, and had against us past,
But that the *scambling* and unquiet time
Did push it out of further question. *Shakes. Henry* V.

He was no sooner entered into the town but a *scambling* soldier clapt hold of his bridle, which he thought was in a begging or a drunken fashion. *Wotton.*

2. To shift aukwardly.

Some *scambling* shifts may be made without them. *More.*

To SCA'MBLE. *v. a.* To mangle; to maul.

My wood was cut in patches, and other parts of it *scambled* and cut before it was at its growth. *Mortimer.*

SCA'MBLER. *n. s.* [Scottish.] A bold intruder upon one's generosity or table.

SCA'MBLINGLY. *adv.* [from *scambling.*] With turbulence and noise; with intrusive audaciousness.

SCAMMO'NIATE. *adj.* [from *scammony.*] Made with scammony.

It may be excited by a local, *scammoniate*, or other acrimonious medicines. *Wiseman's Surgery.*

SCA'MMONY. *n. s.* [Latin; *scammonée*, French.] A concreted resinous juice, light, tender, friable, of a greyish-brown colour, and disagreeable odour. It flows upon incision of the root of a kind of convolvulus, that grows in many parts of Asia. *Trevoux.*

To SCA'MPER. *v. n.* [*schampen*, Dutch; *scampare*, Italian.] To fly with speed and trepidation.

A fox seized upon the fawn, and fairly *scampered* away with him. *L'Estrange.*

You will suddenly take a resolution, in your cabinet of Highlanders, to *scamper* off with your new crown. *Addison.*

Be quick, nay very quick, or he'll approach,
And as you're *scamp'ring* stop you in your coach. *King.*

To SCAN. *v. a.* [*scandre*, French; *scando*, Latin.]

1. To examine a verse by counting the feet.

Harry, whose tuneful and well measur'd song
First taught our English musick how to span
Words with just note and accent, not to *scan*
With Midas' ears, committing short and long. *Milton.*

They *scan* their verses upon their fingers, run after conceits and glaring thoughts. *Walsh.*

2. To examine nicely.

So he goes to heav'n,
And so am I reveng'd: that would be *scann'd*. *Shakes. Ham.*

The rest the great architect
Did wisely to conceal; and not divulge
His secrets to be *scann'd* by them, who ought
Rather admire. *Milton's Paradise Lost, b.* viii.

Every man has some guilts, which he desires should not be rigorously *scanned*; and therefore, by the rule of charity and justice, ought not to do that which he would not suffer. *Government of the Tongue.*

At the final reckoning, when all mens actions shall be *scanned* and judged, the great king shall pass his sentence, according to the good men have done, or neglected to do. *Calam.*

Sir Roger exposing his palm, they crumpled it into all shapes, and diligently *scanned* every wrinkle that could be made in it. *Addison.*

The actions of men in high stations are all conspicuous, and liable to be *scanned* and sifted. *Atterbury.*

In full fruition of successful pow'r,
One moment and one thought might let him *scan*
The various turns of life, and fickle state of man. *Prior.*

SCA'NDAL. *n. s.* [σκάνδαλον; *scandle*, French.]

1. Offence given by the faults of others.

His lustful orgies he enlarg'd
Even to the hill of *scandal*, by the grove
Of Moloch homicide. *Milton's Paradise Lost, b.* i.

2. Reproachful aspersion; opprobrious censure; infamy.

If black *scandal*, or foul-fac'd reproach,
Attend the sequel of your imposition,
Your meer enforcement shall acquittance me
From all the impure blots and stains thereof. *Shak. R.* III.

My known virtue is from *scandal* free,
And leaves no shadow for your calumny. *Dryd. Aurengz.*

In the case of *scandal*, we are to reflect how men ought to judge. *Rogers's Sermons.*

To SCA'NDAL. *v. a.* [from the noun.] To treat opprobriously; to charge falsely with faults.

You repin'd,
Scandal'd the suppliants; for the people call'd them
Time-pleasers, flatterers. *Shakesp. Coriolanus.*

I do fawn on men, and hug them hard,
And after *scandal* them. *Shak. Julius Cæsar.*

To SCA'NDALIZE. *v. a.* [σκανδαλίζω; *scandaliser*, French; from *scandal*.]

1. To offend by some action supposed criminal.

I demand who they are whom we *scandalize* by using harmless things? Among ourselves, that agree in this use, no man will say that one of us is offensive and scandalous unto another. *Hooker.*

It had the excuse of some bashfulness, and care not to *scandalize* others. *Hammond on Fundamentals.*

Whoever considers the injustice of some ministers, in those intervals of parliament, will not be *scandalized* at the warmth and vivacity of those meetings. *Clarendon.*

Many were *scandalized* at the personal slander and reflection flung out by *scandalizing* libellers. *Addison.*

2. To reproach; to disgrace; to defame.

Thou do'st appear to *scandalize*
The publick right, and common cause of kings. *Daniel.*

SCA'NDALOUS. *adj.* [*scandaleux*, French; from *scandal.*]

1. Giving publick offence.

Nothing *scandalous* or offensive unto any, especially unto the church of God: all things in order, and with seemliness. *Hooker.*

Something savouring
Of tyranny, which will ignoble make you,
Yea, *scandalous* to the world. *Shakesp. Winter's Tale.*

2. Opprobrious; disgraceful.

3. Shameful; openly vile.

You know the *scandalous* meanness of that proceeding, which was used. *Pope.*

SCA'NDALOUSLY. *adv.* [from *scandalous.*]

1. Censoriously; opprobriously.

Shun their fault, who, *scandalously* nice,
Will needs mistake an author into vice. *Pope.*

2. Shamefully; ill to a degree that gives publick offence.

His discourse at table was *scandalously* unbecoming the dignity of his station; noise, brutality, and obsceneness. *Swift.*

SCA'NDALOUSNESS. *n. s.* [from *scandalous.*] The quality of giving publick offence.

SCA'NSION. *n. s.* [*scansio*, Latin.] The act or practice of scanning a verse.

To SCANT. *v. a.* [ᵹeſcænan, Saxon, to break; *skaaner*, Danish, to spare.] To limit; to straiten.

You think
I will your serious and great business *scant*,
For she is with me. *Shakespeare's Othello.*

They need rather to be *scanted* in their nourishment than replenished, to have them sweet. *Bacon's Nat. History.*

We might do well to think with ourselves, what time of stay we would demand, and he bade us not to *scant* ourselves. *Bacon.*

Looking on things through the wrong end of the perspective, which *scants* their dimensions, we neglect and contemn them. *Glanv. Sceps.*

Starve

Starve them,
For fear the rankneſs of the ſwelling womb
Should *ſcant* the paſſage and confine the room. *Dryden.*

I am *ſcanted* in the pleaſure of dwelling on your actions. *Dryden's Fables, Dedication.*

SCANT. *adj.* [from the verb.]

1. Wary; not liberal; parcimonious.

From this time,
Be ſomewhat *ſcanter* of your maiden preſence. *Shakeſp.*

2. Not plentiful; ſcarce; leſs than what is proper or competent.

White is a penurious colour, and where moiſture is *ſcant*: ſo blue violets, and other flowers, if they be ſtarved, turn pale and white. *Bacon's Natural Hiſtory.*

A ſingle violet tranſplant:
The ſtrength, the colour, and the ſize,
All which before was poor and *ſcant*,
Redoubles ſtill and multiplies. *Donne.*

To find out that,
In ſuch a *ſcant* allowance of ſtar-light,
Would over-taſk the beſt land-pilot's art. *Milton.*

SCANT. *adv.* [from the adjective.] Scarcely; hardly.

The people, beſide their travail, charge, and long attendance, received of the bankers *ſcant* twenty ſhillings for thirty. *Camden's Remains.*

We *ſcant* read in any writer, that there have been ſeen any people upon the ſouth coaſt. *Abbot's Deſcript. of the World.*

A wild pamphlet, beſides other malignities, would *ſcant* allow him to be a gentleman. *Wotton.*

O'er yonder hill does *ſcant* the dawn appear. *Gay.*

SCA'NTILY. *adv.* [from *ſcanty.*]

1. Sparingly; niggardly.

He ſpoke
Scantily of me, when perforce he could not
But pay me terms of honour. *Shakeſp. Ant. and Cleop.*

2. Narrowly; not plentifully.

SCA'NTINESS. *n. ſ.* [from *ſcanty.*]

1. Narrowneſs; want of ſpace; want of compaſs.

Virgil has ſometimes two of them in a line; but the *ſcantineſs* of our heroick verſe is not capable of receiving more than one. *Dryden.*

2. Want of amplitude or greatneſs.

Alexander was much troubled at the *ſcantineſs* of nature itſelf, that there were no more worlds for him to diſturb. *South.*

SCA'NTLET. *n. ſ.* [corrupted, as it ſeems, from *ſcantling.*] A ſmall pattern; a ſmall quantity; a little piece.

While the world was but thin, the ages of mankind were longer; and as the world grew fuller, ſo their lives were ſucceſſively reduced to a ſhorter *ſcantlet*, 'till they came to that time of life which they now have. *Hale.*

SCA'NTLING. *n. ſ.* [*eſchantillon*, French; *ciantellino*, Italian.]

1. A quantity cut for a particular purpoſe.

'Tis hard to find out a woman that's of a juſt *ſcantling* for her age, humour, and fortune, to make a wife of. *L'Eſtrange.*

2. A certain proportion.

The ſucceſs,
Although particular, ſhall give a *ſcantling*
Of good or bad unto the general. *Shak. Troil. and Creſſ.*

3. A ſmall quantity.

Reduce deſires to narrow *ſcantlings* and ſmall proportions. *Taylor's Rule of living holy.*

A *ſcantling* of wit lay gaſping for life, and groaning beneath a heap of rubbiſh. *Dryden.*

In this narrow *ſcantling* of capacity, we enjoy but one pleaſure at once. *Locke.*

SCA'NTLY. *adv.* [from *ſcant.*]

1. Scarcely; hardly.

England, in the opinion of the popes, was preferred, becauſe it contained in the eccleſiaſtical diviſion two large provinces, which had their ſeveral *legati nati*; whereas France had *ſcantly* one. *Camden's Remains.*

2. Narrowly; penuriouſly; without amplitude.

My eager love, I'll give myſelf the lye;
The very hope is a full happineſs,
Yet *ſcantly* meaſures what I ſhall poſſeſs. *Dryden.*

SCA'NTNESS. *n. ſ.* [from *ſcant.*] Narrowneſs; meanneſs; ſmalneſs.

He was a man of a fierce ſpirit, and of no evil diſpoſition, ſaving that he thought *ſcantneſs* of eſtate too great an evil. *Hayward.*

Did we but compare the miſerable *ſcantneſs* of our capacities with the vaſt profundity of things, truth and modeſty would teach us wary language. *Glanv. Scepſ.*

SCA'NTY. *adj.* [The ſame with *ſcant.*]

1. Narrow; ſmall; wanting amplitude; ſhort of quantity ſufficient.

As long as one can increaſe the number, he will think the idea he hath a little too *ſcanty* for poſitive infinity. *Locke.*

His dominions were very narrow and *ſcanty*; for he had not the poſſeſſion of a foot of land, 'till he bought a field of the ſons of Heth. *Locke.*

Now *ſcantier* limits the proud arch confine,
And ſcarce are ſeen the proſtrate Nile and Rhine;
A ſmall Euphrates through the piece is roll'd,
And little eagles wave their wings in gold. *Pope.*

2. Small; poor; not copious; not ample.

Their language being *ſcanty*, and accommodated only to the few neceſſaries of a needy ſimple life, had no words in it to ſtand for a thouſand. *Locke.*

There remained few marks of the old tradition, ſo they had narrow and *ſcanty* conceptions of providence. *Woodward.*

They with ſuch *ſcanty* wages pay
The bondage and the ſlavery of years. *Swift.*

3. Sparing; niggardly; parcimonious.

In illuſtrating a point of difficulty, be not too *ſcanty* of words, but rather become copious in your language. *Watts.*

To SCAPE. *v. a.* [contracted from *eſcape.*] To eſcape; to avoid; to ſhun; not to incur; to fly.

What, have I *ſcaped* love-letters in the holyday time of my beauty, and am I now a ſubject for them? *Shakeſpeare.*

I doubt not but to die a fair death, if I *ſcape* hanging. *Shak.*

What can '*ſcape* the eye
Of God all-ſeeing? *Milton.*

To SCAPE. *v. n.* To get away from hurt or danger.

Could they not fall unpity'd on the plain,
But ſlain revive, and, taken, *ſcape* again. *Dryden.*

SCAPE. *n. ſ.* [from the verb.]

1. Eſcape; flight from hurt or danger; the act of declining or running from danger; accident of ſafety.

I ſpoke of moſt diſaſtrous chances,
Of hair-breadth *ſcapes* in th' imminent deadly breach. *Shak.*

2. Means of eſcape; evaſion.

Having purpos'd falſhood, you
Can have no way but falſhood to be true!
Vain lunatick, againſt theſe *ſcapes* I could
Diſpute, and conquer, if I would. *Donne.*

3. Negligent freak.

No natural exhalation in the ſky,
No *ſcape* of nature, no diſtemper'd day,
But they will pluck away its nat'ral cauſe,
And call them meteors, prodigies, and ſigns. *Shakeſpeare.*

4. Looſe act of vice or lewdneſs.

A bearne! a very pretty bearne! ſure ſome *ſcape*: though I am not bookiſh, yet I can read waiting-gentlewoman in the *ſcape*. *Shakeſp. Winter's Tale.*

Thou lurk'dſt
In valley or green meadow, to way-lay
Some beauty rare, Caliſto, Clymene:
Too long thou laid'ſt thy *ſcapes* on names ador'd. *Milton.*

SCA'PULA. n. ſ. [Latin.] The ſhoulder-blade.

The heat went off from the parts, and ſpread up higher to the breaſt and *ſcapula*. *Wiſeman.*

SCA'PULAR. }
SCA'PULARY. } *adj.* [*ſcapulaire*, Fr. from *ſcapula*, Lat.] Relating or belonging to the ſhoulders.

The humours diſperſed through the branches of the axillary artery to the *ſcapulary* branches. *Wiſeman of Ulcers.*

The viſcera were counterpoiſed with the weight of the *ſcapular* part. *Derham.*

SCAR. *n. ſ.* [from *eſchar*, *eſcare*, French; ἐσχάρα.] A mark made by a hurt or fire; a cicatrix.

Scratch thee but with a pin, and there remains
Some *ſcar* of it. *Shakeſp. As you like it.*

The ſoft delicious air,
To heal the *ſcars* of theſe corroſive fires,
Shall breathe her balm. *Milton.*

It may be ſtruck out of the omniſciency of God, and leave no *ſcar* nor blemiſh behind. *More.*

This earth had the beauty of youth and blooming nature, and not a wrinkle, *ſcar*, or fracture on all its body. *Burnet.*

In a hemorrhage from the lungs ſtypticks are often inſignificant; and if they could operate upon the affected part, ſo far as to make a *ſcar*, when that fell off, the diſeaſe would return. *Arbuthnot on Diet.*

To SCAR. *v. a.* [from the noun.] To mark as with a ſore or wound.

Yet I'll not ſhed her blood,
Nor *ſcar* that whiter ſkin of her's than ſnow,
And ſmooth as monumental alabaſter. *Shakeſp. Othello.*

SCA'RAB. *n. ſ.* [*ſcarabée*, Fr. *ſcarabæus*, Latin.] A beetle; an inſect with ſheathed wings.

A ſmall *ſcarab* is bred in the very tips of elm-leaves: theſe leaves may be obſerved to be dry and dead, as alſo turgid, in which lieth a dirty, whitiſh, rough maggot, from which proceeds a beetle. *Derham's Phyſico-Theology.*

SCA'RAMOUCH. *n. ſ.* [*eſcarmouche*, Fr.] A buffoon in motly dreſs.

It makes the ſolemnities of juſtice pageantry, and the bench reverend poppets, or *ſcaramouches* in ſcarlet. *Collier.*

SCARCE. *adj.* [*ſcarſo*, Italian; *ſchaers*, Dutch.]

1. Not plentiful.

A Swede will no more ſell you his hemp for leſs ſilver, becauſe you tell him ſilver is *ſcarcer* now in England, and therefore

fore risen one fifth in value, than a tradesman of London will sell his commodity cheaper to the Isle of Man, because money is *scarce* there. *Locke.*

2. Rare; not common.

The *scarcest* of all is a *Pescennius Niger* on a medallion well preserved. *Addison.*

SCARCE. } SCA'RCELY. } *adv.* [from the adjective.]

1. Hardly; scantly.

A thing which we so little hoped to see, that even they which beheld it done *scarcely* believed their own senses. *Hooker.*

When we our betters see bearing our woes,
We *scarcely* think our miseries our foes. *Shak. King Lear.*

Age, which unavoidably is but one remove from death, and consequently should have nothing about it but what looks like a decent preparation for it, *scarce* ever appears, of late days, but in the high mode, the flaunting garb, and utmost gaudery of youth. *South.*

You neither have enemies, nor can *scarce* have any. *Dryd.*

2. With difficulty.

He *scarcely* knew him, striving to disown
His blotted form, and blushing to be known. *Dryden.*

Slowly he sails, and *scarcely* stems the tides;
The pressing water pours within her sides. *Dryden.*

SCA'RCENESS. } SCA'RCITY. } *n. s.* [from *scarce.*]

1. Smalness of quantity; not plenty; penury.

Scarcity and want shall shun you;
Ceres' blessing so is on you. *Shakespeare.*

Raphael writes thus concerning his Galatea: to paint a fair one, 'tis necessary for me to see many fair ones; but, because there is so great a *scarcity* of lovely women, I am constrained to make use of one certain idea, which I have formed in my fancy. *Dryden's Dufresnoy.*

Corn does not rise or fall by the differences of more or less plenty of money, but by the plenty and *scarcity* that God sends. *Locke.*

In this grave age, when comedies are few,
We crave your patronage for one that's new,
And let the *scarceness* recommend the fare. *Addison.*

They drink very few liquors that have not lain in fresco, insomuch that a *scarcity* of snow would raise a mutiny at Naples. *Addison.*

2. Rareness; infrequency; not commonness.

They that find fault with our store, should be least willing to reprove our *scarcity* of thanksgivings. *Hooker.*

Since the value of an advantage is enhanced by its *scarceness*, it is hard not to give a man leave to love that most which is most serviceable. *Collier on Pride.*

To SCARE. *v. a.* [*scorare*, Italian. *Skinner.*] To fright; to frighten; to affright; to terrify; to strike with sudden fear.

They have *scared* away two of my best sheep, which, I fear, the wolf will sooner find than the master. *Shakespeare.*

Poor Tom hath been *scared* out of his good wits. *Shakesp.*

My grained ash an hundred times hath broke,
And *scar'd* the moon with splinters. *Shak. Coriolanus.*

The noise of thy cross-bow
Will *scare* the herd, and so my shoot is lost. *Shakes. H.* VI.

Scarecrows are set up to keep birds from corn and fruit; and some report that the head of a wolf, whole, dried, and hanged up in a dovehouse, will *scare* away vermin. *Bacon.*

The wing of the Irish was so grievously either galled or *scared* therewith, that being strangers, and in a manner neutrals, they had neither good heart to go forward, nor good liking to stand still, nor good assurance to run away. *Hayward.*

The light
Waves threaten now, as that was *scar'd* by fire. *Waller.*

One great reason why mens good purposes so often fail, is, that when they are devout, or *scared*, they then in the general resolve to live religiously. *Calamy's Sermons.*

Let wanton wives by death be *scar'd*;
But, to my comfort, I'm prepar'd. *Prior.*

SCA'RECROW. *n. s.* [*scare* and *crow.*] An image or clapper set up to fright birds: thence any vain terrour.

Thereat the *scarecrow* waxed wond'rous proud,
Through fortune of his first adventure fair,
And with big thundering voice revil'd him loud. *Fa. Queen.*

No eye hath seen such *scarecrows*: I'll not march through Coventry with them, that's flat. *Shakesp. Henry* IV.

We must not make a *scarecrow* of the law,
Setting it up to fear the birds of prey,
And let it keep one shape, 'till custom make it
Their pearch, and not their terrour. *Shakespeare.*

Many of those great guns, wanting powder and shot, stood but as cyphers and *scarecrows*. *Raleigh.*

A *scarecrow* set to frighten fools away. *Dryden.*

SCA'REFIRE. *n. s.* [*scare* and *fire.*] A fright by fire; a fire breaking out so as to raise terrour.

The drum and trumpet, by their several sounds, serve for many kind of advertisements; and bells serve to proclaim a *scarefire*, and in some places water-breaches. *Holder.*

SCARF. *n. s.* [*escharfe*, French.] Any thing that hangs loose upon the shoulders or dress.

The matrons flung their gloves,
Ladies and maids their *scarfs* and handkerchiefs,
Upon him as he pass'd. *Shakesp. Coriolanus.*

Will you wear the garland about your neck, or under your arm, like a lieutenant's *scarf?* *Shakespeare.*

Iris there, with humid bow,
Waters th' odorous banks, that blow
Flowers of more mingled hew
Than her purfled *scarf* can show. *Milton.*

Titian, in his triumph of Bacchus, having placed Ariadne on one of the borders of the picture, gave her a *scarf* of a vermilion colour upon a blue drapery. *Dryden.*

The ready nymphs receive the crying child;
They swath'd him with their *scarfs*. *Dryden.*

My learned correspondent writes a word in defence of large *scarves*. *Spectator.*

Put on your hood and *scarf*, and take your pleasure. *Swift.*

To SCARF. *v. a.* [from the noun.]

1. To throw loosely on.

My sea-gown *scarft* about me, in the dark
Grop'd I to find them out. *Shakesp. Hamlet.*

2. To dress in any loose vesture.

How like a younker, or a prodigal,
The *scarfed* bark puts from her native bay,
Hugg'd and embraced by the strumpet wind! *Shakespeare.*

Come, feeling night,
Scarf up the tender eye of pitiful day. *Shak. Macbeth.*

SCA'RFSKIN. *n. s.* [*scarf* and *skin.*] The cuticle; the epidermis; the outer scaly integuments of the body.

The *scarfskin*, being uppermost, is composed of several lays of small scales, which lie thicker according as it is thicker in one part of the body than another: between these the excretory ducts of the miliary glands of the true skin open. *Cheyne.*

SCARIFICA'TION. *n. s.* [*scarificatio*, Lat. *scarification*, French; from *scarify.*] Incision of the skin with a lancet, or such like instrument. It is most practised in cupping. *Quincy.*

Hippocrates tells you, that, in applying of cups, the *scarification* ought to be made with crooked instruments. *Arbuthnot.*

SCARIFICA'TOR. *n. s.* [from *scarify.*] One who scarifies.

SCA'RIFIER. *n. s.* [from *scarify.*]

1. He who scarifies.

2. The instrument with which scarifications are made.

To SCA'RIFY. *v. a.* [*scarifico*, Lat. *scarifier*, Fr.] To let blood by incisions of the skin, commonly after the application of cupping-glasses.

Washing the salts out of the eschar, and *scarifying* it, I dressed it. *Wiseman's Surgery.*

You quarter foul language upon me, without knowing whether I deserve to be cupped and *scarified* at this rate. *Spectator.*

SCA'RLET. *n. s.* [*escarlate*, French; *scarlato*, Ital.] A colour deeply red, but not shining; cloath dyed with a scarlet colour.

If we live thus tamely,
To be thus jaded by a piece of *scarlet*,
Farewel nobility. *Shakespeare's Henry* VIII.

As a bull
Amid' the circus roars; provok'd from far
By sight of *scarlet* and a sanguine war. *Dryden.*

Would it not be insufferable for a learned professor, and that which his *scarlet* would blush at, to have his authority of forty years standing in an instant overturned. *Locke.*

SCA'RLET. *adj.* [from the noun.] Of the colour of scarlet; red deeply died.

I conjure thee,
By her high forehead and her *scarlet* lip. *Shak. Ro. and Jul.*

Thy ambition,
Thou *scarlet* sin, robb'd this bewailing land
Of noble Buckingham. *Shak. Henry* VIII.

The Chinese, who are of an ill complexion, being olivaster, paint their cheeks *scarlet*. *Bacon.*

The *scarlet* honour of your peaceful gown. *Dryden.*

SCA'RLETBEAN. *n. s.* [*scarlet* and *bean.*] A plant.

The *scarletbean* has a red husk, and is not the best to eat in the shell, as kidneybeans; but is reputed the best to be eaten in Winter, when dry and boiled. *Mortimer's Husbandry.*

SCA'RLETOAK. *n. s.* The ilex. A species of oak.

SCA'RMAGE. } SCA'RMOGE. } *n. s.* [For skirmish. *Spenser.*]

Such cruel game my *scarmages* disarms;
Another war, and other weapons I,
Do love, when love does give his sweet alarms. *Fa. Queen.*

SCARP. *n. s.* [*escarpe*, French.] The slope on that side of a ditch which is next to a fortified place, and looks towards the fields. *Dict.*

SCATCH. *n. s.* [*escache*, French.] A kind of horsebit for bridles. *Bailey.*

SCA'TCHES. *n. s.* [*chasses*, French.] Stilts to put the feet in to walk in dirty places. *Bailey.*

SCATE. *n. s.* [*skidor*, Swedish; *skid*, Islandick.] A kind of wooden shoe, with a steel plate underneath, on which they slide over the ice.

 To

To Scate. *v. n.* [from the noun.] To ſlide on ſcates.

Scate. *n. ſ.* [*ſquatus*, Latin.] A fiſh of the ſpecies of thornback.

Sca'tebrous. *adj.* [from *ſcatebræ*, Latin.] Abounding with ſprings. *Dict.*

To SCATH. *v. a.* [ꞅceaðan, ꞅcaðan, Saxon; *ſchaeden*, Dut.] To waſte; to damage; to deſtroy.

As when heaven's fire
Hath *ſcath'd* the foreſt oaks, or mountain pines,
With ſinged top their ſtately growth, though bare,
Stands on the blaſted heath. *Milton's Parad. Loſt*, *b.* i.

Scath. *n. ſ.* [ꞅceað, Saxon.] Waſte; damage; miſchief; depopulation. *Scath* in Scotland denotes ſpoil or damage: as, he bears the *ſca'h* and the ſcorn. A proverb.

She ſuborned hath
This crafty meſſenger, with letters vain,
To work new woe and unprovided *ſcath*. *Fairy Queen.*

The ear that budded fair is burnt and blaſted,
And all my hoped gain is turn'd to *ſcath*. *Spenſer.*

He bore a ſpiteful mind againſt king Edward, doing him all the *ſ ath* that he could, and annoying his territories. *Spenſer.*

My proud one doth work the greater *ſcath*,
Through ſweet allurement of her lovely hue. *Spenſer.*

They placed them in Rhodes, where daily doing great *ſcath* to the Turk, the great warrior Soliman, with a mighty army, ſo overlaid them, that he won the iſland from them. *Knolles.*

Still preſerv'd from danger, harm, and *ſcath*,
By many a ſea and many an unknown ſhore. *Fairfax.*

Sca'thful. *adj.* [from *ſcath*.] Miſchievous; deſtructive.

A bawbling veſſel was he captain of,
For ſhallow draught, and bulk unprizable,
With which ſuch *ſcathful* grapple did he make,
That very envy, and the tongue of loſs,
Cried fame and honour on him. *Shakeſp. Twelfth Night.*

To SCA'TTER. *v. a.* [ꞅcaꞇeꞃan, Saxon; *ſchatteren*, Dutch.]

1. To throw looſely about; to ſprinkle.

Where cattle paſtur'd late, now *ſcatter'd* lies
With carcaſes and arms th' enſanguin'd field. *Milton.*

Teach the glad hours to *ſcatter*, as they fly,
Soft quiet, gentle love, and endleſs joy. *Prior.*

Corruption, ſtill
Voracious, ſwallow'd what the liberal hand
Of bounty *ſcatter'd* o'er the ſavage year. *Thomſon.*

2. To diſſipate; to diſperſe.

A king, that ſitteth in the throne of judgment, *ſcattereth* away all evil with his eyes. *Prov.* xx. 8.

The Lord ſhall cauſe his glorious voice to be heard with *ſcattering* and tempeſt and ſtones. *Iſ.* xxx. 30.

Samuel came not to Gilgal, and the people were *ſcattered* from Saul. 1 *Sa.* xiii. 8.

Adam by this from the cold ſudden damp
Recovering, and his *ſcatter'd* ſp'rits return'd. *Milton.*

3. To ſpread thinly.

Why ſhould my muſe enlarge on Libyan ſwains,
Their *ſcatter'd* cottages and ample plains. *Dryden.*

To Sca'tter. *v. n.* To be diſſipated; to be diſperſed.

Sound diffuſeth itſelf in rounds; but if that which would *ſcatter* in open air, be made to go into a canal, it gives greater force to the ſound. *Bacon.*

The ſun
Shakes from his noon-day throne the *ſcattering* clouds. *Thom.*

Sca'tteringly. *adv.* [from *ſcattering*.] Looſely; diſperſedly.

The Spaniards have here and there *ſcatteringly*, upon the ſea-coaſts, ſet up ſome towns. *Abbot.*

Thoſe drops of prettineſs, *ſcatteringly* ſprinkled amongſt the creatures, were deſigned to defecate and exalt our conceptions, not to inveigle or detain our paſſions. *Boyle.*

Sca'tterling. *n. ſ.* [from *ſcatter*.] A vagabond; one that has no home or ſettled habitation.

Such loſels and *ſcatterlings* cannot eaſily, by any ordinary officer, be gotten, when challenged for any ſuch fact. *Spenſer.*

Gathering unto him all the *ſcatterlings* and outlaws out of all the woods and mountains, in which they long had lurked, he marched forth into the Engliſh pale. *Spenſer on Ireland.*

Scatu'rient. *adj.* [*ſcaturiens*, Latin.] Springing as a fountain. *Dict.*

Scaturi'ginous. *adj.* [from *ſcaturigo*, Latin.] Full of ſprings or fountains. *Dict.*

Sca'venger. *n. ſ.* [from ꞅcaꝼan, to ſhave, perhaps to ſweep, Saxon.] A petty magiſtrate, whoſe province is to keep the ſtreets clean.

Since it is made a labour of the mind, as to inform mens judgments, and move their affections, to reſolve difficult places of Scripture, to decide and clear off controverſies, I cannot ſee how to be a butcher, *ſcavenger*, or any other ſuch trade, does at all qualify men for this work. *South's Sermons.*

Faſting's nature's *ſcavenger*. *Baynard.*

Dick the *ſcavenger*, with equal grace,
Flirts from his cart the mud in Walpole's face. *Swift.*

SCE'LERAT. *n. ſ.* [French; *ſceleratus*, Latin.] A villain; a wicked wretch. A word introduced unneceſſarily from the French by a Scottiſh author.

Scelerats can by no arts ſtifle the cries of a wounded conſcience. *Cheyne.*

Sce'nary. *n. ſ.* [from *ſcene*.]

1. The appearances of place or things.

He muſt gain a reliſh of the works of nature, and be converſant in the various *ſcenary* of a country life. *Addiſon.*

2. The repreſentation of the place in which an action is performed.

The progreſs of the ſound, and the *ſcenary* of the bordering regions, are imitated from Æn. vii. on the ſounding the horn of Alecto. *Pope.*

3. The diſpoſition and conſecution of the ſcenes of a play.

To make a more perfect model of a picture, is, in the language of poets, to draw up the *ſcenary* of a play. *Dryden.*

SCENE. *n. ſ.* [*ſcæna*, Latin; σκηνὴ; *ſcene*, French.]

1. The ſtage; the theatre of dramatick poetry.

Cedar and pine, and fir and branching palm,
A ſylvan *ſcene*; and as the ranks aſcend
Shade above ſhade, a woody theatre
Of ſtatelieſt view. *Milton.*

2. The general appearance of any action; the whole contexture of objects; a diſplay; a ſeries; a regular diſpoſition.

Now prepare thee for another *ſcene*. *Milton.*

A mute *ſcene* of ſorrow, mixt with fear;
Still on the table lay the unfiniſh'd cheer. *Dryden.*

A larger *ſcene* of action is diſplay'd,
And, riſing hence, a greater work is weigh'd. *Dryden.*

Ev'ry ſev'ral place muſt be
A *ſcene* of triumph and revenge to me. *Dryden.*

When riſing Spring adorns the mead,
A charming *ſcene* of nature is diſplay'd. *Dryden.*

Eternity! thou pleaſing, dreadful thought!
Through what variety of untry'd beings,
Through what new *ſcenes* and changes muſt we paſs! *Addiſ.*

About eight miles diſtance from Naples lies a very noble *ſcene* of antiquities: what they call Virgil's tomb is the firſt. *Addiſon on Italy.*

Say, ſhepherd, ſay, are theſe reflections true?
Or was it but the woman's fear that drew
This cruel *ſcene*, unjuſt to love and you. *Prior.*

3. Part of a play.

It ſhall be ſo my care
To have you royally appointed, as if
The *ſcene* you play were mine. *Shakeſp. Winter's Tale.*

Our author would excuſe theſe youthful *ſcenes*
Begotten at his entrance. *Granville.*

4. So much of an act of a play as paſſes between the ſame perſons in the ſame place.

If his characters were good,
The *ſcenes* entire, and freed from noiſe and blood,
The action great, yet circumſcrib'd by time,
The words not forc'd, but ſliding into rhime,
He thought, in hitting theſe, his buſineſs done. *Dryden.*

5. The place repreſented by the ſtage.

The king is ſet from London, and the *ſcene*
Is now tranſported to Southampton. *Shakeſp. Hen.* V.

6. The hanging of the theatre adapted to the play.

The alteration of *ſcenes* feeds and relieves the eye, before it be full of the ſame object. *Bacon.*

Sce'nick. *adj.* [*ſcenique*, Fr. from *ſcene*.] Dramatick; theatrical.

With *ſcenick* virtue charm the riſing age. *Anonym.*

Scenogra'phical. *adj.* [σκηνὴ and γράφω.] Drawn in perſpective.

Scenogra'phically. *adv.* [from *ſcenographical*.] In perſpective.

If the workman be ſkilled in perſpective, more than one face may be repreſented in our diagram *ſcenographically*. *Mort.*

Sce'nography. *n. ſ.* [σκηνὴ and γράφω; *ſcenographie*, Fr.] The art of perſpective.

SCENT. *n. ſ.* [*ſentir*, to ſmell, French.]

1. The power of ſmelling; the ſmell.

A hunted hare treads back her mazes, croſſes and confounds her former track, and uſes all poſſible methods to divert the *ſcent*. *Watts's Improvement of the Mind.*

2. The object of ſmell; odour good or bad.

Belman cried upon it at the meereſt loſs,
And twice to-day pick'd out the dulleſt *ſcent*. *Shakeſpeare.*

The plague, they report, hath a *ſcent* of the ſmell of a mellow apple. *Bacon.*

Good earth, newly turned up, hath a freſhneſs and good *ſcent*. *Bacon.*

Good *ſcents* do purify the brain,
Awake the fancy, and the wits refine. *Davies.*

Partake
The ſeaſon, prime for ſweeteſt *ſcents* and airs. *Milton.*

Exulting, 'till he finds their nobler ſenſe
Their diſproportion'd ſpeed does recompenſe;
Then curſes his conſpiring feet, whoſe *ſcent*
Betrays that ſafety which their ſwiftneſs lent. *Denham.*

Chearful health,
His duteous handmaid, through the air improv'd,
With laviſh hand diffuſes *ſcents* ambroſial. *Prior.*

3. Chace followed by the ſmell.

He gained the obſervations of innumerable ages, and travelled upon the ſame *ſcent* into Æthiopia. *Temple.*

To Scent. *v. a.* [from the noun.]

1. To smell; to perceive by the nose.

So *scented* the grim feature, and upturn'd
His nostrils wide into the murky air,
Sagacious of his quarry from so far. *Milton's Par. Lost.*

2. To perfume; or to imbue with odour good or bad.

Balm, from a silver box distill'd around,
Shall all bedew the roots, and *scent* the sacred ground. *Dryd.*
He spies
His op'ning hounds, and now he hears their cries;
A gen'rous pack, or to maintain the chace,
Or snuff the vapour from the *scented* grass. *Addison.*

Sce'ntless. *adj.* [from *scent.*] Inodorous; having no smell.

SCE'PTRE. *n. s.* [*sceptrum*, Latin; *sceptre*, Fr.] The ensign of royalty born in the hand.

Nor shall proud Lancaster usurp my right,
Nor hold the *sceptre* in his childish fist. *Shak. Henry* VI.
Thou *sceptre*'s heir,
That thus affect'st a sheephook. *Shakespeare.*
How, best of kings, do'st thou a *sceptre* bear!
How, best of poets, do'st thou laurel wear!
But two things rare the fates had in their store,
And gave thee both, to shew they could no more. *B. Johns.*
The *sceptre* bearers lent
Their free attendance. *Chapman's Odyssey.*

The parliament presented those acts which were prepared by them to the royal *sceptre*, in which were some laws restraining the extravagant power of the nobility. *Clarendon.*

The court of Rome has, in other instances, so well attested its good managery, that it is not credible crowns and *sceptres* are conferred gratis. *Decay of Piety.*

Sce'ptred. *adj.* [from *sceptre.*] Bearing a sceptre.

The *sceptred* heralds call
To council, in the city-gates. *Milton's Paradise Lost.*
To Britain's queen the *scepter'd* suppliant bends,
To her his crowns and infant race commends. *Tickel.*

Sce'ptick. *n. s.* See Skeptick.

Sche'dule. *n. s.* [*schedula*, Latin; *schedule*, French.]

1. A small scroll.

The first published *schedules* being brought to a grave knight, he read over an unsavory sentence or two, and delivered back the libel. *Hooker.*

All ill, which all
Prophets or poets spake, and all which shall
B' annex'd in *schedules* unto this by me,
Fall on that man. *Donne.*

2. A little inventory.

I will give out *schedules* of my beauty: it shall be inventoried, and every particle and utensil label'd to my will. *Shak.*

Sche'matism. *n. s.* [σχηματισμός.] Combination of the aspects of heavenly bodies; particular form or disposition of a thing.

Every particle of matter, whatever form or *schematism* it puts on, must in all conditions be equally extended, and therefore take up the same room. *Creech.*

Sche'matist. *n. s.* [from *scheme.*] A projector; one given to forming schemes.

SCHEME. *n. s.* [σχῆμα.]

1. A plan; a combination of various things into one view, design, or purpose; a system.

Were our senses made much quicker, the appearance and outward *scheme* of things would have quite another face to us, and be inconsistent with our well being. *Locke.*

We shall never be able to give ourselves a satisfactory account of the divine conduct, without forming such a *scheme* of things as shall at once take in time and eternity. *Atterbury.*

2. A project; a contrivance; a design.

The haughty monarch was laying *schemes* for suppressing the ancient liberties, and removing the ancient boundaries of kingdoms. *Atterbury's Sermons.*

He forms the well-concerted *scheme* of mischief;
'Tis fix'd, 'tis done, and both are doom'd to death. *Rowe.*

The stoical *scheme* of supplying our wants by lopping of our desires, is like cutting off our feet when we want shoes. *Swift.*

3. A representation of the aspects of the celestial bodies; any lineal or mathematical diagram.

It hath embroiled the endeavours of astrology in the erection of *schemes*, and the judgment of death and diseases. *Brown's Vulgar Errours.*

It is a *scheme* and face of heaven,
As th' aspects are dispos'd this even. *Hudibras.*

Sche'mer. *n. s.* [from *scheme.*] A projector; a contriver.

Sche'sis. *n. s.* [σχέσις.] An habitude; state of any thing with respect to other things.

If that mind which has existing in itself from all eternity all the simple essences of things, and consequently all their possible *scheses* or habitudes, should ever change, there would arise a new *schesis* in the mind, which is contrary to the supposition. *Norris.*

Sci'rrhus. *n. s.* [*scirrhe*, French. This should be written *skirrhus*, not merely because it comes from σκίῤῥος, but because *c* in English has before *e* and *i* the sound of *s.* See Skeptick.] An indurated gland.

Any of these three may degenerate into a *scirrhus*, and that *scirrhus* into a cancer. *Wiseman of Tumours.*

Schi'rrhous. *adj.* [from *scirrhus.*] Having a gland indurated.

How they are to be treated when they are strumous, *scirrhous*, or cancerous, you may see. *Wiseman.*

Scirrho'sity. *n. s.* [from *scirrhous.*] An induration of the glands.

The difficulty of breathing, occasioned by *scirrhosities* of the glands, is not to be cured. *Arbuthnot on Diet.*

SCHISM. *n. s.* [σχίσμα; *schisme*, Fr.] A separation or division in the church of God.

Set bounds to our passions by reason, to our errours by truth, and to our *schisms* by charity. *King Charles.*

Oppose *schisms* by unity, hypocrisy by sober piety, and debauchery by temperance. *Spratt's Sermons.*

When a *schism* is once spread, there grows at length a dispute which are the schismaticks: in the sense of the law the *schism* lies on that side which opposes itself to the religion of the state. *Swift.*

Schisma'tical. *adj.* [*schismatique*, Fr. from *schismatick.*] Implying schism; practising schism.

By these tumults all factions, seditions, and *schimatical* proposals against government, ecclesiastical and civil, must be backed. *King Charles.*

Here bare anathema's fall but like so many *bruta fulmina* upon the obstinate and *schismatical*, who are like to think themselves shrewdly hurt by being cut off from that body which they chuse not to be of, and so being punished into a quiet enjoyment of their beloved separation. *South's Sermons.*

Schisma'tically. *adv.* [from *schismatical.*] In a schismatical manner.

Schi'smatick. *n. s.* [from *schism.*] One who separates from the true church.

No known heretick nor *schismatick* should be suffered to go into those countries. *Bacon.*

Thus you behold the *schismaticks* bravado's:
Wild speaks in squibs, and Calamy in granado's. *Butler.*

The *schismaticks* united in a solemn league and covenant to alter the whole system of spiritual government. *Swift.*

To Schi'smatize. *v. a.* [from *schism.*] To commit the crime of schism; to make a breach in the communion of the church.

SCHO'LAR. *n. s.* [*scho'aris*, Latin; *ecolier*, French.]

1. One who learns of a master; a disciple.

Many times that which deserveth approbation would hardly find favour, if they which propose it were not to profess themselves *scholars*, and followers of the ancients. *Hooker.*

The *scholars* of the Stagyrite,
Who for the old opinion fight,
Would make their modern friends confess
The diff'rence but from more to less. *Prior.*

2. A man of letters.

This same *scholar*'s fate, *res angusta domi*, hinders the promoting of learning. *Wilkins's Math. Magic.*

To watch occasions to correct others in their discourse, and not slip any opportunity of shewing their talents, *scholars* are most blamed for. *Locke.*

3. A pedant; a man of books.

To spend too much time in studies, is sloth; to make judgment wholly by their rules, is the humour of a *scholar*: they perfect nature, and are perfected by experience. *Bacon.*

4. One who has a lettered education.

My cousin William is become a good *scholar*: he is at Oxford still, is he not? *Shakesp. Henry* VI.

Scho'larship. *n. s.* [from *scholar.*]

1. Learning; literature; knowledge.

It pitied my very heart to think that a man of my master's understanding, and great *scholarship*, who had a book of his own in print, should talk so outragiously. *Pope.*

2. Literary education.

This place should be school and university, not needing a remove to any other house of *scholarship*. *Milton.*

3. Exhibition or maintenance for a scholar. *Ainsworth.*

Schola'stical. *adj.* [*scholasticus*, Latin.] Belonging to a scholar or school.

Schola'stically. *adv.* [from *scholastick.*] According to the niceties or method of the schools.

No moralists or casuists, that treat *scholastically* of justice, but treat of gratitude, under that general head, as a part of it. *South's Sermons.*

Schola'stick. *adj.* [from *schola*, Latin; *scholastique*, French.]

1. Pertaining to the school; practised in schools.

I would render this intelligible to every rational man, however little versed in *scholastick* learning. *Digby on Bodies.*

Scholastick education, like a trade, does so fix a man in a particular way, that he is not fit to judge of any thing that lies out of that way. *Burnet's Theory of the Earth.*

2. Befitting the school; suitable to the school; pedantick; needlesly subtle.

The

The favour of proposing there, in convenient sort, whatsoever ye can object, which thing I have known them to grant of *scholastick* courtesy unto strangers, never hath nor ever will be denied you. *Hooker.*

Sir Francis Bacon was wont to say, that those who left useful studies for useless *scholastick* speculations, were like the Olympick gamesters, who abstained from necessary labours, that they might be fit for such as were not so. *Bacon.*

Both sides charge the other with idolatry, and that is a matter of conscience, and not a *scholastick* nicety. *Stillingfleet.*

SCHO'LIAST. *n. s.* [*scholiaste*, French; *scholiastes*, Latin.] A writer of explanatory notes.

The title of this satyr, in some ancient manuscripts, was the reproach of idleness; though in others of the *scholiasts* 'tis inscribed against the luxury of the rich. *Dryden.*

What Gellius or Stobæus cook'd before,
Or chew'd by blind old *scholiasts* o'er and o'er. *Dunciad.*

SCHO'LION. } *n. s.* [Latin.] A note; an explanatory ob-
SCHO'LIUM. } servation.

Hereunto have I added a certain gloss or *scholion*, for the exposition of old words, and harder phrases, which manner of glossing and commenting will seem strange in our language. *Spenser.*

Some cast all their metaphysical and moral learning into the method of mathematicians, and bring every thing relating to those abstracted or practical sciences under theorems, problems, postulates, *scholiums*, and corollaries. *Watts.*

SCHO'LY. *n. s.* [*scholie*, Fr. *scholium*, Latin.] An explanatory note. This word, with the verb following, is, I fancy, peculiar to the learned *Hooker.*

He therefore, which made us to live, hath also taught us to pray, to the end, that speaking unto the Father in the Son's own prescript form, without *scholy* or gloss of ours, we may be sure that we utter nothing which God will deny. *Hooker.*

That *scholy* had need of a very favourable reader, and a tractable, that should think it plain construction, when to be commanded in the word, and grounded upon the word, are made all one. *Hooker.*

To SCHO'LY. *v. n.* [from the noun.] To write expositions.

The preacher should want a text, whereupon to *scholy*. *Hooker.*

SCHOOL. *n. s.* [*schola*, Latin; *ecole*, French.]

1. A house of discipline and instruction.

Their age the same, their inclinations too,
And bred together in one *school* they grew. *Dryden.*

2. A place of literary education.

My end being private, I have not expressed my conceptions in the language of the *schools*. *Digby.*

Writers on that subject have turned it into a composition of hard words, trifles, and subtilties, for the mere use of the *schools*, and that only to amuse men with empty sounds. *Watts.*

3. A state of instruction.

The calf breed to the rural trade,
Set him betimes to *school*, and let him be
Instructed there in rules of husbandry. *Dryden.*

4. System of doctrine as delivered by particular teachers.

No craz'd brain could ever yet propound,
Touching the soul, so vain and fond a thought;
But some among these masters have been found,
Which in their *schools* the self-same thing had taught. *Davies.*

Let no man be less confident in his faith, concerning the great blessings God designs in these divine mysteries, by reason of any difference in the several *schools* of Christians, concerning the consequent blessings thereof. *Taylor.*

5. The age of the church, and form of theology succeeding that of the fathers.

The first principles of Christian religion should not be farced with *school* points and private tenets. *Sanderson.*

A man may find an infinite number of propositions in books of metaphysicks, *school* divinity, and natural philosophy, and know as little of God, spirits, or bodies, as he did before. *Locke.*

To SCHOOL. *v. a.* [from the noun.]

1. To instruct; to train.

Una her besought to be so good
As in her virtuous rules to *school* her knight. *Fa. Queen.*

He's gentle, never *school'd*, and yet learned. *Shakespeare.*

2. To teach with superiority; to tutor.

You shall go with me;
I have some private *schooling* for you both. *Shakespeare.*

Cousin, *school* yourself; but for your husband,
He's noble, wise, judicious. *Shakes. Macbeth.*

School your child,
And ask why God's anointed he revil'd. *Dryden.*

If this be *schooling*, 'tis well for the considerer: I'll engage that no adversary of his shall in this sense ever *school* him. *Att.*

SCHO'OLBOY. *n. s.* [*school* and *boy.*] A boy that is in his rudiments at school.

Schoolboys tears take up
The glasses of my sight. *Shakespeare.*

He grins, smacks, shrugs, and such an itch endures,
As 'prentices or *schoolboys*, which do know
Of some gay sport abroad, yet dare not go. *Donne.*

A *schoolboy* brought his mother a book he had stolen. *L'Estr.*

Once he had heard a *schoolboy* tell,
How Semele of mortal race
By thunder died. *Swift.*

SCHO'OLDAY. *n. s.* [*school* and *day.*] Age in which youth is sent to school.

Is all forgot?
All *schooldays* friendship, childhood, innocence? *Shakesp.*

SCHO'OLFELLOW. *n. s.* [*school* and *fellow.*] One bred at the same school.

Thy flatt'ring method on the youth pursue;
Join'd with his *schoolfellows* by two and two:
Persuade them first to lead an empty wheel,
In length of time produce the lab'ring yoke. *Dryden.*

The emulation of *schoolfellows* often puts life and industry into young lads. *Locke.*

SCHO'OLHOUSE. *n. s.* [*school* and *house.*] House of discipline and instruction.

Fair Una 'gan Fidelia fair request,
To have her knight unto her *schoolhouse* plac'd. *Spenser.*

SCHO'OLMAN. *n. s.* [*school* and *man.*]

1. One versed in the niceties and subtilties of academical disputation.

The king, though no good *schoolman*, converted one of them by dispute. *Bacon.*

Unlearn'd, he knew no *schoolman's* subtle art;
No language, but the language of the heart. *Pope.*

2. One skilled in the divinity of the school.

If a man's wit be not apt to distinguish or find differences, let him study the *schoolmen*. *Bacon.*

To *schoolmen* I bequeath my doubtfulness,
My sickness to physicians. *Donne.*

Men of nice palates could not relish Aristotle, as he was drest up by the *schoolmen*. *Baker.*

Let subtle *schoolmen* teach these fiends to fight,
More studious to divide than to unite. *Pope.*

SCHOOLMA'STER. *n. s.* [*school* and *master.*] One who presides and teaches in a school.

I, thy *schoolmaster*, have made thee more profit
Than other princes can, that have more time
For vainer hours, and tutors not so careful. *Shakespeare.*

Adrian VI. was sometime *schoolmaster* to Charles V. *Knolles.*

The ancient sophists and rhetoricians lived 'till they were an hundred years old; and so likewise did many of the grammarians and *schoolmasters*, as Orbilius. *Bacon.*

A father may see his children taught, though he himself does not turn *schoolmaster*. *South's Sermons.*

SCHO'OLMISTRESS. *n. s.* [*school* and *mistress.*] A woman who governs a school.

Such precepts I have selected from the most considerable which we have received from nature, that exact *schoolmistress*. *Dryden's Dufresnoy.*

My *schoolmistress*, like a vixen Turk,
Maintains her lazy husband. *Gay's What d'ye Call it.*

SCHREIGHT. *n. s.* A fish. *Ainsworth.*

SCI'AGRAPHY. *n. s.* [*sciagraphie*, French; σκιαγραφία. This should be written with a *k.*]

1. [In architecture.] The profile or section of a building, to shew the inside thereof. *Bailey.*

2. [In astronomy.] The art of finding the hour of the day or night by the shadow of the sun, moon, or stars. *Bailey.*

SCI'ATHERICAL. } *adj.* [*sciaterique*, Fr. σκιαθηρικός.] Be-
SCI'ATHERICK. } longing to a sun-dial. *Dict.* This should be written *skiatherical.*

There were also, from great antiquity, *sciatherical* or sundials, by the shadow of a stile or gnomon denoting the hours of the day; an invention ascribed unto Anaxamines by Pliny. *Brown's Vulg. Errours.*

SCIA'TICA. } *n. s.* [*sciatique*, French; *ischiadica passio*, Latin.]
SCIA'TICK. } The hip gout.

Which of your hips has the most profound *sciatica*? *Shakes.*

Thou cold *sciatica*,
Cripple our senators, that their limbs may halt
As lamely as their manners. *Shakesp. Timon.*

The Scythians, using continual riding, were generally molested with the *sciatica*, or hip gout. *Brown's Vulg. Err.*

Rack'd with *sciatick*, martyr'd with the stone,
Will any mortal let himself alone? *Pope.*

SCIA'TICAL. *adj.* [from *sciatica.*] Afflicting the hip.

In obstinate *sciatical* pains, blistering and cauteries have been found effectual. *Arbuthnot.*

SCI'ENCE. *n. s.* [*science*, French; *scientia*, Latin.]

1. Knowledge.

If we conceive God's sight or *science*, before the creation of the world, to be extended to all and every part of the world, seeing every thing as it is, his prescience or foresight of any action of mine, or rather his *science* or sight, from all eternity, lays no necessity on any thing to come to pass, any more than my seeing the sun move hath to do in the moving of it. *Hamm.*

2. Certainty grounded on demonstration.

So you arrive at truth, though not at *science*. *Berkley.*

3. Art attained by precepts, or built on principles.

Science perfects genius, and moderates that fury of the fancy which cannot contain itself within the bounds of reason. *Dryd.*

4. Any art or species of knowledge.

No *science* doth make known the first principles, whereon it buildeth; but they are always taken as plain and manifest in themselves, or as proved and granted already, some former knowledge having made them evident. *Hooker.*

Whatsoever we may learn by them, we only attain according to the manner of natural *sciences*, which mere discourse of wit and reason findeth out. *Hooker.*

I present you with a man
Cunning in musick and the mathematicks,
To instruct her fully in those *sciences*. *Shakespeare.*

The indisputable mathematicks, the only *science* heaven hath yet vouchsafed humanity, have but few votaries among the slaves of the Stagirite. *Glanv. Sceps.*

5. One of the seven liberal arts, grammar, rhetorick, logick, arithmetick, musick, geometry, astronomy.

Good sense, which only is the gift of heav'n,
And though no *science*, fairly worth the sev'n. *Pope.*

Scie'ntial. *adj.* [from *science.*] Producing science.

From the tree her step she turn'd;
But first low reverence done, as to the pow'r
That dwelt within; whose presence had infus'd
Into the plant *sciential* sap, deriv'd
From nectar, drink of gods. *Milton's Paradise Lost.*

Scienti'fical. } *adj.* [*scientifique*, Fr. *scientia* and *facio*, Lat.]
Scienti'fick. } Producing demonstrative knowledge; producing certainty.

Natural philosophy proceeding from settled principles, therein is expected a satisfaction from *scientifical* progressions, and such as beget a sure or rational belief. *Brown's Vulg. Err.*

No where are there more quick, inventive, and penetrating capacities, fraught with all kind of *scientifical* knowledge. *Howel.*

No man, who first trafficks into a foreign country, has any *scientifick* evidence that there is such a country, but by report, which can produce no more than a moral certainty; that is, a very high probability, and such as there can be no reason to except against. *South's Sermons.*

The systems of natural philosophy that have obtained, are to be read more to know the hypotheses, than with hopes to gain there a comprehensive, *scientifical*, and satisfactory knowledge of the works of nature. *Locke.*

Scienti'fically. *adv.* [from *scientifical.*] In such a manner as to produce knowledge.

Sometimes it rests upon testimony, because it is easier to believe than to be *scientifically* instructed. *Locke.*

Sci'mitar. *n. s.* [See Cimeter.] A short sword with a convex edge.

I'll heat his blood with Greekish wine to-night,
Which with my *scimitar* I'll cool to-morrow. *Shakespeare.*

Sci'ney *Clise.* *n. s.* A species of violet. *Ainsworth.*

Scink. *n. s.* A cast calf. *Ainsworth.* In Scotland and in London they call it *slink*.

To SCINTI'LLATE. *v. n.* [*scintillo*, Latin.] To sparkle; to emit sparks.

Scintilla'tion. *n. s.* [*scintillatio*, Lat. from *scintillate.*] The act of sparkling; sparks emitted.

He saith the planets *scintillation* is not seen, because of their propinquity. *Glanv. Sceps.*

These *scintillations* are not the accension of the air upon the collision of two hard bodies, but rather the inflammable effluences discharged from the bodies collided. *Brown.*

Scio'list. *n. s.* [*sciolus*, Latin.] One who knows many things superficially.

'Twas this vain idolizing of authors which gave birth to that silly vanity of impertinent citations: these ridiculous fooleries signify nothing to the more generous discerners, but the pedantry of the affected *sciolists*. *Glanv. Sceps.*

These passages, in that book, were enough to humble the presumption of our modern *sciolists*, if their pride were not as great as their ignorance. *Temple.*

Sci'olous. *adj.* [*sciolus*, Latin.] Superficially or imperfectly knowing.

I could wish these *sciolous* zelotists had more judgment joined with their zeal. *Howel.*

Scio'machy. *n. s.* [*schiamachie*, Fr. σκία and μαχὴ.] Battle with a shadow. This should be written *skiamachy*.

To avoid this *sciomachy*, or imaginary combat of words, let me know, sir, what you mean by the name of tyrant? *Cowley.*

Scion. *n. s.* [*scion*, French.] A small twig taken from one tree to be engrafted into another.

Sweet maid, we marry
A gentle *scion* to the wildest stock;
And make conceive a bark of baser kind,
By bud of nobler race. *Shakesp. Winter's Tale.*

March is drawn in his left hand blossoms, and *scions* upon his arm. *Peacham.*

The *scions* are best of an old tree. *Mortimer's Husbandry.*

SCIRE FACIAS. *n. s.* [Latin.] A writ judicial, in law, most commonly to call a man to shew cause unto the court, whence it is sent, why execution of a judgment passed should not be made. This writ is not granted before a year and a day is passed, after the judgment given. *Cowel.*

Sci'ssible. *adj.* [from *scissus*, Latin.] Capable of being divided smoothly by a sharp edge.

The differences of impressible and not impressible, *scissible* and not *scissible*, and many other passions of matter, are plebeian notions. *Bacon.*

Sci'ssile. *adj.* [*scissile*, Fr. *scissilis*, Latin.] Capable of being cut or divided smoothly by a sharp edge.

Animal fat is a sort of amphibious substance, *scissile* like a solid, and resolveable by heat. *Arbuthnot.*

Sci'ssion. *n. s.* [*scission*, French; *scissio*, Latin.] The act of cutting.

Nerves may be wounded by *scission* or puncture: the former way they are usually cut through, and wholly cease from action. *Wiseman's Surgery.*

Sci'ssor. *n. s.* [This word is variously written, as it is supposed to be derived by different writers; of whom some write *cisors*, from *cædo*, or *incido*; others *scissors*, from *scindo*; and some *cisars*, *cizars*, or *scissars*, *ciseaux*, Fr.] A small pair of sheers, or blades moveable on a pivot, and intercepting the thing to be cut.

His beard they have sing'd off with brands of fire;
And ever, as it blaz'd, they threw on him
Great pails of puddled mire to quench the hair:
My master preaches patience to him, and the while
His man with *scissars* nicks him for a fool. *Shakespeare.*

Wanting the *scissars*, with these hands I'll tear,
If that obstruct my flight, this load of hair. — *Prior.*

When the lawyers and tradesmen brought extravagant bills, sir Roger wore a pair of *scissars* in his pocket, with which he would snip a quarter of a yard off nicely. *Arbuthnot.*

Sci'ssure. *n. s.* [*scissum*, Latin.] A crack; a rent; a fissure.

The breach seems like the *scissures* and ruptures of an earthquake, and threatens to swallow all that attempt to close it, and reserves its cure only for omnipotence. *Decay of Piety.*

SCLERO'TICK. *adj.* [*sclerotique*, Fr. σκληρὸς.] Hard: an epithet of one of the coats of the eye.

The ligaments observed in the inside of the *sclerotick* tunicles of the eye, serve instead of a muscle, by their contraction, to alter the figure of the eye. *Ray on the Creation.*

Sclero'ticks. *n. s.* [from the adjective.] Medicines which harden and consolidate the parts they are applied to. *Quincy.*

To Scoat. } *v. a.* To stop a wheel by putting a stone or
To Scotch. } piece of wood under it before. *Bailey.*

To SCOFF. *v. n.* [*schoppen*, Dutch.] To treat with insolent ridicule; to treat with contumelious language. With *at.*

Of two noblemen of the West of England, the one was given to *scoff*, but kept ever royal cheer in his house; the other would ask of those that had been at his table, Tell truly, was there never a flout or dry blow given? *Bacon.*

There is no greater argument of a light and inconsiderate person, than prophanely to *scoff at* religion. *Tillotson.*

Such is love,
And such the laws of his fantastick empire,
The wanton boy delights to bend the mighty,
And *scoffs at* the vain wisdom of the wise. *Rowe.*

Scoff. *n. s.* [from the verb.] Contemptuous ridicule; expression of scorn; contumelious language.

Our answer therefore to their reasons is no; to their *scoffs*, nothing. *Hooker.*

With *scoffs* and scorns, and contumelious taunts,
In open market-place produc'd they me. *Shakes. H. VI.*

How could men surrender up their reason to flattery, more abusive and reproachful than the rudest *scoffs* and the sharpest invectives? *South.*

Some little souls, that have got a smattering of astronomy or chemistry, for want of a due acquaintance with other sciences, make a *scoff* at them all, in comparison of their favourite science. *Watts.*

Sco'ffer. *n. s.* [from *scoff.*] Insolent ridiculer; saucy scorner; contumelious reproacher.

I must tell you friendly in your ear,
Sell when you can; you are not for all markets:
Cry the man mercy, love him, take his offer;
Foul is most foul, being found to be a *scoffer*. *Shakesp.*

Divers have herded themselves amongst these profane *scoffers*, not that they are convinced by their reasons, but terrified by their contumelies. *Government of the Tongue.*

Consider what the apostle tells these *scoffers* they were ignorant of, not that there was a deluge; but he tells them, that they were ignorant that the heavens and the earth of old were so and so constituted. *Burnet's Theory of the Earth.*

Sco'ffingly. *adv.* [from *scoffing.*] In contempt; in ridicule.

Aristotle applied this hemistick *scoffingly* to the sycophants at Athens. *Broome's Notes to the Odyssey.*

To Scold. *v. n.* [*scholden*, Dutch.] To quarrel clamorously and rudely.

Pardon me, 'tis the first time that ever
I'm forc'd to *scold*. *Shakes. Coriolanus.*

The one as famous for a *scolding* tongue,
As the other is for beauteous modesty. *Shakespeare.*

They attacked me, some with piteous moans, others grinning and only shewing their teeth, others ranting, and others *scolding* and reviling. *Stillingfleet.*

Pallas meets the queen of love;
For gods, we are by Homer told,
Can in celestial language *scold.* *Swift.*

Scolding and cursing are her common conversation. *Swift.*

SCOLD. *n. s.* [from the verb.] A clamourous, rude, mean, low, foul-mouthed woman.

A shrew in domestick life, is now become a *scold* in politicks. *Addison's Freeholder.*

Sun-burnt matrons mending old nets;
Now singing shrill, and scolding oft between;
Scolds answer foul-mouth'd *scolds.* *Swift.*

SCO'LLOP. *n. s.* [Written properly *scallop.*] A pectinated shell-fish.

SCOLOPE'NDRA. *n. s.* [*scolopendre*, French; σκολόπενδρα.]

1. A sort of venomous serpent.
2. [*Scolopendrium*, Latin.] An herb. *Ainsworth.*

SCOMM. *n. s.* [Perhaps from *scomma*, Latin.] A buffoon. A word out of use, and unworthy of revival.

The *scomms*, or buffoons of quality, are wolvish in conversation. *L'Estrange.*

SCONCE. *n. s.* [*schantz*, German.]

1. A fort; a bulwark.

Such fellows are perfect in the great commanders names, and they will learn you by rote where services were done; at such and such a *sconce*, at such a breach. *Shak. Henry V.*

2. The head: perhaps as being the *acropolis*, or citadel of the body. A low word.

Why does he suffer this rude knave now to knock him about the *sconce* with a dirty shovel, and will not tell him of his action of battery? *Shakesp. Hamlet.*

3. A pensile candlestick, generally with a looking-glass to reflect the light.

Golden *sconces* hang upon the walls,
To light the costly suppers and the balls. *Dryden's Lucret.*

Triumphant Umbriel, on a *sconce*'s height,
Clapp'd his glad wings, and sat to view the fight. *Pope.*

Put candles into *sconces.* *Swift's Direct. to the Butler.*

To SCONCE. *v. a.* [A word used in the universities, and derived plausibly by *Skinner*, whose etymologies are generally rational, from *sconce*, as it signifies the head; to *sconce* being to fix a fine on any one's head.] To mulct; to fine. A low word which ought not to be retained.

SCOOP. *n. s.* [*schoepe*, Dutch.]

1. A kind of large ladle; a vessel with a long handle used to throw out liquor.

They turn upside down hops on malt-kilns, when almost dry, with a *scoop.* *Mortimer's Husbandry.*

Endeavour with thy *scoop*, or fingers, to force the stone outwards. *Sharp's Surgery.*

2. A sweep; a stroke. Perhaps it should be *sweep.*

Oh hell-kite!
What, all my pretty chickens and their dam,
At one fell *scoop!* *Shakesp. Macbeth.*

To SCOOP. *v. a.* [*schoepen*, Dutch.]

1. To lade out.

As by the brook he stood,
He *scoop'd* the water from the crystal flood. *Dryden's Æn.*

2. This word seems to have not been understood by *Thomson.*

Melted Alpine snows
The mountain cisterns fill, those ample stores
Of water *scoop'd* among the hollow rocks. *Thomson.*

3. To empty by lading.

If some penurious source by chance appear'd,
Scanty of waters, when you *scoop'd* it dry,
And offer'd the full helmet up to Cato,
Did he not dash th' untasted moisture from him? *Addison.*

4. To carry off in any thing hollow.

A spectator would think this circular mount had been actually *scooped* out of that hollow space. *Spectator.*

Her fore-feet are broad, that she may *scoop* away much earth at a time. *Addison.*

5. To cut hollow, or deep.

Whatever part of the harbour they *scoop* in, it has an influence on all the rest; for the sea immediately works the whole bottom to a level. *Addison on Italy.*

Those carbuncles the Indians will *scoop*, so as to hold above a pint. *Arbuthnot on Coins.*

To his single eye, that in his forehead glar'd
Like a full moon, or a broad burnish'd shield,
A forky staff we dext'rously apply'd,
Which, in the spacious socket turning round,
Scoopt out the big round gelly from its orb. *Addison.*

It much conduces how to scare
The little race of birds, that hop
From spray to spray, *scooping* the costliest fruit,
Insatiate, undisturb'd. *Phillips.*

The genius of the place
Or helps th' ambitious hill the heav'n to scale,
Or *scoops* in circling theatres the vale. *Pope.*

SCO'OPER. *n. s.* [from *scoop.*] One who scoops.

SCOPE. *n. s.* [*scopus*, Latin.]

1. Aim; intention; drift.

Your *scope* is as mine own,
So to inforce or qualify the laws,
As to your soul seems good. *Shak. Meas. for Measure.*

His coming hither hath no farther *scope*
Than for his lineal royalties, and to beg
Infranchisement immediate on his knees. *Shak. R. II.*

Had the whole *scope* of the author been answerable to his title, he would have only undertaken to prove what every man is convinced of; but the drift of the pamphlet is to stir up our compassion towards the rebels. *Addison's Freeholder.*

2. Thing aimed at; mark; final end.

The *scope* of all their pleading against man's authority is to overthrow such laws and constitutions in the church, as depending thereupon, if they should therefore be taken away, would leave neither face nor memory of church to continue long in the world. *Hooker.*

Now was time
To aim their counsels to the fairest *scope.* *Hubberd's Tale.*

We should impute the war to the *scope* at which it aimeth. *Raleigh.*

He, in what he counsels, and in what excels,
Mistrustful, grounds his courage on despair,
And utter dissolution, as the *scope*
Of all his aim. *Milton's Paradise Lost.*

3. Room; space; amplitude of intellectual view.

An heroick poet is not tied to a bare representation of what is true, but that he might let himself loose to visionary objects, which may give him a freer *scope* for imagination. *Dryden.*

These theorems being admitted into opticks, there would be *scope* enough of handling that science voluminously, after a new manner; not only by teaching those things which tend to the perfection of vision, but also by determining mathematically all kinds of phenomena of colours which could be produced by refraction. *Newton's Opt.*

4. Liberty; freedom from restraint.

If this constrain them to grant that their axiom is not to take any place, save in those things only where the church hath larger *scope*, it resteth that they search out some stronger reason. *Hooker.*

Ah, cut my lace asunder,
That my pent heart may have some *scope* to beat,
Or else I swoon with this dead killing news. *Shakespeare.*

5. Liberty beyond just limits; licence.

Sith 'twas my fault to give the people *scope*,
'Twould be my tyranny to strike and gall them,
For what I bid them do. *Shakespeare.*

Being moody, give him line and *scope*,
'Till that his passions, like a whale on ground,
Confound themselves with working. *Shakesp. Henry IV.*

6. Act of riot; sally.

As surfeit is the father of much fast,
So every *scope*, by the immoderate use,
Turns to restraint. *Shakespeare.*

7. Extended quantity.

The *scopes* of land granted to the first adventurers were too large, and the liberties and royalties were too great for subjects. *Davies on Ireland.*

8. It is out of use, except in the three first senses.

SCO'PULOUS. *adj.* [*scopulosus*, Latin.] Full of rocks. *Dict.*

SCORBU'TICAL. } *n. s.* [*scorbutique*, Fr. from *scorbutus*, Latin.]
SCORBU'TICK. } Diseased with the scurvy.

A person about forty, of a full and *scorbutical* body, having broke her skin, endeavoured the curing of it; but observing the ulcer sanious, I proposed digestion. *Wiseman.*

Violent purging hurts *scorbutick* constitutions; lenitive substances relieve. *Arbuthnot.*

SCORBU'TICALLY. *adv.* [from *scorbutical.*] With tendency to the scurvy; in the scurvy.

A woman of forty, *scorbutically* and hydropically affected, having a sordid ulcer, put herself into my hand. *Wiseman.*

SCORCE. *n. s.* This word is used by *Spenser* for discourse, or power of reason.

Lively vigour rested in his mind,
And recompensed him with a better *scorce*;
Weak body well is chang'd for mind's redoubled force. *F. Q.*

To SCORCH. *v. a.* [ꞅcoꞃcneꝺ, Saxon, burnt]

1. To burn superficially.

Fire *scorcheth* in frosty weather. *Bacon's Nat. History.*

The ladies gasp'd, and scarcely cou'd respire;
The breath they drew, no longer air, but fire;
The fainty knights were *scorch'd.* *Dryden.*

2. To burn.

Power was given to *scorch* men with fire. *Rev.* xvi. 8.

The same that left thee by the cooling stream,
Safe from sun's heat; but *scorch'd* with beauty's beam. *Fairf.*

You look with ſuch contempt on pain,
That languiſhing you conquer more:
So lightnings which in ſtorms appear,
Scorch more than when the ſkies are clear. *Waller.*

The ſame beams that ſhine, *ſcorch* too. *South.*

I rave,
And, like a giddy bird in dead of night,
Fly round the fire that *ſcorches* me to death. *Dryden.*

He from whom the nations ſhould receive
Juſtice and freedom, lies himſelf a ſlave;
Tortur'd by cruel change of wild deſires,
Laſh'd by mad rage, and *ſcorch'd* by brutal fires. *Prior.*

To Scorch. *v. n.* To be burnt ſuperficially; to be dried up.

To ſee the chariot of the ſun
So near the *ſcorching* country run. *Roſcommon.*

The love was made in Autumn, and the hunting followed properly, when the heats of that *ſcorching* country were declining. *Dryden.*

Scatter a little mungy ſtraw or fern amongſt your ſeedlings, to prevent the roots from *ſcorching*, and to receive the moiſture that falls. *Mortimer's Husbandry.*

Sco'rching *Fennel. n. ſ.* A plant.

SCO'RDIUM. n. ſ. [Latin.] An herb. *Ainſworth.*

SCORE. *n. ſ.* [*ſkora*, Iſlandick, a mark, cut, or notch.]

1. A notch or long inciſion.

Our forefathers had no other books but the *ſcore* and the tally: thou haſt cauſed printing to be uſed. *Shakeſ. Henry* VI.

2. A line drawn.

3. An account, which, when writing was leſs common, was kept by marks on tallies, or by lines of chalk.

He's worth no more:
They ſay he parted well, and paid his *ſcore*. *Shakeſp. Macb.*

Does not the air feed the flame? And does not the flame warm and enlighten the air? Does not the earth quit *ſcores* with all the elements, in the fruits that iſſue from it. *South.*

4. Account kept of ſomething paſt.

Univerſal deluges have ſwept all away, except two or three perſons who begun the world again upon a new *ſcore*. *Tillotſon.*

5. Debt imputed.

That thou do'ſt love her, ſtrikes ſome *ſcores* away
From the great compt. *Shakeſp. All's well that ends well.*

He can win widows and pay *ſcores*,
Out-flatter favourites, or out-lie either
Jovius or Surius, or both together. *Donne.*

6. Reaſon; motive.

The knight, upon the fore-nam'd *ſcore*,
In queſt of Sidrophel advancing,
Was now in proſpect of the manſion. *Hudibras.*

He had been prentice to a brewer,
But left the trade, as many more
Have lately done on the ſame *ſcore*. *Hudibras.*

A lion, that had got a politick fit of ſickneſs, wrote the fox word how glad he ſhould be of his company, upon the *ſcore* of ancient friendſhip. *L'Eſtrange.*

If your terms are moderate, we'll never break off upon that *ſcore*. *Collier on Pride.*

7. Sake; account; reaſon referred to ſome one.

You act your kindneſs on Cydaria's *ſcore*. *Dryden.*

Kings in Greece were depoſed by their people upon the *ſcore* of their arbitrary proceedings. *Swift.*

8. Twenty. I ſuppoſe, becauſe twenty, being a round number, was diſtinguiſhed on tallies by a long ſcore.

How many *ſcore* of miles may we well ride
'Twixt hour and hour? *Shakeſ. Cymbeline.*

The fewer ſtill you name, you wound the more;
Bond is but one; but Harpax is a *ſcore*. *Pope.*

For ſome *ſcores* of lines there is a perfect abſence of that ſpirit of poeſy. *Watts.*

9. *A ſong in* Score. The words with the muſical notes of a ſong annexed.

To Score. *v. a.*

1. To ſet down as a debt.

Madam, I know when
Inſtead of five you *ſcor'd* me ten. *Swift.*

2. To impute; to charge.

Your follies and debauches change
With ſuch a whirl, the poets of your age
Are tir'd, and cannot *ſcore* 'em on the ſtage;
Unleſs each vice in ſhort-hand they indite,
Ev'n as notcht prentices whole ſermons write. *Dryden.*

3. To mark by a line.

Haſt thou appointed where the moon ſhould riſe,
And with her purple light adorn the ſkies?
Scor'd out the bounded ſun's obliquer ways,
That he on all might ſpread his equal rays? *Sandys.*

SCO'RIA. n. ſ. [Latin.] Droſs; recrement.

The *ſcoria*, or vitrified part, which moſt metals, when heated or melted, do continually protrude to the ſurface, and which, by covering the metals in form of a thin glaſſy ſkin, cauſes theſe colours, is much denſer than water. *Newt. Opt.*

Sco'rious. *adj.* [from *ſcoria*, Lat.] Droſſy; recrementitious.

By the fire they emit many droſſy and *ſcorious* parts. *Brown.*

To SCORN. *v. a* [*ſchernen*, Dutch; *eſcorner*, French.] To deſpiſe; to ſlight; to revile; to vilify; to contemn.

My friends *ſcorn* me; but mine eye poureth out tears unto God. *Job* xvi. 20.

To Scorn. *v. n.* To ſcoff.

He ſaid mine eyes were black, and my hair black;
And now, I am remember'd, *ſcorn'd* at me. *Shakeſpeare.*

Our ſoul is filled with the *ſcorning* of thoſe that are at eaſe, and with the contempt of the proud. *Pſ.* cxxiii. 4.

I've ſeen the morning's lovely ray
Hover o'er the new-born day,
With roſy wings ſo richly bright,
As if he *ſcorn'd* to think of night. *Craſhaw.*

Fame, that delights around the world to ſtray,
Scorns not to take our Argos in her way. *Pope's Statius.*

Scorn. *n. ſ.* [*eſcorne*, old Fr. from the verb.] Contempt; ſcoff; ſlight; act of contumely.

If he do fully prove himſelf the honeſt ſhepherd Menalcas his brother and heir, I know no reaſon why you ſhould think *ſcorn* of him. *Sidney.*

Unto thee will I cry, O Lord: think no *ſcorn* of me, leſt if thou make as tho' thou heareſt not, I become like them that go down into the pit. *Pſ.* xxviii. 1.

We were better parch in Africk's ſun,
Than in the pride and ſalt *ſcorn* of his eyes. *Shakeſpeare.*

Why ſhould you think that I ſhould woo in *ſcorn*?
Scorn and deriſion never come in tears. *Shakeſpeare.*

If we draw her not unto us, ſhe will laugh us to *ſcorn*. *Jud.*

Diogenes was aſked in *ſcorn*, what was the matter that philoſophers haunted rich men, and not rich men philoſophers? He anſwered, becauſe the one knew what they wanted, the others did not. *Bacon.*

Whoſoever hath any thing in his perſon that induces contempt, hath alſo a perpetual ſpur to reſcue himſelf from *ſcorn*: therefore all deformed perſons are bold, as being on their own defence as expoſed to *ſcorn*. *Bacon.*

Every ſullen frown and bitter *ſcorn*,
But fann'd the fuel that too faſt did burn. *Dryden.*

Is it not a moſt horrid ingratitude, thus to make a *ſcorn* of him that made us? *Tillotſon.*

Numidia's grown a *ſcorn* among the nations
For breach of publick vows. *Addiſon's Cato.*

Sco'rner. *n. ſ.* [from *ſcorn*.]

1. Contemner; deſpiſer.

They are very active, vigilant in their enterpriſes, preſent in perils, and great *ſcorners* of death. *Spenſer on Ireland.*

2. Scoffer; ridiculer.

The *ſcorner* ſhould conſider, upon the ſight of a cripple, that it was only the diſtinguiſhing mercy of heaven that kept him from being one too. *L'Eſtrange.*

They, in the *ſcorner's* or the judge's ſeat,
Dare to condemn the virtue which they hate. *Prior.*

Sco'rnful. *adj.* [*ſcorn* and *full*.]

1. Contemptuous; inſolent.

Th' enamour'd deity
The *ſcornful* damſel ſhuns. *Dryden.*

2. Acting in defiance.

With him I o'er the hills had run,
Scornful of Winter's froſt and Summer's ſun. *Prior.*

Sco'rnfully. *adv.* [from *ſcornful*.] Contemptuouſly; inſolently.

He us'd us *ſcornfully*: he would have ſhew'd us
His marks of merit, wounds receiv'd for's country. *Shakeſ.*

The ſacred rights of the Chriſtian church are *ſcornfully* trampled on in print, under an hypocritical pretence of maintaining them. *Atterbury's Sermons.*

Sco'rpion. *n. ſ.* [*ſcorpion*, French; *ſcorpio*, Latin.]

1. A reptile much reſembling a ſmall lobſter, but that his tail ends in a point with a very venomous ſting.

Well, fore-warning winds
Did ſeem to ſay, ſeek not a *ſcorpion's* neſt. *Shakeſp. H.VI.*

Full of *ſcorpions* is my mind, dear wife. *Shak. Macbeth.*

If he ſhall aſk an egg, will he offer him a *ſcorpion*? *Lu.* xi.

2. One of the ſigns of the zodiack.

The ſqueezing crab and ſtinging *ſcorpion* ſhine. *Dryden.*

3. A ſcourge ſo called from its cruelty.

My father hath chaſtiſed you with whips, but I will chaſtiſe you with *ſcorpions*. *1 Kings* xii. 11.

4. [*Scorpius*, Latin.] A ſea fiſh. *Ainſworth.*

Scorpion *Sena. n. ſ.* [*emerus*, Latin.] A plant.

The characters are: it hath leaves like thoſe of the colutea: the flowers are papilionaceous; the pods are ſlender, and contain two or three cylindrical-ſhaped ſeeds in each. *Miller.*

Scorpion *Graſs.*
Scorpion's *Tail.* } *n. ſ.* Herbs. *Ainſworth.*
Scorpion *Wort.*

Scot. *n. ſ.* [*écot*, French.]

1. Shot; payment.

2. Scot *and Lot.* Pariſh payments.

'Twas time to counterfeit, or that hot termagant Scot had paid me *ſcot and lot* too. *Shakeſp. Henry* IV.

Protogenes, hiſtorians note,
Liv'd there a burgeſs, *ſcot and lot.* *Prior.*

The chief point that has puzzled the freeholders, as well as those that pay *scot and lot*, for about these six months, is, whether they would rather be governed by a prince that is obliged by law to be good, or by one who, if he pleases, may plunder or imprison. *Addison.*

To SCOTCH. *v. a.* To cut with shallow incisions.

He was too hard for him directly: before Corioli, he *scotcht* and notcht him like a carbonado. *Shakesp. Coriolanus.*

SCOTCH. *n. s.* [from the verb.] A slight cut; a shallow incision.

We'll beat 'em into bench-holes: I have yet room for six *scotches* more. *Shakesp. Ant. and Cleopatra.*

Give him four *scotches* with a knife, and then put into his belly and these *scotches* sweet herbs. *Walton's Angler.*

SCOTCH *Collops*, or *Scotched Collops*. *n. s.* [from *To scotch*, or cut.] Veal cut into small pieces.

SCOTCH *Hoppers*. *n. s.* A play in which boys hop over lines or scotches in the ground.

Children being indifferent to any thing they can do, dancing and *scotch hoppers* would be the same thing to them. *Locke.*

SCO'TOMY. *n. s.* [σκότωμα.] A dizziness or swimming in the head, causing dimness of sight, wherein external objects seem to turn round. *Ains.* and *Bailey.*

SCO'TTERING. A provincial word which denotes, in Herefordshire, a custom among the boys of burning a wad of pease-straw at the end of harvest. *Bailey.*

SCO'VEL. *n. s.* [*scopa*, Latin.] A sort of mop of clouts for sweeping an oven; a maulkin. *Ains.* and *Bailey.*

SCO'UNDREL. *n. s.* [*scondaruolo*, Italian, a hider. *Skinner.*] A mean rascal; a low petty villain.

Now to be baff'd by a *scoundrel*,
An upstart sect'ry, and a mungrel. *Hudibras.*

Scoundrels as these wretched Ombites be,
Canopus they exceed in luxury. *Tate.*

Go, if your ancient but ignoble blood
Has crept through *scoundrels* ever since the flood,
Go, and pretend your family is young;
Nor own your fathers have been fools so long. *Pope.*

To SCOUR. *v. a.* [*skurer*, Danish; *schceuren*, Dutch.]

1. To rub hard with any thing rough, in order to clean the surface.

I were better to be eaten to death with a rust, than to be *scour'd* to nothing with perpetual motion. *Shakesp. Hen.* IV.

By dint of sword his crown he shall increase,
And *scour* his armour from the rust of peace. *Dryden's Æn.*

Part *scour* the rusty shields with seam, and part
New grind the blunted ax, and point the dart. *Dryden.*

Some blamed Mrs. Bull for grudging a quarter of a pound of soap and sand to *scour* the rooms. *Arbuthnot.*

Poor Vadius, long with learned spleen devour'd,
Can taste no pleasure since his shield was *scour'd*. *Pope.*

2. To purge violently.

3. To cleanse; to bleach; to whiten; to blanche.

In some lakes the water is so nitrous, as, if foul clothes be put into it, it *scoureth* them of itself; and, if they stay, they moulder away. *Bacon's Natural History.*

A garden-worm should be well *scoured* eight days in moss, before you fish with him. *Walton's Angler.*

Beneath the lamp her tawdry ribbons glare,
The new *scour'd* manteau, and the slattern air. *Gay.*

4. To remove by scouring.

Never came reformation in a flood
With such a heady current, *scouring* faults;
Nor ever hydra-headed wilfulness
So soon did lose his seat, and all at once,
As in this king. *Shakesp. Henry* V.

I will wear a garment all of blood,
And stain my favour in a bloody mask,
Which, wash'd away, shall *scour* my shame with it. *Shak.*

Then, in the clemency of upward air,
We'll *scour* our spots, and the dire thunder's scar. *Dryden.*

5. To range in order to catch or drive away something; to clear away.

The kings of Lacedemon having set out some gallies, under the charge of one of their nephews, to *scour* the sea of the pyrates, they met us. *Sidney.*

Divers are kept continually to *scour* these seas, infested greatly by pirates. *Sandys.*

If with thy guards thou *scour'st* the streets by night,
And do'st in murders, rapes, and spoils delight,
Please not thyself the flatt'ring crowd to hear,
'Tis fulsome stuff. *Dryden's Pers.*

6. To pass swiftly over.

Sometimes
He *scours* the right hand coast, sometimes the left. *Milton.*

Not half the number in their seats are found,
But men and steeds lie grov'ling on the ground;
The points of spears are stuck within the shield,
The steeds without their riders *scour* the field,
The knights unhors'd. *Dryden.*

When Ajax strives some rock's vast weight to throw,
The line too labours, and the words move slow;
Not so when swift Camilla *scours* the plain,
Flies o'er th' unbending corn, and skims along the main.
Pope's Essay on Criticism.

To SCOUR. *v. n.*

1. To perform the office of cleaning domestick utensils.

I keep his house, and was to wring, brew, bake, *scour*, dress meat, and make the beds. *Shakespeare.*

2. To clean.

Warm water is softer than cold; for it *scoureth* better. *Bac.*

3. To be purged or lax.

Some apothecaries, upon stamping coloquintida, have been put into a great *scouring* by the vapour only. *Bacon.*

Convulsion and *scouring*, they say, do often cause one another. *Graunt's Bills of Mortality.*

If you turn sheep into wheat or rye to feed, let it not be too rank, lest it make them *scour*. *Mortimer's Husbandry.*

4. To rove; to range.

Barbarossa, thus *scouring* along the coast of Italy, struck an exceeding terror into the minds of the citizens of Rome. *Knoll.*

5. To run here and there.

The enemy's drum is heard, and fearful *scouring*
Doth choak the air with dust. *Shak. Timon.*

6. To run with great eagerness and swiftness; to scamper.

She from him fled with all her pow'r,
Who after her as hastily 'gan to *scour*. *Fairy Queen.*

I saw men *scour* so on their way: I ey'd them
Even to their ships. *Shakes. Winter's Tale.*

Word was brought him, in the middle of his schemes, that his house was robbed; and so away he *scours* to learn the truth. *L'Estrange.*

If they be men of fraud, they'll *scour* off themselves, and leave those that trust them to pay the reckoning. *L'Estrange.*

So four fierce coursers, starting to the race,
Scour through the plain, and lengthen ev'ry pace;
Nor reins, nor curbs, nor threat'ning cries they fear,
But force along the trembling charioteer. *Dryden.*

As soon as any foreign object presses upon the sense, those spirits, which are posted upon the out-guards, immediately take the alarm, and *scour* off to the brain, which is the head quarters. *Collier.*

Swift at her call her husband *scour'd* away,
To wreak his hunger on the destin'd prey. *Pope.*

SCO'URER. *n. s.* [from *scour.*]

1. One that cleans by rubbing.

2. A purge.

3. One who runs swiftly.

SCOURGE. *n. s.* [*escourgee*, French; *scoreggia*, Italian; *corrigia*, Latin.]

1. A whip; a lash; an instrument of discipline.

When he had made a *scourge* of small cords, he drove them all out of the temple. *Jo.* ii. 15.

The *scourge*
Inexorable, and the torturing hour,
Calls us to penance. *Milton.*

2. A punishment; a vindictive affliction.

What *scourge* for perjury
Can this dark monarchy afford false Clarence? *Shakespeare.*

See what a *scourge* is laid upon your hate,
That heav'n finds means to kill your joys with love. *Shak.*

Famine and plague are sent as *scourges* for amendment. 2 *Esd.*

2. One that afflicts, harrasses, or destroys. Thus *Attila* was called *flagellum Dei.*

Is this the *scourge* of France?
Is this the Talbot so much fear'd abroad,
That with his name the mothers still their babes? *Sh. H.*VI.

Such conquerors are not the favourites, but *scourges* of God, the instruments of that vengeance. *Atterbury's Sermons.*

In all these trials I have born a part;
I was myself the *scourge* that caus'd the smart. *Pope.*

Immortal Jove,
Let kings no more with gentle mercy sway,
Or bless a people willing to obey,
But crush the nations with an iron rod,
And every monarch be the *scourge* of God. *Pope.*

3. A whip for a top.

If they had a top, the *scourge* stick and leather strap should be left to their own making. *Locke.*

To SCOURGE. *v. a.* [from the noun.]

1. To lash with a whip; to whip.

The gods are just, and of our pleasant vices
Make instruments to *scourge* us. *Shakesp. King Lear.*

Others had trial of cruel mockings and *scourgings*. *Hebr.*

Is it lawful for you to *scourge* a Roman, and uncondemned?
Acts xxii. 25.

He *scourg'd* with many a stroke the indignant waves.
Milton's Paradise Lost.

When a professor of any religion is set up to be laughed at, this cannot help us to judge of the truth of his faith, any better than if he were *scourged*. *Watts.*

2. To

2. To punish; to chastise; to chasten; to castigate with any punishment or affliction.

Seeing that thou hast been *scourged* from heaven, declare the mighty power of God. *2 Mac.* iii. 34.

He doth *scourge*, and hath mercy. *Tob.* iii. 2.

He will *scourge* us for our iniquities, and will have mercy again. *Tob.* xiii. 5.

SCO'URGER. *n. s.* [from *scourge.*] One that scourges; a punisher or chastiser.

To SCOURSE. *v. a.* To exchange one thing for another; to swap. *Ainsw.* It seems a corruption of *scorsa*, Ital. exchange; and hence a *horse scourser*.

SCOUT. *n. s.* [*escout*, Fr. from *escouter*; *auscultare*, Lat. to listen; *scolta*, Italian.] One who is sent privily to observe the motions of the enemy.

Are not the speedy *scouts* return'd again,
That dogg'd the mighty army of the dauphin? *Shakesp.*

As when a *scout*,
Through dark and desert ways with peril gone
All night, at last, by break of cheerful dawn,
Obtains the brow of some high-climbing hill. *Milton.*

This great vessel may have lesser cabins, wherein *scouts* may be lodged for the taking of observations. *Wilkins.*

The *scouts* to sev'ral parts divide their way,
To learn the natives names, their towns, explore
The coasts. *Dryden's Æn.*

To SCOUT. *v. n.* [from the noun.] To go out in order to observe the motions of an enemy privately.

Oft on the bordering deep
Encamp their legions; or with obscure wing
Scout far and wide into the realm of night,
Scorning surprize. *Milton.*

As a hunted panther casts about
Her glaring eyes, and pricks her list'ning ears to *scout*,
So she, to shun his toils, her cares employ'd. *Dryden.*

Command a party out,
With a strict charge not to engage, but *scout*. *Dryden.*

To SCOWL. *v. n.* [ꞅcylian, to squint, Saxon; *skeela sig*, to look sour, Islandick.] To frown; to pout; to look angry, sour, or sullen.

Miso, having now her authority increased, came with *scowling* eyes to deliver a slavering good-morrow to the two ladies. *Sidney.*

With bent louring brows, as she would threat,
She *scowl'd* and frowned with froward countenance. *F. Q.*

Even so, or with much more contempt, mens eyes
Did *scowl* on Richard. *Shakespeare's Richard* II.

Not a courtier,
Although they wear their faces to the bent
Of the king's look, but hath a heart that is
Glad at the thing they *scowl* at. *Shakesp. Cymbeline.*

The dusky clouds o'erspread
Heav'n's cheerful face, the low'ring element
Scowls o'er the darken'd landschape snow or show'r. *Milton.*

Fly, fly, prophane fogs! far hence fly away,
With your dull influence; it is for you
To sit and *scowl* upon night's heavy brow. *Crashaw.*

In rueful gaze
The cattle stand, and on the *scowling* heavens
Cast a deploring eye. *Thomson's Summer.*

SCOWL. *n. s.* [from the verb.] Look of sullenness or discontent; gloom.

I've seen the morning's lovely ray
Hover o'er the new-born day,
With rosy wings so richly bright,
As if he scorn'd to think of night;
When a ruddy storm, whose *scowl*
Made heaven's radiant face look foul,
Call'd for an untimely night,
To blot the newly-blossom'd light. *Crashaw.*

SCO'WLINGLY. *adv.* [from *scowl.*] With a frowning and sullen look.

To SCRA'BBLE. *v. n.* [*krabbelen*, *scraffelen*, to scrape or scratch, Dutch.] To paw with the hands.

He feigned himself mad in their hands, and *scrabbled* on the doors of the gate. *1 Sa.* xxi. 13.

SCRAG. *n. s.* [*scraghe*, Dutch.] Any thing thin or lean.

SCRA'GGED. *adj.* [This seems corrupted from *cragged.*] Rough; uneven; full of protuberances or asperities.

Is there then any physical deformity in the fabrick of a human body, because our imagination can strip it of its muscles and skin, and shew us the *scragged* and knotty backbone? *Bentley's Sermons.*

SCRA'GGEDNESS. } *n. s.* [from *scragged.*]
SCRA'GGINESS. } *n. s.* [from *scraggy.*]

1. Leanness; marcour.
2. Unevenness; roughness; ruggedness.

SCRA'GGY. *n. s.* [from *scrag.*]

1. Lean; marcid; thin.

Such a constitution is easily known by the body being lean, warm, hairy, *scraggy*, and dry, without a disease. *Arbuthnot.*

2. [Corrupted from *craggy.*] Rough; rugged; uneven.

From a *scragey* rock, whose prominence
Half overshades the ocean, hardy men,
Fearless of rending winds and dashing waves,
Cut sampire. *Phillips.*

To SCRA'MBLE. *v. n.* [The same with *scrabble*; *scraffelen*, Dutch.]

1. To catch at any thing eagerly and tumultuously with the hands; to catch with haste preventive of another; to contend tumultuously which shall catch any thing.

England now is left
To tug and *scramble*, and to part by th' teeth
The unow'd interest of proud swelling state. *Shakespeare.*

Of other care they little reck'ning make,
Than how to *scramble* at the shearer's feast,
And shove away the worthy bidden guest. *Milton.*

It is not to be supposed, that, when such a tree was shaking, there would be no *scrambling* for the fruit. *Stillingfleet.*

They must have *scrambled* with the wild beasts for crabs and nuts. *Ray on the Creation.*

2. To climb by the help of the hands: as, he *scrambled* up that rock.

SCRA'MBLE. *n. s.* [from the verb.]

1. Eager contest for something, in which one endeavours to get it before another.

As they were in the middle of their gambols, some body threw a handful of apples among them, that set them presently together by the ears upon the *scramble*. *L'Estrange.*

Because the desire of money is constantly almost every where the same, its vent varies very little, but as its greater scarcity enhances its price and increases the *scramble*. *Locke.*

2. Act of climbing by the help of the hands.

SCRA'MBLER. *n. s.* [from *scramble.*]

1. One that scrambles.

All the little *scramblers* after fame fall upon him. *Addison.*

2. One that climbs by help of the hands.

To SCRANCH. *v. a.* [*schrantzer*, Dutch.] To grind somewhat crackling between the teeth. The Scots retain it.

SCRA'NNEL. *adj.* [Of this word I know not the etymology, nor any other example.] Vile; worthless. Perhaps grating by the sound.

When they list, their lean and flashy songs
Grate on their *scrannel* pipes of wretched straw. *Milton.*

SCRAP. *n. s.* [from *scrape*, a thing scraped or rubbed off.]

1. A small particle; a little piece; a fragment.

It is an unaccountable vanity to spend all our time raking into the *scraps* and imperfect remains of former ages, and neglecting the clearer notices of our own. *Glanv.*

Trencher esquires spend their time in hopping from one great man's table to another's, only to pick up *scraps* and intelligence. *L'Estrange.*

Languages are to be learned only by reading and talking, and not by *scraps* of authors got by heart. *Locke.*

No rag, no *scrap*, of all the beau, or wit,
That once so flutter'd, and that once so writ. *Pope.*

I can never have too many of your letters: I am angry at every *scrap* of paper lost. *Pope.*

2. Crumb; small particles of meat left at the table.

The contract you pretend with that base wretch,
One bred of alms, and foster'd with cold dishes,
With *scraps* o' th' court, is no contract. *Shak. Cymbeline.*

The attendants puff a court up beyond her bounds, for their own *scraps* and advantage. *Bacon.*

On bones, on *scraps* of dogs let me be fed,
My limbs uncover'd, and expos'd my head
To bleakest colds. *Granv.*

What has he else to bait his traps,
Or bring his vermin in, but *scraps*?
The offals of a church distrest,
A hungry vicarage. *Swift.*

3. A small piece of paper. This is properly *scrip*.

Pregnant with thousands flits the *scrap* unseen,
And silent sells a king, or buys a queen. *Pope.*

To SCRAPE. *v. a.* [ꞅcneopan, Saxon; *schrapen*, Dutch; *'sascrôpitigh*, Erse; *cravn*, Welsh.]

1. To deprive of the surface by the light action of a sharp instrument, used with the edge almost perpendicular.

These hard woods are more properly *scraped* than planed. *Mox.*

2. To take away by scraping; to eraze.

They shall destroy the walls, and I will *scrape* her dust, and make her like the top of a rock. *Ezek.* xxvi. 4.

Bread for a toast lay on the coals; and, if toasted quite through, *scrape* off the burnt side, and serve it up. *Swift.*

3. To act upon any surface with a harsh noise.

The chiming clocks to dinner call;
A hundred footsteps *scrape* the marble hall. *Pope.*

4. To gather by great efforts, or penurious or trifling diligence.

Let the government be ruined by his avarice, if, by the same avarice, he can *scrape* together so much as to make his peace. *South's Sermons.*

Unhappy those who hunt for a party, and *scrape* together out of every author all those things only which favour their own tenets. *Watts.*

5. *To* SCRAPE *Acquaintance.* A low phrase. To curry favour, or insinuate into one's familiarity.

To SCRAPE. *v. n.*

1. To make a harsh noise.
2. To play ill on a fiddle.
3. To make an aukward bow. *Ainsworth.*

SCRAPE. *n. s.* [*skrap*, Swedish.] Difficulty; perplexity; distress. This is a low word.

SCRA'PER. *n. s.* [from *scrape.*]

1. Instrument with which any thing is scraped.

Never clean your shoes on the *scraper*, but in the entry, and the *scraper* will last the longer. *Swift.*

2. A miser; a man intent on getting money; a scrapepenny.

Be thrifty, but not covetous; therefore give
Thy need, thine honour, and thy friend his due:
Never was *scraper* brave man. Get to live,
Then live, and use it; else it is not true
That thou hast gotten: surely use alone
Makes money not a contemptible stone. *Herbert.*

3. A vile fiddler.

Out! ye sempiternal *scrapers.* *Cowley.*

Have wild boars or dolphins the least emotion at the most elaborate strains of your modern *scrapers*, all which have been tamed and humanized by ancient musicians? *Arbuthnot.*

SCRAT. *n. s.* [ꞅcꞃıττa, Saxon.] An hermaphrodite. *Skinner* and *Junius.*

To SCRATCH. *v. a.* [*kratzen*, Dutch.]

1. To tear or mark with slight incisions ragged and uneven.

The lab'ring swain
Scratch'd with a rake a furrow for his grain,
And cover'd with his hand the shallow seed again. *Dryden.*

A sort of small sand-coloured stones, so hard as to *scratch* glass. *Grew's Musæum.*

2. To tear with the nails.

How can I tell but that his talons may
Yet *scratch* my son, or rend his tender hand. *Fa. Queen.*

I should have *scratch'd* out your unseeing eyes,
To make my master out of love with thee. *Shakespeare.*

I had rather hear my dog bark at a crow, than a man swear he loves me.

——Keep your ladyship still in that mind! so some gentleman or other shall 'scape a predestinate *scratcht* face.

——*Scratching* could not make it worse, an 'twere such a face as yours were. *Shak. Much Ado about Nothing.*

Scots are like witches: do but whet your pen,
Scratch 'till the blood come, they'll not hurt you then. *Cleav.*

To wish that there were nothing but such dull tame things in the world, that will neither bite nor *scratch*, is as childless as to wish there were no fire in nature. *More.*

Unhand me, or I'll *scratch* your face;
Let go, for shame. *Dryden.*

3. To wound slightly.
4. To hurt slightly with any thing pointed or keen.

Daphne, roaming through a thorny wood,
Scratching her legs, that one shall swear she bleeds. *Shakes.*

5. To rub with the nails.

Francis Cornfield did *scratch* his elbow, when he had sweetly invented to signify his name St. Francis, with a friary cowl in a corn field. *Camden.*

Other mechanical helps Aretæus uses to procure sleep, particularly the *scratching* of the temples and the ears. *Arbuthnot.*

Be mindful, when invention fails,
To *scratch* your head, and bite your nails. *Swift.*

6. To write or draw aukwardly.

If any of their labourers can *scratch* out a pamphlet, they desire no wit, style, or argument. *Swift.*

SCRATCH. *n. s.* [from the verb.]

1. An incision ragged and shallow.

The coarse file cuts deep, and makes deep *scratches* in the work; and before you can take out those deep *scratches* with your finer cut files, those places where the risings were when your work was forged, may become dents to your hammer dents. *Moxon's Mech. Exer.*

The smaller the particles of those substances are, the smaller will be the *scratches*, by which they continually fret and wear away the glass until it be polished; but be they never so small, they can wear away the glass no otherwise than by grating and scratching it, and breaking the protuberances: and therefore polish it no otherwise than by bringing its roughness to a very fine grain, so that the *scratches* and frettings of the surface become too small to become visible. *Newton's Opt.*

2. Laceration with the nails.

These nails with *scratches* shall deform my breast,
Lest by my look or colour be express'd
The mark of aught high-born, or ever better dress'd. *Prior.*

3. A slight wound.

The valiant beast turning on her with open jaws, she gave him such a thrust through his breast, that all the lion could do was with his open paw to tear off the mantle and sleeve of Zelmane, with a little *scratch* rather than a wound. *Sidney.*

Heav'n forbid a shallow *scratch* should drive
The prince of Wales from such a field as this. *Shak. H.* IV.

SCRA'TCHER. *n. s.* [from *scratch.*] He that scratches.

SCRA'TCHES. *n. s.* Cracked ulcers or scabs in a horse's foot. *Ains.*

SCRA'TCHINGLY. *adv.* [from *scratching.*] With the action of scratching.

Making him turn close to the ground, like a cat, when *scratchingly* she wheels about after a mouse. *Sidney.*

SCRAW. *n. s.* [Irish and Erse.] Surface or scurf.

Neither should that odious custom be allowed of cutting *scraws*, which is flaying off the green surface of the ground to cover their cabins, or make up their ditches. *Swift.*

To SCRAWL. *v. a.* [I suppose to be corrupted from *scrabble.*]

1. To draw or mark irregularly or clumsily.
2. To write unskilfully and inelegantly.

Peruse my leaves through ev'ry part,
And think thou see'st its owner's heart,
Scrawl'd o'er with trifles thus, and quite
As hard, as senseless, and as light. *Swift.*

Think not your verses sterling,
Though with a golden pen you *scrawl*,
And scribble in a Berlin. *Swift.*

3. [From *crawl.*] To creep like a reptile. *Ains.*

SCRAWL. *n. s.* [from the verb.] Unskilful and inelegant writing.

The left hand will make such a *scrawl*, that it will not be legible. *Arbuthn. Hist. of John Bull.*

Mr. Wycherly, hearing from me how welcome his letters would be, writ to you, in which I inserted my *scrawl.* *Pope.*

SCRA'WLER. *n. s.* [from *scrawl.*] A clumsy and inelegant writer.

SCRAY. *n. s.* A bird called a sea-swallow. *Ains.* and *Bailey.*

SCRE'ABLE. *adj.* [*screabilis*, Latin.] That which may be spit out. *Bailey.*

To SCREAK. *v. n.* [Properly *creak*, or *shriek*, from *skrige*, Dan.] To make a shrill or hoarse noise. *Bailey.*

To SCREAM. *v. n.* [ꞅꞃeman. Saxon.]

1. To cry out shrilly, as in terrour or agony.

Soon a whirlwind rose around,
And from afar he heard a *screaming* sound,
As of a dame distress'd, who cry'd for aid,
And fill'd with loud laments the secret shade. *Dryden.*

The fearful matrons raise a *screaming* cry,
Old feeble men with fainter groans reply;
A jarring sound results, and mingles in the sky. *Dryden.*

If chance a mouse creeps in her sight,
Can finely counterfeit a fright;
So sweetly *screams*, if it comes near her,
She ravishes all hearts to hear her. *Swift.*

2. To cry shrilly.

I heard the owl *scream*, and the crickets cry. *Shakesp.*

SCREAM. *n. s.* [from the verb.] A shrill quick loud cry of terrour or pain.

Our chimneys were blown down; and, as they say,
Lamentings heard i' th' air, strange *screams* of death. *Shak.*

Then flash'd the livid lightning from her eyes,
And *screams* of horror rend th' affrighted skies. *Pope.*

To SCREECH. *v. n.* [*skrækia*, to cry, Islandick.]

1. To cry out as in terrour or anguish.

Screeching is an appetite of expelling that which suddenly strikes the spirits. *Bacon.*

2. To cry as a night owl: thence called a screechowl.

SCREECH. *n. s.* [from the verb.]

1. Cry of horrour and anguish.
2. Harsh horrid cry.

The birds obscene, that nightly flock'd to taste,
With hollow *screechs* fled from the dire repast;
And ravenous dogs, allur'd by scented blood,
And starving wolves, ran howling to the wood. *Pope.*

SCREE'CHOWL. *n. s.* [*screech* and *owl.*] An owl that hoots in the night, and whose voice is supposed to betoken danger, misery, or death.

Deep night,
The time of night when Troy was set on fire,
The time when *screechowls* cry, and bandogs howl. *Shakesp.*

Let him, that will a *screechowl* ay be call'd,
Go into Troy, and say there, Hector's dead. *Shakespeare.*

By the *screechowl's* dismal note,
By the black night raven's throat,
I charge thee, Hob. *Drayton.*

Jupiter, though he had hung the balance, and given it a jog to weigh down Turnus, sent the *screechowl* to discourage him. *Dryden.*

O, that *screechowl* at the window! we shall be pursued immediately. *Dryden's Don Sebastian.*

Sooner shall *screechowls* bask in sunny day,
Than I forget my shepherd's wonted love. *Gay.*

SCREEN. *n. s.* [*escran*, French.]

1. Any thing that affords shelter or concealment.

Now near enough: your leavy *screens* throw down,
And show like those you are. *Shakes. Macbeth.*

Some ambitious men seem as *screens* to princes in matters of danger and envy. *Bacon.*

Our

Our people, who transport themselves, are settled in those interjacent tracts, as a *screen* against the insults of the savages. *Swift.*

My juniors by a year,
Who wisely thought my age a *screen*,
When death approach'd, to stand between,
The *screen* remov'd, their hearts are trembling. *Swift.*

2. Any thing used to exclude cold or light.

When there is a *screen* between the candle and the eye, yet the light passeth to the paper whereon one writeth. *Bacon.*

One speaks the glory of the British queen,
And one describes a charming Indian *screen*. *Pope.*

Ladies make their old cloaths into patchwork for *screens* and stools. *Swift.*

3. A riddle to sift sand.

To SCREEN. *v. a.* [from the noun.]

1. To shelter; to conceal; to hide.

Back'd with a ridge of hills,
That *screen'd* the fruits of th' earth and seats of men,
From cold Septentrion blasts. *Milt. Par. Regain'd.*

A good magistrate's retinue of state *screens* him from the dangers, which he is to incur for the sake of it. *Atterbury.*

This gentle deed shall fairly be set foremost,
To *screen* the wild escapes of lawless passion. *Rowe.*

2. [*Cerno crevi*, Latin.] To sift; to riddle.

Let the cases be filled with natural earth, taken the first half spit, from just under the turf of the best pasture ground, mixed with one part of very mellow soil *screened*. *Evelyn.*

SCREW. *n. s.* [*scroeve*, Dutch; *escrou*, French.] One of the mechanical powers, which is defined a right cylinder cut into a furrowed spiral: of this there are two kinds, the male and female; the former being cut convex, so that its threads rise outwards; but the latter channelled on its concave side, so as to receive the former. *Quincy.*

The *screw* is a kind of wedge, that is multiplied or continued by a helical revolution about a cylinder, receiving its motion not from any stroak, but from a vectis at one end of it. *Wilkins's Math. Magick.*

After your apples are ground, commit them to the *screw* press, which is the best. *Mortimer's Husbandry.*

To SCREW. *v. a.* [from the noun.]

1. To turn by a screw.

If we should fail.—
——We fail!
But *screw* your courage to the sticking place,
And we'll not fail. *Shakesp. Macbeth.*

Some, when the press by utmost vigour *screw'd*,
Has drain'd the pulpous mass, regale their swine
With the dry refuse. *Phillips.*

2. To fasten with a screw.

To *screw* your lock on the door, make wide holes, big enough to receive the shank of the screw. *Moxon.*

3. To deform by contorsions.

Sometimes a violent laughter *screw'd* his face,
And sometimes ready tears dropp'd down apace. *Cowley.*

With *screwed* face, and doleful whine, they ply you with senseless harangues against human inventions on the one hand, and loud outcries for a further reformation on the other. *South.*

He *screw'd* his face into a harden'd smile,
And said Sebastian knew to govern slaves. *Dryden.*

Let others *screw* their hypocritick face,
She shews her grief in a sincerer place. *Swift.*

4. To force; to bring by violence.

He resolved to govern by subaltern ministers, who *screwed* up the pins of power too high. *Howel's Vocal Forest.*

No discourse can be administered, but they will try to turn the tide, and draw it all into their own channel; or they will *screw* in here and there some intimations of what they said or did. *Government of the Tongue.*

The rents of land in Ireland, since they have been so enormously raised and *screwed* up, may be computed to be about two millions. *Swift.*

5. To squeeze; to press.

6. To oppress by extortion.

Our country landlords, by unmeasurable *screwing* and racking their tenants, have already reduced the miserable people to a worse condition than the peasants in France. *Swift.*

SCREW *Tree. n. s.* [*isora*, Latin.] A plant of the East and West Indies.

To SCRI'BBLE. *v. a.* [*scribo*, *scribillo*, Latin.]

1. To fill with artless or worthless writing.

How gird the sphere
With centrick and eccentrick, *scribbl'd* o'er
Cycle and epicycle, orb in orb. *Milton's Paradise Lost.*

2. To write without use or elegance.

To SCRI'BBLE. *v. n.* To write without care or beauty.

If a man should affirm, that an ape casually meeting with pen, ink and paper, and falling to *scribble*, did happen to write exactly the Leviathan of Hobbes, would an atheist believe such a story? And yet he can easily digest things as incredible as that. *Bently.*

If Mævius *scribble* in Apollo's spite,
There are, who judge still worse than he can write. *Pope.*

Leave flattery to fulsome dedicators,
Whom, when they praise, the world believes no more
Than when they promise to give *scribbling* o'er. *Pope.*

SCRI'BBLE. *n. s.* [from the verb.] Worthless writing.

By solemnly endeavouring to countenance my conjectures, I might be thought dogmatical in a hasty *scribble*. *Boyle.*

If it struck the present taste, it was soon transferred into the plays and current *scribbles* of the week, and became an addition to our language. *Swift.*

SCRI'BBLER. *n. s.* [from *scribble*.] A petty author; a writer without worth.

The most copious writers are the arrantest *scribblers*, and in so much talking the tongue runs before the wit. *L'Estrange.*

The actors represent such things as they are capable, by which they and the *scribbler* may get their living. *Dryden.*

The *scribbler*, pinch'd with hunger, writes to dine,
And to your genius must conform his line. *Granv.*

To affirm he had cause to apprehend the same treatment with his father, is an improbable scandal flung upon the nation by a few bigotted French *scribblers*. *Swift.*

No body was concerned or surprised, if this or that *scribbler* was proved a dunce. *Letter to Pope's Dunciad.*

SCRIBE. *n. s.* [*scribe*, French; *scriba*, Latin.]

1. A writer.

Hearts, tongues, figures, *scribes*, bards, poets, cannot
Think, speak, cast, write, sing, number, ho!
His love to Antony. *Shak. Ant. and Cleopatra.*

My master, being the *scribe* to himself, should write the letter. *Shakespeare.*

A certain *scribe* came and said, master, I will follow thee. *Mat.* viii. 19.

We are not to wonder, if he thinks not fit to make any perfect and unerring *scribes*. *Grew's Cosmol.*

The following letter comes from some notable young female *scribe*. *Spectator.*

2. A publick notary. *Ainsworth.*

SCRI'MER. *n. s.* [*escrimeur*, French.] A gladiator; a fencing master. Not in use.

The *scrimers* of their nation,
He swore, had neither motion, guard, nor eye,
If you oppos'd them. *Shakesp. Hamlet.*

SCRINE. *n. s.* [*scrinium*, Latin.] A place in which writings or curiosities are reposited.

Help then, O holy virgin,
Thy weaker novice to perform thy will;
Lay forth, out of thine everlasting *scrine*,
The antique rolls which there lie hidden still. *Fa. Queen.*

SCRIP. *n. s.* [*skræppa*, Islandick.]

1. A small bag; a satchel.

Come, shepherd, let us make an honourable retreat; though not with bag and baggage, yet with *scrip* and scrippage. *Shak.*

He'd in requittal ope his leathern *scrip*,
And shew me simples of a thousand names,
Telling their strange and vigorous faculties. *Milton.*

2. [From *scriptio*, Latin, as it seems.] A schedule; a small writing.

Call them generally man by man, according to the *scrip*. *Shakespeare's Midsummer Night's Dream.*

Bills of exchange cannot pay our debts abroad, 'till *scrips* of paper can be made current coin. *Locke.*

SCRI'PPAGE. *n. s.* [from *scrip*.] That which is contained in a scrip. *Dict.*

SCRI'PTORY. *adj.* [*scriptorius*, Latin.] Written; not orally delivered. *Swift.*

SCRI'PTURAL. *adj.* [from *scripture*.] Contained in the Bible; biblical.

By creatures, the *scriptural* use of that word determines it sometimes to men. *Atterbury.*

SCRI'PTURE. *n. s.* [*scriptura*, Latin.]

1. Writing.

It is not only remembered in many *scriptures*, but famous for the death and overthrow of Crassus. *Raleigh.*

2. Sacred writing; the Bible.

With us there is never any time bestowed in divine service, without the reading of a great part of the holy *scripture*, which we account a thing most necessary. *Hooker.*

The devil can cite *scripture* for his purpose:
An evil soul producing holy witness,
Is like a villain with a smiling cheek. *Shakespeare.*

There is not any action which a man ought to do, or to forbear, but the *scripture* will give him a clear precept, or prohibition for it. *South.*

Forbear any discourse of other spirits, 'till his reading the *scripture* history put him upon that enquiry. *Locke.*

Scripture proof was never the talent of these men, and 'tis no wonder they are foiled. *Atterbury.*

Why are *scripture* maxims put upon us, without taking notice of *scripture* examples, that lie cross 'em? *Atterbury.*

The author of nature and the *scriptures* has expresly enjoined, that he who will not work, shall not eat. *Seed's Serm.*

SCRI'VENER.

SCRI'VENER. *n. s.* [*scrivano*, Latin.]

1. One who draws contracts.

We'll pass the business privately and well:
Send for your daughter by your servant here,
My boy shall fetch the *scrivener*. *Shakesf. Tam. of the Shrew.*

2. One whose business is to place money at interest.

How happy in his low degree,
Who leads a quiet country life,
And from the griping *scrivener* free? *Dryden's Horace.*

I am reduced to beg and borrow from *scriveners* and usurers, that suck the heart and blood. *Arbuthn. Hist. of John Bull.*

SCRO'FULA. *n. s.* [from *scrofa*, Latin, a sow, as χοιράς.] A depravation of the humours of the body, which breaks out in sores commonly called the king's evil.

If matter in the milk dispose to coagulation, it produces a *scrofula*. *Wiseman of Tumours.*

SCRO'FULOUS. *adj.* [from *scrofula*.] Diseased with the scrofula.

Scrofulous persons can never be duly nourished; for such as have tumours in the parotides often have them in the pancreas and mesentery. *Arbuthnot on Aliments.*

English consumptions generally proceed from a *scrofulous* disposition. *Arbuthnot.*

What would become of the race of men in the next age, if we had nothing to trust to, beside the *scrofulous* consumptive production furnished by our men of wit and pleasure? *Swift.*

SCROLL. *n. s.* [Supposed by *Minshew* to be corrupted from *roll*; by *Skinner* derived from *escrouelle*, a shrimp given by the heralds: whence parchment, wrapped up into a resembling form, has the same name. It may be observed, that a gaoler's list of prisoners is *escrou*.] A writing wrapped up.

His chamber all was hanged about with rolls,
And old records from ancient times deriv'd;
Some made in books, some in long parchment *scrolls*,
That were all worm-eaten, and full of canker holes. *Spens.*

Accept this *scroll*,
Which, in right of Richard Plantagenet,
We do exhibit to your majesty. *Shakesp. H. VI.*

See'st thou this letter, take it up,
And give the king this fatal plotted *scroll*. *Shakes. Tit. Andr.*

We'll add a royal number to the dead,
Gracing the *scroll*, that tells of this war's loss,
With slaughter coupled to the name of kings. *Shakespeare.*

Here is the *scroll* of every man's name, which is thought fit through all Athens to play in our interlude. *Shakespeare.*

A Numidian priest, bellowing out certain superstitious charms, cast divers *scrolls* of paper on each side the way, wherein he cursed and banned the Christians. *Knolles.*

He drew forth a *scroll* of parchment, and delivered it to our foremost man. *Bacon.*

Such follow him, as shall be register'd;
Part good, part bad: of bad the longer *scroll*. *Milton.*

With this epistolary *scroll*,
Receive the partner of my inmost soul. *Prior.*

Yet if he wills, may change or spoil the whole;
May take yon' beauteous, mystick, starry roll,
And burn it, like an useless parchment *scroll*. *Prior.*

SCROYLE. *n. s.* [This word I remember only in *Shakespeare*: it seems derived from *escrouelle*, French, a scrofulous swelling; as he calls a mean fellow a *scab* from his itch, or a *patch* from his raggedness.] A mean fellow; a rascal; a wretch.

The *scroyles* of Angiers flout you kings,
And stand securely on their battlements,
As in a theatre. *Shakespeare's King John.*

To SCRUB. *v. a.* [*schrubben*, Dutch.] To rub hard with some '`ing coarse and rough.

.h wrinkles as a skilful hand would draw
For an old grandam ape, when, with a grace,
She sits at squat, and *scrubs* her leathern face. *Dryden.*

She never would lay aside the use of brooms and *scrubbing* brushes. *Arbuthnot.*

Now Moll had whirl'd her mop with dext'rous airs,
Prepar'd to *scrub* the entry and the stairs. *Swift.*

SCRUB. *n. s.* [from the verb.]

1. A mean fellow, either as he is supposed to scrub himself for the itch, or as he is employed in the mean offices of scouring away dirt.

2. Any thing mean or despicable.

With a dozen large vessels my vault shall be stor'd;
No little *scrub* joint shall come on my board. *Swift.*

3. A worn out broom. *Ainsworth.*

SCRU'BBED. } *adj.* [*scrubet*, Danish.] Mean; vile; worth-
SCRU'BBY. } less; dirty; sorry.

I gave it to a youth,
A kind of boy, a little *scrubbed* boy,
No higher than thyself. *Shak. Merchant of Venice.*

The *scrubbiest* cur in all the pack,
Can set the mastiff on your back. *Swift.*

The scene a wood, produc'd no more
Than a few *scrubby* trees before. *Swift.*

SCRUFF. *n. s.* The same, I suppose, with *scurf*, by a metathesis usual in pronunciation.

SCRU'PLE. *n. s.* [*scrupule*, French; *scrupulus*, Latin.]

1. Doubt; difficulty of determination; perplexity: generally about minute things.

Macduff, this noble passion,
Child of integrity, hath from my soul
Wip'd the black *scruples*, reconcil'd my thoughts
To your good truth. *Shakespeare's Macbeth.*

Nothing did more fill foreign nations with admiration of his succession, than the consent of all estates of England for the receiving of the king without the least *scruple*, pause, or question. *Bacon.*

For the matter of your confession, let it be severe and serious; but yet so as it may be without any inordinate anxiety, and unnecessary *scruples*, which only intangle the soul. *Taylor.*

Men make no *scruple* to conclude, that those propositions, of whose knowledge they can find in themselves no original, were certainly the impress of God and nature upon their minds, and not taught them by any one else. *Locke.*

2. Twenty grains; the third part of a dram.

Milk one ounce, oil of vitriol a *scruple*, doth coagulate; the milk at the bottom, where the vitriol goeth. *Bacon.*

3. Proverbially, any small quantity.

Nature never lends
The smallest *scruple* of her excellence,
But, like a thrifty goddess, she determines
Herself the glory of a creditor. *Shakesp. Meas. for Meas.*

To SCRU'PLE. *v. n.* [from the noun.] To doubt; to hesitate.

He *scrupled* not to eat
Against his better knowledge; not deceiv'd,
But fondly overcome with female charms. *Milt. Par. Lost.*

SCRU'PLER. *n. s.* [from *scruple*.] A doubter; one who has scruples.

The scruples which many publick ministers would make of the worthiness of parents to have their children baptised, forced such questioned parents, who did not believe the necessity of having their children baptised by such *scruplers*, to carry their children unto other ministers. *Graunt's Bills of Mortality.*

SCRUPULO'SITY. *n. s.* [from *scrupulous*.]

1. Doubt; minute and nice doubtfulness.

Amongst ourselves there was some question moved, by reason of a few mens *scrupulosity* touching certain things. *Hooker.*

The one sort they warned to take heed, that *scrupulosity* did not make them rigorous in giving unadvised sentence against their brethren which were free; the other, that they did not become scandalous, by abusing their liberty and freedom to the offence of their weak brethren, which were scrupulous. *Hook.*

So careful, even to *scrupulosity*, were they to keep their sabbath, that they must not only have a time to prepare them for that, but a further time also to prepare them for their very preparations. *South.*

2. Fear of acting in any manner; tenderness of conscience.

The first sacrilege is looked on with some horror; but when they have once made the breach, their *scrupulosity* soon retires. *Decay of Piety.*

SCRU'PULOUS. *adj.* [*scrupuleux*, French; *scrupulosus*, Latin; from *scruple*.]

1. Nicely doubtful; hard to satisfy in determinations of conscience.

They warned them that they did not become scandalous, by abusing their liberty, to the offence of their weak brethren which were *scrupulous*. *Hooker.*

Some birds, inhabitants of the waters, whose blood is cold as fishes, and their flesh is so like in taste, that the *scrupulous* are allowed them on fish-days. *Locke.*

2. Given to objections; captious.

Equality of two domestick pow'rs
Breeds *scrupulous* faction. *Shakesp. Ant. and Cleopatra.*

3. Nice; doubtful.

As the cause of a war ought to be just, so the justice of that cause ought to be evident; not obscure, not *scrupulous*. *Bacon's holy War.*

4. Careful; vigilant; cautious.

I have been the more *scrupulous* and wary, in regard the inferences drawn from these observations are of some importance. *Woodward.*

SCRU'PULOUSLY. *adv.* [from *scrupulous*.] Carefully; nicely; anxiously.

The duty consists not *scrupulously* in minutes and half hours. *Taylor.*

Henry V. manifestly derived his courage from his piety, and was *scrupulously* careful not to ascribe the success of it to himself. *Addison's Freeholder.*

SCRU'PULOUSNESS. *n. s.* [from *scrupulous*.] The state of being scrupulous.

SCRU'TABLE. *adj.* [from *scrutor*, Latin.] Discoverable by inquiry.

Shall we think God so *scrutable*, or ourselves so penetrating, that none of his secrets can escape us? *Decay of Piety.*

SCRUTA'TION. *n. s.* [*scrutor*, Latin.] Search; examination; inquiry. *Dict.*

SCRUTA'TOR. *n. s.* [*scrutateur*, Fr. from *scrutor*, Lat.] Enquirer; searcher; examiner.

In process of time, from being a simple *scrutator*, an archdeacon became to have jurisdiction more amply. *Ayliffe.*

Scru'tinous. *adj.* [from *scrutiny.*] Captious; full of inquiries. A word little used.

Age is froward, uneasy, *scrutinous*,
Hard to be pleas'd, and parcimonious. *Denham.*

SCRU'TINY. *n. s.* [*scrutinium*, Latin.] Enquiry; search; examination with nicety.

In the *scrutinies* for righteousness and judgment, when it is inquired whether such a person be a good man or no, the meaning is not, what does he believe or hope, but what he loves. *Taylor's Rule of living holy.*

I thought thee worth my nearer view
And narrower *scrutiny*, that I might learn
In what degree or meaning thou art call'd
The son of God. *Milton's Paradise Regain'd.*

They that have designed exactness and deep *scrutiny*, have taken some one part of nature. *Hale.*

Their difference to measure, and to reach,
Reason well rectify'd must nature teach;
And these high *scrutinies* are subjects fit
For man's all-searching and enquiring wit. *Denham.*

We are admonished of want of charity towards others, and want of a Christian *scrutiny* and examination into ourselves. *L'Estrange.*

When any argument of great importance is managed with that warmth, which a serious conviction of it generally inspires, somewhat may easily escape, even from a wary pen, which will not bear the test of a severe *scrutiny*. *Atterbury.*

These, coming not within the *scrutiny* of human senses, cannot be examined by them, or attested by any body. *Locke.*

To Scru'tinize. } *v. a.* [from *scrutiny.*] To search; to examine.
To Scru'tiny. }

The compromissarii should chuse according to the votes of such, whose votes they were obliged to *scrutinize*. *Ayliffe.*

Scruto'ire. *n. s.* [for *scritoire*, or *escritoire.*] A case of drawers for writings.

I locked up these papers in my *scrutoire*, and my *scrutoire* came to be unlocked. *Prior.*

To Scruze. *v. a.* [Perhaps from *screw*. This word, though now disused by writers, is still preserved, at least in its corruption, *to scrouge*, in the *London* jargon.] To squeeze; to compress.

Though up he caught him 'twixt his puissant hands,
And having *scruzed* out of his carrion corse
The loathful life, now loos'd from sinful bands,
Upon his shoulders carried him. *Fairy Queen.*

To SCUD. *v. n.* [*squittire*, Italian; *skutta*, Swedish; *skiótur*, swift, Islandick.] To fly; to run away with precipitation.

The vote was no sooner passed, but away they *scudded* to the next lake. *L'Estrange.*

The frighted satyrs, that in woods delight,
Now into plains with prick'd-up ears take flight;
And *scudding* thence, while they their horn-feet ply,
About their sires the little sylvans cry. *Dryden.*

Away the frighted spectre *scuds*,
And leaves my lady in the suds. *Swift.*

To Scu'ddle. *v. n.* [from *scud.*] To run with a kind of affected haste or precipitation. A low word.

Scuffle. *n. s.* [This word is derived by *Skinner* from *shuffle.*] A confused quarrel; a tumultuous broil.

His captain's heart,
In the *scuffles* of great fights hath burst
The buckles on his breast. *Shakesp. Ant. and Cleopatra.*

Avowed atheists, placing themselves in the seat of the scorner, take much pleasing divertisement, by deriding our eager *scuffles* about that which they think nothing. *Decay of Piety.*

The dog leaps upon the serpent, and tears it to pieces; but in the *scuffle* the cradle happened to be overturned. *L'Estrange.*

Popish missionaries mix themselves in these dark *scuffles*, and animate the mob to such outrages and insults. *Addison.*

To Scu'ffle. *v. n.* [from the noun.] To fight confusedly and tumultuously.

I must confess I've seen, in former days,
The best knights in the world, and *scuffled* in some frays. *Drayton.*

A gallant man had rather fight to great disadvantages in the field, in an orderly way, than *scuffle* with an undisciplined rabble. *King Charles.*

To SCULK. *v. n.* [*sculcke*, Danish] To lurk in hiding places; to lie close.

It has struck on a sudden into such a reputation, that it scorns any longer to *sculk*, but owns itself publickly. *Gov. of Tongue.*

Fearing to be seen, within a bed
Of coleworts he conceal'd his wily head;
There *sculk'd* 'till afternoon, and watch'd his time. *Dryden.*

My prophets and my sophists finish'd here
Their civil efforts of the verbal war:
Not so my rabbins and logicians yield;
Retiring still they combat; from the field
Of open arms unwilling they depart,
And *sculk* behind the subterfuge of art. *Prior.*

No news of Phyl.! the bridegroom came,
And thought his bride had *sculk'd* for shame;
Because her father us'd to say
The girl had such a bashful way. *Swift.*

The immediate publishers thereof lay *sculking* under the wings of an act of parliament. *Letter to Publisher of the Dunc.*

Scu'lker. *n. s.* [from *sculk.*] A lurker; one that hides himself for shame or mischief.

Scull. *n. s.* [It is derived by *Skinner* from *shell*, in some provinces called *shull*; as *testa* and *teste*, or *tête*, signify the head. Mr. *Lye* observes more satisfactorily, that *skola* is in Islandick the *skull* of an animal.]

1. The bone which incases and defends the brain; the arched bone of the head.

Fractures of the *scull* are at all times very dangerous, as the brain becomes affected from the pressure. *Sharp*

2. A small boat; a cockboat. [See Sculler.]

3. One who rows a cockboat.

Like caitiff vile, that for misdeed
Rides with his face to rump of steed;
Or rowing *scull*, he's fain to love,
Look one way and another move. *Hudibras.*

4. [Sceole, Saxon, an assembly.] In *Milton*'s style, a shoal or vast multitude of fish.

Each bay
With fry innumerable swarm, and shoals
Of fish, that with their fins and shining scales
Glide under the green wave, in *sculls* that oft
Bank the mid sea. *Milton.*

Scu'llcap. *n. s.* [*scull* and *cap.*]

1. A headpiece.

2. A nightcap.

Scu'ller. *n. s.* [Of this word I know not the etymology. *Skiola* is in Islandick a vessel, and *escueille* in French a dish.]

1. A cockboat; a boat in which there is but one rower.

Her soul already was consign'd to fate,
And shiv'ring in the leaky *sculler* sate. *Dryden.*

They hire the *sculler*, and, when once aboard,
Grow sick, and damn the climate like a lord. *Pope.*

2. One that rows a cockboat.

Scu'llery. *n. s.* [from *skiola*, a vessel, Islandick; or *escueille*, French, a dish.] The place where common utensils, as kettles or dishes, are cleaned and kept.

Pyreicus was famous for counterfeiting base things, as pitchers, a *scullery*, and setting rogues together by the ears. *Peach.*

Scu'llion. *n. s.* [from *escueille*, French, a dish.] The lowest domestick servant, that washes the kettles and the dishes in the kitchen.

I must, like a whore, unpack my heart with words,
And fall a cursing like a very drab,
A *scullion*, fye upon't! foh! about my brain. *Shak. Hamlet.*

If the gentleman hath lain there, get the cook, the stablemen, and the *scullion*, to stand in his way. *Swift.*

To Sculp. *v. a.* [*sculpo*, Latin; *sculper*, Fr.] To carve; to engrave. A word not in use.

Oh, that the tenor of my just complaint
Were *sculpt* with steel on rocks of adamant! *Sandys.*

Scu'lptile. *adj.* [*sculptilis*, Latin.] Made by carving.

In a silver medal is upon one side Moses horned, and on the reverse the commandment against *sculptile* images. *Brown.*

Scu'lptor. *n. s.* [*sculptor*, Latin; *sculpteur*, Fr.] A carver; one who cuts wood or stone into images.

Thy shape's in every part
So clean, as might instruct the *sculptor*'s art. *Dryden.*

The Latin poets give the epithets of *trisidum* and *trisulcum* to the thunderbolt, from the *sculptors* and painters that lived before them, that had given it three forks. *Addison.*

Scu'lpture. *n. s.* [*sculptura*, Latin; *sculpture*, French.]

1. The art of carving wood, or hewing stone into images.

Then *sculpture* and her sister arts revive,
Stones leap'd to form, and rocks began to live. *Pope.*

2. Carved work.

Nor did there want
Cornice or freeze with bossy *sculptures* graven. *Milton.*

There too, in living *sculpture*, might be seen
The mad affection of the Cretan queen. *Dryden.*

3. The act of engraving.

To Scu'lpture. *v. a.* [from the noun.] To cut; to engrave.

Gold, silver, ivory vases *sculptur'd* high,
There are who have not. *Pope.*

Scum. *n. s.* [*escume*, French; *schiuma*, Italian; *skum*, Danish; *schuym*, Dutch.]

1. That which rises to the top of any liquor.

The rest had several offices assign'd;
Some to remove the *scum* as it did rise;
Others to bear the same away did mind;
And others it to use according to his kind. *Fairy Queen.*

The salt part of the water doth partly rise into a *scum* on the top, and partly goeth into a sediment in the bottom. *Bacon.*

Gather'd like *scum*, and settl'd to itself,
Self-fed and self-consum'd. *Milton.*

Away,

Away, ye *scum*,
That still rise upmost when the nation boils. *Dryden.*
They mix a med'cine to foment their limbs,
With *scum* that on the molten silver swims. *Dryden.*

2. The dross; the refuse; the recrement; that part which is to be thrown away.

There flocked unto him all the *scum* of the Irish out of all places, that e're long he had a mighty army. *Spenser.*

Some forty gentlemen excepted, had we the very *scum* of the world, such as their friends thought it an exceeding good gain to be discharged. *Raleigh's Essays.*

I told thee what would come
Of all thy vapouring, base *scum*. *Hudibras.*
The Scythian and Egyptian *scum*
Had almost ruin'd Rome. *Roscommon.*
You'll find, in these hereditary tales,
Your ancestors the *scum* of broken jayls. *Dryden's Juven.*

The great and innocent are insulted by the *scum* and refuse of the people. *Addison's Freeholder.*

To SCUM. *v. a.* [from the noun.] To clear off the scum. Commonly written and spoken *skim.*

A second multitude
Severing each kind, and *scum'd* the bullion dross. *Milton.*
Hear, ye sullen powers below;
Hear, ye taskers of the dead:
You that boiling cauldrons blow,
You that *scum* the molten lead. *Dryd. and Lee's Oedipus.*

What corns swim upon the top of the brine, *scum* off. *Mort.*

SCU'MMER. *n. s.* [*escumoir*, French.] A vessel with which liquor is scummed, commonly called a *skimmer.*

SCUPPER *Holes.* *n. s.* [*schoepen*, Dutch, to draw off.] In a ship, small holes on the deck, through which water is carried into the sea. The leathers over those holes are called *scupper* leathers, and the nails with which they are fastened *scupper* nails. *Bailey.*

SCURF. *n. s.* [ꞅcupꝼ, Saxon; *skurfa*, Islandick; *skurff*, Danish; *skorf*, Swedish; *schorft*, Dutch.]

1. A kind of dry miliary scab.

Her crafty head was altogether bald,
And, as in hate of honourable eld,
Was overgrown with *scurf* and filthy scald. *Fairy Queen.*
The virtue of his hands
Was lost among Pactolus' sands,
Against whose torrent while he swims,
The golden *scurf* peels off his limbs. *Swift.*

2. A soil or stain adherent.

Then are they happy, when by length of time
The *scurf* is worn away of each committed crime,
No speck is left. *Dryden.*

3. Any thing sticking on the surface.

There stood a hill, whose grisly top
Shone with a glossy *scurf*. *Milton.*

Upon throwing in a stone the water boils; and at the same time are seen little flakes of *scurf* rising up. *Addison.*

SCU'RFINESS. *n. s.* [from *scurf.*] The state of being scurfy.

SCU'RRIL. *adj.* [*scurrilis*, Latin.] Low; mean; grosly opprobrious; loudly jocose.

With him, Patroclus,
Upon a lazy bed, the live-long day
Breaks *scurril* jests. *Shakesp. Troilus and Cressida.*

Nothing conduces more to letters than to examine the writings of the ancients, provided the plagues of judging and pronouncing against them be away; such as envy, bitterness, precipitation, impudence, and *scurril* scoffing. *Ben. Johnson.*

Thou mov'st me more by barely naming him,
Than all thy foul unmanner'd *scurril* taunts. *Dryden.*

SCURRI'LITY. *n. s.* [*scurrilité*, Fr. *scurrilitas*, Lat.] Grossness of reproach; loudness of jocularity; mean buffoonery.

Good master Holofernes, purge; so it shall please you to abrogate *scurrility*. *Shakespeare.*

Banish *scurrility* and profaneness, and restrain the licentious insolence of poets. *Dryden.*

SCU'RRILOUS. *adj.* [*scurrilis*, Latin.] Grosly opprobrious; using such language as only the license of a buffoon can warrant; loudly jocular; vile; low.

Yet is not their goodness so intolerable, as, on the contrary side, the *scurrilous* and more than satyrical immodesty of Martinism. *Hooker.*

Let him approach singing.
—Forewarn him that he use no *scurrilous* words in's tunes.
Shakespeare's Winter's Tale.

How often is a person, whose intentions are to do good by the works he publishes, treated in as *scurrilous* a manner as if he were an enemy to mankind? *Addison's Freeholder.*

Their characters have been often treated with the utmost barbarity and injustice by *scurrilous* and enraged orators. *Swift.*

SCU'RRILOUSLY. *adv.* [from *scurrilous.*] With gross reproach; with low buffoonery; with lewd merriment.

Such men there are, who have written *scurrilously* against me, without any provocation. *Dryden.*

It is barbarous incivility *scurrilously* to sport with that which others count religion. *Tillotson.*

SCU'RVILY. *adv.* [from *scurvy.*] Vilely; basely; coarsely. It is seldom used but in a ludicrous sense.

Look i' your glass now,
And see how *scurvily* that countenance shews;
You would be loth to own it. *Ben. Johns. Catiline.*

This alters the whole complexion of an action, that would otherwise look but very *scurvily*, and makes it perfect. *South.*

The clergy were never more learned, or so *scurvily* treated. *Swift.*

SCU'RVY. *n. s.* [from *scurf*. This word was, I believe, originally an adjective.]

The *scurvy* is a distemper of the inhabitants of cold countries, and amongst those such as inhabit marshy, fat, low, moist soils, near stagnating water, fresh or salt; invading chiefly in the Winter such as are sedentary, or live upon salted or smoaked flesh and fish, or quantities of unfermented farinaceous vegetables, and drink bad water. *Arbuthnot.*

SCU'RVY. *adj.* [from *scurf*, *scurfy*, *scurvy.*]

1. Scabbed; covered with scabs; diseased with the scurvy.

Whatsoever man be *scurvy* or scabbed. *Lev.* xxi. 20.

2. Vile; bad; sorry; worthless; contemptible; offensive.

I know him for a man divine and holy;
Not *scurvy*, nor a temporary meddler. *Shakespeare.*
This is a very *scurvy* tune to sing to a man's funeral. *Shakesp.*
He spoke *scurvy* and provoking terms
Against your honour. *Shakespeare.*

A crane, which is but *scurvy* meat, lays but two eggs. *Chey.*

It would be convenient to prevent the excess of drink, with that *scurvy* custom of taking tobacco. *Swift.*

SCU'RVYGRASS. *n. s.* [*scurvy* and *grass.*] The spoonwort. A plant.

The flower consists of four leaves, which are disposed in form of a cross: from the flower-cup arises the pointal, which becomes an almost globular fruit, divided into two cells by an intermediate partition, to which the valves adhere on both sides, and are furnished with many round seeds. *Miller.*

'SCUSES. For excuses.

I shifted him away,
And laid good *'scuses* on your exstasy. *Shakesp. Othello.*

SCUT. *n. s.* [*skott*, Islandick.] The tail of those animals whose tails are very short, as a hare.

In the hare it is aversely seated, and in its distension inclines unto the coccix or *scut*. *Brown's Vulgar Errours.*

He fled to earth; but first it cost him dear,
He left his *scut* behind, and half an ear. *Swift.*

SCU'TCHEON. *n. s.* [*scuccione*, Italian, from *scutum*, Lat.] The shield represented in heraldry; the ensigns armorial of a family. See ESCHUTCHEON.

And thereto had she that *scutcheon* of her desires, supported by certain badly diligent ministers. *Sidney.*

Your *scutcheons*, and your signs of conquest, shall
Hang in what place you please. *Shak. Ant. and Cleopatra.*
Honour is a meer *scutcheon*. *Shakesp. Henry* IV.
The chiefs about their necks the *scutcheons* wore,
With orient pearls and jewels powder'd o'er. *Dryden.*

SCUTE'LLATED. *adj.* [*scutella*, Lat.] Divided into small surfaces.

It seems part of the *scutellated* bone of a sturgeon, being flat, of a porous or cellular constitution. *Woodward.*

SCU'TIFORM. *adj.* [*scutiformis*, Latin.] Shaped like a shield.

SCU'TTLE. *n. s.* [*scutella*, Latin; *scutell*, Celt. *Ainsw.*]

1. A wide shallow basket, so named from a dish or platter which it resembles in form.

A *scuttle* or skrein to rid soil fro' the corn. *Tusser.*

The earth and stones they are fain to carry from under their feet in *scuttles* and baskets. *Hakewill on Providence.*

2. A small grate.

To the hole in the door have a small *scuttle*, to keep in what mice are there. *Mortimer's Husbandry.*

3. [From *scud.*] A quick pace; a short run; a pace of affected precipitation.

She went with an easy *scuttle* out of the shop. *Spectator.*

To SCU'TTLE. *v. n.* [from *scud* or *scuddle.*] To run with affected precipitation.

The old fellow *scuttled* out of the room. *Arbuthnot.*

To SDEIGN. *v. a.* [*Spenser. Sdegnare*, Ital. *Milton*, for *disdain.*]

Lifted up so high,
I *sdeign'd* subjection. *Milton.*

SDE'IGNFUL. *adj.* Contracted for *disdainful.*

They now, puft up with *sdeignful* insolence,
Despise the brood of blessed sapience. *Spenser.*

SEA. *n. s.* [ꞅæ, Saxon; *see*, or *zee*, Dutch.]

1 The ocean; the water opposed to the land.

Will all great Neptune's ocean wash this blood
Clean from my hand? No, this my hand will rather
Thy multitudinous *sea* incarnardine,
Making the green one red. *Shakesp. Macbeth.*
The rivers run into the *sea*. *Carew.*
He made the *sea*, and all that is therein. *Ex.* xx. 11.
So do the winds and thunders cleanse the air,
So working *seas* settle and purge the wine. *Davies.*
Amphibious between *sea* and land
The river horse. *Milton.*

Some leviathan,
Haply ſlumb'ring on the Norway foam,
The pilot of ſome ſmall night-founder'd ſkiff
Deeming ſome iſland, oft as ſeamen tell,
With fixed anchor in his ſcaly rind,
Moors by his ſide under the lee, while night
Inveſts the *ſea*. *Milton.*

Small fragments of ſhells, broken by ſtorms on ſome ſhores, are uſed for manuring of *ſea* land. *Woodward.*

They put to *ſea* with a fleet of three hundred ſail. *Arbuthn.*

Sea racing dolphins are train'd for our motion,
Moony tides ſwelling to roll us aſhore. *Dryden's Albion.*

But like a rock unmov'd, a rock that braves
The raging tempeſt, and the riſing waves,
Propp'd on himſelf he ſtands: his ſolid ſide
Waſh off the *ſea* weeds, and the ſounding tides. *Dryden.*

The *ſea* could not be much narrower than it is, without a great loſs to the world. *Bentley.*

So when the firſt bold veſſel dar'd the *ſeas*,
High on the ſtern the Thracian rais'd his ſtrain,
While Argo ſaw her kindred trees
Deſcend from Pelion to the main. *Pope.*

2. A collection of water; a lake.

Jeſus walking by the *ſea* of Galilee, ſaw two brethren. *Mat.* iv. 18.

3. Proverbially for any large quantity.

That *ſea* of blood which hath in Ireland been barbarouſly ſhed, is enough to drown in eternal infamy and miſery the malicious author and inſtigator of its effuſion. *King Charles.*

4. Any thing rough and tempeſtuous.

To ſorrow abandon'd, but worſe felt within,
And in a troubled *ſea* of paſſion toſt. *Milton.*

5. *Half* SEAS *over.* Half drunk.

The whole magiſtracy was pretty well diſguiſed before I gave 'em the ſlip: our friend the alderman was *half ſeas over* before the bonfire was out. *Spectator.*

SEA is often uſed in compoſition, as will appear in the following examples.

SE'ABEAT. [*ſea* and *beat.*] Daſhed by the waves of the ſea.

The ſovereign of the ſeas he blames in vain,
That once *ſeabet* will to ſea again. *Spenſer's Paſtorals.*

Darkneſs cover'd o'er
The face of things: along the *ſeabeat* ſhore
Satiate we ſlept. *Pope's Odyſſey.*

SEABO'AT. *n. ſ.* [*ſea* and *boat.*] Veſſel capable to bear the ſea.

Shipwrecks were occaſioned by their ſhips being bad *ſeaboats*, and themſelves but indifferent ſeamen. *Arbuthnot.*

SEABO'RN. *adj.* [*ſea* and *born.*] Born of the ſea; produced by the ſea.

Like Neptune and his *ſeaborn* niece, ſhall be
The ſhining glories of the land and ſea. *Waller.*

All theſe in order march, and marching ſing
The warlike actions of their *ſeaborn* king. *Dryden.*

SEABO'Y. *n. ſ.* [*ſea* and *boy.*] Boy employed on ſhipboard.

Can'ſt thou, O partial ſleep, give thy repoſe
To the wet *ſeaboy* in an hour ſo rude,
And in the calmeſt and the ſtilleſt night
Deny it to a king? *Shakeſpeare.*

SEABRE'ACH. *n. ſ.* [*ſea* and *breach.*] Irruption of the ſea by breaking the banks.

To an impetuous woman, tempeſts and *ſeabreaches* are nothing. *L'Eſtrange.*

SEABREE'ZE. *n. ſ.* [*ſea* and *breeze.*] Wind blowing from the ſea.

Hedges, in moſt places, would be of great advantage to ſhelter the graſs from the *ſeabreeze.* *Mortimer.*

SEABU'ILT. *adj.* [*ſea* and *built.*] Built for the ſea.

Borne each by other in a diſtant line,
The *ſeabuilt* forts in dreadful order move. *Dryden.*

SEACA'BBAGE. *n. ſ.* [*crambe*, Latin.] Seacolewort. A plant.

It hath fleſhy leaves like thoſe of the cabbage. *Miller.*

SE'AHOLLY. *n. ſ.* [*eryngium*, Latin.] A plant.

The ſpecies are, *ſeaholly*, or eryngo. Common eryngo, &c. The roots of the firſt are candied, and ſent to London for medicinal uſe, being the true eryngo.

SE'ACALF. *n. ſ.* [*ſea* and *calf.*] The ſeal.

The *ſeacalf*, or ſeal, is ſo called from the noiſe he makes like a calf: his head comparatively not big, ſhaped rather like an otter's, with teeth like a dog's, and muſtaches like thoſe of a cat: his body long, and all over hairy: his forefeet, with fingers clawed, but not divided, yet fit for going: his hinder feet, more properly fins, and fitter for ſwimming, as being an amphibious animal. The female gives ſuck, as the porpeſs, and other viviparous fiſhes. *Grew's Muſæum.*

SE'ACAP. *n. ſ.* [*ſea* and *cap.*] Cap made to be worn on ſhipboard.

I know your favour well,
Though now you have no *ſeacap* on your head. *Shakeſp.*

SE'ACHART. *n. ſ.* [*ſea* and *chart.*] Map on which only the coaſts are delineated.

The ſituation of the parts of the earth are better learned by a map or *ſeachart*, than reading the deſcription. *Watts.*

SEACOA'L. *n. ſ.* [*ſea* and *coal.*] Coal, ſo called not becauſe found in the ſea, but becauſe brought to *London* by ſea; pitcoal.

We'll have a poſſet ſoon at the latter end of a *ſeacoal* fire. *Shakeſpeare.*

Seacoal laſts longer than charcoal. *Bacon.*

This pulmonique indiſpoſition of the air is very much heightened, where a great quantity of *ſeacoal* is burnt. *Harv.*

SE'ACOAST. *n. ſ.* [*ſea* and *coaſt.*] Shore; edge of the ſea.

The venturous mariner that way,
Learning his ſhip from thoſe white rocks to ſave,
Which all along the ſouthern *ſeacoaſt* lay;
For ſafety's ſake that ſame his ſeamark made,
And nam'd it Albion. *Fairy Queen.*

Upon the *ſeacoaſt* are many parcels of land, that would pay well for the taking in. *Mortimer's Husbandry.*

SE'ACOMPASS. *n. ſ.* [*ſea* and *compaſs.*] The card and needle of mariners.

The needle in the *ſeacompaſs* ſtill moving but to the northpoint only, with moveor immotus, notified the reſpective conſtancy of the gentleman to one only. *Camden's Remains.*

SE'ACOW. *n. ſ.* [*ſea* and *cow.*] The manatee.

The *ſeacow* is a very bulky animal, of the cetaceous kind. It grows to fifteen feet long, and to ſeven or eight in circumference: its head is like that of a hog, but longer, and more cylindrick: its eyes are ſmall, and it has no external ears, but only two little apertures in the place of them; yet its ſenſe of hearing is very quick. Its lips are thick, and it has two long tuſks ſtanding out. It has two fins, which ſtand forward on the breaſt like hands, whence the Spaniards firſt called it manatee. The female has two round breaſts placed between the pectoral fins. The ſkin is very thick and hard, and not ſcaly, but hairy. This creature lives principally about the mouths of the large rivers in Africa, the Eaſt Indies, and America, and feeds upon vegetables. Its fleſh is white like veal, and very well taſted. The lapis manati, which is of a fine clean white colour, and bony texture, is properly the os petroſum of this animal. This ſtone has been ſuppoſed to be a powerful amulet, but is now neglected. *Hill's Mat. Med.*

SEADO'G. *n. ſ.* [*ſea* and *dog.*] Perhaps the ſhark.

Fierce *ſeadogs* devour the mangl'd friends. *Roſcommon.*

When, ſtung with hunger, ſhe embroils the flood,
The *ſeadog* and the dolphin are her food. *Pope's Odyſſey.*

SEAFA'RER. *n. ſ.* [*ſea* and *fare.*] A traveller by ſea; a mariner.

They ſtifly refuſed to vail their bonnets by the ſummons of thoſe towns, which is reckoned intolerable contempt by the better enabled *ſeafarers.* *Carew.*

A wand'ring merchant, he frequents the main,
Some mean *ſeafarer* in purſuit of gain;
Studious of freight, in naval trade well ſkill'd;
But dreads th' athletick labours of the field. *Pope.*

SEAFA'RING. *adj.* [*ſea* and *fare.*] Travelling by ſea.

My wife faſten'd him unto a ſmall ſpare maſt,
Such as *ſeafaring* men provide for ſtorms. *Shakeſpeare.*

It was death to divert the ſhips of *ſeafaring* people, againſt their will, to other uſes than they were appointed. *Arbuthnot.*

SEAFE'NNEL. The ſame with SAMPHIRE, which ſee.

SE'AFIGHT. *n. ſ.* [*ſea* and *fight.*] Battle of ſhips; battle on the ſea.

Seafights have been often final to the war; but this is when princes ſet up their reſt upon the battles. *Bacon.*

They were full of drink at the time of their *ſeafights.* *Wiſeman's Surgery.*

If our ſenſe of hearing were a thouſand times quicker than it is, we ſhould, in the quieteſt retirement, be leſs able to ſleep than in the middle of a *ſeafight.* *Locke.*

This fleet they recruited with two hundred ſail, whereof they loſt ninety-three in a *ſeafight.* *Arbuthnot on Coins.*

SEAFO'WL. *n. ſ.* [*ſea* and *fowl.*] Birds that live at ſea.

The bills of curlews, and many other *ſeafowl*, are very long, to enable them to hunt for the worms. *Derham.*

A *ſeafowl* properly repreſents the paſſage of a deity over the ſeas. *Broome's Notes to the Odyſſey.*

A length of ocean and unbounded ſky,
Which ſcarce the *ſeafowl* in a year o'er fly. *Pope.*

SE'AGIRT. *adj.* [*ſea* and *girt.*] Girded or incircled by the ſea.

Neptune, beſides the ſway
Of every ſalt flood and each ebbing ſtream,
Took in by lot, 'twixt high and nether Jove,
Imperial rule of all the *ſeagirt* iſles. *Milton.*

Telemachus, the blooming heir
Of *ſeagirt* Ithaca, demands my care:
'Tis mine to form his green unpractis'd years
In ſage debates. *Pope.*

SE'AGULL. *n. ſ.* [*ſea* and *gull.*] A water fowl.

Seagulls, when they flock together from the ſea towards the ſhores, foreſhow rain and wind. *Bacon's Nat. Hiſtory.*

Bitterns,

Bitterns, herons, and *seagulls*, are great enemies to fish. *Mortimer's Husbandry.*

SE'AGREEN. *adj.* [*sea* and *green.*] Resembling the colour of the distant sea; cerulean.

White, red, yellow, blue, with their several mixtures, as green, scarlet, purple, and *seagreen*, come in only by the eyes. *Locke.*

Upon his urn reclin'd,
His *seagreen* mantle waving in the wind,
The god appear'd. *Pope.*

SE'AGREEN. *n. s.* Saxifrage. A plant.

SE'AGULL. *n. s.* A sea bird. *Ainsworth.*

SE'AHEDGEHOG. *n. s.* [*sea*, *hedge*, and *hog.*] A kind of sea shell-fish.

The *seahedgehog* is inclosed in a round shell, fashioned as a loaf of bread, wrought and pinched, and guarded by an outer skin full of prickles, as the land urchin. *Carew.*

SE'AHOG. *n. s.* [*sea* and *hog.*] The porpus.

SE'AHOLM. *n. s.* [*sea* and *holm.*]

1. A small uninhabited island.
2. Seaholly. A kind of sea weed.

Cornwal bringeth forth greater store of *seaholm* and samphire than any other county. *Carew.*

SE'AHORSE. *n. s.* [*sea* and *horse.*]

1. The *seahorse* is a fish of a very singular form, as we see it dried, and of the needlefish kind. It is about four or five inches in length, and nearly half an inch in diameter in the broadest part. Its colour, as we see it dried, is a deep reddish brown; and its tail is turned round under the belly. It is found about the Mediterranean, and has been celebrated for medicinal virtues; but is at present wholly neglected. *Hill's Materia Med.*
2. The morse.

Part of a large tooth, round and tapering: a tusk of the morse, or waltrons, called by some the *seahorse*. *Woodward.*

3. The medical and the poetical *seahorse* seem very different. By the seahorse *Dryden* means probably the hippopotamus.

By 'em
Seahorses, flound'ring in the slimy mud,
Toss'd up their heads, and dash'd the ooze about 'em. *Dry.*

SE'AMAID. *n. s.* [*sea* and *maid.*] Mermaid.

Certain stars shot from their spheres,
To hear the *seamaids* musick. *Shakespeare.*

SE'AMAN. *n. s.* [*sea* and *man.*]

1. A sailor; a navigator; a mariner.

She, looking out,
Beholds the fleet, and hears the *seamen* shout. *Denham.*

Seamen, through dismal storms, are wont
To pass the oyster-breeding Hellespont. *Evelyn.*

The whole poem was first written, and now sent you from a place where I have not so much as the converse of any *seaman*. *Dryden.*

Æneas order'd
A stately tomb, whose top a trumpet bore,
A soldier's fauchion, and a *seaman's* oar;
Thus was his friend interr'd. *Dryden.*

By undergoing the hazards of the sea, and the company of common *seamen*, you make it evident you will refuse no opportunity of rendering yourself useful. *Dryden.*

Had they applied themselves to the increase of their strength by sea, they might have had the greatest fleet and the most *seamen* of any state in Europe. *Addison.*

2. Merman; the male of the mermaid.

Seals live at land and at sea, and porpuses have the warm blood and intrails of a hog, not to mention mermaids, or *seamen*. *Locke.*

SEAMA'RK. *n. s.* [*sea* and *mark.*] Point or conspicuous place distinguished at sea, and serving the mariners as directions of their course.

Those white rocks,
Which all along the southern seacoast lay,
Threat'ning unheedy wreck and rash decay,
For safety's sake his *seamark* made,
And nam'd it Albion. *Fairy Queen.*

Though you do see me weapon'd,
Here is my journey's end, here is my butt,
The very *seamark* of my utmost sail. *Shakesp. Othello.*

They were executed at divers places upon the seacoast, for *seamarks* or lighthouses, to teach Perkins's people to avoid the coast. *Bacon's Henry VII.*

They are remembered with a brand of infamy fixt upon them, and set as *seamarks* for those who observe them to avoid. *Dryden.*

The fault of others sway,
He set as *seamarks* for himself to shun. *Dryden.*

SEAME'W. *n. s.* [*sea* and *mew.*] A fowl that frequents the sea.

An island salt and bare,
The haunt of seals, and orcks, and *seamews* clang. *Milton.*

The chough, the *seamew*, the loquacious crow,
Scream aloft. *Pope's Odyssey.*

SE'AMONSTER. *n. s.* [*sea* and *monster.*] Strange animal of the sea.

Seamonsters give suck to their young. *Lam.* iv. 3.

Where luxury once reign'd, *seamonsters* whelp. *Milton.*

SE'ANYMPH. *n. s.* [*sea* and *nymph.*] Goddess of the sea.

Virgil, after Homer's example, gives us a transformation of Æneas's ship into *seanymphs*. *Broome.*

SE'AONION. *n. s.* An herb. *Ainsworth.*

SE'AOOSE. *n. s.* [*sea* and *oose.*] The mud in the sea or shore.

All *seaoose*, or oosy mud, and the mud of rivers, are of great advantage to all sorts of land. *Mortimer.*

SE'APIECE. *n. s.* [*sea* and *piece.*] A picture representing any thing at sea.

Great painters often employ their pencils upon *seapieces*. *Addison's Spectator.*

SE'APOOL. *n. s.* [*sea* and *pool.*] A lake of salt water.

I have often heard it wished, that all that land were a *seapool*. *Spenser on Ireland.*

SE'APORT. *n. s.* [*sea* and *port.*] A harbour.

SE'ARISQUE. *n. s.* [*sea* and *risque.*] Hazard at sea.

He was so great an encourager of commerce, that he charged himself with all the *searisque* of such vessels as carried corn to Rome in the Winter. *Arbuthnot.*

SE'AROCKET. *n. s.* A plant. *Miller.*

SE'AROOM. *n. s.* [*sea* and *room.*] Open sea; spacious main.

There is *searoom* enough for both nations, without offending one another, and it would exceedingly support the navy. *Bacon's Advice to Villiers.*

The bigger whale like some huge carrack lay,
Which wanteth *searoom* with her foes to play. *Waller.*

SEARO'VER. *n. s.* [*sea* and *rove.*] A pirate.

SE'ASHARK. *n. s.* [*sea* and *shark.*] A ravenous seafish.

Witches mummy, maw and gulf
Of the ravening salt *seashark*. *Shakespeare.*

SE'ASHELL. *n. s.* [*sea* and *shell.*] Shells found on the shore.

Seashells are great improvers of sour or cold land. *Mortim.*

SE'ASHORE. *n. s.* [*sea* and *shore.*] The coast of the sea.

That *seashore* where no more world is found,
But foaming billows breaking on the ground. *Dryden.*

Fournier gives an account of an earthquake in Peru, that reached three hundred leagues along the *seashore*. *Burnet.*

To say a man has a clear idea of any quantity, without knowing how great it is, is as reasonable as to say he has the positive idea of the number of the sands on the *seashore*. *Locke.*

SE'ASICK. *adj.* [*sea* and *sick.*] Sick, as new voyagers on the sea.

She began to be much *seasick*, extremity of weather continuing. *Shakespeare.*

Barbarossa was not able to come on shore, for that he was, as they said, *seasick*, and troubled with an ague. *Knolles.*

In love's voyage nothing can offend;
Women are never *seasick*. *Dryden's Juvenal.*

Weary and *seasick*, when in thee confin'd;
Now, for thy safety, cares distract my mind. *Swift.*

SE'ASIDE. *n. s.* [*sea* and *side.*] The edge of the sea.

Their camels were without number, as the sand by the *seaside*. *Jud.* vii. 12.

There disembarking on the green *seaside*,
We land our cattle, and the spoil divide. *Pope.*

SE'ASERPENT. *n. s.* [*sea* and *serpent.*] Serpent generated in the water.

SEASE'RVICE. *n. s.* [*sea* and *service.*] Naval war.

You were pressed for the *seaservice*, and got off with much ado. *Swift's Direct. to Servants.*

SEASU'RGEON. *n. s.* [*sea* and *surgeon.*] A chirurgeon employed on shipboard.

My design was to help the *seasurgeon*. *Wiseman's Surgery.*

SEASURRO'UNDED. *adj.* [*sea* and *surround.*] Encircled by the sea.

To *seasurrounded* realms the gods assign
Small tract of fertile lawn, the least to mine. *Pope.*

SEATE'RM. *n. s.* [*sea* and *term.*] Word of art used by the seamen.

I agree with you in your censure of the *seaterms* in Dryden's Virgil, because no terms of art, or cant words, suit the majesty of epick poetry. *Pope.*

SEAWA'TER. *n. s.* [*sea* and *water.*] The salt water of the sea.

By digging of pits in the seashore, he did frustrate the laborious works of the enemies, which had turned the *seawater* upon the wells of Alexandria. *Bacon's Nat. History.*

I took off the dressings, and bathed the member with *seawater*. *Wiseman.*

Seawater has many gross, rough, and earthy particles in it, as appears from its saltness; whereas fresh water is more pure and unmixt. *Broome's Notes on the Odyssey.*

SEAL. *n. s.* [seol, sele, Saxon; *seel*, Danish.] The seacalf. See SEACALF.

The *seal* or soyle is in make and growth not unlike a pig, ugly faced, and footed like a moldwarp: he delighteth in musick, or any loud noise, and thereby is trained to shew himself above water: they also come on land. *Carew.*

An island salt and bare,
The haunt of *seals* and orcs, and seamaws clang. *Milton.*

SEAL. *n. s.* [ꞅiᵹel, Saxon; *sigillum*, Latin.]

1. A stamp engraved with a particular impression, which is fixed upon the wax that closes letters, or affixed as a testimony.

The king commands you
To render up the great *seal*. *Shakesp. Henry* VIII.

If the organs of perception, like wax overhardened with cold, will not receive the impression of the *seal*; or, like wax of a temper too soft, will not hold it; or else supposing the wax of a temper fit, but the *seal* not applied with a sufficient force to make a clear impression: in any of these cases the print left by the *seal* will be obscure. *Locke.*

The same
His grandsire wore about his neck
In three *seal* rings, which after, melted down,
Form'd a vast buckle for his widow's gown. *Pope.*

2. The impression made in wax.

'Till thou can'st rail the *seal* from off my bond,
Thou but offend'st thy lungs to speak so loud. *Shakesp.*

Solyman shewed him his own letters, asking him if he knew not that hand, and if he knew not that *seal*. *Knolles.*

He saw his monkey picking the *seal* wax from a letter. *Arb.*

3. Any act of confirmation.

They their fill of love
Took largely, of their mutual guilt the *seal*. *Milton.*

To SEAL. *v. a.* [from the noun.]

1. To fasten with a seal.

He that brings this love to thee,
Little knows this love in me;
And by him *seal* up thy mind. *Shakesp. As you like it.*

I have seen her rise from her bed, take forth paper, fold it, write upon't, and afterwards *seal* it. *Shakespeare.*

2. To confirm or attest by a seal.

God join'd my heart to Romeo's; thou our hands;
And ere this hand, by thee to Romeo *seal'd*,
Shall be the label to another deed,
Or my true heart with treacherous revolt
Turn to another, this shall slay them both. *Shakespeare,*

3. To confirm; to ratify; to settle.

My soul is purg'd from grudging hate,
And with my hand I *seal* our true hearts love. *Shak. R.* III.

When I have performed this, and *sealed* to them this fruit, I will come into Spain. *Rom.* xv. 28.

4. To shut; to close.

Seal up your lips, and give no words, but mum! *Shakes.*

At my death
Thou hast *seal'd* up my expectation. *Shakesp. Henry* IV.

The root of evil is *sealed* up from you. 2 *Esdr.* viii. 53.

The sense is like the sun; for the sun *seals* up the globe of heaven, and opens the globe of earth: so the sense doth obscure heavenly things, and reveals earthly things. *Bacon.*

Back to th' infernal pit I drag thee chain'd,
And *seal* thee so, as henceforth not to scorn
The facil gates of hell too slightly barr'd. *Milton.*

5. To mark with a stamp.

You'd rail upon the hostess,
And say you would present her at the leet,
Because she bought stone jugs, and no *seal'd* quarts. *Shakes.*

To SEAL. *v. n.* To fix a seal.

I will *seal* unto this bond. *Shakespeare.*

We make a sure covenant and write it, and our princes and priests *seal* unto it. *Neh.* ix. 38.

SE'ALER. *n. s.* [from *seal*.] One that seals.

SE'ALINGWAX. *n. s.* [*seal* and *wax*.] Hard wax made of rosin used to seal letters.

The prominent orifice was closed with *sealingwax*. *Boyle.*

SEAM. *n. s.* [ꞅeam, Saxon; *zoom*, Dutch.]

1. The edge of cloath where the threads are doubled; the suture where the two edges are sewed together.

In velvet white as snow the troop was gown'd,
The *seams* with sparkling emeralds set around. *Dryden.*

Precepts should be so finely wrought together in the same piece, that no coarse *seam* may discover where they join. *Add.*

2. The juncture of planks in a ship.

With boiling pitch the *seams* instops,
Which, well laid o'er, the salt sea waves withstand. *Dryd.*

3. A cicatrix; a scar.

4. [ꞅeam, Saxon, a load.] A measure; a vessel in which things are held; eight bushels of corn. *Ainsworth.*

5. [Seme, Saxon; *saim*, Welsh; *sain*, French.] Tallow; grease; hog's lard.

Shall the proud lord,
That bastes his arrogance with his own *seam*,
Be worshipp'd? *Shakesp. Troilus and Cressida.*

Part scour the rusty shields with *seam*, and part
New grind the blunted ax. *Dryden's Æn.*

To SEAM. *v. a.* [from the noun.]

1. To join together by suture, or otherwise.

2. To mark; to scar with a long cicatrix.

Seam'd o'er with wounds, which his own sabre gave. *Pope.*

Say, has the small or greater pox
Sunk down her nose, or *seam'd* her face? *Swift.*

SE'AMLESS. *adj.* [from *seam*.] Having no seam.

SE'AMRENT. *n. s.* [*seam* and *rent*.] A separation of any thing where it is joined; a breach of the stitches.

SE'AMSTRESS. *n. s.* [ꞅeameꞅꞇꞃe, Saxon.] A woman whose trade is to sew.

They wanted food and raiment; so they took
Religion for their *seamstress* and their cook. *Cleave'and.*

SE'AMY. *adj.* [from *seam*.] Having a seam; shewing the seam.

Some such squire he was,
That turn'd your wit the *seamy* side without,
And made me to suspect you. *Shak. Othello.*

SEAN. *n. s.* [ꞅeᵹne, Saxon; *sagena*, Latin.] A net. Sometimes written *seine*, or *saine*.

SEAR. *adj.* [ꞅeaꞅan, Saxon, to dry.] Dry; not any longer green. *Spenser* uses it.

I have liv'd long enough: my May of life
Is fall'n into the *sear*, the yellow leaf. *Shak. Macbeth.*

Ye myrtles brown, with ivy never *sear*. *Milton.*

Some may be cherished in dry places, as in *sear* wood. *Ray.*

To SEAR. *v. a.* [ꞅeaꞅan, Saxon.] To burn; to cauterize.

The scorching flame sore singed all his face,
And through his armour all his body *sear'd*. *Fairy Queen.*

Some shall depart from the faith, speaking lies, having their conscience *seared* with a hot iron. 1 *Tim.* iv. 2.

Cherish veins of good humour, and *sear* up those of ill. *Temp.*

I'm *sear'd* with burning steel, 'till the scorch'd marrow
Fries in the bones. *Rowe's Royal Convert.*

SE'ARBREACH. *n. s.* [*sear* and *breach*.] Perhaps *sealreach*.

'Tis one thing for a man to be firm against honest dangers; but to run his head against stone walls, or to put his shoulders to a *searbreach*, to attempt insuperable difficulties, would be just the moral of the ram in the fable. *L'Estrange*

SE'ARCLOATH. *n. s.* [ꞅaꞃclaꝺ, Saxon, from ꞅaꞃ, pain, and claꝺ, a plaster; so that *cerecloath*, as it is now written, from *cera*, wax, seems to be wrong.] A plaster; a large plaster.

Bees wax is the ground of all *searcloath* salves. *Mortimer.*

To SEARCE. *v. a.* [*sasser*, French.] To sift finely.

Put the finely *searced* powder of alabaster into a flat-bottomed and well heated brass vessel. *Boyle.*

For the keeping of meal, bolt and *searce* it from the bran. *Mortimer's Husbandry.*

SEARCE. *n. s.* A sieve; a bolter.

SEA'RCER. *n. s.* [from *searce*.] He who searces.

To SEARCH. *v. a.* [*chercher*, French.]

1. To examine; to try; to explore; to look through.

Help to *search* my house this one time: if I find not what I seek, let me for ever be your table sport. *Shakespeare.*

They returned from *searching* of the land. *Num.* xiii. 25.

Through the void immense
To *search* with wand'ring quest a place foretold. *Milton.*

2. To inquire; to seek.

Now clear I understand
What oft my steddiest thoughts have *search'd* in vain. *Milt.*

Enough is left besides to *search* and know. *Milton.*

Draw up some valuable meditations from the depths of the earth, and *search* them through the vast ocean. *Watts.*

3. To probe as a chirurgeon.

Alas, poor shepherd! *searching* of thy wound,
I have, by hard adventure, found my own. *Shakespeare.*

With this good sword,
That ran through Cæsar's bowels, *search* this bosom. *Shak.*

For the divisions of Reuben there were great *searchings* of heart. *Judg.* v. 16.

The signs of wounds penetrating are discovered by the proportion of the *searching* candle, or probe which enters into the cavity. *Wiseman's Surgery.*

4. *To* SEARCH *out.* To find by seeking.

Who went before you, to *search* you *out* a place to pitch your tents in? *Deutr.* i. 33.

They may sometimes be successful to *search out* truth. *Watts.*

To SEARCH. *v. n.*

1. To make a search.

Satisfy me once more; once more *search* with me. *Shakes.*

To ask or *search* I blame thee not. *Milton.*

2. To make inquiry.

Those who seriously *search* after or maintain truth, should study to deliver themselves without obscurity or equivocation. *Locke.*

It suffices that they have once with care sifted the matter, and *searched* into all the particulars that could give any light to the question. *Locke.*

With piercing eye some *search* where nature plays,
And trace the wanton through her darksome maze. *Tickel.*

3. To seek; to try to find.

Your husband's coming, woman, to *search* for a gentleman that is here now in the house. *Shak. Merry Wives of Windsor.*

We in vain *search* for that constitution within a fly, upon which depend those powers we observe in them. *Locke.*

SEARCH. *n. s.* [from the verb.]

1. Inquiry by looking into every suspected place.

The orb he roam'd
With narrow *search*, and with inspection deep. *Milton.*

2. Inquiry;

2. Inquiry; examination; act of ſeeking.

His reaſons are as two grains of wheat hid in two buſhels of chaff: you ſhall ſeek all day ere you find them, and when you have them they are not worth the *ſearch*. *Shakeſpeare.*

Who great in *ſearch* of God and nature grow,
They beſt the wiſe Creator's praiſe declare. *Dryden.*

Now mourn thy fatal *ſearch*;
It is not ſafe to have too quick a ſenſe. *Dryden.*

The mind ſets itſelf on work in *ſearch* of ſome hidden idea, and turns the eye of the ſoul upon it. *Locke.*

By the philoſophical uſe of words, I mean ſuch an uſe as conveys the preciſe notions of things, which the mind may be ſatisfied with in its *ſearch* after knowledge. *Locke.*

The parents, after a long *ſearch* for the boy, gave him for drowned in a canal. *Addiſon.*

This common practice carries the heart aſide from all that is honeſt in our *ſearch* after truth. *Watts.*

3. Queſt; purſuit.

If zealous love ſhould go in *ſearch* of virtue,
Where ſhould he find it purer than in Blanch? *Shakeſp.*

Stay him from his intendment, or brook ſuch diſgrace well as he ſhall run into; in that it is a thing of his own *ſearch*, and altogether againſt my will. *Shakeſp. As you like it.*

Nor did my *ſearch* of liberty begin,
'Till my black hairs were chang'd upon my chin. *Dryden.*

SE'ARCHER. *n. ſ.* [from *ſearch*.]

1. Examiner; inquirer; trier.

The Agarenes that ſeek wiſdom upon earth, the authors of fables, and *ſearchers* out of underſtanding. *Bar.* iii. 23.

The *ſearchers* found a marvellous difference between the Anakims and themſelves. *Raleigh.*

Religion has given us a more juſt idea of the divine nature: he whom we appeal to is truth itſelf, the great *ſearcher* of hearts, who will not let fraud go unpuniſhed, or hold him guiltleſs that taketh his name in vain. *Addiſon.*

In vain we lift up our preſumptuous eyes
To what our Maker to their ken denies:
The *ſearcher* follows faſt; the object flies. *Prior.*

Avoid the man who practiſes any thing unbecoming a free and open *ſearcher* after truth. *Watts.*

2. Officer in London appointed to examine the bodies of the dead, and report the cauſe of death.

The *ſearchers*, who are ancient matrons ſworn to their office, repair to the place where the dead corps lies, and by view of the ſame, and by other inquiries, examine by what diſeaſe the corps died. *Graunt's Bills of Mortality.*

SE'ASON. *n. ſ.* [*ſaiſon*, French.]

1. One of the four parts of the year, Spring, Summer, Autumn, Winter.

The faireſt flowers o' th' *ſeaſon*
Are our carnations and ſtreak'd gillyflowers. *Shakeſp.*

Then Summer, Autumn, Winter did appear;
And Spring was but a *ſeaſon* of the year. *Dryden.*

We ſaw, in ſix days travelling, the ſeveral *ſeaſons* of the year in their beauty. *Addiſon on Italy.*

2. A time as diſtinguiſhed from others.

He's noble, wiſe, judicious, and beſt knows
The fits o' th' *ſeaſon*. *Shak. Macbeth.*

The *ſeaſon* prime for ſweeteſt ſcents and airs. *Milton.*

3. A fit time; an opportune concurrence.

At *ſeaſon* fit let her with thee partake. *Milton.*

All buſineſs ſhould be done betimes; and there's as little trouble of doing it in *ſeaſon* too, as out of *ſeaſon*. *L'Eſtrange.*

For active ſports, for pleaſing reſt,
This is the time to be poſſeſt;
The beſt is but in *ſeaſon* beſt. *Dryden.*

I would indulge the gladneſs of my heart!
Let us retire: her grief is out of *ſeaſon*. *Philips.*

There is no *ſeaſon* to which ſuch thoughts as theſe are more ſuitable. *Atterbury.*

The *ſeaſon* when to come, and when to go,
To ſing, or ceaſe to ſing, we never know. *Pope.*

4. A time not very long.

We'll ſlip you for a *ſeaſon*, but our jealouſy
Do's yet depend. *Shakeſ. Cymbeline.*

5. [From the verb.] That which gives a high reliſh.

You lack the *ſeaſon* of all natures, ſleep. *Shak. Macbeth.*

To SE'ASON. *v. a.* [*aſſaiſſonner*, French.]

1. To mix with food any thing that gives a high reliſh.

Every oblation of thy meat-offering ſhalt thou *ſeaſon* with ſalt. *Lev.* ii. 13.

They *ſeaſoned* every ſacrifice, whereof a greater part was eaten by the prieſts. *Brown's Vulgar Errours.*

For breakfaſt and ſupper, milk and milk-pottage are very fit for children; only let them be *ſeaſoned* with ſugar. *Locke.*

The wiſe contriver,
To keep the waters from corruption free,
Mixt them with ſalt, and *ſeaſon'd* all the ſea. *Blackmore.*

2. To give a reliſh to.

You *ſeaſon* ſtill with ſports your ſerious hours;
For age but taſtes of pleaſures, youth devours. *Dryden.*

The proper uſe of wit is to *ſeaſon* converſation, to repreſent what is praiſeworthy to the greateſt advantage, and to expoſe the vices and follies of men. *Tillotſon.*

3. To qualify by admixture of another ingredient.

Mercy is above this ſcepter'd ſway;
It is an attribute to God himſelf;
And earthly pow'r does then ſhew likeſt God's,
When mercy *ſeaſons* juſtice. *Shak. Merchant of Venice.*

Seaſon your admiration but a while,
With an attentive ear, 'till I deliver
This marvel to you. *Shak. Hamlet.*

4. To imbue; to tinge or taint.

Whatever thing
The ſcythe of time mows down, devour unſpar'd,
'Till I, in man reſiding, through the race
His thoughts, his looks, words, actions, all infect,
And *ſeaſon* him thy laſt and ſweeteſt prey. *Milton's Pa. Loſt.*

Secure their religion, *ſeaſon* their younger years with prudent and pious principles. *Taylor.*

Sin, taken into the ſoul, is like a liquor poured into a veſſel; ſo much of it as it fills, it alſo *ſeaſons*: the touch and tincture go together. *South.*

5. To fit for any uſe by time or habit; to mature.

The crow doth ſing as ſweetly as the lark,
When neither is attended; and, I think,
The nightingale, if ſhe ſhould ſing by day,
When ev'ry gooſe is cackling, would be thought
No better a muſician than the wren:
How many things by ſeaſon *ſeaſon'd* are,
To their right praiſe and true perfection. *Shakeſpeare.*

Who in want a hollow friend doth try,
Directly *ſeaſons* him his enemy. *Shakeſpeare.*

We charge you, that you have contriv'd to take
From Rome all *ſeaſon'd* office, and to wind
Yourſelf unto a power tyrannical. *Shakeſp. Coriolanus.*

The archers of his guard ſhot two arrows every man together againſt an inch board of well *ſeaſoned* timber. *Hayward.*

His plenteous ſtores do *ſeaſon'd* timber ſend;
Thither the brawny carpenters repair. *Dryden.*

A man ſhould harden and *ſeaſon* himſelf beyond the degree of cold wherein he lives. *Addiſon.*

To SE'ASON. *v. n.* To be mature; to grow fit for any purpoſe.

Carpenters rough plane boards for flooring, that they may ſet them by to *ſeaſon*. *Moxon's Mech. Exerc.*

SE'ASONABLE. *adj.* [*ſaiſon*, French.] Opportune; happening or done at a proper time; proper as to time.

Mercy is *ſeaſonable* in the time of affliction, as clouds of rain in the time of drought. *Ecclus.* v. 2.

If ever it was *ſeaſonable* to preach courage in the deſpiſed abuſed cauſe of Chriſt, it is now, when his truths are reformed into nothing, when the hands and hearts of his faithful miniſters are weakened. *South's Sermons.*

SE'ASONABLENESS. *n. ſ.* [from *ſeaſonable*.] Opportuneneſs of time; propriety with regard to time.

A Britiſh freeholder would very ill diſcharge his part, if he did not acknowledge the excellency and *ſeaſonableneſs* of thoſe laws by which his country has been recovered out of its confuſions. *Addiſon's Freeholder.*

SE'ASONABLY. *adv.* [from *ſeaſonable*.] Properly with reſpect to time.

This is that to which I would moſt earneſtly, moſt *ſeaſonably* adviſe you all. *Sprat's Sermons.*

SE'ASONER. *n. ſ.* [from *To ſeaſon*.] He who ſeaſons or gives a reliſh to any thing.

SE'ASONING. *n. ſ.* [from *ſeaſon*.] That which is added to any thing to give it a reliſh.

Breads we have of ſeveral grains, with divers kinds of leavenings and *ſeaſonings*; ſo that ſome do extremely move appetites, and ſome do nouriſh ſo as divers do live of them alone. *Bacon.*

Some abound with words, without any *ſeaſoning* or taſte of matter. *Ben. Johnſon.*

A foundation of good ſenſe, and a cultivation of learning, are required to give a *ſeaſoning* to retirement, and make us taſte the bleſſing. *Dryden.*

Political ſpeculations are of ſo dry and auſtere a nature, that they will not go down with the publick without frequent *ſeaſonings*. *Addiſon's Freeholder.*

The publick accept a paper which has in it none of thoſe *ſeaſonings* that recommend the writings which are in vogue among us. *Addiſon's Spectator.*

Many vegetable ſubſtances are uſed by mankind as *ſeaſonings*, which abound with a highly exalted aromatick oil; as thyme and ſavory. *Arbuthnot on Aliments.*

SEAT. *n. ſ.* [*ſedes*, Latin; *ſett*, old German. *Skinner.*]

1. A chair, bench, or any thing on which one may ſit.

The ſons of light
Haſted, reſorting to the ſummons high,
And took their *ſeats*. *Milton's Paradiſe Loſt.*

The lady of the leaf ordain'd a feaſt,
And made the lady of the flow'r her gueſt;
When, lo, a bow'r aſcended on the plain,
With ſudden *ſeats* ordain'd, and large for either train. *Dryd.*

2. Chair of state; throne; post of authority; tribunal.

With due observance of thy goodly *seat*,
Great Agamemnon, Nestor shall supply
Thy latest words. *Shakesp. Troilus and Cressida.*

Thus we debase
The nature of our *seats*, and make the rabble
Call our cares fears. *Shak. Coriolanus.*

Whatsoever be the manner of the world's end, most certain it is an end it shall have, and as certain that then we shall appear before the judgment *seat* of Christ, that every man may receive according to that which he hath done in his body, whether it be good or evil. *Hakewill on Providence.*

3. Mansion; residence; dwelling; abode.

It were enough in reason to succour with victuals, and other helps, a vast multitude, compelled by necessity to seek a new *seat*, or to direct them unto a country able to receive them. *Raleigh.*

O earth, how like to heav'n! if not prefer'd
Most justly, *seat* worthier of gods, as built
With second thoughts, reforming what was old! *Milton.*

In Alba he shall fix his royal *seat*;
And, born a king, a race of kings beget. *Dryden.*

Has Winter caus'd thee, friend, to change thy *seat*,
And seek in Sabine air a warm retreat? *Dryden.*

The promis'd *seat* of empire shall again
Cover the mountain, and command the plain. *Prior.*

4. Situation; site.

The fittest and the easiest to be drawn
To our society, and to aid the war,
The rather for their *seat*, being next borderers
On Italy. *Ben. Johnson's Catiline.*

He that builds a fair house upon an ill *seat*, committeth himself to prison. *Bacon.*

A church by Strand-bridge, and two bishops houses, were pulled down to make a *seat* for his new building. *Hayward.*

It followeth now that we find out the *seat* of Eden; for in it was Paradise by God planted. *Raleigh.*

To Seat. *v. a* [from the noun.]

1. To place on seats; to cause to sit down.

The guests were no sooner *seated* but they entered into a warm debate. *Arbuthnot.*

2. To place in a post of authority, or place of distinction.

Thus high was king Richard *seated.* *Shak. R.* III.

Not Babylon,
Nor great Alcairo, such magnificence
Equal'd in all their glories to inshrine
Belus or Serapis their gods, or *seat*
Their kings. *Milton.*

A spirit of envy or opposition makes mankind uneasy to see others of the same species *seated* above them in a sort of perfection. *Pope.*

3. To fix in any particular place or situation; to settle.

Should one family or one thousand hold possession of all the southern undiscovered continent, because they had *seated* themselves in Nova Guiana. *Raleigh.*

By no means build too near a great neighbour, which were, in truth, to be as unfortunately *seated* on the earth as Mercury is in the heavens; for the most part ever in combustion, or obscurity, under brighter beams than his own. *Wotton.*

4. To fix; to place firm.

Why do I yield to that suggestion,
Whose horrid image doth upfix my hair,
And make my *seated* heart knock at my ribs,
Against the use of nature. *Shak. Macbeth.*

From their foundations loosening to and fro,
They pluck'd the *seated* hills. *Milton.*

Se'award. *adv.* [*sea* and peapꝺ, Saxon.] Towards the sea.

The rock rush'd *seaward* with impetuous roar,
Ingulf'd, and to th' abyss the boaster bore. *Pope.*

Se'cant. *n. s.* [*secans*, Latin; *secante*, Fr.] In geometry, the right line drawn from the centre of a circle, cutting and meeting with another line called the tangent without it. *Dict.*

To SECE'DE. *v. n.* [*secedo*, Latin.] To withdraw from fellowship in any affair.

Sece'der. *n. s.* [from *secede.*] One who discovers his disapprobation of any proceedings by withdrawing himself.

To Sece'rn. *v. a.* [*secerno*, Latin.] To separate finer from grosser matter; to make the separation of substances in the body.

Birds are commonly better meat than beasts, because their flesh doth assimilate more finely, and *secerneth* more subtilly. *Bacon's Natural History.*

The pituite or mucus *secerned* in the nose and windpipe, is not an excrementitious but a laudable humour, necessary for defending those parts, from which it is *secerned*, from excoriations. *Arbuthnot.*

Sece'ssion. *n. s.* [*secessio*, Latin.]

1. The act of departing.

The accession of bodies upon, or *secession* thereof from the earth's surface, perturb not the equilibration of either hemisphere. *Brown.*

2. The act of withdrawing from councils or actions.

Se'cle. *n. s.* [*siecle*, French; *seculum*, Latin.] A century.

Of a man's age, part he lives in his father's life-time, and part after his son's birth; and thereupon it is wont to be said that three generations make one *secle*, or hundred years in the genealogies. *Hammond's Pract. Catech.*

To Seclu'de. *v. a.* [*secludo*, Latin.] To confine from; to shut up apart; to exclude.

None is *secluded* from that function of any degree, state, or calling. *Whitgifte.*

Some parts of knowledge God has thought fit to *seclude* from us, to fence them not only, as he did the interdicted tree, by precept and commination, but with difficulties and impossibilities. *Decay of Piety.*

The number of birds described may be near five hundred, and the number of fishes, *secluding* shell-fish, as many; but if the shell-fish be taken in, more than six times the number. *Ray on the Creation.*

Inclose your tender plants in your conservatory, *secluding* all entrance of cold. *Evelyn's Kalendar.*

Let eastern tyrants from the light of heaven
Seclude their bosom slaves. *Thomson.*

SE'COND. *n. s.* [*second*, French; *secundus*, Latin. It is observable that the English have no ordinal of *two*, as the Latins and the nations deriving from them have none of *duo*. What the Latins call *secundus*, from *sequor*, the Saxons term oꝥeꞃ, or æꝼꞇeꞃa.]

1. The next in order to the first; the ordinal of two.

Sunk were their hearts with horror of the crime,
Nor needed to be warn'd a *second* time,
But bore each other back. *Dryden.*

2. Next in value or dignity; inferiour.

I shall not speak superlatively of them, lest I be suspected of partiality; but this I may truly say, they are *second* to none in the Christian world. *Bacon's Advice to Villiers.*

None I know
Second to me, or like; equal much less. *Milton.*

My eyes are still the same; each glance, each grace,
Keep their first lustre, and maintain their place,
Not *second* yet to any other face. *Dryden.*

Not these huge bolts, by which the giants slain,
Lay overthrown on the Phlegrean plain;
'Twas of a lesser mould and lighter weight;
They call it thunder of a *second* rate. *Addison.*

By a sad train of miseries alone
Distinguish'd long, and *second* now to none. *Pope.*

Persons of *second* rate merit in their own country, like birds of passage, thrive here, and fly off when their employments are at an end. *Swift.*

Se'cond-hand. *n. s.* Possession received from the first possessor.

Se'cond-hand is sometimes used adjectively. Not original; not primary.

Some men build so much upon authorities, they have but a *second-hand* or implicit knowledge. *Locke.*

They are too proud to cringe to *second-hand* favourites in a great family. *Swift to Gay.*

At Second-hand. In imitation; in the second place of order; by transmission; not primarily; not originally.

They pelted them with satyrs and epigrams, which perhaps had been taken up at first only to make their court, and *at second-hand* to flatter those who had flattered their king. *Temple.*

In imitation of preachers *at second-hand*, I shall transcribe from Bruyere a piece of raillery. *Tatler.*

Spurious virtue in a maid;
A virtue but *at second-hand.* *Swift.*

Se'cond. *n. s.* [*second*, French; from the adjective.]

1. One who accompanies another in a duel to direct or defend him.

Their *seconds* minister an oath,
Which was indifferent to them both,
That on their knightly faith and troth
No magick them supplied;
And sought them that they had no charms,
Wherewith to work each other's harms,
But came with simple open arms
To have their causes tried. *Drayton's Nymphid.*

Their first encounters were very furious, 'till after some toil and bloodshed they were parted by the *seconds.* *Addison.*

Personal brawls come in as *seconds* to finish the dispute of opinion. *Watts.*

2. One who supports or maintains; a supporter; a maintainer.

He propounded the duke as a main cause of divers infirmities in the state, being sure enough of *seconds* after the first onset. *Wotton.*

Courage, when it is only a *second* to injustice, and falls on without provocation, is a disadvantage to a character. *Collier.*

3. A *second* minute, the *second* division of an hour by sixty; the sixtieth part of a minute.

Four flames of an equal magnitude will be kept alive the space of sixteen *second* minutes, though one of these flames alone, in the same vessel, will not last above twenty-five or at most thirty *seconds.* *Wilkins's Math. Magic.*

Sounds move above 1140 English feet in a *second* minute of time, and in seven or eight minutes of time about 100 English miles. *Locke.*

To SE'COND. *v. a.* [*seconder*, Fr. *secundo*, Lat. from the noun.]

1. To support; to forward; to assist; to come in after the act as a maintainer.

The authors of the former opinion were presently *seconded* by other wittier and better learned, who being loth that the form of church polity, which they sought to bring in, should be otherwise than in the highest degree accounted of, took first an exception against the difference between church polity and matters of necessity to salvation. *Hooker.*

Though we here fall down,
We have supplies to *second* our attempt;
If they miscarry, theirs shall *second* them. *Shak. Henry* VI.

I to be the power of Israel's God
Avow, and challenge Dagon to the test,
Off'ring to combat thee his champion bold,
With th' utmost of his godhead *seconded.* *Milton.*

Familiar Ovid tender thoughts inspires,
And nature *seconds* all his soft desires. *Roscommon.*

If in company you offer something for a jest, and no body *seconds* you in your laughter, you may condemn their taste; but in the mean time you make a very indifferent figure. *Swift.*

In human works, though labour'd on with pain,
A thousand movements scarce one purpose gain;
In God's, one single can its ends produce,
Yet serves to *second* too some other use. *Pope.*

2. To follow in the next place.

You some permit
To *second* ills with ills. *Shakespeare.*

Having formerly discoursed of a maritimal voyage, I think it not impertinent to *second* the same with some necessary relations concerning the royal navy. *Raleigh.*

He saw his guileful act
By Eve, though all unweeting, *seconded*
Upon her husband. *Milton's Paradise Lost.*

Sin is usually *seconded* with sin; and a man seldom commits one sin to please, but he commits another to defend himself. *South's Sermons.*

SE'COND *Sight. n. s.* The power of seeing things future, or things distant: supposed inherent in some of the Scottish islanders.

As he was going out to steal a sheep, he was seised with a fit of *second sight:* the face of the country presented him with a wide prospect of new scenes, which he had never seen before. *Addison's Freeholder.*

SE'COND *sighted. adj.* [from *second sight.*] Having the second sight.

Sawney was descended of an ancient family, renowned for their skill in prognosticks: most of his ancestors were *second sighted*, and his mother but narrowly escaped for a witch. *Add.*

SE'CONDARILY. *adv.* [from *secondary.*] In the second degree; in the second order; not primarily; not originally; not in the first intention.

These atoms make the wind primarily tend downwards, though other accidental causes impel them *secondarily* to a sloping motion. *Digby.*

He confesses that temples are erected, and festivals kept, to the honour of saints, at least *secondarily.* *Stillingfleet.*

It is primarily generated out of the effusion of melancholick blood, or *secondarily* out of the dregs and remainder of a phlegmonous or œdematick tumour. *Harvey.*

SE'CONDARINESS. *n. s.* [from *secondary*] The state of being secondary.

That which is peculiar and discriminative, must be taken from the primariness and *secondariness* of the perception. *Norr.*

SE'CONDARY. *adj.* [*secundarius*, Latin.]

1. Not primary; not of the first intention; not of the first rate; next to the first.

Two are the radical differences: the *secondary* differences are as four. *Bacon's Natural History.*

Wheresoever there is moral right on the one hand, no *secondary* right can discharge it. *L'Estrange.*

Gravitation is the powerful cement which holds together this magnificent structure of the world, which stretcheth the North over the empty space, and hangeth the earth upon nothing, to transfer the words of Job from the first and real cause to the *secondary.* *Bentley.*

If the system had been fortuitously formed by the convening matter of a chaos, how is it conceivable that all the planets, both primary and *secondary*, should revolve the same way from the West to the East, and that in the same plane? *Bentl.*

2. Acting by transmission or deputation.

That we were form'd then, say'st thou? and the work
Of *secondary* hands, by task transfer'd
From father to his son? *Milton's Paradise Lost, b.* v.

As in a watch's fine machine,
Though many artful springs are seen,
The added movements which declare
How full the moon, how old the year,
Derive their *secondary* pow'r
From that which simply points the hour. *Prior.*

3. A *secondary* fever is that which arises after a crisis, or the discharge of some morbid matter, as after the declension of the small pox or measles. *Quincy.*

SE'CONDARY. *n. s.* [from the adjective.] A delegate; a deputy.

SE'CONDLY. *adv.* [from *second.*] In the second place.

First she hath disobeyed the law, and *secondly* trespassed against her husband. *Ecclus.* xxiii. 23.

First, metals are more durable than plants; and *secondly*, they are more solid and hard. *Bacon.*

The house of commons in Ireland, and, *secondly*, the privy council, addressed his majesty against these half-pence. *Swift.*

SE'CONDRATE. *n. s.* [*second* and *rate.*]

1. The second order in dignity or value.

They call it thunder of the *secondrate.* *Addison's Ovid.*

2. It is sometimes used adjectively, one of the second order. A colloquial licence.

He was not then a *secondrate* champion, as they would have him, who think fortitude the first virtue in a hero. *Dryden.*

SE'CRECY. *n. s.* [from *secret.*]

1. Privacy; state of being hidden.

That's not suddenly to be perform'd,
But with advice and silent *secrecy.* *Shak. Henry* VI.

The lady Anne,
Whom the king hath in *secrecy* long married,
This day was view'd in open as his queen. *Shakes. H.*VIII.

In nature's book of infinite *secrecy*,
A little can I read. *Shakesp. Ant. and Cleopatra.*

2. Solitude; retirement.

Thou in thy *secrecy*, although alone,
Best with thyself accompany'd, seek'st not
Social communication. *Milton's Parad. Lost.*

There is no such thing as perfect *secrecy*, to encourage a rational mind to the perpetration of any base action; for a man must first extinguish and put out the great light within him, his conscience; he must get away from himself, and shake off the thousand witnesses which he always carries about him, before he can be alone. *South's Sermons.*

3. Forbearance of discovery.

It is not with publick as with private prayer: in this rather *secrecy* is commanded than outward shew; whereas that being the publick act of a whole society, requireth accordingly more care to be had of external appearance. *Hooker.*

4. Fidelity to a secret; taciturnity inviolate; close silence.

SE'CRET. *adj.* [*secret*, French; *secretus*, Latin.]

1. Kept hidden; not revealed; concealed; private.

The *secret* things belong unto the Lord our God; but those things which are revealed belong unto us. *Deutr.* xxix. 29.

2. Retired; private; unseen.

Thou open'st wisdom's way,
And giv'st access, though *secret* she retire:
And I perhaps am *secret.* *Milton.*

3. Faithful to a secret entrusted.

Secret Romans, that have spoke the word,
And will not palter? *Shakesp. Julius Cæsar.*

4. Unknown; not discovered: as, a *secret* remedy.

5. Privy; obscene.

SE'CRET. *n. s.* [*secret*, French; *secretum*, Latin.]

1. Something studiously hidden.

Infected minds
To their deaf pillows will discharge their *secrets.* *Shakesp.*

There is no *secret* that they can hide from thee. *Ezek.* xxviii.

We not to explore the *secrets* ask
Of his eternal empire. *Milton.*

2. A thing unknown; something not yet discovered.

All blest *secrets*,
All you unpublish'd virtues of the earth. *Shakes. King Lear.*

All *secrets* of the deep, all nature's works. *Milton.*

The Romans seem not to have known the *secret* of paper-credit. *Arbuthnot.*

3. Privacy; secrecy.

Bread eaten in *secret* is pleasant. *Prov.* ix. 17.

In *secret*, riding through the air she comes. *Milton.*

To SE'CRET. *v. a.* [from the noun.] To keep private.

Great care is to be used of the clerks of the council, for the *secreting* of their consultations. *Bacon's Advice to Villiers.*

SE'CRETARISHIP. *n. s.* [*secretaire*, Fr. from *secretary.*] The office of a secretary.

SE'CRETARY. *n. s.* [*secretaire*, Fr. *secretarius*, low Latin.] One entrusted with the management of business; one who writes for another.

Call Gardiner to me, my new *secretary.* *Shakesp.*

That which is most of all profitable is acquaintance with the *secretaries*, and employed men of ambassadors. *Bacon.*

Cottington was *secretary* to the prince. *Clarendon.*

To SECRE'TE. *v. a.* [*secretus*, Latin.]

1. To put aside; to hide.

2. [In the animal œconomy.] To secern; to separate.

SECRE'TION. *n. s.* [from *secretus*, Latin.]

1. That part of the animal œconomy that consists in separating the various fluids of the body.

2. The fluid secreted.

SECRETI'TIOUS. *adj.* [from *secretus*, Latin.] Parted by animal secretion.

They have a similitude or contrariety to the *secretitious* humours in taste and quality. *Floyer on the Humours.*

SE'CRETIST. *n. s.* [from *secret.*] A dealer in secrets.

Some things I have not yet thought fit so plainly to reveal, not out of any envious design of having them buried with me, but that I may barter with those *secretists*, that will not part with one secret but in exchange for another. *Boyle.*

SE'CRETLY. *adv.* [from *secret.*] Privately; privily; not openly; not publickly; not so as to be known.

Give him this letter, do it *secretly*. *Shakespeare.*

Those thoughts are not wholly mine; but either they are *secretly* in the poet, or may be fairly deduced from him. *Dryd.*

Now *secretly* with inward grief she pin'd;
Now warm resentments to his griefs he join'd. *Addison.*

Some may place their chief satisfaction in giving *secretly* what is to be distributed; others, in being the open and avowed instruments of making such distributions. *Atterbury.*

SE'CRETNESS. *n. s.* [from *secret.*]

1. State of being hidden.
2. Quality of keeping a secret.

I could muster up
My giants and my witches too,
Which are vast constancy and *secretness*. *Donne.*

SE'CRETORY. *adj.* [from *secretus*, Latin.] Performing the office of secretion.

All the glands are a congeries of vessels complicated together, whereby they give the blood time to separate through the capillary vessels into the *secretory*, which afterwards exonerate themselves into one duct. *Ray.*

SECT. *n. s.* [*secte*, French; *secta*, Latin, from *sectando.*]

1. A body of men following some particular master, or united in some settled tenets. Often in a bad sense.

We'll wear out,
In a wall'd prison, packs and *sects* of great ones,
That ebb and flow by th' moon. *Shakesp. King Lear.*

The greatest vicissitude of things is the vicissitude of *sects* and religions: the true religion is built upon the rock; the rest are tossed upon the waves of time. *Bacon's Essays.*

The jealous *sects* that dare not trust their cause
So far from their own will as to the laws,
You for their umpire and their synod take. *Dryden.*

The academics were willing to admit the goods of fortune into their notion of felicity; but no *sects* of old philosophers did ever leave a room for greatness. *Dryden.*

A *sect* of free thinkers is a sum of ciphers. *Bentley.*

2. In *Shakespeare* it seems to be misprinted for *set.*

Of our unbitted lusts, I take this that you call love to be a *sect* or cion. *Shakesp. Othello.*

SE'CTARISM. *n. s.* [from *sect.*] Disposition to petty sects in opposition to things established.

Nothing hath more marks of schism and *sectarism* than this presbyterian way. *King Charles.*

SE'CTARY. *n. s.* [*sectaire*, French; from *sect.*]

1. One who divides from publick establishment, and joins with those distinguished by some particular whims.

My lord, you are a *sectary*,
That's the plain truth. *Shakesp.*

Romish catholick tenets are inconsistent, on the one hand, with the truth of religion professed and protested by the church of England, whence we are called protestants; and the anabaptists, and separatists, and *sectaries*, on the other hand, whose tenets are full of schism, and inconsistent with monarchy. *Bac.*

The number of *sectaries* does not concern the clergy in point of interest or conscience. *Swift.*

2. A follower; a pupil.

The *sectaries* of my celestial skill,
That wont to be the world's chief ornament,
And learned imps that wont to shoot up still,
They under keep. *Spenser.*

SECTA'TOR. *n. s.* [*sectateur*, Fr. *sectator*, Latin.] A follower; an imitator; a disciple.

Hereof the wiser sort and the best learned philosophers were not ignorant, as Cicero witnesseth, gathering the opinion of Aristotle and his *sectators.* *Raleigh.*

SE'CTION. *n. s.* [*section*, French; *sectio*, Latin.]

1. The act of cutting or dividing.

In the *section* of bodies, man, of all sensible creatures, has the fullest brain to his proportion. *Wotton.*

2. A part divided from the rest.
3. A small and distinct part of a writing or book.

Instead of their law, which they might not read openly, they read of the prophets, that which in likeness of matter came nearest to each *section* of their law. *Hooker.*

The production of volatile salts I reserve 'till I mention them in another *section.* *Boyle.*

Without breaking in upon the connection of his language, it is hardly possible to give a distinct view of his several arguments in distinct *sections.* *Locke.*

SE'CTOR. *n. s.* [*secteur*, French.] In geometry.

Sector is an instrument made of wood or metal, with a joint, and sometimes a piece to turn out to make a true square, with lines of sines, tangents, secants, equal parts, rhumbs, polygons, hours, latitudes, metals and solids. It is generally useful in all the practical parts of the mathematicks, and particularly contrived for navigation, surveying, astronomy, dialling, and projection of the sphere. All the lines of the *sector* can be accommodated to any radius, which is done by taking off all divisions parallelwise, and not lengthwise; the ground of which practice is this, that parallels to the base of any plain triangle, bear the same proportion to it as the parts of the legs above the parallel do to the whole legs. *Harris.*

SE'CULAR. *adj.* [*secularis*, Latin; *seculier*, French.]

1. Not spiritual; relating to affairs of the present world; not holy; worldly.

This in every several man's actions of common life, appertaineth unto moral; in publick and politick *secular* affairs, unto civil wisdom. *Hooker.*

Then shall they seek t' avail themselves of names,
Places, and titles; and with these to join
Secular pow'r, though feigning still to act
By spiritual. *Milton's Paradise Lost.*

2. [In the church of *Rome.*] Not bound by monastick rules.

Those northern nations easily embraced the religion of those they subdued, and by their devotion gave great authority and reverence, and thereby ease to the clergy both *secular* and regular. *Temple.*

In France vast numbers of ecclesiasticks, *secular* and religious, live upon the labours of others. *Addison.*

3. [*Seculaire*, Fr.] Happening or coming once in a *secle* or century.

The *secular* year was kept but once in a century. *Addison.*

SECULA'RITY. *n. s.* [from *secular.*] Worldliness; attention to the things of the present life.

Littleness and *secularity* of spirit is the greatest enemy to contemplation. *Burnet's Theory of the Earth.*

To SE'CULARIZE. *v. a.* [*seculariser*, Fr. from *secular.*]

1. To convert from spiritual appropriations to common use.
2. To make worldly.

SE'CULARLY. *adv.* [from *secular.*] In a worldly manner.

SE'CULARNESS. *n. s.* [from *secular.*] Worldliness.

SE'CUNDINE. *n. s.* [*secondines*, *secondes*, Fr. *secundæ*, viz. *partes quod nascentem infantem sequantur.* Ainsw.] The membrane in which the embryo is wrapped; the after-birth.

The casting of the skin is by the ancients compared to the breaking of the *secundine*, or cawl, but not rightly; for the *secundine* is but a general cover, not shaped according to the parts, but the skin is. *Bacon's Nat. History.*

Future ages lie
Wrapp'd in their sacred *secundine* asleep. *Cowley.*

If the fætus be taken out of the womb inclosed in the *secundines*, it will continue to live, and the blood to circulate. *Ray.*

SECU'RE. *adj.* [*securus*, Latin.]

1. Free from fear; exempt from terrour; easy; assured.

Confidence then bore thee on *secure*
To meet no danger. *Milton.*

One maid she had, belov'd above the rest;
Secure of her, the secret she confess'd. *Dryden.*

In Lethe's lake souls long oblivion taste;
Of future life *secure*, forgetful of the past. *Dryden.*

But thou, *secure* of soul, unbent with woes;
The more thy fortune frowns, the more oppose. *Dryden.*

We live and act as if we were perfectly *secure* of the final event of things, however we may behave ourselves. *Atterbury.*

The portion of their wealth they design for the uses of the poor, they may throw into one of these publick repositories, *secure* that it will be well employed. *Atterbury.*

It concerns the most *secure* of his strength, to pray to God not to expose him to an enemy. *Rogers.*

2. Careless; wanting caution; wanting vigilance.
3. Free from danger; safe.

Let us not then suspect our happy state,
As not *secure* to single or combin'd. *Milton.*

Messapus next,
Secure of steel, and fated from the fire,
In pomp appears. *Dryden.*

4. It has sometimes *of* before the object in all its senses; but more properly *from* before *evil*, or the *cause of evil.*

Haply too *secure* of our discharge
From penalty. *Milton.*

Secure from fortune's blows,
Secure of what I cannot lose,
In my small pinnace I can sail. *Dryden's Horace.*

To SECU'RE. *v. a.* [from the adjective.]

1. To make certain; to put out of hazard; to ascertain.

Nothing left
That might his happy state *secure*,
Secure from outward force. *Milton.*

I spread a cloud before the victor's sight,
Sustain'd the vanquish'd, and *secur'd* his flight;
Ev'n then *secur'd* him, when I fought with joy
The vow'd destruction of ungrateful Troy. *Dryden.*

Actions have their preference, not according to the transient pleasure or pain that accompanies or follows them here, but as they serve to *secure* that perfect durable happiness hereafter. *Locke.*

Truth and certainty are not *secured* by innate principles; but men are in the same uncertain floating estate with as without them. *Locke.*

That prince who shall be so wise as by established laws of liberty to *secure* protection to the honest industry of mankind, against the oppression of power, will quickly be too hard for his neighbours. *Locke.*

Deeper to wound, she shuns the fight;
She drops her arms to gain the field:
Secures her conquest by her flight,
And triumphs when she seems to yield. *Prior.*

Nothing can be more artful than the address of Ulysses: he *secures* himself of a powerful advocate, by paying an ingenuous and laudable deference to his friend. *Broome.*

2. To protect; to make safe.

Where two or three sciences are pursued at the same time, if one of them be dry, as logick, let another be more entertaining, to *secure* the mind from weariness. *Watts.*

3. To insure.

4. To make fast.

SECU'RELY. *adv.* [from *secure.*] Without fear; carelesly; without danger; safely.

Love, that had now long time *securely* slept
In Venus' lap, unarmed then and naked,
'Gan rear his head, by Clotho being waked. *Spenser.*

'Tis done like Hector, but *securely* done,
A little proudly, and great deal misprizing
The knight oppos'd. *Shakesp. Troilus and Cressida.*

His daring foe *securely* him defy'd. *Milton.*

A soul that can *securely* death defy,
And count it nature's privilege to die. *Dryden's Juven.*

We upon our globe's last verge shall go,
And view the ocean leaning on the sky;
From thence our rolling neighbours we shall know,
And on the lunar world *securely* pry. *Dryden.*

Whether any of the reasonings are inconsistent, I *securely* leave to the judgment of the reader. *Atterbury.*

SECU'REMENT. *n. s.* [from *secure.*] The cause of safety; protection; defence.

They, like Judas, desire death; Cain, on the contrary, grew afraid thereof, and obtained a *securement* from it. *Brown.*

SECU'RITY. *n. s.* [*securité*, Fr. *securitas*, Lat. from *secure.*]

1. Carelessness; freedom from fear.

Marvellous *security* is always dangerous, when men will not believe any bees to be in a hive, until they have a sharp sense of their stings. *Hayward.*

2. Vitious carelessness; confidence; want of vigilance.

There is scarce truth enough alive to make societies secure; but *security* enough to make fellowships accurst. *Shakespeare.*

How senseless then, and dead a soul hath he,
Which thinks his soul doth with his body die;
Or thinks not so, but so would have it be,
That he might sin with more *security.* *Davies.*

3. Protection; defence.

If the providence of God be taken away, what *security* have we against those innumerable dangers to which human nature is continually exposed? *Tillotson.*

4. Any thing given as a pledge or caution; insurance; assurance for any thing.

When they had taken *security* of Jason, they let them go. *Acts* xvii 9.

It is possible for a man, who hath the appearance of religion, to be wicked and an hypocrite; but it is impossible for a man, who openly declares against religion, to give any reasonable *security* that he will not be false and cruel. *Swift.*

Exchequer bills have been generally reckoned the surest and most sacred of all *securities.* *Swift's Examiner.*

The Romans do not seem to have known the secret of paper credit, and *securities* upon mortgages. *Arbuthnot on Coins.*

5. Safety; certainty.

Some, who gave their advice for entering into a war, alleged that we should have no *security* for our trade, while Spain was subject to a prince of the Bourbon family. *Swift.*

SEDA'N. *n. s.* [from *sedes*, Latin.] A kind of portable coach; a chair.

Some beg for absent persons, feign them sick,
Close mew'd in their *sedans* for want of air,
And for their wives produce an empty chair. *Dryden.*

By a tax of Cato's it was provided, that women's wearing cloaths, ornament and *sedan*, exceeding 121 *l.* 1 *s.* 10 *d.* halfpenny, should pay 30 *s.* in the hundred pound value. *Arbuthn.*

SEDA'TE. *adj.* [*sedatus*, Latin.] Calm; quiet; still; unruffled; undisturbed; serene.

With count'nance calm and soul *sedate*,
Thus Turnus. *Dryden's Æn.*

Disputation carries away the mind from that calm and *sedate* temper which is so necessary to contemplate truth. *Watts.*

SEDA'TELY. *adv.* [from *sedate*] Calmly; without disturbance.

That has most weight with them that appears *sedately* to come from their parents reason. *Locke.*

SEDA'TENESS. *n. s.* [from *sedate.*] Calmness; tranquillity; serenity; freedom from disturbance.

There is a particular *sedateness* in their conversation and behaviour that qualifies them for council, with a great intrepidity that fits them for action. *Addison on the War.*

SE'DENTARINESS. *n. s.* [from *sedentary.*] The state of being sedentary; inactivity.

SE'DENTARY. *adj.* [*sedentaire*, French; *sedentario*, Italian; *sedentarius*, from *sedeo*, Latin.]

1. Passed in sitting still; wanting motion or action.

A *sedentary* life, appropriate to all students, crushes the bowels; and, for want of stirring the body, suffers the spirits to lie dormant. *Harvey on Consumptions.*

The blood of labouring people is more dense and heavy than of those who live a *sedentary* life. *Arbuthnot.*

2. Torpid; inactive; sluggish; motionless.

The *sedentary* earth,
That better might with far less compass move,
Serv'd by more noble than herself, attains
Her end without least motion. *Milton.*

'Till length of years
And *sedentary* numbness, craze my limbs
To a contemptible old age obscure. *Milton's Agonistes.*

The soul, considered abstractedly from its passions, is of a remiss *sedentary* nature, slow in its resolves, and languishing in its executions. *Addison's Spectator.*

SEDGE. *n. s.* [ꞅæcᵹ, Saxon; whence, in the provinces, a narrow flag is called a *sag* or *seg.*] A growth of narrow flags; a narrow flag

T' one layeth for turf and for *sedge.* *Tusser.*

The current, that with gentle murmur glides,
Thou know'st, being stopp'd, impatiently doth rage;
But when his fair course is not hindered,
He makes sweet musick with th' enamel'd stones,
Giving a gentle kiss to every *sedge*
He overtaketh in his pilgrimage;
And so by many winding nooks he strays,
With willing sport, to the wild ocean. *Shakespeare.*

Adonis, painted by a running brook,
And Cytherea all in *sedges* hid;
Which seem to move and wanton with her breath,
Even as the waving *sedges* play with wind. *Shakespeare.*

In hotter countries a fly called lucciole, that shineth as the glow-worm, is chiefly upon fens and marshes; yet is not seen but in the height of Summer, and *sedge* or other green of the fens give as good shade as bushes. *Bacon.*

He hid himself in the *sedges* adjoining. *Sandys.*

My bonds I brake,
Fled from my guards, and in a muddy lake,
Amongst the *sedges*, all the night lay hid. *Denham.*

Niphates, with inverted urn,
And drooping *sedge*, shall his Armenia mourn. *Dryden.*

SE'DGY. *adj.* [from *sedge.*] Overgrown with narrow flags.

On the gentle Severn's *sedgy* bank,
In single opposition, hand to hand,
He did confound the best part of an hour,
In changing hardiment with great Glendower. *Shak. H.* IV.

Old father Thames rais'd up his reverend head,
But fear'd the fate of Simoeis would return:
Deep in his ooze he sought his *sedgy* bed,
And shrunk his waters back into his urn. *Dryden.*

SE'DIMENT. *n. s.* [*sediment*, French; *sedimentum*, Lat.] That which subsides or settles at the bottom.

The salt water rises into a kind of scum on the top, and partly goeth into a *sediment* in the bottom, and so is rather a separation than an evaporation. *Bacon's Nat. History.*

It is not bare agitation, but the *sediment* at the bottom, that troubles and defiles the water. *South's Sermons.*

That matter sunk not down 'till last of all, settling at the surface of the *sediment*, and covering all the rest. *Woodward.*

SEDI'TION. *n. s.* [*sedition*, Fr. *seditio*, Latin.] A tumult; an insurrection; a popular commotion; an uproar.

That sunshine brew'd a show'r for him,
That wash'd his father's fortunes forth of France,
And heap'd *sedition* on his crown at home. *Shak. H.* VI.

In soothing them we nourish, 'gainst our senate,
The cockle of rebellion, insolence, *sedition.* *Shak. Coriolan.*

SEDI'TIOUS. *adj.* [*seditieux*, Fr. *seditiosus*, Latin.] Factious with tumult; turbulent.

The cause, why I have brought this army hither,
Is to remove proud Somerset from the king,
Seditious to his grace and to the state. *Shakesp. H.* VI.

Very many of the nobility in Edenborough, at that time, did not appear yet in this *seditious* behaviour. *Clarendon.*

Thou return'st
From flight, *seditious* angel. *Milton.*

But if she has deform'd this earthly life
With murd'rous rapine and *seditious* strife,
In everlasting darkness must she lie;
Still more unhappy that she cannot die. *Prior.*

SEDI'TIOUSLY. *adv.* [from *seditious.*] Tumultuously; with factious turbulence.

SEDI'TIOUSNESS. *n. s.* [from *seditious.*] Turbulence; disposition to sedition.

To

To SEDU'CE. *v. a.* [*seduco*, Latin; *seduire*, French.] To draw aside from the right; to tempt; to corrupt; to deprave; to mislead; to deceive.

'Tis meet
That noble minds keep ever with their likes;
For who so firm that cannot be *seduc'd*? *Shakesp. Jul. Cæs.*

Me the gold of France did not *seduce*,
Although I did admit it as a motive,
The sooner to effect what I intended. *Shakesp. H.* V.

A beauty-waining and distressed widow,
Seduc'd the pitch and height of all his thoughts
To base declension. *Shakesp. R.* III.

In the latter times some shall depart from the faith, giving heed to *seducing* spirits. 1 *Tim.* iv. 1.

I shall never gratify the spightfulness of a few with any sinister thoughts of all their allegiance, whom pious frauds have *seduced*. *King Charles.*

Subtle he needs must be who could *seduce*
Angels. *Milton.*

Nor let false friends *seduce* thy mind to fame,
By arrogating Johnson's hostile name;
Let father Flecknoe fire thy mind with praise,
And uncle Ogleby thy envy raise. *Dryden.*

SEDU'CEMENT. *n. s.* [from *seduce.*] Practice of seduction; art or means used in order to seduce.

To season them, and win them early to the love of virtue and true labour, ere any flattering *seducement* or vain principle seize them wandering, some easy and delightful book of education should be read to them. *Milton on Education.*

Her hero's dangers touch'd the pitying pow'r,
The nymph's *seducements*, and the magick bow'r. *Pope.*

SEDU'CER. *n. s.* [from *seduce.*] One who draws aside from the right; a tempter; a corrupter.

Grant it me, O king; otherwise a *seducer* flourishes, and a poor maid is undone. *Shakespeare.*

There is a teaching by restraining *seducers*, and so removing the hindrances of knowledge. *South.*

The soft *seducer*, with enticing looks,
The bellowing rivals to the fight provokes. *Dryden.*

He whose firm faith no reason could remove,
Will melt before that soft *seducer*, love. *Dryden.*

SEDU'CIBLE. *adj.* [from *seduce.*] Corruptible; capable of being drawn aside.

The vicious example of ages past poisons the curiosity of these present, affording a hint of sin unto *seducible* spirits. *Brown's Vulg. Errours.*

We owe much of our errour to the power which our affections have over our so easy *seducible* understandings. *Glanv.*

SEDU'CTION. *n. s.* [*seduction*, Fr. *seductus*, Latin.] The act of seducing; the act of drawing aside.

Whatsoever mens faith, patience, or perseverance were, any remarkable indulgence to this sin, the *seduction* of Balaam, were sure to bring judgments. *Hammond.*

To procure the miseries of others in those extremities, wherein we hold an hope to have no society ourselves, is a strain above Lucifer, and a project beyond the primary *seduction* of hell. *Brown's Vulgar Errours.*

Whereby is evident the easy *seduction* of men, neither inquiring into the verity of the substance, nor reforming upon repugnance of circumstances. *Brown's Vulg. Err.*

The deceiver soon found out this soft place of Adam's, and innocency itself did not secure him from this way of *seduction*. *Glanv. Sceps.*

Helen ascribes her *seduction* to Venus, and mentions nothing of Paris. *Pope.*

A woman who is above flattery, and despises all praise, but that which flows from the approbation of her own heart, is, morally speaking, out of reach of *seduction*. *Clarissa.*

SEDU'LITY. *n. s.* [*sedulitas*, Latin.] Diligent assiduity; laboriousness; industry; application; intenseness of endeavour.

Man oftentimes pursues, with great *sedulity* and earnestness, that which cannot stand him in any stead for vital purpose. *Hooker.*

Let there be but the same propensity and bent of will to religion, and there will be the same *sedulity* and indefatigable industry in mens enquiries into it. *South.*

SE'DULOUS. *adj.* [*sedulus*, Latin.] Assiduous; industrious; laborious; diligent; painful.

Not *sedulous* by nature to indite
Wars, hitherto the only argument
Heroick deem'd. *Milton's Paradise Lost.*

What signifies the sound of words in prayer, without the affection of the heart, and a *sedulous* application of the proper means that may naturally lead us to such an end. *L'Estrange.*

The goat, now bright amidst her fellow stars,
Kind Amalthæa reach'd her teat, distent
With milk, thy early food: the *sedulous* bee
Distill'd her honey on thy purple lips. *Prior.*

The bare majority of a few representatives is often procured by great industry and application, wherein those who engage in the pursuits of malice are much more *sedulous* than such as would prevent them. *Swift.*

SE'DULOUSLY. *adv.* [from *sedulous.*] Assiduously; industriously; laboriously; diligently; painfully.

The ritual, preceptive, prophetick, and all other parts of sacred writ, were most *sedulously*, most religiously guarded by them. *Government of the Tongue.*

All things by experience
Are most improv'd; then *sedulously* think
To meliorate thy stock, no way or rule
Be unessay'd. *Philips.*

SE'DULOUSNESS. *n. s.* [from *sedulous.*] Assiduity; assiduousness; industry; diligence.

SEE. *n. s.* [*sedes*, Latin.] The seat of episcopal power; the diocess of a bishop.

You, my lord archbishop,
Whose *see* is by a civil peace maintain'd,
Whose beard the silver hand of peace hath touch'd,
Whose learning and good letters peace hath tutor'd,
Whose white investments figure innocence,
The dove and every blessed spirit of peace;
Wherefore do you so ill translate yourself
Out of the speech of peace, that bears such grace,
Into the harsh and boist'rous tongue of war? *Shakes. H.IV.*

It is a safe opinion for their *sees*, empires, and kingdoms; and for themselves, if they be wise. *Bacon.*

The pope would use these treasures, in case of any great calamity that should endanger the holy *see*. *Addison.*

Episcopal revenues were so low reduced, that three or four *sees* were often united to make a tolerable competency. *Swift.*

To SEE. *v. a.* preter. *I saw*; part. pass. *seen.* [ʃeon, Saxon; *sien*, Dutch.]

1. To perceive by the eye.

Dear son Edgar,
Might I but live to *see* thee in my touch,
I'd say I had eyes again. *Shakes. King Lear.*

I was bowed down at the hearing of it; I was dismayed at the *seeing* of it. *Is.* xxi. 3.

I speak that which I have *seen* with my father, and ye do that which you have *seen* with yours. *Jo* viii. 38.

He'll lead the life of gods, and be
By gods and heroes *seen*, and gods and heroes *see*. *Dryden.*

It was a right answer of the physician to his patient, that had sore eyes: If you have more pleasure in the taste of wine than in the use of your sight, wine is good for you; but if the pleasure of *seeing* be greater to you than that of drinking, wine is naught. *Locke.*

I *see* her sober over a sampler. *Pope.*

2. To observe; to find.

Seven other kine came up, lean fleshed, such as I never *saw* for badness. *Gen.* xli. 19.

Such command we had,
To *see* that none thence issu'd forth a spy. *Milton.*

Give them first one simple idea, and *see* that they perfectly comprehend it, before you go any farther. *Locke.*

The thunderbolt we *see* used by the greatest poet of Augustus's age, to express irresistible force in battle. *Addison.*

3. To discover; to descry.

Who is so gross
As cannot *see* this palpable device?
Yet who so bold but says he *sees* it not?
When such ill dealings must be *seen* in thought. *Shakespeare.*

4. To converse with.

The main of them may be reduced to language, and to an improvement in wisdom and prudence by *seeing* men, and conversing with people of different tempers and customs. *Locke.*

5. To attend; to remark.

I had a mind to *see* him out, and therefore did not care for contradicting him. *Addison's Freeholder.*

To SEE. *v. n.*

1. To have the power of sight; to have by the eye perception of things distant.

Who maketh the *seeing* or the blind? have not I the Lord? *Ex.* iv. 11.

Air hath some secret degree of light; otherwise cats and owls could not *see* in the night. *Bacon's Natural History.*

Could you *see* into my secret soul,
There you might read your own dominion doubled. *Dryden.*

2. To discern without deception.

Many sagacious persons will find us out, will look under our mask, and *see* through all our fine pretensions, and discern the absurdity of telling the world that we believe one thing when we do the contrary. *Tillotson.*

You may *see* into the spirit of them all, and form your pen from those general notions. *Felton.*

3. To enquire; to distinguish.

See whether fear doth make thee wrong her. *Shakesp.*

4. To be attentive.

Mark and perform it, *see'st* thou; for the fail
Of any point in't shall be death. *Shakespeare.*

5. To scheme; to contrive.

Cassio's a proper man: let me *see* now;
To get his place. *Shakespeare's Othello.*

SEE.

Sᴇᴇ. *interjection.* [Originally the imperative of the verb *ſee.*] Lo; look; obſerve; behold.

See, ſee! upon the banks of Boyne he ſtands,
By his own view adjuſting his commands. *Halifax.*
See! the ſole bliſs heav'n could on all beſtow,
Which who but feels can taſte, but thinks can know? *Pope.*

See what it is to have a poet in your houſe. *Pope.*

SEED. *n. ſ.* [ꞅæꝺ, Saxon; *ſeed*, Daniſh; *ſaed*, Dutch.]

1. The organiſed particle produced by plants and animals, from which new plants and animals are generated.

If you can look into the *ſeeds* of time,
And ſay which grain will grow and which will not,
Speak then to me. *Shakeſpeare's Macbeth.*

Seed of a year old is the beſt, though ſome *ſeed* and grains laſt better than others. *Bacon's Nat. Hiſtory.*

That every plant has its *ſeed* is an evident ſign of divine providence. *More.*

Did they ever ſee any herbs, except thoſe of the graſs-leaved tribe, come up without two *ſeed* leaves; which to me is an argument that they came all of *ſeed*, there being no reaſon elſe why they ſhould produce two *ſeed* leaves different from the ſubſequent. *Ray.*

Juſt gods! all other things their like produce;
The vine ariſes from her mother's juice:
When feeble plants or tender flow'rs decay,
They to their *ſeed* their images convey. *Prior.*

In the ſouth part of Staffordſhire they go to the north for *ſeed* corn. *Mortimer.*

2. Firſt principle; original.

The *ſeed* of whatſoever perfect virtue groweth from us, is a right opinion touching things divine. *Hooker.*

3. Principle of production.

Praiſe of great acts he ſcatters as a *ſeed*,
Which may the like in coming ages breed. *Waller.*

4. Progeny; offspring; deſcendants.

Next him king Lear in happy peace long reign'd;
But had no iſſue male him to ſucceed,
But three fair daughters, which were well uptrain'd
In all that ſeemed fit for kingly *ſeed.* *Fairy Queen.*

The thing doth touch
The main of all your ſtates, your blood, your *ſeed.* *Daniel.*

When God gave Canaan to Abraham, he thought fit to put his *ſeed* into the grant too. *Locke.*

5. Race; generation; birth.

Of mortal *ſeed* they were not held,
Which other mortals ſo excel'd;
And beauty too in ſuch exceſs,
As your's, Zelinda! claims no leſs. *Waller.*

To Sᴇᴇᴅ. *v. n.* [from the noun.] To grow to perfect maturity ſo as to ſhed the ſeed.

Whate'er I plant, like corn on barren earth,
By an equivocal birth,
Seeds and runs up to poetry. *Swift.*

They pick up all the old roots, except what they deſign for ſeed, which they let ſtand to *ſeed* the next year. *Mortimer.*

Sᴇ'ᴇᴅᴄᴀᴋᴇ. *n. ſ.* [*ſeed* and *cake.*] A ſweet cake interſperſed with warm aromatick ſeeds.

Remember, wife,
The *ſeedcake*, the paſties, and furmenty pot. *Tuſſer.*

Sᴇᴇᴅʟɪᴘ. } *n. ſ.* A veſſel in which the ſower carries his
Sᴇᴇᴅʟᴏᴘ. } ſeed. *Ainſworth.*

Sᴇ'ᴇᴅᴘᴇᴀʀʟ. *n. ſ.* [*ſeed* and *pearl.*] Small grains of pearl.

In the diſſolution of *ſeedpearl* in ſome acid menſtruum, if a good quantity of the little pearls be caſt in whole, they will be carried in ſwarms from the bottom to the top. *Boyle.*

Sᴇ'ᴇᴅᴘʟᴏᴛ. *n. ſ.* [*ſeed* and *plot.*] The ground on which plants are ſowed to be afterwards tranſplanted.

To counſel others, a man muſt be furniſhed with an univerſal ſtore in himſelf to the knowledge of all nature: that is the matter and *ſeedplot*; there are the ſeats of all argument and invention. *Ben. Johnſon.*

Humility is a *ſeedplot* of virtue, eſpecially Chriſtian, which thrives beſt when 'tis deep rooted in the humble lowly heart. *Hammond.*

It will not be unuſeful to preſent a full narration of this rebellion, looking back to thoſe paſſages by which the *ſeedplots* were made and framed, from whence thoſe miſchiefs have ſucceſſively grown. *Clarendon.*

Sᴇ'ᴇᴅᴛɪᴍᴇ. *n. ſ.* [*ſeed* and *time.*] The ſeaſon of ſowing.

While the earth remaineth, *ſeedtime* and harveſt ſhall not ceaſe. *Gen.* viii. 22.

If he would have two tributes in one year, he muſt give them two *ſeedtimes*, and two harveſts. *Bacon.*

The firſt rain fell upon the *ſeedtime* about October, and was to make the ſeed to root; the latter was to fill the ear. *Brown.*

Their very *ſeedtime* was their harveſt, and by ſowing tares they immediately reaped gold. *Decay of Piety.*

Day and night,
Seedtime and harveſt, heat and hoary froſt,
Shall hold their courſe, 'till fire purge all things. *Milton.*

He that too curiouſly obſerves the face of the heavens, by miſſing his *ſeedtime*, will loſe the hopes of his harveſt. *Atterb.*

Sᴇ'ᴇᴅʟɪɴɢ. *n. ſ.* [from *ſeed.*] A young plant juſt riſen from the ſeed.

Carry into the ſhade ſuch *ſeedlings* or plants as are for their choiceneſs reſerved in pots. *Evelyn's Kalendar.*

Sᴇ'ᴇᴅɴᴇꜱꜱ. *n. ſ.* [from *ſeed.*] Seedtime; the time of ſowing.

Bloſſoming time
From the *ſeedneſs* the bare fallow brings
To teeming foyſon. *Shakeſ. Meaſure for Meaſure.*

Sᴇ'ᴇᴅꜱᴍᴀɴ. *n. ſ.* [*ſeed* and *man.*] The ſower; he that ſcatters the ſeed.

The higher Nilus ſwells
The more it promiſes: as it ebbs, the *ſeedſman*
Upon the ſlime and ooze ſcatters his grain,
And ſhortly comes to harveſt. *Shak. Ant. and Cleopat.*

Sᴇᴇ'ᴅʏ. *adj.* [from *ſeed.*] Abounding with ſeed.

Sᴇᴇ'ɪɴɢ. *n. ſ.* [from *ſee.*] Sight; viſion.

Love adds a precious *ſeeing* to the eye. *Shakeſpeare.*

Sᴇᴇ'ɪɴɢ. } *adv.* [*vû que*, French; from *ſee.* It would be
Sᴇᴇ'ɪɴɢ *that.* } more grammatically written, as in French, *ſeen that*, or *provided that.*] Since; ſith; it being ſo that.

Why ſhould not they be as well victualled for ſo long time, as the ſhips are uſually for a year, *ſeeing* it is eaſier to keep victuals on land than water? *Spenſer on Ireland.*

How ſhall they have any trial of his doctrine, learning, and ability to preach, *ſeeing that* he may not publickly either teach or exhort, becauſe he is not yet called to the miniſtry? *Whitgifte.*

Seeing every nation affords not experience and tradition enough for all kind of learning, therefore we are taught the languages of thoſe people who have been moſt induſtrious after wiſdom. *Milton on Education.*

Seeing they explained the phenomena of viſion, imagination, and thought, by certain thin fleeces of atoms that flow from the ſurfaces of bodies, and by their ſubtlety penetrate any obſtacle, and yet retain the exact lineaments of the ſeveral bodies from which they proceed: in conſequence of this hypotheſis they maintained, that we could have no phantaſy of any thing, but what did really ſubſiſt either intire or in its ſeveral parts. *Bentley's Sermons.*

To SEEK. *v. a.* pret. *I ſought*; part. paſſ. *ſought.* [ꞅecan, Sax. *ſoecken*, Dutch.]

1. To look for; to ſearch for.

He did range the town to *ſeek* me out. *Shakeſpeare.*
I have a venturous fairy, that ſhall *ſeek*
The ſquirrel's hoard, and fetch thee thence new nuts. *Shak.*

Becauſe of the money returned in our ſacks, are we brought in, that he may *ſeek* occaſion againſt us, and take us for bondmen. *Gen.* xliii. 18.

He *ſeeketh* unto him a cunning workman, to prepare a graven image. *Iſ.* xl. 20.

Seek thee a man which may go with thee. *Tob.* v. 3.

The king meant not to *ſeek* out nor to decline fighting with them, if they put themſelves in his way. *Clarendon.*

Sweet peace, where do'ſt thou dwell?
I humbly crave,
Let me once know;
I *ſought* thee in a ſecret cave,
And aſk'd if peace were there. *Herbert.*

So fatal 'twas to *ſeek* temptations out!
Moſt confidence has ſtill moſt cauſe to doubt. *Dryden.*

We muſt *ſeek* out ſome other original of power for the government of politicks than this of Adam, or elſe there will be none at all in the world. *Locke.*

2. To ſolicit; to endeavour to gain.

Others tempting him, *ſought* of him a ſign. *Lu.* xi. 16.

The young lions roar after their prey, and *ſeek* their meat from God. *Pſ.* civ. 21.

God hath bid dwell far off all anxious cares,
And not moleſt us, unleſs we ourſelves
Seek them with wandering thoughts. *Milton.*

Oft our alliance other lands deſir'd,
And what we *ſeek* of you, of us requir'd. *Dryden.*

3. To go to find.

Let us *ſeek* death, or, he not found, ſupply
His office. *Milton.*

Dardanus, though born
On Latian plains, yet *ſought* the Phrygian ſhore. *Dryden.*

Like fury ſeiz'd the reſt; the progreſs known,
All *ſeek* the mountains, and forſake the town. *Dryden.*

Since great Ulyſſes *ſought* the Phrygian plains,
Within theſe walls inglorious ſilence reigns. *Pope.*

Indulge one labour more,
And *ſeek* Atrides on the Spartan ſhore. *Pope.*

4. To purſue by ſecret machinations.

I had a ſon,
Now outlaw'd from my blood; he *ſought* my life. *Shakeſp.*

David ſaw that Saul was come out to *ſeek* his life. 1 *Sa.* xxiii.

To Sᴇᴇᴋ. *v. n.*

1. To make ſearch; to make inquiry; to endeavour.

Seek ye out of the book of the Lord, and read. *Iſ.* xxxiv.

Why ſhould he mean me ill, or *ſeek* to harm? *Milton.*

Aſk

Ask not what pains, nor further *seek* to know
Their process, or the forms of law below. *Dryden.*

I have been forced to relinquish that opinion, and have endeavoured to *seek* after some better reason. *Addison's Spectat.*

2. To make pursuit.

Violent men have *sought* after my soul. *Ps.* lxxxvi. 14.

If thy brother's ox or sheep go astray, it shall be with thee until thy brother *seek* after it. *Deut.* xxii. 2.

3. To apply to; to use solicitation.

All the earth *sought* to Solomon, to hear his wisdom. 1 *K.*

Unto his habitation shall ye *seek*, and thither thou shalt come. *Deutr.* xii. 5.

4. To endeavour after.

Being a man of experience, he wished by wisdom to order that which the young prince *sought* for by war. *Knolles.*

To SEEK. [An adverbial mode of speech.] At a loss; without measures, knowledge, or experience.

Being brought and transferred from other services abroad, though they be of good experience in those, yet in these they will be new to *seek*; and before they have gathered experience, they shall buy it with great loss to his majesty. *Spenser.*

Unpractis'd, unprepar'd, and still to *seek*. *Milton.*

But they misplace them all;
And are as much to *seek* in other things,
As he that only can design a tree,
Would be to draw a shipwreck. *Roscommon.*

SEE'KER. *n. s.* [from *seek*.] One that seeks; an inquirer.

Though I confess that in philosophy I'm a *seeker*, yet cannot believe that a sceptick in philosophy must be one in divinity. *Glanv.*

A language of a very witty volatile people, *seekers* after novelty, and abounding with variety of notions. *Locke.*

SEE'KSORROW. *n. s.* [*seek* and *sorrow*.] One who contrives to give himself vexation.

Afield they go, where many lookers be,
And thou *seeksorrow*, Klaius, them among:
Indeed thou saidst it was thy friend to see,
Strephon, whose absence seem'd unto thee long. *Sidney.*

To SEEL. *v. a.* [*seeller*, to seal, French.] To close the eyes. A term of falconry, the eyes of a wild or haggard hawk being for a time seeled or closed.

Now she brought them to see a *seeled* dove, who the blinder she was, the higher she strave. *Sidney.*

As gentle hind, whose sides with cruel steel
Through lanced, her bleeding life does rain;
While the sad pang approaching she does feel,
Brays out her latest breath, and up her eyes doth *seel*. *F. Q.*

Mine eyes no more on vanity shall feed,
But *seeled* up with death shall have their deadly meed. *F. Q.*

Come, *seeling* night,
Scarf up the tender eye of pitiful day. *Shakesp. Macbeth.*

Some ambitious men seem as screens to princes in matters of danger and envy; for no man will take such parts, unless he be like the *seeled* dove, that mounts and mounts, because he cannot see about him. *Bacon.*

Since, blinded with ambition, he did soar
Like a *seeled* dove, his crime shall be his punishment,
To be depriv'd of sight. *Denham's Sophy.*

To SEEL. *v. n.* [ꞅyllan, Saxon.] To lean on one side.

When a ship *seels* or rowls in foul weather, the breaking loose of ordnance is a thing very dangerous. *Raleigh.*

SEE'LY. *adj.* [from ꞅeel, lucky time, Saxon.]

1. Lucky; happy.

My *seely* sheep like well below,
For they been hale enough and trow,
And liken their abode. *Spenser.*

2. Silly; foolish; simple. *Spenser.*

Peacock and turkie, that nibbles off top,
Are very ill neighbours to *seely* poor hop. *Tusser.*

To SEEM. *v. n.* [*sembler*, French; unless it has a Teutonick original, as *seemly* certainly has.]

1. To appear; to make a show; to have semblance.

My lord, you've lost a friend, indeed;
And I dare swear, you borrow not that face
Of *seeming* sorrow; it is sure your own. *Shakesp. H.* IV.

Speak: we will not trust our eyes
Without our ears: thou art not what thou *seem'st*. *Shakes.*

So spake th' Omnipotent; and with his words
All *seem'd* well pleas'd; all *seem'd*, but were not all. *Milton.*

In holy nuptials ty'd;
A *seeming* widow, and a secret bride. *Dryden.*

Observe the youth
Already *seems* to snuff the vital air. *Dryden's Æn.*

2. To have the appearance of truth.

It *seems* to me, that the true reason why we have so few versions which are tolerable, is because there are so few who have all the talents requisite for translation. *Dryden*

3. In *Shakespeare*, to *seem*, perhaps signifies to be beautiful.

Sir, there she stands:
If aught within that little *seeming* substance
May fitly like your grace,
She's there, and she is your's. *Shakesp. King Lear.*

4. *It* SEEMS. A phrase hard to be explained. It sometimes signifies that there is an appearance, though no reality; but generally it is used ironically to condem the thing mentioned, like the Latin *scilicet*, or the old English *forsooth*. *Id mihi datur negotii* scilicet. *This*, it seems, *is to be my task.*

The earth by these, 'tis said,
This single crop of men and women bred;
Who, grown adult, so chance, *it seems*, enjoin'd,
Did male and female propagate. *Blackmore's Creation.*

5. It is sometimes a slight affirmation.

A prince of Italy, *it seems*, entertained his mistress upon a great lake. *Addison's Guardian.*

The raven, urg'd by such impertinence,
Grew passionate, *it seems*, and took offence. *Addison.*

He had been a chief magistrate; and had, *it seems*, executed that high office justly and honourably. *Atterbury.*

It seems that when first I was discovered sleeping on the ground, the emperor had early notice. *Gulliver.*

6. It appears to be.

Here's another discontented paper,
Found in his pocket too; and this, *it seems*,
Rodorigo meant t' have sent. *Shakesp. Othello*

It seems the camel's hair is taken by painters for the skin with the hair on. *Brown's Vulgar Errours.*

SEE'MER. *n. s.* [from *seem*.] One that carries an appearance.

Angelo scarce confesses
That his blood flows, or that his appetite
Is more to bread than stone: hence shall we see,
If pow'r change purpose, what our *seemers* be. *Shakespeare.*

SEE'MING. *n. s.* [from *seem*.]

1. Appearance; show; semblance.

All good *seeming*,
By thy revolt, oh husband, shall be thought
Put on for villainy. *Shakesp. Cymbeline.*

Give him heedful note;
And, after, we will both our judgments join
In censure of his *seeming*. *Shak. Hamlet.*

2. Fair appearance.

For you there's rosemary and rue; these keep
Seeming and savour all the Winter long. *Shakespeare.*

3. Opinion.

Nothing more clear unto their *seeming*, than that a new Jerusalem, being often spoken of in Scripture, they undoubtedly were themselves that new Jerusalem. *Hooker.*

His persuasive words impregn'd
With reason to her *seeming*. *Milton.*

SEE'MINGLY. *adv.* [from *seeming*.] In appearance; in show; in semblance.

To this her mother's plot,
She, *seemingly* obedient, likewise hath
Made promise to the doctor. *Shak. Merry Wives of Winds.*

They to their viands fell, not *seemingly*
The angels, nor in mist. *Milton.*

I have touched upon them, though *seemingly* collateral to my scope; and yet I think they are more than *seemingly* so, since they pertinently illustrate my design. *Glanv. Sceps.*

The city dame was so well bred, as *seemingly* to take all in good part. *L'Estrange.*

The king and haughty empress, to our wonder,
If not aton'd, yet *seemingly* at peace. *Dryden.*

This the father *seemingly* complied with; but afterwards refusing, the son was likewise set aside. *Addison's Freeholder.*

They depend often on remote and *seemingly* disproportioned causes. *Atterbury.*

SEE'MINGNESS. *n. s.* [from *seeming*.] Plausibility; fair appearance.

The *seemingness* of those reasons persuades us on the other side. *Digby.*

SEE'MLINESS. *n. s.* [from *seemly*.] Decency; handsomeness; comeliness; grace; beauty.

When substantialness combineth with delightfulness, *seemliness* with portliness, and currentness with stayedness, how can the language sound other than full of sweetness? *Camden.*

SEE'MLY. *adj.* [*soommeligt*, Danish, from *soome*, Islandick, honour or decency.] Decent; becoming; proper; fit.

Suspence of judgment and exercise of charity were safer and *seemlier* for Christian men, than the hot pursuit of these controversies. *Hooker.*

I am a woman, lacking wit
To make a *seemly* answer to such persons. *Shakes. H.* VIII.

The wife safest and *seemliest* by her husband stays. *Milton.*

May we enjoy
Our humid products, and with *seemly* draughts
Enkindle mirth and hospitable love. *Phillips.*

SEE'MLY. *adv.* [from the adjective.] In a decent manner; in a proper manner.

There, *seemly* rang'd in peaceful order, stood
Ulysses' arms, now long disus'd to blood. *Pope.*

SEEN. *adj.* [from *see*.] Skilled; versed.

Petruchio shall offer me, disguis'd in sober robes,
To old Baptista as a schoolmaster
Well *seen* in musick. *Shakespeare.*

Noble

Noble Boyle, not leſs in nature *ſeen*,
Than his great brother read in ſtates and men. *Dryden.*

SE'ER. *n. ſ.* [from *ſee.*]

1. One who ſees.

We are in hopes that you may prove a dreamer of dreams, and a *ſeer* of viſions. *Addiſon's Spectator.*

2. A prophet; one who foreſees future events.

How ſoon hath thy prediction, *ſeer* bleſt!
Meaſur'd this tranſient world the race of time,
'Till time ſtand fix'd? *Milton's Paradiſe Loſt, b.* xii.

By day your frighted *ſeers*
Shall call for fountains to expreſs their tears,
And wiſh their eyes were floods: by night from dreams
Of opening gulphs, black ſtorms, and raging flames,
Starting amaz'd, ſhall to the people ſhow
Emblems of heav'nly wrath and myſtick types of woe. *Pri.*

SEE'RWOOD. *n. ſ.* See SEARWOOD. Dry wood.

Caught, like dry ſtubble fir'd, or like *ſearwood*;
Yet from the wound enſu'd no purple flood,
But look'd a bubbling maſs of frying blood. *Dryden.*

SEE'SAW. *n. ſ.* [from *ſaw.*] A reciprocating motion.

His wit all *ſee-ſaw*, between that and this;
Now high, now low, now maſter up, now miſs,
And he himſelf one vile antitheſis. *Pope.*

To SEE'SAW. *v. n.* [from *ſaw.*] To move with a reciprocating motion.

Sometimes they were like to pull John over, then it went all of a ſudden again on John's ſide; ſo they went *ſeeſawing* up and down, from one end of the room to the other. *Arbut.*

To SEETH. *v. a.* preterite *I ſod* or *ſeethed*; part. paſſ. *ſodden.* [ſeoðan, Saxon; *ſoeden*, Dutch.] To boil; to decoct in hot liquor.

The Scythians uſed to *ſeeth* the fleſh in the hide, and ſo do the northern Iriſh. *Spenſer.*

Go, ſuck the ſubtile blood o' th' grape,
'Till the high fever *ſeeth* your blood to froth,
And ſo 'ſcape hanging. *Shakeſpeare's Timon.*

Set on the great pot, and *ſeeth* pottage for the ſons of the prophets. *2 Kings* iv.

To SEETH. *v. n.* To be in a ſtate of ebullition; to be hot.

The boiling baths at Cairbadon,
Which *ſeeth* with ſecret fire eternally,
And in their entrails, full of quick brimſton,
Nouriſh the flames, which they are warm'd upon. *Fa. Qu.*

I will make a complimental aſſault upon him; for my buſineſs *ſeeths*. *Shakeſ. Troilus and Creſſida.*

Lovers and madmen have their *ſeething* brains,
Such ſhaping fantaſies, that apprehend
More than cool reaſon ever comprehends. *Shakeſpeare.*

The prieſt's ſervant came, while the fleſh was in *ſeething*, with a fleſh-hook, and ſtuck it into the pan. *1 Sa.* ii. 13.

SEE'THER. *n. ſ.* [from *ſeeth.*] A boiler; a pot.

The fire thus form'd, ſhe ſets the kettle on;
Like burniſh'd gold the little *ſeether* ſhone. *Dryden.*

SE'GMENT. *n. ſ.* [*ſegment*, French; *ſegmentum*, Lat.] A figure contained between a chord and an arch of the circle, or ſo much of the circle as is cut off by that chord.

Even unto a parallel ſphere, and ſuch as live under the poles for half a year, ſome *ſegments* may appear at any time, and under any quarter, the ſun not ſetting, but walking round. *Brown's Vulgar Errours.*

Their *ſegments* or arcs, which appeared ſo numerous, for the moſt part exceeded not the third part of a circle. *Newton.*

SE'GNITY. *n. ſ.* [from *ſegnis*, Latin.] Sluggiſhneſs; inactivity. *Dict.*

To SE'GREGATE. *v. a.* [*ſegrego*, Latin; *ſegreger*, French.] To ſet apart; to ſeparate from others.

SEGREGA'TION. *n. ſ.* [*ſegregation*, Fr. from *ſegregate.*] Separation from others.

What ſhall we hear of this?
——A *ſegregation* of the Turkiſh fleet;
For do but ſtand upon the foaming ſhore,
The chiding billows ſeem to pelt the clouds. *Shak. Othello.*

SEIGNEU'RIAL. *adj.* [from *ſeignior.*] Inveſted with large powers; independant.

Thoſe lands were *ſeigneurial.* *Temple.*

SE'IGNIOR. *n. ſ.* [from *ſenior*, Latin; *ſeigneur*, Fr.] A lord. The title of honour given by Italians.

SE'IGNIORY. *n. ſ.* [*ſeigneurie*, Fr. from *ſeignior.*] A lordſhip; a territory.

O'Neal never had any *ſeigniory* over that country, but what by incroachment he got upon the Engliſh. *Spenſer.*

Were you not reſtor'd
To all the duke of Norfolk's *ſeigniories?* *Shakeſp. H.* IV.

Hoſea, in the perſon of God, ſayeth of the Jews, they have reigned, but not by me; they have ſet a *ſeigniory* over themſelves: which place proveth plainly, that there are governments which God doth not avow. *Bacon.*

William Marſhal, earl of Pembroke, being lord of all Leinſter, had royal juriſdiction throughout that province, and every one of his five ſons enjoyed that *ſeigniory* ſucceſſively. *Davies on Ireland.*

SE'IGNORAGE. *n. ſ.* [*ſeigneuriage*, Fr. from *ſeignior.*] Authority; acknowledgment of power.

They brought work to the mint, and a part of the money coined to the crown for *ſeignorage.* *Locke.*

To SE'IGNORISE. *v. a.* [from *ſeignior.*] To lord over.

As fair he was as Cytherea's make,
As proud as he that *ſeignoriſeth* hell. *Fairfax.*

SEINE. *n. ſ.* [ſegne, Saxon; *ſeine*, *ſenne*, *ſeme*, French.] A net uſed in fiſhing.

They have cock-boats for paſſengers, and *ſeine* boats for taking of pilchards. *Carew.*

SE'INER. *n. ſ.* [from *ſeine.*] A fiſher with nets.

Seiners complain with open mouth, that theſe drovers work much prejudice to the commonwealth of fiſhermen, and reap ſmall gain to themſelves. *Carew's Survey of Cornwal.*

To SEIZE. *v. a.* [*ſaiſir*, French.]

1. To take poſſeſſion of; to graſp; to lay hold on; to faſten on.

In her ſad breaſt the prince's fortunes rowl,
And hope and doubt alternate *ſeize* her ſoul. *Pope.*

2. To take forcible poſſeſſion of by law.

An eſcheator of London had arreſted a clothier that was outlawed, and *ſeized* his goods. *Camden.*

It was judged by the higheſt kind of judgment, that he ſhould be baniſhed, and his whole eſtate confiſcated and *ſeized*, and his houſes pulled down. *Bacon.*

3. To make poſſeſſed.

So th' one for wrong, the other ſtrives for right:
As when a griffin, *ſeized* of his prey,
A dragon fierce encount'reth in his flight,
Through wildeſt air making his idle way. *Fa. Queen.*

So Pluto, *ſeiz'd* of Proſerpine, convey'd
To hell's tremenduous gloom th' affrighted maid,
There grimly ſmil'd, pleas'd with the beauteous prize,
Nor envy'd Jove his ſunſhine and his ſkies. *Addiſ. Cato.*

To SEIZE. *v. n.* To fix the graſp or the power on any thing.

Faireſt Cordelia,
Thee and thy virtues here I *ſeize* upon:
Be't lawful I take up what's caſt away? *Shakeſp. K. Lear.*

Where there is a deſign of ſupplanting, that neceſſarily requires another of accuſing: even Jezebel projects not to *ſeize* on Naboth's vineyard without a precedent charge. *Dec. of Piety.*

SE'IZIN. *n. ſ.* [*ſaiſine*, French.]

1. [In law.] Is of two ſorts: *ſeiſin* in fact, and *ſeiſin* in law. *Seiſin* in fact, is when a corporal poſſeſſion is taken: *ſeiſin* in law, is when ſomething is done which the law accounteth a *ſeiſin*, as an inrolment. This is as much as a right to lands and tenements, though the owner be by wrong diſſeized of them. *Cowel.*

2. The act of taking poſſeſſion.

Every indulged ſin gives Satan livery and *ſeiſin* of his heart, and a power to diſpoſe of it as he pleaſes. *Decay of Piety.*

Seiſin is the ſame in the canon law as livery and *ſeiſin* at the common law. *Ayliffe's Parergon.*

3. The things poſſeſſed.

Many recoveries were had as well by heirs as ſucceſſors of the *ſeizin* of their predeceſſors. *Hale.*

SE'IZURE. *n. ſ.* [from *ſeize.*]

1. The act of ſeizing.

2. The thing ſeized.

Sufficient that thy pray'rs are heard, and death,
Then due by ſentence when thou did'ſt tranſgreſs,
Defeated of his *ſeizure*, many days
Giv'n thee of grace. *Milton's Paradiſe Loſt.*

3. The act of taking forcible poſſeſſion.

Thy lands, and all things that thou do'ſt call thine,
Worth *ſeizure*, do we ſeize into our hands. *Shakeſpeare.*

In the general town he maintained a *ſeizure*, and poſſeſſion of the whole. *Wotton.*

Henry continued to burn proteſtants, after he had caſt off the pope; and his *ſeizure* of eccleſiaſtical revenues cannot be reckoned as a mark of the church's liberty. *Swift.*

4. Gripe; poſſeſſion.

And ſhall theſe hands, ſo lately purg'd of blood,
Unyoke this *ſeizure*, and this kind regreet? *Shakeſpeare.*

Make o'er thy honour by a deed of truſt,
And give me *ſeizure* of the mighty wealth. *Dryden.*

5. Catch.

Let there be no ſudden *ſeizure* of a lapſed ſyllable to play upon it. *Watts.*

SE'LCOUTH. *adj.* [ſeld, rare, Sax. and *couth*, known.] Uncommon. *Spenſer.* The ſame with *uncouth.*

SE'LDOM. *adv.* [ſeldan, rarely; ſeldoꞃ, more rarely; ſeldoꞅt, moſt rarely. Seldan is ſuppoſed to be contracted from ſeldæn, or ſeld; rare, and ƿænne, when, Saxon. *Selden*, Dutch; *ſeltan*, German.] Rarely; not often; not frequently.

Wiſdom and youth are *ſeldom* joined in one; and the ordinary courſe of the world is more according to Job's obſervation, who giveth men advice to ſeek wiſdom amongſt the ancients, and in the length of days underſtanding. *Hooker.*

There is true joy conveyed to the heart by preventing grace, which pardoning grace *ſeldom* gives. *South's Sermons.*

Where

Where the flight of fancy is managed with good judgment, the *ſeldomer* it is ſeen it is the more valuable. *Grew.*

SE'LDOMNESS. *n. ſ.* [from *ſeldom.*] Uncommonneſs; infrequency; rareneſs; rarity. Little uſed.

Degrees of well-doing there could be none, except perhaps in the *ſeldomneſs* and oftenneſs of doing well. *Hooker.*

SE'LDSHOWN. *adj.* [*ſeld* and *ſhown.*] Seldom exhibited to view.

Seldſhown flamins
Do preſs among the popular throngs. *Shakeſp. Coriolanus.*

To SELE'CT. *v. a.* [*ſelectus*, Latin.] To chuſe in preference to others rejected.

The footmen, *ſelected* out of all the provinces, were greatly diminiſhed, being now ſcarce eight thouſand ſtrong. *Knolles.*

The pious chief
A hundred youths from all his train *ſelects.* *Dryden.*

SELE'CT. *adj.* [from the verb.] Nicely choſen; choice; culled out on account of ſuperiour excellence.

To the nuptial bow'r
I led her, bluſhing like the morn: all heav'n,
And happy conſtellations, on that hour
Shed their *ſelecteſt* influence. *Milton's Parad. Loſt.*

Select from vulgar herds, with garlands gay,
A hundred bulls aſcend the ſacred way. *Prior.*

SELE'CTION. *n. ſ.* [*ſelectio*, Lat. from *ſelect.*] The act of culling or chuſing; choice.

While we ſingle out ſeveral diſhes, and reject others, the *ſelection* ſeems but arbitrary. *Brown's Vulgar Errours.*

SELE'CTNESS. *n. ſ.* [from *ſelect.*] The ſtate of being ſelect.

SELE'CTOR. *n. ſ.* [from *ſelect.*] He who ſelects.

SELENOGRA'PHICAL. } *adj.* [*ſelenographique*, Fr. from *ſelenography.*] Belonging to ſelenography.
SELENOGRA'PHICK. }

SELE'NOGRAPHY. *n. ſ.* [*ſelenographie*, Fr. σελήνη and γράφω.] A deſcription of the moon.

Hevelius, in his accurate *ſelenography*, or deſcription of the moon, hath well tranſlated the known appellations of regions, ſeas, and mountains, unto the parts of that luminary. *Brown.*

SELF. *pronoun.* plur. *ſelves.* [*ſilba*, Gothick; ꞅẏlꝼ, ꞅẏlꝼa, Sax. *ſelf*, *ſelve*, Dutch.]

1. Its primary ſignification ſeems to be that of an adjective: very; particular; this above others; ſometimes, one's own.

Shoot another arrow that *ſelf* way
Which you did ſhoot the firſt. *Shakeſp. Merch. of Ven.*

The cruel miniſters, by *ſelf* and violent hands,
Took off her life. *Shakeſpeare.*

On theſe *ſelf* hills the air is ſo thin, that it is not ſufficient to bear up the body of a bird. *Raleigh.*

At that *ſelf* moment enters Palamon
The gate of Venus. *Dryden.*

2. It is united both to the perſonal pronouns, and to the neutral pronoun *it*, and is always added when they are uſed reciprocally, or return upon themſelves: as, *I did not hurt* him, *he hurt* himſelf; *the people hiſs* me, *but I clap* myſelf; *thou loveſt* thyſelf, *though the world ſcorns* thee.

Self is that conſcious thinking thing, which is ſenſible or conſcious of pleaſure and pain, capable of happineſs and miſery, and ſo is concerned for *itſelf*, as far as that conſciouſneſs extends. *Locke.*

3. It is ſometimes uſed emphatically in the nominative caſe: as, *myſelf* will decide it; I *myſelf* will come; *himſelf* ſhall revenge it. This uſe of *ſelf*, thus compounded, without the pronoun perſonal, is chiefly poetical.

4. Compounded with *him*, a pronoun ſubſtantive, *ſelf* is in appearance an adjective: joined to *my*, *thy*, *our*, *your*, pronoun adjectives, it ſeems a ſubſtantive. Even when compounded with *him* it is at laſt found to be a ſubſtantive, by its variation in the plural, contrary to the nature of Engliſh adjectives, as *himſelf*, *themſelves.*

5. *Myſelf*, *himſelf*, *themſelves*, and the reſt, may, contrary to the analogy of *my*, *him*, *them*, be uſed as nominatives.

6. It often adds only emphaſis and force to the pronoun with which it is compounded.

Next to the knowledge of God, this knowledge of our *ſelves* ſeems moſt worthy of our endeavour. *Hale.*

The fondneſs we have for ſelf, and the relation which other things have to our *ſelves*, furniſhes another long rank of prejudices. *Watts.*

7. It ſignifies the individual, as ſubject to his own contemplation or action.

The ſpark of noble courage now awake,
And ſtrive your excellent *ſelf* to excel. *Fairy Queen.*

Since conſciouſneſs always accompanies thinking, and it is that that makes every one to be what he calls *ſelf*, and thereby diſtinguiſhes himſelf from all other thinking things; in this alone conſiſts perſonal identity, *i. e.* the ſameneſs of a rational being. *Locke.*

It is by the conſciouſneſs it has of its preſent thoughts and actions, that it is *ſelf* to it *ſelf* now, and ſo will be the ſame *ſelf*, as far as the ſame conſciouſneſs can extend to actions paſt or to come. *Locke.*

8. It is much uſed in compoſition, which it is proper to explain by a train of examples. It is to be obſerved, that its compoſition in *Shakeſpeare* is often harſh.

Then held ſhe her tongue, and caſt down a *ſelf* accuſing look, finding that in her ſelf ſhe had ſhot out of the bow of her affection a more quick opening of her mind, than ſhe minded to have done. *Sidney.*

Alas! while we are wrapt in foggy miſt
Of our *ſelf*-love, ſo paſſions do deceive,
We think they hurt when moſt they do aſſiſt. *Sidney.*

'Till Strephon's plaining voice him nearer drew,
Where by his words his *ſelf*-like caſe he knew. *Sidney.*

Ah! where was firſt that cruel cunning found,
To frame of earth a veſſel of the mind,
Where it ſhould be to *ſelf*-deſtruction bound? *Sidney.*

Before the door ſat *ſelf*-conſuming care,
Day and night keeping wary watch and ward. *Fa. Queen.*

My ſtrange and *ſelf*-abuſe,
Is the initiate fear that wants hard uſe. *Shakeſ. Macbeth.*

I have heard ſo much,
And with Demetrius thought t' have ſpoke thereof;
But being over-full of *ſelf*-affairs,
My mind did loſe it. *Shakeſp. Midſum. Night's Dream.*

Nor know I aught
By me that's ſaid or done amiſs this night,
Unleſs *ſelf*-charity be ſometimes a vice,
And to defend ourſelves it be a ſin,
When violence aſſails us. *Shakeſpeare's Othello.*

He walks, and that *ſelf*-chain about his neck,
Which he forſwore. *Shakeſpeare.*

It is in my power, in one *ſelf*-born hour,
To plant and o'erwhelm cuſtom. *Shakeſp. Winter's Tale.*

His treaſons will ſit bluſhing in his face,
Not able to endure the ſight of day,
But *ſelf*-affrighted tremble at his ſin. *Shak. Rich.* II.

The ſtars above us govern our conditions;
Elſe one *ſelf*-mate and mate could not beget
Such different iſſues. *Shakeſpeare.*

I'm made of that *ſelf*-metal as my ſiſter,
And prize me at her worth. *Shak. King Lear.*

In my ſchool-days, when I had loſt one ſhaft,
I ſhot his fellow of the *ſelf*-ſame flight
The *ſelf*-ſame way, with more adviſed watch,
To find the other forth. *Shakeſpeare.*

He may do ſome good on her:
A peeviſh *ſelf*-will'd harlotry it is. *Shak. Romeo and Juliet.*

But leſt myſelf be guilty of *ſelf*-wrong,
I'll ſtop mine ears againſt the mermaid's ſong. *Shakeſpeare.*

He conjunct and flatt'ring his diſpleaſure,
Tript me behind: being down, inſulted, rail'd,
Got praiſes of the king,
For him attempting who was *ſelf*-ſubdu'd. *Shakeſpeare.*

The Everlaſting fixt
His canon 'gainſt *ſelf*-ſlaughter. *Shak. Hamlet.*

Know if his laſt purpoſe hold,
Or whether ſince he is adviſ'd by aught
To change the courſe? He's full of alteration,
And *ſelf*-reproving. *Shakeſ. King Lear.*

More or leſs to others paying,
Than by *ſelf*-offences weighing;
Shame to him whoſe cruel ſtriking,
Kills for faults of his own liking! *Shakeſpeare.*

Bellona's bridegroom, lapt in proof,
Confronted him with *ſelf*-capariſons,
Point againſt point rebellious, arm 'gainſt arm,
Curbing his laviſh ſpirit. *Shak. Macbeth.*

Self-love, my liege, is not ſo vile a ſin
As *ſelf*-neglecting. *Shakeſ. Henry* V.

Anger is like
A full hot horſe, who, being allow'd his way,
Self-mettle tires him. *Shakeſpeare.*

His lords deſire him to have borne
His bruiſed helmet and his bended ſword
Before him through the city; he forbids it,
Being free from vainneſs and *ſelf*-glorious pride. *Shakeſp.*

You promis'd
To lay aſide *ſelf*-harming heavineſs,
And entertain a cheerful diſpoſition. *Shakeſ. Rich.* III.

In their anger they ſlew a man, and in their *ſelf*-will they digged down a wall. *Gen.* xlix. 6.

The moſt ordinary cauſe of a ſingle life is liberty, eſpecially in certain *ſelf*-pleaſing and humorous minds, which are ſo ſenſible of every reſtraint as to think their girdles and garters to be bonds and ſhackles. *Bacon.*

Haſt thou ſet up nothing in competition with God; no pride, pleaſure, profit, *ſelf*-love, or *ſelf*-intereſt of thy own? *Duppa.*

Up through the ſpacious palace paſſed ſhe,
To where the king's proudly repoſed head,
If any can be ſoft to tyranny,
And *ſelf*-tormenting ſin, had a ſoft bed. *Craſhaw.*

With a joyful willingness these *self*-loving reformers took possession of all vacant preferments, and with reluctance others parted with their beloved colleges and subsistence. *Walton.*

Repent the sin; but if the punishment
Thou can'st avoid, *self*-preservation bids. *Milton.*

Him fast sleeping soon he found,
In labyrinth of many a round *self*-roll'd. *Milton.*

Oft times nothing profits more
Than *self*-esteem, grounded on just and right,
Well manag'd. *Milton's Paradise Lost.*

Self-knowing, and from thence
Magnanimous, to correspond with heav'n. *Milton.*

So virtue giv'n for lost,
Deprest and overthrown, as seem'd,
Like that *self*-begotten bird,
In th' Arabian woods embost,
That no second knows nor third,
And lay ere while a holocaust,
From out her ashy womb now teem'd. *Milton's Agonist.*

He sorrows now, repents, and prays contrite,
My motions in him: longer than they move,
His heart I know how variable and vain,
Self-left. *Milton.*

Seneca approves this *self*-homicide. *Hakewill.*

Thyself from flatt'ring *self*-conceit defend,
Nor what thou do'st not know, to know pretend. *Denham.*

Man's that savage beast, whose mind,
From reason to *self*-love declin'd,
Delights to prey upon his kind. *Denham.*

Farewel, my tears;
And my just anger be no more confin'd
To vain complaints, or *self*-devouring silence. *Denham.*

They are yet more mad to think that men may go to rest by death, though they die in *self*-murder, the greatest sin. *Graunt's Bills of Mortality.*

Are not these strange *self*-delusions, and yet attested by common experience? *South's Sermons.*

If the image of God is only sovereignty, certainly we have been hitherto much mistaken, and hereafter are to beware of making ourselves unlike God, by too much *self*-denial and humility. *South's Sermons.*

If a man would have a devout, humble, sin-abhorring, *self*-denying frame of spirit, he cannot take a more efficacious course to attain it than by praying himself into it. *South.*

Let a man apply himself to the difficult work of *self*-examination by a strict scrutiny into the whole estate of his soul. *South's Sermons.*

A fatal *self*-imposture, such as defeats the design, and destroys the force of all religion. *South's Sermons.*

When he intends to bereave the world of an illustrious person, he may cast him upon a bold *self*-opinioned physician, worse than his distemper, who shall make a shift to cure him into his grave. *South's Sermons.*

Neglect of friends can never be proved rational, 'till we prove the person using it omnipotent and *self*-sufficient, and such as can never need any mortal assistance. *South.*

By all human laws, as well as divine, *self*-murder has ever been agreed on as the greatest crime. *Temple.*

A *self*-conceited fop will swallow any thing. *L'Estrange.*

From Atreus though your ancient lineage came;
Yet my *self*-conscious worth, your high renown,
Your virtue, through the neighb'ring nations blown. *Dryd.*

He has given you all the commendation which his *self*-sufficiency could afford to any. *Dryden.*

Below yon sphere
There hangs the ball of earth and water mixt,
Self-center'd and unmov'd. *Dryden's State of Innocence.*

All these receive their birth from other things,
But from himself the phoenix only springs;
Self-born, begotten by the parent flame
In which he burn'd, another and the same. *Dryden.*

The burning fire that shone so bright,
Flew off all sudden with extinguish'd light,
And left one altar dark, a little space;
Which turn'd *self*-kindled, and renew'd the blaze. *Dryden.*

Thou first, O king! release the rights of sway;
Pow'r, *self*-restrain'd, the people best obey. *Dryden.*

Eighteen and nineteen are equal to thirty-seven, by the same *self*-evidence that one and two are equal to three. *Locke.*

A contradiction of what has been said, is a mark of yet greater pride and *self*-conceitedness, when we take upon us to set another right in his story. *Locke.*

I am as justly accountable for any action done many years since, appropriated to me now by this *self*-consciousness, as I am for what I did the last moment. *Locke.*

Each intermediate idea agreeing on each side with those two, it is immediately placed between: the ideas of men and *self*-determination appear to be connected. *Locke.*

This *self*-existent being hath the power of perfection, as well as of existence in himself; for he that is above, or existeth without, any cause, that is, hath the power of existence in himself, cannot be without the power of any possible existence. *Grew's Cosm. Sacr.*

Body cannot be *self*-existent, because it is not *self*-movent; for motion is not of the essence of body, because we may have a definitive conception of body, abstracted from that of motion: wherefore motion is something else besides body, and something without which a body may be conceived to exist. *Grew's Cosmol. Sac.*

Confidence, as opposed to modesty, and distinguished from decent assurance, proceeds from *self*-opinion, occasioned by ignorance or flattery. *Collier of Confidence.*

Bewilder'd I, my author cannot find,
'Till some first cause, some *self*-existent mind,
Who form'd, and rules all nature, is assign'd. *Blackm.*

If a first body may to any place
Be not determin'd in the boundless space,
'Tis plain it then may absent be from all,
Who then will this a *self*-existence call? *Blackmore.*

Shall nature, erring from her first command,
Self-preservation fall by her own hand? *Granville.*

Low nonsense is the talent of a cold phlegmatick temper: a writer of this complexion gropes his way softly amongst *self*-contradiction, and grovels in absurdities. *Addison.*

This fatal hypocrisy and *self*-deceit is taken notice of in these words, Who can understand his errours? Cleanse thou me from secret faults. *Addison's Spectator.*

The guilt of perjury is so *self*-evident, that it was always reckoned amongst the greatest crimes, by those who were only governed by the light of reason. *Addison.*

Self-sufficiency proceeds from inexperience. *Addison.*

Men had better own their ignorance than advance doctrines which are *self*-contradictory. *Spectator.*

Light, which of all bodies is nearest allied to spirit, is also most diffusive and *self*-communicative. *Norris.*

Thus we see in bodies, the more of kin they are to spirit in subtilty and refinement, the more spreading are they and *self*-diffusive. *Norris.*

God, who is an absolute spiritual act, and who is such a pure light as in which there is no darkness, must needs be infinitely *self*-imparting and communicative. *Norris.*

Every animal is conscious of some individual, *self*-moving, *self*-determining principle. *Pope and Arbuthn. Mart. Scrib.*

Nick does not pretend to be a gentleman: he is a tradesman, a *self*-seeking wretch. *Arbuthn. John Bull.*

By the blast of *self*-opinion mov'd,
We wish to charm, and seek to be belov'd. *Prior.*

Living and understanding substances do most clearly demonstrate to philosophical inquirers the necessary *self*-existence, power, wisdom, and beneficence of their maker. *Bentley's Sermons.*

If it can intrinsically stir itself, and either commence or alter its course, it must have a principle of *self*-activity, which is life and sense. *Bentley's Sermons.*

This desire of existence is a natural affection of the soul; 'tis *self*-preservation in the highest and truest meaning. *Bentley.*

The philosophers, and even the Epicureans, maintained the *self*-sufficiency of the Godhead, and seldom or never sacrificed at all. *Bentley's Sermons.*

Matter is not endued with *self*-motion, nor with a power to alter the course in which it is put: it is merely passive, and must ever continue in that state it is settled in. *Cheyne.*

I took not arms, 'till urg'd by *self*-defence,
The eldest law of nature. *Rowe's Ambit. Stepmother.*

His labour and study would have shewn his early mistakes, and cured him of *self*-flattering delusions. *Watts.*

This is not to be done in a rash and *self*-sufficient manner; but with an humble dependance on divine grace, while we walk among snares. *Watts.*

The religion of Jesus, with all its *self*-denials, virtues, and devotions, is very practicable. *Watts.*

I heard in Crete, this island's name;
For 'twas in Crete, my native soil, I came
Self-banish'd thence. *Pope's Odyssey.*

Achilles's courage is furious and untractable; that of Ajax is heavy and *self*-confiding. *Pope.*

I doom, to fix the gallant ship,
A mark of vengeance on the sable deep;
To warn the thoughtless *self*-confiding train,
No more unlicens'd thus to brave the main. *Pope.*

What is loose love? a transient gust,
A vapour fed from wild desire,
A wand'ring *self*-consuming fire. *Pope.*

In dubious thought the king awaits,
And *self*-considering, as he stands, debates. *Pope.*

By mighty Jove's command,
Unwilling have I trod this pleasing land;
For who *self*-mov'd with weary wing would sweep
Such length of ocean? *Pope.*

They who reach Parnassus' lofty crown,
Employ their pains to spurn some others down;
And while *self*-love each jealous writer rules,
Contending wits become the sport of fools. *Pope.*

It may be thought that Ulysses here is too ostentatious, and that he dwells more than modesty allows upon his own accomplishments; but *self*-praise is sometimes no fault. *Broome.*

No wonder such a spirit, in such a situation, is provoked beyond the regards of religion or *self*-conviction. *Swift.*

SE'LFHEAL. *n. s.* [*brunella*, Latin.] A plant. The same with SANICLE, which see.

SE'LFISH. *adj.* [from *self.*] Attentive only to one's own interest; void of regard for others.

What could the most aspiring *selfish* man desire more, were he to form the notion of a being to whom he would recommend himself, than such a knowledge as can discover the least appearance of perfection, and such a goodness as will proportion a reward to it? *Addison's Spectator.*

Passions, though *selfish*, if their means be fair,
List under reason, and deserve her care;
Those that imparted court a nobler aim,
Exalt their kind, and take some virtue's name. *Pope.*

SE'LFISHNESS. *n. s.* [from *selfish.*] Attention to his own interest, without any regard to others; self-love.

This sublimer love, being, by an intimate conjunction with its object, throughly refined from all base dross of *selfishness* and interest, nobly begets a perfect submission of our wills to the will of God. *Boyle's Seraphick Love.*

SE'LFISHLY. *adv.* [from *selfish.*] With regard only to his own interest; without love of others.

He can your merit *selfishly* approve,
And shew the sense of it without the love. *Pope.*

SE'LFSAME. *adj.* [*self* and *same.*] Numerically the same.

I have no great cause to look for other than the *self-same* portion and lot, which your manner hath been hitherto to lay on them that concur not in opinion with you. *Hooker, Pref.*

Flight pursu'd one way the *self-same* hour. *Milton.*

I have been base,
Base ev'n to him from whom I did receive
All that a son could to a parent give:
Behold me punish'd in the *self-same* kind;
Th' ungrateful does a more ungrateful find. *Dryden.*

SE'LION. *n. s.* [*selio*, low Latin.] A ridge of land. *Ainsw.*

SELL. *pronoun.* [for *self.*] *Sell* is retained in Scotland for self, and *sells* in the plural for selves.

They turn round like grindle-stones,
Which they dig out fro' the dells,
For their bairns bread, wives and *sells.* *Ben. Johnson.*

SELL. *n. s.* [*selle*, French; *sella*, Latin.] A saddle.

Turning to that place, in which
He left his lofty steed with golden *sells*,
And goodly gorgeous barbes, him found not there. *F. Qu.*

To SELL. *v. a.* [ſyllan, Saxon; *sela*, Islandick.] To give for a price; the word correlative to buy; to vend.

The Midianites *sold* him unto Egypt, unto Potiphar. *Gen.*

Let us *sell* him to the Ishmaelites. *Gen.* xxxvii. 27.

The first tenth part I gave to the sons of Aaron, and another I *sold* away. *Tob.* i. 7.

All the inns and publick houses are obliged to furnish themselves with corn, which is *sold* out at a much dearer rate than 'tis bought up. *Addison on Italy.*

You have made an order that ale should be *sold* for three half-pence a quart. *Swift.*

To SELL. *v. n.* To have commerce or traffick with one.

I will buy with you, *sell* with you; but I will not eat with you. *Shakesp. Merchant of Venice.*

Consult not with a buyer of *selling.* *Ecclus.* xxxvii. 11.

SE'LLANDER. *n. s.* A dry scab in a horse's hough or pastern. *Ainsworth.*

SE'LLER. *n. s.* [from *sell.*] The person that sells; vender.

To things of sale a *seller's* praise belongs. *Shakespeare.*

The name of the agent, of the *seller*, notary, and witnesses, are in both instruments. *Addison on Italy.*

SE'LVAGE. *n. s.* [Of this word I know not the etymology. *Skinner* thinks *selvage* is said as *salvage*, from its saving the cloath.] The edge of cloath where it is closed by complicating the threads.

Make loops of blue upon the edge of the one curtain from the *selvage* in the coupling. *Ex.* xxvi. 4.

SELVES. The plural of *self.*

Consciousness being interrupted, and we losing sight of our past *selves*, doubts are raised whether we are the same. *Locke.*

SE'MBLABLE. *adj.* [*semblable*, French.] Like; resembling.

Then be abhorr'd
All feasts, societies, and throngs of men!
His *semblable*, yea himself, Timon disdains. *Shakespeare.*

With *semblable* reason we might expect a regularity in the winds. *Brown's Vulgar Errours.*

SE'MBLABLY. *adv.* [from *semblable.*] With resemblance.

A gallant knight he was, his name was Blunt;
Semblably furnish'd like the king himself. *Shakesp. H. IV.*

SE'MBLANCE. *n. s.* [*semblance*, Fr. from *semblant.*]

1. Likeness; resemblance; similitude; representation.

Solicit Henry with her wond'rous praise;
Bethink thee on her virtues, that surmount
Her natural graces, that extinguish art:
Repeat their *semblance* often. *Shakespeare.*

She's but the sign and *semblance* of her honour:
Behold how like a maid she blushes here!
O, what authority and shew of truth
Can cunning sin cover itself withal! *Shakespeare.*

He with high words, that bore
Semblance of worth, not substance, gently rais'd
Their fainting courage, and dispell'd their fears. *Milton.*

This last effort brought forth the opinion, that these bodies are not what they seem to be; that they are no shells, but mere sportings of active nature, and only *semblances* or imitations of shells. *Woodward.*

It is not his meaning that we put on the outward face and *semblance* of virtue, only to conceal and disguise our vice. *Rog.*

2. Appearance; show; figure.

Be you the soldier; for you likest are,
For manly *semblance* and for skill in war. *Spenser.*

Their *semblance* kind, and mild their gestures were,
Peace in their hands, and friendship in their face. *Fairfax.*

All that fair and good in thy divine
Semblance, and in thy beauty's heav'nly ray,
United I beheld. *Milt. Par. Lost.*

SE'MBLANT. *adj.* [*semblant*, French.] Like; resembling; having the appearance of any thing. Little used.

In despite of age, of impious flame,
And eating time, thy picture, like thy fame,
Entire may last; that as their eyes survey
The *semblant* shade, men yet unborn may say,
Thus great, thus gracious look'd Britannia's queen;
Her brow thus smooth, her look was thus serene. *Prior.*

SE'MBLANT. *n. s.* Show; figure; resemblance; representation. Not in use.

Her purpose was not such as she did feign,
Ne yet her person such as it was seen;
But under simple shew, and *semblant* plain,
Lurks false Duessa, secretly unseen. *Fairy Queen.*

Full lively is the *semblant*, tho' the substance dead. *Spens.*

SE'MBLATIVE. *adj.* [from *semblant.*] Suitable; accommodate; fit; resembling.

Diana's lip
Is not more smooth and ruby; thy small pipe
Is as the maiden's organ, shrill and sound;
And all is *semblative* a woman's part. *Shak. Twelfth Night.*

To SE'MBLE. *v. n.* [*sembler*, French.] To represent; to make a likeness. Little used.

Let Europe, sav'd, the column high erect,
Than Trajan's higher, or than Antonine's,
Where *sembling* art may carve the fair effect,
And full atchievement of thy great designs. *Prior.*

SEMI. *n. s.* [Latin.] A word which, used in composition, signifies half: as *semicircle*, half a circle.

SE'MIANNULAR. *adj.* [*semi* and *annulus*, a ring.] Half round.

Another boar tusk, somewhat slenderer, and of a *semiannular* figure. *Grew's Musæum.*

SE'MIBREF. *n. s.* [*semibreve*, French.]

Semibref is a note in musick relating to time, and is the last in augmentation. It is commonly called the master-note, or measure-note, or time-note, as being of a certain determinate measure or length of time by itself; and all the other notes of augmentation and diminution are adjusted to its value. *Harris.*

He takes my hand, and as a still which stays
A *semibref*, 'twixt each drop, he niggardly,
As loth to enrich me, so tells many a lye. *Donne.*

SEMICI'RCLE. *n. s.* [*semicirculus*, Lat. *semi* and *circle.*] A half round; part of a circle divided by the diameter.

Black brows
Become some women best, so they be in a *semicircle*,
Or a half-moon, made with a pen. *Shakespeare.*

Has he given the lye
In circle, or oblique, or *semicircle*,
Or direct parallel? *Shakespeare.*

The chains that held my left leg gave me the liberty of walking backwards and forwards in a *semicircle.* *Swift.*

SEMICI'RCLED. } *adj.* [*semi* and *circular.*] Half round.
SEMICI'RCULAR. }

The firm fixure of thy foot would give an excellent motion to thy gait, in a *semicircled* farthingale. *Shakespeare.*

The rainbow is caused by the rays of the sun falling upon a rorid and opposite cloud, whereof some reflected, others refracted, beget the *semicircular* variety we call the rainbow. *Brown's Vulgar Errours.*

The seas are inclosed between the two *semicircular* moles that surround it. *Addison on Italy.*

SEMICO'LON. *n. s.* [*semi* and κῶλον.] Half a colon; a point made thus [;] to note a greater pause than that of a comma.

SEMIDIA'METER. *n. s.* [*semi* and *diameter.*] Half the line which, drawn through the centre of a circle, divides it into two equal parts; a ſtreight line drawn from the circumference to the center of a circle.

Their difference is as little conſiderable as a *ſemidiameter* of the earth in two meaſures of the higheſt heaven, the one taken from the ſurface of the earth, the other from its centre: the diſproportion is juſt nothing. *More.*

The force of this inſtrument conſiſts in the diſproportion of diſtance betwixt the *ſemidiameter* of the cylinder and the *ſemidiameter* of the rundle with the ſpokes. *Wilkins.*

SEMIDIAPHANE'ITY. *n. s.* [*ſemi* and *diaphaneity.*] Half tranſparency; imperfect tranſparency.

The tranſparency or *ſemidiaphaneity* of the ſuperficial corpuſcles of bigger bodies may have an intereſt in the production of their colours. *Boyle on Colours.*

SEMIDIA'PHANOUS. *adj.* [*ſemi* and *diaphanous.*] Half tranſparent; imperfectly tranſparent.

Another plate, finely variegated with a *ſemidiaphanous* grey or ſky, yellow and brown. *Woodward on Foſſils.*

SE'MIDOUBLE. *n. s.* [*ſemi* and *double.*] In the Romiſh breviary, ſuch offices and feaſts as are celebrated with leſs ſolemnity than the double ones, but yet with more than the ſingle ones. *Bailey.*

SEMIFLO'SCULOUS. *adj.* [*ſemi* and *floſculus,* Latin.] Having a ſemifloret. *Bailey.*

SE'MIFLORET. *n. s.* [*ſemi* and *floret.*] Among floriſts, an half flouriſh, which is tubulous at the beginning like a floret, and afterwards expanded in the form of a tongue. *Bailey.*

SEMIFLU'ID. *adj.* [*ſemi* and *fluid.*] Imperfectly fluid.

Phlegm, or petuite, is a ſort of *ſemifluid,* it being ſo far ſolid that one part draws along ſeveral other parts adhering to it, which doth not happen in a perfect fluid, and yet no part will draw the whole maſs, as happens in a perfect ſolid. *Arb.*

SEMILU'NAR. } *adj.* [*ſemilunaire,* Fr. *ſemi* and *luna,* Latin.]
SEMILU'NARY. } Reſembling in form a half moon.

The eyes are guarded with a *ſemilunar* ridge. *Grew.*

SE'MIMETAL. *n. s.* [*ſemi* and *metal.*] Half metal; imperfect metal.

Semimetals are metallick foſſils, heavy, opake, of a bright glittering ſurface, and not malleable under the hammer; ſuch as quickſilver, antimony, cobalt, with the arſenicks, biſmuth, zink, with its ore calamine: to theſe may be added the ſemimetallick recrements, ſuch as tutty and pampholyx. *Hill.*

SEMINA'LITY. *n. s.* [from *ſemen,* Latin.]

1. The nature of ſeed.

As though there were a *ſeminality* in urine, or that, like the ſeed, it carried with it the idea of every part, they fooliſhly conceive we viſibly behold therein the anatomy of every particle. *Brown's Vulgar Errours.*

2. The power of being produced.

In the ſeeds of wheat there lieth obſcurely the *ſeminality* of darnel. *Brown's Vulgar Errours.*

SE'MINAL. *adj.* [*ſeminal,* French; *ſeminis,* Latin.]

1. Belonging to ſeed.

2. Contained in the ſeed; radical.

Had our ſenſes never preſented us with thoſe obvious *ſeminal* principles of apparent generations, we ſhould never have ſuſpected that a plant or animal would have proceeded from ſuch unlikely materials. *Glanv. Sceps.*

Though we cannot prolong the period of a commonwealth beyond the decree of heaven, or the date of its nature, any more than human life beyond the ſtrength of the *ſeminal* virtue, yet we may manage a ſickly conſtitution, and preſerve a ſtrong one. *Swift.*

SE'MINARY. *n. s.* [*ſeminaire,* Fr. *ſeminarium* from *ſemino,* Lat.]

1. The ground where any thing is ſown to be afterwards tranſplanted.

Some, at the firſt tranſplanting trees out of their *ſeminaries,* cut them off about an inch from the ground, and plant them like quickſet. *Mortimer's Husbandry.*

2. The place or original ſtock whence any thing is brought.

This ſtratum is ſtill expanded at top of all, ſerving for a common integument, and being the *ſeminary* or promptuary that furniſheth forth matter for the formation and increment of animal and vegetable bodies. *Woodward.*

3. Seminal ſtate.

The hand of God, who firſt created the earth, hath wiſely contrived them in their proper *ſeminaries,* and where they beſt maintain the intention of their ſpecies. *Brown's Vulgar Errours.*

4. Original; firſt principles.

Nothing ſubminiſtrates apter matter to be converted into peſtilent *ſeminaries,* ſooner than ſteams of naſty folks and beggars. *Harvey on the Plague.*

5. Breeding place; place of education, from whence ſcholars are tranſplanted into life.

It was the ſeat of the greateſt monarchy, and the *ſeminary* of the greateſt men of the world, whilſt it was heathen. *Bacon.*

The inns of court muſt be the worſt inſtituted *ſeminaries* in any Chriſtian country. *Swift.*

SEMINA'TION. *n. s.* [from *ſemino,* Latin.] The act of ſowing.

SEMINI'FICAL. } *adj.* [*ſemen* and *facio,* Latin.] Productive of
SEMINI'FICK. } ſeed.

We are made to believe, that in the fourteenth year males are *ſeminifical* and pubeſcent; but he that ſhall inquire into the generality, will rather adhere unto Ariſtotle. *Brown.*

SEMINIFICA'TION. *n. s.*

Seminification is the propagation from the ſeed or ſeminal parts. *Hale's Origin of Mankind.*

SEMIOPA'COUS. *adj.* [*ſemi* and *opacus,* Latin.] Half dark.

Semiopacous bodies are ſuch as, looked upon in an ordinary light, and not held betwixt it and the eye, are not wont to be diſcriminated from the reſt of opacous bodies. *Boyle.*

SEMIPE'DAL. *adj.* [*ſemi* and *pedis,* Latin.] Containing half a foot.

SEMIPERSPI'CUOUS. *adj.* [*ſemi* and *perſpicuus,* Latin.] Half tranſparent; imperfectly clear.

A kind of amethyſtine flint, not compoſed of cryſtals or grains; but one intire maſſy ſtone, *ſemiperſpicuous,* and of a pale blue, almoſt of the colour of ſome cow's horns. *Grew.*

SEMIO'RDINATE. *n. s.* [In conick ſections.] A line drawn at right angles to and biſſected by the axis, and reaching from one ſide of the ſection to another; the half of which is properly the *ſemiordinate,* but is now called the ordinate. *Harris.*

SEMIPELLU'CID. *adj.* [*ſemi* and *pellucidus,* Latin.] Half clear; imperfectly tranſparent.

A light grey *ſemipellucid* flint, of much the ſame complexion with the common Indian agat. *Woodward.*

SE'MIPROOF. *n. s.* [*ſemi* and *proof.*] The proof of a ſingle evidence. *Bailey.*

SEMIQUA'DRATE. } *n. s.* [In aſtronomy.] An aſpect of the
SEMIQUA'RTILE. } planets when diſtant from each other forty five degrees, or one ſign and a half. *Bailey.*

SEMIQUA'VER. *n. s.* [In muſick.] A note containing half the quantity of the quaver. *Bailey.*

SEMIQUI'NTILE. *n. s.* [In aſtronomy.] An aſpect of the planets when at the diſtance of thirty-ſix degrees from one another. *Bailey.*

SEMISE'XTILE. *n. s.* [In aſtronomy.] A ſemiſixth; an aſpect of the planets when they are diſtant from each other one twelfth part of a circle, or thirty degrees. *Bailey.*

SEMISPHE'RICAL. *adj.* [*ſemi* and *ſpherical.*] Belonging to half a ſphere. *Bailey.*

SEMISPHERO'IDAL. *adj.* [*ſemi* and *ſpheroidal.*] Formed like a half ſpheroid.

SEMITE'RTIAN. *n. s.* [*ſemi* and *tertian.*] An ague compounded of a tertian and a quotidian. *Bailey.*

The natural product of ſuch a cold moiſt year are tertians, *ſemitertians,* and ſome quartans. *Arbuthnot on Air.*

SEMITO'NE. *n. s.* [*ſemiton,* French.] In muſick, one of the degrees of concinuous intervals of concords. *Bailey.*

SEMIVO'WEL. *n. s.* [*ſemi* and *vowel.*] A conſonant which makes an imperfect ſound, or does not demand a total occluſion of the mouth.

When Homer would repreſent any agreeable object, he makes uſe of the ſmootheſt vowels and moſt flowing *ſemivowels.* *Broome's Notes to the Odyſſey.*

SE'MPERVIVE. *n. s.* [*ſemper* and *vivus,* Latin, that is, always alive.] A plant.

The greater *ſempervive* will put out branches two or three years; but they wrap the root in an oil cloth once in half a year. *Bacon.*

SEMPITE'RNAL. *adj.* [*ſempiternel,* Fr. *ſempiternus,* from *ſemper* and *æternus,* Latin.]

1. Eternal in futurity; having beginning, but no end.

Thoſe, though they ſuppoſe the world not to be eternal, *a parte ante,* are not contented to ſuppoſe it to be *ſempiternal,* or eternal *a parte poſt;* but will carry up the creation of the world to an immenſe antiquity. *Hale.*

2. In poetry it is uſed ſimply for eternal.

Should we the long depending ſcale aſcend
Of ſons and fathers, will it never end?
If 'twill, then muſt we through the order run,
To ſome one man whoſe being ne'er begun;
If that one man was *ſempiternal,* why
Did he, ſince independant, ever die? *Blackmore.*

SEMPITE'RNITY. *n. s.* [*ſempiternitas,* Latin.] Future duration without end.

The future eternity, or *ſempiternity* of the world, being admitted, though the eternity *a parte ante* be denied, there will be a future infinity for the emanation of the divine goodneſs. *Hale.*

SE'MSTRESS. *n. s.* [ſeameſtre, Saxon.] A woman whoſe buſineſs is to ſew; a woman who lives by her needle.

Two hundred *ſemſtreſſes* were employed to make me ſhirts, and linnen for bed and table, which they were forced to quilt together in ſeveral folds. *Gulliver's Travels.*

The tuck'd up *ſemſtreſs* walks with haſty ſtrides. *Swift.*

SE'NARY. *adj.* [*ſenarius, ſeni,* Latin.] Belonging to the number ſix; containing ſix.

SENATE.

SE'NATE. *n. ſ.* [*ſenatus*, Latin; *ſenat*, French.] An aſſembly of counſellors; a body of men ſet apart to conſult for the publick good.

We debaſe
The nature of our ſeats, which will in time break ope
The locks o' th' *ſenate*, and bring in the crows
To peck the eagles. *Shak. Coriolanus.*

There they ſhall found
Their government, and their great *ſenate* chuſe. *Milton.*

He had not us'd excurſions, ſpears, or darts,
But counſel, order, and ſuch aged arts;
Which, if our anceſtors had not retain'd,
The *ſenate*'s name our council had not gain'd. *Denham.*

Gallus was welcom'd to the ſacred ſtrand,
The *ſenate* riſing to ſalute their gueſt. *Dryden.*

SE'NATEHOUSE. *n. ſ.* [*ſenate* and *houſe*.] Place of publick council.

The nobles in great earneſtneſs are going
All to the *ſenatehouſe*; ſome news is come. *Shakeſpeare.*

SE'NATOR. *n. ſ.* [*ſenator*, Latin; *ſenateur*, French.] A publick counſellor.

Moſt unwiſe patricians,
You grave but reckleſs *ſenators*. *Shakeſp. Coriolanus.*

As if to ev'ry fop it might belong,
Like *ſenators*, to cenſure, right or wrong. *Granville.*

SENATO'RIAL. } *adj.* [*ſenatorius*, Lat. *ſenatorial*, *ſenatorien*, Fr.]
SENATO'RIAN. } Belonging to ſenators; befitting ſenators.

To SEND. *v. a.* [*ſandgan*, Gothick; ꞅenꝺan, Saxon; *ſenden*, Dutch.]

1. To diſpatch from one place to another.

There ſhalt thou ſerve thine enemies, which the Lord ſhall *ſend* againſt thee, in hunger and in thirſt. *Deutr.* xxviii. 48.

Send our brother with us, and we will go down. *Gen.* xliii.

His citizens *ſent* a meſſage after him, ſaying, we will not have this man to reign over us. *Lu.* xix. 14.

The meſſenger came, and ſhewed David all that Joab had *ſent* him for. 2 *Sa.* xi. 22.

My overſhadowing ſpirit and might with thee
I *ſend* along. *Milton.*

His wounded men he firſt *ſends* off to ſhore. *Dryden.*

Servants, *ſent* on meſſages, ſtay out ſomewhat longer than the meſſage requires. *Swift.*

2. To commiſſion by authority to go and act.

There have been commiſſions
Sent down among them, which have flow'd the heart
Of all their loyalties. *Shakeſ. Henry* VIII.

3. To grant as from a diſtant place: as, if God *ſend* life.

I pray thee *ſend* me good ſpeed this day, and ſhew kindneſs unto my maſter. *Gen.* xxiv. 12.

O *ſend* out thy light and thy truth; let them lead me. *Pſ.*

4. To inflict, as from a diſtance.

The Lord ſhall *ſend* upon thee curſing, vexation, and rebuke, in all that thou ſetteſt thine hand unto. *Deutr.* xxviii.

5. To emit; to immit; to produce.

The water *ſends* forth plants that have no roots fixed in the bottom, being almoſt but leaves. *Bacon's Nat. Hiſtory.*

The ſenſes *ſend* in only the influxes of material things, and the imagination and memory preſent only their pictures or images, when the objects themſelves are abſent. *Cheyne.*

6. To diffuſe; to propagate.

When the fury took her ſtand on high,
A hiſs from all the ſnaky tire went round:
The dreadful ſignal all the rocks rebound,
And through the Achaian cities *ſend* the ſound. *Pope.*

7. To let fly; to caſt or ſhoot.

To SEND. *v. n.*

1. To deliver or diſpatch a meſſage.

I have made bold to *ſend* in to your wife:
My ſuit is that ſhe will to Deſdemona
Procure me ſome acceſs. *Shakeſp. Othello.*

They could not attempt their perfect reformation in church and ſtate, 'till thoſe votes were utterly aboliſhed; therefore they *ſent* the ſame day again to the king. *Clarendon.*

2. *To* SEND *for*. To require by meſſage to come, or cauſe to be brought.

Go with me ſome few of you, and ſee the place; and then you may *ſend for* your ſick, which bring on land. *Bacon.*

He *ſent for* me; and, while I rais'd his head,
He threw his aged arms about my neck,
And, ſeeing that I wept, he preſs'd me cloſe. *Dryden.*

SE'NDER. *n. ſ.* [from *ſend*.] He that ſends.

This was a merry meſſage.
—We hope to make the *ſender* bluſh at it. *Shak. H.* V.

Love that comes too late,
Like a remorſeful pardon ſlowly carried,
To the great *ſender* turns a ſour offence. *Shakeſpeare.*

Beſt with the beſt, the *ſender*, not the ſent. *Milton.*

SENE'SCENCE. *n. ſ.* [*ſeneſco*, Latin.] The ſtate of growing old; decay by time.

The earth and all things will continue in the ſtate wherein they now are, without the leaſt *ſeneſcence* or decay, without jarring, diſorder, or invaſion of one another. *Woodward.*

SE'NESCHAL. *n. ſ.* [*ſeneſchal*, French, of uncertain original.]

1. One who had in great houſes the care of feaſts, or domeſtick ceremonies.

John earl of Huntingdon, under his ſeal of arms, made ſir John Arundel, of Trerice, *ſeneſchal* of his houſhold, as well in peace as in war. *Carew's Survey of Cornwal.*

Marſhal'd feaſt,
Serv'd up in hall with ſewers and *ſeneſchals*;
The ſkill of artifice, or office, mean! *Milton's Par. Loſt.*

The *ſeneſchal* rebuk'd, in haſte withdrew;
With equal haſte a menial train purſue. *Pope's Odyſſey.*

2. It afterwards came to ſignify other offices.

SE'NGREEN. *n. ſ.* A plant. *Ainſworth.*

SE'NILE. *adj.* [*ſenilis*, Latin.] Belonging to old age; conſequent on old age.

My green youth made me very unripe for a taſk of that nature, whoſe difficulty requires that it ſhould be handled by a perſon in whom nature, education, and time have happily matched a *ſenile* maturity of judgment with youthful vigour of fancy. *Boyle on Colours.*

SE'NIOR. *n. ſ.* [*ſenior*, Latin.]

1. One older than another; one who on account of longer time has ſome ſuperiority.

How can you admit your *ſeniors* to the examination or allowing of them, not only being inferior in office and calling, but in gifts alſo? *Whitgifte.*

2. An aged perſon.

A *ſenior* of the place replies,
Well read, and curious of antiquities. *Dryden.*

SENIO'RITY. *n. ſ.* [from *ſenior*.] Elderſhip; priority of birth.

As in all civil inſurrections the ringleader is looked on with a peculiar ſeverity, ſo, in this caſe, the firſt provoker has, by his *ſeniority* and primogeniture, a double portion of the guilt. *Government of the Tongue.*

He was the elder brother, and Ulyſſes might be conſigned to his care, by the right due to his *ſeniority*. *Broome.*

SE'NNA. *n. ſ.* [*ſena*, Latin.] A phyſical tree.

The flower, for the moſt part, conſiſts of five leaves, which are placed orbicularly, and expand in form of a roſe: the pointal afterwards becomes a plain, incurved, bivalve pod, which is full of ſeeds, each being ſeparated by a double thin membrane. The ſpecies are three. The third ſort, that uſed in medicine, is at preſent very rare. *Miller.*

What rhubarb, *ſenna*, or what purgative drug,
Would ſcour theſe Engliſh hence! *Shak. Macbeth.*

Senna tree is of two ſorts: the baſtard *ſenna*, and the ſcorpion *ſenna*, both which yield a pleaſant leaf and flower. *Mort.*

SE'NNIGHT. *n. ſ.* [Contracted from *ſevennight*.] The ſpace of ſeven nights and days; a week. See FORTNIGHT.

Time trots hard with a young maid between the contract of her marriage and the day it is ſolemnized: if the interim be but a *ſennight*, time's pace is ſo hard that it ſeems the length of ſeven years. *Shakeſp. As you like it.*

SENO'CULAR. *adj.* [*ſeni* and *oculus*, Latin.] Having ſix eyes.

Moſt animals are binocular, ſpiders octonocular, and ſome *ſenocular*. *Derham's Phyſico-Theology.*

SENSA'TION. *n. ſ.* [*ſenſation*, French; *ſenſatio*, ſchool Latin.] Perception by means of the ſenſes.

Diverſity of conſtitution, or other circumſtances, vary the *ſenſations*; and to them of Java pepper is cold. *Glanv. Scepſ.*

The brain, diſtempered by a cold, beating againſt the root of the auditory nerve, and protracted to the tympanum, cauſes the *ſenſation* of noiſe. *Harvey on Conſumptions.*

This great ſource of moſt of the ideas we have, depending wholly upon our ſenſes, and derived by them to the underſtanding, I call *ſenſation*. *Locke.*

When we are aſleep, joy and ſorrow give us more vigorous *ſenſations* of pain or pleaſure than at any other time. *Addiſon.*

The happieſt, upon a fair eſtimate, have ſtronger *ſenſations* of pain than pleaſure. *Rogers.*

SENSE. *n. ſ.* [*ſens*, French; *ſenſus*, Latin.]

1. Faculty or power by which external objects are perceived; the ſight; touch; hearing; ſmell; taſte.

This pow'r is *ſenſe*, which from abroad doth bring
The colour, taſte, and touch, and ſcent, and ſound,
The quantity and ſhape of ev'ry thing
Within earth's centre, or heav'n's circle found:
And though things ſenſible be numberleſs,
But only five the *ſenſe*'s organs be;
And in thoſe five, all things their forms expreſs,
Which we can touch, taſte, feel, or hear or ſee. *Davies.*

Then is the ſoul a nature, which contains
The pow'r of *ſenſe* within a greater pow'r,
Which doth employ and uſe the *ſenſe*'s pains;
But ſits and rules within her private bow'r. *Davies.*

Both contain
Within them ev'ry lower faculty
Of *ſenſe*, whereby they hear, ſee, ſmell, touch, taſte. *Milt.*

Of the five *ſenſes*, two are uſually and moſt properly called the *ſenſes* of learning, as being moſt capable of receiving communication of thought and notions by ſelected ſigns; and theſe are hearing and ſeeing. *Holder's Elements of Speech.*

There's

2. Perception by the senses; sensation.

In a living creature, though never so great, the *sense* and the affects of any one part of the body instantly make a transcursion throughout the whole. *Bacon's Natural History.*

If we had nought but *sense*, then only they
Should have found minds which have their senses sound;
But wisdom grows when senses do decay,
And folly most in quickest *sense* is found. *Davies.*

Such is the mighty swiftness of your mind,
That, like the earth's, it leaves the *sense* behind. *Dryden.*

3. Perception of intellect; apprehension of mind.

This Basilius, having the quick *sense* of a lover, took as though his mistress had given him a secret reprehension. *Sidn.*

God, to remove his ways from human *sense*,
Plac'd heav'n from earth so far. *Milton.*

Why hast thou added *sense* of endless woes? *Milton.*

4. Sensibility; quickness or keenness of perception.

He should have liv'd,
Save that his riotous youth, with dangerous *sense*,
Might in the times to come have ta'en revenge. *Shakesp.*

5. Understanding; soundness of faculties; strength of natural reason.

Opprest nature sleeps:
This rest might yet have balm'd thy broken *senses*. *Shakes.*

God hath endued mankind with powers and abilities, which we call natural light and reason, and common *sense*. *Bentley.*

There's something previous ev'n to taste; 'tis *sense*,
Good *sense*, which only is the gift of heav'n,
And, though no science, fairly worth the sev'n:
A light within yourself you must perceive;
Jones and Le Nôtre have it not to give. *Pope.*

6. Reason; reasonable meaning.

He raves; his words are loose
As heaps of sand, and scattering wide from *sense*:
You see he knows not me, his natural father;
That now the wind is got into his head,
And turns his brains to frenzy. *Dryd. Spanish Fryar.*

7. Opinion; notion; judgment.

I speak my private but impartial *sense*
With freedom, and, I hope, without offence. *Roscommon.*

8. Consciousness; conviction.

In the due *sense* of my want of learning, I only make a confession of my own faith. *Dryden.*

9. Moral perception.

Some are so hardened in wickedness, as to have no *sense* of the most friendly offices. *L'Estrange.*

10. Meaning; import.

In this *sense* to be preserved from all sin is not impossible. *Hooker, b.* v.

My hearty friends,
You take me in too dolorous a *sense*. *Shakespeare.*

This comes out of a haughty presumption, that because we are encouraged to believe that in some *sense* all things are made for man, that therefore they are not made at all for themselves. *More's Antidote against Atheism.*

All before Richard I. is before time of memory; and what is since, is, in a legal *sense*, within the time of memory. *Hale.*

In one *sense* it is, indeed, a building of gold and silver upon the foundation of Christianity. *Tillotson.*

When a word has been used in two or three *senses*, and has made a great inroad for error, drop one or two of those *senses*, and leave it only one remaining, and affix the other *senses* or ideas to other words. *Watts's Logick.*

SE'NSED. *part.* [from *sense.*] Perceived by the senses. A word not in use.

Let the sciolist tell me, why things must needs be so as his individual senses represent them: is he sure that objects are not otherwise *sensed* by others, than they are by him? And why must his sense be the infallible criterion? It may be, what is white to us, is black to negroes. *Glanv. Sceps.*

SE'NSEFUL. *adj.* [from *sense* and *full.*] Reasonable; judicious.

Men, otherwise *senseful* and ingenious, quote such things out of an author as would never pass in conversation. *Norris.*

SE'NSELESS. *adj.* [from *sense.*]

1. Wanting sense; wanting life; void of all life or perception.

The charm and venom, which they drunk,
Their blood with secret filth infected hath,
Being diffused through the *senseless* trunk,
That through the great contagion direful deadly stunk. *F. Q.*

The ears are *senseless* that should give us hearing,
To tell him his commandment is fulfill'd. *Shak. Hamlet.*

You blocks, you worse than *senseless* things! *Shakesp.*

It is as repugnant to the idea of *senseless* matter, that it should put into itself sense, perception, and knowledge, as it is repugnant to the idea of a triangle, that it should put into itself greater angles than two right ones. *Locke.*

2. Unfeeling; wanting perception.

The *senseless* grave feels not your pious sorrows. *Rowe.*

3. Unreasonable; stupid; doltish; blockish.

They would repent this their *senseless* perverseness when it would be too late, and when they found themselves under a power that would destroy them. *Clarendon.*

If we be not extremely foolish, thankless, or *senseless*, a great joy is more apt to cure sorrow than a great trouble is. *Taylor.*

The great design of this authour's book is to prove this, which I believe no man in the world was ever so *senseless* as to deny. *Tillotson.*

She saw her favour was misplac'd;
The fellows had a wretched taste:
She needs must tell them to their face,
They were a *senseless* stupid race. *Swift.*

4. Contrary to true judgment; contrary to reason.

It is a *senseless* thing, in reason, to think that one of these interests can stand without the other, when, in the very order of natural causes, government is preserved by religion. *South.*

Other creatures, as well as monkeys, little wiser than they, destroy their young by *senseless* fondness, and too much embracing. *Locke.*

5. Wanting sensibility; wanting quickness or keenness of perception.

To draw Mars like a young Hippolytus, with an effeminate countenance, or that hot-spurred Harpalice in Virgil, proceedeth from a *senseless* and overcold judgment. *Peacham.*

6. Wanting knowledge; unconscious. With *of.*

The wretch is drench'd too deep;
His soul is stupid, and his heart asleep,
Fatten'd in vice; so callous and so gross,
He sins and sees not, *senseless of* his loss. *Dryden.*

Hear this,
You unhous'd, lawless, rambling libertines,
Senseless of any charm in love, beyond
The prostitution of a common bed. *Southerne.*

SE'NSELESSLY. *adv.* [from *senseless.*] In a senseless manner; stupidly; unreasonably.

If any one should be found so *senselessly* arrogant as to suppose man alone knowing and wise, but yet the product of mere ignorance and chance, and that all the rest of the universe acted only by that blind hap-hazard, I shall leave with him that very rational and emphatical rebuke of Tully. *Locke.*

SE'NSELESSNESS. *n. s.* [from *senseless.*] Folly; unreasonableness; absurdity; stupidity.

The *senselessness* of the tradition of the crocodile's moving his upper jaw, is plain from the articulation of the occiput with the neck, and the nether jaw with the upper. *Grew.*

SENSIBI'LITY. *n. s.* [*sensibilité*, French.]

1. Quickness of sensation.

Modesty is a kind of quick and delicate feeling in the soul: it is such an exquisite *sensibility*, as warns a woman to shun the first appearance of every thing hurtful. *Addison's Spectator.*

2. Quickness of perception.

SE'NSIBLE. *adj.* [*sensible*, French; *sensilis*, Latin.]

1. Having the power of perceiving by the senses.

Would your cambrick were as *sensible* as your finger, that you might leave pricking it for pity. *Shakespeare.*

These be those discourses of God, whose effects those that live witness in themselves; the *sensible* in their *sensible* natures, the reasonable in their reasonable souls. *Raleigh.*

A blind man conceives not colours, but under the notion of some other *sensible* faculty. *Glanv. Sceps.*

2. Perceptible by the senses.

By reason man attaineth unto the knowledge of things that are and are not *sensible*: it resteth, therefore, that we search how man attaineth unto the knowledge of such things unsensible as are to be known. *Hooker.*

Is this a dagger which I see before me,
The handle tow'rd my hand? Come, let me clutch thee:
I have thee not, and yet I see thee still:
Art thou not, fatal vision, *sensible*
To feeling as to sight? *Shakesp. Macbeth.*

The space left and acquired in every *sensible* moment in such slow progressions, is so inconsiderable, that it cannot possibly move the sense. *Glanv. Sceps.*

It is manifest that the heavens are void of all *sensible* resistance, and by consequence of all *sensible* matter. *Newton.*

The far greater part of men are no otherwise moved than by sense, and have neither leisure nor ability so far to improve their power of reflection, as to be capable of conceiving the divine perfections, without the assistance of *sensible* objects. *Rogers's Sermons.*

Air is *sensible* to the touch by its motion, and by its resistance to bodies moved in it. *Arbuthnot on Air.*

3. Perceived by the mind.

Idleness was punished by so many stripes in publick, and the disgrace was more *sensible* than the pain. *Temple.*

4. Perceiving by either mind or senses; having perception by the mind or senses.

This must needs remove
The *sensible* of pain. *Milton.*

I saw you in the East at your first arising: I was as soon *sensible* as any of that light, when just shooting out, and beginning to travel upwards to the meridian. *Dryden.*

I do not say there is no soul in man, because he is not *sensible* of it in his sleep; but I do say, he cannot think at any time, waking or sleeping, without being *sensible* of it. *Locke.*

The versification is as beautiful as the description complete; every ear must be *sensible* of it. *Broome's Notes on the Odyss.*

5. Having moral perception; having the quality of being affected by moral good or ill.

If thou wert *sensible* of courtesy,
I should not make so great a shew of zeal. *Shakespeare.*

6. Having quick intellectual feeling; being easily or strongly affected.

Even I, the bold, the *sensible* of wrong,
Restrain'd by shame, was forc'd to hold my tongue. *Dryd.*

7. Convinced; persuaded. A low use.

They are very *sensible* that they had better have pushed their conquests on the other side of the Adriatick; for then their territories would have lain together. *Addison.*

8. In low conversation it has sometimes the sense of reasonable; judicious; wise.

I have been tired with accounts from *sensible* men, furnished with matters of fact, which have happened within their own knowledge. *Addison.*

SE'NSIBLENESS. *n. s.* [from *sensible.*]

1. Possibility to be perceived by the senses.
2. Actual perception by mind or body.
3. Quickness of perception; sensibility.

The *sensibleness* of the eye renders it subject to pain, as also unfit to be dressed with sharp medicaments. *Sharp.*

4. Painful consciousness.

There is no condition of soul more wretched than that of the senseless obdurate sinner, being a kind of numbness of soul; and, contrariwise, this feeling and *sensibleness*, and sorrow for sin, the most vital quality. *Hammond.*

5. Judgment; reasonableness. An use not admitted but in conversation.

SE'NSIBLY. *adv.* [from *sensible.*]

1. Perceptibly to the senses.

He is your brother, lords; *sensibly* fed
Of that self-blood, that first gave life to you. *Shakespeare.*

A sudden pain in my right foot increased *sensibly.* *Temple.*

The salts of human urine may, by the violent motion of the blood, be turned alkaline, and even corrosive; and so they affect the fibres of the brain more *sensibly* than other parts. *Arb.*

2. With perception of either mind or body.
3. Externally; by impression on the senses.

That church of Christ, which we properly term his body mystical, can be but one; neither can that one be *sensibly* discerned by any, inasmuch as the parts thereof are some in heaven already with Christ. *Hooker.*

4. With quick intellectual perception.
5. In low language, judiciously; reasonably.

SE'NSITIVE. *adj.* [*sensitif*, French.] Having sense or perception, but not reason.

The *sensitive* faculty may have a *sensitive* love of some *sensitive* objects, which though moderated so as not to fall into sin; yet, through the nature of man's sense, may express itself more sensitively towards that inferior object than towards God: this is a piece of human frailty. *Hammond.*

All the actions of the *sensitive* appetite are in painting called passions, because the soul is agitated by them, and because the body suffers and is sensibly altered. *Dryden.*

Bodies are such as are endued with a vegetative soul, as plants; a *sensitive* soul, as animals; or a rational soul, as the body of man. *Ray.*

SE'NSITIVE *Plant. n. s.* [*mimosa*, Latin.] A plant.

The flower consists of one leaf, which is shaped like a funnel, having many stamina in the centre: these flowers are collected into a round head: from the bottom of the flower rises the pistillum, which afterwards becomes an oblong flat-jointed pod, which opens both ways, and contains in each partition one roundish seed. Of this plant the humble plants are a species, which are so called, because, upon being touched, the pedicle of their leaves falls downward; but the leaves of the *sensitive plant* are only contracted. *Miller.*

Vegetables have many of them some degrees of motion, and, upon the different application of other bodies to them, do very briskly alter their figure and motion, and so have obtained the name of *sensitive plants*, from a motion which has some resemblance to that which in animals follows upon sensation. *Locke.*

Whence does it happen, that the plant which well
We name the *sensitive*, should move and feel?
Whence know her leaves to answer her command,
And with quick horrour fly the neighb'ring hand? *Prior.*

The *sensitive plant* is so call'd, because, as soon as you touch it, the leaf shrinks. *Mortimer.*

SE'NSITIVELY. *adv.* [from *sensitive.*] In a sensitive manner.

The sensitive faculty, through the nature of man's sense, may express itself more *sensitively* towards an inferior object than towards God: this is a piece of frailty. *Hammond.*

SENSO'RIUM. }
SE'NSORY. } *n. s.* [Latin.]

1. The part where the senses transmit their perceptions to the mind; the seat of sense.

Spiritual species, both visible and audible, will work upon the *sensories*, though they move not any other body. *Bacon.*

As sound in a bell or musical string, or other sounding body, is nothing but a trembling motion, and the air nothing but that motion propagated from the object, in the *sensorium* 'tis a sense of that motion under the form of sound. *Newton.*

Is not the *sensory* of animals the place to which the sensitive substance is present, and into which the sensible species of things are carried through the nerves of the brain, that there they may be perceived by their immediate presence to that substance? *Newton's Opt.*

2. Organ of sensation.

That we all have double *sensories*, two eyes, two ears, is an effectual confutation of this atheistical sophism. *Bentley.*

SE'NSUAL. *adj.* [*sensuel*, French.]

1. Consisting in sense; depending on sense; affecting the senses.

Men in general are too partial, in favour of a *sensual* appetite, to take notice of truth when they have found it. *L'Estr.*

Far as creation's ample range extends,
The scale of *sensual*, mental pow'rs ascends. *Pope.*

2. Pleasing to the senses; carnal; not spiritual.

The greatest part of men are such as prefer their own private good before all things, even that good which is *sensual* before whatsoever is most divine. *Hooker.*

3. Devoted to sense; lewd; luxurious.

From amidst them rose
Belial, the dissolutest spirit that fell,
The *sensuallest*; and, after Asmodai,
The fleshliest incubus. *Paradise Regain'd.*

No small part of virtue consists in abstaining from that wherein *sensual* men place their felicity. *Atterbury.*

SE'NSUALIST. *n. s.* [from *sensual.*] A carnal person; one devoted to corporal pleasures.

Let atheists and *sensualists* satisfy themselves as they are able; the former of which will find, that, as long as reason keeps her ground, religion neither can nor will lose her's. *South.*

SENSUA'LITY. *n. s.* [from *sensual.*] Devotedness to the senses; addiction to brutal and corporal pleasures.

But you are more intemperate in your blood
Than Venus, or those pamper'd animals
That rage in savage *sensuality.* *Shakespeare.*

Kill not her quick'ning pow'r with surfeitings;
Mar not her sense with *sensuality*:
Cast not her serious wit on idle things;
Make not her free will slave to vanity. *Davies.*

Sensuality is one kind of pleasure, such an one as it is. *South.*

They avoid dress, lest they should have affections tainted by any *sensuality*, and diverted from the love of him who is to be the only comfort and delight of their whole beings. *Addis.*

Impure and brutal *sensuality* was too much confirmed by the religion of those countries, where even Venus and Bacchus had their temples. *Bentley.*

To SE'NSUALIZE. *v. a.* [from *sensual.*] To sink to sensual pleasures; to degrade the mind into subjection to the senses.

Not to suffer one's self to be *sensualized* by pleasures, like those who were changed into brutes by Circe. *Pope.*

SE'NSUALLY. *adv.* [from *sensual.*] In a sensual manner.

SE'NSUOUS. *adj.* [from *sense.*] Tender; pathetick; full of passion.

To this poetry would be made precedent, as being less subtile and fine; but more simple, *sensuous*, and passionate. *Milt.*

SENT. The participle passive of *send.*

I make a decree that all Israel go with thee; forasmuch as thou art *sent* of the king. *Ezr.* vii. 14.

SE'NTENCE. *n. s.* [*sentence*, French; *sententia*, Latin.]

1. Determination or decision, as of a judge civil or criminal.

The rule of voluntary agents on earth is the *sentence* that reason giveth, concerning the goodness of those things which they are to do. *Hooker.*

If we have neither voice from heaven, that so pronounceth of them, neither *sentence* of men grounded upon such manifest and clear proof, that they, in whose hands it is to alter them, may likewise infallibly, even in heart and conscience, judge them so; upon necessity to urge alteration, is to trouble and disturb without necessity. *Hooker.*

How will I give *sentence* against them. *Jer.* iv. 12.

If matter of fact breaks out with too great an evidence to be denied, why, still there are other lenitives, that friendship will apply, before it will be brought to the decretory rigours of a condemning *sentence.* *South's Sermons.*

Let him set out some of Luther's works, that by them we may pass *sentence* upon his doctrines. *Atterbury.*

2. It is usually spoken of condemnation pronounced by the judge; doom.

By the consent of all laws, in capital causes, the evidence must be full and clear; and if so, where one man's life is in question, what say we to a war, which is ever the *sentence* of death upon many? *Bacon's holy War.*

What rests but that the mortal *sentence* pass? *Milton.*

3. A maxim; an axiom, generally moral.

A *sentence* may be defined a moral instruction couched in a few words. *Broome's Notes on the Odyssey.*

4. A short paragraph; a period in writing.
An excellent spirit, knowledge, understanding, and shewing of hard *sentences* were found in Daniel. *Dan.* v. 12.

To SE'NTENCE. *v. a.* [*sentencier*, Fr. from the noun.]
1. To pass the last judgment on any one.
After this cold consid'rance, *sentence* me;
And, as you are a king, speak in your state,
What I have done that misbecame my place. *Shakesp.*
Came the mild judge and intercessor both,
To *sentence* man. *Milton.*
2. To condemn.
Could that decree from our brother come?
Nature herself is *sentenc'd* in your doom:
Piety is no more. *Dryden.*
Idleness, *sentenced* by the decurions, was punished by so many stripes. *Temple.*

SENTENTIO'SITY. *n. s.* [from *sententious.*] Comprehension in a sentence.
Vulgar precepts in morality carry with them nothing above the line, or beyond the extemporary *sententiosity* of common conceits with us. *Brown's Vulg. Errours.*

SENTE'NTIOUS. *adj.* [*sentencieux*, Fr. from *sentence.*] Abounding with short sentences, axioms, and maxims, short and energetick.
He is very swift and *sententious.* *Shakesp. As you like it.*
Eyes are vocal, tears have tongues:
Sententious showers! O let them fall;
Their cadence is rhetorical. *Crashaw.*
Eloquence, with all her pomp and charms,
Foretold us useful and *sententious* truths. *Waller.*
How he apes his sire,
Ambitiously *sententious.* *Addison's Cato.*
The making of those figures being tedious, and requiring much room, put men first upon contracting them; as by the most ancient Egyptian monuments it appears they did: next, instead of *sententious* marks, to think of verbal, such as the Chinese still retain. *Grew's Cosmol.*

SENTE'NTIOUSLY. *adv.* [from *sententious.*] In short sentences; with striking brevity.
They describe her in part finely and elegantly, and in part gravely and *sententiously*: they say, look how many feathers she hath, so many eyes she hath underneath. *Bacon's Essays.*
Nausicaa delivers her judgment *sententiously*, to give it more weight. *Broome.*

SENTE'NTIOUSNESS. *n. s.* [from *sententious.*] Pithiness of sentences; brevity with strength.
The Medea I esteem for the gravity and *sententiousness* of it, which he himself concludes to be suitable to a tragedy. *Dryd.*

SE'NTERY. *n. s.* [This is commonly written *sentry*, corrupted from *sentinel.*] One who is set to watch in a garrison, or in the outlines of an army.
What strength, what art can then
Suffice, or what evasion bear him safe
Through the strict *senteries*, and stations thick
Of angels watching round. *Milton.*

SE'NTIENT. *adj.* [*sentiens*, Latin.] Perceiving; having perception.
This acting of the *sentient* phantasy is performed by a presence of sense, as the horse is under the sense of hunger, and that without any formal syllogism presseth him to eat. *Hale.*

SE'NTIENT. *n. s.* [from the adjective.] He that has perception.
If the *sentient* be carried, *passibus æquis*, with the body, whose motion it would observe, supposing it regular, the remove is insensible. *Glanv. Sceps.*

SE'NTIMENT. *n. s.* [*sentiment*, French.]
1. Thought; notion; opinion.
The consideration of the reason, why they are annexed to so many other ideas, serving to give us due *sentiments* of the wisdom and goodness of the sovereign Disposer of all things, may not be unsuitable to the main end of these enquiries. *Loc.*
Alike to council or th' assembly came,
With equal souls and *sentiments* the same. *Pope.*
2. The sense considered distinctly from the language or things; a striking sentence in a composition.

SE'NTINEL. *n. s.* [*sentinelle*, French, from *sentio*, Lat.] One who watches or keeps guard to prevent surprise.
Norfolk, hie thee to thy charge;
Use careful watch, chuse trusty *sentinels.* *Shakesp. R.* III.
Counsellors are not commonly so united, but that one counsellor keepeth *sentinel* over another; so that if any do counsel out of faction or private ends, it commonly comes to the king's ear. *Bacon's Essays.*
First, the two eyes, which have the seeing pow'r,
Stand as one watchman, spy, or *sentinel*,
Being plac'd aloft, within the head's high tow'r;
And though both see, yet both but one thing tell. *Davies.*
Love to our citadel resorts,
Through those deceitful sallyports;
Our *sentinels* betray our forts. *Denham.*
The senses are situate in the head, as *sentinels* in a watchtower, to receive and convey to the soul the impressions of external objects. *Ray on the Creation.*

Perhaps they had *sentinels* waking while they slept; but even this would be unsoldierlike. *Broome's Notes on the Odyssey.*

SE'NTRY. *n. s.* [Corrupted, I believe, from *sentinel.*]
1. A watch; a sentinel; one who watches in a garrison, or army, to keep them from surprise.
If I do send, dispatch
Those *sentries* to our aid; the rest will serve
For a short holding. *Shakesp. Coriolanus.*
The youth of hell strict guard may keep,
And set their *sentries* to the utmost deep. *Dryden.*
One goose they had, 'twas all they could allow,
A wakeful *sentry*, and on duty now. *Dryden.*
2. Guard; watch; the duty of a sentry.
Here toils and death, and death's half brother, sleep,
Forms terrible to view, their *sentry* keep. *Dryden.*
Thou, whose nature cannot sleep,
O'er my slumbers *sentry* keep;
Guard me 'gainst those watchful foes,
Whose eyes are open while mine close. *Brown.*

SEPARABI'LITY. *n. s.* [from *separable.*] The quality of admitting disunion or discerption.
Separability is the greatest argument of real distinction. *Glan.*
The greatest argument of real distinction is *separability*, and actual separation; for nothing can be separated from itself. *Norris.*

SE'PARABLE. *adj.* [*separable*, Fr. *separabilis*, Lat. from *separate.*]
1. Susceptive of disunion; discerptible.
2. Possible to be disjoined from something.
Expansion and duration have this farther agreement, that though they are both considered by us as having parts, yet their parts are not *separable* one from another. *Locke.*
The infusions and decoctions of plants contain the most *separable* parts of the plants, and convey not only their nutritious but medicinal qualities into the blood. *Arbuthnot.*

SE'PARABLENESS. *n. s.* [from *separable.*] Capableness of being separable.
Trials permit me not to doubt of the *separableness* of a yellow tincture from gold. *Boyle.*

To SE'PARATE. *v. a.* [*separo*, Latin; *separer*, French.]
1. To break; to divide into parts.
2. To disunite; to disjoin.
I'll to England.
——To Ireland, I: our *separated* fortunes
Shall keep us both the safer. *Shakesp. Macbeth.*
Resolv'd,
Rather than death, or aught than death more dread,
Shall *separate* us. *Milton.*
3. To sever from the rest.
Can a body be inflammable, from which it would puzzle a chymist to *separate* an inflammable ingredient? *Boyle.*
Death from sin no power can *separate.* *Milton.*
4. To set apart; to segregate.
Separate me Barnabas and Saul, for the work whereunto I have called them. *Acts* xiii. 2.
David *separated* to the service those who should prophesy. *1 Chron.* xxv. 1.
5. To withdraw.
Separate thyself from me: if thou wilt take the left, I will go to the right. *Gen.* xiii. 9.

To SE'PARATE. *v. n.* To part; to be disunited.
When there was not room enough for their herds to feed, they by consent *separated*, and enlarged their pasture. *Locke.*

SE'PARATE. *adj.* [from the verb.]
1. Divided from the rest.
Eve *separate* he wish'd. *Milton.*
'Twere hard to conceive an eternal watch, whose pieces were never *separate* one from another, nor ever in any other form. *Burnet's Theory of the Earth.*
In a secret vale the Trojan sees
A *sep'rate* grove. *Dryden.*
2. Disunited from the body; disengaged from corporeal nature.
Whatever ideas the mind can receive and contemplate without the help of the body, it can retain without the help of the body too; or else the soul, or any *separate* spirit, will have but little advantage by thinking. *Locke.*

SE'PARATELY. *adv.* [from *separate.*] Apart; singly; not in union; distinctly; particularly.
It is of singular use to princes, if they take the opinions of their council, both *separately* and together; for private opinion is more free, but opinion before others is more reserved. *Bac.*
If you admit of many figures, then conceive the whole together, and not every thing *separately* and in particular. *Dryden.*

SE'PARATENESS. *n. s.* [from *separate.*] The state of being separate.

SEPARA'TION. *n. s.* [*separatio*, Lat. *separation*, Fr. from *separate.*]
1. The act of separating; disjunction.
They have a dark opinion, that the soul doth live after the *separation* from the body. *Abbot.*
Any part of our bodies, vitally united to that which is conscious in us, makes a part of ourselves; but upon *separation* from the vital union, by which that consciousness is communicated,

nicated, that which a moment since was part of ourselves, is now no more so. *Locke.*

2. The state of being separate; disunion.

As the confusion of tongues was a mark of *separation*, so the being of one language was a mark of union. *Bacon.*

3. The chimical analysis, or operation of disuniting things mingled.

A fifteenth part of silver, incorporate with gold, will not be recovered by any matter of *separation*, unless you put a greater quantity of silver, which is the last refuge in *separations*. *Bacon.*

4. Divorce; disjunction from a married state.

Did you not hear
A buzzing of a *separation*
Between the king and Cath'rine? *Shakespeare.*

SE'PARATIST. *n. s.* [*separatiste*, Fr. from *separate.*] One who divides from the church; a schismatick; a seceder.

The anabaptists, *separatists*, and sectaries tenets are full of schism, and inconsistent with monarchy. *Bacon.*

Our modern *separatists* pronounce all those heretical, or carnal, from whom they have withdrawn. *Decay of Piety.*

Says the *separatist*, if those, who have the rule over you, should command you any thing about church affairs, you ought not, in conscience, to obey them. *South's Sermons.*

SEPARA'TOR. *n. s.* [from *separate.*] One who divides; a divider.

SE'PARATORY. *adj.* [from *separate.*] Used in separation.

The most conspicuous gland of an animal is the system of the guts, where the lacteals are the emissary vessels, or *separatory* ducts. *Cheyne's Phil. Prin.*

SEPILI'BLE. *adj.* [*sepio*, Lat.] That may be buried. *Bailey.*

SE'PIMENT. *n. s.* [*sepimentum*, Lat.] A hedge; a fence. *Bail.*

SEPOSI'TION. *n. s.* [*sepono*, Latin.] The act of setting apart; segregation.

SEPT. *n. s.* [*septum*, Latin.] A clan; a race; a generation. A word used only with regard or allusion to Ireland, and, I suppose, Irish.

This judge, being the lord's brehon, adjudgeth a better share unto the lord of the soil, or the head of that *sept*, and also unto himself for his judgment a greater portion, than unto the plaintiffs. *Spenser on Ireland.*

The true and ancient Russians, a *sept* whom he had met with in one of the provinces of that vast empire, were white like the Danes. *Boyle.*

The English forces were ever too weak to subdue so many warlike nations, or *septs*, of the Irish as did possess this island. *Davies on Ireland.*

SEPTA'NGULAR. *adj.* [*septem* and *angulus*, Latin.] Having seven corners or sides.

SEPTE'MBER. *n. s.* [Latin; *Septembre*, French.] The ninth month of the year; the seventh from March.

September hath his name as being the seventh month from March: he is drawn with a merry and cheerful countenance, in a purple robe. *Peacham on Drawing.*

SE'PTENARY. *adj.* [*septenarius*, Lat.] Consisting of seven.

Every controversy has seven questions belonging to it; tho' the order of nature seems too much neglected by a confinement to this *septenary* number. *Watts.*

SE'PTENARY. *n. s.* The number seven.

The days of men are cast up by *septenaries*, and every seventh year conceived to carry some altering character in temper of mind or body. *Brown's Vulgar Errours.*

These constitutions of Moses, that proceed so much upon a *septenary*, or number of seven, have no reason in the nature of the thing. *Burnet.*

SEPTE'NNIAL. *adj.* [*septennis*, Latin.]

1. Lasting seven years.

2. Happening once in seven years.

Being once dispensed with for his *septennial* visit, by a holy instrument from Petropolis, he resolved to govern them by subaltern ministers. *Howel's Vocal Forest.*

With weekly libels and *septennial* ale,
Their wish is full, to riot and to rail. *Anonym.*

SEPTE'NTRION. *n. s.* [Fr. *septentrio*, Latin.] The North.

Thou art as opposite to every good,
As the antipodes are unto us,
Or as the South to the *Septentrion*. *Shakesp. Hen.* VI.

SEPTE'NTRION. } *adj.* [*septentrionalis*, Latin; *septentrional*,
SEPTE'NTRIONAL. } French.] Northern.

Back'd with a ridge of hills,
That screen'd the fruits of th' earth and seats of men
From cold *septentrion* blasts. *Milton's Par. Regain'd.*

If the Spring
Preceding should be destitute of rain,
Or blast *septentrional* with brushing wings
Sweep up the smoaky mists and vapours damp,
Then woe to mortals. *Philips.*

SEPTENTRIONA'LITY. *n. s.* [from *septentrional.*] Northerliness.

SEPTE'NTRIONALLY. *adv.* [from *septentrional.*] Towards the North; northerly.

If they be powerfully excited, and equally let fall, they commonly sink down, and break the water, at that extreme whereat they were *septentrionally* excited. *Brown.*

To SEPTENTRIO'NATE. *v. n.* [from *septentrio*, Lat.] To tend northerly.

Steel and good iron, never excited by the loadstone, *septentrionate* at one extreme, and australize at another. *Brown.*

SE'PTICAL. *adj.* [σηπτικός.] Having power to promote or produce putrefaction.

As a *septical* medicine, Galen commended the ashes of a salamander. *Brown's Vulgar Errours.*

SEPTILA'TERAL. *adj.* [*septem* and *lateris*, Lat.] Having seven sides.

By an equal interval they make seven triangles, the bases whereof are the seven sides of a *septilateral* figure, described within a circle. *Brown's Vulgar Errours.*

SEPTUA'GENARY. *adj.* [*septuagenarius*, Lat. *septuagenaire*, Fr.] Consisting of seventy.

The three hundred years of John of times, or Nestor, cannot afford a reasonable encouragement beyond Moses's *septuaginary* determination. *Brown's Vulgar Errours.*

SEPTUAGE'SIMAL. *adj.* [*septuagesimus*, Latin.] Consisting of seventy.

In our abridged and *septuagesimal* age, it is very rare to behold the fourth generation. *Brown's Vulgar Errours.*

SE'PTUAGINT. *n. s.* [*septuaginta*, Latin.] The old Greek version of the Old Testament, so called as being supposed the work of seventy-two interpreters.

Which way soever you try, you shall find the product great enough for the extent of this earth; and if you follow the *septuagint* chronology, it will still be far higher. *Burnet.*

SE'PTUPLE. *adj.* [*septuplex*, Latin.] Seven times as much. A technical term.

SEPU'LCHRAL. *adj.* [*sepulcral*, Fr. *sepulcralis*, from *sepulchrum*, Lat.] Relating to burial; relating to the grave; monumental.

Whilst our souls negotiate there,
We like *sepulchral* statues lay;
All day the same our postures were,
And we said nothing all the day. *Donne.*

Mine eye hath found that sad *sepulchral* rock,
That was the casket of heav'n's richest store. *Milton.*

Sepulchral lies our holy walls to grace,
And new-year odes. *Pope's Dunciad.*

SE'PULCHRE. *n. s.* [*sepulcre*, Fr. *sepulchrum*, Lat.] A grave; a tomb.

To entail him and's heirs unto the crown,
What is it but to make thy *sepulchre?* *Shak. Henry* VI.

Flies and spiders get a *sepulchre* in amber, more durable than the monument and embalming of any king. *Bacon.*

There where the virgin's son his doctrine taught,
His miracles, and our redemption wrought;
Where I, by thee inspir'd, his praises sung,
And on his *sepulchre* my offering hung. *Sandys.*

Perpetual lamps for many hundred years have continued burning, without supply, in the *sepulchres* of the ancients. *Wilk.*

If not one common *sepulchre* contains
Our bodies, or one urn our last remains,
Yet Ceyx and Alcyone shall join. *Dryden.*

To SEPU'LCHRE. *v. a.* [from the noun. It is accented on the second syllable by *Shakespeare* and *Milton*; on the first, more properly, by *Johnson* and *Prior.*] To bury; to entomb.

Go to thy lady's grave, and call her thence;
Or, at the least, in her's *sepulchre* thine. *Shakesp.*

I am glad to see that time survive,
Where merit is not *sepulcher'd* alive;
Where good men's virtues them to honours bring,
And not to dangers. *Ben. Johnson.*

Thou so *sepulcher'd* in such pomp do'st lie,
That kings for such a tomb would wish to die. *Milton.*

Disparted streams shall from their channels fly,
And, deep surcharg'd, by sandy mountains lie,
Obscurely *sepulcher'd*. *Prior.*

SE'PULTURE. *n. s.* [*sepulture*, Fr. *sepultura*, Lat.] Interment; burial.

That Niobe, weeping over her children, was turned into a stone, was nothing else but that during her life she erected over her *sepultures* a marble tomb of her own. *Brown.*

Where we may royal *sepulture* prepare;
With speed to Melesinda bring relief,
Recall her spirits, and moderate her grief. *Dryden.*

In England *sepulture*, or burial of the dead, may be deferred and put off for the debts of the person deceased. *Ayliffe.*

SEQUA'CIOUS. *adj.* [*sequacis*, Latin.]

1. Following; attendant.

Orpheus could lead the savage race,
And trees uprooted left their place,
Sequacious of the lyre;
But bright Cecilia rais'd the wonder higher:
When to her organ vocal breath was giv'n,
An angel heard and straight appear'd,
Mistaking earth for heav'n. *Dryden.*

Above thoſe ſuperſtitious horrours that enſlave
The fond *ſequacious* herd, to myſtick faith
And blind amazement prone, th' enlighten'd few
The glorious ſtranger hail! *Thomſon.*

2. Ductile; pliant.

In the greater bodies the forge was eaſy, the matter being ductile and *ſequacious*, and obedient to the hand and ſtroke of the artificer, and apt to be drawn, formed, or moulded. *Ray.*

SEQUA'CITY. *n. ſ.* [from *ſequax*, Latin.] Ductility; toughneſs.

Matter, whereof creatures are produced, hath a cloſeneſs, lentor, and *ſequacity*. *Bacon's Natural Hiſtory.*

SE'QUEL. *n. ſ.* [*ſequelle*, French; *ſequela*, Latin.]

1. Concluſion; ſucceeding part.

If black ſcandal or foul-fac'd reproach
Attend the *ſequel* of your impoſition,
Your meer enforcement ſhall acquittance me. *Shak. R. III.*

Was he not a man of wiſdom? Yes, but he was poor: but was he not alſo ſucceſsful? True, but ſtill he was poor: and once grant this, and you cannot keep off that unavoidable *ſequel* in the next verſe, the poor man's wiſdom is deſpiſed. *South's Sermons.*

2. Conſequence; event.

Let any principal thing, as the ſun or the moon, but once ceaſe, fail, or ſwerve, and who doth not eaſily conceive that the *ſequel* thereof would be ruin both to itſelf and whatſoever dependeth on it? *Hooker.*

In theſe he put two weights,
The *ſequel* each of parting and of fight. *Milton's Par. Loſt.*

3. Conſequence inferred; conſequentialneſs.

What *ſequel* is there in this argument? An archdeacon is the chief deacon: ergo, he is only a deacon. *Whitgifte.*

SE'QUENCE. *n. ſ.* [from *ſequor*, Latin.]

1. Order of ſucceſſion.

How art thou a king,
But by fair *ſequence* and ſucceſſion? *Shakeſp. R. II.*

2. Series; arrangement; method.

The cauſe proceedeth from a precedent *ſequence*, and ſeries of the ſeaſons of the year. *Bacon's Nat. Hiſtory.*

SE'QUENT. *adj.* [*ſequens*, Latin.]

1. Following; ſucceeding.

Let my tryal be mine own confeſſion:
Immediate ſentence then, and *ſequent* death,
Is all the grace I beg. *Shakeſ. Meaſ. for Meaſure.*

There he dies, and leaves his race
Growing into a nation; and now grown,
Suſpected to a *ſequent* king, who ſeeks
To ſtop their overgrowth. *Milton's Paradiſe Loſt.*

2. Conſequential.

SE'QUENT. *n. ſ.* [from the adjective.] A follower. Not in uſe.

Here he hath framed a letter to a *ſequent* of the ſtranger queen's, which accidentally miſcarried. *Shakeſpeare.*

To SEQUE'STER. *v. a.* [*ſequeſtrer*, Fr. *ſecreſtar*, Spaniſh; *ſequeſtro*, low Latin.]

1. To ſeparate from others for the ſake of privacy.

Why are you *ſequeſter'd* from all your train? *Shakeſp.*

To the which place a poor *ſequeſter'd* ſtag,
That from the hunter's aim had ta'en a hurt,
Did come to languiſh. *Shak. As you like it.*

In ſhady bow'r,
More *ſacred* and *ſequeſter'd*, though but feign'd,
Pan or Sylvanus never ſlept. *Milton.*

Ye ſacred Nine! that all my ſoul poſſeſs,
Whoſe raptures fire me, and whoſe viſions bleſs,
Bear me, oh bear me to *ſequeſter'd* ſcenes
Of bow'ry mazes, and ſurrounding greens. *Pope.*

2. To put aſide; to remove.

Although I had wholly *ſequeſtered* my civil affairs, yet I ſet down, out of long continued experience in buſineſs, and converſation in books, what I thought pertinent to this affair. *Bacon.*

3. To withdraw; to ſegregate.

A thing as ſeaſonable in grief as in joy, as decent being added unto actions of greateſt weight and ſolemnity, as being uſed when men moſt *ſequeſter* themſelves from action. *Hooker.*

4. To ſet aſide from the uſe of the owner to that of others.

5. To deprive of poſſeſſions.

It was his taylor and his cook, his fine faſhions and his French ragou's, which *ſequeſtered* him; and, in a word, he came by his poverty as ſinfully as ſome uſually do by their riches. *South.*

SEQUE'STRABLE. *adj.* [from *ſequeſtrate.*]

1. Subject to privation.

2. Capable of ſeparation.

Hartſhorn, and divers other bodies belonging to the animal kingdom, abound with a not uneaſily *ſequeſtrable* ſalt. *Boyle.*

To SEQUE'STRATE. *v. n.* To ſequeſter; to ſeparate from company.

In general contagions more periſh for want of neceſſaries than by the malignity of the diſeaſe, they being *ſequeſtrated* from mankind. *Arbuthnot on Air.*

SEQUESTRA'TION. *n. ſ.* [*ſequeſtration*, Fr. from *ſequeſtrate.*]

1. Separation; retirement.

His addiction was to courſes vain;
I never noted in him any ſtudy,
Any retirement, any *ſequeſtration*
From open haunts and popularity. *Shak. Henry V.*

There muſt be leiſure, retirement, ſolitude, and a *ſequeſtration* of a man's ſelf from the noiſe and toils of the world; for truth ſcorns to be ſeen by eyes too much fixt upon inferior objects. *South's Sermons.*

2. Diſunion; disjunction.

The metals remain unſevered, the fire only dividing the body into ſmaller particles, hindering reſt and continuity, without any *ſequeſtration* of elementary principles. *Boyle.*

3. State of being ſet aſide.

Since Henry Monmouth firſt began to reign,
Before whoſe glory I was great in arms,
This loathſome *ſequeſtration* have I had. *Shakeſp. H. VI.*

4. Deprivation of the uſe and profits of a poſſeſſion.

If there be a ſingle ſpot in the glebe more barren, the rector or vicar may be obliged, by the caprice or pique of the biſhop, to build upon it, under pain of *ſequeſtration*. *Swift.*

SEQUESTRA'TOR. *n. ſ.* [from *ſequeſtrate.*] One who takes from a man the profit of his poſſeſſions.

I am fallen into the hands of publicans and *ſequeſtrators*, and they have taken all from me. *Taylor.*

SERA'GLIO. *n. ſ.* [Italian, perhaps of Oriental original. The *g* is loſt in the pronunciation.] A houſe of women kept for debauchery.

There is a great deal more ſolid content to be found in a conſtant courſe of well living, than in the voluptuouſneſs of a *ſeraglio*. *Norris.*

SE'RAPH. *n. ſ.* [שׂראף.] One of the orders of angels.

He is infinitely more remote in the real excellency of his nature, from the higheſt and perfecteſt of all created beings, than the pureſt *ſeraph* is from the moſt contemptible part of matter, and conſequently muſt infinitely exceed what our narrow underſtandings can conceive of him. *Locke.*

As full, as perfect in vile man that mourns,
As the rapt *ſeraph* that adores and burns. *Pope.*

SERA'PHICAL. } *adj.* [*ſeraphique*, French; from *ſeraph.*] Angelick; angelical.
SERA'PHICK. }

Love is curious of little things, deſiring to be of angelical purity, of perfect innocence, and *ſeraphical* fervour. *Taylor.*

Seraphick arms and trophies. *Milton.*

'Tis to the world a ſecret yet,
Whether the nymph, to pleaſe her ſwain,
Talks in a high romantick ſtrain;
Or whether he at laſt deſcends
To like with leſs *ſeraphick* ends. *Swift.*

SE'RAPHIM. *n. ſ.* [This is properly the plural of *ſeraph*, and therefore cannot have *s* added; yet, in compliance with our language, *ſeraphims* is ſometimes written.] Angels of one of the heavenly orders.

To thee cherubim and *ſeraphim* continually do cry. *Com. Pr.*

Then flew one of the *ſeraphims* unto me, having a live coal in his hand. *Iſ. vi. 6.*

Of *ſeraphim* another row. *Milton.*

SERE. *adj.* [ꞅeaꞃian, Saxon, to dry.] Dry; withered; no longer green. See SEAR.

The muſes, that were wont green bays to wear,
Now bringen bitter elder-branches *ſere*. *Spenſer.*

He is deformed, crooked, old, and *ſere*,
Ill-fac'd, worſe bodied, ſhapeleſs every where;
Vicious, ungentle. *Shakeſp. Comedy of Errours.*

Ere this diurnal ſtar
Leave cold the night, how we his gather'd beams
Reflected, may with matter *ſere* foment. *Milton.*

They *ſere* wood from the rotten hedges took,
And ſeeds of latent fire from flints provoke. *Dryden.*

On a *ſere* branch,
Low bending to the bank, I ſat me down,
Muſing and ſtill. *Rowe's Royal Convert.*

SERE. *n. ſ.* [Of this word I know not the etymology, nor, except from this paſſage, the meaning. Can it come, like *ſheers*, from ꞅcyꞃan, Saxon, to cut?] Claw; talon.

Two eagles,
That, mounted on the winds, together ſtill
Their ſtrokes extended; but arriving now
Amidſt the council, over every brow
Shook their thick wings, and threatning death's cold fears,
Their necks and cheeks tore with their eager *ſeres* *Chapm.*

SERENA'DE. *n. ſ.* [*ſerenade*, Fr. *ſerenata*, Italian, whence, in *Milton*, *ſerenate*, from *ſerenus*, Latin, the lovers commonly attending their miſtreſſes in fair nights.] Muſick or ſongs with which ladies are entertained by their lovers in the night.

Mixt dance, or wanton maſk, or midnight ball,
Or *ſerenate*, which the ſtarv'd lover ſings
To his proud fair; beſt quitted with diſdain. *Milton.*

Fooliſh ſwallow, what do'ſt thou
So often at my window do,
With thy tuneleſs *ſerenade*? *Cowley.*

Shall I the neighbours nightly reſt invade,
At her deaf doors, with ſome vile *ſerenade?* *Dryden.*

Will. fancies he never ſhould have been the man he is, had not he broke windows, and diſturbed honeſt people with his midnight *ſerenades*, when he was a young fellow. *Addiſon.*

To SERENA'DE. *v. a.* [from the noun.] To entertain with nocturnal muſick.

He continued to *ſerenade* her every morning, 'till the queen was charmed with his harmony. *Spectator.*

SERE'NE. *adj.* [*ſerein*, French; *ſerenus*, Latin.]

1. Calm; placid; quiet.

Spirits live inſpher'd
In regions mild, of calm and *ſerene* air. *Milton.*
The moon, *ſerene* in glory, mounts the ſky. *Pope.*

2. Unruffled; undiſturbed; even of temper; peaceful or calm of mind; ſhewing a calm mind.

There wanted yet a creature might erect
His ſtature, and upright with front *ſerene*
Govern the reſt. *Milton.*

Exciting them, by a due remembrance of all that is paſt, unto future circumſpection, and a *ſerene* expectation of the future life. *Grew's Coſmol.*

Gutta SERE'NA. *n. ſ.* An obſtruction in the optick nerve.

Theſe eyes that roll in vain,
So thick a drop *ſerene* hath quench'd their orbs. *Milton.*

SERE'NE. *n. ſ.* [from the adjective.] A calm damp evening.

Where ever death doth pleaſe t' appear,
Seas, *ſerenes*, ſwords, ſhot, ſickneſs, all are there. *Ben. Johnſ.*

To SERE'NE. *v. a.* [*ſerener*, French; *ſereno*, Latin.]

1. To calm; to quiet.

2. To clear; to brighten. Not proper.

Take care
Thy muddy bev'rage to *ſerene*, and drive
Precipitant the baſer ropy lees. *Philips.*

SERE'NELY. *adv.* [from *ſerene*.]

1. Calmly; quietly.

The ſetting ſun now ſhone *ſerenely* bright. *Pope.*

2. With unruffled temper; coolly.

Whatever practical rule is generally broken, cannot be ſuppoſed innate; it being impoſſible that men would, without ſhame or fear, confidently and *ſerenely* break a rule, which they could not but evidently know that God had ſet up. *Locke.*

The nymph did like the ſcene appear,
Serenely pleaſant, calmly fair:
Soft fell her words as flew the air. *Prior.*

SERE'NENESS. *n. ſ.* [from *ſerene*.] Serenity.

SERE'NITUDE. *n. ſ.* [from *ſerene*.] Calmneſs; coolneſs of mind. Not in uſe.

From the equal diſtribution of the phlegmatick humour, will flow quietude and *ſerenitude* in the affections. *Wotton.*

SERE'NITY. *n. ſ.* [*ſerenité*, Fr. from *ſerenus*, Latin.]

1. Calmneſs; temperature.

In the conſtitution of a perpetual equinox, the beſt part of the globe would be deſolate; and as to that little that would be inhabited, there is no reaſon to expect that it would conſtantly enjoy that admired calm and *ſerenity*. *Bentley.*

Pure *ſerenity* apace
Induces thought, and contemplation ſtill. *Thomſon.*

2. Peace; quietneſs; not diſturbance.

A general peace and *ſerenity* newly ſucceeded a general trouble and cloud throughout all his kingdoms. *Temple.*

3. Evenneſs of temper; coolneſs of mind.

I cannot ſee how any men ſhould ever tranſgreſs thoſe moral rules, with confidence and *ſerenity*, were they innate, and ſtamped upon their minds. *Locke.*

SERGE. *n. ſ.* [*ſerge*, French; *xerga*, Spaniſh, which *Covairuvias* derives from *xirica*, Arabick; *Skinner* from *ſerge*, German, a mat.] A kind of cloath.

The ſame wool one man felts into a hat, another weaves into cloath, another into kerſey or *ſerge*, and another into arras. *Hale.*

Ye weavers, all your ſhuttles throw,
And bid broad-cloaths and *ſerges* grow. *Gay.*

SE'RGEANT. *n. ſ.* [*ſergent*, French; *ſergente*, Italian, from *ſervicus*, Latin.]

1. An officer whoſe buſineſs it is to execute the commands of magiſtrates.

Had I but time, as this fell *ſergeant*, death,
Is ſtrict in his arreſt, oh, I could tell. *Shakeſ. Hamlet.*

When it was day the magiſtrates ſent the *ſergeants*, ſaying, let theſe men go. *Acts* xvi. 35.

2. A petty officer in the army.

This is the *ſergeant*,
Who, like a good and hardy ſoldier, fought. *Shakeſ. Macb.*

3. A lawyer of the higheſt rank under a judge.

None ſhould be made *ſergeants*, but ſuch as probably might be held fit to be judges afterwards. *Bacon.*

4. It is a title given to ſome of the king's ſervants: as, *ſergeant chirurgeons.*

SE'RGEANTRY. *n. ſ.* [from *ſergeant*.]

Grand *ſergeantry* is that where one holdeth lands of the king by ſervice, which he ought to do in his own perſon unto him: as to bear the king's banner or his ſpear, or to lead his hoſt, or to be his marſhal, or to blow a horn, when he ſeeth his enemies invade the land; or to find a man at arms to fight within the four ſeas, or elſe to do it himſelf; or to bear the king's ſword before him at his coronation, or on that day to be his ſewer, carver, butler, or chamberlain. Petit *ſergeantry* is where a man holdeth land of the king, to yield him yearly ſome ſmall thing toward his wars: as a ſword, dagger, bow, knife, ſpear, pair of gloves of mail, a pair of ſpurs, or ſuch like. *Cowel.*

SE'RGEANTSHIP. *n. ſ.* [from *ſergeant*.] The office of a ſergeant.

SE'RIES. *n. ſ.* [*ſerie*, Fr. *ſeries*, Latin.]

1. Sequence; order.

Draw out that antecedent, by reflecting briefly upon the text as it lies in the *ſeries* of the epiſtle. *Ward of Infidelity.*

The chaſms of the correſpondence I cannot ſupply, having deſtroyed too many letters to preſerve any *ſeries*. *Pope.*

2. Succeſſion; courſe.

This is the *ſeries* of perpetual woe,
Which thou, alas, and thine are born to know. *Pope.*

SE'RIOUS. *adj.* [*ſerieux*, Fr. *ſerius*, Latin.]

1. Grave; ſolemn; not volatile; not light of behaviour.

2. Important; weighty; not trifling.

I'll hence to London on a *ſerious* matter. *Shakeſ. H. VI.*
There's nothing *ſerious* in mortality;
All is but toys. *Shakeſp. Macbeth.*

SE'RIOUSLY. *adv.* [from *ſerious*.] Gravely; ſolemnly; in earneſt; without levity.

It cannot but be matter of very dreadful conſideration to any one, ſober and in his wits, to think *ſeriouſly* with himſelf, what horror and confuſion muſt needs ſurprize that man, at the laſt day of account, who had led his whole life by one rule, when God intends to judge him by another. *South.*

All laugh to find
Unthinking plainneſs ſo o'erſpread thy mind,
That thou could'ſt *ſeriouſly* perſuade the crowd
To keep their oaths, and to believe a god. *Dryden.*

Juſtin Martyr, Tertullian, Lactantius, and Arnobius, tell us, that this martyrdom firſt of all made them *ſeriouſly* inquiſitive into that religion, which could endue the mind with ſo much ſtrength, and overcome the fear of death, nay, raiſe an earneſt deſire of it, though it appeared in all its terrors. *Addiſ.*

SE'RIOUSNESS. *n. ſ.* [from *ſerious*.] Gravity; ſolemnity; earneſt attention.

That ſpirit of religion and *ſeriouſneſs* vaniſhed all at once, and a ſpirit of libertiniſm and profaneneſs ſtarted up in the room of it. *Atterbury's Sermons.*

The youth was received at the door by a ſervant, who then conducted him with great ſilence and *ſeriouſneſs* to a long gallery, which was darkened at noon-day. *Addiſon's Spectator.*

SERMOCINA'TION. *n. ſ.* [*ſermocinatio*, Latin.] The act or practice of making ſpeeches.

SERMOCINA'TOR. *n. ſ.* [*ſermocinor*, Latin.] A preacher; a ſpeechmaker.

Theſe obſtreperous *ſermocinators* make eaſy impreſſion upon the minds of the vulgar. *Howel.*

SE'RMON. *n. ſ.* [*ſermon*, Fr. *ſermo*, Lat.] A diſcourſe of inſtruction pronounced by a divine for the edification of the people.

As for our *ſermons*, be they never ſo ſound and perfect, God's word they are not, as the *ſermons* of the prophets were; no, they are but ambiguouſly termed his word, becauſe his word is commonly the ſubject whereof they treat, and muſt be the rule whereby they are framed. *Hooker.*

This our life, exempt from publick haunt,
Finds tongues in trees, books in the running brooks,
Sermons in ſtones, and good in every thing. *Shakeſpeare.*

In his *ſermons* unto the ſoldiers, and in open talk with the nobility, it ſhould ſeem that he himſelf had been enough to have overthrown the Turks. *Knolles's Hiſtory of the Turks.*

Sermons he heard, yet not ſo many
As left no time to practiſe any:
He heard them reverently, and then
His practice preach'd them o'er again. *Craſhaw.*

Many, while they have preached Chriſt in their *ſermons*, have read a lecture of atheiſm in their practice. *South.*

His preaching much, but more his practice wrought;
A living *ſermon* of the truths he taught. *Dryden.*

To SE'RMON. *v. a.* [*ſermoner*, Fr. from the noun.]

1. To diſcourſe as in a ſermon.

Some would rather have good diſcipline delivered plainly by way of precept, or *ſermoned* at large, than thus cloudily inwrapped in allegorical deviſes. *Spenſer.*

2. To tutor; to teach dogmatically; to leſſon.

Come, *ſermon* me no farther:
No villainous bounty yet hath paſt my heart. *Shak. Timon.*

SE'RMOUNTAIN, or *Seſeli*. *n. ſ.* [*ſilex*, Lat.] A plant.

It hath a roſe and umbellated flower, conſiſting of ſeveral leaves, which are ranged orbicularly, and reſt on the empalement, which becomes a fruit compoſed of two large oblong furrowed ſeeds, having foliaceous ridges on one ſide. To theſe notes muſt be added, that the lobes of the leaves are large, long, and intire, excepting their extremity, where they are ſlightly cut into three parts. *Miller.*

Sero'sity. *n. s.* [*serosité*, Fr.] Thin or watery part of the blood.

In these the salt and lixiviated *serosity* is divided between the guts and the bladder; but it remains undivided in birds. *Brown.*

The tumour of the throat, which occasions the difficulty of swallowing and breathing, proceeds from a *serosity* obstructing the glands, which may be watery, œdematose, and schirrous, according to the viscosity of the humour. *Arbuthnot.*

SE'ROUS. *adj.* [*sereux*, French; *serosus*, Latin.]

1. Thin; watery. Used of the part of the blood which separates in congelation from the grumous or red part.

2. Adapted to the serum.

This disease is commonly an extravasation of serum, received in some cavity of the body; for there may be also a dropsy by a dilatation of the *serous* vessels, as that in the ovarium. *Arbuthnot on Diet.*

SE'RPENT. *n. s.* [*serpens*, Latin.] An animal that moves by undulation without legs. They are often venomous. They are divided into two kinds; the *viper*, which brings young, and the *snake*, that lays eggs.

She was arrayed all in lily white,
And in her right hand bore a cup of gold,
With wine and water filled up to the height;
In which a *serpent* did himself enfold,
That horror made to all that did behold. *Fairy Queen.*

She struck me with her tongue,
Most *serpent* like, upon the very heart. *Shakesp. K. Lear.*

They, or under ground, or circuit wide,
With *serpent* error wand'ring, found their way. *Milton.*

Haply piercing through the dark disguise,
The chief I challeng'd: he whose practis'd wit
Knew all the *serpent* mazes of deceit,
Eludes my search. *Pope's Odyssey.*

Se'rpentine. *adj.* [*serpentinus*, Lat. from *serpent*.]

1. Resembling a serpent.

I craved of him to lead me to the top of this rock, with meaning to free him from so *serpentine* a companion as I am. *Sidney.*

This of ours is described with legs, wings, a *serpentine* and winding tail, and a crest or comb somewhat like a cock. *Brown.*

Nothing wants, but that thy shape
Like his, and colour *serpentine*, may shew
Thy inward fraud. *Milton's Paradise Lost.*

The figures and their parts ought to have a *serpentine* and flaming form naturally: these sorts of outlines have, I know not what of life and seeming motion in them, which very much resembles the activity of the flame and serpent. *Dryden.*

2. Winding like a serpent; anfractuous.

Nor can the sun
Perfect a circle, or maintain his way
One inch direct; but where he rose to-day
He comes no more, but with a cozening line
Steals by that point, and so is *serpentine*. *Donne.*

His hand the adorned firmament display'd,
Those *serpentine*, yet constant motions made. *Sandys.*

How many spacious countries does the Rhine,
In winding banks, and mazes *serpentine*,
Traverse, before he splits in Belgia's plain,
And, lost in sand, creeps to the German main? *Blackmore.*

Se'rpentine. *n. s.* An herb. *Ainsworth.*

Se'rpentine *Stone.* *n. s.*

There were three species of this stone known among the ancients, all resembling one another, and celebrated for the same virtues. They were all of the marble kind: the one was green, variegated with spots of black, thence called the black ophites; another, called the white ophites, was green also, but variegated with spots of white: the third was called tephria, and was of a grey colour, variegated with small black spots. The first species was chiefly used in medicine, and found by the ancients only in Egypt; but it is frequent in the desarts of Arabia, in the islands of the Archipelago, in Italy, and we have whole quarries of it in Wales. The ancients tell us, that it was a certain remedy against the poison of the bite of serpents; but it is now justly rejected. *Hill's Mat. Med.*

Accept in good part a bottle made of a *serpentine stone*, which hath the quality to give any wine or water, that shall be infused therein for four and twenty hours, the taste and operation of the spaw-water, and is very medicinable for the cure of the spleen and gravel. *Wotton.*

Se'rpents *Tongue.* *n. s.* An herb. *Ainsworth.*

Se'rpet *n. s.* A basket. *Ainsworth.*

Serpi'ginous. *adj.* [from *serpigo*, Latin.] Diseased with a serpigo.

The skin behind her ear downwards became *serpiginous*, and was covered with white scales. *Wiseman.*

SERPI'GO. *n. s.* [Latin.] A kind of tetter.

For thy own bowels, which do call thee sire,
Do curse the gout, *serpigo*, and the rheum,
For ending thee no sooner. *Shakespeare.*

She had a node with pains on her right leg, and a *serpigo* on her right hand. *Wiseman.*

To **Serr.** *v. a.* [*serrer*, French.] To drive hard together; to crowd into a little space. Not received into use, nor deserving reception.

The frowning and knitting of the brows is a gathering or *serring* of the spirits, to resist in some measure; and also this knitting will follow upon earnest studying, though it be without dislike. *Bacon's Nat. History.*

Heat attenuates and sends forth the spirit of a body, and upon that the more gross parts contract and *serr* themselves together. *Bacon.*

Se'rrate. } *adj.* [*serratus*, Latin.] Formed with jags or
Se'rrated. } indentures like the edge of a saw.

All that have *serrate* teeth are carnivorous. *Ray.*

The common heron hath long legs for wading, a long neck answerable thereto to reach prey, a wide throat to pouch it, and long toes with strong hooked talons, one of which is remarkably *serrate* on the edge. *Derham's Physico-Theology.*

This stick is usually knotted, and always armed: one of them with a curious shark's tooth near an inch long, and indented or *serrated* on both edges: a scurvy weapon. *Grew.*

Serra'tion. *n. s.* [from *serra*, Latin.] Formation in the shape of a saw.

Se'rrature. *n. s.* [from *serra*, Latin.] Indenture like teeth of saws.

These are serrated on the edges; but the *serratures* are deeper and grosser than in any of the rest. *Woodward.*

To **Se'rry.** *v. a.* [*serrer*, French; *serrato*, Italian.] To press close; to drive hard together. For *serry Bacon* uses *serr*; but neither *serr* nor *serry* are received.

With them rose
A forest huge of spears; and thronging helms
Appear'd, and *serried* shields in thick array,
Of death immeasurable. *Milton's Paradise Lost.*

Foul dissipation follow'd, and forc'd rout;
Nor serv'd it to relax their *serried* files. *Milton's Par. Lost.*

Se'rvant. *n. s.* [*servant*, French; *servus*, Latin.]

1. One who attends another, and acts at his command. The correlative of master.

We are one in fortune; both
Fell by our *servants*, by those men we lov'd most. *Shakesp.*

I had rather be a country *servant* maid,
Than a great queen with this condition. *Shak. R. III.*

He disdain'd not
Thenceforth the form of *servant* to assume. *Milton.*

For master or for *servant* here to call
Was all alike, where only two were all. *Dryden.*

2. One in a state of subjection. Unusual.

Being unprepar'd,
Our will became the *servant* to defect,
Which else should free have wrought. *Shak. Macbeth.*

3. A word of civility used to superiours or equals.

This subjection, due from all men to all men, is something more than the compliment of course, when our betters tell us they are our humble *servants*, but understand us to be their slaves. *Swift.*

To **Se'rvant.** *v. a.* [from the noun.] To subject. Not in use.

My affairs
Are *servanted* to others: though I owe
My revenge properly, remission lies
In Volscian breasts. *Shakesp. Coriolanus.*

To **SERVE.** *v. a.* [*servir*, French; *servio*, Latin.]

1. To attend at command.

Because thou art my brother, should'st thou therefore *serve* me for nought? *Gen.* xxix. 15.

A goddess among gods ador'd, and *serv'd*
By angels numberless, thy daily train. *Milton.*

2. To obey servilely or meanly.

When wealthy, shew thy wisdom not to be
To wealth a servant, but make wealth *serve* thee. *Denham.*

3. To supply with food ceremoniously.

Others, pamper'd in their shameless pride,
Are *serv'd* in plate, and in their chariots ride. *Dryden.*

4. To bring as a menial attendant.

Bid them cover the table, *serve* in the meat, and we will come in to dinner. *Shakesp. Merch. of Venice.*

Soon after our dinner was *served* in, which was right good viands, both for bread and meat: we had also drink of three sorts, all wholsome and good. *Bacon.*

Besmeared with the horrid juice of sepia, they danced a little in phantastick postures, retired a while, and then returned *serving* up a banquet as at solemn funerals. *Taylor.*

Some part he roasts; then *serves* it up so drest,
And bids me welcome to this humble feast:
Mov'd with disdain,
I with avenging flames the palace burn'd. *Dryden.*

The same mess should be *served* up again for supper, and breakfast next morning. *Arbuthn. History of John Bull.*

5. To be subservient or subordinate to.

Bodies bright and greater should not *serve*
The less not bright. *Milton.*

6. To supply with any thing.

They that *serve* the city, shall *serve* it out of all the tribes of Israel. *Ezek.* xlviii. 19.

7. To obey in military actions.
8. To be ſufficient to.

If any ſubject, intereſt, or fancy has recommended, their reaſoning is after their faſhion; it *ſerves* their turn. *Locke.*

9. To be of uſe to; to aſſiſt.

When a ſtorm of a ſad miſchance beats upon our ſpirits, turn it into ſome advantage, by obſerving where it can *ſerve* another end, either of religion or prudence. *Taylor.*

10. To promote.

He conſider'd every creature
Moſt opportune might *ſerve* his wiles. *Milton.*

11. To comply with.

They think herein we *ſerve* the time, becauſe thereby we either hold or ſeek preferment. *Hooker.*

12. To ſatisfy; to content.

As the former empty plea *ſerved* the ſottiſh Jews, this equally *ſerves* theſe to put them into a fool's paradiſe, by feeding their hopes, without changing their lives. *South.*

Nothing would *ſerve* them then but riding. *L'Eſtrange.*

One half-pint bottle *ſerves* them both to dine,
And is at once their vinegar and wine. *Pope.*

13. To ſtand inſtead of any thing to one.

The dull flat falſhood *ſerves* for policy,
And in the cunning, truth itſelf's a lye. *Pope.*

14. [*Se ſervirde*, French.] *To* SERVE *himſelf of.* To make uſe of. A mere Galliciſm.

A complete brave man muſt know ſolidly the main end he is in the world for; and withal how to *ſerve himſelf* of the divine's high contemplations, of the metaphyſician's ſubtile ſpeculations, and of the natural philoſopher's minute obſervations. *Digby on the Soul.*

They would *ſerve themſelves* of this form. *Taylor.*

I will *ſerve myſelf* of this conceſſion. *Chillingworth.*

It is much more eaſy for men to *ſerve* their own ends of thoſe principles, which they do not put into men, but find there *Tillotſon's Sermons.*

If they elevate themſelves, 'tis only to fall from a higher place, becauſe they *ſerve themſelves* of other men's wings, neither underſtanding their uſe nor virtue. *Dryden's Dufreſn.*

15. To requite: as, he *ſerved* me ungratefully.
16. [In divinity.] To worſhip the Supreme Being.

Matters hid leave to God, him *ſerve* and fear. *Milton.*

17. *To* SERVE *a warrant.* To ſeize an offender, and carry to juſtice.

To SERVE. *v. n.*

1. To be a ſervant, or ſlave.

Iſrael *ſerved* for a wife, and for a wife he kept ſheep. *Hoſ.*

We will give thee this alſo, for the ſervice which thou ſhalt *ſerve* with me. *Gen.* xx. 27.

2. To be in ſubjection.

Thou haſt made me to *ſerve* with thy ſins; thou haſt wearied me with thine iniquities. *Iſ.* xliii. 24.

3. To attend; to wait.

Martha was cumbered about much *ſerving*, and ſaid, Lord, do'ſt thou not care that my ſiſter hath left me to *ſerve* alone? *Luke* x. 40.

4. To act in war.

Both more or leſs have given him the revolt;
And none *ſerve* with but conſtrained things,
Whoſe hearts are abſent too. *Shakeſp. Macbeth.*

Many noble gentlemen came out of all parts of Italy, who had before been great commanders, but now *ſerved* as private gentlemen without pay. *Knolles's Hiſtory of the Turks.*

5. To produce the end deſired.

The look bewrayed, that as ſhe uſed theſe ornaments, not for herſelf, but to prevail with another, ſo ſhe feared that all would not *ſerve*. *Sidney.*

6. To be ſufficient for a purpoſe.

Take it, ſhe ſaid; and when your needs require,
This little brand will *ſerve* to light your fire. *Dryden.*

7. To ſuit; to be convenient.

We have the ſummary of all our griefs,
When time ſhall *ſerve* to ſhew in articles. *Shakeſp. H.* IV.

Yet time *ſerves*, wherein you may redeem
Your baniſh'd honours. *Shakeſ. H.* IV.

As occaſion *ſerves*, this noble queen
And prince ſhall follow with a freſh ſupply. *Shakeſ. H.* VI.

Read that; 'tis with the royal ſignet ſign'd,
And given me by the king, when time ſhould *ſerve*,
To be perus'd by you. *Dryden's Spaniſh Fryar.*

8. To conduce; to be of uſe.

Churches, as every thing elſe, receive their chief perfection from the end whereunto they *ſerve*. *Hooker.*

Our ſpeech to worldly ſuperiors we frame in ſuch ſort as *ſerveth* beſt to inform and perſuade the minds of them, who otherwiſe neither could nor would greatly regard our neceſſities. *Hooker.*

Prieſts *ſerve* unto the example and ſhadow of heavenly things. *Hebr.* viii. 5.

Who leſſens thee, againſt his purpoſe *ſerves*
To manifeſt the more thy might. *Milton.*

Faſhion is, for the moſt part, nothing but the oſtentation of riches; and therefore the high price of what *ſerves* to that, rather encreaſes than leſſens its vent. *Locke.*

Firſt inveſtigate the variety of motions and figures made by the organs which *ſerve* for articulation, and the variety of matter to which thoſe articulations are ſeverally applied. *Hold.*

Our victory only *ſerved* to lead us on to further viſionary proſpects. *Swift.*

9. To officiate or miniſter.

SE'RVICE. *n. ſ.* [*ſervice*, Fr. *ſervitium*, Latin.]

1. Menial office; low buſineſs done at the command of a maſter.

The baniſh'd Kent, who in diſguiſe
Follow'd his king, and did him *ſervice*
Improper for a ſlave. *Shakeſp. K. Lear.*

2. Attendance of a ſervant.

Both fell by our ſervants, by thoſe men we lov'd moſt:
A moſt unnatural and faithleſs *ſervice*. *Shakeſp.*

3. Place; office of a ſervant.

I have ſerved prince Florizel; but now I am out of *ſervice*. *Shakeſpeare.*

By oppreſſing and betraying me,
Thou might'ſt have ſooner got another *ſervice*. *Shakeſ.*

Theſe that accuſe him are a yoke of his diſcarded men; very rogues, now they be out of *ſervice*. *Shakeſp.*

A court, properly a fair, the end of it trade and gain; for none would go to *ſervice* that thinks he has enough to live well of himſelf. *Temple.*

4. Any thing done by way of duty to a ſuperior.

That *ſervice* is not *ſervice*, ſo being done,
But being ſo allow'd. *Shakeſp. Cymbeline.*

This poem was the laſt piece of *ſervice* I did for my maſter King Charles. *Dryden.*

5. Attendance on any ſuperiour.

Madam, I entreat true peace of you,
Which I will purchaſe with my duteous *ſervice*. *Shakeſp.*

Riches gotten by *ſervice*, tho' it be of the beſt riſe, yet when gotten by flattery, may be placed amongſt the worſt. *Bacon.*

6. Profeſſion of reſpect uttered or ſent.

I am a woman, lacking wit,
To make a ſeemly anſwer to ſuch perſons,
Pray do my *ſervice* to his majeſty. *Shakeſp. Hen.* VIII.

7. Obedience; ſubmiſſion.

Thou nature, art my Goddeſs; to thy law
My *ſervices* are bound. *Shakeſp. K. Lear.*

God requires no man's *ſervice* upon hard and unreaſonable Terms. *Tillotſ. Serm.*

8. Act on the performance of which poſſeſſion depends.

Altho' they built caſtles and made freeholders, yet were there no tenures and *ſervices* reſerved to the crown; but the lords drew all the reſpect and dependency of the common people unto themſelves. *Davies's State of Ireland.*

9. Actual duty; office.

The order of human ſociety cannot be preſerved, nor the *ſervices* requiſite to the ſupport of it be ſupplied, without a diſtinction of ſtations, and a long ſubordination of offices. *Roger.*

10. Employment; buſineſs.

If ſtations of power and truſt were conſtantly made the rewards of virtue, men of great abilities would endeavour to excel in the duties of a religious life, in order to qualify themſelves for publick *ſervice*. *Swift.*

11. Military duty.

When he cometh to experience of *ſervice* abroad, or is put to a piece or pike, he maketh a worthy ſoldier. *Spenſer.*

At the parliament at Oxford his youth and want of experience in ſea *ſervice* had ſomewhat been ſhrewdly touched, even before the ſluices of popular liberty were yet ſet open. *Wotton's Buckingham.*

12. A military atchievement.

Such fellows will learn you by rote where *ſervices* were done, at ſuch and ſuch a breach. *Shakeſp. Hen.* V.

13. Purpoſe; uſe.

All the veſſels of the king's houſe are not for uſes of honour, ſome be common ſtuff, and for mean *ſervices*, yet profitable. *Spelman.*

14. Uſeful office; advantage.

The ſtork's plea, when taken in a net, was the *ſervice* ſhe did in picking up venemous creatures. *L'Eſtrange.*

The clergy prevent themſelves from doing much *ſervice* to religion, by affecting ſo much to converſe with each other, and caring ſo little to mingle with the laity. *Swift.*

Gentle ſtreams viſit populous towns in their courſe, and are at once of ornament and *ſervice* to them. *Pope.*

15. Favour.

To thee a woman's *ſervices* are due,
My fool uſurps my body. *Shakeſp. K. Lear.*

16. Publick office of devotion.

According to this form of theirs, it muſt ſtand for a rule, no ſermon, no *ſervice*. *Hooker.*

If that very *ſervice* of God in the Jewiſh ſynagogues, which our Lord did approve and ſanctify with his own preſence, had ſo large portions of the law and prophets, together with the many prayers and pſalms read day by day, as equal in a manner the length of ours, and yet in that reſpect was

was never thought to deserve blame; is it now an offence that the like measure of time is bestowed in the like manner? *Hooker.*

I know no necessity why private and single abilities should quite justle out and deprive the church of the joint abilities and concurrent gifts of many learned and godly men, such as the composers of the *service*-book were. *K. Charles.*

The congregation was discomposed, and divine *service* broken off. *Watts.*

18. Course; order of dishes.

Cleopatra made Antony a supper sumptuous and royal; howbeit there was no extraordinary *service* seen on the board. *Hakewill.*

19. A tree and fruit. [*sorbus*, Latin.]

The flower consists of several leaves, which are placed orbicularly, and expand in form of a rose, whose flower-cup afterwards becomes a fruit shaped like a pear or medlar: to which must be added, pennated leaves like that of the ash. *Miller.*

October is drawn in a garment of yellow and carnation; in his left hand a basket of *services*, medlars, and other fruits that ripen late. *Peacham.*

SE'RVICEABLE. *adj.* [*servissable*, old French, from *service.*]

1. Active; diligent; officious.

He was sent to the King's court, with letters from that officer, containing his own *serviceable* diligence in discovering so great a personage; adding withal more than was true of his conjectures. *Sidney.*

I know thee well, a *serviceable* villain;
As duteous to the vices of thy mistress
As badness could desire. *Shakesp. K. Lear.*

2. Useful; beneficial.

Religion hath force to qualify all sorts of men, and to make them, in publick affairs, the more *serviceable*; governors the apter to rule with conscience; inferiors, for conscience sake, the willinger to obey. *Hooker.*

So your father charg'd me at our parting,
Be *serviceable* to my son. *Shakesp.*

His own inclinations were to confine himself to his own business, and be *serviceable* to religion and learning. *Atterbury.*

A book to justify the revolution, archbishop Tillotson recommended to the king as the most *serviceable* treatise could have been published then. *Swift.*

SE'RVICEABLENESS. *n. s.* [from *serviceable.*]

1. Officiousness; activity.

He might continually be in her presence, shewing more humble *serviceableness* and joy to content her than ever before. *Sidney.*

2. Usefulness; beneficialness.

All action being for some end, its aptness to be commanded or forbidden, must be founded upon its *serviceableness* or disserviceableness to some end. *Norris.*

SE'RVILE. *adj.* [*servil*, French; *serviles*, Latin.]

1. Slavish; dependant; mean.

Fight and die, is death destroying death:
Where fearing dying, pays death *servile* breath. *Shakesp.*

From imposition of strict laws to free
Acceptance of large grace, from *servile* fear
To filial. *Milton.*

Ev'n fortune rules no more a *servile* land,
Where exil'd tyrants still by turns command. *Pope.*

2. Fawning; cringing.

The most *servile* flattery is lodged the most easily in the grossest capacity; for their ordinary conceit draweth a yielding to their greaters, and then have they not wit to discern the right degrees of duty. *Sidney.*

She must bend the *servile* knee,
And fawning take the splendid robber's boon. *Thomson.*

SE'RVILELY. *adv.* [from *servile.*] Meanly; slavishly.

T' each changing news, they chang'd affections bring,
And *servilely* from fate expect a King. *Dryd. Aurengzebe.*

He affects a singularity in his actions and thoughts, rather than *servilely* to copy from the wisest. *Swift.*

SE'RVILENESS. } *n. s.* [from *servile.*]
SERVI'LITY. }

1. Slavishness; involuntary obedience.

What, besides this unhappy *servility* to custom, can possibly reconcile men that own christianity, to a practice widely distant from it? *Govern. of the Tongue.*

2. Meanness; dependance; baseness.

The angels and dæmons, those by their subserviency, and these by the *servility* of their obedience, manifestly declared Christ and his apostles to be vested with an authority derived from their Lord. *West.*

3. Slavery, the condition of a slave.

To be a queen in bondage, is more vile
Than is a slave in base *servility*;
For princes should be free. *Shakesp. Hen. VI.*

SE'RVING-MAN. *n. s.* [*serve* and *man.*] A menial servant.

Your niece did more favours to the duke's *serving-man*, than ever she bestowed on me. *Shakesp. Twelfth Night.*

Just in the nick; the cook knock'd thrice,
And all the waiters in a trice
His summons did obey;
Each *serving-man*, with dish in hand,
March'd boldly up, like our train'd band,
Presented and away. *Suckling.*

With Dennis you did ne'er combine,
Not you, to steal your master's wine;
Except a bottle now and then,
To welcome brother *serving-men*. *Swift.*

SE'RVITOR. *n. s.* [*serviteur*, French.]

1. Servant; attendant. A word obsolete.

This workman, whose *servitor* nature is, being only one, the heathens imagining to be more, gave him in the sky the name of Jupiter; in the air, of Juno; in the water, of Neptune; in the earth, of Vesta; and Ceres. *Hooker.*

Your trusty and most valiant *servitor*,
With his free duty recommends you thus. *Shakesp.*

Thus are poor *servitors*,
When others sleep upon their quiet beds,
Constrain'd to watch in darkness, rain and cold. *Shakesp.*

Our Norman conqueror gave away to his *servitors* the lands and possessions of such as did oppose his invasion. *Davies.*

Fearful commenting
Is leaden *servitor* to dull delay;
Delay leads impotent and snail-pac'd beggary. *Shakesp.*

My noble queen, let former grudges pass,
And henceforth I am thy true *servitor*. *Shakesp. Hen. VI.*

2. One of the lowest order in the university.

His learning is much of a size with his birth and education; no more of either than what a poor hungry *servitor* can be expected to bring with him from his college. *Swift.*

SE'RVITUDE. *n. s.* [*servitude*, French; *servitus*, Latin.]

1. Slavery; state of a slave; dependance.

Aristotle speaketh of men, whom nature hath framed for the state of *servitude*, saying, they have reason so far forth as to conceive when others direct them. *Hooker.*

You would have sold your king to slaughter,
His princes and his peers to *servitude*,
His subjects to oppression and contempt. *Shakesp. Hen. V.*

Tho' it is necessary, that some persons in the world should be in love with a splendid *servitude*, yet certainly they must be much beholding to their own fancy, that they can be pleased at it; for he that rises up early, and goes to bed late, only to receive addresses, is really as much abridged in his freedom, as he that waits to present one. *South Sermons.*

Unjustly thou deprav'st it with the name
Of *servitude*, to serve whom God ordains,
Or nature: God and nature bid the same,
When he who rules is worthiest. *Milton.*

2. Servants collectively.

After him a cum'brous train
Of herds, and flocks, and numerous *servitude*. *Milton.*

SE'RUM. *n. s.* [Latin.]

1. The thin and watry part that separates from the rest in any liquor, as in milk from the cream.

2. The part of the blood, which in coagulation separates from the grume.

Blood is the most universal juice in an animal body: the red part of it differs from the *serum*, the *serum* from the lymph, the lymph from the nervous juice, and that from the several other humours separated in the glands. *Arbuthnot.*

SESQUIA'LTER. } *adj.* [*sesquialtere*, Fr. *sesquialter*, Lat.]
SESQUIA'LTERAL. }

In geometry, is a ratio, where one quantity or number contains another once and half as much more, as 6 and 9. *Dict.*

In all the revolutions of the planets about the sun, and of the secondary planets about the primary ones, the periodical times is in a *sesquialter* proportion to the mean distance. *Cheyne.*

As the six primary planets revolve about the sun, so the secondary ones are moved about them in the same *sesquialteral* proportion of their periodical motions to their orbs. *Bentley.*

SE'SQUIPLICATE. *adj.* [In mathematicks.] Is the proportion one quantity or number has to another, in the ratio of one half.

The periodical times of the planets are in *sesquiplicate* proportion, and not a duplicate proportion of the distances from the center or the radii; and consequently the planets cannot be carried about by an harmonically circulating fluid. *Cheyne's Phil. Prin.*

SE'SQUIPEDAL. } *adj.* [*sesquipedalis*, Latin.] Containing
SESQUIPEDA'LIAN. } a foot and a half.

As for my own part, I am but a *sesquipedal*, having only six foot and a half of stature. *Addis. Guard.*

Hast thou ever measured the gigantick Ethiopian, whose stature is above eight cubits high, or the *sesquipedalian* pigmey? *Arbuth and Pope's Mart. Scrib.*

SESQUITE'RTIAN. [in mathematicks.] Having such a ratio, as that one quantity or number contains another once and one third part more; as between 6 and 8. *Dict.*

Sess. *n. s.* [for *assess*, *cess*, or *cense*.] Rate; cess charged; tax.

His army was so ill paid and governed, as the English suffered more damage by the *sess* of his soldiers than they gained profit or security by abating the pride of their enemies. *Davies's Hist. of Ireland.*

Se'ssion. *n. s.* [*session*, French; *sessio*, Latin.]

1. The act of sitting.

He hath as man, not as God only, a supreme dominion over quick and dead; for so much his ascension into heaven, and his *session* at the right-hand of God do import. *Hooker.*

Many, tho' they concede a table-gesture, will hardly allow this usual way of *session*. *Brown's Vulg. Errors.*

2. An assembly of magistrates or senators.

They are ready t'appear
Where you shall hold your *session*. *Shakesp. K. Lear.*

Summon a *session* that we may arraign
Our most disloyal lady. *Shakesp.*

The old man mindful still of moan,
Weeping, thus bespake the *session*. *Chapman's Hom. Odys.*

Of their *session* ended they bid cry
The great result. *Milton.*

Call'd to council all the Achaian states,
Nor herald sworn the *session* to proclaim. *Pope's Odys.*

3. The space for which an assembly sits, without intermission or recess.

It was contrary to the course of parliament, that any bill that had been rejected should be again preferred the same *session*. *Clarendon.*

The second Nicene council affords us plentiful assistance, in the first *session*, wherein the pope's vicar declares that Meletius was ordained by Arian bishops, and yet his ordination was never questioned. *Stillingfleet.*

Many decrees are enacted, which at the next *session* are repealed. *Norris.*

4. A meeting of justices: as the sessions of the peace.

Se'sterce. *n. s.* [*sesterce*, French; *sestertium*, Latin.] Among the Romans, a sum of about 8 l. 1 s. 5 d. half-penny *sterling*. *Dict.*

Several of them would rather chuse a sum in *sesterces*, than in pounds *sterling*. *Addison on Medals.*

To SET. *v. a.* preterite *I set*; part. pass. *I am set.* [*Satgan*, or *satyan*, Gothick; settan, Saxon; *setten*, Dutch.]

1. To place; to put in any situation or place; to put.

E're I could
Give him that parting kiss which I had *set*
Betwixt two charming words, comes in my father. *Shakes.*

But that my admirable dexterity of wit, counterfeiting the action of an old woman, delivered me, the knave constable had *set* me i' th' common stocks for a witch. *Shakesp.*

They that are younger have me in derision, whose fathers I would have disdained to have *set* with the dogs of my flock. *Job.* xxx. 1.

He that hath received his testimony, hath *set* to his seal, that God is true. *John* iii. 33.

They have *set* her a bed in the midst of the slain. *Ezek.* xxxii.

God *set* them in the firmament, to give light upon the earth. *Gen.* i. 17.

In their *setting* of their threshold by my thresholds, they have defiled my holy name. *Ezek.* xliii. 8.

I have *set* thee for a tower among my people. *Jer.* vi. 27.

By his aid aspiring
To *set* himself in glory above his peers. *Milton.*

She *sets* the bar that causes all my pain;
One gift refused, makes all their bounty vain. *Dryd.*

The lives of the revealers may be justly enough *set* over against the revelation, to find whether they agree. *Atterb.*

2. To put into any condition, state, or posture.

They thought the very disturbance of things established an hire sufficient to *set* them on work. *Hooker.*

That man that sits within a monarch's heart,
Would he abuse the count'nance of the king,
Alack! what mischiefs might he *set* abroach? *Shakesp.*

Our princely general,
Will give you audience; and wherein
It shall appear that your demands are just,
You shall enjoy them; ev'ry thing *set* off
That might so much as think you enemies. *Shakesp.*

This present enterprize *set* off his head,
I do not think a braver gentleman
Is now alive. *Shakesp. Hen.* IV.

Ye caused every man his servant, whom he had *set* at liberty, to return. *Jer.* xxxiv. 16.

Every sabbath ye shall *set* it in order. *Lev.* xxiv. 8.

I am come to *set* a man at variance against his father. *Mat.*

Thou shalt pour out into all those vessels, and *set* aside that which is full. 2 *Kings* iv. 4.

The beauty of his ornament he *set* in majesty, but they made images; therefore have I *set* it far from them. *Ezek.*

The gates of thy land shall be *set* wide open. *Nah.* iii. 13.

The fathers have eaten a sour grape, and the children's teeth are *set* on edge. *Jer.* xxxi. 20.

The tongue defileth the whole body, and *setteth* on fire the course of nature, and is *set* on fire of hell. *Ja.* iii. 6.

The shipping might be *set* on work by fishing, by transportations from port to port. *Bacon.*

This wheel *set* on going, did pour a war upon the Venetians with such a tempest, as Padua and Trevigi were taken from them. *Bacon.*

That this may be done with the more advantage, some hours must be *set* apart for this examination. *Duppa.*

Finding the river fordable at the foot of the bridge, he *set* over his horse. *Hayward.*

Equal success had *set* these champions high,
And both resolv'd to conquer, or to die. *Waller.*

Nothing renders a man so inconsiderable; for it *sets* him above the meaner sort of company, and makes him intolerable to the better. *Govern. of the Tongue.*

Some are reclaimed by punishment, and some are *set* right by good nature. *L'Estrange.*

The fire was form'd, she *sets* the kettle on. *Dryd.*

Leda's present came,
To ruin Troy, and *set* the world on flame. *Dryd.*

Set calf betimes to school, and let him be
Instructed there in rules of husbandry. *Dryd.*

Over labour'd with so long a course,
'Tis time to set at ease the smoking horse. *Dryd.*

The punish'd crime shall *set* my soul at ease,
And murm'ring manes of my friend appease. *Dryd.*

Jove call'd in haste
The son of Maia with severe decree,
To kill the keeper, and to *set* her free. *Dryd.*

If such a tradition were at any time endeavoured to be *set* on foot, it is not easy to imagine how it should at first gain entertainment. *Tillotson.*

When the father looks sour on the child, every body else should put on the same coldness, till forgiveness asked, and a reformation of his fault has *set* him right again, and restored him to his former credit. *Locke on Educat.*

His practice must by no means cross his precepts, unless he intend to *set* him wrong. *Locke on Educat.*

If the fear of absolute and irresistible power *set* it on upon the mind, the idea is likely to sink the deeper. *Locke.*

When he has once chosen it, it raises desire that proportionably gives him uneasiness which determines his will, and *sets* him at work in pursuit of his choice, on all occasions. *Locke.*

This river,
When nature's self lay ready to expire,
Quench'd the dire flame that *set* the world on fire. *Addis.*

The many hospitals every where erected, serve rather to encourage idleness in the people than to *set* them at work. *Add.*

A couple of lovers agreed at parting, to *set* aside one half hour in the day to think of each other. *Addis.*

Your fortunes place you far above the necessity of learning, but nothing can *set* you above the ornament of it. *Felton.*

Their first movement and impressed motions demand the impulse of an almighty hand to *set* them agoing. *Cheyne.*

Men of quality look upon it as one of their distinguishing privileges, not to *set* other people at ease, with the loss of the least of their own. *Pope.*

That the wheels were but small, may be guessed from a custom they have of taking them off, and *setting* them on. *Pope.*

Be frequent in *setting* such causes at work, whose effects you desire to know. *Watts.*

3. To make motionless; to fix immoveably.

Struck with the sight, inanimate she seems,
Set are her eyes, and motionless her limbs. *Garth.*

4. To fix; to state by some rule.

Hereon the prompter falls to flat railing in the bitterest terms; which the gentleman with a *set* gesture and countenance still soberly related, until the ordinary, driven at last into a mad rage, was fain to give over. *Carew.*

The town of Bern has handsome fountains planted, at *set* distances, from one end of the streets to the other. *Addison.*

5. To regulate; to adjust.

In court they determine the king's good by his desires, which is a kind of *setting* the sun by the dial. *Suckling.*

God bears a different respect to places *set* apart and consecrated to his worship, to what he bears to places designed to common uses. *South.*

Our palates grow into a liking of the seasoning and cookery, which by custom they are *set* to. *Locke.*

He rules the church's blest dominions,
And *sets* men's faith by his opinions. *Prior.*

Against experience he believes,
He argues against demonstration;
Plead's when his reason he deceives,
And *sets* his judgment by his passion. *Prior.*

6. To fit to musick; to adapt with notes.

Set thy own songs, and sing them to thy lute. *Dryden.*

Grief he tames that fetters it in verse;
But when I have done so,
Some man, his art or voice to show,
Doth *set* and sing my pain;
And by delighting many, frees again
Grief, which verse did restrain. *Donne.*

I had one day *set* the hundredth psalm, and was singing the first line, in order to put the congregation into the tune. *Spect.*

7. To plant, not sow.

Whatsoever fruit useth to be *set* upon a root or a slip, if it be sown, will degenerate. *Bacon's Nat. History.*

I prostrate fell,
To shrubs and plants my vile devotion paid,
And *set* the bearded leek to which I pray'd. *Prior.*

8. To intersperse or mark with any thing.

As with stars, their bodies all
And wings were *set* with eyes. *Milton.*

High on their heads, with jewels richly *set*,
Each lady wore a radiant coronet. *Dryden.*

The body is smooth on that end, and on this 'tis *set* with ridges round the point. *Woodward.*

9. To reduce from a fractured or dislocated state.

Can honour *set* to a leg? no: or an arm? no: honour hath no skill in surgery then? no. *Shakesp. Henry IV.*

Considering what an orderly life I had led, I only commanded that my arm and leg should be *set*, and my body anointed with oil. *G. Herbert.*

The fracture was of both the focils of the left leg: he had been in great pain from the time of the *setting*. *Wiseman.*

Credit is gained by course of time, and seldom recovers a strain; but if broken, is never well *set* again. *Temple.*

10. To fix the affection; to determine the resolution.

Set your affection on things above, not on things on the earth. *Col.* iii. 2.

They should *set* their hope in God, and not forget his works. *Ps.* lxxviii. 7.

Because sentence against an evil work is not executed speedily, the heart of men is fully *set* in them to do evil. *Eccl.*

Set to work millions of spinning worms,
That in their green shops weave the smooth hair'd silk
To deck her sons. *Milt.*

Set not thy heart
Thus overfond on that which is not thine. *Milton.*

When we are well, our hearts are *set*,
Which way we care not, to be rich or great. *Denham.*

Our hearts are so much *set* upon the value of the benefits received, that we never think of the bestower. *L'Estrange.*

These bubbles of the shallowest, emptiest sorrow,
Which children vent for toys, and women rain
For any trifle their fond hearts are *set* on. *Dryd. and Lee.*

Should we *set* our hearts only upon these things, and be able to taste no pleasure but what is sensual, we must be extremely miserable when we come unto the other world, because we should meet with nothing to entertain ourselves. *Tillotson.*

No sooner is one action dispatched, which we are *set* upon, but another uneasiness is ready to *set* us on work. *Locke.*

Minds, altogether *set* on trade and profit, often contract a certain narrowness of temper. *Addison.*

Men take an ill-natured pleasure in disappointing us in what our hearts are most *set* upon. *Addison's Spectator.*

An Englishman, who has any degree of reflection, cannot be better awakened to a sense of religion in general, than by observing how the minds of all mankind are *set* upon this important point, and how every nation is attentive to the great business of their being. *Addison.*

I am much concerned when I see young gentlemen of fortune so wholly *set* upon pleasures, that they neglect all improvements in wisdom and knowledge. *Addison.*

11. To predetermine; to settle.

We may still doubt whether the Lord, in such indifferent ceremonies as those whereof we dispute, did frame his people of *set* purpose unto any utter dissimilitude with Egyptians, or with any other nation. *Hooker.*

He remembers only the name of Conon, and forgets the other on *set* purpose, to shew his country swain was no great scholar. *Dryden.*

12. To establish; to appoint; to fix.

Of all helps for due performance of this service, the greatest is that very *set* and standing order itself, which, framed with common advice, hath for matter and form prescribed whatsoever is herein publickly done. *Hooker.*

It pleased the king to send me, and I *set* him a time. *Neh.* ii.

Am I a sea, or a whale, that thou *settest* a watch over me? *Job* vii. 12.

He *setteth* an end to darkness, and searcheth out all perfection. *Job* xxviii. 3.

In studies, whatsoever a man commandeth upon himself, let him *set* hours for it; but whatsoever is agreeable to his nature, let him take no care for any *set* times: for his thoughts will fly to it of themselves, so as the spaces of other business or studies will suffice. *Bacon.*

For using *set* and prescribed forms, there is no doubt but that wholsome words, being known, are aptest to excite judicious and fervent affections. *King Charles.*

His seed, when is not *set*, shall bruise my head. *Milton.*

Though *set* form of prayer be an abomination,
Set forms of petitions find great approbation. *Denham.*

Set places and *set* hours are but parts of that worship we owe. *South.*

That law cannot keep men from taking more use than you *set*, the want of money being that alone which regulates its price, will appear, if we consider how hard it is to *set* a price upon unnecessary commodities; but how impossible it is to *set* a rate upon victuals in a time of famine. *Locke.*

Set him such a task, to be done in such a time. *Locke.*

As in the subordinations of government the king is offended by any insults to an inferior magistrate, so the sovereign ruler of the universe is affronted by a breach of allegiance to those whom he has *set* over us. *Addison.*

Take *set* times of meditating on what is future. *Atterbury.*

Should a man go about, with never so *set* study and design, to describe such a natural form of the year as that which is at present established, he could scarcely ever do it in so few words that were so fit. *Woodward.*

13. To exhibit; to display; to propose. With *before*.

Through the variety of my reading, I *set before* me many examples both of ancient and later times. *Bacon.*

Reject not then what offer'd means: who knows
But God hath *set before* us, to return thee
Home to thy country and his sacred house? *Milton.*

Long has my soul desir'd this time and place,
To *set before* your sight your glorious race. *Dryden.*

All that can be done is to *set* the thing *before* men, and to offer it to their choice. *Tillotson.*

A spacious veil from his broad shoulders flew,
That *set* th' unhappy Phaeton to view:
The flaming chariot and the steeds it shew'd,
And the whole fable in the mantle glow'd. *Addison.*

When his fortune *sets before* him all
The pomps and pleasures that his soul can wish,
His rigid virtue will accept of none. *Addison's Cato.*

He supplies his not appearing in the present scene of action, by *setting* his character *before* us, and continually forcing his patience, prudence, and valour upon our observation. *Broome.*

14. To value; to estimate; to rate.

Be you contented
To have a son *set* your decrees at nought?
To pluck down justice from your awful bench,
To trip the course of law? *Shakes. H. IV.*

The backwardness parents shew in divulging their faults, will make them *set* a greater value on their credit themselves, and teach them to be the more careful to preserve the good opinion of others. *Locke.*

If we act by several broken views, and will not only be virtuous, but wealthy, popular, and every thing that has a value *set* upon it by the world, we shall live and die in misery. *Addis.*

Have I not *set* at nought my noble birth,
A spotless fame, and an unblemish'd race,
The peace of innocence, and pride of virtue?
My prodigality has giv'n thee all. *Rowe's Jane Shore.*

Though the same sun, with all diffusive rays,
Blush in the rose and in the diamond blaze,
We prize the stronger effort of his pow'r,
And always *set* the gem above the flow'r. *Pope.*

15. To stake at play.

What sad disorders play begets!
Desp'rate and mad, at length he *sets*
Those darts, whose points make gods adore. *Prior.*

16. To offer a wager at dice to another.

Who *sets* me else? I'll throw at all. *Shakesp. R. II.*

17. To fix in metal.

Think so vast a treasure as your son
Too great for any private man's possession;
And him too rich a jewel to be *set*
In vulgar metal, or vulgar use. *Dryden.*

He may learn to cut, polish, and *set* precious stones. *Locke.*

18. To embarrass; to distress; to perplex. [This is used, I think, by mistake, for *beset*: as,

Adam, hard *beset*, replied. *Milton.*]

Those who raise popular murmurs and discontents against his majesty's government, that they find so very few and so very improper occasions for them, shew how hard they are *set* in this particular, represent the bill as a grievance. *Addis.*

19. To fix in an artificial manner, so as to produce a particular effect.

The proud have laid a snare for me, they have *set* gins. *Ps.*

20. To apply to something.

Unto thy brother thou shalt not lend upon usury, that the Lord may bless thee in all that thou *settest* thine hand to. *Deut.*

With whate'er gall thou *set'st* thyself to write,
Thy inoffensive satires never bite. *Dryden.*

21. To fix the eyes.

I will *set* mine eyes upon them for good, and bring them again to this land. *Jer.* xxiv. 6.

Joy

Joy ſalutes me when I *ſet*
My bleſt eyes on Amoret. *Waller.*

22 To offer for a price.

There is not a more wicked thing than a covetous man; for ſuch an one *ſetteth* his own ſoul to ſale. *Eccluſ.* x. 9.

23. To place in order; to frame.

After it was framed, and ready to be *ſet* together, he was, with infinite labour and charge, carried by land with camels, through that hot and ſandy country, from Caire to Suetia. *Knolles's Hiſtory of the Turks.*

24. To ſtation; to place.

Cœnus has betray'd
The bitter truths that our looſe court upbraid:
Your friend was *ſet* upon you for a ſpy,
And on his witneſs you are doom'd to die. *Dryden.*

25. To oppoſe.

Will you *ſet* your wit to a fool's? *Shakeſpeare.*

26. To bring to a fine edge: as, to *ſet* a razor.

27. *To* SET *about.* To apply to.

They ſhould make them play-games, or endeavour it, and *ſet* themſelves *about* it. *Locke.*

28. *To* SET *againſt.* To place in a ſtate of enmity or oppoſition.

The terrors of God do *ſet* themſelves in array *againſt* me. *Job* vi. 4.

The king of Babylon *ſet* himſelf *againſt* Jeruſalem. *Ezek.*

The devil hath reaſon to *ſet* himſelf *againſt* it; for nothing is more deſtructive to him than a ſoul armed with prayer. *Duppa.*

There ſhould be ſuch a being as aſſiſts us againſt our worſt enemies, and comforts us under our ſharpeſt ſufferings, when all other things *ſet* themſelves *againſt* us. *Tillotſon.*

29. *To* SET *againſt.* To oppoſe; to place in rhetorical oppoſition.

This periſhing of the world in a deluge is *ſet againſt*, or compared with, the periſhing of the world in the conflagration. *Burnet's Theory of the Earth.*

30. *To* SET *apart.* To neglect for a ſeaſon.

They highly commended his forwardneſs, and all other matters for that time *ſet apart.* *Knolles.*

31. *To* SET *aſide.* To omit for the preſent.

Set your knighthood and your ſoldierſhip *aſide*, and give me leave to tell you that you lie in your throat. *Shakeſp. H.* IV.

In 1585 followed the proſperous expedition of Drake and Carlile into the Weſt Indies; in the which I *ſet aſide* the taking of St. Jago and St. Domingo in Hiſpaniola, as ſurprizes rather than encounters. *Bacon.*

My higheſt intereſt is not to be deceived about theſe matters; therefore, *ſetting aſide* all other conſiderations, I will endeavour to know the truth, and yield to that. *Tillotſon.*

32. *To* SET *aſide.* To reject.

I'll look into the pretenſions of each, and ſhew upon what ground 'tis that I embrace that of the deluge, and *ſet aſide* all the reſt. *Woodward's Nat. Hiſtory.*

No longer now does my neglected mind
Its wonted ſtores and old ideas find:
Fix'd judgment there no longer does abide,
To taſte the true, or *ſet* the falſe *aſide.* *Prior.*

33. *To* SET *aſide.* To abrogate; to annul.

Several innovations, made to the detriment of the Engliſh merchant, are now intirely *ſet aſide.* *Addiſon.*

There may be
Reaſons of ſo much pow'r and cogent force,
As may ev'n *ſet aſide* this right of birth:
If ſons have rights, yet fathers have 'em too. *Rowe.*

He ſhows what abſurdities follow upon ſuch a ſuppoſition, and the greater thoſe abſurdities are, the more ſtrongly do they evince the falſity of that ſuppoſition from whence they flow, and conſequently the truth of the doctrine *ſet aſide* by that ſuppoſition. *Atterbury.*

34. *To* SET *by.* To regard; to eſteem.

David behaved himſelf more wiſely than all, ſo that his name was much *ſet by.* 1 *Sa.* xviii. 30.

35. *To* SET *by.* To reject or omit for the preſent.

You ſhall hardly edify me, that thoſe nations might not, by the law of nature, have been ſubdued by any nation that had only policy and moral virtue; though the propagation of the faith, whereof we ſhall ſpeak in the proper place, were *ſet by*, and not made part of the caſe. *Bacon.*

36. *To* SET *down.* To mention; to explain; to relate in writing.

They have *ſet down*, that a roſe ſet by garlick is ſweeter, becauſe the more fetid juice goeth into the garlick. *Bacon.*

Some rules were to be *ſet down* for the government of the army. *Clarendon.*

I ſhall *ſet down* an account of a diſcourſe I chanced to have with one of theſe rural ſtateſmen. *Addiſon.*

37. *To* SET *down.* To regiſter or note in any book or paper; to put in writing.

Let thoſe that play your clowns ſpeak no more than is *ſet down* for them. *Shakeſp. Hamlet.*

Every man, careful of virtuous converſation, ſtudious of ſcripture, and given unto any abſtinence in diet, was *ſet down* in his calendar of ſuſpected Priſcilianiſts. *Hooker.*

Take
One half of my commiſſion, and *ſet down*
As beſt thou art experienc'd, ſince thou know'ſt
Thy country's ſtrength and weakneſs. *Shak Coriolanus.*

The reaſons that led me into the meaning which prevailed on my mind, are *ſet down.* *Locke.*

An eminent inſtance of this, to ſhew what uſe can do, I ſhall *ſet down.* *Locke.*

I cannot forbear *ſetting down* the beautiful deſcription Claudian has made of a wild beaſt, newly brought from the woods, and making its firſt appearance in a full amphitheatre. *Addiſon.*

38. *To* SET *down.* To fix on a reſolve.

Finding him ſo reſolutely *ſet down*, that he was neither by fair nor foul means, but only by force, to be removed out of his town, he incloſed the ſame round. *Knolles.*

39. *To* SET *down.* To fix; to eſtabliſh.

This law we may name eternal, being that order which God before all others hath *ſet down* with himſelf, for himſelf to do all things by. *Hooker.*

40. *To* SET *forth.* To publiſh; to promulgate; to make appear.

My willing love,
The rather by theſe arguments of fear,
Set forth in your purſuit. *Shakeſ. Twelfth Night.*

The poems, which have been ſo ill *ſet forth* under his name, are as he firſt writ them. *Waller.*

41. *To* SET *forth.* To raiſe; to ſend out.

Our merchants, to their great charges, *ſet forth* fleets to deſcry the ſeas. *Abbot.*

The Venetian admiral had a fleet of ſixty gallies, *ſet forth* by the Venetians. *Knolles's Hiſt. of the Turks.*

They agreed, all with one conſent, at a prefixed day, to ſend unto Vienna ſuch warlike forces, as they had in any time before *ſet forth*, for the defence of the Chriſtian religion. *Knolles's Hiſtory of the Turks.*

When poor Rutilus ſpends all his worth,
In hopes of *ſetting* one good dinner *forth*,
'Tis downright madneſs. *Dryden's Juvenal.*

42. *To* SET *forth.* To diſplay; to explain.

As for words to *ſet forth* ſuch lewdneſs, it is not hard for them to give a goodly and painted ſhew thereunto, borrowed even from the praiſes proper to virtue. *Spenſer.*

So little have theſe falſe colours diſhonoured painting, that they have only ſerved to *ſet forth* her praiſe, and to make her merit further known. *Dryden's Dufreſnoy.*

43. *To* SET *forth.* To arrange; to place in order.

Up higher to the plain, where we'll *ſet forth*
In beſt appointment all our regiments. *Shakeſp. K. John.*

44. *To* SET *forth.* To ſhow; to exhibit.

To render our errours more monſtrous, and what unto a miracle *ſets forth* the patience of God, he hath endeavoured to make the world believe he was God himſelf. *Browne.*

Whereas it is commonly *ſet forth* green or yellow, it is inclining to white. *Brown's Vulg. Err.*

To *ſet forth* great things by ſmall. *Milton.*

The two humours of a chearful truſt in providence, and a ſuſpicious diffidence of it, are very well *ſet forth* here for our inſtruction. *L'Eſtrange.*

45. *To* SET *forward.* To advance; to promote.

They yield that reading may *ſet forward*, but not begin the work of ſalvation. *Hooker.*

Amongſt them there are not thoſe helps which others have, to *ſet* them *forward* in the way of life. *Hooker.*

In the external form of religion, ſuch things as are apparently or can be ſufficiently proved effectual, and generally fit to *ſet forward* godlineſs, either as betokening the greatneſs of God, or as beſeeming the dignity of religion, or as concurring with celeſtial impreſſions in the minds of men, may be reverently thought of. *Hooker.*

They mar my path, they *ſet forward* my calamity. *Job.*

Dung or chalk, applied ſeaſonably to the roots of trees, doth *ſet* them *forwards.* *Bacon's Nat. Hiſtory.*

46. *To* SET *in.* To put in a way to begin.

If you pleaſe to aſſiſt and *ſet* me *in*, I will recollect myſelf. *Collier.*

47. *To* SET *off.* To decorate; to recommend; to adorn; to embelliſh. It anſwers to the French *relever.*

Like bright metal on a ſullen ground,
My reformation, glittering o'er my fault,
Shall ſhew more goodly, and attract more eyes,
Than that which hath no foil to *ſet* it *off.* *Shak. H.* IV.

The prince put thee into my ſervice for no other reaſon than to *ſet* me *off.* *Shakeſp. Henry* IV.

Neglect not the examples of thoſe that have carried themſelves ill in the ſame place; not to *ſet off* thyſelf by taxing their memory, but to direct thyſelf what to avoid. *Bacon.*

May you be happy, and your ſorrows paſt
Set off thoſe joys I wiſh may ever laſt. *Waller.*

The figures of the groupes muſt contraſt each other by their ſeveral poſitions: thus in a play ſome characters muſt be raiſed to oppoſe others, and to *ſet* them *off.* *Dryden.*

The men, whoſe hearts are aimed at, are the occaſion that one part of the face lies under a kind of diſguiſe, while the other is ſo much *ſet off*, and adorned by the owner. *Addiſon.*

Their women are perfect miſtreſſes in ſhewing themſelves to the beſt advantage: they are always gay and ſprightly, and *ſet off* the worſt faces with the beſt airs. *Addiſon.*

The general good ſenſe and worthineſs of his character, makes his friends obſerve theſe little ſingularities as foils, that rather *ſet off* than blemiſh his good qualities. *Addiſon.*

The work will never take, if it is not *ſet off* with proper ſcenes. *Addiſon.*

Claudian *ſets off* his deſcription of the Eridanus with all the poetical ſtories. *Addiſon on Italy.*

48. *To* SET *on* or *upon.* To animate; to inſtigate; to incite.

You had either never attempted this change, *ſet on* with hope, or never diſcovered it, ſtopt with diſpair. *Sidney.*

He upbraids Iago, that he made him
Brave me upon the watch; whereon it came
That I was caſt; and even now he ſpake
Iago *ſet* him *on.* *Shakeſp. Othello.*

Thou, traitor, haſt *ſet on* thy wife to this. *Shakeſpeare.*

Baruch *ſetteth* thee *on* againſt us, to deliver us unto the Chaldeans. *Jer.* xliii. 3.

He ſhould be thought to be mad, or *ſet on* and employed by his own or the malice of other men to abuſe the duke. *Claren.*

In oppoſition ſits
Grim death, my ſon and foe, who *ſets* them *on.* *Milton.*

The vengeance of God, and the indignation of men, will join forces againſt an inſulting baſeneſs, when backed with greatneſs and *ſet on* by miſinformation. *South's Serm.*

The ſkill uſed in dreſſing up power, will ſerve only to give a greater edge to man's natural ambition: what can this do but *ſet* men *on* the more eagerly to ſcramble? *Locke.*

A prince's court introduces a kind of luxury, that *ſets* every particular perſon *upon* making a higher figure than is conſiſtent with his revenue. *Addiſon.*

49. *To* SET *on* or *upon.* To attack; to aſſault.

There you miſſing me, I was taken up by pyrates, who putting me under board priſoner, preſently *ſet upon* another ſhip, and maintaining a long fight, in the end put them all to the ſword. *Sidney.*

Caſſio hath here been *ſet on* in the dark:
He's almoſt ſlain, and Rodorigo dead. *Shakeſ. Othello.*

So other foes may *ſet upon* our back. *Shakeſp. H.* VI.

Alphonſus, captain of another of the galleys, ſuffering his men to ſtraggle too far into the land, was *ſet upon* by a Turkiſh pyrate, and taken. *Knolles.*

Of one hundred ſhips there came ſcarce thirty to work: howbeit with them, and ſuch as came daily in, we *ſet upon* them, and gave them the chace. *Bacon's War with Spain.*

If I had been *ſet upon* by villains, I would have redeemed that evil by this which I now ſuffer. *Taylor.*

When once I am *ſet upon*, 'twill be too late to be whetting when I ſhould be fighting. *L'Eſtrange.*

When ſome rival power invades a right,
Flies *ſet on* flies, and turtles turtles fight. *Garth's Diſpenſ.*

50. *To* SET *on.* To employ as in a taſk.

Set on thy wife t' obſerve. *Shakeſp. Othello.*

51. *To* SET *on* or *upon.* To fix the attention; to determine to any thing with ſettled and full reſolution.

It becomes a true lover to have your heart more *ſet upon* her good than your own, and to bear a tenderer reſpect to her honour than your ſatisfaction. *Sidney.*

Some I found wond'rous harſh,
Contemptuous, proud, *ſet on* revenge and ſpite. *Milton.*

52. *To* SET *out.* To aſſign; to allot.

The reſt, unable to ſerve any longer, or willing to fall to thrift, ſhould be placed in part of the lands by them won, at better rate than others, to whom the ſame ſhall be *ſet out.* *Spenſ.*

The ſquaring of a man's thoughts to the lot that providence has *ſet out* for him is a bleſſing. *L'Eſtrange.*

53. *To* SET *out.* To publiſh.

I will uſe no other authority than that excellent proclamation *ſet out* by the king in the firſt year of his reign, and annexed before the book of Common Prayer. *Bacon.*

If all ſhould be *ſet out* to the world by an angry whig, the conſequence muſt be a confinement of our friend for ſome months more to his garret. *Swift.*

54. *To* SET *out.* To mark by boundaries or diſtinctions of ſpace.

Time and place, taken thus for determinate portions of thoſe infinite abyſſes of ſpace and duration, *ſet out*, or ſuppoſed to be diſtinguiſhed from the reſt by known boundaries, have each a twofold acceptation. *Locke.*

55. *To* SET *out.* To adorn; to embelliſh.

An ugly woman, in a rich habit *ſet out* with jewels, nothing can become. *Dryden.*

56. *To* SET *out.* To raiſe; to equip.

The Venetians pretend they could *ſet out*, in caſe of great neceſſity, thirty men of war, a hundred gallies, and ten galeaſſes. *Addiſon on Italy.*

57. *To* SET *out.* To ſhow; to diſplay; to recommend.

Barbaroſſa, in his diſcourſes concerning the conqueſt of Africk, *ſet* him *out* as a moſt fit inſtrument for ſubduing the kingdom of Tunis. *Knolles.*

I could *ſet out* that beſt ſide of Luther, which our author, in the picture he has given us of him, has thrown into ſhade, that he might place a ſuppoſed deformity more in view. *Atterb.*

58. *To* SET *out.* To ſhow; to prove.

Thoſe very reaſons *ſet out* how heinous his ſin was. *Atterb.*

59. *To* SET *up.* To erect; to eſtabliſh newly.

There are many excellent inſtitutions of charity lately *ſet up*, and which deſerve all manner of encouragement, particularly thoſe which relate to the careful and pious education of poor children. *Atterbury's Sermons.*

Who could not win the miſtreſs, woo'd the maid,
Set up themſelves, and drove a ſep'rate trade. *Pope.*

60. *To* SET *up.* To build; to erect.

Their ancient habitations they neglect,
And *ſet up* new: then, if the echo like not
In ſuch a room, they pluck down thoſe. *Ben. Johnſon's Catil.*

Jacob took the ſtone, that he had for his pillow, and *ſet* it *up* for a pillar. *Gen.* xxviii. 18.

Saul *ſet* him *up* a place, and is paſſed on, and gone down to Gilgal. 1 *Sa.* xv. 12.

Such delight hath God in men
Obedient to his will, that he vouchſafes
Among them to *ſet up* his tabernacle. *Milton's Paradiſe Loſt.*

Images were not *ſet up* or worſhipped among the heathens, becauſe they ſuppoſed the gods to be like them. *Stillingfleet.*

Statues were *ſet up* to all thoſe who had made themſelves eminent for any noble action. *Dryden.*

I ſhall ſhew you how to *ſet up* a forge, and what tools you muſt uſe. *Moxon's Mech. Exer.*

Patrons, who ſneak from living worth to dead,
With-hold the penſion, and *ſet up* the head. *Pope.*

61. *To* SET *up.* To raiſe; to exalt; to put in power.

He was ſkilful enough to have lived ſtill, if knowledge could be *ſet up* againſt mortality. *Shakeſpeare.*

I'll tranſlate the kingdom from the houſe of Saul, and *ſet up* the throne of David over Iſrael. 2 *Sa.* iii. 10.

Of thoſe that lead theſe parties, if you could take off the major number, the leſſer would govern; nay, if you could take off all, they would *ſet up* one, and follow him. *Suckling.*

Homer took all occaſions of *ſetting up* his own countrymen the Grecians, and of undervaluing the Trojan chiefs. *Dryd.*

Whatever practical rule is generally broken, it cannot be ſuppoſed innate; it being impoſſible that men ſhould, without ſhame or fear, ſerenely break a rule which they could not but evidently know that God had *ſet up.* *Locke.*

62. *To* SET *up.* To place in view.

He hath taken me by my neck, ſhaken me to pieces, and *ſet* me *up* for his mark. *Job* xvi. 12.

Scarecrows are *ſet up* to keep birds from corn and fruit. *Bac.*

Thy father's merit *ſets* thee *up* to view,
And ſhows thee in the faireſt point of light,
To make thy virtues or thy faults conſpicuous. *Addiſon.*

63. *To* SET *up.* To place in repoſe; to fix; to reſt.

Whilſt we *ſet up* our hopes here, we do not ſo ſeriouſly, as we ought, conſider that God has provided another and better place for us. *Wake.*

64. *To* SET *up.* To raiſe by the voice.

My right eye itches, ſome good luck is near;
Perhaps my Amaryllis may appear;
I'll *ſet up* ſuch a note as ſhe ſhall hear. *Dryden.*

65. *To* SET *up.* To advance; to propoſe to reception.

The authors that *ſet up* this opinion were not themſelves ſatisfied with it. *Burnet's Theory of the Earth.*

66. *To* SET *up.* To raiſe to a ſufficient fortune.

In a ſoldier's life there's honour to be got, and one lucky hit *ſets up* a man for ever. *L'Eſtrange.*

To SET. *v. n.*

1. To fall below the horizon, as the ſun at evening.

The ſun was *ſet.* *Gen.* xxviii. 11.

Whereas the *ſetting* of the pleiades and ſeven ſtars is deſigned the term of Autumn and the beginning of Winter, unto ſome latitudes theſe ſtars do never *ſet.* *Brown's Vulgar Err.*

That ſun once *ſet*, a thouſand meaner ſtars
Gave a dim light to violence and wars. *Waller.*

Now the latter watch of waſting night,
And *ſetting* ſtars, to kindly reſt invite. *Dryden's Æn.*

Not thicker billows beat the Libyan main,
When pale Orion *ſets* in wintry rain,
Than ſtand theſe troops. *Dryden's Æn.*

My eyes no object met,
But diſtant ſkies that in the ocean *ſet.* *Dryden's Ind. Emp.*

The Julian eagles here their wings diſplay,
And there like *ſetting* ſtars the Decii lay. *Garth's Ovid.*

2. To be fixed hard.

A gathering and ſerring of the ſpirits together to reſiſt, maketh the teeth to *ſet* hard one againſt another. *Bacon.*

3. To be extinguiſhed or darkened, as the ſun at night.

Ahijah could not ſee; for his eyes were *ſet*, by reaſon of his age. 1 *Kings* xiv. 4.

4. To

4. To fit musick to words.

That I might sing it, madam, to a tune,
Give me a note: your ladyship can *set*.
—As little by such toys as may be possible. *Shakespeare.*

5. To become not fluid.

That fluid substance in a few minutes begins to *set*, as the tradesmen speak; that is, to exchange its fluidity for firmness. *Boyle.*

6. To begin a journey.

So let him land,
And solemnly see him *set* on to London. *Shakesp H. V.*
On Wednesday next, Harry, thou shalt *set* forward;
On Thursday we ourselves will march. *Shakespeare.*
The king is *set* from London, and the scene
Is now transported to Southampton. *Shakesf. Hen. V.*

7. To go, or pass, or put one's self into any state or posture.

The faithless pirate soon will *set* to sea,
And bear the royal virgin far away. *Dryden.*
When *sets* he forward?
—He is near at hand. *Dryden's Ind Emp.*

He with forty of his gallies, in most warlike manner appointed, *set* forward with Solyman's ambassador towards Constantinople. *Knolles's History of the Turks.*

8. To catch birds with a dog that *sets* them, that is, lies down and points them out; and with a large net.

When I go a hawking or *setting*, I think myself beholden to him that assures me, that in such a field there is a covey of partridges. *Boyle.*

9. To plant, not sow.

In gard'ning ne'er this rule forget,
To sow dry, and *set* wet. *Old Proverb.*

10. It is commonly used in conversation for *sit*, which, though undoubtedly barbarous, is sometimes found in authors.

If they *set* down before's, 'fore they remove,
Bring up your army. *Shakespeare.*

11. To apply one's self.

If he *sets* industriously and sincerely to perform the commands of Christ, he can have no ground of doubting but it shall prove successful to him. *Hammond.*

12. *To* Set *about.* To fall to; to begin.

We find it most hard to convince them, that it is necessary now, at this very present, to *set about* it: we are thought a little too hot and hasty, when we press wicked men to leave their sins to-day, as long as they have so much time before them to do it in. *Calamy's Sermons.*

How preposterous is it, never to *set about* works of charity, whilst we ourselves can see them performed? *Atterbury.*

13. *To* Set *in.* To fix in a particular state.

When the weather was *set in* to be very bad, I have taken a whole day's journey to see a gallery furnished by great masters. *Addison's Spectator.*

As November *set in* with keen frosts, so they continued through the whole of that month, without any other alteration than freezing with more or less severity, as the winds changed. *Ellis's Voyage.*

A storm accordingly happened the following day; for a southern monsoon began to *set in*. *Gulliver's Travels.*

14. *To* Set *on* or *upon.* To begin a march, journey, or enterprize.

Be't your charge
To see perform'd the tenor of our word:
Set on. *Shakespeare's Henry IV.*

He that would seriously *set upon* the search of truth, ought to prepare his mind with a love of it. *Locke.*

The understanding would presently obtain the knowledge it is about, and then *set upon* some new inquiry. *Locke.*

15. *To* Set *on.* To make an attack.

Hence every leader to his charge;
For on their answer we will *set on* them. *Shak. Hen. IV.*

16. *To* Set *out.* To have beginning.

If any invisible casualty there be, it is questionable whether its activity only *set out* at our nativity, and began not rather in the womb. *Brown's Vulg. Errours.*

The dazzling lustre to abate,
He *set* not *out* in all his pomp and state,
Clad in the mildest lightning. *Addison.*

17. *To* Set *out.* To begin a journey.

At their *setting out* they must have their commission from the king. *Bacon.*

I shall put you in mind where you promised to *set out*, or begin your first stage. *Hammond.*

Me thou think'st not slow,
Who since the morning-hour *set out* from heav'n,
Where God resides, and ere mid-day arriv'd
In Eden. *Milton's Parad. Lost.*
My soul then mov'd the quicker pace;
Your's first *set out*, mine reach'd her in the race. *Dryden.*

These doctrines, laid down for foundations of any science, were called principles, as the beginnings from which we must *set out*, and look no farther backwards. *Locke.*

He that *sets out* upon weak legs will not only go farther, but grow stronger too, than one who with firm limbs only sits still. *Locke.*

For these reasons I shall *set out* for London to-morrow. *Add.*

Look no more on man in the first stage of his existence, in his *setting out* for eternity. *Addison.*

If we slacken our arms, and drop our oars, we shall be hurried back to the place from whence we first *set out*. *Addison.*

18. *To* Set *out.* To begin the world.

Eudoxus, at his first *setting out*, threw himself into court. *Addison's Spectator.*

Eugenio *set out* from the same university, and about the same time with Corusodes. *Swift.*

19. *To* Set *to.* To apply himself to.

I may appeal to some, who have made this their business, whether it go not against the hair with them to *set to* any thing else. *Government of the Tongue.*

20. *To* Set *up.* To begin a trade openly.

We have stock enough to *set up* with, capable of infinite advancement, and yet no less capable of total decay. *Decay of Piety.*

A man of a clear reputation, though his bark be split, yet he saves his cargo; has something left towards *setting up* again, and so is in capacity of receiving benefit not only from his own industry, but the friendship of others. *Gov. of the Tongue.*

Those who have once made their court to those mistresses without portions, the muses, are never like to *set up* for fortunes. *Pope.*

This habit of writing and discoursing was acquired during my apprenticeship in London, and a long residence there after I had *set up* for myself. *Swift.*

21. *To* Set *up.* To begin a project of advantage.

Eumenes, one of Alexander's captains, *setting up* for himself after the death of his master, persuaded his principal officers to lend him great sums; after which they were forced to follow him for their own security. *Arbuthnot.*

A severe treatment might tempt them to *set up* for a republick. *Addison on Italy.*

22. *To* Set *up.* To profess publickly.

Scow'ring the watch grows out of fashion wit;
Now we *set up* for tilting in the pit. *Dryden.*
Can Polyphemus, or Antiphates,
Who gorge themselves with man,
Set up to teach humanity, and give,
By their example, rules for us to live? *Dryd. Juvenal.*

It is found by experience, that those men who *set up* for morality, without regard to religion, are generally but virtuous in part. *Swift.*

Set. *part. adj.* [from the verb.] Regular; not lax; made in consequence of some formal rule.

Rude am I in my speech,
And little bless'd with the *set* phrase of peace. *Shak. Othello.*
Th' inditement of the good lord Hastings,
In a *set* hand fairly is ingross'd. *Shakes. Richard III.*

He would not perform that service by the hazard of one *set* battle, but by dallying off the time. *Knolles.*

Set speeches, and a formal tale,
With none but statesmen and grave fools prevail. *Dryden.*
In ten *set* battles have we driv'n back
These heathen Saxons, and regain'd our earth. *Dryden.*

What we hear in conversation has this general advantage over *set* discourses, that in the latter we are apt to attend more to the beauty and elegance of the composure than to the matter delivered. *Rogers.*

Set. *n. s.* [from the verb.]

1. A number of things suited to each other; a number of things of which one cannot conveniently be separated from the rest.

Sensations and passions seem to depend upon a particular *set* of motions. *Collier.*

All corpuscles of the same *set* or kind agree in every thing. *Woodward.*

'Tis not a *set* of features or complexion,
The tincture of a skin, that I admire. *Addison.*

I shall here lay together a new *set* of remarks, and observe the artifices of our enemies to raise such prejudices. *Addison.*

Homer introduced that monstrous character to show the marvellous, and paint it in a new *set* of colours. *Broome.*

He must change his comrades;
In half the time he talks them round,
There must another *set* be found. *Swift.*

They refer to those criticks who are partial to some particular *set* of writers to the prejudice of others. *Pope.*

Perhaps there is no man, nor *set* of men, upon earth, whose sentiments I intirely follow. *Watts.*

2. Any thing not sown, but put in a state of some growth into the ground.

'Tis raised by *sets* or berries, like white thorn, and lies the same time in the ground. *Mortimer's Husbandry.*

3. The apparent fall of the sun, or other bodies of heaven, below the horizon.

The weary sun hath made a golden *set*;
And, by the bright track of his firy car,
Gives signal of a goodly day to-morrow. *Shak. R. III.*
When the battle's lost and won.
—That will be ere *set* of sun. *Shakesp. Macbeth.*

Before *set* of sun that day, I hope to reach my Winter-quarters. *Atterbury to Pope.*

4. A wager at dice.
That was but civil war, an equal *set*,
Where piles with piles, and eagles eagles fight. *Dryden.*

5. A game.
Have I not here the best cards for the game,
To win this easy match plaid for a crown?
And shall I now give o'er the yielded *set*? *Shakespeare.*
When we have match'd our rackets to these balls,
We will, in France, play a *set*
Shall strike his father's crown into the hazard. *Shak. H. V.*

SETA'CEOUS. *adj* [*seta*, Latin.] Bristly; set with strong hairs; consisting of strong hairs.

The parent insect, with its stiff *setaceous* tail, terebrates the rib of the leaf when tender, and makes way for its egg into the very pith. *Derham.*

SE'TON. *n. s.* [*seton*, French, from *seta*, Latin.]

A *seton* is made when the skin is taken up with a needle, and the wound kept open by a twist of silk or hair, that humours may vent themselves. Farriers call this operation in cattle rowelling. *Quincy.*

I made a *seton* to give a vent to the humour. *Wiseman.*

If the sinus be of great length depending, make a perforation in the lower part by a *seton*-needle with a twisted silk. *Wiseman's Surgery.*

SETTE'E. *n. s.* A large long seat with a back to it.

SE'TTER. *n. s.* [from *set*.]

1. One who sets.

When he was gone I cast this book away: I could not look upon it but with weeping eyes, in remembering him who was the only *setter* on to do it. *Ascham.*

Shameless Warwick, peace!
Proud *setter* up and puller down of kings! *Shakesp. H. VI.*

He seemeth to be a *setter* forth of strange gods. *Acts* xvii.

2. A dog who beats the field, and points the bird for the sportsmen.

3. A man who performs the office of a setting dog, or finds out persons to be plundered.

Another set of men are the devil's *setters*, who continually beat their brains how to draw in some innocent unguarded heir into their hellish net, learning his humour, prying into his circumstances, and observing his weak side. *South.*

SE'TTERWORT. *n. s.* An herb; a species of hellebore.

SE'TTING *Dog. n. s.* [*cane sentacchione*, Ital. *setting* and *dog*.] A dog taught to find game, and point it out to the sportsman.

Will obliges young heirs with a *setting dog* he has made himself. *Addison.*

SE'TTLE. *n. s.* [ꞅetol, Sax.] A seat; a bench; something to sit on.

From the bottom to the lower *settle* shall be two cubits. *Ezek.* xliii. 14.

The man, their hearty welcome first exprest,
A common *settle* drew for either guest,
Inviting each his weary limbs to rest. *Dryden.*

To SE'TTLE. *v. a.* [from the noun.]

1. To place in any certain state after a time of fluctuation or disturbance.

I will *settle* you after your old estates, and will do better unto you than at your beginnings. *Ezek.* xxxvi. 11.

In hope to find
Better abode, and my afflicted powers
To *settle* here. *Milton.*

2. To fix in any way of life.
The father thought the time drew on
Of *settling* in the world his only son. *Dryden.*

3. To fix in any place.
Settl'd in his face I see
Sad resolution. *Milton.*

4. To establish; to confirm.
Justice submitted to what Abra pleas'd:
Her will alone could *settle* or revoke,
And law was fix'd by what she latest spoke. *Prior.*

5. To determine; to affirm; to free from ambiguity.

This exactness will be judged troublesome, and therefore most men will think they may be excused from *settling* the complex ideas of mixed modes so precisely in their minds. *Locke.*

Medals give a very great light to history, in confirming such passages as are true in old authors, and *settling* such as are told after different manners. *Addison.*

6. To fix; to make certain or unchangeable.
His banish'd gods restor'd to rites divine,
And *settl'd* sure succession in his line. *Dryden's Æn.*

If you will not take some care to *settle* our language, and put it into a state of continuance, your memory shall not be preserved above an hundred years, further than by imperfect tradition. *Swift.*

7. To fix; not to suffer to continue doubtful in opinion, or desultory and wavering in conduct.

This, by a *settled* habit in things, whereof we have frequent experience, is performed so quick, that we take that for the perception of our sensation which is an idea formed by our judgment. *Locke.*

A pamphlet that talks of slavery, France, and the pretender; they desire no more: it will *settle* the wavering, and confirm the doubtful. *Swift.*

8. To make close or compact.

Cover ant-hills up, that the rain may *settle* the turf before the Spring. *Mortimer's Husbandry.*

9. To fix unalienably by legal sanctions.

I have given him the parsonage of the parish, and, because I know his value, have *settled* upon him a good annuity for life. *Addison's Spectator.*

10. To fix inseparably.

Exalt your passion by directing and *settling* it upon an object, the due contemplation of whose loveliness may cure perfectly all hurts received from mortal beauty. *Boyle.*

11. To affect so as that the dregs or impurities sink to the bottom.
So do the winds and thunders cleanse the air;
So working seas *settle* and purge the wine. *Davies.*

12. To compose; to put into a state of calmness.

When thou art *settling* thyself to thy devotions, imagine thou hearest thy Saviour calling to thee, as he did to Martha, Why art thou so careful? *Duppa.*

To SE'TTLE. *v. n.*

1. To subside; to sink to the bottom and repose there.
This is mere moral babble, and direct
Against the canon laws of our foundation:
I must not suffer this; yet 'tis the lees
And *settlings* of a melancholy blood. *Milton.*

2. To lose motion or fermentation; to deposite fæces at the bottom.
Your fury then boil'd upward to a foam;
But since this message came, you sink and *settle*,
As if cold water had been pour'd upon you. *Dryden.*

A government, upon such occasions, is always thick before it *settles*. *Addison's Freeholder.*

3. To fix one's self; to establish a residence.

The Spinetæ, descended from the Pelesgi, *settled* at the mouth of the river Po. *Arbuthnot.*

4. To chuse a method of life; to establish a domestick state.
As people marry now, and *settle*,
Fierce love abates his usual mettle;
Worldly desires, and houshold cares,
Disturb the godhead's soft affairs. *Prior.*

5. To become fixed so as not to change.

The wind came about and *settled* in the West, so as we could make no way. *Bacon.*

6. To quit an irregular and desultory for a methodical life.

7. To take any lasting state.

That country became a gained ground by the mud brought down by the Nilus, which *settled* by degrees into a firm land. *Brown's Vulgar Errours.*

According to laws established by the divine wisdom, it was wrought by degrees from one form into another, 'till it *settled* at length into an habitable earth. *Burnet.*

Chyle, before it circulates with the blood, is whitish: by the force of circulation it runs through all the intermediate colours, 'till it *settles* in an intense red. *Arbuthnot.*

8. To rest; to repose.

When time hath worn out their natural vanity, and taught them discretion, their fondness *settles* on its proper object. *Spect.*

Warm'd in the brain the brazen weapon lies,
And shades eternal *settle* o'er his eyes. *Pope.*

9. To grow calm.
'Till the fury of his highness *settle*,
Come not before him. *Shakespeare's Winter's Tale.*

10. To make a jointure for a wife.
He sighs with most success that *settles* well. *Garth.*

11. To crack as work sinks.

One part being moist, and the other dry, occasions its *settling* more in one place than another, which causes cracks and *settlings* in the wall. *Mortimer's Husbandry.*

SE'TTLEDNESS. *n. s.* [from *settle*.] The state of being settled; confirmed state.

What one party thought to rivet to a *settledness* by the strength and influence of the Scots, that the other rejects and contemns. *King Charles.*

SE'TTLEMENT. *n. s.* [from *settle*.]

1. The act of settling; the state of being settled.

2. The act of giving possession by legal sanction.
My flocks, my fields, my woods, my pastures take,
With *settlement* as good as law can make. *Dryden.*

3. A

3. A jointure granted to a wife.

Strephon sigh'd so loud and strong,
He blew a *settlement* along;
And bravely drove his rivals down
With coach and six, and house in town. *Swift.*

4. Subsidence; dregs.

Fullers earth left a thick *settlement.* *Mortimer's Husbandry.*

5. Act of quitting a roving for a domestick and methodical life.

Every man living has a design in his head upon wealth, power, or *settlement* in the world. *L'Estrange.*

6. A colony; a place where a colony is established.

SE'TWAL. *n. s.* An herb. *Dict.*

SE'VEN. *adj.* [ſeoꝼon, Saxon.]

1. Four and three; one more than six. It is commonly used in poetry as one syllable.

Let ev'ry man be master of his time
'Till *seven* at night. *Shakesp. Macbeth.*

Of every clean beast thou shalt take to thee by *sevens.* *Gen.*

Pharmis, king of the Medes, it is said, he overthrew and cruelly murdered, with his *seven* children. *Raleigh.*

Sev'n bullocks, yet unyok'd, for Phœbus chuse;
And for Diana *sev'n* unspotted ewes. *Dryden's Æn.*

SE'VENFOLD. *adj.* [*seven* and *fold.*] Repeated seven times; having seven doubles.

Upon this dreadful beast with *sevenfold* head,
He set the false Duessa for more awe and dread. *Fa. Queen.*

The *sevenfold* shield of Ajax cannot keep
The battery from my heart. *Shakes. Ant. and Cleopat.*

Not for that silly old morality,
That as these links were knit, our loves should be,
Mourn I, that I thy *sevenfold* chain have lost,
Nor for the luck's sake, but the bitter cost. *Donne.*

What if the breath that kindled those grim fires
Awak'd, should blow them into *sevenfold* rage. *Milton.*

Fair queen,
Who sway'st the sceptre of the Pharian isle,
And *sev'nfold* falls of disemboguing Nile. *Dryden.*

SE'VENFOLD. *adv.* Seven times.

Whosoever slayeth Cain, vengeance shall be taken on him *sevenfold.* *Gen.* iv. 15.

Wrath meet thy flight *sevenfold.* *Milton.*

SE'VENNIGHT. *n. s.* [*seven* and *night.*]

1. A week; the time from one day of the week to the next day of the same denomination preceding or following; a week, numbered according to the practice of the old northern nations, as in *fortnight.*

Rome was either more grateful to the beholders, or more noble in itself, than justs with the sword and lance, maintained for a *sevennight* together. *Sidney.*

Iago's footing here anticipates our thoughts
A *se'nnight's* speed. *Shak. Othello.*

Shining woods, laid in a dry room, within a *sevennight* lost their shining. *Bacon's Natural History.*

2. We use still the word *sevennight* or *se'nnight* in computing time: as, it happened on Monday was *sevennight,* that is, *on the Monday before last Monday*; it will be done on Monday *sevennight,* that is, *on the Monday after next Monday.*

This comes from one of those untucker'd ladies whom you were so sharp upon on Monday was *se'ennight.* *Addis.*

SE'VENSCORE. *adj.* [*Seven* and *score.*] Seven times twenty; an hundred and forty.

The old countess of Desmond, who lived till she was *sevenscore* years old, did dentire twice or thrice; casting her old teeth, and others coming in their place. *Bacon.*

SE'VENTEEN. *adj.* [ſeoꝼontyne, Saxon.] Seven and ten; seven added to ten.

SE'VENTEENTH. *adj.* [ſeoꝼonteoþa, Saxon.] The seventh after the tenth; the ordinal of seventeen.

In the six hundredth year of Noah's life, the second month, the *seventeenth* day, were all the fountains of the great deep broken up. *Gen.* vii. 11.

The conquest of Ireland was perfected by the king in the *seventeenth* year of his reign. *Judge Hale.*

SE'VENTH. *adj.* [ſeoꝼoþa, Saxon.] The ordinal of seven; the first after the sixth.

The child born in the *seventh* month doth commonly well. *Bacon.*

So Pharaoh, or some greater king than he,
Provided for the *seventh* necessity:
Taught from above his magazines to frame;
That famine was prevented e'er it came. *Dryd.*

2. Containing one part in *seven.*

Thy air is like the first:
A third is like the former. Filthy hags!
Why do you shew me this? A fourth? Start, eye!
What! will the line stretch to the crack of doom?
Another yet? A *seventh!* I'll see no more. *Shakesp.*

SE'VENTHLY. *adv.* [From *seventh.*] In the seventh place; an ordinal adverb.

Seventhly, living bodies have sense, which plants have not. *Bacon.*

SE'VENTIETH. *adj.* [From *seventy.*] The tenth seven times repeated; the ordinal of seventy.

SE'VENTY. *adj.* [Hanbreoꝼontiᵹ, Saxon.] Seven times ten.

Worthy Marcius,
Had we no quarrel else to Rome, but that
Thou art thence banish'd, we would master all,
From twelve to *seventy.* *Shakesp. Coriolanus.*

We call not that death immature, if a man lives till *seventy.* *Taylor.*

The weight of *seventy* winters prest him down,
He bent beneath the burthen of a crown. *Dryd.*

In the Hebrew, there is a particle consisting but of one single letter, of which there are reckoned up *seventy* several significations. *Locke.*

To SE'VER. *v. a.* [*sevrer,* French; *separo,* Latin.]

1. To part by violence from the rest.

Forgetful queen, who *severed* that bright head,
Which charm'd two mighty monarchs to her bed. *Granv.*

2. To divide; to part; to force asunder.

They are not so far disjoined and *severed,* but that they come at length to meet. *Hooker.*

Fortune, divorce
Pomp from the bearer, 'tis a suff'rance panging,
As soul and body's *sev'ring.* *Shakesp. Hen.* VIII.

Our force by land
Hath nobly held; our *sever'd* navy too
Have knit again, and float. *Shakesp. Ant. and Cleop.*

What thou art is mine:
Our state cannot be *sever'd,* we are one,
One flesh; to lose thee were to lose myself. *Milton.*

3. To separate; to put in different orders or places.

The angels shall *sever* the wicked from among the just. *Mat.*

He, with his guide, the farther fields attain'd;
Where *sever'd* from the rest the warrior souls remain'd. *Dryd.*

4. To separate by chimical operation.

This axiom is of large extent, and would be *severed* and refined by trial. *Bacon.*

5. To disjoin, to disunite.

Look, love, what envious streaks
Do lace the *severing* clouds in yonder east. *Shakesp.*

How stiff is my vile sense,
That I stand up and have ingenious feeling
Of my huge sorrows! better I were distract,
So should my thoughts be *sever'd* from my griefs;
And woes by wrong imaginations, lose
The knowledge of themselves. *Shakesp.*

The medical virtues lodge in some one or other of its principles, and may therefore usefully be sought for in that principle *sever'd* from the others. *Boyle.*

6. To keep distinct; to keep apart.

Three glorious suns, each one a perfect sun;
Not separated with the racking clouds,
But *sever'd* in a pale clear-shining sky. *Shakesp.*

I will *sever* Goshen, that no swarms of flies shall be there. *Exod.* viii. 22.

To SE'VER. *v. n.* To make a separation; to make a partition.

The Lord shall *sever* between the cattle of Israel and of Egypt. *Exod.* ix. 4.

There remains so much religion, as to know how to *sever* between the use and abuse of things. *K. Charles.*

Better from me thou *sever* not. *Milton.*

SE'VERAL *adj.* [from *sever.*]

1. Different; distinct; unlike one another.

Divers sorts of beasts came from *several* parts to drink; and so being refreshed, fall to couple, and many times with *several* kinds. *Bacon's Nat. Hist.*

The conquest of *Ireland* was made piece and piece, by *several* attempts, in *several* ages. *Davies's Hist. of Ireland.*

Four *several* armies to the field are led,
Which high in equal hopes four princes head. *Dryd.*

2. Divers; many. It is used in any number not large, and more than two.

This country is large, having in it many people, and *several* kingdoms. *Abbot's Descript. of the World.*

This else to *several* spheres thou must ascribe. *Milton.*

We might have repaired the losses of one campaign by the advantages of another, and after *several* victories gained over us, might have still kept the enemy from our gates. *Addis.*

3. Particular; single.

Each *several* ship a victory did gain,
As Rupert, or as Albemarle were there. *Dryd.*

4. Distinct; appropriate.

The parts and passages of state are so many, as to express them fully, would require a *several* treatise. *Davies's Ireland.*

Like things to like, the rest to *several* place
Disparted. *Milton.*

Each might his *sev'ral* province well command,
Would all but stoop to what they understand. *Pope.*

SE'VERAL. *n. s.* [from the *adj.*]

1. A state of separation; or partition. This substantive has a plural.

More

More profit is quieter found
Where pastures in *several* be,
Of one silly aker of ground
Than champion maketh of three. *Tusser. Husband.*

2. Each particular singly taken.

This by some *severals*
Of head-piece extraordinary, lower messes
Perchance are to this business purblind. *Shakesp.*

There was not time enough to hear
The *severals*. *Shakesp.*

That will appear to be a methodical successive observation of these *severals*, as degrees and steps preparative the one to the other. *Hammond's Fundamentals.*

Several of them neither rose from any conspicuous family, nor left any behind them. *Addison's Freeholer.*

3. Any inclosed or separate place.

They had their *several* for heathen nations, their *several* for the people of their own nation, their *several* for men, their *several* for women, their *several* for their priests, and for the high priest alone their *several*. *Hooker.*

4. Inclosed ground.

There was a nobleman that was lean of visage, but immediately after his marriage he grew pretty plump and fat. One said to him, your lordship doth contrary to other married men; for they at first wax lean, and you wax fat. Sir Walter Raleigh stood by and said, there is no beast, that if you take him from the common, and put him into the *several*, but will wax fat. *Bacon.*

SE'VERALLY. *adv.* [from *several.*] Distinctly; particularly; separately; apart from others.

Consider angels each of them *severally* in himself, and their law is, all ye his angels praise him. *Hooker.*

Nature and scripture, both jointly and not *severally*, either of them, be so compleat, that unto everlasting felicity we need not the knowledge of any thing more than these two may easily furnish our minds with. *Hooker.*

Th' apostles could not be confin'd
To these or those, but *severally* design'd
Their large commission round the world to blow. *Dryd.*

We ought not so much to love likeness as beauty, and to chuse from the fairest bodies *severally* the fairest parts. *Dryd.*

Others were so very small and close together, that I could not keep my eye stedy on them *severally* so as to number them. *Newt. Opt.*

SE'VERALTY. *n.s.* [from *several.*] State of separation from the rest.

The jointure or advancement of the lady was the third part of the principality of Wales, the dukedom of Cornwal, and earldom of Chester, to be set forth in *severalty*. *Bacon.*

Having considered the apertions in *severalty*, according to their particular requisites, I am now come to the casting and contexture of the whole work. *Wotton.*

SE'VERANCE. *n.s.* [from *sever.*] Separation; partition.

Those rivers enclose a neck of land, in regard of his fruitfulness, not unworthy of a *severance*. *Carew's Survey of Cornw.*

SEVE'RE. *n.s.* [*severe*, French; *severus*, Latin.]

1. Sharp; apt to punish; censorious; apt to blame; hard; rigorous.

Let your zeal, if it must be expressed in anger, be always more *severe* against thy self than against others. *Taylor.*

Soon mov'd with touch of blame, thus Eve:
What words have pass'd thy lips, Adam *severe?* *Milton.*

What made the church of Alexandria be so *severe* with Origen for, but holding the incence in his hands, which those about him cast from thence upon the altar? yet for this he was cast out of the church. *Stillingfleet.*

2. Rigid; austere; morose; harsh; not indulgent.

Am I upbraided? not enough *severe*
It seems, in thy restraint. *Milton.*

In his looks serene,
When angry most he seem'd and most *severe*,
What else but favour shone? *Milton.*

Nor blame *severe* his choice,
Warbling the Grecian woes. *Pope's Odyssey.*

3. Cruel; inexorable.

His *severe* wrath shall he sharpen for a sword. *Wisd.*

4. Regulated by rigid rules; strict.

Truth, wisdom, sanctitude, *severe* and pure,
Severe, but in true filial freedom plac'd. *Milton.*

5. Exempt from all levity of appearance; grave; sober; sedate.

Your looks must alter, as your subject does,
From kind to fierce, from wanton to *severe*. *Waller.*

6. Not lax; not airy; close; strictly methodical; rigidly exact.

His grave rebuke,
Severe in youthful beauty, added grace. *Milton.*

Their beauty I leave it rather to the delicate wit of poets, than venture upon so nice a subject with my *severer* style. *More.*

7. Painful; afflictive.

8. Close; concise; not luxuriant.

The Latin, a most *severe* and compendious language, often expresses that in one word, which modern tongues cannot in more. *Dryden.*

These piercing fires as soft as now *severe*. *Milton.*

SEVE'RELY. *adv.* [from *severe.*]

1. Painfully; afflictively.

We have wasted our strength to attain ends different from those for which we undertook the war, and often to effect others which after a peace, we may *severely* repent. *Swift.*

2. Ferociously; horridly.

More formidable Hydra stands within;
Whose jaws with iron teeth *severely* grin. *Dryd.*

SEVE'RITY. *n.s.* [*severitas*, Latin.]

1. Cruel treatment; sharpness of punishment.

I laugh to see your ladyship so fond,
To think that you have ought but Talbot's shadow
Whereon to practise your *severity*. *Shakesp.*

He shall be thrown down the Tarpeian rock
With rigorous hands; he hath resisted law,
And therefore law shall scorn him further trial
Than the *severity* of publick power,
Which he so sets at nought. *Shakesp. Coriolanus.*

Never were so great rebellions expiated with so little blood; as for the *severity* used upon those taken in Kent, it was but upon a scum of people. *Bacon.*

There is a difference between an ecclesiastical censure and *severity*: for under a censure we only include excommunication, suspension, and an interdict; but under an ecclesiastical *severity*, every other punishment of the church is intended; but according to some, a censure and a *severity* is the same. *Ayliffe.*

2. Hardness; power of distressing.

Though nature hath given insects sagacity to avoid the winter cold, yet its *severity* finds them out. *Hale's Orig. of Mank.*

3. Strictness; rigid accuracy.

Confining myself to the *severity* of truth, becoming, I must pass over many instances of your military skill. *Dryd.*

4. Rigour; austerity; harshness; want of mildness; want of indulgence.

SE'VOCATION. *n.s.* [*sevoco*, Latin.] The act of calling aside.

To SEW for *sue*. *Spenser.* To follow.

To SEW. *v.n.* [*suo*, Latin.] To any thing by the use of the needle.

A time to rent and a time to *sew*. *Eccl.* iii. 7.

To SEW. *v.a.* To join by threads drawn with a needle.

No man *seweth* a piece of new cloth on an old garment. *Mark.* ii. 21.

To SEW *up*. To inclose in any thing sewed.

If ever I said loose bodied gown, *sew* me *up* in the skirts of it. *Shakespeare's Taming of the Shrew.*

My transgression is sealed up in a bag, and thou *sewest up* mine iniquity. *Job.* xiv. 17.

To SEW. *v.a.* To drain a pond for the fish. *Ainsworth.*

SEWER. *v.n.* [*escuyer trenchant*, French; or *asseour*, old French; from *asseoir*, to set down; for those officers set the dishes on the table. *Newton's Milton.*]

1. An officer who serves up a feast.

Marshall'd feast,
Serv'd up in hall with *sewers* and seneshals:
The skill of artifice or office mean. *Milt.*

The cook and *sewer*, each his talent tries,
In various figures scenes of dishes rise:

2. [From *issue*, *issuer.*] *Cowel.* A passage for water to run through, now corrupted to *shore*.

The fenmen hold that the *sewers* must be kept so, as the water may not stay too long in the spring till the weeds and sedge be grown up. *Bacon.*

Men suffer their private in judgment to be drawn into the common *sewer*, or stream of the present vogue. *K. Charles.*

As one who long in populous city pent,
Where houses thick, and *sewers* annoy the air,
Forth issuing on a summer's morn, to breathe
Among the pleasant villages and farms
Adjoin'd, from each thing met conceives delight. *Milt.*

3. He that uses a needle.

SEX. *n.s.* [*sexe*, French; *sexus*, Latin.]

1. The property by which any animal is male or female.

These two great *sexes* animate the world. *Milton.*

Under his forming hands a creature grew,
Manlike, but different *sex*. *Milton.*

2. Womankind; by way of emphasis.

Unhappy *sex!* whose beauty is your snare;
Expos'd to trials; made too frail to bear. *Dryd.*

Shame is hard to be overcome; but if the *sex* once get the better of it, it gives them afterwards no more trouble. *Garth.*

SE'XAGENARY. *adj.* [*sexagenaire*, French; *sexagenarius*, Latin.] Aged sixty years.

SEXAGE'SIMA. *n.s.* [Latin.] The second Sunday before Lent.

SEXAGE'SIMAL. *adj.* [from *sexagesimus*, Latin.] Sixtieth; numbred by sixties.

SEXA'NGLED. } *adj.* [from *sex* and *angular*, Latin.] Having
SEXA'NGULAR. } six corners or angles; hexagonal.

Snow *sexangular*, at least of starry and many pointed figure.

The grubs from their *sexangular* abode
Crawl out unfinish'd like the maggot's brood. *Dryd.*

SEXA'NGULARLY. *adv.* [from *sexangular.*] With six angles; hexagonally.

SEXE'NNIAL. *adj.* [*sex* and *annus*, Latin.] Lasting six years; happening once in six years.

SE'XTAIN. *n. ſ.* [from *ſextans, ſex*, Latin.] A ſtanza of ſix lines.

SE'XTANT. *n. ſ.* [*ſextant*, French.] The ſixth part of a circle.

SE'XTARY. *n. ſ.* A pint and a half.

SE'XTARY. } *n. ſ.* The ſame as ſacriſty; a veſtry. *Dict.*
SE'XTRY. }

SE'XTILE. *adj* [*ſextilis*, Latin.] Is ſuch a poſition or aſpect of two planets, when at 60 degrees diſtant, or at the diſtance of two ſigns from one another, and is marked thus *. *Har.*

Planetary motions and aſpects,
In *ſextile*, ſquare, and trine, *Milton.*

The moon receives the duſky light we diſcern in its *ſextile* aſpect from the earth's benignity. *Glanville.*

SE'XTON. *n. ſ.* [corrupted from *ſacriſtan.*] An under-officer of the church, whoſe buſineſs is to dig graves.

A ſtool and cuſhion for the *ſexton*. *Shakeſp.*

When any dies, then by tolling a bell, or beſpeaking a grave of the *ſexton*, the ſame is known to the ſearchers correſponding with the ſaid *ſexton*. *Graunt.*

SE'XTONSHIP. *n. ſ.* [from *ſexton.*] The office of a ſexton.

They may get a diſpenſation to hold the clerkſhip and *ſextonſhip* of their own pariſh in commendam. *Swift.*

SEXTU'PLE. *adj* [*ſextuplus*, Latin.] Sixfold; ſix times told.

Man's length being a perpendicular from the vertex unto the ſole of the foot is *ſextuple* unto his breadth, or a right line drawn from the ribs of one ſide to another. *Brown.*

To SHAB. *v.n.* To play mean tricks; a low barbarous cant word.

SHA'BBILY. *adv.* [from *ſhabby.*] Meanly; reproachfully; deſpicably; paltrily. A cant word.

SHA'BBINESS. *n. ſ.* [from *ſhabby.*] Meanneſs; paltrineſs.

He exchanged his gay *ſhabbineſs* of cloaths fit for a much younger man, to warm ones that would be decent for a much older one. *Addiſ. Spectator.*

SHA'BBY. *adj.* [A word that has crept into converſation and low writing; but ought not to be admitted into the language.] Mean; paltry.

The dean was ſo *ſhabby*, and look'd like a ninny,
That the captain ſuppos'd he was curate to Jenny. *Swift.*

To SHA'CKLE. *v. a.* [from the noun, *ſhackles, ſhaeckelen*, Dutch.] To chain; to fetter; to bind.

It is great,
To do that thing that ends all other deeds;
Which *ſhackles* accidents, and bolts up change. *Shakeſp.*

You muſt not *ſhackle* and tie him up with rules about indifferent matters. *Locke.*

No trivial price
Should ſet him free, or ſmall ſhould be my praiſe
To lead him *ſhackled*. *Philips.*

So the ſtretch'd cord the *ſhackled* dancer tries,
As prone to fall as impotent to riſe. *Smith.*

SHA'CKLES. *n. ſ.* wanting the ſingular. [ꞅeacul, Saxon, *ſchaeckels*, Dutch.] Fetters; gyves; chains for priſoners.

Himſelf he frees by ſecret means unſeen,
His *ſhackles* empty left, himſelf eſcaped clean. *Fa. Queen.*

A ſervant commonly is leſs free in mind than in condition; his very will ſeems to be in bonds and *ſhackles*, and deſire itſelf under durance and captivity. *South's Sermons.*

The forge in fetters only is employed;
Our iron mines exhauſted and deſtroyed
In *ſhackles*. *Dryd. Juv.*

SHAD. *n. ſ.* A kind of fiſh.

SHADE. *n. ſ.* [ꞅcabu, Saxon; *ſchade*, Dutch.]

1. The cloud or opacity made by interception of the light.

Spring no obſtacle found here nor *ſhade*,
But all ſunſhine. *Milton.*

2. Darkneſs; obſcurity.

The weaker light unwillingly declin'd,
And to prevailing *ſhades* the murmuring world reſign'd. *Roſc.*

3. Coolneſs made by interception of the ſun.

Antigonus, when told that the enemy had ſuch volleys of arrows that hid the ſun, ſaid, that falls out well; for this is hot weather, and ſo we ſhall fight in the *ſhade*. *Bacon.*

That high mount of God whence light and *ſhade*
Shine both. *Milton.*

4. An obſcure place, properly in a grove or cloſe wood by which the light is excluded.

Let us ſeek out ſome deſolate *ſhade*, and there
Weep our ſad boſoms empty. *Shakeſp.*

Regions of ſorrow, doleful *ſhades*. *Milton.*

Then to the deſart takes his flight;
Where ſtill from *ſhade* to *ſhade* the ſon of God,
After forty days faſting, had remain'd. *Milton.*

The pious prince then ſeeks the *ſhade*,
Which hides from ſight his venerable maid. *Dryd.*

5. Screen cauſing an excluſion of light or heat; umbrage.

Let the arched knife
Well ſharpen'd now aſſail the ſpreading *ſhades*
Of vegetables, and their thirſty limbs diſſever. *Philips.*

In Brazil are trees which kill thoſe that ſit under their *ſhade* in a few hours. *Arbuthnot.*

6. Protection; ſhelter.

7. The parts of a picture not brightly coloured.

'Tis ev'ry painter's art to hide from ſight,
And caſt in *ſhades* what ſeen would not delight. *Dryd.*

8. A colour; gradation of light.

White, red, yellow, blue, with their ſeveral degrees, or *ſhades* and mixtures, as green come in only by the eyes. *Locke.*

9. The figure formed upon any ſurface correſponding to the body by which the light is intercepted.

Envy will merit as its *ſhade* purſue. *Pope.*

10. The ſoul ſeparated from the body; ſo called as ſuppoſed by the ancients to be perceptible to the ſight, not to the touch. A ſpirit; a ghoſt; manes.

To Trachin ſwift as thought the flitting *ſhade*
Thro' air his momentary journey made. *Dryd.*

Ne'er to theſe chambers where the mighty reſt,
Since their foundation, came a nobler gueſt;
Nor e'er was to the bow'rs of bliſs convey'd
A fairer ſpirit or more welcome *ſhade*. *Tickell.*

To SHADE. *v. a.* [from the noun.]

1. To overſpread with opacity.

Thou *ſhad'ſt*
The full blaze of thy beams, and through a cloud
Thy ſkirts appear. *Milton.*

2. To cover from the light or heat; to overſpread.

A ſeraph ſix wings wore to *ſhade*
His lineaments divine. *Milton.*

And after theſe, came arm'd with ſpear and ſhield
An hoſt ſo great, as cover'd all the field:
And all their foreheads like the knights before,
With lawrels ever-green were *ſhaded* o'er. *Dryd.*

I went to crop the ſylvan ſcenes,
And *ſhade* our altars with their leafy greens. *Dryd.*

Sing, while beſide the *ſhaded* tomb I mourn,
And with freſh bays her rural ſhrine adorn. *Pope's Wint.*

3. To ſhelter; to hide.

E're in our own houſe I do *ſhade* my head,
The good patricians muſt be viſited. *Shakeſp.*

4. To protect; to cover; to ſcreen.

Leave not the faithful ſide
That gave thee being, ſtill *ſhades* thee and protects. *Milt.*

5. To mark with different gradations of colours.

The portal ſhone, inimitable on earth
By model, or by *ſhading* pencil drawn. *Milton.*

6. To paint in obſcure colours.

SHA'DINESS. *n. ſ.* [from *ſhady*] The ſtate of being ſhady; umbrageouſneſs.

SHA'DOW. *n. ſ.* [ꞅcabu, Saxon; *ſchaduwe*, Dutch.]

1. The repreſentation of a body by which the light is intercepted.

Poor Tom! proud of heart, to ride over four inch'd bridges, to courſe his own *ſhadow* for a traitor. *Shakeſp.*

Life's but a walking *ſhadow*, a poor player,
That ſtruts and frets his hour upon the ſtage,
And then is heard no more. *Shakeſp.*

Such a nature,
Tickl'd with good ſucceſs, diſdains the *ſhadow*
Which he treads on at noon. *Shakeſp.*

The body, tho' it moves, yet not changing perceivable diſtance with ſome other bodies, the thing ſeems to ſtand ſtill, as in the hands of clocks, and *ſhadows* of ſun-dials. *Locke.*

2. Opacity; darkneſs; ſhade.

By the revolution of the ſkies
Night's ſable *ſhadows* from the ocean riſe. *Denham.*

His countrymen probably lived within the ſhake of the earthquake and *ſhadow* of the eclipſe. *Addiſon.*

3. Shelter made by any thing that intercepts the light, heat, or influence of the air.

In ſecret *ſhadow* from the ſunny ray,
On a ſweet bed of lillies ſoftly laid. *Fa. Queen.*

Here father, take the *ſhadow* of this tree
For your good hoſt. *Shakeſp. K. Lear.*

4. Obſcure place.

To the ſecret *ſhadows* I retire,
To pay my penance till my years expire. *Dryd.*

5. Dark part of a picture.

A *ſhadow* is a diminution of the firſt and ſecond light. The firſt light is that which proceeds immediately from a lightned body, as the beams of the ſun. The ſecond is an accidental light ſpreading itſelf into the air or medium proceeding from the other. *Shadows* are threefold: the firſt is a ſingle *ſhadow*, and the leaſt of all; and is proper to the plain ſurface where it is not wholly poſſeſſed of the light. The ſecond is the double *ſhadow*, and it is uſed when the ſurface begins once to forſake your eye, as in columns. The third *ſhadow* is made by croſſing over your double *ſhadow* again, which darkneth by a third part. It is uſed for the inmoſt *ſhadow*, and fartheſt from the light, as in gulfs, wells, and caves. *Peacham.*

After great lights there muſt be great *ſhadows*. *Dryden.*

6. Any thing perceptible only to the ſight; a ghoſt; a ſpirit, or ſhade.

Hence, terrible *ſhadow*!
Unreal mock'ry, hence! *Shakeſp.*

7. An imperfect and faint repreſentation: oppoſed to ſubſtance.

If ſubſtance might be call'd that *ſhadow* ſeem'd. *Milt.*

In the glorious lights of heaven we perceive a *ſhadow* of his divine countenance. *Raleigh.*

Without the least impulse or *shadow* of fate. *Milton.*
Amongst the creatures are particular excellencies scattered, which are some *shadows* of the divine perfections. *Tillotson.*

8. Inseparable companion.
Sin and her *shadow*, death. *Milton.*
Thou my *shadow*
Inseparable must with me be long. *Milton.*

9. Type; mystical representation.
Types and *shadows* of that destin'd seed. *Milton.*

10. Protection; shelter; favour.
Keep me under the *shadow* of thy wings. *Psalms.*

To SHA'DOW. *v. a.* [from the noun.]

1. To cover with opacity.
The warlike elf much wondered at this tree,
So fair and great, that *shadowed* all the ground. *Fa. Q.*
The Assyrian was a cedar with fair branches, and with a *shadowing* shroud. *Ezek.* xxxi. 3.

2. To cloud; to darken.
Mislike me not for my complexion;
The *shadow'd* livery of the burning sun
To whom I am a neighbour. *Shakesp.*

3. To make cool or gently gloomy by interception of the light or heat.
A gentle south-west wind comes creeping over flowery fields and *shadowed* waters in the extreme heat of summer. *Sidney.*

4. To conceal under cover; to hide; to screen.
Let every soldier hew him down a bough,
And bear't before him; thereby shall we *shadow*
The number of our host, and make discov'ry
Err in report of us. *Shakesp.*

5. To protect; to screen from danger; to shroud.
God shall forgive you Cœur de Lion's death,
The rather, that you give his offspring life,
Shadowing their right under your wings of war. *Shakesp.*

6. To mark with various gradations of colour, or light.
Turnsoil is made of old linnen rags dried, and laid in a saucer of vinegar, and set over a chafing dish of coals till it boil; then wring it into a shell, and put it into a little gum arabick: it is good to *shadow* carnations, and all yellows. *Peach.*
From a round globe of any uniform colour, the idea imprinted in our minds is of a flat circle, variously *shadowed* with different degrees of light coming to our eyes. *Locke.*
More broken scene, made up of an infinite variety of inequalities and *shadowings*, that naturally arise from an agreeable mixture of hills, groves, and vallies. *Addis.*

7. To paint in obscure colours.
If the parts be too much distant, so that there be void spaces which are deeply *shadowed*, then place in those voids some fold to make a joining of the parts. *Dryd. Dufresnoy.*

8. To represent imperfectly.
Whereat I wak'd and found
Before mine eyes all real, as the dream
Had lively *shadow'd*. *Milton Parad. Lost.*
Augustus is *shadowed* in the person of Æneas. *Dryd.*
I have *shadowed* some part of your virtues under another name. *Dryd.*

9. To represent typically.
Many times there are three things said to make up the substance of a sacrament; namely, the grace which is thereby offered, the element which *shadoweth* or signifieth grace, and the word which expresseth what is done by the element. *Hook.*
The shield being to defend the body from weapons, aptly *shadows* out to us the continence of the emperor, which made him proof to all the attacks of pleasure. *Addison.*

SHA'DOWY. *adj.* [from *shadow.*]

1. Full of shade; gloomy.
This *shadowy* desart, unfrequented woods,
I better brook than flourishing peopled towns. *Shakesp.*
With *shadowy* verdure flourish'd high,
A sudden youth the groves enjoy. *Fenton.*

2. Not brightly luminous.
More pleasant light
Shadowy sets off the face of things. *Milton.*

3. Faintly representative; typical.
When they see
Law can discover sin, but not remove
Save by those *shadowy* expiations weak,
The blood of bulls and goats; they may conclude
Some blood more precious must be paid for man. *Milt.*

4. Unsubstantial; unreal.
Milton has brought into his poems two actors of a *shadowy* and fictitious nature, in the persons of sin and death; by which he hath interwoven in his fable a very beautiful allegory. *Addis.*

5. Dark; opake.
By command, e're yet dim night
Her *shadowy* cloud withdraws, I am to haste
Homeward. *Milt. Parad. Lost.*

SHA'DY. *adj.* [from *shade.*]

1. Full of shade; mildly gloomy.
The wakeful bird
Sings darkling, and in *shadiest* covert hid
Tunes her nocturnal note. *Milt. Parad. Lost.*
Stretch'd at ease you sing your happy loves,
And Amarillis fills the *shady* groves. *Dryd*

2. Secure from the glare of light; or sultriness of heat.
Cast it also that you may have rooms *shady* for summer, and warm for winter. *Bacon.*

SHAFT. *n. s.* [ꞅceaꝼꞇ, Saxon.]

1. An arrow; a missive weapon.
To pierce pursuing shield,
By parents train'd, the Tartars wild are taught,
With *shafts* shot out from their back-turned bow. *Sidney.*
Who in the spring, from the new sun,
Already has a fever got,
Too late begins those *shafts* to shun,
Which Phœbus thro' his veins has shot. *Waller.*
They are both the archer and *shaft* taking aim afar off, and then shooting themselves directly upon the desired mark. *More.*
So lofty was the pile, a Parthian bow
With vigour drawn, must send the *shaft* below. *Dryd.*
O'er thee the secret *shaft*
That wastes at midnight, or th'undreaded hour
Of noon, flies harmless. *Thomson.*

2. [*Shaft*, Dutch.] A narrow, deep, perpendicular pit.
They sink a *shaft* or pit of six foot in length. *Carew.*
The fulminating damp, upon its accension, gives a crack like the report of a gun, and makes an explosion so forcible as to kill the miners, and force bodies of great weight from the bottom of the pit up through the *shaft*. *Woodward.*
Suppose a tube, or as the miners call it, a *shaft*, were sunk from the surface of the earth to the center. *Arbuthnot.*

3. Any thing strait; the spire of a church.
Practise to draw small and easy things, as a cherry with the leaf, the *shaft* of a steeple *Peacham.*

SHAG. *n. s.* [ꞅceacga, Saxon.]

1. Rough wooly hair.
Full often like a *shag*-hair'd crafty kern,
Hath he conversed with the enemy;
And given me notice of their villanies. *Shakesp.*
Where is your husband?
He's a traitor.
Thou lie'st thou *shag*-ear'd villain. *Shakesp.*
From the *shag* of his body, the shape of his legs, his having little or no tail, the slowness of his gate, and his climbing up of trees, he seems to come near the bear kind. *Grew.*
True Witney broad cloth, with its *shag* unshorn,
Be this the horseman's fence. *Gay.*

2. A kind of cloth.

SHAG. *n. s.* A sea bird.
Among the first sort we reckon *shags*, duck, and mallard. *Car.*

SHA'GGED. } *adj.* [from *shag.*]
SHA'GGY. }

1. Ruggedly; hairy.
They change their hue, with haggar'd eyes they stare,
Lean are their looks, and *shagged* are their hair. *Dryd.*
A lion's hide he wears;
About his shoulders hangs the *shaggy* skin,
The teeth and gaping jaws severely grin. *Dryd.*
From the frosty north
The early valiant Swede draws forth his wings,
In battailous array, while Volga's stream
Sends opposite, in *shaggy* armour clad
Her borderers; on mutual slaughter bent. *Philips.*

2. Rough; rugged.
They pluck'd the seated hills with all their load,
Rocks, waters, woods, and by the *shaggy* tops
Uplifting bore them in their hands. *Milt. Parad. Lost.*
There, where very desolation dwells,
By grots and caverns *shagg'd* with horrid shades,
She may pass on with unblench'd majesty,
Be it not done in pride. *Milt.*
Through Eden went a river large,
Nor chang'd his course, but through the *shaggy* hill
Pass'd underneath ingulph'd. *Milton.*
How would the old king smile
To see you weigh the paws when tip'd with gold,
And throw the *shaggy* spoils about your shoulders. *Addis.*
Ye rugged rocks! which holy knees have worn,
Ye grots and caverns *shagg'd* with horrid thorn. *Pope.*

SHAGRE'EN. *n. s.* [*chagrin*, French.] The skin of a kind of fish, or skin made rough in imitation of it.

To SHA'GREEN. *v. a.* [*chagriner*, French.] To irritate; to provoke. Both should be written *chagrin*.

To SHAIL. *v. n.* To walk sideways; a low word.
Child, you must walk strait, without skiewing and *shailing* to every step you set. *L'Estrange.*

To SHAKE. *v. a.* preterit, *shook*; part. pass. *shaken*, or *shook*. [ꞅceacan, Saxon; *shecken*, Dutch.]

1. To put into a vibrating motion; to move with quick returns backwards and forwards; to agitate.
Who honours not his father,
Henry the fifth that made all France to quake,
Shake he his weapon at us, and pass by. *Shakesp.*
I will *shake* mine hand upon them, and they shall be a spoil to their servants. *Zech.* ii 9.
I *shook* my lap and said, so God *shake* out every man from his house, even thus be he *shaken* out and emptied. *Neh.* v.

The

The ſtars fell unto the earth, even as a fig-tree caſteth her untimely figs when ſhe is *ſhaken* of a mighty wind. *Rev.* vi.

He *ſhook* the ſacred honours of his head:
With terror trembled heav'n's ſubſiding hill,
And from his *ſhaken* curls ambroſial dews diſtil. *Dryden.*

She firſt her huſband on the poop eſpies,
Shaking his hand at diſtance on the main;
She took the ſign, and *ſhook* her hand again. *Dryden.*

2. To make to totter or tremble.

The rapid wheels *ſhake* heav'n's baſis. *Milton.*

Let France acknowledge that her *ſhaken* throne
Was once ſupported, ſir, by you alone. *Roſcommon.*

3. To throw down by a violent motion.

Macbeth is ripe for *ſhaking*, and the powers above
Put on their inſtruments. *Shakeſp.*

The tyrannous breathing of the North
Shakes all our buds from blowing. *Shakeſpeare.*

When ye depart, *ſhake* off the duſt of your feet. *Mat.* x.

He looked at his book, and, holding out his right leg, put it into ſuch a quivering motion, that I thought he would have *ſhaked* it off. *Tatler.*

4. To throw away; to drive off.

'Tis our firſt intent
To *ſhake* all cares and buſineſs from our age,
Conferring them on younger ſtrengths, whilſt we
Unburthen'd crawl towards death. *Shakeſpeare.*

5. To weaken; to put in danger.

When his doctrines grew too ſtrong to be *ſhook* by his enemies, they perſecuted his reputation. *Atterbury.*

6. To drive from reſolution; to depreſs; to make afraid.

A ſly and conſtant knave, not to be *ſhak'd*. *Shakeſ. Cymb.*

This reſpite *ſhook*
The boſom of my conſcience. *Shakeſ. Henry* VIII.

Be not ſoon *ſhaken* in mind, or troubled, as that the day of Chriſt is at hand. 2 *Theſ.* ii. 2.

Not my firm faith
Can by his fraud be *ſhaken* or ſeduc'd. *Milton.*

7. *To* SHAKE *hands.* This phraſe, from the action uſed among friends at meeting and parting, ſometimes ſignifies to *join with*, but commonly to *take leave of.*

With the ſlave,
He ne'er *ſhook hands*, nor bid farewel to him,
'Till he unſeam'd him from the nape to th' chops. *Shakeſp.*

Nor can it be ſafe to a king to tarry among them who are *ſhaking hands* with their allegiance, under pretence of laying faſter hold of their religion. *King Charles.*

8. *To* SHAKE *off.* To rid himſelf of; to free from; to diveſt of.

Be pleas'd that I *ſhake off* theſe names you give me:
Antonio never yet was thief or pirate. *Shakeſpeare.*

If I could *ſhake off* but one ſeven years,
From theſe old arms and legs,
I'd with thee every foot. *Shakeſp. Coriolanus.*

Say, ſacred bard! what could beſtow
Courage on thee, to ſoar ſo high?
Tell me, brave friend! what help'd thee ſo
To *ſhake off* all mortality? *Waller.*

Him I reſerved to be anſwered by himſelf, after I had *ſhaken off* the leſſer and more barking creatures. *Stillingfleet.*

Can I want courage for ſo brave a deed?
I've *ſhook* it *off*: my ſoul is free from fear. *Dryden.*

Here we are free from the formalities of cuſtom and reſpect: we may *ſhake off* the haughty impertinent. *Collier.*

How does thy beauty ſmooth
The face of war, and make even horrour ſmile!
At ſight of thee my heart *ſhakes off* its ſorrows. *Addiſon.*

To SHAKE. *v. n.*

1. To be agitated with a vibratory motion.

Darts are counted as ſtubble: he laugheth at the *ſhaking* of a ſpear. *Job* xli. 29.

2. To totter.

3. To tremble; to be unable to keep the body ſtill.

Thy ſight, which ſhould
Make our eyes flow with joy, hearts dance with comforts,
Conſtrains them weep, and *ſhake* with fear and ſorrow. *Shak.*

What ſaid the wench, when he roſe up again?
—Trembled and *ſhook*; for why, he ſtamp'd,
As if the vicar meant to cozen him. *Shakeſpeare.*

A *ſhaking* through their limbs they find,
Like leaves ſaluted by the wind. *Waller.*

4. To be in terrour; to be deprived of firmneſs.

He ſhort of ſuccours, and in deep deſpair,
Shook at the diſmal proſpect of the war. *Dryd. Æn.*

SHAKE. *n. ſ.* [from the verb.]

1. Concuſſion.

If that thy fame with ev'ry toy be pos'd,
'Tis a thin web, which poiſonous fancies make;
But the great ſoldier's honour was compos'd
Of thicker ſtuff, which could endure a *ſhake*:
Wiſdom picks friends; civility plays the reſt,
A toy ſhunn'd cleanly paſſeth with thee beſt. *Herbert.*

The freeholder is the baſis of all other titles: this is the ſubſtantial ſtock, without which they are no more than bloſſoms that would fall away with every *ſhake* of wind. *Addiſon.*

2. Vibratory motion.

Several of his countrymen probably lived within the *ſhake* of the earthquake, and the ſhadow of the eclipſe, which are recorded by this author. *Addiſon.*

3. Motion given and received.

Our ſalutations were very hearty on both ſides, conſiſting of many kind *ſhakes* of the hand. *Addiſon.*

SHA'KER. *n. ſ.* [from *ſhake.*] The perſon or thing that ſhakes.

Go then, the guilty at thy will chaſtiſe,
He ſaid; the *ſhaker* of the earth replies. *Pope's Odyſſey.*

SHALE. *n. ſ.* [Corrupted, I think, for *ſhell.*] A huſk; the caſe of ſeeds in ſiliquous plants.

Behold yon poor and ſtarved band,
And your fair ſhew ſhall ſuck away their ſouls,
Leaving them but the *ſhales* and huſks of men. *Shakeſp.*

SHALL. *v. defective.* [ſceal, Sax. is originally I *owe*, or I *ought*. In *Chaucer, the faithe I* ſhall *to God*, means *the faith I* owe *to God*: thence it became a ſign of the future tenſe. The French uſe *devoir, dois, doit*, in the ſame manner, with a kind of future ſignification; and the Swedes have *ſkall*, and the Iſlanders *ſkal*, in the ſame ſenſe. It has no tenſes but *ſhall* future, and *ſhould* imperfect.

The explanation of *ſhall*, which foreigners and provincials confound with *will*, is not eaſy; and the difficulty is increaſed by the poets, who ſometimes give to *ſhall* an emphatical ſenſe of *will*: but I ſhall endeavour, *craſſâ Minervâ*, to ſhow the meaning of *ſhall* in the future tenſe.]

1. *I* SHALL *love.* It will ſo happen that I muſt love; I am reſolved to love.

2. SHALL *I love?* Will it be permitted me to love? Will you permit me to love? Will it happen that I muſt love?

3. *Thou* SHALT *love.* I command thee to love; it is permitted thee to love: [in poetry or ſolemn diction] it will happen that thou muſt love.

4. SHALT *thou love?* Will it happen that thou muſt love? Will it be permitted to thee to love?

5. *He* SHALL *love.* It will happen that he muſt love; it is commanded him that he love.

It is a mind, that *ſhall* remain a poiſon where it is.
——*Shall* remain!
Hear you this triton of the minnows? Mark you
His abſolute *ſhall?* *Shakeſp. Coriolanus.*

See Romulus the great:
This prince a prieſteſs of your blood *ſhall* bear,
And like his ſire in arms he *ſhall* appear. *Dryden's Æn.*

That he *ſhall* receive no benefit from Chriſt, is the affirmation whereon all his deſpair is founded; and the one way of removing this diſmal apprehenſion, is to convince him that Chriſt's death, and the benefits thereof, either do, or, if he perform the condition required of him, *ſhall* certainly belong to him. *Hammond's Fundamentals.*

6. SHALL *he love?* Is it permitted him to love? In ſolemn language, Will it happen that he muſt love?

7. The plural perſons follow the ſignification of the ſingulars.

SHA'LLOON. *n. ſ.* A ſlight woollen ſtuff.

In blue *ſhalloon* ſhall Hannibal be clad,
And Scipio trail an Iriſh purple plaid. *Swift.*

SHA'LLOP. *n. ſ.* [*chaloupe*, French.] A ſmall boat.

You were reſolved, after your arrival into Oroonoque, to paſs to the mine; and, to that end, you deſired to have ſir John Fearne's *ſhallop*: I do not allow of that courſe, becauſe ye cannot land ſo ſecretly but that ſome Indians on the river ſide may diſcover you, who giving knowledge of your paſſage to the Spaniards, you may be cut off before you can recover your boat. *Raleigh.*

There with your *ſhallop* ſtay:
The game's not loſt; I have one card to play. *Waller.*

Our hero ſet
In a ſmall *ſhallop*, fortune in his debt;
So near a hope of crowns and ſcepters, more
Than ever Priam, when he flouriſh'd, wore. *Waller.*

SHA'LLOW. *adj.* [This word is probably compounded of *ſhoal* and *low.*]

1. Not deep; having the bottom at no great diſtance from the ſurface or edge.

I had been drowned, but that the ſhore was ſhelvy and *ſhallow*; a death that I abhor. *Shakeſ. Merry Wives of Windſ.*

That inundation, though it were *ſhallow*, had a long continuance, whereby they of the vale, that were not drowned, periſhed for want of food. *Bacon.*

The like opinion he held of Meotis Palus, that by the floods of Tanais, and earth brought down thereby, it grew obſervably *ſhallower* in his days, and would in proceſs of time become a firm land. *Brown's Vulgar Errours.*

I am made a *ſhallow* forded ſtream,
Seen to the bottom: all my clearneſs ſcorn'd,
And all my faults expos'd. *Dryden's All for Love.*

Shallow brooks, that flow'd ſo clear,
The bottom did the top appear. *Dryden.*

In *ſhallow* furrows vines ſecurely grow. *Dryden.*

2. Not

2. Not intellectually deep; not profound; not very knowing or wise; empty; trifling; futile; silly.

I'll shew my mind,
According to my *shallow* simple skill. *Shakespeare.*
This is a very *shallow* monster:
Afraid of him? A very *shallow* monster,
The man i' th' moon! A most poor credulous monster. *Shak.*

The king was neither so *shallow* nor so ill advertised as not to perceive the intention of the French king, for the investing himself of Britaigne. *Bacon's Henry VII.*

Uncertain and unsettled he remains,
Deep verst in books, and *shallow* in himself. *Milton.*

One would no more wonder to see the most *shallow* nation of Europe the most vain, than to find the most empty fellows in every nation more conceited than the rest. *Addison.*

3. Not deep of sound.

If a virginal were made with a double concave, the one all the length of the virginal, and the other at the end of the strings, as the harp hath, it must make the sound perfecter, and not so *shallow* and jarring. *Bacon.*

SHA'LLOW. *n. s.* [from the adjective.] A shelf; a sand; a flat; a shoal; a place where the water is not deep.

I should not see the sandy hour-glass run,
But I should think of *shallows* and of flats;
And see my wealthy Andrew dock'd in sand,
Veiling her high top lower than her ribs,
To kiss her burial. *Shakesp. Coriolanus.*

A swift stream is not heard in the channel, but upon *shallows* of gravel. *Bacon's Nat. History.*

Having but newly left those grammatick flats and *shallows*, where they stuck unreasonably, to learn a few words with lamentable construction, and now on the sudden transported, to be tost with their unballasted wits in fathomless and unquiet deeps of controversy, they do grow into hatred of learning. *Milt.*

You that so oft have sounded
And fathom'd all his thoughts, that know the deeps
And *shallows* of his heart, should need no instruments
To advance your ends. *Denham.*

In arms of the sea, and among islands, there is no great depth, and some places are plain *shallows*. *Burnet.*

He sounds and fathoms him, to find
The *shallows* of his soul. *Dryd. Spanish Fryar.*

The wary Dutch
Behind their treach'rous *shallows* now withdraw,
And there lay snares to catch the British host. *Dryden.*

Three more fierce Eurus in his angry mood
Dash'd on the *shallows* of the moving sand,
And in mid ocean left them moor'd a-land. *Dryd. Æn.*

Their spawn being lighter than the water, there it would not sink to the bottom, but be buoyed up by it, and carried away to the *shallows*. *Ray on the Creation.*

With the use of diligence, and prudent conduct, he may decline both rocks and *shallows*. *Norris.*

The sea could not be much narrower than it is, without a great loss to the world; and must we now have an ocean of mere flats and *shallows*, to the utter ruin of navigation? *Bentley.*

SHA'LLOWBRAINED. *adj.* [*shallow* and *brain.*] Foolish; futile; trifling; empty.

It cannot but be matter of just indignation to all good men to see a company of lewd *shallowbrained* huffs making atheism, and contempt of religion, the sole badge of wit. *South.*

SHA'LLOWLY. *adv.* [from *shallow.*]

1. With no great depth.

The load lieth open on the grass, or but *shallowly* covered. *Carew.*

2. Simply; foolishly.

Most *shallowly* did you these arms commence,
Fondly brought here, and foolishly sent hence:
Strike up our drums, pursue the scatter'd stray. *Shakespeare.*

SHA'LLOWNESS. *n. s.* [from *shallow.*]

1. Want of depth.

2. Want of thought; want of understanding; futility; silliness; emptiness.

By it do all things live their measur'd hour:
We cannot ask the thing which is not there,
Blaming the *shallowness* of our request. *Herbert.*

I cannot wonder enough at the *shallowness* and impertinent zeal of the vulgar sort in Druina, who were carried away with such an ignorant devotion for his successes, when it little concerned their religion or security. *Howel.*

SHALM. *n. s.* [German.] A kind of musical pipe.

Every captain was commanded to have his soldiers in readiness to set forward upon the sign given, which was by the sound of a *shalm* or hoboy. *Knolles's Hist. of the Turks.*

SHALT. Second person of *shall.*

To SHAM. *v. n.* [*shommi*, Welsh, to cheat.]

1. To trick; to cheat; to fool with a fraud; to delude with false pretences. A low word.

Men tender in point of honour, and yet with little regard to truth, are sooner wrought upon by shame than by conscience, when they find themselves fooled and *shammed* into a conviction. *L'Estrange.*

2. To obtrude by fraud or folly.

We must have a care that we do not, for want of laying things and things together, *sham* fallacies upon the world for current reason. *L'Estrange.*

Then all your wits that flear and *sham*,
Down from Don Quixote to Tom Tram,
From whom I jests and puns purloin,
And slily put them off for mine,
Fond to be thought a country wit. *Prior.*

SHAM. *n. s.* [from the verb.] Fraud; trick; delusion; false pretence; imposture. A low word.

No *sham* so gross but it will pass upon a weak man, that is pragmatical and inquisitive. *L'Estrange.*

It goes a great way when natural curiosity and vulgar prejudice shall be assisted with the *shams* of astrological judgments. *L'Estrange.*

He that first brought the *sham*, wheedle, or banter in use, put together, as he thought fit, those ideas he made it stand for. *Locke.*

That in the sacred temple needs would try
Without a fire th' unheated gums to fry,
Believe who will the solemn *sham*, not I. *Addison.*

SHAM. *adj.* False; counterfeit; fictitious; pretended.

Never join the fray,
Where the *sham* quarrel interrupts the way. *Gay.*

SHA'MBLES. *n. s.* [Of uncertain etymology. *Scannaglia*, Ital.]

1. The place where butchers kill or sell their meat; a butchery.

Far be the thoughts of this from Henry's heart,
To make a *shambles* of the parliament-house. *Shak. H. VI.*
I hope my noble lord esteems me honest.
—Oh, ay, as summer-flies are in the *shambles*,
That quicken ev'n with blowing. *Shakesp. Othello.*

He warned a flock of sheep, that were driving to the *shambles*, of their danger; and, upon uttering some sounds, they all fled. *Arbuthnot.*

2. It is here improperly used.

When the person is made the jest of the mob, or his back the *shambles* of the executioner, there is no more conviction in the one than in the other. *Watts.*

SHA'MBLING. *adj.* [See SCAMBLING.] Moving aukwardly and irregularly. A low bad word.

By that *shambling* in his walk, it should be my rich banker, Gomez, whom I knew at Barcelona. *Dryd. Span. Fryar.*

So when nurse Nokes to act young Ammon tries,
With *shambling* legs, long chin, and foolish eyes,
With dangling hands he strokes th' imperial robe,
And with a cuckold's air commands the globe. *Smith.*

SHAME. *n. s.* [ꞅceam, Saxon; *schaemte*, Dutch.]

1. The passion felt when reputation is supposed to be lost; the passion expressed sometimes by blushes.

Lamenting sorrow did in darkness lye,
And *shame* his ugly face did hide from living eye. *Fa. Qu.*
Peace, peace, for *shame*, if not for charity.
—Urge neither charity nor *shame* to me:
Uncharitably with me have you dealt,
And shamefully my hopes by you are butcher'd:
My charity is outrage, life my *shame*;
And in my *shame* still lives my sorrow's rage. *Shak. R. III.*
Hide, for *shame*,
Romans, your grandsires images,
That blush at their degenerate progeny. *Dryden.*

In the schools men are allowed, without *shame*, to deny the agreement of ideas; or out of the schools, from thence have learned, without *shame*, to deny the connection of ideas. *Locke.*

2. The cause or reason of shame; disgrace; ignominy.

The more *shame* for him that he sends it me;
For I have heard him say a thousand times,
His Julia gave it him at his departure. *Shakespeare.*

Aaron had made them naked unto their *shame* amongst their enemies. *Ex.* xxxii. 25.

God deliver the world from such guides, who are the *shame* of religion. *South.*

This jest was first of the other house's making,
And, five times try'd, has never fail'd of taking;
For 'twere a *shame* a poet should be kill'd,
Under the shelter of so broad a shield. *Dryden.*
O *shame* to manhood! shall one daring boy
The scheme of all our happiness destroy? *Pope's Odyssey.*

3. Reproach.

A foul *shame* is upon the thief. *Ecclus.* v. 14.
Applause
Turn'd to exploding hiss, triumph to *shame*,
Cast on themselves from their own mouths. *Milton.*

To SHAME. *v. a.* [from the noun.]

1. To make ashamed; to fill with shame.

To tell thee of whom deriv'd,
Were shame enough to *shame* thee, wert thou not shameless. *Sh.*
If thou hast power to raise him, bring him hither,
And I've power to *shame* him hence:
Oh, while you live tell truth and *shame* the devil. *Shakesp.*
Hyperbolus by suffering did traduce
The ostracism, and *sham'd* it out of use. *Cleaveland.*

Despoil'd
Of all our good, *sham'd*, naked, miserable. *Milton.*

What hurt can there be in all the slanders and disgraces of this world, if they are but the arts and methods of providence to *shame* us into the glories of the next. *South.*

Were there but one righteous man in the world, he would hold up his head with confidence and honour; he would *shame* the world, and not the world him. *South.*

He in a loathsome dungeon doom'd to lie,
In bonds retain'd his birthright liberty,
And *sham'd* oppression, 'till it set him free. *Dryden.*
The coward bore the man immortal spite,
Who *sham'd* him out of madness into flight. *Dryden.*
Who *shames* a scribbler, breaks a cobweb through;
He spins the slight self-pleasing thread a-new. *Pope.*

2. To disgrace.

Certes, sir knight, ye been too much to blame,
Thus for to blot the honour of the dead,
And with foul cowardice his carcass *shame*. *Fairy Queen.*
So bent, the more shall *shame* him his repulse. *Milton.*

To SHAME. *v. n.* To be ashamed.

Great shame it is, thing so divine in view,
Made for to be the world's most ornament,
To make the bait her gazers to embrew;
Good *shames* to be to ill an instrument. *Spenser.*
Sham'st thou not, knowing whence thou art extraught,
To let thy tongue detect thy base-born heart? *Shakespeare.*

To the trunk of it authors give such a magnitude, as I *shame* to repeat. *Raleigh's History of the World.*

Auster spy'd him,
Cruel Auster thither hy'd him;
And with the rush of one rude blast,
Sham'd not spitefully to waste
All his leaves, so fresh, so sweet,
And lay them trembling at his feet. *Crashaw.*

SHA'MEFACED. *adj.* [*shame* and *face.*] Modest; bashful; easily put out of countenance.

Philoclea, who blushing and withal smiling, making shamefacedness pleasing, and pleasure *shamefaced*, tenderly moved her feet, unwonted to feel the naked ground. *Sidney.*

Conscience is a blushing *shamefac'd* spirit, that mutinies in a man's bosom: it fills one full of obstacles. *Shak. R. III.*

A man may be *shamefaced*, and a woman modest, to the degree of scandalous. *L'Estrange.*

Your *shamefac'd* virtue shunn'd the people's praise,
And senate's honours. *Dryden.*

From this time we may date that remarkable turn in the behaviour of our fashionable Englishmen, that makes them *shamefaced* in the exercise of those duties which they were sent into the world to perform. *Addison's Freeholder.*

SHAMEFA'CEDLY. *adv.* [from *shamefaced.*] Modestly; bashfully.

SHAMEFA'CEDNESS. *n. s.* [from *shamefaced.*] Modesty; bashfulness; timidity.

Dorus, when he had sung this, having had all the while a free beholding of the fair Pamela, could well have spared such horrour, and defended the assault he gave unto her face with bringing a fair stain of *shamefacedness* into it. *Sidney.*

Why wonder ye,
Fair sir, at that which ye so much embrace?
She is the fountain of your modesty;
You shamefac'd are, but *shamefastness* itself is she. *Fa. Qu.*

None but fools, out of *shamefacedness*, hide their ulcers, which, if shown, might be healed. *Dryden's Dufresnoy.*

SHA'MEFUL. *adj.* [*shame* and *full.*] Disgraceful; ignominious; infamous; reproachful.

Phœbus flying so most *shameful* sight,
His blushing face in foggy cloud implies,
And hides for shame. *Fairy Queen.*
This all through that great princess pride did fall,
And came to *shameful* end. *Fairy Queen.*
For this he shall live hated, be blasphem'd,
Seiz'd on by force, judg'd, and to death condemn'd,
A *shameful* and accurst! *Milton.*

His naval preparations were not more surprising than his quick and *shameful* retreat; for he returned to Carthage with only one ship, having fled without striking one stroke. *Arbuth.*

The knave of diamonds tries his wily arts,
And wins, O *shameful* chance! the queen of hearts. *Pope.*

SHA'MEFULLY. *adv.* [from *shameful.*] Disgracefully; ignominiously; infamously; reproachfully.

None but that saw, quoth he, would ween for truth,
How *shamefully* that maid he did torment. *Fairy Queen.*
But I his holy secret
Presumptuously have publish'd, impiously,
Weakly at least, and *shamefully*. *Milton's Agonistes.*

Would she *shamefully* fail in the last act in this contrivance of the nature of man? *More.*

Those who are ready enough to confess him, both in judgment and profession, are, for the most part, very prone to deny him *shamefully* in their doings. *South's Sermons.*

SHA'MELESS. *adj.* [from *shame.*] Wanting shame; wanting modesty; impudent; frontless; immodest; audacious.

To tell thee whence thou cam'st, of whom deriv'd,
Were shame enough to shame thee, wert thou not *shameless*. *Shakespeare's Henry VI.*
Beyond imagination is the wrong
That she this day hath, *shameless*, thrown on me. *Shakesp.*

The *shameless* denial hereof by some of their friends, and the more *shameless* justification by some of their flatterers, makes it needful to exemplify, which I had rather forbear. *Ral.*

God deliver the world from such hucksters of souls, the very shame of religion, and the *shameless* subverters of morality. *South's Sermons.*

Such *shameless* bards we have; and yet 'tis true,
There are as mad abandon'd criticks too. *Pope.*

SHA'MELESSLY. *adv.* [from *shameless.*] Impudently; audaciously; without shame.

The king to-day, as one of the vain fellows, *shamelessly* uncovereth himself. 2 *Sa.* vi. 20.

He must needs be *shamelessly* wicked that abhors not this licentiousness. *Hale.*

SHA'MELESSNESS. *n. s.* [from *shameless.*] Impudence; want of shame; immodesty.

Being most impudent in her heart, she could, when she would, teach her cheeks blushing, and make shamefastness the cloak of *shamelessness*. *Sidney.*

He that blushes not at his crime, but adds *shamelessness* to his shame, hath nothing left to restore him to virtue. *Taylor.*

SHA'MMER. *n. s.* [from *sham.*] A cheat; an impostor. A low word.

SHA'MOIS. *n. s.* [*chamois*, French.] See CHAMOIS. A kind of wild goat.

I'll bring thee
To clust'ring filberds, and sometimes I'll get thee
Young *shamois* from the rocks. *Shakespeare.*

SHA'MROCK. *n. s.* The Irish name for three leaved grass.

If they found a plot of watercresses, or *shamrocks*, there they flocked as to a feast for the time. *Spenser on Ireland.*

SHANK. *n. s.* [ſceanca, Saxon; *schenckel*, Dutch.]

1. The middle joint of the leg; that part which reaches from the ankle to the knee.

Eftsoons her white strait legs were altered
To crooked crawling *shanks*, of marrow emptied;
And her fair face to foul and loathsome hue,
And her fine corps to a bag of venom grew. *Spenser.*
The sixth age shifts
Into the lean and slipper'd pantaloon,
With spectacles on nose, and pouch on side;
His youthful hose, well sav'd, a world too wide
For his shrunk *shanks*. *Shak. As you like it.*

A stag says, if these pitiful *shanks* of mine were but answerable to this branching head, I can't but think how I should defy all my enemies. *L'Estrange.*

2. The bone of the leg.

Shut me nightly in a charnel-house,
O'er cover'd quite with dead men's rattling bones,
With reeky *shanks*, and yellow chapless skulls. *Shakespeare.*

3. The long part of any instrument.

The *shank* of a key, or some such long hole, the punch cannot strike, because the *shank* is not forged with substance sufficient. *Moxon.*

SHA'NKED. *adj.* [from *shank.*] Having a shank.

SHA'NKER. *n. s.* [*chancre*, French.] A venereal excrescence.

To SHAPE. *v. a.* preter. *shaped*; part. pass. *shaped* and *shapen.* [ſcyppan, Saxon; *scheppen*, Dutch.]

1. To form; to mould with respect to external dimensions.

I that am not *shap'd* for sportive tricks,
Nor made to court an am'rous looking-glass;
I, that am rudely stampt, and want love's majesty,
To strut before a wanton ambling nymph. *Shakes. R. III.*

Those nature hath *shaped* with a great head, narrow breast, and shoulders sticking out, seem much inclined to a consumption. *Harvey.*

Mature the virgin was, of Egypt's race;
Grace *shap'd* her limbs, and beauty deck'd her face. *Prior.*
The faultless form,
Shap'd by the hand of harmony. *Thomson.*

2. To mould; to cast; to regulate; to adjust.

Drag the villain hither by the hair,
Nor age nor honour shall *shape* privilege. *Shakesp. Tit. And.*

Mr. Candish, when without hope, and ready to *shape* his course by the East homewards, met a ship which came from the Philippines. *Raleigh.*

To the stream, when neither friends nor force,
Nor speed nor art avail, he *shapes* his course. *Denham.*
Charm'd by their eyes, their manners I acquire,
And *shape* my foolishness to their desire. *Prior.*

3. To image; to conceive.

Lovers and madmen have their seething brains,
Such *shaping* fantasies that apprehend
More than cool reason ever apprehends. *Shakesp.*

It is my nature's plague
To ſpy into abuſe, and oft my jealouſy
Shapes faults that are not. *Shakeſ. Othello.*

When fancy hath formed and *ſhaped* the perfecteſt ideas of bleſſedneſs, our own more happy experiences of greater muſt diſabuſe us. *Boyle.*

4. To make; to create. Obſolete.

I was *ſhapen* in iniquity, and in ſin did my mother conceive me. *Pſ.* li. 5.

SHAPE. *n. ſ.* [from the verb.]

1. Form; external appearance.

He beat me grievouſly in the *ſhape* of a woman; for in the *ſhape* of a man, maſter Brook, I fear not Goliah with a weaver's beam. *Shakeſpeare.*

The *ſhapes* of the locuſts were like unto horſes prepared for battle. *Rev.* ix. 7.

The other *ſhape*,
If *ſhape* it may be call'd that *ſhape* had none,
Diſtinguiſhable in member, joint, or limb. *Milton.*

In vegetables and animals the *ſhape* we moſt fix on, and are moſt led by. *Locke.*

2. Make of the trunk of the body.

Firſt a charming *ſhape* enſlav'd me,
An eye then gave the fatal ſtroke;
'Till by her wit Corinna ſav'd me,
And all my former fetters broke. *Addiſon.*

3. Being, as moulded into ſhape.

Before the gates there ſat
On either ſide a formidable *ſhape*. *Milton's Paradiſe Loſt.*

4. Idea; pattern.

Thy heart
Contains of good, wiſe, juſt, the perfect *ſhape*. *Milton.*

5. It is now uſed in low converſation for manner.

SHA'PELESS. *adj.* [from *ſhape.*] Wanting regularity of form; wanting ſymmetry of dimenſions.

You are born
To ſet a form upon that indigeſt,
Which he hath left ſo *ſhapeleſs* and ſo rude. *Shakeſpeare.*
He is deformed, crooked, old and ſere;
Ill-fac'd, worſe-bodied, *ſhapeleſs* ev'ry where. *Shakeſpeare.*
What fools were here,
Diſguis'd like Muſcovites in *ſhapeleſs* gear? *Shakeſpeare.*
Thrice had I lov'd thee,
Before I knew thy face or name;
So in a voice, ſo in a *ſhapeleſs* flame,
Angels affect us oft, and worſhipp'd be. *Donne.*
Now the victor ſtretch'd his eager hand,
Where the tall nothing ſtood, or ſeem'd to ſtand;
A *ſhapeleſs* ſhade, it melted from his ſight,
Like forms in clouds, or viſions of the night! *Pope.*
Some objects pleaſe our eyes,
Which out of nature's common order riſe,
The *ſhapeleſs* rock, or hanging precipice. *Pope.*

SHA'PESMITH. *n. ſ.* [*ſhape* and *ſmith.*] One who undertakes to improve the form of the body. A burleſque word.

No *ſhapeſmith* yet ſet up and drove a trade,
To mend the work that providence had made. *Garth.*

SHA'PELINESS. *n. ſ.* [from *ſhapely.*] Beauty or proportion of form.

SHA'PELY. *adv.* [from *ſhape.*] Symmetrical; well formed.

SHARD. *n. ſ.* [*ſchaerde*, Triſick.]

1. A fragment of an earthen veſſel.

For charitable prayers,
Shards, flints, and pebbles ſhould be thrown on her;
Yet here ſhe is allow'd her virgin chants,
Her maiden ſtrewments. *Shak. Hamlet.*

2. [*Chard.*] A plant.

Shards or mallows for the pot,
Keep the looſen'd body ſound. *Dryden's Horace.*

3. It ſeems in *Spenſer* to ſignify a frith or ſtrait.

Upon that ſhore he ſpied Atin ſtand,
There by his maſter left, when late he far'd
In Phedria's fleet bark, over that per'lous *ſhard*. *Fa. Queen.*

4. A ſort of fiſh.

SHA'RDBORN. *adj.* [*ſhard* and *born.*] Born or produced among broken ſtones or pots. Perhaps *ſhard* in *Shakeſpeare* may ſignify the ſheaths of the wings of inſects.

Ere to black Hecat's ſummons
The *ſhardborn* beetle with his drowſy hums
Hath rung night's yawning peal, there ſhall be done
A deed of dreadful note. *Shakeſpeare.*

SHA'RDED. *adj.* [from *ſhard.*] Inhabiting ſhards.

Often ſhall we find
The *ſharded* beetle in a ſafer hold,
Than is the full-wing'd eagle. *Shakeſpeare's Cymbeline.*

To SHARE. *v. n.* [ꞅceaꞃan, ꞅcyꞃan, Saxon.]

1. To divide; to part among many.

Good fellows all,
The lateſt of my wealth I'll *ſhare* amongſt you. *Shakeſpeare.*

Any man may make trial of his fortune, provided he acknowledge the lord's right, by *ſharing* out unto him a toll. *Carew.*

Well may he then to you his cares impart,
And *ſhare* his burden where he *ſhares* his heart. *Dryden.*

In the primitive times the advantage of prieſthood was equally *ſhared* among all the order, and none of that character had any ſuperiority. *Collier.*

Though the weight of a falſhood would be too heavy for one to bear, it grows light in their imaginations when it is *ſhared* among many. *Addiſon's Spectator.*

Suppoſe I *ſhare* my fortune equally between my children and a ſtranger, will that unite them? *Swift.*

2. To partake with others.

The captain, half of whoſe ſoldiers are dead, and the other quarter never muſtered or ſeen, comes ſhortly to demand payment of his whole account; where, by good means of ſome great ones, and privy *ſharings* with the officers of other ſome, he receiveth his debt. *Spenſer on Ireland.*

In vain does valour bleed,
While avarice and rapine *ſhare* the land. *Milton.*
Go, ſilently enjoy your part of grief,
And *ſhare* the ſad inheritance with me. *Dryden.*
Wav'd by the wanton winds his banner flies,
All maiden white, and *ſhares* the people's eyes. *Dryden.*
This was the prince decreed
To *ſhare* his ſceptre. *Dryden's Æn.*
Not a love of liberty, nor thirſt of honour,
Drew you thus far; but hopes to *ſhare* the ſpoil
Of conquer'd towns and plunder'd provinces. *Addiſ. Cato.*
All night it rains, the ſhews return with day;
Great Jove with Cæſar *ſhares* his ſov'reign ſway. *Logic.*

3. To cut; to ſeparate; to ſheer. [From ꞅceaꞃ, Saxon.]

With ſwift wheel reverſe deep ent'ring *ſhar'd*
All his right ſide. *Milton.*
Scalp, face, and ſhoulders the keen ſteel divides,
And the *ſhar'd* viſage hangs on equal ſides. *Dryden.*

To SHARE. *v. n.* To have part; to have a dividend.

I am the prince of Wales; and think not, Percy,
To *ſhare* with me in glory any more. *Shakeſ. Henry IV.*
Had greater haſte theſe ſacred rites prepar'd,
Some guilty mouths had in your triumphs *ſhar'd*;
But this untainted year is all your own. *Dryden.*

A right of inheritance gave every one a title to *ſhare* in the goods of his father. *Locke.*

This is Dutch partnerſhip, to *ſhare* in all our beneficial bargains, and exclude us wholly from theirs. *Swift.*

SHARE. *n. ſ.* [from the verb.]

1. Part; allotment; dividend.

If every juſt man, that now pines with want,
Had but a moderate and beſeeming *ſhare*,
Of that which lewdly-pamper'd luxury
Now heaps upon ſome with vaſt exceſs. *Milton.*

They went a hunting, and every one to go *ſhare* and *ſhare* like in what they took. *L'Eſtrange.*

The ſubdued territory was divided into greater and ſmaller *ſhares*, beſides that reſerved to the prince. *Temple.*

I'll give you arms; burn, raviſh, and deſtroy:
For my own *ſhare* one beauty I deſign;
Engage your honours that ſhe ſhall be mine. *Dryden.*
While fortune favour'd,
I made ſome figure; nor was my name
Obſcure, nor I without my *ſhare* of fame. *Dryd. Æn.*
The youths have equal *ſhare*
In Marcia's wiſhes, and divide their ſiſter. *Addiſ. Cato.*
In poets, as true genius is but rare,
True taſte as ſeldom is the critick's *ſhare*. *Pope.*

He who doth not perform that part aſſigned him, is a very miſchievous member of the publick; becauſe he takes his *ſhare* of the profit, and yet leaves his *ſhare* of the burden to be born by others. *Swift.*

2. A part.

Theſe, although they bear a *ſhare* in the diſcharge, yet have different offices in the compoſition. *Brown's Vulgar Errours.*

3. [Sceaꞃ, Saxon.] The blade of the plow that cuts the ground.

Nor laws they knew, nor manners, nor the care
Of lab'ring oxen, nor the ſhining *ſhare*. *Dryden.*
Then let him mark the ſheep, or whet the ſhining *ſhare*. *Dryden's Virgil's Georg.*
Great cities ſhall with walls be compaſs'd round,
And ſharpen'd *ſhares* ſhall vex the fruitful ground. *Dryden.*
Incumbent o'er the ſhining *ſhare*
The maſter leans, removes th' obſtructive clay. *Thomſon.*

For clay the coulter is long and bending, and the *ſhare* narrow. *Mortimer.*

SHA'REBONE. *n. ſ.* [*ſhare* and *bone.*] The os pubis; the bone that divides the trunk from the limbs.

The cartilage bracing together the two oſſa pubis, or *ſharebones*, Bartholine ſaith, is twice thicker and laxer in women than men. *Derham.*

SHA'RER. *n. ſ.* [from *ſhare.*]

1. One who divides, or apportions to others; a divider.

2. A partaker; one who participates any thing with others.

Moſt it ſeem'd the French king to import,
As *ſharer* in his daughter's injury. *Daniel's Civil War.*

People not allowed to be *ſharers* with their companions in good fortune, will hardly agree to be *ſharers* in bad. *L'Eſtr.*

An

An overgrown estate falling into the hands of one that has many children, it is broken into so many portions as render the *sharers* rich enough. *Addison.*

You must have known it.
—Indeed I did, then favour'd by the king,
And by that means a *sharer* in the secret. *Rowe.*

If, by taking on himself human nature at large, he hath a compassionate and tender sense of the infirmities of mankind in general, he must needs, in a peculiar manner, feel and commiserate the infirmities of the poor, in which he himself was so eminent a *sharer*. *Atterbury's Sermons.*

I suffer many things as an author militant, whereof in your days of probation you have been a *sharer*. *Pope to Swift.*

SHARK. *n. s.* [*canis charcharias*, Latin.]

1. A voracious sea-fish.

His jaws horrifick arm'd with threefold fate,
The direful *shark*. *Thomson's Summer.*

2. A greedy artful fellow; one who fills his pockets by sly tricks.

David's messengers are sent back to him, like so many *sharks* and runnagates, only for endeavouring to compliment an ill-nature out of itself, and seeking that by petition which they might have commanded by their sword. *South's Sermons.*

3. Trick; fraud; petty rapine.

Wretches who live upon the *shark*, and other mens sins, the common poisoners of youth, equally desperate in their fortunes and their manners, and getting their very bread by the damnation of souls. *South's Sermons.*

To SHARK. *v. a.* To pick up hastily or slily.

Young Fontinbras,
Of unimproved mettle, hot and full,
Hath in the skirts of Norway, here and there,
Shark'd up a list of landless resolutes. *Shakesp. Hamlet.*

To SHARK. *v. n.*

1. To play the petty thief.

The fly leads a lazy, voluptuous, scandalous, *sharking* life, hateful wherever she comes. *L'Estrange.*

2. To cheat; to trick. *Ainsworth.*

There are cheats by natural inclination as well as by corruption: nature taught this boy to *shark*, not discipline. *L'Est.*

The old generous English spirit, which heretofore made this nation so great in the eyes of all the world, seems utterly extinct; and we are degenerated into a mean, *sharking*, fallacious, undermining converse, there being a snare and a trapan almost in every word we hear, and every action we see. *South.*

SHARP. *adj.* [ſceaɲp, Saxon; *scherpe*, Dutch.]

1. Keen; piercing; having a keen edge; having an acute point; not blunt.

She hath tied
Sharp tooth'd unkindness like a vulture here. *Shakespeare.*

In Ireland have I seen this stubborn Cade
Oppose himself against a troop of kerns;
And fought so long, 'till that his thighs with darts
Were almost like a *sharp* quill'd porcupine. *Shak. H. VI.*

Thy tongue deviseth mischiefs, like a *sharp* razor working deceitfully. *Ps.* lii. 2.

With edged grooving tools they cut down and smoothen away the extuberances left by the *sharp* pointed grooving tools, and bring the work into a perfect shape. *Moxon's Mech. Ex.*

2. Terminating in a point or edge; not obtuse.

The form of their heads is narrow and *sharp*, that they may the better cut the air in their swift flight. *More.*

There was seen some miles in the sea a great pillar of light, not *sharp*, but in form of a column or cylinder, rising a great way up towards heaven. *Bacon.*

To come near the point, and draw unto a *sharper* angle, they do not only speak and practise truth, but really desire its enlargement. *Brown's Vulgar Errours.*

Their embryon atoms
Light arm'd or heavy, *sharp*, smooth, light or slow. *Milton.*

It is so much the firmer by how much broader the bottom and *sharper* the top. *Temple.*

In shipping such as this, the Irish kern,
And untaught Indian, on the stream did glide,
Ere *sharp* keel'd boats to stem the flood did learn,
Or fin-like oars did spread from either side. *Dryden.*

3. Acute of mind; witty; ingenious; inventive.

Now as fine in his apparel as if he would make me in love with a cloak, and verse for verse with the *sharpest* witted lover in Arcadia. *Sidney.*

If we had nought but sense, each living wight,
Which we call brute, would be more *sharp* than we. *Davies.*

Sharp to the world, but thoughtless of renown,
They plot not on the stage, but on the town. *Dryden.*

There is nothing makes men *sharper*, and sets their hands and wits more at work, than want. *Addison on Italy.*

Many other things belong to the material world, wherein the *sharpest* philosophers have never yet arrived at clear and distinct ideas. *Watts.*

4. Quick, as of sight or hearing.

As the *sharpest* eye discerneth nought,
Except the sun-beams in the air do shine;
So the best soul, with her reflecting thought,
Sees not herself, without some light divine. *Davies.*

To *sharp* ey'd reason this would seem untrue;
But reason I through love's false opticks view. *Dryden.*

5. Sour without astringency; sour but not austere; acid.

So we, if children young diseased we find,
Anoint with sweets the vessel's foremost parts,
To make them taste the potions *sharp* we give;
They drink deceiv'd, and so deceiv'd they live. *Fa. Qu.*

Sharp tasted citrons Median climes produce;
Bitter the rind, but generous is the juice. *Dryden.*

Different simple ideas are sometimes expressed by the same word, as sweet and *sharp* are applied to the objects of hearing and tasting. *Watts.*

6. Shrill; piercing the ear with a quick noise; not flat.

In whistling you contract the mouth, and, to make it more *sharp*, men use their finger. *Bacon's Nat. History.*

Let one whistle at the one end of a trunk, and hold your ear at the other, and the sound strikes so *sharp* as you can scarce endure it. *Bacon.*

For the various modulation of the voice, the upper end of the windpipe is endued with several cartilages to contract or dilate it, as we would have our voice flat or *sharp*. *Ray.*

7. Severe; harsh; biting; sarcastick.

If he should intend his voyage towards my wife, I would turn her loose to him; and what he gets more of her than *sharp* words, let it lie on my head. *Shakespeare.*

How often may we meet with those who are one while courteous, but within a small time after are so supercilious, *sharp*, troublesome, fierce and exceptious, that they are not only short of the true character of friendship, but become the very sores and burdens of society! *South.*

Cease contention: be thy words severe,
Sharp as he merits; but the sword forbear. *Dryden.*

8. Severe; quick to punish; cruel; severely rigid.

There, gentle Hermia, may I marry thee;
And to that place the *sharp* Athenian law
Cannot pursue us. *Shakespeare.*

9. Eager; hungry; keen upon a quest.

My faulcon now is *sharp* and passing empty,
And, 'till she stoop, she must not be full gorg'd;
For then she never looks upon her lure. *Shakespeare.*

The *sharp* desire I had
Of tasting. *Milton.*

10. Painful; afflictive.

That she may feel
How *sharper* than a serpent's tooth it is,
To have a thankless child. *Shakesp. King Lear.*

He caused his father's friends to be cruelly tortured; grieving to see them live to whom he was so much beholden, and therefore rewarded them with such *sharp* payment. *Knolles.*

Death becomes
His final remedy; and after life
Try'd in *sharp* tribulation, and refin'd
By faith, and faithful works. *Milt. Paradise Lost, b.* xi.

It is a very small comfort that a plain man, lying under a *sharp* fit of the stone, receives from this sentence. *Tillotson.*

11. Fierce; ardent; fiery.

Their piety feign'd,
In *sharp* contest of battle found no aid. *Milton.*

A *sharp* assault already is begun;
Their murdering guns play fiercely on the walls. *Dryden.*

12. Attentive; vigilant.

Sharp at her utmost ken she cast her eyes,
And somewhat floating from afar descries. *Dryden.*

Is a man bound to look out *sharp* to plague himself, and to take care that he slips no opportunity of being unhappy? *Collier.*

A clergyman, established in a competent living, is not under the necessity of being so *sharp* and exacting. *Swift.*

13. Acrid; biting; pinching; piercing, as the cold.

The windpipe is continually moistened with a glutinous humour, issuing out of small glandules in its inner coat, to fence it against the *sharp* air. *Ray.*

Nor here the sun's meridian rays had pow'r,
Nor wind *sharp* piercing, nor the rushing show'r,
The verdant arch so close its texture kept. *Pope's Odyssey.*

14. Subtile; nice; witty; acute.

Sharp and subtile discourses procure very great applause; but being laid in the balance with that which sound experience plainly delivereth, they are overweighed. *Hooker.*

The instances you mention are the strongest and *sharpest* that can be urged. *Digby.*

15. [Among workmen.] Hard.

They make use of the *sharpest* sand, that being best for mortar, to lay bricks and tiles in. *Moxon's Mech. Exer.*

16. Emaciated; lean.

His visage drawn he felt to *sharp* and spare. *Milton.*

SHARP. *n. s.* [from the adjective.]

1. A sharp or acute sound.

It is the lark that sings so out of tune,
Straining harsh discords and unpleasing *sharps*. *Shakespeare.*

2. A pointed weapon; small sword; rapier.

If butchers had but the manners to go to *sharps*, gentlemen would be contented with a rubber at cuffs. *Collier.*

To

To Sharp. *v. a.* [from the noun.] To make keen.

Whom the whetstone *sharps* to eat,
They cry, milstones are good meat. *Ben. Johnson.*

To Sharp. *v. n.* [from the noun.] To play thievish tricks.

I live upon what's my own, whereas your scandalous life is only cheating or *sharping*, one half of the year, and starving the other. *L'Estrange.*

To Sha'rpen. *v. a.* [from *sharp*.]

1. To make keen; to edge; to point.

The weaker their helps are, the more their need is to *sharpen* the edge of their own industry. *Hooker.*

The Israelites went down to the Philistines to *sharpen* every man his share and his coulter. 1 *Sam.* xiii. 20.

His severe wrath shall he *sharpen* for a sword. *Wisd.* v. 20.

The grating of a saw when *sharpen'd*, offends so much as it setteth the teeth on edge. *Bacon.*

Th' squadron bright, *sharp'ning* in mooned horns
Their phalanx. *Milton.*

It may contribute to his misery, heighten the anguish, and *sharpen* the sting of conscience, and so add fury to the everlasting flames, when he shall reflect upon the abuse of wealth and greatness. *South's Sermons.*

No: 'tis resistance that inflames desire;
Sharpens the darts of love, and blows the fire. *Dryd.*

E're ten moons had *sharpen'd* either horn,
To crown their bliss, a lovely boy was born. *Dryd.*

Her nails are *sharpen'd* into pointed claws,
Her hands bear half her weight and turn to paws. *Addis.*

2. To make quick, ingenious, or acute.

Overmuch quickness of wit, either given by nature, or *sharpen'd* by study, doth not commonly bring greatest learning, best manners, or happiest life in the end. *Ascham.*

3. To make quicker of sense.

Th' air *sharpen'd* his visual ray
To objects distant far. *Milton.*

4. To make eager or hungry.

Epicurean cooks
Sharpen with cloyless sauce his appetite. *Shakesp.*

Such an assurance as will *sharpen* mens desires and quicken their endeavours for obtaining a lesser good, ought to inspire men with more vigour in pursuit of what is greater. *Tillot.*

4. To make fierce or angry.

Mine enemy *sharpeneth* his eyes upon me. *Job* xvi. 9.

5. To make biting, or sarcastick.

My haughty soul would swell;
Sharpen each word, and threaten in my eyes. *Smith.*

6. To make less flat; more piercing to the ears.

Enclosures not only preserve sound, but encrease and *sharpen* it. *Bacon.*

7. To make sour.

Sha'rper. *n. s.* [from *sharp*.] A tricking fellow; a petty thief; a rascal.

Sharpers, as pikes, prey upon their own kind. *L'Estrange.*

He should retrench what he lost to *sharpers*, and spent upon puppet-plays, to apply it to that use. *Arbuth.*

I only wear it in a land of Hectors,
Thieves, supercargo's, *sharpers*, and directors. *Pope.*

Sha'rply. *adv.* [from *sharp*.]

1. With keenness; with good edge or point.

2. Severely; rigorously; roughly.

They are more *sharply* to be chastised and reformed than the rude Irish, which being very wild at the first, are now become more civil. *Spenser.*

3. Keenly; acutely; vigorously.

The mind and memory are more *sharply* exercised in comprehending another man's things than our own. *Ben. Johnson.*

4. Afflictively; painfully.

At the arrival of the English embassadors the soldiers were *sharply* assailed with wants. *Hayward.*

5. With quickness.

You contract your eye when you would see *sharply*; and erect your ear when you would hear attentively. *Bacon.*

6. Judiciously; acutely; wittily.

Sharpness. *n. s.* [from *sharp*.]

1. Keeness of edge or point.

Palladius neither suffering us nor himself to take in hand the party till the afternoon; when we were to fight in troops, not differing otherwise from earnest, but that the *sharpness* of the weapons was taken away. *Sidney.*

A second glance came gliding like the first;
And he who saw the *sharpness* of the dart,
Without defence receiv'd it in his heart. *Dryd.*

2. Not obtuseness.

Force consisteth in the roundings and raisings of the work, according as the limbs do more or less require it; so as the beholder shall spy no *sharpness* in the bordering lines. *Wotton.*

3. Sourness without austereness.

There is a *sharpness* in vinegar, and there is a *sharpness* in pain, in sorrow, and in reproach; there is a sharp eye, a sharp wit, and a sharp sword: but there is not one of these severe *sharpnesses* the same as another of them; and a sharp east wind is different from them all. *Watts's Logick.*

Provoking sweat extremely, and taking away all *sharpness* from whatever you put in, must be of good effect in the cure of the gout. *Temple.*

4. Severity of language; satyrical sarcasm.

There's gold for thee,
Thou must not take my former *sharpness* ill,
I will employ thee back again. *Shakesp.*

Some did all folly with just *sharpness* blame,
While others laugh'd and scorn'd them into shame;
But, of these two, the last succeeded best,
As men aim rightest when they shoot in jest. *Dryd.*

This is a subject of which it is hard to speak without satyrical *sharpness* and particular reflections on many churches of christians. *Sprat.*

The *sharpness* of his satyr, next to himself, falls most heavily on his friends. *Dryden.*

5. Painfulness; afflictiveness.

At this time
We sweat and bleed; the friend hath lost his friend;
And the best quarrels in the heat are curst
By those that feel their *sharpness*. *Shakesp.*

Not a single death only that then attended this profession; but the terror and *sharpness* of it was redoubled in the manner and circumstances. *South.*

6. Intellectual acuteness; ingenuity; wit.

Till Arianism had made it a matter of great *sharpness*, and subtilty of wit to be a sound believing christian, men were not curious what syllables or particles of speech they used. *Hook.*

The daring of the soul proceeds from thence,
Sharpness of wit and active diligence. *Dryd.*

The son returned with strength of constitution, *sharpness* of understanding, and skill in languages. *Addison.*

7. Quickness of senses.

If the understanding or faculty of the soul be like unto bodily sight, not of equal *sharpness* in all; what can be more convenient than that, even as the dark-sighted man is directed by the clear about things visible, so likewise in matters of deeper discourse the wise in heart doth shew the simple where his way lieth. *Hooker.*

Sharp-set. [*sharp* and *set*.] Eager; vehemently desirous.

Basilius forced her to stay, tho' with much ado, she being *sharp-set* upon the fulfilling of a shrewd office, in overlooking Philoclea. *Sidney.*

An eagle *sharp-set*, looking about her for her prey, spy'd a leveret. *L'Estrange.*

Our senses are *sharp-set* on pleasures. *L'Estrange.*

A comedy of Johnson's, not Ben, held seven nights; for the town is *sharp-set* on new plays. *Pope.*

Sharp-visaged. *adj.* [*sharp* and *visaged*.] Having a sharp countenance.

The Welsh that inhabit the mountains are commonly *sharp-visaged*. *Hale's Orig. of Mankind.*

Sharp-sighted. *adj.* [*sharp* and *sight*.] Having quick sight.

If she were the body's quality,
Then would she be with it sick, maim'd, and blind;
But we perceive, where these privations be,
An healthy, perfect, and *sharp-sighted* mind. *Davies.*

I am not so *sharp-sighted* as those who have discerned this rebellion contriving from the death of Q. Elizabeth. *Clarend.*

Your majesty's clear and *sharp-sighted* judgment has as good a title to give law in matters of this nature, as in any other. *Denham.*

Nothing so fierce but love will soften, nothing so *sharp-sighted* in other matters but it throws a mist before the eyes on't. *L'Est.*

To Sha'tter. *v. a.* [*schetteren*, Dutch.]

1. To break at once into many pieces; to break so as to scatter the parts.

He rais'd a sigh so piteous and profound,
That it did seem to *shatter* all his bulk,
And rend his being. *Shakesp.*

Ye myrtles brown, with ivy never sear,
I come to pluck your berries harsh and crude,
And with forc'd fingers rude
Shatter your leaves before the mellowing year. *Milt.*

They escape dissolution, because they can scarce ever meet with an agent minute, and swiftly enough moved, to *shatter* or dissociate the combined parts. *Boyle.*

A monarchy was *shattered* to pieces, and divided amongst revolted subjects, into a multitude of little governments. *Locke.*

Black from the stroke above, the smouldring pine
Stands as a *shatter'd* trunk. *Thoms. Summer.*

2. To dissipate; to make incapable of close and continued attention.

A man of a loose, volatile and *shattered* humour, thinks only by fits and starts. *Norris.*

To Sha'tter. *v. n.* To be broken, or to fall, by any force applied, into fragments.

Of bodies, some are fragil; and some are tough and not fragil; and in the breaking, some fragil bodies break but where the force is; some *shatter* and fly in many places. *Bacon.*

Sha'tter. *n. s.* [from the verb.] One part of many into which any thing is broken at once.

Stick

Stick the candle ſo looſe, that it will fall upon the glaſs of the ſconce and break it into *ſhatters*. *Swift.*

SHA'TTERBRAINED. } *adj.* [from *ſhatter brain* and *pate.*] In-
SHA'TTERPATED. } attentive; not conſiſtent. A low word.

SHA'TTERY. *adj.* [from *ſhatte*.] Diſunited; not compact; eaſily falling into many parts; looſe of texture.

A brittle *ſhattery* ſort of ſpar, found in form of a white ſand chiefly in the perpendicular fiſſures amongſt the ores of metal. *Woodward.*

To SHAVE. *v. a.* preterit *ſhaved*, part. *ſhaved* or *ſhaven*. [ſceapan, Saxon; *ſchaeven*, Dutch.]

1. To pare off with a razor.

He that is to be cleanſed ſhall *ſhave* off all his hair. *Levit.*

Zelim was the firſt of the Ottomans that did *ſhave* his beard: a baſhaw aſk'd why he alter'd the cuſtom of his predeceſſors? He anſwered, becauſe you baſhaws may not lead me by the beard, as you did them. *Bacon.*

Doſt thou not know this *ſhaven* pate? Truly it is a great man's head. *Knolles's Hiſt. of the Turks.*

I cauſed the hair of his head to be *ſhaved* off. *Wiſeman.*

2. To pare cloſe to the ſurface.

Sweet bird!
Thee chauntreſs, oft the woods among,
I wooe to hear the evening ſong:
And miſſing thee, I walk unſeen
On the dry ſmooth *ſhaven* green. *Milt.*
The bending ſcythe
Shaves all the ſurface of the waving green. *Gay.*

3. To ſkim by paſſing near, or ſlightly touching.

He *ſhaves* with level wing the deep; then ſoars
Up to the fiery concave tow'ring high. *Milton.*

4. To cut in thin ſlices.

Make ſome medley of earth, with ſome other plants bruis'd or *ſhaven* in leaf or root. *Bacon.*

5. To ſtrip; to oppreſs by extortion; to pillage.

SHA'VELING. *n. ſ.* [from *ſhave.*] A man ſhaved; a friar, or religious. Uſed in contempt.

Of elfes, there be no ſuch things; only by bald fryars and knaviſh *ſhavelings* ſo feigned. *Spenſer.*

SHA'VER. *n. ſ.* [from *ſhave.*]

1. A man that practiſes the art of *ſhaving*.

2. A man cloſely attentive to his own intereſt.

My lord
Was now diſpos'd to crack a jeſt,
And bid friend Lewis go in queſt;
This Lewis is a cunning *ſhaver*. *Swift.*

3. A robber; a plunderer.

They fell all into the hands of the cruel mountain people, living for the moſt part by theft, and waiting for wrecks, as hawks for their prey: by theſe *ſhavers* the Turks were ſtript of all they had. *Knolles.*

SHA'VING. *n. ſ.* [from *ſhave.*] Any thin ſlice pared off from any body.

Take lignum aloes in groſs *ſhavings*, ſteep them in ſack, changed twice, till the bitterneſs be drawn forth; then take the *ſhavings* forth and dry them in the ſhade, and beat them to powder. *Bacon.*

By electrick bodies I do not conceive only ſuch as take up *ſhavings*, ſtraws, and light bodies, but ſuch as attract all bodies palpable whatſoever. *Brown's Vulgar Errours.*

The *ſhavings* are good for the fining of wine. *Mort.*

SHAW. *n. ſ.* [ſcua, Saxon; *ſchawe*, Dutch; *ſkugga*, Iſlandick.] A thicket; a ſmall wood. A tuft of trees near Lichfield is called Gentle *ſhaw*.

SHA'BANDER. *n. ſ.* [among the Perſians.] A great officer; a viceroy. *Bailey.*

SHA'WFOWL. *n. ſ.* [*ſhaw* and *fowl.*] An artificial fowl made by fowlers on purpoſe to ſhoot at.

SHA'WM. *n. ſ.* [from *ſchawme*, Teutonick.] A hautboy; a cornet.

With trumpets alſo and *ſhawms*. *Pſalm Common Prayer.*

SHE. *pronoun.* In oblique caſes *her*. [*ſi*, Gothick; ſeo, Sax. *ſche*, old Engliſh.]

1. The female pronoun demonſtrative: the woman; the woman before mentioned.

She, of whom the ancients ſeem'd to propheſy,
When they call'd virtues by the name of *ſhe*;
She, in whom virtue was ſo much refin'd,
That for allay unto ſo pure a mind
She took the weaker ſex. *Donne.*
This once diſclos'd,
The ladies did change favours, and then we
Following the ſigns, woo'd but the ſign of *ſhe*. *Shakeſp.*
What, at any time, have you heard *her* ſay? *Shakeſp.*
The moſt upright of mortal men was he;
The moſt ſincere, and holy woman, *ſhe*. *Dryden.*

2. It is ſometimes uſed for a woman abſolutely, with ſome degree of contempt.

The *ſhes* of Italy ſhall not betray
Mine intereſt, and his honour. *Shakeſpear's Cymbeline.*
Lady, you are the cruell'ſt *ſhe* alive,
If you will lead theſe graces to the grave,
And leave the world no copy. *Shakeſpeare's Twelfth Night.*
I was wont
To load my *ſhe* with knacks, I wou'd have ranſack'd
The pedlar's ſilken treaſury, and have pour'd it
To her acceptance. *Shakeſpeare's Winter's Tale.*

3. The female; not the male.

I would outſtare the ſterneſt eyes that look,
Pluck the young ſucking cubs from the *ſhe* bear
To win thee, lady. *Shakeſp. Merchant of Venice.*
Let us do it with no ſhew of fear;
No, with no more, than if we heard that England
Were buſied with a Whitſon morris-dance;
For my good liege, *ſhe* is ſo idly king'd,
That fear attends her not. *Shakeſp. Hen. V.*
The nightingale, if *ſhe* would ſing by day,
When every gooſe is cackling, wou'd be thought
No better a muſician than the wren. *Shakeſpeare.*

He-lions are hirſute, and have great manes, the *ſhes* are ſmooth like cats. *Bacon.*

Stand it in Judah's chronicles confeſt,
That David's ſon, by impious paſſion mov'd,
Smote a *ſhe*-ſlave, and murder'd what he lov'd. *Prior.*

SHEAF. *n. ſ. ſheaves* plural. [ſceap, Saxon; *ſchoof*, Dutch.]

1. A bundle of ſtalks of corn bound together, that the ears may dry.

Theſe be the *ſheaves* that honour's harveſt bears,
The ſeed thy valiant acts, the world the field. *Fairfax.*
He beheld a field,
Part arable and tilth; whereon were *ſheaves*
New-reap'd: the other part ſheep-walks and folds. *Milt.*
The reaper fills his greedy hands,
And binds the golden *ſheaves* in brittle bands. *Dryden.*
I pitch'd the *ſheaves* (oh could I do ſo now)
Which ſhe in rows pil'd. *Gay's Paſtorals.*

2. Any bundle or collection held together.

She vaniſh'd;
The *ſheaf* of arrows ſhook and rattled in the caſe. *Dryden.*

In the knowledge of bodies, we muſt glean what we can; ſince we cannot, from a diſcovery of their real eſſences, graſp at a time whole *ſheaves*; and in bundles comprehend the nature of whole ſpecies. *Locke.*

To SHEAL. *v. a.* To ſhell. See SHALE.

Thou art a *ſhealed* peaſcod. *Shakeſp. K. Lear.*

To SHEAR. preter. *ſhore*, or *ſheared*; part. paſſ. *ſhorn*. [ſceapan, ſcypen, Saxon.]

1. To clip or cut by interception between two blades moving on a rivet.

So many days, my ews have been with young;
So many weeks, e're the poor fools will yean;
So many months, e're I ſhall *ſheer* the fleece. *Shakeſp.*
I am ſhepherd to another man,
And do not *ſheer* the fleeces that I graze. *Shakeſp.*
Laban went to *ſheer* his ſheep. *Gen.* xxxi. 19.

When wool is new *ſhorn*, they ſet pails of water by in the ſame room to increaſe its weight. *Bacon's Nat. Hiſt.*

To lay my head and hollow pledge
Of all my ſtrength, in the laſcivious lap
Of a deceitful concubine, who *ſhore* me,
Like a tame weather, all my precious fleece. *Milton.*
The ſame ill taſte of ſenſe wou'd ſerve to join
Dog foxes in the yoak, and *ſheer* the ſwine. *Dryden.*
May'ſt thou henceforth ſweetly ſleep,
Sheer, ſwains, oh *ſheer* your ſofteſt ſheep
To ſwell his couch. *Gay.*
O'er the congenial duſt injoin'd to *ſhear*
The graceful curl, and drop the tender tear. *Pope.*

2. To cut.

The ſharp and toothed edge of the nether chap ſtrikes into a canal cut into the bone of the upper; and the toothed protuberance of the upper into a canal in the nether: by which means he eaſily *ſheers* the graſs whereon he feeds. *Grew.*

SHEAR. } *n. ſ.* [from the verb. It is ſeldom uſed in the
SHEARS. } ſingular, but is found once in *Dryden.*]

1. An inſtrument to cut, conſiſting of two blades moving on a pin, between which the thing cut is intercepted. *Shears* are large, and *ſciſſars* a ſmaller inſtrument of the ſame kind.

Alas, thought Philoclea to herſelf, your *ſheers* come too late to clip the bird's wings that already is flown away. *Sidney.*

Why do you bend ſuch ſolemn brows on me?
Think you I bear the *ſhears* of deſtiny?
Have I commandment on the pulſe of life? *Shakeſpeare.*
The fates prepar'd their ſharpen'd *ſheers*. *Dryd.*
When the fleece is ſhorn,
Then their defenceleſs limbs the brambles tear;
Short of their wool, and naked from the *ſheer*. *Dryden.*
That people live and die, I knew,
An hour ago, as well as you;
And if fate ſpins us longer years,
Or is in haſte to take the *ſheers*,
I know, we muſt both fortunes try,
And bear our evils, wet or dry. *Prior.*

How happy ſhould we be if we had the privilege of employing the *ſheers* for want of a mint, upon foreign gold, by clipping it into half crowns. *Swift.*

Fate urg'd the *sheers* and cut the sylph in twain,
But airy substance soon unites again. *Pope.*
Beneath the *shears* they felt no lasting smart,
They lost but fleeces, while I lost a heart. *Gay.*

2. The denomination of the age of sheep.

When sheep is one *shear*, they will have two broad teeth before; when two *shear*, four; when three, six; when four, eight: and after that, their mouths break. *Mortimer.*

3. Any thing in the form of the blades of *sheers*.

4. Wings, in *Spenser*.

Two sharp-wing'd *sheers*
Deck'd with divers plumes, like painted jays,
Were fix'd at his back to cut his airy ways. *Spenser.*

SHEARD *n. s.* [ſceanꝺ, Sax.] A fragment. It is now commonly written *shard*, and applied only to fragments of earthen ware.

In the bursting of it, not a *sherd* to take fire from the hearth, or to take water out of the pit. *Isa.* xxx. 14.

SHEA'RER. *n. s.* [from *shear*.] One that clips with shears; particularly one that fleeces sheep.

Of other care they little reck'ninng make,
Than how to scramble at the *shearers* feast,
And shove away the worthy bidden guest. *Milton.*

Was he to be led as a lamb to the slaughter, patient and resigned as a sheep before her *shearers*? *Rogers.*

SHEA'RMAN. *n. s.* [*shear* and *man*.] He that *shears*.

Thy father was a plaisterer,
And thou thyself a *shearman*. *Shakespeare.*

SHEA'RWATER. *n. s.* A fowl. *Ainsworth.*

SHEATH. *n. s.* [ſcæðe, Saxon.] The case of any thing; the scabbard of a weapon.

The dead knight's sword out of his *sheath* he drew,
With which he cut a lock off all their hair. *Fa. Queen.*
Doth not each look a flash of light'ning feel,
Which spares the body's *sheath*, yet melts the steel? *Cleav.*
Swords, by the lightning's subtile force distill'd,
And the cold *sheath* with running metal fill'd. *Addison.*

To SHEATH. } *v. a.* [from the noun.]
To SHEATHE. }

1. To inclose in a *sheath* or scabbard; to inclose in any case.

This drawn but now against my sovereign's breast,
Before 'tis *sheath'd*, shall give him peace and rest. *Waller.*

Those active parts of a body are of differing natures when *sheath'd* up, or wedged in amongst others in the texture of a concrete; and when extricated from these impediments. *Boyle.*

In his hair one hand he wreaths,
His sword, the other, in his bosom *sheaths*. *Denham.*
Is this her hate to him, his love to me!
'Tis in my breast she *sheaths* her dagger now. *Dryden.*
The left foot naked, when they march to fight,
But in a bull's raw hide they *sheath* the right. *Dryden.*

The leopard, and all of this kind as goes, keeps the claws of his forefeet turned up from the ground and *sheathed* in the skin of his toes, whereby he preserves them sharp for rapine, extending them only when he leaps at the prey. *Grew.*

Other substances opposite to acrimony are called demulcent or mild; because they blunt or *sheath* those sharp salts as pease, and beans. *Arbuthnot.*

2. To fit with a *sheath*.

There was no ink to colour Peter's hat,
Walter's dagger was not come from *sheathing*. *Shak.*

3. To defend the main body by an outward covering.

It were to be wished that the whole navy throughout were *sheathed* as some are. *Raleigh.*

SHEATHWI'NGED. *adj.* [*sheath* and *wing*.] Having hard cases which are folded over the wings.

Some insects fly with four wings, as all vaginipennous, or *sheathwinged* insects, as beetles and dorrs. *Brown's Vulg. Er.*

SHEA'THY. *adj.* [from *sheath*.] Forming a sheath.

With a needle put aside the short and *sheathy* cases on earwigs backs, and you may draw forth two wings. *Brown.*

SHE'CKLATON. *n. s.*

He went to fight against the giant in his robe of *shecklaton*, which is that kind of gilded leather with which they use to embroider the Irish jackets. *Spenser.*

To SHED. *v. a.* [ſceban, Saxon.]

1. To effuse; to pour out; to spill.

The painful service, and the drops of blood
Shed for my thankless country are requited
But with that surname of Coriolanus. *Shakespeare.*
Cromwell, I did not think to *shed* a tear
In all my miseries. *Shakesp.*

Without *shedding* of blood is no remission. *Heb.* ix. 22.

For this is my blood which is *shed* for many, for the remission of sins. *Matth.* xxvi. 28.

Some think one gen'ral soul fills ev'ry brain,
As the bright sun *sheds* light in ev'ry star. *Davies.*
Around its entry nodding poppies grow,
And all cool simples that sweet rest bestow;
Night from the plants their sleepy virtue drains,
And passing, *sheds* it on the silent plains. *Dryden.*
You seem'd to mourn another lover dead,
My sighs you gave him, and my tears you *shed*. *Dryden.*
Unhappy man! to break the pious laws
Of nature, pleading in his children's cause:
'Tis love of honour, and his country's good;
The consul, not the father, *sheds* the blood. *Dryden.*
In these lone walls, their days eternal bound,
These moss-grown domes with spiry turrets crown'd,
Where awful arches make a noon-day night,
And the dim windows *shed* a solemn light;
Thy eyes diffus'd a reconciling ray,
And gleams of glory brighten'd all the day. *Pope.*

2. To scatter; to let fall.

Trees that bring forth their leaves late, and cast them late, are more lasting than those that sprout their leaves early, or *shed* them betimes. *Bacon's Nat. Hist.*

So the returning year be blest,
As his infant months bestow,
Springing wreaths for William's brow;
As his summer's youth shall *shed*
Eternal sweets around Maria's head. *Prior.*

To SHED. *v. n.* To let fall its parts.

White oats are apt to *shed* most as they lie, and black as they stand. *Mortimer's Husbandry.*

SHED. *n. s.* [supposed by *Skinner* to be corrupted from *shade*.]

1. A slight temporary covering.

The first Aletes born in lowly *shed*,
Of parents base, a rose sprung from a bride. *Fairfax.*
Though he his house of polish'd marble build,
With jasper floor'd, and carved cedar ceil'd;
Yet shall it ruin like the moth's frail cell,
Or *sheds* of reeds, which summer's heat repel. *Sandys.*
So all our minds with his conspire to grace
The Gentiles great apostle, and deface
Those state-obscuring *sheds*, that like a chain
Seem'd to confine and fetter him again. *Waller.*
In such a season born, when scarce a *shed*
Could be obtain'd to shelter him or me
From the bleak air. *Parad. Regain'd.*
Those houses then were caves, or homely *sheds*,
With twining osiers fenc'd, and moss their beds. *Dryden.*
An hospitable house they found,
A homely *shed*; the roof, not far from ground
Was thatch'd with reeds and straw together bound. *Dryd.*
Then out he steals, and finds where by the head,
Their horse hung fasten'd underneath a *shed*. *Betterton.*
Her various kinds by various fortunes led,
Commence acquaintance, underneath a *shed*. *Swift.*

2. In composition. Effusion; as blood-*shed*.

SHE'DDER. *n. s.* [from *shed*.] A spiller; one who sheds.

A *shedder* of blood shall surely die. *Ezek.* xviii. 10.

SHEEN. } *adj.* [This was probably only the old pronunciation
SHEE'NY. } of *shine*]. Bright; glittering; shewy. A word now not in use.

That lewd ribbald, with vile lust advanc'd,
Laid first his filthy hands on virgin clean,
To spoil her dainty corse so fair and *sheen*. *Fa. Queen.*
When he was all dight, he took his way
Into the forest, that he might be seen
Of the wild beasts, in his new glory *sheen*. *Hubberd's Tale.*
Now they never meet in grove or green,
By fountain clear, or spangled star-light *sheen*. *Shakespeare.*
Up arose each warrior bold and brave,
Glistering in filed steel and armour *sheen*. *Fairfax.*
Out of the hierarchies of angels *sheen*,
The gentle Gabriel call'd he from the rest. *Fairfax.*
By the rushy fringed bank,
Where grows the willow and the osier dank,
My sliding chariot stays,
Which set with agat, or the azure *sheen*,
Of turcois blue, and emerald green. *Milton.*
Or did of late earth's sons besiege the wall
Of *sheeny* heav'n. *Milton.*

SHEEN. *n. s.* [from the adjective.] Brightness; splendour.

Mercy will sit between,
Thron'd in celestial *sheen*. *Milton.*
Far above, in spangled *sheen*,
Celestial Cupid, her fam'd son advanc'd,
Holds his dear Psyche sweet entranc'd. *Milton.*

SHEEP. *n. s.* plural likewise *sheep*. [ſceap, Saxon; of which the plural was ſeep; *schaep*, Dutch.]

1. The animal that bears wool: remarkable for its usefulness and innocence.

Fire the brambles, snare the birds, and steep
In wholesome water-falls the fleecy *sheep*. *Dryden.*

Of substances there are two sorts of ideas; one of single substances, as they exist separately, as a man or *sheep*. *Locke.*

2. In contempt. A foolish silly fellow. *Ainsworth.*

To SHEEPBI'TE. *v. n.* [*sheep* and *bite*.] To use petty thefts.

Shew your knave's visage, with a pox to you; shew your *sheepbiting* face, and be hanged. *Shakespeare.*

SHEE'PBITER. *n. s.* [from *sheepbite*.] A petty thief.

His gate like a *sheepbiter* fleering aside. *Tusser.*

Wouldſt thou not be glad to have the niggardly raſcally *ſheepbiter* come to ſome notable ſhame. *Shakeſpeare.*

There are political *ſheepbiters* as well as paſtoral: betrayers of publick truſts, as well as of private. *L'Eſtrange.*

SHEE'PCOT. *n. ſ.* [*ſheep* and *cot.*] A little incloſure for *ſheep.*

Bedlam beggars, with roaring voices,
From low farms, *ſheepcots* and mills
Inforce their charity. *Shakeſp. K. Lear.*

Up to a hill anon his ſteps he rear'd,
From whoſe high top to ken the proſpect round,
If cottage were in view, *ſheepcot* or herd;
But cottage, herd, or *ſheepcot* none he ſaw. *Milton.*

SHEEPFO'LD. *n. ſ.* [*ſheep* and *fold.*] The place where ſheep are incloſed.

The bear, the lion, terrors of the plain,
The *ſheepfold* ſcatter'd and the ſhepherd ſlain. *Prior.*

SHEE'PHOOK. *n. ſ.* [*ſheep* and *hook.*] A hook faſtened to a pole by which ſhepherds lay hold on the legs of their ſheep.

The one carried a croſier of balm-wood, the other a paſtoral ſtaff of cedar like a *ſheep-hook.* *Bacon's New Atlantis.*

If you dare think of deſerving our charms,
Away with your *ſheephook*, and take to your arms. *Dryden.*

SHEE'PISH. *adj.* [from *ſheep.*] Baſhful; over-modeſt; timorouſly and meanly diffident.

Wanting change of company, he will, when he comes abroad, be a *ſheepiſh* or conceited creature. *Locke.*

SHEE'PISHNESS. *n. ſ.* [from *ſheepiſh.*] Baſhfulneſs; mean and timorous diffidence.

Thy gentry bleats, as if thy native cloth
Transfus'd a *ſheepiſhneſs* into thy ſtory. *Herbert.*

Sheepiſhneſs and ignorance of the world, are not conſequences of being bred at home. *Locke.*

Without ſucceſs, let a man be never ſo hardy, he will have ſome degree of *ſheepiſhneſs.* *Grew.*

SHEE'PMASTER. *n. ſ.* [*ſheep* and *maſter.*] An owner of *ſheep.*

A nobleman was a great graſier, and a great *ſheepmaſter.* *Bacon.*

SHEEPSHEA'RING. *n ſ.* [*ſheep* and *ſhear.*] The time of ſhearing ſheep; the feaſt made when ſheep are ſhorn.

There happening a ſolemn feſtivity, ſuch as the *ſheepſhearings* uſed to be, David begs ſome ſmall repaſt. *South.*

SHEEPS EYE. *n. ſ.* [*ſheep* and *eye*] A modeſt diffident look, ſuch as lovers caſt at their miſtreſſes.

Caſt a *ſheep's eye* behind you: in before me. *Dryden.*

SHEEPWA'LK. *n. ſ.* [*ſheep* and *walk.*] Paſture for ſheep.

He beheld a field,
Part arable and tilth; whereon were ſheaves
New reap'd; the other part *ſheepwalks* and folds. *Milt.*

SHEER. *adj.* [ſcyn, Saxon.] Pure; clear; unmingled.

If ſhe ſay, I am not fourteen pence on the ſcore for *ſheer* ale, ſcore me up for the lying'ſt rogue in Chriſtendom. *Shak.*

Sheer argument is not the talent of the man; little wreſted ſentences are the bladders which bear him up, and he ſinks downright, when he once pretends to ſwim without them. *Atterbury.*

SHEER. *adv.* [from the adjective.] Clean; quick; at once.

Thrown by angry Jove
Sheer o'er the cryſtal battlements; from morn
To noon he fell, from noon to dewy eve,
A ſummer's day; and with the ſetting ſun,
Drop'd from the zenith, like a falling ſtar,
On Lemnos. *Milton.*

The ſword of Satan, with ſteep force to ſmite
Deſcending, and in half cut *ſheer.* *Milton.*

Due entrance he diſdain'd, and in contempt
At one ſlight bound high overleap'd all bound
Of hill or higheſt wall, and *ſheer* within
Lights on his feet. *Milton.*

To SHEER. *v. a.* [See SHEAR.]

I keep my birth-day; ſend my Phillis home
At *ſheering*-time. *Dryden.*

To SHEER *off. v n.* To ſteal away; to ſlip off clandeſtinely.

SHEERS. *n. ſ.* [See SHEARS.]

SHEET. *n. ſ.* [ſceat, Saxon.]

1. A broad and large piece of linen.

He ſaw heaven opened, and a veſſel deſcending unto him, as a great *ſheet*, knit at the four corners. *Acts* x. 11.

2. The linen of a bed.

If I die before thee, ſhroud me
In one of theſe ſame *ſheets.* *Shakeſpeare.*

You think none but your *ſheets* are privy to your wiſhes. *Sha.*

Some unequal bride in nobler *ſheets*
Receives her lord. *Dryden.*

3. *Ecoutes*, French; *ecboten*, Dutch.] In a ſhip are ropes bent to the clews of the ſails, which ſerve in all the lower ſails to hale or round off the clew of the ſail; but in topſails they draw the ſail cloſe to the yard arms. *Dict.—Dryden* ſeems to underſtand it otherwiſe.

The little word behind the back, and undoing whiſper, like pulling off a *ſheet*-rope at ſea, ſlackens the ſail. *Suckling.*

Fierce Boreas drove againſt his flying ſails,
And rent the *ſheets.* *Dryden.*

4. As much paper as is made in one body.

As much love in rhime,
As could be cramm'd up in a *ſheet* of paper.
Writ on both ſides the leaf, margin and all. *Shakeſpeare.*

When I firſt put pen to paper, I though a! I ſhould have to ſay would have been contained in one *ſheet* of paper. *Locke.*

I let the refracted light fall perpendicularly upon a *ſheet* of white paper upon the oppoſite wall. *Newton's Opticks.*

5. A ſingle complication or fold of paper in a book.

6. Any thing expanded.

Such *ſheets* of fire, ſuch burſts of horrid thunder
I never remember to have heard. *Shakeſpeare's K. Lear.*

Rowling thunder roars,
And *ſheets* of lightning blaſt the ſtanding field. *Dryden.*

An azure *ſheet* it ruſhes broad,
And from the loud reſounding rocks below,
Daſh'd in a cloud of foam. *Thomſon.*

SHEET-*anchor. n. ſ.* [*ſheet* and *anchor.*] In a ſhip is the largeſt anchor; which, in ſtreſs of weather, is the mariners laſt refuge, when an extraordinary ſtiff gale of wind happens. *Bailey.*

To SHEET *v. a.* [from the noun.]

1. To furniſh with *ſheets.*

2. To enfold in a *ſheet.*

3. To cover as with a *ſheet.*

Like the ſtag when ſnow the paſture *ſheets*,
The barks of trees thou browſed'ſt. *Shakeſpeare.*

SHE'KEL. *n. ſ.* [שקל.] An ancient Jewiſh coin equal to four Attick drachms, or four Roman denarii, in value about 2. s 6d. ſterling. *Dict.*

The Jews, albeit they deteſted images, yet imprinted upon their *ſheckle* on one ſide the golden pot which had the manna, and on the other Aaron's rod. *Camden.*

The huge iron head ſix hundred *ſhekels* weighed,
And of whole bodies but one wound it made,
Able death's worſt command to overdoe
Deſtroying life at once and carcaſe too. *Cowley.*

This coat of mail weighed five thouſand *ſhekels* of braſs. *Broome.*

SHE'LDAPLE. *n. ſ.* A chaffinch.

SHE'LDRAPE. *n. ſ.* A bird that preys upon fiſhes.

SHELF. *n. ſ.* [ſcylf, Saxon; *ſcelf*, Dutch.] A board fixed againſt a ſupporter, ſo that any thing may be placed upon it.

About his *ſhelves*
A beggarly account of empty boxes. *Shakeſp.*

Bind faſt, or from their *ſhelves*
Your books will come and right themſelves. *Swift.*

You have the pleaſure of the proſpect whenever you take it from your *ſhelf*, and the ſolid caſh you ſold it for. *Blount.*

2. A ſand bank in the ſea; a rock under ſhallow water.

Our tranſported ſouls ſhall congratulate each other their having now fully eſcaped the numerous rocks, *ſhelves*, and quick-ſands. *Boyle.*

Near the *ſhelves* of Circe's ſhores they run,
A dang'rous coaſt. *Dryden.*

He call'd his money in;
But the prevailing love of pelf
Soon ſplit him on the former *ſhelf*,
He put it out again. *Dryden.*

3. The plural is analogically *ſhelves*; *Dryden* has *ſhelfs*, probably by negligence.

He ſeiz'd the helm, his fellows cheer'd,
Turn'd ſhort upon the *ſhelfs* and madly ſteer'd. *Dryden.*

SHE'LFY. *adj.* [from *ſhelf.*]

1. Full of hidden rocks or banks; full of dangerous ſhallows.

Glides by the ſyren's cliffs a *ſhelfy* coaſt,
Long infamous for ſhips and ſailors loſt,
And white with bones. *Dryden.*

2. I know not well the meaning in this paſſage, perhaps rocky.

The tillable fields are in ſome places ſo tough, that the plough will ſcarcely cut them; and in ſome ſo *ſhelfy* that the corn hath much ado to faſten its root. *Carew.*

SHELL. *n. ſ.* [ſcyll, ſceall, Saxon; *ſchale*, *ſchelle*, Dutch.]

1. The hard covering of any thing; the external cruſt.

The ſun is as the fire, and the exterior earth is as the *ſhell* of the eolipile, and the abyſs as the water within it; now when the heat of the ſun had pierced thro' the *ſhell* and reach'd the waters, it rarefy'd them. *Burn. Theo. of the Earth.*

Whatever we fetch from under ground is only what is lodged in the *ſhell* of the earth. *Locke.*

2. The covering of a teſtaceous or cruſtaceous animal.

Her women wear
The ſpoils of nations in an ear;
Chang'd for the treaſure of a *ſhell*,
And in their looſe attires do ſwell. *Ben. Johnſ. Catiline.*

Albion
Was to Neptune recommended;
Peace and plenty ſpread the ſails:
Venus, in her *ſhell* before him,
From the ſands in ſafety bore him. *Dryden's Albion.*

The *ſhells* ſerved as moulds to this ſand, which, when conſolidated, and afterwards freed from its inveſtient *ſhell*, is of the ſame ſhape as the cavity of the *ſhell.* *Woodward.*

He,

He, whom ungrateful Athens could expel,
At all times just, but when he sign'd the *shell*. *Pope.*

3. The covering of the seeds of siliquous plants.

Some fruits are contained within a hard *shell*, being the seeds of the plants. *Arbuthnot.*

4. The covering of kernels.

Chang'd loves are but chang'd sorts of meat;
And when he hath the kernel eat,
Who doth not throw away the *shell*? *Donne.*

5. The covering of an egg.

I think him as a serpent's egg,
Which, hatch'd, would, as his kind, grow mischievous,
And kill him in the *shell*. *Shakesp. Julius Cæsar.*

6. The outer part of an house.

The marquis of Medina Sidonia made the *shell* of a house, that would have been a very noble building, had he brought it to perfection. *Addison on Italy.*

7. It is used for a musical instrument in poetry, from *testudo*, Latin; the first lyre being said to have been made by straining strings over the shell of a tortoise.

Less than a god they thought there could not dwell
Within the hollow of that *shell*,
That spoke so sweetly. *Dryden.*

8. The superficial part.

So devout are the Romanists about this outward *shell* of religion, that if an altar be moved, or a stone of it broken, it ought to be reconsecrated. *Ayliffe's Parergon.*

To SHELL. *v. a.* [from the noun.] To take out of the shell; to strip of the shell.

To SHELL. *v. n.*

1. To fall off as broken shells.

The ulcers were cured, and the scabs *shelled* off. *Wiseman.*

2. To cast the shell.

SHE'LLDUCK. *n. s.* A kind of wild duck.

To preserve wild ducks, and *shellducks*, have a place walled in with a pond. *Mortimer's Husbandry.*

SHE'LLFISH. *n. s.* [*shell* and *fish*.] Fish invested with a hard covering, either testaceous, as oysters, or crustaceous, as lobsters.

The shells, being found, were so like those they saw upon their shores, that they never questioned but that they were the exuviæ of *shellfish*, and once belonged to the sea. *Woodward.*

SHE'LLY. *adj.* [from *shell*.]

1. Abounding with shells.

The ocean rolling, and the *shelly* shore,
Beautiful objects, shall delight no more. *Prior.*

2. Consisting of shells.

The conceit of Anaximander was, that the first men and all animals were bred in some warm moisture, inclosed in crustaceous skins, as lobsters; and so continued 'till their *shelly* prisons, growing dry and breaking, made way for them. *Bentley.*

SHE'LTER. *n. s.* [Of this word the etymology is unknown: *Skinner* deduces it from *shell*, *Davies* from ʃcylb, a shield, Saxon.]

1. A cover from any external injury or violence.

We hear this fearful tempest sing,
Yet seek no *shelter* to avoid the storm. *Shakesp. R. II.*

They wish'd the mountains now might be again
Thrown on them, as a *shelter* from his ire. *Milton.*

Heroes of old, when wounded, *shelter* sought;
But he who meets all dangers with disdain,
Ev'n in their face his ship to anchor brought,
And steeple high stood propt upon the main. *Dryden.*

They may learn experience, and avoid a cave as the worst *shelter* from rain, when they have a lover in company. *Dryd.*

The healing plant shall aid,
From storms a *shelter*, and from heat a shade. *Pope.*

2. A protector; a defender; one that gives security.

Thou hast been a *shelter* for me, and a strong tower from the enemy. *Ps.* lxi. 3.

3. The state of being covered; protection; security.

Low at his foot a spacious plain is plac'd,
Between the mountain and the stream embrac'd;
Which shade and *shelter* from the hill derives,
While the kind river wealth and beauty gives. *Denham.*

To SHE'LTER. *v. a.* [from the noun.]

1. To cover from external violence.

We besought the deep to *shelter* us. *Milton.*

Those ruins *shelter'd* once his sacred head,
When he from Wor'ster's fatal battle fled,
Watch'd by the genius of this royal place. *Dryden.*

2. To defend; to protect; to succour with refuge; to harbour.

What endless honour shall you gain,
To save and *shelter* Troy's unhappy train. *Dryden's Æn.*

3. To betake to cover.

They *sheltered* themselves under a rock. *Abbot.*

Comfort thyself with such thoughts, chiefly when all earthly comforts fail thee: then do thou particularly retreat to those considerations, and *shelter* thyself under them. *Atterbury.*

4. To cover from notice.

In vain I strove to check my growing flame,
Or *shelter* passion under friendship's name;
You saw my heart. *Prior.*

To SHE'LTER. *v. n.*

1. To take shelter.

There the Indian herdsman, shunning heat,
Shelters in cool. *Milton.*

2. To give shelter.

Then seeks the farthest ooze, the *shelt'ring* weed,
The cavern'd bank, his old secure abode. *Thomson.*

SHE'LTERLESS. *adj.* [from *shelter*.] Harbourless; without home or refuge.

Now sad and *shelterless*, perhaps, she lies,
Where piercing winds blow sharp. *Rowe's Jane Shore.*

SHE'LVING. *adj.* [from *shelf*.] Sloping; inclining; having declivity.

Her chamber is aloft, far from the ground;
And built so *shelving*, that one cannot climb it,
Without apparent hazard of his life. *Shakespeare*

Amidst the brake a hollow den was found,
With rocks and *shelving* arches vaulted round. *Addison.*

SHE'LVY. *adj.* [from *shelf*.] Shallow; rocky; full of banks.

I had been drowned, but that the shore was *shelvy* and shallow. *Shakesp. Merry Wives of Windsor.*

To SHEND. *v. a.* preter. and part. pass. *shent*. [ʃcenðan, Saxon; *schenden*, Dutch.]

1. To ruin; to spoil; to mischief.

Provide for thy wife, or else look to be *shent*,
Good milchcow for Winter, another for Lent. *Tusser.*

Shepherds, should it not *yshent*
Your roundels fresh, to hear a doleful verse
Of Rosalind, that Colin made? *Spenser.*

Such a dream I had of dire portent,
That much I fear my body will be *shent*;
It bodes I shall have wars. *Dryden.*

2. To disgrace; to degrade; to blame.

Debateful strife, and cruel enmity,
The famous name of knighthood foully *shend*. *Fa. Queen.*

Sore bruised with the fall, he slow uprose,
And all enraged thus, thus him loudly *shent*,
Disleal knight, whose coward courage chose
To wreak itself on beast. *Fairy Queen.*

My tongue and soul in this be hypocrites,
How in my words soever she be *shent*,
To give them seals never my soul consent. *Shakesp. Haml.*

3. To overpower; to crush; to surpass.

She pass'd the rest as Cynthia doth *shend*
The lesser stars. *Spenser.*

4. It is, though used by *Dryden*, wholly obsolete.

SHE'PHERD. *n. s.* [ʃceap, sheep, and hýnð, a keeper, Saxon, ʃceapahýnð.]

1. One who tends sheep in the pasture.

I am *shepherd* to another man,
And do not sheer the fleeces that I graze. *Shakespeare.*

A *shepherd* next
More meek came with the firstlings of his flock. *Milton.*

2. A swain; a rural lover.

If that the world and love were young,
And truth in ev'ry *shepherd*'s tongue,
These pretty pleasures might me move
To live with thee, and be thy love. *Raleigh.*

3. One who tends the congregation; a pastor.

Lead up all those who heard thee, and believ'd;
'Midst thy own flock, great *shepherd*, be receiv'd,
And glad all heav'n with millions thou hast sav'd. *Prior.*

SHE'PHERDESS. *n. s.* [from *shepherd*.] A woman that tends sheep; a rural lass.

She put herself into the garb of a *shepherdess*, and in that disguise lived many years; but discovering herself a little before her death, did profess herself the happiest person alive, not for her condition, but in enjoying him she first loved; and that she would rather, ten thousand times, live a *shepherdess* in contentment and satisfaction. *Sidney.*

These your unusual weeds, to each part of you
Do give a life: no *shepherdess*, but Flora
Peering in April's front. *Shakesp. Winter's Tale.*

She like some *shepherdess* did shew,
Who sat to bathe her by a river's side. *Dryden.*

His dorick dialect has an incomparable sweetness in its clownishness, like a fair *shepherdess* in her country russet. *Dryden.*

SHEPHERDS *Needle*. *n. s.* [*scandix*, Lat.] Venus comb. An herb.

SHEPHERDS *Purse*, or *Pouch*. *n. s.* [*bursa pastoris*, Latin.] A common weed.

SHE'PHERDS *Rod*. *n. s.* Teasel, of which plant it is a species.

SHE'PHERDISH. *adj.* [from *shepherd*.] Resembling a shepherd; suiting a shepherd; pastoral; rustick. Not in use.

He would have drawn her eldest sister, esteemed her match for beauty, in her *shepherdish* attire. *Sidney.*

She saw walking from her-ward a man in *shepherdish* apparel. *Sidney.*

SHE'RBET. *n. s.* [*sharbat*, Arabick.] The juice of lemons or oranges mixed with water and sugar. *Dict.*

They prefer our beer above all other drinks; and considering that water is with the rareſt, eſpecially in this clime, the deareſt of *ſherbets*, and plenty of barley, it would prove infinitely profitable to ſuch as ſhould bring in the uſe thereof. *Sand.*

SHERD. *n. ſ.* [ſceaрo, Saxon.] The fragment of broken earthen ware.

The trivet-table of a foot was lame;
She thruſts beneath the limping leg a *ſherd*. *Dryden.*

SHE'RIFF. *n. ſ.* [ſcyreзeрefa, Saxon, from ſcyre, a ſhire, and reve, a ſteward. It is ſometimes pronounced *ſhrieve*, which ſome poets have injudiciouſly adopted.] An officer to whom is intruſted in each county the execution of the laws.

A great pow'r of Engliſh and of Scots
Are by the *ſheriff* of Yorkſhire overthrown. *Shakeſp.*

Concerning miniſters of juſtice, the high *ſheriffs* of the counties have been very ancient in this kingdom. *Bacon.*

Now may'rs and *ſhrieves* all huſh'd and ſatiate lay. *Pope.*

SHE'RIFFALTY.
SHE'RIFFDOM.
SHE'RIFFSHIP.
SHE'RIFFWICK. } *n. ſ.* [from *ſheriff.*] The office or juriſdiction of a ſheriff.

There was a reſumption of patents of gaols, and reannexing of them to the *ſheriffwicks*; privileged officers being no leſs an interruption of juſtice than privileged places. *Bacon.*

SHE'RRIS.
SHE'RRIS *Sack*.
SHE'RRY. } *n. ſ.* [from *Xeres*, a town of *Andaluſia* in *Spain*.] A kind of ſweet Spaniſh wine.

Your *ſherris* warms the blood, which before, cold and ſettled, left the liver white, which is the badge of puſilanimity; but the *ſherris* makes it courſe from the inwards to the parts extreme. *Shakeſpeare.*

Good *ſherris ſack* aſcends me into the brain, dries me there all the fooliſh dull vapours, and makes it apprehenſive. *Shak.*

SHEW. See SHOW.

SHIDE. *n ſ.* [from ſceaban, to divide, Saxon.] A board; a cutting. *Skinner.*

SHIELD. *n ſ.* [ſcylb, Saxon.]

1. A buckler; a broad piece of defenſive armour held on the left arm to ward off blows.

Now put your *ſhields* before your hearts, and fight
With hearts more proof than *ſhields*. *Shakeſp. Coriolanus.*

2. Defence; protection.

3. One that gives protection or ſecurity.

The terror of the Trojan field,
The Grecian honour, ornament, and *ſhield*,
High on a pile th' unconquer'd chief is plac'd. *Dryden.*

To SHIELD. *v. a.* [from the noun.]

1. To cover with a ſhield.

2. To defend; to protect; to ſecure.

Were't my fitneſs to let theſe hands obey my boiling blood,
They're apt enough to diſlocate and tear
Thy fleſh and bones: howe'er
A woman's ſhape doth *ſhield* thee. *Shakeſ. King Lear.*

Shouts of applauſe ran ringing through the field,
To ſee the ſon the vanquiſh'd father *ſhield*. *Dryden.*

Hear one that comes to *ſhield* his injur'd honour,
And guard his life with hazard of her own. *Smith.*

3. To keep off; to defend againſt.

Out of their cold caves and frozen habitations, into the ſweet ſoil of Europe, they brought with them their uſual weeds, fit to *ſhield* the cold, to which they had been inured. *Spenſer.*

My lord, I muſt intreat the time alone.
—God *ſhield* I ſhould diſturb devotion. *Shakeſpeare.*

To SHIFT. *v. n.* [Of this word the original is obſcure: *ſkipta*, Runick, is to change.]

1. To change place.

Vegetables being fixed to the ſame place, and ſo not able to *ſhift* and ſeek out after proper matter for their increment, it was neceſſary that it ſhould be brought to them. *Woodward.*

2. To change; to give place to other things.

If the ideas of our minds conſtantly change and *ſhift*, in a continual ſucceſſion, it would be impoſſible for a man to think long of any one thing. *Locke.*

3. To change cloaths, particularly the linen.

She begs you juſt would turn you while ſhe *ſhifts*. *Young.*

4. To find ſome expedient; to act or live though with difficulty.

We cannot *ſhift*: being in, we muſt go on. *Daniel.*

Men in diſtreſs will look to themſelves, and leave their companions to *ſhift* as well as they can. *L'Eſtrange.*

Since we deſire no recompence nor thanks, we ought to be diſmiſſed, and have leave to *ſhift* for ourſelves. *Swift.*

5. To practiſe indirect methods.

All thoſe ſchoolmen, though they were exceeding witty, yet better teach all their followers to *ſhift* than to reſolve by their diſtinctions. *Raleigh.*

6. To take ſome method for ſafety.

Nature inſtructs every creature how to *ſhift* for itſelf in caſes of danger. *L'Eſtrange.*

To SHIFT. *v. a.*

1. To change; to alter.

It was not levity, but abſolute neceſſity, that made the fiſh *ſhift* their condition. *L'Eſtrange.*

Come, aſſiſt me, muſe obedient;
Let us try ſome new expedient;
Shift the ſcene for half an hour,
Time and place are in thy pow'r. *Swift.*

2. To transfer from place to place.

Pare ſaffron between the two St. Mary's days,
Or ſet or go *ſhift* it that knoweſt the ways. *Tuſſer.*

3. To put by ſome expedient out of the way.

I *ſhifted* him away,
And laid good 'ſcuſes on your ecſtaſy. *Shakeſ. Othello.*

The wiſdom of all theſe latter times, in princes affairs, is rather fine deliveries, and *ſhiftings* of dangers and miſchiefs, when they are near, than ſolid and grounded courſes to keep them aloof. *Bacon.*

4. To change in poſition.

Neither uſe they ſails, nor place their oars in order upon the ſides; but carrying the oar looſe, *ſhift* it hither and thither at pleaſure. *Raleigh.*

Where the wind
Veers oft, as oft ſhe ſteers and *ſhifts* her ſail. *Milton.*

We ſtrive in vain againſt the ſeas and wind;
Now *ſhift* your ſails. *Dryden's Æn.*

5. To change, as cloaths.

I would adviſe you to *ſhift* a ſhirt: the violence of action hath made you reek as a ſacrifice. *Shakeſ. Cymbeline.*

6. To dreſs in freſh cloaths.

As it were to ride day and night, and not to have patience to *ſhift* me. *Shak. Henry IV.*

7. *To* SHIFT *off.* To defer; to put away by ſome expedient.

The moſt beautiful parts muſt be the moſt finiſhed, the colours and words moſt choſen: many things in both, which are not deſerving of this care, muſt be *ſhifted off*, content with vulgar expreſſions. *Dryden's Dufreſnoy.*

Struggle and contrive as you will, and lay your taxes as you pleaſe, the traders will *ſhift* it *off* from their own gain. *Locke.*

By various illuſions of the devil they are prevailed on to *ſhift off* the duties, and neglect the conditions, on which ſalvation is promiſed. *Rogers's Sermons.*

SHIFT. *n. ſ.* [from the verb.]

1. Expedient found or uſed with difficulty; difficult means.

She redoubling her blows, drave the ſtranger to no other *ſhift* than to ward and go back; at that time ſeeming the image of innocency againſt violence. *Sidney.*

If I get down, and do not break my limbs,
I'll find a thouſand *ſhifts* to get away. *Shakeſ. K. John.*

This perfect artifice and accuracy might have been omitted, and yet they have made *ſhift* to move up and down in the water. *More's Antidote againſt Atheiſm.*

Not any boaſt of ſkill, but extreme *ſhift*
How to regain my ſever'd company,
Compell'd me to awake the courteous echo,
To give me anſwer from her moſſy couch. *Milton.*

A faſhionable hypocriſy ſhall be called good manners, ſo we make a *ſhift* ſomewhat to legitimate the abuſe. *L'Eſtrange.*

Thoſe little animals provide themſelves with wheat; but they can make *ſhift* without it. *Addiſon.*

Our herbals are ſufficiently ſtored with plants, and we have made a tolerable *ſhift* to reduce them to claſſes. *Baker.*

2. Indirect expedient; mean refuge; laſt recourſe.

The very cuſtom of ſeeking ſo particular aid and relief at the hands of God, doth, by a ſecret contradiction, withdraw them from endeavouring to help themſelves, even by thoſe wicked *ſhifts*, which they know can never have his allowance whoſe aſſiſtance their prayers ſeek. *Hooker.*

To ſay, where the notions cannot fitly be reconciled, that there wanteth a term, is but a *ſhift* of ignorance. *Bacon.*

Slow to reſolve, but in performance quick;
So true, that he was aukward at a trick;
For little ſouls on little *ſhifts* rely. *Dryden.*

3. Fraud; artifice; ſtratagem.

Know ye not Ulyſſes' *ſhifts*?
Their ſwords leſs danger carry than their gifts. *Denham.*

4. Evaſion; eluſory practice.

As long as wit, by whetting itſelf, is able to find out any *ſhift*, be it never ſo ſlight, whereby to eſcape out of the hands of preſent contradiction, they are never at a ſtand. *Hooker.*

Of themſelves, for the moſt part, they are ſo cautious and wily-headed, eſpecially being men of ſo ſmall experience and practice in law matters, that you would wonder whence they borrow ſuch ſubtilities and ſly *ſhifts*. *Spenſer.*

Here you ſee your commiſſion; this is your duty, theſe are your diſcouragements: never ſeek for *ſhifts* and evaſions from worldly afflictions: this is your reward, if you perform it; this your doom, if you decline it. *South.*

5. A woman's linen.

SHI'FTER. *n. ſ.* [from *ſhift*.] One who plays tricks; a man of artifice.

'Twas ſuch a *ſhifter*, that, if truth were known,
Death was half glad when he had got him down. *Milton.*

SHI'FTLESS. *adj.* [from *ſhift*.] Wanting expedients; wanting means to act or live.

For

For the poor *shiftless* irrationals, it is a prodigious act of the great Creator's indulgence, that they are all ready furnished with such cloathing. *Derham's Physico-Theology.*

SHI'LLING. *n. s.* [scylling, Sax. and Erse; *schelling*, Dut.] A coin of various value in different times. It is now twelve pence.

Five of these pence made their *shilling*, which they called *scilling*, probably from *scilingus*, which the Romans used for the fourth part of an ounce; and forty-eight of these *scillings* made their pound, and four hundred of these pounds were a legacy for a king's daughter, as appeareth by the last will of king Alfred. *Camden's Remains.*

The very same *shilling* may at one time pay twenty men in twenty days, and at another rest in the same hands one hundred days. *Locke.*

SHILL-I-SHALL-I. A corrupt reduplication of *shall I?* The question of a man hesitating. To stand *shill-I-shall-I*, is to continue hesitating and procrastinating.

I am somewhat dainty in making a resolution, because when I make it, I keep it: I don't stand *shill-I shall-I* then; if I say't, I'll do't. *Congreve's Way of the World.*

SHI'LY. *adv.* [from *shy.*] Not familiarly; not frankly.

SHIN. *n. s.* [scina, Saxon; *schien*, German.] The forepart of the leg.

I bruised my *shin* the other day with playing at sword and dagger. *Shakesp. Merry Wives of Windsor.*

The *shin* bone, from the knee to the instep, is made by shadowing one half of the leg with a single shadow. *Peacham.*

His leg, then broke,
Had got a deputy of oak;
For when a *shin* in fight is cropt,
The knee with one of timber's propt. *Hudibras.*

As when to an house we come,
To know if any one's at home,
We knock; so one must kick your *shin*,
Ere he can find your soul's within. *Anonymous.*

To SHINE. *v. n.* preterite *I shone, I have shone*; sometimes *I shined, I have shined.* [scinan, Saxon; *schijnen*, Dutch.]

1. To have bright resplendence; to glitter; to glisten; to gleam.

To-day the French,
All clinquant, all in gold, like heathen gods,
Shone down the English; and to-morrow
Made Britain India: ev'ry man that stood,
Shew'd like a mine. *Shakespeare.*

True paradise inclos'd with *shining* rock. *Milton.*

We can dismiss thee ere the morning *shine.* *Milton.*

Fair daughter, blow away these mists and clouds,
And let thy eyes *shine* forth in their full lustre. *Denham.*

The sun *shines* when he sees it. *Locke.*

2. To be without clouds.

The moon *shines* bright: in such a night as this,
When the sweet wind did gently kiss the trees,
And they did make no noise. *Shak. Merch. of Venice.*

How bright and goodly *shines* the moon!
The moon! the sun: it is not moonlight now. *Shakesp.*

Two men stood by them in *shining* garments. *Lu.* xxiv. 4.

Clear pools greatly comfort the eyes when the sun is overcast, or when the moon *shineth.* *Bacon.*

3. To be glossy.

They are waxen fat, they *shine.* *Jer.* v. 28.

Fish with their fins and *shining* scales. *Milton.*

The colour and *shining* of bodies is nothing but the different arrangement and refraction of their minute parts. *Locke.*

4. To be gay; to be splendid.

So proud she *shined* in her princely state,
Looking to heaven; for earth she did disdain,
And sitting high. *Fairy Queen.*

5. To be beautiful.

Of all th' enamel'd race, whose silv'ry wing
Waves to the tepid zephyrs of the Spring,
Or swims along the fluid atmosphere,
Once brightest *shin'd* this child of heat and air. *Dunciad.*

6. To be eminent or conspicuous.

If there come truth from them,
As upon thee, Macbeth, their speeches *shine*,
Why, by the verities on thee made good,
May they not be my oracles as well? *Shakespeare.*

Her face was veil'd; yet to my fancied sight
Love, sweetness, goodness, in her person *shin'd*
So clear, as in no face with more delight. *Milton.*

Cato's soul
Shines out in every thing she acts or speaks;
While winning mildness and attractive smiles
Dwell in her looks, and, with becoming grace,
Soften the rigour of her father's virtues. *Addison.*

The reformation, in its first establishment, produced its proper fruits, and distinguished the whole age with *shining* instances of virtue and morality. *Addison's Freeholder.*

The courtier smooth, who forty years had *shin'd*
An humble servant to all human kind. *Pope.*

Few are qualified to *shine* in company; but it is in most mens power to be agreeable. *Swift.*

7. To be propitious.

The Lord make his face *shine* upon thee, and be gracious. *Num.* vi. 25.

8. To enlighten corporeally and externally.

The light of righteousness hath not *shined* unto us, and the sun of righteousness rose not upon us. *Wisd.* v. 6.

Celestial light
Shine inward, and the mind through all her powers
Irradiate. *Milton.*

SHINE. *n. s.* [from the verb.]

1. Fair weather.

Be it fair or foul, or rain or *shine.* *Dryden.*

He will accustom himself to heat and cold, and *shine* and rain; all which if a man's body will not endure, it will serve him to very little purpose. *Locke.*

2. Brightness; splendour; lustre. It is a word, though not unanalogical, yet ungraceful, and little used.

He that has inured his eyes to that divine splendour, which results from the beauty of holiness, is not dazzled with the glittering *shine* of gold, and considers it as a vein of the same earth he treads on. *Decay of Piety.*

Say, in what mortal soil thou deign'st to grow?
Fair op'ning to some court's propitious *shine*,
Or deep with di'monds in the flaming mine? *Pope.*

SHI'NESS. *n. s.* [from *shy.*] Unwillingness to be tractable or familiar.

An incurable *shiness* is the vice of Irish horses, and is hardly ever seen in Flanders, because the Winter forces the breeders there to house and handle their colts. *Temple.*

They were famous for their justice in commerce, but extreme *shiness* to strangers: they exposed their goods with the price marked upon them, and then retired. *Arbuthnot.*

SHI'NGLE. *n. s.* [*schindel*, Germ.] A thin board to cover houses.

The best to cleave, is the most useful for pales, laths, *shingles*, and wainscot. *Mortimer's Husbandry.*

SHI'NGLES. *n. s.* Wants singul. [*cingulum*, Latin; *zona morbus*, Plinio.] A kind of tetter or herpes that spreads itself round the loins.

Such are used successfully in erysipelas and *shingles*, by a slender diet of decoctions of farinaceous vegetables, and copious drinking of cooling liquors. *Arbuthnot on Diet.*

SHI'NY. *adj.* [from *shine.*] Bright; splendid; luminous.

When Aldeboran was mounted high,
Above the *shiny* Cassiopeia's chain,
One knocked at the door, and in would fare. *Fa. Queen.*

The night
Is *shiny*, and they say we shall embattle
By th' second hour o' th' morn. *Shak. Ant. and Cleopatra.*

While from afar we heard the cannons play,
Like distant thunder on a *shiny* day,
For absent friends we were asham'd to fear. *Dryden.*

SHIP. [scip, scyp, Saxon; *schap*, Dutch.] A termination noting quality or adjunct, as *lordship*; or office, as *stewardship*.

SHIP. *n. s.* [scip, Saxon; *schippen*, Dutch.] A ship may be defined a large hollow building, made to pass over the sea with sails. *Watts.*

All my followers to the eager foe
Turn back, and fly like *ships* before the wind. *Shak. H. VI.*

There made forth to us a small boat, with about eight persons in it, whereof one of them had in his hand a tipstaff, who made aboard our *ship.* *Bacon.*

Two other *ships* loaded with victuals were burnt, and some of the men saved by their shipboats. *Knolles.*

Nor is indeed that man less mad than these,
Who freights a *ship* to venture on the seas,
With one frail interposing plank to save
From certain death, roll'd on by ev'ry wave. *Dryden.*

Instead of a *ship*, he should levy upon his country such a sum of money, and return the same to the treasurer of the navy: hence that tax had the denomination of *ship*-money, by which accrued the yearly sum of two hundred thousand pounds. *Clarendon.*

A *ship*-carpenter of old Rome could not have talked more judiciously. *Addison.*

To SHIP. *v. a.* [from the noun.]

1. To put into a ship.

My father at the road
Expects my coming, there to see me *shipp'd.* *Shakesp.*

The emperor, *shipping* his great ordnance, departed down the river. *Knolles's Hist. of the Turks.*

All the timber whereof was cut down in the mountains of Cilicia, and *shipped* in the bay of Attalia, from whence it was by sea transported to Pelusium. *Knolles.*

A breeze from shore began to blow,
The sailors *ship* their oars, and cease to row;
Then hoist their yards a-trip, and all their sails
Let fall. *Dryden.*

2. To transport in a ship.

Andronicus, would thou wert *shipt* to hell,
Rather than rob me of the people's hearts. *Shakespeare.*

The

The sun no sooner shall the mountains touch,
But we will *ship* him hence. *Shakesp. Hamlet.*

In Portugal men spent with age, so as they cannot hope for above a year of life, *ship* themselves away in a Brazil fleet. *Temple.*

A single leaf can waft an army o'er,
Or *ship* off senates to some distant shore. *Pope.*

The canal that runs from the sea into the Arno gives a convenient carriage to all goods that are to be *shipped* off. *Addis.*

SHI'PBOARD. *n. s.* [*ship* and *board.* See BOARD.]

1. This word is seldom used but in adverbial phrases: *a shipboard, on shipboard*, in a ship.

Let him go *on shipboard*, and the mariners will not leave their starboard and larboard. *Bramhall.*

Friend,
What do'st thou make *a shipboard?* To what end? *Dryden.*

Ovid, writing from *on shipboard* to his friends, excused the faults of his poetry by his misfortunes. *Dryden.*

2. The plank of a ship.

They have made all thy *shipboards* of fir-trees, and brought cedars from Lebanon to make masts. *Ezek.* xxvii. 5.

SHI'PBOY. *n. s.* [*ship* and *boy.*] Boy that serves in a ship.

Few or none know me: if they did,
This *shipboy*'s semblance hath disguis'd me quite. *Shakesp.*

SHI'PMAN. *n. s.* [*ship* and *man.*] Sailor; seaman.

I myself have the very points they blow,
All the quarters that they know
I' th' *shipman*'s card. *Shakesp. Macbeth.*

Hiram sent in the navy *shipmen* that had knowledge of the sea. *1 Kings* ix. 27.

SHI'PMASTER. *n. s.* Master of the ship.

The *shipmaster* came to him, and said unto him, what meanest thou, O sleeper! arise, call upon thy God. *Jon.* i. 6.

SHI'PPING. *n. s.* [from *ship.*]

1. Vessels of navigation.

Before Cæsar's invasion of this land, the Britons had not any *shipping* at all, other than their boats of twigs covered with hides. *Raleigh.*

The numbers and courage of our men, with the strength of our *shipping*, have for many ages past made us a match for the greatest of our neighbours at land, and an overmatch for the strongest at sea. *Temple.*

Fishes first to *shipping* did impart;
Their tail the rudder, and their head the prow. *Dryden.*

2. Passage in a ship.

They took *shipping* and came to Capernaum, seeking for Jesus. *Jo.* vi. 24.

SHI'PWRECK. *n. s.* [*ship* and *wreck.*]

1. The destruction of ships by rocks or shelves.

Bold were the men, which on the ocean first
Spread their new sails, when *shipwreck* was the worst. *Waller.*

We are not to quarrel with the water for inundations and *shipwrecks.* *L'Estrange.*

This sea war cost the Carthaginians five hundred quinquiremes, and the Romans seven hundred, including their *shipwrecks.* *Arbuthnot.*

2. The parts of a shattered ship.

They might have it in their own country, and that by gathering up the *shipwrecks* of the Athenian and Roman theatres. *Dryden.*

3. Destruction; miscarriage.

Holding faith and a good conscience, which some having put away, concerning faith, have made *shipwreck.* *1 Tim.* i.

To SHI'PWRECK. *v. a.* [from the noun.]

1. To destroy by dashing on rocks or shallows.

Whence the sun 'gins his reflection,
Shipwrecking storms and direful thunders break. *Shakesp.*

2. To make to suffer the dangers of a wreck.

Thou that can'st still the raging of the seas,
Chain up the winds, and bid the tempests cease,
Redeem my *shipwreck'd* soul from raging gusts
Of cruel passion and deceitful lusts. *Prior.*

A square piece of marble shews itself to have been a little pagan monument of two persons who were *shipwrecked.* *Addis.*

3. To throw by loss of the vessel.

Shipwreck'd upon a kingdom, where no pity,
No friends, no hope! no kindred weep for me. *Shakesp.*

SHI'PWRIGHT. *n s.* [*ship* and *wright.*] A builder of ships.

Why such impress of *shipwrights*, whose sore task
Does not divide the Sunday from the week. *Shakesp.*

A miserable shame it were for our *shipwrights*, if they did not exceed all others in the setting up of our royal ships. *Ral.*

Vast numbers of ships in our harbours, and *shipwrights* in our sea-port towns. *Swift.*

The Roman fleet, although built by *shipwrights*, and conducted by pilots, both without experience, defeated that of the Carthaginians. *Arbuthnot.*

As when a *shipwright* stands his workmen o'er,
Who ply the wimble some huge beam to bore,
Urg'd on all hands it nimbly spins about,
The grain deep piercing, 'till it scoops it out. *Pope.*

SHIRE. *n. s.* [ꞅciꞃ, from ꞅciꞃan, to divide, Sax. *skyre*, Erse.] A division of the kingdom; a county; so much of the kingdom as is under one sheriff.

His blazing eyes, like two bright shining shields,
Did burn with wrath, and sparkled living fire;
As two broad beacons, set in open fields,
Send forth their flames far off to every *shire.* *Fa. Queen.*

The noble youths from distant *shires* resort. *Prior.*

SHIRT. *n. s.* [*skiert*, Danish; ꞅcẏꞃc, ꞅcẏꞃic, Saxon.] The under linen garment of a man.

Shift a *shirt*: the violence of action hath made you reek as a sacrifice. *Shakesp. Cymbeline.*

I take but two *shirts* out with me, and I mean not to sweat extraordinarily. *Shakesp. Henry* IV.

When we lay next us what we hold most dear,
Like Hercules, envenom'd *shirts* we wear,
And cleaving mischiefs. *Dryden.*

Several persons in December had nothing over their shoulders but their *shirts.* *Addison on Italy.*

To SHIRT. *v. a.* [from the noun.] To cover; to clothe as in a shirt.

Ah! for so many souls, as but this morn
Were cloath'd with flesh, and warm'd with vital blood,
But naked now, or *shirted* but with air. *Dryden.*

SHI'RTLESS. *adj.* [from *shirt.*] Wanting a shirt.

Linsey-woolsey brothers,
Grave mummers! sleeveless some, and *shirtless* others. *Pope.*

SHI'TTAH. } *n. s.* A sort of precious wood, of which *Moses*
SHI'TTIM. } made the greatest part of the tables, altars, and planks belonging to the tabernacle. The wood is hard, tough, smooth, without knots, and extremely beautiful. It grows in Arabia. *Calmett.*

I will plant in the wilderness the *shittah*-tree. *Is.* xli. 19.

Bring me an offering of badgers skins and *shittim*-wood. *Ex.*

SHI'TTLECOCK. *n. s.* [Commonly and perhaps as properly *shuttlecock.* Of *shittle* or *shuttle* the etymology is doubtful: *Skinner* derives it from *schutteln*, German, to shake; or ꞅceaꞇan, Saxon, to throw. He thinks it is called a cock from its feathers. Perhaps it is properly *shuttlecork*, a cork driven to and fro, as the instrument in weaving, and softened by frequent and rapid utterance from *cork* to *cock.*] A cork stuck with feathers, and driven by players from one to another with battledoors.

You need not discharge a cannon to break the chain of his thoughts: the pat of a *shittlecock*, or the creaking of a jack, will do his business. *Collier.*

SHIVE. *n. s.* [*schyve*, Dutch.]

1. A slice of bread.

Easy it is
Of a cut loaf to steal a *shive.* *Shakesp. Titus Andronicus.*

2. A thick splinter, or lamina cut off from the main substance.

Shavings made by the plane are in some things differing from those *shives*, or thin and flexible pieces of wood, that are obtained by borers. *Boyle.*

To SHI'VER. *v. n.* [*schawren*, German.] To quake; to tremble; to shudder, as with cold or fear.

Any very harsh noise will set the teeth on edge, and make all the body *shiver.* *Bacon.*

What religious palsy's this,
Which makes the boughs divest their bliss?
And that they might her footsteps straw,
Drop their leaves with *shivering* awe. *Cleaveland.*

Why stand we longer *shivering* under fear? *Milton.*

The man that *shiver'd* on the brink of sin,
Thus steel'd and harden'd, ventures boldly in. *Dryden.*

He described this march to the temple with so much horror, that he *shivered* every joint. *Addison.*

Give up Laius to the realms of day,
Whose ghost, yet *shiv'ring* on Cocytus' sand,
Expects its passage to the farther strand. *Pope.*

Prometheus is laid
On icy Caucasus to *shiver*,
While vultures eat his growing liver. *Swift.*

To SHI'VER. *v. n.* [from *shive.*] To fall at once into many parts or shives.

Had'st thou been aught but goss'mer, feathers, air,
So many fathom down precipitating,
Thou'd'st *shiver'd* like an egg. *Shakes. King John.*

Upon the breaking and *shivering* of a great state, you may be sure to have wars. *Bacon.*

The natural world, should gravity once cease, or be withdrawn, would instantly *shiver* into millions of atoms. *Woodw.*

To SHI'VER. *v. a.* To break by one act into many parts; to shatter.

The ground with *shiver'd* armour strown. *Milton.*

Show'rs of granado's rain, by sudden burst
Disploding murd'rous bowels; fragments of steel
A thousand ways at once, the *shiver'd* orbs
Fly diverse, working torment. *Philips.*

SHI'VER. *n. s.* [from the verb.] One fragment of many into which any thing is broken.

He would pound thee into *shivers* with his fist, as a sailor breaks a bisket. *Shakesp. Troilus and Cressida.*

As brittle as the glory is the face;
For there it is crack'd in an hundred *shivers.* *Shakespeare.*

If you strike a solid body that is brittle, it breaketh not only where the immediate force is, but breaketh all about into *shivers* and fritters. *Bacon's Nat. History.*

Surging waves against a solid rock,
Though all to *shivers* dash'd, th' assault renew,
Vain batt'ry, and in froth or bubbles end. *Milton.*

SHI'VERY. *adj.* [from *shiver.*] Loose of coherence; incompact; easily falling into many fragments.

There were observed incredible numbers of these shells thus flatted, and extremely tender; in *shivery* stone. *Woodward.*

SHO'ADSTONE. *n. s.*

Shoadstone is a small stone, smooth without, of a dark liver colour, and of the same colour within, only with the addition of a faint purple. It is a fragment broke of an iron vein. *Woodward on Fossils.*

Certain tin-stones ly on the face of the ground which they call *shoad*, as shed from the main load, and made somewhat round by the water. *Carew's Survey of Cornwall.*

The loads or veins of metal were by this action of the departing water made easy to be found out by the *shoads*, or trains of metallick fragments born off from them, and lying in trains from those veins towards the sea, in the same course that water falling thence would take. *Woodward.*

SHOAL. *n. s.* [ſcole, Saxon.

1. A croud; a great multitude; a throng.

When there be great *shoals* of people, which go on to populate, without foreseeing means of sustentation: once in an age they discharge a portion of their people upon other nations. *Bacon.*

A league is made against such routs and *sholes* of people as have utterly degenerated from nature. *Bacon.*

The vices of a prince draw *sholes* of followers, when his virtue leaves him the more eminent, because single. *Decay of Piety.*

A *shoal* of silver fishes glides
And plays about the barges. *Waller.*

God had the command of famine, whereby he could have carried them off by *shoals.* *Woodward.*

Around the goddess roll
Broad hats, and hoods, and caps, a sable *shoal*,
Thick, and more thick the black blocade extends. *Pope.*

2. A shallow; a sand bank.

The haven's mouth they durst not enter, for the dangerous *shoals.* *Abbot's Descript. of the World.*

He heaves them off the *sholes.* *Dryden.*

The depth of your pond should be six foot; and on the sides some *sholes* for the fish to lay their spawn. *Mortimer.*

To SHOAL. *v. n.* [from the noun.]

1. To croud; to throng.

The wave-sprung entrails, about which fausens and fish
did *shole.* *Chapman.*

2. To be shallow; to grow shallow.

What they met
Solid, or slimy, as in raging sea,
Tost up and down, together crouded drove,
From each side *shoaling* tow'rds the mouth of hell. *Milton.*

SHOAL. *adj.* Shallow; obstructed or incumbered with banks.

SHOA'LINESS. *n. s.* [from *shoaly.*] Shallowness; frequency of shallow places.

SHOA'LY. *adj.* [from *shoal.*] Full of shoals; full of shallow places.

Those who live
Where, with his *shoaly* foords Vulturnus roars. *Dryden.*

The watchful heroe felt the knocks, and found
The tossing vessel sail'd on *shoaly* ground. *Dryden.*

SHOCK. *n. s.* [*choc*, French; *schocken*, Dutch.]

1. Conflict; mutual impression of violence; violent concourse.

Thro' the *shock*
Of fighting elements on all sides round
Environ'd, wins his way. *Milton.*

2. Concussion; external violence.

It is inconceptible how any such man that hath stood the *shock* of an eternal duration, without corruption or alteration, should after be corrupted or altered. *Judge Hale.*

These strong unshaken mounds resist the *shocks*
Of tides and seas tempestuous, while the rocks,
That secret in a long continu'd vein
Pass through the earth, the pon'drous pile sustain. *Black.*

Such is the haughty man, his tow'ring soul,
'Midst all the *shocks* and injuries of fortune,
Rises superior and looks down on Cæsar. *Addison.*

Long at the head of his few faithful friends,
He stood the *shock* of a whole host of foes. *Addison.*

The tender apples from their parents rent,
By stormy *shocks* must not neglected lye,
The prey of worms. *Philips.*

3. The conflict of enemies.

The adverse legions, not less hideous join'd
The horrid *shock.* *Milton.*

Those that run away are in more danger than the others that stand the *shock.* *L'Estrange.*

The mighty force
Of Edward twice o'erturn'd their desp'rate king:
Twice he arose, and join'd the horrid *shock.* *Philips.*

4. Offence; impression of disgust.

Fewer *shocks* a statesman gives his friend. *Young.*

5. [*Schocke* old Dutch.] A pile of sheaves of corn.

Corn tithed, sir parson, together to get,
And cause it on *shocks* to be by and by set. *Tuss.*

In a full age, like as a *shock* of corn cometh in, in his season. *Job.*

Thou, full of days, like weighty *shocks* of corn,
In season reap'd, shall to thy grave be born. *Sandys.*

Behind the master walks, builds up the *shocks*,
Feels his heart heave with joy. *Thomson.*

6. [from *shagg.*] A rough dog.

I would fain know why a *shock* and a hound are not distinct species. *Locke.*

To SHOCK. *v. a.* [*schocken*, Dutch.

1. To shake by violence.

These her princes are come home again:
Come the three corners of the world in arms,
And we will *shock* them. *Shakesp. K. John.*

2. To offend; to disgust.

Supposing verses are never so beautiful, yet if they contain any thing that *shocks* religion or good manners, they are
Versus inopes rerum nugæque canoræ. *Dryden.*

Those who in reading Homer are *shock'd* that 'tis always a lion, may as well be angry that 'tis always a man. *Pope.*

My son,
I bade him love, and bid him now forbear:
If you have any kindness for him, still
Advise him not to *shock* a father's will. *Dryden.*

To SHOCK. *v. n.* To be offensive.

The French humour, in regard of the liberties they take in female conversations, is very *shocking* to the Italians, who are naturally jealous. *Addison's Remarks on Italy.*

To SHOCK. *v. n.* [from the noun.] To build up piles of sheaves.

Reap well, scatter not, gather clean that is shorn,
Bind fast, *shock* apace, have an eye to thy corn. *Tusser.*

SHOD. for *shoed*, the preterit and participle passive of to *shoe.*

Strong exeltreed cart that is clouted and *shod.* *Tusser.*

SHOE. *n. s.* plural *shoes*, anciently *shoon.* [ſceo, ſeoe, Saxon; *schoe*, Dutch.] The cover of the foot.

Your hose should be ungarter'd, your *shoe* untied, and every thing about you demonstrating a careless desolation. *Shakesp.*

Spare none but such as go in clouted *shoon*,
For they are thrifty honest men. *Shakesp. Hen. VI.*

This hollow cylinder is fitted with a sucker, upon which is nailed a good thick piece of tanned *shoe*-leather. *Boyle.*

Unknown and like esteem'd, and the dull swain
Treads on it daily with his clouted *shoon*,
And yet more medic'nal than that moly
That Hermes once to wise Ulysses gave;
He call'd it hæmony. *Milton.*

I was in pain, pulled of my *shoe*, and some ease that gave me. *Temple.*

To SHOE. *v. a.* preterit, I *shod*; participle passive *shod.* [from the noun.]

1. To fit the foot with a *shoe.*

The smith's note for *shoeing* and plough irons. *Shakesp.*

He doth nothing but talk of his horse; and makes it a great appropriation to his own good parts, that he can *shoe* him himself. *Shakespeare.*

Tell your master that the horses want *shoeing.* *Swift.*

2. To cover at the bottom.

The wheel compos'd of crickets bones,
And daintily made for the nonce,
For fear of rattling on the stones,
With thistle down they *shod* it. *Drayt.*

SHOE'BOY. *n. s.* [*shoe* and *boy.*] A boy that cleans *shoes.*

If I employ a *shoeboy*, is it in view to his advantage, or my own convenience? *Swift.*

How each the publick good pursues,
Make all true patriots up to *shoeboys*,
Huzza their brethren. *Swift.*

SHOE'ING-HORN. *n. s.* [*shoe* and *horn.*]

1. A horn used to facilitate the admission of the foot into a narrow *shoe.*

2. Any thing by which a transaction is facilitated; any thing used as a medium. In contempt.

Most of our fine young ladies retain in their service supernumerary and insignificant fellows which they use like whifflers, and commonly call *shoeing-horns.* *Spectator.*

I have been an arrant *shoeing-horn* for above these twenty years. I served my mistress in that capacity above five of the number before she was shod. Though she had many who made their applications to her, I always thought myself the best shoe in her shop. *Spectator.*

SHOEMA'KER. *n. s.* [*shoe* and *maker.*] One whose trade is to make shoes.

A cobler or *shoemaker* may find some little fault with the latchet of a shoe that an Appelles had painted, when the whole figure is such, as none but an Appelles could paint. *Watts.*

SHOE'TYE. *n. s.* [*shoe* and *tye.*] The ribband with which women tie their *shoes*.

Madam, I do as is my duty,
Honour the shadow of your *shoetye*. *Hudibras.*

SHOG. *n. s.* [from *shock.*] Violent concussion.

Another's diving bow he did adore,
Which, with a *shog*, casts all the hair before. *Dryden.*

He will rather have the primitive man to be produced, in a kind of digesting balneum, where all the heavier lees may subside, and a due æquilibrium be maintained, not disturbed by any such rude and violent *shogs* that would ruffle and break all the little stamina of the embryon. *Bentley.*

To SHOG. *v. a.* To shake; to agitate by sudden interrupted impulses.

After it is washed, they put the remnant into a wooden dish, the which they softly *shog* to and fro in the water, until the earthy substance be flitted away. *Carew.*

SHONE. The preterite of *shine*.

All his father in him *shone*. *Milton.*

SHOOK. The preterite and in poetry participle passive of *shake*.

Taxallan *shook* by Montezuma's pow'rs,
Has, to resist his forces, call'd in ours. *Dryden.*

To SHOOT. *v. a* preterite, I *shot*; participle, *shot* or *shotten*. [ʃceotan, Saxon.]

1. To discharge any thing so as to make it fly with speed or violence.

Light
Shoots far into the bosom of dim night
A glimmering dawn. *Milton.*

2. To discharge from a bow or gun.

I owe you much, and like a witless youth,
That which I owe is lost; but if you please
To *shoot* an arrow that self way
Which you did *shoot* the first, I do not doubt
To find both. *Shakespeare.*

This murtherous shaft that's *shot*
Hath not yet lighted; and our safest way
Is to avoid the aim. *Shakespeare.*

3. To let off.

The men *shoot* strong shoots with their bows. *Abbot.*

The two ends of a bow *shot* off, fly from one another. *Boyle.*

Men who know not hearts, should make examples;
Which like a warning-piece, must be *shot* off,
To fright the rest from crimes. *Dryden.*

4. To strike with any thing *shot*.

Not an hand shall touch the mount, but he shall be stoned or *shot* thro'. *Exod.* xix. 13.

The liquid air his moving pinions wound,
And, in the moment, *shoot* him on the ground. *Dryden.*

5. To emit new parts, as a vegetable.

None of the trees exalt themselves, neither *shoot* up their top among the thick boughs. *Ezek.* xxxi. 14.

A grain of mustard groweth up and *shooteth* out great branches. *Mark.* iv. 32.

Tell like a tall old oak, how learning *shoots*,
To heaven her branches, and to hell her roots. *Denham.*

6. To emit; to dart or thrust forth.

Ye bucks, who pluck the flow'rs,
Beware the secret snake that *shoots* a sting. *Dryden.*

The last had a star upon its breast, which *shot* forth pointed beams of a peculiar lustre. *Addison.*

Fir'd by the torch of noon, to tenfold rage,
Th' infuriate hill forth *shoots* the pillar'd flame. *Thomson.*

7. To push suddenly.

I have laugh'd sometimes when I have reflected on those men who have *shot* themselves into the world; some bolting out upon the stage with vast applause, and some hissed off, quitting it with disgrace. *Dryden.*

8. To push forward.

They that see me *shoot* out the lip, they shake the head. *Ps.*

9. To fit to each other by pianing; a workman's term.

Strait lines in joiner's language are called a joint; that is two pieces of wood that are *shot*, that is plained or else paired with a pairing chissel. *Moxon.*

10. To pass through with swiftness.

Thus having said, she sinks beneath the ground,
With furious haste, and *shoots* the Stygian sound. *Dryden.*

To SHOOT. *v. n.*

1. To perform the act of *shooting*.

The archers have sorely grieved him and *shot* at him. *Gen.*

When he has *shot* his best, he is sure that none ever did *shoot* better. *Temple.*

When you *shoot*, and shut one eye,
You cannot think he would deny
To lend the t'other friendly aid,
Or wink, as coward and afraid. *Prior.*

2. To germinate; to increase in vegetable growth.

Such trees as love the sun do not willingly descend far into the earth; and therefore they are commonly trees that *shoot* up much. *Bacon.*

Onions, as they hang, will *shoot* forth. *Bacon.*

The tree at once both upward *shoots*,
And just as much grows downward to the roots. *Cleav.*

The monarch oak, the patriarch of the trees,
Shoots rising up, and spreads by slow degrees. *Dryden.*

Nor will the wither'd stock be green again,
But the wild olive *shoots* and shades the ungrateful plain. *Dr.*

New creatures rise,
A moving mass at first, and short of thighs;
Till *shooting* out with legs and imp'd with wings. *Dryden.*

The corn laid up by ants would *shoot* under ground, if they did not bite off all the buds; and therefore it will produce nothing. *Addison.*

This valley of the Tirol lies enclosed on all sides by the Alps, though its dominions *shoot* out into several branches among the breaks of the mountains. *Addison's Italy.*

Express'd juices of plants, boiled into the consistence of a syrup, and set into a cool place, the essential salt will *shoot* upon the sides of the vessels. *Arbuthnot on Aliments.*

A wild, where weeds and flow'rs promiscuous *shoot*,
Or garden, tempting with forbidden fruit. *Pope.*

3. To form itself into any shape.

If the menstruum be over charged, metals will *shoot* into chrystals. *Bacon.*

Although exhaled and placed in cold conservatories, it will chrystalize and *shoot* into glaceous bodies. *Brown's Vulg. Er.*

That rude mass will *shoot* itself into several forms, till it make an habitable world: the steady hand of Providence being the invisible guide of all its motions. *Burnet's Theory of the Earth.*

4. To be emitted.

There *shot* a streaming lamp along the sky,
Which on the winged light'ning seem'd to fly. *Dryden.*

Tell them that the rays of light *shoot* from the sun to our earth, at the rate of one hundred and eighty thousand miles in the second of a minute, they stand aghast at such talk. *Watts.*

The grand ætherial bow
Shoots up immense. *Thomson.*

5. To protuberate; to jet out.

The land did *shoot* out with a very great promontory, bending that way. *Abbot's Descript. of the World.*

6. To pass as an arrow.

Thy words *shoot* thro' my heart,
Melt my resolves, and turn me all to love. *Addison.*

7. To become any thing suddenly.

Let me but live to shadow this young plant
From blites and storms: he'll soon *shoot* up a heroe. *Dryd.*

8. To move swiftly along.

A *shooting* star in autumn thwarts the night. *Milton.*

A shining harvest either host displays,
And *shoots* against the sun with equal rays. *Dryden.*

At first she flutters, but at length she springs,
To smoother flight, and *shoots* upon her wings. *Dryden.*

The broken air loud whistling as she flies,
She stops and listens, and *shoots* forth again,
And guides her pinions by her young ones cries. *Dryden.*

Heav'n's imperious queen *shot* down from high,
At her approach the brazen hinges fly,
The gates are forc'd. *Dryden.*

She downward glides,
Lights in Fleet-ditch, and *shoots* beneath the tides. *Gay.*

Where the mob gathers, swiftly *shoot* along,
Nor idly mingle in the noisy throng. *Gay.*

At the summons roll'd her eyes around,
Not half so swiftly *shoots* along in air,
The gliding light'ning. *Pope.*

9. To feel a quick pain.

SHOOT. *n. s.* [from the verb.]

1. The act or impression of any thing emitted from a distance.

The Turkish bow giveth a very forcible *shoot*, insomuch as the arrow, hath pierced a steel target two inches thick; but the arrow if headed with wood, hath been known to pierce thro' a piece of wood of eight inches thick. *Bacon.*

2. The act of striking, or endeavouring to strike with a missive weapon discharged by any instrument.

The noise of thy cross-bow
Will scare the herd, and so my *shoot* is lost. *Shakesp.*

But come the bow; now mercy goes to kill,
And shooting well is then accounted ill.
Thus will I save my credit in the *shoot*,
Not wounding, pity would not let me do't. *Shakespeare.*

As a country fellow was making a *shoot* at a pigeon, he trode upon a snake that bit him. *L'Estrange.*

3. [*Scheuten*, Dutch.] Branches issuing from the main stock.

They will not come just on the tops where they were cut, but out of those *shoots* which were water boughs. *Bacon.*

I saw them under a green mantling vine,
Plucking ripe clusters from the tender *shoots*. *Milton.*

Prune off superfluous branches and *shoots* of this second spring; but expose not the fruit without leaves sufficient. *Evel.*

The

The hook she bore,
To lop the growth of the luxuriant year,
To decent form the lawless *shoots* to bring,
And teach th'obedient branches where to spring. *Pope.*

Now, should my praises owe their truth
To beauty, dress, or paint, or youth,
'Twere grafting on an annual stock
That must our expectations mock;
And making one luxuriant *shoot*,
Die the next year for want of root. *Swift.*

SHOO'TER. *n. s.* [from *shoot.*] One that shoots; an archer; a gunner.

The *shooter* ewe, the broad-leav'd sycamore. *Fairfax.*

We are *shooters* both, and thou dost deign
To enter combat with us, and contest
With thine own clay. *Herbert.*

The King with gifts a vessel stores;
And next, to reconcile the *shooter* God,
Within her hollow sides the sacrifice he stow'd. *Dryden.*

SHOP. *n. s.* [sceop, Saxon, a magazine; *eschoppe*, French; *shopa*, low Latin.] *Ainsworth.*

1. A place where any thing is sold.

Our windows are broke down,
And we for fear compell'd to shut our *shops*. *Shakespeare.*

Your most grave belly thus answer'd;
True is it, my incorporate friends,
That I receive the general food at first,
Which you do live upon; and fit it is,
Because I am the store-house and the *shop*
Of the whole body. *Shakespeare's Macbeth.*

In his needy *shop* a tortoise hung,
An alligator stuft, and other skins
Of ill-shap'd fishes; and about his shelves
A beggarly account of empty boxes. *Shakespeare.*

Scarce any sold in *shops* could be relied on as faithfully prepared. *Boyle.*

His *shop* is his element, and he cannot with any enjoyment of himself live out of it. *South's Sermons.*

2. A room in which manufactures are carried on.

We have divers mechanical arts and stuffs made by them; and *shops* for such as are not brought into vulgar use. *Bacon.*

SHOPBOA'RD. *n. s.* [*shop* and *board.*] Bench on which any work is done.

That beastly rabble, that came down
From all the garrets in the town,
And stalls, and *shopboards*, in vast swarms,
With new-chalk'd bills, and rusty arms. *Hudibras.*

It dwells not in shops or work-houses; nor till the late age was it ever known, that any one served seven years to a smith or a taylor, that he should commence doctor or divine from the *shopboard* or the anvil; or from whistling to a team, come to preach to a congregation. *South's Sermons.*

SHO'PBOOK. *n. s.* [*shop* and *book.*] Book in which a tradesman keeps his accounts.

They that have wholly neglected the exercise of their understandings, will be as unfit for it as one unpractised in figures to cast up a *shopbook*. *Locke.*

SHOPKEE'PER. *n. s.* [*shop* and *keep.*] A trader who sells in a shop; not a merchant who only deals by wholesale.

Nothing is more common than to hear a *shopkeeper* desiring his neighbour to have the goodness to tell him what is a clock. *Addison.*

SHO'PMAN. *n. s.* [*shop* and *man.*] A petty trader.

Garth, gen'rous as his muse, prescribes and gives,
The *shopman* sells, and by destruction lives. *Dryden.*

SHORE. the preterit of *shear.*

I'm glad thy father's dead:
Thy match was mortal to him, and pure grief
Shore his old thread in twain. *Shakespeare.*

SHORE. *n. s.* [score, Saxon.]

1. The coast of the sea.

Sea cover'd sea;
Sea without *shore*. *Milton.*

2. The bank of a river. A licentious use.

Beside the fruitful *shore* of muddy Nile,
Upon a sunny bank outstretched lay,
In monstrous length a mighty crocodile. *Spenser.*

3. A drain; properly *sewer*.

4. [*Schooren*, Dutch; to prop.] The support of a building; a buttress.

When I use the word *shore*, I may intend thereby a coast of land near the sea, or a drain to carry off water, or a prop to support a building. *Watts's Logick.*

To SHORE. *v. a.* [*schooren*, Dutch.]

1. To prop; to support.

They undermined the wall, and as they wrought, *shored* it up with timber. *Knolles.*

He did not much strengthen his own subsistence in court, but stood there on his own feet, for the most of his allies rather leaned upon him than *shored* him up. *Wotton.*

There was also made a *shoring* or under-propping act for the benevolence; to make the sums which any person had agreed to pay, leviable by course of law. *Bacon's Hen. VII.*

2. To set on shore. Not in use.

I will bring these two blind ones aboard him; if he think it fit to *shore* them again let him call me rogue. *Shakespeare.*

SHO'RELESS. *adj.* [from *shore.*] Having no coast.

This ocean of felicity is so *shoreless* and bottomless, that all the saints and angels cannot exhaust it. *Boyle.*

SHO'RLING. *n. s.* [from *shear*, *shore.*] The felt or skin of a sheep shorn.

SHORN. The participle passive of *shear.*

So rose the Danite strong,
Shorn of his strength. *Milton.*

Vile shrubs are *shorn* for browze: the tow'ring height
Of unctuous trees are torches for the night. *Dryden.*

He plunging downward shot his radiant head;
Dispell'd the breathing air that broke his flight;
Shorn of his beams, a man to mortal sight. *Dryden.*

SHORT. *adj.* [sceort, Saxon.]

1. Not long; commonly not long enough.

Weak though I am of limb, and *short* of sight,
Far from a lynx, and not a giant quite,
I'll do what Mead and Cheselden advise,
To keep these limbs, and to preserve these eyes. *Pope.*

2. Not long in space or extent.

This less voluble earth,
By *shorter* flight to the east, had left him there. *Milton.*

Though *short* my stature, yet my name extends
To heaven itself, and earth's remotest ends. *Pope.*

3. Not long in time or duration.

They change the night into day: the light is *short*, because of darkness. *Job* xvii. 12.

Nor love thy life, nor hate, but what thou liv'st,
Live well, how long or *short* permit to heav'n. *Milton.*

Short were her marriage joys: for in the prime
Of youth her lord expir'd before his time. *Dryden.*

4. Repeated by quick iterations.

Her breath then *short*, seem'd loth from home to pass,
Which more it mov'd, the more it sweeter was. *Sidney.*

Thy breath comes *short*, thy darted eyes are fixt
On me for aid, as if thou wert pursu'd. *Dryden.*

My breath grew *short*, my beating heart sprung upward,
And leap'd and bounded in my heaving bosom. *Smith.*

5. Not attaining an end; not reaching the purposed point; not adequate; not equal.

Immoderate praises, the foolish lover thinks *short* of his mistress, though they reach far beyond the heavens. *Sidney.*

Some cottons here grow, but *short* in worth unto those of Smyrna. *Sandys.*

The Turks give you a quantity rather exceeding than *short* of your expectation. *Sandys.*

Since higher I fall *short*, on him who next
Provokes my envy. *Milton.*

I know them not; not therefore am I *short*
Of knowing what I ought. *Milton's Paradise Reg.*

To attain
The height and depth of thy eternal ways,
All human thoughts come *short*, supreme of things. *Milton.*

O glorious trial of exceeding love,
Engaging me to emulate! but *short*
Of thy perfection, how shall I attain. *Milton.*

To place her in Olympus' top a guest,
Among th' immortals, who with nectar feast;
That poor would seem, that entertainment *short*
Of the true splendor of her present court. *Waller.*

We err, and come *short* of science, because we are so frequently misled by the evil conduct of our imaginations. *Glan.*

That great wit has fallen *short* in his account. *More.*

As in many things the knowledge of philosophers was *short* of the truth, so almost in all things their practice fell *short* of their knowledge: the principles by which they walked were as much below those by which they judged, as their feet were below their head. *South's Sermons.*

He wills not death should terminate their strife;
And wounds, if wounds ensue, be *short* of life. *Dryden.*

Virgil exceeds Theocritus in regularity and brevity, and falls *short* of him in nothing but simplicity and propriety of style. *Pope.*

Where reason came *short*, revelation discovered on which side the truth lay. *Locke.*

Defect in our behaviour, coming *short* of the utmost gracefulness, often escapes our observation. *Locke.*

If speculative maxims have not an actual universal assent from all mankind, practical principles come *short* of an universal reception. *Locke.*

Men express their universal ideas by signs; a faculty which beasts come *short* in. *Locke.*

The people fall *short* of those who border upon them, in strength of understanding. *Addison.*

A neutral indifference falls *short* of that obligation they lie under, who have taken such oaths. *Addison.*

When I made these, an artist undertook to imitate it; but using another way of polishing them, he fell much *short* of what I had attained to, as I afterwards understood. *Newton.*

It

It is not credible that the Phœnicians, who had established colonies in the Persian gulph, stopt *short*, without pushing their trade to the Indies. *Arbuthnot.*

Doing is expressly commanded, and no happiness allowed to any thing *short* of it. *South's Sermons.*

The signification of words will be allowed to fall much *short* of the knowledge of things. *Baker.*

6. Not far distant in time.

He commanded those, who were appointed to attend him, to be ready by a *short* day. *Clarendon.*

7. Defective; imperfect.

8. Scanty; wanting.

The English were inferior in number, and grew *short* in their provisions. *Hayward.*

They *short* of succours, and in deep despair,
Shook at the dismal prospect of the war. *Dryden.*

9. Not fetching a compass.

So soon as ever they were gotten out of the hearing of the cock, the lion turned *short* upon him, and tore him to pieces. *L'Estrange.*

He seiz'd the helm, his fellows cheer'd,
Turn'd *short* upon the shelves, and madly steer'd. *Dryden.*
For turning *short*, he struck with all his might
Full on the helmet of th' unwary knight. *Dryden.*

10. Not going so far as was intended.

As one condemn'd to leap a precipice,
Who sees before his eyes the depth below,
Stops *short*. *Dryden.*

11. Defective as to quantity.

When the fleece is shorn,
When their defenceless limbs the brambles tear,
Short of their wool, and naked from the sheer. *Dryden.*

12. Narrow; contracted.

Men of wit and parts, but of *short* thoughts and little meditation, are apt to distrust every thing for a fancy. *Burnet.*

They, since their own *short* understandings reach
No farther than the present, think ev'n the wise
Like them disclose the secrets of their breasts. *Rowe.*

13. Brittle; friable.

His flesh is not firm, but *short* and tasteless. *Walton.*

Marl from Derbyshire was very fat, though it had so great a quantity of sand, that it was so *short*, that, if you wet it, you could not work it into a ball, or make it hold together. *Mortimer's Husbandry.*

14. Not bending.

The lance broke *short*, the beast then bellow'd loud,
And his strong neck to a new onset bow'd. *Dryden.*

SHORT. *n. s.* [from the adjective.] A summary account.

The *short* and long is our play is prefer'd. *Shakesp.*

In *short*, she makes a man of him at sixteen, and a boy all his life after. *L'Estrange.*

If he meet with no reply, you may conclude that I trust to the goodness of my cause: the *short* on't is, 'tis indifferent to your humble servant whatever your party says. *Dryden.*

From Medway's pleasing stream
To Severn's roar be thine:
In *short*, restore my love, and share my kingdom. *Dryden.*

The proprieties and delicacies of the English are known to few: 'tis impossible even for a good wit to understand and practise them, without the help of a liberal education and long reading; in *short*, without wearing off the rust which he contracted while he was laying in a stock of learning. *Dryden.*

The *short* is, to speak all in a word, the possibility of being found in a salvable state cannot be sufficiently secured, without a possibility of always persevering in it. *Norris.*

To see whole bodies of men breaking a constitution; in *short*, to be encompassed with the greatest dangers from without, to be torn by many virulent factions within, then to be secure and senseless, are the most likely symptoms, in a state, of sickness unto death. *Swift.*

SHORT. *adv.* [It is, I think, only used in composition.] Not long.

Beauty and youth,
And sprightly hope and *short*-enduring joy. *Dryden.*

One strange draught prescribed by Hippocrates, for a *short*-breathed man, is half a gallon of hydromel, with a little vinegar. *Arbuthnot.*

To SHO'RTEN. *v. a.* [from *short.*]

1. To make short, either in time or space.

Because they see it is not generally fit, or possible, that churches should frame thanksgivings answerable to each petition, they *shorten* somewhat the reins of their censure. *Hooker.*

Would you have been so brief with him, he would
Have been so brief with you, to *shorten* you,
For taking so the head, the whole head's length. *Shakesp.*

To *shorten* its ways to knowledge, and make each perception more comprehensive, it binds them into bundles. *Locke.*

None shall dare
With *shorten'd* sword to stab in closer war,
But in fair combat. *Dryden.*

War, and luxury's more direful rage,
Thy crimes have brought, to *shorten* mortal breath,
With all the num'rous family of death. *Dryden.*

Whatever *shortens* the fibres, by insinuating themselves into their parts, as water in a rope, contracts. *Arbuthnot.*

2. To contract; to abbreviate.

We *shorten'd* days to moments by love's art,
Whilst our two souls
Perceiv'd no passing time, as if a part
Our love had been of still eternity. *Suckling.*

3. To confine; to hinder from progression.

To be known, *shortens* my laid intent;
My boon I make it, that you know me not. *Shakespeare.*

Here where the subject is so fruitful, I am *shortened* by my chain, and can only see what is forbidden me to reach. *Dryd.*

4. To cut off; to defeat.

The Irish dwell altogether by their septs, so as they may conspire what they will; whereas if there were English placed among them, they should not be able to stir but that it should be known, and they *shortened* according to their demerits. *Spens.*

5. To lop.

Dishonest with lopt arms the youth appears,
Spoil'd of his nose, and *shorten'd* of his ears. *Dryden.*

SHO'RTHAND. *n. s.* [*short* and *hand.*] A method of writing in compendious characters.

Your follies and debauches change
With such a whirl, the poets of your age
Are tir'd, and cannot score them on the stage,
Unless each vice in *shorthand* they indite,
Ev'n as notcht 'prentices whole sermons write. *Dryden.*

Boys have but little use of *shorthand*, and should by no means practise it, 'till they can write perfectly well. *Locke.*

In *shorthand* skill'd, where little marks comprise
Whole words, a sentence in a letter lies. *Creech.*

As the language of the face is universal, so 'tis very comprehensive: no laconism can reach it: 'tis the *shorthand* of the mind, and crowds a great deal in a little room. *Collier.*

SHO'RTLIVED. *adj.* [*short* and *live.*] Not living or lasting long.

Unhappy parent of a *shortliv'd* son!
Why loads he this embitter'd life with shame? *Dryden.*
The joyful *shortliv'd* news soon spread around,
Took the same train. *Dryden.*

Some vices promise a great deal of pleasure in the commission; but then, at best, it is but *shortlived* and transient, a sudden flash presently extinguished. *Calamy's Sermons.*

The frequent alterations in publick proceedings, the variety of *shortlived* favourites that prevailed in their several turns under the government of her successors, have broken us into these unhappy distinctions. *Addison's Freeholder.*

A piercing torment that *shortlived* pleasure of your's must bring upon me, from whom you never received any offence. *Addison's Spectator.*

All those graces
The common fate of mortal charms may find;
Content our *shortliv'd* praises to engage,
The joy and wonder of a single age. *Addison.*

Admiration is a *shortlived* passion, that immediately decays upon growing familiar with its object, unless it be still fed with fresh discoveries. *Addison.*

In youth alone its empty praise we boast;
But soon the *shortliv'd* vanity is lost. *Pope.*
Then palaces shall rise; the joyful son
Shall finish what his *shortliv'd* sire begun. *Pope.*

SHO'RTLY. *adv.* [from *short.*]

1. Quickly; soon; in a little time.

I must leave thee, love, and *shortly* too. *Shakesp.*
Thou art no friend to God, or to the king:
Open the gates, or I'll shut thee out *shortly*. *Shak. H. VI.*

The armies came *shortly* in view of each other. *Clarendon.*

The time will *shortly* come, wherein you shall more rejoice for that little you have expended for the benefit of others, than in that which by so long toil you shall have saved. *Calamy.*

He celebrates the anniversary of his father's funeral, and *shortly* after arrives at Cumæ. *Dryden.*

Ev'n he, whose soul now melts in mournful lays,
Shall *shortly* want the gen'rous tear he pays. *Pope.*

2. In a few words; briefly.

I could express them more *shortly* this way than in prose, and much of the force, as well as grace of arguments, depends on their conciseness. *Pope.*

SHO'RTNESS. *n. s.* [from *short.*]

1. The quality of being short, either in time or space:

I'll make a journey twice as far, t' enjoy
A second night of such sweet *shortness*, which
Was mine in Britain. *Shakesp. Cymbeline.*

They move strongest in a right line, which is caused by the *shortness* of the distance. *Bacon's Natural History.*

I will not trouble my readers with the *shortness* of the time in which I writ it. *Dryden.*

May

May they not justly to our climes upbraid
Shortness of night, and penury of shade? *Prior.*

2. Fewness of words; brevity; conciseness.

The necessity of *shortness* causeth men to cut off impertinent discourses, and to comprise much matter in few words. *Hooker, b. v.*

Sir, pardon me in what I have to say,
Your plainness and your *shortness* please me well. *Shakesp.*

3. Want of retention.

Whatsoever is above these proceedeth of *shortness* of memory, or of want of a stayed attention. *Bacon.*

4. Deficience; imperfection.

Another account of the *shortness* of our reason, and easiness of deception, is the forwardness of our understanding's assent to slightly examined conclusions. *Glanv. Sceps.*

From the instances I had given of human ignorance, to our *shortness* in most things else, 'tis an easy inference. *Glanv.*

It may be easily conceived, by any that can allow for the lameness and *shortness* of translations, out of languages and manners of writing differing from ours. *Temple.*

SHO'RTRIBS. *n. s.* [*short* and *ribs.*] The bastard ribs; the ribs below the sternum.

A gentleman was wounded in a duel: the rapier entered into his right side, slanting by his *shortribs* under the muscles. *Wiseman's Surgery.*

SHO'RTSIGHTED. *adj.* [*short* and *sight.*]

1. Unable by the convexity of the eye to see far.

Shortsighted men see remote objects best in old age, and therefore they are accounted to have the most lasting eyes. *Newton's Opt.*

2. Unable by intellectual sight to see far.

The foolish and *shortsighted* die with fear
That they go no where, or they know not where. *Denham.*

Other propositions were designed for snares to the *shortsighted* and credulous. *L'Estrange.*

SHO'RTSIGHTEDNESS. *n. s.* [*short* and *sight.*]

1. Defect of sight, proceeding from the convexity of the eye.

2. Defect of intellectual sight.

Cunning is a kind of *shortsightedness*, that discovers the minutest objects which are near at hand, but is not able to discern things at a distance. *Addison's Spectator.*

SHO'RTWAISTED. *adj.* [*short* and *waist.*] Having a short body.

Duck-legg'd, *shortwaisted*; such a dwarf she is,
That she must rise on tip-toes for a kiss. *Dryden's Juv.*

SHO'RTWINDED. *adj.* [*short* and *wind.*] Shortbreathed; asthmatick; breathing by quick and faint reciprocations.

Sure he means brevity in breath; *shortwinded.* *Shak. H.* IV.

So shaken as we are, so wan with care,
Find we a time for frighted peace to pant,
And breathe *shortwinded* accents of new broils,
To be commenc'd in strands afar. *Shakes. H.* IV.

With this the Mede *shortwinded* old men eases,
And cures the lungs unsavory diseases. *May's Virgil.*

SHO'RTWINGED. *adj.* [*short* and *wing.*] Having short wings. Hawks are divided into long and short winged.

Shortwing'd, unfit himself to fly,
His fear foretold foul weather. *Dryden.*

SHO'RY. *adj.* [from *shore.*] Lying near the coast.

There is commonly a declivity from the shore to the middle part of the channel, and those *shory* parts are generally but some fathoms deep. *Burnet's Theory of the Earth.*

SHOT. The preterite and participle passive of *shoot*.

On the other side a pleasant grove
Was *shot* up high, full of the stately tree
That dedicated is to Olympick Jove. *Fairy Queen.*

Their tongue is as an arrow *shot* out, it speaketh deceit. *Jer.* ix. 8.

The fortifier of Pendennis made his advantage of the commodiousness afforded by the ground, and *shot* rather at a safe preserving the harbour from sudden attempts of little fleets, than to withstand any great navy. *Carew.*

He only thought to crop the flow'r,
New *shot* up from a vernal show'r. *Milton.*

From before her vanish'd night,
Shot through with orient beams. *Milton's Paradise Lost.*

Sometimes they *shot* out in length like rivers, and sometimes they flew into remote countries in colonies. *Burnet.*

The same metal is naturally *shot* into quite different figures, as quite different kinds of them are of the same figure. *Woodw.*

Prone on ocean in a moment flung,
Stretch'd wide his eager arms, and *shot* the seas along. *Pope.*

SHOT. *n. s.* [*schot*, Dutch; from *shoot.*]

1. The act of shooting.

A *shot* unheard gave me a wound unseen. *Sidney.*

Proud death!
What feast is tow'rd in thy infernal cell,
That thou so many princes at a *shot*
So bloodily hast struck? *Shakes. Hamlet.*

2. The missive weapon emitted by any instrument.

I shall here abide the hourly *shot*
Of angry eyes. *Shakesp. Cymbeline.*

At this booty they were joyful, for that they were supplied thereby with good store of powder and *shot*. *Hayward.*

Above one thousand great *shot* were spent upon the walls, without any damage to the garrison. *Clarendon.*

He caused twenty *shot* of his greatest cannon to be made at the king's army. *Clarendon.*

Impatient to revenge the fatal *shot*,
His right hand doubly to his left succeeds. *Dryden.*

3. The flight of a shot.

She sat over against him, a good way off, as it were a bow *shot*. *Gen.* xxi. 16.

4. [*Escot*, French.] A sum charged; a reckoning.

A man is never welcome to a place, 'till some certain *shot* be paid, and the hostess say welcome. *Shakespeare.*

As the fund of our pleasure, let each pay his *shot*;
Far hence be the sad, the lewd fop, and the sot. *Ben. Johns.*

Shepherd, leave decoying,
Pipes are sweet a Summer's day;
But a little after toying,
Women have the *shot* to pay. *Dryden.*

He touch'd the pence when others touch'd the pot;
The hand that sign'd the mortgage paid the *shot*. *Swift.*

SHOTE. *n. s.* [ꞅceoꞇa, Saxon.] A fish.

The *shote*, peculiar to Devonshire and Cornwal, in shape and colour resembleth the trout; howbeit, in bigness and goodness cometh far behind him. *Carew.*

SHO'TFREE. *adj.* [*shot* and *free.*] Clear of the reckoning.

Though I could 'scape *shotfree* at London, I fear the shot here: here's no scoring but upon the pate. *Shakesp. H.* IV.

SHO'TTEN. *adj.* [from *shoot.*] Having ejected the spawn.

Go thy ways, old Jack; die when thou wilt, if good manhood be not forgot upon the earth, then am I a *shotten* herring. *Shak. Henry* IV.

Ask for what price thy venal tongue was sold!
Tough wither'd treuffles, ropy wine, a dish
Of *shotten* herrings, or stale stinking fish. *Dryden.*

To SHOVE. *v. a.* [ꞅcupan, Saxon; *schuyven*, Dutch.]

1. To push by main strength.

The hand could pluck her back, that *shov'd* her on. *Shak.*

In the corrupted currents of this world,
Offence's gilded hand may *shove* by justice;
And oft the wicked prize itself
Buys out the law. *Shakespeare.*

I sent your grace
The parcels and particulars of our grief,
The which hath been with scorn *shov'd* from the court. *Shak.*

Of other care they little reck'ning make,
Than how to scramble at the shearers feast,
And *shove* away the worthy bidden guest. *Milton.*

There the British Neptune stood,
Beneath them to submit th' officious flood,
And with his trident *shov'd* them off the sand. *Dryden.*

Shoving back this earth on which I sit,
I'll mount. *Dryd. Tyrannick Love.*

A strong man was going to *shove* down St. Paul's cupola. *Arb.*

2. To drive a boat by a pole that reaches to the bottom of the water.

3. To push; to rush against.

He used to *shove* and elbow his fellow-servants to get near his mistress, when money was a-paying or receiving. *Arbuthn.*

Behold a rev'rend sire
Crawl through the streets, *shov'd* on or rudely press'd
By his own sons. *Pope.*

You've play'd and lov'd, and eat and drank your fill;
Walk sober off, before a sprightlier age
Come titt'ring on, and *shove* you from the stage. *Pope.*

Make nature still incroach upon his plan,
And *shove* him off as far as e'er we can. *Pope.*

Eager to express your love,
You ne'er consider whom you *shove*,
But rudely press before a duke. *Swift.*

To SHOVE. *v. n.*

1. To push forward before one.

The seamen towed, and I *shoved* 'till we arrived within forty yards of the shore. *Gulliver's Travels.*

2. To move in a boat, not by oars but a pole.

He grasp'd the oar,
Receiv'd his guests aboard, and *shov'd* from shore. *Garth.*

SHOVE. *n. s.* [from the verb.] The act of shoving; a push.

I was forced to swim behind, and push the boat forward with one of my hands; and the tide favouring me, I could feel the ground: I rested two minutes, and then gave the boat another *shove*. *Gulliver's Travels.*

SHO'VEL. *n. s.* [ꞅcofl, Saxon; *schoeffel*, Dutch.] An instrument consisting of a long handle and broad blade with raised edges.

A handbarrow, wheelbarrow, *shovel* and spade. *Tusser.*

The brag of the Ottoman, that he would throw Malta into the sea, might be performed at an easier rate than by the *shovels* of his Janizaries. *Glanv. Sceps.*

To Sho'vel. *v. a.* [from the noun.]

1. To throw or heap with a shovel.

I thought
To die upon the bed my father dy'd,
To lie close by his honest bones; but now
Some hangman must put on my shrowd, and lay me
Where no priest *shovels* in dust. *Shakes. Winter's Tale.*

2. To gather in great quantities.

Ducks *shovel* them up as they swim along the waters; but divers insects also devour them. *Derham.*

Sho'velboard. *n. s.* [*shovel* and *board.*] A long board on which they play by sliding metal pieces at a mark.

So have I seen, in hall of lord,
A weak arm throw on a long *shovelboard*;
He barely lays his piece. *Dryden.*

Sho'veller, or *Shovelard. n. s.* [from *shovel.*] A bird.

Shoveller, or spoonbill: the former name the more proper, the end of the bill being broad like a shovel, but not concave like a spoon, but perfectly flat. *Grew's Musæum.*

Pewets, gulls, and *shovellers* feed upon flesh, and yet are good meat. *Bacon.*

This formation of the wizzon is not peculiar to the swan, but common unto the platea, or *shovelard*, a bird of no musical throat. *Brown's Vulgar Errours.*

Shough. *n. s.* [for *shock.*] A species of shaggy dog; a shock.

In the catalogue ye be for men,
As hound and greyhounds, mungrels, spaniels, curs,
Shoughs, water-rugs, and demi-wolves are 'cleped
All by the name of dogs. *Shak. Macbeth.*

Should. *v n.* [*scude*, Dutch; ꞅceolꝺan, Saxon.]

1. This is a kind of auxiliary verb used in the conjunctive mood, of which the signification is not easily fixed.
2. *I* Should *go.* It is my business or duty to go.
3. *If I* Should *go.* If it happens that I go.
4. *Thou* Should'st *go.* Thou oughtest to go.
5. *If thou* Should'st *go.* If it happens that thou goest.
6. The same significations are found in all the other persons singular and plural.

Let not a desperate action more engage you
Than safety *should.* *Ben. Johnson's Catiline.*

Some praises come of good wishes and respects, when by telling men what they are, they represent to them what they *should* be. *Bacon.*

To do thee honour I will shed their blood,
Which the just laws, if I were faultless, *should.* *Waller.*
So subjects love just kings, or so they *should.* *Dryden.*
I conclude, that things are not as they *should* be. *Swift.*

7. Should *be.* A proverbial phrase of slight contempt or irony.

The girls look upon their father as a clown, and the boys think their mother no better than she *should be.* *Addison.*

8. There is another signification now little in use, in which *should* has scarcely any distinct or explicable meaning. *It should be* differs in this sense very little from *it is.*

There is a fabulous narration, that in the northern countries there *should be* an herb that groweth in the likeness of a lamb, and feedeth upon the grass. *Bacon's Nat. History.*

SHO'ULDER. *n. s.* [ꞅculꝺꞃe, Saxon; *scholder*, Dutch.]

1. The joint which connects the arm to the body.

I have seen better faces in my time,
Than stand on any *shoulder* that I see
Before me. *Shakespeare.*

If I have lifted up my hand against the fatherless, when I saw my help in the gate, then let mine arm fall from my *shoulder*-blade, and mine arm be broken from the bone. *Job* xxxi. 22.

It is a fine thing to be carried on mens *shoulders*; but give God thanks that thou art not forced to carry a rich fool upon thy *shoulders*, as those poor men do. *Taylor.*

The head of the *shoulder*-bone being round, is inserted into so shallow a cavity in the scapula, that, were there no other guards for it, it would be thrust out upon every occasion. *Wise.*

2. The upper joint of the foreleg.

We must have a *shoulder* of mutton for a property. *Shakesp.*

He took occasion, from a *shoulder* of mutton, to cry up the plenty of England. *Addison's Freeholder.*

3. The upper part of the back.

Emily dress'd herself in rich array;
Fresh as the month, and as the morning fair,
Adown her *shoulders* fell her length of hair. *Dryden.*

4. The shoulders are used as emblems of strength, or the act of supporting.

Ev'n as thou wilt, sweet Warwick, let it be;
For on thy *shoulders* do I build my seat. *Shakesp. H.* VI.
The king has cur'd me; and from these *shoulders*,
These ruin'd pillars, out of pity taken
A load would sink a navy. *Shakesp. Henry* VIII.

5. A rising part; a prominence.

When you rivet a pin into a hole, your pin must have a *shoulder* to it thicker than the hole is wide, that the *shoulder* slip not through the hole as well as the shank. *Moxon.*

To Sho'ulder. *v. a.* [from the noun.]

1. To push with insolence and violence.

The rolling billows beat the ragged shore,
As they the earth would *shoulder* from her seat. *Fairy Queen.*

Dudman, a well-known foreland to most sailors, here *shoulders* out the ocean, to shape the same a large bosom between itself. *Carew's Survey of Cornwal.*

You debase yourself,
To think of mixing with th' ignoble herd:
What, shall the people know their god-like prince
Headed a rabble, and profan'd his person,
Shoulder'd with filth? *Dryden.*

So vast the navy now at anchor rides,
That underneath it the press'd waters fail,
And, with its weight, it *shoulders* off the tides. *Dryden.*

Around her numberless the rabble flow'd,
Should'ring each other, crowding for a view. *Rowe's J. Shore.*

When Hopkins dies, a thousand lights attend
The wretch, who living sav'd a candle's end;
Should'ring God's altar a vile image stands,
Belies his features, nay extends his hands. *Pope.*

2. To put upon the shoulder.

Archimedes's lifting up Marcellus's ships finds little more credit than that of the giants *shouldering* mountains. *Glanv.*

Sho'ulderbelt. *n. s.* [*shoulder* and *belt.*] A belt that comes across the shoulder.

Thou hast an ulcer, which no leech can heal,
Though thy broad *shoulderbelt* the wound conceal. *Dryden.*

Sho'ulderclapper. *n. s.* [*shoulder* and *clap.*] One who affects familiarity, or one that mischiefs privily.

A fiend, a fury, pitiless and rough;
A back friend, a *shoulderclapper*, one that commands
The passages of alleys. *Shak. Comedy of Errours.*

Sho'uldershotten. *adj.* [*shoulder* and *shot.*] Strained in the shoulder.

His horse waid in the back, and *shouldershotten.* *Shakesp.*

Sho'ulderslip. *n. s.* [*shoulder* and *slip.*] Dislocation of the shoulder.

The horse will take so much care of himself as to come off with only a strain or a *shoulderslip.* *Swift.*

To SHOUT. *v. n.* [A word of which no etymology is known.]

To cry in triumph or exhortation.

They *shouted* thrice: what was the last cry for? *Shakesp.*
Shout unto God with the voice of triumph. *Ps.* xlvii. 1.
It is not the voice of them that *shout* for mastery. *Ex.* xxxii.
The *shouting* for thy summer fruits and harvest is fallen. *Is.*

He storms and *shouts*; but flying bullets now
To execute his rage appear too slow:
They miss, or sweep but common souls away;
For such a loss Opdam his life must pay. *Waller.*

There had been nothing but howlings and *shoutings* of poor naked men, belabouring one another with snagged sticks. *More.*

All clad in skins of beasts the jav'lin bear,
And shrieks and *shoutings* rend the suff'ring air. *Dryden.*

What hinders you to take the man you love?
The people will be glad, the soldier *shout*;
And Bertran, though repining, will be aw'd. *Dryden.*

Shout. *n. s.* [from the verb.] A loud and vehement cry of triumph or exhortation.

Thanks, gentle citizens:
This general applause, and chearful *shout*,
Argues your wisdom and your love to Richard. *Shakespeare.*

The Rhodians, seeing the enemy turn their backs, gave a great *shout* in derision. *Knolles's History of the Turks.*

Then he might have dy'd of all admir'd,
And his triumphant soul with *shouts* expir'd. *Dryden.*

Sho'uter. *n. s.* [from *shout.*] He who shouts.

A peal of loud applause rang out,
And thinn'd the air, 'till even the birds fell down
Upon the *shouters* heads. *Dryden's Cleomenes.*

To SHOW. *v. a.* pret. *showed* and *shown*; part. pass. *shown.* [ꞅceapan, Saxon; *schowen*, Dutch. This word is frequently written *shew*; but since it is always pronounced and often written *show*, which is favoured likewise by the Dutch *schowen*, I have adjusted the orthography to the pronunciation.]

1. To exhibit to view.

If I do feign,
O let me in my present wildness die,
And never live to *shew* th' incredulous word
The noble change that I have purposed. *Shakes. H.* IV.

Shew me a token for good, that they which hate me may see it. *Ps.* lxxxvi. 17.

Wilt thou *shew* wonders to the dead? Shall the dead arise and praise thee? *Ps.* lxxxviii. 10.

Men should not take a charge upon them that they are not fit for, as if singing, dancing, and *shewing* of tricks, were qualifications for a governor. *L'Estrange.*

2. To give proof of; to prove.

This I urge to *show*
Invalid that which thee to doubt it mov'd. *Milton.*

I'll to the citadel repair,
And *show* my duty by my timely care. *Dryden.*

Achates' diligence his duty *shows.* *Dryden.*

3. To publish; to make publick; to proclaim.

Ye are a chosen generation, that ye should *shew* forth the praises of him who hath called you out of darkness. 1 *Pet.* ii.

4. To make known.
I raised thee up to *shew* in thee my power. *Ex.* ix. 16.
I shall no more speak in proverbs, but *shew* you plainly of the Father. *Jo.* xvi. 25.
Nothing wants but that thy shape may *show*
Thy inward fraud. *Milton.*
5. To point the way; to direct.
She taking him for some cautious city patient, that came for privacy, *shews* him into the dining-room. *Swift.*
6. To offer; to afford.
To him that is afflicted, pity should be *shewed* from his friend. *Job.* vi. 14.
Felix, willing to *shew* the Jews a pleasure, left Paul bound. *Acts* xxiv. 27.
Thou shalt utterly destroy them; make no covenant with them, nor *shew* mercy unto them. *Deutr.* vii. 2.
7. To explain; to expound.
Forasmuch as knowledge and *shewing* of hard sentences, and dissolving of doubts, were found in the same, Daniel let him be called. *Dan.* v. 12.
8. To teach; to tell.
I'm sent to *show* thee what shall come. *Milton.*

To Show. *v. n.*
1. To appear; to look; to be in appearance.
She *shews* a body rather than a life,
A statue than a brother. *Shakesp. Ant. and Cleopatra.*
Just such she *shows* before a rising storm. *Dryden.*
Still on we press; and here renew the carnage,
So great, that, in the stream, the moon *show'd* purple. *Philips.*
2. To have appearance.
My lord of York, it better *shew'd* with you,
When that your flock assembled by the bell,
Encircled you to hear with rev'rence
Your exposition on the holy text,
Than now to see you here an iron man,
Cheering a rout of rebels with your drum. *Shak. Henry* IV.

Show. *n. s.* [from the verb.]
1. A spectacle; something publickly exposed to view for money.
I do not know what she may produce me; but, provided it be a *show*, I shall be very well satisfied. *Addison.*
The dwarf kept the gates of the *show* room. *Arbuthnot.*
2. Superficial appearance.
Mild heav'n
Disapproves that care, though wise in *show*,
That with superfluous burden loads the day. *Milton.*
3. Ostentatious display.
Nor doth his grandeur and majestick *show*
Of luxury, though call'd magnificence,
Allure mine eye. *Milton's Par. Regain'd.*
Stand before her in a golden dream;
Set all the pleasures of the world to *show*,
And in vain joys let her loose spirits flow. *Dryden.*
The radiant sun
Sends from above ten thousand blessings down,
Nor is he set so high for *show* alone. *Granville.*
Never was a charge, maintained with such a *show* of gravity, which had a slighter foundation. *Atterbury.*
4. Object attracting notice.
The city itself makes the noblest *show* of any in the world: the houses are most of them painted on the outside, so that they look extremely gay and lively. *Addison.*
5. Splendid appearance.
Jesus, rising from his grave,
Spoil'd principalities and pow'rs, triumph'd
In open *show*, and with ascension bright
Captivity led captive. *Milton.*
6. Semblance; likeness.
When devils will their blackest sins put on,
They do suggest at first with heav'nly *shows*. *Shak. Othello.*
He through pass'd the midst unmark'd,
In *show* plebeian angel militant. *Milton.*
7. Speciousness; plausibility.
The places of Ezechiel have some *show* in them; for there the Lord commandeth the Levites, which had committed idolatry, to be put from their dignity, and serve in inferior ministries. *Whitgifte.*
The kindred of the slain forgive the deed;
But a short exile must for *show* precede. *Dryden.*
8. External appearance.
Shall I say O Zelmane? Alas, your words be against it. Shall I say prince Pyrocles? Wretch that I am, your *show* is manifest against it. *Sidney.*
Fierce was the fight on the proud Belgians side,
For honour, which they seldom sought before;
But now they by their own vain boasts were ty'd,
And forc'd, at least in *shew*, to prize it more. *Dryden.*
9. Exhibition to view.
I have a letter from her;
The mirth whereof's so larded with my matter,
That neither singly can be manifested,
Without the *shew* of both. *Shakespeare.*
10. Pomp; magnificent spectacle.
As for triumphs, masks, feasts, and such *shews*, men need not be put in mind of them. *Bacon.*
11. Phantoms; not realities.
What you saw was all a fairy *show*;
And all those airy shapes you now behold,
Were human bodies once. *Dryden.*
12. Representative action.
Florio was so overwhelmed with happiness, that he could not make a reply, but expressed in dumb *show* those sentiments of gratitude that were too big for utterance. *Addison.*

Sho'wbread, or *Shewbread.* *n. s.* [*show* and *bread.*] Among the Jews, they thus called loaves of bread that the priest of the week put every Sabbath-day upon the golden table, which was in the sanctum before the Lord. They were covered with leaves of gold, and were twelve in number, representing the twelve tribes of Israel. They served them up hot, and at the same time took away the stale ones, and which could not be eaten but by the priest alone. This offering was accompanied with frankincense and salt. *Calmet.*
Set upon the table *showbread* before me. *Ex.* xxv. 30.

SHO'WER. *n. s.* [*scheure*, Dutch.]
1. Rain either moderate or violent.
If the boy have not a woman's gift,
To rain a *shower* of commanded tears,
An onion will do well for such a shift. *Shakespeare.*
The ancient cinnamon was, while it grew, the dryest; and in *showers* it prospered worst. *Bacon.*
2. Storm of any thing falling thick.
I'll set thee in a *shower* of gold, and hail
Rich pearls upon them. *Shakes. Ant. and Cleopatra.*
With *show'rs* of stones he drives them far away;
The scatt'ring dogs around at distance bay. *Pope.*
3. Any very liberal distribution.
He and myself
Have travell'd in the great *shower* of your gifts,
And sweetly felt it. *Shakesp. Timon.*

To Shower. *v. a.* [from the noun.]
1. To wet or drown with rain.
Serve they as a flow'ry verge, to bind
The fluid skirts of that same wat'ry cloud,
Lest it again dissolve, and *show'r* the earth? *Milton.*
The sun more glad impress'd his beams,
Than in fair evening cloud, or humid bow,
When God hath *show'r'd* the earth. *Milton's Paradise Lost.*
Cæsar's favour,
That *show'rs* down greatness on his friends, will raise me
To Rome's first honours. *Addison's Cato.*
2. To pour down.
These, lull'd by nightingales, embracing slept;
And on their naked limbs the flow'ry roof
Shower'd roses, which the morn repair'd. *Milton's Par. Lost.*
3. To distribute or scatter with great liberality.
After this fair discharge, all civil honours having *showered* on him before, there now fell out great occasion to action. *Wotton's Life of the Duke of Buckingham.*

To Sho'wer. *v. n.* To be rainy.

Sho'wery. *adj.* [from *shower.*] Rainy.
A hilly field, where the stubble is standing, set on fire in the *showery* season, will put forth mushrooms. *Bacon.*
Murranus came from Anxur's *show'ry* height,
With ragged rocks and stony quarries white,
Seated on hills. *Addison on Italy.*
The combat thickens, like the storm that flies
From westward, when the *show'ry* winds arise. *Addison.*

Sho'wish, or *Showy.* *adj.* [from *show.*]
1. Splendid; gaudy.
The escutcheons of the company are *showish*, and will look magnificent. *Swift.*
2. Ostentatious.
Men of warm imaginations neglect solid and substantial happiness for what is *showy* and superficial. *Addison.*

Shown. pret. and part. pass. of *To show.* Exhibited.
Mercy *shown* on man by him seduc'd. *Milton.*

Shrank. The preterite of *shrunk.*
The children of Israel eat not of the sinew which *shrank* upon the hollow of the thigh. *Gen.* xxxii. 32.

To Shred. *v. a.* pret. *shred.* [ꞅcꞃeadan, Saxon.] To cut into small pieces. Commonly used of cloath or herbs.
It hath a number of short cuts or *shreadings*, which may be better called wishes than prayers. *Hooker.*
One gathered wild gourds, and *shred* them. 2 *Kings* iv. 39.
Where did you whet your knife to-night, he cries,
And *shred* the leeks that in your stomach rise? *Dryd. Juv.*

Shred. *n. s.* [from the verb.]
1. A small piece cut off.
Gold, grown somewhat churlish by recovering, is made more pliant by throwing in *shreds* of tanned leather. *Bacon.*
The mighty Tyrian queen, that gain'd
With subtle *shreds* a tract of land,
Did leave it with a castle fair
To his great ancestor. *Hudibras.*

His

His panegyrick is made up of half a dozen *shreds*, like a schoolboy's theme, beaten general topicks. *Swift.*

A beggar might patch up a garment with such *shreds* as the world throws away. *Pope.*

2. A fragment.

They said they were an hungry; sigh'd forth proverbs,
That hunger broke stone walls; that dogs must eat:
And with these *shreds* they vented their complainings. *Shak.*

Shreds of wit and senseless rhimes
Blunder'd out a thousand times. *Swift.*

SHREW. *n. s.* [*schreyen*, German, to clamour.] A peevish, malignant, clamorous, spiteful, vexatious, turbulent woman. [It appears in *Robert* of *Gloucester*, that this word signified anciently any one perverse or obstinate of either sex.]

There dede of hem vor hunger a thousand and mo,
And yat nolde the *screwen* to none pes go. *Robert of Gloucester.*

Be merry, my wife has all;
For women are *shrews* both short and tall. *Shak. H. IV.*

By this reckoning he is more *shrew* than she. *Shakespeare.*

A man had got a *shrew* to his wife, and there could be no quiet in the house for her. *L'Estrange.*

Her sallow cheeks her envious mind did shew,
And ev'ry feature spoke aloud the *shrew*. *Dryden.*

Every one of them, who is a *shrew* in domestick life, is now become a scold in politicks. *Addis. Freeholder.*

SHREWD. *adj.* [Contracted from *shrewed.*]

1. Having the qualities of a shrew; malicious; troublesome; mischievous.

Her eldest sister is so curst and *shrewd*,
That 'till the father rids his hands of her,
Your love must live a maid. *Shakespeare.*

2. Maliciously sly; cunning; more artful than good.

It was a *shrewd* saying of the old monk, that two kind of prisons would serve for all offenders, an inquisition and a bedlam: if any man should deny the being of a God, and the immortality of the soul, such a one should be put into the first, as being a desperate heretick; but if any man should profess to believe these things, and yet allow himself in any known wickedness, such a one should be put into bedlam. *Tillotson.*

A spiteful saying gratifies so many little passions, that it meets with a good reception; and the man who utters it is looked upon as a *shrewd* satirist. *Addison.*

Corruption proceeds from employing those who have the character of *shrewd* worldly men, instead of such as have had a liberal education, and trained up in virtue. *Addison.*

3. Bad; ill-betokening.

Scarce any man passes to a liking of sin in others, but by first practising it himself; and consequently we may take it for a *shrewd* indication, and sign, whereby to judge of those who have sinned with too much caution, to suffer the world to charge sins directly upon their conversation. *South's Serm.*

4. Painful; pinching; dangerous; mischievous.

Every of this number,
That have endur'd *shrewd* nights and days with us,
Shall share the good of our returned fortune. *Shakespeare.*

When a man thinks he has a servant, he finds a traitor that eats his bread, and is readier to do him a mischief, and a *shrewd* turn, than an open adversary. *South's Sermons.*

No enemy is so despicable but he may do a body a *shrewd* turn. *L'Estrange.*

SHRE'WDLY. *adv.* [from *shrewd.*]

1. Mischievously; destructively.

This practice hath most *shrewdly* past upon thee. *Shakesp.*

At Oxford, his youth and want of experience in maritime service, had somewhat been *shrewdly* touched, even before the sluices of popular liberty were set open. *Wotton.*

2. Vexatiously. It is used commonly of slight mischief, or in ironical expression.

The obstinate and schismatical are like to think themselves *shrewdly* hurt, forsooth, by being cut off from that body which they choose not to be of. *South's Sermons.*

This last allusion rubb'd upon the sore;
Yet seem'd she not to winch, tho' *shrewdly* pain'd. *Dryden.*

3. With strong suspicion.

Four *per cent.* encreases not the number of lenders; as any man at first hearing will *shrewdly* suspect it. *Locke.*

SHRE'WDNESS. *n. s.* [from *shrewd.*]

1. Sly cunning; archness.

Her garboiles, which not wanted *shrewdness* of policy too, did you too much disquiet. *Shakespeare.*

The neighbours round admire his *shrewdness*,
For songs of loyalty and lewdness. *Swift.*

2. Mischievousness; petulance.

SHRE'WISH. *adj.* [from *shrew.*] Having the qualities of a shrew; froward; petulantly clamorous.

Angelo, you must excuse us;
My wife is *shrewish* when I keep not hours. *Shakespeare.*

SHRE'WISHLY. *adv.* [from *shrewish.*] Petulantly; peevishly; clamorously; frowardly.

He speaks very *shrewishly*; one would think his mother's milk were scarce out of him. *Shakespeare.*

SHRE'WISHNESS. *n. s.* [from *shrewish.*] The qualities of a shrew; frowardness; petulance; clamorousness.

I have no gift in *shrewishness*,
I am a right maid for my cowardice;
Let her not strike me. *Shakespeare.*

SHRE'WMOUSE. *n. s.* [ꞅcꞃeapa, Saxon.] A mouse of which the bite is generally supposed venomous, and to which vulgar tradition assigns such malignity, that she is said to lame the foot over which she runs. I am informed that all these reports are calumnious, and that her feet and teeth are equally harmless with those of any other little mouse. Our ancestors however looked on her with such terrour, that they are supposed to have given her name to a scolding woman, whom for her venom they call a *shrew.*

To SHRIEK. *v. n.* [*skrieger*, Danish; *scricciolare*, Italian.] To cry out inarticulately with anguish or horrour; to scream.

On top whereof ay dwelt the ghastly owl,
Shrieking his baleful note. *Fa. Queen.*

It was the owl that *shriek'd*, the fatal belman
Which gives the sternest good-night. *Shakespeare.*

Were I the ghost that walk'd,
I'd *shriek*, that even your ears should rift to hear me. *Shak.*

In a dreadful dream
I saw my lord so near destruction,
Then *shriek't* myself awake. *Denham.*

Hark! Peace!
At this she *shriek'd* aloud; the mournful train
Eccho'd her grief. *Dryden's Knight's Tale.*

Why did you *shriek* out? *Dryden's Spanish Fryar.*

SHRIEK. *n. s.* [*skrieg*, Danish; *scriccio*, Italian.] An inarticulate cry of anguish or horrour.

Una hearing evermore
His rueful *shrieks* and groanings, often tore
Her guiltless garments, and her golden hair,
For pity of his pain. *Fa. Queen.*

Time has been my senses wou'd have cool'd,
To hear a night *shriek*, and my fell of hair
Wou'd at a dismal treatise rouse and stir
As life were in't. *Shakespeare's Macbeth.*

The corps of Almon, and the rest are shown,
Shrieks, clamours, murmurs, fill the frighted town. *Dryd.*

SHRIFT. *n. s.* [ꞅcꞃiꝼt, Saxon.] Confession made to a priest. A word out of use.

Off with
Bernardine's head: I will give a present *shrift*,
And will advise him for a better place. *Shakespeare.*

My lord shall never rest;
I'll watch him tame, and talk him out:
His bed shall seem a school, his board a *shrift*. *Shakesp.*

The duke's commands were absolute,
Therefore my lord, address you to your *shrift*,
And be yourself; for you must die this instant. *Rowe.*

SHRIGHT, for *shrieked.* *Spenser.*

SHRILL. [A word supposed to be made *per onomatopœiam*, in imitation of the thing expressed, which indeed it images very happily.] Sounding with a piercing, tremulous, or vibratory sound.

Thy hounds shall make the welkin answer them,
And fetch *shrill* echoes from the hollow earth. *Shakespeare.*

I have heard
The cock that is the trumpet to the morn,
Doth with his lofty and *shrill* sounding throat
Awake the god of day. *Shakespeare's Hamlet.*

Have I fall'n,
From the dread summit of this chalky bourn!
Look up a height, the *shrill* gorg'd lark so far
Cannot be seen or heard. *Shakespeare's K. Lear.*

Upsprings the lark,
Shrill voic'd and loud, the messenger of morn. *Thomson.*

To SHRILL. *v. n.* [from the adjective.] To pierce the ear with sharp and quick vibrations of sound.

The sun of all the world is dim and dark;
O heavy herse,
Break we our pipes that *shrill'd* as loud as lark,
O careful verse. *Spenser.*

Hark how the minstrels 'gin to *shrill* aloud
Their merry musick that resounds from far,
The pipe, the tabor, and the trembling crowd
That well agree withouten breach or jar. *Spenser.*

A *shrilling* trumpet sounded from on high,
And unto battle bade themselves address. *Shakespeare.*

Here, no clarion's *shrilling* note
The muse's green retreat can pierce;
The grove, from noisy camps remote,
Is only vocal with my verse. *Fenton's Ode to Lord Gower.*

The females round,
Maids, wives, and matrons mix a *shrilling* sound. *Pope.*

SHRI'LLY. *adv.* [from *shrill.*] With a shrill noise.

SHRI'LLNESS. *n. s.* [from *shrill.*] The quality of being shrill.

Shrimp. *n. s.* [*schrumpe*, a wrinkle, German; *scrympe*, Danish.]

1. A small crustaceous vermiculated fish.

Of shell-fish there are wrinkles, *shrimps*, crabs. *Carew.*

Hawks and gulls can at a great height see mice on the earth, and *shrimps* in the waters. *Derham.*

2. A little wrinkled man; a dwarf. In contempt.

It cannot be, this weak and writhled *shrimp*
Should strike such terrour in his enemies. *Shakespeare.*

He hath found,
Within the ground,
At last, no *shrimp*,
Whereon to imp
His jolly club. *Ben. Johnson.*

Shrine. *n. s.* [ſcrin, Saxon; *scrinium*, Latin.] A case in which something sacred is reposited.

You living powers enclos'd in stately *shrine*
Of growing trees; you rural gods that wield
Your scepters here, if to your cares divine
A voice may come, which troubled soul doth yield. *Sidney.*

All the world come
To kiss this *shrine*, this mortal breathing saint. *Shakespeare.*

Come offer at my *shrine* and I will help thee. *Shakesp.*

They often plac'd
Within his sanctu'ry itself their *shrines*,
Abominations! and with cursed things
His holy rites profan'd. *Milton.*

Falling on his knees before her *shrine*,
He thus implor'd her pow'r. *Dryden.*

Lovers are in rapture at the name of their fair idol; they lavish out all their incense upon that *shrine*, and cannot bear the thought of admitting a blemish therein. *Watts.*

To **Shrink.** *v. n.* preterite, *I shrunk*, or *shrank*; participle, *shrunken.* [ſcrincan, Saxon.]

1. To contract itself into less room; to shrivel; to be drawn together by some internal power.

But to be still hot summer's tantlings, and
The *shrinking* slaves of winter. *Shakespeare's Cymbeline.*

I am a scribbled form, drawn with a pen
Upon a parchment, and against this fire
Do I *shrink* up. *Shakespeare's K. John.*

I have not found that water, by mixture of ashes, will *shrink* or draw into less room. *Bacon's Nat. History.*

Ill-weav'd ambition how much art thou *shrunk*!
When that this body did contain a spirit,
A kingdom for it was too small a bound:
But now two paces of the vilest earth
Is room enough. *Shakespeare.*

2. To withdraw as from danger.

The noise encreases,
She comes, and feeble nature now I find
Shrinks back in danger, and forsakes my mind. *Dryden.*

Am I become so monstrous, so disfigur'd,
That nature stands agast;
And the fair light which gilds this new made orb,
Shorn of his beams, *shrinks* in. *Dryden.*

Love is a plant of the most tender kind,
That *shrinks* and shakes with ev'ry ruffling wind. *Granv.*

All fibres have a contractile power, whereby they shorten; as appears if a fibre be cut transversly, the ends *shrink*, and make the wound gape. *Arbuthnot.*

Philosophy that touch'd the heav'ns before,
Shrinks to her hidden cause, and is no more. *Pope.*

3. To express fear, horrour, or pain, by shrugging, or contracting the body.

There is no particular object so good, but it may have the shew of some difficulty or unpleasant quality annexed to it, in respect whereof the will may *shrink* and decline it. *Hooker.*

The morning cock crew loud,
And at the found it *shrunk* in haste away,
And vanish'd from our sight. *Shakespeare's Hamlet.*

I'll embrace him with a soldier's arm,
That he shall *shrink* under my courtesy. *Shakespeare.*

When he walks, he moves like an engine,
And the ground *shrinks* before his treading. *Shakespeare.*

4. To fall back as from danger.

Many *shrink*, which at the first would dare,
And be the foremost men to execute. *Daniel's Civil War.*

I laugh, when those who at the spear are bold
And vent'rous, if that fail them, *shrink* and fear
To endure exile, ignominy, bonds. *Milton.*

If a man accustoms himself to slight those first motions to good, or *shrinkings* of his conscience from evil, conscience will by degrees grow dull and unconcerned. *South's Sermons.*

The sky *shrunk* upward with unusual dread,
And trembling Tyber div'd beneath his bed. *Dryden.*

The gold-fraught vessel which mad tempests beat,
He sees now vainly make to his retreat;
And, when from far the tenth wave does appear,
Shrinks up in silent joy, that he's not there. *Dryden.*

The fires but faintly lick'd their prey,
Then loath'd their impious food, and would have *shrunk* away. *Dryden.*

Fall on: behold a noble beast at bay,
And the vile huntsmen *shrink*. *Dryden.*

Inuring children to suffer some pain, without *shrinking*, is a way to gain firmness and courage. *Locke.*

What happier natures *shrink* at with affright,
The hard inhabitant contends is right. *Pope.*

To **Shrink.** *v. a.* participle pass *shrunk*, *shrank*, or *shrunken.* To make to shrink. Not in use.

O mighty Cæsar! d'ost thou lye so low?
Are all thy conquests, glories, triumphs, spoils,
Shrunk to this little measure? *Shakespeare.*

The sixth age shifts
Into the lean and slipper'd pantaloon.
His youthful hose well sav'd, a world too wide
For his *shrunk* shank. *Shakespeare.*

If he lessens the revenue, he will also *shrink* the necessity. *Taylor.*

Keep it from coming too long, lest it should *shrink* the corn in measure. *Mortimer.*

Shrink *n. s.* [from the verb.]

1. Corrugation; contraction into less compass.

There is, in this, a crack, which seems a *shrink*, or contraction in the body since it was first formed. *Woodward.*

2. Contraction of the body from fear or horrour.

This publick death, receiv'd with such a chear,
As not a sigh, a look, a *shrink* bewrays
The least felt touch of a degenerous fear. *Daniel's Civ. War.*

Shri'nker. *n. s.* [from *shrink.*] He who shrinks.

Shri'valty. *n. s.* Corrupted for **She'riffalty**, which see.

To **Shrive.** *v. a.* [ſcrifan, Saxon.] To hear at confession.

What, talking with a priest, lord chamberlain?
Your friends at Pomfret they do need a priest,
Your honour hath no *shriving* work in hand. *Shakespeare.*

He *shrives* this woman,
Else ne'er could he so long protract his speech. *Shakesp.*

If he had the condition of a saint, and the complexion of a devil, I had rather he should *shrive* me than wive me. *Shak.*

Shrive but their title, and their moneys poize,
A laird and twenty pence pronounc'd with noise,
When constru'd but for a plain yeoman go,
And a good sober two pence, and well so. *Cleaveland.*

To **Shri'vel.** *v. n.* [*schrompelen*, Dutch.] To contract itself into wrinkles.

Leaves, if they *shrivel* and fold up, give them drink. *Evel.*

If she smelled to the freshest nosegay, it would *shrivel* and wither as it had been blighted. *Arbuthnot.*

To **Shri'vel.** *v. a.* To contract into wrinkles.

He burns the leaves, the scorching blast invades
The tender corn, and *shrivels* up the blades. *Dryden.*

When the fiery suns too fiercely play,
And *shrivel'd* herbs on with'ring stems decay.
The wary ploughman, on the mountain's brow,
Undams his watry stores. *Dryden.*

Shri'ver. *n. s.* [from *shrive.*] A confessor.

The ghostly father now hath done his shrift,
When he was made a *shriver* 'twas for shift. *Shakesp.*

Shroud. *n. s.* [ſcruꝺ, Saxon.

1. A shelter; a cover.

It would warm his spirits,
To hear from me you had left Antony,
And put yourself under his *shroud*, the universal landlord. *Shakesp. Ant. and Cleop.*

By me invested with a vail of clouds,
And swaddled, as new-born, in sable *shrouds*,
For these a receptacle I design'd. *Sandys.*

The winds
Blow moist and keen, shattering the graceful locks
Of these fair spreading trees; which bids us seek
Some better *shroud*, some better warmth, to cherish
Our limbs benumb'd. *Milton's Paradise Lost.*

2. The dress of the dead; a winding-sheet.

Now the wasted brands do glow;
Whilst the screech owl screeching loud,
Puts the wretch that lies in woe
In remembrance of a *shroud.* *Shakespeare.*

3. The sail ropes. It seems to be taken sometimes for the sails.

I turned back to the mast of the ship; there I found my sword among some of the *shrouds.* *Sidney.*

The visitation of the winds,
Who take the ruffian billows by the top,
Curling their monstrous heads, and hanging them
With deafning clamours in the slipp'ry *shrouds*,
That with the hurley death itself awakes. *Shakespeare.*

The tackle of my heart is crackt and burnt;
And all the *shrowds* wherewith my life should sail,
Are turned to one little hair. *Shakespeare.*

A weather-

A weather-beaten vessel holds
Gladly the port, tho' *shrouds* and takle torn. *Milton.*
The flaming *shrouds* so dreadful did appear,
All judg'd a wreck could no proportion bear. *Dryden.*
The cries of men are mix'd with rattling *shrouds*,
Seas dash on seas, and clouds encounter clouds. *Dryden.*
He summons strait his denizens of air;
The lucid squadrons round the sails repair:
Soft o'er the *shrouds* aerial whispers breathe,
That seem'd but zephyrs. *Pope.*

To SHROUD. *v. a.* [from the noun.]

1. To shelter; to cover from danger.

Under your beams I will me safely *shroud*. *Fa. Queen.*

He got himself with his fellows to the town of Mege, in hope to *shroud* himself, until such time as the rage of the people were appeased. *Knolles's Hist. of the Turks.*

The governors of Corfu caused the suburbs, which were very great, to be plucked down, for fear that the Turks *shrouding* themselves in them, should with more ease besiege the town. *Knolles's Hist. of the Turks.*

One of these trees, with all his young ones, may *shroud* four hundred horsemen. *Raleigh.*

Besides the faults men commit, with this immediate avowed aspect upon their religion, there are others which slily *shroud* themselves under the skirt of its mantle. *Decay of Piety.*

So Venus, from prevailing Greeks did *shroud*
The hope of Rome, and sav'd him in a cloud. *Waller.*

2. To dress for the grave.

If I die before thee, *shroud* me
In one of these same sheets. *Shakespeare's Othello.*

The antient Egyptian mummies were *shrouded* in a number of folds of linen, besmeared with gums, like serecloth. *Bacon.*

Whoever comes to *shroud* me, do not harm
That subtile wreath of hair about mine arm. *Donne.*

3. To clothe; to dress.

4. To cover or conceal.

That same evening, when all *shrouded* were
In careless sleep, all, without care or fear,
They fell upon the flock. *Spenser.*

Under this thick-grown brake we'll *shroud* ourselves,
For through this land anon the deer will come,
And in this covert will we make our stand,
Culling the principal. *Shakespeare's Hen.* VI.

Moon, slip behind some cloud: some tempest rise,
And blow out all the stars that light the skies,
To *shroud* my shame. *Dryden.*

Thither the loud tumultuous winds resort,
And on the mountain keep their boist'rous court,
That in thick show'rs her rocky summit *shrouds*,
And darkens all the broken view with clouds. *Addison.*

5. To defend; to protect.

To SHROUD. *v. n.* To harbour; to take shelter.

If your stray attendance be yet lodg'd,
Or *shroud* within these limits, I shall know
Ere morrow wake. *Milton.*

SHRO'VETIDE. } *n. s.* [from *shrove*, the preterite of *shrive*.]
SHRO'VETUESDAY. } The time of confession; the day before Ash-wednesday or Lent, on which anciently they went to confession.

At *shrovetide* to shroving. *Tusser.*

SHRUB. *n. s.* [ſcribbe, Saxon.]

1. A bush; a small tree.

Trees generally shoot up in one great stem or body; and then at a good distance from the earth spread into branches; thus gooseberries and currans are *shrubs*; oaks and cherries are trees. *Locke.*

He came unto a gloomy glade,
Cover'd with boughs and *shrubs* from heav'n's light. *Fa. Q.*
Th' humble *shrub* and bush with frizled hair. *Milton.*
All might have been as well brushwood and *shrubs*. *More.*

Comedy is a representation of common life, in low subjects, and is a kind of juniper, a *shrub* belonging to the species of cedar. *Dryden.*

I've liv'd
Amidst these woods, gleaning from thorns and *shrubs*
A wretched sustenance. *Addison.*

2. [A cant word.] Spirit, acid, and sugar mixed.

SHRU'BBY. *adj.* [from *shrub*.]

1. Resembling a shrub.

Plants appearing weathered, *shrubby* and curled, are the effects of immoderate wet. *Mortimer's Husbandry.*

2 Full of shrubs; bushy.

Gentle villager,
What readiest way would bring me to that place?
Due west it rises from this *shrubby* point. *Milton.*

On that cloud-piercing hill
Plinlimmon, the goats their *shrubby* browze
Gnaw pendent. *Philips.*

To SHRUGG. *v. n.* [*schricken, Dutch*; to tremble.] To express horror or dissatisfaction by motion of the shoulders or whole body.

Like a fearful deer that looks most about when he comes to the best feed, with a *shrugging* kind of tremor through all her principal parts, she gave these words. *Sidney.*

The touch of the cold water made a pretty kind of *shrugging* come over her body like the twinkling of the fairest among the fixed stars. *Sidney.*

Be quick, thou wert best
To answer other business; *shrug'st* thou malice? *Shakesp.*

He grins, smacks, *shrugs*, and such an itch endures,
As prentices or school boys which do know
Of some gay sport abroad, yet dare not go. *Donne.*

They grin, they *shrug*,
They bow, they snarl, they scratch, they hug. *Swift.*

To SHRUG. *v. a.* To contract or draw up.

He *shrugs* his shoulders when you talk of securities. *Addison.*
Zealots will *shrug* up their shoulders. *Blount.*

He *shrug'd* his sturdy back,
As if he felt his shoulders ake. *Hudibras.*

SHRUG. *n. s.* [from the verb.] A motion of the shoulders usually expressing dislike or aversion.

And yet they ramble not to learn the mode,
How to be drest, or how to lisp abroad,
To return knowing in the Spanish *shrug*. *Cleaveland.*

As Spaniards talk in dialogues,
Of heads and shoulders, nods and *shrugs*. *Hudibras.*

Put on the critick's brow, and sit
At Will's, the puny judge of wit.
A nod, a *shrug*, a scornful smile,
With caution us'd may serve a while. *Swift.*

SHRUNK. The preterite and part. passive of *shrink*.

Leaving the two friends alone, I *shrunk* aside to the Banqueting house where the pictures were. *Sidney.*

The wicked *shrunk* for fear of him, and all the workers of iniquity were troubled. *1 Maccabees.*

SHRU'NKEN. The part. passive of *shrink*.

She weighing the decaying plight,
And *shrunken* sinews of her chosen knight;
Would not a while her forward course pursue. *Fa. Queen.*

If there were taken out of mens minds, vain opinions, it would leave the minds of a number of men, poor *shrunken* things, full of melancholy. *Bacon.*

To SHU'DDER. *v. a.* [*schuddren*, Dutch.] To quake with fear, or with aversion.

All the other passions fleet to air,
As doubtful thoughts, and rash embrac'd despair,
And *shudd'ring* fear. *Shakespeare.*

The fright was general; but the female band
With horror *shudd'ring* on a heap they run. *Dryden.*

I love,—alas! I *shudder* at the name,
My blood runs backward, and my fault'ring tongue
Sticks at the sound. *Smith.*

Cæsar will shrink to hear the words thou utter'st,
And *shudder* in the midst of all his conquests. *Addison.*

Youth's bold courage cools,
Each *shudd'ring* owns the genius of the schools. *Dunciad.*

To SHUFFLE. *v. a.* [ſcyfeling, Saxon, a bustle, a tumult.]

1. To throw into disorder; to agitate tumultuously, so as that one thing takes the place of another; to confuse; to throw together tumultuously.

When the heavens *shuffle* all in one,
The torrid, with the frozen zone,
Then, sybil, thou and I will greet. *Cleaveland.*

From a new *shuffling* and disposition of the component particles of a body, might not nature compose a body dissoluble in water. *Boyle.*

In most things good and evil lie *shuffled*, and thrust up together in a confused heap; and it is study which must draw them forth and range them. *South's Sermons.*

When lots are *shuffled* together in a lap or pitcher, what reason can a man have to presume, that he shall draw a white stone rather than a black. *South's Sermons.*

A glimpse of moonshine sheath'd with red,
A *shuffled*, sullen and uncertain light
That dances thro' the clouds and shuts again. *Dryden.*

Children should not lose the consideration of human nature in the *shufflings* of outward conditions. The more they have, the better humoured they should be taught to be. *Locke.*

We shall in vain, *shuffling* the little money we have from one another's hands, endeavour to prevent our wants; decay of trade will quickly waste all the remainder. *Locke.*

These vapours soon, miraculous event,
Shuff'd by chance, and mix'd by accident.
Shuff'd and entangl'd in their race,
They clasp each other. *Blackmore.*

He has *shuffled* the two ends of the sentence together, and by taking out the middle, makes it speak just as he would have it. *Atterbury.*

'Tis in no wise strange that such a one should believe, that things were blindly *shuffled* and hurled about in the world; that the elements were at constant strife with each other. *Wood.*

2. To

2. To remove, or put by with some artifice or fraud.

I can no other answer make, but thanks;
And oft good turns
Are *shuffled* off with such uncurrent pay. *Shakespeare.*

Her mother,
Now firm for doctor Caius, hath appointed
That he shall likewise *shuffle* her away. *Shakespeare.*

If any thing hits, we take it to ourselves; if it miscarries, we *shuffle* it off to our neighbours. *L'Estrange.*

It was contrived by your enemies, and *shuffled* into the papers that were seiz'd. *Dryden.*

If, when a child is questioned for any thing, he persists to *shuffle* it off with a falshood, he must be chastised. *Locke.*

3. To shake; to divest.

In that sleep of death, what dreams may come,
When we have *shuffled* off this mortal coil,
Must give us pause. *Shakespeare.*

4. To change the position of cards with respect to each other.

The motions of *shuffling* of cards or casting of dice, are very light. *Bacon.*

We sure in vain the cards condemn,
Ourselves both cut and *shuff'd* them. *Prior.*

5. To form tumultuously, or fraudulently.

They sent forth their precepts to convent them before a court of commission, and there used to *shuffle* up a summary proceeding by examination, without trial of jury. *Bacon.*

He *shuffled* up a peace with the cedar, in which the Bumelians were excluded. *Howel.*

To SHUFFLE. *v. n.*

1. To throw the cards into a new order.

A sharper both *shuffles* and cuts. *L'Estrange.*

Cards we play
A round or two, when us'd, we throw away,
Take a fresh pack, nor is it worth our grieving
Who cuts or *shuffles* with our dirty leaving. *Granville.*

2. To play mean tricks; to practise fraud; to evade fair questions.

I myself, leaving the fear of heaven on the left hand, and hiding mine honour in my necessit , am fain to *shuffle*. *Shak.*

I have nought to do with that *shuffling* sect, that doubt eternally, and question all things. *Glanvil's Defence.*

The crab advised his companion to give over *shuffling* and doubling, and practise good faith. *L'Estrange.*

It is an unhappiness that children should be so much addicted to the humour of *shuffling*. *L'Estrange.*

If a steward be suffered to run on, without bringing him to a reckoning, such a sottish forbearance will teach him to *shuffle*, and strongly tempt him to be a cheat. *South.*

To these arguments concerning the novelty of the earth, there are some *shuffling* excuses made. *Burn. Theory of the Earth.*

Tho' he durst not directly break his appointment, he made many a *shuffling* excuse. *Arbuthnot's Hist. of John Bull.*

3. To struggle; to shift.

Your life, good master,
Must *shuffle* for itself. *Shakespeare's Cymbeline.*

4. To move with an irregular gait.

Mincing poetry,
'Tis like the forc'd gait of a *shuffling* nag. *Shakespeare.*

SHUFFLE *n. s.* [from the verb.]

1. The act of disordering things, or making them take confusedly the place of each other.

Is it not a firmer foundation for contentment, to believe that all things were at first created, and are continually disposed for the best, than that the whole universe is mere bungling, nothing effected for any purpose, but all ill-favouredly cobled and jumbled together, by the unguided agitation and rude *shuffle* of matter. *Bentley's Sermons.*

2. A trick; an artifice.

The gifts of nature are beyond all shams and *shuffles*. *L'Estr.*

SHU'FFLECAP. *n. s.* [*shuffle* and *cap*.] A play at which money is shaken in a hat.

He lost his money at chuck farthing, *shufflecap*, and all-fours. *Arbuthnot's Hist of John Bull.*

SHU'FFLER. *n. s.* [from *shuffle*.] He who plays tricks or shuffles.

SHU'FFLINGLY. *adv.* [from *shuffle*.] With an irregular gait.

I may go *shufflingly*, for I was never before walked in trammels; yet I shall drudge and moil at constancy, 'till I have worn off the hitching in my pace. *Dryden.*

To SHUN. *v. a.* [ascunian, Saxon] To avoid; to decline; to endeavour to escape; to eschew.

Consider death in itself, and nature teacheth Christ to *shun* it *Hooker.*

The lark! *shuns* on lofty boughs to build,
Her humble nest lies silent in the field. *Waller.*

Birds and beasts can fly their foe:
So chanticleer, who never saw a fox,
Yet *shun'd* him as a sailor *shuns* the rocks. *Dryden.*

Cato will train thee up to great
And virtuous deeds: do but observe him well,
Thou'lt *shun* misfortunes, or thou'lt learn to bear them. *Addis.*

SHU'NLESS. *adj.* [from *shun*.] Inevitable; unavoidable.

Alone he enter'd
The mortal gate of the city, which he painted
With *shunless* destiny. *Shakespeare's Coriolanus.*

To SHUT. *v. a.* preterite, *I shut*; part. passive. *shut*. [scittan, Saxon; *schutten*, Dutch.]

1. To close so as to prohibit ingress or regress; to make not open.

Kings shall *shut* their mouths at him. *Isaiah* lii. 15.

To a strong tower fled all the men and women, and *shut* it to them, and gat them up to the top. *Judges* ix. 51.

We see more exquisitely with one eye *shut* than with both open; for that the spirits visual unite more, and become stronger. *Bacon's Natural History.*

She open'd. but to *shut*
Excell'd her pow'r; the gates wide open stood. *Milton.*

2. To inclose; to confine.

Before faith came, we were kept under the law *shut* up unto the faith, which should afterwards be revealed. *Gal.* iii.

They went in male and female of all flesh; and the Lord *shut* him in *Gen* vii. 16.

3. To prohibit; to bar.

Shall that be *shut* to man, which to the beast
Is open? *Milton.*

4. To exclude.

On various seas, not only lost,
But *shut* from ev'ry shoar, and barr'd from ev'ry coast. *Dryd.*

5. To contract; not to keep expanded.

Harden not thy heart, nor *shut* thine hand from thy poor brother. *Deut.* xv. 7.

6. *To* SHUT *out*. To exclude; to deny admission.

Beat in the reed,
The juster you drive it to *shut off* the rain. *Tusser's Husb.*

In such a night
To *shut* me out? pour on I will endure. *Shakespeare.*

Wisdom at one entrance quite *shut out* *Milton.*

He in his walls confin'd,
Shut out the woes which he too well divin'd. *Dryden's Æn.*

Sometimes the mind fixes itself with so much earnestness on the contemplation of some objects, that it *shuts out* all other thoughts. *Locke.*

7. *To* SHUT *up*. To close; to confine. Up is sometimes little more than emphatical

Thou hast known my soul in adversities; and not *shut* me *up* into the hand of the enemy *Psalms* xxxi. 8.

Woe unto you scribes; for you *shut up* the kingdom of heaven against men. *Matth.* xxiii. 13.

Dangerous rocks *shut up* the passage. *Raleigh.*

What barbarous ustoms!
Shut up a desart shore to drowning men.
And drive us to the cruel seas. *Dryden's Æneid.*

A loss at sea, a fit of sickness, are trifles, when we consider whole families put to the sword, wretches *shut up* in dungeons. *Addison's Spectator.*

His mother *shut up* half the rooms in the house, in which her husband or son had died. *Addison.*

Lucullus, with a great fleet, *shut up* Mithridates in Pitany. *Arbuthnot on Coins.*

8. *To* SHUT *up*. To conclude;

The king's a bed,
He is *shut* up in measureless content. *Shakesp. Macbeth.*

Altho' he was patiently heard as he delivered his embassage; yet, in the *shutting up* of all, he received no more but an insolent answer. *Knolles's History of the Turks.*

To leave you blest, I would be more accurst,
Than death can make me; for death ends our woes,
And the kind grave *shuts up* the mournful scene. *Dryden.*

When the scene of life is *shut up*, the slave will be above his master, if he has acted better. *Collier of Envy.*

To SHUT. *v. n.* To be closed; to close itself.

SHUT. Participial adjective. Rid; clear; free.

We must not pray in one breath to find a thief, and in the next to get *shut* of him. *L'Estrange.*

SHUT. *n. s.* [from the verb.]

1. Close; act of shutting.

I sought him round his palace, made enquiry
Of all the slaves: but had for answer,
That since the *shut* of evening none had seen him. *Dryden.*

2. Small door or cover.

The wind gun is charged by the forcible compression of air, the imprisoned air serving, by the help of little falls or *shuts* within, to stop the vents by which it was admitted. *Wilk.*

In a very dark chamber, at a round hole, about one third part of an inch broad, made in the *shut* of a window, I placed a glass prism. *Newton's Opticks.*

There were no *shuts* or stopples made for the animal's ears, that any loud noise might awaken it. *Ray's Creation.*

SHU'TTER. *n. s.* [from *shut*.]

1. One that shuts.

2. A

2. A cover; a door.

The wealthy,
In lofty litters born, read and write,
Or sleep at ease, the *shutters* make it night. *Dryden's Juven.*

SHU'TTLE. *n. s.* [*schietspoele*, Dutch; *skutul*, Islandick.] The instrument with which the weaver shoots the cross threads.

I know life is a *shuttle*. *Shak. Merry Wives of Windsor.*

Like *shuttles* through the loom, so swiftly glide
My feather'd hours. *Sandys.*

What curious loom does chance by ev'ning spread!
With what fine *shuttle* weave the virgin's thread,
Which like the spider's net hangs o'er the mead! *Blackm.*

SHU'TTLECOCK. *n. s.* [See SHITTLECOCK.] A cork stuck with feathers, and beaten backward and forward.

With dice, with cards, with balliards far unfit,
With *shuttlecocks* misseeming manly wit. *Hubberd's Tale.*

SHY. *adj.* [*schowe*, Dutch; *schifo*, Italian.]

1. Reserved; not familiar; not free of behaviour.

She is represented in such a *shy* retiring posture, and covers her bosom with one of her hands. *Addison's Guardian.*

What makes you so *shy*, my good friend? There's no body loves you better than I. *Arbuthn. Hist. of John Bull.*

2. Cautious; wary; chary.

I am very *shy* of employing corrosive liquors in the preparation of medicines. *Boyle.*

We are not *shy* of assent to celestial informations, because they were hid from ages. *Glanv. Sceps.*

We grant, although he had much wit,
H' was very *shy* of using it,
As being loth to wear it out,
And therefore bore it not about. *Hudibras.*

3. Keeping at a distance; unwilling to approach.

A *shy* fellow was the duke; and, I believe, I know the cause of his withdrawing. *Shakesp. Measure for Measure.*

The bruise imposthumated, and afterwards turned to a stinking ulcer, which made every body *shy* to come near her. *Arbuthnot's History of John Bull.*

The horses of the army, having been daily led before me, were no longer *shy*, but would come up to my very feet, without starting. *Gulliver's Travels.*

But when we come to seize th' inviting prey,
Like a *shy* ghost, it vanishes away. *Norris.*

4. Suspicious; jealous; unwilling to suffer near acquaintance.

Princes are, by wisdom of state, somewhat *shy* of their successors; and there may be supposed in queens regnant a little proportion of tenderness that way more than in kings. *Wotton.*

I know you *shy* to be oblig'd,
And still more loth to be oblig'd by me. *Southern.*

SI'BILANT. *adj.* [*sibilans*, Latin.] Hissing.

It were easy to add a nasal letter to each of the other pair of lisping and *sibilant* letters. *Holder's Elements of Speech.*

SIBILA'TION. *n. s.* [from *sibilo*, Latin.] A hissing sound.

Metals, quenched in water, give a *sibilation* or hissing sound. *Bacon's Natural History.*

A pipe, a little moistened on the inside, maketh a more solemn sound than if the pipe were dry; but yet with a sweet degree of *sibilation* or purling. *Bacon's Nat. History.*

SI'CAMORE. *n. s.* [*sicamorus*, Latin.] A tree.

Of trees you have the palm, olive, and *sicamore*. *Peacham.*

To SI'CCATE. *v. a.* [*sicco*, Latin.] To dry.

SICCA'TION. *n. s.* [from *siccate*.] The act of drying.

SICCI'FICK. *adj.* [*siccus* and *fio*, Latin.] Causing driness.

SI'CCITY. *n. s.* [*siccité*, Fr. *siccitas*, from *siccus*, Latin.] Driness; aridity; want of moisture.

That which is coagulated by a firy *siccity* will suffer coliquation from an aqueous humidity, as salt and sugar. *Brown's Vulgar Errours.*

The reason some attempt to make out from the *siccity* and driness of its flesh. *Brown's Vulgar Errours.*

In application of medicaments consider what degree of heat and *siccity* is proper. *Wiseman's Surgery.*

SICE. *n. s.* [*six*, French.] The number six at dice.

My study was to cog the dice,
And dext'rously to throw the lucky *sice*;
To shun ames-ace, that swept my stakes away. *Dryden.*

SICH. *adj.* Such. See SUCH.

I thought the soul would have made me rich;
But now I wote it is nothing *sich*;
For either the shepherds been idle and still,
And led of their sheep what they will. *Spenser's Pastorals.*

SICK. *adj.* [ꞅeoc, Saxon; *sieck*, Dutch.]

1. Afflicted with disease.

'Tis meet we all go forth,
To view the *sick* and feeble parts of France. *Shak. H. V.*

In poison there is physick; and this news,
That would, had I been well, have made me *sick*,
Being *sick*, hath in some measure made me well. *Shakesp.*

Cassius, I am *sick* of many griefs. *Shakesp. Jul. Cæsar.*

Ammon was so vexed, that he fell *sick* for Tamar. 2 *Sa.* iii.

Where's the stoick can his wrath appease,
To see his country *sick* of Pym's disease? *Cleaveland.*

Despair
Tended the *sick*, busiest from couch to couch. *Milton.*

A spark of the man-killing trade
Fell *sick*. *Dryden's Pers.*

Nothing makes a more ridiculous figure in a man's life, than the disparity we often find in him *sick* and well. *Pope.*

2. Disordered in the organs of digestion; ill in the stomach.

3. Corrupted.

What we oft do best,
By *sick* interpreters, or weak ones, is
Not ours, or not allow'd: what worst, as oft
Hitting a grosser quality, is cried up
For our best act. *Shakesp. Henry VIII.*

4. Disgusted.

I do not, as an enemy to peace,
Troop in the throngs of military men.
But rather shew a-while like fearful war,
To diet rank minds *sick* of happiness,
And purge th' obstructions, which begin to stop
Our very veins of life. *Shakespeare.*

He was not so *sick* of his master as of his work. *L'Estrange.*

Why will you break the sabbath of my days,
Now *sick* alike of envy and of praise? *Pope.*

To SICK. *v. n.* [from the noun.] To sicken; to take a disease. Not in use.

A little time before
Our great grandsire Edward *sick'd* and died. *Shakesp. H. IV.*

To SI'CKEN. *v. a.* [from *sick*.]

1. To make sick; to disease.

Why should one earth, one clime, one stream, one breath,
Raise this to strength, and *sicken* that to death? *Prior.*

2. To weaken; to impair.

Kinsmen of mine have
By this so *sicken'd* their estates, that never
They shall abound as formerly. *Shak. Henry VIII.*

To SI'CKEN. *v. n.*

1. To grow sick; to fall into disease.

I know the more one *sickens*, the worse he is. *Shakespeare.*

The judges that sat upon the jail, and those that attended, *sickened* upon it, and died. *Bacon.*

Meerly to drive away the time, he *sicken'd*,
Fainted, and died; nor would with ale be quicken'd. *Milt.*

2. To be satiated; to be filled to disgust.

Though the treasure
Of nature's germins tumble all together,
Even 'till destruction *sicken*, answer me
To what I ask you. *Shakesp. Macbeth.*

3. To be disgusted, or disordered with abhorrence.

The ghosts repine at violated night,
And curse th' invading sun, and *sicken* at the sight. *Dryden.*

4. To grow weak; to decay; to languish.

Ply'd thick and close, as when the fight begun,
Their huge unwieldy navy wastes away:
So *sicken* waining moons too near the sun,
And blunt their crescents on the edge of day. *Dryden.*

Abstract what others feel, what others think;
All pleasures *sicken*, and all glories sink. *Pope.*

SI'CKER. *adj.* [*sicr*, Welsh; *seker*, Dutch.] Sure; certain; firm.

Being some honest curate, or some vicar,
Content with little, in condition *sicker*. *Hubberd's Tale.*

SI'CKER. *adv.* Surely; certainly.

Sicker thou's but a lazy loord,
And rekes much of thy swink,
That with fond terms and witless words,
To bleer mine eyes do'st think. *Spenser.*

SI'CKLE. *n. s.* [ꞅicol, Saxon; *sickel*, Dutch, from *secale*, or *sicula*, Latin.] The hook with which corn is cut; a reaping hook.

God's harvest is even ready for the *sickle*, and all the fields yellow long ago. *Spenser on Ireland.*

Time should never,
In life or death, their fortunes sever;
But with his rusty *sickle* mow
Both down together at a blow. *Hudibras.*

When corn has once felt the *sickle*, it has no more benefit from the sunshine. *South's Sermons.*

O'er whom time gently shakes his wings of down,
'Till with his silent *sickle* they are mown. *Dryden.*

SI'CKLEMAN. } *n. s.* [from *sickle*.] A reaper.
SI'CKLER. }

You sunburnt *sicklemen*, of August weary,
Come hither from the furrow, and be merry. *Shakespeare.*

Their *sicklers* reap the corn another sows. *Sandys.*

SI'CKLINESS. *n. s.* [from *sickly*.] Disposition to sickness; habitual disease.

Impute
His words to wayward *sickliness* and age. *Shakes. R. II.*

Next compare the *sickliness*, healthfulness, and fruitfulness of the several years. *Graunt.*

SI'CKLY. *adv.* [from *sick.*] Not in health.

We wear our health but *sickly* in his life,
Which in his death were perfect. *Shakesp. Macbeth.*

SI'CKLY. *adj.* [from *sick.*]

1. Not healthy; not sound; not well; somewhat disordered.

I'm fall'n out with more headier will,
To take the indispos'd and *sickly* fit
For the sound man. *Shakespeare's King Lear.*

Bring me word, boy, if thy lord looks well;
For he went *sickly* forth. *Shakesp. Julius Cæsar.*

A pleasing cordial, Buckingham,
Is this thy vow unto my *sickly* heart. *Shakesp. R. III.*

The moon grows *sickly* at the sight of day,
And early cocks have summon'd me away. *Dryden.*

Time seems not now beneath his years to stoop,
Nor do his wings with *sickly* feathers droop. *Dryden.*

Would we know what health and ease are worth, let us ask one that is *sickly*, or in pain, and we have the price. *Grew.*

There affectation, with a *sickly* mien,
Shows in her cheek the roses of eighteen;
Practis'd to lisp, and hang the head aside,
Faints into airs, and languishes with pride. *Pope.*

When on my *sickly* couch I lay,
Impatient both of night and day,
Then Stella ran to my relief. *Swift.*

2. Faint; weak; languid.

To animate the doubtful fight,
Namur in vain expects that ray;
In vain France hopes the *sickly* light
Should shine near William's fuller day. *Prior.*

To SI'CKLY. *v. a.* [from the adjective.] To make diseased; to taint with the hue of disease. Not in use.

The native hue of resolution
Is *sicklied* o'er with the pale cast of thought. *Shakespeare.*

SI'CKNESS. *n. s.* [from *sick.*]

1. State of being diseased.

I do lament the *sickness* of the king,
As loth to lose him. *Shakesp. Rich. III.*

2. Disease; malady.

My people are with *sickness* much enfeebled,
My numbers lessen'd. *Shakesp. Henry V.*

Himself took our infirmities, and bare our *sicknesses*. *Mat.*

When I say every *sickness* has a tendency to death, I mean every individual *sickness* as well as every kind. *Watts.*

Trust not too much your now resistless charms;
Those age or *sickness* soon or late disarms. *Pope.*

3. Disorder in the organs of digestion.

SIDE. *n. s.* [ꞅiᵭe, Saxon; *sijde*, Dutch.]

1. The parts of animals fortified by the ribs.

When two boars with rankling malice meet,
Their gory *sides* fresh bleeding fiercely fret. *Fairy Queen.*

The clamour much,
Ere the soft fearful people to the flood
Commit their woolly *sides*. *Thomson.*

2. Any part of any body opposed to any other part.

The tables were written on both their *sides*, on the one *side* and on the other. *Ex.* xxxii. 15.

The force of these outward streams might well enough serve for the turning of the screw, if it were so that both its *sides* would equiponderate. *Wilkins.*

3. The right or left.

4. Margin; edge; verge.

Or where Hydaspes' wealthy *side*
Pays tribute to the Persian pride. *Roscommon.*

Poor wretch! on stormy seas to lose thy life;
For now the flowing tide
Had brought the body nearer to the *side*. *Dryden.*

The temple of Diana chaste,
A sylvan scene, with various greens was drawn,
Shades on the *sides*, and in the midst a lawn. *Dryden.*

I could see persons dressed in glorious habits, with garlands upon their heads, lying down by the *sides* of fountains. *Addis.*

5. Any kind of local respect.

They looking back, all the eastern *side* beheld
Of Paradise. *Milton.*

If our substance be indeed divine,
And cannot cease to be, we are at worst
On this *side* nothing. *Milton.*

6. Party; interest; faction; sect.

To take the widow,
Exasperates, makes mad her sister Goneril;
And hardly shall I carry out my *side*,
Her husband being alive. *Shakesp. King Lear.*

Their weapons only
Seem'd on our *side*; but for their spirits and souls,
This word rebellion, it had froze them up,
As fish are in a pond. *Shakesp. Henry IV.*

Favour, custom, and at last number, will be on the *side* of grace. *Sprat.*

Men he always took to be
His friends, and dogs his enemy;
Who never so much hurt had done him,
As his own *side* did falling on him. *Hudibras.*

In the serious part of poetry the advantage is wholly on Chaucer's *side*. *Dryden.*

That person, who fills their chair, has justly gained the esteem of all *sides* by the impartiality of his behaviour. *Addis.*

Let not our James, though foil'd in arms, despair,
Whilst on his *side* he reckons half the fair. *Tickell.*

Some valuing those of their own *side*, or mind,
Still make themselves the measure of mankind:
Fondly we think we honour merit then,
When we but praise ourselves in other men. *Pope.*

He from the taste obscene reclaims our youth,
And sets the passions on the *side* of truth;
Forms the soft bosom with the gentlest art,
And pours each human virtue in the heart. *Pope.*

7. Any part placed in contradistinction or opposition to another. It is used of persons, or propositions respecting each other.

There began a sharp and cruel fight, many being slain and wounded on both *sides*. *Knolles's Hist. of the Turks.*

The plague is not easily received by such as continually are about them that have it: on the other *side*, the plague taketh soonest hold of those that come out of a fresh air. *Bacon.*

I am too well satisfied of my own weakness to be pleased with any thing I have written; but, on the other *side*, my reason tells me, that what I have long considered may be as just as what an ordinary judge will condemn. *Dryden.*

My secret wishes would my choice decide;
But open justice bends to neither *side*. *Dryden.*

It is granted on both *sides*, that the fear of a Deity doth universally possess the minds of men. *Tillotson's Sermons.*

Two nations still pursu'd
Peculiar ends, on each *side* resolute
To fly conjunction. *Philips.*

SIDE. *adj.* [from the noun.] Lateral; oblique; not direct; being on either side.

They presume that the law doth speak with all indifferency, that the law hath no *side* respect to their persons. *Hooker.*

Take of the blood, and strike it on the two *side* posts, and on the upper door post of the houses. *Ex.* xii. 7.

People are sooner reclaimed by the *side* wind of a surprize, than by downright admonition. *L'Estrange.*

One mighty squadron with a *side* wind sped. *Dryden.*

The parts of water, being easily separable from each other, will, by a *side* motion, be easily removed, and give way to the approach of two pieces of marble. *Locke.*

What natural agent could turn them aside, could impel them so strongly with a transverse *side* blow against that tremendous weight and rapidity, when whole worlds are a falling. *Bentley's Sermons.*

He not only gives us the full prospects, but several unexpected peculiarities, and *side* views, unobserved by any painter but Homer. *Pope's Preface to the Iliad.*

My secret enemies could not forbear some expressions, which by a *side* wind reflected on me. *Swift.*

To SIDE. *v. n.* [from the noun.] To take a party; to engage in a faction.

Vex'd are the nobles who have *sided*
In his behalf. *Shakesp. Coriolanus.*

All rising to great place is by a winding stair; and if there be factions, it is good to *side* a man's self whilst rising, and balance himself when placed. *Bacon.*

As soon as discontents drove men into *sidings*, as ill humours fall to the disaffected part, which causes inflammations, so did all who affected novelties adhere to that side. *King Charles.*

Terms rightly conceived, and notions duly fitted to them, require a brain free from all inclination to *siding*, or affection to opinions for the authors sakes, before they be well understood. *Digby on Bodies.*

Not yet so dully desperate
To *side* against ourselves with fate;
As criminals, condemn'd to suffer,
Are blinded first, and then turn'd over. *Hudibras.*

The princes differ and divide;
Some follow law, and some with beauty *side*. *Granville.*

It is pleasant to see a verse of an old poet revolting from its original sense, and *siding* with a modern subject. *Addison.*

All *side* in parties, and begin th' attack. *Pope.*

Those who pretended to be in with the principles upon which her majesty proceeded, either absented themselves where the whole cause depended, or *sided* with the enemy. *Swift.*

The equitable part of those who now *side* against the court, will probably be more temperate. *Swift.*

SI'DEBOARD. *n. s.* [*side* and *board.*] The side table on which conveniencies are placed for those that eat at the other table.

At a stately *sideboard* by the wine
That fragrant smell diffus'd. *Milt. Paradise Regain'd.*

No *sideboards* then with gilded plate were dress'd,
No sweating slaves with massive dishes press'd. *Dryden.*

The

The snow white damask ensigns are display'd,
And glitt'ring salvers on the *sideboard* laid. *King.*
The shining *sideboard*, and the burnish'd plate,
Let other ministers, great Anne, require. *Prior.*

Scipio Africanus brought from Carthage to Rome, in silver vessels, to the value of 11966*l.* 15*s.* 9*d.* a quantity exceeded afterwards by the *sideboards* of many private tables. *Arbuthnot.*

SI'DEBOX. *n. s.* [*side* and *box.*] Seat for the ladies on the side of the theatre.

Why round our coaches crowd the white-glov'd beaus?
Why bows the *sidebox* from its inmost rows? *Pope.*

SI'DEFLY. *n. s.* An insect.

From a rough whitish maggot, in the intestinum rectum of horses, the *sidefly* proceeds. *Derham's Physico-Theology.*

To SI'DLE. *v. n.* [from *side.*] To go with the body the narrowest way.

The chaffering with dissenters is but like opening a few wickets, and leaving them no more than one can get in at a time, and that not without stooping and *sidling*, and squeezing his body. *Swift.*

I passed very gently and *sidling* through the two principal streets. *Gulliver's Travels.*

A fellow nailed up maps in a gentleman's closet, some *sidling*, and others upside down, the better to adjust them to the pannels. *Swift.*

SI'DELONG. *adj.* [*side* and *long.*] Lateral; oblique; not in front; not direct.

She darted from her eyes a *sidelong* glance,
Just as she spoke, and, like her words, it flew;
Seem'd not to beg what she then bid me do. *Dryden.*
The deadly wound is in thy soul:
When thou a tempting harlot do'st behold,
And when she casts on thee a *sidelong* glance,
Then try thy heart, and tell me if it dance? *Dryden.*

The reason of the planets motions in curve lines is the attraction of the sun, and an oblique or *sidelong* impulse. *Locke.*

The kiss snatch'd hasty from the *sidelong* maid. *Thomson.*

SI'DELONG. *adv.*

1. Laterally; obliquely; not in pursuit; not in opposition.

As if on earth
Winds under ground, or waters, forcing way,
Sidelong had push'd a mountain from his seat,
Half sunk with all his pines. *Milton's Paradise Lost.*
As a lion, bounding in his way,
With force augmented bears against his prey,
Sidelong to seize. *Dryden's Ceyx and Alcyone.*

2. On the side.

If it prove too wet, lay your pots *sidelong*; but shade those which blow from the afternoon sun. *Evelyn's Kalendar.*

SI'DER. *n. s.* See CIDER.

SI'DERAL. *adj.* [from *sidus*, Latin.] Starry; astral.

These changes in the heav'ns, though slow, produc'd
Like change on sea, and land; *sideral* blast,
Vapour and mist, and exhalation hot,
Corrupt and pestilent! *Milton's Paradise Lost.*
The musk gives
Sure hopes of racy wine, and in its youth,
Its tender nonage, loads the spreading boughs
With large and juicy offspring, that defies
The vernal nippings and cold *sideral* blasts. *Philips.*

SI'DERATED. *adj.* [from *sideratus*, Latin.] Blasted; planet struck.

Parts cauterized, gangrenated, *siderated*, and mortified, become black; the radical moisture, or vital sulphur, suffering an extinction. *Brown's Vulgar Errours.*

SIDERA'TION. *n. s.* [*sideration*, French; *sideratio*, Latin.] A sudden mortification, or, as the common people call it, a blast; or a sudden deprivation of sense, as in an apoplexy.

The contagious vapour of the very eggs produce a mortification or *sideration* in the parts of plants on which they are laid. *Ray on the Creation.*

SI'DESADDLE. *n. s.* [*side* and *saddle.*] A woman's seat on horseback.

SI'DESMAN. *n. s.* [*side* and *man.*] An assistant to the churchwarden.

A gift of such goods, made by them with the consent of the *sidesmen* or vestry, is void. *Ayliffe's Parergon.*

SI'DEWAYS. } *adv.* [from *side* and *way*, or *wise.*] Laterally;
SI'DEWISE. } on one side.

The fair blossom hangs the head
Sideways, as on a dying bed;
And those pearls of dew she wears,
Prove to be presaging tears. *Milton.*

If in the third experiment the image of the sun should be drawn out into an oblong form, either by a dilatation of every ray, or by any other casual inequality of the refractions, the same oblong image would, by a second refraction made *sideways*, be drawn out as much in breadth by the like dilatation of the rays, or other casual inequality of the refraction *sideways.* *Newton's Opt.*

SIEGE. *n. s.* [*siege*, French.]

1. The act of besetting a fortified place; a leaguer.

Our castle's strength
Will laugh a *siege* to scorn: here let them lie,
'Till famine eat them up. *Shakesp. Macbeth.*

It seemed, by the manner of their proceeding, that the Turks purposed rather by long *siege* than by assault to take the town. *Knolles's History of the Turks.*

The more I see pleasures about me, so much more I feel
Torment within me, as from the hateful *siege*
Of contraries. *Milton's Paradise Lost, b.* ix.

2. Any continued endeavour to gain possession.

Beat away the busy meddling fiend,
That lays strong *siege* unto this wretch's soul,
And from his bosom purge this black despair. *Shakes. H.* VI.

Give me so much of your time, in exchange of it, as to lay an amiable *siege* to the honesty of Ford's wife. *Shakesp.*

Love stood the *siege*, and would not yield his breast. *Dryd.*

3. [*Siege*, French.] Seat; throne. Obsolete.

Drawing to him the eyes of all around,
From lofty *siege* began these words aloud to sound. *Fa. Qu.*

4. Place; class; rank. Obsolete.

I fetch my life and being
From men of royal *siege.* *Shakesp. Othello.*
Your sum of parts
Did not together pluck such envy from him,
As did that one, and that in my regard
Of the unworthiest *siege.* *Shakesp. Hamlet.*

5. [*Siege*, French.] Stool.

It entereth not the veins, but taketh leave of the permeant parts, as the mouths of the meseraicks, and accompanieth the inconvertible portion unto the *siege.* *Brown's Vulg. Errours.*

To SIEGE. *v. a.* [*sieger*, Fr. from the noun.] To besiege. A word not now in use.

Him he had long opprest with tort,
And fast imprisoned in *sieged* fort. *Fairy Queen.*

SIEVE. *n. s.* [from *sift.*] Hair or lawn strained upon a hoop, by which flower is separated from bran, or fine powder from coarse; a boulter; a searce.

Thy counsel
Falls now into my ears as profitless
As water in a *sieve.* *Shakespeare.*
In a *sieve* I'll thither sail,
And like a rat without a tail,
I'll do—I'll do—I'll do. *Shakesp. Macbeth.*

An innocent found a *sieve*, and presently fell to stopping the holes. *L'Estrange.*

If life sunk through you like a leaky *sieve*,
Accuse yourself you liv'd not while you might. *Dryden.*

To SIFT. *v. a.* [ꞅiꝼꞇan, Saxon; *siften*, Dutch.]

1. To separate by a sieve.

In the *sifting* of such favour all that came out could not be expected to be pure meal, but must have a mixture of padar and bran. *Wotton.*

2. To separate; to part.

When yellow sands are *sifted* from below,
The glitt'ring billows give a golden show. *Dryden.*

3. To examine; to try.

We have *sifted* your objections against those pre-eminences royal. *Hooker, Preface.*

All which the wit of Calvin could from thence draw, by *sifting* the very utmost sentence and syllable, is no more than that certain speeches seem to intimate, that all Christian churches ought to have their elderships. *Hooker.*

I fear me, if thy thoughts were *sifted*,
The king thy sovereign is not quite exempt
From envious malice of thy swelling heart. *Shak. Hen.* VI.
As near as I could *sift* him on that argument. *Shakesp.*
Opportunity I here have had
To try thee, *sift* thee, and confess have found thee
Proof against all temptation as a rock
Of adamant. *Milton's Paradise Regain'd.*

One would think, that every member who embraces with vehemence the principles of either of these parties, had thoroughly *sifted* and examined them, and was secretly convinced of their preference to those he rejects. *Addison.*

SI'FTER. *n. s.* [from *sift.*] He who sifts.

SIG was used by the Saxons for victory: *Sigbert*, famous for victory; *Sigward*, victorious preserver; *Sigard*, conquering temper: and almost in the same sense are Nicocles, Nicomachus, Nicander, Victor, Victorinus, Vincentius, &c. *Gibson.*

To SIGH. *v. n.* [ꞅican, ꞅiceꞇꞇan, Saxon; *suchten*, Dutch.]

To emit the breath audibly, as in grief.

I lov'd the maid I married; never man
Sigh'd truer breath. *Shakesp. Coriolanus.*
I'll not be made a soft and dull-ey'd fool,
To shake the head, relent, and *sigh*, and yield
To Christian intercessors. *Shakes. Merch. of Venice.*

He *sighed* deeply in his spirit, and saith, why doth this generation seek after a sign? *Mar.* viii. 12.

For the oppression of the poor, for the *sighing* of the needy will I arise. *Ps.* xii. 5.

Happier

Happier he,
Who ſeeks not pleaſure through neceſſity,
Than ſuch as once on ſlipp'ry thrones were plac'd,
And chaſing, *ſigh* to think themſelves are chas'd. *Dryden.*
The nymph too longs to be alone;
Leaves all the ſwains, and *ſighs* for one. *Prior.*
Thus *ſighed* he away the melancholy night. *Arb. and Pope.*

To SIGH. *v. a.* To lament; to mourn. Not in uſe.
Ages to come, and men unborn,
Shall bleſs her name, and *ſigh* her fate. *Prior.*

SIGH. *n. ſ.* [from the verb] A violent and audible emiſſion of the breath which has been long retained, as in ſadneſs.

Full often has my heart ſwoln with keeping my *ſighs* impriſoned; full often have the tears I drove back from mine eyes, turned back to drown my heart. *Sidney.*

Love is a ſmoke rais'd with the fume of *ſighs*;
Being purg'd, a fire ſparkling in lovers eyes. *Shakeſpeare.*
What a *ſigh* is there! The heart is ſorely charg'd. *Shakeſp.*

Laughing, if loud, ends in a deep *ſigh*; and all pleaſures have a ſting in the tail, though they carry beauty on the face. *Taylor.*

In Venus' temple, on the ſides were ſeen
Iſſuing *ſighs*, that ſmok'd along the wall. *Dryden.*

SIGHT. *n. ſ.* [ȝeſiðe, Saxon; *ſicht*, *geſicht*, Dutch.]

1. Perception by the eye; the ſenſe of ſeeing.

If bees go forth right to a place, they muſt needs have *ſight*. *Bacon.*

O loſs of *ſight*, of thee I moſt complain!
Blind among enemies, O worſe than chains,
Dungeon or beggary, decrepit age! *Milton's Agoniſtes.*
Things inviſible to mortal *ſight*. *Milton.*
'Tis ſtill the ſame, although their airy ſhape
All but a quick poetick *ſight* eſcape. *Denham.*
My eyes are ſomewhat dimiſh grown;
For nature, always in the right,
To your decays adapts my *ſight*. *Swift.*

2. Open view; a ſituation in which nothing obſtructs the eye.
Undaunted Hotſpur
Brings on his army, eager unto fight,
And plac'd the ſame before the king in *ſight*. *Daniel.*
Æneas caſt his wond'ring eyes around,
And all the Tyrrhene army had in *ſight*,
Stretch'd on the ſpacious plain from left to right. *Dryden.*
I met Brutidius in a mortal fright;
He's dipt for certain, and plays leaſt in *ſight*. *Dryd. Juven.*

3. Act of ſeeing or beholding.
Nine things to *ſight* required are;
The pow'r to ſee, the light, the viſible thing,
Being not too ſmall, too thin, too nigh, too far,
Clear ſpace and time, the form diſtinct to bring. *Davies.*
Mine eye purſu'd him ſtill, but under ſhade
Loſt *ſight* of him. *Milton's Paradiſe Loſt, b.* iv.
What form of death could him affright,
Who unconcern'd, with ſtedfaſt *ſight*,
Could view the ſurges mounting ſteep,
And monſters rolling in the deep! *Dryden's Horace.*

Having little knowledge of the circumſtances of thoſe St. Paul writ to, it is not ſtrange that many things lie concealed to us, which they who were concerned in the letter underſtood at firſt *ſight*. *Locke.*

4. Notice; knowledge.

It was writ as a private letter to a perſon of piety, upon an aſſurance that it ſhould never come to any one's *ſight* but her own. *Wake.*

5. Eye; inſtrument of ſeeing.
From the depth of hell they lift their *ſight*,
And at a diſtance ſee ſuperior light. *Dryden.*

6. Aperture pervious to the eye, or other point fixed to guide the eye: as, the *ſights* of a quadrant.
Their armed ſtaves in charge, their beavers down,
Their eyes of fire ſparkling through *ſights* of ſteel. *Shakeſp.*

7. Spectacle; ſhow; thing wonderful to be ſeen.
Thus are my eyes ſtill captive to one *ſight*;
Thus all my thoughts are ſlaves to one thought ſtill. *Sidney.*
Them ſeem'd they never ſaw a *ſight* ſo fair
Of fowls ſo lovely, that they ſure did deem
Them heavenly born. *Spenſer.*
Not an eye
But is a-weary of thy common *ſight*,
Save mine, which hath deſir'd to ſee thee more. *Shakeſp.*

Moſes ſaid, I will turn aſide and ſee this great *ſight*, why the buſh is not burnt. *Ex.* iii. 3.

I took a felucca at Naples to carry me to Rome, that I might not run over the ſame *ſights* a ſecond time. *Addiſon.*

Not proud Olympus yields a nobler *ſight*,
Though gods aſſembled grace his tow'ring height,
Than what more humble mountains offer here,
Where, in their bleſſings, all thoſe gods appear. *Pope.*
Before you paſs th' imaginary *ſights*
Of lords and earls, and dukes and garter'd knights,
While the ſpread fan o'erſhades your cloſing eyes,
Then give one flirt, and all the viſion flies. *Pope.*

SI'GHTED. *adj.* [from *ſight*.] Seeing in a particular manner. It is uſed only in compoſition, as *quickſighted*, *ſhortſighted*.

As they might, to avoid the weather, pull the joints of the coach up cloſe, ſo they might put each end down, and remain as diſcovered and open*ſighted* as on horſeback. *Sidney.*

The king was very quick*ſighted* in diſcerning difficulties, and raiſing objections, and very ſlow in maſtering them. *Claren.*

SI'GHTFULNESS. *n. ſ.* [from *ſight* and *full*.] Perſpicuity; clearneſs of ſight. Not in uſe.
But ſtill, although we fail of perfect rightfulneſs,
Seek we to tame theſe childiſh ſuperfluities;
Let us not wink, though void of pureſt *ſightfulneſs*. *Sidney.*

SI'GHTLESS. *adj.* [from *ſight*.]

1. Wanting ſight; blind.
The latent tracts, the giddy heights explore,
Of all who blindly creep, or *ſightleſs* ſoar. *Pope.*

2. Not ſightly; offenſive to the eye; unpleaſing to look at.
Full of unpleaſing blots and *ſightleſs* ſtains,
Patch'd with foul moles, and eye-offending marks. *Shak.*

SI'GHTLY. *adj.* [from *ſight*.] Pleaſing to the eye; ſtriking to the view.
It lies as *ſightly* on the back of him,
As great Alcides ſhews upon an aſs. *Shakeſp. K. John.*

Their having two eyes and two ears ſo placed, is more *ſightly* and uſeful. *More's Antidote againſt Atheiſm.*

A great many brave *ſightly* horſes were brought out, and only one plain nag that made ſport. *L'Eſtrange.*

We have thirty members, the moſt *ſightly* of all her majeſty's ſubjects: we elected a preſident by his height. *Addiſon.*

SI'GIL. *n. ſ.* [*ſigillum*, Latin.] Seal.
Sorceries to raiſe th' infernal pow'rs,
And *ſigils* fram'd in planetary hours. *Dryd. Knight's Tale.*

SIGN. *n. ſ.* [*ſigne*, French; *ſignum*, Latin.]

1. A token of any thing; that by which any thing is ſhown.

Signs muſt reſemble the things they ſignify. *Hooker.*

Signs for communication may be contrived from any variety of objects of one kind appertaining to either ſenſe. *Holder.*

To expreſs the paſſions which are ſeated in the heart by outward *ſigns*, is one great precept of the painters, and very difficult to perform. *Dryden's Dufreſnoy.*

When any one uſes any term, he may have in his mind a determined idea which he makes it the *ſign* of, and to which he ſhould keep it ſteadily annexed. *Locke.*

2. A wonder; a miracle.

If they will not hearken to the voice of the firſt *ſign*, they will not believe the latter *ſign*. *Ex.* iv. 8.

Cover thy face that thou ſee not; for I have ſet thee for a *ſign* unto Iſrael. *Ezek.* xii. 6.

Compell'd by *ſigns* and judgments dire. *Milton.*

3. A picture hung at a door, to give notice what is ſold within:
I found my miſs, ſtruck hands, and pray'd him tell,
To hold acquaintance ſtill, where he did dwell;
He barely nam'd the ſtreet, promis'd the wine;
But his kind wife gave me the very *ſign*. *Donne.*
Underneath an alehouſe' paltry *ſign*. *Shakeſp. H.* VI.
True ſorrow's like to wine,
That which is good does never need a *ſign*. *Suckling.*

Wit and fancy are not employed in any one article ſo much as that of contriving *ſigns* to hang over houſes. *Swift.*

4. A monument; a memorial.

The fire devoured two hundred and fifty men, and they became a *ſign*. *Num.* xxvi. 10.

5. A conſtellation in the zodiack.
There ſtay until the twelve celeſtial *ſigns*
Have brought about their annual reckoning. *Shakeſpeare.*

Now did the *ſign* reign, and the conſtellation was come, under which Perkin ſhould appear. *Bacon's Henry* VII.

After ev'ry foe ſubdu'd, the ſun
Thrice through the *ſigns* his annual race ſhall run. *Dryden.*

6. Note of reſemblance.

7. Enſign.
The enſign of Meſſiah blaz'd,
Aloft by angels borne, his *ſign* in heaven. *Milton.*

8. Typical repreſentation; ſymbol.

The holy ſymbols or *ſigns* are not barely ſignificative; but what they repreſent is as certainly delivered to us as the ſymbols themſelves. *Brerewood.*

9. A ſubſcription of one's name: as, a *ſign* manual.

To SIGN. *v. a.* [*ſigno*, Latin.]

1. To mark.
You *ſign* your place and calling in full ſeeming
With meekneſs and humility; but your heart
Is cramm'd with arrogancy. *Shakeſp. Henry* VIII.

2. [*Signer*, French.] To ratify by hand or ſeal.
Be pleas'd to *ſign* theſe papers: they are all
Of great concern! *Dryden's Cleomenes.*

3. To betoken; to ſignify; to repreſent typically.

The ſacraments and ſymbols are juſt ſuch as they ſeem; but becauſe they are made to be ſigns of a ſecret myſtery, they receive the names of what themſelves do *ſign*. *Taylor.*

SI'GNAL. *n. ſ.* [*ſignal*, French; *ſennale*, Spaniſh.] Notice given by a ſign; a ſign that gives notice.

The weary sun hath made a golden set,
And, by the bright track of his firy car,
Gives *signal* of a goodly day to-morrow. *Shakesp. R. III.*

Scarce the dawning day began to spring,
As at a *signal* giv'n, the streets with clamours ring. *Dryden.*

SI'GNAL. *adj.* [*signal*, French.] Eminent; memorable; remarkable.

He was esteemed more by the parliament, for the *signal* acts of cruelty committed upon the Irish. *Clarendon.*

The Thames frozen twice in one year, so as men to walk on it, is a very *signal* accident. *Swift.*

SIGNA'LITY. *n. s.* [from *signal.*] Quality of something remarkable or memorable.

Of the ways whereby they enquired and determined its *signality*, the first was natural, arising from physical causes. *Brown.*

It seems a *signality* in providence, in erecting your society in such a juncture of dangerous humours. *Glanv. Sceps. Pref.*

To SI'GNALIZE. *v. a.* [*signaler*, French.] To make eminent; to make remarkable.

Many, who have endeavoured to *signalize* themselves by works of this nature, plainly discover that they are not acquainted with the most common systems of arts and sciences. *Addison's Spectator.*

Some one eminent spirit, having *signalized* his valour and fortune in defence of his country, or by the practice of popular arts at home, becomes to have great influence on the people. *Swift.*

SI'GNALLY. *adv.* [from *signal.*] Eminently; remarkably; memorably.

Persons *signally* and eminently obliged, yet missing of the utmost of their greedy designs in swallowing both gifts and giver too, instead of thanks for received kindnesses, have betook themselves to barbarous threatnings. *South's Sermons.*

SIGNA'TION. *n. s.* [from *signo*, Latin.] Sign given; act of betokening.

A horseshoe Baptista Porta hath thought too low a *signation*, he raised unto a lunary representation. *Brown.*

SI'GNATURE. *n. s.* [*signature*, Fr. *signatura*, from *signo*, Lat.]

1. A sign or mark impressed upon any thing; a stamp; a mark.

The brain being well furnished with various traces, *signatures*, and images, will have a rich treasure always ready to be offered to the soul. *Watts.*

That natural and indelible *signature* of God, which human souls, in their first origin, are supposed to be stampt with, we have no need of in disputes against atheism. *Bentley.*

Vulgar parents cannot stamp their race
With *signatures* of such majestick grace. *Pope's Odyssey.*

2. A mark upon any matter, particularly upon plants, by which their nature or medicinal use is pointed out.

All bodies work by the communication of their nature, or by the impression and *signatures* of their motions: the diffusion of species visible, seemeth to participate more of the former, and the species audible of the latter. *Bacon's Nat. History.*

Some plants bear a very evident *signature* of their nature and use. *More against Atheism.*

Seek out for plants, and *signatures*,
To quack of universal cures. *Hudibras.*

Herbs are described by marks and *signatures*, so far as to distinguish them from one another. *Baker on Learning.*

3. Proof; evidence.

The most despicable pieces of decayed nature are curiously wrought with eminent *signatures* of divine wisdom. *Glanv.*

Some rely on certain marks and *signatures* of their election, and others on their belonging to some particular church or sect. *Rogers's Sermons.*

4. [Among printers.] Some letter or figure to distinguish different sheets.

SI'GNATURIST. *n. s.* [from *signature.*] One who holds the doctrine of signatures.

Signaturists seldom omit what the ancients delivered, drawing unto inference received distinctions. *Brown.*

SI'GNET. *n. s.* [*signette*, French.] A seal commonly used for the seal-manual of a king.

I've been bold,
For that I knew it the most gen'ral way,
To them to use your *signet* and your name. *Shakesp. Timon.*

Here is the hand and seal of the duke: you know the character, I doubt not, and the *signet*. *Shakesp. Meas. for Meas.*

Give thy *signet*, bracelets, and staff. *Gen.* xxxviii. 18.

He delivered him his private *signet*. *Knolles.*

He knew my pleasure to discharge his bands:
Proof of my life my royal *signet* made,
Yet still he arm'd. *Dryden's Aurengzebe.*

The impression of a *signet* ring. *Ayliffe's Parergon.*

SIGNI'FICANCE. } *n. s.* [from *signify.*]
SIGNI'FICANCY. }

1. Power of signifying; meaning.

Speaking is a sensible expression of the notions of the mind by discriminations of utterance of voice, used as signs, having by consent several determinate *significancies*. *Holder.*

If he declares he intends it for the honour of another, he takes away by his words the *significance* of his action. *Stillingfl.*

2. Force; energy; power of impressing the mind.

The clearness of conception and expression, the boldness maintained to majesty, the *significancy* and sound of words, not strained into bombast, must escape our transient view upon the theatre. *Dryden.*

As far as this duty will admit of privacy, our Saviour hath enjoined it in terms of particular *significancy* and force. *Atterb.*

I have been admiring the wonderful *significancy* of that word persecution, and what various interpretations it hath acquired. *Swift.*

3. Importance; moment; consequence.

How fatal would such a distinction have proved in former reigns, when many a circumstance of less *significancy* has been construed into an overt act of high treason? *Addison.*

SIGNI'FICANT. *adj.* [*significant*, Fr. *significans*, Latin.]

1. Expressive of something beyond the external mark.

Since you are tongue-ty'd, and so loth to speak,
In dumb *significants* proclaim your thoughts. *Shakesp. H. VI.*

2. Betokening; standing as a sign of something.

It was well said of Plotinus, that the stars were *significant*, but not efficient. *Raleigh.*

3. Expressive or representative in an eminent degree; forcible to impress the intended meaning.

Whereas it may be objected, that to add to religious duties such rites and ceremonies as are *significant*, is to institute new sacraments. *Hooker.*

Common life is full of this kind of *significant* expressions, by knocking, beckoning, frowning, and pointing; and dumb persons are sagacious in the use of them. *Holder on Speech.*

The Romans joined both devices, to make the emblem the more *significant*; as, indeed, they could not too much extol the learning and military virtues of this emperor. *Addison.*

4. Important; momentous. A low word.

SIGNI'FICANTLY. *adv.* [from *significant.*] With force of expression.

Christianity is known in Scripture by no name so *significantly* as by the simplicity of the Gospel. *South's Sermons.*

SIGNIFICA'TION. *n. s.* [*signification*, French; *significatio*, Latin; from *signify.*]

1. The act of making known by signs.

A lye is properly a species of injustice, and a violation of the right of that person to whom the false speech is directed; for all speaking, or *signification* of one's mind, implies an act or address of one man to another. *South.*

2. Meaning expressed by a sign or word.

An adjective requireth another word to be joined with him, to shew his *signification*. *Accidence.*

Brute animals make divers motions to have several *significations*, to call, warn, cherish, and threaten. *Holder.*

SIGNI'FICATIVE. *adj.* [*significatif*, Fr. from *signify.*]

1. Betokening by an external sign.

The holy symbols or signs are not barely *significative*, but what by divine institution they represent and testify unto our souls, is truly and certainly delivered unto us. *Brerewood.*

2. Forcible; strongly expressive.

Neither in the degrees of kindred they were destitute of *significative* words; for whom we call grandfather, they called ealdfader; whom we call great-grandfather, they called thirdafader. *Camden's Remains.*

SIGNI'FICATORY. *n. s.* [from *signify.*] That which signifies or betokens.

Here is a double *significatory* of the spirit, a word and a sign. *Taylor.*

To SI'GNIFY. *v. a.* [*signifier*, French; *significo*, Latin.]

1. To declare by some token or sign.

The maid from that ill omen turn'd her eyes,
Nor knew what *signify'd* the boding sign,
But found the pow'rs displeas'd. *Dryden.*

Those parts of nature, into which the chaos was divided, they *signified* by dark and obscure names; as the night, tartarus, and oceanus. *Burnet's Theory of the Earth.*

2. To mean; to express.

Life's but a walking shadow; a poor player,
That struts and frets his hour upon the stage,
And then is heard no more! It is a tale,
Told by an ideot, full of sound and fury,
Signifying nothing! *Shakespeare's Macbeth.*

Stephano, *signify*
Within the house your mistress is at hand. *Shakespeare.*

3. To import; to weigh. This is seldom used but interrogatively, *what signifies?* or with *much, little,* or *nothing.*

Though he that sins frequently, and repents frequently, gives reason to believe his repentances before God *signify nothing*; yet that is nothing to us. *Taylor.*

What signifies the splendor of courts, considering the slavish attendances that go along with it? *L'Estrange.*

He hath one way more, which although it *signify little* to men of sober reason, yet unhappily hits the suspicious humour of men, that governors have a design to impose. *Tillotson.*

If the first of these fail, the power of Adam, were it never so great, will *signify nothing* to the present societies in the world. *Locke.*

What

What signifies the people's consent in making and repealing laws, if the person who administers hath no tie. *Swift.*

4. To make known.

I'll to the king, and *signify* to him,
That thus I have resign'd to you my charge. *Shakesp. R.* III.

He sent and *signified* it by his angel unto John. *Rev.* i. 1.

The government should *signify* to the protestants of Ireland, that want of silver is not to be remedied. *Swift.*

To SI'GNIFY. *v. n.* To express meaning with force.

If the words be but comely and *signifying*, and the sense gentle, there is juice; but where that wanteth, the language is thin. *Ben. Johnson.*

SI'GNIORY. *n. s.* [*seignoria*, Italian.] Lordship; dominion.

If ancient sorrow be most reverent,
Give mine the benefit of *signiory*,
And let my griefs frown on the upper hand. *Shakesp. R.* III.

At that time
Through all the *signiories* it was the first,
And Prospero the prime duke. *Shakesp. Tempest.*

The earls, their titles and their *signiories*
They must restore again. *Daniel's Civil War.*

My brave progenitors, by valour, zeal,
Gain'd those high honours, princely *signiories*,
And proud prerogatives. *West.*

SI'GNPOST. *n. s.* [*sign* and *post*.] That upon which a sign hangs.

He should share with them in the preserving
A shed or *signpost*. *Ben. Johnson's Catiline.*

This noble invention of our author's hath been copied by so many *signpost* dawbers, that now 'tis grown fulsome, rather by their want of skill than by the commonness. *Dryden.*

SI'KER. *adv.* The old word for *sure*, or *surely*. *Spenser.*

SI'KERNESS. *n. s.* [from *siker*.] Sureness; safety.

SI'LENCE. *n. s.* [*silence*, French; *silentium*, Latin.]

1. The state of holding peace.

Unto me men gave ear, and waited and kept *silence* at my counsel. *Job* xxix. 21.

I suffer not a woman to teach, nor to usurp authority over the man, but to be in *silence*. 1 *Tim.* ii. 12.

First to himself he inward *silence* broke. *Milton.*

2. Habitual taciturnity; not loquacity.

I think the best grace of wit will shortly turn into *silence*,
And discourse grow commendable in none but parrots. *Shak.*

3. Secrecy.

4. Stilness; not noise.

Here all their rage, and ev'n their murmurs cease,
And sacred *silence* reigns, and universal peace. *Pope.*

5. Not mention.

Thus fame shall be atchiev'd,
And what most merits fame in *silence* hid. *Milton.*

SI'LENCE. *interj.* An authoritative restraint of speech.

Sir, have pity; I'll be his surety.—
—*Silence:* one word more
Shall make me chide thee, if not hate thee. *Shakespeare.*

To SI'LENCE. *v. a.* [from the noun] To still; to oblige to hold peace.

We must suggest the people, that to's pow'r
He wou'd have made them mules, *silenc'd* their pleaders, and
Dispropertied their freedoms. *Shakespeare.*

The ambassador is *silenc'd*. *Shakespeare's Hen.* VIII.

Silence that dreadful bell; it frights the isle
From her propriety. *Shakespeare's Othello.*

This passed as an oracle, and *silenced* those that moved the question. *Bacon's Hen.* VII.

Thus could not the mouths of worthy martyrs be *silenced*, who being exposed unto wolves, gave loud expressions of their faith, and were heard as high as heaven. *Brown's Vulgar Err.*

This would *silence* all further opposition. *Clarendon.*

Since in dark sorrow I my days did spend,
I could not *silence* my complaints. *Denham.*

These dying lovers, and their floating sons,
Suspend the fight and *silence* all our guns. *Waller.*

Had they duly considered the extent of infinite knowledge and power, these would have *silenced* their scruples, and they had adored the amazing mystery. *Rogers's Sermons.*

If it please him altogether to *silence* me, so that I shall not only speak with difficulty, but wholly be disabled to open my mouth, to any articulate utterance; yet I hope he will give me grace, even in my thoughts, to praise him. *Wake.*

The thund'rer spoke, nor durst the queen reply;
A reverend horror *silenc'd* all the sky. *Pope's Iliad.*

SI'LENT. *adj.* [*silens*, Latin.]

1. Not speaking; mute.

O my God, I cry in the day time, and in the night season I am not *silent*. *Psalms* xxii. 2.

Silent, and in face
Confounded long they sat as stricken mute. *Milton.*

Be not *silent* to me: lest if thou be *silent*, I become like those that go down into the pit. *Psalms* xxviii. 1.

2. Not talkative; not loquacious.

Ulysses, adds he, was the most eloquent and most *silent* of men; he knew that a word spoken never wrought so much good as a word conceal'd. *Notes on the Odyssey.*

3. Still; having no noise.

Deep night, dark night, the *silent* of the night,
The time of night when Troy was set on fire,
The time when screech-owls cry, and ban-dogs howl. *Shak.*

Now is the pleasant time,
The cool, the *silent*, save where silence yields
To the night-warbling bird. *Milton.*

4. Wanting efficacy. I think an Hebraism.

Second and instrumental causes, together with nature itself, without that operative faculty which God gave them, would become *silent*, virtueless and dead. *Raleigh's History.*

The sun to me is dark,
And *silent* as the moon,
When she deserts the night,
Hid in her vacant interlunar cave. *Milton.*

5. Not mentioning.

This new created world, whereof in hell
Fame is not *silent*. *Milton.*

SI'LENTLY. *adv.* [from *silent*.]

1. Without speech.

When with one three nations join to fight,
They *silently* confess that one more brave. *Dryden.*

For me they beg, each *silently*
Demands thy grace, and seems to watch thy eye. *Dryden.*

2. Without noise.

You to a certain victory are led;
Your men all arm'd stand *silently* within. *Dryden.*

3. Without mention.

The difficulties remain still, till he can show who is meant by right heir, in all those cases where the present possessor hath no son: this he *silently* passes over. *Locke.*

SILI'CIOUS. *adj.* [from *cilicium*.] It should be therefore written *cilicious*. Made of hair.

The *silicious* and hairy vests of the strictest orders of friars, derive their institution from St. John and Elias. *Brown.*

SILI'CULOSE. *adj.* [*silicula*, Latin.] Husky; full of husks. *Dict.*

SILI'GINOSE. *adj.* [*siliginosus*, Latin.] Made of fine wheat. *Dict.*

SI'LIQUA. n. s. [Latin]

1. [With gold finers.] A carat of which six make a scruple.

2. [*Silique*, French, with botanists.] The seed-vessel, husk, cod, or shell of such plants as are of the pulse kind. *Dict.*

SI'LIQUOSE. } *adj.* [from *siliqua*, Latin.] Having a pod, or
SI'LIQUOUS. } capsula.

All the tetrapetalous *siliquose* plants are alkalescent. *Arbuth.*

SILK. *n. s.* [ꞅeolc, Saxon.]

1. The thread of the worm that turns afterwards to a butterfly.

The worms were hallow'd that did breed the *silk*;
And it was dy'd in mummy, which the skilful
Conserv'd of maiden's hearts. *Shakespeare's Othello.*

2. The stuff made of the worms thread.

Let not the creaking of shoes, or rustling of *silks* betray thy poor heart to woman. *Shakespeare.*

He caused the shore to be covered with Persian *silk* for him to tread upon. *Knolles.*

Without the worm, in Persian *silks* we shine. *Waller.*

SI'LKEN. *adj.* [from *silk*.]

1. Made of *silk*.

Men counsel and give comfort to that grief
Which they themselves not feel; but tasting it,
Their counsel turns to passion, which before
Would give preceptial medicine to rage;
Fetter strong madness in a *silken* thread;
Charm ach with air, and agony with words. *Shakespeare.*

Now, will we revel it
With *silken* coats, and caps, and golden rings. *Shakespeare.*

She weeps,
And words address'd seem tears dissolv'd,
Wetting the borders of her *silken* veil. *Milton.*

2. Soft; tender.

Full many a lady fair, in court full oft
Beholding them, him secretly envide,
And wisht that two such fans, so *silken* soft,
And golden fair, her love would her provide. *Spenser.*

All the youth of England are on fire,
And *silken* dalliance in the wardrobe lies. *Shakesp. Hen.* V.

For then the hills with pleasing shades are crown'd,
And sleeps are sweeter on the *silken* ground. *Dryden.*

Dress up virtue in all the beauties of oratory, and you will find the wild passions of men too violent to be restrained by such mild and *silken* language. *Watts's Improv. of the Mind.*

3. Dressed in silk.

Shall a beardless boy,
A cocker'd, *silken* wanton, brave our fields,
And flesh his spirit in a warlike soil,
Mocking the air with colours idly spread,
And find no check? *Shakespeare's King John.*

SILKME'RCER. *n. s.* [*silk* and *mercer*.] A dealer in silk.

SILKWEA'VER. *n. s.* [*silk* and *weaver*.] One whose trade is to weave silken stuffs.

True English hate your monsieurs paltry arts;
For you are all *silk-weavers* in your hearts. *Dryden.*

The Chinese are ingenious *silk-weavers*. *Watts.*

SI'LKWORM. *n. s.* [*silk* and *worm*.] The worm that spins silk.

Grasshoppers eat up the green of whole countries, and *silkworms* devour leaves swiftly. *Bacon's Natural History.*

Broad were the banners, and of snowy hue,
A purer web the *silk-worm* never drew. *Dryden.*

SI'LKY. *adj.* [from *silk*.]

1. Made of silk.

2. Soft; pliant.

These kind of knaves, in plainness,
Harbour more craft, and more corrupter ends
Than twenty *silky* ducking observants,
That stretch their duties nicely. *Shakespeare's K. Lear.*

SILL. *n. s.* [ſyl, Sax. *sueil*, French; *sulle*, Dutch; *sulgan*, to found, Gothick.] The timber or stone at the foot of the door.

The farmer's goose,
Grown fat with corn and sitting still,
Can scarce get o'er the barn-door *sill*:
And hardly waddles forth. *Swift.*

SI'LLABUB. *n. s.* [This word has exercised the etymologists. *Minshew* thinks it corrupted from *swillingbubbles*. *Junius* omits it. *Henshaw*, whom *Skinner* follows, deduces it from the Dutch *sulle*, a pipe, and *buyck*, a paunch; because *sillabubs* are commonly drunk through a spout, out of a jug with a large belly. It seems more probably derived from *esil*, in old English *vinegar*, *esil a bouc*, *vinegar for the mouth*, vinegar made pleasant.] Curds made by milking upon vinegar.

Joan takes her neat rubb'd pail, and now
She trips to milk the sand-red cow;
Where, for some sturdy foot-ball swain,
Joan strokes a *sillabub* or twain. *Wotton.*

A feast,
By some rich farmer's wife and sister drest,
Might be resembled to a sick man's dream,
Where all ideas huddling run so fast,
That *sillabubs* come first, and soups the last. *King.*

SI'LLILY. *adv.* [from *silly*.] In a silly manner; simply; foolishly.

I wonder, what thou and I
Did, till we lov'd? were we not wean'd till then,
But suck'd on childish pleasures *sillily*?
Or slumber'd we in the seven sleepers den? *Donne.*

We are caught as *sillily* as the bird in the net. *L'Estrange.*

Do, do, look *sillily*, good colonel; 'tis a decent melancholy after an absolute defeat. *Dryden's Spanish Friar.*

SI'LLINESS. *n. s.* [from *silly*.] Simplicity; weakness; harmless folly.

The *sillyness* of the person does not derogate from the dignity of his character. *L'Estrange.*

SI'LLY. *adj.* [*selig*, German. *Skinner*.]

1. Harmless; innocent; inoffensive; plain; artless.

2. Weak; helpless.

After long storms,
In dread of death and dangerous dismay,
With which my *silly* bark was toss'd sore,
I do at length descry the happy shore. *Spenser.*

3. Foolish; witless.

Perhaps their loves, or else their sheep,
Was that did their *silly* thoughts so busy keep. *Milton.*

The meanest subjects censure the actions of the greatest prince; the *silliest* servants, of the wisest master. *Temple.*

I have no discontent at living here; besides what arises from a *silly* spirit of liberty, which I resolve to throw off. *Swift.*

Such parts of writings as are stupid or *silly*, false or mistaken, should become subjects of occasional criticism. *Watts.*

SI'LLYHOW. *n. s.* [Perhaps from ſelig, happy, and heofd, the head.] The membrane that covers the head of the fœtus.

Great conceits are raised, of the membranous covering called the *sillyhow*, sometimes found about the heads of children upon their birth. *Brown's Vulgar Errours.*

SILT. *n. s.* Mud; slime.

Several trees of oak and fir stand in firm earth below the moor, near Thorny, in all probability covered by inundation, and the *silt* and moorish earth exaggerated upon them. *Hale.*

SI'LVAN. *adj.* [from *silva*, Latin.] Woody; full of woods.

Betwixt two rows of rocks, a *silvan* scene
Appears above, and groves for ever green. *Dryden.*

SI'LVER. *n. s.* [ſeolfeꝛ, Saxon; *silver*, Dutch.]

1. *Silver* is a white and hard metal, next in weight to gold. *Watts's Logick.*

2. Any thing of soft splendour.

Pallas, piteous of her plaintive cries,
In slumber clos'd her *silver*-streaming eyes. *Pope.*

3. Money made of silver.

SI'LVER. *adj.*

1. Made of silver.

Put my *silver* cup in the sack's mouth. *Gen.* xliv. 2.

Hence had the huntress Dian her dread bow,
Fair *silver*-shafted queen for ever chaste. *Milton.*

The *silver*-shafted goddess of the place. *Pope's Odyssey.*

3. White like silver.

Of all the race of *silver*-winged flies
Was none more favourable, nor more fair,
Than Clarion. *Spenser.*

Old Salisbury, shame to thy *silver* hair,
Thou mad misleader of thy brain-sick son. *Shakespeare.*

The great in honour are not always wise,
Nor judgment under *silver* tresses lies. *Sandys.*

Others on *silver*-lakes and rivers bath'd
Their downy breast. *Milton.*

3. Having a pale lustre.

So sweet a kiss the golden sun gives not
To those fresh morning drops upon the rose,
As thy eye beams, when their fresh rays have smote
The night of dew that on my cheeks down flows;
Nor shines the *silver* moon one half so bright,
Through the transparent bosom of the deep,
As doth thy face through tears of mine give light. *Shakespeare.*

4. Soft of voice. This phrase is Italian, *voce argentina*.

From all their groves, which with the heavenly noises,
Of their sweet instruments were wont to sound,
And th' hollow hills, from which their *silver* voices
Were wont redoubled ecchoes to rebound,
Did now rebound with nought but rueful cries,
And yelling shrieks thrown up into the skies. *Spenser.*

It is my love that calls upon my name,
How *silver* sweet sound lovers tongues by night,
Like softest musick to attending ears. *Shakespeare.*

To SI'LVER. *v. a.* [from the noun.]

1. To cover superficially with silver.

There be fools alive, I wis,
Silver'd o'er, and so was this. *Shakespeare.*

The splendour of silver is more pleasing to some eyes, than that of gold; as in cloth of silver, and *silver'd* rapiers. *Bacon.*

Silvering will fully and canker more than gilding. *Bacon.*

A gilder shewed me a ring *silver'd* over with mercurial fumes, which he was then to restore to its native yellow. *Boyle.*

2. To adorn with mild lustre.

Here retir'd the sinking billows sleep,
And smiling calmness *silver'd* o'er the deep. *Pope.*

SI'LVERBEATER. *n. s.* [*silver* and *beat*.] One that foliates silver.

Silverbeaters chuse the finest coin, as that which is most extensive under the hammer. *Boyle.*

SI'LVERLING. *n. s.*

A thousand vines, at a thousand *silverlings*, shall be for briars and thorns. *Isaiah* vii. 23.

SI'LVERLY. *adv.* [from *silver*.] With the appearance of silver.

Let me wipe off this honourable dew
That *silverly* doth progress on thy cheeks. *Shakespeare.*

SI'LVERSMITH. *n. s.* [*silver* and *smith*.] One that works in silver.

Demetrius a *silversmith*, made shrines for Diana. *Acts* xix.

SI'LVERTHISTLE. }
SI'LVERWEED. } *n. s.* Plants.

SI'LVERTREE. *n. s.* [*conocarpodendron*, Latin.] A plant.

The leaves throughout the year are of a fine silver colour; it hath an apetalous flamineous flower, which is surrounded by a number of long leaves immediately under the flower-cup, which consists of five narrow leaves; these are succeeded by cones, in shape like those of the larchtree; the seeds are each of them included in a square cell. *Miller.*

SI'LVERY. *adj.* [from *silver*.] Besprinkled with silver.

A gritty stone, with small spangles of a white *silvery* talc in it. *Woodward on Fossils.*

Of all th' enamel'd race whose *silv'ry* wing
Waves to the tepid zephyrs of the spring,
Once brightest shin'd this child of heat and air. *Dunciad.*

SI'MAR. *n. s.* [*simarre*, French.] A woman's robe.

The ladies dress'd in rich *simars* were seen,
Of Florence sattin, flower'd with white and green. *Dryden.*

SI'MILAR. }
SI'MILARY. } *adj.* [*similaire*, French; from *similis*, Latin.]

1. Homogeneous; having one part like another.

Minerals appear to the eye to be perfectly *similar*, as metals; or at least to consist but of two or three distinct ingredients, as cinnabar. *Boyle.*

2. Resembling; having resemblance.

The laws of England, relative to those matters, were the original and exemplar from whence those *similar* or parallel laws of Scotland were derived. *Hale's Hist. of Com. Law of En.*

SIMILA'RITY. *n. s.* [from *similar*.] Likeness.

The blood and chyle are intimately mixed, and by attrition attenuated; by which the mixture acquires a greater degree of fluidity and *similarity*, or homogeneity of parts. *Arbuthnot.*

SI'MILE. *n. s.* [*simile*, Latin.] A comparison by which any thing is illustrated or aggrandized.

Their rhimes,
Full of protest, of oath, and big compare,
Want *similes*. *Shakespeare's Troilus and Cressida.*

Lucentio slip'd me, like his greyhound,
Which runs himself, and catches for his master:
A good swift *simile*, but something currish. *Shakespeare.*

In

In argument,
Similes are like songs in love,
They much describe; they nothing prove. *Prior.*

Poets, to give a loose to a warm fancy, not only expatiate in their *similes*, but introduce them too frequently. *Garth.*

SIMI'LITUDE. *n. s.* [*similitude*, French; *similitudo*, Latin.]

1. Likeness; resemblance.

Similitude of substance would cause attraction, where the body is wholly freed from the motion of gravity; for then lead would draw lead. *Bacon's Natural History.*

Our immortal souls, while righteous, are by God himself beautified with the title of his own image and *similitude*. *Ral.*

Let us make man in our image, man
In our *similitude*, and let them rule
Over the fish and fowl. *Milton.*

Similitude to the Deity was not regarded in the things they gave divine worship to, and looked on as symbols of the god they worshipped. *Stillingfleet.*

If we compare the picture of a man, drawn at the years of seventeen, with that of the same person at the years of threescore, hardly the least trace or *similitude* of one face can be found in the other. *South's Sermons.*

Fate some future bard shall join,
In sad *similitude* of griefs to mine,
Condemn'd whole years in absence to deplore,
And image charms he must behold no more. *Pope.*

2. Comparison; simile.

Plutarch, in the first of his tractates, by sundry *similitudes*, shews us the force of education. *Wotton.*

Tasso, in his *similitudes*, never departed from the woods; that is, all his comparisons were taken from the country. *Dryd.*

SI'MITAR. *n. s.* [See CI'METER.] A crooked or falcated sword with a convex edge.

To SI'MMER. *v. n.* [A word made probably from the sound, but written by *Skinner*, *simber*.] To boil gently; to boil with a gentle hissing.

Place a vessel in warm sand, increasing the heat by degrees, till the spirit *simmer* or boil a little. *Boyle.*

Their vital heat and moisture may always not only *simber* in one sluggish tenour, but sometimes boil up higher, and seeth over; the fire of life being more than ordinarily kindled upon some emergent occasion. *More's Antidote against Atheism.*

SI'MNEL. [*n. s.* [*simnellus*, low Latin.] A kind of sweet bread or cake.

SIMONI'ACK. *n. s.* [*simoniaque*, French; *simoniacus*, Latin.] One who buys or sells preferment in the church.'

If the bishop alleges that the person presented is a *simoniac*, or unlearned, they are to proceed to trial. *Ayliffe.*

SIMONI'ACAL. *adj.* [from *simoniac.*] Guilty of buying or selling ecclesiastical preferment.

Add to your criminals the *simoniacal* ladies, who seduce the sacred order into the difficulty of breaking their troth. *Spect.*

SI'MONY. *n. s.* [*simonie*, French; *simonia*, Latin.] The crime of buying or selling church preferment.

One that by suggestion
Tied all the kingdom; *simony* was fair play,
His own opinion was his law. *Shakespeare's Henry* VIII.

Many papers remain in private hands, of which one is of *simony*; and I wish the world might see it, that it might undeceive some patrons, who think they have discharged that great trust to God and man, if they take no money for a living, though it may be parted with for other ends less justifiable. *Walton's Life of Bishop Sanderson.*

No *simony* nor sinecure is known;
There works the bee, no honey for the drone. *Garth.*

To SIMPER. *v. n.* [from ꞅymbelan, Saxon, to keep holiday, *Skinner*. He derives *simmer* from the same word, and confirms his etymology by writing it *simber*. It is perhaps derived from *simmer*, as it may seem to imitate the dimples of water gently boiling.] To smile; generally to smile foolishly.

A made countenance about her mouth between *simpering* and smiling, her head bowed somewhat down, seemed to languish with over much idleness. *Sidney.*

I charge you, O men, for the love you bear to women, as I perceive by your *simpering* none of you hate them, to like as much as pleases them. *Shakespeare's As you like it.*

Stars above *simper* and shine,
As having keys unto thy love, while poor I pine. *Herbert.*

Let then the fair one beautifully cry,
Drest in smiles of sweet Cecilia shine,
With *simp'ring* angels, palms and harps divine. *Pope.*

SI'MPER. *n. s.* [from the verb.] Smile; generally a foolish smile.

The wit at his elbow stared him in the face, with so bewitching a grin, that the whistler relaxed his fibres into a kind of *simper*, and at length burst out into an open laugh. *Add.*

Great Tibbald nods: the proud Parnassian sneer,
The conscious *simper*, and the jealous leer,
Mix on his look. *Pope's Dunciad.*

SI'MPLE. *adj.* [*simplex*, Latin; *simple*, French.]

1. Plain; artless; unskilled; undesigning; sincere; harmless.

Were it not to satisfy the minds of the *simpler* sort of men, these nice curiosities are not worthy the labour which we bestow to answer them. *Hooker.*

They meet upon the way,
A *simple* husbandman in garments grey. *Hubberd's Tale.*

I am a *simple* woman, much too weak
T' oppose your cunning. *Shakespeare's Hen.* VIII.

O Ethelinda,
My heart was made to fit and pair with thine,
Simple and plain, and fraught with artless tenderness. *Rowe.*

2. Uncompounded; unmingled; single; only one; plain; not complicated.

To make the compound pass for the rich metal *simple*, is an adulteration or counterfeiting. *Bacon.*

Simple philosophically signifies single, but vulgarly foolish. *Watts.*

Among substances some are called *simple*, some compound, whether taken in a philosophical or vulgar sense. *Watt.*

If we take *simple* and compound in a vulgar sense, then all those are *simple* substances which are generally esteemed uniform in their natures: so every herb is called a *simple*, and every metal a mineral; though the chymist perhaps may find all his several elements in each of them. *Watts's Logicks.*

Let Newton, pure intelligence, whom God
To mortals lent, to trace his boundless works,
From laws, sublimely *simple*, speak thy fame
In all philosophy. *Thomson's Summer.*

3. Silly; not wise; not cunning.

The *simple* believeth every word; but the prudent man looketh well to his going. *Prov.* xv.

I would have you wise unto that which is good, and *simple* concerning evil. *Rom.* xvi. 19.

Dick, *simple* odes too many show
My servile complaisance to Cloe. *Prior.*

SI'MPLE. *n. s.* [*simple*, French.] A single ingredient in a medicine; a drug. It is popularly used for an *herb*.

Of *simples* in these groves that grow,
We'll learn the perfect skill;
The nature of each herb to know,
Which cures, and which can kill. *Drayton's Q. of Cynthia.*

Our foster nurse of nature is repose,
The which he lacks; that to provoke in him,
Are many *simples* operative, whose power
Will close the eye of anguish. *Shakespeare's K. Lear.*

He would ope his leathern scrip,
And shew me *simples* of a thousand names,
Telling their strange and vigorous faculties *Milton.*

What virtue is in this remedy lies in the naked *simple* itself, as it comes over from the Indies. *Temple.*

Around its entries nodding poppies grow,
And all cool *simples* that sweet rest bestow;
Night from the plants their sleepy virtue drains,
And passing, sheds it on the silent plains. *Dryden.*

Med'cine is mine: what herbs and *simples* grow
In fields and forests, all their pow'rs I know,
And am the great physician call'd. *Dryden.*

To SIMPLE. *v. n.* To gather simples.

As once the foaming boar he chas'd,
Lascivious Circe well the youth survey'd,
As *simpling* on the flow'ry hills he stray'd. *Garth.*

SI'MPLESS. *n. s.* [*simplesse*, French.] Simplicity; silliness; folly. An obsolete word.

Their weeds been not so nighly were,
Such *simplesse* mought them shend,
They been yclad in purple and pall,
They reign and rulen over all. *Spenser's Pastorals.*

SI'MPLENESS. *n. s.* [from *simple.*] The quality of being simple.

I will hear that play:
For never any thing can be amiss,
When *simpleness* and duty tender it. *Shakespeare.*

Such perfect elements may be found in these four known bodies that we call pure ones; for they are least compounded, and approach most to the *simpleness* of the elements. *Digby.*

SIMPLE'R. *n. s.* [from *simple.*] A simplist. An herbarist.

SI'MPLETON. *n. s.* [from *simple.*] A silly mortal; a trifler; a foolish fellow. A low word.

A country farmer sent his man to look after an ox; the *simpleton* went hunting up and down till he found him in a wood. *L'Estrange.*

Those letters may prove a discredit, as lasting as mercenary scribblers, or curious *simpletons* can make it. *Pope.*

SIMPLI'CITY. *n. s.* [*simplicitas*, Latin; *simplicité*, French.]

1. Plainness; artlessness; not subtilty; not cunning; not deceit.

The sweet-minded Philoclea was in their degree of well doing, to whom the not knowing of evil serveth for a ground of virtue, and hold their inward powers in better form, with an unspotted *simplicity*, than many who rather cunningly seek to know what goodness is, than willingly take unto themselves the following of it. *Sidney.*

In

In low *ſimplicity*,
He lends out money *gratis*, and brings down
The rate of uſance. *Shakeſpeare.*

Marquis Dorſet, a man for his harmleſs *ſimplicity*, neither miſliked nor much regarded, was created Duke. *Haywood.*

Suſpicion ſleeps
At wiſdom's gate, and to *ſimplicity*
Reſigns her charge. *Milton.*

Of manners gentle, of affections mild;
In wit a man, *ſimplicity* a child. *Pope.*

Beauty is their own,
The feeling heart, *ſimplicity* of life,
And elegance and taſte. *Thomſon's Summer.*

The native elegance and *ſimplicity* of her manners, were accompanied with real benevolence of heart. *Female Quixote.*

2. Plainneſs; not ſubtilty; not abſtruſeneſs.

They keep the reverend *ſimplicity* of ancienter times. *Hooker.*

Thoſe enter into farther ſpeculations herein, which is the itch of curioſity, and content not themſelves with the *ſimplicity* of that doctrine, within which this church hath contained herſelf. *Hammond's Fundamentals.*

3. Plainneſs; not finery.

They repreſent our poet, when he left Mantua for Rome, dreſſed in his beſt habit, too fine for the place whence he came, and yet retaining part of its *ſimplicity*. *Dryden.*

4. Singleneſs; not compoſition; ſtate of being uncompounded.

Mandrakes afford a papaverous and unpleaſant odour in the leaf or apple, as is diſcoverable in their *ſimplicity* and mixture. *Brown's Vulg. Errours.*

We are led to conceive that great machine of the world, to have been once in a ſtate of greater *ſimplicity* than now it is, as to conceive a watch once in its firſt and ſimple materials. *Burnet.*

5. Weakneſs; ſillineſs.

Many that know what they ſhould do, would nevertheleſs diſſemble it, and to excuſe themſelves, pretend ignorance and *ſimplicity*, which now they cannot. *Hooker.*

How long ye ſimple ones will ye love *ſimplicity*? and fools hate knowledge? *Prov.* i. 22.

Si'mplist. *n. ſ.* [from *ſimple*.] One ſkilled in ſimples.

A plant ſo unlike a roſe, it hath been miſtaken by ſome good *ſimpliſts* for amomum. *Brown's Vulg. Errours.*

Si'mply. *adv.* [from *ſimple*.]

1. Without art; without ſubtlety; plainly; artleſly.

Accompliſhing great things by things deem'd weak;
Subverting worldy ſtrong and worldly wiſe,
By *ſimply* meek. *Milton's Paradiſe Loſt.*

2. Of itſelf; without addition.

This queſtion about the changing of laws concerneth only ſuch laws as are poſitive, and do make that now good or evil, by being commanded or forbidden, which otherwiſe of itſelf were not *ſimply* the one or the other. *Hooker.*

3. Merely; ſolely.

Under man, no creature in the world is capable of felicity and bliſs; becauſe their chiefeſt perfection conſiſteth in that which is beſt for them, but not in that which is *ſimply* beſt, as ours doth. *Hooker.*

I will eat and drink, and ſleep as ſoft
As captain ſhall; *ſimply* the thing I am
Shall make me live. *Shakeſpeare.*

To ſay, or to do ought with memory and imitation, no purpoſe or reſpect ſhould ſooner move us, than *ſimply* the love of God and of mankind. *Milton.*

4. Fooliſhly; ſillily.

Si'mular. *n. ſ.* [from *ſimulo*, Latin.] One that counterfeits.

Hide thee, thou bloody hand,
Thou perjurer, thou *ſimular* of virtue,
That art inceſtuous. *Shakeſpeare's King Lear.*

Simula'tion. *n. ſ.* [*ſimulation*, French; *ſimulatio* from *ſimulo*, Latin.] That part of hypocriſy which pretends that to be which is not.

Simulation is a vice riſing of a natural falſeneſs, or fearfulneſs; or of a mind that hath ſome main faults; which becauſe a man muſt needs diſguiſe, it maketh him practiſe *ſimulation*. *Bacon.*

For the unqueſtionable virtues of her perſon and mind, he well expreſſed his love in an act and time of no *ſimulation* towards his end, bequeathing her all his manſion-houſes, and a power to diſpoſe of his whole perſonal eſtate. *Wotton.*

For diſtinction ſake, a deceiving by word is commonly called a lie; and deceiving by actions, geſtures, or behaviour, is called *ſimulation* or hypocriſy. *South's Sermons.*

Simulta'neous. *adj.* [*ſimultaneus*, Latin.] Acting together; exiſting at the ſame time.

If the parts may all change places at the ſame time, without any reſpect of priority or poſteriority to each other's motion, why may not bullets, cloſely crouded in a box, move by a like mutual and *ſimultaneous* exchange? *Glanville.*

Sin. *n. ſ.* [ſyn, Saxon.]

1. An act againſt the laws of God; a violation of the laws of religion.

How haſt thou the heart,
Being a divine, a ghoſtly confeſſor,
A *ſin* abſolver, and my friend profeſt,
To mangle me with that word baniſhment. *Shakeſpeare.*

But thoſe that ſleep, and think not on their *ſins*,
Pinch them. *Shakeſpeare's Merry Wives of Windſor.*

Thou knoweſt, Lord, that I am pure from all *ſin* with man. *Tob.* iii. 14.

2. Habitual negligence of religion.

Sin, death, and hell, have ſet their marks upon him,
And all their miniſters attend on him. *Shakeſpeare.*

Diſhoneſt ſhame
Of nature's works: honour diſhonourable!
Sin-bred! how have ye troubled all mankind? *Milton.*

Is there no means, but that a *ſin*-ſick land
Should be let blood with ſuch a boiſt'rous hand? *Daniel.*

Vice or virtue chiefly imply the relation of our actions to men in this world: *ſin* and holineſs rather imply their relation to God and the other world. *Watts's Logick.*

Light from her thought, as ſummer's careleſs robe,
Fell each affection of this *ſin*-worn globe. *Brooke.*

3. It is uſed by *Shakeſpeare* emphatically for a man enormouſly wicked.

Thy ambition,
Thou ſcarlet *ſin*, robb'd this bewailing land
Of noble Buckingham. *Shakeſpeare's Henry* VIII.

To Sin. *v. n.* [from the noun.]

1. To neglect the laws of religion; to violate the laws of religion.

Stand in awe and *ſin* not. *Pſalms* iv. 4.

Many alſo have periſh'd, err'd, and *ſinn'd* for women. *Eſdr.*

He ſhall aſk, and he ſhall give him life for them that *ſin* not unto death. 1 *John* v. 16.

2. To offend againſt right.

I am a man,
More *ſinn'd* againſt than *ſinning*. *Shakeſpeare.*

And who but wiſhes to invert the laws
Of order, *ſins* againſt th' eternal cauſe. *Pope's Eſſay on Man.*

Si'nworm. *n. ſ.* [*ſin* and *worm*.] A vile ſinful creature.

I would not ſoil theſe pure ambroſial weeds,
With the rank vapours of the *ſin-worn* mould. *Milton.*

Since. *adv.* [formed by contraction from *ſithence*, or *ſith thence*, from ſiðe, Saxon.]

1. Becauſe that.

Since the cleareſt diſcoveries we have of other ſpirits, beſides God and our own ſouls, are imparted by revelation, the information of them ſhould be taken from thence. *Locke.*

Since truth and conſtancy are vain,
Since neither love, nor ſenſe of pain,
Nor force of reaſon can perſuade,
Then let example be obey'd. *Granville.*

2. From the time that.

Am not I thine aſs, upon which thou haſt ridden ever *ſince* I was thine unto this day? *Numb.* xxii. 30.

He is the moſt improved mind *ſince* you ſaw him, that ever was, without ſhifting into a new body. *Pope.*

3. Ago; before this.

About two years *ſince*, it ſo fell out, that he was brought to a great lady's houſe. *Sidney.*

Spies held me in chaſe, that I was forc'd to wheel
Three or four miles about; elſe had I, ſir,
Half an hour *ſince*, brought my report. *Shakeſp. Coriolanus.*

A law was made no longer *ſince* than the twenty eighth of Henry the eighth. *Davies's Hiſt. of Ireland.*

How many ages *ſince* has Virgil writ? *Roſcommon.*

Since. *prepoſition.* After; reckoning from ſome time paſt to the time preſent.

He *ſince* the morning hour ſet out from heav'n. *Milton.*

If ſuch a man ariſe, I have a model by which he may build a nobler poem than any extant *ſince* the ancients. *Dryden.*

Since're. *adj.* [*ſincerus*, Latin; *ſincere*, French.]

1. Unhurt; uninjured.

He try'd a tough well choſen ſpear;
Th' inviolable body ſtood *ſincere*. *Dryden.*

2. Pure; unmingled.

Pardon my tears, 'tis joy which bids them flow:
A joy which never was *ſincere* till now;
That which my conqueſt gave, I could not prize,
Or 'twas imperfect till I ſaw your eyes. *Dryden.*

The pleaſures of ſenſe beaſts taſte *ſincere* and pure always, without mixture or allay, without being diſtracted in the purſuit, or diſquieted in the uſe of them. *Atterbury.*

Animal ſubſtances differ from vegetable, in that being reduced to aſhes, they are perfectly inſipid, and in that there is no *ſincere* acid in any animal juice. *Arbuthnot on Aliments.*

3. Honeſt; undiſſembling; uncorrupt.

This top proud fellow,
Whom from the flow of gall I name not, but
From *ſincere* motions by intelligence
I do know to be corrupt. *Shakeſpeare's Hen.* VIII.

Nor troubled at theſe tidings from the earth,
Which your *ſincereſt* care could not prevent;
Foretold ſo lately what would come to paſs,
When firſt this temper croſs'd the gulf from hell. *Milton.*

In English I would have all Gallicisms avoided, that our tongue may be *sincere*, and that we may keep to our own language. *Felton on the Classicks.*

SINCE'RELY. *adv.* [from *sincere*.] Honestly; without hypocrisy; with purity of heart.

The purer and perfecter our religion is, the worthier effects it hath in them who stedfastly and *sincerely* embrace it. *Hooker.*

That you may, fair lady,
Perceive I speak *sincerely*, the king's majesty
Does purpose honour to you. *Shakesp. Henry VIII.*

In your whole reasoning, keep your mind *sincerely* intent in the pursuit of truth. *Watts's Logick.*

SINCE'RENESS. } SINCE'RITY. } *n. s.* [*sincerité*, French; from *sincere*.]

1. Honesty of intention; purity of mind.

Jesus Christ has purchased for us terms of reconciliation, who will accept of *sincerity* instead of perfection; but then this *sincerity* implies our honest endeavours to do our utmost. *Rogers.*

2. Freedom from hypocrisy.

In thy consort cease to fear a foe;
For thee she feels *sincerity* of woe. *Pope's Odyssey.*

SI'NDON. *n. s.* [Latin.] A fold; a wrapper.

There were found a book and a letter, both written in fine parchment, and wrapped in *sindons* of linen. *Bacon.*

SI'NE. *n. s.* [*sinus*, Latin.] A right *sine*, in geometry, is a right line drawn from one end of an arch perpendicularly upon the diameter drawn from the other end of that arch; or it is half the chord of twice the arch. *Harris.*

Whatever inclinations the rays have to the plane of incidence, the *sine* of the angle of incidence of every ray, considered apart, shall have to the *sine* of the angle of refraction a constant ratio. *Cheyne's Phil. Princ.*

SI'NECURE. *n. s.* [*sine*, without, and *cura*, care, Latin.] An office which has revenue without any employment.

A *sinecure* is a benefice without cure of souls. *Ayliffe.*

No symony nor *sinecure* were known,
Nor would the bee work honey for the drone. *Garth.*

SI'NEW. *n. s.* [ꞅenpe, Saxon; *senewen*, Dutch.]

1. A tendon; the ligament by which the joints are moved.

The torrent roar'd, and we did buffet it
With lusty *sinews*. *Shakesp. Julius Cæsar.*

The rooted fibres rose, and from the wound
Black bloody drops distill'd upon the ground:
Mute and amaz'd, my hair with terror stood;
Fear shrunk my *sinews*, and congeal'd my blood. *Dryden.*

A *sinew* cracked, seldom recovers its former strength. *Locke.*

2. Applied to whatever gives strength or compactness: as, money is the *sinews* of war.

Some other *sinews* there are, from which that overplus of strength in persuasion doth arise. *Hooker.*

Such discouraging of men in the ways of an active conformity to the church's rules, cracks the *sinews* of government; for it weakens and damps the spirits of the obedient. *South.*

In the principal figures of a picture the painter is to employ the *sinews* of his art; for in them consists the principal beauties of his work. *Dryden's Dufresnoy.*

3. Muscle or nerve.

The feeling pow'r, which is life's root,
Through ev'ry living part itself doth shed
By *sinews*, which extend from head to foot;
And, like a net, all o'er the body spread. *Davies.*

To SINEW. *v. a.* [from the noun.] To knit as by sinews. Not in use.

Ask the lady Bona for thy queen;
So shalt thou *sinew* both these lands together. *Shak. H. VI.*

SI'NEWED. *adj.* [from *sinew*.]

1. Furnished with sinews.

Strong *sinew'd* was the youth, and big of bone. *Dryden.*

2. Strong; firm; vigorous.

He will the rather do it, when he sees
Ourselves well *sinewed* to our defence. *Shakes. King John.*

SI'NEWSHRUNK. *adj.* [*sinew* and *shrunk*.] A horse is said to be *sinewshrunk* when he has been over-ridden, and so fatigued that he becomes gaunt-bellied by a stiffness and contraction of the two sinews which are under his belly. *Farriers Dict.*

SI'NEWY. *adj.* [from *sinew*.]

1. Consisting of a sinew; nervous. The nerves and sinews are in poetry often confounded, from *nervus*, Latin, which signifies a sinew.

The *sinewy* thread my brain lets fall
Through every part,
Can tie those parts, and make me one of all. *Donne.*

2. Strong; nervous; vigorous; forcible.

And for thy vigour, bull-bearing Milo his addition yields
To *sinewy* Ajax. *Shakespeare's Troilus and Cressida.*

Worthy fellows, and like to prove
Most *sinewy* swordsmen. *Shakespeare.*

The northern people are large, fair-complexioned, strong, *sinewy*, and couragious. *Hale's Origin of Mankind.*

Fainting as he reach'd the shore,
He dropt his *sinewy* arms: his knees no more
Perform'd their office. *Pope's Odyssey.*

SI'NFUL. *adj.* [*sin* and *full*.]

1. Alien from God; not holy; unsanctified.

Drive out the *sinful* pair,
From hallow'd ground th' unholy. *Milton.*

2. Wicked; not observant of religion; contrary to religion. It is used both of persons and things.

Thrice happy man, said then the father grave,
Whose staggering steps thy steddy hand doth lead,
And shews the way his *sinful* soul to save,
Who better can the way to heaven aread? *Fairy Queen.*

It is great sin to swear unto a sin;
But greater sin to keep a *sinful* oath. *Shakesp. Henry VI.*

Nature herself, though pure of *sinful* thought,
Wrought in her so, that, seeing me, she turn'd. *Milton.*

The stoicks looked upon all passions as *sinful* defects and irregularities, as so many deviations from right reason, making passion to be only another word for perturbation. *South.*

SI'NFULLY. *adv.* [from *sinful*.] Wickedly; not piously; not according to the ordinance of God.

All this from my remembrance brutish wrath
Sinfully pluckt, and not a man of you
Had so much grace to put it in my mind. *Shakesp. R. III.*

The humble and contented man pleases himself innocently and easily, while the ambitious man attempts to please others *sinfully* and difficultly, and perhaps unsuccessfully too. *South.*

SI'NFULNESS. *n. s.* [from *sinful*.] Alienation from God; neglect or violation of the duties of religion; contrariety to religious goodness.

I am sent
To shew thee what shall come in future days
To thee, and to thy offspring: good with bad
Expect to hear; supernal grace contending
With *sinfulness* of men. *Milton.*

Peevishness, the general fault of sick persons, is equally to be avoided for the folly and *sinfulness*. *Wake.*

To SING. *v. n.* preterite *I sang*, or *sung*; participle pass. *sung*. [ꞅingan, Saxon; *singia*, Islandick; *singhen*, Dutch.]

1. To form the voice to melody; to articulate musically.

Orpheus with his lute made trees,
And the mountain tops that freeze,
Bow themselves when he did *sing*:
To his musick plants and flowers
Ever sprung, as sun and showers
There had made a lasting spring. *Shakes. Henry VIII.*

Then they for sudden joy did weep,
And some for sorrow *sung*. *Shakes. King Lear.*

They rather had beheld
Dissentious numbers pestering streets, than see
Our tradesmen *singing* in their shops, and going
About their functions friendly. *Shakesp. Coriolanus.*

The morning stars *sang* together. *Job.*

Then shall the trees of the wood *sing* out at the presence of the Lord. *1 Chro. xvi. 33.*

Their airy limbs in sports they exercise,
Some in heroick verse divinely *sing*. *Dryden.*

2. To utter sweet sounds inarticulately.

The time of the *singing* of birds is come. *Cant. ii. 12.*

You will sooner bind a bird from *singing* than from flying. *Bac.*

Join voices all ye birds,
That *singing* up to heav'n's gate ascend. *Milton.*

And parrots, imitating human tongue,
And *singing* birds, in silver cages hung. *Dryden's Ovid.*

Oh! were I made, by some transforming pow'r,
The captive bird that *sings* within thy bow'r,
Then might my voice thy list'ning ears employ,
And I those kisses he receives enjoy. *Pope's Summer.*

3. To make any small or shrill noise.

A man may hear this shower *sing* in the wind. *Shakespeare.*

You leaden messengers,
Fly with false aim; pierce the still moving air,
That *sings* with piercing; do not touch my lord. *Shakesp.*

We hear this fearful tempest *sing*. *Shakespeare.*

4. To tell in poetry.

Bid her exalt her melancholy wing,
And rais'd from earth, and sav'd from passion, *sing*
Of human hope by cross event destroy'd,
Of useless wealth and greatness unenjoy'd. *Prior.*

To SING. *v. a.*

1. To relate or mention in poetry.

All the prophets in their age the times
Of great Messiah *sing*. *Milton.*

Arms and the man I *sing*. *Dryden's Æn.*

Well might he *sing* the day he could not fear,
And paint the glories he was sure to wear. *Smith.*

2. To celebrate; to give praises to.

3. To utter harmoniously.

Incles, caddisses, cambricks, lawns, why
He *sings* them over as they were gods and goddesses. *Shakes.*

They that wasted us required of us mirth, saying, *sing* us one of the songs of Zion. *Ps. cxxxvii. 3.*

How could we to his godhead *sing*
Forc'd hallelujahs? *Milton.*

To Singe. *v. a.* [ſænȝan, Saxon; *ſenghen*, Dutch.] To ſcorch; to burn ſlightly or ſuperficially.

They bound the doctor,
Whoſe beard they have *ſing'd* off with brands of fire. *Shak.*

You ſulph'rous and thought executing fires,
Singe my white head. *Shakeſpeare.*

Drake, in the vaunting ſtile of a ſoldier, would call this enterprize the *ſingeing* of the king of Spain's beard. *Bacon.*

That neither was *ſinged* in the combuſtion of Phaeton, nor overwhelmed by the inundation of Deucalion. *Brown.*

They leave a *ſinged* bottom all involv'd
With ſtench and ſmoke. *Milton's Paradiſe Loſt.*

I *ſinged* the toes of an ape through a burning-glaſs, and he never would endure it after. *L'Eſtrange.*

Thus riding on his curls he ſeem'd to paſs
A rolling fire along, and *ſinge* the graſs. *Dryden.*

Si'nger. *n. ſ.* [from *ſing*.] One that ſings; one whoſe profeſſion or buſineſs is to ſing.

His filching was like an unſkilful *ſinger*, he kept not time. *Shakeſp. Merry Wives of Windſor.*

I gat me men *ſingers* and women *ſingers*, and the delights of the ſons of men. *Eccl.* ii. 8.

To the chief *ſinger* on my ſtringed inſtruments. *Hab.* iii.

Thy heart no ruder than the rugged ſtone,
I might, like Orpheus, with my num'rous moan
Melt to compaſſion: now my trait'rous ſong
With thee conſpires to do the *ſinger* wrong. *Waller.*

Cockbirds amongſt ſinging birds are ever the better *ſingers*, becauſe they are more lively. *Bacon's Natural Hiſtory.*

The birds know how to chuſe their fare;
To peck this fruit they all forbear:
Thoſe cheerful *ſingers* know not why
They ſhould make any haſte to die. *Waller.*

The Grecian tragedy was at firſt nothing but a chorus of *ſingers*. *Dryden.*

Si'ngingmaster. *n. ſ.* [*ſing* and *maſter*.] One who teaches to ſing.

He employed an itinerant *ſingingmaſter* to inſtruct them rightly in the tunes of the pſalms. *Addiſon's Spectator.*

SI'NGLE. *adj.* [*ſingulus*, Latin.]

1. One; not double; not more than one.

The words are clear and eaſy, and their originals are of *ſingle* ſignification without any ambiguity. *South.*

Some were *ſingle* acts, though each compleat;
But ev'ry act ſtood ready to repeat. *Dryden.*

Then Theſeus join'd with bold Pirithous came,
A *ſingle* concord in a double name. *Dryden.*

High Alba,
A lonely deſart, and an empty land,
Shall ſcarce afford, for needful hours of reſt,
A *ſingle* houſe to their benighted gueſt. *Addiſon on Italy.*

Where the poeſy or oratory ſhines, a *ſingle* reading is no ſufficient to ſatisfy a mind that has a true taſte; nor can we make the fulleſt improvement of them without proper reviews. *Watts's Improvement of the Mind.*

2. Particular; individual.

As no *ſingle* man is born with a right of controuling the opinions of all the reſt, ſo the world has no title to demand the whole time of any particular perſon. *Pope.*

If one *ſingle* word were to expreſs but one ſimple idea, and nothing elſe, there would be ſcarce any miſtake. *Watts.*

3. Not compounded.

As ſimple ideas are oppoſed to complex, and *ſingle* ideas to compound, ſo propoſitions are diſtinguiſhed: the Engliſh tongue has ſome advantage above the learned languages, which have no uſual word to diſtinguiſh *ſingle* from ſimple. *Watts.*

4. Alone; having no companion; having no aſſiſtant.

Servant of God, well haſt thou fought
The better fight, who *ſingle* haſt maintain'd
Againſt revolted multitudes the cauſe of truth. *Milton.*

His wiſdom ſuch,
Three kingdoms wonder, and three kingdoms fear,
Whilſt *ſingle* he ſtood forth. *Denham.*

In ſweet poſſeſſion of the fairy place,
Single and conſcious to myſelf alone,
Of pleaſures to th' excluded world unknown. *Dryden.*

5. Unmarried.

Is the *ſingle* man therefore bleſſed? no: as a walled town is more worthier than a village, ſo is the forehead of a married man more honourable than the bare brow of a batchelor. *Shak.*

Pygmalion
Abhorr'd all womankind, but moſt a wife;
So *ſingle* choſe to live, and ſhunn'd to wed,
Well pleas'd to want a conſort of his bed. *Dryden.*

6. Not complicated; not duplicated.

To make flowers double is effected by often removing them into new earth; as, on the contrary, double flowers, by neglecting and not removing, prove *ſingle*. *Bacon's Nat. Hiſt.*

7. Pure; uncorrupt; not double minded; ſimple. A ſcriptural ſenſe.

The light of the body is the eye: if thine eye be *ſingle*, thy whole body ſhall be full of light. *Mat.* vi. 22.

8. That in which one is oppoſed to one.

He, when his country, threaten'd with alarms,
Shall more than once the Punick bands affright,
Shall kill the Gauliſh king in *ſingle* fight. *Dryden's Æn.*

To Si'ngle. *v. a.* [from the adjective.]

1. To chuſe out from among others.

I ſaw him in the battle range about,
And how he *ſingled* Clifford forth. *Shakeſ. Henry* VI.

Every man may have a peculiar favour, which although not perceptible unto man, yet ſenſible unto dogs, who hereby can *ſingle* out their maſter in the dark. *Brown.*

Do'ſt thou already *ſingle* me? I thought
Gyves and the mill had tam'd thee. *Milton's Agoniſtes.*

Begin, auſpicious boy, to caſt about
Thy infant eyes, and with a ſmile thy mother *ſingle* out. *Dry.*

Single the lowlieſt of the am'rous youth;
Aſk for his vows, but hope not for his truth. *Prior.*

2. To ſequeſter; to withdraw.

Yea ſimply, ſaith Baſil, and univerſally, whether it be in works of nature, or of voluntary choice, I ſee not any thing done as it ſhould be, if it be wrought by an agent *ſingling* itſelf from conſorts. *Hooker.*

3. To take alone.

Many men there are, than whom nothing is more commendable when they are *ſingled*; and yet, in ſociety with others, none leſs fit to anſwer the duties which are looked for at their hands. *Hooker.*

4. To ſeparate.

Hardly they heard, which by good hunters *ſingled* are. *Sidn.*

Si'ngleness. *n. ſ.* [from *ſingle*.] Simplicity; ſincerity; honeſt plainneſs.

It is not the deepneſs of their knowledge, but the *ſingleneſs* of their belief, which God accepteth. *Hooker.*

Si'ngly. *adv.* [from *ſingle*.]

1. Individually; particularly.

If the injured perſon be not righted, every one of them is wholly guilty of the injuſtice, and therefore bound to reſtitution *ſingly* and intirely. *Taylor's Rule of living holy.*

They tend to the perfection of human nature, and to make men *ſingly* and perſonally good, or tend to the happineſs of ſociety. *Tillotſon's Sermons.*

2. Only; by himſelf.

Look thee, 'tis ſo; thou *ſingly* honeſt man,
Here take: the gods out of my miſery
Have ſent thee treaſure. *Shakeſ. Timon of Athens.*

3. Without partners or aſſociates.

Belinda
Burns to encounter two advent'rous knights,
At ombre *ſingly* to decide their doom. *Pope.*

4. Honeſtly; ſimply; ſincerely.

SI'NGULAR. *adj.* [*ſingulier*, Fr. *ſingularis*, Latin.]

1. Single; not complex; not compound.

That idea which repreſents one particular determinate thing is called a *ſingular* idea, whether ſimple, complex, or compound. *Watts.*

2. [In grammar.] Expreſſing only one; not plural.

If St. Paul's ſpeaking of himſelf in the firſt perſon *ſingular* has ſo various meanings, his uſe of the firſt perſon plural has a greater latitude. *Locke.*

3. Particular; unexampled.

So *ſingular* a ſadneſs
Muſt have a cauſe as ſtrange as the effect. *Denham's Sophy.*

Doubtleſs, if you are innocent, your caſe is extremely hard, yet it is not *ſingular*. *Female Quixote.*

4. Having ſomething not common to others. It is commonly uſed in a ſenſe of diſapprobation, whether applied to perſons or things.

His zeal
None ſeconded, as *ſingular* and raſh. *Milton.*

It is very commendable to be *ſingular* in any excellency, and religion is the greateſt excellency: to be *ſingular* in any thing that is wiſe and worthy is not a diſparagement, but a praiſe. *Tillotſ.*

5. Alone; that of which there is but one.

Theſe buſts of the emperors and empreſſes are all very ſcarce, and ſome of them almoſt *ſingular* in their kind. *Addiſ.*

Singula'rity. *n. ſ.* [*ſingularité*, Fr. from *ſingular*.]

1. Some character or quality by which one is diſtinguiſhed from others.

Pliny addeth this *ſingularity* to that ſoil, that the ſecond year the very falling down of the ſeeds yieldeth corn. *Raleigh.*

Though, according to the practice of the world, it be ſingular for men thoroughly to live up to the principles of their religion, yet *ſingularity* in this matter is a ſingular commendation of it. *Tillotſon's Sermons.*

I took notice of this little figure for the *ſingularity* of the inſtrument: it is not unlike a violin. *Addiſon on Italy.*

2. Any thing remarkable; a curioſity.

Your gallery
Have we paſs'd through, not without much content
In many *ſingularities*; but we ſaw not
That which my daughter came to look upon,
The ſtatue of her mother. *Shak. Winter's Tale.*

3. Particular privilege or prerogative.

St. Gregory, being himself a bishop of Rome, and writing against the title of universal bishop, saith thus: none of all my predecessors ever consented to use this ungodly title; no bishop of Rome ever took upon him this name of *singularity*. *Hooker.*

4. Character or manners different from those of others.

The spirit of *singularity* in a few ought to give place to publick judgment. *Hooker.*

Singularity in sin puts it out of fashion, since to be alone in any practice seems to make the judgment of the world against it; but the concurrence of others is a tacit approbation of that in which they concur. *South.*

To Si'ngularize. *v. a.* [*se singulariser*, Fr. from *singular.*] To make single.

Si'ngularly. *adv.* [from *singular.*] Particularly; in a manner not common to others.

Solitude and singularity can neither daunt nor disgrace him, unless we could suppose it a disgrace to be *singularly* good. *South.*

Si'ngult. *n. s.* [*singultus*, Latin.] A sigh. *Spenser.*

Si'nister. *adj.* [*sinister*, Latin.]

1. Being on the left hand; left; not right; not dexter.

My mother's blood
Runs on the dexter cheek, and this *sinister*
Bounds in my sire's. *Shak. Troilus and Cressida.*

Captain Spurio, with his cicatrice, an emblem of war, here on his *sinister* cheek. *Shak. All's well that ends well.*

But a rib, crooked by nature, bent, as now appears,
More to the part *sinister* from me drawn. *Milton's Pa. Lost.*

The spleen is unjustly introduced to invigorate the *sinister* side, which, being dilated, would rather infirm and debilitate it. *Brown's Vulgar Errours.*

In his *sinister* hand, instead of ball,
He plac'd a mighty mug of potent ale. *Dryden.*

2. Bad; perverse; corrupt; deviating from honesty; unfair.

Is it so strange a matter to find a good thing furthered by ill men of a *sinister* intent and purpose, whose forwardness is not therefore a bridle to such as favour the same cause with a better and sincere meaning. *Hooker.*

The duke of Clarence was soon after by *sinister* means made clean away. *Spenser on Ireland.*

When are there more unworthy men chosen to offices, when is there more strife and contention about elections, or when do partial and *sinister* affections more utter themselves, than when an election is committed to many? *Whitgifte.*

He professes to have received no *sinister* measure from his judge, but most willingly humbles himself to the determination of justice. *Shakes. Measure for Measure.*

Those may be accounted the left hands of courts; persons that are full of nimble and *sinister* tricks and shifts, whereby they pervert the plain courses of courts, and bring justice into oblique lines and labyrinths. *Bacon's Essays.*

The just person has given the world an assurance, by the constant tenor of his practice, that he makes a conscience of his ways, and that he scorns to undermine another's interest by any *sinister* or inferior arts. *South.*

3. [*Sinistre*, French.] Unlucky; inauspicious.

Tempt it again: that is thy act, or none:
What all the several ills that visit earth,
Brought forth by night, with a *sinister* birth,
Plagues, famine, fire, could not reach unto,
The sword, nor surfeits, let thy fury do. *Ben. Johnson.*

SI'NISTROUS. *adj.* [*sinister*, Latin.] Absurd; perverse; wrong-headed.

A knave or fool can do no harm, even by the most *sinistrous* and absurd choice. *Bentley.*

Si'nistrously. *adv.* [from *sinistrous.*]

1. With a tendency to the left.

Many in their infancy are *sinistrously* disposed, and divers continue all their life left-handed, and have but weak and imperfect use of the right. *Brown's Vulgar Errours.*

2. Perversely; absurdly.

To SINK *v. n.* pret *I sunk*, anciently *sank*; part. *sunk* or *sunken.* [ſencan, Saxon; *senken*, German.]

1. To fall down through any medium; not to swim; to go to the bottom.

Make his chronicle as rich with prize,
As is the oozy bottom of the sea
With *sunken* wreck and sumless treasuries. *Shakesp. H. V.*

In with the river *sunk*, and with it rose,
Satan, involv'd in rising mist; then sought
Where to lie hid. *Milton's Paradise Lost, b. ix.*

He swims or *sinks*, or wades, or creeps or flies. *Milton.*

The pirate *sinks* with his ill-gotten gains,
And nothing to another's use remains. *Dryden.*

Supposing several in a tempest will rather perish than work, would it not be madness in the rest to chuse to *sink* together, rather than do more than their share? *Addison on the War.*

2. To fall gradually.

The arrow went out at his heart, and he *sunk* down in his chariot. 2 *Kings* ix. 24.

3. To enter or penetrate into any body.

David took a stone and slang it, and smote the Philistine, that the stone *sunk* into his forehead. 1 *Sa.* xvii. 49.

4. To lose height; to fall to a level.

In vain has nature form'd
Mountains and oceans to oppose his passage;
He bounds o'er all, victorious in his march;
The Alps and Pyreneans *sink* before him. *Addison's Cato.*

5. To lose or want prominence.

What were his marks?——A lean cheek, a blue eye and *sunken.* *Shakesp. As you like it.*

Deep dinted wrinkles on her cheeks she draws;
Sunk are her eyes, and toothless are her jaws. *Dryden.*

6. To be overwhelmed or depressed.

Our country *sinks* beneath the yoke;
It weeps, it bleeds, and each new day a gash
Is added to her wounds. *Shakesp. Macbeth.*

They arraign'd shall *sink*
Beneath thy sentence. *Milton.*

But if you this ambitious pray'r deny,
Then let me *sink* beneath proud Arcite's arms;
And, I once dead, let him possess her charms. *Dryden.*

7. To be received; to be impressed.

Let these sayings *sink* down into your ears. *Lu.* ix. 44.

Truth never *sinks* into these mens minds, nor gives any tincture to them. *Locke.*

8. To decline; to decrease; to decay.

This republick has been much more powerful than it is at present, as it is still likelier to *sink* than increase in its dominions. *Addison on Italy.*

Let not the fire *sink* or slacken, but increase. *Mortimer.*

9. To fall into rest or indolence.

Would'st thou have me *sink* away
In pleasing dreams, and lose myself in love,
When every moment Cato's life's at stake? *Addison's Cato.*

10. To fall into any state worse than the former; to tend to ruin.

Nor urg'd the labours of my lord in vain,
A *sinking* empire longer to sustain. *Dryden's Æn.*

To Sink. *v. a.*

1. To put under water; to disable from swimming or floating.

A small fleet of English made an hostile invasion or incursion, upon their havens and roads, and fired, *sunk*, and carried away ten thousand ton of their great shipping, besides smaller vessels. *Bacon.*

2. To delve; to make by delving.

At Saga in Germany they dig up iron in the fields by *sinking* ditches two foot deep, and in the space of ten years the ditches are digged again for iron since produced. *Boyle.*

Near Geneva are quarries of freestone, that run under the lake: when the water is at lowest, they make within the borders of it a little square, inclosed within four walls: in this square they *sink* a pit, and dig for freestone. *Addison.*

3. To depress; to degrade.

A mighty king I am, an earthly god;
I raise or *sink*, imprison or set free;
And life or death depends on my decree. *Prior.*

Trifling painters or sculptors bestow infinite pains upon the most insignificant parts of a figure, 'till they *sink* the grandeur of the whole. *Pope's Essay on Homer.*

4. To plunge into destruction.

Heav'n bear witness,
And if I have a conscience let it *sink* me,
Ev'n as the ax falls, if I be not faithful. *Shakespeare.*

5. To make to fall.

These are so far from raising mountains, that they overturn and fling down some before standing, and undermine others, *sinking* them into the abyss. *Woodward.*

6. To bring low; to diminish in quantity.

When on the banks of an unlook'd-for stream,
You *sunk* the river with repeated draughts,
Who was the last in all your host that thirsted? *Addison.*

7. To crush; to overbear; to depress.

That Hector was in certainty of death, and depressed with the conscience of an ill cause: if you will not grant the first of these will *sink* the spirit of a hero, you'll at least allow the second may. *Pope.*

8. To lessen; to diminish.

They catch at all opportunities of ruining our trade, and *sinking* the figure which we make. *Addison on the War.*

I mean not that we should *sink* our figure out of covetousness, and deny ourselves the proper conveniences of our station, only that we may lay up a superfluous treasure. *Rogers.*

9. To make to decline.

Thy cruel and unnatural lust of power
Has *sunk* thy father more than all his years,
And made him wither in a green old age. *Rowe.*

To labour for a *sunk* corrupted state. *Lyttleton.*

10. To suppress; to conceal; to intervert.

If sent with ready money to buy any thing, and you happen to be out of pocket, *sink* the money, and take up the goods on account. *Swift's Rules to Servants.*

Sink. *n. s.* [ſinc, Saxon.]

1. A drain; a jakes.

Should by the cormorant belly be restrain'd,
Who is the *sink* o' th' body. *Shakesp. Coriolanus.*

Bad humours gather to a bile, or as divers kennels flow to one *ſink*, ſo in ſhort time their numbers increaſed. *Hayward.*

Gather more filth than any *ſink* in town. *Granville.*

Returning home at night, you'll find the *ſink*
Strike your offended ſenſe with double ſtink. *Swift.*

2. Any place where corruption is gathered.

What *ſink* of monſters, wretches of loſt minds,
Mad after change, and deſperate in their ſtates,
Wearied and gall'd with their neceſſities,
Durſt have thought it? *Ben. Johnſon's Catiline.*

Our ſoul, whoſe country's heav'n and God her father,
Into this world, corruption's *ſink*, is ſent;
Yet ſo much in her travail ſhe doth gather,
That ſhe returns home wiſer than ſhe went. *Donne.*

SI'NLESS. *adj.* [from *ſin.*] Exempt from ſin.

Led on, yet *ſinleſs*, with deſire to know,
What nearer might concern him, how this world
Of heav'n, and earth conſpicuous, firſt began. *Milton.*

At that taſted fruit,
The ſun, as from Thyeſtean banquet, turn'd
His courſe; elſe how had the world
Inhabited, though *ſinleſs*, more than now
Avoided pinching cold, and ſcorching heat? *Milton.*

Infernal ghoſts and helliſh furies round
Environ'd thee; ſome howl'd, ſome yell'd, ſome ſhriek'd,
Some bent at thee their fiery darts, while thou
Satt'ſt unappal'd in calm and *ſinleſs* peace. *Milton.*

No thoughts like mine his *ſinleſs* ſoul profane,
Obſervant of the right. *Dryden's Ovid.*

Did God, indeed, inſiſt on a *ſinleſs* and unerring obſervance of all this multiplicity of duties; had the Chriſtian diſpenſation provided no remedy for our lapſes, we might cry out with Balaam, Alas! who ſhould live, if God did this? *Rogers.*

SI'NLESSNESS. *n. ſ.* [from *ſinleſs.*] Exemption from ſin.

We may the leſs admire at his gracious condeſcenſions to thoſe, the *ſinleſſneſs* of whoſe condition will keep them from turning his vouchſafements into any thing but occaſions of joy and gratitude. *Boyle's Seraphick Love.*

SI'NNER. *n. ſ.* [from *ſin.*]

1. One at enmity with God; one not truly or religiouſly good.

Let the boldeſt *ſinner* take this one conſideration along with him, when he is going to ſin, that whether the ſin he is about to act ever comes to be pardoned or no, yet, as ſoon as it is acted, it quite turns the balance, puts his ſalvation upon the venture, and makes it ten to one odds againſt him. *South.*

2. An offender; a criminal.

Here's that which is too weak to be a *ſinner*, honeſt water, which ne'er left man i' th' mire. *Shakeſpeare's Timon.*

Over the guilty then the fury ſhakes
The ſounding whip, and brandiſhes her ſnakes,
And the pale *ſinner* with her ſiſters takes. *Dryden's Æn.*

Thither, where *ſinners* may have reſt, I go,
Where flames refin'd in breaſts ſeraphick glow. *Pope.*

Whether the charmer *ſinner* it or ſaint it,
If folly grows romantick, I muſt paint it. *Pope.*

SI'NOFFERING. *n. ſ.* [*ſin* and *offering.*] An expiation or ſacrifice for ſin.

The fleſh of the bullock ſhalt thou burn without the camp: it is a *ſinoffering*. *Ex.* xxix. 14.

SI'NOPER, or *Sinople. n. ſ.* A ſpecies of earth; ruddle. *Ainſ.*

To SI'NUATE. *v. a.* [*ſinuo*, Latin.] To bend in and out.

Another was very perfect, ſomewhat leſs with the margin, and more *ſinuated*. *Woodward on Foſſils.*

SINUA'TION. *n. ſ.* [from *ſinuate.*] A bending in and out.

The human brain is, in proportion to the body, much larger than the brains of brutes, in proportion to their bodies, and fuller of anfractus, or *ſinuations*. *Hale's Origin of Mankind.*

SI'NUOUS. *adj.* [*ſinueux*, French, from *ſinus*, Latin.] Bending in and out.

Try with what diſadvantage the voice will be carried in an horn, which is a line arched; or in a trumpet, which is a line retorted; or in ſome pipe that were *ſinuous*. *Bacon.*

Theſe, as a line, their long dimenſion drew,
Streaking the ground with *ſinuous* trace. *Milt. Parad. Loſt.*

In the diſſections of horſes, in the concave or *ſinuous* part of the liver, whereat the gall is uſually ſeated in quadrupeds, I diſcover an hollow, long, and membranous ſubſtance. *Brown's Vulgar Errours.*

SI'NUS. *n. ſ.* [Latin.]

1. A bay of the ſea; an opening of the land.

Plato ſuppoſeth his Atlantis to have ſunk all into the ſea: whether that be true or no, I do not think it impoſſible that ſome arms of the ſea, or *ſinus's*, might have had ſuch an original. *Burnet's Theory of the Earth.*

2. Any fold or opening.

To SIP. *v. a.* [ſypan, Saxon; *ſippen*, Dutch.]

1. To drink by ſmall draughts; to take at one appoſition of the cup to the mouth no more than the mouth will contain.

Soft yielding minds to water glide away,
And *ſip* with nymphs their elemental tea. *Pope.*

2. To drink in ſmall quantities.

Find out the peaceful hermitage;
The hairy gown and moſſy cell,
Where I may ſit and rightly ſpell
Of ev'ry ſtar that heav'n doth ſhew,
And every herb that *ſips* the dew. *Milton.*

3. To drink out of.

The winged nation o'er the foreſt flies:
Then ſtooping on the meads and leafy bow'rs,
They ſkim the floods and *ſip* the purple flow'rs. *Dryden.*

To SIP. *v. n.* To drink a ſmall quantity.

She rais'd it to her mouth with ſober grace;
Then *ſipping*, offer'd to the next. *Dryden's Æn.*

SIP. *n. ſ.* [from the verb.] A ſmall draught; as much as the mouth will hold.

Her face o' fire
With labour, and the thing ſhe took to quench it
She would to each one *ſip*. *Shakeſp. Winter's Tale.*

One *ſip* of this
Will bathe the drooping ſpirits in delight,
Beyond the bliſs of dreams. *Milton.*

SI'PHON. *n. ſ.* [σίφον; *ſipho*, Lat. *ſiphon*, Fr.] A pipe through which liquors are conveyed.

Beneath th' inceſſant weeping of theſe drains
I ſee the rocky *ſiphons* ſtretch'd immenſe,
The mighty reſervoirs of harden'd chalk,
Of ſtiff compacted clay. *Thomſon's Autumn.*

SI'PPER. *n. ſ.* [from *ſip.*] One that ſips.

SI'PPET. *n. ſ.* [from *ſip.*] A ſmall ſop.

SIR. *n. ſ.* [*ſire*, Fr. *ſeignior*, Ital. *ſenor*, Spaniſh; *ſenior*, Latin.]

1. The word of reſpect in compellation.

Speak on, *ſir*,
I dare your worſt objections: if I bluſh,
It is to ſee a nobleman want manners. *Shakeſp. H.* VIII.

But, *ſirs*, be ſudden in the execution;
Withal obdurate; do not let him plead. *Shakeſp. R.* III.

Sir king,
This man is better than the man he ſlew. *Shakeſpeare.*

At a banquet the ambaſſador deſired the wiſe men to deliver every one of them ſome ſentence or parable, that he might report to his king, which they did: only one was ſilent, which the ambaſſador perceiving, ſaid to him, *ſir*, let it not diſpleaſe you; why do not you ſay ſomewhat that I may report? He anſwered, report to your lord, that there are that can hold their peace. *Bacon's Apophthegms.*

2. The title of a knight or baronet. This word was anciently ſo much held eſſential, that the Jews in their addreſſes expreſſed it in Hebrew characters.

Sir Horace Vere, his brother, was the principal in the active part. *Bacon's War with Spain.*

The court forſakes him, and *ſir* Balaam hangs. *Pope.*

3. It is ſometimes uſed for *man.*

I have adventur'd
To try your taking of a falſe report, which hath
Honour'd with confirmation your great judgment,
In the election of a *ſir* ſo rare. *Shakeſp. Cymbeline.*

4. A title given to the loin of beef, which one of our kings knighted in a fit of good humour.

He loſt his roaſt-beef ſtomach, not being able to touch a *ſir*-loin which was ſerved up. *Addiſon.*

And the ſtrong table groans
Beneath the ſmoaking *ſir*-loin, ſtretch'd immenſe
From ſide to ſide. *Thomſon's Autumn.*

It would be ridiculous, indeed, if a ſpit which is ſtrong enough to turn a *ſir*-loin of beef, ſhould not be able to turn a lark. *Swift.*

SIRE. *n. ſ.* [*ſire*, French; *ſenior*, Latin.]

1. A father, in poetry.

He, but a duke, would have his ſon a king,
And raiſe his iſſue like a loving *ſire*. *Shakeſp. Henry* VI.

Cowards father cowards, and baſe things *ſire* the baſe. *Shak.*

A virgin is his mother, but his *ſire*
The pow'r of the Moſt High. *Milton's Paradiſe Loſt.*

And now I leave the true and juſt ſupports
Of legal princes and of honeſt courts,
Whoſe *ſires*, great part'ners in my father's cares,
Saluted their young king at Hebron crown'd. *Prior.*

Whether his hoary *ſire* he ſpies,
While thouſand grateful thoughts ariſe,
Or meets his ſpouſe's fonder eye. *Pope's Chorus to Brutus.*

2. It is uſed in common ſpeech of beaſts: as, the horſe had a good *ſire*, but a bad dam.

3. It is uſed in compoſition: as, grand-*ſire*, great-grand-*ſire*.

SI'REN. *n. ſ.* [Latin.] A goddeſs who enticed men by ſinging, and devoured them; any miſchievous enticer.

Oh train me not, ſweet mermaid, with thy note,
To drown me in thy ſiſter's flood of tears:
Sing, *ſiren*, to thyſelf, and I will dote;
Spread o'er the ſilver waves thy golden hair,
And as a-bed I'll take thee, and there lie. *Shakeſpeare.*

SIRI'ASIS. *n. ſ.* [σιϱίασις.] An inflammation of the brain and its membrane, through an exceſſive heat of the ſun. *Dict.*

SI'RIUS. *n. s.* [Latin.] The dogstar.

SIRO'CCO. *n. s.* [Italian; *syrus ventus*, Latin.] The south east or Syrian wind.

Forth rush the levant and the ponent winds,
Eurus and Zephyr, with their lateral noise,
Sirocco and Libecchio. *Milton.*

SI'RRAH. *n. s.* [*sir, ha! Minshew.*] A compellation of reproach and insult.

Go, *sirrah*, to my cell;
Take with you your companions: as you look
To have my pardon, trim it handsomely. *Shakes. Tempest.*

Sirrah, There's no room for faith, troth, or honesty in this bosom of thine. *Shakespeare's Henry* IV.

It runs in the blood of your whole race, *sirrah*, to hate our family. *L'Estrange.*

Guess how the goddess greets her son,
Come hither, *sirrah*; no, begone. *Prior.*

SI'ROP. } *n. s.* [Arabick] The juice of vegetables boiled
SI'RUP. } with sugar.

Shall I, whose ears her mournful words did seize,
Her words in *sirup* laid of sweetest breath,
Relent. *Sidney.*

Not poppy, nor mandragora,
Nor all the drowsy *sirups* of the world
Shall ever med'cine thee to that sweet sleep,
Which thou owed'st yesterday. *Shakespeare's Othello.*

And first, behold this cordial jalap here,
That flames and dances in his crystal bounds,
With spirits of balm, and fragrant *syrops* mixt. *Milton.*

Those expressed juices contain the true essential salt of the plant; for if they be boiled into the consistence of a *syrup*, and set in a cool place, the essential salt of the plant will shoot upon the sides of the vessels. *Arbuthnot.*

SI'RUPED. *adj.* [from *sirup.*] Sweet, like sirup; bedewed with sweets.

Yet when there haps a honey fall,
We'll lick the *syrupt* leaves:
And tell the bees that their's is gall. *Drayton's Q. of Cynthia.*

SI'RUPY. *adj.* [from *sirup.*] Resembling sirup.

Apples are of a *sirupy* tenacious nature. *Mortimer.*

SISE. *n. s.* [contracted from *assize.*]

You said, if I returned next *size* in lent,
I should be in remitter of your grace. *Donne.*

SI'SKIN. *n. s.* A bird; a green finch.

SI'STER. *n. s.* ꞅpeoꞅꞇeꞃ, Saxon; *zuster*, Dutch.]

1. A woman born of the same parents; correlative to brother.

Her *sister* began to scold. *Shakesp. Taming of the Shrew.*

I have said to corruption, thou art my father: to the worm, thou art my mother and my *sister*. *Job.* xvii. 14.

2. One of the same faith; a christian. One of the same nature, human being.

If a brother or *sister* be naked, and destitute of food, and you say unto them, depart in peace, be you warmed and filled: notwithstanding you give them not those things which are needful to the body, what doth it profit? *James* ii. 15.

3. A woman of the same kind.

He chid the *sisters*,
And bade them speak to him. *Shakespeare's Macbeth.*

4. One of the same kind; one of the same office.

The women, who would rather wrest the laws,
Than let a *sister*-plaintiff lose the cause,
As judges on the bench more gracious are,
And more attent to brothers of the bar,
Cry'd one and all, the suppliant should have right:
And to the grandame hag adjudg'd the knight. *Dryden.*

There grew two olives, closest of the grove,
With roots entwin'd, and branches interwove:
Alike their leaves, but not alike they smil'd
With *sister*-fruits: one fertile, one was wild. *Pope.*

SI'STER *in law. n. s.* A husband or wife's sister.

Thy *sister in law* is gone back unto her people: return thou after thy *sister in law*. *Ruth* i. 15.

SI'STERHOOD. *n. s.* [from *sister.*]

1. The office or duty of a sister.

She abhorr'd
Her proper blood, and left to do the part
Of *sisterhood*, to do that of a wife. *Daniel's Civil War.*

2. A set of sisters.

3. A number of women of the same order.

I speak,
Wishing a more strict restraint
Upon the *sisterhood*, the votarists of Saint Clare. *Shakesp.*

A woman who flourishes in her innocence, amidst that spite and rancour which prevails among her exasperated *sisterhood*, appears more amiable. *Addison's Freeholder.*

SI'STERLY. *adj.* [from *sister.*] Like a sister; becoming a sister.

After much debatement,
My *sisterly* remorse confutes mine honour,
And I did yield to him. *Shakespeare.*

To SIT. *v. n.* preterite, *I sat.* [*sitan*, Gothick; ꞅiꞇꞇan, Sax. *setten*, Dutch.]

1. To rest upon the buttocks.

There were stays on each side of the *sitting* place. 1 *Chron.*

He *sat* for alms at the beautiful gate. *Acts* iii. 10.

Their wives do *sit* beside them carding wool. *May's Virgil.*

Aloft in awful state,
The godlike hero *sat*
On his imperial throne. *Dryden.*

2. To perch.

All new fashions be pleasant to me,
I will have them whether I thrive or thee,
Now I am a frisker, all men on me look,
What should I do but *sit* cock on the hoop?
What do I care if all the world me fail,
I will have a garment reach to my tail. *Bourd.*

3. To be in a state of rest, or idleness.

Shall your brethren go to war, and shall ye *sit* here? *Num.*

Why *sit* we here each other viewing idly. *Milton.*

4. To be in any local position.

I should be still
Plucking the grass to know where *sits* the wind:
Peering in maps for ports. *Shakesp. Merch. of Venice.*

Those
Appointed to *sit* there had left their charge. *Milton.*

The ships are ready, and the wind *sits* fair. *A. Philips.*

5. To rest as a weight or burthen.

Your brother's death *sits* at your heart. *Shakespeare.*

When God lets loose upon us a sickness, if we fear to die, then the calamity *sits* heavy on us. *Taylor.*

To toss and fling, and to be restless, only galls our sores, and makes the burden that is upon us *sit* more uneasy. *Tillotson.*

Fear, the last of ills, remain'd behind,
And horrour, heavy *sat* on every mind. *Dryden.*

Our whole endeavours are intent to get rid of the present evil, as the first necessary condition to our happiness. Nothing, as we passionately think, can equal the uneasiness that *sits* so heavy upon us. *Locke.*

6. To settle; to abide.

That this new comer shame,
There *sit* not and reproach us. *Milton.*

When Thetis blush'd, in purple not her own,
And from her face the breathing winds were blown;
A sudden silence *sate* upon the sea,
And sweeping oars, with struggling, urg'd their way. *Dryd.*

He to the void advanc'd his pace,
Pale horrour *sat* on each Arcadian face. *Dryden.*

7. To brood; to incubate.

As the partridge *sitteth* on eggs, and hatcheth them not, so he that getteth riches not by right, shall leave them in the midst of his days. *Jer.* xvii. 11.

The egg laid and sever'd from the body of the hen, hath no more nourishment from the hen; but only a quickening heat when she *sitteth*. *Bacon's Natural History.*

She mistakes a piece of chalk for an egg, and *sits* upon it in the same manner. *Addison.*

8. To be adjusted; to be with respect to fitness or unfitness, decorum or indecorum.

This new and gorgeous garment, majesty,
Sits not so easy on me as you think. *Shakespeare.*

Heav'n knows,
By what by-paths, and indirect crook'd ways
I met this crown; and I myself know well,
How troublesome it *sate* upon my head;
To thee it shall descend with better quiet. *Shakespeare.*

Your preferring that to all other considerations does, in the eyes of all men, *sit* well upon you. *Locke.*

9. To be placed in order to be painted.

One is under no more obligation to extol every thing he finds in the author he translates, than a painter is to make every face that *sits* to him handsome. *Garth.*

10. To be in any situation or condition.

As a farmer cannot husband his ground so well, if he *sit* at a great rent; so the merchant cannot drive his trade so well, if he *sit* at great usury. *Bacon.*

Suppose all the church-lands were thrown up to the laity; would the tenants *sit* easier in their rents than now? *Swift.*

11. To be fixed, as an assembly;

12. To be placed at the table.

Whether is greater he that *sitteth* at meat, or he that serveth? *Luke* xxii. 27.

13. To exercise authority.

The judgment shall *sit*, and take away his dominion. *Dan.*

Asses are ye that *sit* in judgment. *Judges* v. 10.

Down to the golden Chersonese, or where
The Persian in Echatan *sate*. *Milton.*

One council *sits* upon life and death, the other is for taxes, and a third for the distributions of justice. *Addison.*

Assert, ye fair ones, who in judgment *sit*,
Your ancient empire over love and wit. *Rowe.*

14. To be in any solemn assembly as a member.

Three hundred and twenty men *sat* in council daily. 1 *Mac.*

15. *To* SIT *down*. *Down* is little more than emphatical.

Go and *sit down* to meat. *Luke* xvii. 7.

When

When we *sit down* to our meal, we need not suspect the intrusion of armed uninvited guests. *Decay of Piety.*

16. *To* SIT *down.* To begin a siege.

Nor would the enemy have *sate* down before it, till they had done their business in all other places. *Clarendon.*

17. *To* SIT *down.* To rest; to cease satisfied.

Here we cannot *sit down*, but still proceed in our search, and look higher for a support. *Rogers.*

18. *To* SIT *down.* To settle; to fix abode.

From besides Tanais, the Goths, Huns, and Getes *sat down.* *Spenser.*

19. *To* SIT *out.* To be without engagement or employment.

They are glad, rather than *sit out*, to play very small game, and to make use of arguments, such as will not prove a bare inexpediency. *Bp. Sanderson's Judgment.*

20. *To* SIT *up.* To rise from lying to sitting.

He that was dead, *sat up*, and began to speak. *Luke* vii.

21. *To* SIT *up.* To watch; not to go to bed.

Be courtly,
And entertain, and feast, *sit up*, and revel;
Call all the great, the fair and spirited dames
Of Rome about thee, and begin a fashion
Of freedom. *Ben. Johnson.*

Some *sit up* late at winter-fires, and fit
Their sharp-edg'd tools. *May.*

Most children shorten that time by *sitting up* with the company at night. *Locke.*

To SIT. *v. a.*

1. To keep the seat upon.

Hardly the muse can *sit* the head-strong horse,
Nor would she, if she could, check his impetuous force. *Prior.*

2. [When the reciprocal pronoun follows *sit*, it seems to be an active verb.] To place on a seat.

The happiest youth viewing his progress through,
What perils past, what crosses to ensue,
Would shut the book, and *sit him* down and die. *Shakesp.*

He came to visit us, and calling for a chair, *sat him* down, and we sat down with him. *Bacon.*

Thus fenc'd,
But not at rest or ease of mind,
They *sat them* down to weep. *Milton.*

3. To be settled to do business.

The court was *sat* before sir Roger came, but the justices made room for the old knight at the head of them. *Addison.*

SITE. *n. s.* [*situs*, Latin.]

1. Situation; local position.

The city self he strongly fortifies,
Three sides by *site* it well defenced has. *Fairfax.*

Manifold streams of goodly navigable rivers, as so many chains, environed the same *site* and temple. *Bacon.*

If we consider the heart in its constituent parts, we shall find nothing singular, but what is in any muscle. 'Tis only the *site* and posture of their several parts that give it the form and functions of a heart. *Bentley.*

Before my view appear'd a structure fair,
Its *site* uncertain if on earth or air. *Pope.*

2. It is taken by *Thomson* for posture, or situation of a thing with respect to itself: but improperly.

And leaves the semblance of a lover fix'd
In melancholy *site*, with head declin'd,
And love-dejected eyes. *Thomson's Spring.*

SI'TFAST. *n. s.* [*sit* and *fast.*]

A hard knob growing under the saddle. *Farrier's Dict.*

SITH. *adv.* [ꞅiðe, Saxon.] Since; seeing that. Obsolete.

What ceremony of odours used about the bodies of the dead! after which custom notwithstanding, *sith* it was their custom, our Lord was contented that his own most precious blood should be intombed. *Hooker.*

Not I, my lord; *sith* true nobility
Warrants these words in princely courtesie. *Shakespeare.*

I thank you for this profit, and from hence
I'll love no friend, *sith* love breeds such offence. *Shakesp.*

SITHE. *n. s.* [ꞅiðe, Saxon. This word is very variously written by authors: I have chosen the orthography which is at once most simple and most agreeable to etymology.] The instrument of mowing; a crooked blade joined at right angles to a long pole.

Let fame, that all hunt after in their lives,
Live registred upon our brazen tombs;
And then grace us in the disgrace of death:
When, spight of cormorant-devouring time,
Th' endeavour of this present breath may buy
That honour which shall 'bate his *scythe's* keen edge;
And make us heirs of all eternity. *Shakespeare.*

Time is commonly drawn upon tombs, in gardens, and other places, an old man, bald, winged with a *sithe*, and an hour-glass. *Peacham on Drawing.*

There rude impetuous rage does storm and fret;
And there, as master of this murd'ring brood,
Swinging a huge *scithe*, stands impartial death,
With endless business almost out of breath. *Crashaw.*

The milk-maid singeth blithe,
And the mower whets his *scithe.* *Milton.*

The brazen trumpets kindle rage no more;
But useless lances into *sythes* shall bend,
And the broad faulchion in a plough-share end. *Pope.*

Grav'd o'er their seats the form of time was found,
His *scythe* revers'd, and both his pinions bound. *Pope.*

But, Stella, say, what evil tongue
Reports you are no longer young?
That time sits with his *sythe* to mow
Where erst sat Cupid with his bow. *Swift.*

Echo no more returns the chearful sound
Of sharpening *scythe.* *Thomson's Summer.*

SI'THENCE. *adv.* [Now contracted to *since.* See SINCE.] Since; in latter times.

This over-running and wasting of the realm was the beginning of all the other evils which *sithence* have afflicted that land. *Spenser's State of Ireland.*

SITHES. *n. s.* Times. *Spenser.*

SI'THNESS. *adv.* Since. *Spenser.*

SI'TTER. *n. s.* [from *sit.*]

1. One that sits.

The Turks are great *sitters*, and seldom walk; whereby they sweat less, and need bathing more. *Bacon.*

2. A bird that broods.

The oldest hens are reckoned the best *sitters*; and the youngest the best layers. *Mortimer's Husbandry.*

SI'TTING. *n. s.* [from *sit.*]

1. The posture of sitting on a seat.

2. The act of resting on a seat.

Thou knowest my down-*sitting* and mine up rising. *Psal.*

3. A time at which one exhibits himself to a painter.

Few good pictures have been finished at one *sitting*; neither can a good play be produced at a heat. *Dryden.*

4. A meeting of an assembly.

I'll write you down;
The which shall point you forth at every *sitting*,
What you must say. *Shakespeare.*

I wish it may be at that *sitting* concluded, unless the necessity of the time press it. *Bacon.*

5. A course of study unintermitted.

For the understanding of any one of St. Paul's epistles, I read it all through at one *sitting.* *Locke.*

6. A time for which one sits without rising.

What more than madness reigns,
When one short *sitting* many hundred drains,
And not enough is left him to supply
Board-wages, or a footman's livery. *Dryden.*

7. Incubation.

Whilst the hen is covering her eggs, the male bird takes his stand upon a neighbouring bough, and amuses her with his songs during the whole time of her *sitting.* *Addison.*

SI'TUATE. *part. adj.* [from *situs*, Latin.]

1. Placed with respect to any thing else.

He was resolved to chuse a war, rather than to have Bretagne carried by France, being so great and opulent a duchy, and *situate* so opportunely to annoy England. *Bacon.*

Within a trading town they long abide,
Full fairly *situate* on a haven's side. *Dryden's Nun's Priest.*

The eye is a part so artificially composed, and commodiously *situate*, as nothing can be contrived better for use, ornament, or security. *Ray on the Creation.*

2. Placed; consisting.

Earth hath this variety from heav'n,
Of pleasure *situate* in hill and dale. *Milton's Parad. Lost.*

SITUA'TION. *n. s.* [from *situate*; *situation*, French.]

1. Local respect; position.

Prince Cesarini has a palace in a pleasant *situation*, and set off with many beautiful walks. *Addison's Italy.*

2. Condition; state.

Though this is a *situation* of the greatest ease and tranquillity in human life, yet this is by no means fit to be the subject of all men's petitions to God. *Roger's Sermons.*

SIX. *n. s.* [*six*, French.] Twice three; one more than five.

No incident in the piece or play but must carry on the main design; all things else are like *six* fingers to the hand, when nature can do her work with five. *Dryden.*

That of *six* hath many respects in it, not only for the days of the creation, but its natural consideration, as being a perfect number. *Brown's Vulgar Errours.*

SIX *and seven.* *n. s.* To be *at six and seven*, is to be in a state of disorder and confusion.

All is uneven,
And every thing is left *at six and seven.* *Shakespeare.*

In 1588, there sat in the see of Rome a fierce thundring friar, that would set all *at six and seven*, or at six and five, if you allude to his name. *Bacon.*

What blinder bargain e're was driv'n,
Or wager laid *at six and seven.* *Hudibras.*

John once, turned his mother out of doors, to his great sorrow; for his affairs went on *at sixes and sevens.* *Arbuthnot.*

The goddess would no longer wait;
But raising from her chair of state,
Left all below *at six and seven*,
Harness'd her doves and flew to heav'n. *Swift.*

SI'XPENCE. *n. ſ.* [*ſix* and *pence.*] A coin; half a ſhilling.

Where have you left the money that I gave you?
Oh!—*ſixpence* that I had. *Shakeſpeare.*

The wiſeſt man might bluſh,
If D—lov'd *ſixpence* more than he. *Pope.*

SIXSCO'RE. *adj.* [*ſix* and *ſcore.*] Six times twenty.

Sixſcore and five miles it containeth in circuit. *Sandys.*

The crown of Spain hath enlarged the bounds thereof within this laſt *ſixſcore* years, much more than the Ottomans. *Bacon.*

SIXTEE'N. *adj.* [ſixtyne, Saxon.] Six and ten.

I have been begging *ſixteen* years in court. *Shakeſpeare.*

It returned the voice thirteen times; and I have heard of others that it would return *ſixteen* times. *Bacon.*

If men lived but twenty years, we ſhould be ſatisfied if they died about *ſixteen* or eighteen. *Taylor.*

SI'XTEENTH. *adj.* [ſixteoþa, Saxon.] The ſixth after the tenth; the ordinal of ſixteen.

The firſt lot came forth to Jehoiarib, the *ſixteenth* to Immer. 1 *Chron.* xxiv. 14.

SIXTH. *adj.* [ſixta, Saxon.] The firſt after the fifth; the ordinal of ſix.

You are more clement than vile men,
Who of their broken debtors take
A *ſixth*, letting them thrive again. *Shakeſpeare.*

There ſucceeded to the kingdom of England James the *ſixth*, then king of Scotland. *Bacon.*

SIXTH. *n. ſ.* [from the adjective.] A ſixth part.

Only the other half would have been a tolerable ſeat for rational creatures, and five *ſixths* of the whole globe would have been rendered uſeleſs. *Cheyne's Philoſ. Principles.*

SI'XTHLY. *adv.* [from *ſix.*] In the ſixth place.

Sixthly, living creatures have more diverſity of organs than plants. *Bacon.*

SI'XTIETH. *adj.* ſixteogoþa, Saxon.] The tenth ſix times repeated; the ordinal of ſixty.

Let the appearing circle of the fire be three foot diameter, and the time of one entire circulation of it the *ſixtieth* part of a minute, in a whole day there will be but 86400 ſuch parts. *Digby on Bodies.*

SI'XTY. *adj.* [ſixtig, Saxon.] Six times ten.

When the boats were come within *ſixty* yards of the pillar, they found themſelves all bound, and could go no farther. *Bacon.*

Of which 7 times 9, or the year 63, is conceived to carry with it the moſt conſiderable fatality. *Brown's Vulg. Errours.*

SIZE. *n. ſ.* [perhaps rather *ciſe*, from *incida*, Latin; or from *aſſiſe*, French.] Bulk; quantity of ſuperficies; comparative magnitude.

I ever narrified my friends,
With all the *ſize* that verity
Would without lapſing ſuffer. *Shakeſpeare's Coriolanus.*

If any decayed ſhip be new made, it is more fit to make her a *ſize* leſs than bigger. *Raleigh.*

The diſtance judg'd for ſhot of ev'ry *ſize*,
The linſtocks touch, the pond'rous ball expires. *Dryden.*

Objects near our view are thought greater than thoſe of a larger *ſize*, that are more remote. *Locke.*

The martial goddeſs,
Like thee, Telemachus, in voice and *ſize*,
With ſpeed divine, from ſtreet to ſtreet ſhe flies;
She bids the mariners prepare to ſtand. *Pope's Odyſſey.*

2. [*Aſſiſe*, old French.] A ſettled quantity. In the following paſſage it ſeems to ſignify the allowance of the table: whence they ſay a *ſizer* at Cambridge.

'Tis not in thee
To cut off my train, to ſcant my *ſizes*,
And, in concluſion, to oppoſe the bolt
Againſt my coming in. *Shakeſpeare's King Lear.*

3. Figurative bulk; condition.

This agrees too in the contempt of men of a leſs *ſize* and quality. *L'Eſtrange.*

They do not conſider the difference between elaborate diſcourſes, delivered to princes or parliaments, and a plain ſermon, intended for the middling or lower *ſize* of people. *Swift.*

4. [*Siſa*, Italian.] Any viſcous or glutinous ſubſtance.

To SIZE. *v. a.* [from the noun.]

1. To adjuſt, or arrange according to ſize.

The foxes weigh the geeſe they carry,
And ere they venture on a ſtream,
Know how to *ſize* themſelves and them. *Hudibras.*

Two troops ſo match'd were never to be found,
Such bodies built for ſtrength, of equal age,
In ſtature *ſiz'd*. *Dryden's Knights Tale.*

2. [From *aſſiſe.*] To ſettle; to fix.

There was a ſtatute for diſperſing the ſtandard of the exchequer throughout England; thereby to *ſize* weights and meaſures. *Bacon's Henry* VII.

3. To cover with glutinous matter; to beſmear with ſize.

SI'ZED. *adj.* [from *ſize.*] Having a particular magnitude.

What my love is, proof hath made you know,
And as my love is *ſiz'd*, my fear is ſo. *Shakeſpeare.*

That will be a great horſe to a Welſhman, which is but a ſmall one to a Fleming; having, from the different breed of their countries, taken ſeveral *ſized* ideas, to which they compare their great and their little. *Locke.*

SI'ZEABLE. *adj.* [from *ſize.*] Reaſonably bulky.

He ſhould be purged, ſweated, vomited, and ſtarved, till he come to a *ſizeable* bulk. *Arbuthnot.*

SIZER. or *Servitor. n. ſ.* A certain rank of ſtudents in the univerſities.

They make a ſcramble for degree:
Maſters of all ſorts and of all ages,
Keepers, ſub-*ſiſers*, lackeys, pages. *Bp. Corbet.*

SI'ZERS. *n. ſ.* See SCISSARS.

A buttrice and pincers, a hammer and naile,
An apron and *ſizers* for head and for taile. *Tuſſer.*

SI'ZINESS. *n. ſ.* [from *ſizy.*] Glutinouſneſs; viſcoſity.

In rheumatiſms, the *ſizineſs* paſſes off thick contents in the urine, or glutinous ſweats. *Floyer on the Humours.*

Cold is capable of producing a *ſizineſs* and viſcoſity in the blood. *Arbuthnot.*

SI'ZY. *adj.* [from *ſize.*] Viſcous; glutinous.

The blood is *ſizy*, the alkaleſcent ſalts in the ſerum producing coriaceous concretions. *Arbuthnot on Diet.*

SKA'DDLE. *n. ſ.* [ſceaðniſſe, Saxon.] Hurt; damage. *Dict.*

SKA'DDONS. *n. ſ.* The embryos of bees. *Bailey.*

SKEIN. *n. ſ.* [*eſcaigne*, French.] A knot of thread or ſilk wound and doubled.

Why art thou then exaſperate, thou idle immaterial *ſkein* of ſley'd ſilk, thou taſſel of a prodigal's purſe? *Shakeſp.*

Our ſtile ſhould be like a *ſkein* of ſilk, to be found by the right thread, not ravell'd or perplexed. Then all is a knot, a heap. *Ben. Johnſon.*

Beſides, ſo lazy a brain as mine is, grows ſoon weary when it has ſo entangled a *ſkein* as this to unwind. *Digby.*

SKAI'NSMATE. *n. ſ.* [I ſuppoſe from *ſkain*, or *ſkean*, a knife, and *mate*, a meſſmate.] It is remarkable that *mes*, Dutch, is a knife.

Scurvy knave, I am none of his flirt gills;
I am none of his *ſkainſmates*. *Shakeſpeare's Romeo and Juliet.*

SKATE. *n. ſ.* [ſceadda, Saxon.]

1. A flat ſea fiſh.

2. A ſort of ſhoe armed with iron, for ſliding on the ice.

They ſweep
On ſounding *ſkates* a thouſand different ways,
In circling poiſe ſwift as the winds. *Thomſon.*

SKEAN. *n. ſ.* [Iriſh and Erſe; ſagene, Saxon.] A ſhort ſword; a knife.

Any diſpoſed to do miſchief, may under his mantle privily carry his head-piece, *ſkean*, or piſtol, to be always ready. *Spenſer.*

The Iriſh did not fail in courage or fierceneſs, but being only armed with darts and *ſkeines*, it was rather an execution than a fight upon them. *Bacon's Henry* VII.

SKEG *n. ſ.* A wild plum.

SKE'GGER. *n ſ.*

Little ſalmons called *ſkeggers*, are bred of ſuch ſick ſalmon that might not go to the ſea, and though they abound, yet never thrive to any bigneſs. *Walton's Angler.*

SKE'LETON. *n. ſ.* [σκελετὸς, Greek.]

1. [In anatomy.] The bones of the body preſerved together as much as can be in their natural ſituation. *Quincey.*

When rattling bones together fly,
From the four corners of the ſky;
When ſinews o'er the *ſkeletons* are ſpread,
Thoſe cloth'd with fleſh, and life inſpires the dead. *Dryden.*

A *ſkeleton*, in outward figure,
His meagre corps, though full of vigour,
Would halt behind him were it bigger. *Swift.*

2. The compages of the principal parts.

The great ſtructure itſelf, and its great integrals, the heavenly and elementary bodies, are framed in ſuch a poſition and ſituation, the great *ſkeleton* of the world. *Hale.*

The ſchemes of any of the arts or ſciences may be analyzed in a ſort of *ſkeleton*, and repreſented upon tables, with the various dependencies of their ſeveral parts. *Watts.*

SKE'LLUM. *n. ſ.* [*ſkelm*, German.] A villain; a ſcoundrel. *Skin.*

SKEP. *n. ſ.* [ſcephen, lower Saxon, to draw.]

1. *Skep* is a ſort of baſket, narrow at the bottom, and wide at the top to fetch corn in.

A pitchforke, a doongforke, ſeeve, *ſkep*, and a bin. *Tuſſer.*

2. In Scotland, the repoſitories where the bees lay their honey is ſtill called *ſkep.*

SK'EPTICK. *n. ſ.* [σκέπτομαι, Gr. *ſceptique*, French.] One who doubts, or pretends to doubt of every thing.

Bring the cauſe unto the bar; whoſe authority none muſt diſclaim, and leaſt of all thoſe *ſcepticks* in religion. *Dec. of Piety.*

Survey
Nature's extended face, then *ſcepticks* ſay,
In this wide field of wonders can you find
No art. *Blackmore.*

With too much knowledge for the *ſcepticks* ſide,
With too much weakneſs for the ſtoicks pride,
Man hangs between. *Pope's Eſſay on Man.*

The dogmatist is sure of every thing, and the *sceptick* believes nothing. *Watts's Logick.*

SKE'PTICAL. *adj.* [from *skeptick.*] Doubtful; pretending to universal doubt.

May the Father of mercies confirm the *sceptical* and wavering minds, and so prevent us that stand fast, in all our doings, and further us with his continual help. *Bentley.*

SKE'PTICISM. *n. s.* [*scepticisme*, French, from *sceptick.*] Universal doubt; pretence or profession of universal doubt.

I laid by my natural diffidence and *scepticism* for a while, to take up that dogmatick way. *Dryden.*

SKETCH. *n. s.* [*schedula*, Latin.] An outline; a rough draught; a first plan.

I shall not attempt a character of his present majesty, having already given an imperfect *sketch* of it. *Addison.*

As the lightest *sketch*, if justly trac'd,
Is by ill colouring but the more disgrac'd,
So by false learning is good sense defac'd. *Pope.*

To SKETCH. *v. n.* [from the noun.]

1. To draw, by tracing the outline.

If a picture is daubed with many glaring colours, the vulgar eye admires it; whereas he judges very contemptuously of some admirable design *sketched* out only with a black pencil, though by the hand of Raphael. *Watts's Logick.*

2. To plan, by giving the first or principal notion.

The reader I'll leave in the midst of silence, to contemplate those ideas which I have only *sketch'd*, and which every man must finish for himself. *Dryden's Dufresnoy.*

SKE'WER. *n. s.* [*skere*, Danish.] A wooden or iron pin, used to keep meat in form.

Sweet breeds and collops were with *skewers* prick'd
About the sides. *Dryden's Iliad.*

From his rug the *skewer* he takes,
And on the stick ten equal notches makes. *Swift.*

I once may overlook,
A *skewer* sent to table by my cook. *King.*

Send up meat well stuck with *skewers*, to make it look round; and an iron *skewer*, when rightly employed, will make it look handsomer. *Swift's Directions to the Cook.*

To SKEWER. *v. a.* [from the noun.] To fasten with skewers.

SKIFF. *n. s.* [*esquife*, French; *scapha*, Lat.] A small light boat.

If in two *skiffs* of cork, a loadstone and steel be placed within the orb of their activities, the one doth not move, the other standing still; but both steer into each other. *Brown's Vulgar Errours.*

In a poor *skiff* he pass'd the bloody main,
Choak'd with the slaughter'd bodies of his train. *Dryden.*

On Garrway cliffs
A savage race by shipwreck fed,
Lie waiting for the founder'd *skiffs*,
And strip the bodies of the dead. *Swift.*

SKI'LFUL. *adj.* [*skill* and *full.*] Knowing; qualified with skill; possessing any art; dexterous; able.

His father was a man of Tyre, *skilful* to work in gold and silver. *2 Chron.* ii. 14.

They shall call the husbandman to mourning, and such as are *skilful* of lamentation, to wailing. *Amos* v. 16.

Will Vafer is *skilful* at finding out the ridiculous side of a thing, and placing it in a new light. *Tatler.*

Say, Stella, feel you no content,
Reflecting on a life well spent;
Your *skilful* hand employ'd to save
Despairing wretches from the grave:
And then supporting with your store
Those whom you dragg'd from death before. *Swift.*

Instructors should not only be *skilful* in those sciences which they teach; but have skill in the method of teaching, and patience in the practice. *Watts's Improvement of the Mind.*

SKI'LFULLY. *adv.* [from *skilful.*] With skill; with art; with uncommon ability; dexterously.

As soon as he came near me, in fit distance, with much fury, but with fury *skilfully* guided, he ran upon me. *Sidney.*

Ulysses builds a ship with his own hands, as *skilfully* as a shipwright. *Broome.*

SKI'LFULNESS. *n. s.* [from *skilful.*] Art; ability; dextrousness.

He fed them according to the integrity of his heart, and guided them by the *skilfulness* of his hands. *Psalms* lxxviii. 72.

SKILL. *n. s.* [*skil*, Islandick.]

1. Knowledge of any practice or art; readiness in any practice; knowledge; dexterity; artfulness.

Skill in the weapon is nothing without sack. *Shakespeare.*

You have
As little *skill* to fear, as I have purpose
To put you to't. *Shakespeare.*

Oft nothing profits more
Than self-esteem grounded on just and right,
Well manag'd; of that *skill* the more thou know'st,
The more she will acknowledge thee her head. *Milton.*

I will from wond'rous principles ordain
A race unlike the first, and try my *skill* again. *Dryden.*

Phocion the Athenian general, then ambassador from the state, by his great wisdom and *skill* at negotiations, diverted Alexander from the conquest of Athens, and restored the Athenians to his favour. *Swift.*

2. Any particular art.

Learned in one *skill*, and in another kind of learning unskilful. *Hooker.*

To SKILL. *v. n.* [*skilia*, Islandick.]

1. To be knowing in; to be dextrous at.

They that *skill* not of so heavenly matter,
All that they know not, envy or admire. *Spenser.*

The overseers were all that could *skill* of instruments of musick. *2 Chron.* xxxiv. 12.

One man of wisdom, experience, learning, and direction, may judge better in those things that he can *skill* of, than ten thousand others that be ignorant. *Whitgifte.*

2. [*Skilia*, Islandick, signifies to distinguish.] To differ; to make difference; to interest; to matter. Not in use.

Whether the commandments of God in scripture be general or special, it *skilleth* not. *Hooker.*

What *skills* it, if a bag of stones or gold
About thy neck do drown thee? raise thy head,
Take stars for money; stars not to be told,
By any art: yet to be purchas'd.
None is so wastful as the scraping dame,
She loseth three for one; her soul, rest, fame. *Herbert.*

He intending not to make a summer business of it, but a resolute war, without term prefixed, until he had recovered France, it *skilled* not much when he began the war, especially having Calais at his back where he might winter. *Bacon.*

SKI'LLED. *adj.* [from *skill.*] Knowing; dextrous; acquainted with.

Of these nor *skilled* nor studious. *Milton.*

Moses, in all the Egyptian arts was *skill'd*,
When heav'nly power that chosen vessel fill'd. *Denham.*

He must be very little *skill'd* in the world, who thinks that a voluble tongue shall accompany only a good understanding. *Locke.*

SKI'LLESS. *adj.* [from *skill.*] Wanting art. Not in use.

Nor have I seen
More that I may call men than you:
How features are abroad I'm *skilless* of. *Shakespeare.*

Jealously what might befal your travel,
Being *skilless* in these parts; which to a stranger
Unguided and unfriended, often prove
Rough and unhospitable. *Shakespeare's Twelfth Night.*

Thy wit, that ornament to shape and love,
Misshapen in the conduct of them both,
Like powder in a *skilless* soldier's flask
Is set on fire. *Shakespeare's Romeo and Juliet.*

SKI'LLET. *n. s.* [*escuellette*, French.] A small kettle or boiler.

When light-wing'd toys
Of feather'd Cupid foil with wanton dullness
My speculative and offic'd instruments,
Let house-wives make a *skillet* of my helm,
And all indign and base adversities
Make head against my estimation. *Shakespeare's Othello.*

Break all the wax, and in a kettle or *skillet* set it over a soft fire. *Mortimer's Husbandry.*

SKILT. *n. s.* [A word used by *Cleaveland*, of which I know not either the etymology or meaning.]

Smeitymnus! ha! what art?
Syriack? Or Arabick? Or Welsh? What *skilt*?
Ape all the bricklayers that Babel built. *Cleaveland.*

To SKIM. *v. a.* [properly to *scum*, from *scum*; *escume*, French.]

1. To clear off from the upper part, by passing a vessel a little below the surface.

My coz Tom, or his coz Mary,
Who hold the plough or *skim* the dairy,
My fav'rite books, and pictures sell. *Prior.*

2. To take by skimming.

She boils in kettles must of wine, and *skims*
With leaves the dregs that overflow the brims. *Dryden.*

His principal studies were after the works of Titian, whose cream he has *skimm'd*. *Dryden's Dufresnoy.*

The surface of the sea is covered with its bubbles, while it rises, which they *skim* off into their boats, and afterwards separate in pots. *Addison.*

Whilome I've seen her *skim* the cloated cream,
And press from spongy curds the milky stream. *Gay.*

3. To brush the surface slightly; to pass very near the surface.

Nor seeks in air her humble flight to raise,
Content to *skim* the surface of the seas. *Dryden.*

The swallow *skims* the river's watry face. *Dryden.*

A winged eastern blast just *skimming* o'er
The ocean's brow, and sinking on the shore. *Prior.*

4. To cover superficially. Improper.

Dang'rous flats in secret ambush lay,
Where the false tides *skim* o'er the cover'd land,
And seamen with dissembled depths betray. *Dryden.*

To Skim. *v. n.* To pass lightly; to glide along.

Thin airy shapes o'er the furrows rise,
A dreadful scene! and *skim* before his eyes. *Addison.*

When Ajax strives some rock's vast weight to throw,
The line too labours, and the words move slow;
Not so when swift Camilla scours the plain,
Flies o'er th' unbending corn, and *skims* along the main. *Pope.*

Such as have active spirits, who are ever *skimming* over the surface of things with a volatile spirit, will fix nothing in their memory. *Watts's Improvement of the Mind.*

They *skim* over a science in a very superficial survey, and never lead their disciples into the depths of it. *Watts.*

The boat, light *skimming*, stretch'd his oary wings. *Thoms.*

Ski'mbleskamble. *adj.* [A cant word formed by reduplication from *scamble.*] Wandering; wild.

A couching lion and a ramping cat,
And such a deal of *skimbleskamble* stuff,
As puts me from my faith. *Shakespeare.*

Ski'mmer. *n. s.* [from *skim.*] A shallow vessel with which the scum is taken off.

Wash your wheat in three or four waters, stirring it round; and with a *skimmer*, each time, take off the light. *Mortimer.*

Sk'immilk. *n. s.* [*skim* and *milk.*] Milk from which the cream has been taken.

Then cheese was brought: says Slouch, this e'en shall roll;
This is *skimmilk*, and therefore it shall go. *King.*

Skin. *n. s.* [*skind*, Danish.]

1. The natural covering of the flesh. It consists of the *cuticle*, outward skin, or scarf skin, which is thin and insensible, and the *cutis*, or inner skin, extremely sensible.

The body is consumed to nothing, the *skin* feeling rough and dry like leather. *Harvey on Consumptions.*

The priest on *skins* of off'rings takes his ease,
And nightly visions in his slumber sees. *Dryden's Æn.*

2. Hide; pelt; that which is taken from animals to make parchment or leather.

3. The body; the person.

We meet with many of these dangerous civilities, wherein 'tis hard for a man to save both his *skin* and his credit. *L'Estr.*

To Skin. *v. a.* [from the noun.]

1. To flay; to strip or divest of the skin.

The beavers run to the door to make their escape, are there intangled in the nets, seized by the Indians, and immediately *skinned*. *Ellis's Voyage.*

2. To cover with the skin.

It will but *skin* and film the ulcerous place,
Whilst rank corruption, mining all within,
Infects unseen. *Shakespeare.*

Authority, though it err like others,
Has yet a kind of medicine in itself,
That *skins* the vice o' th' top. *Shakesp. Meas. for Meas.*

The wound was *skinned*; but the strength of his thigh was not restored. *Dryden.*

It only patches up and *skins* it over, but reaches not to the bottom of the sore. *Locke.*

The last stage of healing, or *skinning* over, is called cicatrization. *Sharp's Surgery.*

3. To cover superficially.

What I took for solid earth was only heaps of rubbish, *skinned* over with a covering of vegetables. *Addison.*

Skink. *n. s.* [scenc, Saxon.]

1. Drink; any thing potable.

2. Pottage.

Scotch *skink*, which is a pottage of strong nourishment, is made with the knees and sinews of beef, but long boiled: jelly also of knuckles of veal. *Bacon's Nat. History.*

To Skink. *v. n.* [scencan, Saxon.] To serve drink. Both noun and verb are wholly obsolete.

Ski'nker. *n. s.* [from *skink.*] One that serves drink.

I give thee this pennyworth of sugar, clapt even now into my hand by an under *skinker*; one that never spake other English in his life, than eight shillings and six pence, and you are welcome, sir. *Shakesp. Henry IV.*

Hang up all the poor hop-drinkers,
Cries old Sym, the king of *skinkers*. *Ben. Johnson.*

His mother took the cup the clown had fill'd:
The reconciler bowl went round the board,
Which, empty'd, the rude *skinker* still restor'd. *Dryden.*

Ski'nned. *adj.* [from *skin.*] Having the nature of skin or leather; hard; callous.

When the ulcer becomes foul, and discharges a nasty ichor, the edges in process of time tuck in, and, growing *skinned* and hard, give it the name of callous. *Sharp's Surgery.*

Ski'nner. *n. s.* [from *skin.*] A dealer in skins.

Ski'nniness. *n. s.* [from *skinny.*] The quality of being skinny.

Ski'nny. *adj.* [from *skin.*] Consisting only of skin; wanting flesh.

Her choppy finger laying
Upon her *skinny* lips. *Shakesp. Macbeth.*

Least the asperity of these cartilages of the windpipe should hurt the gullet, which is tender, and of a *skinny* substance, these annulary gristles are not made round; but where the gullet touches the windpipe, there, to fill up the circle, is only a soft membrane, which may easily give way. *Ray on the Creation.*

His fingers meet
In *skinny* films, and shape his oary feet. *Addison's Ovid.*

To Skip. *v. n.* [*squittire*, Italian; *esquirer*, French. I know not whether it may not come from *scape.*]

1. To fetch quick bounds; to pass by quick leaps; to bound lightly and joyfully.

Was not Israel a derision unto thee? Was he found among thieves? For since thou spakest of him, thou *skippedst* for joy. *Jer.* xlviii. 27.

The queen, bound with love's powerful'st charm,
Sat with Pigwiggen arm in arm:
Her merry maids, that thought no harm,
About the room were *skipping*. *Drayton.*

At spur or switch no more he *skipt*,
Or mended pace, than Spaniard whipt. *Hudibras.*

The earth-born race
O'er ev'ry hill and verdant pasture stray,
Skip o'er the lawns, and by the rivers play. *Blackmore.*

John *skipped* from room to room, ran up stairs and down stairs, peeping into every cranny. *Arbuthn. Hist. of J. Bull.*

Thus each hand promotes the pleasing pain,
And quick sensations *skip* from vein to vein. *Pope's Dunciad.*

The lamb thy riot dooms to bleed to-day,
Had he thy reason, would he *skip* and play? *Pope.*

2. To pass without notice.

Pope Pius II. was wont to say, that the former popes did wisely to set the lawyers a-work to debate, whether the donation of Constantine the Great to Sylvester of St. Peter's patrimony were good or valid in law or no; the better to *skip* over the matter in fact, whether there was ever any such thing at all or no. *Bacon's Apophthegms.*

A gentleman made it a rule, in reading, to *skip* over all sentences where he spied a note of admiration at the end. *Swift.*

To Skip. *v. a.* [*esquirer*, French.] To miss; to pass.

Let not thy sword *skip* one:
Pity not honour'd age for his white beard;
He is an usurer. *Shakesp. Timon of Athens.*

Although to engage very far in such a metaphysical speculation were unfit, when I only endeavour to explicate fluidity, yet we dare not quite *skip* it over, lest we be accused of overseeing it. *Boyle.*

They who have a mind to see the issue may *skip* these two chapters, and proceed to the following. *Burnet.*

Skip. *n. s.* [from the verb.] A light leap or bound.

He looked very curiously upon himself, sometimes fetching a little *skip*, as if he had said his strength had not yet forsaken him. *Sidney.*

You will make so large a *skip* as to cast yourself from the land into the water. *More's Antidote against Atheism.*

Sk'ipjack. *n. s.* [*skip* and *jack.*] An upstart.

The want of shame or brains does not presently entitle every little *skipjack* to the board's-end in the cabinet. *L'Estr.*

Ski'pkennel. *n. s.* [*skip* and *kennel.*] A lackey; a footboy.

Ski'pper. *n. s.* [*schipper*, Dutch.] A shipmaster or shipboy.

Are not you afraid of being drowned too? No, not I, says the *skipper*. *L'Estrange.*

No doubt you will return very much improved.——Yes, refined like a Dutch *skipper* from a whale-fishing. *Congreve.*

Ski'ppet. *n. s.* [Probably from *skiff.*] A small boat.

Upon the bank they sitting did espy
A dainty damsel, dressing of her hair,
By whom a little *skippet* floating did appear. *Fairy Queen.*

Ski'rmish. *n. s.* [from *ys* and *carm*, Welsh, the shout of war: whence *ysgarm*, and *ysgarmes*, old British words. *Maes a n ew 'sgarmes a wnan*, says an ancient writer. *Escarmouche*, French.]

1. A slight fight: less than a set battle.

One battle, yes, a *skirmish* more there was
With adverse fortune fought by Cartismand;
Her subjects most revolt. *Philips's Briton.*

2. A contest; a contention.

There is a kind of merry war betwixt signior Benedick and her: they never meet but there's a *skirmish* of wit. *Shakesp.*

These *skirmishes* expire not with the first propugners of the opinions: they perhaps began as single duellers; but then they soon have their partisans and abettors, who not only enhance, but intail the feud to posterity. *Decay of Piety.*

To Ski'rmish. *v. n.* [*escarmoucher*, French; from the noun.] To fight loosely; to fight in parties before or after the shock of the main battle.

Ready to charge, and to retire at will;
Though broken, scatter'd, fled, they *skirmish* still. *Fairfax.*

A gentleman volunteer, *skirmishing* with the enemy before Worcester, was run through his arm in the middle of the biceps with a sword, and shot with a musket-bullet in the same shoulder. *Wiseman's Surgery.*

I'll pass by the little *skirmishings* on either side. *Atterbury.*

Ski'rmisher. *n. s.* [from *skirmish.*] He who skirmishes. *Ains.*

To Skirre. *v. a.* [This word seems to be derived from scir, Saxon, pure, clean; unless it shall be rather deduced from σκιῤῥόω.] To scour; to ramble over in order to clear.

Send

Send out more horses, *skirre* the country round;
Hang those that talk of fear. *Shakesp. Macbeth.*

To SKIRRE. *v. n.* To scour; to scud; to run in haste.

We'll make them *skirre* away as swift as stones
Enforced from the old Assyrian slings. *Shakesp. Henry V.*

SKI'RRET. *n. s.* [*sisarum*, Latin.] A plant.

It produces its flowers in an umbel, which consists of several leaves placed circularly, and expanded in form of a rose: the empalement afterward becomes a fruit, composed of two narrow seeds, that are gibbous, and furrowed on one side, but plain on the other. The roots are shaped like long turneps, and are joined to one head. *Miller.*

Skirrets are a sort of roots propagated by seed. *Mortimer.*

SKIRT. *n. s.* [*skiorte*, Swedish.]

1. The loose edge of a garment; that part which hangs loose below the waist.

It's but a nightgown in respect of yours; cloth of gold and cuts, side sleeves and *skirts*, round underborne with a bluish tinsel. *Shakesp. Much Ado about Nothing.*

As Samuel turned about to go away, he laid hold upon the *skirt* of his mantle, and it rent. 1 *Sa.* xv. 27.

2. The edge of any part of the dress.

A narrow lace, or a small *skirt* of ruffled linen, which runs along the upper part of the stays before, and crosses the breast, being a part of the tucker, is called the modesty-piece. *Addison.*

3. Edge; margin; border; extreme part.

He should seat himself at Athie, upon the *skirt* of that unquiet country. *Spenser on Ireland.*

Ye mists, that rise
From hill or steaming lake, dusky or grey,
'Till the sun paint your fleecy *skirts* with gold,
In honour to the world's great Author rise. *Milton.*

Though I fled him angry, yet recall'd
To life prolong'd, and promis'd race, I now
Gladly behold, though but his utmost *skirts*
Of glory, and far off his steps adore. *Milt. Parad. Lost.*

The northern *skirts* that join to Syria have entered into the conquests or commerce of the four great empires; but that which seems to have secured the other is the stony and sandy desarts, through which no army can pass. *Temple.*

Upon the *skirts*
Of Arragon our squander'd troops he rallies. *Dryden.*

To SKIRT. *v. a.* [from the noun.] To border; to run along the edge.

Temple *skirteth* this hundred on the waste side. *Carew.*

Of all these bounds,
With shadowy forests and with champions rich'd,
With plenteous rivers and wide *skirted* meads,
We make thee lady. *Shakespeare.*

The middle pair
Skirted his loins and thighs with downy gold. *Milton.*

A spacious circuit on the hill there stood,
Level and wide, and *skirted* round with wood. *Addison.*

SKI'TTISH. *adj.* [*skye*, Danish; *schew*, Dutch.]

1. Shy; easily frighted

A restiff *skittish* jade had gotten a trick of rising, starting, and flying out at his own shadow. *L'Estrange.*

2. Wanton; volatile; hasty; precipitate.

Now expectation, tickling *skittish* spirits,
Sets all on hazard. *Shakespeare.*

He still resolv'd, to mend the matter,
T' adhere and cleave the obstinater;
And still the *skittisher* and looser,
Her freaks appear'd to sit the closer. *Hudibras.*

3. Changeable; fickle.

Some men sleep in *skittish* fortune's hall,
While others play the ideots in her eyes. *Shakespeare.*

Such as I am, all true lovers are;
Unstaid and *skittish* in all notions else,
Save in the constant image of the creature
That is belov'd. *Shak. Twelfth Night.*

SKI'TTISHLY. *adv.* [from *skittish*.] Wantonly; uncertainly; fickly.

SKI'TTISHNESS. *n. s.* [from *skittish*.] Wantonness; fickleness.

SKONCE. *n. s.* [See SCONCE.]

Reinard ransacketh every corner of his wily *skonce*, and bestirreth the utmost of his nimble stumps to quit his coat from their jaws. *Carew.*

SKREEN, *n. s.* [*escran*, *escrein*, French, which *Minshew* derives from *secerniculum*, Latin. *Nimis violenter ut solet*, says *Skinner*, which may be true as to one of the senses; but if the first sense of *skreen* be a kind of coarse *sieve or riddle*, it may perhaps come, if not from *cribrum*, from some of the descendants of *cerno*.]

1. A riddle or coarse sieve.

A skuttle or *skreen* to rid soil fro' the corn. *Tusser.*

2. Any thing by which the sun or weather is kept off.

3. Shelter; concealment.

Fenc'd from day, by night's eternal *skreen*;
Unknown to heav'n, and to myself unseen. *Dryden.*

To SKREEN. *v. a.* [from the noun.]

1. To riddle; to sift. A term yet used among masons when they sift sand for mortar.

2. To shade from sun or light, or weather.

3. To keep off light or weather.

The curtains closely drawn, the light to *skreen*:
Thus cover'd with an artificial night,
Sleep did his office. *Dryden.*

The waters mounted up into the air: their interposition betwixt the earth and the sun *skreen* and fence off the heat, otherwise insupportable. *Woodward's Natural History.*

4. To shelter; to protect.

Ajax interpos'd
His sevenfold shield, and *skreen'd* Laertes' son,
When the insulting Trojans urg'd him sore. *Philips.*

He that travels with them is to *skreen* them, and get them out when they have run themselves into the briars. *Locke.*

His majesty encouraged his subjects to make mouths at their betters, and afterwards *skreened* them from punishment. *Spect.*

The scales, of which the scarf-skin is composed, are designed to fence the orifices of the secretory ducts of the miliary glands, and to *skreen* the nerves from external injuries. *Cheyne.*

SKUE. *adj.* [Of this word there is found no satisfactory derivation.] Oblique; sidelong. It is most used in the adverb *askue*.

Several have imagined that this *skue* posture of the axis is a most unfortunate thing; and that if the poles had been erect to the plane of the ecliptick, all mankind would have enjoyed a very paradise. *Bentley.*

To SKULK. *v. n.* To hide; to lurk in fear or malice.

Discover'd, and defeated of your prey,
You *skulk'd* behind the fence, and sneak'd away. *Dryden.*

SKULL. *n. s.* [*skiola*, Islandick; *skatti*, Islandick, a head.]

1. The bone that incloses the head: it is made up of several pieces, which, being joined together, form a considerable cavity, which contain the brain as in a box, and it is proportionate to the bigness of the brain. Its figure is round, and a little depressed on its sides. The several pieces, of which the skull is composed, are joined together by sutures, which makes it less apt to break: these pieces or bones are six proper and two common, and each is made up of two tables, or laminæ, between which there is a thin and spongious substance, made of some bony fibres, which come from each lamina, called in Greek διπλοε, and in Latin *meditullium*. In it are a great many veins and arteries, which bring blood for the nourishment of the bones. The tables are hard and solid, because in them the fibres of the bones are close to one another. The *diploe* is soft, because the bony fibres are at a greater distance from one another. The external lamina is smooth, and covered with the pericranium: the internal is likewise smooth; but on it are several furrows, made by the pulse of the arteries of the dura mater, whilst the cranium was soft and yielding. *Quincy.*

Some lay in dead mens *skulls*; and in those holes,
Where eyes did once inhabit, there were crept,
As 'twere in scorn of eyes, reflecting gems. *Shakes. R. III.*

With redoubled strokes he plies his head;
But drives the batter'd *skull* within the brains. *Dryden.*

2. [Sceole, Saxon, a company.] A shoal. See SCULL.

Repair to the river where you have seen them swim in *skulls* or shoals. *Walton.*

SKU'LLCAP. *n. s.* A headpiece.

SKU'LLCAP. *n. s.* [*cassida*, Latin.] A plant.

The florets are longish, one in each ala of the leaves: the upper leaf is galeated like an helmet, with two auricles adjoining: the under leaf, for the most part, is divided into two: the calyx, having a cover, contains a fruit resembling the heel of a slipper or shoe. *Miller.*

SKY. *n. s.* [*sky*, Danish.]

1. The region which surrounds this earth beyond the atmosphere. It is taken for the whole region without the earth.

The mountains their broad backs upheave
Into the clouds, their tops ascend the *sky*. *Milton.*

The maids of Argos, who with frantick cries,
And imitated lowings, fill'd the *skies*. *Roscommon.*

Raise all thy winds, with night involve the *skies*,
Sink, or disperse. *Dryden's Æn.*

2. The heavens.

The thunderer's bolt you know,
Sky planted, batters all rebelling coasts. *Shakesp. Cymbeline.*

What is this knowledge but the *sky* stol'n fire,
For which the thief still chain'd in ice doth sit. *Davies.*

Wide is the fronting gate, and rais'd on high,
With adamantine columns threats the *sky*. *Dryden.*

3. The weather.

Thou wert better in thy grave, than to answer with thy uncovered body this extremity of the *skies*. *Shakesp. K. Lear.*

SKY'EY. *adj.* [from *sky*. Not very elegantly formed.] Ethereal.

A breath thou art,
Servile to all the *skiey* influences,
That do this habitation, where thou keep'st,
Hourly afflict. *Shakesp. Measure for Measure.*

Sky'colour. *n. s.* [*sky* and *colour.*] An azure colour; the colour of the sky.

A solution as clear as water, with only a light touch of *sky-colour*, but nothing near so high as the ceruleous tincture of silver. *Boyle.*

Sky'coloured. *adj.* [*sky* and *colour.*] Blue; azure; like the sky.

This your Ovid himself has hinted, when he tells us that the blue water nymphs are dressed in *skycoloured* garments. *Add.*

Sky'dyed. *adj.* [*sky* and *dye.*] Coloured like the sky.

There figs, *skydyed*, a purple hue disclose. *Pope.*

Sky'ed. *adj.* [from *sky.*] Envelloped by the skies. This is unusual and unauthorised.

The pale deluge floats
O'er the *sky'd* mountain to the shadowy vale. *Thomson.*

Sky'ish. *adj.* [from *sky.*] Coloured by the ether; approaching the sky.

Of this flat a mountain you have made,
T' o'ertop old Pelion, or the *skyish* head
Of blue Olympus. *Shakesp. Hamlet.*

Sky'lark. *n. s.* [*sky* and *lark.*] A lark that mounts and sings.

He next proceeded to the *skylark*, mounting up by a proper scale of notes, and afterwards falling to the ground with a very easy descent. *Spectator.*

Sky'light. *n. s.* [*sky* and *light.*] A window placed in a room, not laterally, but in the cieling.

A monstrous fowl dropt through the *skylight*, near his wife's apartment. *Arbuthn. and Pope's Mart. Scriblerus.*

Sky'rocket. *n. s.* [*sky* and *rocket.*] A kind of firework, which flies high and burns as it flies.

I considered a comet, or in the language of the vulgar a blazing star, as a *skyrocket* discharged by an hand that is almighty. *Addison.*

Slab. *n. s.*

1. A puddle. *Ainsworth.*
2. A plane of stone: as, a marble *slab.*

Slab. *adj.* [A word, I suppose, of the same original with *slabber*, or *slaver.*] Thick; viscous; glutinous.

Nose of Turk, and Tartar's lips;
Finger of birth-strangl'd babe,
Ditch-deliver'd by a drab;
Make the gruel thick and *slab.* *Shakesp. Macbeth.*

To Sla'bber. *v. n.* [*slabben*, *slabberen*, Dutch.]

1. To let the spittle fall from the mouth; to drivel.
2. To shed or pour any thing.

To Sla'bber. *v. a.*

1. To smear with spittle.

He *slabbered* me all over, from cheek to cheek, with his great tongue. *Arbuthnot's History of John Bull.*

2. To shed; to spill.

The milk pan and cream pot so *slabber'd* and sost,
That butter is wanting, and cheese is half lost. *Tusser.*

Sla'bberer. *n. s.* [from *slabber.*] He who slabbers.

Sla'bby. *adj.* [The same with *slab.*]

1. Thick; viscous.

In the cure of an ulcer, with a moist intemperies, *slabby* and greasy medicaments are to be forborn, and drying to be used. *Wiseman's Surgery.*

2. Wet; floody.

When waggish boys the stunted besom ply,
To rid the *slabby* pavements, pass not by. *Gay.*

SLACK. *adj.* [ꞅleac, Saxon; *slaken*, Islandick; *yslack*, Welsh; *laxus*, Latin.]

1. Not tense; not hard drawn; loose.

The vein in the arm is that which Aretæus commonly opens; and he gives a particular caution in this case to make a *slack* compression, for fear of exciting a convulsion. *Arbuthn.*

2. Remiss; not diligent; not eager; not fervent.

Thus much help and furtherance is more yielded, in that, if so be our zeal and devotion to Godward be *slack*, the alacrity and fervour of others serveth as a present spur. *Hooker.*

Seeing his soldiers *slack* and timorous, he reproved them of cowardice and treason. *Knolles.*

Nor were it just, would he resume that shape,
That *slack* devotion should his thunder 'scape. *Waller.*

Rebellion now began, for lack
Of zeal and plunder, to grow *slack.* *Hudibras.*

3. Not violent; not rapid.

Their pace was formal, grave, and *slack*:
His nimble wit out-ran the heavy pack. *Dryden.*

A handful of *slack* dried hops spoil many pounds, by taking away their pleasant smell. *Mortimer's Husbandry.*

4. Relaxed; weak; not holding fast.

All his joints relax'd:
From his *slack* hand the garland wreath'd for Eve
Down dropp'd, and all the faded roses shed. *Milton.*

To Slack. } *v. n.* [from the adjective.
To Sla'cken. }

1. To be remiss; to neglect.

When thou shalt vow a vow unto the Lord, *slack* not to pay it. *Deutr.* xxiii. 21.

2. To lose the power of cohesion.

The fire, in lime burnt, lies hid, so that it appears to be cold; but water excites it again, whereby it *slacks* and crumbles into fine powder. *Moxon's Mech. Exer.*

3. To abate.

Whence these raging fires
Will *slacken*, if his breath stir not their flames. *Milton.*

4. To languish; to fail; to flag. *Ainsworth.*

To Slack. } *v. a.*
To Sla'cken. }

1. To loosen; to make less tight.

Ah generous youth, that wish forbear;
Slack all thy sails, and fear to come. *Dryden.*

Had Ajax been employ'd, our *slacken'd* sails
Had still at Aulis waited happy gales. *Dryden.*

2. To relax; to remit.

This makes the pulses beat, and lungs respire;
This holds the sinews like a bridle's reins,
And makes the body to advance, retire,
To turn or stop, as she them *slacks* or strains. *Davies.*

Taught power's due use to people and to kings,
Taught nor to *slack* nor strain its tender strings. *Pope.*

3. To ease; to mitigate. *Philips* seems to have used it by mistake for *slake.*

Men, having been brought up at home under a strict rule of duty, always restrained by sharp penalties from lewd behaviour, so soon as they come thither, where they see laws more slackly tended, and the hard restraint, which they were used unto, now *slacked*, they grow more loose. *Spenser.*

If there be cure or charm
To respite or deceive, or *slack* the pain
Of this ill mansion. *Milton's Paradise Lost.*

On our account has Jove,
Indulgent, to all moons some succulent plant
Allow'd, that poor helpless man might *slack*
His present thirst, and matter find for toil. *Philips.*

4. To remit for want of eagerness.

My guards
Are you, great pow'rs, and th' unbated strength
Of a firm conscience; which shall arm each step
Ta'en for the state, and teach me *slack* no pace. *Ben. Johns.*

With such delay well pleas'd, they *slack* their course. *Milt.*

5. To cause to be remitted.

You may sooner by imagination quicken or *slack* a motion, than raise or cease it; as it is easier to make a dog go slower than make him stand still. *Bacon.*

This doctrine must supersede and *slacken* all industry and endeavour, which is the lowest degree of that which hath been promised to be accepted by Christ; and leave nothing to us to deliberate or attempt, but only to obey our fate. *Hammond.*

Extol not riches then, the toil of fools,
The wise man's cumbrance, if not snare; more apt
To *slacken* virtue, and abate her edge,
Than prompt her to do aught may merit praise. *Milton.*

Balls of this metal *slack'd* Atlanta's pace,
And on the am'rous youth bestow'd the race. *Waller.*

One conduces to the poet's aim, which he is driving on in every line: the other *slackens* his pace, and diverts him from his way. *Dryden.*

6. To relieve; to unbend.

Here have I seen the king, when great affairs
Gave leave to *slacken* and unbend his cares,
Attended to the chase by all the flow'r
Of youth, whose hopes a nobler prey devour. *Denham.*

7. To with-hold; to use less liberally.

He that so generally is good, must of necessity hold his virtue to you, whose worthiness would stir it up where it wanted, rather than *slack* it where there is such abundance. *Shakesp.*

8. To crumble; to deprive of the power of cohesion.

Some unslacked lime cover with ashes, and let it stand 'till rain comes to *slack* the lime; then spread them together. *Mort.*

9. To neglect.

Why might not you, my lord, receive attendance
From those that she calls servants, or from mine?
—If then they chanc'd to *slack* ye,
We could controul them. *Shakesp. King Lear.*

This good chance, that thus much favoureth,
He *slacks* not. *Daniel's Civil War.*

Slack not the good presage, while heav'n inspires
Our minds to dare, and gives the ready fires. *Dryden.*

10. To repress; to make less quick or forcible.

I should be griev'd, young prince, to think my presence
Unbent your thoughts, and *slacken'd* 'em to arms. *Addison.*

Slack. *n. s.* [from the verb *To slack.*] Small coal; coal broken in small parts.

Sla'ckly. *adv.* [from *slack.*]

1. Loosely; not tightly; not closely.
2. Negligently; remissly.

That a king's children should be so convey'd,
So *slackly* guarded, and the search so slow
That could not trace them. *Shakespeare's Cymbeline.*

SLA'CKNESS. *n. s.* [from *slack.*]

1. Looseness; not tightness.

2. Negligence; inattention; remissness.

It concerneth the duty of the church by law to provide, that the looseness and *slackness* of men may not cause the commandments of God to be unexecuted. *Hooker.*

These thy offices,
So rarely kind, are as interpreters
Of my behind-hand *slackness.* *Shak. Winter's Tale.*

From man's effeminate *slackness* it begins,
Who should better hold his place
By wisdom, and superior gifts receiv'd. *Milton's Par. Lost.*

3. Want of tendency.

When they have no disposition to shoot out above their lips, there is a *slackness* to heal, and a cure is very difficultly effected. *Sharp's Surgery.*

4. Weakness; not force; not intenseness.

Through the *slackness* of motion, or long banishment from the air, it might gather some aptness to putrefy. *Brerewood.*

SLAG. *n. s.* The dross or recrement of metal.

Not only the calces but the glasses of metal may be of differing colours from the natural colour of the metal, as I have observed about the glass or *slag* of copper. *Boyle.*

SLAIE. *n. s.* A weaver's reed. *Ainsworth.*

SLAIN The participle passive of *slay.*

The *slain* of the Lord shall be many. *Is.* lxvi. 16.

The king grew vain,
Fought all his battles o'er again;
And thrice he routed all his foes, and thrice he slew the *slain.* *Dryden.*

To SLAKE. *v. a.* [from *slack, Skinner*; from *slock,* Islandick, to quench, Mr. *Lye.*]

1. To quench; to extinguish.

He did always strive
Himself with salves to health for to restore,
And *slake* the heavenly fire that raged evermore. *Fa. Queen.*

If I digg'd up thy forefathers graves,
And hung their rotten coffins up in chains,
It could not *slake* mine ire, nor ease my heart. *Shakes. H.VI.*

She with her cold hand *slakes*
His spirits, the sparks of life, and chills his heart. *Crashaw.*

From Iülus' head
A lambent flame arose, which gently spread
Around his brows, and on his temples fed:
Amaz'd, with running water we prepare
To quench the sacred fire, and *slake* his hair. *Dryden.*

The fragrant fruit from bending branches shake,
And with the crystal stream their thirst at pleasure *slake.* *Blackmore's Creation.*

Coarse are his meals, the fortune of the chace;
Amidst the running stream he *slakes* his thirst. *Addis. Cato.*

2. It is used of lime, so that it is uncertain whether the original notion of *To slack* or *slake* lime be to powder or quench it.

That which he saw happened to be fresh lime, and gathered before any rain had fallen to *slake* it. *Woodward.*

To SLAKE. *v. n.* [This is apparently from *slack.*] To grow less tense; to be relaxed.

If she the body's nature did partake,
Her strength would with the body's strength decay;
But when the body's strongest sinews *slake,*
Then is the soul most active, quick, and gay. *Davies.*

To SLAM. *v. a.* [*lema,* Islandick; *schlagen,* Dutch.] To slaughter; to crush. A word not used but in low conversation.

To SLA'NDER. *v. a.* [*esclaundrie,* French; *scandalum,* Latin.] To censure falsely; to belie.

Slander Valentine
With falshood, cowardice, and poor descent. *Shakespeare.*

He hath *slandered* thy servant unto the king. 2 *Sa.* xix. 27.

Give me leave to speak as earnestly in truly commending it, as you have done in untruly and unkindly defacing and *slandering* it. *Whitgifte.*

Thou do'st with lies the throne invade,
By practice harden'd in thy *slandering* trade;
Obtending heav'n for whate'er ills befal,
And sputt'ring under specious names thy gall. *Dryden.*

Of all her dears she never *slander'd* one,
But cares not if a thousand are undone. *Dryden.*

SLA'NDER. *n. s.* [from the verb.]

1. False invective.

When *slanders* do not live in tongues;
When cut-purses come not to throngs. *Shak. K. Lear.*

Since that, we hear he is in arms,
We think not so;
Yet charge the consul with our harms,
That let him go:
So in our censure of the state
We still do wander,
And make the careful magistrate
The mark of *slander.* *Ben. Johnson's Catiline.*

2. Disgrace; reproach.

Thou *slander* of thy heavy mother's womb!
Thou loathed issue of thy father's loins. *Shakesp. R.* III.

3. Disreputation; ill name.

You shall not find me, daughter,
After the *slander* of most step-mothers,
Ill-ey'd unto you. *Shakespeare.*

SLA'NDERER. *n. s.* [from *slander.*] One who belies another; one who lays false imputations on another.

In your servants suffer any offence against yourself rather than against God: endure not that they should be railers or *slanderers,* tell-tales or sowers of dissension. *Taylor.*

Thou shalt answer for this, thou *slanderer.* *Dryden.*

SLA'NDEROUS. *adj.* [from *slander.*]

1. Uttering reproachful falshoods.

What king so strong
Can tie the gall up in the *slanderous* tongue? *Shakespeare.*

To me belongs
The care to shun the blast of *sland'rous* tongues:
Let malice, prone the virtuous to defame,
Thus with vile censure taint my spotless name. *Pope.*

2. Containing reproachful falshoods; calumnious.

I was never able 'till now to choke the mouth of such detractors, with the certain knowledge of their *slanderous* untruths. *Spenser on Ireland.*

We lay these honours on this man,
To ease ourselves of divers *sland'rous* loads. *Shak. Jul. Cæs.*

As by flattery a man opens his bosom to his mortal enemy, so by detraction and a *slanderous* misreport he shuts the same to his best friends. *South.*

SLA'NDEROUSLY. *adv.* [from *slanderous.*] Calumniously; with false reproach.

I may the better satisfy them who object these doubts, and *slanderously* bark at the courses which are held against that traiterous earl and his adherents. *Spenser on Ireland.*

They did *slanderously* object,
How that they durst not hazard to present
In person their defences. *Daniel's Civil War.*

SLANG. The preterite of *sling.*

David *slang* a stone, and smote the Philistine. 1 *Sa.* xvii.

SLANK. *n. s.* An herb. *Ainsworth.*

SLANT. / SLA'NTING. *adj.* [from *slanghe,* a serpent, Dutch. *Skinner.*] Oblique; not direct; not perpendicular.

Late the clouds
Justling, or push'd with winds, rude in their shock,
Tine the *slant* lightning; whose thwart flame driv'n down,
Kindles the gummy bark of fir and pine. *Milton's Paradise Lost.*

The sun round the globe describes th' Æquator line,
By which wise means he can the whole survey
With a direct or with a *slanting* ray,
In the succession of a night and day. *Blackmore.*

SLA'NTLY. / SLA'NTWISE. *adv.* [from *slant.*] Obliquely; not perpendicularly; slope.

Some maketh a hollowness half a foot deep,
With fower sets in it, set *slantwise* asleep. *Tusser's Husband.*

SLAP. *n. s.* [*schlap,* German.] A blow. Properly with the hand open, or with something rather broad than sharp.

The laugh, the *slap,* the jocund curse go round. *Thomson.*

SLAP. *adv.* [from the noun.] With a sudden and violent blow.

Peg's servants complained; and if they offered to come into the warehouse, then strait went the yard *slap* over their noddle. *Arbuthnot's History of John Bull.*

To SLAP. *v a.* [from the noun.] To strike with a slap.

Dick, who thus long had passive sat,
Here stroak'd his chin, and cock'd his hat;
Then *slapp'd* his hand upon the board,
And thus the youth put in his word. *Prior.*

SLA'PDASH. *interj.* [from *slap* and *dash.*] All at once: as any thing broad falls with a *slap* into the water, and *dashes* it about. A low word.

And yet, *slapdash,* is all again
In ev'ry sinew, nerve, and vein. *Prior.*

To SLASH. *v. a.* [*slasa,* to strike, Islandick.]

1. To cut; to cut with long cuts.

2. To lash. *Slash* is improper.

Daniel, a sprightly swain, that us'd to *slash*
The vig'rous steeds that drew his lord's calash,
To Peggy's side inclin'd. *King.*

To SLASH. *v. n.* To strike at random with a sword; to lay about him.

The knights with their bright burning blades
Broke their rude troops, and orders did confound,
Hewing and *slashing* at their idle shades. *Fairy Queen.*

Not that I'd lop the beauties from his book,
Like *slashing* Bentley with his desp'rate hook. *Pope.*

SLASH. *n. s.* [from the verb.]

1. Cut; wound.

Some few received some cuts and *slashes* that had drawn blood. *Clarendon.*

2. A cut in cloath.

What! this a sleeve?
Here's snip and nip, and cut, and slish and *slash,*
Like to a censor in a barber's shop. *Shakespeare.*

Diſtinguiſh'd *ſlaſhes* deck the great,
As each excels in birth or ſtate:
His oylet-holes are more and ampler;
The king's own body was a ſampler. *Prior.*

SLATCH. *n. ſ.* [A ſea term.] The middle part of a rope or cable that hangs down looſe. *Bailey.*

SLATE. *n. ſ.* [from *ſlit*: *ſlate* is in ſome counties a crack; or from *eſclate*, a tile, French.] A grey foſſile ſtone, eaſily broken into thin plates, which are uſed to cover houſes, or to write upon.

A ſquare cannot be ſo truly drawn upon a *ſlate* as it is conceived in the mind. *Grew's Coſmol.*

A ſmall piece of a flat *ſlate* the ants laid over the hole of their neſt, when they foreſaw it would rain. *Addiſon's Spect.*

To SLATE. *v. a.* [from the noun.] To cover the roof; to tile.

Sonnets and elegies to Chloris,
Would raiſe a houſe about two ſtories,
A lyrick ode would *ſlate*. *Swift.*

SLA'TER. *n. ſ.* [from *ſlate*.] One who covers with ſlates or tiles.

SLA'TTERN. *n. ſ.* [*ſlaetti*, Swediſh.] A woman negligent, not elegant or nice.

Without the raiſing of which ſum,
You dare not be ſo troubleſome
To pinch the *ſlatterns* black and blue,
For leaving you their work to do. *Hudibras.*

We may always obſerve, that a goſſip in politicks is a *ſlattern* in her family. *Addiſon's Freeholder.*

The ſallow ſkin is for the ſwarthy put,
And love can make a *ſlattern* of a ſlut. *Dryden.*

Beneath the lamp her tawdry ribbans glare,
The new-ſcour'd manteau and the *ſlattern* air. *Gay.*

SLA'TY. *adj.* [from *ſlate*.] Having the nature of ſlate.

All the ſtone that is *ſlaty*, with a texture long, and parallel to the ſite of the ſtratum, will ſplit only lengthways, or horizontally; and, if placed in any other poſition, 'tis apt to give way, ſtart, and burſt, when any conſiderable weight is laid upon it. *Woodward on Foſſils.*

SLAVE. *n. ſ.* [*eſclave*, French. It is ſaid to have its original from the *Slavi*, or *Sclavonians*, ſubdued and ſold by the *Venetians*.] One mancipated to a maſter: not a freeman; a dependant.

The baniſh'd Kent, who in diſguiſe
Follow'd his enemy king, and did him ſervice
Improper for a *ſlave*. *Shakeſp. King Lear.*

Thou elviſh markt, abortive, rooting hog!
Thou that waſt ſeal'd in thy nativity
The *ſlave* of nature, and the ſon of hell. *Shakeſp. R.* III.

Of gueſts he makes them *ſlaves*
Inhoſpitably. *Milton.*

Slaves to our paſſions we become, and then
It grows impoſſible to govern men. *Waller.*

The condition of ſervants was different from what it is now, they being generally *ſlaves*, and ſuch as were bought and ſold for money. *South.*

Perſpective a painter muſt not want; yet without ſubjecting ourſelves ſo wholly to it, as to become *ſlaves* of it. *Dryden.*

To-morrow, ſhould we thus expreſs our friendſhip,
Each might receive a *ſlave* into his arms:
This ſun perhaps, this morning ſun's the laſt,
That e'er ſhall riſe on Roman liberty. *Addiſon's Cato.*

To SLAVE. *v. n.* [from the noun.] To drudge; to moil; to toil.

Had women been the makers of our laws,
The men ſhould *ſlave* at cards from morn to night. *Swift.*

SLA'VER. *n. ſ.* [*ſaliva*, Latin; *ſlæfa*, Iſlandick.] Spittle running from the mouth; drivel.

Mathiolus hath a paſſage, that a toad communicates its venom not only by urine, but by the humidity and *ſlaver* of its mouth, which will not conſiſt with truth. *Brown.*

Of all mad creatures, if the learn'd are right,
It is the *ſlaver* kills, and not the bite. *Pope.*

To SLA'VER. *v. n.* [from the noun.]

1. To be ſmeared with ſpittle.

Should I
Slaver with lips, as common as the ſtairs
That mount the capitol; join gripes with hands
Made hard with hourly falſhood as with labour. *Shakeſp.*

2. To emit ſpittle.

Miſo came with ſcowling eyes to deliver a *ſlavering* good-morrow to the two ladies. *Sidney.*

Why muſt he ſputter, ſpawl, and *ſlaver* it,
In vain, againſt the people's fav'rite? *Swift.*

To SLA'VER. *v. a.* To ſmear with drivel.

Twitch'd by the ſlave he mouths it more and more,
'Till with white froth his gown is *ſlaver'd* o'er. *Dryden.*

SLA'VERER. *n. ſ.* [*ſlabbaerd*, Dutch; from *ſlaver*.] One who cannot hold his ſpittle; a driveller; an ideot.

SLA'VERY. *n. ſ.* [from *ſlave*.] Servitude; the condition of a ſlave; the offices of a ſlave.

If my diſſentings were out of errour, weakneſs, or obſtinacy in me, yet no man can think it other than the badge and method of *ſlavery*, by ſavage rudeneſs and importunate obtruſions of violence to have the miſt of his errour diſpelled. *King Charles.*

SLA'UGHTER. *n. ſ.* [onƿlauȝt, Saxon, from ƿlæȝan, ƿleȝan, to ſtrike or kill.] Maſſacre; deſtruction by the ſword.

Sinful Macduff,
They were all ſtruck for thee!
Not for their own demerits, but for mine,
Fell *ſlaughter* on their ſouls. *Shakeſp. Macbeth.*

On each hand *ſlaughter* and gigantick deeds. *Milton.*

The pair you ſee,
Now friends below, in cloſe embraces join;
But when they leave the ſhady realms of night,
With mortal heat each other ſhall purſue:
What wars, what wounds, what *ſlaughter* ſhall enſue? *Dryd.*

To SLA'UGHTER. *v. a.* [from the noun.] To maſſacre; to ſlay; to kill with the ſword.

Your caſtle is ſurpriz'd, your wife and babes
Savagely *ſlaughter'd*. *Shakeſp. Macbeth.*

SLA'UGHTERHOUSE. *n. ſ.* [*ſlaughter* and *houſe*.] Houſe in which beaſts are killed for the butcher.

Away with me, all you whoſe ſouls abhor
Th' uncleanly ſavour of a *ſlaughterhouſe*;
For I am ſtifl'd with the ſmell of ſin. *Shakeſpeare.*

SLA'UGHTERMAN. *n. ſ.* [*ſlaughter* and *man*.] One employed in killing.

The mad mothers with their howls confus'd
Do break the clouds; as did the wives of Jewry,
At Herod's bloody hunting *ſlaughtermen*. *Shak. Hen.* V.

Ten chas'd by one,
Are now each one the *ſlaughterman* of twenty. *Shakeſpeare.*

See, thou fight'ſt againſt thy countrymen;
And join'ſt with them, will be thy *ſlaughtermen*. *Shak. H.*VI.

SLA'UGHTEROUS. *adj.* [from *ſlaughter*.] Deſtructive; murderous.

I have ſupt full with horrours:
Direneſs familiar to my *ſlaughterous* thoughts
Cannot once ſtart me. *Shakeſ. Macbeth.*

SLA'VISH. *adj.* [from *ſlave*.] Servile; mean; baſe; dependant.

A thing
More *ſlaviſh* did I ne'er, than anſwering
A ſlave without a knock. *Shakeſp. Cymbeline.*

You have among you many a purchas'd ſlave,
Which, like your aſſes, and your dogs and mules,
You uſe in abject and in *ſlaviſh* part,
Becauſe you bought them. *Shak. Merchant of Venice.*

I believe
That he, the ſupreme God, t' whom all things ill
Are but as *ſlaviſh* officers of vengeance,
Would ſend a gliſt'ring guardian, if need were,
To keep my life and honour unaſſail'd. *Milton.*

Thoſe are the labour'd births of *ſlaviſh* brains;
Not the effect of poetry, but pains. *Denham.*

Slaviſh bards our mutual loves rehearſe
In lying ſtrains and ignominious verſe. *Prior.*

SLA'VISHLY. *adv.* [from *ſlaviſh*.] Servilely; meanly.

SLA'VISHNESS. *n. ſ.* [from *ſlaviſh*.] Servility; meanneſs.

To SLAY. *v. a.* preter. *ſlew*; part. paſſ. *ſlain*. [*ſlahan*, Gothick; ƿlean, Sax. *ſlachten*, Dutch, to ſtrike.] To kill; to butcher; to put to death.

Her father's brother
Would be her lord; or ſhall I ſay her uncle?
Or he that *ſlew* her brothers and her uncle? *Shak. R.* III.

Tyrant, ſhew thy face:
If thou be'ſt *ſlain*, and with no ſtroke of mine,
My wife and children's ghoſts will haunt me ſtill. *Shakeſp.*

The deadly-handed Clifford *ſlew* my ſteed. *Shak. H.* VI.

I ſaw under the altar the ſouls of them that were *ſlain* for the word of God. *Rev.* vi. 2.

Thus there was killing of young and old, and *ſlaying* of virgins and infants. 2 *Mac.* v. 13.

Slay and make ready. *Gen.* xliii. 16.

Wrath killeth the fooliſh man, and envy *ſlayeth* the ſilly one. *Job* v. 2.

They *ſlew* ten thouſand men. *Judg.* i. 4.

Of Trojan chiefs he view'd a numerous train;
All much lamented, all in battle *ſlain*. *Dryden's Æn.*

Abraham
By blood and battles muſt his pow'r maintain,
And *ſlay* the monarchs, ere he rule the plain. *Prior.*

SLA'YER. *n. ſ.* [from *ſlay*.] Killer; murderer; deſtroyer.

Witneſs the guiltleſs blood poured oft on ground;
The crowned often ſlain, the *ſlayer* crown'd. *Fairy Queen.*

They ſlew thoſe that were *ſlayers* of their countrymen. *Abb.*

The *ſlayer* of himſelf yet ſaw I there;
The gore congeal'd was clotted in his hair:
With eyes half clos'd and gaping mouth he lay,
And grim as when he breath'd his ſullen ſoul away. *Dryden.*

SLEAVE. *n. ſ.* [Of this word I know not well the meaning: *ſleave* ſilk is explained by *Gou'dman floccus ſericus*, a lock of ſilk; and the women ſtill ſay *ſleave the ſilk*, for *untwiſt* it. *Ainſworth* calls

calls a weaver's shuttle or reed a *slay*. *To sley* is to part a twist into single fibres.]

I on a fountain light,
Whose brim with pinks was platted,
The banks with daffadillies dight
With grass like *sleave* was matted. *Drayton's Cynthia.*

SLEAZY. *adj.* [often written *sleezy.*] Weak; wanting substance. This seems to be of the same race with *sleave*, or from to *sley*.

SLED. *n. s.* [*slæd*, Danish; *sledde*, Dutch.] A carriage drawn without wheels.

The *sled*, the tumbril, hurdles, and the flail,
These all must be prepar'd. *Dryden.*

SLE'DDED. *adj.* [from *sled.*] Mounted on a sled.

So frown'd he once when in an angry parle,
He smote the *sledded* Polack on the ice. *Shakespeare.*

SLEDGE. *n. s.* [ꞅlecz, Saxon; *sleggia*, Islandick.]

1. A large heavy hammer.

They him spying, both with greedy force,
At once upon him ran, and him beset,
With strokes of mortal steel, without remorse,
And on his shield like iron *sledges* bet. *Fairy Queen.*

The painful smith, with force of fervent heat,
The hardest iron soon doth mollify,
That with his heavy *sledge* he can it beat,
And fashion to what he it list apply. *Spenser.*

The uphand *sledge* is used by under workmen, when the work is not of the largest, yet requires help to batter and draw it out: they use it with both their hands before them, and seldom lift their hammer higher than their head. *Moxon.*

Aristotle ascribes it unto the swiftness of that motion; but it would follow that the quick stroak of a light hammer should be of greater efficacy, than any softer and more gentle striking of a great *sledge*. *Wilkins's Mathematical Magick.*

2. A carriage without wheels, or with very low wheels; properly a *sled*. See SLED.

In Lancashire, they use a sort of *sledge* made with thick wheels, to bring their marl out, drawn with one horse. *Mort.*

SLEEK. *n. s.* [*sleych*, Dutch.] Smooth; nitid; glossy.

Let me have men about me that are fat,
Sleek-headed men, and such as sleep a-nights. *Shakespeare.*

Envy!
How eagerly ye follow my disgrace,
As if it fed ye; and how *sleek* and wanton
Y' appear in ev'ry thing may bring my ruin. *Shakespeare.*

Yet are the men more loose than they,
More kemb'd, and bath'd, and rub'd, and trim'd,
More *sleek'd*, more soft, and slacker limb'd. *Ben. Johnson.*

What time the groves were clad in green,
The fields all drest in flowers,
And that the *sleek*-hair'd nymphs were seen,
To seek them summer bowers. *Drayton.*

The purest pasteboard, with a *sleek* stone rub smooth, and as even as you can. *Peacham.*

As in gaze admiring, oft he bow'd
His turret crest, and *sleek* enamel'd neck,
Fawning. *Milton's Paradise Lost.*

Those rugged names to our like mouths grow *sleek*,
That would have made Quintilian stare and gasp. *Milton.*

Thy head and hair are *sleek*,
And then thou kemb'st the tuzzes on thy cheek. *Dryden.*

So *sleek* her skin, so faultless was her make,
Ev'n Juno did unwilling pleasure take
To see so fair a rival. *Dryden.*

To SLEEK. *v. a.* [from the adjective.]

1. To comb smooth and even.

By dead Parthenope's dear tomb,
And fair Ligea's golden comb,
Wherewith she sits on diamond rocks,
Sleeking her soft alluring locks. *Milton.*

2. To render soft, smooth, or glossy.

Gentle my lord, *sleek* o'er your rugged looks;
Be bright and jovial 'mong your guests to night. *Shakesp.*

She does *sleek*
With crumbs of bread and milk, and lies a-nights
In her neat gloves. *Ben. Johnson's Catiline.*

A sheet of well *sleeked* marble paper did not cast any of its distinct colours upon the wall. *Boyle.*

The persuasive rhetorick
That *sleek'd* his tongue, and won so much on Eve,
So little here, nay lost. *Milton.*

A cruise of fragrance, form'd of burnish'd gold,
Odour divine! whose soft refreshing streams
Sleek the smooth skin, and scent the snowy limbs. *Pope.*

SLEE'KLY. *adv.* [from *sleek.*] Smoothly; glossily.

Let their heads be *sleekly* comb'd, and their blue coats brush'd. *Shakespeare's Taming of the Shrew.*

To SLEEP. *v. n.* [*slepan*, Gothick; ꞅlæpan, Saxon; *slaepen*, Dutch.]

1. To take rest, by suspension of the mental powers.

I've watch'd and travell'd hard:
Some time I shall *sleep* out; the rest I'll whistle. *Shakesp.*

Where's Pede?—go you, and where you find a maid,
That, ere she *sleep*, hath thrice her prayers said,
Rein up the organs of her fantasy;
Sleep she as sound as careless infancy;
But those that *sleep*, and think not on their sins,
Pinch them, arms, legs, backs, shoulders, sides, and shins.
Shakespeare's Merry Wives of Windsor.

If the man be poor, thou shalt not *sleep* with his pledge. *Deut.*

Sleep on now, and take your rest; behold the hour is at hand. *Matth.* xxvi. 45.

Peace, good reader! do not weep;
Peace! the lovers are asleep:
They, sweet turtles! folded lie,
In the last knot that love could tie.
Let them *sleep*, let them *sleep* on,
Till this stormy night be gone,
And the eternal morrow dawn,
Then the curtains will be drawn,
And they waken with that light,
Whose day shall never *sleep* in night. *Crashaw.*

Those who at any time *sleep* without dreaming, can never be convinced that their thoughts are for four hours busy without their knowing it. *Locke.*

2. To rest; to be motionless.

Steel, if thou turn thine edge, or cut not out the burly-bon'd clown in chines of beef ere thou *sleep* in thy sheath, I beseech Jove on my knees thou mayst be turned into hob-nails. *Shakespeare's Henry VI.*

How sweet the moonlight *sleeps* upon this bank!
Here will we sit, and let the sounds of musick
Creep in our ears. *Shakespeare's Merch. of Venice.*

The giddy ship, betwixt the winds and tides,
Forc'd back and forwards, in a circle rides,
Stunn'd with the different blows; then shoots amain,
Till counterbuff'd she stops, and *sleeps* again. *Dryden.*

3. To live thoughtlessly.

We *sleep* over our happiness, and want to be rouzed into a quick thankful sense of it. *Atterbury.*

4. To be dead; death being a state from which man will some time awake.

If we believe that Jesus died and rose again, even so them also which *sleep* in Jesus will God bring with him. 1 *Thess.*

A person is said to be dead to us, because we cannot raise from the grave; though he only *sleeps* unto God, who can raise from the chamber of death. *Ayliffe's Parergon.*

5. To be inattentive; not vigilant.

Heav'n will one day open
The king's eyes, that so long have *slept* upon
This bold, bad man. *Shakespeare's Henry VIII.*

6. To be unnoticed, or unattended.

You ever
Have wish'd the *sleeping* of this business, never
Desir'd it to be stirr'd. *Shakespeare's Henry VIII.*

SLEEP. *n. s.* [from the verb.] Repose; rest; suspension of the mental powers; slumber.

Methought I heard a voice cry sleep no more!
Macbeth doth murder *sleep*; the innocent *sleep*;
Sleep that knits up the ravell'd sleeve of care;
The birth of each day's life, sore labour's bath,
Balm of hurt minds, great nature's second course,
Chief nourisher in life's feast. *Shakespeare's Macbeth.*

Cold calleth the spirits to succour; and therefore they cannot so well close and go together in the head, which is ever requisite to *sleep*. And for the same cause, pain and noise hinder *sleep*; and darkness furthereth *sleep*. *Bacon.*

Beasts that sleep in winter, as wild bears, during their *sleep* wax very fat, though they eat nothing. *Bacon.*

His fasten'd hands the rudder keep,
And fix'd on heav'n, his eyes repel invading *sleep*. *Dryden.*

Hermes o'er his head in air appear'd,
His hat adorn'd with wings disclos'd the god,
And in his hand the *sleep*-compelling rod. *Dryden.*

Infants spend the greatest part of their time in *sleep*, and are seldom awake but when hunger calls for the teat, or some pain forces the mind to perceive it. *Locke.*

SLEE'PER. *n. s.* [from *sleep.*]

1. One who sleeps; one who is not awake.

Sound musick; come my queen, take hand with me,
And rock the ground whereon these *sleepers* be. *Shakesp.*

What's the business,
That such an hideous trumpet calls to parley
The *sleepers* of the house? *Shakespeare's Macbeth.*

In some countries, a plant which shutteth in the night, openeth in the morning, and openeth wide at noon; the inhabitants say is a plant that sleepeth. There be *sleepers* enow then; for almost all flowers do the like. *Bacon.*

Night is indeed the province of his reign;
Yet all his dark exploits no more contain
Than a spy taken, and a *sleeper* slain. *Dryden.*

He must be no great eater, drinker, nor *sleeper*, that will discipline his senses, and exert his mind: every worthy undertaking requires both. *Grew.*

2. A

2. A lazy inactive drone.
3. That which lies dormant, or without effect.
Let penal laws, if they have been *sleepers* of long, or if grown unfit for the present time, be by wise judges confined in the execution. *Bacon.*
4. A fish. *Ainsworth.*

SLEE'PILY. *adv.* [from *sleepy.*]
1. Drowsily; with desire to sleep.
2. Dully; lazily.
I rather chuse to endure the wounds of those darts, which envy casteth at novelty, than to go on safely and *sleepily* in the easy ways of ancient mistakings. *Raleigh.*
3. Stupidly.
He would make us believe that Luther in these actions pretended to authority, forgetting what he had *sleepily* owned before. *Atterbury.*

SLEE'PINESS. *n. s.* [from *sleepy.*] Drowsiness; disposition to sleep; inability to keep awake.
Watchfulness precedes too great *sleepiness*, and is the most ill boding symptom of a fever. *Arbuthnot.*

SLEE'PLESS. *adj.* [from *sleep.*] Wanting sleep.
The field
To labour calls us, now with sweat impos'd,
Though after *sleepless* night. *Milton's Paradise Lost.*
While pensive poets painful vigils keep,
Sleepless themselves to give their readers sleep. *Pope.*

SLEE'PY. *adj.* [from *sleep.*]
1. Drowsy; disposed to sleep.
2. Not awake.
Why did you bring these daggers from the place?
They must lie there. Go, carry them and smear
The *sleepy* grooms with blood. *Shakespeare's Macbeth.*
She wak'd her *sleepy* crew,
And rising hasty, took a short adieu. *Dryden.*
3. Soporiferous; somniferous; causing sleep.
We will give you *sleepy* drinks, that your senses unintelligent of our insufficience, may, though they cannot praise us, as little accuse us. *Shakespeare's Winter's Tale.*
Let such bethink them, if the *sleepy* drench
Of that forgetful lake benumb not still. *Milton.*
I sleeped about eight hours, and no wonder; for the physicians had mingled a *sleepy* potion in the wine. *Gulliver.*

SLEET. *n. s.* [perhaps from the Danish, *slet.*] A kind of smooth small hail or snow, not falling in flakes, but single particles.
Now van to van the foremost squadrons meet,
The midmost battles hastning up behind,
Who view, far off, the storm of falling *sleet*,
And hear their thunder rattling in the wind. *Dryden.*
Perpetual *sleet* and driving snow
Obscure the skies, and hang on herds below.
Huge oxen stand inclos'd in wintry walls
Of snow congeal'd. *Dryden.*
Rains would have been poured down, as the vapours became cooler; next *sleet*, then snow, and ice, and frost. *Cheyne.*

To SLEET. *v. n.* [from the noun.] To snow in small particles, intermixed with rain.

SLEE'TY. *adj.* [from the noun.] Bringing sleet.

SLEEVE. *n. s.* [rlyp, Saxon.]
1. The part of a garment that covers the arms.
Once my well-waiting eyes espy'd my treasure,
With *sleeves* turn'd up, loose hair, and breast enlarged,
Her father's corn, moving her fair limbs, measure. *Sidney.*
The deep smock *sleeve*, which the Irish women use, they say, was old Spanish; and yet that should seem rather to be an old English fashion: for in armory, the fashion of the Manche, which is given in arms, being nothing else but a *sleeve*, is fashioned much like to that *sleeve*. And knights, in ancient times, used to wear their mistress's or love's *sleeve* upon their arms; sir Launcelot wore the *sleeve* of the fair maid of Asteloth in a tourney. *Spenser's Ireland.*
Your hose should be ungarter'd, your *sleeve* unbutton'd, your shoe untied, demonstrating a careless desolation. *Shakesp.*
You would think a smock a she-angel, he so chants to the *sleeve*-band, and the work about the square on't. *Shakespeare.*
He was cloathed in cloth, with wide *sleeves* and a cape. *Bacon.*
In velvet white as snow the troop was gown'd,
Their hoods and *sleeves* the same. *Dryden.*
2. *Sleeve*, in some provinces, signifies a knot or skein of silk, which is by some very probably supposed to be its meaning in the following passage. [See SLEAVE.]
Methought I heard a voice cry, sleep no more!
Macbeth doth murder sleep; the innocent sleep;
Sleep that knits up the ravell'd *sleeve* of care,
The birth of each day's life. *Shakespeare.*
3. *Sleeve*, Dutch, signifies a cover; any thing spread over; which seems to be the sense of *sleeve* in the proverbial phrase.
A brace of sharpers laugh at the whole roguery in their *sleeves*. *L'Estrange.*
Men know themselves utterly void of those qualities which the impudent sycophant ascribes to them, and in his *sleeve* laughs at them for believing. *South's Sermons.*
John laughed heartily in his *sleeve* at the pride of the esquire. *Arbuthnot's Hist. of John Bull.*
4. To hang on a *sleeve*; to make dependent.
It is not for a man which doth know, or should know what orders, and what peaceable government requireth, to ask why we should hang our judgment upon the church's *sleeve*, and why in matters of orders more than in matters of doctrine. *Hooker.*
5. [*Lolligo*, Latin.] A fish. *Ainsworth.*

SLEE'VED. *adj.* [from *sleeve.*] Having sleeves.

SLEE'VELESS. *adj.* [from *sleeve.*]
1. Wanting sleeves; having no sleeves.
His cloaths were strange, though coarse, and black, tho' bare;
Sleeveless his jerkin was, and it had been
Velvet, but 'twas now, so much ground was seen,
Become tufftaffaty. *Donne.*
They put on long *sleeveless* coats of home-spun cotton. *Sandys.*
Behold yon isle by palmers, pilgrims trod,
Grave mummers! *sleeveless* some, and shirtless others. *Pope.*
2. Wanting reasonableness; wanting propriety; wanting solidity. [This sense, of which the word has been long possessed, I know not well how it obtained; *Skinner* thinks it properly *liveless* or *lifeless*: to this I cannot heartily agree, though I know not what better to suggest. Can it come from *sleeve*, a knot, or *skein*, and so signify *unconnected, hanging ill together*? or from *sleeve*, a cover; and therefore means *plainly absurd*; foolish without palliation?]
This *sleeveless* tale of transubstantiation was brought into the world by that other fable of the multipresence. *Hall.*
My landlady quarrelled with him for sending every one of her children on a *sleeveless* errand, as she calls it. *Spectator.*

SLEIGHT. *n. s.* [*slagd*, cunning, Islandick.] Artful trick; cunning artifice; dexterous practice; as sleight of hand; the tricks of a juggler. This is often written, but less properly, *slight.*
He that exhorted to beware of an enemy's policy, doth not give counsel to be impolite; but rather to be all prudent foresight, lest our simplicity be over-reached by cunning *sleights*. *Hooker.*
Fair Una to the red cross knight
Betrothed is with joy;
Though false Duessa it to bar,
Her false *sleights* do employ. *Fairy Queen.*
Upon the corner of the moon,
There hangs a vap'rous drop, profound;
I'll catch it ere it come to ground;
And that distill'd by magick *sleights*,
Shall raise such artificial sprights,
As, by the strength of their illusion
Shall draw him on to his confusion. *Shakespeare's Macbeth.*
Out stept the ample size
Of mighty Ajax, huge in strength; to him, Laertes' son,
That crafty one as huge in *sleight*. *Chapman.*
She could not so convey
The massy substance of that idol great,
What *sleight* had she the wardens to betray?
What strength to heave the goddess from her seat? *Fairf.*
In the wily snake
Whatever *sleights*, none would suspicious mark,
As from his wit, and native subtilty
Proceeding. *Milton.*
Doubtless the pleasure is as great
Of being cheated, as to cheat;
As lookers on feel most delight,
That least perceive the juggler's *sleight*. *Hudibras.*
Good humour is but a *sleight* of hand, or a faculty making truths look like appearances, or appearances like truths. *L'Estrange.*
When we hear death related, we are all willing to favour the *sleight*, when the poet does not too grossly impose upon us. *Dryden.*
While innocent he scorns ignoble flight,
His honest friends preserve him by a *sleight*. *Swift.*

SLEINE. *n. s.* [This word is apparently misprinted for *seine.*] Is a net of about forty fathoms in length, with which they encompass a part of the sea, and draw the same on land by two ropes fastned at its ends, together with such fish as lighteth within his precinct. *Carew.*

SLE'NDER. *adj.* [*slinder*, Dutch.]
1. Thin; small in circumference compared with the length; not thick.
So thick the roses bushing round
About her glow'd; half stooping to support
Each flow'r of *slender* stalk. *Milton.*
2. Small in the waist; having a fine shape.
What *slender* youth bedew'd with liquid odours,
Courts thee on roses in some pleasant cave. *Milton.*
Beauteous Helen shines among the rest,
Tall, *slender*, straight, with all the graces blest. *Dryden.*

3. Not bulky; slight; not strong.

Love in these labyrinths his slaves detains,
And mighty hearts are held in *slender* chains. *Pope.*

4. Small; inconsiderable; weak.

Yet they, who claim the general assent of the whole world unto that which they teach, and do not fear to give very hard and heavy sentence upon as many as refuse to embrace the same, must have special regard, that their first foundations and grounds be more than *slender* probabilities. *Hooker.*

Where joy most revels, grief doth most lament;
Grief joys, joy grieves, on *slender* accident. *Shakespeare.*

Positively to define that season, there is no *slender* difficulty. *Brown's Vulgar Errours.*

It is a very *slender* comfort that relies upon this nice distinction, between things being troublesome, and being evils; when all the evil of affliction lies in the trouble it creates to us. *Tillotson.*

5. Sparing; less than enough: as, a *slender* estate and *slender* parts.

At my lodging,
The worst is this, that at so *slender* warning,
You're like to have a thin and *slender* pittance. *Shakesp.*

In obstructions inflammatory, the aliment ought to be cool, *slender*, thin, diluting. *Arbuthnot.*

6. Not amply supplied.

The good Ostorius often deign'd
To grace my *slender* table with his presence. *Philips.*

SLE'NDERLY. *adv.* [from *slender.*]

1. Without bulk.
2. Slightly; meanly.

If the debt be not just, we know not what may be deemed just, neither is it a sum to be *slenderly* regarded. *Hayward.*

If I have done well, it is that which I desired; but if *slenderly* and meanly, it is that which I could attain to. 2 *Mac.*

SLE'NDERNESS. *n. s.* [from *slender.*]

1. Thinness; smallness of circumference.

Small whistles give a sound because of their extreme *slenderness*, whereby the air is more pent than in a wider pipe. *Bacon's Natural History.*

Their colours arise from the thinness of the transparent parts of the feathers; that is from the *slenderness* of the very fine hairs or capillamenta, which grow out of the sides of the grosser lateral branches or fibres of those feathers. *Newton.*

2. Want of bulk or strength.

It is preceded by a spitting of blood, occasioned by its acrimony, and too great a projectile motion, with *slenderness* and weakness of the vessels. *Arbuthnot on Diet.*

3. Slightness; weakness; inconsiderableness.

The *slenderness* of your reasons against the book, together with the inconveniencies that must of necessity follow, have procured a great credit unto it. *Whitgifte.*

4. Want of plenty.

SLEPT. The preterite of *sleep.*

Silence! coeval with eternity,
Thou wert ere nature first began to be,
'Twas one vast nothing all, and all *slept* fast in thee. *Pope.*

SLEW. The preterite of *slay.*

He *slew* Hamet, a great commander among the Numidians, and chased Benchades and Amida, two of their greatest princes, out of the country. *Knolles's History of the Turks.*

To SLEY. *v. n.* [See to SLEAVE.] To part or twist into threads.

Why art thou then exasperate, thou immaterial skein of *sley'd* silk? *Shakespeare.*

To SLICE. *v. n.* [ꞅliꞇan, Saxon.]

1. To cut into flat pieces.

Their cooks make no more ado, but *slicing* it into little gobbets, prick it on a prong of iron, and hang it in a furnace. *Sandys's Journey.*

The residue were on foot, well furnished with jack and skull, pikes and *slicing* swords, broad, thin, and of an excellent temper. *Hayward.*

2. To cut into parts.

Nature lost one by thee, and therefore must
Slice one in two to keep her number just. *Cleaveland.*

3. To cut off.

When hungry thou stood'st staring, like an oaf,
I *slic'd* the luncheon from the barley loaf. *Gay.*

4. To cut; to divide.

Ambitious princes and tyrants *slice* the earth among them. *Burnet's Theory of the Earth.*

SLICE. *n. s.* [ꞅliꞇe, Saxon; from the verb.]

1. A broad piece cut off.

Hacking of trees in their bark, both downright and across, so as you may make them rather in *slices* than in continued hacks, doth great good to trees. *Bacon.*

You need not wipe your knife to cut bread; because in cutting a *slice* or two it will wipe itself. *Swift.*

He from out the chimney took,
A flitch of bacon off the hook,
And freely, from the fattest side,
Cut out large *slices* to be fry'd. *Swift.*

2. A broad piece.

Then clap four *slices* of pilaster on't,
That lac'd with bits of rustick, makes a front. *Pope.*

3. A broad head fixed in a handle; a peel; a spatula.

The pelican hath a beak broad and flat, much like the *slice* of apothecaries, with which they spread plaisters. *Hakewill.*

When burning with the iron in it, with the *slice*, clap the coals upon the outside close together, to keep the heat in. *Mox.*

SLICK. *adj.* [*slickt*, Dutch. See SLEEK.]

Glass attracts but weakly; some *slick* stones, and thick glasses indifferently. *Brown's Vulgar Errours.*

SLID. The preterite of *slide.*

At first the silent venom *slid* with ease,
And seiz'd her cooler senses by degrees. *Dryden's Æneid.*

SLI'DDEN. The participle passive of *slide.*

Why is this people *slidden* back, by a perpetual backsliding? *Jer* viii. 5.

To SLI'DDER. *v. n.* [*slidderen*, Dutch.] To slide with interruption.

Go thou from me to fate,
Now die: with that he dragg'd the trembling sire,
Slidd'ring through clotted blood. *Dryden.*

To SLIDE. *v. n.* *slid*, preterite; *slidden*, participle pass. [ꞅliðan, ꞅliðenðe, sliding, Saxon; *slijden*, Dutch; *ys-lithe*, Welsh.]

1. To pass along smoothly; to slip; to glide.

Sounds do not only *slide* upon the surface of a smooth body, but communicate with the spirits in the pores of the body. *Bacon's Natural History.*

Ulysses, Stheneleus, Tisander *slide*
Down by a rope, Machaon was their guide. *Denham.*

2. To move without change of the foot.

Oh Ladon, happy Ladon, rather *slide* than run by her, lest thou shouldst make her legs slip from her. *Sidney.*

Smooth *sliding* without step. *Milton.*

He that once sins, like him that *slides* on ice,
Goes swiftly down the slippery ways of vice:
Though conscience checks him, yet those rubs gone o'er,
He *slides* on smoothly, and looks back no more. *Dryden.*

3. To pass inadvertently.

Make a door and a bar for thy mouth: beware thou *slide* not by it. *Ecclus* xxviii. 26.

4. To pass unnoticed.

In the princess I could find no apprehension of what I said or did, but with a calm carelessness, letting every thing *slide* justly, as we do by their speeches, who neither in matter nor person do any way belong unto us. *Sidney.*

5. To pass along by silent and unobserved progression.

Thou shalt
Hate all, shew charity to none;
But let the famisht flesh *slide* from the bone,
Ere thou relieve the beggar. *Shakespeare.*

Then no day void of bliss, of pleasure leaving,
Ages shall *slide* away without perceiving. *Dryden.*

Rescue me from their ignoble hands:
Let me kiss yours when you my wound begin,
Then easy death will *slide* with pleasure in. *Dryden.*

Their eye *slides* over the pages, or the words *slide* over their eyes, and vanish like a rhapsody of evening tales. *Watts.*

6. To pass silently and gradually from good to bad.

Nor could they have *slid* into those brutish immoralities of life, had they duly manured those first practical notions and dictates of right reason. *South.*

7. To pass without difficulty or obstruction.

Such of them should be retained as *slide* easily of themselves into English compounds, without violence to the ear. *Pope.*

Begin with sense, of ev'ry art the soul,
Parts answ'ring parts shall *slide* into a whole;
Nature shall join you, time shall make it grow
A work to wonder at. *Pope.*

8. To move upon the ice by a single impulse, without change of feet.

The gallants dancing by the river side,
They bathe in summer, and in winter *slide.* *Waller.*

9. To fall by errour.

The discovering and reprehension of these colours cannot be done but out of a very universal knowledge of things, which so cleareth man's judgment, as it is the less apt to *slide* into any errour. *Bacon.*

10. To be not firm.

Ye fair!
Be greatly cautious of your *sliding* hearts. *Thomson.*

11. To pass with a free and gentle course or flow.

To SLIDE. *v. a.* To put imperceptibly.

Little tricks of sophistry by *sliding* in, or leaving out such words as entirely change the question, should be abandoned by all fair disputants. *Watts.*

SLIDE. *n. s.* [from the verb.]

1. Smooth and easy passage.

We have some *slides* or relishes of the voice or strings, continued without notes, from one to another, rising or falling, which are delightful. *Bacon's Natural History.*

Kings that have able men of their nobility shall find ease in employing them, and a better *slide* into their business; for people naturally bend to them. *Bacon.*

2. Flow; even course.

There be, whose fortunes are like Homer's verses, that have a *slide* and easiness more than the verses of other poets. *Bac.*

SLI'DER. *n. s.* [from *slide.*] He who slides.

SLIGHT. *adj.* [*slicht*, Dutch.]

1. Small; worthless; inconsiderable.

Is Cæsar with Antonius priz'd so *slight*? *Shakespeare.*

Their arms, their arts, their manners I disclose,
Slight is the subject, but the praise not small,
If heav'n assist, and Phœbus hear my call. *Dryden.*
Slight is the subject, but not so the praise;
If she inspire, and he approve my lays. *Pope.*

2. Not important; not cogent; weak.

Some firmly embrace doctrines upon *slight* grounds, some upon no grounds, and some contrary to appearance. *Locke.*

3. Negligent; not vehement; not done with effect.

The shaking of the head is a gesture of *slight* refusal. *Bacon.*

He in contempt
At one *slight* bound high overleap'd all bound. *Milton.*

4. Foolish; weak of mind.

No beast ever was so *slight*
For man, as for his God, to fight. *Hudibras.*

5. Not strong; thin; as a *slight* silk.

SLIGHT. *n. s.* [from the adjective.]

1. Neglect; contempt; act of scorn.

People in misfortune construe unavoidable accidents into *slights* or neglects. *Clarissa.*

2. Artifice; cunning practice. See SLEIGHT.

As boisterous a thing as force is, it rarely atchieves any thing but under the conduct of fraud. *Slight* of hand has done that, which force of hand could never do. *South.*

After Nic had bambouzled John a while, what with *slight* of hand, and taking from his own score, and adding to John's, Nic brought the balance to his own side. *Arbuthnot.*

To SLIGHT. *v. a.* [from the adjective.]

1. To neglect; to disregard.

Beware lest they transgress and *slight* that sole command. *Milton.*

You cannot expect your son should have any regard for one whom he sees you *slight*. *Locke.*

2. To throw carelessly, unless in this passage to *slight* be the same with to *fling*.

The rogues *slighted* me into the river, with as little remorse as they would have drowned puppies. *Shakespeare.*

3. [*Slighten*, Dutch.] To overthrow; to demolish. *Junius*, *Skinner*, and *Ainsworth*.

4. *To* SLIGHT *over*. To treat or perform carelessly.

These men, when they have promised great matters, and failed most shamefully, if they have the perfection of boldness, will but *slight* it *over*, and no more ado. *Bacon's Essays.*

His death and your deliverance
Were themes that ought not to be *slighted over*: *Dryden.*

SLI'GHTER. *n. s.* [from *slight.*] One who disregards.

SLI'GHTINGLY. *adv.* [from *slighting.*] Without reverence; with contempt.

If my sceptick speaks *slightingly* of the opinions he opposes, I have done no more than became the part. *Boyle.*

SLI'GHTLY. *adv.* [from *slight.*]

1. Negligently; without regard.

Words, both because they are common, and do not so strongly move the fancy of man, are for the most part but *slightly* heard. *Hooker.*

Leave nothing fitting for the purpose
Untouch'd, or *slightly* handled in discourse. *Shakespeare.*
You were to blame
To part so *slightly* with your wife's first gift. *Shakespeare.*

The letter-writer dissembles his knowledge of this restriction, and contents himself *slightly* to mention it towards the close of his pamphlet. *Atterbury.*

2. Scornfully; contemptuously.

Long had the Gallick monarch uncontroul'd,
Enlarg'd his borders, and of human force
Opponent *slightly* thought. *Philips.*

3. Weakly; without force.

Scorn not the facil gates of hell too *slightly* barr'd. *Milton.*

4. Without worth.

SLI'GHTNESS. *n. s.* [from *slight.*]

1. Weakness; want of strength.

2. Negligence; want of attention; want of vehemence.

Where gentry, title, wisdom,
Cannot conclude but by the yea and no
Of gen'ral ignorance, it must omit
Real necessities, and give way the while
T' unstable *slightness*. *Shakespeare's Coriolanus.*

What strong cries must they be that shall drown so loud a clamour of impieties? and how does it reproach the *slightness* of our sleepy heartless addresses? *Decay of Piety.*

SLI'LY. *adv.* [from *sly.*] Cunningly; with cunning secrecy; with subtile covertness.

Were there a serpent seen with forked tongue,
That *slily* glided towards your majesty,
It were but necessary you were wak'd. *Shakespeare.*
He, closely false and *slily* wise,
Cast how he might annoy them most from far. *Fairfax.*

Satan, like a cunning pick-lock, *slily* robs us of our grand treasure. *Decay of Piety.*

With this he did a herd of goats controul;
Which by the way he met, and *slily* stole:
Clad like a country swain *Dryden.*
May hypocrites,
That *slily* speak one thing, another think,
Hateful as hell, pleas'd with the relish weak,
Drink on unwarned, till by inchanting cups
Infatuate, they their wily thoughts disclose,
And through intemperance grow a while sincere. *Philips.*

SLIM. *adv.* [A cant word as it seems, and therefore not to be used.] Slender; thin of shape.

A thin *slim*-gutted fox made a hard shift to wriggle his body into a henroost; and when he had stuft his guts well, squeezed hard to get out again; but the hole was too little. *L'Estr.*

I was jogg'd on the elbow by a *slim* young girl of seventeen. *Addison.*

SLIME. *n. s.* [ſlim, Saxon; *sligm*, Dutch.] Viscous mire; any glutinous substance.

The higher Nilus swells
The more it promises: as it ebbs, the seedsman
Upon the *slime* and ooze scatters his grain. *Shakespeare.*
Brick for stone, and *slime* for mortar. *Gen.*
The vale of Siddim was full of *slime*-pits. *Gen.* xiv. 10.

God, out of his goodness, caused the wind to blow, to dry up the abundant *slime* and mud of the earth, and make the land more firm, and to cleanse the air of thick vapours and unwholsome mists. *Raleigh.*

Some plants grow upon the top of the sea, from some concretion of *slime* where the sun beateth hot, and the sea stirreth little. *Bacon's Natural History.*

And with Asphaltick *slime*, broad as the gate,
Deep to the roots of hell, the gather'd beach
They fasten'd. *Milton's Paradise Lost.*
Now dragon grown; larger than whom the sun
Engender'd in the Pythian vale on *slime*,
Huge Python! *Milton's Paradise Lost.*
O foul descent! I'm now constrain'd
Into a beast, to mix with bestial *slime*,
This essence to incarnate and imbrute. *Milton.*

SLI'MINESS. *n. s.* [from *slimy.*] Viscosity; glutinous matter.

By a weak fermentation a pendulous *sliminess* is produced, which answers a pituitous state. *Floyer.*

SLI'MY. *adj.* [from *slime.*]

1. Overspread with slime.

My bended hook shall pierce
Their *slimy* jaws; and, as I draw them up,
I'll think them every one an Antony. *Shakespeare.*
Some lay in dead men's skulls; and in those holes,
Where eyes did once inhabit, there were crept,
As 'twere in scorn of eyes, reflecting gems,
That woo'd the *slimy* bottom of the deep,
And mock'd the dead bones that lay scatter'd by. *Shak.*

They have cobwebs about them, which is a sign of a *slimy* dryness. *Bacon.*

The rest are all by bad example led,
And in their father's *slimy* tract they tread. *Dryden.*

Eels for want of exercise, are fat and *slimy*. *Arbuthnot.*

Shoals of slow house-bearing do snails creep
O'er the ripe fruitage, paring *slimy* tracks
In the sleek rind. *Philips.*
The swallow sweeps
The *slimy* pool to build his hanging house. *Thomson.*

2. Viscous; glutinous.

Then both from out hell-gates, into the waste,
Wide anarchy of chaos, damp and dark,
Hovering upon the waters, what they met
Solid or *slimy*, as in raging sea,
Tost up and down, together crowded drove. *Milton.*
From their groins they shed
A *slimy* juice by false conception bred. *Dryden.*

The astrological undertakers would raise men like vegetables, out of some fat and *slimy* soil, well digested by the kindly heat of the sun, and impregnated with the influence of the stars. *Bentley.*

SLI'NESS. *n. s.* [from *sly.*] Designing artifice.

By an excellent faculty in mimickry, my correspondent can assume my air, and give my taciturnity a *slyness*, which diverts more than any thing I could say. *Addison.*

SLING. *n. s.* [ſlingan, Saxon; *slingen*, Dutch.]

1. A missive weapon made by a strap and two strings; the stone is lodged in the strap, and thrown by loosing one of the strings.

The arrow cannot make him flee: *sling* stones are turned with him into stubble. *Job* xli. 28.

Dreads he the twanging of the archer's ſtring?
Or ſinging ſtones from the Phœnician *ſling?* *Sandys.*

Slings have ſo much greater ſwiftneſs than a ſtone thrown from the hand, by how much the end of the *ſling* is farther off from the ſhoulder-joint, the center of motion. *Wilkins.*

The Tuſcan king
Laid by the lance, and took him to the *ſling*;
Thrice whirl'd the thong around his head, and threw
The heated lead, half melted as it flew. *Dryden's Æn.*

Whirl'd from a *ſling*, or from an engine thrown,
Amidſt the foes, as flies a mighty ſtone,
So flew the beaſt. *Dryden's Ovid.*

2. A throw; a ſtroke.

'Till cram'd and gorg'd, nigh burſt
With ſuck'd and glutted offal, at one *ſling*
Of thy victorious arm, well-pleaſing ſon. *Milt. Par. Loſt.*

3. A kind of hanging bandage.

To Sling. *v. a.* [from the noun.]

1. To throw by a ſling.

2. To throw; to caſt. Not very proper.

Ætna's entrails fraught with fire,
That now caſts out dark fumes and pitchy clouds,
Incenſt, or tears up mountains by the roots,
Or *ſlings* a broken rock aloft in air. *Addiſon.*

3. To hang looſely by a ſtring.

From rivers drive the kids, and *ſling* your hook;
Anon I'll waſh 'em in the ſhallow brook. *Dryden.*

4. To move by means of a rope.

Cœnus I ſaw amidſt the ſhouts
Of mariners, and buſy care to *ſling*
His horſes ſoon aſhore. *Dryden's Cleomenes.*

They *ſlung* up one of their largeſt hogſheads, then rolled it towards my hand, and beat out the top. *Gulliver's Travels.*

Sli'nger. *n. ſ.* [from *ſling.*] One who ſlings or uſes the ſling.

The *ſlingers* went about it, and ſmote it. 2 *Kings* iii. 25.

To Slink. *v. n.* preter. *ſlunk.* [ꞅlıŋgan, Saxon, to creep.] To ſneak; to ſteal out of the way.

We will *ſlink* away in ſupper-time, diſguiſe us at my lodging, and return all in an hour. *Shakeſp. Merch. of Venice.*

As we do turn our backs
From our companion, thrown into his grave,
So his familiars from his buried fortunes
Slink away. *Shakeſp. Timon of Athens.*

He, after Eve ſeduc'd, unminded *ſlunk*
Into the wood faſt by. *Milton's Paradiſe Loſt.*

Not far from hence doth dwell
A cunning man, hight Sidrophel,
To whom all people far and near
On deep importances repair;
When braſs and pewter hap to ſtray,
And linen *ſlinks* out of the way. *Hudibras.*

She *ſlunk* into a corner, where ſhe lay trembling 'till the company went their way. *L'Eſtrange.*

He would pinch the children in the dark, and then *ſlink* into a corner, as if no body had done it. *Arbuthn. Hiſt. of J. Bull.*

A weaſel once made ſhift to *ſlink*
In at a corn-loft through a chink;
But having amply ſtuff'd his ſkin,
Could not get out as he got in. *Pope's Epiſt. of Horace.*

We have a ſuſpicious, fearful, and conſtrained countenance, often turning back, and *ſlinking* through narrow lanes. *Swift.*

To Slink. *v. a.* To caſt; to miſcarry of. A low word.

To prevent a mare's *ſlinking* her foal, in ſnowy weather keep her where ſhe may have good ſpring-water to drink. *Mort.*

To SLIP. *v. n.* [ꞅlıpan, Saxon; *ſlippen*, Dutch.]

1. To ſlide; not to tread firm.

If a man walks over a narrow bridge, when he is drunk, it is no wonder that he forgets his caution while he overlooks his danger; but he who is ſober, and views that nice ſeparation between himſelf and the devouring deep, ſo that, if he ſhould *ſlip*, he ſees his grave gaping under him, ſurely muſt needs take every ſtep with horrour and the utmoſt caution. *South.*

A ſkilful dancer on the ropes *ſlips* willingly, and makes a ſeeming ſtumble, that you may think him in great hazard, while he is only giving you a proof of his dexterity. *Dryden.*

If after ſome diſtinguiſh'd leap
He drops his pole, and ſeems to *ſlip*,
Straight gath'ring all his active ſtrength,
He riſes higher half his length. *Prior.*

2. To ſlide; to glide.

Oh Ladon, happy Ladon! rather ſlide than run by her, leſt thou ſhouldſt make her legs *ſlip* from her. *Sidney.*

They trim their feathers, which makes them oily and ſlippery, that the water may *ſlip* off them. *Mortimer's Huſbandry.*

3. To move or fly out of place.

Sometimes the ancle-bone is apt to turn out on either ſide, by reaſon of relaxation, which though you reduce, yet, upon the leaſt walking on it, the bone *ſlips* out again. *Wiſeman.*

4. To ſneak; to ſlink.

From her moſt beaſtly company
I 'gan refrain, in mind to *ſlip* away,
Soon as appear'd ſafe opportunity. *Spenſer.*

When Judas ſaw that his hoſt *ſlipt* away, he was ſore troubled. 1 *Mac.* ix. 7.

I'll *ſlip* down out of my lodging. *Dryden's Don Sebaſtian.*

Thus one tradeſman *ſlips* away,
To give his partner fairer play. *Prior.*

5. To glide; to paſs unexpectedly or imperceptibly.

The banks of either ſide ſeeming arms of the loving earth, that fain would embrace it, and the river a wanton nymph, which ſtill would *ſlip* from it. *Sidney.*

The bleſſing of the Lord ſhall *ſlip* from thee, without doing thee any good, if thou haſt not ceaſed from doing evil. *Taylor.*

Slipping from thy mother's eye thou went'ſt
Alone into the temple; there was found
Among the graveſt rabbies diſputant,
On points and queſtions fitting Moſes' chair. *Milton.*

Thrice around his neck his arms he threw,
And thrice the flitting ſhadow *ſlipp'd* away,
Like winds or empty dreams that fly the day. *Dryden.*

Though with pale cheeks, wet beard, and dropping hair,
None but my Ceyx could appear ſo fair,
I would have ſtrain'd him with a ſtrict embrace;
But through my arms he *ſlipt*, and vaniſh'd from the place. *Dryden.*

When a corn *ſlips* out of their paws, they take hold of it again. *Addiſon's Spectator.*

Wiſe men watch every opportunity, and retrieve every miſpent hour which has *ſlipped* from them. *Rogers.*

I will impute no defect to thoſe two years which have *ſlipped* by ſince. *Swift to Pope.*

6. To fall into fault or errour.

If he had been as you,
And you as he, you would have *ſlipt* like him;
But he, like you, would not have been ſo ſtern. *Shakeſpeare.*

One *ſlippeth* in his ſpeech, but not from his heart. *Eccluſ.*

An eloquent man is known far and near; but a man of underſtanding knoweth when he *ſlippeth.* *Eccluſ.* xxi. 7.

7. To creep by overſight.

Some miſtakes may have *ſlipt* into it; but others will be prevented by the names being now ſet at length. *Adv. to Dunciad.*

8. To eſcape; to fall away out of the memory.

By the hearer it is ſtill preſumed, that if they be let *ſlip* for the preſent, what good ſoever they contain is loſt, and that without all hope of recovery. *Hooker.*

The mathematician proceeds upon propoſitions he has once demonſtrated; and though the demonſtration may have *ſlipt* out of his memory, he builds upon the truth. *Addiſon.*

Uſe the moſt proper methods to retain the ideas you have acquired; for the mind is ready to let many of them *ſlip*, unleſs ſome pains be taken to fix them upon the memory. *Watts.*

To Slip. *v. a.*

1. To convey ſecretly.

In his officious attendance upon his miſtreſs he tried to *ſlip* a powder into her drink. *Arbuthn. Hiſt. of John Bull.*

2. To loſe by negligence.

You are not now to think what's beſt to do,
As in beginnings; but what muſt be done,
Being thus enter'd; and *ſlip* no advantage
That may ſecure you. *Ben. Johnſon's Catiline.*

Let us not *ſlip* th' occaſion, whether ſcorn
Or ſatiate fury yield it from our foe. *Milton.*

One ill man may not think of the miſchief he could do, or *ſlip* the occaſion. *L'Eſtrange.*

To *ſlip* the market, when thus fairly offered, is great imprudence. *Collier.*

For watching occaſions to correct others in their diſcourſe, and not to *ſlip* any opportunity of ſhewing their talents, ſcholars are moſt blamed. *Locke.*

Thus far my author has *ſlipt* his firſt deſign; not a letter of what has been yet ſaid promoting any ways the trial. *Atterb.*

3. To part twigs from the main body by laceration.

The runners ſpread from the maſter-roots, and have little ſprouts or roots to them, which, being cut four or five inches long, make excellent ſets: the branches alſo may be *ſlipped* and planted. *Mortimer's Huſbandry.*

4. To eſcape from; to leave ſlily.

This bird you aim'd at, though you hit it not.
—Oh, ſir, Lucentio *ſlipp'd* me like his greyhound,
Which runs himſelf, and catches for his maſter. *Shakeſp.*

5. To let looſe.

On Eryx altars lays
A lamb new fallen to the ſtormy ſeas;
Then *ſlips* his haulſers, and his anchors weighs. *Dryden.*

6. To let a dog looſe.

The impatient greyhound, *ſlipt* from far,
Bounds o'er the glebe, to courſe the fearful hare. *Dryden.*

7. To throw off any thing that holds one.

Forced to alight, my horſe *ſlipped* his bridle, and ran away. *Swift.*

8. To paſs over negligently.

If our author gives us a liſt of his doctrines, with what reaſon can that about indulgences be *ſlipped* over? *Atterbury.*

SLIP. *n. s.* [from the verb.]
1. The act of slipping; false step.
2. Errour; mistake; fault.

There put on him
What forgeries you please: marry, none so rank
As may dishonour him.
But, sir, such wanton, wild, and usual *slips*,
As are most known to youth and liberty. *Shakespeare.*

Of the promise there made, our master hath failed us, by *slip* of memory, or injury of time. *Wotton's Architecture.*

This religious affection, which nature has implanted in man, would be the most enormous *slip* she could commit. *More's Antidote against Atheism.*

One casual *slip* is enough to weigh down the faithful service of a long life. *L'Estrange.*

Alonzo, mark the characters;
And if th' impostor's pen have made a *slip*,
That shews it counterfeit, mark that and save me. *Dryden.*

Lighting upon a very easy *slip* I have made, in putting one seemingly indifferent word for another, that discovery opened to me this present view. *Locke.*

Any little *slip* is more conspicuous and observable in a good man's conduct than in another's, as it is not of a piece with his character. *Addison's Spectator.*

3. A twig torn from the main stock.

In truth, they are fewer, when they come to be discussed by reason, than otherwise they seem, when by heat of contention they are divided into many *slips*, and of every branch an heap is made. *Hooker.*

The *slips* of their vines have been brought into Spain. *Abb.*

Adoption strives with nature, and choice breeds
A native *slip* to us from foreign seeds. *Shakespeare.*

Thy mother took into her blameful bed
Some stern untutor'd churl, and noble stock
Was graft with crab-tree *slip*, whose fruit thou art. *Shakes.*

Trees are apparelled with flowers or herbs by boring holes in their bodies, and putting into them earth holpen with muck, and setting seeds or *slips* of violets in the earth. *Bacon.*

So have I seen some tender *slip*,
Sav'd with care from Winter's nip,
The pride of her carnation train,
Pluck'd up by some unheedy swain. *Milton.*

The lab'rer cuts
Young *slips*, and in the soil securely puts. *Dryden.*

They are propagated not only by the seed, but many also by the root, and some by *slips* or cuttings. *Ray on the Creation.*

4. A leash or string in which a dog is held.

I see you stand like greyhounds in the *slips*,
Straining upon the start. *Shakesp. Henry V.*

God is said to harden the heart permissively, but not operatively, nor effectively; as he who only lets loose a greyhound out of the *slip*, is said to hound him at the hare. *Bramh.*

5. An escape; a desertion. I know not whether *to give the slip*, be not originally taken from a dog that runs and leaves the string or *slip* in the leader's hand.

The more shame for her goodyship,
To give so near a friend the *slip*. *Hudibras.*

The daw did not like his companion, and gave him the *slip*, and away into the woods. *L'Estrange.*

Their explications are not your's, and will give you the *slip*. *Locke.*

6. A long narrow piece.

Between these eastern and western mountains lies a *slip* of lower ground, which runs across the island. *Addison.*

SLI'PBOARD. *n. s.* [*slip* and *board.*] A board sliding in grooves.

I ventured to draw back the *slipboard* on the roof, contrived on purpose to let in air. *Gulliver's Travels.*

SLI'PKNOT. *n. s.* [*slip* and *knot.*] A bowknot; a knot easily untied.

They draw off so much line as is necessary, and fasten the rest upon the line-rowl with a *slipknot*, that no more line turn off. *Moxon's Mech. Exer.*

In large wounds a single knot first; over this a little linen compress, on which is to be made another single knot, and then a *slipknot*, which may be loosened upon inflammation. *Sharp's Surgery.*

SLI'PPER, or *Slipshoe*. *n. s.* [from *slip.*] A shoe without leather behind, into which the foot slips easily.

A gown made of the finest wool,
Which from our pretty lambs we pull;
Fair lined *slippers* for the cold,
With buckles of the purest gold;
A belt of straw and ivy buds,
With coral clasps, and amber studs. *Raleigh.*

If he went abroad too much, she'd use
To give him *slippers*, and lock up his shoes. *King.*

Thrice rung the bell, the *slipper* knock'd the ground,
And the press'd watch return'd a silver sound. *Pope.*

SLI'PPER. *adj.* [ꞅlıpuꞃ, Saxon.] Slippery; not firm. Obsolete. Perhaps never in use but for poetical convenience.

A trustless state of earthly things, and *slipper* hope
Of mortal men, that swinke and sweat for nought. *Spenser.*

SLI'PPERINESS. *n. s.* [from *slippery.*]
1. State or quality of being slippery; smoothness; glibness.

We do not only fall by the *slipperiness* of our tongues, but we deliberately discipline them to mischief. *Gov. of the Tongue.*

The schirrus may be distinguished by its want of inflammation in the skin, its smoothness, and *slipperiness* deep in the breast. *Sharp's Surgery.*

2. Uncertainty; want of firm footing.

SLI'PPERY. *adj.* [ꞅlıpuꞃ, Saxon; *sliperig*, Swedish.]
1. Smooth; glib.

They trim their feathers, which makes them oily and *slippery*, that the water slips off. *Mortimer.*

Oily substances only lubricate and make the bowels *slippery*. *Arbuthnot.*

2. Not affording firm footing.

Did you know the art o' th' court,
As hard to leave as keep; whose top to climb,
Is certain falling; or so *slipp'ry*, that
The fear's as bad as falling. *Shakesp. Cymbeline.*

His promise to trust to as *slippery* as ice. *Tusser.*

Their way shall be as *slippery* ways in the darkness. *Jer.* xxiii.

The *slipp'ry* tops of human state,
The gilded pinacles of fate. *Cowley.*

The higher they are raised, the giddier they are; the more *slippery* is their standing, and the deeper the fall. *L'Estrange.*

The highest hill is the most *slipp'ry* place,
And fortune mocks us with a smiling face. *Denham.*

Beauty, like ice, our footing does betray;
Who can tread sure on the smooth *slippery* way? *Dryden.*

3. Hard to hold; hard to keep.

Thus surely bound, yet be not overbold,
The *slipp'ry* god will try to loose his hold;
And various forms assume, to cheat thy sight,
And with vain images of beasts affright. *Dryden's Georg.*

4. Not standing firm.

When they fall, as being *slipp'ry* standers,
The love that lean'd on them as *slipp'ry* too,
Doth one pluck down another, and together
Die in the fall. *Shakes. Troilus and Cressida.*

5. Uncertain; changeable; mutable; instable.

Oh world, thy *slippery* turns! Friends now fast sworn,
Whose double bosoms seem to wear one heart,
Whose hours, whose bed, whose meal and exercise,
Are still together; who twine, as 'twere, in love
Unseparable, shall within this hour,
On a dissension of a doit, break out
To bitterest enmity. *Shakespeare.*

He looking down
With scorn or pity on the *slippery* state
Of kings, will tread upon the neck of fate. *Denh. Sophy.*

6. Not certain in its effect.

One sure trick is better than a hundred *slippery* ones. *L'Estr.*

7. [*Lubrique*, French.] Not chaste.

My wife is *slippery*. *Shakesp. Winter's Tale.*

SLI'PPY. *adv.* [from *slip.*] Slippery; easily sliding. A barbarous provincial word.

The white of an egg is ropy, *slippy*, and nutritious. *Floyer.*

SLI'PSHOD. *adj.* [*slip* and *shod.*] Having the shoes not pulled up at the heels, but barely slipped on.

The *slipshod* 'prentice from his master's door
Had par'd the dirt, and sprinkled round the floor. *Swift.*

SLI'PSLOP. *n. s.* Bad liquor. A low word formed by reduplication of *slop*.

SLISH. *n. s.* A low word formed by reduplicating *slash*.

What! this a sleeve?
Here's snip and nip, and *slish* and slash,
Like to a censor in a barber's shop. *Shakespeare.*

To SLIT. *v. a.* pret. and part. *slit* and *slitted*. [ꞅlıtan, Saxon.] To cut longwise.

To make plants medicinable *slit* the root, and infuse into it the medicine; as hellebore, opium, scammony, and then bind it up. *Bacon's Nat. History.*

The deers of Arginusa had their ears divided, casioned at first by *slitting* the ears. *Brown's Vulgar Errours.*

Had it hit
The upper part of him, the blow
Had *slit*, as sure as that below. *Hudibras.*

We *slit* the preternatural body open. *Wiseman's Surgery.*

A liberty might be left to the judges to inflict death, or some notorious mark, by *slitting* the nose, or brands upon the cheeks. *Temple.*

If a tinned or plated body, which, being of an even thickness, appears all over of an uniform colour, should be *slit* into threads, or broken into fragments of the same thickness with the plate, I see no reason why every thread or fragment should not keep its colour. *Newton's Opt.*

He took a freak
To *slit* my tongue, and make me speak. *Swift.*

SLIT. *n. s.* [ꞅlıt, Saxon.] A long cut, or narrow opening.

In St James's fields is a conduit of brick, unto which joineth a low vault, and at the end of that a round house of stone; and in the brick conduit there is a window, and in the round

round house a *slit* or rift of some little breadth: if you cry out in the rift, it will make a fearful roaring at the window. *Bacon.*

Where the tender rinds of trees disclose
Their shooting gems, a swelling knot there grows:
Just in that place a narrow *slit* we make,
Then other buds from bearing trees we take;
Inserted thus, the wounded rind we close. *Dryden.*

I found, by looking through a *slit* or oblong hole, which was narrower than the pupil of my eyes, and held close to it parallel to the prisms, I could see the circles much distincter, and visible to a far greater number, than otherwise. *Newton.*

To SLIVE. } *v. a.* [ꞅliꝼan, Saxon.] To split; to divide
To SLI'VER. } longwise; to tear off longwise.

Liver of blaspheming Jew,
Gall of goat, and *slips* of yew,
Sliver'd in the moons eclipse. *Shakesp. Macbeth.*

SLI'VER. *n. s.* [from the verb.] A branch torn off. *Sliver*, in Scotland, still denotes a slice cut off: as, he took a large *sliver* of the beef.

There on the pendant boughs, her coronet weed
Clamb'ring to hang, an envious *sliver* broke,
When down her weedy coronet and herself
Fell in the weeping brook. *Shak. Hamlet.*

SLOATS. *n. s.* Of a cart, are those underpieces which keep the bottom together. *Bailey.*

SLO'BBER. *n. s.* [*glavoerio*, Welsh.] Slaver. See SLAVER.

To SLOCK. *v. n.* [*slock*, to quench, Swedish and Scottish.] To slake; to quench.

SLOE. *n. s.* [ꞅla, Saxon; *slaae*, Danish.] The fruit of the blackthorn, a small wild plum.

The fair pomgranate might adorn the pine,
The grape the bramble, and the *sloe* the vine. *Blackmore.*

When you fell your underwoods, sow haws and *slows* in them, and they will furnish you, without doing of your woods any hurt. *Mortimer's Husbandry.*

SLOOP. *n. s.* A small ship.

To SLOP. *v. a.* [from *lap*, *lop*, *slop*.] To drink grosly and greedily.

SLOP. *n. s.* [from the verb.] Mean and vile liquor of any kind. Generally some nauseous or useless medicinal liquor.

The sick husband here wanted for neither *slops* nor doctors. *L'Estrange.*

But thou, whatever *slops* she will have bought,
Be thankful. *Dryden's Juvenal.*

SLOP. *n. s.* [ꞅlop, Saxon; *sloove*, Dutch, a covering.] Trowsers; open breeches.

What said Mr. Dombledon about the sattin for my short cloak and *slops*? *Shakesp. Henry IV.*

SLOPE. *adj.* [This word is not derived from any satisfactory original. *Junius* omits it: *Skinner* derives it from *slap*, lax, Dutch; and derives it from the curve of a loose rope. Perhaps its original may be latent in *loopen*, Dutch, to run, *slope* being easy to the runner.] Oblique; not perpendicular. It is generally used of acclivity or declivity; forming an angle greater or less with the plane of the horizon.

Where there is a greater quantity of water, and space enough, the water moveth with a *sloper* rise and fall. *Bacon.*

Murm'ring waters fall
Down the *slope* hills, dispers'd, or in a lake,
That to the fringed bank with myrtle crown'd
Her crystal mirror holds, unite their streams. *Milton.*

SLOPE. *n. s.* [from the adjective.]

1. An oblique direction; any thing obliquely directed.
2. Declivity; ground cut or formed with declivity.

Growing upon *slopes* is caused for that moss, as it cometh of moisture, so the water must but slide, not be in a pool. *Bac.*

My lord advances with majestick mien,
And when up ten steep *slopes* you've dragg'd your thighs,
Just at his study door he'll bless your eyes. *Pope.*

SLOPE. *adv.* Obliquely; not perpendicularly.

Uriel
Return'd on that bright beam, whose point now rais'd
Bore him *slope* downward to the sun, now fall'n. *Milton.*

To SLOPE. *v. a.* [from the adjective.] To form to obliquity or declivity; to direct obliquely.

Though bladed corn be lodg'd, and trees blown down,
Though palaces and pyramids do *slope*
Their heads to their foundations. *Shakesp. Macbeth.*

On each hand the flames
Driv'n backward *slope* their pointing spires, and rowl'd
In billows, leave i' th' midst a horrid vale. *Milt. Par. Lost.*

The star, that rose at evening bright,
Toward heav'n's descent had *slop'd* his westering wheel. *Milt.*

All night I slept, oblivious of my pain;
Aurora dawn'd, and Phœbus shin'd in vain:
Nor 'till oblique he *slop'd* his evening ray,
Had Somnus dry'd the balmy dews away. *Pope's Odyssey.*

To SLOPE. *v. n.* To take an oblique or declivous direction.

Betwixt the midst and these the gods assign'd
Two habitable seats for human kind,
And cross their limits cut a *sloping* way,
Which the twelve signs in beauteous order sway. *Dryden.*

Upstarts a palace, lo! th' obedient base
Slopes at its foot, the woods its sides embrace. *Pope.*

There is a strait hole in every ants nest half an inch deep, and then it goes down *sloping* into a place where they have their magazine. *Addison's Spectator.*

SLO'PENESS. *n. s.* [from *slope*.] Obliquity; declivity; not perpendicularity.

The Italians give the cover a graceful pendence of *slopeness*, dividing the whole breadth into nine parts, whereof two shall serve for the elevation of the highest ridge. *Wotton's Architect.*

SLO'PEWISE. *adj.* [*slope* and *wise*.] Obliquely; not perpendicularly.

The Wear is a frith, reaching *slopewise* through the Ose from the land to low water mark, and having in it a bent or cod with an eye-hook; where the fish entering, upon their coming back with the ebb, are stopped from issuing out again, forsaken by the water, and left dry on the Ose. *Carew.*

SLO'PINGLY. *adv.* [from *sloping*.] Obliquely; not perpendicularly.

These atoms do not descend always perpendicularly, but sometimes *slopingly*. *Digby on the Soul.*

SLO'PPY. *adj.* [from *slop*.] Miry and wet: perhaps rather *slabby*. See SLAB.

To SLOT. *v. a.* [*slughen*, Dutch.] To strike or clash hard.

SLOT. *n. s.* [*slod*, Islandick.] The track of a deer.

SLOTH. *n. s.* [ꞅlæpð, ꞅlepð, Saxon. It might therefore be not improperly written *sloath*, but that it seems better to regard the orthography of the primitive *slow*.]

1. Slowness; tardiness.

These cardinals trifle with me: I abhor
This dilatory *sloth* and tricks of Rome. *Shak. Henry VIII.*

2. Laziness; sluggishness; idleness.

False of heart, light of ear, bloody of hand,
Hog in *sloth*, fox in stealth. *Shakesp. King Lear.*

They change their course to pleasure, ease, and *sloth*. *Milt.*

Industry approach'd,
And rous'd him from his miserable *sloth*. *Thomson's Autumn.*

3. An animal.

The *sloth* is an animal of so slow a motion, that he will be three or four days at least in climbing up and coming down a tree; and to go the length of fifty paces on plain ground, requires a whole day. *Grew.*

SLO'THFUL. *adj.* [*sloth* and *full*.] Idle; lazy; sluggish; inactive; indolent; dull of motion.

He that is *slothful* in his work, is brother to him that is a great waster. *Prov.* xviii. 9.

The desire of the *slothful* killeth him; for his hands refuse to labour. *Prov.* xxi. 25.

To vice industrious; but to nobler deeds
Timorous and *slothful*. *Milton.*

Flora commands those nymphs and knights,
Who liv'd in *slothful* ease and loose delights,
Who never acts of honour durst pursue,
The men inglorious knights, the ladies all untrue. *Dryden.*

The very soul of the *slothful* does effectually but lie drowsing in his body, and the whole man is totally given up to his senses. *L'Estrange.*

SLO'THFULLY. *adv.* [from *slothful*.] With sloth.

SLO'THFULNESS. *n. s.* [from *slothful*.] Idleness; laziness; sluggishness; inactivity.

To trust to labour without prayer, argueth impiety and prophaneness; it maketh light of the providence of God: and although it be not the intent of a religious mind, yet it is the fault of those men whose religion wanteth light of a mature judgment to direct it, when we join with our prayer *slothfulness* and neglect of convenient labour. *Hooker.*

Slothfulness casteth into a deep sleep, and an idle soul shall suffer hunger. *Prov.* xix. 15.

SLOUCH. *n. s.* [*sloff*, Danish, stupid.]

1. A downcast look; a depression of the head. In Scotland, an ungainly gait, as also the person whose gait it is.

Our doctor has every quality that can make a man useful; but, alas! he hath a sort of *slouch* in his walk. *Swift.*

2. A man who looks heavy and clownish.

Begin thy carrols then, thou vaunting *slouch*;
Be thine the oaken staff, or mine the pouch. *Gay.*

To SLOUCH. *v. n.* [from the noun.] To have a downcast clownish look.

SLO'VEN. *n. s.* [*sloef*, Dutch; *yslyvn*, Welsh, nasty, shabby.] A man indecently negligent of cleanliness; a man dirtily dressed.

The ministers came to church in handsome holiday apparel, and that himself did not think them bound by the law of God to go like *slovens*. *Hooker.*

Affect in things about thee cleanliness,
That all may gladly board thee as a flow'r:
Slovens take up their stock of noisomeness
Beforehand, and anticipate their last hour. *Herbert.*

For as when *slovens* do amiss
At others doors. *Hudibras.*

You

You laugh, half beau, half *sloven* if I stand;
My wig half powder, and all snuff my band. *Pope.*

SLO'VENLINESS. *n. s.* [from *slovenly.*] Indecent negligence of dress; neglect of cleanliness.

Slovenliness is the worst sign of a hard student, and civility the best exercise of the remiss; yet not to be exact in the phrase of compliment, or gestures of courtesy. *Wotton.*

SLO'VENLY. *adj.* [from *sloven.*] Negligent of dress; negligent of neatness; not neat; not cleanly.

Æsop at last found out a *slovenly* lazy fellow, lolling at his ease, as if he had nothing to do. *L'Estrange.*

SLO'VENLY. *adv.* [from *sloven.*] In a coarse inelegant manner.

As I hang my cloaths on somewhat *slovenly*, I no sooner went in but he frowned upon me. *Pope.*

SLO'VENRY. *n. s.* [from *sloven.*] Dirtiness; want of neatness.

Our gayness and our gilt are all besmirch'd
With rainy marching in the painful field:
There's not a piece of feather in our host,
And time hath worn us into *slovenry.* *Shakesp. H. V.*

SLOUGH. *n. s.* [ꞅloᵹ, Saxon.]

1. A deep miry place; a hole full of dirt.

The Scots were in a fallow field, whereinto the English could not enter, but over a cross ditch and a *slough*; in passing whereof many of the English horse were plunged, and some mired. *Hayward.*

The ways being foul, twenty to one,
He's here stuck in a *slough*, and overthrown. *Milton.*

A carter had laid his waggon fast in a *slough.* *L'Estrange.*

2. The skin which a serpent casts off at his periodical renovation.

Thy fates open their hands, let thy blood and spirit embrace them; and to inure thyself to what thou art like to be, cast thy humble *slough*, and appear fresh. *Shak. Twelfth Night.*

When the mind is quicken'd,
The organs, though defunct and dead before,
Break up their drowsy grave, and newly move,
With casted *slough* and fresh legerity. *Shakespeare.*

As the snake, roll'd in a flow'ry bank,
With shining checker'd *slough*, doth sting a child,
That for the beauty thinks it excellent. *Shak. Hen. VI.*

Oh let not sleep my closing eyes invade
In open plains, or in the secret shade,
When he, renew'd in all the speckl'd pride
Of pompous youth, has cast his *slough* aside;
And in his Summer liv'ry rolls along,
Erect and brandishing his forky tongue. *Dryden.*

The *slough* of an English viper, that is, the cuticula, they cast off twice every year, at spring and fall: the separation begins at the head, and is finished in twenty-four hours. *Grew.*

The body, which we leave behind in this visible world, is as the womb or *slough* from whence we issue, and are born into the other. *Grew's Cosmol.*

3. The part that separates from a foul sore.

At the next dressing I found a *slough* come away with the dressings, which was the sordes. *Wiseman on Ulcers.*

SLO'UGHY. *adj.* [from *slough.*] Miry; boggy; muddy.

That custom should not be allowed of cutting scraws in low grounds *sloughy* underneath, which turn into bog. *Swift.*

SLOW. *adj.* [ꞅlap, ꞅleap, Saxon; *sleeuw*, Frisick.]

1. Not swift; not quick of motion; not speedy; not having velocity; wanting celerity.

Me thou think'st not *slow*,
Who since the morning hour set out from heav'n,
Where God resides, and on mid-day arriv'd
In Eden, distance inexpressible. *Milton.*

Where the motion is so *slow* as not to supply a constant train of fresh ideas to the senses, the sense of motion is lost. *Locke.*

2. Late; not happening in a short time.

These changes in the heav'ns, though *slow*, produc'd
Like change on sea and land, sidereal blast. *Milton.*

3. Not ready; not prompt; not quick.

I am *slow* of speech, and a *slow* tongue. *Ex.* iv. 10.

Mine ear shall not be *slow*, mine eye not shut. *Milton.*

The *slow* of speech make in dreams unpremeditated harangues, or converse readily in languages that they are but little acquainted with. *Addison.*

4. Dull; inactive; tardy; sluggish.

Fix'd on defence, the Trojans are not *slow*
To guard their shore from an expected foe. *Dryden.*

5. Not hasty; acting with deliberation; not vehement.

The Lord is merciful, and *slow* to anger. *Common Prayer.*

He that is *slow* to wrath is of great understanding. *Prov.*

6. Dull; heavy in wit.

The politick and wise
Are sly *slow* things with circumspective eyes. *Pope.*

SLOW, in composition, is an adverb, *slowly.*

This *slow*-pac'd soul, which late did cleave
T' a body, and went but by the body's leave,
Twenty perchance or thirty mile a day,
Dispatches in a minute all the way
'Twixt heav'n and earth. *Donne.*

To the shame of *slow*-endeavouring art
Thy easy numbers flow. *Milton.*

This day's death denounc'd, if ought I see,
Will prove no sudden, but a *slow*-pac'd evil,
A long day's dying to augment our pain. *Milton's Par. Lost.*

For eight *slow*-circling years by tempests tost. *Pope.*

Some demon urg'd
T' explore the fraud with guile oppos'd to guile,
Slow-pacing thrice around th' insidious pile. *Pope.*

To SLOW. *v. a.* [from the adjective.] To omit by dilatoriness; to delay; to procrastinate. Not in use.

Now do you know the reason of this haste?
—I would I knew not why it should be *slow'd.* *Shakespeare.*

SLO'WLY. *adv.* [from *slow.*]

1. Not speedily; not with celerity; not with velocity.

The gnome rejoicing bears her gift away,
Spreads his black wings, and *slowly* mounts to day. *Pope.*

2. Not soon; not early; not in a little time.

The poor remnant of human seed peopled their country again *slowly*, by little and little. *Bacon.*

Our fathers bent their baneful industry
To check a monarchy that *slowly* grew;
But did not France or Holland's fate forsee,
Whose rising pow'r to swift dominion flew. *Dryden.*

We oft our *slowly* growing works impart,
While images reflect from art to art. *Pope.*

3. Not hastily; not rashly.

4. Not promptly; not readily.

5. Tardily; sluggishly.

The chapel of St. Laurence advances so very *slowly*, that 'tis not impossible but the family of Medicis may be extinct before their burial place is finished. *Addison on Italy.*

SLO'WNESS. *n. s.* [from *slow.*]

1. Smalness of motion; not speed; want of velocity; absence of celerity or swiftness.

Providence hath confined these human arts, that what any invention hath in the strength of its motion, is abated in the *slowness* of it; and what it hath in the extraordinary quickness of its motion, must be allowed for in the great strength that is required unto it. *Wilkins's Math. Magic.*

Motion is the absolute mode of a body, but swiftness or *slowness* are relative ideas. *Watts.*

2. Length of time in which any thing acts or is brought to pass; not quickness.

Tyrants use what art they can to increase the *slowness* of death. *Hooker.*

3. Dulness to admit conviction or affection.

Christ would not heal their infirmities, because of the hardness and *slowness* of their hearts, in that they believed him not. *Bentley's Sermons.*

4. Want of promptness; want of readiness.

5. Deliberation; cool delay.

6. Dilatoriness; procrastination.

SLO'WWORM. *n. s.* [ꞅlapẏꞃm, Saxon.] The blind worm; a small viper, venomous, but scarcely mortal.

Though we have found formed snakes in the belly of the cæcilia, or *slowworm*, yet may the viper emphatically bear the name. *Brown's Vulgar Errours.*

To SLU'BBER. *v. a.* [Probably from *lubber.*]

1. To do any thing lazily, imperfectly, or with idle hurry.

Nature shewed she doth not like men, who *slubber* up matters of mean account. *Sidney.*

Bassanio told him, he would make some speed
Of his return: he answer'd, do not so,
Slubber not business for my sake. *Shakesp. Merch. of Venice.*

As they are *slubbered* over, the malignity that remains will show itself in some chronick disease, or in some species of the *lues venerea.* *Wiseman's Surgery.*

2. To stain; to daub. [This seems to be from *slobber*, *slabber*, or *slaver.*]

You must be content to *slubber* the gloss of your new fortunes, with this more stubborn and boisterous expedition. *Shak.*

3. To cover coarsely or carelesly.

A man of secret ambitious ends, and proportionate counsels, smothered under the habit of a scholar, and *slubbered* over with a certain rude and clownish fashion, that had the semblance of integrity. *Wotton.*

SLU'BBERDEGULLION. *n. s.* [I suppose a cant word without derivation.] A paltry, dirty, sorry wretch.

Quoth she, although thou hast deserv'd,
Base *slubberdegullion*, to be serv'd
As thou did'st vow to deal with me,
If thou had'st got the victory. *Hudibras.*

SLUDGE. *n. s.* [I suppose from ꞅloᵹ, slough, Saxon.] Mire; dirt mixed with water.

The earth I made a mere soft *sludge* or mud. *Mortimer.*

SLUG. *n. s.* [*slug*, Danish, and *slock*, Dutch, signify a glutton, and thence one that has the sloth of a glutton.]

1. An idler; a drone; a slow, heavy, sleepy, lazy wretch.

Fie, what a *slug* is Hastings, that he comes not! *Shakesp.*

2. An hindrance; an obstruction.

Usury dulls and damps all improvements, wherein money would be stirring, if it were not for this *slug.* *Bacon.*

3. A kind of ſlow creeping ſnail.
4. [Slecȝ, an hammerhead, Saxon.] A cylindrical or oval piece of metal ſhot from a gun.

When fractures are made with bullets or *ſlugs*, there the ſcalp and cranium are driven in together. *Wiſeman's Surgery.*

As, forc'd from wind-guns, lead itſelf can fly,
And pond'rous *ſlugs* cut ſwiftly through the ſky. *Pope.*

To Slug. *v. n.* [from the noun.] To lie idle; to play the drone; to move ſlowly.

All he did was to deceive good knights,
And draw them from purſuit of praiſe and fame,
To *ſlug* in ſloth and ſenſual delights,
And end their days with irrenowned ſhame. *Fairy Queen.*

He lay not all night *ſlugging* in a cabbin under his mantle, but uſed commonly to keep others waking to defend their lives. *Spenſer.*

One went *ſlugging* on with a thouſand cares. *L'Eſtrange.*

Slu'ggard. *n. ſ.* [from *ſlug.*] An idler; a drone; an inactive lazy fellow.

Cry mercy, lords, and watchful gentlemen,
That you have ta'en a tardy *ſluggard* here. *Shakeſp. R. III.*

Up, up, ſays avarice; thou ſnor'ſt again,
Stretcheſt thy limbs; and yawn'ſt, but all in vain:
The tyrant lucre no denial takes;
At his command th' unwilling *ſluggard* wakes. *Dryden.*

Sprightly May commands our youth to keep
The vigils of her night, and breaks their *ſluggard* ſleep. *Dry.*

To Slu'ggardize. *v. a.* [from *ſluggard.*] To make idle; to make droniſh.

Rather ſee the wonders of the world abroad,
Than, living dully *ſluggardiz'd* at home,
Wear out thy youth with ſhapeleſs idleneſs. *Shakeſpeare.*

Slu'ggish. *adj.* [from *ſlug.*] Dull; drowſy; lazy; ſlothful; idle; inſipid; ſlow; inactive; inert.

Sluggiſh idleneſs, the nurſe of ſin,
Upon a ſlothful aſs he choſe to ride. *Fairy Queen.*

The dull billows, thick as troubled mire,
Whom neither wind out of their ſeat could force,
Nor tides did drive out of their *ſluggiſh* ſource. *Spenſer.*

One, bolder than the reſt,
With his broad ſword provok'd the *ſluggiſh* beaſt. *Waller.*

Matter, being impotent, *ſluggiſh*, and inactive, hath no power to ſtir or move itſelf. *Woodward.*

Slu'ggishly. *adv.* [from *ſluggiſh.*] Dully; not nimbly; lazily; idly; ſlowly.

Slu'ggishness. *n. ſ.* [from *ſluggiſh.*] Dulneſs; ſloth; lazineſs; idleneſs; inertneſs.

The moſt of mankind are inclined by her thither, if they would take the pains; no leſs than birds to fly, and horſes to run; which, if they loſe, it is thro' their own *ſluggiſhneſs*, and by that means become her prodigies, not her children. *B. Johnſ.*

It is of great moment to teach the mind to ſhake off its *ſluggiſhneſs*, and vigorouſly employ itſelf about what reaſon ſhall direct. *Locke.*

SLUICE. *n. ſ.* [*ſluyſe*, Dutch; *eſcluſe*, French; *ſcluſa*, Italian.] A watergate; a floodgate; a vent for water.

Two other precious drops that ready ſtood,
Each in their cryſtal *ſluice*, he ere they fell
Kiſs'd, as the gracious ſigns of ſweet remorſe,
And pious awe, that fear'd to have offended. *Milton.*

Divine Alpheus, who, by ſecret *ſluice*,
Stole under ſeas to meet his Arethuſe. *Milton.*

If we receive them all, they were more than ſeven; if only the natural *ſluices*, they were fewer. *Brown's Vulgar Errours.*

As waters from her *ſluices*, flow'd
Unbounded ſorrow from her eyes:
And ſent her wailings to the ſkies. *Prior.*

To Sluice. *v. a.* [from the noun.] To emit by floodgates.

Like a traitor coward,
Sluic'd out his inn'cent ſoul through ſtreams of blood. *Shak.*

Veins of liquid ore *ſluic'd* from the lake. *Milton.*

You wrong me, if you think I'll ſell one drop
Within theſe veins for pageants; but let honour
Call for my blood, I'll *ſluice* it into ſtreams;
Turn fortune looſe again to my purſuit,
And let me hunt her through embattl'd foes
In duſty plains; there will I be the firſt. *Dryd. Span. Fryar.*

Slu'icy. *adj.* [from *ſluice.*] Falling in ſtreams as from a ſluice or floodgate.

And oft whole ſheets deſcend of *ſluicy* rain,
Suck'd by the ſpongy clouds from off the main:
The lofty ſkies at once come pouring down,
The promis'd crop and golden labours drown. *Dryden.*

To SLU'MBER. *v. n.* [ſlumeꝛan, Saxon; *ſluymeren*, Dutch.]
1. To ſleep lightly; to be not awake nor in profound ſleep.

He that keepeth Iſrael ſhall neither *ſlumber* nor ſleep. *Pſ.*

Conſcience wakes deſpair that *ſlumber'd* *Milton.*

2. To ſleep; to repoſe. *Sleep* and *ſlumber* are often confounded.

God ſpeaketh, yet man perceiveth it not: in a dream, in a viſion of the night, when deep ſleep falleth upon men, in *ſlumberings* upon the bed. *Job* xxxiii. 15.

Have ye choſen this place,
After the toil of battle, to repoſe
Your wearied virtue, for the uſe you find
To *ſlumber* here. *Milton.*

3. To be in a ſtate of negligence and ſupineneſs.

To Slu'mber. *v. a.*
1. To lay to ſleep.
2. To ſtupify; to ſtun.

Then up he took the *ſlumbered* ſenſeleſs corſe,
And ere he could out of his ſwoon awake,
Him to his caſtle brought. *Fairy Queen.*

To honeſt a deed after it was done, or to *ſlumber* his conſcience in the doing, he ſtudied other incentives. *Wotton.*

Slu'mber. *n. ſ.* [from the verb.]
1. Light ſleep; ſleep not profound.

And for his dreams, I wonder he's ſo fond
To truſt the mock'ry of unquiet *ſlumbers*. *Shakeſp. R. III.*

From careleſſneſs it ſhall fall into *ſlumber*, and from a *ſlumber* it ſhall ſettle into a deep and long ſleep; 'till at laſt, perhaps, it ſhall ſleep itſelf into a lethargy, and that ſuch an one that nothing but hell and judgment ſhall awaken it. *South.*

Labour and reſt, that equal periods keep;
Obedient *ſlumbers* that can wake and weep. *Pope.*

2. Sleep; repoſe.

Boy! Lucius! faſt aſleep? It is no matter;
Enjoy the honey-heavy dew of *ſlumber*. *Shakeſ. Jul. Cæſ.*

Love denies
Reſt to my ſoul, and *ſlumber* to my eyes:
Three days I promis'd to attend my doom,
And two long days and nights are yet to come. *Dryden.*

Slu'mberous. } *adj.* [from *ſlumber.*]
Slu'mbery. }

1. Inviting to ſleep; ſoporiferous; cauſing ſleep.

The timely dew of ſleep,
Now falling with ſoft *ſlumb'rous* weight, inclines
Our eyelids. *Milton*

While penſive in the ſilent *ſlumb'rous* ſhade,
Sleep's gentle pow'rs her drooping eyes invade;
Minerva, life-like, on embodied air
Impreſs'd the form of Iphthema. *Pope's Odyſſey.*

There every eye with *ſlumb'rous* chains ſhe bound,
And daſh'd the flowing goblets to the ground. *Pope.*

2. Sleepy; not waking.

A great perturbation in nature! to receive at once the benefit of ſleep, and do the effects of watching: in this *ſlumbery* agitation, what have you heard her ſay? *Shakeſp. Macbeth.*

Slung. The preterite and participle paſſive of *ſling*.

Slunk. The preterite and participle paſſive of *ſlink*.

Silence accompany'd; for beaſt, and bird,
They to their graſſy couch, theſe to their neſts,
Were *ſlunk*. *Milton's Paradiſe Loſt, b.* iv.

Back to the thicket *ſlunk*
The guilty ſerpent, and well might; for Eve,
Intent now wholly on her taſte, nought elſe
Regarded. *Milton's Paradiſe Loſt.*

To SLUR. *v. a.* [*ſloorig*, Dutch, naſty; *ſloore*, a ſlut.]
1. To ſully; to ſoil; to contaminate.
2. To paſs lightly; to balk; to miſs.

The atheiſts laugh in their ſleeves, and not a little triumph to ſee the cauſe of theiſm thus betrayed by its profeſſed friends, and the grand argument *ſlurred* by them, and ſo their work done to their hands. *Cudworth.*

Studious to pleaſe the genius of the times,
With periods, points, and tropes he *ſlurs* his crimes;
He robb'd not, but he borrow'd from the poor,
And took but with intention to reſtore. *Dryden.*

3. To cheat; to trick.

What was the publick faith found out for,
But to *ſlur* men of what they fought for? *Hudibras.*

Come, ſeven's the main,
Cries Ganymede: the uſual trick:
Seven, *ſlur* a ſix; eleven, a nick. *Prior.*

Slur. *n. ſ.* [from the verb.] Faint reproach; ſlight diſgrace.

Here's an ape made a king, for ſhewing tricks; and the fox is then to put a *ſlur* upon him, in expoſing him for ſport to the ſcorn of the people. *L'Eſtrange.*

No one can rely upon ſuch an one, either with ſafety to his affairs, or without a *ſlur* to his reputation; ſince he that truſts a knave has no other recompence, but to be accounted a fool for his pains. *South's Sermons.*

SLUT. *n. ſ.* [*ſlodde*, Dutch.]
1. A dirty woman.

Cricket, to Windſor chimneys ſhalt thou leap:
Where fires thou find'ſt unrak'd, and hearths unſwept,
There pinch the maids as blue as bilberry;
Our radiant queen hates *ſluts* and ſluttery. *Shakeſpeare.*

The fallow ſkin is for the ſwarthy put,
And love can make a ſlattern of a *ſlut*. *Dryden.*

The veal's all rags, the butter's turn'd to oil;
And thus I buy good meat for *ſluts* to ſpoil. *King.*

2. A word of slight contempt to a woman.

Hold up, you *sluts*,
Your aprons mountant; you're not othable,
Although I know you'll swear. *Shakesp. Timon.*

The frogs were ready to leap out of their skins for joy, 'till one crafty old *slut* in the company advised them to consider a little better on't. *L'Estrange.*

SLU'TTERY. *n. s.* [from *slut.*] The qualities or practice of a slut.

Slut'ry, to such neat excellence oppos'd,
Should make desire vomit emptiness. *Shakesp. Cymbeline.*

Where fires thou find'st unrak'd, and hearths unswept,
There pinch the maids as blue as bilberry;
Our radiant queen hates sluts and *slutt'ry.* *Shakespeare.*

These make our girls their *sluttery* rue,
By pinching them both black and blue;
And put a penny in their shoe,
The house for cleanly sweeping. *Drayton.*

A man gave money for a black, upon an opinion that his swarthy colour was rather *sluttery* than nature, and the fault of his master that kept him no cleaner. *L'Estrange.*

SLU'TTISH. *adj.* [from *slut.*] Nasty; not nice; not cleanly; dirty; indecently negligent of cleanliness.

All preparations both for food and lodging such as would make one detest niggardness, it is so *sluttish* a vice. *Sidney.*

Albeit the mariners do covet store of cabbins, yet indeed they are but *sluttish* dens that breed sickness in peace, serving to cover stealths, and in fight are dangerous to tear men with their splinters. *Raleigh's Essays.*

Fortune's displeasure is but *sluttish*, if it smell so strongly as thou speak'st of: I will henceforth eat no fish of fortune's buttering. *Shakesp. All's well that ends well.*

The nastiness of that nation, and *sluttish* course of life, hath much promoted the opinion, occasioned by their servile condition at first, and inferior ways of parsimony ever since. *Brown.*

Slothful disorder fill'd his stable,
And *sluttish* plenty deck'd her table. *Prior.*

SLU'TTISHLY. *adv.* [from *sluttish.*] In a sluttish manner; nastily; dirtily.

SLU'TTISHNESS. *n. s.* [from *sluttish.*] The qualities or practice of a slut; nastiness; dirtiness.

That is only suitable in laying a foul complexion upon a filthy favour, setting forth both in *sluttishness.* *Sidney.*

I look on the instinct of this noisome and troublesome creature, the louse, of searching out foul and nasty clothes to harbour and breed in, as an effect of divine providence, designed to deter men and women from *sluttishness* and sordidness, and to provoke them to cleanliness and neatness. *Ray on the Creation.*

SLY. *adj.* [ſliδ, Saxon, slippery and metaphorically deceitful; *slægur*, Islandick.] Meanly artful; secretly insidious; cunning.

For my *sly* wyles and subtile craftiness,
The title of the kingdom I possess. *Hubberd's Tale.*

And for I doubt the Greekish monarch *sly*,
Will use with him some of his wonted craft. *Fairfax.*

His proud step he scornful turn'd,
And with *sly* circumspection. *Milton's Paradise Lost.*

Envy is a cursed plant: some fibres of it are rooted almost in every man's nature, and it works in a *sly* and imperceptible manner. *Watts.*

It is odious in a man to look *sly* and leering at a woman. *Clarissa.*

SLY'LY. *adv.* [from *sly.*] With secret artifice; insidiously.

To SMACK. *v. n.* [ſmæcꝃan, Saxon; *smacken*, Dutch.]

1. To have a taste; to be tinctured with any particular taste.
2. To have a tincture or quality infused.

All sects, all ages, *smack* of this vice, and he
To die for it! *Shakesp. Measure for Measure.*

He is but a bastard to the time,
That doth not *smack* of observation. *Shakesp. King John.*

3. To make a noise by separation of the lips strongly pressed together, as after a taste.
4. To kiss with a close compression of the lips, so as to be heard when they separate.

She kiss'd with *smacking* lip the snoring lout;
For such a kiss demands a pair of gloves. *Gay.*

He gives a *smacking* buss. *Pope.*

To SMACK. *v. a.*

1. To kiss.

So careless flowers, strow'd on the waters face,
The curled whirlpools suck, *smack*, and embrace,
Yet drown them. *Donne.*

2. To make any quick smart noise.

SMACK. *n. s.* [*smaeck*, Dutch; from the verb.]

1. Taste; savour.
2. Tincture; quality from something mixed.

The child, that sucketh the milk of the nurse, learns his first speech of her; the which, being the first inured to his tongue, is ever after most pleasing unto him, insomuch, that though he afterwards be taught English, yet the *smack* of the first will always abide with him. *Spenser.*

Your lordship, though not clean past your youth, hath yet some *smack* of age in you, some relish of the saltness of time, and have a care of your health. *Shakesp. Henry IV.*

It caused the neighbours to rue, that a petty *smack* only of popery opened a gap to the oppression of the whole. *Carew.*

As the Pythagorean soul
Runs through all beasts, and fish and fowl,
And has a *smack* of ev'ry one,
So love does, and has ever done. *Hudibras.*

3. A pleasing taste.

Stack pease upon hovel;
To cover it quickly let owner regard,
Lest dove and the cadow there finding a *smack*,
With ill stormy weather do perish thy stack. *Tusser.*

4. A small quantity; a taste.

Trembling to approach
The little barrel, which he fears to broach,
H' essays the wimble, often draws it back,
And deals to thirsty servants but a *smack.* *Dryden's Pers.*

5. The act of parting the lips audibly, as after a pleasing taste.
6. A loud kiss.

He took
The bride about the neck, and kist her lips
With such a clamorous *smack*, that at the parting
All the church echo'd. *Shakesp. Taming of the Shrew.*

I saw the lecherous citizen turn back
His head, and on his wife's lip steal a *smack.* *Donne.*

7. [Snacca, Saxon; *snecra*, Islandick.] A small ship.

SMALL. *adj.* [ſmall, Saxon; *smal*, Dutch; *smaar*, Islandick.]

1. Little in quantity; not great.

For a *small* moment have I forsaken thee, but with great mercies will I gather thee. *Is.* liv. 7.

Death only this mysterious truth unfolds,
The mighty soul how *small* a body holds. *Dryden's Juven.*

All numeration is but still the adding of one unit more, and giving to the whole together a distinct name, whereby to distinguish it from every *smaller* or greater multitude of units. *Locke.*

The ordinary *smallest* measure we have is looked on as an unit in number. *Locke.*

The danger is less when the quantity of the fluids is too *small*, than when it is too great; for a *smaller* quantity will pass where a larger cannot, but not contrariwise. *Arbuthnot.*

Good cooks cannot abide fiddling work: such is the dressing of *small* birds, requiring a world of cookery. *Swift.*

2. Slender; exile; minute.

After the earthquake a fire, and after the fire a still *small* voice. 1 *Kings* xix. 12.

Your sin and calf I burnt, and ground it very *small*, 'till it was as *small* as dust. *Deutr.* ix. 21.

Those wav'd their limber fans
For wings, and *smallest* lineaments exact. *Milton.*

Small grained sand is esteemed the best for the tenant, and the large for the landlord and land. *Mortimer's Husbandry.*

3. Little in degree.

There arose no *small* stir about that way. *Acts* xix. 23.

4. Little in importance; petty; minute.

Is it a *small* matter that thou hast taken my husband? *Gen.*

Narrow man being fill'd with little shares,
Courts, city, church, are all shops of *small* wares;
All having blown to sparks their noble fire,
And drawn their sound gold ingot into wire. *Donne.*

Some mens behaviour is like a verse, wherein every syllable is measured: how can a man comprehend great matters that breaketh his mind too much to *small* observations? *Bacon.*

5. Little in the principal quality, as *small* beer; not strong; weak.

Go down to the cellar to draw ale or *small* beer. *Swift.*

SMALL. *n. s.* [from the adjective.] The small or narrow part of any thing. It is particularly applied to the part of the leg below the calf.

Her garment was cut after such a fashion, that though the length of it reached to the ancles, yet in her going one might sometimes discern the *small* of her leg. *Sidney.*

Into her legs I'd have love's issues fall,
And all her calf into a gouty *small.* *Suckling.*

His excellency, having mounted on the *small* of my leg, advanced forwards. *Gulliver's Travels.*

SMA'LLAGE. *n. s.* [from *small age*, because it soon withers. *Skinner.*] A plant. It is a species of parsley, and a common weed by the sides of ditches and brooks. *Miller.*

Smallage is raised by slips or seed, which is redish, and pretty big, of a roundish oval figure; a little more full and rising on one side than the other, and streaked from one end to the other. *Mortimer's Husbandry.*

SMA'LLCOAL. *n. s.* [*small* and *coal.*] Little wood coals used to light fires.

A *smallcoal* man, by waking one of these distressed gentlemen, saved him from ten years imprisonment. *Spectator.*

When *smallcoal* murmurs in the hoarser throat,
From smutty dangers guard thy threaten'd coat. *Gay.*

SMA'LLCRAFT. *n. s.* [*small* and *craft.*] A little vessel below the denomination of ship.

Shall he before me sign, whom t'other day
A *smallcraft* vessel hither did convey;
Where stain'd with prunes, and rotten figs, he lay. *Dryd.*

SMALLPO'X. *n. s.* [*small* and *pox.*] An eruptive distemper of great malignity; *variolæ*.

He fell sick of the *smallpox*. *Wiseman.*

SMA'LLY. *adv.* [from *small.*] In a little quantity; with minuteness; in a little or low degree.

A child that is still, and somewhat hard of wit, is never chosen by the father to be made a scholar, or else when he cometh to the school, is *smally* regarded. *Ascham.*

SMA'LNESS. *n. s.* [from *small.*]

1. Littleness; not greatness.

The parts in glass are evenly spread, but are not so close as in gold; as we see by the easy admission of light, and by the *smalness* of the weight. *Bacon's Natural History.*

2. Littleness; want of bulk; minuteness; exility.

Whatsoever is invisible, in respect of the fineness of the body, or the *smalness* of the parts, or subtilty of the motion, is little enquired. *Bacon's Natural History.*

The *smalness* of the rays of light may contribute very much to the power of the agent by which they are refracted. *Newt.*

3. Want of strength; weakness.

SMALT. *n. s.*

A beautiful blue substance, produced from two parts of zaffre being fused with three parts common salt, and one part potash. *Hill on Fossils.*

To make a light purple, mingle ceruse with logwood water; and moreover turnsoil with lac mingled with *smalt* of bice. *Peacham.*

SMA'RAGDINE. *adj.* [*smaragdinus*, Latin.] Made of emerald; resembling emerald.

SMART. *n. s.* [ꞅmeoꞃꞇa, Saxon; *smert*, Dutch; *smarta*, Swedish.]

1. Quick, pungent, lively pain.

Then her mind, though too late, by the *smart*, was brought to think of the disease. *Sidney.*

2. Pain, corporal or intellectual.

Mishaps are master'd by advice discreet,
And counsel mitigates the greatest *smart*. *Fairy Queen.*

It increased the *smart* of his present sufferings, to compare them with his former happiness. *Atterbury.*

To SMART. *v. n.* [ꞅmeoꞃꞇan, Saxon; *smerten*, Dutch.]

1. To feel quick lively pain.

When a man's wounds cease to *smart*, only because he has lost his feeling, they are nevertheless mortal. *South.*

Human blood, when first let, is mild, and will not make the eye or a fresh wound *smart*. *Arbuthnot.*

2. To feel pain of body or mind.

He that is surety for a stranger shall *smart* for it. *Prov.*

No creature *smarts* so little as a fool.
Let peals of laughter, Codrus! round thee break,
Thou unconcern'd can'st hear the mighty crack. *Pope.*

SMART. *adj.* [from the noun.]

1. Pungent; sharp; causing smart.

How *smart* a lash that speech doth give my conscience? *Shakespeare.*

To the fair he fain would quarter show,
His tender heart recoils at every blow;
If unawares he gives too *smart* a stroke,
He means but to correct, and not provoke. *Granville.*

2. Quick; vigorous; active.

That day was spent in *smart* skirmishes, in which many fell. *Clarendon.*

This sound proceeded from the nimble and *smart* percussions of the ambient air, made by the swift and irregular motions of the particles of the liquors. *Boyle.*

3. Producing any effect with force and vigour.

After show'rs,
The stars shine *smarter*, and the moon adorns,
As with unborrow'd beams, her sharpen'd horns. *Dryden.*

4. Acute; witty.

It was a *smart* reply that Augustus made to one that ministred this comfort of the fatality of things: this was so far from giving any ease to his mind, that it was the very thing that troubled him. *Tillotson.*

5. Brisk; vivacious; lively.

You may see a *smart* rhetorician turning his hat in his hands, during the whole course of his harangue. A deaf man would think he was cheapening a beaver. *Addison.*

SMART. *n. s.* A fellow affecting briskness and vivacity. A cant word.

SMA'RTLY. *adv.* [from *smart.*] After a smart manner; sharply; briskly; vigorously; wittily.

The art, order, and gravity of those proceedings, where short, severe, constant rules were set, and *smartly* pursued, made them less taken notice of. *Clarendon.*

SMA'RTNESS. *n. s.* [from *smart.*]

1. The quality of being smart; quickness; vigour.

What interest such a *smartness* in striking the air hath in the production of sound, may in some measure appear by the motion of a bullet, and that of a switch or other wand, which produce no sound, if they do but slowly pass through the air; whereas if the one do smartly strike the air, and the other be shot out of a gun, the celerity of their percussions on the air puts it into an undulating motion, which, reaching the ear, produces an audible noise. *Boyle.*

2. Liveliness; briskness; wittiness.

I defy all the clubs to invent a new phrase, equal in wit, humour, *smartness* or politeness, to my set. *Swift.*

SMATCH. *n. s.* [corrupted from *smack.*]

1. Taste; tincture; twang.

Thou art a fellow of a good respect;
Thy life hath had some *smatch* of honour in't. *Shakespeare.*

Some nations have a peculiar guttural or nasal *smatch* in their language. *Holder's Elements of Speech.*

These salts have somewhat of a nitrous taste, but mixt with a *smatch* of a vitriolick. *Grew.*

2. [*Cœruleo*, Latin.] A bird.

To SMA'TTER. *v. n.* [It is supposed to be corrupted from *smack* or *taste.*]

1. To have a slight taste; to have a slight, superficial, and imperfect knowledge.

Such a practice gives a slight *smattering* of several sciences, without any solid knowledge. *Watts.*

Since, by a little *smattering* in learning, and great conceit of himself, he has lost his religion, may he find it again by harder study and an humbler mind. *Bentley.*

2. To talk superficially or ignorantly.

In proper terms, such as men *smatter*,
When they throw out and miss the matter. *Hudibras.*

Of state affairs you cannot *smatter*;
Are aukward when you try to flatter. *Swift.*

SMA'TTER. *n. s.* [from the verb.] Superficial or slight knowledge.

All other sciences were extinguished during this empire, excepting only a *smatter* of judicial astrology. *Temple.*

SMA'TTERER. *n. s.* [from *smatter.*] One who has a slight or superficial knowledge.

These few who preserve any rudiments of learning, are, except one or two *smatterers*, the clergy's friends. *Swift.*

To SMEAR. *v. a.* [ꞅmeꞃan, Saxon; *smeeren*, Dutch.]

1. To overspread with something viscous and adhesive; to besmear.

If any such be here, that love this painting,
Wherein you see me *smear'd*,
If any think brave death outweighs bad life,
Let him wave thus. *Shakespeare's Othello.*

Then from the mountain hewing timber tall,
Began to build a vessel of huge bulk,
Smear'd round with pitch. *Milton.*

Smear'd as she was with black Gorgonean blood,
The fury sprang above the Stygian flood. *Dryden.*

2. To soil; to contaminate.

Why had I not, with charitable hand,
Took up a beggar's issue at my gates?
Who *smeered* thus, and mir'd with infamy,
I might have said no part of it is mine. *Shakespeare.*

SMEA'RY. *adj.* [from *smear.*] Dawby; adhesive.

A *smeary* foam works o'er my grinding jaws,
And utmost anguish shakes my lab'ring frame. *Rowe.*

SMEATH. *n. s.* A sea fowl.

To SMEETH. or *smutch.* *v. a.* [ꞅmiðe, Saxon.] To smoke; to blacken with smoke.

SME'GMATICK. *adj.* [σμῆγμα.] Soapy; detersive. *Dict.*

To SMELL. *v. a.* [Of this word the etymology is very obscure. *Skinner*, the most acute of all etymologists, derives it from *smoel*, warm, Dutch; because smells are encreased by heat.]

1. To perceive by the nose.

Their neighbours hear the same musick, or *smell* the same perfumes with themselves: for here is enough. *Collier.*

2. To find out by mental sagacity.

The horse *smelt* him out, and presently a crochet came in his head how to countermine him. *L'Estrange.*

To SMELL. *v. n.*

1. To strike the nostrils.

The king is but a man as I am: the violet *smells* to him as it doth to me; all his senses have but human conditions. *Shak.*

The daintiest smells of flowers are out of those plants whose leaves *smell* not. *Bacon's Natural History.*

2. To have any particular scent.

Honey in Spain *smelleth* apparently of the rosemary or orange, from whence the bee gathereth it. *Bacon.*

A work of this nature is not to be performed upon one leg, and should *smell* of oil if duly handled. *Brown.*

If you have a silver saucepan, and the butter *smells* of smoak, lay the fault upon the coals. *Swift.*

3. To have a particular tincture or smack of any quality.

My unsoil'd name, the austereness of my life,
Will so your accusation overweigh,
That you shall stifle in your own report,
And *smell* of calumny. *Shakespeare.*

Down with the nose, take the bridge quite away
Of him that his particular to forefend,
Smells from the general weal. *Shakespeare.*

A man

A man ſo *ſmelling* of the people's lee,
The court receiv'd him firſt for charity. *Dryden.*

4. To practiſe the act of ſmelling.

Whoſoever ſhall make like unto that, to *ſmell* thereto, ſhall be cut off. *Exod.* xxx. 38.

I had a mind to know, whether they would find out the treaſure, and whether *ſmelling* enabled them to know what is good for their nouriſhment. *Addiſon's Spectator.*

SMELL. *n. ſ.* [from the verb.]

1. Power of ſmelling; the ſenſe of which the noſe is the organ.

Next, in the noſtrils ſhe doth uſe the *ſmell*,
As God the breath of life in them did give;
So makes he now this pow'r in them to dwell,
To judge all airs, whereby we breathe, and live. *Davies.*

2. Scent; power of affecting the noſe.

The ſweeteſt *ſmell* in the air is the white double violet, which comes twice a-year. *Bacon.*

All ſweet *ſmells* have joined with them ſome earthy or crude odours. *Bacon.*

Pleaſant *ſmells* are not confined unto vegetables, but found in divers animals. *Brown's Vulgar Errours.*

There is a great variety of *ſmells*, though we have but a few names for them: the *ſmell* of a violet and of muſk, both ſweet, are as diſtinct as any two *ſmells*. *Locke.*

SME'LLER. *n. ſ.* [from *ſmell.*] He who ſmells.

SME'LLFEAST. *n. ſ.* [*ſmell* and *feaſt.*] A paraſite; one who haunts good tables.

The ant lives upon her own, honeſtly gotten; whereas the fly is an intruder, and a common *ſmellfeaſt* that ſpunges upon other people's trenchers. *L'Eſtrange.*

SMELT. The preterite and participle paſſ. of *ſmell.*

SMELT. *n. ſ.* [ꞅmelt, Saxon.] A ſmall ſea fiſh.

Of round fiſh there are brit, ſprat, barn, *ſmelts.* *Carew.*

To SMELT. *v. a.* [*ſmalta*, Iſlandick; *ſmelten*, Dutch.] To melt oar, ſo as to extract the metal.

A ſort of earth, of a duſky red colour, found chiefly in iron mines. Some of this earth contains as much iron as to render it worth *ſmelting.* *Woodward.*

SME'LTER. *n. ſ.* [from *ſmelt.*] One who melts oar.

The *ſmelters* come up to the aſſayers. *Woodward on Foſſils.*

To SMERK. *v. a.* [ꞅmercian, Saxon.] To ſmile wantonly.

Certain gentlemen of the gown, whoſe aukward, ſpruce, prim, ſneering, and *ſmirking* countenances have got good preferment by force of cringing. *Swift.*

SMERKY. } *adj.* Nice; ſmart; jaunty.
SMIRK. }

Seeſt, how bragg yon bullock bears,
So *ſmirk*, ſo ſmooth his pricked ears:
His horns been as brade as rainbow bent,
His dew-lap as lith as laſs of Kent. *Spenſer.*

SME'RLIN. *n. ſ.* A fiſh. *Ainſworth.*

SMI'CKET. *n. ſ.* [Diminutive of *ſmock*, *ſmocket*, *ſmicket.*] The under garment of a woman.

To SMIGHT. For *ſmite.*

As when a griffon, ſeized of his prey,
A dragon fierce encountreth in his flight,
Through wideſt air making his idle way,
That would his rightful ravin rend away:
With hideous horror both together *ſmight*,
And ſouce ſo ſore that they the heavens affray. *Fa. Queen.*

To SMILE. *v. n.* [*ſmuylen*, Dutch.]

1. To contract the face with pleaſure; to expreſs gladneſs by the countenance.

I would, while it was *ſmiling* in my face,
Have pluckt my nipple from his boneleſs gums. *Shakeſpeare.*

The goddeſs of the mountain *ſmiled* upon her votaries, and cheared them in their paſſage to her palace. *Tatler.*

'Twas what I ſaid to Crags and Child,
Who prais'd my modeſty, and *ſmil'd.* *Pope.*

2. To expreſs ſlight contempt.

Our king replied, which ſome will *ſmile* at now, but according to the learning of that time. *Camden.*

3. To look gay or joyous.

Let their heirs enrich their time
With *ſmiling* plenty and fair proſp'rous days. *Shakeſpeare.*

All things *ſmil'd*,
Birds on the branches warbling. *Milton.*

4. To be favourable; to be propitious.

Then let me not let paſs
Occaſion which now *ſmiles.* *Milton.*

SMILE. *n. ſ.* [from the verb.] A ſlight contraction of the face; a look of pleaſure, or kindneſs.

I frown upon him, yet he loves me ſtill.—
—Oh that your frowns would teach my *ſmiles* ſuch ſkill.
Shakeſpeare's Midſummer Night's Feaſt.

No man marks the narrow ſpace
'Twixt a priſon and a *ſmile.* *Wotton.*

Sweet intercourſe
Of looks and *ſmiles*: for *ſmiles* from reaſon flow,
To brute denied, and are of love the food. *Milton.*

SMI'LINGLY. *adv.* [from *ſmiling.*] With a look of pleaſure.

His flaw'd heart,
'Twixt two extremes of paſſion, joy and grief,
Burſt *ſmilingly.* *Shakeſpeare's King Lear.*

Carneades ſtopping him *ſmilingly*, told him, we are not ſo forward to loſe good company *Boyle.*

To SMILT. *v. n.* [corrupted from *ſmelt*, or *melt.*]

Having too much water, many corns will *ſmilt*, or have their pulp turned into a ſubſtance like thick cream. *Mortimer.*

To SMIRCH. *v. a.* [from *murk* or *murcky.*] To cloud; to duſk; to ſoil.

I'll put myſelf in poor and mean attire,
And with a kind of umber *ſmirch* my face. *Shakeſpeare.*

Like the ſhaven Hercules in the *ſmirch* worm-eaten tapeſtry. *Shakeſpeare.*

To SMIRK. See SMERK.

SMIT. The participle paſſive of *ſmite.*

Fir'd with the views this glitt'ring ſcene diſplays,
And *ſmit* with paſſion for my country's praiſe,
My artleſs reed attempts this lofty theme,
Where ſacred Iſis rolls her ancient ſtream. *Tickell.*

To SMITE. *v. a.* preterite *ſmote*; participle paſſ. *ſmit*, *ſmitten.* [ꞅmitan, Saxon; *ſmijten*, Dutch.]

1. To ſtrike; to reach with a blow.

So ſweet a kiſs the golden ſun gives not
To thoſe freſh morning drops upon the roſe,
As thy eye beams, when their freſh rays have *ſmote*
The night of dew that on my cheeks down flows. *Shak.*

I have *ſmitten* mine hand at thy diſhoneſt gain. *Ezek.*

2. To kill; to deſtroy.

The ſervants of David had *ſmitten* of Benjamin's men, ſo that three hundred and threeſcore died. 2 *Sam.* ii. 31.

God *ſmote* him for his errour, and he died. 2 *Sam.* vi.

3. To afflict; to chaſten A ſcriptural expreſſion.

Let us not miſtake God's goodneſs, nor imagine, becauſe he *ſmites* us, that we are forſaken by him. *Wake.*

4. To blaſt.

5. To affect with any paſſion.

I wander where the muſes haunt,
Clear ſpring, or ſhady grove, or ſunny hill,
Smit with the love of ſacred ſong. *Milton.*

See what the charms that *ſmite* the ſimple heart,
Not touch'd by nature, and not reach'd by art. *Pope.*

Smit with the love of ſiſter arts we came,
And met congenial, mingling flame with flame. *Pope.*

To SMITE. *v. n.* To ſtrike; to collide.

The heart melteth, and the knees *ſmite* together. *Nahum.*

SMI'TER. *n. ſ.* [from *ſmite.*] He who ſmites.

I gave my back to the *ſmiters*, and my cheeks to them that pluck off the hair. *Iſa.* l. 6.

SMITH. *n. ſ.* [ꞅmiꝺ, Saxon; *ſmeth*, German; *ſmid*, Dutch; from ꞅmitan, Saxon, to beat.]

1. One who forges with his hammer; one who works in metals.

He doth nothing but talk of his horſe, and can ſhoe him. I am afraid, my lady, his mother, played falſe with a *ſmith.*
Shakeſpeare's Merchant of Venice.

Lawleſs man, the anvil dares profane,
And forge that ſteel by which a man is ſlain:
Which earth at firſt for plough ſhares did afford;
Nor yet the *ſmith* had learn'd to form a ſword. *Tate.*

The ordinary qualities obſervable in iron, or a diamond, that make their true complex idea, a *ſmith* or a jeweler commonly knows better than a philoſopher. *Locke.*

2. He that makes or effects any thing.

The doves repented, though too late,
Become the *ſmiths* of their own fooliſh fate. *Dryden.*

SMI'THCRAFT. *n. ſ.* [ꞅmiꝺcꞃæꝼꞇ, Sax.] The art of a ſmith.

Inventors of paſtorage, *ſmithcraft*, and muſick. *Raleigh.*

SMI'THERY. *n. ſ.* [from *ſmith.*] The ſhop of a ſmith.

SMI'THING. *n. ſ.* [from *ſmith.*] *Smithing* is an art manual, by which an irregular lump, or ſeveral lumps of iron is wrought into an intended ſhape. *Moxon's Mechanical Exerciſe.*

SMI'THY. *n. ſ.* [ꞅmiꝺꝺe, Saxon.] The ſhop of a ſmith.

His blazing locks ſent forth a crackling ſound,
And hiſs'd, like red hot iron, within the *ſmithy* drown'd.
Dryden.

SMITT. *n. ſ.* The fineſt of the clayey ore, made up into balls, they uſe for marking of ſheep, and call it *ſmitt.* *Woodward.*

SMI'TTEN. The participle paſſive of *ſmite.* Struck; blaſted; killed; affected with paſſion.

And the flax and the barley was *ſmitten*, but the wheat and the rye not. *Exod.* ix. 31.

How agree the kettle and the earthen pot together? for if the one be *ſmitten* againſt the other, it ſhall be broken. *Ecclus.*

The third part of the ſun was *ſmitten.* *Rev.* viii. 12.

We did eſteem him ſtricken, *ſmitten* of God and afflicted. *Iſa.* liii. 4.

Tempt not the Lord thy God, he ſaid, and ſtood:
But Satan *ſmitten* with amazement fell. *Milton.*

By the advantages of a good perſon and a pleaſing converſation, he made ſuch an impreſſion in her heart as could not be effaced; and he was himſelf no leſs *ſmitten* with Conſtantia. *Addiſon.*

SMOCK. *n. s.* [ſmoc, Saxon.]

1. The under garment of a woman; a shift.

Her body covered with a light taffeta garment, so cut, as the wrought *smock* came through it in many places. *Sidney.*

How do'st thou look now? oh ill-starr'd wench!
Pale as thy *smock*! when we shall meet at compt;
This look of thine will hurl my soul from heav'n. *Shakesp.*

Their apparel was linnen breeches, and over that a *smock* close girt unto them with a towel. *Sandys.*

Though Artemisia talks by fits,
Of councils, classicks, fathers, wits;
Reads Malbranche, Boyle, and Locke:
Yet in some things, methinks, she fails,
'Twere well, if she would pair her nails,
And wear a cleaner *smock*. *Swift.*

2. *Smock* is used in a ludicrous kind of composition for any thing relating to women.

At *smock* treason, matron, I believe you;
And if I were your husband; but when I
Trust to your cob-web bosoms any other,
Let me there die a fly, and feast you, spider. *Ben. Johnson.*

Plague on his *smock*-loyalty!
I hate to see a brave bold fellow sotted,
Made sour and senseless, turn'd to whey by love. *Dryden.*

SMOCKFA'CED. *adj.* [*smock* and *face.*] Palefaced; maidenly.]

Old chiefs reflecting on their former deeds,
Disdain to rust with batter'd invalids;
But active in the foremost ranks appear,
And leave young *smockfac'd* beaux to guard the rear. *Fenton.*

SMOKE. *n. s.* [*ys-mwg*, Welsh; ſmec, ſmoec, Saxon; *smoock*, Dutch.] The visible effluvium, or sooty exhalation from any thing burning.

She might utter out some *smoke* of those flames wherewith else she was not only burned, but smothered. *Sidney.*

May you a better feast never behold,
You knot of mouth-friends: *smoke*, and lukewarm water,
Is your perfection. *Shakespeare.*

Stand off, and let me take the air,
Why should the *smoke* pursue the fair? *Cleaveland.*

He knew 'twas caused by *smoke*, but not by flame. *Cowley.*

All involv'd with stench and *smoke*.
As *smoke* that rises from the kindling fires, *Milton.*
Is seen this moment, and the next expires. *Prior.*

Smoke passing through flame cannot but grow red hot, and red hot *smoke* can appear no other than flame. *Newton.*

To SMOKE. *v. n.* [from the noun.]

1. To emit a dark exhalation by heat.

When the sun went down, a *smoking* furnace and a burning lamp passed between those pieces. *Gen.* xv. 17.

Brave Macbeth
Disdaining fortune, with his brandish'd steel,
Which *smoak'd* with bloody execution,
Like valour's minion carved out his passage,
'Till he had fac'd the slaves. *Shakespeare's Macbeth.*

Queen Margaret saw
Thy murd'rous faulchion *smoking* in his blood. *Shakespeare.*

To him no temple stood nor altar *smok'd*. *Milton.*

For Venus, Cytherea was invok'd,
Altars for Pallas to Athena *smok'd*. *Granville.*

2. To burn; to be kindled. A scriptural term.

The anger of the Lord shall *smoak* against that man. *Deut.*

3. To move with such swiftness as to kindle; to move very fast so as to raise dust like smoke.

Aventinus drives his chariot round;
Proud of his steeds he *smokes* along the field;
His father's hydra fills the ample shield. *Dryden's Æn.*

With hasty hand the ruling reins he drew,
He lash'd the coursers, and the coursers flew;
Beneath the bending yoke alike they held
Their equal pace, and *smoak'd* along the field. *Pope.*

4. To smell, or hunt out.

He hither came t'observe and *smoke*
What courses other riskers took. *Hudibras.*

I began to *smoke* that they were a parcel of mummers, and wondred that none of the Middlesex justices took care to lay some of them by the heels. *Addison's Freeholder.*

5. To use tobacco.

6. To suffer to be punished.

Maugre all the world will I keep safe,
Or some of you shall *smoke* for it in Rome. *Shakespeare.*

To SMOKE. *v. a.*

1. To scent by smoke, or dry in smoke.

Frictions of the back-bone with flannel, *smoaked* with penetrating aromatical substances, have proved effectual. *Arbuthnot.*

2. To smell out; to find out.

He was first *smok'd* by the old lord Lafeu; when his disguise and he is parted, tell me what a sprat you shall find him? *Shakespeare's All's well that ends well.*

Tom Tattle passes for an impertinent, and Will. Trippet begins to be *smoked*, in case I continue this paper. *Addis. Spect.*

3. To sneer; to ridicule to the face.

Smoke the fellow there. *Congreve.*

To SMOKE-*dry.* *v. a.* [*smoke* and *dry.*] To dry by smoke.

Smoke-dry the fruit, but not if you plant them. *Mortimer.*

SMO'KER. *n. s.* [from *smoke.*]

1. One that dries or perfumes by smoke.

2. One that uses tobacco.

SMO'KELESS. *adj.* [from *smoke.*] Having no smoke.

Tenants with sighs the *smokeless* tow'rs survey,
And turn th' unwilling steed another way. *Pope.*

SMO'KY. *adj.* [from *smoke.*]

1. Emitting smoke; fumid.

O he's as tedious
As a tir'd horse, or as a railing wife,
Worse than a *smoky* house. *Shakespeare.*

Victorious to the top aspires,
Involving all the wood in *smoky* fires. *Dryden.*

2. Having the appearance or nature of smoke.

London appears in a morning drowned in a black cloud, and all the day after smothered with *smoky* fog, the consequence whereof proves very offensive to the lungs. *Harvey.*

If blast septentrional with brushing wings
Sweep up the *smoky* mists, and vapours damp,
Then woe to mortals. *Philips.*

3. Noisome with smoke.

Courtesy
Is sooner found in lowly sheds,
With *smoky* rafters, than in tap'stry halls
And courts of princes. *Milton.*

Morpheus, the humble god, that dwells
In cottages and *smoky* cells,
Hates gilded roofs and beds of down;
And though he fears no prince's frown,
Flies from the circle of a crown. *Denham*

SMOOTH. [ſmeð, ſmoeð, Saxon; *mwyth*, Welsh.]

1. Even on the surface; not rough; level; having no asperities.

Behold Esau my brother is a hairy man, and I am a *smooth* man. *Gen.* xxvii. 11.

Missing thee, I walk unseen,
On the dry *smooth*-shaven green,
To behold the wandring moon,
Riding near her highest noon. *Milton.*

The outlines must be *smooth*, imperceptible to the touch, and even without eminences or cavities. *Dryden.*

Nor box nor limes, without their use,
Smooth-grain'd, and proper for the turner's trade:
Which curious hands may carve and steel with ease invade. *Dryden.*

2. Evenly spread; glossy.

He for the promis'd journey bids prepare
The *smooth*-hair'd horses, and the rapid car. *Pope.*

3. Equal in pace; without starts or obstruction.

By the hand he took me rais'd,
And over fields and waters, as in air,
Smooth-sliding without step. *Milton.*

The fair-hair'd queen of love
Descends *smooth*-gliding from the courts above. *Pope.*

4. Flowing; soft; not harsh.

Smooth Adonis from his rock
Ran purple to the sea. *Milton.*

When sage Minerva rose,
From her sweet lips *smooth* elocution flows. *Gay.*

So, Dick adept, tuck back thy hair;
And I will pour into thy ear
Remarks, which none did e'er disclose,
In *smooth*-pac'd verse or hobling prose. *Prior.*

5. Bland; mild; adulatory.

The subtle fiend,
Though inly stung with anger and disdain,
Dissembled, and this answer *smooth* return'd. *Milt. Par. Reg.*

This *smooth* discourse and mild behaviour oft
Conceal a traitor. *Addison.*

He was *smooth*-tongued, gave good words, and seldom lost his temper. *Arbuthnot's Hist. of J. Bull.*

The madding monarchs to compose
The Pylian prince, the *smooth*-speech'd Nestor, rose. *Tickel.*

To SMOOTH. *v. a.* [from the adjective.]

1. To level; to make even on the surface.

This man's a flatt'rer? if one be,
So are they all; for every greeze of fortune
Is *smooth'd* by that below. *Shakespeare.*

The carpenter encouraged the goldsmith, and he that *smootheth* with the hammer him that smote the anvil. *Isa.* xli.

Now on the wings of winds our course we keep;
For God had *smooth'd* the waters of the deep. *Pope's Odyss.*

2. To work into a soft uniform mass.

It brings up again into the mouth that which it had swallowed, and chewing it, grinds and *smooths* it, and afterwards swallows it into another stomach. *Ray on the Creation.*

The board on which we sit
Is not so smooth as are thy verses, *Swift.*

3. To make easy; to rid from obstructions.

Thou, Abelard! the last sad office pay,
And *smooth* my passage to the realms of day. *Pope.*

4. To

4. To make flowing; to free from harshness.

In their motions harmony divine
So *smooths* her charming tones. *Milton.*

All your muse's softer art display,
Let Carolina *smooth* the tuneful lay;
Lull with Amelia's liquid name the Nine,
And sweetly flow through all the royal line. *Pope.*

5. To palliate; to soften.

Had it been a stranger, not my child,
To *smooth* his fault, I would have been more mild. *Shakesp.*

6. To calm; to mollify.

Now breathe we, lords; good fortune bids us pause,
And *smooth* the frowns of war with peaceful looks. *Shakesp.*

Each perturbation *smooth'd* with outward calm. *Milton.*

Smiling she seem'd, and full of pleasing thought,
From ocean as she first began to rise,
And *smooth'd* the ruffled seas, and clear'd the skies. *Dryden.*

7. To ease.

Restor'd it soon will be; the means prepar'd,
The difficulty *smooth'd*, the danger shar'd:
Be but yourself. *Dryden.*

8. To flatter; to soften with blandishments.

Because I cannot flatter and look fair,
Smile in men's faces, *smooth*, deceive and cog,
Duck with French nods, and apish courtesy,
I must be held a rancorous enemy. *Shakespeare.*

To SMO'OTHEN. *v. a.* [A bad word among mechanicks for *smooth.*] To make even and smooth.

With edged grooving tools they cut down and *smoothen* the extuberances left. *Moxon's Mech. Exer.*

SMO'OTHFACED. *adj.* [*smooth* and *face.*] Mild looking; having a soft air.

O, shall I say I thank you, gentle wife?
—Not so, my lord; a twelve-month and a day,
I'll mark no words that *smoothfac'd* wooers say. *Shakespeare.*

Let their heirs
Enrich their time to come with *smoothfac'd* peace,
With smiling plenty, and fair prosp'rous days. *Shak. R.* III.

SMO'OTHLY. *adv.* [from *smooth.*]

1. Not roughly; evenly.
2. With even glide.

The musick of that murm'ring spring
Is not so mournful as the strains you sing;
Nor rivers winding through the vales below
So sweetly warble, or so *smoothly* flow. *Pope.*

3. Without obstruction; easily; readily.

Had Joshua been mindful, the fraud of the Gibeonites could not so *smoothly* have past unespied 'till there was no help. *Hook.*

4. With soft and bland language.

SMO'OTHNESS. *n. s.* [from *smooth.*]

1. Evenness on the surface; freedom from asperity.

The purling, which proceeds of inequality, is bred between the *smoothness* of the inward surface of the pipe, which is wet, and the rest that remaineth dry. *Bacon's Natural History.*

A countryman feeding his flock by the seaside, it was so delicate a fine day, that the *smoothness* of the water tempted him to set up for a merchant. *L'Estrange.*

The nymph is all into a laurel gone,
The *smoothness* of her skin remains alone. *Dryden.*

2. Softness or mildness on the palate.

Fallacious drink! ye honest men beware,
Nor trust its *smoothness*; the third circling glass
Suffices virtue. *Philips.*

3. Sweetness and softness of numbers.

As French has more fineness and *smoothness* at this time, so it had more compass, spirit, and force in Montaigne's age. *Temp.*

Virgil, though smooth, where *smoothness* is required, is so far from affecting it, that he rather disdains it; frequently using synalephas, and concluding his sense in the middle of his verse. *Dryden.*

4. Blandness and gentleness of speech.

She is too subtle for thee; and her *smoothness*,
Her very silence, and her patience,
Speak to the people, and they pity her. *Shakespeare.*

SMOTE. The preterite of *smite.*

Death with a trident *smote.* *Milton.*

To SMO'THER. *v. a.* [ꞅmoꞃan, Saxon.]

1. To suffocate with smoke, or by exclusion of the air.

She might give passage to her thoughts, and so as it were utter out some smoke of those flames, wherewith else she was not only burned but *smothered.* *Sidney.*

We *smother'd*
The most replenished sweet work of nature,
That from the prime creation e'er she fram'd. *Shakespeare.*

We are enow yet living in the field,
To *smother* up the English in our throngs. *Shakesp. Hen.* V.

She was warmed with the graceful appearance of the hero: she *smothered* those sparkles out of decency, but conversation blew them up into a flame. *Dryden's Æn. Dedication.*

The helpless traveller, with wild surprise,
Sees the dry desart all around him rise,
And *smother'd* in the dusty whirlwind dies. *Addison's Cato.*

2. To suppress.

Lewd and wicked custom, beginning perhaps at the first amongst few, afterwards spreading into greater multitudes; and so continuing; from time may be of force, even in plain things, to *smother* the light of natural understanding. *Hooker.*

SMO'THER. *n. s.* [from the verb.]

1. A state of suppression.

This unfortunate prince, after a long *smother* of discontent, and hatred of many of his nobility and people, breaking forth at times into seditions, was at last distressed by them. *Bacon.*

A man were better relate himself to a statue, than suffer his thoughts to pass in *smother.* *Bacon.*

Nothing makes a man suspect much, more than to know little; and therefore men should procure to know more, and not to keep their suspicions in *smother.* *Bacon's Essays.*

2. Smoke; thick dusk.

Thus must I from the smoke into the *smother*,
From tyrant duke into a tyrant brother. *Shakespeare.*

Where yon disorder'd heap of ruin lies,
Stones rent from stones, where clouds of dust arise,
Amid' that *smother* Neptune holds his place. *Dryd. Æn.*

The greater part enter only like mutes to fill the stage, and spend their taper in smoke and *smother.* *Collier on Fame.*

To SMO'THER. *v. n.* [from the noun.]

1. To smoke without vent.

Hay and straw have a very low degree of heat; but yet close and *smothering*, and which drieth not. *Bacon's Nat. History.*

2. To be suppressed or kept close.

The advantage of conversation is such, that, for want of company, a man had better talk to a post than let his thoughts lie smoking and *smothering.* *Collier of Friendship.*

SMO'ULDERING. } [This word seems a participle; but I know
SMO'ULDRY. } not whether the verb *smoulder* be in use: ꞅmoꞃan, Saxon, to smother; *smoel*, Dutch, hot.] Burning and smoking without vent.

None can breathe, nor see, nor hear at will,
Through *smouldry* cloud of duskish stinking smoke,
That th' only breath him daunts who hath escap'd the stroke. *Fairy Queen.*

In some close pent room it crept along,
And, *smould'ring* as it went, in silence fed;
'Till th' infant monster, with devouring strong,
Walk'd boldly upright with exalted head. *Dryden.*

SMUG. *adj.* [*smuck*, dress, *smucken*, to dress, Dutch.] Nice; spruce; dressed with affectation of niceness, but without elegance.

There I have a bankrupt for a prodigal, who dares scarce shew his head on the Rialto; a beggar, that used to come so *smug* upon the mart. *Shak. Merchant of Venice.*

He who can make your visage less horrid, and your person more *smug*, is worthy some good reception. *Spectator.*

To SMU'GGLE. *v. a.* [*smockelen*, Dutch.] To import or export goods without paying the customs.

SMU'GGLER. *n. s.* [from *smuggle.*] A wretch, who, in defiance of justice and the laws, imports or exports goods either contraband or without payment of the customs.

SMU'GLY. *adv.* [from *smug.*] Neatly; sprucely.

Lilies and roses will quickly appear,
And her face will look wond'rous *smugly.* *Gay.*

SMU'GNESS. *n. s.* [from *smug.*] Spruceness; neatness.

SMUT. *n. s.* [ꞅmitta, Saxon; *smette*, Dutch.]

1. A spot made with soot or coal.
2. Must or blackness gathered on corn; mildew.

Farmers have suffered by smutty wheat, when such will not sell for above five shillings a bushel; whereas that which is free from *smut* will sell for ten. *Mortimer's Husbandry.*

3. Obscenity.

To SMUT. *v. a.* [from the noun.]

1. To stain; to mark with soot or coal.

He is far from being *smutted* with the soil of atheism. *More.*

A fuller had invitation from a collier to live with him: he gave him a thousand thanks; but, says he, as fast as I make any thing clean, you'll be *smutting* it again. *L'Estrange.*

The inside is so *smutted* with dust and smoke, that neither the marble, silver, nor brass works shew themselves. *Addis. on Italy.*

I am wonderfully pleased to see my tenants play their innocent tricks, and *smutting* one another. *Addison.*

2. To taint with mildew.

Mildew falleth upon corn, and *smutteth* it. *Bacon.*

To SMUT. *v. n.* To gather must.

White red-eared wheat is good for clays, and bears a very good crop, and seldom *smuts.* *Mortimer.*

To SMUTCH. *v. a.* [from *smut.*] To black with smoke.

Has't *smutch'd* thy nose?
They say it's a copy out of mine. *Shakesp. Winter's Tale.*

Have you seen but a bright lily grow,
Before rude hands have touch'd it?
Ha' you mark'd but the fall o' the snow,
Before the soil hath *smutch'd* it? *Ben. Johnson's Underwoods.*

SMU'TTILY. *adv.* [from *smutty.*]

1. Blackly; smokily.
2. Obscenely.

SMU'TTINESS. *n. s.* [from *smutty.*]
1. Soil from smoke.
My vines and peaches, upon my best south walls, were apt to a soot or *smuttiness* upon their leaves and upon their fruits, which were good for nothing. *Temple.*
2. Obscenenefs.
SMU'TTY. *adj.* [from *smut.*]
1. Black with smoke or coal.
The *smutty* grain,
With sudden blaze diffus'd, inflames the air. *Milton.*
The *smutty* wainscot full of cracks. *Swift.*
He was a *smutty* dog yesterday, and cost me near two hours to wash the ink off his face. *Pope.*
2. Tainted with mildew.
Smutty corn will sell dearer at one time than the clean at another. *Locke.*
3. Obscene; not modest.
The place is a censure of a profane and *smutty* passage in the Old Batchelor. *Collier.*
SNACK. *n. s.* [from *snatch.*] A share; a part taken by compact.
If the master gets the better on't, they come in for their *snack.* *L'Estrange.*
For four times talking, if one piece thou take,
That must be cantled, and the judge go *snack.* *Dryden.*
All my demurs but double his attacks;
At last he whispers, "Do, and we go *snacks.*" *Pope.*
SNA'COT *n. s.* A fish. *Ainsworth.*
SNA'FFLE. *n. s.* [*snavel*, Dutch, the nose.] A bridle which crosses the nose.
The third o' th' world is your's, which with a *snaffle*
You may pace easy; but not such a wife. *Shakespeare.*
Sooth him with praise;
This, from his weaning, let him well be taught,
And then betimes in a soft *snaffle* wrought. *Dryden's Georg.*
To SNA'FFLE. *v. a.* [from the noun.] To bridle; to hold in a bridle; to hold; to manage.
SNAG. *n. s.* [Of this word I know not the etymology or original.]
1. A jag, or sharp protuberance.
The one her other leg had lame,
Which with a staff, all full of little *snags*,
She did disport, and impotence her name. *Fairy Queen.*
The coat of arms,
Now on a naked *snag* in triumph born,
Was hung on high. *Dryden's Æn.*
2. A tooth left by itself, or standing beyond the rest.
In China none hold women sweet,
Except their *snags* are black as jet:
King Chihu put nine queens to death,
Convict on statute, iv'ry teeth. *Prior.*
SNA'GGED. } *adj.* [from *snag.*] Full of snags; full of sharp
SNA'GGY. } protuberances; shooting into sharp points.
His stalking steps are stay'd
Upon a *snaggy* oak, which he had torn
Out of his mother's bowels, and it made
His mortal mace, wherewith his foemen he dismay'd. *Spens.*
Naked men belabouring one another with *snagged* sticks, or dully falling together by the ears at fisty-cuffs. *More.*
SNAIL. *n. s.* [snæȝl, Saxon; *snegel*, Dutch.]
1. A slimy animal which creeps on plants, some with shells on their backs.
I can tell why a *snail* has a house.—Why?—Why, to put's head in; not to give it away to his daughters, and leave his horns without a case. *Shakes. King Lear.*
Fearful commenting
Is leaden servitor to dull delay;
Delay leads impotent and *snail* pac'd beggary. *Shak. R.* III.
The patch is kind enough, but a huge feeder:
Snail slow in profit, but he sleeps by day
More than the wild cat. *Shakespeare.*
Seeing the *snail*, which every where doth roam,
Carrying his own house still, still is at home,
Follow, for he is easy-pac'd, this *snail*
Be thine own palace, or the world's thy gaol. *Donne.*
A river *snail*-shell decayed, shewed spar within. *Woodward.*
There may be as many ranks of beings in the invisible world superior to us, as we ourselves are superior to all the ranks of being beneath us in this visible world, even though we descend below the *snail* and the oyster. *Watts.*
2. A name given to a drone from the slow motion of a snail.
Why prat'st thou to thyself, and answer'st not?
Dromio, thou drone, thou *snail*, thou slug, thou sot! *Shak.*
SNA'IL-CLAVER, or *Snail-trefoil.* *n. s.* An herb. *Ainsworth.*
SNAKE. *n. s.* [snaca, Saxon; *snake*, Dutch.] A serpent of the oviparous kind, distinguished from a viper. The snake's bite is harmless. *Snake* in poetry is a general name for a viper.
Glo'ster's shew beguiles him;
As the *snake*, roll'd in a flow'ry bank,
With shining checker'd slough, doth sting a child,
That for the beauty thinks it excellent. *Shakes. Hen.* VI.

We have scotch'd the *snake*, not kill'd it:
She'll close, and be herself; whilst our poor malice
Remains in danger of her former teeth. *Shakesp. Macbeth.*
The parts must have their outlines in waves, resembling the gliding of a *snake* upon the ground: they must be smooth and even. *Dryden's Dufresnoy.*
Nor chalk, nor crumbling stones, the food of *snakes*
That work in hollow earth their winding tracks. *Dryden.*
SNA'KEROOT. *n. s.* [*snake* and *root.*] A species of birthwort growing in Virginia and Carolina. See RATTLESNAKE-ROOT.
SNA'KESHEAD *Iris.* *n. s.* [*hermodactylus*, Latin.] A plant.
The characters are: it hath a lily-shaped flower, of one leaf, shaped exactly like an iris; but has a tuberose root, divided into two or three dugs, like oblong bulbs. *Miller.*
SNA'KEWEED, or *Bistort.* *n. s.* [*bistorta*, Latin.] A plant.
It flowers in May; and, if the season proves moist, will continue to produce new spikes of flowers 'till August: it may be propagated by planting the roots in a moist shady border, and will soon furnish the ground with plants. *Miller.*
SNA'KEWOOD. *n. s.* [from *snake* and *wood.*]
What we call *snakewood* is properly the smaller branches of the root of a tall strait tree growing in the island of Timor, and other parts of the East. It has no remarkable smell; but is of an intensely bitter taste. The Indians are of opinion, that it is a certain remedy for the bite of the hooded serpent, and from thence its name of *lignum colubrinum*, or *snakewood.* We very seldom use it. *Hill's Mat. Med.*
SNA'KY. *adj.* [from *snake.*]
1. Serpentine; belonging to a snake; resembling a snake.
Venomous tongue, tipt with vile adder's sting,
Of that self kind with which the furies fell
Their *snaky* heads do comb. *Spenser.*
The true lovers knot had its original from *nodus Herculaneus*, or Hercules's knot, resembling the *snaky* complication in the caduceus, or rod of Hermes. *Brown's Vulgar Errours.*
So to the coast of Jordan he directs
His easy steps, girded with *snaky* wiles. *Milton's Par. Reg.*
2. Having serpents.
Look, look unto this *snaky* rod,
And stop your ears against the charming god. *Ben. Johnson.*
In his hand
He took caduceus, his *snaky* wand. *Hubberd's Tale.*
What was that *snaky*-headed gorgon shield
That wise Minerva wore, unconquer'd virgin,
Wherewith she freez'd her foes to congeal'd stone? *Milton.*
His flying hat was fasten'd on his head;
Wings on his heels were hung, and in his hand
He holds the virtue of the *snaky* wand. *Dryden.*
To SNAP. *v. a.* [The same with *knap.*]
1. To break at once; to break short.
If the chain of necessity be no stronger, but that it may be *snapped* so easily in sunder; if his will was no otherwise determined from without himself, but only by the signification of your desire, and my modest intreaty, then we may conclude, human affairs are not always governed by absolute necessity. *Bramh. against Hobbs.*
Light is broken like a body, as when 'tis *snapped* in pieces by a tougher body. *Digby.*
Dauntless as death, away he walks;
Breaks the doors open, *snaps* the locks;
Searches the parlour, chamber, study,
Nor stops 'till he has culprit's body. *Prior.*
2. To strike with a knacking noise, snap, or sharp knap.
The bowzy sire
First shook from out his pipe the seeds of fire,
Then *snapt* his box. *Dunciad.*
3. To bite.
A gentleman passing by a coach, one of the horses *snapt* off the end of his finger. *Wiseman's Surgery.*
All mungrel curs bawl, snarl, and *snap*, where the foe flies before him. *L'Estrange.*
A notion generally received, that a lion is dangerous to all women who are not virgins, may have given occasion to a foolish report, that my lion's jaws are so contrived as to *snap* the hands of any of the female sex, who are not thus qualified. *Addison's Spectator.*
He *snaps* deceitful air with empty jaws,
The subtle hare darts swift beneath his paws. *Gay.*
4. To catch suddenly and unexpectedly.
Sir Richard Graham tells the marquis he would *snap* one of the kids, and make some shift to carry him close to their lodgings. *Wotton.*
Some with a noise and greasy light
Are *snapt*, as men catch larks at night. *Butler.*
You should have thought of this before you was taken; for now you are in no danger to be *snapt* singing again. *L'Estr.*
Did I not see you, rascal, did I not!
When you lay snug to *snap* young Damon's goat? *Dryden.*
Belated seem on watch to lie,
And *snap* some cully passing by. *Swift.*

5. [*Snappen*,

5. [*Snappen*, Dutch.] To treat with sharp language.

Capoch'd your rabbins of the synod,
And *snapp'd* their canons with a why not. *Hudibras.*

A surly ill-bred lord
That chides and *snaps* her up at every word. *Granville.*

To Snap. *v. n.*

1. To break short; to fall asunder.

Note the ship's sicknesses, the mast
Shak'd with an ague, and the hold and waist
With a salt dropsy clogg'd; and our tacklings
Snapping, like to too high-stretch'd treble strings. *Donne.*

The backbone is divided into so many vertebres for commodious bending, and not one intire rigid bone, which, being of that length, would have been often in danger of *snapping* in sunder. *Ray on the Creation.*

If your steel be too hard, that is, too brittle, if it be a spring, it will not bow; but with the least bending it will *snap* asunder. *Moxon's Mech. Exer.*

The makers of these needles should give them a due temper; for if they are too soft they will bend, and if they are too brittle they *snap*. *Sharp's Surgery.*

2. To make an effort to bite with eagerness.

If the young dace be a bait for the old pike, I see no reason but I may *snap* at him. *Shakesp. Henry IV.*

We *snap* at the bait without ever dreaming of the hook that goes along with it. *L'Estrange.*

Towzer *snaps*
At people's heels with frothy chaps. *Swift.*

Snap. *n. s.* [from the verb.]

1. The act of breaking with a quick motion.
2. A greedy fellow.

He had no sooner said out his say, but up rises a cunning *snap*, then at the board. *L'Estrange.*

3. A quick eager bite.

With their bills, thwarted crosswise at the end, they would cut an apple in two at one *snap*. *Carew.*

4. A catch; a theft.

Sna'pdragon, or *Calf's snout*. *n. s.* [*antirrhinum*, Latin.]

1. A plant.
2. A kind of play, in which brandy is set on fire, and raisins thrown into it, which those who are unused to the sport are afraid to take out; but which may be safely snatched by a quick motion, and put blazing into the mouth, which being closed, the fire is at once extinguished.

Sna'pper. *n. s.* [from *snap*.] One who snaps.

My father named me Autolicus, being letter'd under Mercury; who, as I am, was likewise a *snapper* up of unconsider'd trifles. *Shakesp. Winter's Tale.*

Sna'ppish. *adj.* [from *snap*.]

1. Eager to bite.

The *snappish* cur, the passenger's annoy,
Close at my heel with yelping treble flies. *Swift.*

They lived in the temple; but were such *snappish* curs, that they frighted away most of the votaries. *Spectator.*

2. Peevish; sharp in reply.

Sna'ppishly. *adv.* [from *snappish*.] Peevishly; tartly.

Sna'ppishness. *n. s.* [from *snappish*.] Peevishness; tartness.

Sna'psack. *n. s.* [*snappsack*, Swedish.] A soldier's bag.

Snare. *n. s.* [*snara*, Swedish and Islandick; *snare*, Danish; *snoor*, Dutch.]

1. Any thing set to catch an animal; a gin; a net.

O poor hapless nightingale, thought I,
How sweet thou sing'st, how near the deadly *snare*. *Milton.*

2. Any thing by which one is intrapped or intangled.

This I speak for your own profit, not that I may cast a *snare* upon you. 1 *Cor.* vii. 35.

A fool's mouth is his destruction, and his lips are the *snare* of his soul. *Prov.* xviii. 7.

Propound to thyself a constant rule of living, which though it may not be fit to observe scrupulously, lest it become a *snare* to thy conscience, or endanger thy health, yet let not thy rule be broken. *Taylor's Rule of living holy.*

For thee ordain'd a help, became thy *snare*. *Milton.*

Beauty, wealth, and wit,
And prowess, to the pow'r of love submit;
The spreading *snare* for all mankind is laid,
And lovers all betray, or are betray'd. *Dryden.*

To Snare. *v. a.* [from the noun.] To intrap; to intangle.

Glo'ster's shew
Beguiles him, as the mournful crocodile
With sorrow *snares* relenting passengers. *Shakesp. H. VI.*

The wicked is *snared* in the work of his own hands. *Ps.* ix.

Warn all creatures from thee
Henceforth, lest that too heav'nly form, pretended
To hellish falshood, *snare* them. *Milton's Paradise Lost.*

To SNARL. *v. n.* [*snarren*, Dutch.]

1. To growl as an angry animal; to gnarre.

What! were you *snarling* all before I came,
Ready to catch each other by the throat,
And turn you all your hatred now on me? *Shakesp. R. III.*

He is born with teeth!
And so I was; which plainly signify'd
That I should *snarl*, and bite, and play the dog. *Shak. H. VI.*

The she's even of the savage herd are safe:
All, when they *snarl* or bite, have no return
But courtship from the male. *Dryden's Don Sebastian.*

Now, for the bare pick'd bone of majesty,
Doth dogged war bristle his angry crest,
And *snarleth* in the gentle eyes of peace. *Shakesp. K. John.*

An angry cur
Snarls while he feeds. *Dryd. and Lee's Oedipus.*

2. To speak roughly; to talk in rude terms.

'Tis malicious and unmanly to *snarl* at the little lapses of a pen, from which Virgil himself stands not exempted. *Dryden.*

The honest farmer and his wife,
Two years declin'd from prime of life,
Had struggled with the marriage-noose,
As almost ev'ry couple does:
Sometimes my plague! sometimes my darling!
Kissing to-day, to-morrow *snarling*. *Prior.*

Where hast thou been *snarling* odious truths, and entertaining company with discourse of their diseases? *Congreve.*

To Snarl. *v. a.* To intangle; to embarrass. I know not that this sense is well authorised.

Confused *snarled* consciences render it difficult to pull out thread by thread. *Decay of Piety.*

Sna'rler. *n. s.* [from *snarl*.] One who snarls; a growling, surly, quarrelsome, insulting fellow.

Should stupid libels grieve your mind,
You soon a remedy may find;
Lie down obscure, like other folks,
Below the lash of *snarlers* jokes. *Swift.*

Sna'ry. *adj.* [from *snare*.] Intangling; insidious.

Spiders in the vault their *snary* webs have spread. *Dryden.*

Snast. *n. s.* The snuff of a candle.

It first burned fair, 'till some part of the candle was consumed, and the sawdust gathering about the *snast*; but then it made the *snast* big and long, and burn duskishly, and the candle wasted in half the time of the wax pure. *Bacon's Nat. History.*

To SNATCH. *v. a.* [*snacken*, Dutch]

1. To seize any thing hastily.

A virtuous mind should rather wish to depart this world with a kind of treatable dissolution, than to be suddenly cut off in a moment; rather to be taken than *snatched* away from the face of the earth. *Hooker.*

Death,
So *snatch'd*, will not exempt us from the pain. *Milton.*

Life's stream hurries all too fast:
In vain sedate reflections we would make,
When half our knowledge we must *snatch*, not take. *Pope.*

She *snatch'd* a sheet of Thule from her bed:
Sudden she flies, and whelms it o'er the pyre;
Down sink the flames. *Pope's Dunciad.*

They, sailing down the stream,
Are *snatch'd* immediate by the quick-ey'd trout
Of darting salmon. *Thomson's Summer.*

2. To transport or carry suddenly.

He had scarce performed any part of the office of a bishop in the diocess of London, when he was *snatched* from thence, and promoted to Canterbury. *Clarendon.*

Oh nature!
Inrich me with the knowledge of thy works,
Snatch me to heaven. *Thomson's Autumn.*

To Snatch. *v. n.* To bite, or catch eagerly at something.

Lords will not let me: if I had a monopoly on't, they would have part on't; nay, the ladies too will be *snatching*. *Shakesp. King Lear.*

He shall *snatch* on the right hand, and be hungry. *Is.* ix. 20.

Lycus, swifter of his feet,
Runs, doubles, winds and turns, amidst the war;
Springs to the walls, and leaves his foes behind,
And *snatches* at the beam he first can find. *Dryden's Æn.*

Snatch. *n. s.* [from the verb.]

1. A hasty catch.
2. A short fit of vigorous action.

After a shower to weeding a *snatch*;
More easily weed with the root to dispatch. *Tusser.*

3. A small part of any thing; a broken part.

She chaunted *snatches* of old tunes,
As one incapable of her own distress. *Shakesp. Hamlet.*

In this work attempts will exceed performances, it being composed by *snatches* of time, as medical vacations would permit. *Brown's Vulgar Errours.*

4. A broken or interrupted action; a short fit.

The *snatches* in his voice,
And burst of speaking, were as his. *Shakesp. Cymbeline.*

They move by fits and *snatches*; so that it is not conceivable how they conduce unto a motion, which, by reason of its perpetuity, must be regular and equal. *Wilkins's Dædalus.*

We have often little *snatches* of sunshine and fair weather in the most uncomfortable parts of the year. *Spectator.*

5. A quip; a shuffling answer.

Come, leave your *snatches*, and yield me a direct answer. *Shakesp. Measure for Measure.*

SNA'TCHER. *n. s.* [from *snatch.*] One that snatches, or takes any thing in haste.

They of those marches
Shall be a wall sufficient to defend
Our inland from the pilfering borderers.
——We do not mean the coursing *snatchers* only,
But fear the main intendment of the Scot. *Shakesp. H. V.*

SNA'TCHINGLY. *adv.* [from *snatching.*] Hastily; with interruption.

To SNEAK. *v. n.* [snican, Saxon; *snige*, Danish.]

1. To creep slily; to come or go as if afraid to be seen.

Once the eagle, England, being in prey,
To her unguarded nest the weazel, Scot,
Comes *sneaking*, and so sucks her princely eggs. *Shakespeare.*

Sneak not away, sir; for the friar and you
Must have a word anon: lay hold on him. *Shakespeare.*

Discover'd, and defeated of your prey,
You skulk'd behind the fence, and *sneak'd* away. *Dryden.*

I ought not to turn my back, and to *sneak* off in silence, and leave the truth to lie baffled, bleeding, and slain. *Watts.*

He *sneak'd* into the grave,
A monarch's half and half a harlot's slave. *Dunciad.*

Are you all ready? Here's your musick here:
Author, *sneak* off; we'll tickle you, my dear. *Moore.*

2. To behave with meanness and servility; to crouch; to truckle.

I need salute no great man's threshold, *sneak* to none of his friends to speak a good word for me to my conscience. *South.*

Nothing can support minds drooping and *sneaking*, and inwardly reproaching them, from a sense of their own guilt, but to see others as bad. *South's Sermons.*

When int'rest calls off all her *sneaking* train,
When all th' oblig'd desert, and all the vain,
She waits, or to the scaffold, or the cell,
When the last ling'ring friend has bid farewel. *Pope.*

Tom struts a soldier, open, bold, and brave;
Will *sneaks* a scriv'ner, an exceeding knave. *Pope.*

SNE'AKER. *n. s.* A large vessel of drink.

I have just left the right worshipful and his myrmidons about a *sneaker* of five gallons. *Spectator.*

SNE'AKING. *participial adj.* [from *sneak.*]

1. Servile; mean; low.

2. Covetous; niggardly; meanly parcimonious.

SNE'AKINGLY. *adv.* [from *sneaking.*] Meanly; servilely.

Do all things like a man, not *sneakingly*:
Think the king sees thee still. *Herbert.*

While you *sneakingly* submit,
And beg our pardon at our feet,
Discourag'd by your guilty fears
To hope for quarter for your ears. *Hudibras.*

SNE'AKUP. *n. s.* [from *sneak.*] A cowardly, creeping, insidious scoundrel. Obsolete.

The prince is a jack, a *sneakup*; and, if he were here, I would cudgel him like a dog, if he would say so. *Shak. H. IV.*

To SNEAP. *v. a.* [This word seems a corruption of *snib*, or of *snap*, to reprimand. Perhaps *snap* is in that sense from *snib*, *snibbe*, Danish.

Men shulde him *snibbe* bitterly. *Chaucer.*]

1. To reprimand; to check.

2. To nip.

What may
Breed upon our absence, may there blow
No *sneaping* winds at home. *Shakespeare.*

SNEAP. *n. s.* [from the verb.] A reprimand; a check.

My lord, I will not undergo this *sneap* without reply: you call honourable boldness impudent sauciness: if a man will court'sy and say nothing, he is virtuous. *Shakesp. Henry IV.*

To SNEB. *v. a.* [Properly to *snib.* See SNEAP.] To check; to chide; to reprimand.

Which made this foolish briar wax so bold,
That on a time he cast him to scold,
And *snebbe* the good oak, for he was old. *Spenser.*

To SNEER. *v. n.* [This word is apparently of the same family with *snore* and *snort.*]

1. To show contempt by looks: *naso suspendere adunco.*

2. To insinuate contempt by covert expressions.

The wolf was by, and the fox in a *sneering* way advised him not to irritate a prince against his subjects. *L'Estrange.*

I could be content to be a little *sneered* at in a line, for the sake of the pleasure I should have in reading the rest. *Pope.*

If there has been any thing expressed with too much severity, it will fall upon those *sneering* or daring writers of the age against religion, who have left reason and decency. *Watts.*

3. To utter with grimace.

I have not been *sneering* fulsome lies, and nauseous flattery, at a little tawdry whore. *Congreve.*

4. To show aukward mirth.

I had no power over one muscle in their faces, though they *sneered* at every word spoken by each other. *Tatler.*

SNEER. *n. s.* [from the verb.]

1. A look of contemptuous ridicule.

Did not the *sneer* of more impartial men
At sense and virtue, balance all agen. *Pope.*

2. An expression of ludicrous scorn.

Socrates or Cæsar might have a fool's coat clapt upon them, and in this disguise neither the wisdom of the one nor the majesty of the other could secure them from a *sneer*. *Watts.*

To SNEEZE. *v. n.* [nieṡan, Saxon; *niesen*, Dutch.] To emit wind audibly by the nose.

If one be about to *sneeze*, rubbing the eyes 'till tears run will prevent it; for that the humour descending to the nostrils is diverted to the eyes. *Bacon.*

If the pain be more intense and deeper within amongst the membranes, there will be an itching in the palate and nostrils, with frequent *sneezing*. *Wiseman's Surgery.*

To thee Cupid *sneez'd* aloud;
And every lucky omen sent before,
To meet thee landing on the Spartan shore. *Dryden.*

If any thing oppress the head, it hath a power to free itself by *sneezing*. *Ray on the Creation.*

Violent *sneezing* produceth convulsions in all the muscles of respiration: so great an alteration can be produced only by the tickling of a feather; and if the action of *sneezing* should be continued by some very acrid substance, it will produce headach, universal convulsions, fever, and death. *Arbuthnot.*

An officer put the sharp end of his half-pike a good way up into my nostril, which tickled my nose like a straw, and made me *sneeze* violently. *Gulliver's Travels.*

SNEEZE. *n. s.* [from the verb.] Emission of wind audibly by the nose.

I heard the rack
As earth and sky would mingle; but
These flaws, though mortals fear them
As dangerous to the pillar'd frame of heav'n,
Are to the main as wholsome as a *sneeze*
To man's less universe, and soon are gone. *Milt. Par. Reg.*

We read in Godignus, that upon a *sneeze* of the emperor of Monomotapa, there past acclamations successively through the city. *Brown's Vulgar Errours.*

SNE'EZEWORT. *n. s.* [*ptarmica*, Latin.] A plant.

It hath radiated flowers, whose disk consists of many florets; but the borders are composed of half florets: the embryoes are lodged in the flowercup, which is scaly, each of which becomes one slender seed. *Miller.*

SNET. *n. s.* [Among hunters.] The fat of a deer. *Dict.*

SNEW. The old preterite of *To snow.* *Dict.*

To SNIB. *v. a.* [*snibbe*, Danish. See SNEAP.] To check; to nip; to reprimand.

Asked for their pass by every squib,
That list at will them to revile or *snib.* *Hubberd's Tale.*

SNICK *and Snee. n. s.* A combat with knives.

Among the Dunkirkers, where *snick and snee* was in fashion, a boatswain with some of our men drinking together, became quarrelsome: one of our men beat him down; then kneeling upon his breast, he drew out a knife, sticking in his sash, and cut him from the ear towards the mouth. *Wiseman's Surgery.*

To SNI'CKER, or *Snigger. v. n.* To laugh slily, wantonly, or contemptuously; to laugh in one's sleeve. *Dict.*

To SNIFF. *v. n.* [*sniffa*, Swedish.] To draw breath audibly up the nose.

So then you look'd scornful, and *snift* at the dean,
As, who should say, now am I skinny and lean? *Swift.*

To SNI'GGLE. *v. n.*

Sniggling is thus performed: in a warm day, when the water is lowest, take a strong small hook, tied to a string about a yard long; and then into one of the holes, where an eel may hide herself, with the help of a short stick put in your bait leisurely, and as far as you may conveniently: if within the sight of it, the eel will bite instantly, and as certainly gorge it: pull him out by degrees. *Walton's Angler.*

To SNIP. *v. a.* [*snippen*, Dutch.] To cut at once with scissars.

The sinus should be laid open, which was *snipt* up about two inches with a pair of probe-scissars, and the incised lips dressed. *Wiseman's Surgery.*

When tradesmen brought extravagant bills, sir Roger used to bargain to cut off a quarter of a yard: he wore a pair of scissars for this purpose, and would *snip* it off nicely. *Arbuthnot.*

Putting one blade of the scissars up the gut, and the other up the wound, *snip* the whole length of the fistula. *Sharp.*

SNIP. *n. s.* [from the verb.]

1. A single cut with scissars.

What! this a sleeve?
Here's *snip* and nip, and cut, and slish and slash,
Like to a censor in a barber's shop. *Shakespeare.*

The ulcer would not cure farther than it was laid open; therefore with one *snip* more I laid it open to the very end. *Wise.*

2. A small shred.

Those we keep within compass by small *snips* of emplast, hoping to defend the parts about; but, in spite of all, they will spread farther. *Wiseman's Surgery.*

3. A

3. A ſhare; a ſnack. A low word.

He found his friend upon the mending hand, which he was glad to hear, becauſe of the *ſnip* that he himſelf expected upon the dividend. *L'Eſtrange.*

SNIPE. *n. ſ.* [*ſneppe*, German; ꞅnıꞇe, Saxon; *yſnit*, Welſh.]

1. A ſmall fen fowl with a long bill.

The external evident cauſes of the atra bilis are a high fermenting diet; as old cheeſe, birds feeding in fens, as geeſe, ducks, woodcocks, *ſnipes*, and ſwans. *Floyer.*

2. A fool; a blockhead.

Thus do I ever make my fool my purſe;
For I mine own gain'd knowledge ſhould profane,
If I ſhould time expend with ſuch a *ſnipe*,
But for my ſport and profit. *Shakeſp. Othello.*

SNI'PPER. *n. ſ.* [from *ſnip.*] One that ſnips.

SNI'PPET. *n. ſ.* [from *ſnip.*] A ſmall part; a ſhare.

Witches ſimpling, and on gibbets
Cutting from malefactors *ſnippets*;
Or from the pill'ry tips of ears. *Hudibras.*

SNI'PSNAP. *n. ſ.* [A cant word formed by reduplication of *ſnap.*] Tart dialogue.

Dennis and diſſonance, and captious art,
And *ſnipſnap* ſhort, and interruption ſmart. *Pope's Dunciad.*

SNITE. *n. ſ.* [ꞅnıꞇa, Saxon.] A ſnipe. This is perhaps the true name; but *ſnipe* prevails.

Of tame birds Cornwal hath doves, geeſe, and ducks: of wild, quail, rail, *ſnite*, and wood-dove. *Carew.*

To SNITE. *v. a.* [ꞅnȳꞇan, Saxon.] To blow the noſe.

Nor would any one be able to *ſnite* his noſe, or to ſneeze; in both which the paſſage of the breath through the mouth, being intercepted by the tongue, is forced to go through the noſe. *Grew's Coſmol.*

SNI'VEL. *n. ſ.* [*ſnavel, ſnevel*, German.] Snot; the running of the noſe.

To SNI'VEL. *v. n.* [from the noun.]

1. To run at the noſe.

2. To cry as children.

Funeral tears are hired out as mourning cloaks; and whether we go to our graves *ſniveling* or ſinging, 'tis all mere form. *L'Eſtrange.*

Away goes he *ſniveling* and yelping, that he had dropt his ax into the water. *L'Eſtrange.*

SNI'VELLER. *n. ſ.* [from *ſnivel.*] A weeper; a weak lamenter.

He'd more lament when I was dead,
Than all the *ſnivellers* round my bed. *Swift.*

To SNORE. *v. n.* [*ſnorcken*, Dutch.] To breathe hard through the noſe, as men in ſleep.

I did unreverently blame the gods,
Who wake for thee, though thou *ſnore* for thyſelf. *B. Johnſ.*

Whoſe railing heroes, and whoſe wounded gods,
Makes ſome ſuſpect he *ſnores* as well as nods. *Roſcommon.*

He may lie quietly in his ſhades, and *ſnore* on to doomſday for me; unleſs I ſee farther reaſon of diſturbing his repoſe. *Stillingfleet.*

Is not yonder Proteus' cave?
It is; and in it lies the god aſleep;
And *ſnoring* by
We may deſcry
The monſters of the deep. *Dryden's Albion.*

'Twas Acme's and Septimius' life;
The lady ſigh'd, the lover *ſnor'd.* *Prior.*

The giant, gorg'd with fleſh, and wine, and blood,
Lay ſtretcht at length, and *ſnoring* in his den,
Belching raw gobbets from his maw, o'ercharg'd
With purple wine and cruddl'd gore confus'd. *Addiſon.*

SNORE. *n. ſ.* [ꞅnoꞃa, Saxon; from the verb.] Audible reſpiration of ſleepers through the noſe.

The ſurfeited grooms
Do mock their charge with *ſnores*: I've drugg'd their poſſets. *Shakeſpeare's Macbeth.*

To SNORT. *v. n.* [*ſnorcken*, Dutch.] To blow through the noſe as a high mettled horſe.

The *ſnorting* of his horſes was heard. *Jer.* viii. 16.

The fiery war-horſe paws the ground,
And *ſnorts* and trembles at the trumpet's ſound. *Addiſon.*

From their full racks the gen'rous ſteeds retire,
Dropping ambroſial foams and *ſnorting* fire. *Addiſon's Ovid.*

He with wide noſtrils, *ſnorting*, ſkims the wave. *Thomſon.*

SNOT. *n. ſ.* [ꞅnoꞇe, Saxon; *ſnot*, Dutch.] The mucus of the noſe.

Thus, when a greedy ſloven once has thrown
His *ſnot* into the meſs, 'tis all his own. *Swift.*

SNO'TTY. *adj.* [from *ſnot.*] Full of ſnot.

This ſquire South my huſband took in a dirty *ſnotty*-noſed boy. *Arbuthnot.*

SNOUT. *n. ſ.* [*ſnuyt*, Dutch.]

1. The noſe of a beaſt.

His noſe in the air, his *ſnout* in the ſkies. *Tuſſer.*

In ſhape a beagle's whelp throughout,
With broader forehead, and a ſharper *ſnout.* *Dryden.*

2. The noſe of a man, in contempt.

Her ſubtle *ſnout*
Did quickly wind his meaning out. *Hudibras.*

But when the date of Nock was out,
Off dropt the ſympathetick *ſnout.* *Hudibras.*

What Ethiop lips he has,
How foul a *ſnout*; and what a hanging face! *Dryd. Juven.*

Charm'd with his eyes, and chin, and *ſnout*,
Her pocket-glaſs drew ſlily out;
And grew enamour'd with her phiz,
As juſt the counterpart of his. *Swift.*

3. The noſel or end of any hollow pipe.

SNO'UTED. *adj.* [from *ſnout.*] Having a ſnout.

Snouted and tailed like a boar, and footed like a goat. *Grew.*

SNOW. *n. ſ.* [ꞅnap, Saxon; *ſnee*, Dutch.] The ſmall particles of water frozen before they unite into drops. *Locke.*

Benaiah ſlew a lion in a pit, in time of *ſnow.* 2 *Sa.* xxiii.

Drought and heat conſume *ſnow* waters. *Job* xxiv. 19.

He gives the Winter's *ſnow* her airy birth,
And bids her virgin fleeces clothe the earth. *Sandys.*

To SNOW. *v. n.* [ꞅnapan, Saxon; *ſneeuwen*, Dutch.] To have ſnow fall.

To SNOW. *v. a.* To ſcatter like ſnow.

If thou be'ſt born to ſee ſtrange ſights,
Ride ten thouſand days and nights,
'Till age *ſnow* white hairs on thee. *Donne.*

SNO'WBALL. *n. ſ.* [*ſnow* and *ball.*] A round lump of congelated ſnow.

They paſſed to the eaſt-riding of Yorkſhire, their company daily increaſing, like a *ſnowball* in rolling. *Hayward.*

His bulky folly gathers as it goes,
And, rolling o'er you, like a *ſnowball* grows. *Dryden.*

A *ſnowball* having the power to produce in us the ideas of white, cold, and round, the powers, as they are in the *ſnowball*, I call qualities; and as they are ſenſations in our underſtandings, ideas. *Locke.*

SNO'WBROTH. *n. ſ.* [*ſnow* and *broth*] Very cold liquor.

Angelo, a man whoſe blood
Is very *ſnowbroth*, one who never feels
The wanton ſtings and motions of the ſenſe. *Shakeſpeare.*

SNO'WDROP. *n. ſ.* [*narciſſoleucoium*, Latin.] An early flower.

The flower is, for the moſt part, compoſed of ſix leaves, in form of a lily, which are ſometimes equal, and ſometimes unequal and pendulous: the empalement becomes a roundiſh fruit, which is divided into three cells, and full of roundiſh ſeeds: to which may be anded, it hath a bulbous root. *Miller.*

When we tried the experiment with the leaves of thoſe purely white flowers that appear about the end of Winter, called *ſnowdrops*, the event was not much unlike that newly mentioned. *Boyle on Colours.*

The little ſhape, by magick pow'r,
Grew leſs and leſs, contracted to a flow'r;
A flow'r, that firſt in this ſweet garden ſmil'd,
To virgins ſacred, and the *ſnowdrop* ſtyl'd. *Tickell.*

SNOW-WHITE. *adj.* [*ſnow* and *white.*] White as ſnow.

A *ſnow-white* bull ſhall on your ſhore be ſlain;
His offer'd entrails caſt into the main. *Dryden's Æn.*

SNO'WY. *adj.* [from *ſnow.*]

1. White like ſnow.

So ſhews a *ſnowy* dove trooping with crows,
As yonder lady o'er her fellows ſhews. *Shakeſpeare.*

Now I ſee thy jolly train:
Snowy headed Winter leads,
Spring and Summer next ſucceeds;
Yellow Autumn brings the rear;
Thou art father of the year. *Rowe.*

The bluſhing ruby on her *ſnowy* breaſt,
Render'd its panting whiteneſs more confeſt. *Prior.*

2. Abounding with ſnow.

Theſe firſt in Crete
And Ida known; thence on the *ſnowy* top
Of cold Olympus rul'd the middle air. *Milton's Par. Loſt.*

As when the Tartar from his Ruſſian foe,
By Aſtracan, over the *ſnowy* plains,
Retires. *Milton's Paradiſe Loſt.*

SNUB. *n. ſ.* [from *ſnebbe*, Dutch, a noſe, or *knubel*, a joint of the finger.] A jag; a ſnag; a knot in wood.

Lifting up his dreadful club on high,
All arm'd with ragged *ſnubs* and knotty grain,
Him thought at firſt encounter to have ſlain. *Fairy Queen.*

To SNUB. *v. a.* [Rather *To ſnib.* See SNEAP, SNEB, SNIB.]

1. To check; to reprimand.

2. To nip.

Near the ſeaſhores the heads and boughs of trees run out far to landward; but toward the ſea are ſo *ſnubbed* by the winds, as if their boughs had been pared or ſhaven off. *Ray.*

To SNUB. *v. n.* [*ſnuffen*, Dutch.] To ſob with convulſion.

To SNUDGE. *v. n.* [*ſniger*, Daniſh.] To lie idle, cloſe, or ſnug.

Now he will fight it out, and to the wars;
Now eat his bread in peace,
And *snudge* in quiet; now he scorns increase;
Now all day spares. *Herbert.*

SNUFF. *n. s.* [*snuf*, Dutch, snot.]

1. Snot. In this sense it is not used.

2. The useless excrescence of a candle: whence *moucher la chandelle.*

My great affliction,
If I could bear longer, and not fall
To quarrel with your opposeless wills,
My *snuff* and loathed part of nature should
Burn itself out. *Shakesp. King Lear.*

But dearest heart, and dearer image, stay!
Alas! true joys at best are dreams enough:
Though you stay here, you pass too fast away;
For even at first life's taper is a *snuff.* *Donne.*

The *snuff*-dishes shall be of pure gold. *Ex.* xxv. 38.

If the liquor be of a close and glutinous consistency, it may burn without any *snuff*, as we see in camphire, and some other bituminous substances; and most of the ancient lamps were of this kind, because none have been found with such wicks. *Wilk.*

3. A candle almost burnt out.

Lamentable!
To hide me from the radiant sun, and solace
I' th' dungeon by a *snuff.* *Shakesp. Cymbeline.*

4. The fired wick of a candle remaining after the flame.

A torch, *snuff* and all, goes out in a moment, when dipped into the vapour. *Addison on Italy.*

5. Resentment expressed by snifting; perverse resentment.

What hath been seen
Either in *snuffs* or packings of the duke's,
Or the hard rein which both of them have borne
Against the old kind king. *Shakesp. King Lear.*

Jupiter took *snuff* at the contempt, and punished him: he sent him home again. *L'Estrange.*

6. Powdered tobacco taken by the nose.

Just where the breath of life his nostrils drew,
A charge of *snuff* the wily virgin threw;
The gnomes direct to ev'ry atom just
The pungent grains of titillating dust. *Pope.*

To SNUFF. *v. a.* [*snuffen*, Dutch.]

1. To draw in with the breath.

A heifer will put up her nose, and *snuff* in the air against rain. *Bacon.*

With delight he *snuff'd* the smell
Of mortal change on earth. *Milton's Paradise Lost.*

He *snuffs* the wind, his heels the sand excite;
But when he stands collected in his might,
He roars and promises a more successful fight. *Dryden.*

The youth,
Who holds the nearest station to the light,
Already seems to *snuff* the vital air,
And leans just forward on a shining spear. *Dryden's Æn.*

My troops are mounted; their Numidian steeds
Snuff up the wind, and long to scour the desart. *Addison.*

My nag's greatest fault was *snuffing* up the air about Brackdenstown, whereby he became such a lover of liberty, that I could scarce hold him in. *Swift.*

2. To scent.

The cow looks up, and from afar can find
The change of heav'n, and *snuffs* it in the wind. *Dryden.*

For thee the bulls rebellow through the groves,
And tempt the stream, and *snuff* their absent loves. *Dryden.*

O'er all the blood-hound boasts superior skill,
To scent, to view, to turn, and boldly kill!
His fellows vain alarms rejects with scorn,
True to the master's voice, and learned horn:
His nostrils oft, if ancient fame sing true,
Trace the sly felon through the tainted dew:
Once *snuff'd*, he follows with unalter'd aim,
Nor odours lure him from the chosen game;
Deep-mouth'd he thunders, and inflam'd he views,
Springs on relentless, and to death pursues. *Tickell.*

3. To crop the candle.

The late queen's gentlewoman!
To be her mistress' mistress!
This candle burns not clear: 'tis I must *snuff* it,
And out it goes. *Shakesp. Henry* VIII.

Against a communion-day our lamps should be better dressed, and our lights *snuffed*, and our religion more active. *Taylor's worthy Communicant.*

You have got
An office for your talents fit,
To *snuff* the lights, and stir the fire,
And get a dinner for your hire. *Swift.*

To SNUFF. *v. n.*

1. To snort; to draw breath by the nose.

The fury fires the pack, they *snuff*, they vent,
And feed their hungry nostrils with the scent. *Dryd. Æn.*

Says Humpus, sir, my master bad me pray
Your company to dine with him to-day:
He *snuffs*, then follows, up the stairs he goes,
Never pulls off his hat, nor cleans his shoes. *King.*

2. To snift in contempt.

Ye said, what a weariness is it, and ye have *snuff'd* at it. *Mal.* ii. 13.

SNU'FFBOX. *n. s.* [*snuff* and *box.*] The box in which snuff is carried.

If a gentleman leaves a *snuffbox* on the table, and goeth away, lock it up as part of your vails. *Swift.*

Sir Plume, of amber *snuffbox* justly vain,
And the nice conduct of a clouded cane. *Pope.*

SNU'FFERS. *n. s.* [from *snuff.*] The instrument with which the candle is clipped.

When you have snuffed the candle, leave the *snuffers* open. *Swift's Directions to the Butler.*

To SNU'FFLE. *v. n.* [*snuffelen*, Dutch.] To speak through the nose; to breath hard through the nose.

A water-spaniel came down the river, shewing that he hunted for a duck; and with a *snuffling* grace, disdaining that his smelling force could not as well prevail through the water as through the air, waited with his eye to see whether he could espy the duck's getting up again. *Sidney.*

Bagpipes of the loudest drones,
With *snuffling* broken-winded tones,
Whose blasts of air in pockets shut,
Sound filthier than from the gut. *Hudibras.*

It came to the ape to deliver his opinion, who smelt and *snuffled*, and considered on't. *L'Estrange.*

One clad in purple,
Eats and recites some lamentable rhyme;
Some senseless Phillis in a broken note,
Snuffling at nose, and croaking in his throat. *Dryden.*

To SNUG. *v. n.* [*sniger*, Dutch.] To lie close; to snudge.

There *snugging* well, he well appear'd content,
So to have done amiss, so to be shent. *Sidney.*

As the loving couple lay *snugging* together, Venus, to try if the cat had changed her manners with her shape, turned a mouse loose into the chamber. *L'Estrange.*

SNUG. *adj.* [from the verb.]

1. Close; free from any inconvenience.

They spy'd a country farm,
Where all was *snug*, and clean, and warm;
For woods before, and hills behind,
Secur'd it both from rain and wind. *Prior.*

2. Close; out of notice.

At Will's
Lie *snug*, and hear what criticks say. *Swift.*

3. Slily or insidiously close.

Did I not see you, rascal, did I not!
When you lay *snug* to snap young Damon's goat? *Dryden.*

To SNU'GGLE. *v. n.* [from *snug.*] To lie close; to lie warm.

SO. *adv.* [ꞅpa, Saxon; *soo*, Dutch; *so*, German.]

1. In like manner. It answers to *as* either preceding or following. Noting comparison.

As whom the fables feign of monstrous size,
Titanian or earthborn that warr'd on Jove,
So stretch'd out huge in length the arch fiend lay. *Milton.*

Thick *as* autumnal leaves that strew the brooks
In Valombrosa, where th' Etrurian shades
High over-arch'd embow'r, *so* thick bestrewn
Abject and lost lay these. *Milton.*

Tir'd at first sight with what the muse imparts,
In fearless youth we tempt the heights of arts;
So pleas'd at first the tow'ring Alps we try,
Mount o'er the vales, and seem to tread the sky. *Pope.*

As into air the purer spirits flow,
And sep'rate from their kindred dregs below,
So flew her soul to its congeneal place. *Pope.*

2. To such a degree.

Why is his chariot *so* long in coming? *Judg.* v. 28.

Can nothing great, and at the height,
Remain *so* long, but its own weight
Will ruin it? Or is't blind chance
That still desires new states t' advance. *Ben. Johns. Catiline.*

Amoret, my lovely foe,
Tell me where thy strength does lie;
Where the pow'r that charms us *so*,
In thy soul, or in thy eye? *Waller.*

I viewed in my mind, *so* far as I was able, the beginning and progress of a rising world. *Burnet's Theory of the Earth.*

Since then our Arcite is with honour dead,
Why should we mourn that he *so* soon is freed. *Dryden.*

Upon our first going into a company of strangers, our benevolence or aversion rises towards several particular persons, before we have heard them speak, or *so* much as know who they are. *Addison's Spectator.*

We think our fathers fools, *so* wise we're grown:
Our wiser sons, no doubt, will think us so. *Pope.*

3. In fuch a manner.
4. It is regularly anfwered by *as* or *that*, but they are fometimes omitted.

So frown'd the mighty combatants, that hell
Grew darker at their frown. *Milton.*

There's no fuch thing, as that we beauty call,
It is meer cofenage all;
For though fome long ago
Lik'd certain colours mingl'd *fo* and *fo*,
That doth not tie me now from chufing new. *Suckling.*

There is fomething equivalent in France and Scotland; *fo* as 'tis a very hard calumny upon our foil to affirm that *fo* excellent a fruit will not grow here. *Temple.*

We may be certain that man is not a creature that hath wings; becaufe this only concerns the manner of his exiftence; and we feeing what he is, may certainly know that he is not *fo* or *fo*. *Locke.*

I fhall minutely tell him the fteps by which I was brought into this way, that he may judge whether I proceeded rationally, if *fo* be any thing in my example is worth his notice. *Locke.*

This gentleman is a perfon of good fenfe, and knows that he is very much in fir Roger's efteem, *fo that* he lives in the family rather as a relation than dependent. *Addifon.*

5. In the fame manner.

Of fuch examples add me to the roll;
Me eafily indeed mine may neglect,
But God's propos'd deliverance not *fo*. *Milton.*

To keep up the tutor's authority, ufe him with great refpect yourfelf, and caufe all your family to do *fo* too. *Locke.*

According to the multifarioufnefs of this immutability, *fo* are the poffibilities of being. *Norris.*

6. Thus; in this manner.

Not far from thence the mournful fields appear,
So call'd from lovers that inhabit there. *Dryden.*
Does this deferve to be rewarded *fo*?
Did you come here a ftranger or a foe? *Dryden.*

It concerns every man, with the greateft feriousnefs, to enquire into thofe matters whether they be *fo* or not. *Tillotfon.*

No nation ever complained they had too broad, too deep, or too many rivers; they underftand better than *fo*, how to value thofe ineftimable gifts of nature. *Bentley.*

So when the firft bold veffel dar'd the feas,
High on the ftern the Thracian rais'd his ftrain. *Pope.*

Whether this be from an habitual motion of the animal fpirits, or from the alteration of the conftitution, by fome more unaccountable way, this is certain that *fo* it is. *Locke.*

7. Therefore; for this reafon; in confequence of this.

The god, though loth, yet was conftrain'd t'obey;
For longer time than that, no living wight,
Below the earth, might fuffer'd be to ftay:
So back again him brought to living light. *Fairy Queen.*

If he fet induftrioufly and fincerely to perform the commands of Chrift, he can have no ground of doubting but it fhall prove fuccefsful to him, and *fo* all that he hath to do is to endeavour by prayer and ufe of the means, to qualify himfelf for this bleffed condition. *Hammond's Fundamentals.*

Some are fall'n, to difobedience fall'n;
And *fo* from heav'n to deepeft hell. *Milton's Paradife Loft.*

God makes him in his own image an intellectual creature, and *fo* capable of dominion. *Locke.*

8. On thefe terms; noting a conditional petition: anfwered by *as*.

O goddefs! tell what I would fay,
Thou know'ft it, and I feel too much to pray,
So grant my fuit, *as* I enforce my might,
In love to be thy champion. *Dryden's Knight's Tale.*

Here then exchange we mutually forgivenefs:
So may the guilt of all my broken vows,
My perjuries to thee be all forgotten;
As here my foul acquits thee of my death,
As here I part without an angry thought. *Rowe.*

So may kind rains their vital moifture yield,
And fwell the future harveft of thy field. *Pope.*

9. Provided that; on condition that; *modo.*

Be not fad:
Evil into the mind of God or man
May come and go, *fo* unapprov'd, and leave
No fpot or blame behind. *Milton's Paradife Loft.*

So the doctrine be but wholfome and edifying, though there fhould be a want of exactnefs in the manner of fpeaking or reafoning, it may be overlooked. *Atterbury.*

Too much of love thy haplefs friend has prov'd,
Too many giddy foolifh hours are gone;
May the remaining few know only friendfhip:
So thou, my deareft, trueft, beft Alicia,
Vouchfafe to lodge me in thy gentle heart,
A partner there; I will give up mankind. *Rowe.*

10. In like manner; noting conceffion of one propofition and affumption of another, anfwering to *as*.

As a war fhould be undertaken upon a juft motive, *fo* a prince ought to confider the condition he is in when he enters on it. *Swift.*

11. It fometimes anfwers to the word or fentence going before, and returns the fenfe.

Who thinks his wife is virtuous, though not *fo*,
Is pleas'd and patient till the truth he know. *Denham.*

Angling is fomething like poetry, men are to be born *fo*. *Walton's Angler.*

One may as well fay, that the conflagration fhall be only national, as to fay that the deluge was *fo*. *Burnet.*

However foft within themfelves they are,
To you they will be valiant by defpair;
For having once been guilty, well they know
To a revengeful prince they ftill are *fo*. *Dryden.*
He was great ere fortune made him *fo*. *Dryden.*

I laugh at every one, faid an old cynick, who laughs at me. Do you *fo*? replied the philofopher; then you live the merrieft life of any man in Athens. *Addifon.*

They are beautiful in themfelves, and much more *fo* in that noble language peculiar to that great poet. *Addifon.*

Common-place books have been long ufed by induftrious young divines, and ftill continue *fo*. *Swift.*

As to his ufing ludicrous expreffions, my opinion is, that they are not *fo*. *Pope.*

The bleft to-day is as completely *fo*,
As who began a thoufand years ago. *Pope.*

12. Thus it is; this is the ftate.

How forrow fhakes him!
So, now the tempeft tears him up by th' roots,
And on the ground extends the noble ruin. *Dryden.*

13. At this point; at this time.

When
With wild wood-leaves and weeds I ha' ftrew'd his grave,
And on it faid a century of prayers,
Such as I can, twice o'er, I'll weep and figh;
And, leaving *fo* his fervice, follow you. *Shakefpeare.*

14. It notes a kind of abrupt beginning. Well.

O, *fo*, and had you a council
Of ladies too? who was your fpeaker,
Madam? *Ben. Johnfon's Catiline.*

15. It fometimes is little more than an expletive, though it implies fome latent or furd comparifon.

An aftringent is not quite *fo* proper, where relaxing the urinary paffages is neceffary. *Arbuthnot.*

16. A word of affumption; thus be it.

There is Percy; if your father will do me any honour, *fo*; if not, let him kill the next Percy himfelf. *Shakefpeare.*

I will never bear a bafe mind: if it be my deftiny, *fo*: if it be not, *fo*. No man is too good to ferve his prince. *Shak.*

17. A form of petition.

Ready are th' appellant and defendant,
The armourer and his man, to enter the lifts,
So pleafe your highnefs to behold the fight. *Shakefpeare.*

18. So *much as.* However much. This is, I think, an irregular expreffion.

So much as you admire the beauty of his verfe, his profe is full as good. *Pope.*

19. So *fo.* An exclamation after fome thing done or known.

I would not have thee linger in thy pain:
So fo. *Shakefpeare's Othello.*
So fo; it works: now miftrefs, fit you faft. *Dryden.*

20. So *fo.* [*cofi cofi*, Italian.] Indifferently; not much amifs nor well.

He's not very tall; yet for his years he's tall;
His leg is but *fo fo*: and yet 'tis well. *Shakefpeare.*

Deliver us from the naufeous repetition of As and So, which fome *fo fo* writers, I may call them fo, are continually founding in our ears. *Felton on the Claffick.*

21. So *then.* Thus then it is that; therefore.

So then the Volfcians ftand; but as at firft
Ready, when time fhall prompt them, to make road
Upon's again. *Shakefpeare's Coriolanus.*

To a war are required a juft quarrel, fufficient forces, and a prudent choice of the defigns: *fo then*, I will firft juftify the quarrel, balance the forces, and propound variety of defigns. *Bacon's War with Spain.*

To Soak. *v. n.* [ſocian, Saxon.]

1. To lie fteeped in moifture.

For thy conceit in *foaking* will draw in
More than the common blocks. *Shakefpeare.*

2. To enter by degrees into pores.

Lay a heap of earth in great frofts upon a hollow veffel, putting a canvafs between, and pour water upon it, fo as to *foak* through: it will make a harder ice in the veffel, and lefs apt to diffolve than ordinarily. *Bacon.*

Rain *foaking* into the ftrata, which lie near the furface, bears with it all fuch moveable matter as occurs. *Woodward.*

3. To drink gluttonoufly and intemperately. This is a low term.

Let a drunkard fee that his health decays, his eftate waftes, yet the habitual thirft after his cups drives him to the tavern, though he has in his view the lofs of health and plenty; the leaft of which he confeffes is far greater than the tickling of his palate with a glafs of wine, or the idle chat of a *foaking* club. *Locke.*

To

To SOAK. *v. a.*

1. To macerate in any moisture; to steep; to keep wet till moisture is imbibed; to drench.

Many of our princes
Lie drown'd and *soak'd* in mercenary blood:
So do our vulgar drench their peasant limbs
In blood of princes. *Shakespeare's Hen.* V.

Their land shall be *soaked* with blood. *Isa.* xxxiv. 7.

There deep Galesus *soaks* the yellow sands *Dryden.*

Thou whose life's a dream of lazy pleasure:
'Tis all thy bus'ness, bus'ness how to shun
To bask thy naked body in the sun;
Suppling thy stiffen'd joints with fragrant oil;
Then in thy spacious garden walk a while,
To suck the moisture up and *soak* it in. *Dryden.*

Wormwood, put into the brine you *soak* your corn in, prevents the birds eating it. *Mortimer.*

2. To drain; to exhaust. This seems to be a cant term.

Plants that draw much nourishment from the earth, and *soak* and exhaust it, hurt all things that grow by them. *Bacon.*

A greater sparer than a saver; for though he had such means to accumulate, yet his forts, and his garrisons, and his feastings, wherein he was only sumptuous, could not but *soak* his exchequer. *Wotton.*

SOAP. *n. s.* [ſape, Saxon; *sapo*, Latin.] A substance used in washing, made of a lixivium of vegetable alkaline ashes and any unctuous substance.

Soap is a mixture of a fixed alkaline salt and oil; its virtues are cleansing, penetrating, attenuating, and resolving; and any mixture of any oily substance with salt may be called a *soap*. *Arbuthnot on Aliments.*

He is like a refiner's fire, and like fullers *soap*. *Malachi.*

A bubble blown with water, first made tenacious by dissolving a little *soap* in it, after a while will appear tinged with a great variety of colours. *Newton's Opticks.*

Soap-earth is found in great quantity on the land near the banks of the river Hermus, seven miles from Smyrna. *Woodw.*

Soap-ashes are much commended, after the *soap*-boilers have done with them, for cold or sour lands. *Mortimer.*

As rain-water diminishes their salt, so the moistening of them with chamber-lee or *soap*-suds adds thereto. *Mortimer.*

SOAPBOI'LER. *n. s.* [*soap* and *boil.*] One whose trade is to make *soap*.

A *soapboiler* condoles with me on the duties on castle-soap. *Addison's Spectator.*

SOAPWORT. *n. s.* Is a species of campion. *Miller.*

To SOAR. *v. n.* [*sorare*, Italian.]

1. To fly aloft; to tower; to mount; properly to fly without any visible action of the wings.

Feather'd soon and fledg'd,
They summ'd their pens, and *soaring* th' air sublime,
With clang despis'd the ground. *Milton.*

2. To mount intellectually; to tower with the mind.

'Tis but a base ignoble mind
That mounts no higher than a bird can *soar*. *Shakespeare.*

How high a pitch his resolution *soars*. *Shakespeare.*

Valour *soars* above
What the world calls misfortune and afflictions. *Addison.*

3. To rise high.

Who aspires must down as low
As high he *soar'd*. *Milton.*

Flames rise and sink by fits; at last they *soar*
In one bright blaze, and then descend no more. *Dryden.*

When swallows fleet *soar* high, and sport in air,
He told us that the welkin would be clear. *Gay.*

SOAR. *n. s.* [from the verb.] Towering flight.

Within *soar*
Of tow'ring eagles, to all the fowls he seems
A phœnix. *Milton.*

To SOB. *v. n.* [ſeob, ʒeab, complaining, Saxon. Perhaps it is a mere *onomatopœia* copied from the sound.] To heave audibly with convulsive sorrow; to sigh with convulsion.

When thy warlike father, like a child,
Told the sad story of my father's death,
He twenty times made pause to *sob* and weep. *Shakespeare.*

As if her life and death lay on his saying,
Some tears she shed, with sighs and *sobbings* mixt,
As if her hopes were dead through his delaying. *Fairfax.*

She sigh'd, she *sobb'd*, and furious with despair,
She rent her garments, and she tore her hair. *Dryden.*

When children have not the power to obtain their desire, they will, by their clamour and *sobbing*, maintain their title to it. *Locke on Education.*

He *sobbing* sees
The glades, mild-opening to the golden day. *Thomson.*

SOB. *n. s.* [from the verb.] A convulsive sigh; a convulsive act of respiration obstructed by sorrow.

Break heart, or choak with *sobs* my hated breath;
Do thy own work, admit no foreign death. *Dryden.*

There oft are heard the notes of infant woe,
The short thick *sob*, loud scream, and shriller squall. *Swift.*

A wond'rous bag with both her hands she binds:
There she collects the force of female lungs,
Sighs, *sobs*, and passions, and the war of tongues. *Pope.*

To SOB. *v. a.* To soak. A cant word.

The tree being *sobbed* and wet, swells. *Mortimer.*

SO'BER. *adj.* [*sobrius*, Latin; *sobre*, French.]

1. Temperate, particularly in liquours; not drunken.

Live a *sober*, righteous, and godly life. *Common Prayer.*

The vines give wine to the drunkard as well as to the *sober* man. *Taylor's Worthy Communicant.*

No *sober* temperate person, whatsoever other sins he may be guilty of, can look with complacency upon the drunkenness and sottishness of his neighbour. *South's Sermons.*

2. Not overpowered by drink.

A law there is among the Grecians, whereof Pittacus is author; that he which being overcome with drink did then strike any man, should suffer punishment double, as much as if he had done the same being *sober*. *Hooker.*

3. Not mad; right in the understanding.

Another, who had a great genius for tragedy, following the fury of his natural temper, made every man and woman in his plays stark raging mad: there was not a *sober* person to be had; all was tempestuous and blustering. *Dryden.*

No *sober* man would put himself into danger, for the applause of escaping without breaking his neck. *Dryden.*

4. Regular; calm; free from inordinate passion.

This same young *sober*-blooded boy a man cannot make him laugh. *Shakespeare.*

Cieca travelled all over Peru, and is a grave and *sober* writer. *Abbot's Description of the World.*

Young men likewise exhort to be *sober* minded. *Tit.* ii. 6.

The governour of Scotland being of great courage, and *sober* judgment, amply performed his duty both before the battle and in the field. *Hayward.*

These confusions disposed men of any *sober* understanding to wish for peace. *Clarendon.*

Among them some *sober* men confessed, that as his majesty's affairs then stood, he could not grant it. *Clarendon.*

To these, that *sober* race of men, whose lives
Religious, titled them the sons of God,
Shall yield up all their virtue, all their fame
Ignobly to the trains and to the smiles
Of these fair atheists. *Milton.*

5. Serious; solemn; grave.

Petruchio shall
Offer me, disguis'd in *sober* robes,
To old Baptista as a schoolmaster. *Shakespeare.*

Come, civil night,
Thou *sober*-suited matron, all in black. *Shakespeare.*

Twilight grey
Had in her *sober* liv'ry all things clad. *Milton.*

What parts gay France from *sober* Spain,
A little rising rocky chain:
Of men born south or north th' hill,
Those seldom move; these ne'er stand still. *Prior.*

Swift and he despis'd the farce of state,
The *sober* follies of the wise and great. *Pope.*

See her *sober* over a sampler, or gay over a jointed baby. *Pope.*

To SO'BER. *v. a.* [from the adjective.] To make sober.

A little learning is a dang'rous thing;
Drink deep, or taste not the Pierian spring;
There shallow draughts intoxicate the brain,
And drinking largely *sobers* us again. *Pope.*

SO'BERLY. *adv.* [from *sober.*]

1. Without intemperance.
2. Without madness.
3. Temperately; moderately.

Let any prince think *soberly* of his forces, except his militia of natives be valiant soldiers. *Bacon.*

4. Cooly; calmly.

Whenever children are chastised, let it be done without passion, and *soberly* laying on the blows slowly. *Locke.*

SO'BERNESS. *n. s.* [from *sober.*]

1. Temperance in drink.

Keep my body in temperance, *soberness*, and chastity. *Common Prayer.*

2. Calmness; freedom from enthusiasm; coolness.

A person noted for his *soberness* and skill in spagyrical preparations, made Helmont's experiment succeed very well. *Boyle.*

The *soberness* of Virgil might have shewn him the difference. *Dryden's Dufresnoy.*

SOBRI'ETY. *n. s.* [from *sobrieté*, French; *sobrius*, Latin.]

1. Temperance in drink; soberness.

Drunkenness is more uncharitable to the soul, and in scripture is more declaimed against than gluttony; and *sobriety* hath obtained to signify temperance in drinking. *Taylor.*

2. Present freedom from the power of strong liquour.
3. General temperance.

In setting down the form of common prayer, there was no need that the book should mention either the learning of a fit, or the unfitness of an ignorant minister, more than that he which describeth the manner how to pitch a field, should speak of moderation and *sobriety* in diet. *Hooker.*

4 Freedom from inordinate passion.

The libertine could not prevail on men of virtue and *sobriety* to give up their religion. *Rogers.*

5. Calmness; coolness.

We will enquire with all *sobriety* and severity, whether there be in the footsteps of nature, any such transmission of immateriate virtues and what the force of imagination is. *Bacon's Natural History.*

Sobriety in our riper years is the effect of a well concocted warmth; but where the principles are only phlegm, what can be expected but an insipid manhood, and stupid old infancy? *Dryden.*

If sometimes Ovid appears too gay, there is a secret gracefulness of youth which accompanies his writings, though the stayedness and *sobriety* of age be wanting. *Dryden.*

6. Seriousness; gravity.

Mirth makes them not mad;
Nor *sobriety* sad. *Denham.*

So'ccage *n. s.* [*soc*, French, a ploughshare; *soccagium*, barbarous Latin.] In law, is a tenure of lands for certain inferiour or husbandly services to be performed to the lord of the fee. All services due for land being knight's service, or *soccage*; so that whatever is not knight's service, is *soccage*. This *soccage* is of three kinds; a *soccage* of free tenure, where a man holdeth by free service of twelve pence a-year for all manner of services. *Soccage* of ancient tenure is of land of ancient demesne, where no writ original shall be sued, but the writ *secundum consuetudinem manerii*. *Soccage* of base tenure is where those that hold it may have none other writ but the *monstraverunt*; and such sockmen hold not by certain service. *Cowel.*

The lands are not holden at all of her majesty, or not holden in chief, but by a mean tenure in *soccage*, or by knight's service. *Bacon.*

SO'CIABLE. *adj.* [*sociable*, French; *sociabilis*, Latin.]

1. Fit to be conjoined.

Another law toucheth them as they are *sociable* parts united into one body; a law which bindeth them each to serve unto other's good, and all to prefer the good of the whole before whatsoever their own particular. *Hooker.*

2. Ready to unite in a general interest.

To make man mild, and *sociable* to man;
To cultivate the wild licentious savage
With wisdom, discipline. *Addison's Cato.*

3. Friendly; familiar; conversible.

Them thus employ'd, beheld
With pity heav'n's high King, and to him call'd
Raphael, the *sociable* spirit, that deign'd
To travel with Tobias. *Milton.*

4. Inclin'd to company.

In children much solitude and silence I like not, nor any thing born before his time, as this must needs be in that *sociable* and exposed age. *Wotton.*

So'ciableness. [from *sociable*.]

1. Inclination to company and converse.

Such as would call her friendship love, and feign
To *sociableness* a name profane. *Donne.*

The two main properties of man are contemplation and *sociableness*, or love of converse. *More.*

2. Freedom of conversation; good fellowship.

He always used courtesy and modesty, disliked of none; sometimes *sociableness* and fellowship well lik'd by many. *Hayw.*

So'ciably. *adv.* [from *sociable*.] Conversibly; as a companion.

Yet not terrible,
That I should fear; nor *sociably* mild,
As Raphael, that I should much confide;
But solemn and sublime. *Milton's Paradise Lost.*

SO'CIAL. *adj.* [*socialis*, Latin.]

1. Relating to a general or publick interest; relating to society.

To love our neighbour as ourselves is such a fundamental truth for regulating human society, that by that alone one might determine all the cases in *social* morality. *Locke.*

2. Easy to mix in friendly gaiety; companionable.

Withers adieu! yet not with thee remove
Thy martial spirit or thy *social* love. *Pope.*

3. Consisting in union or converse with another.

Thou in thy secrecy although alone,
Best with thy self accompany'd, seek'st not
Social communication. *Milton.*

So'cialness. [from *social*.] The quality of being social.

Soci'ety. *n. s.* [*societé*, French; *societas*, Latin.]

1. Union of many in one general interest.

2. Numbers united in one interest; community.

As the practice of piety and virtue is agreeable to our reason, so is it for the interest of private persons and publick *societies*. *Tillotson.*

3. Company; converse.

To make *society*
The sweeter welcome, we will keep ourself
Till supper time alone. *Shakespeare's Macbeth.*

Whilst I was big in clamour, came there a man,
Who having seen me in my worser state,
Shunn'd my abhorr'd *society*. *Shakespeare's K. Lear.*

Solitude sometimes is best *society*,
And short retirement urges sweet return. *Milton.*

4. Partnership; union on equal terms.

Among unequals what *society* can sort? *Milton.*
Heav'n's greatness no *society* can bear;
Servants he made, and those thou want'st not here. *Dryden.*

Sock. *n. s.* [*soccus*, Latin; socc, Saxon; *socke*, Dutch.]

1. Something put between the foot and shoe.

Ere I lead this life long, I'll sow nether *socks*, and mend them, and foot them too. *Shakespeare's Henry IV.*

A physician, that would be mystical, prescribeth for the rheum to walk continually upon a camomile alley; meaning he should put camomile within his *socks*. *Bacon.*

2. The shoe of the ancient comick actors, taken in poems for comedy, and opposed to buskin or tragedy.

Then to the well trod stage anon,
If Johnson's learned *sock* be on,
Or sweetest Shakespeare, fancy's child,
Warble his native wood-notes wild. *Milton.*

Great Fletcher never treads in buskins here,
Nor greater Johnson dares in *socks* appear;
But gentle Simkin just reception finds
Amidst the monument of vanish'd minds. *Dryden.*

On two figures of actors in the villa Mathei at Rome, we see the fashion of the old *sock* and larva. *Addison.*

So'cket. *n. s.* [*souchette*, French]

1. Any hollow pipe; generally the hollow of a candlestick.

Two goodly beacons set in watches stead,
Therein gave light, and flam'd continually;
For they of living fire most subtilly
Were made, and set in silver *sockets* bright. *Fairy Queen.*

She at your flames would soon take fire,
And like a candle in the *socket*
Dissolve. *Hudibras.*

The nightly virgin sees
When sparkling lamps their sputt'ring light advance,
And in the *sockets* oily bubbles dance. *Dryden.*

The stars amaz'd ran backward from the sight,
And, shrunk within their *sockets*, lost their light. *Dryden.*

Two dire comets
In their own plague, and fire have breath'd their last,
Or dimly in their sinking *sockets* frown. *Dryden.*

To nurse up the vital flame as long as the matter will last, is not always good husbandry; it is much better to cover it with an extinguisher of honour, than let it consume till it burns blue, and lies agonizing within the *socket*, and at length goes out in no perfume. *Collier.*

2. The receptacle of the eye.

His eye-balls in their hollow *sockets* sink;
Bereft of sleep he loths his meat and drink;
He withers at his heart, and looks as wan
As the pale spectre of a murder'd man. *Dryden.*

3. Any hollow that receives something inserted.

The *sockets* and supporters of flowers are figured; as in the five brethren of the rose, and *sockets* of gillyflowers. *Bacon.*

Gomphosis is the connection of a tooth to its *socket*. *Wise.*

As the weight leans wholly upon the axis, the grating and rubbing of these axes against the *sockets* wherein they are placed, will cause some inaptitude and resistency to that rotation of the cylinder which would otherwise ensue. *Wilkins.*

On either side the head produce an ear,
And sink a *socket* for the shining share. *Dryden.*

Socketchisel. *n. s.*

Carpenters, for their rougher work, use a stronger sort of chisels, and distinguish them by the name of *socketchisels*; their shank made with a hollow socket a-top, to receive a strong wooden sprig made to fit into the socket. *Moxon.*

Socle. *n. s.* [With architects.] A flat square member, under the bases of pedestals of statues and vases: it serves as a foot or stand. *Bailey.*

So'cman, or *Soccager*. *n. s.* [socaƿman, Saxon.] A sort of tenant that holds lands and tenements by soccage tenure, of which there are three kinds. See Soccage. *Cowel.*

So'come. *n. s.* [In the old law, and in Scoland.] A custom of tenants being obliged to grind their corn at their lord's mill. *Bailey.*

Sod. *n. s.* [*sod*, Dutch.] A turf; a clod.

The sexton shall green *sods* on thee bestow;
Alas the sexton is thy banker now. *Swift.*

Here fame shall dress a sweeter *sod*,
Than fancy's feet have ever trod. *Collins.*

Sod. The preterite of *seethe*.

Never caldron *sod*
With so much fervour, fed with all the store
That could enrage it. *Chapman.*

Jacob *sod* pottage, and Esau came from the field faint. *Gen.* xxv. 29.

Soda'lity. *n. s.* [*sodalitas*, Latin.] A fellowship; a fraternity.

A new confraternity was instituted in Spain, of the slaves of the blessed virgin, and this *sodality* established with large indulgencies. *Stillingfleet.*

SO'DDEN. [The participle passive of *seethe.*] Boiled; seethed.

Can *sodden* water, their barley broth,
Decoct their cold blood to such valiant heat? *Shakespeare.*

Sodden business! there's a stew'd phrase indeed. *Shakesp.*

Thou *sodden*-witted lord; thou hast no more brain than I have in my elbows. *Shakespeare's Troilus and Cressida.*

Try it with milk *sodden*, and with cream. *Bacon.*

Mix it with *sodden* wines and raisins. *Dryden.*

To SO'DER. *v. a.* [*souder*, French; *souderen*, Dutch. It is generally written *solder*, from *soldare*, Italian; *solidare*, Latin.] To cement with some metallick matter.

He that smootheth with the hammer, encourageth him that smote the anvil, saying, it is ready for *sodering.* *Isa.* xli.

SO'DER. *n. s.* Metallick cement.

Still the difficulty returns, how these hooks were made: what is it that fastens this *soder*, and links these first principles of bodies into a chain? *Collier on Pride.*

SOE. *n. s.* [*sae*, Scottish.] A large wooden vessel with hoops, for holding water; a cowl.

A pump grown dry will yield no water; but pouring a little into it first, for one bason full you may fetch up as many *soe*-fills. *More.*

SOE'VER. *adv.* [*so* and *ever.*] A word properly joined with a pronoun or adverb, as whosoever; whatsoever; howsoever.

What great thing *soever* a man proposed to do in his life, he should think of atchieving it by fifty. *Temple.*

What love *soever* by an heir is shown,
Or you could ne'er suspect my loyal love. *Dryden.*

SO'FA. *n. s.* [I believe an eastern word.] A splended seat covered with carpets.

The king leaped off from the *sofa* on which he sat, and cried out, 'tis my Abdallah! *Guardian.*

SOFT. *adj.* [ꞅoꝼt, Saxon; *saft*, Dutch.]

1. Not hard.

Hard and *soft* are names we give things, only in relation to the constitutions of our own bodies; that being called hard, which will put us to pain sooner than change figure, by the pressure of any part of our bodies; and that *soft*, which changes the situation of its parts upon an easy touch. *Locke.*

Some bodies are hard, and some *soft*: the hardness is caused by the jejuneness of the spirits, which if a greater degree, make them not only hard, but fragil. *Bacon.*

Hot and cold were in one body fixt,
And *soft* with hard, and light with heavy mixt. *Dryden.*

2. Not rugged; not rough.

What went ye out for to see? a man clothed in *soft* raiment? behold, they that wear *soft* raiment are in kings houses. *Matth.*

3. Ductile; not unchangeable of form.

Spirits can either sex assume; so *soft*
And uncompounded is their essence pure. *Milton.*

4. Facile; flexible; not resolute; yielding.

A few divines of so *soft* and servile tempers as disposed them to so sudden acting and compliance. *K. Charles.*

One king is too *soft* and easy; another too fiery. *L'Estrange.*

5. Tender; timorous.

What he hath done famously, he did it to that end; tho' *soft* conscienced men can be content to say, it was for his country. *Shakespeare's Coriolanus.*

However *soft* within themselves they are,
To you they will be valiant by despair. *Dryden.*

Curst be the verse, how well soe'er it flow,
That tends to make one worthy man my foe;
Give virtue scandal, innocence a fear,
Or from the *soft* ey'd virgin steal a tear. *Pope.*

6. Mild; gentle; kind; not severe.

Would my heart were flint like Edward's;
Or Edward's *soft* and pitiful like mine. *Shakespeare.*

Our torments may become as *soft* as now severe. *Milton.*

Yet *soft* his nature, though severe his lay,
His anger moral, and his wisdom gay. *Pope.*

7. Meek; civil; complaisant.

Say,
Thou art their soldier, and being bred in broils,
Hast not the *soft* way, which thou do'st confess
Were fit for thee to use, as they to claim
In asking their good loves. *Shakespeare's Coriolanus.*

8. Placid; still; easy.

On her *soft* axle while she paces even,
She bears thee *soft* with the smooth air along. *Milton.*

There *soft*-extended, to the murmuring sound
Of the high porch, Ulysses sleeps profound. *Pope.*

9. Effeminate; viciously nice.

This sense is also mistress of an art
Which to *soft* people sweet perfumes doth sell;
Though this dear art doth little good impart,
Since they smell best, that do of nothing smell. *Davies.*

An idle and *soft* course of life is the source of criminal pleasures. *Notes on the Odyssey.*

10. Delicacy; elegantly tender.

Her form more *soft* and feminine *Milton.*
Less winning *soft*, less amiably mild. *Milton.*

11. Weak; simple.

The deceiver soon found this *soft* place of Adam's, and innocency itself did not secure him. *Glanville.*

12. Gentle; not loud; not rough.

Her voice was ever *soft*,
Gentle and low, an excellent thing in women. *Shakespeare.*

The Dorian mood of flutes and *soft* recorders. *Milton.*

When some great and gracious monarch dies,
Soft whispers first, and mournful murmurs rise
Among the sad attendants; then the sound
Soon gathers voice. *Dryden.*

Soft whispering thus to Nestor's son,
His head reclin'd, young Ithacus begun. *Pope.*

13. Smooth; flowing.

The solemn nightingale tun'd her *soft* lays. *Milton.*

Soft were my numbers, who could take offence,
When smooth description held the place of sense. *Pope.*

Hark, the numbers *soft* and clear
Gently steal upon the ear. *Pope.*

14. Not forcible; not violent.

Sleep falls with *soft* slumb'rous weight. *Milton.*

SOFT. *interj.* Hold; stop; not so fast.

But *soft*, I pray you; did King Richard then
Proclaim my brother. *Shakespeare's Hen.* IV.

Oh, come in Æmilia;
Soft, by and by, let me the curtains draw. *Shakespeare.*

But *soft*, my muse, the world is wide,
And all at once was not descry'd. *Suckling.*

To SO'FTEN. *v. a.* [from *soft.*]

1. To make soft; to make less hard.

Bodies, into which the water will enter, long seething will rather *soften* than indurate. *Bacon's Natural History.*

Their arrow's point they *soften* in the flame,
And sounding hammers break its barbed frame. *Gay.*

2. To intenerate; to make less fierce or obstinate; to mollify.

I will *soften* stony hearts. *Milton.*

Our friends see not our faults, or conceal them, or *soften* them by their representation. *Addison.*

I would correct the harsh expressions of one party, by *softening* and reconciling methods. *Watts.*

3. To make easy; to compose; to make placid; to mitigate; to palliate; to alleviate.

Call round her tomb each object of desire,
Bid her be all that chears or *softens* life,
The tender sister, daughter, friend, and wife. *Pope.*

Musick the fiercest griefs can charm;
Musick can *soften* pain to ease,
And make despair and madness please. *Pope.*

4. To make less harsh.

He bore his great commission in his look,
But sweetly temper'd awe, and *soften'd* all he spoke. *Dryd.*

To SO'FTEN. *v. n.*

1. To grow less hard.

Many bodies, that will hardly melt, will *soften*; as iron in the forge. *Bacon's Natural History.*

2. To grow less obdurate, cruel, or obstinate.

He may *soften* at the sight of the child;
The silence often of pure innocence
Persuades, when speaking fails. *Shakespeare.*

SO'FTLY. *adv.* [from *soft.*]

1. Without hardness.

2. Not violently; not forcibly.

Solid bodies, if very *softly* percussed, give no sound; as when a man treadeth very *softly* upon boards. *Bacon.*

3. Not loudly.

Ahab rent his cloaths, and went *softly.* 1 *Kings* xxi. 27.

In this dark silence *softly* leave the town,
And to the general's tent direct your steps. *Dryden.*

4. Gently; placidly.

Death will dismiss me,
And lay me *softly* in my native dust,
To pay the forfeit of ill-manag'd trust. *Dryden.*

She with a wreath of myrtle crowns the head,
And *softly* lays him on a flow'ry bed. *Dryden's Æneid.*

5. Mildly; tenderly.

The king must die;
Though pity *softly* plead within my soul,
Yet he must die, that I may make you great. *Dryden.*

SO'FTNER. *n. s.* [from *soft.*]

1. That which makes soft.

2. One who palliates.

Those *softners*, and expedient-mongers, shake their heads so strongly, that we can hear their pockets jingle. *Swift.*

SO'FTNESS. *n. s.* [from *soft.*]

1. The quality of being soft.

2. Quality contrary to hardness.

Softness cometh by the greater quantity of spirits, which ever induce yielding and cession; and by the more equal spreading

ing of the tangible parts, which thereby are more sliding and following; as in gold *Bacon's Natural History.*

3. Mildneſs; kindneſs.

A wiſe man, when there is a neceſſity of expreſſing any evil actions, ſhould do it by a word that has a ſecondary idea of kindneſs or *ſoftneſs*; or a word that carries in it rebuke and ſeverity. *Watts's Logick.*

4. Civility; gentleneſs.

Improve theſe virtues, with a *ſoftneſs* of manners, and a ſweetneſs of converſation. *Dryden.*

5. Effeminacy; vicious delicacy.

So long as idleneſs is quite ſhut out from our lives, all the ſins of wantonneſs, *ſoftneſs*, and effeminacy are prevented; and there is but little room for temptation. *Taylor.*

He was not delighted with the *ſoftneſſes* of the court. *Clarend.*

6. Timorouſneſs; puſillanimity.

This virtue could not proceed out of fear or *ſoftneſs*; for he was valiant and active. *Bacon's Henry VII.*

Saving a man's ſelf, or ſuffering, if with reaſon, is virtue: if without it, is *ſoftneſs*, or obſtinacy. *Grew.*

7. Quality contrary to harſhneſs.

Softneſs of ſounds is diſtinct from the exility of ſounds. *Bac.*

8. Facility; gentleneſs; candour; eaſineſs to be affected.

Such was the ancient ſimplicity and *ſoftneſs* of ſpirit, which ſometimes prevailed in the world, that they whoſe words were even as oracles amongſt men, ſeemed evermore loth to give ſentence againſt any thing publickly received in the church of God. *Hooker.*

9. Mildneſs; meekneſs.

For contemplation he and valour form'd,
For *ſoftneſs* ſhe and ſweet attractive grace. *Milton.*

Her ſtubborn look
This *ſoftneſs* from thy finger took. *Waller.*

SOHO. *interj.* A form of calling from a diſtant place.

To SOIL. *v. a.* [ſylian, Saxon; *ſoelen*, old German; *ſouiller*, French.]

1. To foul; to dirt; to pollute; to ſtain; to ſully.

A ſilly man in ſimple weeds forlorn,
And *ſoiled* with duſt of the long dried way. *Fairy Queen.*

Although ſome hereticks have abuſed this text, yet the ſun is not *ſoiled* in paſſage. *Bacon's Holy War.*

If I *ſoil*
Myſelf with ſin, I then but vainly toil. *Sandys.*

I would not *ſoil* theſe pure ambroſial weeds,
With the rank vapours of this ſin-worm mould. *Milton.*

Bad fruit of knowledge, if this be to know,
Which leaves us naked thus, of honour void,
Of innocence, of faith, of purity,
Our wonted ornaments now *ſoil'd* and ſtain'd. *Milton.*

One who cou'd n't for a taſte o' th' fleſh come in,
Licks the *ſoil'd* earth,
While reeking with a mangled Ombit's blood. *Tate.*

If the eye-glaſs be tincted faintly with the ſmoke of a lamp or torch, to obſcure the light of the ſtar, the fainter light in the circumference of the ſtar ceaſes to be viſible, and the ſtar, if the glaſs be ſufficiently *ſoiled* with ſmoke, appears ſomething more like a mathematical point. *Newton.*

An abſent hero's bed they ſought to *ſoil*,
An abſent hero's wealth they made their ſpoil. *Pope.*

2. To dung; to manure.

Men now preſent, juſt as they *ſoil* their ground, not that they love the dirt, but that they expect a crop. *South.*

SOIL. *n. ſ.* [from the verb.]

1. Dirt; ſpot; pollution; foulneſs.

By indirect ways
I met this crown; and I myſelf know well
How troubleſome it ſate upon my head:
To thee it ſhall deſcend with better quiet;
For all the *ſoil* of the atchievement goes
With me into the earth. *Shakeſpeare's Henry.* IV.

That would be a great *ſoil* in the new gloſs of your marriage. *Shakeſpeare.*

Vexed I am with paſſions,
Which give ſome *ſoil* perhaps to my behaviour. *Shakeſpeare.*

I would have the *ſoil* of her fair rape
Wip'd off. *Shakeſpeare.*

A lady's honour muſt be touch'd,
Which, nice as ermines, will not bear a *ſoil.* *Dryden.*

2. [*Sol*, French; *ſolum*, Latin.] Ground; earth, conſidered with relation to its vegetative qualities.

Judgment may be made of waters by the *ſoil* whereupon they run. *Bacon's Natural Hiſtory.*

Her ſpots thou ſee'ſt
As clouds, and clouds may rain, and rain produce
Fruits in her ſoften'd *ſoil.* *Milton's Paradiſe Loſt.*

The firſt cauſe of a kingdom's thriving is the fruitfulneſs of the *ſoil*, to produce the neceſſaries and conveniencies of life; not only for the inhabitants, but for exportation. *Swift.*

3. Land; country.

Dorſet, that with a fearful ſoul
Leads diſcontented ſteps in foreign *ſoil*,
This fair alliance ſhall call home
To high promotions. *Shakeſpeare.*

O unexpected ſtroke, worſe than of death!
Muſt I thus leave thee, paradiſe! thus leave
Thee, native *ſoil!* theſe happy walks and ſhades;
Fit haunts of gods. *Milton.*

4. Dung; compoſt.

The haven has been ſtopped up by the great heaps of dirt that the ſea has thrown into it; for all the *ſoil* on that ſide of Ravenna has been left there inſenſibly by the ſea. *Addiſ.*

Improve land by manure, dung, and other ſort of *ſoils.* *Mortimer's Huſbandry.*

SOI'LINESS. *n. ſ.* [from *ſoil.*] Stain; foulneſs.

Make proof of the incorporation of ſilver and tin, whether it yield no *ſoilineſs* more than ſilver. *Bacon.*

SOI'LURE. *n. ſ.* [from *ſoil.*] Stain; pollution.

He merits well to have her,
Not making any ſcruple of her *ſoilure.* *Shakeſpeare.*

To SO'JOURN. *v. n.* [*ſejourner*, French; *ſeggiornare*, Italian.] To dwell any where for a time; to live as not at home; to inhabit as not in a ſettled habitation. Almoſt out of uſe.

If, till the expiration of your month,
You will return and *ſojourn* with my ſiſter,
Diſmiſſing half your train, come then to me. *Shakeſpeare.*

Th' advantage of his abſence took the king,
And in the mean time *ſojourn'd* at my father's. *Shakeſp.*

How comes it he is to *ſojourn* with you? how creeps acquaintance? *Shakeſpeare's Cymbeline.*

Here dwells he; though he *ſojourn* every where
In progreſs, yet his ſtanding houſe is here. *Donne.*

The *ſojourning* of Iſrael, who dwelt in Egypt, was four hundred and thirty years. *Exod.* xii. 40.

The ſoldiers firſt aſſembled at Newcaſtle, and there *ſojourned* three days. *Hayward.*

To *ſojourn* in that land
He comes invited. *Milton's Paradiſe Loſt.*

He who *ſojourns* in a foreign country, refers what he ſees abroad to the ſtate of things at home *Atterbury.*

SO'JOURN. *n. ſ.* [*ſejour*, French, from the verb.] A temporary reſidence; a caſual and no ſettled habitation. This word was anciently accented on the laſt ſyllable: *Milton* accents it indifferently.

The princes, France and Burgundy,
Long in our court have made their am'rous *ſojourn.* *Shakeſp.*

Thee I reviſit now,
Eſcap'd the Stygian pool, though long detain'd
In that obſcure *ſojourn.* *Milton's Paradiſe Loſt.*

Scarce view'd the Galilean towns,
And once a-year Jeruſalem, few days
Short *ſojourn.* *Milton's Paradiſe Regained.*

SO'JOURNER. *n. ſ.* [from *ſojourn.*] A temporary dweller.

We are ſtrangers and *ſojourners*, as were all our fathers: our days on earth are as a ſhadow. *1 Chron.* xxix. 16.

Waves o'erthrew
Buſiris, and his Memphian chivalry,
While with perfidious hatred they purſu'd
The *ſojourners* of Goſhen. *Milton's Paradiſe Loſt.*

Not for a night, or quick revolving year,
Welcome an owner, not a *ſojourner.* *Dryden.*

To SO'LACE. *v. a.* [*ſolacier*, old French; *ſolazzare*, Italian; *ſolatium*, Latin.] To comfort; to cheer; to amuſe.

We will with ſome ſtrange paſtime *ſolace* them. *Shakeſpeare.*

The birds with ſong
Solac'd the woods. *Milton.*

To SOLACE. *v. n.* To take comfort; to be recreated. The neutral ſenſe is obſolete.

Give me leave to go;
Sorrow would *ſolace*, and my age would eaſe. *Shak. H.* VI.

One poor and loving child,
But one thing to rejoice and *ſolace* in,
And cruel death hath catch'd it from my ſight. *Shakeſpeare.*

Were they to be rul'd, and not to rule,
This ſickly land might *ſolace* as before. *Shakeſp. R.* III.

SO'LACE. *n. ſ.* [*ſolatium*, Latin. Comfort; pleaſure; alleviation; that which gives comfort or pleaſure; recreation; amuſement.

If we have that which is meet and right, although they be glad, we are not to envy them this their *ſolace*; we do not think it a duty of ours to be in every ſuch thing their tormentors. *Hooker.*

Therein ſat a lady freſh and fair,
Making ſweet *ſolace* to herſelf alone;
Sometimes ſhe ſung as loud as lark in air,
Sometimes ſhe laugh'd, that nigh her breath was gone. *F. Q.*

Great joy he promis'd to his thoughts, and new
Solace in her return. *Milton's Paradiſe Loſt.*

If I would delight my private hours
With muſick or with poem, where ſo ſoon
As in our native language can I find
That *ſolace*? *Milton's Paradiſe Regain'd.*

Though sight be lost,
Life yet hath many *solaces*, enjoy'd
Where other senses want not their delights,
At home in leisure and domestick ease,
Exempt from many a care and chance, to which
Eye-sight exposes daily men abroad. *Milton's Agonistes.*

Through waters, and through flames I'll go,
Suff'rer and *solace* of thy woe. *Prior.*

SOLA'NDER. *n. s.* [*soulandres*, Fr.] A disease in horses. *Dict.*

SO'LAR. }
SO'LARY. } *adj.* [*solaire*, French; *solaris*, Latin.]

1. Being of the sun.

The corpuscles that make up the beams of light be *solary* effluviums, or minute particles of some ethereal substance, thrusting on one another from the lucid body. *Boyle.*

Instead of golden fruits,
By genial show'rs and *solar* heat supply'd,
Unsufferable Winter hath defac'd
Earth's blooming charms, and made a barren waste. *Blackm.*

2. Belonging to the sun.

They denominate some herbs *solar*, and some lunar. *Bacon.*

Scripture hath been punctual in other records, concerning *solary* miracles. *Brown's Vulgar Errours.*

3. Born under or in the predominant influence of the sun.

The cock was pleas'd to hear him speak so fair,
And proud beside, as *solar* people are. *Dryden.*

4. Measured by the sun.

The rule to find the moon's age, on any day of any *solar* month, cannot shew precisely an exact account of the moon, because of the inequality of the motions of the sun and moon, and the number of days of the *solar* months. *Holder on Time.*

SOLD. The preterite and participle passive of *sell.*

SOLD. *n. s.* [*souldee*, old French. *Trevoux.*] Military pay; warlike entertainment.

But were your will her *sold* to entertain,
And number'd be amongst knights of maidenhead,
Great guerdon, well I wot, should you remain,
And in her favour high be reckoned. *Fairy Queen.*

SO'LDAN. *n. s.* [for *sultan.*] The emperor of the Turks.

They at the *soldan*'s chair defy'd the best. *Milton.*

SO'LDANEL. *n. s.* [*soldanella*, Latin.] A plant.

It grows on the Alps, and several other mountainous places of Italy, Germany, and Hungary. They are plants of humble growth, seldom rising above six or eight inches high: their round leaves grow close to the ground, from between which the flower-stems arise, each of which have four or five flowers, of a fine blue colour, or of a snow-white, which hang down, and are shaped like bells. *Miller.*

To SO'LDER. *v. a.* [*souder*, Fr. *soldare*, Ital. *solidare*, Latin.] See SODER.

1. To unite or fasten with any kind of metallick cement.

A concave sphere of gold, filled with water, and *soldered* up, has, upon pressing the sphere with great force, let the water squeeze through it, and stand all over its outside in multitudes of small drops like dew, without bursting or cracking the body of the gold. *Newton's Opt.*

2. To mend; to unite any thing broken.

It booteth them not thus to *solder* up a broken cause, whereof their first and last discourses will fall asunder. *Hooker.*

Wars 'twixt you twain would be
As if the world should cleave, and that slain men
Should *solder* up the rift. *Shakes. Ant. and Cleopatra.*

Thou visible god,
That *sould'rest* close impossibilities,
And mak'st them kiss! *Shakesp. Timon.*

Learn'd he was in med'c'nal lore;
For by his side a pouch he wore,
Replete with strange hermetick powder,
That wounds nine miles point-blank would *solder. Hudibras.*

The naked cynick's jar ne'er flames; if broken,
'Tis quickly *solder'd*, or a new bespoken. *Dryd. jun. Juv.*

At the Restoration the presbyterians, and other sects, did all unite and *solder* up their several schemes, to join against the church. *Swift.*

SO'LDER. *n. s.* [from the verb.] Metallick cement.

Goldsmiths say, the coarsest stuff
Will serve for *solder* well enough. *Swift.*

SO'LDERER. *n. s.* [from *solder.*] One that solders or mends.

SO'LDIER. *n. s.* [*soldat*, Fr. from *solidarius*, low Latin, of *solidus*, a piece of money, the pay of a soldier; *souldée*, French.]

1. A fighting man; a warriour. Originally one who served for pay.

Your sister is the better *soldier*. *Shakes. King Lear.*

Good Siward,
An older and a better *soldier* none. *Shakesp. Macbeth.*

A *soldier*,
Full of strange oaths, and bearded like a pard,
Jealous in honour, sudden and quick in quarrel,
Seeking the bubble reputation
Ev'n in the cannon's mouth. *Shakespeare.*

This attempt
I'm *soldier* to, and will abide it with
A prince's courage. *Shakes. Cymbeline.*

I have not yet forgot I am a king:
If I have wrong'd thee, charge me face to face;
I have not yet forgot I am a *soldier*. *Dryd. Don Sebastian.*

2. It is generally used of the common men, as distinct from the commanders.

It were meet that any one, before he came to be a captain, should have been a *soldier*. *Spenser on Ireland.*

SO'LDIERLIKE. } *adj.* [*soldier* and *like.*] Martial; warlike;
SO'LDIERLY. } military; becoming a soldier.

Although at the first they had fought with beastly fury rather than any *soldierly* discipline, practice had now made them comparable to the best. *Sidney.*

I will maintain the word with my sword to be a *soldier like* word, and a word of good command. *Shakes. Henry IV.*

They according to a *soldierly* custom, in cases of extremity, by interchange of a kiss by every of them upon the swords of others, sealed a resolution to maintain the place *Hayward.*

Enemies as well as friends confessed, that it was as *soldierly* an action as had been performed on either side. *Clarendon.*

SO'LDIERSHIP. *n. s.* [from *soldier.*] Military character, martial qualities behaviour becoming a soldier.

Thy father and myself in friendship
First tried our *soldiership*: he did look far
Into the service of the time, and was
Discipled of the brav'st. *Shak. All's well that ends well.*

By sea you throw away
The absolute *soldiership* you have by land,
Distract your army, which doth most consist
Of war-mark'd footmen. *Shakespeare.*

SO'LDIERY. *n. s.* [from *soldier.*]

1. Body of military men; soldiers collectively.

The Memphian *soldiery*,
That swell'd the Erythrean wave, when wall'd,
The unfroze waters marvellously stood. *Philips.*

I charge not the *soldiery* with ignorance and contempt of learning, without allowing exceptions. *Swift.*

2. Soldiership; martial skill.

Offering him, if he would exercise his courage in *soldiery*, he would commit some charge unto him under his lieutenant Philanax. *Sidney.*

SOLE. *n. s.* [*solum*, Latin.]

1. The bottom of the foot.

I will only be bold with Benedict for his company; for from the crown of his head to the *sole* of his foot he is all mirth. *Shakesp. Much Ado about Nothing.*

Tickling is most in the *soles* of the feet: the cause is the rareness of being touched there. *Bacon's Nat. History.*

The *soals* of the feet have great affinity with the head and the mouth of the stomach; as going wet-shod, to those that use it not, affecteth both. *Bacon's Natural History.*

Such resting found the *sole* of unblest feet. *Milton.*

In the make of the camel's foot, the *sole* is flat and broad, being very fleshy, and covered only with a thick, soft, and somewhat callous skin; but very fit to travel in sandy places. *Ray on the Creation.*

2. The foot.

To redeem thy woful parent's head
From tyrant's rage and ever-dying dread,
Hast wander'd through the world now long a day,
Yet ceasest not thy weary *soles* to lead. *Fairy Queen.*

3. The bottom of the shoe.

Nay, gentle Romeo, we must have you dance.
—Not I, believe me: you have dancing shoes,
With nimble *soles*. *Shakesp. Romeo and Juliet.*

A trade that, I hope, I may use with a safe conscience; which is, indeed, sir, a mender of bad *soles*. *Shakespeare's Julius Cæsar.*

On fortune's cap we are not the very button —Nor the *soles* of her shoe. *Shakespeare's Hamlet.*

The caliga was a military shoe, with a very thick *sole*, tied above the instep with leather thongs. *Arbuthnot on Coins.*

4. The part of any thing that touches the ground.

The strike-block is a plane shorter than the jointer, having its *sole* made exactly flat and straight, and is used for the shooting of a short joint. *Moxon's Mech. Exer.*

Elm is proper for mills, *soles* of wheels, and pipes. *Mortim.*

5. A kind of sea-fish.

Of flat fish, rays, thornbacks, *soles*, and flowks. *Carew.*

To SOLE. *v. a.* [from the noun.] To furnish with soles: as, to *sole* a pair of shoes.

His feet were *soled* with a treble tuft of a close short tawney down. *Grew's Musæum.*

SOLE. *adj.* [*sol*, old French; *solus*, Latin.]

1. Single; only.

Take not upon thee to be judge alone: there is no *sole* judge but only one: say not to others, receive my sentence, when their authority is above thine. *Hooker.*

Orpheus every where expressed the infinite and *sole* power of one God, though he used the name of Jupiter. *Raleigh.*

To me shall be the glory *sole* among
Th' infernal pow'rs. *Milton's Paradise Lost.*

A rattling tempest through the branches went,
That stripp'd them bare, and one *sole* way they rent. *Dryd.*
He, *sole* in power, at the beginning said,
Let sea and air, and earth and heav'n be made:
And it was so; and when he shall ordain
In other sort, has but to speak again,
And they shall be no more. *Prior.*

2. [In law.] Not married.

Some others are such as a man cannot make his wife, though he himself be *sole* and unmarried. *Ayliffe.*

SO'LECISM. *n. s.* [σολοικισμὸς.] Unfitness of one word to another; impropriety in language. A barbarism may be in one word, a solecism must be of more.

There is scarce a *solecism* in writing which the best author is not guilty of, if we be at liberty to read him in the words of some manuscript. *Addison.*

SO'LELY. *adv.* [from *sole.*] Singly; only.

You knew my father well, and in him me,
Left *solely* heir to all his lands. *Shak. Taming of the Shrew.*
This night's great business
Shall to all our nights and days to come
Give *solely* sovereign sway and masterdom. *Shakespeare.*

That the intemperate heat of the clime *solely* occasions this complexion, experience admits not. *Brown's Vulgar Errours.*

This truth is pointed chiefly, if not *solely*, upon sinners of the first rate, who have cast off all regard for piety. *Atterbury.*

SO'LEMN. *adj.* [*solemnel*, French; *solemnis*, Latin.]

1. Anniversary; observed once a year with religious ceremonies.

The worship of this image was advanced, and a *solemn* supplication observed every year. *Stillingfleet.*

2. Religiously grave.

His holy rites and *solemn* feasts profan'd. *Milton.*

3. Awful; striking with seriousness.

Then 'gan he loudly through the house to call,
But no one care to answer to his cry;
There reigned a *solemn* silence over all. *Fairy Queen.*
To 'swage with *solemn* touches troubled thoughts. *Milt.*
Nor then the *solemn* nightingale ceas'd warbling. *Milton.*

4. Grave; affectedly serious.

When Steele reflects upon the many *solemn* strong barriers to our succession of laws and oaths, he thinks all fear vanisheth: so do I, provided the epithet *solemn* goes for nothing; because though I have heard of a *solemn* day, and a *solemn* coxcomb, yet I can conceive no idea of a *solemn* barrier. *Swift.*

SO'LEMNESS. } *n. s.* [*solemnité*, French; from *solemn.*]
SOLE'MNITY. }

1. Ceremony or rite annually performed.

Great was the cause; our old *solemnities*
From no blind zeal or fond tradition rise;
But, sav'd from death, our Argives yearly pay
These grateful honours to the god of day. *Pope.*

2. Religious ceremony.

3. Awful ceremony or procession.

The lady Constance,
Some speedy messenger bid repair
To our *solemnity*. *Shakesp. King John.*
The moon, like to a silver bow,
New bent in heaven, shall behold the night
Of our *solemnities*. *Shakespeare.*

There may be great danger in using such compositions in churches, at arraignments, plays, and *solemnities*. *Bacon.*

What fun'ral pomp shall floating Tiber see,
When rising from his bed he views the sad *solemnity*! *Dryd.*

Though the forms and *solemnities* of the last judgment may bear some resemblance to those we are acquainted with here, yet the rule of proceeding shall be very different. *Atterbury.*

4. Manner of acting awfully serious.

With much more skilful cruelty, and horrible *solemnity*, he caused each thing to be prepared for his triumph of tyranny. *Sid.*

5. Gravity; steady seriousness.

The stateliness and gravity of the Spaniards shews itself in the *solemnity* of their language. *Addison's Spectator.*

6. Awful grandeur; grave stateliness; sober dignity.

A diligent decency was in Polycletus, above others; to whom though the highest praise be attributed by the most, yet some think he wanted *solemness*. *Wotton's Architecture.*

7. Affected gravity.

Pr'ythee, Virgilia, turn thy *solemness* out o' door,
And go along with us. *Shakesp. Coriolanus.*

This speech ended with a *solemnity* of accent. *Fem. Quixote.*

SOLEMNIZA'TION. *n. s.* [from *solemnize.*] The act of solemnizing; celebration.

Soon followed the *solemnization* of the marriage between Charles and Anne dutchess of Bretagne, with whom he received the dutchy of Bretagne. *Bacon's Henry* VII.

To SO'LEMNIZE. *v. a.* [*solemniser*, French; from *solemn.*]

1. To dignify by particular formalities; to celebrate.

Dorilaus in a great battle was deprived of life; his obsequies being no more *solemnized* by the tears of his partakers than the blood of his enemies. *Sidney.*

Baptism to be administred in one place, and marriage *solemnized* in another. *Hooker.*

Then 'gan they sprinkle all the parts with wine,
And made great feast to *solemnize* that day. *Fairy Queen.*

The multitude of the celestial host were heard to *solemnize* his miraculous birth. *Boyle's Seraphick Love.*

Their choice nobility and flower
Met from all parts to *solemnize* this feast. *Milton's Agonist.*

2. To perform religiously once a year.

What commandment the Jews had to celebrate their feast of dedication is never spoken of in the law, yet *solemnized* even by our Saviour himself. *Hooker.*

SO'LEMNLY. *adv.* [from *solemn.*]

1. With annual religious ceremonies.

2. With formal gravity and stateliness.

There are, in points of wisdom and sufficiency, that do nothing or little very *solemnly*. *Bacon's Essays.*

3. With formal state.

Let him land,
And *solemnly* see him set on to London. *Shakesp. H. V.*

4. With affected gravity.

The ministers of state, who gave us law,
In corners, with selected friends, withdraw;
There in deaf murmurs *solemnly* are wise,
Whisp'ring like winds, ere hurricanes arise. *Dryden.*

5. With religious seriousness.

To demonstrate how much men are blinded by their own partiality, I do *solemnly* assure the reader, that he is the only person from whom I ever heard that objection. *Swift.*

To SOLI'CIT. *v. a.* [*solicito*, Latin.]

1. To importune; to intreat.

If you bethink yourself of any crime,
Unreconcil'd as yet to heav'n and grace,
Solicit for it straight. *Shakesp. Othello.*
We heartily *solicit*
Your gracious self to take on you the charge
And kingly government of this your land. *Shak. R.* III.
How he *solicits* heav'n
Himself best knows; but strangely visited people,
The mere despair of surgery, he cures. *Shakespeare.*
This in obedience hath my daughter shewn me,
And, more above, hath his *solicitings*,
As they fell out by time, by means and place,
All given to mine ear. *Shakesp. Hamlet.*
Did I request thee, Maker! from my clay,
To mold me man? Did I *solicit* thee
From darkness to promote me? *Milt. Par. Lost, b.* x.
The guardian of my faith so false did prove,
As to *solicit* me with lawless love. *Dryden's Aurengzebe.*

2. To call to action; to summon; to awake; to excite.

This supernatural *soliciting*
Cannot be ill, cannot be good. *Shakes. Macbeth.*
Solicit Henry with her wond'rous praise;
Bethink thee on her virtues that surmount
Her nat'ral graces, that extinguish art. *Shakesp. H.* VI.
That fruit *solicited* her longing eye. *Milton.*

Sounds and some tangible qualities *solicit* their proper senses, and force an entrance to the mind. *Locke.*

He is *solicited* by popular custom to indulge himself in forbidden liberties. *Rogers's Sermons.*

3. To implore; to ask.

With that she wept again, 'till he again *soliciting* the conclusion of her story, then must you, said she, know the story of Amphialus. *Sidney.*

4. To attempt; to try to obtain.

I view my crime, but kindle at the view,
Repent old pleasures, and *solicit* new. *Pope.*

5. To disturb; to disquiet. A Latinism.

Solicit not thy thoughts with matters hid. *Milton.*
I find your love, and would reward it too;
But anxious fears *solicit* my weak breast. *Dryd. Span. Fryar.*

SOLICITA'TION. *n. s.* from *solicit.*]

1. Importunity; act of importuning.

I can produce a man
Of female seed, far abler to resist
All his *solicitations*, and at length
All his vast force, and drive him back to hell. *Parad. Reg.*

2. Invitation; excitement.

Children are surrounded with new things, which, by a constant *solicitation* of their senses, draw the mind constantly to them. *Locke.*

SOLI'CITOR. *n. s.* [from *solicit.*]

1. One who petitions for another.

Be merry, Cassio;
For thy *solicitor* shall rather die,
Than give thy cause away. *Shakesp. Othello.*

Honest minds will consider poverty as a recommendation in the person who applies himself to them, and make the justice of his cause the most powerful *solicitor* in his behalf. *Addison.*

2. One who does in Chancery the business which is done by attorneys in other courts.

For the king's attorney and *solicitor* general, their continual use for the king's service requires men every way fit. *Bacon.*

SOLI'CITOUS.

SOLI'CITOUS. *adj.* [*solicitus*, Latin.] Anxious; careful; concerned. It has commonly *about* before that which causes anxiety; sometimes *for* or *of*. *For* is proper before something to be obtained.

Our hearts are pure, when we are not *solicitous* of the opinion and censures of men, but only that we do our duty. *Tayl.*

Enjoy the present, whatsoever it be, and be not *solicitous* for the future. *Taylor's Rule of living holy.*

The colonel had been intent upon other things, and not enough *solicitous* to finish the fortifications. *Clarendon.*

In providing money for disbanding the armies, upon which they were marvelously *solicitous*, there arose a question. *Clarend.*

They who were in truth zealous for the preservation of the laws, were *solicitous* to preserve the king's honour from any indignity, and his regal power from violation. *Clarendon.*

Laud attended on his majesty, which he would have been excused from, if that design had not been in view, to accomplish which he was *solicitous* for his advice. *Clarendon.*

There kept their watch the legions, while the grand
In council sat, *solicitous* what chance
Might intercept their emperour sent. *Milton's Par. Lost.*

Without sign of boast, or sign of joy,
Solicitous and blank, he thus began. *Milton's Parad. Reg.*

No man is *solicitous* about the event of that which he has in his power to dispose of. *South's Sermons.*

You have not only been careful of my fortune, the effect of your nobleness, but you have been *solicitous* of my reputation, which is that of your kindness. *Dryden.*

The tender dame, *solicitous* to know
Whether her child should reach old age or no,
Consults the sage Tiresias. *Addison.*

SOLI'CITOUSLY. *adv.* [from *solicitous.*] Anxiously; carefully.

The medical art being conversant about the health and life of man, doctrinal errours in it are to be *solicitously* avoided. *Boyle.*

He would surely have as *solicitously* promoted their learning, as ever he obstructed it. *Decay of Piety.*

SOLI'CITUDE. *n. s.* [*solicitudo*, Latin.] Anxiety; carefulness.

In this, by comparison, we behold the many cares and great labours of worldly men, their *solicitude* and outward shews, and publick ostentation, their pride, and vanities. *Raleigh.*

If they would but provide for eternity with the same *solicitude*, and real care, as they do for this life, they could not fail of heaven. *Tillotson's Sermons.*

They are to be known by a wonderful *solicitude* for the reputation of their friends. *Tatler.*

SOLI'CITRESS. *n. s.* [Feminine of *solicitor.*] A woman who petitions for another.

I had the most earnest *solicitress*, as well as the fairest; and nothing could be refused to my lady Hyde. *Dryden.*

SO'LID. *adj.* [*solidus*, Latin; *solide*, French.]

1. Not liquid; not fluid.

Land that ever burn'd
With *solid*, as the lake with liquid fire. *Milton.*

2. Not hollow; full of matter; compact; dense.

I hear his thund'ring voice resound,
And trampling feet that shake the *solid* ground. *Dryden.*

3. Having all the geometrical dimensions.

In a *solid* foot are 1728 *solid* inches, weighing 76 pound of rain water. *Arbuthnot on Coins.*

4. Strong; firm.

The duke's new palace is a noble pile built after this manner, which makes it look very *solid* and majestick. *Addison.*

5. Sound; not weakly.

If persons devote themselves to science, they should be well assured of a *solid* and strong constitution of body, to bear the fatigue. *Watts's Improvement of the Mind.*

6. Real; not empty; true; not fallacious.

This might satisfy sober and wise men, not with soft and specious words, but with pregnant and *solid* reasons. *K. Charles.*

The earth may of *solid* good contain
More plenty than the sun. *Milton.*

7. Not light; not superficial; grave; profound.

These, wanting wit, affect gravity, and go by the name of *solid* men; and a *solid* man is, in plain English, a *solid* solemn fool. *Dryden.*

SO'LID. *n. s.* [In physick.] The part containing the fluids.

The first and most simple *solids* of our body are perhaps merely terrestrial, and incapable of any change or disease. *Arb.*

SOLI'DITY. *n. s.* [*solidité*, Fr. *soliditas*, Lat. from *solid.*]

1. Fulness of matter; not hollowness.

2. Firmness; hardness; compactness; density.

That which hinders the approach of two bodies, when they are moving one towards another, I call *solidity*. *Locke.*

The stone itself, whether naked or invested with earth, is not by its *solidity* secured, but washed down. *Woodward.*

3. Truth; not fallaciousness; intellectual strength; certainty.

The most known rules are placed in so beautiful a light, that they have all the graces of novelty; and make the reader, who was before acquainted with them, still more convinced of their truth and *solidity*. *Addison's Spectator.*

His fellow-peers have attended to his eloquence, and have been convinced by the *solidity* of his reasoning. *Prior.*

SO'LIDLY. *adv.* [from *solid.*]

1. Firmly; densely; compactly.

2. Truly; on good grounds.

A complete brave man ought to know *solidly* the main end he is in the world for. *Digby.*

I look upon this as a sufficient ground for any rational man to take up his religion upon, and which I defy the subtlest atheist in the world *solidly* to answer; namely, that it is good to be sure. *South.*

SO'LIDNESS. *n. s.* [from *solid.*] Solidity; firmness; density.

It beareth misseltoe: the cause may be the closeness and *solidness* of the wood and pith of the oak. *Bacon.*

It is built with that unusual *solidness*, that it seems he intended to make a sacrifice to perpetuity, and to contest with the iron teeth of time. *Howel's Vocal Forest.*

SOLIDU'NGULOUS. *adj.* [*solidus* and *ungula*, Latin.] Whole-hoofed.

It is set down by Aristotle and Pliny, that an horse and all *solidungulous* or whole-hoofed animals have no gall, which we find repugnant unto reason. *Brown's Vulgar Errours.*

SOLIFI'DIAN. *n. s.* [*solus* and *fides*, Latin.] One who supposes only faith, not works, necessary to justification.

It may be justly feared, that the title of fundamentals, being ordinarily confined to the doctrines of faith, hath occasioned that great scandal in the church of God, at which so many myriads of *solifidians* have stumbled, and fallen irreversibly, by conceiving heaven a reward of true opinions. *Hammond.*

SOLI'LOQUY. *n. s.* [*soliloque*, Fr. *solus* and *loquor*, Lat.] A discourse made by one in solitude to himself.

The whole poem is a *soliloquy*: Solomon is the person that speaks: he is at once the hero and the author; but he tells us very often what others say to him. *Prior.*

He finds no respite from his anxious grief,
Then seeks from his *soliloquy* relief. *Garth's Dispensatory.*

If I should own myself in love, you know lovers are always allowed the comfort of *soliloquy*. *Spectator.*

SO'LIPEDE. *n. s.* [*solus* and *pedes*, Lat.] An animal whose feet are not cloven.

Solipedes, or firm footed animals, as horses, asses, and mules, are in mighty number. *Brown's Vulgar Errours.*

SOLITA'IRE. *n. s.* [*solitaire*, French.]

1. A recluse; a hermit.

Often have I been going to take possession of tranquillity, when your conversation has spoiled me for a *solitaire*. *Pope.*

2. An ornament for the neck.

SO'LITARILY. *adv.* [from *solitary.*] In solitude; with loneliness; without company.

How should that subsist *solitarily* by itself, which hath no substance, but individually the very same whereby others subsist with it. *Hooker.*

Feed thy people with thy rod, the flock of thine heritage, which dwell *solitarily* in the wood. *Mic.* vii. 14.

SO'LITARINESS. *n. s.* [from *solitary.*] Solitude; forbearance of company; habitual retirement.

There is no cause to blame the prince for sometimes hearing them: the blame-worthiness is, that to hear them he rather goes to *solitariness* than makes them come to company. *Sidney.*

You subject yourself to *solitariness*, the sly enemy that doth most separate a man from well doing. *Sidney.*

At home in wholsome *solitariness*,
My piteous soul began the wretchedness
Of suitors at the court to mourn. *Donne.*

SO'LITARY. *adj.* [*solitaire*, French; *solitarius*, Latin.]

1. Living alone; not having company.

Those rare and *solitary*, these in flocks. *Milton.*
Satan explores his *solitary* flight. *Milton.*
Him fair Lavinia
Shall breed in groves to lead a *solitary* life. *Dryden's Æn.*

2. Retired; remote from company.

In respect that it is *solitary*, I like it very well; but in respect that it is private, it is a very vile life. *Shakespeare.*

3. Gloomy; dismal.

Let that night be *solitary*, let no joyful voice come therein. *Job.*

4. Single.

Nor did a *solitary* vengeance serve: the cutting off one head is not enough; the eldest son must be involved. *K. Charles.*

Relations alternately relieve each other, their mutual concurrences supporting their *solitary* instabilities. *Brown.*

SO'LITARY. *n. s.* [from the adjective.] One that lives alone; an hermit.

You describe so well your heremitical state of life, that none of the ancient anchorites could go beyond you, for a cave, with a spring, or any of the accommodations that befit a *solitary*. *Pope's Letters.*

SO'LITUDE. *n. s.* [*solitude*, French; *solitudo*, Latin.]

1. Lonely life; state of being alone.

It had been hard to have put more truth and untruth together, in few words, than in that speech; whosoever is delighted with *solitude*, is either a wild beast or a god. *Bacon.*

What call'ſt thou *ſolitude?* Is not the earth
With various living creatures, and the air,
Repleniſh'd, and all theſe at thy command
To come, and play before thee? *Milton's Paradiſe Loſt.*

Such only can enjoy the country who are capable of thinking when they are there: then they are prepared for *ſolitude*, and in that *ſolitude* is prepared for them. *Dryden.*

2. A lonely place; a deſert.

SO'LLAR. *n. ſ.* [*ſolarium*, low Latin.] A garret.

Some ſkilfully drieth their hops on a kel,
And ſome on a *ſollar*, oft turning them wel. *Tuſſer.*

SO'LO. *n. ſ.* [Italian.] A tune played by a ſingle inſtrument.

SO'LOMON'S *Loaf. n. ſ.* A plant.

SO'LOMON'S *Seal. n. ſ.* [*polygonatum*, Lat.] A plant.

SO'LSTICE. *n. ſ.* [*ſolſtice*, French; *ſolſtitium*, Latin.]

1. The point beyond which the ſun does not go; the tropical point; the point at which the day is longeſt in Summer, or ſhorteſt in Winter.

2. It is taken of itſelf commonly for the Summer ſolſtice.

The ſun, aſcending unto the northern ſigns, begetteth firſt a temperate heat in the air, which by his approach unto the *ſolſtice* he intendeth, and by continuation increaſeth the ſame even upon declination. *Brown's Vulgar Errours.*

Let the plowmen's prayer
Be for moiſt *ſolſtices*, and Winters fair. *May's Virgil.*

SOLSTI'TIAL. *adj.* [*ſolſticial*, French; from *ſolſtice.*]

1. Belonging to the ſolſtice.

Obſerving the dog-days ten days before and after the equinoctial and *ſolſtitial* points, by this obſervation alone, are exempted a hundred days. *Brown's Vulgar Errours.*

2. Happening at the ſolſtice.

From the North to call
Decrepit Winter; from the South to bring
Solſtitial Summer's heat. *Milton's Paradiſe Loſt.*

The fields labour'd with thirſt; Aquarius had not ſhed
His wonted ſhowers, and Sirius parch'd with heat
Solſtitial the green herbs. *Philips.*

SO'LVIBLE. *adj.* [from *ſolve.*] Poſſible to be cleared by reaſon or inquiry.

Intellective memory I call an act of the intellective faculty, becauſe it is wrought by it, though I do not inquire how or where, becauſe it is not *ſolvible.* *Hale's Origin of Mankind.*

SO'LUBLE. *adj.* [*ſolubilis*, Latin.] Capable of diſſolution or ſeparation of parts.

Sugar is a *ſal oleoſum*, being *ſoluble* in water and fuſible in fire. *Arbuthnot.*

SOLUBI'LITY. *n. ſ.* [from *ſoluble.*] Suſceptiveneſs of ſeparation of parts.

This cannot account for the indiſſolvable coherence of ſome bodies, and the fragility and *ſolubility* of others. *Glanv. Sceps.*

To SOLVE. *v. a.* [*ſolvo*, Latin.] To clear; to explain; to untie an intellectual knot.

He would *ſolve* high diſpute
With conjugal careſſes. *Milton.*

Do thou, my ſoul, the deſtin'd period wait,
When God ſhall *ſolve* the dark decrees of fate;
His now unequal diſpenſations clear,
And make all wiſe and beautiful appear. *Tickell.*

It is mere trifling to raiſe objections, merely for the ſake of anſwering and *ſolving* them. *Watts.*

SO'LVENCY. *n. ſ.* [from *ſolvent.*] Ability to pay.

SO'LVENT. *adj.* [*ſolvens*, Latin.]

1. Having the power to cauſe diſſolution.

When diſſolved in water, it is not by the eye diſtinguiſhable from the *ſolvent* body, and appears as fluid. *Boyle.*

2. Able to pay debts contracted.

SO'LUND-GOOSE. *n. ſ.* A fowl.

A *ſolund-gooſe* is in bigneſs and feather very like a tame gooſe, but his bill longer, and ſomewhat pointed; his wings alſo much longer, being two yards over. *Grew.*

A Scot, when from the gallow-tree let looſe,
Drops into Styx, and turns a *ſoland-gooſe.* *Cleaveland.*

SOLU'TION. *n. ſ.* [*ſolution*, French; *ſolutio*, Latin.]

1. Diſruption; breach; disjunction; ſeparation.

In all bodies there is an appetite of union, and evitation of *ſolution* of continuity. *Bacon's Nat. Hiſtory.*

2. Matter diſſolved; that which contains any thing diſſolved.

Aretæus, to procure ſleep, recommends a *ſolution* of opium in water to foment the forehead. *Arbuthnot on Coins.*

When ſalt of Tartar *per deliquium*, poured into the *ſolution* of any metal, precipitates the metal, and makes it fall down to the bottom of the liquor in the form of mud, does not this argue that the acid particles are attracted more ſtrongly by the ſalt of tartar than by the metal, and by the ſtronger attraction go from the metal to the ſalt of tartar? *Newton's Opt.*

3. Reſolution of a doubt; removal of an intellectual difficulty.

Something yet of doubt remains,
Which only thy *ſolution* can reſolve. *Milton's Parad. Loſt.*

They give the reins to wand'ring thoughts,
'Till by their own perplexities involv'd
They ravel more, ſtill leſs reſolv'd,
But never find ſelf-ſatisfying *ſolution.* *Milton's Agoniſtes.*

With hope and fear
The woman did the new *ſolution* hear;
The man diffides in his own augury,
And doubts. *Dryden.*

This will inſtruct you to give a plainer *ſolution* of any difficulties that may attend the theme, and refute objections. *Watts.*

SO'LUTIVE. *adj.* [from *ſolvo*, Latin.] Laxative; cauſing relaxation.

Though it would not be ſo abſterſive, opening, and *ſolutive* as mead, yet it will be more lenitive in ſharp diſeaſes. *Bacon.*

SOMATO'LOGY. *n. ſ.* [σῶμα and λέγω.] The doctrine of bodies.

SOME. A termination of many adjectives, which denote quality or property of any thing. It is generally joined with a ſubſtantive: as *gameſome.* [*ſaam*, Dutch.]

SOME. *adj.* [ſom, ſum, Saxon; *ſums*, Gothick; *ſum*, Germ. *ſom*, Daniſh; *ſom*, *ſommig*, Dutch.]

1. More or leſs, noting an indeterminate quantity.

We landed ſome hundred men, where we found *ſome* freſh water. *Raleigh.*

2. More or fewer, noting an indeterminate number.

Let me leave *ſome* of the folk that are with me. *Gen.* xxxiii.

Firſt go with me *ſome* few of you, and ſee the place, and how it may be made convenient for you; and then ſend for your ſick. *Bacon.*

3. Certain perſons. *Some* is often uſed abſolutely for ſome people; part.

Some to the ſhores do fly,
Some to the woods, or whither fear adviſ'd;
But running from, all to deſtruction hye. *Daniel.*

Not in the neighbouring moon as *ſome* have dream'd. *Milt.*

Your edicts *ſome* reclaim from ſins,
But moſt your life and bleſt example wins. *Dryden.*

4. *Some* is oppoſed to *ſome*, or to *others.*

It may be that the queen's treaſure, in ſo great occaſions of diſburſements, is not always ſo ready; but being paid as it is, now *ſome*, and then *ſome*, it is no great impoveriſhment to her coffers. *Spenſer on Ireland.*

5. It is added to a number, to ſhow that the number is uncertain and conjectural.

Being encountered with a ſtrong ſtorm *ſome* eight leagues to the weſtward of Scilly, I held it the office of a commander to take a port. *Raleigh.*

At the higher end of a creek Milbrook lurketh between two hills, a village of *ſome* eighty houſes. *Carew.*

Old mens ſpirits viſual, contrary to thoſe of purblind men, unite not, but when the object is at *ſome* good diſtance. *Bacon.*

Sir Edward Poinings, after he had continued at Sluice *ſome* good while, returned unto the king, then before Buloigne. *Bac.*

The number ſlain on the rebels part were *ſome* two thouſand. *Bacon.*

He bore away the prize to the admiration of *ſome* hundreds. *Addiſon.*

Your good-natur'd gods, they ſay,
Deſcend *ſome* twice or thrice a day. *Prior.*

Paint, patches, jewels laid aſide,
At night aſtronomers agree,
The evening has the day bely'd,
And Phyllis is *ſome* forty-three. *Prior.*

6. One; any without determining which.

The pilot of *ſome* ſmall night founder'd ſkiff. *Milton.*

SO'MEBODY. *n. ſ.* [*ſome* and *body.*]

1. One; not nobody; a perſon indiſcriminate and undetermined.

O that ſir John were come, he would make this a bloody day to *ſomebody.* *Shakeſp. Henry IV.*

Jeſus ſaid *ſomebody* hath touched me; for I perceive that virtue is gone out of me. *Lu.* viii. 46.

If there be a tacit league, it is againſt ſomewhat or *ſomebody*: who ſhould they be? Is it againſt wild beaſts? No. It is againſt ſuch routs and ſhoals of people as have utterly degenerated from the laws of nature. *Bacon.*

We muſt draw in *ſomebody*, that may ſtand
'Twixt us and danger. *Denham's Sophy.*

The hopes that what he has muſt come to *ſomebody*, and that he has no heirs, have that effect, that he has every day three or four invitations. *Addiſon's Spectator.*

2. A perſon of conſideration.

Theudas roſe up, boaſting himſelf to be *ſomebody.* *Acts* v.

SO'MEDEAL. *adv.* [ſumdeal, Saxon.] In ſome degree. Obſolete.

Siker now I ſee thou ſpeak'ſt of ſpite,
All for thou lackeſt *ſomedele* their delight. *Spenſer.*

SO'MERSAULT. } *n. ſ.* [*Somerſet* is the corruption. *Sommer*, a
SO'MERSET. } beam, and *ſault*, French, a leap.] A leap by which a jumper throws himſelf from a beam, and turns over his head.

SO'MEHOW. *adj.* [*ſome* and *how.*] One way or other; I know not how.

The veſicular cells may be for receiving the arterial and nervous juices, that, by their action upon one another, they may be ſwelled *ſomehow*, ſo as to ſhorten the length of every fibril. *Cheyne.*

SOMETHING. *n. s.* [sumðing, Saxon.]

1. Not nothing, though it appears not what; a thing or matter indeterminate.

When fierce Bavar
Did from afar the British chief behold,
Betwixt despair and rage, and hope and pain,
Something within his warring bosom roll'd. *Prior.*

The force of the air upon the pulmonary artery is but small, in respect of that of the heart; but it is still *something*. *Arbuthnot on Aliments.*

You'll say the whole world has *something* to do, *something* to talk of, *something* to wish for, and *something* to be employed about; but pray put all these *somethings* together, and what is the sum total but just nothing. *Pope's Letters.*

Here she beholds the chaos dark and deep,
Where nameless *somethings* in their causes sleep. *Pope.*

2. More or less.

Something yet of doubt remains. *Milton.*

Years following years steal *something* ev'ry day,
At least they steal us from ourselves away. *Pope.*

3. Part.

Something of it arises from our infant state. *Watts.*

4. Distance not great.

I will acquaint you with the perfect spy o' th' time; for't must be done to-night, and *something* from the palace. *Shakesp.*

SO'METHING. *adv.* In some degree.

The pain went away upon it; but he was *something* discouraged by a new pain falling some days after upon his elbow on the other side. *Temple.*

SO'METIME. *adv.* [*some* and *time.*] Once; formerly.

What art thou that usurp'st this time of night,
Together with that fair and warlike form,
In which the majesty of buried Denmark
Did *sometime* march? *Shakesp. Hamlet.*

Good *sometime* queen, prepare thee hence for France. *Sh.*

SO'METIMES. *adv.* [*some* and *times.*]

1. Not never; now and then; at one time or other.

'Twill render me more equal, *sometime* superior. *Milton.*

It is good that we *sometimes* be contradicted, and that we always bear it well; for perfect peace cannot be had in this world. *Taylor.*

2. At one time, opposed to *sometimes*, or to *another time*.

The body passive is better wrought upon at *sometimes* than at others. *Bacon's Natural History.*

Sometimes the one, and *sometimes* the other, may be glanced upon in these scripture descriptions. *Burnet.*

He writes not always of a piece, but *sometimes* mixes trivial things with those of greater moment: *sometimes* also, though not often, he runs riot, and knows not when he has said enough. *Dryden's Fables, Preface.*

SO'MEWHAT. *n. s.* [*some* and *what.*]

1. Something; not nothing, though it be uncertain what.

Upon the sea *somewhat* methought did rise
Like blueish mists. *Dryden's Indian Emperor.*

He that shuts his eyes against a small light, on purpose to avoid the sight of *somewhat* that displeases him, would, for the same reason, shut them against the sun. *Atterbury.*

2. More or less.

Concerning every of these, *somewhat* Christ hath commanded, which must be kept 'till the world's end: on the contrary side, in every of them *somewhat* there may be added, as the church judges it expedient. *Hooker.*

These salts have *somewhat* of a nitrous taste, but mixt with a smatch of vitriolick. *Grew.*

3. Part greater or less.

Somewhat of his good sense will suffer in this transfusion, and much of the beauty of his thoughts will be lost. *Dryden.*

SO'MEWHAT. *adv.* In some degree.

Holding of the breath doth help *somewhat* to cease the hiccough. *Bacon's Natural History.*

He is *somewhat* arrogant at his first entrance, and is too inquisitive through the whole; yet these imperfections hinder not our compassion. *Dryden.*

SO'MEWHERE. *adv.* [*some* and *where.*] In one place or other; not nowhere.

Hopeless and forelorn
They are return'd, and *somewhere* live obscurely. *Denham.*

Compressing two prisms hard together, that their sides, which by chance were a very little convex, might *somewhere* touch one another, I found the place in which they touched to become absolutely transparent, as if they had there been one continued piece of glass. *Newton's Opt.*

Does something still, and *somewhere* yet remain,
Reward or punishment? *Prior.*

Of the dead we must speak gently; and therefore, as Mr. Dryden says *somewhere*, peace be to its manes. *Pope.*

SO'MEWHILE. *n. s.* [*some* and *while.*] Once; for a time. Out of use.

Though under colour of the shepherds *somewhile*,
There crept in wolves full of fraud and guile,
That often devoured their own sheep,
And often the shepherd that did 'em keep. *Spenser's Past.*

SOMNI'FEROUS. *adj.* [*somnifere*, Fr. *somnifer*, Latin.] Causing sleep; procuring sleep; soporiferous; dormitive.

I wish for some *somniferous* potion, that might force me to sleep away the intermitted time, as it does with men in sorrow. *Walton's Angler.*

SOMNI'FICK. *adj.* [*somnus* and *facio*, Latin.] Causing sleep.

SO'MNOLENCY. *n. s.* [*somnolentia*, Latin.] Sleepiness; inclination to sleep.

SON. *n. s.* [*sunus*, Gothick; suna, Saxon; *sohn*, German; *son*, Swedish; *sone*, Dutch; *syn*, Sclavonian.]

1. A male born of one or begotten by one; correlative to father or mother.

She had a *son* for her cradle, ere she had a husband for her bed. *Shakesp. King Lear.*

Cast out this bondwoman and her *son*. *Gen.* xxi. 10.

He compares the affection of the Divine Being to the indulgence of a wise father, who would have his *sons* exercised with labour and pain, that they may gather strength. *Addison.*

2. Descendant however distant: as, the *sons* of *Adam*.

I am the *son* of the wise, the *son* of ancient kings. *Is.* xix.

3. Compellation of an old to a young man, or of a confessor to his penitent.

Be plain, good *son*, and homely in thy drift;
Riddling confession finds but riddling shrift. *Shakespeare.*

4. Native of a country.

Britain then
Sees arts her savage *sons* controul. *Pope.*

5. The second person of the Trinity.

If thou be the *son* of God, come down. *Mat.* xxvii. 40.

6. Product of any thing.

Our imperfections prompt our corruption, and loudly tell us we are *sons* of earth. *Brown's Vulgar Errours.*

Earth's tall *sons*, the cedar, oak, and pine,
Their parents undecaying strength declare. *Blackmore.*

7. In scripture, *sons* of pride, and *sons* of light, denoting some quality. 'Tis a Hebraism.

This new fav'rite
Of heav'n, this man of clay, *son* of despite. *Milton.*

SON-IN-LAW. *n. s.* One married to one's daughter.

If virtue no benighted beauty lack,
Your *son-in-law* is far more fair than black. *Shak. Othello.*

A foreign *son-in-law* shall come from far,
Whose race shall bear aloft the Latian name. *Dryd. Æn.*

SO'NSHIP. *n. s.* [from *son.*] Filiation; the character of a son.

The apostle to the Hebrews makes afflictions not only incident but necessary to Christianity, the badge and cognizance of *sonship*. *Decay of Piety.*

SONA'TA. *n. s.* [Italian.] A tune.

He whistled a Scotch tune, and an Italian *sonata*. *Addison.*

Could Pedro, think you, make no trial
Of a *sonata* on his viol,
Unless he had the total gut,
Whence every string at first was cut. *Prior.*

SONG. *n. s.* [from gesungen, Saxon.]

1. Any thing modulated in the utterance.

Noise other than the sound of dance and *song*. *Milton.*

He first thinks fit no sonnetter advance
His censure farther than the *song* or dance. *Dryden.*

2. A poem to be modulated by the voice; a ballad.

Pardon, goddess of the night,
Those that flew thy virgin knight;
For the which, with *songs* of woe,
Round about his tomb they go! *Shakespeare.*

In her days ev'ry man shall sing
The merry *songs* of peace to all his neighbours. *Sh. H.* VIII.

3. A poem; lay; strain.

The bard that first adorn'd our native tongue,
Tun'd to his British lyre this ancient *song*. *Dryden.*

4. Poetry; poesy.

This subject for heroick *song* pleas'd me. *Milton.*

Names memorable long,
If there be force in virtue, or in *song*. *Pope.*

5. Notes of birds.

The lark, the messenger of day,
Saluted in her *song* the morning grey. *Dryden.*

6. *An old* SONG. A trifle.

I do not intend to be thus put off with an *old song*. *More.*

A hopeful youth, newly advanced to great honour, was forced by a cobler to resign all for an *old song*. *Addison.*

SO'NGISH. *adj.* [from *song.*] Containing songs; consisting of songs. A low word.

The *songish* part must abound in the softness and variety of numbers, its intention being to please the hearing. *Dryden.*

SO'NGSTER. *n. s.* [from *song.*] A singer. Used of human singers, it is a word of slight contempt.

The pretty *songsters* of the Spring with their various notes did seem to welcome him as he passed. *Howel.*

Some *songsters* can no more sing in any chamber but their own, than some clerks read in any book but their own. *L'Estr.*

Either *songster* holding out their throats,
And folding up their wings, renew'd their notes. *Dryden.*

SO'NGSTRESS. *n. s.* [from *song*.] A female singer.
Through the soft silence of the listening night,
The sober-suited *songstress* trills her lay. *Thomson's Summer.*

SO'NNET. *n. s.* [*sonnet*, French; *sonnetto*, Italian.]

1. A short poem consisting of fourteen lines, of which the rhymes are adjusted by a particular rule. It is not very suitable to the English language, and has not been used by any man of eminence since *Milton*.

A book was writ of late call'd Tetrachordon,
And woven close, both matter, form, and stile;
The subject new: it walk'd the town a-while,
Numb'ring good intellects, now seldom por'd on:
Cries the stall-reader, Bless us, what a word on
A title-page is this! and some in file
Stand spelling false, while one might walk to Mile-
End-green. Why is it harder, sirs, than Gordon,
Colkitto, or Macdonnel, or Galasp?
Those rugged names to our like mouths grow sleek,
That would have made Quintilian stare and gasp:
Thy age like ours, soul of sir John Cheek,
Hated not learning worse than toad or asp,
When thou taught'st Cambridge and king Edward
Greek. *Milton.*

2. A small poem.

Let us into the city presently,
To sort some gentlemen well skill'd in musick;
I have a *sonnet* that will serve the turn. *Shakespeare.*

SONNETTE'ER. *n. s.* [*sonnetier*, French; from *sonnet*.] A small poet, in contempt.

Assist me, some extemporal god of rhime; for I am sure I shall turn *sonnetteer*. *Shakesp. Love's Labour's Lost.*

He first thinks fit no *sonnetteer* advance
His censure farther than the song or dance. *Dryden.*

There are as many kinds of gardening as of poetry: your makers of parterres and flower-gardens are epigrammatists and *sonnetteers* in this art. *Spectator.*

What woful stuff this madrigal would be,
In some starv'd hackney *sonnetteer* or me?
But let a lord once own the happy lines,
How the wit brightens! how the style refines! *Pope.*

SONI'FEROUS. *adj.* [*sonus* and *fero*, Latin.] Giving or bringing sound.

This will appear, let the subject matter of sounds be what it will; either the atmosphere, or the etherial part thereof, or *soniferous* particles of bodies. *Derham.*

SONORI'FICK. *adj.* [*sonorus* and *facio*, Lat.] Producing sound.

If he should ask me why a clock strikes, and points to the hour; and I should say, it is by an indicating form and *sonorifick* quality, this would be unsatisfactory. *Watts's Logick.*

SONO'ROUS *adj.* [*sonore*, French; *sonorus*, Latin.]

1. Loud sounding; giving loud or shrill sound. Bodies are distinguished as *sonorous* or *unsonorous*.

All the while
Sonorous metal blowing martial sounds;
At which the universal host up-sent
A shout that tore hell's concave. *Milton's Paradise Lost.*

2. High sounding; magnificent of sound.

The Italian opera, amidst all the meanness and familiarity of the thoughts, has something beautiful and *sonorous* in the expression. *Addison on Italy.*

SONO'ROUSLY. *adv.* [from *sonorous*.] With high sound; with magnificence of sound.

SONO'ROUSNESS. *n. s.* [from *sonorous*.]

1. The quality of giving sound.

Enquiring of a maker of viols and lutes of what age he thought lutes ought to be, to attain their full and best seasoning for *sonorousness*, he replied, that in some twenty years would be requisite, and in others forty. *Boyle.*

2. Magnificence of sound.

SOON. *adv.* [*suns*, Gothick; ſona, Saxon; *saen*, Dutch.]

1. Before long time be past; shortly after any time assigned or supposed.

Nor did they not perceive their evil plight,
Yet to their gen'ral's voice they *soon* obey'd. *Milton.*
You must obey me, *soon* or late;
Why should you vainly struggle with your fate? *Dryden.*

2. Early; before any time supposed: opposed to late.

O boy! thy father gave thee life too *soon*,
And hath bereft thee of thy life too late. *Shakes. Hen.* VI.

Do this, that I may be restored to you the *sooner*. *Heb.* xiii.

How is it that you are come so *soon* to-day? *Ex.* ii. 18.

The earlier stayeth for the later, and not that the later cometh *sooner*. *Bacon's Nat. History.*

3. Readily; willingly.

I would as *soon* see a river winding through woods and meadows, as when it is tossed up in so many whimsical figures at Versailles. *Addison's Guardian.*

4. It has in *Sidney* the signification of an adjective, whether licentiously or according to the custom of his time.

He hath preserved Argalus alive, under pretence of having him publickly executed after these wars, of which they hope for a *soon* and prosperous issue. *Sidney.*

5. SOON *as*. Immediately; at the very time.

As *soon as* he came nigh unto the camp, he saw the calf and the dance. *Ex.* xxxii. 19.

Nor was his virtue poison'd, *soon as* born,
With the too early thoughts of being king. *Dryden.*

SOONLY. *adv.* [from *soon*.] Quickly; speedily. This word I remember in no other place; but if *soon* be, as it seems once to have been, an adjective, *soonly* is proper.

A mason meets with a stone that wants no cutting, and, *soonly* approving of it, places it in his work. *More.*

SO'OPBERRY. *n. s.* [*sapindus*, Latin] A plant.

It hath a flower, which for the most part is composed of four leaves, expanding in form of a rose; from whose four-leaved empalement arises the pointal, which afterward becomes a spherical fruit, inclosing a nut of the same form. *Miller.*

SOOT. *n. s.* [ſoꞇ, Saxon; *sot*, Islandick; *soet*, Dutch.] Condensed or embodied smoke.

Soot, though thin spread in a field, is a very good compost. *Bacon.*

If the fire be not kept within the tunnel of the chimney, and some appointed to sweep down the *soot*, the house will be in danger of burning. *Howel.*

Oft they assay'd,
Hunger and thirst constraining; drugg'd as oft
With hatefullest disrelish, writh'd their jaws,
With *soot* and cinders fill'd. *Milton's Paradise Lost.*
Our houshold gods, that droop upon our hearths,
Each from his venerable face shall brush
The Macedonian *soot*, and shine again. *Dryd. Cleomenes.*

SO'OTED. *adj.* [from *soot*.] Smeared, manured, or covered with soot.

The land was *sooted* before. *Mortimer.*

SO'OTERKIN. *n. s.* A kind of false birth fabled to be produced by the Dutch women from sitting over their stoves.

When Jove was, from his teeming head,
Of wit's fair goddess brought to-bed,
There follow'd at his lying-in,
For after-birth, a *sooterkin*. *Swift.*

SOOTH. *n. s.* [ſoð, Saxon.] Truth; reality. Obsolete.

Sir, understand you this of me in *sooth*,
Th' youngest daughter, whom you hearken for,
Her father keeps from all access of suitors,
Until the eldest sister first be wed. *Shakespeare.*
That e'er this tongue of mine,
That laid the sentence of dread banishment
On yond proud man, should take it off again
With words of *sooth*. *Shakes. Richard* II.
He looks like *sooth*: he says he loves my daughter;
I think so too; for never gaz'd the moon
Upon the water, as he'll stand and read
My daughter's eyes. *Shakesp. Winter's Tale.*

If I have any skill in soothsaying, as in *sooth* I have none, it doth prognosticate that I shall change caps. *Camden's Rem.*

The very *sooth* of it is, that an ill habit has the force of an ill fate. *L'Estrange.*

I did not mean to chide you;
For, *sooth* to say, I hold it noble in you
To cherish the distress'd. *Rowe.*

SOOTH. *adj.* [ſoð, Saxon.] Pleasing; delightful.

Some other means I have,
Which once of Melibæus old I learn'd,
The *soothest* shepherd that e'er pip'd on plains. *Milton.*

To SOOTH. *v. a.* [ᵹeſoðian, Saxon.]

1. To flatter; to please with blandishments.

In *soothing* them, we nourish 'gainst our senate
The cockle of rebellion, insolence, sedition. *Shakespeare.*
Can I *sooth* tyranny?
Seem pleas'd to see my royal master murder'd,
His crown usurp'd, a distaff in the throne? *Dryden.*
By his fair daughter is the chief confin'd,
Who *sooths* to dear delight his anxious mind;
Successless all her soft caresses prove,
To banish from his breast his country's love. *Pope's Odyssey.*
Thinks he that Memnon, soldier as he is,
Thoughtless and dull, will listen to his *soothing*? *Rowe.*
I've try'd the force of every reason on him,
Sooth'd and caress'd, been angry, *sooth'd* again;
Laid safety, life, and interest in his sight;
But all are vain, he scorns them all for Cato. *Addis. Cato.*

2. To calm; to soften; to mollify.

The beldame
Sooths her with blandishments, and frights with threats. *Dry.*

3. To gratify; to please.

This calm'd his cares; *sooth'd* with his future fame,
And pleas'd to hear his propagated name. *Dryden.*

SO'OTHER. *n. s.* [from *sooth*.] A flatterer; one who gains by blandishments.

I cannot flatter: I defy
The tongues of *soothers*. *Shakesp. Henry* IV.

To SOOTHSA'Y. *v. n.* [*sooth* and *say*.] To predict; to foretell.

A damsel, possessed with a spirit of divination, met us, which brought her masters much gain by *soothsaying*. *Acts* xvi.

SOOTHSAY'ER.

Soothsa'yer. *n. s.* [from *soothsay.*] A foreteller; a predicter; a prognosticator.

Scarce was Musidorus made partaker of this oft blinding light, when there were found numbers of *soothsayers* who affirmed strange and incredible things should be performed by that child. *Sidney.*

A *soothsayer* bids you beware the ides of March. *Shakesp.*

He was animated to expect the papacy by the prediction of a *soothsayer*, that one should succeed pope Leo, whose name should be Adrian, an aged man of mean birth, and of great learning and wisdom. *Bacon's Henry* VII.

Soo'tiness. *n. s.* [from *sooty.*] The quality of being sooty; fuliginousness.

Soo'ty. *adj.* [from *soot.*]

1. Breeding soot.

By fire of *sooty* coal th' alchymist turns
Metals to gold. *Milton.*

2. Consisting of soot; fuliginous.

There may be some chymical way so to defecate this oil, that it shall not spend into a *sooty* matter. *Wilkins.*

3. Black; dark; dusky.

All the grisly legions that troop
Under the *sooty* flag of Acheron;
Harpies and hydras and all monstrous forms. *Milton.*
Swift on his *sooty* pinions flits the gnome,
And in a vapour reach'd the gloomy dome. *Pope.*

Sop. *n. s.* [ꞅop, Saxon; *sopa*, Spanish; *soppe*, Dutch.]

1. Any thing steeped in liquour to be eaten.

The bounded waters
Would lift their bosoms higher than the shores,
And make a *sop* of all this solid globe. *Shakespeare.*

Draw, you rogue; for though it be night, yet the moon shines: I'll make a *sop* o'th' moonshine of you. *Shakespeare.*

Sops in wine, quantity for quantity, inebriate more than wine of itself. *Bacon's Natural History.*

The prudent Sibyl had before prepar'd
A *sop*, in honey steep'd, to charm the guard,
Which mix'd with powerful drugs, she cast before
His greedy grinning jaws, just op'd to roar. *Dryden.*

Ill nature is not to be cured with a *sop*; but quarrelsome men, as well as quarrelsome curs, are worse for fair usage. *L'Estrange.*

2. Any thing given to pacify, from the *sop* given to Cerberus.

To Cerberus they give a *sop*,
His tripple barking mouth to stop. *Swift.*

To Sop. *v. a.* To steep in liquour.

Sope. *n. s.* [See Soap.]

Soph. *n. s.* [from *sophista*, Latin.] A young man who has been two years at the university.

Three Cambridge *sophs*, and three pert templars came,
The same their talents, and their tastes the same;
Each prompt to query, answer and debate,
And smit with love of poesy and prate. *Pope's Dunciad.*

So'phi. *n. s.* [Persian.] The emperor of Persia.

By this scimitar
That slew the *sophi* and a Persian prince. *Shakespeare.*
A fig for the sultan and *sophi.* *Congreve.*

So'phism. *n. s.* [*sophisma*, Latin.] A fallacious argument; an unsound subtilty; a fallacy.

When a false argument puts on the appearance of a true one, then it is properly called a *sophism* or fallacy. *Watts.*

So'phist. *n. s.* [*sophista*, Latin.] A professor of philosophy.

The court of Crœsus is said to have been much resorted by the *sophists* of Greece in the happy beginning of his reign. *Tem.*

So'phister. *n. s.* [*sophiste*, French; *sophista*, Latin.]

1. A disputant fallaciously subtle; an artful but insidious logician.

A subtle traitor needs no *sophister*. *Shakespeare's Hen.* VI.

If a heathen philosopher bring arguments from reason, which none of our atheistical *sophisters* can confute, for the immortality of the soul, I hope they will so weigh the consequences, as neither to talk, nor live, as if there was no such thing. *Denham.*

Not all the subtle objections of *sophisters* and rabbies, against the gospel, so much prejudiced the reception of it, as the reproach of those crimes with which they aspersed the assemblies of christians. *Rogers's Sermons.*

2. A professor of philosophy; a sophist. This sense is antiquated.

Alcidimus the *sophister* hath many arguments to prove, that voluntary and extemporal far excelleth premeditated speech. *Hooker.*

Sophi'stical. *adj.* [*sophistique*, Fr. from *sophist.*] Fallaciously subtle; logically deceitful.

Neither know I whether I should prefer for madness, and *sophistical* couzenage, that the same body of Christ should be in a thousand places at once of this sublunary world. *Hall.*

When the state of the controversy is well understood, the difficulty will not be great in giving answers to all his *sophistical* cavils. *Stillingfleet.*

That may seem a demonstration for the present, which to posterity will appear a more *sophistical* knot. *More.*

Sophi'stically. *adv.* [from *sophistical.*] With fallacious subtilty.

Bolingbroke argues most *sophistically*. *Swift.*

To Sophi'sticate. *v. a.* [*sophistiquer*, Fr. from *sophist.*] To adulterate; to corrupt with something spurious.

If the passions of the mind be strong, they easily *sophisticate* the understanding, they make it apt to believe upon every slender warrant, and to imagine infallible truth, where scarce any probable shew appeareth. *Hooker.*

Here's three of us are *sophisticated*. *Shakespeare.*

Divers experiments succeeded not, because they were at one time tried with genuine materials, and at another time with *sophisticated* ones. *Boyle.*

The only persons amongst the heathens, who *sophisticated* nature and philosophy, were the Stoicks; who affirmed a fatal, unchangeable concatenation of causes, reaching even to the elicite acts of man's will. *South's Sermons.*

Yet the rich cullies may their boasting spare;
They purchase but *sophisticated* ware:
'Tis prodigality that buys deceit,
Where both the giver and the taker cheat. *Dryden.*

The eye hath its coats and humours transparent and colourless, lest it should tinge and *sophisticate* the light that it lets in by a natural jaundice. *Bentley.*

Sophi'sticate. *part. adj.* [from the verb.] Adulterate; not genuine.

Since then a great part of our scientifical treasure is most likely to be adulterate, though all bears the image and superscription of truth; the only way to know what is *sophisticate* and what is not so, is to bring all to the examen of the touchstone. *Glanville.*

So truth, when only one supply'd the state,
Grew scarce and dear, and yet *sophisticate*. *Dryden.*

Sophistica'tion. *n. s.* [*sophistication*, Fr. from *sophisticate.*] Adulteration; not genuineness.

Sophistication is the act of counterfeiting or adulterating any thing with what is not so good, for the sake of unlawful gain. *Quincy.*

The drugs and simples sold in shops, generally are adulterated by the fraudulent avarice of the sellers, especially if the preciousness may make their *sophistication* very beneficial. *Boyle.*

Besides easy submission to *sophistications* of sense, we have inability to prevent the miscarriages of our junior reasons. *Glanv.*

Sophistica'tor. *n. s.* [from *sophisticate.*] Adulterator; one that makes things not genuine.

So'phistry. *n. s.* [from *sophist.*] Fallacious ratiocination.

His *sophistry* prevailed; his father believed. *Sidney.*

These men have obscured and confounded the natures of things, by their false principles and wretched *sophistry*; tho' an act be never so sinful, they will strip it of its guilt. *South.*

To S'oporate. *v. n.* [*soporo*, Latin.] To lay asleep. *Dict.*

Sopori'ferous. *adj.* [*sopor* and *fero.*] Productive of sleep; causing sleep; narcotick; opiate; dormitive; somniferous; anodyne; sleepy.

The particular ingredients of those magical ointments are opiate and *soporiferous*; for anointing of the forehead, neck, feet, and back-bone, procures dead sleeps. *Bacon.*

While the whole operation was performing, I lay in a profound sleep, by the force of that *soporiferous* medicine infused into my liquor. *Gulliver's Travels.*

Sopori'ferousness. *n. s.* [from *soporiferous.*] The quality of causing sleep.

Sopori'fick. *adj.* [*sopor* and *facio.*] Causing sleep; opiate; narcotick.

The colour and taste of opium are, as well as its *soporifick* or anodyne virtues, mere powers depending on its primary qualities. *Locke.*

So'pper. *n. s.* [from *sop.*] One that steeps any thing in liquor.

So'rbile. *adj.* [from *sorbeo*, Latin.] That may be drunk or sipped.

Sorbi'tion. *n. s.* [*sorbitio*, Latin.] The act of drinking or sipping.

Sorbs. *n. s.* [*sorbum*, Lat.] The berries of the sorb or service-tree.

So'rcerer. *n. s.* [*sorcier*, French; *sortiarius*, low Latin.] A conjurer; an enchanter; a magician.

They say this town is full of cozenage,
As nimble jugglers that deceive the eye,
Drug-working *sorcerers* that change the mind,
Soul-killing witches that deform the body,
And many such like libertines of sin. *Shakespeare.*

The weakness of the power of witches upon kings and magistrates may be ascribed to the weakness of imagination; for it is hard for a witch or a *sorcerer* to put on a belief that they can hurt such. *Bacon's Natural History.*

He saw a fable *sorcerer* arise,
All sudden gorgon's hiss and dragon's glare,
And ten horn'd fiends. *Pope.*

The Egyptian *sorcerers* contended with Moses; but the wonders which Moses wrought did so far transcend the power of magicians, as made them confess it was the finger of God. *Watts's Logick.*

SO'RCERESS. *n. s.* [Female of *sorcerer.*] A female magician; an enchantress.

Bring forth that *sorceress* condemn'd to burn. *Shakesp.*

Divers witches and *sorceresses* have fed upon man's flesh, to aid their imagination with high and foul vapours. *Bacon.*

The snaky *sorceress* that sat
Just by hell-gate, and kept the fatal key,
Ris'n, and with hideous outcry rush'd between. *Milton.*

How cunningly the *sorceress* displays
Her own transgressions, to upbraid me, mine. *Milton.*

SO'RCERY. *n. s.* Magick; enchantment; conjuration; witchcraft; charms.

This witch Sycorax,
For mischiefs manifold, and *sorceries* terrible,
Was banish'd. *Shakespeare.*

Adders wisdom I have learn'd
To fence my ear against thy *sorceries.* *Milton.*

Actæon has long tracts of rich soil; but had the misfortune in his youth to fall under the power of *sorcery.* *Tatler.*

SORD. *n. s.* [from *sward.*] Turf; grassy ground.

This is the prettiest low-born lass that ever ran on the green *sord.* *Shakespeare's Winter's Tale.*

An altar of grassy *sord.* *Milton.*

SO'RDES. *n. s.* [Latin.] Foulness; dregs.

The sea washes off the *soil* and *sordes* wherein mineral mosses were involved and concealed, and thereby renders them more conspicuous. *Woodward.*

SO'RDET. } *n. s.* *sourdine,* French; *sordina,* Italian.] A small
SO'RDINE. } pipe put into the mouth of a trumpet to make it found lower or shriller. *Bailey.*

SO'RDID. *adj.* [*sordidus,* Latin.]

1. Foul; gross; filthy; dirty.

There Charon stands
A *sordid* god, down from his hoary chin
A length of beard descends, uncomb'd, unclean. *Dryden.*

2. [*Sordide,* French.] Intellectually dirty; mean; vile; base.

It is strange since the priests office heretofore was always splendid, that it is now looked upon as a piece of religion, to make it low and *sordid.* *South's Sermons.*

3. [*Sordide,* French.] Covetous; niggardly.

He may be old,
And yet not *sordid,* who refuses gold. *Denham.*

If one should cease to be generous and charitable, because another is *sordid* and ungrateful, it would be much in the power of vice to extinguish christian virtues. *L'Estrange.*

SO'RDIDLY. *adv.* [from *sordid.*] Meanly; poorly; covetously;

SO'RDIDNESS. *n. s.* [from *sordid.*]

1. Meanness; baseness.

I omit the madnesses of Caligula's delights, and the execrable *sordidness* of those of Tiberius. *Cowley.*

2. Nastiness; not neatness.

Providence deters people from sluttishness and *sordidness,* and provokes them to cleanliness. *Ray.*

SORE. *n. s.* [ꞅaꞃ, Saxon; *saur,* Danish.] A place tender and painful; a place excoriated; an ulcer. It is not used of a wound, but of a breach of continuity, either long continued or from internal cause: to be a *sore,* there must be an excoriation; a tumour or bruise is not called a *sore* before some disruption happen.

Let us hence provide
A salve for any *sore* that may betide. *Shakespeare's Hen. VI.*

It is a bad exchange to wound a man's own conscience, to salve state *sores.* *King Charles.*

Receipts abound; but searching all thy store,
The best is still at hand to launce the *sore,*
And cut the head; for till the core be found
The secret vice is fed and gathers ground. *Dryden.*

By these all festring *sores* her councils heal,
Which time or has disclos'd, or shall reveal. *Dryden.*

Lice and flies, which have a most wonderful instinct to find out convenient places for the hatching and nourishment of their young, lay their eggs upon *sores.* *Bentley.*

SORE. *adj.* [from the noun.]

1. Tender to the touch.

We can ne'er be sure,
Whether we pain or not endure;
And just so far are *sore* and griev'd,
As by the fancy is believ'd. *Hudibras.*

While *sore* of battle, while our wounds are green,
Why should we tempt the doubtful dye again. *Dryden.*

It was a right answer of the physician to his patient, that had *sore* eyes, if you have more pleasure in the taste of wine than in the use of your sight, wine is good; but if the pleasure of seeing be greater to you than that of drinking, wine is naught. *Locke.*

2. Tender in the mind; easily vexed.

Malice and hatred are very fretting and vexatious, and apt to make our minds *sore* and uneasy; but he that can moderate these affections will find ease in his mind. *Tillotson.*

Laugh at your friends, and if your friends are *sore,*
So much the better, you may laugh the more. *Pope.*

3. Violent with pain; afflictively vehement. See SORE. adverb.

Threescore and ten I can remember well,
Within the volume of which time I've seen
Hours dreadful, and things strange; but this *sore* night
Hath trifled former knowings. *Shakespeare.*

I will persevere in my course of loyalty, though the conflict be *sore* between that and my blood. *Shakespeare's K. Lear.*

My loins are filled with a *sore* disease; and there is no whole part in my body. *Common Prayer.*

Sore hath been their fight,
As likeliest was, when two such foes met arm'd. *Milton.*

Gentle lady, may thy grave
Peace and quiet ever have;
After this day's travel *sore*
Sweet rest seize thee evermore. *Milton.*

They are determin'd to live up to the holy rule, though *sore* evils and great temporal inconveniencies should attend the discharge of their duty. *Atterbury.*

4. Criminal. Out of use.

To lapse in fullness
Is *sorer* than to lie for need; and falshood
Is worse in kings than beggars. *Shakespeare's Cymbeline.*

5. [From *saur,* French.]

The buck is called the first year a fawn; the second, a pricket; the third, a sorel; and the fourth year, a *sore.* *Shak.*

SORE. *adv.* [This the etymologists derive from *seer,* Dutch; but *seer* means only an intenseness of any thing; *sore* almost always includes pain.] With painful or dangerous vehemence; a very painful degree; with afflictive violence or pertinacity. It is now little used.

Thine arrows stick fast in me, and thy hand presseth me *sore.* *Common Prayer.*

The knight, then lightly leaping to the prey,
With mortal steel him smote again so *sore,*
That headless his unweildy body lay. *Fairy Queen.*

He this and that, and each man's blow
Doth eye, defend, and shift, being laid to *sore.* *Daniel.*

Though iron hew and mangle *sore,*
Would wounds and bruises honour more. *Hudibras.*

Distrust shook *sore* their minds. *Milton.*

So that Palamon were wounded *sore,*
Arcite was hurt as much. *Dryden's Knights Tale.*

Sore-sigh'd the knight, who this long sermon heard:
At length, considering all, his heart he chear'd. *Dryden.*

How, Didius, shall a Roman *sore* repuls'd
Greet your arrival to this distant isle?
How bid you welcome to these shatter'd legions? *A. Philips.*

SO'REHON. } *n. s.* [Irish and Scottish.] A kind of arbitrary
SORN. } exaction or servile tenure, formerly in Scotland, as likewise in Ireland; whenever a chieftan had a mind to revel, he came down among the tenants with his followers, by way of contempt called in the lowlands giliwitfitts, and lived on free quarters; so that ever since, when a person obtrudes himself upon another, stays at his house, and hangs upon him for bed and board, he is said to *sorn,* or be a *sorner.* *Macbean.*

They exact upon them all kind of services; yea, and the very wild exactions, coignie, livery, and *sorehon*; by which they poll and utterly undo the poor tenants and freeholders under them. *Spenser's Ireland.*

SO'REL. *n. s.* [Diminutive of *sore.*]

The buck is called the first year a fawn; the second, a pricket; the third, a *sorel.* *Shakespeare.*

SO'RELY. *adv.* [from *sore.*]

1. With a great degree of pain or distress.

Here's the smell of the blood still; all the perfumes of Arabia will not sweeten this little hand. Oh! oh! oh!—What a sigh is there? the heart is *sorely* overcharged. *Shakespeare.*

The warrior train,
Though most were *sorely* wounded, none were slain. *Dryden.*

2. With vehemence dangerous or afflictive.

I have done ill,
Of which I do accuse myself so *sorely,*
That I will enjoy no more. *Shakespeare.*

SO'RENESS. *n. s.* [from *sore.*] Tenderness of a hurt.

He that, whilst the *soreness* of his late pangs of conscience remains, finds himself a little indisposed for sin, presently concludes repentance hath had its perfect work. *Decay of Piety.*

My foot began to swell, and the pain asswaged, though it left such a *soreness,* that I could hardly suffer the cloaths of my bed. *Temple.*

SORI'TES. *n. s.* [σωρείτης.] Properly an heap. An argument where one proposition is accumulated on another.

Chrysippus the Stoick invented a kind of argument, consisting of more than three propositions, which is called *sorites,* or a heap. *Dryden.*

Sorites is when several middle terms are chosen to connect one another successively in several propositions, till the last proposition connects its predicate with the first subject. Thus, all men of revenge have their souls often uneasy; uneasy souls are a plague to themselves; now to be one's own plague is folly in the extreme. *Watts's Logick.*

SORO'RICIDE. *n. s.* [*soror* and *cædo.*] The murder of a sister.

So'RRAGE. *n. s.* The blades of green wheat or barley. *Dict.*

So'RRANCE. *n. s.* [In farriery.] Any disease or sore in horses. *Dict.*

So'RREL. *n. s.* [ſuɲe, Saxon; *sorel*, French.] This plant agrees with the dock in all its characters, and only differs in having an acid taste. *Miller.*

Of all roots of herbs the root of *sorrel* goeth the farthest into the earth. It is a cold and acid herb that loveth the earth, and is not much drawn by the sun. *Bacon.*

Acid austere vegetables contract and strengthen the fibres, as all kinds of *sorrel*, the virtues of which lie in acid astringent salt, a sovereign antidote against the putrescent bilious alkali. *Arbuthnot on Aliments.*

So'RRILY. *adv.* [from *sorry.*] Meanly; poorly; despicably; wretchedly; pitiably.

Thy pipe, O Pan, shall help though I sing *sorrily.* *Sidney.*

So'RRINESS. *n. s.* [from *sorry.*] Meanness; wretchedness; pitiableness; despicableness.

So'RROW. *n. s.* [*sorg*, Danish.] Grief; pain for something past; sadness; mourning. Sorrow is not commonly understood as the effect of present evil, but of lost good.

Sorrow is uneasiness in the mind, upon the thought of a good lost, which might have been enjoyed longer; or the sense of a present evil. *Locke.*

Sorrow on thee, and all the pack of you;
That triumph thus upon my misery! *Shakespeare.*
A world of woe and *sorrow.* *Milton.*
Some other hour I will to tears allow;
But having you, can show no *sorrow* now. *Dryden.*

To So'RROW. *v. n.* [*saurgan*, Gothick; ſoɲʒian, Sax.] To grieve; to be sad; to be dejected.

The miserable change, now at my end,
Lament, nor *sorrow* at. *Shakesp. Antony and Cleopatra.*
Where-ever sorrow is relief wou'd be,
If you do *sorrow* at my grief in love,
By giving love, your sorrow and my grief
Were both extermin'd. *Shakespeare.*

Now I rejoice, not that ye were made sorry, but that ye *sorrowed* to repentance. 2 *Cor.* vii. 9.

I neither fear to die nor desire to live; and having mastered all grief in myself, I desire no man to *sorrow* for me. *Hayw.*

Send them forth, though *sorrowing*, yet in peace. *Milton.*

Sad the prince explores
The neighb'ring main, and *sorrowing* treads the shores. *Pope.*

So'RROWED. *adj.* [from *sorrow.*] Accompanied with sorrow. Out of use.

Now the publick body, which doth seldom
Play the recanter, feeling in itself
A lack of Timon's aid, hath sense withal
Of its own fall, restraining aid to Timon;
And sends forth us to make their *sorrowed* tender. *Shakesp.*

So'RROWFUL. *adj.* [*sorrow* and *full.*]

1. Sad for something past; mournful; grieving.

Blessed are they which have been *sorrowful* for all thy scourges; for they shall rejoice for thee, when they have seen all thy glory. *Tob.* xiii. 14.

2. Deeply serious. Not in use.

Hannah said, no, my lord, I am a woman of a *sorrowful* spirit: I have poured out my soul before the Lord. 1 *Sam.*

3. Expressing grief; accompanied with grief.

The things that my soul refused to touch are as my *sorrowful* meat. *Job.* vi. 7.

So'RRY. *adj.* [ſaɲiʒ, Saxon.]

1. Grieved for something past. It is generally used of slight or casual miscarriages or vexations, but sometimes of greater things. It does not imply any long continuance of grief.

O, forget
What we are *sorry* for ourselves in thee. *Timon of Athens.*

The king was *sorry*: nevertheless for the oath's sake he commanded the Baptist's head to be given her. *Matth.* xiv. 9.

I'm *sorry* for thee, friend; 'tis the duke's pleasure. *Shak.*

We are *sorry* for the satire interspersed in some of these pieces, upon a few people, from whom the highest provocations have been received. *Swift.*

2. [From *saur*, filth, Islandick.] Vile; worthless; vexatious.

A salt and *sorry* rheum offends me:
Lend me thy handkerchief. *Shakespeare's Othello.*
How now, why do you keep alone?
Of *sorriest* fancies your companions making,
Using those thoughts, which should, indeed, have died
With them they think on. *Shakespeare's Macbeth.*

If the union of the parts consist only in rest, it would seem that a bag of dust would be of as firm a consistence as that of marble; and Bajazet's cage had been but a *sorry* prison. *Glanv.*

Coarse complexions,
And cheeks of *sorry* grain will serve to ply
The sampler, and to teize the housewife's wool. *Milton.*

How vain were all the ensigns of his power, that could not support him against one slighting look of a *sorry* slave! *L'Est.*

If this innocent had any relation to his Thebais, the poet might have found some *sorry* excuse for detaining the reader. *Dryden.*

If such a slight and *sorry* business as that could produce one organical body, one might reasonably expect, that now and then a dead lump of dough might be leavened into an animal. *Bentley's Sermons.*

SORT. *n. s.* [*sorte*, French.]

1. A kind; a species.

Disfigur'd more than spirit of happy *sort.* *Milton.*

A substantial and unaffected piety, not only gives a man a credit among the sober and virtuous, but even among the vicious *sort* of men. *Tillotson.*

These three *sorts* of poems should differ in their numbers, designs, and every thought. *Walsh.*

Endeavouring to make the signification of specifick names clear, they make their specifick ideas of the *sorts* of substances of a few of those simple ideas found in them. *Locke.*

2. A manner; a form of being or acting.

Flowers in such *sort* worn, can neither be smelt nor seen well by those that wear them. *Hooker.*

That I may laugh at her in equal *sort*
As she doth laugh at me, and makes my pain her sport. *Spenser's Sonnet.*

Rheum and Shimshai wrote after this *sort.* *Ezra* iv. 8.

To Adam in what *sort* shall I appear? *Milton.*

3. A degree of any quality.

I have written the more boldly unto you, in some *sort*, as putting you in mind. *Rom.* xv. 15.

I shall not be wholly without praise, if in some *sort* I have copied his stile. *Dryden.*

4. A class, or order of persons.

The one being a thing that belongeth generally unto all, the other, such as none but the wiser and more judicious *sort* can perform. *Hooker.*

I have bought
Golden opinions from all *sorts* of people. *Shakespeare.*

Hospitality to the better *sort*, and charity to the poor, two virtues that are never exercised so well as when they accompany each other. *Atterbury's Sermons.*

5. A company; a knot of people.

Mine eyes are full of tears: I cannot see;
And yet salt water blinds them not so much,
But they can see a *sort* of traitors here. *Shakespeare.*

6. Rank; condition above the vulgar.

Is signior Montanto returned from the wars?—I know none of that name, lady; there was none such in the army of any *sort.* *Shakespeare's Much ado about Nothing.*

7. [*Sort*, Fr. *sortes*, Latin.] A lot. Out of use.

Make a lott'ry,
And by decree, let blockish Ajax
Draw the *sort* to fight with Hector. *Shakespeare.*

8. A pair; a set.

The first *sort* by their own suggestion fell. *Milton.*

To SORT. *v. a.* [*Sortiri*, Lat. *assortire*, Italian.]

1. To separate into distinct and proper classes.

These they *sorted* into their several times and places; some to begin the service of God with, and some to end; some to be interlac'd between the divine readings of the law and prophets. *Hooker.*

I come to thee for charitable licence,
To *sort* our nobles from our common men. *Shakespeare.*

A piece of cloth made of white and black threads though the whole appear neither white nor black, but grey; yet each remains what it was before, if the threads were pulled asunder, and *sorted* each colour by itself. *Boyle.*

Shell-fish have been, by some of the ancients, compared and *sorted* with the insects. *Bacon's Natural History.*

With this desire, she hath a native might
To find out ev'ry truth, if she had time;
Th' innumerable effects to *sort* aright,
And by degrees from cause to cause to climb. *Davies.*

The number of simple ideas, that make the nominal essence of the lowest species, or first *sorting* of individuals, depends on the mind of man. *Locke.*

The rays which differ in refrangibility may be parted and *sorted* from one another, and that either by refraction, or by reflexion. *Newton's Opticks.*

But grant that actions best discover man,
Take the most strong and *sort* them as you can;
The few that glare, each character must mark:
You balance not the many in the dark. *Pope.*

2. To reduce to order from a state of confusion.

Let me not be light;
For a light wife doth make a heavy husband;
And never be Bassanio so from me;
But God *sort* all! *Shakespeare's Merch. of Venice.*

3. To conjoin; to put together in distribution.

For, when she *sorts* things present with things past,
And thereby things to come doth oft foresee;
When she doth doubt at first, and chuse at first,
These acts her own, without her body be. *Davies.*

4. To cull; to chuse; to select.

Send his mother to his father's houſe,
That he may *ſort* her out a worthy ſpouſe. *Chapman.*

To SORT. *v. n.*

1. To be joined with others of the ſame ſpecies.

Nor do metals only *ſort* and herd with metals in the earth, and minerals with minerals; but both in common together. *Woodward.*

2. To conſort; to join.

The illiberality of parents towards their children, makes them baſe and *ſort* with any company. *Bacon.*

3. To ſuit; to fit.

A man cannot ſpeak to a ſon but as a father; whereas a friend may ſpeak as the caſe requires, and not as it *ſorteth* with the perſon. *Bacon.*

They are happy whoſe natures *ſort* with their vocations. *Bacon.*

Among unequals, what ſociety
Can *ſort*, what harmony, or true delight?
Which muſt be mutual, in proportion due,
Giv'n, and receiv'd. *Milton's Paradiſe Loſt.*

The Creator calling forth by name
His mighty angels, gave them ſeveral charge,
As *ſorted* beſt with preſent things. *Milton's Paradiſe Loſt.*

For diff'rent ſtiles with diff'rent ſubjects *ſort*,
As ſeveral garbs with country, town, and court. *Pope.*

4. To terminate; to iſſue.

It *ſorted* not to any fight of importance, but to a retreat. *Bacon's War with Spain.*

5. To have ſucceſs.

The ſlips of their vines have been brought into Spain, but they have not *ſorted* to the ſame purpoſe as in their native country. *Abbot's Deſcription of the World.*

It was tried in a blown bladder, whereunto fleſh and a flower were put, and it *ſorted* not; for dry bladders will not blow, and new bladders further putrefaction. *Bacon.*

6. To fall out. [from *ſort*, a lot, or *ſortir*, to iſſue, French.]

And ſo far am I glad it did ſo *ſort*,
As this their jangling I eſteem a ſport. *Shakeſpeare.*

Princes cannot gather this fruit, except they raiſe ſome perſons to be companions; which many times *ſorteth* to inconvenience. *Bacon.*

SO'RTAL. *adj.* A word formed by *Locke*, but not yet received.

As things are ranked under names, into ſorts or ſpecies only as they agree to certain abſtract ideas, the eſſence of each ſort comes to be nothing but that idea which the *ſortal*, if I may ſo call it from ſort, as I do general from *genus*, name ſtands for. *Locke.*

SO'RTANCE. *n. ſ.* [from *ſort.*] Suitableneſs; agreement.

I have received
New dated letters from Northumberland,
Their cold intent, thus:
Here doth he wiſh his perſon, with ſuch power
As might hold *ſortance* with his quality,
The which he could not levy. *Shakeſpeare's Henry IV.*

SO'RTILEGE. *n. ſ.* [*ſortilege*, Fr. *ſortilegium*, Latin.] The act or practice of drawing lots.

SO'RTMENT. *n. ſ.* [from *ſort.*]

1. The act of ſorting; diſtribution.
2. A parcel ſorted or diſtributed.

To SOSS. *v. n.* [A cant word.] To ſit lazily on a chair; to fall at once into a chair.

The winter ſky began to frown,
Poor Stella muſt pack off to town;
From wholeſome exerciſe and air,
To *ſoſſing* in an eaſy chair. *Swift.*

SOT. *n. ſ.* [ꞅot, Saxon; *ſot*, French; *ſot*, Dutch.]

1. A blockhead; a dull ignorant ſtupid fellow; a dolt.

Of Glo'ſter's treachery,
And of the loyal ſervice of his ſon,
When I inform'd him, then he call'd me *ſot*;
And told me I had turn'd the wrong ſide out. *Shakeſpeare.*

This by his tongue being made his miſtreſs' picture,
And then a mind put in't, either our braggs
Were crackt of kitchen trulls, or his deſcription
Prov'd us unſpeaking *ſots.* *Shakeſpeare.*

Tell him that no hiſtory or antiquity can match his conduct; and preſently the *ſot*, becauſe he knows neither hiſtory nor antiquity, ſhall begin to meaſure himſelf by himſelf, which is the only ſure way for him not to fall ſhort. *South's Sermons.*

2. A wretch ſtupified by drinking.

Every ſign
That calls the ſtaring *ſots* to naſty wine. *Roſcommon.*

A ſurly ill-bred lord,
That chides and ſnaps her up at every word:
A brutal *ſot*; who while ſhe holds his head,
With drunken filth bedaubs the nuptial bed. *Granville.*

To SOT. *v. a.* To ſtupify; to beſot.

Pox on his loyalty!
I hate to ſee a brave bold fellow *ſotted*,
Made ſour and ſenſeleſs, turn'd to whey by love;
A driveling hero, fit for a romance. *Dryden's Span. Friar.*

The potion
Turns his brain and ſtupifies his mind;
The *ſotted* moon-calf gapes. *Dryden.*

To SOT. *v. n.* To tipple to ſtupidity.

SO'TTISH. *adj.* [from *ſot.*]

1. Dull; ſtupid; ſenſeleſs; infatuate; doltiſh.

All's but naught:
Patience is *ſottiſh*, and impatience does
Become a dog that's mad. *Shakeſpeare's Ant. and Cleopatra.*

Upon the report of his approach, more than half fell away and diſperſed; the reſidue, being more deſperate or more *ſottiſh*, did abide in the field, of whom many were ſlain. *Hayward.*

He gain'd a king
Ahaz his *ſottiſh* conqueror. *Milton.*

'Tis *ſottiſh* to offer at things that cannot be brought about. *L'Eſtrange.*

How ignorant are *ſottiſh* pretenders to aſtrology. *Swift.*

2. Dull with intemperance.

SO'TTISHLY. *adv.* [from *ſottiſh.*] Stupidly; dully; ſenſeleſsly.

Northumberland *ſottiſhly* mad with over great fortune, procured the King by his letters patent under the great ſeal, to appoint the lady Jane to ſucceed him in the inheritance of the crown. *Hayward.*

Atheiſm is impudent in pretending to philoſophy, and ſuperſtition *ſottiſhly* ignorant in fancying that the knowledge of nature tends to irreligion. *Glanville.*

So *ſottiſhly* to loſe the pureſt pleaſures and comforts of this world, and forego the expectation of immortality in another; and ſo deſperately to run the riſk of dwelling with everlaſting burnings, plainly diſcovers itſelf to be the moſt pernicious folly and deplorable madneſs in the world. *Bentley.*

SO'TTISHNESS. *n. ſ.* [from *ſottiſh.*] Dullneſs; ſtupidity; inſenſibility.

Few conſider what a degree of *ſottiſhneſs* and confirmed ignorance men may ſin themſelves into. *South's Sermons.*

No ſober temperate perſon can look with any complacency upon the drunkenneſs and *ſottiſhneſs* of his neighbour. *South.*

The firſt part of the text, the folly and *ſottiſhneſs* of Atheiſm, will come home to their caſe; ſince they make ſuch a noiſy pretence to wit and ſagacity. *Bentley's Sermons.*

SO'VEREIGN. *adj.* [*ſouverain*, French; *ſovrano*, Spaniſh.]

1. Supreme in power; having no ſuperiour.

As teaching bringeth us to know that God is our ſupreme truth; ſo prayer teſtifieth that we acknowledge him our *ſovereign* good. *Hooker.*

You, my *ſovereign* lady,
Cauſeleſs have laid diſgraces on my head. *Shakeſp. Hen. IV.*

None of us who now thy grace implore,
But held the rank of *ſovereign* queen before,
Till giddy chance, whoſe malice never bears
That mortal bliſs ſhould laſt for length of years,
Caſt us headlong from our high eſtate. *Dryden.*

Whether Eſau, then, were a vaſſal to Jacob, and Jacob his *ſovereign* prince by birth right, I leave the reader to judge. *Locke.*

2. Supremely efficacious.

A memorial of their fidelity and zeal, a *ſovereign* preſervative of God's people from the venomous infection of hereſy. *Hooker.*

The moſt *ſovereign* preſcription in Galen is but empirick; and to this preſervative of no better report than a horſe drench. *Shakeſpeare's Coriolanus.*

Love-wounded Protheus,
My boſom, as a bed,
Shall lodge thee, till thy wound be throughly heal'd,
And thus I ſearch it with a *ſov'reign* kiſs. *Shakeſpeare.*

A water we call water of paradiſe, by that we do to it, is made very *ſovereign* for health. *Bacon.*

Like the ſcum ſtarv'd men did draw
From parboil'd ſhoes and boots, and all the reſt
Which were with any *ſovereign* fatneſs bleſt. *Donne.*

Be cool, my friend, and hear my muſe diſpenſe
Some *ſovereign* comforts drawn from common ſenſe. *Dryden.*

SO'VEREIGN. *n. ſ.* Supreme lord.

O, let my *ſovereign* turn away his face,
And bid his ears a little while be deaf. *Shakeſpeare.*

By my *ſovereign*, and his fate, I ſwear,
Renown'd for faith in peace, for force in war,
Oft our alliance other lands deſir'd. *Dryden.*

SO'VEREIGNLY. *adv.* [from *ſovereign.*] Supremely; in the higheſt degree.

He was *ſovereignly* lovely in himſelf. *Boyle.*

SO'VEREIGNTY. *n. ſ.* [*ſouverainetè*, French.] Supremacy; higheſt place; ſupreme power; higheſt degree of excellence.

Give me pardon,
That I, your vaſſal, have employed and pain'd
Your unknown *ſovereignty.* *Shakeſpeare.*

Happy were England, would this virtuous prince
Take on his grace the *ſov'reignty* thereof. *Shakeſpeare.*

To give laws unto a people, to inſtitute magiſtrates and officers over them; to puniſh and pardon malefactors; to have the sole authority of making war and peace, are the true marks of *sovereignty*. *Davies.*

A mighty hunter thence he shall be stil'd
Before the Lord; as in despite of heav'n,
Or from heav'n, claiming second *sov'reignty*. *Milton.*

Nothing does so gratify a haughty humour, as this piece of usurped *sovereignty* over our brethren. *Govern. of the Tongue.*

Jove's own tree,
That holds the woods in awful *sov'reignty*,
Requires a depth of lodging in the ground;
High as his topmost boughs to heav'n ascend,
So low his roots to hell's dominion tend. *Dryden.*

I well foresee, whene'er thy suit I grant,
That I my much lov'd *sov'reignty* shall want,
And her new beauty may thy heart invade. *Dryden.*

Let us above all things possess our souls with awful apprehensions of the majesty and *sovereignty* of God. *Rogers.*

Alexander's Grecian colonies in the Indies were almost exterminated by Sandrocottus; Seleucus recovered the *sovereignty* in some degree, but was forced to abandon to him the country along the Indus. *Arbuthnot on Coins.*

SOUGH. *n. s.* [from *sous*, French.] A subterraneous drain.

Yet could not such mines, without great pains, and charges, if at all, be wrought; the delfs would be so flown with waters, it being impossible to make any addits or *soughs* to drain them, that no gins or machines could suffice to lay and keep them dry. *Ray on the Creation.*

Another of like sort, was found in sinking a *sough*-pit at Haigh in Lancashire. *Woodward.*

SOUGHT. The preterite and participle pass. of *seek*.

I am *sought* of them that asked not for me: I am found of them that *sought* me not. *Isa.* lxv. 1.

The works of the Lord are great, *sought* out of all them that have pleasure therein. *Psal.* cxi. 2.

SOUL. *n. s.* [rapel, Sax. *sael*, Dan. *sual*, Islandick; *siel*, Dutch.]

1. The immaterial and immortal spirit of man.

When death was overcome, he opened heaven as well to the believing Gentiles as Jews: heaven till then was no receptacle to the *souls* of either. *Hooker.*

Fie, fie, unreverent tongue! to call her bad,
Whose sov'reignty so oft thou hast preferr'd
With twenty thousand *soul*-confirming oaths. *Shakespeare.*

Perhaps, for want of food, the *soul* may pine;
But that were strange, since all things bad and good;
Since all God's creatures, mortal and divine;
Since God himself is her eternal food. *Davies.*

He remembered them of the promises, seals and oaths, which by publick authority had passed for concluding this marriage, that these being religious bonds betwixt God and their *souls*, could not by any politick act of state be dissolved. *Hayward.*

Eloquence the *soul*, song charms the sense. *Milton.*

2. Vital principle.

They say this town is full of cozenage,
Drug-working sorcerers that change the mind;
Soul-killing witches that deform the body;
And many such like libertines of sin. *Shakespeare.*

Thou almost mak'st me waver in my faith,
To hold opinion with Pythagoras,
That *souls* of animals infuse themselves
Into the trunks of men. *Shakesp. Merch. of Venice.*

Thou sun, of this great world both eye and *soul*. *Milton.*

Join voices all ye living *souls!* ye birds,
That singing up to heav'n-gate ascend,
Bear on your wings, and in your notes his praise. *Milton.*

In common discourse and writing, we leave out the words vegetative, sensitive, and rational; and make the word *soul* serve for all these principles. *Watts.*

3. Spirit; essence; quintessence; principal part.

He has the very *soul* of bounty. *Shakespeare.*
Charity the *soul* of all the rest. *Milton.*

4. Interiour power.

There is some *soul* of goodness in things evil,
Would men observingly distil it out. *Shakespeare.*

5. A familiar appellation expressing the qualities of the mind.

Three wenches where I stood, cry'd:
" Alas, good *soul!*" *Shakespeare's Julius Cæsar.*

This is a poor mad *soul*; and she says up and down the town, that her eldest son is like you. *Shakesp. Hen.* IV.

The poor *soul* sat singing by a sycamore tree,
Sing all a green willow:
Her hand on her bosom, her head on her knee. *Shakesp.*

Unenlarged *souls* are disgusted with the wonders of the microscope, discovering animals which equal not a peppercorn. *Watts.*

6. Human being.

The moral is the case of every *soul* of us. *L'Estrange.*

Keep the poor *soul* no longer in suspense,
Your change is such as does not need defence. *Dryden.*

It is a republick; there are in it a hundred burgeois, and about a thousand *souls*. *Addison's Italy.*

My state of health none care to learn;
My life is here no *soul's* concern. *Swift.*

7. Active power.

Earth, air and seas, through empty space would rowl,
And heav'n would fly before the driving *soul*. *Dryden.*

8. Spirit; fire; grandeur of mind.

9. Intelligent being in general.

Every *soul* in heav'n shall bend the knee. *Milton.*

SOU'LED. *adj.* [from *soul.*] Furnished with mind.

Griping, and still tenacious of thy hold,
Wou'd'st thou the Grecian chiefs, though largely *soul'd*,
Shou'd give the prizes they had gain'd before. *Dryden.*

SOU'LLESS. *adj.* [from *soul.*] Mean; low; spiritless.

Slave, *soulless* villain, dog, O rarely base! *Shakespeare.*

SOU'LSHOT. *n. s.* [*soul* and *shot.*] Something paid for a soul's requiem among the Romanists.

In the Saxon times there was a funeral duty to be paid, called *pecunia sepulchralis & symbolum animæ*, and a Saxon *soul-shot*. *Ayliffe's Parergon.*

SOUND. *adj.* [runb, Saxon.]

1. Healthy; hearty; not morbid; not diseased; not hurt.

I am fall'n out with my more headier will,
To take the indispos'd and sickly fit
For the *sound* man. *Shakespeare's King Lear.*

He hath a heart as *sound* as a bell, and his tongue is the clapper; for what his heart thinks, his tongue speaks. *Shak.*

He hath received him safe and *sound*. *Luke* xv. 27.

We can preserve
Unhurt our minds, and understanding *sound*. *Milton.*

The king visits all around,
Comforts the sick, congratulates the *sound*;
Honours the princely chiefs. *Dryden.*

But Capys, and the rest of *sounder* mind,
The fatal present to the flames design'd,
Or to the deep. *Dryden.*

When a word, which originally signifies any particular object, is attributed to several other objects, on account of some evident reference or relation to the original idea, this is peculiarly called an analogical word; so a *sound* or healthy pulse, a *sound* digestion, *sound* sleep, are all so called, with reference to a *sound* and healthy constitution; but if you speak of *sound* doctrine, or *sound* speech, this is by way of resemblance to health, and the words are metaphorical. *Watts's Logick.*

2. Right; not erroneous.

Whom although to know be life, and joy to make mention of his name; yet our *soundest* knowledge is to know that we know him not as indeed he is, neither can know him: and our safest eloquence concerning him is silence. *Hooker.*

Let my heart be *sound* in thy statutes, that I be not ashamed. *Psal.* cxix. 80.

The rules are *sound* and useful, and may serve your devotion. *Wake.*

3. Stout; strong; lusty.

The men are very strong and able of body; and therefore either give *sound* strokes with their clubs wherewith they fight, or else shoot strong shots with their bows. *Abbot.*

4. Valid; not failing.

They reserved their titles, tenures, and signiories whole and *sound* to themselves. *Spenser's Ireland.*

5. Fast; hearty. It is applied to sleep.

New wak'd from *soundest* sleep,
Soft on the flow'ry herb I found me laid
In balmy sweat. *Milton's Paradise Lost.*

SOUND. *adv.* Soundly; heartily; completely fast.

The messenger approaching to him spake,
But his waste words return'd to him in vain;
So *sound* he slept that nought might him awake. *Fa. Queen.*

SOUND. *n. s.* [*sonde*, French.] A shallow sea, such as may be sounded.

The *sound* of Denmark, where ships pay toll. *Camden.*

Wake,
Behold I come, sent from the Stygian *sound*,
As a dire vapour that had cleft the ground,
T' ingender with the night, and blast the day. *Ben. Johnson.*

Him young Thoosa bore, the bright increase
Of Phorcys, dreaded in the *sounds* and seas. *Pope.*

SOUND. *n. s.* [*sonde*, Fr.] A probe, an instrument used by chirurgeons to feel what is out of reach of the fingers.

The patient being laid on a table, pass the *sound* till it meet with some resistance. *Sharp's Surgery.*

To SOUND. *v. a.*

1. To search with a plummet; to try depth.

In this secret there is a gulf, which while we live we shall never *sound*. *Hooker.*

You are, Hastings, much too shallow
To *sound* the bottom of the after-times. *Shakesp. Hen.* IV.

2. To try; to examine.

Has he never before *sounded* you in this business. *Shakespeare.*

Invites these lords, and those he meant to *sound*. *Daniel.*

I was in jest,
And by that offer meant to *sound* your breast. *Dryden.*

I've *sounded* my Numidians, man by man,
And find 'em ripe for a revolt. *Addison's Cato.*

To

To Sound. *v. n.* To try with the sounding line.

The shipmen deemed that they drew near to some country and *sounded* and found it near twenty fathoms. *Acts* xxvii.

Beyond this we have no more a positive distinct notion of, infinite space than a mariner has of the depth of the sea, where having let down a large portion of his *sounding*-line, he reaches no bottom. *Locke.*

Sound. *n. s.* The cuttle-fish. *Ainsworth.*

Sound. *n. s.* [*son*, French; *sonus*, Latin.]

1. Any thing audible; a noise; that which is perceived by the ear.

Heaps of huge words uphoarded hideously
With horrid *sound*, though having little sense,
And thereby wanting due intelligence,
Have marred the face of goodly poesy,
And made a monster of their fantasy. *Spenser.*

Come, sisters, cheer we up his sprights,
And shew the best of our delights;
I'll charm the air to give a *sound*,
While you perform your antick round. *Shakesp. Macbeth.*

Dash a stone against a stone in the bottom of the water, and it maketh a *sound*: so a long pole struck upon gravel in the bottom of the water, maketh a *sound*. *Bacon's Nat. Hist.*

The warlike *sound* of trumpets loud. *Milton.*

Whene'er he spoke his voice was heard around,
Loud as a trumpet with a silver *sound*. *Dryden.*

That which is conveyed into the brain by the ear is called *sound*; though, 'till it affect the perceptive part, it be nothing but motion. *Locke.*

2. Mere empty noise opposed to meaning.

He contented himself with doubtful and general terms, which might make no ill *sound* in mens ears. *Locke.*

Let us consider this proposition as to its meaning; for it is the sense and not *sound* that must be the principle. *Locke.*

To Sound. *v. n.*

1. To make a noise; to emit a noise.

From you *sounded* out the word of the Lord. 1 *Thes.* i. 8.

Trumpet once more to *sound* at general doom. *Milton.*

That with one blast through the whole house does bound,
And first taught speaking-trumpets how to *sound*. *Dryden.*

Thither the silver *sounding* lyres
Shall call the smiling loves and young desires. *Pope.*

2. To exhibit by likeness of sound.

Why do you start, and seem to fear
Things that do *sound* so fair? *Shakespeare.*

They being told there was small hope of ease
To be expected to their evils from hence,
Were willing at the first to give an ear
To any thing that *sounded* liberty. *Ben. Johnson's Catiline.*

This relation *sounds* rather like a chymical dream than a philosophical truth. *Wilkins's Math. Magic.*

To Sound. *v. a.*

1. To cause to make a noise; to play on.

And many nymphs about them flocking round,
And many tritons, which their horns did *sound*. *Spenser.*

Michael bid *sound*
Th' archangel trumpet. *Milton.*

Misenus lay; none so renown'd
The warrior trumpet in the field to *sound*;
With breathing brass to kindle fierce alarms,
And rouze to dare their fate in honourable arms. *Dryden.*

2. To betoken or direct by a sound.

Once Jove from Ida did both hosts survey,
And, when he pleas'd to thunder, part the fray;
Here heav'n in vain that kind retreat should *sound*,
The louder cannon had the thunder drown'd. *Waller.*

3. To celebrate by sound.

Sun, *sound* his praise. *Milton.*

So'undboard. *n. s.* [*sound* and *board.*] Board which propagates the sound in organs.

Try it without any *soundboard* along, only harpwise at one end of the string. *Bacon's Natural History.*

As in an organ, from one blast of wind,
To many a row of pipes the *soundboard* breathes. *Milton.*

So'unding. *adj.* [from *sound.*] Sonorous; having a magnificent sound.

Obsolete words may then be revived, when more *sounding* or more significant than those in practice. *Dryden.*

So'undly. *adv.* [from *sound.*]

1. Healthily; heartily.

2. Lustily; stoutly; strongly.

When Duncan is asleep,
Whereto the rather shall this hard day's journey
Soundly invite him. *Shakesp. Macbeth.*

They did ply
My feet and hands with cords, and to the mast
With other halsers made me *soundly* fast. *Chapman's Odyssey.*

Who had so often in your aid
So many ways been *soundly* paid;
Came in at last for better ends. *Hudibras.*

Have no concern,
Provided Punch, for there's the jest,
Be *soundly* maul'd, and plague the rest. *Swift.*

Their nobility and gentry are one half ruined, banished, or converted: they all *soundly* feel the smart of the last Irish war. *Swift.*

3. Truly; rightly.

The wisest are always the readiest to acknowledge, that *soundly* to judge of a law is the weightiest thing which any man can take upon him. *Hooker.*

The doctrine of the church of England, expressed in the thirty-nine articles, is so *soundly* and orthodoxly settled, as cannot be questioned without extreme danger to our religion. *Bacon.*

4. Fast; closely.

Now when that idle dream was to him brought,
Unto that elfen knight he bad him fly,
Where he slept *soundly*, void of evil thought. *Fairy Queen.*

When the succession of ideas ceases, our perception of duration ceases with it, which every one experiments whilst he sleeps *soundly*. *Locke.*

Sou'ndness. *n. s.* [from *sound.*]

1. Health; heartiness.

I would I had that corporal *soundness* now,
As when thy father and myself in friendship
First tried our soldiership. *Shakespeare.*

2. Truth; rectitude; incorrupt state.

In the end, very few excepted, all became subject to the sway of time: other odds there was none amongst them, saving only that some fell sooner away, and some later from the *soundness* of belief. *Hooker.*

Lesly is misled in his politicks; but he hath given proof of his *soundness* in religion. *Swift.*

3. Strength; solidity.

This presupposed, it may stand then very well with strength and *soundness* of reason, even thus to answer. *Hooker.*

Soup. *n. s.* [*soupe*, French.] Strong decoction of flesh for the table.

Spongy morells in strong ragousts are found,
And in the *soup* the slimy snail is drown'd. *Gay's Trivia.*

Let the cook daub the back of the footman's new livery, or, when he is going up with a dish of *soup*, let her follow him softly with a ladle-full. *Swift.*

SOUR. *n. s.* [ꞅuꞃ, ꞅuꞃiᵹ, Saxon; *sur*, Welsh.]

1. Acid; austere; pungent on the palate with astringency, as vinegar, or unripe fruit.

All *sour* things, as vinegar, provoke appetite. *Bacon.*

Their drink is *sour*. *Hos.* iv. 18.

But let the bounds of licences be fix'd,
Not things of disagreeing natures mix'd,
Not sweet with *sour*, nor birds with serpents join'd. *Dryden.*

2. Harsh of temper; crabbed; peevish; morose; severe.

He was a scholar,
Lofty and *sour* to them that lov'd him not. *Shakes. H* VIII.

A man of pleasant and popular conversation, rather free than *sour* and reserved. *Wotton's Life of the Duke of Buckingham.*

Tiberius, otherwise a very *sour* man, would punctually perform this rite unto others, and expect the same. *Brown.*

He said a *sour* thing to Laura the other day. *Tatler.*

Sullen and *sour*, with discontented mien
Jocasta frown'd. *Pope.*

3. Afflictive; painful.

Let me embrace these *sour* adversities;
For wise men say it is the wisest course. *Shakesp. H. VI.*

4. Expressing discontent.

The lord treasurer often looked on me with a *sour* countenance. *Gulliver's Travels.*

Sour. *n. s.* [from the adjective.] Acid substance.

A thousand *sours* to temper with one sweet,
To make it seem more dear and dainty. *Spenser.*

To Sour. *v. a.*

1. To make acid.

His angelick nature had none of that carnal leven which ferments to the *souring* of ours. *Decay of Piety.*

Thus kneaded up with milk, the new made man
His kingdom o'er his kindred world began;
'Till knowledge misapply'd, misunderstood,
And pride of empire, *sour'd* his balmy blood. *Dryden.*

One passion, with a different turn,
Makes wit inflame or anger burn:
So the sun's heat, with diff'rent pow'rs,
Ripens the grape, the liquor *sours*. *Swift.*

2. To make harsh.

Tufts of grass *sour* land. *Mortimer's Husbandry.*

3. To make uneasy; to make less pleasing.

Hail, great king!
To *sour* your happiness, I must report
The queen is dead. *Shakes. Cymbeline.*

He brought envy, malice, and ambition into Paradise, which *soured* to him the sweetness of the place. *Dryden.*

4. To make discontented.

Not my own disgrace
Hath ever made me *sour* my patient cheek,
Or bend one wrinkle on my sovereign's face. *Shakespeare.*

Three crabbed mouths had *ſour'd* themſelves to death,
Ere I could make thee open thy white hand. *Shakeſpeare.*

To Sour. *v. n.*

1. To become acid.

Aſſes milk, when it *ſours* in the ſtomach, and whey, turned ſour, will purge ſtrongly. *Arbuthnot on Diet.*

2. To grow peeviſh or crabbed.

They keep out melancholy from the virtuous, and hinder the hatred of vice from *ſouring* into ſeverity. *Addiſon.*

If I turn my eyes from them, or ſeem diſpleaſed, they *ſour* upon it. *Spectator.*

Source. *n. ſ.* [*ſource*, French.]

1. Spring; fountain; head.

Kings that rule
Behind the hidden *ſources* of the Nile. *Addiſon's Cato.*

2. Original; firſt courſe.

This ſecond *ſource* of men, while yet but few,
With ſome regard to what is juſt and right,
Shall lead their lives. *Milton's Parad. Loſt.*

This is the true *ſource* and original of this miſchief. *South.*

Of himſelf is none;
But that eternal Infinite, and One,
Who never did begin, who ne'er can end,
On him all beings, as their *ſource*, depend. *Dryden.*

3. Firſt producer.

Famous Greece,
That *ſource* of art and cultivated thought,
Which they to Rome, and Romans hither brought. *Waller.*

So'urish. *adj.* [from *ſour.*] Somewhat ſour.

By diſtillation we obtain a *ſouriſh* ſpirit, which will diſſolve coral. *Boyle.*

So'urly. *adv.* [from *ſour.*]

1. With acidity.

2. With acrimony.

The ſtern Athenian prince
Then *ſourly* ſmil'd. *Dryden's Knight's Tale.*

So'urness. *n. ſ.* [from *ſour.*]

1. Acidity; auſtereneſs of taſte.

Sourneſs conſiſteth in ſome groſſneſs of the body, and incorporation doth make the mixture of the body more equal, which induceth a milder taſte. *Bacon's Natural Hiſtory.*

I' th' Spring, like youth, it yields an acid taſte;
But Summer doth, like age, the *ſourneſs* waſte. *Denham.*

He knew
For fruit the grafted pear-tree to diſpoſe,
And tame to plumbs the *ſourneſs* of the ſloes. *Dryd. Virgil.*

Of acid or ſour one has a notion from taſte, *ſourneſs* being one of thoſe ſimple ideas which one cannot deſcribe. *Arbuthn.*

Has life no *ſourneſs*, drawn ſo near its end? *Pope.*

2. Aſperity; harſhneſs of temper.

Pelagius carped at the curious neatneſs of mens apparel in thoſe days, and, through the *ſourneſs* of his diſpoſition, ſpoke ſomewhat too hardly thereof. *Hooker.*

He was never thought to be of that ſuperſtitious *ſourneſs*, which ſome men pretend to in religion. *King Charles.*

Her religion is equally free from the weakneſs of ſuperſtition and the *ſourneſs* of enthuſiaſm: it is not of an uncomfortable melancholy nature. *Addiſon's Freeholder.*

So'ursop. *n. ſ.* [*guanabanus*, Latin.] Cuſtard-apple.

It grows in ſeveral parts of the Spaniſh Weſt-Indies, where it is cultivated for its fruits. *Miller.*

Sous. *n. ſ.* [*ſol*, French.] A ſmall denomination of money.

Souse. *n. ſ.* [*ſout*, ſalt, Dutch.]

1. Pickle made of ſalt.

2. Any thing kept parboiled in ſalt-pickle.

And he that can rear up a pig in his houſe,
Hath cheaper his bacon, and ſweeter his *ſouſe.* *Tuſſer.*

All-ſaints, do lay for pork and *ſouſe*,
For ſprats and ſpurlings for your houſe. *Tuſſer.*

To Souse. *v. a.* [from the noun.]

1 To parboil, and ſteep in pickle.

Oil, though it ſtink, they drop by drop impart;
But *ſouſe* the cabbage with a bounteous heart. *Pope.*

2. To throw into water. A ludicrous ſenſe.

They *ſouſed* me into the Thames with as little remorſe as they drown blind puppies. *Shakeſpeare.*

Who thoſe were that run away,
And yet gave out th' had won the day;
Although the rabble *ſous'd* them for't,
O'er head and ears in mud and dirt. *Butler.*

They *ſouſed* me over head and ears in water when a boy, ſo that I am now one of the moſt caſe-hardened of the Ironſides. *Addiſon's Guardian.*

To Souse. *v. n.* [Of this word I know not the original.] To fall as a bird on its prey.

Thus on ſome ſilver ſwan, or tim'rous hare,
Jove's bird comes *ſouſing* down from upper air;
Her crooked tallons truſs the fearful prey,
Then out of ſight ſhe ſoars. *Dryden's Æn.*

Jove's bird will *ſouſe* upon the tim'rous hare,
And tender kids with his ſharp talons tear. *Dryden, jun.*

To Souse. *v. a.* To ſtrike with ſudden violence, as a bird ſtrikes his prey.

The gallant monarch is in arms;
And like an eagle o'er his airy tow'rs,
To *ſouſe* annoyance that comes near his neſt. *Shakeſpeare.*

Souse. *adv.* With ſudden violence. A low word.

So'uterrain. *n. ſ.* [*ſouterrain*, French.] A grotto or cavern in the ground. Not Engliſh.

Defences againſt extremities of heat, as ſhade, grottoes, or *ſouterrains*, are neceſſary preſervatives of health. *Arbuthnot.*

SOUTH. *n. ſ.* [ꞅuð, Saxon; *ſuyd*, Dutch; *ſud*, French.]

1. The part where the ſun is to us at noon.

Eaſt and Weſt have no certain points of heaven, but North and *South* are fixed; and ſeldom the far ſouthern people have invaded the northern, but contrariwiſe. *Bacon.*

2. The ſouthern regions of the globe.

The queen of the *South.* *Bible.*

From the North to call
Decrepit Winter, from the *South* to bring
Solſtitial Summer's heat. *Milton.*

3. The wind that blows from the South.

All the contagion of the *South* light on you,
You ſhames of Rome, you! *Shakeſp. Coriolanus.*

The North-eaſt ſpends its rage, and now
Th' effuſive *South* warms the wide air. *Thomſon's Spring.*

South. *adj.* [from the noun.] Southern; meridional.

One inch of delay more is a *ſouth* ſea off diſcovery. *Shakeſ.*

How thy garments are warm, when he quieteth the earth by the *ſouth* wind. *Job* xxxvii. 17.

Mean while the *ſouth* wind roſe, and with black wings
Wide hovering, all the clouds together drove. *Milton.*

South. *adv.*

1. Towards the South.

His regiment lies half a mile
South from the mighty power of the king. *Shak. R.* III.

2. From the South.

Such fruits as you appoint for long keeping, gather in a fair and dry day, and when the wind bloweth not *ſouth.* *Bacon.*

So'uthing. *adj.* [from the noun.] Going towards the South.

I will conduct thee on thy way,
When next the *ſouthing* ſun inflames the day. *Dryden.*

Not far from hence, if I obſerv'd aright
The *ſouthing* of the ſtars and polar light,
Sicilia lies. *Dryden's Æn.*

Southea'st. *n. ſ.* [*South* and *Eaſt.*] The point between the Eaſt and South; the point of Winter ſunriſe.

The planting of trees warm upon a wall againſt the South, or *Southeaſt* ſun, doth haſten their ripening; and the *Southeaſt* is found better than the Southweſt. *Bacon.*

The three ſeas of Italy, the Inferiour towards the *Southeaſt*, the Ionian towards the South, and the Adriatick on the North-eaſt ſide, were commanded by three different nations. *Arbuth.*

So'utherly. *adj.* [from *South.*]

1. Belonging to any of the points denominated from the South; not abſolutely ſouthern.

2. Lying towards the South.

Unto ſuch as live under the Pole that is only north which is above them, that is only *ſoutherly* which is below them. *Brown.*

Two other country bills give us a view of the moſt eaſterly, weſterly, and *ſoutherly* parts of England. *Graunt.*

3. Coming from about the South.

I am but mad north, northweſt: when the wind is *ſoutherly*,
I know a hawk from a handſaw. *Shakeſ. Hamlet.*

So'uthern. *adj.* [ꞅuðeꞃne, Saxon; from *South.*]

1. Belonging to the South; meridional.

Why mourn I not for thee,
And with the *ſouthern* clouds contend in tears? *Shak. H.* VI.

2. Lying towards the South.

3. Coming from the South.

Mens bodies are heavier when *ſouthern* winds blow than when northern. *Bacon's Natural Hiſtory.*

Frowning Auſter ſeeks the *ſouthern* ſphere,
And rots with endleſs rain th' unwholſome year. *Dryden.*

So'uthernwood. *n. ſ.* [ꞅuðeꞃnpuðu, Saxon; *abrotanum*, Lat.]

This plant agrees in moſt parts with the wormwood, from which it is not eaſy to ſeparate it. *Miller.*

So'uthmost. *adj.* [from *South.*] Fartheſt toward the South.

Next Chemos, th' obſcene dread of Moab's ſons,
From Aroar to Nebo, and the wild
Of *ſouthmoſt* Abarim. *Milton.*

So'uthsay. *n. ſ.* [Properly *ſoothſay.*] Prediction.

All thoſe were idle thoughts and fantaſies,
Devices, dreams, opinions unſound,
Shews, viſions, *ſouthſays*, and prophecies,
And all that feigned is, as leaſings, tales, and lies. *Fa. Qu.*

To So'uthsay. *v. n.* [See Soothsay.] To predict.

Young men, hovering between hope and fear, might eaſily be carried into the ſuperſtition of *ſouthſaying* by names. *Camden.*

Southsay'er. *n. ſ.* [Properly *ſoothſayer.* See Soothsayer.] A predicter.

So'uthward. *adv.* [from *South.*] Towards the South.

Countries are more fruitful to the *ſouthward* than in the northern parts. *Raleigh's Hiſtory of the World.*

A priſoner in a room twenty foot ſquare, is at liberty to walk twenty foot *ſouthward*, but not northward. *Locke.*

Every

Every life, from the dreary months,
Flies conscious *southward*. *Thomson's Winter.*

SOUTHWE'ST. *n. s.* [*South* and *West.*] Point between the South and West; Winter sun-set.

Phenice is an haven of Crete, and lieth toward the *Southwest.* *Acts* xxvii. 12.

The planting of trees warm upon a wall against the South, or Southeast sun, doth hasten their coming on and ripening; and the Southeast is found to be better than the *Southwest*, tho' the *Southwest* be the hotter coast. *Bacon's Natural History.*

SOUVENANCE. *n. s.* [French.] Remembrance; memory. A French word which with many more is now happily disused.

If thou wilt renounce thy miscreance,
Life will I grant thee for thy valiance,
And all thy wrongs will wipe out of my *souvenance*. *Spens.*

Gave wond'rous great countenance to the knight,
That of his way he had no *souvenance*,
Nor care of vow'd revenge. *Spenser.*

SOW. *n. s.* [ꞅuᵹn, Saxon; *soeg*, *souwe*, Dutch.]

1. A female pig; the female of a boar.

Boars have great fangs, *sows* much less. *Bacon's Nat. Hist.*

A *sow* beneath an oak shall lye along,
And white herself, and white her thirty young. *Dryden.*

For which they scorn and hate them worse
Than dogs and cats do *sow* gelders. *Hudibras.*

The *sow* gelder's horn has something musical in it, but this is seldom heard. *Addison's Spectator.*

2. Perhaps from *sow* might come *swine*, ꞅpina, Saxon.

And was't thou fain
To hovel thee with *swine*, and rogues forlorn,
In short and musty straw? *Shakesp. King Lear.*

3. An oblong mass of lead. *Ainsworth.*

4. An insect; a millepede. *Ainsworth.*

SO'WBREAD. *n. s.* [*cyclamen*, Latin.] A plant.

It hath a thick round fleshy root: the flowers arise singly upon pedicles from the root, which consist of one leaf, divided into five or six segments, which are reflexed almost to the bottom, where they are divided: the pointal of the flower becomes a round membranaceous fruit, which contains roundish seeds. *Miller.*

To SOW. *v. n.* [*saian*, Gothick; ꞅapan, Saxon; *saeyen*, Dutch.] To scatter seed in order to a harvest.

The one belongeth unto them that seek, the other unto them that have found happiness: they that pray do but yet *sow*, they that give thanks declare they have reaped. *Hooker.*

The vintage shall reach unto the *sowing* time. *Lev.* xxvi. 5.

They that *sow* in tears, shall reap in joy. *Ps.* cxxvi. 5.

He that *soweth* to his flesh, shall reap corruption; but he that *soweth* to the spirit, shall reap life everlasting. *Gal.* vi. 8.

Sow to yourselves in righteousness, and reap in mercy. *Hos.*

To SOW. *v. a.* part. pass. *sown.*

1. To scatter in the ground in order to growth; to propagate by seed.

Like was not to be found,
Save in that soil where all good things did grow,
And freely sprung out of the fruitful ground
As incorrupted nature did them *sow*. *Fairy Queen.*

From Ireland come I with my strength,
And reap the harvest which that rascal *sow'd*. *Shakes. H.* VI.

I *sow* my law in you, and it shall bring fruit in you. 2 *Esdr.*

Many plants, which grow in the hotter countries, being set in the colder, will, being *sown* of seeds late in the Spring, come up and abide most part of the Summer. *Bacon.*

The intellectual faculty is a goodly field, capable of great improvement; and it is the worst husbandry in the world to *sow* it with trifles or impertinencies. *Hale's Origin of Mankind.*

When to turn
The fruitful soil, and when to *sow* the corn,
I sing, Mecænas. *Dryden's Georg.*

The proud mother views her precious brood,
And happier branches, which she never *sow'd*. *Dryden.*

2. To spread; to propagate.

Frowardness is in his heart: he deviseth mischief continually, he *soweth* discord. *Prov.* vi. 14.

To *sow* a jangling noise of words unknown. *Milton.*

Since then they stand secur'd by being join'd:
It were worthy a king's head, to *sow* division,
And seeds of jealousy, to loose those bonds. *Rowe.*

Born to afflict my Marcia's family,
And *sow* dissention in the hearts of brothers. *Addis. Cato.*

3. To impregnate or stock with seed.

He shall give the rain of thy seed, that thou shalt *sow* the ground withal. *Is.* xxx. 23.

4. To besprinkle.

He *sow'd* with stars the heav'n thick as a field. *Milton.*

Morn now *sow'd* the earth with orient pearl. *Milton.*

To SOW. *v. a.* For *sew.*

Some tree, whose broad smooth leaves together *sow'd*,
And girded on, may cover round. *Milton.*

To SOWCE. *v. a.* To throw into the water. See SOUSE.

He *sowced* me up to the middle in the pond. *L'Estrange.*

SO'WER. *n. s.* [from *sow.*]

1. He that sprinkles the seed.

A *sower* went forth to sow. *Mat* xiii. 3.

It is thrown round, as grain by a skilful *sower*. *Derham.*

2. A scatterer.

Terming Paul and his doctrine a *sower* of words, a very babbler or trifler. *Hakewill on Providence.*

3. A breeder; a promoter.

They are *sowers* of suits, which make the court swell, and the country pine. *Bacon.*

SO'WINS. *n. s.* Flummery, somewhat sour'd and made of oatmeal.

These *sowins*, that is, flummery, being blended together, produce good yeast. *Mortimer's Husbandry.*

See where Norah with the *sowins* comes. *Swift.*

To SOWL. *v. a.* [from *sow*, as hogs are pulled by dogs, *Skinner*; from *sole*, a strap, a rein, *Kennet.*] To pull by the ears.

He'll go and *sowl* the porter of Rome-gates by th' ears. *Shak.*

SOWN. The participle of *sow*. It is barbarously used by *Swift* for *sewed.*

An hundred and fifty of their beds, *sown* together, made up the breadth and length. *Gulliver.*

SO'WTHISTLE. *n. s.* A weed.

Sowthistles though coneys eat, yet sheep and cattle will not touch; the milk of which rubbed on warts weareth them away, which sheweth it is corrosive. *Bacon.*

SPAAD. *n. s.* A kind of mineral.

English talc, of which the coarser sort is called plaister or parget; the finer, *spaad*, earth-flax, or salamander's hair. *Woodward's Met. Foss.*

SPACE. *n. s.* [*spatium*, Latin.]

1. Room; local extension.

Space is the relation of distance between any two bodies or points. *Locke.*

Oh, undistinguish'd *space* of woman's wit!
A plot upon her virtuous husband's life,
And the exchange my brother. *Shak. King Lear.*

This which yields or fills all *space*. *Milton.*

Pure *space* is capable neither of resistance nor motion. *Locke.*

Space and motion can never be actually infinite: they have a power only and a capacity of being increased without end; so that no *space* can be assigned so vast, but still a larger may be imagined; no motion so swift or languid, but a greater velocity or slowness may still be conceived. *Bentley.*

2. Any quantity of place.

I would not be the villain that thou think'st
For the whole *space* that's in the tyrant's grasp,
And the rich East to boot. *Shakes. Macbeth.*

There was but two ways to escape; the one through the woods about ten miles *space* to Walpo. *Knolles.*

In such a great ruin, where the fragments are great and hard, it is not possible they should be so adjusted in their fall, but that they would lie hollow, and many unfilled *spaces* would be intercepted amongst them. *Burnet.*

Measuring first with careful eyes
The *space* his spear could reach, aloud he cries. *Dryden.*

3. Quantity of time.

Nine times the *space* that measures day and night
To mortal men, he with his horrid crew
Lay vanquish'd, rolling in the fiery gulph,
Confounded, though immortal. *Milton.*

In a lever the motion can be continued only for so short a *space*, as may be answerable to that little distance betwixt the fulciment and the weight. *Wilkins's Math. Mag.*

God may defer his judgments for a time, and give a people a longer *space* of repentance: he may stay 'till the iniquities of a nation be full; but sooner or later they have reason to expect his vengeance. *Tillotson's Sermons.*

The lives of great men cannot be writ with any tolerable degree of elegance or exactness, within a short *space* after their decease. *Addison's Freeholder.*

4. A small time; a while.

Sith for me ye fight, to me this grace
Both yield, to stay your deadly strife a *space*. *Fairy Queen.*

Compassion quell'd
His best of man, and gave him up to tears
A *space*, 'till firmer thoughts restrain'd excess. *Milton.*

SPA'CIOUS. *adj.* [*spacieux*, Fr. *spatiosus*, Latin.] Wide; extensive; roomy; not narrow.

The former buildings, which were but mean, contented them not: *spacious* and ample churches they erected throughout every city. *Hooker.*

Convey your pleasures in a *spacious* plenty;
And yet seem cold. *Shakes.*

Merab with *spacious* beauty fills the sight,
But too much awe chastis'd the bold delight. *Cowley.*

Like an English gen'ral will I die,
And all the ocean make my *spacious* grave:
Women and cowards on the land may lie;
The sea's a tomb that's proper for the brave. *Dryden.*

SPA'CIOUSNESS. *n. s.* [from *spacious.*] Roominess; wide extension.

SPA'DDLE.

SPA'DDLE. *n. s.* [Diminutive of *spade.*] A little spade.

Others destroy moles with a *spaddle*, waiting in the mornings and evenings for them. *Mortimer's Husbandry.*

SPADE. *n. s.* [ꞅpaꝺ, Saxon; *spade*, Islandick and Dutch.]

1. The instrument of digging.

Take the air of the earth new turned up, by digging with the *spade*, or standing by him that diggeth. *Bacon.*

Many learned men affirm, that some isthmes have been eat through by the sea, and others cut by the *spade*. *Brown.*

His next advance was to the soldier's trade,
Where if he did not nimbly ply the *spade*,
His surly officer ne'er fail'd to crack
His knotty cudgel on his tougher back. *Dryden.*

Here nature never diff'rence made
Between the sceptre and the *spade*. *Swift.*

2. A deer three years old. *Ainsworth.*

3. A suit of cards.

SPA'DICEOUS. *adj.* [*spadiceus*, Latin.]

Of those five Scaliger beheld, though one was *spadiceous*, or of a light red, and two inclining to red, yet was there not any of this complexion among them. *Brown's Vulgar Errours.*

SPADI'LLE. *n. s.* [*spadille*, or *espadille*, French.] The ace of spades at ombre.

SPAGY'RICK. *adj.* [*spagyricus*, Lat. A word coined by *Paracelsus* from *spaher*, a searcher, Teutonick.] Chymical.

SPA'GYRIST. *n. s.* A chymist.

This change is so unexampled, that though among the more curious *spagyrists* it be very well known, yet many naturalists cannot easily believe it. *Boyle.*

SPAKE. The old preterite of *speak.*

So *spake* the archangel Michael, then paus'd. *Milton.*

SPALL. *n. s.* [*espaule*, French.] Shoulder. Out of use.

Their mighty strokes their haberions dismay'd,
And naked made each others manly *spalles*. *Fairfax.*

SPALT, or *Spelt. n. s.* A white, scaly, shining stone, frequently used to promote the fusion of metals. *Bailey.*

SPAN. *n. s.* [ꞅpan, ꞅponne, Saxon; *spanna*, Ital. *span*, Dutch.]

1. The space from the end of the thumb to the end of the little finger extended.

A foot, the length of it, is a sixth part of the statute; a *span*, one eight; a palm, or hand's breadth, one twenty-fourth; a thumb's breadth, or inch, one seventy-second; and a fore-finger's breadth one ninety-sixth. *Holder on Time.*

Will you with counters sum
The vast proportion of his infinite?
And buckle in a waste most fathomless,
With *spans* and inches so diminutive
As fears and reasons? *Shakesp. Troilus and Cressida.*

Sum how brief the life of man
Runs his erring pilgrimage,
That the stretching of a *span*
Buckles in his sum of age. *Shakespeare.*

When I removed the one, although but at the distance of a *span*, the other would stand like Hercules's pillar. *Brown.*

2. Any short duration.

You have scarce time
To steal from spiritual leisure a brief *span*,
To keep your earthly audit. *Shakesp. Henry* VIII.

The virgin's part, the mother and the wife,
So well she acted in this *span* of life. *Waller.*

Then conscience, unrestrain'd by fears, began
To stretch her limits, and extend the *span*. *Dryden.*

Life's but a *span*, I'll ev'ry inch enjoy. *Farqhuar.*

To SPAN. *v. a.*

1. To measure by the hand extended.

Oft on the well-known spot I fix my eyes,
And *span* the distance that between us lies. *Tickell.*

2. To measure.

My surveyor is false; the o'er great cardinal
Hath shew'd him gold; my life is *spann'd* already. *Shakesp.*

This soul doth *span* the world, and hang content
From either pole unto the centre;
Where in each room of the well-furnish'd tent
He lies warm, and without adventure. *Herbert.*

Harry, whose tuneful and well-measur'd song
First taught our English musick how to *span*
Words with just note and accent, not to scan
With Midas' ears, counting short and long. *Milton.*

SPAN. The preterite of *spin.* See SPIN.

Together furiously they ran,
That to the ground came horse and man;
The blood out of their helmets *span*,
So sharp were their encounters. *Drayton's Nymphid.*

SPA'NCOUNTER. } *n. s.* [from *span*, *counter* and *farthing.*] A
SPA'NFARTHING. } play at which money is thrown within a span or mark.

Tell the king, that for his father's sake, Henry V. in whose time boys went to *spancounter* for French crowns, I am content he shall reign. *Shakespeare's Henry* VI.

Boys shall not play
At *spancounter* or blowpoint, but shall pay
Toll to some courtier. *Donne.*

His chief solace is to steal down, and play at *spanfarthing* with the page. *Swift.*

SPANG. *n. s.* [*spange*, Dutch.] This word seems to have signified a cluster of shining bodies.

The colours that shew best by candlelight are white, carnation, and a kind of sea-water green; and ouches or *spangs*, as they are of no great cost, so they are of most glory. *Bacon.*

SPA'NGLE. *n. s.* [*spange*, German, a buckle, a locket: whence *ober spangen*, ear-rings.]

1. A small plate or boss of shining metal.

2. Any thing sparkling and shining.

As hoary frost with *spangles* doth attire
The mossy branches of an oak half dead. *Fairy Queen.*

Thus in a starry night fond children cry
For the rich *spangles* that adorn the sky. *Waller.*

The twinkling *spangles*, the ornaments of the upper world, lose their beauty and magnificence: vulgar spectators see them but as a confused huddle of petty illuminants. *Glanville.*

That now the dew with *spangles* deck'd the ground,
A sweeter spot of earth was never found. *Dryden.*

To SPA'NGLE. *v. a.* [from the noun.] To besprinkle with spangles or shining bodies.

They never meet in grove or green,
By fountain clear, or *spangled* starlight sheen. *Shakespeare.*

What stars do *spangle* heaven with such beauty,
As those two eyes become that heavenly face. *Shakespeare.*

Unpin that *spangled* breastplate which you wear,
That th' eyes of busy fools may be stopt there. *Donne.*

Four faces each
Had, like a double Janus; all their shape
Spangled with eyes, more numerous than those
Of Argus. *Milton's Par. Lost.*

Then appear'd
Spangling the hemisphere, then first adorn'd
With the bright luminaries, that set and rose. *Milton.*

The spacious firmament on high,
With all the blue etherial sky,
And *spangl'd* heav'ns, a shining frame,
Their great Original proclaim. *Addison's Spectator.*

SPA'NIEL. *n. s.* [*hispaniolus*, Latin; *espagneul*, French.]

1. A dog used for sports in the field, remarkoble for sagacity and obedience.

Divers days I followed his steps 'till I found him, having newly met with an excellent *spaniel* belonging to his dead companion. *Sidney.*

There are arts to reclaim the wildest men, as there are to make *spaniels* fetch and carry: chide 'em often, and feed 'em seldom. *Dryden's Spanish Fryar.*

2. A low, mean, sneaking fellow; a courtier; a dedicator; a pensioner; a dependant; a placeman.

I mean sweet words,
Low crooked curtesies, and base *spaniel* fawning. *Shakesp.*
I am your *spaniel*; and, Demetrius,
The more you beat me I will fawn on you. *Shakespeare.*

To SPA'NIEL. *v. n.* [from the noun.] To fawn on; to play the spaniel.

The hearts
That *spaniel'd* me at heels, to whom I gave
Their wishes, do discandy and melt their sweets
On blossoming Cæsar. *Shakespeare.*

SPANISH *Broom. n. s.* [*genista juncea*, Lat.] A plant so called, as being a native of Spain: it hath pliant branches, leaves placed alternately, flowers of the pea-bloom kind, succeeded by smooth pods, containing several kidney-shaped seeds in each. *Miller.*

SPANISH *Nut. n. s.* [*sisyrinchium*, Latin.] A plant.

It hath a flower resembling the iris, from whence it differs in having a double root, one lying over another, after the same manner as those of crocus and gladiolus. *Miller.*

SPA'NKER. *n. s.* A small coin.

Your cure too costs you but a *spanker*. *Denham.*

SPA'NNER. *n. s.* The lock of a fusee or carabine. *Bailey.*

My prince's court is now full of nothing but buff-coats, *spanners*, and musket-rests. *Howel.*

SPAR. *n. s.*

1. Marcasite.

Spar is a mixed body, consisting of crystal incorporated sometimes with *lac lunæ*, and sometimes with other mineral, stony, earthy, or metallick matter. *Woodward.*

Some stones, as *spar* of lead, dissolved in proper menstruums, become salts. *Newton's Opt.*

2. [*Sparre*, Dutch.] A small beam; the bar of a gate.

To SPAR. *v. n.* To fight with prelusive strokes.

To SPAR. *v. a.* [ꞅpannan, Saxon; *sperren*, German.] To shut; to close; to bar.

And if he chance come when I am abroad,
Sparre the yate fast for fear of fraud;
Ne for all his worst, nor for his best,
Open the door at his request. *Spenser's Pastorals.*

Six gates i' th' city with massy staples,
And corresponsive and fulfilling bolts,
Spar up the sons of Troy. *Shakespeare.*

Yet for she yode thereat half agast,
And Kiddie the door *sparred* after her fast. *Spenser.*

SPA'RABLE. *n.s.* [ꞅpappan, Saxon, to fasten.] Small nails.

SPA'RADRAP. *n.s.* [In pharmacy.] A cerecloth.

With application of the common *sparadrap* for issues, this ulcer was by a fontanel kept open. *Wiseman's Surgery.*

To SPARE. *v. a.* [ꞅpapan, Saxon; *sparen*, Dutch; *espargne*, French.]

1. To use frugally; not to waste; not to consume.

Thou thy father's thunder didst not *spare*. *Milton.*

2. To have unemployed; to save from any particular use.

All the time he could *spare* from the necessary cares of his weighty charge he bestowed on prayer, and serving of God: he oftentimes spent the night alone in church-praying, his head-piece, gorget, and gauntlets lying by him. *Knolles.*

He had no bread to *spare*. *L'Estrange.*

Only the foolish virgins entertained this foolish conceit, that there might be an overplus of grace sufficient to supply their want; but the wise knew not of any that they had to *spare*, but supposed all that they had little enough. *Tillotson.*

Let a pamphlet come in a proper juncture, and every one who can *spare* a shilling shall be a subscriber. *Swift.*

3. To do without; to lose willingly.

I could have better *spar'd* a better man. *Shak. Hen.* IV.

For his mind, I do not care,
That's a toy that I could *spare*;
Let his title be but great,
His clothes rich, and band sit neat. *Ben. Johnson.*

Sense of pleasure we may well
Spare out of life perhaps, and not repine;
But pain is perfect misery. *Milton.*

Now she might *spare* the ocean, and oppose
Your conduct to the fiercest of her foes. *Waller.*

The fair blessing we vouchsafe to send;
Nor can we *spare* you long, tho' often we may lend. *Dryd.*

4. To omit; to forbear.

We might have *spar'd* our coming. *Milton.*

Be pleas'd your politicks to *spare*;
I'm old enough, and can myself take care. *Dryden.*

5. To use tenderly; to forbear; to treat with pity; not to afflict; not to destroy; to use with mercy.

Spare us, good Lord. *Common Prayer.*

Who will set the discipline of wisdom over mine heart, that they *spare* me not for my ignorances? *Ecclus* xxiii. 2.

Doth not each look a flash of lightning feel!
Which *spares* the body's sheath, but melts the steel. *Cleavel.*

Dim sadness did not *spare*
Celestial visages. *Milton.*

Less pleasure take brave minds in battles won
Than in restoring such as are undone:
Tygers have courage, and the rugged bear;
But man alone can whom he conquers *spare*. *Waller.*

Spare me one hour! O *spare* me but a moment. *Irene.*

6. To grant; to allow; to indulge.

Set me in the remotest place,
That Neptune's frozen arms embrace;
Where angry Jove did never *spare*
One breath of kind and temperate air. *Roscommon.*

7. To forbear to inflict or impose.

Spare my remembrance; 'twas a guilty day;
And still the blush hangs here. *Dryd. All for Love.*

O spare this great, this good, this aged king,
And *spare* your soul the crime! *Dryden's Spanish Fryar.*

Spare my sight the pain
Of seeing what a world of tears it costs you. *Dryden.*

To SPARE. *v. n.*

1. To live frugally; to be parcimonious; to be not liberal.

H' has wherewithal: in him
Sparing would show a worse sin than ill doctrine. *Shakesp.*

Those wants, which they rather feared than felt, would well enough be overcome by *sparing* and patience. *Knolles.*

Our labours late and early every morning,
Midst Winter frosts, then clad and fed with *sparing*,
Rise to our toils. *Otway.*

God has not been so *sparing* to men to make them barely two-legged creatures, and left it to Aristotle to make them rational. *Locke.*

When they discover the passionate desire of fame in the ambitious man, they become *sparing* and saving in their commendations; they envy him the satisfaction of an applause. *Addis.*

Now a reservoir to keep and *spare*,
The next a fountain spouting through his heir. *Pope.*

No statute in his favour says
How free or frugal I shall pass my days;
Who at some times spend, at others *spare*,
Divided between carelessness and care. *Pope.*

2. To forbear; to be scrupulous.

His soldiers *spared* not to say that they should be unkindly dealt with, if they were defrauded of the spoil. *Knolles.*

In these relations, although he be more *sparing*, his predecessors were very numerous. *Brown's Vulgar Errours.*

To pluck and eat my fill I *spar'd* not. *Milton.*

3. To use mercy; to forgive; to be tender.

Their king, out of a princely feeling, was *sparing* and compassionate towards his subjects. *Bacon.*

SPARE. *adj.*

1. Scanty; not abundant; parcimonious.

He was *spare*, but discreet of speech; better conceiving than delivering; equally stout and kind. *Carew's Surv. of Cornwal.*

Men ought to beware, that they use not exercise and a *spare* diet both. *Bacon's Natural History.*

Join with thee calm peace and quiet;
Spare fast, that oft with gods doth diet. *Milton.*

The masters of the world were bred up with *spare* diet; and the young gentlemen of Rome felt no want of strength, because they ate but once a day. *Locke.*

2. Superfluous; unwanted.

If that no *spare* cloths he had to give,
His own coat he would cut, and it distribute glad. *F. Q.*

As any of our sick waxed well, he might be removed; for which purpose there were set forth ten *spare* chambers. *Bacon.*

Learning seems more adapted to the female world than to the male, because they have more *spare* time upon their hands, and lead a more sedentary life. *Addison's Spectator.*

In my *spare* hours you've had your part;
Ev'n now my servile hand your sovereign will obeys. *Norr.*

3. Lean; wanting flesh; macilent.

O give me your *spare* men, and spare me the great ones. *Sh.*

If my name were liable to fear,
I do not know the man I should avoid
So soon as that *spare* Cassius. *Shakesp. Julius Cæsar.*

His visage drawn he felt to sharp and *spare*,
His arms clung to his ribs. *Milton's Parad. Lost.*

SPARE. *n.s.* [from the verb.] Parcimony; frugal use; husbandry. Not in use.

Our victuals failed us, though we had made good *spare* of them. *Bacon.*

SPA'RER. *n.s.* [from *spare.*] One who avoids expence.

By nature far from profusion, and yet a greater *sparer* than a saver; for though he had such means to accumulate, yet his forts, garrisons, and his feastings, wherein he was only sumptuous, could not but soak his Exchequer. *Wotton.*

SPA'RERIB. *n.s.* [*spare* and *rib.*] Some part cut off from the ribs: as, a *sparerib* of pork.

SPARGEFA'CTION. *n.s.* [*spargo*, Lat.] The act of sprinkling.

SPA'RING. *adj.* [from *spare.*]

1. Scarce; little.

Of this there is with you *sparing* memory or none; but we have large knowledge thereof. *Bacon.*

2. Scanty; not plentiful.

If much exercise, then use a plentiful diet; and if *sparing* diet, then little exercise. *Bacon.*

Good air, solitary groves, and *sparing* diet, sufficient to make you fancy yourself one of the fathers of the desert. *Pope.*

3. Parcimonious; not liberal.

Virgil being so very *sparing* of his words, and leaving so much to be imagined by the reader, can never be translated as he ought in any modern tongue. *Dryden.*

Though *sparing* of his grace, to mischief bent,
He seldom does a good with good intent. *Dryden.*

SPA'RINGLY. *adv.* [from *sparing.*]

1. Not abundantly.

Give us leave freely to render what we have in charge;
Or shall we *sparingly* shew you far off
The dauphin's meaning? *Shakesp. Henry* V.

The borders whereon you plant fruit-trees should be large, and set with fine flowers; but thin and *sparingly*, lest they deceive the trees. *Bacon's Essays.*

2. Frugally; parcimoniously; not lavishly.

Speech of touch towards others should be *sparingly* used; for discourse ought to be as a field, without coming home to any man. *Bacon's Essays.*

High titles of honour were in the king's minority *sparingly* granted, because dignity then waited on desert. *Hayward.*

Commend but *sparingly* whom thou do'st love;
But less condemn whom thou do'st not approve. *Denham.*

The morality of a grave sentence, affected by Lucan, is more *sparingly* used by Virgil. *Dryden.*

3. With abstinence.

Christians are obliged to taste even the innocent pleasures of life but *sparingly*. *Atterbury.*

4. Not with great frequency.

Our sacraments, which had been frequented with so much zeal, were approached more *sparingly*. *Atterbury's Sermons.*

5. Cautiously; tenderly.

SPARK. *n.s.* [ꞅpeanca, Saxon; *sparke*, Dutch.]

1. A small particle of fire, or kindled matter.

If any marvel how a thing, in itself so weak, could import any great danger, they must consider not so much how small the *spark* is that flieth up, as how apt things about it are to take fire. *Hooker.*

I am about to weep; but thinking that
We are a queen, my drops of tears I'll turn
To *sparks* of fire. *Shakespeare.*

I was

I was not forgetful of the *ſparks* which ſome mens diſtempers formerly ſtudied to kindle in parliaments. *K. Charles.*

In this deep quiet, from what ſource unknown,
Thoſe ſeeds of fire that fatal birth diſcloſe:
And firſt, few ſcatt'ring *ſparks* about were blown,
Big with the flames that to our ruin roſe. *Dryden.*

Oh, may ſome *ſpark* of your celeſtial fire
The laſt, the meaneſt of your ſons inſpire. *Pope.*

2. Any thing ſhining.

We have, here and there, a little clear light, ſome *ſparks* of bright knowledge. *Locke.*

3. Any thing vivid or active.

If any *ſpark* of life be yet remaining,
Down, down to hell, and ſay, I ſent thee thither. *Shakeſp.*

4. A lively, ſhowy, ſplendid, gay man. It is commonly uſed ontempt.

How many huffing *ſparks* have we ſeen, that in the ſame day have been both the idols and the ſcorn of the ſame ſlaves? *L'Eſtrange.*

A *ſpark* like thee, of the mankilling trade
Fell ſick. *Dryden.*

As for the diſputes of ſharpers, we don't read of any proviſions made for the honours of ſuch *ſparks*. *Collier.*

The fineſt *ſparks*, and cleaneſt beaux
Drip from the ſhoulders to the toes. *Prior.*

I who have been the poet's *ſpark* to day,
Will now become the champion of his play. *Granville.*

Unlucky as Fungoſo in the play,
Theſe *ſparks* with aukward vanity diſplay
What the fine gentlemen wore yeſterday. *Pope.*

To SPARK. *v. n.* [from the noun] To emit particles of fire; to ſparkle. Not in uſe.

Fair is my love,
When the roſe in her cheek appears,
Or in her eyes the fire of love doth *ſpark*. *Spenſer.*

SPA'RKFUL. *adj.* [*ſpark* and *full.*] Lively; briſk; airy.

Hitherto will our *ſparkful* youth laugh at their great grandfather's Engliſh, who had more care to do well than to ſpeak minion-like. *Camden's Remains.*

SPA'RKISH. *adj.* [from *ſpark.*]

1. Airy; gay. A low word.

Is any thing more *ſparkiſh* and better humour'd than Venus's accoſting her ſon in the deſarts of Libya? *Walſh.*

2. Showy; well dreſſed; fine.

A daw, to be *ſparkiſh*, trick'd himſelf up with all the gay feathers he could muſter. *L'Eſtrange.*

SPA'RKLE *n. ſ.* [from *ſpark.*]

1. A ſpark; a ſmall particle of fire.

He with repeated ſtrokes
Of claſhing flints, their hidden fires provokes;
Short flame ſucceeds, a bed of wither'd leaves
The dying *ſparkles* in their fall receives:
Caught into life, in fiery fumes they riſe,
And, fed with ſtronger food, invade the ſkies. *Dryden.*

2. Any luminous particle.

To detract from the dignity thereof, were to injure ev'n God himſelf, who being that light which none can approach unto, hath ſent out theſe lights whereof we are capable, even as ſo many *ſparkles* reſembling the bright fountain from which they riſe. *Hooker.*

When reaſon's lamp, which, like the ſun in ſky,
Throughout man's little world her beams did ſpread,
Is now become a *ſparkle* which doth lie
Under the aſhes, half extinct and dead. *Davies.*

Ah then! thy once lov'd Eloiſa ſee!
It will be then no crime to gaze on me.
See from my cheek the tranſient roſes die,
See the laſt *ſparkle* languiſh in my eye. *Pope.*

To SPA'RKLE. *v. n.* [from the noun.]

1. To emit ſparks.

2. To iſſue in ſparks.

The bold deſign
Pleas'd highly thoſe infernal ſtates, and joy
Sparkled in all their eyes. *Milton.*

3. To ſhine; to glitter.

A hair ſeen in a microſcope loſes its former colour, and is in a great meaſure pellucid, with a mixture of ſome bright *ſparkling* colours, ſuch as appear from the refraction of diamonds. *Locke.*

Politulus is a fine young gentleman, who *ſparkles* in all the ſhining things of dreſs and equipage. *Watts.*

SPA'RKLINGLY. *adv.* [from *ſparkling.*] With vivid and twinkling luſtre.

Diamonds ſometimes would look more *ſparklingly* than they were wont, and ſometimes far more dull than ordinary. *Boyle.*

SPA'RKLINGNESS. *n. ſ.* [from *ſparkling.*] Vivid and twinkling luſtre.

I have obſerved a manifeſtly greater clearneſs and *ſparklingneſs* at ſome times than at others, though I could not refer it to the ſuperficial clearneſs or foulneſs of the ſtone. *Boyle.*

SPA'RROW. *n. ſ.* [ſpeaꞃꞃa, Saxon.] A ſmall bird.

Diſmay'd not this
Macbeth and Banquo? Yes,
As *ſparrows*, eagles; or the hare, the lion. *Shakeſpeare.*

There is great probability that a thouſand *ſparrows* will fly away at the ſight of a hawk among them. *Watts.*

SPA'RROWHAWK, or *ſparhawk. n. ſ.* [ſpeaꞃhaꝼoc, Saxon] The female of the muſket hawk. *Hanmer.*

SPA'RROWGRASS. *n. ſ.* [Corrupted from *aſparagus.*]

Your infant peaſe to *ſparrowgraſs* prefer,
Which to the ſupper you may beſt defer. *King.*

SPA'RRY. *adj.* [from *ſpar.*] Conſiſting of ſpar.

In which manner ſpar is uſually found herein, and other minerals; or ſuch as are of ſome obſervable figure; of which ſort are the *ſparry* ſtriæ, or icicles called ſtalactitæ. *Woodw.*

SPASM. *n. ſ.* [*ſpaſme*, Fr. σπάσμα.] Convulſion; violent and involuntary contraction of any part.

All the maladies
Of ghaſtly *ſpaſm*, or racking torture, qualms
Of heart ſick agony. *Milton.*

Wounds are ſubject to pain, inflammation, *ſpaſm*. *Wiſeman.*

Carminative things dilute and relax; becauſe wind occaſions a *ſpaſm* or convulſion in ſome part. *Arbuthnot.*

SPA'SMODICK. *adj.* [*ſpaſmodique*, Fr. from *ſpaſm.*] Convulſive.

SPAT. The preterite of *ſpit*.

And when he had *ſpat* on the ground, he anointed his eyes. *Goſpel.*

SPAT. *n. ſ.* The young ſhell-fiſh.

A reticulated film found upon ſea-ſhells, and uſually ſuppoſed to be the remains of the veſicles of the *ſpat* of ſome ſort of ſhell-fiſh. *Woodward on Foſſils.*

To SPA'TIATE. *v. n.* [*ſpatior*, Latin.] To rove; to range; to ramble at large.

Wonder cauſeth aſtoniſhment, or an immoveable poſture of the body, cauſed by the fixing of the mind upon one cogitation, whereby it doth not *ſpatiate* and tranſcur. *Bacon.*

Confined to a narrow chamber, he could *ſpatiate* at large through the whole univerſe. *Bentley.*

To SPA'TTER. *v. a.* [ſpaꞇ, ſpit, Saxon.]

1. To ſprinkle with dirt, or any thing offenſive.

The pavement ſwam in blood, the walls are
Were *ſpatter'd* o'er with brains. *Addiſon.*

2. To throw out any thing offenſive.

His forward voice now is to ſpeak well of his friend; his backward voice is to *ſpatter* foul ſpeeches, and to detract. *Shak.*

3. To aſperſe; to defame.

To SPA'TTER. *v. n.* To ſpit; to ſpatter as at any thing nauſeous taken into the mouth.

They fondly thinking to allay
Their appetite with guſt, inſtead of fruit
Chew'd bitter aſhes, which th' offended taſte
With *ſpattering* noiſe rejected. *Milton.*

SPATTERDASHES. *n. ſ.* [*ſpatter* and *daſh.*] Coverings for the legs by which the wet is kept off.

SPA'TTLING *Poppy. n. ſ.* White behen. A plant which is a ſpecies of campion. *Miller.*

SPA'TULA. *n. ſ.* [*ſpatha*, *ſpathula*, Latin.] A ſpattle or ſlice.

Spatula is an inſtrument uſed by apothecaries and ſurgeons in ſpreading plaiſters or ſtirring medicines together. *Quincy.*

In raiſing up the hairy ſcalp ſmooth with my *ſpatula*, I could diſcover no fault in the bone. *Wiſeman's Surgery.*

SPA'VIN. *n. ſ.* [*eſpavent*, Fr. *ſpavano*, Italian.] This diſeaſe in horſes is a bony excreſcence or cruſtas hard as a bone, that grows on the inſide of the hough, not far from the elbow, and is generated of the ſame matter by which the bones or ligaments are nouriſhed: it is at firſt like a tender griſtle, but by degrees comes to hardneſs. *Farrier's Dict.*

They've all new legs and lame ones; one would take it,
That never ſaw them pace before, the *ſpavin*,
And ſpringhalt reign'd among them. *Shakeſpeare.*

If it had been a *ſpavin*, and the aſs had petitioned for another farrier, it might have been reaſonable. *L'Eſtrange.*

SPAW. *n. ſ.* [from *Spaw* in Germany.] A place famous for mineral waters; any mineral water.

To SPAWL. *v. n.* [ſpœꞇlian, to ſpit, Saxon.] To throw moiſture out of the mouth.

He who does on iv'ry tables dine,
His marble floors with drunken *ſpawlings* ſhine. *Dryden.*

What miſchief can the dean have done him,
That Traulus calls for vengeance on him?
Why muſt he ſputter, *ſpawl*, and ſlaver it,
In vain againſt the people's fav'rite. *Swift.*

SPAWL. *n. ſ.* ſpaꞇl, Saxon.] Spittle; moiſture ejected from the mouth.

Of ſpittle ſhe luſtration makes;
Then in the *ſpawl* her middle finger dips,
Anoints the temple, forehead, and the lips. *Dryden.*

SPAWN. *n. ſ.* [*ſpene*, *ſpenne*, Dutch.]

1. The eggs of fiſh, or of frogs.

Maſters of the people,
Your multiplying *ſpawn* how can he flatter
That's thouſand to one good one? *Shakeſpeare's Coriolanus.*

God

God ſaid, let the waters generate
Reptile, with *ſpawn* abundant, living ſoul! *Milton.*

These ponds, in ſpawning time abounded with frogs, and a great deal of *ſpawn*. *Ray on the Creation.*

2. Any product or offspring. In contempt.

'Twas not the *ſpawn* of ſuch as theſe
That dy'd with Punick blood the conquer'd ſeas,
And quaſht the ſtern Æacides.. *Roſcommon.*

This atheiſtical humour was the *ſpawn* of the groſs ſuperſtitions of the Romiſh church and court. *Tillotſon.*

To SPAWN. *v. a.* [from the noun.]

1. To produce as fiſhes do eggs.

Some report a ſea-maid *ſpawn'd* him. *Shakeſpeare.*

2. To generate; to bring forth. In contempt.

What practices ſuch principles as theſe may *ſpawn*, when they are laid out to the ſun, you may determine. *Swift.*

To SPAWN. *v. n.*

1. To iſſue as eggs from fiſh.

2. To iſſue; to proceed. In contempt.

It is ſo ill a quality, and the mother of ſo many ill ones that *ſpawn* from it, that a child ſhould be brought up in the greateſt abhorrence of it. *Locke.*

SPAW'NER. *n. ſ.* [from *ſpawn.*] The female fiſh.

The barbel, for the preſervation of their ſeed, both the *ſpawner* and the melter cover their ſpawn with ſand. *Walton.*

To SPAY. *v. a.* [*ſpado*, Latin.] To caſtrate female animals.

Be dumb you beggars of the rhyming trade,
Geld your looſe wits, and let your muſe be *ſpay'd*. *Cleavel.*

The males muſt be gelt, and the ſows *ſpay'd*; the *ſpay'd* they eſteem as the moſt profitable, becauſe of the great quantity of fat upon the inwards. *Mortimer's Huſbandry.*

To SPEAK. *v. n.* [Preterite, *ſpake* or *ſpoke*; participle paſſive, *ſpoken*; ſpecan, Saxon; *ſpreken*, Dutch.]

1. To utter articulate ſounds; to expreſs thoughts by words.

Speaking is nothing elſe than a ſenſible expreſſion of the notions of the mind, by ſeveral diſcriminations of utterance of voice, uſed as ſigns, having by conſent ſeveral determinate ſignificancies. *Holder.*

Hannah *ſpake* in her heart, only her lips moved, but her voice was not heard. 1 *Sam.* i. 13.

2. To harangue; to make a ſpeech.

Many of the nobility made themſelves popular by *ſpeaking* in parliament, againſt thoſe things which were moſt grateful to his majeſty, and which ſtill paſſed notwithſtanding their contradiction. *Clarendon.*

Therſites, though the moſt preſumptuous Greek,
Yet durſt not for Achilles' armour *ſpeak*. *Dryden.*

3. To talk for or againſt; to diſpute.

A knave ſhould have ſome countenance at his friend's requeſt. An honeſt man, ſir, is able to *ſpeak* for himſelf when a knave is not. *Shakeſpeare's Henry* IV.

The general and his wife are talking of it;
And ſhe *ſpeaks* for you ſtoutly. *Shakeſpeare's Othello.*

When he had no power,
He was your enemy; ſtill *ſpake* againſt
Your liberties and charters. *Shakeſpeare's Coriolanus.*

4. To diſcourſe; to make mention.

Were ſuch things here as we do *ſpeak* about?
Or have we eaten of the inſane root,
That takes the reaſon priſoner. *Shakeſpeare's King Lear.*

Lot went out and *ſpake* unto his ſons in law. *Gen.* xix. 14.

The fire you *ſpeak* of,
If any flames of it approach my fortunes,
I'll quench it not with water, but with ruin. *Ben. Johnſon.*

They could never be loſt, but by an univerſal deluge which has been *ſpoken* to already. *Tillotſon's Sermons.*

Lucan *ſpeaks* of a part of Cæſar's army that came to him, from the Leman-lake, in the beginning of the civil war. *Addiſ.*

Had Luther *ſpoke* up to this accuſation, yet Chryſoſtom's example would have been his defence. *Atterbury.*

4. To give ſound.

Make all your trumpets *ſpeak*, give them all breath,
Thoſe clam'rous harbingers of blood and death. *Shakeſp.*

5. *To* SPEAK *with.* To addreſs; to converſe with.

Thou can'ſt not fear us, Pompey, with thy ſails,
We'll *ſpeak with* thee at ſea. *Shakeſp. Ant. and Cleopatra.*

I *ſpake with* one that came from thence,
That freely render'd me theſe news for true. *Shakeſpeare.*

Nicholas was by a herald ſent for to come into the great baſſa; Solyman diſdaining to *ſpeak with* him himſelf. *Knolles.*

To SPEAK. *v. a.*

1. To utter with the mouth; to pronounce.

Saul *ſpake* not any think that day. 1 *Sam.* xx. 26.

Mordecai had *ſpoken* good. *Eſth.* vii. 9.

Conſider of it, take advice, and *ſpeak* your minds. *Judges.*

They ſat down with him upon the ground, and none *ſpake* a word. *Job* ii. 13.

When divers were hardened, and believed not, but *ſpake* evil of that way before the multitude, he departed. *Acts* xix. 9.

You, from my youth,
Have known and try'd me, *ſpeak* I more than truth? *Sandys.*

What you keep by you, you may change and mend,
But words once *ſpoke* can never be recall'd. *Waller.*

Under the tropick is our language *ſpoke*,
And part of Flanders hath receiv'd our yoke. *Waller.*

He no where *ſpeaks* it out, or in direct terms calls them ſubſtances. *Locke.*

Colours *ſpeak* all languages, but words are underſtood only by ſuch a people or nation. *Spectator.*

2. To proclaim; to celebrate.

It is my father's muſick
To *ſpeak* your deeds, not little of his care
To have them recompenſed. *Shakeſpeare's Winter's Tale.*

3. To addreſs; to accoſt.

If he have need of thee, he will deceive thee, ſmile upon thee, put thee in hope, *ſpeak* thee fair, and ſay, what wanteſt thou? *Ecclus* xiii. 6.

4. To exhibit.

Let heav'n's wide circuit *ſpeak*
The Maker's high magnificence. *Milton.*

SPEA'KABLE. *adj.* [from *ſpeak.*]

1. Poſſible to be ſpoken.

2. Having the power of ſpeech.

Say,
How cam'ſt thou *ſpeakable* of mute. *Milton.*

SPEA'KER. *n. ſ.* [from *ſpeak.*]

1. One that ſpeaks.

Theſe fames grew ſo general, as the authors were loſt in the generality of *ſpeakers*. *Bacon's Henry* VII.

In converſation or reading, find out the true ſenſe, idea which the *ſpeaker* or writer affixes to his words. *Watts's Logick.*

Common *ſpeakers* have only one ſet of ideas, and one ſet of words to cloath them in; and theſe are always ready at the mouth. *Swift.*

2. One that ſpeaks in any particular manner.

Horace's phraſe is *torret jecur*;
And happy was that curious *ſpeaker*. *Prior.*

3. One that celebrates, proclaims, or mentions.

After my death, I wiſh no other herald,
No other *ſpeaker* of my living actions
To keep mine honour from corruption. *Shakeſpeare.*

4. The prolocutor of the commons.

I have diſabled myſelf like an elected *ſpeaker* of the houſe. *Dryd*

SPEA'KING *Trumpet. n. ſ.* A ſtentorophonick inſtrument; a trumpet by which the voice may be propagated to a great diſtance.

That with one blaſt through the whole houſe does bound,
And firſt taught *ſpeaking trumpet* how to ſound. *Dryden.*

SPEAR. *n. ſ.* [*yſ-per*, Welſh; ſpere, Saxon; *ſpere*, Dutch; *ſpare*, old French; *ſparum*, low Lat.]

1. A long weapon with a ſharp point, uſed in thruſting or throwing; a lance.

Th' Egyptian, like a hill, himſelf did rear,
Like ſome tall tree; upon it ſeem'd a *ſpear*. *Cowley.*

Nor wanted in his graſp
What ſeem'd both ſhield and *ſpear*. *Milton.*

The flying *ſpear*
Sung innocent, and ſpent its force in air. *Pope.*

The rous'd up lion, reſolute and ſlow,
Advances full on the protended *ſpear*. *Thomſon.*

2. A lance generally with prongs, to kill fiſh.

The borderers watching, until they be paſt up into ſome narrow creek, below them, caſt a ſtrong corded net athwart the ſtream, with which, and their loud ſhouting, they ſtop them from retiring, until the ebb have abandoned them to the hunter's mercy, who, by an old cuſtom, ſhare them with ſuch indifferency, as if a woman with child be preſent, the babe in her womb is gratified with a portion: a point alſo obſerved by the *ſpear*-hunters in taking of ſalmons. *Carew.*

To SPEAR. *v. a.* [from the noun.] To kill or pierce with a ſpear.

To SPEAR. *v. n.* To ſhoot or ſprout. This is commonly written *ſpire*.

Let them not lie leſt they ſhould *ſpear*, and the air dry and ſpoil the ſhoot. *Mortimer's Huſbandry.*

SPEA'RGRASS. *n. ſ.* [*ſpear* and *graſs.*] Long ſtiff graſs.

Tickle our noſes with *ſpeargraſs* to make them bleed; and then beſlubber our garments with it. *Shakeſpeare's Henry* IV.

SPEA'RMAN. *n. ſ* [*ſpear* and *man.*] One who uſes a lance in fight.

The *ſpearman's* arm by thee, great God, directed,
Sends forth a certain wound. *Prior.*

SPEA'RMINT. *n. ſ.* A plant; a ſpecies of mint.

SPEA'RWORT. *n. ſ.* An herb. *Ainſworth.*

SPE'CIAL. *adj.* [*ſpecial*, Fr. *ſpecialis*, Latin.]

1. Noting a ſort or ſpecies.

A *ſpecial* idea is called by the ſchools a ſpecies. *Watts.*

2. Particular; peculiar.

Moſt commonly with a certain *ſpecial* grace of her own, wagging her lips, and grinning inſtead of ſmiling. *Sidney.*

The ſeveral books of ſcripture having had each ſome ſeveral occaſion and particular purpoſe which cauſed them to be written, the contents thereof are according to the exigence of that *ſpecial* end whereunto they are intended. *Hooker.*

Of all men alive
I never yet beheld that *special* face,
Which I could fancy more than any other. *Shakespeare.*
Nought so vile that on the earth doth live,
But to the earth some *special* good doth give. *Shakespeare.*

Our Saviour is represented every where in scripture, as the *special* patron of the poor and the afflicted, and as laying their interests to heart more nearly than those of any other of his members. *Atterbury's Sermons.*

3. Appropriate; designed for a particular purpose.

O Neal, upon his marriage with a daughter of Kildare, was made denizen by a *special* act of parliament. *Davies.*

4. Extraordinary; uncommon.

That which necessity of some *special* time doth cause to be enjoined, bindeth no longer than during that time, but doth afterward become free. *Hooker.*

Though our charity should be universal, yet as it cannot be actually exercised, but on particular times, so it should be chiefly on *special* opportunities. *Spratt's Sermons.*

He bore
A paunch of the same bulk before;
Which still he had a *special* care
To keep well cramm'd with thrifty fare. *Hudibras.*

5. Chief in excellence.

The king hath drawn
The *special* head of all the land together. *Shakes. Henry* IV.

SPE'CIALLY. *adv.* [from *special.*]

1. Particularly above others.

Specially the day that thou stoodest before the Lord. *Deutr.*
A brother beloved, *specially* to me. *Phil.* xvi.

2. Not in a common way; peculiarly.

If there be matter of law that carries any difficulty, the jury may, to deliver themselves from an attaint, find it *specially.* *Hale.*

SPE'CIALTY. } *n. s.* [*specialité*, French; from *special.*] Particularity.
SPECIA'LITY. }

On these two general heads all other *specialties* are dependent. *Hooker.*

The packet is not come,
Where that and other *specialties* are bound. *Shakespeare.*
Speciality of rule hath been neglected. *Shakespeare.*

When men were sure, that in case they rested upon a bare contract without *speciality*, the other party might wage his law, they would not rest upon such contracts without reducing the debt into a *speciality* which accorded many suits. *Hale.*

SPE'CIES. *n. s.* [*species*, Latin.]

1. A sort; a subdivision of a general term.

A special idea is called by the schools a *species*; it is one common nature that agrees to several singular individual beings: so horse is a special idea or *species* as it agrees to Bucephalus, Trot, and Snowball. *Watts.*

2. Class of nature; single order of beings.

He intendeth only the care of the *species* or common natures, but letteth loose the guard of individuals or single existencies. *Brown's Vulgar Errours.*

For we are animals no less,
Although of different *species.* *Hudibras.*
Thou nam'st a race which must proceed from me,
Yet my whole *species* in myself I see. *Dryden.*

A mind of superior or meaner capacities than human would constitute a different *species*, though united to a human body in the same laws of connexion: and a mind of human capacities would make another *species*, if united to a different body in different laws of connexion. *Bentley's Sermons.*

3. Appearance to the senses; any visible or sensible representation.

An apparent diversity between the *species* visible and audible is, that the visible doth not mingle in the medium, but the audible doth. *Bacon.*

It is a most certain rule, how much any body hath of colour, so much hath it of opacity, and by so much the more unfit it is to transmit the *species.* *Ray on the Creation.*

The *species* of the letters illuminated with blue were nearer to the lens than those illuminated with deep red by about three inches, or three and a quarter; but the *species* of the letters illuminated with indigo and violet appeared so confused and indistinct, that I could not read them. *Newton's Opticks.*

4. Representation to the mind.

Wit in the poet, or wit-writing is no other than the faculty of imagination in the writer, which searches over all the memory for the *species* or ideas of those things which it designs to represent. *Dryden.*

5. Show; visible exhibition.

Shews and *species* serve best with the common people. *Bacon.*

6. Circulating money.

As there was in the time of the greatest splendour of the Roman empire, a less quantity of current *species* in Europe than there is now, Rome possessed a much greater proportion of the circulating *species* of its time than any European city. *Arbuthnot on Coins.*

7. Simples that have place in a compound.

SPECI'FICAL. } *adj.* [*specifique*, French; *species* and *facio.*]
SPECI'FICK. }

1. That which makes a thing of the species of which it is.

That thou to truth the perfect way may'st know,
To thee all her *specifick* forms I'll show. *Denham.*

The understanding, as to the exercise of this power, is subject to the command of the will, though as to the *specifick* nature of its acts it is determined by the object. *South.*

By whose direction is the nutriment so regularly distributed into the respective parts, and how are they kept to their *specifick* uniformities? *Glanville.*

These principles I consider not as occult qualities, supposed to result from the *specifick* forms of things, but as general laws of nature by which the things themselves are formed; their truth appearing to us by phænomena, though their causes be not yet discovered. *Newton's Opticks.*

As all things were formed according to these *specifical* platforms, so their truth must be measured from their conformity to them. *Norris.*

Specifick gravity is the appropriate and peculiar gravity or weight, which any species of natural bodies have, and by which they are plainly distinguishable from all other bodies of different kinds. *Quincey.*

The *specifick* qualities of plants reside in their native spirit, oil and essential salt: for the water, fixt salt and earth appear to be the same in all plants. *Arbuthnot.*

Specifick difference is that primary attribute which distinguishes each species from one another, while they stand ranked under the same general nature or genus. Though wine differs from other liquids, in that it is the juice of a certain fruit, yet this is but a general or generick difference; for it does not distinguish wine from cyder or perry: the *specifick* difference of wine therefore is its pressure from the grape; as cyder is pressed from apples, and perry from pears. *Watts.*

2. [In medicine.] Appropriated to the cure of some particular distemper. It is usually applied to the *arcana*, or medicines that work by occult qualities.

The operation of purging medicines have been referred to a hidden propriety, a *specifical* virtue, and the like shifts of ignorance. *Bacon's Natural History.*

If she would drink a good decoction of sarsa, with the usual *specificks*, she might enjoy a good health. *Wiseman.*

SPECI'FICALLY. *adv.* [from *specifick.*] In such a manner as to constitute a species; acording to the nature of the species.

His faith must be not only living, but lively too; it must be put into a posture by a particular exercise of those several virtues that are *specifically* requisite to a due performance of this duty. *South's Sermons.*

Human reason doth not only gradually, but *specifically* differ from the fantastick reason of brutes, which have no conceit of truth, as an aggregate of divers simple conceits, nor of any other universal. *Grew.*

He must allow that bodies were endowed with the same affections then as ever since; and that, if an ax head be supposed to float upon water which is *specifically* lighter, it had been supernatural. *Bentley.*

To SPECI'FICATE. *v. a.* [from *species* and *facio.*] To mark by notation of distinguishing particularities.

Man, by the instituted law of his creation, and the common influence of the divine goodness, is enabled to act as a reasonable creature, without any particular, *specificating*, concurrent, new imperate act of the divine special providence. *Hale.*

SPECIFICATION, *n. s.* [from *specifick*; *specification*, Fr.]

1. Distinct notation; determination by a peculiar mark.

This *specification* or limitation of the question hinders the disputers from wandering away from the precise point of enquiry. *Watts's Improvement of the Mind.*

2. Particular mention.

The constitution here speaks generally without the *specification* of any place. *Ayliffe's Parergon.*

To SPE'CIFY. *v. a.* [from *species*; *specifier*, Fr.] To mention; to show by some particular marks of distinction.

As the change of such laws as have been *specified* is necessary, so the evidence that they are such, must be great. *Hooker.*

St. Peter doth not *specify* what these waters were. *Burnet.*

He has there given us an exact geography of Greece, where the countries, and the uses of their soils are *specified.* *Pope.*

SPE'CIMEN. *n. s.* [*specimen*, Latin.] A sample; a part of any thing exhibited that the rest may be known.

Several persons have exhibited *specimens* of this art before multitudes of beholders. *Addison's Spectator.*

SPE'CIOUS. *adj.* [*specieux*, Fr. *speciosus*, Latin.]

1. Showy; pleasing to the view.

The rest, far greater part,
Will deem in outward rites and *specious* forms,
Religion satisfy'd. *Milton.*

She next I took to wife,
O that I never had! fond wish too late!
Was in the vale of Sorec, Dalila,
That *specious* monster, my accomplish'd snare. *Milton.*

2. Plausible;

2. Plauſible; ſuperficially, not ſolidly right; ſtriking at firſt view.

Bad men boaſt
Their *ſpecious* deeds on earth which glory excites,
Or cloſe ambition varniſh'd o'er with zeal. *Milton.*

Somewhat of *ſpecious* they muſt have to recommend themſelves to princes; for folly will not eaſily go down in its natural form. *Dryden.*

Temptation is of greater danger, becauſe it is covered with the *ſpecious* names of good nature and good manners. *Rogers.*

This is the only *ſpecious* objection which our Romiſh adverſaries urge againſt the doctrine of this church in the point of celebacy. *Atterbury.*

SPE'CIOUSLY. *adv.* [from *ſpecious.*] With fair appearance.

Piety is oppoſed to hypocriſy and unſincerity; eſpecially to that perſonated devotion under which any kind of impiety is wont to be diſguiſed, and put off more *ſpeciouſly.* *Hammond.*

SPECK. *n. ſ.* [ſpecec, Saxon.] A ſmall diſcoloration; a ſpot.

Every *ſpeck* does not blind a man. *Govern. of the Tongue.*

Then are they happy, when
No *ſpeck* is left of their habitual ſtains;
But the pure æther of the ſoul remains. *Dryden's Æneid.*

To SPECK. *v. a.* To ſpot; to ſtain in drops.

Flow'r
Carnation, purple, azure, or *ſpeck'd* with gold. *Milton.*

SPECKLE. *n. ſ.* [from *ſpeck.*] Small ſpeck; little ſpot.

To SPECKLE. *v. a.* [from the noun.] To mark with ſmall ſpots.

So dreadfully he towards him did paſs,
Forelifting up aloft his *ſpeckled* breaſt,
And often bounding on the bruiſed graſs,
As for great joy of his new comen gueſt. *Fairy Queen.*

Speckl'd vanity
Will ſicken ſoon and die,
And leprous ſin will melt from earthly mould. *Milton.*

Saw'ſt thou not late a *ſpeckl'd* ſerpent rear
His gilded ſpires to climb on yon fair tree?
Before this happy minute I was he. *Dryden.*

The ſmiling infant in his hand ſhall take
The creſted baſiliſk and *ſpeckled* ſnake;
Pleas'd the green luſtre of the ſcales ſurvey,
And with their forky tongue and pointleſs ſting ſhall play. *Pope's Meſſiah.*

The tortoiſe here and elephant unite,
Transform'd to combs, the *ſpeckl'd* and the white. *Pope.*

SPECKT, or *ſpeight, n. ſ.* A woodpecker. *Ainſworth.*

SPE'CTACLE. *n. ſ.* [*ſpectacle*, Fr. *ſpectaculum*, Latin.]

1. A ſhow; a gazing ſtock; any thing exhibited to the view as eminently remarkable.

In open place produc'd they me,
To be a publick *ſpectacle* to all. *Shakeſp. Henry* VI.

We are made a *ſpectacle* unto angels, and men. 1 *Cor.* iv. 9.

2. Any thing perceived by the ſight.

Forth riding underneath the caſtle wall,
A dunghill of dead carcaſes he ſpy'd,
The dreadful *ſpectacle* of that ſad houſe of pride. *Fa. Queen.*

When pronouncing ſentence, ſeem not glad,
Such *ſpectacles*, though they are juſt, are ſad. *Denham.*

3. [In the plural.] Glaſſes to aſſiſt the ſight.

The ſixth age ſhifts
Into the lean and ſlipper'd pantaloon,
With *ſpectacles* on noſe and pouch on ſide. *Shakeſpeare.*

We have helps for the ſight far above *ſpectacles* and glaſſes. *Bacon.*

It is no fault in the *ſpectacles* that the blind man ſees not. *Glanville's Apology.*

Shakeſpeare was naturally learned: he needed not the *ſpectacles* of books to read nature; he looked inwards and found her there. *Dryden on Dramatick Poeſy.*

The firſt *ſpectacle*-maker did not think that he was leading the way to the diſcovery of new planets. *Grew.*

This is the reaſon of the decay of ſight in old men, and ſhews why their ſight is mended by *ſpectacles.* *Newton.*

This day, then let us not be told,
That you are ſick and I grown old;
Nor think on our approaching ills,
And talk of *ſpectacles* and pills. *Swift.*

SPE'CTACLED. *adj.* [from the noun.] Furniſhed with ſpectacles.

All tongues ſpeak of him, and the bleared ſights
Are *ſpectacled* to ſee him. *Shakeſpeare's Coriolanus.*

SPECTA'TION. *n. ſ.* [*ſpectatio*, Latin.] Regard; reſpect.

This ſimple *ſpectation* of the lungs is differenced from that which concomitates a pleuriſy. *Harvey.*

SPECTA'TOR. *n. ſ.* [*ſpectateur*, Fr. *ſpectator*, Latin.] A looker on; a beholder.

More
Than hiſtory can pattern, though devis'd
And play'd, to take *ſpectators.* *Shakeſpeare.*

If it proves a good repaſt to the *ſpectators*, the diſh pays the ſhot. *Shakeſpeare's Cymbeline.*

An old gentleman mounting on horſeback got up heavily; but deſired the *ſpectators* that they would count fourſcore and eight before they judged him. *Dryden.*

He mourns his former vigour loſt ſo far,
To make him now *ſpectator* of a war. *Dryden.*

What pleaſure hath the owner more than the *ſpectator?* *Seed.*

SPE'CTRE. *n. ſ.* [*ſpectre*, Fr. *ſpectrum*, Latin.] Apparition; appearance of perſons dead.

The ghoſts of traitors from the bridge deſcend,
With bold fanatick *ſpectres* to rejoice. *Dryden.*

The very poetical uſe of the word for a *ſpectre*, doth imply an exact reſemblance to ſome real being it repreſents. *Stilling.*

Theſe are nothing but *ſpectres* the underſtanding raiſes to itſelf to flatter its own lazineſs. *Locke.*

SPECTA'TORSHIP. *n. ſ.* [from *ſpectator.*] Act of beholding.

Thou ſtand'ſt i' th' ſtate of hanging, or of ſome death more long in *ſpectatorſhip*, and crueller in ſuffering. *Shakeſpeare.*

SPE'CTRUM. *n. ſ.* [Latin.] An image; a viſible form.

This priſm had ſome veins running along within the glaſs, from the one end to the other, which ſcattered ſome of the ſun's light irregularly, but had no ſenſible effect in encreaſing the length of the coloured *ſpectrum.* *Newton's Opticks.*

SPE'CULAR. *n. ſ.* [*ſpecularis*, Latin.]

1. Having the qualities of a mirrour or looking glaſs.

It were but madneſs now t' impart
The ſkill of *ſpecular* ſtone. *Donne.*

Quickſilver may by the fire alone, in glaſs-veſſels, be turned into a red body; and from this red body may be obtained a mercury, bright and *ſpecular* as before. *Boyle.*

A ſpeculum of metal without glaſs, made ſome years ſince for optical uſes, and very well wrought, produced none of thoſe rings; and thence I underſtood that theſe rings ariſe not from *ſpecular* ſurface alone, but depend upon the two ſurfaces of the plate of glaſs whereof the ſpeculum was made, and upon the thickneſs of the glaſs between them. *Newton.*

2. Aſſiſting ſight. Improper.

The hidden way
Of nature would'ſt thou know, how firſt ſhe frames
All things in miniature? thy *ſpecular* orb
Apply to well diſſected kernels; lo!
In each obſerve the ſlender threads
Of firſt-beginning trees. *Philips.*

To SPE'CULATE. *v. n.* [*ſpeculer*, Fr. *ſpeculor*, Lat.] To meditate; to contemplate; to take a view of any thing with the mind.

Conſider the quantity, and not *ſpeculate* upon an intrinſecal relation. *Digby on Bodies.*

As our news-writers record many facts which afford great matter of ſpeculation, their readers *ſpeculate* accordingly, and by their variety of conjectures become conſummate ſtateſmen. *Addiſon.*

To SPE'CULATE. *v. a.* To conſider attentively; to look through with the mind.

Man was not meant to gape, or look upward with the eye, but to have his thoughts ſublime; and not only behold, but *ſpeculate* their nature with the eye of the underſtanding. *Brown's Vulgar Errours.*

SPECULA'TION. *n. ſ.* [*ſpeculation*, Fr. from *ſpeculate.*]

1. Examination by the eye; view.

2. Examiner; ſpy. This word is found no where elſe, and probably is here miſprinted for *ſpeculator.*

They who have, as who have not, whom their great ſtars
Throne and ſet high? ſervants
Which are to France the ſpies and *ſpeculations*,
Intelligent of our ſtate. *Shakeſpeare's King Lear.*

3. Mental view; intellectual examination; contemplation.

In all theſe things being fully perſuaded, that what they did, it was obedience to the will of God, and that all men ſhould do the like; there remained after *ſpeculation*, practice whereunto the whole world might be framed. *Hooker.*

Thenceforth to *ſpeculations* high or deep,
I turn'd my thoughts; and with capacious mind
Conſider'd all things viſible. *Milton.*

News-writers afford matter of *ſpeculation.* *Addiſon.*

4. A train of thoughts formed by meditation.

From him Socrates derived the principles of morality, and moſt part of his natural *ſpeculations.* *Temple.*

5. Mental ſcheme not reduced to practice.

This terreſtrial globe, which before was only round in *ſpeculation*, has ſince been ſurrounded by the fortune and boldneſs of many navigators. *Temple.*

6. Power of ſight. Not in uſe.

Thy bones are marrowleſs; thy blood is cold;
Thou haſt no *ſpeculation* in thoſe eyes
Thou ſtar'ſt with. *Shakeſpeare.*

SPE'CULATIVE. *adj.* [*ſpeculatif*, Fr. from *ſpeculate.*]

1. Given to ſpeculation; contemplative.

If all other uſes were utterly taken away, yet the mind of man being by nature *ſpeculative* and delighted with contemplation in itſelf, they were to be known even for meer knowledge ſake. *Hooker.*

It encourages *ſpeculative* perſons who have no turn of mind to encreaſe their fortunes. *Addiſon.*

2. Theo-

2. Theoretical; notional; ideal; not practical.

Some take it for a *speculative* platform, that reason and nature would that the best should govern, but no wise to create a right. *Bacon's holy War.*

SPE'CULATIVELY. *adv.* [from *speculative.*]

1. Contemplatively; with meditation.
2. Ideally; notionally; theoretically; not practically.

SPECULA'TOR. *n. s.* [from *speculate.*]

1. One who forms theories.

He is dexterous in puzzling others, if they be not throughpaced *speculators* in those great theories. *More.*

2. [*Speculateur*, French.] An observer; a contemplator.

Although lapidaries and questuary enquirers affirm it, yet the writers of minerals, and natural *speculators*, conceive the stones which bear this name to be a mineral concretion. *Brown.*

3. A spy; a watcher.

All the boats had one *speculator*, to give notice when the fish approached. *Broome's Notes on the Odyssey.*

SPE'CULATORY. *adj.* [from *speculate.*] Exercising speculation.

SPE'CULUM. *n. s.* [Latin.] A mirrour; a looking-glass; that in which representations are formed by reflection.

A rough and coloured object may serve for a *speculum*, to reflect the artificial rainbow. *Boyle on Colours.*

SPED. The preterite and part. passive of *speed.*

His horse full of windgalls, *sped* with the spavins, and rayed with the yellows. *Shakespeare.*

Barbarossa, *sped* of that he desired, staid not long at Constantinople, but shaped his course towards Italy. *Knolles.*

With all his harness soon the god was *sped*;
His flying hat, wings on his heels. *Dryden.*

SPEECH. *n. s.* [from *speak.*]

1. The power of articulate utterance; the power of expressing thoughts by vocal words.

There is none comparable to the variety of instructive expressions by *speech*, wherewith a man alone is endowed, for the communication of his thoughts. *Holder on Speech.*

Though our ideas are first acquired by various sensations and reflections, yet we convey them to each other by the means of certain sounds, or written marks, which we call words; and a great part of our knowledge is both obtained and communicated by these means, which are called *speech.* *Watts.*

2. Language; words considered as expressing thoughts.

In *speech* be eight parts. *Accidence.*

The acts of God to human ears
Cannot without process of *speech* be told. *Milton.*

3. Particular language as distinct from others.

There is neither *speech* nor language, but their voices are heard among them. *Ps. Common Prayer.*

4. Any thing spoken.

A plague upon your epileptick visage!
Smile you my *speeches* as I were a fool. *Shakesp. K. Lear.*

5. Talk; mention.

The duke did of me demand
What was the *speech* among the Londoners,
Concerning the French journey. *Shakespeare.*

Speech of a man's self ought to be seldom. *Bacon's Essays.*

6. Oration; harangue.

The constant design of these orators, in all their *speeches*, was to drive some one particular point. *Swift.*

7. Liberty to speak.

I, with leave of *speech* implor'd, reply'd. *Milton.*

SPE'ECHLESS. *adj.* [from *speech.*]

1. Deprived of the power of speaking; made mute or dumb.

He fell down, foam'd at mouth, and was *speechless.* *Shakesp.*

The great god Pan hath broken his pipes, and Apollo's priests are become *speechless.* *Raleigh.*

A single vision transports them: it finds them in the eagerness and height of their devotion; they are *speechless* for the time that it continues, and prostrate when it departs. *Dryden.*

Speechless with wonder, and half dead with fear. *Addison.*

2. Mute; dumb.

I kneel'd before him;
'Twas very faintly he said rise: dismiss'd me
Thus, with his *speechless* hand. *Shakesp. Coriolanus.*

From her eyes
I did receive fair *speechless* messages. *Shakespeare.*

He that never hears a word spoken, it is no wonder he remain *speechless*; as any one must do, who from an infant should be bred up among mutes. *Holder's Elements of Speech.*

To SPEED. *v. n.* pret. and part. pass. *sped* and *speeded.* [*spoeden*, Dutch.]

1. To make haste; to move with celerity.

So well they *sped* that they be come at length
Unto the place whereas the Paynim lay,
Devoid of outward sense and native strength,
Covered with charmed cloud from view of day. *Fa. Queen.*

Do you think me a swallow, an arrow, or a bullet? Have I, in my poor and cold motion, the expedition of thought? I *speeded* hither with the very extremest inch of possibility. *Shak.*

If pray'rs
Could alter high decrees, I to that place
Would *speed* before thee, and be louder heard. *Milton.*

See where Idwall *speeds!* a trusty soldier. *A. Philips.*

2. [Spebran, to grow rich, Saxon.] To have success.

Make me not sighted like the basilisk:
I've look'd on thousands, who have *sped* the better
By my regard, but kill'd none so. *Shakesp. Winter's Tale.*

Now if this suit lay in Bianca's pow'r,
How quickly should you *speed.* *Shakespeare.*

Macicaus shewed them what an offence it was rashly to depart out of the city, which might be unto them dangerous, although they should *speed* never so well. *Knolles.*

When first this tempter cross'd the gulph from hell,
I told you then he should prevail, and *speed*
In his bad errand. *Milton.*

These were violators of the first temple, and those that profaned and abused the second *sped* no better. *South.*

3. To have any condition good or bad.

Ships heretofore in seas like fishes *sped*,
The mightiest still upon the smallest fed. *Waller.*

To SPEED. *v. a.*

1. To dispatch in haste.

The tyrant's self, a thing unused, began
To feel his heart relent with meer compassion;
But not dispos'd to ruth or mercy then,
He *sped* him thence home to his habitation. *Fairfax.*

2. To furnish in haste.
3. To dispatch; to destroy; to kill.

With a *speeding* thrust his heart he found;
The lukewarm blood came rushing thro' the wound. *Dryd.*

A dire dilemma! either way I'm *sped*;
If foes, they write; if friends, they read me dead. *Pope.*

4. To mischief; to ruin.
5. To hasten; to put into quick motion.

She,
Hearing so much, will *speed* her foot again,
Led hither by pure love. *Shakesp. All's well that ends well.*

Satan, tow'rd the coast of earth beneath,
Down from th' ecliptick *sped* with hop'd success,
Throws his steep flight in many an airy wheel. *Milton.*

The priest reply'd no more,
But *sped* his steps along the hoarse resounding shore. *Dryden.*

6. To execute; to dispatch.

Judicial acts are all those writings and matters which relate to judicial proceedings, and are *sped* in open court at the instance of one or both of the parties. *Ayliffe's Parergon.*

7. To assist; to help forward.

Lucina
Reach'd her midwife hands to *speed* the throws. *Dryden.*

Propitious Neptune steer'd their course by night
With rising gales, that *sped* their happy flight. *Dryden.*

Speed the soft intercourse from soul to soul,
And waft a sigh from Indus to the Pole. *Pope.*

8. To make prosperous.

If any bring not this doctrine, receive him not into your house, neither bid him God *speed.* *St. Paul.*

Timon is shrunk, indeed;
And he, that's once deny'd, will hardly *speed.* *Shakesp.*

SPEED. *n. s.* [*spoed*, Dutch.]

1. Quickness; celerity.

Earth receives
As tribute, such a sumless journey brought
Of incorporeal *speed*, her warmth and light;
Speed! to describe whose swiftness number fails. *Milton.*

We observe the horse's patient service at the plough, his *speed* upon the highway, his docibleness, and desire of glory. *More.*

2. Haste; hurry; dispatch.

When they strain to their utmost *speed*, there is still the wonted distance between them and their aims: all their eager pursuits bring them no acquests. *Decay of Piety.*

3. The course or pace of a horse.

He that rides at high *speed*, and with a pistol, kills a sparrow flying. *Shakesp. Henry IV.*

4. Success; event.

The prince your son, with mere conceit and fear
Of the queen's *speed*, is gone. *Shakespeare.*

O Lord, I pray thee send me good *speed.* *Gen.* xxiv. 12.

SPE'EDILY. *adv.* [from *speedy.*] With haste; quickly.

Post *speedily* to your husband,
Shew him this letter. *Shakesp. King Lear.*

Send *speedily* to Bertran; charge him strictly
Not to proceed. *Dryden's Spanish Fryar.*

SPE'EDINESS. *n. s.* [from *speedy.*] The quality of being speedy.

SPE'EDWELL. *n. s.* [*veronica*, Latin.] Fluellin. A plant.

The leaves grow opposite by pairs: the calyx consists of one leaf, which is divided into four parts, expanding in form of a star: the flower consists of one leaf, divided into four segments, expanding in a circular order: when the flower decays, the ovary becomes a membranaceous fruit, divided into two cells, shaped like an heart, and filled with seeds, sometimes small, and at other times large and thick. *Miller.*

In a ſcarcity in Silesia a rumour was ſpread of its raining millet-seed; but 'twas found to be only the ſeeds of the ivy-leaved *ſpeedwell*, or ſmall henbit. *Derham's Phyſico-Theology.*

SPE'EDY. *adj.* [from *ſpeed.*] Quick; ſwift; nimble; quick of diſpatch.

How near's the other army?
—Near, and on *ſpeedy* foot: the main deſcry
Stands on the hourly thought. *Shakeſp. King Lear.*

Back with *ſpeedieſt* ſail
Zophiel, of cherubim the ſwifteſt wing,
Came flying. *Milton's Paradiſe Loſt.*

Let it be enough what thou haſt done,
When ſpotted deaths ran arm'd through ev'ry ſtreet,
With poiſon'd darts, which not the good could ſhun,
The *ſpeedy* could outfly, or valiant meet. *Dryden.*

SPELL. *n. ſ.* [ſpel, Saxon, a word.]

1. A charm conſiſting of ſome words of occult power. Thus *Horace* uſes *words*:

Sunt verba & voces *quibus hunc lenire dolorem*
Poſſis.

Start not; her actions ſhall be holy:
You hear my *ſpell* is lawful: do not ſhun her,
Until you ſee her die again; for then
You kill her double. *Shakeſp. Winter's Tale.*

Some have delivered the polity of ſpirits, that they ſtand in awe of charms, *ſpells*, and conjurations, letters, characters, notes, and daſhes. *Brown's Vulgar Errours.*

Thou durſt not thus diſparage glorious arms,
Had not *ſpells*
And black enchantments, ſome magician's art,
Arm'd thee or charm'd thee ſtrong. *Milton's Agoniſtes.*

Begin, begin, the myſtick *ſpell* prepare. *Milton.*

Yourſelf you ſo excel,
When you vouchſafe to breathe my thought,
That like a ſpirit with this *ſpell*
Of my own teaching, I am caught. *Waller.*

Mild Lucina
Then reach'd her midwife hands to ſpeed the throes,
And ſpoke the pow'rful *ſpells* that babes to birth diſcloſe. *Dry.*

2. A turn of work.

Their toil is ſo extreme as they cannot endure it above four hours in a day, but are ſucceeded by *ſpells*: the reſidue of the time they wear out at coytes and kayles. *Carew.*

To SPELL. *v. a.* [*ſpellen*, Dutch.]

1. To write with the proper letters.

In the criticiſm of *ſpelling*, the word *ſatire* ought to be with *i*, and not with *y*; and if this be ſo, then it is falſe *ſpelled* throughout. *Dryden's Juvenal, Dedication.*

2. To read by naming letters ſingly.

I never yet ſaw man,
How wiſe, how noble, young, how rarely featur'd,
But ſhe would *ſpell* him backward; if fair fac'd,
She'd ſwear the gentleman ſhould be her ſiſter. *Shakeſp.*

3. To charm.

I have you faſt:
Unchain your ſpirits now with *ſpelling* charms,
And try if they can gain your liberty. *Shak. Henry VI.*

This gather'd in the planetary hour,
With noxious weeds, and *ſpell'd* with words of pow'r,
Dire ſtepdames in the magick bowl infuſe. *Dryden.*

To SPELL. *v. n.*

1. To form words of letters.

What ſmall knowledge was, in them did dwell;
And he a god, who could but read or *ſpell*. *Dryden.*

By paſting on the vowels and conſonants on the ſides of four dice, he has made this a play for his children, whereby his eldeſt ſon in coats, has played himſelf into *ſpelling*. *Locke.*

The Latin, being written of the ſame character with the mother-tongue, by the aſſiſtance of a *ſpelling* book, it is legible. *Spectator.*

Another cauſe, which hath maimed our language, is a fooliſh opinion that we ought to *ſpell* exactly as we ſpeak. *Swift.*

2. To read.

If I read aught in heav'n,
Or heav'n write aught of fate, by what the ſtars,
Voluminous or ſingle characters,
In their conjunction met, give me to *ſpell*,
Sorrows and labours, oppoſition, hate,
Attends thee. *Milton's Paradiſe Loſt.*

When gowns, not arms, repell'd
The fierce Epirote, and the African bold,
Whether to ſettle peace, or to unfold
The drift of hollow ſtates, hard to be *ſpell'd*. *Milton.*

And may at laſt my weary age
Find out the peaceful hermitage,
Where I may ſit and rightly *ſpell*
Of every ſtar that heav'n doth ſhew,
And every herb that ſips the dew. *Milton.*

3. To read unſkilfully.

As to his underſtanding, they bring him in void of all notion, a rude unwritten blank; ſent into the world only to read and *ſpell* out a God in the works of creation. *South.*

To SPELT. *v. n.* To ſplit; to break. A bad word.

Feed geeſe with oats, *ſpelted* beans, barley-meal, or ground malt mixed with beer. *Mortimer's Huſbandry.*

SPE'LTER. *n. ſ.* A kind of ſemi-metal.

Metals in fuſion do not flame for want of a copious fume, except *ſpelter*, which fumes copiouſly, and thereby flames. *Newt.*

To SPEND. *v. a.* [ſpendan, Saxon; *ſpendere*, Italian.]

1. To conſume; to exhauſt; to lay out.

Our cannons malice vainly ſhall be *ſpent*
Againſt th' invulnerable clouds. *Shakeſpeare.*

I will very gladly *ſpend* and be *ſpent* for you. 2 *Cor.* xii. 15.

There is oil in the dwelling of the wiſe, but a fooliſh man *ſpendeth* it up. *Prov.* xxi. 20.

We muſt exaſperate
Th' almighty Victor to *ſpend* all his rage. *Milton.*

Thus labour could at firſt begin a title of property in the common things of nature, and *ſpending* it upon our uſes bound it. *Locke.*

Money is brought into England by nothing but *ſpending* here leſs of foreign commodities than what we carry to market can pay for. *Locke.*

2. To beſtow as expence; to expend.

Wherefore do ye *ſpend* money for that which is not bread? *Iſ.* lv. 2.

Eleutherius, perceiving that he was unwilling to *ſpend* any more time upon the debate, thought not fit to make any mention to him of the propoſed opinion. *Boyle.*

3. To effuſe.

Coward dogs
Moſt *ſpend* their mouths, when what they ſeem to threaten
Runs far before them. *Shakeſ. Henry V.*

4. To ſquander; to laviſh.

They bend their bows, they whirl their ſlings around;
Heaps of *ſpent* arrows fall, and ſtrew the ground. *Dryden.*

The whole of our reflections terminate in this, what courſe we are to take to paſs our time; ſome to get, and others to *ſpend* their eſtates. *Wake.*

5. To paſs.

When we can intreat an hour to ſerve,
Would *ſpend* it in ſome words upon that buſineſs,
If you would grant the time. *Shakeſ. Macbeth.*

They *ſpend* their days in wealth, and in a moment go down to the grave. *Job* xxi. 13.

He *ſpends* his life with his wife, and remembereth neither father nor mother. 1 *Eſdr.* iv. 21.

When he was of riper years, for his farther accompliſhment, he *ſpent* a conſiderable part of his time in travelling. *Pope.*

6. To waſte; to wear out.

In thoſe paſtoral paſtimes a great many days were *ſpent*, to follow their flying predeceſſors. *Sidney.*

The waves aſcended and deſcended, 'till their violence being *ſpent* by degrees, they ſettled at laſt. *Burnet's Theo. of the Earth.*

The winds are rais'd, the ſtorm blows high;
Be it your care, my friends, to keep it up
In its full fury, and direct it right,
'Till it has *ſpent* itſelf on Cato's head. *Addiſon's Cato.*

7. To fatigue; to harraſs.

Nothing but only the hope of ſpoil did relieve them, having ſcarce clothes to cover their nakedneſs, and their bodies *ſpent* with long labour and thirſt. *Knolles's Hiſtory of the Turks.*

Or come your ſhipping in our ports to lay,
Spent and diſabled in ſo long a way? *Dryden's Æn.*

Our walls are thinly mann'd, our beſt men ſlain;
The reſt, an heartleſs number, *ſpent* with watching,
And harraſs'd out with duty. *Dryden.*

Some *ſpent* with toil, ſome with deſpair oppreſs'd,
Leap'd headlong from the heights, the flames conſum'd the reſt. *Dryden's Æn.*

Thou oft haſt ſeen me
Wreſtling with vice and faction; now thou ſee'ſt me
Spent, overpower'd, deſpairing of ſucceſs. *Addiſon's Cato.*

To SPEND. *v. n.*

1. To make expence.

Henceforth your tongue muſt *ſpend* at leſſer rate,
Than in its flames to wrap a nation's fate. *Dryden.*

He *ſpends* as a perſon who knows that he muſt come to a reckoning. *South.*

2. To prove in the uſe.

Butter *ſpent* as if it came from the richer ſoil. *Temple.*

3. To be loſt or waſted.

The ſound *ſpendeth* and is diſſipated in the open air; but in ſuch concaves it is conſerved and contracted. *Bacon.*

On mountains, it may be, many dews fall, that *ſpend* before they come to the valleys. *Bacon.*

4. To be employed to any uſe.

There have been cups and an image of Jupiter made of wild vines; for the vines that they uſe for wine are ſo often cut, that their ſap *ſpendeth* into the grapes. *Bacon.*

SPE'NDER. *n. ſ.* [from *ſpend.*]

1. One who ſpends.

Let not your recreations be laviſh *ſpenders* of your time; but healthful, ſhort, and apt to refreſh you. *Taylor.*

2. A prodigal; a laviſher.

Biſhop Morton told the commiſſioners, who were to levy the benevolence, if they met with any that were ſparing, tell them that they muſt needs have, becauſe they laid up; and if they were *ſpenders*, they muſt needs have, becauſe it was ſeen in their port and manner of living. *Bacon's Henry* VII.

SPE'NDTHRIFT. *n. ſ.* [*ſpend* and *thrift.*] A prodigal; a laviſher.

Bitter cold weather ſtarved both the bird and the *ſpendthrift*. *L'Eſtrange.*

Some fawning uſurer does feed
With preſent ſums th' unwary *ſpendthrift*'s need. *Dryden.*

Moſt men, like *ſpendthrift* heirs, judge a little in hand better than a great deal to come. *Locke.*

The ſon, bred in ſloth, becomes a *ſpendthrift*, a profligate, and goes out of the world a beggar. *Swift.*

SPE'RABLE. *adj.* [*ſperabilis*, Latin.] Such as may be hoped.

We may caſt it away, if it be found but a bladder, and diſcharge it of ſo much as is vain and not *ſperable*. *Bacon.*

SPERM. *n. ſ.* [*ſperme*, Fr. *ſperma*, Lat.] Seed; that by which the ſpecies is continued.

Some creatures bring forth many young ones at a burthen, and ſome but one: this may be cauſed by the quantity of *ſperm* required, or by the partitions of the womb which may ſever the *ſperm*. *Bacon.*

There is required to the preparation of the *ſperm* of animals a great apparatus of veſſels, many ſecretions, concoctions, reflections, and circulations. *Ray.*

SPERMACE'TI. *n. ſ.* [Latin.] Corruptedly pronounced *parmaſitty*.

A particular ſort of whale affords the oil whence this is made; and that is very improperly called *ſperma*, becauſe it is only the oil which comes from the head of which it can be made. It is changed from what it is naturally, the oil itſelf being very brown and rank. The peculiar property of it is to ſhoot into flakes, not much unlike the cryſtallization of ſalts; but in this ſtate 'tis yellow, and has a certain rankneſs, from which it is freed by ſqueezing it between warm metalline plates in a preſs, and afterwards expoſing the remainder to the open air: at length it becomes perfectly pure, inodorous, flaky, ſmooth, white, and in ſome meaſure tranſparent. *Quincy.*

SPERMA'TICAL. } *adj.* [*ſpermatique*, Fr. from *ſperm.*]
SPERMA'TICK. }

1. Seminal; conſiſting of ſeed.

The primordials of the world are not mechanical, but *ſpermatical* or vital. *More's Divine Dialogues.*

Metals and ſundry meteors rude ſhapes have no need of any particular principle of life, or *ſpermatical* form, diſtinct from the reſt or motion of the particles of the matter. *More.*

2. Belonging to the ſperm.

The moiſture of the body, which did before irrigate the parts, is drawn down to the *ſpermatical* veſſels. *Bacon.*

Two different ſexes muſt concur to their generation: there is in both a great apparatus of *ſpermatick* veſſels, wherein the more ſpirituous part of the blood is by many digeſtions and circulations exalted into ſperm. *Ray on the Creation.*

To SPE'RMATIZE. *v. n.* [from *ſperm.*] To yield ſeed.

Ariſtotle affirming that women do not *ſpermatize*, and confer a receptacle rather than eſſential principles of generation, deductively includes both ſexes in mankind. *Brown.*

SPERMATOCE'LE. *n. ſ.* [σπέρμα and κηλή.] A rupture cauſed by the contraction of the ſeminal veſſels, and the ſemen falling into the ſcrotum. *Bailey.*

SPERMO'LOGIST. *n. ſ.* [σπερμολόγος.] One who gathers or treats of ſeeds. *Dict.*

To SPERSE. *v. a.* [*ſperſus*, Latin.] To diſperſe; to ſcatter. A word not now in uſe.

The wrathful wind,
Which blows cold ſtorms, burſt out of Scythian mew
That *ſperſt* thoſe clouds, and in ſo ſhort as thought
This dreadful ſhape was vaniſhed to nought. *Spenſer.*
He making ſpeedy way through *ſperſed* air,
And through the world of waters wide and deep,
To Morpheus' houſe doth haſtily repair. *Fairy Queen.*

To SPET. *v. a.* To bring or pour abundantly. [*Spet* in Scotland is a ſuperabundance of water: as, that tide or freſh was a high *ſpet.*]

Myſterious dame,
That ne'er art call'd, but when the dragon womb
Of Stygian darkneſs *ſpets* her thickeſt gloom,
And makes one blot of all the air,
Stop thy cloudy ebon chair. *Milton.*

To SPEW. *v. a.* [ſpepan, Saxon; *ſpeuwen*, Dutch.]

1. To vomit; to eject from the ſtomach.

A ſwordfiſh ſmall him from the reſt did ſunder,
That in his throat him pricking ſoftly under
His wide abyſs, him forced forth to *ſpew*,
That all the ſea did roar like heaven's thunder,
And all the waves were ſtain'd with filthy hue. *Spenſer.*

2. To eject; to caſt forth.

When earth with ſlime and mud is cover'd o'er,
Or hollow places *ſpew* their wat'ry ſtore. *Dryden's Georg.*
When yellow ſands are ſifted from below,
The glitt'ring billows give a golden ſhow;
And when the fouler bottom *ſpews* the black,
The Stygian dye the tainted waters take. *Dryden.*

3. To eject with loathing.

Keep my ſtatutes, and commit not any of theſe abominations, that the land *ſpew* not you out. *Lev.* xviii. 28.

Contentious ſuits ought to be *ſpewed* out, as the ſurfeit of courts. *Bacon's Eſſays.*

To SPEW. *v. n.* To vomit; to eaſe the ſtomach.

He could have haul'd in
The drunkards, and the noiſes of the inn;
But better 'twas that they ſhould ſleep or *ſpew*,
Than in the ſcene to offend or him or you. *Ben. Johnſon.*

SPE'WY. *adj.* [from *ſpew.*] A provincial word.

The lower vallies in wet Winters are ſo *ſpewy*, that they know not how to feed them. *Mortimer's Husbandry.*

To SPHA'CELATE. *v. a.* [from *ſphacelus*, medical, Latin.] To affect with a gangrene.

The long retention of matter *ſphacelates* the brain. *Sharp.*

To SPHA'CELATE. *v. n.* To mortify; to ſuffer the gangrene.

The ſkin, by the great diſtenſion, having been rendered very thin, will, if not taken away, *ſphacelate*, and the reſt degenerate into a cancerous ulcer. *Sharp's Surgery.*

SPHA'CELUS. *n. ſ.* [σφάκελος; *ſphacele*, Fr.] A gangrene; a mortification.

It is the ground of inflammation, gangrene, *ſphacelus*. *Wiſem.*

SPHERE. *n. ſ.* [*ſphere*, French; *ſphæra*, Latin.]

1. A globe; an orbicular body; a body of which the center is at the ſame diſtance from every point of the circumference.

Firſt the ſun, a mighty *ſphere*, he fram'd. *Milton.*

2. Any globe of the mundane ſyſtem.

What if within the moon's fair ſhining *ſphere*,
What if in every other ſtar unſeen,
Of other worlds he happily ſhould hear? *Fairy Queen.*
And then mortal ears
Had heard the muſick of the *ſpheres*. *Dryden.*

3. A globe repreſenting the earth or ſky.

Two figures on the ſides emboſs'd appear; }
Conon, and what's his name who made the *ſphere*, }
And ſhew'd the ſeaſons of the ſliding year. *Dryden.* }

4. Orb; circuit of motion.

Half unſung, but narrower bound
Within the viſible diurnal *ſphere*. *Milton.*

5. Province; compaſs of knowledge or action; employment. [From the *ſphere* of activity aſcribed to the power emanating from bodies.]

To be call'd into a huge *ſphere*, and not to be ſeen to move in't. *Shakeſp. Ant. and Cleopatra.*

Of enemies he could not but contract good ſtore, while moving in ſo high a *ſphere*, and with ſo vigorous a luſtre. *K. C.*

Every man, verſed in any particular buſineſs, finds fault with theſe authors, ſo far as they treat of matters within his *ſphere*. *Addiſon's Freeholder.*

Ye know the *ſpheres* and various taſks aſſign'd
By laws eternal to the æthereal kind. *Pope.*

To SPHERE. *v. a.* [from the noun.]

1. To place in a ſphere.

The glorious planet Sol,
In noble eminence enthron'd and *ſpher'd*
Amidſt the reſt, whoſe med'cinable eye
Corrects the ill aſpects of planets evil. *Shakeſpeare.*

2. To form into roundneſs.

Light from her native Eaſt
To journey through the airy gloom began,
Spher'd in a radiant cloud; for yet the ſun
Was not. *Milton's Paradiſe Loſt.*

SPHE'RICAL. } *adj.* [*ſpherique*, French; from *ſphere.*]
SPHE'RICK. }

1. Round; orbicular; globular.

What deſcent of waters could there be in a *ſpherical* and round body, wherein there is nor high nor low. *Raleigh.*

Though ſounds ſpread round, ſo that there is an orb or *ſpherical* area of the ſound, yet they go fartheſt in the forelines from the firſt local impulſion of the air. *Bacon.*

By diſcernment of the moiſture drawn up in vapours, we muſt know the reaſon of the *ſpherical* figures of the drops. *Glan.*

A fluid maſs neceſſarily falls into a *ſpherical* ſurface. *Keil.*

Where the central nodule was globular, the inner ſurface of the firſt cruſt would be *ſpherick*; and if the cruſt was in all parts of the ſame thickneſs, that whole cruſt would be *ſpherical*. *Woodward on Foſſils.*

2. Planetary; relating to orbs of the planets.

We make guilty of our diſaſters the ſun, the moon, and ſtars, as if we were villains by *ſpherical* predominance. *Shakeſ.*

SPHE'RICALLY. *adv.* [from *ſpherical.*] In form of a ſphere.

SPHE'RICALNESS. } *n. ſ.* [from *ſphere.*] Roundneſs; rotundity.
SPHE'RICITY. }

Such bodies receive their figure and limits from ſuch lets as hinder them from attaining to that *ſphericalneſs* they aim at. *Dig.*

Water conſiſts of ſmall, ſmooth, ſpherical particles: their ſmoothneſs makes 'em ſlip eaſily upon one another; the *ſphericity*

ricity keeps 'em from touching one another in more points than one. *Cheyne's Phil. Princ.*

SPHE'ROID. *n. s.* [σφαῖρα and εἶδος; *spheroide*, Fr.] A body oblong or oblate, approaching to the form of a sphere.

They are not solid particles, by the necessity they are under to change their figures into oblong *spheroids*, in the capillary vessels. *Cheyn's Phil. Princ.*

SPHEROI'DICAL. *adj.* [from *spheroid.*] Having the form of a spheroid.

If these corpuscles be *spheroidical*, or oval, their shortest diameters must not be much greater than those of light. *Cheyne.*

SPHE'RULE. *n. s.* [*sphærula*, Latin.] A little globe.

Mercury is a collection of exceeding small, vastly heavy *spherules*. *Cheyne's Phil. Princ.*

SPHINX. *n. s.* [σφίγξ.]

The *sphinx* was a famous monster in Egypt, that remained by conjoined Nilus, having the face of a virgin, and the body of a lion. *Peacham on Drawing.*

SPI'AL. *n. s.* [*espial*, Fr.] A spy; a scout; a watcher. Obsolete.

His ears be as *spials*, alarum to crie. *Tusser's Husbandry.*

He privy *spials* plac'd in all his way,
To weet what course he takes, and how he fares. *Fa. Qu.*

For he by faithful *spial* was assured
That Egypt's king was forward on his way. *Fairfax.*

Their trust towards them hath rather been as to good *spials* and good whisperers, than good magistrates and officers. *Bac.*

SPICE. *n. s.* [*espice*, French.]

1. A vegetable production, fragrant to the smell and pungent to the palate; an aromatick substance used in sauces.

Dang'rous rocks,
Which, touching but my gentle vessel's side,
Would scatter all the *spices* on the stream. *Shakespeare.*

Is not manhood, learning, gentleness, and virtue, the *spice* and salt that seasons a man? *Shakesp. Troil. and Cressida.*

The traffick of the *spice*-merchants. *1 Kings* x. 15.

Garlick, the northern *spice*, is in mighty request among the Indians. *Temple.*

High sauces and rich *spices* are fetched from the Indies. *Baker.*

2. A small quantity, as of spice to the thing seasoned.

Think what they have done,
And then run stark mad; for all
Thy by-gone fooleries were but *spices* of it. *Shakespeare.*

It containeth singular relations, not without some *spice* or sprinkling of all learning. *Brown's Vulgar Errours.*

So in the wicked there's no vice,
Of which the saints have not a *spice*. *Hudibras.*

To SPICE. *v. a.* [from the noun.] To season with spice; to mix with aromatick bodies.

His mother was a votress of my order,
And in the *spiced* Indian air by night
Full often she hath gossip'd by my side. *Shakespeare.*

These hymns may work on future wits, and so
May great-grand-children of thy praises grow;
And so, though not revive, embalm and *spice*
The world, which else would putrify with vice. *Donne.*

What though some have a fraught
Of cloves and nutmegs, and in cinnamon sail,
If thou hast wherewithal to *spice* a draught,
When griefs prevail? *Herbert.*

SPI'CER. *n. s.* [from *spice.*] One who deals in spice.

Names have been derived from occupations, as Salter and *Spicer*. *Camden.*

SPI'CERY. *n. s.* [*espiceries*, French; from *spice.*]

1. The commodity of spices.

Their camels were loaden with *spicery*, and balm and myrrh. *Raleigh's History of the World.*

She in whose body
The western treasure, eastern *spicery*,
Europe and Africk, and the unknown rest,
Were easily found. *Donne.*

2. A repository of spices.

The *spicery*, the cellar and its furniture, are too well known to be here insisted upon. *Addison on Italy.*

SPICK *and* SPAN. [This word I should not have expected to have found authorised by a polite writer. *Span-new* is used by *Chaucer*, and is supposed to come from spannan, to stretch, Sax. *expandere*, Lat. whence *span*. *Span-new* is therefore originally used of cloath new extended or dressed at the clothiers, and *spick and span* is newly extended on the *spikes* or tenters: it is however a low word.] Quite new; now first used.

While the honour, thou hast got,
Is *spick and span* new, piping hot,
Strike her up bravely. *Butler.*

They would have these reduced to nothing, and then others created *spick and span* new out of nothing. *Burnet.*

I keep no antiquated stuff;
But *spick and span* I have enough. *Swift.*

SPI'CKNEL. *n. s.* The herb maldmony or bearwort. *Dict.*

SPI'CY. *adj.* [from *spice.*]

1. Producing spice; abounding with aromaticks.

For them the Idumæan balm did sweat,
And in hot Ceilon *spicy* forests grew. *Dryden.*

2. Aromatick; having the qualities of spice.

Off at sea north-east winds blow
Sabæan odour, from the *spicy* shore
Of Araby the blest, with such delay
Well pleas'd they slack their course, and many a league,
Chear'd with the grateful smell, old ocean smiles. *Milton.*

The regimen in this disease ought to be of *spicy* and cephalick vegetables, to dispel the viscosity. *Arbuthnot on Diet.*

Under southern skies exalt their sails,
Led by new stars, and borne by *spicy* gales! *Pope.*

SPI'COSITY. *n. s.* [*spica*, Latin.] The quality of being spiked like ears of corn; fulness of ears. *Dict.*

SPI'DER. *n. s.* [*Skinner* thinks this word softened from *spinder*, or *spinner*, from *spin*: *Junius*, with his usual felicity, dreams that it comes from σπίζειν, to extend; for the spider extends his web. Perhaps it comes from *spieden*, Dutch; *speyden*, Danish, to spy, to lye upon the catch. Don, bona, Saxon, is a *beetle*, or properly an *humble bee*, or *stingless bee*. May not *spider* be *spy dor*, the insect that watches the *dor*?] The animal that spins a web for flies.

More direful hap betide that hated wretch,
Than I can wish to adders, *spiders*, toads. *Shakespeare.*

The *spider*'s web to watch we'll stand,
And when it takes the bee,
We'll help out of the tyrant's hand
The innocent to free. *Drayton.*

Insidious, restless, watchful *spider*,
Fear no officious damsel's broom;
Extend thy artful fabrick wider,
And spread thy banners round my room:
While I thy curious fabrick stare at,
And think on hapless poet's fate,
Like thee confin'd to noisome garret,
And rudely banish'd rooms of state. *Dr. Littleton.*

The *spider*'s touch how exquisitely fine!
Feels at each thread, and lives along the line. *Pope.*

SPI'DERWORT. *n. s.* [*phalangium*, Latin.] A plant with a lily-flower, composed of six petals. *Miller.*

SPI'GNEL. *n. s.* [*meum*, Latin.] A plant.

The characters are: it is an umbelliferous plant, with very narrow leaves: the seeds are large, oblong, and striated. To which may be added, it hath a perennial root. It is medicinal. *Miller.*

SPI'GOT. *n. s.* [*spijcker*, Dutch.] A pin or peg put into the faucet to keep in the liquor.

Base Hungarian wight, wilt thou the *spigot* wield. *Shakes.*

Take out the *spigot*, and clap the point in your mouth. *Sw.*

SPIKE. *n. s.* [*spica*, Latin.]

1. An ear of corn.

Drawn up in ranks and files, the bearded *spikes*
Guard it from birds as with a stand of pikes. *Denham.*

Suffering not the yellow beards to rear,
He tramples down the *spikes*, and intercepts the year. *Dryd.*

The gleaners,
Spike after *spike*, their sparing harvest pick. *Thomson.*

2. A long nail of iron or wood; a long rod of iron sharpened: so called from its similitude to an ear.

For the body of the ships, no nation equals England for the oaken timber; and we need not borrow of any other iron for *spikes*, or nails to fasten them. *Bacon.*

The head of your medal would be seen to more advantage, if it were placed on a *spike* of the tower. *Dryden.*

He wears on his head the *corona radiata*, another type of his divinity: the *spikes* that shoot out represent the rays of the sun. *Addison.*

SPIKE. *n. s.* The name of a plant. This is a smaller species of lavender.

The oil of *spike* is much used by our artificers in their varnishes; but it is generally adulterated. *Hill's Mat. Med.*

To SPIKE. *v. a.* [from the noun.]

1. To fasten with long nails.

Lay long planks upon them, pinned or *spiked* down to the pieces of oak on which they lie. *Moxon's Mech. Exer.*

Lay long planks upon them, *spiking* or pinning them down fast. *Mortimer's Husbandry.*

2. To set with spikes.

A youth, leaping over the *spiked* pales, was suddenly frighted down, and in his falling he was catched by those spikes. *Wisem.*

SPI'KENARD. *n. s.* [*spica nardi*, Latin.] A plant, and the oil or balsam produced from the plant.

There are three sorts of spikenard. 1. The Indian spikenard is most famous: it is a congeries of fibrous substances adhering to the upper part of the root, of an agreeable aromatick and bitterish taste: it grows plentifully in Java. It has been known to the medical writers of all ages. 2. Celtick spikenard is an oblong root, of an irregular figure, a fragrant and aromatick but not very pleasant smell. It had its name from Celtick Gaul, and is still found in great abundance on the Alpine and Pyrenean mountains. 3. Mountain spikenard is a moderately large oblong root of a plant of the valerian kind, its smell and qualities resembling those of the Celtick spikenard. *Hill's Mat. Med.*

A woman having an alabaſter box of ointment of *ſpikenard*, brake and poured it on his head. *Mar.* xiv. 3.

He caſt into the pile bundles of myrrh, and ſheaves of *ſpikenard*, enriching it with every ſpicy ſhrub. *Spectator.*

Spill. *n. ſ.* [*ſpijlen*, Dutch.]

1. A ſmall ſhiver of wood, or thin bar of iron.

The oyſters, beſides gathering by hand, have a peculiar dredge, which is a thick ſtrong net, faſtened to three *ſpills* of iron, and drawn at the boat's ſtern. *Carew.*

Have near the bunghole a little venthole, ſtopped with a *ſpill.* *Mortimer.*

2. A ſmall quantity of money. I know not whence derived.

The biſhops, who conſecrated this ground, were wont to have a *ſpill* or ſportule from the credulous laity. *Ayliffe.*

To SPILL. *v. a.* [ſpillan, Saxon; *ſpillen*, Dutch; *ſpilla*, Iſlandick.]

1. To ſhed; to loſe by ſhedding.

Be ſatisfied, dear God, with our true blood,
Which, as thou know'ſt, unjuſtly muſt be *ſpilt.* *Shakeſp.*

Friend or brother,
He forfeits his own blood that *ſpills* another. *Shak. Timon.*

Themſelves exact their cruelty,
And I conſtrained am this blood to *ſpill. Daniel's Civil War.*

They having *ſpill'd* much blood, and done much waſte,
Subduing nations; and atchiev'd thereby
Fame in the world, high titles, and rich prey,
Shall change their courſe to pleaſure, eaſe, and ſloth. *Milton.*

Sichæus' blood, by his falſe brother *ſpilt*,
I have reveng'd. *Denham.*

Medea muſt not draw her murth'ring knife,
And *ſpill* her childrens blood upon the ſtage. *Roſcommon.*

Orbellan did diſgrace
With treach'rous deeds our mighty mother's race;
And to revenge his blood, ſo juſtly *ſpilt*,
What is it leſs than to partake his guilt? *Dryden.*

Nor the Centaurs tale
Be here repeated; how, with luſt and wine
Inflam'd, they fought and *ſpilt* their drunken ſouls
At feaſting hour. *Philips.*

2. To deſtroy; to miſchief.

Thus is our thought with pain of thiſtle tilled,
Thus be our nobleſt parts dried up with ſorrow;
Thus is our mind with too much minding *ſpilled.* *Sidney.*

Why are ye ſo fierce and cruel?
Is it becauſe your eyes have power to kill?
Then know that mercy is the Mighty's jewel,
And greater glory think to ſave than *ſpill.* *Spenſer.*

Thou all-ſhaking thunder,
Crack nature's mould, all germins *ſpill* at once
That make ingrateful man. *Shakeſ. King Lear.*

Be not angry with theſe fires;
For then their threats will kill me:
Nor look too kind on my deſires;
For then my hopes will *ſpill* me. *Ben. Johnſon.*

All bodies are with other bodies fill'd;
But ſhe receives both heav'n and earth together:
Nor are their forms by raſh encounters *ſpill'd*;
For there they ſtand, and neither toucheth either. *Davies.*

3. To throw away.

This ſight ſhall damp the raging ruffian's breaſt,
The poiſon *ſpill*, and half-drawn ſword arreſt. *Tickell.*

To Spill. *v. n.*

1. To waſte; to be laviſh.

Thy father bids thee ſpare, and chides for *ſpilling.* *Sidney.*

2. To be ſhed; to be loſt by being ſhed.

He was ſo topfull of himſelf, that he let it *ſpill* on all the company: he ſpoke well indeed, but he ſpoke too long. *Watts.*

Spi'ller. *n. ſ.* [I know not whence derived.] A kind of fiſhing line.

In harbour they are taken by *ſpillers* made of a cord, to which divers ſhorter are tied at a little diſtance, and to each of theſe a hook is faſtened with a bait: this *ſpiller* they ſink in the ſea where thoſe fiſhes have their accuſtomed haunt. *Carew.*

Spilth. *n. ſ.* [from *ſpill.*] Any thing poured out or waſted.

Our vaults have wept with drunken *ſpilth* of wine. *Shakeſp.*

To SPIN. *v. a.* preter. *ſpun* or *ſpan*; part. *ſpun.* [ſpinnan, Sax. *ſpinnen*, Dutch.]

1. To draw out into threads.

The women *ſpun* goats hair. *Ex.* xxxv. 26.

2. To form threads by drawing out and twiſting any filamentous matter.

You would be another Penelope; yet they ſay all the yarn ſhe *ſpun*, in Ulyſſes's abſence, did but fill Ithaca full of moths. *Shakeſpeare's Coriolanus.*

The fates but only *ſpin* the coarſer clue;
The fineſt of the wool is left for you. *Dryden.*

3. To protract; to draw out.

By one delay after another they *ſpin* out their whole lives, 'till there's no more future left before 'em. *L'Eſtrange.*

If his cure lies among the lawyers let nothing be ſaid againſt intangling property, *ſpinning* out cauſes, and ſqueezing clients. *Collier.*

Why ſhould Rome fall a moment ere her time?
No, let us draw her term of freedom out
In its full length, and *ſpin* it to the laſt. *Addiſon's Cato.*

4. To form by degrees; to draw out tediouſly.

I paſſed lightly over many particulars, on which learned and witty men might *ſpin* out large volumes. *Digby.*

Men of large thoughts and quick apprehenſions are not to expect any thing here, but what, being *ſpun* out of my own coarſe thoughts, is fitted to men of my own ſize. *Locke.*

The lines are weak, another's pleas'd to ſay;
Lord Fanny *ſpins* a thouſand ſuch a day. *Pope.*

To Spin. *v. n.*

1. To exerciſe the art of ſpinning.

We can fling our legs and arms upwards and downwards, backwards, forwards, and round, as they that *ſpin.* *More.*

Ten thouſand ſtalks their various bloſſoms ſpread;
Peaceful and lowly in their native ſoil,
They neither know to *ſpin*, nor care to toil. *Prior.*

For this Alcides learn'd to *ſpin*,
His club laid down, and lion's ſkin. *Prior.*

2. [*Spingare*, Italian.] To ſtream out in a thread or ſmall current.

Together furiouſly they ran,
That to the ground came horſe and man;
The blood out of their helmets *ſpan*,
So ſharp were their encounters. *Drayton's Nymphid.*

3. To move round as a ſpindle.

Whether the ſun, predominant in heav'n,
Riſe on the earth, or earth riſe on the ſun,
He from the Eaſt his flaming road begin,
Or ſhe from Weſt her ſilent courſe advance
With inoffenſive pace, that *ſpinning* ſleeps
On her ſoft axle, while ſhe paces ev'n
And bears thee ſoft with the ſmooth air along,
Solicit not thy thoughts. *Milton's Paradiſe Loſt, b.* viii.

As when a ſhipwright ſtands his workmen o'er,
Who ply the wimble ſome huge beam to bore;
Urg'd on all hands it nimbly *ſpins* about,
The grain deep piercing 'till it ſcoops it out. *Pope.*

Spi'nach. }
Spi'nage. } *n. ſ.* [*ſpinachia*, Latin.] A plant.

It hath an apetalous flower, conſiſting of many ſtamina included in the flower-cup, which are produced in ſpikes upon the male plants which are barren; but the embryoes are produced from the wings of the leaves on the female plants, which afterward become roundiſh or angular ſeeds, which, in ſome ſorts, have thorns adhering to them. *Miller.*

Spinage is an excellent herb crude, or boiled. *Mortimer.*

Spi'nal. *adj.* [*ſpina*, Latin.] Belonging to the back bone.

All *ſpinal*, or ſuch as have no ribs, but only a back bone, are ſomewhat analogous thereto. *Brown's Vulgar Errours.*

Thoſe ſolids are entirely nervous, and proceed from the brain, and *ſpinal* marrow, which by their bulk appear ſufficient to furniſh all the ſtamina or threads of the ſolid parts. *Arb.*

Deſcending careleſs from his couch, the fall
Lux'd his joint neck and *ſpinal* marrow bruis'd. *Philips.*

Spi'ndle. *n. ſ.* [ſpinbl, ſpinbel, Saxon.]

1. The pin by which the thread is formed, and on which it is conglomerated.

Bodies fibrous by moiſture incorporate with other thread, eſpecially if there be a little wreathing; as appeareth by the twiſting of thread, and twirling about of *ſpindles.* *Bacon.*

Sing to thoſe that hold the vital ſheers,
And turn the adamantine *ſpindle* round
On which the fate of gods and men is wound. *Milton.*

Upon a true repentance, God is not ſo fatally tied to the *ſpindle* of abſolute reprobation as not to keep his promiſe, and ſeal merciful pardons. *Dr. Jaſper Maine.*

So Pallas from the duſty field withdrew,
And when imperial Jove appear'd in view,
Reſum'd her female arts, the *ſpindle* and the clew;
Forgot the ſcepter ſhe ſo well had ſway'd,
And with that mildneſs, ſhe had rul'd, obey'd. *Stepney.*

Do you take me for a Roman matron,
Bred tamely to the *ſpindle* and the loom? *A. Philips.*

2. A long ſlender ſtalk.

The *ſpindles* muſt be tied up, and, as they grow in height, rods ſet by them, leſt by their bending they ſhould break. *Mort.*

3. Any thing ſlender. In contempt.

Repoſe yourſelf, if thoſe *ſpindle* legs of yours will carry you to the next chair. *Dryden's Spaniſh Friar.*

The marriage of one of our heireſſes with an eminent courtier gave us *ſpindle* ſhanks and cramps. *Tatler.*

To Spi'ndle. *v. n.* [from the noun.] To ſhoot into a long ſmall ſtalk.

Another ill accident in drought is the *ſpindling* of the corn, which with us is rare, but in hotter countries common; inſomuch as the word calamity was firſt derived from calamus, when the corn could not get out of the ſtalk. *Bacon.*

When the flowers begin to *ſpindle*, all but one or two of the biggeſt, at each root, ſhould be nipped off. *Mortimer.*

SPINDLESHA'NKED. *adj.* [*spindle* and *shank.*] Having small legs.

Her lawyer is a little rivelled, *spindleshanked* gentleman. *Addis.*

SPI'NDLETREE. *n. s.* Prickwood. A plant.

SPINE. *n. s.* [*spina*, Latin.] The back bone.

The rapier entered his right side, reaching within a finger's breadth of the *spine.* *Wiseman's Surgery.*

There are who think the marrow of a man,
Which in the *spine*, while he was living, ran;
When dead, the pith corrupted, will become
A snake, and hiss within the hollow tomb. *Dryden.*

SPI'NEL. *n. s.* A sort of mineral. *Spinel*-ruby is of a bright rosy red; it is softer than the rock or balass ruby. *Woodward.*

SPI'NET. *n. s.* [*espinette*, French.] A small harpsichord, an instrument with keys.

When miss delights in her *spinnet*,
A fiddler may his fortune get. *Swift.*

SPINI'FEROUS. *adj.* [*spina* and *fero*, Latin.] Bearing thorns.

SPI'NNER. *n. s.* [from *spin.*]

1. One skilled in spinning.

A practised *spinner* shall spin a pound of wool worth two shillings for sixpence. *Graunt.*

2. A garden spider with long jointed legs.

Weaving spiders come not here:
Hence you long leg'd *spinners*, hence. *Shakespeare.*

SPI'NNING *Wheel. n. s.* [from *spin.*] The wheel by which, since the disuse of the rock, the thread is drawn.

My *spinning wheel* and rake,
Let Susan keep for her dear sister's sake. *Gay.*

SPINNY. *adj.* I suppose *small, slender.* A barbarous word.

They plow it early in the year, and then there will come some *spinny* grass that will keep it from scalding in summer. *Mortimer's Husbandry.*

SPI'NOSITY. *n. s.* [*spinosus*, Latin.] Crabbedness; thorny or briary perplexity.

Philosophy consisted of nought but dry *spinosities*, lean notions, and endless altercations about things of nothing. *Glanv.*

SPI'NOUS. *adj.* [*spinosus*, Latin.] Thorny; full of thorns.

SPI'NSTER. *n. s.* [from *spin.*]

1. A woman that spins.

The *spinsters* and the knitters in the sun,
And the free maids that weave their thread with bones,
Do use to chant it. *Shakespeare's Twelfth Night.*

2. [In law.] The general term for a girl or maiden woman.

One Michael Cassio,
That never set a squadron in the field,
Nor the division of a battle knows
More than a *spinster.* *Shakespeare's Othello.*

I desire that a yearly annuity of twenty pounds shall be paid to Rebecca Dingley of the city of Dublin, *spinster*, during her life. *Swift.*

SPI'NSTRY. *n. s.* [from *spinster.*] The work of spinning.

SPI'NY. *adj.* [*spina*, Latin.] Thorny; briary; perplexed; difficult; troublesome.

The first attempts are always imperfect; much more in so difficult and *spiny* an affair as so nice a subject. *Digby.*

SPI'RACLE. [*spiraculum*, Latin.] A breathing hole; a vent; a small aperture.

Most of these *spiracles* perpetually send forth fire, more or less. *Woodward.*

SPI'RAL. *adj.* [*spirale*, Fr. from *spira*, Latin.] Curve; winding; circularly involved.

The process of the fibres in the ventricles, running in *spiral* lines from the tip to the base of the heart, shews that the systole of the heart is a muscular constriction, as a purse is shut by drawing the strings contrary ways. *Ray.*

Why earth or sun diurnal stages keep?
In *spiral* tracts why through the zodiack creep? *Blackmore.*

The intestinal tube affects a straight, instead of a *spiral* cylinder. *Arbuthnot on Aliments.*

SPI'RALLY. *adv.* [from *spiral.*] In a spiral form.

The sides are composed of two orders of fibres running circularly or *spirally* from base to tip. *Ray on the Creation.*

SPI'RE. *n. s.* [*spira*, Latin; *spira*, Italian; *spira*, Swedish.]

1. A curve line; any thing wreathed or contorted; a curl; a twist; a wreath.

His head
Crested aloft, and carbuncle his eyes;
With burnish'd neck of verdant gold, erect
Amidst his circling *spires*, that on the grass
Floated redundant. *Milton.*

A dragon's fiery form belied the god,
Sublime on radiant *spires* he rode. *Dryden.*

Air seems to consist of *spires* contorted into small spheres, through the interstices of which the particles of light may freely pass; it is light, the solid substance of the *spires* being very small in proportion to the spaces they take up. *Cheyne.*

2. Any thing growing up taper; a round pyramid, so called perhaps because a line drawn round and round in less and less circles, would be a spire; a steeple.

With glist'ring *spires* and pinnacles adorn'd. *Milton.*

He cannot make one *spire* of grass more or less than he hath made. *Hale's Orig. of Mankind.*

These pointed *spires* that wound the ambient sky,
Inglorious change! shall in destruction lie. *Prior.*

3. The top or uppermost point.

'Twere no less than a traducement to silence, that
Which to the *spire* and top of praises vouch'd,
Wou'd seem but modest. *Shakespeare.*

To SPIRE. *v. n.* [from the noun.]

1. To shoot up pyramidically.

It will grow to a great bigness; but it is not so apt to *spire* up as the other sorts, being more inclined to branch into arms. *Mortimer's Husbandry.*

2. [*Spiro*, Latin.] To breathe. Not in use. *Spenser.*

SPI'RIT. *n. s.* [*spiritus*, Latin.]

1. Breath; wind in motion.

All purges have in them a raw *spirit* or wind, which is the principal cause of tension in the stomach. *Bacon.*

The balmy *spirit* of the western breeze.

2. [*Esprit*, Fr.] An immaterial substance.

Spirit is a substance wherein thinking, knowing, doubting, and a power of moving do subsist. *Locke.*

I shall depend upon your constant friendship; like the trust we have in benevolent *spirits*, who, though we never see or hear them, we think are constantly praying for us. *Pope.*

She is a *spirit*; yet not like air, or wind;
Nor like the spirits about the heart, or brain;
Nor like those spirits which alchymists do find,
When they in ev'ry thing seek gold in vain;
For she all natures under heav'n doth pass,
Being like those *spirits* which God's bright face do see,
Or like himself whose image once she was,
Though now, alas! she scarce his shadow be;
For of all forms she holds the first degree,
That are to gross material bodies knit;
Yet she herself is bodyless and free;
And though confin'd is almost infinite. *Davies.*

If we seclude space, there will remain in the world but matter and mind, or body and *spirit.* *Watts's Logick.*

3. The soul of man.

The *spirit* shall return unto God that gave it. *Bible.*

Look, who comes here! a grave unto a soul,
Holding th' eternal *spirit* 'gainst her will
In the vile prison of afflicted breath. *Shakespeare's K. John.*

4. An apparition.

They were terrified, and supposed that they had seen a *spirit.* *Luke* xxiv. 37.

Perhaps you might see the image, and not the glass; the former appearing like a *spirit* in the air. *Bacon.*

Whilst young, preserve his tender mind from all impressions of *spirits* and goblins in the dark. *Locke.*

5. Temper; habitual disposition of mind.

He sits
Upon their tongues a various *spirit*, to rase
Quite out their native language. *Milton.*

That peculiar law of christianity which forbids revenge, no man can think it grievous who considers the restless torment of a malicious and revengeful *spirit.* *Tillotson.*

Nor once disturb their heav'nly *spirits*
With Scapin's cheats, or Cæsar's merits. *Prior.*

6. Ardour; courage; elevation; vehemence of mind.

'Tis well blown, lads;
This morning, like the *spirit* of a youth
That means to be of note, begins betimes. *Shakespeare.*

Farewel the big war,
The *spirit* stirring drum, th' ear piercing fife. *Shakespeare.*

7. Genius; vigour of mind.

More ample *spirit* than hitherto was wont,
Here needs me, whiles the famous ancestors
Of my most dreaded sovereign I recount,
By which all earthly princes she doth far surmount. *Fa. Q.*

To a mighty work thou goest, O king,
That equal *spirits* and equal pow'rs shall bring. *Daniel.*

A wild Tartar, when he spies
A man that's handsome, valiant, wise,
If he can kill him, thinks t' inherit
His wit, his beauty, and his *spirit.* *Butler.*

The noblest *spirit* or genius cannot deserve enough of mankind, to pretend to the esteem of heroick virtue. *Temple.*

A perfect judge will read each work of wit,
With the same *spirit* that its author writ:
Survey the whole, nor seek slight fault to find,
Where nature moves, and rapture warms the mind. *Pope.*

8. Turn of mind; power of mind moral or intellectual.

You were us'd
To say extremity was the trier of *spirits*,
That common chances common men could bear. *Shakesp.*

I ask but half thy mighty *spirit* for me. *Cowley.*

9. Intellectual powers distinct from the body.

These discourses made so deep impression upon the mind and *spirit* of the prince, whose nature was inclined to adventures, that he was transported with the thought of it. *Clarendon.*

In *spirit* perhaps he also saw
Rich Mexico, the seat of Montezume. *Milton.*

10. Sen-

10. Sentiment; perception.
You are too great to be by me gainsaid:
Your *spirit* is too true, your fears too certain. *Shakespeare.*
11. Eagerness; desire.
God has changed mens tempers with the times, and made a *spirit* of building succeed a *spirit* of pulling down. *South.*
12. Man of activity; man of life, fire and enterprise.
The watry kingdom is no bar
To stop the foreign *spirits*, but they come. *Shakespeare*
13. Persons distinguished by qualities of the mind. A French word, happily growing obsolete.
Such *spirits* as he desired to please, such would I chuse for my judges. *Dryden.*
14. That which gives vigour or cheerfulness to the mind; the purest part of the body bordering, says *Sydenham*, on immateriality. In this meaning it is commonly written with the plural termination.
Though thou didst but jest:
With my vex'd *spirits* I cannot take a truce,
But they will quake. *Shakespeare's King John.*
When I sit and tell
The warlike feats I've done, his *spirits* fly out
Into my story. *Shakespeare's Cymbeline.*
Alas! when all our lamps are burn'd,
Our bodies wasted, and our *spirits* spent,
When we have all the learned volumes turn'd,
Which yield men's wits both help and ornament;
What can we know, or what can we discern? *Davies.*
To sing thy praise, wou'd heav'n my breath prolong,
Infusing *spirits* worthy such a song,
Not Thracian Orpheus should transcend my lays. *Dryden.*
By means of the curious lodgment and inosculation of the auditory nerves, the orgasms of the *spirits* should be allayed. *Derham.*
In some fair body thus the secret soul
With *spirits* feeds, with vigour fills the whole;
Each motion guides, and ev'ry nerve sustains,
Itself unseen, but in the effects remains. *Pope.*
The king's party, called the cavaliers, began to recover their *spirits*. *Swift.*
15. The likeness; essential qualities.
Italian pieces will appear best in a room where the windows are high, because they are commonly made to a descending light, which of all other doth set off mens faces in their truest *spirit*. *Wotton.*
16. Any thing eminently pure and refined.
Nor doth the eye itself,
That most pure *spirit* of sense, behold itself. *Shakespeare.*
17. That which hath power or energy.
All bodies have *spirits* and pneumatical parts within them; but the main difference between animate and inanimate are, that the *spirits* of things animate are all continued within themselves, and branched in veins as blood is; and the *spirits* have also certain seats where the principal do reside, and whereunto the rest do resort; but the *spirits* in things inanimate are shut in and cut off by the tangible parts, as air in snow. *Bacon's Natural History.*
18. An inflammable liquour raised by distillation.
What the chymists call *spirit*, they apply the name to so many differing things, that they seem to have no settled notion of the thing. In general, they give the name of *spirit* to any distilled volatile liquour. *Boyle.*
All *spirits*, by frequent use, destroy, and at last extinguish the natural heat of the stomach. *Temple.*
In distillations, what trickles down the sides of the receiver, if it will not mix with water, is oil; if it will, it is *spirit*. *Arbuthnot on Aliments.*
19. It may be observed, that in the old poets *spirit* was commonly a monosyllable, being written *spright* or *sprite*.
The charge thereof unto a courteous *spright*
Commanded was. *Spenser.*
To SPI'RIT. *v. a.*
1. To animate or actuate as a spirit.
So talk'd the *spirited* sly snake. *Milton's Par. Lost.*
2. To excite; to animate; to encourage.
He will be faint in any execution of such a counsel, unless *spirited* by the unanimous decrees of a general diet. *Temple.*
Civil dissensions never fail of introducing and *spiriting* the ambition of private men. *Swift on the Cont. in Athens and Rome.*
Many officers and private men *spirit* up and assist those obstinate people to continue in their rebellion. *Swift.*
3. To draw; to entice.
In the southern coast of America, the southern point of the needle varieth toward the land, as being disposed and *spirited* that way, by the meridional and proper hemisphere. *Brown.*
The ministry had him *spirited* away, and carried abroad as a dangerous person. *Arbuthnot and Pope.*
SPI'RITALLY. *adv.* [from *spiritus*, Latin.] By means of the breath.
Conceive one of each pronounced *spiritally*, the other vocally. *Holder's Elements of Speech.*
SPI'RITED. *adj.* [from *spirit.*] Lively; vivacious; full of fire.
Dryden's translation of Virgil is noble and *spirited*. *Pope.*
SPI'RITEDNESS. *n. s.* [from *spirited.*] Disposition or make of mind.
He showed the narrow *spiritedness*, pride, and ignorance of pedants. *Addison.*
SPI'RITFULNESS. *n. s.* [from *spirit* and *full.*] Sprightliness; liveliness.
A cocks crowing is, a tone that corresponds to singing, attesting his mirth and *spiritfulness*. *Harvey.*
SPI'RITLESS. *adj.* [from *spirit.*] Dejected; low; deprived of vigour; wanting courage; depressed.
A man so faint, so *spiritless*,
So dull, so dead in look, so woe begone,
Drew Priam's curtain. *Shakespeare's Henry.* IV.
Of their wonted vigour left them drain'd,
Exhausted, *spiritless*, afflicted, fall'n. *Milton's Paradise Lost.*
Nor did all Rome, grown *spiritless*, supply
A man that for bold truth durst bravely die. *Dryden.*
Art thou so base, so *spiritless* a slave?
Not so he bore the fate to which you doom'd him. *Smith.*
SPI'RITOUS. *adj.* [from *spirit.*]
1. Refined; defecated; advanced near to spirit.
More refin'd, more *spiritous* and pure,
As nearer to him plac'd, or nearer tending. *Milton.*
2. Fine; ardent; active.
SPI'RITOUSNESS. *n. s.* [from *spiritous.*] Fineness and activity of parts.
They, notwithstanding the great thinness and *spiritousness* of the liquor, did, before they broke, lift up the upper surface, and for a moment form a thin film like a small hemisphere. *Boyle.*
SPIRI'TUAL. *adj.* [*spirituel*, Fr. from *spirit.*]
1. Distinct from matter; immaterial; incorporeal.
Echo is a great argument of the *spiritual* essence of sounds; for if it were corporeal, the repercussion should be created by like instruments with the original sound. *Bacon.*
Both visibles and audibles in their working emit no corporeal substance into their mediums, but only carry certain *spiritual* species. *Bacon.*
All creatures, as well *spiritual* as corporeal, declare their absolute dependence upon the first author of all beings, the only self-existent God. *Bentley.*
2. Mental; intellectual.
The same disaster has invaded his *spirituals*; the passions rebel; and there are so many governours, that there can be no government. *South.*
3. Not gross; refined from external things; relative only to the mind.
Some who pretend to be of a more *spiritual* and refined religion, spend their time in contemplation, and talk much of communion with God. *Calamy's Sermons.*
4. Not temporal; relating to the things of heaven; ecclesiastical.
Place man in some publick society, civil or *spiritual*. *Hooker.*
Thou art reverend,
Touching thy *spiritual* function, not thy life. *Shakespeare.*
I have made an offer to his majesty,
Upon our *spiritual* convocation,
As touching France, to give a greater sum
Than ever at one time the clergy did. *Shakespeare.*
Spiritual armour, able to resist
Satan's assaults. *Milton.*
The clergy's business lies among the laity; nor is there a more effectual way to forward the salvation of mens souls, than for *spiritual* persons to make themselves as agreeable as they can in the conversations of the world. *Swift.*
SPIRI'TUALITY. *n. s.* [from *spiritual.*]
1. Incorporeity; immateriality; essence distinct from matter.
If this light be not spiritual, yet it approacheth nearest unto *spirituality*; and if it have any corporality, then of all other the most subtile and pure. *Raleigh.*
2. Intellectual nature.
A pleasure made for the soul; suitable to its *spirituality*, and equal to all its capacities. *South's Sermons.*
3. [*Spiritualié*, Fr.] Acts independent of the body; pure acts of the soul; mental refinement.
Many secret indispositions and aversions to duty will steal upon the soul, and it will require both time and close application of mind to recover it to such a frame, as shall dispose it for the *spiritualities* of religion. *South's Sermons.*
4. That which belongs to any one as an ecclesiastick.
Of common right, the dean and chapter are guardians of the *spiritualities*, during the vacancy of a bishoprick. *Ayliffe.*
SPI'RITUALTY. *n. s.* [from *spiritual.*] Ecclesiastical body.
We of the *spiritualty*
Will raise your highness such a mighty sum,
As never did the clergy at one time. *Shakespeare.*
SPIRITUALIZA'TION. *n. s.* [from *spiritualize.*] The act of spiritualizing.
To SPI'RITUALIZE. *v. a.* [*spiritualiser*, Fr. from *spirit.*] To refine the intellect; to purify from the feculencies of the world.
This would take it much out of the care of the soul, to *spiritualize* and replenish it with good works. *Hammond.*

We begin our survey from the lowest dregs of sense, and so ascend to our more *spiritualized* selves. *Glanville.*

As to the future glory in which the body is to partake, that load of earth which now engages to corruption, must be calcined and *spiritualized*, and thus be clothed upon with glory. *Decay of Piety.*

If man will act rationally, he cannot admit any competition between a momentary satisfaction, and an everlasting happiness, as great as God can give, and our *spiritualized* capacities receive. *Rogers's Sermons.*

SPIRI'TUALLY. *adv.* [from *spiritual*] Without corporeal grossness; with attention to things purely intellectual.

In the same degree that virgins live more *spiritually* than other persons, in the same degree is their virginity a more excellent state. *Taylor's Rule of holy Living.*

SPIRI'TUOUS. *adj.* [*spiritueux*, Fr. from *spirit.*]

1. Having the quality of spirit, tenuity and activity of parts.

More refin'd, more *spirituous* and pure,
As to him nearer tending. *Milton.*

The most *spirituous* and most fragrant part of the plant exhales by the action of the sun. *Arbuthnot.*

2. Lively; gay; vivid; airy.

It may appear airy and *spirituous*, and fit for the welcome of chearful guests. *Wotton's Architecture.*

SPIRITUO'SITY. } *n. s.* [from *spirituous.*] The quality of being spirituous; tenuity and activity.
SPIRITUOU'SNESS. }

To SPIRT. *v. n.* [*spruyten*, Dutch, to shoot up, *Skinner*; *spritta*, Swedish, to fly out. *Lye.*] To spring out in a sudden stream; to stream out by intervals.

Bottling of beer, while new and full of spirit, so that it *spirteth* when the stopple is taken forth, maketh the drink more quick and windy. *Bacon's Natural History.*

Thus the small jett, which hasty hands unlock,
Spirts in the gard'ner's eyes who turns the cock. *Pope.*

To SPIRT. *v. a.* To throw out in a jet.

When weary Proteus
Retir'd for shelter to his wonted caves,
His finny flocks about their shepherd play,
And rowling round him, *spirt* the bitter sea. *Dryden.*
When rains the passage hide,
Oft the loose stones *spirt* up a muddy tide
Beneath thy careless foot. *Gay.*

To SPI'RTLE. *v. a.* [A corruption of *spirt.*] To dissipate.

The terraqueous globe would, by the centrifugal force of that motion, be soon dissipated and *spirtled* into the circumambient space, was it not kept together by this noble contrivance of the Creator. *Derham's Physico-Theology.*

SPI'RY. *adj.* [from *spire.*]

1. Pyramidal.

Waste sandy valleys, once perplex'd with thorn,
The *spiry* firr, and shapely box adorn. *Pope's Messiah.*
In these lone walls, their days eternal bound,
These moss-grown domes with *spiry* turrets crown'd,
Where awful arches make a noon-day night,
And the dim windows shed a solemn light;
Thy eyes diffus'd a reconciling ray,
And gleams of glory brighten'd all the day. *Pope.*

2. Wreathed; curled.

Hid in the *spiry* volumes of the snake,
I lurk'd within the covert of a brake. *Dryden.*

SPISS. *adj.* [*spissus*, Latin.] Close; firm; thick.

From his modest and humble charity, virtues which rarely cohabit with the swelling windiness of much knowledge, issued this *spiss* and dense, yet polished; this copious, yet concise treatise of the variety of languages. *Brerewood.*

SPI'SSITUDE. *n. s.* [from *spissus*, Latin.] Grossness; thickness.

Drawing wine or beer from the lees, called racking, it will clarify the sooner; for though the lees keep the drink in heart, and make it lasting, yet they cast up some *spissitude*. *Bacon.*

Spissitude is subdued by acrid things, and acrimony by inspissating. *Arbuthnot on Aliments.*

SPIT. *n. s.* [ꞅpitan, Saxon; *spit*, Dutch; *spedo*, Italian.]

1. A long prong on which meat is driven to be turned before the fire.

A goodly city is this Antium;
'Tis I that made thy widows: then know me not,
Lest that thy wives with *spits*, and boys with stones
In puny battle slay me. *Shakespeare's Coriolanus.*

They may be contrived to the moving of sails in a chimney corner, the motion of which may be applied to the turning of a *spit*. *Wilkins's Mathematical Magick.*

With Peggy Dixon thoughtful sit,
Contriving for the pot and *spit*. *Swift.*

2. Such a depth of earth as is pierced by one action of the spade.

Where the earth is washed from the quick, face it with the first *spit* of earth dug out of the ditch. *Mortimer.*

To SPIT. *v. a.* Preterite *spat*; participle pass. *spit*, or *spitted.* [from the noun.]

1. To put upon a spit.

I see my cousin's ghost
Seeking out Romeo, that did *spit* his body
Upon a rapier's point. *Shakespeare's Romeo and Juliet.*

2. To thrust through.

I *spitted* frogs, I crush'd a heap of emmets. *Dryden.*

To SPIT. *v. a.* [ꞅpætan, Saxon; *spytter*, Danish.] To eject from the mouth.

A large mouth, indeed,
That *spits* forth death, and mountains, rocks and seas.
Shakespeare's King John.
Commissions which compel from each
The sixth part of his substance, makes bold mouths,
Tongues *spit* their duties out, and cold hearts freeze
Allegiance in them. *Shakespeare.*

To SPIT. *v. n.* To throw out spittle or moisture of the mouth.

Very good orators, when they are here, will *spit*. *Shakesp.*
I dare meet Surrey,
And *spit* upon him whilst I say he lies. *Shakesp. Rich.* II.
You *spit* upon me last Wednesday,
You spurn'd me such a day. *Shakespeare's Merch. of Venice.*
The watry kingdom, whose ambitious head
Spits in the face of heaven, is no bar
To stop the foreign spirits; but they come. *Shakespeare.*

He *spat* on the ground, made clay of the spittle, and anointed the eyes of the blind man. *John* ix. 6.

A maid came from her father's house to one of the tribunals of the Gentiles, and declaring herself a Christian, *spit* in the judge's face. *South.*

A drunkard men abhor, and would even *spit* at him, were it not for fear he should something more than *spit* at them. *South's Sermons.*

Spit on your finger and thumb, and pinch the snuff till the candle goes out. *Swift's Rules for the Servants.*

SPI'TTAL. *n. s.* [Corrupted from *hospital.*] A charitable foundation. In use only in the phrases, *a spittal sermon*, and *rob not the spittal.*

To SPI'TCHCOCK. *v. a.* To cut an eel in pieces and roast him. Of this word I find no good etymology.

No man lards salt pork with orange peel,
Or garnishes his lamb with *spitchcockt* eel. *King.*

SPITE. *n. s.* [*spijt*, Dutch; *despit*, French.]

1. Malice; rancour; hate; malignity; malevolence.

This breeding rather *spite* than shame in her, or, if it were a shame, a shame not of the fault, but of the repulse, she did thirst for a revenge. *Sidney.*

Bewray they did their inward boiling *spite*,
Each stirring others to revenge their cause. *Daniel.*
Done all to spite
The great Creator; but their *spite* still serves
His glory to augment. *Milton's Paradise Lost.*
Be gone, ye criticks, and restrain your *spite*,
Codrus writes on, and will for ever write. *Pope.*

2. SPITE *of*, or *In* SPITE *of.* Notwithstanding; in defiance of. It is often used without any malignity of meaning.

Blessed be such a preacher, whom God made use of to speak a word in season, and saved me in *spite of* the world, the devil, and myself. *South.*

In spite of me I love, and see too late
My mother's pride must find my mother's fate. *Dryden.*
For thy lov'd sake, *spite of* my boding fears,
I'll meet the danger which ambition brings. *Rowe.*
My father's fate,
In spite of all the fortitude that shines
Before my face in Cato's great example,
Subdues my soul, and fills my eyes with tears. *Addis. Cato.*

In spite of all applications the patient grew worse every day. *Arbuthnot.*

To SPITE. *v. a.* [from the noun.]

1. To mischief; to treat maliciously; to vex; to thwart malignantly.

Beguil'd, divorced, wronged, *spighted*, slain,
Most detestable death, by thee. *Shakespeare.*
I'll sacrifice the lamb that I do love,
To *spight* a raven's heart within a dove. *Shakespeare.*

2. To fill with spite; to offend.

So with play did he a good while fight against the fight of Zelmane, who, more *spited* with that courtesy, that one that did nothing should be able to resist her, burned away with choler any motions which might grow out of her own sweet disposition. *Sidney.*

Darius, *spited* at the magi, endeavoured to abolish not only their learning but their language. *Temple.*

SPI'TEFUL. *adj.* [*spite* and *full.*] Malicious; malignant.

The Jews were the deadliest and *spitefullest* enemies of Christianity that were in the world, and in this respect their orders to be shunned. *Hooker.*

All you have done
Hath been but for a wayward son,
Spightful and wrathful. *Shakes. Macbeth.*

Contempt is a thing made up of an undervaluing of a man, upon a belief of his utter uselessness, and a *spiteful* endeavour to engage the rest of the world in the same slight esteem of him. *South's Sermons.*

The *spiteful* stars have shed their venom down,
And now the peaceful planets take their turn. *Dryden.*

SPI'TEFULLY. *adv.* [from *spiteful.*] Maliciously; malignantly.

Twice false Evadne, *spitefully* forsworn!
That fatal beast like this I would have torn. *Waller.*

Vanessa sat,
Scarce list'ning to their idle chat,
Further than sometimes by a frown,
When they grew pert, to pull them down;
At last she *spitefully* was bent
To try their wisdom's full extent. *Swift.*

SPI'TEFULNESS. *n. s.* [from *spiteful.*] Malice; malignity; desire of vexing.

It looks more like *spitefulness* and ill-nature, than a diligent search after truth. *Keil against Burnet.*

SPI'TTED. *adj.* [from *spit.*] Shot out into length.

Whether the head of a deer, that by age is more *spitted*, may be brought again to be more branched. *Bacon.*

SPI'TTER. *n. s.* [from *spit.*]
1. One who puts meat on a spit.
2. One who spits with his mouth.
3. A young deer. *Ainsworth.*

SPI'TTLE. *n. s.* [Corrupted from *hospital*, and therefore better written *spital*, or *spittal.*] Hospital. It is still retained in Scotland.

To the *spittle* go,
And from the powd'ring tub of infamy
Fetch forth the lazar kite of Cressid's kind. *Shakes. H. V.*

This is it
That makes the waned widow wed again;
She whom the *spittle* house, and ulcerous sores,
Would cast the gorge at, this embalms and spices
To th' April-day again. *Shakesp. Timon.*

Cure the *spittle* world of maladies. *Cleaveland.*

SPI'TTLE. *n. s.* [ꞅpœtlian, Saxon.] Moisture of the mouth.

The saliva or *spittle* is an humour of eminent use. *Ray.*

Mænas and Atys in the mouth were bred,
And never hatch'd within the lab'ring head;
No blood from bitten nails those poems drew,
But churn'd like *spittle* from the lips they flew. *Dryden.*

The *spittle* is an active liquor, immediately derived from the arterial blood: it is saponaceous. *Arbuthnot.*

A genius for all stations fit,
Whose meanest talent is his wit;
His heart too great, though fortune little,
To lick a rascal statesman's *spittle.* *Swift.*

SPI'TVENOM. *n. s.* [*spit* and *venom.*] Poison ejected from the mouth.

The *spitvenom* of their poisoned hearts breaketh out to the annoyance of others. *Hooker.*

SPLANCHNO'LOGY. *n. s.* [*splanchnologie*, French; σπλάγχνα and λόγος.] A treatise or description of the bowels. *Dict.*

To SPLASH. *v. a.* [*plaska*, Swedish. They have both an affinity with *plash.*] To daub with dirt in great quantities.

SPLA'SHY. *adj.* [from *splash.*] Full of dirty water; apt to daub.

SPLA'YFOOT. *adj.* [*splay* or *display* and *foot.*] Having the foot turned inward.

Though still some traces of our rustick vein,
And *splayfoot* verse remain'd, and will remain. *Pope.*

SPLA'YMOUTH. *n. s.* [*splay* and *mouth.*] Mouth widened by design.

All authors to their own defects are blind:
Had'st thou but Janus-like a face behind,
To see the people when *splaymouths* they make,
To mark their fingers pointed at thy back,
Their tongues loll'd out a foot. *Dryden.*

SPLEEN. *n. s.* [*splen*, Latin.]
1. The milt; one of the viscera, of which the use is scarcely known. It is supposed the seat of anger and melancholy.

If the wound be on the left hypochondrium, under the short ribs, you may conclude the *spleen* wounded. *Wiseman.*

2. Anger; spite; ill-humour.

If she must teem,
Create her child of *spleen*, that it may live
And be a thwart disnatur'd torment to her. *Shakespeare.*

Charge not in your *spleen* a noble person,
And spoil your nobler soul. *Shakespeare.*

Kind pity checks my *spleen*; brave scorn forbids
Those tears to issue, which swell my eye-lids. *Donne.*

All envy'd; but the Thestyan brethren show'd
The least respect; and thus they vent their *spleen* aloud:
Lay down those honour'd spoils. *Dryden.*

In noble minds some dregs remain,
Not yet purg'd off, of *spleen* and sour disdain. *Pope.*

3. A fit of anger.

Brief as the lightning in the collied night,
That, in a *spleen*, unfolds both heav'n and earth;
And, ere a man hath power to say, behold!
The jaws of darkness do devour it up. *Shakespeare.*

4. Melancholy; hypochondriacal vapours.

Spleen, vapours, and small-pox above them all. *Pope.*
Bodies chang'd to recent forms by *spleen.* *Pope.*

SPLE'ENED. *adj.* [from *spleen.*] Deprived of the spleen.

Animals *spleened* grow salacious. *Arbuthnot.*

SPLE'ENFUL. *adj.* [*spleen* and *full.*] Angry; peevish; fretful; melancholy.

The commons, like an angry hive of bees
That want their leader, scatter up and down;
Myself have calm'd their *spleenful* mutiny. *Shak. H.* VI.

The chearful soldiers, with new stores supply'd,
Now long to execute their *spleenful* will. *Dryden.*

If you drink tea upon a promontory that over-hangs the sea, the whistling of the wind is better musick to contented minds than the opera to the *spleenful.* *Pope.*

SPLE'ENLESS. *adj.* [from *spleen.*] Kind; gentle; mild. Obsolete.

Mean time flew our ships, and streight we fetcht
The syren's isle; a *spleenless* wind so stretcht
Her wings to waft us, and so urg'd our keel. *Chapman.*

SPLE'ENWORT. *n. s.* [*spleen* and *wort.*] Miltwaste. A plant.

The leaves and fruit are like those of the fern; but the pinnulæ are eared at their basis. *Miller.*

Safe pass'd the gnome through this fantastick band,
A branch of healing *spleenwort* in his hand. *Pope.*

SPLE'ENY. *adj.* [from *spleen.*] Angry; peevish.

What though I know her virtuous,
And well deserving; yet I know her for
A *spleeny* Lutheran, and not wholsome to
Our cause. *Shakesp. Henry* VIII.

SPLE'NDENT. *adj.* [*splendens*, Latin.] Shining; glossy; having lustre.

They assigned them names from some remarkable qualities, that is very observable in their red and *splendent* planets. *Brown.*

Metallick substances may, by reason of their great density, reflect all the light incident upon them, and so be as opake and *splendent* as it's possible for any body to be. *Newton.*

SPLE'NDID. *adj.* [*splendide*, Fr. *splendidus*, Latin.] Showy; magnificent; sumptuous; pompous.

Unacceptable, though in heav'n, our state
Of *splendid* vassalage. *Milton.*

Deep in a rich alcove the prince was laid,
And slept beneath the pompous colonade:
Fast by his side Pisistratus lay spread,
In age his equal, on a *splendid* bed. *Pope's Odyssey.*

SPLE'NDIDLY. *adv.* [from *splendid.*] Magnificently; sumptuously; pompously.

Their condition, though it look *splendidly*, yet when you handle it on all sides, it will prick your fingers. *Taylor.*

You will not admit you live *splendidly*, yet it cannot be denied but that you live neatly and elegantly. *More.*

How he lives and eats,
How largely gives, how *splendidly* he treats. *Dryden.*

He, of the royal store
Splendidly frugal, sits whole nights devoid
Of sweet repose. *Philips.*

SPLE'NDOUR. *n. s.* [*splendeur*, French; *splendor*, Latin.]
1. Lustre; power of shining.

Splendour hath a degree of whiteness, especially if there be a little repercussion; for a looking-glass, with the steel behind, looketh whiter than glass simple. *Bacon's Natural History.*

The dignity of gold above silver is not much; the *splendour* is alike, and more pleasing to some eyes, as in cloth of silver. *Bacon's Phys. Remarks.*

The first symptoms are a chilness, a certain *splendour* or shining in the eyes, with a little moisture. *Arbuthnot.*

2. Magnificence; pomp.

Romulus, being to give laws to his new Romans, found no better way to procure an esteem and reverence to them, than by first procuring it to himself by *splendour* of habit and retinue. *South's Sermons.*

'Tis use alone that sanctifies expence,
And *splendour* borrows all her rays from sense. *Pope.*

SPLE'NETICK. *adj.* [*splenetique*, French.] Troubled with the spleen; fretful; peevish.

Horace purged himself from these *splenetick* reflections in odes and epodes, before he undertook his satyrs. *Dryden.*

This daughter silently lowers, t'other steals a kind look at you, a third is exactly well behaved, and a fourth a *splenetick.* *Tatler.*

You humour me when I am sick;
Why not when I am *splenetick*? *Pope.*

SPLE'NICK. *adj.* [*splenique*, French; *splen*, Latin.] Belonging to the spleen.

Suppose the spleen obstructed in its lower parts and *splenick* branch, a potent heat causeth the orgasmus to boil. *Harvey.*

The *splenick* vein hath divers cells opening into it near its extremities in human bodies; but in quadrupeds the cells open into the trunks of the *splenick* veins. *Ray on the Creation.*

SPLE'NISH. *adj.* [from *spleen.*] Fretful; peevish.

Yourselves you must engage,
Somewhat to cool your *splenish* rage,
Your grievous thirst, and to asswage,
That first you drink this liquor. *Drayton.*

SPLENITIVE. *adj.* [from *spleen.*] Hot; fiery; passionate. Not in use.

Take thy fingers from my throat;
For though I am not *splenitive* and rash,
Yet I have in me something dangerous. *Shakes. Hamlet.*

SPLENT. *n. s.* [Or perhaps *splint*; *spinella*, Italian.]

Splents is a callous hard substance, or an insensible swelling, which breeds on or adheres to the shank-bone, and when it grows big spoils the shape of the leg. When there is but one, it is called a single *splent*; but when there is another opposite to it on the outside of the shank-bone, it is called a pegged or pinned *splent*. *Farrier's Dict.*

To SPLICE. *v. a.* [*splissen*, Dutch; *plico*, Latin.] To join the two ends of a rope without a knot.

SPLINT. *n. s.* [*splinter*, Dutch.] A thin piece of wood or other matter used by chirurgeons to hold the bone newly set in its place.

The ancients, after the seventh day, used *splints*, which not only kept the members steady, but straight; and of these some are made of tin, others of scabbard and wood, sowed up in linnen cloths. *Wiseman's Surgery.*

To SPLINT. } *v. a.* [from the noun.]
To SPLI'NTER. }

1. To secure by splints.

This broken joint intreat her to *splinter*, and this crack of your love shall grow stronger than it was before. *Shak. Othello.*

2. To shiver; to break into fragments.

SPLI'NTER. *n. s.* [*splinter*, Dutch.]

1. A fragment of any thing broken with violence.

He was slain upon a course at tilt, one of the *splinters* of Montgomery's staff going in at his bever. *Bacon.*

Amidst whole heaps of spices lights a ball,
And now their odours arm'd against them flie;
Some preciously by shatter'd porcelain fall,
And some by aromatick *splinters* die. *Dryden.*

2. A thin piece of wood.

A plain Indian fan, used by the meaner sort, made of the small stringy parts of roots, spread out in a round flat form, and so bound together with a *splinter* hoop, and strengthened with small bars on both sides. *Grew's Musæum.*

To SPLI'NTER. *v. n.* [from the noun.] To be broken into fragments.

To SPLIT. *v. a.* pret. *split.* [*spletten*, *splitten*, Dutch.]

1. To cleave; to rive; to divide longitudinally in two.

Do't, and thou hast the one half of my heart;
Do't not, thou *split'st* thine own. *Shak. Winter's Tale.*
Mine own tongue *splits* what it speaks. *Shakespeare.*
That self-hand
Hath, with the courage which the heart did lend it,
Splitted the heart. *Shakesp. Ant. and Cleopatra.*
Wer't thou serv'd up two in one dish, the rather
To *split* thy sire into a double father? *Cleaveland.*
When cold Winter *split* the rocks in twain,
He stript the bearsfoot of its leafy growth. *Dryden.*

A skull so hard, that it is almost as easy to *split* a helmet of iron as to make a fracture in it. *Ray on the Creation.*

This effort is in some earthquakes so vehement, that it *splits* and tears the earth, making cracks or chasms in it some miles. *Woodward.*

2. To divide; to part.

Their logick has appeared the mere art of wrangling, and their metaphysicks the skill of *splitting* an hair, of distinguishing without a difference. *Watts's Improv. of the Mind.*

One and the same ray is by refraction disturbed, shattered, dilated, and *split*, and spread into many diverging rays. *Newt.*

He instances Luther's sensuality and disobedience; two crimes which he has dealt with, and to make the more solemn shew he *split* 'em into twenty. *Atterbury.*

Oh, would it please the gods to *split*
Thy beauty, size, and years, and wit,
No age could furnish out a pair
Of nymphs so graceful, wise, and fair;
With half the lustre of your eyes,
With half your wit, your years, and size. *Swift.*

3. To dash and break on a rock.

God's desertion, as a full and violent wind, drives him in an instant, not to the harbour, but on the rock where he will be irrecoverably *split*. *Decay of Piety.*

Those who live by shores, with joy behold
Some wealthy vessel *split* or stranded nigh;
And from the rocks leap down for shipwreck'd gold,
And seek the tempests which the others fly. *Dryden.*

4. To divide; to break into discord.

In states notoriously irreligious, a secret and irresistible power *splits* their counsels, and smites their most refined policies with frustration and a curse. *South's Sermons.*

To SPLIT. *v. n.*

1. To burst in sunder; to crack; to suffer disruption.

A huge vessel of exceeding hard marble *split* asunder by congealed water. *Boyle.*

What is't to me,
Who never sail on her unfaithful sea,
If storms arise and clouds grow black,
If the mast *split*, and threaten wrack? *Dryden.*
The road that to the lungs this store transmits,
Into unnumber'd narrow channels *splits*. *Blackmore.*
Each had a gravity would make you *split*,
And shook his head at M—y as a wit. *Pope.*

2. To be broken against rocks.

After our ship did *split*,
When you, and the poor number sav'd with you,
Hung on our driving boat. *Shakespeare.*

These are the rocks on which the sanguine tribe of lovers daily *split*, and on which the politician, the alchymist, and projector are cast away. *Addison's Spectator.*

The seamen spied a rock, and the wind was so strong that we were driven directly upon it, and immediately *split*. *Gulliv.*

SPLI'TTER. *n. s.* [from *split.*] One who splits.

How should we rejoice, if, like Judas the first,
Those *splitters* of parsons in sunder should burst! *Swift.*

SPLU'TTER. *n. s.* Bustle; tumult. A low word.

To SPOIL. *v. a.* [*spolio*, Latin; *spolier*, French.]

1. To rob; to take away by force.

Ye took joyfully the *spoiling* of your goods, knowing in yourselves that ye have in heaven an enduring substance. *Heb.*

This mount
With all his verdure *spoil'd*, and trees adrift. *Milton.*

2. To plunder; to strip of goods.

Yielding themselves upon the Turks faith, for the safeguard of their liberty and goods, they were most injuriously *spoiled* of all that they had. *Knolles's History of the Turks.*

Thou shalt not gain what I deny to yield,
Nor reap the harvest, though thou *spoil'st* the field. *Prior.*
My sons their old unhappy sire despise,
Spoil'd of his kingdom, and depriv'd of eyes. *Pope.*

3. To corrupt; to mar; to make useless. [This is properly *spill*, ꞅpillan, Saxon.]

Beware lest any man *spoil* you, through philosophy and vain deceit. *Col.* ii. 8.

Spiritual pride *spoils* many graces. *Taylor.*

To SPOIL. *v. n.*

1. To practice robbery or plunder.

England was infested with robbers and outlaws, which, lurking in woods, used often to break forth to rob and *spoil*. *Spenser on Ireland.*

They which hate us *spoil* for themselves. *Ps.* xliv. 14.

2. To grow useless; to be corrupted.

He that gathered a hundred bushels of acorns, or apples, had thereby a property in them: he was only to look that he used them before they *spoiled*, else he robbed others. *Locke.*

SPOIL. *n. s.* [*spolium*, Latin.]

1. That which is taken by violence; that which is taken from an enemy; plunder; pillage; booty.

The cry of Talbot serves me for a sword;
For I have loaden me with many *spoils*,
Using no other weapon but his name. *Shakesp. Hen.* VI.
Where the cleaver chops the heifer's *spoil*,
Thy breathing nostril hold. *Gay's Trivia.*

2. The act of robbery; robbery; waste.

The man that hath not musick in himself,
Nor is not mov'd with concord of sweet sounds,
Is fit for treasons, stratagems, and *spoils*. *Shakespeare.*
Go and speed!
Havock, and *spoil*, and ruin are my gain. *Milt. Parad. Lost.*

3. Corruption; cause of corruption.

Company, villainous company, hath been the *spoil* of me. *Shakespeare.*

4. The slough; the cast-off skin of a serpent.

Snakes, the rather for the casting of their *spoil*, live 'till they be old. *Bacon.*

SPO'ILER. *n. s.* [from *spoil.*]

1. A robber; a plunderer; a pillager.

Such ruin of her manners Rome
Doth suffer now, as she's become
Both her own *spoiler* and own prey. *Ben. Johns. Catiline.*

Providence, where it loves a nation, concerns itself to own and assert the interest of religion, by blasting the *spoilers* of religious persons and places. *South's Sermons.*

Came you, then, here, thus far, thro' waves, to conquer,
To waste, to plunder, out of meer compassion?
Is it humanity that prompts you on?
Happy for us, and happy for you *spoilers*,
Had your humanity ne'er reach'd our world! *A. Philips.*

2. One who mars or corrupts any thing.

SPO'ILFUL. *adj.* [*spoil* and *full.*] Wasteful; rapacious.

Having oft in battle vanquished
Those *spoilful* Picts, and swarming Easterlings,
Long time in peace his realm established. *Fairy Queen.*

SPOKE. *n. s.* [ꞅpaca, Saxon; *speiche*, German.] The bar of a wheel that passes from the nave to the felly.

All you gods,
In general synod take away her power;
Break all the *spokes* and fellies of her wheel,
And bowl the round nave down the hill of heav'n. *Shakes.*

No heir e'er drove so fine a coach;
The *spokes*, we are by Ovid told,
Were silver, and the axle gold. *Swift.*

SPOKE. The preterite of *speak*.

They *spoke* best in the glory of their conquest. *Sprat.*

SPOKEN. Participle passive of *speak*.

Wouldst thou be *spoken* for to the king? 2 *Kings* iv. 13.

The original of these signs for communication is found in *viva voce*, in *spoken* language. *Holder's Elements of Speech.*

SPO'KESMAN. *n. s.* [*spoke* and *man.*] One who speaks for another.

'Tis you that have the reason.
—To do what?
—To be a *spokesman* from madam Silvia: *Shakespeare.*

He shall be thy *spokesman* unto the people. *Ex.* iv. 16.

To SPO'LIATE. *v. a.* [*spolio*, Lat.] To rob; to plunder. *Dict.*

SPOLIA'TION. *n. s.* [*spoliation*, French; *spoliatio*, Latin.] The act of robbery or privation.

An ecclesiastical benefice is sometimes void *de jure & facto*, and sometimes *de facto*, and not *de jure*; as when a man suffers a *spoliation* by his own act. *Ayliffe's Parergon.*

SPO'NDEE. *n. s.* [*spondée*, French; *spondæus*, Latin.] A foot of two long syllables.

We see in the choice of the words the weight of the stone, and the striving to heave it up the mountain: Homer clogs the verse with *spondees*, and leaves the vowels open. *Broome.*

SPO'NDYLE. *n. s.* [σπονδυλ©; *spondile*, Fr. *spondylus*, Latin.] A vertebra; a joint of the spine.

It hath for the spine or back-bone a cartilaginous substance, without any *spondyles*, processes, or protuberances. *Brown.*

SPONGE. *n. s.* [*spongia*, Latin.] A soft porous substance supposed by some the nidus of animals. It is remarkable for sucking up water.

Sponges are gathered from the sides of rocks, being as a large but tough moss. *Bacon.*

They opened and washed part of their *sponges*. *Sandys.*

Great officers are like *sponges*: they suck 'till they are full, and, when they come once to be squeezed, their very heart's blood come away. *L'Estrange.*

To SPONGE. *v. a.* [from the noun.] To blot; to wipe away as with a sponge.

Except between the words of translation and the mind of Scripture itself there be contradiction, very little difference should not seem an intolerable blemish necessarily to be *spunged* out. *Hooker.*

To SPONGE. *v. n.* To suck in as a sponge; to gain by mean arts.

The ant lives upon her own honesty; whereas the fly is an intruder, and a common smell-feast, that *spunges* upon other people's trenchers. *L'Estrange.*

Here wont the dean, when he's to seek,
To *spunge* a breakfast once a week. *Swift.*

SPO'NGER. *n. s.* [from *sponge.*] One who hangs for a maintenance on others.

A generous rich man, that kept a splendid and open table, would try which were friends, and which only trencher-flies and *spungers*. *L'Estrange.*

SPO'NGINESS. *n. s.* [from *spongy.*] Softness and fulness of cavities like a sponge.

The lungs are exposed to receive all the droppings from the brain: a very fit cistern, because of their *sponginess*. *Harvey.*

SPO'NGIOUS. *adj.* [*spongieux*, French; from *sponge.*] Full of small cavities like a sponge.

All thick bones are hollow or *spongeous*, and contain an oleaginous substance in little vesicles, which by the heat of the body is exhaled through these bones to supply their fibres. *Chey.*

SPO'NGY. *adj.* [from *sponge.*]

1. Soft and full of small interstitial holes.

The lungs are the most *spongy* part of the body, and therefore ablest to contract and dilate itself. *Bacon's Nat. History.*

A *spongy* excrescence groweth upon the roots of the laser-tree, and upon cedar, very white, light, and friable, called agarick. *Bacon's Natural History.*

The body of the tree being very *spongy* within, though hard without, they easily contrive into canoes. *More.*

Into earth's *spungy* veins the ocean sinks,
Those rivers to replenish which he drinks. *Denham.*

Return, unhappy swain!
The *spungy* clouds are fill'd with gath'ring rain. *Dryden.*

Her bones are all very *spongy*, and more remarkably those of a wild bird, which flies much, and long together. *Grew.*

2. Wet; drenched; soaked; full like a sponge.

When their drenched natures lie as in a death,
What cannot you and I perform upon
Th' unguarded Duncan? What not put upon
His *spungy* officers, who shall bear the guilt. *Shakesp.*

SPONK. *n. s.* A word in Edinburgh which denotes a match, or any thing dipt in sulphur that takes fire: as, any *sponks* will ye buy? Touchwood.

SPO'NSAL. *adj.* [*sponsalis*, Latin.] Relating to marriage.

SPO'NSION. *n. s.* [*sponsio*, Latin.] The act of becoming surety for another.

SPO'NSOR. *n. s.* [Latin.] A surety; one who makes a promise or gives security for another.

In the baptism of a male there ought to be two males and one woman, and in the baptism of a female child two women and one man; and these are called *sponsors* or sureties for their education in the true Christian faith. *Ayliffe's Parergon.*

The *sponsor* ought to be of the same station with the person to whom he becomes surety. *Broome.*

SPONTA'NEITY. *n. s.* [*spontaneitas*, school Lat. *spontaneité*, Fr. from *spontaneous.*] Voluntariness; willingness; accord uncompelled.

Necessity and *spontaneity* may sometimes meet together, so may *spontaneity* and liberty; but real necessity and true liberty can never. *Bramh. against Hobbs.*

Strict necessity they simple call;
It so binds the will, that things foreknown
By *spontaneity* not choice are done. *Dryden.*

SPONTA'NEOUS. *adj.* [*spontanée*, French; from *sponte*, Lat.] Voluntary; not compelled; acting without compulsion or restraint; acting of itself; acting of its own accord.

Many analogal motions in animals, though I cannot call them voluntary, yet I see them *spontaneous*: I have reason to conclude, that these are not simply mechanical. *Hale.*

They now came forth
Spontaneous; for within them spirit mov'd
Attendant on their lord. *Milton.*

While John for nine-pins does declare,
And Roger loves to pitch the bar,
Both legs and arms *spontaneous* move,
Which was the thing I meant to prove. *Prior.*

Begin with sense, of ev'ry art the soul,
Parts answering parts shall slide into a whole;
Spontaneous beauties all around advance,
Start ev'n from difficulty, strike from chance,
Nature shall join you, time shall make it grow. *Pope.*

SPONTA'NEOUSLY. *adv.* [from *spontaneous.*] Voluntarily; of its own accord.

This would be as impossible as that the lead of an edifice should naturally and *spontaneously* mount up to the roof, while lighter materials employ themselves beneath it. *Bentley.*

Whey turns *spontaneously* acid, and the curd into cheese as hard as a stone. *Arbuthnot on Aliments.*

SPONTA'NEOUSNESS. *n. s.* [from *spontaneous.*] Voluntariness; freedom of will; accord unforced.

The sagacities and instincts of brutes, the *spontaneousness* of many of their animal motions, are not explicable without supposing some active determinate power connexed to and inherent in their spirits, of a higher extraction than the bare natural modification of matter. *Hale's Origin of Mankind.*

SPOOL. *n. s.* [*spuhl*, German; *spohl*, Dutch.] A small piece of cane or reed, with a knot at each end; or a piece of wood turned in that form to wind yarn upon; a quill.

To SPOOM. *v. n.* [Probably from *spume*, or *foam*, as a ship driven with violence spumes, or raises a foam.]

When virtue *spooms* before a prosperous gale,
My heaving wishes help to fill the sail. *Dryden.*

SPOON. *n. s.* [*spaen*, Dutch; *spone*, Danish; *spoonn*, Islandick.] A concave vessel with a handle, used in eating liquids.

Would'st thou drown thyself,
Put but a little water in a *spoon*,
And it shall be as all the ocean,
Enough to stifle such a villain up. *Shakesp. King John.*

This is a devil, and no monster: I will leave him; I have no long *spoon*. *Shakesp. Tempest.*

Or o'er cold coffee trifle with the *spoon*,
Count the slow clock, and dine exact at noon. *Pope.*

SPO'ONBILL. *n. s.* [*spoon* and *bill.*] A bird.

The shoveller, or *spoonbill*; the former name the more proper, the end of the bill being broad like a shovel; but not concave like a spoon, but perfectly flat. *Grew's Musæum.*

Ducks and geese have such long broad bills to quaffer in water and mud; to which we may reckon the bill of the *spoonbill*. *Derham's Physico-Theology.*

SPO'ONFUL. *n. s.* [*spoon* and *full.*]

1. As much as is generally taken at once in a spoon. A medical spoonful is half an ounce.

Prescribe him, before he do use the receipt, that he take such a pill, or a *spoonful* of liquor. *Bacon.*

2. Any small quantity of liquid.

Surely the choice and measure of the materials of which the whole body is composed, and what we take daily by pounds, is at least of as much importance as of what we take seldom, and only by grains and *spoonfuls*. *Arbuthnot.*

SPO'ONMEAT. *n. s.* [*spoon* and *meat.*] Liquid food; nourishment taken with a spoon.

We prescribed a slender diet, allowing only *spoonmeats*. *Wise.*

Wretched
Are mortals born to sleep their lives away!
Go back to what thy infancy began,
Eat pap and *spoonmeat*; for thy gugaws cry,
Be sullen, and refuse the lullaby. *Dryden's Pers.*

Diet

Diet most upon *spoonmeats*, as veal, or cock-broths. *Harv.*

SPOO'NWORT, or *Scurvygrass. n. s.* See SCURVYGRASS.

To SPOON. *v. n.* In sea language, is when a ship being under sail in a storm cannot bear it, but is obliged to put right before the wind. *Bailey.*

SPORA'DICAL. *adj.* [σποραδικὸς; *sporadique*, French.]

A *sporadical* disease is an endemial disease, what in a particular season affects but few people. *Arbuthnot.*

SPORT. *n. s.* [*sport*, a make-game, Islandick.]

1. Play; diversion; game; frolick and tumultuous merriment.

Her *sports* were such as carried riches of knowledge upon the stream of delight. *Sidney.*

As flies to wanton boys, are we to th' gods;
They kill us for their *sport.* *Shakespeare's K. Lear.*

If I suspect without cause, why then make *sport* at me; then let me be your jest. *Shakespeare.*

When their hearts were merry, they said, call for Samson, that he may make us *sport*; and they called for him, and he made them *sport.* *Judg.* xvi. 25.

As a mad-man who casteth fire-brands, arrows and death; so is the man that deceiveth his neighbour, and saith, am not I in *sport?* *Prov.* xxvi. 19.

The discourse of fools is irksome, and their *sport* is in the wantonness of sin. *Ecclus* xxvii. 13.

2. Mock; contemptuous mirth.

They had his messengers in derision and made a *sport* of his prophets. 1 *Esdr.* i. 51.

To make *sport* with his word, and to endeavour to render it ridiculous, by turning that holy book into raillery, is a direct affront to God. *Tillotson's Sermons.*

3. That with which one plays.

Each on his rock transfix'd, the *sport* and prey
Of wrecking whirlwinds. *Milton.*

Commit not thy prophetick mind
To flitting leaves, the *sport* of every wind,
Lest they disperse in air. *Dryden.*

4. Play; idle gingle.

An author who should introduce such a *sport* of words upon our stage, would meet with small applause. *Broome.*

5. Diversion of the field, as of fowling, hunting, fishing.

Now for our mountain *sport*, up to yon hill,
Your legs are young. *Shakespeare's Cymbeline.*

The king, who was excessively affected to hunting, and the *sports* of the field, had a great desire to make a great park for red as well as fallow deer, between Richmond and Hampton court. *Clarendon.*

To SPORT. *v. a.* [from the noun.]

1. To divert; to make merry.

The poor man wept and bled, cried and prayed, while they *sported* themselves in his pain, and delighted in his prayers as the argument of their victory. *Sidney.*

Away with him, and let her *sport* herself
With that she's big with. *Shakespeare's Winter's Tale.*

Against whom do ye *sport* yourselves? against whom make ye a wide mouth, and draw out the tongue? *Isa.* lvii. 4.

What pretty stories these are for a man of his seriousness to *sport* himself withal! *Atterbury.*

Let such writers go on at their dearest peril, and *sport* themselves in their own deceivings. *Watts.*

2. To represent by any kind of play.

Now *sporting* on thy lyre the love of youth,
Now virtuous age and venerable truth;
Expressing justly Sappho's wanton art
Of odes, and Pindar's more majestick part. *Dryden.*

To SPORT. *v. n.*

1. To play; to frolick; to game; to wanton.

They *sporting* with quick glance,
Shew to the sun their wav'd coats dropt with gold. *Milton.*

Larissa, as she *sported* at this play, was drowned in the river Peneus. *Broome's Notes on the Odyssey.*

2. To trifle.

If any man turn religion into raillery, by bold jests, he renders himself ridiculous, because he *sports* with his own life. *Till.*

SPO'RTFUL. *adj.* [*sport* and *full.*] Merry; frolick; wanton; ludicrous; done in jest.

How with a *sportful* malice it was follow'd,
May rather pluck on laughter than revenge. *Shakespeare.*

His highness, even in such a slight and *sportful* damage, had a noble sense of just dealing. *Wotton.*

Down he alights among the *sportful* herd
Of those four-footed kinds. *Milton.*

Behold your own Ascanius, while he said,
He drew his glitt'ring helmet from his head,
In which the youth to *sportful* arms he led. *Dryden.*

They are no *sportful* productions of the soil, but did once belong to real and living fishes; seeing each of them doth exactly resemble some other shell on the sea-shore. *Bentley.*

A catalogue of this may be had in Albericus Gentilis; which, because it is too *sportful*, I forbear to mention. *Baker.*

SPORTFULLY. *adv.* [from *sportful.*] Wantonly; merrily.

SPO'RTFULNESS. *n. s.* [from *sportful.*] Wantonness; play; merriment; frolick.

The otter got out of the river, and inweeded himself so, as the ladies lost the further marking of his *sportfulness.* *Sidney.*

SPO'RTIVE. *adj.* [from *sport.*] Gay; merry; frolick; wanton; playful; ludicrous.

I am not in a *sportive* humour now;
Tell me, and dally not, where is the money? *Shakespeare.*

Is it I
That drive thee from the *sportive* court, where thou
Was't shot at with fair eyes, to be the mark
Of smoky muskets? *Shakespeare's All's well that ends well.*

While thus the constant pair alternate said,
Joyful above them and around them play'd
Angels and *sportive* loves, a numerous crowd,
Smiling they clapt their wings, and low they bow'd. *Prior.*

We must not hope wholly to change their original tempers, nor make the gay, pensive and grave; nor the melancholy, *sportive*, without spoiling them. *Locke.*

No wonder savages or subjects slain,
Were equal crimes in a despotick reign;
Both doom'd alike for *sportive* tyrants bled,
But subjects starv'd while savages were fed. *Pope.*

SPO'RTIVENESS. *n. s.* [from *sportive.*] Gaiety; play; wantonness.

Shall I conclude her to be simple, that has her time to begin, or refuse *sportiveness* as freely as I have? *Walton's Angler.*

SPO'RTSMAN. *n. s.* [*sport* and *man.*] One who pursues the recreations of the field.

Manilius lets us know the pagan hunters had Meleager for their patron, as the Christians have their St. Hubert: he speaks of the constellation which makes a good *sportsman.* *Addison.*

SPO'RTULE. *n. s.* [*sportule*, French; *sportula*, Latin.] An alms; a dole.

The bishops, who consecrated the ground, had a spill or *sportule* from the credulous laity. *Ayliffe's Parergon.*

SPOT. *n. s.* [*spette*, Danish; *spotte*, Flemish.]

1. A blot; a mark made by discoloration.

This three years day, these eyes, though clear
To outward view of blemish or of *spot*,
Bereft of sight, their seeing have forgot. *Milton.*

A long series of ancestors shews the native lustre with advantage; but if he any way degenerate from his line, the least *spot* is visible on ermine. *Dryden.*

2. A taint; a disgrace; a reproach.

3. I know not well the meaning of *spot* in this place, unless it be a scandalous woman; a disgrace to her sex.

Let him take thee,
And hoist thee up to the shouting plebeians;
Follow his chariot, like the greatest *spot*
Of all thy sex. *Shakespeare's Antony and Cleopatra.*

4. A small extent of place.

That *spot* to which I point is paradise,
Adam's abode, those lofty shades his bow'r. *Milton.*

He, who with Plato, shall place beatitude in the knowledge of God, will have his thoughts raised to other contemplations than those who looked not beyond this *spot* of earth, and those perishing things in it. *Locke.*

About one of these breathing passages is a *spot* of myrtles, that flourish within the steam of these vapours. *Addison.*

Abdallah converted the whole mountain into a kind of garden, and covered every part of it with plantations or *spots* of flowers. *The Guardian.*

He that could make two ears of corn grow upon a *spot* of ground where only one grew before, would deserve better of mankind than the whole race of politicians. *Gulliver.*

5. Any particular place.

I would be busy in the world, and learn,
Not like a coarse and useless dunghill weed,
Fix'd to one *spot*, and rot just as I grow. *Otway.*

As in this grove I took my last farewel,
As on this very *spot* of earth I fell,
So she my prey becomes ev'n here. *Dryden.*

Here Adrian fell: upon that fatal *spot*
Our brother died. *Granville.*

6. *Upon the* SPOT. Immediately; without changing place. [*Sur le champ.*]

The lion did not chop him up immediately *upon the spot*; and yet he was resolved he should not escape. *L'Estrange.*

It was determined *upon the spot*, according as the oratory on either side prevailed. *Swift.*

To SPOT. *v. a.* [from the noun.]

1. To mark with discolorations; to maculate.

They are polluted off'rings, more abhorr'd
Than *spotted* livers in the sacrifice. *Shakespeare.*

Have you not seen a handkerchief,
Spotted with strawberries in your wife's hand? *Shakespeare.*

But serpents now more amity maintain;
From *spotted* skins the leopard does refrain:
No weaker lion's by a stronger slain. *Tate's Juvenal.*

I counted the patches on both sides, and found the tory patches to be about twenty stronger than the whig; but next morning the whole puppet-show was filled with faces *spotted* after the whiggish manner. *Addison's Spectator.*

2. To corrupt; to disgrace; to taint.

This vow receive, this vow of God's maintain,
My virgin life, no *spotted* thoughts shall stain. *Sidney.*

The people of Armenia have retained the christian faith, from the time of the apostles; but at this day it is *spotted* with many absurdities. *Abbot's Descript. of the World.*

SPO'TLESS. *adj.* [from *spot.*]

1. Free from spots.
2. Free from reproach or impurity; immaculate; pure; untainted.

So much fairer
And *spotless* shall mine innocence arise,
When the king knows my truth. *Shakespeare.*

I dare my life lay down, that the queen is *spotless*
In th' eyes of heaven. *Shakespeare's Winter's Tale.*

You grac'd the sev'ral parts of life,
A *spotless* virgin, and a faultless wife. *Waller.*

We sometimes wish that it had been our lot to live and converse with Christ, to hear his divine discourses, and to observe his *spotless* behaviour; and we please ourselves perhaps with thinking, how ready a reception we should have given to him and his doctrine. *Atterbury.*

Eternal sunshine of the *spotless* mind,
Each pray'r accepted, and each wish resign'd. *Pope.*

SPO'TTER. *n. s.* [from *spot.*] One that spots; one that maculates.

SPO'TTY. *adj.* [from *spot.*] Full of spots; maculated.

The moon whose orb
Through optick glass the Tuscan artist views
In Valombrosa to descry new lands,
Rivers or mountains on her *spotty* globe. *Milton.*

SPOU'SAL. *adj.* [from *spouse.*] Nuptial; matrimonial; conjugal; connubial; bridal.

There shall we consummate our *spousal* rites. *Shakespeare.*

Hope's chast kiss wrongs no more joy's maidenhead,
Than *spousal* rites prejudice the marriage bed. *Crashaw.*

This other in her prime of love,
Spousal embraces vitiated with gold. *Milton.*

Sleep'st thou, careless of the nuptial day?
Thy *spousal* ornament neglected lies;
Arise, prepare the bridal train, arise. *Pope's Odyssey.*

SPOU'SAL. *n. s.* [*espousailles*, Fr. *sponsalia*, Latin.] Marriage; nuptials.

As man and wife, being two, are one in love,
So be there 'twixt your kingdoms such a *spousal*,
That never may ill office, or fell jealousy
Thrust in between the paction of these kingdoms,
To make divorce of their incorporate league. *Shakespeare.*

The amorous bird of night
Sung *spousal*, and bid haste the ev'ning star,
On his hill top to light the bridal lamp. *Milton.*

The *spousals* of Hippolita the queen,
What tilts and tourneys at the feast were seen. *Dryden.*

Ætherial musick did her death prepare,
Like joyful sounds of *spousals* in the air:
A radiant light did her crown'd temples gild. *Dryden.*

SPOUSE. *n. s.* [*sponsa*, *sponsus*, Latin; *espouse*, French.] One joined in marriage; a husband or wife.

She is of good esteem;
Beside so qualified as may beseem
The *spouse* of any noble gentleman. *Shakespeare.*

At once farewel, O faithful *spouse!* they said;
At once th'encroaching rhinds their closing lips invade. *Dryd.*

SPOU'SED. *adj.* [from the noun.] Wedded; espoused; joined together as in matrimony.

They led the vine
To wed her elm; she *spous'd* about him twins
Her marriageable arms. *Milton.*

SPOU'SELESS. *adj.* [from *spouse.*] Wanting a husband or wife.

To tempt the *spouseless* queen with am'rous wiles,
Resort the nobles from the neigh'bring isles. *Pope.*

SPOUT. *n. s.* [from *spuyt*, Dutch.]

1. A pipe, or mouth of a pipe or vessel out of which any thing is poured.

She gasping to begin some speech, her eyes
Became two *spouts.* *Shakespeare's Winter's Tale.*

In whales that breathe, lest the water should get unto the lungs, an ejection thereof is contrived by a fistula or *spout* at the head. *Brown's Vulgar Errours.*

If you chance it to lack,
Be it claret or sack,
I'll make this snout
To deal it about,
Or this to run out,
As it were from a *spout.* *Ben. Johnson.*

As waters did in storms, now pitch runs out,
As lead, when a fir'd church becomes one *spout.* *Donne.*

In Gaza they couch vessels of earth in their walls to gather the wind from the top, and to pass it down in *spouts* into rooms. *Bacon.*

Let the water be fed by some higher than the pool, and delivered into it by fair *spouts*, and then discharged by some equality of bores that it stay little. *Bacon.*

In this single cathedral the very *spouts* are loaded with ornaments. *Addison on Italy.*

From silver *spouts* the grateful liquors glide,
And China's earth receives the smoking tide. *Pope.*

2. Water falling in a body; a cataract, such as is seen in the hot climates when clouds sometimes discharge all their water at once.

Not the dreadful *spout*,
Which shipmen do the hurricano call,
Constring'd in mass by the almighty sun,
Shall dizzy with more clamour Neptune's ear
In his descent, than shall my prompted sword
Falling on Diomede. *Shakespeare's Troilus and Cressida.*

The force of these motions pressing more in some places than in others, there would fall not showers, but great *spouts* or cascades of water. *Burnet's Theory of the Earth.*

To SPOUT. *v. a.* [from the noun.] To pour with violence, or in a collected body as from a spout.

We will bear home that lusty blood again,
Which here we came to *spout* against your town. *Shakesp.*

I intend two fountains, the one that sprinkleth or *spouteth* water, the other a fair receipt of water. *Bacon.*

She swims in blood, and blood does *spouting* throw
To heav'n, that heav'n mens cruelties might know. *Waller.*

Next on his belly floats the mighty whale;
He twists his back, and rears his threatning tail:
He *spouts* the tide. *Creech.*

To SPOUT. *v. n.* To issue as from a spout.

They laid them down hard by the murmuring musick of certain waters, which *spouted* out of the side of the hills. *Sidney.*

No hands cou'd force it thence, so fixt it stood,
Till out it rush'd, expell'd by streams of *spouting* blood. *Dryd.*

It *spouts* up out of deep wells, and flies forth at the tops of them, upon the face of the ground. *Woodward.*

All the glittering hill
Is bright with *spouting* rills. *Thomson's Autumn.*

To SPRAIN. *v. a.* [Corrupted from *strain.*] To stretch the ligaments of a joint without dislocation of the bone.

Should the big last extend the shoe too wide,
The sudden turn may stretch the swelling vein,
Thy cracking joint unhinge, or ancle *sprain.* *Gay.*

SPRAIN. *n. s.* [from the verb.] Extension of ligaments without dislocation of the joint.

I was in pain, and thought it was with some *sprain* at tennis. *Temple.*

SPRAINTS. *n. s.* The dung of an otter. *Dict.*

SPRANG. The preterite of *spring.*

Mankind *sprang* from one common original; whence this tradition would be universally diffused. *Tillotson.*

SPRAT. *n. s.* [*sprot*, Dutch.] A small sea fish.

So oft in feasts with costly changes clad,
To crammed maws a *sprat* new stomach brings. *Sidney.*

All-saints do lay for porke and sowse,
For *sprats* and spurlings for their house *Tusser.*

Of round fish there are brit, *sprat*, barn, smelts. *Carew.*

To SPRAWL. *v. n.* [*spradle*, Danish; *spartelen*, Dutch.]

1. To struggle as in the convulsions of death.

Hang the child, that he may see it *sprawl*;
A sight to vex the father's soul. *Shakespeare.*

Some lie *sprawling* on the ground,
With many a gash and bloody wound. *Hudibras.*

2. To tumble with agitation and contortion of the limbs.

The birds were not fledged; but upon *sprawling* and struggling to get clear of the flame, down they tumbled. *L'Estrange.*

Telamon hap'd to meet
A rising root that held his fasten'd feet;
So down he fell, whom *sprawling* on the ground,
His brother from the wooden gyves unbound. *Dryden.*

Hence, long before the child can crawl,
He learns to kick, and wince, and *sprawl.* *Prior.*

Did the stars do this feat once only, which gave beginning to human race? who were there then in the world, to observe the births of those first men, and calculate their nativities, as they *sprawled* out of ditches? *Bentley.*

He ran, he leapt into a flood,
There *sprawl'd* a while, and scarce got out,
All cover'd o'er with slime. *Swift.*

SPRAY. *n. s.* [Of the same race with *sprit* and *sprout.*]

1. The extremity of a branch.

At sight whereof each bird that sits on *spray*,
And every beast that to his den was fled,
Come forth afresh out of their late dismay,
And to the light lift up their drooping head. *Hubberd's Tale.*

Thus droops this lofty pine, and hangs his *sprays*;
Thus Eleanor's pride dies in her younger days. *Shakespeare.*

In hewing Rutland, when his leaves put forth,
Clifford set his murth'ring knife to the root,
From whence that tender *spray* did sweetly spring. *Shakesp.*

The wind that whistles through the *sprays*,
Maintains the consort of the song;
And hidden birds with native lays,
The golden sleep prolong. *Dryden.*

2. The

2. The foam of the sea, commonly written *spry*.

Winds raise some of the salt with the *spray*. *Arbuthnot.*

To SPREAD. *v. a.* [ꞅꝑꞃeꝺan, Saxon; *spreyden*, Dutch.]

1. To extend; to expand; to make to cover or fill a larger space than before.

He bought a field where he had *spread* his tent. *Gen.* xxxiii.

Rizpah *spread* sackloth for her upon the rock. 2 *Sam.* xxi.

Make the trees more tall, more *spread*, and more hasty than they use to be. *Bacon's Natural History.*

Silver *spread* into plates is brought from Tarshish. *Jer.* x.

2. To cover by extension.

Her cheeks their freshness lose and wonted grace,
And an unusual paleness *spreads* her face. *Granville.*

3. To cover over.

The workman melteth a graven image, and the goldsmith *spreadeth* it over with gold. *Isa.* xl. 19.

4. To stretch; to extend.

Spread o'er the silver waves thy golden hair. *Shakespeare.*

He arose from kneeling, with his hands *spread* up to heaven, and he blessed the congregation. 1 *Kings* viii. 54.

The stately trees fast *spread* their branches. *Milton.*

Deep in a rich alcove the prince was laid,
Fast by his side Pisistratus lay *spread*,
In age his equal, on a splendid bed. *Pope.*

5. To publish; to divulge; to disseminate.

They, when departed, *spread* abroad his fame in all that country. *Matth.* ix. 31.

6. To emit as effluvia or emanations; to diffuse.

Their course thro' thickest constellations held,
They *spread* their bane. *Milton.*

To SPREAD. *v. n.* To extend or expand itself.

Can any understand the *spreadings* of the clouds, or the noise of his tabernacle? *Job* xxxvi. 29.

The princes of Germany had but a dull fear of the greatness of Spain, upon a general apprehension only of their *spreading* and ambitious designs. *Bacon.*

Plants, if they *spread* much, are seldom tall. *Bacon.*

Great Pan, who wont to chase the fair,
And lov'd the *spreading* oak, was there. *Addison's Cato.*

The valley opened at the farther end *spreading* forth into an immense ocean. *Addison.*

SPREAD. *n. s.* [from the verb.]

1. Extent; compass.

I have got a fine *spread* of improveable lands, and am already ploughing up some, fencing others. *Addison.*

2. Expansion of parts.

No flower hath that *spread* of the woodbind. *Bacon.*

SPREA'DER. *n. s.* [from *spread*.]

1. One that spreads.

By conforming ourselves we should be *spreaders* of a worse infection than any we are likely to draw from Papists by our conformity with them in ceremonies. *Hooker.*

2. Publisher; divulger; disseminator.

If it be a mistake, I desire I may not be accused for a *spreader* of false news. *Swift.*

SPRENT. *part.* [from *sprene*, to sprinkle, ꞅꝑꞃenᵹan, ꞅꝑꞃenan, Saxon; *sprengen*, Dutch.] Sprinkled. Obsolete.

O lips, that kiss'd that hand, with my tears *sprent*. *Sidney.*

SPRIG. *n. s.* [*ysbrig*, Welsh, so *Davies*: but it is probably of the same race with *spring*.] A small branch; a spray.

The substance is true ivy, after it is taken down, the friends of the family are desirous to have some *sprig* to keep. *Bacon.*

Our chilling climate hardly bears
A *sprig* of bays in fifty years;
While ev'ry fool his claim alledges,
As if it grew in common hedges. *Swift.*

SPRIG *Chrystal. n. s.*

In perpendicular fissures, chrystal is found in form of an hexangular column, adhering at one end to the stone, and near the other lessening gradually, till it terminates in a point: this is called by lapidaries *sprig* or rock *chrystal*. *Woodward.*

SPRI'GGY. *adj.* [from *sprig*.] Full of small branches.

SPRIGHT. *n. s.* [Contraction of *spirit*, *spiritus*, Latin: it was anciently written *sprete* or *spryte*; and *spirit*, as now written, was long considered in verse as a monosyllable: this word should therefore be spelled *sprite*, and its derivatives *spritely*, *spriteful*; but custom has determined otherwise.]

1. Spirit; shade; soul; incorporeal agent.

She doth display
The gate with pearls and rubies richly dight,
Through which her words so wise do make their way,
To bear the message of her *spright*. *Spenser.*

Forth he called out of deep darkness dread,
Legions of *sprights*, the which like little flies,
Flutt'ring about his ever damned head,
Await whereto their service he applies. *Fairy Queen.*

While with heav'nly charity she spoke,
A streaming blaze the silent shadows broke;
The birds obscene to forests wing'd their flight,
And gaping graves received the guilty *spright*. *Dryden.*

Of these am I who thy protection claim,
A watchful *sprite*. *Pope.*

2. Walking spirit; apparition.

The ideas of goblins and *sprights* have no more to do with darkness than light; yet let but a foolish maid inculcate these often on the mind of a child, possibly he shall never be able to separate them again. *Locke.*

3. Power which gives cheerfulness or courage.

O chastity, the chief of heav'nly lights,
Which mak'st us most immortal shape to wear,
Hold thou my heart, establish thou my *sprights*:
To only thee my constant course I bear,
Till spotless soul unto thy bosom fly,
Such life to lead, such death I vow to die. *Sidney.*

4. An arrow.

We had in use for sea fight short arrows called *sprights*, without any other heads save wood sharpened; which were discharged out of muskets, and would pierce through the sides of ships where a bullet would not. *Bacon's Natural History.*

To SPRIGHT. *v. a.* To haunt as a spright. A ludicrous use.

I am *sprighted* with a fool. *Shakespeare's Cymbeline.*

SPRI'GHTFUL. *adj.* [*spright* and *full*.] Lively; brisk; gay; vigorous.

The spirit of the time shall teach me speed.—
—Spoke like a *sprightful* noble gentleman. *Shakespeare.*

Happy my eyes when they behold thy face:
My heavy heart will leave its doleful beating,
At sight of thee, and bound with *sprightful* joys. *Otway.*

SPRI'GHTFULLY. *adv.* [from *sprightful*.] Briskly; vigorously.

Norfolk, *sprightfully* and bold,
Stays but the summons of the appellant's trumpet. *Shakesp.*

SPRI'GHTLINESS. *n. s.* [from *sprightly*.] Liveliness; briskness; vigour; gaiety; vivacity.

The soul is clogged when she acts in conjunction with a companion so heavy; but in dreams, observe with what a *sprightliness* and alacrity does she exert herself. *Addison.*

SPRI'GHTLY. *adj.* [from *spright*.] Gay; brisk; lively; vigorous; airy; vivacious.

Produce the wine that makes us bold,
And *sprightly* wit and love inspires. *Dryden.*

When now the *sprightly* trumpet, from afar,
Had giv'n the signal of approaching war. *Dryden.*

Each morn they wak'd me with a *sprightly* lay:
Of opening heav'n they sung, and gladsome day. *Prior.*

The *sprightly* Sylvia trips along the green;
She runs, but hopes she does not run unseen. *Pope.*

To SPRING. *v. n.* Preterite *sprung* or *sprang*, anciently *sprong*. [ꞅꝑꞃinᵹan, Sax. *springen*, Dutch.]

1. To arise out of the ground and grow by vegetative power.

All blest secrets,
All you unpublish'd virtues of the earth,
Spring with my tears; be aidant and remediate
In the good man's distress. *Shakespeare.*

To his musick, plants and flowers
Ever *sprung*, as sun and showers
There had made a lasting spring. *Shakespeare's Henry* VIII.

To satisfy the desolate ground, and cause the bud of the tender herb to *spring* forth. *Job* xxxviii. 27.

Other fell on good ground, and did yield fruit that *sprang* up and encreased. *Mark* iv. 8.

Tell me, in what happy fields
The thistle *springs*, to which the lily yields? *Pope.*

2. To begin to grow.

That the nipples should be made with such perforations as to admit passage to the milk, when drawn, otherwise to retain it; and the teeth of the young not *sprung*, are effects of providence. *Ray.*

3. To proceed as from seed.

Ye shall eat this year such things as grow of themselves; and in the second year that which *springeth* of the same. 2 *Kings.*

Much more good of sin shall *spring*. *Milton.*

4. To come into existence; to issue forth.

Had'st thou sway'd as kings should do,
Giving no ground unto the house of York,
They never then had *sprung* like summer flies. *Shakespeare.*

Ev'n thought meets thought, ere from the lips it part,
And each warm wish *springs* mutual from the heart. *Pope.*

5. To arise; to appear.

When the day began to *spring*, they let her go. *Judges.*

To them which sat in the region and shadow of death, light is *sprung* up. *Matth.* iv. 16.

6. To issue with effect or force.

Swift fly the years, and rise th' expected morn;
Oh *spring* to light: auspicious babe be born. *Pope.*

7. To proceed as from ancestors.

How youngly he began to serve his country,
How long continued; and what stock he *springs* of;
The noble house of Marcius. *Shakespeare's Coriolanus.*

Our Lord *sprang* out of Judea. *Heb.* vii. 14.

All these
Shall, like the brethren *sprung* of dragon's teeth,
Ruin each other, and he fall amongst 'em. *Ben. Johnson.*

Heroes of old, by rapine, and by spoil,
In search of fame did all the world embroil;

Thus

Thus to their gods, each then ally'd his name,
This *ſprang* from Jove, and that from Titan came. *Granv.*

8. To proceed as from a ground, cauſe, or reaſon.

They found new hope to ſpring
Out of deſpair. *Milton.*

Some have been deceived into an opinion, that the inheritance of rule over men, and property in things, *ſprang* from the ſame original, and were to deſcend by the ſame rules. *Locke.*

Do not blaſt my *ſpringing* hopes
Which thy kind hand has planted in my ſoul. *Rowe.*

9. To grow; to thrive.

What makes all this but Jupiter the king,
At whoſe command we periſh and we *ſpring:*
Then 'tis our beſt, ſince thus ordain'd to die,
To make a virtue of neceſſity. *Dryden's Knight's Tale.*

10. To bound; to leap; to jump.

Some ſtrange commotion
Is in his brain; he bites his lip, and ſtarts;
Stops on a ſudden, looks upon the ground,
Then lays his finger on his temple; ſtrait
Springs out into faſt gait, then ſtops again. *Shak. H.* VIII.

I *ſprang* not more in joy at firſt hearing he was a man child, than now in firſt ſeeing he had proved himſelf a man. *Shakeſ.*

He called for a light, and *ſprang* in and fell before Paul. *Acts.*

When heav'n was nam'd, they loos'd their hold again;
Then *ſprung* ſhe forth, they follow'd her amain. *Dryden.*

Afraid to ſleep;
Her blood all fever'd, with a furious leap
She *ſprung* from bed. *Dryden.*

Nor lies ſhe long; but as her fates ordain,
Springs up to life, and freſh to ſecond pain,
Is ſav'd to-day, to-morrow to be ſlain. *Dryden.*

See, aw'd by heaven, the blooming Hebrew flies
Her artful tongue, and more perſuaſive eyes;
And *ſpringing* from her diſappointed arms,
Prefers a dungeon to forbidden charms. *Blackmore.*

The mountain ſtag, that *ſprings*
From height to height, and bounds along the plains,
Nor has a maſter to reſtrain his courſe;
That mountain ſtag would Vanoe rather be,
Than be a ſlave. *Philips's Briton.*

11. To fly with elaſtick power.

A link of horſehair, that will eaſily ſlip, faſten to the end of the ſtick that *ſprings.* *Mortimer's Husbandry.*

12. To riſe from a covert.

My doors are hateful to my eyes,
Fill'd and damm'd up with gaping creditors,
Watchful as fowlers when their game will *ſpring.* *Otway.*

A covey of partridges *ſpringing* in our front, put our infantry in diſorder. *Addiſon.*

13. To iſſue from a fountain.

Iſrael's ſervants digged in the valley, and found a well of *ſpringing* water. *Gen.* xxvi. 19.

Let the wide world his praiſes ſing,
Where Tagus and Euphrates *ſpring;*
And from the Danube's froſty banks to thoſe
Where from an unknown head great Nilus flows. *Roſcomm.*

14. To proceed as from a ſource.

Fly, fly, prophane fogs! far hence fly away,
Taint not the pure ſtreams of the *ſpringing* day
With your dull influence: 'tis for you
To ſit and ſcoule upon night's heavy brow. *Craſhaw.*

15. To ſhoot; to iſſue with ſpeed and violence.

Then ſhook the ſacred ſhrine, and ſudden light
Sprung thro' the vaulted roof, and made the temple bright:
The pow'r, behold! the pow'r in glory ſhone,
By her bent bow and her keen arrows known. *Dryden.*

The friendly gods a *ſpringing* gale enlarg'd,
The fleet ſwift tilting o'er the ſurges flew,
Till Grecian cliffs appeared. *Pope.*

To Spring. *v. a.*

1. To ſtart; to rouſe game.

Thus I reclaim'd my buzzard love to fly
At what, and when, and how, and where I choſe:
Now negligent of ſport I lie;
And now, as other fawkners uſe,
I *ſpring* a miſtreſs, ſwear, write, ſigh, and dye,
And the game kill'd, or loſt, go talk or lie. *Donne.*

That *ſprung* the game you were to ſet,
Before you had time to draw the net. *Hudibras.*

A large cock-pheaſant he *ſprung* in one of the neighbouring woods. *Addiſon's Spectator.*

Here I uſe a great deal of diligence before I can *ſpring* any thing; whereas in town, whilſt I am following one character, I am croſſed by another, that they puzzle the chace. *Addiſon.*

See how the well-taught pointer leads the way!
The ſcent grows warm; he ſtops, he *ſprings* the prey. *Gay.*

2. To produce to light.

The nurſe, ſurpriz'd with fright,
Starts and leaves her bed, and *ſprings* a light. *Dryden.*

Thus man by his own ſtrength to heav'n would ſoar,
And would not be oblig'd to God for more:
Vain, wretched creature, how art thou miſled,
To think thy wit theſe godlike notions bred!
Theſe truths are not the product of thy mind,
But dropt from heaven, and of a nobler kind:
Reveal'd religion firſt inform'd thy ſight,
And reaſon ſaw not, 'till faith *ſprung* the light. *Dryden.*

He that has ſuch a burning zeal, and *ſprings* ſuch mighty diſcoveries, muſt needs be an admirable patriot. *Collier.*

3. To make by ſtarting a plank.

People diſcharge themſelves of burdenſome reflections, as of the cargo of a ſhip that has *ſprung* a leak. *L'Eſtrange.*

No more accuſe thy pen; but charge the crime
On native ſloth, and negligence of time:
Beware the publick laughter of the town,
Thou *ſpring'ſt* a leak already in thy crown. *Dryden.*

Whether ſhe *ſprung* a leak, I cannot find,
Or whether ſhe was overſet with wind,
But down at once with all her crew ſhe went. *Dryden.*

4. To diſcharge a mine.

Our miners diſcovered ſeveral of the enemies mines, who have *ſprung* divers others which did little execution. *Tatler.*

I *ſprung* a mine, whereby the whole neſt was overthrown. *Addiſon's Spectator.*

5. To contrive as a ſudden expedient; to offer unexpectedly.

The friends to the cauſe *ſprang* a new project, and it was advertiſed that the criſis could not appear 'till the ladies had ſhewn their zeal againſt the pretender. *Swift.*

6. To produce haſtily.

7. To paſs by leaping. A barbarous uſe.

Unbeſeeming ſkill
To *ſpring* the fence, to rein the prancing ſteed. *Thomſon.*

Spring. *n. ſ.* [from the verb.]

1. The ſeaſon in which plants ſpring and vegetate; the vernal ſeaſon.

Orpheus with his lute made trees,
And the mountain-tops, that freeze,
Bow themſelves when he did ſing:
To his muſick, plants and flowers
Ever ſprung, as ſun and ſhowers
There had made a laſting *Spring.* *Shakeſp. Hen.* VIII.

The *Spring* viſiteth not theſe quarters ſo timely as the eaſtern parts. *Carew.*

Come, gentle *Spring,* ethereal mildneſs come,
And from the boſom of yon dropping cloud
Upon our plains deſcend. *Thomſon's Spring.*

2. An elaſtick body; a body which when diſtorted has the power of reſtoring itſelf to its former ſtate.

This may be better performed by the ſtrength of ſome ſuch *ſpring* as is uſed in watches: this *ſpring* may be applied to one wheel, which ſhall give an equal motion to both the wings. *Wilkins's Math. Magic.*

The *ſpring* muſt be made of good ſteel, well tempered; and the wider the two ends of the *ſpring* ſtand aſunder, the milder it throws the chape of the vice open. *Moxon's Mech. Exer.*

He that was ſharp-ſighted enough to ſee the configuration of the minute particles of the *ſpring* of a clock, and upon what peculiar impulſe its elaſtick motion depends, would no doubt diſcover ſomething very admirable. *Locke.*

3. Elaſtick force.

Heav'ns, what a *ſpring* was in his arm, to throw!
How high he held his ſhield, and roſe at ev'ry blow! *Dryd.*

Bodies which are abſolutely hard, or ſo ſoft as to be void of elaſticity, will not rebound from one another: impenetrability makes them only ſtop. If two equal bodies meet directly *in vacuo,* they will by the laws of motion ſtop where they meet, loſe their motion, and remain in reſt, unleſs they be elaſtick, and receive new motion from their *ſpring.* *Newton.*

The ſoul is gathered within herſelf, and recovers that *ſpring* which is weakened, when ſhe operates more in concert with the body. *Addiſon.*

In adult perſons, when the fibres cannot any more yield, they muſt break, or loſe their *ſpring.* *Arbuthnot.*

4. Any active power; any cauſe by which motion is produced or propagated.

My heart ſinks in me while I hear him ſpeak,
And every ſlacken'd fibre drops its hold,
Like nature letting down the *ſprings* of life;
So much the name of father awes me ſtill. *Dryden.*

Nature is the ſame, and man is the ſame; has the ſame affections and paſſions, and the ſame *ſprings* that give them motion. *Rymer.*

Our author ſhuns by vulgar *ſprings* to move
The hero's glory, or the virgin's love. *Pope's Prol. to Cato.*

5. A leap; a bound; a jump; a violent effort; a ſudden ſtruggle.

The pris'ner with a *ſpring* from priſon broke:
Then ſtretch'd his feather'd fans with all his might,
And to the neighb'ring maple wing'd his flight. *Dryden.*

With what a *ſpring* his furious ſoul broke looſe,
And left the limbs ſtill quivering on the ground! *Add. Cato.*

6. A

6. A leak; a ſtart of plank.

Each petty hand
Can ſteer a ſhip becalm'd; but he that will
Govern, and carry her to her ends, muſt know
His tides, his currents; how to ſhift his ſails,
Where her *ſprings* are, her leaks, and how to ſtop 'em.
Ben. Johnſon's Catiline.

7. A fountain; an iſſue of water from the earth.

Now ſtop thy *ſprings*; my ſea ſhall ſuck them dry,
And ſwell ſo much the higher by their ebb. *Shakeſp. H. VI.*

Springs on the tops of hills paſs through a great deal of pure earth, with leſs mixture of other waters. *Bacon's Nat. Hiſt.*

When in th' effects ſhe doth the cauſes know,
And ſeeing the ſtream, thinks where the *ſpring* doth riſe;
And ſeeing the branch, conceives the root below:
Theſe things ſhe views without the body's eyes. *Davies.*

He adds the running *ſprings* and ſtanding lakes,
And bounding banks for winding rivers makes. *Dryden.*

Nile hears him knocking at his ſevenfold gates,
And ſeeks his hidden *ſpring*, and fears his nephews fates. *Dry.*

He bathed himſelf in cold *ſpring* water in the midſt of Winter. *Locke.*

The water that falls down from the clouds, ſinking into beds of rock or clay, breaks out in *ſprings*, commonly at the bottom of hilly ground. *Locke.*

8. A ſource; that by which any thing is ſupplied.

To that great ſpring, which doth great kingdoms move,
The ſacred *ſpring*, whence right and honour ſtreams;
Diſtilling virtue, ſhedding peace and love
In every place, as Cynthia ſheds her beams. *Davies.*

I move, I ſee, I ſpeak, diſcourſe, and know,
Though now I am, I was not always ſo:
Then that from which I was, muſt be before,
Whom, as my *ſpring* of being, I adore. *Dryden.*

Rolling down through ſo many barbarous ages, from the *ſpring* of Virgil, it bears along with it the filth of the Goths and Vandals. *Dryden.*

He has a ſecret *ſpring* of ſpiritual joy, and the continual feaſt of a good conſcience within, that forbids him to be miſerable. *Bentley.*

9. Riſe; beginning.

About the *ſpring* of the day Samuel called Saul to the top of the houſe. *1 Sa.* ix. 26.

10. Courſe; original.

The firſt *ſprings* of great events, like thoſe of great rivers, are often mean and little. *Swift.*

SPRING. *adv.* [from the noun.] With elaſtick vigour.

Before the bull ſhe pictur'd winged love,
With his young brother ſport, light fluttering
Upon the waves, as each had been a dove;
The one his bow and ſhafts, the other *ſpring*
A burning tead about his head did move,
As in their ſire's new love both triumphing. *Spenſer.*

SPRI'NGAL. *n. ſ.* A youth. *Spenſer.*

SPRINGE. *n. ſ.* [from *ſpring.*] A gin; a nooſe which faſtened to any elaſtick body catches by a ſpring or jerk.

As a woodcock to my own *ſpringe*, Oſrick,
I'm juſtly kill'd with mine own treachery.
Shakeſpeare's Hamlet.

Let goats for food their loaded udders lend;
But neither *ſpringes*, nets, nor ſnares employ. *Dryden.*

With hairy *ſpringes* we the birds betray,
Slight lines of hair ſurprize the finny prey. *Pope.*

SPRI'NGER. *n. ſ.* [from *ſpring.*] One who rouſes game.

SPRI'NGINESS. *n. ſ.* [from *ſpringy.*] Elaſticity; power of reſtoring itſelf.

Where there is a continued endeavour of the parts of a body to put themſelves into another ſtate, the progreſs may be much more ſlow, ſince it was a great while before the texture of the corpuſcles of the ſteel were ſo altered as to make them loſe their former *ſpringineſs*. *Boyle.*

The air is a thin fluid body, endowed with elaſticity and *ſpringineſs*, capable of condenſation and rarefaction. *Bentley.*

SPRI'NGHALT. *n. ſ.* [*ſpring* and *halt.*] A lameneſs by which the horſe twiches up his legs.

They've all new legs, and lame ones; one would take it,
That never ſaw them pace before, the ſpavin
And *ſpringhalt* reign'd among them. *Shakeſp. Henry* VIII.

SPRI'NGTIDE. *n. ſ.* [*ſpring* and *tide.*] Tide at the new moon; high tide.

Love, like *ſpringtides*, full and high,
Swells in every youthful vein;
But each tide does leſs ſupply,
'Till they quite ſhrink in again:
If a flow in age appear,
'Tis but rain, and runs not clear. *Dryd. Tyrannick Love.*

Moſt people die when the moon chiefly reigns; that is, in the night, or upon or near a *ſpringtide*. *Grew's Coſmol.*

SPRI'NGLE. *n. ſ.* [from *ſpring.*] A ſpringe; an elaſtick nooſe.

Woodcocks arrive firſt on the north coaſt, where every plaſh-ſhoot ſerveth for *ſpringles* to take them. *Carew.*

To SPRI'NGLE. *v. n.* Miſprinted, I ſuppoſe, for *ſprinkle.*

This is Timon's laſt,
Who, ſtuck and ſpangled with your flatteries,
Waſhes it off, and *ſpringles* in your faces
Your reeking villany. *Shakeſp. Timon of Athens.*

SPRI'NGY. *adj.* [from *ſpringe.*]

1. Elaſtick; having the power of reſtoring itſelf.

Had not the Maker wrought the *ſpringy* frame,
Such as it is to fan the vital flame,
The blood, defrauded of its nitrous food,
Had cool'd and languiſh'd in th' arterial road;
While the tir'd heart had ſtrove, with fruitleſs pain,
To puſh the lazy tide along the vein. *Blackm. Creation.*

This vaſt contraction and expanſion ſeems unintelligible, by feigning the particles of air to be *ſpringy* and ramous, or rolled up like hoops, or by any other means than a repulſive power. *Newton.*

Though the bundle of fibres which conſtitute the muſcles may be ſmall, the fibres may be ſtrong and *ſpringy*. *Arbuthnot.*

If our air had not been a *ſpringy* body, no animal could have exerciſed the very function of reſpiration; and yet the ends of reſpiration are not ſerved by that ſpringineſs, but by ſome other unknown quality. *Bentley's Sermons.*

2. [From *ſpring.*] Full of ſprings or fountains. Not uſed.

Where the ſandy or gravelly lands are *ſpringy* or wet, rather marl them for graſs than corn. *Mortimer's Huſbandry.*

To SPRI'NKLE. *v. a.* [*ſprinkelen*, Dutch.]

1. To ſcatter; to diſperſe in ſmall maſſes.

Take handfuls of aſhes of the furnace, and let Moſes *ſprinkle* it towards the heaven. *Ex.* ix. 8.

2. To ſcatter in drops.

Sprinkle water of purifying upon them. *Num.* viii. 7.

3. To beſprinkle; to waſh, wet, or duſt by ſprinkling.

Let us draw near with a true heart, in full aſſurance of faith, having our hearts *ſprinkled* from an evil conſcience. *Heb.*

Wings he wore
Of many a colour'd plume *ſprinkled* with gold. *Milton.*

The prince, with living water *ſprinkl'd* o'er
His limbs and body; then approach'd the door,
Poſſeſs'd the porch. *Dryden's Æn.*

To SPRI'NKLE. *v. n.* To perform the act of ſcattering in ſmall drops.

The prieſt ſhall *ſprinkle* of the oil with his finger. *Lev.* xiv.

Baptiſm may well enough be performed by *ſprinkling*, or effuſion of water. *Ayliffe's Parergon.*

When dext'rous damſels twirl the *ſprinkling* mop,
And cleanſe the ſpatter'd ſaſh, and ſcrub the ſtairs,
Know Saturday appears. *Gay's Trivia.*

To SPRIT. *v. a.* [ſpꞃyꞇꞇan, Saxon; *ſpruyten*, Dutch.] To throw out; to eject with force. Commonly *ſpirt.*

Toads ſometimes exclude or *ſprit* out a dark and liquid matter behind, and a venomous condition there may be perhaps therein; but it cannot be called their urine. *Brown.*

To SPRIT. *v. n.* [ſpꞃyꞇꞇan, Saxon; *ſpruyten*, Dutch.] To ſhoot; to germinate; to ſprout.

SPRIT. *n. ſ.* [from the verb.] Shoot; ſprout.

The barley, after it has been couched four days, will ſweat a little, and ſhew the chit or *ſprit* at the root-end of the corn. *Mortimer's Huſbandry.*

SPRI'TSAIL. *n. ſ.* [*ſprit* and *ſail.*] The ſail which belongs to the boltſprit-maſt. *Dict.*

Our men quitted themſelves of the fireſhip, by cutting the *ſpritſail* tackle off with their ſhort hatchets. *Wiſeman.*

SPRITE. *n. ſ.* [Contracted from *ſpirit.*] A ſpirit; an incorporeal agent.

The *ſprites* of fiery termagants in flame
Mount up, and take a ſalamander's name. *Pope.*

SPRI'TEFULLY. *adv.* [See SPRIGHTFULLY.] Vigorouſly; with life and ardour.

The Grecians *ſpritefully* drew from the darts the corſe,
And hearſt it, bearing it to fleet. *Chapman's Iliads.*

SPRONG. The preterite of *ſpring.* Obſolete.

Not miſtruſting, 'till theſe new curioſities *ſprong* up, that ever any man would think our labour herein miſpent, or the time waſtefully conſumed. *Hooker.*

To SPROUT. *v. n.* [ſpꞃyꞇꞇan, Saxon; *ſpruyten*, Dutch.]

1. To ſhoot by vegetation; to germinate.

Try whether theſe things in the *ſprouting* do increaſe weight, by weighing them before they are hanged up; and afterwards again, when they are *ſprouted*. *Bacon.*

That leaf faded, but the young buds *ſprouted* on, which afterwards opened into fair leaves. *Bacon's Natural Hiſtory.*

We find no ſecurity to prevent germination, having made trial of grains, whoſe ends, cut off, have notwithſtanding *ſprouted*. *Brown's Vulgar Errours.*

Old Baucis is by old Philemon ſeen
Sprouting with ſudden leaves of ſprightly green. *Dryden.*

Hence *ſprouting* plants enrich the plain and wood:
For phyſick ſome, and ſome deſign'd for food. *Blackmore.*

Envy'd Britannia, ſturdy as the oak
Which on her mountain top ſhe proudly bears,
Eludes the ax, and *ſprouts* againſt the ſtroke,
Strong from her wounds, and greater by her wars. *Prior.*

24 Y Rub

Rub malt between your hands to get the come or *sprouting* clean away. *Mortime's Husbandry.*

2. To shoot into ramifications.

Vitriol is apt to *sprout* with moisture. *Bacon.*

3. To grow.

Th' enliv'ning dust its head begins to rear,
And on the ashes *sprouting* plumes appear. *Tickell.*

SPROUT. *n. s.* [from the verb.] A shoot of a vegetable.

Stumps of trees, lying out of the ground, will put forth *sprouts* for a time. *Bacon.*

Early ere the odorous breath of morn
Awakes the slumbering leaves, or tassel'd horn
Shakes the high thicket, haste I all about,
Number my ranks, and visit every *sprout.* *Milton.*

To this kid, taken out of the womb, were brought in the tender *sprouts* of shrubs; and, after it had tasted, began to eat of such as are the usual food of goats. *Ray on the Creation.*

SPRUCE. *adj.* [*Skinner* derives this word from *preux*, French; but he proposes it with hesitation: *Junius* thinks it comes from *sprout*; *Casaubon* trifles yet more contemptibly. I know not whence to deduce it, except from *pruce*. In ancient books we find furniture of *pruce* a thing costly and elegant, and thence probably came *spruce.*] Nice; trim; neat without elegance.

The tree
That wraps that crystal in a wooden tomb,
Shall be took up *spruce*, fill'd with diamond. *Donne.*

Thou wilt not leave me in the middle street,
Tho' some more *spruce* companion thou do'st meet. *Donne.*

Along the crisped shades and bow'rs
Revels the *spruce* and jocund Spring;
The graces, and the rosy-bosom'd hours,
Thither all their bounties bring. *Milton.*

I must not slip into too *spruce* a style for serious matters; and yet I approve not that dull insipid way of writing practised by many chymists. *Boyle.*

He put his band and beard in order,
The *sprucer* to accost and board her. *Hudibras.*

He is so *spruce*, that he can never be genteel. *Tatler.*

This Tim makes a strange figure with that ragged coat under his livery: can't he go *spruce* and clean? *Arbuthnot.*

To SPRUCE. *v. n.* [from the noun.] To dress with affected neatness.

SPRU'CEBEER. *n. s.* [from *spruce*, a kind of fir.] Beer tinctured with branches of fir.

In ulcers of the kidneys *sprucebeer* is a good balsamick. *Arb.*

SPRU'CELEATHER. *n. s.* [Corrupted for *Prussian leather.*] *Ains.*

The *leather* was of *Pruce.* *Dryden's Fables.*

SPRU'CENESS. *n. s.* [from *spruce.*] Neatness without elegance.

SPRUNG. The preterite and participle passive of *spring.*

Tall Norway fir, their masts in battle spent,
And English oaks, *sprung* leaks, and planks, restore. *Dryd.*

Now from beneath Maleas' airy height,
Aloft she *sprung*, and steer'd to Thebes her flight. *Pope.*

Who *sprung* from kings shall know less joy than I. *Pope.*

SPRUNT. *n. s.* Any thing that is short and will not easily bend.

SPUD. *n. s.* A short knife.

My love to Sheelah is more firmly fixt,
Than strongest weeds that grow these stones betwixt:
My *spud* these nettles from the stones can part,
No knife so keen to weed thee from my heart. *Swift.*

SPU'LLERS *of Yarn. n. s.* Are such as are employed to see that it be well spun, and fit for the loom. *Dict.*

SPUME. *n. s.* [*spuma*, Latin.] Foam; froth.

Materials dark and crude,
Of spirituous and fiery *spume*, 'till touch'd
With heaven's ray, and temper'd, they shoot forth
So beauteous, op'ning to the ambient light. *Milton.*

Waters frozen in pans, after their dissolution, leave a froth and *spume* upon them, which are caused by the airy parts diffused by the congealable mixture. *Brown's Vulgar Errours.*

To SPUME. *v. n.* [*spumo*, Latin.] To foam; to froth.

SPU'MOUS. } *adj.* [*spumeus*, Latin; from the noun.] Frothy;
SPU'MY. } foamy.

The cause is the putrefaction of the body by unnatural heat: the putrifying parts suffer a turgescence, and becoming airy and *spumous*, ascend into the surface of the water. *Brown.*

Not with more madness, rolling from afar,
The *spumy* waves proclaim the wat'ry war;
And mounting upwards with a mighty roar,
March onwards, and insult the rocky shore. *Dryden.*

The *spumous* and florid state of the blood, in passing through the lungs, arises from its own elasticity, and its violent motion, the aerial particles expanding themselves. *Arbuthnot.*

SPUN. The preterite and part. pass. of *spin.*

The nymph nor *spun*, nor dress'd with artful pride;
Her vest was gather'd up, her hair was ty'd. *Addison.*

SPUNGE. *n. s.* [*spongia*, Latin.] A sponge. See SPONGE.

When he needs what you have glean'd, it is but squeezing you, and, *spunge*, you shall be dry again. *Shakesp. Hamlet.*

Considering the motion that was impressed by the painter's hand upon the *spunge*, compounded with the specifick gravity of the *spunge* and the resistance of the air, the *spunge* did mechanically and unavoidably move in that particular line of motion. *Bentley's Sermons.*

To SPUNGE. *v. n.* [Rather *To sponge.*] To hang on others for maintenance.

This will maintain you, with the perquisite of *spunging* while you are young. *Swift to Gay.*

SPU'NGINGHOUSE. *n. s.* [*spunge* and *house.*] A house to which debtors are taken before commitment to prison, where the bailiffs sponge upon them, or riot at their cost.

A bailiff kept you the whole evening in a *spunginghouse. Sw.*

SPU'NGY. *adj.* [from *spunge.*]

1. Full of small holes, and soft like a spunge.

Some English wool, vex'd in a Belgian loom,
And into cloth of *spungy* softness made,
Did into France or colder Denmark roam,
To ruin with worse air our staple trade. *Dryden.*

2. Wet; moist; watery.

There is no lady of more softer bowels,
More *spungy* to suck in the sense of fear. *Shakespeare.*

I saw Jove's bird, the Roman eagle, wing'd
From the *spungy* South to this part of the West,
There vanish'd in the sun-beams. *Shakes. Cymbeline.*

3. Drunken; wet with liquor.

What cannot we put upon
His *spungy* officers? *Shakespeare.*

SPUNK. *n. s.* Rotten wood; touchwood. See SPONK.

To make white powder, the best way is by the powder of rotten willows: *spunk*, or touchwood prepared, might perhaps make it russet. *Brown's Vulgar Errours.*

SPUR. *n. s.* [ꞅpuꞃa, Sax. *spore*, Danish, Islandick, and Dutch; *esperon*, French.]

1. A sharp point fixed in the rider's heel, with which he pricks his horse to drive him forward.

He borrowing that homely armour for want of a better, had come upon the *spur* to redeem Philoclea's picture. *Sidney.*

Whether the body politick be
A horse whereon the governour doth ride,
Who, newly in the seat, that it may know
He can command it, lets it straight feel the *spur.* *Shakesp.*

He presently set *spurs* to his horse, and departed with the rest of the company. *Knolles's History of the Turks.*

Was I for this entitled, sir,
And girt with rusty sword and *spur*,
For fame and honour to wage battle? *Hudibras.*

2. Incitement; instigation.

Seeing then that nothing can move, unless there be some end, the desire whereof provoketh unto motion, how should that divine power of the soul, that spirit of our mind, ever stir itself into action, unless it have also the like *spur*? *Hooker.*

What need we any *spur*, but our own cause,
To prick us to redress? *Shakes. Julius Cæsar.*

His laws are deep, and not vulgar; not made upon the *spur* of a particular occasion, but out of providence of the future, to make his people more and more happy. *Bacon.*

Reward is the *spur* of virtue in all good arts, all laudable attempts; and emulation, which is the other *spur*, will never be wanting, when particular rewards are proposed. *Dryden.*

The chief, if not only, *spur* to human industry and action, is uneasiness. *Locke.*

The former may be a *spur* to the latter, 'till age makes him in love with the study, without any childish bait. *Cheyne.*

3. A stimulus; a prick; any thing that galls and teazes.

Grief and patience, rooted in him both,
Mingle their *spurs* together. *Shakes. Cymbeline.*

4. The sharp points on the legs of a cock with which he fights.

Of birds the bill is of like matter with the teeth: as for their *spur*, it is but a nail. *Bacon.*

Animals have natural weapons to defend and offend; some talons, some claws, some *spurs* and beaks. *Ray.*

5. Any thing standing out; a snag.

The strong bas'd promontory
Have I made shake, and pluckt up by the *spurs*
The pine and cedar. *Shakespeare.*

To SPUR. *v. a.* [from the noun.]

1. To prick with the spur; to drive with the spur.

My friend, who always takes care to cure his horse of starting fits, *spurred* him up to the very side of the coach. *Addison.*

Your father, when he mounted,
Rein'd 'em in strongly, and he *spurr'd* them hard. *Dryden.*

Who would be at the trouble of learning, when he finds his ignorance is caressed? But when you brow-beat and maul them, you make them men; for though they have no natural mettle, yet, if they are *spurred* and kicked, they will mend their pace. *Collier on Pride.*

2. To instigate; to incite; to urge forward.

Lovers break not hours,
Unless it be to come before their time:
So much they *spur* their expedition. *Shakespeare.*

Let the awe he has got upon their minds be so tempered with the marks of good-will, that affection may *spur* them to their duty. *Locke.*

3. To

3. To drive by force.
Love will not be *spurr'd* to what it loaths. *Shakespeare.*

To SPUR. *v. n.*

1. To travel with great expedition.
With backward bows the Parthians shall be there,
And, *spurring* from the fight, confess their fear:
A double wreath shall crown our Cæsar's brows. *Dryden.*

2. To press forward.
Ascanius took th' alarm, while yet he led,
And *spurring* on, his equals soon o'erpass'd. *Dryd. Æn.*
Some bold men, though they begin with infinite ignorance and errour, yet, by *spurring* on, refine themselves. *Grew.*

SPU'RGALLED. *adj.* [*spur* and *gall.*] Hurt with the spur.
I was not made a horse,
And yet I bear a burthen like an ass,
Spurgall'd and tir'd, by jaunting Bolingbroke. *Shakespeare.*
What! shall each *spurgall'd* hackney of the day,
Or each new pension'd sycophant, pretend
To break my windows, if I treat a friend. *Pope.*

SPURGE. *n. s.* [*espurge*, French; *spurgie*, Dutch, from *purgo*, Latin.] A plant violently purgative. *Spurge* is a general name in English for all milky purgative plants. *Skinner.*
The flower consists of one leaf, of the globous bell shape, cut into several moon-shaped segments, and encompassed by two little leaves, which seem to perform the office of a flower-cup: the pointal is for the most part triangular, which rises from the bottom of the flower, and becomes a fruit of the same shape, divided into three cells, each containing an oblong seed. Every part of the plant abounds with a milky juice. There are seventy-one species of this plant, of which wart-wort is one. The first sort, called broad-leaved spurge, is a biennial plant, and used in medicine under the name of cataputia minor. The milky juice in these plants is used by some to destroy warts; but particular care should be taken in the application, because it is a strong caustick. *Miller.*
The leaves of cataputia, or *spurge*, being plucked upwards or downwards, perform their operations by purge or vomit; is a strange conceit, ascribing unto plants positional operations. *Brown's Vulgar Errours.*

SPURGE *Laurel*, or *Mezereon.* *n. s.* [*thymelæa*, Latin.] A plant.
The characters are: the flower consists of one leaf; is, for the most part, funnel-shaped, and cut into four segments; from whose centre rises the pointal, which afterward becomes an oval fruit, which is in some full of juice, but in others is dry. In each is contained one oblong seed. It is a rough purge. *Miller.*

SPU'RIOUS. *adj.* [*spurius*, Latin.]

1. Not genuine; counterfeit; adulterine.
The coin that shows the first is generally rejected as *spurious*, nor is the other esteemed more authentick by the present Roman medalists. *Addison on Italy.*
If any thing else has been printed, in which we really had any hand, it is loaded with *spurious* additions. *Swift.*

2. Not legitimate; bastard.
Your Scipio's, Cæsar's, Pompey's, and your Cato's,
These gods on earth, are all the *spurious* brood
Of violated maids. *Addison's Cato.*

SPU'RLING. *n. s.* [*esperlan*, French.] A small sea-fish.
All-saints, do lay for porke and sowse,
For sprats and *spurlings* for your house. *Tusser.*

To SPURN. *v. a.* [ꞅpoꞃnan, Saxon.]

1. To kick; to strike or drive with the foot.
They suppos'd I could rend bars of steel,
And *spurn* in pieces posts of adamant. *Shakes. Henry VI.*
Say my request's unjust,
And *spurn* me back; but if it be not so,
Thou art not honest. *Shakespeare's Coriolanus.*
You that did void your rheum upon my beard,
And foot me as you *spurn* a stranger cur
Over your threshold. *Shak. Merchant of Venice.*
He in the surging smoke
Uplifted *spurn'd* the ground. *Milton.*
So was I forc'd
To do a sovereign justice to myself,
And *spurn* thee from my presence. *Dryden's Don Sebastian.*
Then will I draw up my legs, and *spurn* her from me with my foot. *Addison's Spectator.*
A milk-white bull shall at your altars stand,
That threats a fight, and *spurns* the rising sand. *Pope.*
When Athens sinks by fates unjust,
When wild barbarians *spurn* her dust. *Pope.*
Now they, who reach Parnassus' lofty crown,
Employ their pains to *spurn* some others down. *Pope.*

2. To reject; to scorn; to put away with contempt; to disdain.
In wisdom I should ask your name;
But since thy outside looks so fair and warlike,
What safe and nicely I might well delay,
By rule of knighthood, I disdain and *spurn*. *Shakespeare.*

3. To treat with contempt.
Domesticks will pay a more chearful service, when they find themselves not *spurned*, because fortune has laid them at their masters feet. *Locke.*

To SPURN. *v. n.*

1. To make contemptuous opposition; to make insolent resistance.
A son to blunt the sword
That guards the peace and safety of your person;
Nay more, to *spurn* at your most royal image. *Shakesp.*
I, Pandulph, do religiously demand
Why thou against the church, our holy mother,
So wilfully do'st *spurn*? *Shakesp. King John.*
Instruct me why
Vanoc should *spurn* against our rule, and stir
The tributary provinces to war. *Philips's Briton.*

2. To toss up the heels; to kick or struggle.
The drunken chairman in the kennel *spurns*,
The glasses shatters, and his charge o'erturns. *Gay.*

SPURN. *n. s.* [from the verb.] Kick; insolent and contemptuous treatment.
The insolence of office, and the *spurns*
That patient merit of th' unworthy takes. *Shakesp. Hamlet.*

SPU'RNEY. *n. s.* A plant.

SPU'RRER. *n. s.* [from *spur.*] One who uses spurs.

SPU'RRIER. *n. s.* [from *spur.*] One who makes spurs.

SPU'RRY. *n. s.* [*spergula*, Latin.] A plant.
Spurry seed is sown in the low countries in Summer, the first time in May, that it may flower in June and July; and in August the seed is ripe. *Mortimer's Husbandry.*

To SPURT. *v. n.* [See *To* SPIRT.] To fly out with a quick stream.
If from a puncture of a lancet, the manner of the *spurting* out of the blood will shew it. *Wiseman's Surgery.*

SPU'RWAY. *n. s.* [*spur* and *way.*] A horseway; a bridle-road; distinct from a road for carriages.

SPUTA'TION. *n. s.* [*sputum*, Latin.] The act of spitting.
A moist consumption receives its nomenclature from a moist *sputation*, or expectoration: a dry one is known by its dry cough. *Harvey on Consumptions.*

To SPU'TTER. *v. n.* [*sputo*, Latin.]

1. To emit moisture in small flying drops.
If a manly drop or two fall down,
It scalds along my cheeks, like the green wood,
That, *sputt'ring* in the flame, works outward into tears. *Dry.*

2. To fly out in small particles with some noise.
The nightly virgin, while her wheel she plies,
Foresees the storms impending in the skies,
When sparkling lamps their *sputt'ring* light advance,
And in the sockets oily bubbles dance. *Dryden.*

3. To speak hastily and obscurely, as with the mouth full; to throw out the spittle by hasty speech.
A pinking owl sat *sputtering* at the sun, and asked him what he meant to stand staring her in the eyes. *L'Estrange.*
They could neither of them speak their rage; and so fell a *sputtering* at one another, like two roasting apples. *Congreve.*
Though he *sputter* through a session,
It never makes the least impression;
Whate'er he speaks for madness goes. *Swift.*

To SPU'TTER. *v. a.* To throw out with noise and hesitation.
Thou do'st with lies the throne invade,
Obtending heav'n for whate'er ills befall;
And *sputt'ring* under specious names thy gall. *Dryden.*
In the midst of caresses, and without the least pretended incitement, to *sputter* out the basest accusations! *Swift.*

SPU'TTERER. *n. s.* [from *sputter.*] One that sputters.

SPY. *n. s.* [*yspio*, Welsh; *espion*, French; *spie*, Dutch; *speculator*, Latin. It is observed by a German, that *spy* has been in all ages a word by which the eye, or office of the eye, has been expressed: thus the *Arimaspians* of old, fabled to have but one eye, were so called from *ari*, which, among the nations of *Caucasus*, still signifies *one*, and *spi*, which has been received from the old Asiatick languages for an *eye*, *sight*, or one that *sees.*] One sent to watch the conduct or motions of others; one sent to gain intelligence in an enemy's camp or country.
We'll hear poor rogues
Talk of court news, and we'll talk with them too,
And take upon's the mystery of things,
As if we were God's *spies*. *Shakesp. King Lear.*
Spies of the Volscians
Held me in chace, that I was forc'd to wheel
Three or four miles about. *Shakespeare's Coriolanus.*
Every corner was possessed by diligent *spies* upon their master and mistress. *Clarendon.*
I come no *spy*,
With purpose to explore, or to disturb,
The secrets of your realm. *Milton's Paradise Lost.*
Such command we had,
To see that none thence issu'd forth a *spy*,
Or enemy, while God was in his work. *Milton.*
Nothing lies hid from radiant eyes;
All they subdue become their *spies*:
Secrets, as chosen jewels, are
Presented to oblige the fair. *Waller.*

O'er my men I'll set my careful *spies*,
To watch rebellion in their very eyes. *Dryden.*

These wretched *spies* of wit must then confess,
They take more pains to please themselves the less. *Dryden.*

Those who attend on their state, are so many *spies* placed upon them by the publick to observe them nearly. *Atterbury.*

To SPY. *v. a.* [See SPY. *n. s.*]

1. To discover by the eye at a distance, or in a state of concealment; to espy.

Light hath no tongue, but is all eye;
If it could speak as well as *spy*,
This were the worst that it could say,
That being well I fain would stay. *Donne.*

As tiger *spy'd* two gentle fawns. *Milton.*

A countryman *spied* a snake under a hedge, half frozen to death. *L'Estrange.*

My brother Guyomar, methinks, I *spy*:
Haste in his steps, and wonder in his eye. *Dryden.*

One in reading skip'd over all sentences where he *spy'd* a note of admiration. *Swift.*

2. To discover by close examination.

Let a lawyer tell he has *spy'd* some defect in an entail, how solicitous are they to repair that errour. *Decay of Piety.*

3. To search or discover by artifice.

Moses sent to *spy* out Jaazer, and took the villages. *Numb.*

To SPY. *v. n.* To search narrowly.

It is my nature's plague
To *spy* into abuse; and oft my jealousy
Shapes faults that are not. *Shakespeare's Othello.*

SPY'BOAT. *n. s.* [*spy* and *boat.*] A boat sent out for intelligence.

Giving the colour of the sea to their *spyboats* to keep them from being discovered, came from the Veneti. *Arbuthnot.*

SQUAB. *adj.* [I know not whence derived.]

1. Unfeathered; newly hatched.

Why must old pidgeons, and they stale, be drest,
When there's so many *squab* ones in the nest. *King.*

2. Fat; thick and stout; awkwardly bulky.

The nappy ale goes round,
Nor the *squab* daughter nor the wife were nice,
Each health the youths began, Sim pledg'd it twice. *Bettert.*

SQUAB. *n. s.* A kind of sofa or couch; a stuffed cushion.

On her large *squab* you find her spread,
Like a fat corpse upon a bed. *Swift.*

SQUAB. *adv.* With a heavy sudden fall; plump and flat. A low word.

The eagle took the tortoise up into the air, and dropt him down, *squab*, upon a rock, that dashed him to pieces. *L'Estr.*

SQUA'BPIE. *n. s.* [*squab*, and *pie.*] A pie made of many ingredients.

Cornwal *squabpie*, and Devon whitepot brings,
And Leister beans and bacon, food of kings. *King.*

To SQUAB. *v. n.* To fall down plump or flat; to squelsh or squash.

SQUA'BBISH. *adj.* [from *squab.*] Thick; heavy; fleshy.

Diet renders them of a *squabbish* or lardy habit of body. *Harvey.*

To SQUA'BBLE. *v. n.* [*kiabla*, Swedish.] To quarrel; to debate peevishly; to wrangle; to fight.. A low word.

Drunk? and speak parrot? and *squabble?* swagger? oh, thou invincible spirit of wine! *Shakespeare's Othello.*

I thought it not improper in a *squabbling* and contentious age, to detect the vanity of confiding ignorance. *Glanville.*

If there must be disputes, is not *squabbling* less inconvenient than murder? *Collier on Duelling.*

The sense of these propositions is very plain, though logicians might *squabble* a whole day, whether they should rank them under negative or affirmative. *Watts's Logick.*

SQUA'BBLE. *n. s.* [from the verb.] A low brawl; a petty quarrel.

In popular factions, pragmatick fools commonly begin the *squabble*, and crafty knaves reap the benefit. *L'Estrange.*

A man whose personal courage is suspected, is not to drive squadrons before him; but may be allowed the merit of some *squabble*, or throwing a bottle at his neighbour's head. *Arbuth.*

SQUA'BBLER. *n. s.* [from *squabble.*] A quarrelsome fellow; a brawler.

SQUA'DDRON. *n. s.* [*escadron*, Fr. *squadrone*, Italian, from *quadratus*, Latin.]

1. A body of men drawn up square.

Those half rounding guards
Just met, and closing stood in *squadron* join'd. *Milton.*

2. A part of an army; a troop.

Nothing the Moors were more afraid of, than in a set battle to fight with *squadrons* coming orderly on. *Knolles.*

Then beauteous Atys, with Iulus bred,
Of equal age, the second *squadron* led. *Dryden.*

3. Part of a fleet, a certain number of ships.

Rome could not maintain its dominion over so many provinces, without *squadrons* ready equipt. *Arbuthnot.*

SQUA'DRONED. *adj.* [from *squadron.*] Formed into squadrons.

They gladly thither haste; and by a choir
Of *squadron'd* angels hear his carol sung. *Milt. Par. Lost.*

SQUA'LID. *adj.* [*squalidus*, Latin.] Foul; nasty; filthy.

A doleful case desires a doleful song,
Without vain art or curious compliments,
And *squalid* fortune into baseness flowing,
Doth scorn the pride of wonted ornaments. *Spenser.*

Uncomb'd his locks, and *squalid* his attire,
Unlike the trim of love and gay desire. *Dryden's Knights Tale.*

All these Cocytus bounds with *squalid* reeds,
With muddy ditches and with deadly weeds. *Dryden.*

To SQUALL. *v. n.* [*squala*, Swedish.] To scream out as a child or woman frighted.

In my neighbourhood, a very pretty prattling shoulder of veal *squalls* out at the sight of a knife. *Spectator.*

I put five into my coat pocket, and as to the sixth I made a countenance as if I would eat him alive. The poor man *squalled* terribly. *Swift.*

Cornelius sunk back on a chair; the guests stood astonished; the infant *squawl'd.* *Arbuthnot and Pope.*

SQUALL. *n. s.* [from the verb.]

1. Loud scream.

There oft are heard the notes of infant woe,
The short thick sob, loud scream, and shriller *squall.* *Swift.*

2. Sudden gust of wind. A sailor's word.

SQUA'LLER. *n. s.* [from *squall.*] Screamer; one that screams.

SQUA'LOR. *n. s.* [Latin.] Coarseness; nastiness; want of cleanliness and neatness.

Take heed that their new flowers and sweetness do not as much corrupt as the others dryness and *squalor.* *Ben. Johnson.*

What can filthy poverty give else, but beggary, fulsome nastiness, *squalor*, ugliness, hunger, and thirst? *Burton.*

SQUA'LLY. *adj.* [from *squall*] Windy; gusty. A sailor's word.

SQUA'MOUS. *adj.* [*squameus*, Latin.] Scaly; covered with scales.

The sea was replenished with fish, of the cartilaginous and *squamose*, as of the testaceous and crustaceous kinds. *Woodw.*

Those galls and balls are produced, in the gems of oak, which may be called *squamous* oak cones. *Derham's Physico-Theology.*

To SQUA'NDER. *v. a.* [*verschwenden*, Teutonick.]

1. To scatter lavishly; to spend profusely; to throw away in idle prodigality.

We *squander* away some part of our fortune at play. *Atterb.*

They often *squander'd*, but they never gave. *Savage.*

Never take a favourite waiting maid, to insinuate how great a fortune you brought, and how little you are allowed to *squander.* *Swift.*

Then, in plain prose, were made two sorts of men,
To *squander* some, and some to hide agen. *Pope.*

True friends would rather see such thoughts as they communicate only to one another, than what they *squander* about to all the world. *Pope.*

How uncertain it is, whether the years we propose to ourselves shall be indulged to us, uncertain whether we shall have power or even inclination to improve them better than those we now *squander* away. *Rogers.*

2. To scatter; to dissipate; to disperse.

He hath an argosie bound to Tripolis, another to the Indies, and other ventures he hath *squandered* abroad. *Shakespeare.*

The troops we *squander'd* first, again appear
From sev'ral quarters, and enclose the rear. *Dryden.*

He is a successful warrior,
And has the soldiers hearts: upon the skirts
Of Arragon our *squander'd* troops he rallies. *Dryden.*

SQUA'NDERER. *n. s.* [from *squander.*] A spendthrift; a prodigal; a waster; a lavisher.

Plenty in their own keeping, teaches them from the beginning, to be *squanderers* and wasters. *Locke.*

SQUARE. *adj.* [*ysgwâr*, Welsh; *quadratus*, Latin.]

1. Cornered; having right angles.

All the doors and posts were *square*, with the windows. *Kings.*

Water and air the varied form confound;
The straight looks crooked, and the *square* grows round. *Prior.*

2. Forming a right angle.

This instrument is for striking lines *square* to other lines or streight sides, and try the squareness of their work. *Moxon.*

3. Cornered; having angles of whatever content; as three square, five square.

Catching up in haste his three *square* shield,
And shining helmet, soon him buckled to the field. *Spenser.*

The clavicle is a crooked bone, in the figure of an S, one end of which being thicker and almost three *square*, is inserted into the first bone of the sternon. *Wiseman's Surgery.*

4. Parallel; exactly suitable.

She's a most triumphant lady, if report be *square* to her. *Shak.*

5. Strong; stout; well set. As, a *square* man.

6. Equal; exact; honest; fair. As, *square* dealing.

All have not offended;
For those that were, it is not *square* to take
On those that are, revenge; crimes, like to lands,
Are not inherited. *Shakespeare's Timon of Athens.*

7. [In geometry.] *Square* root of any number is that which, multiplied by it self, produces the *square*, as 4 is the *square* root of 16; because $4 \times 4 = 16$; and likewise 6 the *square* root of 36, as $6 \times 6 = 36$.

SQUARE.

SQUARE. *n. s.* [*quadra*, Latin.]

1. A figure with right angles and equal sides.

Then did a sharped spire of diamond bright,
Ten feet each way in *square* appear to me,
Justly proportion'd up unto his height,
So far as archer might his level see. *Spenser.*

Rais'd of grassy turf their table was;
And on her ample *square* from side to side
All Autumn pil'd. *Milton.*

2. An area of four sides, with houses on each side.

The statue of Alexander VII. stands in the large *square* of the town. *Addison's Remarks on Italy.*

3. Content of an angle.

In rectangle triangles the *square* which is made of the side that subtendeth the right angle, is equal to the *squares* which are made of the sides, containing the right angle. *Brown.*

4. A rule or instrument by which workmen measure or form their angles.

5. Rule; regularity; exact proportion; justness of workmanship or conduct.

In St. Paul's time the integrity of Rome was famous: Corinth many ways reproved: they of Galatia much more out of *square*. *Hooker.*

The whole ordinance of that government was at first evil plotted, and through other oversights came more out of *square*, to that disorder which it is now come unto. *Spenser's Ireland.*

I have not kept my *square*, but that to come
Shall all be done by th' rule. *Shakesp. Antony and Cleopatra.*

Nothing so much setteth this art of influence out of *square* and rule as education. *Raleigh.*

6. Squadron; troops formed square.

He alone
Dealt on lieutenantry, and no practice had
In the brave *squares* of war. *Shakespeare.*

Our superfluous lacqueys and our peasants,
Who in unnecessary action swarm
About our *squares* of battle, were enow
To purge this field of such a hilding foe. *Shakespeare.*

7. A *square* number is when another called its root can be exactly found, which multiplied by itself produces the square. The following example is not accurate.

Advance thy golden mountains to the skies,
On the broad base of fifty thousand rise;
Add one round hundred, and if that's not fair,
Add fifty more, and bring it to a *square*. *Pope.*

8. Quaternion; number four.

I profess
Myself an enemy to all other joys
Which the most precious *square* of sense possesses,
And find I am alone felicitate
In your love. *Shakespeare.*

9. Level; equality.

Men should sort themselves with their equals; for a rich man that converses upon the *square* with a poor man, shall certainly undoe him. *L'Estrange.*

We live not on the *square* with such as these,
Such are our betters who can better please. *Dryden.*

10. Quartile; the astrological situation of planets, distant ninety degrees from each other.

To th' other five
Their planetary motions, and aspects,
In sextile, *square*, and trine and opposite
Of noxious efficacy. *Milton's Paradise Lost.*

11. Rule; conformity. A proverbial use.

I shall break no *squares* whether it be so or not. *L'Estrange.*

12. SQUARES *go*. The game proceeds. Chessboards being full of squares.

One frog looked about him to see how *squares* went with their new king. *L'Estrange.*

To SQUARE. *v. a.* [*quadro*, Latin; from the noun.]

1. To form with right angles.

He employs not on us the hammer and the chizzel, with an intent to wound or mangle us, but only to *square* and fashion our hard and stubborn hearts. *Boyle's Seraphick Love.*

2. To reduce to a square.

Circles to *square*, and cubes to double,
Wou'd give a man excessive trouble. *Prior.*

3. To measure; to reduce to a measure.

Stubborn criticks, apt, without a theme
For depravation, to *square* all the sex
By Cressid's rule. *Shakespeare's Troilus and Cressida.*

4. To adjust; to regulate; to mould; to shape.

Dreams are toys;
Yet for this once, yea superstitiously,
I will be *squar'd* by this. *Shakespeare's Winter's Tale.*

How franticly I *square* my talk! *Shakespeare.*

Thou'rt said to have a stubborn soul,
That apprehends no further than this world,
And *squar'st* thy life accordingly. *Shakespeare.*

God has designed us a measure of our undertakings; his word and law, by the proportions whereof we are to *square* our actions. *Decay of Piety.*

The oracle was inforced to proclaim Socrates to be the wisest man in the world, because he applied his studies to the moral part, the *squaring* men's lives. *Hammond.*

His preaching much, but more his practice wrought;
A living sermon of the truths he taught;
For this by rules severe his life he *squar'd*,
That all might see the doctrine which they heard. *Dryden.*

This must convince all such who have, upon a wrong interpretation, presumed to *square* opinions by theirs, and have in loud exclamations shewn their abhorrence of university education. *Swift.*

5. To accommodate; to fit.

Eye me, blest providence, and *square* my trial
To my proportion'd strength. *Milton.*

6. To respect in quartile.

O'er libra's sign a crowd of foes prevails,
The icy goat and crab that *square* the scales. *Creech.*

Some professions can equally *square* themselves to, and thrive under all revolutions of government. *South's Sermons.*

To SQUARE. *v. n.*

1. To suit with; to fit with.

I set them by the rule, and, as they *square*,
Or deviate from undoubted doctrine, fare. *Dryden.*

His description *squares* exactly to lime. *Woodward.*

These marine bodies do not *square* with those opinions, but exhibit phænomena that thwart them. *Woodward.*

2. To quarrel; to go to opposite sides. Obsolete.

Are you such fools
To *square* for this? would it offend you then
That both should speed! *Shakespeare's Titus Andronicus.*

But they do *square*, that all their elves for fear
Creep into acorn cups, and hide them there. *Shakespeare.*

SQUA'RENESS. *n. s.* [from *square*.] The state of being square.

This instrument is for striking lines square to other lines or straight lines, and try the *squareness* of their work. *Moxon.*

Motion, *squareness*, or any particular shape, are the accidents of body. *Watts's Logick.*

SQUASH. *n. s.* [from *quash*.]

1. Any thing soft and easily crushed.

Not yet old enough for a man, nor young enough for a boy; as a *squash* is before it is a peascod, or a coddling, when it is almost an apple. *Shakespeare's Twelfth Night.*

2. [*Melopepo*.] A plant.

The characters are, it hath the whole appearance of a pumpion or gourd; from which this differs in its fruit, which is roundish, fleshy, streaked, angular, and for the most part divided into five partitions, inclosing flat seeds adhering to a spongy placenta. *Miller.*

Squash is an Indian kind of pumpion that grows apace. *Boyle.*

3. Any thing unripe; any thing soft. In contempt.

How like I then was to this kernel,
This *squash*, this gentleman. *Shakespeare's Winter's Tale.*

4. A sudden fall.

Since they will overload my shoulders, I shall throw down the burden with a *squash* among them. *Arbuthnot.*

5. A shock of soft bodies.

My fall was stopped by a terrible *squash* that sounded louder than the cataract of Niagara. *Gulliver's Travels.*

To SQUASH. *v. a.* To crush into pulp.

To SQUAT. *v. n.* [*quattare*, Italian.] To sit cowering; to sit close to the ground.

SQUAT. *adj.* [from the verb.]

1. Cowering; close to the ground.

Him there they found,
Squat like a toad, close at the ear of Eve. *Milton.*

Her dearest com'rades never caught her
Squat on her hams. *Swift.*

2. Short and thick; having one part close to another, as those of an animal contracted and cowering.

The squill-insect is so called from some similitude to the squill-fish: the head is broad and *squat*. *Grew.*

Alma in verse, in prose, the mind,
By Aristotle's pen defin'd,
Throughout the body *squat* or tall,
Is *bonâ fide*, all in all. *Prior.*

SQUAT. *n. s.*

1. The posture of cowering or lying close.

A stitch-fall'n cheek that hangs below the jaw;
Such wrinkles as a skilful hand would draw
For an old grandam ape, when with a grace
She sits at *squat*, and scrubs her leathern face. *Dryden.*

2. A sudden fall.

Bruises, *squats* and falls, which often kill others, can bring little hurt to those that are temperate. *Herbert.*

SQUAT. *n. s.* A sort of mineral.

The *squat* consists of tin ore and spar incorporated. *Woodw.*

To SQUEAK. *v. n.* [*sqwaka*, Swedish.]

1. To set up a sudden dolorous cry; to cry out with pain.

2. To cry with a shrill acute tone.

The sheeted dead
Did *squeak* and gibber in the Roman streets. *Shakespeare.*

Cart wheels *squeak* not when they are liquored. *Bacon.*

I see the new Arion sail,
The lute still trembling underneath thy nail:
At thy well sharpen'd thumb from shore to shore,
The trebles *squeak* for fear, the bases roar. *Dryden.*

Blunderbusses planted in every loop-hole, go off constantly at the *squeaking* of a fiddle and the thrumming of a guitar. *Dryden's Spanish Friar.*

Who can endure to hear one of the rough old Romans *squeaking* through the mouth of an eunuch? *Addison.*

How like brutes organs are to ours;
They grant, if higher pow'rs think fit,
A bear might soon be made a wit;
And that for any thing in nature,
Pigs might *squeak* love-odes, dogs bark satyr. *Prior.*

In florid impotence he speaks,
And as the prompter breathes, the puppet *squeaks.* *Pope.*

Zoilus calls the companions of Ulysses the *squeaking* pigs of Homer. *Pope's Odyssey.*

3. To break silence or secrecy for fear or pain.

If he be obstinate, put a civil question to him upon the rack, and he *squeaks*, I warrant him. *Dryden's Don Sebastian.*

SQUEAK. *n. s.* [from the verb.] A shrill quick cry; a cry of pain.

Ran cow and calf, and family of hogs,
In panick horrour of pursuing dogs:
With many a deadly grunt and doleful *squeak*,
Poor swine! as if their pretty hearts wou'd break. *Dryden.*

To SQUEAL. *v. n.* [*sqwala*, Swedish.] To cry with a shrill sharp voice; to cry with pain. *Squeak* seems a short sudden cry, and *squeal* a cry continued.

SQUEA'MISH. *adj.* [for *quawmish* or *qualmish*, from *qualm.*] Nice; fastidious; easily disgusted; having the stomach easily turned; being apt to take offence without much reason. It is used always in dislike either real or ironical.

Yet, for countenance sake, he seemed very *squeamish* in respect of the charge he had of the princess Pamela. *Sidney.*

Quoth he, that honour's very *squeamish*,
That takes a basting for a blemish;
For what's more honourable than scars,
Or skin to tatters rent in wars? *Hudibras.*

His musick is rustick, and perhaps too plain,
The men of *squeamish* taste to entertain. *Southern.*

It is rare to see a man at once *squeamish* and voracious. *South.*

There is no occasion to oppose the ancients and the moderns, or to be *squeamish* on either side. He that wisely conducts his mind in the pursuit of knowledge, will gather what lights he can from either. *Locke.*

SQUEA'MISHNESS. *n. s.* [from *squeamish.*] Niceness; delicacy; fastidiousness.

The thorough-pac'd politician must presently laugh at the *squeamishness* of his conscience, and read it another lecture. *South's Sermons.*

Upon their principles they may revive the worship of the host of heaven; it is but conquering a little *squeamishness* of stomach. *Stillingfleet.*

To administer this dose, fifty thousand operators, considering the *squeamishness* of some stomachs, and the peevishness of young children, is but reasonable. *Swift.*

To SQUEEZE. *v. a.* [cpiran, Saxon; *ys-gwasgu*, Welsh.]

1. To press; to crush between two bodies.

It is applied to the *squeezing* or pressing of things downwards, as in the presses for printing. *Wilkins.*

The sinking of the earth would make an extraordinary convulsion of the air, and that crack must so shake or *squeeze* the atmosphere, as to bring down all the remaining vapours. *Burnet's Theory of the Earth.*

He reap'd the product of his labour'd ground,
And *squeez'd* the combs with golden liquor crown'd. *Dryden.*

None acted mournings forc'd to show,
Or *squeeze* his eyes to make the torrent flow. *Dryden.*

When Florio speaks, what virgin could withstand,
If gentle Damon did not *squeeze* her hand? *Pope.*

2. To oppress; to crush; to harass by extortion.

In a civil war people must expect to be crushed and *squeezed* toward the burden. *L'Estrange.*

3. To force between close bodies.

To SQUEEZE. *v. n.*

1. To act or pass, in consequence of compression.

A concave sphere of gold fill'd with water and solder'd up, upon pressing the sphere with great force, let the water *squeeze* through it, and stand all over its outside in multitudes of small drops, like dew, without bursting or cracking the body of the gold. *Newton's Opticks.*

What crowds of these, impenitently bold,
In sounds and jingling syllables grown old,
Still run on poets, in a raging vein,
Ev'n to the dregs and *squeezings* of the brain. *Pope.*

2. To force way through close bodies.

Many a publick minister comes empty in; but when he has crammed his guts, he is fain to *squeeze* hard before he can get off. *L'Estrange.*

SQUEEZE. *n. s.* [from the verb.] Compression; pressure.

A subtile artist stands with wond'rous bag,
That bears imprison'd winds, of gentler sort
Than those that erst Laertes' son enclos'd:
Peaceful they sleep; but let the tuneful *squeeze*
Of lab'ring elbow rouse them, out they fly
Melodious, and with spritely accents charm. *Philips.*

SQUELCH. *n. s.* Heavy fall. A low ludicrous word.

He tore the earth which he had sav'd
From *squelch* of knight, and storm'd and rav'd. *Hudibras.*

So soon as the poor devil had recovered the *squelch*, away he scampers, bawling like mad. *L'Estrange.*

SQUIB. *n. s.* [*schieben*, German, to push forward. This etymology, though the best that I have found, is not very probable.]

1. A small pipe of paper filled with wildfire. Used in sport.

The armada at Calais, sir Walter Raleigh was wont prettily to say, were suddenly driven away with *squibs*; for it was no more than a stratagem of fire-boats manless, and sent upon them. *Bacon's War with Spain.*

The forest of the south, compareth the French valour to a *squib*, or fire of flax, which burns and crackles for a time, but suddenly extinguishes. *Howel's Vocal Forest.*

Lampoons, like *squibs*, may make a present blaze;
But time, and thunder, pay respect to bays. *Waller.*

Furious he begins his march,
Drives rattling o'er a brazen arch;
With *squibs* and crackers arm'd to throw
Among the trembling crowd below. *Swift.*

2. Any petty fellow.

Asked for their pass by every *squib*,
That list at will them to revile or snib. *Spenser.*

The *squibs*, in the common phrase, are called libellers. *Tatler.*

SQUILL. *n. s.* [*squilla, scilla*, Latin; *squille*, Fr.]

1. A plant.

It hath a large acrid bulbous root like an onion; the leaves are broad; the flowers are like those of ornithogalum; or the starry hyacinth: they grow in a long spike, and come out before the leaves. *Miller.*

Seed or kernels of apples and pears put into a *squill*, which is like a great onion, will come up earlier than in the earth itself. *Bacon's Natural History.*

'Twill down like oxymel of *squills*. *Roscommon.*

The self same atoms
Can, in the trufle, furnish out a feast;
And nauseate, in the scaly *squill*, the taste. *Garth.*

2. A fish.

3. An insect.

The *squill*-insect is so called from some similitude to the *squill*-fish, in having a long body covered with a crust, composed of several rings: the head broad and squat. *Grew.*

SQUI'NANCY. *n. s.* [*squinance, squinancie*, Fr. *squinatia*, Italian.] An inflammation in the throat; a quinsey.

It is used for *squinancies* and inflammations of the throat; whereby it seemeth to have a mollifying and lenifying virtue. *Bacon's Natural History.*

In a *squinancy* there is danger of suffocation. *Wiseman.*

SQUINT. *adj.* [*squinte*, Dutch, oblique, transverse.] Looking obliquely; looking not directly; looking suspiciously.

Where an equal poise of hope and fear
Does arbitrate the event, my nature is
That I incline to hope rather than fear,
And gladly banish *squint* suspicion. *Milton.*

To SQUINT. *v. n.* To look obliquely; to look not in a direct line of vision.

Some can *squint* when they will; and children set upon a table with a candle behind them, both eyes will move outwards, as affecting to see the light, and so induce *squinting*. *Bacon's Natural History.*

Not a period of this epistle but *squints* towards another over against it. *Pope.*

To SQUINT. *v. a.*

1. To form the eye to oblique vision.

This is the foul Flibertigibbet; he gives the web and the pin, *squints* the eye, and makes the hairlip. *Shakespeare.*

2. To turn the eye obliquely.

Perkin began already to *squint* one eye upon the crown, and another upon the sanctuary. *Bacon's Henry VII.*

SQUI'NTEYED. *adj.* [*squint* and *eye.*]

1. Having the sight directed oblique.

He was so *squinteyed*, that he seemed spitefully to look upon them whom he beheld. *Knolles's History of the Turks.*

2. Indirect; oblique; malignant.

This is such a false and *squinteyed* praise,
Which seeming to look upwards on his glories,
Looks down upon my fears. *Denham.*

SQUINTIFE'GO. *adj.* Squinting. A cant word.

The timbrel and the *squintifego* maid
Of Isis awe thee; lest the gods for sin,
Should, with a swelling dropsy stuff thy skin. *Dryden.*

I re-

To Squiny. *v. n.* To look asquint. A cant word.

I remember thine eyes well enough:
Do'st thou *squiny* at me? *Shakespeare's King Lear.*

Squire. *n. s.* [Contraction of *esquire*; *escuyer*, French. See Esquire.]

1. A gentleman next in rank to a knight.

He will maintain you like a gentlewoman.—Ay, that I will, come cut and long tail under the degree of a *squire*. *Shakesp.*

The rest are princes, barons, knights, *squires*,
And gentlemen of blood. *Shakespeare's Henry V.*

2. An attendant on a noble warriour.

Old Butes' form he took, Anchises' *squire*
Now left to rule Ascanius. *Dryden's Æneid.*

Knights, *squires*, and steeds must enter on the stage. *Pope.*

3. An attendant at court.

Return with her—
I could as well be brought
To knee his throne, and *squire*-like pension beg,
To keep base life a-foot. *Shakespeare's King Lear.*

Squi'rrel. *n. s.* [*escurueil*, French; *sciurus*, Latin.] A small animal that lives in woods, remarkable for leaping from tree to tree.

One chanc'd to find a nut,
In the end of which a hole was cut,
Which lay upon a hazel-root,
There scatter'd by a *squirrel*:
Which out the kernel gotten had;
When quoth this fay, dear queen be glad,
Let Oberon be ne'er so mad,
I'll set you safe from peril. *Drayton.*

To SQUIRT. *v. a.* To throw out in a quick stream. Of uncertain etymology.

Sir Roger she mortally hated, and used to hire fellows to *squirt* kennel water upon him as he passed along. *Arbuthnot.*

To Squirt. *v. n.* To prate; to let fly. Low cant.

You are so given to *squirting* up and down, and chattering, that the world would say, I had chosen a jack-pudding for a prime minister. *L'Estrange.*

Squirt. *n. s.* [from the verb.]

1. An instrument by which a quick stream is ejected.

He with his *squirt*-fire cou'd disperse
Whole troops. *Hudibras.*

There is war declared by a lord; his weapons are a pin to scratch, and a *squirt* to bespatter. *Pope.*

2. A small quick stream.

Water those with *squirts* of an infusion of the medicine in dunged water. *Bacon's Natural History.*

Squi'rter. *n. s.* [from *squirt.*] One that plies a squirt.

The *squirters* were at it with their kennel water, for they were mad for the loss of their bubble. *Arbuthnot.*

To STAB. *v. a.* [*staven*, old Dutch.]

1. To pierce with a pointed weapon.

Be't lawful, that I invocate thy ghost,
To hear the lamentations of poor Anne,
Wife to thy Edward, to thy slaughter'd son;
Stabb'd by the self same hand that made these wounds. *Shak.*

Thou hid'st a thousand daggers in thy thoughts,
Which thou hast whetted on thy stony heart,
To *stab* at my frail life. *Shakespeare's Henry IV.*

None shall dare
With shorten'd sword to *stab* in closer war;
But in fair combat fight. *Dryden's Knights Tale.*

Killing a man with a sword or a hatchet, are looked on as no distinct species of action; but if the point of the sword first enter the body, it passes for a distinct species where it has a distinct name; as in England, where it is called *stabbing*. *Locke.*

Porcius, think, thou seest thy dying brother
Stabb'd at his heart, and all besmear'd with blood,
Storming at thee! *Addison's Cato.*

2. To wound mortally or mischievously.

He speaks poinards, and every word *stabs*. *Shakespeare.*

What tears will then be shed!
Then, to compleat her woes, will I espouse
Hermione:—'twill *stab* her to the heart! *A. Philips.*

Stab. *n. s.* [from the verb.]

1. A stab or wound with a sharp pointed weapon.

The elements
Of whom your swords are temper'd, may as well
Wound the loud winds, or with bemockt at *stabs*
Kill the still closing waters. *Shakespeare.*

Cleander,
Unworthy was thy fate, thou first of warriours,
To fall beneath a base assassin's *stab*. *Rowe.*

2. A dark injury; a sly mischief.

3. A stroke; a blow.

He had a suitable scripture ready to repell them all; every pertinent text urged home being a direct *stab* to a temptation. *South's Sermons.*

Sta'bber. *n. s.* [from *stab.*] One who stabs; a privy murderer.

STABI'LIMENT. *n. s.* [from *stabilis*, Latin.] Support; firmness; act of making firm.

They serve for *stabiliment*, propagation and shade. *Derham.*

Stabi'lity. *n. s.* [*stabilité*, Fr. from *stabilitas*, Latin.]

1. Stableness; steadiness; strength to stand.

By the same degrees that either of these happen, the *stability* of the figure is by the same lessened. *Temple.*

These mighty girders which the fabrick bind,
These ribs robust and vast in order join'd,
Such strength and such *stability* impart,
That storms above, and earthquakes under ground
Break not the pillars. *Blackmore.*

He began to try
This and that hanging stone's *stability*. *Cotton.*

2. Fixedness; not fluidity.

Since fluidness and *stability* are contrary qualities, we may conceive that the firmness or *stability* of a body consists in this, that the particles which compose it do so rest, or are intangled, that there is among them a mutual cohesion. *Boyle.*

3. Firmness of resolution.

Sta'ble. *adj.* [*stable*, Fr. *stabilis*, Latin.]

1. Fixed; able to stand.

2. Steady; constant; fixed in resolution or conduct.

If man would be unvariable,
He must be like a rock or stone, or tree;
For ev'n the perfect angels were not *stable*,
But had a fall more desperate than we. *Davies.*

He perfect, *stable*; but imperfect we,
Subject to change. *Dryden's Knights Tale.*

3. Strong; fixed in state.

This region of chance and vanity, where nothing is *stable*, nothing equal; nothing could be offered to-day but what tomorrow might deprive us of. *Rogers's Sermons.*

STA'BLE. *n. s.* [*stabulum*, Latin.] A house for beasts.

I will make Rabbah a *stable* for camels. *Ezra* xxv. 5.

To Sta'ble. *v. n.* [*stabulo*, Latin.] To kennel; to dwell as beasts.

In their palaces,
Where luxury late reign'd, sea monsters whelp'd
And *stabled*. *Milton.*

Sta'bleboy. } *n. s.* [*stable* and *boy*, or *man.*] One who attends in the stable.
Sta'bleman. }

As soon as you alight at the inn, deliver your horses to the *stableboy*. *Swift.*

If the gentleman hath lain a night, get the *stablemen* and the scullion to stand in his way. *Swift's Directions to the Butler.*

I would with jockeys from Newmarket dine,
And to rough riders give my choicest wine;
I would caress some *stableman* of note,
And imitate his language and his coat. *Bramston.*

Sta'bleness. *n. s.* [from *stable.*]

1. Power to stand.

2. Steadiness; constancy; stability.

The king becoming graces,
As justice, verity, temp'rance, *stableness*,
Bounty, persev'rance, I have no relish of them. *Shakespeare.*

Sta'blestand. *n. s.* [In law.] Is one of the four evidences or presumptions, whereby a man is convinced to intend the stealing of the king's deer in the forest: and this is when a man is found at his standing in the forest with a cross bow bent, ready to shoot at any deer; or with a long bow, or else standing close by a tree with greyhounds in a leash ready to slip. *Cowel.*

I'll keep my *stablestand* where I lodge my wife, I'll go in couples with her. *Shakespeare.*

To Sta'blish. *v. a.* [*establir*, Fr. *stabilio*, Latin.] To establish; to fix; to settle.

Then she began a treaty to procure,
And *stablish* terms betwixt both their requests. *Fairy Queen.*

Stop effusion of our Christian blood,
And *stablish* quietness on ev'ry side. *Shakesp. Hen.* VI.

Comfort your hearts, and *stablish* you in every good work. 2 *Thess.* ii. 17.

Poor hereticks in love there be,
Which think to *stablish* dangerous constancy;
But I have told them, since you will be true,
You shall be true to them who're false to you. *Donne.*

His covenant sworn
To David, *stablish'd* as the days of heav'n. *Milton.*

Stack. *n. s.* [*stacca*, Italian.]

1. A large quantity of hay, corn, or wood, heaped up regularly together.

Against every pillar was a *stack* of billets above a man's height, which the watermen that bring wood down the Seine laid there. *Bacon's Natural History.*

While the marquis and his servant on foot were chasing the kid about the *stack*, the prince from horseback killed him with a pistol. *Wotton's Buckingham.*

While the cock
To the *stack* or the barn-door
Stoutly struts his dame before. *Milton.*

Stacks of moist corn grow hot by fermentation. *Newton.*

An inundation, says the fable,
O'erflow'd a farmer's barn and stable;
Whole ricks of hay and *stacks* of corn
Were down the sudden current born. *Swift.*

2. A

2. A number of chimneys or funnels ſtanding together.
A maſon making a *ſtack* of chimneys, the foundation of the houſe ſunk. *Wiſeman's Surgery.*

To STACK. *v. a.* [from the noun.] To pile up regularly in ricks.
So likewiſe a hovel will ſerve for a room,
To *ſtack* on the peaſe. *Tuſſer.*
The prices of *ſtacking* up of wood I ſhall give you. *Mort.*

STACTE. *n. ſ.* An aromatick; the gum that diſtills from the tree which produces myrrh.
Take ſweet ſpices, *ſtacte*, and galbanum. *Ex.* xxx. 34.

STA'DLE. *n. ſ.* [ſtaðel, Saxon, a foundation.]
1. Any thing which ſerves for ſupport to another.
2. A ſtaff; a crutch.
He cometh on, his weak ſteps governing
And aged limbs on cypreſs *ſtadle* ſtout,
And with an ivy twine his waiſt is girt about. *Fa. Queen.*
3. A tree ſuffered to grow for coarſe and common uſes, as poſts or rails. Of this meaning I am doubtful.
Leave growing for *ſtaddles* the likelieſt and beſt,
Though ſeller and buyer diſpatched the reſt. *Tuſſer.*
Coppice-woods, if you leave in them *ſtaddles* too thick, will run to buſhes and briars, and have little clean underwood. *Bac.*

To STA'DLE. *v. a.* [from the noun.] To furniſh with ſtadles.
Firſt ſee it well fenced, ere hewers begin;
Then ſee it well *ſtadled* without and within. *Tuſſer.*

STA'DTHOLDER. *n. ſ.* [*ſtadt* and *houden*, Dutch.] The chief magiſtrate of the United Provinces.

STAFF. *n. ſ.* plur. *ſtaves.* [ſtæf, Saxon; *ſtaff*, Daniſh; *ſtaf*, Dutch.]
1. A ſtick with which a man ſupports himſelf in walking.
It much would pleaſe him,
That of his fortunes you would make a *ſtaff*
To lean upon. *Shakeſp. Ant. and Cleopatra.*
Grant me and my people the benefit of thy chaſtiſements, that thy rod as well as thy *ſtaff* may comfort us. *K. Charles.*
Is it probable that he, who had met whole armies in battle, ſhould now throw away his *ſtaff*, out of fear of a dog. *Broome.*
2. A prop; a ſupport.
Hope is a lover's *ſtaff*; walk hence with that,
And manage it againſt deſpairing thoughts. *Shakeſpeare.*
The boy was the very *ſtaff* of my age, my very prop. *Shak.*
3. A ſtick uſed as a weapon; a club; the handle of an edged or pointed weapon. A *club* properly includes the notion of weight, and the *ſtaff* of length.
I cannot ſtrike at wretched kernes, whoſe arms
Are hir'd to bear their *ſtaves*. *Shakeſp. Macbeth.*
He that bought the ſkin ran greater riſque than t'other that ſold it, and had the worſe end of the *ſtaff*. *L'Eſtrange.*
With forks and *ſtaves* the felon they purſue. *Dryden.*
4. Any long piece of wood.
He forthwith from the glitt'ring *ſtaff* unfurl'd
Th' imperial enſign. *Milton.*
To his ſingle eye, that in his forehead glar'd
Like a full moon, or a broad burniſh'd ſhield,
A forky *ſtaff* we dext'rouſly apply'd,
Which, in the ſpacious ſocket turning round,
Scoopt out the big round gelly from its orb. *Addiſon.*
5. An enſign of an office; a badge of authority.
Methought this *ſtaff*, mine office-badge in court,
Was broke in twain. *Shakeſp. Henry* VI.
All his officers brake their *ſtaves*; but at their return new *ſtaves* were delivered unto them. *Hayward on Edward* VI.
6. [*Stef*, Iſlandick.] A ſtanza; a ſeries of verſes regularly diſpoſed, ſo as that, when the ſtanza is concluded, the ſame order begins again.
Cowley found out that no kind of *ſtaff* is proper for an heroick poem, as being all too lyrical; yet though he wrote in couplets, where rhyme is freer from conſtraint, he affects half verſes. *Dryden.*

STA'FFISH. *adj.* [from *ſtaff.*] Stiff; harſh. Obſolete.
A wit in youth not over dull, heavy, knotty, and lumpiſh, but hard, tough, and though ſomewhat *ſtaffiſh*, both for learning and whole courſe of living, proveth always beſt. *Aſcham.*

STA'FFTREE. *n. ſ.* A ſort of ever green privet.

STAG. *n. ſ.* [Of this word I find no derivation.] The male red deer; the male of the hind.
To the place a poor ſequeſtred *ſtag*,
That from the hunter's aim had ta'en a hurt,
Did come to languiſh. *Shakeſp. As you like it.*
The ſwift *ſtag* from under ground
Bore up his branching head. *Milton.*
Th' inhabitants of ſeas and ſkies ſhall change,
And fiſh on ſhore, and *ſtags* in air ſhall range. *Dryden.*
The *ſtag*
Hears his own feet, and thinks they ſound like more,
And fears his hind legs will o'ertake his fore. *Pope.*

STAGE. *n. ſ.* [*eſtage*, French.]
1. A floor raiſed to view on which any ſhow is exhibited.
2. The theatre; the place of ſcenick entertainments.
And much good do't you then,
Brave pluſh and velvet men:
Can feed on ort; and, ſafe in your *ſtage* clothes,
Dare quit, upon your oaths,
The ſtagers and the *ſtage* wrights too. *Ben. Johnſon.*
Thoſe two Mytilene brethren, baſely born, crept out of a ſmall galliot unto the majeſty of great kings. Herein admire the wonderful changes and chances of theſe worldly things, now up, now down, as if the life of man were not of much more certainty than a *ſtage* play. *Knolles's Hiſt. of the Turks.*
I maintain, againſt the enemies of the *ſtage*, that patterns of piety, decently repreſented, may ſecond the precepts. *Dryd.*
One Livius Andronicus was the firſt *ſtage* player in Rome. *Dryden's Juvenal, Dedication.*
Knights, ſquires, and ſteeds muſt enter on the *ſtage*. *Pope.*
Among ſlaves, who exerciſed polite arts, none ſold ſo dear as *ſtage* players or actors. *Arbuthnot on Coins.*
3. Any place where any thing is publickly tranſacted or performed.
When we are born, we cry that we are come
To this great *ſtage* of fools. *Shakeſp. King Lear.*
4. A place in which reſt is taken on a journey; as much of a journey as is performed without intermiſſion. [*Statio*, Latin.]
I ſhall put you in mind where it was you promiſed to ſet out, or begin your firſt *ſtage*; and beſeech you to go before me my guide. *Hammond's Pract. Catech.*
Our next *ſtage* brought us to the mouth of the Tiber. *Add.*
From thence compell'd by craft and age,
She makes the head her lateſt *ſtage*. *Prior.*
By opening a paſſage from Muſcovy to China, and marking the ſeveral *ſtages*, it was a journey of ſo many days. *Baker.*
5. A ſingle ſtep of gradual proceſs.
The changes and viciſſitude in wars are many; but chiefly in the ſeats or *ſtages* of the war, the weapons, and the manner of the conduct. *Bacon's Eſſays.*
We muſt not expect that our journey through the ſeveral *ſtages* of this life ſhould be all ſmooth and even. *Atterbury.*
To prepare the ſoul to be a fit inhabitant of that holy place to which we aſpire, is to be brought to perfection by gradual advances through ſeveral hard and laborious *ſtages* of diſcipline. *Rogers's Sermons.*
The firſt *ſtage* of healing, or the diſcharge of matter, is by ſurgeons called digeſtion. *Sharp's Surgery.*

To STAGE. *v. a.* [from the noun.] To exhibit publickly. Out of uſe.
I love the people;
But do not like to *ſtage* me to their eyes:
Though it do well, I do not reliſh well
Their loud applauſe. *Shakeſp. Meaſure for Meaſure.*
The quick comedians
Extemp'rally will *ſtage* us, and preſent
Our Alexandrian revels. *Shakeſp. Ant. and Cleopatra.*

STA'GECOACH. *n. ſ.* [*ſtage* and *coach.*] A coach that keeps its ſtages; a coach that paſſes and repaſſes on certain days for the accommodation of paſſengers.
The ſtory was told me by a prieſt, as we travelled in a *ſtagecoach*. *Addiſon.*
When late their miry ſides *ſtagecoaches* ſhow,
And their ſtiff horſes through the town move ſlow,
Then let the prudent walker ſhoes provide. *Gay.*

STA'GEPLAY. *n. ſ.* [*ſtage* and *play.*] Theatrical entertainment.
This rough-caſt unhewn poetry was inſtead of *ſtageplays* for one hundred and twenty years. *Dryden's Juv. Dedication.*

STA'GER. *n. ſ.* [from *ſtage.*]
1. A player.
You ſafe in your ſtage clothes,
Dare quit, upon your oaths,
The *ſtagers* and the ſtage wrights too. *Ben. Johnſon.*
2. One who has long acted on the ſtage of life; a practitioner; a perſon of cunning.
I've heard old cunning *ſtagers*
Say, fools for argument uſe wagers. *Hudibras.*
One experienced *ſtager*, that had baffled twenty traps and tricks before, diſcovered the plot. *L'Eſtrange.*
Some *ſtagers* of the wiſer ſort
Made all theſe idle wonderments their ſport:
But he, who heard what ev'ry fool could ſay,
Would never fix his thought, but trim his time away. *Dryd.*
One cries out, theſe *ſtagers*
Come in good time to make more work for wagers. *Dryd.*
Be by a parſon cheated!
Had you been cunning *ſtagers*,
You might yourſelves be treated
By captains and by majors. *Swift.*

STA'GEVIL. *n. ſ.* A diſeaſe in horſes. *Dict.*

STA'GGARD. *n. ſ.* [from *ſtag.*] A four year old ſtag. *Ainſw.*

To STA'GGER. *v. n.* [*ſtaggeren*, Dutch.]
1. To reel; not to ſtand or walk ſteadily.
He began to appear ſick and giddy, and to *ſtagger*; after which he fell down as dead. *Boyle.*
He ſtruck with all his might
Full on the helmet of th' unwary knight:
Deep was the wound; he *ſtagger'd* with the blow. *Dryden.*

Them

Them revelling the Tentyrites invade,
By giddy heads and *staggering* legs betray'd:
Strange odds! where cropsick drunkards must engage
An hungry foe. *Tate's Juvenal.*

The immediate forerunners of an apoplexy are a vertigo, *staggering*, and loss of memory. *Arbuthnot.*

2. To faint; to begin to give way.

The enemy *staggers*: if you follow your blow, he falls at your feet; but if you allow him respite, he will recover his strength. *Addison.*

3. To hesitate; to fall into doubt; to become less confident or determined.

A man may, if he were fearful, *stagger* in this attempt. *Shak.*

He *staggered* not at the promise of God through unbelief; but was strong in faith. *Rom.* iv. 20.

Three means to fortify belief are experience, reason, and authority: of these the most potent is authority; for belief upon reason, or experience, will *stagger*. *Bacon.*

No hereticks desire to spread
Their light opinions, like these Epicures;
For so their *stagg'ring* thoughts are comforted,
And other mens assent their doubt assures. *Davies.*

If thou confidently depend on the truth of this, without any doubting or *staggering*, this will be accepted by God. *Hamm.*

But let it inward sink and drown my mind:
Falshood shall want its triumph: I begin
To *stagger*; but I'll prop myself within. *Dryden.*

To Sta'gger. *v. a.*

1. To make to stagger; to make to reel.

That hand shall burn in never-quenching fire,
That *staggers* thus my person. *Shakesp. Richard* II.

2. To shock; to alarm; to make less steady or confident.

The question did at first so *stagger* me,
Bearing a state of mighty moment in't. *Shak. Henry* VIII.

When a prince fails in honour and justice, 'tis enough to *stagger* his people in their allegiance. *L'Estrange.*

Whosoever will read the story of this war, will find himself much *staggered*, and put to a kind of riddle. *Howel.*

The shells being lodged with the belemnites, selenites, and other like natural fossils, it was enough to *stagger* a spectator, and make him ready to entertain a belief that these were so too. *Woodward.*

Sta'ggers. *n. s.* [from the verb.]

1. A kind of horse apoplexy.

His horse past cure of the fives, stark spoil'd with the *staggers*. *Shakesp. Taming of the Shrew.*

2. Madness; wild conduct; irregular behaviour. Out of use.

I will throw thee from my care for ever
Into the *staggers*, and the careless lapse
Of youth and ignorance. *Shak. All's well that ends well.*

Sta'gnancy. *n. s.* [from *stagnant.*] The state of being without motion or ventilation.

STA'GNANT. *adj.* [*stagnans*, Latin.] Motionless; still; not agitated; not flowing; not running.

What does the flood from putrefaction keep?
Should it be *stagnant* in its ample seat,
The sun would through it spread destructive heat. *Blackm.*

'Twas owing to this hurry and action of the water that the sand now was cast into layers, and not to a regular settlement, from a water quiet and *stagnant*. *Woodward.*

Immur'd and busied in perpetual sloth,
That gloomy slumber of the *stagnant* soul. *Irene.*

To STA'GNATE. *v. n.* [*stagnum*, Latin.] To lye motionless; to have no course or stream.

The water which now arises must have all *stagnated* at the surface, and could never possibly have been refunded forth upon the earth, had not the strata been thus raised up. *Woodw.*

The aliment moving through the capillary tubes *stagnates*, and unites itself to the vessel through which it flows. *Arbuthn.*

Where creeping waters ooze,
Where marshes *stagnate*. *Thomson.*

Stagna'tion. *n. s.* [from *stagnate.*] Stop of course; cessation of motion.

As the Alps surround Geneva on all sides, they form a vast bason, where there would be a constant *stagnation* of vapours, did not the north wind scatter them from time to time. *Addison.*

To what great ends subservient is the wind?
Behold, where e'er this active vapour flies,
It drives the clouds, and agitates the skies:
This from *stagnation* and corruption saves
Th' aerial ocean's ever-rolling waves. *Blackmore's Creation.*

Staid. *participial adjective.* [from *stay.*] Sober; grave; regular; composed; not wild; not volatile.

Put thyself
Into a 'haviour of less fear, ere wildness
Vanquish my *staider* senses. *Shakespeare's Cymbeline.*

This seems to our weaker view,
O'erlaid with black *staid* wisdom's hue. *Milton.*

I should not be a persuader to them of studying much in the Spring, after three years that they have well laid their grounds; but to ride out, with prudent and *staid* guides, to all the quarters of the land. *Milton on Education.*

I am the more at ease in sir Roger's family, because it consists of sober and *staid* persons. *Addison.*

Sta'idness. *n. s.* [from *staid.*] Sobriety; gravity; regularity; contrariety to wildness.

The boiling blood of youth, fiercely agitating the fluid air, hinders that serenity and fixed *staidness* which is necessary to so severe an intentness. *Glanv. Sceps.*

If sometimes he appears too gay, yet a secret gracefulness of youth accompanies his writings, though the *staidness* and sobriety of age be wanting. *Dryd. Preface to Ovid.*

To STAIN. *v. a.* [*ystaenio*, Welsh, from *ys* and *taenu*.
Rhag Gwyar or Gnawd,
Afar *ystaenawd*. *Taliessyn*, an old British poet.]

1. To blot; to spot; to maculate.

Lend me a looking-glass;
If that her breath will mist or *stain* the stone,
Why then she lives. *Shakespeare's King Lear.*

From the gash a stream
His armour *stain'd*, ere while so bright. *Milton.*

Embrace again, my sons: be foes no more,
Nor *stain* your country with your children's gore. *Dryden.*

2. To disgrace; to spot with guilt or infamy.

Of honour void, of innocence, of faith, of purity,
Our wonted ornaments now soil'd and *stain'd*. *Milton.*

Stain. *n. s.* [from the verb.]

1. Blot; spot; discoloration.

Nor death itself can wholly wash their *stains*;
But long contracted filth ev'n in the soul remains:
The reliques of inveterate vice they wear,
And spots of sin. *Dryden's Æn.*

We no where meet with a more pleasing show than what appears in the heavens at the rising and setting of the sun, which is wholly made up of those different *stains* of light that shew themselves in clouds of a different situation. *Addison.*

Swift trouts diversify'd with crimson *stains*,
And pikes, the tyrants of the wat'ry plains. *Pope.*

2. Taint of guilt or infamy.

To solemn actions of royalty and justice their suitable ornaments are a beauty: are they only in religion a *stain*? *Hooker.*

Our opinion, concerning the force and virtue which such places have, is, I trust, without any blemish or *stain* of heresy. *Hooker.*

Then heav'n and earth renew'd, shall be made pure
To sanctity, that shall receive no *stain*. *Milton's Par. Lost.*

Ulysses bids his friends to cast lots; for if he had made the choice himself, they whom he had rejected might have judged it a *stain* upon them for want of merit. *Broome.*

3. Cause of reproach; shame.

Hereby I will lead her that is the praise, and yet the *stain* of all womankind. *Sidney.*

Sta'iner. *n. s.* [from *stain.*] One who stains; one who blots.

Sta'inless. *adj.* [from *stain.*]

1. Free from blots or spots.

The phenix wings are not so rare
For faultless length and *stainless* hue. *Sidney.*

2. Free from sin or reproach.

I cannot love him;
Yet I suppose him virtuous, know him noble,
Of great estate, of fresh and *stainless* youth. *Shakespeare.*

STAIR. *n. s.* [ꞅᵹæᵹeꞃ, Saxon; *steghe*, Dutch.] Steps by which we rise an ascent from the lower part of a building to the upper. *Stair* was anciently used for the whole order of steps; but *stair* now, if it be used at all, signifies, as in *Milton*, only one flight of steps.

A good builder to a high tower will not make his *stair* upright, but winding almost the full compass about, that the steepness be the more insensible. *Sidney.*

How many cowards, whose hearts are all as false
As *stairs* of sand, wear yet upon their chins
The beards of Hercules and frowning Mars! *Shakespeare.*

Slaver with lips as common as the *stairs*
That mount the Capitol. *Shakesp.*

I would have one only goodly room above *stairs*, of some forty foot high. *Bacon's Essays.*

Sir James Tirrel repairing to the Tower by night, attended by two servants, stood at the *stair*-foot, and sent these two villains to execute the murder. *Bacon.*

There being good *stairs* at either end, they never went through each other's quarters. *Clarendon.*

The *stairs* were such as whereon Jacob saw
Angels ascending and descending. *Milton's Parad. Lost.*

Satan now on the lower *stair*,
That scal'd by steps of gold to heav'n gate,
Looks down with wonder at the sudden view
Of all this world. *Milton's Parad. Lost.*

Trembling he springs,
As terror had increas'd his feet with wings;
Nor staid for *stairs*; but down the depth he threw
His body: on his back the door he drew. *Dryden.*

Sta'ircase. *n. s.* [*stair* and *case.*] The part of a fabrick that contains the stairs.

To make a complete *ſtaircaſe* is a curious piece of architecture. *Wotton.*

I cannot forbear mentioning a *ſtaircaſe*, where the eaſineſs of the aſcent, the diſpoſition of the lights, and the convenient landing, are admirably contrived. *Addiſon on Italy.*

STAKE. *n. ſ.* [ſtaca, Saxon; *ſtaeck*, Dutch; *eſtaca*, Spaniſh.]

1. A poſt or ſtrong ſtick fixed in the ground.

The more I ſhaked the *ſtake*, which he had planted in the ground of my heart, the deeper ſtill it ſunk into it. *Sidney.*

His credit in the world might ſtand the poor town in great ſtead, as hitherto their miniſters foreign eſtimation hath been the beſt *ſtake* in their hedge. *Hooker.*

He wanted pikes to ſet before his archers;
Inſtead whereof ſharp *ſtakes*, pluckt out of hedges,
They pitched in the ground. *Shakeſp. Henry VI.*

In France the grapes that make the wine grow upon low vines bound to ſmall *ſtakes*, and the raiſed vines in arbors make but verjuice. *Bacon's Natural Hiſtory.*

Or ſharpen *ſtakes*, or head the forks, or twine
The ſallow twigs to tie the ſtraggling vine. *Dryden.*

2. A piece of wood.

While he whirl'd in fiery circles round
The brand, a ſharpen'd *ſtake* ſtrong Dryas found,
And in the ſhoulder's joint inflicts the wound. *Dryden.*

3. Any thing placed as a paliſade or fence.

That hollow I ſhould know: what are you, ſpeak?
Come not too near, you fall on iron *ſtakes* elſe. *Milton.*

4. The poſt to which a beaſt is tied to be baited.

We are at the *ſtake*,
And bay'd about with many enemies. *Shakeſp. Jul. Cæſar.*

Have you not ſet mine honour at the *ſtake*,
And baited it with all th' unmuzzled thoughts
That tyrannous heart can think? *Shak. Twelfth Night.*

5. Any thing pledged or wagered. I know not well whence it has this meaning.

'Tis time ſhort pleaſure now to take,
Of little life the beſt to make,
And manage wiſely the laſt *ſtake*. *Cowley.*

O then, what intereſt ſhall I make
To ſave my laſt important *ſtake*,
When the moſt juſt have cauſe to quake! *Roſcommon.*

He ventures little for ſo great a *ſtake*. *More.*

Th' increaſing ſound is borne to either ſhore,
And for their *ſtakes* the throwing nations fear. *Dryden.*

The game was ſo contrived, that one particular caſt took up the whole *ſtake*; and when ſome others came up, you laid down. *Arbuthnot.*

6. The ſtate of being hazarded, pledged, or wagered.

When he heard that the lady Margaret was declared for it, he ſaw plainly that his kingdom muſt again be put to the *ſtake*, and that he muſt fight for it. *Bacon's Henry VII.*

Are not our liberties, our lives,
The laws, religion, and our wives,
Enough at once to lie at *ſtake*,
For cov'nant and the cauſe's ſake? *Hudibras.*

Of my crown thou too much care do'ſt take;
That which I value more, my love's at *ſtake*. *Dryden.*

Hath any of you a great intereſt at *ſtake* in a diſtant part of the world? Hath he ventured a good ſhare of his fortune? *Att.*

Every moment Cato's life's at *ſtake*. *Addiſ. Cato.*

7. The *ſtake* is a ſmall anvil, which ſtands upon a ſmall iron foot on the work-bench, to remove as occaſion offers; or elſe it hath a ſtrong iron ſpike at the bottom let into ſome place of the work-bench, not to be removed. Its office is to ſet ſmall cold work ſtraight upon, or to cut or punch upon with the cold chiſſel or cold punch. *Moxon's Mech. Exer.*

To STAKE. *v. a.* [from the noun.]

1. To faſten, ſupport, or defend with poſts ſet upright.

Stake and bind up your weakeſt plants and flowers againſt the winds, before they in a moment proſtrate a whole year's labour. *Evelyn's Kalendar.*

2. To wager; to hazard; to put to hazard.

Is a man betrayed in his neareſt concerns? The cauſe is, he relied upon the ſervices of a pack of villains, who deſigned nothing but their own game, and to *ſtake* him while they play'd for themſelves. *South.*

Perſons, after their priſons have been flung open, have choſen rather to languiſh in their dungeons than *ſtake* their miſerable lives on the ſucceſs of a revolution. *Addiſon.*

They durſt not *ſtake* their preſent and future happineſs on their own chimerical imaginations. *Addiſon.*

I'll *ſtake* yon' lamb that near the fountain plays,
And from the brink his dancing ſhade ſurveys. *Pope.*

STALACTITES. *n. ſ.* [from σαλαζω.]

Stalactites is only ſpar in the ſhape of an icicle, accidentally formed in the perpendicular fiſſures of the ſtone. *Woodward.*

STALA'CTICAL. *adj.* Reſembling an icicle.

A cave was lined with thoſe *ſtalactical* ſtones on the top and ſides. *Derham's Phyſico-Theology.*

STALAGMI'TES. *n. ſ.* Spar formed into the ſhape of drops. *Woodward's Meth. Foſſ.*

STALE. *adj.* [*ſtelle*, Dutch.]

1. Old; long kept; altered by time. *Stale* is not uſed of perſons otherwiſe than in contempt.

This, Richard, is a curious caſe·
Suppoſe your eyes ſent equal rays
Upon two diſtant pots of ale,
Not knowing which was mild or *ſtale*;
In this ſad ſtate your doubtful choice
Would never have the caſting voice. *Prior.*

A *ſtale* virgin ſets up a ſhop in a place where ſhe is not known. *Spectator.*

2. Uſed 'till it is of no uſe or eſteem; worn out of regard or notice.

The duke regarded not the muttering multitude, knowing that rumours grow *ſtale* and vaniſh with time. *Hayward.*

About her neck a pacquet mail,
Fraught with advice, ſome freſh, ſome *ſtale*. *Butler.*

Many things beget opinion; ſo doth novelty: wit itſelf, if *ſtale*, is leſs taking. *Grew's Coſmol.*

Pompey was a perfect favourite of the people; but his pretenſions grew *ſtale* for want of a timely opportunity of introducing them upon the ſtage. *Swift.*

They reaſon and conclude by precedent,
And own *ſtale* nonſenſe which they ne'er invent. *Pope.*

STALE. *n. ſ.* [from ſtælan, Saxon, to ſteal.]

1. Something exhibited or offered as an allurement to draw others to any place or purpoſe.

His heart being wholly delighted in deceiving us, we could never be warned; but rather one bird caught, ſerved for a *ſtale* to bring in more. *Sidney.*

Still as he went he crafty *ſtales* did lay,
With cunning trains him to entrap unwares;
And privy ſpials plac'd in all his way,
To weet what courſe he takes, and how he fares. *Fa. Qu.*

The trumpery in my houſe bring hither,
For *ſtale* to catch theſe thieves. *Shakeſp. Tempeſt.*

Had he none elſe to make a *ſtale* but me?
I was the chief that rais'd him to the crown,
And I'll be chief to bring him down again. *Shakeſ. H.VI.*

A pretence of kindneſs is the univerſal *ſtale* to all baſe projects: by this men are robbed of their fortunes, and women of their honour. *Government of the Tongue.*

It may be a vizor for the hypocrite, and a *ſtale* for the ambitious. *Decay of Piety.*

This eaſy fool muſt be my *ſtale*, ſet up
To catch the people's eyes: he's tame and merciful;
Him I can manage. *Dryden's Don Sebaſtian.*

2. In *Shakeſpeare* it ſeems to ſignify a proſtitute.

I ſtand diſhonour'd, that have gone about
To link my dear friend to a common *ſtale*. *Shakeſpeare.*

3. [From *ſtale*, adj.] Urine; old urine.

4. Old beer; beer ſomewhat acidulated.

5. [*Stele*, Dutch, a ſtick.] A handle.

It hath a long *ſtale* or handle, with a button at the end for one's hand. *Mortimer's Huſbandry.*

To STALE. *v. a.* [from the adjective] To wear out; to make old.

Age cannot wither her, nor cuſtom *ſtale*
Her infinite variety. *Shakeſp. Ant. and Cleopatra.*

Were I a common laugher, or did uſe
To *ſtale* with ordinary oaths my love
To every new proteſtor. *Shakeſp. Julius Cæſar.*

A barren-ſpirited fellow, one that feeds
On abject orts and imitations;
Which, out of uſe, and *ſtal'd* by other men,
Begin his faſhion. *Shakeſp. Julius Cæſar.*

To STALE. *v. n.* [from the noun.] To make water.

Having ty'd his beaſt t' a pale,
And taken time for both to *ſtale*. *Hudibras.*

STA'LELY. *adv.* [from *ſtale*.] Of old; long time.

All your promis'd mountains
And ſeas I am ſo *ſtalely* acquainted with. *Ben. Johnſon.*

STA'LENESS. *n. ſ.* [from *ſtale*.] Oldneſs; ſtate of being long kept; ſtate of being corrupted by time.

The beer and wine, as well within water as above, have not been palled; but ſomewhat better than bottles of the ſame drinks and *ſtaleneſs*, kept in a cellar. *Bacon's Nat. Hiſtory.*

Provided our landlord's principles were ſound, we did not take any notice of the *ſtaleneſs* of his proviſions. *Addiſon.*

To STALK. *v. n.* [ſtealcan, Saxon.]

1. To walk with high and ſuperb ſteps. It is uſed commonly in a ſenſe of diſlike.

His monſtrous enemy
With ſturdy ſteps came *ſtalking* in his ſight. *Fairy Queen.*

Shall your city call us lord,
In that behalf which we challeng'd it?
Or ſhall we give the ſignal to our rage,
And *ſtalk* in blood to our poſſeſſion? *Shakeſp. K. John.*

Unfold th' eternal door:
You ſee before the gate what *ſtalking* ghoſt
Commands the guard, what ſentries keep the poſt. *Dryden.*

Bertran

Bertran
Stalks close behind her, like a witch's fiend
Pressing to be employ'd. *Dryden's Spanish Fryar.*

They pass their precious hours in plays and sports,
'Till death behind came *stalking* on unseen. *Dryden.*

With manly mien he *stalk'd* along the ground;
Nor wanted voice bely'd, nor vaunting sound. *Dryden.*

Then *stalking* through the deep
He fords the ocean, while the topmost wave
Scarce reaches up his middle side. *Addison.*

'Tis not to *stalk* about, and draw fresh air
From time to time. *Addison's Cato.*

Vexatious thought still found my flying mind,
Nor bound by limits, nor to place confin'd;
Haunted my nights, and terrify'd my days;
Stalk'd through my gardens, and pursu'd my ways,
Nor shut from artful bow'r, nor lost in winding maze. *Pri.*

Scornful turning from the shore
My haughty step, I *stalk'd* the valley o'er. *Pope's Odyssey.*

2. To walk behind a stalking horse or cover.

The king asked how far it was to a certain town: they said six miles. Half an hour after he asked again: one said six miles and a half. The king alighted out of his coach, and crept under the shoulder of his led horse: and when some asked his majesty what he meant, I must *stalk*, said he; for yonder town is shy, and flies me. *Bacon's Apophthegms.*

STALK. *n. s.* [from the verb.]

1. High, proud, wide, and stately step.

Behind it forth there leapt
An ugly fiend, more foul than dismal day;
The which with monstrous *stalk* behind him stept,
And ever as he went due watch upon him kept. *Fa. Queen.*

Great Milton next, with high and haughty *stalks*,
Unfetter'd in majestick numbers walks. *Addison.*

2. [*Stele*, Dutch.] The stem on which flowers or fruits grow.

A stock-gillyflower, gently tied on a stick, put into a steep glass full of quicksilver, so that the quicksilver cover it; after five days you will find the flower fresh, and the *stalk* harder and less flexible than it was. *Bacon.*

Small store will serve, where store,
All seasons, ripe for use hangs on the *stalk*. *Milton.*

That amber attracts not basil is wholly repugnant unto truth; for if the leaves thereof, or dried *stalks*, be stripped unto small straws, they arise unto amber, wax, and other electricks, no otherways than those of wheat and rye. *Brown.*

Roses unbid, and ev'ry fragrant flow'r,
Flew from their *stalks* to strew thy nuptial bow'r. *Dryden.*

3. The stem of a quill.

Viewed with a glass, they appear made up of little bladders, like those in the plume or *stalk* of a quill. *Grew.*

STAL'KINGHORSE. *n. s.* [*stalking* and *horse*.] A horse either real or fictitious by which a fowler shelters himself from the sight of the game; a mask; a pretence.

Let the counsellor give counsel not for faction but for conscience, forbearing to make the good of the state the *stalkinghorse* of his private ends. *Hakewill on Providence.*

Hypocrisy is the devil's *stalkinghorse*, under an affectation of simplicity and religion. *L'Estrange.*

STA'LKY. *adj.* [from *stalk*.] Hard like a stalk.

It grows upon a round stalk, and at the top bears a great *stalky* head. *Mortimer.*

STALL. *n. s.* [ꞅꞇeal, Saxon; *stal*, Dutch; *stalla*, Italian.]

1. A crib in which an ox is fed, or where any horse is kept in the stable.

A herd of oxen then he carv'd, with high rais'd heads, forg'd all
Of gold and tin, for colour mixt, and bellowing from their *stall*,
Rusht to their pastures. *Chapman's Iliad.*

Duncan's horses,
Beauteous and swift, the minions of the race,
Turn'd wild in nature, broke their *stalls*, flung out,
Contending 'gainst obedience. *Shakes. Macbeth.*

Solomon had forty thousand *stalls* of horses. *1 Kings iv.*

His fellow sought what lodging he could find;
At last he found a *stall* where oxen stood. *Dryden.*

2. A bench or form where any thing is set to sale.

Stalls, bulks, windows,
Are smother'd up, leads fill'd, and ridges hors'd
With variable complections; all agreeing
In earnestness to see him. *Shakesp. Coriolanus.*

They are nature's coarser wares that lie on the *stall*, exposed to the transient view of every common eye. *Glanv.*

Bess Hoy first found it troublesome to bawl,
And therefore plac'd her cherries on a *stall*. *King.*

How pedlars *stalls* with glitt'ring toys are laid,
The various fairings of the country maid. *Gay.*

Harley, the nation's great support,
Returning home one day from court,
Observ'd a parson near Whitehall,
Cheap'ning old authors on a *stall*. *Swift.*

3. [*Stall*, Swedish; *stal*, Armorick.] A small house or shed in which certain trades are practised.

All these together in one heap were thrown,
Like carcases of beasts in butcher's *stall*;
And in another corner wide were strown
The antique ruins of the Roman's fall. *Fairy Queen.*

4. The seat of a dignified clergyman in the choir.

The pope creates a canon beyond the number limited, and commands the chapter to assign unto such canon a *stall* in the choir and place in the chapter. *Ayliffe's Parergon.*

The dignified clergy, out of mere humility, have called their thrones by the names of *stalls*. *Warburton.*

To STALL. *v. a.* [from the noun.]

1. To keep in a stall or stable.

For such encheason, if you go nie,
Few chimneys reeking you will espy;
The fat ox, that wont ligg in the stall,
Is now fast *stalled* in his crumenal. *Spenser's Pastorals.*

For my part, he keeps me rustically at home; or, to speak more properly, sties me here at home unkept: for call you that keeping, for a gentleman of my birth, that differs not from the *stalling* of an ox? *Shakespeare.*

Nisus the forest pass'd,
And Alban plains, from Alba's name so call'd,
Where king Latinus then his oxen *stall'd*. *Dryden.*

2. [For *install*.] To invest.

Long may'st thou live to wail thy children's loss;
And see another as I see thee now,
Deck'd in thy rights, as thou art *stall'd* in mine. *Shakesp.*

To STALL. *v. n.*

1. To inhabit; to dwell.

We could not *stall* together in the world. *Shakespeare.*

2. To kennel.

STA'LLFED. *adj.* [*stall* and *fed*.] Fed not with grass but dry feed.

Stallfed oxen, and crammed fowls, are often diseased in their livers. *Arbuthnot on Aliments.*

STA'LLWORN. *adj.* [*stall* and *worn*.] Long kept in the stable. But it is probably a mistake for *stalworth*, [ꞅꞇapelpeꞃð, Saxon, stout.]

His *stallworn* steed the champion stout bestrode. *Shakesp.*

STA'LLION. *n. s.* [*ysdalwyn*, an old Welch word: the one is derived from the other; but which from which I cannot certainly tell. *Wotton.* *Estallion*, French; *stallone*, Italian; *stalhengst*, Dutch. *Junius* thinks it derived from ꞅꞇælan, to leap.] A horse kept for mares.

The present defects are breeding without choice of *stallions* in shape or size. *Temple.*

If fleet Dragon's progeny at last
Prove jaded, and in frequent matches cast,
No favour for the *stallion* we retain,
And no respect for the degen'rate strain. *Dryden.*

I will not ask him one of his Egyptians;
No, let him keep 'em all for slaves and *stallions*. *Dryden.*

STA'MINA. *n. s.* [Latin.]

1. The first principles of any thing.
2. The solids of a human body.
3. [In botany.] Those little fine threads or capillaments which grow up within the flowers of plants, encompassing round the style, and on which the apices grow at their extremities.

STA'MINEOUS. *adj.* [*stamineus*, Latin.]

1. Consisting of threads.
2. Stamineous flowers.

Stamineous flowers are so far imperfect as to want those coloured leaves which are called petala, and consist only of the stylus and the stamina; and such plants as do bear these *stamineous* flowers Ray makes to constitute a large genus of plants: these he divides into such as, first, have their fruit or seed totally divided from the flower; and these are such plants as are said to be of different sexes: the reason of which is, that from the said seed some plant shall arise with flowers and no fruit, and others with fruit and no flowers; as hops, hemp, stinging nettles. 2. Such as have their fruit only a little disjointed from their flowers; as the ricinus, and the heliotropium tricoccon. 3. Such as have their fruit immediately contiguous, or adhering to their flower. 4. Such whose flowers adhere to the top or uppermost of the seed; as the beta, asarum, and alchimilla.

STA'MMEL. *n. s.* Of this word I know not the meaning.

Reedhood, the first that doth appear
In *stammel*: scarlet is too dear. *Ben. Johnson.*

To STA'MMER. *v. n.* [ꞅꞇamen, a stammerer, Saxon; *stamelen*, *stameren*, to stammer, Dutch.] To speak with unnatural hesitation; to utter words with difficulty.

Sometimes to her news of myself to tell
I go about; but then is all my best
Wry words, and *stamm'ring*, or else doltish dumb:
Say then, can this but of enchantment come? *Sidney.*

I would thou could'st *stammer*, that thou might'st pour out of thy mouth, as wine comes out of a narrow-mouth'd bottle, either too much at once, or none at all. *Shakespeare.*

She *stammers*; oh what grace in lisping lies!
If she says nothing, to be sure she's wise. *Dryden.*

Lagean juice,
Which *stammering* tongues and stagg'ring feet produce. *Dryd.*

Cornelius hoped he would come to *stammer* like Demosthenes. *Arbuthn. Mart. Scrib.*

Your hearers would rather you should be less correct, than perpetually *stammering*, which is one of the worst solecisms in rhetorick. *Swift.*

STA'MMERER. *n. s.* [from *stammer.*] One who speaks with hesitation.

A *stammerer* cannot with moderation hope for the gift of tongues, or a peasant to become learned as Origen. *Taylor.*

To STAMP *v. a.* [*stampen*, Dutch; *stamper*, Danish.]

1. To strike by pressing the foot hastily downwards.

If Arcite thus deplore
His suff'rings, Palamon yet suffers more:
He frets, he fumes, he stares, he *stamps* the ground;
The hollow tow'r with clamours rings around. *Dryden.*

2. To pound; to beat as in a mortar.

I took the calf you had made, burnt it with fire, and *stamped* and ground it very small. *Deutr.* ix. 21.

Some apothecaries, upon *stamping* of coloquintida, have been put into a great scouring by the vapour only. *Bacon.*

3. [*Estamper*, French; *stampare*, Italian; *estampar*, Spanish.] To impress with some mark or figure.

Height of place is intended only to *stamp* the endowments of a private condition with lustre and authority. *South.*

Here swells the shelf with Ogilby the great;
There, *stamp'd* with arms, Newcastle shines complete. *Pope.*

4. To fix a mark by impressing it.

Out of mere ambition, you have made
Your holy hat be *stampt* on the king's coin. *Shakespeare.*

These prodigious conceits in nature spring out of framing abstracted conceptions, instead of those easy and primary notions which nature *stamps* alike in all men of common sense. *Digby on Bodies.*

There needs no positive law or sanction of God to *stamp* an obliquity upon such a disobedience. *South's Sermons.*

No constant reason of this can be given, but from the nature of man's mind, which hath this notion of a deity born with it, and *stamped* upon it; or is of such a frame, that in the free use of itself it will find out God. *Tillotson.*

Though God has given us no innate ideas of himself, though he has *stampt* no original characters on our minds, wherein we may read his being; yet having furnished us with those faculties our minds are endowed with, he hath not left himself without witness. *Locke.*

Can they perceive the impressions from things without, and be at the same time ignorant of those characters which nature herself has taken care to *stamp* within? *Locke.*

What titles had they had, if nature had not
Strove hard to thrust the worst deserving first,
And *stamp'd* the noble mark of eldership
Upon their baser metal? *Rowe's Ambitious Stepmother.*

What an unspeakable happiness would it be to a man engaged in the pursuit of knowledge, if he had but a power of *stamping* his best sentiments upon his memory in indelible characters? *Watts.*

5. To make by impressing a mark.

If two penny weight of silver, marked with a certain impression, shall here in England be equivalent to three penny weight marked with another impression, they will not fail to *stamp* pieces of that fashion, and quickly carry away your silver. *Locke.*

6. To mint; to form; to coin.

We are bastards all;
And that most venerable man, which
I did call my father, was I know not where
When I was *stampt*. *Shakesp. Cymbeline.*

To STAMP. *v. n.* To strike the foot suddenly downward.

What a fool art thou,
A ramping fool, to brag, to *stamp*, and swear,
Upon my party! Thou cold-blooded slave,
Hast thou not spoke like thunder on my side? *Shakespeare.*

The men shall howl at the noise of the *stamping* of the hoofs of his strong horses. *Jer.* xlvii. 3.

There is such an echo among the old ruins and vaults, that, if you *stamp* but a little louder than ordinary, you hear the sound repeated. *Addison's Spectator.*

He cannot bear th' astonishing delight,
But starts, exclaims, and *stamps*, and raves and dies. *Dennis.*

They got to the top, which was flat and even, and *stamping* upon it, they found it was hollow. *Gulliver's Travels.*

STAMP. *n. s.* [*estampe*, French; *stampa*, Italian.]

1. Any instrument by which a hollow impression is made.

Some other nymphs, with colours faint
And pencil slow, may Cupid paint,
And a weak heart in time destroy:
She has a *stamp*, and prints the boy. *Waller.*

'Tis gold so pure,
It cannot bear the *stamp* without allay. *Dryden.*

2. A mark set on any thing; impression.

That sacred name gives ornament and grace,
And, like his *stamp*, makes basest metals pass:
'Twere folly now a stately pile to raise,
To build a playhouse, while you throw down plays. *Dryd.*

Ideas are imprinted on the memory; some by an object affecting the senses only; others, that have more than once offered themselves, have yet been little taken notice of; the mind, intent only on one thing, not settling the *stamp* deep into itself. *Locke.*

3. A thing marked or stamped.

The mere despair of surgery he cures;
Hanging a golden *stamp* about their necks,
Put on with holy prayers. *Shakesp. Macbeth.*

4. A picture cut in wood or metal; a picture made by impression; a cut; a plate.

At Venice they put out very curious *stamps* of the several edifices, which are most famous for their beauty and magnificence. *Addison on Italy.*

5. A mark set upon things that pay customs to the government.

Indeed the paper *stamp*
Did very much his genius cramp;
And since he could not spend his fire,
He now intended to retire. *Swift.*

6. A character of reputation, good or bad, fixed upon any thing.

The persons here reflected upon are of such a peculiar *stamp* of impiety, that they seem formed into a kind of diabolical society for the finding out new experiments in vice. *South.*

Where reason or scripture is expressed for any opinion, we may receive it as of divine authority; but it is not the strength of our own persuasions which can give it that *stamp*. *Locke.*

7. Authority; currency; value derived from any suffrage or attestation.

Of the same *stamp* is that which is obtruded upon us, that an adamant suspends the attraction of the loadstone. *Brown.*

The common people do not judge of vice or virtue by morality, or the immorality, so much as by the *stamp* that is set upon't by men of figure. *L'Estrange.*

8. Make; cast; form.

If speaking truth
In this fine age were not thought flatt'ry,
Such attribution should this Douglas have,
As not a soldier of this season's *stamp*
Should go so general current through the world. *Shakesp.*

When one man of an exemplary improbity charges another of the same *stamp* in a court of justice, he lies under the disadvantage of a strong suspicion. *L'Estrange.*

Let a friend to the government relate to him a matter of fact, he gives him the lye in every look; but if one of his own *stamp* should tell him that the king of Sweden would be suddenly at Perth, he hugs himself at the good news. *Addison.*

STA'MPER. *n. s.* [from *stamp.*] An instrument of pounding.

From the stamping-mill it passeth through the crazing-mill; but of late times they mostly use wet *stampers*. *Carew.*

STAN, amongst our forefathers, was the termination of the superlative degree: so *Athelstan*, most noble; *Betstan*, the best; *Leofstan*, the dearest; *Wistan*, the wisest; *Dunstan*, the highest. *Gibson's Camden.*

To STANCH. *v. a.* [*estancher*, French; *stagnare*, Italian.] To stop blood; to hinder from running.

Iron or a stone, laid to the neck, doth *stanch* the bleeding of the nose. *Bacon's Natural History.*

Of veins of earth medicinal are terra lemnia, terra sigillata, communis, and bolus armenus; whereof terra lemnia is the chief: the virtues of them are for curing of wounds, *stanching* of blood, and stopping of fluxes and rheums. *Bacon.*

Leeches, inwardly taken, fasten upon the veins, and occasion an effusion of blood, which cannot be easily *stanched*. *Brown's Vulgar Errours.*

He fought to hinder fighting, and assay'd
To *stanch* blood by breathing of the vein. *Dryden.*

To STANCH. *v. n.* To stop.

A woman touched the hem of his garment, and immediately her issue *stanched*. *Lu.* viii. 44.

STANCH. *adj.* [This seems to come from the verb.]

1. Sound; such as will not run out.

What we endeavoured in vain may be performed by some virtuoso, that shall have *stancher* vessels, and more sunny days. *Boyle.*

2. Firm; sound of principle; trusty; hearty; determined.

The standing absurdity, without the belief of which no man is reckoned a *stanch* churchman, is that there is a calf's-head club. *Addison.*

In politicks, I hear, you're *stanch*,
Directly bent against the French. *Prior.*

Each *staunch* polemick stubborn as a rock,
Each fierce logician still expelling Locke,
Came whip and spur. *Dunciad.*

3. Strong; not to be broken.

If I knew
What hoop would hold us *ſtaunch* from edge to edge
O' th' world, I would purſue it. *Shak. Ant. and Cleopatra.*

You will loſe their love: this is to be kept *ſtanch*, and carefully watched. *Locke.*

STA'NCHION. *n. ſ.* [*eſtançon*, French.] A prop; a ſupport.

STA'NCHLESS. *adj.* [from *ſtanch.*] Not to be ſtopped.

There grows,
In my moſt ill compos'd affection, ſuch
A *ſtanchleſs* avarice, that, were I king,
I ſhould cut off the nobles for their lands. *Shakeſ. Macbeth.*

To STAND. *v. n.* preterite *I ſtood, I have ſtood.* [ƿtanban, Gothick and Saxon; *ſtaen*, Dutch; *ſtare*, Italian; *eſtar*, Spaniſh; *ſtare*, Latin.]

1. To be upon the feet; not to ſit or lie down.
2. To be not demoliſhed or overthrown.

What will they then? what but unbuild
A living temple, built by faith to *ſtand?* *Milton.*

3. To be placed as an edifice.

This poet's tomb *ſtood* on the other ſide of Naples, which looks towards Veſuvio. *Addiſon on Italy.*

4. To remain erect; not to fall.

Chariot and charioteer lay overturn'd,
And fiery foaming ſteeds: what *ſtood*, recoil'd
O'erweary'd, through the faint ſatanick hoſt
Defenſive ſcarce, or with pale fear ſurpris'd
Fled ignominious. *Milton's Paradiſe Loſt.*

5. To become erect.

The rooted fibres roſe, and from the wound
Black bloody drops diſtill'd upon the ground:
Mute, and amaz'd, my hair with horror *ſtood*;
Fear ſhrunk my ſenſes, and congeal'd my blood. *Dryden.*

Her hair *ſtood* up; convulſive rage poſſeſs'd
Her trembling limbs. *Dryden's Æn.*

6. To ſtop; to halt; not to go forward.

The leaders, having charge from you to *ſtand*,
Will not go off until they hear you ſpeak. *Shakeſ. H.* VI.

Sun in Gideon *ſtand*,
And thou moon in the vale of Ajalon. *Milton.*

Mortal, who this forbidden path
In arms preſum'ſt to tread, I charge thee *ſtand*,
And tell thy name. *Dryden's Æn.*

7. To be at a ſtationary point without progreſs or regreſſion.

This nation of Spain runs a race ſtill of empire, when all other ſtates of Chriſtendom *ſtand* at a ſtay. *Bacon.*

Immenſe the pow'r, immenſe were the demand;
Say, at what part of nature will they *ſtand?* *Pope.*

8. To be in a ſtate of firmneſs, not vacillation.

Commonwealths by virtue ever *ſtood.* *Davies.*

To *ſtand* or fall,
Free in thine own arbitrement it lies. *Milton.*

My mind on its own centre *ſtands* unmov'd,
And ſtable as the fabrick of the world,
Propt on itſelf. *Dryden.*

9. To be in any poſture of reſiſtance or defence.

Seeing how lothly oppoſite I *ſtood*
To his unnat'ral purpoſe, in fell motion
With his prepared ſword he charges home
My unprovided body. *Shakeſp. King Lear.*

From enemies heav'n keep your majeſty;
And when they *ſtand* againſt you, may they fall. *Shakeſp.*

10. To be in a ſtate of hoſtility; to keep the ground.

If he would preſently yield, Barbaroſſa promiſed to let him go free; but if he ſhould *ſtand* upon his defence, he threatened to make him repent his fooliſh hardineſs. *Knolles.*

The king granted the Jews to gather themſelves together, and *ſtand* for their life. *Eſth.* viii. 11.

We are often conſtrained to *ſtand* alone againſt the ſtrength of opinion. *Brown's Preface to Vulgar Errours.*

It was by the ſword they ſhould die, if they *ſtood* upon defence; and by the halter, if they ſhould yield. *Hayward.*

11. Not to yield; not to fly; not to give way.

Who before him *ſtood* ſo to it? for the Lord brought his enemies unto him. *Ecclus* xlvi. 3.

Put on the whole armour of God, that ye may be able to *ſtand* againſt the wiles of the devil. *Eph.* vi. 11.

Their lives and fortunes were put in ſafety, whether they *ſtood* to it or ran away. *Bacon's Henry* VII.

12. To ſtay; not to fly.

At the ſoldierly word *ſtand* the flyers halted a little. *Clarend.*

13. To be placed with regard to rank or order.

Amongſt liquids endued with this quality of relaxing, warm water *ſtands* firſt. *Arbuthnot on Aliments.*

Theology would truly enlarge the mind, were it ſtudied with that freedom and that ſacred charity which it teaches: let this therefore *ſtand* always chief. *Watts.*

14. To remain in the preſent ſtate.

If meat make my brother offend, I will eat no fleſh while the world *ſtandeth.* 1 *Cor.* viii. 13.

That ſots and knaves ſhould be ſo vain
To wiſh their vile reſemblance may remain;
And *ſtand* recorded, at their own requeſt,
To future days a libel or a jeſt. *Dryden.*

15. [*Eſtar*, Spaniſh.] To be in any particular ſtate; to be: emphatically expreſſed.

The ſea,
Aw'd by the rod of Moſes ſo to *ſtand*,
Divided. *Milton.*

Accompliſh what your ſigns foreſhow:
I *ſtand* reſign'd, and am prepar'd to go. *Dryden's Æn.*

He ſtruck the ſnakes, and *ſtood* again
New ſex'd, and ſtrait recover'd into man. *Addiſon.*

They expect to be favoured, who *ſtand* not poſſeſſed of any one of thoſe qualifications that belonged to him. *Atterbury.*

Some middle prices ſhew us in what proportion the value of their lands *ſtood*, in regard to thoſe of our own country. *Arbuth.*

God, who ſees all things intuitively, does not want theſe helps: he neither *ſtands* in need of logick nor uſes it. *Baker.*

Perſians and Greeks like turns of nature found,
And the world's victor *ſtood* ſubdu'd by ſound. *Pope.*

Narrow capacities, imagining the great capable of being diſconcerted by little occaſions, frame their malignant fables accordingly, and *ſtand* detected by it, as by an evident mark of ignorance. *Pope's Eſſay on Homer.*

16. Not to become void; to remain in force.

God was not ignorant that the judges, whoſe ſentence in matters of controverſy he ordained ſhould *ſtand*, oftentimes would be deceived. *Hooker.*

A thing within my boſom tells me,
That no conditions of our peace can *ſtand.* *Shakeſ. H.* IV.

I will puniſh you, that ye may know that my words ſhall ſurely *ſtand* againſt you for evil. *Jer* xliv. 29.

My mercy will I keep for him, and my covenant ſhall *ſtand* faſt with him. *Pſ.* lxxxix. 28.

17. To conſiſt; to have its being or eſſence.

That could not make him that did the ſervice perfect, as pertaining to the conſcience, which *ſtood* only in meats and drinks. *Heb.* ix. 10.

18. To be with reſpect to terms of a contract.

The hirelings *ſtand* at a certain wages. *Carew*

19. To have a place.

If it *ſtand*
Within the eye of honour, be aſſured
My purſe, my perſon, my extremeſt means,
Lie all unlock'd to your occaſions. *Shak. Merch. of Venice.*

My very enemy's dog,
Though he had bit me, ſhould have *ſtood* that night
Againſt my fire. *Shakeſp. King Lear.*

A philoſopher diſputed with Adrian the emperor, and did it but weakly: one of his friends, that *ſtood* by, ſaid, Methinks you were not like yourſelf laſt day in argument with the emperor; I could have anſwered better myſelf. Why, ſaid the philoſopher, would you have me contend with him that commands thirty legions? *Bacon.*

This excellent man, who *ſtood* not upon the advantage-ground before, provoked men of all qualities. *Clarendon.*

Chariots wing'd
From th' armoury of God, where *ſtand* of old
Myriads. *Milton.*

We make all our addreſſes to the promiſes, hug and careſs them, and in the interim let the commands *ſtand* by neglected. *Decay of Piety.*

20. To be in any ſtate at the time preſent.

Oppreſt nature ſleeps:
This reſt might yet have balm'd thy broken ſenſes,
Which *ſtand* in hard cure. *Shak. King Lear.*

So it *ſtands*; and this I fear at laſt,
Hume's knavery will be the dutcheſs' wreck. *Shak. H.* VI.

Our company aſſembled, I ſaid, My dear friends, let us know ourſelves, and how it *ſtandeth* with us. *Bacon.*

Gardiner was made king's ſolicitor, and the patent, formerly granted to Saint-John, *ſtood* revoked. *Clarendon.*

Why *ſtand* we longer ſhivering under fears? *Milton.*

As things now *ſtand* with us, we have no power to do good after that illuſtrious manner our Saviour did. *Calamy's Serm.*

21. To be in a permanent ſtate.

The broil doubtful long *ſtood*,
As two ſpent ſwimmers that do cling together,
And choke their art. *Shakeſpeare.*

I in thy perſevering ſhall rejoice,
And all the bleſt *ſtand* faſt. *Milton.*

22. To be with regard to condition or fortune.

I *ſtand* in need of one whoſe glories may
Redeem my crimes, ally me to his fame. *Dryden.*

23. To have any particular reſpect.

Here ſtood he in the dark, his ſharp ſword out,
Mumbling of wicked charms, conj'ring the moon
To *ſtand*'s auſpicious miſtreſs. *Shakeſp. King Lear.*

An utter unſuitableneſs diſobedience has to the relation which man neceſſarily *ſtands* in towards his Maker. *South.*

24. To be without action.
25. To depend; to reſt; to be ſupported.

This reply *ſtandeth* all by conjectures. *Whitgifte.*

 The

The presbyterians of the kirk, less forward to declare their opinion in the former point, *stand* upon the latter only. *Sanderf.*

He that will know, must by the connexion of the proofs see the truth and the ground it *stands* on. *Locke.*

26. To be with regard to state of mind.

Stand in awe and sin not: commune with your own heart upon your bed, and be still. *Psal.* iv. 4.

I desire to be present, and change my voice, for I *stand* in doubt of you. *Gal.* iv. 20.

27. To succeed; to be acquitted; to be safe.

Readers, by whose judgment I would *stand* or fall, would not be such as are acquainted only with the French and Italian criticks. *Addison's Spectator.*

28. To be with respect to any particular.

Cæsar entreats,
Not to consider in what case thou *stand'st*
Further than he is Cæsar. *Shakesp. Ant. and Cleopatra.*

To heav'n I do appeal,
I have lov'd my king and common-weal;
As for my wife, I know not how it *stands*. *Shak. Henry* VI.

29. To be resolutely of a party.

The cause must be presumed as good on our part as on theirs, till it be decided who have *stood* for the truth, and who for errour. *Hooker.*

Shall we sound him?
I think, he will *stand* very strong with us. *Shakespeare.*

Who will rise up or *stand* up for me against the workers of iniquity? *Psalm* xciv. 16.

30. To be in the place; to be representative.

Chilon said, that kings friends and favourites were like casting counters; that sometimes *stood* for one, sometimes for ten. *Bacon.*

I will not trouble myself, whether these names *stand* for the same thing, or really include one another. *Locke.*

Their language being scanty, had no words in it to *stand* for a thousand. *Locke.*

31. To remain; to be fixed.

Watch ye, *stand* fast in the faith, quit you like men, be strong. 1 *Cor.* xvi. 13.

How soon hath thy prediction, seer blest!
Measur'd this transient world, the race of time,
Till time *stand* fix'd. *Milton.*

32. To hold a course.

Behold on Latian shores a foreign prince!
From the same parts of heav'n his navy *stands*,
To the same parts on earth his army lands. *Dryden.*

Full for the port the Ithacensians *stand*,
And furl their sails, and issue on the land. *Pope's Odyssey.*

33. To have direction towards any local point.

The wand did not really *stand* to the metals, when placed under it, or the metalline veins. *Boyle.*

34. To offer as a candidate.

He *stood* to be elected one of the proctors for the university. *Sanderson's Life.*

35. To place himself; to be placed.

The fool hath planted in his memory
An army of good words; and I do know
A many fools that *stand* in better place,
Garnish'd like him, that for a tricksy word
Defy the matter. *Shakespeare's Merch. of Venice.*

He was commanded by the duke to *stand* aside and expect his answer. *Knolles's History of the Turks.*

I *stood* between the Lord and you, to shew you the Lord's word. *Deuter.* v. 5.

Stand by when he is going. *Swift's Directions to the Butler.*

36. To stagnate; not to flow.

Where Ufens glides along the lowly lands,
Or the black water of Pomptina *stands*. *Dryden.*

37. To be with respect to chance.

Yourself, renowned prince, then *stood* as fair
As any comer I have look'd on,
For my affection. *Shakespeare's Merchant of Venice.*

Each thinks he *stands* fairest for the great lot, and that he is possessed of the golden number. *Addison's Spectator.*

He was a gentleman of considerable practice at the bar, and *stood* fair for the first vacancy on the bench. *Rowe.*

38. To remain satisfied.

Though Page be a secure fool, and *stand* so firmly on his wife's frailty, yet I cannot put off my opinion so easily. *Shak.*

39. To be without motion.

I'll tell you who time ambles withal, who time gallops withal.—Whom *stands* it still withal?—With lawyers in the vacation; for they sleep between term and term, and then they perceive not how time moves. *Shakespeare.*

40. To make delay.

They will suspect they shall make but small progress, if, in the books they read, they must *stand* to examine and unravel every argument. *Locke.*

41. To insist; to dwell with many words, or much pertinacity.

To *stand* upon every point, and be curious in particulars, belongeth to the first author of the story. 2 *Maccab.* ii. 30.

It is so plain that it needeth not to be *stood* upon. *Bacon.*

42. To be exposed.

Have I lived to *stand* in the taunt of one that makes fritters of English. *Shakespeare's Merry Wives of Windsor.*

43. To persist; to persevere.

Never *stand* in a lie when thou art accused, but ask pardon and make amends. *Taylor's Rule of holy Living.*

The emperor *standing* upon the advantage he had got by the seisure of their fleet, obliged them to deliver. *Gulliver's Travels.*

Hath the prince a full commission,
To hear, and absolutely to determine
Of what conditions we shall *stand* upon? *Shak. Henry* IV.

44. To persist in a claim.

It remains,
To gratify his noble service, that
Hath thus *stood* for his country. *Shakespeare's Coriolanus.*

45. To adhere; to abide.

Despair would *stand* to the sword,
To try what friends would do, or fate afford. *Daniel.*

46. To be consistent.

His faithful people, whatsoever they rightly ask, the same shall they receive, so far as may *stand* with the glory of God and their own everlasting good; unto either of which it is no virtuous man's purpose to seek any thing prejudicial. *Hooker.*

Some instances of fortune cannot *stand* with some others; but if you desire this, you must lose that. *Taylor.*

It *stood* with reason that they should be rewarded liberally out of their own labours since they received pay. *Davies.*

Sprightly youth and close application will hardly *stand* together. *Felton.*

47. *To* STAND *by*. To support; to defend; not to desert.

The ass hoped the dog would *stand by* him, if set upon by the wolf. *L'Estrange.*

If he meet with a repulse, we must throw off the fox's skin, and put on the lion's: come, gentlemen, you'll *stand by* me. *Dryden's Spanish Friar.*

Our good works will attend and *stand by* us at the hour of death. *Calamy.*

48. *To* STAND *by*. To be present without being an actor.

Margaret's curse is fall'n upon our heads,
For *standing by* when Richard kill'd her son. *Shakespeare.*

49. *To* STAND *by*. To repose on; to rest in.

The world is inclined to *stand by* the Arundelian marble. *Pope's Essay on Homer.*

50. *To* STAND *for*. To propose one's self a candidate.

How many *stand for* consulships?—three; but 'tis thought of every one Coriolanus will carry it. *Shakespeare.*

If they were jealous that Coriolanus had a design on their liberties when he *stood for* the consulship, it was but just that they should give him a repulse. *Dennis.*

51. *To* STAND *for*. To maintain; to profess to support.

Those which *stood for* the presbytery thought their cause had more sympathy with the discipline of Scotland, than the hierarchy of England. *Bacon.*

Freedom we all *stand for*. *Ben. Johnson.*

52. *To* STAND *off*. To keep at a distance.

Stand off, and let me take my fill of death. *Dryden.*

53. *To* STAND *off*. Not to comply.

Stand no more *off*,
But give thyself unto my sick desires. *Shakespeare.*

54. *To* STAND *off*. To forbear friendship or intimacy.

Our bloods pour'd altogether
Would quite confound distinction; yet *stand off*
In differences so mighty. *Shakespeare.*

Such behaviour frights away friendship, and makes it *stand off* in dislike and aversion. *Collier of Friendship.*

Though nothing can be more honourable than an acquaintance with God, we *stand off* from it, and will not be tempted to embrace it. *Atterbury.*

55. *To* STAND *off*. To have relief; to appear protuberant or prominent.

Picture is best when it *standeth off*, as if it were carved; and sculpture is best when it appeareth so tender as if it were painted; when there is such a softness in the limbs, as if not a chisel had hewed them out of stone, but a pencil had drawn and stroaked them in oil. *Wotton's Architecture.*

56. *To* STAND *out*. To hold resolution; to hold a post; not to yield a point.

King John hath reconcil'd
Himself to Rome; his spirit is come in,
That so *stood out* against the holy church. *Shakespeare.*

Pomtinius knows not you,
While you *stand out* upon these traiterous terms. *Ben. John.*

Let not men flatter themselves, that though they find it difficult at present to combat and *stand out* against an ill practice; yet that old age would do that for them, which they in their youth could never find in their hearts to do for themselves. *South's Sermons.*

Scarce can a good natured man refuse a compliance with the solicitations of his company, and *stand out* against the raillery of his familiars. *Rogers's Sermons.*

56. To

57. *To* STAND *out.* Not to comply; to secede.

Thou shalt see me at Tullus' face:
What, art thou stiff? *stand'st out?* *Shakespeare.*

If the ladies will *stand out*, let them remember that the jury is not all agreed. *Dryden.*

58. *To* STAND *out.* To be prominent or protuberant.

Their eyes *stand out* with fatness. *Ps.* lxxiii. 7.

59. *To* STAND *to.* To ply; to persevere.

Palinurus, cry'd aloud,
What gusts of weather from that gath'ring cloud
My thoughts presage! ere that the tempest roars,
Stand to your tackles, mates, and stretch your oars. *Dryden.*

60. *To* STAND *to.* To remain fixed in a purpose; to abide by a contract or assertion.

He that will pass his land,
As I have mine, may set his hand
And heart unto this deed, when he hath read;
And make the purchase spread
To both our goods if he *to* it will *stand.* *Herbert.*

I still *stand to* it, that this is his sense, as will appear from the design of his words. *Stillingfleet.*

As I have no reason to *stand to* the award of my enemies; so neither dare I trust the partiality of my friends. *Dryden.*

61. *To* STAND *under.* To undergo; to sustain.

If you unite in your complaints,
And force them with a constancy, the cardinal
Cannot *stand under* them. *Shakespeare's H.* VIII.

62. *To* STAND *up.* To arise in order to gain notice.

When the accusers *stood up*, he brought none accusation of such things as I supposed. *Acts* xxv. 18.

63. *To* STAND *up.* To make a party.

When we *stood up* about the corn, he himself stuck not to call us the many-headed monster. *Shakespeare's Coriolanus.*

64. *To* STAND *upon.* To concern; to interest.

Does it not *stand* me now *upon?* *Shakespeare's Hamlet.*

The king knowing well that it *stood* him *upon*: by how much the more he had hitherto protracted the time, by so much the sooner to dispatch with the rebels. *Bacon.*

It *stands* me much *upon*
T' enervate this objection. *Hudibras.*

Does it not *stand* them *upon*, to examine upon what grounds they presume it to be a revelation from God. *Locke.*

65. *To* STAND *upon.* To value; to take pride.

Men *stand* very much *upon* the reputation of their understandings, and of all things hate to be accounted fools: the best way to avoid this imputation is to be religious. *Tillotson.*

We highly esteem and *stand* much *upon* our birth, though we derive nothing from our ancestors but our bodies; and it is useful to improve this advantage, to imitate their good examples. *Ray on the Creation.*

66. *To* STAND *upon.* To insist.

A rascally, yea—forsooth, knave, to bear a gentleman in hand, and then *stand upon* security. *Shakespeare.*

To STAND. *v. a.*

1. To endure; to resist without flying or yielding.

None durst *stand* him;
Here, there, and every where, enrag'd he flew. *Shakespeare.*
Love *stood* the siege, and wou'd not yield his breast. *Dryd.*

Oh! had bounteous heav'n
Bestow'd Hippolitus on Phædra's arms,
So had I *stood* the shock of angry fate. *Smith's Phæd. and Hip.*

That not for fame, but virtue's better end,
He *stood* the furious foe, the timid friend,
The damning critick. *Pope.*

2. To await; to abide; to suffer.

Bid him disband the legions,
Submit his actions to the publick censure,
And *stand* the judgment of a Roman senate. *Addison's Cato.*

3. To keep; to maintain with *ground.*

Turning at the length, he *stood* his ground,
And miss'd his friend. *Dryden.*

STAND. *n. s.* [from the verb.]

1. A station; a place where one waits standing.

I have found you out a *stand* most fit,
Where you may have such 'vantage on the duke,
He shall not pass you. *Shakespeare's Measure for Measure.*

In this covert will we make a *stand*,
Culling the principal of all the deer. *Shakespeare.*

Then from his lofty *stand* on that high tree,
Down he alights among the sportful herds. *Milton.*

The princely hierarch
In their bright *stand* there left his pow'rs, to seize
Possession of the garden. *Milton's Paradise Lost.*

The male bird, whilst the hen is covering her eggs, generally takes his *stand* upon a neighbouring bough and diverts her with his songs during her sitting. *Addison's Spectator.*

I took my *stand* upon an eminence which was appointed for a general rendezvous of these female carriers, to look into their several ladings. *Addison's Spectator.*

Three persons entered into a conspiracy to assassinate Timoleon, as he was offering up his devotions in a certain temple: in order to it they took their several *stands* in the most convenient places. *Addison.*

When just as by her *stand* Arsaces past,
The window by design or chance fell down,
And to his view expos'd her blushing beauties. *Rowe.*

The urchin from his private *stand*
Took aim, and shot with all his strength. *Swift.*

2. Rank; post; station.

Father, since your fortune did attain
So high a *stand*; I mean not to descend. *Daniel.*

3. A stop; a halt.

A race of youthful and unhandled colts
Fetching mad bounds, bellowing and neighing;
If any air of musick touch their ears,
You shall perceive them make a mutual *stand*;
Their savage eyes turn'd to a modest gaze. *Shakespeare.*

The earl of Northampton followed the horse so closely, that they made a *stand*, when he furiously charged and routed them. *Clarendon.*

Once more the fleeting soul came back,
T' inspire the mortal frame,
And in the body took a doubtful *stand*,
Hov'ring like expiring flame,
That mounts and falls by turns. *Dryden.*

At every turn she made a little *stand*,
And thrust among the thorns her lily hand
To draw the rose. *Dryden.*

4. Stop; interruption.

The greatest part of trade is driven by young merchants, upon borrowing at interest; so as, if the usurer either call in, or keep back his money, there will ensue presently a great *stand* of trade. *Bacon.*

Should this circulation cease, the formation of bodies would be at an end, and nature at a perfect *stand.* *Woodward.*

5. The act of opposing.

We are come off
Like Romans; neither foolish in our *stands*,
Nor cowardly in retire. *Shakespeare.*

6. Highest mark; stationary point; point from which the next motion is regressive.

Our sons but the same things can wish and do,
Vice is at *stand* and at the highest flow:
Then, satire, spread thy sails; take all the winds can blow. *Dryden.*

In the beginning of summer the days are at a *stand*, with little variation of length or shortness; because the diurnal variation of the sun partakes more of a right line than of a spiral. *Dryden.*

The sea, since the memory of all ages, hath continued at a *stand*, without considerable variation. *Bentley.*

7. A point beyond which one cannot proceed.

Every part of what we would,
Must make a *stand* at what your highness will. *Shakespeare.*

When fam'd Varelst this little wonder drew,
Flora vouchsav'd the growing work to view;
Finding the painter's science at a *stand*,
The goddess snatch'd the pencil from his hand:
And finishing the piece, she smiling said,
Behold one work of mine that ne'er shall fade. *Prior.*

8. Difficulty; perplexity; embarassment; hesitation.

A fool may so far imitate the mein of a wise man, as at first to put a body to a *stand* what to make of him. *L'Estrange.*

The well-shap'd changeling is a man, has a rational soul, tho' it appear not: this is past doubt. Make the ears a little longer, then you begin to boggle: make the face yet narrower, and then you are at a *stand.* *Locke.*

9. A frame or table on which vessels are placed.

Such squires are only fit for country towns,
To stink of ale, and dust a *stand* with clowns;
Who, to be chosen for the land's protectors,
Tope and get drunk before the wise electors. *Dryden.*

After supper a *stand* was brought in, with a brass vessel full of wine, of which he that pleas'd might drink; but no liquour was forced. *Dryden's Life of Cleomenes.*

STA'NDARD. *n. s.* [*estendart*, French.]

1. An ensign in war, particularly the ensign of the horse.

His armies, in the following day,
On those fair plains their *standards* proud display. *Fairfax.*

Erect the *standard* there of ancient night,
Yours be the advantage all, mine the revenge. *Milton.*

Behold Camillus loaded home,
With *standards* well redeem'd and foreign foes o'ercome. *Dryden.*

To their common *standard* they repair;
The nimble horsemen scour the fields of air. *Dryden.*

2. [From *stand.*] That which is of undoubted authority; that which is the test of other things of the same kind.

The dogmatist gives the lie to all dissenting apprehenders, and proclaims his judgment the fittest intellectual *standard.* *Glanville.*

The

The heavenly motions are more ſtated than the terreſtrial models, and are both originals and *ſtandards*. *Holder.*

Theſe are our meaſures of length, but I cannot call them *ſtandards*; for *ſtandard* meaſures muſt be certain and fixed. *Holder on Time.*

When people have brought the queſtion of right and wrong to a falſe *ſtandard*, there follows an envious malevolence. *L'Eſtrange.*

The Romans made thoſe times the *ſtandard* of their wit, when they ſubdued the world. *Sprat.*

From theſe ancient *ſtandards* I deſcend to our own hiſtorians. *Felton.*

When I ſhall propoſe the *ſtandard* whereby I give judgment, any may eaſily inform himſelf of the quantity and meaſure of it. *Woodward.*

The court which uſed to be the *ſtandard* of propriety, and correctneſs of ſpeech, ever ſince continued the worſt ſchool in England for that accompliſhment. *Swift.*

First follow nature, and your judgment frame,
By her juſt *ſtandard* which is ſtill the ſame. *Pope.*

3. That which has been tried by the proper teſt.

The Engliſh tongue, if refined to a certain *ſtandard*, perhaps might be fixed for ever. *Swift.*

In comely rank call ev'ry merit forth;
Imprint on ev'ry act its *ſtandard*-worth. *Prior.*

4. A ſettled rate.

That preciſe weight and fineneſs, by law appropriated to the pieces of each denomination, is called the *ſtandard*. *Locke.*

The device of King Henry VII. was profound in making farms of a *ſtandard*, that is, maintained with ſuch a proportion of lands as may breed a ſubject to live in convenient plenty. *Bacon.*

A *ſtandard* might be made, under which no horſe ſhould be uſed for draught: this would enlarge the breed of horſes. *Temp.*

By the preſent *ſtandard* of the coinage, ſixty two ſhillings is coined out of one pound weight of ſilver. *Arbuthnot.*

5. A ſtanding ſtem or tree.

A *ſtandard* of a damaſk roſe with the root on, was ſet upright in an earthen pan, full of fair water, half a foot under the water, the *ſtandard* being more than two foot above it. *Bacon's Natural Hiſtory.*

Plant fruit of all ſorts and *ſtandard*, mural, or ſhrubs which loſe their leaf. *Evelyn's Kalender.*

In France part of their gardens is laid out for flowers, others for fruits; ſome *ſtandards*, ſome againſt walls. *Temple.*

STA'NDARDBEARER. *n. ſ.* [*ſtandard* and *bear.*] One who bears a ſtandard or enſign.

They ſhall be as when a *ſtandardbearer* fainteth. *Iſa.* x. 18.

Theſe are the *ſtandardbearers* in our contending armies, the dwarfs and ſquires who carry the impreſſes of the giants or knights. *Spectator.*

STA'NDCROP. *n. ſ.* An herb. *Ainſworth.*

STA'NDEL. *n. ſ.* [from *ſtand.*] A tree of long ſtanding.

The Druinians were nettled to ſee the princely *ſtandel* of their royal oak return with a branch of willows. *Howel.*

STA'NDER. *n. ſ.* [from *ſtand*:]

1. One who ſtands.
2. A tree that has ſtood long.

The young ſpring was pitifully nipt and over-trodden by very beaſts; and alſo the faireſt *ſtanders* of all were rooted up and caſt into the fire. *Aſcham's Schoolmaſter.*

3. STA'NDER *by.* One preſent; a mere ſpectator.

Explain ſome ſtatute of the land to the *ſtanders by*. *Hooker.*

I would not be a *ſtander by* to hear
My ſovereign miſtreſs clouded ſo, without
My preſent vengeance taken. *Shakeſpeare.*

When a gentleman is diſpoſed to ſwear, it is not for any *ſtanders by* to curtail his oaths. *Shakeſpeare's Cymbeline.*

The *ſtanders by* ſee clearly this event,
All parties ſay, they're ſure, yet all diſſent. *Denham.*

The *ſtanders by* ſuſpected her to be a ducheſs.. *Addiſon.*

STA'NDERGRASS. *n. ſ.* An herb. *Ainſworth.*

STA'NDING. *part. adj.* [from *ſtand.*]

1. Settled; eſtabliſhed.

Standing armies have the place of ſubjects, and the government depends upon the contented and diſcontented humours of the ſoldiers. *Temple.*

Laugh'd all the pow'rs who favour tyranny,
And all the *ſtanding* army of the ſky. *Dryden.*

Money being looked upon as the *ſtanding* meaſure of other commodities, men conſider it as a *ſtanding* meaſure, though when it has varied its quantity, it is not ſo. *Locke.*

Such a one, by pretending to diſtinguiſh himſelf from the herd, becomes a *ſtanding* object of raillery. *Addiſon.*

The common *ſtanding* rules of the goſpel are a more powerful means of conviction than any miracle. *Atterbury.*

Great *ſtanding* miracle that heav'n aſſign'd!
'Tis only thinking gives this turn of mind. *Pope.*

2. Laſting; not tranſitory.

The landlord had ſwelled his body to a prodigious ſize, and worked up his complexion to a *ſtanding* crimſon by his zeal. *Addiſon's Freeholder.*

3. Stagnant; not running.

He turned the wilderneſs into a *ſtanding* water. *Pſal.* cvii.

This made their flowing ſhrink
From *ſtanding* lake to tripping ebb. *Milton.*

4. Placed on feet.

There's his chamber,
His *ſtanding* bed and truckle bed. *Shakeſpeare.*

STA'NDING. *n. ſ.* [from *ſtand.*]

1. Continuance; long poſſeſſion of an office, character, or place.

Nothing had been more eaſy than to command a patron of a long *ſtanding*. *Dryden.*

Although the ancients were of opinion that Egypt was formerly ſea; yet this tract of land is as old, and of as long a *ſtanding* as any upon the continent of Africa. *Woodward.*

I wiſh your fortune had enabled you to have continued longer in the univerſity, till you were of ten years *ſtanding*. *Swift.*

2. Station; place to ſtand in.

Such ordnance as he brought with him, becauſe it was fitter for ſervice in field than for battery, did only beat down the battlements, and ſuch little *ſtandings*. *Knolles's Hiſt. of the Turks.*

His coming is in ſtate, I will provide you a good *ſtanding* to ſee his entry. *Bacon.*

3. Power to ſtand.

I ſink in deep mire, where there is no *ſtanding*. *Pſal.* lxix.

4. Rank; condition.

How this grace
Speaks his own *ſtanding*? what a mental power
This eye ſhoots forth? how big imagination
Moves in this lip. *Shakeſpeare's Timon of Athens.*

5. Competition; candidateſhip.

His former *ſtanding* for a proctor's place, and being diſappointed, muſt prove much diſpleaſing. *Walton.*

STA'NDISH. *n. ſ.* [*ſtand* and *diſh.*] A caſe for pen and ink.

A grubſtreet patriot does not write to ſecure, but get ſomething: ſhould the government be overturned he has nothing to loſe but an old *ſtandiſh*. *Addiſon.*

I bequeath to Dean Swift eſq; my large ſilver *ſtandiſh*, conſiſting of a large ſilver plate, an ink-pot, and a ſand-box. *Swift.*

STANG. *n. ſ.* [ſtænᵹ, Saxon.] A perch.

Theſe fields were intermingled with woods of half a *ſtang*, and the talleſt tree appeared to be ſeven feet high. *Swift.*

STANK. *adj.* Weak; worn out.

Diggon, I am ſo ſtiff and ſo *ſtank*,
That unneth I may ſtand any more,
And how the weſtern wind bloweth ſore,
Beating the withered leaf from the tree. *Spenſer.*

STANK. The preterite of *ſtink*.

The fiſh in the river died, and the river *ſtank*. *Exod.* vii.

STA'NNARY. *adj.* [from *ſtannum*, Latin.] Relating to the tinworks.

A ſteward keepeth his court once every three weeks: they are termed *ſtannary* courts of the Latin *ſtannum*, and hold plea of action of debt or treſpaſs about white or black tin. *Carew.*

STA'NZA. *n. ſ.* [*ſtanza*, Ital. *ſtance*, Fr.] A number of lines regularly adjuſted to each other; ſo much of a poem as contains every variation of meaſure or relation of rhyme. *Stanza* is originally a room of a houſe, and came to ſignify a ſubdiviſion of a poem; a ſtaff.

Horace confines himſelf ſtrictly to one ſort of verſe or *ſtanza* in every ode. *Dryden.*

In quatrains, the laſt line of the *ſtanza* is to be conſidered in the compoſition of the firſt. *Dryden.*

Before his ſacred name flies ev'ry fault,
And each exalted *ſtanza* teems with thought. *Pope.*

STAPLE. *n. ſ.* [*eſtape*, Fr. *ſtapel*, Dutch.]

1. A ſettled mart; an eſtabliſhed emporium.

A *ſtaple* of romance and lies,
Falſe tears, and real perjuries. *Prior.*

The cuſtoms of Alexandria were very great, it having been the *ſtaple* of the Indian trade. *Arbuthnot on Coins.*

Tyre, Alexander the Great ſacked, and eſtabliſhing the *ſtaple* at Alexandria, made the greateſt revolution in trade that ever was known. *Arbuthnot.*

2. I know not the meaning in the following paſſage.

Henry II. granted liberty of coining to certain abbies, allowing them one *ſtaple*, and two puncheons at a rate. *Camden.*

STAPLE. *adj.* [from the noun.]

1. Settled; eſtabliſhed in commerce.

Some Engliſh wool, vex'd in a Belgian loom,
And into cloth of ſpungy ſoftneſs made:
Did into France or colder Denmark roam,
To ruin with worſe ware our *ſtaple* trade. *Dryden.*

2. According to the laws of commerce.

What needy writer would not ſolicit to work under ſuch maſters, who will take off their ware at their own rates, and trouble not themſelves to examine whether it be *ſtaple* or no? *Swift.*

STA'PLE. *n. ſ.* [ſtapul, Saxon, a prop.] A loop of iron; a bar bent and driven in at both ends.

I have ſeen *ſtaples* of doors and nails born. *Peacham.*

The ſilver ring ſhe pull'd, the door reclos'd:
The bolt, obedient to the ſilken cord,
To the ſtrong *ſtaple*'s inmoſt depth reſtor'd,
Secur'd the valves. *Pope's Odyſſey.*

STAR. *n. ſ.* [ſteorra, Saxon; *ſterre*, Dutch.]

1. One of the luminous bodies that appear in the nocturnal ſky.

Then let the pebbles on the hungry beech
Fillop the *ſtars*;
Murdering impoſſibility, to make
What cannot be, ſlight work. *Shakeſp. Coriolanus.*

When an aſtronomer uſes the word *ſtar* in its ſtrict ſenſe, it is applied only to the fixt *ſtars*; but in a large ſenſe it includes the planets. *Watts.*

Hither the Syracuſan's art tranſlates
Heaven's form, the courſe of things and human fates;
Th' included ſpirit ſerving the *ſtar* deck'd ſigns,
The living work in conſtant motions winds. *Hakewill.*

As from a cloud his fulgent head,
And ſhape *ſtar* bright, appear'd. *Milton.*

2. The pole-ſtar.

Well, if you be not turn'd Turk, there is no more ſailing by the *ſtar*. *Shak. Much Ado about Nothing.*

3. Configuration of the planets ſuppoſed to influence fortune.

From forth the fatal loins of theſe two foes,
A pair of *ſtar* croſt lovers take their life. *Shakeſpeare.*

We are apt to do amiſs, and lay the blame upon our *ſtars* or fortune. *L'Eſtrange.*

4. A mark of reference; an aſteriſk.

Remarks worthy of riper obſervation, note with a marginal *ſtar*. *Watts.*

STAR *of Bethlehem. n. ſ.* [*ornithogalum*, Latin.] A plant.

The characters are: it hath a lily-flower, compoſed of ſix petals, or leaves ranged circularly, whoſe centre is poſſeſſed by the pointal, which afterwards turns to a roundiſh fruit, which is divided into three cells, and filled with roundiſh ſeeds: to which muſt be added, it hath a bulbous or tuberoſe root, in which it differs from ſpiderwort. *Miller.*

STA'RAPPLE. *n. ſ.* A plant.

It hath an open bell-ſhaped flower, conſiſting of one leaf, and cut into ſeveral ſegments towards the top; from whoſe cup ariſes the pointal, which afterwards becomes a globular or olive-ſhaped ſoft fleſhy fruit, incloſing a ſtone of the ſame ſhape. This plant grows in the warmeſt parts of America, where the fruit is eaten by way of deſert. It grows to the height of thirty or forty feet, and has a ſtrait ſmooth ſtem, regularly beſet with branches, which are adorned with leaves of a ſhining green colour on their upper ſides, but of a ruſſet colour underneath: from the ſetting on of the footſtalks of the leaves come out the flowers, which have no great beauty, but are ſucceeded by the fruit, which is about the ſize of a large apple, and of the ſame ſhape. *Miller.*

STA'RBOARD. *n. ſ.* [ſteorbord, Saxon.] Is the right-hand ſide of the ſhip, as larboard is the left. *Harris.*

On ſhipboard the mariners will not leave their *ſtarboard* and larboard, becauſe ſome one accounts it gibriſh. *Bramh.*

STARCH. *n. ſ.* [from *ſtarc*, Teutonick, ſtiff.] A kind of viſcous matter made of flower or potatoes, with which linen is ſtiffened, and was formerly coloured.

Has he
Diſlik'd your yellow *ſtarch*, or ſaid your doublet
Was not exactly Frenchified. *Fletcher's Queen of Corinth.*

With *ſtarch* thin laid on, and the ſkin well ſtretched, prepare your ground. *Peacham on Drawing.*

To STARCH. *v. a.* [from the noun.] To ſtiffen with ſtarch.

Her goodly countenance I've ſeen
Set off with kerchief *ſtarch'd* and pinners clean. *Gay.*

STA'RCHAMBER. *n. ſ.* [*camera ſtellata*, Latin.] A kind of criminal court of equity. Now aboliſhed.

I'll make a *ſtarchamber* matter of it: if he were twenty ſir John Falſtaffs, he ſhall not abuſe Robert Shallow, eſq; *Shakeſ.*

STA'RCHED *adj.* [from *ſtarch.*]

1. Stiffened with ſtarch.

2. Stiff; preciſe; formal.

Does the Goſpel any where preſcribe a *ſtarched* ſqueezed countenance, a ſtiff formal gait, or a ſingularity of manners. *Swift.*

STA'RCHER. *n. ſ.* [from *ſtarch.*] One whoſe trade is to ſtarch.

STA'RCHLY. *adv.* [from *ſtarch.*] Stiffly; preciſely.

STA'RCHNESS. *n. ſ.* [from *ſtarch.*] Stiffneſs; preciſeneſs.

To STARE. *v. n.* [ſtarian, Saxon; *ſterren*, Dutch.]

1. To look with fixed eyes; to look with wonder, impudence, confidence, ſtupidity, or horrour.

Her modeſt eyes, abaſhed to behold
So many gazers, as on her do *ſtare*,
Upon the lowly ground affixed are. *Spenſer.*

Their *ſtaring* eyes, ſparkling with fervent fire,
And ugly ſhapes, did nigh the man diſmay,
That, were it not for ſhame, he would retire. *Fa. Queen;*

Look not big, nor *ſtare* nor fret:
I will be maſter of what is mine own. *Shakeſpeare.*

They were never ſatisfied with *ſtaring* upon their maſts, ſails, cables, ropes, and tacklings. *Abbot.*

I hear
The tread of many feet ſteering this way;
Perhaps my enemies, who come to *ſtare*
At my affliction, and perhaps t' inſult. *Milton's Agoniſtes.*

A ſatyr that comes *ſtaring* from the woods,
Muſt not at firſt ſpeak like an orator. *Waller.*

And while he *ſtares* around with ſtupid eyes,
His brows with berries and his temples dies. *Dryden.*

What do'ſt thou make a ſhipboard?
Art thou of Bethlem's noble college free?
Stark *ſtaring* mad, that thou ſhould'ſt tempt the ſea? *Dryd.*

Struggling, and wildly *ſtaring* on the ſkies
With ſcarce recover'd ſight. *Dryden's Æn.*

Trembling the miſcreant ſtood;
He *ſtar'd* and roll'd his haggard eyes around. *Dryden.*

Break out in crackling flames to ſhun thy ſnare,
Or hiſs a dragon, or a tyger *ſtare*. *Dryden's Virgil.*

Why do'ſt thou not
Try the virtue of that gorgon face,
To *ſtare* me into ſtatue? *Dryden.*

I was unluckily prevented by the preſence of a bear, which, as I approached with my preſent, threw his eyes in my way, and *ſtared* me out of my reſolution. *Addiſon's Guardian.*

The wit at his elbow gave him a touch upon the ſhoulder, and *ſtared* him in the face with ſo bewitching a grin, that the whiſtler relaxed his fibres. *Addiſon.*

Narciſſa
Has paid a tradeſman once, to make him *ſtare*. *Pope.*

Gods! ſhall the raviſher diſplay your hair,
While the fops envy and the ladies *ſtare*. *Pope.*

Through nature and through art ſhe rang'd,
And gracefully her ſubject chang'd:
In vain; her hearers had no ſhare
In all ſhe ſpoke, except to *ſtare*. *Swift.*

2. *To* STARE *in the face.* To be undeniably evident.

Is it poſſible for people, without ſcruple to offend againſt the law, which they carry about them in indelible characters, and that *ſtares* them *in the face*, whilſt they are breaking it? *Locke.*

3. To ſtand out.

Take off all the *ſtaring* ſtraws and jaggs in the hive, and make them ſmooth. *Mortimer's Huſbandry.*

STARE. *n. ſ.* [from the verb.]

1. Fixed look.

The balls of his broad eyes roll'd in his head,
And glar'd betwixt a yellow and a red:
He look'd a lion with a gloomy *ſtare*,
And o'er his eyebrows hung his matted hair. *Dryden.*

2. [*Sturnus*, Latin.] Starling. A bird.

STA'RER. *n. ſ.* [from *ſtare.*] One who looks with fixed eyes.

One ſelf-approving hour whole years outweighs
Of ſtupid *ſtarers*, and of loud huzza's. *Pope.*

STA'RFISH. *n. ſ.* [*ſtar* and *fiſh.*] A fiſh branching out into ſeveral points.

This has a ray of one ſpecies of Engliſh *ſtarfiſh*. *Woodw.*

STARGA'ZER. *n. ſ.* [*ſtar* and *gaze.*] An aſtronomer, or aſtrologer. In contempt.

Let the aſtrologers, the *ſtargazers*, and the monthly prognoſticators, ſtand up and ſave thee. *Iſ.* xlvii. 13.

A *ſtargazer*, in the height of his celeſtial obſervations, ſtumbled into a ditch. *L'Eſtrange.*

STA'RHAWK. *n. ſ.* [*aſtur*, Latin.] A ſort of hawk. *Ainſw.*

STARK. *adj.* [ſtearc, ſtræc, Saxon; *ſterck*, Dutch.]

1. Stiff; ſtrong; rugged.

His heavy head devoid of careful cark,
Whoſe ſenſes all were ſtraight benumed and *ſtark*. *Fa. Qu.*

Many a nobleman lies *ſtark* and ſtiff
Under the hoofs of vaunting enemies. *Shakeſ. H. IV.*

The North is not ſo *ſtark* and cold. *Ben. Johnſon.*

So ſoon as this ſpring is become *ſtark* enough, it breaks the caſe in two, and ſlings the ſeed. *Derham's Phyſico-Theology.*

2. Deep; full.

Conſider the *ſtark* ſecurity
The commonwealth is in now; the whole ſenate
Sleepy, and dreaming no ſuch violent blow. *Ben. Johnſon.*

3. Mere; ſimple; plain; groſs.

To turn *ſtark* fools, and ſubjects fit
For ſport of boys, and rabble wit. *Hudibras.*

He pronounces the citation *ſtark* nonſenſe. *Collier.*

STARK. *adv.* Is uſed to intend or augment the ſignification of a word: as *ſtark mad*, mad in the higheſt degree. It is now little uſed but in low language.

Then are the beſt but *ſtark* naught; for open ſuſpecting others, comes of ſecret condemning themſelves. *Sidney.*

The fruitful-headed beaſt, amaz'd
At flaſhing beams of that ſun-ſhiny ſhield,
Became *ſtark* blind, and all his ſenſes doz'd,
That down he tumbled. *Spenſer.*

Men and women go *ſtark* naked. *Abbot.*

He

He is *ſtark* mad, who ever ſays
That he hath been in love an hour. *Donne.*

Thoſe ſeditious, that ſeemed moderate before, became deſperate, and thoſe who were deſperate ſeemed *ſtark* mad; whence tumults, confuſed hollowings and howlings. *Hayw.*

Who, by the moſt cogent arguments, will diſrobe himſelf at once of all his old opinions, and turn himſelf out *ſtark* naked in queſt of new notions? *Locke.*

In came ſquire South, all dreſſed up in feathers and ribbons, *ſtark* ſtaring mad, brandiſhing his ſword. *Arbuthnot.*

STA'RKLY. *adv.* [from *ſtark.*] Stiffly; ſtrongly.

As faſt lock'd up in ſleep as guiltleſs labour,
When it lies *ſtarkly* in the traveller's bones. *Shakeſpeare.*

STA'RLESS. *adj.* [from *ſtar.*] Having no light of ſtars.

A boundleſs continent,
Dark, waſte, and wild, under the frown of night,
Starleſs expos'd. *Milton's Paradiſe Loſt, b.* iii.

Cato might give them furlo's for another world;
But we, like ſentries, are oblig'd to ſtand
In *ſtarleſs* nights, and wait th' appointed hour. *Dryden.*

STA'RLIGHT. *n. ſ.* [*ſtar* and *light*] Luſtre of the ſtars.

Now they never meet in grove or green,
By fountain clear or ſpangled *ſtarlight* ſheen. *Shakeſpeare.*

Nor walk by moon,
Or glittering *ſtarlight*, without thee is ſweet. *Milton.*

They danc'd by *ſtarlight* and the friendly moon. *Dryden.*

STA'RLIGHT. *adj.* Lighted by the ſtars.

Owls, that mark the ſetting ſun, declare
A *ſtarlight* evening and a morning fair. *Dryden's Virg.*

STA'RLIKE. *adj.* [*ſtar* and *like.*]

1. Stellated; having various points reſembling a ſtar in luſtre.

Nightſhade-tree riſes with a wooden ſtem, green-leaved, and has *ſtarlike* flowers. *Mortimer's Husbandry.*

2. Bright; illuſtrious.

The having turned many to righteouſneſs ſhall confer a *ſtarlike* and immortal brightneſs. *Boyle's Seraphick Love.*

Theſe reaſons mov'd her *ſtarlike* huſband's heart;
But ſtill he held his purpoſe to depart. *Dryden.*

STA'RLING. *n. ſ.* [ſtærling, Saxon.] A ſmall ſinging bird.

I will have a *ſtarling* taught to ſpeak
Nothing but Mortimer, and give it him,
To keep his anger ſtill in motion. *Shak. Henry* IV.

STA'RPAVED. *adj.* [*ſtar* and *pave.*] Studded with ſtars.

In progreſs through the road of heav'n *ſtarpav'd.* *Milton.*

STA'RPROOF. *adj.* [*ſtar* and *proof.*] Impervious to ſtarlight.

Under the ſhady roof
Of branching elm *ſtarproof.* *Milton.*

STAR-READ. *n. ſ.* [*ſtar* and *read.*] Doctrine of the ſtars; aſtronomy. *Spenſer.*

STA'RRED. *adj.* [from *ſtar.*]

1. Influenced by the ſtars with reſpect to fortune.

My third comfort,
Starr'd moſt unluckily, is from my breaſt
Hal'd out to murder. *Shakeſp. Winter's Tale.*

2. Decorated with ſtars.

That *ſtarr'd* Ethiop queen, that ſtrove
To ſet her beauty's praiſe above
The ſea-nymphs. *Milton.*

He furious hurl'd againſt the ground
His ſceptre *ſtarr'd* with golden ſtuds around. *Pope.*

STA'RRY. *adj.* [from *ſtar.*]

1. Decorated with ſtars.

Daphne wond'ring mounts on high,
Above the clouds, above the *ſtarry* ſky! *Pope.*

2. Conſiſting of ſtars; ſtellar.

Such is his will, that paints
The earth with colours freſh,
The darkeſt ſkies with ſtore
Of *ſtarry* lights. *Spenſer.*

Heav'n and earth's compacted frame,
And flowing waters, and the *ſtarry* flame,
And both the radiant lights, one common ſoul
Inſpires and feeds, and animates the whole. *Dryden.*

3. Reſembling ſtars.

Tears had dimm'd the luſtre of her *ſtarry* eyes. *Shak. Illuſt.*

STA'RRING. *adj.* [*ſtellans*, Latin; from *ſtar.*] Shining with ſtellar light; blazing with ſparkling light.

Such his fell glances as the fatal light
Of *ſtarring* comets that look kingdoms dead. *Craſhaw.*

STA'RSHOOT. *n. ſ.* [*ſtar* and *ſhoot.*] An emiſſion from a ſtar.

I have ſeen a good quantity of that jelly, by the vulgar called a *ſtarſhoot*, as if it remained upon the extinction of a falling ſtar. *Boyle.*

To START. *v. n.* [*ſtartzen*, German.]

1. To feel a ſudden and involuntary twitch or motion of the animal frame, on the apprehenſion of danger.

Starting is an apprehenſion of the thing feared, and in that kind it is a motion of ſhrinking; and likewiſe an inquiſition, in the beginning, what the matter ſhould be, and in that kind it is a motion of erection, and therefore, when a man would liſten ſuddenly to any thing, he *ſtarteth*; for the *ſtarting* is an erection of the ſpirits to attend. *Bacon's Natural Hiſtory.*

A ſhape appear'd
Bending to look on me: I *ſtarted* back;
It *ſtarted* back. *Shakeſpeare.*

I *ſtart* as from ſome dreadful dream,
And often aſk myſelf if yet awake. *Dryden's Span. Fryar.*

As his doubts decline,
He dreads juſt vengeance, and he *ſtarts* at ſin. *Dryden.*

He *ſtarts* at every new appearance, and is always waking and ſolicitous for fear of a ſurprize. *Collier on Covetouſneſs.*

2. To riſe ſuddenly.

Charm'd by theſe ſtrings, trees *ſtarting* from the ground
Have follow'd with delight the powerful ſound. *Roſcommon.*

They *ſtarting* up beheld the heavy ſight. *Dryden.*

The mind often works in ſearch of ſome hidden idea, though ſometimes they *ſtart* up in our minds of their own accord. *Locke.*

Might Dryden bleſs once more our eyes,
New Blackmores and new Milbourns muſt ariſe;
Nay, ſhould great Homer lift his awful head,
Zoilus again would *ſtart* up from the dead. *Pope.*

3. To move with ſudden quickneſs.

The flowers, call'd out of their beds,
Start and raiſe up their drowſy heads. *Cleaveland.*

A ſpirit fit to *ſtart* into an empire,
And look the world to law. *Dryden's Cleomenes.*

She at the ſummons roll'd her eyes around,
And ſnatch'd the *ſtarting* ſerpents from the ground. *Pope.*

4. To ſhrink; to winch.

What trick, what *ſtarting* hole, can'ſt thou find out to hide thee from this open ſhame? *Shakeſp. Henry* IV.

With tryal fire touch me his finger end;
If he be chaſte, the flame will back deſcend,
And turn him to no pain; but if he *ſtart*,
It is the fleſh of a corrupted heart. *Shakeſpeare.*

5. To deviate.

The lords and gentlemen take all the meaneſt ſort upon themſelves; for they are beſt able to bring them in, whenſoever any of them *ſtarteth* out. *Spenſer on Ireland.*

I rank him with the prodigies of fame,
With things which *ſtart* from nature's common rules,
With bearded infants, and with teeming mules. *Creech.*

Keep your ſoul to the work when ready to *ſtart* aſide, unleſs you will be a ſlave to every wild imagination. *Watts.*

6. To ſet out from the barrier at a race.

It ſeems to be rather a *terminus a quo* than a true principle, as the *ſtarting* poſt is none of the horſe's legs. *Boyle.*

Should ſome god tell me, that I ſhould be born
And cry again, his offer I ſhould ſcorn;
Aſham'd, when I have ended well my race,
To be led back to my firſt *ſtarting* place. *Denham.*

When from the goal they *ſtart*,
The youthful charioteers with heaving heart
Ruſh to the race. *Dryden's Virg. Georg.*

The clangor of the trumpet gives the ſign;
At once they *ſtart*, advancing in a line. *Dryden.*

7. To ſet out on any purſuit.

Fair courſe of paſſion, where two lovers *ſtart*,
And run together, heart ſtill yokt with heart. *Waller.*

People, when they have made themſelves weary, ſet up their reſt upon the very ſpot where they *ſtarted.* *L'Eſtrange.*

When two *ſtart* into the world together, he that is thrown behind, unleſs his mind proves generous, will be diſpleaſed with the other. *Collier.*

To START. *v. a.*

1. To alarm; to diſturb ſuddenly.

Direneſs, familiar to my ſlaught'rous thoughts,
Cannot once *ſtart* me. *Shakeſpeare.*

Being full of ſupper and diſtemp'ring draughts,
Upon malicious bravery do'ſt thou come
To *ſtart* my quiet. *Shakeſpeare's Othello.*

The very print of a fox-foot would have *ſtarted* ye. *L'Eſtr.*

2. To make to ſtart or fly haſtily from a hiding place.

The blood more ſtirs
To rouze a lion than to *ſtart* a hare. *Shakeſpeare.*

I *ſtarted* from its vernal bow'r
The riſing game, and chac'd from flow'r to flow'r. *Pope.*

3. To bring into motion; to produce to view or notice; to produce unexpectedly.

Conjure with 'em!
Brutus will *ſtart* a ſpirit as ſoon as Cæſar. *Shakeſpeare.*

It was unadviſedly done, when I was enforcing a weightier deſign, to *ſtart* and follow another of leſs moment. *Sprat.*

Inſignificant cavils may be *ſtarted* againſt every thing that is not capable of mathematical demonſtration. *Addiſon.*

I was engaged in converſation upon a ſubject which the people love to *ſtart* in diſcourſe. *Addiſon's Freeholder.*

4. To diſcover; to bring within purſuit.

The ſenſual men agree in purſuit of every pleaſure they can *ſtart.* *Temple.*

5. To put ſuddenly out of place.

One, by a fall in wreſtling, *ſtarted* the end of the clavicle from the ſternon. *Wiſeman's Surgery.*

STA

START. *n. ſ.* [from the verb.]

1. A motion of terrour; a ſudden twitch or contraction of the frame from fear or alarm.

> Theſe flaws and *ſtarts* would well become
> A woman's ſtory at a Winter's fire,
> Authoriz'd by her grandam. *Shakeſpeare.*
> The fright awaken'd Arcite with a *ſtart*;
> Againſt his boſom bounc'd his heaving heart. *Dryden.*

2. A ſudden rouſing to action; excitement.

> How much had I to do to calm his rage!
> Now fear I this will give it *ſtart* again. *Shakeſ. Hamlet.*

3. Sally; vehement eruption; ſudden effuſion.

> Thou art like enough, through vaſſal fear,
> Baſe inclination, and the *ſtart* of ſpleen,
> To fight againſt me under Percy's pay. *Shakeſpeare.*

Several *ſtarts* of fancy off-hand, look well enough; but bring them to the teſt, and there is nothing in 'em. *L'Eſtrange.*

> Are they not only to diſguiſe our paſſions,
> To ſet our looks at variance with our thoughts,
> To check the *ſtarts* and ſallies of the ſoul? *Addiſon's Cato.*

We were well enough pleaſed with this *ſtart* of thought. *Add.*

4. Sudden fit; intermitted action.

> Methought her eyes had croſt her tongue;
> For ſhe did ſpeak in *ſtarts* diſtractedly. *Shakeſpeare.*
> Thy forms are ſtudied arts,
> Thy ſubtile ways be narrow ſtraits;
> Thy curteſy but ſudden *ſtarts*;
> And what thou call'ſt thy gifts are baits. *Ben. Johnſon.*

Nature does nothing by *ſtarts* and leaps, or in a hurry; but all her motions are gradual. *L'Eſtrange.*

An ambiguous expreſſion, a little chagrin, or a *ſtart* of paſſion, is not enough to take leave upon. *Collier.*

5. A quick ſpring or motion.

In ſtrings, the more they are wound up and ſtrained, and thereby give a more quick *ſtart* back, the more treble is the ſound; and the ſlacker they are, or leſs wound up, the baſer is the ſound. *Bacon's Natural Hiſtory.*

Both cauſe the ſtring to give a quicker *ſtart*. *Bacon.*

How could water make thoſe viſible *ſtarts* upon freezing, but by ſome ſubtile freezing principle which as ſuddenly ſhoots into it. *Grew's Coſmol. Sac.*

6. Firſt emiſſion from the barrier; act of ſetting out.

> You ſtand like greyhounds in the ſlips,
> Straining upon the *ſtart*. *Shakeſp. Henry V.*
> All leapt to chariot,
> And every man then for the *ſtart* caſt in his proper lot. *Chap.*

If a man deal with another upon conditions, the *ſtart* of firſt performance is all. *Bacon.*

7. *To get the* START. To begin before another; to obtain advantage over another.

> *Get the ſtart* of the majeſtick world. *Shakeſ. Jul. Cæſ.*

All pretorian courts, if any of the parties be laid aſleep, under pretence of arbitrement, and the other party, during that time, doth cautelouſly *get the ſtart* and advantage at common law, yet the pretorian court will ſet back all things in *ſtatu quo prius.* *Bacon's War with Spain.*

> Doubtleſs ſome other heart
> Will *get the ſtart*;
> And, ſtepping in before,
> Will take poſſeſſion of the ſacred ſtore
> Of hidden ſweets. *Craſhaw.*
> Ere the knight could do his part,
> The ſquire had *got* ſo much *the ſtart*,
> H' had to the lady done his errand,
> And told her all his tricks aforehand. *Hudibras.*

She might have forſaken him, if he had not *got the ſtart* of her. *Dryden's Æn. Dedication.*

The reaſon why the mathematicks and mechanick arts have ſo much *got the ſtart* in growth of other ſciences, may be reſolved into this, that their progreſs hath not been retarded by that reverential awe of former diſcoverers. *Glanville.*

The French year has *got the ſtart* of ours more in the works of nature than the new ſtile. *Addiſon.*

STA'RTER. *n. ſ.* [from *ſtart.*] One that ſhrinks from his purpoſe.

> Stand to it boldly, and take quarter,
> To let thee ſee I am no *ſtarter*. *Hudibras.*

STA'RTINGLY. *adv.* [from *ſtarting.*] By ſudden fits; with frequent intermiſſion.

> Why do you ſpeak ſo *ſtartingly* and raſh. *Shak. Othello.*

To STA'RTLE. *v. n.* [from *ſtart.*] To ſhrink; to move on feeling a ſudden impreſſion of alarm or terrour.

> The *ſtartling* ſteed was ſeiz'd with ſudden fright,
> And bounding o'er the pommel caſt the knight. *Dryden.*
> Why ſhrinks the ſoul
> Back on herſelf, and *ſtartles* at deſtruction? *Addiſ. Cato.*
> My frighted thoughts run back,
> And *ſtartle* into madneſs at the ſound. *Addiſon's Cato.*

To STA'RTLE. *v. a.* To fright; to ſhock; to impreſs with ſudden terrour, ſurpriſe, or alarm.

They would find occaſions enough, upon the account of his known affections to the king's ſervice, from which it was not poſſible to remove or *ſtartle* him. *Clarendon.*

Wilmot had more ſcruples from religion to *ſtartle* him, and would not have attained his end by any groſs act of wickedneſs. *Clarendon.*

> Such whiſp'ring wak'd her, but with *ſtartled* eye
> On Adam. *Milton.*
> To hear the lark begin his flight,
> And ſinging *ſtartle* the dull night
> From his watch-tower in the ſkies,
> 'Till the dappled dawn doth riſe. *Milton.*

The ſuppoſition that angels aſſume bodies needs not *ſtartle* us, ſince ſome of the moſt ancient and moſt learned fathers ſeemed to believe that they had bodies. *Locke.*

> Inceſt! Oh name it not!
> The very mention ſhakes my inmoſt ſoul:
> The gods are *ſtartled* in their peaceful manſions,
> And nature ſickens at the ſhocking ſound. *Smith.*

His books had been ſolemnly burnt at Rome as heretical: ſome people, he found, were *ſtartled* at it; ſo he was forced boldly to make repriſals, to buoy up their courage. *Atterbury.*

> Now the leaf
> Inceſſant ruſtles, from the mournful grove
> Oft *ſtartling* ſuch as ſtudious walk below,
> And ſlowly circles through the waving air. *Thomſon.*

STA'RTLE. *n. ſ.* [from the verb.] Sudden alarm; ſhock; ſudden impreſſion of terrour.

After having recovered from my firſt *ſtartle*, I was very well pleaſed at the accident. *Spectator.*

STA'RTUP. *n. ſ.* [*ſtart* and *up.*] One that comes ſuddenly into notice.

> That young *ſtartup* hath all the glory of my overthrow. *Sh.*

To STARVE. *v. n.* [ſteaꞃꝼan, Saxon; *ſterven*, Dutch, to die.]

1. To periſh; to be deſtroyed. Obſolete.

> To her came meſſage of the murderment,
> Wherein her guiltleſs friends ſhould hopeleſs *ſtarve.* *Fairfax.*

2. To periſh with hunger. It has *with* or *for* before the cauſe, *of* leſs properly.

Were the pains of honeſt induſtry, and of *ſtarving* with hunger and cold, ſet before us, no body would doubt which to chuſe. *Locke.*

An animal that *ſtarves* of hunger, dies feveriſh and delirious. *Arbuthnot.*

3. To be killed with cold.

> Have I ſeen the naked *ſtarve* for cold,
> While avarice my charity controll'd? *Sandys.*

4. To ſuffer extreme poverty.

> Sometimes virtue *ſtarves* while vice is fed:
> What then! Is the reward of virtue bread? *Pope.*

5. To be deſtroyed with cold.

Had the ſeeds of the pepper-plant been born from Java to theſe northern countries, they muſt have *ſtarved* for want of ſun. *Woodward's Natural Hiſtory.*

To STARVE. *v. a.*

1. To kill with hunger.

> I cannot blame his couſin king,
> That wiſh'd him on the barren mountains *ſtarv'd.* *Shakeſp.*
> Hunger and thirſt, or guns and ſwords,
> Give the ſame death in different words:
> To puſh this argument no further,
> To *ſtarve* a man in law is murther. *Prior.*

If they had died through faſting, when meat was at hand, they would have been guilty of *ſtarving* themſelves. *Pope.*

2. To ſubdue by famine.

> Thy deſires
> Are wolfiſh, bloody, *ſtarv'd*, and ravenous. *Shakeſpeare.*
> He would have worn her out by ſlow degrees,
> As men by faſting *ſtarve* th' untam'd diſeaſe. *Dryden.*

Attalus endeavoured to *ſtarve* Italy, by ſtopping their convoy of proviſions from Africa. *Arbuthnot on Coins.*

3. To kill with cold.

> From beds of raging fire to *ſtarve* in ice
> Their ſoft ethereal warmth, and there to pine
> Immoveable, infix'd, and frozen round. *Milton's Par. Loſt.*

4. To deprive of force or vigour.

The powers of their minds are *ſtarved* by diſuſe, and have loſt that reach and ſtrength which nature fitted them to receive. *Locke.*

STA'RVELING. *n. ſ.* [from *ſtarve.*] An animal thin and weak for want of nouriſhment.

If I hang, I'll make a fat pair of gallows; for old ſir John hangs with me, and he's no *ſtarveling.* *Shakeſpeare.*

> Now thy alms is giv'n, the letter's read;
> The body riſen again, the which was dead;
> And thy poor *ſtarveling* bountifully fed. *Donne.*

The fat ones would be making ſport with the lean, and calling them *ſtarvelings.* *L'Eſtrange.*

> The thronging cluſters thin
> By kind avulſion; elſe the *ſtarv'ling* brood,
> Void of ſufficient ſuſtenance, will yield
> A ſlender Autumn. *Philips.*

Poor

Poor *starveling* bard, how small thy gains!
How unproportion'd to thy pains! *Swift.*

STA'RWORT. *n. s.* [*aster*, Latin.] See ELECAMPANE.

It hath a fibrous root: the leaves for the most part intire, and placed alternately on the branches: the stalks are branched; the flowers radiated, specious, and have a scaly cup: the seeds are inclosed in a downy substance. *Miller.*

STA'TARY. *adj.* [from *status*, Latin.] Fixed; settled.

The set and *statary* times of pairing of nails, and cutting of hair, is but the continuation of ancient superstition. *Brown.*

STATE. *n. s.* [*status*, Latin.]

1. Condition; circumstances of nature or fortune.

I do not
Infer as if I thought my sister's *state*
Secure. *Milton.*

Relate what Latium was,
Declare the past and present *state* of things. *Dryden's Æn.*

Like the papists is your poets *state*,
Poor and disarm'd. *Pope.*

2. Modification of any thing.

Keep the *state* of the question in your eye. *Boyle.*

3. Stationary point; crisis; height; point from which the next movement is regression.

The deer that endureth the womb but eight months, and is compleat at six years, cannot live much more than thirty, as having passed two general motions; that is, its beginning and increase; and having but two more to run through, that is, its *state* and declination. *Brown's Vulgar Errours.*

Tumours have their several degrees and times; as beginning, augment, *state*, and declination: *Wiseman.*

4. [*Estat*, French.] Estate; signiory; possession.

Strong was their plot,
Their *states* far off, and they of wary wit. *Daniel.*

5. The community; the publick; the commonwealth.

If any thing more than your sport
Did move your greatness, and this noble *state*,
To call on him, he hopes it is no other
But for your health sake. *Shakesp. Troilus and Cressida.*

A *state's* anger
Should not take knowledge either of fools or women.
Ben. Johnson't Catiline.

I hear her talk of *state* matters and the senate. *Ben. Johns.*

What he got by fortune,
It was the *state* that now must make his right. *Daniel.*

The *state* hath given you licence to stay on land for the space of six weeks. *Bacon.*

It is better the kingdom should be in good estate, with particular loss to many of the people, than that all the people should be well, and the *state* of the kingdom altogether lost. *Hayward.*

It is a bad exchange to wound a man's own conscience, thereby to salve *state* sores. *King Charles.*

For you we stay'd, as did the Grecian *state*
'Till Alexander came. *Waller.*

Since they all live by begging, it were better for the *state* to keep them. *Graunt.*

These are the realms of unrelenting fate;
And awful Rhadamanthus rules the *state*:
He hears and judges. *Dryden's Æn.*

6. Hence *single state* in *Shakespeare* for individuality.

My thought, whose murther yet is but fantastical,
Shakes so my *single state* of man, that function
Is smother'd in surmise. *Shakesp. Macbeth.*

7. A republick; a government not monarchical.

They feared nothing from a *state* so narrow in compass of land, and so weak, that the strength of their armies has ever been made up of foreign troops. *Temple.*

8. Rank; condition; quality.

Fair dame, I am not to you known,
Though in your *state* of honour I am perfect. *Shakesp.*
High *state* the bed is where misfortune lies. *Fairfax.*

9. Solemn pomp; appearance of greatness.

When in triumphant *state* the British muse,
True to herself, shall barb'rous aid refuse. *Roscommon.*

There kings receiv'd the marks of sov'reign pow'r:
In *state* the monarchs march'd, the lictors bore
The awful axes and the rods before. *Dryden's Æn.*

Let my attendants wait: I'll be alone,
Where least of *state*, where most of love is shown. *Dryden.*

To appear in their robes would be a troublesome piece of *state*. *Collier.*

At home surrounded by a servile crowd,
Prompt to abuse, and in detraction loud;
Abroad begirt with men, and swords, and spears,
His very *state* acknowledging his fears. *Prior.*

10. Dignity; grandeur.

She instructed him how he should keep *state*, and yet with a modest sense of his misfortunes.
Bacon's Henry VII.

The swan rows her *state* with oary feet. *Milton.*

He was staid, and in his gait
Preserv'd a grave majestick *state*. *Butler.*

Such cheerful modesty, such humble *state*,
Moves certain love. *Waller.*

Can this imperious lord forget to reign,
Quit all his *state*, descend, and serve again. *Pope's Statius.*

11. A seat of dignity.

This chair shall be my *state*, this dagger my sceptre, and this cushion my crown. *Shakes. Henry IV.*

As she affected not the grandeur of a *state* with a canopy, she thought there was no offence in an elbow-chair. *Arbuthn.*

The brain was her study, the heart her *state* room. *Arbuth.*

12. A canopy; a covering of dignity.

Over the chair is a *state* made round of ivy, somewhat whiter than ours; and the *state* is curiously wrought with silver and silk. *Bacon.*

His high throne, under *state*
Of richest texture spread, at th' upper end
Was plac'd. *Milton's Paradise Lost.*

13. A person of high rank. Obsolete.

She is a dutchess, a great *state*. *Latymer.*

14. The principal persons in the government.

The bold design
Pleas'd highly those infernal *states*. *Milton.*

15. Joined with another word it signifies publick.

I am no courtier, nor versed in *state*-affairs: my life hath rather been contemplative than active. *Bacon.*

Council! What's that? a pack of bearded slaves,
The scavengers that sweep *states* nusances,
And are themselves the greatest. *Dryden's Cleomenes.*

I am accused of reflecting upon great *states*-folks. *Swift.*

To STATE. *v. a.* [*constater*, French.]

1. To settle; to regulate.

This is so *stated* a rule, that all casuists press it in all cases of damage. *Decay of Piety.*

This is to *state* accounts, and looks more like merchandize than friendship. *Collier of Friendship.*

He is capable of corruption who receives more than what is the *stated* and unquestioned fee of his office. *Addison.*

2. To represent in all the circumstances of modification.

Many other inconveniences are consequent to this *stating* of this question; and particularly that, by those which thus *state* it, there hath never yet been assigned any definite number of fundamentals. *Hammond on Fundamentals.*

Its present state *stateth* it to be what it now is. *Hale.*

Were our case *stated* to any sober heathen, he would never guess why they who acknowledge the necessity of prayer, and confess the same God, may not ask in the same form.
Decay of Piety.

To *state* it fairly, imitation is the most advantageous way for a translator to shew himself, but the greatest wrong which can be done to the memory of the dead. *Dryden.*

I pretended not fully to *state*, much less demonstrate, the truth contained in the text. *Atterbury.*

STA'TELINESS. *n. s.* [from *stately*.]

1. Grandeur; majestick appearance; august manner; dignity.

We may collect the excellency of the understanding then by the glorious remainders of it now, and guess at the *stateliness* of the building by the magnificence of its ruins. *South.*

For *stateliness* and majesty what is comparable to a horse?
More's Antidote against Atheism.

2. Appearance of pride; affected dignity.

She hated *stateliness*; but wisely knew
What just regard was to her title due. *Betterton.*

STA'TELY. *adj.* [from *state*.]

1. August; grand; lofty; elevated; majestick; magnificent.

A *statelier* pyramid to her I'll rear,
Than Rhodope's or Memphis' ever was. *Shak. Hen. VI.*

These regions have abundance of high cedars, and other *stately* trees casting a shade. *Raleigh's History of the World.*

Truth, like a *stately* dome, will not shew herself at the first visit. *South.*

He many a walk travers'd
Of *stateliest* covert, cedar, pine, or palm. *Milton.*

2. Elevated in mien or sentiment.

He maintains majesty in the midst of plainness, and is *stately* without ambition, which is the vice of Lucan. *Dryden.*

STA'TELY. *adv.* [from the adjective.] Majestically.

Ye that *stately* tread or lowly creep. *Milton.*

STA'TESMAN. *n. s.* [*state* and *man*.]

1. A politician; one versed in the arts of government.

It looks grave enough
To seem a *statesman*. *Ben. Johnson's Epigr.*

The corruption of a poet is the generation of a *statesman*. *Pope.*

2. One employed in publick affairs.

If such actions may have passage free,
Bond-slaves and pagans shall our *statesmen* be. *Shak. Othello.*

It is a weakness which attends high and low; the *statesman* who holds the helm, as well as the peasant who holds the plough. *South's Sermons.*

A British minister must expect to see many friends fall off, whom he cannot gratify, since, to use the phrase of a late *statesman*, the pasture is not large enough. *Addison.*

Here

Here Britain's *statesmen* oft the fall foredoom
Of foreign tyrants, and of nymphs at home. *Pope.*

STA'TESWOMAN. *n. s.* [*state* and *woman.*] A woman who meddles with publick affairs. In contempt.

How she was in debt, and where she meant
To raise fresh sums: she's a great *stateswoman!* *B. Johnson.*

Several objects may innocently be ridiculed, as the passions of our *stateswomen.* *Addison.*

STA'TICAL. } *adj.* [from the noun.] Relating to the science
STA'TICK. } of weighing.

A man weigheth some pounds less in the height of Winter, according to experience, and the *statick* aphorisms of Sanctorius. *Brown's Vulgar Errours.*

If one by a *statical* engine could regulate his insensible perspiration, he might often, by restoring of that, foresee, prevent, or shorten a fit of the gout. *Arbuthnot on Diet.*

STA'TICKS. *n. s.* [στατικὴ; *statique*, Fr.] The science which considers the weight of bodies.

This is a catholick rule of *staticks*, that if any body be bulk for bulk heavier than a fluid, it will sink to the bottom; and if lighter, it will float upon it, having part extant, and part immersed, as that so much of the fluid as is equal in bulk to the immersed part be equal in gravity to the whole. *Bentley.*

STA'TION. *n. s.* [*station*, French; *statio*, Latin.]

1. The act of standing.

Their manner was to stand at prayer, whereupon their meetings unto that purpose on those days had the names of *stations* given them. *Hooker.*

2. A state of rest.

All progression is performed by drawing on or impelling forward some part which was before in *station* or at quiet, where there are no joints. *Brown's Vulgar Errours.*

3. A place where any one is placed.

In *station* like the herald, Mercury,
New-lighted on a heav'n-kissing hill. *Shakesp. Timon.*

The seditious remained within their *station*, which, by reason of the nastiness of the beastly multitude, might more fitly be termed a kennel than a camp. *Hayward.*

The planets in their *station* list'ning stood. *Milton.*

To single *stations* now what years belong,
With planets join'd, they claim another song. *Creech.*

4. Post assigned; office.

Michael in either hand leads them out of Paradise, the fiery serpent waving behind them, and the cherubims taking their *stations* to guard the place. *Milton.*

5. Situation; position.

The fig and date, why love they to remain
In middle *station* and an even plain;
While in the lower marsh the gourd is found,
And while the hill with olive-shade is crown'd? *Prior.*

6. Employment; office.

No member of a political body so mean, but it may be useful in some *station* or other. *L'Estrange.*

They believe that the common size of human understanding is fitted to some *station* or other. *Swift.*

Whether those who are leaders of a party arrive at that *station* more by a sort of instinct, or influence of the stars, than by the possession of any great abilities, may be a point of much dispute. *Swift.*

7. Character; state.

Far the greater part have kept their *station.* *Milton.*

8. Rank; condition of life.

I can be contented with an humbler *station* in the temple of virtue, than to be set on the pinnacle. *Dryden.*

To STA'TION. *v. a.* [from the noun] To place in a certain post, rank, or place.

STA'TIONARY. *adj.* [from *station.*] Fixed; not progressive.

The same harmony and *stationary* constitution, as it happened in many species, so doth it fall out in individuals. *Brown.*

Between the descent and ascent, where the image seemed *stationary*, I stopped the prism, and fixed it in that posture, that it should be moved no more. *Newton's Opt.*

STA'TIONER. *n. s.* [from *station*]

1. A bookseller.

Some modern tragedies are beautiful on the stage, and yet Tryphon the *stationer* complains they are seldom asked for in his shop. *Dryden.*

With authors, *stationers* obey'd the call;
Glory and gain th' industrious tribe provoke,
And gentle dulness ever loves a joke. *Pope's Dunciad.*

2. A seller of paper.

STA'TIST. *n. s.* [from *state*] A statesman; a politician; one skilled in government.

I once did hold it, as our *statists* do,
A baseness to write fair; and labour'd much
How to forget that learning. *Shakesp. Hamlet.*

I do believe,
Statist though I am none, nor like to be,
That this shall prove a war. *Shakes. Cymbeline.*

Their orators thou then extoll'st, as those
The top of eloquence, *statists* indeed,
And lovers of their country. *Milton's Paradise Reg.*

STA'TUARY. *n. s.* [*statuaire*, French; from *statua*, Latin.]

1. The art of carving images or representations of life.

The northern nations, that overwhelmed it by their numbers, were too barbarous to preserve the remains of learning more carefully than they did those of architecture and *statuary*. *Temple.*

2. One that practises or professes the art of making statues.

On other occasions the *statuaries* took their subjects from the poets. *Addison.*

How shall any man, who hath a genius for history, undertake such a work with spirit and chearfulness, when he considers that he will be read with pleasure but a very few years? This is like employing an excellent *statuary* to work upon mouldering stone. *Swift.*

STA'TUE. *n. s.* [*statue*, Fr. *statua*, Latin.] An image; a solid representation of any living being.

The princess heard of her mother's *statue*, a piece many years in doing, and now newly perform'd by that rare Italian master. *Shakesp. Winter's Tale.*

They spake not a word;
But like dumb *statues*, or unbreathing stones,
Star'd each on other. *Shakespeare's Richard III.*

Architects propounded unto Alexander to cut the mountain Athos into the form of a *statue*, which in his right hand should hold a town capable of containing ten thousand men, and in his left a vessel to receive all the water that flowed from the mountain. *Wilkins's Math. Magick.*

A *statue* of Polycletus, called the rule, deserves that name for having so perfect an agreement in all its parts, that it is not possible to find a fault in it. *Dryden's Dufresnoy.*

To STA'TUE. *v. a.* [from the noun.] To place as a statue.

Thou shalt be worshipp'd, kiss'd, lov'd and ador'd;
And were there sense in his idolatry,
My substance should be *statued* in thy stead. *Shakespeare.*

STA'TURE. *n. s.* [*stature*, Fr. *statura*, Latin.] The height of any animal.

What *stature* we attain at seven years we sometimes double, most times come short of at one and twenty. *Brown.*

A creature who might erect
His *stature*, and upright with front serene
Govern the rest. *Milton.*

Foreign men of mighty *stature* came. *Dryden.*

Thyself but dust, thy *stature* but a span;
A moment thy duration, foolish man! *Prior.*

We have certain demonstration from Egyptian mummies, and Roman urns and rings, and measures and edifices, and many other antiquities, that human *stature* has not diminished for above two thousand years. *Bentley's Sermons.*

STA'TUTABLE. *adj.* [from *statute.*] According to statute.

I met with one who was three inches above five feet, the *statutable* measure of that club. *Addison's Guardian.*

STA'TUTE. *n. s.* [*statut*, French; *statutum*, Latin.] A law; an edict of the legislature.

Not only the common law, but also the *statutes* and acts of parliament were specially intended for its benefit. *Spenser.*

Blood hath been shed,
Ere human *statute* purg'd the gen'ral weal. *Shakespeare.*

There was a *statute* against vagabonds; wherein note the dislike the parliament had of goaling them as chargeable and pesterous. *Bacon.*

Know the *statutes* of heaven and laws of eternity, those immutable rules of justice. *Tillotson's Sermons.*

O queen, indulg'd by favour of the gods,
To build a town, with *statutes* to restrain
The wild inhabitant beneath thy reign. *Dryden's Æneid.*

To STAVE. *v. a.* In the plural *staves.* [from *staff.*]

1. To break in pieces; used originally of barrels made of small parts or staves.

If irreverent expression, or a thought too wanton are crept into my verses, let them be *stav'd* or forfeited like contrabanded goods. *Dryden.*

2. To push off as with a staff.

How can they escape the contagion of the writings, whom the virulency of the calumnies have not *staved* off, from reading. *Ben. Johnson.*

The condition of a servant *staves* him off to a distance; but the gospel speaks nothing but allurement, attraction, and invitation. *South's Sermons.*

3. To pour out by breaking the cask.

The feared disorders that might ensue thereof have been an occasion that divers times all the wine in the city hath been *staved.* *Sandys's Travels.*

4. To furnish with rundles or staves.

This was the shameful end of Aloysus Grittus, Solyman's deputy in Hungary; who climbing too fast up the evil *staved* ladder of ambition, suddenly fell, and never rose more. *Knolles.*

To STAVE. *v. n.* To fight with staves.

Equal shame and envy stirr'd
I' th' enemy, that one shou'd beard
So many warriours, and so stout,
As he had done, and *stav'd* it out. *Hudibras.*

To STAVE *and Tail. v. a.* To part dogs by interposing a staff, and by pulling the tail.

The

The conquering foe they soon assail'd,
First Trulla *stav'd*, and Cerdon *tail'd*. *Hudibras.*

STAVES. *n. s.* The plural of *staff*.

All in strange manner arm'd,
Some rustick knives, some *staves* in fire warmed. *Fairy Qu.*

They tie teasils up in bundles or *staves*. *Mortimer's Husband.*

STA'VESACRE. *n. s.* Larkspur. A plant.

To STAY. *v. n.* [*staen*, Dutch.]

1. To continue in a place; to forbear departure.

Macbeth, we *stay* upon your leisure. *Shakespeare's Macbeth.*

If she do bid me pack, I'll give her thanks,
As though she bid me *stay* by her a week. *Shakespeare.*

Would ye tarry for them till they were grown? would ye *stay* for them from having husbands? *Ruth* i. 13.

Not after resurrection shall he *stay*
Longer on earth than certain times t'appear. *Milton.*

He did ordain that as many might depart as would; but as many as would *stay* should have very good means to live from the state. *Bacon.*

They flocked in such multitudes, that they not only *stayed* for their resort, but discharged divers. *Hayward.*

Th' injur'd sea, which from her wonted place,
To gain some acres, avarice did force,
If the new banks neglected once decay,
No longer will from her old channel *stay*. *Waller.*

Stay, I command you, *stay* and hear me first. *Dryden.*

Nor must he *stay* at home, because he must be back again by one and twenty. The father cannot *stay* any longer. *Locke.*

Every plant has its atmosphere, which hath various effects on those who *stay* near them. *Arbuthnot on Aliments.*

Servants sent on messages *stay* out longer than the message requires. *Swift.*

2. To continue in a state.

The flames augment, and *stay*
At their full height, then languish to decay. *Dryden.*

3. To wait; to attend.

I'll tell thee my whole device
When I am in my coach, which *stays* for us. *Shakespeare.*

We for his royal presence only *stay*
To end the rites. *Dryden.*

I *stay* for Turnus, whose devoted head
Is owing to the living and the dead;
My son and I expect it from his hand. *Dryden.*

4. To stop; to stand still.

When she list pour out her larger spright,
She would command the hasty sun to *stay*,
Or backward turn his course. *Fairy Queen.*

Perkin Warbeck, finding that when matters once go down the hill, they *stay* not without a new force, resolved to try some exploit upon England. *Bacon.*

Satan
Throws his steep flight in many an airy wheel,
Nor *stay'd*, till on Niphates' top he lights. *Milton.*

5. To dwell; to be long.

Nor will I *stay*
On Amphix, or what deaths he dealt that day. *Dryden.*

I must *stay* a little on one action, which preferred the relief of others to the consideration of yourself. *Dryden.*

6. To rest confidently.

Because ye trust in oppression, and *stay* thereon, this shall be as a breach ready to fall. *Isa.* xxx. 12.

They call themselves of the holy city, and *stay* themselves upon God. *Isa.* xlviii. 2.

To STAY. *v. a.*

1. To stop; to withold; to repress.

All that may *stay* their minds from thinking that true which they heartily wish were false, but cannot think it so without some scruple. *Hooker.*

The Syrens sang to allure them into danger; but Orpheus sang so well that he *staid* them. *Raleigh's History of the World.*

He took nothing but a bit of bread to *stay* his stomach. *Locke.*

To *stay* these sudden gusts of passion
That hurry you from reason, rest assur'd
The secret of your love lives with me only. *Rowe.*

Stay her stomach with these half hundred plays, till I can procure her a romance big enough to satisfy her great soul with adventures. *Pope.*

Why cease we then the wrath of heaven to *stay*?
Be humbled all. *Pope.*

2. To delay; to obstruct; to hinder from progression.

The joyous time will not be *stay'd*
Unless she do him by the forelock take. *Spenser.*

Your ships are *staid* at Venice. *Shakespeare.*

Unto the shore, with tears, with sighs, with moan,
They him conduct; cursing the bounds that *stay*
Their willing feet, that would have further gone. *Daniel.*

I will bring thee where no shadow *stays*
Thy coming, and thy soft embraces. *Milton's Paradise Lost.*

I was willing to *stay* my reader on an argument that appears to me new. *Locke.*

3. To keep from departure.

If as a prisoner I were here, you might
Have then insisted on a conqueror's right,
And *stay'd* me here. *Dryden.*

4. [*Estayer*, French.] To prop; to support; to hold up.

On this determination we might *stay* ourselves without further proceeding herein. *Hooker.*

Aaron and Hur *stayed* up his hands, the one on the one side and the other on the other. *Exod.* xvii. 12.

Sallows and reeds for vineyards useful found,
To *stay* thy vines. *Dryden.*

STAY. *n. s.* [*estaye*, French.]

1. Continuance in a place; forbearance of departure.

Determine,
Or for her *stay* or going; the affair cries haste. *Shakespeare.*

Should judges make a longer *stay* in a place than usually they do; a day more in a county would be a very good addition. *Bacon.*

Her long with ardent look his eye pursu'd,
Delighted! but desired more her *stay*. *Milton.*

The Thracian youth invades
Orpheus returning from th' Elysian shades,
Embrace the hero, and his *stay* implore. *Waller.*

So long a *stay* will make
The jealous king suspect we have been plotting. *Denham.*

What pleasure hop'st thou in my *stay*,
When I'm constrain'd and wish myself away? *Dryden.*

When the wine sparkles,
Make haste, and leave thy business and thy care,
No mortal int'rest can be worth thy *stay*. *Dryden.*

2. Stand; cessation of progression.

Bones, after full growth, continue at a *stay*; teeth stand at a *stay*, except their wearing. *Bacon.*

Affairs of state seemed rather to stand at a *stay*, than to advance or decline. *Heyward.*

Made of sphere-metal, never to decay,
Until his revolution was at *stay*. *Milton.*

Almighty crowd! thou shorten'st all dispute;
Nor faith nor reason make thee at a *stay*,
Thou leap'st o'er all. *Dryden's Medal.*

3. A stop; an obstruction; a hindrance from progress.

His fell heart thought long that little way,
Griev'd with each step, tormented with each *stay*. *Fairfax.*

4. Restraint; prudence; caution.

Many just and temperate provisos, well shewed and foretokened the wisdom, *stay* and moderation of the king. *Bacon.*

With prudent *stay* he long deferr'd
The rough contention. *Philips.*

5. A fixed state.

Who have before, or shall write after thee,
Their works though toughly laboured will be
Like infancy or age to man's firm *stay*,
Or early and late twilights to mid-day. *Donne.*

Alas, what *stay* is there in human state!
And who can shun inevitable fate? *Dryden.*

6. A prop; a support.

Obedience of creatures unto the law of nature is the *stay* of the whole world. *Hooker.*

What surety of the world, what hope, what *stay*,
What this was once a king, and now is clay. *Shakespeare.*

My only strength, and *stay*! forlorn of thee,
Whither shall I betake me?—where subsist? *Milton.*

Trees serve as so many *stays* for their vines, which hang like garlands from tree to tree. *Addison's Remarks on Italy.*

7. Tackling. [See STAYS]

With *stays* and cordage last he rig'd a ship,
And roll'd on leavers, launch'd her in the deep. *Pope.*

8. [In the plural.] Boddice.

No stubborn *stays* her yielding shape embrace. *Gay.*

9. Steadiness of conduct.

STA'YED. *part. adj.* [from *stay*.]

1. Fixed; settled; serious; not volatile.

For her son,
In her own hand the crown she kept in store,
Till riper years he raught, and stronger *stay*. *Fa. Queen.*

Whatsoever is above these proceedeth of shortness of memory, or of want of a *stayed* and equal attention. *Bacon.*

He was well *stayed*, and in his gate
Preserv'd a grave majestick state. *Hudibras.*

A *stayed* man and wife are seldom so indolent as not to find consolation in each other. *Pope.*

2. Stopped.

STA'YEDLY. *adv.* [from *stayed*.] Composedly; gravely; prudently; soberly; calmly; judiciously.

SLA'YEDNESS. *n. s.* [from *stayed*.]

1. Solidity; weight.

When substantialness combineth with delightfulness, and currantness with *stayedness*, how can the language sound other than most full of sweetness. *Camden's Remains.*

2. Com-

2. Composure; prudence; gravity; judiciousness.

STA'YER. *n. s.* [from *stay.*] One who stops, holds or supports.

May Jove, the guardian of the capitol,
He, the great *stayer* of our troops in rout,
Fulfil your hopes, and animate the cohorts. *A. Philips.*

STA'YLACE. *n. s.* [*stay* and *lace.*] A lace with which women fasten their boddice.

A *stay'ace* from England should become a topick for censure at visits. *Swift.*

STAYS. *n. s.* Without singular.

1. Boddice; a kind of stiff waistcoat made of whalebone, worn by ladies.

2. Ropes in a ship to keep the mast from falling aft. All masts, topmasts, and flagstaves have *stays*, except the spritsail topmast: the mainmast, foremast, with the masts belonging to them, have also back *stays*, which help to keep the mast from pitching forward or overboard. *Harris.*

They were come upon the *stays*, when one of the sailors descried a galley. *Sidney.*

3. Any support; any thing that keeps another extended.

Weavers stretch your *stays* upon the weft. *Dryden.*

STEAD. *n. s.* [ꞅꞇeꝺ, Saxon.]

1. Place. Obsolete.

Fly therefore, fly this fearful *stead* anon,
Lest thy fool hardize work thy sad confusion. *Fairy Queen.*

They nigh approached to the *stead*
Where as those maremaids dwelt. *Spenser's Fairy Queen.*

The term of life is limited,
Ne may a man prolong nor shorten it;
The soldier may not move from watchful *stead*,
Nor leave his stand until his captain bed. *Fairy Queen.*

2. Room; place which another had or might have.

If we had simply taken them clean away, or else removed them, so as to place in their *stead* others, we had done worse. *Hooker.*

There fell down many slain, and they dwelt in their *steads* until the captivity. 1 *Chron.* v. 22.

Nor do the bold'st attempts bring forth
Events still equal to their worth;
But sometimes fail, and in their *stead*
Fortune and cowardice succeed. *Butler.*

Jealousy then fir'd his soul,
And his face kindled like a burning coal;
Now cold despair succeeding in her *stead*,
To livid paleness turns the glowing red. *Dryden.*

3. Use; help. *To stand in stead*; to be of great use; to help; to advantage.

A compleat man hath some parts, whereof the want could not deprive him of his essence; yet to have them *standeth* him *in* singular *stead*, in respect of special uses. *Hooker.*

He makes his understanding the warehouse of lumber rather than a repository of truth, which will *stand* him *in stead* when he has occasion for it. *Locke.*

The smallest act of charity shall *stand* us *in* great *stead*. *Atterbury's Sermons.*

4. The frame of a bed.

The genial bed,
Sallow the feet, the borders and the *sted*. *Dryden.*

STEAD, *sted*, being in the name of a place that is distant from any river, comes from the Saxon ꞅꞇeꝺ, ꞅꞇyꝺ, a place; but if it be upon a river or harbour, it is to be derived from ꞅꞇaꝺe, a shore or station for ships. *Gibson's Camden.*

To STEAD. *v. a.* [from the noun.]

1. To help; to advantage; to support; to assist. A word somewhat obsolete.

We are neither in skill, nor ability of power greatly to *stead* you. *Sidney.*

It nothing *steads* us
To chide him from our eves. *Shakespeare.*

Rich garments, linnens, stuffs, and necessaries,
Which since have *steaded* much. *Shakespeare's Tempest.*

Madam, so it *stead* you I will write. *Shakespeare.*

Can you so *stead* me
As bring me to the sight of Isabella. *Shakespeare.*

Your friendly aid and counsel much may *stead* me. *Rowe.*

2. To fill the place of another. Obsolete.

We shall advise this wronged maid to *stead* up your appointment, and go in your place. *Shakespeare.*

STEA'DFAST. *adj.* [*stead* and *fast.*]

1. Fast in place; firm; fixed.

Such was this giant's fall, that seem'd to shake
This *stedfast* globe of earth, as it for fear did quake. *F. Qu.*

Laws ought to be like stony tables, plain, *steadfast*, and immoveable. *Spenser's State of Ireland.*

2. Constant; resolute.

I hope her stubborn heart to bend,
And that it then more *stedfast* will endure. *Spenser.*

A generation that set not their heart aright, and whose spirit was not *stedfast* with God. *Psal.* lxxviii. 8.

Be faithful to thy neighbour in his poverty; abide *stedfast* unto him in the time of his trouble. *Ecclus.* xxii. 23.

Him resist *stedfast* in the faith. 1 *Pet.* v. 9.

What form of death could him affright,
Who unconcern'd, with *stedfast* sight
Cou'd view the surges mounting steep,
And monsters rolling in the deep? *Dryden.*

STEA'DFASTLY. *adv.* [from *stedfast.*] Firmly; constantly.

God's omniscience *steadfastly* grasps the greatest and most slippery uncertainties. *South's Sermons.*

In general, *stedfastly* believe that whatever God hath revealed is infallibly true. *Wake's Preparation for Death.*

STEA'DFASTNESS. *n. s.* [from *steadfast.*]

1. Immutability; fixedness.

So hard these heavenly beauties be enfir'd,
As things divine, least passions do impress,
The more of steadfast minds to be admir'd,
The more they stayed be on *stedfastness*. *Spenser.*

2. Firmness; constancy; resolution.

STEA'DILY. *adv.* [from *steady.*]

1. Without tottering; without shaking.

Sin has a tendency to bring men under evils, unless hindered by some accident which no man can *steadily* build upon. *South's Sermons.*

2. Without variation or irregularity.

So *steadily* does fickle fortune steer
Th' obedient orb that it should never err. *Blackmore.*

STEA'DINESS. *n. s.* [from *steady.*]

1. State of being not tottering nor easily shaken.

2. Firmness; constancy.

John got the better of his cholerick temper, and wrought himself up to a great *steadiness* of mind, to pursue his interest through all impediments. *Arbuthnot.*

3. Consistent unvaried conduct.

Steadiness is a point of prudence as well as of courage. *L'Est.*

A friend is useful to form an undertaking, and secure *steadiness* of conduct. *Collier of Friendship.*

STEA'DY. *adj.* [ꞅꞇæꝺiᵹ, Saxon.]

1. Firm; fixed; not tottering.

Their feet *steady*, their hands diligent, their eyes watchful, and their hearts resolute. *Sidney.*

He sails 'tween worlds and worlds with *steady* wing. *Milt.*

Steer the bounding bark with *steady* toil,
When the storm thickens and the billows boil. *Pope.*

2. Not wavering; not fickle; not changeable with regard to resolution or attention.

Now clear I understand,
What oft my *steadiest* thoughts have search'd in vain. *Milton.*

Steady to my principles, and not dispirited with my afflictions, I have, by the blessing of God, overcome all difficulties. *Dryden's Æneid.*

A clear sight keeps the understanding *steady*. *Locke.*

STEAK *n. s.* [*styck*, Islandick and Erse, a piece; *steka*, Swedish, to boil.] A slice of flesh broiled or fried; a collop.

The surgeon protested he had cured him very well, and offered to eat the first *stake* of him. *Tatler.*

Fair ladies who contrive
To feast on ale and *steaks*. *Swift.*

To STEAL. *v. a.* Preterite *I stole*, part. pass. *stolen.* [ꞅꞇelan, Saxon; *stelen*, Dutch.]

1. To take by theft; to take clandestinely; to take without right. To *steal* generally implies secrecy, to *rob*, either secrecy or violence.

Thou ran'st a tilt in honour of my love,
And *stol'st* away the ladies hearts of France. *Shakespeare.*

There are some shrewd contents in yon same paper,
That *steal* the colour from Bassanio's cheek;
Some dear friend dead. *Shakespeare's Merch. of Venice.*

How should we *steal* silver or gold? *Gen.* xliv. 8.

A schoolboy finding a bird's nest, shews it his companion and he *steals* it. *Shakespeare.*

2. To withdraw or convey without notice.

The law of England never was properly applied to the Irish, by a purposed plot of government, but as they could insinuate and *steal* themselves under the same by their humble carriage and submission. *Spenser.*

Let us shift away, there's warrant in that theft
Which *steals* itself when there's no mercy left. *Shakespeare.*

Variety of objects has a tendency to *steal* away the mind from its steady pursuit of any subject. *Watts.*

3. To gain or effect by private means.

Young Lorenzo
Stole her soul with many vows of faith,
And ne'er a true one. *Shakespeare.*

Were it not that my fellow schoolmaster
Doth watch Bianca's steps so narrowly,
'Twere good to *steal* our marriage. *Shakespeare.*

They hate nothing so much as being alone, for fear some affrighting apprehensions should *steal* or force their way in. *Calamy.*

To STEAL. *v. n.*

1. To withdraw privily; to pass silently.

Fixt of mind to avoid further entreaty, and to fly all company, one night she *stole* away. *Sidney.*

My

My lord of Amiens and myself
Did *steal* behind him as he lay along
Under an oak. *Shakespeare.*

I cannot think it,
That he would *steal* away so guilty like,
Seeing you coming. *Shakespeare's Othello.*

The most peaceable way, if you take a thief, is to let him shew what he is, and *steal* out of your company. *Shakespeare.*

At time that lover's flights doth still conceal,
Through Athens' gate have we devis'd to *steal.* *Shakesp.*

In my conduct shall your ladies come,
From whom you now must *steal* and take no leave. *Shak.*

Others weary of the long journey, lingering behind, were *stolen* away; and they which were left, moiled with dirt and mire. *Knolles.*

A bride
Should vanish from her cloaths into her bed,
As souls from bodies *steal* and are not spy'd. *Donne.*

The vapour of charcoal hath killed many; and it is the more dangerous, because it cometh without any ill smell, and *stealeth* on by little and little. *Bacon's Natural History.*

A soft and solemn breathing sound,
Rose like a steam of rich distill'd perfumes,
And *stole* upon the air, that even silence
Was took ere she was ware. *Milton.*

As wise artists mix their colours so,
That by degrees they from each other go;
Black *steals* unheeded from the neighb'ring white,
So on us *stole* our blessed change. *Dryden.*

At a time when he had no steward, he *stole* away. *Swift.*

Now his fierce eyes with sparkling fury glow,
Now sighs *steal* out when tears begin to flow. *Pope.*

2. To practise theft; to play the thief; to take any thing thievishly; to have the habit of thieving.

Stealing is the taking from another what is his, without his knowledge or allowance. *Locke.*

The good humour is to *steal* at a minute's rest.——Convey, the wise it call; *steal!* a fico for the phrase! *Shakespeare.*

STEA'LER. *n. s.* [from *steal.*] One who steals; a thief.

The transgression is in the *stealer.* *Shakespeare.*

STEA'LINGLY. *adv.* [from *stealing.*] Slily; by invisible motion; by secret practice.

They were diverse motions, they did so *stealingly* slip one into another, as the latter part was ever in hand before the eye could discern the former was ended. *Sidney.*

STEALTH. *n. s.* [from *steal.*]

1. The act of stealing; theft.

The owner proveth the *stealth* to have been committed upon him by such an outlaw, and to have been found in the possession of the prisoner. *Spenser's State of Ireland.*

The *stealth* of mutual entertainment
With character too gross is written on Juliet. *Shakespeare.*

In the secret dark that none reproves,
Their pretty *stealths* shall work, and snares shall spread. *Spenser.*

The gods persuaded Mercury,
Their good observer, to his *stealth.* *Chapman's Iliad.*

2. The thing stolen.

On his back a heavy load he bare
Of nightly *stealths*, and pillage several. *Fairy Queen.*

Store of cabbins are but sluttish dens, that breed sickness in peace, serving to cover *stealths*, and in fight are dangerous to tear men with splinters. *Raleigh.*

3. Secret act; clandestine practice. *By stealth* means secretly; clandestinely; with desire of concealment: but, like *steal*, is often used in a good sense.

The wisdom of the same spirit borrowed from melody that pleasure, which mingled with heavenly mysteries, causeth the smoothness and softness of that which toucheth the ear, to convey as it were by *stealth* the treasure of good things into man's mind. *Hooker.*

I feel this youth's perfections,
With an invisible and subtile *stealth*,
To creep in at mine eyes. *Shakespeare's Twelfth Night.*

The monarch blinded with desire of wealth,
With steel invades his brother's life by *stealth*
Before the sacred altar. *Dryden.*

Let humble Allen, with an aukward shame,
Do good by *stealth*, and blush to find it fame. *Pope.*

STEA'LTHY. *adj.* [from *stealth.*] Done clandestinely; performed by stealth.

Now wither'd murder with his *stealthy* pace,
Moves like a ghost. *Shakespeare's Macbeth.*

STEAM. *n. s.* [steme, Saxon.] The smoke or vapour of any thing moist and hot.

Sweet odours are, in such a company as there is *steam* and heat, things of great refreshment. *Bacon.*

His offering soon propitious fire from heaven
Consum'd with nimble glance and grateful *steam.* *Milton.*

While the temple smoak'd with hallow'd *steam*,
They wash the virgin. *Dryden.*

Such the figure of a feast
Which, were it not for plenty and for *steam*,
Might be resembled to a sick man's dream. *King.*

Some it bears in *steams* up into the air, and this in such a quantity as to be manifest to the smell, especially the sulphur. *Woodward's Natural History.*

To STEAM. *v. n.* [steman, Saxon.]

1. To smoke or vapour with moist heat.

Scarcely had Phœbus in the gloomy east,
Got harnassed his fiery-footed team,
Ne rear'd above the earth his flaming crest
When the last deadly smoke aloft did *steam.* *Fairy Queen.*

See, see, my brother's ghost hangs hovering there,
O'er his warm blood, that *steams* into the air. *Dryden.*

O wretched we! Why were we hurry'd down
This lubrick and adult'rate age;
Nay, added fat pollutions of our own,
T' increase the *steaming* ordures of the stage? *Dryden.*

Let the crude humours dance
In heated brass, *steaming* with fire intense. *Philips.*

These minerals not only issue out at these larger exits, but *steam* forth through the pores of the earth, occasioning sulphureous and other offensive stenches. *Woodward.*

2. To send up vapours.

Ye mists that rise from *steaming* lake. *Milton.*

3. To pass in vapours.

The dissolved amber plainly swam like a thin film upon the liquour, whence it *steamed* away into the air. *Boyle.*

STEAN for *stone.* *Spenser.*

STEATO'MA. *n. s.* [στεάτωμα.]

If the matter in a wen resembles milk-curds, the tumour is called atheroma; if like honey, meliceris; and if composed of fat, *steatoma.* *Sharp's Surgery.*

STEED. *n. s.* [steda, Saxon.] A horse for state or war.

My noble *steed* I give him,
With all his trim belonging. *Shak. Macbeth.*

Impresses quaint, caparisons and *steeds.* *Milton.*

Stout are our men, and warlike are our *steeds.* *Waller.*

She thought herself the trembling dame who fled,
And him the grisly ghost that spurr'd th' infernal *steed.* *Dryd.*

Who, like our active African, instructs
The fiery *steed*, and trains him to his hand? *Addison's Cato.*

See! the bold youth strain up the threat'ning steep;
Hang o'er their coursers heads with eager speed,
And earth rolls back beneath the flying *steed.* *Pope.*

STEEL. *n. s.* [stal, Saxon; *stael*, Dutch.]

1. Steel is a kind of iron, refined and purified by the fire with other ingredients, which renders it white, and its grain closer and finer than common iron. Steel, of all other metals, is that susceptible of the greatest degree of hardness, when well tempered; whence its great use in the making of tools and instruments of all kinds. *Chambers.*

Steel is made from the purest and softest iron, by keeping it red-hot, stratified with coal-dust and wood-ashes, or other substances that abound in the phlogiston, for several hours in a close furnace. It may also be made by fusion, and several other ways; but they are greatly in the wrong who prefer *steel* to iron for medicinal purposes. *Hill's Mat. Medica.*

At her back a bow and quiver gay,
Stuff'd with *steel*-headed darts wherewith she quell'd
The savage beasts in her victorious play. *Fairy Queen.*

With mighty bars of long enduring brass
The *steel*-bound doors and iron gates he ties. *Fairfax.*

A looking-glass, with the *steel* behind, looketh whiter than glass simple. *Bacon's Natural History.*

Diamonds, though hard bodies, will not ready strike fire with *steel*, much less with one another; nor a flint easily with a *steel*, if they both be wet; the sparks being then quenched in their eruption. *Brown's Vulgar Errours.*

Both were of shining *steel*, and wrought so pure
As might the strokes of two such arms endure. *Dryden.*

2. It is often used metonymically for weapons or armour.

Brave Macbeth with his brandish'd *steel*
Which smok'd with bloody execution,
Carv'd out his passage till he had fac'd the slave. *Shakespeare.*

A grove of oaks,
Whose polish'd *steel* from far severely shines,
Are not so dreadful as this beauteous queen. *Dryden.*

He sudden as the word,
In proud Plexippus' bosom plunged the sword;
Toxeus amaz'd, and with amazement slow,
Stood doubting; and while doubting thus he stood,
Receiv'd the *steel* bath'd in his brother's blood. *Dryden.*

3. Chalybeate medicines.

After relaxing, *steel* strengthens the solids, and is likewise an antiacid. *Arbuthnot.*

4. It is used proverbially for hardness: as heads of *steel.*

To STEEL. *v. a.* [from the noun.]

1. To point or edge with steel.

Add proof unto mine armour with thy prayers,
And with thy blessings *steel* my lance's point. *Shak. R. II.*

2. To make hard or firm. It is used, if it be applied to the mind, very often in a bad sense.

Lies well *steel'd* with weighty arguments. *Shakespeare.*

So service shall with *steeled* fingers toil,
And labour shall refresh itself with hope. *Shakespeare's H. V.*

From his metal was his party *steel'd*;
Which once in him rebated, all the rest
Turn'd on themselves, like dull and heavy lead. *Shakesp.*

O God of battles! *steel* my soldiers hearts,
Possess them not with fear. *Shakespeare's Henry V.*

Why will you fight against so sweet a passion,
And *steel* your heart to such a world of charms? *Addison.*

Man, foolish man!
Scarce know'st thou how thyself began;
Yet *steel'd* with study'd boldness, thou dar'st try
To send thy doubted reason's dazled eye
Through the mysterious gulph of vast immensity. *Prior.*

Let the *steel'd* Turk be deaf to matrons cries,
See virgins ravish'd with relentless eyes. *Tickell.*

STEE'LY. *adj.* [from *steel.*]

1. Made of steel.

Thy brother's blood the thirsty earth hath drunk,
Broach'd with the *steely* point of Clifford's lance. *Shakesp.*

Here smokes his forge, he bares his sinewy arm,
And early strokes the sounding anvil warm;
Around his shop the *steely* sparkles flew,
As for the steed he shap'd the bending shoe. *Gay.*

2. Hard; firm.

That she would unarm her noble heart of that *steely* resistance against the sweet blows of love. *Sidney.*

STEE'LYARD. *n. s.* [*steel* and *yard.*] A kind of balance, in which the weight is moved along an iron rod, and grows heavier as it is removed farther from the fulorum.

STEEN, *or* Stean. *n. s.* A fictious vessel of clay or stone. *Ainsworth.*

STEEP. *adj.* [ſteap, Saxon.] Rising or descending with little inclination.

He now had conquer'd Anxur's *steep* ascent. *Addison.*

STEEP. *n. s* Precipice; ascent or descent approaching to perpendicularity.

As that Theban monster that propos'd
Her riddle, and him, who solv'd it not, devour'd;
That once found out and solv'd, for grief and spight
Cast herself headlong from the Ismenian *steep*. *Milton.*

As high turrets for their airy *steep*
Require foundations, in proportion deep;
And lofty cedars as far upwards shoot,
As to the neather heavens they drive the root;
So low did her secure foundation lie,
She was not humble, but humility. *Dryden.*

Instructs the beast to know his native force,
To take the bit between his teeth, and fly
To the next headlong *steep* of anarchy. *Dryden.*

We had on each side naked rocks and mountains, broken into a thousand irregular *steeps* and precipices. *Addison.*

Leaning o'er the rails, he musing stood,
And view'd below the black canal of mud,
Where common shores a lulling murmur keep,
Whose torrents rush from Holborn's fatal *steep*. *Gay.*

To STEEP. *v. a.* [*stippen*, Dutch.] To soak; to macerate; to imbue; to dip.

When his brother saw the red blood trail
Adown so fast, and all his armour *steep*,
For very fellness loud he 'gan to weep. *Spenser.*

He, like an adder, lurking in the weeds,
His wandring thought in deep desire does *steep*;
And his frail eye with spoil of beauty feeds. *Fairy Queen.*

A napkin *steeped* in the harmless blood
Of sweet young Rutland. *Shakespeare's Henry VI.*

Present to her, as sometime Marg'ret
Did to thy father, *steep'd* in Rutland's blood,
A handkerchief; which, say to her, did drain
The purple tide from her sweet brother's body. *Shakesp.*

The conquering wine hath *steep'd* our sense
In soft and delicate Lethe. *Shakespeare.*

Many dream not to find, neither deserve,
And yet are *steep'd* in favours. *Shakespeare's Cymbeline.*

Four days will quickly *steep* themselves in night:
Four nights will quickly dream away the time. *Shakespeare.*

Most of the *steepings* are cheap things, and the goodness of the crop is a great matter of gain. *Bacon.*

Whole droves of minds are by the driving god
Compell'd to drink the deep Lethean flood:
In large forgetful draughts to *steep* the cares
Of their past labours and their irksome years. *Dryden.*

Wheat *steeped* in brine twelve hours prevents the smuttiness. *Mortimer's Husbandry.*

STEE'PLE. *n. s.* [ſteopl, ſtypel, Saxon.] A turret of a church generally furnished with bells. A spire.

Blow, winds, and crack your cheeks; rage, blow!
You cataracts and hurricanoes spout
Till you have drench'd our *steeples*, drown'd the cocks. *Shakespeare.*

What was found in many places, and preached for wheat fallen on the ground from the clouds, was but the seed of ivy-berries, and though found in *steeples* or high places, might be conveyed thither or muted by birds. *Brown's Vulgar Errours.*

A raven I saw yesterday *steeple*-high, just over your house. *L'Estrange.*

They, far from *steeples* and their sacred sound,
In fields their sullen conventicles found. *Dryden.*

STEE'PLY. *adv.* [from *steep.*] With precipitous declivity.

STEE'PNESS. *n. s.* [from *steep.*] Precipitous declivity.

The craggedness or *steepness* of that mountain maketh many parts of it inaccessible. *Brerewood on Language.*

Lord Lovel swam over Trent on horseback, but could not recover the farther side, by reason of the *steepness* of the bank, and so was drowned. *Bacon's Henry VII.*

Vineyards, meadows, and cornfields lie on the borders, and run up all the sides of the Alps, where the barrenness of the rocks, or the *steepness* of the ascent will suffer them. *Addison.*

STEE'PY. *adj.* [from *steep.*] Having a precipitous declivity. A poetical word for *steep*.

Who hath dispos'd, but thou, the winding way,
Where springs down from the *steepy* craggs do beat. *Wotton.*

A prophet some, and some a poet cry,
From *steepy* Othrys' top to Pylus drove
His herd; and for his pains enjoy'd his love. *Dryden.*

No more, my goats, shall I behold you climb
The *steepy* cliffs, or crop the flow'ry thyme! *Dryden.*

STEER. *n. s.* [ſtyre, ſteor, ſtiore. Saxon; *stier*, Dutch.] A young bullock.

They think themselves half exempted from law and obedience; and having once tasted freedom, do, like a *steer* that hath been long out of his yoke, grudge and repine ever after to come under rule again. *Spenser's Ireland.*

Lacaon, Neptune's priest,
With solemn pomp then sacrific'd a *steer*. *Dryden.*

Nor has the *steer*,
At whose strong chest the deadly tiger hangs,
E'er plow'd for him. *Thomson.*

To STEER. *v. a.* [ſteoran, ſtyran, Sax. *stieren*, Dutch.] To direct; to guide in a passage.

A comely palmer, clad in black attire,
Of ripest years, and hairs all hoary gray,
That with a staff his feeble steps did *steer*,
Lest his long way his aged limbs should tire. *Fairy Queen.*

If a pilot cannot see the pole star it can be no fault in him to *steer* his course by such stars as do best appear to him. *K. Ch.*

To STEER. *v. n.* To direct a course.

As when a ship by skilful steersman wrought,
Nigh river's mouth, or foreland, where the wind
Veers oft, as oft so *steers*, and shifts her sail. *Milton.*

In a creature, whose thoughts are more than the sands, and wider than the ocean, fancy and passion must needs run him into strange courses, if reason, which is his only star and compass be not that he *steers* by. *Locke.*

STEE'RAGE. *n. s.* [from *steer.*]

1. The act or practice of steering.

2. Direction; regulation of a course.

He that hath the *steerage* of my course,
Direct my suit. *Shakespeare's Romeo and Juliet*

Having got his vessel launched and set afloat, he committed the *steerage* of it to such as he thought capable of conducting it. *Spectator.*

3. That by which any course is guided.

His costly frame
Inscrib'd to Phœbus, here he hung on high,
The *steerage* of his wings, and cut the sky. *Dryden.*

4. Regulation, or management of any thing.

You raise the honour of the peerage,
Proud to attend you at the *steerage*. *Swift.*

5. The stern or hinder part of the ship.

STEE'RSMATE. } *n. s. steer* and *man*, or *mate.*] A pilot; one
STEE'RSMAN. } who steers a ship.

What pilot so expert but needs must wreck,
Embark'd with such a *steersmate* at the helm? *Milton.*

In a storm, though the vessel be pressed never so hard, a skilful *steersman* will yet bear up against it. *L'Estrange.*

Through it the joyful *steersman* clears his way,
And comes to anchor in his inmost bay. *Dryden.*

STEGANO'GRAPHIST. *n. s.* [στεγανὸς and γράφω.] He who practises the art of secret writing. *Bailey.*

STEGANO'GRAPHY. *n. s.* [στεγανὸς and γράφω.] The art of secret writing by characters or cyphers, intelligible only to the persons who correspond one with another. *Bailey.*

STEGNO'TICK. *adj.* [στεγνωτικὸς.] Binding; rendering costive. *Bailey.*

STE'LE. *n. s.* [ſtela, Sax. *stele*, Dutch.] A stalk; a handle.

STE'LLAR. *adj.* [from *stella.*] Astral; relating to the stars.

In part shed down
Their *stellar* virtue, on all kinds that grow
On earth; made hereby apter to receive
Perfection from the sun's more potent ray. *Milton.*

Salt dissolved, upon fixation, returns to its affected cubes, and regular figures of minerals, as the hexagonal of chrystal, and *stellar* figure of the stone asteria. *Glanville.*

STE'LLATE. *adj.* [*stellatus*, Latin.] Pointed in the manner of a painted star.

One making a regulus of antimony, without iron, found his regulus adorned with a more conspicuous star than I have seen in several *stellate* regulus's of antimony and mars. *Boyle.*

STELLA'TION. *n. s.* [from *stella*.] Emission of light as from a star.

STELLI'FEROUS. *adj.* [*stella* and *fero*.] Having stars. *Dict.*

STE'LLION. *n. s.* [*stellio*, Latin.] A newt. *Ainsworth.*

STE'LLIONATE. *n. s.* [*stellionat*, French; *stellionatus*, Latin.] A kind of crime which is committed [in law] by a deceitful selling of a thing otherwise than it really is: as, if a man should sell that for his own estate which is actually another man's.

It discerneth of crimes of *stellionate*, and the inchoations towards crimes capital, not actually committed. *Bacon.*

STEM. *n. s.* [*stemma*, Latin.]

1. The stalk; the twig.

Two lovely berries molded on one *stem*,
So with two seeming bodies, but one heart. *Shakespeare.*

After they are first shot up thirty foot in length, they spread a very large top, having no bough nor twig in the trunk or *stem*. *Raleigh's History of the World.*

Set them aslope a reasonable depth, and then they will put forth many roots, and so carry more shoots upon a *stem*. *Bacon.*

This, ere it was in th' earth,
God made, and ev'ry herb, before it grew
On the green *stem*. *Milt. Parad. Lost.*

The *stem* thus threaten'd and the sap in thee,
Drops all the branches of that noble tree. *Waller:*

Farewell, you flow'rs, whose buds with early care
I watch'd, and to the chearful sun did rear:
Who now shall bind your *stems*? or, when you fall,
With fountain streams your fainting souls recall? *Dryden.*

The low'ring Spring with lavish rain
Beats down the slender *stem* and bearded grain. *Dryden.*

2. Family; race; generation. Pedigrees are drawn in the form of a branching tree.

This is a *stem*
Of that victorious stock, and let us fear
His native mightiness. *Shakespeare's Henry V.*

I will assay her worth to celebrate,
And so attend ye toward her glittering state;
Where ye may all, that are of noble *stem*,
Approach. *Milton.*

Whosoever will undertake the imperial diadem, must have of his own wherewith to support it; which is one of the reasons that it hath continued these two ages and more in that *stem*, now so much spoken of. *Howel's Vocal Forest.*

Do'st thou in hounds aspire to deathless fame?
Learn well their lineage and their ancient *stem*. *Tickell.*

3. [*Stammen*, Swedish.] The prow or forepart of a ship.

Orante's barque, ev'n in the hero's view,
From *stem* to stern, by waves was overborn. *Dryden.*

To STEM. *v. a.* [*stæmma*, Islandick.] To oppose a current; to pass cross or forward notwithstanding the stream.

They on the trading flood,
Through the wide Ethiopian to the cape
Ply, *stemming* nightly tow'rd the Pole. *Milt. Par. Lost.*

Above the deep they raise their scaly crests,
And *stem* the flood with their erected breasts. *Denham.*

In shipping such as this, the Irish kern
And untaught Indian, on the stream did glide,
Ere sharp-keel'd boats to *stem* the flood did learn,
Or fin-like oars did spread from either side. *Dryden.*

At length Erasmus, that great injur'd name,
Stemm'd the wild torrent of a barb'rous age,
And drove those holy Vandals off the stage. *Pope.*

STENCH. *n. s.* [from ſtencan, Saxon.]

1. A stink; a bad smell.

Death, death; oh amiable and lovely death!
Thou odoriferous *stench*, sound rottenness,
Arise forth from thy couch of lasting night. *Shakes. K. John.*

So bees with smoke, and doves with noisome *stench*,
Are from their hives, and houses, driv'n away. *Shakespeare.*

Physicians by the *stench* of feathers cure the rising of the mother. *Bacon's Nat. History.*

The ministery will be found the salt of the earth, the only thing that keeps societies of men from *stench* and corruption. *South's Sermons.*

The hoary Nar,
Corrupted with the *stench* of sulphur flows,
And into Tiber's streams th' infected current throws. *Addis.*

2. I find it used once for a good smell.

Black bulls and bearded goats on altars lie,
And clouds of sav'ry *stench* involve the sky. *Dryden.*

To STENCH. *v. a.* [from the noun.]

1. To make to stink.

The foulness of the ponds only *stencheth* the water. *Mortim.*

2. [For *staunch*, corruptly.] To stop; to hinder to flow.

They had better skill to let blood than *stench* it. *K. Charles.*

Restringents to *stench* and incrassatives to thicken the blood. *Harvey on Consumptions.*

STENO'GRAPHY. *n. s.* [στενὸς and γράφω.] Short-hand.

O the accurst *stenography* of state!
The princely eagle shrunk into a bat. *Cleaveland.*

STENTOROPHO'NICK. *adj.* [from *Stentor*, the Homerical herald, whose voice was as loud as that of fifty men, and φωνὴ, a voice.] Loudly speaking or sounding.

Of this *stentorophonick* horn of Alexander there is a figure preserved in the Vatican. *Derham's Physico-Theology.*

To STEP. *v. n.* [ſτæppan, Saxon; *stappen*, Dutch.]

1. To move by a single change of the place of the foot.

Whosoever first after the troubling the water *stepped* in, was made whole. *Jo.* v. 4.

One of our nation hath proceeded so far, that he was able, by the help of wings, in a running pace to *step* constantly ten yards at a time. *Wilkins's Math. Mag.*

2. To advance by a sudden progression.

Ventidius lately
Bury'd his father, by whose death he's *stepp'd*
Into a great estate. *Shakesp. Timon of Athens.*

3. To move mentally.

When a person is hearing a sermon, he may give his thoughts leave to *step* back so far as to recollect the several heads. *Watts.*

They are *stepping* almost three thousand years back into the remotest antiquity, the only true mirrour of that ancient world. *Pope's Preface to the Iliad.*

4. To go; to walk.

I am in blood
Stept in so far, that, should I wade no more,
Returning were as tedious as go o'er. *Shakesp. Macbeth.*

The old poets *step* in to the assistance of the medalist. *Addis.*

5. To take a short walk.

See where he comes: so please you, *step* aside;
I'll know his grievance. *Shakesp. Romeo and Juliet.*

My brothers, when they saw me wearied out,
Stepp'd, as they said, to the next thicket-side
To bring me berries. *Milton.*

When your master wants a servant who happens to be abroad, answer, that he had but just that minute *stept* out. *Swift's Directions to Servants.*

6. To walk gravely and slowly.

Pyrrhus, the most ancient of all the bashaws, *stept* forth, and, appealing unto his mercies, earnestly requested him to spare his life. *Knolles's History of the Turks.*

When you *stepp'd* forth, how did the monster rage,
In scorn of your soft looks and tender age! *Cowley.*

Home the swain retreats,
His flock before him *stepping* to the fold. *Thomson's Summer.*

STEP. *n. s.* [ſτæp, Saxon; *stap*, Dutch.]

1. Progression by one removal of the foot.

Thou sound and firm-set earth,
Hear not my *steps*, which way they walk. *Shakesp. Macbeth.*

Ling'ring perdition, worse than any death
Can be at once, shall *step* by *step* attend
You and your ways. *Shakespeare's Tempest.*

Who was the first to explore th' untrodden path,
When life was hazarded in every *step*? *Addison's Cato.*

2. One remove in climbing; hold for the foot; a stair.

While Solyman lay at Buda, seven bloody heads of bishops, slain in the battle, were all set in order upon a wooden *step*. *Knolles's History of the Turks.*

The breadth of every single *step* or stair should be never less than one foot, nor more than eighteen inches. *Wotton.*

Those heights where William's virtue might have staid,
And on the subject world look'd safely down,
By Marlbro' pass'd, the props and *steps* were made
Sublimer yet to raise his queen's renown. *Prior.*

It was a saying among the ancients, truth lies in a well; and, to carry on this metaphor, we may justly say, that logick does supply us with *steps*, whereby we may go down to reach the water. *Watts.*

3. Quantity of space passed or measured by one removal of the foot.

The gradus, a Roman measure, may be translated a *step*, or the half of a passus or pace. *Arbuthnot on Coins.*

4. A small length; a small space.

There is but a *step* between me and death. 1 *Sa.* xx. 3.

5. Walk; passage.

O may thy pow'r, propitious still to me,
Conduct my *steps* to find the fatal tree
In this deep forest. *Dryden's Æn.*

6. Progression; act of advancing.

To derive two or three general principles of motion from phænomena, and afterwards to tell us how the properties and actions of all corporeal things follow from those manifest principles, would be a very great *step* in philosophy, though the causes of those principles were not yet discovered. *Newton.*

One injury is best defended by a second, and this by a third: by these *steps* the old masters of the palace in France became masters of the kingdom; and by these *steps* a general, during pleasure, might have grown into a general for life, and a general for life into a kings *Swift.*

The querist must not proceed too swiftly towards the determination of his point, that he may with more ease draw the learner to those principles *step* by *step*, from whence the final conclusion will arise. *Watts.*

7. Footstep; print of the foot.

From hence Astrea took her flight, and here
The prints of her departing *steps* appear. *Dryden's Virgil.*

8. Gait; manner of walking.

Sudden from the golden throne
With a submissive *step* I hasted down;
The glowing garland from my hair I took,
Love in my heart, obedience in my look. *Prior.*

9. Action; instance of conduct.

The reputation of a man depends upon the first *steps* he makes in the world. *Pope.*

STEP, in composition, signifies one who is related only by marriage. [Steop, Saxon, from stepan, to *deprive* or *make an orphan*: for the Saxons not only said a *step-mother*, but a *step-daughter*, or *step-son*; to which it indeed, according to this etymology, more properly belongs: but as it is now seldom applied but to the mother, it seems to mean, in the mind of those who use it, a woman who has *stepped* into the vacant place of the true mother.]

How should their minds chuse but misdoubt, lest this discipline, which always you match with divine doctrine as her natural and true sister, be found unto all kinds of knowledge a *step-mother*. *Hooker.*

His wanton *step-dame* loved him the more;
But when she saw her offered sweets refuse,
Her love she turn'd to hate. *Fairy Queen.*

You shall not find me, daughter,
After the slander of most *step-mothers*,
Ill-ey'd unto you. *Shakes. Cymbeline.*

A father cruel, and a *step-dame* false. *Shakespeare.*

Cato the elder, being aged, buried his wife, and married a young woman: his son came to him, and said, Sir, what have I offended, that you have brought a *step-mother* into your house? The old man answered, Nay, quite the contrary, son; thou pleasest me so well, as I would be glad to have more such. *Bacon.*

The name of *step-dame*, your practis'd art,
By which you have estrang'd my father's heart,
All you have done against me, or design,
Shows your aversion, but begets not mine. *Dryd. Aurengz.*

A *step-dame* too I have, a cursed she,
Who rules my hen-peck'd sire, and orders me. *Dryden.*

Any body would have guessed miss to have been bred up under the influence of a cruel *step-dame*, and John to be the fondling of a tender mother. *Arbuthn. Hist. of John Bull.*

STE'PPINGSTONE. *n. s.* [*step* and *stone*.] Stone laid to catch the foot, and save it from wet or dirt.

Like *steppingstones* to save a stride,
In streets where kennels are too wide. *Swift.*

STERCORA'CEOUS. *adj.* [*stercoraceus*, Latin.] Belonging to dung; partaking of the nature of dung.

Green juicy vegetables, in a heap together, acquire a heat equal to that of a human body; then a putrid *stercoraceous* taste and odour, in taste resembling putrid flesh, and in smell human fæces. *Arbuthnot on Aliments.*

STERCORA'TION. *n. s.* [from *stercora*, Latin.] The act of dunging; the act of manuring with dung.

The first help is *stercoration*: the sheeps dung is one of the best, and next the dung of kine, and that of horses. *Bacon.*

Stercoration is seasonable. *Evelyn's Kalendar.*

The exteriour pulp of the fruit serves not only for the security of the seed, whilst it hangs upon the plant, but, after it is fallen upon the earth, for the *stercoration* of the soil, and promotion of the growth, though not the first germination of the seminal plant. *Ray on the Creation.*

STEREO'GRAPHY. *n. s.* [στερεὸς and γράφω; *stereographie*, Fr.] The art of drawing the forms of solids upon a plane. *Harris.*

STEREO'METRY. *n. s.* [στερεὸς and μετρέω; *stereometrie*, French.] The art of measuring all sorts of solid bodies. *Harris.*

STE'RIL. *adj.* [*sterile*, French; *sterilis*, Latin] Barren; unfruitful; not productive; wanting fecundity.

Our elders say,
The barren, touched in this holy chase,
Shake off their *steril* curse. *Shakesp. Julius Cæsar.*

Thy sea marge *steril*, and rocky hard. *Shakes. Tempest.*

In very *steril* years corn sown will grow to another kind. *Bacon's Natural History.*

To separate seeds, put them in water: such as are corrupted and *steril* swim. *Brown's Vulgar Errours.*

She is grown *steril* and barren, and her births of animals are now very inconsiderable. *More's Antidote against Atheism.*

When the vegetative stratum was once washed off by rains, the hills would have become barren, the strata below yielding only mere *sterile* and mineral matter, such as was inept for the formation of vegetables. *Woodward.*

STERI'LITY. *n. s.* [*sterilité*, French; *sterilitas*, from *sterilis*, Latin.] Barrenness; want of fecundity; unfruitfulness.

Spain is thin sown of people, by reason of the *sterility* of the soil, and because their natives are exhausted by so many employments in such vast territories. *Bacon's War with Spain.*

An eternal *sterility* must have possessed the world, where all things had been fastened everlastingly with the adamantine chains of specifick gravity, if the Almighty had not said, Let the earth bring forth grass, the herb yielding seed, and the fruit-tree yielding fruit. *Bentley's Sermons.*

He had more frequent occasion for repetition than any poet; yet one cannot ascribe this to any *sterility* of expression, but to the genius of his times, which delighted in these reiterated verses. *Pope's Essay on Homer.*

To STE'RILIZE. *v. a.* [from *steril*.] To make barren; to deprive of fecundity, or the power of production.

May we not as well suppose the *sterilizing* the earth was suspended for some time, 'till the deluge became the executioner of it? *Woodward's Natural History.*

Go! *sterilize* the fertile with thy rage. *Savage.*

STE'RLING. *adj.* [Of this word many derivations have been offered; the most probable of which is that offered by *Camden*, who derives it from the *Easterlings*, who were employed as coiners.]

1. An epithet by which genuine English money is discriminated.

The king's treasure of store, that he left at his death, amounted unto eighteen hundred thousand pounds *sterling*. *Bacon's Henry* VII.

Several of them would rather chuse to count out a sum in sesterces than in pounds *sterling*. *Addison.*

2. Genuine; having past the test.

There is not one single witty phrase in this collection, which hath not received the stamp and approbation of one hundred years: he may therefore be secure to find them all genuine, *sterling*, and authentick. *Swift's Polite Conversation.*

STE'RLING. *n. s.* [*sterlingum*, low Lat. from the adjective.]

1. English coin; money.

This visionary various projects tries,
And knows that to be rich is to be wise:
By useful observation he can tell
The sacred charms that in true *sterling* dwell;
How gold makes a patrician of a slave,
A dwarf an Atlas, a Thersites brave. *Garth.*

Great name, which in our rolls recorded stands,
Leads honours, and protects the learned bands,
Accept this offering to thy bounty due,
And Roman wealth in English *sterling* view. *C. Arbuthnot.*

2. Standard rate.

STERN. *adj.* [styrn, Saxon.]

1. Severe of countenance; truculent of aspect.

Why look you still so *stern* and tragical. *Shakes. H.* VI.

I would outstare the *sternest* eyes that look,
Outbrave the heart most daring on the earth,
Pluck the young sucking cubs from the she-bear,
Yea, mock the lion when he roars for prey,
To win thee, lady. *Shakes. Merchant of Venice.*

It shall not be amiss here to present the *stern* but lively countenance of this so famous a man. *Knolles's Hist. of the Turks.*

Gods and men
Fear'd her *stern* frown, and she was queen o' th' woods. *Milt.*

2. Severe of manners; harsh; unrelenting; cruel.

My sometime general,
I've seen thee *stern*, and thou hast oft beheld
Heart-hard'ning spectacles. *Shakesp. Coriolanus.*

Women are soft, mild, pitiful, and flexible;
Thou *stern*, obdurate, flinty, rough, remorseless. *Shakesp.*

The common executioner,
Whose heart th' accustom'd sight of death makes hard,
Falls not the ax upon the humbled neck,
But first begs pardon: will you *sterner* be
Than he that deals and lives by bloody drops? *Shakespeare.*

Did this in Cæsar seem ambitious?
When that the poor have cry'd, Cæsar hath wept;
Ambition should be made of *sterner* stuff. *Shak. Jul. Cæs.*

Then shall the war, and *stern* debate and strife
Immortal, be the bus'ness of my life;
And in thy fane the dusty spoils among,
High on the burnish'd roof, my banner shall be hung. *Dryd.*

How *stern* as tutors, and as uncles hard,
We lash the pupil and defraud the ward. *Dryden's Pers.*

3. Hard; afflictive.

If wolves had at thy gate howl'd that *stern* time,
Thou shouldst have said, Go, porter, turn the key,
All cruels else subscrib'd. *Shakesp. King Lear.*

STERN. *n. s.* [steor, Saxon. Of the same original with *steer*.]

1. The hind part of the ship where the rudder is placed.

Let a barbarous Indian, who had never seen a ship, view the separate and disjointed parts, as the prow and *stern*, the ribs, masts, ropes, and shrouds, he would form but a very lame idea of it. *Watts's Improvement of the Mind.*

They

They turn their heads to ſea, their *ſterns* to land. *Dryd.*

2. Poſt of management; direction.

The king from Eltam I intend to ſend,
And ſit at chiefeſt *ſtern* of publick weal. *Shakeſ. H. VI.*

3. The hinder part of any thing.

She all at once her beaſtly body raiſed,
With doubled forces high above the ground,
Though wrapping up her wreathed *ſtern* around. *Fa. Queen.*

STE'RNAGE. *n. ſ.* [from *ſtern.*] The ſteerage or ſtern. Not uſed.

Grapple your minds to *ſternage* of this navy,
And leave your England as dead midnight ſtill. *Shakeſpeare.*

STE'RNLY. *adj.* [from *ſtern.*] In a ſtern manner; ſeverely; truculently.

Sternly he pronounc'd
The rigid interdiction. *Milton's Parad. Loſt.*

Yet ſure thou art not, nor thy face the ſame,
Nor thy limbs moulded in ſo ſoft a frame;
Thou look'ſt more *ſternly*, do'ſt more ſtrongly move,
And more of awe thou bear'ſt, and leſs of love. *Dryden.*

STE'RNNESS. *n. ſ.* [from *ſtern.*]

1. Severity of look.

Of ſtature huge, and eke of courage bold,
That ſons of men amaz'd their *ſternneſs* to behold. *Spenſer.*

How would he look to ſee his work ſo noble
Wildly bound up! or how
Should I, in theſe my borrow'd flaunts, behold
The *ſternneſs* of his preſence! *Shakeſpeare.*

2. Severity or harſhneſs of manners.

I have *ſternneſs* in my ſoul enough
To hear of ſoldiers work. *Dryden's Cleomenes.*

STE'RNON. *n. ſ.* [στέρνον.] The breaſt-bone.

A ſoldier was ſhot in the breaſt through the *ſternon*. *Wiſeman.*

STERNUTA'TION. *n. ſ.* [*ſternutatio*, Latin.] The act of ſneezing.

Sternutation is a convulſive ſhaking of the nerves and muſcles, firſt occaſioned by an irritation of thoſe in the noſtrils. *Quincy.*

Concerning *ſternutation*, or ſneezing, and the cuſtom of ſaluting upon that motion, it is generally believed to derive its original from a diſeaſe wherein *ſternutation* proved mortal, and ſuch as ſneezed died. *Brown's Vulgar Errours.*

STERNU'TATIVE. *adj.* [*ſternutatif*, Fr. from *ſternuto*, Latin.] Having the quality of ſneezing.

STERNU'TATORY. *n. ſ.* [*ſternutatoire*, Fr. from *ſternuto*, Lat.] Medicine that provokes to ſneeze.

Phyſicians, in perſons near death, uſe *ſternutatories*, or ſuch medicines as provoke unto ſneezing; when if the faculty ariſe, and *ſternutation* enſueth, they conceive hopes of life. *Brown.*

STE'VEN. *n. ſ.* [ſtefen, Saxon.] A cry, or loud clamour.

Ne ſooner was out, but ſwifter than thought,
Faſt by the hide, the wolf Lowder caught;
And had not Roffy renne to the *ſteven*,
Lowder had been ſlain thilke ſame even. *Spenſer.*

To STEW. *v. a.* [*eſtuver*, French; *ſtoven*, Dutch.] To ſeeth any thing in a ſlow moiſt heat.

Ere I was riſen from the place, that ſhow'd
My duty kneeling, came a reeking poſt,
Stew'd in his haſte, half breathleſs. *Shakeſp. King Lear.*

I bruiſed my ſkin with playing at ſword and dagger with a maſter of fence, three veneys for a diſh of *ſtew'd* prunes. *Shak.*

To STEW. *v. n.* To be ſeethed in a ſlow moiſt heat.

STEW. *n. ſ.* [*eſtuve*, French; *ſtufa*, Italian; *eſtufa*, Spaniſh.]

1. A bagnio; a hot-houſe.

As burning Ætna from his boiling *ſtew*
Doth belch out flames, and rocks in pieces broke,
And ragged ribs of mountains molten new,
Enwrapt in coal-black clouds and filthy ſmoke. *Fa. Queen.*

The Lydians were inhibited by Cyrus to uſe any armour, and give themſelves to baths and *ſtews*. *Abbot.*

2. A brothel; a houſe of proſtitution. [This ſignification is by ſome imputed to this, that there were licenſed brothels near the *ſtews* or fiſhponds in Southwark; but probably *ſtew*, like bagnio, took a bad ſignification from bad uſe.]

There be that hate harlots, and never were at the *ſtews*; that abhor falſhood, and never brake promiſe. *Aſcham.*

My buſineſs in this ſtate
Made me a looker-on here in Vienna,
Where I have ſeen corruption boil and bubble,
'Till it o'er-run the *ſtew*. *Shakeſpeare.*

With them there are no *ſtews*, no diſſolute houſes, no curteſans. *Bacon's New Atlantis.*

Her, though ſeven years ſhe in the *ſtews* had laid,
A nunnery durſt receive and think a maid
And though in childbirth's labour ſhe did lie,
Midwives would ſwear 'twere but a tympany. *Donne.*

What mod'rate fop would rake the park or *ſtews*,
Who among troops of faultleſs nymphs can chuſe? *Roſcom.*

Making his own houſe a *ſtews*, a bordel, and a ſchool of lewdneſs, to inſtill the rudiments of vice into the unwary flexible years of his poor children. *South's Sermons.*

3. [*Stowen*, Dutch, to ſtore.] A ſtorepond; a ſmall pond where fiſh are kept for the table.

STE'WARD. *n. ſ.* [ſtiƿarð, Saxon.]

1. One who manages the affairs of another.

There ſat yclad in red,
Down to the ground, a comely perſonage,
That in his hand a white rod managed;
He *ſteward* was, hight diet, ripe of age,
And in demeanour ſober, and in council ſage. *Fa. Queen.*

Whilſt I have gold, I'll be his *ſteward* ſtill. *Shak. Timon.*

Take on you the charge
And kingly government of this your land;
Not as protector, *ſteward*, ſubſtitute,
Or lowly factor for another's gain. *Shakeſ. Richard III.*

How is it that I hear this of thee? Give an account of thy ſtewardſhip; for thou mayeſt be no longer *ſteward*. *Lu.* xvi.

When a *ſteward* defrauds his lord, he muſt connive at the reſt of the ſervants while they are following the ſame practice. *Swift.*

What can be a greater honour than to be choſen one of the *ſtewards* and diſpenſers of God's bounty to mankind? What can give a generous ſpirit more complacency than to conſider, that great numbers owe to him, under God, their ſubſiſtence, and the good conduct of their lives? *Swift.*

2. An officer of ſtate.

The duke of Suffolk is the firſt, and claims
To be high *ſteward*. *Shakeſpeare.*

STE'WARDSHIP. *n. ſ.* [from *ſteward.*] The office of a ſteward.

The earl of Worceſter
Hath broke his ſtaff, reſign'd his *ſtewardſhip*. *Shakeſp. R. II.*

Shew us the hand of God
That hath diſmiſs'd us from our *ſtewardſhip*. *Shakeſpeare.*

If they are not employed to ſuch purpoſes, we are falſe to our truſt, and the *ſtewardſhip* committed to us, and ſhall be one day ſeverely accountable to God for it. *Calamy's Sermons.*

STI'BIAL. *adj.* [from *ſtibium*, Latin.] Antimonial.

The former depend upon a corrupt incinerated melancholy, and the latter upon an aduſt *ſtibial* or eruginous ſulphur. *Harv.*

STI'CADOS. *n. ſ.* [*ſticadis*, Latin.] An herb. *Ainſworth.*

STICK. *n. ſ.* [ſticca, Saxon; *ſtecco*, Italian; *ſteck*, Dutch.] A piece of wood ſmall and long.

Onions as they hang will ſhoot forth, and ſo will the herb orpin, with which in the country they trim their houſes, binding it to a lath or *ſtick* ſet againſt a wall. *Bacon's Nat. Hiſtory.*

Some ſtrike from claſhing flints their fiery ſeed,
Some gather *ſticks* the kindled flames to feed. *Dryden.*

To STICK. *v. a.* preterite *ſtuck*; participle paſſ. *ſtuck*. [ſtican, Saxon.] To faſten on ſo as that it may adhere.

Two troops in fair array one moment ſhow'd;
The next, a field with fallen bodies ſtrow'd:
The points of ſpears are *ſtuck* within the ſhield,
The ſteeds without their riders ſcour the field,
The knights unhors'd. *Dryden.*

Would our ladies, inſtead of *ſticking* on a patch againſt their country, ſacrifice their necklaces againſt the common enemy, what decrees ought not to be made in their favour? *Addiſon.*

Oh for ſome pedant reign,
Some gentle James to bleſs the land again;
To *ſtick* the doctor's chair unto the throne,
Give law to words, or war with words alone. *Pope.*

To STICK. *v. n.*

1. To adhere; to unite itſelf by its tenacity or penetrating power.

I will cauſe the fiſh of thy rivers to *ſtick* unto thy ſcales. *Ez.*

The green caterpillar breedeth in the inward parts of roſes not blown, where the dew *ſticketh*. *Bacon.*

Though the ſword be put into the ſheath, we muſt not ſuffer it there to ruſt, or *ſtick* ſo faſt as that we ſhall not be able to draw it readily, when need requires. *Raleigh.*

2. To be inſeparable; to be united with any thing. Generally in an ill ſenſe.

Now does he feel
His ſecret murthers *ſticking* on his hands. *Shakeſp. Macbeth.*

He is often ſtigmatized with it, as a note of infamy, to *ſtick* by him whilſt the world laſteth. *Sanderſon.*

In their quarrels they proceed to calling names, 'till they light upon one that is ſure to *ſtick*. *Swift.*

3. To reſt upon the memory painfully.

The going away of that which had ſtaid ſo long, doth yet *ſtick* with me. *Bacon's Natural Hiſtory.*

4. To ſtop; to loſe motion.

I ſhudder at the name!
My blood runs backward, and my fault'ring tongue
Sticks at the ſound. *Smith's Phædra and Hippolitus.*

5. To reſiſt emiſſion.

Wherefore could I not pronounce amen?
I had moſt need of bleſſing, and amen
Stuck in my throat. *Shakeſp. Macbeth.*

6. To be conſtant; to adhere with firmneſs.

The knave will *ſtick* by thee, I can aſſure thee that: he will not out, he is true bred. *Shakeſpeare's Henry* IV.

The firſt contains a *ſticking* faſt to Chriſt, when the Chriſtian profeſſion is perſecuted; and the ſecond a riſing from ſin, as he roſe, to a new Chriſtian life. *Hammond.*

Some *ſtick* to you, and ſome to t'other ſide. *Dryden.*

They could not but conclude, that to be their intereſt, and being ſo convinced, purſue it and *ſtick* to it. *Tillotſon.*

The advantage will be on our ſide, if we *ſtick* to its eſſentials. *Addiſon's Freeholder.*

7. To be troubleſome by adhering.

I am ſatisfied to trifle away my time, rather than let it *ſtick* by me. *Pope's Letters.*

8. To remain; not to be loſt.

Proverbial ſentences are formed into a verſe, whereby they *ſtick* upon the memory. *Watts.*

9. To dwell upon; not to forſake.

If the matter be knotty, the mind muſt ſtop and buckle to it, and *ſtick* upon it with labour and thought, and not leave it 'till it has maſtered the difficulty. *Locke.*

Every man, beſides occaſional affections, has beloved ſtudies which the mind will more cloſely *ſtick* to. *Locke.*

10. To cauſe difficulties or ſcruple.

This is the difficulty that *ſticks* with the moſt reaſonable of thoſe who, from conſcience, refuſe to join with the Revolution. *Swift.*

11. To ſcruple; to heſitate.

It is a good point of cunning for a man to ſhape the anſwer he would have in his own words and propoſitions; for it makes the other party *ſtick* the leſs. *Bacon.*

The church of Rome, under pretext of expoſition of Scripture, doth not *ſtick* to add and alter. *Bacon.*

Rather than impute our miſcarriages to our own corruption, we do not *ſtick* to arraign providence itſelf. *L'Eſtrange.*

Every one without heſitation ſuppoſes eternity, and *ſticks* not to aſcribe infinity to duration. *Locke.*

That two bodies cannot be in the ſame place is a truth that no body any more *ſticks* at, than at this maxim, that it is impoſſible for the ſame thing to be, and not to be. *Locke.*

To *ſtick* at nothing for the publick intereſt is repreſented as the refined part of the Venetian wiſdom. *Addiſon on Italy.*

Some *ſtick* not to ſay, that the parſon and attorney forged a will. *Arbuthnot.*

12. To be ſtopped; to be unable to proceed.

If we ſhould fail.
——We fail!
But ſcrew your courage to the *ſticking* place,
And we'll not fail. *Shakeſpeare's Macbeth.*

They never doubted the commons; but heard all *ſtuck* in the lords houſe, and deſired the names of thoſe who hindered the agreement between the lords and commons. *Clarendon.*

He threw: the trembling weapon paſs'd
Through nine bull-hides, each under other plac'd
On his broad ſhield, and *ſtuck* within the laſt. *Dryden.*

13. To be embarraſſed; to be puzzled.

Where they *ſtick*, they are not to be farther puzzled by putting them upon finding it out themſelves. *Locke.*

They will *ſtick* long at part of a demonſtration, for want of perceiving the connexion of two ideas, that, to one more exerciſed, is as viſible as any thing. *Locke.*

Souls a little more capacious can take in the connexion of a few propoſitions; but if the chain be prolix, here they *ſtick* and are confounded. *Watts's Improvement of the Mind.*

14. *To* STICK *out.* To be prominent with deformity.

His fleſh is conſumed away that it cannot be ſeen, and his bones that were not ſeen *ſtick out.* *Job* xxxiii. 21.

15. *To* STICK *out.* To be unemployed.

TO STICK. *v. a.* [ſtician, Saxon; *ſteken*, Dutch.]

1. To ſtab; to pierce with a pointed inſtrument.

The Heruli, when their old kindred fell ſick, *ſtuck* them with a dagger. *Grew.*

2. To fix upon a pointed body.

3. To faſten by transfixion.

Her death!
I'll ſtand betwixt: it firſt ſhall pierce my heart:
We will be *ſtuck* together on his dart. *Dryd. Tyran. Love.*

4. To ſet with ſomething pointed.

A lofty pile they rear;
The fabrick's front with cypreſs twigs they ſtrew,
And *ſtick* the ſides with boughs of baleful yew. *Dryden.*

STI'CKINESS. *n. ſ.* [from *ſticky.*] Adheſive quality; viſcoſity; glutinouſneſs; tenacity.

TO STI'CKLE. *v. n.* [from the practice of prizefighters, who placed ſeconds with ſtaves or *ſticks* to interpoſe occaſionally.]

1. To take part with one ſide or other.

Fortune, as ſhe's wont, turn'd fickle,
And for the foe began to *ſtickle.* *Hudibras.*

2. To conteſt; to altercate; to contend rather with obſtinacy than vehemence.

Let them go to't, and *ſtickle*,
Whether a conclave, or a conventicle. *Cleaveland.*

Heralds *ſtickle*, who got who,
So many hundred years ago. *Hudibras.*

3. To trim; to play faſt and looſe; to act a part between oppoſites.

When he ſees half of the Chriſtians killed, and the reſt in a fair way of being routed, he *ſtickles* betwixt the remainder of God's hoſt and the race of fiends. *Dryden's Juv. Dedication.*

STI'CKLEBAG. *n. ſ.* [Properly *ſtickleback*, from *ſtick*, to prick.] The ſmalleſt of freſh-water fiſh.

A little fiſh called a *ſticklebag*, without ſcales, hath his body fenced with ſeveral prickles. *Walton's Angler.*

STI'CKLER. *n. ſ.* [from *ſtickle.*]

1. A ſideſman to fencers; a ſecond to a duelliſt; one who ſtands to judge a combat.

Baſilius came to part them, the *ſtickler*'s authority being unable to perſuade cholerick hearers; and part them he did. *Sidn.*

Baſilius, the judge, appointed *ſticklers* and trumpets, whom the others ſhould obey. *Sidney.*

Our former chiefs, like *ſticklers* of the war,
Firſt fought t' inflame the parties, then to poiſe:
The quarrel lov'd, but did the cauſe abhor;
And did not ſtrike to hurt, but made a noiſe. *Dryden.*

2. An obſtinate contender about any thing.

Quercetanus, though the grand *ſtickler* for the *tria prima*, has this conceſſion of the irreſolubleneſs of diamonds. *Boyle.*

The inferior tribe of common women have, in moſt reigns, been the profeſſed *ſticklers* for ſuch as have acted againſt the true intereſt of the nation. *Addiſon's Freeholder.*

The tory or high church clergy were the greateſt *ſticklers* againſt the exorbitant proceedings of king James II. *Swift.*

All place themſelves in the liſt of the national church, though they are great *ſticklers* for liberty of conſcience. *Swift.*

STI'CKY. *adj.* [from *ſtick.*] Viſcous; adheſive; glutinous.

Herbs which laſt longeſt are thoſe of ſtrong ſmell and with a *ſticky* ſtalk. *Bacon's Natural Hiſtory.*

STIFF. *adj* [ſtıꝼ, Saxon; *ſtiff*, Daniſh; *ſtyf*, Swediſh; *ſtifur*, Iſlandick; *ſtijf*, Dutch.]

1. Rigid; inflexible; reſiſting flexure; not flaccid; not limber; not eaſily flexible; not pliant.

They riſing on *ſtiff* pinions tower
The mid aerial ſky. *Milton.*

The glittering robe
Hung floating looſe, or *ſtiff* with mazy gold. *Thomſon.*

2. Not ſoft; not giving way; not fluid; not eaſily yielding to the touch.

Still leſs and leſs my boiling ſpirits flow;
And I grow *ſtiff* as cooling metals do. *Dryd. Indian Emp.*

Mingling with that oily liquor, they were wholly incorporate, and ſo grew more *ſtiff* and firm, making but one ſubſtance. *Burnet's Theory of the Earth.*

3. Strong; not eaſily reſiſted.

On a *ſtiff* gale
The Theban ſwan extends his wings. *Denham.*

4. Hardy; ſtubborn; not eaſily ſubdued.

How *ſtiff* is my vile ſenſe,
That I ſtand up, and have ingenious feeling
Of my huge ſorrows! Better I were diſtract! *Shakeſpeare.*

5. Obſtinate; pertinacious.

We neither allow unmeet nor purpoſe the *ſtiff* defence of any unneceſſary cuſtom heretofore received. *Hooker.*

Yield to others when there is cauſe; but it is a ſhame to ſtand *ſtiff* in a fooliſh argument. *Taylor.*

A war enſues, the Cretans own their cauſe,
Stiff to defend their hoſpitable laws. *Dryden.*

6. Harſh; not written with eaſe; conſtrained.

7. Formal; rigorous in certain ceremonies; not diſengaged in behaviour; ſtarched; affected.

The French are open, familiar, and talkative; the Italians *ſtiff*, ceremonious, and reſerved. *Addiſon on Italy.*

8. In *Shakeſpeare* it ſeems to mean ſtrongly maintained, or aſſerted with good evidence.

This is *ſtiff* news. *Shakeſpeare.*

TO STI'FFEN. *v. a.* [ſtıꝼıan, Saxon.]

1. To make ſtiff; to make inflexible; to make unpliant.

When the blaſt of war blows in our ears,
Stiffen the ſinews, ſummon up the blood,
Diſguiſe fair nature with hard favour'd rage. *Shakeſ. H. V.*

He *ſtiffened* his neck, and hardened his heart from turning unto the Lord. 2 *Chron.* xxxvi. 13.

The poor, by them diſrobed, naked lie,
Veil'd with no other covering but the ſky;
Expos'd to *ſtiff'ning* froſts, and drenching ſhowers,
Which thicken'd air from her black boſom pours. *Sandys.*

Her eyes grow *ſtiffen'd*, and with ſulphur burn. *Dryden.*

2. To make obſtinate.

Her *ſtiff'ning* grief,
Who ſaw her children ſlaughter'd all at once,
Was dull to mine. *Dryden and Lee.*

TO STI'FFEN. *v. n.*

1. To grow ſtiff; to grow rigid; to become unpliant.

Aghaſt, aſtoniſh'd, and ſtruck dumb with fear,
I ſtood; like briſtles roſe my *ſtiff'ning* hair. *Dryden.*

Fix'd in astonishment I gaze upon thee,
Like one just blasted by a stroke from heaven,
Who pants for breath, and *stiffens* yet alive;
In dreadful looks, a monument of wrath. *Addison's Cato.*

2. To grow hard; to be hardened.
The tender soil, then *stiffening* by degrees,
Shut from the bounded earth the bounding seas. *Dryden.*

3. To grow less susceptive of impression; to grow obstinate.
Some souls, we see,
Grow hard and *stiffen* with adversity. *Dryden.*

STIFFHEA'RTED. *adj.* [*stiff* and *heart.*] Obstinate; stubborn; contumacious.
They are impudent children, and *stiffhearted. Ezek.* ii.

STI'FFLY. *adv.* [from *stiff.*] Rigidly; inflexibly; stubbornly.
In matters divine, it is still maintained *stiffly*, that they have no stiffnecked force. *Hooker.*
I commended them that stood so *stiffly* for the Lord. 2 *Esdr.*
The Indian fig of itself multiplieth from root to root, the plenty of the sap and the softness of the stalk making the bough, being overloaden and not *stiffly* upheld, to weigh down. *Bacon.*

STI'FFNECKED. *adj.* [*stiff* and *neck.*] Stubborn; obstinate; contumacious.
An infinite charge to her majesty, to send over such an army as should tread down all that standeth before them on foot, and lay on the ground all the *stiffnecked.* *Spenser.*
This *stiffneck'd* pride, nor art nor force can bend,
Nor high-flown hopes to reason's lure descend. *Denham.*

STI'FFNESS. *n. s.* [from *stiff.*]
1. Rigidity; inflexibility; hardness; ineptitude to bend.
The *stiffness* and dryness of iron to melt, must be holpen by moistening or opening it. *Bacon.*
The willow bows and recovers, the oak is stubborn and inflexible; and the punishment of that *stiffness* is one branch of the allegory. *L'Estrange.*
2. Ineptitude to motion.
The pillars of this frame grow weak,
My sinews slacken, and an icy *stiffness*
Benumbs my blood. *Denham.*
3. Tension; not laxity.
To try new shrouds, one mounts into the wind,
And one below, their ease or *stiffness* notes. *Dryden.*
4. Obstinacy; stubbornness; contumaciousness.
The vices of old age have the *stiffness* of it too; and as it is the unfittest time to learn in, so the unfitness of it to unlearn will be found much greater. *South's Sermons.*
Firmness or *stiffness* of the mind is not from adherence to truth, but submission to prejudice. *Locke.*
These hold their opinions with the greatest *stiffness*; being generally the most fierce and firm in their tenets. *Locke.*
5. Unpleasing formality; constraint.
All this religion sat easily upon him, without any of that *stiffness* and constraint, any of those forbidding appearances which disparage the actions of the sincerely pious. *Atterbury.*
6. Rigorousness; harshness.
There fill yourself with those most joyous sights;
But speak no word to her of these sad plights,
Which her too constant *stiffness* doth constrain. *Spenser.*
7. Manner of writing, not easy but harsh and constrained.
Rules and critical observations improve a good genius, where nature leadeth the way, provided he is not too scrupulous; for that will introduce a *stiffness* and affectation, which are utterly abhorrent from all good writing. *Felton.*

To STIFLE. *v. a.* [*estoufer*, French.]
1. To oppress or kill by closeness of air; to suffocate.
Where have you been broiling?
—Among the croud i' th' abbey, where a finger
Cou'd not be wedg'd in more; I am *stifled*
With the mere rankness of their joy. *Shakespeare.*
Pray'r against his absolute decree,
No more avails than breath against the wind;
Blown *stifling* back on him that breathes it forth. *Milton.*
That part of the air that we drew out, left the more room for the *stifling* steams of the coals to be received into it. *Boyle.*
Stifled with kisses a sweet death he dies. *Dryden.*
At one time they keep their patients so close and warm, as almost to *stifle* them with care; and all on a sudden, the cold regimen is in vogue. *Baker.*
I took my leave, being half *stifled* with the closeness of the room. *Swift's Account of Partridge's Death.*
2. To keep in; to hinder from emission.
Whilst bodies become coloured by reflecting or transmitting this or that sort of rays more copiously than the rest, they stop and *stifle* in themselves the rays which they do not reflect or transmit. *Newton's Opticks.*
3. To extinguish by hindering communication.
4. To extinguish by artful or gentle means.
Every reasonable man will pay a tax with chearfulness for *stifling* a civil war in its birth. *Addison's Freeholder.*
5. To suppress; to conceal.
If't prove thy fortune, Polydore, to conquer,
Trust me, and let me know thy love's success,
That I may ever after *stifle* mine. *Otway's Orphan.*

These conclusions have been acknowledged by the disputers themselves, till with labour and study they had *stifled* their first convictions. *Rogers.*
You excel in the art of *stifling* and concealing your resentment. *Swift.*

STI'GMA. *n. s.* [*stigma*, Latin.]
1. A brand; a mark with a hot iron.
2. A mark of infamy.

STIGMA'TICAL. } *adj.* [from *stigma.*] Branded or marked
STI'GMATICK. } with some token of infamy.
Foul *stigmatick*, that's more than thou can'st tell. *Shak.*
Thou'rt like a foul mishapen *stigmatick*,
Mark'd by the destinies to be avoided. *Shakespeare.*
He is deformed, crooked, old and sere,
Vicious, ungentle, foolish, blunt, unkind,
Stigmatical in making, worse in mind. *Shakespeare.*

To STI'GMATIZE. *v. a.* [*stigmatiser*, French, from *stigma.*] To mark with a brand; to disgrace with a note of reproach.
Men of learning who take to business, discharge it with greater honesty than men of the world; because the former in reading have been used to find virtue extolled and vice *stigmatized*, while the latter have seen vice triumphant and virtue discountenanced. *Addison.*
Sour enthusiasts affect to *stigmatize* the finest and most elegant authors both ancient and modern, as dangerous to religion. *Addison's Freeholder.*
The privileges of juries should be ascertained, and whoever violates them *stigmatized* by publick censure. *Swift.*

STI'LAR. *adj.* [from *stile.*] Belonging to the stile of a dial.
At fifty one and a half degrees, which is London's latitude, make a mark, and laying a ruler to the center of the plane and to this mark, draw a line for the *stilar* line. *Moxon.*

STILE. *n. s.* [ſtigele, from ſtigan, Sax. to climb.]
1. A set of steps to pass from one enclosure to another.
There comes my master and another gentleman from Frogmare over the *stile* this way. *Shakespeare.*
If they draw several ways, they be ready to hang themselves upon every gate or *stile* they come at. *L'Estrange.*
The little strutting pile,
You see just by the church-yard *stile.* *Swift.*
2. [*Stile*, Fr.] A pin to cast the shadow in a sun dial.
Erect the *stile* perpendicularly over the substilar line, so as to make an angle with the dial plane equal to the elevation of the pole of your place. *Moxon's Mech. Exercise.*

STILE'TTO. *n. s.* [Italian; *stilet*, Fr.] A small dagger, of which the blade is not edged but round, with a sharp point.
When a senator should be torn in pieces, he hired one, who entering into the senate-house, should assault him as an enemy to the state; and stabbing him with *stilettoes* leave him to be torn by others. *Hakewill on Providence.*

To STILL. *v. a.* [ſtillan, Sax. *stillen*, Dutch.]
1. To silence; to make silent.
Is this the scourge of France?
Is this the Talbot so much fear'd abroad,
That with his name the mothers *still* their babes. *Shakesp.*
2. To quiet; to appease.
In all refrainings of anger, it is the best remedy to make a man's self believe, that the opportunity of revenge is not yet come; but that he foresees a time for it, and so to *still* himself in the mean time, and reserve it. *Bacon.*
3. To make motionless.
He having a full sway over the water, had power to *still* and compose it, as well as to move and disturb it. *Woodward.*
The third fair morn now blaz'd upon the main,
Then glassy smooth lay all the liquid plain,
The winds were hush'd, the billows scarcely curl'd,
And a dead silence *still'd* the watry world. *Pope.*

STILL. *adj.* [*stil*, Dutch.]
1. Silent; uttering no noise. It is well observed by *Junius*, that *st* is the sound commanding silence.
We do not act, that often jest and laugh:
'Tis old but true, *still* swine eat all the draugh. *Shakesp.*
Your wife Octavia, with her modest eyes,
And *still* conclusion, shall acquire no honour,
Demuring upon me. *Shakespeare's Antony and Cleopatra.*
The storm was laid, the winds retir'd,
Obedient to thy will;
The sea that roar'd at thy command,
At thy command was *still.* *Addison.*
2. Quiet; calm.
Atin when he spied
Thus in *still* waves of deep delight to wade,
Fiercely approaching to him loudly cry'd. *Fairy Queen.*
From hence my lines and I depart,
I to my soft *still* walks, they to my heart;
I to the nurse, they to the child of art. *Donne.*
Religious pleasure moves gently, and therefore constantly. It does not affect by rapture, but is like the pleasure of health, which is *still* and sober. *South's Sermons.*

Hope

Hope quickens all the *still* parts of life, and keeps the mind awake in her most remiss and indolent hours. *Addison.*

Silius Italicus has represented it as a very gentle and *still* river, in the beautiful description he has given of it. *Addison.*

How all things listen, while thy muse complains;
Such silence waits on philomela's strains,
In some *still* ev'ning, when the whisp'ring breeze
Pants on the leaves, and dies upon the trees. *Pope.*

3. Motionless.

Gyrecia sit *still*, but with no still pensiveness. *Sidney.*

Though the body really moves, yet not changing perceiveable distance with other bodies, as fast as the ideas of our minds follow in train, the thing seems to stand *still*, as we find in the hands of clocks. *Locke.*

That in this state of ignorance, we short-sighted creatures might not mistake true felicity, we are endowed with a power to suspend any particular desire. This is standing *still* where we are not sufficiently assured. *Locke.*

This stone, O Sysiphus, stands *still*;
Ixion rests upon his wheel. *Pope.*

STILL. *n. s.* Calm; silence.

Herne the hunter,
Sometime a keeper here in Windsor forest,
Doth all the winter time at *still* of mid-night,
Walk round about an oak with ragged horns. *Shakespeare.*

He had never any jealousy with his father, which might give occasion of altering court or council upon the change; but all things pass'd in a *still*. *Bacon's Henry VII.*

STILL. *adv.* [ꞅtille, Saxon.]

1. To this time; till now.

It hath been anciently reported, and is *still* received, that extreme applauses of great multitudes have so rarified the air, that birds flying over have fallen down. *Bacon.*

Thou, O matron!
Here dying to the shore hast left thy name:
Cajeta *still* the place is call'd from thee,
The nurse of great Æneas' infancy. *Dryden's Æneid.*

2. Nevertheless; notwithstanding.

The desire of fame betrays the ambitious man into indecencies that lessen his reputation; he is *still* afraid lest any of his actions should be thrown away in private. *Addison.*

3. In an encreasing degree.

As God sometimes addresses himself in this manner to the hearts of men; so, if the heart will receive such motions by a ready compliance, they will return more frequently, and *still* more and more powerfully. *South.*

The moral perfections of the Deity, the more attentively we consider them, the more perfectly *still* shall we know them. *Atterbury.*

4. Always; ever; continually.

Unless God from heaven did by vision *still* shew them what to do, they might do nothing. *Hooker.*

My brain I'll prove the female to my soul;
My soul, the father; and these two beget
A generation of *still*-breeding thoughts. *Shakespeare.*

Whom the disease of talking *still* once possesseth, he can never hold his peace. *Ben. Johnson.*

He told them, that if their king were *still* absent from them, they would at length crown apes. *Davies on Ireland.*

Chymists would be rich, if they could *still* do in great quantities, what they have sometimes done in little. *Boyle.*

Trade begets trade, and people go much where many people are already gone: so men run *still* to a crowd in the streets, though only to see. *Temple.*

The fewer *still* you name, you wound the more,
Bond is but one; but Harpax is a score. *Pope.*

5. After that.

In the primitive church, such as by fear being compelled to sacrifice to strange gods, after repented, and kept *still* the office of preaching the gospel. *Whitgifte.*

6. In continuance.

I with my hand at midnight held your head;
And, like the watchful minutes to the hour,
Still and anon chear'd up the heavy time,
Saying, what want you? *Shakespeare's King John.*

STILL. *n. s.* [from *distil.*] A vessel for distillation; an alembick.

Nature's confectioner, the bee,
Whose suckets are moist alchimy;
The *still* of his refining mold,
Minting the garden into gold. *Cleaveland.*

In distilling hot spirits, if the head of the *still* be taken off, the vapour which ascends out of the *still* will take fire at the flame of a candle, and the flame will run along the vapour from the candle to the *still*. *Newton's Opticks.*

This fragrant spirit is obtained from all plants in the least aromatick, by a cold *still*, with a heat not exceeding that of summer. *Arbuthnot on Aliments.*

To STILL. *v. a.* [from *distil.*] To distil; to extract or operate upon by distillation.

To STILL. *v. n.* [*stillo*, Latin.] To drop; to fall in drops. Out of use.

His sceptre 'gainst the ground he threw,
And tears *still'd* from him which mov'd all the crew. *Chapm.*

Short thick sobs, whose thund'ring volleys float,
And roul themselves over her lubric throat
In panting murmurs, *still'd* out of her breast,
That ever-bubbling spring. *Crashaw.*

STILLATI'TIOUS. *adj.* [*stillatitius*, Latin.] Falling in drops; drawn by a still.

STI'LLATORY. *n. s.* [from *still* or *distil*]

1. An alembick; a vessel in which distillation is performed.

In all *stillatories*, the vapour is turned back upon itself, by the encounter of the sides of the *stillatory*. *Bacon.*

2. The room in which stills are placed; laboratory

All offices that require heat, as kitchins, *stillatories*, stoves, should be meridional. *Wotton's Architecture.*

These are nature's *stillatories*, in whose caverns the ascending vapours are congealed to that universal aquavitæ, that good fresh water. *More's Antidote against Atheism.*

STI'LLBORN. *adj.* [*still* and *born.*] Born lifeless; dead in the birth.

Grant that our hopes, yet likely of fair birth,
Should be *stillborn*; and that we now possest
The utmost man of expectation; we are
A body strong enough to equal with the king. *Shak.*

Many casualties were but matter of sense, as whether a child were abortive or *stillborn*. *Graunt's Bills of Mortality.*

The pale assistants on each other star'd,
With gaping mouths for issuing words prepar'd:
The *stillborn* sounds upon the palate hung,
And dy'd imperfect on the falt'ring tongue. *Dryden.*

I know a trick to make you thrive;
O, 'tis a quaint device!
Your *stillborn* poems shall revive,
And scorn to wrap up spice. *Swift.*

STI'LLICIDE. *n. s.* [*stillicidium*, Latin.] A succession of drops.

The *stillicides* of water, if there be water enough to follow, will draw themselves into a small thread; because they will not discontinue. *Bacon's Natural History.*

STILLICI'DIOUS. *adj.* [from *stillicide.*] Falling in drops.

Crystal is found sometimes in rocks, and in some places not unlike the stirious or *stillicidious* dependencies of ice. *Brown.*

STI'LLNESS. *n. s.* [from *still.*]

1. Calm; quiet.

How sweet the moonlight sleeps upon this bank!
Here will we sit, and let the sounds of musick
Creep in our ears; soft *stillness* and the night
Become the touches of sweet harmony. *Shakespeare.*

When black clouds draw down the lab'ring skies,
And horrid *stillness* first invades the ear;
And in that silence we the tempest fear. *Dryden.*

Virgil, to heighten the horrour of Æneas' passing by this coast, has prepared the reader by Cajeta's funeral and the *stillness* of the night. *Dryden.*

If a house be on fire, those at next door may escape, by the *stillness* of the weather. *Swift.*

2. Silence; taciturnity.

The gravity and *stillness* of your youth
The world hath noted. *Shakespeare's Othello.*

STI'LLSTAND. *n. s.* [*still* and *stand.*] Absence of motion.

The tide swell'd up unto his height,
Then makes a *stillstand*, running neither way. *Shakespeare.*

STI'LLY. *adv.* [from *still.*]

1. Silently; not loudly.

From camp to camp, through the foul womb of night,
The hum of either army *stilly* sounds. *Shakesp. Henry V.*

2. Calmly; not tumultuously.

STILTS. *n. s.* [*styltor*, Swedish; *stelten*, Dutch; ꞅceacan.] Supports on which boys raise themselves when they walk.

Some could not be content to walk upon the battlements, but they must put themselves upon *stilts*. *Howel's Eng. Tears.*

The heron and such like fowl live of fishes, walk on long *stilts* like the people in the marshes. *More's Ant. against Atheism.*

Men must not walk upon *stilts*. *L'Estrange.*

To STI'MULATE. *v. a.* [*stimulo*, Latin.]

1. To prick.

2. To prick forward; to excite by some pungent motive.

3. [In physick.] To excite a quick sensation, with a derivation towards the part.

Extreme cold *stimulates*, producing first a rigour, and then a glowing heat; those things which *stimulate* in the extreme degree excite pain. *Arbuthnot on Diet.*

Some medicines lubricate and others both lubricate and *stimulate*. *Sharp.*

STIMULA'TION. *n. s.* [*stimulatio*, Latin.] Excitement; pungency.

Some persons, from the secret *stimulations* of vanity or envy, despise a valuable book, and throw contempt upon it by wholesale. *Watts's Improvement of the Mind.*

To STING. *v. a.* Preterite, *I stung*, participle passive *stung*, and *stung*. [stingan, Saxon; *stungen*, sore pricked, Islandick.]

1. To pierce or wound with a point darted out, as that of wasps or scorpions.

The snake, rolled in a flow'ry bank,
With shining checker'd slough, doth *sting* a child
That for the beauty thinks it excellent. *Shakespeare.*

That snakes and vipers *sting* and transmit their mischief by the tail is not easily to be justified, the poison lying about the teeth and communicated by the bite. *Brown's Vulgar Errours.*

2. To pain acutely.

His unkindness
That stript her from his benediction, turn'd her
To foreign casualties, gave her dear right,
To his doghearted daughters: these things *sting* him
So venomously, that burning shame detains him
From his Cordelia. *Shakespeare.*

No more I wave
To prove the hero.—Slander *stings* the brave. *Pope.*

Sting. *n. s.* [from the verb.]

1. A sharp point with which some animals are armed, and which is commonly venomous.

Serpents have venomous teeth, which are mistaken for their *sting*. *Bacon's Natural History.*

His rapier was a hornet's *sting*,
It was a very dangerous thing:
For if he chanc'd to hurt the king,
It would be long in healing. *Drayton.*

2. Any thing that gives pain.

The Jews receiving this book originally with such *sting* in it, shews that the authority was high. *Forbes.*

3. The point in the last verse.

It is not the jerk or *sting* of an epigram, nor the seeming contradiction of a poor antithesis. *Dryden.*

Sti'ngily. *adv.* [from *stingy*.] Covetously.

Sti'nginess. *n. s.* [from *stingy*.] Avarice; covetousness; niggardliness.

Sti'ngless. *adj.* [from *sting*.] Having no sting.

He hugs this viper when he thinks it *stingless*. *Decay of Piety.*

Sti'ngo. *n. s.* [from the sharpness of the taste.] Old beer. A cant word.

Sti'ngy. *adj.* [A low cant word. In this word, with its derivatives, the *g* is pronounced as in *gem*.] Covetous; niggardly; avaricious.

A *stingy* narrow hearted fellow that had a deal of choice fruit, had not the heart to touch it till it began to be rotten. *L'Estrange.*

He relates it only by parcels, and wont give us the whole, which forces me to bespeak his friends to engage him to lay aside that *stingy* humour, and gratify the publick at once. *Arbuthnot's History of J. Bull.*

To STINK. *v. n.* Preterite *I stunk* or *stank.* [stincan, Saxon; *stincken*, Dutch.] To emit an offensive smell, commonly a smell of putrefaction.

John, it will be *stinking* law for his breath. *Shakespeare.*

When the children of Ammon saw that they *stank* before David, they sent and hired Syrians. 2 *Sam.* x. 6.

What a fool art thou, to leave thy mother for a nasty *stinking* goat? *L'Estrange.*

Most of smells want names; sweet and *stinking* serve our turn for these ideas, which is little more than to call them pleasing and displeasing. *Locke.*

Chloris, this costly way to *stink* give o'er,
'Tis throwing sweet into a common shore;
Not all Arabia would sufficient be,
Thou smell'st not of thy sweets, they *stink* of thee. *Granv.*

Stink. *n. s.* [from the verb.] Offensive smell.

Those *stinks* which the nostrils straight abhor are not most pernicious, but such airs as have some similitude with man's body, and so betray the spirits. *Bacon's Natural History.*

They share a sin; and such proportions fall,
That, like a *stink*, 'tis nothing to them all. *Dryden.*

By what criterion do ye eat, d'ye think?
If this is priz'd for sweetness, that for *stink*. *Pope.*

Sti'nkard. *n. s.* [from *stink*.] A mean stinking paltry fellow.

Sti'nker. *n. s.* [from *stink*.] Something intended to offend by the smell.

The air may be purified by burning of stinkpots or *stinkers* in contagious lanes. *Harvey.*

Sti'nkingly. *adv.* [from *stinking*.] With a stink.

Can'st thou believe thy living is a life,
So *stinkingly* depending? *Shakespeare.*

Sti'nkpot. *n. s.* [*stink* and *pot*.] An artificial composition offensive to the smell.

The air may be purified by fires of pitch-barrels, especially in close places, by burning of *stinkpots*. *Harvey.*

To Stint. *v. a.* [*stynta*, Swed. *stunta*, Islandick.] To bound; to limit; to confine; to restrain; to stop.

The reason hereof is the end which he hath proposed, and the law whereby his wisdom hath *stinted* the effects of his power in such sort, that it doth not work infinitely, but correspondently unto that end for which it worketh. *Hooker.*

Then hopeless, heartless, 'gan the cunning thief,
Persuade us die, to *stint* all further strife. *Fairy Queen.*

Nature wisely *stints* our appetite,
And craves no more than undisturb'd delight. *Dryden.*

I shall not go about to extenuate the latitude of the curse upon the earth, or *stint* it only to the production of weeds, but give it its full scope in an universal diminution of the fruitfulness of the earth. *Woodward.*

A supposed heathen deity might be so poor in his attributes, so *stinted* in his knowledge, that a Pagan might hope to conceal his perjury from his notice. *Addison.*

Few countries, which, if well cultivated, would not support double their inhabitants, and yet fewer where one third are not extremely *stinted* in necessaries. *Swift.*

Stint. *n. s.* [from the verb.]

1. Limit; bound; restraint.

We must come at the length to some pause: for if every thing were to be desired for some other without any *stint*, there could be no certain end proposed unto our actions, we should go on we know not whither. *Hooker.*

Touching the *stint* or measure thereof, rites and ceremonies, and other external things of the like nature being hurtful unto the church, either in respect of their quality, or in regard of their number; in the former there could be no doubt or difficulty what would be done; their deliberation in the latter was more difficult. *Hooker.*

The exteriours of mourning, a decent funeral, and black habits are the usual *stints* of common husbands. *Dryden.*

2. A proportion; a quantity assigned.

Our *stint* of woe
Is common; every day, a sailor's wife,
The masters of some merchant, and the merchant
Have just our theme of woe. *Shakespeare.*

He that gave the hint,
This letter for to print,
Must also pay the *stint*. *Denham.*

How much wine drink you in a day? my *stint* in company is a pint at noon. *Swift.*

STIPEND. *n. s.* [*stipendium*, Latin.] Wages; settled pay.

All the earth,
Her kings and tetrarchs are their tributaries;
People and nations pay them hourly *stipends*. *Ben. Johnson.*

St. Paul's zeal was expressed in preaching without any offerings or *stipend*. *Taylor.*

Stipe'ndiary. *adj.* [*stipendiarius*, Latin.] Receiving salaries; performing any service for a stated price.

His great *stipendiary* prelates came with troops of evil appointed horsemen not half full. *Knolles's Hist. of the Turks.*

Place rectories in the remaining churches, which are now served only by *stipendiary* curates. *Swift.*

Stipe'ndiary. *n. s.* [*stipendiaire*, Fr. *stipendiarius*, Latin.] One who performs any service for a settled payment.

This whole country is called the kingdom of Tunis; the king whereof is a kind of *stipendary* unto the Turk. *Abbot.*

Sti'ptick. } *adj.* [στυπτικός.] Having the power to staunch
Sti'ptical. } blood; astringent. This by analogy should be written *styptick*.

There is a sowr *stiptick* salt diffused through the earth, which passing a concoction in plants, becometh milder. *Brown.*

From spirit of salt, carefully dephlegmed and removed into lower glasses, having gently abstracted the whole, there remained in the bottom, and the neck of the retort, a great quantity of a certain dry and *stiptical* substance, mostly of a yellowish colour. *Boyle.*

In an effusion of blood, having dossils ready dipt in the royal *stiptick*, we applied them. *Wiseman's Surgery.*

To STIPULATE. *v. n.* [*stipulor*, Latin; *stipuler*, Fr.] To contract; to bargain; to settle terms.

The Romans very much neglected their maritime affairs; for they *stipulated* with the Carthaginians to furnish them with ships for transport and war. *Arbuthnot.*

Stipula'tion. *n. s.* [*stipulation*, Fr. from *stipulate*.] Bargain;

We promise obediently to keep all God's commandments; the hopes given by the gospel depend on our performance of that *stipulation*. *Rogers's Sermons.*

To STIR. *v. a.* [styrian, Saxon; *stooren*, Dutch.]

1. To move; to remove from its place.

My foot I had never yet in five days been able to *stir* but as it was lifted. *Temple.*

Other spirits
Shoot through their tracts, and distant muscles fill:
This sov'reign, by his arbitrary nod,
Restrains or sends his ministers abroad,
Swift and obedient to his high command
They *stir* a finger, or they lift a hand. *Blackmore.*

2. To agitate; to bring into debate.

Preserve the right of thy place, but *stir* not questions of jurisdiction, and rather assume thy right in silence than voice it with claims. *Bacon.*

One judgment in parliament, that cases of that nature ought to be determined according to the common law, is of greater weight than many cases to the contrary, wherein the question was not *stirred*: yea, even though it should be *stirred* and the contrary affirmed. *Hale.*

3. To incite; to instigate; to animate.

With him is come the mother queen;
An Até *stirring* him to blood and strife. *Shakespeare.*

If you *stir* these daughters hearts
Against their father, fool me not so much
To bear it tamely. *Shakespeare's King Lear.*

The soldiers love her brother's memory;
And for her sake some mutiny will *stir*. *Dryden.*

4. *To* STIR *up*. To incite; to animate; to instigate.

This would seem a dangerous commission, and ready to *stir up* all the Irish in rebellion. *Spenser's Ireland.*

The greedy thirst of royal crown,
That knows no kindred, no regards, no right,
Stirred Porrex *up* to put his brother down. *Spenser.*

God *stirred* him *up* another adversary. 1 *Kings* xi. 23.

The words of Judas were very good, and able to *stir* them *up* to valour. 2 *Maccab.* xiv. 17.

Having overcome and thrust him out of his kingdom, he *stirred up* the Christians and Numidians against him. *Knolles.*

The vigorous spirit of Montrose *stirred* him *up* to make some attempt whether he had any help or no. *Clarendon.*

The improving of his own parts and happiness *stir* him *up* to so notable a design. *More's Antid. against Atheism.*

To *stir up* vigour in him, employ him in some constant bodily labour. *Locke.*

Thou with rebel insolence did'st dare
To own and to protect that hoary ruffian,
To *stir* the factious rabble *up* to arms. *Rowe.*

The use of the passions is to *stir it up*, and put it upon action, to awake the understanding and to enforce the will. *Addison.*

5. *To* STIR *up*. To put in action.

Hell is moved for thee to meet thee at thy coming; it *stirreth up* the dead for thee. *Isa.* xiv. 9.

Such mirth the jocund flute or gamesome pipe
Stirs up among the loose unletter'd hinds. *Milton.*

To STIR. *v. n.*

1. To move one's self; to go out of the place; to change place.

No power he had to *stir* nor will to rise. *Fairy Queen.*

They had the semblance of great bodies behind on the other side of the hill, the falshood of which would have been manifest as soon as they should move from the place where they were, and from whence they were therefore not to *stir*. *Clarendon.*

2. To be in motion; not to be still; to pass from inactivity to motion.

The great Judge of all knows every different degree of human improvement, from these weak *stirrings* and tendencies of the will, which have not yet formed themselves into regular purposes, to the last entire consummation of a good habit. *Addison's Spectator.*

3. To become the object of notice.

If they happen to have any superiour character, they fancy they have a right to talk freely upon every thing that *stirs* or appears. *Watts.*

4. To rise in the morning. This is a colloquial and familiar use.

If the gentlewoman that attends the general's wife be *stirring*, tell her, there's one Cassio entreats of her a little favour of speech. *Shakespeare's Othello.*

STIR. *n. s.* [*stur*, Runick, a battle; *ystwrf*, noise, Welsh.]

1. Tumult; bustle.

What halloing and what *stir* is this to-day?
These are my mates, that make their wills their law,
Have some unhappy passenger in chace. *Shakespeare.*

He hath spun a fair thread, to make all this *stir* for such a necessity as no man ever denied. *Bp. Bramhall.*

Tell, said the soldier, miserable sir,
Why all these words, this clamour and this *stir*,
Why do disputes in wrangling spend the day? *Denham.*

Silence is usually worse than the fiercest and loudest accusations; since it proceeds from a kind of numbness or stupidity of conscience, and an absolute dominion obtained by sin over the soul, so that it shall not so much as dare to complain or make a *stir*. *South's Sermons.*

The great *stirs* of the disputing world are but the conflicts of the humours. *Glanville.*

After all this *stir* about them they are good for nothing. *Til.*

Consider, after so much *stir* about genus and species, how few words we have yet settled definitions of. *Locke.*

2. Commotion; publick disturbance; tumultuous disorder; seditious uproar.

Whensoever the earl shall die, all those lands are to come unto her majesty; he is like to make a foul *stir* there, though of himself of no power, yet through supportance of some others who lie in the wind. *Spenser's Ireland.*

He did make these *stirs*, grieving that the name of Christ was at all brought into those parts. *Abbot.*

Being advertised of some *stirs* raised by his unnatural sons in England, he departed out of Ireland without striking a blow. *Davies.*

Raphael, thou hear'st what *stir* on earth,
Satan from hell 'scap'd through the darksome gulf
Hath rais'd in paradise, and how disturb'd
This night the human pair. *Milton.*

3. Agitation; conflicting passion.

He did keep
The deck, with glove or hat, or handkerchief,
Still waving, as the *stirs* and fits of 's mind
Could best express how slow his soul sail'd on,
How swift his ship. *Shakespeare's Cymbeline.*

STI'RIOUS. *adj.* [from *stiria*, Latin.] Resembling icicles.

Chrystal is found sometimes in rocks, and in some places not much unlike the *stirious* or stillicidious dependencies of ice. *Brown's Vulgar Errours.*

STIRP. *n. s.* [*stirps*, Latin.] Race; family; generation. Not used.

Sundry nations got footing in that land, of the which there yet remain divers great families and *stirps*. *Spenser.*

Democracies are less subject to sedition than when there are *stirps* of nobles. *Bacon.*

All nations of might and fame resorted hither; of whom we have some *stirps* and little tribes with us at this day. *Bacon.*

STI'RRER. *n. s.* [from *stir*.]

1. One who is in motion; one who puts in motion.

2. A riser in the morning.

Come on; give me your hand, sir; an early *stirrer*. *Shak.*

3. An inciter; an instigator.

4. STIRRER *up*. An inciter; an instigator.

A perpetual spring, not found elsewhere but in the Indies only, by reason of the sun's neighbourhood, the life and *stirrer up* of nature in a perpetual activity. *Raleigh.*

Will it not reflect on thy character, Nic, to turn barreter in thy old days; a *stirrer up* of quarrels betwixt thy neighbours? *Arbuthnot.*

STI'RRUP. *n. s.* [stigerap, stirap, from stigan, Saxon, to climb, and rap, a cord.] An iron hoop suspended by a strap, in which the horseman sets his foot when he mounts or rides.

Neither is his manner of mounting unseemly, though he lack *stirrups*; for in his getting up, his horse is still going, whereby he gaineth way: and therefore the *stirrup* was called so in scorn, as it were a stay to get up, being derived of the old English word *sty*; which is to get up, or mount. *Spenser.*

Hast thou not kiss'd my hand, and held my *stirrup*? *Shak.*

His horse hipped with an old mothy saddle, the *stirrups* of no kindred. *Shakesp. Taming of the Shrew.*

Between the *stirrup* and the ground,
Mercy I ask'd, mercy I found. *Camden's Remains.*

At this the knight began to chear up,
And raising up himself on *stirrup*,
Cry'd out Victoria. *Hudibras.*

To STITCH. *v. a.* [*sticke*, Danish; *sticken*, Dutch.]

1. To sew, to work on with a needle.

2. To join; to unite, generally with some degree of clumsiness or inaccuracy.

Having *stitched* together these animadversions touching architecture and their ornaments, contemplative spirits are as restless as active. *Wotton.*

3. *To* STITCH *up*. To mend what was rent.

It is in your hand as well to *stitch up* his life again, as it was before to rent it. *Sidney.*

I with a needle and thread *stitch'd up* the artery and the wound. *Wiseman's Surgery.*

To STITCH. *v. n.* To practise needlework.

STITCH *n. s.* [from the verb.]

1. A pass of the needle and thread through any thing.

2. [From stician, Saxon.] A sharp lancinating pain.

If you desire the spleen, and will laugh yourself into *stitches*, follow me; yond gull Malvolio is turned heathen, a very renegado. *Shakesp. Twelfth Night.*

A simple bloody sputation of the lungs is differenced from a pleurisy, which is ever painful, and attended with a *stitch*. *Harvey on Consumption.*

3. In *Chapman* it seems to mean furrows or ridges, and perhaps has the same meaning in the following passage of *Dryden*, which otherwise I do not understand.

Many men at plow he made, and drave earth here and there,
And turn'd up *stitches* orderly. *Chapman's Iliads.*

A *stitch*-fall'n cheek, that hangs below the jaw,
Such wrinkles as a skilful hand would draw,
For an old grandam ape. *Dryden.*

STI'TCHERY. *n. s.* [from *stitch*.] Needlework. In contempt.

Come lay aside your *stitchery*; play the idle housewife with me this afternoon. *Shakespeare's Othello.*

STITCHWORT. *n. s.* Camomile. *Ainsworth.*

STI'THY. *n. s.* [*stedie*, Islandick; stið, hard, Saxon.]

1. An anvil; the iron body on which the smith forges his work.

My imaginations are as foul
As Vulcan's *stithy*. *Shakespeare's Hamlet.*

To

To Stive. *v. a.* [Suppoſed of the ſame original with *ſtew.*]
1. To ſtuff up cloſe.
You would admire, if you ſaw them *ſtive* it in their ſhips. *Sandys's Journey.*
2. To make hot or ſultry.
His chamber was commonly *ſtived* with friends or ſuitors of one kind or other. *Wotton.*
Stoat. *n. ſ.* A ſmall ſtinking animal.
Sto'cah. *n. ſ.* [Iriſh; *ſtochk*, Erſe.] An attendant; a wallet-boy; one who runs at a horſeman's foot; a horſeboy.
He holdeth himſelf a gentleman, and ſcorneth to work, which he ſaith is the life of a peaſant; but thenceforth becometh an horſeboy, or a *ſtocah* to ſome kern, inuring himſelf to his ſword, and the gentlemanly trade of ſtealing. *Spenſer.*
Stocca'do. *n. ſ.* [*ſtoccato*, from *ſtocco*, a rapier, Italian.] A thruſt with the rapier.
I have heard the Frenchman hath good ſkill in his rapier.—You ſtand on diſtance, your paſſes, *ſtoccado's*, and I know not what. *Shakeſpeare's Merry Wives of Windſor.*
STOCK. *n. ſ.* [ſtoc, Saxon; *ſtock*, Dutch; *eſtoc*, French.]
1. The trunk; the body of a plant.
That furious beaſt
His precious horn, ſought of his enemies,
Strikes in the *ſtock*, ne thence can be releas'd. *Fa. Queen.*
There is hope of a tree, if cut down, that it will ſprout again, though the root wax old in the earth, and the *ſtock* die in the ground. *Job* xiv. 8.
2. The trunk into which a graft is inſerted.
The cion over-ruleth the *ſtock* quite; and the *ſtock* is but paſſive only, and giveth aliment but no motion to the graft. *Bacon's Natural Hiſtory.*
As fruits, ungrateful to the planter's care,
On ſavage *ſtocks* inſerted, learn to bear;
The ſureſt virtues thus from paſſions ſhoot,
Wild nature's vigour working at the root. *Pope.*
3. A log; a poſt.
That they kept thy truth ſo pure of old,
When all our fathers worſhipp'd *ſtocks* and ſtones,
Forget not. *Milton.*
Why all this fury? What's the matter,
That oaks muſt come from Thrace to dance?
Muſt ſtupid *ſtocks* be taught to flatter?
And is there no ſuch wood in France? *Prior.*
4. A man proverbially ſtupid.
What tyranny is this, my heart to thrall,
And eke my tongue with proud reſtraint to tie,
That neither I may ſpeak nor think at all,
But like a ſtupid *ſtock* in ſilence die? *Spenſer.*
While we admire
This virtue and this moral diſcipline,
Let's be no ſtoicks, nor no *ſtocks*. *Shakeſpeare.*
5. The handle of any thing.
6. A ſupport of a ſhip while it is building.
Freſh ſupplies of ſhips,
And ſuch as fitted ſince the fight had been,
Or new from *ſtocks* were fall'n into the road. *Dryden.*
7. [*Stocco*, a rapier, Italian.] A thruſt; a ſtoccado.
To ſee thee here, to ſee thee there; to ſee thee paſs thy puncto, thy *ſtock*, thy reverſe. *Shakeſpeare.*
8. Something made of linen; a cravat; a cloſe neckcloth. Anciently a ſtocken.
His lackey with a linen *ſtock* on one leg, and a kerſey boot-hoſe on the other. *Shak. Taming of the Shrew.*
9. A race; a lineage; a family.
Say what *ſtock* he ſprings of.—
—The noble houſe of Marcius. *Shakeſ. Coriolanus.*
His early virtues to that ancient *ſtock*
Gave as much honour as from thence he took. *Waller.*
The like ſhall ſing
All propheſy, that of the royal *ſtock*
Of David, ſo I name this king, ſhall riſe
A ſon, the woman's ſeed. *Milton.*
Thou haſt ſeen one world begin, and end,
And man, as from a ſecond *ſtock*, proceed. *Milton.*
To no human *ſtock*
We owe this fierce unkindneſs; but the rock,
That cloven rock produc'd thee. *Waller.*
Thy mother was no goddeſs, nor thy *ſtock*
From Dardanus; but in ſome horrid rock,
Perfidious wretch, rough Caucaſus thee bred. *Denham.*
10. The principal; capital ſtore; fund already provided.
Prodigal men
Feel not their own *ſtock* waſting. *Ben. Johnſ. Catiline.*
Let the exportation of home commodities be more in value than the importation of foreign; ſo the *ſtock* of the kingdom ſhall yearly increaſe; for then the balance of trade muſt be returned in money or bullion. *Bacon's Advice to Villiers.*
A king, againſt a ſtorm, muſt foreſee to a convenient *ſtock* of treaſure. *Bacon.*
'Tis the place where God promiſes and delights to diſpenſe larger proportions of his favour, that he may fix a mark of honour on his ſanctuary, and recommend it to the ſons of men, upon the *ſtock* of their own intereſt as well as his own glory. *South.*
Some honour of your own acquire;
Add to that *ſtock*, which juſtly we beſtow,
Of thoſe bleſt ſhades to whom you all things owe. *Dryden.*
Yet was ſhe not profuſe; but fear'd to waſte,
And wiſely manag'd that the *ſtock* might laſt;
That all might be ſupply'd, and ſhe not grieve,
When crouds appear'd, ſhe had not to relieve;
Which to prevent, ſhe ſtill increas'd her ſtore;
Laid up, and ſpar'd, that ſhe might give the more. *Dryden.*
Beneath one law bees live,
And with one common *ſtock* their traffick drive:
All is the ſtate's, the ſtate provides for all. *Dryden's Georg.*
If parents die without actually transferring their right to another, why does it not return to the common *ſtock* of mankind? *Locke.*
When we brought it out it took ſuch a quantity of air into its lungs, that it ſwelled almoſt twice as big as before; and it was perhaps on this *ſtock* of air that it lived a minute longer the ſecond time. *Addiſon on Italy.*
Be ready to give, and glad to diſtribute, by ſetting apart ſomething out of thy *ſtock* for the uſe of ſome charities. *Atterb.*
Of thoſe ſtars, which our imperfect eye
Has doom'd and fix'd to one eternal ſky,
Each by a native *ſtock* of honour great,
May dart ſtrong influence, and diffuſe kind heat. *Prior.*
They had law-ſuits; but, though they ſpent their income, they never mortgaged the *ſtock*. *Arbuthnot.*
11. Quantity; ſtore; body.
A great benefit ſuch a natural hiſtory, as may be confided in, will prove to the whole *ſtock* of learned mankind. *Glanv.*
Nor do thoſe ills on ſingle bodies prey;
But oftner bring the nation to decay,
And ſweep the preſent *ſtock* and future hope away. *Dryd.*
He propoſes to himſelf no ſmall *ſtock* of fame in future ages, in being the firſt who has undertaken this deſign. *Arbuthnot.*
12. A fund eſtabliſhed by the government, of which the value riſes and falls by artifice or chance.
An artificial wealth of funds and *ſtocks* was in the hands of thoſe who had been plundering the publick. *Swift.*
Stateſman and patriot ply alike the *ſtocks*,
Peereſs and butler ſhare alike the box. *Pope.*
To Stock. *v. a.* [from the noun.]
1. To ſtore; to fill ſufficiently.
If a man will commit ſuch rules to his memory, and *ſtock* his mind with portions of Scripture anſwerable to all the heads of duty, his conſcience can never be at a loſs. *South.*
I, who before with ſhepherds in the groves,
Sung to my oaten pipe their rural loves,
Manur'd the glebe, and *ſtock'd* the fruitful plain. *Dryden.*
The world begun to be *ſtocked* with people, and human induſtry drained thoſe uninhabitable places. *Burnet.*
Springs and rivers are by large ſupplies continually *ſtocked* with water. *Woodward.*
2. To lay in ſtore.
3. To put in the ſtocks. See Stocks.
Call not your ſtocks for me: I ſerve the king,
On whoſe employment I was ſent to you:
You ſhall do ſmall reſpect, ſhew too bold malice
Againſt the grace and perſon of my maſter,
Stocking his meſſenger. *Shakeſp. King Lear.*
4. *To* Stock *up.* To extirpate.
The wild boar not only ſpoils her branches, but *ſtocks up* her roots. *Decay of Piety.*
Sto'ckdove. *n. ſ.* Ringdove.
Stockdoves and turtles tell their am'rous pain,
And, from the lofty elms, of love complain. *Dryden.*
Sto'ckfish. *n. ſ.* [*ſtockeviſch*, Dutch.] Dried cod, ſo called from its hardneſs.
Stockgi'llyflower. *n. ſ.* [*leucoium*, Latin.] A plant.
The characters are: the flower is compoſed, for the moſt part, of four leaves, which are placed in form of a croſs: out of the flower-cup riſes the pointal, which becomes a long flat pod, divided into two cells by an intermediate partition, to which the valves adhere on both ſides, and are furniſhed with flat ſmooth ſeeds, which are orbicular, and bordered round their edges: to which may be added, the flowers are ſpecious, and ſweet ſmelling. *Miller.*
The *ſtockgillyflowers* are commonly biennial plants, and there are many different ſpecies of them, including the various ſorts of wallflowers, of which the common ſort grows on the walls of ruinous houſes, and is uſed in medicine. The Ravenal wallflower is remarkable for the beauty and ſweetneſs of its flower. *Hill.*
Sto'cking. *n. ſ.* The covering of the leg.
In his firſt approach before my lady he will come to her in yellow *ſtockings*, and 'tis a colour ſhe abhors. *Shakeſpeare.*
By the loyalty of that town he procured ſhoes, *ſtockings*, and money for his ſoldiers. *Clarendon.*

Unlefs we fhould expect that nature fhould make jerkins and *ftockings* grow out of the ground, what could fhe do better than afford us fo fit materials for cloathing as the wool of fheep? *More's Antidote againft Atheifm.*

He fpent half a day to look for his odd *ftocking*, when he had them both upon a leg. *L'Eftrange.*

See how he rolls his *ftockings!* *Spectator.*

At am'rous Flavio is the *ftocking* thrown,
That very night he longs to lie alone. *Pope.*

The families of farmers live in filth and naftinefs, without a fhoe or *ftocking* to their feet. *Swift.*

To STO'CKING. *v. a.* [from the noun.] To drefs in ftockings.

Stocking'd with loads of fat town-dirt, he goes. *Dryden.*

STO'CKJOBBER. *n. f.* [*ftock* and *job.*] A low wretch who gets money by buying and felling fhares in the funds.

The *ftockjobber* thus from 'Change-alley goes down,
And tips you the freeman a wink;
Let me have but your vote to ferve for the town,
And here is a guinea to drink. *Swift.*

STO'CKISH. *adj.* [from *ftock.*] Hard; blockifh.

The poet
Did feign that Orpheus drew trees, ftones, and floods;
Since nought fo *ftockifh*, hard, and full of rage,
But mufick for the time doth change his nature. *Shakefp.*

STO'CKLOCK. *n. f.* [*ftock* and *lock.*] Lock fixed in wood.

There are locks for feveral purpofes; as ftreet-door locks, called *ftocklocks*; chamber-door-locks, called fpring-locks, and cupboard-locks. *Moxon's Mech. Exer.*

STOCKS. *n. f.* [Commonly without fingular.] Prifon for the legs.

Fetch forth the *ftocks*:
As I have life and honour, there fhall he fit 'till noon. *Shak.*

Tom is whipt from tything to tything, *ftock*-punifh'd, and imprifoned. *Shakefpeare's King Lear.*

I have fat in the *ftocks* for the puddings he hath ftol'n, otherwife he had been executed. *Shakefp. Two Gent. of Verona.*

Matrimony is expreffed by a young man ftanding, his legs being faft in a pair of *ftocks*. *Peacham.*

The *ftocks* hinder his legs from obeying the determination of his mind, if it would transfer his body to another place. *Locke.*

STOCKSTI'L. *adj.* [*ftock* and *ftill.*] Motionlefs as logs.

Our preachers ftand *ftockftill* in the pulpit, and will not fo much as move a finger to fet off the beft fermon. *Addifon.*

STO'ICK. *n. f.* [στωικός; *ftoique*, Fr.] A philofopher who followed the fect of Zeno; holding the neutrality of external things.

While we admire
This virtue, and this moral difcipline,
Let's be no *ftoicks*, nor no ftocks, I pray. *Shakefpeare.*

STOKE, *ftoak*, feem to come from the Saxon ſtocce, fignifying the ftock or body of a tree. *Gibfon's Camden.*

STOLE. *n. f.* [*ftola*, Latin.] A long veft.

Over all a black *ftole* fhe did throw,
As one that inly mourned. *Fairy Queen.*

The folemn feaft of Ceres now was near,
When long white linen *ftoles* the matrons wear. *Dryden.*

STOLE. The preterite of *fteal.*

A factor *ftole* a gem away. *Pope.*

STOLEN. Participle paffive of *fteal.*

Stolen waters are fweet, and bread eaten in fecret is pleafant. *Prov.* ix. 17.

STOLI'DITY. *n. f.* [*ftolidus*, Lat. *ftolidité*, French.] Stupidity; want of fenfe.

Thefe are the fools in the text, indocile untractable fools, whofe *ftolidity* can baffle all arguments. *Bentley.*

STO'MACH. *n. f.* [*eftomach*, French; *ftomachus*, Latin.]

1. The ventricle in which food is digefted.

If you're fick at fea,
Or *ftomach* qualm'd at land, a dram of this
Will drive away diftemper. *Shakefpeare's Cymbeline.*

This filthy fimile, this beaftly line,
Quite turns my *ftomach*. *Pope.*

2. Appetite; defire of food.

Tell me, what is't that takes from thee
Thy *ftomach*, pleafure, and thy golden fleep? *Shakefpeare.*

Will fortune never come with both hands full,
But write her fair words ftill in fouleft letters?
She either gives a *ftomach*, and no food,
Such are the poor in health; or elfe a feaft,
And takes away the *ftomach*; fuch the rich,
That have abundance and enjoy it not. *Shakef. Hen.* IV.

As appetite or *ftomach* to meat is a fign of health in the body, fo is this hunger in the foul a vital quality, an evidence of fome life of grace in the heart; whereas decay of appetite, and the no manner of *ftomach*, is a moft defperate prognoftick. *Hammond.*

3. Inclination; liking.

He which hath no *ftomach* to this fight,
Let him depart. *Shakef. Henry* V.

The unufual diftance of time made it fubject to every man's note, that it was an act againft his *ftomach*, and put upon him by neceffity of ftate. *Bacon's Henry* VII.

The very trade went againft his *ftomach*. *L'Eftrange.*

4. [*Stomachus*, Latin.] Anger; refolution.

Difdain he called was, and did difdain
To be fo call'd, and who fo did him call:
Stern was his look, and full of *ftomach* vain,
His portance terrible, and ftature tall. *Fairy Queen.*

Is't near dinner-time?——I would it were,
That you might kill your *ftomach* on your meat,
And not upon your maid. *Shak. Two Gent. of Verona.*

Inftead of trumpet and of drum,
That makes the warrior's *ftomach* come. *Butler.*

5. Sullennefs; refentment.

Some of the chiefeft laity profeffed with greater *ftomach* their judgments, that fuch a difcipline was little better than popifh tyranny difguifed under a new form. *Hooker.*

Arius, a fubtile witted and a marvellous fair-fpoken man, was difcontented that one fhould be placed before him in honour, whofe fuperior he thought himfelf in defert, becaufe through envy and *ftomach* prone unto contradiction. *Hooker.*

They plainly faw, that when *ftomach* doth ftrive with wit, the match is not equal. *Hooker.*

Whereby the ape in wond'rous *ftomach* wox,
Strongly encouraged by the crafty fox. *Hubberd's Tale.*

That nobles fhould fuch *ftomachs* bear!
I myfelf fight not once in forty year. *Shakef. Henry* VI.

It ftuck in the camel's *ftomach*, that bulls fhould be armed with horns, and that a creature of his fize fhould be left defencelefs. *L'Eftrange.*

Not courage but *ftomach* that makes people break rather than they will bend. *L'Eftrange.*

This fort of crying proceeding from pride, obftinacy, and *ftomach*, the will, where the fault lies, muft be bent. *Locke.*

6. Pride; haughtinefs.

He was a man
Of an unbounded *ftomach*, ever ranking
Himfelf with princes. *Shakefpeare's Henry* VIII.

To STO'MACH. *v. a.* [*ftomachor*, Latin.] To refent; to remember with anger and malignity.

Believe not all; or, if you muft believe,
Stomach not all. *Shakefp. Ant. and Cleopatra.*

Jonathan loved David, and the people applauded him; only Saul *ftomached* him, and therefore hated him. *Hall's Contempl.*

The lion began to fhew his teeth, and to *ftomach* the affront. *L'Eftrange's Fables.*

To STO'MACH. *v. n.* To be angry.

Let a man, though never fo juftly, oppofe himfelf unto thofe that are difordered in their ways, and what one amongft them commonly doth not *ftomach* at fuch contradiction, ftorm at reproof, and hate fuch as would reform them? *Hooker.*

STO'MACHED. *adj.* [from *ftomach.*] Filled with paffions of refentment.

High *ftomach'd* are they both, and full of ire;
In rage deaf as the fea, hafty as fire. *Shakefpeare.*

STO'MACHER. *n. f.* [from *ftomach.*] An ornamental covering worn by women on the breaft.

Golden quoifs and *ftomachers*,
For my lads to give their dears. *Shakefp. Winter's Tale.*

Inftead of a *ftomacher*, a girding of fackcloth. *If.* iii. 24.

Thou marry'ft every year
The lyrick lark and the grave whifpering dove,
The fparrow that neglects his life for love,
The houfhold bird with the red *ftomacher*. *Donne.*

STO'MACHFUL. *adj.* [*ftomachofus*, Latin; *ftomach* and *full.*] Sullen; ftubborn; perverfe.

A *ftomachful* boy put to fchool, the whole world could not bring to pronounce the firft letter. *L'Eftrange.*

Obftinate or *ftomachful* crying fhould not be permitted, becaufe it is another way of encouraging thofe paffions which 'tis our bufinefs to fubdue. *Locke.*

STO'MACHFULNESS. *n. f.* [from *ftomachful.*] Stubbornnefs; fullennefs; obftinacy.

STOMA'CHICAL. } *adj.* [*ftomachique*, Fr.] Relating to the ftomach; pertaining to the ftomach.
STOMA'CHICK. }

An hypochondriack confumption is an extenuation, occafioned by an infarction and obftruction of the *ftomachick* veffels through melancholy humours. *Harvey.*

By a catarrh the *ftomachical* ferment is vitiated. *Floyer.*

STOMA'CHICK. *n. f.* [from *ftomach.*] A medicine for the ftomach.

STO'MACHOUS. *adj.* [from *ftomach.*] Stout; angry; fullen; obftinate. Obfolete.

That ftranger knight in prefence came,
And goodly falved them; but nought again
Him anfwered, as courtefy became;
But with ftern looks, and *ftomachous* difdain,
Gave figns of grudge and difcontentment vain. *Fa. Queen.*

STOND. *n. f.* [for *ftand.*]

1. Poft; ftation.

On th' other fide, th' affieged caftle's ward
Their ftedfaft *ftonds* did mightily maintain. *Fairy Queen.*

2. Stop; indifpofition to proceed.

There be not *ftonds* nor reftivenefs in a man's nature; but the wheels of his mind keep way with the wheels of his fortune. *Bacon's Effays.*

STONE. *n. s.* [*stains*, Gothick; ꞅtan, Saxon; *steen*, Dutch.]

1. Stones are bodies insipid, hard, not ductile or malleable, nor soluble in water. *Woodward's Meth. Foss.*

We understand by the term *stones* fossile bodies, solid, not ductile under the hammer, fixed in the fire, not easily melted in it, and not to be dissolved by water. *Stones* are arranged under two distinct series, the softer and the harder. Of the softer *stones* there are three general distinctions. 1. The foliaceous or flaky, as talk. 2. The fibrose, as the asbestus. 3. The granulated, as the gypsum. Of the harder stones there are also three general distinctions. 1. The opake stones, as limestone. 2. The semi-pellucid, as agate. 3. The pellucid, as crystal and the gems. *Hill's Mat. Med.*

Should I go to church, and see the holy edifice of *stone*,
And not bethink me strait of dang'rous rocks! *Shakespeare.*

The English used the *stones* to reinforce the pier. *Hayward.*

2. Piece of stone cut for building.

He shall bring forth the head *stone* with shoutings. *Zech.* iv.

3. Gem; precious stone.

I thought I saw
Wedges of gold, great anchors, heaps of pearl,
Inestimable *stones*, unvalu'd jewels. *Shakesp. Rich.* III.

4. Any thing made of stone.

Lend me a looking-glass;
If that her breath will mist or stain the *stone*,
Why then she lives. *Shakespeare.*

5. Calculous concretion in the kidneys or bladder; the disease arising from a calculus.

A specifick remedy for preventing of the *stone* I take to be the constant use of alehoof-ale. *Temple.*

A gentleman supposed his difficulty in urining proceeded from the *stone*. *Wiseman's Surgery.*

6. The case which in some fruits contains the seed.

To make fruits without core or *stone* is a curiosity. *Bacon.*

7. Testicle.

8. A weight containing fourteen pounds.

Does Wood think that we will sell him a *stone* of wool for his counters? *Swift.*

9. STONE is used by way of exaggeration.

What need you be so boist'rous rough?
I will not struggle, I will stand *stone* still. *Shakesp. K. John.*

And there lies Whacum by my side,
Stone dead, and in his own blood dy'd. *Hudibras.*

The fellow held his breath, and lay *stone* still, as if he was dead. *L'Estrange.*

She had got a trick of holding her breath, and lying at her length for *stone* dead. *L'Estrange.*

The cottages having taken a country-dance together, had been all out, and stood *stone* still with amazement. *Pope.*

10. *To leave no* STONE *unturned.* To do every thing that can be done for the production or promotion of any effect.

Women, that *left no stone unturn'd*
In which the cause might be concern'd,
Brought in their children's spoons and whistles,
To purchase swords, carbines, and pistols. *Hudibras.*

He crimes invented, *left unturn'd no stone*
To make my guilt appear, and hide his own. *Dryden.*

STONE. *adj.* Made of stone.

Present her at the leet,
Because she bought *stone* jugs, and no seal'd quarts. *Shakesp.*

To STONE. *v. a.* [from the noun.]

1. To pelt or beat or kill with stones.

These people be almost ready to *stone* me. *Ex.* xvii. 4.

Crucifixion was a punishment unknown to the Jewish laws, among whom the *stoning* to death was the punishment for blasphemy. *Stephens's Sermons.*

2. To harden.

Oh perjur'd woman! thou do'st *stone* my heart;
And mak'st me call what I intend to do,
A murder, which I thought a sacrifice. *Shakesp. Othello.*

STO'NEBREAK. *n. s.* An herb. *Ainsworth.*

STO'NECHATTER. *n. s.* A bird. *Ainsworth.*

STO'NECROP. *n. s.* A sort of tree.

Stonecrop tree is a beautiful tree, but not common. *Mortim.*

STO'NECUTTER. *n. s.* [from *stone* and *cutter.*] One whose trade is to hew stones.

A *stonecutter*'s man had the vesiculæ of his lungs so stuffed with dust, that, in cutting, the knife went as if through a heap of sand. *Derham's Physico-Theology.*

My prosecutor provided me a monument at the *stonecutter*'s, and would have erected it in the parish-church. *Swift.*

STO'NEFERN. *n. s.* A plant. *Ainsworth.*

STO'NEFLY. *n. s.* An insect. *Ainsworth.*

STO'NEFRUIT. *n. s.* [*stone* and *fruit.*] Fruit of which the seed is covered with a hard shell enveloped in the pulp.

We gathered ripe apricocks and ripe plums upon one tree, from which we expect some other sorts of *stonefruit*. *Boyle.*

STO'NEHAWK. *n. s.* A kind of hawk. *Ainsworth.*

STO'NEHORSE. *n. s.* [*stone* and *horse.*] A horse not castrated.

Where there is most arable land, *stonehorses* or geldings are more necessary. *Mortimer's Husbandry.*

STO'NEPIT. *n. s.* [*stone* and *pit.*] A quarry; a pit where stones are dug.

There's one found in a *stonepit*. *Woodward.*

STO'NEPITCH. *n. s.* [from *stone* and *pitch.*] Hard inspissated pitch.

The Egyptian mummies are reported to be as hard as *stonepitch*. *Bacon's Nat. History.*

STO'NEPLOVER. *n. s.* A bird. *Ainsworth.*

STO'NESMICKLE. *n. s.* A bird. *Ainsworth.*

STO'NEWORK. *n. s.* [*stone* and *work.*] Building of stone.

They make two walls with flat stones, and fill the space with earth, and so they continue the *stonework*. *Mortimer.*

STO'NINESS. *n. s.* [from *stony.*] The quality of having many stones.

The name Hexton owes its original to the *stoniness* of the place. *Hearne.*

Small gravel or *stoniness* is found therein. *Mortimer.*

STO'NY. *adj.* [from *stone.*]

1. Made of stone.

Nor *stony* tower, nor walls of beaten brass,
Can be retentive to the strength of spirit. *Shak. Jul. Cæs.*

With love's light wings did I o'erperch these walls;
For *stony* limits cannot hold love out. *Shak. Rom. and Jul.*

Nor slept the winds
Within their *stony* caves, but rush'd abroad
From the four hinges of the world, and fell
On the vext wilderness, whose tallest pines,
Though rooted deep as high and sturdiest oaks,
Bow'd their stiff necks, loaden with stormy blasts,
Or torn up sheer. *Milton's Paradise Regain'd.*

Here the marshy grounds approach your fields,
And there the soil a *stony* harvest yields. *Dryden's Virgil.*

As in spires he stood, he turn'd to stone;
The *stony* snake retain'd the figure still his own. *Dryden.*

They suppose these bodies to be only water petrified, or converted into these sparry or *stony* icicles. *Woodward.*

2. Abounding with stones.

From the *stony* Mænalus
Bring your flocks, and live with us. *Milton.*

3. Petrifick.

Now let the *stony* dart of senseless cold
Pierce to my heart, and pass through every side. *F. Queen.*

4. Hard; inflexible; unrelenting.

The *stony* hardness of too many patrons hearts, not touched with any feeling in this case. *Hooker.*

Thou art come to answer
A *stony* adversary, an inhuman wretch
Uncapable of pity. *Shakes. Merchant of Venice.*

Eight yards of uneven ground is threescore and ten miles a-foot with me, and the *stony* hearted villains know it. *Shakes.*

At this sight
My heart is turn'd to stone; and while 'tis mine,
It shall be *stony*. *Shakes. Henry* VI.

I will clear their senses dark,
What may suffice, and soften *stony* hearts
To pray, repent, and bring obedience due. *Milt. Par. Lost.*

Indiff'rence, clad in wisdom's guise,
All fortitude of mind supplies;
For how can *stony* bowels melt,
In those who never pity felt? *Swift.*

STOOD. The preterite of *To stand.*

Adam, at the news,
Heart-struck with chilling gripe of sorrow *stood*. *Milton.*

STOOL. *n. s.* [*stols*, Gothick; ꞅtol, Saxon; *stoel*, Dutch.]

1. A seat without a back, so distinguished from a chair.

If a chair be defined a seat for a single person, with a back belonging to it, then a *stool* is a seat for a single person without a back. *Watts's Logick.*

Thou fearful fool,
Why takest not of the same fruit of gold?
Ne sittest down on that same silver *stool*,
To rest thy weary person in the shadow cold? *Fa. Queen.*

Now which were wise, and which were fools?
Poor Alma sits between two *stools*:
The more she reads, the more perplext. *Prior.*

2. Evacuation by purgative medicines.

There be medicines that move *stools*, and not urine; some other urine, and not *stools*: those that purge by *stool*, are such as enter not at all, or little, into the mesentery veins; but either at the first are not digestible by the stomach, and therefore move immediately downwards to the guts; or else are afterwards rejected by the mesentery veins, and so turn likewise downwards to the guts. *Bacon's Natural History.*

The peristaltick motion, or repeated changes of contraction and dilatation, is not in the lower guts, else one would have a continual needing of going to *stool*. *Arbuthnot on Aliments.*

3. STOOL *of Repentance*, or *cutty stool*, in the kirks of Scotland, is somewhat analogous to the pillory. It is elevated above the congregation. In some places there may be a seat in it; but it is generally without, and the person stands therein who has been guilty of fornication, for three Sundays in the forenoon; and after sermon

sermon is called upon by name and surname, the beadle or kirk-officer bringing the offender, if refractory, forwards to his post; and then the preacher proceeds to admonition. Here too are set to publick view adulterers; only these are habited in a coarse canvas, analogous to a hairy or monastick vest, with a hood to it, which they call the sack or sackcloth, and that every Sunday throughout a year, or longer.

Unequal and unreasonable judgment of things brings many a great man to the *stool of repentance*. *L'Estrange.*

STO'OLBALL. *n. s.* [*stool* and *ball.*] A play where balls are driven from stool to stool.

While Betty dances on the green,
And Susan is at *stoolball* seen. *Prior.*

To STOOP. *v. n.* [ꞅꞇupian, Saxon; *stuypen*, Dutch.]

1. To bend down; to bend forward.

Like unto the boughs of this tree he bended downward, and *stooped* toward the earth. *Raleigh.*

2. To lean forward standing or walking.

When Pelopidas and Ismenias were sent to Artaxerxes, Pelopidas did nothing unworthy; but Ismenias let fall his ring to the ground, and, *stooping* for that, was thought to make his adoration. *Stillingfleet.*

He *stooping* open'd my left side, and took
From thence a rib. *Milton.*

3. To yield; to bend; to submit.

I am the son of Henry the fifth,
Who made the dauphin and the French to *stoop*. *Shakesp.*
Mighty in her ships stood Carthage long,
And swept the riches of the world from far;
Yet *stoop'd* to Rome, less wealthy, but more strong. *Dryd.*

4. To descend from rank or dignity.

He that condescended so far, and *stooped* so low, to invite and to bring us to heaven, will not refuse us a gracious reception there. *Boyle's Seraphick Love.*

Where men of great wealth *stoop* to husbandry, it multiplieth riches exceedingly. *Bacon.*

5. To yield; to be inferiour.

Death his death-wound shall then receive,
And *stoop* inglorious. *Milton.*
These are arts, my prince,
In which your Zama does not *stoop* to Rome. *Addison.*

6. To sink from resolution or superiority; to condescend.

They, whose authority is required unto the satisfying of your demand, do think it both dangerous to admit such concourse of divided minds, and unmeet that their laws, which, being once solemnly established, are to exact obedience of all men and to constrain thereunto, should so far *stoop* as to hold themselves in suspence from taking any effect upon you, 'till some disputer can persuade you to be obedient. *Hooker.*

7. To come down on prey as a falcon.

The bird of Jove *stoop'd* from his airy tour,
Two birds of gayest plume before him drove. *Milton.*

8. To alight from the wing.

Satan ready now
To *stoop* with wearied wings and willing feet,
On the bare outside of this world. *Milton.*
Twelve swans behold in beauteous order move,
And *stoop* with closing pinions from above. *Dryden.*

9. To sink to a lower place.

Cow'ring low
With blandishment, each bird *stoop'd* on his wing. *Milton.*

STOOP. *n. s.* [from the verb.]

1. Act of stooping; inclination downward.

2. Descent from dignity or superiority.

Can any loyal subject see
With patience such a *stoop* from sovereignty?
An ocean pour'd upon a narrow brook? *Dryden.*

3. Fall of a bird upon his prey.

Now will I wander through the air,
Mount, make a *stoop* at ev'ry fair. *Waller.*

An eagle made a *stoop* at him in the middle of his exaltation, and carried him away. *L'Estrange.*

4. [Stoppa, Saxon; *stoope*, Dutch.] A vessel of liquor.

Come, lieutenant, I have a *stoop* of wine; and here without are a brace of gallants, that would fain have a measure to the health of Othello. *Shakesp. Othello.*

There's nothing more in me, sir, but may be squeez'd out without racking, only a *stoop* or two of wine. *Denham.*

A caldron of fat beef, and *stoop* of ale,
On the huzzaing mob shall more prevail,
Than if you give them, with the nicest art,
Ragousts of peacocks brains, or filbert tart. *King.*

STO'OPINGLY. *adv.* [from *stooping.*] With inclination downwards.

Nani was noted to tread softly, to walk *stoopingly*, and raise himself from benches with laborious gesture. *Wotton.*

To STOP. *v. a.* [*estouper*, Fr. *stoppare*, Ital. *stoppen*, Dutch.]

1. To hinder from progressive motion.

From the oracle
They will bring all; whose spiritual counsel had
Shall *stop* or spur me. *Shakespeare.*
Can any dresses find a way
To *stop* th' approaches of decay,
And mend a ruin'd face? *Dorset.*

2. To hinder from any change of state, whether to better or worse.

3. To hinder from action.

As the truth of Christ is in me, no man shall *stop* me of this boasting. *2 Cor.* xi. 10.

4. To put an end to the motion or action of any thing.

Friend, 'tis the duke's pleasure,
Whose disposition, all the world well knows,
Will not be rubb'd nor *stopp'd*. *Shakes. King Lear.*
Almon falls, pierc'd with an arrow from the distant war:
Fix'd in his throat the flying weapon stood,
And *stopp'd* his breath, and drank his vital blood. *Dryden.*

5. To suppress.

Every bold sinner, when about to engage in the commission of any known sin, should arrest his confidence, and *stop* the execution of his purpose with this question: Do I believe that God has denounced death to such a practice, or do I not? *South.*

He, on occasion of *stopping* my play, did me a good office at court, by representing it as long ago designed. *Dryden.*

6. To regulate musical strings with the fingers.

In instruments of strings, if you *stop* a string high, whereby it hath less scope to tremble, the sound is more treble, but yet more dead. *Bacon's Natural History.*

7. To close any aperture.

Smite every fenced city, *stop* all wells of water, and mar land with stones. *2 Kings* iii. 19.

They pulled away the shoulder, and *stopped* their ears, that they should not hear. *Zech.* vii. 11.

A hawk's bell, the holes *stopped* up, hang by a thread within a bottle-glass, and *stop* the glass close with wax. *Bacon.*

His majesty *stopped* a leak that did much harm. *Bacon.*

Stoppings and suffocations are dangerous in the body. *Bacon.*

They first raised an army with this design, to *stop* my mouth or force my consent. *King Charles.*

Celsus gives a precept about bleeding, that when the blood is good, which is to be judged by the colour, that immediately the vein should be *stopped*. *Arbuthnot.*

8. To obstruct; to encumber.

Mountains of ice that *stop* th' imagin'd way. *Milton.*

To STOP. *v. n.* To cease to go forward.

Some strange commotion
Is in his brain: he bites his lip, and starts;
Stops on a sudden, looks upon the ground,
Then lays his finger on his temple; strait
Springs out into fast gait, then *stops* again. *Shak. H.* VIII.

When men pursue their thoughts of space, they *stop* at the confines of body, as if space were there at an end. *Locke.*

If the rude throng pour on with furious pace,
And hap to break thee from a friend's embrace,
Stop short, nor struggle through. *Gay.*

STOP. *n. s.* [from the verb.]

1. Cessation of progressive motion.

Thought's the slave of time, and life time's fool;
And time, that takes survey of all the world,
Must have a *stop*. *Shakespeare.*
The marigold, whose courtier's face
Ecchoes the sun, and doth unlace
Her at his rise, at his full *stop*
Packs and shuts up her gawdy shop,
Mistakes her cue, and doth display. *Cleaveland.*

A lion, ranging for his prey, made a *stop* on a sudden at a hideous yelling noise, which startled him. *L'Estrange.*

2. Hindrance of progress; obstruction.

In weak and tender minds we little know what misery this strict opinion would breed, besides the *stops* it would make in the whole course of all mens lives and actions. *Hooker.*

These gates are not sufficient for the communication between the walled city and its suburbs, as daily appears by the *stops* and embarrasses of coaches near both these gates. *Graunt.*

My praise the Fabii claim,
And thou great hero, greatest of thy name,
Ordain'd in war to save the sinking state,
And, by delays, to put a *stop* to fate. *Dryden's Æn.*

Occult qualities put a *stop* to the improvement of natural philosophy, and therefore have been rejected. *Newton's Opt.*

Brokers hinder trade, by making the circuit which the money goes larger, and in that circuit more *stops*, so that the returns must necessarily be slower and scantier. *Locke.*

Female zeal, though proceeding from so good a principle, if we may believe the French historians, often put a *stop* to the proceedings of their kings, which might have ended in a reformation. *Addison's Freeholder.*

3. Hindrance of action.

'Tis a great step towards the mastery of our desires to give this *stop* to them, and shut them up in silence. *Locke.*

4. Cessation of action.

Look you to the guard to-night:
Let's teach ourselves that honourable *stop*,
Not to outsport discretion. *Shakespeare.*

5. Interruption.

Thou art full of love and honesty,
And weigh'st thy words before thou giv'st them breath;
Therefore these *stops* of thine fright me the more. *Shakesp.*

6. Prohibition

6. Prohibition of sale.

If they should open a war, they foresee the consumption France must fall into by the *stop* of their wine and salts, wholly taken off by our two nations. *Temple.*

7. That which obstructs; obstacle; impediment.

The proud Duessa, full of wrathful spight
And fierce disdain to be affronted so,
Inforc'd her purple beast with all her might,
That *stop* out of the way to overthrow. *Fairy Queen.*

On indeed they went: but O! not far;
A fatal *stop* travers'd their headlong course. *Daniel.*

Blessed be that God who cast rubs, *stops*, and hindrances in my way, when I was attempting the commission of such a sin. *South's Sermons.*

So melancholy a prospect should inspire us with zeal to oppose some *stop* to the rising torrent, and check this overflowing of ungodliness. *Rogers.*

8. Instrument by which the sounds of wind musick are regulated.

You would play upon me, you would seem to know my *stops*; you would pluck out the heart of my mystery. *Shakesp.*

Blest are those,
Whose blood and judgment are so well comming'd,
That they are not a pipe for fortune's finger,
To sound what *stop* she please. *Shakesp. Hamlet.*

The harp
Had work, and rested not; the solemn pipe,
And dulcimer, all organs of sweet *stop*. *Milt. Par. Lost.*

The sound
Of instruments, that made melodious chime,
Was heard of harp and organ; and who mov'd
Their *stops*, and chords, was seen; his volant touch
Instinct through all proportions, low and high,
Fled, and pursu'd transverse the resonant fugue. *Milton.*

A variety of strings may be observed on their harps, and of *stops* on their tibiæ; which shews the little foundation that such writers have gone upon, who, from a short passage in a classick author, have determined the precise shape of the ancient musical instruments, with the exact number of their pipes, strings, and *stops*. *Addison on Italy.*

9. Regulation of musical chords by the fingers.

The further a string is strained, the less superstraining goeth to a note; for it requireth good winding of a string before it will make any note at all: and in the *stops* of lutes, the higher they go, the less distance is between the frets. *Bacon.*

10. The act of applying the stops in musick.

Th' organ-sound a time survives the *stop*,
Before it doth the dying note give up. *Daniel's Civil War.*

11. A point in writing, by which sentences are distinguished.

Even the iron-pointed pen,
That notes the tragick dooms of men,
Wet with tears still'd from the eyes
Of the flinty destinies,
Would have learn'd a softer style,
And have been asham'd to spoil
His life's sweet story by the haste
Of a cruel *stop* ill-plac'd. *Crashaw.*

STO'PCOCK. *n. s.* [*stop* and *cock.*] A pipe made to let out liquor, stopped by a turning cock.

No man could spit from him without it, but would drivel like some paralytick or fool; the tongue being as a *stopcock* to the air, 'till upon its removal the spittle is driven away. *Grew.*

STO'PPAGE. *n. s.* [from *stop.*] The act of stopping; the state of being stopped.

The effects are a *stoppage* of circulation by too great a weight upon the heart, and suffocation. *Arbuthnot.*

The *stoppage* of a cough, or spitting, increases phlegm in the stomach. *Floyer on the Humours.*

STO'PPLE, or *Stopper. n. s.* [from *stop.*] That by which any hole or the mouth of any vessel is filled up.

Bottles swinged, or carried in a wheel-barrow upon rough ground, fill not full, but leave some air; for if the liquor come close to the *stopple*, it cannot flower. *Bacon.*

There were no shuts or *stopples* made for the ears, that any loud or sharp noise might awaken it, as also a soft and gentle murmur provoke it to sleep. *Ray on the Creation.*

STO'RAXTREE. *n. s.* [*styrax*, Latin.]

1. A tree.

The flower consists of one leaf, shaped like a funnel, and cut into several segments, out of whose flower-cup rises the pointal, which is fixed like a nail in the forepart of the flower: this afterwards becomes a roundish fleshy fruit, including one or two seeds in hard shells. *Miller.*

2. A resinous and odoriferous gum.

I yielded a pleasant odour like the best myrrh, as galbanum, and sweet *storax*. *Ecclus* xxiv. 15.

STORE. *n. s.* [*stôr*, in old Swedish and Runick, is *much*, and is prefixed to other words to intend their signification; *stor*, Danish; *stoor*, Islandick, is *great*. The Teutonick dialects nearer to English seem not to have retained this word.]

1. Large number; large quantity; plenty.

The ships are fraught with *store* of victuals, and good quantity of treasure. *Bacon.*

None yet, but *store* hereafter from the earth
Up hither like aereal vapours flew,
Of all things transitory and vain, when sin
With vanity had fill'd the works of men. *Milt. Par. Lost.*

Jove, grant me length of life, and years good *store*
Heap on my bended back. *Dryden's Juvenal.*

2. A stock accumulated; a supply hoarded.

We liv'd
Supine amidst our flowing *store*,
We slept securely, and we dreamt of more. *Dryden.*

Thee, goddess, thee, Britannia's isle adores:
How has she oft exhausted all her *stores*,
How oft in fields of death thy presence sought?
Nor thinks the mighty prize too dearly bought. *Addison.*

Their minds are richly fraught
With philosophick *stores*. *Thomson.*

3. The state of being accumulated; hoard.

Is not this laid up in *store* with me, and sealed up among my treasures? *Deutr.* xxxii. 34.

Divine Cecilia came,
Inventress of the vocal frame:
The sweet enthusiast from her sacred *store*
Enlarg'd the former narrow bounds,
And added length to solemn sounds. *Dryden.*

4. Storehouse; magazine.

Sulphurous and nitrous foam,
Concocted and adusted, they reduc'd
To blackest grain, and into *store* convey'd. *Milton.*

STORE. *adj.* Hoarded; laid up; accumulated.

What floods of treasure have flowed into Europe by that action, so that the cause of Christendom is raised since twenty times told: of this treasure the gold was accumulate and *store* treasure; but the silver is still growing. *Bacon's Holy War.*

To STORE. *v. a.* [from the noun.]

1. To furnish; to replenish.

Wise Plato said the world with men was *stor'd*,
That succour each to other might afford. *Denham.*

Her face with thousand beauties blest;
Her mind with thousand virtues *stor'd*;
Her pow'r with boundless joy confest,
Her person only not ador'd. *Prior.*

2. To stock against a future time.

Some were of opinion that it were best to stay where they were, until more aid and store of victuals were come; but others said the enemy were but barely *stored* with victuals, and therefore could not long hold out. *Knolles's Hist. of the Turks.*

One having *stored* a pond of four acres with carps, tench, and other fish, and only put in two small pikes, at seven years end, upon the draught, not one fish was left, but the two pikes grown to an excessive bigness. *Hale.*

The mind reflects on its own operations about the ideas got by sensation, and thereby *stores* itself with a new set of ideas, which I call ideas of reflection. *Locke.*

To *store* the vessel let the care be mine,
With water from the rocks and rosy wine,
And life-sustaining bread. *Pope's Odyssey.*

3. To lay up; to hoard.

Let the main part of the corn be a common stock, laid in and *stored* up, and then delivered out in proportion. *Bacon.*

STO'REHOUSE. *n. s.* [*store* and *house.*] Magazine; treasury; place in which things are hoarded and reposited against a future time.

By us it is willingly confessed, that the Scripture of God is a *storehouse* abounding with inestimable treasures of wisdom and knowledge, in many kinds over and above things in this kind barely necessary. *Hooker.*

They greatly joyed merry tales to feign,
Of which a *storehouse* did with her remain. *Fairy Queen.*

Suffer us to famish, and their *storehouses* cramm'd with grain! *Shakesp. Coriolanus.*

Joseph opened all the *storehouses*, and sold unto the Egyptians. *Gen.* xli. 56.

To these high pow'rs a *storehouse* doth pertain,
Where they all arts and gen'ral reasons lay;
Which in the soul, ev'n after death, remain,
And no Lethean flood can wash away. *Davies.*

My heart hath been a *storehouse* long of things
And sayings laid up, portending strange events. *Parad. Reg.*

The image of God was resplendent in man's practical understanding, namely that *storehouse* of the soul, in which are treasured up the rules of action and the seeds of morality. *South's Sermons.*

As many different sounds as can be made by single articulations, so many letters there are in the *storehouse* of nature. *Hold.*

STO'RER. *n. s.* [from *store.*] One who lays up.

STO'RIED. *adj.* [from *story.*] Adorned with historical pictures.

Let my due feet never fail
To walk the studious cloisters pale,
And love the high embowed roof,
With antick pillar massy proof,
And *storied* windows richly dight,
Casting a dim religious light. *Milton.*

Some

Some greedy minion or imperious wife,
The trophy'd arches, *ſtory'd* halls invade. *Pope.*

STORK. *n. ſ.* [ꞅꞇoꞃc, Saxon.] A bird of paſſage famous for the regularity of its departure.

Its beak and legs are long and red; it feeds upon ſerpents, frogs, and inſects: its plumage would be quite white, were not the extremity of its wings, and alſo ſome part of its head and thighs black: it ſits for thirty days and lays but four eggs. Formerly they would not eat the *ſtork*; but at preſent it is much eſteemed for the deliciouſneſs of its fleſh: they go away in the middle of Auguſt, and return in ſpring. *Calmet.*

The *ſtork* in the heaven knoweth her appointed times. *Jer.*

STO'RKSBILL. *n. ſ.* An herb. *Ainſworth.*

STORM. *n. ſ.* [*yſtorm*, Welſh; ꞅꞇoꞃm, Saxon; *ſtorm*, Dutch; *ſtormo*, Italian.]

1. A tempeſt; a commotion of the elements.

O turn thy rudder hitherward a while,
Here may thy *ſtorm*-beat veſſel ſafely ride. *Spenſer.*

We hear this fearful tempeſt ſing,
Yet ſeek no ſhelter to avoid the *ſtorm.* *Shakeſpeare.*

Them ſhe upſtays, mindleſs the while
Herſelf, though faireſt unſupported flower,
From her beſt prop ſo far and *ſtorm* ſo nigh. *Milton.*

Sulphurous hail ſhot after us in *ſtorm.* *Milton.*

Then ſtay my child! *ſtorms* beat and rolls the main;
Oh, beat thoſe *ſtorms* and roll the ſeas in vain. *Pope.*

2. Aſſault on a fortified place.

How by *ſtorm* the walls were won,
Or how the victor ſack'd and burnt the town. *Dryden.*

3. Commotion; ſedition; tumult; clamour; buſtle.

Whilſt I in Ireland nouriſh a mighty band,
I will ſtir up in England ſome black *ſtorm.* *Shakeſpeare.*

Her ſiſter
Began to ſcold and raiſe up ſuch a *ſtorm*,
That mortal ears might hardly endure the din. *Shakeſp.*

4. Affliction; calamity; diſtreſs.

5. Violence; vehemence; tumultuous force.

As oft as we are delivered from thoſe either imminent or preſent calamities, againſt the *ſtorm* and tempeſt whereof we all inſtantly craved favour from above, let it be a queſtion what we ſhould render unto God for his bleſſings, univerſally, ſenſibly, and extraordinarily beſtowed. *Hooker.*

To STORM. *v. a.* [from the noun.] To attack by open force.

From ploughs and harrows ſent to ſeek renown,
They fight in fields, and *ſtorm* the ſhaken town. *Dryden.*

There the brazen tow'r was *ſtorm'd* of old,
When Jove deſcended in almighty gold. *Pope.*

To STORM. *v. n.*

1. To raiſe tempeſts.

So now he *ſtorms* with many a ſturdy ſtoure,
So now his bluſtering blaſt each coaſt doth ſcoure. *Spenſer.*

2. To rage; to fume; to be loudly angry.

Hoarſe, and all in rage,
As mock'd they *ſtorm.* *Milton's Paradiſe Loſt.*

When you return, the maſter *ſtorms*, the lady ſcolds. *Swift.*

While thus they rail, and ſcold, and *ſtorm*,
It paſſes but for common form. *Swift.*

STO'RMY. *adj.* [from *ſtorm.*]

1. Tempeſtuous.

Bellowing clouds burſt with a *ſtormy* ſound,
And with an armed winter ſtrew the ground. *Addiſon's Italy.*

The tender apples from their parents rent
By *ſtormy* ſhocks, muſt not neglected lie. *Philips.*

2. Violent; paſſionate.

The *ſtormy* ſultan rages at our ſtay. *Irene.*

STO'RY. *n. ſ.* ꞅꞇoꞃ, Saxon; *ſtorie*, Dutch; *ſtoria*, Italian; ἱϛορία.]

1. Hiſtory; account of things paſt.

The fable of the dividing of the world between the three ſons of Saturn, aroſe from the true *ſtory* of the dividing of the earth between the three brethren the ſons of Noah. *Raleigh.*

Thee I have heard relating what was done
Ere my remembrance: now hear me relate
My *ſtory* which perhaps thou haſt not heard. *Milton.*

To king Artaxerxes, thy ſervants Rathumnus the *ſtory*-writer, and Smellius the ſcribe. 1 *Eſdr.* ii. 17.

The four great monarchies make the ſubject of ancient *ſtory*, and are related by the Greek and Latin authors. *Temple.*

Governments that once made ſuch a noiſe, as founded upon the deepeſt counſels and the ſtrongeſt force; yet by ſome ſlight miſcarriage which let in ruin upon them, are now ſo utterly extinct, that nothing remains of them but a name; nor are there the leaſt traces of them to be found but only in *ſtory.* *South's Sermons.*

2. Small tale; petty narrative; account of a ſingle incident.

In the road between Bern and Soleurre, a monument erected by the republick of Bern, tells us the *ſtory* of an Engliſhman not to be met with in any of our own writers. *Addiſon.*

3. An idle or trifling tale; a petty fiction.

Theſe flaws and ſtarts, would well become
A woman's *ſtory* at a winter's fire,
Authoris'd by her grandame. *Shakeſpeare's Macbeth.*

This ſcene had ſome bold Greek or Britiſh bard
Beheld of old, what *ſtories* had we heard
Of fairies, ſatyrs, and the nymphs their dames,
Their feaſts, their revels, and their am'rous flames. *Denham.*

My maid left on the table one of her *ſtory*-books, which I found full of ſtrange impertinence, of poor ſervants who came to be ladies. *Swift.*

4. [ꞅꞇoꞃ, place, Saxon.] A floor; a flight of rooms.

Avoid enormous heights of ſeven *ſtories*, as well as irregular forms, and the contrary fault of low diſtended fronts. *Wotton.*

Sonnets or elegies to Chloris,
Might raiſe a houſe about two *ſtories*;
A lyrick ode wou'd ſlate; a catch
Would tile; an epigram would thatch. *Swift.*

To STORY. *v. a.* [from the noun.]

1. To tell in hiſtory; to relate.

How worthy he is, I will leave to appear hereafter, rather than *ſtory* him in his own hearing. *Shakeſpeare's Cymbeline.*

'Tis not vain or fabulous
What the ſage poets, taught by th' heav'nly muſe,
Story'd of old in high immortal verſe,
Of dire chimera's and enchanted iſles,
And rifted rocks; whoſe entrance leads to hell. *Milton.*

It is *ſtoried* of the brazen Coloſſus, in the iſland of Rhodes, that it was ſeventy cubits high; the thumbs of it being ſo big, that no man could graſp one of them about with both his arms. *Wilkins.*

Recite them, nor in erring pity fear,
To wound with *ſtoried* griefs the filial ear. *Pope.*

2. To range one under another.

Becauſe all the parts of an undiſturbed fluid are of equal gravity, or gradually placed or *ſtoried* according to the difference of it; any concretion that can be ſuppoſed to be naturally and mechanically made in ſuch a fluid, muſt have a like ſtructure of its ſeveral parts; that is, either be all over of a ſimilar gravity, or have the more ponderous parts nearer to its baſis. *Bentley's Sermons.*

STO'RYTELLER. *n. ſ.* [*ſtory* and *tell.*] One who relates tales; An hiſtorian. In contempt.

In ſuch a ſatire all would ſeek a ſhare,
And every fool will fancy he is there;
Old *ſtorytellers* too muſt pine and die,
To ſee their antiquated wit laid by;
Like her, who miſs'd her name in a lampoon,
And griev'd to find herſelf decay'd ſo ſoon. *Dryden.*

Company will be no longer peſtered with dull, dry, tedious *ſtorytellers.* *Swift's Polite Converſation.*

STOVE. *n. ſ.* [*ſtoo*, Iſlandick, a fire place; ꞅꞇoꝼa, Saxon; *eſtuve*, French; *ſtove*, Dutch.]

1. A hot houſe; a place artificially made warm.

Fiſhermen who make holes in the ice, to dip up ſuch fiſh with their nets as reſort thither for breathing, light on ſwallows congealed in clods, of a ſlimy ſubſtance, and carrying them home to their *ſtoves*, the warmth recovereth them to life and flight. *Carew's Survey of Cornwall.*

The heat which ariſes out of the leſſer ſpiracles brings forth nitre and ſulphur; ſome of which it affixes to the tops and ſides of the grotto's, which are uſually ſo hot as to ſerve for natural *ſtoves* or ſweating vaults. *Woodward.*

The moſt proper place for unction is a *ſtove.* *Wiſeman.*

2. A place in which fire is made, and by which heat is communicated.

If the ſeaſon prove exceeding piercing, in your great houſe kindle ſome charcoals; and when they have done ſmoaking, put them into a hole ſunk a little into the floor, about the middle of it. This is the ſafeſt *ſtove.* *Evelyn.*

To STOVE *v. a.* [from the noun.] To keep warm in a houſe artificially heated.

For December, January, and the latter part of November, take ſuch things as are green all winter; orange trees, lemon trees, and myrtles, if they be *ſtoved*; and ſweet marjoram warm ſet. *Bacon.*

To STOUND. *v. n.* [*ſtunde*, I grieved, Iſlandick.]

1. To be in pain or ſorrow. Out of uſe.

2. For *ſtun'd.* *Spenſer.*

STOUND. *n. ſ.* [from the verb.]

1. Sorrow; grief; miſhap. Out of uſe. The *Scots* retain it.

Begin and end the bitter baleful *ſtound*,
If leſs than that I fear. *Fair. Queen.*

The fox his copeſmate found,
To whom complaining his unhappy *ſtound*,
He with him far'd ſome better chance to find. *Hubberd.*

2. Aſtoniſhment; amazement.

Thus we ſtood as in a *ſtound*,
And wet with tears, like dew, the ground. *Gay.*

3. Hour; time; ſeaſon. *Spenſer.*

STOUR. *n. ſ.* [*ſtur*, Runick, a battle; ꞅꞇeoꞃan, Saxon, to diſturb.] Aſſault; incurſion; tumult. Obſolete.

And he that harrow'd hell with heavy *ſtour*,
The faulty ſouls from thence brought to his heavenly bowr. *Fairy Queen.*

Love, that long ſince has to thy mighty powre
Per force ſubdu'd my poor captived heart,
And raging now therein with reſtleſs *ſtowre*,
Do'ſt tyrannize in every weaker part. *Spenſer.*

The giant ſtruck ſo mainly mercileſs,
That cou'd have overthrown a ſtonny tower,
And were not heavenly grace that him did bleſs,
He had been pouldered all as thin as flower,
But he was wary of that deadly *ſtowre*. *Fairy Queen.*

STOUT. *n. ſ.* [*ſtout*, Dutch; *ſtolz*, proud, German; *ſtautan*, Gothick, is to ſtrike.]

1. Strong; luſty; valiant.

When I was young,
I do remember how my father ſaid,
A *ſtouter* champion never handled ſword. *Shakeſ. Hen.* VI.

Some captain of the land or fleet,
Stout of his hands, but of a ſoldier's wit;
Cries, I have ſenſe to ſerve my turn, in ſtore,
And he's a raſcal who pretends to more. *Dryden.*

2. Brave; bold; intrepid.

The *ſtout*-hearted are ſpoiled, they have ſlept their ſleep. *Pſal.* lxxvi. 5.

He loſt the character of a bold, *ſtout*, and magnanimous man, which he had been long reputed to be. *Clarendon.*

3. Obſtinate; pertinacious; reſolute; proud.

The lords all ſtand,
To clear their cauſe, moſt reſolutely *ſtout*. *Daniel.*

There virtue and *ſtout* honour paſs'd the guard,
Thoſe only friends that could not be debar'd. *Bathurſt.*

4. Strong; firm.

The *ſtouteſt* veſſel to the ſtorm gave way,
And ſuck'd through looſen'd planks the ruſhing ſea. *Dryden.*

STOUT. *n. ſ.* A cant name for ſtrong beer.

Should but his muſe deſcending drop
A ſlice of bread and mutton chop,
Or kindly, when his credit's out,
Surpriſe him with a pint of *ſtout*;
Exalted in his mighty mind,
He flies and leaves the ſtars behind. *Swift.*

STOU'TLY. *adv.* [from *ſtout.*] Luſtily; boldly; obſtinately.

STOU'TNESS. *n. ſ.* [from *ſtout.*]

1. Strength; valour.

2. Boldneſs; fortitude.

His baſhfulneſs in youth was the very true ſign of his virtue and *ſtoutneſs* after. *Aſcham's Schoolmaſter.*

3. Obſtinacy; ſtubborneſs.

Come all to ruin, let
Thy mother rather feel thy pride, than fear
Thy dangerous *ſtoutneſs*: for I mock at death
With as ſtout heart as thou. *Shakeſpeare's Coriolanus.*

To STOW. *v. a.* [ꞅꞇop, Sax. *ſtoe*, old Friſick, a place; *ſtowen*, Dutch; to lay up.] To lay up; to repoſite in order; to lay in the proper place.

Foul thief! where haſt thou *ſtow'd* my daughter? *Shak.*

I'th'holſters of the ſaddle-bow,
Two aged piſtols he did *ſtow*. *Hudibras.*

Some *ſtow* their oars, or ſtop the leaky ſides. *Dryden.*

All the patriots of their ancient liberties were beheaded, *ſtowed* in dungeons, or condemned to work in the mines. *Ad.*

The goddeſs ſhov'd the veſſel from the ſhores,
And *ſtow'd* within its womb the naval ſtores. *Pope.*

STOW'AGE. *n. ſ.* [from *ſtow.*]

1. Room for laying up.

In every veſſel there is *ſtowage* for immenſe treaſures, when the cargo is pure bullion, or merchandize of as great a value. *Addiſon on the State of the War.*

2. The ſtate of being laid up.

'Tis plate of rare device, and jewels
Of rich and exquiſite form, their value's great;
And I am ſomething curious, being ſtrange,
To have them in ſafe *ſtowage*. *Shakeſpeare's Cymbeline.*

STOWE, *ſtoe*. Whether ſingly or jointly are the ſame with the Saxon ꞅꞇop, a place. *Gibſon's Camden.*

STRA'BISM. *n. ſ.* [*ſtrabiſme*, Fr. στραβισμὸς.] A ſquinting; act of looking aſquint.

To STRA'DDLE. *v. n.* [Suppoſed to come from *ſtriddle* or *ſtride.*] To ſtand or walk with the feet removed far from each other to the right and left.

Let man ſurvey himſelf, diveſted of artificial charms, and he will find himſelf a forked *ſtradling* animal, with bandy legs. *Arbuthnot and Pope.*

To STRA'GGLE. [Of this word no etymology is known; it is probably a frequentative of *ſtray*, from *ſtravviare*, Italian, of *extraviam*, Latin.]

1. To wander without any certain direction; to rove; to ramble.

But ſtay, like one that thinks to bring his friend
A mile or two, and ſees the journey's end:
I *ſtraggle* on too far. *Suckling.*

Having paſſed the Syrens, they came between Scylla and Charybdis, and the *ſtraggling* rocks, which ſeemed to caſt out great ſtore of flames and ſmoke. *Raleigh.*

A wolf ſpied out a *ſtraggling* kid, and purſued him. *L'Eſtr.*

Children, even when they endeavour their utmoſt, cannot keep their minds from *ſtraggling*. *Locke.*

2. To wander diſperſedly.

He likewiſe enriched poor *ſtraggling* ſoldiers with great quantity. *Shakeſpeare's Timon of Athens.*

They found in Burford ſome of the *ſtraggling* ſoldiers, who out of wearineſs ſtayed behind. *Clarendon.*

From *ſtraggling* mountaineers for publick good,
To rank in tribes, and quit the ſavage wood;
Houſes to build, and them contiguous make,
For cheerful neighbourhood and ſafety's ſake. *Tate.*

3. To exuberate; to ſhoot too far.

Were they content to prune the laviſh vine,
Of *ſtraggling* branches, and improve the wine,

Trim off the ſmall ſuperfluous branches on each ſide of the hedge that *ſtraggle* too far out. *Mortimer's Huſbandry.*

4. To be diſperſed; to be apart from any main body; to ſtand ſingle.

Wide was his pariſh, not contracted cloſe
In ſtreets, but here and there a *ſtraggling* houſe;
Yet ſtill he was at hand. *Dryden.*

STRA'GGLER. *n. ſ.* [from *ſtraggle.*]

1. A wanderer; a rover; one who forſakes his company; one who rambles without any ſettled direction.

The laſt ſhould keep the countries from paſſage of *ſtragglers* from thoſe parts, whence they uſe to come forth, and oftentimes uſe to work much miſchief. *Spenſer's Ireland.*

Let's whip theſe *ſtragglers* o'er the ſeas again,
Laſh hence theſe over-weening rags of France,
Theſe famiſh'd beggars. *Shakeſpeare's Richard* III.

His pruning hook corrects the vines,
And the looſe *ſtragglers* to their ranks confines. *Pope.*

Bottles miſſing are ſuppoſed to be half ſtolen by *ſtragglers*, and the other half broken. *Swift.*

2. Any thing that puſhes beyond the reſt, or ſtands ſingle.

Let thy hand ſupply the pruning knife,
And crop luxuriant *ſtragglers*, nor be loth
To ſtrip the branches of their leafy growth. *Dryden.*

STRAIGHT. *adj.* [*ſtrack*, old Dutch. It is well obſerved by *Ainſworth*, that for *not* crooked we ought to write *ſtraight*, and for narrow *ſtrait*; but for *ſtreight*, which is ſometimes found, there is no good authority.]

1. Not crooked; right.

Beauty made barren the ſwell'd boaſt
Of him that beſt could ſpeak; feature, laming
The ſhrine of Venus, or *ſtraight*-pight Minerva. *Shakeſpeare.*

A hunter's horn and cornet is oblique; yet they have likewiſe *ſtraight* horns; which, if they be of the ſame bore with the oblique, differ little in ſound, ſave that the *ſtraight* require ſomewhat a ſtronger blaſt. *Bacon's Natural Hiſtory.*

There are many ſeveral ſorts of crooked lines; but there is one only which is *ſtraight* *Dryden.*

Water and air the varied form confound;
The *ſtraight* looks crooked, and the ſquare grows round. *Prior.*

When I ſee a *ſtrait* ſtaff appear crooked while half under the water, the water gives me a falſe idea. *Watts's Logick.*

2. Narrow; cloſe. This ſhould properly be *ſtrait*, *eſtroit*, Fr. [See STRAIT.]

Queen Elizabeth uſed to ſay of her inſtructions to great officers, that they were like to garments, *ſtrait* at the firſt putting on, but did by and by wear looſe enough. *Bacon.*

STRAIGHT. *adv.* [*ſtrax*, Daniſh; *ſtrack*, Dutch.] Immediately; directly. This ſenſe is naturally derived from the adjective, as a *ſtraight* line is the ſhorteſt line between two points.

If the devil come and roar for them,
I will not ſend them. I will after *ſtraight*,
And tell him ſo. *Shakeſpeare's Henry* IV.

Thoſe ſtinks which the noſtrils *ſtraight* abhor and expel, are not the moſt pernicious. *Bacon's Natural Hiſtory.*

With chalk I firſt deſcribe a circle here,
Where the ætherial ſpirits muſt appear:
Come in, come in; for here they will be *ſtrait*:
Around, around the place I fumigate. *Dryden.*

I know thy generous temper well,
Fling but the appearance of diſhonour on it,
It *ſtraight* takes fire, and mounts into a blaze. *Addiſon.*

To STRAI'GHTEN. *v. a.* [from *ſtraight.*] To make not crooked; to make ſtraight.

A crooked ſtick is not *ſtraightened* except it be as far bent on the clean contrary ſide. *Hooker.*

Of our ſelves being ſo apt to err, the only way which we have to *ſtraighten* our paths is, by following the rule of his will, whoſe footſteps naturally are right. *Hooker.*

STRAI'GHTNESS. *n. ſ.* [from *ſtraight.*] Rectitude; the contrary to crookedneſs.

Some are for maſts, as fir and pine, becauſe of their length and *ſtraightneſs*. *Bacon's Natural Hiſtory.*

STRAI'GHTWAYS. *adv.* [*ſtraight* and *way.* Immediately; ſtraight.

Let me here for ay in peace remain,
Or *ſtraightway* on that laſt long voyage fare. *Fairy Queen.*
Soon as he entred was, the door *ſtraightway*
Did ſhut. *Fairy Queen.*
Thus ſtands my ſtate, 'twixt Cade and York diſtreſt;
Like to a ſhip, that, having 'ſcap'd a tempeſt,
Is *ſtraitway* claim'd and boarded with a pirate. *Shakeſp.*
Blood will I draw on thee, thou art a witch,
And *ſtraightway* give thy ſoul to him thou ſerv'ſt. *Shakeſpeare.*

The Turks *ſtraightway* breaking in upon them, made a bloody fight. *Knolles.*

As ſoon as iron is out of the fire, it deadeth *ſtraightways.* *Bacon's Natural Hiſtory.*

The ſound of a bell is ſtrong; continueth ſome time after the percuſſion; but ceaſeth *ſtraightways* if the bell or ſtring be touched. *Bacon's Natural Hiſtory.*

The ſun's power being in thoſe months greater, it then *ſtraightways* hurries ſteams up into the atmoſphere. *Woodward.*

To STRAIN. *v. a.* [*eſtreindre*, French.]

1. To ſqueeze through ſomething.

Their aliment ought to be light, rice boiled in whey and *ſtrained.* *Arbuthnot on Diet.*

2. To purify by filtration.

Earth doth not *ſtrain* water ſo finely as ſand. *Bacon.*

3. To ſqueeze in an embrace.

I would have *ſtrain'd* him with a ſtrict embrace;
But through my arms he ſlipt and vaniſh'd. *Dryden.*
Old Evander, with a cloſe embrace,
Strain'd his departing friend; and tears o'erflow his face. *Dryden's Æneid.*

4. To ſprain; to weaken by too much violence.

The jury make no more ſcruple to paſs againſt an Engliſhman and the queen, though it be to *ſtrain* their oaths, than to drink milk unſtrained. *Spenſer's State of Ireland.*

Prudes decay'd about may tack,
Strain their necks with looking back. *Swift.*

5. To put to its utmoſt ſtrength.

By this we ſee in a cauſe of religion, to how deſperate adventures men will *ſtrain* themſelves for relief of their own part, having law and authority againſt them. *Hooker.*

Too well I wote my humble vaine,
And how my rhimes been rugged and unkempt;
Yet as I con my cunning I will *ſtrain.* *Spenſer.*
Thus mine enemy fell,
And thus I ſet my foot on's neck;—even then
The princely blood flows in his cheek, he ſweats,
Strains his young nerves, and puts himſelf in poſture
That acts my words. *Shakeſpeare's Cymbeline.*
My earthly by his heavenly overpower'd,
Which it had long ſtood under, *ſtrain'd* to th' height
In that celeſtial colloquy ſublime,
As with an object that excels the ſenſe,
Dazled and ſpent, ſunk down. *Milton's Parad. Loſt.*
The lark and linnet ſing with rival notes;
They *ſtrain* their warbling throats,
To welcome in the ſpring. *Dryden.*
Nor yet content, ſhe *ſtrains* her malice more,
And adds new ills to thoſe contriv'd before. *Dryden.*

It is the worſt ſort of good huſbandry for a father not to *ſtrain* himſelf a little for his ſon's breeding. *Locke.*

Our words flow from us in a ſmooth continued ſtream, without thoſe *ſtrainings* of the voice, motions of the body, and majeſty of the hand, which are ſo much celebrated in the orators of Greece and Rome. *Atterbury.*

Strain'd to the root, the ſtooping foreſt pours
A ruſtling ſhower of yet untimely leaves. *Thomſon.*

6. To make ſtrait or tenſe.

A bigger ſtring more *ſtrained*, and a leſſer ſtring leſs *ſtrained*, may fall into the ſame tone. *Bacon.*

Thou, the more he varies forms, beware
To *ſtrain* his fetters with a ſtricter care. *Dryden's Virgil.*

7. To puſh beyond the proper extent.

See they ſuffer death,
But in their deaths remember they are men,
Strain not the laws to make their torture grievous. *Addiſon.*

There can be no other meaning in this expreſſion, however ſome may pretend to *ſtrain* it. *Swift.*

8. To force; to conſtrain; to make uneaſy or unnatural.

The lark ſings ſo out of tune,
Straining harſh diſcords and unpleaſing ſtrains. *Shakeſpeare.*
He talks and plays with Fatima, but his mirth
Is forc'd and *ſtrain'd*: in his looks appears
A wild diſtracted fierceneſs. *Denham.*

To STRAIN. *v. n.* To make violent efforts.

To build his fortune I will *ſtrain* a little,
For 'tis a bond in men. *Shakeſp. Timon of Athens.*
You ſtand like greyhounds in the ſlips,
Straining upon the ſtart. *Shakeſp. Hen.* V.
They *ſtrain*,
That death may not them idly find t' attend
Their certain laſt, but work to meet their end. *Daniel.*

Straining with too weak a wing,
We needs will write epiſtles to the king. *Pope.*

2. To be filtred by compreſſion.

Cæſar thought that all ſea ſands had natural ſprings of freſh water: but it is the ſea water; becauſe the pit filled according to the meaſure of the tide, and the ſea water paſſing or *ſtraining* through the ſands leaveth the ſaltneſs behind them. *Bacon.*

STRAIN. *n. ſ.* [from the verb.]

1. An injury by too much violence.

Credit is gained by cuſtom, and ſeldom recovers a *ſtrain*; but if broken, is never well ſet again. *Temple.*

In all pain there is a deformity by a ſolution of continuity, as in cutting; or a tendency to ſolution, as in convulſions or *ſtrains.* *Grew.*

2. [ſtrenge, Saxon.] Race; generation; deſcent. *Spenſer.*

Thus far I can praiſe him; he is of a noble *ſtrain*,
Of approv'd valour. *Shakeſpeare.*
Twelve Trojan youths, born of their nobleſt *ſtrains*,
I took alive: and, yet enrag'd, will empty all their veins
Of vital ſpirits. *Chapman's Iliad.*
Why do'ſt thou falſly feign
Thyſelf a Sidney? from which noble *ſtrain*
He ſprung, that could ſo far exalt the name
Of love. *Waller.*
Turn then to Pharamond, and Charlemagne,
And the long heroes of the Gallick *ſtrain.* *Prior.*

3. Hereditary diſpoſition.

Amongſt theſe ſweet knaves and all this courteſy! the *ſtrain* of man's bred out into baboon and monkey. *Shakeſpeare.*

Intemperance and luſt breed diſeaſes, which propagated, ſpoil the *ſtrain* of a nation. *Tillotſon.*

4. A ſtile or manner of ſpeaking.

According to the genius and *ſtrain* of the book of Proverbs, the words wiſdom and righteouſneſs are uſed to ſignify all religion and virtue. *Tillotſon's Sermons.*

In our liturgy are as great *ſtrains* of true ſublime eloquence, as are any where to be found in our language. *Swift.*

Macrobius ſpeaks of Hippocrates' knowlege in very lofty *ſtrains.* *Baker.*

5. Song; note; ſound.

Wilt thou love ſuch a woman? what, to make thee an inſtrument, and play falſe *ſtrains* upon thee. *Shakeſpeare.*

Orpheus ſelf may heave his head
From golden ſlumber on a bed
Of heap'd Elyſian flowers, and hear
Such *ſtrains* as would have won the ear
Of Pluto, to have quite ſet free
His half-regain'd Eurydice. *Milton.*
Their heav'nly harps a lower *ſtrain* began,
And in ſoft muſick mourn the fall of man. *Dryden.*
When the firſt bold veſſel dar'd the ſeas,
High on the ſtern the Thracian rais'd his *ſtrain*,
While Argo ſaw her kindred trees
Deſcend from Pelion to the main. *Pope's St. Cecilia.*

6. Rank; character.

But thou who lately of the common *ſtrain*,
Wert one of us, if ſtill thou do'ſt retain
The ſame ill habits, the ſame follies too,
Still thou art bound to vice, and ſtill a ſlave *Dryden.*

7. Turn; tendency.

Becauſe hereticks have a *ſtrain* of madneſs, he applied her with ſome corporal chaſtiſements, which with reſpite of time might haply reduce her to good order. *Hayward.*

8. Manner of violent ſpeech or action.

You have ſhew'd to-day your valiant *ſtrain*,
And fortune led you well. *Shakeſp. King Lear.*

Such take too high a *ſtrain* at the firſt, and are magnanimous more than tract of years can uphold, as was Scipio Africanus, of whom Livy ſaith, *ultima primis cedebant.* *Bacon.*

STRAINER. *n. ſ.* [from *ſtrain.*] An inſtrument of filtration.

The excrementitious moiſture paſſeth in birds through a finer and more delicate *ſtrainer* than it doth in beaſts; for feathers paſs through quills, and hair through ſkin. *Bacon.*

Shave the goat's ſhaggy beard, leſt thou too late
In vain ſhould'ſt ſeek a *ſtrainer* to diſpart
The huſky terrene dregs from purer muſt. *Philips.*

The ſtomach and inteſtines are the preſs, and the lacteal veſſels the *ſtrainers* to ſeparate the pure emulſion from its feces. *Arb.*

Theſe when condens'd, the airy region pours
On the dry earth, in rain or gentle ſhowers,
Th' inſinuating drops ſink through the ſand,
And paſs the porous *ſtrainers* of the land. *Blackmore.*

STRAIT. *adj.* [*eſtroit*, French; *ſtretto*, Italian.]

1. Narrow; cloſe; not wide.

Witneſſes, like watches go
Juſt as they're ſet, too faſt or ſlow;
And where in conſcience they're *ſtreight* lac'd,
'Tis ten to one that ſide is caſt. *Hudibras.*

2. Cloſe; intimate.

He, forgetting all former injuries, had received that naughty Plexirtus into a *ſtraight* degree of favour, his goodneſs being as apt to be deceived, as the other's craft was to deceive. *Sidney.*

3. Strict; rigorous.

Therefore hold I *strait* all thy commandments; and all false ways I utterly abhor. *Psalms, Common Prayer.*

Fugitives are not relieved by the profit of their lands in England, for there is a *straighter* order taken. *Spenser.*

He now, forsooth, takes on him to reform
Some certain edicts, and some *strait* decrees
That lay too heavy on the commonwealth. *Shakespeare.*

4. Difficult; distressful.

Proceed no *straiter* 'gainst our uncle Glo'ster,
Than from the evidence of good esteem,
He be approv'd in practice culpable. *Shakesp. Henry VI.*

5. It is used in opposition to crooked, but is then more properly written *straight.* [See STREIGHT.]

A bell or a cannon may be heard beyond a hill which intercepts the sight of the sounding body, and sounds are propagated as readily through crooked pipes as through *streight* ones. *Newton's Opticks.*

STRAIT. *n. s.*

1. A narrow pass, or frith.

Plant garrisons to command the *streights* and narrow passages. *Spenser.*

Honour travels in a *streight* so narrow,
Where one but goes abreast. *Shakespeare's Troil. and Cressida.*

Fretum Magellanicum, or Magellan's *Straits.* *Abbot.*

They went forth unto the *straits* of the mountain. *Judith.*

The Saracens brought together with their victories their language and religion into all that coast of Africk, even from Egypt to the *streights* of Gibraltar. *Brerewood on Languages.*

2. Distress; difficulty.

The independent party which abhorred all motions towards peace, were in as great *streights* as the other how to carry on their designs. *Clarendon.*

It was impossible to have administred such advice to the king, in the *streight* he was in, which being pursued might not have proved inconvenient. *Clarendon.*

Thyself
Bred up in poverty, and *streights* at home,
Lost in a desart here, and hunger-bit. *Milton's Paradise Reg.*

Thus Adam, sore beset! reply'd,
O heav'n! in evil *streight* this day I stand
Before my Judge. *Milton's Paradise Lost.*

Let no man who owns a Providence grow desperate under any calamity or *strait* whatsoever, but compose the anguish of his thoughts upon this one consideration, that he comprehends not those strange unaccountable methods by which Providence may dispose of him. *South's Sermons.*

Some modern authors observing what *straits* they have been put to in all ages, to find out water enough for Noah's flood, say, Noah's flood was not universal, but a national inundation. *Burnet's Theory of the Earth.*

'Tis hard with me, whatever choice I make,
I must not merit you, or must forsake:
But in this *streight*, to honour I'll be true,
And leave my fortune to the gods and you. *Dryden.*

Cæsar sees
The *streights* to which you're driven, and as he knows
Cato's high worth, is anxious for your life. *Addison's Cato.*

Ulysses made use of the pretence of natural infirmity to conceal the *straits* he was in at that time in his thoughts. *Broome.*

To STRAIT. *v. a.* [from the noun.] To put to difficulties.

If your lass
Interpretation should abuse, and call this
Your lack of love or bounty; you were *straited*
For a reply, at least, if you make care
Of happy holding her. *Shakespeare's Winter's Tale.*

To STRAI'TEN. *v. a.* [from *strait.*]

1. To make narrow.

The city of Sion has a secure haven, yet with something a dangerous entrance, *straitened* on the north side by the sea-ruined wall of the mole. *Sandys's Journey.*

If this be our condition, thus to dwell
In narrow circuit, *straiten'd* by a foe,
Subtile or violent. *Milton's Paradise Lost.*

Whatever *straitens* the vessels, so as the channels become more narrow, must heat; therefore strait cloaths and cold baths, heat. *Arbuthnot on Diet.*

2. To contract; to confine.

The *straitning* and confining the profession of the common law, must naturally extend and enlarge the jurisdiction of the church. *Clarendon.*

The landed man finds him aggrieved by the falling of his rents, and the *streightning* of his fortune, whilst the monied man keeps up his gain. *Locke.*

Feeling can give us a notion of all ideas that enter at the eye, except colours; but it is very much *streightened* and confined to the number, bulk, and distance of its objects. *Addison.*

The causes which *straiten* the British commerce, will enlarge the French. *Addison's State of the War.*

3. To make tight; to intend.

Stretch them at their length,
And pull the *streighten'd* cords with all your strength. *Dryd.*

Morality, by her false guardians drawn,
Chicane in furs, and casuistry in lawn,
Gasps, as they *straiten* at each end the cord,
And dies when dulness gives her page the word. *Dunciad.*

4. To deprive of necessary room.

Waters when *straitned* as in the falls of bridges, give a roaring noise. *Bacon's Natural History.*

He could not be *streightned* in room or provisions, or compelled to fight. *Clarendon.*

Several congregations find themselves very much *straitned*, and if the mode encrease, I wish it may not drive many ordinary women into meetings. *Addison's Spectator.*

5. To distress; to perplex.

Men by continually striving and fighting to enlarge their bounds, and encroaching upon one another, seem to be *straitned* for want of room. *Ray.*

STRAI'TLY. *adv.* [from *strait.*]

1. Narrowly.

2. Strictly; rigorously.

Those laws he *straitly* requireth to be observed without breach or blame. *Hooker.*

3. Closely; intimately.

STRAI'TNESS. *n. s.* [from *strait.*]

1. Narrowness.

The town was hard to besiege, and uneasy to come unto, by reason of the *straitness* of all the places. 2 *Maccab.* xii.

It is a great errour, and a narrowness or *straitness* of mind, if any man think that nations have nothing to do one with another, except there be an union in sovereignty, or a conjunction in pact. *Bacon's Holy War.*

The *straitness* of my conscience will not give me leave to swallow down such camels. *King Charles.*

2. Strictness; rigour.

If his own life answer the *straitness* of his proceeding, it shall become him well. *Shakespeare.*

Among the Romans, the laws of the twelve tables did exclude the females from inheriting, and had many other *straitnesses* and hardships which were successively remedied. *Hale.*

3. Distress; difficulty.

4. Want; scarcity.

The *straitness* of the conveniences of life amongst them had never reached so far, as to the use of fire, till the Spaniards brought it amongst them. *Locke.*

STRAITLA'CED. *adj.* [*strait* and *lace.*] Stiff; constrained; without freedom.

Let nature have scope to fashion the body as she thinks best; we have few well-shaped that are *straitlaced*, or much tamper'd with. *Locke on Education.*

STRAKE. The obsolete preterite of *strike.* Struck.

Did'st thou not see a bleeding hind
Whose right haunch earst my stedfast arrow *strake.* *Spenser.*

Fearing lest they should fall into the quick-sands, they *strake* sail, and so were driven. *Acts* xxvii. 17.

STRAND. *n. s.* [ꞅꞇꞃanꝺ, Saxon; *strande*, Dutch; *strend*, Islandick.] The verge of the sea or of any water.

I saw sweet beauty in her face;
Such as the daughter of Agenor had,
That made great Jove to humble him to her hand,
When with his knees he kiss'd the Cretan *strand.* *Shakesp.*

Some wretched lines from this neglected hand,
May find my hero on the foreign *strand*,
Warm'd with new fires. *Prior.*

To STRAND. *v. a.* [from the noun.] To drive or force upon the shallows.

Tarchon's alone was lost, and *stranded* stood,
Stuck on a bank, and beaten by the flood. *Dryden's Æneid.*

I have seen of both those kinds from the sea, but so few that they can only be such as have strayed from their main residence, and been accidentally intercepted and *stranded* by great storms. *Woodward on Fossils.*

Some from the *stranded* vessel force their way,
Fearful of fate they meet it in the sea;
Some who escape the fury of the wave,
Sicken on earth, and sink into a grave. *Prior.*

STRANGE. *adj.* [*estrange*, French; *extraneus*, Latin.]

1. Foreign; of another country.

I do not contemn the knowledge of *strange* and divers tongues. *Ascham's Schoolmaster.*

The natural subjects of the state should bear a sufficient proportion to the *strange* subjects that they govern. *Bacon.*

2. Not domestick.

As the man loves least at home to be,
That hath a sluttish house, haunted with sprites;
So she, impatient her own faults to see,
Turns from herself, and in *strange* things delights. *Davies.*

3. Wonderful; causing wonder.

It is evident, and it is one of the *strangest* secrets in sounds, that the whole sound is not in the whole air only; but is also in every small part of the air. *Bacon's Natural History.*

Sated at length, ere long I might perceive
Strange alteration in me. *Milton.*

It

It is *strange* they should be so silent in this matter, when there were so many occasions to speak of it, if our Saviour had plainly appointed such an infallible judge of controversies. *Till.*

Strange to relate, from young Iülus' head
A lambent flame arose, which gently spread
Around his brows, and on his temples fed. *Dryden's Æn.*

Strange to relate, the flames, involv'd in smoke
Of incense, from the sacred altar broke. *Dryden's Æn.*

3. Odd; irregular; not according to the common way.

Desire my man's abode, where I did leave him:
He's *strange* and peevish. *Shakesp. Cymbeline.*

A *strange* proud return you may think I make you, madam, when I tell you it is not from every body I would be thus obliged. *Suckling.*

4. Unknown; new.

Long custom had inured them to the former kind alone, by which the latter was new and *strange* in their ears. *Hooker.*

Here is the hand and seal of the duke: you know the character, I doubt not; and the signet is not *strange* to you. *Shak.*

Joseph saw his brethren, but made himself *strange* unto them. *Gen.* xlii. 7.

Here passion first I felt,
Commotion *strange!* *Milton:*

5. Remote.

She makes it *strange*, but she would be best pleas'd
To be so anger'd with another letter. *Shakespeare.*

6. Uncommonly good or bad.

This made David to admire the law of God at that *strange* rate, and to advance the knowledge of it above all other knowledge. *Tillotson.*

7. Unacquainted.

They were now, like sand without lime, ill bound together, at a gaze, looking *strange* one upon another, not knowing who was faithful. *Bacon.*

STRANGE. *interj.* An expression of wonder.

Strange! what extremes should thus preserve the snow,
High on the Alps, or in deep caves below. *Waller.*

Strange! that fatherly authority should be the only original of government, and yet all mankind not know it. *Locke.*

To STRANGE. *v. n.* [from the adjective.] To wonder; to be astonished.

Were all the assertions of Aristotle such as theology pronounceth impieties, which we *strange* not at from one, of whom a father saith, *Nec Deum coluit, nec curavit.* *Glanv.*

STRA'NGELY. *adv.* [from *strange.*]

1. With some relation to foreigners.

As by strange fortune
It came to us, I do in justice charge thee
That thou commend it *strangely* to some place,
Where chance may nurse or end it. *Shakesp. Winter's Tale.*

2. Wonderfully; in a way to cause wonder, but with a degree of dislike.

My former speeches have but hit your thoughts,
Which can interpret farther: only, I say,
Things have been *strangely* borne. *Shakesp. Macbeth.*

How *strangely* active are the arts of peace,
Whose restless motions less than wars do cease;
Peace is not freed from labour, but from noise;
And war more force, but not more pains, employs. *Dryden.*

We should carry along with us some of those virtuous qualities, which we were *strangely* careless if we did not bring from home with us. *Sprat's Sermons.*

In a time of affliction the remembrance of our good deeds will *strangely* cheer and support our spirits. *Calamy.*

STRA'NGENESS. *n. s.* [from *strange.*]

1. Foreignness; the state of belonging to another country.

If I will obey the Gospel, no distance of place, no *strangeness* of country can make any man a stranger to me. *Sprat.*

2. Uncommunicativeness; distance of behaviour.

Ungird thy *strangeness*, and tell me what I shall vent to my lady. *Shakes. Twelfth Night.*

Will you not observe
The *strangeness* of his alter'd countenance? *Shakes. H. VI.*

3. Remoteness from common apprehension; uncouthness.

Men worthier than himself
Here tend the savage *strangeness* he puts on;
And undergo, in an observing kind,
His humourous predominance. *Shakesp. Troil. and Cressida.*

This raised greater tumults and boilings in the hearts of men, than the *strangeness* and seeming unreasonableness of all the former articles. *South's Sermons.*

4. Mutual dislike.

In this peace there was an article that no Englishman should enter into Scotland, and no Scottishman into England, without letters commendatory: this might seem a means to continue a *strangeness* between the nations; but it was done to lock in the borderers. *Bacon.*

5. Wonderfulness; power of raising wonder.

If a man, for curiosity or *strangeness* sake, would make a puppet pronounce a word, let him consider the motion of the instruments of voice, and the like sounds made in inanimate bodies. *Bacon's Natural History.*

STRA'NGER. *n. s.* [*estranger*, French.]

1. A foreigner; one of another country.

I am a most poor woman, and a *stranger*,
Born out of your dominions; having here
No judge indiff'rent. *Shakesp. Henry VIII.*

Your daughter hath made a gross revolt;
Tying her duty, beauty, wit and fortunes
To an extravagant and wheeling *stranger*
Of here and every where. *Shakespeare.*

There is no place in Europe so much frequented by *strangers*, whether they are such as come out of curiosity, or such who are obliged to attend the court of Rome. *Addison on Italy.*

Melons on beds of ice are taught to bear,
And *strangers* to the sun yet ripen here. *Granville.*

After a year's inter-regnum from the death of Romulus, the senate of their own authority chose a successor, and a *stranger*, merely upon the fame of his virtues. *Swift.*

2. One unknown.

Strangers and foes do sunder, and not kiss. *Shakespeare.*

You did void your rheum upon my beard,
And foot me, as you spurn a *stranger* cur
Over your threshold. *Shakesp. Merchant of Venice.*

We ought to acknowledge, that no nations are wholly aliens and *strangers* the one to the other. *Bacon.*

That *stranger* guest the Taphean realm obeys. *Pope.*

They came, and near him plac'd the *stranger* guest. *Pope.*

3. A guest; one not a domestick.

He will vouchsafe
This day to be our guest: bring forth and pour
Abundance, fit to honour and receive
Our heavenly *stranger*. *Milton.*

4. One unacquainted.

My child is yet a *stranger* in the world;
She hath not seen the change of fourteen years. *Shakesp.*

I was no *stranger* to the original: I had also studied Virgil's design, and his disposition of it. *Dryden.*

5. One not admitted to any communication or fellowship.

I unspeak my detraction; here abjure
The taints and blames upon myself,
For *strangers* to my nature. *Shakesp. Macbeth.*

To STRA'NGER. *v. a.* [from the noun.] To estrange; to alienate.

Will you with those infirmities she owes,
Dower'd with our curse, and *stranger'd* with our oath,
Take her or leave her? *Shakespeare.*

To STRA'NGLE. *v. a.* [*strangulo*, Latin.]

1. To choak; to suffocate; to kill by intercepting the breath.

His face is black and full of blood;
His eye-balls farther out, than when he liv'd;
Staring full ghastly, like a *strangled* man. *Shakes. H. VI.*

Shall I not then be stifled in the vault,
To whose foul mouth no healthsome air breathes in,
And there be *strangled* ere my Romeo comes? *Shakespeare.*

Do'st thou not know that thou hast *strangled* thine husbands? *Tob.* iii. 8.

The lion did tear in pieces enough for his whelps, and *strangled* for his lionesses, and filled his holes with prey. *Neh.*

So heinous a crime was the sin of adultery, that our Saxon ancestors compelled the adulteress to *strangle* herself; and he who debauched her was to be hanged over her grave. *Ayliffe.*

2. To suppress; to hinder from birth or appearance.

By th' clock, 'tis day;
And yet dark night *strangles* the travelling lamp:
Is't night's predominance, or the day's shame? *Shak. Macb.*

STRA'NGLER. *n. s.* [from *strangle.*] One who strangles.

The band that seems to tie their friendship together, will be the very *strangler* of their amity. *Shak. Ant. and Cleopatra.*

STRA'NGLES. *n. s.* [from *strangle.*] Swellings in a horse's throat.

STRANGULA'TION. *n. s.* [from *strangle.*] The act of strangling; suffocation; the state of being strangled.

A spunge is mischievous, not in itself, for its powder is harmless; but because, being received into the stomach, it swelleth, and, occasioning its continual distension, induceth a *strangulation*. *Brown's Vulgar Errours.*

The reduction of the jaws is difficult, and, if they be not timely reduced, there happen paralysis and *strangulation*. *Wise.*

STRA'NGURY. *n. s.* [στραγγουρία; *stranguríe*, French.] A difficulty of urine attended with pain.

STRAP. *n. s.* [*stroppe*, Dutch; *stroppa*, Italian.] A narrow long slip of cloath or leather.

These cloaths are good enough to drink in, and so be these boots too; an' they be not, let them hang themselves in their own *straps*. *Shakesp. Twelfth Night.*

I found but one husband, a lively cobler, that kicked and spurred all the while his wife was carrying him on; and had scarce passed a day without giving her the discipline of the *strap*. *Addison's Spectator.*

STRAPPA'DO. *n. s.* Chastisement by blows.

Were I at the *strappado*, or all the racks in the world, I would not tell you on compulsion. *Shakespeare.*

STRA'PPING. *adj.* Vast; large; bulky. Used of large men or women in contempt.

STRATA. n. ſ. [The plural of *ſtratum*, Latin.] Beds; layers. A philoſophical term.

The terreſtrial matter is diſpoſed into *ſtrata*, or layers, placed one upon another; in like manner as any earthy ſediment, ſettling down from a fluid, will naturally be. *Woodward.*

With how much wiſdom are the *ſtrata* laid,
Of different weight and of a different kind,
Of ſundry forms for ſundry ends deſign'd! *Blackmore.*

STRA'TAGEM. *n. ſ.* [στράτηγημα; *ſtratageme*, French.]

1. An artifice in war; a trick by which an enemy is deceived.

John Talbot, I did ſend for thee,
To tutor thee in *ſtratagems* of war. *Shakeſp. Henry* VI.
Ev'ry minute now
Should be the father of ſome *ſtratagem*. *Shakeſ. Henry* IV.

2. An artifice; a trick by which ſome advantage is obtained.

Rouſe up your courage, call up all your counſels,
And think on all thoſe *ſtratagems* which nature
Keeps ready to encounter ſudden dangers. *Denham's Sophy.*
Thoſe oft are *ſtratagems* which errours ſeem;
Nor is it Homer nods, but we who dream. *Pope.*

To STRA'TIFY. *v. a.* [*ſtratifier*, Fr. from *ſtratum*, Lat.] To range in beds or layers. A chymical term.

STRATUM. *n. ſ.* [Latin.] A bed; a layer. A term of philoſophy.

Another was found in a perpendicular fiſſure of a *ſtratum* of ſtone in Langron iron-mine, Cumberland. *Woodward.*

Drill'd through the ſandy *ſtratum*, every way
The waters with the ſandy *ſtratum* riſe. *Thomſon.*

STRAW. *n. ſ.* [ſtreop, Saxon; *ſtroo*, Dutch.]

1. The ſtalk on which corn grows, and from which it is threſhed.

I can counterfeit the deep tragedian,
Tremble and ſtart at wagging of a *ſtraw*,
Intending deep ſuſpicion. *Shakeſp. Richard* III.
Plate ſin with gold,
And the ſtrong lance of juſtice hurtleſs breaks;
Arm it in rags, a pigmy's *ſtraw* doth pierce it. *Shakeſpeare.*

Apples in hay and *ſtraw* ripened apparently; but the apple in the *ſtraw* more. *Bacon's Natural Hiſtory.*

My new *ſtraw* hat, that's trimly lin'd with green,
Let Peggy wear. *Gay's Paſtorals.*
More light he treads, more tall he ſeems to riſe,
And ſtruts a *ſtraw* breadth nearer to the ſkies. *Tickell.*

2. Any thing proverbially worthleſs.

Thy arms, thy liberty, beſide
All that's on th' outſide of thy hide,
Are mine by military law,
Of which I will not bate one *ſtraw*. *Hudibras.*

'Tis not a *ſtraw* matter whether the main cauſe be right or wrong. *L'Eſtrange.*

STRA'WBERRY. *n. ſ.* [*fragaria*, Latin.] A plant.

It hath a perennial fibroſe root: the leaves are veined, growing upon each footſtalk; the ſtalks trail upon the ground: the cup of the flower conſiſts of one leaf, divided into ten equal parts, and expands in form of a ſtar: the flower conſiſts, for the moſt part, of five leaves, expanded in form of a roſe, and having many ſtamina in the middle, round the baſe of the ovary: the fruit is globoſe or oval, and conſiſts of a fleſhy eatable pulp, full of protuberances. The ſpecies are ſeven. *Mill.*

The *ſtrawberry* grows underneath the nettle,
And wholeſome berries thrive and ripen beſt,
Neighbour'd by fruit of baſer quality. *Shak. Henry* V.
Content with food, which nature freely bred,
On wildings and on *ſtrawberries* they fed. *Dryden.*

Strawberries, by their fragrant ſmell, ſeem to be cordial: the ſeeds obtained by ſhaking the ripe fruit in Winter, are an excellent remedy againſt the ſtone. The juice of *ſtrawberries* and limmons in ſpring-water is an excellent drink in bilious fevers. *Arbuthnot on Diet.*

STRA'WBERRY *Tree.* *n. ſ.* [*arbutus*, Latin.]

It is ever green, the leaves roundiſh and ſerrated on the edges: the flowers conſiſt of one leaf, and ſhaped like a pitcher: the fruit is of a fleſhy ſubſtance, and very like a ſtrawberry; divided into five cells, which contain many ſmall feeds. *Miller.*

STRA'WBUILT. *adj.* [*ſtraw* and *built.*] Made up of ſtraw.

They on the ſmoothed plank,
The ſuburb of their *ſtrawbuilt* citadel,
New rubb'd with balm, expatiate. *Milton.*

STRA'WCOLOURED. *adj.* [*ſtraw* and *colour.*] Of a light yellow.

I will diſcharge it in your *ſtrawcolour'd* beard. *Shakeſpeare.*

STRA'WWORM. *n. ſ.* [*ſtraw* and *worm.*] A worm bred in ſtraw.

STRA'WY. *adj.* [from *ſtraw.*] Made of ſtraw; conſiſting of ſtraw.

There the *ſtrawy* Greeks, ripe for his edge,
Fall down before him, like the mower's ſwath. *Shakeſpeare.*

In a field of corn, blown upon by the wind, there will appear waves of a colour differing from that of the reſt; the wind, by depreſſing ſome of the ears, and not others, makes the one reflect more from the lateral and *ſtrawy* parts than the reſt. *Boyle on Colours.*

To STRAY. *v. n.* [*ſtroe*, Daniſh, to ſcatter; *ſtravviare*, Italian, to wander.]

1. To wander; to rove.

My eye, deſcending from the hill, ſurveys
Where Thames among the wanton valley *ſtrays*. *Denham.*
Lo, the glad gales o'er all her beauties *ſtray*,
Breathe on her lips, and in her boſom play. *Pope.*

2. To rove out of the way; to range beyond the proper limits.

What grace hath thee now hither brought this way?
Or doen thy feeble feet unweeting hither *ſtray*. *Fai. Queen.*
No: where can I *ſtray*,
Save back to England? all the world's my way. *Shakeſp.*
Hath not elſe his eye
Stray'd his affection in unlawful love? *Shakeſpeare.*
She doth *ſtray* about
By holy croſſes, where ſhe kneeling prays
For happy wedlock hours. *Shakeſpeare.*
Wand'reſt thou within this lucid orb,
And *ſtray'd* from thoſe fair fields of light above,
Amidſt this new creation want'ſt a guide
To reconduct thy ſteps? *Dryden.*

3. To err; to deviate from the right.

We have erred and *ſtrayed*. *Common Prayer.*

STRAY. *n. ſ.* [from the verb.]

1. Any creature wandering beyond its limits; any thing loſt by wandering.

She hath herſelf not only well defended,
But taken and impounded as a *ſtray*
The king of Scots. *Shakeſpeare's Henry* V.
Should I take you for a *ſtray*,
You muſt be kept a year and day. *Hudibras.*

When he has traced his talk through all its wild rambles, let him bring home his *ſtray*; not like the loſt ſheep with joy, but with tears of penitence. *Government of the Tongue.*

Seeing him wander about, I took him up for a *ſtray*. *Dryd.*

He cries out, neighbour, haſt thou ſeen a *ſtray*
Of bullocks and of heifers paſs this way? *Addiſon.*

2. Act of wandering.

I would not from your love make ſuch a *ſtray*,
To match you where I hate. *Shakeſpeare.*

STREAK. *n. ſ.* [ſꞇꞃice, Saxon; *ſtreke*, Dutch; *ſtricia*, Ital.] A line of colour different from that of the ground.

The Weſt yet glimmers with ſome *ſtreaks* of day;
Now ſpurs the lated traveller apace,
To gain the timely inn. *Shak. Macbeth.*
What mean thoſe colour'd *ſtreaks* in heav'n,
Diſtended, as the brow of God appeas'd? *Milton.*
The night comes on, we eager to purſue
'Till the laſt *ſtreaks* of dying day withdrew,
And doubtful moonlight did our rage deceive. *Dryden.*
Ten wildings have I gather'd for my dear;
How ruddy, like your lips, their *ſtreaks* appear! *Dryden.*
While the fantaſtick tulip ſtrives to break
In two-fold beauty, and a parted *ſtreak*. *Prior.*

To STREAK. *v. a.* [from the noun.]

1. To ſtripe; to variegate in hues; to dapple.

Mark what Jacob did;
When all the yeanlings which were *ſtreak'd* and pied,
Should fall as Jacob's hire. *Shak Merchant of Venice.*

A mule, admirably *ſtreaked* and dapped with white and black. *Sandys's Journey.*

To-morrow, ere freſh morning *ſtreak* the Eaſt,
With firſt approach of light we muſt be ris'n,
And at our pleaſant labour, to reform
Yon flow'ry arbours. *Milton.*
Now let us leave this earth, and lift our eye
To the large convex of yon azure ſky:
Behold it like an ample curtain ſpread,
Now *ſtreak'd* and glowing with the morning red;
Anon at noon in flaming yellow bright,
And chuſing ſable for the peaceful night. *Prior.*

2. To ſtretch. Obſolete.

She lurks in midſt of all her den, and *ſtreaks*
From out a ghaſtly whirlpool all her necks;
Where, glotting round her rock, to fiſh ſhe falls. *Chapman.*

STRE'AKY. *adj* [from *ſtreak.*] Striped; variegated by hues.

When the hoary head is hid in ſnow,
The life is in the leaf, and ſtill between
The fits of falling ſnows appears the *ſtreaky* green. *Dryden.*

STREAM. *n. ſ.* [ſꞇꞃeam, Sax. *ſtraum*, Iſlandick; *ſtroom*, Dut.]

1. A running water; the courſe of running water; current.

As plays the ſun upon the glaſſy *ſtream*,
Twinkling another counterfeited beam. *Shakeſ. Hen.* VI.

He brought *ſtreams* out of the rock, and cauſed waters to run down like rivers. *Pſ.* lxxviii. 16.

Had their cables of iron chains had any great length, they had been unportable; and, being ſhort, the ſhips muſt have ſunk at an anchor in any *ſtream* of weather. *Raleigh.*

Thus from one common ſource our *ſtreams* divide;
Ours is the Trojan, yours th' Arcadian ſide. *Dryden.*
Divided intereſts, while thou think'ſt to ſway,
Draw like two brooks thy middle *ſtream* away. *Dryden.*

2. Any

2. Any thing issuing from a head, and moving forward with continuity of parts.

The breath of the Lord is like a *stream* of brimstone. *Is.*

You, Drances, never want a *stream* of words. *Dryden.*

The *stream* of beneficence hath, by several rivulets which have since fallen into it, wonderfully enlarged its current. *Att.*

3. Any thing forcible and continued.

The very *stream* of his life, and the business he hath helmed, must give him a better proclamation. *Shakespeare.*

It is looked upon as insolence for a man to adhere to his own opinion, against the current *stream* of antiquity. *Locke.*

To STREAM. *v. n.* [*streyma*, Islandick.]

1. To flow; to run in a continuous current.

On all sides round
Streams the black blood, and smokes upon the ground. *Pope.*

2. To flow with a current; to pour out water in a stream; to be overflown.

Then grateful Greece with *streaming* eyes would raise
Historick marbles to record his praise. *Pope.*

3. To issue forth with continuance.

Now to impartial love, that god most high,
Do my sighs *stream.* *Shakes. All's well that ends well.*

To STREAM. *v. a.* To mark with colours or embroidery in long tracks.

The herald's mantle is *streamed* with gold. *Bacon.*

STRE'AMER. *n. s.* [from *stream.*] An ensign; a flag; a pennon; any thing flowing loosely from a stock.

His brave fleet
With silken *streamers*, the young Phœbus fanning. *Shakes.*

The rosy morn began to rise,
And wav'd her saffron *streamer* through the skies. *Dryden.*

Brave Rupert from afar appears,
Whose waving *streamers* the glad general knows. *Dryden.*

The man of sense his meat devours;
But only smells the peel and flow'rs:
And he must be an idle dreamer,
Who leaves the pie, and gnaws the *streamer.* *Prior.*

STRE'AMY. *adj.* [from *stream.*]

1. Abounding in running water.

Arcadia,
However *streamy* now, adust and dry,
Deny'd the goddess water: where deep Melas,
And rocky Cratis flow, the chariot smoak'd
Obscure with rising dust. *Prior.*

2. Flowing with a current.

Before him flaming his enormous shield,
Like the broad sun, illumin'd all the field;
His nodding helm emits a *streamy* ray. *Pope's Iliad.*

STREET. *n. s.* [ꞅꞇꞃæꞇ, Saxon; *straz*, German; *strada*, Spanish and Ital. *streede*, Danish; *straet*, Dutch; *stratum*, Lat.]

1. A way, properly a paved way, between two rows of houses.

He led us through fair *streets*; and all the way we went there were gathered people on both sides, standing in a row. *Bacon.*

The *streets* are no larger than allies. *Sandys.*

When night
Darkens the *streets*, then wander forth the sons
Of Belial, flown with insolence and wine;
Witness the *streets* of Sodom. *Milton.*

The Italians say the ancients always considered the situation of a building, whether it were high or low, in an open square, or in a narrow *street*, and more or less deviated from their rule of art. *Addison on Italy.*

When you tattle with some crony servant in the same *street*, leave your own *street*-door open. *Swift.*

2. Proverbially, a publick place.

That there be no leading into captivity, and no complaining in our *streets.* *Psalm* cxliv. 14.

Our publick ways would be so crowded, that we should want *street*-room. *Addison's Spectator.*

Let us reflect upon what we daily see practised in the world, and can we believe, if an apostle of Christ appeared in our *streets*, he would retract his caution, and command us to be conformed to the world? *Rogers's Sermons.*

STRE'ETWALKER. *n. s.* [*street* and *walk.*] A common prostitute that offers herself to sale in the open street.

STRENGTH. *n. s.* [ꞅꞇꞃenᵹð, Saxon.]

1. Force; vigour; power of the body.

Thy youth, thy *strength*, thy beauty, which will change
To wither'd, weak, and grey. *Milton.*

Th' insulting Trojan came,
And menac'd us with force, our fleet with flame:
Was it the *strength* of this tongue-valiant lord,
In that black hour, that sav'd you from the sword? *Dryden.*

2. Power of endurance; firmness; durability; toughness; hardness.

Not founded on the brittle *strength* of bones. *Milton.*

3. Vigour of any kind; power of any kind.

The allies, after a successful Summer, are too apt, upon the *strength* of it, to neglect their preparations for the ensuing campaign. *Addison.*

4. Power of mind; force of any mental faculty.

Aristotle's large views, acuteness and penetration of thought, and *strength* of judgment, few have equalled. *Locke.*

He enjoyed the greatest *strength* of good-sense, and the most exquisite taste of politeness. *Addison.*

5. Potency of liquours.

6. Fortification; fortress.

The rashness of talking should not only be retarded by the guard of our heart, but fenced in by certain *strengths* placed in the mouth. *Ben. Johnson's Discoveries.*

He thought
This inaccessible high *strength* to have seiz'd. *Milton.*

Betray'd in all his *strengths*, the wood beset;
All instruments, all arts of ruin met. *Denham.*

7. Support; maintenance of power.

What they boded would be a mischief to us, you are providing shall be one of our principal *strengths.* *Sprat's Sermons.*

8. Armament; force; power.

What is his *strength* by land? *Shakesp. Ant. and Cleopat.*

Nor was there any other *strength* designed to attend about his highness than one regiment. *Clarendon.*

9. Persuasive prevalence; argumentative force.

This presupposed, it may then stand very well with *strength* and soundness of reason, thus to answer. *Hooker.*

To STRENGTH. *v. a.* To strengthen. Not used.

Edward's happy-order'd reign, most fertile breeds
Plenty of mighty spirits, to *strength* his state. *Daniel.*

To STRE'NGTHEN. *v. a.* [from *strength.*]

1. To make strong.

2. To confirm; to establish.

Let us rise up and build: so they *strengthened* their hands for this work. *Neh.* ii. 18.

Authority is by nothing so much *strengthened* and confirmed as by custom; for no man easily distrusts the things which he and all men have been always bred up to. *Temple.*

Thee, bold Longinus! all the Nine inspire,
And bless your critick with a poet's fire:
An ardent judge, who, zealous in his trust,
With warmth gives sentence, yet is always just;
Whose own example *strengthens* all his laws,
And is himself that great sublime he draws. *Pope.*

3. To animate; to fix in resolution.

Charge Joshua, and encourage him and *strengthen* him. *Deut.*

4. To make to increase in power or security.

Let noble Warwick, Cobham, and the rest,
With powerful policy *strengthen* themselves. *Shakesp. H.* VI.

They sought the *strengthening* of the heathen. 1 *Mac.* vi.

To STRE'NGTHEN. *v. n.* To grow strong.

Oh men for flatt'ry and deceit renown'd!
Thus when y' are young ye learn it all like him,
'Till as your years increase, that *strengthens* too,
T' undo poor maids. *Otway's Orphan.*

STRE'NGTHENER. } *n. s.* [from *strengthen*: by contraction
STRE'NGTHNER. } *strengthner.*]

1. That which gives strength; that which makes strong.

Garlick is a great *strengthner* of the stomach upon decays of appetite or indigestion. *Temple.*

2. [In medicine.] Strengtheners add to the bulk and firmness of the solids: cordials are such as drive on the vital actions; but these such as confirm the stamina. *Quincy.*

STRE'NGTHLESS. *adj.* [from *strength*]

1. Wanting strength; deprived of strength.

Yet are these feet, whose *strengthless* stay is numb,
Unable to support this lump of clay. *Shakesp. Henry* VI.

As the wretch, whose fever-weaken'd joints,
Like *strengthless* hinges, buckle under life,
Impatient of his fit, breaks like a fire
Out of his keeper's arms. *Shakes. Henry* IV.

2. Wanting potency; weak. Used of liquours.

This liquor must be inflammable or not, and yet subtile and pungent, which may be called spirit; or else *strengthless* or insipid, which may be named phlegm. *Boyle.*

STRE'NUOUS. *adj.* [*strenuus*, Latin.]

1. Brave; bold; active; valiant.

Nations grown corrupt
Love bondage more than liberty;
Bondage with ease than *strenuous* liberty. *Milton's Agonistes.*

2. Zealous; vehement.

He resolves to be *strenuous* for taking off the test, against the maxims of all wise Christian governments, which always had some established religion, leaving at best a toleration to others. *Swift to Pope.*

Citizens within the bills of mortality have been *strenuous* against the church and crown. *Swift.*

STRE'NUOUSLY. *adv.* [from *strenuous.*]

1. Vigorously; actively.

Many can use both hands, yet will there divers remain that can *strenuously* make use of neither. *Brown's Vulgar Errours.*

2. Zealously; vehemently; with ardour.

Writers dispute *strenuously* for the liberty of conscience, and inveigh largely against all ecclesiasticks under the name of high church. *Swift.*

STRE'PEROUS. *adj.* [*strepo*, Latin.] Loud; noisy.

Porta conceives, because in a *streperous* eruption it riseth against fire, it doth therefore resist lightning. *Brown.*

STRESS. *n. s.* [ꞅꞇꞃece, Saxon, violence; or from *distress*.]
1. Importance; important part.
A body may as well lay too little as too much *stress* upon a dream; but the less we heed them the better. *L'Estrange.*
The *stress* of the fable lies upon the hazard of having a numerous stock of children. *L'Estrange.*
This, on which the great *stress* of the business depends, would have been made out with reasons sufficient. *Locke.*
Consider how great a *stress* he laid upon this duty, while upon earth, and how earnestly he recommended it. *Atterbury.*
2. Violence; force, either acting or suffered.

By *stress* of weather driv'n,
At last they landed. *Dryden's Æn.*

Though the faculties of the mind are improved by exercise, yet they must not be put to a *stress* beyond their strength. *Locke.*

To STRESS. *v. a.* [Evidently from *distress*.] To distress; to put to hardships or difficulties.

Stirred with pity of the *stressed* plight
Of this sad realm. *Fairy Queen.*

To STRETCH. *v. a.* [ꞅꞇꞃecan, Saxon; *strecken*, Dutch.]
1. To extend; to spread out to a distance.
The *stretching* out of his wings shall fill the breadth of thy land. *Is.* viii. 8.
Stretch thine hand unto the poor. *Ecclus* vii. 32.
Take thy rod, and *stretch* out thine hand. *Ex.* vii. 19.
2. To elongate, or strain to a greater space.
3. To expand; to display.

Leviathan on the deep,
Stretch'd like a promontory, sleeps. *Milton.*

What more likely to *stretch* forth the heavens, and lay the foundation of the earth, than infinite power? *Tillotson.*
4. To strain to the utmost.

This kiss, if it durst speak,
Would *stretch* thy spirits up into the air. *Shak. K. Lear.*

5. To make tense.

So the *stretch'd* cord the shackl'd dancer tries. *Smith.*

6. To carry by violence farther than is right: as, to *stretch* a text.

To STRETCH. *v. n.*
1. To be extended.
Idolatry is a horrible sin, yet doth repentance *stretch* unto it. *Whitgifte.*

A third is like the former: a fourth? start eye!
What! will the line *stretch* out to th' crack of doom? *Shak.*
This to rich Ophir's rising morn is known,
And *stretch'd* out far to the burnt swarthy zone. *Cowley.*
Your dungeon *stretching* far and wide beneath. *Milton.*

2. To bear extension without rupture.
The inner membrane, that involved the liquors of the egg, because it would *stretch* and yield, remained unbroken. *Boyle.*
3. To sally beyond the truth.
What an allay do we find to the credit of the most probable event, that is reported by one who uses to *stretch*? *Gov. Tongue.*

STRETCH. *n. s.* [from the verb.]
1. Extension; reach; occupation of more space.

At all her *stretch* her little wings she spread,
And with her feather'd arms embrac'd the dead:
Then flickering to his pallid lips, she strove
To print a kiss. *Dryden's Ceyx and Alcyo.*

Disruption, as strong as they are, the bones would be in some danger of, upon a great and sudden *stretch* or contortion, if they were dry. *Ray on the Creation.*
2. Force of body extended.

He thought to swim the stormy main,
By *stretch* of arms the distant shore to gain. *Dryden's Æn.*

3. Effort; struggle: from the act of running.
Those put a lawful authority upon the *stretch* to the abuse of power, under the colour of prerogative. *L'Estrange.*
Upon this alarm we made incredible *stretches* towards the South, to gain the fastnesses of Preston. *Addison.*
4. Utmost extent of meaning.
Quotations, in their utmost *stretch*, can signify no more than that Luther lay under severe agonies of mind. *Atterbury.*
5. Utmost reach of power.

This is the utmost *stretch* that nature can,
And all beyond is fulsome, false, and vain. *Granville.*

STRE'TCHER. *n. s.* [from *stretch*.]
1. Any thing used for extension.
Tooth in the stretching course two inches with the *stretcher* only. *Moxon.*
2. The timber against which the rower plants his feet.

This fiery speech inflames his fearful friends,
They tug at ev'ry oar, and ev'ry *stretcher* bends. *Dryden.*

To STREW. *v. a.* [The orthography of this word is doubtful: it is generally written *strew*, and I have followed custom; but *Skinner* likewise proposes *strow*, and *Junius* writes *straw*. Their reasons will appear in the word from which it may be derived. *Strawan*, Gothick; *stroyen*, Dutch; ꞅꞇꞃeapian, Sax. *strawen*, German; *stròer*, Danish. Perhaps *strow* is best, being that which reconciles etymology with pronunciation.]
1. To spread by being scattered.

The snow which does the top of Pindus *strew*,
Did never whiter shew. *Spenser.*
Is thine alone the seed that *strews* the plain?
The birds of heav'n shall vindicate their grain. *Pope.*

2. To spread by scattering.

I thought thy bride-bed to have deck'd, sweet maid,
And not have *strew'd* thy grave. *Shakes. Hamlet.*
Here be tears of perfect moan,
Wept for thee in Helicon;
And some flowers and some bays,
For thy herse, to *strew* the ways. *Milton.*

3. To scatter loosely.
The calf he burnt in the fire, ground it to powder, and *strawed* it upon the water, and made Israel drink of it. *Ex.*

With furies and nocturnal orgies fir'd,
Whom ev'n the savage beasts had spar'd, they kill'd,
And *strew'd* his mangled limbs about the field. *Dryden.*

STRE'WMENT. *n. s.* [from *strew*.] Any thing scattered in decoration.

Her death was doubtful.—For charitable prayers,
Shards, flints, and pebbles should be thrown on her;
Yet here she is allow'd her virgin chants,
Her maiden *strewments*, and the bringing home
Of bell and burial. *Shakes. Hamlet.*

STRIÆ. n. s. [Latin.] In natural history, the small channels in the shells of cockles and scallops.
The salt, leisurely permitted to shoot of itself in the liquor, exposed to the open air, did shoot into more fair crystalline *striæ*, than those that were gained out of the remaining part of the same liquor by a more hasty evaporation. *Boyle.*

STRI'ATE. } *adj.* [from *striæ*, Latin; *strié*, French.] Formed
STRI'ATED. } in striæ.
These effluviums fly by *striated* atoms and winding particles, as Des Cartes conceiveth, or glide by streams attracted from either pole unto the equator. *Brown's Vulgar Errours.*
Des Cartes imagines this earth once to have been a sun, and so the centre of a lesser vortex, whose axis still kept the same posture, by reason of the *striate* particles finding no fit pores for their passages, but only in this direction. *Ray.*
Crystal, when incorporated with the fibrous talcs, shews, if broke, a *striated* or fibrous texture, like those talcs. *Woodw.*

STRI'ATURE. *n. s.* [from *striæ*; *strieure*, Fr.] Disposition of striæ.
Parts of tuberous hæmatitæ shew several varieties in the crusts, *striature*, and texture of the body. *Woodward.*

STRICK. *n. s.* [στρίγξ; *strix*, Latin.] A bird of bad omen.

The ill fac'd owl, death's dreadful messenger,
The hoarse night-raven, trump of doleful drere,
The leather-winged bat, day's enemy,
The rueful *strick*, still waiting on the bier. *Fairy Queen.*

STRI'CKEN. The ancient participle of *strike*.
The cunningest mariners were so conquered by the storm, as they thought it best with *stricken* sails to yield to be governed by it. *Sidney.*

That shall I shew, as sure as hound
The *stricken* deer doth challenge by the bleeding wound. *F. Q.*

Abraham and Sarah were old, and well *stricken* in age. *Gen.*
With blindness were these *stricken*. *Wisd.* xix. 17.
Parker and Vaughan, having had a controversy touching certain arms, were appointed to run some courses, when Parker was *stricken* into the mouth at the first course. *Bacon.*
Though the earl of Ulster was of greater power than any other subject in Ireland, yet was he so far *stricken* in years, as that he was unable to manage the martial affairs. *Davies.*

STRI'CKLE, or *Strickless*, or *Stritchel*. *n. s.* That which strikes the corn to level it with the bushel. *Ainsworth.*

STRICT. *adj.* [*strictus*, Latin.]
1. Exact; accurate; rigorously nice.

Thou'lt fall into deception unaware,
Not keeping *strictest* watch. *Milton.*
As legions in the field their front display,
To try the fortune of some doubtful day,
And move to meet their foes with sober pace,
Strict to their figure, though in wider space. *Dryden.*
He checks the bold design;
And rules as *strict* his labour'd works confine,
As if the Stagyrite o'erlook'd each line. *Pope.*

2. Severe; rigorous; not mild; not indulgent.

Implore her, in my voice, that she make friends
To the *strict* deputy. *Shakes. Measure for Measure.*
Thy will
By nature free, not over-rul'd by fate
Inextricable, or *strict* necessity. *Milton.*

If a *strict* hand be kept over children from the beginning, they will in that age be tractable; and if, as they grow up, the rigour be, as they deserve it, gently relaxed, former restraints will increase their love. *Locke.*

Numa the rites of *strict* religion knew;
On ev'ry altar laid the incense due. *Prior.*

3. Confined; not extensive.
As they took the compass of their commission *stricter* or larger, so their dealings were more or less moderate. *Hooker.*
4. Close; tight.

The god, with speedy pace,
Just thought to strain her in a *strict* embrace. *Dryden.*

The

The fatal noose performed its office, and with most *strict* ligature squeezed the blood into his face. *Arbuthnot.*

5. Tense; not relaxed.

We feel our fibres grow *strict* or lax according to the state of the air. *Arbuthnot.*

STRI'CTLY. *adv.* [from *strict.*]

1. Exactly; with rigorous accuracy.

The other parts being grosser, composed not only water, *strictly* so called, but the whole mass of liquid bodies. *Burnet.*

Charge him *strictly*
Not to proceed, but wait my farther pleasure. *Dryden.*

2. Rigorously; severely; without remission or indulgence.

In the discharge of thy place, set before thee the best examples; and after a time set before thee thine own, and examine thyself *strictly* whether thou didst not best at first. *Bacon.*

God may with the greatest justice *strictly* require endeavours from us, and without any inconsistency with his goodness inflict penalties on those who are wanting. *Rogers's Sermons.*

A weak prince again disposed the people to new attempts, which it was the clergy's duty to endeavour to prevent, if some of them had not proceeded upon a topick that, *strictly* followed, would enslave all mankind. *Swift.*

3. Closely; with tenseness.

STRI'CTNESS. *n. s.* [from *strict.*]

1. Exactness; rigorous accuracy; nice regularity.

I could not grant too much or distrust too little to men, that pretended singular piety and religious *strictness*. *K. Charles.*

Such of them as cannot be concealed connive at, though in the *strictness* of your judgment you cannot pardon. *Dryden.*

Who were made privy to the secrets of heaven, but such as performed his revealed will at an higher rate of *strictness* than the rest? *South.*

Though in *strictness* our Saviour might have pleaded exemption from the Jewish tribute, he exerted his divine power in a miracle to pay it. *Rogers.*

2. Severity; rigour.

These commissioners proceeded with such *strictness* and severity as did much obscure the king's mercy. *Bacon's Hen.* VII.

3. Closeness; tightness; not laxity.

STRI'CTURE. *n. s.* [from *strictura*, Latin, a spark.]

1. A stroke; a touch.

The God of nature implanted in their vegetable natures certain passive *strictures*, or signatures of that wisdom which hath made and ordered all things with the highest reason. *Hale.*

2. Contraction; closure by contraction.

As long as there is thirst, with a free passage by urine, and *stricture* of the vessels, so long is water safely taken. *Arbuthnot.*

3. A slight touch upon a subject; not a set discourse.

STRIDE. *n. s.* [ꞅꞇꞃæde, Saxon.] A long step; a step taken with great violence; a wide divarication of the legs.

I'll speak between the change of man and boy,
With a reed voice, and turn two mincing steps
Into a manly *stride*. *Shakes. Merchant of Venice.*

The monster moved on with horrid *strides*. *Milton.*

Her voice theatrically loud,
And masculine her *stride*. *Swift.*

To STRIDE. *v. n.* preter. *I strode* or *strid*; part. pass. *stridden.* [from the noun.]

1. To walk with long steps.

Mars in the middle of the shining shield
Is grav'd, and *strides* along the liquid field. *Dryden.*

To Jove, or to thy father Neptune, pray,
The brethren cry'd, and instant *strode* away. *Pope.*

2. To stand with the legs far from each other.

To STRIDE. *v. a.* To pass by a step.

See him *stride*
Vallies wide. *Arbuthnot.*

STRI'DULOUS. *adj.* [*stridulus*, Latin.] Making a small noise.

It arises from a small and *stridulous* noise, which, being firmly rooted, maketh a divulsion of parts. *Brown.*

STRIFE. *n. s.* [from *strive.*]

1. Contention; contest; discord.

I and my people were at great *strife* with the children of Ammon. *Judg.* xii. 2.

Some preach Christ even of envy and *strife*, and some of good-will. *Phil.* i. 15.

He is proud, knowing nothing; but doating about questions and *strife* of words. 1 *Tim.* vi. 4.

These vows, thus granted, rais'd a *strife* above
Betwixt the god of war and queen of love:
She granting first, had right of time to plead;
But he had granted too, and would recede. *Dryden.*

2. Opposition of nature or appearance; contrariety; contrast.

Artificial *strife*
Lives in those touches, livelier than life. *Shakespeare.*

How passion's well accorded *strife*
Makes all the harmony of life. *Johnson.*

STRI'FEFUL. *adj.* [*strife* and *full.*] Contentious; discordant.

Th' ape was *strifeful* and ambitious,
And the fox guileful and most covetous. *Hubberd's Tale.*

I know not what new creation may creep forth from the *strifeful* heap of things, into which, as into a second chaos, we are fallen. *Dr. Maine.*

STRI'GMENT. *n. s.* [*strigmentum*, from *stringo*, Lat. to scrape.] Scraping; recrement.

Many, besides the *strigments* and sudorous adhesions from mens hands, acknowledge that nothing proceedeth from gold in its usual decoction. *Brown's Vulgar Errours.*

To STRIKE. *v. a.* preter. *I struck* or *strook*; part. pass. *struck*, *strucken*, *stricken*. [aꞅꞇꞃican, Saxon; *streichen*, German; *adstrykia*, Islandick; *stricker*, Danish.]

1. To act upon by a blow; to hit with a blow.

He at Philippi kept
His sword e'en like a dancer, while I *struck*
The lean and wrinkled Cassius. *Shakesp. Ant. and Cleopat.*

We will deliver you the cause,
Why I, that did love Cæsar when I *struck* him,
Proceeded thus. *Shakesp. Julius Cæsar.*

I must
But wail his fall, whom I myself *struck* down. *Shak. Macb.*

2. To dash; to throw by a quick motion.

The blood *strike* on the two side-posts. *Ex.* xii. 7.

3. To notify by the sound of a hammer on a bell.

The Windsor bell hath *struck* twelve. *Shakesp.*

A judicious friend moderates the pursuit, gives the signal for action, presses the advantage, and *strikes* the critical minute. *Collier of Friendship.*

4. To stamp; to impress.

The memory in some men is very tenacious; but yet there seems to be a constant decay of all our ideas, even of those which are *struck* deepest, and in minds the most retentive. *Loc.*

5. To punish; to afflict.

To punish the just is not good, nor to *strike* princes for equity. *Prov.* xvii. 26.

6. To contract; to lower; to vale. It is only used in the phrases to *strike sail*, or to *strike a flag*.

How many nobles then would hold their places,
That must *strike sail* to spirits of vile sort! *Shakes. H.* IV.

To this all differing passions and interests should *strike sail*, and like swelling streams, running different courses, should yet all make haste into the sea of common safety. *Temple.*

They *strike sail* where they know they shall be mastered, and murder where they can with safety. *Dryden.*

Now, did I not so near my labours end,
Strike sail, and hast'ning to the harbour tend,
My song to flow'ry gardens might extend. *Dryden.*

7. To alarm; to put into emotion.

The rest, *struck* with horror stood,
To see their leader cover'd o'er with blood. *Waller.*

Jack Straw at London-stone, with all his rout,
Struck not the city with so loud a shout. *Dryden.*

His virtues render our assembly awful
They *strike* with something like religious fear. *Addis. Cato.*

Did'st thou but view him right, should'st see him black
With murder, treason, sacrilege, and crimes
That *strike* my soul with horror but to name them. *Addison.*

We are no sooner presented to any one we never saw before, but we are immediately *struck* with the idea of a proud, a reserved, an affable or a good natured man. *Addison.*

Nice works of art *strike* and surprise us most upon the first view; but the better we are acquainted with them, the less we wonder. *Atterbury.*

Court virtues bear, like gems, the highest rate,
Born where heav'n's influence scarce can penetrate;
In life's low vale, the soil the virtues like,
They please as beauties, here as wonders *strike*. *Pope.*

8. [*Fœdus ferire.*] To make a bargain.

Sign but his peace, he vows he'll ne'er again
The sacred names of fops and beaus profane:
Strike up the bargain quickly; for I swear,
As times go now, he offers very fair. *Dryden.*

I come to offer peace; to reconcile
Past enmities; to *strike* perpetual leagues
With Vanoc. *A. Philips's Briton.*

9. To produce by a sudden action.

The court paved, *striketh* up a great heat in summer, and much cold in winter. *Bacon.*

Waving wide her myrtle wand,
She *strikes* an universal peace through sea and land. *Milton.*

Take my caduceus!
With this the infernal ghosts I can command,
And *strike* a terror through the Stygian strand. *Dryden.*

10. To affect suddenly in any particular manner.

When verses cannot be understood, nor a man's good wit seconded with the forward child understanding; it *strikes* a man more dead than a great reckoning in a little room. *Shakesp.*

Strike her young bones,
Ye taking airs, with lameness. *Shakespeare.*

He that is *stricken* blind cannot forget
The precious treasure of his eye-sight lost. *Shakespeare.*

So ceas'd the rival crew, when Purcell came,
They sung no more, or only sung his fame;
Struck dumb, they all admir'd. *Dryden.*

Humility disarms envy, and *strikes* it dead. *Collier.*

Then do not *strike* him dead with a denial,
But hold him up in life. *Addison's Cato.*

11. To

11. To cause to sound by blows. With *up* only emphatical.

The drums presently *striking up* a march, they plucked up their ensigns, and forward they go. *Knolles.*

Strike up the drums, and let the tongue of war
Plead for our int'rest, and our being here. *Shakespeare.*

12. To forge; to mint.

Some very rare coins *struck* of a pound weight, of gold and silver, Constantine sent to Chilperick. *Arbuthnot.*

13. It is used in the participle, I know not well how, for *advanced in years.*

The king
Is wise and virtuous, and his noble queen
Well *struck* in years; fair and not jealous. *Shakespeare.*

14. *To* STRIKE *off.* To erase from a reckoning or account.

Deliver Helen, and all damage else
Shall be *struck off.* *Shakespeare's Troilus and Cressida.*

I have this while with leaden thoughts been prest;
But I shall in a more convenient time
Strike off this score of absence. *Shakespeare's Othello.*

Ask mens opinions: Scoto now shall tell
How trade encreases, and the world goes well:
Strike off his pension by the setting sun,
And Britain, if not Europe, is undone. *Pope.*

15. *To* STRIKE *off.* To separate as by a blow.

Germany had *stricken off* that which appeared corrupt in the doctrine of the church of Rome; but seemed nevertheless in discipline still to retain therewith great conformity. *Hooker.*

They followed so fast that they overtook him, and without further delay *struck off* his head. *Knolles.*

He was taken prisoner by Surinas, lieutenant-general for the king of Parthia, who *stroke off* his head. *Hakewell.*

A mass of water would be quite *struck off* and separate from the rest, and tost through the air like a flying river. *Burnet's Theory of the Earth.*

16. *To* STRIKE *out.* To produce by collision.

My thoughtless youth was wing'd with vain desires;
My manhood long misled by wand'ring fires,
Follow'd false lights; and when their glimpse was gone,
My pride *struck out* new sparkles of her own. *Dryden.*

17. *To* STRIKE *out.* To blot; to efface.

By expurgatory animadversions, we might *strike out* great numbers of hidden qualities, and having once a conceded list, with more safety attempt their reasons. *Brown.*

To methodize is as necessary as to *strike out.* *Pope.*

18. *To* STRIKE *out.* To bring to light.

19. *To* STRIKE *out.* To form at once by a quick effort.

Whether thy hand *strike out* some free design,
Where life awakes and dawns at ev'ry line,
Or blend in beauteous tints the colour'd mass,
And from the canvass call the mimick face. *Pope.*

To STRIKE. *v. n.*

1. To make a blow.

I in mine own woe charm'd,
Could not find death, where I did hear him groan;
Nor feel him where he *struck.* *Shakespeare's Cymbeline.*

It pleased the king
To *Strike* at me upon his misconstruction;
When he tript me behind. *Shakespeare's King Lear.*

He wither'd all their strength before he *strook.* *Dryden.*

2. To collide; to clash.

Holding a ring by a thread in a glass, tell him that holdeth it, it shall *strike* so many times against the side of the glass, and no more. *Bacon's Natural History.*

3. To act by repeated percussion.

Bid thy mistress when my drink is ready,
She *strike* upon the bell. *Shakespeare's Macbeth.*

Those antique minstrels, sure, were Charles like kings,
Cities their lutes, and subjects hearts their strings;
On which with so divine a hand they *strook,*
Consent of motion from their breath they took. *Waller.*

4. To sound by the stroke of a hammer.

Cæsar, 'tis *strucken* eight. *Shakespeare.*

Deep thoughts will often suspend the senses so far, that about a man clocks may *strike* and bells ring, which he takes no notice of. *Grew.*

5. To make an attack.

Is not the king's name forty thousand names?
Arm, arm, my name; a puny subject *strikes*
At thy great glory. *Shakespeare's Richard* II.

When by their designing leaders taught
To *strike* at power, which for themselves they sought:
The vulgar gull'd into rebellion arm'd,
Their blood to action by their prize was warm'd. *Dryden.*

6. To act by external influx.

Consider the red and white colours in porphyre; hinder light but from *striking* on it, and its colours vanish. *Locke.*

7. To sound with blows.

Whilst any trump did sound, or drum *struck* up,
His sword did ne'er leave striking in the field. *Shakespeare.*

8. To be dashed upon shallows; to be stranded.

The admiral galley wherein the emperor was, *struck* upon a sand, and there stuck fast. *Knolles.*

9. To pass with a quick or strong effect.

Now and then a glittering beam of wit or passion *strikes* through the obscurity of the poem: any of these effect a present liking, but not a lasting admiration. *Dryden.*

10. To pay homage, as by lowering the sail.

We see the wind sit sore upon our sails;
And yet we *strike* not, but securely perish. *Shakespeare.*

I'd rather chop this hand off at a blow,
And with the other fling it at thy face,
Than bear so low a sail, to *strike* to thee. *Shakespeare.*

The interest of our kingdom is ready to *strike* to that of your poorest fishing towns: it is hard you will not accept our services. *Swift.*

11. To be put by some sudden act or motion into any state; to break forth.

It *struck* on a sudden into such reputation, that it scorns any longer to sculk, but owns itself publickly. *Gov. of the Tongue.*

12. *To* STRIKE *in with.* To conform; to suit itself to; to join with at once.

Those who by the prerogative of their age, should frown youth into sobriety, imitate and *strike in with* them, and are really vitious that they may be thought young. *South.*

They catch at every shadow of relief, *strike in* at a venture *with* the next companion, and so the dead commodity be taken off, care not who be the chapman. *Norris.*

The cares or pleasures of the world *strike in with* every thought. *Addison.*

He immediately *struck in with* them, but described this march to the temple with so much horrour, that he shivered every joint. *Addison's Freeholder.*

13. *To* STRIKE *out.* To spread or rove; to make a sudden excursion.

In this plain was the last general rendezvous of mankind; and from thence they were broken into companies and dispersed, the several successive generations, like the waves of the sea over-reaching one another, and *striking out* farther and farther upon the land. *Burnet's Theory of the Earth.*

When a great man *strikes out* into a sudden irregularity, he needs not question the respect of a retinue. *Collier of Popularity.*

STRIKE. *n. s.* A bushel; a dry measure of capacity.

Wing, cartnave and bushel, peck, *strike* ready at hand. *Tusser's Husbandry.*

STRI'KEBLOCK. *n. s.* Is a plane shorter than the jointer, having its sole made exactly flat and straight, and is used for the shooting of a short joint. *Moxon's Mechanical Exercise.*

STRI'KER. *n. s.* [from *strike.*] One that strikes

A bishop then must be blameless, not given to wine, no *striker.* *1 Tim.* iii. 3.

He thought with his staff to have struck the *striker.* *Sandys.*

The *striker* must be dense, and in its best velocity. *Digby.*

STRI'KING. *part. adj.* [from *strike.*] Affecting; surprising.

STRING. *n. s.* [ꞅꞇꞃınᵹ, Saxon; *streng,* German and Danish; *stringhe* Dutch; *stringo,* Latin.]

1. A slender rope; a small cord; any slender and flexible band; a riband; any thing tied.

Any lower bullet hanging upon the other above it, must be conceived, as if the weight of it were in that point where its *string* touches the upper. *Wilkins's Dedalus.*

Round Ormond's knee thou ty'st the mystick *string,*
That makes the knight companion to the king. *Prior.*

2. A thread on which any things are filed.

Their priests pray by their beads, having a *string* with a hundred of nutshels upon it; and the repeating of certain words with them they account meritorious. *Stillingfleet.*

3. Any set of things filed on a line.

I have caught two of these dark undermining vermin, and intend to make a *string* of them, in order to hang them up in one of my papers. *Addison's Spectator.*

4. The chord of a musical instrument.

The *string* that jars
When rudely touch'd, ungrateful to the sense,
With pleasure feels the master's flying fingers,
Swells into harmony, and charms the hearers. *Rowe.*

By the appearance they make in marble, there is not one *string*-instrument that seems comparable to our violins. *Addis.*

5. A small fibre.

Duckweed putteth forth a little *string* into the water, from the bottom. *Bacon.*

In pulling broom up, the least *strings* left behind will grow. *Mortimer's Husbandry.*

6. A nerve; a tendon.

The most piteous tale which in recounting,
His grief grew puissant, and the *strings* of life
Began to crack: *Shakespeare's King Lear.*

The *string* of his tongue loosed. *Mark* xxvii. 35.

7. The nerve of the bow.

The wicked bend their bow, they make ready their arrows upon the *string.* *Psalm* xi. 2.

8. Any concatenation or series, as *a* string *of propositions.*

9. *To have two* STRINGS *to the bow.* To have two views or two expedients; to have double advantage, or double security.

No

No lover has that pow'r
T' enforce a desperate amour,
As he that has two *strings* to's bow,
And burns for love and money too. *Hudibras.*

To STRING. *v. a.* Preterite *I strung*, part. pass. *strung*. [from the noun.]

1. To furnish with strings.
Has not wise nature *strung* the legs and feet
With firmest nerves, design'd to walk the street? *Gay.*

2. To put a stringed instrument in tune.
Here the muse so oft her harp has *strung*,
That not a mountain rears its head unsung. *Addison.*

3. To file on a string.
Men of great learning or genius are too full to be exact; and therefore chuse to throw down their pearls in heaps before the reader, rather than be at the pains of *stringing* them. *Spect.*

4. To make tense.
Toil *strung* the nerves, and purified the blood. *Dryden.*

STRI'NGED. *adj.* [from *string*.] Having strings; produced by strings.
Praise him with *stringed* instruments and organs. *Psalms.*
Divinely warbl'd voice,
Answering the *stringed* noise,
As all their souls in blissful rapture took. *Milton.*

STRINGENT. *adj.* [*stringens*, Latin.] Binding; contracting.

STRI'NGHALT. *n. s.* [*string* and *halt*.]
Stringhalt is a sudden twitching and snatching up of the hinder leg of a horse much higher than the other, or an involuntary or convulsive motion of the muscles that extend or bend the hough. *Farrier's Dict.*

STRI'NGLESS. *adj.* [from *string*.] Having no strings.
Nothing; all is said;
His tongue is now a *stringless* instrument,
Words, life, and all, old Lancaster hath spent. *Shakespeare.*

STRI'NGY. *adj.* [from *string*.] Fibrous; consisting of small threads.
A plain Indian fan, made of the small *stringy* parts of roots spread out in a round flat form. *Grew.*

To STRIP. *v. a.* [*streopen*, Dutch; beſtꞃıpꞇe, stripped, Sax.]

1. To make naked; to deprive of covering.
They began to *strip* her of her cloaths when I came in among them. *Sidney.*
They *stript* Joseph out of his coat. *Gen.* xxxvii. 23.
Scarce credible it is how soon they were *stript* and laid naked on the ground. *Hayward.*
Hadst thou not committed
Notorious murder on those thirty men
At Askelon, who never did thee harm,
Then like a robber *strip'dst* them of their robes. *Milton.*
You cloath all that have no relation to you, and *strip* your master that gives you food. *L'Estrange.*
A rattling tempest through the branches went,
That *stript* them bare. *Dryden's Knights Tale.*
He saw a beauteous maid
With hair dishevel'd, issuing through the shade,
Stript of her cloaths. *Dryden.*
He left the pillagers, to rapine bred,
Without controul to *strip* and spoil the dead. *Dryden.*
The bride was put in form to bed;
He follow'd *stript*. *Swift.*

2. To deprive; to divest.
The apostle in exhorting men to contentment, although they have in this world no more than bare food and raiment, giveth us to understand that those are even the lowest of things necessary, that if we should be *stript* of all these things, without which we might possibly be, yet these must be left. *Hooker.*
We *strip* and divest ourselves of our own will, and give ourselves entirely up to the will of God. *Duppa.*
It is difficult to lead another by words into the thoughts of things, *stripped* of those specifick differences we give them. *Locke.*
One would imagine these to be the expressions of a man blessed with ease and affluence, not of one just *stript* of all those advantages, and plunged in the deepest miseries; and now sitting naked upon a dunghil. *Atterbury.*

3. To rob; to plunder; to pillage.
That which lays a man open to an enemy, and that which *strips* him of a friend, equally attacks him in all those interests that are capable of being weakned by the one and supported by the other. *South's Sermons.*

4. To peel; to decorticate.
If the leaves or dried stocks be *stripped* into small straws, they arise unto amber, wax, and other electerics, no other ways than those of wheat or rye. *Brown's Vulgar Errours.*

5. To deprive of all.
When some fond easy fathers *strip* themselves before they lie down to their long sleep, and settle their whole estates upon their sons, has it not been seen that the father has been requited with beggary? *South's Sermons.*

6. To take off covering.
He *stript* off his cloaths. 1 *Sam.* xix. 24.
Logick helps us to *strip* off the outward disguise of things, and to behold and judge of them in their own nature. *Watts.*

7. To cast off.
His unkindness
That *stript* her from his benediction, turn'd her
To foreign casualties, gave her dear rights
To her doghearted daughters: these things sting him. *Shakesp.*

8. To separate from something adhesive or connected.
Amongst men who examine not scrupulously their own ideas, and *strip* them not from the marks men use for them, but confound them with words, there must be endless dispute. *Locke.*

STRIP. *n. s.* [Probably for *stripe*.] A narrow shred.
These two apartments were hung in close mourning, and only a *strip* of bays round the other rooms. *Swift.*

To STRIPE. *v. a.* [*strepen*, Dutch.] To variegate with lines of different colours.

STRIPE. *n. s.* [*strepe*, Dutch.]

1. A lineary variation of colour. This seems to be the original notion of the word.
Gardeners may have three roots among an hundred that are rare, as purple and carnation of several *stripes*. *Bacon.*

2. A shred of a different colour.
One of the most valuable trimmings of their cloaths was a long *stripe* sowed upon the garment, called latus clavus. *Arbuth.*

3. A weal; or discolouration made by a lash or blow.
Cruelty marked him with inglorious *stripes*. *Thomson.*

4. A blow; a lash.
A body cannot be so torn with *stripes*, as a mind with remembrance of wicked actions. *Hayward.*
To those that are yet within the reach of the *stripes* and reproofs of their own conscience; I would address that they would not seek to remove themselves from that wholsome discipline. *Decay of Piety.*

STRI'PLING. *n. s.* [Of uncertain etymology.] A youth; one in the state of adolescence.
'Thwart the lane,
He, with two *striplings*, lads, more like to run
The country base, than to commit such slaughter,
Made good the passage. *Shakespeare's Cymbeline.*
Now a *stripling* cherub he appears,
Not of the prime, yet such as in his face
Youth smil'd cœlestial. *Milton's Paradise Lost.*
Compositions on any important subjects are not matters to be wrung from poor *striplings*, like blood out of the nose, or the plucking of untimely fruit. *Milton on Education.*
As when young *striplings* whip the top for sport,
On the smooth pavement of an empty court;
The wooden engine whirls. *Dryden's Æneid.*
As every particular member of the body is nourished with a several qualified juice, so children and *striplings*, old men and young men must have divers diets. *Arbuthnot on Aliments.*

To STRIVE. *v.n.* Preterite *I strove*, anciently *I strived*; part. pass. *striven*. [*streven*, Dutch; *estriver*, French.]

1. To struggle; to labour; to make an effort.
The immutability of God they *strive* unto, by working after one and the same manner. *Hooker*
Many brave young minds have, through hearing the praises and eulogies of worthy men, been stirred up to affect the like commendations, and so *strive* to the like deserts. *Spenser.*
Strive with me in your prayers to God for me. *Rom.* xv.
So have I *strived* to preach the gospel. *Rom.* xv. 20.

2. To contest; to contend; to struggle in opposition to another: with *against* or *with* before the person opposed.
Do as adversaries do in law,
Strive mightily, but eat and drink as friends. *Shakespeare.*
Thou art caught, because thou hast *striven* against the Lord. *Jer.* l. 24.
Strive for the truth unto death. *Ecclus* iv. 28.
Why dost thou *strive* against him? *Job* xxxiii. 13.
Charge them that they *strive* not about words to no profit. 2 *Tim.* ii. 14.
Avoid contentions and *strivings* about the law. *Tit.* iii. 9.
This is only warrantable conflict for the trial of our faith; so that these *strivings* are not a contending with superior powers. *L'Estrange.*
Thus does every wicked man that contemns God, who can save or destroy him who *strives* with his Maker. *Tillotson.*
Now private pity *strove* with publick hate,
Reason with rage, and eloquence with fate. *Denham.*
If intestine broils alarm the hive,
For two pretenders oft for empire *strive*,
The vulgar in divided factions jar;
And murm'ring sounds proclaim the civil war. *Dryden.*

3. To vie; to be comparable to; to emulate; to contend in excellence.
Nor that sweet grove
Of Daphne by Orontes, and the inspir'd
Castalian spring, might with this paradise
Of Eden *strive*. *Milton's Parad. Lost.*

STRI'VER. *n. s.* [from *strive*.] One who labours; one who contends.

STRO'KAL. *n. s.* An instrument used by glass makers. *Bailey.*

STROKE, or *Strook*. Old preterite of *strike*, now commonly *struck*.

 He

He hoodwinked with kindneſs, leaſt of all men knew who *ſtroke* him. *Sidney.*

STROKE. *n. ſ.* [from *ſtrook*, the preterite of *ſtrike*]

1. A blow; a knock; a ſudden act of one body upon another.

Th' oars were ſilver,
Which to the tune of flutes kept *ſtroke*, and made
The water which they beat to follow faſter,
As amorous of their *ſtrokes*. *Shakeſp. Ant. and Cleopatra.*

2. A hoſtile blow.

As cannons overcharg'd with double cracks,
So they redoubled *ſtrokes* upon the foe. *Shakeſpeare.*

He entered and won the whole kingdom of Naples, without ſtriking *ſtroke*. *Bacon.*

His white-man'd ſteeds that bow'd beneath the yoke,
He chear'd to courage with a gentle *ſtroke*,
Then urg'd his fiery chariot on the foe,
And riſing, ſhook his lance in act to throw. *Dryden.*

Both were of ſhining ſteel, and wrought ſo pure,
As might the *ſtrokes* of two ſuch arms endure. *Dryden.*

I had a long deſign upon the ears of Curl, but the rogue would never allow me a fair *ſtroke* at them, though my penknife was ready. *Swift.*

3. A ſudden diſeaſe or affliction.

Take this purſe, thou whom the heav'ns plagues
Have humbled to all *ſtrokes*. *Shakeſp. King Lear.*

4. The ſound of the clock.

What is't o'clock?—
Upon the *ſtroke* of four. *Shakeſpeare's Richard III.*

5. The touch of a pencil.

Oh, laſting as thoſe colours may they ſhine!
Free as thy *ſtroke*, yet faultleſs as thy line. *Pope.*

6. A touch; a maſterly or eminent effort.

Another in my place would take it for a notable *ſtroke* of good breeding, to compliment the reader. *L'Eſtrange.*

The boldeſt *ſtrokes* of poetry, when managed artfully, moſt delight the reader. *Dryden's State of Innocence.*

As he purchaſed the firſt ſucceſs in the preſent war, by forcing, into the ſervice of the confederates, an army that was raiſed againſt them, he will give one of the finiſhing *ſtrokes* to it, and help to conclude the great work. *Addiſon.*

A verdict more puts me in poſſeſſion of my eſtate, I queſtion not but you will give it the finiſhing *ſtroke*. *Arbuthnot.*

Iſiodore's collection was the great and bold *ſtroke*, which in its main parts has been diſcovered to be an impudent forgery. *Baker's Reflections on Learning.*

7. An effect ſuddenly or unexpectedly produced.

8. Power; efficacy.

Theſe having equal authority for inſtruction of the young prince, and well agreeing, bare equal *ſtroke* in divers faculties. *Hayward.*

Perfectly opacous bodies can but reflect the incident beams, thoſe that are diaphanous refract them too, and that refraction has ſuch a *ſtroke* in the production of colours, generated by the trajection of light through drops of water, that exhibit a rainbow through divers other tranſparent bodies. *Boyle.*

He has a great *ſtroke* with the reader when he condemns any of my poems, to make the world have a better opinion of them. *Dryden.*

The ſubtile effluvia of the male ſeed have the greateſt *ſtroke* in generation. *Ray.*

To STROKE. *v. a.* [ſtracan, Saxon.]

1. To rub gently with the hand by way of kindneſs or endearment; to ſooth.

Thus children do the ſilly birds they find
With *ſtroaking* hurt, and too much cramming kill. *Sidney.*

The ſenior weaned, his younger ſhall teach,
More *ſtroken* and made of, when ought it doth aile,
More gentle ye make it for yoke or the paile. *Tuſſer.*

Thy praiſe or diſpraiſe is to me alike,
One doth not *ſtroke* me, nor the other ſtrike. *Ben. Johnſ.*

He ſet forth a proclamation *ſtroaking* the people with fair promiſes, and humouring them with invectives againſt the king and government. *Bacon.*

He dry'd the falling drops, and yet more kind,
He *ſtrok'd* her cheeks. *Dryden.*

Come, let us practiſe death,
Stroke the grim lion till he grow familiar. *Dryden.*

She pluck'd the riſing flow'rs, and fed
The gentle beaſt, and fondly *ſtroak'd* his head. *Addiſon.*

2. To rub gently in one direction.

When the big-udder'd cows with patience ſtand,
Waiting the *ſtrokings* of the damſel's hand. *Gay.*

To STROLL. *v. n.* To wander; to ramble; to rove; to be a vagrant.

She's mine, and thine, and *ſtrolling* up and down. *Granv.*

Your wine lock'd up, your butler *ſtroll'd* abroad. *Pope.*

Theſe mothers *ſtrole*, to beg ſuſtenance for their helpleſs infants. *Swift.*

STRO'LLER. *n. ſ.* [from *ſtroll.*] A vagrant; a wanderer; a vagabond.

Two brother-hermits, ſaints by trade,
Diſguis'd in tatter'd habits, went
To a ſmall village down in Kent;
Where, in the *ſtrollers* canting ſtrain,
They begg'd from door to door in vain. *Swift.*

The men of pleaſure, who never go to church, form their ideas of the clergy from a few poor *ſtrollers* they often obſerve in the ſtreets. *Swift.*

STROND. *n. ſ.* [from *ſtrand.*] The beach; the bank of the water.

So looks the *ſtrond* whereon th' imperious flood
Hath left a witneſs'd uſurpation. *Shakeſpeare's H. IV.*

STRONG. *adj.* [ſtrang, Saxon.]

1. Vigorous; forceful; of great ability of body.

Though 'gan the villain wax ſo fierce and *ſtrong*,
That nothing may ſuſtain his furious force,
He caſt him down to ground, and all along
Drew him through dirt and mire. *Fairy Queen.*

The *ſtrong*-wing'd Mercury ſhould fetch thee up,
And ſet thee by Jove's ſide. *Shakeſpeare's Ant. and Cleopatra.*

That our oxen may be *ſtrong* to labour. *Pſal.* cxliv. 14.

The Marſian and Sabellian race,
Strong limb'd and ſtout. *Dryden.*

Orſes the *ſtrong* to greater ſtrength muſt yield;
He, with Parthenius, were by Rapo kill'd. *Dryden.*

2. Fortified; ſecure from attack.

Within Troy's *ſtrong* immures
The raviſh'd Helen with wanton Paris ſleeps. *Shakeſpeare.*

An army of Engliſh engaged in the midſt, between an army of a greater number, freſh and in vigour on the one ſide, and a town *ſtrong* in fortification, and *ſtrong* in men on the other. *Bacon's War with Spain.*

It is no matter how things are, ſo a man obſerve but the agreement of his own imaginations, and talk conformably, it is all truth: ſuch caſtles in the air will be as *ſtrong* holds of truth as the demonſtrations of Euclid. *Locke.*

3. Powerful; mighty.

While there was war between the houſes of Saul and David, Abner made himſelf *ſtrong* for Saul. 2 *Sam.* iii. 6.

The merchant-adventurers being a *ſtrong* company, and well underſet with rich men and good order, held out bravely. *Bacon.*

Thoſe that are *ſtrong* at ſea may eaſily bring them to what terms they pleaſe. *Addiſon.*

The weak, by thinking themſelves *ſtrong*, are induced to proclaim war againſt that which ruins them; and the *ſtrong*, by conceiting themſelves weak, are thereby rendered as uſeleſs as if they really were ſo. *South's Sermons.*

4. Supplied with forces.

When he was not ſix and twenty *ſtrong*,
Sick in the world's regard, wretched and low,
My father gave him welcome to the ſhore. *Shak. Hen. IV.*

He was, at his riſing from Exeter, between ſix and ſeven thouſand *ſtrong*. *Bacon.*

In Britain's lovely iſle a ſhining throng
War in his cauſe, a thouſand beauties *ſtrong*. *Tickell.*

5. Hale; healthy.

Better is the poor being ſound and *ſtrong* in conſtitution, than a rich man afflicted in his body. *Ecclus* xxx. 14.

6. Forcibly acting in the imagination.

This is one of the *ſtrongeſt* examples of a perſonation that ever was. *Bacon.*

7. Ardent; eager; poſitive; zealous.

Her mother, ever *ſtrong* againſt that match,
And firm for doctor Caius, hath appointed,
That he ſhall ſhuffle her away. *Shakeſp. Mer. Wives of Wind.*

In choice of committees for ripening buſineſs for the council, it is better to chuſe indifferent perſons, than to make an indifferency, by putting in thoſe that are *ſtrong* on both ſides. *Bacon.*

The knight is a much *ſtronger* tory in the country than in town, which is neceſſary for the keeping up his intereſt. *Add.*

8. Full; having any quality in a great degree; affecting the ſight or ſmell forcibly.

Add with Cecropian thyme *ſtrong*-ſcented centaury. *Dryd.*

By mixing ſuch powders we are not to expect a *ſtrong* and full white, ſuch as is that of paper; but ſome duſky obſcure one, ſuch as might ariſe from a mixture of light and darkneſs, or from white and black, that is, a grey or dun, or ruſſet brown. *Newton's Opticks.*

Thus ſhall there be made two bows of colours, an interior and *ſtronger*, by one reflexion in the drops, and an exterior and fainter by two; for the light becomes fainter by every reflexion. *Newton's Opticks.*

9. Potent; intoxicating.

Get *ſtrong* beer to rub your horſes heels. *Swift.*

10. Having a deep tincture; affecting the taſte forcibly.

Many of their propoſitions favour very *ſtrong* of the old leaven of innovations. *King Charles.*

11. Affecting the ſmell powerfully.

The prince of Cambay's daily food
Is aſps, and baſiliſk and toad,
Which makes him have ſo *ſtrong* a breath,
Each night he ſtinks a queen to death. *Hudibras.*

The

The heat of a human body, as it grows more intense, makes the urine smell more *strong*. *Arbuthnot.*

12. Hard of digestion; not easily nutrimental.

Strong meat belongeth to them that are of full age. *Hebr.*

13. Furnished with abilities for any thing.

I was *stronger* in prophecy than in criticism. *Dryden.*

14. Valid; confirmed.

In process of time, an ungodly custom grown *strong*, was kept as a law. *Wisdom* xiv. 16.

15. Violent; vehement; forcible.

In the days of his flesh he offered up prayers, with *strong* crying and tears. *Heb.* v. 7.

The scriptures make deep and *strong* impressions on the minds of men: and whosoever denies this, as he is in point of religion atheistical, so in understanding brutish. *J. Corbet.*

16. Cogent; conclusive.

Messengers
Of *strong* prevailment in unharden'd youth. *Shakespeare.*

What *strong* cries must they be that shall drown so loud a clamour of impieties. *Decay of Piety.*

Produce your cause; bring forth your *strong* reasons. *Isa.*

17. Able; skilful; of great force of mind.

There is no English soul
More *stronger* to direct you than yourself,
If with the sap of reason you would quench,
Or but allay the fire of passion. *Shakesp. Henry* VIII.

18. Firm; compact; not soon broken.

Full on his ankle fell the pond'rous stone,
Burst the *strong* nerves, and crash'd the solid bone. *Pope.*

19. Forcibly written; comprising much meaning in few words.

STRONGFI'STED. *adj.* [*strong* and *fist*.] Stronghanded.

John, who was pretty *strongfisted*, gave him such a squeeze as made his eyes water. *Arbuthnot.*

STRO'NGHAND. *n. s.* [*strong* and *hand*.] Force; violence.

When their captain dieth, if the seniory should descend to his child, and an infant, another would thrust him out by *stronghand*, being then unable to defend his right. *Spenser.*

They wanting land wherewith to sustain their people, and the Tuscans having more than enough, it was their meaning to take what they needed by *stronghand*. *Raleigh.*

STRO'NGLY. *adv.* [from *strong*.]

1. Powerfully; forcibly.

The colewort is an enemy to any plant, because it draweth *strongly* the fattest juice of the earth. *Bacon's Natural History.*

The dazzling light
Had flash'd too *strongly* on his aking sight. *Addison.*

Water impregnated with salt attenuates *strongly*. *Arbuthnot.*

When the attention is *strongly* fixed to any subject, all that is said concerning it makes a deeper impression. *Watts.*

2. With strength; with firmness; in such a manner as to last; in such a manner as not easily to be forced.

Great Dunsinane he *strongly* fortifies. *Shakespeare.*
Let the foundations be *strongly* laid. *Ezra* vi. 3.

3. Vehemently; forcibly; eagerly.

All these accuse him *strongly*. *Shakespeare.*

The ruinous consequences of Wood's patent have been *strongly* represented by both houses. *Swift.*

STRO'NGWATER. *n. s.* [*strong* and *water*.] Distilled spirits.

Metals receive in readily *strongwaters*; and *strongwaters* do readily pierce into metals and stones: and some will touch upon gold, that will not touch upon silver. *Bacon's Nat. Hist.*

STROOK. The preterite of *strike*, used in poetry for *struck*.

A sudden tempest from the desart flew,
With horrid wings, and thunder'd as it blew:
Then whirling round, the quoins together *strook*. *Sandys.*

That conqu'ring look
When next beheld, like light'ning *strook*
My blasted soul, and made me bow. *Waller.*

He, like a patient angler, ere he *strook*,
Would let them play a while upon the hook. *Dryden.*

STROPHE. *n. s.* [*strophe*, Fr. στροφὴ.] A stanza.

STROVE. The preterite of *strive*.

Having quite lost the way of nobleness, he *strove* to climb to the height of terribleness. *Sidney.*

To STROUT. *v. n.* [*strussen*, German.] To swell with an appearance of greatness; to walk with affected dignity; to strut. This is commonly written *strut*, which seems more proper.

To STROUT. *v. a.* To swell out; to puff out; to enlarge by affectation.

I will make a brief list of the particulars in an historical truth nowise *strouted*, nor made greater by language. *Bacon.*

To STROW. *v. n.* [See to STREW.]

1. To spread by being scattered.

Angel forms lay entranc'd,
Thick as autumnal leaves that *strow* the brooks
In Valombrosa. *Milton's Paradise Lost.*

2. To spread by scattering; to besprinkle.

All the ground
With shiver'd armour *strown*. *Milton's Paradise Lost.*

Come, shepherds come, and *strow* with leaves the plain;
Such funeral rites your Daphnis did ordain. *Dryden.*

With osier floats the standing water *strow*,
With massy stones make bridges if it flow. *Dryden.*

3. To spread.

There have been three years dearth of corn, and every place *strow'd* with beggars. *Swift.*

4. To scatter; to throw at random.

Synah, can I tell thee more?
And of our ladies bowre;
But little need to *strow* my store,
Suffice this hill of our. *Spenser.*

The tree in storms
The glad earth about her *strows*,
With treasure from her yielding boughs. *Waller.*

Possession kept the beaten road,
And gatherd all his brother *strow'd*. *Swift.*

To STROWL. *v. n.* To range; to wander. [See STROLL.]

'Tis she who nightly *strowls* with saunt'ring pace. *Gay.*

To STROY. *v. a.* [For *destroy*.]

Dig garden, *stroy* mallow, now may you at ease. *Tusser.*

STRUCK. The old preterite and participle passive of *strike*.

This message bear: the Trojans and their chief
Bring holy peace, and beg the king's relief;
Struck with so great a name, and all on fire,
The youth replies; whatever you require. *Dryden.*

In a regular plantation, I can place myself in its several centers, so as to view all the walks *struck* from them. *Spectator.*

High on his car Sesostris *struck* my view,
Whom scepter'd slaves in golden harness drew. *Pope.*

Some to conceit alone their taste confine,
And glitt'ring thoughts *struck* out at ev'ry line. *Pope.*

STRU'CKEN. The old participle passive of *strike*.

Down fell the duke, his joints dissolv'd asunder,
Blind with the light, and *strucken* dead with wonder. *Fairf.*

All liquours *strucken* make round circles, and dash. *Bacon.*

Silent, and in face
Confounded, long they sat, as *strucken* mute. *Milton.*

STRU'CTURE. [*structure*, Fr. *structura*, from *structus*, Latin.]

1. Act of building; practice of building.

His son builds on, and never is content,
Till the last farthing is in *structure* spent. *Dryden.*

2. Manner of building; form; make.

Several have gone about to inform them, but for want of insight into the *structure* and constitution of the terraqueous globe, have not given satisfaction. *Woodward.*

3. Edifice; building.

Ecbatana her *structure* vast there shews,
And Hecatompylos her hundred gates. *Milton.*

High on a rock of ice the *structure* lay. *Pope.*
There stands a *structure* of majestick frame. *Pope.*

STRUDE. *or Strode. n. s.* A stock of breeding mares. *Baily.*

To STRU'GGLE. *v. n.* [Of uncertain etymology.]

1. To labour; to act with effort.

2. To strive; to contend; to contest.

No man is guilty of an act of intemperance but he might have forborn it; not without some trouble from the *strugglings* of the contrary habit, but still the thing was possible. *South.*

In the time of Henry VIII. differences of religion tore the nation into two mighty factions, and, under the name of Papist and Protestant, *struggled* in her bowels with many various events. *Temple.*

I repent, like some despairing wretch,
That boldly plunges in the frightful deep,
Then pants, and *struggles* with the whirling waves;
And catches every slender reed to save him. *Smith.*

3. To labour in difficulties; to be in agonies or distress.

Strong virtue, like strong nature, *struggles* still,
Exerts itself, and then throws off the ill. *Dryden.*

'Tis wisdom to beware
And better shun the bait, than *struggle* in the snare. *Dryden.*

If men *struggle* through as many troubles to be miserable as to be happy; my readers may be persuaded to be good. *Spect.*

He *struggling* groans beneath the cruel hands
Even of the clowns he feeds. *Thomson.*

STRU'GGLE. *n. s.* [from the verb.]

1. Labour; effort.

2. Contest; contention.

When, in the division of parties, men only strove for the first place in the prince's favour, an honest man might look upon the *struggle* with indifference. *Addison.*

It began and ended without any of those unnatural *struggles* for the chair, which have disturbed the peace of this great city. *Atterbury.*

3. Agony; tumultuous distress.

STRUMA. n. s. [Latin.] A glandular swelling; the king's evil.

A gentlewoman had a *struma* about the instep, very hard and deep about the tendons. *Wiseman's Surgery.*

STRU'MOUS. *adj.* [from *struma*.] Having swelling in the glands.

How to treat them when *strumous*, scirrhous, or cancerous. *Wiseman.*

STRU'MPET. *n. s.* A whore; a prostitute. Of doubtful original.

Stropo vieux mot *palliardise*. Stuprum, Lat. *Trevoux.*

How like a younker or a prodigal
The skarfed bark puts from her native bay,

Hugg'd

Hugg'd and embraced by the *ſtrumpet* wind!
How like a prodigal doth ſhe return,
Lean, rent, and beggar'd by the *ſtrumpet* wind. *Shakeſp.*
Ne'er could the *ſtrumpet*,
With all her double vigour, art and nature,
Once ſtir my temper, but this virtuous maid
Subdues me quite. *Shakeſp. Meaſure for Meaſure.*
If to preſerve this veſſel for my lord
From any other, foul, unlawful touch,
Be not to be a *ſtrumpet*, I am none. *Shakeſpeare's Othello.*

Common fame is as falſe and impudent as a common *ſtrumpet*. *L'Eſtrange.*

Honour had his due;
Before the holy prieſt my vows were ty'd:
So came I not a *ſtrumpet* but a bride. *Dryden.*

To STRU'MPET. *v. a.* To make a whore; to debauch.
If we two be one, and thou play falſe,
I do digeſt the poiſon of thy fleſh,
Being *ſtrumpeted* by the contagion. *Shakeſpeare.*

STRUNG. The preterite and participle paſſive of *ſtring.*
The *ſtrung* bow points out the Cynthian queen. *Gay.*

To STRUT. *v. n.* [*ſtruſſen*, German.]

1. To walk with affected dignity; to ſwell with ſtatelineſs.
Adore our errours, laugh at's while we *ſtrut*
To our confuſion. *Shakeſpeare's Ant. and Cleopatra.*
Does he not hold up his head and *ſtrut* in his gait? *Shakeſp.*
Though thou *ſtrut* and paint,
Yet art thou both ſhrunk up and old. *Ben. Johnſon.*
The falſe ſyren
Struts on the waves, and ſhews the brute below. *Dryden.*
We will be with you ere the crowing cock
Salutes the light, and *ſtruts* before his feather'd flock. *Dryd.*

2. To ſwell; to protuberate.
The goats with *ſtrutting* dugs ſhall homeward ſpeed. *Dryd.*
The pow'r appeas'd, with winds ſuffic'd the ſail,
The bellying canvaſs *ſtrutted* with the gale. *Dryden.*
As thy *ſtrutting* bags with money riſe,
The love of gain is of an equal ſize. *Dryden.*

STRUT. *n. ſ.* [from the verb.] An affectation of ſtatelineſs in the walk.

Certain gentlemen of the gown, by ſmirking countenances and an ungainly *ſtrut* in their walk, have got preferment. *Swift.*

STUB. *n. ſ.* [ſteb, Sax. *ſtubbe*, Daniſh; *ſtob*, Dutch; *ſtipes*, Latin.]

1. A thick ſhort ſtock left when the reſt is cut off.

Dametas guided the horſes ſo ill, that the wheel coming over a great *ſtub* of a tree, overturned the coach. *Sidney.*

All about, old ſtocks and *ſtubs* of trees,
Whereon nor fruit nor leaf was ever ſeen,
Did hang upon the ragged rocky knees. *Fairy Queen.*
To buy at the *ſtub* is the beſt for the buyer,
More timely proviſion, the cheaper is fire. *Tuſſer.*

Upon cutting down of an old timber tree, the *ſtub* hath put out ſometimes a tree of another kind. *Bacon's Nat. Hiſtory.*

We here
Live on tough roots and *ſtubs*, to thirſt inur'd,
Men to much miſery and hardſhips born. *Milton.*
Prickly *ſtubs* inſtead of trees are found,
Or woods with knots and knares deform'd and old;
Headleſs the moſt, and hideous to behold. *Dryd. Knights Tale.*

2. A log; a block.

You ſhall have more adoe to drive our dulleſt and lazieſt youth, our ſtocks and *ſtubs*, from the infinite deſire of ſuch a happy nurture, than we have now to haul our choiceſt wits to that aſinine feaſt of ſow-thiſtles and brambles. *Milton.*

To STUB. *v. a.* [from the noun.] To force up; to extirpate.

His two tuſks ſerve for fighting and feeding; by the help whereof he *ſtubs* up edible roots out of the ground, or tears off the bark of trees. *Grew's Muſæum.*

The other tree was griev'd,
Grew ſcrubby, dry'd a-top, was ſtunted;
So the next parſon *ſtubb'd* and burnt it. *Swift.*

STU'BBED. *adj.* [from *ſtub.*] Truncated; ſhort and thick.
A pain he in his head-piece feels,
Againſt a *ſtubbed* tree he reels,
And up went poor Hobgoblin's heels. *Drayton.*
To ſpight the coy nymphs,
Hang upon our *ſtubbed* horns
Garlands, ribbons, and fine poeſies. *Ben. Johnſon.*

STU'BBEDNESS. *n. ſ.* [from *ſtubbed.*] The ſtate of being ſhort, thick, and truncated.

STU'BBLE. *n. ſ.* [*eſtouble*, Fr. *ſtoppel*, Dutch; *ſtipula*, Latin.] The ſtalks of corn left in the field by the reaper.
This ſuggeſted
At ſome time, when his ſoaring inſolence
Shall reach the people, will be the fire
To kindle their dry *ſtubble*, and their blaze
Shall darken him for ever *Shakeſpeare.*

If a ſmall red flower in the *ſtubble*-fields, called the wincopipe, open in the morning, you may be ſure of a fair day. *Bacon.*

His ſucceeding years afford him little more than the *ſtubble* of his own harveſt. *Dryden.*

Thrice happy Duck, employ'd in threſhing *ſtubble*,
Thy toil is leſſen'd and thy profits double. *Swift.*

After the firſt crop is off they plow in the wheat *ſtubble*. *Mortimer's Huſbandry.*

STU'BBORN. *adj.* [This word, of which no obvious etymology appears, is derived by *Minſhew* from *ſtoutborn*, referred by *Junius* to ςιβαρὸς, and deduced better by Mr. *Lye*, from *ſtub*, perhaps from *ſtub-horn.*]

1. Obſtinate; inflexible; contumacious.
The queen is obſtinate,
Stubborn to juſtice, apt t' accuſe it, and
Diſdainful to be tried by't. *Shakeſpeare's Henry VIII.*
You *ſtubborn* antient knave, you reverend braggart,
We'll teach you.— *Shakeſpeare's King Lear.*

He believed he had ſo humbled the garriſon, that they would be no longer ſo *ſtubborn*. *Clarendon.*

2. Perſiſting; perſevering; ſteady.

All this is to be had only from the epiſtles themſelves, with *ſtubborn* attention, and more than common application. *Locke.*

3. Stiff; not pliable; inflexible; not eaſily admitting impreſſion.
Strifeful Atin in their *ſtubborn* mind,
Coals of contention and hot vengeance tin'd. *Spenſer.*
Love ſoftens me, and blows up fires which paſs
Through my tough heart, and melt the *ſtubborn* maſs. *Dryd.*
I'll not flatter this tempeſtuous king,
But work his *ſtubborn* ſoul a nobler way. *Dryden.*
Take a plant of *ſtubborn* oak,
And labour him with many a ſturdy ſtroak. *Dryden.*

4. Hardy; firm.
Patience under torturing pain,
Where *ſtubborn* ſtoicks would complain. *Swift.*

5. Harſh; rough; rugged.

We will not oppoſe any thing that is hard and *ſtubborn*, but by a ſoft anſwer deaden their force. *Burnet.*

6. In all its uſes it commonly implies ſomething of a bad quality.

STU'BBORNLY. *adv.* [from *ſtubborn.*] Obſtinately; contumaciouſly; inflexibly.
Stubbornly he did repugn the truth,
About a certain queſtion in the law. *Shakeſp. H. VI.*

He wilfully neglects his book, and *ſtubbornly* refuſes any thing he can do. *Locke.*

So cloſe they cling, ſo *ſtubbornly* retire,
Their love's more violent than the chymiſt's fire. *Garth.*

STU'BBORNNESS. *n. ſ.* [from *ſtubborn.*] Obſtinacy; vicious ſtoutneſs; contumacy; inflexibility.
Happy is your grace,
That can tranſlate the *ſtubbornneſs* of fortune
Into ſo quiet and ſo ſweet a ſtyle. *Shakeſp. As you like it.*

He choſe a courſe leaſt ſubject to envy, between ſtiff *ſtubbornneſs* and filthy flattery. *Hayward.*

Patriots, in peace, aſſert the people's right,
With noble *ſtubbornneſs* reſiſting might. *Dryden.*

Stubbornneſs, and an obſtinate diſobedience, muſt be maſtered with blows. *Locke.*

It failed, partly by the accidents of a ſtorm, and partly by the *ſtubbornneſs* or treachery of that colony for whoſe relief it was deſigned. *Swift.*

STU'BBY. *adj.* [from *ſtub.*] Short and thick; ſhort and ſtrong.

The baſe is ſurrounded with a garland of black and *ſtubby* briſtles. *Grew's Muſæum.*

STU'BNAIL. *n. ſ.* [*ſtub* and *nail.*] A nail broken off; a ſhort thick nail.

STUCCO. *n. ſ.* [Ital. *ſtuc*, Fr.] A kind of fine plaſter for walls.
Palladian walls, Venetian doors,
Groteſco roofs, and *ſtucco* floors. *Pope.*

STUCK. The preterite and participle paſſive of *ſtick.*

I had a paſs with rapier, ſcabbard and all, and he gives me the *ſtuck* in with ſuch a mortal motion, that it is inevitable. *Shakeſpeare's Twelfth Night.*

What more infamous brands have records *ſtuck* upon any, than thoſe who uſed the beſt parts for the worſt ends? *Decay of Piety.*

The partners of their crime will learn obedience,
When they look up and ſee their fellow-traitors
Stuck on a fork. *Addiſon.*
When the polypus from forth his cave,
Torn with full force, reluctant beats the wave,
His ragged claws are *ſtuck* with ſtones and ſands. *Pope.*
Stuck o'er with titles, and hung round with ſtrings,
That thou may'ſt be by kings, or whores of kings. *Pope.*

STUCKLE *n. ſ.* [*ſtook*, Scottiſh.] A number of ſheaves laid together in the field to dry. *Ainſworth.*

STUD. *n. ſ.* [ſtudu, Saxon.]

1. A poſt; a ſtake. In ſome ſuch meaning perhaps it is to be taken in the following paſſage, which I do not underſtand.

A barn in the country, that hath one ſingle *ſtud*, or one height of *ſtuds* to the roof, is two ſhillings a foot. *Mortimer.*

2. A nail with a large head driven for ornament; any ornamental knob or protuberance.

Handles

Handles were to add,
For which he now was making *studs*. *Chapman's Iliad.*
A belt of straw, and ivy buds,
With coral clasps and amber *studs*. *Raleigh.*
Crystal and myrrhine cups emboss'd with gems,
And *studs* of pearl. *Milton's Paradise Regain'd.*
Upon a plane are several small oblong *studs*, placed regularly in a quincunx order. *Woodward on Fossils.*
A desk he had of curious work,
With glitt'ring *studs* about. *Swift.*
3. [Stode, Saxon; *stod*, Islandick, is a stallion.] A collection of breeding horses and mares.
In the *studs* of Ireland, where care is taken, we see horses bred of excellent shape, vigour, and size. *Temple.*
To Stud. *v. a.* [from the noun.] To adorn with studs or shining knobs.
Thy horses shall be trapp'd,
Their harness *studded* all with gold and pearl. *Shakespeare.*
A silver *studded* ax, alike bestow'd. *Dryden's Æn.*
Stu'dent. *n. s.* [*studens*, Latin.] A man given to books; a scholar; a bookish man.
Keep a gamester from dice, and a good *student* from his book. *Shakesp. Merry Wives of Windsor.*
This grave advice some sober *student* bears,
And loudly rings it in his fellow's ears. *Dryden's Pers.*
A *student* shall do more in one hour, when all things concur to invite him to any special study, than in four at a dull season. *Watts's Logick.*
I slightly touch the subject, and recommend it to some *student* of the profession. *Arbuthnot on Coins.*
Stu'died. *adj.* [from *study*.]
1. Learned; versed in any study; qualified by study.
He died
As one that had been *studied* in his death,
To throw away the dearest thing he ow'd,
As 'twere a careless trifle. *Shakespeare.*
I am well *studied* for a liberal thanks,
Which I do owe you. *Shak. Ant. and Cleopatra.*
It will be fit that some man, reasonably *studied* in the law, go as chancellor. *Bacon.*
2. Having any particular inclination. Out of use.
A prince should not be so loosely *studied* as to remember so weak a composition. *Shakespeare.*
Stu'dier. *n. s.* [from *study*.] One who studies.
Lipsius was a great *studier* of the stoical philosophy: upon his death-bed his friend told him, that he needed not use arguments to persuade him to patience, the philosophy which he had studied would furnish him; he answers him, Lord Jesus, give me Christian patience. *Tillotson.*
There is a law of nature, as intelligible to a rational creature and *studier* of that law, as the positive laws of commonwealths. *Locke.*
Stu'dious. *adj.* [*studieux*, French; *studiosus*, Latin.]
1. Given to books and contemplation; given to learning.
A proper remedy for wandering thoughts, he that shall propose, would do great service to the *studious* and contemplative part of mankind. *Locke.*
2. Diligent; busy.
Studious to find new friends, and new allies. *Tickell.*
3. Attentive to; careful.
The people made
Stout for the war, and *studious* of their trade. *Dryden.*
There are who, fondly *studious* of increase,
Rich foreign mold on their ill-natur'd land
Induce. *Philips.*
4. Contemplative; suitable to meditation.
Let my due feet never fail
To walk the *studious* cloister's pale. *Milton.*
Him for the *studious* shade
Kind nature form'd. *Thomson's Summer.*
Stu'diously. *adv.* [from *studious*.]
1. Contemplatively; with close application to literature.
2. Diligently; carefully; attentively.
On a short pruning hook his head reclines,
And *studiously* surveys his gen'rous wines. *Dryden's Æn.*
All of them *studiously* cherished the memory of their honourable extraction. *Atterbury.*
Stu'diousness. *n. s.* [from *studious*.] Addiction to study.
STU'DY. *n. s.* [*estude*, French; *studium*, Latin.]
1. Application of mind to books and learning.
Study gives strength to the mind; conversation, grace. *Temp.*
Engage the mind in *study* by a consideration of the divine pleasures of truth and knowledge. *Watts.*
2. Perplexity; deep cogitation.
Th' idea of her life shall sweetly creep
Into his *study* of imagination. *Shak. Much Ado about Nothing.*
The king of Castile, a little confused, and in a *study*, said, that can I not do with my honour. *Bacon's Henry VII.*
3. Attention; meditation; contrivance.
What can happen
To me above this wretchedness? All your *studies*
Make me a curse like this. *Shakesp. Henry VIII.*
Just men they seem'd, and all their *study* bent
To worship God aright, and know his works. *Milton.*
4. Any particular kind of learning.
Studies serve for delight in privateness and retiring, for ornament in discourse, and for ability in the judgment and disposition of business. *Bacon's Essays.*
5. Apartment set off for literary employment.
Get me a taper in my *study*, Lucius. *Shakes. Jul. Cæs.*
Knock at the *study*, where, they say, he keeps,
To ruminate strange plots. *Shakesp. Titus Andronicus.*
Let all *studies* and libraries be towards the East. *Wotton.*
Some servants of the king visited the lodgings of the accused members, and sealed up their *studies* and trunks. *Clarendon.*
Both adorn'd their age;
One for the *study*, t'other for the stage. *Dryden.*
To Stu'dy. *v. n.* [*studeo*, Latin; *estudier*, French.]
1. To think with very close application; to muse.
I found a moral first, and then *studied* for a fable. *Swift.*
2. To endeavour diligently.
Study to be quiet, and do your own business. 1 *Thes.* iv. 11.
To Stu'dy. *v. a.*
1. To apply the mind to.
Nothing lovelier can be found
In woman, than to *study* houshold good. *Milton.*
If a gentleman be to *study* any language, it ought to be that of his own country. *Locke.*
2. To consider attentively.
He hath *studied* her well, and translated her out of honesty into English. *Shakesp. Merry Wives of Windsor.*
Study thyself: what rank, or what degree,
The wise Creator has ordain'd for thee. *Dryden's Pers.*
You have *studied* every spot of ground in Flanders, which has been the scene of battles and sieges. *Dryden.*
3. To learn by application.
You could, for a need, *study* a speech of some dozen lines, which I would set down. *Shakesp. Hamlet.*
STUFF. *n. s.* [*stoffe*, Dutch; *estoffe*, French.]
1. Any matter or body.
Let Phidias have rude and obstinate *stuff* to carve: though his art do that it should, his work will lack that beauty, which otherwise in fitter matter it might have had. *Hooker.*
The workman on his *stuff* his skill doth show,
And yet the *stuff* gives not the man his skill. *Davies.*
Of brick, and of that *stuff*, they cast to build
A city and tow'r. *Milton.*
Pierce an hole near the inner edge, because the triangle hath there most substance of *stuff*. *Moxon's Mech. Exer.*
2. Materials out of which any thing is made.
Thy verse swells with *stuff* so fine and smooth,
That thou art even natural in thine art. *Shakesp. Timon.*
Cæsar hath wept;
Ambition should be made of sterner *stuff*. *Shakes. Jul. Cæs.*
Success or loss, what is or is not, serves
As *stuff* for these two to make paradoxes. *Shakespeare.*
Thy father, that poor rag,
Must be thy subject, who in spight put *stuff*
To some she-beggar, and compounded thee
Poor rogue hereditary. *Shakespeare's Timon.*
Degrading prose explains his meaning ill,
And shews the *stuff*, and not the workman's skill. *Roscom.*
3. Furniture; goods.
Fare away to get our *stuff* aboard. *Shakespeare.*
He took away locks, and gave away the king's *stuff*. *Hayw.*
Groaning waggons loaded high
With *stuff*. *Cowley's Davideis.*
4. That which fills any thing.
With some sweet oblivious antidote
Cleanse the stuff'd bosom of that perilous *stuff*
Which weighs upon the heart. *Shakespeare.*
5. Essence; elemental part.
Though in the trade of war I have slain men,
Yet do I hold it very *stuff* o' th' conscience
To do no contriv'd murther. *Shakesp. Othello.*
6. Any mixture or medicine.
I did compound for her
A certain *stuff*, which, being ta'en, would seize
The present power of life. *Shakesp. Cymbeline.*
7. Cloth or texture of any kind.
8. Textures of wool thinner and slighter than cloath.
Let us turn the wools of the land into cloaths and *stuffs* of our own growth, and the hemp and flax growing here into linen cloth and cordage. *Bacon's Advice to Villiers.*
9. Matter or thing. In contempt.
O proper *stuff*!
This is the very painting of your fear. *Shakes. Macbeth.*
Such *stuff* as madmen
Tongue and brain not. *Shakespeare.*
At this fusty *stuff*
The large Achilles, on his prest bed lolling,
From his deep chest laughs out a loud applause. *Shakesp.*
Please not thyself the flatt'ring crowd to hear,
'Tis fulsome *stuff* to feed thy itching ear. *Dryden's Pers.*

Anger would indite
Such woful *stuff* as I or Shadwell write. *Dryden's Juven.*
To-morrow will be time enough
To hear such mortifying *stuff*. *Swift.*

The free things that among rakes pass for wit and spirit, must be shocking *stuff* to the ears of persons of delicacy. *Clariss.*

10. It is now seldom used in any sense but in contempt or dislike.

To Stuff. *v. a.* [from the noun.]

1. To fill very full with any thing.

When we've *stuff'd*
These pipes, and these conveyances of blood,
With wine and feeding, we have suppler souls. *Shakespeare.*
If I find him comforting the king,
It will *stuff* his suspicion more fully. *Shakespeare.*
Though plenteous, all too little seems
To *stuff* this maw, this vast unhide-bound corps. *Milton.*

What have we more to do than to *stuff* our guts with these figs? *L'Estrange.*

This crook drew hazel-boughs adown,
And *stuff'd* her apron wide with nuts so brown. *Gay.*

2. To fill to uneasiness.

With some oblivious antidote
Cleanse the *stuff'd* bosom of that perilous stuff
Which weighs upon the heart. *Shakespeare.*

3. To thrust into any thing.

Put roses into a glass with a narrow mouth, *stuffing* them close together, but without bruising, and they retain smell and colour fresh a year. *Bacon's Natural History.*

4. To fill by being put into any thing.

Grief fills the room up of my absent child,
Lies in his bed, walks up and down with me,
Stuffs out his vacant garments with his form. *Shakespeare.*
With inward arms the dire machine they load,
And iron bowels *stuff* the dark abode. *Dryden's Æn.*
A bed,
The *stuffing* leaves, with hides of bears o'erspread. *Dryden.*

5. To swell out by something thrust in.

I will be the man that shall make you great.——I cannot perceive how, unless you give me your doublet, and *stuff* me out with straw. *Shakesp. Henry IV.*

The gods for sin
Should with a swelling dropsy *stuff* thy skin. *Dryden.*
Officious Baucis lays
Two cushions *stuff'd* with straw, the seat to raise. *Dryden.*

6. To fill with something improper or superfluous.

It is not usual among the best patterns to *stuff* the report of particular lives with matter of publick record. *Wotton.*

Those accusations are *stuffed* with odious generals, that the proofs seldom make good. *Clarendon.*

For thee I dim these eyes, and *stuff* this head
With all such reading as was never read. *Pope.*

7. To obstruct the organs of scent or respiration.

These gloves the count sent me; they are an excellent perfume.——I am *stufft*, cousin, I cannot smell. *Shakespeare.*

8. To fill meat with something of high relish.

She went for parsly to *stuff* a rabbet. *Shakespeare.*

He aim'd at all, yet never could excel
In any thing but *stuffing* of his veal. *King's Cookery.*

9. To form by stuffing.

An eastern king put a judge to death for an iniquitous sentence, and ordered his hide to be *stuffed* into a cushion, and placed upon the tribunal. *Swift.*

To Stuff. *v. n.* To feed gluttonously.

Wedg'd in a spacious elbow-chair,
And on her plate a treble share,
As if she ne'er could have enough,
Taught harmless man to cram and *stuff*. *Swift.*

Stu'ffing. *n. s.* [from *stuff*.]

1. That by which any thing is filled.

Rome was a farrago out of the neighbouring nations; and Greece, though one monarchy under Alexander, yet the people that were the *stuffing* and materials thereof, existed before. *Hale.*

2. Relishing ingredients put into meat.

Arrach leaves are very good in pottage and *stuffings*. *Mort.*

Stuke, or *Stuck*. *n. s.* [*stuc*, French; *stucco*, Italian.] A composition of lime and marble, powdered very fine, commonly called plaister of Paris, with which figures and other ornaments resembling sculpture are made. *Bailey.*

Stulm. *n. s.* A shaft to draw water out of a mine. *Bailey.*

Stulti'loquence. *n. s.* [*stultus* and *loquentia*, Lat.] Foolish talk. *Dict.*

Stum. *n. s.* [*stum*, Swedish, supposed to be contracted from *mustum*, Latin.]

1. Wine yet unfermented; the cremor or froth on must.

An unctuous clammy vapour, that arises from the *stum* of grapes, when they lie mashed in the vat, puts out a light, when dipped into it. *Addison on Italy.*

2. New wine used to raise fermentation in dead and vapid wines.

Let our wines without mixture or *stum* be all fine,
Or call up the master, and break his dull noddle. *B. Johns.*

3. Wine revived by a new fermentation.

Drink ev'ry letter on't in *stum*,
And make it brisk champaigne become. *Hudibras.*

To Stum. *v. a.* [from the noun.] To renew wine by mixing fresh wine and raising a new fermentation.

Vapid wines are put upon the lees of noble wines to give them spirit, and we *stum* our wines to renew their spirits. *Floy.*

To STU'MBLE. *v. n.* [This word *Junius* derives from *stump*, and says the original meaning is to *strike* or *trip against a stump*. I rather think it comes from *tumble*.]

1. To trip in walking.

When she will take the rein, I let her run;
But she'll not *stumble*. *Shakesp. Winter's Tale.*

A headstall being restrained to keep him from *stumbling*, hath been often burst. *Shak. Taming of the Shrew.*

As we pac'd along
Upon the giddy footing of the hatches,
Methought that Glo'ster *stumbled*; and, in falling,
Struck me, that sought to stay him, overboard. *Shakesp.*

The way of the wicked is as darkness: they know not at what they *stumble*. *Prov.* iv. 19.

Cover'd o'er with blood,
Which from the patriot's breast in torrents flow'd,
He faints: his steed no longer hears the rein;
But *stumbles* o'er the heap his hand had slain. *Prior.*

2. To slip; to err; to slide into crimes or blunders.

He that loveth his brother, abideth in the light, and there is none occasion of *stumbling* in him. 1 *Jo.* ii. 10.

This my day of grace
They who neglect and scorn, shall never taste;
But hard be harden'd, blind be blinded more,
That they may *stumble* on, and deeper fall. *Milton.*

3. To strike against by chance; to light on by chance.

This extreme dealing had driven her to put herself with a great lady of that country, by which occasion she had *stumbled* upon such mischances as were little for the honour of her or her family. *Sidney.*

What man art thou, that, thus bescreen'd in night,
So *stumblest* on my counsel. *Shak. Romeo and Juliet.*

A mouse, bred in a chest, dropped out over the side, and *stumbled* upon a delicious morsel. *L'Estrange.*

Ovid *stumbled*, by some inadvertency, upon Livia in a bath. *Dryden.*

Many of the greatest inventions have been accidentally *stumbled* upon by men busy and inquisitive. *Ray.*

Write down *p* and *b*, and make signs to him to endeavour to pronounce them, and guide him by shewing him the motion of your own lips; by which he will, with a little endeavour, *stumble* upon one of them. *Holder's Elements of Speech.*

To Stu'mble. *v. a.*

1. To obstruct in progress; to make to trip or stop.

2. To make to boggle; to offend.

Such terms amus'd them all,
And *stumbled* many. *Milton's Paradise Lost.*

One thing more *stumbles* me in the very foundation of this hypothesis. *Locke.*

Stu'mble. *n. s.* [from the verb.]

1. A trip in walking.

2. A blunder; a failure.

One *stumble* is enough to deface the character of an honourable life. *L'Estrange.*

Stu'mbler. *n. s.* [from *stumble*.] One that stumbles.

Be sweet to all: is thy complexion sour?
Then keep such company; make them thy allay:
Get a sharp wife, a servant that will low'r;
A *stumbler* stumbles least in rugged way. *Herbert.*

Stu'mblingblock. } *n. s.* [from *stumble*.] Cause of stumbling;
Stu'mblingstone. } cause of errour; cause of offence.

We preach Christ crucified, unto the Jews a *stumblingblock*, and unto the Greeks foolishness. 1 *Cor.* i. 23.

This *stumblingstone* we hope to take away. *Burnet.*

Shakespeare is a *stumblingblock* to these rigid criticks. *Spectat.*

STUMP. *n. s.* [*stumpe*, Danish; *stompe*, Dutch; *stompen*, Dan. to lop.] The part of any solid body remaining after the rest is taken away.

He struck so strongly, that the knotty sting
Of his huge tail he quite in sunder cleft;
Five joints thereof he hew'd, and but the *stump* him left. *Spens.*

Your colt's tooth is not cast yet.—Not while I have a *stump*. *Shakespeare.*

He through the bushes scrambles;
A *stump* doth trip him in his pace;
Down comes poor Hob upon his face,
Amongst the briers and brambles. *Drayton's Nymphid.*
Who, 'cause they're wasted to the *stumps*,
Are represented best by rumps. *Hudibras.*

A coach-horse snapt off the end of his finger, and I dressed the *stump* with common digestive. *Wiseman's Surgery.*

A poor ass, now wore out to the *stumps*, fell down under his load. *L'Estrange.*

Against a *stump* his tusks the monster grinds,
And in the sharpen'd edge new vigour finds. *Dryden.*

A tongue

A tongue might have ſome reſemblance to the *ſtump* of a feather. *Grew's Muſæum.*

Worn to the *ſtumps* in the ſervice of the maids, 'tis thrown out of doors, or condemned to kindle a fire. *Swift.*

STU'MPY. *adj.* [from *ſtump.*] Full of ſtumps; hard; ſtiff; ſtrong. A bad word.

They burn the ſtubble, which, being ſo *ſtumpy*, they ſeldom plow in. *Mortimer.*

To STUN. *v. a.* [ſtunan, Saxon, geſtun, noiſe.]

1. To confound or dizzy with noiſe.

An univerſal hubbub wild
Of *ſtunning* ſounds, and voices all confus'd,
Aſſaults his ear. *Milton.*

Still ſhall I hear, and never quit the ſcore,
Stunn'd with hoarſe Codrus' Theſeid o'er and o'er. *Dryden.*

Too ſtrong a noiſe *ſtuns* the ear, and one too weak does not act upon the organ. *Cheyne.*

So Alma, weary'd of being great,
And nodding in her chair of ſtate,
Stunn'd and worn out with endleſs chat,
Of Will did this, and Nan ſaid that. *Prior.*

Shouts as thunder loud afflict the air,
And *ſtun* the birds releas'd. *Prior.*

The Britons, once a ſavage kind,
Deſcendents of the barbarous Huns,
With limbs robuſt, and voice that *ſtuns*,
You taught to modulate their tongues,
And ſpeak without the help of lungs. *Swift.*

2. To make ſenſeleſs or dizzy with a blow.

One hung a pole-ax at his ſaddle-bow,
And one a heavy mace to *ſtun* the foe. *Dryden.*

STUNG. The preterite and participle paſſive of *ſting.*

To both theſe ſiſters have I ſworn my love:
Each jealous of the other, as the *ſtung*
Are of the adder. *Shakeſ. King Lear.*

With envy *ſtung*, they view each other's deeds,
The fragrant work with diligence proceeds. *Dryden's Æn.*

STUNK. The preterite of *ſtink.*

To STUNT. *v. a.* [*ſtunta*, Iſlandick.] To hinder from growth.

Though this uſage *ſtunted* the girl in her growth, it gave her a hardy conſtitution; ſhe had life and ſpirit. *Arbuthnot.*

There he ſtopt ſhort, nor ſince has writ a tittle,
But has the wit to make the moſt of little;
Like *ſtunted* hide-bound trees, that juſt have got
Sufficient ſap at once to bear and rot. *Pope.*

The tree grew ſcrubby, dry'd a-top and *ſtunted*,
And the next parſon ſtubb'd and burnt it. *Swift.*

STUPE. *n. ſ.* [*ſtupa*, Latin.] Cloath or flax dipped in warm medicaments, and applied to a hurt or ſore.

A fomentation was by ſome pretender to ſurgery applied with coarſe woollen *ſtupes*, one of which was bound upon his leg. *Wiſeman's Surgery.*

To STUPE. *v. a.* [from the noun.] To foment; to dreſs with ſtupes.

The eſcar divide, and *ſtupe* the part affected with wine. *Wiſem.*

STUPEFA'CTION. *n. ſ.* [*ſtupefaction*, Fr *ſtupefactus*, Lat.] Inſenſibility; dulneſs; ſtupidity; ſluggiſhneſs of mind; heavy folly.

All reſiſtance of the dictates of conſcience brings a hardneſs and *ſtupefaction* upon it. *South.*

She ſent to ev'ry child
Firm impudence, or *ſtupefaction* mild;
And ſtrait ſucceeded, leaving ſhame no room,
Cibberian forehead, or Cimmerian gloom. *Dunciad.*

STUPEFA'CTIVE. *adj.* [from *ſtupefactus*, Latin; *ſtupefactif*, Fr.] Cauſing inſenſibility; dulling; obſtructing the ſenſes; narcotick; opiate.

It is a gentle fomentation, and hath a very little mixture of ſome *ſtupefactive.* *Bacon's Natural Hiſtory.*

Opium hath a *ſtupefactive* part, and a heating part; the one moving ſleep, the other a heat. *Bacon.*

STUPE'NDOUS. *adj.* [*ſtupendus*, Lat.] Wonderful; amazing; aſtoniſhing.

All thoſe *ſtupendous* acts deſervedly are the ſubject of a hiſtory, excellently written in Latin by a learned prelate. *Claren.*

Great joy was at their meeting, and at ſight
Of that *ſtupendous* bridge his joy increas'd. *Milton.*

Portents and prodigies their ſouls amaz'd;
But moſt, when this *ſtupendous* pile was rais'd. *Dryden.*

Mortals, fly this curſt deteſted race:
A hundred of the ſame *ſtupendous* ſize,
A hundred Cyclops live among the hills. *Addiſon.*

Our numbers can ſcarce give us an idea of the vaſt quantity of ſyſtems in this *ſtupendous* piece of architecture. *Cheyne.*

STU'PID. *adj.* [*ſtupide*, French; *ſtupidus*, Latin.]

1. Dull; wanting ſenſibility; wanting apprehenſion; heavy; ſluggiſh of underſtanding.

O that men ſhould be ſo *ſtupid* grown
As to forſake the living God. *Milton.*

Men, boys and women, *ſtupid* with ſurpriſe,
Where e'er ſhe paſſes, fix their wond'ring eyes. *Dryden.*

If I by chance ſucceed,
Know, I am not ſo *ſtupid*, or ſo hard,
Not to feel praiſe, or fame's deſerv'd reward. *Dryden.*

With wild ſurpriſe
A moment *ſtupid*, motionleſs he ſtood. *Thomſon.*

2. Performed without ſkill or genius.

Wit, as the chief of virtue's friends,
Diſdains to ſerve ignoble ends:
Obſerve what loads of *ſtupid* rhimes
Oppreſs us in corrupted times. *Swift.*

STUPI'DITY. *n. ſ.* [*ſtupidité*, Fr. *ſtupiditas*, Latin.] Dulneſs; heavineſs of mind; ſluggiſhneſs of underſtanding.

Shadwel alone, of all my ſons, is he
Who ſtands confirm'd in full *ſtupidity.* *Dryden.*

STU'PIDLY. *adv.* [from *ſtupid.*]

1. With ſuſpenſion or inactivity of underſtanding.

That ſpace the evil one abſtracted ſtood
From his own evil, and for the time remain'd
Stupidly good. *Milton's Paradiſe Loſt.*

2. Dully; without apprehenſion.

On the ſhield there was engraven maps of countries, which Ajax could not comprehend, but looked on as *ſtupidly* as his fellow-beaſt the lion. *Dryden's Fables, Dedicat.*

STU'PIFIER. *n. ſ.* [from *ſtupify.*] That which cauſes ſtupidity.

To STU'PIFY. *v. a.* [*ſtupefacio*, Latin. This word ſhould therefore be ſpelled *ſtupefy*; but the authorities are againſt it.]

To make ſtupid; to deprive of ſenſibility; to dull.

It is not malleable; but yet is not fluent, but *ſtupified.* *Bac.*

Thoſe
Will *ſtupify* and dull the ſenſe a while. *Shakeſp. Cymbeline.*

Pounce it into the quickſilver, and ſo proceed to the *ſtupifying.* *Bacon.*

Conſider whether that method, uſed to quiet ſome conſciences, does not *ſtupefy* more. *Decay of Piety.*

The fumes of his paſſion do as really intoxicate his diſcerning faculty, as the fumes of drink diſcompoſe and *ſtupify* the brain of a man overcharged with it. *South.*

Envy, like a cold poiſon, benumbs and *ſtupifies*; and conſcious of its own impotence, folds its arms in deſpair. *Collier.*

STU'POR. *n. ſ.* [Latin; *ſtupeur*, French.] Suſpenſion or diminution of ſenſibility.

A pungent pain in the region of the kidneys, a *ſtupor*, or dull pain in the thigh and colick, are ſymptoms of an inflammation of the kidneys. *Arbuthnot on Diet.*

To STU'PRATE. *v. a.* [*ſtupro*, Latin.] To raviſh; to violate.

STUPRA'TION. *n. ſ.* [*ſtupratio*, from *ſtupro*, Lat.] Rape; violation.

Stupration muſt not be drawn into practice. *Brown.*

STU'RDILY. *adv.* [from *ſturdy.*]

1. Stoutly; hardily.

2. Obſtinately; reſolutely.

Then withdraw
From Cambridge, thy old nurſe; and, as the reſt,
Here toughly chew and *ſturdily* digeſt
Th' immenſe vaſt volumes of our common law. *Donne.*

STU'RDINESS. *n. ſ.* [from *ſturdy.*]

1. Stoutneſs; hardineſs.

Sacrifice not his innocency to the attaining ſome little ſkill of buſtling for himſelf, by his converſation with vitious boys, when the chief uſe of that *ſturdineſs*, and ſtanding upon his own legs, is only for the preſervation of his virtue. *Locke.*

2. Brutal ſtrength.

STU'RDY. *adv.* [*eſtourdi*, French.]

1. Hardy; ſtout; brutal; obſtinate. It is always uſed of men with ſome diſagreeable idea of coarſeneſs or rudeneſs.

This muſt be done, and I would fain ſee
Mortal ſo *ſturdy* as to gainſay. *Hudibras.*

A *ſturdy* hardened ſinner ſhall advance to the utmoſt pitch of impiety with leſs reluctance than he took the firſt ſteps, whilſt his conſcience was yet vigilant and tender. *Atterbury.*

Aw'd by that houſe, accuſtom'd to command,
The *ſturdy* kerns in due ſubjection ſtand,
Nor bear the reins in any foreign hand. *Dryden.*

2. Strong; forcible.

The ill-apparelled knight now had gotten the reputation of ſome *ſturdy* lout, he had ſo well defended himſelf. *Sidney.*

Ne ought his *ſturdy* ſtrokes might ſtand before,
That high trees overthrew, and rocks in pieces tore. *F. Q.*

3. Stiff; ſtout.

He was not of any delicate contexture, his limbs rather *ſturdy* than dainty. *Wotton.*

Sturdieſt oaks
Bow'd their ſtiff necks, loaden with ſtormy blaſts,
Or torn up ſheer. *Milton's Par. Reg.*

STU'RGEON. *n. ſ.* [*ſturio*, *turſio*, Latin.] A ſea-fiſh.

It is part of the ſcutellated bone of a *ſturgeon*, being flat, of a porous or cellular conſtitution on one ſide, the cells being worn down, and ſmooth on the other. *Woodward.*

STURK. *n. ſ.* [ſtyrc, Saxon.] A young ox or heifer. *Bailey.*

Thus they are ſtill called in Scotland.

To STUT. } *v. n.* [*ſtutten*, to hinder, Dutch.] To ſpeak
To STU'TTER. } with heſitation; to ſtammer.

Divers *ſtut*: the cauſe is the refrigeration of the tongue, whereby it is leſs apt to move; and therefore naturals *ſtut.* *Bacon.*

STU'TTER.

STU'TTER. } *n. s.* [from *stut.*] One that speaks with hesita-
STU'TTERER. } tion; a stammerer.

Many *stutters* are very cholerick, choler inducing a dryness in the tongue. *Bacon's Natural History.*

STY. *n. s.* [ꞅꞇıᵹe, Saxon.]

1. A cabbin to keep hogs in.

Tell Richmond,
That in the *sty* of this most bloody boar,
My son George Stanley is frank'd up in hold. *Shakes. R. III.*

When her hogs had miss'd their way,
Th' untoward creatures to the *sty* I drove,
And whistl'd all the way. *Gay.*

May thy black pigs lie warm in little *sty*,
And have no thought to grieve them 'till they die. *King.*

2. Any place of bestial debauchery.

They all their friends and native home forget,
To roll with pleasure in a sensual *sty*. *Milton.*

With what ease
Might'st thou expel this monster from his throne,
Now made a *sty*. *Milton's Paradise Regain'd.*

To STY. *v. a.* [from the noun.] To shut up in a sty.

Here you *sty* me
In this hard rock, while you do keep from me
The rest of th' island. *Shakespeare's Tempest.*

To STY. *v. n.* To soar; to ascend. *Spenser.*

STY'GIAN. *adj.* [*stygius*, Latin.] Hellish; infernal; pertaining to Styx, one of the poetical rivers of hell.

At that so sudden blaze the *Stygian* throng
Bent their aspect. *Milton.*

STYLE. *n. s.* [*stylus*, Latin.]

1. Manner of writing with regard to language.

Happy
That can translate the stubbornness of fortune
Into so quiet, and so sweet a *style*. *Shakespeare.*

Their beauty I will rather leave to poets, than venture upon so tender and nice a subject with my severer *style*. *More.*

Proper words in proper places, make the true definition of a *stile*. *Swift.*

Let some lord but own the happy lines,
How the wit brightens, and the *style* refines. *Pope.*

2. Manner of speaking appropriate to particular characters.

No *style* is held for base, where love well named is. *Sidney.*

There was never yet philosopher,
That could endure the toothach patiently,
However they have writ the *style* of gods,
And make a pish at chance and sufferance. *Shakespeare.*

3. Title; appellation.

Ford's a knave, and I will aggravate his *stile*; thou shalt know him for knave and cuckold. *Shakespeare.*

The king gave them in his commission the *style* and appellation which belonged to them. *Clarendon.*

O virgin! or what other name you bear
Above that *style*; O more than mortal fair!
Let not an humble suppliant sue in vain. *Dryden's Æn.*

Propitious hear our pray'r,
Whether the *style* of Titan please thee more,
Whose purple rays th' Achæmenes adore. *Pope's Statius.*

4. Course of writing. Unusual.

While his thoughts the ling'ring day beguile,
To gentle Arcite let us turn our *style*. *Dryden.*

5. A pointed iron used anciently in writing on tables of wax.

6. Any thing with a sharp point, as a graver; the pin of a dial.

Placing two *stiles* or needles of the same steel, touched with the same loadstone, when the one is removed but half a span, the other would stand like Hercules's pillars. *Brown.*

7. The stalk which rises from amid the leaves of a flower.

Style is the middle prominent part of the flower of a plant, which adheres to the fruit or seed: 'tis usually slender and long, whence it has its name. *Quincy.*

The figure of the flower-leaves, stamina, apices, *stile*, and seed-vessel. *Ray.*

8. STYLE *of Court*, is properly the practice observed by any court in its way of proceeding. *Ayliffe's Parergon.*

To STYLE. *v. a.* [from the noun.] To call; to term; to name.

The chancellor of the Exchequer they had no mind should be *styled* a knight. *Clarendon.*

Err not that so shall end
The strife which thou call'st evil, but we *style*
The strife of glory. *Milton's Paradise Lost.*

Fortune's gifts, my actions
May *stile* their own rewards. *Denham's Sophy.*

Whoever backs his tenets with authorities, thinks he ought to carry the cause, and is ready to *stile* it impudence in any one who shall stand out. *Locke.*

His conduct might have made him *stil'd*
A father, and the nymph his child. *Swift.*

STY'PTICK. *adj.* [στυπτικὸς; *styptique*, Fr. This is usually written *stiptick.* See STIPTICK.] The same as astringent; but generally expresses the most efficacious sort of astringents, or those which are applied to stop hæmorrhages. *Quincy.*

Fruits of trees and shrubs contain phlegm, oil, and an essential salt, by which they are sharp, sweet, sour or *styptick.* *Arbuthnot on Aliments.*

STYPTI'CITY. *n. s.* [Properly *stipticity.*] The power of stanching blood.

Catharticks of mercurials precipitate the viscidities by their *stypticity*, and mix with all animal acids. *Floyer.*

To STY'THY. *v. a.* [See STITHY.] To forge on an anvil.

By the forge that *stythy'd* Mars his helm,
I'll kill thee every where, yea, o'er and o'er. *Shakespeare.*

SUA'SIBLE. *adj.* [from *suadeo*, Latin.] Easy to be persuaded.

SUA'SIVE. *adj.* [from *suadeo*, Lat.] Having power to persuade.

It had the passions in perfect subjection; and though its command over them was but *suasive* and political, yet it had the force of coaction, and despotical. *South's Sermons.*

SUA'SORY. *adj.* [*suasorius*, Latin.] Having tendency to persuade.

SUA'VITY. *n. s.* [*suavité*, French; *suavitas*, Latin.]

1. Sweetness to the senses.

She desired them for rarity, pulchritude, and *suavity.* *Brown.*

2. Sweetness to the mind.

SUB, in composition, signifies a subordinate degree.

SUBA'CID. *adj.* [*sub* and *acidus*, Latin.] Sour in a small degree.

The juice of the stem is like the chyle in the animal body, not sufficiently concocted by circulation, and is commonly *subacid* in all plants. *Arbuthnot on Aliment.*

SUBA'CRID. *adj.* [*sub* and *acrid.*] Sharp and pungent in a small degree.

The green choler of a cow tasted sweet, bitter, *subacrid*, or a little pungent, and turned syrup of violets green. *Floyer.*

To SUBA'CT. *v. a.* [*subactus*, Latin.] To reduce; to subdue.

Tangible bodies have no pleasure in the consort of air, but endeavour to *subact* it into a more dense body. *Bacon.*

SUBA'CTION. *n. s.* [*subactus*, Latin.] The act of reducing to any state, as of mixing two bodies completely, or beating any thing to a very small powder.

There are of concoction two periods: the one assimilation, or absolute conversion and *subaction*; the other maturation; whereof the former is most conspicuous in living creatures, in which there is an absolute conversion and assimilation of the nourishment into the body. *Bacon's Natural History.*

SU'BALTERN. *adj.* [*subalterne*, French.] Inferiour; subordinate; that which in different respects is both superiour and inferiour. It is used in the army of all officers below a captain.

There had like to have been a duel between two *subalterns*, upon a dispute which should be governor of Portsmouth. *Add.*

Love's *subalterns*, a duteous band,
Like watchmen round their chief appear;
Each had his lanthorn in his hand,
And Venus, mask'd, brought up the rear. *Prior.*

One, while a *subaltern* officer, was every day complaining against the pride of colonels towards their officers; yet after he received his commission for a regiment, he confessed the spirit of colonelship was coming fast upon him, and it daily increased to his death. *Swift.*

This sort of universal ideas, which may either be considered as a genus or species, is called *subaltern.* *Watts.*

SUBALTE'RNATE. *adj.* [*subalternus*, Latin.] Succeeding by turns. *Dict.*

SUBASTRI'NGENT. *adj.* [*sub* and *astringent.*] Astringent in a small degree.

SUBBE'ADLE. *n. s.* [*sub* and *beadle.*] An under beadle.

They ought not to execute those precepts by simple messengers, or *subbeadles*, but in their own persons. *Ayliffe's Parerg.*

SUBCELE'STIAL. *adj.* [*sub* and *celestial.*] Placed beneath the heavens.

The most refined glories of *subcelestial* excellencies are but more faint resemblances of these. *Glanv. Sceps.*

SUBCHA'NTER. *n. s.* [*sub* and *chanter*; *succentor*, Lat.] The deputy of the precentor in a cathedral.

SUBCLA'VIAN. *adj.* [*sub* and *clavus*, Latin.]

Subclavian is applied to any thing under the armpit or shoulder, whether artery, nerve, vein, or muscle. *Quincy.*

The liver, though seated on the right side, yet, by the *subclavian* division, doth equi-distantly communicate its activity unto either arm. *Brown's Vulgar Errours.*

The chyle first mixeth with the blood in the *subclavian* vein, and enters with it into the heart, where it is very imperfectly mixed, there being no mechanism nor fermentation to convert it into blood, which is effected by the lungs. *Arb.*

SUBCONSTELLA'TION. *n. s.* [*sub* and *constellation.*] A subordinate or secondary constellation.

As to the picture of the seven stars, if thereby be meant the pleiades, or *subconstellation* upon the back of Taurus, with what congruity they are described in a clear night an ordinary eye may discover. *Brown's Vulgar Errours.*

SUBCO'NTRARY. *adj.* [*sub* and *contrary.*] Contrary in an inferiour degree.

If two particular propositions differ in quality, they are *subcontraries*; as, some vine is a tree: some vine is not a tree. These may be both true together, but they can never be both false. *Watts.*

SUBCONTRA'CTED. *part. adj.* [*sub* and *contracted.*] Contracted after a former contract.

Your claim,
I bar it in the interest of my wife;
'Tis she is *subcontracted* to this lord,
And I her husband contradict your banes. *Shakesp. K. Lear.*

SUBCUTA'NEOUS. *adj.* [*sub* and *cutaneous.*] Lying under the skin.

SUBDE'ACON. *n. s.* [*subdeaconus*, Latin.]

In the Romish church they have a *subdeacon*, who is the deacon's servant. *Ayliffe's Parergon.*

SUBDE'AN. *n. s.* [*subdecanus*, Lat.] The vicegerent of a dean.

Whenever the dean and chapter confirm any act, that such confirmation may be valid, the dean must join in person, and not in the person of a deputy or *subdean* only. *Ayliffe.*

SUBDECU'PLE. *adj.* [*sub* and *decuplus*, Lat.] Containing one part of ten.

SUBDERISO'RIOUS. *adj.* [*sub* and *derisor.*] Scoffing or ridiculing with tenderness and delicacy.

This *subderisorious* mirth is far from giving any offence to us: it is rather a pleasant condiment of our conversation. *More.*

SUBDITI'TIOUS. *adj.* [*subdititius*, Latin.] Put secretly in the place of something else.

To SUBDIVE'RSIFY. *v. a.* [*sub* and *diversify.*] To diversify again what is already diversified.

The same wool one man felts into a hat, another weaves it into cloth, another into arras; and these variously *subdiversified* according to the fancy of the artificer. *Hale.*

To SU'BDIVIDE. *v. a.* [*subdiviser*, French; *sub* and *divide.*] To divide a part into yet more parts.

In the rise of eight, in tones, there be two beemols, or half notes; so as if you divide the tones equally, the eight is but seven whole and equal notes; and if you *subdivide* that into half notes, as in the stops of a lute, it maketh the number thirteen. *Bacon's Nat. History.*

When Brutus and Cassius were overthrown, soon after Antonius and Octavianus brake and *subdivided.* *Bacon.*

The glad father glories in his child,
When he can *subdivide* a fraction. *Roscommon.*

When the progenies of Cham and Japhet swarmed into colonies, and those colonies were *subdivided* into many others, in time their descendants lost the primitive rites of divine worship, retaining only the notion of one deity. *Dryden.*

SUBDIVI'SION. *n. s.* [*subdivision*, French; from *subdivide.*]

1. The act of subdividing.

When any of the parts of any idea are farther divided, in order to a clear explication of the whole, this is called a *subdivision*; as when a year is divided into months, each month into days, and each day into hours, which may be farther subdivided into minutes and seconds. *Watts's Logick.*

2. The parts distinguished by a second division.

How can we see such a multitude of souls cast under so many *subdivisions* of misery, without reflecting on the absurdity of a government that sacrifices the happiness of so many reasonable beings to the glory of one? *Addison.*

In the decimal table the *subdivisions* of the cubit, as span, palm, and digit, are deduced from the shorter cubit. *Arbuthn.*

SU'BDOLOUS. *adj.* [*subdolus*, Latin.] Cunning; subtle; sly.

To SUBDU'CE. }
To SUBDU'CT. } *v. a.* [*subduco*, *subductus*, Latin.]

1. To withdraw; to take away.

Or nature fail'd in me, and left some part
Not proof enough such object to sustain;
Or from my side *subducting*, took perhaps
More than enough. *Milton's Paradise Lost.*

2. To substract by arithmetical operation.

Take the other operation of arithmetick, subduction: if out of that supposed infinite multitude of antecedent generations we should *subduce* ten, the residue must be less by ten than it was before, and yet still the quotient must be infinite. *Hale.*

SUBDU'CTION. *n. s.* [from *subduct.*]

1. The act of taking away.

Possibly the Divine Beneficence subducting that influence, which it communicated from the time of their first creation, they were kept in a state of immortality 'till that moment of the *subduction.* *Hale's Origin of Mankind.*

2. Arithmetical substraction.

Suppose we take the other operation of arithmetick, *subduction*: if out of that infinite multitude of antecedent generations we should subduct ten, the residue must be less by ten than it was before that *subduction*, and yet still the quotient be infinite. *Hale.*

To SUBDU'E. *v. a.* [from *subdo*, or *subjugo*, Latin.]

1. To crush; to oppress; to sink; to overpower.

Nothing could have *subdu'd* nature
To such a lowness, but his unkind daughters. *Shakespeare.*

Them that rose up against me, hast thou *subdued* under me. 2 *Sa.* xxii. 40.

If aught were worthy to *subdue*
The soul of man. *Milton.*

2. To conquer; to reduce under a new dominion.

Be fruitful, and replenish the earth, and *subdue* it. *Gen.* i. 28.

Augustus Cæsar *subdued* Egypt to the Roman empire. *Peach.*

To overcome in battle, and *subdue*
Nations, and bring home spoils. *Milton.*

The Romans made those times the standard of their wit, when they *subdued* the world. *Sprat.*

3. To tame; to subact.

Nor is't unwholsome to *subdue* the land
By often exercise; and where before
You broke the earth, again to plow. *May's Virgil.*

SUBDU'EMENT. *n. s.* [from *subdue.*] Conquest. A word not used, nor worthy to be used.

I have seen thee,
As hot as Perseus, spur thy Phrygian steed,
Bravely despising forfeits and *subduements.* *Shakespeare.*

SUBDU'ER. *n. s.* [from *subdue.*] Conquerour; tamer.

Great god of might, that reigneth in the mind,
And all the body to thy hest do'st frame;
Victor of gods, *subduer* of mankind,
That do'st the lions and fell tygers tame,
Who can express the glory of thy might? *Spenser.*

Their curious eye
Discerns their great *subduer's* awful mien
And corresponding features fair. *Philips.*

Figs are great *subduers* of acrimony, useful in hoarseness and coughs, and extremely emollient. *Arbuthnot.*

SUBDU'PLE. } *adj.* [*subduple*, Fr. *sub* and *duplus*, Latin.]
SUBDU'PLICATE. } Containing one part of two.

As one of these under pulleys doth abate half of that heaviness which the weight hath in itself, and cause the power to be in a *subduple* proportion unto it, so two of them do abate half of that which remains, and cause a subquadruple proportion, and three a subsextuple. *Wilkins's Math. Mag.*

The motion generated by the forces in the whole passage of the body or thing through that space, shall be in a *subduplicate* proportion of the forces. *Newton's Opt.*

SUBJA'CENT. *adj.* [*subiacens*, Latin.] Lying under.

The superficial parts of rocks and mountains are washed away by rains, and borne down upon the *subjacent* plains. *Wood.*

To SUBJE'CT. *v. a.* [*subjectus*, Latin.]

1. To put under.

The angel led them direct, and down the cliff as fast
To the *subjected* plain. *Milton.*

The medal bears each form and name:
In one short view, *subjected* to our eye,
Gods, emp'rors, heroes, sages, beauties lie. *Pope.*

2. To reduce to submission; to make subordinate; to make submissive.

Think not, young warriors, your diminish'd name
Shall lose of lustre, by *subjecting* rage
To the cool dictates of experienc'd age. *Dryden.*

3. To enslave; to make obnoxious.

I live on bread like you, feel want like you,
Taste grief, need friends, like you. *Subjected* thus,
How can you say to me, I am a king? *Shakesp. Rich.* II.

I see thee, in that fatal hour,
Subjected to the victor's cruel pow'r,
Led hence a slave. *Dryden.*

The blind will always be led by those that see, or fall into the ditch: and he is the most *subjected*, the most enslaved, who is so in his understanding. *Locke.*

4. To expose; to make liable.

If the vessels yield, it *subjects* the person to all the inconveniencies of an erroneous circulation. *Arbuthnot.*

5. To submit; to make accountable.

God is not bound to *subject* his ways of operation to the scrutiny of our thoughts, and confine himself to do nothing but what we must comprehend. *Locke.*

6. To make subservient.

Subjected to his service angel-wings. *Milton.*

SU'BJECT. *adj.* [*subjectus*, Latin.]

1. Placed or situated under.

Th' eastern tower,
Whose height commands, as *subject*, all the vale
To see the fight. *Shakesp. Troilus and Cressida.*

2. Living under the dominion of another.

Esau was never *subject* to Jacob, but founded a distinct people and government, and was himself prince over them. *Locke.*

3. Exposed; liable; obnoxious.

Most *subject* is the fattest soil to weeds;
And he the noble image of my youth
Is overspread with them. *Shakespeare.*

All human things are *subject* to decay,
And when fate summons, monarchs must obey. *Dryden.*

4. Being that on which any action operates, whether intellectual or material.

I enter into the *subject* matter of my discourse. *Dryden.*

SU'BJECT. *n. s.* [*sujet*, French.]

1. One who lives under the dominion of another.

Every *subject's* duty is the king's,
But every *subject's* soul is his own. *Shakespeare's Henry* V.

Never *subject* long'd to be a king,
As I do long and wish to be a *subject.* *Shakesp. Henry* VI.

The

The *subject* must obey his prince, because God commands it, human laws require it. *Swift.*

Those I call *subjects* which are governed by the ordinary laws and magistrates of the sovereign. *Davies.*

Were *subjects* so but only by their choice,
And not from birth did forc'd dominion take.
Our prince alone would have the publick voice. *Dryden.*

2. That on which any operation either mental or material is performed.

Now spurs the lated traveller apace,
To gain the timely inn, and near approaches
The *subject* of our watch. *Shakespeare's Macbeth.*

This *subject* for heroick song pleas'd me. *Milton.*

Here he would have us fix our thoughts; nor are they too dry a *subject* for our contemplation. *Decay of Piety.*

I will not venture on so nice a *subject* with my severer style. *More.*

Make choice of a *subject* beautiful and noble, which being capable of all the graces that colours, and elegance of design can give, shall afford a perfect art, an ample field of matter wherein to expatiate. *Dryden.*

The *subject* of a proposition is that concerning which any thing is affirmed or denied. *Watts's Logick.*

My real design is, that of publishing your praises to the world; not upon the *subject* of your noble birth. *Swift.*

3. That in which any thing inheres or exists.

Anger is certainly a kind of baseness, as it appears well in the weakness of those *subjects* in whom it reigns, children, women, old folks, sick folks. *Bacon.*

4. [In Grammar.] The nominative case to a verb, is called by Grammarians the *subject* of the verb. *Clarke's Lat. Gram.*

SUBJE'CTION. *n. s.* [from *subject.*]

1. The act of subduing.

After the conquest of the kingdom and *subjection* of the rebels, enquiry was made who there were that fighting against the king had saved themselves by flight. *Hale.*

2. [*Sujettion*, Fr.] The state of being under government.

Because the *subjection* of the body to the will is by natural necessity, the *subjection* of the will unto God voluntary; we therefore stand in need of direction after what sort our wills and desires may be rightly conformed to his. *Hooker.*

How hard it is now for him to frame himself to *subjection*, that having once set before his eyes the hope of a kingdom, hath found encouragement. *Spenser.*

Both in *subjection* now to sensual appetite. *Milton.*

SUBJE'CTIVE. *adj.* [from *subject.*] Relating not to the object but the subject.

Certainty, according to the schools, is distinguished into objective and *subjective*: objective is when the proposition is certainly true in itself; and *subjective*, when we are certain of the truth of it. *Watts.*

SUBINGRE'SSION. *n. s.* [*sub* and *ingressus*, Latin.] Secret entrance.

The pressure of the ambient air is strengthened upon the accession of the air sucked out; which, forceth the neighbouring air to a violent *subingression* of its parts. *Boyle.*

To SUBJOI'N. *v. a.* [*sub* and *joindre*, French; *subjungo*, Latin.] To add at the end; to add afterwards.

He makes an excuse from ignorance, the only thing that could take away the fault; namely, that he knew not that he was the high-priest, and *subjoins* a reason. *South's Sermons.*

SUBITA'NEOUS. *adj.* [*subitaneus*, Latin.] Sudden; hasty.

To SU'BJUGATE. *v. a.* [*subjuguer*, Fr. *subjugo*, Latin.] To conquer; to subdue; to bring under dominion by force.

O fav'rite virgin that hast warm'd the breast,
Whose sov'reign dictates *subjugate* the east! *Prior.*

He *subjugated* a king, and called him his vassal. *Baker.*

SUBJUGA'TION. *n. s.* [from *subjugate.*] The act of subduing.

This was the condition of the learned part of the world, after their *subjugation* by the Turks. *Hale.*

SUBJU'NCTION. *n. s.* [from *subjungo*, Latin.] The state of being subjoined; the act of subjoining.

The verb undergoes in Greek a different formation; and in dependence upon, or *subjunction* to some other verb. *Clarke.*

SUBJU'NCTIVE. *adj.* [*subjunctivus*, Latin; *subjonctif*, Fr.]

1. Subjoined to something else.

2. [In Grammar.]

The verb undergoes in Greek a different formation, to signify the same intentions as the indicative, yet not absolutely but relatively to some other verb, which is called the *subjunctive* mood. *Clarke.*

SU'BLAPSARY. *adj.* [*sub* and *lapsus*, Latin.] Done after the fall of man.

SUBLA'TION. *n. s.* [*sublatio*, Latin.] The act of taking away.

SUBLEVA'TION. *n. s.* [*sublevo*, Latin.] The act of raising on high.

SUBLI'MABLE. *adj.* [from *sublime.*] Possible to be sublimed.

SUBLI'MABLENESS. *n. s.* [from *sublimable.*] Quality of admitting sublimation.

He obtained another concrete as to taste and smell, and easy *sublimableness*, as common salt armoniack. *Boyle.*

SU'BLIMATE. *n. s.* [from *sublime.*]

1. Any thing raised by fire in the retort.

Enquire the manner of subliming, and what metals endure subliming, and what body the *sublimate* makes. *Bacon.*

2. Quicksilver raised in the retort.

The particles of mercury uniting with the acid particles of spirit of salt compose mercury *sublimate*, and with the particles of sulphur, cinnaber. *Newton's Opticks.*

To SU'BLIMATE. *v. a.* [from *sublime.*]

1. To raise by the force of chemical fire.

2. To exalt; to heighten; to elevate.

Not only the gross and illiterate souls, but the most aerial and *sublimated* are rather the more proper fuel for an immaterial fire. *Decay of Piety.*

The precepts of Christianity are so excellent and refined, and so apt to cleanse and *sublimate* the more gross and corrupt, as shews flesh and blood never revealed it. *Decay of Piety.*

SUBLIMA'TION. *n. s.* [*sublimation*, Fr. from *sublimate.*]

1. A chemical operation which raises bodies in the vessel by the force of fire.

Sublimation differs very little from distillation, excepting that in distillation, only the fluid parts of bodies are raised, but in this the solid and dry; and that the matter to be distilled may be either solid or fluid, but *sublimation* is only concerned about solid substances. There is also another difference, namely, that rarefaction, which is of very great use in distillation, has hardly any room in *sublimation*; for the substances which are to be sublimed being solid are incapable of rarefaction; and so it is only impulse that can raise them. *Quincy.*

Separation is wrought by weight, as in the settlement of liquors, by heat, by precipitation or *sublimation*; that is a calling of the several parts up or down, which is a kind of attraction. *Bacon's Natural History.*

Since oil of sulphur per campanam is of the same nature with oil of vitriol, may it not be inferred that sulphur is a mixture of volatile and fixed parts so strongly cohering by attraction, as to ascend together by *sublimation*. *Newt. Opt.*

2. Exaltation: elevation; act of heightning or improving.

She turns
Bodies to spirits, by *sublimation* strange. *Davies.*

Shall he pretend to religious attainments, who is defective and short in moral, which are but the rudiments and first draught of religion, as religion is the perfection, refinement, and *sublimation* of morality? *South.*

SUBLI'ME. *adj.* [*sublimis*, Latin.]

1. High in place; exalted aloft.

They sum'd their pens, and soaring th' air *sublime*
With clang despis'd the ground. *Milton.*

Sublime on these a tow'r of steel is rear'd,
And dire Tisiphone there keeps the ward. *Dryden.*

2. High in excellence; exalted by nature.

My earthly strained to the height
In that celestial colloquy *sublime*. *Milton.*

Can it be, that souls *sublime*
Return to visit our terrestrial clime;
And that the gen'rous mind releas'd by death,
Can cover lazy limbs? *Dryden.*

3. High in stile or sentiment; lofty; grand.

Easy in stile, thy work in sense *sublime*. *Prior.*

4. Elevated by joy.

All yet left of that revolted rout,
Heav'n-fall'n, in station stood or just array,
Sublime with expectation. *Milton.*

Their hearts were jocund and *sublime*,
Drunk with idolatry, drunk with wine. *Milton.*

5. Haughty; proud.

He was *sublime*, and almost tumorous in his looks and gestures. *Wotton.*

SUBLI'ME. *n. s.* The grand or lofty stile. *The sublime* is a Gallicism, but now naturalized.

Longinus strengthens all his laws,
And is himself the great *sublime* he draws. *Pope.*

The *sublime* rises from the nobleness of thoughts, the magnificence of the words, or the harmonious and lively turn of the phrase; the perfect *sublime* arises from all three together. *Addis.*

To SUBLI'ME. *v. a.* [*sublimer*, Fr. from the adjective.]

1. To raise by a chemical fire.

Study our manuscripts, those myriads
Of letters, which have past 'twixt thee and me,
Thence write our annals, and in them lessons be
To all, whom love's *subliming* fire invades. *Donne.*

2. To raise on high.

Although thy trunk be neither large nor strong,
Nor can thy head, not helpt, itself *sublime*,
Yet, like a serpent, a tall tree can climb. *Denham.*

3. To exalt; to heighten; to improve.

Flow'rs, and then fruit,
Man's nourishment, by gradual scale *sublim'd*
To vital spirits aspire. *Milton.*

The fancies of most are moved by the inward springs of the corporeal machine, which even in the most *sublimed* intellectuals is dangerously influential. *Glanville.*

Art

Art being ſtrengthened by the knowledge of things, may paſs into nature by ſlow degrees, and ſo be *ſublimed* into a pure genius which is capable of diſtinguiſhing betwixt the beauties of nature and that which is low in her. *Dryden's Dufreſnoy.*

Meanly they ſeek the bleſſing to confine,
And force that ſun but on a part to ſhine;
Which not alone the ſouthern wit *ſublimes*,
But ripens ſpirits in cold northern climes. *Pope.*

To SUBLI'ME. *v. n.* To riſe in the chemical veſſel by the force of fire.

The particles of ſal ammoniack in ſublimation carry up the particles of antimony, which will not *ſublime* alone. *Newt. Opt.*

This ſalt is fixed in a gentle fire, and *ſublimes* in a great one. *Arbuthnot on Aliments.*

SUBLI'MELY. *adv.* [from *ſublime.*] Loftily; grandly.

This fuſtian's ſo *ſublimely* bad;
It is not poetry, but proſe run mad. *Pope.*

SUBLI'MITY. *n. ſ.* [from *ſublime*; *ſublimité*, Fr. *ſublimitas*, Lat.]

1. Height of place; local elevation.

2. Height of nature; excellence.

As religion looketh upon him who in majeſty and power is infinite, as we ought we account not of it, unleſs we eſteem it even according to that very height of excellency which our hearts conceive, when divine *ſublimity* itſelf is rightly conſidered. *Hooker.*

In reſpect of God's incomprehenſible *ſublimity* and purity, this is alſo true, that God is neither a mind, nor a ſpirit like other ſpirits, nor a light ſuch as can be diſcerned. *Raleigh.*

3. Loftineſs of ſtyle or ſentiment.

Milton's diſtinguiſhing excellence lies in the *ſublimity* of his thoughts, in the greatneſs of which he triumphs over all the poets, modern and ancient, Homer only excepted. *Addiſon.*

SUBLI'NGUAL. *adj.* [*ſublingual*, French; *ſub* and *lingua*, Lat.] Placed under the tongue.

Thoſe ſubliming humours ſhould be intercepted, before they mount to the head, by *ſublingual* pills. *Harvey on Conſumption.*

SUBLU'NAR. } *adj.* [*ſublunaire*, Fr. *ſub* and *luna*, Latin.] Si-
SU'BLUNARY. } tuated beneath the moon; earthly; terreſtrial; of this world.

Dull *ſublunary* lovers, love,
Whoſe ſoul is ſenſe, cannot admit
Of abſence, 'cauſe it doth remove
The thing which elemented it. *Donne.*

Night meaſur'd, with her ſhadowy cone,
Half way up hill this vaſt *ſublunar* vault. *Milton.*

Through ſeas of knowledge we our courſe advance,
Diſcov'ring ſtill new worlds of ignorance;
And theſe diſcov'ries make us all confeſs
That *ſublunary* ſcience is but gueſs. *Denham.*

The celeſtial bodies above the moon being not ſubject to chance, remained in perpetual order, while all things *ſublunary* are ſubject to change. *Dryden's Dufreſnoy.*

Ovid had warn'd her to beware
Of ſtrolling gods, whoſe uſual trade is,
Under pretence of taking air,
To pick up *ſublunary* ladies. *Swift.*

SU'BMARINE. *adj.* [*ſub* and *mare.*] Lying or acting under the ſea.

This contrivance may ſeem difficult, becauſe theſe *ſubmarine* navigators will want winds and tides for motion, and the ſight of the heavens for direction. *Wilkins.*

Not only the herbaceous and woody *ſubmarine* plants, but alſo the lithophyta affect this manner of growing, as I obſerved in corals. *Ray on the Creation.*

To SUBME'RGE. *v. a.* [*ſubmerger*, Fr. *ſubmergo*, Lat.] To drown; to put under water.

So half my Egypt were *ſubmerg'd* and made
A ciſtern for ſcal'd ſnakes. *Shakeſpeare's Ant. and Cleopatra.*

SUBME'RSION. *n. ſ.* [*ſubmerſion*, Fr. from *ſubmerſus*, Latin.] The act of drowning; ſtate of being drowned.

The great Atlantick iſland is mentioned in Plato's Timæus, almoſt contiguous to the weſtern parts of Spain and Africa, yet wholly ſwallowed up by that ocean: which if true, might afford a paſſage from Africa to America by land before that *ſubmerſion*. *Hale's Origination of Mankind.*

To SUBMI'NISTER. } *v. a.* [*ſubminiſtro*, Latin.] To ſup-
To SUBMI'NISTRATE. } ply; to afford. A word not much in uſe.

Some things have been diſcovered, not only by the induſtry of mankind, but even the inferiour animals have *ſubminiſtred* unto man the invention of many things, natural, artificial, and medicinal. *Hale's Original of Mankind.*

Nothing *ſubminiſtrates* apter matter to be converted into peſtilent ſeminaries, than ſteams of naſty folks. *Harvey.*

To SUBMI'NISTER. *v. n.* To ſubſerve.

Our paſſions, as fire and water, are good ſervants, but bad maſters, and *ſubminiſter* to the beſt and worſt of purpoſes. *L'Eſtrange.*

SUBMI'SS. *adj.* [from *ſubmiſſus*, Lat.] Humble; ſubmiſſive; obſequious.

King James mollified by the biſhop's *ſubmiſs* and eloquent letters, wrote back, that though he were in part moved by his letters, yet he ſhould not be fully ſatisfied except he ſpake with him. *Bacon's Henry VII.*

Nearer his preſence, Adam, though not aw'd,
Yet with *ſubmiſs* approach, and reverence meek,
As to a ſuperior nature, bowed low. *Milton's Par. Loſt.*

Rejoicing, but with awe,
In adoration at his feet I fell
Submiſs: he rear'd me. *Milton.*

SUBMI'SSION. *n. ſ.* [*ſoumiſſion*, Fr. from *ſubmiſſus*, Latin.]

1. Delivery of himſelf to the power of another.

Submiſſion, Dauphin! 'tis a meer French word,
We Engliſh warriors wot not what it means. *Shakeſpeare.*

2. Acknowledgement of inferiority or dependance; humble or ſuppliant behaviour.

In all *ſubmiſſion* and humility,
York doth preſent himſelf unto your highneſs. *Shakeſpeare.*

Great prince, by that *ſubmiſſion* you'll gain more
Than e'er your haughty courage won before. *Halifax.*

3. Acknowledgment of a fault; confeſſion of errour.

Be not as extreme in *ſubmiſſion*, as in offence. *Shakeſpeare.*

4. Obſequiouſneſs; reſignation; obedience.

No duty in religion is more juſtly required by God Almighty than a perfect *ſubmiſſion* to his will in all things. *Temple.*

SUBMI'SSIVE. *adj.* [*ſubmiſſus*, Lat.] Humble; teſtifying ſubmiſſion or inferiority.

On what *ſubmiſſive* meſſage art thou ſent? *Shakeſpeare.*

Her at his feet *ſubmiſſive* in diſtreſs
He thus with peaceful words uprais'd. *Milton.*

Sudden from the golden throne,
With a *ſubmiſſive* ſtep I haſted down;
The glowing garland from my hair I took,
Love in my heart, obedience in my look. *Prior.*

SUBMI'SSIVELY. *adv.* [from *ſubmiſſive.*] Humbly; with confeſſion of inferiority.

The goddeſs,
Soft in her tone, *ſubmiſſively* replies. *Dryden's Æneid.*

Speech ev'n there *ſubmiſſively* withdraws
From rights of ſubjects, and the poor man's cauſe;
Then pompous ſilence reigns, and ſtills the noiſy laws. *Pope.*

SUBMI'SSIVENESS. *n. ſ.* [from *ſubmiſſive.*] Humility; confeſſion of fault, or inferiority.

If thou ſin in wine and wantonneſs,
Boaſt not thereof, nor make thy ſhame thy glory;
Frailty gets pardon by *ſubmiſſiveneſs*,
But he that boaſts, ſhuts that out of his ſtory:
He makes flat war with God, and doth defy,
With his poor clod of earth, the ſpacious ſky. *Herbert.*

SUBMI'SSLY. *adv.* [from *ſubmiſs.*] Humbly; with ſubmiſſion.

Humility conſiſts, not in wearing mean cloaths, and going ſoftly and *ſubmiſsly*, but in hearty mean opinion of thy ſelf. *Taylor.*

To SUBMI'T. *v. a.* [*ſoumettre*, Fr. *ſubmitto*, Latin.]

1. To let down; to ſink.

Sometimes the hill *ſubmits* itſelf a while
In ſmall deſcents, which do its height beguile,
And ſometimes mounts, but ſo as billows play,
Whoſe riſe not hinders, but makes ſhort our way. *Dryden.*

Neptune ſtood,
With all his hoſts of waters at command,
Beneath them to *ſubmit* th' officious flood,
And with his trident ſhov'd them off the ſand. *Dryden.*

2. To ſubject; to reſign without reſiſtance to authority.

Return to thy miſtreſs, and *ſubmit* thyſelf under her hands. *Gen.* xvi. 9.

Will ye *ſubmit* your neck, and chuſe to bend
The ſupple knee? *Milton.*

3. To leave to diſcretion; to refer to judgment.

Whether the condition of the clergy be able to bear a heavy burden, is *ſubmitted* to the houſe. *Swift.*

To SUBMI'T. *v. n.* To be ſubject; to acquieſce in the authority of another; to yield.

To thy huſband's will
Thine ſhall *ſubmit*: he over thee ſhall rule. *Milton.*

Our religion requires from us, not only to forego pleaſure, but to *ſubmit* to pain, affliction, diſgrace, and even death. *Rogers's Sermons.*

SUBMU'LTIPLE. *n. ſ.* A *ſumbmultiple* number or quantity is that which is contained in another number, a certain number of times exactly: thus 3 is *ſubmultiple* of 21, as being contained in it ſeven times exactly. *Harris.*

SUBOCTA'VE. } *adj.* [*ſub* and *octavus*, Lat. and *octuple.*] Con-
SUBOCTU'PLE. } taining one part of eight.

As one of theſe under pulleys abates half of that heavineſs of the weight, and cauſes the power to be in a ſubduple proportion, ſo two of them abate half of that which remains, and cauſe a ſubquadruple proportion, three a ſubſextuple, four a *ſuboctuple*. *Wilkins's Mathematical Magick.*

Had they erected the cube of a foot for their principal concave, and geometrically taken its *ſuboctave*, the congius, from the cube of half a foot, they would have divided the congius into eight parts, each of which would have been regularly

larly the cube of a quarter foot, their well-known palm: this is the course taken for our gallon, which has the pint for its *suboctave*. *Arbuthnot on Coins.*

SUBO'RDINACY. } *n. s.* [from *subordinate.*] *Subordinacy* is the
SUBO'RDINANCY. } proper and analogical word.

1. The state of being subject.

Pursuing the imagination through all its extravagancies, is no improper method of correcting, and bringing it to act in *subordinacy* to reason. *Spectator.*

2. Series of subordination.

The *subordinancy* of the government changing hands so often, makes an unsteddiness in the pursuit of the publick interests. *Temple.*

SUBO'RDINATE. *adj.* [*sub* and *ordinatus*, Latin.]

1. Inferiour in order; in nature; in dignity or power.

It was *subordinate*, not enslaved to the understanding; not as a servant to a master, but as a queen to her king, who acknowledges a subjection, and yet retains a majesty. *South's Sermons.*

Whether dark presages of the night proceed from any latent power of the soul, during her abstraction, or from any operation of *subordinate* spirits, has been a dispute. *Addison.*

2. Descending in a regular series.

The two armies were assigned to the leading of two generals, rather courtiers than martial men, yet assisted with *subordinate* commanders of great experience. *Bacon.*

His next *subordinate*
Awak'ning, thus to him in secret spake. *Milton.*

These carry such plain characters of disagreement or affinity, that the several kinds and *subordinate* species of each are easily distinguished. *Woodward.*

To SUBO'RDINATE. *v. a.* [*sub* and *ordino*, Latin.] To range under another. Not in use, but proper and elegant.

If I have *subordinated* picture and sculpture to architecture as their mistress, so there are other inferior arts subordinate to them. *Wotton.*

SUBO'RDINATELY. *adv.* [from *subordinate.*] In a series regularly descending.

It being the highest step of ill, to which all others *subordinately* tend, one would think it could be capable of no improvement. *Decay of Piety.*

SUBORDINA'TION. *n. s.* [*subordination*, Fr. from *subordinate.*]

1. The state of being inferior to another.

Nor can a council national decide,
But with *subordination* to her guide. *Dryden.*

2. A series regularly descending.

If we would suppose a ministry, where every single person was of distinguished piety, and all great officers of state and law diligent in chusing persons, who in their several *subordinations* would be obliged to follow the examples of their superiors, the empire of irreligion would be soon destroyed. *Swift.*

To SUBO'RN. *v. a.* [*suborner*, Fr. *suborno*, Latin.]

1. To procure privately; to procure by secret collusion.

His judges were the self-same men by whom his accusers were *suborned*. *Hooker.*

Fond wretch, thou know'st not what thou speak'st,
Or else thou art *suborn'd* against his honour
In hateful practice. *Shakespeare.*

Reason may meet
Some specious object, by the foe *suborn'd*;
And fall into deception. *Milton.*

His artful bosom heaves dissembl'd sighs;
And tears *suborn'd* fall dropping from his eyes. *Prior.*

2. To procure by indirect means.

Behold
Those who by ling'ring sickness lose their breath,
And those who by despair *suborn* their death. *Dryden.*

SUBORNA'TION. *n. s.* [*subornation*, Fr. from *suborn.*] The crime of procuring any to do a bad action.

Thomas earl of Desmond was, through false *subornation* of the Queen of Edward IV. brought to his death at Tredagh most unjustly. *Spenser's Ireland.*

You set the crown
Upon the head of this forgetful man,
And for his sake wear the detested blot
Of murd'rous *subornation*. *Shakesp. Hen.* IV.

The fear of punishment in this life will preserve men from few vices, since some of the blackest often prove the surest steps to favour; such as ingratitude, hypocrisy, treachery, and *subornation*. *Swift.*

SUBO'RNER. *n. s.* [*suborneur*, Fr. from *suborn.*] One that procures a bad action to be done.

SUBPOE'NA. *n. s.* [*sub* and *pœna*, Latin.] A writ commanding attendance in a court under a penalty.

SUBQUADRU'PLE. *adj.* [*sub* and *quadruple.*] Containing one part of four.

As one of these under pulleys abates half of that heaviness the weight hath in itself, and causes the power to be in a subduple proportion unto it, so two of them abate half of that which remains, and cause a *subquadruple* proportion. *Wilkins's Mathematical Magick.*

SUBQUINTU'PLE. *adj.* [*sub* and *quintuple.*] Containing one part of five.

If unto the lower pulley there were added another, then the power would be unto the weight in a *subquintuple* proportion. *Wilkins's Mathematical Magick.*

SUBRE'CTOR. *n. s.* [*sub* and *rector.*] The rector's vicegerent.

He was chosen *subrector* of the college. *Walton.*

SUBRE'PTION. *n. s.* [*subreption*, Fr. *subreptus*, Lat.] The act of obtaining a favour by surprize or unfair representation. *Dict.*

SUBREPTI'TIOUS. *adj.* [*surreptice*, French; *surreptitius*, Latin.] Fraudulently obtained from a superior, by concealing some truth, which, if known, would have prevented the grant. *Bailey.*

To SUBSCRI'BE. *v. a.* [*souscrire*, Fr. *subscribo*, Latin.]

1. To give consent to, by underwriting the name.

They united by *subscribing* a covenant, which they pretended to be no other than had been *subscribed* in the reign of King James, and that his Majesty himself had *subscribed* it; by which imposition people of all degrees engaged themselves in it. *Clarendon.*

The reader sees the names of those persons by whom this letter is *subscribed*. *Addison.*

2. To attest by writing the name.

Their particular testimony ought to be better credited, than some other *subscribed* with an hundred hands. *Whitgifte.*

3. To contract; to limit. Not used.

The king gone to night! *subscrib'd* his pow'r!
Confin'd to exhibition! all is gone. *Shakespeare.*

To SUBSCRI'BE. *v. n.*

1. To give consent.

Osius, with whose hand the Nicene creed was set down, and framed for the whole Christian world to *subscribe* unto, so far yielded in the end, as even with the same hand to ratify the Arrians confession. *Hooker.*

Advise thee what is to be done,
And we will all *subscribe* to thy advice. *Shakespeare.*

If wolves had at thy gate howl'd that stern time,
Thou should'st have said, go porter, turn the key,
All cruels else *subscrib'd*. *Shakespeare's King Lear.*

So spake much humbled Eve; but fate
Subscrib'd not: nature first gave signs, impress'd
On bird, beast, air. *Milton's Parad. Lost.*

2. To promise a stipulated sum for the promotion of any undertaking.

SUBSCRI'BER. *n. s.* [from *subscriptio*, Lat.]

1. One who subscribes.

2. One who contributes to any undertaking.

Let a pamphlet come out upon a demand in a proper juncture, every one of the party who can spare a shilling shall be a *subscriber*. *Swift.*

SUBSCRI'PTION. *n. s.* [from *subscriptio*, Latin.]

1. Any thing underwritten.

The man asked, are ye Christians? We answered we were; fearing the less because of the cross we had seen in the *subscription*. *Bacon.*

2. Consent or attestation given by underwriting the name.

3. The act or state of contributing to any undertaking.

The work he ply'd;
Stocks and *subscriptions* pour on ev'ry side. *Pope.*
South-sea *subscriptions* take who please,
Leave me but liberty. *Pope.*

4. Submission; obedience. Not in use.

I tax not you, you elements, with unkindness;
I never gave you kingdom, call'd you children,
You owe me no *subscription*. *Shakespeare's King Lear.*

SUBSE'CTION. *n. s.* [*sub* and *sectio*, Latin.] A subdivision of a larger section into a lesser. A section of a section. *Dict.*

SU'BSEQUENCE. *n. s.* [from *subsequor*, Latin.] The state of following; not precedence.

By this faculty we can take notice of the order of precedence and *subsequence* in which they are past. *Grew.*

SUBSE'CUTIVE. *adj.* [from *subsequor*.] Following in train.

SUBSEPTU'PLE. *adj.* [*sub* and *septuplus*, Latin.] Containing one of seven parts.

If unto this lower pully there were added another, then the power would be unto the weight in a subquintuple proportion; if a third, a *subseptuple*. *Wilkins.*

SU'BSEQUENT. *adj.* [*subsequent*, Fr. *subsequens*, Latin. This word is improperly pronounced long in the second syllable by *Shakespeare.*] Following in train; not preceding.

In such indexes, although small pricks
To their *subsequent* volumes, there is seen
The baby figure of the giant mass
Of things to come, at large. *Shakesp. Troil. and Cressida.*

The *subsequent* words come on before the precedent vanish. *Bacon.*

Why does each consenting sign
With prudent harmony combine
In turns to move, and *subsequent* appear
To gird the globe and regulate the year? *Prior.*

This

This article is introduced as *subsequent* to the treaty of Munster, made about 1648, when England was in the utmost confusion. *Swift.*

SUBSE'QUENTLY. *adv.* [from *subsequent.*] Not so as to go before; so as to follow in train.

To men in governing most things fall out accidentally, and come not into any compliance with their preconceived ends; but they are forced to comply *subsequently*, and to strike in with things as they fall out, by postliminious after-applications of them to their purposes. *South's Sermons.*

To SUBSE'RVE. *v. a.* [*subservio*, Latin.] To serve in subordination; to serve instrumentally.

Not made to rule,
But to *subserve* where wisdom bears command. *Milton.*

It is a greater credit to know the ways of captivating nature, and making her *subserve* our purposes, than to have learned all the intrigues of policy. *Glanville.*

The memory hath no special part of the brain devoted to its own service, but uses all those parts which *subserve* our sensations, as well as our thinking powers. *Walsh.*

SUBSE'RVIENCE. } *n. s.* [from *subserve.*] Instrumental fitness
SUBSE'RVIENCY. } or use.

Wicked spirits may by their cunning, carry farther in a seeming confederacy or *subserviency* to the designs of a good angel. *Dryden.*

We cannot look upon the body, wherein appears so much fitness, use, and *subserviency* to infinite functions, any otherwise than as the effect of contrivance. *Bentley.*

There is an immediate and agil *subservience* of the spirits to the empire of the soul. *Hale's Originat. of Mankind.*

There is a regular subordination and *subserviency* among all the parts to beneficial ends. *Cheyne's Philosophical Principles.*

SUBSE'RVIENT. *adj.* [*subserviens*, Latin.] Subordinate; instrumentally useful.

Philosophers and common heathens believed one God, to whom all things are referred; but under this God they worshipped many inferior and *subservient* gods. *Stillingfleet.*

These ranks of creatures are *subservient* one to another, and the most of them serviceable to man. *Ray.*

While awake, we feel none of those motions continually made in the disposal of the corporeal principles *subservient* herein. *Grew.*

Sense is *subservient* unto fancy, fancy unto intellect. *Grew.*

We are not to consider the world as the body of God; he is an uniform being, void of organs, members or parts, and they are his creatures subordinate to him, and *subservient* to his will. *Newton's Opticks.*

Most criticks, fond of some *subservient* art,
Still make the whole depend upon a part;
They talk of principles, but notions prize,
And all to one lov'd folly sacrifice. *Pope.*

SUBSE'XTUPLE. *adj.* [*sub* and *sextuplus*, Latin.] Containing one part of six.

One of these under pullies abates half of that heaviness the weight hath, and causes the power to be in a subduple proportion unto it, two of them a subquadruple proportion, three a *subsextuple.* *Wilkins's Mathematical Magick.*

To SUBSI'DE. *v. n.* [*subsido*, Latin.] To sink; to tend downwards.

He shook the sacred honours of his head
With terror trembled heav'ns *subsiding* hill,
And from his shaken curls ambrosial dews distill. *Dryden.*
Now Jove suspends his golden scales in air,
Weighs the mens wits against the lady's hair;
The doubtful beam long nods from side to side:
At length the wits mount up, the hairs *subside.* *Pope.*

SUBSI'DENCE. } *n. s.* [from *subside.*] The act of sinking; ten-
SUBSI'DENCY. } dency downward.

This gradual *subsidency* of the abyss would take up a considerable time. *Burnet's Theory of the Earth.*

This miscellany of bodies being determined to *subsidence* merely by their different specifick gravities, all those which had the same gravity subsided at the same time. *Woodward.*

By the alternate motion of those air-bladders, whose surfaces are by turns freed from mutual contact, and by a sudden *subsidence* meet again by the ingress and egress of the air, the liquour is still farther attenuated. *Arbuthnot.*

SUBSI'DIARY. *adj.* [*subsidiaire*, Fr. *subsidiarius*, Lat. from *subsidy.*] Assistant; brought in aid.

Bitter substances burn the blood, and are a sort of *subsidiary* gall. *Arbuthnot on Aliments.*

SU'BSIDY. *n. s.* [*subside*, Fr. *subsidium*, Latin.] Aid, commonly such as is given in money.

They advised the king to send speedy aids, and with much alacrity granted a great rate of *subsidy.* *Bacon.*

'Tis all the *subsidy* the present age can raise. *Dryden.*

It is a celebrated notion of a patriot, that a house of commons should never grant such *subsidies* as give no pain to the people, lest the nation should acquiesce under a burden they did not feel. *Addison*

To SUBSI'GN. *v. a.* [*subsigno*, Latin.] To sign under.

Neither have they seen any deed before the conquest, but *subsigned* with crosses and single names without surnames. *Camd.*

To SUBSI'ST. *v. n.* [*subsister*, Fr. *subsisto*, Latin.]

1. To continue; to retain the present state or condition.

Firm we *subsist*, but possible to swerve. *Milton.*

The very foundation was removed, and it was a moral impossibility that the republick could *subsist* any longer. *Swift.*

2. To have means of living; to be maintained.

He shone so powerfully upon me, that like the heat of a Russian summer, he ripened the fruits of poetry in a cold climate; and gave me wherewithal to *subsist* in the long winter which succeeded. *Dryden.*

Let us remember those that want necessaries, as we ourselves should have desired to be remembred, had it been our sad lot to *subsist* on other mens charity. *Atterbury.*

3. To inhere; to have existence.

Though the general natures of these qualities are sufficiently distant from one another, yet when they come to *subsist* in particulars, and to be clothed with several accidents, then the discernment is not so easy. *South's Sermons.*

SUBSI'STENCE, *or Subsistency. n. s.* [*subsistance*, Fr. from *subsist.*]

1. Real being.

The flesh, and the conjunction of the flesh with God began both at one instant, his making and taking to himself our flesh was but one act; so that in Christ there is no personal *subsistence* but one, and that from everlasting. *Hooker.*

We know as little how the union is dissolved, that is the chain of these differing *subsistencies* that compound us, as how it first commenced. *Glanville.*

Not only the things had *subsistence*, but the very images were of some creatures existing. *Stillingfleet.*

2. Competence; means of supporting life.

His viceroy could only propose to himself a comfortable *subsistence* out of the plunder of his province *Addison.*

SUBSI'STENT. *adj. subsistens*, Latin.] Having real being.

Such as deny spirits *subsistent* without bodies, will with difficulty affirm the separate existence of their own. *Brown.*

These qualities are not *subsistent* in those bodies, but are operations of fancy begotten in something else. *Bentley.*

SU'BSTANCE. *n. s.* [*substance*, Fr, *substantia*, Latin.]

1. Being; something existing; something of which we can say that it is.

Since then the soul works by herself alone,
Springs not from sense, nor humours well agreeing,
Her nature is peculiar, and her own;
She is a *substance*, and a perfect being. *Davies.*
The strength of gods,
And this empyreal *substance* cannot fail. *Milton.*

2. That which supports accidents.

What creatures there inhabit, of what mold,
And *substance.* *Milton.*

Every being is considered as subsisting in and by itself, and then it is called a *substance*; or it subsists in and by another, and then it is called a mode or manner of being. *Watts.*

3. The essential part.

It will serve our turn to comprehend the *substance*, without confining ourselves to scrupulous exactness in form. *Digby.*

This edition is the same in *substance* with the Latin. *Burn.*

They are the best epitomes, and let you see with one cast of the eye the *substance* of a hundred pages. *Addison.*

4. Something real, not imaginary; something solid, not empty.

Shadows to night
Have struck more terror to the soul of Richard,
Than can the *substance* of ten thousand soldiers
Arm'd in proof and led by shallow Richard. *Shakespeare.*
He the future evil shall no less
In apprehension than in *substance* feel. *Milton.*
Heroick virtue did his actions guide,
And he the *substance*, not th' appearance chose:
To rescue one such friend he took more pride,
Than to destroy whole thousands of such foes. *Dryden.*

5. Body; corporeal nature.

Between the parts of opake and coloured bodies are many spaces, either empty or replenished with mediums of other densities; as water between the tinging corpuscles wherewith any liquor is impregnated, air between the aqueous globules that constitute clouds or mists, and for the most part spaces void of both air and water; but yet perhaps not wholly void of all *substance* between the parts of hard bodies. *Newton.*

The qualities of plants are more various than those of animal *substances.* *Arbuthnot on Aliments.*

6. Wealth; means of life.

He hath eaten me out of house and home, and hath put all my *substance* into that fat belly of his, but I will have some of it out again. *Shakespeare's Henry IV.*

We are destroying many thousand lives, and exhausting our *substance*, but not for our own interest. *Swift.*

SUBSTA'NTIAL. *adj.* [*substantielle*, Fr. from *substance.*]

1. Real; actually existing.

If this atheist would have his chance to be a real and *substantial* agent, he is more stupid than the vulgar. *Bentley.*

2. True;

2. True; solid; real; not merely seeming.

O blessed! blessed night! I am afraid,
Being in night, all this is but a dream;
Too flattering sweet to be *substantial*. *Shakespeare.*

To give thee being, I lent
Out of my side to thee, nearest my heart,
Substantial life. *Milton.*

If happiness be a *substantial* good,
Not fram'd of accidents, nor subject to them,
I err'd to seek it in a blind revenge. *Denham.*

Time, as a river, hath brought down to us what is more light and superficial, while things more solid and *substantial* have been immersed. *Glanville.*

The difference betwixt the empty vanity of ostentation, and the *substantial* ornaments of virtue. *L'Estrange.*

Observations are the only sure grounds whereon to build a lasting and *substantial* philosophy. *Woodward.*

A solid and *substantial* greatness of soul, looks down with neglect on the censures and applauses of the multitude. *Addison.*

3. Corporeal; material.

Now shine these planets with *substantial* rays?
Does innate lustre gild their measur'd days? *Prior.*

The sun appears flat like a plate of silver, the moon as big as the sun, and the rainbow a large *substantial* arch in the sky, all which are gross falshoods. *Watts.*

4. Strong; stout; bulky.

Substantial doors,
Cross-barr'd and bolted fast, fear no assault. *Milton.*

5. Responsible; moderately wealthy.

Trials of crimes and titles of right shall be made by verdict of a jury, chosen out of the honest and most *substantial* freeholders. *Spenser on Ireland.*

The merchants, and *substantial* citizens, cannot make up more than a hundred thousand families. *Addison on the War.*

SUBSTA'NTIALS. *n. s.* [Without singular.] Essential parts.

Although a custom introduced against the *substantials* of an appeal be not valid, as that it should not be appealed to a superior, but to an inferior judge, yet a custom may be introduced against the accidentals of an appeal. *Ayliffe's Parergon.*

SUBSTANTIA'LITY. *n. s.* [from *substantial.*]

1. The state of real existence.

2. Corporeity; materiality.

Body cannot act on any thing but by motion; motion cannot be received but by quantity and matter: the soul is a stranger to such gross *substantiality*, and owns nothing of these. *Glanv. Sceps.*

SUBSTA'NTIALLY. *adv.* [from *substantial.*]

1. In manner of a substance; with reality of existence.

In him his Father shone *substantially* express'd. *Milton.*

2. Strongly; solidly.

Having so *substantially* provided for the North, they promised themselves they should end the war that Summer. *Clarendon.*

3. Truly; solidly; really; with fixed purpose.

The laws of this religion would make men, if they would truly observe them, *substantially* religious towards God, chaste and temperate. *Tillotson.*

4. With competent wealth.

SUBSTA'NTIALNESS. *n. s.* [from *substantial.*]

1. The state of being substantial.

2. Firmness; strength; power of holding or lasting.

When *substantialness* combineth with delightfulness, fulness with fineness, how can the language which consisteth of these sound other than most full of sweetness? *Camden's Remains.*

In degree of *substantialness* next above the dorique, sustaining the third, and adorning the second story. *Wotton.*

To SUBSTA'NTIATE. *v. a.* [from *substance.*] To make to exist.

The accidental of any act is said to be whatever advenes to the act itself already *substantiated*. *Ayliffe's Parergon.*

SU'BSTANTIVE. *n. s.* [*substantif*, French; *substantivum*, Latin.] A noun betokening the thing, not a quality.

Claudian perpetually closes his sense at the end of a verse, commonly called golden, or two *substantives* and two adjectives with a verb betwixt them. *Dryden.*

SUBSTA'NTIVE. *adj.* [*substantivus*, Latin.]

1. Solid; depending only on itself. Not in use.

He considered how sufficient and *substantive* this land was to maintain itself, without any aid of the foreigner. *Bacon.*

2. Betokening existence.

One is obliged to join many particulars in one proposition, because the repetition of the *substantive* verb would be tedious. *Arb.*

To SU'BSTITUTE. *v. a.* [*substituer*, Fr. *substitutus*, from *sub* and *statuo*, Latin.] To put in the place of another.

In the original designs of speaking, a man can *substitute* none for them that can equally conduce to his honour. *Gov. of Tongue.*

If a swarthy tongue
Is underneath his humid palate hung,
Reject him and *substitute* another. *Dryden.*

Some few verses are inserted or *substituted* in the room of others. *Congreve.*

SU'BSTITUTE. *n. s.* [*substitut*, Fr. from the verb.] One placed by another to act with delegated power.

Were you sworn to the duke, or to the deputy?
——To him and his *substitutes*. *Shakespeare.*

You've taken up,
Under the counterfeited zeal of God,
The subjects of his *substitute*, my father,
And here upswarm'd them. *Shakesp. Henry IV.*

Hast thou not made me here thy *substitute*,
And these inferior far beneath me set? *Milton.*

Providence delegates to the supreme magistrate the same power for the good of men, which that supreme magistrate transfers to those several *substitutes* who act under him. *Addis.*

SUBSTITU'TION. *n. s.* [*substitution*, Fr. from *substitute.*] The act of placing any person or thing in the room of another; the state of being placed in the room of another.

He did believe
He was the duke, from *substitution*,
And executing th' outward face of royalty,
With all prerogative. *Shakesp. Tempest.*

Nor sal, sulphur, or mercury can be separated from any perfect metals; for every part, so separated, may easily be reduced into perfect metal without *substitution* of that which chymists imagine to be wanting. *Bacon's Phys. Rem.*

To SUBSTRA'CT. *v. a.* [*subtraho*, Lat. *soustraction*, French.]

1. To take away part from the whole.

2. To take one number from another.

SUBSTRA'CTION. *n. s.* [*soubstraire*, *soubstraction*, French.]

1. The act of taking away part from the whole.

I cannot call this piece Tully's nor my own, being much altered not only by the change of the style, but by addition and *substraction*. *Denham.*

2. [In arithmetick.] The taking of a lesser number out of a greater of like kind, whereby to find out a third number, being or declaring the inequality, excess, or difference between the numbers given. *Cocker's Arithmetick.*

SUBSTRU'CTION. *n. s.* [*substructio*, from *sub* and *struo*, Latin.] Underbuilding.

To found our habitation firmly, examine the bed of earth upon which we build, and then the underfillings, or *substruction*, as the ancients called it. *Wotton's Architecture.*

SUBSTY'LAR. *adj.* [*sub* and *stylus.*] *Substylar* line is, in dialing, a right line, whereon the gnomon or style of a dial is erected at right angles with the plane. *Dict.*

Erect the style perpendicularly over the *substilar* line, so as to make an angle with the dial-plane equal to the elevation of the pole of your place. *Moxon's Mech. Exer.*

SUBSU'LTIVE. } *adj.* [*subsultus*, Latin.] Bounding; moving
SUBSU'LTORY. } by starts.

SUBSU'LTORILY. *adv.* [from *subsultory.*] In a bounding manner.

The spirits spread even, and move not *subsultorily*; for that will make the parts close and pliant. *Bacon's Natural History.*

SUBTA'NGENT. *n. s.* In any curve, is the line which determines the intersection of the tangent in the axis prolonged. *Dict.*

To SUBTE'ND. *v. a.* [*sub* and *tendo*, Latin.] To be extended under.

In rectangles and triangles the square, which is made of the side that *subtendeth* the right angle, is equal to the squares which are made of the sides containing the right angle. *Brown.*

From Aries rightways draw a line, to end
In the same round, and let that line *subtend*
An equal triangle: now since the lines
Must three times touch the round, and meet three signs,
Where e'er they meet in angles, those are trines. *Creech.*

SUBTE'NSE. *n. s.* [*sub* and *tensus*, Latin.] The chord of an arch; that which is extended under any thing.

SU'BTER. [Latin.] In composition, signifies *under*.

SUBTERFLU'ENT. } *adj.* [*subterfluo*, Latin.] Running under.
SUBTE'RFLUOUS. }

SUBTERFU'GE. *n. s.* [*supterfuge*, French; *subter* and *fugio*, Lat.] A shift; an evasion; a trick.

The king cared not for *subterfuges*, but would stand envy, and appear in any thing that was to his mind. *Bacon.*

Notwithstanding all their sly *subterfuges* and studied evasions, yet the product of all their endeavours is but as the birth of the labouring mountains, wind and emptiness. *Glanv.*

Affect not little shifts and *subterfuges* to avoid the force of an argument. *Watts.*

SUBTERRA'NEAL. } *adj.* [*sub* and *terra*, Lat. *sousterraine*, Fr.
SUBTERRA'NEAN. } *Subterranean* or *subterraneous* is the word
SU'BTERRANEOUS. } now used.] Lying under the earth; placed
SU'BTERRANY. } below the surface.

Metals are wholly *subterrany*, whereas plants are part above earth, and part under. *Bacon's Natural History.*

In *subterranies*, as the fathers of their tribes, are brimstone and mercury. *Bacon's Natural History.*

The force
Of *subterranean* wind transports a hill
Torn from Pelorus, or the shatter'd side
Of thund'ring Ætna, whose combustible
And fuel'd entrails thence conceiving fire,
Sublim'd with mineral fury, aid the winds. *Milton.*

Alteration proceeded from the change made in the neighbouring *subterraneal* parts by that great conflagration. *Boyle.*

Tell by what paths, what *subterranean* ways,
Back to the fountain's head the sea conveys
The refluent rivers. *Blackmore.*

Let my soft minutes glide obscurely on,
Like *subterraneous* streams, unheard, unknown. *Norris.*

This *subterraneous* passage was not at first designed so much for a highway as for a quarry. *Addison.*

Rous'd within the *subterranean* world,
Th' expanding earthquake unresisted shakes
Aspiring cities. *Thomson.*

SUBTERRA'NITY. *n. s.* [*sub* and *terra*, Lat.] A place under ground. Not in use.

We commonly consider *subterranities*, not in contemplations, sufficiently respective unto the creation. *Brown.*

SU'BTILE. *adj.* [*subtile*, Fr. *subtilis*, Lat. This word is often written *subtle.*]

1. Thin; not dense; not gross.

From his eyes the fleeting fair
Retir'd, like *subtle* smoke dissolv'd in air. *Dryden's Georg.*

Deny Des Cart his *subtile* matter,
You leave him neither fire nor water. *Prior.*

Is not the heat conveyed through the vacuum by the vibrations of a much *subtiler* medium than air, which, after the air was drawn out, remained in the vacuum? *Newton's Opt.*

2. Nice; fine; delicate; not coarse.

But of the clock which in our breasts we bear,
The *subtile* motions we forget the while. *Davies.*

Thou only know'st her nature, and her pow'rs;
Her *subtile* form thou only can'st define. *Davies.*

I do distinguish plain
Each *subtile* line of her immortal face. *Davies.*

3. Piercing; acute.

Pass we the slow disease and *subtile* pain,
Which our weak frame is destin'd to sustain;
The cruel stone, the cold catarrh. *Prior.*

4. Cunning; artful; sly; subdolous. In this sense it is now commonly written *subtle.*

Arrius, a priest in the church of Alexandria, a *subtile* witted and a marvellous fair spoken man, was discontented that one should be placed before him in honour, whose superior he thought himself in desert, because through envy and stomach prone unto contradiction. *Hooker.*

Think you this York
Was not incensed by his *subtle* mother,
To taunt and scorn you? *Shakesp. Richard* III.

O *subtile* love, a thousand wiles thou hast
By humble suit, by service, or by hire,
To win a maiden's hold. *Fairfax.*

A woman, an harlot and *subtile* of heart. *Prov.* vii. 10.

Nor thou his malice, and false guile, contemn:
Subtile he needs must be, who could seduce
Angels. *Milton's Paradise Lost.*

5. Deceitful.

Like a bowl upon a *subtle* ground,
I've tumbled past the throw. *Shakesp. Coriolanus.*

6. Refined; acute beyond exactness.

Things remote from use, obscure and *subtle.* *Milton.*

SU'BTILELY. *adv.* [from *subtile.*]

1. Finely; not grossly.

The constitution of the air appeareth more *subtilly* by worms in oak-apples than to the sense of man. *Bacon.*

In these plaisters the stone should not be too *subtilely* powdered; for it will better manifest its attraction in more sensible dimensions. *Brown's Vulgar Errours.*

The opakest bodies, if *subtilely* divided, as metals dissolved in acid menstruums, become perfectly transparent. *Newton.*

2. Artfully; cunningly.

By granting this, add the reputation of loving the truth sincerely to that of having been able to oppose it *subtilely.* *Boyle.*

Others have sought to ease themselves of affliction by disputing *subtilly* against it, and pertinaciously maintaining that afflictions are no real evils. *Tillotson's Sermons.*

SU'BTILENESS. *n. s.* [from *subtile.*]

1. Fineness; rareness.
2. Cunning; artfulness.

To SUBTI'LIATE. *v. a.* [from *subtile.*] To make thin.

A very dry and warm or *subtiliating* air opens the surface of the earth. *Harvey on the Plague.*

SUBTILIA'TION. *n. s.* [*subtiliation*, French; from *subtiliate.*] The act of making thin.

By *subtiliation* and rarefaction the oil contained in grapes, if distilled before it be fermented, becomes spirit of wine. *Boyle.*

SU'BTILTY. *n. s.* [*subtilité*, French; from *subtile.*]

1. Thinness; fineness; exility of parts.

The *subtilties* of particular sounds may pass through small crannies not confused, but its magnity not so well. *Bacon.*

How shall we this union well express?
Nought ties the soul, her *subtilty* is such. *Davies.*

The corporeity of all bodies being the same, and *subtilty* in all bodies being essentially the same thing, could any body by *subtilty* become vital, then any degree of *subtilty* would produce some degree of life. *Grew's Cosmol.*

Bodies the more of kin they are to spirit in *subtilty* and refinement, the more spreading and self-diffusive are they. *Norris.*

2. Nicety.

Whatsoever is invisible, in respect of the fineness of the body, or *subtilty* of the motion, is little enquired. *Bacon.*

3. Refinement; too much acuteness.

You prefer the reputation of candour before that of *subtilty.* *Boyle.*

Intelligible discourses are spoiled by too much *subtilty* in nice divisions. *Locke.*

Greece did at length a learned race produce,
Who needful science mock'd, and arts of use;
Mankind with idle *subtilties* embroil,
And fashion systems with romantick toil. *Blackmore.*

They give method, and shed *subtilty* upon their author. *Bak.*

4. Cunning; artifice; slyness.

Finding force now faint to be,
He thought grey hairs afforded *subtilty.* *Sidney.*

The rudeness and barbarity of savage Indians knows not so perfectly to hate all virtues as some mens *subtilty.* *K. Charles.*

Sleights proceeding
As from his wit and native *subtlety.* *Milton.*

SUBTILIZA'TION. *n. s.* [from *subtilize.*]

1. Subtilization is making any thing so volatile as to rise readily in steam or vapour. *Quincy.*

Fluids have their resistances proportional to their densities, so that no *subtilization*, division of parts, or refining can alter these resistances. *Cheyne's Phil. Princ.*

2. Refinement; superfluous acuteness.

To SU'BTILIZE. *v. a.* [*subtilizer*, French; from *subtile.*]

1. To make thin; to make less gross or coarse.

Chyle, being mixed with the choler and pancreatick juices, is further *subtilized*, and rendered so fluid and penetrant, that the thinner and finer part easily finds way in at the streight orifices of the lacteous veins. *Ray on the Creation.*

Body cannot be vital; for if it be, then is it so either as *subtilized* or organized, moved or endowed with life. *Grew.*

2. To refine; to spin into useless niceties.

The most obvious verity is *subtilized* into niceties, and spun into a thread indiscernible by common opticks. *Glanville.*

To SUBTI'LIZE. *v. n.* To talk with too much refinement.

Qualities and moods some modern philosophers have *subtilized* on. *Digby on Bodies.*

SU'BTLE. *adj.* [Written often for *subtile*, especially in the sense of cunning.] Sly; artful; cunning.

Some *subtle* headed fellow will put some quirk, or devise some evasion, whereof the rest will take hold. *Spenser.*

Shall we think the *subtle* witted French
Conj'rers and forc'rers, that, afraid of him,
By magick verse have thus contriv'd his end? *Shak. H.* VI.

The serpent, *subtlest* beast of all the field. *Milton.*

The Arabians were men of a deep and *subtle* wit. *Sprat.*

SU'BTLY. *adv.* [from *subtle.*]

1. Slily; artfully; cunningly.

Thou see'st how *subtly* to detain thee I devise;
Inviting thee to hear, while I relate. *Milton's Parad. Lost.*

2. Nicely; delicately.

In the nice bee, what sense so *subtly* true,
From pois'nous herbs extracts the healing dew! *Pope.*

To SU'BTRACT. *v. a.* [*subtractio*, Latin. They who derive it from the Latin write *subtract*; those who know the French original, write *substract*, which is the common word.] To withdraw part from the rest.

Reducing many things unto charge, which, by confusion, became concealed and *subtracted* from the crown. *Davies.*

What is *subtracted* or subducted out of the extent of the divine perfection, leaves still a quotient infinite. *Hale.*

The same swallow, by the *subtracting* daily of her eggs, lay nineteen successively, and then gave over. *Ray.*

SUBTRA'CTION. *n. s.* See SUBSTRACTION.

SU'BTRAHEND. *n. s.* [*subtrahendum*, Lat.] The number to be taken from a larger number.

SUBTRI'PLE. *adj.* [*subtriple*, Fr. *sub* and *triplus*, Latin.] Containing a third or one part of three.

The power will be in a *subtriple* proportion to the weight. *Wilkins's Math. Magic.*

SUBVENTA'NEOUS. *adj.* [*subventaneus*, Lat.] Addle; windy.

Suitable unto the relation of the mares in Spain, and their *subventaneous* conceptions from the western wind. *Brown.*

To SU'BVERSE. *v. a.* [*subversus*, Latin.] To subvert. *Spenser* uses *subverst* in the same sense.

Empires *subvers'd*, when ruling fate has struck
Th' unalterable hour. *Thomson's Autumn.*

SUBVE'RSION. *n. s.* [*subversion*, Fr. *subversus*, Latin.] Overthrow; ruin; destruction.

These seek *subversion* of thy harmless life. *Shak. H.* VI.

It is far more honourable to suffer, than to prosper in their ruin and *subversion.* *King Charles.*

These things refer to the opening and shutting the abyss, with the dissolution or *subversion* of the earth. *Burnet.*

Laws have been often abused, to the oppression and the *subversion* of that order they were intended to preserve. *Rogers.*

SUBVE'RSIVE. *adj.* [from *subvert.*] Having tendency to overturn.

Lying is a vice *subversive* of the very ends and design of conversation. *Rogers.*

To SU'BVERT. *v. a.* [*subvertir*, French; *subverto*, Latin.]

1. To overthrow; to overturn; to destroy; to turn upside down.

God, by things deem'd weak,
Subverts the worldly strong and worldly wise. *Milton.*

No proposition can be received for divine revelation, if contradictory to our clear intuitive knowledge; because this would *subvert* the principles of all knowledge *Locke.*

Trees are *subverted* or broken by high winds. *Mortimer.*

2. To corrupt; to confound.

Strive not about words to no purpose, but to the *subverting* of the hearers. 2 *Tim.* ii. 14.

SUBVE'RTER. *n. s.* [from *subvert.*] Overthrower; destroyer.

O traytor! worse than Simon was to Troy;
O vile *subverter* of the Gallick reign,
More false than Gano was to Charlemagne. *Dryden.*

SU'BURB. *n. s.* [*suburbium*, Latin.]

1. Building without the walls of a city.

There's a trim rabble let in: are all these your faithful friends o' th' *suburbs?* *Shakespeare's Henry* VIII.

What can be more to the disvaluation of the power of the Spaniard, than to have marched seven days in the heart of his countries, and lodged three nights in the *suburbs* of his principal city? *Bacon's War with Spain.*

2. The confines; the outpart.

The *suburbs* of my jacket are so gone,
I have not left one skirt to sit upon. *Cleaveland.*

They on the smoothed plank,
The *suburb* of their strawbuilt citadel,
Expatiate. *Milton.*

When our fortunes are violently changed, our spirits are unchanged, if they always stood in the *suburbs* and expectation of sorrows. *Taylor.*

SUBU'RBAN. *adj.* [*suburbanus*, Latin; from *suburb.*] Inhabiting the suburb.

Poor clinches the *suburban* muse affords,
And Panton waging harmless war with words. *Dryden.*

SUBWO'RKER. *n. s.* [*sub* and *worker.*] Underworker; subordinate helper.

He that governs well leads the blind; but he that teaches gives him eyes: and it is glorious to be a *subworker* to grace, in freeing it from some of the inconveniences of original sin. *South.*

SUCCEDA'NEOUS. *adj.* [*succedaneus*, Lat.] Supplying the place of something else.

Nor is Ætius strictly to be believed when he prescribeth the stone of the otter as a *succedaneous* unto castoeum. *Brown.*

I have not discovered the menstruum: I will present a *succedaneous* experiment made with a common liquor. *Boyle.*

SUCCEDA'NEUM. n. s. [Latin.] That which is put to serve for something else.

To SU'CCEED. *v. n.* [*succeder*, French; *succedo*, Latin.]

1. To follow in order.

If I were now to die,
'Twere to be most happy; for I fear,
My soul hath her consent so absolute,
That not another comfort like to this
Succeeds in unknown fate. *Shakes. Othello.*

Those of all ages to *succeed* will curse my head. *Milton.*

2. To come into the place of one who has quitted.

Workmen let it cool by degrees in such relentings of nealing heats, lest it should shiver in pieces by a violent *succeeding* of air in the room of the fire. *Digby on Bodies.*

Enjoy 'till I return
Short pleasures; for long woes are to *succeed.* *Milton.*

If the father left only daughters, they equally *succeeded* to him in copartnership, without prelation or preference of the eldest to a double portion. *Hale.*

Revenge *succeeds* to love, and rage to grief. *Dryden.*

While these limbs the vital spirit feeds,
While day to night, and night to day *succeeds*,
Burnt-off'rings morn and ev'ning shall be thine,
And fires eternal in thy temples shine. *Dryden.*

These dull harmless makers of lampoons are yet of dangerous example to the publick: some witty men may *succeed* to their designs, and, mixing sense with malice, blast the reputation of the most innocent. *Dryden.*

The pretensions of Saul's family, who received his crown from the immediate appointment of God, ended with his reign; and David, by the same title, *succeeded* in his throne, to the exclusion of Jonathan. *Locke.*

3. To obtain one's wish; to terminate an undertaking in the desired effect.

'Tis almost impossible for poets to *succeed* without ambition: imagination must be raised by a desire of fame to a desire of pleasing. *Dryden.*

This address I have long thought owing; and if I had never attempted, I might have been vain enough to think I might have *succeeded.* *Dryden.*

A knave's a knave to me in ev'ry state;
Alike my scorn, if he *succeed* or fail:
Sporus at court, or Japhet in a jail. *Pope.*

4. To terminate according to wish.

If thou deal truly, thy doings shall prosperously *succeed* to thee. *Tob.* iv. 6.

This was impossible for Virgil to imitate, because of the severity of the Roman language: Spencer endeavoured it in Sheperd's Kalendar; but neither will it *succeed* in English. *Dry.*

5. To go under cover.

Please that silvan scene to take,
Where whistling winds uncertain shadows make;
Or will you to the cooler cave *succeed*,
Whose mouth the curling vines have overspread. *Dryden.*

To SU'CCEED. *v. a.*

1. To follow; to be subsequent or consequent to.

In that place no creature was hurtful unto man, and those destructive effects they now discover *succeeded* the curse, and came in with thorns and briars. *Brown's Vulgar Errours.*

2. To prosper; to make successful.

Now frequent trines the happier lights among,
And high-rais'd Jove from his dark prison freed,
Those weights took off that on his planet hung,
Will gloriously the new laid works *succeed.* *Dryden.*

Succeed my wish, and second my design,
The fairest Deiopeia shall be thine,
And make thee father of a happy line. *Dryden's Æn.*

SUCCE'EDER. *n. s.* [from *succeed.*] One who follows; one who comes into the place of another.

Why should calamity be full of words?
—Windy attorneys to their client woes,
Airy *succeeders* of intestate joys,
Poor breathing orators of miseries! *Shakes. R.* III.

Now this great *succeeder* all repairs,
He builds up strength and greatness for his heirs,
Out of the virtues that adorn'd his blood. *Daniel.*

Nature has so far imprinted it in us, that should the envy of predecessors deny the secret to *succeeders*, they yet would find it out. *Suckling.*

They make one man's particular fancies, perhaps failings, confining laws to others, and convey them to their *succeeders*, who afterwards misname all unobsequiousness as presumption. *Boyle.*

SU'CCESS. *n. s.* [*succes*, French; *successus*, Latin.]

1. The termination of any affair happy or unhappy. *Success* without any epithet is commonly taken for good success.

For good *success* of his hands, he asketh ability to do of him that is most unable. *Wisd.* xiii. 19.

Perplex'd and troubled at his bad *success*
The tempter stood. *Milton.*

Not Lemuel's mother with more care
Did counsel or instruct her heir;
Or teach, with more *success*, her son
The vices of the time to shun. *Waller.*

Every reasonable man cannot but wish me *success* in this attempt, because I undertake the proof of that which it is every man's interest that it should be true. *Tillotson's Sermons.*

Whilst malice and ingratitude confess,
They've strove for ruin long without *success.* *Garth.*

Gas sulphuris may be given with *success* in any disease of the lungs. *Arbuthnot on Diet.*

Military *successes*, above all others, elevate the minds of a people. *Atterbury's Sermons.*

2. Succession. Obsolete.

All the sons of these five brethren reigned
By due *success*, and all their nephews late,
Even thrice eleven descents, the crown retained. *Spenser.*

SUCCE'SSFUL. *adj.* [*success* and *full.*] Prosperous; happy; fortunate.

They were terrible alarms to persons grown wealthy by a long and *successful* imposture, by persuading the world that men might be honest and happy, though they never mortified any corrupt appetites. *South's Sermons.*

H' observ'd the illustrious throng,
Their names, their fates, their conduct and their care
In peaceful senates and *successful* war. *Dryden.*

The early hunter
Blesses Diana's hand, who leads him safe
O'er hanging cliffs; who spreads his net *successful*,
And guides the arrow through the panther's heart. *Prior.*

SUCCE'SSFULLY. *adv.* [from *successful.*] Prosperously; luckily; fortunately.

He is too young, yet he looks *successfully.* *Shakespeare.*

They would want a competent instrument to collect and convey their rays *successfully*, or so as to imprint the species with any vigour on a dull prejudicate faculty. *Hammond.*

The rule of imitating God can never be *successfully* proposed but upon Christian principles; such as that this world is a place not of rest, but of discipline. *Atterbury.*

A reformation

A reformation *successfully* carried on in this great town, would in time spread itself over the whole kingdom. *Swift.*

Bleeding, when the expectoration goes on *successfully*, suppresseth it. *Arbuthnot on Diet.*

SUCCE'SSFULNESS. *n. s.* [from *successful.*] Happy conclusion; desired event; series of good fortune.

An opinion of the *successfulness* of the work is as necessary to found a purpose of undertaking it, as the authority of commands, or the persuasiveness of promises. *Hammond.*

SUCCE'SSION. *n. s.* [*succession*, French; *successio*, Latin.]

1. Consecution; series of one thing or person following another.

St. Augustine, having reckoned up a great number of the bishops of Rome, saith, in all this order of *succession* of bishops there is not one found a Donatist. *Hooker.*

Reflection on appearances of several ideas, one after another, in our minds, furnishes us with the idea of *succession.* *Locke.*

Let a cannon-bullet pass through a room, and take with it any limb of a man, it is clear that it must strike successively the two sides of the room, touch one part of the flesh first, and another after, and so in *succession.* *Locke.*

2. A series of things or persons following one another.

These decays in Spain have been occasioned by so long a war with Holland; but most by two *successions* of inactive princes. *Bacon.*

The smallest particles of matter may cohere by the strongest attractions, and compose bigger particles of weaker virtue; and many of these may cohere and compose bigger particles, whose virtue is still weaker; and so on for divers *successions*, until the progression end in the biggest particles, on which the operations in chymistry and the colours of natural bodies depend. *Newton's Opt.*

3. A lineage; an order of descendants.

Cassibelan,
And his *succession*, granted Rome a tribute. *Shakesp. Cymbel.*
A long *succession* must ensue;
And his next son the clouded ark of God
Shall in a glorious temple enshrine. *Milt Par. Lost.*

4. The power or right of coming to the inheritance of ancestors.

What people is so void of common sense,
To vote *succession* from a native prince? *Dryden.*

SUCCE'SSIVE. *adj.* [*successif*, French.]

1. Following in order; continuing a course or consecution uninterrupted.

Three with fiery courage he assails,
And each *successive* after other quails,
Still wond'ring whence so many kings should rise. *Daniel.*
God hath set
Labour and rest, as day and night, to men
Successive. *Milt. Par. Lost.*

God, by reason of his eternal indivisible nature, is by one single act of duration present to all the *successive* portions of time, and all successively existing in them. *South.*

Send the *successive* ills through ages down,
And let each weeping father tell his son. *Prior.*

2. Inherited by succession. Not in use.

Countrymen,
Plead my *successive* title with your swords.
Shakespeare's Titus Andronicus.

The empire being elective, and not *successive*, the emperors, in being, made profit of their own times. *Raleigh.*

SUCCE'SSIVLEY. *adv.* [*successivement*, Fr. from *successive.*] In uninterrupted order; one after another.

Three sons he left,
All which *successively* by turns did reign. *Fairy Queen.*
Is it upon record? or else reported
Successively from age to age? *Shakesp. Richard III.*

That king left only by his six wives three children, who reigned *successively*, and died childless. *Bacon.*

We that measure times by first and last,
The sight of things *successively* do take,
When God on all at once his view doth cast,
And of all times doth but one instant make. *Davies.*

I inclined the paper to the rays very obliquely, that the most refrangible rays might be more copiously reflected than the rest, and the whiteness at length changed *successively* into blue, indigo, and violet. *Newton's Opt.*

No such motion of the same atom can be all of it existent at once: it must needs be made gradually and *successively*, both as to place and time, seeing that body cannot at the same instant be in more places than one. *Bentley's Sermons.*

SUCCE'SSIVENESS. *n. s.* [from *successive.*] The state of being successive.

All the notion we have of duration is partly by the *successiveness* of its own operations, and partly by those external measures that it finds in motion. *Hale.*

SUCCE'SSLESS. *adj.* [from *success.*] Unlucky; unfortunate; failing of the event desired.

The hopes of thy *successless* love resign. *Dryden.*

The Bavarian duke,
Bold champion! brandishing his Noric blade,
Best temper'd steel, *successless* prov'd in field. *Philips.*
Passion unpity'd, and *successless* love,
Plant daggers in my heart. *Addison's Cato.*
Successless all her soft caresses prove,
To banish from his breast his country's love. *Pope.*

SU'CCESSOUR. *n. s.* [*successeur*, French; *successor*, Latin. This is sometimes pronounced *succéssour*, with the accent in the middle.] One that follows in the place or character of another; correlative to *predecessour.*

This king by this queen had a son of tender age, but of great expectation, brought up in the hope of themselves, and already acceptation of the inconstant people, as *successor* of his father's crown. *Sidney.*

The *successor* of Moses in prophecies. *Ecclus.* xlvi. 1.

The fear of what was to come from an unacknowledged *successour* to the crown, clouded much of that prosperity then, which now shines in chronicle. *Clarendon.*

The second part of confirmation is the prayer and benediction of the bishop, the *successour* of the apostles in this office. *Hammond on Fundamentals.*

The surly savage offspring disappear,
And curse the bright *successor* of the year;
Yet crafty kind with daylight can dispense. *Dryden.*
Whether a bright *successor*, or the same. *Tate.*

The descendants of Alexander's *successors* cultivated navigation in some lesser degree. *Arbuthnot.*

SUCCI'NCT. *adj.* [*succinct*, French; *succinctus*, Latin.]

1. Tucked or girded up; having the cloaths drawn up to disengage the legs.

His habit fit for speed *succinct.* *Milton's Par. Lost.*
His vest *succinct* then girding round his waist,
Forth rush'd the swain. *Pope.*
Four knaves in garbs *succinct.* *Pope.*

2. Short; concise; brief.

A strict and *succinct* stile is that where you can take nothing away without loss, and that loss manifest. *Ben. Johnson.*

Let all your precepts be *succinct* and clear,
That ready wits may comprehend them soon. *Roscommon.*

SUCCI'NCTLY. *adv.* [from *succinct.*] Briefly; concisely; without superfluity of diction.

I shall present you very *succinctly* with a few reflections that most readily occur. *Boyle.*

I'll recant, when France can shew me wit
As strong as ours, and as *succinctly* writ. *Roscommon.*

SU'CCORY. *n. s.* [*cichorium*, Latin.] A plant.

It is one of the milky plants, with a plain radiated flower: the flowers are produced from the sides of the branches, at the setting off of the branches upon short footstalks: the cup of the flower is like a contracted seed-vessel: the seeds are angular, umbilicated, and shaped somewhat like a wedge. *Miller.*

A garden-sallad
Of endive, radishes, and *succory.* *Dryden.*

The medicaments to diminish the milk are lettuce, purslane, endive, and *succory.* *Wiseman of Tumours.*

To SU'CCOUR. *v. a.* [*secourir*, French; *succurro*, Lat.] To help; to assist in difficulty or distress; to relieve.

As that famous queen
Of Amazons, whom Pyrrhus did destroy,
Did shew herself in great triumphant joy,
To *succour* the weak state of sad afflicted Troy. *Fa. Qu.*

A grateful beast will stand upon record, against those that in their prosperity forget their friends, that to their loss and hazard stood by and *succoured* them in their adversity. *L'Estr.*

SU'CCOUR. *n. s.* [from the verb; *secours*, French.]

1. Aid; assistance; relief of any kind; help in distress.

My father,
Flying for *succour* to his servant Banister,
Being distress'd, was by that wretch betray'd. *Shakespeare.*
Here's a young maid with travel oppress'd,
And faints for *succour.* *Shakespeare.*

2. The person or things that bring help.

Fear nothing else but a betraying of *succours* which reason offereth. *Wisd.* xvii. 12.

Our watchful general had discern'd from far
The mighty *succour* which made glad the foe. *Dryden.*

SU'CCOURER. *n. s.* [from *succour.*] Helper; assistant; reliever.

She hath been a *succourer* of many. *Ro.* xvi. 2.

SU'CCOURLESS. *adj.* [from *succour.*] Wanting relief; void of friends or help.

Succourless and sad,
She with extended arms his aid implores. *Thomson.*

SU'CCULENCY. *n. s.* [from *succulent.*] Juiciness.

SU'CCULENT. *adj.* [*succulent*, French; *succulentus*, Latin.] Juicy; moist.

These plants have a strong, dense, and *succulent* moisture, which is not apt to exhale. *Bacon.*

Divine Providence has spread her table every where, not with a juiceless green carpet, but with *succulent* herbage and nourishing grass, upon which most beasts feed. *More.*

On our account has Jove,
Indulgent, to all lands some *succulent* plant
Allotted, that poor helpless man might slack
His present thirst. *Philips.*

To Succu'mb. *v. n.* [*succumbo*, Latin; *succomber*, French.] To yield; to sink under any difficulty. Not in use, except among the Scotch.

To their wills we must *succumb*,
Quocunque trahunt, 'tis our doom. *Hudibras.*

Succu'ssation. *n. s.* [*succusso*, Latin.] A trot.

They move two legs of one side together, which is tolutation or ambling, or lift one foot before and the cross foot behind, which is *succussation* or trotting. *Brown's Vulgar Err.*

They rode, but authors do not say
Whether tolutation or *succussation*. *Butler.*

Succu'ssion. *n. s.* [*succussio*, Latin.]

1. The act of shaking.

When any of that risible species were brought to the doctor, and when he considered the spasms of the diaphragm, and all the muscles of respiration, with the tremulous *succussion* of the whole human body, he gave such patients over. *Mart. Scrib.*

2. [In physick.] Is such a shaking of the nervous parts as is procured by strong stimuli, like sternutatories, friction, and the like, which are commonly used in apoplectick affections.

Such. *pronoun.* [*sulleiks*, Gothick; *sulk*, Dutch; ſpilc, Saxon.]

1. Of that kind; of the like kind. With *as* before the thing to which it relates, when the thing follows: as, *such* a power *as* a king's; *such* a gift *as* a kingdom.

'Tis *such* another fitchew! marry, a perfum'd one. *Shakes.*

Can we find *such* a one *as* this, in whom the spirit of God is? *Gen.* xli. 38.

The works of the flesh are manifest, *such* are drunkenness, revelings, and *such* like. *Gal.* v. 21.

You will not make this a general rule to debar *such* from preaching of the Gospel *as* have thro' infirmity fallen. *Whitgift.*

Such another idol was Manah, worshipped between Mecca and Medina, which was called a rock or stone. *Stillingfleet.*

Such precepts *as* tend to make men good, singly considered, may be distributed into *such as* enjoin piety towards God, or *such as* require the good government of ourselves. *Tillotson.*

If my song be *such*,
That you will hear and credit me too much,
Attentive listen. *Dryden.*

Such are the cold Riphean race, and *such*
The savage Scythian. *Dryden's Virg. Georg.*

As to be perfectly just is an attribute in the Divine Nature, to be so to the utmost of our abilities is the glory of a man: *such* an one, who has the publick administration, acts like the representative of his Maker. *Addison.*

You love a verse, take *such as* I can send. *Pope.*

2. The same that. With *as*.

This was the state of the kingdom of Tunis at *such* time *as* Barbarossa, with Solyman's great fleet, landed in Africk. *Knoll.*

3. Comprehended under the term premised.

That thou art happy, owe to God;
That thou continu'st *such*, owe to thyself. *Milton.*

To assert that God looked upon Adam's fall as a sin, and punished it as *such*, when, without any antecedent sin, he withdrew that actual grace, upon which it was impossible for him not to fall, highly reproaches the essential equity of the Divine Nature. *South.*

No promise can oblige a prince so much,
Still to be good, as long to have been *such*. *Dryden.*

4. A manner of expressing a particular person or thing.

I saw him yesterday
With *such* and *such*. *Shakesp. Hamlet.*

If you repay me not on *such* a day,
In *such* a place, *such* sum or sums, as are
Express'd in the condition, let the forfeit
Be an equal pound of your flesh. *Shak. Merch. of Venice.*

I have appointed my servants to *such* and *such* place. 1 *Sam.*

Scarce this word death from sorrow did proceed,
When in rush'd one, and tells him *such* a knight
Is new arriv'd. *Daniel's Civil War.*

Himself overtook a party of the army, consisting of three thousand horse and foot, with a train of artillery, which he left at *such* a place, within three hours march of Berwick. *Clarend.*

The same sovereign authority may enact a law, commanding *such* or *such* an action to-day, and a quite contrary law forbidding the same to-morrow. *South's Sermons.*

Those artists who propose only the imitation of *such* or *such* a particular person, without election of those ideas beforementioned, have often been reproached for that omission. *Dryden's Dufresnoy.*

To SUCK. *v. a.* [ſucan, Saxon; *sugo*, *suctum*, Latin; *succer*, French.]

1. To draw by making a rarefaction of the air.

2. To draw in with the mouth.

The cup of astonishment thou shalt drink, and *suck* it out. *Ezek.* xxiii. 34.

We'll hand in hand to the dark mansions go,
Where, *sucking* in each other's latest breath,
We may transfuse our souls. *Dryden.*

Still she drew
The sweets from ev'ry flow'r, and *suck'd* the dew. *Dryden.*

Transfix'd as o'er Castalia's streams he hung,
He *suck'd* new poisons with his triple tongue. *Pope's Statius.*

3. To draw the teat of a female.

Desire, the more he *suck'd*, more sought the breast,
Like dropsy folk still drink to be a-thirst. *Sidney.*

A bitch will nurse young foxes in place of her puppies, if you can get them once to *suck* her so long that her milk may go through them. *Locke.*

Did a child *suck* every day a new nurse, it would be no more affrighted with the change of faces at six months old than at sixty. *Locke.*

4. To draw with the milk.

Thy valiantness was mine, thou *suck'dst* it from me;
But own thy pride thyself. *Shakes. Coriolanus.*

5. To empty by sucking.

A fox lay with whole swarms of flies *sucking* and galling of him. *L'Estrange.*

Bees on tops of lilies feed,
And creep within their bells to *suck* the balmy seed. *Dryden.*

6. To draw or drain.

I can *suck* melancholy out of a song, as a weazel *sucks* eggs. *Shakespeare.*

Pumping hath tir'd our men;
Seas into seas thrown, we *suck* in again. *Donne.*

A cubical vessel of brass is filled an inch and a half in half an hour; but because it *sucks* up nothing as the earth doth, take an inch for half an hour's rain. *Burnet.*

Old ocean, *suck'd* through the porous globe,
Had long ere now forsook his horrid bed. *Thomson.*

To Suck. *v. n.*

1. To draw by rarefying the air.

Continual repairs, the least defects in *sucking* pumps are constantly requiring. *Mortimer's Husbandry.*

2. To draw the breast.

Such as are nourished with milk find the paps, and *suck* at them; whereas none of those that are not designed for that nourishment ever offer to *suck*. *Ray on the Creation.*

I would
Pluck the young *sucking* cubs from the she-bear,
To win thee, lady. *Shakesp. Merchant of Venice.*

Why did the knees prevent me? or why the breasts that I should *suck*? *Job* iii. 12.

A nursing father beareth with the *sucking* child. *Numb.* xi.

3. To draw; imbibe.

The crown had *sucked* too hard, and now being full, was like to draw less. *Bacon's Henry* VIII.

All the under passions,
As waters are by whirl-pools suck'd and drawn,
Were quite devoured in the vast gulph of empire. *Dryden.*

Suck. *n. s.* [from the verb.]

1. The act of sucking.

I hoped, from the descent of the quick-silver in the tube, upon the first *suck*, that I should be able to give a nearer guess at the proportion of force betwixt the pressure of the air and the gravity of quick-silver. *Boyle.*

2. Milk given by females.

They draw with their *suck* the disposition of their nurses. *Spenser.*

I have given *suck* and know
How tender 'tis to love the babe that milks me. *Shakespeare.*

Those first unpolish'd matrons
Gave *suck* to infants of gigantick mold. *Dryden.*

It would be inconvenient for birds to give *suck*. *Ray.*

Su'cker. *n. s.* [*suceur*, French; from *suck*.]

1. Any thing that draws.

2. The embolus of a pump.

Oil must be poured into the cylinder that the *sucker* may slip up and down in it more smoothly. *Boyle.*

The ascent of waters is by *suckers* or forcers, or something equivalent thereunto. *Wilkins's Dædalus.*

3. A round piece of leather, laid wet on a stone, and drawn up in the middle, rarifies the air within, which pressing upon its edges, holds it down to the stone.

One of the round leathers wherewith boys play, called *suckers*, not above an inch and half diameter, being well soaked in water, will stick and pluck a stone of twelve pounds up from the ground. *Grew's Musæum.*

4. A pipe through which any thing is sucked.

Mariners aye ply the pump,
So they, but chearful, unfatigu'd, still move
The draining *sucker*. *Philips.*

5. A young twig shooting from the stock. This word was perhaps originally *surcle*, [*surculus*, Latin.]

The cutting away of *suckers* at the root and body, doth make trees grow high. *Bacon's Natural History.*

Out of this old root a *sucker* may spring, that with a little shelter and good seasons, may prove a mighty tree. *Ray.*

SU'CKET. *n. s.* [from *suck*] A sweet meat.

Nature's confectioner, the bee,
Whose *suckets* are moist alchimy;
The still of his refining mold,
Minting the garden into gold. *Cleaveland.*

SU'CKINGBOTTLE. *n. s.* [*suck* and *bottle.*] A bottle which to children supplies the want of a pap.

He that will say, children join these general abstract speculations with their *suckingbottles*, has more zeal for his opinion, but less sincerity. *Locke.*

To SUCKLE. *v. a.* [from *suck.*] To nurse at the breast.

The breast of Hecuba,
When she did *suckle* Hector, look'd not lovelier. *Shakespeare.*
She nurses me up and *suckles* me. *L'Estrange.*
Two thriving calves she *suckles* twice a-day. *Dryden.*

The Roman soldiers bare on their helmets the first history of Romulus, who was begot by the god of war, and *suckled* by a wolf. *Addison on Italy.*

SU'CKLING. *n. s.* [from *suck.*] A young creature yet fed by the pap.

I provide a *suckling*,
That ne'er had nourishment but from the teat. *Dryden.*

Young animals participate of the nature of their tender aliment, as *sucklings* of milk. *Arbuthnot on Aliments.*

SU'CTION. *n. s.* [from *suck*; *succion*, Fr.] The act of sucking.

Sounds exteriour and interiour may be made by *suction*, as by emission of the breath. *Bacon.*

Though the valve were not above an inch and a half in diameter, yet the weight kept up by *suction*, or supported by the air, and what was cast out of it weighed about ten pounds. *Boyle.*

Cornelius regulated the *suction* of his child. *Arbuthnot.*

SUDA'TION. *n. s.* [*sudo*, Latin.] Sweat.

SU'DATORY. *n. s.* [*sudo*, Latin.] Hot house; sweating bath.

SU'DDEN. *adj.* [*soudain*, French; ꞅoben, Saxon.]

1. Happening without previous notice; coming without the common preparatives; coming unexpectedly.

We have not yet set down this day of triumph;
To-morrow, in my judgment, is too *sudden.* *Shakespeare.*

There was never any thing so *sudden* but Cæsar's thrasonical brag, of I came, saw and overcame. *Shakespeare.*

Herbs *sudden* flower'd,
Opening their various colours. *Milton.*

2. Hasty; violent; rash; passionate; precipitate. Not in use.

I grant him
Sudden, malicious, smacking of ev'ry sin. *Shakespeare.*

SU'DDEN. *n. s.*

1. Any unexpected occurrence; surprise. Not in use.

Parents should mark the witty excuses of their children at *suddains* and surprisals, rather than pamper them. *Wotton.*

2. *On or of a* SUDDEN, *or upon a Sudden.* Sooner than was expected; without the natural or commonly accustomed preparatives.

Following the flyers at the very heels,
With them he enters, who *upon the sudden*
Clapt to their gates. *Shakespeare's Macbeth.*
How art thou lost, how *on a sudden* lost? *Milton.*

They keep their patients so warm as almost to stifle them, and all *on a sudden* the cold regimen is in vogue. *Baker.*

When you have a mind to leave your master, grow rude and saucy *of a sudden*, and beyond your usual behaviour. *Swift.*

SU'DDENLY. *adv.* [from *sudden.*] In an unexpected manner; without preparation; hastily.

You shall find three of your Argosies
Are richly come to harbour *suddenly.* *Shakespeare.*
If thou can'st accuse,
Do it without invention *suddenly.* *Shakesp. Henry VI.*

If elision of the air made the sound, the touch of the bell or string could not extinguish so *suddenly* that motion. *Bacon.*

To the pale foes they *suddenly* draw near,
And summon them to unexpected fight. *Dryden.*
She struck the warlike spear into the ground,
Which sprouting leaves did *suddenly* enclose,
And peaceful olives shaded as they rose. *Dryden.*

SU'DDENNESS. *n. s.* [from *sudden.*] State of being sudden; unexpected presence; manner of coming or happening unexpectedly.

All in the open hall amazed stood,
At *suddeness* of that unwary sight,
And wond'red at his breathless hasty mood. *Fairy Queen.*

He speedily run forward, counting his *suddenness* his most advantage that he might overtake the English. *Spenser.*

The rage of people is like that of the sea, which once breaking bounds, overflows a country with that *suddenness* and violence as leaves no hopes of flying. *Temple.*

SUDORI'FICK. [*sudorifique*, Fr. *sudor* and *facio*, Latin.] Provoking or causing sweat.

Physicians may do well when they provoke sweat in bed by bottles, with a decoction of *sudorifick* herbs in hot water. *Bacon.*

Exhaling the most liquid parts of the blood by *sudorifick* or watery evaporations brings it into a morbid state. *Arbuthnot.*

SUDORI'FICK. *n. s.* A medicine promoting sweat.

As to *sudorificks*, consider that the liquid which goes off by sweat is often the most subtile part of the blood. *Arbuthnot.*

SU'DOROUS. *adj.* [from *sudor*, Latin.] Consisting of sweat.

Beside the strigments and *sudorous* adhesions from mens hands, nothing proceedeth from gold in the usual decoction thereof. *Brown's Vulgar Errours.*

SUDS. *n. s.* [from ꞅeoban, to seeth; whence ꞅobben, Saxon.]

1. A lixivium of soap and water.

2. *To be in the* SUDS. A familiar phrase for being in any difficulty.

To SUE. *v. a.* [*suiver*, French.]

1. To prosecute by law.

If any *sue* thee at the law, and take away thy coat, let him have thy cloke also. *Mat. v. 40.*

2. To gain by legal procedure.

Nor was our blessed Saviour only our propitiation to die for us, but he is still our advocate, continually interceding with his Father in the behalf of all true penitents, and *suing* out a pardon for them in the court of heaven. *Calamy.*

To SUE. *v. n.* To beg; to entreat; to petition.

Full little knowest thou that hast not try'd,
What hell it is in *suing* long to bide. *Hubberd's Tale.*
If me thou deign to serve and *sue*,
At thy command lo all these mountains be. *Spenser.*
When maidens *sue*,
Men give like gods. *Shakespeare*
We were not born to *sue* but command. *Shakespeare.*

Ambassadors came unto him as far as the mouth of the Euphrates, *suing* unto him for peace. *Knolles.*

For this, this only favour let me *sue*,
Refuse it not: but let my body have
The last retreat of human kind, a grave. *Dryden's Æneid.*
Despise not then, that in our hands bear we
These holy boughs, and *sue* with words of pray'r. *Dryden.*
'Twill never be too late,
To *sue* for chains, and own a conqueror. *Addison's Cato.*
The fair Egyptian
Courted with freedom now the beauteous slave,
Now falt'ring *sued*, and threatning now did rave. *Blackm.*
By adverse destiny constrain'd to *sue*
For counsel and redress, he *sues* to you. *Pope's Odyssey.*

SU'ET. *n. s.* [*suet*, an old French word, according to *Skinner.*] A hard fat, particularly that about the kidneys.

The steatoma being *suet*, yields not to escaroticks. *Wisem.*

SU'ETY. *adj.* [from *suet.*] Consisting of suet; resembling suet.

If the matter forming a wen, resembles fat or a *suety* substance, it is called steatoma. *Sharp's Surgery.*

To SU'FFER. *v. a.* [*suffero*, Latin; *souffrir*, French.]

1. To bear; to undergo; to feel with sense of pain.

A man of great wrath shall *suffer* punishment. *Prov. xix.*

A woman *suffered* many things of physicians, and spent all she had. *Mark v. 26.*

Obedience impos'd,
On penalty of death, and *suffering* death. *Milton.*

2. To endure; to support; not to sink under.

Our spirit and strength entire
Strongly to *suffer* and support our pains. *Milton.*

3. To allow; to permit; not to hinder.

He wond'red that your Lordship
Would *suffer* him to spend his youth at home. *Shakespeare.*
Oft have I seen a hot o'erweening cur,
Run back and bite, because he was withheld;
Who being *suffered*, with the bear's fell paw,
Hath clapt his tail betwixt his legs and cry'd. *Shakespeare.*
My duty cannot *suffer*
T' obey in all your daughter's hard commands. *Shakespeare.*

Rebuke thy neighbour, and not *suffer* sin upon him. *Lev.*

I *suffer* them to enter and possess. *Milton.*

He that will *suffer* himself to be informed by observation, will find few signs of a soul accustomed to much thinking in a new born child. *Locke.*

4. To pass through; to be affected by.

The air now must *suffer* change. *Milton.*

To SU'FFER. *v. n.*

1. To undergo pain or inconvenience.

My breast I arm to overcome by *suffering.* *Milton.*

Prudence and good breeding are in all stations necessary; and most young men *suffer* in the want of them. *Locke.*

2. To undergo punishment.

The father was first condemned to *suffer* upon a day appointed, and the son afterwards the day following. *Clarendon.*

He thus
Was forc'd to *suffer* for himself and us!
Heir to his father's sorrows with his crown. *Dryden.*

3. To be injured.

Publick business *suffers* by private infirmities, and kingdoms fall into weaknesses by the diseases or decays of those that manage them. *Temple.*

SU'FFERABLE. *adj.* [from *suffer.*] Tolerable; such as may be endured.

it is *sufferable* in any to use what liberty they list in their own writing, but the contracting and extending the lines and sense of others would appear a thankless office. *Wotton.*

SU'FFERABLY. *adv.* [from *sufferable.*] Tolerably; so as to be endured.

An infant Titan held she in her arms;
Yet *sufferably* bright, the eye might bear
The ungrown glories of his beamy hair. *Addison.*

SU'FFERANCE. *n. s.* [from *suffer*, *souffrance*, French.]

1. Pain; inconvenience; misery.

He must not only die,
But thy unkindness shall the death draw out
To ling'ring *sufferance*. *Shakespeare's Measure for Measure.*

How much education may reconcile young people to pain and *sufferance*, the examples of Sparta shew. *Locke on Education.*

2. Patience; moderation.

He thought t'have slain her in his fierce despight,
But hasty heat tempering with *sufferance* wise,
He staid his hand. *Fairy Queen.*

He hath given excellent *sufferance* and vigorousness to the sufferers, arming them with strange courage. *Taylor.*

And should I touch it nearly, bear it
With all the *suff'rance* of a tender friend. *Otway's Orphan.*

3. Toleration; permission; not hindrance.

In process of time, somewhiles by *sufferance*, and somewhiles by special leave and favour, they erected to themselves oratories not in any sumptuous or stately manner. *Hooker.*

Most wretched man
That to affections does the bridle lend;
In their beginning they are weak and wan,
But soon through *sufferance* grow to fearful end. *Fairy Queen.*

Some villains of my court
Are in consent and *sufferance* in this. *Shakespeare.*

Both gloried to have 'scap'd the Stygian flood,
As gods, and by their own recover'd strength;
Not by the *suff'rance* of supernal pow'r. *Milton's Par. Lost.*

SU'FFERER. *n. s.* [from *suffer.*]

1. One who endures or undergoes pain or inconvenience.

This evil on the Philistines is fall'n,
The *sufferers* then will scarce molest us here;
From other hands we need not much to fear. *Milton.*

And when his love was bounded in a few,
That were unhappy that they might be true,
Made you the fav'rite of his last sad times,
That is, a *suff'rer* in his subjects crime. *Dryden.*

She returns to me with joy in her face, not from the sight of her husband, but from the good luck she has had at cards; and if she has been a loser, I am doubly a *sufferer* by it: she comes home out of humour, because she has been throwing away my estate. *Addison's Spectator.*

The history of civil wars and rebellions does not make such deep and lasting impressions, as events of the same nature in which we or our friends have been *sufferers*. *Addison.*

2. One who allows; one who permits.

SU'FFERING. *n. s.* [from *suffer.*] Pain suffered.

Rejoice in my *sufferings* for you. *Col.* i. 24.

With what strength, what steadiness of mind,
He triumphs in the midst of all his *sufferings?* *Addison.*

We may hope the *sufferings* of innocent people, who have lived in that place which was the scene of rebellion, will secure from the like attempts. *Addison.*

It increased the smart of his present *sufferings* to compare them with his former happiness. *Atterbury.*

To SUFFI'CE. *v. n.* [*suffire*, French; *sufficio*, Latin.] To be enough; to be sufficient; to be equal to the end or purpose.

If thou ask me why, *sufficeth*, my reasons are good. *Shakesp.*

A strong and succulent moisture is able, without drawing help from the earth, to *suffice* the sprouting of the plant. *Bac.*

To recount almighty works
What words or tongue of seraph can *suffice*,
Or heart of man *suffice* to comprehend. *Milton's Par. Lost.*

The indolency we have, *sufficing* for our present happiness, we desire not to venture the change: being content; and that is enough. *Locke.*

He lived in such temperance, as was enough to make the longest life agreeable; and in such a course of piety, as *sufficed* to make the most sudden death so also. *Pope*

To SUFFI'CE. *v. a.*

1. To afford; to supply.

Thou king of horned floods, whose plenteous urn
Suffices fatness to the fruitful corn,
Shall share my morning song and evening vows. *Dryden.*

The pow'r appeas'd, with winds *suffic'd* the sail;
The bellying canvas strutted with the gale. *Dryden.*

2. To satisfy.

Israel, let it *suffice* you of all your abominations. *Ezek.*

Parched corn she did eat and was *sufficed*, and left. *Ruth.*

Let it *suffice* thee that thou know'st us happy. *Milton.*

When the herd *suffic'd*, did late repair
To ferny heaths, and to the forest lare. *Dryden.*

He our conqueror left us this our strength,
That we may so *suffice* his vengeful ire. *Milton.*

SUFFI'CIENCY. *n. s.* [*suffisance*, Fr. from *sufficient.*]

1. State of being adequate to the end proposed.

'Tis all mens office to speak patience
To those that wring under the load of sorrow;
But no man's virtue nor *sufficiency*
To be so moral, when he shall endure
The like himself. *Shakespeare.*

His *sufficiency* is such, that he and pbestows ossesses, his plenty being unexhausted. *Boyle.*

2. Qualification for any purpose.

I am not so confident of my own *sufficiency*, as not willingly to admit the counsel of others. *King Charles.*

The bishop, perhaps an Irishman, being made judge by that law, of the *sufficiency* of the ministers, may dislike the Englishman as unworthy. *Spenser's Ireland.*

Their pensioner De Wit was a minister of the greatest authority and *sufficiency* ever known in their state. *Temple.*

3. Competence; enough.

An elegant *sufficiency*, content. *Thomson.*

4. Supply equal to want.

The most proper subjects of dispute, are questions not of the very highest importance, nor of the meanest kind; but rather the intermediate questions between them: and there is a large *sufficiency* of them in the sciences. *Watts's Improv. of the Mind.*

5. It is used by *Temple* for that conceit which makes a man think himself equal to things above him: and is commonly compounded with *self.*

Sufficiency is a compound of vanity and ignorance. *Temple.*

SUFFI'CIENT. *adj.* [*suffisant*, Fr. *sufficiens*, Latin.]

1. Equal to any end or purpose; enough; competent; not deficient.

Sufficient unto the day is the evil thereof. *Mat.* vi. 34.

Heaven yet retains
Number *sufficient* to possess her realms. *Milton.*

Man is not *sufficient* of himself to his own happiness. *Tillot.*

It is *sufficient* for me, if, by a discourse something out of the way, I shall have given occasion to others to cast about for new discoveries. *Locke.*

She would ruin me in silks, were not the quantity that goes to a large pin-cushion *sufficient* to make her a gown and petticoat. *Addison.*

Sufficient benefice is what is competent to maintain a man and his family, and maintain hospitality; and likewise to pay and satisfy such dues belonging to the bishop. *Ayliffe's Parergon.*

Seven months are a *sufficient* time to correct vice in a Yahoo. *Swift.*

2. Qualified for any thing by fortune or otherwise.

In saying he is a good man, understand me, that he is *sufficient*. *Shakespeare's Merchant of Venice.*

SUFFI'CIENTLY. *adv.* [from *sufficient.*] To a sufficient degree; enough.

If religion did possess sincerely and *sufficiently* the hearts of all men, there would need be no other restraint from evil. *Hooker.*

Seem I to thee *sufficiently* possess'd
Of happiness? *Milton.*

All to whom they are proposed, are by his grace *sufficiently* moved to attend and assent to them; *sufficiently*, but not irresistibly; for if all were irresistibly moved, all would embrace them, and if none were *sufficiently* moved, none would embrace them. *Rogers's Sermons.*

SUFFISANCE [French.] Excess; plenty. Obsolete.

There him rests in riotous *suffisance*
Of all his gladfulness and kingly joyance. *Spenser.*

To SU'FFOCATE. *v. a.* [*suffoquer*, Fr. *suffoco*, Latin.] To choak by exclusion or interception of air.

Let gallows gape for dog, let man go free,
And let not hemp his windpipe *suffocate*. *Shakespeare.*

This chaos, when degree is *suffocate*,
Follows the choaking. *Shakespeare's Troilus and Cressida.*

Air but momentally remains in our bodies, only to refrigerate the heart, which being once performed, lest being self-heated again, it should *suffocate* that part, it hasteth back the same way it passed. *Brown's Vulgar Errours.*

A swelling discontent is apt to *suffocate* and strangle without passage. *Collier of Friendship.*

All involv'd in smoke, the latent foe
From every cranny *suffocated* falls. *Thomson.*

SUFFOCA'TION. *n. s.* [*suffocation*, Fr. from *suffocate.*] The act of choaking; the state of being choaked.

Diseases of stoppings and *suffocations* are dangerous. *Bacon.*

White consists in an equal mixture of all the primitive colours, and black in a *suffocation* of all the rays of light. *Cheyne.*

Mushrooms are best corrected by vinegar; some of them being poisonous, operate by *suffocation*, in which the best remedy is wine or vinegar and salt, and vomiting as soon as possible. *Arbuthnot on Diet.*

SU'FFOCATIVE. *adj.* [from *suffocate.*] Having the power to choak.

From rain, after great frosts in the winter, glandulous tumours, and *suffocative* catarrhs proceed. *Arbuthnot on Air.*

SU'FFRAGAN. *n. s.* [*suffragant*, Fr. *suffraganeus*, Latin.] A bishop considered as subject to his metropolitan.

Suffragan bishops shall have more than one riding apparitor. *Ayliffe's Parergon.*

Becket,

Becket, archbishop of Canterbury, insolently took upon him to declare five articles void, in his epistle to his *suffragans*. *Hale.*

To SU'FFRAGATE. *v. n.* [*suffragor*, Latin.] To vote with; to agree in voice with.

No tradition could universally prevail, unless there were some common congruity of somewhat inherent in nature, which suits and *suffragates* with it, and closeth with it. *Hale.*

SU'FFRAGE. *n. s.* [*suffrage*, Fr. *suffragium*, Latin.] Vote; voice given in a controverted point.

Noble confederates, thus far is perfect,
Only your *suffrages* I will expect
At the assembly for the chusing of consuls. *Ben. Johnson.*

They would not abet by their *suffrages* or presence the designs of those innovations. *King Charles.*

The fairest of our island dare not commit their cause against you to the *suffrage* of those who most partially adore them. *Addison.*

Fabius might joy in Scipio, when he saw
A beardless consul made against the law;
And join his *suffrage* to the votes of Rome. *Dryden.*

This very variety of sea and land, hill and dale, is extremely agreeable, the ancients and moderns giving their *suffrages* unanimously herein. *Woodward's Natural History.*

Lactantius and St. Austin confirm by their *suffrage* the observation made by the heathen writers. *Atterbury.*

SUFFRA'GINOUS. *adj.* [*suffrago*, Latin.] Belonging to the knee joint of beasts.

In elephants, the bought of the forelegs is not directly backward, but laterally, and somewhat inward; but the hough or *suffraginous* flexure behind, rather outward. *Brown.*

SUFFUMIGA'TION. *n. s.* [*suffumigation*, Fr. *suffumigo*, Lat.] Operation of fumes raised by fire.

If the matter be so gross as it yields not to remedies, it may be attempted by *suffumigation*. *Wiseman's Surgery.*

SUFFU'MIGE. *n. s.* [*suffumigo*, Lat.] A medical fume.

For external means, drying *suffumiges* or smoaks are prescribed with good success; they are usually composed out of frankincense, myrrh, and pitch. *Harvey.*

To SUFFU'SE. *v. a.* [*suffusus*, Latin.] To spread over with something expansible, as with a vapour or a tincture.

Suspicions, and fantastical surmise,
And jealousy *suffus'd* with jaundice in her eyes. *Dryden.*

To that recess,
When purple light shall next *suffuse* the skies,
With me repair. *Pope.*

Instead of love-enliven'd cheeks,
With flowing rapture bright, dark looks succeed,
Suffus'd and glaring with untender fire. *Thomson.*

SUFFU'SION. *n. s.* [*suffusion*, French; from *suffuse*.]

1. The act of overspreading with any thing.
2. That which is suffused or spread.

A drop serene hath quench'd their orbs,
Or dim *suffusion* veil'd. *Milton.*

The disk of Phœbus, when he climbs on high
Appears at first but as a bloodshot eye;
And when his chariot downward draws to bed,
His ball is with the same *suffusion* red. *Dryden.*

To those that have the jaundice or like *suffusion* of eyes, objects appear of that colour. *Ray.*

SUG. *n. s.* [*sugo*, Latin, to suck.]

Many have sticking on them *sugs*, or trout-lice, which is a kind of worm like a clove or pin, with a big head, and sticks close to him and sucks his moisture. *Walton.*

SU'GAR. *n. s.* [*sucre*, French; *saccharum*, Latin.]

1. The native salt of the *sugar*-cane, obtained by the expression and evaporation of its juice. *Quincy.*

All the blood of Zelmane's body stirred in her, as wine will do when *sugar* is hastily put into it. *Sidney.*

Lumps of *sugar* lose themselves, and twine
Their subtile essence with the soul of wine. *Crashaw.*

A grocer in London gave for his rebus a *sugar*-loaf standing upon a flat steeple. *Peacham.*

Saccharum candidum shoots into angular figures, by placing a great many slender sticks a-cross a vessel of liquid *sugar*. *Grew's Musæum.*

If the child must have *sugar*-plums when he has a mind, rather than be out of humour: why, when he is grown up, must he not be satisfied too with wine? *Locke.*

In a *sugar*-baker's drying room, where the air was heated, fifty four degrees beyond that of a human body, a sparrow died in two minutes. *Arbuthnot on Air.*

A piece of some geniculated plant, seeming to be part of a *sugar*-cane. *Woodward on Fossils.*

2. Any thing proverbially sweet.

Your fair discourse has been as *sugar*,
Making the hard way sweet and delectable. *Shakespeare.*

3. A chymical dry chrystallization.

Sugar of lead, though made of that insipid metal, and four salt of vinegar, has in it a sweetness surpassing that of common *sugar*. *Boyle.*

To SU'GAR. *v. a.* [from the noun.]

1. To impregnate or season with sugar.

Short thick sobs
In panting murmurs, still'd out of her breast,
That ever-bubbling spring, the *sugar'd* nest
Of her delicious soul, that there does lie,
Bathing in streams of liquid melody. *Crashaw.*

2. To sweeten.

Thou would'st have plung'd thyself
In general riot, and never learn'd
The icy precepts of respect, but followed
The *sugar'd* game before thee. *Shakespeare's Timon of Athens.*

With devotion's visage,
And pious actions we do *sugar* o'er
The devil himself. *Shakespeare.*

His glosing sire his errand daily said,
And *sugar'd* speeches whisper'd in mine ear. *Fairfax.*

Who casts out threats, no man deceives,
But flatt'ry still in *sugar'd* words betrays,
And poison in high tasted meats conveys. *Denham.*

SU'GGARY. *adj.* [from *sugar*.] Sweet; tasting of sugar.

With the *sugg'ry* sweet thereof allure
Chaste ladies ears to phantasies impure. *Spenser.*

To SUGGEST. *v. a.* [*suggero*, *suggestum*, Lat. *suggerer*, Fr.]

1. To hint; to intimate; to insinuate good or ill; to tell privately.

Are you not asham'd?
What spirit *suggests* this imagination? *Shakespeare.*

I could never have suffered greater calamities, by denying to sign that justice my conscience *suggested* to me. *K. Charles.*

These Romish casuists speak peace to the consciences of men, by *suggesting* something to them, which shall satisfy their minds notwithstanding a known, actual, avowed continuance of their sins. *South's Sermons.*

Some ideas make themselves way, and are *suggested* to the mind by all the ways of sensation and reflexion. *Locke.*

Reflect upon the different state of the mind in thinking, which those instances of attention, reverie and dreaming naturally enough *suggest*. *Locke.*

Search for some thoughts thy own *suggesting* mind,
And others dictated by heav'nly pow'r,
Shall rise spontaneous. *Pope's Odyssey.*

This the feeling heart
Wou'd naturally *suggest*. *Thomson.*

2. To seduce; to draw to ill by insinuation. Out of use.

When devils will their blackest sins put on,
They do *suggest* at first with heav'nly shows. *Shakespeare.*
Knowing that tender youth is soon *suggested*,
I nightly lodge her in an upper tower. *Shakespeare.*

3. To inform secretly. Out of use.

We must *suggest* the people, in what hatred
He still hath held them, that to's pow'r he would
Have made them mules. *Shakespeare's Coriolanus.*

SUGGE'STION. *n. s.* [[*suggestion*, Fr. from *suggest*.] Private hint; intimation; insinuation; secret notification.

It allayeth all base and earthly cogitations, banisheth and driveth away those evil secret *suggestions* which our invisible enemy is always apt to minister. *Hooker.*

I met lord Bigot and lord Salisbury,
And other more going to seek the grave
Of Arthur, who, they say, is kill'd to night
On your *suggestion*. *Shakespeare's King John.*

He was a man
Of an unbounded stomach, ever ranking
Himself with princes: one that by *suggestion*
Tied all the kingdom. *Shakespeare's Henry VIII.*

The native and untaught *suggestions* of inquisitive children. *Locke.*

Another way is letting the mind, upon the *suggestion* of any new notion, run after similies. *Locke.*

To SU'GGILATE. *v. a.* [*suggillo*, Latin.] To beat black and blue; to make livid by a bruise.

The head of the os humeri was bruised, and remained *suggilated* long after. *Wiseman's Surgery.*

SU'ICIDE. *n. s.* [*suicidium*, Latin.] Self-murder; the horrid crime of destroying one's self.

Child of despair, and *suicide* my name. *Savage.*

To be cut off by the sword of injured friendship is the most dreadful of all deaths, next to *suicide*. *Clarissa.*

SUI'LLAGE. *n. s.* [*souillage*, French.] Drain of filth. Obsolete.

When they have chosen the plot, and laid out the limits of the work, some Italians dig wells and cisterns, and other conveyances for the *suillage* of the house. *Wotton.*

SUING. *n. s.* [This word seems to come from *suer*, to sweat, French; it is perhaps peculiar to *Bacon*.] The act of soaking through any thing.

Note the percolation or *suing* of the verjuice through the wood; for verjuice of itself would never have passed through the wood. *Bacon.*

SUIT. *n. s.* [*suite*, French.]

1. A set; a number of things correspondent one to the other.

We, ere the day, two *suits* of armour sought,
Which borne before him, on his steed he brought. *Dryd.*

2. Cloaths made one part to answer another.

What a beard of the general's cut, and a horrid *suit* of the camp will do among foaming bottles and ale-wash'd wits is wonderful. *Shakespeare's Henry V.*

Him all repute
For his device in handsoming a *suit*;
To judge of lace, pink, panes, print, cut and plait,
Of all the court to have the best conceit. *Donne.*

His majesty was supplied with three thousand *suits* of cloaths, with good proportions of shoes and stockings. *Clarendon.*

3. Consecution; series; regular order.

Every five and thirty years the same kind and *suite* of weathers comes about again, as great frost, great wet, great droughts, warm winters, summers with little heat; and they call it the prime *Bacon.*

4. *Out of* SUITS. Having no correspondence. A metaphor, I suppose, from cards.

Wear this for me; one *out of suits* with fortune,
That would give more, but that her hand lacks means. *Shak.*

5. [*Suite*, French.] Retinue; company. Obsolete.

Plexirtus's ill-led life, and worse gotten honour, should have tumbled together to destruction, had there not come in Tydeus and Telenor, with fifty in their *suite* to his defence. *Sidney.*

6. [From *To Sue.*] A petition; an address of entreaty.

Mine ears against your *suits* are stronger than
Your gates against my force. *Shakespeare.*

She gallops o'er a courtier's nose;
And then dreams be of smelling out a *suit*. *Shakespeare.*

Had I a *suit* to Mr. Shallow, I would humour his men with the imputation of being near their master. *Shakespeare.*

Many shall make *suit* unto thee. *Job* xi. 19.

My mind, neither with pride's itch, nor yet hath been
Poison'd with love to see or to be seen;
I had no *suit* there, nor new suit to shew:
Yet went to court. *Donne.*

7. Courtship.

He that hath the steerage of my course,
Direct my *suit*. *Shakespeare's Romeo and Juliet.*

Their determinations are to return to their home and to trouble you with no more *suit*, unless you may be won by some other sort than your father's imposition. *Shakespeare.*

8. In *Spenser* it seems to signify pursuit; prosecution.

High amongst all knights hast hung thy shield,
Thenceforth the *suit* of earthly conquest shoone,
And wash thy hands from guilt of bloody field: *Spenser.*

9. [In law.] *Suit* is sometimes put for the instance of a cause, and sometimes for the cause itself deduced in judgment. *Ayliffe.*

All that had any *suits* in law came unto them. *Susanna.*

Wars are *suits* of appeal to the tribunal of God's justice, where there are no superiors on earth to determine the cause. *Bacon's War with Spain.*

Involve not thyself in the *suits* and parties of great personages. *Taylor's Guide to Devotion.*

To Alibech alone refer your *suit*,
And let his sentence finish your dispute. *Dryden.*

John Bull was flattered by the lawyers that his *suit* would not last above a year, and that before that time he would be in quiet possession of his business. *Arbuthnot.*

To SUIT. *v. a.* [from the noun.]

1. To fit; to adapt to something else.

Suit the action to the word, the word to the action, with this special observance, that you o'erstep not the modesty of nature. *Shakespeare's Hamlet.*

The matter and manner of their tales, and of their telling, are so *suited* to their different educations and humours, that each would be improper in any other. *Dryden.*

2. To be fitted to; to become.

Compute the gains of his ungovern'd zeal,
Ill *suits* his cloth the praise of railing well. *Dryden.*

Her purple habit sits with such a grace
On her smooth shoulders, and so *suits* her face. *Dryden.*

If different sects should give us a list of those innate practical principles, they would set down only such as *suited* their distinct hypotheses. *Locke.*

Raise her notes to that sublime degree,
Which *suits* a song of piety and thee. *Prior.*

3. To dress; to clothe.

Such a Sebastian was my brother too,
So went he *suited* to his watry tomb:
If spirits can assume both form and suit,
You come to fright us. *Shakespeare's Twelfth Night.*

Be better *suited*;
These weeds are memories of those misfortunes:
I pr'ythee put them off to worser hours. *Shakespeare.*

I'll disrobe me
Of these Italian weeds, and *suit* myself
As do's a Briton peasant. *Shakespeare's Cymbeline.*

To SUIT. *v. n.* To agree; to accord.

The one intense, the other still remiss,
Cannot well *suit* with either; but soon prove
Tedious alike. *Milton.*

The place itself was *suiting to* his care,
Uncouth and savage as the cruel fair. *Dryden.*

Pity does *with* a noble nature *suit*. *Dryden.*

Constraint does ill *with* love and beauty *suit*. *Dryden.*

This he says, because it *suits with* his hypothesis, but proves it not. *Locke.*

Give me not an office
That *suits with* me so ill; thou know'st my temper. *Addis.*

SUI'TABLE. *adj.* [from *suit.*] Fitting; according with; agreeable to.

Through all those miseries, in both there appeared a kind of nobleness not *suitable* to that affliction. *Sidney.*

What he did purpose, it was the pleasure of God that Solomon his son should perform, in manner *suitable* to their present and ancient state. *Hooker.*

To solemn acts of royalty and justice, their *suitable* ornaments are a beauty; are they only in religion a stain? *Hook.*

It is very *suitable* to the principles of the Roman Church; for why should not their science as well as service be in an unknown tongue? *Tillotson.*

As the blessings of God upon his honest industry had been great, so he was not without intentions of making *suitable* returns in acts of charity. *Atterbury.*

Expression is the dress of thought, and still
Appears more decent, as more *suitable*;
A vile conceit in pompous words express'd,
Is like a clown in regal purple dress'd. *Pope.*

SUI'TABLENESS. *n. s.* [from *suitable.*] Fitness; agreeableness.

In words and styles, *suitableness* makes them acceptable and effective. *Glanville.*

With ordinary minds, it is the *suitableness*, not the evidence of a truth that makes it to be yielded to; and it is seldom that any thing practically convinces a man that does not please him first. *South's Sermons.*

He creates those sympathies and *suitablenesses* of nature that are the foundation of all true friendship, and by his providence brings persons so affected together. *South's Sermons.*

Consider the laws themselves, and their *suitableness* or unsuitableness to those to whom they are given. *Tillotson.*

SUI'TABLY. *adv.* [from *suitable.*] Agreeably; according to.

Whosoever speaks upon a certain occasion may take any text suitable thereto; and ought to speak *suitably* to that text. *South's Sermons.*

Some rank deity, whose filthy face
We *suitably* o'er stinking stables place. *Dryden.*

SUIT *Covenant.* [In law.] Is where the ancestor of one man has covenanted with the ancestor of another to sue at his court. *Bailey.*

SUIT *Court.* [In law.] Is the court in which tenants owe attendance to their lord. *Bailey.*

SUIT *Service.* [In law.] Attendance which tenants owe to the court of their lord. *Bailey.*

SUI'TER. }
SUI'TOR. } *n. s.* [from *suit.*]

1. One that sues; a petitioner; a supplicant.

As humility is in *suiters* a decent virtue, so the testification thereof, by such effectual acknowledgments, not only argueth a sound apprehension of his supereminent glory and majesty before whom we stand, but putteth also into his hands a kind of pledge or bond for security against our unthankfulness. *Hook.*

She hath been a *suitor* to me for her brother,
Cut off by course of justice. *Shakes. Meas. for Measure.*

My piteous soul began the wretchedness
Of *suitors* at court to mourn, *Donne.*

Not only bind thine own hands, but bind the hand of *suitors* also from offering. *Bacon.*

Yet their port
Not of mean *suitors*; nor important less
Seem'd their petition, than when the ancient pair
Deucalion and chaste Pyrrha, to restore
The race of mankind drown'd, before the shrine
Of Themis stood devout. *Milton's Paradise Lost.*

I challenge nothing;
But I'm an humble *suitor* for these prisoners. *Denham.*

My lord, I come an humble *suitor* to you. *Rowe.*

2. A woer; one who courts a mistress.

I would I could find in my heart that I had not a hard heart; for truly I love none.

——A dear happiness to women! they would else have been troubled with a pernicious *suitor*. *Shakespeare.*

He passed a year at Goodby under the counsels of his mother, and then became a *suitor* at London to sir Roger Ashton's daughter. *Wotton's Life of the Duke of Buckingham.*

By many *suitors* sought, she mocks their pains,
And still her vow'd virginity maintains. *Dryden.*

He drew his seat, familiar, to her side,
Far from the *suitor* train, a brutal crowd. *Pope's Odyssey.*

SUI'TRESS.

SUI'TRESS. *n. s.* [from *suiter.*] A female supplicant.

'Twere pity
That could refuse a boon to such a *suitress*;
Y' have got a noble friend to be your advocate. *Rowe.*

SU'LCATED. *adj.* [*sulcus*, Latin.] Furrowed.

All are much chopped and *sulcated* by their having lain exposed on the top of the clay to the weather, and to the erosion of the vitriolick matter mixed amongst the clay. *Woodward.*

SULL. *n. s.* A plough. *Ainsworth.*

SU'LLEN. *adj.* [Of this word the etymology is obscure.]

1. Gloomily angry; sluggishly discontented.

Wilmot continued still *sullen* and perverse, and every day grew more insolent. *Clarendon.*

A man in a jail is *sullen* and out of humour at his first coming in. *L'Estrange.*

Forc'd by my pride, I my concern suppress'd;
Pretended drowsiness, and wish of rest;
And *sullen* I forsook th' imperfect feast. *Prior.*

If we sit down *sullen* and inactive, in expectation that God should do all, we shall find ourselves miserably deceived. *Rog.*

2. Mischievous; malignant.

Such *sullen* planets at my birth did shine,
They threaten every fortune mixt with mine. *Dryden.*

The *sullen* fiend her sounding wings display'd,
Unwilling left the night, and sought the nether shade. *Dryd.*

3. Intractable; obstinate.

Things are as *sullen* as we are, and will be what they are, whatever we think of them. *Tillotson's Sermons.*

4. Gloomy; dark; cloudy; dismal.

Why are thine eyes fixt to the *sullen* earth,
Gazing at that which seems to dim thy sight? *Shak. H. VI.*

Night with her *sullen* wings to double shade,
The desart fowls in their clay nests were couch'd,
And now wild beasts came forth the woods to roam. *Milt.*

A glimpse of moon-shine, streak'd with red;
A shuffled, *sullen*, and uncertain light,
That dances through the clouds, and shuts again. *Dryden.*

No cheerful breeze this *sullen* region knows;
The dreaded East is all the wind that blows. *Pope.*

5. Heavy; dull; sorrowful.

Be thou the trumpet of our wrath,
And *sullen* presage of your own decay. *Shakes. K. John.*

SU'LLENLY. *adv.* [from *sullen.*] Gloomily; malignantly; intractably.

To say they are framed without the assistance of some principle that has wisdom in it, and that they come to pass from chance, is *sullenly* to assert a thing because we will assert it. *More's Antidote against Atheism.*

He in chains demanded more
Than he impos'd in victory before:
He *sullenly* reply'd, he could not make
These offers now. *Dryden's Indian Emperor.*

The gen'ral mends his weary pace,
And *sullenly* to his revenge he sails;
So glides some trodden serpent on the grass,
And long behind his wounded volume trails. *Dryden.*

SU'LLENNESS. *n. s.* [from *sullen.*] Gloominess; moroseness; sluggish anger; malignity; intractability.

Speech being as rare as precious, her silence without *sullenness*, her modesty without affectation, and her shamefastness without ignorance. *Sidney.*

To fit my *sullenness*,
He to another key his stile doth dress. *Donne.*

In those vernal seasons, when the air is calm and pleasant, it were an injury and *sullenness* against nature not to go out, and see her riches. *Milton.*

Quit not the world out of any hypocrisy, *sullenness*, or superstition, but out of a sincere love of true knowledge and virtue. *More.*

With these comforts about me, and *sullenness* enough to use no remedy, monsieur Zulichem came to see me. *Temple.*

SU'LLENS. *n. s.* [Without singular.] Morose temper; gloominess of mind. A burlesque word.

Let them die that age, and *sullens* have. *Shakespeare.*

SU'LLIAGE. *n. s.* [from *sully.*] Pollution; filth; stain of dirt; foulness.

Require it to make some restitution to his neighbour for what it has detracted from it, by wiping off that *sulliage* it has cast upon his fame. *Government of the Tongue.*

Calumniate stoutly; for though we wipe away with never so much care the dirt thrown at us, there will be left some *sulliage* behind. *Decay of Piety.*

To SU'LLY. *v. a.* [*souiller*, French.] To soil; to tarnish; to dirt; to spot.

Silvering will *sully* and canker more than gilding. *Bacon.*

The falling temples which the gods provoke,
And statues *sully'd* yet with sacrilegious smoke. *Roscommon.*

He's dead, whose love had *sully'd* all your reign,
And made you empress of the world in vain. *Dryden.*

Lab'ring years shall weep their destin'd race,
Charg'd with ill omens, *sully'd* with disgrace. *Prior.*

Let there be no spots to *sully* the brightness of this solemnity. *Atterbury's Sermons.*

Ye walkers too, that youthful colours wear,
Three *sullying* trades avoid with equal care;
The little chimney-sweeper skulks along,
And marks with sooty stains the heedless throng. *Gay.*

SU'LLY. *n. s.* [from the verb.] Soil; tarnish; spot.

You laying these light *sullies* on my son,
As 'twere a thing a little soil'd i' th' working. *Shakesp.*

A noble and triumphant merit breaks through little spots and *sullies* in his reputation. *Addison's Spectator.*

SU'LPHUR. *n. s.* [Latin.] Brimstone.

In his womb was hid metallick ore,
The work of *sulphur*. *Milton.*

Sulphur is produced by incorporating an oily or bituminous matter with the fossil and salt. *Woodward.*

Thence nitre, *sulphur*, and the fiery steam
Of fat bitumen. *Thomson.*

SULPHU'REOUS. } *adj.* [*sulphureus*, Latin.] Made of brimstone; having the qualities of brimstone; containing sulphur; impregnated with sulphur.
SU'LPHUROUS. }

My hour is almost come,
When I to *sulphurous* and tormenting flames
Must render up myself. *Shakesp. Hamlet.*

Dart and javelin, stones and *sulphurous* fire. *Milton.*

Is not the strength and vigour of the action between light and *sulphureous* bodies, observed above, one reason why *sulphureous* bodies take fire more readily, and burn more vehemently than other bodies do? *Newton's Opt.*

The fury heard, while on Cocytus' brink,
Her snakes unty'd *sulphureous* waters drink. *Pope.*

No *sulphureous* glooms
Swell'd in the sky, and sent the lightning forth. *Thomson.*

SULPHU'REOUSNESS. *n. s.* [from *sulphureous.*] The state of being sulphureous.

SU'LPHURWORT. *n. s.* The same with HOGSFENEL.

SU'LPHURY. *adj.* [from *sulphur.*] Partaking of sulphur.

SU'LTAN. *n. s.* [Arabick.] The Turkish emperour.

By this scimitar,
That won three fields of *sultan* Solyman. *Shakespeare.*

SU'LTANA. } *n. s.* [from *sultan.*] The queen of an Eastern emperour.
SU'LTANESS. }

Turn the *sultana*'s chambermaid. *Cleaveland.*

Lay the tow'ring *sultaness* aside. *Irene.*

SU'LTANRY. *n. s.* [from *sultan.*] An Eastern empire.

I affirm the same of the *sultanry* of the Mamalukes, where slaves, bought for money, and of unknown descent, reigned over families of freemen. *Bacon.*

SU'LTRINESS. *n. s.* [from *sultry.*] The state of being sultry; close and cloudy heat.

SU'LTRY. *adj.* [This is imagined by *Skinner* to be corrupted from *sulphury*, or *sweltry.*] Hot without ventilation; hot and close; hot and cloudy.

It is very *sultry* and hot. *Shakesp. Hamlet.*

The *sultry* breath
Of tainted air had cloy'd the jaws of death. *Sandys.*

Such as born beneath the burning sky,
And *sultry* sun betwixt the tropicks lie. *Dryden's Æn.*

Our foe advances on us,
And envies us even Lybia's *sultry* desarts. *Addison's Cato.*

Then would *sultry* heats and a burning air have scorched and chapped the earth, and galled the animal tribes in houses or dens. *Cheyne.*

SUM. *n. s.* [*summa*, Latin; *somme*, French.]

1. The whole of any thing; many particulars aggregated to a total.

We may as well conclude so of every sentence, as of the whole *sum* and body thereof. *Hooker.*

How precious are thy thoughts unto me, O God! how great is the *sum* of them. *Ps.* cxxxix. 17.

Th' Almighty Father, where he sits
Shrin'd in his sanctuary of heav'n secure,
Consulting on the *sum* of things, foreseen
This tumult, and permitted all, advis'd. *Milton.*

Such and no less is he, on whom depends
The *sum* of things. *Dryden.*

Weighing the *sum* of things with wise forecast,
Solicitous of publick good. *Philips.*

2. Quantity of money.

I did send to you
For certain *sums* of gold, which you deny'd me. *Shakesp.*

Britain, once despis'd, can raise
As ample *sums* as Rome in Cæsar's days. *C. Arbuthnot.*

3. [*Somme*, Fr.] Compendium, abridgment; the whole abstracted.

This, in effect, is the *sum* and substance of that which they bring by way of opposition against those orders, which we have common with the church of Rome. *Hooker.*

They replenished the hearts of the nearest unto them with words of memorable consolation, strengthened men in the fear of God, gave them wholsome instructions of life, and confirmed them in true religion: in *sum*, they taught the world no less virtuously how to die, than they had done before how to live. *Hooker.*

This

This having learn'd, thou haſt attain'd the *ſum*
Of wiſdom. *Milton.*

In *ſum*, no man can have a greater veneration for Chaucer than myſelf. *Dryden.*

Thy *ſum* of duty let two words contain;
Be humble, and be juſt. *Prior.*

In *ſum*, the Goſpel, conſidered as a law, preſcribes every virtue to our conduct, and forbids every ſin. *Rogers.*

4. The amount; the reſult of reaſoning or computation.

I appeal to the readers, whether the *ſum* of what I have ſaid be not this. *Tillotſon.*

5. Height; completion.

Thus I have told thee all my ſtate, and brought
My ſtory to the *ſum* of earthly bliſs,
Which I enjoy. *Milt. Paradiſe Loſt.*

In ſaying ay or no, the very ſafety of our country, and the *ſum* of our well-being, lies. *L'Eſtrange.*

To SUM. *v. a.* [*ſommer*, French; from the noun.]

1. To compute; to collect particulars into a total; to caſt up. It has *up* emphatical.

You caſt th' event of war,
And *ſumm'd* th' account of chance. *Shak. Henry* IV.

The high prieſt may *ſum* the ſilver brought in. 2 *Kings* xxii.

In ſickneſs time will ſeem longer without a clock than with it; for the mind doth value every moment, and then the hour doth rather *ſum up* the moments than divide the day. *Bacon.*

He that would reckon up all the accidents preferments depend upon, may as well undertake to count the ſands, or *ſum up* infinity. *South.*

2. To compriſe; to comprehend; to collect into a narrow compaſs.

So lovely fair!
That what ſeem'd fair in all the world, ſeem'd now
Mean, or in her *ſumm'd* up, in her contain'd. *Milton.*

To conclude, by *ſumming* up what I would ſay concerning what I have, and what I have not been, in the following paper I ſhall not deny that I pretended not to write an accurate treatiſe of colours, but an occaſional eſſay. *Boyle.*

Go to the ant, thou ſluggard, in few words *ſums* up the moral of this fable. *L'Eſtrange.*

This Atlas muſt our ſinking ſtate uphold;
In council cool, but in performance bold:
He *ſums* their virtues in himſelf alone,
And adds the greateſt, of a loyal ſon. *Dryden's Aurengz.*

A fine evidence *ſumm'd* up among you! *Dryden.*

4. [In falconry.] To have feathers full grown.

With proſperous wing full *ſumm'd*. *Milton.*

SU'MACH-TREE. *n. ſ.* [*ſumach*, French.]

The flower conſiſts of five leaves in a circular order, in form of a roſe; from whoſe flower-cup riſes the pointal, which afterward becomes a veſſel, containing one ſeed: the flowers grow in bunches, and the leaves either winged or have three lobes. The flowers are uſed in dying, and the branches for tanning, in America. *Miller.*

SU'MLESS. *adj.* [from *ſum.*] Not to be computed.

Make his chronicle as rich with prize,
As is the ouzy bottom of the ſea
With ſunken wreck and *ſumleſs* treaſuries. *Shak. Hen.* V.

A *ſumleſs* journey of incorporeal ſpeed. *Milton.*

Above, beneath, around the palace ſhines,
The *ſumleſs* treaſure of exhauſted mines. *Pope.*

SU'MMARILY. *adv.* [from *ſummary.*] Briefly; the ſhorteſt way.

The decalogue of Moſes declareth *ſummarily* thoſe things which we ought to do; the prayer of our Lord, whatſoever we ſhould requeſt or deſire. *Hooker.*

While we labour for theſe demonſtrations out of Scripture, and do *ſummarily* declare the things which many ways have been ſpoken, be contented quietly to hear, and do not think my ſpeech tedious. *Hooker.*

When the parties proceed *ſummarily*, and they chuſe the ordinary way of proceeding, the cauſe is made plenary. *Ayl.*

SU'MMARY. *adj.* [*ſommaire*, French; from *ſum.*] Short; brief; compendious.

The judge
Directed them to mind their brief,
Nor ſpend their time to ſhew their reading,
She'd have a *ſummary* proceeding. *Swift.*

SU'MMARY. *n. ſ.* [from the adj.] Compendium; abridgment.

We are enforc'd from our moſt quiet ſphere
By the rough torrent of occaſion;
And have the *ſummary* of all our griefs,
When time ſhall ſerve, to ſhew in articles. *Shakeſ. H.* IV.

In that comprehenſive *ſummary* of our duty to God, there is no expreſs mention thereof. *Rogers.*

SU'MMER. *n. ſ.* [ſumeꞃ, Saxon; *ſomer*, Dutch.]

1. The ſeaſon in which the ſun arrives at the hither ſolſtice.

Sometimes hath the brighteſt day a cloud;
And, after *Summer*, evermore ſucceeds
The barren Winter with his nipping cold. *Shakeſ. H.* VI.

Can't ſuch things be,
And overcome us like a *Summer's* cloud,
Without our ſpecial wonder? *Shakeſp. Macbeth.*

Two hundred loaves of bread, and an hundred bunches of raiſins, and an hundred of *Summer* fruits. 2 *Sa.* xvi.

He was ſitting in a *Summer* parlour. *Judg.* iii. 20.

In all the liveries deck'd of *Summer's* pride. *Milton.*

They marl and ſow it with wheat, giving it a *Summer* fallowing firſt, and next year ſow it with peaſe. *Mortimer.*

Dry weather is beſt for moſt *Summer* corn. *Mortimer.*

The dazzling roofs,
Reſplendent as the blaze of *Summer* noon,
Or the pale radiance of the midnight moon. *Pope.*

Child of the ſun,
See ſultry *Summer* comes. *Thomſon's Summer.*

2. [*Trabs ſummaria.*] The principal beam of a floor.

Oak, and the like true hearty timber, may be better truſted in croſs and tranſverſe works for *ſummers*, or girders, or binding beams. *Wotton.*

Then enter'd ſin, and with that ſycamore,
Whoſe leaves firſt ſhelter'd man from drought and dew,
Working and winding ſlily evermore,
The inward walls and *ſummers* cleft and tore;
But grace ſhor'd theſe, and cut that as it grew. *Herbert.*

To SU'MMER. *v. n.* [from the noun.] To paſs the Summer.

The fowls ſhall *ſummer* upon them, and all the beaſts ſhall winter upon them. *Iſ.* xviii. 6.

To SU'MMER. *v. a.* To keep warm.

Maids well *ſummer'd*, and warm kept, are like flies at Bartholomew-tide, blind, though they have their eyes. *Shakeſp.*

SU'MMERHOUSE. *n. ſ.* [from *Summer* and *houſe.*] An apartment in a garden uſed in the Summer.

I'd rather live
With cheeſe and garlick, in a windmill, far,
Than feed on cates, and have him talk to me,
In any *ſummerhouſe* in Chriſtendom. *Shakeſ. Henry* IV.

With here a fountain, never to be play'd,
And there a *ſummerhouſe*, that knows no ſhade. *Pope.*

There is ſo much virtue in eight volumes of Spectators, ſuch a reverence of things ſacred, ſo many valuable remarks for our conduct in life, that they are not improper to lie in parlours or *ſummerhouſes*, to entertain our thoughts in any moments of leiſure. *Watts.*

SU'MMERSAULT. } *n. ſ.* [*ſoubreſault*, French. *Somerſet* is a
SU'MMERSET. } corruption.] A high leap in which the heels are thrown over the head.

Some do the *ſummerſault*,
And o'er the bar like tumblers vault. *Hudibras.*

Frogs are obſerved to uſe divers *ſummerſaults*. *Walton.*

The treaſurer cuts a caper on the ſtrait rope: I have ſeen him do the *ſummerſet* upon a trencher fixed on the rope, which is no thicker than a common packthread. *Gulliver's Travels.*

SU'MMIT. *n. ſ.* [*ſummitas*, Lat.] The top; the utmoſt height.

Have I fall'n or no?
——From the dread *ſummit* of this chalky bourn!
Look up a-height, the ſhrill-gorg'd lark ſo far
Cannot be ſeen or heard. *Shakeſ. King Lear.*

Ætna's heat, that makes the *ſummit* glow,
Enriches all the vales below. *Swift.*

To SU'MMON. *v. a.* [*ſummoneo*, Latin.]

1. To call with authority; to admoniſh to appear; to cite.

Cateſby, ſound lord Haſtings,
And *ſummon* him to-morrow to the Tower. *Shak. R.* III.

The courſe of method *ſummoneth* me to diſcourſe of the inhabitants. *Carew's Survey of Cornwal.*

The tirſan is aſſiſted by the governour of the city, where the feaſt is celebrated, and all the perſons of both ſexes are *ſummoned* to attend. *Bacon.*

Rely on what thou haſt of virtue, *ſummon* all. *Milton.*

Nor trumpets *ſummon* him to war,
Nor drums diſturb his morning ſleep. *Dryden.*

Love, duty, ſafety, *ſummon* us away;
'Tis nature's voice, and nature we obey. *Pope.*

2. To excite; to call up; to raiſe. With *up* emphatical.

When the blaſt of war blows in our ears,
Stiffen the ſinews, *ſummon up* the blood. *Shakeſ. Henry* V.

SU'MMONER. *n. ſ.* [from *ſummon.*] One who cites; one who ſummons.

Cloſe pent-up guilts
Rive your concealing continents, and aſk
Theſe dreadful *ſummoners* grace. *Shakeſp. King Lear.*

SU'MMONS. *n. ſ.* [from the verb.] A call of authority; admonition to appear; citation.

What are you?
Your name, your quality, and why you anſwer
This preſent *ſummons?* *Shakeſ. King Lear.*

He ſent to ſummon the ſeditious, and to offer pardon; but neither *ſummons* nor pardon was any thing regarded. *Hayw.*

The ſons of light
Haſted, reſorting to the *ſummons* high,
And took their ſeats. *Milton's Paradiſe Loſt.*

Strike your ſails at *ſummons*, or prepare
To prove the laſt extremities of war. *Dryden.*

SU'MPTER. *n. ſ.* [*ſommier*, French; *ſomaro*, Italian.] A horſe that carries the cloaths or furniture.

Return with her!
Persuade me rather to be a slave and *sumpter*
To this detested groom. *Shakesp. King Lear.*
With full force his deadly bow he bent,
And feather'd fates among the mules and *sumpters* sent. *Dry.*
Two *sumpter* mules, bred of large Flanders mares. *Mortimer's Husbandry.*

SU'MPTION. *n. s.* [from *sumptus*, Latin.] The act of taking.

The *sumption* of the mysteries does all in a capable subject. *Taylor.*

SU'MPTUARY. *adj.* [*sumptuarius*, Latin.] Relating to expence; regulating the cost of life.

To remove that material cause of sedition, which is want and poverty in the estate, serveth the opening and well balancing of trade, the banishing of idleness, the repressing of waste and excess by *sumptuary* laws. *Bacon.*

SUMPTUO'SITY. *n. s.* [from *sumptuous.*] Expensiveness; costliness.

He added *sumptuosity*, invented jewels of gold and stone, and some engines for the war. *Raleigh.*

SU'MPTUOUS. *adj.* [*sumptuosus*, from *sumptus*, Lat.] Costly; expensive; splendid.

We see how most Christians stood then affected, how joyful they were to behold the *sumptuous* stateliness of houses built unto God's glory. *Hooker.*

We are too magnificent and *sumptuous* in our tables and attendance. *F. Atterbury.*

SU'MPTUOUSLY. *adv.* [from *sumptuous.*] Expensively; with great cost.

This monument five hundred years hath stood,
Which I have *sumptuously* re-edified. *Shak Titus Andronicus.*

Ethelwold, bishop of Winchester, in a famine, sold all the rich vessels and ornaments of the church, to relieve the poor with bread; and said, there was no reason that the dead temples of God should be *sumptuously* furnished, and the living temples suffer penury. *Bacon's Apophthegms.*

A good employment will make you live tolerably in London, or *sumptuously* here. *Swift.*

SU'MPTUOUSNESS. *n. s.* [from *sumptuous.*] Expensiveness; costliness.

I will not fall out with those that can reconcile *sumptuousness* and charity. *Boyle.*

SUN. *n. s.* [*sunno*, Gothick; ſunna, ſunne, Saxon; *son*, Dut.]

1. The luminary that makes the day.

Doth beauty keep which never *sun* can burn,
Nor storms do turn? *Sidney.*
Bid her steal into the pleached bow'r,
Where honeysuckles, ripen'd by the *sun*,
Forbid the sun to enter. *Shakespeare.*

Though there be but one *sun* existing in the world, yet the idea of it being abstracted, so that more substances might each agree in it, it is as much a sort as if there were as many *suns* as there are stars. *Locke.*

2. A sunny place; a place eminently warmed by the sun.

This place has choice of *sun* and shade. *Milton.*

3. Any thing eminently splendid.

I will never consent to put out the *sun* of sovereignty to posterity, and all succeeding kings. *King Charles.*

4. *Under the* SUN. In this world. A proverbial expression.

There is no new thing *under the sun.* *Eccl.* i. 9.

To SUN. *v. a.* [from the noun.] To insolate; to expose to the sun; to warm in the sun.

The cry to shady delve him brought at last,
Where Mammon earst did *sun* his treasury. *Fairy Queen.*
What aim'st thou at? delicious fare;
And then to *sun* thyself in open air. *Dryden's Pers.*

SU'NBEAM. *n. s.* [*sun* and *beam.*] Ray of the sun.

The Roman eagle, wing'd
From the spungy South to this part of the West,
Vanish'd in the *sunbeams.* *Shakes. Cymbeline.*
Gliding through the ev'n
On a *sunbeam.* *Milton's Paradise Lost.*

There was a God, a being distinct from this visible world; and this was a truth wrote with a *sunbeam*, legible to all mankind, and received by universal consent. *South.*

SU'NBEAT. *part. adj.* [*sun* and *beat.*] Shone on by the sun.

Its length runs level with th' Atlantic main,
And wearies fruitful Nilus to convey
His *sunbeat* waters by so long a way. *Dryden's Juv. Sat.*

SU'NBRIGHT. *adj.* [*sun* and *bright.*] Resembling the sun in brightness.

Gathering up himself out of the mire,
With his uneven wings did fiercely fall
Upon his *sunbright* shield. *Fairy Queen.*
Now would I have thee to my tutor:
How and which way I may bestow myself,
To be regarded in her *sunbright* eye. *Shakespeare.*
High in the midst, exalted as a God,
Th' apostate in his *sunbright* chariot sat,
Idol of majesty divine! inclos'd
With flaming cherubims, and golden shields. *Milton.*

SUNBU'RNING. *n. s.* [*sun* and *burning.*] The effect of the sun upon the face.

If thou can'st love a fellow of this temper, Kate, whose face is not worth *sunburning*, let thine eye be thy cook. *Shakes.*

The heat of the sun may darken the colour of the skin, which we call *sunburning.* *Boyle.*

SU'NBURNT. *participial adj.* [*sun* and *burnt.*] Tanned; discoloured by the sun.

Where such radiant lights have shone,
No wonder if her cheeks be grown
Sunburnt with lustre of her own. *Cleaveland.*
Sunburnt and swarthy though she be,
She'll fire for Winter nights provide. *Dryden.*
How many nations of the *sunburnt* soil
Does Niger bless? how many drink the Nile? *Blackmore.*

One of them, older and more *sunburnt* than the rest, told him he had a widow in his line of life. *Addison.*

SU'NCLAD. *part. adj.* [*sun* and *clad.*] Clothed in radiance; bright.

SU'NDAY. *n. s.* [*sun* and *day.*] The day anciently dedicated to the sun; the first day of the week; the Christian sabbath.

If thou wilt needs thrust thy neck into a yoke, wear the print of it, and sigh away *Sundays.* *Shakespeare.*

An' she were not kin to me, she would be as fair on Friday as Helen is on *Sunday.* *Shakesp. Troilus and Cressida.*

At prime they enter'd on the *Sunday* morn;
Rich tap'stry spread the streets. *Dryden.*

To SU'NDER. *v. a.* [ſyndpran, Saxon.] To part; to separate; to divide.

Vexation almost stops my breath,
That *sundred* friends greet in the hour of death. *Shakesp.*
It is *sundred* from the main land by a sandy plain. *Carew.*
She that should all parts to reunion bow,
She that had all magnetick force alone,
To draw and fasten *sundred* parts in one. *Donne.*
A *sundred* clock is piecemeal laid,
Not to be lost, but by the maker's hand
Repolish'd, without error then to stand. *Donne.*
When both the chiefs are *sunder'd* from the fight,
Then to the lawful king restore his right. *Dryden's Virgil.*
Th' enormous weight was cast,
Which Crantor's body *sunder'd* at the waist. *Dryden.*
Bears, tigers, wolves, the lion's angry brood,
Whom heav'n endu'd with principles of blood,
He wisely *sundred* from the rest, to yell
In forests. *Dryden.*
Bring me lightning, give me thunder;
—Jove may kill, but ne'er shall *sunder.* *Granville.*

SU'NDER. *n. s.* [ſunbeр, Saxon.] Two; two parts.

He breaketh the bow, and cutteth the spear in *sunder.* *Ps.*

SU'NDEW. *n. s.* An herb. *Ainsworth.*

SUNDI'AL. *n. s.* [*dial* and *sun.*] A marked plate on which the shadow points the hour.

All your graces no more you shall have,
Than a *sundial* in a grave. *Donne.*

The body, though it really moves, yet not changing perceivable distance, seems to stand still; as is evident in the shadows of *sundials.* *Locke.*

SU'NDRY. *adj.* [ſunbeр, Saxon.] Several; more than one.

That law, which, as it is laid up in the bosom of God, we call eternal, receiveth, according unto the different kind of things which are subject unto it, different and *sundry* kinds of names. *Hooker.*

Not of one nation was it peopled, but of *sundry* people of different manners. *Spenser.*

He caused him to be arrested upon complaint of *sundry* grievous oppressions. *Davies.*

How can she several bodies know,
If in herself a body's form she bear?
How can a mirrour *sundry* faces show,
If from all shapes and forms it be not clear? *Davies.*

I have composed *sundry* collects, as the Adventual, Quadragesimal, Paschal or Pentecostal. *Sanderson.*

Sundry foes the rural realm surround. *Dryden.*
Sundry in all manual arts are as wonderful. *Locke.*

SU'NFLOWER. *n. s.* [*corona solis*, Latin.] A plant.

The characters are: it hath a squamous cup; the flowers are radiated like the great starwort; the embryoes of the seeds are distinguished by little imbricated leaves in the disk; the top of the ovary is crowned with two small leaves; the seeds are pushed out from the bottom of the flower, leaving a vacuity which appears very like a honeycomb. *Miller.*

SU'NFLOWER, *Little.* *n. s.* [*helianthemum*, Latin.] A plant.

The characters are: the flower-cup consists of three leaves; the flower, for the most part, of five leaves, placed orbicularly, and expanded in form of a rose; the pointal of the flower becomes a globular fruit, which divides into three parts, having three cells, which are filled with roundish seeds fixed to small capillaments. *Miller.*

Sung. The preterite and participle passive of *sing*.
A larger rock then heaving from the plain,
He whirl'd it round, it *sung* across the main. *Pope.*
From joining stones the city sprung,
While to his harp divine Amphion *sung*. *Pope.*

Sunk. The preterite and participle passive of *sink*.
We have large caves: the deepest are *sunk* six hundred fathom, and some digged and made under great hills. *Bacon.*
Thus we act and thus we are,
Or toss'd by hope or *sunk* by care. *Prior.*
Sunk in Thalestris' arms the nymph he found. *Pope.*
His spirit quite *sunk* with those reflections that solitude and disappointments bring, he is utterly undistinguished and forgotten. *Swift.*

Su'nless. *adj.* [from *sun*.] Wanting sun; wanting warmth.
He thrice happy on the *sunless* side,
Beneath the whole collected shade reclines. *Thomson.*

Su'nlike. *adj.* [*sun* and *like*.] Resembling the sun.
The quantity of light in this bright luminary, and in the *sunlike* fixt stars, must be continually decreasing. *Cheyne.*

Su'nny. *adj.* [from *sun*.]
1. Resembling the sun; bright.
She saw Duessa *sunny* bright,
Adorn'd with gold and jewels shining clear. *Fairy Queen.*
The eldest, that Fidelia hight,
Like *sunny* beams threw from her crystal face. *Fai. Queen.*
My decay'd fair
A *sunny* look of his would soon repair. *Shakespeare.*
The chemist feeds
Perpetual flames, whose unresisted force
O'er sand and ashes and the stubborn flint
Prevailing, turns into a fusile sea,
That in his furnace bubbles *sunny* red. *Philips.*
2. Exposed to the sun; bright with the sun.
About me round I saw
Hill, dale, and shady woods, and *sunny* plains,
And liquid lapse of murm'ring streams. *Milton's Par. Lost.*
Him walking on a *sunny* hill he found,
Back'd on the North and West by a thick wood. *Milton.*
The filmy gossamer now flits no more,
Nor halcyons bask on the short *sunny* shore. *Dryden.*
But what avail her unexhausted stores,
Her blooming mountains and her *sunny* shores,
With all the gifts that heaven and earth impart,
The smiles of nature, and the charms of art,
While proud oppression in her vallies reigns,
And tyranny usurps her happy plains? *Addison.*
3. Coloured by the sun.
Her *sunny* locks
Hang on her temples like a golden fleece. *Shakespeare.*

Su'nrise. } *n. s.* [*sun* and *rising*.] Morning; the appearance of the sun.
Sunri'sing. }
Send out a pursuivant
To Stanley's regiment; bid him bring his power
Before *sunrising*. *Shakesp. Richard III.*
In those days the giants of Libanus mastered all nations, from the *sunrising* to the sunset. *Raleigh's Hist. of the World.*
They intend to prevent the *sunrising*. *Walton's Angler.*
We now believe the Copernican system; yet, upon ordinary occasions, we shall still use the popular terms of *sunrise* and sunset. *Bentley.*

Su'nset. *n. s.* [*sun* and *set*.] Close of the day; evening.
When the sun sets the air doth drizzle dew;
But for the *sunset* of my brother's son
It rains downright. *Shakespeare.*
The stars are of greater use than for men to gaze on after *sunset*. *Raleigh.*
At *sunset* to their ship they make return,
And snore secure on deck 'till rosy morn. *Dryden.*
He observant of the parting ray,
Eyes the calm *sunset* of thy various day
Through fortune's cloud. *Pope.*

Su'nshine. *n. s.* [*sun* and *shine*.] Action of the sun; place where the heat and lustre of the sun are powerful.
That man that sits within a monarch's heart,
And ripens in the *sunshine* of his favour,
Would he abuse the count'nance of the king,
Alack, what mischiefs might be set abroach,
In shadow of such greatness? *Shakesp. Henry IV.*
He had been many years in that *sunshine*, when a new comet appeared in court. *Clarendon.*
Sight no obstacle found here, nor shade,
But all *sunshine*, as when his beams at noon
Culminate from th' equator. *Milton.*
I that in his absence
Blaz'd like a star of the first magnitude,
Now in his brighter *sunshine* am not seen. *Denham's Sophy.*
Nor can we this weak show'r a tempest call,
But drops of heat that in the *sunshine* fall. *Dryden.*
The cases prevent the bees getting abroad upon every *sunshine* day. *Mortimer's Husbandry.*
The more favourable you are to me, the more distinctly I see my faults: spots and blemishes are never so plainly discovered as in the brightest *sunshine*. *Pope.*

Su'nshiny. *adj.* [from *sunshine*. It was anciently accented on the second syllable.]
1. Bright with the sun.
About ten in the morning, in *sunshiny* weather, we took several sorts of paper stained. *Boyle.*
2. Bright like the sun.
The fruitful-headed beast, amaz'd
At flashing beams of that *sunshiny* shield,
Became stark blind, and all his senses daz'd,
That down he tumbled. *Fairy Queen.*

To Sup. *v. a.* [*super*, Norman French; ȷupan, Saxon; *soepen*, Dutch.] To drink by mouthfuls; to drink by little at a time; to sip.
Then took the angry witch her golden cup,
Which still she bore replete with magick arts,
Death and despair did many thereof *sup*. *Spenser.*
There find a purer air
To feed my life with; there I'll *sup*
Balm and nectar in my cup. *Crashaw.*
We saw it smelling to every thing set in the room, and when it had smelt to them all, it *supped* up the milk. *Ray.*
He call'd for drink; you saw him *sup*
Potable gold in golden cup. *Swift.*

To SUP. *v. n.* [*souper*, French.] To eat the evening meal.
You'll *sup* with me?
—Anger's my meat; I *sup* upon myself,
And so shall starve with feeding. *Shakesp. Coriolanus.*
I have *supt* full with horrours;
Direness, familiar to my slaught'rous thoughts,
Cannot once start me. *Shakesp. Macbeth.*
When they had *supped*, they brought Tobias in. *Tob.* viii.
I see all the pilgrims in the Canterbury tales as distinctly as if I had *supped* with them. *Dryden.*
Late returning home, he *supp'd* at ease. *Dryden.*

To Sup. *v. a.* To treat with supper.
He's almost *supp'd*; why have you left the chamber. *Shak.*
Sup them well, and look unto them all. *Shakespeare.*
Let what you have within be brought abroad,
To *sup* the stranger. *Chapman's Odyssey.*

Sup. *n. s.* [from the verb.] A small draught; a mouthful of liquour.
Tom Thumb had got a little *sup*,
And Tomalin scarce kist the cup. *Drayton.*
A pigeon saw the picture of a glass with water in't, and flew eagerly up to't for a *sup* to quench her thirst. *L'Estrange.*
The least transgression of your's, if it be only two bits and one *sup* more than your stint, is a great debauch. *Swift.*

Super, in composition, notes either more than another, or more than enough, or on the top.

Su'perable. *adj.* [*superabilis*, Lat. *superable*, French.] Conquerable; such as may be overcome.

Su'perableness. *n. s.* [from *superable*.] Quality of being conquerable.

To Superabou'nd. *v. n.* [*super* and *abound*.] To be exuberant; to be stored with more than enough.
This case returneth again at this time, except the clemency of his majesty *superabound*. *Bacon.*
She *superabounds* with corn, which is quickly convertible to coin. *Howel.*

Superabu'ndance. *n. s.* [*super* and *abundance*.] More than enough; great quantity.
The precipitation of the vegetative terrestrial matter at the deluge amongst the sand, was to retrench the luxury and *superabundance* of the productions of the earth. *Woodward.*

Superabu'ndant. *adj.* [*super* and *abundant*.] Being more than enough.
So much *superabundant* zeal could have no other design than to damp that spirit raised against Wood. *Swift.*

Superabu'ndantly. *adv.* [from *superabundant*.] More than sufficiently.
Nothing but the uncreated Infinite can adequately fill and *superabundantly* satisfy the desire. *Cheyne.*

To Supera'dd. *v. n.* [*superaddo*, Latin.] To add over and above; to join any thing so as to make it more.
The peacock laid it extremely to heart that he had not the nightingale's voice *superadded* to the beauty of plumes. *L'Estr.*
The schools dispute, whether in morals the external action *superadds* any thing of good or evil to the internal elicit act of the will; but certainly the enmity of our judgments is wrought up to an high pitch before it rages in an open denial. *South.*
The strength of any living creature, in those external motions, is something distinct from and *superadded* unto its natural gravity. *Wilkins's Math. Mag.*

Superaddi'tion. *n. s.* [*super* and *addition*.]
1. The act of adding to something else.
The fabrick of the eye, its safe and useful situation, and the *superaddition* of muscles, are a certain pledge of the existence of God. *More.*
2. That which is added.
Of these, much more than of the Nicene *superadditions*, it

may be affirmed, that being the explications of a father of the church, and not of a whole universal council, they were not necessary to be explicitly acknowledged. *Hammond.*

An animal, in the course of hard labour, seems to be nothing but vessels: let the same animal continue long in rest, it will perhaps double its weight and bulk: this *superaddition* is nothing but fat. *Arbuthnot.*

SUPERADVE'NIENT. *adj.* [*superadveniens*, Latin.]
1. Coming to the increase or assistance of something.

The soul of man may have matter of triumph, when he has done bravely by a *superadvenient* assistance of his God. *More.*

2. Coming unexpectedly.

To SUPERA'NNUATE. *v. a.* [*super* and *annus*, Lat.] To impair or disqualify by age or length of life.

If such depravities be yet alive, deformity need not despair, nor will the eldest hopes be ever *superannuated*. *Brown.*

When the sacramental test was put in execution, the justices of peace through Ireland, that had laid down their commissions, amounted only to a dozen, and those of the lowest fortune, and some of them *superannuated*. *Swift.*

To SUPERA'NNUATE. *v. n.* To last beyond the year. Not in use.

The dying of the roots of plants that are annual, is by the over-expence of the sap into stalk and leaves, which being prevented, they will *superannuate*. *Bacon's Natural History.*

SUPERANNUA'TION. *n. s.* [from *superannuate*.] The state of being disqualified by years.

SUPE'RB. *adj.* [*superbe*, French; *superbus*, Latin.] Grand; pompous; lofty; august; stately; magnificent.

SUPE'RB-LILY. *n. s.* [*methonica*, Lat.] A flower.

SUPERCA'RGO. *n. s.* [*super* and *cargo*.] An officer in the ship whose business is to manage the trade.

I only wear it in a land of Hectors,
Thieves, *supercargo's*, sharpers. *Pope.*

SUPERCELE'STIAL. *adj.* [*super* and *celestial*] Placed above the firmament.

I dare not think that any *supercelestial* heaven, or whatsoever else, not himself, was increate and eternal. *Raleigh.*

Many were for fetching down I know not what *supercelestial* waters for the purpose. *Woodward's Nat. History.*

SUPERCI'LIOUS. *adj.* [from *supercilium*, Latin.] Haughty; dogmatical; dictatorial; arbitrary; despotick; overbearing.

Those who are one while courteous, within a small time after are so *supercilious*, fierce, and exceptious, that they are short of the true character of friendship. *South.*

Several *supercilious* criticks will treat an author with the greatest contempt, if he fancies the old Romans wore a girdle. *Addison.*

SUPERCI'LIOUSLY. *adv.* [from *supercilious*.] Haughtily; dogmatically; contemptuously.

He, who was a punctual man in point of honour, received this address *superciliously* enough, sent it to the king without performing the least ceremony. *Clarendon.*

SUPERCI'LIOUSNESS. *n. s.* [from *supercilious*.] Haughtiness; contemptuousness.

SUPERCONCE'PTION. *n. s.* [*super* and *conception*.] A conception made after another conception.

Those *superconceptions*, where one child was like the father, the other like the adulterer, seem idle. *Brown's Vulgar Errours.*

SUPERCO'NSEQUENCE. *n. s.* [*super* and *consequence*.] Remote consequence.

Not attaining the deuteroscopy, and second intention of the words, they omit their *superconsequences* and coherences. *Brown.*

SUPERCRE'SCENCE. *n. s.* [*super* and *cresco*, Lat.] That which grows upon another growing thing.

Wherever it groweth it maintains a regular figure, like other *supercrescences*, and like such as, living upon the stock of others, are termed parasitical plants. *Brown's Vulgar Errours.*

SUPERE'MINENCE. } *n. s.* [*super* and *emineo*, Latin.] Uncom-
SUPERE'MINENCY. } mon degree of eminence; eminence above others though eminent.

The archbishop of Canterbury, as he is primate over all England and metropolitan, has a *supereminency*, and even some power over the archbishop of York. *Ayliffe's Parergon.*

SUPERE'MINENT. *adj.* [*super* and *eminent*.] Eminent in a high degree.

As humility is in suiters a decent virtue, so the testification thereof by such effectual acknowledgments not only argueth a sound apprehension of his *supereminent* glory and majesty before whom we stand, but putteth also into his hands a kind of pledge or bond for security against our unthankfulness. *Hooker.*

To SUPERE'ROGATE. *v. n.* [*super* and *erogatio*, Lat.] To do more than duty requires.

So by an abbey's skeleton of late,
I heard an eccho *supererogate*
Through imperfection, and the voice restore,
As if she had the hiccup o'er and o'er. *Cleaveland.*

Aristotle acted his own instructions, and his obsequious sectators have *supererogated* in observance. *Glanv. Sceps.*

SUPEREROGA'TION. *n. s.* [from *supererogate*.] Performance of more than duty requires.

There is no such thing as works of *supererogation*; that no man can do more than needs, and is his duty to do, by way of preparation for another world. *Tillotson's Sermons.*

SUPERE'ROGATORY. *adj.* [from *supererogate*.] Performed beyond the strict demands of duty.

Supererogatory services, and too great benefits from subjects to kings, are of dangerous consequence. *Howel.*

SUPERE'XCELLENT. *adj.* [*super* and *excellent*.] Excellent beyond common degrees of excellence.

We discern not the abuse: suffer him to persuade us that we are as gods, something so *superexcellent*, that all must reverence and adore. *Decay of Piety.*

SUPEREXCRE'SCENCE. *n. s.* [*super* and *excrescence*.] Something superfluously growing.

As the escar separated between the scarifications, I rubbed the *superexcrescence* of flesh with the vitriol stone. *Wiseman.*

To SUPERFE'TATE. *v. n.* [*super* and *fœtus*, Latin.] To conceive after conception.

The female brings forth twice in one month, and so is said to *superfetate*, which, saith Aristotle, is because her eggs are hatched in her one after another. *Grew's Musæum.*

SUPERFETA'TION. *n. s.* [*superfetation*, French; from *superfetate*.] One conception following another, so that both are in the womb together, but come not to their full time for delivery together. *Quincy.*

Superfetation must be by abundance of sap in the bough that putteth it forth. *Bacon's Natural History.*

If the *superfetation* be made with considerable intermission, the latter most commonly becomes abortive; for the first being confirmed, engrosseth the aliment from the other. *Brown.*

SU'PERFICE. *n. s.* [*superficie*, Fr. *superficies*, Latin.] Outside; surface.

Then if it rise not to the former height
Of *superfice*, conclude that soil is light. *Dryden.*

SUPERFI'CIAL. *adj.* [*superficiel*, Fr. from *superficies*, Latin.]
1. Lying on the surface; not reaching below the surface.

That, upon the *superficial* ground, heat and moisture cause putrefaction, in England is found not true. *Bacon.*

From these phænomena several have concluded some general rupture in the *superficial* parts of the earth. *Burnet.*

There is not one infidel living so ridiculous as to pretend to solve the phænomena of sight, or cogitation, by those fleeting *superficial* films of bodies. *Bentley.*

2. Shallow; contrived to cover something.

This *superficial* tale
Is but a preface to her worthy praise. *Shakes. Henry VI.*

3. Shallow; not profound; smattering, not learned.

That knowledge is so very *superficial*, and so ill-grounded, that it is impossible for them to describe in what consists the beauty of those works. *Dryden.*

SUPERFICIA'LITY. *n. s.* [from *superficial*.] The quality of being superficial.

By these salts the colours of bodies receive degrees of lustre or obscurity, *superficiality* or profundity. *Brown.*

SUPERFI'CIALLY. *adv.* [from *superficial*]
1. On the surface; not below the surface.
2. Without penetration; without close heed.

Perspective hath been with some diligence inquired; but the nature of sounds in general hath been *superficially* observed. *Bacon's Natural History.*

His eye so *superficially* surveys
These things, as not to mind from whence they grow,
Deep under ground. *Milton's Paradise Lost.*

3. Without going deep; without searching to the bottom of things.

You have said well;
But on the cause and question now in hand,
Have gloz'd but *superficially*. *Shakesp. Troilus and Cressida.*

I have laid down *superficially* my present thoughts. *Dryden.*

SUPERFI'CIALNESS. *n. s.* [from *superficial*.]
1. Shallowness; position on the surface.
2. Slight knowledge; false appearance; show without substance.

SUPERFI'CIES. *n. s.* [Latin.] Outside; surface; superfice.

He on her *superficies* stretch'd his line. *Sandys.*

A convex mirrour makes objects in the middle to come out from the *superficies*: the painter must, in respect of the light and shadows of his figures, give them more relievo. *Dryden.*

SUPERFI'NE. *adj.* [*super* and *fine*.] Eminently fine.

Some, by this journey of Jason, understand the mystery of the philosopher's stone: to which also other *superfine* chymists draw the twelve labours of Hercules. *L'Estrange.*

If you observe your cyder, by interposing it between a candle and your eye, to be very transparent, it may be called *superfine*. *Mortimer's Husbandry.*

SUPERFLU'ITANCE. *n. s.* [*super* and *fluito*, Latin.] The act of floating above.

Sperma ceti, which is a *superfluitance* on the sea, is not the sperm of a whale. *Brown's Vulgar Errours.*

SUPERFLU'ITANT. *adj.* [*superfluitans*, Lat.] Floating above.

A chalky earth, beaten and steeped in water, affordeth a cream or fatness on the top, and a gross subsidence at the bottom: out of the cream, or *superfluitance*, the finest dishes are made; out of the residence, the coarser. *Brown.*

SUPERFLU'ITY. *n. f.* [*fuperfluité*, Fr. from *fuperfluous.*] More than enough; plenty beyond ufe or neceffity.

Having this way eafed the church, as they thought, of *fuperfluity*, they went on till they had plucked up even thofe things which alfo had taken a great deal deeper root. *Hooker.*

They are as fick that furfeit with too much, as they that ftarve with nothing; therefore it is no mean happinefs to be feated in the mean: *fuperfluity* comes fooner by white hairs, but competency lives longer. *Shakefpeare.*

A quiet mediocrity is ftill to be preferred before a troubled *fuperfluity.* *Suckling.*

Like the fun, let bounty fpread her ray,
And fhine that *fuperfluity* away. *Pope.*

SUPE'RFLUOUS. *adj.* [*fuper* and *fluo*, Lat. *fuperflu*, Fr.] Exuberant; more than enough; unneceffary; offenfive by being more than fufficient.

I think it *fuperfluous* to ufe any words of a fubject fo praifed in itfelf as it needs no praifes. *Sidney.*

When a thing ceafeth to be available unto the end which gave it being, the continuance of it muft then appear *fuperfluous.* *Hooker.*

Our *fuperfluous* lacqueys and our peafants,
Who in unneceffary action fwarm
About our fquares of battle. *Shakefpeare's Henry* V.

A proper title of a peace, and purchas'd
At a *fuperfluous* rate. *Shakefpeare.*

As touching the miniftring to the faints, it is *fuperfluous* to write. 2 *Cor.* ix. i.

Horace will our *fuperfluous* branches prune,
Give us new rules, and fet our harp in tune. *Rofcommon.*

If ye know,
Why afk ye, and *fuperfluous* begin
Your meffage, like to end as much in vain? *Milton.*

SUPE'RFLUOUSNESS. *n. f.* [from *fuperfluous.*] The ftate of being fuperfluous.

SU'PERFLUX. *n. f.* [*fuper* and *fluxus*, Latin.] That which is more than is wanted.

Take phyfick, pomp;
Expofe thyfelf to feel what wretches feel,
That thou may'ft fhake the *fuperflux* to them. *Shakefpeare.*

SUPERHU'MAN. *adj.* [*fuper* and *humanus*, Latin.] Above the nature or power of man.

SUPERIMPREGNA'TION. *n. f.* [*fuper* and *impregnation.*] Superconception; fuperfetation.

SUPERINCU'MBENT. *n. f.* [*fuper* and *incumbens*, Latin.] Lying on the top of fomething elfe.

It is fometimes fo extremely violent, that it forces the *fuperincumbent* ftrata; breaks them all throughout, and thereby perfectly undermines and ruins their foundations. *Woodward.*

To SUPERINDU'CE. *v. a.* [*fuper* and *induco*, Latin.]

1. To bring in as an addition to fomething elfe.

Relation is not contained in the real exiftence of things, but fomething extraneous and *fuperinduced.* *Locke.*

In children, favages, and ill-natured people, learning not having caft their native thoughts into new moulds, nor by *fuperinducing* foreign doctrines, confounded thofe fair characters nature had written, their innate notions might lie open. *Locke.*

2. To bring on as a thing not originally belonging to that on which it is brought.

To *fuperinduce* any virtue upon a perfon, take the living creature in which that virtue is moft eminent. *Bacon.*

Cuftom and corruption *fuperinduce* upon us a kind of neceffity of going on as we began. *L'Eftrange.*

Father is a notion *fuperinduced* to the fubftance or man, and refers only to an act of that thing called man, whereby he contributed to the generation of one of his own kind, let man be what it will. *Locke.*

Long cuftom of finning *fuperinduces* upon the foul new and abfurd defires, like the diftemper of the foul, feeding only upon filth and corruption. *South's Sermons.*

SUPERINDU'CTION. *n. f.* [from *fuper* and *induce.*] The act of fuperinducing.

A good inclination is but the firft rude draught of virtue; the *fuperinduction* of ill habits quickly deface it. *South.*

SUPERINJE'CTION. *n. f.* [*fuper* and *injection.*] An injection fucceeding upon another. *Dict.*

SUPERINSTITU'TION. *n. f.* [*fuper* and *inftitution.*] [In law.] One inftitution upon another; as if A be inftituted and admitted to a benefice upon a title, and B be inftituted and admitted by the prefentation of another. *Bailey.*

To SUPERINTE'ND. *v. a.* [*fuper* and *intend.*] To overfee; to overlook; to take care of others with authority.

The king will appoint a council who may *fuperintend* the works of this nature, and regulate what concerns the colonies. *Bacon's Advice to Villiers.*

This argues defign, and a *fuperintending* wifdom, power and providence in this fpecial bufinefs of food. *Derham.*

Angels, good or bad, muft be furnifhed with prodigious knowledge, to overfee Perfia and Grecia of old; or if any fuch *fuperintend* the affairs of Great Britain now. *Watts.*

SUPERINTE'NDENCE. } *n. f.* [from *fuper* and *intend.*] Superiour care; the act of overfeeing with authority.
SUPERINTE'NDENCY. }

Such an univerfal *fuperintendency* has the eye and hand of providence over all, even the moft minute and inconfiderable things. *South's Sermons.*

The divine providence, which hath a vifible refpect to the being of every man, is yet more obfervable in its *fuperintendency* over focieties. *Grew.*

An admirable indication of the divine *fuperintendence* and management. *Derham.*

SUPERINTE'NDENT. *n. f.* [*fuperintendant*, Fr. from *fuperintend.*] One who overlooks others authoritatively.

Next to Brama, one Deuendre is the *fuperintendent* deity, who hath many more under him. *Stillingfleet.*

The world pays a natural veneration to men of virtue, and rejoice to fee themfelves conducted by thofe who act under the care of a fupreme being, and who think themfelves accountable to the great Judge and *Superintendent* of human affairs. *Addifon.*

SUPERIO'RITY. *n. f.* [from *fuperiour.*] Pre-eminence; the quality of being greater or higher than another in any refpect.

Bellarmine makes the formal act of adoration to be fubjection to a fuperiour; but he makes the mere apprehenfion of excellency to include the formal reafon of it; whereas mere excellency without *fuperiority* doth not require any fubjection but only eftimation. *Stillingfleet.*

The perfon who advifes, does in that particular exercife a *fuperiority* over us, thinking us defective in our conduct or underftanding. *Addifon's Spectator.*

SUPE'RIOUR. *adj.* [*fuperieur*, Fr. *fuperior*, Latin.]

1. Higher; greater in dignity or excellence; preferable or preferred to another.

In commending another you do yourfelf right; for he that you commend is either *fuperiour* to you in that you commend, or inferiour; if he be inferiour, if he be to be commended, you much more: if he be *fuperiour*, if he be not to be commended, you much lefs glorious. *Bacon.*

Although *fuperior* to the people, yet not *fuperior* to their own voluntary engagements once paffed from them. *Taylor.*

Heaven takes part with the oppreffed, and tyrants are upon their behaviour to a *fuperior* power. *L'Eftrange.*

Superior beings above us, who enjoy perfect happinefs, are more fteadily determined in their choice of good than we, and yet they are not lefs happy or lefs free than we are. *Locke.*

He laughs at men of far *fuperiour* underftandings to his, for not being as well dreffed as himfelf. *Swift.*

2. Upper; higher locally.

By the refraction of the fecond prifm, the breadth of the image was not encreafed, but its *fuperiour* part, which in the firft prifm fuffered the greater refraction, and appeared violet and blue, did again in the fecond prifm fuffer a greater refraction than its inferiour part which appeared red and yellow. *Newton's Opticks.*

3. Free from emotion or concern; unconquered.

From amidft them forth he pafs'd,
Long way through hoftile fcorn; which he fuftain'd
Superior, nor of violence fear'd ought. *Milton.*

Here paffion firft I felt,
Commotion ftrange! in all enjoyments elfe
Superior and unmov'd. *Milton.*

There is not in earth a fpectacle more worthy than a great man *fuperiour* to his fufferings. *Addifon's Spectator.*

SUPE'RIOUR. *n. f.* One more excellent or dignified than another.

Thofe under the great officers of ftate, have more frequent opportunities for the exercife of benevolence than their *fuperiours.* *Addifon's Spectator.*

SUPERLA'TION. *n. f.* [*fuperlatio*, Latin.] Exaltation of any thing beyond truth or propriety.

There are words that as much raife a ftyle as others can deprefs it; *fuperlation* and overmuchnefs amplifies: it may be above faith, but not above a mean. *Ben. Johnfon.*

SUPE'RLATIVE. *adj.* [*fuperlatif*, Fr. *fuperlativus*, Latin.]

1. Implying or expreffing the higheft degree.

It is an ufual way to give the *fuperlative* unto things of eminence; and when a thing is very great, prefently to define it to be the greateft of all. *Brown's Vulgar Errours.*

Some have a violent and turgid manner of talking and thinking; they are always in extremes, and pronounce concerning every thing in the *fuperlative.* *Watts.*

2. Rifing to the higheft degree.

The high court of parliament in England is *fuperlative.* *Bacon's Advice to Villiers.*

Martyrdoms I reckon amongft miracles; becaufe they feem to exceed the ftrength of human nature; and I may do the like of *fuperlative* and admirable holinefs. *Bacon.*

The generality of its reception is with many the perfuading argument of its *fuperlative* defert; and common judges meafure excellency by numbers. *Glanville.*

Ingratitude and compassion never cohabit in the same breast; which shews the *superlative* malignity of this vice, and the baseness of the mind in which it dwells. *South's Sermons.*

SUPE'RLATIVELY. *adv.* [from *superlative.*]

1. In a manner of speech expressing the highest degree.

I shall not speak *superlatively* of them; but that I may truly say, they are second to none in the Christian world. *Bacon.*

2. In the highest degree.

Tiberius was bad enough in his youth; but *superlatively* and monstrously so in his old age. *South's Sermons.*

The Supreme Being is a spirit most excellently glorious, *superlatively* powerful, wise and good, Creator of all things. *Bent.*

SUPE'RLATIVENESS. *n. s.* [from *superlative.*] The state of being in the highest degree.

SUPERLU'NAR *adj.* [*super* and *luna.*] Not sublunary; placed above the moon; not of this world.

The mind, in metaphysicks, at a loss,
May wander in a wilderness of moss;
The head that turns at *superlunar* things,
Pois'd with a tail, may steer on Wilkins' wings. *Dunciad.*

SUPE'RNAL. *adj.* [*supernus*, Latin.]

1. Having an higher position; locally above us.

By heaven and earth was meant the solid matter and substance, as well of all the heavens and orbs *supernal*, as of the globe of the earth and waters which covered it *Raleigh.*

2. Relating to things above; placed above; cælestial; heavenly.

That *supernal* Judge that stirs good thoughts
In any breast of strong authority,
To look into the bolts and stains of right, *Shakespeare.*
He with frequent intercourse
Thither will send his winged messengers,
On errands of *supernal* grace. *Milton.*
Both glorying to have 'scap'd the Stygian flood,
As gods, and by their own recover'd strength,
Not by the suff'rance of *supernal* pow'r. *Milton.*

SUPERNA'TANT. *adj.* [*supernatans*, Latin.] Swimming above.

Whilst the substance continued fluid, I could shake it with the *supernatant* menstruum, without making between them any true union. *Boyle.*

SUPERNATA'TION. *n. s.* [from *supernato*, Latin.] The act of swimming on the top of any thing.

Touching the *supernatation* of bodies, take of aquafortis two ounces, of quicksilver two drams, the dissolution will not bear a flint as big as a nutmeg. *Bacon's Nat. History.*

Bodies are differenced by *supernatation*, as floating on water; for chrystal will sink in water, as carrying in its own bulk a greater ponderosity than the space of any water it doth occupy; and will therefore only swim in molten metal and quicksilver. *Brown's Vulgar Errours.*

SUPERNA'TURAL. *adj.* [*super* and *natural.*] Being above the powers of nature.

There resteth either no way unto salvation, or if any, then surely a way which is *supernatural*, a way which could never have entered into the heart of a man, as much as once to conceive or imagine, if God himself had not revealed it extraordinarily; for which cause we term it the mystery or secret way of salvation. *Hooker.*

When *supernatural* duties are necessarily exacted, natural are not rejected as needless. *Hooker.*

The understanding is secured by the perfection of its own nature, or by *supernatural* assistance. *Tillotson.*

What mists of providence are these,
Through which we cannot see?
So saints by *supernatural* power set free
Are left at last in martyrdom to die. *Dryden.*

SUPERNA'TURALLY. *adv.* [from *supernatural.*] In a manner above the course or power of nature.

The Son of God came to do every thing in miracle, to love *supernaturally*, and to pardon infinitely, and even to lay down the Sovereign while he assumed the Saviour. *South's Sermons.*

SUPERNU'MERARY. *adj.* [*supernumeraire*, Fr. *super* and *numerus*, Lat.] Being above a stated, a necessary, an usual, or a round number.

Well if thrown out, as *supernumerary*
To my just number found! *Milton's Paradise Lost.*

In sixty three years there may be lost eighteen days, omitting the intercalation of one day every fourth year, allowed for this quadrant or six hours *supernumerary.* *Brown.*

The odd or *supernumerary* six hours are not accounted in the three years after the leap-year. *Holder.*

The produce of this tax is adequate to the services for which it is designed, and the additional tax is proportioned to the *supernumerary* expence this year. *Addison's Freeholder.*

Antiochus Eupator began to augment his fleet; but the Roman senate ordered his *supernumerary* vessels to be burnt. *Arbuthnot on Coins.*

A *supernumerary* canon is one who does not receive any of the profits or emoluments of the church, but only lives and serves there on a future expectation of some prebend. *Ayliffe.*

SU'PERPLANT. *n. s.* [*super* and *plant.*] A plant growing upon another plant.

No *superplant* is a formed plant but misletoe. *Bacon.*

To SUPERPO'NDERATE. *v. a.* [*super* and *pondero*, Latin.] To weigh over and above. *Dict.*

SUPERPROPO'RTION. *n. s.* [*super* and *proportio*, Latin.] Overplus of proportion.

No defect of velocity, which requires as great a *superproportion* in the cause, can be overcome in an instant. *Digby.*

SUPERPURGA'TION. *n. s.* [*superpurgation*, Fr. *super* and *purgation.*] More purgation than enough.

There happening a *superpurgation*, he declined the repeating of that purge. *Wiseman's Surgery.*

SUPERREFLE'XION. *n. s.* [*super* and *reflexion.*] Reflexion of an image reflected.

Place one glass before and another behind, you shall see the glass behind with the image within the glass before, and again the glass before in that, and divers such *superreflexions*, till the species speciei at last die. *Bacon's Natural History.*

SUPERSA'LIENCY. *n. s.* [*super* and *salio*, Latin; this were better written *supersiliency.*] The act of leaping upon any thing.

Their coition is by *supersaliency*, like that of horses. *Brown.*

To SUPERSCRI'BE. *v. a.* [*super* and *scribo*, Latin.] To inscribe upon the top or outside.

Fabretti and others believe, that by the two fortunes were only meant in general the goddess who sent prosperity or afflictions, and produce in their behalf an ancient monument, *superscribed.* *Addison.*

SUPERSCRI'PTION. *n. s.* [*super* and *scriptio*, Latin.]

1. The act of superscribing.

2. That which is written on the top or outside.

Doth this churlish *superscription*
Portend some alteration in good will. *Shakespeare's H. VI.*

Read me the *superscription* of these letters; I know not which is which. *Shakespeare's Timon of Athens.*

Let me love her my fill
No *superscriptions* of fame,
Of honour or good name,
No thought but to improve
The gentle and quick approaches of my love. *Suckling.*
I learn of my experience, not by talk,
How counterfeit a coin they are who friends
Bear in their *superscription*; in prosperous days
They swarm, but in adverse withdraw their head. *Milton.*
It is enough her stone
May honour'd be with *superscription*
Of the sole lady, who had pow'r to move
The great Northumberland. *Waller.*

To SUPERSE'DE. *v. a.* [*super* and *sedeo*, Latin.] To make void or inefficacious by superiour power; to set aside.

Passion is the drunkenness of the mind; and therefore in its present workings not controlable by reason; for as much as the proper effect of it is, for the time, to *supersede* the workings of reason. *South's Sermons.*

In this genuine acceptation of chance, nothing is supposed that can *supersede* the known laws of natural motion. *Bentley.*

SUPERSE'DEAS. [In law.] Is a writ which lieth in divers and sundry cases; in all which it signifies a command or request to stay or forbear the doing of that which in appearance of law were to be done, were it not for the cause whereupon the writ is granted: for example, a man regularly is to have surety of peace against him of whom he will swear that he is afraid; and the justice required hereunto cannot deny him: yet if the party be formerly bound to the peace, in chancery or elsewhere, this writ lieth to stay the justice from doing that, which otherwise he might not deny. *Cowel.*

The far distance of this county from the court, hath heretofore afforded it a *supersedeas* from takers and purveyours. *Carew's Survey of Cornwall.*

SUPERSE'RVICEABLE. *adj.* [*super* and *serviceable.*] Over officious; more than is necessary or required.

A glass-gazing, *superserviceable* finical rogue. *Shakespeare.*

SUPERSTI'TION. *n. s.* [*superstition*, Fr. *superstitio*, Latin.]

1. Unnecessary fear or scruples in religion; observance of unnecessary and uncommanded rites or practices; religion without morality.

They the truth
With *superstitions* and traditions taint. *Milton.*
A rev'rent fear, such *superstition* reigns
Among the rude, ev'n then possess'd the swains. *Dryden.*

2. False religion; reverence of beings not proper objects of reverence; false worship.

They had certain questions against him of their own *superstition.* *Acts* xxv. 19.

3. Over-nicety; exactness too scrupulous.

SUPERSTI'TIOUS. *adj.* [*superstitieux*, Fr. *superstitiosus*, Latin.] Addicted to superstition; full of idle fancies or scruples with regard to religion.

At the kindling of the fire, and lighting of candles, they say certain prayers, and use some other *superstitious* rites, which shew that they honour the fire and the light. *Spenser.*

Have I
Been out of fondness *superstitious* to him?
And am I thus rewarded? *Shakespeare's Henry VIII.*

Nature's own work it seem'd, nature taught art,
And to a *superstitious* eye the haunt
Of wood-gods and wood-nymphs. *Milton.*

A venerable wood,
Where rites divine were paid, whose holy hair
Was kept and cut with *superstitious* care. *Dryden.*

2. Over accurate; scrupulous beyond need.

SUPERSTI'TIOUSLY. *adv.* [from *superstitious.*] In a superstitious manner.

There reigned in this island a king, whose memory of all others we most adore; not *superstitiously*, but as a divine instrument. *Bacon.*

Neither of these methods should be too scrupulously, and *superstitiously* pursued. *Watts's Logick.*

To SUPERSTRAI'N. *v. a.* [*super* and *strain.*] To strain beyond the just stretch.

In the straining of a string, the further it is strained, the less *superstraining* goeth to a note. *Bacon.*

To SUPERSTRU'CT. *v. a* [*superstruo*, *superstructus*, Latin.] To build upon any thing.

Two notions of fundamentals may be conceived, one signifying that whereon our eternal bliss is immediately *superstructed*, the other whereon our obedience to the faith of Christ is founded. *Hammond.*

If his habit of sin have not corrupted his principles, the vitious Christian may think it reasonable to reform, and the preacher may hope to *superstruct* good life upon such a foundation. *Hammond's Fundamentals.*

This is the only proper basis on which to *superstruct* first innocency and then virtue. *Decay of piety.*

SUPERSTRU'CTION. *n. s.* [from *superstruct.*] An edifice raised on any thing.

I want not to improve the honour of the living by impairing that of the dead; and my own profession hath taught me not to erect new *superstructions* upon an old ruin. *Denham.*

SUPERSTRU'CTIVE. *adj.* [from *superstruct.*] Built upon something else.

He that is so sure of his particular election, as to resolve he can never fall, must necessarily resolve, that what were drunkenness in another, is not so in him, and nothing but the removing his fundamental error can rescue him from the *superstructive*, be it never so gross. *Hammond.*

SUPERSTRU'CTURE. *n. s.* [*super* and *structure.*] That which is raised or built upon something else.

He who builds upon the present, builds upon the narrow compass of a point; and where the foundation is so narrow, the *superstructure* cannot be high and strong too. *South's Sermons.*

Purgatory was not known in the primitive church, and is a *superstructure* upon the Christian religion. *Tillotson.*

You have added to your natural endowments the *superstructures* of study. *Dryden.*

SUPERSUBSTA'NTIAL. *adj.* [*super* and *substantial.*] More than substantial.

SUPERVACA'NEOUS. *adj.* [*supervacaneus*, Lat.] Superfluous; needless; unnecessary; serving to no purpose. *Dict.*

SUPERVACA'NEOUSLY. *adv.* [from the adjective.] Needlesly.

SUPERVACA'NEOUSNESS. *n. s.* [from the adjective.] Needlessness. *Bailey.*

To SUPERVE'NE. *v. n.* [*supervenio*, Lat.] To come as an extraneous addition.

Such a mutual gravitation can never *supervene* to matter, unless impressed by a divine power. *Bentley's Sermons.*

SUPERVE'NIENT. *adj.* [*superveniens*, Latin.] Added; additional.

If it were unjust to murder John, the *supervenient* oath did not extenuate the fact, or oblige the jurer unto it. *Brown.*

That branch of belief was in him *supervenient* to Christian practice, and not all Christian practice built on that. *Ham.*

SUPERVE'NTION. *n. s.* [from *supervene.*] The act of supervening.

To SUPERVI'SE. *v. a.* [*super* and *visus*, Latin.] To overlook; to oversee; to intend.

M. Bayle speaks of the vexation of the *supervising* of the press, in terms so feeling that they move compassion. *Congreve.*

SUPERVI'SOR. *n. s.* [from *supervise.*] An overseer; an inspector; a superintendant.

A *supervisor* may signify an overseer of the poor, an inspector of the customs, a surveyor of the high ways, a *supervisor* of the excise. *Watts's Logick.*

How satisfy'd, my lord!
Would you be *supervisor*, grossly gape on? *Shakespeare.*

I am informed of the author and *supervisors* of this pamphlet. *Dryden.*

To SUPERVI'VE. *v. n.* [*super* and *vivo*, Lat.] To overlive; to outlive.

Upon what principle can the soul be imagined to be naturally mortal, or what revolutions in nature will it not be able to resist and *supervive*. *Clarke.*

SUPINA'TION. *n. s.* [*supination*, Fr from *supino*, Latin.] The act of lying with the face upward.

SUPI'NE. *adj.* [*supinus*, Latin.]

1. Lying with the face upward.

Upon these divers positions in man, wherein the spine can only be at right lines with the thigh, arise those remarkable postures, prone, *supine*, and erect. *Brown's Vulgar Errours.*

At him he lanc'd his spear, and pierc'd his breast;
On the hard earth the Lycian knock'd his head,
And lay *supine*; and forth the spirit fled. *Dryden.*

What advantage hath a man by this erection above other animals, the faces of most of them being more *supine* than ours. *Ray on the Creation.*

2. Leaning backwards with exposure to the sun.

If the vine,
On rising ground be plac'd or hills *supine*,
Extend thy loose battalions. *Dryden.*

3. Negligent; careless; indolent; drousy; thoughtless; inattentive.

These men suffer by their absence, silence, negligence, or *supine* credulity. *King Charles.*

Supine amidst our flowing store
We slept securely. *Dryden.*

Supine in Sylvia's snowy arms he lies,
And all the busy cares of life defies. *Tatler.*

He became pusillanimous and *supine*, and openly exposed to any temptation. *Woodward.*

SU'PINE. *n. s.* [*supin*, French; *supinum*, Latin.] In Grammar a term signifying a particular kind of verbal noun.

SUPI'NELY. *adv.* [from *supine.*]

1 With the face upward.

2. Drowsily; thoughtlesly; indolently.

Who on the beds of sin *supinely* lie,
They in the summer of their age shall die. *Sandys.*

The old imprison'd king,
Whose lenity first pleas'd the gaping crowd;
But when long try'd, and found *supinely* good,
Like Æsop's log, they leapt upon his back. *Dryden.*

He panting on thy breast *supinely* lies,
While with thy heav'nly form he feeds his famish'd eyes. *Dryden's Lucretius.*

Beneath a verdant laurel's shade,
Horace, immortal bard, *supinely* laid. *Prior.*

Wilt thou then repine
To labour for thyself? and rather chuse
To lie *supinely*, hoping heaven will bless
Thy slighted fruits, and give thee bread unearn'd *Philips.*

SUPI'NENESS. *n. s.* [from *supine.*]

1. Posture with the face upward.

2. Drowsiness; carelessness; indolence.

When this door is open to let dissenters in, considering their industry and our *supineness*, they may in a very few years grow to a majority in the house of commons. *Swift.*

SUPI'NITY. *n. s.* [from *supine.*]

1. Posture of lying with the face upwards.

2. Carelessness; indolence; thoughtlessness.

The fourth cause of errour is a *supinity* or neglect of enquiry, even in matters wherein we doubt, rather believing than going to see. *Brown's Vulgar Errours.*

SUPPEDA'NEOUS. *adj.* [*sub* and *pes*, Latin.] Placed under the feet.

He had slender legs, but encreased by riding after meals; that is, the humour descended upon their pendulosity, they having no support or *suppedaneous* stability. *Brown.*

SU'PPER. *n. s.* [*souper*, French. See SUP.] The last meal of the day; the evening repast.

To-night we hold a solemn *supper*. *Shakespeare.*

I'll to my book:
For yet, ere *supper*-time must I perform
Much business. *Shakespeare's Tempest.*

Th' hour of *supper* comes unearn'd. *Milton.*

SU'PPERLESS. *adj.* [from *supper.*] Wanting supper; fasting at night.

Suppose a man's going *supperless* to bed, should introduce him to the table of some great prince. *Spectator.*

She ey'd the bard, where *supperless* he sat,
And pin'd. *Pope.*

To SUPPLA'NT. *v. a.* [*supplanter*, French; *sub* and *planta*, Latin.]

1. To trip up the heels.

His legs entwining
Each other, till *supplanted* down he fell;
A monstrous serpent on his belly prone. *Milton.*

The thronging populace with hasty strides
Obstruct the easy way; the rocking town
Supplants their footsteps; to and fro they reel. *Philips.*

2. To displace by stratagem; to turn out.

It is Philoclea his heart is set upon; it is my daughter I have borne to *supplant* me. *Sidney.*

Upon a just survey, take Titus' part,
And so *supplant* us for ingratitude. *Shakespeare.*

3. To displace; to overpower; to force away.

If it be fond, call it a woman's fear;
Which fear, if better reasons can *supplant*,
I will subscribe, and say, I wrong'd the duke. *Shakespeare.*

Suppla'nter. *n. s.* [from *supplant.*] One that supplants; one that displaces.

SUPPLE. *adj.* [*souple*, French.]

1. Pliant; flexible.

The joints are more *supple* to all feats of activity in youth than afterwards. *Bacon.*

Will ye submit your necks, and chuse to bend
The *supple* knee? *Milton's Parad. Lost.*

And sometimes went, and sometimes ran
With *supple* joints, as lively vigour led. *Milton.*

No women are apter to spin linen well than the Irish, who labouring little in any kind with their hands, have their fingers more *supple* and soft than other women of the poorer condition in England. *Temple.*

2. Yielding; soft; not obstinate.

When we've stuff'd
These pipes and these conveyances of blood
With wine and feeding, we have *suppler* souls
Than in our priestlike fasts. *Shakespeare.*

Ev'n softer than thy own, of *suppler* kind,
More exquisite of taste, and more than man refin'd. *Dryden.*

If punishment reaches not the mind, and makes not the will *supple*, it hardens the offender. *Locke.*

3. Flattering; fawning; bending.

There is something so *supple* and insinuating in this absurd unnatural doctrine, as makes it extremely agreeable to a prince's ear. *Addison.*

4. That which makes supple.

Each part depriv'd of *supple* government,
Shall stiff, and stark, and cold appear, like death. *Shakesp.*

To Supple. *v. a.* [from the adjective.]

1. To make pliant; to make soft; to make flexible.

Poultices allaying pain, drew down the humours, and *suppled* the parts, thereby making the passages wider. *Temple.*

To *supple* a carcass, drench it in water. *Arbuthnot.*

2. To make compliant.

Knaves having by their own importunate suit,
Convinc'd or *suppl'd* them, they cannot chuse,
But they must blab. *Shakespeare's Othello.*

A mother persisting till she had bent her daughter's mind, and *suppled* her will, the only end of correction, she established her authority thoroughly ever after. *Locke on Education.*

To Supple. *v. n.* To grow soft; to grow pliant.

The stones
Did first the rigour of their kind expel,
And *suppled* into softness as they fell. *Dryden.*

SU'PPLEMENT. *n. s.* [*supplement*, Fr. *supplementum*, Latin.] Addition to any thing by which its defects are supplied.

Unto the word of God, being in respect of that end for which God ordained it, perfect, exact, and absolute in itself, we do not add reason as a *supplement* of any maim or defect therein, but as a necessary instrument, without which we could not reap by the scriptures perfection that fruit and benefit which it yieldeth. *Hooker.*

His blood will atone for our imperfection, his righteousness be imputed in *supplement* to what is lacking in ours. *Rogers.*

Suppleme'ntal. } *adj.* [from *supplement.*] Additional; such
Suppleme'ntary. } as may supply the place of what is lost or wanting.

Supplemental acts of state were made to supply defects of laws; and so tonnage and poundage were collected. *Clarendon.*

Divinity would not then pass the yard and loom, nor preaching be taken in as an easier *supplementary* trade, by those that disliked the pains of their own. *Decay of Piety.*

Provide his brood next Smithfield fair,
With *supplemental* hobby horses;
And happy be their infant courses. *Prior.*

Su'ppleness. *n. s.* [*souplesse*, Fr. from *supple.*]

1. Pliantness; flexibility; readiness to take any form.

The fruit is of a pleasant taste, caused by the *suppleness* and gentleness of the juice, being that which maketh the boughs also so flexible. *Bacon's Natural History.*

2. Readiness of compliance; facility.

Study gives strength to the mind, conversation grace; the first apt to give stiffness, the other *suppleness*. *Temple.*

A compliance and *suppleness* of their wills, being by a steady hand introduced by parents, will seem natural to them, preventing all occasions of struggling. *Locke.*

Su'ppletory. *n. s.* [*suppletorium*, Latin.] That which is to fill up deficiencies.

That *suppletory* of an implicit belief is by Romanists conceived sufficient for those not capable of an explicit. *Hamm.*

Su'ppliant. *adj.* [*suppliant*, Fr.] Entreating; beseeching; precatory; submissive.

To those legions your levy
Must be *suppliant*. *Shakespeare's Cymbeline.*

To bow and sue for grace with *suppliant* knee. *Milton.*

The rich grow *suppliant*, and the poor grow proud;
Those offer mighty gain, and these ask more. *Dryden.*

Constant to his first decree,
To bow the haughty neck, and raise the *suppliant* knee. *Prior.*

Su'ppliant. *n. s.* [from the adjective.] An humble petitioner; one who begs submissively.

A petition from a Florentine I undertook,
Vanquish'd thereto by the fair grace and speech
Of the poor *suppliant*. *Shakespeare.*

When corn was given them gratis, you repin'd;
Scandal'd the *suppliants* for the people, call'd them
Time-pleasers, flatterers. *Shakespeare's Coriolanus.*

Hourly suitors come:
The east with incense and the west with gold,
Will stand like *suppliants* to receive her doom. *Dryden.*

Spare this life, and hear thy *suppliant's* prayer. *Dryden.*

Su'pplicant. *n. s.* [from *supplicate.*] One that entreats or implores with great submission; an humble petitioner.

The prince and people of Nineveh assembling themselves as a main army of *supplicants*, God did not withstand them. *Hooker.*

The wise *supplicant*, though he prayed for the condition he thought most desirable, yet left the event to God. *Rogers.*

Abraham, instead of indulging the *supplicant* in his desire of new evidence, refers him to what his brethren had. *Atterbury.*

To SU'PPLICATE. *v. n.* [*supplier*, Fr. *supplico*, Lat. from *supplex.*] To implore; to entreat; to petition submissively and humbly.

Many things a man cannot with any comeliness say or do, a man cannot brook to *supplicate* or beg. *Bacon.*

Thither the kingdoms and the nations come,
In *supplicating* crowds to learn their doom. *Addison.*

Supplica'tion. *n. s.* [*supplication*, Fr. from *supplicate.*]

1. Petition humbly delivered; entreaty.

My lord protector will come this way by and by, and then we may deliver our *supplications* in the quill. *Shakespeare.*

My mother bows,
As if Olympus to a mole-hill should
In *supplication* nod. *Shakesp. Coriolanus.*

2. Petitionary worship; the adoration of a suppliant or petitioner.

Praying with all prayer and *supplication*, with all perseverance and *supplication* for all saints. *Eph.* vi. 18.

Bend thine ear
To *supplication*; hear his sighs though mute. *Milton.*

These prove the common practice of the worship of images in the Roman church, as to the rites of *supplication* and adoration, to be as extravagant as among the heathens. *Stilling.*

We should testify our dependence upon God, and our confidence of his goodness by constant prayers and *supplications* for mercy. *Tillotson.*

To Supply'. *v. a.* [*suppleo*, Lat. *suppleer*, French.]

1. To fill up as any deficiencies happen.

Out of the fry of these rakehell horseboys are their kearn *supplied* and maintained. *Spenser.*

2. To give something wanted; to yield; to afford.

They were princes that had wives, sons, and nephews; and yet all these could not *supply* the comfort of friendship. *Bacon.*

I wanted nothing fortune could *supply*,
Nor did she slumber 'till that hour deny. *Dryden.*

3. To relieve.

Although I neither lend nor borrow,
Yet, to *supply* the ripe wants of my friend,
I'll break a custom. *Shakesp. Merchant of Venice.*

4. To serve instead of.

Burning ships the banish'd sun *supply*,
And no light shines but that by which men die. *Waller.*

5. To give or bring, whether good or bad.

Nearer care *supplies*
Sighs to my breast, and sorrow to my eyes. *Prior.*

6. To fill any room made vacant.

Upstart creatures to *supply* our vacant room. *Milton.*

The sun was set; and Vesper, to *supply*
His absent beams, had lighted up the sky. *Dryden.*

7. To accommodate; to furnish.

While trees the mountain-tops with shades *supply*,
Your honour, name, and praise shall never die. *Dryden.*

The reception of light must be *supplied* by some open form of the fabrick. *Wotton.*

My lover, turning away several old servants, *supplied* me with others from his own house. *Swift.*

Supply'. *n. s.* [from the verb.] Relief of want; cure of deficiencies.

I mean that now your abundance may be a *supply* for their want, that their abundance also may be a *supply* for your want. 2 *Cor.* viii. 14.

Art from that fund each just *supply* provides,
Works without show, and without pomp presides. *Pope.*

To SUPPO'RT. *v. a.* [*supporter*, French; *supportare*, Ital.]

1. To sustain; to prop; to bear up.

Stooping to *support* each flow'r of tender stalk. *Milton.*

The palace built by Picus, vast and proud,
Supported by a hundred pillars stood. *Dryden.*

The original community of all things appearing from this donation of God, the sovereignty of Adam, built upon his private dominion, must fall, not having any foundation to *support* it. *Locke.*

2. To endure any thing painful without being overcome.

Strongly to suffer and *support* our pains. *Milton.*
Could'st thou *support* that burden? *Milton.*

This fierce demeanour, and his insolence,
The patience of a god could not *support*. *Dryden.*

3. To endure.

She scarce awake her eyes could keep,
Unable to *support* the fumes of sleep. *Dryden.*

None can *support* a diet of flesh and water without acids, as salt, vinegar, and bread, without falling into a putrid fever. *Arbuthnot on Aliments.*

4. To sustain; to keep from fainting.

With inward consolations recompens'd,
And oft *supported*. *Milton.*

SUPPO'RT. *n. s.* [*support*, French; from the verb.]

1. Act or power of sustaining.

Though the idea we have of a horse or stone be but the collection of those several sensible qualities which we find united in them, yet, because we cannot conceive how they should subsist alone, we suppose them existing in and supported by some common subject, which *support* we denote by the name substance, though it be certain we have no clear idea of that *support*. *Locke.*

2. Prop; sustaining power.

3. Necessaries of life.

4. Maintainance; supply.

SUPPO'RTABLE. *adj.* [*supportable*, French; from *support.*] Tolerable; to be endured. It may be observed that *Shakespeare* accents the first syllable.

As great to me, as late; and, *supportable*
To make the dear loss, have I means much weaker
Than you may call to comfort you. *Shak. Tempest.*

Alterations in the project of uniting Christians might be very *supportable*, as things in their own nature indifferent. *Sw.*

I wish that whatever part of misfortunes they must bear, may be rendered *supportable* to them. *Pope.*

SUPPO'RTABLENESS. *n. s.* [from *supportable.*] The state of being tolerable.

SUPPO'RTANCE. } *n. s.* [from *support.*] Maintenance; support.
SUPPORTA'TION. } Both these words are obsolete.

Give some *supportance* to the bending twigs. *Shakespeare.*

His quarrel he finds scarce worth talking of, therefore draw for the *supportance* of his vow. *Shakesp. Twelfth Night.*

The benefited subject should render some small portion of his gain, for the *supportation* of the king's expence. *Bacon.*

SUPPO'RTER. *n. s.* [from *support.*]

1. One that supports.

You must walk by us upon either hand,
And good *supporters* are you. *Shakes. Meas. for Measure.*

Because a relation cannot be founded in nothing, and the thing here related as a *supporter*, or a support, is not represented to the mind by any distinct idea. *Locke.*

2. Prop; that by which any thing is borne up from falling.

More might be added of helms, crests, mantles, and *supporters*. *Camden.*

The sockets and *supporters* of flowers are figured. *Bacon.*

We shall be discharged of our load; but you, that are designed for beams and *supporters*, shall bear. *L'Estrange.*

There is no loss of room at the bottom, as there is in a building set upon *supporters*. *Mortimer's Husbandry.*

3. Sustainer; comforter.

The saints have a companion and *supporter* in all their miseries. *South's Sermons.*

4. Maintainer; defender.

The beginning of the earl of Essex I must attribute in great part to my lord of Leicester; but yet as an introducer or *supporter*, not as a teacher. *Wotton.*

All examples represent ingratitude as sitting in its throne, with pride at its right hand, and cruelty at its left; worthy *supporters* of such a reigning impiety. *South.*

Love was no more, when loyalty was gone,
The great *supporter* of his awful throne. *Dryden.*

SUPPO'SABLE. *adj.* [from *suppose.*] That may be supposed.

Invincible ignorance is, in the far greatest number of men, ready to be confronted against the necessity of their believing all the severals of any *supposable* catalogue. *Hammond.*

SUPPO'SAL. *n. s.* [from *suppose.*] Position without proof; imagination; belief.

Young Fortinbras,
Holding a weak *supposal* of our worth,
Thinks our state to be out of frame. *Shakespeare.*

Little can be looked for towards the advancement of natural theory, but from those that are likely to mend our prospect: the defect of events, and sensible appearances, suffer us to proceed no further towards science, than to imperfect guesses and timorous *supposals*. *Glanv. Sceps. Preface.*

Interest, with a Jew, never proceeds but upon *supposal* at least of a firm and sufficient bottom. *South.*

Artful men endeavour to entangle thoughtless women by bold *supposals* and offers. *Clarissa.*

To SUPPO'SE. *v. a.* [*supposer*, French; *suppono*, Latin.]

1. To lay down without proof; to advance by way of argument or illustration without maintaining the truth of the position.

Suppose some so negligent that they will not be brought to learn by gentle ways, yet it does not thence follow that the rough discipline of the cudgel is to be used to all. *Locke.*

2. To admit without proof.

This is to be entertained as a firm principle, that when we have as great assurance that a thing is, as we could possibly, *supposing* it were, we ought not to make any doubt of its existence. *Tillotson.*

3. To imagine; to believe without examination.

Tell false Edward, thy *supposed* king,
That Lewis of France is sending over maskers. *Shakesp.*

Let not my lord *suppose* that they have slain all the king's sons; for Ammon only is slain. 2 *Sa.* xiii. 32.

I *suppose* we should compel them to a quick result. *Milton.*

4. To require as previous to itself.

This *supposeth* something, without evident ground. *Hale.*

One falshood always *supposes* another, and renders all you can say suspected. *Female Quixote.*

SU'PPOSE. *n. s.* [from the verb.] Supposition; position without proof; unevidenced conceit.

That we come short of our *suppose* so far,
That after sev'n years siege, yet Troy-walls stand? *Shakesp.*

Is Egypt's safety, and the king's, and your's,
Fit to be trusted on a bare *suppose*
That he is honest? *Dryden's Cleomenes.*

SUPPO'SER. *n. s.* [from *suppose.*] One that supposes.

Thou hast by marriage made thy daughter mine,
While counterfeit *supposers* bleer'd thine eyne. *Shakespeare.*

SUPPOSI'TION. *n. s.* [*supposition*, French; from *suppose.*] Position laid down; hypothesis; imagination yet unproved.

In saying he is a good man, understand me that he is sufficient; yet his means are in *supposition*. *Shakespeare.*

Sing, syren, for thyself, and I will dote;
Spread o'er the silver waves thy golden hairs,
And as a bed I'll take thee, and there lye;
And in that glorious *supposition* think
He gains by death, that hath such means to die. *Shakesp.*

This is only an infallibility upon *supposition*, that if a thing be true, it is impossible to be false. *Tillotson.*

Such an original irresistible notion is neither requisite upon *supposition* of a Deity, nor is pretended to by religion. *Bentley.*

SUPPOSITI'TIOUS. *adj.* [from *suppositus*, *supposititius*, Lat.] Not genuine; put by a trick into the place or character belonging to another.

The destruction of Mustapha was so fatal to Solyman's line, as the succession of the Turks from Solyman is suspected to be of strange blood; for that Selymus II. was thought to be *supposititious*. *Bacon.*

It is their opinion that no man ever killed his father; but that, if it should ever happen, the reputed son must have been illegitimate, *supposititious*, or begotten in adultery. *Addison.*

Some alterations in the globe tend rather to the benefit of the earth, and its productions, than their destruction, as all these *supposititious* ones manifestly would do. *Woodward.*

SUPPOSITI'TIOUSNESS. *n. s.* [from *supposititious.*] State of being counterfeit.

SUPPO'SITIVELY. *adv.* [from *suppose.*] Upon supposition.

The unreformed sinner may have some hope *suppositively*, if he do change and repent: the honest penitent may hope positively. *Hammond.*

SUPPO'SITORY. *n. s.* [*suppositoire*, Fr. *suppositorium*, Latin.] A kind of solid clyster.

Nothing relieves the head more than the piles, therefore *suppositories* of honey, aloes, and rock-salt ought to be tried. *Arb.*

To SU'PPRESS. *v. a.* [*supprimo*, *suppressus*, Lat. *supprimer*, Fr.]

1. To crush; to overpower; to overwhelm; to subdue; to reduce from any state of activity or commotion.

Glo'ster would have armour out of the Tower,
To crown himself king and *suppress* the prince. *Shak. H.VI.*

Every rebellion, when it is *suppressed*, doth make the subject weaker, and the prince stronger. *Davies on Ireland.*

Sir William Herbert, with a well armed and ordered company, set sharply upon them; and oppressing some of the forwardest of them by death, *suppressed* the residue by fear. *Hayw.*

2. To conceal; not to tell; not to reveal.

Things not reveal'd, which th' invisible King,
Only omniscient, hath *suppress'd* in night. *Milton.*

Still she *suppresses* the name, and this keeps him in a pleasing suspense; and, in the very close of her speech, she indirectly mentions it. *Broome's Notes on the Odyssey.*

3. To

3. To keep in; not to let out.

Well did'st thou, Richard, to *suppress* thy voice;
For had the passions of thy heart burst out,
I fear we should have seen decypher'd there
More ranc'rous spight, more furious raging broils. *Shakesp.*

SUPPRE'SSION. *n. s.* [*suppression*, Fr. *suppressio*, Lat. from *suppress.*]
1. The act of suppressing.
2. Not publication.

You may depend upon a *suppression* of these verses. *Pope.*

SUPPRE'SSOR. *n. s.* [from *suppress.*] One that suppresses, crushes, or conceals.

To SU'PPURATE. *v. a.* [from *pus puris*, Lat. *suppurer*, Fr.] To generate *pus* or matter.

This disease is generally fatal: if it *suppurates* the pus, it is evacuated into the lower belly, where it produceth putrefaction. *Arbuthnot on Diet.*

To SU'PPURATE. *v. n.* To grow to pus.

SUPPURA'TION. *n. s.* [*suppuration*, French; from *suppurate.*]
1. The ripening or change of the matter of a tumour into pus.

If the inflammation be gone too far towards a *suppuration*, then it must be promoted with suppuratives, and opened by incision. *Wiseman.*

This great attrition must produce a great propensity to the putrescent alkaline condition of the fluids, and consequently to *suppurations*. *Arbuthnot on Aliments.*

2. The matter suppurated.

The great physician of souls sometimes cannot cure without cutting us: sin has festered inwardly, and he must launce the imposthume, to let out death with the *suppuration*. *South.*

SU'PPURATIVE. *adj.* [*suppuratif*, French; from *suppurate.*] Digestive; generating matter.

SUPPUTA'TION. *n. s.* [*supputation*, French; *supputo*, Latin.] Reckoning; account; calculation; computation.

From these differing properties of day and year arise difficulties in carrying on and reconciling the *supputation* of time in long measures. *Holder on Time.*

The Jews saw every day their Messiah still farther removed from them; that the promises of their doctors, about his speedy manifestations, were false; that the predictions of the prophets, whom they could now no longer understand, were covered with obscurity; that all the *supputations* of time either terminated in Jesus Christ, or were without a period. *West.*

To SUPPU'TE. *v. a.* [from *supputo*, Latin.] To reckon; to calculate.

SU'PRA, [Latin] in composition, signifies *above*, or *before*.

SUPRALA'PSARY. *adj.* [*supra* and *lapsus*, Latin.] Antecedent to the fall of man.

SUPRAVU'LGAR. *adj.* [*supra* and *vulgar.*] Above the vulgar.

None of these motives can prevail with a man to furnish himself with *supravulgar* and noble qualities. *Collier.*

SUPRE'MACY. *n. s.* [from *supreme.*] Highest place; highest authority; state of being supreme.

No appeal may be made unto any one of higher power, in as much as the order of your discipline admitteth no standing inequality of courts, no spiritual judge to have any ordinary superior on earth, but as many *supremacies* as there are parishes and several congregations. *Hooker.*

As we under heav'n are supreme head,
So, under him, that great *supremacy*,
Where we do reign, we will alone uphold. *Shakesp. K. John.*

I am asham'd that women
Seek for rule, *supremacy*, and sway,
When they are bound to serve, love, and obey. *Shakesp.*

Put to proof his high *supremacy*,
Whether upheld by strength, or chance, or fate. *Milton.*

Henry VIII. had no intention to change religion: he continued to burn protestants after he had cast off the pope's *supremacy*. *Swift.*

You're formed by nature for this *supremacy*, which is already granted from the distinguishing character of your writing. *Dryden to Dorset.*

To deny him this *supremacy* is to dethrone the Deity, and give his kingdom to another. *Rogers.*

From some wild curs that from their masters ran,
Abhorring the *supremacy* of man,
In woods and caves the rebel race began. *Dryden.*

SUPRE'ME. *adj.* [*supremus*, Latin.]
1. Highest in dignity; highest in authority. It may be observed that *superiour* is used often of local elevation, but *supreme* only of intellectual or political.

As no man serveth God, and loveth him not; so neither can any man sincerely love God, and not extremely abhor that sin which is the highest degree of treason against the *supreme* Guide and Monarch of the whole world, with whose divine authority and power it investeth others. *Hooker.*

The god of soldiers,
With the consent of *supreme* Jove, inform
Thy thoughts with nobleness. *Shakesp. Coriolanus.*

This strength, the seat of Deity *supreme*. *Milton.*

The monarch oak, the patriarch of the trees,
Shoots rising up, and spreads by slow degrees;
Three centuries he grows, and three he stays
Supreme in state, and in three more decays. *Dryden.*

2. Highest; most excellent.

My soul akes
To know, when two authorities are up,
Neither *supreme*, how soon confusion
May enter 'twixt the gap of both. *Shakesp. Coriolanus.*

No single virtue we could most commend,
Whether the wife, the mother, or the friend;
For she was all in that *supreme* degree,
That as no one prevail'd, so all was she. *Dryden.*

To him both heav'n
The right had giv'n,
And his own love bequeath'd *supreme* command. *Dryden.*

SUPRE'MELY. *adv.* [from the adjective.] In the highest degree.

The starving chemist in his golden views
Supremely blest, the poet in his muse. *Pope.*

SUR. [*sur*, French.] In composition, means *upon* or *over and above.*

SU'RADDITION. *n. s.* [*sur* and *addition.*] Something added to the name.

He serv'd with glory and admir'd success,
So gain'd the *suraddition*, Leonatus. *Shak. Cymbeline.*

SU'RAL. *adj.* [from *sura*, Latin.] Being in the calf of the leg.

He was wounded in the inside of the calf of his leg, into the *sural* artery. *Wiseman's Surgery.*

SU'RANCE. *n. s.* [from *sure.*] Warrant; security; assurance.

Give some *surance* that thou art revenge;
Stab them, or tear them on thy chariot-wheels. *Shakesp.*

To SURBA'TE. *v. a.* [*solbatir*, French.] To bruise and batter the feet with travel; to harrass; to fatigue.

Their march they continued all that night, the horsemen often alighting, that the foot might ride, and others taking many of them behind them; however they could not but be extremely weary and *surbated*. *Clarendon.*

Chalky land *surbates* and spoils oxens feet. *Mortimer.*

SURBE'T. The participle passive of *surbeat.*

A bear and tyger being met
In cruel fight on Lybick ocean wide,
Espy a traveller with feet *surbet*,
Whom they in equal prey hope to divide. *Fairy Queen.*

To SURCE'ASE. *v. n.* [*sur* and *cesser*, French; *cesso*, Latin.]
1. To be at an end; to stop; to cease; to be no longer in use or being.

Small favours will my prayers increase:
Granting my suit, you give me all;
And then my prayers must needs *surcease*;
For I have made your godhead fall. *Donne.*

2. To leave off; to practise no longer; to refrain finally.

To fly altogether from God, to despair, that creatures unworthy shall be able to obtain any thing at his hands, and under that pretence to *surcease* from prayers, as bootless or fruitless offices, were to him no less injurious than pernicious to our own souls. *Hooker.*

Nor did the British squadrons now *surcease*
To gall their foes o'erwhelm'd. *Philips.*

To SURCEA'SE. *v. a.* To stop; to put to an end. Obsolete.

All pain hath end, and every war hath peace;
But mine no price, nor prayer, may *surcease*. *Spenser.*

SURCEA'SE. *n. s.* Cessation; stop.

It might very well agree with your principles, if your discipline were fully planted, even to send out your writs of *surcease* unto all courts of England for the most things handled in them. *Hooker.*

SURCHA'RGE. *n. s.* [*surcharge*, French; from the verb.] Overburthen; more than can be well born.

The air, after receiving a charge, doth not receive a *surcharge*, or greater charge, with like appetite as it doth the first. *Bacon's Natural History.*

An object of *surcharge* or excess destroyeth the sense; as the light of the sun, the eye; a violent sound near the ear, the hearing. *Bacon's Natural History.*

The moralists make this raging of a lion to be a *surcharge* of one madness upon another. *L'Estrange.*

To SURCHA'RGE. *v. a.* [*surcharger*, French.] To overload; to overburthen.

They put upon every portion of land a reasonable rent, which they called Romescot, the which might not *surcharge* the tenant or freeholder. *Spenser on Ireland.*

Tamas was returned to Tauris, in hope to have suddenly surprised his enemy, *surcharged* with the pleasures of so rich a city. *Knolles's History of the Turks.*

More remov'd,
Lest heav'n *surcharg'd* with potent multitude,
Might hap to move new broils. *Milton's Paradise Lost.*

He ceas'd, discerning Adam with such joy
Surcharg'd, as had, like grief, been dew'd in tears
Without the vent of words. *Milton's Paradise Lost.*

When graceful sorrow in her pomp appears,
Sure she is dress'd in Melesinda's tears:
Your head reclin'd, as hiding grief from view,
Droops like a rose *surcharg'd* with morning dew. *Dryden.*

SURCHA'RGER. *n. s.* [from *surcharge.*] One that overburthens.

SURCI'NGLE. *n. s.* [*sur* and *cingulum*, Latin.]
1. A girth with which the burthen is bound upon a horse.
2. The girdle of a cassock.

Justly he chose the *surcingle* and gown. *Marvel.*

SU'RCLE. *n. s.* [*surculus*, Latin.] A shoot; a twig; a sucker. Not in general use.

It is an arboreous excrescence, or superplant, which the tree cannot assimilate, and therefore sprouteth not forth in boughs and *surcles* of the same shape unto the tree. *Brown.*

The basilica dividing into two branches below the cubit, the outward sendeth two *surcles* unto the thumb. *Brown.*

SU'RCOAT. *n. s.* [*surcot*, old French; *sur* and *coat.*] A short coat worn over the rest of the dress.

The honourable habiliments, as robes of state, parliament-robes, the *surcoat*, and mantle. *Camden.*

The commons were besotted in excess of apparel, in wide *surcoats* reaching to their loins. *Camden.*

That day in equal arms they fought for fame;
Their swords, their shields, their *surcoats* were the same. *Dry.*

SURD. *adj.* [*surdus*, Latin.]
1. Deaf; wanting the sense of hearing.
2. Unheard; not perceived by the ear.
3. Not expressed by any term.

SURE. *adj.* [*seure*, French.]
1. Certain; unfailing; infallible.

The testimony of the Lord is *sure*, and giveth wisdom unto the simple. *Psalm* xix. 7.

Who knows,
Let this be good, whether our angry foe
Can give it, or will ever? How he can,
Is doubtful; that he never will, is *sure*. *Milt. Parad. Lost.*

2. Certainly doomed.

Our coin beyond sea is valued according to the silver in it: sending it in bullion is the safest way, and the weightiest is *sure* to go. *Locke.*

3. Confident; undoubting; certainly knowing.

Friar Laurence met them both;
Him he knew well, and guess'd that it was she;
But, being mask'd, he was not *sure* of it. *Shakespeare.*

Let no man seek what may befall;
Evil he may be *sure*. *Milton.*

The youngest in the morning are not *sure*
That 'till the night their life they can secure. *Denham.*

While sore of battle, while our wounds are green,
Why would we tempt the doubtful dye agen?
In wars renew'd, uncertain of success,
Sure of a share, as umpires of the peace. *Dryden.*

If you find nothing new in the matter, I am *sure* much less will you in the stile. *Wake.*

Be silent always, when you doubt your sense;
And speak, though *sure*, with seeming diffidence. *Pope.*

4. Safe; firm; certain; past doubt or danger.

Thy kingdom shall be *sure* unto thee, after that thou shalt have known that the heavens do rule. *Dan.* iv. 26.

He bad me make *sure* of the bear, before I sell his skin. *L'Est.*

They would make others on both sides *sure* of pleasing, in preference to instruction. *Dryden's Dufresnoy.*

They have a nearer and *surer* way to the felicity of life, by tempering their passions, and reducing their appetites. *Temple.*

A peace cannot fail us, provided we make *sure* of Spain. *Temple.*

Revenge is now my joy; he's not for me,
And I'll make *sure* he ne'er shall be for thee. *Dryden.*

I bred you up to arms, rais'd you to power,
All to make *sure* the vengeance of this day,
Which even this day has ruin'd. *Dryd. Spanish Fryar.*

Make Cato *sure*, and give up Utica,
Cæsar will ne'er refuse thee such a trifle. *Addison's Cato.*

They have reason to make all actions worthy of observation, which are *sure* to be observed. *Atterbury.*

5. Firm; stable; not liable to failure.

Thou the garland wear'st successively;
Yet though thou stand'st more *sure* than I could do,
Thou art not firm enough. *Shakesp. Henry* IV.

I wish your horses swift and *sure* of foot,
And so I do commend you to their backs. *Shakes. Macbeth.*

Virtue, dear friend, needs no defence;
The *surest* guard is innocence. *Roscommon.*

Partition firm and *sure* the waters to divide. *Milton.*

Doubting thus of innate principles, men will call pulling up the old foundations of knowledge and certainty: I persuade myself that the way I have pursued, being conformable to truth, lays those foundations *surer*. *Locke.*

To prove a genuine birth,
On female truth assenting faith relies:
Thus manifest of right, I build my claim,
Sure founded on a fair maternal fame. *Pope's Odyssey.*

6. *To be* SURE. Certainly. This is a vitious expression: more properly *be sure.*

Objects of sense would then determine the views of all such, *to be sure*, who conversed perpetually with them. *Atterbury.*

Though the chymist could not calcine the *caput mortuum*, to obtain its fixed salt, *to be sure* it must have some. *Arbuthnot.*

SURE. *adv.* [*surement*, French.] Certainly; without doubt; doubtless. It is generally without emphasis; and, notwithstanding its original meaning, expresses rather doubt than assertion.

Something, *sure*, of state
Hath puddled his clear spirit. *Shakespeare.*

Her looks were flush'd, and sullen was her mien,
That *sure* the virgin goddess, had she been
Aught but a virgin, must the guilt have seen. *Addison.*

Sure the queen would wish him still unknown:
She loaths, detests him, flies his hated presence. *Smith.*

Sure, upon the whole, a bad author deserves better usage than a bad critick. *Pope.*

SUREFO'OTED. *adj.* [*sure* and *foot.*] Treading firmly; not stumbling.

True earnest sorrows, rooted miseries,
Anguish in grain, vexations ripe and blown,
Surefooted griefs, solid calamities. *Herbert.*

SU'RELY. *adv.* [from *sure.*]
1. Certainly; undoubtedly; without doubt. It is often used rather to intend and strengthen the meaning of the sentence, than with any distinct and explicable meaning.

In the day that thou eatest thereof thou shalt *surely* die. *Gen.*

Thou *surely* hadst not come sole fugitive. *Milton.*

He that created something out of nothing, *surely* can raise great things out of small. *South.*

The curious have thought the most minute affairs of Rome worth notice; and *surely* the consideration of their wealth is at least of as great importance as grammatical criticisms. *Arb.*

2. Firmly; without hazard.

He that walketh righteously, walketh *surely.*

SU'RENESS. *n. s.* [from *sure.*] Certainty.

He diverted himself with the speculation of the seed of coral; and for more *sureness* he repeats it. *Woodward.*

SU'RETISHIP. *n. s.* [from *surety.*] The office of a surety or bondsman; the act of being bound for another.

Hath not the greatest slaughter of armies been effected by stratagem? And have not the fairest estates been destroyed by *suretiship?* *South.*

Idly, like prisoners, which whole months will swear
That only *suretiship* hath brought them there. *Donne.*

If here not clear'd, no *suretyship* can bail
Condemned debtors from th' eternal gaol. *Denham.*

SU'RETY. *n. s.* [*sureté*, French.]
1. Certainty; indubitableness.

There the princesses determining to bathe, thought it was so privileged a place as no body durst presume to come thither; yet, for the more *surety*, they looked round about. *Sidney.*

Know of a *surety* that thy seed shall be a stranger. *Gen.* xv.

2. Foundation of stability; support.

We our state
Hold, as you your's, while our obedience holds;
On other *surety* none. *Milton.*

3. Evidence; ratification; confirmation.

She call'd the saints to *surety*,
That she would never put it from her finger,
Unless she gave it to yourself. *Shakespeare.*

4. Security against loss or damage; security for payment.

There remains unpaid
A hundred thousand more, in *surety* of the which
One part of Acquitain is bound to us. *Shakespeare.*

5. Hostage; bondsman; one that gives security for another; one that is bound for another.

That you may well perceive I have not wrong'd you,
One of the greatest in the Christian world
Shall be my *surety*. *Shakesp. All's well that ends well.*

I will be *surety* for him; of my hand shalt thou require him. *Gen.* xliii. 9.

Yet be not *surety*, if thou be a father;
Love is a personal debt: I cannot give
My children's right, nor ought he take it. *Herbert.*

All, in infancy, are by others presented with the desires of the parents, and intercession of *sureties*, that they may be early admitted by baptism into the school of Christ. *Hammond.*

SU'RFACE. *n. s.* [*sur* and *face*, French.] Superficies; outside; superfice. It is accented by *Milton* on the last syllable.

Which of us who beholds the bright *surface*
Of this ethereous mold, whereon we stand. *Milton.*

All their *surfaces* shall be truly plain, or truly spherical, and look all the same way, so as together to compose one even *surface*. *Newton's Opt.*

Errours like straws upon the *surface* flow;
He who would search for pearls must dive below. *Dryden.*

To SU'RFEIT. *v. a.* [from *sur* and *faire*, French, *to do more than enough, to overdo.*] To feed with meat or drink to satiety and sickness; to cram overmuch.

The *surfeited* grooms
Do mock their charge with snores. *Shakespeare.*

To Su'rfeit. *v. n.* To be fed to satiety and sickness.

The commonwealth is sick of their own choice;
Their over-greedy love hath *surfeited.* *Shakesp. Henry IV.*

They are as sick that *surfeit* with too much, as they that starve with nothing. *Shakesp. Merchant of Venice.*

Take heed lest your hearts be overcharged with *surfeiting* and drunkenness. *Luke* xxi. 34.

Though some had so *surfeited* in the vineyards, and with the wines, that they had been left behind, the generosity of the Spaniards sent them all home. *Clarendon.*

They must be let loose to the childish play they fancy, which they should be weaned from, by being made to *surfeit* of it. *Locke.*

Su'rfeit. *n. s.* [from the verb.] Sickness or satiety caused by overfulness.

When we are sick in fortune, often the *surfeits* of our own behaviour, we make guilty of our disasters the sun, the moon and stars. *Shakesp. King Lear.*

How ill white hairs become a fool and jester!
I have long dream'd of such a kind of man,
So *surfeit* swell'd, so old, and so profane. *Shakesp. H. IV.*

Now comes the sick hour that his *surfeit* made;
Now shall he try his friends that flatter'd him. *Shak. R. II.*

Thou'st years upon thee, and thou art too full
Of the wars *surfeits* to go rove with one
That's yet unbruis'd. *Shakes. Coriolanus.*

Why, disease, do'st thou molest
Ladies, and of them the best?
Do not men grow sick of rites,
To thy altars, by their nights
Spent in *surfeits?* *Ben. Johnson.*

Surfeits many times turn to purges, both upwards and downwards. *Bacon's Natural History.*

Peace, which he lov'd in life, did lend
Her hand to bring him to his end;
When age and death call'd for the score,
No *surfeits* were to reckon for. *Crashaw:*

Our father
Has ta'en himself a *surfeit* of the world,
And cries, it is not safe that we should taste it. *Otway.*

Su'rfeiter. *n. s.* [from *surfeit.*] One who riots; a glutton.

I did not think
This am'rous *surfeiter* would have donn'd his helm
For such a petty war. *Shak. Ant. and Cleopatra.*

Su'rfeitwater. *n. s.* [*surfeit* and *water.*] Water that cures surfeits.

A little cold-distilled poppywater, which is the true *surfeit-water,* with ease and abstinence, often ends distempers in the beginning. *Locke.*

Surge. *n. s.* [from *surgo,* Latin.] A swelling sea; wave rolling above the general surface of the water; billow; wave.

The realm was left, like a ship in a storm, amidst all the raging *surges,* unruled and undirected of any. *Spenser.*

The wind-shak'd *surge,* with high and monstrous main,
Seems to cast water on the burning bear,
And quench the guards of the ever-fired pole:
I never did like molestation view
On the enchafed flood. *Shakesp. Othello.*

He trod the water,
Whose enmity he flung aside, and breasted
The *surge* most swoln that met him. *Shakesp. Tempest.*

It was formerly famous for the unfortunate loves of Hero and Leander, drowned in the uncompassionate *surges.* *Sandys.*

The sulph'rous hail
Shot after us in storm, o'erblown, hath laid
The fiery *surge,* that from the precipice
Of heav'n receiv'd us falling. *Milton's Paradise Lost.*

He sweeps the skies, and clears the cloudy North:
He flies aloft, and with impetuous roar
Pursues the foaming *surges* to the shore. *Dryden.*

Thetis, near Ismena's swelling flood,
With dread beheld the rolling *surges* sweep
In heaps his slaughter'd sons into the deep. *Pope.*

To Surge. *v. n.* [from *surgo,* Latin.] To swell; to rise high.

From midst of all the main
The *surging* waters like a mountain rise. *Fairy Queen.*

He, all in rage, his sea-god sire besought,
Some cursed vengeance on his son to cast;
From *surging* gulfs two monsters straight were brought. *F. Q.*

Up from the bottom turn'd by furious winds
And *surging* waves, as mountains, to assault
Heav'n's height, and with the centre mix the pole. *Milton.*

Not with indented wave,
Prone on the ground, as since; but on his rear,
Circular base of rising folds, that tower'd
Fold above fold, a *surging* maze! *Milton's Parad. Lost.*

Surging waves against a solid rock,
Though all to shivers dash'd, th' assault renew,
Vain batt'ry, and in froth or bubbles end. *Milton.*

Su'rgeon. *n. s.* [Corrupted by conversation from *chirurgeon.*] One who cures by manual operation; one whose duty is to act in external maladies by the direction of the physician.

The wound was past the cure of a better *surgeon* than myself, so as I could but receive some few of her dying words. *Sid.*

I meddle with no woman's matters; but withal, I am a *surgeon* to old shoes. *Shakesp. Julius Cæsar.*

He that hath wounded his neighbour, is tied to the expences of the *surgeon,* and other incidences. *Taylor.*

Though most were sorely wounded, none were slain:
The *surgeons* soon despoil'd them of their arms,
And some with salves they cure. *Dryden.*

Su'rgeonry. } *n. s.* [for *chirurgery.*] The act of curing by
Su'rgery. } manual operation.

It would seem very evil *surgery* to cut off every unsound part of the body, which, being by other due means recovered, might afterwards do good service. *Spenser.*

But strangely visited people,
The mere despair of *surgery,* he cures. *Shakesp. Macbeth.*

They are often tarr'd over with the *surgery* of our sheep, and would you have us kiss tar? *Shakespeare.*

Su'rgy. *adj.* [from *surge.*] Rising in billows.

What cause hath led you to the Spartan court?
Do publick or domestick cares constrain
This toilsome voyage o'er the *surgy* main? *Pope.*

Su'rlily. *adv.* [from *surly.*] In a surly manner.

Su'rliness. *n. s.* [from *surly.*] Gloomy moroseness; sour anger.

Thus pale they meet; their eyes with fury burn;
None greets; for none the greeting will return;
But in dumb *surliness,* each arm'd with care,
His foe profest, as brother of the war. *Dryden.*

Su'rling. *n. s.* [from *surly.*] A sour morose fellow. Not used.

These sour *surlings* are to be commended to sieur Gaulard. *Camden.*

SU'RLY. *adj.* [from ꞅup, sour, Saxon.] Gloomily morose; rough; uncivil; sour; silently angry.

'Tis like you'll prove a jolly *surly* groom,
That take it on you at the first so roundly. *Shakespeare.*

That *surly* spirit, melancholy,
Had bak'd thy blood, and made it heavy thick,
Which else runs tickling up and down the veins,
Making that ideot laughter keep mens eyes,
And strain their cheeks to idle merriment. *Shakes. K. John.*

Against the Capitol I met a lion,
Who glar'd upon me, and went *surly* by,
Without annoying me. *Shakesp. Julius Cæsar.*

Repuls'd by *surly* grooms, who wait before
The sleeping tyrant's interdicted door. *Dryden.*

What if among the courtly tribe
You lost a place, and sav'd a bribe?
And then in *surly* mood came here
To fifteen hundred pounds a year,
And fierce against the whigs harangu'd? *Swift.*

The zephyrs floating loose, the timely rains,
Now soften'd into joy the *surly* storms. *Thomson's Summer.*

To Surmi'se. *v. a.* [*surmise,* French.] To suspect; to image imperfectly; to imagine without certain knowledge.

Man coveteth what exceedeth the reach of sense, yea somewhat above capacity of reason, somewhat divine and heavenly, which with hidden exultation it rather *surmiseth* than conceiveth; somewhat it seeketh, and what that is directly it knoweth not; yet very intentive desire thereof doth so incite it, that all other known delights and pleasures are laid aside, and they give place to the search of this but only suspected desire. *Hooker.*

Of questions and strifes of words cometh envy, railings, and evil *surmisings.* 1 *Tim.* vi. 4.

Surmise not
His presence to these narrow bounds confin'd. *Milton.*

It wasted nearer yet, and then she knew
That what before she but *surmis'd,* was true. *Dryden.*

This change was not wrought by altering the form or position of the earth, as was *surmised* by a very learned man, but by dissolving it. *Woodward.*

Surmi'se. *n. s.* [*surmise,* French.] Imperfect notion; suspicion; imagination not supported by knowledge.

To let go private *surmises,* whereby the thing itself is not made better or worse; if just and allowable reasons might lead them to do as they did, then are these censures frustrate. *Hook.*

They were by law of that proud tyranness,
Provok'd with wrath, and envy's false *surmise,*
Condemned to that dungeon merciless,
Where they should live in woe, and die in wretchedness. *F. Q.*

Aaron is gone; and my compassionate heart
Will not permit my eyes once to behold
The thing, whereat it trembles by *surmise.* *Shakespeare.*

My thought, whose murthering yet is but fantastical,
Shakes so my single state of man, that function
Is smother'd in *surmise.* *Shakesp. Macbeth.*

We double honour gain
From his *surmise* prov'd false. *Milton.*

No sooner did they espy the English turning from them, but they were of opinion that they fled towards their shipping: this *surmise* was occasioned, for that the English ships removed the day before. *Hayward.*

Hence guilty joys, distastes, *surmises*,
False oaths, false tears, deceits, disguises. *Pope.*

No man ought to be charged with principles he actually disowns, unless his practices contradict his profession; not upon small *surmises*. *Swift.*

To SURMO'UNT. *v. a.* [*surmonter*, French.]

1. To rise above.

The mountains of Olympus, Atho, and Atlas, over-reach and *surmount* all winds and clouds. *Raleigh.*

2. To conquer; to overcome.

Though no resistance was made, the English had much ado to *surmount* the natural difficulties of the place the greatest part of one day. *Hayward.*

He hardly escaped to the Persian court; from whence, if the love of his country had not *surmounted* its base ingratitude to him, he had many invitations to return at the head of the Persian fleet; but he rather chose a voluntary death. *Swift.*

3. To surpass; to exceed.

What *surmounts* the reach
Of human sense, I shall delineate so,
By lik'ning spiritual to corporeal forms,
As may express them best. *Milton's Paradise Lost.*

SURMO'UNTABLE. *adj.* [from *surmount.*] Conquerable; superable.

SU'RMULLET. *n. s.* [*mugil*, Lat.] A sort of fish. *Ainsworth.*

SU'RNAME. *n. s.* [*surnom*, French.]

1. The name of the family; the name which one has over and above the Christian name.

Many which were mere English joined with the Irish against the king, taking on them Irish habits and customs, which could never since be clean wiped away; of which sort be most of the *surnames* that end in *an*, as Hernan, Shinan, and Mungan, which now account themselves natural Irish. *Spenser.*

He, made heir not only of his brother's kingdom, but of his virtues and haughty thoughts, and of the *surname* also of Barbarossa, began to aspire unto the empire of all that part of Africk. *Knolles's History of the Turks.*

The epithets of great men, monsieur Boileau is of opinion, were in the nature of *surnames*, and repeated as such. *Pope.*

2. An appellation added to the original name.

Witness may
My *surname* Coriolanus: the painful service,
The extreme dangers, and the drops of blood
Shed for my thankless country, are requited
But with that *surname*. *Shak. Coriolanus.*

To SU'RNAME. *v. a.* [*surnommer*, Fr. from the noun.] To name by an appellation added to the original name.

The people of Rome have by common voice,
In election for the Roman empire,
Chosen Andronicus, *surnamed* Pius. *Shak. Titus Andronicus.*

Another shall subscribe with his hand unto the Lord, and *surname* himself by the name of Israel. *Is.* xliv. 5.

Pyreicus, only famous for counterfeiting earthen pitchers, a scullery, rogues together by the ears, was *sirnamed* Rupographus. *Peacham on Drawing.*

How he, *surnam'd* of Africa, dismiss'd
In his prime youth the fair Iberian maid. *Milton.*

God commanded man what was good; but the devil *surnamed* it evil, and thereby baffled the command. *South.*

To SURPA'SS. *v. a.* [*surpasser*, French.] To excel; to exceed; to go beyond in excellence.

The climate's delicate,
Fertile the isle, the temple much *surpassing*
The common praise it bears. *Shak. Winter's Tale.*

O, by what name, for thou above all these,
Above mankind, or aught than mankind higher,
Surpassest far my naming! how may I
Adore thee, author of this universe? *Milton.*

Achilles, Homer's hero, in strength and courage *surpassed* the rest of the Grecian army. *Dryden.*

A nymph of late there was,
Whose heav'nly form her fellows did *surpass*,
The pride and joy of fair Arcadia's plains. *Dryden.*

Under or near the Line are mountains, which, for bigness and number, *surpass* those of colder countries, as much as the heat there *surpasses* that of those countries. *Woodward.*

SURPA'SSING. *participial adj.* [from *surpass.*] Excellent in an high degree.

O thou! that with *surpassing* glory crown'd,
Look'st from thy sole dominion like the god
Of this new world. *Milton's Paradise Lost.*

His miracles proved him to be sent from God, not more by that infinite power that was seen in them, than by that *surpassing* goodness they demonstrated to the world. *Calamy.*

SU'RPLICE. *n. s.* [*surpelis*, *surplis*, Fr. *superpellicium*, Lat.] The white garb which the clergy wear in their acts of ministration.

It will wear the *surplice* of humility over the black gown of a big heart. *Shakes. All's well that ends well.*

The cinctus gabinus is a long garment, not unlike a *surplice*, which would have trailed on the ground, had it hung loose, and was therefore gathered about the middle with a girdle. *Addison.*

SU'RPLUS. } *n. s.* [*sur* and *plus*, French.] A supernume-
SURPLU'SAGE. } rary part; overplus; what remains when use is satisfied.

If then thee list my offered grace to use,
Take what thou please of all this *surplusage*;
If thee list not, leave have thou to refuse. *Spenser.*

That you have vouchsaf'd my poor house to visit,
It is a *surplus* of your grace. *Shakespeare.*

When the price of corn falleth, men give over *surplus* tillage, and break no more ground. *Carew's Survey of Cornwall.*

We made a substance so disposed to fluidity, that by so small an agitation as only the *surplusage* of that which the ambient air is wont to have about the middle even of a Winter's day, above what it hath in the first part. *Boyle.*

The officers spent all, so as there was no *surplusage* of treasure; and yet that all was not sufficient. *Davies.*

Whatsoever degrees of assent one affords a proposition beyond the degrees of evidence, it is plain all that *surplusage* of assurance is owing not to the love of truth. *Locke.*

SURPRI'SAL. } *n. s.* [*surprise*, French; from the verb.]
SURPRI'SE. }

1. The act of taking unawares; the state of being taken unawares.

Parents should mark heedfully the witty excuses of their children, especially at suddains and *surprisals*; but rather mark than pamper them. *Wotton.*

This let him know,
Lest, wilfully transgressing, he pretend
Suprisal, unadmonish'd, unforewarn'd. *Milton's Par. Lost.*

I set aside the taking of St. Jago and St. Domingo in Hispaniola, as *surprizes* rather than encounters. *Bacon.*

This strange *surprisal* put the knight
And wrathful squire into a fright. *Hudibras.*

There is a vast difference between them, as vast as between inadvertency and deliberation, between *surprize* and set purpose. *South.*

2. A dish, I suppose, which has nothing in it.

Few care for carving trifles in disguise,
Or that fantastick dish some call *surprise*. *King's Cookery.*

3. Sudden confusion or perplexity.

To SURPRI'SE. *v. a.* [*surpris*, French, from *surprendre.*]

1. To take unawares; to fall upon unexpectedly.

The castle of Macduff I will *surprise*,
Seize upon Fife, give to the edge o' th' sword
His wife, his babes. *Shakespeare's Macbeth.*

Now do our ears before our eyes,
Like men in mists,
Discover who'd the state *surprize*,
And who resists. *Ben. Johnson.*

Bid her well beware,
Lest, by some fair appearing good *surpris'd*,
She dictate false, and misinform the will. *Milton.*

How shall he keep, what, sleeping or awake,
A weaker may *surprise*, a stronger take? *Pope.*

Who can speak
The mingled passions that *surpriz'd* his heart! *Thomson.*

2. To astonish by something wonderful.

People were not so much frighted as *surprized* at the bigness of the camel. *L'Estrange.*

3. To confuse or perplex by something sudden.

Up he starts, discover'd and *surpris'd*. *Milton.*

SURPRI'SING. *participial adj.* [from *surprise.*] Wonderful; raising sudden wonder or concern.

The greatest actions of a celebrated person, however *surprising* and extraordinary, are no more than what are expected from him. *Addison's Spectator.*

SURPRI'SINGLY. *adv.* [from *surprising.*] To a degree that raises wonder; in a manner that raises wonder.

If out of these ten thousand, we should take the men that are employed in publick business, the number of those who remain will be *surprizingly* little. *Addison.*

SU'RQUEDRY. *n. s.* [*sur* and *cuider*, old Fr. to think.] Overweening; pride; insolence. Obsolete.

They overcommen, were deprived
Of their proud beauty, and the one moiety
Transform'd to fish for their bold *surquedry*. *Fairy Queen.*

Late-born modesty
Hath got such root in easy waxen hearts,
That men may not themselves their own good parts
Extol, without suspect of *surquedry*. *Donne.*

SURREBU'TTER. *n. s.* [In law.] A second rebutter; answer to a rebutter. A term in the courts.

SURREJOI'NDER. *n. s.* [*surrejoindre*, French.] [In law.] A second defence of the plaintiff's action, opposite to the rejoinder of the defendant, which the civilians call *triplicatio*. *Bailey.*

To SURRE'NDER. *v. a.* [*surrendre*, old French.]

1. To yield up; to deliver up.

Solemn dedication of churches serve not only to make them publick, but further also to *surrender* up that right which otherwise

otherwise their founders might have in them, and to make God himself their owner. *Hooker.*

2. To deliver up an enemy.

Ripe age bade him *surrender* late,
His life and long good fortune unto final fate. *Fairfax.*

He willing to *surrender* up the castle, forbade his soldiers to have any talk with the enemy. *Knolles.*

To SURRE'NDER. *v. n.* To yield; to give ones self up.

This mighty Archimedes too *surrenders* now. *Glanville.*

SURRE'NDER. }
SURRE'NDRY. } *n. s.* [from the verb.]

1. The act of yielding.

Our general mother, with eyes
Of conjugal attraction unreprov'd,
And meek *surrender*, half-embracing lean'd
On our first father. *Milton's Paradise Lost.*

Having mustered up all the forces he could, the clouds above and the deeps below, he prepares for a *surrender*; asserting, from a mistaken computation, that all these will not come up to near the quantity requisite. *Woodward.*

Juba's *surrender*
Would give up Africk unto Cæsar's hands. *Addison.*

2. The act of resigning or giving up to another.

If our father carry authority with such disposition as he bears, this last *surrender* of his will but offend us. *Shakespeare.*

That hope quickly vanished upon the undoubted intelligence of that *surrender*. *Clarendon.*

As oppressed states made themselves homagers to the Romans to engage their protection, so we should have made an entire *surrendry* of ourselves to God, that we might have gained a title to his deliverances. *Decay of Piety.*

In passing a thing away by deed of gift, are required a *surrender* on the giver's part, of all the property he has in it; and to the making of a thing sacred, this *surrender* by its right owner is necessary. *South's Sermons.*

SURRE'PTION. *n. s.* [*surreptus*, Latin.] Surprise; sudden and unperceived invasion.

Sins compatible with a regenerate estate, are sins of a sudden *surreption*. *Hammond.*

SURREPTI'TIOUS. *adj.* [*surreptitius*, Latin.] Done by stealth; gotten or produced fraudulently.

Scaliger hath not translated the first; perhaps supposing it *surreptitious*, or unworthy so great an assertion. *Brown.*

The Masorites numbred not only the sections and lines, but even the words and letters of the Old Testament, the better to secure it from *surreptitious* practices. *Govern. of the Tongue.*

A correct copy of the Dunciad, the many *surreptitious* ones have rendered necessary. *Letter to Publ. of Pope's Dunciad.*

SURREPTI'TIOUSLY. *adv.* [from *surreptitious.*] By stealth; fraudulently.

Thou hast got it more *surreptitiously* than he did, and with less effect. *Govern. of the Tongue.*

To SU'RROGATE. *v. a.* [*surrogo*, Latin.] To put in the place of another.

SU'RROGATE. *n. s.* [*surrogatus*, Latin.] A deputy; a delegate; the deputy of an ecclesiastical judge.

To SURROU'ND. *v. a.* [*surronder*, Fr.] To environ; to encompass; to enclose on all sides.

Yelling monsters that with ceaseless cry
Surround me, as thou sawest. *Milton.*

Cloud and ever-during dark
Surrounds me, from the cheerful ways of men
Cut off. *Milton.*

Bad angels seen
On wing under the burning cope of hell,
'Twixt upper, neather, and *surrounding* fires. *Milton.*

As the bodies that *surround* us diversly affect our organs, the mind is forced to receive the impressions. *Locke.*

SURSO'LID. [In algebra.] The fourth multiplication or power of any number whatever taken as the root. *Trevoux.*

SURSO'LID *Problem.* [In mathematicks.] That which cannot be resolved but by curves of a higher nature than a conick section. *Harris.*

SURTOU'T. *n. s.* [French.] A large coat worn over all the rest.

The *surtout* if abroad you wear,
Repels the rigour of the air;
Would you be warmer, if at home
You had the fabrick, and the loom? *Prior.*

Sir Roger she mortally hated, and used to hire fellows to squirt kennel-water upon him, so that he was forced to wear a *surtout* of oiled cloth, by which means he came home pretty clean, except where the *surtout* was a little scanty. *Arbuthnot.*

To SURVE'NE. *v. a.* [*survenir*, Fr.] To supervene; to come as an addition.

Hippocrates mentions a suppuration that *survenes* lethargies, which commonly terminates in a consumption. *Harvey.*

To SURVE'Y. *v. a.* [*surveoir*, old French.]

1. To overlook; to have under the view; to view as from a higher place.

Round he *surveys*, and well might where he stood,
So high above. *Milton.*

Though with those streams he no resemblance hold,
Whose foam is amber and their gravel gold;
His genuine and less guilty wealth t'explore,
Search not his bottom, but *survey* his shore. *Denham.*

2. To oversee as one in authority.

3. To view as examining.

The husbandman's self came that way,
Of custom to *survey* his ground,
And his trees of state incompass round. *Spenser.*

Early abroad he did the world *survey*,
As if he knew he had not long to stay. *Waller.*

With such alter'd looks
All pale and speechless, he *survey'd* me round. *Dryden.*

SURVE'Y. *n. s.* [from the verb.] View; prospect.

Her stars in all their vast *survey*
Useless besides! *Milton.*

Under his proud *survey* the city lies,
And like a mist beneath a hill doth rise. *Denham.*

No longer letted of his prey,
He leaps up at it with enrag'd desire,
O'erlooks the neighbours with a wide *survey*,
And nods at ev'ry house his threat'ning fire. *Dryden.*

SURVEY'OR. *n. s.* [from *survey.*]

1. An overseer; one placed to superintend others.

Were't not madness then,
To make the fox *surveyor* of the fold? *Shakesp. Henry VI.*

Bishop Fox was not only a grave counsellor for war or peace, but also a good *surveyor* of works. *Bacon's Henry VII.*

2. A measurer of land.

Should we survey
The plot of situation, and the model;
Question *surveyors*, know our own estate,
How able such a work to undergo,
To weigh against his opposite. *Shakespeare's Henry IV.*

Decempeda was a measuring rod for taking the dimensions of buildings; from hence came decempedator, for a *surveyor*, used by Cicero. *Arbuthnot on Aliments.*

SURVEY'ORSHIP. *n. s.* [from *surveyor.*] The office of a surveyor.

To SUR'VIEW. *v. a.* [*surveoir*, old French.] To overlook; to have in view. Not in use.

That turret's frame most admirable was,
Like highest heaven compassed round,
And lifted high above this earthly mass,
Which it *surview'd*, as hills do lower ground. *Fairy Queen.*

To SURVI'VE. *v. n.* [*supervivo*, Latin; *survivre*, Fr.]

1. To live after the death of another.

Those that *survive*, let Rome reward with love. *Shak.*

Try pleasure,
Which when no other enemy *survives*,
Still conquers all the conquerors. *Denham.*

2. To live after any thing.

Now that he is dead, his immortal fame *surviveth*, and flourisheth in the mouths of all people. *Spenser.*

The love of horses which they had alive,
And care of chariots after death *survive*. *Dryden.*

The rhapsodies, called the characteristicks, would never have *survived* the first edition, if they had not discovered so strong a tincture of infidelity. *Watts.*

3. To remain alive.

No longer now that golden age appears,
When patriarch-wits *surviv'd* a thousand years;
Now length of fame, our second life, is lost,
And bare threescore is all ev'n that can boast;
Our sons their father's failing language see,
And such as Chaucer is, shall Dryden be. *Pope.*

To SURVI'VE. *v. a.* To outlive.

I'll assure her of
Her widowhood, be it that she *survives* me,
In all my lands and leases whatsoever. *Shakespeare.*

SURVI'VER. *n. s.* [from *survive.*] One who outlives another.

Your father lost a father,
That father, his; and the *survivor* bound
In filial obligation, for some term,
To do obsequious sorrow. *Shakespeare's Hamlet.*

Although some died, the father beholding so many descents, the number of *survivors* must still be very great. *Brown.*

I did discern
From his *survivors*, I could nothing learn. *Denham.*

Her majesty is heir to the *survivor* of the late king. *Swift.*

SURVI'VERSHIP. *n. s.* [from *surviver.*] The state of outliving another.

Such offices granted in reversion were void, unless where the grant has been by *survivership*. *Ayliffe's Parergon.*

SUSCEPTIBI'LITY. *n. s.* [from *susceptible.*] Quality of admitting; tendency to admit.

The *susceptibility* of those influences, and the effects thereof is the general providential law whereby other physical beings are governed. *Hale.*

SUSCE'PTIBLE. *adj.* [*susceptible*, Fr. *Prior* has accented this improperly on the first syllable.] Capable of admitting.

He moulded him platonically to his own idea, delighting first in the choice of the materials, because he found him *susceptible* of good form. *Wotton.*

In their tender years they are more *susceptible* of virtuous impressions than afterwards, when solicited by vulgar inclinations. *L'Estrange.*

Children's minds are narrow, and usually *susceptible* but of one thought at once. *Locke on Education.*

Blow with empty words the *susceptible* flame. *Prior.*

SUSCE'PTION. *n. s.* [*susceptus*, Latin.] Act of taking.

A canon, promoted to holy orders, before he is of a lawful age for the *susception* of orders, shall have a voice in the chapter. *Ayliffe's Parergon.*

SUSCE'PTIVE. *adj.* [from *susceptus*, Lat. this word is more analogical, though less used than *susceptible.*] Capable to admit.

Since our nature is so *susceptive* of errours on all sides, it is fit we should have notices given us how far other persons may become the causes of false judgments. *Watts's Logick.*

SUSCI'PIENCY. *n. s.* [from *suscipient.*] Reception; admission.

SUSCI'PIENT. *n. s.* [*suscipiens*, Latin.] One who takes; one that admits or receives.

To SU'SCITATE. *v. n.* [*susciter*, French; *suscito*, Lat.] To rouse; to excite.

It concurreth but unto predisposed effects, and only *suscitates* those forms whose determinations are seminal, and proceed from the idea of themselves. *Brown's Vulgar Errours.*

SUSCITA'TION. *n. s.* [*suscitation*, Fr. from *suscitate.*] The act of rousing or exciting.

To SUSPE'CT. *v. a.* [*suspicio*, *suspectum*, Lat.]

1. To imagine with a degree of fear and jealousy what is not known.

Nothing makes a man *suspect* much, more than to know little; and therefore men should remedy suspicion by procuring to know more. *Bacon.*

Let us not then *suspect* our happy state,
As not secure. *Milton.*

From her hand I could *suspect* no ill. *Milton.*

2. To imagine guilty without proof.

Though many poets may *suspect* themselves for the partiality of parents to their youngest children, I know myself too well to be ever satisfied with my own conceptions. *Dryden.*

Some would persuade us that body and extension are the same thing, which change the signification of words, which I would not *suspect* them of, they having so severely condemned the philosophy of others. *Locke.*

3. To hold uncertain.

I cannot forbear a story which is so well attested, that I have no manner of reason to *suspect* the truth. *Addison.*

To SUSPE'CT. *v. n.* To imagine guilt.

If I *suspect* without cause, why then let me be your jest. *Shakespeare's Merry Wives of Windsor.*

SUSPE'CT. *part. adj.* [*suspect*, French.] Doubtful.

Sordid interests or affectation of strange relations are not like to render your reports *suspect* or partial. *Glanville.*

SUSPE'CT. *n. s.* [from the verb.] Suspicion; imagination without proof. Obsolete.

No fancy mine, no other wrong *suspect*,
Make me, O virtuous shame, thy laws neglect. *Sidney.*

The sale of offices and towns in France,
If they were known, as the *suspect* is great,
Would make thee quickly hop without a head. *Shakespeare.*

My most worthy master, in whose breast
Doubt and *suspect*, alas, are plac'd too late,
You should have fear'd false times, when you did feast. *Shak.*

There be so many false prints of praise, that a man may justly hold it a *suspect*. *Bacon.*

Nothing more jealous than a favourite towards the waining-time and *suspect* of satiety. *Wotton.*

They might hold sure intelligence
Among themselves, without *suspect* t'offend. *Daniel.*

If the king ends the differences, and takes away the *suspect*, the case will be no worse than when two duellists enter the field. *Suckling.*

To SUSPE'ND. *v. a.* [*suspendre*, French; *suspendo*, Latin.]

1. To hang; to make to hang by any thing.

As 'twixt two equal armies fate
Suspends uncertain victory;
Our souls, which to advance our state,
Were gone out, hung 'twixt her and me. *Donne.*

It is reported by Ruffinus, that in the temple of Serapis, there was an iron chariot *suspended* by loadstones; which stones removed, the chariot fell and was dashed to pieces. *Brown.*

2. To make to depend upon.

God hath in the scripture *suspended* the promise of eternal life upon this condition, that without obedience and holiness of life no man shall ever see the Lord. *Tillotson.*

3. To interrupt; to make to stop for a time.

The harmony
Suspended hell, and took with ravishment
The thronging audience. *Milton.*

The guard nor fights nor flies; their fate so near,
At once *suspends* their courage and their fear. *Denham.*

This is the hinge on which turns the liberty of intellectual beings, in their steady prosecution of true felicity, that they can *suspend* this prosecution in particular cases, till they have looked before them. *Locke.*

4. To delay; to hinder from proceeding.

Suspend your indignation against my brother, till you can derive from him better testimony of his intent. *Shakespeare.*

His answer did the nymph attend;
Her looks, her sighs, her gestures all did pray him;
But Godfrey wisely did his grant *suspend*,
He doubts the worst, and that a while did stay him. *Fairf.*

To themselves I left them;
For I *suspend* their doom. *Milton.*

The reasons for *suspending* the play were ill founded. *Dryden.*

The British dame, famed for resistless grace,
Contends not now but for the second place;
Our love *suspended*, we neglect the fair,
For whom we burn'd, to gaze adoring here. *Granvil.*

A man may *suspend* his choice from being determined for or against the thing proposed, till he has examined whether it be really of a nature to make him happy or no. *Locke.*

5. To debar for a time from the execution of an office or enjoyment of a revenue.

Good men should not be *suspended* from the exercise of their ministry, and deprived of their livelihood for ceremonies, which are on all hands acknowledged indifferent. *Sanderson.*

The bishop of London was summoned for not *suspending* Dr. Sharp. *Swift.*

SUSPE'NSE. *n. s.* [*suspens*, French; *suspensus*, Latin.]

1. Uncertainty; delay of certainty or determination; indetermination.

Till this be done, their good affection towards the safety of the church is acceptable; but the way they prescribe us to preserve it by, must rest in *suspense*. *Hooker.*

Such true joy's *suspense*
What dream can I present to recompense? *Waller.*

Ten days the prophet in *suspense* remain'd,
Would no man's fate pronounce; at last constrain'd
By Ithacus, he solemnly design'd
Me for the sacrifice. *Denham.*

In propositions, where though the proofs in view are of most moment, yet there are sufficient grounds to suspect that there is fallacy, or proofs as considerable to be produced on the contrary side, there *suspense* or dissent are often voluntary. *Locke.*

2. Act of withholding the judgment.

Whatever necessity determines to the pursuit of real bliss, the same necessity establishes *suspense*, deliberation and scrutiny, whether its satisfaction misleads from our true happiness. *Locke.*

3. Privation for a time; impediment for a time.

4. Stop in the midst of two opposites.

For thee the fates, severely kind, ordain
A cool *suspense* from pleasure or from pain. *Pope.*

SUSPE'NSE. *adj.* [*suspensus*, Latin.]

1. Held from proceeding.

The self-same orders allowed, but yet established in more wary and *suspense* manner, as being to stand in force till God should give the opportunity of some general conference what might be best for every of them afterwards to do; had both prevented all occasion of just dislike which others might take, and reserved a greater liberty unto the authors themselves, of entring unto further consultation afterwards. *Hooker.*

The great light of day yet wants to run
Much of his race, though steep, *suspense* in heav'n
Held by thy voice. *Milton's Paradise Lost.*

2. Held in doubt; held in expectation.

This said, he sat; and expectation held
His looks *suspense*, awaiting who appear'd
To second or oppose. *Milton.*

SUSPE'NSION. *n. s.* [*suspension*, Fr. from *suspend.*]

1. Act of making to hang on any thing.

2. Act of making to depend on any thing.

3. Act of delaying.

Had we had time to pray,
With thousand vows and tears we should have sought,
That sad decree's *suspension* to have wrought. *Waller.*

4. Act of withholding or balancing the judgment.

In his Indian relations, wherein are contained incredible accounts, he is surely to be read with *suspension*; these are they which weakned his authorities with former ages, for he is seldom mentioned without derogatory parentheses. *Brown.*

The mode of the will, which answers to dubitation, may be called *suspension*; and that which in the fantastick will is obstinacy, is constancy in the intellectual. *Grew.*

5. Interruption; temporary cessation.

Nor was any thing done for the better adjusting things in the time of that *suspension*, but every thing left in the same state of unconcernedness as before. *Clarendon.*

SUSPE'NSORY. *adj.* [*suspensoire*, Fr. *suspensus*, Lat.] That by which a thing hangs.

There are several parts peculiar to brutes which are wanting in man, as the seventh or *suspensory* muscle of the eye. *Ray.*

SUSPI'CION. *n. s.* [*suspicion*, Fr. *suspicio*, Lat.] The act of suspecting; imagination of something ill without proof.

This *suspicion* Miso for the hoggish shrewdness of her brain, and Mopsa for a very unlikely envy she hath stumbled upon. *Sidney.*

Suspicions amongst thoughts are like bats amongst birds, they ever fly by twilight; they are to be repressed, or at the least well guarded, for they cloud the mind. *Bacon.*

Suspicion all our lives shall be stuck full of eyes;
For treason is but trusted like a fox,
Who ne'er so tame, so cherish'd and lock'd up,
Will have a wild trick of his ancestors. *Shakespeare.*

Though wisdom wake, *suspicion* sleeps
At wisdom's gate; and to simplicity
Resigns her charge, while goodness thinks no ill
Where no ill seems. *Milton's Parad. Lost.*

SUSPI'CIOUS. *adj.* [*suspiciosus*, Latin.]

1. Inclined to suspect; inclined to imagine ill without proof.

Nature itself, after it has done an injury, will for ever be *suspicious*, and no man can love the person he suspects. *South's Sermons.*

A wise man will find us to be rogues by our faces; we have a *suspicious*, fearful, constrained countenance, often turning and slinking through narrow lanes. *Swift.*

2. Liable to suspicion; giving reason to imagine ill.

They, because the light of his candle too much drowned theirs, were glad to lay hold on so colourable matter, and exceeding forward to traduce him as an author of *suspicious* innovations. *Hooker.*

I spy a black *suspicious* threat'ning cloud,
That will encounter with our glorious sun. *Shakespeare.*

Authors are *suspicious*, nor greedily to be swallowed, who pretend to deliver antipathies, sympathies, and the occult abstrusities of things. *Brown's Vulgar Errours.*

His life
Private, unactive, calm, contemplative,
Little *suspicious* to any king. *Milton.*

Many mischievous insects are daily at work, to make people of merit *suspicious* of each other. *Pope.*

SUSPI'CIOUSLY. *adv.* [from *suspicious*.]

1. With suspicion.

2. So as to raise suspicion.

His guard entering the place, found Plangus with his sword in his hand, but not naked, but standing *suspiciously* enough, to one already suspicious. *Sidney.*

SUSPI'CIOUSNESS. *n. s.* [from *suspicious*.] Tending to suspicion.

To make my estate known seemed impossible, by reason of the *suspiciousness* of Miso, and my young mistress. *Sidney.*

SUSPIRA'TION. *n. s.* [*suspiratio* from *suspiro*, Latin.] Sigh; act of fetching the breath deep.

Not customary suits of solemn black,
Nor windy *suspiration* of forc'd breath
That can denote me truly. *Shakespeare.*

In deep *suspirations* we take more large gulphs of air to cool our heart, overcharged with love or sorrow. *More.*

To SUSPI'RE. *v. n.* [*suspiro*, Latin.]

1. To sigh; to fetch the breath deep.

2. It seems in *Shakespeare* to mean only, to begin to breath; perhaps mistaken for *respire*.

Since the birth of Cain, the first male child,
To him that did but yesterday *suspire*,
There was not such a gracious creature born. *Shakespeare.*

To SUSTAI'N. *v. a.* [*soustenir*, Fr. *sustineo*, Latin.]

1. To bear; to prop; to hold up.

The largeness and lightness of her wings and tail *sustain* her without lassitude. *More.*

Vain is the force of man,
To crush the pillars that the pile *sustain*. *Dryden's Æneid.*

2. To support; to keep from sinking under evil.

The admirable curiosity and singular excellency of this design will *sustain* the patience, and animate the industry of him who shall undertake it. *Holder.*

If he have no comfortable expectations of another life to *sustain* him under the evils in this world, he is of all creatures the most miserable. *Tillotson.*

3. To maintain; to keep.

What food
Will he convey up thither to *sustain*
Himself and army? *Milton.*

But it on her, not she on it depends;
For she the body doth *sustain* and cherish. *Davies.*

My labour will *sustain* me. *Milton.*

4. To help; to relieve; to assist.

They charged on pain of perpetual displeasure, neither to entreat for him, or any way *sustain* him. *Shakespeare.*

His sons who seek the tyrant to *sustain*,
And long for arbitrary lords again,
He dooms to death, asserting publick right. *Dryden's Æn.*

5. To bear; to endure.

Were it I thought death menac'd would ensue
This my attempt, I would *sustain* alone
The worst, and not persuade thee. *Milton.*

Can Ceyx then *sustain* to leave his wife,
And unconcern'd forsake the sweets of life. *Dryden.*

Shall Turnus then such endless toil *sustain*,
In fighting fields, and conquer towns in vain. *Dryden.*

The mind stands collected within herself, and *sustains* the shock with all the force which is natural to her; but a heart in love has its foundations sapped. *Addison.*

6. To bear without yielding.

Sacharissa's beauty's wine,
Which to madness doth incline;
Such a liquor as no brain
That is mortal can *sustain*. *Waller.*

7. To suffer; to bear as inflicted.

If you omit
The offer of this time, I cannot promise,
But that you shall *sustain* more new disgraces,
With these you bear already. *Shakespeare's Henry VIII.*

SUSTAI'NABLE. *adj.* [*soustenable*, Fr. from *sustain*.] That may be sustained.

SUSTAI'NER. *n. s.* [from *sustain*.]

1. One that props; one that supports.

2. One that suffers; a sufferer.

Thyself hast a *sustainer* been
Of much affliction in my cause. *Chapman's Iliad.*

SU'STENANCE. *n. s.* [*soustenance*, Fr.]

1. Support; maintenance.

Scarcely allowing himself fit *sustenance* of life, rather than he would spend those goods for whose sake only he seemed to joy in life. *Sidney.*

There are unto one end sundry means; as for the *sustenance* of our bodies many kinds of food, many sorts of raiment to clothe our nakedness. *Hooker.*

Is then the honour of your daughter of greater moment to her, than to my daughter her's, whose *sustenance* it was? *Add.*

2. Necessaries of life; victuals.

The experiment cost him his life for want of *sustenance*. *L'E.*

The ancients were inventers of all arts necessary to life and *sustenance*, as plowing and sowing. *Temple.*

SUSTENTA'TION. *n. s.* [*sustentation*, Fr. from *sustento*, Latin.]

1. Support; preservation from falling.

These steams once raised above the earth, have their ascent and *sustentation* aloft promoted by the air. *Boyle.*

2. Support of life; use of victuals.

A very abstemious animal, by reason of its frigidity, and latitancy in the winter, will long subsist without a visible *sustentation*. *Brown's Vulgar Errours.*

3. Maintenance.

When there be great shoals of people, which go on to populate, without foreseeing means of life and *sustentation*; it is of necessity that once in an age they discharge a portion of their people upon other nations. *Bacon.*

SUSURRA'TION. *n. s.* [from *susurro*, Latin.] Whisper; soft murmur.

SUTE. *n. s.* [for *suite*.] Sort.

Touching matters belonging to the church of Christ, this we conceive that they are not of one *sute*. *Hooker.*

SU'TLER. *n. s.* [*soeteler*, Dutch; *sudler*, German.] A man that sells provisions and liquour in a camp.

I shall *sutler* be
Unto the camp, and profits will accrue. *Shakesp. Hen. V.*

Send to the *sutler's*; there you're sure to find
The bully match'd with rascals of his kind. *Dryden.*

SU'TURE. *n. s.* [*sutura*, Latin.]

1. A manner of sewing or stitching, particularly of stitching wounds.

Wounds, if held in close contact for some time, reunite by inosculation: to maintain this situation, several sorts of *sutures* have been invented; those now chiefly described are the interrupted, the glovers, the quill'd, the twisted and the dry *sutures*, but the interrupted and twisted are almost the only useful ones. *Sharp's Surgery.*

2. *Suture* is a particular articulation: the bones of the cranium are joined to one another by four *sutures*. *Quincy.*

Many of our vessels degenerate into ligaments, and the *sutures* of the skull are abolished in old age. *Arbuthnot.*

SWAB. *n. s.* [*swabb*, Swedish.] A kind of mop to clean floors.

To SWAB. *v. a.* [ꞅpebban, Saxon.] To clean with a mop. It is now used chiefly at sea.

He made him *swab* the deck. *Shelvock's Voyage.*

SWA'BBER. *n. s.* [*swabber*, Dutch.] A sweeper of the deck.

The master, the *swabber*, the boatswain and I,
Lov'd Mall, Meg, and Marrian, and Margery. *Shak.*

Was any thing wanting to the extravagance of this degenerate age, but the making a tarpawlin and a *swabber* the hero of a tragedy. *Dennis.*

To SWA'DDLE. *v. a.* [ꞅpeðan, Saxon.]

1. To swathe; to bind in cloaths, generally used of binding new-born children.

Invested by a veil of clouds,
And *swadled* as new-born in sable shrouds;
For these a receptacle I design'd. *Sandys.*

How soon doth man decay!
When cloths are taken from a chest of sweets,
To *swaddle* infants, whose young breath
Scarce knows the way;
Those clouts are little winding-sheets,
Which do consign and send them unto death. *Herbert.*

They *swaddled* me up in my night-gown with long pieces of linen, 'till they had wrapt me in about an hundred yards of swathe. *Addison.*

2. To beat; to cudgel. A low ludicrous word.
Great on the bench, great in the saddle,
That could as well bind o'er as *swaddle*. *Hudibras.*

SWA'DDLE. *n. s.* [from the verb.] Cloaths bound round the body.

I begged them to uncase me: no, no, say they; and upon that carried me to one of their houses, and put me to bed in all my *swaddles*. *Addison.*

SWA'DDLINGBAND. SWA'DDLINGCLOATH. SWA'DDLINGCLOUT. } *n. s.* [from *swadle*.] Cloath wrapped round a new-born child.

From thence a fairy thee unweeting reft,
There as thou slept'st in tender *swaddlingband*,
And her base elfin brood, there for thee left,
Such men do changelings call, so changed by fairies theft. *Fairy Queen.*

That great baby you see there is not yet out of his *swadling-clouts*. *Shakesp. Hamlet.*

The *swadlingbands* were purple, wrought with gold. *Dryd.*

To SWAG. *v. n.* [ꞅiȝan, Saxon; *sweigia*, Islandick.] To sink down by its weight; to lay heavy.

They are more apt, in *swagging* down, to pierce with their points, than in the jacent posture, and crevice the wall. *Wott.*

Being a tall fish, and with his sides much compressed, he hath a long fin upon his back, and another answering to it on his belly; by which he is the better kept upright, or from *swagging* on his sides. *Grew.*

To SWAGE. *v. a.* [from *asswage*.] To ease; to soften; to mitigate.

Apt words have pow'r to *swage*
The tumours of a troubled mind,
And are as balm to fester'd wounds. *Milton.*

Nor wanting pow'r to mitigate and *swage*,
With solemn touches, troubled thoughts, and chase
Anguish, and doubt, and fear from mortal minds. *Milton.*

I will love thee,
Though my distracted senses should forsake me,
I'd find some intervals, when my poor heart
Should *swage* itself, and be let loose to thine. *Otway.*

To SWA'GGER. *v. n.* [*swadderen*, Dutch, to make a noise; ꞅpeȝan, Saxon.] To bluster; to bully; to be turbulently and tumultuously proud and insolent.

Drunk? squabble? *swagger?* and discourse fustian with one's own shadow? Oh thou invincible spirit of wine! *Shak.*

'Tis the gage of one that I should fight withal, if he be alive; a rascal that *swagger'd* with me last night. *Shakespeare.*

Oft a terrible oath, with a *swaggering* accent sharply twang'd off, gives manhood more approbation than proof itself. *Shak.*

The lesser size of mortals love to *swagger* for opinions, and to boast infallibility of knowledge. *Glanv. Sceps.*

Many such asses in the world huff, look big, stare, dress, cock, and *swagger* at the same noisy rate. *L'Estrange.*

He chuck'd,
And scarcely deign'd to set a foot to ground,
But *swagger'd* like a lord. *Dryden.*

Confidence, how weakly soever founded, hath some effect upon the ignorant, who think there is something more than ordinary in a *swaggering* man that talks of nothing but demonstration. *Tillotson.*

To be great, is not to be starched, and formal, and supercilious; to *swagger* at our footmen, and browbeat our inferiors. *Collier on Pride.*

What a pleasure is it to be victorious in a cause? to *swagger* at the bar? for a lawyer I was born, and a lawyer I will be. *Arbuthnot's History of John Bull.*

SWA'GGERER. *n. s.* [from *swagger*.] A blusterer; a bully; a turbulent noisy fellow.

He's no *swaggerer*, hostess; a tame cheater: you may stroke him as gently as a puppy greyhound. *Shakesp. Henry IV.*

SWA'GGY. *adj.* [from *swag*.] Dependent by its weight.

The beaver is called animal ventricosum, from his *swaggy* and prominent belly. *Brown's Vulgar Errours.*

SWAIN. *n. s.* [ꞅpein, Saxon and Runick.]

1. A young man.
That good knight would not so nigh repair,
Himself estranging from their joyance vain,
Whose fellowship seem'd far unfit for warlike *swain*. *F. Q.*

2. A country servant employed in husbandry.
It were a happy life
To be no better than a homely *swain*. *Shak. Henry VI.*

3. A pastoral youth.
Blest *swains!* whose nymphs in ev'ry grace excel;
Blest nymphs! whose *swains* those graces sing so well. *Pope.*

SWA'INMOTE. *n. s.* [*swainmotus*, law Lat.] A court touching matters of the forest, kept by the charter of the forest thrice in the year. This court of *swainmote* is as incident to a forest, as the court of piepowder is to a fair. The *swainmote* is a court of freeholders within the forest. *Cowel.*

To SWALE. To SWEAL. } *v. a.* [ꞅpelan, Saxon, to kindle.] To waste or blaze away; to melt: as, *the candle* swales.

SWA'LLET. *n. s.* Among the tin-miners, water breaking in upon the miners at their work. *Bailey.*

SWA'LLOW. *n. s.* [ꞅpalepe, Saxon.] A small bird of passage, or, as some say, a bird that lies hid and sleeps in the Winter.

The *swallow* follows not Summer more willingly than we your lordship. *Shak. Timon of Athens.*

Daffodils,
That come before the *swallow* dares. *Shakespeare.*

The *swallows* make use of celandine, and the linnet of euphragia. *More.*

When *swallows* fleet soar high and sport in air,
He told us that the welkin would be clear. *Gay.*

The *swallow* sweeps
The slimy pool, to build his hanging house
Intent. *Thomson's Spring.*

To SWA'LLOW. *v. a.* [ꞅpelȝan, Saxon; *swelgen*, Dutch.]

1. To take down the throat.
I *swallow* down my spittle. *Job* vii. 19.

If little faults
Shall not be wink'd at, how shall we stretch our eye,
Whose capital crimes chew'd, *swallow'd*, and digested,
Appear before us? *Shakespeare's Henry V.*

Men are, at a venture, of the religion of the country; and must therefore *swallow* down opinions, as silly people do empiricks pills, and have nothing to do but believe that they will do the cure. *Locke.*

2. To receive without examination.
Consider and judge of it as a matter of reason, and not *swallow* it without examination as a matter of faith. *Locke.*

3. To engross; to appropriate.
Far be it from me, that I should *swallow* up or destroy. 2 *Sa.*

Homer excels all the inventors of other arts in this, that he has *swallowed* up the honour of those who succeeded him. *Pope.*

4. To absorb; to take in; to sink in any abyss; to engulph.
Though you untie the winds, and let them fight
Against the churches, though the yesty waves
Confound and *swallow* navigation up. *Shakespeare.*

I may be pluck'd into the *swallowing* womb
Of this deep pit, poor Bassianus' grave. *Shak. Tit. Andron.*

Death is *swallowed* up in victory. 1 *Cor.* xv. 54.

If the earth open her mouth and *swallow* them up, ye shall understand that these men have provoked the Lord. *Num.* xvi.

In bogs *swallow'd* up and lost. *Milton.*

He hid many things from us, not that they would *swallow* up our understanding, but divert our attention from what is more important. *Decay of Piety.*

Nature would abhor
To be forced back again upon herself,
And like a whirlpool *swallow* her own streams. *Dryden and Lee's Oedipus.*

Should not the sad occasion *swallow* up
My other cares, and draw them all into it? *Addison.*

Cities overturn'd,
And late at night in *swallowing* earthquake sunk. *Thomson.*

5. To devour; to destroy.
The necessary provision for life *swallows* the greatest part of their time. *Locke.*

Corruption *swallow'd* what the liberal hand
Of bounty scatter'd. *Thomson's Autumn.*

6. To be lost in any thing; to be given up.
The priest and the prophet are *swallowed* up of wine. *Is.*

SWA'LLOW. *n. s.* [from the verb.] The throat; voracity.

Had this man of merit and mortification been called to account for his ungodly *swallow*, in gorging down the estates of helpless widows and orphans, he would have told them that it was all for charitable uses. *South.*

SWA'LLOWTAIL. *n. s.* A species of willow.

The shining willow they call *swallowtail*, because of the pleasure of the leaf. *Bacon's Natural History.*

SWA'LLOWWORT. *n. s.* A plant.

SWAM. The preterite of *swim*.

SWAMP. *n. s.* [*swamms*, Gothick; ꞅpam, Saxon; *suamm*, Islandick; *swamme*, Dutch; *suomp*, Danish; *swamp*, Swedish.] A marsh; a bog; a fen.

SWA'MPY. *adj.* [from *swamp*.] Boggy; fenny.
Swampy fens breathe destructive myriads. *Thomson.*

SWAN. *n. s.* [ꞅpan, Saxon; *suan*, Danish; *swaen*, Dutch.]

The swan is a large water-fowl, that has a long and very straight neck, and is very white, excepting when it is young. Its legs and feet are black, as is its bill, which is like that of a goose, but something rounder, and a little hooked at the lower end of it: the two sides below its eyes are black and shining like ebony. Swans use wings like sails, which catch the wind, so that they are driven along in the water. They feed upon herbs and some sort of grain like a goose, and some are said to have lived three hundred years. There is a species of swans with the feathers of their heads, towards the breast, marked at the ends with a gold colour inclining to red. The swan is reckoned by Moses among the unclean creatures; but it was consecrated to Apollo the god of musick, because it was said to sing melodiously when it was near expiring; a tradition generally received, but fabulous. *Calmet.*

With untainted eye
Compare her face with some that I shall show,
And I will make thee think thy *swan* a crow. *Shakespeare.*

Let musick sound, while he doth make his choice;
Then if he lose, he makes a *swan* like end. *Shakespeare.*

I have seen a *swan*,
With bootless labour, swim against the tide,
And spend her strength with over-matching waves. *Shakesp.*

The birds easy to be drawn are planipedes, or water-fowl, as the mallard, goose, and *swan.* *Peacham on Drawing.*

The fearful matrons raise a screaming cry,
Old feeble men with fainter groans reply;
A jarring sound results, and mingles in the sky,
Like that of *swans* remurm'ring to the floods. *Dryden.*

The idea, which an Englishman signifies by the name *swan*, is a white colour, long neck, black beak, black legs, and whole feet, and all these of a certain size, with a power of swimming in the water, and making a certain kind of noise. *Locke.*

SWA'NSKIN. *n. s.* [*swan* and *skin.*] A kind of soft flannel, imitating for warmth the down of a swan.

SWAP. *adv.* [*ad suipa*, to do at a snatch, Islandick.] Hastily; with hasty violence: as, he did it *swap.* A low word.

To SWAP. *v. a.* To exchange. See *To* SWOP.

SWARD. *n. s.* [*sward*, Swedish.]

1. The skin of bacon.

2. The surface of the ground: whence *green sward*, or *green sword.*

Water, kept too long, loosens and softens the *sward*, makes it subject to rushes and coarse grass. *Note on Tusser.*

The noon of night was past, when the foe
Came dreadless o'er the level *swart*, that lies
Between the wood and the swift streaming Ouse. *A. Philips.*

To plant a vineyard in July, when the earth is very dry and combustible, plow up the *swarth*, and burn it. *Mortimer.*

SWARE. The preterite of *swear.*

SWARM. *n. s.* [ꞅpeaꞃm, Saxon; *swerm*, Dutch.]

1. A great body or number of bees or other small animals, particularly those bees that migrate from the hive.

A *swarm* of bees that cut the liquid sky,
Upon the topmost branch in clouds alight. *Dryden's Æn.*

2. A multitude; a croud.

From this *swarm* of fair advantages,
You grip'd the general sway into your hand,
Forgot your oath to us at Doncaster. *Shakespeare.*

If we could number up those prodigious *swarms* that had settled themselves in every part of it, they would amount to more than can be found. *Addison on Italy.*

To SWARM. *v. n.* [ꞅpeaꞃman, Saxon; *swermen*, Dutch.]

1. To rise as bees in a body, and quit the hive.

All hands employ'd,
Like labouring bees on a long Summer's day;
Some found the trumpet for the rest to *swarm.* *Dryden.*

Swarm'd on a rotten stick the bees I spy'd. *Gay.*

When bees hang in *swarming* time, they will presently rise, if the weather hold. *Mortimer's Husbandry.*

2. To appear in multitudes; to croud; to throng.

The merciless Macdonel,
The multiplying villanies of nature
Do *swarm* upon. *Shakesp. Macbeth.*

Our superfluous lacqueys, and our peasants,
Who in unnecessary action *swarm*
About our squares of battle. *Shakesp. Henry V.*

What a multitude of thoughts at once
Awaken'd in me *swarm*, while I consider
What from within I feel myself, and hear
What from without comes often to my ears. *Milton.*

Then mounts the throne, high plac'd before the shrine;
In crowds around the *swarming* people join. *Dryden's Æn.*

3. To be crouded; to be over-run; to be thronged.

These garrisons you have now planted throughout all Ireland, and every place *swarms* with soldiers. *Spenser.*

Her lower region *swarms* with all sort of fowl, her rivers with fish, and her seas with whole shoals. *Howel.*

Those days *swarmed* with fables, and from such grounds took hints for fictions, poisoning the world ever after. *Brown.*

4. To breed multitudes.

Not so thick *swarm'd* once the soil
Bedropp'd with blood of Gorgon. *Milton's Paradise Lost.*

SWART. } *adj.* [*swarts*, Gothick; ꞅpeaꞃꞇ, Saxon; *swart*,
SWARTH. } Dutch.]

1. Black; darkly brown; tawney.

A nation strange, with visage *swart*,
And courage fierce, that all men did affray,
Through the world then swarmed in every part. *F. Queen.*

A man
Of *swarth* complexion, and of crabbed hue,
That him full of melancholy did shew. *Fairy Queen.*

Whereas I was black and *swart* before;
With those clear rays which she infus'd on me,
That beauty am I blest with, which you see. *Shak. H. VI.*

No goblin, or *swart* fairy of the mine,
Hath hurtful power o'er true virginity. *Milton.*

2. In *Milton* it seems to signify black; gloomy; malignant.

Ye valleys low,
On whose fresh lap the *swart* star sparely looks. *Milton.*

To SWART. *v. a.* [from the noun.] To blacken; to dusk.

The heat of the sun may *swart* a living part, or even black a dead or dissolving flesh. *Brown's Vulgar Errours.*

SWA'RTHILY. *adv.* [from *swarthy.*] Blackly; duskily; tawnily.

SWA'RTHINESS. *n. s.* [from *swarthy.*] Darkness of complexion; tawniness.

SWA'RTHY. *adj.* [See SWART.] Dark of complexion; black; dusky; tawney.

Set me where, on some pathless plain,
The *swarthy* Africans complain. *Roscommon.*

Though in the torrid climates the common colour is black or *swarthy*, yet the natural colour of the temperate climates is more transparent and beautiful. *Hale's Origin of Mankind.*

Here *swarthy* Charles appears, and there
His brother with dejected air. *Addison.*

Did they know Cato, our remotest kings
Would pour embattled multitudes about him;
Their *swarthy* hosts would darken all our plains,
Doubling the native horrour of the war,
And making death more grim. *Addison's Cato.*

SWASH. *n. s.* [A cant word.] A figure, whose circumference is not round, but oval; and whose moldings lie not at right angles, but oblique to the axis of the work. *Moxon.*

To SWASH. *v. n.* To make a great clatter or noise: whence *swashbuckler.*

We'll have a *swashing* and a martial outside,
As many other mannish cowards have,
That do outface it with their semblances. *Shakespeare.*

Draw, if you be men: Gregory, remember thy *swashing* blow. *Shak. Romeo and Juliet.*

SWA'SHER. *n. s.* [from *swash.*] One who makes a show of valour or force of arms.

I have observed these three *swashers*; three such anticks do not amount to a man. *Shakes. Henry V.*

SWATCH. *n. s.* A swathe. Not in use.

One spreadeth those bands so in order to lie,
As barlie in *swatches* may fill it thereby. *Tusser.*

SWATH. *n. s.* [*swade*, Dutch.]

1. A line of grass cut down by the mower.

With tossing and raking, and setting on cox,
Grasse, lately in *swathes*, is meat for an ox. *Tusser.*

The strawy Greeks, ripe for his edge,
Fall down before him, like the mower's *swath.* *Shakesp.*

As soon as your grass is mown, if it lie thick in the *swath*, neither air nor sun can pass freely through it. *Mortimer.*

2. A continued quantity.

An affection'd ass, that cons state without book, and utters it by great *swaths.* *Shak. Twelfth Night.*

3. [Spedan, to bind, Saxon.] A band; a fillet.

An Indian comb, a stick whereof is cut into three sharp and round teeth four inches long: the other part is left for the handle, adorned with fine straws laid along the sides, and lapped round about it in several distinct *swaths.* *Grew.*

They swaddled me up in my night-gown with long pieces of linen, which they folded about me, 'till they had wrapped me in above an hundred yards of *swathe.* *Addison's Spectator.*

To SWATHE. *v. a.* [ꞅpeðan, Saxon.] To bind, as a child with bands and rollers.

Thrice hath this Hotspur, Mars in *swathing* cloaths,
This infant warriour, and his enterprizes,
Discomfited great Douglas. *Shak. Henry IV.*

He had two sons; the eldest of them at three years old,
I' th' *swathing* cloaths the other, from their nursery
Were stol'n. *Shakesp. Cymbeline.*

Their children are never *swathed*, or bound about with any thing, when they are first born; but are put naked into the bed with their parents to lie. *Abbot's Descript. of the World.*

Swath'd in her lap the bold nurse bore him out,
With olive branches cover'd round about. *Dryden.*

Master's feet are *swath'd* no longer,
If in the night too oft he kicks,
Or shows his loco-motive tricks. *Prior.*

To SWAY. *v. a.* [*schweben*, German, to move.]

1. To wave in the hand; to move or weild with facility: as, to *sway* the scepter.

Glancing fire out of the iron play'd,
As sparkles from the anvil rise,
When heavy hammers on the wedge are *sway'd.* *Fai. Queen.*

2. To bias; to direct to either side.

Heav'n forgive them, that so much have *sway'd*
Your majesty's good thoughts away from me. *Shakespeare.*

I took your hands; but was, indeed,
Sway'd from the point, by looking down on Cæsar. *Shakes.*

The only way t' improve our own,
By dealing faithfully with none;
As bowls run true by being made
On purpose false, and to be *sway'd*. *Hudibras.*

3. To govern; to rule; to overpower; to influence.

The lady's mad; yet if 'twere so,
She could not *sway* her house, command her followers,
With such a smooth, discreet, and stable bearing. *Shakesp.*

The will of man is by his reason *sway'd*;
And reason says, you are the worthier maid. *Shakespeare.*

On Europe thence, and where Rome was to *sway*
The world. *Milton's Paradise Lost.*

A gentle nymph, not far from hence,
That with moist curb *sways* the smooth Severn stream,
Sabrina is her name. *Milton.*

Take heed lest passion *sway*
Thy judgment to do ought, which else free will
Would not admit. *Milton's Paradise Lost.*

The judgment is *swayed* by passion, and stored with lubricous opinions, instead of clearly conceived truths. *Glanv.*

This was the race
To *sway* the world, and land and sea subdue. *Dryden.*

With these I went,
Nor idle stood with unassisting hands,
When savage beasts, and mens more savage bands,
Their virtuous toil subdu'd; yet those I *sway'd*
With pow'rful speech: I spoke, and they obey'd. *Dryden.*

When examining these matters, let not temporal and little advantages *sway* you against a more durable interest. *Tillotson.*

To Sway. *v. n.*

1. To hang heavy; to be drawn by weight.

In these personal respects, the balance *sways* on our part. *Bac.*

2. To have weight; to have influence.

The example of sundry churches, for approbation of one thing, doth *sway* much; but yet still as having the force of an example only, and not of a law. *Hooker.*

3. To bear rule; to govern.

The mind I *sway* by, and the heart I bear,
Shall never sagg with doubt, nor shake with fear. *Shakesp.*

Had'st thou *sway'd* as kings should do,
They never then had sprung like summer flies. *Shakesp.*

Aged tyranny *sways* not as it hath power, but as it is suffered. *Shakesp. King Lear.*

Here thou shalt monarch reign;
There did'st not: there let him still victor *sway*. *Milton.*

Sway. *n. s.* [from the verb.]

1. The swing or sweep of a weapon.

To strike with huge two-handed *sway*. *Milton.*

2. Any thing moving with bulk and power.

Are not you mov'd, when all the *sway* of earth
Shakes like a thing unfirm? *Shak. Julius Cæsar.*

Expert
When to advance, or stand, or turn the *sway*
Of battle. *Milton.*

3. Power; rule; dominion.

This sort had some fear that the filling up the seats in the consistory, with so great number of laymen, was but to please the minds of the people, to the end they might think their own *sway* somewhat. *Hooker.*

In the end, very few excepted, all became subject to the *sway* of time: other odds there was none, saving that some fell sooner, and some later, from the soundness of belief. *Hook.*

Only retain
The name and all th' addition to a king;
The *sway*, revenue, execution of th' hest,
Beloved sons, be yours. *Shakes. King Lear.*

Her father counts it dangerous
That she should give her sorrow so much *sway*,
And in his wisdom hastes our marriage,
To stop the inundation of her tears. *Shakespeare.*

Too truly Tamerlane's successors they;
Each thinks a world too little for his *sway*. *Dryd. Aurengz.*

When vice prevails, and impious men bear *sway*,
The post of honour is a private station. *Addison's Cato.*

4. Influence; direction.

An evil mind in authority doth not only follow the *sway* of the desires already within it, but frames to itself new desires, not before thought of. *Sidney.*

They rush along, the rattling woods give way,
The branches bend before their sweepy *sway*. *Dryden.*

To SWEAR. *v. n.* preter. *swore* or *sware*; part. pass. *sworn.* [*swaran*, Gothick; ꞅpeꞃian, Saxon; *sweeren*, Dutch.]

1. To obtest some superiour power; to utter an oath.

If a man vow a vow unto the Lord, or *swear* an oath to bind his soul with a bond, he shall not break his word. *Num.*

Thee, thee an hundred languages shall claim,
And savage Indians *swear* by Anna's name. *Tickel.*

2. To declare or promise upon oath.

We shall have old *swearing*
That they did give the rings away to men;
But we'll outface them, and outswear them too. *Shakespeare.*

I gave my love a ring, and made him *swear*
Never to part with it; and here he stands,
I dare be sworn for him, he would not leave it,
Nor pluck it from his finger. *Shakespeare.*

I would have kept my word;
But, when I *swear*, it is irrevocable. *Shakes. Henry VI.*

Jacob said, *swear* to me; and he *sware* unto him. *Gen.*

Bacchus taken at Rhodes by Demetrius Poliorcetes, which he so esteemed, that, as Plutarch reports, he *sware* he had rather lose all his father's images than that table. *Peacham.*

3. To give evidence upon oath.

At what ease
Might corrupt minds procure knaves as corrupt
To *swear* against you? *Shak. Henry VIII.*

4. To obtest the great name profanely.

Because of *swearing* the land mourneth. *Jer.* xxiii. 10.

Obey thy parents, keep thy word justly;
Swear not. *Shakes. King Lear.*

None so nearly disposed to scoffing at religion as those who have accustomed themselves to *swear* on trifling occasions. *Till.*

To Swear. *v. a.*

1. To put to an oath.

Moses took the bones of Joseph; for he had straitly *sworn* the children of Israel. *Ex.* xiii. 19.

Swom ashore, man, like a duck; I can swim like a duck, I'll be *sworn*. *Shakespeare's Tempest.*

Let me *swear* you all to secrecy;
And, to conceal my shame, conceal my life. *Dryden.*

2. To declare upon oath.

3. To obtest by an oath.

Now by Apollo, king, thou *swear'st* thy gods in vain.
——O vassal! miscreant! *Shakespeare.*

Swe'arer. *n. s.* [from *swear.*] A wretch who obtests the great name wantonly and profanely.

And must they all be hang'd that swear and lie?
——Every one.
——Who must hang them?
——Why, the honest men.
—Then the liars and *swearers* are fools; for there are liars and *swearers* enow to beat the honest men and hang them up. *Shak.*

Take not his name, who made thy mouth, in vain:
It gets thee nothing, and hath no excuse:
Lust and wine plead a pleasure, avarice a gain;
But the cheap *swearer* through his open sluice
Lets his soul run for nought. *Herbert.*

Of all men a philosopher should be no *swearer*; for an oath, which is the end of controversies in law, cannot determine any here, where reason only must induce. *Brown.*

It is the opinion of our most refined *swearers*, that the same oath or curse cannot, consistently with true politeness, be repeated above nine times in the same company by the same person. *Swift's Polite Conversation.*

SWEAT. *n. s.* [ꞅpeat, Saxon; *sweet*, Dutch.]

1. The matter evacuated at the pores by heat or labour.

Sweat is salt in taste; for that part of the nourishment which is fresh and sweet, turneth into blood and flesh; and the *sweat* is that part which is excerned. *Bacon.*

Some insensible effluvium, exhaling out of the stone, comes to be checked and condensed by the air on the superficies of it, as it happens to *sweat* on the skins of animals. *Boyle.*

Soft on the flow'ry herb I found me laid
In balmy *sweat*. *Milton.*

When Lucilius brandishes his pen,
And flashes in the face of guilty men,
A cold *sweat* stands in drops on ev'ry part,
And rage succeeds to tears, revenge to smart. *Dryden.*

Sweat is produced by changing the balance between the fluids and solids, in which health consists, so as that projectile motion of the fluids overcome the resistance of the solids. *Arb.*

2. Labour; toil; drudgery.

This painful labour of abridging was not easy, but a matter of *sweat* and watching. *2 Mac.* ii. 26.

The field
To labour calls us, now with *sweat* impos'd. *Milton.*

What from Johnson's oil and *sweat* did flow,
Or what more easy nature did bestow
On Shakespeare's gentler muse, in thee full grown
Their graces both appear. *Denham.*

3. Evaporation of moisture.

Beans give in the mow; and therefore those that are to be kept are not to be thrashed 'till March, that they have had a thorough *sweat* in the mow. *Mortimer's Husbandry.*

To Sweat. *v. n.* preterite *swet*, *sweated*; particip. pass. *sweaten.* [from the noun.]

1. To be moist on the body with heat or labour.

Shall I say to you,
Let them be free, marry them to your heirs?
Why *sweat* they under burdens? *Shak. Merch. of Venice.*

Mistress

Miſtreſs Page at the door, *ſweating* and blowing, and looking wildly, would needs ſpeak with you. *Shakeſpeare.*

When he was brought again to the bar, to hear
His knell rung out, his judgment, he was ſtirr'd
With ſuch an agony, he *ſweat* extremely. *Shak. H.* VIII.

About this time in autumn, there reigned in the city and other parts of the kingdom a diſeaſe then new; which, of the accidents and manner thereof they called the *ſweating* ſickneſs. *Bacon's Henry* VII.

A young tall ſquire
Did from the camp at firſt before him go;
At firſt he did, but ſcarce could follow ſtrait,
Sweating beneath a ſhield's unruly weight. *Cowley.*

2. To toil; to labour; to drudge.

How the drudging goblin *ſwet*
To earn his cream-bowl duly ſet;
When in one night, ere glimpſe of morn,
His ſhadowy flail hath threſh'd the corn. *Milton.*

Our author, not content to ſee
That others write as careleſly as he;
Though he pretends not to make things complete,
Yet, to pleaſe you, he'd have the poets *ſweat.* *Waller.*

3. To emit moiſture.

Wainſcots will *ſweat* ſo that they will run with water. *Bacon.*

In cold evenings there will be a moiſture or *ſweating* upon the ſtool. *Mortimer.*

To SWEAT. *v. a.* To emit as ſweat.

Greaſe that's *ſweaten*
From the murtherer's gibbet, throw
Into the flame. *Shakeſpeare's Macbeth.*

For him the rich Arabia *ſweats* her gum. *Dryden.*

SWEA'TER. *n. ſ.* [from *ſweat*] One who ſweats.

SWEA'TY. *adj.* [from *ſweat.*]

1. Covered with ſweat; moiſt with ſweat.

The rabblement houted and clap'd their chop'd hands, and threw up their *ſweaty* night-caps. *Shakeſp. Julius Cæſar.*

A *ſweaty* reaper from his tillage brought
Firſt-fruits, the green ear, and the yellow ſheaf. *Milton.*

2. Conſiſting of ſweat.

And then, ſo nice, and ſo genteel,
Such cleanlineſs from head to heel;
No humours groſs, or frowſy ſteams,
No noiſome whiffs, or *ſweaty* ſtreams. *Swift.*

3. Laborious; toilſome.

Thoſe who labour
The *ſweaty* forge, who edge the crooked ſcythe,
Bend ſtubborn ſteel, and harden gleening armour,
Acknowledge Vulcan's aid. *Prior.*

To SWEEP. *v. a.* [ſpapan, Saxon.]

1. To drive away with a beſom.

2. To clean with a beſom.

What woman, having ten pieces of ſilver, if ſhe loſe one, doth not *ſweep* the houſe, and ſeek diligently 'till ſhe find it? *Lu.* xv. 8.

3. To carry with pomp.

Let frantick Talbot triumph for a while,
And, like a peacock, *ſweep* along his tail. *Shak. H.* VI.

4. To drive or carry off with celerity and violence.

Though I could,
With barefac'd power, *ſweep* him from my ſight,
And bid my will avouch it; yet I muſt not. *Shakeſpeare.*

The river of Kiſhon *ſwept* them away. *Judges* v.

The bluſtering winds ſtriving for victory, *ſwept* the ſnow from off the tops of thoſe high mountains, and caſt it down unto the plains in ſuch abundance, that the Turks lay as men buried alive. *Knolles's Hiſtory of the Turks.*

Flying bullets now
To execute his rage appear too ſlow;
They miſs or *ſweep* but common ſouls away;
For ſuch a loſs Opdam his life muſt pay. *Waller.*

My looking is the fire of peſtilence,
That *ſweeps* at once the people and the prince. *Dryden.*

I have already *ſwept* the ſtakes, and with the common good fortune of proſperous gameſters can be content to ſit. *Dryden.*

Is this the man who drives me before him
To the world's ridge, and *ſweeps* me off like rubbiſh? *Dryd.*

Fool! time no change of motion knows;
With equal ſpeed the torrent flows
To *ſweep* fame, pow'r, and wealth away:
The paſt is all by death poſſeſt,
And frugal fate that guards the reſt,
By giving, bids them live, to day. *Fenton.*

A duke holding in a great many hands, drew a huge heap of gold; but never obſerved a ſharper, who under his arm *ſwept* a great deal of it into his hat. *Swift.*

5. To paſs over with celerity and force.

6. To rub over.

Their long deſcending train
With rubies edg'd, and ſapphires *ſwept* the plain. *Dryden.*

7. To ſtrike with long ſtroke.

Deſcend ye nine; deſcend and ſing;
The breathing inſtruments inſpire,
Wake into voice each ſilent ſtring,
And *ſweep* the ſounding lyre. *Pope.*

To SWEEP. *v. n.*

1. To paſs with violence, tumult, or ſwiftneſs.

Haſte me to know it, that I with wings as ſwift
As meditation or the thoughts of love
May *ſweep* to my revenge. *Shakeſpeare.*

A poor man that oppreſſeth the poor, is like a *ſweeping* rain which leaveth no food. *Prov.* xxviii. iii.

Before tempeſtuous winds ariſe,
Stars ſhooting through the darkneſs gild the night
With *ſweeping* glories and long trails of light. *Dryden.*

2. To paſs with pomp; to paſs with an equal motion.

She *ſweeps* it through the court with troops of ladies,
More like an empreſs than duke Humphrey's wife. *Shak.*

In gentle dreams I often will be by,
And *ſweep* along before your cloſing eye. *Dryden.*

3. To move with a long reach.

Nor always errs; for oft the gauntlet draws
A *ſweeping* ſtroke along the crackling jaws. *Dryden.*

SWEEP. *n. ſ.* [from the verb.]

1. The act of ſweeping.

2. The compaſs of any violent or continued motion.

A door drags when by its ill hanging on its hinges, or by the ill boarding of the room the bottom edge of the door rides in its *ſweep* upon the floor. *Moxon's Mechan. Exerciſe.*

Lion-hearted Richard like a torrent ſwell'd
With wintry tempeſts, that diſdains all mounds,
Breaking away impetuous, and involves
Within its *ſweep*, trees, houſes, men. *Philips.*

3. Violent deſtruction.

In countries ſubject to great epidemical *ſweeps*, men may live very long, but where the proportion of the chronical diſtemper is great, it is not likely to be ſo. *Graunt.*

4. Direction of any motion not rectilinear.

Having made one inciſion a little circularly, begin a ſecond, bringing it with an oppoſite *ſweep* to meet the other. *Sharp.*

SWEE'PINGS. *n. ſ.* [from *ſweep.*] That which is ſwept away.

Should this one broomſtick enter the ſcene, covered with duſt, though the *ſweepings* of the fineſt lady's chamber, we ſhould deſpiſe its vanity. *Swift.*

SWEE'PNET. *n. ſ.* [*ſweep* and *net.*] A net that takes in a great compaſs.

She was a *ſweepnet* for the Spaniſh ſhips, which happily fell into her net. *Camden.*

SWEE'PSTAKE. *n. ſ.* [*ſweep* and *ſtake.*] A man that wins all.

Is't writ in your revenge,
That *ſweepſtake* you will draw both friend and foe,
Winner and loſer. *Shakeſpeare.*

SWEE'PY. *adj.* [from *ſweep.*] Paſſing with great ſpeed and violence over a great compaſs at once.

They ruſh along, the rattling woods give way,
The branches bend before their *ſweepy* ſway. *Dryden.*

SWEET. *adj.* [ſpete, Sax. *ſoet,* Dutch.]

1. Pleaſing to any ſenſe.

Sweet expreſſes the pleaſant perceptions of almoſt every ſenſe: ſugar is *ſweet*, but it hath not the ſame ſweetneſs as muſick; nor hath muſick the ſweetneſs of a roſe, and a ſweet proſpect differs from them all: nor yet have any of theſe the ſame ſweetneſs as diſcourſe, counſel, or meditation hath; yet the royal Pſalmiſt ſaith of a man, we took *ſweet* counſel together; and of God, my meditation of him ſhall be *ſweet.* *Watts.*

2. Luſcious to the taſte.

This honey taſted ſtill is ever *ſweet.* *Davies.*

3. Fragrant to the ſmell.

Balm his foul head with warm diſtilled waters,
And burn *ſweet* wood to make the lodging *ſweet.* *Shakeſp.*

Where a rainbow hangeth over or toucheth, there breatheth a *ſweet* ſmell; for that this happeneth but in certain matters which have ſome ſweetneſs which the dew of the rainbow draweth forth. *Bacon.*

Shred very ſmall with thime *ſweet*-margory and a little winter ſavoury. *Walton's Angler.*

The balmy zephyrs, ſilent ſince her death,
Lament the ceaſing of a *ſweeter* breath. *Pope.*

The ſtreets with treble voices ring,
To ſell the bounteous product of the ſpring;
Sweet-ſmelling flow'rs, and elders early bud. *Gay.*

4. Melodious to the ear.

The dulcimer, all organs of *ſweet* ſtop. *Milton.*

Her ſpeech is grac'd with *ſweeter* ſound
Than in another's ſong is found. *Waller.*

No more the ſtreams their murmurs ſhall forbear
A *ſweeter* muſick than their own to hear;
But tell the reeds, and tell the vocal ſhore,
Fair Daphne's dead, and muſick is no more. *Pope.*

5. Pleasing to the eye.

Heav'n bless thee!
Thou hast the *sweetest* face I ever look'd on. *Shakespeare.*

6. Not salt.

The white of an egg, or blood mingled with salt water, gathers the saltness and maketh the water *sweeter*; this may be by adhesion. *Bacon's Natural History.*

The sails drop with rain,
Sweet waters mingle with the briny main. *Dryden.*

7. Not sour.

Time changeth fruits from more sour to more *sweet*; but contrariwise liquors, even those that are of the juice of fruit, from more *sweet* to more sour. *Bacon's Natural History.*

Trees whose fruit is acid last longer than those whose fruit is *sweet*. *Bacon.*

When metals are dissolved in acid menstruums, and the acids in conjunction with the metal act after a different manner, so that the compound has a different taste, much milder than before, and sometimes a *sweet* one; is it not because the acids adhere to the metallick particles, and thereby lose much of their activity. *Newton's Opticks.*

8. Mild; soft; gentle.

Let me report to him
Your *sweet* dependency, and you shall find
A conqu'ror that will pray in aid for kindness. *Shakesp.*

The Peleiades shedding *sweet* influence. *Milton.*

Mercy has, could mercy's self be seen,
No *sweeter* look than this propitious queen. *Waller.*

9. Grateful; pleasing.

Sweet interchange of hill and valley. *Milton.*

Euryalus,
Than whom the Trojan host
No fairer face or *sweeter* air could boast. *Dryden's Æneid.*

10. Not stale; not stinking: as, *that meat is* sweet.

SWEET. *n. s.*

1. Sweetness; something pleasing.

Pluck out
The multitudinous tongue, let them not lick
The *sweet* which is their poison. *Shakespeare's Coriolanus.*

What softer sounds are these salute the ear,
From the large circle of the hemisphere,
As if the center of all *sweets* met here! *Ben. Johnson.*

Hail! wedded love,
Perpetual fountain of domestick *sweets!* *Milton.*

Taught to live
The easiest way; nor with perplexing thoughts
To interrupt the *sweet* of life. *Milton's Paradise Lost.*

Now since the Latian and the Trojan brood
Have tasted vengeance, and the *sweets* of blood,
Speak. *Dryden's Æneid.*

Can Ceyx then sustain to leave his wife,
And unconcern'd forsake the *sweets* of life? *Dryden.*

We have so great an abhorrence of pain, that a little of it extinguishes all our pleasures; a little bitter mingled in our cup leaves no relish of the *sweet*. *Locke.*

Love had ordain'd that it was Abra's turn
To mix the *sweets*, and minister the urn. *Prior.*

2. A word of endearment.

Sweet! leave me here a while
My spirits grow dull, and fain I would beguile
The tedious day with sleep. *Shakespeare.*

Wherefore frowns my *sweet?*
Have I too long been absent from these lips? *Ben. Johnson.*

3. A perfume.

As in perfumes,
'Tis hard to say what scent is uppermost;
Nor this part musick or civet can we call,
Or amber, but a rich result of all:
So she was all a *sweet*. *Dryden.*

Flowers
Innumerable, by the soft south-west
Open'd, and gather'd by religious hands,
Rebound their *sweets* from th' odoriferous pavement. *Prior.*

SWEE'TBREAD. *n. s.* The pancreas of the calf.

Never tie yourself always to eat meats of easy digesture, as veal, pullets, or *sweetbreads*. *Harvey on Consumption.*

Sweetbreed and collops were with skewers prick'd
About the sides; imbibing what they deck'd. *Dryden.*

When you roast a breast of veal, remember your sweetheart the butler loves a *sweetbread*. *Swift.*

SWEE'TBRIAR. *n. s.* [*sweet* and *briar.*] A fragrant shrub.

For March come violets and peach-tree in blossom, the cornelian-tree in blossom, and *sweetbriar*. *Bacon.*

SWEE'TBROOM. *n. s.* An herb. *Ainsworth.*

SWEE'TCICELY. *n. s.* [*Myrrhus.*] A plant.

The characters are; it is an umbelliferous plant, with a rose-shaped flower, consisting of several unequal petals or flower-leaves that are placed circularly, and rest upon the empalement, which turns to a fruit, composed of two seeds resembling a bird's bill, channelled and gibbous on one side, but plain on the other. *Miller.*

To SWEE'TEN. *v. a.* [from *sweet.*]

1. To make sweet.

The world the garden is, she is the flow'r
That *sweetens* all the place; she is the guest
Of rarest price. *Sidney.*

Here is the smell of the blood still: all the perfumes of Arabia will not *sweeten* this little hand. *Shakespeare.*

Give me an ounce of civet to *sweeten* my imagination. *Shakespeare's King Lear.*

With fairest flow'rs Fidele,
I'll *sweeten* thy sad grave. *Shakespeare's Cymbeline.*

Be humbly minded, know your post;
Sweeten your tea, and watch your toast. *Swift.*

2. To make mild or kind.

All kindnesses descend upon such a temper, as rivers of fresh waters falling into the main sea; the sea swallows them all, but is not changed or *sweetened* by them. *South's Sermons.*

3. To make less painful.

She the sweetness of my heart, even *sweetens* the death which her sweetness brought upon me. *Sidney.*

Thou shalt secure her helpless sex from harms,
And she thy cares will *sweeten* with her charms. *Dryden.*

Interest of state and change of circumstances may have *sweetened* these reflections to the politer sort, but impressions are not so easily worn out of the minds of the vulgar. *Addison.*

Thy mercy *sweet'ned* ev'ry soil,
Made ev'ry region please;
The hoary Alpin hills it warm'd,
And smooth'd the Tyrrhene seas. *Addison's Spectator.*

4. To palliate; to reconcile.

These lessons may be gilt and *sweetened* as we order pills and potions, so as to take off the disgust of the remedy. *L'Estr.*

5. To make grateful or pleasing.

I would have my love
Angry sometimes, to *sweeten* off the rest
Of her behaviour. *Ben. Johnson's Catiline.*

6. To soften; to make delicate.

Corregio has made his memory immortal, by the strength he has given to his figures, and by *sweetening* his lights and shadows, and melting them into each other so happily, that they are even imperceptible. *Dryden's Dufresnoy.*

To SWEE'TEN. *v. n.* To grow sweet.

Where a wasp hath bitten in a grape, or any fruit, it will *sweeten* hastily. *Bacon's Natural History.*

SWEE'TENER. *n. s.* [from *sweeten.*]

1. One that palliates; one that represents things tenderly.

But you who, till your fortune's made,
Must be a *sweet'ner* by your trade,
Must swear he never meant us ill. *Swift.*

Those softners, *sweetners*, and compounders, shake their heads so strongly, that we can hear their pockets jingle. *Swift.*

2. That which contemporates acrimony.

Powder of crabs eyes and claws, and burnt egg-shells are prescribed as *sweetners* of any sharp humours. *Temple.*

SWEE'THEART. *n. s.* [*sweet* and *heart.*] A lover or mistress.

Mistress retire yourself
Into some covert; take your *sweethearts*
And pluck o'er your brows. *Shakespeare.*

Sweetheart, you are now in an excellent good temperality, and your colour, I warrant you, is as red as any rose. *Shak.*

One thing, *Sweetheart*, I will ask,
Take me for a new-fashion'd mask. *Cleaveland.*

A wench was wringing her hands and crying; she had newly parted with her *sweetheart*. *L'Estrange.*

Pry'thee, *sweetheart*, how go matters in the house where thou hast been? *L'Estrange.*

She interprets all your dreams for these,
Foretells th' estate, when the rich uncle dies,
And sees a *sweetheart* in the sacrifice. *Dryden's Juvenal.*

SWEE'TING. *n. s.* [from *sweet.*]

1. A sweet luscious apple.

A child will chuse a *sweeting* because it is presently fair and pleasant, and refuse a runnet, because it is then green, hard and sour. *Ascham's Schoolmaster.*

2. A word of endearment.

Trip no further, pretty *sweeting*;
Journeys end in lovers meeting. *Shakespeare.*

SWEE'TISH. *adj.* [from *sweet.*] Somewhat sweet.

They esteemed that blood pituitous naturally, which abounded with an exceeding quantity of *sweetish* chyle. *Floyer.*

SWEE'TLY. *adv.* [from *sweet.*] In a sweet manner; with sweetness.

The best wine for my beloved goeth down *sweetly*. *Cant.*

He bore his great commission in his look;
But *sweetly* temper'd awe, and soften'd all he spoke. *Dryden.*

No poet ever *sweetly* sung,
Unless he were like Phœbus young;
Nor ever nymph inspir'd to rhyme,
Unless like Venus in her prime. *Swift.*

SWEE'TMEAT. *n. s.* [*sweet* and *meat.*] Delicacies made of fruits preserved with sugar.

Mopsa, as glad as of *sweetmeats* to go of such an errand, quickly returned. *Sidney.*

Why all the charges of the nuptial feast,
Wine and deserts, and *sweetmeats* to digest. *Dryden.*

There was plenty, but the dishes were ill sorted; whole pyramids of *sweetmeats* for boys and women, but little solid meat for men. *Dryden.*

Make your transparent *sweetmeats* truly nice,
With Indian sugar and Arabian spice. *King's Cookery.*

If a child cries for any unwholsome fruit, you purchase his quiet by giving him a less hurtful *sweetmeat*: this may preserve his health, but spoils his mind. *Locke.*

At a lord mayor's feast, the *sweetmeats* do not make their appearance till people are cloyed with beef and mutton. *Addison.*

They are allowed to kiss the child at meeting and parting; but a professor, who always stands by, will not suffer them to bring any presents of toys or *sweetmeats*. *Gulliver's Travels.*

SWEE'TNESS. *n. s.* [from *sweet.*] The quality of being sweet in any of its senses; fragrance; melody; lusciousness; deliciousness; agreeableness; delightfulness; gentleness of manners; mildness of aspect.

She the *sweetness* of my heart, even sweetning the death which her *sweetness* brought upon me. *Sidney.*

The right form, the true figure, the natural colour that is fit and due to the dignity of a man, to the beauty of a woman, to the *sweetness* of a young babe. *Ascham.*

O our lives *sweetness!*
That we the pain of death would hourly bear,
Rather than die at once. *Shakespeare's King Lear.*

Where a rainbow toucheth, there breatheth forth a sweet smell: for this happeneth but in certain matters, which have in themselves some *sweetness*, which the gentle dew of the rainbow draweth forth. *Bacon.*

Serene and clear harmonious Horace flows,
With *sweetness* not to be exprest in prose. *Roscommon.*

Suppose two authors equally sweet, there is a great distinction to be made in *sweetness*; as in that of sugar and that of honey. *Dryden.*

This old man's talk, though honey flow'd
In every word, would now lose all its *sweetness*. *Addison.*

Leave such to tune their own dull rhymes, and know
What's roundly smooth, or languishingly flow;
And praise the easy vigor of a line,
Where Denham's strength and Waller's *sweetness* join. *Pope.*

A man of good education, excellent understanding, and exact taste; these qualities are adorned with great modesty and a most amiable *sweetness* of temper. *Swift.*

SWEE'TWILLIAM. } *n. s.* Plants. They are a species of gilli-
SWEE'TWILLOW } flowers. [See CLOVE GILLIFLOWERS.]

SWEE'TWILLOW. *n. s.* Gale or Dutch myrtle.

The leaves are placed alternately on the branches: it hath male flowers which are produced at the wings of the leaves; are naked, and grow in a longish spike: the fruit, which is produced in separate trees, is of a conical figure, and squamose, containing one seed in each scale. *Miller.*

To SWELL. *v. n.* Participle pass. *swollen.* [ꝩpellan, Sax. *swellen*, Dutch.]

1. To grow bigger; to grow turgid; to extend the parts.

Propitious Tyber smooth'd his wat'ry way,
He roll'd his river back, and pois'd he stood,
A gentle *swelling* and a peaceful flood. *Dryden's Æneid.*

2. To tumify by obstruction.

But strangely visited people,
All *swol'n* and ulc'rous; pitiful to the eye,
The meer despair of surgery he cures. *Shakespeare's Macbeth.*

Forty years didst thou sustain them in the wilderness, so that their cloaths waxed not old, and their feet *swelled* not. *Nehem.* ix. 21.

Swol'n is his breast; his inward pains encrease,
All means are us'd, and all without success. *Dryden.*

3. To be exasperated.

My pity hath been balm to heal their wounds,
My mildness hath allay'd their *swelling* griefs. *Shakespeare.*

4. To look big.

Here he comes, *swelling* like a turkey-cock. *Shakespeare.*

Peleus and Telephus exil'd and poor,
Forget their *swelling* and gigantick words. *Roscommon.*

5. To protuberate.

This iniquity shall be as a breach ready to fall, *swelling* out in a high wall. *Isa.* xxx. 13.

6. To rise into arrogance; to be elated.

In all things else above our humble fate,
Your equal mind yet *swells* not into state. *Dryden.*

7. To be inflated with anger.

I will help every one from him that *swelleth* against him, and will set him at rest. *Psalms* xii. 6.

We have made peace of enmity
Between these *swelling* wrong incensed peers. *Shakespeare.*

The hearts of princes kiss obedience,
So much they love it; but to stubborn spirits
They *swell* and grow as terrible as storms. *Shakespeare.*

8. To grow upon the view.

O for a muse of fire, that would ascend
The brightest heaven of invention!
A kingdom for a stage, princes to act,
And monarchs to behold the *swelling* scene. *Shakespeare.*

9. It implies commonly a notion of something wrong.

Your youth admires
The throws and *swellings* of a Roman soul,
Cato's bold flights, th' extravagance of virtue. *Addison.*

Immoderate valour *swells* into a fault. *Addison's Cato.*

To SWELL. *v. a.*

1. To cause to rise or encrease; to make tumid.

Wind, blow the earth into the sea,
Or *swell* the curled waters 'bove the main. *Shakespeare.*

You who supply the ground with seeds of grain,
And you who *swell* those seeds with kindly rain. *Dryden.*

2. To aggravate; to heighten.

It is low ebb with his accuser, when such peccadillos are put to *swell* the charge. *Atterbury.*

3. To raise to arrogance.

All these miseries proceed from the same natural causes, which have usually attended kingdoms *swolen* with long plenty, pride, and excess. *Clarendon.*

SWELL. *n. s.* [from the verb.] Extension of bulk.

The swan's down-feather
That stands upon the *swell* at full of tide,
And neither way inclines. *Shakesp. Antony and Cleopatra.*

The king of men, *swoln* with pride,
Refus'd his presents, and his prayers deny'd. *Dryden.*

SWE'LLING. *n. s.* [from *swell.*]

1. Morbid tumour.

2. Protuberance; prominence.

The superficies of such plates are not even, but have many cavities and *swellings*, which how shallow soever do a little vary the thickness of the plate. *Newton's Opticks.*

3. Effort for a vent.

My heart was torn in pieces to see the husband suppressing and keeping down the *swellings* of his grief. *Tatler.*

To SWELT. *v. n.* To puff in sweat, if that be the meaning.

Chearful blood in faintness chill did melt,
Which like a fever fit through all his body *swelt*. *Fa. Queen.*

To SWE'LTER. *v. n.* [This is supposed to be corrupted from *sultry.*]

1. To be pained with heat.

If the sun's excessive heat
Makes our bodies *swelter*,
To an osier hedge we get
For a friendly shelter;
There we may
Think and pray,
Before death
Stops our breath. *Walton's Angler.*

To SWE'LTER. *v. a.* To parch, or dry up with heat.

Some would always have long nights and short days; others again long days and short nights; one climate would be scorched and *sweltered* with everlasting dog-days, while an eternal December blasted another. *Bentley's Sermons.*

SWE'LTRY. *adj.* [from *swelter.*] Suffocating with heat.

SWEPT. The participle and preterite of *sweep.*

To SWERD. *v. n.* To breed a green turf. [See to SWARD.]

The clays that are long in *swerding*, and little subject to weeds, are the best land for clover. *Mortimer.*

To SWERVE. *v. n.* [*swerven*, Saxon and Dutch.]

1. To wander; to rove.

A maid thitherward did run,
To catch her sparrow which from her did *swerve*. *Sidney.*

The *swerving* vines on the tall elms prevail,
Unhurt by southern show'rs or northern hail. *Dryden.*

2. To deviate; to depart from rule, custom or duty.

That which angels do clearly behold, and without any *swerving* observe, is a law celestial and heavenly. *Hooker.*

Howsoever these *swervings* are now and then incident into the course of nature, nevertheless so constantly the laws of nature are by natural agents observed, that no man denieth; but those things which nature worketh are wrought either always, or for the most part after one and the same manner. *Hooker.*

The ungodly have laid a snare for me; but yet I *swerve* not from thy commandments. *Common Prayer.*

Were I crown'd the most imperial monarch,
Thereof most worthy, were I the fairest youth
That ever made the eye *swerve*,
I would not prize them without her love. *Shakespeare.*

There is a protection very just which princes owe to their servants, when, in obedience to their just commands, upon extraordinary occasions, in the execution of their trusts, they *swerve* from the strict letter of the law. *Clarendon.*

Till then his majesty had not in the least *swerved* from that act of parliament. *Clarendon.*

Annihilation in the course of nature, defect and *swerving* in the creature without the sin of man would immediately follow. *Hakewill on Providence.*

Firm

Firm we subsist, yet possible to *swerve*. *Milton.*

Many who, through the contagion of ill example, *swerve* exceedingly from the rules of their holy faith, yet would upon such an extraordinary warning be brought to comply with them. *Atterbury's Sermons.*

3. To ply; to bend.

Now their mightiest quell'd, the battle *swerv'd*
With many an inroad gor'd. *Milton.*

4. [I know not whence derived.] To climb on a narrow body.

Ten wildings have I gather'd for my dear,
Upon the topmost branch, the tree was high,
Yet nimbly up from bough to bough I *swerv'd*. *Dryden.*
She fled, returning by the way she went,
And *swerv'd* along her bow with swift ascent. *Dryden.*

SWIFT. *adj.* [ſpıꝼt, Saxon.]

1. Moving far in a short time; quick; fleet; speedy; nimble; rapid.

Thou art so far before,
That *swiftest* wing of recompence is slow
To overtake thee. *Shakespeare.*
Yet are these feet, whose strengthless stay is numb,
Unable to support this lump of clay,
Swift-winged with desire to get a grave. *Shakespeare.*

Men of war, whose faces were like the faces of lions, and as *swift* as the roes upon the mountains. *1 Chron.* xii. 8.

We imitate and practise to make *swifter* motions than any out of other muskets. *Bacon.*

To him with *swift* ascent he up return'd. *Milton.*

Things that move so *swift* as not to affect the senses distinctly, with several distinguishable distances of their motion, and so cause not any train of ideas in the mind, are not perceived to move. *Locke.*

It preserves the ends of the bones from incalescency, which they, being solid bodies, would contract from any *swift* motion. *Ray.*

Thy stumbling founder'd jade can trot as high
As any other Pegasus can fly;
So the dull eel moves nimbler in the mud,
Than all the *swift* fin'd racers of the flood. *Dorset.*
Clouded in a deep abyss of light,
While present, too severe for human sight,
Nor staying longer than one *swift*-wing'd night. *Prior.*

Mantiger made a circle round the chamber, and the *swift*-footed martin pursued him. *Arbuthnot.*

There too my son,——ah once my best delight,
Once *swift* of foot, and terrible in fight. *Pope's Odyssey.*
Swift they descend, with wing to wing conjoin'd,
Stretch their broad plumes, and float upon the wind. *Pope.*

2. Ready.

Let every man be *swift* to hear, slow to speak. *Ja.* i. 19.

He made intricate seem straight,
To mischief *swift*. *Milton.*

SWIFT. *n. s.* [from the quickness of their flight.]

1. A bird like a swallow; a martinet.

Swifts and swallows have remarkably short legs, and their toes grasp any thing very strongly. *Derham.*

2. The current of a stream.

He can live in the strongest *swifts* of the water. *Walton.*

SWI'FTLY. *adv.* [from *swift*.] Fleetly; rapidly; nimbly; with celerity; with velocity.

These move *swiftly*, and at great distance; but then they require a medium well-disposed, and their transmission is easily stopped. *Bacon's Natural History.*

Pleas'd with the passage, we slide *swiftly* on,
And see the dangers which we cannot shun. *Dryden.*
In decent order they advance to light;
Yet then too *swiftly* fleet by human sight,
And meditate too soon their everlasting flight. *Prior.*

SWI'FTNESS. *n. s.* [from *swift*.] Speed; nimbleness; rapidity; quickness; velocity; celerity.

Let our proportions for these wars
Be soon collected, and all thing thought upon,
That may with reasonable *swiftness* add
More feathers to our wings. *Shakespeare's Henry V.*
We may outrun
By violent *swiftness* that which we run at;
And lose by over running. *Shakespeare's Henry VIII.*
Speed to describe whose *swiftness* number fails. *Milton.*
Exulting, till he finds their nobler sense
Their disproportion'd speed does recompense;
Then curses his conspiring feet, whose scent
Betrays that safety which their *swiftness* lent. *Denham.*
Such is the mighty *swiftness* of your mind,
That like the earth's, it leaves our sense behind. *Dryden.*

To SWIG. *v. n.* [*swiga*, Islandick.] To drink by large draughts.

To SWILL. *v. a.* [ſpılʒan, Saxon.]

1. To drink luxuriously and grossly.

The wretched, bloody, and usurping boar
That spoil'd your summer fields and fruitful vines,
Swills your warm blood like wash, and makes his trough
In your embowel'd bosoms. *Shakespeare's Richard III.*

The most common of these causes are an hereditary disposition, *swilling* down great quantities of cold watery liquors. *Arbuthnot on Diet.*

Such is the poet, fresh in pay,
The third night's profits of his play;
His morning draughts till noon can *swill*,
Among his brethren of the quill. *Swift.*

2. To wash; to drench.

As fearfully as doth a galled rock
O'erhang and jutty his confounded base,
Swill'd with the wild and wasteful ocean. *Shakespeare.*
With that a German oft has *swill'd* his throat,
Deluded, that imperial Rhine bestow'd
The generous rummer. *Philips.*

3. To inebriate.

I should be loth
To meet the rudeness and *swill'd* insolence
Of such late wassailers. *Milton.*
He drinks a *swilling* draught; and lin'd within,
Will supple in the bath his outward skin. *Dryden.*

SWILL. *n. s.* [from the verb.] Drink, luxuriously poured down.

Give swine such *swill* as you have. *Mortimer.*

Thus as they swim, in mutual *swill* the talk
Reels fast from theme to theme. *Thomson.*

SWILLER. *n. s.* [from *swill*.] A luxurious drinker.

To SWIM. *v. n.* Preterite *swam*, *swom*, or *swum*. [ſpımman, Saxon; *swemmen*, Dutch.]

1. To float on the water; not to sink.

I will scarce think you have *swam* in a gondola. *Shakespeare.*

We have ships and boats for going under water, and brooking of seas; also *swimming*-girdles and supporters. *Bacon.*

2. To move progressively in the water by the motion of the limbs.

Leap in with me into this angry flood,
And *swim* to yonder point. *Shakespeare's Julius Cæsar.*
I have ventur'd,
Like little wanton boys that *swim* on bladders,
These many summers in a sea of glory;
But far beyond my depth. *Shakespeare's Henry VIII.*

The soldiers counsel was to kill the prisoners, lest any of them should *swim* out and escape. *Acts* xxvii. 42.

The rest driven into the lake, where seeking to save their lives by *swimming*, they were slain in coming to land by the Spanish horsemen, or else in their *swimming* shot by the harquebusiers. *Knolles.*

Animals *swim* in the same manner as they go, and need no other way of motion for natation in the water, then for progression upon the land. *Brown's Vulgar Errours.*

The frighted wolf now *swims* among the sheep,
The yellow lion wanders in the deep:
The stag *swims* faster than he ran before. *Dryden.*
Blue Triton gave the signal from the shore,
The ready Nereids heard and *swam* before,
To smooth the seas. *Dryden.*

3. To be conveyed by the stream.

With tenders of our protection of them from the fury of those who would soon drown them, if they refused to *swim* down the popular stream with them. *King Charles.*

I *swom* with the tide, and the water under me was buoyant. *Dryden.*

4. To glide along with a smooth or dizzy motion.

She with pretty and with *swimming* gate
Follying, her womb then rich with my young squire
Would imitate. *Shakespeare.*
A hovering mist came *swimming* o'er his sight,
And seal'd his eyes in everlasting night. *Dryden.*
My slack hand dropt, and all the idle pomp,
Priests, altars, victims *swam* before my sight! *Smith.*
The fainting soul stood ready wing'd for flight,
And o'er his eye-balls *swum* the shades of night. *Pope.*

5. To be dizzy; to be vertiginous.

I am taken with a grievous *swimming* in my head, and such a mist before my eyes, that I can neither hear nor see. *Dryd.*

6. To be floated.

When the heavens are filled with clouds, when the earth *swims* in rain, and all nature wears a lowring countenance, I withdraw myself from these uncomfortable scenes into the visionary worlds of art. *Addison's Spectator.*

Sudden the ditches swell, the meadows *swim*. *Thomson.*

7. To have abundance of any quality; to flow in any thing.

They now *swim* in joy,
Ere long to *swim* at large, and laugh; for which
The world a world of tears must weep. *Milton.*

To SWIM. *v. a.* To pass by swimming.

Sometimes he thought to *swim* the stormy main,
By stretch of arms the distant shore to gain. *Dryden.*

SWIMM. *n. s.* [from the verb.] The bladder of fishes by which they are supported in the water.

The braces have the nature and use of tendons, in contracting the *swim*, and thereby transfusing the air out of one bladder into another, or discharging it from them both. *Grew.*

Swi'mmer. *n. ſ.* [from *ſwim.*]

1. One who ſwims.

Birds find eaſe in the depth of the air, as *ſwimmers* do in a deep water. *Bacon.*

Latiroſtrous and flat billed birds, being generally *ſwimmers*, the organ is wiſely contrived for action. *Brown.*

Life is oft preſerv'd
By the bold *ſwimmer*, in the ſwift illapſe
Of accident diſaſtrous. *Thomſon.*

2. The *ſwimmer* is ſituated in the fore legs of a horſe, above the knees, and upon the inſide, and almoſt upon the back parts of the hind legs, a little below the ham: this part is without hair, and reſembles a piece of hard dry horn. *Farrier's Dict.*

Swi'mmingly. *adv.* [from *ſwimming.*] Smoothly; without obſtruction. A low word.

John got on the battlements, and called to Nick, I hope the cauſe goes on *ſwimmingly.* *Arbuthnot.*

SWINE. *n. ſ.* [ꞅpin, Saxon; *ſwyn*, Dutch. It is probably the plural of ſome old word, and is now the ſame in both numbers.] A hog; a pig. A creature remarkable for ſtupidity and naſtineſs.

O monſtrous beaſt! how like a *ſwine* he lies! *Shakeſp.*

He will be *ſwine* drunk; and in his ſleep he does little harm, ſave to his bedcloaths. *Shakeſpeare.*

Who knows not Circe,
The daughter of the Sun? whoſe charmed cup
Whoever taſted, loſt his upright ſhape,
And downward fell into a groveling *ſwine.* *Milton.*

Had the upper part, to the middle, been of human ſhape, and all below *ſwine*, had it been murder to deſtroy it? *Locke.*

How inſtinct varies in the grov'ling *ſwine*,
Compar'd, half reaſ'ning elephant, with thine! *Pope.*

Swi'nebread. *n. ſ.* A kind of plant; truffles. *Bailey.*

Swi'neherd. *n. ſ.* [ꞅpin and hyꞃꝺ, Saxon.] A keeper of hogs.

There *ſwineherd*, that keepeth the hog. *Tuſſer.*

The whole interview between Ulyſſes and Eumeus has fallen into ridicule: Eumeus has been judged to be of the ſame rank and condition with our modern *ſwineherds.* *Broome.*

Swi'nepipe. *n. ſ.* A bird of the thruſh kind. *Bailey.*

To Swing. *v. n.* [ꞅpingan, Saxon.]

1. To wave too and fro hanging looſely.

I tried if a pendulum would *ſwing* faſter, or continue *ſwinging* longer in our receiver, in caſe of exſuction of the air, than otherwiſe. *Boyle.*

If the coach *ſwung* but the leaſt to one ſide, ſhe uſed to ſhriek ſo loud, that all concluded ſhe was overturned. *Arbuthn.*

Jack hath hanged himſelf: let us go ſee how he *ſwings.* *Arb.*

When the *ſwinging* ſigns your ears offend
With creaking noiſe, then rainy floods impend. *Gay.*

2. To fly backward and forward on a rope.

To Swing. *v. a.* preterite *ſwang*, *ſwung.*

1. To make to play looſely on a ſtring.

2. To whirl round in the air.

His ſword prepar'd
He *ſwang* about his head, and cut the winds. *Shakeſpeare.*

Take bottles and *ſwing* them: fill not the bottles full, but leave ſome air, elſe the liquor cannot play nor flower. *Bacon.*

Swinging a red-hot iron about, or faſtening it unto a wheel under that motion, it will ſooner grow cold. *Brown.*

Swing thee in the air, then daſh thee down,
To th' hazard of thy brains and ſhatter'd ſides. *Milton.*

3. To wave looſely.

If one approach to dare his force,
He *ſwings* his tail, and ſwiftly turns him round. *Dryden.*

Swing. *n. ſ.* [from the verb.]

1. Motion of any thing hanging looſely.

In caſting of any thing, the arms, to make a greater *ſwing*, are firſt caſt backward. *Bacon's Natural Hiſtory.*

Men uſe a pendulum, as a more ſteady and regular motion than that of the earth; yet if any one ſhould aſk how he certainly knows that the two ſucceſſive *ſwings* of a pendulum are equal, it would be very hard to ſatisfy him. *Locke.*

2. A line on which any thing hangs looſe.

3. Influence or power of a body put in motion.

The ram that batters down the wall,
For the great *ſwing* and rudeneſs of his poize,
They place before his hand that made the engine. *Shakeſp.*

In this encyclopædia, and round of knowledge, like the great wheels of heaven, we're to obſerve two circles, that, while we are daily carried about, and whirled on by the *ſwing* and rapt of the one, we may maintain a natural and proper courſe in the ſober wheel of the other. *Brown.*

The deſcending of the earth to this orbit is not upon that mechanical account Carteſius pretends, namely, the ſtrong *ſwing* of the more ſolid globuli that overflow it. *More.*

4. Courſe; unreſtrained liberty; abandonment to any motive.

Facts unjuſt
Commit, even to the full *ſwing* of his luſt. *Chapman.*

Take thy *ſwing*;
For not to take, is but the ſelf-ſame thing. *Dryden.*

Let them all take their *ſwing*
To pillage the king,
And get a blue ribband inſtead of a ſtring. *Swift.*

5. Unreſtrained tendency.

Where the *ſwing* goeth, there follow, fawn, flatter, laugh, and lie luſtily at other mens liking. *Aſcham's Schoolmaſter.*

Theſe exuberant productions only excited and fomented his luſts; ſo that his whole time lay upon his hands, and gave him leiſure to contrive and with full *ſwing* purſue his follies. *Wood.*

Thoſe that are ſo perſuaded, deſire to be wiſe in a way that will gratify their appetites, and ſo give up themſelves to the *ſwing* of their unbounded propenſions. *Glanv. Scepſ. Preface.*

Were it not for theſe, civil government were not able to ſtand before the prevailing *ſwing* of corrupt nature, which would know no honeſty but advantage. *South.*

To SWINGE. *v. a.* [ꞅpingan, Saxon.]

1. To whip; to baſtinade; to puniſh.

Sir, I was in love with my bed: I thank you, you *ſwing'd* me for my love, which makes me the bolder to chide you for your's. *Shakeſ. Two Gent. of Verona.*

This very rev'rend letcher, quite worn out
With rheumatiſms, and crippled with his gout,
Forgets what he in youthful times has done,
And *ſwinges* his own vices in his ſon. *Dryd. jun. Juvenal.*

The printer brought along with him a bundle of thoſe papers, which, in the phraſe of the whig-coffeehouſes, have *ſwinged* off the Examiner. *Swift.*

2. To move as a laſh. Not in uſe.

He, wroth to ſee his kingdom fail,
Swinges the ſcaly horror of his folded tail. *Milton.*

Swinge. *n. ſ.* [from the verb.] A ſway; a ſweep of any thing in motion. Not in uſe.

The ſhallow water doth her force infringe,
And renders vain her tail's impetuous *ſwinge.* *Waller.*

Swi'ngebuckler. *n. ſ.* [*ſwinge* and *buckler.*] A bully; a man who pretends to feats of arms.

You had not four ſuch *ſwingebucklers* in all the inns of court again. *Shakeſp. Henry* IV.

Swi'nger. *n. ſ.* [from *ſwing.*] He who ſwings; a hurler.

Swi'nging. *adj.* [from *ſwinge.*] Great; huge. A low word.

The countryman ſeeing the lion diſarmed, with a *ſwinging* cudgel broke off the match. *L'Eſtrange.*

A good *ſwinging* ſum of John's readieſt caſh went towards building of Hocus's countryhouſe. *Arbuthnot.*

Swi'ngingly. *adv.* [from *ſwinging.*] Vaſtly; greatly.

Henceforward he'll print neither pamphlets nor linen,
And, if ſwearing can do't, ſhall be *ſwingingly* maul'd. *Swift.*

To Swi'ngle. *v. n.* [from *ſwing.*]

1. To dangle; to wave hanging.

2. To ſwing in pleaſure.

Swi'nish. *adj.* [from *ſwine.*] Befitting ſwine; reſembling ſwine; groſs; brutal.

They clepe us drunkards, and with *ſwiniſh* phraſe
Soil our addition. *Shakeſp. Hamlet.*

Swiniſh gluttony
Ne'er looks to heav'n amidſt his gorgeous feaſt;
But, with beſotted baſe ingratitude,
Crams and blaſphemes his feeder. *Milton.*

To Swink. *v. n.* [ꞅpincan, Saxon.] To labour; to toil; to drudge. Obſolete.

Riches, renown, and principality,
For which men *ſwink* and ſweat inceſſantly. *Fairy Queen.*

For they do *ſwink* and ſweat to feed the other,
Who live like lords of that which they do gather. *Hub. Tale.*

To Swink. *v. a.* To overlabour.

The labour'd ox
In his looſe traces from the furrow came,
And the *ſwink'd* hedger at his ſupper ſat. *Milton.*

Swink. *n. ſ.* [ꞅpinc, Saxon.] Labour; toil; drudgery. Obſolete.

Ah, Piers, been thy teeth on edge, to think
How great ſport they gaynen with little *ſwinke*? *Spenſer.*

Thou's but a lazy loorde,
And rekes much of thy *ſwinke.* *Spenſer.*

Switch. *n. ſ.* A ſmall flexible twig.

Fetch me a dozen crabtree ſtaves, and ſtrong ones; theſe are but *ſwitches.* *Shakeſp. Henry* VIII.

When a circle 'bout the wriſt
Is made by beadle exorciſt,
The body feels the ſpur and *ſwitch.* *Hudibras.*

Mauritania, on the fifth medal, leads a horſe with ſomething like a thread; in her other hand ſhe holds a *ſwitch.* *Addiſon.*

To Switch. *v. a.* [from the noun.] To laſh; to jerk.

Lay thy bridle's weight
Moſt of thy left ſide; thy right horſe then *ſwitching*, all thy throat
Spent in encouragements, give him; and all the rein let float. *Chapman's Iliad.*

Swi'vel. *n. ſ.* Something fixed in another body ſo as to turn round in it.

Swo'bber. *n. s.* [See Swabber.]

1. A sweeper of the deck.

Cubb'd in a cabbin, on a mattress laid,
On a brown george with lousy *swobbers* fed. *Dryden.*

2. Four privileged cards that are only incidentally used in betting at the game of whist.

The clergyman used to play at whist and *swobbers*: playing now and then a sober game at whist for pastime, it might be pardoned; but he could not digest those wicked *swobbers*. *Swift.*

Swo'llen. } The participle passive of *swell.*
Swoln. }

Unto his aid she hastily did draw
Her dreadful beast, who, *swoln* with blood of late,
Came ramping forth with proud presumptuous gait. *F. Qu.*

When thus the gather'd storms of wretched love
In my *swoln* bosom with long war had strove,
At length they broke their bounds: at length their force
Bore down whatever met its stronger course;
Laid all the civil bonds of manhood waste,
And scatter'd ruin as the torrent past. *Prior.*

Whereas at first we had only three of these principles, their number is already *swoln* to five. *Baker on Learning.*

Swom. The preterite of *swim.*

I *swom* with the tide, and the water was buoyant under me. *Dryden.*

To Swoon. *v. n.* [aſpunan, Saxon.] To suffer a suspension of thought and sensation; to faint.

So play the foolish throngs with one that *swoons*;
Come all to help him, and so stop the air
By which he should revive. *Shakespeare.*

If thou stand'st not i' th' state of hanging, or of some death more long in spectatorship, and crueler in suffering, behold now presently, and *swoon* for what's to come upon thee. *Shak.*

We see the great and sudden effect of smells in fetching men again, when they *swoon.* *Bacon.*

The most in years *swoon'd* first away for pain;
Then, scarce recover'd, spoke. *Dryden.*

The woman finds it all a trick,
That he could *swoon* when she was sick;
And knows that in that grief he reckon'd
On black-ey'd Susan for his second. *Prior.*

There appeared such an ecstacy in his action, that he seemed ready to *swoon* away in the surprize of joy. *Tatler.*

Swoon. *n. s.* [from the verb.] A lipothymy; a fainting fit.

To Swoop. *v. a.* [I suppose formed from the sound.]

1. To fall at once as a hawk upon his prey.

A fowl in Madagascar, called a ruck, the feathers of whose wings are twelve paces, can with as much ease *swoop* up an elephant as our kites do a mouse. *Wilkins.*

This mould'ring piecemeal in your hands did fall,
And now at last you came to *swoop* it all. *Dryden.*

2. To prey upon; to catch up.

The physician looks with another eye on the medicinal herb than the grazing ox, which *swoops* it in with the common grass. *Glanv. Sceps.*

Swoop. *n. s.* [from the verb.] Fall of a bird of prey upon his quarry.

All my pretty ones?
Did you say all? What, all? O hellkite! all!
What, all my pretty chickens and their dam,
At one fell *swoop?* *Shakes. Macbeth.*

The eagle fell into the fox's quarters, and carried away a whole litter of cubs at a *swoop.* *L'Estrange.*

To Swop. *v. a.* [Of uncertain derivation.] To change; to exchange one thing for another. A low word.

When I drove a thrust home, he put it by,
And cried, as in derision, spare the stripling;
Oh that insulting word! I would have *swopp'd*
Youth for old age, and all my life behind,
To have been then a momentary man. *Dryden's Cleomenes.*

SWORD. *n. s.* [ſpeoꞃd, Saxon; *sweerd*, Dutch.]

1. A weapon used either in cutting or thrusting; the usual weapon of fights hand to hand.

Old unhappy traitor, the *sword* is out
That must destroy thee. *Shakesp. King Lear.*

Each man took his *sword*, and slew all the males. *Gen.*

Euryalus is the only peer that is described with a *sword*, which he gives to Ulysses to repair his injury. *Broome.*

2. Destruction by war.

The *sword* without, and terrour within. *Deut.* xxxii. 25.

3. Vengeance of justice.

4. Emblem of authority.

This I, her *sword* bearer, do carry,
For civil deed and military. *Hudibras.*

Swo'rded. *adj.* [from *sword.*] Girt with a sword.

The *sworded* seraphim
Are seen in glitt'ring ranks with wings display'd. *Milton.*

Swo'rder. *n. s.* [from *sword.*] A cut-throat; a soldier. In contempt.

A Roman *sworder* and banditto slave
Murther'd sweet Tully. *Shakes. Henry VI.*

Cæsar will
Unstate his happiness, and be stag'd to th' shew
Against a *sworder.* *Shakespeare.*

Swo'rdfish. *n. s.* A fish with a long sharp bone issuing from his head.

A *swordfish* small him from the rest did sunder,
That in his throat him pricking softly under,
His wide abyss him forced forth to spew. *Spenser.*

Malpighi observed the middle of the optick nerve of the *swordfish* to be a large membrane, folded, according to its length, in many doubles, like a fan. *Derham's Physico-Theol.*

Our little fleet was now engag'd so far,
That, like the *swordfish* in the whale, they fought;
The combat only seem'd a civil war,
'Till through their bowels we our passage wrought. *Dryd.*

Swo'rdgrass. *n. s.* A kind of sedge; glader. *Ainsw.*

Swo'rdknot. *n. s.* [*sword* and *knot.*] Ribband tied to the hilt of the sword.

Wigs with wigs, *swordknots* with *swordknots* strive,
Beaus banish beaus, and coaches coaches drive. *Pope.*

Swo'rdlaw. *n. s.* Violence; the law by which all is yielded to the stronger.

So violence
Proceeded, and oppression, and *swordlaw*,
Through all the plain, and refuge none was found. *Milton.*

Swo'rdman. *n. s.* [*sword* and *man.*] Soldier; fighting man.

Worthy fellows, and like to prove most sinewy *swordmen.* *Shak. All's well that ends well.*

At Lecca's house,
Among your *swordmen*, where so many associates
Both of thy mischief and thy madness met. *Ben. Johnson.*

Essex was made lieutenant-general of the army, the darling of the *swordmen.* *Clarendon.*

Swo'rdplayer. *n. s.* [*sword* and *play.*] Gladiator; fencer; one who exhibits in publick his skill at the weapons by fighting prizes.

These they called *swordplayers*, and this spectacle a swordfight. *Hakewill on Providence.*

Swore. The preterite of *swear.*

How soon unsay
What feign'd submission *swore.* *Milton.*

Sworn. The participle passive of *swear.*

What does else want credit, come to me,
And I'll be *sworn* 'tis true. *Shakespeare.*

I am *sworn* brother, sweet,
To grim necessity; and he and I
Will keep a league 'till death. *Shak. Richard II.*

They that are mad against me, are *sworn* against me. *Ps.*

He refused not the civil offer of a pharisee, though his *sworn* enemy; and would eat at the table of those who sought his ruin. *Calamy's Sermons.*

To shelter innocence,
The nation all elects some patron-knight,
Sworn to be true to love, and slave to fame,
And many a valiant chief enrols his name. *Granville.*

Swum. Preterite and participle passive of *swim.*

Air, water, earth,
By fowl, fish, beast, was flown, was *swum*, was walk'd
Frequent. *Milton's Paradise Lost.*

Swung. Preterite and participle passive of *swing.*

Her hand within her hair she wound,
Swung her to earth, and dragg'd her on the ground. *Addis.*

Syb. *adj.* [Properly *sib*, ſib, Saxon.] Related by blood. The Scottish dialect still retains it.

If what my grandsire to me said be true,
Siker I am very *syb* to you. *Spenser's Pastorals.*

Sy'camine. } *n. s.* A tree.
Sy'camore. }

Sycamore is our *acer majus*, one of the kinds of maples: it is a quick grower. *Mortimer's Husbandry.*

Under the grove of *sycamore*
I saw your son. *Shakesp. Romeo and Juliet.*

If ye had faith as a grain of mustard-seed, ye might say unto this *sycamine*-tree, be thou plucked up, and it should obey you. *Lu.* xvii. 6.

I was no prophet, but an herdman, and a gatherer of *sycamore* fruit. *Amos* vii. 14.

Go to yonder *sycamore*-tree, and hide your bottle of drink under its hollow root. *Walton's Angler.*

Sycamores with eglantine were spread;
A hedge about the sides, a covering over head. *Dryden.*

SY'COPHANT. *n. s.* [συκοφάντης; *sycophanta*, Latin.] A flatterer; a parasite.

Accusing *sycophants*, of all men, did best sort to his nature; but therefore not seeming *sycophants*, because of no evil they said, they could bring any new or doubtful thing unto him, but such as already he had been apt to determine; so as they came but as proofs of his wisdom, fearful and more secure, while the fear he had figured in his mind had any possibility of event. *Sidney.*

Men

Men know themſelves void of thoſe qualities which the impudent *ſycophant*, at the ſame time, both aſcribes to them, and in his ſleeve laughs at them for believing. *South.*

To SY'COPHANT. *v. n.* [συκοφαντέω; from the noun.] To play the ſycophant. A low bad word.

His *ſycophanting* arts being detected, that game is not to be played the ſecond time; whereas a man of clear reputation, though his barque be ſplit, has ſomething left towards ſetting up again. *Government of the Tongue.*

SYCOPHA'NTICK. *adj.* [from *ſycophant.*] Flattering; paraſitical.

To SY'COPHANTISE. *v. n.* [συκοφαντικὸς; from *ſycophant.*] To play the flatterer. *Dict.*

SYLLA'BICAL. *adj.* [from *ſyllable.*] Relating to ſyllables; conſiſting of ſyllables.

SYLLA'BICALLY. *adv.* [from *ſyllabical.*] In a ſyllabical manner.

SYLLA'BICK. *adj.* [*ſyllabique*, French; from *ſyllable.*] Relating to ſyllables.

SY'LLABLE. *n. ſ.* [συλλαβὴ; *ſyllabe*, French.]

1. As much of a word as is uttered by the help of one vowel, or one articulation.

I heard
Each *ſyllable* that breath made up between them. *Shakeſp.*

There is that property in all letters of aptneſs to be conjoined in *ſyllables* and words, through the voluble motions of the organs from one ſtop or figure to another, that they modify and diſcriminate the voice without appearing to diſcontinue it. *Holder's Elements of Speech.*

2. Any thing proverbially conciſe.

Abraham, Job, and the reſt that lived before any *ſyllable* of the law of God was written, did they not ſin as much as we do in every action not commanded? *Hooker.*

To-morrow, and to-morrow, and to-morrow,
Creeps in this petty pace from day to day,
To the laſt *ſyllable* of recorded time;
And all our yeſterdays have lighted fools
The way to duſty death. *Shakeſ. Macbeth.*

He hath told ſo many melancholy ſtories, without one *ſyllable* of truth, that he hath blunted the edge of my fears. *Swift.*

To SY'LLABLE. *v. a.* [from the noun.] To utter; to pronounce; to articulate. Not in uſe.

Airy tongues that *ſyllable* mens names
On ſands and ſhores, and deſart wilderneſſes. *Milton.*

SY'LLABUB. *n. ſ.* [Rightly SILLABUB, which ſee.] Milk and acids.

No *ſyllabubs* made at the milking pail,
But what are compos'd of a pot of good ale. *Beaumont.*

Two lines would expreſs all they ſay in two pages: 'tis nothing but whipt *ſyllabub* and froth, without any ſolidity. *Felton on the Claſſicks.*

SY'LLABUS. *n. ſ.* [συλλαβὸς.] An abſtract; a compendium containing the heads of a diſcourſe.

SY'LLOGISM. *n. ſ.* [συλλογισμὸς; *ſyllogiſme*, French.] An argument compoſed of three propoſitions: as, *every man thinks; Peter is a man, therefore Peter thinks.*

Unto them a piece of rhetorick is a ſufficient argument of logick, an apologue of Æſop beyond a *ſyllogiſm* in Barbara. *Brown's Vulgar Errours.*

What a miraculous thing ſhould we count it, if the flint and the ſteel, inſtead of a few ſparks, ſhould chance to knock out definitions and *ſyllogiſms?* *Bentley.*

SYLLOGI'STICAL. } *adj.* [συλλογιστικὸς; from *ſyllogiſm.*] Re-
SYLLOGI'STICK. } taining to a ſyllogiſm; conſiſting of a ſyllogiſm.

Though we ſuppoſe ſubject and predicate, and copula, and propoſitions and *ſyllogiſtical* connexions in their reaſoning, there is no ſuch matter; but the intire buſineſs is at the ſame moment preſent with them, without deducing one thing from another. *Hale's Origin of Mankind.*

Though the terms of propoſitions may be complex, yet where the compoſition of the whole argument is thus plain, ſimple, and regular, it is properly called a ſimple ſyllogiſm, ſince the complexion does not belong to the *ſyllogiſtick* form of it. *Watts's Logick.*

SYLLOGI'STICALLY. *adv.* [from *ſyllogiſtical.*] In the form of a ſyllogiſm.

A man knows firſt, and then he is able to prove *ſyllogiſtically*; ſo that ſyllogiſm comes after knowledge, when a man has no need of it. *Locke.*

To SY'LLOGIZE. *v. n.* [*ſyllogiſer*, French; συλλογίζειν.] To reaſon by ſyllogiſm.

Logick is, in effect, an art of *ſyllogizing.* *Baker.*

Men have endeavoured to transform logick into a kind of mechaniſm, and to teach boys to *ſyllogize*, or frame arguments and refute them, without real knowledge. *Watts.*

SY'LVAN. *adj.* [Better *ſilvan.*] Woody; ſhady; relating to woods.

Cedar and pine, and fir and branching palm,
A *ſylvan* ſcene! and as the ranks aſcend,
Shade above ſhade, a woody theatre
Of ſtatelieſt view. *Milton's Paradiſe Loſt.*

Eternal greens the moſſy margin grace,
Watch'd by the *ſylvan* genius of the place. *Pope.*

SY'LVAN. *n. ſ.* [*ſylvain*, French.] A wood-god, or ſatyr.

When the ſun begins to fling
His flaring beams, me, goddeſs, bring
To arched walks of twilight groves,
And ſhadows brown, that *ſylvan* loves,
Of pine or monumental oak. *Milton.*

Her private orchards wall'd on ev'ry ſide;
To lawleſs *ſylvans* all acceſs deny'd. *Pope.*

SY'MBOL. *n. ſ.* [*ſymbole*, French; σύμβολον; *ſymbolum*, Latin.]

1. An abſtract; a compendium; a comprehenſive form.

Beginning with the *ſymbol* of our faith, upon that the author of the gloſs enquires into the nature of faith. *Baker.*

2. A type; that which comprehends in its figure a repreſentation of ſomething elſe.

Salt, as incorruptible, was the *ſymbol* of friendſhip; which, if it caſually fell, was accounted ominous, and their amity of no duration. *Brown's Vulgar Errours.*

Words are the ſigns and *ſymbols* of things; and as, in accounts, ciphers and figures paſs for real ſums, ſo words and names paſs for things themſelves. *South's Sermons.*

The heathens made choice of theſe lights as apt *ſymbols* of eternity, becauſe, contrary to all ſublunary beings, though they ſeem to periſh every night, they renew themſelves every morning. *Addiſon on ancient Medals.*

SYMBO'LICAL. *adj.* [*ſymbolique*, French; συμβολικὸς; from *ſymbol.*] Repreſentative; typical; expreſſing by ſigns.

By this incroachment idolatry firſt crept in, men converting the *ſymbolical* uſe of idols into their proper worſhip, and receiving the repreſentation of things unto them as the ſubſtance and thing itſelf. *Brown.*

The ſacrament is a repreſentation of Chriſt's death, by ſuch *ſymbolical* actions as himſelf appointed. *Taylor.*

SYMBO'LICALLY. *adv.* [from *ſymbolical.*] Typically; by repreſentation.

This diſtinction of animals was hieroglyphical, in the inward ſenſe implying an abſtinence from certain vices, *ſymbolically* intimated from the nature of thoſe animals. *Brown.*

It *ſymbolically* teaches our duty, and promotes charity by a real ſignature and a ſenſible ſermon. *Taylor.*

SYMBOLIZA'TION. *n. ſ.* [from *ſymbolize.*] The act of ſymbolizing; repreſentation; reſemblance.

The hieroglyphical ſymbols of Scripture, excellently intended in the ſpecies of things ſacrificed in the dreams of Pharaoh, are oftentimes racked beyond their *ſymbolizations.* *Brown's Vulgar Errours.*

To SYMBOLI'ZE. *v. n.* [*ſymboliſer*, French; from *ſymbol.*] To have ſomething in common with another by repreſentative qualities.

Our king finding himſelf to *ſymbolize* in many things with that king of the Hebrews, honoured him with the title of this foundation. *Bacon.*

The pleaſing of colour *ſymbolizeth* with the pleaſing of any ſingle tone to the ear; but the pleaſing of order doth *ſymbolize* with harmony. *Bacon's Natural Hiſtory.*

Ariſtotle and the ſchools have taught, that air and water, being *ſymbolizing* elements, in the quality of moiſture, are eaſily tranſmutable into one another. *Boyle.*

They both *ſymbolize* in this, that they love to look upon themſelves through multiplying glaſſes. *Howel.*

I affectedly *ſymbolized* in careleſs mirth and freedom with the libertines, to circumvent libertiniſm. *More.*

The ſoul is ſuch, that it ſtrangely *ſymbolizes* with the thing it mightily deſires. *South's Sermons.*

To SYMBOLI'ZE. *v. a.* To make repreſentative of ſomething.

Some *ſymbolize* the ſame from the myſtery of its colours. *Brown's Vulgar Errours.*

SYMME'TRIAN. *n. ſ.* [from *ſymmetry.*] One eminently ſtudious of proportion.

His face was a thought longer than the exact *ſymmetrians* would allow. *Sidney.*

SYMME'TRICAL. *adj.* [from *ſymmetry.*] Proportionate; having parts well adapted to each other.

SYMME'TRIST. *n. ſ.* [from *ſymmetry.*] One very ſtudious or obſervant of proportion.

Some exact *ſymmetriſts* have been blamed for being too true. *Wotton's Architecture.*

SY'MMETRY. *n. ſ.* [*ſymmetrie*, French; σὺν and μέτρον.] Adaptation of parts to each other; proportion; harmony; agreement of one part to another.

She by whoſe lines proportion ſhould be
Examin'd, meaſure of all *ſymmetry*;
Whom had that ancient ſeen, who thought ſouls made
Of harmony, he would at next have ſaid
That harmony was ſhe. *Donne.*

And in the *ſymmetry* of her parts is found
A pow'r, like that of harmony in ſound. *Waller.*

Symmetry, equality, and correſpondence of parts, is the diſcernment of reaſon, not the object of ſenſe. *More.*

Nor were they only animated by him, but their meaſure and *ſymmetry* were owing to him. *Dryden.*

SYMPATHE'TICAL. } *adj.* [*ſympathetique*, Fr. from *ſympathy.*]
SYMPATHE'TICK. } Having mutual ſenſation; being affected either by what happens to the other; feeling in conſequence of what another feels.

Hereupon are grounded the groſs miſtakes, in the cure of diſeaſes, not only from the laſt medicine and *ſympathetick* receipts, but amulets, charms, and all incantatory applications. *Brown's Vulgar Errours.*

United by this *ſympathetick* bond,
You grow familiar, intimate, and fond. *Roſcommon.*

To confer at the diſtance of the Indies by *ſympathetick* conveyances, may be as uſual to future times as to us in a literary correſpondence. *Glanv. Sceps.*

To you our author makes her ſoft requeſt,
Who ſpeak the kindeſt, and who write the beſt:
Your *ſympathetick* hearts ſhe hopes to move,
From tender friendſhip and endearing love. *Prior.*

All the ideas of ſenſible qualities are not inherent in the inanimate bodies; but are the effects of their motion upon our nerves, and *ſympathetical* and vital paſſions produced within ourſelves. *Bentley.*

SYMPATHE'TICALLY. *adv.* [from *ſympathetick.*] With ſympathy; in conſequence of ſympathy.

To SY'MPATHIZE. *v. n.* [*ſympatiſer*, French; from *ſympathy.*] To feel with another; to feel in conſequence of what another feels; to feel mutually.

The men *ſympathize* with the maſtiffs in robuſtious and rough coming on. *Shakeſpeare.*

The thing of courage,
As rouz'd with rage, with rage doth *ſympathize.* *Shakeſp.*

Nature, in awe to him,
Had doff'd her gaudy trim,
With her great maſter ſo to *ſympathize.* *Milton.*

Green is a pleaſing colour, from a blue and a yellow mixed together, and by conſequence blue and yellow are two colours which *ſympathize.* *Dryden's Dufreſnoy.*

The limbs of his body is to every one a part of himſelf: he *ſympathizes*, and is concerned for them. *Locke.*

Their countrymen were particularly attentive to all their ſtory, and *ſympathized* with their heroes in all their adventures. *Addiſon's Spectator.*

Though the greatneſs of their mind exempts them from fear, yet none condole and *ſympathize* more heartily than they. *Collier on Kindneſs.*

SY'MPATHY. *n. ſ.* [*ſympathie*, French; συμπάθεια.] Fellowfeeling; mutual ſenſibility; the quality of being affected by the affection of another.

A world of earthly bleſſings to my ſoul,
If *ſympathy* of love unite our thoughts. *Shakeſp. H. VI.*

You are not young; no more am I: go to, then, there's *ſympathy*: you are merry, ſo am I; ha! ha! then there's more *ſympathy*: you love ſack, and ſo do I; would you deſire better *ſympathy*? *Shakeſp. Merry Wives of Windſor.*

But what it is,
The action of my life is like it, which I'll keep,
If but for *ſympathy.* *Shakeſ. Cymbeline.*

If there was a *ſympathy* in choice,
War, death, or ſickneſs did lay ſiege to it. *Shakeſpeare.*

I ſtarted back;
It ſtarted back: but pleas'd I ſoon return'd;
Pleas'd it return'd as ſoon, with anſwering looks
Of *ſympathy* and love. *Milton's Paradiſe Loſt.*

They ſaw, but other ſight inſtead, a crowd
Of ugly ſerpents: horror on them fell,
And horrid *ſympathy.* *Milton.*

Or *ſympathy*, or ſome connat'ral force,
Pow'rful at greateſt diſtance to unite,
With ſecret amity, things of like kind,
By ſecreteſt conveyance. *Milt. Paradiſe Loſt.*

There never was any heart truly great and generous, that was not alſo tender and compaſſionate: it is this noble quality that makes all men to be of one kind; for every man would be a diſtinct ſpecies to himſelf, were there no *ſympathy* among individuals. *South's Sermons.*

Can kindneſs to deſert, like your's, be ſtrange?
Kindneſs by ſecret *ſympathy* is ty'd;
For noble ſouls in nature are ally'd. *Dryden.*

There are ſuch aſſociations made in the minds of moſt men, and to this might be attributed moſt of the *ſympathies* and antipathies obſervable in them. *Locke.*

SYMPHO'NIOUS. *adj.* [from *ſymphony.*] Harmonious; agreeing in ſound.

Up he rode,
Follow'd with acclamation and the ſound
Symphonious of ten thouſand harps, that tun'd
Angelick harmonies. *Milton.*

SY'MPHONY. *n. ſ.* [*ſymphonie*, French; σὺν and φωνή.] Concert of inſtruments; harmony of mingled ſounds.

A learned ſearcher from Pythagoras's ſchool, where it was a maxim that the images of all things are latent in numbers, determines the comelieſt proportion between breadths and heights, reducing ſymmetry to *ſymphony*, and the harmony of ſound to a kind of harmony in ſight. *Wotton.*

Speak ye who beſt can tell, ye ſons of light,
Angels! for ye behold him, and with ſongs
And choral *ſymphonies*, day without night,
Circle his throne rejoicing. *Milton's Par. Loſt.*

The trumpets ſound,
And warlike *ſymphony* is heard around;
The marching troops through Athens take their way;
The great earl-marſhal orders their array. *Dryden.*

SY'MPHYSIS. *n. ſ.* [σύν and φύω.]

Symphyſis, in its original ſignification, denotes a connaſcency, or growing together; and perhaps is meant of thoſe bones which in young children are diſtinct, but after ſome years unite and conſolidate into one bone. *Wiſeman.*

SYMPO'SIACK. *adj.* [*ſympoſiaque*, French; συμποσιακός.] Relating to merry makings; happening where company is drinking together.

By deſiring a ſecrecy to words ſpoke under the roſe, we only mean in ſociety and compotation, from the ancient cuſtom of *ſympoſiack* meetings to wear chaplets of roſes about their heads. *Brown's Vulgar Errours.*

In ſome of thoſe *ſympoſiack* diſputations amongſt my acquaintance, I affirmed that the dietetick part of medicine depended upon ſcientifick principles. *Arbuthnot.*

SY'MPTOM. *n. ſ.* [*ſymptome*, French; σύμπτωμα.]

1. Something that happens concurrently with ſomething elſe, not as the original cauſe, nor as the neceſſary or conſtant effect.

2. A ſign; a token.

Ten glorious campaigns are paſſed, and now, like the ſick man, we are expiring with all ſorts of good *ſymptoms.* *Swift.*

SYMPTOMA'TICAL. } *adj.* [*ſymptomatique*, French; from *ſymptom.*]
SYMPTOMA'TICK. } Happening concurrently, or occaſionally.

Symptomatical is often uſed to denote the difference between the primary and ſecondary cauſes in diſeaſes; as a fever from pain is ſaid to be *ſymptomatical*, becauſe it ariſes from pain only; and therefore the ordinary means in fevers are not in ſuch caſes to be had recourſe to, but to what will remove the pain; for when that ceaſes, the fever will ceaſe, without any direct means taken for that. *Quincy.*

By fomentation and a cataplaſm the ſwelling was diſcuſſed; and the fever, then appearing but *ſymptomatical*, leſſened as the heat and pain mitigated. *Wiſeman's Surgery.*

SYMPTOMA'TICALLY. *adv.* [from *ſymptomatical.*] In the nature of a ſymptom.

The cauſes of a bubo are vicious humours abounding in the blood, or in the nerves, excreted ſometimes critically, ſometimes *ſymptomatically.* *Wiſeman.*

SYNAGO'GICAL. *adj.* [from *ſynagogue.*] Pertaining to a ſynagogue.

SY'NAGOGUE. *n. ſ.* [*ſynagogue*, French; συναγωγή.] An aſſembly of the Jews to worſhip.

Go, Tubal, and meet me at our *ſynagogue.* *Shakeſp.*

As his cuſtom was, he went into the *ſynagogue* on the ſabbath. *Goſpel.*

SYNALE'PHA. *n. ſ.* [συναλοιφή.] A contraction or exciſion of a ſyllable in a Latin verſe, by joining together two vowels in the ſcanning or cutting off the ending vowel; as, *ill' ego.* *Bailey.*

Virgil, though ſmooth, is far from affecting it: he frequently uſes *ſynalepha's*, and concludes his ſenſe in the middle of his verſe. *Dryden.*

SYNARTHRO'SIS. *n. ſ.* [σὺν and ἄρθρον.] A cloſe conjunction of two bones.

There is a conſpicuous motion where the conjunction is called diarthroſis, as in the elbow; an obſcure one, where the conjunction is called *ſynarthroſis*, as in the joining of the carpus to the metacarpus. *Wiſeman's Surgery.*

SYNCHONDRO'SIS. *n. ſ.* [σὺν and χόνδρος.]

Synchondroſis is an union by griſtles of the ſternon to the ribs. *Wiſeman.*

SYNCHRO'NICAL. *adj.* [σὺν and χρόνος.] Happening together at the ſame time.

It is difficult to make out how the air is conveyed into the left ventricle of the heart, the ſyſtole and diaſtole of the heart and lungs being far from *ſynchronical.* *Boyle.*

SY'NCHRONISM. *n. ſ.* [σὺν and χρόνος.] Concurrence of events happening at the ſame time.

The coherence and *ſynchroniſm* of all the parts of the Moſaical chronology, after the Flood, bears a moſt regular teſtimony to the truth of his hiſtory. *Hale.*

SY'NCHRONOUS. *adj.* [σὺν and χρόνος.] Happening at the ſame time.

The

The variations of the gravity of the air keep both the solids and fluids in an oscillatory motion, *synchronous* and proportional to their changes. *Arbuthnot on Air.*

SY'NCOPE. *n. s.* [*syncope*, French; συγκοπή.]

1. Fainting fit.

The symptoms attending gunshot wounds are pain, fever, delirium, and *syncope.* *Wiseman.*

2. Contraction of a word by cutting off part.

SY'NCOPIST. *n. s.* [from *syncope.*] Contractor of words.

To outshine all the modern *syncopists*, and thoroughly content my English readers, I intend to publish a Spectator that shall not have a single vowel in it. *Spectator.*

To SYNDI'CATE. *v. n.* [*syndiquer*, French; σὺν and δίκη.] To judge; to pass judgement on; to censure. An unusual word.

Aristotle undertook to censure and *syndicate* his master and all law makers before him. *Hakewill on Providence.*

SY'NDROME. *n. s.* [συνδρομή.] Concurrent action; concurrence.

All things being linked together by an uninterrupted chain of causes, every single motion owns a dependance on such a *syndrome* of prerequired motors. *Glanville's Sceps.*

SYNE'CDOCHE. *n. s.* [*synecdoche*, French; συνεκδοχή.] A figure by which part is taken for the whole, or the whole for part.

Because they are instruments of grace in the hand of God, and by these his holy spirit changes our hearts; therefore the whole work is attributed to them by a *synecdoche*; that is, they do in this manner the work for which God ordained them. *Taylor's Worthy Communicant.*

SYNECDO'CHICAL. *adj.* [from *synecdoche.*] Expressed by a synecdoche; implying a synecdoche.

Should I, Lindamer, bring you into hospitals, and shew you there how many souls, narrowly lodged in *synecdochical* bodies, see their earthen cottages moulder away to dust, those miserable persons, by the loss of one limb after another, surviving but part of themselves, and living to see themselves dead and buried by piecemeal? *Boyle's Seraphick Love.*

SYNNEURO'SIS. *n. s.* [σὺν and νεῦρον.]

Synneurosis is when the connexion is made by a ligament. Of this in symphysis we find instances, in the connexion of the ossa pubis together, especially in women, by a ligamentous substance. In articulations it is either round, as that which unites the head of the os femoris to the coxa; or broad, as the tendon of the patella, which unites it to the os tibiæ. *Wiseman's Surgery.*

SY'NOD. *n. s.* [*synode*, French; σύνοδος.]

1. An assembly, particularly of ecclesiasticks. A provincial *synod* is commonly used, and a general *council.*

The glorious gods sit in hourly *synod* about thy particular prosperity. *Shakesp. Coriolanus.*

Since the mortal and intestine jars
'Twixt thy seditious countrymen and us,
It hath in solemn *synod* been decreed,
T' admit no traffick to our adverse towns. *Shakespeare.*

The opinion was not only condemned by the *synod*, but imputed to the emperor as extreme madness. *Bacon.*

Flea-bitten *synod*, an assembly brew'd
Of clerks and elders ana, like the rude
Chaos of presbyt'ry, where laymen guide
With the tame woolpack clergy by their side. *Cleaveland.*

Well have ye judg'd, well ended long debate,
Synod of gods! and, like to what ye are,
Great things resolv'd. *Milton's Paradise Lost.*

Let us call to *synod* all the blest,
Through heav'n's wide bounds. *Milton.*

The second council of Nice he saith I most irreverently call that wise *synod*; upon which he falls into a very tragical exclamation, that I should dare to reflect so much dishonour on a council. *Stillingfleet.*

Parent of gods and men, propitious Jove!
And you bright *synod* of the pow'rs above,
On this my son your gracious gifts bestow. *Dryden.*

2. Conjunction of the heavenly bodies.

Howe'er love's native hours are set,
Whatever starry *synod* met,
'Tis in the mercy of her eye,
If poor love shall live or die. *Crashaw.*

Their planetary motions and aspects
Of noxious efficacy, and when to join
In *synod* unbenign. *Milton.*

As the planets and stars have, according to astrologers, in their great *synods*, or conjunctions, much more powerful influences on the air than are ascribed to one or two of them out of that aspect; so divers particulars, which, whilst they lay scattered among the writings of several authors, were inconsiderable, when they come to be laid together, may oftentimes prove highly useful to physiology in their conjunctions. *Boyle.*

SY'NODAL. }
SYNO'DICAL. } *adj.* [*synodique*, French; from *synod.*]
SYNO'DICK. }

1. Relating to a synod; transacted in a synod.

St. Athanasius writes a *synodical* epistle to those of Antioch, to compose the differences among them upon the ordination of Paulinus. *Stillingfleet.*

2. [*Synodique*, French.] Reckoned from one conjunction with the sun to another.

The diurnal and annual revolutions of the sun, to us are the measures of day and year; and the *synodick* revolution of the moon measures the month. *Holder.*

The moon makes its *synodical* motion about the earth in twenty-nine days twelve hours and about forty-four minutes. *Locke's Elements of Natural Philosophy.*

SYNO'DICALLY. *adv.* [from *synodical.*] By the authority of a synod or publick assembly.

It shall be needful for those churches *synodically* to determine something in those points. *Saunderson.*

SYNO'NYMA. *n. s.* [Latin; συνώνυμος.] Names which signify the same thing.

To SYNO'NOMISE. *v. a.* [from *synonyma.*] To express the same thing in different words.

This word fortis we may *synonymise* after all these fashions, stout, hardy, valiant, doughty, couragious, adventurous, brave, bold, daring, intrepid. *Camden's Remains.*

SYNONYMO'US. *adj.* [*synonyme*, Fr. συνώνυμος.] Expressing the same thing by different words.

These words consist of two propositions which are not distinct in sense, but one and the same thing variously expressed; for wisdom and understanding are *synonymous* words here. *Tillot.*

Fortune is but a *synonymous* word for nature and necessity. *Bentley's Sermons.*

When two or more words signify the same thing, as wave and billow, mead and meadow, they are usually called *synonymous* words. *Watts's Logick.*

SYNO'NYMY. *n. s.* [συνωνυμία.] The quality of expressing by different words the same thing.

SYNO'PSIS. *n. s.* [σύνοψις.] A general view; all the parts brought under one view.

SYNO'PTICAL. *adj.* [from *synopsis.*] Affording a view of many parts at once.

We have collected so many *synoptical* tables, calculated for his monthly use. *Evelyne's Kalendar.*

SYNTA'CTICAL. *adj.* [from *syntaxis*, Latin.]

1. Conjoined; fitted to each other.

2. Relating to the construction of speech.

SY'NTAX. }
SYNTA'XIS. } *n. s.* [σύνταξις.]

1. A system; a number of things joined together.

They owe no other dependance to the first than what is common to the whole *syntax* of beings. *Glanville.*

2. That part of Grammar which teaches the construction of words.

I can produce a hundred instances to convince any reasonable man that they do not so much as understand common Grammar and *syntax.* *Swift.*

SYNTHE'SIS. *n. s.* [σύνθεσις.] The act of joining, opposed to *analysis.*

The *synthesis* consists in assuming the causes discovered and established as principles, and by them explaining the phænomena proceeding from them, and proving the explanations. *Newton's Opticks.*

SYNTHE'TICK. *adj.* συνθετικός.] Conjoining; compounding; forming composition.

Synthetick method is that which begins with the parts, and leads onward to the knowledge of the whole; it begins with the most simple principles and general truths, and proceeds by degrees to that which is drawn from them or compounded of them; and therefore it is called the method of composition. *Watts's Logick.*

SY'PHON. *n. s.* [This should be written *siphon*; σίφων.] A tube; a pipe.

Take your glass, *syphon*, or crane, and draw it off from its last fæces into small bottles. *Mortimer.*

SY'RINGE. *n. s.* [σύριγξ.] A pipe through which any liquour is squirted.

The heart seems not designed to be the fountain or conservatory of the vital flame, but as a machine to receive the blood from the veins and force it out by the arteries through the whole body as a *syringe* doth any liquor, though not by the same artifice. *Ray.*

To SY'RINGE. *v. a.* [from the noun.]

1. To spout by a syringe.

A flux of blood from the nose, mouth, and eye was stopt by the *syringing* up of oxycrate. *Wiseman's Surgery.*

2. To wash with a syringe.

SY'RINGOTOMY. *n. s.* [σύριγξ and τέτομα.] The act or practice of cutting fistulas or hollow sores.

SY'RTIS.

SY'RTIS. *n. s.* [Latin.] A quick sand; a bog.

A beggy *syrtis*, neither sea, nor good dry land. *Milton.*

SY'STEM. *n. s.* [*systeme*, Fr. σύςημα.]

1. Any complexure or combination of many things acting together.
2. A scheme which reduces many things to regular dependence or co-operation.
3. A scheme which unites many things in order.

Aristotle brings morality into *system*, by treating of happiness under heads, and ranges it in classes according to its different objects, distinguishing virtues into their several kinds which had not been handled systematically before. *Baker.*

The best way to learn any science is to begin with a regular *system*, or a short and plain scheme of that science well drawn up into a narrow compass. *Watts.*

SYSTEMA'TICAL. *adj.* [*systematique*, Fr. συςηματικὸς; from *system.*] Methodical; written or formed with regular subordination of one part to another.

It will be necessary, in a discourse about the formation of the world, to give you a brief account of some of the most principal and *systematical* phænomena that occur in it. *Bentley.*

Now we deal much in essays, and unreasonably despise *systematical* learning; whereas our fathers had a just value for regularity and systems. *Watts.*

SYSTEMA'TICALLY. *adv.* [from *systematical.*] In form of a system.

I treat of the usefulness of writing books of essay, in comparison of that of writing *systematically.* *Boyle.*

Aristotle brings morality into system, and ranges it into classes according to its different objects, distinguishing virtues into their several kinds, which had not been handled *systematically* before. *Baker.*

SY'STOLE. *n. s.* [*systole*, Fr. συςολὴ.]

1. [In anatomy.] The contraction of the heart.

The *systole* resembles the forcible bending of a spring, and the diastole its flying out again to its natural site. *Ray.*

2. [*Systole*, French.] In Grammar, the shortening of a long syllable.

T.

T.

T, A consonant, which, at the beginning and end of words, has always the same sound nearly approaching to the *d*; but before an *i*, when followed by a vowel, has the sound of an obscure *s*: as, *nation*, *salvation*, except when *s* precedes *t*: as, *Christian*, *question*.

TA'BBY. *n. s.* [*tabi*, *tabino*, Italian; *tabis*, French.] A kind of waved silk.

Brocades, and *tabies*, and gauses. *Swift.*

TA'BBY. *adj.* Brinded; brindled; varied with different colours.

A *tabby* cat sat in the chimney-corner. *Addison.*

On her *tabby* rival's face,
She deep will mark her new disgrace. *Prior.*

TABEFA'CTION. *n. s.* [*tabefacio*, Latin.] The act of wasting away.

To TA'BEFY. *v. n.* [*tabefacio*, Latin.] To waste; to be extenuated by disease. In the following example it is improperly a verb active.

Meat eaten in greater quantity than is convenient *tabefies* the body. *Harvey on Consumptions.*

TA'BARD. } *n. s.* [*taberda*, low Latin; *tabard*, Fr.] A long
TA'BERD. } gown; a herald's coat.

TA'BERDER. *n. s.* [from *taberd.*] One who wears a long gown.

TA'BERNACLE. *n. s.* [*tabernacle*, Fr. *tabernaculum*, Lat.]

1. A temporary habitation; a casual dwelling.

They sudden rear'd
Cœlestial *tabernacles*, where they slept
Fann'd with cool winds. *Milton's Par. Lost*, *b.* v.

2. A sacred place; a place of worship.

The greatest conqueror did not only compose his divine odes, but set them to musick: his works, though consecrated to the *tabernacle*, became the national entertainment, as well as the devotion of his people. *Addison's Spect.* N°. 405.

To TA'BERNACLE. *v. n.* [from the noun.] To enshrine; to house.

The word was made flesh, and *tabernacled* amongst us, and we beheld his glory. *John* i. 14.

TA'BID. *adj.* [*tabide*, Fr. *tabidus*, Lat.] Wasted by disease; consumptive.

In *tabid* persons milk is the best restorative, being chyle already prepared. *Arbuthnot on Aliments.*

TA'BIDNESS. *n. s.* [from *tabid.*] Consumptiveness; state of being wasted by disease.

TA'BLATURE. *n. s.* [from *table.*] Painting on walls or ceilings.

TA'BLE. *n. s.* [*table*, Fr. *tabula*, Latin.]

1. Any flat or level surface.

Upon the castle hill there is a bagnio paved with fair *tables* of marble. *Sandys.*

2. A horizontal surface raised above the ground, used for meals and other purposes.

We may again
Give to our *tables* meat, sleep to our nights. *Shakespeare.*

Help to search my house; if I find not what I seek, let me for ever be your *table* sport. *Shakespeare.*

Children at a *table* never asked for any thing, but contentedly took what was given them. *Locke on Education.*

This shuts them out from all *table* conversation, and the most agreeable intercourses. *Addison's Spectator.*

Nor hath the fruit in it any core or kernel; and differing from other apples, yet is a good *table* fruit. *Mortimer.*

The nymph the *table* spread,
Ambrosial cates, with nectar, rosy red. *Pope.*

3. The persons sitting at table, or partaking of entertainment.

Give me some wine, fill full,
I drink to th' general joy of the whole *table*. *Shakespeare.*

4. The fare or entertainment itself: as, *he keeps a good* table.

5. A tablet; a surface on which any thing is written or engraved.

He was the writer of them in the *tables* of their hearts. *Hooker*, *b.* iii.

'Twas pretty, though a plague,
To see him every hour; to sit and draw
His arched brows, his hawking eye, his curls,
In our hearts *table*. *Shakespeare.*

All these true notes of immortality
In our heart's *table* we shall written find. *Davies.*

I prepar'd to pay in verses rude
A most detested act of gratitude:
Ev'n this had been your elegy which now
Is offer'd for your health, the *table* of my vow. *Dryden.*

There are books extant which the atheist must allow of as proper evidence; even the mighty volumes of visible nature, and the everlasting *tables* of right reason; wherein if they do not wilfully shut their eyes, they may read their own folly written by the finger of God in a much plainer and more terrible sentence, than Belshazzar's was by the hand upon the wall. *Bentley's Sermons.*

Among the Romans, the judge or prætor granted administration, not only according to the *tables* of the testament, but even contrary to those *tables*. *Ayliffe's Parergon.*

By the twelve *tables*, only those were called into succession of their parents that were in the parent's power. *Ayliffe.*

6. [*Tableau*, Fr.] A picture, or any thing that exhibits a view of any thing.

I never lov'd myself,
Till now, infixed, I beheld myself
Drawn in the flatt'ring *table* of her eye. *Shakespeare.*

His Jalysus or Bacchus he so esteemed, that he had rather lose all his father's images than that *table*. *Peacham.*

Saint Anthony has a *table* that hangs up to him from a poor peasant, who fancied the saint had saved his neck. *Addis.*

7. An index; a collection of heads; a catalogue; a syllabus.

It might seem impertinent to have added a *table* to a book of so small a volume, and which seems to be itself but a *table*: but it may prove advantagious at once to learn the whole culture of any plant. *Evelyn's Kalender.*

Their learning reaches no farther than the *tables* of contents. *Watts.*

8. A synopsis; many particulars brought into one view.

I have no images of ancestors,
Wanting an ear, or nose; no forged *tables*
Of long descents, to boast false honours from. *B. Johnson.*

9. The palm of the hand.

Mistress of a fairer *table*
Hath not history nor fable. *Benj. Johnson.*

10. Draughts; small pieces of wood shifted on squares.

Monsieur the nice,
When he plays at *tables*, chides the dice. *Shakespeare.*

We are in the world like men playing at *tables*; the chance is not in our power, but to play it, is; and when it is fallen we must manage it as we can. *Taylor.*

11. *To turn the* TABLES. To change the condition or fortune of two contending parties: a metaphor taken from the vicissitude of fortune at gaming tables.

They that are honest would be arrant knaves if the *tables* were *turned*. *L'Estrange.*

If it be thus, the *tables* would be *turned* upon me; but I should only fail in my vain attempt. *Dryden.*

To TA'BLE. *v. n.* [from the noun.] To board; to live at the table of another.

He lost his kingdom, was driven from the society of men to *table* with the beasts, and to graze with oxen. *South.*

You will have no notion of delicacies if you *table* with them; they are all for rank and foul feeding. *Felton.*

To TA'BLE. *v. a.* To make into a catalogue; to set down.

I could have looked on him without admiration, though the catalogue of his endowments had been *tabled* by his side, and I to peruse him by items. *Shakespeare's Cymbeline.*

TA'BLEBEER. *n. s.* [*table* and *beer.*] Beer used at victuals; small beer.

TA'BLEBOOK. *n. s.* [*table* and *book.*] A book on which any thing is graved or written without ink.

What might you think,
If I had play'd the desk or *table-book*. *Shakesp. Hamlet.*

26 A

Nature

Nature wipes clean the *table-book* firſt, and then pourtrays upon it what ſhe pleaſeth. *More's Antidote againſt Atheiſm.*

Put into your *table-book* whatſoever you judge worthy. *Dry.*

Nature's fair *table-book*, our tender ſouls,
We ſcrawl all o'er with old and empty rules,
Stale memorandums of the ſchools. *Swift's Miſcel.*

TA'BLECLOTH. *n. ſ.* [*table* and *cloth.*] Linen ſpread on a table.

I will end with Odo holding maſter doctor's mule, and Anne with her *tablecloth.* *Camden's Remains.*

TA'BLEMAN. *n. ſ.* A man at draughts.

In clericals the keys are lined, and in colleges they uſe to line the *tablemen.* *Bacon's Nat. Hiſt.*

TA'BLER. *n. ſ.* [from *table.*] One who boards. *Ainſ.*

TA'BLETALK. *n. ſ.* [*table* and *talk.*] Converſation at meals or entertainments; table diſcourſe.

Let me praiſe you while I have a ſtomach.
—No, let it ſerve for *tabletalk.* *Shakeſp. Merch. of Venice.*

His fate makes *tabletalk*, divulg'd with ſcorn,
And he a jeſt into his grave is born. *Dryden's Juvenal.*

He improves by the *tabletalk*, and repeats in the kitchen what he learns in the parlour. *Guardian*, N°. 165.

No fair adverſary would urge looſe *table-talk* in controverſy, and build ſerious inferences upon what was ſpoken but in jeſt. *Atterbury.*

TA'BLET. *n. ſ.* [from *table.*]

1. A ſmall level ſurface.
2. A medicine in a ſquare form.

It hath been anciently in uſe to wear *tablets* of arſenick, or preſervatives, againſt the plague; as they draw the venom to them from the ſpirits. *Bacon.*

3. A ſurface written on or painted.

It was by the authority of Alexander, that through all Greece the young gentlemen learned, before all other things, to deſign upon *tablets* of boxen wood. *Dryden.*

The pillar'd marble, and the *tablet* braſs,
Mould'ring, drop the victor's praiſe. *Prior.*

TA'BOUR. *n. ſ.* [*tabourin*, *tabour*, old French.] A ſmall drum; a drum beaten with one ſtick to accompany a pipe.

If you did but hear the pedlar at door, you would never dance again after a *tabour* and pipe. *Shakeſp. Winter's Tale.*

The ſhepherd knows not thunder from a *tabour*,
More than I know the ſound of Marcius' tongue
From every meaner man. *Shakeſp. Coriolanus.*

Morrice-dancers danced a maid marian, and a *tabour* and pipe. *Temple.*

To TA'BOUR. *v. n.* [*taborer*, old French, from the noun.] To ſtrike lightly and frequently.

And her maids ſhall lead her as with the voice of doves, *tabouring* upon their breaſts. *Nah.* ii. 7.

TA'BOURER. *n. ſ.* [from *tabour.*] One who beats the tabour.

Would I could ſee this *tabourer.* *Shakeſpeare.*

TA'BOURET. *n. ſ.* [from *tabour.*] A ſmall drum or tabour.

They ſhall depart the manor before him with trumpets, *tabourets*, and other minſtrelſey. *Spectat.* N°. 607.

TA'BOURINE. *n. ſ.* [French.] A tabour; a ſmall drum.

Trumpeters,
With brazen din blaſt you the city's ear,
Make mingle with our rattling *tabourines*,
That heav'n and earth may ſtrike their ſounds together,
Applauding our approach. *Shakeſp. Antony and Cleopatra.*

TA'BRERE. *n. ſ.* Tabourer. Obſolete.

I ſaw a ſhole of ſhepherds outgo,
Before them yode a luſty *tabrere*,
That to the merry hornpipe plaid,
Whereto they danced. *Spenſer's Paſtorals.*

TA'BRET. *n. ſ.* A tabour.

Wherefore didſt thou ſteal away, that I might have ſent thee away with mirth and with *tabret.* *Gen.* xxxi. 27.

TA'BULAR. *n. ſ.* [*tabularis*, Lat.]

1. Set down in the form of tables or ſynopſes.
2. Formed in ſquares; made into laminæ.

All the nodules that conſiſt of one uniform ſubſtance were formed from a point, as the cruſted ones, nay, and moſt of the ſpotted ones, and indeed all whatever, except thoſe that are *tabular* and plated. *Woodward on Foſſils.*

To TA'BULATE. *v. a.* [*tabula*, Lat.] To reduce to tables or ſynopſes.

TA'BULATED. *adj.* [*tabula*, Lat.] Having a flat ſurface.

Many of the beſt diamonds are pointed with ſix angles, and ſome *tabulated* or plain, and ſquare. *Grew's Muſæum.*

TA'CHE. *n. ſ.* [from *tack.*] Any thing taken hold of; a catch; a loop; a button.

Make fifty *taches* of gold, and couple the curtains together with the *taches.* *Exod.* xxv. 6.

TA'CHYGRAPHY. *n. ſ.* [ταχὺς and γράφω.] The art or practice of quick writing.

TA'CIT. *n. ſ.* [*tacite*, Fr. *tacitus*, Latin.] Silent; implied; not expreſſed by words.

As there are formal and written leagues reſpective to certain enemies, ſo is there a natural and *tacit* confederation amongſt all men, againſt the common enemy of human ſociety, pirates. *Bacon's holy War.*

In elective governments there is a *tacit* covenant, that the king of their own making ſhall make his makers princes. *L'Eſtrange.*

Captiouſneſs not only produces miſbecoming expreſſions and carriage, but is a *tacit* reproach of ſome incivility. *Locke.*

TA'CITLY. *adv.* [from *tacit.*] Silently; without oral expreſſion.

While they are expoſing another's weakneſſes, they are *tacitly* aiming at their own commendations. *Addiſon.*

Indulgence to the vices of men can never be *tacitly* implied, ſince they are plainly forbidden in ſcripture. *Rogers's Serm.*

TACITU'RNITY. *n. ſ.* [*taciturnité*, French; *taciturnitas*, Lat.] Habitual ſilence.

The ſecreteſt of natures
Have not more gift in *taciturnity.* *Shakeſpeare.*

Some women have ſome *taciturnity*,
Some nunneries ſome grains of chaſtity. *Donne.*

Too great loquacity, and too great *taciturnity* by fits. *Arb.*

To TACK. *v. a.* [*tacher.* Breton.]

1. To faſten to any thing.

Of what ſupreme almighty pow'r
Is thy great arm, which ſpans the Eaſt and Weſt,
And *tacks* the centre to the ſphere. *Herbert.*

True freedom you have well defin'd:
But living as you liſt, and to your mind,
And looſely *tack'd*, all muſt be left behind. *Dryden.*

The ſymmetry of cloaths fancy appropriates to the wearer, *tacking* them to the body as if they belonged to it. *Grew.*

Frame with ſticks driven into the ground, ſo as to be covered with the hair-cloth, or a blanket *tacked* about the edges. *Mortimer's Huſbandry.*

If a corner of a hanging wants a nail to faſten it, *tack* it up. *Swift.*

2. To join; to unite; to ſtitch together.

There's but a ſhirt and an half in all my company; and the half ſhirt is two napkins *tack'd* together, and thrown over the ſhoulders like a herald's coat without ſleeves. *Shakeſp.*

I *tack'd* two plays together for the pleaſure of variety. *Dryden.*

They ſerve every turn that ſhall be demanded, in hopes of getting ſome commendam *tacked* to their ſees, to the great diſcouragement of the inferior clergy. *Swift.*

To TACK. *v. n.* [probably from *tackle.*] To turn a ſhip.

This verſeriam they conſtrue to be the compaſs, which is better interpreted the rope that turns the ſhip; as we ſay, makes it *tack* about. *Brown's Vulgar Errours, b.* ii.

Seeing Holland fall into cloſer meaſures with us and Sweden, upon the triple alliance, they have *tacked* ſome points nearer France. *Temple.*

On either ſide they nimbly *tack*,
Both ſtrive to intercept and guide the wind. *Dryden.*

They give me ſigns
To *tack* about, and ſteer another way. *Addiſon.*

TACK. *n. ſ.* [from the verb.]

1. A ſmall nail.
2. The act of turning ſhips at ſea.

At each *tack* our little fleet grows leſs,
And, like maim'd fowl, ſwim lagging on the main. *Dryd.*

3. *To hold* TACK. To laſt; to hold out. *Tack* is ſtill retained in Scotland, and denotes hold or perſevering coheſion.

Martilmas beefe doth *bear* good *tacke*,
When countrey folke do dainties lacke. *Tuſſer.*

If this twig be made of wood
That will hold *tack*, I'll make the fur
Fly 'bout the ears of that old cur. *Hudibras, p.* i.

TA'CKLE. *n. ſ.* [*tacel*, Welſh, an arrow.]

1. An arrow.

The *takil* ſmote and in it went. *Chaucer.*

2. Weapons; inſtruments of action.

She to her *tackle* fell,
And on the knight let fall a peal
Of blows ſo fierce, and preſs'd ſo home,
That he retir'd. *Hudibras, p.* i.

Being at work without catching any thing, he reſolved to take up his *tackle* and be gone. *L'Eſtrange's Fables.*

3. [*Taeckel*, a rope, Dutch.] The ropes of a ſhip.

After at ſea a tall ſhip did appear,
Made all of Heben and white ivory,
The ſails of gold, of ſilk the *tackle* were,
Mild was the wind, calm ſeem'd the ſea to be. *Spenſer.*

At the helm
A ſeeming mermaid ſteers; the ſilken *tackles*
Swell with the touches of thoſe flower-ſoft hands
That yarely frame the office. *Shakeſpeare.*

Thou haſt a grim appearance, and thy face
Bears a command in't; though thy *tackle*'s torn,
Thou ſhew'ſt a noble veſſel. *Shakeſp. Coriolanus.*

A ſtately ſhip
With all her bravery on, and *tackle* trim,
Sails fill'd, and ſtreamers waving,
Courted by all the winds that hold them play. *Milton.*

Ere yet the tempeſt roars
Stand to your *tackle*, mates, and ſtretch your oars. *Dryden.*

If he drew the figure of a ſhip, there was not a rope among the *tackle* that eſcaped him. *Addiſon's Spectator.*

Ta'ckled. *adj.* [from *tackle.*] Made of ropes tacked together.

My man ſhall
Bring thee cords, made like a *tackled* ſtair,
Which to the high top-gallant of my joy
Muſt be my convoy in the ſecret night. *Shakeſpeare.*

Ta'ckling. *n. ſ.* [from *tackle.*]

1. Furniture of the maſt.

They wondered at their ſhips and their *tacklings.* *Abbot.*

Tackling, as ſails and cordage, muſt be foreſeen, and laid up in ſtore. *Bacon's Advice to Villiers.*

Red ſheets of lightning o'er the ſeas are ſpread,
Our *tackling* yield, and wrecks at laſt ſucceed. *Garth.*

2. Inſtruments of action: as, *fiſhing* tackling, *kitchen* tackling.

I will furniſh him with a rod, if you will furniſh him with the reſt of the *tackling*, and make him a fiſher. *Walton.*

Ta'ctical. } *adj.* [τακτικὸς, τάττω; *tactique*, Fr.] Relating
Ta'ctick. } to the art of ranging a battle.

Tac'ticks. *n. ſ.* [τακτικὴ.] The art of ranging men in the field of battle.

When Tully had read the *tacticks*, he was thinking on the bar, which was his field of battle. *Dryden.*

Ta'ctile. *adj.* [*tactile*, Fr. *tactilis*, *tactum*, Lat.] Suſceptible of touch.

We have iron, ſounds, light, figuration, *tactile* qualities; ſome of a more active, ſome of a more paſſive nature. *Hale.*

Tacti'lity. *n. ſ.* [from *tactile.*] Perceptibility by the touch.

Ta'ction. *n. ſ.* [*taction*, Fr. *tactio*, Lat.] The act of touching.

Ta'dpole. *n. ſ.* [taꝺ, *toad*, and pola, *a young one*, Saxon.] A young ſhapeleſs frog or toad, conſiſting only of a body and a tail; a porwiggle.

I'll broach the *tadpole* on my rapier's point. *Shakeſpeare.*

Poor Tom eats the toad and the *tadpole.* *Shakeſpeare.*

The reſult is not a perfect frog but a *tadpole*, without any feet, and having a long tail to ſwim with. *Ray.*

A black and round ſubſtance began to dilate, and after awhile the head, the eyes, the tail to be diſcernable, and at laſt become what the ancients called gyrinus, we a porwigle or *tadpole.* *Brown's Vulgar Errours, b.* iii.

Ta'en, the poetical contraction of *taken.*

Ta'ffeta. *n. ſ.* [*taffetas*, Fr. *taffetar*, Spaniſh.] A thin ſilk.

All hail, the richeſt beauties on the earth!
—Beauties no richer than rich *taffata.* *Shakeſpeare.*

Never will I truſt to ſpeeches penn'd;
Taffata phraſes, ſilken terms preciſe,
Three pil'd hyperboles. *Shakeſp. Love's Labour loſt.*

Some think that a conſiderable diverſity of colours argues an equal diverſity of nature, but I am not of their mind for not to mention the changeable *taffety*, whoſe colours the philoſophers call not real, but apparent. *Boyle on Colours.*

Tag. *n. ſ.* [*tag*, Iſlandiſh, the point of a lance.]

1. A point of metal put to the end of a ſtring.

2. Any thing paltry and mean.

If *tag* and rag be admitted, learned and unlearned, it is the fault of ſome, not of the law. *Whitgift.*

Will you hence
Before the *tag* return, whoſe rage doth rend
Like interrupted waters. *Shakeſpeare's Coriolanus.*

The *tag*-rag people did not clap him and hiſs him. *Shak.*

He invited *tag*, rag, and bob-tail, to the wedding. *L'Eſtr.*

Ta'gtail. *n. ſ.* [*tag* and *tail.*] A worm which has the tail of another colour.

They feed on *tag* worms and lugges. *Carew.*

There are other worms; as the marſh and *tagtail. Walton.*

To Tag. *v. a.* [from the noun.]

1. To fit any thing with an end: as, *to* tag *a lace.*

2. To append one thing to another.

His courteous hoſt
Tags every ſentence with ſome fawning word,
Such as my king, my prince, at leaſt my lord. *Dryden.*

'Tis *tagg'd* with rhyme, like Berecynthian Atys,
The mid-part chimes with art, which never flat is. *Dryd.*

3. The word is here improperly uſed.

Compell'd by you to *tag* in rhimes
The common ſlanders of the times. *Swift.*

4. To join: this is properly *to tack.*

Reſiſtance, and the ſucceſſion of the houſe of Hanover, the whig writers perpetually *tag* together. *Swift's Miſcel.*

Tail. *n. ſ.* [tæȝl, Saxon.]

1. That which terminates the animal behind; the continuation of the vertebræ of the back hanging looſe behind.

Oft have I ſeen a hot o'er-weening cur,
Run back and bite, becauſe he was with-held,
Who, having ſuffer'd with the bear's fell paw,
Hath clapt his *tail* betwixt his legs and cry'd. *Shakeſpeare.*

This ſees the cub, and does himſelf oppoſe,
And men and boats his active *tail* confounds. *Waller.*

The lion will not kick, but will ſtrike ſuch a ſtroke with his *tail*, that will break the back of his encounterer. *More.*

Rouz'd by the laſh of his own ſtubborn *tail*,
Our lion now will foreign foes aſſail. *Dryden.*

The *tail* fin is half a foot high, but underneath level with the *tail.* *Grew.*

2. The lower part.

The Lord ſhall make thee the head, and not the *tail*; and thou ſhalt be above, and not beneath. *Deut.* xxviii. 13.

3. Any thing hanging long; a cat-kin.

Duretus writes a great praiſe of the diſtilled water of thoſe *tails* that hang upon willow trees. *Harvey on Conſumptions.*

4. The hinder part of any thing.

With the helm they turn and ſteer the *tail.* *Butler.*

5. *To turn* Tail. To fly; to run away.

Would ſhe *turn tail* to the heron, and fly quite out another way; but all was to return in a higher pitch. *Sidney.*

To Tail. *v. n.* To pull by the tail.

The conquering foe they ſoon aſſail'd,
Firſt Trulla ſtav'd and Cerdon *tail'd.* *Hudibras, b.* i.

Ta'iled. *adj.* [from *tail.*] Furniſhed with a tail.

Snouted and *tailed* like a boar, footed like a goat. *Grew.*

Ta'illage. *n. ſ.* [*tailler*, French.]

Taillage originally ſignifies a piece cut out of the whole; and, metaphorically, a ſhare of a man's ſubſtance paid by way of tribute. In law, it ſignifies a roll or tax. *Cowel.*

Taille. *n. ſ.*

Taille, the fee which is oppoſite to fee-ſimple, becauſe it is ſo minced or pared, that it is not in his free power to be diſpoſed of who owns it; but is, by the firſt giver, cut or divided from all other, and tied to the iſſue of the donee. This limitation, or *taille*, is either general or ſpecial. *Taille* general is that whereby lands or tenements are limited to a man, and to the heirs of his body begotten; and the reaſon of this term is, becauſe how many ſoever women the tenant, holding by this title, ſhall take to his wives, one after another, in lawful matrimony, his iſſue by them all have a poſſibility to inherit one after the other. *Taile* ſpecial is that whereby lands or tenements be limited unto a man and his wife, and the heirs of their two bodies begotten. *Cowel.*

Tai'lor. *n. ſ.* [*tailleur*, from *tailler*, French, to cut.] One whoſe buſineſs is to make cloaths.

I'll entertain a ſcore or two of *tailors*,
To ſtudy faſhions to adorn my body. *Shakeſp. Rich.* III.

Here's an Engliſh *tailor* come for ſtealing out of a French hoſe: come *tailor*, you may roaſt your gooſe. *Shakeſpeare.*

The knight came to the *tailor*'s to take meaſure of his gown. *Camden.*

The world is come now to that paſs, that the *tailor* and ſhoemaker may cut out what religion they pleaſe. *Howel.*

They value themſelves for this outſide faſhionableneſs of the *tailor's* making. *Locke on Education.*

It was prettily ſaid by Seneca, that friendſhip ſhould not be unript, but unſtitcht, though ſomewhat in the phraſe of a *tailor.* *Collier.*

In Covent-Garden did a *tailor* dwell,
That ſure a place deſerv'd in his own hell. *King.*

To Taint. *v. a.* [*teindre*, French.]

1. To imbue or impregnate with any thing.

The ſpaniel ſtruck
Stiff by the *tainted* gale, with open noſe
Draws full upon the latent prey. *Thomſon.*

2. To ſtain; to ſully.

We come not by the way of accuſation
To *taint* that honour every good tongue bleſſes. *Shakeſp.*

Sirens *taint*
The minds of all men, whom they can acquaint
With their attractions. *Chapman's Odyſſey, b.* xii.

They the truth
With ſuperſtitions and traditions *taint.* *Milton.*

Thoſe pure immortal elements
Eject him *tainted* now, and purge him off
As a diſtemper. *Milton.*

3. To infect.

Nothing *taints* ſound lungs ſooner than inſpiring the breath of conſumptive lungs. *Harvey on Conſumptions.*

Salts in fumes contract the veſicles, and perhaps the *tainted* air may affect the lungs by its heat. *Arbuthnot on Air.*

With wholeſome herbage mixt, the direful bane
Of vegetable venom *taints* the plain. *Pope.*

4. To corrupt.

A ſweet-bread you found it *tainted* or fly-blown. *Swift.*

The yellow tinging plague
Internal viſion *taints.* *Thomſon's Spring.*

5. A corrupt contraction of *attaint.*

To Taint. *v. n.* To be infected; to be touched.

Till Birnam wood remove to Dunſinane
I cannot *taint* with fear. *Shakeſp. Macbeth.*

Taint. *n. ſ.* [*teinte*, Fr. from the verb.]

1. A tincture; a ſtain.

2. An inſect.

There is found in the Summer a ſpider called a *taint*, of a red colour, and ſo little that ten of the largeſt will hardly outweigh a grain. *Brown's Vulgar Errours, b.* iii.

As

As killing as the canker to the roſe,
Or *taint* worm to the weaning herds that graze. *Milton.*

3. Infection.

A father that breeds his ſon at home, can keep him better from the *taint* of ſervants than abroad. *Locke on Education.*

But is no rank, no ſtation, no degree,
From this contagious *taint* of ſorrow free. *Prior.*

4. A ſpot; a ſoil; a blemiſh.

Her offence
Muſt be of ſuch unnatural degree,
That monſters it; or your forevouch'd affection
Fall'n into *taint.* *Shakeſpeare's King Lear.*

Now I
Unſpeak mine own detraction; here abjure
The *taints* and blames I laid upon myſelf. *Shakeſpeare.*

My hellhounds ſhall lick up the draff and filth,
Which man's polluting ſin with *taint* hath ſhed
On what was pure. *Milton.*

TA'INTLESS. *adj.* [from *taint.*] Free from infection.

No humours groſs, or frowzy ſteams,
Could from her *taintleſs* body flow. *Swift's Miſcel.*

TA'INTURE. *n. ſ.* [*tinctura*, Lat. *teinture*, French.] Taint; tinge; defilement.

See here the *tainture* of thy neſt,
And look thyſelf be faultleſs. *Shakeſpeare.*

To TAKE. *v. a.* preterite *took*, part. paſſ. *taken*, ſometimes *took*; *taka*, Iſlandiſh; *ey tek*, I take; *ey took*, I took.]

1. To receive what is offered.

Then *took* I the cup at the Lord's hand, and made all the nations to drink. *Jer.* xxv. 17.

They refuſe to *take* the cup at thine hand to drink. *Jer.*

Be thou adviſ'd, thy black deſign forſake;
Death, or this counſel, from Lucippus *take.* *Waller.*

An honeſt man may *take* a knave's advice,
But idiots only may be cozen'd twice. *Dryden.*

Madam, were I as you, I'd *take* her counſel. *Philips.*

Diſtreſs'd myſelf, like you, confin'd I live,
And therefore can compaſſion *take* and give. *Dryden.*

2. To ſeize what is not given.

In fetters one the barking porter ty'd,
And *took* him trembling from his ſovereign's ſide. *Dryden.*

3. To receive.

No man ſhall *take* the nether or upper milſtone to pledge. *Deut.* xxiv. 6.

4. To receive with good or ill will.

For, what we know muſt be,
Why ſhould we, in our peeviſh oppoſition,
Take it to heart. *Shakeſpeare's Hamlet.*

I will frown as they paſs by, and let them *take* it as they liſt. *Shakeſp. Romeo and Juliet.*

La you! if you ſpeak ill of the devil, how he *takes* it at heart. *Shakeſp. Twelfth Night.*

Damaſco, without any more ado, yielded unto the Turks; which the baſſa *took* in ſo good part, that he would not ſuffer his ſoldiers to enter it. *Knolles's Hiſt. of the Turks.*

The king being in a rage, *took* it grievouſly that he was mocked. 2 *Mac.* vii. 39.

The queen hearing of a declination of monarchy, *took* it ſo ill as ſhe would never after hear of the other's ſuit. *Bacon.*

A following hath ever been a thing civil, and well *taken* in monarchies, ſo it be without too much popularity. *Bacon.*

The diminution of the power of the nobility they *took* very heavily. *Clarendon.*

I hope you will not expect from me things demonſtrated with certainty; but will *take* it well that I ſhould offer at a new thing. *Graunt.*

If I have been a little pilfering, I *take* it bitterly of thee to tell me of it. *Dryden.*

The ſole advice I could give him in conſcience, would be that which he would *take* ill, and not follow. *Swift.*

5. To lay hold on; to catch by ſurprize or artifice.

Who will believe a man that hath no houſe, and lodgeth whereſoever the night *taketh* him? *Eccluſ.* xxxvi. 26.

They ſilenced thoſe who oppoſed them, by traducing them abroad, or *taking* advantage againſt them in the houſe. *Clar.*

Men in their looſe unguarded hours they *take*,
Not that themſelves are wiſe, but others weak. *Pope.*

6. To ſnatch; to ſeize.

I am contented to dwell on the Divine Providence, and *take* up any occaſion to lead me to its contemplation. *Hale.*

7. To make priſoner.

Appoint a meeting with this old fat fellow,
Where we may *take* him, and diſgrace him for it. *Shak.*

King Lear hath loſt, he and his daughter *ta'en.* *Shak.*

This man was *taken* of the Jews, and ſhould have been killed. *Acts* xxii. 27.

They entering with wonderful celerity on every ſide, ſlew and *took* three hundred Janizaries. *Knolles.*

8. To captivate with pleaſure; to delight; to engage.

More than hiſtory can pattern, though deviſ'd
And play'd to *take* ſpectators. *Shakeſpeare.*

I long
To hear the ſtory of your life, which muſt
Take the ear ſtrangely. *Shakeſpeare's Tempeſt.*

Let her not *take* thee with her eyelids. *Prov.* vi. 25.

Yet notwithſtanding, *taken* by Perkin's amiable behaviour, he entertained him as became the perſon of Richard duke of York. *Bacon's Henry* VII.

Their ſong was partial, but the harmony
Suſpended hell, and *took* with raviſhment
The thronging audience. *Milton.*

If I renounce virtue, though naked, then I do it yet more when ſhe is thus beautified on purpoſe to allure the eye, and *take* the heart. *Decay of Piety.*

This beauty ſhines through ſome mens actions, ſets off all that they do, and *takes* all they come near. *Locke.*

Cleombrotus was ſo *taken* with this proſpect, that he had no patience. *Wake.*

9. To ſurprize; to catch.

Wiſe men are overborn when *taken* at a diſadvantage. *Collier of Confidence.*

10. To entrap; to catch in a ſnare.

Take us the foxes, that ſpoil the vines. 2 *Cant.* xv.

11. To underſtand in any particular ſenſe or manner.

The words are more properly *taken* for the air or æther than the heavens. *Raleigh.*

You *take* me right, Eupolis; for there is no poſſibility of an ho[illegible]ar. *Bacon's holy War.*

I [illegible] it, andiron braſs, called white braſs, hath ſome mixture of tin to help the luſtre. *Bacon.*

Why, now you *take* me; theſe are rites
That grace love's days, and crown his nights:
Theſe are the motions I would ſee. *Benj. Johnſon.*

Give them one ſimple idea, and ſee that they *take* it right, and perfectly comprehend it. *Locke.*

Charity *taken* in its largeſt extent, is nothing elſe but the ſincere love of God and our neighbour. *Wake.*

12. To exact.

Take no uſury of him or increaſe. *Lev.* xxv. 36.

13. To get; to have; to appropriate.

And the king of Sodom ſaid unto Abram, give me the perſons, and *take* the goods to thyſelf. *Gen.* xiv. 21.

14. To uſe; to employ.

This man always *takes* time, and ponders things maturely before he paſſes his judgment. *Watts.*

15. To blaſt; to infect.

Strike her young bones,
You *taking* airs with lameneſs. *Shakeſpeare.*

16. To judge in favour of.

The niceſt eye could no diſtinction make
Where lay the advantage, or what ſide to *take.* *Dryden.*

17. To admit any thing bad from without.

I ought to have a care
To keep my wounds from *taking* air. *Hudibras, p.* iii.

18. To get; to procure.

Striking ſtones they *took* fire out of them. 2 *Mac.* x. 3.

19. To turn to; to practiſe.

If any of the family be diſtreſſed, order is taken for their relief: if any be ſubject to vice, or *take* ill courſes, they are reproved. *Bacon's New Atlantis.*

20. To cloſe in with; to comply with.

Old as I am, I *take* thee at thy word,
And will to-morrow thank thee with my ſword. *Dryden.*

She to her country's uſe reſign'd your ſword,
And you, kind lover, *took* her at her word. *Dryden.*

I *take* thee at thy word. *Rowe's Ambitious Stepmother.*

Where any one thought is ſuch, that we have power to *take* it up or lay it by, there we are at liberty. *Locke.*

21. To form; to fix.

Reſolutions *taken* upon full debate, were ſeldom proſecuted with equal reſolution. *Clarendon.*

22. To catch in the hand; to ſeize.

He put forth a hand, and *took* me by a lock of my head. *Ezek.* viii. 3.

I *took* not arms till urg'd by ſelf defence. *Dryden.*

23. To admit; to ſuffer.

Yet thy moiſt clay is pliant to command;
Now *take* the mould; now bend thy mind to feel
The firſt ſharp motions of the forming wheel. *Dryden.*

24. To perform any action.

Peradventure we ſhall prevail againſt him, and *take* our revenge on him. *Jer.* xx. 10.

Uzzah put forth his hand to the ark, and *took* hold of it, for the oxen ſhook it. 2 *Sam.* vi. 6.

Taking my leave of them, I went into Macedonia. 2 *Cor.*

Before I proceed, I would be glad to *take* ſome breath. *Bacon's holy War.*

His wind he never *took* whilſt the cup was at his mouth, but juſtly obſerved the rule of drinking with one breath. *Hakewill on Providence.*

Then call'd his brothers,
And her to whom his nuptial vows were bound;
A long

A long sigh he drew,
And his voice failing, *took* his last adieu. *Dryden's Fab.*
The Sabine Clausus came,
And from afar, at Dryops *took* his aim. *Dryden's Æn.*
Her lovers names in order to run o'er,
The girl *took* breath full thirty times and more. *Dryden.*
Heighten'd revenge he should have *took*;
He should have burnt his tutor's book. *Prior.*

The husband's affairs made it necessary for him to *take* a voyage to Naples. *Addison's Spectator.*

I *took* a walk in Lincoln's Inn Garden. *Tatler.*

The Carthaginian *took* his seat, and Pompey entered with great dignity in his own person. *Tatler.*

I am possessed of power and credit, can gratify my favourites, and *take* vengeance on my enemies. *Swift.*

25. To receive into the mind.

When they saw the boldness of Peter and John, they *took* knowledge of them that they had been with Jesus. *Acts* iv.

It appeared in his face, that he *took* great contentment in this our question. *Bacon.*

Doctor Moore, in his Ethicks, reckons this particular inclination, to *take* a prejudice against a man for his looks, among the smaller vices in morality, and names it a prosopolepsia. *Addison's Spect.* N°. 86.

A student should never satisfy himself with bare attendance on lectures, unless he clearly *takes* up the sense. *Watts.*

26. To go into.

When news were brought that the French king besieged Constance, he posted to the sea-coast to *take* ship. *Camden.*

Tygers and lions are not apt to *take* the water. *Hale.*

27. To go along; to follow; to persue.

The joyful short-liv'd news soon spread around,
Took the same train. *Dryden.*
Observing still the motions of their flight,
What course they *took*, what happy signs they shew. *Dry.*

28. To swallow; to receive.

Consider the insatisfaction of several bodies, and of their appetite to *take* in others. *Bacon's Nat. Hist.*

Turkeys *take* down stones, having found in the gizzard of one no less than seven hundred. *Brown's Vulgar Errours.*

29. To swallow as a medicine.

Tell an ignoramus in place to his face that he has a wit above all the world, and as fulsome a dose as you give him he shall readily *take* it *down*, and admit the commendation, though he cannot believe the thing. *South.*

Upon this assurance he *took* physick. *Locke.*

The glutinous mucilage that is on the outsides of the seeds washed off causes them to *take*. *Mortimer's Husb.*

30. To choose one of more.

Take to thee from among the cherubim
Thy choice of flaming warriors. *Milton.*

Either but one man, or all men are kings: *take* which you please it dissolves the bonds of government. *Locke.*

31. To copy.

Our phænix queen was pourtray'd too so bright,
Beauty alone cou'd beauty *take* so right. *Dryden.*

32. To convey; to carry; to transport.

Carry sir John Falstaff to the fleet,
Take all his company along with him. *Shakesp. Henry* IV.

He sat him down in a street; for no man *took* them into his house to lodging. *Judges* xix. 15.

33. To fasten on; to seize.

Wheresoever he *taketh* him he teareth him; and he foameth. *Mark* ix. 18.

No temptation hath *taken* you, but such as is common to man. 1 *Cor.* x. 13.

When the frost and rain have *taken* them they grow dangerous. *Temple.*

At first they warm, then scorch, and then they *take*,
Now with long necks from side to side they feed;
At length grown strong their mother-size forsake,
And a new colony of flames succeed. *Dryden.*

No beast will eat sour grass till the frost hath *taken* it. *Mort.*

In burning of stubble, take care to plow the land up round the field, that the fire may not *take* the hedges. *Mortimer.*

34. Not to refuse; to accept.

Take no satisfaction for the life of a murderer, he shall be surely put to death. *Num.* xxxv. 31.

Thou *tak'st* thy mother's word too far, said he,
And hast usurp'd thy boasted pedigree. *Dryden.*

He that should demand of him how begetting a child gives the father absolute power over him, will find him answer nothing: we are to *take* his word for this. *Locke.*

Who will not receive clipped money whilst he sees the great receipt of the exchequer admits it, and the bank and goldsmiths will *take* it of him. *Locke.*

35. To adopt.

I will *take* you to me for a people, and I will be to you a God. *Exod.* vi. 7.

36. To change with respect to place.

When he departed, he *took* out two pence, and gave them to the host. *Luke* x. 35.

He put his hand into his bosom; and when he *took* it out, it was leprous. *Exod.* iv. 6.

If you slit the artery, thrust a pipe into it, and cast a strait ligature upon that part containing the pipe, the artery will not beat below the ligature; yet do but *take* it off, and it will beat immediately. *Ray.*

Lovers flung themselves from the top of the precipice into the sea, where they were sometimes *taken* up alive. *Addison.*

37. To separate.

A multitude, how great soever, brings not a man any nearer to the end of the inexhaustible stock of number, where still there remains as much to be added as if none were *taken* out. *Locke.*

The living fabrick now in pieces *take*,
Of every part due observation make;
All which such art discovers. *Blackmore.*

38. To admit.

Let not a widow be *taken* into the number under threescore. 1 *Tim.* v. 9.

Though so much of heav'n appears in my make,
The foulest impressions I easily *take*. *Swift.*

39. To persue; to go in.

He alone,
To find where Adam shelter'd, *took* his way. *Milton.*
To the port she *takes* her way,
And stands upon the margin of the sea. *Dryden.*
Give me leave to seize my destin'd prey,
And let eternal justice *take* the way. *Dryden.*
It was her fortune once to *take* her way
Along the sandy margin of the sea. *Dryden.*

40. To receive any temper or disposition of mind.

They shall not *take* shame. *Mic.* ii. 6.

Thou hast scourged me, and hast *taken* pity on me. *Tob.*

They *take* delight in approaching to God. *Isa.* lviii. 2.

Take a good heart, O Jerusalem. *Bar.* iv. 30.

Men die in desire of some things which they *take* to heart. *Bacon.*

Few are so wicked as to *take* delight
In crimes unprofitable. *Dryden.*

Children, if kept out of ill company, will *take* a pride to behave themselves prettily, perceiving themselves esteemed. *Locke on Education.*

41. To endure; to bear.

I can be as quiet as any body with those that are quarrelsome, and be as troublesome as another when I meet with those that will *take* it. *L'Estrange.*

Won't you then *take* a jest? *Spectator*, N°. 422.

He met with such a reception as those only deserve who are content to *take* it. *Swift's Miscel.*

42. To draw; to derive.

The firm belief of a future judgment, is the most forcible motive to a good life; because *taken* from this consideration of the most lasting happiness and misery. *Tillotson.*

43. To leap; to jump over.

That hand which had the strength, ev'n at your door,
To cudgel you, and make you *take* the hatch. *Shakesp.*

44. To assume.

Fit you to the custom,
And *take* t'ye as your predecessors have,
Your honour with your form. *Shakesp. Coriolanus.*

I *take* liberty to say, that these propositions are so far from having an universal assent, that to a great part of mankind they are not known. *Locke.*

45. To allow; to admit.

Take not any term, howsoever authorized by the language of the schools, to stand for any thing till you have an idea of it. *Locke.*

Chemists *take*, in our present controversy, something for granted which they ought to prove. *Boyle.*

46. To receive with fondness.

I lov'd you still, and *took* your weak excuses,
Took you into my bosom. *Dryden.*

47. To carry out for use.

He commanded them that they should *take* nothing for their journey, save a staff. *Mar.* vi. 8.

48. To suppose; to receive in thought; to entertain in opinion.

This I *take* it
Is the main motive of our preparations. *Shakespeare.*

The spirits that are in all tangible bodies are scarce known. Sometimes they *take* them for vacuum, whereas they are the most active of bodies. *Bacon's Nat. Hist.*

The farmer *took* himself to have deserved as much as any man, in contributing more, and appearing sooner, in their first approach towards rebellion. *Clarendon.*

Is a man unfortunate in marriage? Still it is because he was deceived; and so *took* that for virtue and affection which was nothing but vice in a disguise. *South.*

Our depraved appetites cause us often to *take* that for true imitation of nature which has no resemblance of it. *Dryden.*

So soft his tresses, fill'd with trickling pearl,
You'd doubt his sex, and *take* him for a girl. *Tate.*

Time is *taken* for so much of infinite duration, as is measured out by the great bodies of the universe. *Locke.*

They who would advance in knowledge, should lay down this as a fundamental rule, not to *take* words for things. *Locke.*

Few will *take* a proposition which amounts to no more than this, that God is pleased with the doing of what he himself commands for an innate moral principle, since it teaches so little. *Locke.*

Some tories will *take* you for a whig, some whigs will *take* you for a tory. *Pope.*

As I *take* it, the two principal branches of preaching are, to tell the people what is their duty, and then to convince them that it is so. *Swift.*

49. To direct.

Where injur'd Nisus *takes* his airy course,
Hence trembling Scylla flies and shuns his foe. *Dryden.*

50. To separate for one's self from any quantity; to remove for one's self from any place.

I will *take* of them for priests. *Isa.* lxvi. 21.

Hath God assayed to *take* a nation from the midst of another. *Deut.* iv. 34.

I might have *taken* her to me to wife. *Gen.* xii. 19.

Enoch walked with God, and he was not, for God *took* him. *Gen.* v. 24.

The Lord *took* of the spirit that was upon him, and gave it unto the seventy elders.

Four heifers from his female store he *took*. *Dryden.*

51. Not to leave; not to omit.

The discourse here is about ideas, which he says are real things, and we see in God: in *taking* this along with me, to make it prove any thing to his purpose, the argument must stand thus. *Locke.*

Young gentlemen ought not only to *take* along with them a clear idea of the antiquities on medals and figures, but likewise to exercise their arithmetick in reducing the sums of money to those of their own country. *Arbuthnot on Coins.*

52. To receive payments.

Never a wife leads a better life than she does; do what she will, *take* all, pay all. *Shakespeare.*

53. To obtain by mensuration.

The knight coming to the taylor's to *take* measure of his gown, perceiveth the like gown cloth lying there. *Camden.*

With a two foot rule in his hand measuring my walls, he *took* the dimensions of the room. *Swift.*

54. To withdraw.

Honeycomb, on the verge of threescore, *took* me aside, and asked me whether I would advise him to marry? *Spectat.*

55. To seize with a transitory impulse; to affect so as not to last.

Tiberius, noted for his niggardly temper, only gave his attendants their diet; but once he was *taken* with a fit of generosity, and divided them into three classes. *Arbuthnot.*

56. To comprise; to comprehend.

We always *take* the account of a future state into our schemes about the concerns of this world. *Atterbury.*

Had those who would persuade us that there are innate principles, not *taken* them together in gross, but considered separately the parts, they would not have been so forward to believe they were innate. *Locke.*

57. To have recourse to.

A sparrow *took* a bush just as an eagle made a stoop at an hare. *L'Estrange.*

The cat presently *takes* a tree, and sees the poor fox torn to pieces. *L'Estrange.*

58. To produce; or suffer to be produced.

No purposes whatsoever which are meant for the good of that land will prosper, or *take* good effect. *Spenser.*

59. To catch in the mind.

These do best who *take* material hints to be judged by history. *Locke.*

60. To hire; to rent.

If three ladies, like a luckless play,
Takes the whole house upon the poet's day. *Pope.*

61. To engage in; to be active in.

Question your royal thoughts, make the case yours;
Be now the father, and propose a son;
Behold yourself so by a son disdain'd;
And then imagine me *taking* your part,
And in your pow'r so silencing your son. *Shak. Henry* IV.

62. To suffer; to support.

In streams, my boy, and rivers *take* thy chance,
There swims, said he, thy whole inheritance. *Addison.*

Now *take* your turn; and, as a brother shou'd,
Attend your brother to the Stygian flood. *Dryden's Æn.*

63. To admit in copulation.

Five hundred asses yearly *took* the horse,
Producing mules of greater speed and force. *Sandys.*

64. To catch eagerly.

Drances *took* the word; who grudg'd, long since,
The rising glories of the Daunian prince. *Dryden.*

65. To use as an oath or expression.

Thou shalt not *take* the name of the Lord in vain. *Exod.*

66. To seize as a disease.

They that come abroad after these showers are commonly *taken* with sickness. *Bacon.*

I am *taken* on the sudden with a swimming in my head. *Dryden.*

67. *To* TAKE *away.* To deprive of.

If any *take away* from the book of this prophecy, God shall *take away* his part out of the book of life. *Rev.* xx. 19.

The bill for *taking away* the votes of bishops was called a bill for *taking away* all temporal jurisdiction. *Clarendon.*

Many dispersed objects breed confusion, and *take away* from the picture that grave majesty which gives beauty to the piece. *Dryden.*

You should be hunted like a beast of prey,
By your own law I *take* your life *away*. *Dryden.*

The fun'ral pomp which to your kings you pay,
Is all I want, and all you *take away*. *Dryden's Æn.*

One who gives another any thing, has not always a right to *take* it *away* again. *Locke.*

Not foes nor fortune *takes* this pow'r *away*,
And is my Abelard less kind than they. *Pope.*

68. *To* TAKE *away.* To set aside; to remove.

If we *take away* all consciousness of pleasure and pain, it will be hard to know wherein to place personal identity. *Locke.*

69. *To* TAKE *care.* To be careful; to be solicitous for; to superintend.

Thou shalt not muzzle the ox that treadeth out the corn. Doth God *take care* for oxen? 1 *Cor.* ix. 9.

70. *To* TAKE *care.* To be cautious; to be vigilant.

71. *To* TAKE *course.* To have recourse to measures.

They meant to *take* a *course* to deal with particulars by reconcilements, and cared not for any head. *Bacon.*

The violence of storming is the *course* which God is forced to *take* for the destroying, but cannot, without changing the course of nature, for the converting of sinners. *Hammond.*

72. *To* TAKE *down.* To crush; to reduce; to suppress.

Do you think he is now so dangerous an enemy as he is counted, or that it is so hard to *take* him *down* as some suppose? *Spenser on Ireland.*

Take down their mettle, keep them lean and bare. *Dryd.*

Lacqueys were never so saucy and pragmatical as now, and he should be glad to see them *taken down*. *Addison.*

73. *To* TAKE *down.* To swallow; to take by the mouth.

We cannot *take down* the lives of living creatures, which some of the Paracelsians say, if they could be *taken down*, would make us immortal: the next for subtilty of operation, to take bodies putrefied, such as may be easily taken. *Bacon.*

74. *To* TAKE *from.* To derogate; to detract.

It *takes* not *from* you, that you were born with principles of generosity; but it adds to you that you have cultivated nature. *Dryden.*

75. *To* TAKE *from.* To deprive of.

Conversation will add to their knowledge, but be too apt to *take from* their virtue. *Locke.*

Gentle gods *take* my breath from me. *Shakespeare.*

I will smite thee, and *take* thine head *from* thee. 1 *Sam.*

76. *To* TAKE *heed.* To be cautious; to beware.

Take heed of a mischievous man. *Ecclus.* xi. 33.

Take heed lest passion
Sway thy judgment to do ought. *Milton.*

Children to serve their parents int'rest live,
Take heed what doom against yourself you give. *Dryden.*

77. *To* TAKE *heed to.* To attend.

Nothing sweeter than to *take heed unto* the commandments of the Lord. *Ecclus.* xxiii. 27.

78. *To* TAKE *in.* To comprise; to comprehend.

These heads are sufficient for the explication of this whole matter; *taking in* some additional discourses, which make the work more even. *Burnet's Theory of the Earth.*

This love of our country *takes in* our families, friends, and acquaintance. *Addison.*

The disuse of the tucker has enlarged the neck of a fine woman, that at present it *takes in* almost half the body. *Add.*

Of these matters no satisfactory account can be given by any mechanical hypothesis, without *taking in* the superintendence of the great Creator. *Derham's Physico-Theol.*

79. *To* TAKE *in.* To admit.

An opinion brought into his head by course, because he heard himself called a father, rather than any kindness that he found in his own heart, made him *take* us *in*. *Sidney.*

A great vessel full being drawn into bottles, and then the liquor put again into the vessel, will not fill the vessel again so full as it was, but that it may *take in* more. *Bacon.*

Porter was *taken in* not only as a bed-chamber servant, but as an useful instrument for his skill in the Spanish. *Wotton.*

Let fortune empty her whole quiver on me,
I have a soul, that, like an ample shield,
Can *take in* all; and verge enough for more. *Dryden.*

The sight and touch *take in* from the same object different ideas. *Locke.*

There is the same irregularity in my plantations: I *take in* none that do not naturally rejoice in the soil. *Spectator.*

80. *To*

80. *To* TAKE *in*. To win.

He sent Asan-aga with the Janizaries, and pieces of great ordnance, to *take in* the other cities of Tunis. *Knolles.*

Should a great beauty resolve to *take* me *in* with the artillery of her eyes, it would be as vain as for a thief to set upon a new robbed passenger. *Suckling.*

Open places are easily *taken in*, and towns not strongly fortified make but a weak resistance. *Felton on the Classicks.*

81. *To* TAKE *in*. To receive.

We went before, and sailed unto Assos, there intending to *take in* Paul. *Acts* xx. 13.

That which men *take in* by education is next to that which is natural. *Tillotson's Sermons.*

As no acid is in an animal body but must be *taken in* by the mouth, so if it is not subdued it may get into the blood. *Arbuthnot on Aliments.*

82. *To* TAKE *in*. To receive mentally.

Though a created understanding can never *take in* the fulness of the divine excellencies, yet so much as it can receive is of greater value than any other object. *Hale.*

The idea of extension joins itself so inseparably with all visible qualities, that it suffers to see no one without *taking in* impressions of extension too. *Locke.*

It is not in the power of the most enlarged understanding to frame one new simple idea in the mind, not *taken in* by the ways afore-mentioned. *Locke.*

A man can never have *taken in* his full measure of knowledge before he is hurried off the stage. *Addison's Spect.*

Let him *take in* the instructions you give him in a way suited to his natural inclination. *Watts.*

Some bright genius can *take in* a long train of propositions. *Watts.*

83. *To* TAKE *oath*. To swear.

The king of Babylon is come to Jerusalem, and hath taken of the king's seed, and of him *taken* an *oath*. *Ezek.*

We *take* all *oath* of secrecy, for the concealing of those inventions which we think fit to keep secret. *Bacon.*

84. *To* TAKE *off*. To invalidate; to destroy; to remove.

You must forsake this room and go with us;
Your power and your command is *taken off*,
And Cassio rules in Cyprus. *Shakespeare's Othello.*

The cruel ministers
Took off her life. *Shakespeare.*

If the heads of the tribes can be *taken off*, and the misled multitude return to their obedience, such an extent of mercy is honourable. *Bacon's Advice to Villiers.*

Sena loseth its windiness by decocting; and subtile or windy spirits are *taken off* by incension or evaporation. *Bacon.*

To stop schisms, *take off* the principal authors by winning and advancing them, rather than enrage them by violence. *Bac.*

What *taketh off* the objection is, that in judging scandal we are to look to the cause whence it cometh. *Bishop Sanderson.*

The promises, the terrors, or the authority of the commander, must be the topick whence that argument is drawn; and all force of these is *taken off* by this doctrine. *Hammond.*

It will not be unwelcome to these worthies, who endeavour the advancement of learning, as being likely to find a clear progression when so many untruths are *taken off*. *Brown.*

This *takes* not *off* the force of our former evidence. *Still.*

If the mark, by hindering its exportation, makes it less valuable, the melting pot can easily *take* it *off*. *Locke.*

A man's understanding failing him, would *take off* that presumption most men have of themselves. *Locke.*

It shews virtue in the fairest light, and *takes off* from the deformity of vice. *Addison.*

When we would *take off* from the reputation of an action, we ascribe it to vain glory. *Addison.*

This *takes off* from the elegance of our tongue, but expresses our ideas in the readiest manner. *Addison.*

The justices decreed, to *take off* a halfpeny in a quart from the price of ale. *Swift's Miscel.*

How many lives have been lost in hot blood, and how many likely to be *taken off* in cold. *Blount to Pope.*

Favourable names are put upon ill ideas, to *take off* the odium. *Watts.*

85. *To* TAKE *off*. To with-hold; to withdraw.

He perceiving that we were willing to say somewhat, in great courtesy *took* us *off*, aud condescended to ask us questions. *Bacon.*

Your present distemper is not so troublesome, as to *take* you *off* from all satisfaction. *Wake.*

There is nothing more resty and ungovernable than our thoughts: they will not be directed what objects to pursue, nor be *taken off* from those they have once fixed on; but run away with a man in pursuit of those ideas they have in view, let him do what he can. *Locke.*

Keep foreign ideas from *taking off* our minds from its present pursuit. *Locke.*

86. *To* TAKE *off*. To swallow.

Were the pleasure of drinking accompanied, the moment a man *takes off* his glass, with that sick stomach which, in some men, follows not many hours after, nobody would ever let wine touch his lips. *Locke.*

87. *To* TAKE *off*. To purchase.

Corn, in plenty, the labourer will have at his own rate, else he'll not *take* it *off* the farmer's hands for wages. *Locke.*

The Spaniards having no commodities that we will *take off*, above the value of one hundred thousand pounds *per annum*, cannot pay us. *Locke.*

There is a project on foot for transporting our best wheaten straw to Dunstable, and obliging us to *take off* yearly so many ton of straw hats. *Swift's Miscel.*

88. *To* TAKE *off*. To copy.

Take off all their models in wood. *Addison.*

89. *To* TAKE *off*. To find place for.

The multiplying of nobility brings a state to necessity; and, in like manner, when more are bred scholars than preferments can *take off*. *Bacon's Essays.*

90. *To* TAKE *off*. To remove.

When Moses went in, he *took* the vail *off* until he came out. *Exod.* xxxiv. 34.

If any would reign and take up all the time, let him *take* them *off* and bring others on. *Bacon.*

He has *taken* you *off*, by a peculiar instance of his mercy, from the vanities and temptations of the world. *Wake.*

91. *To* TAKE *order with*. To check; to take course with.

Though he would have turned his teeth upon Spain, yet he was *taken order with* before it came to that. *Bacon.*

92. *To* TAKE *out*. To remove from within any place.

Griefs are green;
And all thy friends which thou must make thy friends
Have but their stings and teeth newly *ta'en out*. *Shakesp.*

93. *To* TAKE *part*. To share.

Take part in rejoicing for the victory over the Turks. *Pope.*

94. *To* TAKE *place*. To prevail; to have effect.

Where arms *take place*, all other pleas are vain;
Love taught me force, and force shall love maintain. *Dry.*

The debt a man owes his father *takes place*, and gives the father a right to inherit. *Locke.*

95. *To* TAKE *up*. To borrow upon credit or interest.

The smooth pates now wear nothing but high shoes; and if a man is through with them in honest *taking up*, they stand upon security. *Shakespeare.*

We *take up* corn for them, that we may eat and live. *Neh.*

When Winter shuts the seas, she to the merchant goes,
Rich crystals of the rock she *takes up* there,
Huge agat vases, and old china ware. *Dryden's Juvenal.*

I have anticipated already, and *taken up* from Boccace before I come to him. *Dryden's Fables.*

Men, for want of due payment, are forced to *take up* the necessaries of life at almost double value. *Swift.*

96. To be ready for; to engage with.

His divisions
Are, one power against the French,
And one against Glendower; perforce, a third
Must *take up* us. *Shakesp. Henry* IV.

97. *To* TAKE *up*. To apply to the use of.

We *took up* arms not to revenge ourselves,
But free the commonwealth. *Addison.*

98. *To* TAKE *up*. To begin.

They shall *take up* a lamentation for me. *Ezek.* xxv. 17.

Princes friendship, which they *take up* upon the accounts of judgment and merit, they most times lay down out of humour. *South's Serm.*

99. *To* TAKE *up*. To fasten with a ligature passed under.

A large vessel opened by incision must be *taken up* before you proceed. *Sharp.*

100. *To* TAKE *up*. To engross; to engage.

Take my esteem,
If from my heart you ask, or hope for more,
I grieve the place is *taken up* before. *Dryden.*

I intended to have left the stage, to which my genius never much inclined me, for a work which would have *taken up* my life in the performance. *Dryden's Juvenal.*

Over-much anxiety in worldly things *takes up* the mind, hardly admitting so much as a thought of heaven. *Duppa.*

To understand fully his particular calling in the commonwealth, and religion, which is his calling, as he is a man, *takes up* his whole time. *Locke.*

Every one knows that mines alone furnish these: but withal, countries stored with mines are poor; the digging and refining of these metals *taking up* the labour, and wasting the number of the people. *Locke.*

We were so confident of success, that most of my fellow-soldiers were *taken up* with the same imaginations. *Addison.*

The following letter is from an artist, now *taken up* with this invention. *Addison.*

There is so much time *taken up* in the ceremony, that before they enter on their subject the dialogue is half ended. *Addison on ancient Medals.*

The affairs of religion and war *took up* Constantine so much, that he had not time to think of trade. *Arbuthnot.*

When the compass of twelve books is *taken up* in these, the reader will wonder by what methods our author could prevent being tedious. *Pope's Essay on Homer.*

101. *To* TAKE *up.* To have final recourse to.

Arnobius asserts, that men of the finest parts and learning, rhetoricians, lawyers, physicians, despising the sentiments they had been once fond of, *took up* their rest in the Christian religion. *Addison on the Christian Religion.*

102. *To* TAKE *up.* To seize; to catch; to arrest.

Though the sheriff have this authority to *take up* all such stragglers, and imprison them; yet shall he not work that terror in their hearts that a marshal will, whom they know to have power of life and death. *Spenser.*

I was *taken up* for laying them down. *Shakespeare.*

You have *taken up*,
Under the counterfeited zeal of God,
The subjects of his substitute, and here upswarm'd them. *Shakespeare.*

103. *To* TAKE *up.* To admit.

The ancients *took up* experiments upon credit, and did build great matters upon them. *Bacon's Nat. Hist.*

104. *To* TAKE *up.* To answer by reproving; to reprimand.

One of his relations *took* him *up* roundly, for stooping so much below the dignity of his profession. *L'Estrange.*

105. *To* TAKE *up.* To begin where the former left off.

The plot is purely fiction; for I *take* it *up* where the history has laid it down. *Dryden's Don Sebastian.*

Soon as the evening shades prevail,
The moon *takes up* the wond'rous tale,
And nightly to the list'ning earth
Repeats the story of her birth. *Addison's Spect.*

106. *To* TAKE *up.* To lift.

Take up these cloaths here quickly:
Where's the cowlstaff? *Shakespeare.*

The least things are *taken up* by the thumb and forefinger; when we would *take up* a greater quantity, we would use the thumb and all the fingers. *Ray.*

Milo *took up* a calf daily on his shoulders, and at last arrived at firmness to bear the bull. *Watts.*

107. *To* TAKE *up.* To occupy.

The people by such thick throngs swarmed to the place, that the chambers which opened towards the scaffold were *taken up*. *Hayward.*

All vicious enormous practices are regularly consequent, where the other hath *taken up* the lodging. *Hammond.*

Committees, for the convenience of the common-council who *took up* the Guild-hall, sat in Grocer's-hall. *Clarendon.*

When my concernment *takes up* no more room than myself, then so long as I know where to breathe, I know also where to be happy. *South's Sermons.*

These things being compared, notwithstanding the room that mountains *take up* on the dry land, there would be at least eight oceans required. *Burnet's Theory of the Earth.*

When these waters were annihilated, so much other matter must be created to *take up* their places. *Burnet.*

Princes were so *taken up* with wars, that few could write or read besides those of the long robes. *Temple.*

The buildings about *took up* the whole space. *Arbuthnot.*

108. *To* TAKE *up.* To accommodate; to adjust.

I have his horse to *take up* the quarrel. *Shakespeare.*

The greatest empires have had their rise from the pretence of *taking up* quarrels, or keeping the peace. *L'Estrange.*

109. *To* TAKE *up.* To comprise.

I prefer in our countryman the noble poem of Palemon and Arcite, which is perhaps not much inferior to the Ilias, only it *takes up* seven years. *Dryden's Fables.*

110. *To* TAKE *up.* To adopt; to assume.

God's decrees of salvation and damnation have been *taken up* by some of the Romish and Reformed churches, affixing them to mens particular entities, absolutely considered. *Hamm.*

The command in war is given to the strongest, or to the bravest; and in peace *taken up* and exercised by the boldest. *Temple.*

Assurance is properly that confidence which a man *takes up* of the pardon of his sins, upon such grounds as the scripture lays down. *South's Sermons.*

The French and we still change, but here's the curse,
They change for better, and we change for worse.
They *take up* our old trade of conquering,
And we are taking their's to dance and sing. *Dryden.*

He that will observe the conclusions men *take up*, must be satisfied they are not all rational. *Locke.*

Celibacy, in the church of Rome, was commonly forced, and *taken up*, under a bold vow. *Atterbury.*

Lewis Baboon had *taken up* the trade of clothier, without serving his time. *Arbuthnot's Hist. of John Bull.*

Every man *takes up* those interests in which his humour engages him. *Pope.*

If those proceedings were observed, morality and religion would soon become fashionable court virtues, and be *taken up* as the only methods to get or keep employments. *Swift.*

111. *To* TAEK *up.* To collect; to exact a tax.

This great bassa was born in a poor country village, and in his childhood taken from his Christian parents, by such as *take up* the tribute children. *Knolles's Hist. of the Turks.*

112. *To* TAKE *upon.* To appropriate to; to assume; to admit to be imputed to.

If I had no more wit than he, to *take* a fault *upon* me that he did, he had been hang'd for't. *Shakespeare.*

He *took* not *on* him the nature of angels, but the seed of Abraham. *Heb.* ii. 16.

For confederates, I will not *take upon* me the knowledge how the princes of Europe, at this day, stand affected towards Spain. *Bacon's War with Spain.*

Would I could your suff'rings bear;
Or once again could some new way invent,
To *take upon* myself your punishment. *Dryden.*

She loves me, ev'n to suffer for my sake;
And on herself would my refusal *take*. *Dryden.*

113. *To* TAKE *upon.* To assume; to claim authority.

These dangerous, unsafe lunes i' th' king! beshrew them,
He must be told on't, and he shall; the office
Becomes a woman best: I'll *take*'t *upon* me. *Shakespeare.*

Look that you *take upon* you as you should. *Shakespeare.*

This every translator *taketh upon* himself to do. *Felton.*

To TAKE. *v. n.*

1. To direct the course; to have a tendency to.

The inclination to goodness, if it issue not towards men, it will *take* unto other things. *Bacon.*

The king began to be troubled with the gout; but the defluxion *taking* also into his breast, wasted his lungs. *Bacon.*

All men being alarmed with it, and in dreadful suspence of the event, some *took* towards the park. *Dryden.*

To shun thy lawless lust the dying bride,
Unwary, *took* along the river's side. *Dryden.*

2. To please; to gain reception.

An apple of Sodom, though it may entertain the eye with a florid white and red, yet fills the hand with stench and foulness: fair in look and rotten at heart, as the gayest and most *taking* things are. *South's Sermons.*

Words and thoughts, which cannot be changed but for the worse, must of necessity escape the transient view upon the theatre; and yet without these a play may *take*. *Dryden.*

Each wit may praise it for his own dear sake,
And hint he writ it, if the thing shou'd *take*. *Addison.*

The work may be well performed, but will never *take* if it is not set off with proper scenes. *Addison's Freeholder.*

May the man grow wittier and wiser by finding that this stuff will not *take* nor please; and since by a little smattering in learning, and great conceit of himself, he has lost his religion, may he find it again by harder study and an humbler mind. *Bentley.*

3. To have the intended or natural effect.

In impressions from mind to mind, the impression *taketh*, but is overcome by the mind passive before it work any manifest effect. *Bacon's Nat. Hist.* N°. 901.

The clods, expos'd to Winter winds, will bake,
For putrid earth will best in vineyards *take*. *Dryden.*

4. To catch; to fix.

When flame *taketh* and openeth, it giveth a noise. *Bacon.*

5. *To* TAKE *after.* To learn of; to resemble; to imitate.

Beasts, that converse
With man, *take after* him, as hogs
Get pigs all th' year, and bitches dogs. *Hudibras, p.* i.

We cannot but think that he has *taken after* a good pattern. *Atterbury.*

6. *To* TAKE *in.* To inclose.

Upon the sea-coast are parcels of land that would pay well for the *taking in*. *Mortimer's Husb.*

7. *To* TAKE *in.* To lessen; to contract: as, *he* took in *his sails.*

8. *To* TAKE *in.* To cheat; to gull: as, *the cunning ones were* taken *in.* A low vulgar phrase.

9. *To* TAKE *in hand.* To undertake.

Till there were a perfect reformation, nothing would prosper that they *took in hand*. *Clarendon, b.* viii.

10. *To* TAKE *in with.* To resort to.

Men once placed *take in with* the contrary faction to that by which they enter. *Bacon's Essays.*

11. *To* TAKE *notice.* To observe.

12. *To* TAKE *notice.* To shew by any act that observation is made.

Some laws restrained the extravagant power of the nobility, the diminution whereof they took very heavily, though at that time they *took* little *notice* of it. *Clarendon.*

13. *To* TAKE *on.* To be violently affected.

Your husband is in his old tunes again; he so *takes on* yonder with me husband, that any madness I ever yet beheld seemed but tameness to this distemper. *Shakespeare.*

In horses, the smell of a dead horse maketh them fly away, and *take on* as if they were mad. *Bacon's Nat. Hist.*

14. *To* TAKE *on*. To grieve; to pine.

How will my mother, for a father's death,
Take on with me, and ne'er be satisfy'd? *Shakesp.*

15. *To* TAKE *to*. To apply to; to be fond of.

Have him understand it as a play of older people, and he will *take to* it of himself. *Locke.*

Miss Betsey won't *take to* her book. *Swift.*

The heirs to titles and large estates could never *take to* their books, yet are well enough qualified to sign a receipt for half a year's rent. *Swift's Miscel.*

Fear *took* hold upon them there, and pain, as of a woman in travail. *Psal.* xlviii. 6.

They sent forth spies, which should feign themselves just men, that they might *take* hold of his words. *Luke* xx. 20.

16. *To* TAKE *to*. To betake to; to have recourse.

If I had *taken to* the church, I should have had more sense than to have turned myself out of my benefice by writing libels. *Dryden.*

The callow storks with lizzard and with snake
Are fed, and soon as e'er to wing they *take*,
At sight those animals for food pursue. *Dryden.*

Men of learning who *take to* business, discharge it generally with greater honesty than men of the world. *Addison.*

17. *To* TAKE *up*. To stop.

The mind of man being naturally timorous of truth, and yet averse to that diligent search necessary to its discovery, it must needs *take up* short of what is really so. *Glanville.*

This grated harder upon the hearts of men, than the strangeness of all the former articles that *took up* chiefly in speculation. *South.*

Sinners at last *take up*, and settle in a contempt of all religion, which is called sitting in the seat of the scornful. *Tillotson's Sermons.*

18. *To* TAKE *up*. To reform.

This rational thought wrought so effectually, that it made him *take up*, and from that time prove a good husband. *Locke.*

19. *To* TAKE *up with*. To be contented with.

The ass *takes up with* that for his satisfaction, which he reckoned upon before for his misfortune. *L'Estrange.*

The law and gospel call aloud for active obedience, and such a piety as *takes* not *up with* idle inclinations, but shows itself in solid instances of practice. *South.*

I could as easily *take up with* that senseless assertion of the Stoicks, that virtues and vices are real bodies and distinct animals, as with this of the atheist, that they can all be derived from the power of mere bodies. *Bentley.*

A poor gentleman ought not to be curate of a parish, except he be cunninger than the devil. It will be difficult to remedy this, because whoever had half his cunning would never *take up with* a vicarage of ten pounds. *Swift.*

In affairs which may have an extensive influence on our future happiness, we should not *take up with* probabilities. *Watts's Logick.*

20. *To* TAKE *up with*. To lodge; to dwell.

Who would not rather *take up with* the wolf in the woods, than make such a clutter in the world? *L'Estrange.*

Are dogs such desirable company to *take up with?* *South.*

His name and credit shall you undertake,
And in my house you shall be friendly lodg'd:

In 1643, the parliament *took upon* them to call an assembly of divines, to settle some church controversies, of which many were unfit to judge. *Sanderson.*

I *take* not *on* me here as a physician:
Nor do I, as an enemy to peace,
Troop in the throngs of military men:
But rather
To purge th' obstructions, which begins to stop
Our very veins of life. *Shakesp. Henry* IV.

21. *To* TAKE *with*. To please.

Our gracious master is a precedent to his own subjects, and seasonable memento's may be useful; and being discretely used, cannot but *take* well *with* him. *Bacon.*

TA'KEN, the participle pass. of *take*.

Thou art *taken* in thy mischief, because thou art bloody. 2 *Sam.* xvi. 8.

He who letteth will let, until he be *taken* out of the way. 2 *Thess.* ii. 7.

It concerns all who think it worth while to be in earnest with their immortal souls, not to abuse themselves with a false confidence: a thing so easily *taken* up, and so hardly laid down. *South's Sermons.*

Scaliger, comparing the two great orators, says, that nothing can be *taken* from Demosthenes, nor added to Tully. *Denham.*

Though he that is full of them thinks it rather an ease than oppression to speak them out, yet his auditors are perhaps as much *taken* up with themselves. *Gov. of the Tongue.*

The object of desire once *ta'en* away,
'Tis then not love, but pity which we pay. *Dryden.*

TA'KER. *n. s.* [from *take*.] He that takes.

He will hang upon him like a disease,
He is sooner caught than the pestilence,
And the *taker* runs presently mad. *Shakespeare.*

The dear sale beyond the seas encreased the number of *takers*, and the *takers* jarring and brawling one with another, and foreclosing the fishes, taking their kind within harbour, decreased the number of the taken. *Carew.*

The far distance of this county from the court hath heretofore afforded it a supersedeas from *takers* and surveyors. *Carew's Survey of Cornwall.*

Berry coffee and the leaf tobacco, of which the Turks are great *takers*, condense the spirits, and make them strong. *Bacon.*

Few like the Fabii or the Scipio's are,
Takers of cities, conquerors in war. *Denham.*

He to betray us did himself betray,
At once the *taker*, and at once the prey. *Denham.*

Seize on the king, and him your prisoner make,
While I, in kind revenge, my *taker* take. *Dryden.*

Rich cullies may their boasting spare,
They purchase but sophisticated ware:
'Tis prodigality that buys deceit,
Where both the giver and the *taker* cheat. *Dryden.*

TA'KING. *n. s.* [from *take*.] Seizure; distress.

What a *taking* was he in, when your husband asked who was in the basket. *Shakespeare.*

She saw in what a *taking*,
The knight was by his furious quaking. *Butler.*

TALE. *n. s.* [tale, from tellan, *to tell*, Saxon.]

1. A narrative; a story. Commonly a slight or petty account of some trifling or fabulous incident: as, *a* tale *of a tub*.

This story prepared their minds for the reception of any *tales* relating to other countries. *Watts.*

2. Oral relation.

My conscience hath a thousand several tongues,
And ev'ry tongue brings in a sev'ral *tale*,
And every *tale* condemns me for a villain. *Shakespeare.*

Life is a *tale*
Told by an idiot, full of sound and fury,
Signifying nothing. *Shakesp. Macbeth.*

Hermia, for aught I could read,
Could ever hear by *tale* or history,
The course of true love never did run smooth. *Shakesp.*

We spend our years as a *tale* that is told. *Psal.* xc. 9.

3. [Talan, *to count*, Saxon.] Number reckoned.

Number may serve your purpose with the ignorant, who measure by *tale* and not by weight. *Hooker.*

For ev'ry bloom his trees in Spring afford,
An autumn apple was by *tale* restor'd. *Dryden's Virgil.*

Both number twice a day the milky dams,
And once she takes the *tale* of all the lambs. *Dryden.*

The herald for the last proclaims
A silence, while they answer'd to their names,
To shun the fraud of musters false;
The *tale* was just. *Dryden's Knight's Tale.*

Reasons of things are rather to be taken by weight than *tale*. *Collier on Cloaths.*

4. Reckoning; numeral account.

In packing, they keep a just *tale* of the number that every hogshead containeth. *Carew.*

Money b'ing the common scale
Of things by measure, weight and *tale*;
In all th' affairs of church and state,
'Tis both the balance and the weight. *Butler.*

Then twelve returned upon the principal pannel, or the *tales*, are sworn to try the same according to their evidence. *Hale.*

5. Information; disclosure of any thing secret.

From hour to hour we ripe and ripe,
And then from hour to hour we rot and rot;
And thereby hangs a *tale*. *Shakespeare.*

Birds live in the air freest, and are aptest by their voice to tell *tales* what they find, and by their flight to express the same. *Bacon.*

TALEBE'ARING. *n. s.* [*tale* and *bear*.] The act of informing; officious or malignant intelligence.

The said Timothy was extremely officious about their mistress's person, endeavouring, by flattery and *talebearing*, to set her against the rest of the servants. *Arbuthnot.*

TALEBE'ARER. *n. s.* [*tale* and *bear*.] One who gives officious or malignant intelligence.

The liberty of a common table is a tacit invitation to all intruders; as buffoons, spies, *talebearers*, flatterers. *L'Estr.*

In great families, some one false, paultry *talebearer*, by carrying stories from one to another, shall inflame the minds, and discompose the quiet of the whole family. *South.*

TA'LENT. *n. s.* [*talentum*, Lat.]

A *talent* signified so much weight, or a sum of money, the value differing according to the different ages and countries. *Arbuthnot.*

Five *talents* in his debt,
His means most short, his creditors most straight. *Shakesp.*

Two tripods caſt in antick mould,
With two great *talents* of the fineſt gold. *Dryden.*

2. Faculty; power; gift of nature. A metaphor borrowed from the talents mentioned in the holy writ.

Many who knew the treaſurer's *talent* in removing prejudice, and reconciling himſelf to wavering affections, believed the loſs of the duke was unſeaſonable. *Clarendon.*

He is chiefly to be conſidered in his three different *talents*, as a critick, ſatyriſt, and writer of odes. *Dryden.*

'Tis not my *talent* to conceal my thoughts,
Or carry ſmiles and ſunſhine in my face,
When diſcontent ſits heavy at my heart. *Addiſon's Cato.*

They are out of their element, and logick is none of their *talent*. *Baker's Reflections on Learning.*

Perſons who poſſeſs the true *talent* of raillery are like comets; they are ſeldom ſeen, and all at once admired and feared. *Female Quixote.*

3. Quality; nature. An improper and miſtaken uſe.

Though the nation generally was without any ill *talent* to the church in doctrine or diſcipline, yet they were not without a jealouſy that popery was not enough diſcountenanced. *Clarendon.*

It is the *talent* of human nature to run from one extreme to another. *Swift.*

TA'LISMAN. *n. ſ.* [I know not whence derived: τέλεσμα, *Skinner.*] A magical character.

If the phyſicians would forbid us to pronounce gout, rheumatiſm, and ſtone, would that ſerve like ſo many *taliſmans* to deſtroy the diſeaſes. *Swift.*

Of *taliſmans* and ſigils knew the power,
And careful watch'd the planetary hour. *Pope.*

TALISMA'NICK. *adj.* [from *taliſman.*] Magical.

The figure of a heart bleeding upon an altar, or held in the hand of a Cupid, has always been looked upon as *taliſmanick* in dreſſes of this nature. *Addiſon's Spect.*

To TALK. *v. n.* [*taelen*, Dutch.]

1. To ſpeak in converſation; to ſpeak fluently and familiarly; not in ſet ſpeeches; to converſe.

I will buy with you, ſell with you, *talk* with you; but I will not eat with you. *Shakſpeare.*

Now is this vice's dagger become a ſquire, and *talks* as familiarly of John of Gaunt as if he had been ſworn brother to him; and he never ſaw him but once. *Shakeſp. Henry* IV.

The princes refrained *talking*, and laid their hand on their mouth. *Job* xxix. 9.

The children of thy people ſtill *talk* againſt thee. *Ezek.*

If I *talk* much, they ſhall lay their hands upon their mouth. *Wiſd.* viii. 12.

Here free from court-compliances he walks,
And with himſelf, his beſt adviſer, *talks.* *Waller.*

As God remembers that we are but fleſh, unable to bear the nearer approaches of divinity, and ſo *talks* with us as once with Moſes through a cloud; ſo he forgets not that he breathed into us breath of life, a vital active ſpirit. *Decay of Piety.*

Mention the king of Spain, he *talks* very notably; but if you go out of the Gazette you drop him. *Addiſon.*

2. To prattle; to ſpeak impertinently.

Hypocrites auſterely *talk*
Of purity. *Milton.*

My heedleſs tongue has *talk'd* away this life. *Rowe.*

3. To give account.

The cryſtalline ſphere, whoſe balance weighs
The trepidation *talk'd.* *Milton.*

The natural hiſtories of Switzerland *talk* much of the fall of theſe rocks, and the great damage done. *Addiſon.*

We will conſider whether Adam had any ſuch heir as our author *talks* of. *Locke.*

4. To ſpeak; to reaſon; to confer.

Let me *talk* with thee of thy judments. *Jer.* xii. 1.

Will ye ſpeak wickedly for God, and *talk* deceitfully for him? *Job* xiii. 7.

It is difficult taſk to *talk* to the purpoſe, and to put life and perſpicuity into our diſcourſes. *Collier on Pride.*

Talking over the things which you have read with your companions fixes them upon the mind. *Watts.*

TALK. *n. ſ.* [from the verb.]

1. Oral converſation; fluent and familiar ſpeech.

We do remember; but our argument
Is all too heavy to admit much *talk.* *Shakeſpeare.*

Perceiving his ſoldiers diſmayed, he forbad them to have any *talk* with the enemy. *Knolles's Hiſt. of the Turks.*

How can he get wiſdom that driveth oxen, is occupied in their labours, and whoſe *talk* is of bullocks? *Ecclus.* xxxviii.

This ought to weigh with thoſe whoſe reading is deſigned for much *talk* and little knowledge. *Locke.*

In various *talk* th' inſtructive hours they paſt,
Who gave the ball, or paid the viſit laſt. *Pope.*

2. Report; rumour.

I hear a *talk* up and down of raiſing our money, as a means to retain our wealth, and keep our money from being carried away. *Locke.*

3. Subject of diſcourſe.

What delight to be by ſuch extoll'd,
To live upon their tongues and be their *talk*,
Of whom to be deſpis'd were no ſmall praiſe? *Milton.*

TALK. *n. ſ.* [*talc*, Fr.]

Stones compoſed of plates are generally parallel, and flexible and elaſtick: as, *talk*, cat-ſilver or glimmer, of which there are three ſorts, the yellow or golden, the white or ſilvery, and the black. *Woodward's Foſſils.*

Venetian *talk* kept in a heat of a glaſs furnace; after all the remaining body, though brittle and diſcoloured, had not loſt much of its bulk, and ſeemed nearer of kin to *talk* than mere earth. *Boyle.*

TA'LKATIVE. *adj.* [from *talk.*] Full of prate; loquacious.

If I have held you overlong, lay hardly the fault upon my old age, which in its diſpoſition is *talkative.* *Sidney.*

This may prove an inſtructive leſſon to the diſaffected, not to build any hopes on the *talkative* zealots of their party. *Addiſon.*

I am aſhamed I cannot make a quicker progreſs in the French, where everybody is ſo courteous and *talkative.* *Add.*

The coxcomb bird ſo *talkative* and grave,
That from his cage cries cuckold, whore, and knave;
Though many a paſſenger he rightly call,
You hold him no philoſopher at all. *Pope.*

TA'LKATIVENESS. *n. ſ.* [from *talkative.*] Loquacity; garrulity; fulneſs of prate.

We call this *talkativeneſs* a feminine vice; but he that ſhall appropriate loquacity to women, may perhaps ſometimes need to light Diogenes's candle to ſeek a man. *Gov. Tongue.*

Learned women have loſt all credit by their impertinent *talkativeneſs* and conceit. *Swift.*

TA'LKER. *n. ſ.* [from *talk.*]

1. One who talks.

Let me give for inſtance ſome of thoſe writers or *talkers* who deal much in the words nature or fate. *Watts.*

2. A loquacious perſon; a pratler.

Keep me company but two years,
Thou ſhalt not know the ſound of thine own tongue.
—Farewel, I'll grow a *talker* for this jeer. *Shakeſpeare.*

If it were deſirable to have a child a more briſk *talker*, ways might be found to make him ſo; but a wiſe father had rather his ſon ſhould be uſeful when a man, than pretty company. *Locke on Education.*

3. A boaſter; a bragging fellow.

The greateſt *talkers* in the days of peace, have been the moſt puſillanimous in the day of temptation. *Taylor.*

TA'LKY. *adj.* [from *talk.*] Conſiſting of talk; reſembling talk.

The *talky* flakes in the ſtrata were all formed before the ſubſidence, along with the ſand. *Woodward on Foſſils.*

TALL. *adj.* [*tâl*, Welſh.]

1. High in ſtature.

Bring word, how *tall* ſhe is. *Shak. Ant. and Cleopatra.*

Two of nobler ſhape,
Erect and *tall.* *Milton.*

2. High; lofty.

Winds ruſh'd abroad
From the four hinges of the world, and fell
On the vext wilderneſs, whoſe *talleſt* pines,
Though rooted deep as high, and ſturdieſt oaks
Bow'd their ſtiff necks. *Milton's Par. Reg. b.* iv.

May they encreaſe as faſt, and ſpread their boughs,
As the high fame of their great owner grows:
May he live long enough to ſee them all
Dark ſhadows caſt, and as his palace *tall!*
Methinks I ſee the love that ſhall be made,
The lovers walking in that am'rous ſhade. *Waller.*

3. Sturdy; luſty.

I'll ſwear thou art a *tall* fellow of thy hands, and that thou wilt not be drunk; but I know thou art no *tall* fellow of thy hands, and that thou wilt be drunk; but I would thou wouldſt be a *tall* fellow of thy hands. *Shakeſp. Winter's Tale.*

TA'LLAGE. *n. ſ.* [*taillage*, French.] Impoſt; exciſe.

The people of Spain were better affected unto Philip than to Ferdinando, becauſe he had impoſed upon them many taxes and *tallages.* *Bacon's Henry* VII.

TA'LLOW. *n. ſ.* [*talge*, Daniſh.] The greaſe or fat of an animal; ſuet.

She's the kitchen wench and all greaſe; and I know not what uſe to put her to, but to make a lamp of her, and run from her by her own light. I warrant her rags, and the *tallow* in them, will burn a Lapland winter. *Shakeſpeare.*

In Cuba and Hiſpaniola are killed divers thouſands, whereof the Spaniards only take the *tallow* or the hide. *Abbot.*

Snuff the candles cloſe to the *tallow*, which will make them run. *Swift.*

To TA'LLOW. *v. a.* [from the noun.] To greaſe; to ſmear with tallow.

TA'LLOWCHANDLER. *n. ſ.* [*tallow* and *chandelier*, Fr.] One who makes candles of tallow, not of wax.

Naſtineſs, and ſeveral naſty trades, as *tallowchandlers*, butchers, and neglect of cleanſing of gutters, are great occaſions of a plague. *Harvey on the Plague.*

TA'LLY. *n. ſ.* [from *tailler*, to cut, Fr.]

1. A ſtick notched or cut in conformity to another ſtick, and uſed to keep accounts by.

So right his judgment was cut fit,
And made a *tally* to his wit. *Hudibras, p.* iii.

The only talents in eſteem at preſent are thoſe of Exchange-Alley; one *tally* is worth a grove of bays. *Garth.*

Have you not ſeen a baker's maid
Between two equal panniers ſway'd?
Her *tallies* uſeleſs lie and idle,
If plac'd exactly in the middle. *Prior.*

From his rug the ſkew'r he takes,
And on the ſtick ten equal notches makes;
With juſt reſentment flings it on the ground,
There take my *tally* of ten thouſand pound. *Swift.*

2. Any thing made to ſuit another.

So ſuited in their minds and perſons,
That they were fram'd the *tallies* for each other:
If any alien love had interpos'd,
It muſt have been an eye-ſore to beholders. *Dryden.*

To TA'LLY. *v. a.* [from the noun.] To fit; to ſuit; to cut out for any thing.

Nor ſiſter either had, nor brother;
They ſeem'd juſt *tally'd* for each other. *Prior.*

They are not ſo well *tallied* to the preſent juncture. *Pope.*

To TA'LLY. *v. n.* To be fitted; to conform; to be ſuitable.

I found pieces of tiles that exactly *tallied* with the channel. *Addiſon's Remarks on Italy.*

TA'LMUD. } *n. ſ.* The book containing the Jewiſh traditions, the rabbinical conſtitutions and explications of the law.
THA'LMUD. }

TA'LNESS. *n. ſ.* [from *tall.*] Height of ſtature; procerity.

An hideous giant, horrible and high,
That with his *talneſs* ſeem'd to threat the ſky. *Fairy Qu.*

The eyes behold ſo many naked bodies, as for *talneſs* of ſtature could hardly be equalled in any country. *Hayward.*

TA'LON. *n. ſ.* [*talon*, French.] The claw of a bird of prey.

It may be tried, whether birds may not be made to have greater or longer *talons.* *Bacon's Nat. Hiſt.*

Upward the noble bird directs his wing,
And tow'ring round his maſter's earth-born foes,
Swift he collects his fatal ſtock of ire,
Lifts his fierce *talon* high, and darts the forked fire. *Prior.*

TA'MARIND *tree. n. ſ.* [*tamarindus*, Lat.]

The flower of the *tamarind tree* conſiſts of ſeveral leaves, which are ſo placed as to reſemble a papilionaceous one in ſome meaſure; but theſe expand circularly, from whoſe many leaved flower-cup riſes the pointal, which afterward becomes a flat pod, containing many flat angular ſeeds ſurrounded with an acid blackiſh pulp. *Miller.*

Lenitives are caſſia, *tamarinds*, manna. *Wiſeman's Surgery.*

Lay me reclin'd
Beneath the ſpreading *tamarind* that ſhakes,
Fan'd by the breeze its fever-cooling fruit. *Thomſon.*

TA'MARISK. *n. ſ.* [*tamariſce*, Lat.]

The flowers of the *tamariſk* are roſaceous, conſiſting of ſeveral leaves, which are placed orbicularly; from whoſe flower-cup riſes the pointal, which afterward becomes a pod, ſomewhat like thoſe of the ſallow, which opens into two parts, and contains ſeveral downy ſeeds. *Miller.*

Tamariſk is a tree that grows tall, and its wood is medicinal. *Mortimer's Huſbandry.*

TA'MBARINE. *n. ſ.* [*tambourin*, Fr.] A tabor; a ſmall drum.

Calliope with muſes moe,
Soon as thy oaten pipe began to ſound,
Their ivory lutes and *tambar nes* forego. *Spenſer's Paſt.*

TAME. *adj.* [tame, Saxon; *taem*, Dutch; *tam*, Daniſh.]

1. Not wild; domeſtick.

Thales the Mileſian ſaid, That of all wild beaſts a tyrant is the worſt, and of all *tame* beaſts a flatterer. *Addiſon.*

2. Cruſhed; ſubdued; depreſſed; dejected; ſpiritleſs; heartleſs.

If you ſhould need a pin,
You could not with more *tame* a tongue deſire it. *Shakeſp.*

And now their pride and mettle is aſleep,
Their courage with hard labour *tame* and dull. *Shakeſp.*

A moſt poor man made *tame* to fortune's blows,
Who by the art of known and feeling ſorrows,
Am pregnant to good pity. *Shakeſp. King Lear.*

Praiſe him each ſavage furious beaſt,
That on his ſtores do daily feaſt;
And you *tame* ſlaves of the laborious plough,
Your weary knees to your Creator bow. *Roſcommon.*

3. Spiritleſs; unanimated: as, a tame *poem.* A low phraſe.

To TAME. *v. n.* [*gatamgan*, Gothick; temean, Saxon; *tammen*, Dutch.]

1. To reduce from wildneſs; to reclaim; to make gentle.

Thoſe that *tame* wild horſes,
Pace 'em not in their hands to make 'em gentle,
But ſtop their mouths with ſtubborn bits. *Shakeſpeare.*

2. To ſubdue; to cruſh; to depreſs; to conquer.

If the heavens do not their viſible ſpirits
Send quickly down to *tame* the offences,
Humanity muſt perforce prey on itſelf. *Shakeſp. King Lear.*

They cannot *tame*
Or overcome their riches! not by making
Baths, orchards, fiſh-pools, letting in of ſeas
Here, and then there forcing them out again. *B. Johnſon.*

A puling cuckold, would drink up
The lees and dregs of a flat *tamed* piece. *Shakeſpeare.*

A race unconquer'd, by their clime made bold,
The Caledonians arm'd with want and cold,
Have been kept for you to *tame.* *Waller.*

TA'MEABLE. *adj.* [from *tame.*] Suſceptive of taming.

Ganzas are ſuppoſed to be great fowls, of a ſtrong flight, and eaſily *tameable*; divers of which may be ſo brought up as to join together in carrying the weight of a man. *Wilkins.*

TA'MELY. *adj.* [from *tame.*] Not wildly; meanly; ſpiritleſly.

True obedience, of this madneſs cur'd,
Stoop *tamely* to the foot of majeſty. *Shakeſ. Henry* IV.

What courage *tamely* could to death conſent,
And not by ſtriking firſt the blow prevent. *Dryden.*

Once a champion of renown,
So *tamely* can you bear the raviſh'd crown? *Dryden.*

Has he given way?
Did he look *tamely* on and let them paſs? *Addiſon.*

Can you love and reverence your prelate, whom you *tamely* ſuffer to be abuſed. *Swift.*

TA'MENESS. *n. ſ.* [from *tame.*]

1. The quality of being tame; not wildneſs.

2. Want of ſpirits; timidity.

Such a conduct muſt appear rather like *tameneſs* than beauty, and expoſe his authority to inſults. *Rogers.*

TA'MER. *n. ſ.* [from *tame.*] Conqueror; ſubduer.

He, great *tamer* of all human art,
Dulneſs! whoſe good old cauſe I yet defend. *Pope.*

TA'MINY. *n. ſ.* A woollen ſtuff.

TA'MKIN. *n. ſ.* The ſtopple of the mouth of a great gun.

To TA'MPER. *v. a.* [of uncertain derivation, derived by *Skinner* from *tempero*, Latin.]

1. To be buſy with phyſick.

'Tis in vain
To *tamper* with your crazy brain,
Without trepanning of your ſkull
As often as the moon's at full. *Hudibras, p.* ii.

He tried waſhes to bring him to a better complexion, but there was no good to be done; the very *tampering* caſt him into a diſeaſe. *L'Eſtrange's Fables.*

2. To meddle; to have to do without fitneſs or neceſſity.

That key of knowledge, which ſhould give us entrance into the receſſes of religion, is by ſo much *tampering* and wrenching made uſeleſs. *Decay of Piety.*

'Tis dang'rous *tampering* with a muſe,
The profits ſmall, and you have much to loſe:
For though true wit adorns your birth or place,
Degenerate lines degrade the attainted race. *Roſcommon.*

Earl Waltheof being overtaken with wine, engaged in a conſpiracy; but repenting next morning, repaired to the king, and diſcovered the whole matter: notwithſtanding which he was beheaded upon the defeat of the conſpiracy, for having but thus far *tampered* in it. *Addiſon's Freeholder.*

3. To deal; to practiſe with.

Others *tamper'd*
For Fleetwood, Deſborough, and Lambert. *Hudibras.*

To TAN. *v. a.* [*tannen*, Dutch; *tannen*, French.]

1. To impregnate or imbue with bark.

A human ſkull covered with the ſkin, having been buried in ſome limy ſoil, was *tanned* or turned into a kind of leather. *Grew's Muſ.*

Black cattle produce tallow, hides, and beef; but the greateſt part of the hides are exported raw for want of bark to *tan* them. *Swift.*

They ſell us their bark at a good price for *tanning* our hides into leather. *Swift's Miſcel.*

2. To imbrown by the ſun.

His face all *tann'd* with ſcorching ſunny ray,
As he had travell'd many a Summer's day
Through boiling ſands of Araby and Ind. *Fa. Qu. b.* i.

Like ſun parch'd quarters on the city gates,
Such is thy *tann'd* ſkin's lamentable ſtate. *Donne.*

A brown for which heaven would diſband
The galaxy, and ſtars be *tann'd.* *Cleaveland.*

TANE for *taken*, *ta'en.*

Two trophees *tane* from th' Eaſt and Weſtern ſhore,
And both thoſe nations twice triumphed o'er. *May's Virg.*

TANG. *n. ſ.* [*tanghe*, Dutch, acrid.]

1. A ſtrong taſte; a taſte left in the mouth.

Sin taken into the ſoul, is like a liquor poured into a veſſel; ſo much of it as it fills it alſo ſeaſons: ſo that although the body of the liquor ſhould be poured out again, yet ſtill it leaves that *tang* behind it. *South's Sermons.*

It is ſtrange that the ſoul ſhould never once recal over any of its pure native thoughts, before it borrowed any thing from the body; never bring into the waking man's view any other ideas but what have a *tang* of the caſk, and derive their original from that union. *Locke.*

2. Reliſh; taſte. A low word.

There was not the leaſt *tang* of religion, which is indeed the worſt affectation in any thing he ſaid or did. *Atterbury.*

3. Something that leaves a ſting or pain behind it.

She had a tongue with a *tang*,
Would cry to a ſailor, go hang. *Shakeſp. Tempeſt.*

4. Sound; tone: this is miſtaken for *tone* or *twang*.

There is a pretty affectation in the Allemain, which gives their ſpeech a different *tang* from ours. *Holder.*

To TANG. *v. n.* [This is, I think, miſtaken for *twang*.] To ring with.

Be oppoſite with a kinſman, ſurly with thy ſervants; let thy tongue *tang* arguments of ſtate; put thyſelf into the trick of ſingularity. *Shakeſp. Twelfth Night.*

TA'NGENT. *n. ſ.* [*tangent*, Fr. *tangens*, Lat.]

Tangent, in trigonometry, is a right line perpendicularly raiſed on the extremity of a radius, and which touches a circle ſo as not to cut it; but yet interſects another line without the circle called a ſecant that is drawn from the centre, and which cuts the arc to which it is a *tangent*. *Trevoux.*

Nothing in this hypotheſis can retain the planets in their orbs, but they would immediately deſert them and the neighbourhood of the ſun, and vaniſh away in *tangents* to their ſeveral circles into the mundane ſpace. *Bentley's Serm.*

TANGIBI'LITY. *n. ſ.* [from *tangible*.] The quality of being perceived by the touch.

TA'NGIBLE. *adj.* [from *tango*, Lat.] Perceptible by the touch.

Tangible bodies have no pleaſure in the conſort of air, but endeavour to ſubact it into a more denſe body. *Bacon.*

By the touch, the *tangible* qualities of bodies are diſcerned, as hard, ſoft, ſmooth. *Locke.*

To TA'NGLE. *v. a.* [See *entangle*.]

1. To implicate; to knit together.
2. To enſnare; to entrap.

She means to *tangle* mine eyes too.
'Tis not your inky brows, your black ſilk hair,
Your bugle eye-balls, nor your cheek of cream. *Shakeſp.*

I do, quoth he, perceive
My king is *tangl'd* in affection to
A creature of the queen's, lady Anne Bullen. *Shakeſpeare.*

You muſt lay lime to *tangle* her deſires
By wailful ſonnets, whoſe compoſed rhimes
Shall be full fraught with ſerviceable vows. *Shakeſpeare.*

If thou retire, the dauphin, well appointed,
Stands with the ſnares of war to *tangle* thee. *Shakeſp.*

Now ly'ſt victorious
Among thy ſlain ſelf-kill'd,
Not willingly, but *tangl'd* in the fold
Of dire neceſſity. *Milton's Agoniſtes.*

Skill'd to retire, and in retiring draw
Hearts after them, *tangl'd* in amorous nets. *Milton.*

With ſubtile cobweb cheats,
They're catch'd in knotted law-like nets;
In which when once they are *entangl'd*,
The more they ſtir, the more they're *tangl'd*. *Hudibras.*

3. To embroil; to embarraſs.

When my ſimple weakneſs ſtrays,
Tangled in forbidden ways:
He, my ſhepherd! is my guide,
He's before me, on my ſide. *Craſhaw.*

To TA'NGLE. *v. n.* To be entangled.

Shrubs and *tangling* buſhes had perplex'd
All path of man or beaſt.

TA'NGLE. *n. ſ.* [from the verb.] A knot of things mingled in one another.

He leading ſwiftly rowl'd
In *tangles*, and made intricate ſeem ſtrait,
To miſchief ſwift. *Milton's Par. Loſt, b.* ix.

Sport with Amaryllis in the ſhade,
Or with the *tangles* of Neæra's hair. *Milton.*

TA'NIST. *n. ſ.* [an Iriſh word; *an taaniſther*, Erſe.]

Preſently after the death of any of their captains, they aſſemble themſelves to chuſe another in his ſtead, and nominate commonly the next brother, and then next to him do they chuſe next of the blood to be *taniſt*, who ſhall next ſucceed him in the ſaid captainry. *Spenſer on Ireland.*

TA'NISTRY. *n. ſ.* [from *taniſh*.]

The Iriſh hold their lands by *taniſtry*, which is no more than a perſonal eſtate for his life-time that is *taniſt*, by reaſon he is admitted thereunto by election. *Spenſer on Ireland.*

If the Iriſh be not permitted to purchaſe eſtates of freeholds, which might deſcend to their children, muſt they not continue their cuſtom of *taniſtry*? which makes all their poſſeſſions uncertain. *Davies on Ireland.*

By the Iriſh cuſtom of *taniſtry*, the chieftains of every country, and the chief of every ſept, had no longer eſtate than for life in their chieferies; and when their chieftains were dead, their ſons, or next heirs, did not ſucceed them, but their *taniſts*, who were elective, and purchaſed their elections by ſtrong hand. *Davies on Ireland.*

TANK. *n. ſ.* [*tanque*, Fr.] A large ciſtern or baſon.

Handle your pruning-knife with dexterity; go tightly to your buſineſs: you have coſt me much, and muſt earn it: here's plentiful proviſion, raſcal; ſallading in the garden and water in the *tank*; and in holy days, the licking of a platter of rice when you deſerve it. *Dryden's Don Sebaſtian.*

TA'NKARD. *n. ſ.* [*tanquaerd*, French; *tankaerd*, Dutch; *tancaird*, Iriſh.] A large veſſel with a cover, for ſtrong drink.

Hath his *tankard* touch'd your brain?
Sure they're fall'n aſleep again. *Benj. Johnſon.*

Marius was the firſt who drank out of a ſilver *tankard*, after the manner of Bacchus. *Arbuthnot on Coins.*

When any calls for ale, fill the largeſt *tankard* cup top full. *Swift.*

TA'NNER. *n. ſ.* [from *tan*.] One whoſe trade is to tan leather.

Tanners uſe that lime which is newly drawn out of the kiln, and not ſlacked with water or air. *Moxon.*

TA'NSY. *n. ſ.* [*tanacetum*, Lat.]

The *tanſy* hath a floſculous flower, conſiſting of many florets, divided into ſeveral ſegments ſitting on the embrio, and contained in a ſquamous and hemiſpherical empalement; the embrio afterward becomes a ſeed not at all downy; to theſe notes muſt be added thick flowers into a gathered head. *Miller.*

TA'NTALISM. *n. ſ.* [from *tantalize*.] A puniſhment like that of Tantalus.

A lively repreſentation of a perſon lying under the torments of ſuch a *tantaliſm*, or platonick hell. *Addiſon's Spectat.*

To TA'NTALIZE. *v. a.* [from *Tantalus*, whoſe puniſhment was to ſtarve among fruits and water which he could not touch.] To torment by the ſhew of pleaſures which cannot be reached.

Thy vain deſires, at ſtrife
Within themſelves, have *tantaliz'd* thy life. *Dryden.*

The maid once ſped was not ſuffered to *tantalize* the male part of the commonwealth. *Addiſon.*

TA'NTIVY. *adv.* [from the note of a hunting horn, ſo expreſſed in articulate ſounds; from *tantâ vi*, ſays *Skinner*.] To ride *tantivy* is to ride with great ſpeed.

TA'NTLING. *n. ſ.* [from *Tantalus*.] One ſeized with hopes of pleaſure unattainable.

Hard life,
To be ſtill hot Summer's *tantlings*, and
The ſhrinking ſlaves of Winter. *Shakeſpeare.*

TA'NTAMOUNT. *n. ſ.* [French.] Equivalent.

If one third of our coin were gone, and ſo men had equally one third leſs money than they have, it muſt be *tantamount*; and what I 'ſcape of one third leſs, another muſt make up. *Locke.*

To TAP. *v. a.* [*tappen*, Dutch; *tapper*, French.]

1. To touch lightly; to ſtrike gently.
2. [*Tappen*, Dutch.] To pierce a veſſel; to broach a veſſel. It is uſed likewiſe of the liquor.

That blood, already like the pelican,
Haſt thou *tapt* out, and drunkenly carouzed. *Shakeſpeare.*

He has been *tapping* his liquors, while I have been ſpilling my blood. *Addiſon.*

Wait with patience till the tumour becomes troubleſome, and then *tap* it with a lancet. *Sharp' Surgery.*

TAP. *n. ſ.* [from the verb.]

1. A gentle blow.

This is the right fencing grace, *tap* for *tap*, and ſo part fair. *Shakeſp. Henry* IV.

Each ſhakes her fan with a ſmile, then gives her right-hand woman a *tap* upon the ſhoulder. *Addiſon's Spect.*

As at hot cockles once I laid me down,
And felt the weighty hand of many a clown,
Buxoma gave a gentle *tap*. *Gay's Paſtorals.*

2. A pipe at which the liquor of a veſſel is let out.

A gentleman was inclined to the knight of Gaſcoigne's diſtemper, upon hearing the noiſe of a *tap* running. *Derham.*

TAPROOT. *n. ſ.* [*tap* and *root*.] The principal ſtem of the root.

Some put under the trees raiſed of ſeed, about four inches below the place where they ſow their ſeeds, a ſmall piece of tile to ſtop the running down of the *taproot*, which occaſions it to branch when it comes to the tile. *Mortimer's Huſb.*

TAPE. *n. ſ.* [tæppan, Saxon.] A narrow fillet or band.

Will you buy any *tape*, or lace for your cap,
My dainty duck, my dear-a? *Shakeſpeare.*

This pouch that's ty'd with *tape*
I'll wager, that the prize ſhall be my due. *Gay.*

On once a flock bed, but repair'd with ſtraw,
With *tape* ty'd curtains never meant to draw. *Pope.*

TA'PER. *n. s.* [tapeꞃ, Saxon.] A wax candle; a light.

Get me a *taper* in my ſtudy, Lucius:
When it is lighted come and call me. *Shakeſpeare.*

My daughter and little ſon we'll dreſs
With rounds of waxen *tapers* on their heads,
And rattles in their hands. *Shakeſpeare.*

If any ſnatch the pure *taper* from my hand, and hold it to the devil, he will only burn his own fingers, but ſhall not rob me of the reward of my good intention. *Taylor.*

There the fair light,
Like hero's *taper* in the window plac'd,
Such fate from the malignant air did find,
As that expoſed to the boiſt'rous wind. *Waller.*

To ſee this fleet
Heav'n, as if there wanted lights above,
For *tapers* made two glaring comets riſe. *Dryden.*

TA'PER. *adj.* [from the form of a taper.] Regularly narrowed from the bottom to the top; pyramidal; conical.

Her *taper* fingers, and her panting breaſt,
He praiſes. *Dryden.*

From the beaver the otter differs in his teeth, which are canine, and in his tail, which is feline, or a long *taper*. *Grew's Muſæum.*

To TA'PER. *v. n.* To grow ſmaller.

The back is made *tapering* in form of a pillar, the lower vertebres being the broadeſt and largeſt; the ſuperior leſſer and leſſer, for the greater ſtability of the trunk. *Ray.*

Such be the dog,
With *tap'ring* tail, that nimbly cuts the wind. *Tickell.*

TA'PESTRY. *n. ſ.* [*tapeſterie*, *tapiſſerie*, *tapis*, Fr. *tapetum*, Lat.] Cloth woven in regular figures.

In the deſk
That's covered o'er with Turkiſh *tapeſtry*,
There is a purſe of ducats. *Shakeſpeare.*

The caſements are with golden tiſſue ſpread,
And horſes hoofs, for earth, on ſilken *tap'ſtry* tread. *Dryd.*

One room is hung with *tapeſtry*, in which are wrought the figures of the great perſons of the family. *Addiſon.*

TA'PET. *n. ſ.* [*tapetia*, Lat.] Worked or figured ſtuff.

To their work they ſit, and each doth chuſe
What ſtory ſhe will for her *tapet* take. *Spenſer.*

TA'PSTER. *n. ſ.* [from *tap*.] One whoſe buſineſs is to draw beer in an alehouſe.

The oath of a lover is no ſtronger than the word of a *tapſter*; they are both the confirmers of falſe reckonings. *Shak.*

Though you change your place, you need not change your trade: I'll be your *tapſter* ſtill. *Shakeſpeare.*

The world is come now to that paſs, that the vintner and *tapſter* may broach what religion they pleaſe; and the apothecary may mingle her as he pleaſes. *Howel.*

Though the painting grows decay'd,
The houſe will never loſe its trade;
Nay, though the treacherous *tapſter* Thomas
Hangs a new angel two doors from us,
In hopes that ſtrangers may miſtake it. *Swift.*

TAR. *n. ſ.* [ꞇaꞃe, Saxon; *tarre*, Dutch; *tiere*, Daniſh.] Liquid pitch; the turpentine of the pine or fir drained out by fire.

Then, foaming *tar*, their bridles they would champ,
And trampling the fine element would fiercely ramp. *Spenſ.*

A man will not loſe a hog for a halfpennyworth of *tar*. *Camden's Remains.*

Some ſtir the melted *tar*. *Thomſon's Summer.*

TAR. *n. ſ.* [from *tar* uſed in ſhips.] A ſailor; a ſeaman in contempt.

In ſenates bold, and fierce in war,
A land commander, and a *tar*. *Swift's Miſcel.*

To TAR. *v. a.* [from the noun.]

1. To ſmear over with tar.
2. To teaze; to provoke. [ταράττω.]

There has been much to do on both ſides; and the nation holds it no ſin to *tarre* them on to controverſy. *Shakeſp.*

Two curs ſhall tame each other; pride alone
Muſt *tar* the maſtiffs on, as 'twere the bone. *Shakeſpeare.*

TARA'NTULA. n. ſ. [Italian; *tarentule*, French.] An inſect whoſe bite is only cured by muſick.

This word, lover, did no leſs pierce poor Pyrocles than the right tune of muſick toucheth him that is ſick of the *tarantula*. *Sidney.*

He that uſes the word *tarantula*, without having any idea of what it ſtands for, means nothing at all by it. *Locke.*

TARDA'TION. *n. ſ.* [*tardo*, Latin.] The act of hindering or delaying.

TA'RDIGRADOUS. *adj.* [*tardigradus*, Lat.] Moving ſlowly.

It is but a ſlow and *tardigradous* animal, preying upon advantage, and otherways may be eſcaped. *Brown.*

TA'RDILY. *adv.* [from *tardy*.] Slowly; ſluggiſhly.

He was indeed the glaſs,
Wherein the noble youth did dreſs themſelves;
Speaking thick, which nature made his blemiſh,
Became the accents of the valiant:
For thoſe that could ſpeak ſlow and *tardily*,
Would turn their own perfection to abuſe,
To ſeem like him. *Shakeſp. Henry IV. p. ii.*

TA'RDITY. *n. ſ.* [*tarditas* from *tardus*, Latin; *tardiveté*, Fr.] Slowneſs; want of velocity.

Suppoſe there may be ſome obſervable *tardity* in the motion of light, and then aſk how we ſhould arrive to perceive it? *Digby.*

Our explication includes time in the notions of velocity and *tardity*. *Digby on the Soul.*

TA'RDINESS. *n. ſ.* [from *tardy*.] Slowneſs; ſluggiſhneſs; unwillingneſs to action or motion.

A *tardineſs* in nature,
Which often leaves the hiſtory unſpoke,
That it intends to do. *Shakeſp. King Lear.*

TA'RDY. *adj.* [*tardus*, Lat. *tardif*, Fr.]

1. Slow; not ſwift.

Nor ſhould their age by years be told,
Whoſe ſouls, more ſwift than motion, climb,
And check the *tardy* flight of time. *Sandy's Paraph.*

2. Sluggiſh; unwilling to action or motion.

Behold that navy which a while before
Provok'd the *tardy* Engliſh cloſe to fight;
Now draw their beaten veſſels cloſe to ſhore,
As larks lie dar'd to ſhun the hobbies flight. *Dryden.*

When certain to o'ercome, inclin'd to ſave,
Tardy to vengeance, and with mercy brave. *Prior.*

3. Dilatory; late; tedious.

You ſhall have letters from me to my ſon
In your behalf, to meet you on the way;
Be not ta'en *tardy* by unwiſe delay. *Shakeſp. Rich. III.*

Death he as oft accus'd
Of *tardy* execution, ſince denounc'd
The day of his offence. *Milton's Par. Loſt, b. x.*

The *tardy* plants in our cold orchards plac'd,
Reſerve their fruit for the next age's taſte:
There a ſmall grain in ſome few months will be
A firm, a lofty and a ſpacious tree. *Waller.*

Tardy of aid, unſeal thy heavy eyes,
Awake, and with the dawning day ariſe. *Dryden.*

You may freely cenſure him for being *tardy* in his payments. *Arbuthnot.*

4. Unwary. A low word.

Yield, ſcoundrel baſe, quoth ſhe, or die,
Thy life is mine, and liberty:
But if thou think'ſt I took thee *tardy*,
And dar'ſt preſume to be ſo hardy,
To try thy fortune o'er a-freſh,
I'll wave my title to thy fleſh. *Hudibras, p. i.*

5. Criminal; offending. A low word.

If they take them *tardy*, they endeavour to humble them by way of repriſal: thoſe ſlips and miſmanagements are uſually ridiculed. *Collier on Pride.*

To TA'RDY. *v. a.* [*tarder*, Fr. from the adjective.] To delay; to hinder.

I choſe
Camillo for the miniſter, to poiſon
My friend Polixenes; which had been done,
But that the good mind of Camillo *tardied*
My ſwift command. *Shakſp. Winter's Tale.*

TARE. *n. ſ.* [from *teeren*, Dutch, to conſume. *Skinner.*] A weed that grows among corn.

Through hatred of *tares* the corn in the field of God is plucked up. *Hooker, b. v.*

The liberal contributions ſuch teachers met with ſerved to invite more labourers, where their ſeed time was their harveſt, and by ſowing *tares* they reaped gold. *Decay of Piety.*

My country neighbours begin not to think of being in general, which is being abſtracted from all its inferior ſpecies, before they come to think of the fly in their ſheep, or the *tares* in their corn. *Locke.*

TARE. n. ſ. [French.] A mercantile word denoting the weight of any thing containing a commodity; alſo the allowance made for it.

TARE, preterite of *tear*.

The women beat their breaſts, their cheeks they *tare*. *Dryden.*

TARGE. } *n. ſ.* [ꞇaꞃᵹa, Saxon; *targe*, Italian; *targe*, French;
TARGET. } *tarian*, Welſh, which ſeems the original of the reſt; *an taargett*, Erſe.] A kind of buckler or ſhield born on the left arm. It ſeems to be commonly uſed for a defenſive weapon leſs in circumference than a ſhield.

Glancing on his helmet made a large
And open gaſh therein, were not his *targe*
That broke the violence. *Fa. Qu.*

I took all their
Seven points in my *target*. *Shakeſp. Henry IV.*

Henceforward will I bear
Upon my *target* three fair ſhining ſuns. *Shakeſp. Hen. VI.*

The arms ſhe uſeth moſt is the *target* to ſhroud herſelf under, and fence away the blow. *Howel's England's Tears.*

Thoſe leaves
They gather'd, broad as Amazonian *targe*. *Milton.*

The

The Greeks the gates approach'd, their *targets* cast
Over their heads, some scaling ladders plac'd
Against the walls. *Derham.*

TA'RGUM. *n. s.* [תרגום.] A paraphrase on the pentateuch in the Chaldee language.

TA'RIFF. *n. s.* [perhaps a Spanish word; *tarif*, Fr.] A cartel of commerce.
This branch of our trade was regulated by a *tariff*, or declaration of the duties of import and export. *Addison.*

TARN. *n. s.* [*tiorn*, Islandick.] A bog; a fen; a marsh; a pool; a quagmire.

To TA'RNISH. *v. a.* [*ternir*, French.] To sully; to soil; to make not bright.
Let him pray for resolution, that he may discover nothing that may discredit the cause, *tarnish* the glory, and weaken the example of the suffering. *Collier.*
Low waves the rooted forest, vex'd, and sheds
What of its *tarnish'd* honours yet remain. *Thomson.*

To TA'RNISH. *v. n.* To lose brightness.
If a fine object should *tarnish* by having a great many see it, or the musick should run mostly into one man's ears, these satisfactions would be made inclosure. *Collier of Envy.*

TARPA'WLING. *n. s.* [from *tar.*]
1. Hempen cloath smeered with tar.
Some the gall'd ropes with dauby marling bind,
Or searcloth masts with strong *tarpawling* coats. *Dryden.*
2. A sailor in contempt.
Was any thing wanting to the extravagance of this age, but the making a living *tarpawlin* and a swabber the hero of a tragedy. *Dennis.*

TA'RRAGON. *n. s.* A plant called herb-dragon.

TA'RRIANCE. *n. s.* [from *tarry.*] Stay; delay; perhaps sojourn.
Dispatch me hence:
Come, answer not; but do it presently,
I am impatient of my *tarriance.* *Shakespeare.*

TA'RRIER. *n. s.* [This should be written *terrier*, from *terre*, French, the earth.]
1. A sort of small dog, that hunts the fox or otter out of his hole.
The fox is earthed; but I shall send my two *tarriers* in after him. *Dryden.*
2. One that tarries or stays.

To TA'RRY. *v. n.* [*targir*, French.]
1. To stay; to continue in a place.
Tarry I here, I but attend on death;
But fly I hence, I fly away from life. *Shakespeare.*
2. To delay; to be long in coming.
Thou art my deliverer, make no *tarrying*, O God. *Psal.*
Who hath woe and redness of eyes? they that *tarry* long at the wine. *Prov.* xxiii. 30.
Tarry ye here for us until we come again. *Exod.* xxiv. 14.
I yet am tender, young, and full of fear,
And dare not die, but fain would *tarry* here. *Dryden.*

To TA'RRY. *v. a.* To wait for.
I will go drink with you, but I cannot *tarry* dinner. *Shak.*

TA'RSEL. *n. s.* A kind of hawk.
Hist! Romeo, hist! O for a falkner's voice;
To lure this *tarsel* gentle back again. *Shakespeare.*
A falc'ner Henry is, when Emma hawks;
With her of *tarsels* and of lures he talks. *Prior.*

TA'RSUS. *n. s.* [In anatomy; *tarse*, Fr.] The space betwixt the lower end of the focil bones of the leg, and the beginning of the five long bones that are jointed with, and bear up, the toes: it comprises seven bones and the three ossa cuneiformia. *Dict.*
An obscure motion, where the conjunction is called synanthrosis; as, in joining the *tarsus* to the metatarsus. *Wiseman.*

TART. *adj.* [ꞇeaꞃꞇ, Saxon; *taertig*, Dutch.]
1. Sour; acid; acidulated; sharp of taste.
2. Sharp; keen; severe.
Why so *tart* a favour
To trumpet such good tidings? *Shakespeare.*
When his humours grew *tart*, as being now in the lees of favour, they brake forth into certain sudden excesses. *Wotton.*

TART. *n. s.* [*tarte*, French; *tarta*, Italian; *taart*, Danish;
A small pie of fruit.
Figures, with divers coloured earths, under the windows of the house on that side near which the garden stands, be but toys; you may see as good sights in *tarts.* *Bacon's Essays.*

TA'RTANE. *n. s.* [*tartana*, Italian; *tartane*, Fr.] A vessel much used in the Mediterranean, with one mast and a three-cornered sail.
I set out from Marseilles to Genoa in a *tartane*, and arrived late at a small French port called Cassis. *Addison.*

TA'RTAR. *n. s.* [*tartarus*, Lat.]
1. Hell. A word used by the old poets, now obsolete.
With this the damned ghosts he governeth,
And furies rules, and *tartare* tempereth. *Spenser.*
He's in *tartar* limbo worse than hell;
A devil in an everlasting garment hath him,
One whose hard heart is button'd up with steel. *Shakesp.*
2. [*Tartre*, Fr.] *Tartar* is what sticks to wine casks, like a hard stone, either white or red, as the colour of the wine from whence it comes: the white is preferable, as containing less dross or earthy parts: the best comes from Germany, and is the *tartar* of the rhenish wine. *Quincy.*
The fermented juice of grapes is partly turned into liquid drops or lees, and partly into that crust or dry feculency that is commonly called *tartar*; and this *tartar* may by the fire be divided into five differing substances, four of which are not acid, and the other not so manifestly acid as the *tartar* itself. *Boyle.*

TARTA'REAN. *adj.* [*tartarus*, Lat.] Hellish.
His throne mix'd with *tartarean* sulphur. *Milton.*

TARTA'REOUS. *n. s.* [from *tartar.*]
1. Consisting of tartar.
In fruits, the *tartareous* parts of the sap are thrown upon the fibres designed for the stone, and the oily upon the seed within it. *Grew's Cosmol.*
2. Hellish.
The spirit of God downward purg'd
The black *tartareous* cold infernal dregs,
Adverse to life. *Milton.*

To TA'RTARIZE. *v. a.* [from *tartar.*] To impregnate with tartar.

TA'RTAROUS. *adj.* [from *tartar.*] Containing tartar; consisting of tartar.

TA'RTLY. *adv.* [from *tart.*]
1. Sharply; sourly; with acidity.
2. Sharply; with poignancy; with severity.
Seneca, an ingenious and sententious writer, was by Caligula called *arena sine calce*, sand without lime. *Walker.*
3. With sourness of aspect.
How *tartly* that gentleman looks!
—He is of a very melancholy disposition. *Shakespeare.*

TA'RTNESS. *n. s.* [from *tart.*]
1. Sharpness; sourness; acidity.
Of these sweets put in three gallons, more or less, into an hogshead, as the *tartness* of your cyder requires. *Mortimer.*
2. Sourness of temper; poignancy of language.
They cannot be too sweet for the king's *tartness.* *Shakesp.*

TASK. *n. s.* [*tasche*, French; *tassa*, Italian.]
1. Something to be done imposed by another.
Relieves me from my *task* of servile toil
Daily in the common prison else enjoin'd me. *Milton.*
2. Employment; business.
His mental powers were equal to greater *tasks.* *Atterbury.*
No happier *task* these faded eyes pursue,
To read and weep is all they now can do. *Pope.*
3. *To* TAKE *to task.* To reprove; to reprimand.
A holy man *took* a soldier *to task* upon the subject of his profession. *L'Estrange.*
He discovered some remains of his nature when he met with a foot-ball, for which Sir Roger *took* him *to task.* *Addis.*

To TASK. *v. a.* [*tascu*, Welsh, or from the noun.] To burthen with something to be done.
He depos'd the king,
Soon after that depriv'd him of his life,
And, in the neck of that, *task'd* the whole state. *Shakesp.*
Forth he goes,
Like to a harvestman, that's *task'd* to mow,
Or all, or lose his hire. *Shakesp. Coriolanus.*
Some things of weight,
That *task* our thoughts, concerning us and France. *Shak.*
I have drunk but one cup to-night, and that was craftily qualified too; and behold what innovation it makes here. I am unfortunate in the infirmity, and dare not *task* my weakness with any more. *Shakesp. Othello.*
Divert thy thoughts at home,
There *task* thy maids, and exercise the loom. *Dryden.*

TA'SKER. } *n. s.* [*task* and *master.*] One who imposes
TA'SKMASTER. } tasks.
All is, if I have grace to use it so,
As ever in my great *taskmaster's* eye. *Milton.*
The service of sin is perfect slavery; and he who will pay obedience to the commands of it, shall find it an unreasonable *taskmaster*, and an unmeasurable exactor. *South.*
Hear, ye sullen powers below;
Hear, ye *taskers* of the dead. *Dryden and Lee.*

TA'SSEL. *n. s.* [*tasse*, French; *tassellus*, low Latin.] An ornamental bunch of silk, or glittering substances.
Then took the squire an horn of bugle small,
Which hung adown his side in twisted gold,
And *tassels* gay. *Fairy Queen, b.* i.
Their heads are tricked with *tassels* and flowers. *Sandys.*

TA'SSEL. } *n. s.* An herb. *Ains.*
TA'ZEL. }

TA'SSELED. *adj.* [from *tassel.*] Adorned with tassels.
Early ere the odorous breath of morn
Awakes the slumb'ring leaves, or *tassel'd* horn
Shakes the high thicket, haste I all about. *Milton.*

TA'SSES. *n. s.* Armour for the thighs. *Ains.*

TA'STABLE. *adj.* That may be tasted; savoury; relishing.
Their distilled oils are fluid, volatile and *tastable.* *Boyle.*

To TASTE. *v. a.* [*taster*, to try, French.]
1. To perceive and distinguish by the palate.
The ruler of the feast *tasted* the water made wine. *John* ii.
2. To try by the mouth; to eat at least in a small quantity.
Bold deed to *taste* it under ban to touch. *Milton.*

3. To

3. To essay first.
Roscetes was seldom permitted to eat any other meat but such as the prince before *tasted* of. *Knolles.*
Thou and I marching before our troops
May *taste* fate to them, mow them out a passage. *Dryden.*
4. To feel; to have perception of.
He should *taste* death for every man. *Heb.* ii. 9.
To Taste. *v. n.*
1. To try by the mouth to eat.
Of this tree we may not *taste* nor touch. *Milton.*
2. To have a smack; to produce on the palate a particular sensation.
When the mouth is out of taste, it maketh things *taste* bitter and loathsome, but never sweet. *Bacon's Nat. Hist.*
When kine feed upon wild garlick, their milk *tasteth* of it. *Bacon.*
If your butter *tastes* of brass, it is your master's fault, who will not allow a silver saucepan. *Swift.*
3. To distinguish intellectually.
Scholars when good sense describing,
Call it *tasting* and imbibing. *Swift.*
4. To relish intellectually; to approve.
Thou, Adam, wilt *taste* no pleasure. *Milton.*
5. To be tinctured, or receive some quality or character.
Ev'ry idle, nice, and wanton reason
Shall, to the king, *taste* of this action. *Shakespeare.*
6. To try the relish of any thing.
The body's life with meats and air is fed,
Therefore the soul doth use the *tasting* pow'r
In veins, which through the tongue and palate spread,
Distinguish ev'ry relish sweet and sour. *Davies.*
7. To have perception of.
Cowards die many times before their deaths;
The valiant never *taste* of death but once. *Shakespeare.*
The *tasting* of death touched the righteous also, and there was a destruction of the multitude in the wilderness. *Wisd.*
8. To take enjoyment.
What hither brought us? not hope here to *taste*
Of pleasure. *Milton.*
Of nature's bounty men forbore to *taste*,
And the best portion of the earth lay waste. *Waller.*
9. To enjoy sparingly.
This fiery game your active youth maintain'd,
Not yet by years extinguish'd, though restrain'd;
You season still with sports your serious hours,
For age but *tastes* of pleasures, youth devours. *Dryden.*
Taste. *n. s.* [from the verb.]
1. The act of tasting; gustation.
Best of fruits, whose *taste* gave elocution. *Milton.*
2. The sense by which the relish of any thing on the palate is perceived.
Bees delight more in one flower than another, and therefore have *taste.* *Bacon's Nat. Hist.*
Delicacies of *taste*, sight, smell. *Milton.*
The tardy plants in our cold orchards plac'd,
Reserve their fruit for the next age's *taste.* *Waller.*
3. Sensibility; perception.
I have almost forgot the *taste* of fears:
The time has been, my senses would have cool'd
To hear a night shriek. *Shakesp. Macbeth.*
Musick in the close,
As the last *taste* of sweets is sweetest last. *Shakesp. R.* II.
4. That sensation which all things taken into the mouth give particularly to the tongue, the papillæ of which are the principal instruments hereof. *Quincy.*
Manna was like coriander seed, white; and the *taste* of it was like wafers made with honey. *Exod.* xvi. 31.
Though there be a great variety of *tastes*, yet, as in smells, they have only some few general names. *Locke.*
5. Intellectual relish or discernment.
Seeing they pretend no quarrel at other psalms which are in like manner appointed to be daily read, why do these so much offend and displease their *tastes?* *Hooker.*
Sion's songs to all true *tastes* excelling,
Where God is prais'd aright. *Milton.*
I have no *taste*
Of popular applause. *Dryden's Spanish Friar.*
As he had no *taste* of true glory, we see him equipped like an Hercules, with a club and a lion's skin. *Addison.*
This metaphor would not have been so general, had there not been a conformity between the mental *taste* and that sensitive taste which gives us a relish of every flavour. *Addison.*
Your way of life, in my *taste*, will be the best. *Pope.*
I see how ill a *taste* for wit and sense prevails in the world. *Swift.*
Pleasure results from a sense to discern, and a *taste* to be affected with beauty. *Seed's Sermons.*
6. An essay; a trial; an experiment. Not in use.
I hope, for my brother's justification, he wrote as an essay or *taste* of my virtue. *Shakespeare.*
7. A small portion given as a specimen.
They thought it not safe to resolve, till they had a *taste* of the people's inclination. *Bacon's Henry* VII.
Besides the prayers mentioned, I shall give only a *taste* of some few recommended to devout persons in the manuals and offices. *Stillingfleet.*
Ta'sted. *adj.* [from *taste.*] Having a particular relish.
Coleworts prosper exceedingly, and are better *tasted*, if watered with salt water. *Bacon's Nat. Hist.* N°. 460.
Ta'ster. *n. s.* [*tasteur*, Fr. from *taste.*]
1. One who takes the first essay of food.
Fair hope! our earlier heav'n! by thee
Young time is *taster* to eternity. *Crashaw.*
Says the fly, Are not all places open to me? Am not I the *taster* to princes in all their entertainments. *L'Estrange.*
Thy tutor be thy *taster*, ere thou eat,
There's poison in thy drink, and in thy meat. *Dryden.*
2. A dram cup. *Ains.*
Ta'steful. *adj.* [*taste* and *full.*] High relished; savoury.
Not *tasteful* herbs that in these gardens rise,
Which the kind soil with milky sap supplies,
Can move. *Pope.*
Ta'steless. *adj.* [from *taste.*]
1. Having no power of perceiving taste.
2. Having no relish or power of stimulating the palate; insipid.
By depurating chemical oils, and reducing them to an elementary simplicity, they could never be made *tasteless.* *Boyle.*
3. Having no power of giving pleasure; insipid.
The understanding cannot, by its natural light, discover spiritual truths; and the corruption of our will and affections renders them *tasteless* and insipid to us. *Rogers's Serm.*
4. Having no intellectual gust.
If by his manner of writing he is heavy and *tasteless*, I throw aside his criticisms. *Addison's Spect.*
Ta'stelessness. *n. s.* [from *tasteless.*]
1. Insipidity; want of relish.
2. Want of perception of taste.
3. Want of intellectual relish.
To Ta'tter. *v. a.* [totæpan, Saxon.] To tear; to rend; to make ragged. *Tattered* is perhaps more properly an adjective.
Through *tatter'd* cloaths small vices do appear,
Robes and furr'd gowns hide all. *Shakesp. King Lear.*
An apothecary late I noted
In *tatter'd* weeds, with overwhelming brows,
Culling of simples. *Shakesp. Rome and Juliet.*
Where wav'd the *tatter'd* ensigns of Ragfair,
A yawning ruin hangs. *Pope.*
In the land of liberty little tyrants rag'd,
Tore from cold wintry limbs the *tatter'd* weed. *Thomson.*
Ta'tter. *n. s.* [from the verb.] A rag; a fluttering rag.
This fable holds from him that sits upon the throne, to the poor devil that has scarce a *tatter.* *L'Estrange.*
Tatterdema'lion. *n. s.* [*tatter* and *I know not what.*] A ragged fellow.
As a poor fellow was trudging along in a bitter cold morning with never a rag, a spark that was warm clad called to this *tatterdemalion*, how he could endure this weather? *L'Estrange.*
To Ta'ttle. *v. n.* [*tateren*, Dutch.] To prate; to talk idly; to use many words with little meaning.
He stands on terms of honourable mind,
Ne will be carried with every common wind
Of court's inconstant mutability,
Ne after every *tattling* fable fly. *Hubberd's Tale.*
The one is too like an image, and says nothing; and the other too like my lady's eldest son, evermore *tattling.* *Shak.*
Excuse it by the *tattling* quality of age, which is always narrative. *Dryden.*
The world is forward enough to *tattle* of them. *Locke.*
Their language is extremely proper to *tattle* in; it is made up of so much repetition and compliment. *Addison.*
Ta'ttle. *n. s.* [from the verb.] Prate; idle chat; trifling talk.
They asked her, how she lik'd the play?
Then told the *tattle* of the day. *Swift's Miscel.*
Such *tattle* often entertains
My lord and me. *Swift.*
A young academick shall dwell upon trade and politicks in a dictatorial stile, while at the same time persons well skilled in those different subjects hear the impertinent *tattle* with a just contempt. *Watts's Improvement of the Mind.*
Ta'ttler. *n. s.* [from *tattle.*] An idle talker; a prater.
Going from house to house, *tatlers*, busy bodies, which are the canker and rust of idleness, as idleness is the rust of time, are reproved by the apostle. *Taylor.*
Tatto'o. *n. s.* [perhaps from *tapotez tous*, Fr. to strike.] The beat of drum by which soldiers are warned to their quarters.
All those whose hearts are loose and low,
Start if they hear but the *tatto.* *Prior.*
Ta'vern. *n. s.* [*taverne*, Fr. *taberna*, Latin.] A house where wine is sold, and drinkers are entertained.
Enquire at London, 'mong the *taverns* there;
For there they say he daily doth frequent,
With unrestrained loose companions. *Shakesp. Rich.* II.
You

You ſhall be called to no more payments; fear no more *tavern* bills, which are often the ſadneſs of parting, as the procuring of mirth. *Shakeſpeare's Cymbeline.*

To reform the vices of this town, all *taverns* and alehouſes ſhould be obliged to diſmiſs their company by twelve at night, and no woman ſuffered to enter any *tavern* or alſehouſe. *Sw.*

TA'VERNER.
TA'VERNKEEPER.
TA'VERNMAN. *n. ſ.* [from *tavern man* or *keep*; *tabernarius*, Latin; *tavernier*, French.] One who keeps a tavern.

After local names, the moſt in number have been derived from occupations; as tailor, archer, *taverner*. *Camden.*

TAUGHT, preterite and part. paſſive of *teach.*

All thy children ſhall be *taught* of the Lord. *Iſa.* liv. 13.

How haſt thou ſatisfy'd me, *taught* to live. *Milton.*

To TAUNT. *v. a.* [*tanſer*, Fr. *Skinner. Tanden*, Dutch, to ſhew teeth. *Minſhew.*]

1. To reproach; to inſult; to revile; to ridicule; to treat with inſolence and contumelies.

When I had at my pleaſure *taunted* her,
She in mild terms begg'd my patience. *Shakeſpeare.*

The bitterneſs and ſtings of *taunting* jealouſy,
Vexatious days, and jarring joyleſs nights,
Have driv'n him forth. *Rowe's Jane Shore.*

2. To exprobrate; to mention with upbraiding.

Rail thou in Fulvia's phraſe, and *taunt* my faults
With ſuch full licence. *Shakeſp. Ant. and Cleopatra.*

TAUNT. *n. ſ.* [from the verb.] Inſult; ſcoff; reproach; ridicule.

With ſcoffs and ſcorns, and contumelious *taunts*,
In open market-place produc'd they me,
To be a publick ſpectacle. *Shakeſp. Henry* VI.

He would avoid ſuch bitter *taunts*,
As in the time of death he gave our father. *Shakeſpeare.*

Julian thought it more effectual to perſecute the Chriſtians by *taunts* and ironies, than by tortures. *Gov. of the Tongue.*

He by vile hands to common uſe debas'd,
Shall ſend them flowing round his drunken feaſt,
With ſacrilegious *taunt*, and impious jeſt. *Prior.*

TA'UNTER. *n. ſ.* [from *taunt.*] One who taunts, reproaches, or inſults.

TA'UNTINGLY. *adv.* [from *taunting.*] With inſult; ſcoffingly; with contumely and exprobration.

It *tauntingly* replied
To th' diſcontented members, th' mutinous parts,
That envied his receipt. *Shakeſp. Coriolanus.*

The wanton goddeſs view'd the warlike maid
From head to foot, and *tauntingly* ſhe ſaid. *Prior.*

TAURICO'RNOUS. *adj.* [*taurus* and *cornu*, Latin.] Having horns like a bull.

Their deſcriptions muſt be relative, or the *tauricornous* picture of the one the ſame with the other. *Brown.*

TAUTOLO'GICAL. *adj.* [*tautologique*, Fr. from *tautology.*] Repeating the ſame thing.

TAUTO'LOGIST. *n. ſ.* [from *tautology.*] One who repeats tediouſly.

TAUTO'LOGY. *n. ſ.* [ταυ̃τολογία; *tautologie*, Fr. ταυ̃το and λόγος.] Repetition of the ſame words, or of the ſame ſenſe in different words.

All ſcience is not *tautology*; the laſt ages have ſhewn us, what antiquity never ſaw, in a dream. *Glanville's Sceps.*

Saint Andre's feet ne'er kept more equal time,
Not ev'n the feet of thy own Pſyche's rhime;
Though they in numbers as in ſenſe excel,
So juſt, ſo like *tautology*, they fell. *Dryden.*

Every paper addreſſed to our beautiful incendiaries, hath been filled with different conſiderations, that enemies may not accuſe me of *tautology*. *Addiſon's Freeholder.*

To TAW. *v. a.* [*touwen*, Dutch; ꞇaƿian, Saxon.] To dreſs white leather commonly called alum leather, in contradiſtinction from *tan* leather, that which is dreſſed with bark.

TAW. *n. ſ.* A marble to play with.

Trembling I've ſeen thee
Mix with children as they play'd at *taw*;
Nor fear the marbles as they bounding flew,
Marbles to them, but rolling rocks to you. *Swift.*

TA'WDRINESS. *n. ſ.* [from *tawdry.*] Tinſel finery; finery too oſtentatious.

A clumſy beau makes his ungracefulneſs appear the more ungraceful by his *tawdrineſs* of dreſs. *Clariſſa.*

TA'WDRY. *adj.* [from Stawdrey, Saint Awdrey, or Saint Etheldred, as the things bought at Saint Etheldred's fair. *Henſhaw, Skinner.*] Meanly ſhewy; ſplendid without coſt; fine without grace; ſhewy without elegance. It is uſed both of things and of perſons wearing them.

Bind your fillets faſt,
And gird in your waſte,
For more fineneſs, with a *tawdrie* lace. *Spenſer's Paſt.*

He has a kind of coxcomb upon his crown, and a few *tawdry* feathers. *L'Eſtrange.*

Old Romulus and father Mars look down,
Your herdſman primitive, your homely clown,
Is turn'd a beau in a looſe *tawdry* gown. *Dryden's Juv.*

He rails from morning to night at eſſenced fops and *tawdry* courtiers. *Addiſon's Spect.* N°. 128.

Her eyes were wan and eager, her dreſs thin and *tawdry*, her mien genteel and childiſh. *Addiſon's Spect.*

TA'WER. *n. ſ.* [from *taw.*] A dreſſer of white leather.

TA'WNY. *adj.* [*tané*, *tanné*, Fr.] Yellow, like things tanned.

This child of fancy that armado hight,
For interim to our ſtudies ſhall relate,
In high born words, the worth of many a knight
From *tawny* Spain, loſt in the world's debate. *Shakeſpeare.*

Eurus his body muſt be drawn the colour of the *tawny* Moor, upon his head a red ſun. *Peacham.*

The *tawny* lion pawing to get free. *Milton.*

Whilſt they make the river Senaga to bound the Moors, ſo that on the ſouth ſide they are black, on the other only *tawny*, they ſeem not to derive it from the ſun. *Brown.*

Where's the worth that ſets this people up
Above your own Numidia's *tawny* ſons? *Addiſon's Cato.*

TAX. *n. ſ.* [*taſg*, Welſh; *taxe*, French; *taxe*, Dutch.]

1. An impoſt; a tribute impoſed; an exciſe: a tallage.

He ſays Horace, being the ſon of a *tax* gatherer or collector, ſmells everywhere of the meanneſs of his birth. *Dryden.*

With wars and *taxes* others waſte their own,
And houſes burn, and houſhold gods deface,
To drink in bowls which glittering gems enchaſe. *Dryden.*

The *tax* upon tillage was two ſhillings in the pound in arable land, and four in plantations: this *tax* was often levied in kind upon corn, and called decumæ or tithes. *Arbuthnot.*

2. [*Taxo*, Lat.] Charge; cenſure.

He could not without grief of heart, and without ſome *tax* upon himſelf and his miniſters for the not executing the laws, look upon the bold licence of ſome pamphlets. *Clarendon.*

To TAX. *v. a.* [*taxer*, Fr. from the noun.]

1. To load with impoſts.

Jehoiakim gave the ſilver and gold to Pharaoh, but he *taxed* the land to give the money. 2 *Kings* xxiii. 35.

2. [*Taxo*, Lat.] To charge; to cenſure; to accuſe. It has *of* or *with* before the fault imputed, and is uſed both of perſons and things.

How many hath he killed? I promiſed to eat all of his killing.——Niece, you *tax* ſignior Benedick too much; but he'll be meet with you. *Shakeſpeare.*

I am not juſtly to be *taxed* with any preſumption for meddling with matters wherein I have no dealing. *Raleigh.*

Tax not divine diſpoſal, wiſeſt men
Have err'd, and by bad women been deceiv'd. *Milton.*

They cannot *tax* others omiſſions towards them without a tacit reproach of their own. *Decay of Piety.*

He *taxed* not Homer nor Virgil for intereſting their gods in the wars of Troy and Italy; neither would he have *taxed* Milton for his choice of a ſupernatural argument. *Dryden.*

Mens virtues I have commended as freely as I have *taxed* their crimes. *Dryden.*

He call'd him back aloud, and *tax'd* his fear;
And ſure enough he heard, but durſt not hear. *Dryden.*

Like ſome rich and mighty murderer,
Too great for priſon which he breaks with gold,
Who freſher for new miſchief does appear,
And dares the world to *tax* him with the old. *Dryden.*

If this be chance, it is extraordinary; and I dare not call it more, for fear of being *taxed* with ſuperſtition. *Dryden.*

If he *taxes* both of long delay,
My guilt is leſs, who ſooner came away. *Dryden.*

This ſalutation cannot be *taxed* with flattery, ſince it was directed to a prince, of whom it had been happy for Rome if he had never been born, or if he had never died. *Addiſon.*

TA'XABLE. *adj.* [from *tax.*] That may be taxed.

TAXA'TION. *n. ſ.* [*taxation*, Fr. *taxatio*, Lat. from *tax.*]

1. The act of loading with taxes; impoſt; tax.

The ſubjects could taſte no ſweeter fruits of having a king than grievous *taxations* to ſome vain purpoſes; laws made rather to find faults than to prevent faults. *Sidney, b.* ii.

I bring no overture of war, no *taxation* of homage; my words are as full of peace as matter. *Shakeſp. Twelfth Night.*

He daily ſuch *taxations* did exact,
As were againſt the order of the ſtate. *Daniel.*

Various news I heard,
Of old miſmanagements, *taxations* new;
All neither wholly falſe, nor wholly true. *Pope.*

2. Accuſation; ſcandal.

My father's love is enough to honour; ſpeak no more of him, you'll be whipt for *taxation* one of theſe days. *Shakeſp.*

TA'XER. *n. ſ.* [from *tax.*] He who taxes.

Theſe rumours begot ſcandal againſt the king, taxing him for a great *taxer* of his people. *Bacon's Henry* VII.

[T]EA. *n. ſ.* [a word, I ſuppoſe, Chineſe; *thé*, Fr.] A Chineſe [p]lant, of which the infuſion has lately been much drunk in [E]urope.

The muſes friend, *tea*, does our fancy aid,
Repreſs thoſe vapours which the head invade. *Waller.*

One

One has a design of keeping an open *tea* table. *Addison.*

I have filled a *tea* pot, and received a dish of it. *Addison.*

He swept down a dozen *tea* dishes. *Spectator.*

Nor will you encourage the common *tea* table talk. *Spect.*

Green leaves of *tea* contain a narcotick juice, which exudes by roasting: this is performed with great care before it is exposed to sale. *Arbuthnot on Aliments.*

Here living *tea* pot stands; one arm held out,
One bent; the handle this, and that the spout. *Pope.*

The mistress of the *tea* shop may give half an ounce. *Sw.*

The fear of being thought pedants hath taken many young divines off from their severer studies, which they have exchanged for plays, in order to qualify them for *tea* tables. *Swift.*

When you sweep, never stay to pick up *tea* spoons. *Swift.*

To TEACH. *v. a.* preter. and part. pass. *taught*, sometimes *teached*, which is now obsolete. [tæcan, Sax.]

1. To instruct; to inform.

The Lord will *teach* us of his ways, and we will walk in his paths. *Isa.* ii. 3.

Teach us by what means to shun
Th' inclement seasons. *Milton.*

2. To deliver any doctrine or art, or words to be learned.

Moses wrote this song, and *taught* it. *Deut.* xxxi. 22.

In vain they worship me, *teaching* for doctrines the commandments of men. *Mat.* xv. 9.

They *teach* all nations what of him they learn'd. *Milton.*

3. To show; to exhibit so as to impress upon the mind.

He is a good divine that follows his own instructions; I can easier *teach* twenty what were good to be done, than to be one of the twenty to follow my own *teaching*. *Shakesp.*

If some men *teach* wicked things, it must be that others should practise them. *South's Sermons.*

4. To tell; to give intelligence.

Huswives are *teached*, instead of a clocke,
How winter night passeth by crowing of cocke. *Tusser.*

To TEACH. *v. n.* To perform the office of an instructor.

I have labour'd,
And with no little study, that my *teaching*,
And the strong course of my authority,
Might go one way. *Shakespeare.*

I am too sudden bold
To *teach*; a teacher ill beseemeth me. *Shakespeare.*

The heads judge for reward, the priests *teach* for hire, and the prophets divine for money. *Mic.* iii. 11.

TE'ACHABLE. *adj.* [from *teach.*] Docile; susceptive of instruction.

We ought to bring our minds free, unbiassed, and *teachable* to learn our religion from the word of God. *Watts.*

TE'ACHABLENESS. *n. s.* [from *teachable.*] Docility; willingness to learn; capacity to learn.

TE'ACHER. *n. s.* [from *teach.*]

1. One who teaches; an instructor; preceptor.

Nature is no sufficient *teacher* what we should do that may attain unto life everlasting. *Hooker, b.* ii.

I went into the temple, there to hear
The *teachers* of our law, and to propose
What might improve my knowledge or their own. *Milton.*

These were notions born with us; such as we were taught without the help of a *teacher*. *South's Sermons.*

Imperious with a *teacher*'s air,
Boastful he claims a right to wisdom's chair. *Blackmore.*

2. One who without regular ordination assumes the ministry.

Dissenting *teachers* are under no incapacity of accepting civil and military employments. *Swift.*

3. A preacher; one who is to deliver doctrine to the people.

For the choice of a governor more sufficient, the *teachers* in all the churches assembled themselves. *Raleigh.*

Wolves shall succeed for *teachers*. *Milton.*

He may teach his diocese who ceases to be able to preach to it; for he may do it by appointing *teachers*, and by a vigilant exacting from them the instruction of their flocks. *South.*

TEAD or *tede*. *n. s.* [*tæda*, Lat.] A torch; a flambeau. Not in use.

A bushy *tead* a groom did light,
And sacred lamp in secret chamber hide. *Fairy Queen.*

Hymen is awake,
And long since ready from his mask to move,
With his bright *tead* that flames with many a flake.
Spenser's Epithalamium.

TEAGUE. *n. s.* A name of contempt used for an Irishman.

TEAL. *n. s.* [*teelingh*, Dutch.] A wild fowl.

Some serve for food to us, and some but to feed themselves; amongst the first sort we reckon the dip-chick, coots, *teal*, wigeon. *Carew's Survey of Cornwall.*

TEAM. *n. s.* [*temo*, the team of a carriage, Latin; tyme, Saxon, a yoke.]

1. A number of horses or oxen drawing at once the same carriage.

Thee a ploughman all unweeting found,
As he his toilsome *team* that way did guide,
And brought thee up in ploughman's state to bide. *F. Qu.*

We fairies that do run
By the triple Hecate's *team*,
From the presence of the sun,
Following darkness like a dream,
Now are frolick. *Shakesp. Midsummer Night's Dream.*

Making such difference betwixt wake and sleep,
As is the diff'rence betwixt day and night,
The hour before the heav'nly harness'd *team*
Begins his golden progress in the East. *Shakesp. Henry* IV.

I am in love; but a *team* of horse shall not pluck that from me, nor who 'tis I love. *Shakespeare.*

After the declining sun
Had chang'd the shadows, and their task was done,
Home with their weary *team* they took their way. *Roscom.*

He heav'd with more than human force to move
A weighty stone, the labour of a *team*. *Dryden.*

In stiff clays they may plow one acre of wheat with a *team* of horse. *Mortimer's Husb.*

2. Any number passing in a line.

Like a long *team* of snowy swans on high,
Which clap their wings, and cleave the liquid sky. *Dryden.*

TEAR. *n. s.* [*ea* in this word is pronounced *ee*; tear, Saxon; *taare*, Danish.]

1. The water which violent passion forces from the eyes.

She comes; and I'll prepare
My *tear* stain'd eyes to see her miseries. *Shakespeare.*

The pretty vaulting sea refus'd to drown me,
Knowing, that thou would'st have me drown'd on shore
With *tears* as salt as sea, through thy unkindness. *Shak.*

Cromwell, I did not think to shed a *tear*
In all my miseries; but thou hast forc'd me.
Lets dry our eyes. *Shakespeare's Henry* VIII.

Tears are the effects of compression of the moisture of the brain upon dilation of the spirits. *Bacon's Nat. Hist.*

She silently a gentle *tear* let fall. *Milton.*

2. Any moisture trickling in drops.

Let Araby extol her happy coast,
Her fragrant flow'rs, her trees with precious *tears*,
Her second harvests. *Dryden.*

TEAR. *n. s.* [from the verb.] A rent; a fissure.

To TEAR. pret. *tore*, anciently *tare*, part. pass. *torn*; [tæran, Saxon; *tara*, Swedish.]

1. To pull in pieces; to lacerate; to rend; to separate by violent pulling.

Come seeling night,
And with thy bloody and invisible hand
Cancel and *tear* to pieces that great bond
Which keeps me pale. *Shakesp. Macbeth.*

The one went out from me; and I said, Surely he is *torn* in pieces, and I saw him not since. *Gen.* xliv. 28.

John *tore* off lord Strutt's servants cloaths: now and then they came home naked. *Arbuthnot's Hist. of John Bull.*

Ambassadors sent to Carthage were like to be *torn* to pieces by the populace. *Arbuthnot.*

2. To laniate; to wound with any sharp point drawn along.

Old with dust deform'd their hoary hair,
The women beat their breasts, their cheeks they *tare*. *Shak.*

Neither shall men *tear* themselves for them in mourning to comfort them for the dead. *Jer.* xvi. 7.

3. To break by violence.

In the midst a *tearing* groan did break
The name of Antony. *Shakesp. Antony and Cleopatra.*

As storms the skies, and torrents *tear* the ground,
Thus rag'd the prince, and scatter'd death around. *Dryden.*

Blush rather, that you are a slave to passion,
Which, like a whirlwind, *tears* up all your virtues,
And gives you not the leisure to consider. *A. Philips.*

4. To divide violently; to shatter.

Is it not as much reason to say, that God destroys fatherly authority, when he suffers one in possession of it to have his government *torn* in pieces, and shared by his subjects. *Locke.*

5. To pull with violence; to drive violently.

He roar'd, he beat his breast, he *tore* his hair. *Dryden.*

From harden'd oak, or from a rock's cold womb,
At least thou art from some fierce tygress come;
Or on rough seas from their foundation *torn*,
Got by the winds, and in a tempest born. *Dryden.*

6. To take away by sudden violence.

Solyman
Rhodes and Buda from the Christians *tore*. *Waller.*

The hand of fate
Has *torn* thee from me, and I must forget thee. *Addison.*

To TEAR. *v. n.* [*tieren*, Dutch.] To fume; to rave; to rant turbulently.

All men transported into outrages for small trivial matters, fall under the inuendo of this bull, that ran *tearing* mad for the pinching of a mouse. *L'Estrange's Fables.*

TE'ARER. *n. s.* [from *to tear.*] He who rends or tears.

TE'ARFALLING. *adj.* [*tear* and *fall.*] Tender; shedding tears.

I am in
So far in blood, that sin will pluck on sin,
Tearfalling pity dwells not in this eye. *Shakespeare.*

TE'ARFUL. *adj.* [*tear* and *full.*] Weeping; full of tears.

Is't meet that he
Should leave the helm, and, like a fearful lad,
With *tearful* eyes add water to the sea? *Shakespeare.*

This clears the cloudy front of wrinkled care,
And drie, the *tearful* sluices of despair:
Charm'd with that virtuous draught th' exalted mind
All sense of woe delivers to the wind. *Pope's Odyssey.*

On Celadon her eye
Fell *tearful*, wetting her disorder'd cheek. *Thomson.*

To TEASE. *v. a.* [tæsan, Saxon.]

1. To comb or unravel wool or flax.
2. To scratch cloth in order to level the nap.
3. To torment with importunity; to vex with assiduous impertinence.

Not by the force of carnal reason,
But indefatigable *teasing*. *Butler.*

My friends always *tease* me about him, because he has no estate. *Spectator*, N°. 475.

After having been present in publick debates, he was *teased* by his mother to inform her of what had passed. *Addison.*

We system-makers can sustain
The thesis, which you grant was plain;
And with remarks and comments *tease* ye,
In case the thing before was easy. *Prior.*

TE'ASEL. *n. s.* [tæsl, Saxon; *dipsacus*, Lat.] A plant.

The flower of the *teasel* hath no proper calyx, but leaves representing the perianthium encompassing the bottom of the head: the little flowers which are produced singly from between the scales, are collected into an head somewhat like a bee-hive; these are succeeded by longish four-cornered seeds: the species are three: one is called carduus fullonum, and is of singular use in raising the knap upon woollen cloth. *Miller.*

TE'ASER. *n. s.* [from *tease.*] Any thing that torments by incessant importunity.

A fly buzzing at his ear, makes him deaf to the best advice. If you would have him come to himself, you must take off his little *teaser*, which holds his reason at bay. *Collier.*

TEAT. *n. s.* [*teth*, Welsh; tit, Saxon; *tette*, Dutch; *teton*, French.] The dug of a beast; anciently the pap of a woman.

Even at thy *teat* thou hadst thy tyranny. *Shakespeare.*

Snows cause a fruitful year, watering the earth better than rain; for the earth sucks it as out of the *teat*. *Bacon.*

When we perceive that bats have *teats*, we infer, that they suckle their younglings with milk. *Brown's Vulgar Errours.*

It more pleas'd my sense
Than smell of sweetest fennel, or the *teats*
Of ewe or goat dropping with milk at even. *Milton.*

Infants sleep, and are seldom awake but when hunger calls for the *teat*. *Locke.*

The goat, how bright amidst her fellow stars,
Kind Amalthea, reach'd her *teat* distent
With milk, thy early food. *Prior.*

TE'CHILY. *adv.* [from *techy.*] Peevishly; fretfully; frowardly.

TE'CHINESS. *n. s.* [from *techy.*] Peevishness; fretfulness.

TE'CHNICAL. *adj.* [τεχνικὸς; *technique*, Fr..] Belonging to arts; not in common or popular use.

In *technical* words, or terms of art, they refrain not from calling the same substance sometimes the sulphur, and sometimes the mercury of a body. *Locke.*

TE'CHY. *adj.* Peevish; fretful; irritable; easily made angry; froward.

I cannot come to Cressid but by Pandar,
And he is as *techy* to be woo'd to woo,
As she is stubborn-chaste against all sute. *Shakespeare.*

When it did taste the wormwood on the nipple, and felt it bitter, pretty fool, to see it *techy*, and fall out with the dug. *Shakespeare's Romeo and Juliet.*

TECTO'NICK. *adj.* [τεκτονικὸς.] Pertaining to building. *Bailey.*

To TED. *v. a.* [teaban, Saxon, to prepare.] To lay grass newly mown in rows.

The smell of grain, or *tedded* grass or kine,
Or dairy, each rural sight, each rural sound. *Milton.*

Hay-makers following the mowers, and casting it abroad, they call *tedding*. *Mortimer's Husb.*

Prudent his fall'n heaps
Collecting, cherish'd with the tepid wreaths
Of *tedded* grass, and the sun's mellowing beams,
Rivall'd with artful heats. *Philips.*

TE'DDER or *tether*. *n. s.* [*tudder*, Dut. *tindt*, a rope, Islandick.]

1. A rope with which a horse is tied in the field that he may not pasture too wide. *Teigher*, Erse.
2. Any thing by which one is restrained.

We lived joyfully, going abroad within our *tedder*. *Bacon.*

We shall have them against the wall; we know the length of their *tedder*, they cannot run far from us. *Child.*

TE DEUM. *n. s.* An hymn of the church, so called from the two first words of the Latin.

The choir,
With all the choicest musick of the kingdom,
Together sung *te deum*. *Shakesp. Henry* VIII.

Te deum was sung at Saint Paul's after the victory. *Bacon.*

TE'DIOUS. *adj.* [*tedieux*, Fr. *tædium*, Latin.]

1. Wearisome by continuance; troublesome; irksome.

That I be not further *tedious* unto thee, hear us of thy clemency a few words. *Acts* xxiv. 4.

The one intense, the other still remiss,
Cannot well suit with either, but soon prove
Tedious alike. *Milton.*

Pity only on fresh objects stays,
But with the *tedious* sight of woes decays. *Dryden.*

2. Wearisome by prolixity.

They unto whom we shall seem *tedious* are in nowise injured by us, because it is in their own hands to spare that labour which they are not willing to endure. *Hooker*, *b.* i.

3. Slow. *Ains.*

Chief mastery to dissect
With long and *tedious* havock fabled knights. *Milton.*

TE'DIOUSLY. *adv.* [from *tedious.*] In such a manner as to weary.

TE'DIOUSNESS. *n. s.* [from *tedious.*]

1. Wearisomeness by continuance.
2. Wearisomeness by prolixity.

In vain we labour to persuade them, that any thing can take away the *tediousness* of prayer, except it be brought to the same measure and form which themselves assign. *Hooker.*

3. Prolixity; length.

Since brevity's the soul of wit,
And *tediousness* the limbs and outward flourishes,
I will be brief. *Shakesp. Hamlet.*

4. Uneasiness; tiresomeness; quality of wearying.

In those very actions whereby we are especially perfected in this life we are not able to persist; forced we are with very weariness, and that often, to interrupt them; which *tediousness* cannot fall into those operations that are in the state of bliss when our union with God is compleat. *Hooker*, *b.* i.

More than kisses, letters mingle souls,
For thus friends absent speak: this ease controuls
The *tediousness* of my life. *Donne.*

She distastes them all within a while;
And in the sweetest finds a *tediousness*. *Davies.*

To TEEM. *v. n.* [team, Saxon, offspring.]

1. To bring young.

If she must *teem*,
Create her child of spleen, that it may live,
And be a thwart disnatur'd torment to her. *Shakespeare.*

2. To be pregnant; to engender young.

Have we more sons? or are we like to have?
Is not my *teeming* date drunk up with time,
And wilt thou pluck my fair son from mine age? *Shakesp.*

When the rising Spring adorns the mead,
Teeming buds and cheerful greens appear. *Dryden.*

There are fundamental truths the basis upon which a great many others rest: these are *teeming* truths, rich in store, with which they furnish the mind, and, like the lights of heaven, give light and evidence to other things. *Locke.*

3. To be full; to be charged as a breeding animal.

We live in a nation where there is scarce a single head that does not *teem* with politicks. *Addison.*

To TEEM. *v. a.*

1. To bring forth; to produce.

What's the newest grief?
Each minute *teems* a new one. *Shakesp. Macbeth.*

Common mother, thou
Whose womb unmeasurable, and infinite breast,
Teems and feeds all. *Shakesp. Timon of Athens.*

The earth obey'd; and strait
Op'ning her fertile womb, *teem'd* at a birth
Innumerous living creatures. *Milton's Par. Lost*, *b.* vii.

The deluge wrought such a change, that the earth did not then *teem* forth its increase, as formerly, of its own accord, but required culture. *Woodward's Nat. Hist.*

2. To pour. A low word, imagined by *Skinner* to come from *tommen*, Danish, *to draw out*; *to pour*. The Scots retain it: as, teem *that water out*; hence *Swift* took this word.

Teem out the remainder of the ale into the tankard, and fill the glass with small beer. *Swift's Directions to the Butler.*

TE'EMFUL. *adj.* [teampul, Saxon.]

2. Pregnant; prolifick.
2. Brimful. *Ains.*

TE'EMER. *n. s.* [from *teem.*] One that brings young.

TE'EMLESS. *adj.* [from *teem.*] Unfruitful; not prolifick.

Such wars, such waste, such fiery tracks of dearth,
Their zeal has left, and such a *teemless* earth. *Dryden.*

TEEN. *n. s.* [tinan, Saxon, *to kindle*; *tenen*, Flemish, *to vex*; teonan, Saxon, *injuries.*] Sorrow; grief.

Arrived there
That barehead knight, for dread and doleful *teen*
Would fain have fled, ne durst approachen near. *Fa. Qu.*

Fry not in heartless grief and doleful *teen*. *Spenser.*

My heart bleeds
To think o' th' *teene* that I have turn'd you to. *Shakesp.*

Eighty odd years of sorrow have I seen,
And each hour's joy wreck'd with a week of *teen*. *Shak.*

To Teen. *v. a.* [from tinan, *to kindle*, Saxon.] To excite; to provoke to do a thing. *Spenser.*

Teens. *n. s.* [from *teen* for *ten.*] The years reckoned by the termination *teen*; as, thirteen, fourteen.

Our author would excuse these youthful scenes,
Begotten at his entrance, in his *teens*;
Some childish fancies may approve the toy,
Some like the muse the more for being a boy. *Granville.*

Teeth, the plural of *tooth.*

Who can open the doors of his face? his *teeth* are terrible round about. *Job* xli. 14.

To Teeth. *v. n.* [from the noun.] To breed teeth; to be at the time of dentition.

When the symptoms of *teething* appear, the gums ought to be relaxed by softening ointment. *Arbuthnot on Diet.*

Te'gument. *n. s.* [*tegumentum*, Latin.] Cover; the outward part. This word is seldom used but in anatomy or physicks.

Clip and trim those tender strings in the fashion of beard, or other hairy *teguments*. *Brown's Vulgar Errours, b.* ii.

Proceed by section, dividing the skin, and separating the *teguments*. *Wiseman's Surgery.*

In the nutmeg another *tegument* is the mace between the green pericarpium and the hard shell. *Ray on the Creation.*

To Teh-he. *v. n.* [a cant word made from the sound.] To laugh with a loud and more insolent kind of cachinnation; to titter.

They laugh'd and *teh-he'd* with derision,
To see them take your deposition. *Hudibras, p.* iii.

Teil *tree. n. s.* [*tilia*, Latin.] The same with linden or lime tree: which see.

A *teiltree* and an oak have their substance in them when they cast their leaves. *Isa.* vi. 13.

Teint. *n s.* [*teinte*, French.] Colour; touch of the pencil.

Glazed colours have a vivacity which can never be imitated by the most brilliant colours, because the different *teints* are simply laid on, each in its place, one after another. *Dryd.*

Te'lary. *adj.* [*tela*, a web, Lat.] Spinning webs.

The pictures of *telary* spiders, and their position in the web, is commonly made lateral, and regarding the horizon; although we shall commonly find it downward, and their heads respecting the center. *Brown's Vulgar Err. b.* v.

TE'LESCOPE. *n. s.* [*telescope*, Fr. τέλος and σκοπέω.] A long glass by which distant objects are viewed.

The *telescope* discovers to us distant wonders in the heavens, and shews the milky way, and the bright cloudy spots, in a very dark sky, to be a collection of little stars. *Watts.*

Telesco'pical. *adj.* [from *telescope.*] Belonging to a telescope; seeing at a distance.

To Tell. *v. a.* preterite and part. pass. *told.* [tellan, Saxon; *taelen, tellen*, Dutch; *talen*, Danish.]

1. To utter; to express; to speak.

I will not eat till I have *told* mine errand. *Gen.* xxiv. 33.

Thy message which might else in *telling* wound,
And in performing end us. *Milton.*

2. To relate; to rehearse; to speak.

I will declare what wise men have *told* from their fathers, and have not hid. *Job* xv. 18.

When Gideon heard the *telling* of the dream, and the interpretation, he worshipped. *Judg.* vii. 13.

He longer will delay to hear thee *tell*
His generation. *Milton.*

You must know; but break, O break my heart,
Before I *tell* my fatal story out,
Th' usurper of my throne is my wife! *Dryden.*

The rest are vanish'd, none repass'd the gate,
And not a man appears to *tell* their fate. *Pope's Odyssey.*

3. To teach; to inform.

He gently ask'd where all the people be,
Which in that stately building wont to dwell,
Who answer'd him full soft, he could not *tell*. *Fa. Qu.*

I *told* him of myself; which was as much
As to have ask'd him pardon. *Shakesp. Ant. and Cleopatra.*

Tell me now, what lady is the same,
To whom you swore a secret pilgrimage,
That you to day promis'd to *tell* me of. *Shakespeare.*

The fourth part of a shekel of silver will I give to the man of God to *tell* us our way. 1 *Sam.* ix. 8.

Saint Paul *telleth* us, we must needs be subject not only for fear, but also for conscience sake. *Bishop Sanderson.*

Tell me how may I know him, how adore. *Milton.*

4. To discover; to betray.

They will *tell* it to the inhabitants. *Num.* xiv. 14.

5. To count; to number.

Here lies the learned Savile's heir,
So early wise, and lasting fair;
That none, except her years they *told*,
Thought her a child, or thought her old. *Waller.*

Numerous fails the fearful only *tell*;
Courage from hearts, and not from numbers grows. *Dryd.*

A child can *tell* twenty before he has any idea of infinite. *Locke.*

She doubts if two and two make four,
Though she has *told* them ten times o'er. *Prior.*

6. To make excuses. A low word.

Tush, never *tell* me, I take it much unkindly,
That thou, Iago, who hast had my purse,
As if the strings were thine, should'st know of this. *Shak.*

To Tell. *v. n.*

1. To give an account; to make report.

I will compass thine altar, O Lord, that I may publish with the voice of thanksgiving, and *tell* of all thy wondrous works. *Psal.* xxvi. 7.

Ye that live and move, fair creatures *tell*,
Tell, if ye saw, how came I thus, how here? *Milton.*

2. *To* Tell *on.* To inform of. A doubtful phrase.

David saved neither man nor woman alive, to bring tidings to Gath, saying, lest they should *tell on* us, saying, so did David. 1 *Sam.* xxvii. 11.

Te'lltale. *n. s.* [*tell* and *tale.*] One who gives malicious information; one who carries officious intelligence.

You speak to Casca, and to such a man
That is no flearing *telltale*. *Shakesp. Julius Cæsar.*

What shall these papers lie like *telltales* here? *Shakesp.*

Let not the heav'ns hear these *telltale* women
Rail on the Lord's anointed. *Shakespeare.*

'Tis done; report displays her *telltale* wings,
And to each ear the news and tidings brings. *Fairfax.*

And to the *telltale* sun descry
Our conceal'd solemnity. *Milton.*

Eurydice and he are prisoners here,
But will not long be so: this *telltale* ghost
Perhaps will clear them both. *Dryden and Lee.*

A *telltale* out of school
Is of all wits the greatest fool. *Swift.*

Te'ller. *n. s.* [from *tell.*]

1. One who tells or relates.
2. One who numbers; a numberer.
3. A *teller* is an officer of the exchequer, of which there are four in number: their business is to receive all monies due to the king, and give the clerk of the pell a bill to charge him therewith: they also pay all persons any money payable to them by the king, by warrant from the auditor of the receipt: they also make books of receipts and payments, which they deliver the lord treasurer. *Cowel.*

Temera'rious. *adj.* [*temeraire*, Fr. *temerarius*, Lat.]

1. Rash; heady.

Resolution without foresight is but a *temerarious* folly; and the consequences of things are the first point to be taken into consideration. *L'Estrange.*

2. Careless; heedless.

Should he find upon one single sheet of parchment, an oration written full of profound sense, adorned with elegant phrase, the wit of man could not persuade him that this was done by the *temerarious* dashes of an unguided pen. *Ray.*

Teme'rity. *n. s.* [*temeritas*, Latin.] Rashness; unreasonable contempt of danger.

The figures are bold even to *temerity*. *Cowly.*

To Te'mper. *v. a.* [*tempero*, Lat. *temperer*, Fr.]

1. To mix so as that one part qualifies the other.

I shall *temper* so
Justice with mercy, as may illustrate most
Them fully satisfy'd, and Thee appease. *Milton.*

2. To compound; to form by mixture.

If you could find out but a man
To bear a poison, I would *temper* it;
That Romeo should upon receipt thereof
Soon sleep in quiet. *Shakesp. Romeo and Juliet.*

3. To mingle.

Prepare the sixth part of an ephah and the third part of an hin of oil, to *temper* with the fine flour. *Ezek.* xlvi. 14.

The good old knight, with a mixture of the father and master of the family, *tempered* the inquiries after his own affairs with kind questions relating to themselves. *Addison.*

4. To beat together to a proper consistence.

Th' uncivil kerns of Ireland are in arms,
And *temper* clay with blood of Englishmen. *Shakespeare.*

The potter *tempering* soft earth, fashioneth every vessel with much labour. *Wisd.* xv. 7.

5. To accommodate; to modify.

Thy sustenance serving to the appetite of the eater, *tempered* itself to every man's liking. *Wisd.* xvi. 21.

These soft fires with kindly heat
Of various influence foment and warm,
Temper or nourish. *Milton.*

6. To soften; to mollify; to assuage; to sooth; to calm.

Solon, in his laws to the Athenians, laboured to *temper* their warlike courages with sweet delights of learning and sciences: so that as much as the one excelled in arms, the other exceeded in knowledge. *Spenser on Ireland.*

With this she wonts to *temper* angry Jove,
When all the gods he threats with thund'ring dart. *Spens.*

Now will I to that old Andronicus,
And *temper* him with all the art I have. *Shakespeare.*

Woman! Nature made thee
To *temper* man: we had been brutes without you. *Otway.*

7. To

7. To form metals to a proper degree of hardneſs.

The ſword
Of Michael from the armoury of God
Was given him *temper'd* ſo, that neither keen
Nor ſolid might reſiſt that edge. *Milton.*

In the *tempering* of ſteel, by holding it but a minute or two longer or leſſer in the other competent heat, gives it very differing tempers as to brittleneſs or toughneſs. *Boyle.*

Repeated peals they hear,
And, in a heav'n ſerene, refulgent arms appear;
Red'ning the ſkies, and glitt'ring all around,
The *temper'd* metals claſh, and yield a ſilver ſound. *Dryd.*

8. To govern. A latiniſm.

With which the damned ghoſts he governeth,
And furies rules, and Tartare *tempereth.* *Hubberd's Tale.*

TE'MPER. *n. ſ.* [from the verb.]

1. Due mixture of contrary qualities.

Nothing better proveth the excellency of this ſoil and *temper* than the abundant growing of the palm trees. *Raleigh.*

Health itſelf is but a kind of *temper*, gotten and preſerved by a convenient mixture of contrarieties. *Arbuthnot.*

2. Middle courſe; mean or medium.

If the eſtates of ſome biſhops were exorbitant before the reformation, the preſent clergy's wiſhes reach no further than that ſome reaſonable *temper* had been uſed inſtead of paring them ſo quick. *Swift's Miſcel.*

3. Conſtitution of body.

This body would be increaſed daily, being ſupplied from above and below, and having done growing, it would become more dry by degrees, and of a *temper* of greater conſiſtency and firmneſs. *Burnet's Theory of the Earth.*

4. Diſpoſition of mind.

Remember with what mild
And gracious *temper* he both heard, and judg'd,
Without wrath or reviling. *Milton's Par. Loſt, b.* x.

This will keep their thoughts eaſy and free, the only *temper* wherein the mind is capable of receiving new informations. *Locke on Education.*

5. Conſtitutional frame of mind.

The brain may deviſe laws for the blood, but a hot *temper* leaps o'er a cold decree. *Shakeſp. Merchant of Venice.*

Our hearts,
Of brothers *temper*, do receive you in
With all kind love. *Shakeſpeare's Julius Cæſar.*

6. Calmneſs of mind; moderation.

Reſtore yourſelves unto your *tempers*, fathers,
And without perturbation hear me ſpeak. *Benj. Johnſon.*

Teach me, like thee, in various nature wiſe,
To fall with dignity, with *temper* riſe. *Pope.*

7. State to which metals are reduced, particularly as to hardneſs.

Here draw I
A ſword, whoſe *temper* I intend to ſtain
With the beſt blood that I can meet withal. *Shakeſp.*

Ithuriel with his ſpear
Touch'd lightly; for no falſhood can endure
Touch of cœleſtial *temper*, but returns
Of force to its own likeneſs: up he ſtarts,
Diſcover'd, and ſurpriz'd. *Milton's Par. Loſt, b.* iv.

Theſe needles ſhould have a due *temper*; for if they are too ſoft, the force exerted to carry them through the fleſh will bend them; if they are too brittle they ſnap. *Sharp.*

TE'MPERAMENT. *n. ſ.* [*temperamentum*, Lat. *temperament*, Fr.]

1. Conſtitution; ſtate with reſpect to the predominance of any quality.

Bodies are denominated hot and cold in proportion to the preſent *temperament* of that part of our body to which they are applied. *Locke.*

2. Medium; due mixture of oppoſites.

The common law has waſted and wrought out thoſe diſtempers, and reduced the kingdom to its juſt ſtate and *temperament.* *Hale.*

TEMPERAME'NTAL. *adj.* [from *temperament.*] Conſtitutional.

That *temperamental* dignotions, and conjecture of prevalent humours, that may be collected from ſpots in our nails, we concede. *Brown's Vulgar Errours.*

Intellectual repreſentations are received with as unequal a fate upon a bare *temperamental* reliſh or diſguſt. *Glanville.*

TE'MPERANCE. *n. ſ.* [*temperantia*, Lat.]

1. Moderation; oppoſed to gluttony and drunkenneſs.

Well obſerve
The rule of not too much; by *temperance* taught
In what thou eat'ſt and drink'ſt; ſeeking from thence
Due nouriſhment, no gluttonous delight. *Milton.*

Temperance, that virtue without pride, and fortune without envy, gives indolence of body and tranquillity of mind; the beſt guardian of youth and ſupport of old age. *Temple.*

Make *temperance* thy companion; ſo ſhall health
Sit on thy brow. *Dodſley's Agriculture.*

2. Patience; calmneſs; ſedateneſs; moderation of paſſion.

His ſenſeleſs ſpeech and doted ignorance,
When as the noble prince had marked well;
He calm'd his wrath with goodly *temperance.* *Fa. Qu.*

What, are you chaf'd?
Aſk God for *temp'rance*, that's th' appliance only
Which your diſeaſe requires. *Shakeſp. Henry* VIII.

TE'MPERATE. *adj.* [*temperatus*, Lat.]

1. Not exceſſive; moderate in degree of any quality.

Uſe a *temperate* heat, for they are ever *temperate* heats that digeſt and mature; wherein we mean *temperate*, according to the nature of the ſubject; for that may be *temperate* to fruits and liquors which will not work at all upon metals. *Bacon.*

His ſleep
Was airy, light, from pure digeſtion bred,
And *temp'rate* vapours bland. *Milton.*

2. Moderate in meat and drink.

I adviſed him to be *temperate* in eating and drinking. *Wiſem.*

3. Free from ardent paſſion.

So hot a ſpeed with ſuch advice diſpos'd;
Such *temp'rate* order in ſo fierce a courſe
Doth want example. *Shakeſpeare.*

She's not froward, but modeſt as the dove:
She is not hot, but *temperate* as the morn. *Shakeſpeare.*

From *temperate* inactivity we are unready to put in execution the ſuggeſtions of reaſon. *Brown's Vulgar Errours.*

TE'MPERATELY. *adv.* [from *temperate.*]

1. Moderately; not exceſſively.

By winds that *temperately* blow,
The bark ſhould paſs ſecure and ſlow. *Addiſon.*

2. Calmly; without violence of paſſion.

Temp'rately proceed to what you would
Thus violently redreſs. *Shakeſpeare.*

3. Without gluttony or luxury.

God eſteems it a part of his ſervice if we eat or drink; ſo it be *temperately*, and as may beſt preſerve health. *Taylor.*

TE'MPERATENESS. *n. ſ.* [from *temperate.*]

1. Freedom from exceſſes; mediocrity.

2. Calmneſs; coolneſs of mind.

Langley's mild *temperateneſs*,
Did tend unto a calmer quietneſs. *Daniel's Civil War.*

TE'MPERATURE. *n. ſ.* [*temperatura*, *tempero*, Latin; *temperature*, French.]

1. Conſtitution of nature; degree of any qualities.

It lieth in the ſame climate, and is of no other *temperature* than Guinea. *Abbot's Deſcription of the World.*

Birds that change countries at certain ſeaſons, if they come earlier, ſhew the *temperature* of weather. *Bacon.*

Memory depends upon the conſiſtence and the *temperature* of the brain. *Watts.*

2. Mediocrity; due balance of contrarieties.

As the world's ſun doth effects beget
Diff'rent, in divers places ev'ry day;
Here Autumn's *temperature*, there Summer's heat,
Here flow'ry Spring-tide, and there Winter gray. *Davies.*

If, inſtead of this variation of heat, we ſuppoſe an equality, or conſtant *temperature* of it before the deluge, the caſe would be much altered. *Woodward's Nat. Hiſt.*

3. Moderation; freedom from predominant paſſion.

In that proud port which her ſo goodly graceth,
Moſt goodly *temperature* you may deſcry. *Spenſer.*

TE'MPERED. *adj.* [from *temper.*] Diſpoſed with regard to the paſſions.

When was my lord ſo much ungently *tempered*,
To ſtop his ears againſt admoniſhment? *Shakeſpeare.*

TE'MPEST. *n. ſ.* [*tempeſte*, Fr. *tempeſtas*, Lat.]

1. The utmoſt violence of the wind; the names by which the wind is called according to the gradual encreaſe of its force ſeems to be, a breeze; a gale; a guſt; a ſtorm; a tempeſt.

I have ſeen *tempeſts*, when the ſcolding winds
Have riv'd the knotty oaks. *Shakeſp. Julius Cæſar.*

Some have been driven by *tempeſt* to the ſouth. *Abbot.*

What at firſt was call'd a guſt, the ſame
Hath now a ſtorm's, anon a *tempeſt*'s name. *Donne.*

We, caught in a fiery *tempeſt*, ſhall be hurl'd
Each on his rock transfix'd. *Milton.*

With clouds and ſtorms
Around thee thrown, *tempeſt* o'er *tempeſt* roll'd,
Thou humbleſt nature with thy northern blaſt. *Thomſon.*

2. Any tumult; commotion; perturbation.

The *tempeſt* in my mind
Doth from my ſenſes take all feeling elſe,
Save what beats there. *Shakeſpeare's King Lear.*

To TE'MPEST. *v. a.* [from the noun.] To diſturb as by a tempeſt.

Part huge of bulk,
Wallowing unweildy, enormous in their gait,
Tempeſt the ocean. *Milton.*

Leviathan, in dreadful ſport,
Tempeſt the looſen'd brine. *Thompſon.*

TE'MPEST-BEATEN. *v. a.* [*tempeſt* and *beat.*] Shattered with ſtorms.

In the calm harbour of her gentle breaſt,
My *tempeſt-beaten* ſoul may ſafely reſt. *Dryden's Aureng.*

TE'MPEST-TOST. *adj.* [*tempeſt* and *toſt.*] Driven about by ſtorms.

Though his bark cannot be loſt,
Yet it ſhall be *tempeſt-toſt.* *Shakeſp. Macbeth.*

TEMPESTI'VITY. *n. ſ.* [*tempeſtivus*, Lat.] Seaſonableneſs.

Since their diſperſion the conſtitutions of countries admit not ſuch *tempeſtivity* of harveſt. *Brown's Vulgar Errours.*

TEMPE'STUOUS. *adj.* [*tempeſtueux*, Fr. from *tempeſt.*] Stormy; turbulent.

Tempeſtuous fortune hath ſpent all her ſpight,
And thrilling ſorrow thrown his utmoſt dart. *Fairy Qu.*

Which of them riſing with the ſun or falling
Should prove *tempeſtuous.* *Milton.*

Her looks grow black as a *tempeſtuous* wind,
Some raging thoughts are rowling in her mind. *Dryden.*

Pompey, when diſſuaded from embarking becauſe the weather was *tempeſtuous*, replied, My voyage is neceſſary, my life is not ſo. *Collier on the Value of Life.*

TE'MPLAR. *n. ſ.* [from the *Temple*, an houſe near the Thames, anciently belonging to the knights *templars*, originally from the temple of Jeruſalem.] A ſtudent in the law.

Wits and *templars* ev'ry ſentence raiſe,
And wonder with a fooliſh face of praiſe. *Pope's Epiſt.*

TE'MPLE. *n. ſ.* [*temple*, Fr. *templum*, Lat.]

1. A place appropriated to acts of religion.

The honour'd gods
Throng our large *temples* with the ſhews of peace. *Shak.*

Here we have no *temple* but the wood, no aſſembly but hornbeaſts. *Shakeſpeare's As you like it.*

Moſt ſacrilegious murther hath broke ope
The lord's anointed *temple*, and ſtole thence
The life o' th' building. *Shakeſpeare's Macbeth.*

This gueſt of Summer,
The *temple* haunting martlet. *Shakeſpeare's Macbeth.*

2. [*Tempora*, Latin.] The upper part of the ſides of the head where the pulſe is felt.

Her ſunny locks
Hang on her *temples* like a golden fleece. *Shakeſpeare.*

We may apply intercipients of maſtich upon the *temples*; frontals alſo may be applied. *Wiſeman's Surgery.*

To procure ſleep, he uſes the ſcratching of the *temples* and ears; that even mollifies wild beaſts. *Arbuthnot.*

The weapon enter'd cloſe above his ear,
Cold through his *temples* glides the whizzing ſpear. *Pope.*

TE'MPLET. *n. ſ.* A piece of timber in a building.

When you lay any timber on brick-work, as linteols over windows, or *templets* under girders, lay them in loam. *Moxon.*

TE'MPORAL. *adj.* [*temporal*, Fr. *temporalis*, low Latin.]

1. Meaſured by time; not eternal.

As there they ſuſtain *temporal* life, ſo here they would learn to make proviſion for eternal. *Hooker.*

2. Secular; not eccleſiaſtical.

This ſceptre ſhews the force of *temporal* power,
The attribute to awe and majeſty,
Wherein doth ſit the dread of kings. *Shakeſpeare.*

All the *temporal* lands, which men devout
By teſtament have given to the church,
Would they ſtrip from us. *Shakeſp. Henry V.*

All *temporal* power hath been wreſted from the clergy, and much of their eccleſiaſtick. *Swift.*

3. Not ſpiritual.

Call not every *temporal* end a defiling of the intention, but only when it contradicts the ends of God, or when it is principally intended: for ſometimes a *temporal* end is part of our duty; and ſuch are all the actions of our calling. *Taylor.*

Our petitions to God with regard to *temporals*, muſt be that medium of convenience proportioned to the ſeveral conditions of life. *Rogers's Serm.*

4. [*Temporal*, Fr.] Placed at the temples, or upper part of the head.

Copious bleeding, by opening the *temporal* arteries, are the moſt effectual remedies for a phrenſy. *Arbuthnot on Aliments.*

TEMPORA'LITY. } *n. ſ.* [*temporalité*, Fr. from *temporal.*] Se-
TE'MPORALS. } cular poſſeſſions; not eccleſiaſtick rights.

Such revenues, lands, and tenements, as biſhops have had annexed to their ſees by the kings and others from time to time, as they are barons and lords of the parliament. *Cowel.*

The reſidue of theſe ordinary finances is caſual, as the *temporalities* of vacant biſhopricks, the profits that grow by the tenures of lands. *Bacon.*

TE'MPORALLY. *adv.* [from *temporal.*] With reſpect to this life.

Sinners who are in ſuch a *temporally* happy condition, owe it not to their ſins, but wholly to their luck. *South.*

TE'MPORALTY. *n. ſ.* [from *temporal.*]

1. The laity; ſecular people.

The pope ſucked out ineſtimable ſums of money, to the intolerable grievance of clergy and *temporalty.* *Abbot.*

2. Secular poſſeſſions.

The king yielded up the point, reſerving the ceremony of homage from the biſhops, in reſpect of the *temporalities*, to himſelf. *Ayliffe.*

TEMPORA'NEOUS. *adj.* [*temporis*, Lat.] Temporary. *Dict.*

TE'MPORARINESS. [from *temporary.*] The ſtate of being temporary; not perpetuity.

TE'MPORARY. *adj.* [*tempus*, Lat.] Laſting only for a limited time.

Theſe *temporary* truces were ſoon made and ſoon broken; he deſired a ſtraiter amity. *Bacon's Henry VII.*

The republick threatened with danger, appointed a *temporary* dictator, who, when the danger was over, retired again into the community. *Addiſon.*

To **TE'MPORIZE.** *v. n.* [*temporiſer*, Fr. *tempus*, Lat.]

1. To delay; to procraſtinate.

If Cupid hath not ſpent all his quiver in Venice, thou wilt quake for this ſhortly.
——I look for an earthquake too then.
——Well, you will *temporize* with the hours. *Shakeſpeare.*

The earl of Lincoln deceived of the country's concourſe, in which caſe he would have *temporized*, reſolved to give the king battle. *Bacon's Henry VII.*

2. To comply with the times or occaſions.

They might their grievance inwardly complain,
But outwardly they needs muſt *temporize.* *Daniel.*

3. To comply: this is improper.

The dauphin is too wilful oppoſite,
And will not *temporize* with my entreaties:
He flatly ſays, he'll not lay down his arms. *Shakeſpeare.*

TEMPORI'ZER. *n. ſ.* [*temporiſeur*, Fr. from *temporize.*] One that complies with times or occaſions; a trimmer.

I pronounce thee a hovering *temporizer*, that
Canſt with thine eyes at once ſee good and evil,
Inclining to them both. *Shakeſ. Winter's Tale.*

TEMSE BREAD. } *n. ſ.* [*temſen*, Dutch; *tamiſe*, Fr. *tame-*
TEMSED BREAD. } *ſare*, Italian, to ſift; *tems*, Dutch; *tamis*, French; *tamiſo*, Italian, a ſieve.] Bread made of flower better ſifted than common.

To **TEMPT.** *v. a.* [*tento*, Lat. *tenter*, Fr.]

1. To ſollicit to ill; to incite by preſenting ſome pleaſure or advantage to the mind; to entice.

'Tis not the king that ſends you to the Tower:
My lady Gray *tempts* him to this harſh extremity. *Shak.*

You ever gentle gods, take my breath from me;
Let not my worſer ſpirit *tempt* me again
To die before you pleaſe. *Shakeſp. King Lear.*

Come together, that Satan *tempt* you not. 1 *Cor.* vii. 5.

He that hath not wholly ſubdued himſelf, is quickly *tempted* and overcome in ſmall things. *Biſhop Taylor.*

Fix'd on the fruit ſhe gaz'd, which to behold
Might *tempt* alone. *Milton.*

The devil can but *tempt* and deceive; and if he cannot deſtroy ſo, his power is at an end. *South.*

O wretched maid!
Whoſe roving fancy would reſolve the ſame
With him, who next ſhould *tempt* her eaſy fame. *Prior.*

2. To provoke.

I'm much too vent'rous
In *tempting* of your patience. *Shakeſp. Henry VIII.*

With-hold
Your talons from the wretched and the bold;
Tempt not the brave and needy to deſpair:
For, though your violence ſhou'd leave 'em bare
Of gold and ſilver, ſwords and darts remain. *Dryden.*

3. It is ſometimes uſed without any notion of evil; to ſollicit; to draw.

Still his ſtrength conceal'd
Which *tempted* our attempt, and wrought our fall. *Milton.*

The rowing crew,
To *tempt* a fare, clothe all their tilts in blue. *Gay.*

4. To try; to attempt.

This from the vulgar branches muſt be torn,
And to fair Proſerpine the preſent born,
Ere leave be giv'n to *tempt* the nether ſkies. *Dryden.*

TEMPTA'TION. *n. ſ.* [*tentation*, Fr. from *tempt.*]

1. The act of tempting; ſollicitation to ill; enticement.

All *temptation* to tranſgreſs repel. *Milt.*

2. The ſtate of being tempted.

When by human weakneſs, and the arts of the tempter, you are led into *temptations*, prayer is the thread to bring you out of this labyrinth. *Duppa.*

3. That which is offered to the mind as a motive to ill.

Set a deep glaſs of rheniſh wine on the contrary caſket; for if the devil be within, and that *temptation* without, he will chooſe it. *Shakeſp. Merchant of Venice.*

Dare to be great without a guilty crown;
View it, and lay the bright *temptation* down:
'Tis baſe to ſeize on all. *Dryden's Aurengzebe.*

TE'MPTABLE. *adj.* [from *tempt.*] Liable to temptation; obnoxious to bad influence.

If the parliament were as *temptable* as any other aſſembly, the managers muſt fail for want of tools to work with. *Swift.*

TE'MPTER. *n. ſ.* [from *tempt.*]

1. One who ſollicits to ill; an enticer.

Theſe women are ſhrewd *tempters* with their tongues.
Shakeſpeare's Henry VI.

Is this her fault or mine?
The *tempter* or the tempted, who ſins moſt?
Not ſhe; nor doth ſhe tempt. *Shak. Meaſ. for Meaſure.*

Thoſe who are bent to do wickedly, will never want *tempters* to urge them on. *Tillotſon.*

My work is done:
She's now the *tempter* to enſnare his heart. *Dryden.*

2. The infernal ſollicitor to evil.

The experience of our own frailties, and the watchfulneſs of the *tempter*, diſcourage us. *Hammond's Fundamentals.*

Foretold what would come to paſs,
When firſt this *tempter* croſs'd the gulf from hell. *Milton.*
To this high mountain's top the *tempter* brought
Our Saviour. *Milton's Par. Reg. b.* iii.

TE'MULENCY. *n. ſ.* [*temulentia*, Lat.] Inebriation; intoxication by liquor.

TE'MULENT. *adj.* [*temulentus*, Lat.] Inebriated; intoxicated as with ſtrong liquors.

TEN. *adj.* [ꞇyn, Saxon; *tien*, Dutch.] The decimal number; twice five; the number by which we multiply numbers into new denominations.

Thou ſhalt have more
Than two *tens* to a ſcore. *Shakeſp. King Lear.*

Ten hath been extolled as containing even, odd, long, and plain, quadrate and cubical numbers; and Ariſtotle obſerved, that Barbarians as well as Greeks uſed a numeration unto *ten*. *Brown's Vulgar Errours, b.* iv.

With twice *ten* ſail I croſs'd the Phrygian ſea,
Scarce ſeven within your harbour meet. *Dryden.*

There's a proud modeſty in merit,
Averſe from begging; and reſolv'd to pay
Ten times the gift it aſks. *Dryden's Cleomenes.*

From the ſoft lyre,
Sweet flute, and *ten* ſtring'd inſtrument, require
Sounds of delight. *Prior.*

Although Engliſh is too little cultivated, yet the faults are nine in *ten* owing to affectation. *Swift's Miſcel.*

TE'NABLE. *adj.* [*tenable*, French.] Such as may be maintained againſt oppoſition; ſuch as may be held againſt attacks.

The town was ſtrong of itſelf, and wanted no induſtry to fortify and make it *tenable*. *Bacon's War with Spain.*

Sir William Ogle ſeized upon the caſtle, and put it into a *tenable* condition. *Clarendon.*

Infidelity has been driven out of all its outworks: the atheiſt has not found his poſt *tenable*, and is therefore retired into deiſm. *Addiſon's Spect.* N. 186.

TENA'CIOUS. *adj.* [*tenax*, Lat.]

1. Graſping hard; inclined to hold faſt; not willing to let go, with *of* before the thing held.

A reſolute *tenacious* adherence to well choſen principles, makes the face of a governor ſhine in the eyes of thoſe that ſee his actions. *South.*

Griping, and ſtill *tenacious of* thy hold,
Wou'd'ſt thou the Grecian chiefs, though largely ſoul'd,
Shou'd give the priſes they had gain'd. *Dryden.*

You reign abſolute over the hearts of a ſtubborn and freeborn people, *tenacious* to madneſs *of* their liberty. *Dryden.*

True love's a miſer; ſo *tenacious* grown,
He weighs to the leaſt grain of what's his own. *Dryden.*

Men are *tenacious of* the opinions that firſt poſſeſs them. *Locke.*

He is *tenacious of* his own property, and ready to invade that of others. *Arbuthnot.*

2. Retentive.

The memory in ſome is very *tenacious*; but yet there ſeems to be a conſtant decay of all our ideas, even of thoſe which are ſtruck deepeſt, and in minds the moſt retentive. *Locke.*

3. [*Tenace*, French.] Having parts diſpoſed to adhere to each other; coheſive.

Three equal round veſſels filled, the one with water, the other with oil, the third with molten pitch, and the liquors ſtirred alike to give them a vortical motion; the pitch by its tenacity will loſe its motion quickly, the oil being leſs *tenacious* will keep it longer, and the water being leſs *tenacious* will keep it longeſt, but yet will loſe it in a ſhort time. *Newt.*

4. Niggardly; cloſe-fiſted; meanly parcimonious. *Ainſ.*

TENA'CIOUSLY. *adv.* [from *tenacious.*] With diſpoſition to hold faſt.

Some things our juvenile reaſons *tenaciouſly* adhere to, which yet our maturer judgments diſallow of. *Glanville.*

TENA'CIOUSNESS. *n. ſ.* [from *tenacious.*] Unwillingneſs to quit, reſign, or let go.

TENA'CITY. *n. ſ.* [*tenacitas*, *tenacité*, Fr. *tenax*, Latin.] Viſcoſity; glutinouſneſs; adheſion of one part to another.

If many contiguous vortices of molten pitch were each of them as large as thoſe which ſome ſuppoſe to revolve about the ſun and fixed ſtars, yet theſe and all their parts would, by their *tenacity* and ſtiffneſs, communicate their motion to one another till they all reſted among themſelves. *Newton.*

Subſtances, whoſe *tenacity* exceeds the powers of digeſtion, will neither paſs, nor be converted into aliment. *Arbuthnot.*

TE'NANCY. *n. ſ.* [*tenanche*, old French; *tenentia*, law Latin; from *tenant.*] Temporary poſſeſſion of what belongs to another.

This duke becomes ſeized of favour by deſcent, though the condition of that eſtate be commonly no more than a *tenancy* at will. *Wotton.*

TE'NANT. *n. ſ.* [*tenant*, French.]

1. One that holds of another; one that on certain conditions has temporary poſſeſſion and uſe of that which is in reality the property of another: correlative to landlord.

I have been your *tenant*,
And your father's *tenant*, theſe fourſcore years. *Shakeſp.*

Such is the mould that the bleſt *tenant* feeds
On precious fruits, and pays his rent in weeds. *Waller.*

Jupiter had a farm long for want of a *tenant*. *L'Eſtrange.*

His cheerful *tenants* bleſs their yearly toil,
Yet to their lord owe more than to the ſoil. *Pope.*

The *tenants* of a manor fall into the ſentiments of their lord. *Watts.*

The father is a tyrant over ſlaves and beggars, whom he calls his *tenants*. *Swift.*

2. One who reſides in any place.

The bear, rough *tenant* of theſe ſhades. *Thomſon.*

To TE'NANT. *v. a.* [from the noun.] To hold on certain conditions.

Sir Roger's eſtate is *tenanted* by perſons who have ſerved him or his anceſtors. *Addiſon's Spect.* N. 107.

TE'NANTABLE. *adj.* [from *tenant.*] Such as may be held by a tenant.

The ruins that time, ſickneſs, or melancholy ſhall bring, muſt be made up at your coſt; for that thing a huſband is but tenant for life in what he holds, and is bound to leave the place *tenantable* to the next that ſhall take it. *Suckling.*

That the ſoul may not be too much incommoded in her houſe of clay, ſuch neceſſaries are ſecured to the body as may keep it in *tenantable* repair. *Decay of Piety.*

TE'NANTLESS. *adj.* [from *tenant.*] Unoccupied; unpoſſeſſed.

O thou, that doſt inhabit in my breaſt,
Leave not the manſion ſo long *tenantleſs*;
Leſt growing ruinous the building fall,
And leave no memory of what it was. *Shakeſpeare.*

TE'NANT-SAW. *n. ſ.* [corrupted, I ſuppoſe, from *tenon-ſaw.*] See TENON.

TENCH. *n. ſ.* [ꞇince, Saxon; *tinca*, Lat.] A pond fiſh.

Having ſtored a very great pond with carps, *tench*, and other pond fiſh, and only put in two ſmall pikes, this pair of tyrants in ſeven years devoured the whole. *Hale.*

To TEND. *v. a.* [contracted from *attend.*]

1. To watch; to guard; to accompany as an aſſiſtant or defender.

Nymphs of Mulla which, with careful heed,
The ſilver ſcaly trouts did *tend* full well. *Spenſer's Epithal.*

Go thou to Richard, and good angels *tend* thee. *Shak.*

Him lord pronounc'd; and O! indignity
Subjected to his ſervice angel wings,
And flaming miniſters to watch and *tend*
Their earthy charge. *Milton.*

He led a rural life, and had command
O'er all the ſhepherds, who about thoſe vales
Tended their numerous flocks. *Dryden and Lee's Oedipus.*

There is a pleaſure in that ſimplicity, in beholding princes *tending* their flocks. *Pope.*

Our humbler province is to *tend* the fair;
To ſave the powder from too rude a gale,
Nor let th' impriſon'd eſſences exhale. *Pope.*

Cic'ly had won his heart;
Cic'ly, the weſtern laſs, that *tends* the kee. *Gay.*

2. To attend; to accompany.

Deſpair
Tended the ſick, buſieſt from couch to couch. *Milton.*

Thoſe with whom I now converſe,
Without a tear will *tend* my herſe. *Swift.*

3. To be attentive to.

Unſuck'd of lamb or kid that *tend* their play. *Milton.*

To TEND. *v. n.* [*tendo*, Lat.]

1. To move towards a certain point or place.

They had a view of the princeſs at a maſk, having overheard two gentlemen *tending* towards that ſight. *Wotton.*

To theſe abodes our fleet Apollo ſends:
Here Dardanus was born, and hither *tends*. *Dryden.*

2. [*Tendre*, French.] To be directed to any end or purpoſe; to aim at.

Admiration ſeiz'd
All heav'n, what this might mean and whither *tend*. *Milt.*

Factions gain their power by pretending common ſafety, and *tending* towards it in the directeſt courſe. *Temple.*

The laws of our religion *tend* to the univerſal happineſs of mankind. *Tillotſon's Sermons.*

3. To contribute.

Many times that which we aſk would, if it ſhould be granted, be worſe for us, and perhaps *tend* to our deſtruction; and then God by denying the particular matter of our prayers, doth grant the general matter of them. *Hammond.*

4. [From *attend.*] To wait; to expect. Out of uſe.

The bark is ready, and the wind at help;
Th' aſſociates *tend*. *Shakeſpeare's Hamlet.*

5. To

5. To attend; to wait as dependants or servants.

She deserves a lord,
That twenty such rude boys might *tend* upon,
And call her hourly mistress. *Shakespeare.*

Give him *tending*,
He brings great news. *Shakespeare.*

Was he not companion with the riotous knights,
That *tend* upon my father. *Shakesp. King Lear.*

6. To attend as something inseparable.

Threefold vengeance *tend* upon your steps! *Shakesp.*

TE'NDANCE. *n. s.* [from *tend.*]

1. Attendance; state of expectation.

Unhappy wight born to disastrous end,
That doth his life in so long *tendance* spend. *Hubberd.*

2. Person; attendant. Out of use.

His lobbies fill with *tendance*,
Rain sacrificial whisp'rings in his ear. *Shakespeare.*

3. Attendance; act of waiting.

She purpos'd,
By watching, weeping, *tendance*, to
O'ercome you with her shew. *Shakesp. Cymbeline.*

4. Care; act of tending.

Nature does require
Her times of preservation, which, perforce,
I her frail son, amongst my brethren mortal,
Must give my *tendance* to. *Shakesp. Henry* VIII.

They at her coming sprung,
And touch'd by her fair *tendance* gladlier grew. *Milton.*

TE'NDENCE. } *n. s.* [from *tend.*]
TE'NDENCY. }

1. Direction or course towards any place or object.

It is not much business that distracts any man; but the want of purity, constancy, and *tendency* towards God. *Taylor.*

Writings of this kind, if conducted with candour, have a more particular *tendency* to the good of their country than any other compositions. *Addison's Freeholder*, N°. 40.

We may acquaint ourselves with the powers and properties, the *tendencies* and inclinations, of body and spirit. *Watts.*

All of them are innocent, and most of them had a moral *tendency*, to soften the virulence of parties, or laugh out of countenance some vice or folly. *Swift.*

2. Direction or course toward any inference or result; drift.

These opinions are of so little moment, that, like motes in the sun, their *tendencies* are little noticed. *Locke.*

TE'NDER. *adj.* [*tendre*, French.]

1. Soft; easily impressed or injured.

The earth brought forth the *tender* grass. *Milton.*
From each *tender* stalk she gathers. *Milton.*

2. Sensible; easily pained; soon sore.

Unneath may she endure the flinty street,
To tread them with her *tender* feeling feet. *Shakespeare.*

Leah was *tender* eyed, but Rachael was well-favoured. *Gen.* xxix. 17.

Our bodies are not naturally more *tender* than our faces; but by being less exposed to the air, they become less able to endure it. *L'Estrange.*

The face when we are born is no less *tender* than any other part of the body: it is use alone hardens it, and makes it more able to endure the cold. *Locke on Education.*

3. Effeminate; emasculate; delicate.

When Cyrus had overcome the Lydians, that were a warlike nation, and devised to bring them to a more peaceable life, instead of their short warlike coat he clothed them in long garments like women, and instead of their warlike musick appointed to them certain lascivious lays, by which their minds were so mollified and abated, that they forgot their former fierceness, and became most *tender* and effeminate. *Spenser on Ireland.*

4. Exciting kind concern.

I love Valentine;
His life's as *tender* to me as my soul. *Shakespeare.*

5. Compassionate; anxious for another's good.

The *tender* kindness of the church it well beseemeth to help the weaker sort, although some few of the perfecter and stronger be for a time displeased. *Hooker, b.* v.

This not mistrust but *tender* love injoins. *Milton.*

Be *tender* hearted and compassionate towards those in want, and ready to relieve them. *Tillotson's Sermons.*

6. Susceptible of soft passions.

Your tears a heart of flint
Might *tender* make, yet nought
Herein they will prevail. *Spenser.*

7. Amorous; lascivious.

What mad lover ever dy'd,
To gain a soft and gentle bride?
Or for a lady *tender* hearted,
In purling streams or hemp departed? *Hudibras, p.* iii.

8. Expressive of the softer passions.

9. Careful not to hurt, with *of*.

The civil authority should be *tender of* the honour of God and religion. *Tillotson's Sermons.*

As I have been *tender of* every particular person's reputation, so I have taken care not to give offence. *Addison.*

10. Gentle; mild; unwilling to pain.

Thy *tender* hefted nature shall not give
Thee o'er to harshness; her eyes are fierce, but thine
Do comfort and not burn. *Shakesp. King Lear.*

You, that are thus so *tender* o'er his follies,
Will never do him good. *Shakesp. Winter's Tale.*

11. Apt to give pain.

In things that are *tender* and unpleasing, break the ice by some whose words are of less weight, and reserve the more weighty voice to come in as by chance. *Bacon.*

12. Young; weak: as, tender *age.*

When yet he was but *tender* bodied, a mother should not sell him. *Shakespeare's Coriolanus.*

To TE'NDER. *v. a.* [*tendre*, French.]

1. To offer; to exhibit; to propose to acceptance.

Some of the chiefest laity professed with greater stomach their judgments, that such a discipline was little better than popish tyranny, disguised and *tendered* unto them. *Hooker.*

I crave no more than what your highness offer'd;
Nor will you *tender* less. *Shakesp. King Lear.*

All conditions, all minds, *tender* down
Their service to lord Timon. *Shakespeare.*

Owe not all creatures by just right to thee
Duty and service, not to stay till bid,
But *tender* all their pow'r? *Milton's Par. Regain'd.*

2. To hold; to esteem.

Tender yourself more dearly;
Or, not to crack the wind of the poor phrase,
Wringing it thus, you'll *tender* me a fool. *Shakespeare.*

3. [From the adjective.] To regard with kindness. Not in use.

I thank you, madam, that you *tender* her:
Poor gentlewoman, my master wrongs her much. *Shak.*

TE'NDER. *n. s.* [from the verb.]

1. Offer; proposal to acceptance.

Then to have a wretched puling fool,
A whining mammet, in her fortune's *tender*,
To answer I'll not wed. *Shak. Romeo and Juliet.*

Think yourself a baby;
That you have ta'en his *tenders* for true pay,
Which are not sterling. *Shakespeare's Hamlet.*

The earl accepted the *tenders* of my service. *Dryden.*

To declare the calling of the Gentiles by a free, unlimited *tender* of the gospel to all. *South's Sermons.*

Our *tenders* of duty every now and then miscarry. *Addison.*

2. [From the adjective.] Regard; kind concern.

Thou hast shew'd thou mak'st some *tender* of my life,
In this fair rescue thou hast brought to me. *Shakespeare.*

TE'NDER-HEARTED. *adj.* [*tender* and *heart.*] Of a soft compassionate disposition.

TE'NDERLING. *n. s.* [from *tender.*]

1. The first horns of a deer.

2. A fondling; one who is made soft by too much kindness.

TE'NDERLY. *adv.* [from *tender.*] In a tender manner; mildly; gently; softly; kindly; without harshness.

Tenderly apply to her
Some remedies for life. *Shakespeare.*

She embrac'd him, and for joy
Tenderly wept. *Milton.*

They are the most perfect pieces of Ovid, and the style *tenderly* passionate and courtly. *Pref. to Ovid.*

Marcus with blushes owns he loves,
And Brutus *tenderly* reproves. *Pope.*

TE'NDERNESS. *n. s.* [*tendresse*, Fr. from *tender.*]

1. The state of being tender; susceptibility of impressions.

Pied cattle are spotted in their tongues, the *tenderness* of the part receiving more easily alterations than other parts of the flesh. *Bacon.*

The difference of the muscular flesh depends upon the hardness, *tenderness*, moisture, or driness of the fibres. *Arbuth.*

2. State of being easily hurt; soreness.

A quickness and *tenderness* of sight could not endure bright sun-shine. *Locke.*

Any zealous for his country, must conquer that *tenderness* and delicacy which may make him afraid of being spoken ill of. *Addison.*

There are examples of wounded persons, that have roared for anguish at the discharge of ordnance, though at a great distance; what insupportable torture then should we be under upon a like concussion in the air, when all the whole body would have the *tenderness* of a wound. *Bentley's Sermons.*

3. Susceptibility of the softer passions.

Weep no more, lest I give cause
To be suspected of more *tenderness*
Than doth become a man. *Shakespeare.*

Well we know your *tenderness* of heart,
And gentle, kind, effeminate remorse
To your kindred. *Shakesp. Richard* III.

With what a graceful *tenderneſs* he loves!
And breathes the ſofteſt, the ſincereſt vows! *Addiſon.*

4. Kind attention; anxiety for the good of another.

Having no children, ſhe did with ſingular care and *tenderneſs* intend the education of Philip and Margaret. *Bacon.*

5. Scrupulouſneſs; caution.

My conſcience firſt receiv'd a *tenderneſs*,
Scruple, and prick, on certain ſpeeches utter'd
By th' biſhop of Bayon. *Shakeſp. Henry* VIII.

Some are unworthily cenſured for keeping their own, whom *tenderneſs* how to get honeſtly teacheth to ſpend diſcreetly; whereas ſuch need no great thriftineſs in preſerving their own who aſſume more liberty in exacting from others. *Wotton.*

True *tenderneſs* of conſcience is nothing elſe but an awful and exact ſenſe of the rule which ſhould direct it; and while it ſteers by this compaſs, and is ſenſible of every declination from it, ſo long it is properly tender. *South.*

6. Cautious care.

There being implanted in every man's nature a great *tenderneſs* of reputation, to be careleſs of it is looked on as a mark of a degenerous mind. *Government of the Tongue.*

7. Soft pathos of expreſſion.

TE'NDINOUS. *adj.* [*tendineux*, Fr. *tendinis*, Latin.] Sinewy; containing tendons; conſiſting of tendons.

Nervous and *tendinous* parts have worſe ſymptoms, and are harder of cure than fleſhy ones. *Wiſeman.*

TE'NDON. *n. ſ.* [*tendo*, Latin.] A ſinew; a ligature by which the joints are moved.

A ſtruma in her inſtep lay very hard and big amongſt the *tendons*. *Wiſeman's Surgery.*

The entrails theſe embrace in ſpiral ſtrings,
Thoſe claſp th' arterial tubes in tender rings;
The *tendons* ſome compacted cloſe produce,
And ſome thin fibres for the ſkin diffuſe. *Blackmore.*

TE'NDRIL *n. ſ.* [*tendrillon*, French.] The claſp of a vine, or other climbing plant.

In wanton ringlets wav'd,
As the vine curls her *tendrils*; which imply'd
Subjection. *Milton's Par. Loſt*, *b.* iv.

So may thy tender bloſſoms fear no blite;
Nor goats with venom'd teeth thy *tendrils* bite. *Dryden.*

The *tendrils* or claſpers of plants are given only to ſuch as have weak ſtalks, and cannot raiſe up or ſupport themſelves. *Ray on the Creation.*

TENE'BRICOSE. } *adj.* [*tenebricoſus*, *tenebroſus*, Latin.] Dark;
TE'NEBROUS. } gloomy.

TENEBRO'SITY. *n. ſ.* [*tenebræ*, Lat.] Darkneſs; gloom.

TE'NEMENT. *n. ſ.* [*tenement*, Fr. *tenementum*, law Latin.] Any thing held by a tenant.

What reaſonable man will not think that the *tenement* ſhall be made much better, if the tenant may be drawn to build himſelf ſome handſome habitation thereon, to ditch and incloſe his ground? *Spenſer on Ireland.*

'Tis policy for father and ſon to take different ſides;
For then lands and *tenements* commit no treaſon. *Dryden.*

Who has informed us, that a rational ſoul can inhabit no *tenement*, unleſs it has juſt ſuch a ſort of frontiſpiece. *Locke.*

Treat on, treat on, is her eternal note,
And lands and *tenements* glide down her throat. *Pope.*

TE'NENT. *n. ſ.* See TENET.

TENE'RITY. *n. ſ.* [*teneritas*, *tener*, Lat.] Tenderneſs. *Ainſ.*

TENE'SMUS. *n. ſ.*

The ſtone ſhutting up the orifice of the bladder, is attended with a *teneſmus*, or needing to go to ſtool. *Arbuthnot.*

TE'NET. *n. ſ.* [from *tenet*, Latin, *he holds*. It is ſometimes written *tenent*, or *they hold.*] Poſition; principle; opinion.

That all animals of the land are in their kind in the ſea, although received as a principle, is a *tenet* very queſtionable. *Brown's Vulgar Errours*, *b.* iii.

While, in church matters, profit ſhall be the touch-ſtone for faith and manners, we are not to wonder if no gainful *tenet* be depoſited. *Decay of Piety.*

This ſavours of ſomething ranker than ſocinianiſm, even the *tenents* of the fifth monarchy, and of ſovereignty founded only upon ſaintſhip. *South's Sermons.*

They wonder men ſhould have miſtook
The *tenets* of their maſter's book. *Prior.*

TE'NNIS. *n. ſ.* [this play is ſuppoſed by *Skinner* to be ſo named from the word *tenez*, take it, hold it, or there it goes, uſed by the French when they drive the ball.] A play at which a ball is driven with a racket.

The barber's man hath been ſeen with him, and the old ornament of his cheek hath already ſtuffed *tennis* balls. *Shak.*

There was he gaming, there o'ertook in's rowſe,
There falling out at *tennis*. *Shakeſp. Hamlet.*

A prince, by a hard deſtiny, became a *tennis* ball long to the blind goddeſs. *Howel's Vocal Foreſt.*

It can be no more diſgrace to a great lord to draw a fair picture, than to play at *tennis* with his page. *Peacham.*

The inſide of the uvea is blacked like the walls of a *tennis* court, that the rays falling upon the retina may not, by being rebounded thence upon the uvea, be returned again; for ſuch a repercuſſion would make the ſight more confuſed. *More's Antidote againſt Atheiſm.*

We conceive not a *tennis* ball to think, and conſequently not to have any volition, or preference of motion to reſt. *Locke.*

We have no exedra for the philoſophers adjoining to our *tennis* court, but there are alehouſes. *Arbuthnot and Pope.*

To TE'NNIS. *v. a.* [from the noun.] To drive as a ball.

Thoſe four gariſons iſſuing forth upon the enemy, will ſo drive him from one ſide to another, and *tennis* him amongſt them, that he ſhall find no where ſafe to keep his feet in, nor hide himſelf. *Spenſer on Ireland.*

TE'NON. *n. ſ.* [French.] The end of a timber cut to be fitted into another timber.

Such variety of parts, ſolid with hollow; ſome with cavities as mortiſes to receive, others with *tenons* to fit them. *Ray.*

The *tenant-jaw* being thin, hath a back to keep it from bending. *Moxon's Mech. Exerciſe.*

TE'NOUR. *n. ſ.* [*tenor*, Lat. *teneur*, Fr.]

1. Continuity of ſtate; conſtant mode; manner of continuity; general currency.

We might perceive his words interrupted continually with ſighs, and the *tenor* of his ſpeech not knit together to one conſtant end, but diſſolved in itſelf, as the vehemency of the inward paſſion prevailed. *Sidney.*

When the world firſt out of chaos ſprang,
So ſmil'd the days, and ſo the *tenor* ran
Of their felicity: a ſpring was there,
An everlaſting ſpring, the jolly year
Led round in his great circle, no winds breath
As now did ſmell of Winter or of death. *Craſhaw.*

Still I ſee the *tenor* of man's woe
Hold on the ſame, from woman to begin. *Milton.*

Does not the whole *tenor* of the divine law poſitively require humility and meekneſs to all men. *Sprat.*

Inſpire my numbers,
Till I my long laborious work complete,
And add perpetual *tenor* to my rhimes,
Deduc'd from nature's birth to Cæſar's times. *Dryden.*

This ſucceſs would look like chance if it were not perpetual, and always of the ſame *tenor*. *Dryden.*

Can it be poiſon! poiſon's of one *tenor*,
Or hot, or cold. *Dryden's Don Sebaſtian.*

There is ſo great an uniformity amongſt them, that the whole *tenor* of thoſe bodies thus preſerved clearly points forth the month of May. *Woodward's Nat. Hiſt.*

In ſuch lays as neither ebb nor flow,
Correctly cold, and regularly low,
That ſhunning faults, one quiet *tenor* keep,
We cannot blame indeed—but we may ſleep. *Pope.*

2. Senſe contained; general courſe or drift.

Has not the divine Apollo ſaid,
Is't not the *tenor* of his oracle,
That king Leontes ſhall not have an heir,
Till his loſt child be found? *Shak. Winter's Tale.*

By the ſtern brow and waſpiſh action,
Which ſhe did uſe as ſhe was writing of it,
It bears an angry *tenor*. *Shakeſp. As you like it.*

Bid me tear the bond.
—When it is paid according to the *tenor*. *Shakeſpeare.*

Reading it muſt be repeated again and again with a cloſe attention to the *tenor* of the diſcourſe, and a perfect neglect of the diviſions into chapters and verſes. *Locke.*

3. A ſound in muſick.

The treble cutteth the air too ſharp to make the ſound equal; and therefore a mean or *tenor* is the ſweeteſt part. *Bacon's Nat. Hiſt.* N°. 173.

TENSE. *adj.* [*tenſus*, Lat.] Stretched; ſtiff; not lax.

For the free paſſage of the ſound into the ear, it is requiſite that the tympanum be *tenſe*, and hard ſtretched, otherwiſe the laxneſs of the membrane will certainly dead and damp the ſound. *Holder.*

TENSE. *n. ſ.* [*temps*, Fr. *tempus*, Lat.]

[In grammar.] *Tenſe*, in ſtrict ſpeaking, is only a variation of the verb to ſignify time. *Clarke.*

As foreſight, when it is natural, anſwers to memory, ſo when methodical it anſwers to reminiſcence, and may be called forecaſt; all of them expreſſed in the *tenſes* given to verbs. Memory ſaith, I did ſee; reminiſcence, I had ſeen; foreſight, I ſhall ſee; forecaſt, I ſhall have ſeen. *Grew.*

Ladies, without knowing what *tenſes* and participles are, ſpeak as properly and as correctly as gentlemen. *Locke.*

He ſhould have the Latin words given him in their firſt caſe and *tenſe*, and ſhould never be left to ſeek them himſelf from a dictionary. *Watts.*

TE'NSENESS. *n. ſ.* [from *tenſe.*] Contraction; tenſion: the contrary to laxity.

Should

Should the pain and *tenseness* of the part continue, the operation must take place. *Sharp's Surgery.*

TE'NSIBLE. *adj.* [*tensus*, Lat.] Capable of being extended.

Gold is the closest, and therefore the heaviest, of metals, and is likewise the most flexible and *tensible*. *Bacon.*

TE'NSILE. *adj.* [*tensilis*, Lat.] Capable of extension.

All bodies ductile and *tensile*, as metals, that will be drawn into wires, have in them the appetite of not discontinuing. *Bacon's Nat. Hist.* N°. 845.

TE'NSION. *n. s.* [*tension*, Fr. *tensus*, Lat.] The act of stretching; not laxation; the state of being stretched; not laxity.

It can have nothing of vocal sound, voice being raised by stiff *tension* of the larynx; and on the contrary, this found by a relaxed posture of the muscles thereof. *Holder.*

Still are the subtle strings in *tension* found,
Like those of lutes, to just proportion wound,
Which of the air's vibration is the force. *Blackmore.*

TE'NSIVE *adj.* [*tensus*, Lat.] Giving a sensation of stiffness or contraction.

From choler is a hot burning pain; a beating pain from the pulse of the artery; a *tensive* pain from distention of the parts by the fulness of humours. *Floyer on Humours.*

TE'NSURE. *n. s.* [*tensus*, Lat.] The act of stretching, or state of being stretched; the contrary to laxation or laxity.

This motion upon pressure, and the reciprocal thereof, motion upon *tensure*, we call motion of liberty, which is, when any body being forced to a preternatural extent, restoreth itself to the natural. *Bacon.*

TENT. *n. s.* [*tente*, French; *tentorium*, Lat.]

1. A soldier's moveable lodging-place, commonly made of canvas extended upon poles.

The Turks, the more to terrify Corfu, taking a hill not far from it, covered the same with *tents*. *Knolles.*

Because of the same craft he wrought with them; for by occupation they were *tent* makers. *Acts* xviii. 23.

2. Any temporary habitation; a pavilion.

He saw a spacious plain, whereon
Were *tents* of various hue: by some were herds
Of cattle grazing. *Milton's Par. Lost*, *b.* xi.

To Chassis' pleasing plains he took his way,
There pitch'd his *tents*, and there resolv'd to stay. *Dryden.*

3. [*Tente*, French.] A roll of lint put into a sore.

Modest doubt is call'd
The beacon of the wise; the *tent* that searches
To th' bottom of the worst. *Shak. Troil. and Cressida.*

A declining orifice keep open by a small *tent* dipt in some medicaments, and after digestion withdraw the *tent* and heal it. *Wiseman's Surgery.*

4. [*Vino tinto*, Spanish.] A species of wine deeply red, chiefly from Gallicia in Spain.

To TENT. *v. n.* [from the noun.] To lodge as in a tent; to tabernacle.

The smiles of knaves
Tent in my cheeks, and schoolboy's tears take up
The glasses of my sight. *Shakespeare.*

To TENT. *v. a.* To search as with a medical tent.

I'll *tent* him to the quick; if he but blench,
I know my course. *Shakesp. Hamlet.*

I have some wounds upon me, and they smart.
—Well might they fester 'gainst ingratitude,
And *tent* themselves with death. *Shakesp. Coriolanus.*

Some surgeons, possibly against their own judgments, keep wounds *tented*, often to the ruin of their patient. *Wiseman.*

TENTA'TION. *n. s.* [*tentation*, French; *tentatio*, Lat.] Trial; temptation.

The first delusion satan put upon Eve, and his whole *tentation*, when he said ye shall not die, was in his equivocation, you shall not incur present death. *Brown's Vulgar Errours.*

TE'NTATIVE. *adj.* [*tentative*, effort, Fr. *tento*, Latin.] Trying; essaying.

TE'NTED. *adj.* [from *tent.*] Covered with tents.

These arms of mine till now have us'd
Their dearest action in the *tented* field. *Shak. Othello.*

The foe deceiv'd, he pass'd the *tented* plain,
In Troy to mingle with the hostile train. *Pope's Odyssey.*

TE'NTER. *n. s.* [*tendo*, *tentus*, Lat.]

1. A hook on which things are stretched.

2. *To be on the* TENTERS. To be on the stretch; to be in difficulties; to be in suspense.

In all my past adventures,
I ne'er was set so on the *tenters*;
Or taken tardy with dilemma,
That ev'ry way I turn does hem me. *Hudibras*, *p.* ii.

To TE'NTER. *v. a.* [from the noun.] To stretch by hooks.

A blown bladder pressed riseth again, and when leather or cloth is *tentered*, it springeth back. *Bacon's N. Hist.* N°. 12.

To TE'NTER. *v. n.* To admit; extension.

Woollen cloth will *tenter*, linen scarcely. *Bacon.*

TENTH. *adj.* [teoþa, Saxon.] First after the ninth; ordinal of ten.

It may be thought the less strange if others cannot do as much at the *tenth* or twentieth trial, as we did after much practice. *Boyle.*

TENTH. *n. s.* [from the adjective.]

1. The tenth part.

Of all the horses,
The treasure in the field atchiev'd, and city,
We render you the *tenth*. *Shakesp. Coriolanus.*

By decimation and a tithed death,
If thy revenges hunger for that food
Which nature loaths, take thou the destin'd *tenth*. *Shak.*

To purchase but the *tenth* of all their store,
Would make the mighty Persian monarch poor. *Dryden.*

Suppose half an ounce of silver now worth a bushel of wheat; but should there be next year a scarcity, five ounces of silver would purchase but one bushel: so that money would be then nine *tenths* less worth in respect of food. *Locke.*

2. Tithe.

With cheerful heart
The *tenth* of thy increase bestow, and own
Heav'n's bounteous goodness, that will sure repay
Thy grateful duty. *Philips.*

3. *Tenths* are that yearly portion or tribute which all livings ecclesiastical yield to the king. The bishop of Rome pretended right to this revenue by example of the high priest of the Jews, who had *tenths* from the Levites, till by Henry the eighth they were annexed perpetually to the crown. *Cowel.*

TE'NTHLY. *adv.* [from *tenth.*] In the tenth place.

TENTI'GINOUS. *adj.* [*tentiginis*, Lat.] Stiff; stretched.

TE'NTWORT. *n. s.* A plant. *Ainſ.*

TENUIFO'LIOUS. *adj.* [*tenuis* and *folium*, Lat.] Having thin leaves.

TENU'ITY. *n. s.* [*tenuité*, French; *tenuitas*, from *tenuis*, Lat.] Thinness; exility; smallness; minuteness; not grossness.

Firs and pines mount of themselves in height without side boughs; partly heat, and partly *tenuity* of juice, sending the sap upwards. *Bacon's Nat. Hist.* N°. 533.

The *tenuity* and contempt of clergymen will soon let them see what a poor carcass they are, when parted from the influence of that supremacy. *King Charles.*

Consider the divers figurings of the brain; the strings or filaments thereof; their difference in *tenuity*, or aptness for motion. *Glanville's Sceps.*

Aliment circulating through an animal body, is reduced to an almost imperceptible *tenuity*, before it can serve animal purposes. *Arbuthnot.*

At the height of four thousand miles the æther is of that wonderful *tenuity*, that if a small sphere of common air, of an inch diameter, should be expanded to the thinness of that æther, it would more than take up the orb of Saturn, which is many million times bigger than the earth. *Bentley.*

TE'NUOUS. *adj.* [*tenuis*, Lat.] Thin; small; minute.

Another way of their attraction is by a *tenuous* emanation, or continued effluvium, which after some distance retracteth unto itself. *Brown's Vulgar Err. b.* ii.

TENURE. *n. s.* [*teneo*, Lat. *tenure*, Fr. *tenura*, law Latin.]

Tenure is the manner whereby tenements are holden of their lords. In Scotland are four *tenures*; the first is pura eleemosina, which is proper to spiritual men, paying nothing for it, but devota animarum suffragia; the second they call feu, which holds of the king, church, barons, or others, paying a certain duty called feudi firma; the third is a holding in blanch by payment of a penny, rose, pair of gilt spurs, or some such thing, if asked; the fourth is by service of ward and relief, where the heir being minor is in the custody of his lord, together with his lands, &c. and land holden in this fourth manner is called feudum de hauberk or haubert, feudum militare or loricatum. *Tenure* in gross is the *tenure* in capite; for the crown is called a seignory in gross, because a corporation of and by itself. *Cowel.*

The service follows the *tenure* of lands; and the lands were given away by the kings of England to those lords. *Spenser.*

The uncertainty of *tenure*, by which all worldly things are held, ministers very unpleasant meditation. *Raleigh.*

Man must be known, his strength, his state,
And by that *tenure* he holds all of fate. *Dryden.*

TEPEFA'CTION. *n. s.* [*tepefacio*, Latin.] The act of warming to a small degree.

TE'PID. *adj.* [*tepidus*, Latin.] Lukewarm; warm in a small degree.

The *tepid* caves, and fens, and shores,
Their brood as numerous hatch. *Milton.*

He with his *tepid* rays the rose renews,
And licks the dropping leaves, and dries the dews. *Dryden.*

Such things as relax the skin are likewise sudorifick; as warm water, friction, and *tepid* vapours. *Arbuthnot.*

TEPI'DITY. *n. s.* [from *tepid.*] Lukewarmness. *Ainſ.*

TE'POR. *n. s.* [*tepor*, Lat.] Lukewarmness; gentle heat.

The small pox, mortal during such a season, grew more favourable by the *tepor* and moisture in April. *Arbuthnot.*

TERATO'LOGY. *n. s.* [τέρας and λέγω.] Bombast, affectation of false sublimity. *Bailey.*

TERCE. *n. s.* [*tierce*, Fr. *triens*, Latin.] A vessel containing forty-two gallons of wine; the third part of a butt or pipe. *Ainsw.*

TEREBI'NTHINATE. } *adj.* [*terebinthine*, Fr. *terebinthum*, Lat.]
TEREBI'NTHINE. } Consisting of turpentine; mixed with turpentine.

Salt serum may be evacuated by urine, by *terebinthinates*; as tops of pine in all our ale. *Floyer.*

To TE'REBRATE. *v. a.* [*terebro*, Latin.] To bore; to perforate; to pierce.

Consider the threefold effect of Jupiter's trisulk, to burn, discuss, and *terebrate*. *Brown's Vulgar Err. b.* ii.

Earth-worms are completely adapted to their way of life, for *terebrating* the earth, and creeping. *Derham.*

TEREBRA'TION. *n. s.* [from *terebrate*.] The act of boring or piercing.

Terebration of trees makes them prosper better; and also it maketh the fruit sweeter and better. *Bacon.*

TERGE'MINOUS. *adj.* [*tergeminus*, Lat.] Threefold.

TERGIVERSA'TION. *n. s.* [*tergum* and *verso*, Lat.]

1. Shift; subterfuge; evasion.

Writing is to be preferred before verbal conferences, as being freer from passions and *tergiversations*. *Bishop Bramhall.*

2. Change; fickleness.

The colonel, after all his *tergiversations*, lost his life in the king's service. *Clarendon.*

TERM. *n. s.* [*terminus*, Latin.]

1. Limit; boundary.

Corruption is a reciprocal to generation; and they two are as nature's two *terms* or boundaries, and the guides to life and death. *Bacon's Nat. Hist.* N°. 328.

2. [*Terme*, Fr.] The word by which a thing is expressed. A word of art.

To apply notions philosophical to plebeian *terms*, or to say, where the notions cannot fitly be reconciled, that there wanteth a *term* or nomenclature for it, be but shifts of ignorance. *Bacon.*

Those parts of nature into which the chaos was divided, they signified by dark and obscure names, which we have expressed in their plain and proper *terms*. *Burnet.*

In painting, the greatest beauties cannot always be expressed for want of *terms*. *Dryden.*

Had the Roman tongue continued vulgar, it would have been necessary, from the many *terms* of art required in trade and in war, to have made great additions to it. *Swift.*

3. Words; language.

Would curses kill, as doth the mandrakes groan,
I would invent as bitter searching *terms*,
As curst, as harsh, as horrible to hear. *Shakespeare.*

God to satan first his doom apply'd,
Though in mysterious *terms*. *Milton.*

4. Condition; stipulation.

Well, on my *terms* thou wilt not be my heir? *Dryden.*

Enjoy thy love, since such is thy desire,
Live though unhappy, live on any *terms*. *Dryden.*

Did religion bestow heaven without any *terms* or conditions, indifferently upon all, there would be no infidel. *Bentley.*

We flattered ourselves with reducing France to our own *terms* by the want of money, but have been still disappointed by the great sums imported from America. *Addison.*

5. [*Termine*, old French.] Time for which any thing lasts; a limited time.

I am thy father's spirit,
Doom'd for a certain *term* to walk the night. *Shakespeare.*

Why should Rome fall a moment ere her time:
No; let us draw her *term* of freedom out
In its full length, and spin it to the last. *Addison.*

6. [In law.] The time in which the tribunals, or places of judgment, are open to all that list to complain of wrong, or to seek their right by course of law or action; the rest of the year is called vacation. Of these *terms* there are four in every year, during which matters of justice are dispatched: one is called Hillary *term*, which begins the twenty-third of January, or, if that be Sunday, the next day following, and ends the twenty-first of February; another is called Easter *term*, which begins eighteen days after Easter, and ends the Monday next after Ascension-day; the third is Trinity *term*, beginning the Friday next after Trinity Sunday, and ending the Wednesday-fortnight after; the fourth is Michaelmas *term*, beginning the sixth of November, or, if that be Sunday, the next day after, and ending the twenty-eighth of November. *Cowel.*

The *term* suiters may speed their business: for the end of these sessions delivereth them space enough to overtake the beginning of the *terms*. *Carew.*

Too long vacation hasten'd on his *term*. *Milton.*

Those men employed as justices daily in *term* time consult with one another. *Hale.*

What are these to those vast heaps of crimes
Which *terms* prolong. *Dryden.*

To TERM. *v. a.* [from the noun.] To name; to call.

Men *term* what is beyond the limits of the universe imaginary space, as if no body existed in it. *Locke.*

TE'RMAGANCY. *n. s.* [from *termagant*.] Turbulence; tumultuousness.

By a violent *termagancy* of temper, she may never suffer him to have a moment's peace. *Barker.*

TE'RMAGANT. *adj.* [tyr and magan, Saxon, *eminently powerful*.]

1. Tumultuous; turbulent.

'Twas time to counterfeit, or that hot *termagant* Scot had paid me scot and lot too. *Shakesp. Henry* IV. *p.* i.

2. Quarrelsome; scolding; furious.

The eldest was a *termagant*, imperious, prodigal, profligate wench. *Arbuthnot's Hist. of John Bull.*

TE'RMAGANT. *n. s.* A scold; a brawling turbulent woman. It appears in *Shakespeare* to have been anciently used of men.

I could have such a fellow whipt for o'erdoing *termagant*; it outherod's Herod. *Shakespeare's Hamlet.*

For zeal's a dreadful *termagant*,
That teaches saints to tear and rant. *Hudibras, p.* iii.

She threw his periwig into the fire: well, said he, thou art a brave *termagant*. *Tatler*, N°. 54.

The sprites of fiery *termagants* in flame
Mount up, and take a salamander's name. *Pope.*

TE'RMER. *n. s.* [from *term*.] One who travels up to the term.

Nor have my title leaf on posts or walls,
Or in cleft sticks, advanced to make calls
For *te mers*, or some clerk-like serving man. *B. Johnson.*

TE'RMINABLE. *adj.* [from *terminate*.] Limitable; that admits of bounds.

To TE'RMINATE. *v. a.* [*termino*, Lat. *terminer*, Fr.]

1. To bound; to limit.

Bodies that are solid, separable, *terminated* and moveable, have all sorts of figures. *Locke.*

2. To put an end to: as, *to* terminate *any difference*.

To TE'RMINATE. *v. n.* To be limited; to end; to have an end; to attain its end.

That God was the maker of this visible world was evident from the very order of causes; the greatest argument by which natural reason evinces a God: it being necessary in such a chain of causes to ascend to, and *terminate* in, some first; which should be the original of motion, and the cause of all other things, but itself be caused by none. *South.*

The wisdom of this world, its designs and efficacy, *te minate* on this side heaven. *South's Sermons.*

Ere I the rapture of my wish renew,
I tell you then, it *terminates* in you. *Dryden's Aurengzebe.*

TERMINA'TION. *n. s.* [from *terminate*.]

1. The act of limiting or bounding.

2. Bound; limit.

Its earthly and salinous parts are so exactly resolved, that its body is left imporous, and not discreted by atomical *terminations*. *Brown's Vulgar Errours, b.* ii.

3. End; conclusion.

4. [In grammar; *terminatio*, Latin; *terminaison*, Fr.] End of words as varied by their significations.

Those rude heaps of words and *terminations* of an unknown tongue, would have never been so happily learnt by heart without some smoothing artifice. *Watts.*

5. Word; term. Not in use.

She speaks poniards, and every word stabs; if her breath were as terrible as her *te minations*, there were no living near her, she would infect to the North star. *Shakespeare.*

TERMI'NTHUS. *n. s.* [τέρμινθος.] A tumour.

Terminthus is of a blackish colour; it breaks, and within a day the pustule comes away in a slough. *Wiseman.*

TE'RMLESS. *adj.* [from *te m*.] Unlimited; boundless.

These betraying lights look not up towards *termless* joys, nor down towards endless sorrows. *Raleigh.*

TE'RMLY. *adv.* [from *te m*.] Term by term; every term.

The fees or allowances that are *termly* given to these deputies I pretermit. *Bacon.*

The clerks are partly rewarded by that means also, besides that *termly* fee which they are allowed. *Bacon.*

TE'RNARY. *adj.* [*ternaire*, Fr. *ternarius*, Lat.] Proceeding by threes; consisting of three.

TE'RNARY. } *n. s.* [*terna ius*, Lat. *ternio*, Lat.] The num-
TE'RNION. } ber three.

These nineteen consonants stood in such confused order, some in *ternaries*, some in pairs, and some single. *Holder.*

TE'RRACE. *n. s.* [*terrace*, French; *terraccia*, Italian.] A small mount of earth covered with grass.

He made her gardens not only within the palaces, but upon *te rasses* raised with earth over the arched roofs, planted with all sorts of fruits. *Temple.*

Fear broke my slumbers, I no longer stay,
But mount the *terrace*, thence the town survey. *Dryden.*

To TE'RRACE. *v. a.* [from the noun.]

The reception of light into the body of the building must now be supplied, by *terracing* any story which is in danger of darkness. *Wotton's Architecture.*

Clermont's *terrac'd* height and Esher's groves. *Thomson.*

TERRA'QUEOUS. *adj.* [*terra* and *aqua*, Latin.] Composed of land and water.

The

The *terraqueous* globe is, to this day, nearly in the same condition that the universal deluge left it. *Woodward.*

TERRE'NE. *adj.* [*terrenus*, Lat.] Earthly; terrestrial.

They think that the same rules of decency which serve for things done unto *terrene* powers, should universally decide what is fit in the service of God. *Hooker, b.* v.

Our *terrene* moon is now eclips'd,
And it portends alone the fall of Antony. *Shakespeare.*

God set before him a mortal and immortal life, a nature cœlestial and *terrene*; but God gave man to himself. *Raleigh.*

Over many a tract
Of heav'n they march'd, and many a province wide,
Tenfold the length of this *terrene*. *Milton's Par. Lost.*

TE'RRE-BLUE. *n. s.* [*terre* and *bleu*, Fr.] A sort of earth.

Terre-blue is a light, loose, friable kind of lapis armenus. *Woodward's Meth. Fossils.*

TE'RRE-VERTE. n. s. [French.] A sort of earth.

Terre-verte owes its colour to a slight admixture of copper. *Woodward's Meth. Fossils.*

Terre-verte, or green earth, is light; it is a mean betwixt yellow ochre and ultramarine. *Dryden's Dufresnoy.*

TE'RREOUS. *adj.* [*terreus*, Lat.] Earthy; consisting of earth.

There is but little similitude betwixt a *terreous* humidity and plantal germinations. *Glanville's Scep.*

According to the temper of the *terreous* parts at the bottom, variously begin intumescencies. *Brown's Vulgar Err.*

TERRE'STRIAL. *adj.* [*terrestris*, Lat.]

1. Earthly; not cœlestial.

Far passing th' height of men *terrestrial*,
Like an huge giant of the Titan race. *Spenser.*

Terrestrial heav'n! danc'd round by other heav'ns
That shine, yet bear their bright officious lamps,
Light above light. *Milton.*

Thou brought'st Briareus with his hundred hands,
So call'd in heav'n; but mortal men below
By his *terrestrial* name Ægeon know. *Dryden.*

2. Consisting of earth; terreous. Improper.

I did not confine these observations to land or *terrestrial* parts of the globe, but extended them to the fluids. *Woodw.*

To TERRE'STRIFY. *v. a.* [*terrestris* and *facio*, Latin.] To reduce to the state of earth.

Though we should affirm, that heaven were but earth celestified, and earth but heaven *terrestrified*; or, that each part above had an influence on its divided affinity below; yet to single out these relations is a work to be effected by revelation. *Brown's Vulgar Errours, b.* iv.

TERRE'STRIOUS. *adj.* [*terrestris*, Lat. *terrestre*, Fr.] Terreous; earthy; consisting of earth.

This variation proceedeth from *terrestrious* eminences of earth respecting the needle. *Brown.*

TE'RRIBLE. *adj.* [*terrible*, Fr. from *terribilis*, Lat.]

1. Dreadful; formidable; causing fear.

Was this a face to be expos'd
In the most *terrible* and nimble stroke
Of quick, cross lightning. *Shakesp. King Lear.*

Fit love for gods
Not *terrible*, though terrour be in love. *Milton.*

Thy native Latium was thy darling care,
Prudent in peace, and *terrible* in war. *Prior.*

2. Great so as to offend: a colloquial hyperbole.

Being indispos'd by the *terrible* coldness of the season, he reposed himself till the weather should mend. *Clarendon.*

I began to be in a *terrible* fear of him, and to look upon myself as a dead man. *Tillotson.*

TE'RRIBLENESS. *n. s.* [from *terrible.*] Formidableness; the quality of being terrible: dreadfulness.

Having quite lost the way of nobleness, he strove to climb to the height of *terribleness*. *Sidney, b.* ii.

Their *terribleness* is owing to the violent contusion and laceration of the parts. *Sharp's Surgery.*

TE'RRIBLY. *n. s.* [from *terrible.*]

1. Dreadfully; formidably; so as to raise fear.

The polish'd steel gleams *terribly* from far,
And every moment nearer shows the war. *Dryden.*

2. Violently; very much.

The poor man squalled *terribly*. *Gulliver's Travels.*

TE'RRIER. *n. s.* [*terrier*, Fr. from *terra*, earth.]

1. A dog that follows his game under-ground.

The fox is earth'd, but I shall send my two *terriers* in after him. *Dryden's Spanish Fryar.*

2. [*Terrier*, Fr.] A survey or register of lands.

King James's canons require that the bishops procure a *terrier* to be taken of such lands. *Ayliffe.*

3. [From *terebro*, Lat.] A wimble; auger or borer. *Ains.*

TERRI'FICK. *adj.* [*terrificus*, Latin.] Dreadful; causing terrour.

The serpent, subtlest beast of all the field,
Of huge extent sometimes, with brazen eyes
And hairy mane *terrifick*. *Milton's Par. Lost, b.* vii.

The British navy through ocean vast
Shall wave her double cross, t' extremest climes
Terrifick. *Philips.*

To TE'RRIFY. *v. a.* [*terror* and *facio*, Latin.] To fright; to shock with fear; to make afraid.

Thou scarest me with dreams, and *terrifiest* me through visions. *Job* vii. 14.

Simon slandered Onias, as if he had *terrified* Heliodorus. 2 *Mac.* iv. 1.

In nothing *terrified* by your adversaries. *Phil.* i. 28.

Neither doth it beseem this most wealthy state to be *terrified* from that which is right with any charges of war. *Knolles.*

The amazing difficulty of his account will rather *terrify* than inform him, and keep him from setting heartily about such a task as he despairs ever to go through with. *South.*

Meteors for various purposes to form;
The breeze to cheer, to *terrify* the storm. *Blackmore.*

TE'RRITORY. *n. s.* [*territorium*, law Latin; *territoire*, Fr.] Land; country; dominion; district.

Linger not in my *territories* longer than swiftest expedition will give thee time to leave our royal court. *Shakespeare.*

They erected a house within their own *territory*, half way between their fort and the town. *Hayward.*

He saw wide *territory* spread
Before him, towns, and rural works between. *Milton.*

Ne'er did the Turk invade our *territory*,
But fame and terror doubl'd still their files. *Denham.*

Arts and sciences took their rise, and flourished only in those small *territories* where the people were free. *Swift.*

TE'RROUR. *n. s.* [*terror*, Lat. *terreur*, Fr.]

1. Fear communicated.

Amaze and *terrour* seiz'd the rebel host. *Milton.*

The thunder when to roll
With *terrour* through the dark aerial hall. *Milton.*

2. Fear received.

It is the cowish *terrour* of his spirit
That dares not undertake. *Shakesp. King Lear.*

They shot thorough both the walls of the town and the bulwark also, to the great *terrour* of the defendants. *Knolles.*

They with conscious *terrours* vex me round. *Milton.*

O sight
Of *terrour*, foul and ugly to behold,
Horrid to think, how horrible to feel. *Milton.*

The pleasures and *terrours* of the main. *Blackmore.*

3 The cause of fear.

Lords of the street, and *terrours* of the way. *Anonym.*

Those enormous *terrours* of the Nile. *Prior.*

So spake the griesly *terrour*. *Milton.*

TERSE. *adj.* [*ters*, Fr. *tersus*, Lat.]

1. Smooth.

Many stones precious and vulgar, although *terse* and smooth, have not this power attractive. *Brown's Vulgar Err.*

2 Cleanly written; neat; elegant without pompousness.

To raw numbers and unfinish'd verse,
Sweet sound is added now to make it *terse*. *Dryden.*

These accomplishments in the pulpit appear by a quaint, *terse*, florid style, rounded into periods without propriety or meaning. *Swift's Miscel.*

TE'RTIAN. *n. s.* [*tertiana*, Lat.] Is an ague intermitting but one day, so that there are two fits in three days.

Tertians of a long continuance do most menace this symptom. *Harvey on Consumptions.*

To TE'RTIATE. *v. a.* [*tertio*, *tertius*, Lat.] To do any thing the third time.

TESSE'LLATED. *adj.* [*tessella*, Lat.] Variegated by squares.

Van Helmont produced a stone very different from the *tessellated* pyrites. *Woodward on Fossils.*

TEST. *n. s.* [*test*, Fr. *testa*, Italian.]

1. The cupel by which refiners try their metals.

2. Trial; examination: as by the cupel.

All thy vexations
Were but my trials of thy love, and thou
Hast strangely stood the *test*. *Shakespeare's Tempest.*

Let there be some more *test* made of my metal,
Before so noble and so great a figure
Be stampt upon it. *Shakesp. Meas. for Measure.*

They who thought worst of the Scots, did not think there would be no fruit or discovery from that *test*. *Clarendon.*

What use of oaths, of promise, or of *test*,
Where men regard no God but interest. *Waller.*

Thy virtue, prince, has stood the *test* of fortune
Like purest gold, that, tortur'd in the furnace,
Comes out more bright, and brings forth all its weight. *Add.*

3. Means of trial.

Whom should my muse then fly to, but the best
Of kings for grace; of poets for my *test*. *B. Johnson.*

To be read herself she need not fear;
Each *test*, and every light, her muse will bear. *Dryden.*

4. That with which any thing is compared in order to prove its genuineness.

Unerring Nature, still divinely bright,
One clear, unchang'd and universal light,
Life, force, and beauty, must to all impart,
At once the source, and end, and *test* of art. *Pope.*

5. Discriminative

5. Discriminative characteristick.

Our penal laws no sons of yours admit,
Our *test* excludes your tribe from benefit. *Dryden.*

6. Judgment; distinction.

Who would excel, when few can make a *test*,
Betwixt indiff'rent writing and the best? *Dryden.*

7. It seems to signify any vessel that holds fire.

Your noble race
We banish not, but they forsake the place:
Our doors are open: True, but ere they come,
You toss your 'censing *test*, and fume the room. *Dryden.*

TESTA'CEOUS. *adj.* [*testaceus*, Lat. *testacée*, Fr.]

1. Consisting of shells; composed of shells.
2. Having continous; not jointed shells; opposed to crustaceous.

Testaceous, with naturalists, is a term given only to such fish whose strong and thick shells are entire, and of a piece; because those which are joined, as the lobsters, are crustaceous: but in medicine all preparations of shells, and substances of the like kind, are thus called. *Quincy.*

Several shells were found upon the shores, of the crustaceous and *testaceous* kind. *Woodward's Nat. Hist.*

The mineral particles in these shells is plainly to be distinguished from the *testaceous* ones, or the texture and substance of the shell. *Woodward's Nat. Hist.*

TE'STAMENT. *n. s.* [*testament*. Fr. *testamentum*, Lat.]

1. A will; any writing directing the disposal of the possessions of a man deceased.

He bringeth arguments from the love which always the testator bore him, imagining that these, or the like proofs, will convict a *testament* to have that in it which other men can nowhere by reading find. *Hooker, b.* iii.

All the temporal lands, which men devout
By *testament* have given to the church,
Would they strip from us. *Shakesp. Henry* V.

He ordained by his last *testament*, that his Æneis should be burnt. *Dryden.*

2. The name of each of the volumes of the holy scripture.

TESTAME'NTARY. *adj.* [*testamentaire*, French; *testamentarius*, Lat.] Given by will; contained in wills.

How many *testamentary* charities have been defeated by the negligence or fraud of executors? by the suppression of a will? the subornation of witnesses, or the corrupt sentence of a judge? *Atterbury's Sermons.*

TE'STATE. *adj.* [*testatus*, Lat.] Having made a will.

By the canon law, the bishop had the lawful distribution of the goods of persons dying *testate* and intestate. *Ayliffe.*

TESTA'TOR. *n. s.* [*testator*, Lat. *testateur*, French.] One who leaves a will.

He bringeth arguments from the love or good-will which always the *testator* bore him. *Hooker, b.* iii.

The same is the case of a *testator* giving a legacy by kindness, or by promise and common right. *Taylor.*

TESTA'TRIX. n. s. [Latin.] A woman who leaves a will.

TE'STED. *adj.* [from *test*.] Tried by a test.

Not with fond shekels of the *tested* gold. *Shakespeare.*

TE'STER. *n. s.* [*teste*, French, a head: this coin probably being distinguished by the head stamped upon it.]

1. A sixpence.

Come manage me your caliver: hold, there is a *tester* for thee. *Shakespeare's Henry* IV. *p.* ii.

A crown goes for sixty pence, a shilling for twelve pence, and a *tester* for sixpence. *Locke.*

Those who bore bulwarks on their backs,
And guarded nations from attacks,
Now practise ev'ry pliant gesture,
Op'ning their trunk for ev'ry *tester*. *Swift's Miscel.*

Young man your days can ne'er be long,
In flow'r of age you perish for a song;
Plums and directors, Shylock and his wife,
Will club their *testers* now to take thy life. *Pope.*

2. The cover of a bed.

TE'STICLE. *n. s.* [*testiculus*, Lat.] Stone.

That a bever, to escape the hunter, bites off his *testicles* or stones, is a tenent very antient. *Brown's Vulg. Err.*

The more certain sign from the pains reaching to the groins and *testicles*. *Wiseman's Surgery.*

TESTIFICA'TION. *n. s.* [*testificatio*, Lat. from *testify*.] The act of witnessing.

When together we have all received those heavenly mysteries wherein Christ imparteth himself unto us, and giveth visible *testification* of our blessed communion with him, we should, in hatred of all heresies, factions, and schisms, declare openly ourselves united. *Hooker, b.* v.

In places solemnly dedicated for that purpose, is a more direct service and *testification* of our homage to God. *South.*

TESTIFICA'TOR. *n. s.* [from *testificor*, Latin.] One who witnesses.

TE'STIFIER. *n. s.* [from *testify*.] One who testifies.

To TE'STIFY. *v. n.* [*testificor*, Lat.] To witness; to prove; to give evidence.

Jesus needed not that any should *testify* of man; for he knew what was in man. *John* ii. 25.

One witness shall not *testify* against any, to cause him t[o] die. *Num.* xxxv. 3[0]

Heaven and earth shall *testify* for us, that you put us t[o] death wrongfully. 1 *Mac.* ii. 47

Th' event was dire,
As this place *testifies*. *Milton's Par. Lost, b.* i

To TE'STIFY. *v. a.* To witness; to give evidence of an[y] point.

We speak that we do know, and *testify* that we have seen and ye receive not our witness. *John* iii. 11

TE'STILY. *adv.* [from *testy*.] Fretfully; peevishly; morosely.

TESTIMO'NIAL. *n. s.* [*testimonial*, Fr. *testimonium*, Lat.] A writing produced by any one as an evidence for himself.

Hospitable people entertain all the idle vagrant reports, an[d] send them out with passports and *testimonials*, and will hav[e] them pass for legitimate. *Government of the Tongue*

It is possible to have such *testimonials* of divine authority a[s] may be sufficient to convince the more reasonable part o[f] mankind, and pray what is wanting in the testimonies o[f] Jesus Christ? *Burnet's Theory of the Earth*

A clerk does not exhibit to the bishop letters missive or *testimonial*, testifying his good behaviour. *Ayliffe*

TE'STIMONY. *n. s.* [*testimonium*, Latin.]

1. Evidence given; proof.

The proof of every thing must be by the *testimony* of such as the parties produce. *Spenser*

If I bring you sufficient *testimony*, my ten thousand ducat[s] are mine. *Shakespeare's Cymbeline*

I could not answer it to the world, if I gave not you[r] lordship my *testimony* of being the best husband. *Dryden*

I must bear this *testimony* to Otway's memory, that th[e] passions are truly touched in his Venice Preserved. *Dryden*

2. Publick evidences.

By his prescript a sanctuary is fram'd,
An ark and in the ark his *testimony*;
The records of his covenant. *Milton*

3. Open attestation; profession.

Thou for the *testimony* of truth hast born
Universal reproach. *Milton*

To TE'STIMONY. *v. a.* To witness. A word not used.

Let him be but *testimonied* in his own bringings forth, and he shall appear a scholar, a statesman, and a soldier. *Shakesp*

TE'STINESS. *n. s.* [from *testy*.] Moroseness.

Testiness is a disposition or aptness to be angry. *Locke.*

TESTU'DINATED. *adj.* [*testudo*, Lat.] Roofed; arched.

TESTUDI'NEOUS. *adj.* [*testudo*, Lat.] Resembling the shell o[f] a tortoise.

TE'STY. *adj.* [*testie*, Fr. *testurdo*, Italian.] Fretful; peevish; apt to be angry.

Lead these *testy* rivals so astray,
As one come not within another's way. *Shakespeare.*

Must I stand and crouch under your *testy* humour? *Shak.*

King Pyrrhus cur'd his splenetick
And *testy* courtiers with a kick. *Hudibras, p.* ii.

Averse or *testy* in nothing they desire. *Locke.*

In all thy humours, whether grave or mellow,
Thou'rt such a touchy, *testy*, pleasing fellow;
Hast so much wit, and mirth, and spleen about thee,
There is no living with thee, nor without thee. *Tatler.*

TE'TCHY. *adj.* Froward; peevish: a corruption of *testy* o[r] *touchy*.

A grievous burthen was thy birth to me,
Tetchy and wayward was thy infancy. *Shak. Rich.* III.

A silly school-boy, coming to say my lesson to the world, that peevish and *tetchy* master. *Graunt.*

TETE A TETE. n. s. [French.] Cheek by jowl.

Long before the squire and dame
Are *tête à tête*. *Prior.*

Deluded mortals, whom the great
Chuse for companions *tête à tête*;
Who at their dinners, en famille,
Get leave to sit whene'er you will. *Swift's Miscel.*

TE'THER. *n. s.* [See TEDDER.] A string by which horses are held from pasturing too wide.

Hamlet is young,
And with a larger *tether* he may walk
Than may be given you. *Shakespeare.*

Fame and censure with a *tether*,
By fate are always link'd together. *Swift's Miscel.*

Imagination has no limits; but where it is confined, we find the shortness of our *tether*. *Swift.*

To TE'THER. *v. a.* [from the noun.] To tie up.

TETRA'GONAL. *adj.* [τετράγωνος.] Four square.

From the beginning of the disease, reckoning on unto the seventh day, the moon will be in a *tetragonal* or quadrate aspect, that is, four signs removed from that wherein the disease began; in the fourteenth day it will be an opposite aspect, and at the end of the third septenary *tetragonal* again. *Brown's Vulgar Errours, b.* iv.

TETRAPE'TALOUS. *adj.* [τέσσαρες and πέταλον.] Are such flowers as consist of four leaves round the style: plants having a *tetrapetalous* flower constitute a distinct kind. *Miller.*

All the *tetrapetalous* siliquose plants are alkalescent. *Arbuth.*

TE'TRARCH. *n. s.* [*tetrarcha*, Lat. *tetrarque*, Fr. τετράρχης.] A Roman governor of the fourth part of a province.

All the earth,
Her kings and *tet archs*, are their tributaries:
People and nations pay them hourly stipends. *B. Johnson.*

TETRA'RCHATE. } *n. s.* [τετραρχία.] A Roman government.
TE'TRARCHY. }

TETRA'STICK. *n. s.* [τετράστιχος.] An epigram or stanza of four verses.

The *tetrastick* obliged Spenser to extend his sense to the length of four lines, which would have been more closely confined in the couplet. *Pope.*

TE'TRICAL. } *adj.* [*tetricus*, Latin; *tetrique*, Fr.] Froward; perverse; sour.
TE'TRICOUS. }

In this the *tetrical* bassa finding him to excel, gave him as a rare gift to Solyman. *Knolles's Hist. of the Turks.*

TE'TTER. *n. s.* [teteꞃ, Saxon.] A scab; a scurf; a ringworm.

A most instant *tetter* bark'd about
Most lazar like, with vile and loathsome crust,
All my smooth body. *Shakesp. Hamlet.*
A scabby *tetter* on their pelts will stick. *Dryden.*

TEW. *n. s.* [*towe*, a hempen rope, Dutch.]
1. Materials for any thing. *Skinner.*
2. An iron chain. *Ainf.*

To TEW. *v. a.* [tapian, Saxon.] To work; to beat so as to soften.

TE'WEL. *n. s.* [*tuyau* or *tuyal*, French.]

In the back of the forge, against the fire-place, is fixed a thick iron plate, and a taper pipe in it above five inches long, called a *tewel*, or *tewel* iron, which comes through the back of the forge; into this *tewel* is placed the bellows. *Moxon.*

To TE'WTAW. *v. a.* [formed from *tew* by reduplication.] To beat; to break.

The method and way of watering, pilling, breaking, and *tewtawing*, of hemp and flax, is a particular business. *Mort.*

TEXT. *n. s.* [*texte*, Fr. *textus*, Lat.]
1. That on which a comment is written.

We expect your next
Shou'd be no comment but a *text*,
To tell how modern beasts are vext. *Waller.*

2. A sentence of scripture.

In religion
What errour but some sober brow
Will bless it, and approve it with a *text*. *Shakespeare.*

His mind he should fortify with some few *texts*, which are home and apposite to his case. *South's Sermons.*

TE'XTILE. *adj.* [*textilis*, Latin.] Woven; capable of being woven.

The placing of the tangible parts in length or tranverse, as in the warp and woof of *textiles*. *Bacon's Nat. Hist.*

The materials of them were not from any herb, as other *textiles*, but from a stone called amiantus. *Wilkins.*

TE'XTMAN. *n. s.* [*text* and *man.*] A man ready in quotation of texts.

Mens daily occasions require the doing of a thousand things, which it would puzzle the best *textman* readily to bethink himself of a sentence in the Bible, clear enough to satisfy a scrupulous conscience of the lawfulness of. *Sanderson.*

TE'XTRINE. *adj.* [*textrina*, Lat.] Relating to weaving.

It is a wonderful artifice how newly hatched maggots, not the parent animal, because she emits no web, nor hath any *textrine* art, can convolve the stubborn leaf, and bind it with the thread it weaves from its body. *Derham.*

TE'XTUARY. *adj.* [from *text.*]
1. Contained in the text.

He extends the exclusion unto twenty days, which in the *textuary* sense is fully accomplished in one. *Brown.*

2. Serving as a text; authoritative.

I see no ground why his reason should be *textuary* to ours, or that God intended him an universal headship. *Glanville.*

TE'XTUARIST. } *n. s.* [*textuaire*, Fr. from *text.*] One ready in the text of scripture; a divine well versed in scripture.
TE'XTUARY. }

TE'XTURE. *n. s.* [*textus*, Lat.]
1. The act of weaving.

Skins, although a natural habit unto all before the invention of *texture*, was something more unto Adam. *Brown.*

2. A web; a thing woven.

Others, far in the grassy dale,
Their humble *texture* weave. *Thomson's Spring.*

3. Manner of weaving with respect either to form or matter.

Under state of richest *texture* spread. *Milton.*
A veil of richest *texture* wrought she wears. *Pope.*

4. Disposition of the parts of bodies; combination of parts.

Spirits not in their liquid *texture* mortal wound
Receive, no more than can third air. *Milton.*

While the particles continue entire, they may compose bodies of the same nature and *texture* now, with water and earth composed of entire particles in the beginning. *Newton.*

THAN. *adv.* [ðanne, Saxon.] A particle placed in comparison after the comparative adverb.

Were we not better to fall once with virtue,
Than draw a wretched and dishonour'd breath. *B. Johnson.*
More true delight in that small ground,
Than in possessing all the earth was found. *Daniel.*

I never met with a more unhappy conjuncture of affairs *than* in the business of that unfortunate earl. *King Charles.*

He lov'd her more *than* plunder. *Congreve.*

I love you for nothing more *than* for the just esteem you have for all the sons of Adam. *Swift.*

THANE. *n. s.* [ðegn, Saxon.] An old title of honour, perhaps equivalent to baron.

By Sinel's death I know I'm *thane* of Glamis;
But how of Cawdor? the *thane* of Cawdor lives. *Shakesp.*

To THANK. *v. a.* [ðancian, Saxon; *dancken*, Dutch; *thanken*, German.]
1. To return acknowledgments for any favour or kindness.

The forlorn soldier, that so nobly fought,
He would have well become this place, and grac'd
The *thankings* of a king. *Shakesp. Cymbeline.*
For your stubborn answer
The king shall know it, and, no doubt, *thank* you. *Shak.*

We *thank* God always for you. *2 Thes.* i. 3.

He was so true a father of his country,
To *thank* me for defending ev'n his foes,
Because they were his subjects. *Dryden's Spanish Fryar.*

2. It is used often in a contrary or ironical sense.

Ill fare our ancestor impure,
For this we may *thank* Adam. *Milton.*
Weigh the danger with the doubtful bliss,
And *thank* yourself, if ought should fall amiss. *Dryden.*

That Portugal hath yet no more than a suspension of arms; they may *thank* themselves, because they came so late into the treaty; and, that they came so late, they may *thank* the whigs, whose false representations they believed. *Swift.*

THANK. } *n. s.* [ðancaꞃ, Saxon; *dancke*, Dutch.] Acknowledgment paid for favour or kindness; expression of gratitude. *Thanks* is commonly used of verbal acknowledgment, *gratitude* of real repayment. It is seldom used in the singular.
THANKS. }

The poorest service is repaid with *thanks*. *Shakespeare.*
Happy be Theseus, our renowned duke.
—*Thanks*, good Egeus, what's the news? *Shakespeare.*

The fool saith, I have no *thank* for all my good deed; and they that eat my bread speak evil of me. *Eccluf.* xx. 16.

He took bread, and gave *thanks* to God in presence of them all. *Acts* xxvii. 35.

Thanks be to God, which giveth us the victory. 1 *Cor.* xv.

Some embrace suits which never mean to deal effectually in them; but they will win a *thank*, or take a reward. *Bacon.*

For this to th' infinitely good we owe
Immortal *thanks*. *Milton.*

THA'NKFUL. *adj.* [ðancꝑul, Saxon.] Full of gratitude; ready to acknowledge good received.

Be *thankful* unto him, and bless his name. *Psal.* c. 4.

In favour, to use men with much difference is good; for it maketh the persons preferred more *thankful*, and the rest more officious. *Bacon's Essays.*

Live, thou great encourager of arts;
Live ever in our *thankful* hearts. *Dryden.*

THA'NKFULLY. *adv.* [from *thankful.*] With lively and grateful sense of good received.

Here is better than the open air; take it *thankfully*. *Shak.*

If you have liv'd, take *thankfully* the past;
Make, as you can, the sweet remembrance last. *Dryden.*

Out of gold how to draw as many distinct substances as I can separate from vitriol, I shall very *thankfully* learn. *Boyle.*

THA'NKFULNESS. *n. s.* [from *thankful.*] Gratitude; lively sense or ready acknowledgment of good received.

He scarcely would give me thanks for what I had done, for fear that *thankfulness* might have an introduction of reward. *Sidney, b.* ii.

Will you give me this maid your daughter?
—As freely, son, as God did give her me.
—Sweet prince, you learn me noble *thankfulness*. *Shakesp.*

The celebration of these holy mysteries being ended, retire with all *thankfulness* of heart for having been admitted to that heavenly feast. *Taylor.*

Thankfulness and submission make us happy. *L'Estrange.*

THA'NKLESS. *adj.* [from *thank.*]
1. Unthankful; ungrateful; making no acknowledgment.

Least so great good, as he for her had wrought,
Should die unknown, and buried be in *thankless* thought.
Fairy Queen, b. i.

May he feel
How sharper than a serpent's tooth it is,
To have a *thankless* child. *Shakesp. King Lear.*

Blest in thy genius, in thy love too blest!
One grateful woman to thy fame supply'd,
What a whole *thankless* land to his deny'd. *Pope.*

2. Not deserving, or not likely, to gain thanks.

The contracting and extending the lines and sense of others, if if the first authors might speak for themselves, would appear a *thankless* office. *Wotton.*

Wage still their wars,
And bring home on thy breast more *thankless* scars. *Crashaw.*

THA'NKLESSNESS. *n. s.* [from *thankless.*] Ingratitude; Failure to acknowledge good received.

Not t' have written then, seems little less
Than worst of civil vices, *thanklessness.* *Donne.*

THANKO'FFERING. *n. s.* [*thank* and *offering.*] Offering paid in acknowledgment of mercy.

A thousand *thank-offerings* are due to that providence which has delivered our nation from these absurd iniquities. *Watts.*

THANKSGI'VING. *n. s.* [*thanks* and *give.*] Celebration of mercy.

These sacred hymns Christianity hath peculiar to itself, the other being songs too of praise and *thanksgiving*, wherewith as we serve God so the Jews likewise. *Hooker, b.* v.

tude; meritorious.

Of old there were songs of praise and *thanksgiving* unto God. *Neh.* xii. 46.

We should acknowledge our obligations to God for the many favours we receive, by continual praises and *thanksgivings.* *Tillotson's Sermons.*

THA'NKWORTHY. *adj.* [*thank* and *worthy.*] Deserving grati-

This is *thankworthy*, if a man endure grief. 1 *Pet.* ii. 19.

If love be compell'd, and cannot chuse,
How can it grateful, or *thank-worthy* prove? *Davies.*

THARM. *n. s.* [ðeaꞃm, Saxon; *darm*, Dutch, the gut.] Intestines twisted for several uses.

THAT, pronoun. [*thata*, Gothick; ðæt, Saxon; *dat*, Dutch.]

1. Not this, but the other.

He wins me by *that* means I told you. *Shakespeare.*
Octavia, not only *that*,
That were excuseable, *that* and thousands more
Of semblable import, but he hath wag'd
New wars against Pompey. *Shakespeare.*

2. Which; relating to an antecedent thing.

You'll rue the time
That clogs me with this answer. *Shakesp. Macbeth.*
Nothing they but dust can show,
Or bones *that* hasten to be so. *Cowley.*

3. Who; relating to an antecedent person.

Saints *that* taught and led the way to heav'n. *Tickel.*

4. It sometimes serves to save the repetition of a word or words foregoing.

I'll know your business, *that* I will. *Shaksp. Henry* IV.

They said, what is *that* to us? see thou to *that.* *Matth.*

Ye defraud, and *that* your brethren. 1 *Cor.* vi. 8.

Yet for all *that*, when they be in the land of their enemies I will not cast them away. *Lev.* xxvi. 44.

They weep as if they meant
That way at least proud Nabas to prevent. *Cowley.*

This runick subject will occur upon *that* of poetry. *Temple.*

What is inviting in this sort of poetry proceeds not so much from the idea of a country life itself, as from *that* of its tranquillity. *Pope.*

5. Opposed to *this* as *the other* to *one.*

This is not fair; nor profitable *that*;
Nor t'other question proper for debate. *Dryden's Persius.*
In this scale gold, in t'other fame does lie,
The weight of *that* mounts this so high. *Cowley.*

6. When *this* and *that* relate to foregoing words, *this* is referred like *hic* or *cecy* to the latter, and *that* like *ille* or *cela* to the former.

7. Such as.

By religion is meant a living up to those principles, *that* is, to act conformably to our best reason, and to live as becomes those who believe a God and a future state. *Tillotson.*

8. That which; what.

Sir, I think the meat wants *that* I have.
——Basting. *Shakesp. Comedy of Errours.*

9. The thing.

The Nazarite hath vowed, besides *that* that his hand shall get. *Num.* vi. 21.

He made *that* art which was a rage. *Cowley.*

10. The thing which then was.

Secure proud Nabas slept,
And dreamt, vain man, of *that* day's barb'rous sport. *Cowley.*

11. By way of eminence.

This is *that* Jonathan, the joy and grace,
That Jonathan in whom does mixt remain
All that fond mothers wish. *Cowley.*
Hence love himself, *that* tyrant of my days. *Cowley.*

12. *In* THAT. As being.

Things are preached not *in that* they are taught, but *in that* they are published. *Hooker, b.* v.

THAT. *conjunction.*

1. Because.

It is not *that* I love you less
Than when before your feet I lay:
But to prevent the sad increase
Of hopeless love, I keep away. *Waller.*

Forgive me *that* I thus your patience wrong. *Cow.*

2. Noting a consequence.

That he should dare to do me this disgrace,
Is fool or coward writ upon my face? *Dry.*

The custom and familiarity of these tongues do someti[...] so far influence the expressions in these epistles, *that* one r[...] observe the force of the Hebrew conjugations. *Lo*[...]

3. Noting indication.

We answered, *that* we held it so agreeable, as we b[...] forgot dangers past and fears to come, *that* we thought [...] hour spent with him was worth years of our former life. *Bacon's New Atla*[...]

4. Noting a final end.

Treat it kindly, *that* it may
Wish at least with us to stay. *Cou*[...]

THATCH. *n. s.* [ðace, Saxon, *straw*, *Skinner*, from ðac, *roof*, in Islandick *thak.* Mr. *Lye.*] Straw laid upon the [...] of a house to keep out the weather.

Hard by a stye, beneath a roof of *thatch*
Dwelt Obloquy, who in her early days
Baskets of fish at Billingsgate did watch,
Cod, whiting, oyster, mackrel, sprat, or plaise. *Sw*[...]

A plough-boy, who has never seen any thing but thatc[...] ed houses, naturally imagines that *thatch* belongs to the v[...] nature of a house. *Wa*[...]

Then came rosy Health from her cottage of *thatch.* *Sm*[...]

To THATCH. *v. a.* [ðaccian, Saxon.] To cover as with stra[...]

Make false hair, and *thatch*
Your poor thin roofs with burthens of the dead. *Shak.*

Moss groweth chiefly upon ridges of houses tiled or *that*[...] *ed.* *Bacon's Nat. Hist.* N°. 5[...]

Then Rome was poor, and there you might behold
The palace *thatch'd* with straw. *Dryd*[...]

Sonnets or elegies to Chloris
Might raise a house above two stories:
A lyrick ode would slate, a catch
Would tile, an epigram would *thatch.* *Sw*[...]

On the cottage *thatch'd*, or lordly roof
Keen fastening. *Thoms*[...]

THA'TCHER. *n. s.* [from *thatch.*] One whose trade is to co[...] houses with straw.

You merit new employments daily;
Our *thatcher*, ditcher, gard'ner, baily. *Swi*[...]

Ash is universal timber; it serves the soldier, seaman, ca[...] penter, *thatcher*, and husbandman. *Mortim.*

To THAW. *v. n.* [ðapan, Saxon; *degen*, Dutch.]

1. To grow liquid after congelation; to melt.

When thy melted maid
His letter at thy pillow hath laid:
If thou begin'st to *thaw* for this,
May my name step in. *Don*[...]

It on firm land
Thaws not but gathers heap, and ruin seems
Of ancient pile; all else deep snow and ice. *Milto*[...]

Having let that ice *thaw* of itself, and frozen the liquor [...] second time, we could not discern any thing. *Boy.*

2. To remit the cold which had caused frost.

To THAW. *v. a.* To melt what was congealed.

Bring me the fairest creature northward born,
Where Phœbus' fire scarce *thaws* the isicles. *Shakespear*[...]

Think not that Cæsar bears such rebel blood,
That will be *thaw'd* from the true quality
With that which melteth fools. *Shakesp. Julius Cæsa*[...]

My love is *thaw'd*,
Which, like a waxen image 'gainst a fire,
Bears no impression of the thing it was. *Shakespear*[...]

Burnish'd steel, that cast a glare
From far, and seem'd to *thaw* the freezing air. *Dryde*[...]

She can unlock
The clasping charm, and *thaw* the numbing spell. *Milto*[...]

Her icy heart is *thaw'd.* *Granvill*[...]

THAW. *n. s.* [from the verb.] Liquefaction of any thing con[...] gealed; warmth such as liquifies congelation.

I was the prince's jester, and duller than a great *thaw.* *Shakesp. Much ado about nothing*

A man of my kidney, that am as subject to heat as but[...] ter; a man of continual dissolution and *thaw.* *Shakespear*[...]

Hardens his stubborn heart, but still as ice
More harden'd after *thaw.* *Milton*[...]

That cold country where discourse doth freeze in the ai[...] all Winter, and may be heard in the next Summer, or at [...] great *thaw.* *Wilkins's Math. Magick*

When sharp frosts had long constrain'd the earth,
A kindly *thaw* unlocks it with cold rain,
First the tender blade peeps. *Dryden*

THE, article. [*de*, Dutch.]

1. The article noting a particular thing.

Your son has paid a soldier's debt;
He only liv'd but till he was a man,
The which no sooner had his prowess confirm'd,
In *the* unshrinking station where he fought,
But like a man he dy'd. *Shakespeare's Macbeth*

He put him in mind of the long pretence he had to be groom of the bed chamber, for *the* which he could not chuſe but ſay, that he had the queen's promiſe. *Clarendon, b.* viii.

Unhappy ſlave, and pupil to a bell,
Unhappy till *the* laſt, *the* kind releaſing knell. *Cowley.*

I'll march *the* muſes Hannibal. *Cowley.*

The fair example of *the* heav'nly lark,
Thy fellow poet, Cowley, mark;
Above *the* ſtars let thy bold muſick ſound,
Thy humble neſt build on *the* ground. *Cowley.*

The fruit
Of that forbidden tree, whoſe mortal taſte
Brought death into *the* world. *Milton.*

Night ſhades the groves, and all in ſilence lie,
All but *the* mournful philomel and I. *Pope.*

2. Before a vowel *e* is commonly cut off in verſe.

Who had *th'* eſpecial engines been to rear
His fortunes up unto *the* ſtate they were. *Daniel.*

Th' adorning thee with ſo much art
Is but a barb'rous ſkill,
'Tis like the pois'ning of a dart,
Too apt before to kill. *Cowley.*

3. Sometimes *he* is cut off.

In this ſcale worth, in *t'other* gold does lie. *Cowley.*

4. In the following paſſage *the* is uſed according to the French idiom.

As all the conſiderable governments among the Alps are commonwealths, ſo it is a conſtitution *the* moſt adapted of any to the poverty of theſe countries. *Addiſon on Italy.*

THEA'TRAL. *adj.* [*theatral*, Fr. *theatralis*, Lat.] Belonging to a theatre.

THE'ATRE. *n. ſ.* [*theatre*, Fr. *theatrum*, Lat.]

1. A place in which ſhews are exhibited; a playhouſe.

This wiſe and univerſal *theatre*,
Preſents more woful pageants than the ſcene
Wherein we play. *Shakeſp. As you like it.*

When the boats came within ſixty yards of the pillar, they found themſelves all bound, yet ſo as they might go about, ſo as they all ſtood as in a *theatre* beholding this light. *Bacon.*

2. A place riſing by ſteps like a theatre.

Shade above ſhade, a woody *theatre*
Of ſtatelieſt view. *Milton.*

In the midſt of this fair valley ſtood
A native *theatre*, which riſing ſlow,
By juſt degrees o'erlook'd the ground below. *Dryden.*

THEA'TRICK. } *adj.* [*theatrum*, Latin.] Scenick; ſuiting a
THEA'TRICAL. } theatre; pertaining to a theatre.

Theatrical forms ſtickle hard for the prize of religion: a diſtorted countenance is made the mark of an upright heart. *Decay of Piety.*

Load ſome vain church with old *theatrick* ſtate,
Turn arcs of triumph to a garden gate. *Pope.*

THEA'TRICALLY. *adv.* [from *theatrical.*] In a manner ſuiting the ſtage.

Dauntleſs her look, her geſture proud,
Her voice *theatrically* loud. *Swift's Miſcel.*

THEE, the oblique ſingular of *thou.*

Poet and ſaint, to *thee* alone were giv'n
The two moſt ſacred names of earth and heav'n. *Cowley.*

THEFT. *n. ſ.* [from *theif.*]

1. The act of ſtealing.

Theft is an unlawful felonious taking away of another man's goods againſt the owner's knowledge or will. *Cowel.*

His *thefts* were too open, his filching was like an unſkilful ſinger, he kept not time. *Shakeſp. Merry Wives of Windſor.*

Their nurſe Euriphile,
Whom for the *theft* I wedded, ſtole theſe children. *Shak.*

2. The thing ſtolen.

If the *theft* be certainly found in his hand alive, whether ox, aſs, or ſheep, he ſhall reſtore double. *Exod.* xxii. 4.

THEIR. *n. ſ.* [ðeopa, *of them*, Saxon.] Of them: the pronoun poſſeſſive, from *they.*

The round world ſhould have ſhook
Lions into civil ſtreets, and citizens into *their* dens. *Shak.*

For the Italians, Dante had begun to file *their* language in verſe before Boccace, who likewiſe received no little help from his maſter Petrarch; but the reformation of *their* proſe was wholly owing to Boccace. *Dryden.*

2. *Theirs* is uſed when any thing comes between the poſſeſſive and ſubſtantive.

Prayer we always have in our power to beſtow, and they never in *theirs* to refuſe. *Hooker, b.* v.

They gave the ſame names to their own idols which the Egyptians did to *theirs.* *Raleigh.*

The penalty to thy tranſgreſſion due,
And due to *theirs* which out of thine will grow. *Milton.*

Nothing but the name of zeal appears,
'Twixt our beſt actions and the worſt of *theirs.* *Denham.*

Vain are our neighbours hopes, and vain their cares,
The fault is more their languages than *their's.* *Roſcommon.*

Which eſtabliſhed law of *theirs* ſeems too ſtrict at firſt, becauſe it excludes all ſecret intrigues. *Dryden.*

And reading wiſh, like *theirs*, our fate and fame. *Pope.*

THEM, the oblique of *they.*

The materials of *them* were not from any herb. *Wilkins.*

THEME. *n. ſ.* [*theme*, Fr. from θέμα.]

1. A ſubject on which one ſpeaks or writes.

Every object of our idea is called a *theme*, whether it be a being or not being. *Watts.*

Two truths are told,
As happy prologues to the ſwelling act
Of the imperial *theme.* *Shakeſpeare's Macbeth.*

When a ſoldier was the *theme*, my name
Was not far off. *Shakeſpeare's Cymbeline.*

O! could I flow like thee, and make thy ſtream
My great example, as it is my *theme*:
Though deep, yet clear; though gentle, yet not dull;
Strong without rage, without o'erflowing full. *Denham.*

Whatever near Eurota's happy ſtream,
With laurels crown'd, had been Apollo's *theme.* *Roſcommon.*

Though Tyber's ſtreams immortal Rome behold,
Though foaming Hermus ſwells with tides of gold,
From heav'n itſelf though ſeven-fold Nilus flows,
And harveſts on a hundred realms beſtows;
Theſe now no more ſhall be the muſe's *themes*,
Loſt in my fame, as in the ſea their ſtreams. *Pope.*

2. A ſhort diſſertation written by boys on any topick.

3. The original word whence others are derived.

Let ſcholars daily reduce the words to their original or *theme*, to the firſt caſe of nouns, or firſt tenſe of verbs. *Watts.*

THEMSE'LVES. *n. ſ.* [See THEY and SELF.]

1. Theſe very perſons.

Whatſoever evil befalleth in that, *themſelves* have made themſelves worthy to ſuffer it. *Hooker, b.* v.

2. The oblique caſe of *they* and *ſelves.*

They open to *themſelves* at length the way. *Milton.*

Waken children out of ſleep with a low call, and give them kind uſage till they come perfectly to *themſelves.* *Locke.*

THEN. *adv.* [*than*, Gothick; ðan, Saxon; *dan*, Dutch.]

1. At that time.

The *then* biſhop of London, Dr. Laud, attended on his majeſty throughout that whole journey. *Clarendon.*

Thee, *then* a boy, with my arms I laid. *Dryden.*

2. Afterwards; immediately afterwards; ſoon afterwards.

If an herb be cut off from the roots in Winter, and *then* the earth be trodden down hard, the roots will become very big in Summer. *Bacon's Nat. Hiſt.* N°. 437.

3. In that caſe; in conſequence.

Had not men been fated to be blind,
Then had our lances pierc'd the treach'rous wood. *Dryden.*

Had fate ſo pleas'd I had been eldeſt born,
And *then* without a crime the crown had worn. *Dryden.*

If all this be ſo, *then* man has a natural freedom. *Locke.*

4. Therefore; for this reaſon.

If *then* his providence
Out of our evil ſeek to bring forth good. *Milton.*

Now *then* be all thy weighty cares away,
Thy jealouſies and fears, and, while you may,
To peace and ſoft repoſe give all the day. *Dryden.*

5. At another time: as *now* and *then*, at one time and other.

Now ſhaves with level wing the deep, *then* ſoars. *Milton.*

One while the maſter is not aware of what is done, and *then* in other caſes it may fall out to be his own act. *L'Eſtr.*

6. That time: it has here the effect of a noun.

Till *then* who knew
The force of thoſe dire arms? *Milton.*

THENCE. *n. ſ.* [contracted, according to *Minſhew*, from *there hence.*]

1. From that place.

Faſt by the oracle of God; I *thence*
Invoke thy aid. *Milton.*

Surat he took, and *thence* preventing fame,
By quick and painful marches thither came. *Dryden.*

2. From that time.

There ſhall be no more *thence* an infant of days. *Iſa.* lxv.

3. For that reaſon.

Not to ſit idle with ſo great a gift
Uſeleſs, and *thence* ridiculous about him. *Milton's Agoniſt.*

4. *From thence* is a barbarous expreſſion, *thence* implying the ſame.

From thence; from him, whoſe daughter
His tears proclaim'd his parting with her; *thence*
We have croſs'd. *Shakeſpeare.*

There plant eyes, all muſt *from thence*
Purge and diſperſe. *Milton.*

THE'NCEFORTH. *adv.* [*thence* and *forth.*]

1. From that time.

Thenceforth this land was tributary made
T' ambitious Rome. *Spenſer.*

They ſhall be placed in Leinſter, and have land given them to live upon, in ſuch ſort as ſhall become good ſubjects, to labour *thenceforth* for their living. *Spenſer on Ireland.*

Wrath ſhall be no more
Thenceforth, but in thy preſence joy entire. *Milton.*

2. *From thenceforth* is a barbarous corruption crept into later books.

Avert
His holy eyes; resolving *from thenceforth*
To leave them to their own polluted ways. *Milton.*

Men grow acquainted with these self-evident truths upon their being proposed; but whosoever does so, finds in himself that he then begins to know a proposition which he knew not before, and which *from thenceforth* he never questions. *Locke.*

THENCEFO'RWARD. *adv.* [*thence* and *forward.*] On from that time.

THE'OCRACY. *n. s.* [*theocratie*, Fr. Θεὸς and κρατέω.] Government immediately superintended by God.

The characters of the reign of Christ are chiefly justice, peace, and divine presence or conduct, which is called *theocracy*. *Burnet's Theory of the Earth.*

THEOCRA'TICAL. *adj.* [*theocratique*, Fr. from *theocracy.*] Relating to a government administered by God.

The government is neither human nor angelical, but peculiarly *theocratical*. *Burnet's Theory of the Earth.*

THEO'DOLITE. *n. s.* A mathematical instrument for taking heights and distances.

THE'OGONY. *n. s.* [*theogonie*, Fr. θεογονία.] The generation of the gods. *Bailey.*

THEOLO'GIAN. *n. s.* [*theologien*, Fr. *theologus*, Latin.] A divine; a professor of divinity.

Some *theologians* defile places erected only for religion by defending oppressions. *Hayward.*

They to their viands fell: nor seemingly
The angel, nor in mist, the common gloss
Of *theologians*, but with keen dispatch
Of real hunger. *Milton's Par. Lost, b.* v.

THEOLO'GICAL. *adj.* [*theologique*, Fr. *theologia*, Lat.] Relating to the science of divinity.

Although some pens have only symbolized the same from the mystery of its colours, yet are there other affections might admit of *theological* allusions. *Brown.*

They generally are extracts of *theological* and moral sentences, drawn from ecclesiastical and other authors. *Swift.*

THEOLO'GICALLY. *adv.* [from *theological.*] According to the principles of theology.

THEO'LOGIST. } *n. s.* [*theologus*, Lat.] A divine; one studious
THEO'LOGUE. } in the science of divinity.

The cardinals of Rome, which are *theologues*, friars, and schoolmen, call all temporal business, of wars, embassages, shirrery, which is under-sheriffries. *Bacon's Essays.*

A *theologue* more by need than genial bent;
Int'rest in all his actions was discern'd. *Dryden.*

It is no more an order, according to popish *theologists*, than the prima tonsura, they allowing only seven ecclesiastical *theologists*. *Ayliffe's Parergon.*

THE'OLOGY. *n. s.* [*theologie*, Fr. θεολογία.] Divinity.

The whole drift of the scripture of God, what is it but only to teach *theology*? *Theology*, what is it but the science of things divine? *Hooker, b.* iii.

She was most dear to the king in regard of her knowledge in languages, in *theology*, and in philosophy. *Hayward.*

The oldest writers of *theology* were of this mind. *Tillotson.*

THE'OMACHIST. *n. s.* He who fights against the gods. *Bailey.*

THE'OMACHY. *n. s.* [Θεὸς and μαχὴ.] The fight against the gods by the giants. *Bailey.*

THEO'RBO. *n. s.* [*tiorba*, Italian; *tuorbe*, Fr.] A large lute for playing a thorough bass, used by the Italians. *Bailey.*

He wanted nothing but a song,
And a well tun'd *theorbo* hung
Upon a bough, to ease the pain
His tugg'd ears suffer'd, with a strain. *Butler.*

THE'OREM. *n. s.* [*theoreme*, Fr. θεώρημα.] A position laid down as an acknowledged truth.

Having found this the head *theorem* of all their discourses, who plead for the change of ecclesiastical government in England, we hold it necessary that the proofs thereof be weighed. *Hooker, b.* ii.

The chief points of morality are no less demonstrable than mathematicks; nor is the subtilty greater in moral *theorems* than in mathematical. *More's divine Dialogues.*

Many observations go to the making up of one *theorem*, which, like oaks fit for durable buildings, must be of many years growth. *Graunt.*

Here are three *theorems*, that from thence we may draw some conclusions. *Dryden's Dufresnoy.*

THEOREMA'TICAL. }
THEOREMA'TICK. } *adj.* [from *theorem.*] Comprised in theorems; consisting in theorems.
THEORE'MICK. }

Theoremick truth, or that which lies in the conceptions we have of things, is negative or positive. *Grew.*

THEORE'TICAL. } *adj.* { [*theoretique*, French; from θεωρητικὸς.] } Speculative;
THEORE'TICK. } { } depending
THEO'RICAL. } { [*theorique*, Fr. from } on theory
THEO'RICK. } { θεωρία.] } or speculation; terminating in theory or speculation; not practical.

When he speaks,
The air, a charter'd libertine, is still;
And the mute wonder lurketh in mens ears,
To steal his sweet and honied sentences:
So that the act and practick part of life
Must be the mistress to this *theorique.* *Shakespe*

The *theorical* part of the inquiry being interwoven w the historical conjectures, the philosophy of colours will promoted by indisputable experiments. *Boyle on Colo*

For *theoretical* learning and sciences there is nothing complete. *Burnet's Theory of the Ea*

THEO'RICK. *n. s.* [from the adjective.] A speculatist; one w knows only speculation, not practice.

The bookish *theorick*,
Wherein the toged consuls can propose
As masterly as he; meer prattle, without practice,
Is all his soldiership. *Shakespeare's Othe*

THEORE'TICALLY. } *adj.* { [from *theoretick.*] } Speculati
THEO'RICALLY. } { [from *theorick.*] } ly; practically.

THE'ORST. *n. s.* [from *theory.*] A speculatist; one given speculation.

The greatest *theorists* have given the preference to such form of government as that which obtains in this kingdon *Addison's Freeholder*, N°.

THE'ORY. *n. s.* [*theorie*, Fr. θεωρία.] Speculation; not pr tice; scheme; plan or system yet subsisting only in the mi

If they had been themselves to execute their own *theory* this church, they would have seen being nearer at hand. *Hooker, b*

In making gold, the means hitherto propounded to eff it are in the practice full of errour, and in the *theory* full unsound imagination. *Bacon's Nat. Hist.* N°. 3

Practice alone divides the world into virtuous and vicio but as to the *theory* and speculation of virtue and vice, m kind are much the same. *South's Serm*

THERAPE'UTICK. *adj.* [θεραπευτικὸς.] Curative; teaching endeavouring the cure of diseases.

Therapeutick or curative physick restoreth the patient i sanity, and taketh away diseases actually affecting. *Brow*

The practice and *therapeutick* is distributed into the cons vative, preservative, and curative. *Harv*

Medicine is justly distributed into prophylactick, or the of preserving health; and *therapeutick*, or the art of restori it. *Wa*

THERE. *adv.* [*thar*, Gothick; ðær, Saxon; *daer*, Dutc *der*, Danish.]

1. In that place.

If they come to sojourn at my house,
I'll not be *there.* *Shakespeare's King Le*

Exil'd by thee from earth to deepest hell,
In brazen bonds shall barb'rous discord dwell;
Gigantick pride, pale terror, gloomy care,
And mad ambition shall attend her *there.* *Po*

2. It is opposed to *here.*

To see thee fight, to see thee traverse, to see thee here, see thee *there.* *Shakesp. Merry Wives of Winds*

Could their relishes be as different *there* as they are he yet the manna in heaven will suit every palate. *Lock*

Darkness *there* might well seem twilight here. *Milt*

3. An exclamation directing something at a distance.

Your fury hardens me.
A guard *there*; seize her. *Dryden's Aurengze*

4. It is used at the beginning of a sentence with the appearan of a nominative case, but serves only to throw the nomin tive behind the verb: as, *a man came*, or *there came a ma* It adds however some emphasis, which, like many oth idioms in every language, must be learned by custom, a can hardly be explained. It cannot always be omitted wit out harshness: as, *in old times* there *was a great king.*

For reformation of errour *there* were that thought it a pa of Christian charity to instruct them. *Hook*

There cannot in nature be a strength so great, as to ma the least moveable to pass in an instant, or all togethe through the least place. *Digby on the So*

There have been that have delivered themselves from the ills by their good fortune or virtue. *Sucklin*

In human actions *there* are no degrees described, but a l titude is indulged. *Bishop Tayl*

Wherever *there* is sense or perception, there some idea actually produced. *Lock*

5. In composition it means *that*: as *thereby, by that.*

THE'REABOUT. } *adv.* [*there* and *about*, *thereabouts* is ther
THE'REABOUTS. } fore less proper.]

1. Near that place.

One speech I lov'd; 'twas Æneas's tale to Dido; ar *thereabout* of it especially, where he speaks of Priam's slaug ter. *Shakesp. Haml*

2. Nearly; near that number, quantity, or state.

Between the twelfth of king John and thirty-sixth of ki Edward the third, containing one hundred and fifty years *thereabouts*, there was a continual bordering war. *Davi*

Find a house to lodge a hundred and fifty persons, where twenty or *thereabout* may be attendants. *Milt*

Son

Some three months ſince, or *thereabout*,
She found me out. *Suckling.*

Water is thirteen times rarer, and its reſiſtance leſs than that of quickſilver *thereabouts*, as I have found by experiments with pendulums. *Newton's Opticks.*

3. Concerning that matter.

As they were much perplexed *thereabout*, two men ſtood by. *Luke* xxiv. 4.

THEREA'FTER. *adv.* [*there* and *after*.] According to that; accordingly.

When you can draw the head indifferent well, proportion the body *thereafter*. *Peacham.*

If food were now before thee ſet,
Wou'dſt thou not eat? *thereafter* as I like
The giver. *Milton.*

THEREA'T. *adj.* [*there* and *at*.]

1. At that; on that account.

Every errour is a ſtain to the beauty of nature; for which cauſe it bluſheth *thereat*, but glorieth in the contrary. *Hooker.*

2. At that place.

Wide is the gate, and broad is the way that leadeth to deſtruction, and many go in *thereat*. *Mat.* vii. 13.

THEREBY'. *adv.* [*there* and *by*.] By that; by means of that; in conſequence of that.

Some parts of our liturgy conſiſt in the reading of the word of God, and the proclaiming of his law, that the people may *thereby* learn what their duties are towards him. *Hooker.*

Therewith at laſt he forc'd him to untie
One of his graſping feet, him to defend *thereby*. *Fa. Qu.*

Being come to the height, they were *thereby* brought to an abſolute neceſſity. *Davies on Ireland.*

Dare to be true; nothing can need a lie,
A fault, which needs it moſt, grows two *thereby*. *Herbert.*

If the paper be placed beyond the focus, and then the red colour at the lens be alternately intercepted and let paſs, the violet on the paper will not ſuffer any change *thereby*. *Newton.*

THE'REFORE. *adv.* [*there* and *fore*.]

1. For that; for this; for this reaſon; in conſequence.

This is the lateſt parley we will admit;
Therefore to our beſt mercy give yourſelves. *Shakeſpeare.*
Falſtaff is dead,
And we muſt yern *therefore*. *Shakeſp. Henry* V.

Therefore ſhall a man leave father and mother and cleave to his wife. *Gen.* ii. 24.

The herd that ſeeks after ſenſual pleaſure is ſoft and unmanly; and *therefore* I compoſe myſelf to meet a ſtorm. *Lucas.*

He bluſhes; *therefore* he is guilty. *Spectator.*

The wreſtlers ſprinkled duſt on their bodies to give better hold: the glory *therefore* was greater to conquer without powder. *Weſt's Pindar.*

2. In return for this; in recompence for this or for that.

We have forſaken all and followed thee, what ſhall we have *therefore*? *Mat.* xix. 27.

THEREFRO'M. *adv.* [*there* and *from*.] From that; from this.

Be ye therefore very couragious to do all that is written in the law, that ye turn not aſide *therefrom*, to the right hand or to the left. *Joſ.* xxiii. 6.

The leaves that ſpring *therefrom* grow white. *Mortimer.*

THEREI'N. *adv.* [*there* and *in*.] In that; in this.

Therein our letters do not well agree. *Shakeſpeare.*

The matter is of that nature, that I find myſelf unable to ſerve you *therein* as you deſire. *Bacon.*

All the earth
To thee, and to thy race, I give: as lords
Poſſeſs it, and all things that *therein* live. *Milton.*

After having well examined them, we ſhall *therein* find many charms. *Dryden's Dufreſnoy.*

THEREINT'O. *adv.* [*there* and *into*.] Into that.

Let not them that are in the countries enter *thereinto*. *Luke.*

Though we ſhall have occaſion to ſpeak of this, we will now make ſome entrance *thereinto*. *Bacon.*

THEREO'F. *adv.* [*there* and *of*.] Of that; of this.

Conſidering how the caſe doth ſtand with this preſent age, full of tongue and weak of brain, behold we yield to the ſtream *thereof*. *Hooker, b.* i.

'Tis vain to think that laſting which muſt end;
And when 'tis paſt, not any part remains
Thereof, but the reward which virtue gains. *Denham.*

I ſhall begin with Greece, where my obſervations ſhall be confined to Athens, though ſeveral inſtances might be brought from other ſtates *thereof*. *Swift.*

THEREO'N. *adv.* [*there* and *on*.] On that.

You ſhall bereave yourſelf
Of my good purpoſes, and put your children
To that deſtruction which I'll guard them from,
If *thereon* you rely. *Shakeſp. Ant. and Cleopatra.*

Peter called to mind the word that Jeſus ſaid; and when he thought *thereon* he wept. *Mark* xiv. 72.

Its foundation is laid *thereon*. *Woodward.*

THE'REOUT. *adv.* [*there* and *out*.] Out of that.

Thereout a ſtrange beaſt with ſeven heads aroſe,
That towns and caſtles under her breaſt did cour. *Spenſer.*

THERETO'.
THEREUNTO'. } *adv.* [*there* and *to*, or *unto*.] To that.

Is it in regard then of ſermons only, that apprehending the goſpel of Chriſt we yield *thereunto* our unfeigned aſſent as to a thing infallibly true. *Hooker, b.* v.

This ſort of baſe people doth not for the moſt part rebel of themſelves, having no heart *thereunto*, but are by force drawn by the grand rebels into their action. *Spenſer on Ireland.*

Next *thereunto* did grow a goodly tree. *Fairy Queen.*

That whereby we reaſon, live and be
Within ourſelves we ſtrangers are *thereto*. *Davies.*

A larger form of ſpeech were ſafer than that which punctually prefixeth a conſtant day *thereto*. *Brown.*

What might his force have done, being brought *thereto*,
When that already gave ſo much to do? *Daniel.*

That it is the appointment of God, might be argument enough to perſuade us *thereunto*. *Tillotſon's Sermons.*

THEREUPO'N. *adv.* [*there* and *upon*.]

1. Upon that; in conſequence of that.

Grace having not in one thing ſhewed itſelf, nor for ſome few days, but in ſuch ſort ſo long continued, our manifold ſins ſtriving to the contrary, what can we leſs *thereupon* conclude, than that God would at leaſt-wiſe, by tract of time, teach the world, that the thing which he bleſſeth cannot but be of him. *Hooker, b.* iv.

He hopes to find you forward
And *thereupon* he ſends you this good news. *Shakeſpeare.*
Let that one article rank with the reſt;
And *thereupon* give me your daughter. *Shakeſp. Henry* V.

Though grants of extraordinary liberties made by a king to his ſubjects do no more diminiſh his greatneſs than when one torch lighteth another, yet many times inconveniencies do ariſe *thereupon*. *Davies on Ireland.*

Children are chid for having failed in good manners, and have *thereupon* reproofs and precepts heaped upon them. *Locke.*

Solon finding the people engaged in two violent factions, of the poor and the rich, and in great confuſion *thereupon*, made due proviſions for ſettling the balance of power. *Swift.*

2. Immediately.

THEREU'NDER. *adv.* [*there* and *under*.] Under that.

Thoſe which come nearer unto reaſon, find paradiſe under the equinoctial line, judging that *thereunder* might be found moſt pleaſure and the greateſt fertility. *Raleigh.*

THEREWI'TH. *adv.* [*there* and *with*.]

1. With that.

Germany had ſtricken off that which appeared corrupt in the doctrine of the church of Rome, but ſeemed in diſcipline ſtill to retain *therewith* very great conformity. *Hooker, b.* iv.

All things without, which round about we ſee,
We ſeek to know, and have *therewith* to do. *Davies.*
Therewith at laſt he forc'd him to untie
One of his graſping feet, him to defend thereby. *Spenſer.*

2. Immediately.

THEREWITHA'L. *adv.* [*there* and *withal*.]

1. Over and above.

Therewithal the execrable act
On their late murther'd king they aggravate. *Daniel.*

2. At the ſame time.

Well, give her that ring, and give *therewithal*
That letter. *Shakeſp. Two Gentlemen of Verona.*

3. With that.

His hideous tail then hurled he about,
And *therewithal* enwrapt the nimble thighs
Of his froth-foamy ſteed. *Spenſer.*

THERI'ACAL. *adj.* [θηριακα; from *theriaca*, Lat.] Medicinal; phyſical.

The virtuous bezoar is taken from the beaſt that feedeth upon the mountains, where there are *theriacal* herbs. *Bacon.*

THERMO'METER. *n. ſ.* [*thermometre*, Fr. θερμὸς and μέτρον.] An inſtrument for meaſuring the heat of the air, or of any matter.

The greateſt heat is about two in the afternoon, when the ſun is paſt the meridian, as is evident from the *thermometer*, or obſervations of the weather-glaſs. *Brown.*

THERMOME'TRICAL. *adj.* [from *thermometer*.] Relating to the meaſure of heat.

His heat raiſes the liquor in the *thermometrical* tubes. *Cheyne.*

THE'RMOSCOPE. *n. ſ.* [*thermoſcope*, Fr. θερμὸς and σκοπέω.] An inſtrument by which the degrees of heat are diſcovered; a thermometer.

By the trial of the *thermoſcope*, fiſhes have more heat than the element which they ſwim in. *Arbuthnot on Aliments.*

THESE, pronoun, the plural of *this*.

1. Oppoſed to *thoſe*.

Did we for *theſe* barbarians plant and ſow
On *theſe*, on *theſe* our happy fields beſtow? *Dryden.*

2. *Theſe* relates to the perſons or things laſt mentioned; and *thoſe* to the firſt.

More rain falls in June and July than in December and January; but it makes a much greater ſhew upon the earth in *theſe* months than in *thoſe*, becauſe it lies longer upon it. *Woodward's Nat. Hiſt. p.* iv.

THE'SIS. *n. s.* [*these*, Fr. θέσις.] A position; something laid down; affirmatively or negatively.

> The truth of what you here lay down,
> By some example should be shewn.
> An honest, but a simple pair,
> May serve to make this *thesis* clear. *Prior.*

THE'SMOTHETE. *n. s.* [*thesmothete*, Fr. θεσμοθέτης; θεσμὸς and τίθημι.] A lawgiver.

THE'URGY. *n. s.* [θεουργία.] The power of doing supernatural things by lawful means, as by prayer to God. *Bailey.*

THEW. *n. s.* [ðeap, Saxon.]

1. Quality; manners; customs; habit of life; form of behaviour.

> Home report these happy news,
> For well yee worthy been for worth and gentle *thewes.*
> *Fairy Queen, b.* i.

> From mother's pap I taken was unfit,
> And streight deliver'd to a fairy knight,
> To be upbrought in gentle *thewes* and martial might.
> *Fairy Queen, b.* i.

2. In *Shakespeare* it seems to signify brawn, or bulk, from the Saxon ðeoh, *the thigh*, or some such meaning.

> Nature crescent does not grow alone
> In *thews* and bulk; but, as this temple waxes,
> The inward service of the mind and soul
> Grows wide withal. *Shakespeare's Hamlet.*

Will you tell me, master Shallow, how to chuse a man? Care I for the limbs, the *thewes*, the stature, bulk and big semblance of a man? give me the spirit, master Shallow. *Shakespeare's Henry* IV.

THE'WED. *adj.* [from *thew.*] Educated; habituated; accustomed.

> But he was wise and wary of her will,
> And ever held his hand upon his heart;
> Yet would not seem so rude, and *thewed* in ill,
> As to despise so courteous seeming part. *Fairy Qu. b.* ii.

THEY. *n. s.* in the oblique case *them*, the plural of *he* or *she*. [ði, Saxon.]

1. The men; the women; the persons.

They are in a most warlike preparation. *Shak. Coriolanus.*

> Why do you keep alone?
> Of sorriest fancies your companions making,
> Using those thoughts, which should indeed have died
> With them *they* think on. *Shakesp. Macbeth.*

> The Spaniard
> Must now confess, if *they* have any goodness,
> The trial just and noble. *Shakespeare.*

> *They* eat on beds of silk and gold,
> At ivory tables, or wood sold
> Dearer than it. *Benj. Johnson's Cataline.*

> *They* know
> To joy the friend and grapple with the foe. *Prior.*

2. Those men; those women: opposed to some others.

> Only *they*,
> That come to hear a merry play,
> Will be deceiv'd. *Shakesp. Henry* VIII.

> 'Tis remarkable, that *they*
> Talk most who have the least to say. *Prior.*

3. It is used indefinitely; as the French *on dit.*

> There, as *they* say, perpetual night is found
> In silence brooding on th' unhappy ground. *Dryden.*

THI'BLE. *n. s.* A slice; a scummer; a spatula. *Ainf.*

THICK. *adj.* [ðicce, Saxon; *dick*, Dutch; *dyck*, Danish; *thickur*, Islandick.]

1. Not thin.

2. Dense; not rare; gross; crass.

God caused the wind to blow, to dry up the abundant slime of the earth, make the land more firm, and cleanse the air of *thick* vapours and unwholesome mists. *Raleigh.*

To warm milk pour spirit of nitre; the milk presently after will become *thicker* than it was. *Arbuthnot on Aliments.*

3. Not clear; not transparent; muddy; feculent.

> Why hast thou lost the fresh blood in thy cheeks,
> And given my treasures and my rights of thee,
> To *thick* ey'd musing and curs'd melancholy? *Shakesp.*

A fermentation makes all the wine in the vessel *thick* or foul; but when that is past, it grows clear of itself. *Temple.*

> Encumber'd in the mud, their oars divide
> With heavy stroaks the *thick* unwieldy tide. *Addison.*

4. Great in circumference; not slender.

My little finger shall be *thicker* than his loins. 1 *Kings* xii.

Thou art waxen fat; thou art grown *thick*, covered with fatness. *Deut.* xxxii. 15.

5. Frequent; in quick succession; with little intermission.

They charged the defendants with their small shot and Turky arrows as *thick* as hail. *Knolles.*

Favours came *thick* upon him, liker main showers than sprinkling drops or dews; for the next St. George's day he was knighted, made gentleman of the king's bed-chamber, and an annual pension given him. *Wotton.*

This being once a week, came too *thick* and too often about. *Spelman.*

> His pills as *thick* as handgranado's flew,
> And where they fell as certainly they slew. *Roscomm*

6. Close; not divided by much space; crowded.

> It brought them to a hollow cave,
> Amid the *thickest* woods. *Fairy Qu. b.*

The people were gathered *thick* together. *Luke* xi. 2

> Not *thicker* billows beat the Libyan main,
> Nor *thicker* harvests on rich Hermus rise,
> Than stand these troops. *Dryden's Æ*

> He fought secure of fortune as of fame;
> Still by new maps the island might be shewn:
> Conquests he strew'd where'er he came,
> *Thick* as the galaxy with stars is sown. *Dryde*

Objects of pain or pleasure do not lie *thick* enough tog ther in life to keep the soul in constant action. *Addis*

7. Not easily pervious; set with things close to each other.

> He through a little window cast his sight,
> Though *thick* of bars that gave a scanty light. *Dryd*

> The speedy horse
> Watch each entrance of the winding wood,
> Black was the forest, *thick* with beech it stood. *Dryde*

> Next the proud palace of Salerno stood
> A mount of rough ascent, and *thick* with wood. *Dryde*

Bring it near some *thick*-headed tree. *Mortime*

8. Coarse; not thin.

It tasteth a little of the wax, which in a pomegranate, some such *thick*-coated fruit, it would not. *Baco*

Thick-leaved weeds amongst the grass will need more dr ing than ordinary grass. *Mortimer's Husbandr*

9. Without proper intervals of articulation.

> Speaking *thick*, which nature made his blemish,
> Became the accents of the valiant,
> To seem like him. *Shakesp. Henry* IV

THICK. *n. s.* [from the adjective.]

1. The thickest part or time when any thing is thickest.

Achimetes having with a mine suddenly blown up a gre part of the wall of the Spanish station, in the *thick* of t dust and smoak presently entered his men. *Knolle*

2. THICK *and thin.* Whatever is in the way.

> Through perils both of wind and limb,
> Through *thick and thin* she followed him. *Hudibra*

> When first the down appears upon his chin,
> For a small sum to swear through *thick and thin.* *Dryde*

THICK. *adv.* [It is not always easy to distinguish the adver from the adjective.]

1. Frequently; fast.

> 'Tis some disaster,
> Or else he would not send so *thick.* *Denham's Soph*

> I hear the trampling of *thick* beating feet;
> This way they move. *Dryden's Don Sebastiar*

2. Closely.

> The neighb'ring plain with arms is cover'd o'er;
> The vale an iron harvest seems to yield,
> Of *thick* sprung lances in a waving field. *Dryder*

A little plat of ground *thick* sown, is better than a grea field which lies fallow. *Norris's Misce*

3. To a great depth.

If you apply it *thick* spread, it will eat to the bone. *Wisem*

> Cato has piercing eyes, and will discern
> Our frauds, unless they're cover'd *thick* with art. *Addison*

4. THICK *and threefold.* In quick succession; in great numbers

They came *thick and threefold* for a time, till one expe rienced stager discovered the plot. *L'Estrange's Fab*

To THI'CKEN. *v. a.* [from *thick.*]

1. To make thick.

2. To make close; to fill up interstices.

Waters evaporated and mounted up into the air, *thicke* and cool it. *Woodward's Nat. Hist*

3. To condense; to concrete.

The white of an egg gradually dissolves by heat, exceed ing a little the heat of a human body; a greater degree o heat will *thicken* it into a white, dark-coloured, dry, viscou mass. *Arbuthnot on Aliments*

4. To strengthen; to confirm.

> 'Tis a shrewd doubt, though it be but a dream;
> And this may help to *thicken* other proofs,
> That do demonstrate thinly. *Shakesp. Othello*

5. To make frequent.

6. To make close or numerous.

To THI'CKEN. *v. n.*

1. To grow thick.

2. To grow dense or muddy.

> Thy lustre *thickens*
> When he shines by. *Shakesp. Ant. and Cleopatra*

3. To concrete; to be consolidated.

> Water stopt gives birth
> To grass and plants, and *thickens* into earth. *Prior*

4. To grow close or numerous.

> The press of people *thickens* to the court,
> Th' impatient crowd devouring the report. *Dryden*

He saw the crowd *thickening*, and desired to know how many there were. *Tatler*

. To grow quick.

The combat *thickens*, like the ſtorm that flies
From weſtward when the ſhow'ry kids ariſe,
Or patt'ring hail comes pouring on the main,
When Jupiter deſcends in harden'd rain. *Addiſon.*

'HI'CKET. *n. ſ.* [ðiccetu, Saxon.] A cloſe knot or tuft of trees; a cloſe wood or copſe.

I drew you hither,
Into the chiefeſt *thicket* of the park. *Shakeſpeare.*

Within a *thicket* I repos'd; and found
Let fall from heav'n a ſleep interminate. *Chapman.*

Chus, or any of his, could not in haſte creep through thoſe deſart regions, which the length of one hundred and thirty years after the flood had fortified with *thickets*, and permitted every buſh and briar, reed and tree, to join themſelves into one main body and foreſt. *Raleigh.*

How often, from the ſteep
Of echoing hill, or *thicket*, have we heard
Cœleſtial voices, to the midnight air,
Sole, or reſponſive, each to other's note,
Singing their great Creator? *Milton.*

My brothers ſtept to the next *thicket* ſide
To bring me berries. *Milton.*

Now Leda's twins
Their trembling lances brandiſh'd at the foe;
Nor had they miſs'd, but he to *thickets* fled,
Conceal'd from aiming ſpears, not pervious to the ſteed. *Dryden.*

I've known young Juba riſe before the ſun,
To beat the *thicket* where the tyger ſlept,
Or ſeek the lion in his dreadful haunts. *Addiſon's Cato.*

'HI'CKLY. *adv.* [from *thick.*] Deeply; to a great quantity.

Mending cracked receivers, having *thickly* overlaid them with diachylon, we could not perceive leaks. *Boyle.*

'HI'CKNESS. *n. ſ.* [from *thick.*]

. The ſtate of being thick; denſity.

. Quantity of matter interpoſed; ſpace taken up by matter interpoſed.

In the darkened room, againſt the hole at which the light entered, I could eaſily ſee through the whole *thickneſs* of my hand the motions of a body placed beyond it. *Boyle.*

. Quantity laid on quantity to ſome conſiderable depth.

Poll a tree, and cover it ſome *thickneſs* with clay on the top, and ſee what it will put forth. *Bacon's Nat. Hiſt.*

. Conſiſtence; groſſneſs; not rareneſs; ſpiſſitude.

Nitre mingled with water to the *thickneſs* of honey, and anointed on the bud after the vine is cut, it will ſprout forth. *Bacon's Nat. Hiſt.* N. 444.

Diſeaſes imagined to come from the *thickneſs* of blood, come often from the contrary cauſe. *Arbuthnot on Aliments.*

. Imperviouſneſs; cloſeneſs.

The banks of the river and the *thickneſs* of the ſhades drew into them all the birds of the country. *Addiſon.*

. Want of ſharpneſs; want of quickneſs.

A perſon found in himſelf, being at ſome times ſubject to a *thickneſs* of hearing, the like effect. *Holder.*

What you write is printed in large letters; otherwiſe between the weakneſs of my eyes and *thickneſs* of hearing, I ſhould loſe the greateſt pleaſure. *Swift.*

'HI'CK-SCULLED. *adj.* Dull; ſtupid.

Pleas'd to hear their *thick-ſcull'd* judges cry,
Well mov'd! oh finely ſaid! *Dryden.*

This downright fighting fool, this *thick-ſcull'd* hero,
This blunt unthinking inſtrument of death,
With plain dull virtue has outgone my wit. *Dryden.*

'HI'CKSET. *adj.* [*thick* and *ſet.*] Cloſe planted.

His eye-balls glare with fire, ſuffus'd with blood,
His neck ſhoots up a *thickſet* thorny wood;
His briſtled back a trench impal'd appears,
And ſtands erected, like a field of ſpears. *Dryden.*

The world is ſo *thickſet* with the numerous productions of the creatures, that beſides the apparent beauty of things view-ed by all, there are thoſe ſecret graces in every part of nature, which ſome few alone have the ſkill to diſcern. *Grew.*

'HI'CKSKIN. *n. ſ.* [*thick* and *ſkin.*] A coarſe groſs man; a numſkul.

The ſhallow'ſt *thickſkin* of that barren ſort,
Who Pyramus preſented in their ſport,
Forſook his ſcene and enter'd in a brake. *Shakeſpeare.*

'HIEF. *n. ſ.* [*thiubs*, Gothick; ðeif, Saxon; *dief*, Dutch. It was anciently written *thieof*, and ſo appeareth to have been of two ſyllables; *thie* was wont to be taken for *thrift*, ſo that *thie of* is he that takes *of* or from a man his *thie*, that is, his *thrift* or *means* whereby he *thrives.*]

. One who takes what belongs to another: *the thief* ſteals by ſecrecy, and *the robber* by violence; but theſe ſenſes are confounded.

Take heed, have open eye; for *thieves* do foot by night. *Shakeſpeare.*

This he ſaid becauſe he was a *thief*, and had the bag. *John.*

Can you think I owe a *thief* my life,
Becauſe he took it not by lawleſs force?
Am I obliged by that t' aſſiſt his rapines,
And to maintain his murders? *Dryden.*

2. An excreſcence in the ſnuff of a candle.

Their burning lamps the ſtorm enſuing ſhow,
Th' oil ſparkles, *thieves* about the ſnuff do grow. *May.*

THIEF-CATCHER. } *n. ſ.* { [*thief* and *catch.*] } One whoſe buſineſs is to detect thieves, and bring them to juſtice.
THIEF-LEADER. } { [*thief* and *lead.*] }
THIEF-TAKER. } { [*thief* and *take.*] }

A wolf paſſed by as the *thief-leaders* were dragging a fox to execution. *L'Eſtrange.*

My ev'nings all I would with ſharpers ſpend,
And make the *thief-catcher* my boſom friend. *Bramſton.*

To THIEVE. *v. n.* [from *thief.*] To ſteal; to practiſe theft.

THI'EVERY. *n. ſ.* [from *thieve.*]

1. The practice of ſtealing.

Ne how to ſcape great puniſhment and ſhame,
For their falſe treaſon and vile *thievery.* *Spenſer.*

Maſter, be one of them; 'tis an honourable kind of *thievery.* *Shakeſpeare.*

Do villainy, do, ſince you profeſs to do't,
Like workmen; I'll example you with *thievery.* *Shakeſp.*

He makes it a help unto *thievery*; for thieves having a deſign upon a houſe, make a fire at the four corners thereof, and caſt therein the fragments of loadſtone, which raiſeth fume. *Brown's Vulg. Errours, b.* ii.

Amongſt the Spartans, *thievery* was a practice morally good and honeſt. *South.*

2. That which is ſtolen.

Injurious time now, with a robber's haſte,
Crams his rich *thiev'ry* up he knows not how. *Shakeſp.*

THI'EVISH. *adj.* [from *thief.*]

1. Given to ſtealing; practiſing theft.

What, would'ſt thou have me go and beg my food?
Or with a baſe and boiſt'rous ſword enforce
A *thieviſh* living on the common road. *Shakeſpeare.*

O *thieviſh* night,
Why ſhould'ſt thou, but for ſome felonious end,
In thy dark lanthorn thus cloſe up the ſtars,
That nature hung in heav'n, and fill'd their lamps
With everlaſting oil, to give due light
To the miſled and lonely traveller? *Milton.*

The *thieviſh* God ſuſpected him, and took
The hind aſide, and thus in whiſpers ſpoke;
Diſcover not the theft. *Addiſon.*

2. Secret; ſly.

Four and twenty times the pilot's glaſs
Hath told the *thieviſh* minutes how they paſs. *Shakeſp.*

THI'EVISHLY. *adv.* [from *thieviſh.*] Like a thief.

They lay not to live by their worke,
But *thieviſhly* loiter and lurke. *Tuſſer's Huſb.*

THI'EVISHNESS. *n. ſ.* [from *thieviſh.*] Diſpoſition to ſteal; habit of ſtealing.

THIGH. *n. ſ.* [ðeoh, Saxon; *thieo*, Iſlandick; *die*, Dutch.]

The *thigh* includes all between the buttocks and the knee. The *thigh* bone is the longeſt of all the bones in the body: its fibres are cloſe and hard: it has a cavity in its middle: it is a little convex and round on its foreſide, but a little hollow, with a long and ſmall ridge on its backſide. *Quincy.*

He touched the hollow of his *thigh*, and it was out of joint. *Gen.* xxxii. 25.

The fleſh diſſolved, and left the *thigh* bone bare. *Wiſeman.*

THILK. pronoun. [þilc, Saxon.] That ſame. Obſolete.

I love *thilk* laſs: alas, why do I love!
She deigns not my good will, but doth reprove,
And of my rural muſick holdeth ſcorn. *Spenſer's Paſt.*

THILL. *n. ſ.* [ðille, Saxon, a piece of timber cut.] The ſhafts of a waggon; the arms of wood between which the laſt horſe is placed.

More eaſily a waggon may be drawn in rough ways if the fore wheels were as high as the hinder wheels, and if the *thills* were fixed under the axis. *Mortimer's Huſb.*

THILL-HORSE. } *n. ſ.* [*thill* and *horſe.*] The laſt horſe; the
THI'LLER. } horſe that goes between the ſhafts.

Whoſe bridle and ſaddle, whitlether and nal,
With collars and harneiſs for *thiller* and al. *Tuſſer.*

What a beard haſt thou got? thou haſt got more hair on thy chin, than Dobbin my *thill* horſe has on his tail. *Shak.*

THI'MBLE. *n. ſ.* [This is ſuppoſed by *Minſhew* to be corrupted from *thumb bell.*] A metal cover by which women ſecure their fingers from the needle when they ſew.

Your ladies and pale viſag'd maids,
Like Amazons, come tripping after drums;
Their *thimbles* into armed gantlets change,
Their needles to lances. *Shakeſp. King John.*

Examine Venus and the Moon,
Who ſtole a *thimble* or a ſpoon. *Hudibras, p.* i.

Veins that run perpendicular to the horizon, have valves ſticking to their ſides like ſo many *thimbles*; which, when the blood preſſes back, ſtop its paſſage, but are compreſſed by the forward motion of the blood. *Cheyne.*

THIME. *n. s.* [*thymus*, Lat. *thym*, Fr.] A fragrant herb from which the bees are supposed to draw honey. This should be written *thyme*, which see.

Fair marigolds, and bees alluring *thyme*. *Spenser*.

THIN. *adj.* [ðinn, Saxon; *thunnur*, Islandick; *dunn*, Dutch.]

1. Not thick.

Beat gold into *thin* plates, and cut it into wires. *Exod.*

2. Rare; not dense.

The hope of the ungodly is like *thin* froth, that is blown away with the wind. *Wisd.* v. 14.

In the day when the air is more *thin*, the sound pierceth better; but when the air is more thick, as in the night, the sound spendeth and spreadeth abroad less. *Bacon.*

Understand the same
Of fish within their wat'ry residence;
Not hither summon'd, since they cannot change
Their element, to draw the *thinner* air. *Milton.*

The waters of Boristhenes are so *thin* and light, that they swim upon the top of the stream of the river Hypanis. *More.*

To warm new milk pour any alkali, the liquor will remain at rest, though it appear somewhat *thinner*. *Arbuthnot.*

3. Not close; separate by large spaces.

He pleas'd the *thin* and bashful audience
Of our well-meaning, frugal ancestors. *Roscommon.*

Thou art weak, and full of art is he;
Else how could he that host seduce to sin,
Whose fall has left the heav'nly nation *thin?* *Dryden.*

Northward, beyond the mountains we will go,
Where rocks lie cover'd with eternal snow,
Thin herbage in the plains, and fruitless fields,
The sand no gold, the mine no silver yields. *Dryden.*

Thin on the tow'rs they stand; and ev'n those few,
A feeble, fainting, and dejected crew. *Dryden.*

Already Cæsar
Has ravag'd more than half the globe; and sees
Mankind grown *thin* by his destructive sword. *Addison.*

4. Not closely compacted or accumulated.

Seven *thin* ears blasted with the east wind sprung up. *Gen.*

Remove the swelling epithets, thick laid
As varnish on a harlot's cheek; the rest
Thin sown with ought of profit or delight. *Milton.*

Thin leaved arbute hazle-graffs receives,
And planes huge apples bear that bore but leaves. *Dryden.*

5. Exile; small.

I hear the groans of ghosts;
Thin, hollow sounds, and lamentable screams. *Dryden.*

6. Not coarse; not gross in substance.

7. Not abounding.

Spain is *thin* sown of people, by reason of the sterility of the soil and the natives being exhausted in such vast territories as they possess. *Bacon.*

Ferrara is very large, but extremely *thin* of people. *Addison.*

8. Not fat; not bulky; lean; slim; slender.

A slim *thin* gutted fox made a hard shift to wriggle his body into a hen-roost, and when he had stuffed his guts well, the hole was too little to get out again. *L'Estrange.*

THIN. *adv.* Not thickly.

Fame is the spur, that the clear spirit doth raise,
That last infirmity of noble mind,
To scorn delights, and live laborious days;
But the fair guerdon when we hope to find,
And think to burst out into sudden blaze,
Comes the blind fury with th' abhorred sheers,
And slits the *thin* spun life. *Milton.*

A country gentlewoman, if it be like to rain, goes not abroad *thin* clad. *Locke.*

To THIN. *v. a.* [from the adjective.]

1. To make thin or rare; not to thicken.

The serum of the blood is neither acid nor alkaline: oil of vitriol thickens, and oil of tartar *thins* it a little. *Arbuthnot.*

2. To make less close or numerous.

The bill against root and branch never passed till both houses were sufficiently *thinned* and overawed. *King Charles.*

T' unload the branches, or the leaves to *thin*
That suck the vital moisture of the vine. *Dryden.*

'Tis Cæsar's sword has made Rome's senate little,
And *thinn'd* its ranks. *Addison's Cato.*

3. To attenuate.

The vapours by the solar heat
Thinn'd and exhal'd rise to their airy seat. *Blackmore.*

THI'NLY. *adv.* [from *thin.*] Not thickly; not closely; not densely; not numerously.

It is commonly opinioned, that the earth was *thinly* inhabited before the flood. *Brown's Vulgar Errours*, *b.* vi.

THINE, pronoun. [*thein*, Gothick; ðin, Saxon; *dijn*, Dutch.] Belonging or relating to thee; the pronoun possessive of *thou*. It is used for *thy* when the substantive is divided from it: as, *this is* thy *house*; thine *is this house*; *this house is* thine.

Thou hast her, France; let her be *thine*, for we
Have no such daughter. *Shakesp. King Lear.*

THINK. *n. s.* [ðinᵹ, Saxon; *ding*, Dutch.]

1. Whatever is; not a person. A general word.

Do not you chide; I have a *thing* for you.
——You have a *thing* for me?
It is a common *thing*—
——Ha?
——To have a foolish wife. *Shakesp. Othello.*

The great master he found busy in packing up his *things* against his departure. *Knolles's Hist. of the Turks.*

The remnant of the meat-offering is a *thing* most holy. *Lev.* ii. 3.

Says the master, you devour the same *things* that they would have eaten, mice and all. *L'Estrange.*

A *thing* by neither man or woman priz'd,
And scarcely known enough to be despis'd. *Dryden.*

I should blush to own so rude a *thing*,
As it is to shun the brother of my king. *Dryden.*

Wicked men, who understand any *thing* of wisdom, may see the imprudence of worldly and irreligious courses. *Tillotson.*

2. It is used in contempt.

I have a *thing* in prose, begun above twenty-eight years ago, and almost finished: it will make a four shilling volume. *Swift.*

3. It is used of persons in contempt, or sometimes with pity.

See, sons, what *things* you are! how quickly nature
Falls to revolt, when gold becomes her object?
For this the foolish over-careful fathers
Have broke their sleeps with thought, their brains with care. *Shakespeare's Henry IV.*

Never any *thing* was so unbred as that odious man. *Congr.*

The poor *thing* sighed, and with a blessing expressed with the utmost vehemence turned from me. *Addison.*

I'll be this abject *thing* no more.
Love give me back my heart again. *Granville.*

4. It is used by *Shakespeare* once in a sense of honour.

I lov'd the maid I married; never man
Sigh'd truer breath: but that I see thee here,
Thou noble *thing!* more dances my wrapt heart. *Shakesp.*

To THINK. *v. n.* preter. *thought.* [*thankgan*, Gothick; ðencean, Saxon; *dencken*, Dutch.]

1. To have ideas; to compare terms or things; to reason; to cogitate; to perform any mental operation.

Thinking, in the propriety of the English tongue, signifies that sort of operation of the mind about its ideas, wherein the mind is active; where it, with some degree of voluntary attention, considers any thing. *Locke.*

What am I? or from whence? for that I am
I know, because I *think*; but whence I came,
Or how this frame of mine began to be,
What other being can disclose to me? *Dryden.*

Those who perceive dully, or retain ideas in their minds ill, will have little matter to *think* on. *Locke.*

It is an opinion that the soul always *thinks*, and that it has the actual perception of ideas in itself constantly, and that actual *thinking* is as inseparable from the soul, as actual extension is from the body. *Locke.*

These are not matters to be slightly and superficially *thought* upon. *Tillotson's Sermons.*

His experience of a good prince must give great satisfaction to every *thinking* man. *Addison's Freeholder.*

2. To judge; to conclude; to determine.

Let them marry to whom they *think* best; only to their father's tribe shall they marry. *Num.* xxxvi. 6.

I fear we shall not find
This long desired king such as was *thought*. *Daniel.*

3. To intend.

Thou *thought'st* to help me, and such thanks I give,
As one near death to those that wish him live. *Shakespeare.*

4. To imagine; to fancy.

Something since his coming forth is *thought* of, which
Imports the kingdom so much fear and danger,
That his return was most requir'd. *Shakesp. King Lear.*

Edmund, I *think*, is gone,
In pity of his misery, to dispatch
His nighted life. *Shakesp. King Lear.*

We may not be startled at the breaking of the exterior earth; for the face of nature hath provoked men to *think* of and observe such a thing. *Burnet's Theory of the Earth.*

Those who love to live in gardens, have never *thought* of contriving a winter garden. *Spectator*, N°. 477.

5. To muse; to meditate.

You pine, you languish, love to be alone,
Think much, speak little, and in speaking sigh. *Dryden.*

6. To recollect; to observe.

We are come to have the warrant.
—Well *thought* upon; I have it here about me. *Shakesp.*

Think upon me, my God, for good, according to all that I have done. *Neh.* v. 19.

7. To judge; to conclude.

If your general acquaintance be among ladies, provided they have no ill reputation, you *think* you are safe. *Swift.*

Still

Still the work was not complete,
When Venus *thought* on a deceit. *Swift's Miſcel.*

The opinions of others whom we know and *think* well of are no ground of aſſent. *Locke.*

To conſider; to doubt.

Any one may *think* with himſelf, how then can any thing live in Mercury and Saturn. *Bentley's Sermons.*

3 THINK. *v. a.*

To imagine; to image in the mind; to conceive.

Royal Lear,
Whom I have ever honour'd as my king,
And as my patron *thought* on in my prayer. *Shakeſpeare.*

Charity *thinketh* no evil. 1 *Cor.* xiii. 5.

To believe; to eſteem.

Me *thought* I ſaw the grave where Laura lay. *Sidney.*

Me *thinketh* the running of the foremoſt is like that of Ahimaaz. 2 *Sam.* xviii. 27.

Nor *think* ſuperfluous others aid. *Milton.*

To THINK *much.* To grudge.

He *thought* not *much* to clothe his enemies. *Milton.*

If we conſider our infinite obligations to God, we have no reaſon to *think* much to ſacrifice to him our deareſt intereſts in this world. *Tillotſon's Sermons.*

To THINK *ſcorn.* To diſdain.

He *thought ſcorn* to lay hands on Mordecai alone. *Eſth.* iii.

HI'NKER. *n. ſ.* [from *think.*] One who thinks in a certain manner.

No body is made any thing by hearing of rules, or laying them up in his memory; practice muſt ſettle the habit: you may as well hope to make a good muſician by a lecture in the art of muſick, as a coherent *thinker*, or ſtrict reaſoner, by a ſet of rules. *Locke.*

If a man had an ill-favoured noſe, deep *thinkers* would impute the cauſe to the prejudice of his education. *Swift.*

HI'NKING. *n. ſ.* [from *think.*] Imagination; cogitation; judgment.

He put it by once; but, to my *thinking*, he would fain have had it. *Shakeſp. Julius Cæſar.*

If we did think,
His contemplations were above the earth,
And fix'd on ſpiritual objects, he ſhould ſtill
Dwell in his muſings; but I am afraid
His *thinkings* are below the moon, nor worth
His ſerious conſidering. *Shakeſp. Henry* VIII.

I heard a bird ſo ſing,
Whoſe muſick, to my *thinking*, pleas'd the king. *Shakeſp.*

I was a man, to my *thinking*, very likely to get a rich widow. *Addiſon's Guard.* N°. 97.

HI'NLY. *n. ſ.* [from *thin.*]

Not thickly.

Not cloſely; not numerouſly.

It is opinioned, that the earth was *thinly* inhabited before the flood. *Brown's Vulgar Errours.*

Our walls are *thinly* mann'd; our beſt men ſlain:
The reſt, an heartleſs number, ſpent with watching. *Dryd.*

HI'NNESS. *n. ſ.* [from *thin.*]

The contrary to thickneſs; exility; tenuity.

Tickling is moſt in the ſoles, arm-holes and ſides, becauſe of the *thinneſs* of the ſkin. *Bacon.*

No breach, but an expanſion,
Like gold to airy *thinneſs* beat. *Donne.*

Tranſparent ſubſtances, as glaſs, water, air, &c. when made very thin by being blown into bubbles, or otherwiſe formed into plates, do exhibit various colours according to their various *thinneſs*, although at a greater thickneſs they appear very clear and colourleſs. *Newton's Opticks.*

Such depend upon a ſtrong projectile motion of the blood, and too great *thinneſs* and delicacy of the veſſels. *Arbuthnot.*

Paucity; ſcarcity.

The buzzard
Invites the feather'd Nimrods of his race,
To hide the *thinneſs* of their flock from ſight,
And all together make a ſeeming goodly flight. *Dryden.*

In country villages pope Leo the ſeventh indulged a practice through the *thinneſs* of the inhabitants, which opened a way for pluralities. *Ayliffe's Parergon.*

Rareneſs; not ſpiſſitude.

Thoſe pleaſures that ſpring from honour the mind can nauſeate, and quickly feel the *thinneſs* of a popular breath. *South.*

HIRD. *adj.* [ðridda, Saxon.] The firſt after the ſecond; the ordinal of three.

This is the *third* time: I hope good luck lies in odd numbers. *Shakeſpeare.*

HIRD. *n. ſ.* [from the adjective.]

The third part.

To thee and thine hereditary ever,
Remain this ample *third* of our fair kingdom. *Shakeſp.*

Men of their broken debtors take a *third*,
A ſixth, a tenth, letting them thrive again. *Shakeſpeare.*

The proteſtant ſubjects of the abbey make up a *third* of its people. *Addiſon.*

No ſentence can ſtand that is not confirmed by two *thirds* of the council. *Addiſon.*

Such clamours are like the feigned quarrels of combined cheats, to delude ſome *third* perſon. *Decay of Piety.*

2. The ſixtieth part of a ſecond.

Divide the natural day into twenty-four equal parts, an hour into ſixty minutes, a minute into ſixty ſeconds, a ſecond into ſixty *thirds.* *Holder on Time.*

THI'RDBOROUGH. *n. ſ.* [*third* and *borough.*] An under-conſtable.

THI'RDLY. *adv.* [from *third.*] In the third place.

Firſt, metals are more durable than plants; ſecondly, they are more ſolid; *thirdly*, they are wholly ſubterrany. *Bacon.*

To THIRL. *v. a.* [ðirlian, Sax.] To pierce; to perforate. *Ainſ.*

THIRST. *n. ſ.* [ðyrſt, Saxon; *dorſt*, Dutch.]

1. The pain ſuffered for want of drink; want of drink.

But fearleſs they perſue, nor can the flood
Quench their dire *thirſt*; alas! they thirſt for blood. *Denh.*

Thus accurs'd,
In midſt of water I complain of *thirſt.* *Dryden.*

Thirſt and hunger denote the ſtate of ſpittle and liquor of the ſtomach. *Thirſt* is the ſign of an acrimony commonly alkaleſcent or muriatick. *Arbuthnot on Aliments.*

2. Eagerneſs; vehement deſire.

Not hope of praiſe, nor *thirſt* of worldly good,
Enticed us to follow this emprize. *Fairfax, b.* ii.

Thou haſt allay'd the *thirſt* I had of knowledge. *Milton.*

Say is't thy bounty, or thy *thirſt* of praiſe. *Granville.*

This is an active and ardent *thirſt* after happineſs, or after a full, beatifying object. *Cheyne.*

3. Draught.

The rapid current, through veins
Of porous earth with kindly *thirſt* up drawn,
Roſe a freſh fountain. *Milton.*

To THIRST. *v. n.* [ðyrſtan, Saxon; *derſten*, Dutch.]

1. To feel want of drink; to be thirſty or athirſt.

They ſhall not hunger nor *thirſt.* *Iſa.* xlix. 10.

The people *thirſted* there for water. *Exod.* xvii. 3.

They as they *thirſted* ſcoop the brimming ſtream. *Milt.*

2. To have a vehement deſire for any thing.

They knew how the ungodly were tormented, *thirſting* in another manner than the juſt. *Wiſd.* xi. 9.

My ſoul *thirſteth* for the living God. *Pſal.* xlii. 2.

Till a man hungers and *thirſts* after righteouſneſs, till he feels an uneaſineſs in the want of it, his will will not be determined to any action in purſuit of this confeſſed, greater good. *Locke.*

But furious *thirſting* thus for gore,
The ſons of men ſhall ne'er approach thy ſhore. *Pope.*

To THIRST. *v. a.* To want to drink.

Untam'd and fierce the tyger ſtill remains:
For the kind gifts of water and of food,
He ſeeks his keeper's fleſh, and *thirſts* his blood. *Prior.*

THI'RSTINESS. *n. ſ.* [from *thirſt.*] The ſtate of being thirſty.

Next they will want a ſucking and ſoaking *thirſtineſs*, or a fiery appetite to drink in the lime. *Wotton.*

THI'RSTY. *adj.* [ðurſtig, Saxon.]

1. Suffering want of drink; pained for want of drink.

Thy brother's blood the *thirſty* earth hath drank,
Broach'd with the ſteely point of Clifford's lance. *Shakeſp.*

Give me a little water to drink, for I am *thirſty.* *Judg.* iv.

Unworthy was thy fate,
To fall beneath a baſe aſſaſſin's ſtab,
Whom all the *thirſty* inſtruments of death
Had in the field of battle ſought in vain. *Rowe.*

2. Poſſeſſed with any vehement deſire: as, *blood* thirſty.

THIRTE'EN. *adj.* [ðreotyne, Saxon.] Ten and three.

Speaking at the one end, I heard it return the voice *thirteen* times. *Bacon's Nat. Hiſt.* N°. 249.

THIRTE'ENTH. *adj.* [from *thirteen*; ðreoteoða, Saxon.] The third after the tenth.

The *thirteenth* part difference bringeth the buſineſs but to ſuch a paſs, that every woman may have an huſband. *Graunt.*

THI'RTIETH. *adj.* [from *thirty*; ðrittegoða, Saxon.] The tenth thrice told; the ordinal of thirty.

Henry ſhall eſpouſe the lady Margaret ere the *thirtieth* of May next enſuing. *Shakeſpeare's Henry* VI. *p.* ii.

A *thirtieth* part of the ſun's revolution. *Hale.*

More will wonder at ſo ſhort an age,
To find a blank beyond the *thirtieth* page. *Dryden.*

THI'RTY. *adj.* [ðrittig, Saxon.] Thrice ten.

I have ſlept fifteen years.
—Ay, and the time ſeems *thirty* unto me. *Shakeſpeare.*

The Claudian aqueduct ran *thirty*-eight miles. *Addiſon.*

THIS. pronoun. [ðiſ, Saxon.]

1. That which is preſent; what is now mentioned.

Bardolph and Nim had more valour than *this*, yet they were both hang'd; and ſo would *this* be, if he durſt ſteal. *Shak.*

Come a little nearer *this* ways. *Shakeſpeare.*

Within *this* three mile may you ſee it coming;
I ſay a moving grove. *Shakeſp. Macbeth.*

Must I endure all *this?* *Shakesp. Julius Cæsar.*

This same shall comfort us concerning our toil. *Gen.* v. 29.

This is not the place for a large reduction. *Hale.*

There is a very great inequality among men as to their internal endowments, and their external conditions, in *this* life. *Calamy's Sermons.*

2. The next future.

Let not the Lord be angry, and I will speak yet but *this* once: peradventure ten shall be found there. *Gen.* xviii. 32.

3. *This* is used for *this time.*

By *this* the vessel half her course had run. *Dryden.*

4. The last past.

I have not wept *this* forty years; but now
My mother comes afresh into my eyes. *Dryden.*

5. It is often opposed to *that.*

As when two winds with rival force contend,
This way and that, the wav'ring sails they bend,
While freezing Boreas and black Eurus blow,
Now here, now there, the reeling vessel throw. *Pope.*

According as the small parts of matter are connected together after *this* or that determinate manner, a body of *this* or that denomination is produced. *Boyle.*

Do we not often hear of *this* or that young heir? are not his riches and his lewdnesses talkt of together? *South's Serm.*

This way and that the impatient captives tend,
And pressing for release the mountains rend. *Dryden.*

6. When *this* and *that* respect a former sentence, *this* relates to the latter, *that* to the former member.

Their judgment in *this* we may not, and in *that* we need not, follow. *Hooker.*

7. Sometimes it is opposed to *the other.*

Consider the arguments which the author had to write *this*, or to design *the other*, before you arraign him. *Dryden.*

With endless pain *this* man persues
What, if he gain'd, he could not use:
And *t'other* fondly hopes to see
What never was, nor e'er shall be. *Prior.*

THI'STLE. *n. s.* [þıſtel, Saxon; *diestel*, Dutch; *carduus*, Lat.] A prickly weed growing in corn fields.

The leaves of the *thistle* grow alternately on the branches, and are prickly; and the heads are, for the most part, squamose and prickly. *Miller.*

Hateful docks, rough *thistles*, kecksies, burs. *Shakesp.*

Get you some carduus benedictus, and lay it to your heart.——There thou prick'st her with a *thistle*. *Shakesp.*

Thorns also and *thistles* it shall bring thee forth. *Milton.*

Tough *thistles* choak'd the fields, and kill'd the corn,
And an unthrifty crop of weeds was born. *Dryden.*

Rie grass will kill *thistles*. *Mortimer's Husb.*

THI'STLE, *golden. n. s.* A plant.

The *golden thistle* hath the appearance of a thistle: the flower consists of many half florets, which rest on the embrios; each of these are separated by a thin leaf, and on the top of each embrio is fastened a little leaf. *Miller.*

THI'STLY. *adj.* [from *thistle.*] Overgrown with thistles.

Wide o'er the *thistly* lawn as swells the breeze,
A whitening shower of vegetable down
Amusive floats. *Thomson's Summer.*

THI'THER. *adv.* [þıðeɲ, Saxon.]

1. To that place: it is opposed to *hither.*

We're coming *thither*. *Shakespeare.*

When, like a bridegroom from the East, the sun
Sets forth; he *thither*, whence he came, doth run. *Denham.*

There Phœnix and Ulysses watch the prey;
And *thither* all the wealth of Troy convey. *Dryden.*

2. To that end; to that point.

THI'THERTO. *adv.* [*thither* and *to.*] To that end; so far.

THI'THERWARD. *adv.* [*thither* and *ward.*] Towards that place.

Ne would he suffer sleep once *thitherward*
Approach, albe his drowsy den were next. *Fairy Qu.*

Madam, he's gone to serve the duke of Florence:
We met him *thitherward*, for thence we came. *Shakesp.*

By quick instinctive motion, up I sprung,
As *thitherward* endeavouring. *Milton's Par. Lost, b.* viii.

The foolish beasts went to the lion's den, leaving very goodly footsteps of their journey *thitherward*, but not the like of their return. *L'Estrange.*

A tuft of daisies on a flow'ry lay
They saw, and *thitherward* they bent their way. *Dryden.*

THO. *adv.* [ðonne, Saxon.]

1. Then. *Spenser.*

2. *Tho'* contracted for *though.*

To THOLE. *v. n.* To wait awhile. *Ainf.*

THONG. *n. s.* [þpang, þpong, Saxon.] A strap, or string of leather.

The Tuscan king
Laid by the lance and took him to the sling;
Thrice whirl'd the *thong* about his head, and threw
The heated lead half melted as it flew. *Dryden's Æn.*

The ancient cestus only consisted of so many large *thongs* about the hand, without any lead at the end. *Addison.*

The smiths and armourers on palfreys ride,
And nails for loosen'd spears, and *thongs* for shields
vide. *Dryden's Knight's*

THORA'CICK. *adj.* [from *thorax.*] Belonging to the brea

The chyle grows grey in the *thoracick* duct. *Arbu*

THO'RAL. *adj.* [from *thorus*, Lat.] Relating to the bed.

The punishment of adultery, according to the R law, was sometimes made by a *thoral* separation. *A*

THORN. *n. s.* [*thaurns*, Gothick; þopn, Saxon; *do* Dutch.]

1. A prickly tree of several kinds.

Thorns and thistles shall it bring forth. *Gen.* iii

2. A prickle growing on the thorn bush.

The most upright is sharper than a *thorn* hedge. *Mi*

Flowers of all hue, and without *thorn* the rose. *M*

3. Any thing troublesome.

The guilt of empire; all its *thorns* and cares
Be only mine. *Southern's Spartan I*

THO'RNAPPLE. *n. s.* A plant.

The *thornapple* is of two sorts; the greater, which up with a strong round stalk, and the lesser differs from other in the smallness of the leaves. *Mort.*

THO'RNBACK. *n. s.* A sea-fish.

The *thornback* when dried tastes of sal ammoniac. *Ar*

THO'RNBUT. *n. s.* A sort of sea-fish, *Ainf.* which he di guishes from thornback. A birt or turbot.

THO'RNY. *adj.* [from *thorn.*]

1. Full of thorns; spiny; rough; prickly.

Not winding ivy, nor the glorious bay;
He wore, sweet head, a *thorny* diadem. *Ran*

The boar's eye-balls glare with fire,
His neck shoots up a thickset *thorny* wood;
His bristled back a trench impal'd appears. *Dr*

The wiser madmen did for virtue toil
A *thorny*, or at best a barren soil. *Dr*

They on the bleaky top
Of rugged hills, the *thorny* bramble crop. *Dr*

2. Pricking; vexatious.

No dislike against the person
Of our good queen, but the sharp *thorny* points
Of my alleged reasons drive this forward. *Shakesp*

3. Difficult; perplexing.

By how many *thorny* and hard ways they are come th unto, by how many civil broils. *Spenser on Ire*

THO'ROUGH. *prepof.* [the word *through* extended into two lables.]

1. By way of making passage or penetration.

2. By means of.

Mark Antony will follow
Thorough the hazards of this untrod state,
With all true faith. *Shakesp. Julius C*

THO'ROUGH. *adj.* [The adjective is always written *thoro* the preposition commonly *through.*]

1. Complete; full; perfect.

The Irish horseboys, in the *thorough* reformation of realm, should be cut off. *Spe*

He did not desire a *thorough* engagement till he had tim reform some whom he resolved never more to trust. *Claren*

A *thorough* translator must be a *thorough* poet. *Dr*

A *thorough* practice of subjecting ourselves to the want others, would extinguish in us pride. *Su*

2. Passing through.

Let all three sides be a double house, without *thor* lights on the sides. *B*

THORO'UGHFARE. *n. s.* [*thorough* and *fare.*] A passage throu a passage without any stop or let.

Th' Hyrcanian deserts are as *thoroughfares* now
For princes to come view fair Portia. *Shakespe*

His body is a passable carcase if he be not hurt: it *thoroughfare* for steel, if it be not hurt. *Shakespe*

Hell, and this world, one realm, one continent
Of easy *thoroughfare*. *Milton's Par. Lost, b*

The ungrateful person is a monster, which is all th and belly; a kind of *thoroughfare*, or common shore for good things of the world to pass into. *South's Serm*

The courts are fill'd with a tumultuous din
Of crouds, or issuing forth, or ent'ring in:
A *thoroughfare* of news; where some devise
Things never heard; some mingle truth with lies. *Dry*

THO'ROUGHLY. *adv.* [from *thorough.*] Completely; fully.

Look into this business *thoroughly*. *Shakespe*

We can never be grieved for their miseries who are *roughly* wicked, and have thereby justly called their calami on themselves. *Dryden's Dufres*

One would think that every member of the commun who embraces with vehemence the principles of either p ty, had *thoroughly* sifted and examined them. *Addi*

They had forgotten their solemn vows as *thoroughly* a they had never made them. *Atterbury's Serm*

THO'ROUGHSPED. *adj.* [*thorough* and *sped.*] Finished in pr ciples; thoroughpaced.

Our *thoroughsped* republick of whigs, which contains the bulk of all hopers, pretenders, and professors, are most highly useful to princes. *Swift.*

HOROUGHPA'CED. *adj.* [*thorough* and *pace.*] Perfect in what is undertaken; complete; thoroughsped. Generally in a bad sense.

When it was proposed to repeal the test clause, the ablest of those who were reckoned the most stanch and *thoroughpaced* whigs fell off at the first mention of it. *Swift.*

HOROUGHSTI'CH. *adv.* [*thorough* and *stitch.*] Completely; fully. A low word.

Perseverance alone can carry us *thoroughstitch.* *L'Estrange.*

HORP. *n. s.*

Thorp, *throp*, *threp*, *trep*, *trop*, are all from the Saxon ðorp, which signifies a village. *Gibson's Camden.*

HOSE. *pron.* the plural of *that.*

Make all our trumpets speak, give them all breath,
Those clam'rous harbingers of blood and death. *Shakesp.*

The fibres of this muscle act as *those* of others. *Cheyne.*

Sure there are poets which did never dream
Upon Parnassus, nor did taste the stream
Of Helicon, we therefore may suppose
Those made not poets, but the poets *those.* *Denham.*

'HOU. *n. s.* [ðu, Saxon; *du*, Dutch; in the oblique cases singular *thee*, ðe, Saxon; in the plural *ye*, ȝe, Saxon; in the oblique cases plural *you*, eop, Saxon.]

The second pronoun personal.

Is this a dagger which I see before me,
The handle tow'rd my hand? Come let me clutch *thee.*
I have *thee* not, and yet I see *thee* still.
Art *thou* not, fatal vision, sensible
To feeling as to sight. *Shakesp. Macbeth.*

I am as like to call *thee* so again,
To spit on *thee* again, to spurn *thee* too,
If *thou* wilt lend this money lend it not
As to thy friend. *Shakesp. Merchant of Venice.*

Thou, if there be a *thou* in this base town,
Who dares with angry Eupolis to frown;
Who at enormous villany turns pale,
And steers against it with a full-blown sail. *Dryden.*

. It is used only in very familiar or very solemn language. When we speak to equals or superiors we say *you*; but in solemn language, and in addresses of worship, we say *thou.*

'o THOU. *v. a.* [from *thou.*] To treat with familiarity.

Taunt him with the licence of ink; if thou *thou'st* him some thrice, it shall not be amiss. *Shakespeare.*

'HOUGH. *conjunction.* [ðeah, Saxon; *thauh*, Gothick.]

. Notwithstanding that; although.

Not that I so affirm, *though* so it seem. *Milton.*

The sound of love makes your soft heart afraid,
And guard itself, *though* but a child invade. *Waller.*

I can desire to perceive those things that God has prepared for those that love him, *though* they be such as eye hath not seen, ear heard, nor hath it entered into the heart of man to conceive. *Locke.*

Though the name of abstracted ideas is attributed to universal ideas, yet this abstraction is not great. *Watts's Logick.*

. *As* THOUGH. As if; like as if.

In the vine were three branches; and it was *as though* it budded. *Gen.* xl. 10.

. It is used in the end of a sentence in familiar language: however; yet.

You shall not quit Cydaria for me:
'Tis dangerous *though* to treat me in this sort,
And to refuse my offers, though in sport. *Dryden.*

A good cause wou'd do well *though*;
It gives my sword an edge. *Dryden's Spanish Fryar.*

'HOUGHT, the *preterite* and *part. pass.* of *think.*

I told him what I *thought.* *Shakespeare's Othello.*

Are my friends embark'd?
Can any thing be *thought* of for their service?
Whilst I yet live, let me not live in vain. *Addison.*

No other tax could have been *thought* of, upon which so much money would have been immediately advanced. *Addis.*

'HOUGHT. *n. s.* [from the preterite of *to think.*]

. The operation of the mind; the act of thinking.

.. Idea; image formed in the mind.

Sulph'rous and *thought* executing fires
Singe my white head. *Shakespeare's King Lear.*

For our instruction to impart
Things above earthly *thought.* *Milton.*

. Sentiment; fancy; imagery.

Thought, if translated truly, cannot be lost in another language; but the words that convey it to our apprehension, which are the image and ornament of that *thought*, may be so ill-chosen as to make it appear unhandsome. *Dryden.*

One may often find as much *thought* on the reverse of a medal as in a canto of Spenser. *Addison on ancient Medals.*

Thoughts come crouding in so fast upon me, that my only difficulty is to choose or to reject. *Dryden.*

The *thoughts* of a soul that perish in thinking. *Locke.*

. Reflection; particular consideration.

Why do you keep alone?
Of sorriest fancies your companions making,
Using those *thoughts* which should indeed have died
With them they think on. *Shakesp. Macbeth.*

5. Conception; preconceived notion.

Things to their *thought*
So unimaginable as hate in heaven. *Milton.*

6. Opinion; judgment.

He that is ready to slip, is as a lamp despised in the *thought* of him that is at ease. *Job* xii. 5.

They communicated their *thoughts* on this subject to each other; and therefore their reasons are little different. *Dryden.*

Thus Bethel spoke, who always speaks his *thought*,
And always thinks the very thing he ought. *Pope.*

7. Meditation; serious consideration.

Pride, of all others the most dangerous fault,
Proceeds from want of sense or want of *thought.* *Roscommon.*

Nor was godhead from her *thought.* *Milton.*

8. Design; purpose.

The *thoughts* I think towards you are *thoughts* of peace, and not evil. *Jer.* xxix. 11.

9. Silent contemplation.

Who is so gross
That cannot see this palpable device?
Yet who so bold, but says, he sees it not?
Bad is the world; and all will come to nought,
When such ill dealings must be seen in *thought.* *Shakesp.*

10. Sollicitude; care; concern.

Let us return, lest he leave caring for the asses and take *thought* for us. 1 *Sam.* ix. 5.

Hawis was put in trouble, and died with *thought* and anguish before his business came to an end. *Bacon's Henry* VII.

Adam took no *thought*, eating his fill. *Milton.*

11. Expectation.

The main descry
Stands on the hourly *thought.* *Shakesp. King Lear.*

12. A small degree; a small quantity.

His face was a *thought* longer than the exact symmetrians would allow. *Sidney.*

If our own be but equal, the law of common indulgence alloweth us to think them at the least half a *thought* the better, because they are our own. *Hooker, b.* iv.

A needle pierced through a globe of cork, cut away by degrees, will swim under water, yet not sink unto the bottom: if the cork be a *thought* too light to sink under the surface, the water may be attenuated with spirits of wine. *Br.*

My giddiness seized me, and though I now totter, yet I think I am a *thought* better. *Swift.*

THO'UGHTFUL. *adj.* [*thought* and *full.*]

1. Contemplative; full of reflection; full of meditation.

On these he mus'd within his *thoughtful* mind,
And then resolv'd what Faunus had divin'd. *Dryden.*

2. Attentive; careful.

Thoughtful of thy gain, I all the live-long day
Consume in meditation deep. *Phillips.*

3. Promoting meditation; favourable to musing.

Unspotted long with human blood:
War, horrid war, your *thoughtful* walks invades,
And steel now glitters in the muses shades. *Pope.*

4. Anxious; sollicitous.

In awful pomp, and melancholy state,
See settled reason on the judgment-seat;
Around her croud distrust, and doubt and fear,
And *thoughtful* foresight, and tormenting care. *Prior.*

THO'UGHTFULLY. *adv.* [from *thoughtful.*] With thought or consideration; with sollicitude.

THO'UGHTFULNESS. *n. s.* [from *thoughtful.*]

1. Deep meditation.
2. Anxiety; sollicitude.

THO'UGHTLESS. *adj.* [from *thought.*]

1. Airy; gay; dissipated.
2. Negligent; careless.

It is something peculiarly shocking to see gray hairs without remorse for the past, and *thoughtless* of the future. *Rogers.*

3. Stupid; dull.

His goodly fabrick fills the eye,
And seems design'd for *thoughtless* majesty:
Thoughtless as monarch oaks that shade the plain,
And spread in solemn state supinely reign. *Dryden.*

THO'UHTLESSLY. *adv.* [from *thought.*] Without thought; carelesly; stupidly.

In restless hurries *thoughtlessly* they live,
At substance oft unmov'd, for shadows grieve. *Garth.*

THO'UGHTLESSNESS. *n. s.* [from *thoughtless.*] Want of thought; absence of thought.

THO'UGHTSICK. *adj.* [*thought* and *sick.*] Uneasy with reflection.

Heav'n's face doth glow
With tristful visage; and, as 'gainst the doom,
Is *thoughtsick* at the act. *Shakesp. Hamlet.*

THO'USAND. *adj.* or *n. s.* [ðusend, Saxon; *duysend*, Dutch.]

1. The number of ten hundred.

About

About three *thouſand* years ago, navigation of the world for remote voyages was greater than at this day. *Bacon.*

2. Proverbially, a great number.

So fair, and *thouſand*, *thouſand* times more fair
She ſeem'd, when ſhe preſented was to ſight. *Fa. Qu.*

For harbour at a *thouſand* doors they knock'd,
Not one of all the *thouſand* but was lock'd. *Dryden.*

Search the herald's roll,
Where thou ſhalt find thy famous pedigree,
Drawn from the root of ſome old Tuſcan tree,
And thou, a *thouſand* off, a fool of long degree. *Dryden.*

Though he regulates himſelf by juſtice, he finds a *thouſand* occaſions for generoſity and compaſſion. *Addiſon's Spect.*

How many *thouſands* pronounce boldly on the affairs of the publick, whom God nor men never qualified for ſuch judgment. *Watts.*

THO'USANDTH. *adj.* [from *thouſand.*] The hundredth ten times told; the ordinal of a thouſand.

He that will divide a minute into a thouſand parts, and break but a part of a *thouſandth* part in the affairs of love, it may be ſaid of him, that Cupid hath clapt him o' th' ſhoulder, but I'll warrant him heart whole. *Shakeſp. As you like it.*

Such is the poet's lot: what luckier fate
Does on the works of grave hiſtorians wait:
More time they ſpend, in greater toils engage,
Their volumes ſwell beyond the *thouſandth* page. *Dryden.*

The French hugonots are many thouſand witneſſes to the contrary; and I wiſh they deſerved the *thouſandth* part of the good treatment they have received. *Swift's Miſcel.*

THOWL. *n. ſ.* A piece of timber by which oars are kept in their places when a rowing. *Ainſ.*

THRALL. *n. ſ.* [þꞃæl, Saxon.]

1. A ſlave; one who is in the power of another.

No *thralls* like them that inward bondage have. *Sidney.*

But ſith ſhe will the conqueſt challenge need,
Let her accept me as her faithful *thrall.* *Spenſer.*

Look gracious on thy proſtrate *thrall.* *Shakeſpeare.*

The two delinquents
That were the ſlaves of drink, and *thralls* of ſleep. *Shak.*

I know I'm one of nature's little kings;
Yet to the leaſt and vileſt things am *thrall.* *Davies.*

That we may ſo ſuffice his vengeful ire,
Or do him mightier ſervice, as his *thralls*
By right of war, whate'er his buſineſs be. *Milton.*

2. Bondage; ſtate of ſlavery or confinement.

And laid about him, till his noſe
From *thrall* of ring and cord broke looſe. *Hudibras, p.* i.

To THRALL. *v. a.* *Spenſer.* [from the noun.] To enſlave; to bring into the power of another.

Let me be a ſlave t' atchieve the maid,
Whoſe ſudden ſight hath *thrall'd* my wounded eye. *Shak.*

Stateſmen purge vice with vice, and may corrode
The bad with bad, a ſpider with a toad.
For ſo ill *thralls* not them, but they tame ill,
And make her do much good againſt her will. *Donne.*

The author of nature is not *thralled* to the laws of nature. *Drummond.*

THRA'LDOM. *n. ſ.* [from *thrall.*] Slavery; ſervitude.

How far am I inferior to thee in the ſtate of the mind? and yet know I that all the heavens cannot bring me to ſuch *thraldom.* *Sidney, b.* i.

He ſwore with ſobs,
That he would labour my delivery.
—Why, ſo he doth, when he delivers you
From this earth's *thraldom* to the joys of heav'n. *Shakeſp.*

This country, in a great part deſolate, groaneth under the Turkiſh *thraldom.* *Sandys.*

He ſhall rule, and ſhe in *thraldom* live. *Dryden.*

They tell us we are all born ſlaves; life and *thraldom* we entered into together, and can never be quit of the one till we part with the other. *Locke.*

THRA'PPLE. *n. ſ.* The windpipe of any animal. They ſtill retain it in the Scottiſh dialect.

To THRASH. *v. a.* [ðaꞃꞅcan, Saxon; *derſchen*, Dutch.]

1. To beat corn to free it from the chaff. This is written variouſly *thraſh* or *threſh*, but *thraſh* is agreeable to etymology.

Firſt *thraſh* the corn, then after burn the ſtraw. *Shakeſp.*

Gideon *threſhed* wheat to hide it. *Judg.* viii. 11.

Here be oxen for burnt ſacrifice, and *threſhing* inſtruments for wood. 2 *Sam.* xxiv. 22.

In the ſun your golden grain diſplay,
And *thraſh* it out, and winnow it by day. *Dryden.*

This is to preſerve the ends of the bones from an incaleſcency, which they being hard bodies would contract from a ſwift motion; ſuch as that of running or *threſhing.* *Ray.*

Out of your clover well dried in the ſun, after the firſt *threſhing*, get what ſeed you can. *Mortimer.*

2. To beat; to drub.

Thou ſcurvy valiant aſs! thou art here but to *thraſh* Trojans, and thou art bought and ſold among thoſe of any wit like a Barbarian ſlave. *Shakeſp. Troil. and Creſſida.*

To THRASH. *v. n.* To labour; to drudge.

I rather wou'd be Mevius, *threſh* for rhimes
Like his, the ſcorn and ſcandal of the times,
Than that Philippick fatally divine,
Which is inſcrib'd the ſecond, ſhould be mine. *Dry*

THRA'SHER. *n. ſ.* [from *thraſh.*] One who thraſhes corn.

Our ſoldiers, like a lazy *thraſher* with a flail,
Fell gently down, as if they ſtruck their friends. *Sha.*

Not barely the plowman's pains, the reaper's and *threſ* toil, and the baker's ſweat, is to be counted into 'the b we eat: the labour of thoſe employed about the utenſils all be charged. *L*

THRA'SHING-FLOOR. *n. ſ.* An area on which corn is bea

In vain the hinds the *threſhing-floor* prepare,
And exerciſe their flails in empty air. *Dry*

Delve of convenient depth your *threſhing-floor*
With temper'd clay, then fill and face it o'er. *Dry*

THRASO'NICAL. *adj.* [from *Thraſo*, a boaſter in old come Boaſtful; bragging.

His humour is lofty, his diſcourſe peremptory, his gen behaviour vain, ridiculous, and *thraſonical.* *Shakeſpe*

There never was any thing ſo ſudden but the fight of rams, and Cæſar's *thraſonical* brag of, I came, ſaw, overcame. *Shakeſp. As you lik*

THRAVE. *n. ſ.* [ðꞃaꝼ, Saxon.]

1. A herd; a drove. Out of uſe.

2. The number of two dozen.

THREAD. *n. ſ.* [þꞃæꝺ, Saxon; *draed*, Dutch.]

1. A ſmall line; a ſmall twiſt.

Let not Bardolph's vital *thread* be cut
With edge of penny cord and vile reproach. *Shakeſpe*

Though the ſlender *thread* of dyed ſilk looked on ſi ſeem devoid of redneſs, yet when numbers of theſe *thr* are brought together, their colour becomes notorious. *B*

He who ſat at a table but with a ſword hanging over head by one ſingle *thread* or hair, ſurely had enough to ch his appetite. *South's Serm*

The art of pleaſing is the ſkill of cutting to a *thread*, twixt flattery and ill-manners. *L'Eſtra*

2. Any thing continued in a courſe; uniform tenor.

The eagerneſs and trembling of the fancy doth not alw regularly follow the ſame even *thread* of diſcourſe, but ſtri upon ſome other thing that hath relation to it. *Bur.*

The gout being a diſeaſe of the nervous parts, makes ſo hard to cure; diſeaſes are ſo as they are more remote the *thread* of the motion of the fluids. *Arbuth*

THRE'ADBARE. *adj.* [*thread* and *bare.*]

1. Deprived of the nap; wore to the naked threads.

Threadbare coat, and cobbled ſhoes he ware. *Fa.*

The clothier means to dreſs the commonwealth, and ſe new nap upon it: ſo he had need; for 'tis *threadbare.* *Sh*

Will any freedom here from you be borne,
Whoſe cloaths are *threadbare*, and whoſe cloaks are tor *Dryden's Juve*

He walk'd the ſtreets, and wore a *threadbare* cloak;
He din'd and ſupp'd at charge of other folk. *Sw.*

2. Worn out; trite.

A hungry lean-fac'd villain,
A mere anatomy, a mountebank,
A *threadbare* juggler, and a fortune-teller. *Shakeſpea*

Many writers of moral diſcourſes run into ſtale topicks a *threadbare* quotations, not handling their ſubject fully a cloſely. *Sw.*

If he underſtood trade, he would not have mentioned t *threadbare* and exploded project. *Child on Tra*

To THREAD. *v. a.* [from the noun.]

1. To paſs through with a thread.

The largeſt crooked needle, with a ligature of the ſize that I have *threaded* it with in taking up the ſpermatick v ſels. *Sharp's Surge.*

2. To paſs through; to pierce through.

Thus out of ſeaſon *threading* dark-ey'd night. *Shake*

Being preſt to th' war,
Ev'n when the nave of the ſtate was touch'd,
They would not *thread* the gates. *Shakeſp. Coriolan.*

THRE'ADEN. *adj.* [from *thread.*] Made of thread.

Behold the *threaden* ſails,
Borne with th' inviſible and creeping wind,
Draw the huge bottoms through the furrow'd ſea. *Sh*

To THREAP. *v. a.* A country word denoting to argue mu or contend. *Ai*

THREAT. *n. ſ.* [from the verb.] Menace; denunciation ill.

There is no terror, Caſſius, in your *threats.* *Shake*

The emperor perceiving that his *threats* were little regar ed, regarded little to threaten any more. *Haywar*

Do not believe
Thoſe rigid *threats* of death: ye ſhall not die. *Milto*

To THREAT. }
To THRE'ATEN. } *v. a.* [þꞃeaꞇian, Saxon: *threat* is ſeldo uſed but in poetry.]

1. To menace; to denounce evil.

Death to be wish'd
Though *threaten'd*, which no worse than this can bring. *Milton.*

2. To menace; to terrify, or attempt to terrify, by denouncing evil.

What *threat* you me with telling of the king?
Tell him and spare not. *Shakesp. Richard* III.

That it spread no further, straitly *threaten* them that they speak henceforth to no man in this name. *Acts* iv. 18.

The void profound
Wide gaping, and with utter loss of being
Threatens him. *Milton.*

Æneas their assault undaunted did abide,
And thus to Lausus, loud with friendly *threat'ning* cry'd. *Dryden's Virgil.*

This day black omens *threat* the brightest fair,
That e'er deserv'd a watchful spirit's care. *Pope.*

3. To menace by action.

Void of fear,
He *threaten'd* with his long protended spear. *Dryden.*

The noise increases as the billows roar,
When rowling from afar they *threat* the shore. *Dryden.*

THR'EATENER. *n. s.* [from *threaten.*] Menacer; one that threatens.

Be stirring as the time; be fire with fire;
Threaten the *threatener*, and outface the brow
Of bragging horrour. *Shakesp. King John.*

The fruit, it gives you life
To knowledge by the *threat'ner?* *Milton's Par. Lost.*

THRE'ATENINGLY. *adv.* [from *threaten.*] With menace; in a threatening manner.

The honour that thus flames in your fair eyes,
Before I speak, too *threat'ningly* replies. *Shakespeare.*

THR'EATFUL. *adj.* [*threat* and *full.*] Full of threats; minacious.

Like as a warlike brigandine applide
To fight, lays forth her *threatful* pikes afore,
The engines which in them sad death do hide. *Spenser.*

THREE. *adj.* [ꝧꞃie, Saxon; *dry*, Dutch; *tri*, Welsh and Erse; *tres*, Lat.] Two and one.

Prove this a prosp'rous day, the *three*-nook'd world
Shall bear the olive freely. *Shakesp. Ant. and Cleopatra.*

If you speak *three* words, it will *three* times report you the whole *three* words. *Bacon's Nat. Hist.* N°. 249.

Great Atreus sons, Tydides fixt above,
With *three*-ag'd Nestor. *Creech's Manilius.*

Jove hurls the *three*-fork'd thunder from above. *Addison.*

These *three* and *three* with osier bands we ty'd. *Pope.*

Down to these worlds I trod the dismal way,
And dragg'd the *three*-mouth'd dog to upper day. *Pope.*

A strait needle, such as glovers use, with a *three*-edged point, useful in sewing up dead bodies. *Sharp.*

2. Proverbially a small number.

Away, thou *three*-inch'd fool; I am no beast. *Shakesp.*

A base, proud, shallow, beggarly, *three*-suited, filthy, worsted stocking knave. *Shakesp. King Lear.*

THRE'EFOLD. *adj.* [ꝧꞃeoꝼealꝺ, Saxon.] Thrice repeated; consisting of three.

A *threefold* cord is not easily broken. *Ecclus.* iv. 12.

By a *threefold* justice the world hath been governed from the beginning: by a justice natural, by which the parents and elders of families governed their children, in which the obedience was called natural piety: again, by a justice divine, drawn from the laws of God; and the obedience was called conscience: and lastly, by a justice civil, begotten by both the former; and the obedience to this we call duty. *Raleigh.*

A *threefold* off'ring to his altar bring,
A bull, a ram, a boar. *Pope's Odyssey.*

THRE'EPENCE. *n. s.* [*three* and *pence.*] A small silver coin valued at thrice a penny.

A *threepence* bow'd would hire me,
Old as I am to queen it. *Shakesp. Henry* VIII.

Laying a caustick, I made an escar the compass of a *threepence*, and gave vent to the matter. *Wiseman's Surgery.*

THRE'EPENNY. *adj.* [*triobolaris*, Lat.] Vulgar; mean.

THRE'EPILE. *n. s.* [*three* and *pile.*] An old name for good velvet.

I, in my time, wore *threepile*, but am out of service. *Shak.*

THREEPI'LED. *adj.* Set with a thick pile; in another place it seems to mean piled one on another.

Thou art good velvet; thou'rt a *threepil'd* piece: I had as lief be English kersey, as be pil'd as thou art. *Shakespeare.*

Threepil'd hyberboles; spruce affectation. *Shakespeare.*

THREESCO'RE. *adj.* [*three* and *score.*] Thrice twenty; sixty.

Threescore and ten I can remember well. *Shakespeare.*

Their lives before the flood were abbreviated after, and contracted unto hundreds and *threescores.* *Brown.*

By chace our long-liv'd fathers earn'd their food;
Toil strung the nerves, and purify'd the blood:
But we their sons, a pamper'd race of men,
Are dwindl'd down to *threescore* years and ten. *Dryden.*

THRENO'DY. *n. s.* [θρηνωδία.] A song of lamentation.

THRE'SHER. *n. s.* properly *thrasher.*

Here too the *thresher* brandishing his flail,
Bespeaks a master. *Dodsley.*

THRE'SHING. See To THRASH.

The careful ploughman doubting stands,
Lest on the *threshing* floor his sheaves prove chaff. *Milton.*

Gideon was taken from *threshing*, as well as Cincinnatus from the plough, to command armies. *Locke on Education.*

THRE'SHOLD. *n. s.* [ꝧꞃeꞅcpalꝺ, Saxon.] The ground or step under the door; entrance; gate; door.

Fair marching forth in honourable wise,
Him at the *threshold* met she well did enterprize. *Spenser.*

Many men, that stumble at the *threshold*,
Are well foretold that danger lurks within. *Shakespeare.*

Not better
Than still at hell's dark *threshold* t' have sat watch,
Unnam'd, undreaded, and thy self half starv'd? *Milton.*

Before the starry *threshold* of Jove's court
My mansion is, where those immortal shapes
Of bright aereal spirits live insphered
In regions mild, of calm and serene air. *Milton.*

There sought the queen's apartment, stood before
The peaceful *threshold*, and besieg'd the door. *Dryden.*

THREW, preterite of *throw.*

A broken rock the force of Pyrrhus *threw*:
Full on his ankle fell the pond'rous stone,
Burst the strong nerves, and crash'd the solid bone. *Pope.*

THRICE. *adv.* [from *three.*]

1. Three times.

Thrice he assay'd it from his foot to draw,
And *thrice* in vain to draw it did assay,
It booted nought to think, to rob him of his prey. *Spenser.*

Thrice within this hour
I saw him down; *thrice* up again and fighting. *Shakesp.*

2. A word of amplification.

Thrice noble lord, let me entreat of you
To pardon me. *Shakesp. Taming of the Shrew.*

Thrice, and four times happy those
That under Ilian walls before their parents dy'd. *Dryden.*

To THRID. *v. a.* [this is corrupted from *thread*; in French *enfiler.*] To slide through a narrow passage.

Some *thrid* the mazy ringlets of her hair,
Some hang upon the pendents of her ear. *Pope.*

THRIFT. *n. s.* [from *thrive.*]

1. Profit; gain; riches gotten; state of prospering.

He came out with all his clowns, horst upon such cart jades, and so furnished, as I thought with myself if that were *thrift*, I wisht none of my friends or subjects ever to thrive. *Sidney, b.* ii.

You some permit
To second ills with ills, each worse than other,
And make them dreaded to the doer's *thrift.* *Shakespeare.*

Had I but the means
To hold a rival place with one of them,
I have a mind presages me such *thrift*,
That I should be fortunate. *Shakesp. Merchant of Venice.*

Should the poor be flatter'd?
No; let the candied tongue lick absurd pomp,
And crook the pregnant hinges of the knee,
Where *thrift* may follow fawning. *Shakesp. Hamlet.*

2. Parsimony; frugality; good husbandry.

The rest unable to serve any longer, or willing to fall to *thrift*, prove very good husbands. *Spenser on Ireland.*

Out of the present sparing and untimely *thrift*, there grow many future inconveniences and continual charge in repairing and re-edifying such imperfect slight-built vessels. *Raleigh.*

Thus heaven, though all-sufficient, shows a *thrift*
In his œconomy, and bounds his gift. *Dryden.*

3. A plant.

The *thrift* is a plant with a flower gathered into an almost spherical head, furnished with a common scaly empalement: this head is composed of several clove-gilliflower flowers, consisting of several leaves in a proper empalement, shaped like a funnel; in like manner the pointal rises out of the same empalement, and afterwards turns to an oblong seed, wrapt up in the empalement, as in an husk. *Miller.*

THRI'FTILY. *adv.* [from *thrifty.*] Frugally; parsimoniously.

Cromartie after fourscore went to his country-house to live *thriftily*, and save up money to spend at London. *Swift.*

THRI'FTINESS. *n. s.* [from *thrifty.*] Frugality; husbandry.

If any other place you have,
Which asks small pains but *thriftiness* to save. *Hubberd.*

Some are censured for keeping their own, whom tenderness how to get honestly teacheth to spend discreetly; whereas such need no great *thriftiness* in preserving their own, who assume more liberty in exacting from others. *Wotton.*

THRI'FTLESS. *adj.* [from *thrift.*] Profuse; extravagant.

They in idle pomp and wanton play
Consumed had their goods and *thriftless* hours,
And thrown themselves into these heavy stowers. *Spenser.*

He ſhall ſpend mine honour with his ſhame,
As *thriftleſs* ſons their ſcraping fathers gold. *Shakeſpear.*

THRI'FTY. *adj.* [from *thrift.*]

1. Frugal; ſparing; not profuſe; not laviſh.

Though ſome men do, as do they would,
Let *thrifty* do, as do they ſhould. *Tuſſer.*

Nature never lends
The ſmalleſt ſcruple of her excellence,
But like a *thrifty* goddeſs ſhe determines
Herſelf the glory of a creditor,
Thanks and uſe. *Shakeſpeare.*

Leſt he ſhould neglect his ſtudies
Like a young heir, the *thrifty* goddeſs,
For fear young maſter ſhould be ſpoil'd,
Would uſe him like a younger child. *Swift.*

I am glad he has ſo much youth and vigour left, of which he hath not been *thrifty*; but wonder he has no more diſcretion. *Swift.*

2. Well-huſbanded.

I have five hundred crowns,
The *thrifty* hire I ſav'd under your father. *Shakeſpeare.*

To THRILL. *v. a.* [þyꞃlian. Saxon; *drilla*, Swediſh.] To pierce; to bore; to penetrate; to drill.

The cruel word her tender heart ſo *thrill'd*,
That ſudden cold did run through every vein,
And ſtormy horrour all her ſenſes fill'd
With dying fit, that down ſhe fell for pain. *Fairy Qu.*

He pierced through his chaffed cheſt
With *thrilling* point of deadly iron brand,
And lanc'd his lordly heart. *Fairy Qu. b.* i.

A ſervant that he bred, *thrill'd* with remorſe,
Oppos'd againſt the act; bending his ſword
To his great maſter. *Shakeſpeare's King Lear.*

Nature, that heard ſuch ſound,
Beneath the hollow round
Of Cynthia's ſeat, the airy region *thrilling*,
Now was almoſt won,
To think her part was done. *Milton.*

To THRILL. *v. n.*

1. To have the quality of piercing.

The knight his *thrillant* ſpear again aſſay'd,
In his braſs-plated body to emboſs. *Fairy Qu. b.* i.

With that, one of his *thrillant* darts he threw,
Headed with ire and vengeable deſpite. *Fairy Qu. b.* ii.

2. To pierce or wound the ear with a ſharp ſound.

The piteous maiden, careful, comfortleſs,
Does throw out *thrilling* ſhrieks, and ſhrieking cries. *Fairy Queen, b.* i.

3. To feel a ſharp tingling ſenſation.

To ſeek ſweet ſafety out,
In vaults and priſons; and to *thrill* and ſhake,
Ev'n at the crying of our nation's crow,
Thinking his voice an armed Engliſhman. *Shakeſpeare.*

Art thou not horribly afraid? Doth not thy blood *thrill* at it? *Shakeſp. Henry* IV. *p.* i.

4. To paſs with a tingling ſenſation.

A faint cold fear *thrills* through my veins,
That almoſt freezes up the heat of life. *Shakeſpeare.*

A ſudden horror chill
Ran through each nerve, and *thrill'd* in ev'ry vein. *Addiſon.*

To THRIVE. *v. n.* pret. *throve.* and ſometimes leſs properly *thrived.* part. *thriven.* [Of this word there is found no ſatiſfactory etymology: in the northern dialect they uſe *throdden, to make grow*; perhaps *throve* was the original word, from *throa*, Iſlandick, *to encreaſe.*] To proſper; to grow rich; to advance in any thing deſired.

He came forth with his clowns horſt on poor cart-jades, and ſo furniſhed, that if this be thrift, I wiſh my ſubjects never *thrive.* *Sidney.*

The better thou *thriveſt*, the gladder am I. *Tuſſer.*

If lord Percy *thrive* not, ere the king
Diſmiſs his power, he means to viſit us. *Shakeſpeare.*

It grew amongſt buſhes, where commonly plants do not *thrive.* *Bacon's Nat. Hiſt.* Nº. 620.

They by vices *thrive*,
Sail on ſmooth ſeas, and at their port arrive. *Sandys.*

O ſon! why ſit we here, each other viewing
Idly, while Satan, our great author, *thrives*
In other worlds, and happier ſeat provides
For us, his offspring dear? *Milton's Par. Loſt, b.* x.

Thoſe who have reſolved upon the *thriving* ſort of piety, ſeldom embark all their hopes in one bottom. *Decay of Piety.*

A careful ſhepherd not only turns his flock into a common paſture, but with particular advertence obſerves the *thriving* of every one. *Decay of Piety.*

Growth is of the very nature of ſome things: to be and to *thrive* is all one with them; and they know no middle ſeaſon between their ſpring and their fall. *South's Serm.*

Experienc'd age in deep deſpair was loſt,
To ſee the rebel *thrive*, the loyal croſt. *Dryden.*

Seldom a *thriving* man turns his land into money to make the greater advantage. *Locke.*

The *thriven* calves in meads their food forſake,
And render their ſweet ſouls before the plenteous rack. *Dryden's Virg.*

A little hope—but I have none.
On air the poor camelions *thrive*,
Deny'd ev'n that my love can live. *Granville.*

Such a care hath always been taken of the city charities, that they have *thriven* and proſpered gradually from their infancy, down to this very day. *Atterbury's Sermons.*

In the fat age of pleaſure, wealth and eaſe,
Sprung the rank weed, and *thriv'd* with large increaſe. *Pope's Eſſay on Criticiſm.*

Diligence and humility is the way to *thrive* in the riches of the underſtanding, as well as in gold. *Watts's Logic.*

THRI'VER. *n. ſ.* [from *thrive.*] One that proſpers; one that grows rich.

He had ſo well improved that little ſtock his father left, as he was like to prove a *thriver* in the end. *Hayward.*

THRI'VINGLY. *adv.* [from *thriving.*] In a proſperous way.

THRO'. contracted by barbarians from *through.*

What thanks can wretched fugitives return,
Who ſcatter'd thro' the world in exile mourn. *Dryden.*

THROAT. *n. ſ.* [ðꞃoꞇe, ðꞃoꞇa, Saxon.]

1. The forepart of the neck; the paſſages of nutriment and breath.

The gold, I give thee, will I melt and pour
Down thy ill-uttering *throat.* *Shakeſpeare.*

Wherefore could I not pronounce, amen?
I had moſt need of bleſſing, and amen
Stuck in my *throat.* *Shakeſpeare's Macbeath.*

2. The main road of any place.

Her honour, and her courage try'd,
Calm and intrepid in the very *throat*
Of ſulphurous war, on Teniers dreadful field. *Thomſon.*

3. *To cut the* THROAT. To murder; to kill by violence.

Theſe bred up amongſt the Engliſhmen, when they become kern, are made more fit *to cut their throats.* *Spenſer.*

A trumpeter that was made priſoner, when the ſoldiers were about *to cut his throat*, ſays, why ſhould you kill a man that kills nobody? *L'Eſtrange.*

THRO'ATPIPE. *n. ſ.* [*throat* and *pipe.*] The weaſon; the windpipe.

THRO'ATWORT. *n. ſ.* [*throat* and *wort.*] A plant.

The *throatwort* hath a funnel-ſhaped flower, conſiſting of one leaf, and cut into ſeveral parts at the top, whoſe empalement becomes a membranaceous fruit, often triangular, and divided into three cells, full of ſmall ſeeds. *Miller.*

To THROB. *v. n.* [from θορυβεῖν, *Minſhew* and *Junius*; formed in imitation of the ſound, *Skinner*; perhaps contracted from *throw up.*]

1. To heave; to beat; to riſe as the breaſt with ſorrow or diſtreſs.

Here may his head live on my *throbbing* breaſt. *Shakeſp.*

My heart *throbs* to know one thing:
Shall Banquo's iſſue ever reign? *Shakeſp. Macbeth.*

'Twas the claſh of ſwords: my troubled heart
Is ſo caſt down, and ſunk amidſt its ſorrows,
It *throbs* with fear, and akes at every ſound. *Addiſon.*

How that warm'd me! How my *throbbing* heart
Leapt to the image of my father's joy,
When you ſhou'd ſtrain me in your folding arms. *Smith.*

2. To beat; to palpitate.

In the depending orifice there was a *throbbing* of the arterial blood, as in an aneuriſm, the blood being choaked in by the contuſed fleſh. *Wiſeman's Surgery.*

THROB. *n. ſ.* [from the verb.] Heave; beat; ſtroke of palpitation.

She ſigh'd from bottom of her wounded breaſt,
And after many bitter *throbs* did throw,
With lips full pale, and fault'ring tongue oppreſt. *Fa. Qu.*

Thou talk'ſt like one who never felt
Th' impatient *throbs* and longings of a ſoul,
That pants and reaches after diſtant good. *Addiſon's Cato.*

THROE. *n. ſ.* [from ðꞃopian, *to ſuffer*, Saxon.]

1. The pain of travail; the anguiſh of bringing children: it is likewiſe written *throw.*

Lucina lent not me her bed,
But took me in my *throes.* *Shakeſp. Cymbeline.*

My womb pregnant, and now exceſſive grown,
Prodigious motion felt and rueful *throes.* *Milton.*

Not knowing 'twas my labour, I complain
Of ſudden ſhootings, and of grinding pains,
My *throes* come thicker and my cries increas'd. *Dryden.*

Reflect on that day, when earth ſhall be again in travail with her ſons, and at one fruitful *throe* bring forth all the generations of learned and unlearned, noble and ignoble duſt. *Rogers's Sermons.*

2. Any extreme agony; the final and mortal ſtruggle.

O man! have mind of that moſt bitter *throe*,
For as the tree does fall ſo lies it ever low. *Fairy Qu.*

To eaſe them of their griefs,
Their fears of hoſtile ſtrokes, their aches, loſſes,

Their

Their pangs of love, with other incident *throes*,
That nature's fragile veſſel doth ſuſtain
In life's uncertain voyage, I will do
Some kindneſs to them. *Shakeſp. Timon of Athens.*

To THROE. *v. a.* [from the noun.] To put in agonies.
The ſetting of thine eye and cheek proclaim a birth,
Which *throes* thee much to yield. *Shakeſp. Tempeſt.*

THRONE. *n. ſ.* [*thronus*, Lat. θρόνος.]

1. A royal ſeat; the ſeat of a king.
Boundleſs intemperance hath been
Th' untimely emptying of the happy *throne*,
And fall of many kings. *Shakeſp. Macbeth.*
Th' eternal father from his *throne* beheld
Their multitude. *Milton.*
Stonehenge once thought a temple, you have found
A *throne* where kings were crown'd. *Dryden.*

2. The ſeat of a biſhop.
In thoſe times the biſhops preached on the ſteps of the altar ſtanding, having not as yet aſſumed the ſtate of a *throne*. *Ayliffe's Parergon.*

To THRONE. *v. a.* [from the noun.] To enthrone; to ſet on a royal ſeat.
They have, as who have not, whom their great ſtars
Thron'd and ſet high? *Shakeſpeare.*
True image of the father, whether *thron'd*
In the boſom of bliſs and light of light,
Conceiving or remote from heav'n, enſhrin'd
In fleſhly tabernacle and human form. *Milton.*
O prince! O chief of many *throned* powers. *Milton.*
Thron'd in glaſs and nam'd it Caroline. *Pope.*

THRONG. *n. ſ.* [ꝥꞃanᵹ, Saxon, from ꝥꞃinᵹan, *to preſs.*] A croud; a multitude preſſing againſt each other.
Let us on heaps go offer up our lives:
We are enow yet living in the field,
To ſmother up the Engliſh in our *throngs*. *Shakeſpeare.*
A *throng*
Of thick ſhort ſobs in thund'ring volleys float,
And roul themſelves over her lubrick throat
In panting murmurs. *Craſhaw.*
This book, the image of his mind,
Will make his name not hard to find:
I wiſh the *throng* of great and good
Made it leſs eas'ly underſtood. *Waller.*
With ſtudious thought obſerv'd th' illuſtrious *throng*,
In nature's order as they paſs'd along;
Their names, their fates. *Dryden's Æn.*

To THRONG. *v. n.* [from the noun.] To croud; to come in tumultuous multitudes.
I have ſeen
The dumb men *throng* to ſee him, and the blind
To hear him ſpeak. *Shakeſpeare's Coriolanus.*
His mother could not longer bear the agitations of ſo many paſſions as *throng'd* upon her, but fell upon his neck, crying out, my ſon. *Tatler,* Nº. 55.

To THRONG. *v. a.* To oppreſs or incommode with crouds or tumults.
I'll ſay, thou haſt gold:
Thou wilt be *throng'd* too ſhortly. *Shakeſpeare.*
The multitude *throng* thee and preſs thee. *Luke* viii. 45.
All acceſs was *throng'd*, the gates
Thick ſwarm'd. *Milton.*

THRO'STLE. *n. ſ.* [ꝥꞃoſtle, Saxon.] The thruſh; a ſmall ſinging bird.
The *throſtle* with his note ſo true,
The wren with little quill. *Shakeſpeare.*
The black-bird and *throſtel* with their melodious voices bid welcome to the cheerful ſpring. *Walton's Angler.*

THRO'TTLE. *n. ſ.* [from *throat.*] The windpipe.
At the upper extreme it hath no larinx or *throttle* to qualify the ſound. *Brown's Vulgar Errours.*

To THRO'TTLE. *v. a.* [from the noun.] To choak; to ſuffocate; to kill by ſtopping the breath.
I have ſeen them ſhiver and look pale,
Make periods in the midſt of ſentences,
Throttle their practis'd accents in their fears,
And, in concluſion, dumbly have broke off. *Shakeſpeare.*
As when Antæus in Iraſſa ſtrove
With Jove's Alcides, and oft foil'd ſtill roſe,
Receiving from his mother earth new ſtrength,
Freſh from his fall and fiercer grapple join'd,
Throttled at length in th' air, expir'd and fell. *Milton.*
His throat half *throttl'd* with corrupted phlegm,
And breathing through his jaws a belching ſteam. *Dryden.*
The *throttling* quinſey 'tis my ſtar appoints,
And rheumatiſm I ſend to rack the joints. *Dryden.*
Throttle thyſelf with an ell of ſtrong tape,
For thou haſt not a groat to attone for a rape. *Swift.*

THROVE, the preterite of *thrive.*
England never *throve* ſo well, nor was there ever brought into England ſo great an increaſe of wealth ſince. *Locke.*

THROUGH. *prep.* [ꝥuꞃh, Saxon; *door*, Dutch; *durch*, German.]

1. From end to end of.
He hath been ſo ſucceſsful with common heads, that he hath led their belief *through* all the works of nature. *Brown.*
A ſimplicity ſhines *through* all he writes. *Dryden.*
Fame of th' aſſerted ſea *through* Europe blown,
Made France and Spain ambitious of his love. *Dryden.*

2. Noting paſſage.
Through the gate of iv'ry he diſmiſs'd
His valiant offspring. *Dryden's Æn.*
The ſame thing happened when I removed the priſm out of the ſun's light, and looking *through* it upon the hole ſhining by the light of the clouds beyond it. *Newton.*

3. By tranſmiſſion.
Through theſe hands this ſcience has paſſed with great applauſe. *Temple.*
Material things are preſented only *through* their ſenſes; they have a real influx on theſe, and all real knowledge of material things is conveyed into the underſtanding *through* theſe ſenſes. *Cheyne's Phil. Principles.*

4. By means of.
The ſtrong *through* pleaſure ſooneſt falls, the weak *through* ſmart. *Fairy Queen, b.* ii.
Something you may deſerve of him *through* me. *Shak.*
By much ſlothfulneſs the building decayeth, and *through* idleneſs of the hands the houſe droppeth *through*. *Eccluſ.* x.
You will not make this a general rule to debar ſuch from preaching the goſpel, as have *through* infirmity fallen. *Whitgift.*
Some *through* ambition, or *through* thirſt of gold,
Have ſlain their brothers, and their country ſold. *Dryden.*
To him, to him 'tis giv'n
Paſſion, and care, and anguiſh to deſtroy:
Through him ſoft peace and plenitude of joy
Perpetual o'er the world redeem'd ſhall flow. *Prior.*

THROUGH. *adv.*

1. From one end or ſide to the other.
You'd be ſo lean, that blaſts of January
Would blow you *through* and *through*. *Shakeſpeare.*
Inquire how metal may be tinged *through* and *through*, and with what, and into what colours? *Bacon.*
Pointed ſatire runs him *through* and *through*. *Oldham.*
To underſtand the mind of him that writ, is to read the whole letter *through*, from one end to the other. *Locke.*

2. To the end of any thing.
Every man brings ſuch a degree of this light into the world with him, that though it cannot bring him to heaven, yet it will carry him ſo far, that if he follows it faithfully he ſhall meet with another light, which ſhall carry him quite *through*. *South's Sermons.*

THRO'UGHBRED. *adj.* [*through* and *bred*, commonly *thorough-bred.*] Completely educated; completely taught.
A *through-bred* ſoldier weighs all preſent circumſtances and all poſſible contingents. *Grew's Coſmol.*

THROUGHLI'GHTED. *adj.* [*through* and *light.*] Lighted on both ſides.
That the beſt pieces be placed where are the feweſt lights; therefore not only rooms windowed on both ends, called *throughlighted*, but with two or more windows on the ſame ſide are enemies to this art. *Wotton's Architecture.*

THRO'UGHLY. *adv.* [from *through*. It is commonly written *thoroughly*, as coming from *thorough.*]

1. Completely; fully; entirely; wholly.
The ſight ſo *throughly* him diſmay'd,
That nought but death before his eyes he ſaw. *Spenſer.*
Rice muſt be *throughly* boiled in reſpect of its hardneſs. *Bac.*
No leſs wiſdom than what made the world can *throughly* underſtand ſo vaſt a deſign. *Tillotſon.*

2. Without reſerve; ſincerely.
Though it be ſomewhat ſingular for men truly and *throughly* to live up to the principles of their religion, yet ſingularity in this is a ſingular commendation. *Tillotſon's Sermons.*

THROUGHO'UT. *prep.* [*through* and *out.*] Quite through; in every part of.
Thus it fareth even clean *throughout* the whole controverſy about that diſcipline which is ſo earneſtly urged. *Hooker.*
There followed after the defeat an avoiding of all Spaniſh forces *throughout* Ireland. *Bacon.*
O for a clap of thunder, as loud
As to be heard *throughout* the univerſe,
To tell the world the fact, and to applaud it. *B. Johnſon.*
Impartially inquire how we have behaved ourſelves *throughout* the courſe of this long war. *Atterbury's Sermons.*

THROUGHO'UT. *adv.* Everywhere; in every part.
Subdue it, and *throughout* dominion hold
Over fiſh of the ſea and fowl of the air. *Milton.*
His youth and age
All of a piece *throughout*, and all divine. *Dryden.*

THROUGHPA'CED. *adj.* [*through* and *pace.*] Perfect; complete.
He is very dextrous in puzzling others, if they be not *throughpaced* ſpeculators in thoſe great theories. *More.*

To THROW. preter. *threw.* part. paſſ. *thrown.* *v. a.* [ꝥꞃapan, Saxon.]

1. To fling; to caſt; to ſend to a diſtant place by any projectile force.

Preianes *threw* down upon the Turks fire and ſcalding oil. *Knolles's Hiſt. of the Turks.*

His head ſhall be *thrown* to thee over the wall. 2 *Sam.* xx.

Shimei *threw* ſtones at him and caſt duſt. 2 *Sam.* xvi. 13.

A poor widow *threw* in two mites, which make a farthing. *Mark* xii. 42.

He fell
From heav'n, they fabled, *thrown* by angry Jove
Sheer o'er the cryſtal battlements. *Milton.*

Calumniate ſtoutly; for though we wipe away with never ſo much care the dirt *thrown* at us, there will be left ſome ſulliage behind. *Decay of Piety.*

Arioſto, in his voyage of Aſtolpho to the moon, has a fine allegory of two ſwans, who, when time had *thrown* the writings of many poets into the river of oblivion, were ever in a readineſs to ſecure the beſt, and bear them aloft into the temple of immortality. *Dryden.*

When Ajax ſtrives ſome rock's vaſt weight to *throw*,
The line too labours, and the words move ſlow. *Pope.*

The air-pump, barometer, and quadrant, were *thrown* out to thoſe buſy ſpirits, as tubs and barrels are to a whale, that he may let the ſhip ſail on while he diverts himſelf with thoſe innocent amuſements. *Addiſon's Spect.*

2. To toſs; to put with any violence or tumult. It always compriſes the idea of haſte, force or negligence.

To threats the ſtubborn ſinner oft is hard,
Wrap'd in his crimes againſt the ſtorm prepar'd;
But when the milder beams of mercy play,
He melts, and *throws* his cumb'rous cloak away. *Dryden.*

The only means for bringing France to our conditions, is to *throw* in multitudes upon them, and overpower them with numbers. *Addiſon's State of the War.*

Labour caſts the humours into their proper channels, *throws* off redundancies, and helps nature. *Addiſon's Spect.*

Make room for merit, by *throwing* down the worthleſs and depraved part of mankind from thoſe conſpicuous ſtations to which they have been advanced. *Addiſon's Spect.* N°. 126.

The iſland Inarime contains, within the compaſs of eighteen miles, a wonderful variety of hills, vales, rocks, fruitful plains, and barren mountains, all *thrown* together in a moſt romantick confuſion. *Berkley to Pope.*

3. To lay careleſly, or in haſte.

His majeſty departed to his chamber, and *threw* himſelf upon his bed, lamenting with much paſſion, and abundance of tears, the loſs of an excellent ſervant. *Clarendon.*

At th' approach of night,
On the firſt friendly bank he *throws* him down,
Or reſts his head upon a rock till morn. *Addiſon's Cato.*

4. To venture at dice.

Learn more than thou troweſt,
Set leſs than thou *throweſt.* *Shakeſp. King Lear.*

5. To caſt; to ſtrip off.

There the ſnake *throws* the enamell'd ſkin,
Weed wide enough to wrap a fairy in. *Shakeſpeare.*

6. To emit in any manner.

To arms; for I have *thrown*
A brave defiance in king Henry's teeth. *Shak. Henry* IV.

One of the Greek orator's antagoniſts reading over the oration that procured his baniſhment, and ſeeing his friends admire it, aſked them, if they were ſo much affected by the bare reading, how much more they would have been alarmed if they had heard him actually *throwing* out ſuch a ſtorm of eloquence. *Addiſon.*

There is no need to *throw* words of contempt on ſuch a practice; the very deſcription of it carries reproof. *Watts.*

7. To ſpread in haſte.

O'er his fair limbs a flow'ry veſt he *threw*,
And iſſu'd like a god to mortal view. *Pope's Odyſſey.*

8. To overturn in wreſtling.

If the ſinner ſhall not only wreſtle with this angel, but *throw* him too, and win ſo complete a victory over his conſcience, that all theſe conſiderations ſhall be able to ſtrike no terrour into his mind, he is too ſtrong for grace. *South.*

9. To drive; to ſend by force.

Myſelf diſtreſt, an exile and unknown,
Debarr'd from Europe, and from Aſia *thrown*,
In Libyan deſarts wander thus alone. *Dryden's Æn.*

When ſeamen are *thrown* upon any unknown coaſt in America, they never venture upon the fruit of any tree, unleſs they obſerve it marked with the pecking of birds. *Addiſon.*

Poor youth! how canſt thou *throw* him from thee?
Lucia, thou know'ſt not half the love he bears thee. *Add.*

10. To make to act at a diſtance.

Throw out our eyes for brave Othello,
Even till we make th' aerial blue
An indiſtinct regard. *Shakeſp. Othello.*

11. To repoſe.

In time of temptation be not buſy to diſpute, but rely upon the concluſion, and *throw* your ſelf upon God, and contend not with him but in prayer. *Taylor's holy living.*

12. To change by any kind of violence.

A new title, or an unſuſpected ſucceſs, *throws* us out of ourſelves, and in a manner deſtroys our identity. *Addiſon.*

To *throw* his language more out of proſe, Homer affects the compound epithets. *Pope.*

13. To turn. [*tornare*, Lat.] *Ainſ.*

14. *To* THROW *away*. To loſe; to ſpend in vain.

He warms 'em to avoid the courts and camps,
Where dilatory fortune plays the jilt
With the brave, noble, honeſt, gallant man,
To *throw* herſelf *away* on fools and knaves. *Otway.*

In vain on ſtudy time *away* we *throw*,
When we forbear to act the things we know. *Denham.*

A man had better *throw away* his care upon any thing elſe than upon a garden on wet or moiſt ground. *Temple.*

Had we but laſting youth and time to ſpare,
Some might be *thrown away* on fame and war. *Dryden.*

He ſigh'd, breath'd ſhort, and wou'd have ſpoke,
But was too fierce to *throw away* the time. *Dryden.*

The next in place and puniſhment are they
Who prodigally *threw* their ſouls *away*;
Fools who, repining at their wretched ſtate,
And loathing anxious life, ſuborn'd their fate. *Dryden.*

In poetry the expreſſion beautifies the deſign; if it be vicious or unpleaſing, the coſt of colouring is *thrown away* upon it. *Dryden's Dufreſnoy.*

The well-meaning man ſhould rather conſider what opportunities he has of doing good to his country, than *throw away* his time in deciding the rights of princes. *Addiſon.*

She *threw away* her money upon roaring bullies, that went about the ſtreets. *Arbuthnot's Hiſt. of John Bull.*

15. *To* THROW *away*. To reject.

He that will *throw away* a good book becauſe it is not gilded, is more curious to pleaſe his eye than underſtanding. *Taylor.*

16. *To* THROW *by*. To reject; to lay aſide as of no uſe.

It can but ſhew
Like one of Juno's diſguiſes; and,
When things ſucceed, be *thrown by*, or let fall. *B. Johnſ.*

He that begins to have any doubt of his tenets, received without examination, ought, in reference to that queſtion, to *throw* wholly *by* all his former notions. *Locke.*

17. *To* THROW *down*. To ſubvert; to overturn.

Muſt one raſh word, th' infirmity of age,
Throw down the merit of my better years:
This the reward of a whole life of ſervice? *Addiſon.*

18. *To* THROW *off*. To expel.

The ſalts and oils in the animal body, as ſoon as they putrefy, are *thrown off*, or produce mortal diſtempers. *Arbuth.*

19. *To* THROW *off*. To reject; to renounce: as, *to* throw off *an acquaintance.*

'Twou'd be better
Cou'd you provoke him to give you th' occaſion,
And then to *throw* him *off*. *Dryden's Spaniſh Fryar.*

Can there be any reaſon why the houſhold of God alone ſhould *throw off* all that orderly dependence and duty, by which all other houſes are beſt governed? *Sprat.*

20. *To* THROW *out*. To exert; to bring forth into act.

She *throws out* thrilling ſhrieks and ſhrieking cries. *Spenſ.*

The gods in bounty work up ſtorms about us,
That give mankind occaſion to exert
Their hidden ſtrength, and *throw out* into practice
Virtues which ſhun the day. *Addiſon.*

21. *To* THROW *out*. To diſtance; to leave behind.

When e'er did Juba, or did Portius, ſhow
A virtue that has caſt me at a diſtance,
And *thrown* me *out* in the purſuits of honour? *Addiſon.*

22. *To* THROW *out*. To eject; to expel.

The other two whom they had *thrown out* they were content ſhould enjoy their exile. *Swift.*

23. *To* THROW *out*. To reject; to exclude.

The oddneſs of the propoſition taught others to reflect a little; and the bill was *thrown out*. *Swift.*

24. *To* THROW *up*. To reſign angrily.

Bad games are *thrown up* too ſoon,
Until they're never to be won. *Hudibras, p.* iii.

Experienced gameſters *throw up* their cards when they know the game is in the enemy's hand, without unneceſſary vexation in playing it out. *Addiſon's Freeholder.*

Life we muſt not part with fooliſhly: it muſt not be *thrown up* in a pet, nor ſacrificed to a quarrel. *Collier.*

25. *To* THROW *up*. To emit; to eject; to bring up.

Judge of the cauſe by the ſubſtances the patient *throws up.* *Arbuthnot.*

To THROW. *v. n.*

1. To perform the act of caſting.

2. To caſt dice.

3. *To* THROW *about*. To caſt about; to try expedients.

Now unto deſpair I 'gin to grow,
And mean for better wind *about to throw.* *Hubberd.*

THROW. *n. ſ.* [from the verb.]

1. A caſt; the act of caſting or throwing.

He heav'd a stone, and rising to the *throw*
He sent it in a whirlwind at the foe;
A tow'r assaulted by so rude a stroke,
With all its lofty battlements had shook. *Addison.*

2. A cast of dice; the manner in which the dice fall when they are cast.

If Hercules and Lichas play at dice
Which is the better man, the greater *throw*
May turn by fortune from the weaker hand:
So is Alcides beaten by his page. *Shakespeare.*

If they err finally, it is like a man's missing his cast when he throws dice for his life; his being, his happiness, and all, is involved in the errour of one *throw*. *South's Sermons.*

Suppose any particular order of the alphabet to be assigned, and the twenty-four letters cast at a venture, so as to fall in a line; it is many million of millions odds to one against any single *throw*, that the assigned order will not be cast. *Bentley's Sermons.*

3. The space to which any thing is thrown.

I have ever narrified my friends,
Like to a bowl upon a subtle ground
I've tumbled past the *throw*; and in his praise
Have, almost, stamp'd the leasing. *Shakesp. Coriolanus.*

The Sirenum Scopuli are two or three sharp rocks that stand about a stone's *throw* from the south side of the island. *Addison.*

4. Stroke; blow.

So fierce he laid about him, and dealt blows
On either side, that neither mail could hold,
Ne shield defend the thunder of his *throws*. *Fa. Queen.*

5. Effort; violent sally.

Your youth admires
The *throws* and swellings of a Roman soul;
Cato's bold flights, the extravagance of virtue. *Addison.*

6. The agony of childbirth: in this sense it is written *throe*. See THROE.

The most pregnant wit in the world never brings forth any thing great without some pain and travail, pangs and *throws* before the delivery. *South's Sermons.*

But when the mother's *throws* begin to come,
The creature, pent within the narrow room,
Breaks his blind prison. *Dryden.*

Say, my friendship wants him
To help me bring to light a manly birth;
Which to the wand'ring world I shall disclose;
Or if he fail me, perish in my *throws*. *Dryden.*

THRO'WER. *n. s.* [from *throw*.] One that throws.

Antigonus,
Since fate, against thy better disposition,
Hath made thy person for the *thrower* out
Of my poor babe;
Places remote enough are in Bohemia,
There weep, or leave it crying. *Shakesp. Winter's Tale.*

THRUM. *n. s.* [*thraum*, Islandick, the end of any thing.]

1. The ends of weavers threads.

2. Any coarse yarn.

There's her *thrum* hat, and her muffler too. *Shakespeare.*

O fates, come, come,
Cut thread and *thrum*,
Quail, crush, conclude and quell. *Shakespeare.*

All moss hath here and there little stalks, besides the low *thrum*. *Bacon's Nat. Hist.* N°. 537.

Wou'd our *thrum*-cap'd ancestors find fault
For want of sugar tongs, or spoons for salt. *King.*

To THRUM. *v. a.* To grate; to play coarsly.

Blunderbusses planted in every loop-hole, go off constantly at the squeaking of a fiddle and the *thrumming* of a guittar. *Dryden's Spanish Fryar.*

THRUSH. *n. s.* [þꞃiꞅc, Saxon.]

1. A small singing bird.

Of singing birds they have linnets, goldfinches, blackbirds and *thrushes*. *Carew's Survey of Cornwall.*

Pain, and a fine *thrush*, have been severally endeavouring to call off my attention; but both in vain. *Pope.*

2. [From *thrust*: as we say, a *push*; a *breaking out*.] By this name are called small, round, superficial ulcerations, which appear first in the mouth; but as they proceed from the obstruction of the emissaries of the saliva, by the lentor and viscosity of the humour, they may affect every part of the alimentary duct except the thick guts: they are just the same in the inward parts as scabs in the skin, and fall off from the inside of the bowels like a crust: the nearer they approach to a white colour the less dangerous. *Arbuthnot on Diet.*

To THRUST. *v. a.* [*trusito*, Lat.]

1. To push any thing into matter, or between close bodies.

Thrust in thy sickle and reap. *Rev.* xiv. 15.

2. To push; to remove with violence; to drive. It is used of persons or things.

They should not only not be *thrust* out, but also have estates and grants of their lands new made to them. *Spenser.*

When the king comes, offer him no violence,
Unless he seek to *thrust* you out by force. *Shakespeare.*

Lock up my doors; and when you hear the drum,
Clamber not you up to the casements then,
Nor *thrust* your head into the publick streets. *Shakespeare.*

When the ass saw the angel, she *thrust* herself unto the wall, and crusht Balaam's foot. *Num.* xxii. 22.

On this condition will I make a covenant with you, that I may *thrust* out all your right eyes. 1 *Sam.* xi. 2.

She caught him by the feet; but Gehazi came near to *thrust* her away. 2 *Kings* iv. 27.

Thou shalt stone him that he die; because he hath sought to *thrust* thee away from the Lord. *Deut.* xiii. 10.

The prince shall not take of the people's inheritance, by oppression to *thrust* them out. *Isa.* xlvi. 18.

Thou Capernaum, which art exalted to heaven, shalt be *thrust* down to hell. *Luke* x. 15.

The sons of Belial shall be as thorns *thrust* away. 2 *Sam.*

Rich, then lord chancellor, a man of quick and lively delivery of speech, but as of mean birth so prone to *thrust* forwards the ruin of great persons, in this manner spake. *Hayw.*

They
In hate of kings shall cast anew the frame,
And *thrust* out Collatine that bore their name. *Dryden.*

To justify his threat, he *thrusts* aside
The croud of centaurs; and redeems the bride. *Dryden.*

3. To stab.

Phineas *thrust* both of them through. *Num.* xxv. 8.

4. To compress.

He *thrust* the fleece together, and wringed the dew out of it. *Judg.* vi. 38.

5. To impel; to urge.

We make guilty of our disasters, the sun, the moon, and stars, as if we were villains on necessity, and all that we are evil in, by a divine *thrusting* on. *Shakesp. King Lear.*

6. To obtrude; to intrude.

Who's there, I say? How dare you *thrust* yourselves
Into my private meditations? *Shakesp. Henry* VIII.

I go to meet
The noble Brutus, *thrusting* this report
Into his ears. *Shakespeare's Julius Cæsar.*

Should he not do as rationally, who, upon this assurance, took physick from any one who had taken on himself the name of physician, or *thrust* himself into that employment. *Locke.*

To THRUST. *v. n.*

1. To make a hostile push; to attack with a pointed weapon.

2. To squeeze in; to put himself into any place by violence.

I'll be a Spartan while I live on earth;
But when in heav'n, I'll stand next Hercules,
And *thrust* between my father and the god. *Dryden.*

3. To intrude.

Not all,
Who like intruders *thrust* into their service,
Participate their sacred influence. *Rowe.*

4. To push forwards; to come violently; to throng; to press.

Young, old, *thrust* there,
In mighty concourse. *Chapman's Odyssey.*

The miserable men which shrunk from the work were again beaten forward, and presently slain; and fresh men still *thrust* on. *Knolles's Hist. of the Turks.*

THRUST. *n. s.* [from the verb.]

1. Hostile attack with any pointed weapon.

Zelmane hearkening to no more, began with such witty fury to pursue him with blows and *thrusts*, that nature and virtue commanded him to look to his safety. *Sidney.*

That *thrust* had been mine enemy indeed,
But that my coat is better than thou know'st. *Shakespeare.*

Polites Pyrrhus, with his lance, pursues,
And often reaches, and his *thrusts* renews. *Dryden.*

2. Assault; attack.

There is one *thrust* at your pure, pretended mechanism. *More's Divine Dialogues.*

THRU'STER. *n. s.* [from *thrust*.] He that thrusts.

THRU'STLE. *n. s.* [from *thrush*.] Thrush; throstle.

No *thrustles* shrill the bramble bush forsake;
No chirping lark the welkin sheen invokes. *Gay.*

To THRYFA'LLOW. *v. a.* [*thrice* and *fallow*.] To give the third plowing in summer.

Thryfallow betime for destroying of weed,
Lest thistle and docke fal a blooming and seed. *Tusser.*

THUMB. *n. s.* [ꞇuma, Saxon.] The short strong finger answering to the other four.

Here I have a pilot's *thumb*,
Wreck'd as homeward he did come. *Shakesp. Macbeth.*

When he is dead you will wear him in *thumb* rings, as the Turks did Scanderbeg. *Dryden.*

Every man in Turkey is of some trade: Sultan Achmet was a maker of ivory rings, which the Turks wear upon their *thumbs* when they shoot their arrows. *Broome.*

It is divided into four fingers bending forwards, and one opposite bending backwards called the *thumb*, to join with them severally or united, whereby it is fitted to lay hold of objects. *Ray on the Creation.*

THU'MB-BAND. *n. ſ.* [*thumb* and *band.*] A twiſt of any materials made thick as a man's thumb.

Tie *thumb-bands* of hay round them. *Mortimer.*

To THUMB. *v. n.* To handle aukwardly.

THUMBSTAL. *n. ſ.* [*thumb* and *ſtall.*] A thimble.

THUMP. *n. ſ.* [*thombo*, Italian.] A hard heavy dead dull blow with ſomething blunt.

And blund'ring ſtill with ſmarting rump,
He gave the knight's ſteed ſuch a *thump*
As made him reel. *Hudibras, p.* i.

Before, behind, the blows are dealt; around
Their hollow ſides the rattling *thumps* reſound. *Dryden.*

Their *thumps* and bruiſes might turn to account, if they could beat each other into good manners. *Addiſon.*

The watchman gave ſo great a *thump* at my door, that I awaked at the knock. *Tatler.*

To THUMP. *v. a.* To beat with dull heavy blows.

Thoſe baſtard Britons whom our fathers
Have in their land beaten, bobb'd, and *thump'd*. *Shakeſp.*

To THUMP. *v. n.* To fall or ſtrike with a dull heavy blow.

A ſtone
Levell'd ſo right, it *thump'd* upon
His manly paunch, with ſuch a force
As almoſt beat him off his horſe. *Hudibras, p.* i.

A watchman at midnight *thumps* with his pole. *Swift.*

THU'MPER. *n. ſ.* [from *thump.*] The perſon or thing that thumps.

THU'NDER. *n. ſ.* [ðunder, ðunor, Saxon; *dunder*, Swediſh; *donder*, Dutch; *tonnere*, Fr.]

Thunder is a moſt bright flame riſing on a ſudden, moving with great violence, and with a very rapid velocity, through the air, according to any determination, upwards from the earth, horizontally, obliquely, downwards, in a right line, or in ſeveral right lines, as it were in ſerpentine tracts, joined at various angles, and commonly ending with a loud noiſe or rattling. *Muſchenbroek.*

2. In popular and poetick language *thunder* is commonly the noiſe, and *lightning* the flaſh; though *thunder* is ſometimes taken for both.

I do not bid the *thunder* bearer ſhoot,
Nor tell tales of thee to high-judging Jove. *Shakeſpeare.*

No more, thou *thunder* maſter, ſhew
Thy ſpite on mortal flies. *Shakeſp. Cymbeline.*

The revenging gods
'Gainſt parricides all the *thunder* bend. *Shakeſpeare.*

The *thunder*
Wing'd with red light'ning and impetuous rage,
Perhaps hath ſpent his ſhafts, and ceaſes now
To bellow through the vaſt and boundleſs deep. *Milton.*

3. Any loud noiſe or tumultuous violence.

So fierce he laid about him, and dealt blows
On either ſide, that neither mail could hold
Ne ſhield defend the *thunder* of his throws. *Spenſer.*

Here will we face this ſtorm of inſolence,
Nor fear the noiſy *thunder*; let it roll,
Then burſt, and ſpend at once its idle rage. *Rowe.*

To THU'NDER. *v. n.* [from the noun.]

1. To make thunder.

His nature is too noble for the world:
He would not flatter Neptune for his trident,
Nor Jove for's power to *thunder*. *Shakeſp. Coriolanus.*

2. To make a loud or terrible noiſe.

So ſoon as ſome few notable examples had *thundered* a duty into the ſubjects hearts, he ſoon ſhewed no baſeneſs of ſuſpicion. *Sidney, b.* ii.

His dreadful name late through all Spain did *thunder*,
And Hercules' two pillars ſtanding near,
Did make to quake and fear. *Spenſer.*

His dreadful voice no more
Would *thunder* in my ears. *Milton.*

Like a black ſheet the whelming billow ſpread,
Burſt o'er the float, and *thunder'd* on his head. *Pope.*

To THU'NDER. *v. a.*

1. To emit with noiſe and terrour.

Oracles ſevere,
Were daily *thunder'd* in our general's ear,
That by his daughter's blood we muſt appeaſe
Diana's kindled wrath. *Dryden.*

2. To publiſh any denunciation or threat.

An archdeacon, as being a prelate, may *thunder* out an eccleſiaſtical cenſure. *Ayliffe.*

THU'NDERBOLT. *n. ſ.* [*thunder* and *bolt*, as it ſignifies an arrow.]

1. Lightning; the arrows of heaven.

If I had a *thunderbolt* in mine eye, I can tell who ſhould down. *Shakeſpeare.*

Let the lightning of this *thunderbolt*, which hath been ſo ſevere a puniſhment to one, be a terrour to all. *K. Charles.*

My heart does beat,
As if 'twere forging *thunderbolts* for Jove. *Denham.*

Who can omit the Gracchi, who declare
The Scipio's worth, thoſe *thunderbolts* of war? *Dryden.*

The moſt remarkable piece in Antonine's pillar, is Jupiter Pluvius ſending down rain on the fainting army of Marcus Aurelius, and *thunderbolts* on his enemies; which is the greateſt confirmation of the ſtory of the Chriſtian legion. *Addiſon.*

2. Fulmination; denunciation properly eccleſiaſtical.

He ſeverely threatens ſuch with the *thunderbolt* of excommunication. *Hakewill on Providence.*

THU'NDERCLAP. *n. ſ.* [*thunder* and *clap.*] Exploſion of thunder.

The kindly bird that bears Jove's *thunderclap*,
One day did ſcorn the ſimple ſcarabee,
Proud of his higheſt ſervice, and good hap,
That made all other fowls his thralls to be. *Spenſer.*

When ſome dreadful *thunderclap* is nigh,
The winged fire ſhoots ſwiftly through the ſky;
Strikes and conſumes ere ſcarce it does appear,
And, by the ſudden ill, prevents the fear. *Dryden.*

When ſuddenly the *thunderclap* was heard,
It took us unprepar'd, and out of guard. *Dryden.*

THU'NDERER. *n. ſ.* [from *thunder.*] The power that thunders.

How dare you, ghoſts,
Accuſe the *thunderer*, whoſe bolt you know,
Sky-planted, batters all rebelling coaſts? *Shakeſpeare.*

Had the old Greeks diſcover'd your abode,
Crete had'nt been the cradle of their god;
On that ſmall iſland they had look'd with ſcorn,
And in Great Britain thought the *thunderer* born. *Waller.*

When the bold Typheus
Forc'd great Jove from his own heav'n to fly,
The leſſer gods that ſhar'd his proſp'rous ſtate,
All ſuffer'd in the exil'd *thunderer*'s fate. *Dryden.*

THU'NDEROUS. *adj.* [from *thunder.*] Producing thunder.

Look in and ſee each bliſsful deity,
How he before the *thunderous* throne doth lie. *Milton.*

THU'NDERSHOWER. *n. ſ.* [*thunder* and *ſhower.*] A rain accompanied with thunder.

The conceit is long in delivering, and at laſt it comes like a *thunderſhower*, full of ſulphur and darkneſs, with a terrible crack. *Stillingfleet.*

In *thunderſhowers* the winds and clouds are oftentimes contrary to one another, eſpecially if hail falls, the ſultry weather below directing the wind one way, and the cold above the clouds another. *Derham's Phyſico-Theol.*

THU'NDERSTONE. *n. ſ.* [*thunder* and *ſtone.*] A ſtone fabulouſly ſuppoſed to be emitted by thunder; thunderbolt.

Fear no more the light'ning flaſh,
Nor th' all-dreaded *thunderſtone*. *Shakeſp. Cymbeline.*

To THU'NDERSTRIKE. *v. a.* [*thunder* and *ſtrike.*] To blaſt or hurt with lightning.

I remained as a man *thunderſtricken*, not daring, nay not able, to behold that power. *Sidney.*

The overthrown he rais'd, and as a herd
Of goats, or tim'rous flock, together throng'd,
Drove them before him *thunderſtruck*. *Milton.*

With the voice divine
Nigh *thunderſtruck*, th' exalted man, to whom
Such high atteſt was giv'n, a while ſurvey'd
With wonder. *Milton's Par. Reg. b.* i.

'Tis ſaid that *thunderſtruck* Enceladus
Lies ſtretch'd ſupine. *Addiſon.*

THURI'FEROUS. *adj.* [*thurifer*, Lat.] Bearing frankincenſe.

THURIFICA'TION. *n. ſ.* [*thuris* and *facio*, Latin.] The act of fuming with incenſe; the act of burning incenſe.

The ſeveral acts of worſhip which were required to be performed to images are proceſſions, genuflections, *thurifications*, deoſculations, and oblations. *Stillingfleet.*

THU'RSDAY. *n. ſ.* [*thorſgday*, Daniſh; from *thor*. *Thor* was the ſon of Odin, yet in ſome of the northern parts they worſhipped the ſupreme deity under his name, attributing the power over all things, even the inferior deities, to him. *Stillingfleet.*] The fifth day of the week.

THUS. *adv.* [ðuſ, Saxon.]

1. In this manner; in this wiſe.

It cannot be that they who ſpeak *thus*, ſhould *thus* judge. *Hooker, b.* v.

The knight him calling, aſked who he was,
Who lifting up his head, him anſwered *thus*. *Fa. Qu.*

I return'd with ſimilar proof enough,
With tokens *thus*, and *thus*. *Shakeſp. Cymbeline.*

To be *thus* is nothing;
But to be ſafely *thus*. *Shakeſpeare's Macbeth.*

I have ſinned againſt the Lord, and *thus* and *thus* have I done. *Joſ.* vii. 23.

That the principle that ſets on work theſe organs, is nothing elſe but the modification of matter *thus* or *thus* poſited, is falſe. *Judge Hale.*

Beware, I warn thee yet, to tell thy griefs
In terms becoming majeſty to hear:
I warn thee *thus*, becauſe I know thy temper
Is inſolent. *Dryden's Don Sebaſtian.*

Thus

4

Thus in the triumphs of soft peace I reign. *Dryden.*

All were attentive to the godlike man,
When from his lofty couch he *thus* began. *Dryden's Æn.*

2. To this degree; to this quantity.

A counsellor of state in Spain said to his master, I will tell your majesty *thus* much for your comfort, your majesty hath but two enemies; whereof the one is all the world, and the other your own ministers. *Bacon.*

He said *thus* far extend, *thus* far thy bounds. *Milton.*

Thus much concerning the first earth, and its production and form. *Burnet's Theory of the Earth.*

No man reasonably pretends to know *thus* much, but he must pretend to know all things. *Tillotson's Sermons.*

This you must do to inherit life; and if you have come up *thus* far, firmly persevere in it. *Wake.*

To THWACK. *v. a.* [ðaccian, Saxon.] To strike with something blunt and heavy; to thresh; to bang; to belabour.

He shall not stay;
We'll *thwack* him hence with distaffs. *Shakespeare.*

Nick fell foul upon John Bull, to snatch the cudgel he had in his hand, that he might *thwack* Lewis with it. *Arbuthnot.*

These long fellows, as sightly as they are, should find their jackets well *thwack'd.* *Arbuthnot.*

THWACK. *n. s.* [from the verb.] A heavy hard blow.

But Talgol first with a hard *thwack*
Twice bruis'd his head, and twice his back. *Hudibras.*

They place several pots of rice, with cudgels in the neighbourhood of each pot; the monkeys descend from the trees, take up the arms, and belabour one another with a storm of *thwacks.* *Addison's Freeholder*, N°. 50.

THWART. *adj.* [ðpyꞃ, Saxon; *dwars*, Dutch.]

1. Transverse; cross to something else.

This else to several spheres thou must ascribe,
Mov'd contrary with *thwart* obliquities. *Milton.*

2. Perverse; inconvenient; mischievous.

To THWART. *v. a.*

1. To cross; to lie or come cross any thing.

Swift as a shooting star
In Autumn *thwarts* the night. *Milton's Par. Lost*, *b.* iv.

Yon stream of light, a thousand ways
Upward and downward *thwarting* and convolv'd. *Thomson.*

2. To cross; to oppose; to traverse; to contravene.

Some sixteen months and longer might have staid,
If crooked fortune had not *thwarted* me. *Shakespeare.*

Lesser had been
The *thwartings* of your dispositions, if
You had not shew'd how you were dispos'd
Ere they lack'd power to cross you. *Shakesp. Coriolanus.*

The understanding and will never disagreed; for the proposals of the one never *thwarted* the inclinations of the other. *South's Sermons.*

The rays both good and bad, of equal pow'r,
Each *thwarting* other made a mingled hour. *Dryden.*

In vain did I the godlike youth deplore,
The more I begg'd, they *thwarted* me the more. *Addison.*

Neptune aton'd, his wrath shall now refrain,
Or *thwart* the synod of the gods in vain. *Pope's Odyssey.*

To THWART. *v. n.* To be opposite.

It is easy to be imagined what reception any proposition shall find, that shall at all *thwart* with these internal oracles. *Locke.*

THWA'RTINGLY. *adv.* [from *thwarting.*] Oppositely; with opposition.

THY. *pronoun.* [ðin, Saxon.] Of thee; belonging to thee; relating to thee.

Whatever God did say,
Is all *thy* clear and smooth uninterrupted way. *Cowley.*

Th' example of the heav'nly lark,
Thy fellow-poet Cowley mark. *Cowley.*

These are *thy* works, parent of good. *Milton.*

THYSE'LF. *pronoun reciprocal.* [*thy* and *self.*]

1. It is commonly used in the oblique cases, or following the verb.

Come high or low,
Thyself and office deftly show. *Shakesp. Macbeth.*

It must and shall be so; content *thyself.* *Shakespeare.*

2. In poetical or solemn language it is sometimes used in the nominative.

These goods *thyself* can on *thyself* bestow. *Dryden.*

THYINE *wood. n. s.* A precious wood.

The merchandize of gold and all *thyine wood* are departed from thee. *Rev.* xviii. 12.

THYME. *n. s.* [*thym*, Fr. *thymus*, Lat.] A plant.

The *thyme* hath a labiated flower, consisting of one leaf, whose upper-lip is erect, and generally split in two, and the under-lip is divided into three parts; out of the flower-cup arises the pointal, accompanied by four embrios, which afterward become so many seeds, inclosed in a husk, which before was the flower-cup; to these marks must be added hard ligneous stalks, and the flowers gathered into heads. *Miller.*

No more, my goats, shall I behold you climb
The steepy cliffs, or crop the flow'ry *thyme.* *Dryden.*

TI'AR. } *n. s.* [*tiare*, Fr. *tiara*, Lat.] A dress for the head;
TIA'RA. } a diadem.

His back was turn'd, but not his brightness hid;
Of beaming sunny rays a golden *tiar*
Circled his head. *Milton's Par. Lost*, *b.* iii.

This royal robe, and this *tiara* wore
Old Priam, and this golden scepter bore
In full assemblies. *Dryden's Æn.*

A *tiar* wreath'd her head with many a fold,
Her waste was circled with a zone of gold. *Pope.*

Fairer she seem'd, distinguish'd from the rest,
And better mien disclos'd, as better drest:
A bright *tiara* round her forehead ty'd,
To juster bounds confin'd its rising pride. *Prior.*

To TICE. *v. a.* [from *entice.*] To draw; to allure.

Lovely enchanting language, sugar-cane,
Honey of roses, whither wilt thou flie?
Hath some fond lover *tic'd* thee to thy bane?
And wilt thou leave the church, and love a stie? *Herbert.*

TICK. *n. s.* [This word seems contracted from *ticket*, a tally on which debts are scored.]

1. Score; trust.

If thou hast the heart to try't,
I'll lend thee back thyself awhile,
And once more for that carcase vile
Fight upon *tick.* *Hudibras*, *p.* i.

When the money is got into hands that have bought all that they have need of, whoever needs any thing else must go on *tick*, or barter for it. *Locke.*

You would see him in the kitchen weighing the beef and butter, paying ready money, that the maids might not run a *tick* at the market. *Arbuthnot's Hist. of John Bull.*

2. [*Tique*, Fr. *teke*, Dutch.] The louse of dogs or sheep.

Would the fountain of your mind were clear again, that I might water an ass at it! I had rather be a *tick* in a sheep, than such a valiant ignorance. *Shakesp. Troil. and Cressida.*

3. The case which holds the feathers of a bed.

To TICK. *v. n.* [from the noun.]

1. To run on score.

2. To trust; to score.

The money went to the lawyers; council wont *tick.* *Arb.*

TI'CKEN. } *n. s.* The same with *tick.* A sort of strong
TI'CKING. } linen for bedding. *Bailey.*

TI'CKET. *n. s.* [*etiquet*, Fr.] A token of any right or debt upon the delivery of which admission is granted, or a claim acknowledged.

There should be a paymaster appointed, of special trust, which should pay every man according to his captain's *ticket*, and the account of the clerk of his band. *Spenser.*

In a lottery with one prize, a single *ticket* is only enriched, and the rest are all blanks. *Collier on Envy.*

Let fops or fortune fly which way they will,
Disdains all loss of *tickets* or codille. *Pope.*

To TI'CKLE. *v. a.* [*titillo*, Lat.]

1. To affect with a prurient sensation by slight touches.

Dissembling courtesy! How fine this tyrant
Can *tickle* where she wounds. *Shakesp. Cymbeline.*

The mind is moved in great vehemency only by *tickling* some parts of the body. *Bacon.*

There is a sweetness in good verse, which *tickles* even while it hurts; and no man can be heartily angry with him who pleases him against his will. *Dryden.*

It is a good thing to laugh at any rate; and if a straw can *tickle* a man, it is an instrument of happiness. *Dryden.*

2. To please by slight gratifications.

Dametas, that of all manners of stile could best conceive of golden eloquence, being withal *tickled* by Musidorus's praises, had his brain so turned, that he became slave to that which he that sued to be his servant offered to give him. *Sidney.*

Expectation *tickling* skittish spirits
Sets all on hazard. *Shakespeare.*

Such a nature
Tickled with good success, disdains the shadow
Which it treads on at noon. *Shakesp. Coriolanus.*

I cannot rule my spleen;
My scorn rebels, and *tickles* me within. *Dryden.*

Dunce at the best; in streets but scarce allow'd
To *tickle*, on thy straw, the stupid crowd. *Dryden.*

A drunkard, the habitual thirst after his cups, drives to the tavern, though he has in his view the loss of health, and perhaps of the joys of another life, the least of which is such a good as he confesses is far greater than the *tickling* of his palate with a glass of wine. *Locke.*

To TI'CKLE. *v. n.* To feel titillation.

He with secret joy therefore
Did *tickle* inwardly in every vein,
And his false heart, fraught with all treason's store,
Was fill'd with hope, his purpose to obtain. *Spenser.*

TI'CKLE.

TI'CKLE. *adj.* [I know not whence to deduce the ſenſe of this word.] Tottering; unfixed; unſtable; eaſily overthrown.

When the laſt O Neal began to ſtand upon ſome *tickle* terms, this fellow, called baron of Dunganon, was ſet up to beard him. *Spenſer on Ireland.*

Thy head ſtands ſo *tickle* on thy ſhoulders, that a milk-maid, if ſhe be in love, may ſigh it off. *Shakeſpeare.*

The ſtate of Normandy
Stands on a *tickle* point, now they are gone. *Shakeſpeare.*

TI'CKLISH. *adj.* [from *tickle.*]

1. Senſible to titillation; eaſily tickled.

The palm of the hand, though it hath as thin a ſkin as the other parts, yet is not *ticklish*, becauſe it is accuſtomed to be touched. *Bacon's Nat. Hiſt.* N°. 766.

2. Tottering; uncertain; unfixed.

Ireland was a *ticklish* and unſettled ſtate, more eaſy to receive diſtempers and mutations than England was. *Bacon.*

Did it ſtand upon ſo *ticklish* and tottering a foundation as ſome mens fancy hath placed it, it would be no wonder ſhould it frequently vary. *Woodward's Nat. Hiſt. p.* i.

3. Difficult; nice.

How ſhall our author hope a gentle fate,
Who dares moſt impudently not tranſlate;
It had been civil in theſe *ticklish* times,
To fetch his fools and knaves from foreign climes. *Swift.*

TI'CKLISHNESS. *n. ſ.* [from *ticklish.*] The ſtate of being ticklish.

TI'CKTACK. *n. ſ.* [*trictac*, Fr.] A game at tables. *Bailey.*

TID. *adj.* [tyððer, Saxon.] Tender; ſoft; nice.

To TI'DDLE. } *v. a.* [from *tid.*] To uſe tenderly; to fondle.
To TI'DDER. }

TIDE. *n. ſ.* [tyð, Saxon; *tijd*, Dutch and Iſlandick.]

1. Time; ſeaſon; while.

There they alight in hope themſelves to hide
From the fierce heat, and reſt their weary limbs a *tide*. *Fairy Queen, b.* i.

They two forth paſſing,
Received thoſe two fair brides, their love's delight,
Which, at the appointed *tide*,
Each one did make his bride. *Spenſer.*

What hath this day deſerv'd,
That it in golden letter ſhould be ſet,
Among the high *tides* in the kalendar. *Shakeſp. K. John.*

At New-year's *tide* following the king choſe him maſter of the horſe. *Wotton.*

2. Alternate ebb and flow of the ſea.

That motion of the water called *tides* is a riſing and falling of the ſea: the cauſe of this is the attraction of the Moon, whereby the part of the water in the great ocean which is neareſt the Moon, being moſt ſtrongly attracted, is raiſed higher than the reſt; and the part oppoſite to it being leaſt attracted, is alſo higher than the reſt; and theſe two oppoſite riſes of the ſurface of the water in the great ocean following the motion of the Moon from Eaſt to Weſt, and ſtriking againſt the large coaſts of the continents, from thence rebounds back again, and ſo makes floods and ebbs in narrow ſeas and rivers. *Locke.*

3. Flood.

As in the *tides* of people once up there want not ſtirring winds to make them more rough, ſo this people did light upon two ringleaders. *Bacon's Henry* VII.

4. Stream; courſe.

Thou art the ruins of the nobleſt man,
That ever lived in the *tide* of times. *Shakeſpeare.*

The rapid currents drive
Towards the retreating ſea their furious *tide*. *Milton.*

But let not all the gold which Tagus hides,
And pays the ſea in tributary *tides*,
Be bribe ſufficient to corrupt thy breaſt,
Or violate with dreams thy peaceful reſt. *Dryden.*

Continual *tide*
Flows from th' exhilarating fount. *Philips.*

To TIDE. *v. a.* [from the noun.] To drive with the ſtream.

Their images, the relicks of the wreck,
Torn from the naked poop, are *tided* back
By the wild waves, and rudely thrown aſhore. *Dryden.*

To TIDE. *v. n.* To pour a flood; to be agitated by the tide.

When, from his dint, the foe ſtill backward ſhrunk,
Wading within the Ouſe, he dealt his blows,
And ſent them, rolling, to the *tiding* Humber. *Philips.*

TI'DEGATE. *n. ſ.* [*tide* and *gate.*] A gate through which the tide paſſes into a baſon. *Bailey.*

TI'DESMAN. *n. ſ.* [*tide* and *man.*] A tidewaiter or cuſtomhouſe officer, who watches on board of merchant ſhips till the duty of goods be paid and the ſhips unloaded. *Bailey.*

TI'DEWAITER. *n. ſ.* [*tide* and *wait.*] An officer who watches the landing of goods at the cuſtomhouſe.

Employments will be in the hands of Engliſhmen; nothing left for Iriſhmen but vicarages and *tidewaiters* places. *Swift.*

TI'DILY. *adv.* [from *tidy.*] Neatly; readily.

TI'DINESS. *n. ſ.* [from *tidy.*] Neatneſs; readineſs.

TI'DINGS. *n. ſ.* [tiðan, Saxon, *to happen, to betide*; *tidende*, Iſlandick.] News; an account of ſomething that has happened.

When her eyes ſhe on the dwarf had ſet,
And ſaw the ſigns that deadly *tidings* ſpake,
She fell to ground for ſorrowful regret. *Fairy Qu. b.* i.

I ſhall make my maſter glad with theſe *tidings*. *Shakeſp.*

They win
Great numbers of each nation to receive,
With joy, the *tidings* brought from heav'n. *Milton.*

Portius, thy looks ſpeak ſomewhat of importance:
What *tidings* doſt thou bring? methinks I ſee
Unuſual gladneſs ſparkling in thy eyes. *Addiſon.*

The meſſenger of theſe glad *tidings*, by whom this covenant of mercy was propoſed and ratified, was the eternal ſon of his boſom. *Rogers's Sermons.*

TI'DY. *adj.* [*tidt*, Iſlandick.]

1. Seaſonable.

If weather be faire and *tidie*, thy grain
Make ſpeedilie carriage, for feare of a raine. *Tuſſer.*

2. Neat; ready.

Whenever by yon barley-mow I paſs,
Before my eyes will trip the *tidy* laſs. *Gay's Paſt.*

3. It ſeems to be here put by miſtake for *untidy*.

Thou whorſon *tidy* Bartholomew boar pig, when wilt thou leave fighting. *Shakeſp. Henry* IV.

To TIE. *v. a.* [tian, tigan, Saxon.]

1. To bind; to faſten with a knot.

Tie the kine to the cart, and bring their calves home from them. 1 *Sam.* vi. 7.

Thouſands of men and women, *tied* together in chains, were, by the cruel Turks, enforced to run as faſt as their horſes. *Knolles's Hiſt. of the Turks.*

2. To knit; to complicate.

We do not *tie* this knot with an intention to puzzle the argument; but the harder it is *tied*, we ſhall feel the pleaſure more ſenſibly when we come to looſe it. *Burnet.*

3. To hold; to faſten.

In bond of virtuous love together *tied*,
Together ſerv'd they, and together died. *Fairfax.*

The intermediate ideas *tie* the extremes ſo firmly together, and the probability is ſo clear, that aſſent neceſſarily follows it. *Locke.*

Certain theorems reſolve propoſitions which depend on them, and are as firmly made out from thence, as if the mind went afreſh over every link of the whole chain that *ties* them to firſt ſelf-evident principles. *Locke.*

4. To hinder; to obſtruct.

Death that hath ta'n her hence to make me wail,
Ties up my tongue and will not let me ſpeak. *Shakeſp.*

Melantius ſtay,
You have my promiſe, and my haſty word
Reſtrains my tongue, but *ties* not up my ſword. *Waller.*

Honour and good-nature may *tie* up his hands; but as theſe would be very much ſtrengthened by reaſon and principle, ſo without them they are only inſtincts. *Addiſon.*

5. To oblige; to conſtrain; to reſtrain; to confine.

Although they profeſs they agree with us touching a preſcript form of prayer to be uſed in the church, they have declared that it ſhall not be preſcribed as a thing whereunto they will *tie* their miniſters. *Hooker, b.* v.

It is the cowiſh terrour of his ſpirit,
That dares not undertake; he'll not feel wrongs
Which *tie* him to an anſwer. *Shakeſp. King Lear.*

Cannot God make any of the appropriate acts of worſhip to become due only to himſelf? cannot he *tie* us to perform them to him. *Stillingfleet.*

They *tie* themſelves ſo ſtrictly to unity of place, that you never ſee in any of their plays a ſcene change in the middle of an act. *Dryden.*

Not *tied* to rules of policy, you find
Revenge leſs ſweet than a forgiving mind. *Dryden.*

No one ſeems leſs *tied* up to a form of words. *Locke.*

The mind ſhould, by ſeveral rules, be *tied* down to this, at firſt, uneaſy taſk; uſe will give it facility. *Locke.*

They have no uneaſy expectations of what is to come, but are ever *tied* down to the preſent moment. *Atterbury.*

A healthy man ought not to *tie* himſelf up to ſtrict rules, nor to abſtain from any ſort of food in common uſe. *Arbuth.*

6. It may be obſerved of *tie*, that it has often the particles *up* and *down* joined to it, which are, for the moſt part, little more than emphatical.

TIE. *n. ſ.* [from the verb.]

1. Knot; faſtening.

2. Bond; obligation.

The rebels that had ſhaken off the great yoke of obedience, had likewiſe caſt away the leſſer *tie* of reſpect. *Bacon.*

No foreſt, cave, or ſavage den,
Holds more pernicious beaſts than men;
Vows, oaths, and contracts, they deviſe,
And tell us they are ſacred *ties*. *Waller.*

'Tis

'Tis not the coarſer *tie* of human law
That binds their peace, but harmony itſelf
Attuning all their paſſions into love. *Thomſon's Spring.*

TIER. *n. ſ.* [*tiere*, *tieire*, old Fr. *tuyer*, Dutch.] A row; a rank.

Fornovius, in his choler, diſcharged a *tier* of great ordnance amongſt the thickeſt of them. *Knolles.*

TIERCE. *n. ſ.* [*tiers*, *tiercier*, Fr.] A veſſel holding the third part of a pipe.

Go now deny his *tierce*. *Benj. Johnſon.*

Wit, like *tierce* claret, when't begins to pall,
Neglected lies, and 's of no uſe at all;
But in its full perfection of decay
Turns vinegar, and comes again in play. *Dorſet.*

TI'ERCET. *n. ſ.* [from *tiers*, Fr.] A triplet; three lines.

TIFF. *n. ſ.* [A low word, I ſuppoſe without etymology.]

1. Liquor; drink.

I, whom griping penury ſurrounds,
And hunger, ſure attendant upon want,
With ſcanty offals, and ſmall acid *tiff*,
Wretched repaſt! my meagre corps ſuſtain. *Phillips.*

2. A fit of peeviſhneſs or ſullenneſs; a pet.

To TIFF. *v. n.* To be in a pet; to quarrel. A low word.

TI'FFANY. *n. ſ.* [*tiffer*, to dreſs up, old Fr. *Skinner.*] Very thin ſilk.

The ſmoak of ſulphur will not black a paper, and is commonly uſed by women to whiten *tiffanies*. *Brown.*

TIGE. *n. ſ.* [in architecture.] The ſhaft of a column from the aſtragal to the capital. *Bailey.*

TI'GER. *n. ſ.* [*tigre*, Fr. *tigris*, Latin.] A fierce beaſt of the leonine kind.

When the blaſt of war blows in your ear,
Then imitate the action of the *tiger*:
Stiffen the ſinews, ſummon up the blood. *Shakeſp. H. V.*

Approach thou like the rugged Ruſſian bear,
The arm'd rhinoceros, or Hyrcanian *tiger*;
Take any ſhape but that, and my firm nerves
Shall never tremble. *Shakeſp. Macbeth.*

This *tiger*-footed rage, when it ſhall find
The harm of unſkain'd ſwiftneſs will, too late,
Tie leaden pounds to's heels. *Shakeſp. Coriolanus.*

Tigris, in the medals of Trajan, is drawn like an old man, and by his ſide a *tiger*. *Peacham on Drawing.*

Has the ſteer,
At whoſe ſtrong cheſt the deadly *tiger* hangs,
E'er plow'd for him. *Thomſon's Spring.*

TIGHT. *adj.* [*dicht*, Dutch.]

1. Tenſe; cloſe; not looſe.

If the centre holes be not very deep, and the pikes fill them not very *tight*, the ſtrength of the ſtring will alter the centre holes. *Moxon's Mech. Exerciſe.*

I do not like this running knot, it holds too *tight*; I may be ſtifled all of a ſudden. *Arbuthnot's Hiſt. of J. Bull.*

Every joint was well grooved; and the door did not move on hinges, but up and down like a ſaſh, which kept my cloſet ſo *tight* that very little water came in. *Gulliver's Travels.*

2. Free from fluttering rags; leſs than neat.

A *tight* maid ere he for wine can aſk,
Gueſſes his meaning and unoils the flaſk. *Dryden's Juv.*

The girl was a *tight* clever wench as any. *Arbuthnot.*

O Thomas, I'll make a loving wife;
I'll ſpin and card, and keep our children *tight*. *Gay.*

Dreſt her again genteel and neat,
And rather *tight* than great. *Swift.*

To TI'GHTEN. *v. a.* [from *tight.*] To ſtraiten; to make cloſe.

TI'GHTER. *n. ſ.* [from *tighten.*] A ribband or ſtring by which women ſtraiten their cloaths.

TI'GHTLY. *adv.* [from *tight.*]

1. Cloſely; not looſely.

2. Neatly; not idly.

Hold, ſirrah, bear you theſe letters *tightly*;
Sail, like my pinnace, to theſe golden ſhores. *Shakeſpeare.*

Handle your pruning-knife with dexterity: *tightly*, I ſay, go *tightly* to your buſineſs; you have coſt me much. *Dryden.*

TI'GHTNESS. *n. ſ.* [from *tight.*] Cloſeneſs; not looſeneſs.

The bones are inflexible, which ariſes from the greatneſs of the number of corpuſcles that compoſe them, and the firmneſs and *tightneſs* of their union. *Woodward on Foſſils.*

TI'GRESS. *n. ſ.* [from *tiger.*] The female of the tiger.

It is reported of the *tigreſs*, that ſeveral ſpots riſe in her ſkin when ſhe is angry. *Addiſon's Spect.* N. 81.

TIKE. *n. ſ.* [*tik*, Swediſh; *teke*, Dutch; *tique*, Fr.]

1. The louſe of dogs or ſheep. See TICK.

Lice and *tikes* are bred by the ſweat cloſe kept, and ſomewhat arefied by the hair. *Bacon's Nat. Hiſt.* N°. 696.

2. It is in *Shakeſpeare* the name of a dog, in which ſenſe it is uſed in Scotland. [from *tijk*, Runick, a little dog.]

Avaunt, you curs!
Hound or ſpaniel, brache or hym,
Or bobtail *tike*, or trundle tail. *Shakeſp. K. Lear.*

TILE. *n. ſ.* [ꞇigle, Saxon; *tegel*, Dutch; *tuile*, Fr. *tegola*, Italian.] Thin plates of baked clay uſed to cover houſes.

The roof is all *tile*, or lead, or ſtone. *Bacon's Nat. Hiſt.*

Earth turned into brick ſerveth for building as ſtone doth; and the like of *tile*. *Bacon's Phyſical Remains.*

In at the window he climbs, or o'er the *tiles*. *Milton.*

Worſe than all the clatt'ring *tiles*, and worſe
Than thouſand padders was the poet's curſe. *Dryden.*

Tile pins made of oak or fir they drive into holes made in the plain *tiles*, to hang them upon their lathing. *Moxon.*

To TILE. *v. a.* [from the noun.]

1. To cover with tiles.

Moſs groweth chiefly upon ridges of houſes *tiled* or thatched. *Bacon's Nat. Hiſt.* N°. 537.

Sonnets or elegies to Chloris
Might raiſe a houſe above two ſtories;
A lyrick ode wou'd ſlate; a catch
Wou'd *tile*, an epigram wou'd thatch. *Swift's Miſcel.*

2. To cover as tiles.

The rafters of my body, bone,
Being ſtill with you, the muſcle, ſinew and vein,
Which *tile* this houſe, will come again. *Donne.*

TI'LER. *n. ſ.* [*tuilier*, Fr. from *tile.*] One whoſe trade is to cover houſes with tiles.

A Flemiſh *tiler*, falling from the top of a houſe upon a Spaniard, killed him; the next of the blood proſecuted his death; and when he was offered pecuniary recompence, nothing would ſerve him but *lex talionis*: whereupon the judge ſaid to him, he ſhould go up to the top of the houſe, and then fall down upon the *tiler*. *Bacon's Apophth.*

TI'LING. *n. ſ.* [from *tile.*] The roof covered with tiles.

They went upon the houſe-top, and let him down through the *tiling* with his couch before Jeſus. *Luke* v. 19.

TILL. *n. ſ.* A money box.

They break up counters, doors and *tills*,
And leave the empty cheſts in view. *Swift.*

TILL. *prep.* [ꞇil, Saxon.] To the time of.

Unhappy ſlave, and pupil to a bell,
Unhappy *till* the laſt, the kind releaſing knell. *Cowley.*

TILL *now.* To the preſent time.

Pleaſure not known *till now.* *Milton.*

TILL *then.* To that time.

The earth *till then* was deſert. *Milton.*

TILL. *conjunction.*

1. To the time.

Wood and rocks had ears
To rapture, *till* the ſavage clamour drown'd
Both harp and voice. *Milton.*

The unity of place we neither find in Ariſtotle, Horace, or any who have written of it, *till* in our age the French poets firſt made it a precept of the ſtage. *Dryden.*

2. To the degree that.

Meditate ſo long *till* you make ſome act of prayer to God, or glorification of him. *Taylor.*

Goddeſs, ſpread thy reign *till* Iſis elders reel. *Pope.*

To TILL. *v. a.* [ꞇylian, Saxon; *tenlen*, Dutch.] To cultivate; to huſband: commonly uſed of the huſbandry of the plow.

This paradiſe I give thee, count it thine,
To *till*, and keep, and of the fruit to eat. *Milton.*

Send him from the garden forth, to *till*
The ground whence he was taken. *Milton's Par. Loſt.*

TI'LLABLE. *adj.* [from *till.*] Arable; fit for the plow.

The *tillable* fields are ſo hilly, that the oxen can hardly take ſure footing. *Carew's Survey of Cornwall.*

TI'LLAGE. *n. ſ.* [from *till.*] Huſbandry; the act or practice of plowing or culture.

Tillage will enable the kingdom for corn for the natives, and to ſpare for exportation. *Bacon.*

A ſweaty reaper from his *tillage* brought
Firſt-fruits, the green ear, and the yellow ſheaf. *Milton.*

Incite them to improve the *tillage* of their country, to recover the bad ſoil, and to remedy the waſte. *Milton.*

Bid the laborious hind,
Whoſe harden'd hands did long in *tillage* toil,
Neglect the promis'd harveſt of the ſoil. *Dryden.*

That there was *tillage* Moſes intimates; but whether beſtowed on all, or only upon ſome parts of that earth, as alſo what ſort of *tillage* that was, is not expreſſed. *Woodward.*

TI'LLER. *n. ſ.* [from *till.*]

1. Huſbandman; ploughman.

They bring in ſea-ſand partly after their nearneſs to the places, and partly by the good huſbandry of the *tiller*. *Carew.*

Abel was a keeper of ſheep, but Cain was a *tiller* of the ground. *Gen.* iv. 2.

The worm that gnaws the ripening fruit, ſad gueſt!
Canker or locuſt hurtful to infeſt
The blade; while huſks elude the *tiller*'s care,
And eminence of want diſtinguiſhes the year. *Prior.*

2. A till; a ſmall drawer.

Search her cabinet, and thou ſhalt find
Each *tiller* there with love epiſtles lin'd. *Dryden's Juv.*

TI'LMAN,

Ti'llyfally. } *adj.* [A word used formerly when any thing
Ti'llyvalley. } said was rejected as trifling or impertinent.

Am not I consanguinious? am not I of her blood? *tillyvalley* lady. *Shakesp. Twelfth Night.*

Tillyfally, sir John, never tell me; your ancient swaggerer comes not in my doors. *Shakesp. Henry* IV. *p.* ii.

Ti'lman. *n. s.* [*till* and *man.*] One who tills; an husbandman.

Good shepherd, good *tilman*, good Jack and good Gil,
Makes husband and huswife their coffers to fil. *Tusser.*

TILT. *n. s.* [ꞇylb, Saxon.]

1. A tent; any covering over head.

The roof of linnen
Intended for a shelter!
But the rain made an ass
Of *tilt* and canvas,
And the snow which you know is a melter. *Denham.*

2. The cover of a boat.

It is a small vessel, like in proportion to a Gravesend *tilt*-boat. *Sandys.*

The rowing crew,
To tempt a fare, clothe all their *tilts* in blue. *Gay.*

3. A military game at which the combatants run against each other with lances on horseback.

His study is his *tilt*-yard, and his loves
Are brazen images of canonized saints. *Shakesp. Henry* IV.

He talks as familiarly of John of Gaunt, as if he had been sworn brother to him; and he never saw him but once in the *tilt*-yard, and then he broke his head. *Shak. H.* IV.

Images representing the forms of Hercules, Apollo, and Diana, he placed in the *tilt*-yard at Constantinople. *Knolles.*

The spousals of Hippolite the queen,
What *tilts* and tourneys at the feast were seen. *Dryden.*

In *tilts* and tournaments the valiant strove,
By glorious deeds to purchase Emma's love. *Prior.*

4. A thrust.

His majesty seldom dismissed the foreigner till he had entertained him with the slaughter of two or three of his liege subjects, whom he very dextrously put to death with the *tilt* of his lance. *Addison's Freeholder*, N°. 10.

To Tilt. *v. a.* [from the noun.]

1. To cover like a tilt of a boat.

2. To carry as in tilts or tournaments.

Ajax interpos'd
His sevenfold shield, and screen'd Laertes' son,
When the insulting Trojans urg'd him sore
With *tilted* spears. *Philips.*

3. To point as in tilts.

Now horrid slaughter reigns,
Sons against fathers *tilt* the fatal lance,
Careless of duty, and their native grounds
Distain with kindred blood. *Philips.*

4. [*Tillen*, Dutch.] To turn up so as to run out.

To Tilt. *v. n.*

1. To run in tilts.

To describe races and games,
Or *tilting* furniture, emblazon'd shields. *Milton.*

2. To fight with rapiers.

Friends all but even now; and then, but now—
Swords out and *tilting* one at other's breasts,
In opposition bloody. *Shakesp. Othello.*

Scow'ring the watch grows out of fashion wit:
Now we set up for *tilting* in the pit,
Where 'tis agreed by bullies, chicken-hearted,
To fright the ladies first, and then be parted. *Dryden.*

It is not yet the fashion for women of quality to *tilt*. *Collier.*

Satire's my weapon, but I'm too discreet
To run a muck, and *tilt* at all I meet;
I only wear it in a land of Hectors. *Pope.*

3. To rush as in combat.

Some say the spirits *tilt* so violently, that they make holes where they strike. *Collier.*

4. To play unsteadily.

The floating vessel swam
Uplifted; and secure with beaked prow
Rode *tilting* o'er the waves. *Milton's Par. Lost*, *b.* xi.

The fleet swift *tilting* o'er the surges flew,
Till Grecian cliffs appear'd. *Pope's Odyssey.*

5. To fall on one side.

As the trunk of the body is kept from *tilting* forward by the muscles of the back, so from falling backward by those of the belly. *Grew's Cosmol. b.* i.

Ti'lter. *n. s.* [from *tilt.*] One who tilts; one who fights.

A puisny *tilter*, that spurs his horse on one side, breaks his staff like a noble goose. *Shakesp. As you like it.*

He us'd the only antique philters,
Deriv'd from old heroick *tilters*. *Hudibras*, *p.* iii.

If war you chuse, and blood must needs be spilt here,
Let me alone to match your *tilter*. *Granville.*

Tilth. *n. s.* [from *till.*] Husbandry; culture.

Bourn, bound of land, *tilth*, vineyard, none;
No use of metal, corn, or wine, or oil. *Shakesp. Tempest.*

Her plenteous womb
Expresseth its full *tilth* and husbandry. *Shakespeare.*

Tilth. *adj.* [from *till.*] Arable; tilled.

He beheld a field,
Part arable and *tilth*; whereon were sheaves
New reap'd. *Milton's Par. Lost*, *b.* xi.

Ti'mber. *n. s.* [ꞇymbꞃian, Saxon, *to build.*]

1. Wood fit for building.

I learn'd of lighter *timber* cotes to frame,
Such as might save my sheep and me from shame. *Spenser.*

For the body of the ships no nation doth equal England for the oaken *timber* wherewith to build them; but there must be a great providence used, that our ship *timber* be not unnecessarily wasted. *Bacon's Advice to Villiers.*

The straw was laid below,
Of chips and sere wood was the second row;
The third of greens, and *timber* newly fell'd. *Dryden.*

There are hardly any countries that are destitute of *timber* of their own growth. *Woodward.*

Upon these walls they plant quick and *timber* trees, which thrive exceedingly. *Mortimer's Husbandry.*

Who set the twigs, shall he remember,
That is in haste to sell the *timber*?
And what shall of thy woods remain,
Except the box that threw the main? *Prior.*

2. The main trunk of a tree.

We take
From every tree, lop, bark, and part o' th' *timber*,
And though we leave it with a root thus hackt,
The air will drink the sap. *Shakespeare.*

3. The main beams of a fabrick.

4. Materials ironically.

Such dispositions are the very errors of human nature, and yet they are the fittest *timber* to make politicks of, like to knee *timber*, that is good for ships to be tossed, but not for houses that shall stand firm. *Bacon.*

To Ti'mber. *v. n.* [from the noun.] To light on a tree. A cant word.

The one took up in a thicket of brush-wood, and the other *timbered* upon a tree hard by. *L'Estrange's Fables.*

To Ti'mber. *v. a.* To furnish with beams or timber.

Ti'mbered. *adj.* [from *timber*; *timbré*, Fr.] Built; formed; contrived.

He left the succession to his second son; not because he thought him the best *timbered* to support it. *Wotton.*

Many heads that undertake learning were never squared nor *timbered* for it. *Brown's Vulgar Errours*, *b.* i.

Ti'mbersow. *n. s.* A worm in wood.

Divers creatures, though they be somewhat loathsome to take, are of this kind; as earth worms, *timbersows*, snails. *Bacon's Nat. Hist.* N°. 692.

Ti'mbrel. *n. s.* [*timbre*, Fr. *tympanum*, Latin.] A kind of musical instrument played by pulsation.

The damsels they delight,
When they their *timbrels* smite,
And thereunto dance and carrol sweet. *Spenser's Epithal.*

In their hands sweet *timbrels* all upheld on hight. *Fa. Q.*

Praise with *timbrels*, organs, flutes;
Praise with violins and lutes. *Sandys's Paraph*

For her through Egypt's fruitful clime renown'd,
Let weeping Nilus hear the *timbrel* sound. *Pope's Statius.*

TIME. *n. s.* [ꞇima, Saxon; *tym*, Erse.]

1. The measure of duration.

This consideration of duration, as set out by certain periods, and marked by certain measures or epochas, is that which most properly we call *time*. *Locke.*

Time is like a fashionable host,
That slightly shakes his parting guest by th' hand,
But with his arms out-stretch'd, as he would fly,
Grasps the incomer. *Shakesp. Troilus and Cressida.*

Come what come may,
Time and the hour runs through the roughest day. *Shakesp.*

Nor will polished amber, although it send forth a gross exhalement, be found *a long time* defective upon the exactest scale. *Brown's Vulgar Errours*, *b.* ii.

Time, which consisteth of parts, can be no part of infinite duration, or of eternity; for then there would be infinite *time* past to day, which to morrow will be more than infinite. *Time* is therefore one thing, and infinite duration is another. *Grew's Cosmol. b.* i.

2. Space of time.

Daniel desired that he would give him *time*, and that he would shew him the interpretation. *Dan.* ii. 16.

He for the *time* remain'd stupidly good. *Milton.*

No *time* is allowed for digressions. *Swift.*

3. Interval.

Pomanders, and knots of powders, you may have continually in your hand; whereas perfumes you can take but at *times*. *Bacon's Nat. Hist.* N°. 929.

4. Season; proper time.

To every thing there is a season, and a *time* to every purpose. *Ecclus.* iii. 1.

They

They were cut down out of *time*, whose foundation was overflown with a flood. *Job* xxii. 16.

He found nothing but leaves on it; for the *time* of figs was not yet. *Mar.* xi. 13.

Knowing the *time*, that it is high *time* to awake out of sleep. *Rom.* xiii. 11.

Short were her marriage joys; for in the prime
Of youth her lord expir'd before his *time*. *Dryden.*

I hope I come in *time*, if not to make,
At least, to save your fortune and your honour:
Take heed you steer your vessel right. *Dryden.*

The *time* will come when we shall be forced to bring our evil ways to remembrance, and then consideration will do us little good. *Calamy's Sermons.*

5. A considerable space of duration; continuance; process of time.

Fight under him, there's plunder to be had;
A captain is a very gainful trade:
And when in service your best days are spent,
In *time* you may command a regiment. *Dryden's Juvenal.*

In *time* the mind reflects on its own operations about the ideas got by sensation, and thereby stores itself with a new set of ideas, ideas of reflection. *Locke.*

One imagines, that the terrestrial matter which is showered down along with rain enlarges the bulk of the earth, and that it will in *time* bury all things under-ground. *Woodward.*

I have resolved to take *time*, and, in spite of all misfortunes, to write you, at intervals, a long letter. *Swift.*

6. Age; particular part of time.

When that company died, what *time* the fire devoured two hundred and fifty men. *Num.* xxvi. 10.

They shall be given into his hand until a *time* and *times*. *Dan.* vii. 25.

If we should impute the heat of the season unto the cooperation of any stars with the sun, it seems more favourable for our *times* to ascribe the same unto the constellation of leo. *Brown's Vulgar Errours*, *b.* iv.

The way to please being to imitate nature, the poets and the painters, in ancient *times*, and in the best ages, have studied her. *Dryden's Dufresnoy.*

7. Past time.

I was the man in th' moon when *time* was. *Shakespeare.*

8. Early time.

Stanley at Bosworth field, though he came *time* enough to save his life, yet he staid long enough to endanger it. *Bacon.*

If they acknowledge repentance and a more strict obedience to be one time or other necessary, they imagine it is *time* enough yet to set about these duties. *Rogers.*

9. Time considered as affording opportunity.

The earl lost no *time*, but marched day and night. *Clarend.*

He continued his delights till all the enemies horse were passed through his quarters; nor did then pursue them in any *time*. *Clarendon*, *b.* viii.

Time is lost, which never will renew,
While we too far the pleasing path pursue,
Surveying nature. *Dryden's Virgil.*

10. Particular quality of the present.

Comets, importing change of *times* and states,
Brandish your crystal tresses in the sky. *Shakespeare.*

All the prophets in their age, the *times*
Of great Messiah sing. *Milton's Par. Lost*, *b.* xii.

If any reply, that the *times* and manners of men will not bear such a practice, that is an answer from the mouth of a professed *time*-server. *South's Sermons.*

11. Particular time.

Give order, that no sort of person
Have, any *time*, recourse unto the princes. *Shakespeare.*

The worst on me must light, when *time* shall be. *Milt.*

A *time* will come when my maturer muse,
In Cæsar's wars a nobler theme shall chuse. *Dryden.*

These reservoirs of snow they cut, distributing them to several shops, that from *time* to *time* supply Naples. *Addison.*

12. Hour of childbirth.

She intended to stay till delivered; for she was within one month of her *time*. *Clarendon.*

The first time I saw a lady dressed in one of these petticoats, I blamed her for walking abroad when she was so near her *time*; but soon I found all the modish part of the sex as far gone as herself. *Addison's Spect.* N°. 127.

13. Repetition of any thing, or mention with reference to repetition.

Four *times* he cross'd the car of night. *Milton.*

Every single particle would have a sphere of void space around it many hundred thousand million million *times* bigger than the dimensions of that particle. *Bentley.*

Lord Oxford I have now the third *time* mentioned in this letter expects you. *Swift.*

14. Musical measure.

Musick do I hear!
Ha, ha! keep *time*. How sour sweet musick is
When *time* is broke and no proportion kept. *Shakespeare.*

You by the help of tune and *time*
Can make that song which was but rime. *Waller.*

On their exalted wings
To the cœlestial orbs they climb,
And with th' harmonious spheres keep *time*. *Denham.*

Heroes who o'ercome, or die,
Have their hearts hung extremely high;
The strings of which in battle's heat
Against their very corslets beat;
Keep *time* with their own trumpet's measure,
And yield them most excessive pleasure. *Prior.*

To TIME. *v. a.* [from the noun.]

1. To adapt to the time; to bring or do at a proper time.

There is no greater wisdom than well to *time* the beginnings and onsets of things. *Bacon's Nat. Hist.*

The *timing* of things is a main point in the dispatch of all affairs. *L'Estrange.*

This 'tis to have a virtue out of season.
Mercy is good, but kings mistake its *timing*. *Dryden.*

A man's conviction should be strong, and so well *tim'd*, that worldly advantages may seem to have no share in it. *Add.*

2. To regulate as to time.

To the same purpose old Epopeus spoke,
Who overlook'd the oars, and *tim'd* the stroke. *Addison.*

3. To measure harmonically.

He was a thing of blood, whose every motion
Was *tim'd* with dying cries. *Shakesp. Coriolanus.*

TI'MEFUL. *adj.* [*time* and *full.*] Seasonable; timely; early.

If this arch-politician find in his pupils any remorse, any feeling of God's future judgments, he persuades them that God hath so great need of mens souls, that he will accept them at any time, and upon any condition; interrupting, by his vigilant endeavours, all offer of *timeful* return towards God. *Raleigh's Hist. of the World*, *b.* i.

TI'MELESS. *adj.* [from *time.*]

1. Unseasonable; done at an improper time.

Nor fits it to prolong the heav'nly feast
Timeless, indecent, but retire to rest. *Pope's Odyssey.*

2. Untimely; immature; done before the proper time.

A pack of sorrows, which would press you down,
If unprevented, to your *timeless* grave. *Shakespeare.*

Noble Gloster's death,
Who wrought it with the king, and who perform'd
The bloody office of his *timeless* end. *Shakesp. Rich.* II.

TI'MELY. *adj.* [from *time.*] Seasonable; sufficiently early.

The West glimmers with some streaks of day,
Now spurs the lated traveller apace
To gain the *timely* inn. *Shakesp. Macbeth.*

Happy were I in my *timely* death;
Could all my travels warrant me they live. *Shakespeare.*

Lest heat should hinder us, his *timely* care
Hath unbesought provided. *Milton.*

I'll to my charge,
And show my duty by my *timely* care. *Dryden.*

TI'MELY. *adv.* [from *time.*] Early; soon.

The beds i' th' East are soft, and thanks to you,
That call'd me *timelier* than my purpose hither. *Shakesp.*

Sent to forewarn
Us *timely* of what else might be our loss. *Milton.*

Timely advis'd, the coming evil shun;
Better not do the deed, than weep it done. *Prior.*

TI'MEPLEASER. *n. s.* [*time* and *please.*] One who complies with prevailing notions whatever they be.

Scandal, the suppliants for the people, call them
Timepleasers, flatterers, foes to nobleness. *Shakespeare.*

TI'MESERVING. *adj.* [*time* and *serve.*] Meanly complying with present power.

If such by trimming and *timeserving*, which are but two words for the same thing, abandon the church of England; this will produce confusion. *South's Sermons.*

TI'MID. *adj.* [*timide*, Fr. *timidus*, Lat.] Fearful; timorous; wanting courage; wanting boldness.

Poor is the triumph o'er the *timid* hare. *Thomson.*

TIMI'DITY. *n. s.* [*timidité*, Fr. *timiditas*, Latin; from *timid.*] Fearfulness; timorousness; habitual cowardice.

The hare figured pusillanimity and *timidity* from its temper. *Brown's Vulgar Errours.*

TI'MOROUS. *adj.* [*timor*, Latin.] Fearful; full of fear and scruple.

Prepossessed heads will ever doubt it, and *timorous* beliefs will never dare to try it. *Brown's Vulgar Err.* *b.* ii.

The infant flames, whilst yet they were conceal'd
In *tim'rous* doubts, with pity I beheld;
With easy smiles dispell'd the silent fear,
That durst not tell me what I dy'd to hear. *Prior.*

TI'MOROUSLY. *adv.* [from *timorous.*] Fearfully; with much fear.

We would have had you heard
The traitor speak, and *tim'rously* confess
The manner and the purpose of his treasons. *Shakespeare.*

Though they had ideas enough to diſtinguiſh gold from a ſtone, and metal from wood, yet they but *timorouſly* ventured on ſuch terms which ſhould pretend to ſignify their real eſſences *Locke.*

Let daſtard ſouls be *timorouſly* wiſe:
But tell them, Pyrrhus knows not how to form
Far-fancy'd ills, and dangers out of ſight. *A. Phillips.*

TI'MOROUSNESS. *n. ſ.* [from *timorous.*] Fearfulneſs.

The clergy, through the *timorouſneſs* of many among them, were refuſed to be heard by their council. *Swift.*

TI'MOUS. *adj.* [from *time.*] Early; timely; not innate.

By a wiſe and *timous* inquiſition, the peccant humours and humouriſts muſt be diſcovered, purged, or cut off. *Bacon.*

TIN. *n. ſ.* [*ten*, Dutch.]

1. One of the primitive metals called by the chemiſts jupiter.

Quickſilver, lead, iron, and *tin*, have opacity or blackneſs. *Peacham on Blazoning.*

Tin ore ſometimes holds about one-ſixth of *tin. Woodward.*

2. Thin plates of iron covered with tin.

To TIN. *v. a.* [from the noun.] To cover with tin.

To keep the earth from getting into the veſſel, he employed a plate of iron *tinned* over and perforated. *Boyle.*

The cover may be *tinned* over only by nailing of ſingle tin plates over it. *Mortimer's Huſbandry.*

New *tinning* a ſaucepan is chargeable. *Swift.*

TI'NCAL. *n. ſ.* A mineral.

The *tincal* of the Perſians ſeems to be the chryſocolla of the ancients, and what our borax is made of. *Woodward.*

To TINCT. *v. a.* [*tinctus*, Lat. *teint*, Fr.]

1. To ſtain; to colour; to ſpot; to die.

Some bodies have a more departible nature than others in colouration; for a ſmall quantity of ſaffron will *tinct* more than a very great quantity of wine. *Bacon.*

Some were *tincted* blue, ſome red, others yellow. *Brown.*

I diſtilled ſome of the *tincted* liquor, and all that came over was as limpid as rock water. *Boyle.*

Thoſe who have preſerved an innocence, would not ſuffer the whiter parts of their ſoul to be diſcoloured or *tincted* by the reflection of one ſin. *Decay of Piety.*

2. To imbue with a taſte.

We have artificial wells made in imitation of the natural, as *tincted* upon vitriol, ſulphur, and ſteel. *Bacon.*

TINCT. *n. ſ.* [from the verb.] Colour; ſtain; ſpot.

That great med'cine hath
With his *tinct* gilded thee. *Shakeſpeare.*

Of evening *tinct*
The purple ſtreaming amethyſt is thine. *Thomſon.*

The firſt ſcent of a veſſel laſts, and the *tinct* the wool firſt appears of. *Benj. Johnſon.*

TI'NCTURE. *n. ſ.* [*teinture*, Fr. *tinctura* from *tinctus*, Lat.]

1. Colour or taſte ſuperadded by ſomething.

The ſight muſt be ſweetly deceived by an inſenſible paſſage from bright colours to dimmer, which Italian artizans call the middle *tinctures. Wotton's Architecture.*

Hence the morning planet gilds her horn,
By *tincture* or reflection they augment
Their ſmall peculiar. *Milton.*

'Tis the fate of princes that no knowledge
Come pure to them, but paſſing through the eyes
And ears of other men, it takes a *tincture*
From every channel. *Denham.*

That beloved thing engroſſes him, and, like a coloured glaſs before his eyes, caſts its own colour and *tincture* upon all the images of things. *South.*

To begin the practice of an art with a light *tincture* of the rules, is to expoſe ourſelves to the ſcorn of thoſe who are judges. *Dryden.*

Malignant tempers, whatever kind of life they are engaged in, will diſcover their natural *tincture* of mind. *Addiſ.*

Few in the next generation who will not write and read, and have an early *tincture* of religion. *Addiſon.*

Sire of her joy and ſource of her delight;
O! wing'd with pleaſure take thy happy flight,
And give each future morn a *tincture* of thy white. *Prior.*

All manners take a *tincture* from our own,
Or come diſcolour'd through our paſſions ſhown. *Pope.*

Have a care leſt ſome darling ſcience ſo far prevail over your mind, as to give a ſovereign *tincture* to all your other ſtudies, and diſcolour all your ideas. *Watts.*

2. Extract of ſome drug made in ſpirits; an infuſion.

In *tinctures* drawn from vegetables, the ſuperfluous ſpirit of wine diſtilled off leaves the extract of the vegetable. *Boyle.*

To TI'NCTURE. *v. a.* [from the noun.]

1. To imbue or impregnate with ſome colour or taſte.

The bright ſun compacts the precious ſtone,
Imparting radiant luſtre like his own:
He *tinctures* rubies with their roſy hue,
And on the ſaphire ſpreads a heavenly blue. *Blackmore.*

A little black paint will *tincture* and ſpoil twenty gay colours. *Watts.*

2. To imbue the mind.

Early were our minds *tinctured* with a diſtinguiſhing ſenſe of good and evil; early were the ſeeds of a divine love, and holy fear of offending, ſown in our hearts. *Atterbury.*

To TIND. *v. a.* [*tendgan*, Gothick; tendan, Saxon.] To kindle; to ſet on fire.

TI'NDER. *n. ſ.* [tynder, tendre, Saxon.] Any thing eminently inflammable placed to catch fire.

Strike on the *tinder* ho!
Give me a taper. *Shakeſp. Othello.*

To theſe ſhameleſs paſtimes were their youth admitted, thereby adding, as it were, fire to *tinder. Hakewill.*

Where ſparks and fire do meet with *tinder*,
Thoſe ſparks more fire will ſtill engender. *Suckling.*

Whoever our trading with England would hinder,
To inflame both the nations do plainly conſpire;
Becauſe Iriſh linen will ſoon turn to *tinder*,
And wool it is greaſy, and quickly takes fire. *Swift.*

TI'NDERBOX. *n. ſ.* [*tinder* and *box.*] The box for holding tinder.

That worthy patriot, once the bellows,
And *tinderbox* of all his fellows. *Hudibras, p.* iii.

He might even as well have employed his time in catching moles, making lanterns and *tinderboxes. Atterbury's Sermons.*

TINE. *n. ſ.* [*tinne*, Iſlandick.]

1. The tooth of a harrow; the ſpike of a fork.

In the ſouthern parts of England they deſtroy moles by traps that fall on them, and ſtrike ſharp *tines* or teeth through them. *Mortimer's Huſbandry.*

2. Trouble; diſtreſs.

The root whereof, and tragical effect,
Vouchſafe, O thou the mournful'ſt muſe of nine,
That wont'ſt the tragick ſtage for to direct,
In funeral complaints and wailful *tine. Spenſer's Muipotmos.*

To TINE. *v. a.* [tynan, Saxon.]

1. To kindle; to light; to ſet on fire.

Strifeful Atin in their ſtubborn mind
Coals of contention and hot vengeance *tin'd. Fa. Qu.*

The clouds
Juſtling or puſh'd with winds, rude in their ſhock,
Tine the ſlant light'ning; whoſe thwart flame driv'n down,
Kindles the gummy bark of fir. *Milton.*

The prieſt with holy hands was ſeen to *tine*
The cloven wood, and pour the ruddy wine. *Dryden.*

2. [tinan, Saxon, *to ſhut.*] To ſhut.

To TINE. *v. n.*

1. To rage; to ſmart. *Spenſer.*

2. To fight.

Eden ſtain'd with blood of many a band
Of Scots and Engliſh both, that *tined* on his ſtrand. *Spenſ.*

To TINGE. *v. a.* [*tingo*, Lat.] To impregnate or imbue with a colour or taſte.

Sir Roger is ſomething of an humouriſt; and his virtues as well as imperfections are *tinged* by a certain extravagance, which makes them particularly his. *Addiſon's Spect.*

A red powder mixed with a little blue, or a blue with a little red, doth not preſently loſe its colour; but a white powder mixed with any colour is preſently *tinged* with that colour, and is equally capable of being *tinged* with any colour whatever. *Newton's Opticks.*

If the eye be *tinged* with any colour, as in the jaundice, ſo as to *tinge* pictures in the bottom of the eye with that colour, all objects appear *tinged* with the ſame colour. *Newton.*

Still lays ſome uſeful bile aſide,
To *tinge* the chyle's inſipid tide;
Elſe we ſhould want both gibe and ſatire,
And all be burſt with pure good-nature. *Prior.*

The infuſions of rhubarb and ſaffron *tinge* the urine with a high yellow. *Arbuthnot on Aliments.*

TI'NGENT. *adj.* [*tingens*, Lat.] Having the power to tinge.

This wood, by the tincture it afforded, appeared to have its coloured part genuine; but as for the white part, it appears much leſs enriched with the *tingent* property. *Boyle.*

TI'NGLASS. *n. ſ.* [*tin* and *glaſs.*] Biſmuth.

To TI'NGLE. *v. n.* [*tingelen*, Dutch.]

1. To feel a ſound, or the continuance of a ſound, in the ears. This is perhaps rather *tinkle.*

When our ear *tingleth*, we uſually ſay that ſomebody is talking of us; which is an ancient conceit. *Brown.*

2. To feel a ſharp quick pain with a ſenſation of motion.

The pale boy ſenator yet *tingling* ſtands. *Pope.*

3. To feel either pain or pleaſure with a ſenſation of motion. The ſenſe of this word is not very well aſcertained.

They ſuck pollution through their *tingling* veins. *Tickell.*

In a palſy, ſometimes the ſenſation or feeling is either totally aboliſhed, or dull with a ſenſe of *tingling. Arbuthnot.*

To TINK. *v. n.* [*tinnio*, Latin; *tincian*, Welſh.] To make a ſharp ſhrill noiſe.

TI'NKER. *n. ſ.* [from *tink*, becauſe their way of proclaiming their trade is to beat a kettle, or becauſe in their tink they make a tinkling noiſe.] A mender of old braſs.

Am not I old Sly's ſon, by education a cardmaker, and now by preſent profeſſion a *tinker. Shakeſpeare.*

My

My copper medals by the pound
May be with learned juſtice weigh'd:
To turn the balance, Otho's head
May be thrown in: and for the mettle
The coin may mend a *tinker*'s kettle. *Prior.*

To TI'NKLE. *v. n.* [*tinter*, Fr. *tinnio*, Latin.]

1. To make a ſharp quick noiſe; to clink.

The daughters of Zion are haughty, and walk with ſtretched out necks, making a *tinkling* with their feet. *Iſa.*

His feeble hand a javelin threw,
Which flutt'ring, ſeem'd to loiter as it flew:
Juſt, and but barely, to the mark it held,
And faintly *tinkl'd* on the brazen ſhield. *Dryden's Æn.*

The ſprightly horſe
Moves to the muſick of his *tinkling* bells. *Dodſley's Agr.*

It ſeems to have been improperly uſed by *Pope.*

The wand'ring ſtreams that ſhine between the hills,
The grots that echo to the *tinkling* rills. *Pope.*

3. To hear a low quick noiſe.

With deeper brown the grove was overſpread,
A ſudden horrour ſeiz'd his giddy head,
And his ears *tinkled*, and the colour fled. *Dryden.*

T'INMAN. *n. ſ.* [*tin* and *man.*] A manufacturer of tin, or iron tinned over.

Didſt thou never pop
Thy head into a *tinman's* ſhop. *Prior.*

TI'NPENNY. *n. ſ.* A certain cuſtomary duty anciently paid to the tithingmen. *Bailey.*

TI'NWORM. *n. ſ.* An inſect. *Bailey.*

TI'NNER. *n. ſ.* [from *tin*; tin, Saxon.] One who works in the tin mines.

The Corniſh men, many of them could for a need live under-ground, that were *tinners.* *Bacon's Henry* VII.

TI'NSEL. *n. ſ.* [*etincelle*, Fr.]

1. A kind of ſhining cloth.

A *tinſel* vail her amber locks did ſhrowd,
That ſtrove to cover what it could not hide. *Fairfax.*

Its but a night-gown in reſpect of your's; cloth of gold and cuts, underborne with a bluiſh *tinſel.* *Shakeſpeare.*

By Thetis' *tinſel* ſlipper'd feet,
And the ſongs of ſirens ſweet. *Milton.*

2. Any thing ſhining with falſe luſtre; any thing ſhewy and of little value.

For favours cheap and common who would ſtrive;
Yet ſcatter'd here and there I ſome behold,
Who can diſcern the *tinſel* from the gold? *Dryden.*

If the man will too curiouſly examine the ſuperficial *tinſel* good, he undeceives himſelf to his own coſt. *Norris.*

No glittering *tinſel* of May fair,
Could with this rod of Sid compare. *Swift.*

Ye *tinſel* inſects, whom a court maintains,
That counts your beauties only by your ſtains,
Spin all your cobwebs o'er the eyes of day,
The muſe's wing ſhall bruſh you all away. *Pope.*

To TI'NSEL. *v. a.* [from the noun.] To decorate with cheap ornaments; to adorn with luſtre that has no value.

Hence you phantaſtick poſtillers in ſong,
My text defeats your art, 'tis nature's tongue,
Scorns all her *tinſoil'd* metaphors of pelf,
Illuſtrated by nothing but herſelf. *Cleaveland.*

She, *tinſell'd* o'er in robes of varying hues,
With ſelf-applauſe her wild creation views,
Sees momentary monſters riſe and fall,
And with her own fool's colours gilds them all. *Pope.*

TINT. *n. ſ.* [*teinte*, Fr. *tinta*, Ital.] A dye; a colour.

Whether thy hand ſtrike out ſome free deſign,
Where life awakes, and dawns at ev'ry line;
Or blend in beauteous *tint* the colour'd maſs,
And from the canvas call the mimick face. *Pope.*

TI'NY. *adj.* [*tint*, *tynd*, Daniſh.] Little; ſmall; puny. A burleſque word.

Some pigeons, Davy, and any pretty little *tiny* kickſhaws. *Shakeſp. Henry* IV.

When that I was a little *tiny* boy,
A fooliſh thing was but a toy. *Shakeſp. Twelfth Night.*

But ah! I fear thy little fancy roves,
On little females and on little loves;
Thy pigmy children, and thy *tiny* ſpouſe,
The baby playthings that adorn thy houſe. *Swift.*

TIP. *n. ſ.* [*tip*, *tipken*, Dutch.] Top; end; point; extremity.

The *tip* no jewel needs to wear,
The *tip* is jewel of the ear. *Sidney, b.* ii.

They touch the beard with the *tip* of their tongue, and wet it. *Bacon's Nat. Hiſt.* N°. 494.

Thrice upon thy fingers *tip*,
Thrice upon thy rubied lip. *Milton.*

All the pleaſure dwells upon the *tip* of his tongue. *South.*

She has fifty private amours, which nobody yet knows any thing of but herſelf, and thirty clandeſtine marriages that have not been touched by the *tip* of the tongue. *Addiſon.*

I no longer look upon lord Plauſible as ridiculous, for admiring a lady's fine *tip* of an ear and pretty elbow. *Pope.*

To TIP. *v. a.* [from the noun.]

1. To top; to end; to cover on the end.

In his hand a reed
Stood waving, *tipp'd* with fire. *Milton's Par. Loſt.*

With truncheon *tipp'd* with iron head,
The warriour to the liſts he led. *Hudibras, p.* i.

How would the old king ſmile
To ſee you weigh the paws, when *tipp'd* with gold,
And throw the ſhaggy ſpoils about your ſhoulders. *Addiſon.*

Quarto's, octavo's ſhape the leſs'ning pyre,
And laſt a little Ajax *tips* the ſpire. *Pope's Dunciad.*

Behold the place, where if a poet
Shin'd in deſcription, he might ſhow it;
Tell how the moon-beam trembling falls,
And *tips* with ſilver all the walls. *Pope's Horace.*

Tipt with jet,
Fair ermines ſpotleſs as the ſnows they preſs. *Thomſon.*

2. To ſtrike ſlightly; to tap.

She writes love letters to the youth in grace,
Nay, *tips* the wink before the cuckold's face. *Dryden.*

The pert jackanapes *tipped* me the wink, and put out his tongue at his grandfather. *Tatler,* N°. 86.

A third rogue *tips* me by the elbow. *Swift.*

Their judgment was, upon the whole,
That lady is the dulleſt ſoul;
Then *tipt* their forehead in a jeer,
As who ſhould ſay, ſhe wants it here. *Swift.*

When I ſaw the keeper frown,
Tipping him with half a crown,
Now, ſaid I, we are alone,
Name your heroes one by one. *Swift.*

TI'PPET. *n. ſ.* [tæppet, Sax.] Something worn about the neck.

His turban was white, with a ſmall red croſs on the top: he had alſo a *tippet* of fine linnen. *Bacon.*

To TI'PPLE. *v. n.* [*tepel*, a dug, old Teutonick.] To drink luxuriouſly; to waſte life over the cup.

Let us grant it is not amiſs to ſit,
And keep the turn of *tippling* with a ſlave,
To reel the ſtreets at noon. *Shakeſp. Ant. and Cleopatra.*

To TI'PPLE. *v. a.* To drink in luxury or exceſs.

While his canting drone-pipe ſcan'd
The myſtick figures of her hand,
He *tipples* palmeſtry, and dines
On all her fortune-telling lines. *Cleaveland.*

To a ſhort meal he makes a tedious grace,
Before the barley-pudding comes in place;
Then bids fall on; himſelf for ſaving charges
A peel'd ſlic'd onion eats, and *tipples* verjuice. *Dryden.*

If a ſlumber haply does invade
My weary limbs, my fancy's ſtill awake,
Thoughtful of drink, and eager in a dream,
Tipples imaginary pots of ale. *Philips.*

TI'PPLE. *n. ſ.* [from the verb.] Drink; liquor.

While the *tipple* was paid for, all went merrily on. *L'Eſtr.*

TI'PPLED. *adj.* [from *tipple.*] Tipſy; drunk.

Merry, we ſail from the Eaſt,
Half *tippled* at a rainbow feaſt. *Dryden.*

TI'PPLER. *n. ſ.* [from *tipple.*] A ſottiſh drunkard; an idle drunken fellow.

TI'PSTAFF. *n. ſ.* [*tip* and *ſtaff.*]

1. An officer with a ſtaff tipped with metal.

2. The ſtaff itſelf ſo tipt.

One had in his hand a tipſtaff of a yellow cane, *tipped* at both ends with blue. *Bacon.*

One had in his hand a *tipſtaff* of a yellow cane, tipped at both ends with blue. *Bacon.*

TI'PSY. *adj.* [from *tipple.*] Drunk; overpowered with exceſs of drink.

The riot of the *tipſy* bacchanals,
Tearing the Thracian ſinger in their rage. *Shakeſpeare.*

Welcome joy and feaſt,
Midnight ſhout and revelry,
Tipſy dance and jollity. *Milton.*

TI'PTOE. *n. ſ.* [*tip* and *toe.*] The end of the toe.

Where the fond ape himſelf uprearing high,
Upon his *tiptoes* ſtalketh ſtately by. *Spenſ. Hubberd's Tale.*

He that outlives this day and comes ſafe home,
Will ſtand a *tiptoe* when this day is nam'd,
And rouze him at the name of Criſpian. *Shakeſpeare.*

Night's candles are burnt out, and jocund day
Stands *tiptoe* on the miſty mountains tops. *Shakeſpeare.*

Religion ſtands on *tiptoe* in our land,
Ready to paſs to the American ſtrand. *Herbert.*

Ten ruddy wildings in the wood I found,
And ſtood on *tiptoes* from the ground. *Dryden.*

TIRE. *n. ſ.* [*tuyr*, Dutch.]

1. Rank; row.

Your loweſt *tire* of ordnance muſt lie four foot clear above water, when all loading is in, or elſe thoſe your beſt pieces will

will be of ſmall uſe at ſea, in any grown weather that makes the billows to riſe. *Raleigh's Eſſays.*

Stood rank'd of ſeraphim another row,
In poſture to diſplode their ſecond *tire*
Of thunder. *Milton's Par. Loſt, b.* vi.

In all thoſe wars there were few triremes, moſt of them being of one *tire* of oars of fifty banks. *Arbuthnot.*

2. [Corrupted from *tiar* or *tiara*, or *attire.*] A head-dreſs.

On her head ſhe wore a *tire* of gold,
Adorn'd with gems and ouches. *Fairy Queen.*

Here is her picture: let me ſee;
If I had ſuch a *tire*, this face of mine
Were full as lovely as is this of hers. *Shakeſpeare.*

The judge of torments, and the king of tears,
Now fills a burniſh'd throne of quenchleſs fire,
And for his old fair robes of light he wears
A gloomy mantle of dark flame, the *tire*
That crowns his hated head on high, appears. *Craſhaw.*

When the fury took her ſtand on high,
A hiſs from all the ſnaky *tire* went round. *Pope.*

3. Furniture; apparatus.

Saint George's worth
Enkindles like deſire of high exploits:
Immediate ſieges, and the *tire* of war
Rowl in thy eager mind. *Philips.*

When they firſt peep forth of the ground, they ſhew their whole *tire* of leaves, then flowers, next ſeeds. *Woodward.*

To TIRE. *v. a.* [tiꞃian, Saxon.]

1. To fatigue; to make weary; to harraſs; to wear out with labour or tedioufneſs.

Tir'd with toil, all hopes of ſafety paſt,
From pray'rs to wiſhes he deſcends at laſt. *Dryden.*

For this a hundred voices I deſire,
To tell thee what a hundred tongues wou'd *tire*;
Yet never could be worthily expreſt,
How deeply thou art ſeated in my breaſt. *Dryden's Perſius.*

2. It has often *out* added to intend the ſignification.

Often a few that are ſtiff do *tire out* a greater number that are more moderate. *Bacon's Eſſays.*

A lonely way
The cheerleſs Albion wander'd half a day;
Tir'd out, at length a ſpreading ſtream he 'ſpy'd. *Tickell.*

3. [From *attire* or *tire*, from *tiara.*] To dreſs the head.

Jezebel painted her face and *tired* her head. 2 *Kings* ix. 30.

To TIRE. *v. n.* [teoꞃian, Saxon.] To fail with wearineſs.

TI'REDNESS. *n. ſ.* [from *tired.*] State of being tired; weari-neſs.

It is not through the *tiredneſs* of the age of the earth, but through our own negligence that it hath not ſatisfied us bountifully. *Hakewill on Providence.*

TI'RESOME. *adj.* [from *tire.*] Weariſome; fatiguing; tedious.

Since the inculcating precept upon precept will prove *tireſome* to the reader, the poet muſt ſometimes relieve the ſubject with a pleaſant and pertinent digreſſion. *Addiſon.*

Nothing is ſo *tireſome* as the works of thoſe criticks who write in a dogmatick way, without language, genius, or imagination. *Addiſon's Spect.* N°. 253.

TI'RESOMENESS. *n. ſ.* [from *tireſome.*] Act or quality of being tireſome.

TI'REWOMAN. *n. ſ.* [*tire* and *woman.*] A woman whoſe buſineſs is to make dreſſes for the head.

Why ſhould they not value themſelves for this outſide faſhionableneſs of the *tirewoman*'s making, when their parents have ſo early inſtructed them to do ſo. *Locke on Education.*

TI'RINGHOUSE. } *n. ſ.* [*tire* and *houſe*, or *room.*] The room in
TI'RINGROOM. } which players dreſs for the ſtage.

This green plot ſhall be our ſtage, this hawthorn brake our *tiringhouſe.* *Shakeſpeare.*

Man's life's a tragedy; his mother's womb,
From which he enters, is the *tiringroom*;
This ſpacious earth the theatre, and the ſtage
That country which he lives in; paſſions, rage,
Folly, and vice, are actors. *Wotton.*

TI'RWIT. *n. ſ.* A bird. *Ainſworth.*

'TIS, contracted for *it is.*

'Tis deſtiny unſhunable. *Shakeſpeare.*

TI'SICK. *n. ſ.* [corrupted from *phthiſick.*] Conſumption; morbid waſte.

TI'SICAL. *adj.* [for *phthiſical.*] Conſumptive.

TI'SSUE. *n. ſ.* [*tiſſue*, Fr. tiꞃan, *to weave*, Norman Saxon.] Cloth interwoven with gold or ſilver.

In their glittering *tiſſues* emblaz'd
Holy memorials, acts of zeal and love,
Recorded eminent. *Milton's Par. Loſt, b.* v.

A robe of *tiſſue*, ſtiff with golden wire;
An upper veſt, once Helen's rich attire;
From Argos by the fam'd adultreſs brought,
With golden flow'rs and winding foliage wrought. *Dryden.*

To TI'SSUE. *v. a.* [from the noun.] To interweave; to variegate.

The chariot was covered with cloth of gold *tiſſued* upon blue. *Bacon's New Atlantis.*

They have been always frank of their bleſſings to countenance any great action; and then, according as it ſhould proſper, to *tiſſue* upon it ſome pretence or other. *Wotton.*

Mercy will ſit between,
Thron'd in cœleſtial ſheen,
With radiant feet the *tiſſued* clouds down ſteering. *Milton.*

TIT. *n. ſ.*

1. A ſmall horſe: generally in contempt.

No ſtoring of paſture with baggagely *tit*,
With ragged, with aged, and evil at hit. *Tuſſer.*

Thou might'ſt have ta'en example
From what thou read'ſt in ſtory;
Being as worthy to ſit
On an ambling *tit*,
As thy predeceſſor Dory. *Denham.*

2. A woman: in contempt.

What does this envious *tit*, but away to her father with a tale. *L'Eſtrange.*

A willing *tit* that will venture her corps with you. *Dryden.*

Short pains for thee, for me a ſon and heir.
Girls coſt as many throes in bringing forth;
Beſide, when born, the *tits* are little worth. *Dryden.*

3. A *titmouſe* or *tomtit.* A bird.

TITBI'T. *n. ſ.* [properly *tidbit*; *tid*, *tender*, and *bit.*] Nice bit; nice food.

John pampered eſquire South with *titbits* till he grew wanton. *Arbuthnot.*

TI'THEABLE. *adj.* [from *tithe.*] Subject to the payment of tithes; that of which tithes may be taken.

The popiſh prieſt ſhall, on taking the oath of allegiance to his majeſty, be entitled to a tenth part or tithe of all things *titheable* in Ireland belonging to the papiſts, within their reſpective pariſhes. *Swift.*

TITHE. *n. ſ.* [teoða, Saxon, *tenth.*]

1. The tenth part; the part aſſigned to the maintenance of the miniſtry.

Many have made witty invectives againſt uſury: they ſay, that it is pity the devil ſhould have God's part, which is the *tithe.* *Bacon.*

Sometimes comes ſhe with a *tithe* pig's tail,
Tickling the parſon as he lies aſleep,
Then dreams he of another benefice. *Shakeſpeare.*

2. The tenth part of any thing.

I have ſearched man by man, boy by boy; the *tithe* of a hair was never loſt in my houſe before. *Shakeſpeare.*

Since the firſt ſword was drawn about this queſtion,
Ev'ry *tithe* ſoul 'mongſt many thouſand diſmes
Hath been as dear as Helen. *Shakeſp. Troil. and Creſſida.*

3. Small part; ſmall portion.

Offenſive wars for religion are ſeldom to be approved, unleſs they have ſome mixture of civil *tithes.* *Bacon.*

To TITHE. *v. a.* [teoðian, Saxon.] To tax; to pay the tenth part.

When I come to the *tithing* of them, I will *tithe* them one with another, and will make an Iriſhman the tithingman. *Spenſer on Ireland.*

By decimation and a *tithed* death,
If thy revenges hunger for that food
Which nature loaths, take thou the deſtin'd tenth. *Shak.*

When thou haſt made an end of *tithing* all the tithes of thine increaſe, the third year, the year of *tithing*, give unto the Levite, ſtranger, fatherleſs and widow. *Deut.* xxvi. 12.

To TITHE. *v. n.* To pay tithe.

For lambe, pig, and calf, and for other the like,
Tithe ſo as thy cattle the lord do not ſtrike. *Tuſſer.*

TI'THER. *n. ſ.* [from *tithe.*] One who gathers tithes.

TI'THYMAL. *n. ſ.* [*tithymalle*, French; *tithymallus*, Lat.] An herb. *Ainſ.*

TI'THING. *n. ſ.* [*tithinga*, law Latin, from *tithe.*]

1. *Tithing* is the number or company of ten men with their families knit together in a ſociety, all of them being bound to the king for the peaceable and good behaviour of each of their ſociety: of theſe companies there was one chief perſon, who, from his office, was called (toothingman) tithingman; but now he is nothing but a conſtable. *Cowel.*

Poor Tom, who is whipt from *tithing* to *tithing*, and ſtock puniſhed and impriſoned. *Shakeſp. King Lear.*

2. Tithe; tenth part due to the prieſt.

Though vicar be bad, or the parſon evil,
Go not for thy *tithing* thyſelf to the devil. *Tuſſer.*

TI'THINGMAN. *n. ſ.* [*tithing* and *man.*] A petty peace officer; an under-conſtable.

His hundred is not at his command further than his prince's ſervice; and alſo every *tithingman* may control him. *Spenſer.*

To TI'TILLATE. *v. n.* [*titillo*, Lat.] To tickle.

Juſt where the breath of life his noſtrils drew,
A charge of ſnuff the wily virgin threw;
The gnomes direct to ev'ry atom juſt,
The pungent grains of *titillating* duſt. *Pope.*

TITILLA'TION.

TITILLA'TION. *n. s.* [*titillation*, French; *titillatio*, Lat. from *titillate*.]

1. The act of tickling.

Tickling causeth laughter: the cause may be the emission of the spirits, and so of the breath, by a flight from *titillation*. *Bacon.*

2. The state of being tickled.

In sweets the acid particles seem so attenuated in the oil as only to produce a small and grateful *titillation*. *Arbuthnot.*

3. Any slight or petty pleasure.

The delights which result from these nobler entertainments our cool thoughts need not be ashamed of, and which are dogged by no such sad sequels as are the products of those *titillations*, that reach no higher than the senses. *Glanville.*

TI'TLARK. *n. s.* A bird.

The smaller birds do the like in their seasons; as the leverock, *titlark*, and linnet. *Walton.*

TI'TLE. *n. s.* [*titelle*, old Fr. *titulus*, Lat.]

1. A general head comprising particulars.

Three draw the experiments of the former four into *titles* and tables for the better drawing of observations; these we call compilers. *Bacon.*

Among the many preferences that the laws of England have above others, I shall single out two particular *titles*, which give a handsome specimen of their excellencies above other laws in other parts or *titles* of the same. *Hale.*

2. An appellation of honour.

To leave his wife, to leave his babes,
His mansion, and his *titles*, in a place
From whence himself does fly? *Shakesp. Macbeth.*

Man over men
He made not lord: such *title* to himself
Reserving. *Milton.*

3. A name; an appellation.

My name's Macbeth.
—The devil himself could not pronounce a *title*
More hateful to mine ear. *Shakesp. Macbeth.*

Ill worthy I such *title* should belong
To me transgressor. *Milton.*

4. The first page of a book, telling its name and generally its subject; an inscription.

This man's brow, like to a *title* leaf,
Foretels the nature of a tragick volume. *Shakespeare.*

Our adversaries encourage a writer who cannot furnish out so much as a *title* page with propriety. *Swift.*

5. A claim of right.

Let the *title* of a man's right be called in question; are we not bold to rely and build upon the judgment of such as are famous for their skill in the laws? *Hooker.*

Is a man impoverished by purchase? it is because he paid his money for a lye, and took a bad *title* for a good. *South.*

'Tis our duty
Such monuments, as we can build, to raise;
Lest all the world prevent what we should do,
And claim a *title* in him by their praise. *Dryden.*

To revenge their common injuries, though you had an undoubted *title* by your birth, you had a greater by your courage. *Dryden.*

Conti would have kept his *title* to Orange. *Addison.*

O the discretion of a girl! she will be a slave to any thing that has not a *title* to make her one. *Southern.*

To TI'TLE. *v. a.* [from the noun.] To entitle; to name; to call.

To these, that sober race of men, whose lives
Religious, *titled* them the sons of God,
Shall yield up all their virtue, all their fame,
Ignobly! *Milton's Par. Lost, b.* xi.

TI'TLELESS. *adj.* [from *title*.] Wanting a name or appellation. Not in use.

He was a kind of nothing, *titleless*,
Till he had forg'd himself a name o' th' fire
Of burning Rome. *Shakesp. Coriolanus.*

TI'TLEPAGE. *n. s.* [*title* and *page*.] The page containing the title of a book.

We should have been pleased to have seen our own names at the bottom of the *titlepage*. *Dryden.*

TI'TMOUSE. or *tit. n. s.* [*tijt*, Dutch, a chick or small bird; *titlingier*, Islandick, a little bird: *tit* signifies *little* in the Teutonick dialects.] A small species of birds.

The nightingale is sovereign of song,
Before him sits the *titmouse* silent be,
And I unfit to thrust in skilful throng,
Should Colin make judge of my foolerie. *Spenser.*

The *titmouse* and the peckers hungry brood,
And Progne with her bosom stain'd in blood. *Dryden.*

To TI'TTER. *v. n.* [formed, I suppose, from the sound.] To laugh with restraint; to laugh without much noise.

In flow'd at once a gay embroider'd race,
And *titt'ring* push'd the pedants off the place. *Dunciad.*

TI'TTER. *n. s.* [from the verb.]

1. A restrained laugh.
2. I know not what it signifies in *Tusser*.

From wheat go and rake out the *titters* or tine,
If eare be not forth, it will rise again fine. *Tusser.*

TI'TTLE. *n. s.* [I suppose from *tit*.] A small particle; a point; a dot.

In the particular which concerned the church, the Scots would never depart from a *tittle*. *Clarendon, b.* viii.

Angels themselves disdaining
T' approach thy temple, give thee in command
What to the smallest *tittle* thou shalt say
To thy adorers. *Paradise Regain'd, b.* i.

They thought God and themselves linked together in so fast a covenant, that although they never performed their part, God was yet bound to make good every *tittle* of his. *South's Sermons.*

Ned Fashion hath been bred about court, and understands to a *tittle* all the punctilios of a drawing-room. *Swift.*

TI'TTLETATTLE. *n. s.* [A word formed from *tattle* by a ludicrous reduplication.] Idle talk; prattle; empty gabble.

As the foe drew near
With love, and joy, and life and dear,
Our don, who knew this *tittletattle*,
Did, sure as trumpet, call to battle. *Prior.*

For every idle *tittletattle* that went about, Jack was suspected for the author. *Arbuthnot's Hist. of J. Bull.*

To TI'TTLETATTLE. *v. n.* [from *tattle*.] To prate idly.

You are full in your *tittletattlings* of Cupid: here is Cupid, and there is Cupid: I will tell you now what a good old woman told me. *Sidney, b.* ii.

TITUBA'TION. *n. s.* [*titubo*, Lat.] The act of stumbling.

TI'TULAR. *adj.* [*titulaire*, Fr. from *titulus*, Lat.] Nominal; having or conferring only the title.

They would deliver up the kingdom to the king of England to shadow their rebellion, and to be *titular* and painted head of those arms. *Bacon's Henry* VII.

Thrones, virtues, powers,
If these magnifick titles yet remain,
Not merely *titular*. *Milton.*

Both Valerius and Austin were *titular* bishops. *Ayliffe.*

TITULA'RITY. *n. s.* [from *titular*.] The state of being titular.

Julius, Augustus, and Tiberius, with great humility received the name of imperator; but their successors retain the same even in its *titularity*. *Brown's Vulgar Errours.*

TI'TULARY. *adj.* [*titulaire*, Fr. from *titulus*, Lat.]

1. Consisting in a title.

The malecontents of his kingdom have not been base nor *titulary* impostors, but of an higher nature. *Bacon's H.* VII.

2. Relating to a title.

William the conqueror, howsoever he used the power of a conqueror to reward his Normans, yet mixed it with a *titulary* pretence, grounded upon the confessor's will. *Bacon.*

TI'TULARY. *n. s.* [from the adj.] One that has a title or right.

The persons deputed for the celebration of these masses were neither *titularies* nor perpetual curates, but persons entirely conductitious. *Ayliffe's Parergon.*

TI'VY. *adj.* [A word expressing speed, from *tantivy*, the note of a hunting horn.]

In a bright moon-shine while winds whistle loud,
Tivy, tivy, tivy, we mount and we fly,
All rocking in a downy white cloud:
And left our leap from the sky should prove too far,
We slide on the back of a new-falling star. *Dryden.*

TO. *adv.* [ꞇo, Saxon; *te*, Dutch.]

1. A particle coming between two verbs, and noting the second as the object of the first.

The delay of our hopes teaches us *to* mortify our desires. *Smallridge.*

2. It notes the intention.

Ambitious fool! with horny hoofs to pass
O'er hollow arches of resounding brass,
To rival thunder. *Dryden's Æn.*

She rais'd a war
In Italy, *to* call me back. *Dryden's All for Love.*

Urg'd by despair, again I go *to* try
The fate of arms, resolv'd in fight *to* die. *Dryden.*

I have done my utmost *to* lead my life so pleasantly as to forget all misfortunes. *Pope.*

3. After an adjective it notes its object.

We ready are *to* try our fortunes
To the last man. *Shakesp. Henry* IV. *p.* ii.

The lawless sword his childrens blood shall shed,
Increast for slaughter, born *to* beg their bread. *Sandys.*

4. Noting futurity.

It is not blood and bones that can be conscious of their own hardness and redness; and we are still *to* seek for something else in our frame that receives those impressions. *Bentley.*

5. { To *and again*. / To *and fro*. } Backward and forward.

Ismay binds and looseth souls condemn'd to woe,
And sends the devils on errands *to and fro*. *Fairfax, b.* ii.

The spirits perverse
With easy intercourse pass *to and fro*,
To tempt or punish mortals. *Milton.*

Dress

Dreſs it not till the ſeventh day, and then move the joint *to and fro*. *Wiſeman's Surgery.*

Maſſes of marble, originally beat off from the ſtrata of the neighbouring rocks, rolled *to and again* till they were rounded to the form of pebbles. *Woodward on Foſſils.*

The winds in diſtant regions blow,
Moving the world of waters *to and fro*. *Addiſon.*

To. *prepoſition.*

1. Noting motion *towards:* oppoſed to *from.*

With that ſhe *to* him afreſh, and ſurely would have put out his eyes. *Sidney, b.* ii.

Tybalt fled;
But by and by comes back *to* Romeo,
And *to*'t they go like light'ning. *Shakeſpeare.*

Give not over ſo; *to* him again, intreat him,
Kneel down before him. *Shakeſp. Meaſ. for Meaſure.*

She's coming; *to* her coz. *Shakeſpeare.*

I'll *to* him again in the name of Brook; he'll tell me all his purpoſe. *Shakeſp. Merry Wives of Windſor.*

I'll *to* the woods among the happier brutes:
Come, let's away. *Smith.*

2. Noting accord or adaptation.

Thus they with ſacred thought
Mov'd on in ſilence *to* ſoft pipes. *Milton's Par. Loſt, b.* i.

3. Noting addreſs or compellation.

To you, my noble lord of Weſtmorland.
——I pledge your grace. *Shakeſp. Henry* V.

Here's *to* you all, gentlemen, and let him that's good-natur'd in his drink pledge me. *Denham's Sophy.*

Now, *to* you, Raymond: can you gueſs no reaſon
Why I repoſe ſuch confidence in you? *Dryden.*

4. Noting attention or application.

Turn out, you rogue! how like a beaſt you lie:
Go buckle *to* the law. *Dryden's Juvenal.*

Sir Roger's kindneſs extends *to* their childrens children. *Addiſon.*

5. Noting addition or accumulation.

Wiſdom he has, and *to* his wiſdom courage;
Temper *to* that, and unto all ſucceſs. *Denham's Sophy.*

6. Noting a ſtate or place whither any one goes.

Take you ſome company and away *to* horſe. *Shakeſp.*

He ſent his coachman's grandchild *to* prentice. *Addiſon.*

7. Noting oppoſition.

No foe unpuniſh'd in the fighting field,
Shall dare thee foot *to* foot with ſword and ſhield. *Dryden.*

8. Noting amount.

There were *to* the number of three hundred horſe, and as many thouſand foot Engliſh. *Bacon's War with Spain.*

9. Noting proportion; noting amount.

Enoch whoſe days were, though many in reſpect of ours, yet ſcarce as three *to* nine in compariſon of theirs with whom he lived. *Hooker, b.* iv.

With theſe bars againſt me,
And yet to win her——all the world *to* nothing. *Shakeſp.*

Twenty *to* one offend more in writing too much than too little; even as twenty *to* one fall into ſickneſs rather by overmuch fulneſs than by any lack. *Aſcham's Schoolmaſter.*

The burial muſt be by the ſmallneſs of the proportion as fifty *to* one; or it muſt be holpen by ſomewhat which may fix the ſilver never to be reſtored when it is incorporated. *Bacon's Phyſical Remains.*

With a funnel filling bottles; *to* their capacity they will all be full. *Benj. Johnſon.*

Phyſicians have two women patients *to* one man. *Graunt.*

When an ambaſſador is diſpatched to any foreign ſtate, he ſhall be allowed *to* the value of a ſhilling a day. *Addiſon.*

Among the ancients the weight of oil was to that of wine as nine *to* ten. *Arbuthnot on Coins.*

Suppoſing them to have an equal ſhare, the odds will be three *to* one on their ſide. *Swift.*

10. Noting poſſeſſion or appropriation.

Still a greater difficulty upon tranſlators riſes from the peculiarities every language hath *to* itſelf. *Felton.*

11. Noting perception.

The flow'r itſelf is glorious to behold,
Sharp *to* the taſte. *Dryden's Virgil.*

12. Noting the ſubject of an affirmation.

I truſt, I may not truſt thee; for thy word
Is but the vain breath of a common man:
Believe me, I do not believe thee, man;
I have a king's oath *to* the contrary. *Shakeſp. King John.*

12. In compariſon of.

All that they did was piety *to* this. *Benj. Johnſon.*

There is no fool *to* the ſinner, who every moment ventures his ſoul. *Tillotſon.*

13. As far as.

Some Americans, otherwiſe of quick parts, could not count *to* one thouſand, nor had any diſtinct idea of it, though they could reckon very well *to* twenty. *Locke.*

Coffee exhales in roaſting *to* the abatement of near one-fourth of its weight. *Arbuthnot on Aliments.*

14. Noting intention.

This the conſul ſees, yet this man lives!
Partakes the publick cares; and with his eye
Marks and points out each man of us *to* ſlaughter. *B. Job.*

15. After an adjective it notes the object.

Draw thy ſword in right.
I'll draw it as apparent *to* the crown,
And in that quarrel uſe it to the death. *Shakeſpeare.*

Fate and the dooming gods are deaf *to* tears. *Dryden.*

All were attentive *to* the godlike man,
When from his lofty couch he thus began. *Dryden.*

16. Noting obligation.

Almanzor is taxed with changing ſides, and what tie has he on him *to* the contrary: he is not born their ſubject, and he is injured by them to a very high degree *Dryden.*

17. Reſpecting.

He's walk'd the way of nature;
And *to* our purpoſes he lives no more. *Shakeſpeare.*

The effects of ſuch a diviſion are pernicious *to* the laſt degree, not only with regard *to* thoſe advantages which they give the common enemy, but *to* thoſe private evils which they produce in every particular. *Addiſon's Spect.* N°. 125.

18. Noting conſequence.

Factions carried too high are much *to* the prejudice of the authority of princes. *Bacon.*

Under how hard a fate are women born,
Priz'd *to* their ruin, or expos'd *to* ſcorn! *Waller.*

Thus, *to* their fame, when finiſh'd was the fight,
The victors from their lofty ſteeds alight. *Dryden.*

Oh frail eſtate of human things,
Now *to* our coſt your emptineſs we know. *Dryden.*

A Britiſh king obliges himſelf by oath to execute juſtice in mercy, and not to exerciſe either *to* the total excluſion of the other. *Addiſon.*

It muſt be confeſſed *to* the reproach of human nature, that this is but too juſt a picture of itſelf. *Broome's Odyſſey.*

19. Towards.

She ſtretch'd her arms *to* heav'n. *Dryden.*

20. Noting preſence.

She ſtill beareth him an invincible hatred, and revileth him *to* his face. *Swift.*

21. Noting effect.

He was wounded tranſverſe the temporal muſcle, and bleeding almoſt *to* death. *Wiſeman.*

By the diſorder in the retreat great numbers were crowded *to* death. *Clarendon.*

Ingenious *to* their ruin, ev'ry age
Improves the act and inſtruments of rage. *Waller.*

To prevent the aſperſion of the Roman majeſty, the offender was whipt *to* death. *Dryden.*

The abuſe reigns chiefly in the country, as I found *to* my vexation when I was laſt there in a viſit I made to a neighbour. *Swift.*

I read my ruin in ev'ry cringing bow and fawning ſmile.
Why with malignant elogies encreaſe
The peoples fears, and praiſe me *to* my ruin? *Smith.*

22. After a verb *to* notes the object.

Give me ſome wine; fill full.
I drink *to* th' general joy of the whole table,
And to our dear friend Banquo. *Shakeſp. Macbeth.*

Had the methods of education been directed *to* their right end, this ſo neceſſary could not have been neglected. *Locke.*

Many of them have expoſed *to* the world the private misfortunes of families. *Pope.*

23. Noting the degree.

This weather-glaſs was ſo placed in the cavity of a ſmall receiver, that only the ſlender part of the pipe, *to* the height of four inches, remained expoſed to the open air. *Boyle.*

Tell her thy brother languiſhes *to* death. *Addiſon.*

A crow though hatched under a hen, and who never has ſeen any of the works of its kind, makes its neſt the ſame, *to* the laying of a ſtick with all the neſts of that ſpecies. *Addiſon.*

If he employs his abilities *to* the beſt advantage, the time will come when the ſupreme governour of the world ſhall proclaim his worth before men and angels. *Addiſon's Spect.*

24. Before *day, to* notes the preſent day; before *morrow*, the day next coming; before *night*, either the preſent night, or night next coming.

Banquo, thy ſoul's flight,
If it find heav'n muſt find it out *to night.* *Shakeſpeare.*

To day they chas'd the boar. *Otway.*

This ought rather to be called a full purpoſe of committing ſin *to day*, than a reſolution of leaving it *to morrow*. *Calamy.*

25. *To day, to night, to morrow*, are uſed, not very properly, as ſubſtantives in the nominative and other caſes.

To morrow, and *to morrow*, and *to morrow*,
Creeps in this petty pace from day to day;
And all our yeſterdays have lighted fools
The way to duſky death. *Shakeſp. Macbeth.*

The father of Solomon's houſe will have private conference with one of you the next day after *to morrow*. *Bacon.*

To

To day is ours, why do we fear?
To day is ours, we have it here;
Let's banish bus'ness, banish sorrow,
To the gods belongs *to morrow*. *Cowley.*
To morrow will deliver all her charms
Into my arms, and make her mine for ever. *Dryden.*
For what *to morrow* shall disclose,
May spoil what you *to night* propose:
England may change, or Cloe stray;
Love and life are for *to day*. *Prior.*

TOAD. *n. s.* [taꝺe, Saxon.] An animal resembling a frog; but the frog leaps, the toad crawls: the toad is accounted venomous, I believe truly.

From th' extreamest upward of thy head,
To the descent and dust below thy foot,
A most *toad*-spotted traitor. *Shakesp. K. Lear.*
I had rather be a *toad*,
And live upon the vapour of a dungeon,
Than keep a corner in the thing I love
For others use. *Shakespeare's Othello.*

In the great plague there were seen, in divers ditches about London, many *toads* that had tails three inches long, whereas *toads* usually have no tails. *Bacon's Nat. Hist.*

In hollow caverns vermin make abode,
The hissing serpent, and the swelling *toad*. *Dryden.*

TO'ADFISH. *n. s.* A kind of sea-fish.

TO'ADFLAX. *n. s.* A plant.

TO'ADSTONE. *n. s.* [*toad* and *stone*.] A concretion supposed to be found in the head of a toad.

The *toadstone* presumed to be found in the head of that animal, is not a thing impossible. *Brown's Vulgar Errours.*

TO'ADSTOOL. *n. s.* [*toad* and *stool*.] A plant like a mushroom.

The grisly *todestool* grown there mought I see,
And loathing paddocks lording on the same. *Spenser.*

Another imperfect plant like a mushroom, but sometimes as broad as a hat, called *toadstool*, is not esculent. *Bacon.*

To TOAST. *v. a.* [*torreo*, *tostum*, Lat.]

1. To dry or heat at the fire.

Put up thy sword betime,
Or I'll so maul you and your *toasting* iron. *Shakespeare.*
His breath stinks with eating *toasted* cheese. *Shakespeare.*

The earth whereof the grass is soon parched with the sun, and *toasted*, is commonly forced earth. *Bacon's Nat. Hist.*

To allure mice I find no other magick, than to draw out a piece of *toasted* cheese. *Brown.*

2. To name when a health is drunk. *To toast* is used commonly when women are named.

Several popish gentlemen *toasted* many loyal healths. *Add.*
We'll try the empire you so long have boasted;
And if we are not prais'd, we'll not be *toasted*. *Prior.*

TOAST. *n. s.* [from the verb.]

1. Bread dried before the fire.

You are both as rheumatick as two dry *toasts*; you cannot one bear with another's confirmities. *Shakesp. Henry* IV.

Every third day take a small *toast* of manchet, dipped in oil of sweet almonds new drawn, and sprinkled with loaf sugar. *Bacon's Physical Remains.*

2. Bread dried and put into liquor.

Where's then the saucy boat
Co-rival'd greatness? or to harbour fled,
Or made a *toast* for Neptune? *Shakesp. Troil. and Cressida.*
Some squire, perhaps, you take delight to rack;
Whose game is whisk, whose treat a *toast* in sack. *Pope.*

3. A celebrated woman whose health is often drunk.

I shall likewise mark out every *toast*, the club in which she was elected, and the number of votes that were on her side. *Addison's Guard.* N°. 107.

Say, why are beauties prais'd and honour'd most,
The wise man's passion, and the vain man's *toast*?
Why deck'd with all that land and sea afford,
Why angels call'd, and angel-like ador'd? *Pope.*

TO'ASTER. *n. s.* [from *toast*.] He who toasts.

We simple *toasters* take delight
To see our women's teeth look white;
And ev'ry saucy ill-bred fellow
Sneers at a mouth profoundly yellow. *Prior.*

TOBA'CCO. *n. s.* [from *Tobaco* or *Tobago* in America.]

The flower of the *tobacco* consists of one leaf, is funnel-shaped, and divided at the top into five deep segments, which expand like a star; the ovary becomes an oblong roundish membranaceous fruit, which is divided into two cells by an intermediate partition, and is filled with small roundish seeds. *Miller.*

It is a planet now I see;
And, if I err not, by his proper
Figure, that's like a *tobacco*-stopper. *Hudibras, p.* ii.

Bread or *tobacco* may be neglected; but reason at first recommends their trial, and custom makes them pleasant. *Locke.*

Salts are to be drained out of the clay by water, before it be fit for the making *tobacco*-pipes or bricks. *Woodward.*

TOB'ACCONIST. *n. s.* [from *tobacco*.] A preparer and vender of tobacco.

TOD. *n. s.* [*totte haar*, a lock of hair, German. *Skinner.* I believe rightly.]

1. A bush; a thick shrub.

Within the ivie *tod*,
There shrouded was the little god;
I heard a busy bustling. *Spenser's Pastorals.*

2. A certain weight of wool, twenty eight pounds.

Every eleven weather *tods*, every *tod* yields a pound and odd shillings. *Shakespeare's Winter's Tale.*

TOE. *n. s.* [ra, Saxon; *teen*, Dutch.] The divided extremities of the feet; the fingers of the feet.

Come all you spirits,
And fill me from the crown to th' *toe*, topful
Of direct cruelty. *Shakesp. Macbeth.*
Sport that wrinkled care derides,
And laughter holding both his sides;
Come and trip it as you go,
On the light fantastick *toe*. *Milton.*
Last to enjoy her sense of feeling,
A thousand little nerves she sends
Quite to our *toes*, and fingers ends. *Prior.*

TOFO'RE. *adv.* [toꝼoꞃan, Saxon.] Before. Obsolete.

It is an epilogue to make plain
Some obscure precedence that hath *tofore* been sain. *Shak.*

So shall they depart the manor with the corn and the bacon *tofore* him that hath won it. *Spectator*, N°. 607.

TOFT. *n. s.* [*toftum*, law Latin.] A place where a messuage has stood. *Cowel and Ains.*

TO'GED. *adj.* [*togatus*, Lat.] Gowned; dressed in gowns.

The bookish theorick,
Wherein the *toged* consuls can propose
As masterly as he; meer prattle, without practice,
Is all his soldiership. *Shakespeare's Othello.*

TOGE'THER. *adv.* [toᵹæꝺeꞃe, Saxon.]

1. In company.

We turn'd o'er many books *together*. *Shakespeare.*
Both *together* went into the wood. *Milton.*

2. Not apart; not in separation.

That king joined humanity and policy *together*. *Bacon.*

3. In the same place.

She lodgeth heat and cold, and moist and dry,
And life and death, and peace and war *together*. *Davies.*

4. In the same time.

While he and I live *together*, I shall not be thought the worst poet. *Dryden.*

5. Without intermission.

The Portuguese expected his return for almost an age *together* after the battle. *Dryden.*

They had a great debate concerning the punishment of one of their admirals, which lasted a month *together*. *Addison.*

6. In concert.

The subject is his confederacy with Henry the eighth, and the wars they made *together* upon France. *Addison on Italy.*

7. In continuity.

Some tree's broad leaves *together* sew'd,
And girded on our loins, may cover round. *Milton.*

8. TOGETHER *with*. In union with; in a state of mixture with.

Take the bad *together with* the good. *Dryden's Juvenal.*

To TOIL. *v. n.* [tilian, Saxon; *tuylen*, Dutch.] To labour; perhaps originally, to labour in tillage.

This Percy was the man nearest my soul;
Who, like a brother, *toil'd* in my affairs,
And laid his love and life under my foot. *Shakespeare.*
Others ill-fated are condemn'd to *toil*
Their tedious life, and mourn their purpose blasted
With fruitless act. *Prior.*
He views the main that ever *toils* below. *Thomson.*

To TOIL. *v. a.*

1. To labour; to work at.

Toil'd out my uncouth passage, forc'd to ride
Th' untractable abyss. *Milton.*

2. To weary; to overlabour.

Then, *toil'd* with works of war, retir'd himself
To Italy. *Shakespeare's Richard* II.

TOIL. *n. s.* [from the verb.]

1. Labour; fatigue.

They live to their great, both *toil* and grief, where the blasphemies of Arians are renewed. *Hooker, b.* v.

Not to irksome *toil*, but to delight
He made us. *Milton.*

2. [*Toile, toiles*, Fr. *tela*, Latin.] Any net or snare woven or meshed.

She looks like sleep,
As she would catch another Antony
In her strong *toil* of grace. *Shakesp. Ant. and Cleopatra.*

He had so placed his horsemen and footmen in the woods, that he shut up the Christians as it were in a *toil*. *Knolles.*

All great spirits
Bear great and sudden change with such impatience
As a Numidian lion, when first caught,
Endures the *toil* that holds him. *Denham's Sophy.*
A fly falls into the *toil* of a spider. *L'Estrange.*
Fantastick honour, thou hast fram'd a *toil*
Thyself, to make thy love thy virtues spoil. *Dryden.*

TO'ILET. *n. s.* [*toilette*, Fr.] A dreſſing table.

The merchant from the exchange returns in peace,
And the long labours of the *toilet* ceaſe. *Pope.*

TO'ILSOME. *n. s.* [from *toil*.] Laborious; weary.

This were it *toilſome*, yet with thee were ſweet. *Milton.*

While here we dwell,
What can be *toilſome* in theſe pleaſant walks? *Milton.*

Abſent or dead, ſtill let a friend be dear,
A ſigh the abſent claims, the dead a tear;
Recal thoſe nights that clos'd thy *toilſome* days,
Still hear thy Parnel in his living lays. *Pope.*

TO'ILSOMENESS. *n. s.* [from *toilſome*.] Weariſomeneſs; laborioufneſs.

TO'KEN. *n. s.* [*taikns*, Gothick; ᵹacn, Saxon; *teycken*, Dutch.]

1. A ſign.

Shew me a *token* for good, that they which hate me may ſee it. *Pſal.* lxxxvi. 17.

2. A mark.

Whereſoever you ſee ingratitude, you may as infallibly conclude, that there is a growing ſtock of ill-nature in that breaſt, as you may know that man to have the plague upon whom you ſee the *tokens*. *South's Sermons.*

3. A memorial of friendſhip; an evidence of remembrance.

Here is a letter from queen Hecuba,
A *token* from her daughter, my fair love. *Shakeſpeare.*

Whence came this?
This is ſome *token* from a newer friend. *Shakeſpeare.*

Pigwiggen gladly would commend
Some *token* to queen Mab to ſend,
Were worthy of her wearing. *Drayton's Nymphid.*

To TO'KEN. *v. a.* [from the noun.] To make known. Not in uſe.

What in time proceeds,
May *token* to the future our paſt deeds. *Shakeſpeare.*

TOLD. pret. and part. paſſ. of *tell*. Mentioned; related.

The acts of God to human ears
Cannot, without proceſs of ſpeech, be *told*. *Milton.*

To TOLE. *v. a.* [This ſeems to be ſome barbarous provincial word.] To train; to draw by degrees.

Whatever you obſerve him to be more frighted at than he ſhould, *tole* him on to by inſenſible degrees, till at laſt he maſters the difficulty. *Locke.*

TO'LERABLE. *adj.* [*tolerable*, Fr. *tolerabilis*, Lat.]

1. Supportable; that may be endured or ſupported.

Yourſelves, who have ſought them, ye ſo excuſe, as that ye would have men to think ye judge them not allowable, but *tolerable* only, and to be borne with, for the furtherance of your purpoſes, till the corrupt eſtate of the church may be better reformed. *Hooker.*

It ſhall be more *tolerable* for Sodom in the day of judgment than for that city. *Mat.* x. 15.

Cold and heat ſcarce *tolerable*. *Milton.*

There is nothing of difficulty in the external performance, but what hypocriſy can make *tolerable* to itſelf. *Tillotſon.*

2. Not excellent; not contemptible; paſſable.

The reader may be aſſured of a *tolerable* tranſlation. *Dryd.*

Princes have it in their power to keep a majority on their ſide by any *tolerable* adminiſtration, till provoked by continual oppreſſions. *Swift.*

TO'LERABLENESS. *n. s.* [from *tolerable*.] The ſtate of being tolerable.

TO'LERABLY. *adv.* [from *tolerable*.]

1. Supportably; in a manner that may be endured.

2. Paſſably; neither well nor ill; moderately well.

Sometimes are found in theſe laxer ſtrata bodies that are ſtill *tolerably* firm. *Woodward's Nat. Hiſt.* p. iii.

The perſon to whom this head belonged laughed frequently, and on particular occaſions had acquitted himſelf *tolerably* at a ball. *Addiſon's Spect.* N°. 275.

TO'LERANCE. *n. s.* [*tolerantia*, Lat. *tolerance*, Fr.] Power of enduring; act of enduring.

Diogenes one froſty morning came into the market-place ſhaking, to ſhew his *tolerance*; many of the people came about him, pitying him: Plato paſſing by, and knowing he did it to be ſeen, ſaid, if you pity him indeed, let him alone to himſelf. *Bacon's Apophth.*

There wants nothing but conſideration of our own eternal weal, a *tolerance* or endurance of being made happy here, and bleſſed eternally. *Hammond's Fundamentals.*

To TO'LERATE. *v. a.* [*tolero*, Lat. *tolerer*, Fr.] To allow ſo as not to hinder; to ſuffer.

Inaſmuch as they did reſolve to remove only ſuch things of that kind as the church might beſt ſpare, retaining the reſidue; their whole counſel is, in this point, utterly condemned, as having either proceeded from the blindneſs of thoſe times, or from negligence, or from deſire of honour and glory, or from an erroneous opinion that ſuch things might be *tolerated* for a while. *Hooker*, b. iv.

We ſhall *tolerate* flying horſes, harpies, and ſatyrs; for theſe are poetical fancies, whoſe ſhaded moralities requite their ſubſtantial falſities. *Brown's Vulgar Errours*, b. v.

Men ſhould not *tolerate* themſelves one minute in any known ſin. *Decay of Piety.*

Crying ſhould not be *tolerated* in children. *Locke.*

We are fully convinced that we ſhall always *tolerate* them, but not that they will *tolerate* us. *Swift.*

TOLERA'TION. *n. s.* [*tolero*, Latin.] Allowance given to that which is not approved.

I ſhall not ſpeak againſt the indulgence and *toleration* granted to theſe men. *South's Sermons.*

TOLL. *n. s.* [This word ſeems derived from *tollo*, Lat. ᵹoll, Saxon; *tol*, Dutch; *told*, Daniſh; *toll*, Welſh; *taille*, Fr.] An exciſe of goods; a ſeizure of ſome part for permiſſion of the reſt.

Toll, in law, has two ſignifications: firſt, a liberty to buy and ſell within the precincts of a manor, which ſeems to import as much as a fair or market; ſecondly, a tribute or cuſtom paid for paſſage. *Cowel.*

Empſon and Dudley the people eſteemed as his horſeleaches, bold men, that took *toll* of their maſter's griſt. *Bac.*

The ſame Pruſias joined with the Rhodians againſt the Byzantines, and ſtopped them from levying the *toll* upon their trade into the Euxine. *Arbuthnot.*

To TOLL. *v. n.* [from the noun.]

1. To pay toll or tallage.

I will buy me a ſon-in-law in a fair, and *toll* for him: for this I'll none of him. *Shakeſp. All's well that ends well.*

Where, when, by whom, and what y' were ſold for,
And in the open market *toll'd* for? *Hudibras*, p. ii.

2. To take toll or tallage.

The meale the more yeeldeth, if ſervant be true,
And miller that *tolleth* takes none but his due. *Tuſſer.*

3. [I know not whence derived.] To ſound as a ſingle bell.

The firſt bringer of unwelcome news
Hath but a loſing office; and his tongue
Sounds ever after as a ſullen bell,
Remember'd *tolling* a departed friend. *Shakeſp. Henry* IV.

Our going to church at the *tolling* of a bell, only tells us the time when we ought to go to worſhip God. *Stillingfleet.*

Toll, toll,
Gentle bell, for the ſoul
Of the pure ones. *Denham.*

You love to hear of ſome prodigious tale,
The bell that *toll'd* alone, or Iriſh whale. *Dryden.*

They give their bodies due repoſe at night:
When hollow murmurs of their ev'ning bells
Diſmiſs the ſleepy ſwains, and *toll* them to their cells. *Dry.*

All the bells *tolled* in different notes. *Pope.*

With horns and trumpets now to madneſs ſwell,
Now ſink in ſorrows with a *tolling* bell. *Pope's Dunciad.*

The maid aſks who the bell *toll'd* for? *Swift.*

To TOLL. *v. a.* [*tollo*, Lat.]

1. To ring a bell.

When any one dies, then by *tolling* or ringing of a bell the ſame is known to the ſearchers. *Graunt.*

2. To take away; to vacate; to annul. A term only uſed in the civil law: in this ſenſe the *o* is ſhort, in the former long.

An appeal from ſentence of excommunication does not ſuſpend it, but then devolves it to a ſuperior judge, and *tolls* the preſumption in favour of a ſentence. *Ayliffe.*

3. To take away. Obſolete.

The adventitious moiſture which hangeth looſe in a body, betrayeth and *tolleth* forth the innate and radical moiſture along with it. *Bacon's Nat. Hiſt.* N°. 365.

TO'LLBOOTH. *n. s.* [*toll* and *booth*.] A priſon. *Ainſ.*

To TO'LLBOOTH. *v. a.* To impriſon in a tollbooth.

To theſe what did he give? why a hen,
That they might *tollbooth* Oxford men. *Biſhop Corbet.*

TOLLGA'THERER. *n. s.* [*toll* and *gather*.] The officer that takes toll.

TO'LSEY. *n. s.* The ſame with *tolbooth*. *Dict.*

TOLUTA'TION. *n. s.* [*toluto*, Latin.] The act of pacing or ambling.

They move *per latera*, that is, two legs of one ſide together, which is *tolutation* or ambling. *Brown's Vulgar Err.*

Authors have not writ
Whether *tolutation* or ſucculſation. *Butler.*

TOMB. *n. s.* [*tombe*, *tombeau*, Fr. *tumba*, low Lat.] A monument in which the dead are encloſed.

Methinks, I ſee thee, now thou art below,
As one dead in the bottom of a *tomb*. *Shakeſpeare.*

Time is drawn upon *tombs* an old man bald, winged, with a ſithe and an hour-glaſs. *Peacham on Drawing.*

Poor heart! ſhe ſlumbers in her ſilent *tomb*,
Let her poſſeſs in peace that narrow room. *Dryden.*

The ſecret wound with which I bleed
Shall lie wrapt up, ev'n in my herſe,
But on my *tomb*-ſtone thou ſhalt read
My anſwer to thy dubious verſe. *Prior.*

To TOMB. *v. a.* [from the noun.] To bury; to entomb.

Souls of boys were there,
And youths, that *tomb'd* before their parents were. *May.*

TO'MBLESS. *adj.* [from *tomb.*] Wanting a tomb; wanting a sepulchral monument.

Lay these bones in an unworthy urn,
Tombless, with no remembrance over them. *Shakespeare.*

TO'MBOY. *n. s.* [*Tom* a diminutive of *Thomas*, and *boy.*] A mean fellow; sometimes a wild coarse girl.

A lady
Fasten'd to an empery, to be partner'd
With *tomboys*, hir'd with that self-exhibition
Which your own coffers yield! *Shakesp. Cymbeline.*

TOME. *n. s.* [Fr. τομὸς.]
1. One volume of many.
2. A book.

All those venerable books of scripture, all those sacred *tomes* and volumes of holy writ, are with such absolute perfection framed. *Hooker.*

TOMTI'T. *n. s.* [See TI'TMOUSE.] A titmouse; a small bird.

You would fancy him a giant when you looked upon him, and a *tomtit* when you shut your eyes. *Spectator.*

TON. *n. s.* [*tonne*, Fr. See TUN.] A measure or weight.

Spain was very weak at home, or very slow to move, when they suffered a small fleet of English to fire, sink, and carry away, ten thousand *ton* of their great shipping. *Bacon.*

TON. } In the names of places, are derived from the Saxon
TUN. } tun, a hedge or wall, and this seems to be from bun, a hill, the towns being anciently built on hills for the sake of defence and protection in times of war. *Gibson's Camden.*

TONE. *n. s.* [*ton*, Fr. *tonus*, Lat.]
1. Note; sound.

Sounds called *tones* are ever equal. *Bacon's Nat. Hist.*

The strength of a voice or sound makes a difference in the loudness or softness, but not in the *tone*. *Bacon's Nat. Hist.*

In their motions harmony divine
So smooths her charming *tones*, that God's own ear
Listens delighted. *Milton's Par. Lost, b.* v.

2. Accent; sound of the voice.

Palamon replies,
Eager his *tone*, and ardent were his eyes. *Dryden.*

3. A whine; a mournful cry.

Made children, with your *tones*, to run for't
As bad as bloody-bones, or Lunsford. *Hudibras, p.* iii.

4. A particular or affected sound in speaking.
5. Elasticity; power of extension and contraction.

Drinking too great quantities of this decoction may weaken the *tone* of the stomach. *Arbuthnot.*

TONG. *n. s.* [See TONGS.] The catch of a buckle. This word is usually written *tongue*, but, as its office is to hold, it has probably the same original with *tongs*, and should therefore have the same orthography.

Their hilts were burnish'd gold, and handle strong
Of mother pearl, and buckled with a golden *tong*. *Fa. Q.*

TONGS. *n. s.* [tang, Saxon; *tang*, Dutch.] An instrument by which hold is taken of any thing: as of coals in the fire.

Another did the dying brands repair
With iron *tongs*, and sprinkled oft the same
With liquid waves. *Fairy Queen, b.* ii.

They turn the glowing mass with crooked *tongs*;
The fiery work proceeds. *Dryden's Æn.*

Get a pair of *tongs* like a smith's *tongs*, stronger and toothed. *Mortimer's Husbandry.*

TONGUE. *n. s.* [tung, Saxon; *tonghe*, Dutch.]
1. The instrument of speech in human beings.

My conscience hath a thousand several *tongue*,
And ev'ry *tongue* brings in a sev'ral tale,
And ev'ry tale condemns me for a villain. *Shakespeare.*

Who with the *tongue* of angels can relate. *Milton.*

The terror of thy power or potent *tongue*. *Milton.*

They are *tongue*-valiant, and as bold as Hercules where there's no danger. *L'Estrange's Fables.*

My ears still ring with noise, I'm vext to death,
Tongue kill'd, and have not yet recover'd breath. *Dryden.*

Tongue-valiant hero, vaunter of thy might,
In threats the foremost; but the lag in fight. *Dryden.*

There have been female Pythagoreans, notwithstanding that philosophy consisted in keeping a secret, and the disciple was to hold her *tongue* five years together. *Addison's Guard.*

I should make but a poor pretence to true learning, if I had not clear ideas under the words my *tongue* could pronounce. *Watts's Improvement of the Mind, p.* i.

2. The organ by which animals lick.

Hiss for hiss returned with forked *tongue*
To forked *tongue*. *Milton.*

3. Speech; fluency of words.

Tongue-doughty giant, how dost thou prove? *Milton.*

Much *tongue* and much judgment seldom go together; for talking and thinking are too quite differing faculties. *L'Estr.*

Parrots, imitating human *tongue*,
And singing-birds in silver cages hung. *Dryden.*

First in the council-hall to steer the state,
And ever foremost in a *tongue* debate. *Dryden's Æn.*

Though they have those sounds ready at their *tongue*'s end, yet there are no determined ideas. *Locke.*

4. Speech, as well or ill used.

Give me thy hand; I am sorry I beat thee: but, while thou liv'st, keep a good *tongue* in thy head. *Shakespeare.*

On evil days though fallen and evil *tongues*. *Milton.*

5. A language.

The Lord shall bring a nation against thee, whose *tongue* thou shalt not understand. *Deut.* xxvii. 49.

With wond'rous gifts endu'd,
To speak all *tongues* and do all miracles. *Milton.*

An acquaintance with the various *tongues* is nothing but a relief against the mischiefs which the building of Babel introduced. *Watts.*

6. Speech as opposed to thoughts.

Let us not love in word, neither in *tongue*, but in deed and in truth. 1 *John* iii. 18.

7. A nation distinguished by their language. A scriptural term.

The Lord shall destroy the *tongue* of the Egyptian sea. *Isa.*

8. A small point: as, *the* tongue *of a balance.*
9. *To hold the* TONGUE. To be silent.

'Tis seldom seen that senators so young
Know when to speak, and when to *hold their tongue*. *Dryd.*

Whilst I live I must not *hold my tongue*,
And languish out old age in his displeasure. *Addison.*

To TONGUE. *v. a.* [from the noun.] To chide; to scold.

But that her tender shame
Will not proclaim against her maiden loss,
How might she *tongue* me. *Shakesp. Meas. for Measure.*

To TONGUE. *v. n.* To talk; to prate.

'Tis still a dream; or else such stuff, as madmen
Tongue, and brain not. *Shakesp. Cymbeline.*

TO'NGUED. *adj.* [from *tongue.*] Having a tongue.

Tongu'd like the night-crow. *Donne.*

TO'NGUELESS. *adj.* [from *tongue.*]
1. Wanting a tongue; speechless.

What *tongueless* blocks, would they not speak? *Shakesp.*

Our grave,
Like Turkish mute, shall have a *tongueless* mouth. *Shak.*

That blood, like sacrificing Abel's, cries,
Even from the *tongueless* caverns of the earth,
To me, for justice. *Shakesp. Richard* II.

2. Unnamed; not spoken of.

One good deed, dying *tongueless*,
Slaughters a thousand waiting upon that. *Shakespeare.*

TO'NGUEPAD. *n. s.* [*tongue* and *pad.*] A great talker.

She who was a celebrated wit at London is, in that dull part of the world, called a *tonguepad*. *Tatler.*

TONGUETI'ED. *adj.* [*tongue* and *tie.*] Having an impediment of speech.

Love, and *tonguety'd* simplicity,
In least speak most to my capacity. *Shakespeare.*

They who have short tongues, or are *tonguetied*, are apt to fall short of the appulse of the tongue to the teeth, and oftner place it on the gums, and say *t* and *d* instead of *th* and *dh*; as moder for mother. *Holder's Elements of Speech.*

He spar'd the blushes of the *tonguety'd* dame. *Tickel.*

TO'NICK. } *adj.* [*tonique*, Fr. τείνω.]
TO'NICAL. }
1. Being extended; being elastick.

Station is no rest, but one kind of motion, relating unto that which physicians, from Galen, do name extensive or *tonical*. *Brown's Vulgar Errours, b.* iii.

2. Relating to tones or sounds.

TO'NNAGE. *n. s.* [from *ton.*] A custom or impost due for merchandise brought or carried in tons from or to other nations, after a certain rate in every ton. *Cowel.*

Tonnage and poundage upon merchandizes were collected, refused to be settled by act of parliament. *Clarendon.*

TO'NSIL. *n. s.* [*tonsille*, Fr. *tonsillæ*, Lat.]

Tonsils or almonds are two round glands placed on the sides of the basis of the tongue, under the common membrane of the fauces, with which they are covered; each of them hath a large oval sinus, which opens into the fauces, and in it there are a great number of lesser ones, which discharge themselves, through the great sinus, of a mucous and slippery matter, into the fauces, larynx, and œsophagus, for the moistening and lubricating these parts. *Quincy.*

TO'NSURE. *n. s.* [*tonsure*, Fr. *tonsura*, Lat.] The act of clipping the hair; the state of being shorn.

The vestals, after having received the *tonsure*, suffered their hair to come again, being here full grown, and gathered under the veil. *Addison.*

TOO. *adv.* [to, Saxon.]
1. Over and above; overmuch; more than enough. It is used to augment the signification of an adjective or adverb to a vicious degree.

Groundless prejudices and weaknesses of conscience, instead of tenderness, mislead *too* many others, *too* many, otherwise good men. *Sprat's Sermons.*

It is *too* much to build a doctrine of so mighty consequence upon so obscure a place of scripture. *Locke.*

These ridiculous stories abide with us *too* long, and *too* far influence the weaker part of mankind. *Watts.*

2. It

2. It is ſometimes doubled to encreaſe its emphaſis; but this reduplication always ſeems harſh, and is therefore laid aſide.

Oh, that this *too too* ſolid fleſh would melt. *Shakeſpeare.*

Sometimes it would be full, and then
Oh! *too too* ſoon decreaſe again;
Eclips'd ſometimes, that 'twou'd ſo fall,
There wou'd appear no hope at all. *Suckling.*

3. Likewiſe; alſo.

See what a ſcourge is laid upon your hate;
And I, for winking at your diſcords *too*,
Have loſt a brace of kinſmen. *Shakeſp. Romeo and Juliet.*

Let on my cup no wars be found,
Leſt thoſe incite to quarrels *too*,
Which wine itſelf enough can do. *Oldham.*

The arriving to ſuch a diſpoſition of mind as ſhall make a man take pleaſure in other mens ſins, is evident from the text and from experience too. *South's Sermons.*

It is better than letting our trade fall for want of current pledges, and better *too* than borrowing money of our neighbours. *Locke.*

Let thoſe eyes that view
The daring crime, behold the vengeance *too*. *Pope.*

TOOK, the preterite, and ſometimes the participle paſſive of *take*.

Thy ſoldiers
All levied in my name, have in my name
Took their diſcharge. *Shakeſp. King Lear.*

He is God in his friendſhip as well as in his nature, and therefore we ſinful creatures are not *took* upon advantages, nor conſumed in our provocations. *South's Sermons.*

Suddenly the thunder-clap
Took us unprepar'd. *Dryden.*

The ſame device encloſed the aſhes of men or boys, maids or matrons; for when the thought *took*, though at firſt it received its riſe from ſuch a particular occaſion, the ignorance of the ſculptors applied it promiſcuouſly. *Addiſon.*

This *took* up ſome of his hours every day. *Spectator.*

The riders would leap them over my hand; and one of the emperor's hunſtmen, upon a large courſer, *took* my foot, ſhoe and all. *Swift.*

Leaving Polybus, I *took* my way
To Cyrrha's temple. *Pope's Statius.*

TOOL. *n. ſ.* [tol, tool, Saxon.]

1. Any inſtrument of manual operation.

In mulberries the ſap is towards the bark only, into which if you cut a little it will come forth; but if you pierce it deeper with a *tool* it will be dry. *Bacon.*

Arm'd with ſuch gard'ning *tools* as art, yet rude,
Guiltleſs of fire had form'd. *Milton's Par. Loſt, b.* ix.

The ancients had ſome ſecret to harden the edges of their *tools*. *Addiſon.*

2. A hireling; a wretch who acts at the command of another.

He'd chooſe
To talk with wits in dirty ſhoes;
And ſcorn the *tools* with ſtars and garters,
So often ſeen careſſing Chartres. *Swift.*

To TOOT. *v. n.* [Of this word, in this ſenſe, I know not the derivation: perhaps totan, Saxon, contracted from toretan, *to know* or *examine*.] To pry; to peep; to ſearch narrowly and ſlily. It is ſtill uſed in the provinces, otherwiſe obſolete.

I caſt to go a ſhooting,
Long wand'ring up and down the land,
With bow and bolts on either hand,
For birds and buſhes *tooting*. *Spenſer's Paſt.*

TOOTH. *n. ſ.* plural *teeth*. [toð, Saxon; *tand*, Dutch.]

The *teeth* are the hardeſt and ſmootheſt bones of the body; they are formed in the cavities of the jaws, and about the ſeventh or eighth month after birth they begin to pierce the edge of the jaw, tear the perioſteum and gums, which being very ſenſible create a violent pain: the *dentes inciſivi*, or fore *teeth* of the upper jaw, appear firſt, and then thoſe of the lower jaw, becauſe they are the thinneſt and the ſharpeſt; after them come out the *canini* or eye *teeth*, and laſt of all the *molares* or grinders, becauſe they are thickeſt and blunteſt: about the ſeventh year of age they are thruſt out by new *teeth* which then begin to ſprout, and if theſe *teeth* be loſt they never grow again; but ſome have been obſerved to ſhed their *teeth* twice: about the one-and-twentieth year the two laſt of the *molares* ſpring up, and they are called *dentes ſapientiæ*. *Quincy.*

Avaunt, you curs!
Be thy mouth or black or white,
Tooth that poiſons if it bite. *Shakeſp. King Lear.*

Deſert deſerves with characters of braſs
A forted reſidence againſt the *tooth* of time,
And razure of oblivion. *Shakeſpeare.*

The *teeth* alone among the bones continue to grow in length during a man's whole life, as appears by the unſightly length of one *tooth* when its oppoſite happens to be pulled out. *Ray on the Creation.*

2. Taſte; palate.

Theſe are not diſhes for thy dainty *tooth*;
What, haſt thou got an ulcer in thy mouth?
Why ſtand'ſt thou picking? *Dryden.*

3. A tine, prong, or blade, of any multifid inſtrument.

The prieſts ſervant came while the fleſh was in ſeething, with a fleſh hook of three *teeth*. 1 *Sam.* ii. 13.

I made an inſtrument in faſhion of a comb, whoſe *teeth*, being in number ſixteen, were about an inch and an half broad, and the intervals of the *teeth* about two inches wide. *Newton's Opticks.*

4. The prominent part of wheels, by which they catch upon correſpondent parts of other bodies.

The edge whereon the *teeth* are is always made thicker than the back, becauſe the back follows the edge. *Moxon.*

In clocks, though the ſcrews and *teeth* be never ſo ſmooth, yet if they be not oiled will hardly move, though you clog them with never ſo much weight; but apply a little oil they whirl about very ſwiftly with the tenth part of the force. *Ray.*

5. TOOTH *and nail.* With one's utmoſt violence; with every means of attack or defence.

A lion and bear were at *tooth and nail* which ſhould carry off a fawn. *L'Eſtrange's Fables.*

6. *To the* TEETH. In open oppoſition.

It warms the very ſickneſs in my heart,
That I ſhall live and tell him *to his teeth*,
Thus diddeſt thou. *Shakeſpeare's Hamlet.*

The action lies
In his true nature, and we ourſelves compell'd,
Ev'n *to the teeth* and forehead of our faults,
To give in evidence. *Shakeſpeare.*

The way to our horſes lies back again by the houſe, and then we ſhall meet 'em full *in the teeth*. *Dryden.*

7. *To caſt in the* TEETH. To inſult by open exprobration.

A wiſe body's part it were not to put out his fire, becauſe his fond and fooliſh neighbour, from whom he borrowed wherewith to kindle it, might *caſt* him therewith *in the teeth*, ſaying, were it not for me thou wouldſt freeze, and not be able to heat thyſelf. *Hooker, b.* iv.

8. *In ſpite of the teeth.* Notwithſtanding threats expreſſed by ſhewing teeth; notwithſtanding any power of injury or defence.

The guiltineſs of my mind drove the groſſneſs of the foppery into a received belief, in *deſpight of the teeth* of all rhime and reaſon, that they were fairies. *Shakeſpeare.*

The only way is not to grumble at the lot they muſt bear *in ſpite of their teeth*. *L'Eſtrange.*

To TOOTH. *v. a.* [from *tooth*.]

1. To furniſh with teeth; to indent.

Then ſaws were *tooth'd*, and ſounding axes made. *Dryd.*

The point hooked down like that of an eagle; and both the edges *toothed*, as in the Indian crow. *Grew's Muſæum.*

Get a pair of tongs like a ſmith's tongs, ſtronger and *toothed* at the end. *Mortimer's Huſbandry.*

2. To lock in each other.

It is common to *tooth* in the ſtretching courſe two inches with the ſtretcher only. *Moxon's Mech. Exerciſe.*

TOOTHA'CH. *n. ſ.* [*tooth* and *ach*.] Pain in the teeth.

There never yet was the philoſopher
That could endure the *toothach* patiently,
However at their eaſe they talk'd like gods. *Shakeſpeare.*

He that ſleeps feels not the *toothach*. *Shakeſp. Cymbeline.*

I have the *toothach*.
——What, ſigh for the *toothach*!
Which is but an humour or a worm. *Shakeſpeare.*

One was grown deſperate with the *toothach*. *Temple.*

TO'OTHDRAWER. *n. ſ.* [*tooth* and *draw*.] One whoſe buſineſs is to extract painful teeth.

Nature with Scots, as *toothdrawers*, hath dealt,
Who uſe to ſtring their teeth upon their belt. *Cleaveland.*

When the teeth are to be diſlocated, a *toothdrawer* is conſulted. *Wiſeman's Surgery.*

TO'OTHED. *adj.* [from *tooth*.] Having teeth.

TO'OTHLESS. *adj.* [from *tooth*.] Wanting teeth; deprived of teeth.

Deep-dinted wrinkles on her cheek ſhe draws,
Sunk are her eyes, and *toothleſs* are her jaws. *Dryden.*

They are fed with fleſh minced ſmall, having not only a ſharp head and ſnout, but a narrow and *toothleſs* ſnout. *Ray.*

TO'OTHPICK. } *n. ſ.* [*tooth* and *pick*.] An inſtrument by
TO'OTHPICKER. } which the teeth are cleanſed from any thing ſticking between them.

I will fetch you a *toothpicker* from the fartheſt inch of Aſia. *Shakeſp. Much ado about nothing.*

He and his *toothpick* at my worſhip's meſs. *Shakeſpeare.*

Preſerve my woods, whereof, if this courſe hold, there will hardly be found in ſome places enough to make a *toothpick*. *Howel's England's Tears.*

Lentiſck excels; if *toothpicks* of the lentiſck be wanting, of a quill then make a *toothpick*. *Sandys.*

Lentiſc

Lentise is a beautiful ever-green, and makes the best *tooth-pickers*. *Mortimer's Husbandry.*

TO'OTHSOME. *adj.* [from *tooth.*] Palatable; pleasing to the taste.

Some are good to be eaten while young, but nothing *toothsome* as they grow old. *Carew.*

TO'OTHSOMENESS. *n. s.* [from *toothsome.*] Pleasantness to the taste.

TO'OTHWORT. *n. s.* [*dentaria*, Lat.] A plant.

The *toothwort* hath a fleshy root, which is scaly, and cut in, as it were, with teeth: the flower consists of four leaves, placed in form of a cross; this is succeeded by a long pod, divided into two cells by an intermediate partition, and when ripe twisted up like a screw, and discharges the seeds with violence. *Miller.*

TOP. *n. s.* [*topp*, Welsh; top, Saxon; *top*, Dutch and Danish; *topper*, a crest, Islandick.]

1. The highest part of any thing.

I should not see the sandy hour-glass run,
But I should think of shallows and of flats,
And see my wealthy Andrew dock'd in sand,
Vailing her high *top* lower than her ribs. *Shakespeare.*

He wears upon his baby brow the round
And *top* of sovereignty. *Shakesp. Macbeth.*

Here Sodom's tow'rs raise their proud *tops* on high,
The tow'rs as well as men outbrave the sky. *Cowley.*

Thou nor on the *top* of old Olympus dwell'st. *Milton.*

That government which takes in the consent of the greatest number of the people, may justly be said to have the broadest bottom; and if it terminate in the authority of one single person, it may be said to have the narrowest *top*, and so makes the firmest pyramid. *Temple.*

Sysiphus no sooner carries his stone up to the *top* of the hill but it tumbles to the bottom. *Addison.*

So up the steepy hill with pain
The weighty stone is rowl'd in vain;
Which having touch'd the *top* recoils,
And leaves the labourer to renew his toils. *Granville.*

Marine bodies are found upon hills, and at the bottom only such as have fallen down from their *tops*. *Woodward.*

2. The surface; the superficies.

Plants that draw much nourishment from the earth hurt all things that grow by them, especially such trees as spread their roots near the *top* of the ground. *Bacon's Nat. Hist.*

Shallow brooks that flow'd so clear,
The bottom did the *top* appear. *Dryden.*

3. The highest place.

He that will not set himself proudly at the *top* of all things, but will consider the immensity of this fabrick, may think, that in other mansions there may be other and different intelligent beings. *Locke.*

What must he expect, when he seeks for preferment, but universal opposition, when he is mounting the ladder, and every hand ready to turn him off when he is at the *top*? *Sw.*

4. The highest person.

How would you be,
If he, which is the *top* of judgment, should
But judge you as you are? *Shakesp. Meas. for Measure.*

5. The utmost degree.

Zeal being the *top* and perfection of so many religious affections, the causes of it must be most eminent. *Sprat.*

If you attain the *top* of your desires in fame, all those who envy you will do you harm; and of those who admire you few will do you good. *Pope.*

The *top* of my ambition is to contribute to that work. *Pope.*

6. The highest rank.

Take a boy from the *top* of a grammar school, and one of the same age bred in his father's family, and bring them into good company together, and then see which of the two will have the more manly carriage. *Locke on Education.*

7. The crown of the head.

All the stor'd vengeance of heaven fall
On her ingrateful *top*! *Shakesp. King Lear.*

Arm'd, say you?
——Arm'd, my lord.
From *top* to toe? *Shakespeare.*

'Tis a per'lous boy,
Bold, quick, ingenious, forward, capable;
He's all the mother's from the *top* to toe. *Shakespeare.*

8. The hair on the crown of the head; the forelock.

Let's take the instant by the forward *top*;
For we are old, and on our quick'st decrees
Th' inaudible and noiseless foot of time
Steals, ere we can effect them. *Shakespeare.*

9. The head of a plant.

The buds made our food are called heads or *tops*; as cabbage heads. *Watts's Logick.*

10. [*Top*, Danish.] An inverted conoid which children set to turn on the point, continuing its motion with a whip.

Since I pluckt geese, play'd truant, and whipt *top*, I knew not what it was to be beaten till lately. *Shakespeare.*

For as whipp'd *tops*, and bandied balls,
The learned hold, are animals:
So horses they affirm to be
Mere engines made by geometry. *Hudibras, p. i.*

As young striplings whip the *top* for sport
On the smooth pavement of an empty court,
The wooden engine flies and whirls about,
Admir'd with clamours of the beardless rout. *Dryden.*

Still humming on their drowsy course they keep,
And lash'd so long, like *tops*, are lash'd asleep. *Pope.*

A *top* may be used with propriety in a similitude by a Virgil, when the sun may be dishonoured by a Mævius. *Broome.*

11. *Top* is sometimes used as an adjective to express lying on the top, or being at the top.

The *top* stones laid in clay are kept together. *Mortimer.*

To TOP. *v. n.* [from the noun.]

1. To rise aloft; to be eminent.

Those long ridges of lofty and *topping* mountains which run East and West, stop the evagation of the vapours to the North and South in hot countries. *Derham's Physico-Theol.*

Some of the letters distinguish themselves from the rest, and *top* it over their fellows; these are to be considered as letters and as cyphers. *Addison on ancient Medals.*

2. To predominate.

The thoughts of the mind are uninterruptedly employed by the determinations of the will, influenced by that *topping* uneasiness while it lasts. *Locke.*

3. To do his best.

But write thy best and *top*, and in each line
Sir Formal's oratory will be thine. *Dryden.*

To TOP. *v. a.*

1. To cover on the top; to tip; to defend or decorate with something extrinsick on the upper part.

The glorious temple rear'd
Her pile, far off appearing like a mount
Of alabaster, *topp'd* with golden spires. *Milton's Par. Reg.*

To him the fairest nymphs do show
Like moving mountains *topt* with snow. *Waller.*

There are other churches in the town, and two or three palaces, which are of a more modern make, and built with a good fancy; I was shown the little notre dame; that is handsomely designed, and *topp'd* with a cupola. *Addison.*

Top the bank with the bottom of the ditch. *Mortimer.*

2. To rise above.

A gourd planted close by a large pine, climbing by the boughs twined about them, till it *topped* and covered the tree. *L'Estrange.*

3. To outgo; to surpass.

He's poor in no one fault, but stor'd with all.
——Especially, in pride.
——And *topping* all others in boasting. *Shakespeare.*

So far he *topp'd* my thought,
That I in forgery of shapes and tricks
Come short of what he did. *Shakespeare.*

I am, cries the envious, of the same nature with the rest: why then should such a man *top* me? where there is equality of kind, there should be no distinction of privilege. *Collier.*

4. To crop.

Top your rose trees a little with your knife near a leaf bud. *Evelyn's Kalendar.*

5. To rise to the top of.

If ought obstruct thy course, yet stand not still,
But wind about till thou hast *topp'd* the hill. *Denham.*

6. To perform eminently: as, *he* tops *his part*. This word, in this sense, is seldom used but on light or ludicrous occasions.

TO'PFUL. *adj.* [*top* and *full.*] Full to the top; full to the brim.

Fill me, from the crown to the toe, *topful*
Of direct cruelty. *Shakespeare's Macbeth.*

'Tis wonderful
What may be wrought out of their discontent;
Now that their souls are *topful* of offence. *Shakespeare.*

Till a considerable part of the air was drawn out of the receiver, the tube continued *topful* of water as at first. *Boyle.*

One was ingenious in his thoughts and bright in his language; but so *topful* of himself, that he let it spill on all the company. *Watts's Improvement of the Mind, p. i.*

Fill the largest tankard-cup *topfull*. *Swift.*

TOPGA'LLANT. *n. s.* [*top* and *gallant.*]

1. The highest sail.

2. It is proverbially applied to any thing elevated.

A rose grew out of another, like honeysuckles, called top and *topgallants*. *Bacon's Nat. Hist.* N°. 646.

I dare appeal to the consciences of *topgallant* sparks. *L'Estr.*

TOPHE'AVY. *adj.* [*top* and *heavy.*] Having the upper part too weighty for the lower.

A roof should not be too heavy nor too light; but of the two extremes a house *topheavy* is the worst. *Wotton's Arch.*

Topheavy drones, and always looking down,
As over-ballasted within the crown,
Mutt'ring betwixt their lips some mystick thing. *Dryden.*

As to stiff gales *topheavy* pines bow low
Their heads, and lift them as they cease to blow. *Pope.*

To'PKNOT. *n. s.* [*top* and *knot.*] A knot worn by women on the top of the head.

This arrogance amounts to the pride of an ass in his trappings; when 'tis but his master's taking away his *topknot* to make an ass of him again. *L'Estrange.*

To'PMAN. *n. s.* [*top* and *man.*] The sawer at the top.

The pit-saw enters the one end of the stuff, the *topman* at the top, and the pitman under him, the *topman* observing to guide the saw exactly in the line. *Moxon's Mech. Exercise.*

To'PMOST. *n. s.* [An irregular superlative formed from *top.*] Uppermost; highest.

A swarm of bees,
Unknown from whence they took their airy flight,
Upon the *topmost* branch in clouds alight. *Dryden's Æn.*
From steep to steep the troops advanc'd with pain,
In hopes at last the *topmost* cliff to gain;
But still by new ascents the mountain grew,
And a fresh toil presented to their view. *Addison.*
Men pil'd on men with active leaps arise,
And build the breathing fabrick to the skies;
A sprightly youth above the *topmost* row,
Points the tall pyramid, and crowns the show. *Addison.*

Toppro'ud. *adj.* [*top* and *proud.*] Proud in the highest degree.

This *top-proud* fellow,
By intelligence I do know
To be corrupt and treasonous. *Shakespeare.*

Topsa'il. *n. s.* [*top* and *sail.*] The highest sail.

Contarenus meeting with the Turk's gallies, which would not vail their *topsails*, fiercely assailed them. *Knolles.*

Strike, strike the *topsail*; let the main-sheet fly,
And furl your sails. *Dryden's Fables.*

TOPA'RCH. *n. s.* [τόπ❧ and αρχὴ.] The principal man in a place.

They are not to be conceived potent monarchs, but *toparchs*, or kings of narrow territories. *Brown's Vulgar Err.*

To'parchy. *n. s.* [from *toparch.*] Command in a small district.

To'paz. *n. s.* [*topase*, Fr. *topazius*, low Lat.] A yellow gem.

The golden stone is the yellow *topaz*. *Bacon's Nat. Hist.*

Can blazing carbuncles with her compare?
The *tophas* sent from scorched Meroe?
Or pearls presented by the Indian sea? *Sandys's Paraph.*
With light's own smile the yellow *topaz* burns. *Thomson.*

To TOPE. *v. n.* [*topff*, German, *an earthen pot*; *toppen*, Dutch, *to be mad.* *Skinner* prefers the latter etymology; *toper*, Fr.] To drink hard; to drink to excess.

If you *tope* in form and treat,
'Tis the sour sauce to the sweet meat,
The fine you pay for being great. *Dryden.*

To'per. *n. s.* [from *tope.*] A drunkard.

Tophaceous. *adj.* [from *tophus*, Lat.] Gritty; stony.

Acids mixed with them precipitate a *tophaceous* chalky matter, but not a cheesy substance. *Arbuthnot.*

To'phet. *n. s.* [תפת Heb. *a drum.*] Hell; a scriptural name.

The pleasant valley of Hinnom, *tophet* thence
And black Gehenna called, the type of hell. *Milton.*

Fire and darkness are here mingled with all other ingredients that make that *tophet* prepared of old. *Burnet.*

To'pical. *adj.* [from τόπ❧.]

1. Relating to some general head.

2. Local; confined to some particular place.

An argument from authority is but a weaker kind of proof; it being but a *topical* probation, and an inartificial argument, depending on naked asseveration. *Brown.*

Evidences of fact can be no more than *topical* and probable. *Hale's Origin of Mankind.*

3. Applied medicinally to a particular part.

A woman, with some unusual hemorrhage, is only to be cured by *topical* remedies. *Arbuthnot.*

To'pically. *adv.* [from *topical.*] With application to some particular part.

This *topically* applied becomes a phænigmus, or rubifying medicine, and is of such fiery parts, that they have of themselves conceived fire and burnt a house. *Brown's Vulgar Err.*

TO'PICK. *n. s.* [*topique*, Fr. τόπ❧.]

1. A general head; something to which other things are referred.

Let them argue over all the *topicks* of divine goodness and human weakness, and whatsoever other pretences sinking sinners catch at to save themselves by, yet how trifling must be their plea! *South's Sermons.*

I might dilate on the difficulties, the temper of the people, the power, arts, and interest of the contrary party; but those are invidious *topicks*, too green in remembrance. *Dryd.*

The principal branches of preaching are, to tell the people what is their duty, and then convince them that it is so: the *topicks* for both are brought from scripture and reason. *Swift.*

All arts and sciences have some general subjects, called *topicks*, or common places; because middle terms are borrowed, and arguments derived from them for the proof of their various propositions. *Watts's Logick.*

2. Things as are externally applied to any particular part.

In the cure of strumæ, the *topicks* ought to be discutient. *Wiseman's Surgery.*

To'pless. *adj.* [from *top.*] Having no top.

He sent abroad his voice,
Which Pallas far off echo'd; who did betwixt them hoise
Shrill tumult to a *topless* height. *Chapman's Iliad.*

Topo'grapher. *n. s.* [τόπ❧ and γράφω.] One who writes descriptions of particular places.

Topo'graphy. *n. s.* [*topographie*, Fr. τόπ❧ and γράφω.] Description of particular places.

That philosophy gives the exactest *topography* of the extramundane spaces. *Glanville's Scep.*

The *topography* of Sulmo in the Latin makes but an aukward figure in the version. *Cromwell.*

To'pping. *adj.* [from *top.*] Fine; noble; gallant. A low word.

The *topping* fellow I take to be the ancestor of the fine fellow. *Tatler.*

To'ppingly. *adj.* [from *topping.*] Fine; gay; gallant; shewy. An obsolete word.

These *toppinglie* ghests be in number but ten,
As welcome to dairie as beares among men. *Tusser.*

To To'pple. *v. n.* [from *top.*] To fall forward; to tumble down.

Though bladed corn be lodged and trees blown down;
Though castles *topple* on their warders heads. *Shakespeare.*
The wisest aunt telling the saddest tale,
Sometime for three-foot stool mistaketh me;
Then slip I from her quite, down *topples* she. *Shakespeare.*

Topsytu'rvy. *adv.* [This *Skinner* fancies to *top* in *turf.*] With the bottom upward.

All suddenly was turned *topsyturvy*, the noble lord eftsoons was blamed, the wretched people pitied, and new counsels plotted. *Spenser on Ireland.*

If we without his help can make a head
To push against the kingdom; with his help
We shall o'erturn it *topsyturvy* down. *Shakesp. Henry IV.*

God told man what was good, but the devil surnamed it evil, and thereby turned the world *topsy-turvy*, and brought a new chaos upon the whole creation. *South's Sermons.*

Man is but a *topsyturvy* creature; his head where his heels should be, grovelling on the earth. *Swift.*

Tor. *n. s.* [ꞇoꞃ, Saxon.]

1. A tower; a turret.

2. A high pointed rock or hill, whence *tor* in the initial syllable of some local names.

Torch. *n. s.* [*torche*, French; *torcia*, Italian; *intortitium*, low Latin.] A wax light generally supposed to be bigger than a candle.

Basilius knew, by the wasting of the *torches*, that the night also was far wasted. *Sidney.*

Here lies the dusky *torch* of Mortimer,
Choak'd with ambition of the meaner sort. *Shakespeare.*
They light the nuptial *torch*, and bid invoke
Hymen. *Milton.*
Never was known a night of such distraction;
Noise so confus'd and dreadful: *torches* gliding
Like meteors, by each other in the streets. *Dryden.*
I'm weary of my part;
My *torch* is out; and the world stands before me
Like a black desart at th' approach of night. *Dryden.*

To'rchbearer. *n. s.* [*torch* and *bear.*] One whose office is to carry a torch.

He did in a genteel manner chastise their negligence, with making them, for that night, the *torchbearers*. *Sidney, b. i.*

To'rchlight. *n. s.* [*torch* and *light.*] Light kindled to supply the want of the sun.

When the emperor Charles had clasped Germany almost in his fist, he was forced to go from Isburg, and, as if in a mask, by *torchlight*, to quit every foot he had gotten. *Bacon.*

If thou like a child didst fear before,
Being in the dark, where thou didst nothing see;
Now I have brought thee *torchlight* fear no more. *Davies.*

To'rcher. *n. s.* [from *torch.*] One that gives light.

Ere the horses of the sun shall bring
Their fiery *torcher* his diurnal ring. *Shakespeare.*

Tore. preterite, and sometimes participle passive of *tear.*

Upon his head an old Scotch cap he wore,
With a plume feather all to pieces *tore.* *Spenser.*

Tore. *v. a.* [Of this word I cannot guess the meaning.]

Proportion according to rowen or *tore* upon the ground; the more *tore* the less hay will do. *Mortimer's Husbandry.*

To Torme'nt. *n. s.* [*tourmenter*, Fr.]

1. To put to pain; to harrass with anguish; to excruciate.

No sleep close up that deadly eye of thine,
Unless it be while some *tormenting* dream
Affrights thee with a hell of ugly devils. *Shakespeare.*
I am glad to be constrain'd to utter what
Torments me to conceal. *Shakesp. Cymbeline.*

Art

Art thou come to *torment* us before the time? *Mat.* viii.

2. To teaze; to vex with importunity.

3. To put into great agitation. [*tormente*, Fr. a great ſtorm.]

They ſoaring on main wing
Tormented all the air. *Milton.*

TO'RMENT. *n. ſ.* [*tourment*, French.]

1. Any thing that gives pain.

They brought unto him all ſick people that were taken with divers diſeaſes and *torments*, and he healed them. *Mat.*

2. Pain; miſery; anguiſh.

3. Penal anguiſh; torture.

No priſoners there, inforc'd by *torments*, cry;
But fearleſs by their old tormentors lie. *Sandys's Paraph.*
Not ſharp revenge, not hell itſelf can find
A fiercer *torment* than a guilty mind,
Which day and night doth dreadfully accuſe,
Condemns the wretch, and ſtill the charge renews. *Dryd.*

TORME'NTOR. *n. ſ.* [from *torment.*]

1. One who torments; one who gives pain.

He called to me for ſuccour, deſiring me at leaſt to kill him, to deliver him from thoſe *tormentors*. *Sidney, b.* ii.

Let his *tormenter* conſcience find him out. *Milton.*

The commandments of God being conformable to the dictates of right reaſon, man's judgment condemns him when he violates any of them; and ſo the ſinner becomes his own *tormentor*. *South's Sermons.*

2. One who inflicts penal tortures.

No priſoners there, enforc'd by torments, cry,
But fearleſs by their old *tormentors* lie. *Sandys on Job.*
Hadſt thou full pow'r to kill,
Or meaſure out his torments by thy will;
Yet, what could'ſt thou, *tormentor*, hope to gain,
Thy loſs continues unrepaid by pain. *Dryden's Juv.*

The ancient martyrs paſſed through ſuch new inventions and varieties of pain as tired their *tormentors*. *Addiſon.*

TO'RMENTIL. *n. ſ.* [*tormentille*, Fr. *tormentilla*, Lat.] Septfoil. A plant.

The root has been uſed for tanning of leather, and accounted the beſt aſtringent in the whole vegetable kingdom. *Miller.*

Refreſh the ſpirits externally by ſome epithemata of balm, bugloſs, with the powder of the roots of *tormentil*. *Wiſeman.*

TORN, part. paſſ. of *tear.*

Ye ſhall not eat any fleſh that is *torn* of beaſts. *Exod.* xxii.

TORNA'DO. *n. ſ.* [*tornado*, Spaniſh.] A hurricane; a whirlwind.

Nimble coruſcations ſtrike the eye,
And bold *tornado*'s bluſter in the ſky. *Garth.*

TORPE'DO. *n. ſ.* [Lat.] A fiſh which while alive, if touched even with a long ſtick, benumbs the hand that ſo touches it, but when dead is eaten ſafely.

TO'RPENT. *adj.* [*torpeus*, Latin.] Benumbed; ſtruck motionleſs; not active; incapable of motion.

A comprehenſive expedient to aſſiſt the frail and *torpent* memory through ſo multifarious an employment. *Evelyn.*

TO'RPID. *adj.* [*torpidus*, Latin.] Numbed; motionleſs; ſluggiſh; not active.

Without heat all things would be *torpid* and without motion. *Ray on the Creation.*

The ſun awakes the *torpid* ſap. *Thomſon's Spring.*

TO'RPIDNESS. *n. ſ.* [from *torpid.*] The ſtate of being torpid.

Though the object about which it is exerciſed be poor, little, and low, yet a man hath this advantage by the exerciſe of this faculty about it, that it keeps it from reſt and *torpidneſs*, it enlargeth and habituates it for a due improvement even about nobler objects. *Hale's Origin of Mankind.*

TO'RPITUDE. *n. ſ.* [from *torpid.*] State of being motionleſs; numbneſs; ſluggiſhneſs.

Some, in their moſt perfect ſtate, ſubſiſt in a kind of *torpitude* or ſleeping ſtate. *Derham.*

TO'RPOR. *n. ſ.* [Latin.] Dulneſs; numbneſs; inability to move; dulneſs of ſenſation.

Motion diſcuſſes the *torpor* of ſolid bodies, which, beſide their motion of gravity, have in them a natural appetite not to move at all. *Bacon's Nat. Hiſt.* N°. 763.

TORREFA'CTION. *n. ſ.* [*torrefaction*, Fr. *torrefacio*, Latin.] The act of drying by the fire.

When torrefied ſulphur makes bodies black, why does *torrefaction* make ſulphur itſelf black. *Boyle on Colours.*

If it have not a ſufficient inſolation it looketh pale; if it be ſunned too long it ſuffereth *torrefaction*. *Brown.*

To TO'RREFY. *v. a.* [*torrifier*, Fr. *torrefacio*, Lat.] To dry by the fire.

In the ſulphur of bodies *torrified* conſiſt the principles of inflammability. *Brown's Vulgar Errours.*

The Africans are more peculiarly ſcorched and *torrefied* from the ſun by addition of dryneſs from the ſoil. *Brown.*

Divers learned men aſſign, for the cauſe of blackneſs, the ſooty ſteam of aduſt, or *torrefied* ſulphur. *Boyle on Colours.*

Torrefied ſulphur makes bodies black; I deſire to know why torrefaction makes ſulphur itſelf black? *Boyle.*

Another cliſter is compoſed of two heminæ of white wine, half a hemina of honey, Ægyptian nitre *torrefied* a quadrant. *Arbuthnot on Coins.*

TO'RRENT. *n. ſ.* [*torrent*, Fr. *torrens*, Lat.]

1. A ſudden ſtream raiſed by ſummer ſhowers.

The near in blood,
Forſake me like the *torrent* of a flood. *Sandys on Job.*
Will no kind flood, no friendly rain,
Diſguiſe the marſhal's plain diſgrace;
No *torrents* ſwell the low Mohayne,
The world will ſay he durſt not paſs. *Prior.*

2. A violent and rapid ſtream; tumultuous current.

Not far from Caucaſus are certain ſteep falling *torrents*, which waſh down many grains of gold, as in many other parts of the world; and the people there inhabiting uſe to ſet many fleeces of wool in theſe deſcents of waters, in which the grains of gold remain, and the water paſſeth through, which Strabo witneſſeth to be true. *Raleigh.*

The memory of thoſe who, out of duty and conſcience, oppoſed that *torrent* which did overwhelm them, ſhould not loſe the recompence due to their virtue. *Clarendon.*

When ſhrivell'd herbs on with'ring ſtems decay,
The wary ploughman, on the mountain's brow,
Undams his wat'ry ſtores, huge *torrents* flow,
Temp'ring the thirſty fever of the field. *Dryden's Georg.*
Eraſmus, that great injur'd name,
Stemm'd the wild *torrent* of a barb'rous age. *Pope.*

TO'RRENT. *adj.* [*torrens*, Lat.] Rolling in a rapid ſtream.

Fierce Phlegeton,
Whoſe waves of *torrent* fire inflame with rage. *Milton.*

TO'RRID. *adj.* [*torride*, Fr. *torridus*, Lat.]

1. Parched; dried with heat.

Galen's commentators mention a twofold dryneſs; the one concomitated with a heat, which they call a *torrid* tabes; the other with a coldneſs, when the parts are conſumed through extinction of their native heat. *Harvey on Conſump.*

2. Burning; violently hot.

This with *torrid* heat,
And vapours as the Libyan air aduſt,
Began to parch that temperate clime. *Milton's Par. Loſt.*

3. It is particularly applied to the regions or zone between the tropicks.

Columbus firſt
Found a temp'rate in a *torrid* zone;
The fev'riſh air fann'd by a cooling breeze. *Dryden.*
Thoſe who amidſt the *torrid* regions live,
May they not gales unknown to us receive?
See daily ſhow'rs rejoice the thirſty earth,
And bleſs the flow'ry buds ſucceeding birth. *Prior.*

TO'RSEL. *n. ſ.* [*torſe*, Fr.] Any thing in a twiſted form.

When you lay any timber on brickwork, as *torſels* for mantle trees to lie on, or lintols over windows, lay them in loam. *Moxon's Mech. Exerciſes.*

TO'RSION. *n. ſ.* [*torſio*, Lat.] The act of turning or twiſting.

TORT. *n. ſ.* [*tort*, Fr. *tortum*, low Latin.] Miſchief; injury; calamity. Obſolete.

Then gan triumphant trumpets ſound on high,
That ſent to heaven the echoed report
Of their new joy, and happy victory
Againſt him that had been long oppreſt with *tort*,
And faſt impriſoned in ſieged fort. *Fa. Qu. b.* i.
He dreadleſs bad them come to court,
For no wild beaſts ſhould do them any *tort*. *Spenſer.*
Your diſobedience and ill managing
Of actions, loſt for want of due ſupport,
Refer I juſtly to a further ſpring,
Spring of ſedition, ſtrife, oppreſſion, *tort*. *Fairfax, b.* i.

TO'RTILE. *n. ſ.* [*tortilis*, Lat.] Twiſted; wreathed.

TO'RTION. *n. ſ.* [from *tortus*, Latin.] Torment; pain. Not in uſe.

All purgers have a raw ſpirit or wind, which is the principal cauſe of *tortion* in the ſtomach and belly. *Bacon.*

TO'RTIOUS. *adj.* [from *tort.*] Injurious; doing wrong. *Spenſ.*

TO'RTIVE. *adj.* [from *tortus*, Lat.] Twiſted; wreathed.

Knots by the conflux of meeting ſap,
Infect the ſound pine, and divert his grain
Tortive and errant from his courſe of growth. *Shakeſpeare.*

TO'RTOISE. *n. ſ.* [*tortue*, French.]

1. An animal covered with a hard ſhell: there are tortoiſes both of land and water.

In his needy ſhop a *tortoiſe* hung,
An alligator ſtuft. *Shakeſpeare.*

A living *tortoiſe* being turned upon its back, not being able to make uſe of its paws for the returning of itſelf, becauſe they could only bend towards the belly, it could help itſelf only by its neck and head; ſometimes one ſide, ſometimes another, by puſhing againſt the ground, to rock itſelf as in a cradle, to find out where the inequality of the ground might permit it to roll its ſhell. *Ray on the Creation.*

2. A form into which the ancient ſoldiers uſed to throw their troops, by bending down and holding their bucklers above their heads ſo that no darts could hurt them.

Their targets in a *tortoiſe* caſt, the foes
Secure advancing, to the turrets roſe. *Dryden's Æn.*

TORTUO'SITY. *n. ſ.* [from *tortuous.*] Wreath; flexure.

Theſe the midwife contriveth unto a knot cloſe unto the body of the infant, from whence enſueth that *tortuoſity*, or complicated nodoſity, called the navel. *Brown's Vulgar Err.*

TO'RTUOUS. *adj.* [*tortueux*, Fr. from *tortuoſus*, *tortus*, Lat.]

1. Twiſted; wreathed; winding.

So vary'd he, and of his *tortuous* train
Curl'd many a wanton wreath. *Milton.*

Aqueous vapours, like a dry wind, paſs through ſo long and *tortuous* a pipe of lead. *Boyle.*

2. Miſchievous. [Thus I explain it, on ſuppoſition that it is derived from *tort*, wrong; but it may mean *crooked:* as we ſay, *crooked* ways for *bad* practices, *crooked* being regularly enough oppoſite to *right*. This in ſome copies is *tortious*, and therefore from *tort.*]

Ne ought he car'd whom he endamaged
By *tortuous* wrong, or whom bereav'd of right. *Fa. Qu.*

TO'RTURE. *n. ſ.* [*torture*, Fr. *tortura*, Lat.]

1. Torments judicially inflicted; pain by which guilt is puniſhed, or confeſſion extorted.

Hecate
Then led me trembling through thoſe dire abodes,
And taught the *tortures* of th' avenging gods. *Dryden.*

2. Pain; anguiſh; pang.

Better be with the dead,
Than on the *torture* of the mind to lie
In reſtleſs extaſy. *Shakeſpeare's Macbeth.*

Ghaſtly ſpaſm or racking *torture*. *Milton.*

To TO'RTURE. *v. a.* [from the noun.]

1. To puniſh with tortures.

Hipparchus my enfranchis'd bondman,
He may at pleaſure whip, or hang, or *torture*. *Shakeſpeare.*

The ſcourge inexorable and the *torturing* hour. *Milton.*

2. To vex; to excruciate; to torment.

Still muſt I cheriſh the dear, ſad remembrance
At once to *torture*, and to pleaſe my ſoul. *Addiſon's Cato.*

3. To keep on the ſtretch.

The bow *tortureth* the ſtring continually, and thereby holdeth it in a continual trepidation. *Bacon's Nat. Hiſt.*

TO'RTURER. *n. ſ.* [from *torture.*] He who tortures; tormenter.

I play the *torturer* by ſmall and ſmall,
To lengthen out the worſt that muſt be ſpoken. *Shakeſp.*

When king Edward the ſecond was amongſt his *torturers*, the more to diſgrace his face, they ſhaved him, and waſhed him with cold water; the king ſaid, well, yet I will have warm water, and ſo ſhed abundance of tears. *Bacon's Apoph.*

Turning our tortures into horrid arms
Againſt the *torturer*. *Milton's Par. Loſt, b.* ii.

TO'RVITY. *n. ſ.* [*torvitas*, Lat.] Sourneſs; ſeverity of countenance.

TO'RVOUS. *adj.* [*torvus*, Lat.] Sour of aſpect; ſtern; ſevere of countenance.

That *torvous* ſour look produced by anger, and that gay and pleaſing countenance accompanying love. *Derham.*

T'ORY. *n. ſ.* [A cant term, derived, I ſuppoſe, from an Iriſh word ſignifying a ſavage.] One who adheres to the antient conſtitution of the ſtate, and the apoſtolical hierarchy of the church of England, oppoſed to a whig.

The knight is more a *tory* in the country than the town, becauſe it more advances his intereſt. *Addiſon.*

To confound his hated coin, all parties and religions join whigs, *tories*. *Swift.*

To TOSE. *v. n.* [Of the ſame original with *teize.*] To comb wool.

To TOSS. *v. a.* [*taſſen*, Dutch; *taſſer*, French, to accumulate; *Minſhew.* Θεῶσαι, to dance; *Meric Caſaubon.* *Toſen*, German, to make a noiſe; *Skinner:* perhaps from *to us*, a word uſed by thoſe who would have any thing thrown to them.]

1. To throw with the hand, as a ball at play.

With this ſhe ſeem'd to play, and as in ſport,
Toſs'd to her love in preſence of the court. *Dryden.*

A ſhepherd diverted himſelf with *toſſing* up eggs and catching them again. *Addiſon.*

2. To throw with violence.

Back do I *toſs* theſe treaſons to thy head. *Shakeſpeare.*

Vulcano's diſcharge forth with the fire not only metallick and mineral matter but huge ſtones, *toſſing* them up to a very great height in the air. *Woodward's Nat. Hiſt. p.* iv.

3. To lift with a ſudden and violent motion.

Behold how they *toſs* their torches on high,
How they point to the Perſian abodes. *Dryden.*

I call'd to ſtop him, but in vain:
He *toſt* his arm aloft, and proudly told me,
He would not ſtay. *Addiſon's Cato.*

So talk too idle buzzing things;
Toſs up their heads, and ſtretch their wings. *Prior.*

4. To agitate; to put into violent motion.

The getting of treaſures by a lying tongue is a vanity *toſſed* to and fro. *Prov.* xxi. 6.

Things will have their firſt or ſecond agitation; if they be not *toſſed* upon the arguments of counſel, they will be *toſſed* upon the waves of fortune, and be full of inconſtancy, doing and undoing. *Bacon's Eſſays.*

Cowls, hoods, and habits, with their wearers *toſt*,
And flutter'd into rags. *Milton.*

I have made ſeveral voyages upon the ſea, often been *toſſed* in ſtorms. *Addiſon's Spect.* N°. 489.

5. To make reſtleſs; to diſquiet.

She did love the knight of the red croſs,
For whoſe dear ſake ſo many troubles her did *toſs*. *F. Qu.*

Calm region once,
And full of peace, now *toſt* and turbulent. *Milton.*

6. To keep in play; to tumble over.

That ſcholar ſhould come to a better knowledge in the Latin tongue than moſt do, that ſpend four years in *toſſing* all the rules of grammar in common ſchools. *Aſcham.*

To TOSS. *v. n.*

1. To fling; to winch; to be in violent commotion.

Dire was the *toſſing!* deep the groans! deſpair
Tended the ſick, buſieſt from couch to couch. *Milton.*

Galen tells us of a woman patient of his whom he found very weak in bed, continually *toſſing* and tumbling from one ſide to another, and totally deprived of her reſt. *Harvey.*

To *toſs* and fling, and to be reſtleſs, only frets and enrages our pain. *Tillotſon.*

And thou, my ſire, not deſtin'd by thy birth,
To turn to duſt and mix with common earth,
How wilt thou *toſs* and rave, and long to die,
And quit thy claim to immortality. *Addiſon's Ovid.*

2. To be toſſed.

Your mind is *toſſing* on the ſea,
There where your argoſies
Do overpeer the petty traffickers. *Shakeſpeare.*

3. *To* TOSS *up*. To throw a coin into the air, and wager on what ſide it ſhall fall.

I'd try if any pleaſure could be found,
In *toſſing up* for twenty thouſand pound. *Brampſton.*

TOSS. *n. ſ.* [from the verb.]

1. The act of toſſing.

The diſcus that is to be ſeen in the hand of the celebrated Caſtor at Don Livio's is perfectly round; nor has it any thing like a fling faſtened to it, to add force to the *toſs*. *Add.*

2. An affected manner of raiſing the head.

His various modes from various fathers follow;
One taught the *toſs*, and one the new French wallow:
His ſword-knot this, his cravat that deſign'd. *Dryden.*

There is hardly a polite ſentence in the following dialogues which doth not require ſome ſuitable *toſs* of the head. *Swift.*

TO'SSEL. *n. ſ.* See TASSEL.

Tie at each lower corner a handful of hops with a piece of packthread to make a *toſſel*, by which you may conveniently lift the bag when full. *Mortimer's Huſbandry.*

TO'SSER. *n. ſ.* [from *toſs.*] One who throws; one who flings and writhes.

TO'SSPOT. *n. ſ.* [*toſs* and *pot.*] A toper and drunkard.

TOST. preterite and part. paſſ. of *toſs*.

In a troubled ſea of paſſion *toſt*. *Milton.*

TO'TAL. *adj.* [*totus*, Lat. *total*, Fr.]

1. Whole; complete; full.

They ſet and riſe;
Leſt *total* darkneſs ſhould by night regain
Her old poſſeſſion, and extinguiſh life. *Milton.*

If all the pains that, for thy Britain's ſake,
My paſt has took, or future life may take,
Be grateful to my queen; permit my pray'r,
And with this gift reward my *total* care. *Prior.*

2. Whole; not divided.

Either to undergo
Myſelf the *total* crime; or to accuſe
My other-ſelf, the partner of my life. *Milton's Par. Loſt.*

TOTA'LITY. *n. ſ.* [*totalité*, Fr.] Complete ſum; whole quantity.

TO'TALLY. *adv.* [from *total.*] Wholly; fully; completely.

The ſound interpreters expound this image of God, of natural reaſon; which, if it be *totally* or moſtly defaced, the right of government doth ceaſe. *Bacon's holy War.*

Charity doth not end with this world, but goes along with us into the next, where it will be perfected: but faith and hope ſhall then *totally* fail; the one being changed into ſight, the other into enjoyment. *Atterbury's Sermons.*

T'OTHER, contracted for *the other*.

To TOTTER. *v. n.* [*tateren*, to ſtagger, Dutch.] To ſhake ſo as to threaten a fall.

What news, in this our *tott'ring* ſtate?
—It is a reeling world indeed, my lord;
And I believe will never ſtand upright. *Shakeſpeare.*

As a bowing wall ſhall ye be, and as a *tottering* fence. *Pſal.*

The foes already have poſſeſs'd the wall,
Troy nods from high, and *totters* to her fall. *Dryden.*

TO'TTERY. } *adj.* [from *totter.*] Shaking; unsteady; dizzy.
TO'TTY. } Neither of those words is used.

Siker thy head very *tottie* is,
So on thy corbe shoulder it leans amisse. *Spenser's Past.*

To TOUCH. *v. a.* [*toucher*, Fr. *tœtsen*, Dutch.]

1. To reach with any thing, so as that there be no space between the thing reached and the thing brought to it.

He so light was at legerdemain,
That what he *touch'd* came not to light again. *Spenser.*

Ye shall not eat nor *touch* it lest ye die. *Gen.* iii. 3.

He brake the withs as a thread of tow is broken when it *toucheth* the fire. *Judg.* xvi. 9.

2. To come to; to attain.

He that is begotten of God keepeth himself, and that wicked one *toucheth* him not. 1 *John* v. 18.

Their impious folly dar'd to prey
On herds devoted to the god of day;
The god vindictive doom'd them never more,
Ah men unbless'd! to *touch* that natal shore. *Pope's Odys.*

3. To try as gold with a stone.

When I have suit,
Wherein I mean to *touch* your love indeed,
It shall be full of poize and difficulty,
And fearful to be granted. *Shakespeare's Othello.*

4. To affect; to relate to.

In ancient times was publickly read first the scripture, as, namely, something out of the books of the prophets of God; some things out of the apostles writings; and, lastly, out of the holy evangelists some things which *touched* the person of our lord Jesus Christ. *Hooker, b.* v.

The quarrel *toucheth* none but us alone;
Betwixt ourselves let us decide it then. *Shakesp. Hen.* VI.

What of sweet
Hath *touch'd* my sense, flat seems to this. *Milton.*

5. To move; to strike mentally; to melt.

I was sensibly *touched* with that kind impression. *Congreve.*

The tender sire was *touch'd* with what he said,
And flung the blaze of glories from his head,
And bid the youth advance. *Addison's Ovid.*

6. To delineate or mark out.

Nature affords at least a glimm'ring light:
The lines, though *touch'd* but faintly, are drawn right. *Pope.*

7. To censure; to animadvert upon.

Doctor Parker, in his sermon before them, *touched* them for their living so near, that they went near to *touch* him for his life. *Hayward.*

8. To infect; to seize slightly.

Pestilent diseases are bred in the Summer; otherwise those *touched* are in most danger in the Winter. *Bacon's Nat. Hist.*

9. To bite; to wear; to have an effect on.

Its face must be very flat and smooth, and so hard, that a file will not *touch* it, as smiths say, when a file will not eat, or race it. *Moxon's Mech. Exercise.*

10. To strike a musical instrument.

They *touch'd* their golden harps, and prais'd. *Milton.*
One dip the pencil, and one *touch* the lyre. *Pope.*

11. To influence by impulse; to impel forcibly.

No decree of mine,
To *touch* with lightest moment of impulse
His free will. *Milton.*

12. To treat of perfunctorily.

This thy last reasoning words *touch'd* only. *Milton.*

13. *To* TOUCH *up.* To repair, or improve by slight strokes, or little emendations.

What he saw was only her natural countenance *touched up* with the usual improvements of an aged coquette. *Addison.*

To TOUCH. *v. n.*

1. To be in a state of junction so that no space is between them.

2. To fasten on; to take effect on.

Strong waters pierce metals, and will *touch* upon gold that will not *touch* upon silver. *Bacon.*

3. *To* TOUCH *at.* To come to without stay.

The next day we *touched* at Sidon. *Acts* xxvii. 3.

Oh fail not to *touch at* Peru;
With gold there our vessel we'll store. *Cowley.*

Civil law and history are studies which a gentleman should not barely *touch at*, but constantly dwell upon. *Locke.*

A fishmonger lately *touched* at Hammersmith. *Spectator.*

4. *To* TOUCH *on.* To mention slightly.

The shewing by what steps knowledge comes into our minds, it may suffice to have only *touched on.* *Locke.*

It is an use no-body has dwelt upon; if the antiquaries have *touched upon* it they immediately quitted it. *Addison.*

5. *To* TOUCH *on* or *upon.* To go for a very short time.

He *touched upon* the Moluccoes. *Abbot's Desc. of the World.*

Which monsters, lest the Trojan's pious host
Should bear, or *touch upon* th' inchanted coast,
Propitious Neptune steer'd their course by night. *Dryden.*

I made a little voyage round the lake, and *touched on* the several towns that lie on its coasts. *Addison on Italy.*

6. *To* TOUCH *on* or *upon.* To mention slightly.

It is impossible to make observations in art or science which have not been *touched upon* by others. *Addison's Spectator.*

TOUCH. *n. s.* [from the verb.]

1. Reach of any thing so that there is no space between the things reaching and reached.

2. The sense of feeling.

O dear son Edgar,
Might I but live to see thee in my *touch*,
I'd say, I had eyes again. *Shakesp. King Lear.*

The spirit of wine, or chemical oils, which are so hot in operation, are to the first *touch* cold. *Bacon's Nat. Hist.*

By *touch* the first pure qualities we learn,
Which quicken all things, hot, cold, moist and dry;
By *touch*, hard, soft, rough, smooth, we do discern;
By *touch*, sweet pleasure, and sharp pain we try. *Davies.*

The spiders *touch* how exquisitely fine!
Feels at each thread, and lives along the line. *Pope.*

The fifth sense is *touch*, a sense over the whole body. *Locke.*

3. The act of touching.

The *touch* of the cold water made a pretty kind of shrugging come over her body, like the twinkling of the fairest among the fixed stars. *Sidney, b.* ii.

The time was once when thou unurg'd wou'd'st vow,
That never *touch* was welcome to thy hand
Unless I touch'd. *Shakespeare.*

With one virtuous *touch*
Th' archchemick sun produces precious things. *Milton.*

4. Examination as by a stone.

To-morrow, good sir Michell, is a day
Wherein the fortune of ten thousand men
Must bide the *touch.* *Shakespeare's Henry* IV.

Ah Buckingham, now do I ply the *touch*,
To try if thou be current gold indeed. *Shakespeare.*

Albeit some of these articles were merely devised, yet the duke being of base gold, and fearing the *touch*, subscribed that he did acknowledge his offences. *Hayward.*

5. Test; that by which any thing is examined.

The law-makers rather respected their own benefit than equity, the true *touch* of all laws. *Carew's Survey of Cornwall.*

6. Proof; tried qualities.

Come my sweet wife, my dearest mother, and
My friends of noble *touch!* when I am forth,
Bid me farewel, and smile. *Shakespeare.*

7. [*Touche*, Fr.] Single act of a pencil upon the picture.

Artificial strife
Lives in those *touches*, livelier than life. *Shakespeare.*

It will be the more difficult for him to conceive when he has only a relation given him, without the nice *touches* which make the graces of the picture. *Dryden.*

Never give the least *touch* with your pencil, till you have well examined your design. *Dryden.*

8. Feature; lineament.

Thus Rosalind of many parts
By heav'nly synod was devis'd;
Of many faces, eyes and hearts,
To have the *touches* dearest priz'd. *Shakesp. As you like it.*

A son was copy'd from his voice so much,
The very same in ev'ry little *touch.* *Dryden.*

9. Act of the hand upon a musical instrument.

Here let the sounds of musick
Creep in our ears; soft stilness and the night
Become the *touches* of sweet harmony. *Shakespeare.*

10. Power of exciting the affections.

Not alone
The death of Fulvia, with more urgent *touches*,
Do strongly speak t' us. *Shakesp. Ant. and Cleopatra.*

Nor wanted power to mitigate and swage,
With solemn *touches*, troubled thoughts. *Milton.*

11. Something of passion or affection.

He which without our nature could not on earth suffer for the world, doth now also, by means thereof, both make intercession to God for sinners, and exercise dominion over all men, with a true, natural, and a sensible *touch* of mercy. *Hooker.*

He loves us not:
He wants the natural *touch.* *Shakespeare.*

12. Particular relation; sensible relation.

Speech of *touch* towards others should be sparingly used; for discourse ought to be as a field, without coming home to any man. *Bacon's Essays.*

13. [*Touche*, Fr.] A stroke.

Our kings no sooner fall out, but their mints make war upon one another; one meets sometimes with very nice *touches* of raillery. *Addison on ancient Medals.*

Another smart *touch* of the author we meet with in the fifth page, where, without any preparation, he breaks out all on a sudden into a vein of poetry. *Addison.*

Though its error may be such,
As Knags and Burgess cannot hit
It yet may feel the nicer *touch*
Of Wicherley's or Congreve's wit. *Prior.*

He gave the little wealth he had
To build a houſe for fools and mad;
To ſhew by one ſatyrick *touch*,
No nation wanted it ſo much. *Swift.*

14. Animadverſion; cenſure.

I never bare any *touch* of conſcience with greater regret. *King Charles.*

Soon mov'd with *touch* of blame, thus Eve,
What words have paſs'd thy lips, Adam, ſevere. *Milton.*

15. Exact performance of agreement.

Touch kept is commended, yet credit to keepe
Is pay and diſpatch him, yer ever ye ſleepe. *Tuſſer.*

Quoth Hudibras, thou offer'ſt much,
But art not able to keep *touch*. *Hudibras, p.* i.

I keep *touch* both with my promiſe to Philopolis, and with my own uſual frugality in theſe kind of collations. *More.*

He was not to expect that ſo perfidious a creature ſhould keep *touch* with him. *L'Eſtrange.*

16. A ſmall quantity intermingled.

Madam, I have a *touch* of your condition,
That cannot brook the accent of reproof. *Shakeſpeare.*

This coming ſtill nearer to an aſpiration, a *touch* of it may perhaps be an ingredient in the rough guttural pronunciation of the Welſh and Iriſh. *Holder's Elements of Speech.*

17. A hint; ſlight notice given.

The king your maſter knows their diſpoſition very well; a ſmall *touch* will put him in mind of them. *Bacon.*

18. A cant word for a ſlight eſſay.

Print my preface in ſuch a form as, in the bookſellers phraſe, will make a ſixpenny *touch*. *Swift.*

To'UCHABLE. *adj.* [from *touch*.] Tangible; that may be touched.

To'UCH-HOLE. *n. ſ.* [*touch* and *hole*.] The hole through which the fire is conveyed to the powder in the gun.

In a piece of ordnance, if you ſpeak in the *touch-hole*, and another lay his ear to the mouth of the piece, the ſound is far better heard than in the open air. *Bacon's Nat. Hiſt.*

To'UCHINESS. *n. ſ.* [from *touching*.] Peeviſhneſs; iraſcibility.

My friends reſented it as a motion not guided with ſuch diſcretion as the *touchineſs* of thoſe times required. *K. Charles.*

To'UCHING. *prep.* [This word is originally a participle of *touch*.] With reſpect, regard, or relation to.

Touching things which belong to diſcipline, the church hath authority to make canons and decrees, even as we read in the apoſtles times it did. *Hooker, b.* iii.

Touching our perſon, ſeek we no revenge;
But we our kingdom's ſafety muſt ſo tender,
Whoſe ruin you three ſought, that to her laws
We do deliver you. *Shakeſpeare's Henry* V.

The heavens and the earth remained in the ſame ſtate in which they were created, as *touching* their ſubſtance, though there was afterwards added multiplicity of perfection in reſpect of beauty. *Raleigh's Hiſt. of the World.*

Touching the debt, he took himſelf to be acquitted thereof. *Hayward.*

Socrates choſe rather to die than renounce or conceal his judgment *touching* the unity of the Godhead. *South.*

To'UCHING. *adj.* [from *touch*.] Pathetick; affecting; moving.

To'UCHINGLY. *adv.* [from *touch*.] With feeling emotion; in a pathetick manner.

This laſt fable ſhows how *touchingly* the poet argues in love affairs. *Garth.*

TOUCHMENOT. *n. ſ.* An herb. *Ainſ.*

To'UCHSTONE. *n. ſ.* [*touch* and *ſtone*; *pierre de touche*, Fr.]

1. Stone by which metals are examined.

Chilon would ſay, that gold was tried with the *touchſtone*, and men with gold. *Bacon's Apophth.*

If he intends to deal clearly, why does he make the *touchſtone* faulty, and the ſtandard uncertain. *Collier.*

2. Any teſt or criterion.

Is not this their rule of ſuch ſufficiency, that we ſhould uſe it as a *touchſtone* to try the orders of the church? *Hooker.*

The work, the *touchſtone* of the nature, is;
And by their operations things are known. *Davies.*

Money ſerves for the *touchſtone* of common honeſty. *L'Eſt.*

Time is the fureſt judge of truth: I am not vain enough to think I have left no faults in this, which that *touchſtone* will not diſcover. *Dryden's Spaniſh Fryar.*

To'UCHWOOD. *n. ſ.* [*touch* and *wood*.] Rotten wood uſed to catch the fire ſtruck from the flint.

A race of reſolute ſtout trees they are, ſo abounding with metal and heat, that they quickly take fire, and become *touchwood*. *Howel's Vocal Foreſt.*

To make white powder, the powder of rotten willows is beſt; ſpunk, or *touchwood* prepared might make it ruſſet. *Br.*

To'UCHY. *adj.* [from *touch*.] Peeviſh; irritable; iraſcible; apt to take fire. A low word.

You are upon a *touchy* point, and therefore treat ſo nice a ſubject with proportionable caution. *Collier on Pride.*

You are ſo *touchy*, and take things ſo hotly, I am ſure there muſt be ſome miſtake in this. *Arbuthnot's Hiſt. of J. Bull.*

TOUGH. *adj.* [toh, Saxon.]

1. Yielding without fracture; not brittle.

Of bodies ſome are fragile, and ſome are *tough*, and not fragile. *Bacon's Nat. Hiſt.*

2. Stiff; not eaſily flexible.

The bow he drew,
And almoſt join'd the horns of the *tough* eugh. *Dryden.*

Fate with nature's law would ſtrive,
To ſhew plain-dealing once an age may thrive;
And when ſo *tough* a frame ſhe could not bend,
Exceeded her commiſſion to befriend. *Dryden.*

3. Not eaſily injured or broken.

O ſides you are too *tough*!
Will you yet hold? *Shakeſpeare.*

A body made of braſs the crone demands
For her lov'd nurſling, ſtrung with nerves of wire,
Tough to the laſt, and with no toil to tire. *Dryden.*

4. Viſcous; clammy; ropy.

To To'UGHEN. *v. n.* [from *tough*.] To grow tough.

Hops off the kiln lay three weeks to cool, give and *toughen*, elſe they will break to powder. *Mortimer's Huſb.*

To'UGHNESS. *n. ſ.* [from *tough*.]

1. Not brittleneſs; flexibility.

To make an induration with *toughneſs*, and leſs fragility, decoct bodies in water for three days; but they muſt be ſuch into which the water will not enter. *Bacon's Nat. Hiſt.*

A well-temper'd ſword is bent at will,
But keeps the native *toughneſs* of the ſteel. *Dryden.*

2. Viſcoſity; tenacity; clammineſs; glutinouſneſs.

In the firſt ſtage the viſcoſity or *toughneſs* of the fluids ſhould be taken off by diluents. *Arbuthnot on Diet.*

3. Firmneſs againſt injury.

I confeſs me knit to thy deſerving with cables of perdurable *toughneſs*. *Shakeſp. Othello.*

TOUPET. *n. ſ.* [Fr.] A curl; an artificial lock of hair.

Remember ſecond-hand *toupees* and repaired ruffles. *Swift.*

TOUR. *n. ſ.* [*tour*, French.]

1. Ramble; roving journey.

I made the *tour* of all the king's palaces. *Addiſon.*

Were it permitted, he'd make the *tour* of the whole ſyſtem of the ſun. *Arbuthnot and Pope's Mart. Scrib.*

2. Turn; revolution. In both theſe ſenſes it is rather French than Engliſh.

Firſt Ptolemy his ſcheme cœleſtial wrought,
And of machines a wild proviſion brought;
Orbs centrick and eccentrick he prepares,
Cycles and epicycles, ſolid ſpheres
In order plac'd, and with bright globes inlaid,
To ſolve the *tours* by heavenly bodies made. *Blackmore.*

3. In *Milton* it is probably tow'r; ſoar; elevation.

The bird of Jove ſtoop'd from his airy *tour*,
Two birds of gayeſt plume before him drove. *Milton.*

To'URNAMENT. }
To'URNEY. } *n. ſ.* [*tournamentum*, low Lat.]

1. Tilt; juſt; military ſport; mock encounter.

They might under the pretence
Of tilts and *tournaments*,
Provide them horſe and armour for defence. *Daniel.*

For juſts, *tourneys*, and barriers, the glories of them are the chariots, wherein challengers make their entry. *Bacon.*

Whence came all thoſe juſts, tiltings, and *tournaments*, ſo much in uſe in theſe parts. *Temple's Miſcel.*

He liv'd with all the pomp he cou'd deviſe,
At tilts and *tournaments* obtain'd the prize,
But found no favour in his lady's eyes. *Dryden.*

The ſpouſals of Hippolita the queen,
What tilts and *tourneys* at the feaſt were ſeen. *Dryden.*

2. *Milton* uſes it ſimply for encounter; ſhock of battle.

With cruel *tournament* the ſquadrons join!
Where cattle paſtur'd late, now ſcatter'd lies
With carcaſſes, and arms, th' inſanguin'd field. *Milton.*

To TOURNEY. *v. n.* [from the noun.] To tilt in the liſts.

An elfin born of noble ſtate,
Well could he *tourney*, and in liſts debate. *F. Qu. b.* ii.

TOURNIQUET. *n. ſ.* [French.] A bandage uſed in amputations, ſtraitened or relaxed by the turn of a handle.

If the orifice does not readily appear, looſen the *tourniquet*, and the effuſion of blood will direct you to it. *Sharp.*

To TOUSE. *v. a.* [probably of the ſame original with *taw*, *teize*, *toſe*.] To pull; to tear; to haul; to drag: whence *touſer* or *towzer*, the name of a maſtiff.

As a bear whom angry curs have *touz'd*,
Having off ſhak'd them and eſcap'd their hands,
Becomes more fell, and all that him withſtands
Treads down and overthrows. *Spenſer.*

Take him hence; to th' rack with him: we'll *towze* you
Joint by joint, but we will know his purpoſe. *Shakeſpeare.*

To *towze* ſuch things as flutter
To honeſt Bounce is bread and butter. *Swift.*

TOW. *n. ſ.* [top, Saxon.] Flax or hemp beaten and combed into a filamentous ſubſtance.

Tow twiſted round the handle of an inſtrument makes it eaſier to be held. *Sharp.*

To Tow. *v. a.* [teon, teohan, Saxon, to lead; *toghen*, old Dutch.] To draw by a rope, particularly through the water.

Thou knew'ſt too well
My heart was to thy rudder ty'd by th' ſtring,
And thou ſhould'ſt *tow* me after. *Shak. Ant. and Cleopatra.*

The ſeamen *towed*, and I ſhoved, till we arrived. *Swift.*

Towa'rd. } Towa'rds. } *prep.* [topanð, Saxon.]

1. In a direction to.

He ſet his face *toward* the wilderneſs. *Num.* xxiv. 1.

The currents drive,
Tow'rds the retreating ſea, their furious tide. *Milton.*

2. Near to: as, the danger now comes *towards* him.

3. With reſpect to; touching; regarding.

We brought them to as great peace between themſelves, as love *towards* us for having made the peace. *Sidney, b.* ii.

Repent you not,
As that the ſin hath brought you to this ſhame,
Which ſorrow's always *tow'rds* ourſelves, not heav'n?
Shakeſp. Meaſure for Meaſure.

His heart relented *towards* her. *Milton.*

By our law, no good is to be left undone *towards* all, not the good of the tongue, the hand, the heart. *South's Sermons.*

4. With tendency to.

This was the firſt alarm England received *towards* any trouble, after it had enjoyed for ſo many years the moſt uninterrupted proſperity. *Clarendon, b.* ii.

5. Nearly; little leſs than.

I am *towards* nine years older ſince I left you. *Swift.*

Towa'rd. } Towa'rds. } *adv.* [It is doubtful whether in this uſe the word be adverb or adjective.] Near; at hand; in a ſtate of preparation.

What might be *toward* that this ſweaty haſte
Doth make the night joint labourer with the day. *Shakeſp.*

Towa'rd. *adj.* Ready to do or learn; not froward.

To'wardliness. *n. ſ.* [from *towardly*.] Docility; compliance; readineſs to do or to learn.

The beauty and *towardlineſs* of theſe children moved her brethren to envy. *Raleigh's Hiſt. of the World.*

To'wardly. *adj.* [from *toward*.] Ready to do or learn; docile; compliant with duty.

Some young *towardly* noblemen or gentlemen were uſually ſent as aſſiſtants or attendants. *Bacon's Advice to Villiers.*

To'wardness. *n. ſ.* [from *toward*.] Docility.

Parents will not throw away the *towardneſs* of a child, and the expence of education upon a profeſſion, the labour of which is encreaſed, and the rewards are vaniſhed. *South.*

To'wel. *n. ſ.* [*touaille*, French; *touaglio*, Italian.] A cloath on which the hands are wiped.

His arm muſt be kept up with a napkin or *towel*. *Wiſeman.*

Th' attendants water for their hands ſupply,
And having waſh'd, with ſilken *towels* dry. *Dryden's Æn.*

To'wer. *n. ſ.* [top, Saxon; *tour*, Fr. *torre*, Italian; *turris*, Latin.]

1. A high building; a building raiſed above the main edifice.

Let us build us a city and a *tower*, whoſe top may reach unto heaven. *Gen.* xi. 4.

2. A fortreſs; a citadel.

3. A high head-dreſs.

I lay trains of amorous intrigues
In *towers*, and curls, and perriwigs. *Hudibras, p.* iii.

4. High flight; elevation.

To To'wer. *v. n.* To ſoar; to fly or riſe high.

On th' other ſide an high rock *tow'red* ſtill. *Spenſer.*

No marvel
My lord protector's hawks do *tower* ſo well. *Shakeſp.*

Circular baſe of riſing folds that *tower'd*
Fold above fold a ſurging maze. *Milton.*

Tow'ring his height, and ample was his breaſt. *Dryden.*

The crooked plough, the ſhare, the *tow'ring* height
Of waggons, and the cart's unweildy weight;
Theſe all muſt be prepar'd. *Dryden's Georg.*

All thoſe ſublime thoughts which *tower* above the clouds, and reach as high as heaven itſelf, take their riſe, not one jot beyond thoſe ideas which ſenſe or reflection have offered for the contemplation of the mind. *Locke.*

To'wer-mustard. *n. ſ.* [*turritis*, Lat.] A plant.

The flower of the *tower-muſtard* conſiſts of four leaves, expanding in form of a croſs, out of whoſe empalement riſes the pointal, which afterward becomes a long, ſmooth pod, growing for the moſt part upright, and opening into two parts, in each of which are many ſmooth ſeeds. *Miller.*

To'wered. *adj.* [from *tower*.] Adorned or defended by towers.

Might ſhe the wiſe Latona be,
Or the *tow'red* Cybele. *Milton's Arcades.*

To'wery. *adj.* [from *tower*.] Adorned or guarded with towers.

Here naked rocks, and empty waſtes were ſeen,
There *tow'ry* cities and the foreſts green. *Pope.*

Riſe, crown'd with lights, imperial Salem riſe!
Exalt thy *tow'ry* head, and lift thy eyes! *Pope's Meſſiah.*

With his *tow'ry* grandeur ſwell their ſtate. *Thomſon.*

Town. *n. ſ.* [tun, Saxon; *tuyn*, Dutch; from tinan, Saxon, *ſhut*.]

1. Any walled collection of houſes.

She let them down by a cord; for her houſe was upon the *town* wall. *Joſ.* ii. 15.

2. Any collection of houſes larger than a village.

Speak the ſpeech trippingly on the tongue: but if you mouth it, as many of our players do, I had as lieve the *town* crier had ſpoke the lines. *Shakeſp. Hamlet.*

Into whatſoever city or *town* ye enter, enquire who in it is worthy, and there abide? *Mat.* x. 11.

Before him *towns* and rural works between. *Milton.*

My friend this inſult ſees,
And flies from *towns* to woods. *Broome.*

3. In England, any number of houſes to which belongs a regular market, and which is not a city or ſee of a biſhop.

4. The court end of London.

A virgin whom her mother's care
Drags from the *town* to wholeſome country air. *Pope.*

5. The people who live in the capital.

He all at once let down,
Stuns with his giddy larum half the *town*. *Pope.*

6. It is uſed by the inhabitants of every town or city: as we ſay, *a new family is come to* town.

There is ſome new dreſs or new diverſion juſt come to *town*. *Law.*

To'wnclerk. *n. ſ.* [*town* and *clerk*.] An officer who manages the publick buſineſs of a place.

The *townclerk* appeaſed the people. *Acts* xix. 35.

Townho'use. *n. ſ.* [*town* and *houſe*.] The hall where publick buſineſs is tranſacted.

A *townhouſe* built at one end will front the church that ſtands at the other. *Addiſon on Italy.*

To'wnship. *n. ſ.* [*town* and *ſhip*.] The corporation of a town; the diſtrict belonging to a town.

I am but a poor petitioner of our whole *townſhip*. *Shakeſp.*

They had built houſes, planted gardens, erected *townſhips*, and made proviſion for their poſterity. *Raleigh.*

To'wnsman. *n. ſ.* [*town* and *man*.]

1. An inhabitant of a place.

Here come the *townſmen* on proceſſion,
Before your highneſs to preſent the man. *Shakeſpeare.*

In the time of king Henry the ſixth, in a fight between the earls of Ormond and Deſmond, almoſt all the *townſmen* of Kilkenny were ſlain. *Davies on Ireland.*

They marched to Newcaſtle, which being defended only by the *townſmen*, was given up to them. *Clarendon, b.* viii.

I left him at the gate firm to your intereſt,
T' admit the *townſmen* at their firſt appearance. *Dryden.*

2. One of the ſame town.

To'wntalk. *n. ſ.* [*town* and *talk*.] Common prattle of a place.

If you tell the ſecret, in twelve hours it ſhall be *towntalk*. *L'Eſtrange.*

To'xical. *adj.* [*toxicum*, Lat.] Poiſonous; containing poiſon.

Toy. *n. ſ.* [*toyen*, *tooghen*, to dreſs with many ornaments, Dutch.]

1. A petty commodity; a trifle; a thing of no value.

Might I make acceptable unto her that *toy* which I had found, following an acquaintance of mine at the plough. *Sidn.*

They exchange for knives, glaſſes and ſuch *toys*, great abundance of gold and pearl. *Abbot.*

Becauſe of old
Thou thyſelf doatd'ſt on womankind, admiring
Their ſhape, their colour, and attractive grace:
None are, thou think'ſt, but taken with ſuch *toys*. *Milton.*

O virtue! virtue! what art thou become,
That men ſhould leave thee for that *toy* a woman. *Dryden.*

2. A plaything; a bauble.

To dally thus with death is no fit *toy*,
Go find ſome other play-fellows, mine own ſweet boy.
Fairy Queen, b. i.

What a profuſion of wealth laid out in coaches, trappings, tables, cabinets, and the like precious *toys*. *Addiſon.*

In Delia's hand this *toy* is fatal found,
Nor could that fabled dart more ſurely wound. *Pope.*

3. Matter of no importance.

'Tis a cockle or a walnut ſhell,
A knack, a *toy*, a trick, a baby's cap. *Shakeſpeare.*

4. Folly; trifling practice; ſilly opinion.

The things which ſo long experience of all ages hath confirmed and made profitable, let us not preſume to condemn as follies and *toys*, becauſe we ſometime know not the cauſe and reaſon of them. *Hooker, b.* iv.

5. Play; ſport; amorous dalliance.

Ye ſons of Venus, play your ſports at will;
For greedy pleaſure, careleſs of your *toys*,
Thinks more upon her paradiſe of joys. *Spenſer's Epithal.*

So ſaid he, and forbore not glance or *toy*
Of amorous intent. *Milton.*

6. Odd story; silly tale.
I never may believe
These antick fables, nor these fairy *toys*. *Shakespeare.*
7. Frolick; humour; odd fancy.
Shall that which hath always received this construction, be now disguised with a *toy* of novelty. *Hooker*, *b.* v.
The very place puts *toys* of desperation,
Without more motive, into every brain,
That looks so many fathoms to the sea,
And hears it roar beneath. *Shakesp. Hamlet.*
To Toy. *v. n.* [from the noun.] To trifle; to dally amourously; to play.
To'yish. *adj.* [from *toy.*] Trifling; wanton.
To'yishness. *n. s.* [from *toyish.*] Nugacity; wantonness.
Your society will discredit that *toyishness* of wanton fancy, that plays tricks with words, and frolicks with the caprices of frothy imagination. *Glanville's Sceps.*
To'yshop. *n. s.* [*toy* and *shop.*] A shop where playthings and little nice manufactures are sold.
Fans, silks, ribbands, laces, and gewgaws, lay so thick together, that the heart was nothing else but a *toyshop*. *Add.*
With varying vanities from every part,
They shift the moving *toyshop* of their heart. *Pope.*
To Toze. *v. a.* [See Towse and Tease.] To pull by violence or impetuosity.
Think'st thou, for that I insinuate, or *toze* from thee thy business, I am therefore no courtier. *Shakespeare.*
Trace. *n. s.* [*trace*, Fr. *traccia*, Italian.]
1. Mark left by any thing passing; footsteps.
These as a line their long dimension drew,
Streaking the ground with sinuous *trace*. *Milton.*
2. Remain; appearance of what has been.
The people of these countries are reported to have lived like the beasts among them, without any *traces* of orders, laws, or religion. *Temple.*
There are not the least *traces* of it to be met, the greatest part of the ornaments being taken from Trajan's arch, and set up to the conqueror. *Addison on Italy.*
The shady empire shall retain no *trace*
Of war, or blood, but in the Sylvan chace. *Pope.*
3. [From *tirasser*, French; *tirassés*, traces.] Harness for beasts of draught.
Her waggon spokes made of long spinner's legs;
The cover, of the wings of grashoppers;
The *traces*, of the smallest spider's web. *Shakespeare.*
The labour'd ox
In his loose *traces* from the furrow came. *Milton.*
While lab'ring oxen, spent with toil and heat,
In their loose *traces* from the field retreat. *Pope:*
Twelve young mules,
New to the plough, unpractis'd in the *trace*. *Pope's Odys.*
To Trace. *v. a.* [*tracer*, Fr. *tracciare*, Italian.]
1. To follow by the footsteps, or remaining marks.
I feel thy power to *trace* the ways
Of highest agents. *Milton.*
You may *trace* the deluge quite round the globe in profane history; and every one of these people have a tale to tell concerning the restauration. *Burnet's Theory of the Earth.*
They do but *trace* over the paths beaten by the ancients, or comment, critick, or flourish upon them. *Temple.*
To this haste of the mind a not due *tracing* of the arguments to their true foundation is owing. *Locke.*
2. To follow with exactness.
That servile path thou nobly dost decline,
Of *tracing* word by word, and line by line. *Denham.*
3. To mark out.
He allows the soul power to *trace* images on the brain, and perceive them. *Locke.*
His pen can *trace* out a true quotation. *Swift.*
4. To walk over.
Men as they *trace*,
Both feet and face one way are wont to lead. *Fa. Qu.*
We do *trace* this alley up and down. *Shakespeare.*
Tra'cer. *n. s.* [from *trace.*] One that traces.
Ambassadors should not be held the *tracers* of a plot of such malice. *Howel.*
Track. *n. s.* [*trac*, old French; *traccia*, Italian.]
1. Mark left upon the way by the foot or otherwise.
Following the *track* of Satan. *Milton.*
Hung by the neck and hair, and dragg'd around,
The hostile spear yet sticking in his wound,
With *tracks* of blood inscrib'd the dusty ground. *Dryden.*
Consider the exterior frame of the globe, if we may find any *tracks* or footsteps of wisdom in its constitution. *Bentley.*
2. A road; a beaten path.
With *track* oblique sidelong he works his way. *Milton.*
Behold Torquatus the same *track* persue,
And next, the two devoted Decii view. *Dryden's Æn.*
To Track. *v. a.* [from the noun.] To follow by the footsteps or marks left in the way.
As shepherd's cur that in dark evening's shade
Hath *tracked* forth some savage beast's treade. *Fa. Queen.*
He was not only a professed imitator of Horace, but a learned plagiary in all the others; you *track* him everywhere in their snow. *Dryden.*
Tra'ckless. *adj.* [from *track.*] Untrodden; marked with no footsteps.
Lost in *trackless* fields of shining day,
Unable to discern the way,
Which Nassau's virtue only cou'd explore. *Prior.*
TRACT. *n. s.* *tractus*, Lat.]
1. Any kind of extended substance.
2. A region; a quantity of land.
Only there are some *tracts* which, by high mountains, are barred from air and fresh wind. *Raleigh.*
Heav'n hides nothing from thy view,
Nor the deep *tract* of hell. *Milton.*
Monte Circeio, by Homer called insula Æea, is a very high mountain joined to the main land by a narrow *tract* of earth. *Addison.*
3. Continuity; any thing protracted, or drawn out to length.
The myrtle flourisheth still; and wonderful it is that for so long a *tract* of time she should still continue fresh. *Howel.*
Your bodies may at last turn all to spirit,
Improv'd by *tract* of time, and wing'd ascend
Ethereal as we. *Milton.*
As in *tract* of speech a dubious word is easily known by the coherence with the rest, and a dubious letter by the whole word; so may a deaf person, having competent knowledge of language, by an acute sagacity by some more evident word discerned by his eye, know the sense. *Holder.*
4. Course; manner of process; unless it means, in this place, rather, discourse; explanation.
The *tract* of every thing
Would, by a good discourser, lose some life
Which action's self was tongue to. *Shakesp. Henry* VIII.
5. It seems to be used by *Shakespeare* for *track*.
The weary sun hath made a golden set,
And, by the bright *tract* of his fiery car,
Gives signal of a goodly day to-morrow. *Shakespeare.*
6. [*Tractatus*, Lat.] A treatise; a small book.
The church clergy at that time writ the best collection of *tracts* against popery that ever appeared. *Swift.*
Tra'ctable. *adj.* [*tractabilis*, Lat. *traitable*, Fr.]
1. Manageable; docile; compliant; obsequious; practicable; governable.
For moderation of those affections growing from the very natural bitterness and gall of adversity, the scripture much alledgeth contrary fruit, which affliction likewise hath, whensoever it falleth on them that are *tractable*, the grace of God's holy spirit concurring therewith. *Hooker*, *b.* v.
Noble Ajax, you are as strong, as valiant, as wise, no less noble, much more gentle, and altogether more *tractable*. *Shakesp. Troilas and Cressida.*
Tractable obedience is a slave
To each incensed will. *Shakesp. Henry* VII.
If thou dost find him *tractable* to us,
Encourage him, and tell him all our reasons;
If he be leaden, icy, cold, unwilling,
Be thou so too. *Shakesp. Rich.* III.
As those who are bent to do wickedly will never want tempters to urge them on in an evil course; so those who yield themselves *tractable* to good motions, will find the spirit of God more ready to encourage them. *Tillotson's Sermons.*
If a strict hand be kept over children from the beginning, they will in that age be *tractable*, and quietly submit to it. *Locke on Education.*
2. Palpable; such as may be handled.
The other measures are of continued quantity visible, and for the most part *tractable*; whereas time is always transient, neither to be seen nor felt. *Holder on Time.*
Tra'ctableness. *n. s.* [from *tractable.*] The state of being tractable; compliance; obsequiousness.
It will be objected, that whatsoever I fansy of childrens *tractableness*, yet many will never apply. *Locke.*
Tra'ctate. *n. s.* [*tractatus*, Latin.] A treatise; a tract; a small book.
Though philosophical *tractates* make enumeration of authors, yet are their reasons usually introduced. *Brown.*
We need no other evidence than Glanville's *tractate*. *Hale.*
Tra'ction. *n. s.* [from *tractus*, Lat.] The act of drawing; the state of being drawn.
The malleus being fixed to an extensible membrane, follows the *traction* of the muscle, and is drawn inwards to bring the terms of that line nearer in proportion as it is curved, and so gives a tension to the tympanum. *Holder.*
Tra'ctile. *n. s.* [*tractus*, Lat.] Capable to be drawn out or extended in length; ductile.
The consistences of bodies are very divers; fragile, tough; flexible, inflexible; *tractile*, or to be drawn forth in length, intractile. *Bacon's Nat. Hist.* N°. 839.
Tracti'lity. *adj.* [from *tractile.*] The quality of being tractile.

Silver, whose ductility and tractility are much inferiour to those of gold, was drawn out to so slender a wire, that a single grain amounted to twenty-seven feet. *Derham.*

TRADE. *n. s.* [*tratta*, Italian.]

1. Traffick; commerce; exchange of goods for other goods, or for money.

Whosoever commands the sea, commands the *trade*; whosoever commands the *trade* of the world, commands the riches of the world, and consequently the world itself. *Ral.*

Trade increases in one place and decays in another. *Temple.*

2. Occupation; particular employment whether manual or mercantile, distinguished from the liberal arts or learned professions.

Appoint to every one that is not able to live of his freehold a certain *trade* of life; the which *trade* he shall be bound to follow. *Spenser on Ireland.*

How dizzy! half way down
Hangs one that gathers samphire, dreadful *trade*. *Shakesp.*
I'll mountebank their loves, and come home belov'd
Of all the *trades* in Rome. *Shakesp. Coriolanus.*

Fear and piety,
Instruction, manners, mysteries, and *trades*,
Decline to your confounding contraries. *Shakespeare.*

The rude Equicolæ
Hunting their sport, and plund'ring was their *trade*. *Dryd.*
Fight under him; there's plunder to be had;
A captain is a very gainful *trade*. *Dryden's Juv.*
The whole division that to Mars pertains,
All *trades* of death, that deal in steel for gains. *Dryden.*

The emperor Pertinax applied himself in his youth to a gainful *trade*; his father, judging him fit for a better employment, had a mind to turn his education another way; the son was obstinate in pursuing so profitable a *trade*, a sort of merchandise of wood. *Arbuthnot on Coins.*

3. Instruments of any occupation.

The shepherd bears
His house and houshold gods, his *trade* of war,
His bow and quiver, and his trusty cur. *Dryden's Virgil.*

4. Any employment not manual; habitual exercise.

Call some of young years to train them up in that *trade*; and so fit them for weighty affairs. *Bacon.*

To TRADE. *v. n.* [from the noun.]

1. To traffick; to deal; to hold commerce.

He commanded these servants to be called, to know how much every man had gained by *trading*. *Luke* xix. 15.

Delos, a sacred place, grew a free port, where nations warring with one another resorted with their goods, and *traded*. *Arbuthnot on Coins.*

Maximinus *traded* with the Goths in the product of his estate in Thracia. *Arbuthnot.*

2. To act merely for money.

Saucy and overbold! how did you dare
To *trade* and traffick with Macbeth,
In riddles and affairs of death? *Shakesp Macbeth.*

3. Having a trading wind.

They on the *trading* flood ply tow'rd the pole. *Milton.*

To TRADE. *v. a.* To sell or exchange in commerce.

They were thy merchants: they *traded* the persons of men and vessels of brass in thy market. *Ezek.* xxvii. 13.

TRADE-WIND. *n. s.* [*trade* and *wind.*] The monsoon; the periodical wind between the tropicks.

Thus to the eastern wealth through storms we go,
But now, the Cape once doubled, fear no more;
A constant *trade-wind* will securely blow,
And gently lay us on the spicey shore. *Dryden.*

His were the projects of perpetuum mobiles, and of increasing the *trade-wind* by vast plantations of reeds. *Arbuth.*

Comfortable is the *trade-wind* to the equatorial parts, without which life would be both short and grievous. *Cheyne.*

TRA'DED. *adj.* [from *trade.*] Versed; practised.

Trust not those cunning waters of his eyes;
For villainy is not without such a rheum:
And he long *traded* in it makes it seem
Like rivers of remorse and innocence. *Shakespeare.*

Eyes and ears,
Two *traded* pilots 'twixt the dangerous shores
Of will and judgment. *Shakesp. Troilus and Cressida.*

TRA'DER. *n. s.* [from *trade.*]

1. One engaged in merchandise or commerce.

Pilgrims are going to Canterbury with rich offerings, and *traders* riding to London with fat purses. *Shakesp. Henry* IV.

Now the victory's won,
We return to our lasses like fortunate *traders*,
Triumphant with spoils. *Dryden.*

Many *traders* will necessitate merchants to trade for less profit, and consequently be more frugal. *Child on Trade.*

That day *traders* sum up the accounts of the week. *Swift.*

2. One long used in the methods of money getting; a practitioner.

TRA'DESFOLK. *n. s.* [*trade* and *folk.*] People employed in trades.

By his advice victuallers and *tradesfolk* would soon get all the money of the kingdom into their hands. *Swift.*

TRA'DESMAN. *n. s.* [*trade* and *man.*] A shopkeeper. A merchant is called a *trader*, but not a tradesman; and it seems distinguished in *Shakespeare* from a man that labours with his hands.

I live by the awl, I meddle with no *tradesmen's* matters. *Shakespeare.*

They rather had beheld
Dissentious numbers pest'ring streets; than see
Our *tradesmen* singing in their shops, and going
About their functions. *Shakesp. Coriolanus.*

Order a trade thither and thence so as some few merchants and *tradesmen*, under colour of furnishing the colony with necessaries, may not grind them. *Bacon.*

Tradesmen might conjecture what doings they were like to have in their respective dealings. *Graunt.*

M. Jordain would not be thought a *tradesman*, but ordered some silk to be measured out to his partner's friends: now I give up my shop. *Prior.*

From a plain *tradesman* with a shop, he is now grown a very rich country gentleman. *Arbuth. Hist. of J. Bull.*

Domesticks in a gentleman's family have more opportunities of improving their minds, than the ordinary *tradesmen*. *Swift.*

Boastful and rough, your first son is a squire;
The next a *tradesman*, meek and much a liar. *Pope's Ep.*

TRA'DEFUL. *adj.* [*trade* and *full.*] Commercial; busy in traffick.

Ye *tradeful* merchants that with weary toil
Do seek most precious things to make your gain,
And both the Indies of their treasure spoil,
What needeth you to seek so far in vain. *Spenser.*

TRADI'TION. *n. s.* [*tradition*, Fr. *traditio*, Lat.]

1. The act or practise of delivering accounts from mouth to mouth without written memorials; communication from age to age.

To learn it we have *tradition*; namely, that so we believe, because both we from our predecessors, and they from theirs, have so received. *Hooker, b.* iii.

2. Any thing delivered orally from age to age.

They the truth
With superstitions and *traditions* taint,
Left only in those written records pure. *Milton.*

Our old solemnities
From no blind zeal, or fond *tradition* rise;
But sav'd from death, our Argives yearly pay
These grateful honours to the God of day. *Pope's Statius.*

TRADI'TIONAL. *adj.* [from *tradition.*]

1. Delivered by tradition; descending by oral communication; transmitted by the foregoing to the following age.

Whence may we have the infallible *traditional* sense of scripture, if not from the heads of their church? *Tillotson.*

If there be any difference in natural parts, it should seem the advantage lies on the side of children born from wealthy parents, the same *traditional* sloth and luxury which render their body weak, perhaps refining their spirits. *Swift.*

2. Observant of traditions, or idle rites. Not used, nor proper.

God forbid
We should infringe the holy privilege
Of sanctuary!
——You are too senseless obstinate, my lord;
Too ceremonious and *traditional*. *Shakesp. Rich.* II.

TRADI'TIONALLY. *adv.* [from *traditional.*]

1. By transmission from age to age.

There is another channel wherein this doctrine is *traditionally* derived from Saint John, namely, from the clergy of Asia. *Burnet's Theory of the Earth.*

2. From tradition without evidence of written memorials.

It crosseth the proverb, and Rome might well be built in a day, if that were true which is *traditionally* related by Strabo, that the great cities Anchiale and Tarsus were built by Sardanapalus both in one day. *Brown's Vulgar Err.*

TRADI'TIONARY. *adj.* [from *tradition.*] Delivered by tradition.

Suppose the same *traditionary* strain
Of rigid manners in the house remain,
Inveterate truth, an old plain Sabine's heart. *Dryden.*

Oral tradition is more uncertain, especially if we may take that to be the *traditionary* sense of texts of scripture. *Tillotson.*

The fame of our Saviour, which in so few years had gone through the whole earth, was confirmed and perpetuated by such records as would preserve the *traditionary* account of him to after-ages. *Addison on the Christian Religion.*

TRA'DITIVE. *adj.* [*traditive*, Fr. from *trado*, Latin.] Transmitted or transmissible from age to age.

Suppose we on things *traditive* divide,
And both appeal to scripture to decide. *Dryd. H. and Pant.*

To TRADU'CE. *v. a.* [*traduco*, Lat. *traduire*, Fr.]

1. To censure; to condemn; to represent as blameable; to calumniate; to decry.

The best stratagem that Satan hath, who knoweth his kingdom to be no one way more shaken than by the publick devout prayers of God's church, is by *traducing* the form and manner of them, to bring them into contempt, and so slack the force of all mens devotion towards them. *Hooker, b.* v.

 Those

Those particular ceremonies which they pretend to be so scandalous, we shall more thoroughly sift, when other things also *traduced* in the publick duties of the church are, together with these, to be touched. *Hooker, b.* iv.

Whilst calumny has such potent abetters, we are not to wonder at its growth: as long as men are malicious and designing they will be *traducing*. *Gov. of the Tongue.*

From that preface he took his hint; though he had the baseness not to acknowledge his benefactor, but instead of it to *traduce* me in libel. *Dryden's Fab.*

2. To propagate; to encrease by deriving one from another.

None are so gross as to contend for this,
That souls from bodies may *traduced* be;
Between whose natures no proportion is,
When root and branch in nature still agree. *Davies.*

From these only the race of perfect animals were propagated and *traduced* over the earth. *Hale.*

Some believe the soul is made by God, some by angels, and some by the generant: whether it be immediately created or *traduced* hath been the great ball of contention to the latter ages. *Glanville's Sceps.*

TRADU'CEMENT. *n. s.* [from *traduce.*] Censure; obloquy.

Rome must know
The value of her own: 'twere a concealment
Worse than a theft, no less than a *traducement*,
To hide your doings. *Shakespeare's Coriolanus.*

TRADU'CER. *n. s.* [from *traduce.*] A false censurer; a calumniator.

TRADU'CIBLE. *adj.* [from *traduce.*] Such as may be derived.

Though oral tradition might be a competent discoverer of the original of a kingdom, yet such a tradition were incompetent without written monuments to derive to us the original laws, because they are of a complex nature, and therefore not orally *traducible* to so great a distance of ages. *Hale.*

TRADU'CTION. *n. s.* [from *traduce.*]

1. Derivation from one of the same kind; propagation.

The patrons of *traduction* accuse their adversaries of affronting the attributes of God; and the asserters of creation impeach them of violence to the nature of things. *Glanville.*

If by *traduction* came thy mind,
Our wonder is the less to find
A soul so charming from a stock so good;
Thy father was transfus'd into thy blood. *Dryden.*

2. Tradition; transmission from one to another.

Touching traditional communication and *traduction* of truths connatural and engraven, I do not doubt but many of them have had the help of that derivation. *Hale.*

3. Conveyance.

Since America is divided on every side by considerable seas, and no passage known by land, the *traduction* of brutes could only be by shipping: though this was a method used for the *traduction* of useful cattle from hence thither, yet it is not credible that bears and lions should have so much care used for their transportation. *Hale's Origin of Mankind.*

4. Transition.

The reports and fugues have an agreement with the figures in rhetorick of repetition and *traduction*. *Bacon.*

TRA'FFICK. *n. s.* [*trafique*, Fr. *traffico*, Italian.]

1. Commerce; merchandising; large trade; exchange of commodities.

Traffick's thy god. *Shakesp. Timon of Athens.*

My father
A merchant of great *traffick* through the world. *Shakesp.*

As the first of these was, for his great wisdom, stiled the English Solomon, he followed the example of that wise king in nothing more than by advancing the *traffick* of his people. *Addison's Freeholder*, N°. 41.

2. Commodities; subject of traffick.

You'll see a draggled damsel
From Billingsgate her fishy *traffick* bear. *Gay.*

To TRA'FFICK. *v. n.* [*trafiquer*, Fr. *trafficare*, Italian.]

1. To practise commerce; to merchandise; to exchange commodities.

They first plant for corn and cattle, and after enlarge themselves for things to *traffick* withal. *Bacon's Advice to Villiers.*

2. To trade meanly or mercenarily.

Saucy and overbold! how did you dare
To trade and *traffick* with Macbeth,
In riddles and affairs of death? *Shakesp. Macbeth.*

How hast thou dar'd to think so vilely of me,
That I would condescend to thy mean arts,
And *traffick* with thee for a prince's ruin? *Rowe.*

TRA'FFICKER. *n. s.* [*trafiqueur*, Fr. from *traffick.*] Trader; merchant.

Your Argosies with portly sail,
Like signiors and rich burghers on the flood,
Do overpeer the petty *traffickers*
That curtsy to them. *Shakesp. Merchant of Venice.*

In it are so many Jews very rich, and so great *traffickers*, that they have most of the English trade in their hands. *Add.*

TRA'GACANTH. *n. s.* [*tragacantha*, Lat.] A sort of gum to which this name has been given, because it proceeds from the incision of the root or trunk of a plant so called. *Trevoux.*

TRAGE'DIAN. *n. s.* [from *tragedy*; *tragœdus*, Lat.]

1. A writer of tragedy.

Many of the poets themselves had much nobler conceptions of the Deity, than to imagine him to have any thing corporeal; as in these verses out of the ancient *tragedian*. *Stillingfleet.*

2. An actor of tragedy.

I can counterfeit the deep *tragedian*;
Speak, and look back, and pry on ev'ry side,
Tremble and start at wagging of a straw,
Intending deep suspicion. *Shakesp. Rich.* III.

To well-lung'd *tragedian*'s rage
They recommend their labours of the stage. *Dryden.*

TRA'GEDY. *n. s.* [*tragedie*, Fr. *tragœdia*, Lat.]

1. A dramatick representation of a serious action.

Thousands more, that yet suspect no peril,
Will now conclude their plotted *tragedy*. *Shakespeare.*

All our *tragedies* are of kings and princes; but you never see a poor man have a part unless it be as a chorus, or to fill up the scenes, to dance, or to be derided. *Taylor's holy living.*

Imitate the sister of painting, *tragedy*; which employs the whole forces of her art in the main action. *Dryden.*

An anthem to their god Dionysus, whilst the goat stood at his altar to be sacrificed, was called the goat-song or *tragedy*. *Rymer's Tragedies of the last Age.*

There to her heart sad *tragedy* addrest
The dagger, wont to pierce the tyrant's breast. *Pope.*

2. Any mournful or dreadful event.

I shall laugh at this,
That they, who brought me in my master's hate,
I live to look upon their *tragedy*. *Shakesp. Rich.* III.

I look upon this now done in England as another act of the same *tragedy* which was lately begun in Scotland. *K. Ch.*

TRA'GICAL.
TRA'GICK. } *adj.* [*tragicus*, Lat. *tragique*, Fr.]

1. Relating to tragedy.

The root whereof and *tragical* effect,
Vouchsafe, O thou the mournfull'st muse of nine,
That wont'st the *tragick* stage for to direct,
In funeral complaints and wailful tine
Reveal to me. *Spenser's Muiopotmos.*

Thy Clarence he is dead that stabb'd my Edward;
And the beholders of this *tragick* play,
Th' adulterer Hastings, Rivers, Vaughan, Gray,
Untimely smother'd in their dusky graves. *Shakesp. R.* III.

2. Mournful; calamitous; sorrowful; dreadful.

A dire induction I am witness to;
And will to France, hoping the consequence
Will prove as bitter, black, and *tragical*. *Shakespeare.*

The gaudy, blabbing, and remorseful day,
Is crept into the bosom of the sea:
And now loud howling wolves arouse the jades,
That drag the *tragick* melancholy night. *Shakesp. Hen.* VI.

Why look you still so stern and *tragical*? *Shakespeare.*

So *tragical* and merited a fate
Shall swallow those who God and justice hate. *Sandys.*

I now must change those notes to *tragick*. *Milton.*

The tale of this song is a pretty *tragical* story; and pleases because it is a copy of nature. *Addison.*

Bid them dress their bloody altars
With every circumstance of *tragick* pomp. *Rowe.*

TRA'GICALLY. *adv.* [from *tragical.*]

1. In a tragical manner; in a manner befitting tragedy.

Juvenal's genius was sharp and eager; and as his provocations were great, he has revenged them *tragically*. *Dryden.*

2. Mournfully; sorrowfully; calamitously.

TRA'GICALNESS. *n. s.* [from *tragical.*] Mournfulness; calamitousness.

Like bold Phaëtons we despise all benefits of the father of light, unless we may guide his chariot; and we moralize the fable as well in the *tragicalness* of the event as in the insolence of the undertaking. *Decay of Piety.*

TRAGICO'MEDY. *n. s.* [*tragicomedie*, Fr. from *tragedy* and *comedy.*] A drama compounded of merry and serious events.

On the world's stage, when our applause grows high,
For acting here life's *tragi-comedy*,
The lookers-on will say we act not well,
Unless the last the former scenes excel. *Denham.*

The faults of that drama are in the kind of it, which is *tragi-comedy*; but it was given to the people. *Dryden.*

We have often had *tragi-comedies* upon the English theatre with success: but in that sort of composition the tragedy and comedy are in distinct scenes. *Gay.*

TRAGICO'MICAL. *adj.* [*tragicomique*, Fr. *tragical* and *comical.*]

1. Relating to tragi-comedy.

The whole art of the *tragi-comical* farce lies in interweaving the several kinds of the drama, so that they cannot be distinguished. *Gay's What d'ye call it.*

2. Consisting of a mixture of mirth with sorrow.

TRAGICO'MICALLY. *adv.* [from *tragicomical.*] In a tragicomical manner.

Laws my Pindarick parents matter'd not,
So I was *tragicomically* got. *Brampston.*

To TRAJE'CT. *v. a.* [*trajectus*, Latin.] To cast through; to throw.

The disputes of those assuming confidents, that think so highly of their attainments, are like the controversy of those in Plato's den, who having never seen but the shadow of an horse *trajected*, eagerly contended, whether its neighing proceeded from its appearing mane or tail. *Glanville's Sceps.*

If there are different kinds of æther, they have a different degree of rarity; by which it becomes so fit a medium for *trajecting* the light of all cœlestial bodies. *Grew's Cosm. b.* i.

If the sun's light be *trajected* through three or more cross prisms successively, those rays which in the first prism are refracted more than others, are in all the following prisms refracted more than others in the same proportion. *Newton.*

TRAJE'CT. *n. s.* [*trajet*, Fr. *trajectus*, Latin.] A ferry; a passage for a water-carriage.

What notes and garments he doth give thee,
Bring to the *traject*, to the common ferry,
Which trades to Venice. *Shakesp. Merchant of Venice.*

TRAJE'CTION. *n. s.* [*trajectio*, Lat.]

1. The act of darting through.

Later astronomers have observed the free motion of such comets as have, by a *trajection* through the æther, wandered through the cœlestial or interstellar part of the universe. *Boyle.*

2. Emission.

The *trajections* of such an object more sharply pierce the martyred soul of John, than afterwards did the nails the crucified body of Peter. *Brown's Vulgar Err. b.* vii.

To TRAIL. *v. a.* [*trailler*, Fr.]

1. To hunt by the track.

2. To draw along the ground.

Beat thou the drum, that it speak mournfully:
Trail your steel pikes. *Shakesp. Coriolanus.*
Faintly he staggered through the hissing throng,
And hung his head, and *trail'd* his legs along. *Dryden.*

3. To draw after in a long floating or waving body.

What boots the regal circle on his head,
That long behind he *trails* his pompous robe,
And, of all monarchs, only grasps the globe? *Pope.*

4. [*Treglen*, Dutch.] To draw; to drag.

Because they shall not *trail* me through their streets
Like a wild beast, I am content to go. *Milton's Agonistes.*
Thrice happy poet, who may *trail*
Thy house about thee like a snail;
Or harness'd to a nag, at ease
Take journies in it like a chaise;
Or in a boat, whene'er thou wilt,
Canst make it serve thee for a tilt. *Swift.*

To TRAIL. *v. n.* To be drawn out in length.

When his brother saw the red blood *trail*
Adown so fast, and all his armour steepe,
For very felness loud he 'gan to weep. *Fairy Qu. b.* ii.
Since the flames pursu'd the *trailing* smoke,
He knew his boon was granted. *Dryden's Knight's Tale.*
From o'er the roof the blaze began to move,
And *trailing* vanish'd in th' Idean grove.
It swept a path in heav'n, and shone a guide,
Then in a steaming stench of sulphur dy'd. *Dryden's Æn.*

TRAIL. *n. s.* [from the verb.]

1. Scent left on the ground by the animal persued; track followed by the hunter.

See but the issue of my jealousy: if I cry out thus upon no *trail*, never trust me when I open again. *Shakespeare.*

How chearfully on the false *trail* they cry!
Oh, this is counter, you false Danish dogs. *Shakespeare.*
I do think, or else this brain of mine
Hunts not the *trail* of policy so sure
As I have us'd to do, that I have found
The very cause of Hamlet's lunacy. *Shakesp. Hamlet.*

2. Any thing drawn to length.

From thence the fuming *trail* began to spread,
And lambent glories danc'd about her head. *Dryden's Æn.*
When light'ning shoots in glitt'ring *trails* along:
It shines, 'tis true, and gilds the gloomy night;
But when it strikes, 'tis fatal. *Rowe's Royal Convert.*

3. Any thing drawn behind in long undulations.

And round about her work she did empale
With a fair border wrought of sundry flow'rs,
Enwoven with an ivy winding *trail*. *Spenser's Muiopotmos.*
A sudden star it shot through liquid air,
And drew behind a radiant *trail* of hair. *Pope.*

To TRAIN. *v. a.* [*trainer*, Fr.]

1. To draw along.

In hollow cube he *train'd*
His devilish enginry. *Milton.*

2. To draw; to entice; to invite.

If but twelve French
Were there in arms, they would be as a call
To *train* ten thousand English to their side. *Shakespeare.*

2. To draw by artifice or stratagem.

For that cause I *train'd* thee to my house. *Shakespeare.*
Oh *train* me not, sweet mermaid, with thy note!
To drown me in thy sister's flood of tears.
Sing, Syren, to thyself, and I will doat:
Spread o'er the silver waves thy golden hair,
And as a bed I'll take thee, and there lie. *Shakespeare.*

3. To draw from act to act by persuasion or promise.

We did *train* him on,
And his corruption being ta'en from us,
We as the spring of all shall pay for all. *Shak. H.* IV.

4. To educate; to bring up: commonly with *up*.

I can speak English,
For I was *train'd up* in the English court. *Shakespeare.*
A most rare speaker,
To nature none more bound; his *training* such
That he may furnish and instruct great teachers. *Shakesp.*

A place for exercise and *training up* of youth in the fashion of the heathen. 2 *Mac.* iv. 9.

Call some of young years to *train* them *up* in that trade, and so fit them for weighty affairs. *Bacon.*

Spirits *train'd* up in feast and song. *Milton.*

The first Christians were by great hardships *trained up* for glory. *Tillotson's Sermons.*

5. To breed, or form to any thing.

Abram armed his *trained* servants born in his house, and pursued. *Gen.* xiv. 14.

The warrior horse here bred he's taught to *train. Dryd.*

The young soldier is to be *trained* on to the warfare of life; wherein care is to be taken that more things be not represented as dangerous than really are so. *Locke.*

TRAIN. *n. s.* [*train*, Fr.]

1. Artifice; stratagem of enticement.

He cast by treaty and by *trains*
Her to persuade. *Fairy Queen, b.* i.
Their general did with due care provide,
To save his men from ambush and from *train. Fairfax.*
This mov'd the king,
To lay to draw him in by any *train. Daniel's Civil War.*
Swol'n with pride into the snare I fell
Of fair fallacious looks, venereal *trains*,
Soft'ned with pleasure and voluptuous life. *Milton's Agon.*
Now to my charms
And to my wily *trains*! I shall ere long
Be well stock'd with as fair a herd as graz'd
About my mother Circe. *Milton.*

The practice begins of crafty men upon the simple and good; these easily follow and are caught, while the others lay *trains* and pursue a game. *Temple.*

2. The tail of a bird.

Contracting their body, and being forced to draw in their fore parts to establish the hinder in the elevation of the *train*, if the fore parts do part and incline to the ground, the hinder grow too weak, and suffer the *train* to fall. *Brown.*

The bird guideth her body with her *train*, and the ship is steered with the rudder. *Hakewill.*

Th' other, whose gay *train*
Adorns him colour'd with the florid hue
Of rainbows and starry eyes. *Milton.*
Rivers now stream and draw their humid *train. Milton.*

The *train* steers their flights, and turns their bodies like the rudder of a ship; as the kite, by a light turning of his *train*, moves his body which way he pleases. *Ray.*

3. The part of a gown that falls behind upon the ground.

A thousand pounds a year, for pure respect!
That promises more thousands: honour's *train*
Is longer than his fore skirts. *Shakesp. Henry* VIII.

Costly followers are not to be liked, lest while a man makes his *train* longer he makes his wings shorter. *Bacon.*

4. A series; a consecution.

Distinct gradual growth in knowledge carries its own light with it, in every step of its progression, in an easy and orderly *train*. *Locke.*

If we reflect on what is observable in ourselves, we shall find our ideas always passing in *train*, one going and another coming, without intermission. *Locke.*

They laboured in vain so far to reach the apostle's meaning, all along in the *train* of what he said. *Locke.*

Some truths result from any ideas, as soon as the mind puts them into propositions; other truths require a *train* of ideas placed in order, a due comparing of them, and deductions made with attention. *Locke.*

What would'st thou have me do? consider well
The *train* of ills our love would draw behind it. *Addison.*

The author of your beings can by a glance of the eye, or a word speaking, enlighten your mind, and conduct you to a *train* of happy sentiments. *Watts.*

5. Process; method; state of procedure.

If things were once in this *train*, if virtue were established as necessary to reputation, and vice not only loaded with infamy, but made the infallible ruin of all mens pretensions, our duty would take root in our nature. *Swift.*

6. A retinue;

6. A retinue; a number of followers or attendants.

My *train* are men of choice and rareſt parts,
That in the moſt exact regard ſupport
The worſhips of their names. *Shakeſpeare.*

Our ſire walks forth, without more *train*
Accompany'd than with his own complete
Perfections. *Milton's Par. Loſt, b.* v.

Thou ſhould'ſt be ſeen
A goddeſs among gods, ador'd, and ſerv'd
By angels numberleſs, thy daily *train.* *Milton's Par. Loſt.*

Faireſt of ſtars, laſt in the *train* of night,
If better thou belong not to the dawn. *Milton's Par. Loſt.*

He comes not with a *train* to move our fear. *Dryden.*

The king's daughter, with a lovely *train*
Of fellow nymphs, was ſporting on the plain. *Addiſon.*

He would put a check to the fury of war, that a ſtop might be put to thoſe ſins which are of its *train.* *Smalridge.*

7. An orderly company; a proceſſion.

Who the knights in green, and what the *train*
Of ladies dreſs'd with daiſies on the plain? *Dryden.*

8. The line of powder reaching to the mine.

Since firſt they fail'd in their deſigns,
To take in heav'n by ſpringing mines;
And with unanſwerable barrels
Of gun-powder, diſpute their quarrels;
Now take a courſe more practicable,
By laying *trains* to fire the rabble. *Hudibras, p.* iii.

Shall he that gives fire to the *train* pretend to waſh his hands of the hurt that's done by the playing of the mine! *L'Eſtrange's Fables.*

9. TRAIN *of artillery.* Cannons accompanying an army.

With an army abundantly ſupplied with a *train of artillery*, and all other proviſions neceſſary, the king advanced towards Scotland. *Clarendon, b.* ii.

TRAINBA'NDS. *n. ſ.* [*train* and *band:* I ſuppoſe for *trained band.*] The militia; the part of a community trained to martial exerciſe.

He directed the *trainbands* of Weſtminſter and Middleſex, which conſiſted of the moſt ſubſtantial houſholders, to attend. *Clarendon.*

Give commiſſion
To ſome bold man, whoſe loyalty you truſt,
And let him raiſe the *trainbands* of the city. *Dryden.*

A council of war was called, wherein we agreed to retreat: but before we could give the word, the *trainbands*, taking advantage of our delay, fled firſt. *Addiſon's Freeholder.*

TRAINO'IL. *n. ſ.* [*train* and *oil.*] Oil drawn by coction from the fat of the whale.

TRA'INY. *adj.* [from *train.*] Belonging to train oil. A bad word.

Here ſteams aſcend,
Where the huge hogſheads ſweat with *trainy oil.* *Gay.*

To TRAIPSE. *v. a.* [A low word, I believe, without any etymology.] To walk in a careleſs or fluttiſh manner.

Two ſlip-ſhod muſes *traipſe* along,
In lofty madneſs, meditating ſong. *Pope.*

TRAIT. *n. ſ.* [*trait*, Fr.] A ſtroke; a touch. Scarce Engliſh.

By this ſingle *trait* Homer marks an eſſential difference between the Iliad and Odyſſey; that in the former the people periſhed by the folly of their kings; in this by their own folly. *Broome's Notes on the Odyſſey.*

TRA'ITOR. *n. ſ.* [*traitre*, Fr. *traditor*, Lat.] One who being truſted betrays.

The law laid that grievous puniſhment upon *traitors*, to forfeit all their lands to the prince, that men might be terrified from committing treaſons. *Spenſer on Ireland.*

If you flatter him, you are a great *traitor* to him. *Bacon.*

I'll put him thus far into the plot, that he ſhould be ſecured as a *traitor*; but when I am out of reach, he ſhall be releaſed. *Dryden's Spaniſh Fryar.*

There is no difference, in point of morality, whether a man calls me *traitor* in one word, or ſays I am one hired to betray my religion and ſell my country. *Swift.*

TRA'ITORLY. *adj.* [from *traitor.*] Treacherous; perfidious.

Theſe *traitorly* raſcals miſeries are to be ſmil'd at, their offences being ſo capital. *Shakeſp. Winter's Tale.*

TRA'ITOROUS. *adj.* [from *traitor.*] Treacherous; perfidious; faithleſs.

What news with him, that *trait'rous* wight? *Daniel.*

Pontinius knows not you,
While you ſtand out upon theſe *traitorous* terms. *B. Johnſ.*

The *traitorous* or treacherous, who have miſled others, he would have ſeverely puniſhed, and the neutrals noted. *Bacon.*

More of his majeſty's friends have loſt their lives in this rebellion than of his *traiterous* ſubjects. *Addiſon's Freeholder.*

TRA'ITOROUSLY. *adv.* [from *traitorous.*] In a manner ſuiting traitors; perfidiouſly; treacherouſly.

Good duke Humphry *traiterouſly* is murther'd
By Suffolk. *Shakeſp. Henry* VI.

Thou bitter ſweet! whom I had laid
Next me, me *traiterouſly* haſt betray'd;
And unſuſpected half inviſibly
At once fled into him, and ſtay'd with me. *Donne.*

They had *traitorouſly* endeavoured to ſubvert the fundamental laws, deprive the king of his regal power, and to place on his ſubjects a tyrannical power. *Clarendon.*

TRA'ITRESS. *n. ſ.* [from *traitor.*] A woman who betrays.

I, what I am, by what I was, o'ercome:
Traitreſs, reſtore my beauty and my charms,
Nor ſteal my conqueſt with my proper arms. *Dryden.*

Nor did my *traitreſs* wife theſe eye-lids cloſe,
Nor decently in death my limbs compoſe. *Pope's Odyſſey.*

By the dire fury of a *traitreſs* wife,
Ends the ſad evening of a ſtormy life. *Pope's Odyſſey.*

TRALATI'TIOUS. *adj.* [from *tranſlatus*, Lat.] Metaphorical; not literal.

TRALATI'TIOUSLY. *adv.* [from *tralatitious.*] Metaphorically; not literally; not according to the firſt intention of the word.

Language properly is that of the tongue directed to the ear by ſpeaking; written language is *tralatitiouſly* ſo called, becauſe it is made to repreſent to the eye the ſame words which are pronounced. *Holder's Elements of Speech.*

To TRALI'NEATE. *v. n.* [*trans* and *line.*] To deviate from any direction.

If you *tralineate* from your father's mind,
What are you elſe but of a baſtard kind?
Do, as your progenitors have done,
And by their virtues prove yourſelf their ſon. *Dryden.*

TRA'MMEL. *n. ſ.* [*tramail*, Fr. *trama, tragula*, Lat.]

1. A net in which birds or fiſh are caught.

The *trammel* differeth not much from the ſhape of the bunt, and ſerveth to ſuch uſe as the wear and haking. *Carew.*

2. Any kind of net.

Her golden locks ſhe roundly did upty
In braided *trammels*, that no looſer hairs
Did out of order ſtray about her dainty ears. *Fairy Qu.*

3. A kind of ſhackles in which horſes are taught to pace.

I may go ſhufflingly at firſt, for I was never before walked in *trammels*; yet I ſhall drudge at conſtancy, till I have worn off the hitching in my pace. *Dryden's Spaniſh Fryar.*

To TRA'MMEL. *v. a.* [from the noun.] To catch; to intercept.

If th' aſſaſſination
Could *trammel* up the conſequence, and catch
With its ſurceaſe ſucceſs. *Shakeſp. Macbeth.*

To TRA'MPLE. *v. a.* [*trampe*, Daniſh.] To tread under foot with pride, contempt, or elevation.

Caſt not your pearls before ſwine, leſt they *trample* them under their feet. *Mat.* vii. 6.

My ſtrength ſhall *trample* thee as mire. *Milton.*

To TRA'MPLE. *v. n.*

1. To tread in contempt.

Diogenes *trampled* on Plato's pride with greater of his own. *Government of the Tongue.*

Your country's gods I ſcorn,
And *trample* on their ignominious altars. *Rowe.*

2. To tread quick and loudly.

I hear his thund'ring voice reſound,
And *trampling* feet that ſhake the ſolid ground. *Dryden.*

TRA'MPLER. *n. ſ.* [from *trample.*] One that tramples.

TRANA'TION. *n. ſ.* [*trano*, Latin.] The act of ſwimming over.

TRANCE. *n. ſ.* [*tranſe*, Fr. *tranſitus*, Lat. It might therefore be written *tranſe.*] An extaſy; a ſtate in which the ſoul is rapt into viſions of future or diſtant things; a temporary abſence of the ſoul from the body.

Gynecia had been in ſuch a *trance* of muſing, that Zelmane was fighting with the lion before ſhe knew of any lion's coming. *Sidney, b.* i.

Rapt with joy reſembling heavenly madneſs,
My ſoul was raviſht quite as in a *trance.* *Spenſer's Sonnet.*

Abſtract as in a *trance* methought I ſaw. *Milton.*

Sudden he ſtarts,
Shook from his tender *trance.* *Thomſon's Spring.*

TRA'NCED. *adj.* [from *trance.*] Lying in a trance or extaſy.

His grief grew puiſſant, and the ſtrings of life
Began to crack. Twice then the trumpets ſounded,
And there I left him *tranc'd.* *Shakeſp. King Lear.*

TRA'NGRAM. *n. ſ.* [A cant word.] An odd intricately contrived thing.

What's the meaning of all theſe *trangrams* and gimcracks? what are you going about, jumping over my maſter's hedges, and running your lines croſs his grounds? *Arbuthnot.*

TRA'NNEL. *n. ſ.* A ſharp pin.

With a ſmall *trannel* of iron, or a large nail grounded to a ſharp point, they mark the brick. *Moxon's Mech. Exer.*

TRA'NQUIL. *adj.* [*tranquille*, Fr. *tranquillus*, Latin.] Quiet; peaceful; undiſturbed.

I had been happy
So I had nothing known. Oh now, for ever
Farewel the *tranquil* mind! farewel content! *Shakeſpeare.*

TRANQUI'LLITY. *n. ſ.* [*tranquillitas*, Latin; *tranquillité*, Fr.] Quiet; peace of mind; peace of condition; freedom from perturbation.

Leave off,
To let a weary wretch from her due reſt,
And trouble dying ſouls *tranquillity*. *Fairy Qu. b.* ii.

You can ſcarce imagine any hero paſſing from one ſtage of life to another with ſo much *tranquillity*, ſo eaſy a tranſition, and ſo laudable a behaviour. *Pope.*

To TRANSA'CT. *v. a.* [*tranſactus*, Lat.]

1. To manage; to negotiate; to conduct a treaty or affairs.
2. To perform; to do; to carry on.

It cannot be expected they ſhould mention particulars which were *tranſacted* amongſt ſome few of the diſciples only, as the transfiguration and the agony. *Addiſon.*

TRANSA'CTION. *n. ſ.* [*tranſaction*, Fr. from *tranſact.*] Negotiation; dealing between man and man; management; affairs; things managed.

It is not the purpoſe of this diſcourſe to ſet down the particular *tranſactions* of this treaty. *Clarendon, b.* viii.

TRANSANIMA'TION. *n. ſ.* [*trans* and *anima.*] Conveyance of the ſoul from one body to another.

If the *tranſanimation* of Pythagoras were true, that the ſouls of men tranſmigrating into ſpecies anſwering their former natures, ſome men cannot eſcape that very brood whoſe ſire Satan entered. *Brown's Vulgar Errours, b.* vii.

To TRANSCE'ND. *v. a.* [*tranſcendo*, Latin.]

1. To paſs; to overpaſs.

It is a dangerous opinion to ſuch popes, as ſhall *tranſcend* their limits and become tyrannical. *Bacon.*

To judge herſelf, ſhe muſt herſelf *tranſcend*,
As greater circles comprehend the leſs. *Davies.*

2. To ſurpaſs; to outgo; to exceed; to excel.

This glorious piece *tranſcends* what he could think;
So much his blood is nobler than his ink. *Waller.*

Theſe are they
Deſerve their greatneſs and unenvy'd ſtand,
Since what they act *tranſcends* what they command. *Denh.*

High though her wit, yet humble was her mind,
As if ſhe cou'd not, or ſhe wou'd not find,
How much her worth *tranſcended* all her kind. *Dryden.*

3. To ſurmount; to riſe above.

Make diſquiſition whether theſe unuſual lights be meteorological impreſſions not *tranſcending* the upper region, or whether to be ranked among celeſtial bodies. *Howel.*

To TRANSCE'ND. *v. n.* To climb. Not in uſe.

To conclude, becauſe things do not eaſily ſink, they do not drown at all, the fallacy is a frequent addition in human expreſſions, which often give diſtinct accounts of proximity, and *tranſcend* from one unto another. *Brown.*

TRANSCE'NDENCE. }
TRANSCE'NDENCY. } *n. ſ.* [from *tranſcend.*]

1. Excellence; unuſual excellence; ſupereminence.
2. Exaggeration; elevation beyond truth.

It is true greatneſs to have in one the frailty of a man, and the ſecurity of a God: this would have done better in poeſy, where *tranſcendencies* are more allowed. *Bacon's Eſſays.*

TRANSCE'NDENT. *adj.* [*tranſcendens*, Lat. *tranſcendant*, Fr.] Excellent; ſupremely excellent; paſſing others.

Thou, whoſe ſtrong hand, with ſo *tranſcendent* worth,
Holds high the rein of fair Parthenope. *Craſhaw.*

There is, in a lawgiver, a habitual and ultimate intention of a more excellent and *tranſcendent* nature. *Biſhop Sanderſon.*

If thou beeſt he——But O! how fal'n, how chang'd
From him who in the happy realms of light,
Cloath'd with *tranſcendent* brightneſs, didſt outſhine
Myriads, though bright. *Milton.*

Oh charming princeſs! Oh *tranſcendent* maid! *A. Phillips.*

The right our Creator has to our obedience is of ſo high and *tranſcendent* a nature, that it can ſuffer no competition; his commands muſt have the firſt and governing influence on all our actions. *Rogers's Sermons.*

TRANSCENDE'NTAL. *adj.* [*tranſcendentalis*, low Lat.]

1. General; pervading many particulars.
2. Supereminent; paſſing others.

Though the Deity perceiveth not pleaſure nor pain, as we do; yet he muſt have a perfect and *tranſcendental* perception of theſe, and of all other things. *Grew's Coſmol. b.* ii.

TRANSCE'NDENTLY. *adv.* [from *tranſcendent.*] Excellently; ſupereminently.

The law of Chriſtianity is eminently and *tranſcendently* called the word of truth. *South's Sermons.*

To TRA'NSCOLATE. *v. a.* [*trans* and *colo*, Latin.] To ſtrain through a ſieve or colander.

The lungs are, unleſs pervious like a ſpunge, unfit to imbibe and *tranſcolate* the air. *Harvey.*

To TRANSCRI'BE. *v. a.* [*tranſcribo*, Lat. *tranſcrire*, Fr.] To copy; to write from an exemplar.

He was the original of all thoſe inventions from which others did but *tranſcribe* copies. *Clarendon.*

The moſt rigid exactors of mere outward purity do but *tranſcribe* the folly of him who pumps very laboriouſly in a ſhip, yet neglects to ſtop the leak. *Decay of Piety.*

If we imitate their repentance as we *tranſcribe* their faults, we ſhall be received with the ſame mercy. *Rogers.*

TRANSCRI'BER. *n. ſ.* [from *tranſcribe.*] A copier; one who writes from a copy.

A coin is in no danger of having its characters altered by copiers and *tranſcribers*. *Addiſon.*

TRA'NSCRIPT. *n. ſ.* [*tranſcript*, Fr. *tranſcriptum*, Latin.] A copy; any thing written from an original.

The Grecian learning was but a *tranſcript* of the Chaldean and Egyptian; and the Roman of the Grecian. *Glanville.*

The decalogue of Moſes was but a *tranſcript*, not an original. *South's Sermons.*

Dictate, O mighty Judge! what thou haſt ſeen
Of cities and of courts, of books and men,
And deign to let thy ſervant hold the pen.
Through ages thus I may preſume to live,
And from the *tranſcript* of thy proſe receive
What my own ſhort-liv'd verſe can never give. *Prior.*

TRANSCRI'PTION. *n. ſ.* [*tranſcription*, Fr. from *tranſcriptus*, Lat.] The act of copying.

The ancients were but men; the practice of *tranſcription* in our days was no monſter in their's: plagiary had not its nativity with printing, but began in times when thefts were difficult. *Brown's Vulgar Errours, b.* i.

The corruptions that have crept into it by many *tranſcriptions* was the cauſe of ſo great difference. *Brerewood.*

TRANSCRI'PTIVELY. *adv.* [from *tranſcript.*] In manner of a copy.

Not a few *tranſcriptively* ſubſcribing their names to other mens endeavours, tranſcribe all they have written. *Brown.*

To TRANSCU'R. *v. n.* [*tranſcurro*, Lat.] To run or rove to and fro.

By fixing the mind on one object, it doth not ſpatiate and *tranſcur*. *Bacon.*

TRANSCU'RSION. *n. ſ.* [from *tranſcurſus*, Lat.] Ramble; paſſage through; paſſage beyond certain limits; extraordinary deviation.

In a great whale, the ſenſe and the affects of any one part of the body inſtantly make a *tranſcurſion* throughout the whole. *Bacon's Nat. Hiſt.*

I have briefly run over *tranſcurſions*, as if my pen had been poſting with them. *Wotton's Life of Buckingham.*

His philoſophy gives them *tranſcurſions* beyond the vortex we breathe in, and leads them through others which are only known in an hypotheſis. *Glanville's Scep.*

I am to make often *tranſcurſions* into the neighbouring foreſts as I paſs along. *Howel.*

If man were out of the world, who were then left to view the face of heaven, to wonder at the *tranſcurſion* of comets. *More's Antidote againſt Atheiſm.*

TRANSE. *n. ſ.* [*tranſe*, Fr. See TRANCE.] A temporary abſence of the ſoul; an ecſtaſy.

Abſtract as in a *tranſe*, methought I ſaw,
Though ſleeping, where I lay, and ſaw the ſhape
Still glorious before whom awake I ſtood. *Milton.*

TRANSELEMENTA'TION. *n. ſ.* [*trans* and *element.*] Change of one element into another.

Rain we allow; but if they ſuppoſe any other *tranſelementation*, it neither agrees with Moſes's philoſophy, nor Saint Peter's. *Burnet's Theory of the Earth.*

TRANSE'XION. *n. ſ.* [*trans* and *ſexus*, Lat.] Change from one ſex to another.

It much impeacheth the iterated *tranſexion* of hares, if that be true which ſome phyſicians affirm, that tranſmutation of ſexes was only ſo in opinion, and that thoſe transfeminated perſons were really men at firſt. *Brown's Vulgar Errours.*

To TRA'NSFER. *v. a.* [*transferer*, Fr. *transfero*, Lat.]

1. To convey, or make over, from one to another.

He that *transfers* the laws of the Lacedemonians to the people of Athens, ſhould find a great abſurdity and inconvenience. *Spenſer's State of Ireland.*

Was't not enough you took my crown away,
But cruelly you muſt my love betray?
I was well pleas'd to have *transferr'd* my right,
And better chang'd your claim of lawleſs might. *Dryden.*

The king,
Who from himſelf all envy would remove,
Left both to be determin'd by the laws,
And to the Grecian chiefs *transferr'd* the cauſe. *Dryden.*

This was one perverſe effect of their ſitting at eaſe under their vines and fig-trees, that they forget from whence that eaſe came, and *transferred* all the honour of it upon themſelves. *Atterbury's Sermons.*

Your ſacred and religious monarchs own,
When firſt they merit, then aſcend the throne:
But tyrants dread you, leſt your juſt decree
Transfer the power and ſet the people free. *Prior.*

By reading we learn not only the actions and the ſentiments of diſtant nations, but *transfer* to ourſelves the knowledge and improvements of the moſt learned men. *Watts.*

2. To remove; to transport.

The king was much moved with this unexpected accident, because it was stirred in such a place where he could not with safety *transfer* his own person to suppress it. *Bacon's H. VII.*

He thirty rowling years the crown shall wear,
Then from Lavinium shall the seat *transfer*. *Dryden.*

TRANSFIGURA'TION. *n. s.* [*transfiguration*, Fr.]

1. Change of form.

In kinds where the discrimination of sexes is obscure, these transformations are more common, and in some without commixture; as in caterpillars or silkworms, wherein there is a visible and triple *transfiguration*. *Brown's Vulgar Errours.*

2. The miraculous change of our blessed Saviour's appearance on the mount.

It cannot be expected that other authors should mention particulars which were transacted amongst some of the disciples; such as the *transfiguration* and the agony in the garden. *Addis.*

Did Raphael's pencil never chuse to fall?
Say, are his works *transfigurations* all? *Blackmore.*

To TRANSFI'GURE. *v. a.* [*transfigurer*, French; *trans* and *figura*, Lat.] To transform; to change with respect to outward appearance.

Jesus was *transfigured* before them, and his face did shine as the sun, and his raiment was white as the light. *Matth.*

I am the more zealous to *transfigure* your love into devotion, because I have observed your passion to have been extremely impatient of confinement. *Boyle.*

The nuptial right his outrage strait attends,
The dow'r desir'd is his *transfigur'd* friends:
The incantation backward she repeats,
Inverts her rod, and what she did defeats. *Garth.*

To TRANSFI'X. *v. a.* [*transfixus*, Lat.] To pierce through.

Amongst these mighty men were women mix'd;
The bold Semiramis, whose sides *transfix'd*
With son's own blade, her foul reproaches spoke. *Fa. Qu.*

With linked thunderbolts
Transfix us to the bottom of this gulph. *Milton's P. Lost.*

Diana's dart
In an unhappy chace *transfix'd* her heart. *Dryden's Homer.*

Nor good Eurytion envy'd him the prize,
Though he *transfix'd* the pigeon in the skies. *Dryden.*

Till fate shall with a single dart
Transfix the pair it cannot part. *Fenton.*

To TRANSFO'RM. *v. a.* [*transformer*, Fr. *trans* and *forma*, Latin.] To metamorphose; to change with regard to external form.

She demanded of him, whether the goddess of those woods had such a power to *transform* every-body. *Sidney, b.* i.

Love is blind, and lovers cannot see
The pretty follies that themselves commit;
For if they could, Cupid himself would blush
To see me thus *transformed* to a boy. *Shakespeare.*

As is the fable of the lady fair,
Which for her lust was turn'd into a cow;
When thirsty to a stream she did repair,
And saw herself *transform'd* she wist not how. *Davies.*

To TRANSFO'RM. *v. n.* To be metamorphosed.

His hair *transforms* to down, his fingers meet
In skinny films and shape his oary feet. *Addison.*

TRANSFORMA'TION. *n. s.* [from *transform.*] Change of shape; act of changing the form; state of being changed with regard to form.

Something you have heard
Of Hamlet's *transformation*; so I call it,
Since not th' exterior, nor the inward man,
Resembles that it was. *Shakesp. Hamlet.*

What beast could'st thou be, that were not subject to a beast?
And what a beast art thou already, and seest not thy loss in *transformation!* *Shakesp. Timon of Athens.*

The mensuration of all manner of curves, and their mutual *transformation*, are not worth the labour of those who design either of the three learned professions. *Watts.*

TRANSFRETA'TION. *n. s.* [*trans* and *fretum*, Latin.] Passage over the sea.

Since the last *transfretation* of king Richard the second, the crown of England never sent over numbers of men sufficient to defend the small territory. *Davies on Ireland.*

To TRANSFU'SE. *v. a.* [*transfusus*, Lat.] To pour out of one into another.

Between men and beasts there is no possibility of social communion; because the well-spring of that communion is a natural delight which man hath to *transfuse* from himself into others, and to receive from others into himself, especially those things wherein the excellency of this kind doth most consist. *Hooker, b.* i.

Transfus'd on thee his ample spirit rests. *Milton.*

When did his muse from Fletcher scenes purloin,
As thou whose Eth'ridge dost *transfuse* to thine?
But so *transfus'd*, as oil and waters flow,
His always floats above, thine sinks below. *Dryden.*

Where the juices are in a morbid state, if one could suppose all the unsound juices taken away and sound juices immediately *transfused*, the sound juices would grow morbid. *Arb.*

TRANSFU'SION. *n. s.* [*transfusion*, Fr. *transfusus*, Lat.] The act of pouring out of one into another.

The crooked part of the pipe was placed in a box, to prevent the loss of the quicksilver that might fall aside in the *transfusion* from the vessel into the pipe. *Boyle.*

Poesy is of so subtile a spirit, that in the pouring out of one language into another it will all evaporate; and if a new spirit be not added in the *transfusion*, there will remain nothing but a *caput mortuum*. *Denham.*

Something must be lost in all *transfusion*, that is, in all translations, but the sense will remain. *Dryden.*

What noise have we had about transplantation of diseases and *transfusion* of blood. *Baker's Reflections on Learning.*

To TRANSGRE'SS. *v. a.* [*transgresser*, French; *transgressus*, Latin.]

1. To pass over; to pass beyond.

Long stood the noble youth oppress'd with awe,
And stupid at the wond'rous things he saw,
Surpassing common faith, *transgressing* nature's law. *Dryd.*

2. To violate; to break.

Let no man doubt but that every thing is well done, because the world is ruled by so good a guide as *transgresseth* not his own law, than which nothing can be more absolute, perfect, and just. *Hooker, b.* i.

This sorrow we must repeat as often as we *transgress* the divine commandments. *Wake's Preparation for Death.*

To TRANSGRE'SS. *v. n.* To offend by violating a law.

I would not marry her, though she were endowed with all Adam had left him before he *transgressed*. *Shakespeare.*

Achan *transgressed* in the thing accursed. 1 *Chron.* ii. 7.

He upbraideth us with our offending the law, and objecteth to our infamy the *transgressings* of our education. *Wisd.*

TRANSGRE'SSION. *n. s.* [*transgression*, Fr. from *transgress.*]

1. Violation of a law; breach of a command.

Shall I abuse this consecrated gift
Of strength, again returning with my hair
After my great *transgression*: so requite
Favour renew'd, and add a greater sin. *Milton.*

All accusation still is founded upon some law; for where there is no law, there can be no *transgression*; and where there can be no *transgression*, there ought to be no accusation. *South's Sermons.*

2. Offence; crime; fault.

What's his fault?
—The flat *transgression* of a school-boy, who, being overjoy'd with finding a bird's nest, shews it his companion, and he steals it.
—Wilt thou make a trust a *transgression?* The *trangression* is in the stealer. *Shakesp. Much ado abeut nothing.*

Teach us, sweet madam, for our rude *transgression*
Some fair excuse. *Shakesp. Love's Labour lost.*

TRANGRE'SSIVE. *adj.* [from *transgress.*] Faulty; culpable; apt to break laws.

Though permitted unto his proper principles, Adam perhaps would have sinned without the suggestion of Satan, and from the *transgressive* infirmities of himself might have erred alone, as well as the angels before him. *Brown.*

TRANGRE'SSOR. *n. s.* [*transgresseur*, French, from *transgress.*] Lawbreaker; violator of command; offender.

He intended the discipline of the church should be applied to the greatest and most splendid *transgressors*, as well as to the punishment of meaner offenders. *Clarendon.*

I go to judge
On earth these thy *transgressors*; but thou know'st
Whoever judg'd, the worst on me must light
When time shall be. *Milton's Par. Lost, b.* x.

Ill-worthy I, such title should belong
To me *transgressor!* who for thee ordain'd
A help, became thy snare. *Milton's Par. Lost, b.* xi.

TRA'NSIENT. *adj.* [*transiens*, Lat.] Soon past; soon passing; short; momentary; not lasting; not durable.

How soon hath thy prediction, seer blest!
Measur'd this *transient* world, the race of time,
Till time stand fix'd. *Milton.*

He that rides post through a country, may, from the *transient* view, tell how in general the parts lie. *Locke.*

Love hitherto a *transient* guest,
Ne'er held possession in his breast. *Swift.*

What is loose love? a *transient* gust,
A vapour fed from wild desire. *Pope.*

TRA'NSIENTLY. *adv.* [from *transient.*] In passage; with a short passage; not extensively.

I touch here but *transiently*, without any strict method, on some few of those many rules of imitating nature which Aristotle drew from Homer. *Dryden.*

TRA'NSIENTNESS. *n. s.* [from *transient.*] Shortness of continuance; speedy passage.

It were to be wished that all words of this sort, as they resemble the wind in fury and impetuousness, so they might do also in transientness and sudden expiration. *Dec. of Piety.*

TRANSI'LIENCE. } *n. s.* [from *transilio*, Lat.] Leap from thing
TRANSI'LIENCY. } to thing.

By unadvised *transiliency* leaping from the effect to its remotest cause, we observe not the connection of more immediate causalities. *Glanville's Scep.*

TRA'NSIT. *n. s.* [*transitus*, Latin.] In astronomy, the passing of any planet just by or under any fixt star; or of the moon in particular, covering or moving close by any other planet. *Harris.*

TRANSI'TION. *n. s.* [*transitio*, Latin.]

1. Removal; passage.

Heat and cold have a virtual *transition* without communication of substance, but moisture not. *Bacon's Nat. Hist.*

As for the mutation of sexes, and *transition* into one another, we cannot deny it in hares, it being observable in man. *Brown's Vulgar Errours, b.* iii.

I have given some intimations of the changes which happen in the interior parts of the earth, I mean the *transitions* and removes of metals and minerals there. *Woodward.*

2. Change.

The spots are of the same colour throughout, there being an immediate *transition* from white to black, and not declining gradually, and mixing as they approach. *Woodward.*

You can scarce imagine any hero passing from one stage of life to another with so easy a *transition*, and so laudable a behaviour. *Pope.*

As once inclos'd in woman's beauteous mould;
Thence, by a soft *transition* we repair,
From earthly vehicles to these of air. *Pope.*

3. [*Transition*, Fr.] Passage in writing or conversation from one subject to another.

Then with *transition* sweet new speech resumes. *Milton.*

Covetousness was none of his faults, but described as a veil over the true meaning of the poet, which was to satyrize his prodigality and voluptuousness, to which he makes a *transition*. *Dryden.*

TRA'NSITIVE. *adj.* [*transitivus*, Lat.]

1. Having the power of passing.

One cause of cold is the contact of cold bodies; for cold is active and *transitive* into bodies adjacent, as well as heat. *Bacon's Nat. Hist.* N°. 70.

2. [In grammar.]

A verb *transitive* is that which signifies an action, conceived as having an effect upon some object; as *ferio terram*, I strike the earth. *Clarke's Latin Grammar.*

TRA'NSITORILY. *adv.* [from *transitory.*] With speedy evanescence; with short continuance.

TRA'NSITORINESS. *n. s.* [from *transitory.*] Speedy evanescence.

TRA'NSITORY. *n. s.* [*transitoire*, Fr. *transitorius*, from *transeo*, Latin.] Continuing but a short time; speedily vanishing.

If we love things have sought; age is a thing
Which we are fifty years in compassing:
If *transitory* things, which soon decay,
Age must be loveliest at the latest day. *Donne.*

Religion prefers those pleasures which flow from the presence of God evermore, infinitely before the *transitory* pleasures of this world. *Tillotson's Sermons.*

To TRANSLA'TE. *v. n.* [*translatus*, Lat.]

1. To transport; to remove.

Since our father is *translated* unto the gods, our will is that they that are in our realm live quietly. 2 *Mac.* xi. 23.

By faith Enoch was *translated* that he should not see death. *Heb.* xi. 5.

Those argent fields
Translated saints or middle spirits hold. *Milton.*

Of the same soil their nursery prepare
With that of their plantation, lest the tree
Translated should not with the soil agree. *Dryden.*

The gods their shapes to winter birds *translate*,
But both obnoxious to their former fate. *Dryden.*

To go to heaven is to be *translated* to that kingdom you have longed for; to enjoy the glories of eternity. *Wake.*

2. It is particularly used of the removal of a bishop from one see to another.

Fisher, bishop of Rochester, when the king would have *translated* him from that poor bishoprick to a better, he refused, saying, he would not forsake his poor little old wife, with whom he had so long lived. *Camden's Remains.*

3. To transfer from one to another; to convey.

I will *translate* the kingdom from the house of Saul, and set up the throne of David. 2 *Sam.* iii. 10.

Because of unrighteous dealings the kingdom is *translated* from one people to another. *Ecclus.* x. 8.

Lucian affirms the souls of usurers, after their death, to be metempsychosed, or *translated* into the bodies of asses, there to remain for poor men to take their pennyworths out of their bones and sides with the cudgel and spur. *Peacham.*

As there are apoplexies from inveterate gouts, the regimen must be to *translate* the morbifick matter upon the extremities of the body. *Arbuthnot.*

Perverse mankind! whose wills, created free,
Charge all their woes on absolute decree;
All to the dooming gods their guilt *translate*,
And follies are miscall'd the crimes of fate. *Pope.*

4. To change.

One do I personate of Timon's frame,
Whom fortune with her iv'ry hand wafts to her,
Whose present grace to present slaves and servants
Translates his rivals. *Shakesp. Timon of Athens.*

Happy is your grace,
That can *translate* the stubbornness of fortune
Into so quiet and so sweet a style. *Shakesp. As you like it.*

5. [*Translater*, old Fr.] To interpret in another language; to change into another language retaining the sense.

I can construe the action of her familiar stile, and the hardest voice of her behaviour, to be englished right, is, I am Sir John Falstaff's.

—He hath studied her well, and *translated* her out of honesty into English. *Shakesp. Merry Wives of Windsor.*

Nor word for word too faithfully *translate*. *Roscommon.*

Read this ere you *translate* one bit
Of books of high renown. *Swift.*

Were it meant that in despite
Of art and nature such dull clods should write,
Bavius and Mævius had been sav'd by fate
For Settle and for Shadwell to *translate*. *Duke.*

6. To explain. A low colloquial use.

There's matter in these sighs, these profound heaves
You must *translate*; 'tis fit we understand them. *Shakesp.*

TRANSLA'TION. *n. s.* [*translatio*, Lat. *translation*, Fr.]

1. Removal; act of removing.

His disease was an asthma; the cause a metastasis or *translation* of humours from his joints to his lungs. *Harvey.*

Translations of morbifick matter arise in acute distempers. *Arbuthnot.*

2. The removal of a bishop to another see.

If part of the people be somewhat in the election, you cannot make them nulls or cyphers in the privation or *translation*. *Bacon's War with Spain.*

The king, the next time the bishop of London came to him, entertained him with this compellation, my lord's grace of Canterbury, you are very welcome; and gave order for all the necessary forms for the *translation*. *Clarendon.*

3. The act of turning into another language; interpretation.

A book of his travels hath been honoured with *translation* into many languages. *Brown's Vulgar Errours, b.* i.

Nor ought a genius less than his that writ,
Attempt *translation*; for transplanted wit,
All the defects of air and soil doth share,
And colder brains like colder climates are. *Denham.*

4. Something made by translation; version.

Of both *translations*, the better I acknowledge that which cometh nearer to the very letter of the very original verity. *Hooker, b.* v.

TRANSLA'TOR. *n. s.* [*translateur*, old Fr. from *translate.*] One that turns any thing into another language.

A new and nobler way thou dost persue,
To make translations and *translators* too. *Denham.*

No translation our own country ever yet produced, hath come up to that of the Old and New Testament; and I am persuaded, that the *translators* of the Bible were masters of an English stile much fitter for that work than any we see in our present writings, the which is owing to the simplicity that runs through the whole. *Swift.*

TRANSLA'TORY. *n. s.* [from *translate.*] Transferring.

The *translatory* is a lie that transfers the merit of a man's good action to another more deserving. *Arbuthnot.*

TRANSLOCA'TION. *n. s.* [*trans* and *locus*, Latin.] Removal of things reciprocally to each others places.

There happened certain *translocations* at the deluge, the matter constituting animal and vegetable substances being dissolved, and mineral matter substituted in its place, and thereby like *translocation* of metals in some springs. *Woodward.*

TRANSLU'CENCY. *n. s.* [from *translucent.*] Diaphaneity; transparency.

Lumps of rock crystal heated red hot, then quenched in fair water, exchanged their *translucency* for whiteness, the ignition and extinction having cracked each lump into a multitude of minute bodies. *Boyle on Colours.*

TRANSLU'CENT. } *adj.* [*trans* and *lucens* or *lucidus* Lat.]
TRANSLU'CID. } Transparent; diaphanous; clear; giving a passage to the light.

In anger the spirits ascend and wax eager; which is seen in the eyes, because they are *translucid*. *Bacon.*

Wherever fountain or fresh current flow'd
Against the eastern ray, *translucent*, pure,
With touch æthereal of heav'n's fiery rod,
I drank. *Milton.*

The golden ewer a maid obsequious brings,
Replenish'd from the cool *translucent* springs. *Pope's Odys.*

TRA'NSMARINE. *adj.* [*transmarinus*, Latin.] Lying on the other side of the sea; found beyond sea.

If she had not been drained this way, she might have made herself mistress of Timaurania, her next *transmarine* neighbour. *Howel's Vocal Forest.*

To TRA'NSMEW. *v. a.* [*transmuto*, Lat. *transmuer*, French.] To transmute; to transform; to metamorphose; to change. Obsolete.

When him list the rascal routs appall,
Men into stones therewith he could *transmew*,
And stones to dust, and dust to nought at all. *Fa. Queen.*

TRA'NSMIGRANT. *adj.* [*transmigrans*, Lat.] Passing into another country or state.

Besides an union in sovereignty, or a conjunction in pacts, there are other implicit confederations, that of colonies or *transmigrants* towards their mother nation. *Bacon's holy War.*

To TRA'NSMIGRATE. *v. n.* [*transmigro*, Lat.] To pass from one place or country into another.

This complexion is maintain'd by generation; so that strangers contract it not, and the natives which *transmigrate* omit it not without commixture. *Brown's Vulgar Errours.*

If Pythagoras's transanimation were true, that the souls of men *transmigrating* into species answering their former natures, some men must live over many serpents. *Brown's Vulg. Err.*

Their souls may *transmigrate* into each other. *Howel.*

Regard
The port of Luna, says our learned bard;
Who, in a drunken dream, beheld his soul
The fifth within the *transmigrating* roll. *Dryden.*

TRANSMIGRA'TION. *n. s.* [*transmigration*, Fr. from *transmigrate*.] Passage from one place or state into another.

The sequel of the conjunction of natures in the person of Christ is no abolishment of natural properties appertaining to either substance, no transition or *transmigration* thereof out of one substance into another. *Hooker, b.* v.

Seeing the earth of itself puts forth plants without seed, plants may well have a *transmigration* of species. *Bacon.*

From the opinion of the metempsychosis, or *transmigration* of the souls of men into the bodies of beasts, most suitable unto their human condition, after his death, Orpheus the musician became a swan. *Brown's Vulgar Errours.*

Easing their passage hence, for intercourse
Of *transmigration*, as their lot shall lead. *Milton.*

'Twas taught by wise Pythagoras,
One soul might through more bodies pass:
Seeing such *transmigration* there,
She thought it not a fable here. *Denham.*

When thou wert form'd, heav'n did a man begin,
But the brute soul by chance was shuffled in:
In woods and wilds thy monarchy maintain,
Where valiant beasts, by force and rapine, reign.
In life's next scene, if *transmigration* be,
Some bear or lion is reserv'd for thee. *Dryden's Aureng.*

TRANSMI'SSION. *n. s.* [*transmission*, Fr. *transmissus*, Latin.] The act of sending from one place to another, or from one person to another.

If there were any such notable *transmission* of a colony hither out of Spain, the very chronicles of Spain would not have omitted so memorable a thing. *Spenser on Ireland.*

Operations by *transmission* of spirits is one of the highest secrets in nature. *Bacon's Nat. Hist.* N°. 236.

In the *transmission* of the sea-water into the pits, the water riseth; but in the *transmission* of the water through the vessels it falleth. *Bacon.*

These move swiftly, but then they require a medium well disposed, and their *transmission* is easily stopped. *Bacon.*

The uvea has a musculous power, and can dilate and contract that round hole in it called the pupil, for the better moderating the *transmission* of light. *More.*

Languages of countries are lost by *transmission* or colonies of a different language. *Hale's Origin of Mankind.*

This enquiry will be of use, as a parallel discovery of the *transmission* of the English laws into Scotland. *Hale.*

Their reflexion or *transmission* depends on the constitution of the air and water behind the glass, and not the striking of the rays upon the parts of the glass. *Newton's Opticks.*

TRANSMI'SSIVE. *adj.* [from *transmissus*, Lat.] Transmitted; derived from one to another.

And still the fire inculcates to his son
Transmissive lessons of the king's renown. *Prior.*

Itself a sun; it with *transmissive* light
Enlivens worlds deny'd to human sight. *Prior.*

Then grateful Greece with streaming eyes would raise
Historick marbles to record his praise;
His praise eternal on the faithful stone,
Had with *transmissive* honour grac'd his son. *Pope.*

To TRANSMI'T. *v. a.* [*transmitto*, Lat. *transmettre*, Fr.] To send from one person or place to another.

By means of writing, former ages *transmit* the memorials of ancient times and things to posterity. *Hale.*

He sent orders to his friend in Spain to sell his estate, and *transmit* the money to him. *Addison's Spect.* N°. 198.

Thus flourish'd love, and beauty reign'd in state,
Till the proud Spaniard gave this glory's date:
Past is the gallantry, the same remains,
Transmitted safe in Dryden's lofty scenes. *Granville.*

Shine forth, ye planets, with distinguish'd light;
Again *transmit* your friendly beams to earth,
As when Britannia joy'd for Anna's birth. *Prior.*

TRANSMI'TTAL. *n. s.* [from *transmit*.] The act of transmitting; transmission.

Besides the *transmittal* to England of two-thirds of the revenues of Ireland, they make our country a receptacle for their supernumerary pretenders to offices. *Swift.*

TRANSMU'TABLE. *adj.* [*transmuable*, Fr. from *transmute*.] Capable of change; possible to be changed into another nature or substance.

It is no easy matter to demonstrate that air is so much as convertible into water; how *transmutable* it is unto flesh may be of deeper doubt. *Brown's Vulg. Err. b.* iii.

The fluids and solids of an animal body are easily *transmutable* into one another. *Arbuthnot on Aliments.*

TRANSMU'TABLY. *adv.* [from *transmute*.] With capacity of being changed into another substance or nature.

TRANSMUTA'TION. *n. s.* [*transmutation*, Fr. *transmutatio*, from *transmuto*, Latin.] Change into another nature or substance. The great aim of alchemy is the transmutation of base metals into gold.

Am not I old Sly's son, by birth a pedlar, by education a cardmaker, by *transmutation* a bear herd. *Shakespeare.*

The *transmutation* of plants one into another, is *inter magnalia naturæ*, for the *transmutation* of species is, in the vulgar philosophy, pronounced impossible; but seeing there appear some manifest instances of it, the opinion of impossibility is to be rejected, and the means thereof to be found out. *Bac.*

The conversion into a body merely new, and which was not before; as silver to gold, or iron to copper, is better called, for distinction sake, *transmutation*. *Bacon.*

The same land suffereth sundry *transmutations* of owners within one term. *Bacon's Office of Alienation.*

The changing of bodies into light, and light into bodies, is very conformable to the course of nature, which seems delighted with *transmutations*. Water, which is a very fluid tasteless salt, she changes by heat into vapour, which is a sort of air, and by cold into ice, which is a hard, pellucid, brittle, fusible stone; and this stone returns into water by heat, and water returns into vapour by cold. *Newton.*

The supposed change of worms into flies is no real *transmutation*; but most of those members, which at last become visible to the eye, are existent at the beginning, artificially complicated together. *Bentley's Sermons.*

To TRANSMU'TE. *v. n.* [*transmuto*, Lat. *transmuer*, French.] To change from one nature or substance to another.

Suidas thinks, that by the golden fleece was meant a golden book of parchment which is of sheeps-skin, and therefore called golden, because it was taught therein how other metals might be *transmuted*. *Raleigh.*

That metals may be *transmuted* one into another I am not satisfied of the fact. *Ray on the Creation.*

Patience sov'reign o'er *transmuted* ill. *Van. of hu. Wishes.*

TRANSMU'TER. *n. s.* [from *transmute*.] One that transmutes.

TRA'NSOM. *n. s.* [*transenna*, Lat.]

1. A thwart beam or lintel over a door.
2. [Among mathematicians.] The vane of an instrument called a cross staff, being a piece of wood fixed across with a square socket upon which it slides. *Bailey.*

TRANSPA'RENCY. *n. s.* [*transparence*, Fr. from *transparent*.] Clearness; diaphaneity; translucence; power of transmitting light.

A poet of another nation would not have dwelt so long upon the clearness and *transparency* of the stream; but in Italy one seldom sees a river that is extremely bright and limpid, most of them being muddy. *Addison.*

Another cause is the greater *transparency* of the vessels occasioned by the thinness and delicacy of their coats. *Arbuth.*

TRANSPA'RENT. *n. s.* [*transparent*, Fr. *trans* and *appareo*, Latin.] Pervious to the light; clear; pellucid; diaphanous; translucent; not opaque.

Nor shines the silver moon one half so bright,
Through the *transparent* bosom of the deep,
As doth thy face through tears of mine give light,
Thou shin'st in every tear that I do weep. *Shakespeare.*

Wait upon him with whom you speak with your eye; for there be many wise men that have secret hearts and *transparent* countenances. *Bacon's Essays*, N°. 23.

Each thought was visible that roll'd within,
As through a crystal case the figur'd hours are seen;
And heav'n did this *transparent* veil provide,
Because she had no guilty thought to hide. *Dryden.*

Her bosom appeared all of chrystal, and so wonderfully *transparent*, that I saw every thought in her heart. *Addison.*

Transparent forms, too fine for mortal sight,
Their fluid bodies half-dissolv'd in light. *Pope.*

TRANSPI'CUOUS.

TRANSPI'CUOUS. *adj.* [*trans* and *ſpecio*, Latin.] Tranſparent; pervious to the ſight.

What if that light,
Sent from her through the wide *tranſpicuous* air,
To the terreſtrial moon be as a ſtar. *Milton.*
Now thy wine's *tranſpicuous*, purg'd from all
Its earthy groſs, yet let it feed awhile
On the fat refuſe. *Philips.*

To TRANSPI'ERCE. *v. n.* [*tranſpercer*, Fr. *trans* and *pierce.*] To penetrate; to make way through; to permeate.

A mind, which through each part infus'd doth paſs,
Faſhions and works, and wholly doth *tranſpierce*
All this great body of the univerſe. *Raleigh's H. of the W.*
His forceful ſpear, which, hiſſing as it flew,
Pierc'd through the yielding planks of jointed wood:
The ſides *tranſpierc'd* return a rattling ſound,
And groans of Greeks inclos'd came iſſuing through the wound. *Dryden's Æn.*

TRANSPIRA'TION. *n. ſ.* [*tranſpiration*, Fr.] Emiſſion in vapour.

That a bullet dipped in oil, by preventing the *tranſpiration* of air, will carry farther, and pierce deeper, my experience cannot diſcern. *Brown's Vulgar Errours, b.* ii.

The *tranſpiration* of the obſtructed fluids is imagined to be one of the ways that an inflammation is removed. *Sharp.*

To TRANSPI'RE. *v. a.* [*tranſpiro*, Lat. *tranſpirer*, French.] To emit in vapour.

To TRANSPI'RE. *v. n.* [*tranſpirer*, Fr.]

1. To be emitted by inſenſible vapour.

The nuts when freſh got are full of a ſoft pulpy matter, which in time *tranſpires*, and paſſes through the ſhell. *Woodward on Foſſils.*

2. To eſcape from ſecreſy to notice: a ſenſe lately innovated from *France*, without neceſſity.

To TRANSPLA'CE. *v. a.* [*trans* and *place.*] To remove; to put into a new place.

It was *tranſplaced* from the left ſide of the Vatican unto a more eminent place. *Wilkins's Math. Magick.*

To TRANSPLA'NT. *v. a.* [*trans* and *planto*, Lat. *tranſplanter*, Fr.]

1. To remove and plant in a new place.

The nobleſt fruits *tranſplanted* in our iſle,
With early hope and fragrant bloſſoms ſmile. *Roſcommon.*
Salopian acres flouriſh with a growth,
Peculiar ſtil'd the Ottley; be thou firſt
This apple to *tranſplant.* *Phillips.*

If any *tranſplant* themſelves into plantations abroad, who are ſchiſmaticks or outlaws, ſuch are not fit to lay the foundation of a new colony. *Bacon's Advice to Villiers.*

2. To remove.

Of light the greater part he took
Tranſplanted from her cloudy ſhrine, and plac'd
In the ſun's orb. *Milton.*

He proſpered at the rate of his own wiſhes, being *tranſplanted* out of his cold barren dioceſe of Saint David's into a warmer climate. *Clarendon.*

TRANSPLANTA'TION. *n. ſ.* [*tranſplantation*, Fr.]

1. The act of tranſplanting or removing to another ſoil.

It is confeſſed, that love changed often doth nothing; nay, it is nothing; for love where it is kept fixed to its firſt object, though it burn not, yet it warms and cheriſhes, ſo as it needs no *tranſplantation*, or change of ſoil, to make it fruitful. *Suckling.*

2. Conveyance from one to another.

What noiſe have we had for ſome years about *tranſplantation* of diſeaſes, and transfuſion of blood. *Baker.*

3. Removal of men from one country to another.

Moſt of kingdoms have throughly felt the calamities of forcible *tranſplantations*, being either overwhelmed by new colonies that fell upon them, or driven, as one wave is driven by another to ſeek new ſeats, having loſt their own. *Raleigh.*

This appears a replication to what Menelaus had offered concerning the *tranſplantation* of Ulyſſes to Sparta. *Broome.*

TRANSPLA'NTER. *n. ſ.* [from *tranſplant.*] One that tranſplants.

To TRANSPO'RT. *v. a.* [*trans* and *porto*, Latin; *tranſporter*, French.]

1. To convey by carriage from place to place.

I came hither to *tranſport* the tidings. *Shakeſpeare.*
Why ſhould ſhe write to Edmund! might not you
Tranſport her purpoſes by word. *Shakeſpeare.*

Impoſe upon men the tranſportation of rivers from one end of the world to the other, which, among other uſes, were made to *tranſport* men. *Raleigh's Hiſt. of the World.*

A ſubterranean wind *tranſports* a hill
Torn from Pilorus. *Milton.*

In the diſturbances of a ſtate, the wiſe Pomponius *tranſported* all the remaining wiſdom and virtue of his country into the ſanctuary of peace and learning. *Dryden.*

2. To carry into baniſhment: as a felon.

We return after being *tranſported*, and are ten times greater rogues than before. *Swift.*

3. To ſentence as a felon to baniſhment.

4. To hurry by violence of paſſion.

You are *tranſported* by calamity
Thither where more attends you, and you ſlander
The helms o' th' ſtate. *Shakeſpeare.*
They laugh as if *tranſported* with ſome fit
Of paſſion. *Milton.*

I ſhew him once *tranſported* by the violence of a ſudden paſſion. *Dryden.*

If an ally not immediately concerned contribute more than the principal party, he ought to have his ſhare in what is conquered; or if his romantick diſpoſition *tranſport* him ſo far as to expect little or nothing, they ſhould make it up in dignity. *Swift.*

5. To put into ecſtaſy; to raviſh with pleaſure.

Here *tranſported* I behold, *tranſported* touch. *Milton.*

Thoſe on whom Chriſt beſtowed miraculous cures were ſo *tranſported* with them, that their gratitude ſupplanted their obedience. *Decay of Piety.*

TRA'NSPORT. *n. ſ.* [*tranſport*, Fr. from the verb.]

1. Tranſportation; carriage; conveyance.

The Romans neglected their maritime affairs; for they ſtipulated with the Carthaginians to furniſh them with ſhips for *tranſport* and war. *Arbuthnot on Coins.*

2. A veſſel of carriage; particularly a veſſel in which ſoldiers are conveyed.

Nor dares his *tranſport* veſſel croſs the waves,
With ſuch whoſe bones are not compos'd in graves. *Dryd.*

Some ſpoke of the men of war only, and others added the *tranſports.* *Arbuthnot on Coins.*

3. Rapture; ecſtaſy.

A truly pious mind receives a temporal bleſſing with *gratitude*, a ſpiritual one with ecſtaſy and *tranſport.* *South's Serm.*

TRANSPO'RTANCE. *n. ſ.* [from *tranſport.*] Conveyance; carriage; removal.

O, be thou my Charon,
And give me ſwift *tranſportance* to thoſe fields,
Where I may wallow in the lilly beds
Propos'd for the deſerver! *Shakeſp. Troilus and Creſſida.*

TRANSPORTA'TION. *n. ſ.* [from *tranſport.*]

1. Removal; conveyance; carriage.

Sir Francis Cottington and Mr. Endymion Porter had been ſent before to provide a veſſel for their *tranſportation.* *Wotton's Life of Buckingham.*

Some were not ſo ſolicitous to provide againſt the plague, as to know whether we had it from the malignity of our own air, or by *tranſportation.* *Dryden.*

2. Baniſhment for felony.

3. Ecſtatick violence of paſſion.

All pleaſures that affect the body muſt needs weary, becauſe they tranſport, and all *tranſportation* is a violence; and no violence can be laſting but determines upon the falling of the ſpirits. *South.*

TRANSPO'RTER. *n. ſ.* [from *tranſport.*] One that tranſports.

The pilchard merchant may reap a ſpeedy benefit by diſpatching, ſaving, and ſelling to the *tranſporters.* *Carew.*

TRANSPO'SAL. *n. ſ.* [from *tranſpoſe.*] The act of putting things in each other's place. *Swift.*

To TRANSPO'SE. *v. a.* [*tranſpoſer*, French; *tranſpoſitum*, Latin.]

1. To put each in the place of other.

The letters of Elizabetha regina *tranſpoſed* ſignify, O England's ſovereign, thou haſt made us happy. *Camden's Rem.*

Tranſpoſe the propoſitions, making the medius terminus the predicate of the firſt and the ſubject of the ſecond. *Locke.*

2. To put out of place.

That which you are my thoughts cannot *tranſpoſe*;
Angels are bright ſtill, though the brighteſt fell. *Shakeſp.*

TRANSPOSI'TION. *n. ſ.* [*tranſpoſition*, Fr. from *tranſpoſe.*]

1. The act of putting one thing in the place of another.

2. The ſtate of being put out of one place into another.

The common centre of gravity in the terraqueous globe is ſteady, and not liable to any accidental *tranſpoſition*, nor hath it ever ſhifted its ſtation. *Woodward's Nat. Hiſt. p.* i.

To TRANSSHA'PE. *v. a.* [*trans* and *ſhape.*] To transform; to bring into another ſhape.

I'll tell thee how Beatrice prais'd thy wit: I ſaid thou hadſt a fine wit; right, ſaid ſhe, a fine little one; nay, ſaid I, he hath the tongues; that I believe, ſaid ſhe; for he ſwore a thing to me on Monday night which he forſwore on Tueſday morning; there's a double tongue: thus did ſhe *tranſſhape* thy particular virtues. *Shakeſp. Much ado about nothing.*

To TRANSUBSTA'NTIATE. *v. a.* [*tranſubſtantier*, Fr.] To change to another ſubſtance.

O ſelf traitor, I do bring
The ſpider love which *tranſubſtantiates* all,
And can convert manna to gall. *Donne.*
Nor ſeemingly, but with keen diſpatch
Of real hunger, and concoctive heat
To *tranſubſtantiate*; what redounds, tranſpires
Through ſpirits with eaſe. *Milton.*

TRANSUBSTANTIA'TION. *n. s.* [*transubstantiation*, Fr.] A miraculous operation believed in the Romish church, in which the elements of the eucharist are supposed to be changed into the real body and blood of CHRIST.

How is a Romanist prepared easily to swallow, not only against all probability, but even the clear evidence of his senses, the doctrine of *transubstantiation?* *Locke.*

TRANSUDA'TION. *n. s.* [from *transude.*] The act of passing in sweat, or perspirable vapour, through any integument.

The drops proceeded not from the *transudation* of the liquors within the glass. *Boyle.*

To TRANSU'DE. *v. n.* [*trans* and *sudo*, Latin.] To pass through in vapour.

Purulent fumes cannot be transmitted throughout the body before the maturation of an aposthem, nor after, unless the humour break; because they cannot *transude* through the bag of an aposthem. *Harvey on Consumptions.*

TRANSVE'RSAL. *adj.* [*transversal*, Fr. *trans* and *versalis*, Lat.] Running crosswise.

An ascending line, direct, as from son to father, or grandfather, is not admitted by the law of England; or in the *transversal* line, as to the uncle or aunt, great-uncle or great-aunt. *Hale.*

TRANSVE'RSALLY. *adv.* [from *transversal.*] In a cross direction.

There are divers subtile enquiries and demonstrations concerning the several proportions of swiftness and distance in an arrow shot vertically, horizontally, or *transversally.* *Wilkins.*

TRANSVE'RSE. *adj.* [*transversus*, Latin.] Being in a cross direction.

His violent touch
Fled and pursu'd *transverse* the resonant fugue. *Milton.*

Part in strait lines, part in *transverse* are found,
One forms a crooked figure, one a round;
The entrails these embrace in spiral strings,
Those clasp th' arterial tubes in tender rings. *Blackmore.*

What natural agent could impel them so strongly with a *transverse* side-blow against that tremendous weight and rapidity, when whole worlds are a falling! *Bentley's Sermons.*

TRANSVE'RSELY. *adv.* [from *transverse.*] In a cross direction.

At Stonehenge the stones lie *transversely* upon each other. *Stillingfleet.*

In all the fibres of an animal there is a contractile power; for if a fibre be cut *transversely*, both the ends shrink and make the wound gape. *Arbuthnot on Aliments.*

TRANSU'MPTION. *n. s.* [*trans* and *sumo*, Latin.] The act of taking from one place to another.

TRAN'TERS. *n. s.* Men who carry fish from the sea-coasts to sell in the inland countries. *Bailey.*

TRAP. *n. s.* [trappe, Saxon; *trape*, Fr. *trappola*, Italian.]

1. A snare set for thieves or vermin.

Die as thou shouldest, but do not die impatiently, and like a fox catched in a *trap.* *Taylor's holy living.*

The *trap* springs and catches the ape by the fingers. *L'Estr.*

2. An ambush; a stratagem to betray or catch unawares.

And lurking closely, in await now lay,
How he might any in his *trap* betray. *Spenser.*

God and your majesty
Protect mine innocence, or I fall into
The *trap* is laid for me. *Shakesp. Henry VIII.*

They continually laid *traps* to ensnare him, and made sinister interpretations of all the good he did. *Calamy.*

He seems a *trap* for charity to lay,
And cons by night his lesson for the day. *Dryden.*

3. A play at which a ball is driven with a stick.

Unruly boys learn to wrangle at *trap*, or rook at span-farthing. *Locke on Education.*

He that of feeble nerves and joints complains,
From nine-pins, coits, and from *trap*-ball abstains. *King.*

To TRAP. *v. a.* [trappan, Saxon.]

1. To ensnare; to catch by a snare or ambush; to take by stratagem.

My brain, more busy than the lab'ring spider,
Weaves tedious snares to *trap* mine enemies. *Shakesp.*

If you require my deeds, with ambush'd arms
I *trapp'd* the foe, or tir'd with false alarms. *Dryden.*

2. [See TRAPPING.] To adorn; to decorate.

The steed that bore him
Was *trapp'd* with polish'd steel, all shining bright,
And covered with th' atchievements of the knight. *Spenser.*

To spoil the dead of weed is sacrilege:
But leave these reliques of his living might
To deck his hearse and *trap* his tomb black steed. *Fa. Qu.*

Lord Lucius presented to you four milk-white horses *trapt* in silver. *Shakesp. Timon of Athens.*

TRAPDO'OR. *n. s.* [*trap* and *door.*] A door opening and shutting unexpectedly.

The arteries which carry from the heart to the several parts have valves which open outward like *trapdoors*, and give the blood a free passage; and the veins, which bring it back to the heart, have valves and *trapdoors* which open inwards, so as to give way into the blood to run into the heart. *Ray.*

To TRAPE. *v. a.* [commonly written *to traipse:* probably of the same original with *drab.*] To run idly and sluttishly about. It is used only of women.

TRAPES. *n. s.* [I suppose from *trape.*] An idle slatternly woman.

He found the sullen *trapes*
Possest with th' devil, worms, and claps. *Hudibras, p.* iii.

From door to door I'd sooner whine and beg,
Than marry such a *trapes.* *Gay's What d'ye call it.*

TRA'PSTICK. *n. s.* [*trap* and *stick.*] A stick with which boys drive a wooden ball.

A foolish swoop between a couple of thick bandy legs and two long *trapsticks* that had no calfs. *Spect.* N. 559.

TRAPE'ZIUM. *n. s.* [τραπέζιον; *trapese*, French.] A quadrilateral figure, whose four sides are not equal, and none of its sides parallel. *Dict.*

Two of the lateral *trapezia* are as broad. *Woodward.*

TRAPEZO'ID. *n. s.* [τραπέζιον and εἶδος; *trapesoide*, Fr.] An irregular figure, whose four sides are not parallel. *Dict.*

TRA'PPINGS. *n. s.* [This word *Minshew* derives from *drap*, French, *cloath.*]

1. Ornaments appendant to the saddle.

Caparisons and steeds,
Bases and tinsel *trappings*, gorgeous knights
At joust and tournament. *Milton.*

2. Ornaments; dress; embellishments; external, superficial, and trifling decoration.

These indeed seem,
But I have that within which passeth shew;
These but the *trappings* and the suits of woe. *Shakespeare.*

He has fair words, rich *trappings*, and large promises; but works only for his master. *L'Estrange.*

The points of honour poets may produce,
Trappings of life, for ornament, not use. *Dryden.*

Such pageantry be to the people shown;
There boast thy horse's *trappings*, and thy own. *Dryden.*

Draw him strictly so,
That all who view the piece may know
He needs no *trappings* of fictitious fame. *Dryden.*

In ships decay'd no mariner confides,
Lur'd by the gilded stern and painted sides;
Yet at a ball unthinking fools delight,
In the gay *trappings* of a birth-day night. *Swift.*

TRASH. *n. s.* [*tros*, Islandick; *drusen*, German.]

1. Any thing worthless; dross; dregs.

Lay hands upon these traitors, and their *trash.* *Shakesp.*

Look what a wardrobe here is for thee!
—Let it alone, thou fool, it is but *trash.* *Shakespeare.*

Who steals my purse, steals *trash*; 'tis something, nothing;
'Twas mine, 'tis his; and has been slave to thousands.
But he that filches from me my good name,
Robs me of that which not enriches him,
And makes me poor indeed. *Shakespeare's Othello.*

More than ten Hollenshed's, or Hall's, or Stow's,
Of trivial houshold *trash* he knows; he knows
When the queen frown'd or smil'd. *Donne.*

The collectors only consider, the greater fame a writer is in possession of, the more *trash* he may bear to have tacked to him. *Swift.*

Weak foolish man! will heav'n reward us there
With the same *trash* mad mortals wish for here? *Pope.*

2. A worthless person.

I suspect this *trash*
To be a party in this injury. *Shakespeare's Othello.*

3. Matter improper for food, frequently eaten by girls in the green sickness.

O that instead of *trash* thou'dst taken steel. *Garth.*

4. I believe that the original signification of *trash* is the loppings of trees, from the verb.

To TRASH. *v. a.*

1. To lop; to crop.

Being once perfected how to grant suits,
How to deny them; whom t' advance, and whom
To *trash* for overtopping. *Shakespeare's Tempest.*

2. To crush; to humble.

Not such as was fit to be imposed on hard-hearted Jews, to encumber and *trash* them, but such as becomes an ingenuous people. *Hammond's Pract. Catechism.*

TRA'SHY. *adj.* [from *trash.*] Worthless; vile; useless.

A judicious reader will discover in his closet that *trashy* stuff, whose glittering deceived him in the action. *Dryden.*

To TRA'VAIL. *v. n.* [*travailler*, Fr.]

1. To labour; to toil.

2. To be in labour; to suffer the pains of childbirth.

I *travail* not, nor bring forth children. *Isa.* xxiii. 4.

She being with child cried, *travailing* in birth, and pained to be delivered. *Rev.* xii. 2.

His heart is in continual labour; it *travails* with the obligation, and is in pangs till it be delivered. *South's Serm.*

To

To TRA'VAIL. *v. a.* To harrass; to tire.

As if all these troubles had not been sufficient to *travail* the realm, a great division fell among the nobility. *Hayward.*

A gleam of light turn'd thitherward in haste
His *travell'd* steps. *Milton.*

TRA'VAIL. *n. s.* [from the verb.]

1. Labour; toil; fatigue.

As every thing of price, so this doth require *travail.* *Hook.*

Such impotent persons as are unable for strong *travail*, are yet able to drive cattle to and fro to their pasture. *Spenser.*

2. Labour in childbirth.

In the time of her *travail* twins were in her. *Gen.* xxxviii.

To procure easy *travails* of women, the intention is to bring down the child, but not too fast. *Bacon's Nat. Hist.*

TRAVE, TRAVE'L, or TRAVI'SE. *n. s.* A wooden frame for shoeing unruly horses. *Ainsworth.*

To TRA'VEL. *v. n.* [This word is generally supposed originally the same with *travail*, and to differ only as particular from general: in some writers the word is written alike in all its senses; but it is more convenient to write *travail* for *labour*, and *travel* for *journey.*]

1. To make journeys: it is used for sea as well as land, though sometimes we distinguish it from *voyage*, a word appropriated to the sea.

In the forest shall ye lodge, O ye *travelling* companies of Dedanim. *Isa.* xxi. 13.

Raphael deign'd to *travel* with Tobias. *Milton.*

Fain wou'd I *travel* to some foreign shore,
So might I to myself myself restore. *Dryden.*

If others believed he was an Egyptian from his knowledge of their rites, it proves at least that he *travelled* there. *Pope.*

2. To pass; to go; to move.

By th' clock 'tis day;
And yet dark night strangles the *travelling* lamp. *Shakesp.*

Time *travels* in divers paces, with divers persons; I'll tell you who time ambles withal, who time trots withal. *Shakesp.*

Thus flying East and West, and North and South,
News *travell'd* with increase from mouth to mouth. *Pope.*

3. To make journeys of curiosity.

Nothing tends so much to enlarge the mind as *travelling*, that is, making a visit to other towns, cities, or countries, beside those in which we were born and educated. *Watts.*

4. To labour; to toil. This should be rather *travail.*

If we labour to maintain truth and reason, let not any think that we *travel* about a matter not needful. *Hooker.*

I've watch'd and *travell'd* hard;
Some time I shall sleep out; the rest I'll whistle. *Shakesp.*

To TRA'VEL. *v. a.*

1. To pass; to journey over.

Thither to arrive I *travel* thus profound. *Milton.*

2. To force to journey.

There are other privileges granted unto most of the corporations, that they shall not be charged with garrisons, and they shall not be *travelled* forth of their own franchises. *Spens.*

TRA'VEL. *n. s.* [*travail*, Fr. from the noun.]

1. Journey; act of passing from place to place.

Love had cut him short,
Confin'd within the purlieus of his court.
Three miles he went, nor farther could retreat,
His *travels* ended at his country-seat. *Dryden.*

Mingled send into the dance
Moments fraught with all the treasures,
Which thy eastern *travel* views. *Prior.*

2. Journey of curiosity or instruction.

Let him spend his time no more at home,
Which would be great impeachment to his age,
In having known no *travel* in his youth. *Shakespeare.*

Travel in the younger sort is a part of education; in the elder a part of experience. *Bacon's Essays*, N°. 18.

A man not enlightened by *travel* or reflexion, grows as fond of arbitrary power, to which he hath been used, as of barren countries, in which he has been born and bred. *Addis.*

3. Labour; toil. This should be *travail:* as in *Daniel.*

He wars with a retiring enemy,
With much more *travail* than with victory. *Daniel.*

What think'st thou of our empire now, though earn'd
With *travel* difficult. *Milton.*

4. Labour in childbirth. This sense belongs rather to *travail.*

Thy mother well deserves that short delight,
The nauseous qualms of ten long months and *travel* to requite. *Dryden's Virg.*

4. TRAVELS. Account of occurrences and observations of a journey into foreign parts.

A book of his *travels* hath been honoured with the translation of many languages. *Brown's Vulgar Errours.*

Histories engage the soul by sensible occurrences; as also voyages, *travels*, and accounts of countries. *Watts.*

TRA'VELLER. *n. s.* [*travailleur*, Fr. from *travel.*]

1. One who goes a journey; a wayfarer.

The weary *traveller* wand'ring that way
Therein did often quench his thirsty heat *Fairy Qu. b.* ii.

A little ease to these my torments give,
Before I go where all in silence mourn,
From whose dark shores no *travellers* return. *Sandys.*

This was a common opinion among the Gentiles, that the gods sometimes assumed human shape, and conversed upon earth with strangers and *travellers.* *Bentley's Sermons.*

2. One who visits foreign countries.

Farewel monsieur *traveller*; look you lisp and wear strange suits, and disable all the benefits of your own country. *Shak.*

The *traveller* into a foreign country knows more by the eye, than he that stayeth at home can by relation of the *traveller.* *Bacon's New Atlantis.*

They are *travellers* newly arrived in a strange country, we should therefore not mislead them. *Locke.*

TRA'VELTAINTED. *adj.* [*travel* and *tainted.*] Harrassed; fatigued with travel.

I have foundered nine score and odd posts: and here, *traveltainted* as I am, have, in my pure and immaculate valour, taken Sir John Coleville. *Shakesp. Henry* IV. *p.* ii.

TRAVERS. adv. [French.] Athwart; across. Not used.

He swears brave oaths, and breaks them bravely, quite *travers*, athwart the heart of his lover. *Shakespeare.*

TRA'VERSE. *adv.* [*a travers*, French.] Crosswise; athwart.

Bring water from some hanging grounds, in long furrows; and from those drawing it *traverse* to spread. *Bacon.*

The ridges of the fallow field lay *traverse.* *Hayward.*

TRAVE'RSE. *prep.* Through crosswise.

He through the armed files
Darts his experienc'd eye, and soon *traverse*
The whole battalion views their order due. *Milton.*

TRA'VERSE. *adj.* [*tranversus*, Lat. *traverse*, Fr.] Lying across; lying athwart.

The paths cut with *traverse* trenches much encumbered the carriages until the pioneers levelled them. *Hayward.*

Oak being strong in all positions, may be trusted in cross and *traverse* work for Summers. *Wotton's Architect.*

TRA'VERSE. *n. s.*

1. Any thing laid or built cross.

The Tirsan cometh with all his generation; and if there be a mother from whom the whole lineage descended, there is a *traverse* placed in a loft where she sitteth. *Bacon.*

Some wind instruments are blown at a small hole in the side, which straiteneth the breath at the first entrance; the rather in respect of their *traverse* and stops above the hole, which performeth the fipple's part. *Bacon.*

2. Something that thwarts, crosses, or obstructs; cross accident; thwarting obstacle. This is a sense rather French than English.

A just and lively picture of human nature in its actions, passions, and *traverses* of fortune. *Dryden.*

He sees no defect in himself, but is satisfied that he should have carried on his designs well enough, had it not been for unlucky *traverses* not in his power. *Locke.*

To TRA'VERSE. *v. a.* [*traverser*, Fr. It was anciently accented on the last syllable.]

1. To cross; to lay athwart.

Myself, and such
As slept within the shadow of your power,
Have wander'd with our *traverst* arms, and breath'd
Our sufferance vainly. *Shakesp. Timon of Athens.*

The parts should be often *traversed* or crossed by the flowing of the folds which loosely encompass them, without sitting too straight. *Dryden's Dufresnoy.*

2. To cross by way of opposition; to thwart with obstacles.

This treatise has, since the first conception thereof, been often *traversed* with other thoughts. *Wotton.*

You save th' expence of long litigious laws,
Where suits are *travers'd*, and so little won,
That he who conquers is but last undone. *Dryden.*

John Bull thought himself now of age to look after his own affairs; Frog resolved to *traverse* this new project, and to make him uneasy in his own family. *Arbuthnot.*

3. To oppose so as to annul. A law term.

Without a good skill in history, and a new geography to understand him aright, one may lose himself in *traversing* the decree. *Baker's Reflections on Learning.*

4. To wander over; to cross.

He many a walk *travers'd*
Of stateliest covert, cedar, pine, or palm. *Milton.*

The lion smarting with the hunter's spear,
Though deeply wounded, no way yet dismay'd;
In sullen fury *traverses* the plain,
To find the vent'rous foe. *Prior.*

Believe me, prince, there's not an African
That *traverses* our vast Numidian desarts
In quest of prey, and lives upon his bow,
But better practises these boasted virtues. *Addison's Cato.*

What seas you *travers'd* and what fields you fought! *Pope.*

5. To survey; to examine thoroughly.

My purpose is to *traverse* the nature, principles, and properties, of this detestable vice, ingratitude. *South's Sermons.*

To TRA'VERSE. *v. n.* To use a posture of opposition in fencing.

To ſee thee fight, to ſee thee *traverſe*, to ſee thee here, to ſee thee there. *Shakeſp. Merry Wives of Windſor.*

TRA'VESTY. *adj.* [*traveſti*, Fr.] Dreſſed ſo as to be made ridiculous; burleſqued.

TRAUMA'TICK. *ad.* [τραυματικὸς.] Vulnerary.

I deterged and diſpoſed the ulcer to incarn, and to do ſo I put the patient into a *traumatick* decoction. *Wiſeman's Surgery.*

TRAY. *n. ſ.* [*tray*, Swediſh.] A ſhallow wooden veſſel in which meat or fiſh is carried.

Sift it into a *tray*, or bole of wood. *Moxon's Mech. Exer.*

No more her care ſhall fill the hollow *tray*,
To fat the guzzling hogs with floods of whey. *Gay.*

TRA'YTRIP. *n. ſ.* A kind of play, I know not of what kind.

Shall I play my freedom at *traytrip*, and become thy bond ſlave. *Shakeſpeare's Twelfth Night.*

TRE'ACHEROUS. *adj.* [from *treachery*.] Faithleſs; perfidious; guilty of deſerting or betraying.

He bad the lion to be remitted
Unto his ſeat, and thoſe ſame *treacherous* vile
Be puniſh'd for their preſumptuous guile. *Hubberd's Tale.*

Deſire in rapture gaz'd awhile,
And ſaw the *treach'rous* goddeſs ſmile. *Swift.*

TRE'ACHEROUSLY. *adv.* [from *treacherous*.] Faithleſsly; perfidiouſly; by treaſon; by ſtratagem.

Then 'gan Carauſius tyrannize anew,
And him Alectus *treacherouſly* ſlew,
And took on him the robe of emperor. *Fairy Qu. b.* ii.

Thou haſt ſlain
The flower of Europe for his chivalry,
And *treacherouſly* haſt thou vanquiſh'd him. *Shakeſpeare.*

Let others freeze with angling reeds,
Or *treacherouſly* poor fiſh beſet,
With ſtrangling ſnare, or winding net. *Donne.*

I treated, truſted you, and thought you mine;
When, in requital of my beſt endeavours,
You *treacherouſly* practis'd to undo me,
Seduc'd my only child, and ſtole her. *Otway.*

They bid him ſtrike, to appeaſe the ghoſt
Of his poor father *treacherouſly* loſt. *Dryden's Juvenal.*

TRE'ACHEROUSNESS. *n. ſ.* [from *treacherous*.] The quality of being treacherous; perfidiouſneſs.

TRE'ACHERY. *n. ſ.* [*tricherie*, French.] Perfidy; breach of faith.

TREA'CHETOR. }
TRE'ACHOUR. } *n. ſ.* [from *tricher*, *tricheur*, Fr.] A traitor; one who betrays; one who violates his faith or allegiance.

Good Claudius with him battle fought,
In which the king was by a *treachetour*
Diſguiſed ſlain. *Fairy Queen, b.* ii.

Where may that *treachour* then be found,
Or by what means may I his footing tract. *Fairy Queen.*

TRE'ACLE. *n. ſ.* [*triacle*, Fr. *triackle*, Dutch; *theriaca*, Lat.]

1. A medicine made up of many ingredients.

The phyſician that has obſerved the medicinal virtues of *treacle*, without knowing the nature of each of the ſixty odd ingredients, may cure many patients with it. *Boyle.*

Treacle water has much of an acid in it. *Floyer.*

2. Moloſſes; the ſpume of ſugar.

To TREAD. *v. n.* pret. *trod.* part. paſſ. *trodden.* [*trudan*, Gothick; tꞃeðan, Saxon; *treden*, Dutch.]

1. To ſet the foot.

He ne'er drinks,
But Timon's ſilver *treads* upon his lip. *Shakeſpeare.*

Thoſe which perfume the air moſt, being trodden upon and cruſhed, are burnet, wild thyme, and water mint; therefore ſet whole alleys of them, to have the pleaſure when you walk or *tread*. *Bacon's Eſſays.*

Thoſe dropping gums
Aſk riddance, if we mean to *tread* with eaſe. *Milton.*

Where'er you *tread* the bluſhing flow'rs ſhall riſe. *Pope.*

2. To trample; to ſet the feet in ſcorn or malice.

Thou
Muſt, as a foreign recreant, be led
With manacles along our ſtreet, or elſe
Triumphantly *tread* on thy country's ruin,
And bear the palm. *Shakeſp. Coriolanus.*

Thou ſhalt *tread* upon their high places. *Deut.* xxxiii. 29.

3. To walk with form or ſtate.

When he walks, he moves like an engine,
And the ground ſhrinks before his *treading*. *Shakeſpeare.*

Ye that ſtately *tread* or lowly creep. *Milton.*

4. To copulate as birds.

When ſhepherds pipe on oaten ſtraws;
When turtles *tread* *Shakeſpeare.*

What diſtance between the *treading* or coupling, and the laying of the egg? *Bacon's Nat. Hiſt.*

They bill, they *tread*, Alcyone compreſs'd,
Seven days ſits brooding on her floating neſt. *Dryden.*

To TREAD. *v. a.*

1. To walk on; to feel under the foot.

Would I had never *trod* this Engliſh earth,
Or felt the flatteries that grow upon it! *Shakeſpeare.*

He dy'd obedient to ſevereſt law;
Forbid to *tread* the promis'd land he ſaw. *Prior.*

2. To preſs under the foot.

Tread the ſnuff out on the floor to prevent ſtinking. *Swift.*

3. To beat; to track.

Full of briars is this working world.
—They are but burs: if we walk not in the *trodden* paths, our very petticoats will catch them. *Shakeſp. As you like it.*

4. To walk on in a formal or ſtately manner.

Methought ſhe *trod* the ground with greater grace. *Dry.*

5. To cruſh under foot; to trample in contempt or hatred.

Through thy name will we *tread* them under that riſe againſt us. *Pſal.* xliv. 5.

Why was I rais'd the meteor of the world,
Hung in the ſkies, and blazing as I travell'd,
'Till all my fires were ſpent; and then caſt downward
To be *trod* out by Cæſar? *Dryden's All for Love.*

6. To put in action by the feet.

They *tread* their wine-preſſes and ſuffer thirſt. *Job* xxiv.

7. To love as the male bird the female.

He feather'd her and *trod* her. *Dryden's Fables.*

TREAD. *n. ſ.* [from the verb.] Footing; ſtep with the foot.

If the ſtreets were pav'd with thine eyes,
Her feet were much too dainty for ſuch *tread*. *Shakeſpeare.*

The quaint mazes in the wanton green,
For want of *tread*, are undiſtinguiſhable. *Milton.*

High above the ground
Their march was, and the paſſive air upbore
Their nimble *tread*. *Milton.*

The dancer on the rope, with doubtful *tread*,
Gets wherewithal to cloath and buy him bread. *Dryden.*

How wert thou wont to walk with cautious *tread*,
A diſh of tea, like milk-pail, on thy head! *Swift.*

2. Way; track; path.

Cromwell is the king's ſecretary: further,
Stands in the gap and *tread* for more preferment. *Shakeſp.*

3. The cocks part in the egg.

TRE'ADER. *n. ſ.* [from *tread*.] He who treads.

The *treaders* ſhall tread out no wine in their preſſes. *Iſa.*

TRE'ADLE. *n. ſ.* [from *tread*.]

1. A part of an engine on which the feet act to put it in motion.

The farther the fore-end of the *treadle* reaches out beyond the fore-ſide of the lathe, the greater will the ſweep of the fore-end of the *treadle* be, and conſequently the more revolutions is made at one tread. *Moxon's Mech. Exerciſes.*

2. The ſperm of the cock.

Whether it is not made out of the garm, or *treadle* of the egg, ſeemeth of leſſer doubt. *Brown's Vulgar Errours.*

At each end of the egg is a *treadle*, formerly thought to be the cock's ſperm. *Derham.*

TRE'ASON. *n. ſ.* [*trahiſon*, French.] An offence committed againſt the dignity and majeſty of the commonwealth: it is divided into high *treaſon* and petit *treaſon*. High *treaſon* is an offence againſt the ſecurity of the commonwealth, or of the king's majeſty, whether by imagination, word, or deed; as to compaſs or imagine *treaſon*, or the death of the prince, or the queen conſort, or his ſon and heir-apparent; or to deflower the king's wife, or his eldeſt daughter unmarried, or his eldeſt ſon's wife; or levy war againſt the king in his realm, or to adhere to his enemies by aiding them; or to counterfeit the king's great ſeal, privy ſeal, or money; or knowingly to bring falſe money into this realm counterfeited like the money of England, and to utter the ſame; or to kill the king's chancellor, treaſurer, juſtice of the one bench, or of the other; juſtices in Eyre, juſtices of aſſize, juſtices of oyer and terminer, when in their place and doing their duty; or forging the king's ſeal manual, or privy ſignet; or diminiſhing or impairing the current money: and, in ſuch *treaſon*, a man forfeits his lands and goods to the king: and it is called *treaſon* paramount. Petit *treaſon* is when a ſervant kills his maſter, a wife her huſband; ſecular or religious kills his prelate: this *treaſon* gives forfeiture to every lord within his own fee: both *treaſons* are capital. *Cowel.*

Man diſobeying,
Diſloyal breaks his fealty, and ſins
Againſt the high ſupremacy of heaven:
To expiate his *treaſon* hath nought left. *Milton.*

He made the overture of thy *treaſons* to us. *Shakeſpeare.*

Athaliah cried, *treaſon*, *treaſon*. 2 *Kings* xi. 14.

TRE'ASONABLE. }
TRE'ASONOUS. } *adj.* [from *treaſon*.] Having the nature or guilt of treaſon. *Treaſonous* is out of uſe.

Him by proofs as clear as founts in July
I know to be corrupt and *treaſonous*. *Shakeſp. Henry* VIII.

Againſt the undivulg'd pretence I fight
Of *treas'nous* malice. *Shakeſpeare's Macbeth.*

Moſt mens heads had been intoxicated with imaginations of plots, and *treaſonable* practices. *Clarendon.*

Were it a draught for June when ſhe banquets,
I wou'd not taſte thy *treaſonous* offer. *Milton.*

A credit to run ten millions in debt without parliamentary ſecurity is dangerous, illegal, and perhaps *treaſonable*. *Swift.*

TRE'ASURE.

TRE'ASURE. *n. s.* [*tresor*, Fr. *thesaurus*, Latin.] Wealth hoarded; riches accumulated.

An inventory, importing
The several parcels of his plate, his *treasure*,
Rich stuffs. *Shakespeare's Henry* VIII.

They built *treasure* cities. *Exod.* i. 11.

He used his laws as well for collecting of *treasure*, as for correcting of manners. *Bacon.*

Gold is *treasure* as well as silver, because not decaying, and never sinking much in value. *Locke.*

To TRE'ASURE. *v. a.* [from the noun.] To hoard; to reposit; to lay up.

After thy hardness and impenitent heart thou *treasurest* up unto thyself wrath against the day of wrath. *Rom.* ii. 5.

Practical principles are *treasured* up in man's mind, that, like the candle of the Lord in the heart of every man, discovers what he is to do, and what to avoid. *South.*

No, my remembrance *treasures* honest thoughts,
And holds not things like thee; I scorn thy friendship. *Rowe.*

Some thought it mounted to the lunar sphere,
Since all things lost on earth are *treasur'd* there. *Pope.*

TRE'ASURER. *n. s.* [from *treasure*; *tresorier*, Fr.] One who has care of money; one who has charge of treasure.

This is my *treasurer*, let him speak
That I have reserv'd nothing. *Shakesp. Ant. and Cleopatra.*

Before the invention of laws, private affections in supreme rulers made their own fancies both their *treasurers* and hangmen, weighing in this balance good and evil. *Raleigh.*

TRE'ASURERSHIP. *n. s.* [from *treasurer.*] Office or dignity of treasurer.

He preferred a base fellow, who was a suitor for the *treasurership*, before the most worthy. *Hakewill.*

TRE'ASUREHOUSE. *n. s.* [*treasure* and *house.*] Place where hoarded riches are kept.

Let there be any grief or disease incident to the soul of men, for which there is not in this *treasurehouse* a present comfortable remedy to be found. *Hooker, b.* v.

Thou silver *treasurehouse*,
Tell me once more, what title dost thou bear? *Shakesp.*

Gather together into your spirit, and its *treasurehouse*, the memory, not only all the promises of God, but also the former senses of the divine favours. *Taylor's holy living.*

TRE'ASURY. *n. s.* [from *treasure*; *tresorerie*, Fr.] A place in which riches are accumulated.

And make his chronicle as rich with prize,
As is the ouzy bottom of the sea
With sunken wreck and sumless *treasuries*. *Shakespeare.*

Thy sumptuous buildings
Have cost a mass of publick *treasury*. *Shakesp. Henry* VI.

And yet I know not how conceit may rob
The *treasury* of life, when life itself
Yields to the theft. *Shakespeare's King Lear.*

He had a purpose to furnish a fair case in that university with choice collections from all parts, like that famous *treasury* of knowledge at Oxford. *Wotton.*

The state of the *treasury* the king best knows. *Temple.*

Physicians, by *treasuries* of just observations, grow to skill in the art of healing. *Watts.*

To TREAT. *v. a.* [*traiter*, Fr. *tracto*, Lat.]

1. To negociate; to settle.

To *treat* the peace, a hundred senators
Shall be commissioned. *Dryden's Æn.*

2. [*Tracto*, Lat.] To discourse on.

3. To use in any manner, good or bad.

He *treated* his prisoner with great harshness. *Spectator.*

Since living virtue is with envy curs'd,
And the best men are *treated* like the worst;
Do thou, just goddess, call our merits forth,
And give each deed th' exact, intrinsick worth. *Pope.*

4. To handle; to manage; to carry on.

Zeuxis and Polygnotus *treated* their subjects in their pictures, as Homer did in his poetry. *Dryden.*

5. To entertain with expence.

To TREAT. *v. n.* [*traiter*, Fr. trahtian, Saxon.]

1. To discourse; to make discussions.

Of love they *treat* till th' ev'ning star appear'd. *Milton.*

Absence, what the poets call death in love, has given occasion to beautiful complaints in those authors who have *treated* of this passion in verse. *Addison's Spect.*

2. To practise negotiation.

The king *treated* with them. 2 *Mac.* xiii. 22.

3. To come to terms of accommodation.

Inform us, will the emp'ror *treat?* *Swift.*

4. To make gratuitous entertainments.

TREAT. *n. s.* [from the verb.]

1. An entertainment given.

This is the ceremony of my fate;
A parting *treat*, and I'm to die in state. *Dryden.*

He pretends a great concern for his country, and insight into matters: now such professions, when recommended by a *treat*, dispose an audience to hear reason. *Collier.*

What tender maid but must a victim fall
For one man's *treat*, but for another's ball? *Pope.*

2. Something given at an entertainment.

Dry figs and grapes, and wrinkled dates were set,
In canisters t' enlarge the little *treat*. *Dryden.*

The King of gods revolving in his mind
Lycaon's guilt and his inhuman *treat*. *Dryden.*

TRE'ATABLE. *adj.* [*traitable*, Fr.] Moderate; not violent.

A virtuous mind should rather wish to depart this world with a kind of *treatable* dissolution, than be suddenly cut off in a moment, rather to be taken than snatched away. *Hooker.*

The heats or the colds of seasons are less *treatable* than with us. *Temple.*

TRE'ATISE. *n. s.* [*tractatus*, Latin.] Discourse; written tractate.

The time has been my fell of hair
Wou'd at a dismal *treatise* rouze, and stir
As life were in't. *Shakespeare.*

Besides the rules given in this *treatise* to make a perfect judgment of good pictures, there is required a long conversation with the best pieces. *Dryden's Dufresnoy.*

TRE'ATMENT. *n. s.* [*traitment*, French.] Usage; manner of using good or bad.

Scarce an humour or character which they have not used; all comes wasted to us: and were they to entertain this age, they could not now make such plenteous *treatment*. *Dryden.*

Accept such *treatment* as a swain affords. *Pope.*

TREATY. *n. s.* [*traité*, Fr.]

1. Negotiation; act of treating.

She began a *treaty* to procure;
And stablish terms betwixt both their requests. *Fa. Qu.*

2. A compact of accommodation relating to publick affairs.

A peace was concluded, being rather a bargain than a *treaty*. *Bacon's Henry* VII.

Echion
Let fall the guiltless weapon from his hand,
And with the rest a peaceful *treaty* makes. *Addison's Ovid.*

3. For entreaty: supplication; petition; solicitation.

He cast by *treaty* and by trains
Her to persuade. *Spenser.*

I must
To the young man send humble *treaties*, dodge,
And palter in the shift of lowness. *Shakespeare.*

TRE'BLE. *adj.* [*triple*, Fr. *triplus*, *triplex*, Lat.]

1. Threefold; triple.

Some I see,
That twofold balls and *treble* sceptres carry. *Shakespeare.*

Who can
His head's huge doors unlock, whose jaws with great
And dreadful teeth in *treble* ranks are set. *Sandys.*

All his malice serv'd but to bring forth
Infinite goodness, grace, and mercy shewn
On man by him seduc'd; but on himself
Treble confusion, wrath, and vengeance pour'd. *Milton.*

A lofty tow'r, and strong on ev'ry side
With *treble* walls. *Dryden's Æn.*

The pious Trojan then his jav'lin sent,
The shield gave way; through *treble* plates it went
Of solid brass. *Dryden's Æn.*

2. Sharp of sound. A musical term.

The sharper or quicker percussion of air causeth the more *treble* sound, and the lower or heavier the more base sound. *Bacon's Nat. Hist.* N°. 179.

To TRE'BLE. *v. a.* [from the adjective; *triplico*, Lat. *tripler*, Fr.] To multiply by three; to make thrice as much.

She conceiv'd, and *trebling* the due time,
Brought forth this monstrous mass. *Spenser.*

I would not be ambitious in my wish,
To wish myself much better; yet for you,
I would be *trebled* twenty times myself,
A thousand times more fair. *Shakesp. Merch. of Venice.*

Aquarius shines with feebler rays,
Four years he *trebles*, and doubles six score days. *Creech.*

To TRE'BLE. *v. n.* To become threefold.

Whoever annually runs out, as the debt doubles and *trebles* upon him, so doth his inability to pay it. *Swift.*

TRE'BLE. *n. s.* A sharp sound.

The *treble* cutteth the air so sharp, as it returneth too swift to make the sound equal; and therefore a mean or tenor is the sweetest. *Bacon.*

The lute still trembles underneath thy nail:
At thy well-sharpen'd thumb from shore to shore,
The *trebles* squeak for fear, the bases roar. *Dryden.*

TRE'BLENESS. *n. s.* [from *treble.*] The state of being treble.

The just proportion of the air percussed towards the baseness or *trebleness* of tones, is a great secret in sounds. *Bacon.*

TRE'BLY. *adv.* [from *treble.*] Thrice told; in threefold number or quantity.

His jav'lin sent,
The shield gave way; through treble plates it went
Of solid brass, of linnen *trebly* roll'd. *Dryden's Æn.*

The seed being so necessary for the maintenance of the several species, it is in some doubly and *trebly* defended. *Ray.*

TREE. *n. s. trie*, Islandick; *tree*, Danish.]

1. A large vegetable rising, with one woody stem, to a considerable height.

Trees and shrubs, of our native growth in England, are distinguished by Ray. 1. Such as have their flowers disjointed and remote from the fruit; and these are, 1. Nuciferous ones; as, the walnut tree, the hazel-nut tree, the beach, the chesnut, and the common oak. 2. Coniferous ones; of this kind are the Scotch firs, male and female; the pine, the common alder tree, and the birch tree. 3. Bacciferous; as, the juniper and yew trees. 4. Lanigerous ones; as, the black, white, and trembling poplar, willows, and osiers of all kinds. 5. Such as bear their seeds, having an imperfect flower, in leafy membranes; as, the horse-bean. 6. Such as have their fruits and flowers contiguous; of these some are pomiferous; as, apples and pears: and some bacciferous; as, the sorb or service tree, the white or hawthorn, the wild rose, sweet brier, currants, the great bilberry bush, honey-suckle, joy. Pruniferous ones, whose fruit is pretty large and soft, with a stone in the middle; as, the black-thorn or sloe tree, the black and white bullace tree, the black cherry, *&c.* Bacciferous ones; as, the strawberry tree in the west of Ireland, misletoe, water elder, the dwarf, a large laurel, the viburnum or way-fairing tree, the dog-berry tree, the sea black thorn, the berry-bearing elder, the privet barberry, common elder, the holy, the buckthorn, the berry-bearing heath, the bramble, and spindle tree or prickwood. Such as have their fruit dry when ripe; as, the bladder nut tree, the box tree, the common elm and ash, the maple, the gaule or sweet willow, common heath, broom, dyers wood, furze or gorse, the lime tree, *&c.* *Miller.*

Sometime we see a cloud that's dragonish,
A forked mountain, or blue promontory
With *trees* upon't, that nod unto the world,
And mock our eyes with air. *Shakesp. Ant. and Cleopatra.*

Who can bid the *tree* unfix his earth-bound root. *Shak.*

It is pleasant to look upon a *tree* in Summer covered with green leaves, decked with blossoms, or laden with fruit, and casting a pleasant shade: but to consider how this *tree* sprang from a little seed, how nature shaped and fed it till it came to this greatness, is a more rational pleasure. *Burnet.*

Trees shoot up in one great stem, and at a good distance from the earth, spread into branches: thus gooseberries are shrubs, and oaks are *trees.* *Locke.*

2. Any thing branched out.

Vain are their hopes who fancy to inherit,
By *trees* of pedigrees, or fame or merit:
Though plodding heralds through each branch may trace
Old captains and dictators of their race. *Dryden.*

TREE *germander. n. s.* A plant.

TREE *of life. n. s.* [*lignum vitæ*, Latin.] An evergreen: the wood is esteemed by turners. *Miller.*

TREE *primrose. n. s.* A plant.

TREEN. old plur. of *tree.*

Well run greenhood, got between
Under the sand-bag he was seen;
Lowting low like a for'ster green,
He knows his tackle and his *treen.* *Benj. Johnson.*

TREEN. *adj.* Wooden; made of wood. Obsolete.

Sir Thomas Rookesby, being controlled for first suffering himself to be served in *treen* cups, answered, these homely cups pay truly for that they contain: I had rather drink out of treen and pay gold and silver, than drink out of gold and silver and make wooden payments. *Camden.*

TRE'FOIL. *n. s.* [*trifolium*, Lat.] A plant.

The *trefoil* hath a papilionaceous flower, consisting of the standard, the wings and keel coming out of the empalement together with the pointal covered with its fringed sheath: it becomes a capsule hidden in the empalement, and full of seeds shaped like a kidney, adhering close to the capsule when ripe: some have flowers consisting of one leaf, and filled with kidney-shaped seeds: to this must be added, that the leaves grow by threes, seldom by four or fives, on a common footstalk. *Miller.*

Hope, by the ancients, was drawn in the form of a sweet and beautiful child, standing upon tiptoes, and a *trefoil*, or three-leaved grass in her hand. *Peacham on Drawing.*

Some sow *trefoil* or rye-grass with their clover. *Mortimer.*

TRE'ILLAGE. n. s. [French.]

Treillage is a contexture of pales to support espalliers, making a distinct inclosure of any part of a garden. *Trevoux.*

There are as many kinds of gardening as of poetry: makers of flower-gardens are epigrammatists and sonneteers, contrivers of bowers, grotto's, *treillages*, and cascades, are romance writers. *Spectator*, N°. 477.

TRE'LLIS. n. s. [French.] Is a structure of iron, wood, or osier, the parts crossing each other like a lattice. *Trevoux.*

To TRE'MBLE. *v. n.* [*trembler*, Fr. *tremo*, Lat.]

1. To shake as with fear or cold; to shiver; to quake; to shudder.

My compassionate heart
Will not permit my eyes once to behold
The thing, whereat it *trembles* by surmise. *Shakespeare.*

God's name
And power thou *tremblest* at. *Shakespeare's Henry* VI.

Shew your slaves how cholerick you are,
And make your bondmen *tremble.* *Shakesp. Julius Cæsar.*

This judgment of the heavens that makes us *tremble*,
Touches us not with pity. *Shakesp. King Lear.*

They shall fear and *tremble.* *Jer.* xxxiii. 9.

When he heard the king, he fell into such a *trembling* that he could hardly speak. *Clarendon.*

Frighted Turnus *trembl'd* as he spoke. *Dryden's Æn.*

He shook the sacred honours of his head,
With terror *trembl'd* heav'n's subsiding hill,
And from his shaken curls ambrosial dews distil. *Dryden.*

Ye powers, revenge your violated altars,
That they who with unhallow'd hands approach
May *tremble.* *Rowe.*

2. To quiver; to totter.

Sinai's grey top shall *tremble.* *Milton.*

We cannot imagine a mass of water to have stood upon the middle of the earth like one great drop, or a *trembling* jelly, and all the places about it dry. *Burnet.*

3. To quaver; to shake as a sound.

Winds make a noise unequally, and sometimes when vehement *tremble* at the height of their blast. *Bacon.*

TRE'MBLINGLY. *adv.* [from *trembling.*] So as to shake or quiver.

Tremblingly she stood,
And on the sudden dropt. *Shakesp. Ant. and Cleopatra.*

Say what the use, were finer opticks giv'n,
Or touch, if *tremblingly* alive all o'er,
To smart and agonize at every pore? *Pope.*

TREME'NDOUS. *adj.* [*tremendus*, Latin.] Dreadful; horrible; astonishingly terrible.

There stands an altar where the priest celebrates some mysteries sacred and *tremendous.* *Tatler*, N°. 57.

In that portal shou'd the chief appear,
Each hand *tremendous* with a brazen spear. *Pope's Odyssey.*

TRE'MOUR. *n. s.* [*tremor*, Lat.]

1. The state of trembling.

He fell into an universal *tremour* of all his joints, that when going his legs trembled under him. *Harvey.*

By its styptick and stimulating quality it affects the nerves, occasioning *tremours.* *Arbuthnot on Aliments.*

2. Quivering or vibratory motion.

These stars do not twinkle when viewed through telescopes which have large apertures: for the rays of light which pass through divers parts of the aperture tremble each of them apart, and by means of their various, and sometimes contrary *tremors* fall at one and the same time upon different points in the bottom of the eye. *Newton.*

TRE'MULOUS. *adj.* [*tremulus*, Lat.]

1. Trembling; fearful.

The tender *tremulous* christian is easily distracted and amazed by them. *Decay of Piety.*

2. Quivering; vibratory.

Breath vocalized, that is, vibrated or undulated, impresses a swift *tremulous* motion in the lips, tongue or palate, which breath passing smooth does not. *Holder.*

As thus th' effulgence *tremulous* I drink,
The lambent light'nings shoot across the sky. *Thomson.*

TRE'MULOUSNESS. *n. s.* [from *tremulous.*] The state of quivering.

TREN. *n. s.* A fish spear. *Ains.*

To TRENCH. *v. a.* [*trancher*, Fr.]

1. To cut.

Safe in a ditch he bides,
With twenty *trenched* gashes on his head. *Shakespeare.*

This weak impress of love is as a figure
Trench'd in ice, which with an hour's heat
Dissolves to water, and doth lose his form. *Shakespeare.*

2. To cut or dig into pits or ditches.

Pioneers with spades and pickax arm'd,
Forerun the royal camp to *trench* a field. *Milton.*

Trench the ground, and make it ready for the Spring. *Evelyn.*

First draw thy faulchion, and on ev'ry side
Trench the black earth a cubit long and wide. *Pope.*

The *trenching* plough or coulter is useful in pasture-ground, to cut out the sides of trenches or drains. *Mortimer.*

TRENCH. *n. s.* [*tranche*, Fr.]

1. A pit or ditch.

On that coast build,
And with a *trench* enclose the fruitful field. *Dryden's Æn.*

When you have got your water up to the highest part of the land, make a small *trench* to carry some of the water in, keeping it always upon a level. *Mortimer's Husb.*

2. Earth thrown up to defend soldiers in their approach to a town, or to guard a camp.

The

The citizens of Corioli have issued forth
And given to Lartius and to Marcius battle:
I saw our party to the *trenches* driven,
And then I came away. *Shakespeare's Coriolanus.*
William carries on the *trench*,
Till both the town and castle yield. *Prior.*

TRE'NCHANT. *adj.* [*trenchant*, Fr.] Cutting; sharp.
He fiercely took his *trenchant* blade in hand,
With which he struck so furious and so fell,
That nothing seem'd the puissance could withstand. *F. Q.*
Against a vanquish'd foe, their swords
Were sharp and *trenchant*, not their words. *Hudibras.*

TRE'NCHER. *n. s* [from *trench*; *trenchoir*, Fr.]
1. A piece of wood on which meat is cut at table.
No more
I'll scrape *trencher*, nor wash dish. *Shakesp. Tempest.*
My estate deserves an heir more rais'd,
Than one which holds a *trencher*. *Shak. Timon of Athens.*
When we find our dogs, we set the dish or *trencher* on the ground. *More's Antidote against Atheism.*
Their homely fare dispatch'd; the hungry band
Invade their *trenchers* next, and soon devour. *Dryden.*
Many a child may have the idea of a square *trencher*, or round plate, before he has any idea of infinite. *Locke.*
2. The table.
How often hast thou,
Fed from my *trencher*, kneel'd down at the board,
When I have feasted. *Shakesp. Henry* VI.
3. Food; pleasures of the table.
It could be no ordinary declension of nature that could bring some men, after an ingenuous education, to place their *summum bonum* upon their *trenchers*, and their utmost felicity in wine. *South's Sermons.*

TRE'NCHERFLY. *n. s.* [*trencher* and *fly*.] One that haunts tables; a parasite.
He found all people came to him promiscuously, and he tried which of them were friends, and which only *trencher-flies* and spungers. *L'Estrange.*

TRE'NCHERMAN. *n. s.* [*trencher* and *man*.] A feeder; an eater.
Palladius assured him, that he had already been more fed to his liking than he could be by the skilfullest *trenchermen* of Media. *Sidney.*
You had musty victuals, and he hath holp to eat it: he's a very valiant *trencherman*; he hath an excellent stomach. *Shakesp. Much ado about nothing.*

TRE'NCHERMATE. *n. s.* [*trencher* and *mate*.] A table companion; a parasite.
Because that judicious learning of the ancient sages doth not in this case serve the turn, these *trenchermates* frame to themselves a way more pleasant; a new method they have of turning things that are serious into mockery, an art of contradiction by way of scorn. *Hooker, b.* v.

To TREND. *v. n.* To tend; to lie in any particular direction. It seems a corruption of *tend*.
The scouts to several parts divide their way,
To learn the natives names, their towns explore
The coasts and *trendings* of the crooked shore. *Dryden.*

TRE'NTALS. *n. s.* [*trente*, Fr.]
Trentals or *trigintals* were a number of masses, to the tale of thirty, said on the same account, according to a certain order instituted by Saint Gregory. *Ayliffe's Parergon.*

TRE'NDLE. *n. s.* [ꞇꞃenbel, Saxon.] Any thing turned round. Now improperly written *trundle*.

TREPA'N. *n. s.* [*trepan*, Fr.]
1. An instrument by which chirurgeons cut out round pieces of the skull.
2. A snare; a stratagem by which any one is ensnared. [Of this signification *Skinner* assigns for the reason, that some English ships in queen Elizabeth's reign being invited, with great shew of friendship, into *Trapani*, a part of Sicily, were there detained.]
But what a thoughtless animal is man,
How very active in his own *trepan*. *Roscommon.*
Can there be any thing of friendship in snares, hooks, and *trepans*. *South's Sermons.*
During the commotion of the blood and spirits, in which passion consists, whatsoever is offered to the imagination in favour of it, tends only to deceive the reason: it is indeed a real *trepan* upon it, feeding it with colours and appearances instead of arguments. *South's Sermons.*

To TREPA'N. *v. a.* [from the noun; *trepaner*, Fr.]
1. To perforate with the trepan.
A putrid matter flowed forth her nostrils, of the same smell with that in *trepanning* the bone. *Wiseman's Surgery.*
Few recovered of those that were *trepanned*. *Arbuthnot.*
2. To catch; to ensnare.
They *trepann'd* the state, and fac'd it down
With plots and projects of our own. *Hudibras, p.* iii.
Those are but *trepanned* who are called to govern, being invested with authority but bereaved of power, which is nothing else but to mock and betray them into a splendid and magisterial way of being ridiculous. *South's Sermons.*

TREPHI'NE. *n. s.* A small trepan; a smaller instrument of perforation managed by one hand.
I shewed a trepan and *trephine*, and gave them liberty to try both upon a skull. *Wiseman's Surgery.*

TREPIDA'TION. *n. s.* [*trepidatio*, Lat.]
1. The state of trembling.
The bow tortureth the string continually, and holdeth it in a continual *trepidation*. *Bacon's Nat. Hist.* N°. 137.
All objects of the senses which are very offensive, cause the spirits to retire; upon which the parts, in some degree, are destitute; and so there is induced in them a *trepidation* and horror. *Bacon's Nat. Hist.* N°. 793.
Moving of th' earth brings harms and fears,
Men reckon what it did and meant;
But *trepidation* of the spheres,
Though greater far, is innocent. *Donne.*
They pass the planets sev'n, and pass the fix'd,
And that crystalline sphere whose balance weighs
The *trepidation* talk'd, and that first-mov'd. *Milton.*
2. State of terrour.
Because the whole kingdom stood in a zealous *trepidation* of the absence of such a prince, I have been the more desirous to research the several passages of the journey. *Wotton.*
His first action of note was in the battle of Lepanto; where the success of that great day, in such *trepidation* of the state, made every man meritorious. *Wotton.*

To TRE'SPASS. *v. n.* [*trespasser*, Fr.]
1. To transgress; to offend.
If they shall confess their trespass which they *trespassed* against me, I will remember my covenant. *Lev.* xxvi. 43.
They not only contradict the general design and particular expresses of the gospel, but *trespass* against all logick. *Norris.*
2. To enter unlawfully on another's ground.
Their morals and œconomy,
Most perfectly they made agree:
Each virtue kept its proper bound,
Nor *trespass'd* on the other's ground. *Prior.*

TRE'SPASS. *n. s.* [*trespas*, Fr.]
1. Transgression; offence.
Your purpos'd low correction
Is such, as basest, and the meanest wretches
For pilf'rings, and most common *trespass*
Are punish'd with. *Shakesp. King Lear.*
The *trespass* money and sin money was the priests. 2 *Kings.*
He shall bring his *trespass* offering for his sin. *Lev.* v. 6.
Will God incense his ire
For such a petty *trespass*? *Milton.*
2. Unlawful entrance on another's ground.

TRE'SPASSER. *n. s.* [from *trespass*.]
1. An offender; a transgressor.
2. One who enters unlawfully on another's ground.
If I come upon another's ground without his licence, or the licence of the law, I am a *trespasser*, for which the owner may have an action of trespass against me. *Walton.*

TRE'SSED. *adj.* [from *tressé*, French.] Knotted or curled.
Nor this nor that so much doth make me mourn,
But for the lad, whom long I lov'd so dear,
Now loves a lass that all his love doth scorn,
He plunged in pain his *tressed* locks doth tear. *Spenser.*

TRE'SSES. *n. s.* without a singular. [*tresse*, Fr. *treccia*, Italian.] A knot or curl of hair.
Hung be the heav'ns with black, yield day to night!
Comets, importing change of times and states,
Brandish your crystal *tresses* in the sky. *Shakespeare.*
Her swelling breast
Naked, met his under the flowing gold
Of her loose *tresses* hid. *Milton.*
Adam had wove
Of choicest flow'rs a garland to adorn
Her *tresses*, and her rural labours crown. *Milton.*
Fair *tresses* man's imperial race ensnare,
And beauty draws us with a single hair. *Pope.*
Then cease, bright nymph! to mourn the ravish'd hair,
Which adds new glory to the shining sphere!
Not all the *tresses* that fair hair can boast,
Shall draw such envy as the lock you lost. *Pope.*

TRE'STLE. *n. s.* [*tresteau*, Fr.]
1. The frame of a table.
2. A moveable form by which any thing is supported.

TRET. *n. s.* [Probably from *tritus*, Lat.] An allowance made by merchants to retailers, which is four pounds in every hundred weight, and four pounds for waste or refuse of a commodity. *Bailey.*

TRE'THINGS. *n. s.* [*trethingi*, low Latin, from *trethu*, Welsh, to tax.] Taxes; imposts.

TREVE'T. *n. s.* [ꞇꞃeꝼeꞇ, Saxon; *trepied*, Fr.] Any thing that stands on three legs: as, a stool.

TREY. *n. s.* [*tres*, Lat. *trois*, Fr.] A three at cards.
White-handed mistress, one sweet word with thee.
——Honey, milk, and sugar; there is three.
——Nay then, two *treys*; metheglin, wort, and malmsey. *Shakesp. Love's Labour lost.*

TRI'ABLE.

Tri'able. *adj.* [from *try.*]

1. Possible to be experimented; capable of trial.

For the more easy understanding of the experiments *triable* by our engine, I insinuated that notion, by which all of them will prove explicable. *Boyle.*

2. Such as may be judicially examined.

No one should be admitted to a bishop's chancellorship without good knowledge in the civil and canon laws, since divers causes *triable* in the spiritual court are of weight. *Ayliffe.*

Tri'ad. *n. s.* [*trias*, Lat. *triade*, Fr.] Three united.

Tri'al. *n. s.* [from *try.*]

1. Test; examination.

With *trial* fire touch me his finger end;
If he be chaste the flame will back descend,
And turn him to no pain; but if he start,
It is the flesh of a corrupted heart. *Shakespeare.*

2. Experience; act of examining by experience.

I leave him to your gracious acceptance,
Whose *trial* shall better publish his commendation. *Shak.*

Skilful gardeners make *trial* of the seeds by putting them into water gently boiled; and if good, they will sprout within half an hour. *Bacon's Nat. Hist.* N°. 520.

3. Experiment; experimental knowledge.

Others had *trial* of cruel mockings and scourgings. *Heb.*

4. Judicial examination.

Trial is used in law for the examination of all causes, civil or criminal, according to the laws of our realm: the *trial* is the issue, which is tried upon the inditement, not the inditement itself. *Cowel.*

He hath resisted law,
And therefore law shall scorn him further *trial*
Than the severity of publick power. *Shakesp. Coriolanus.*

5. Temptation; test of virtue.

Lest our *trial*, when least sought,
May find us both perhaps far less prepar'd,
The willinger I go. *Milton's Par. Lost, b.* ix.

No such company as then thou saw'st
Intended thee; for *trial* only brought,
To see how thou could'st judge of fit and meet. *Milton.*

Every station is exposed to some *trials*, either temptations that provoke our appetites, or disquiet our fears. *Rogers.*

6. State of being tried.

Good shepherd, tell this youth what 'tis to love?
—— It is to be all made of sighs and tears;
It is to be made all of faith and service,
All humbleness, all patience and impatience;
All purity, all *trial*, all observance. *Shakesp. As you like it.*

TRIA'NGLE. *n. s.* [*triangle*, Fr. *triangulum*, Lat.] A figure of three angles.

The three angles of a *triangle* are equal to two right ones. *Locke.*

Tria'ngular. *adj.* [*triangularis*, Lat.] Having three angles.

The frame thereof seem'd partly circular,
And part *triangular*; O work divine!
These two the first and last proportions are. *Fairy Qu.*

Though a round figure be most capacious for the honey, and most convenient for the bee; yet did she not chuse that, because then there must have been *triangular* spaces left void. *Ray on the Creation.*

Tribe. *n. s.* [*tribu*, Fr. *tribus*, Lat. from *trev*, *b* and *v* being labials of promiscuous use in the ancient British words; *trev* from *tir ef*, his lands, is supposed to be Celtick, and used before the Romans had any thing to do with the British government; to prove which Mr. *Rowland* offers many reasons, which he mentions by imagining that *centuriæ* is derived from *trev*, supposing it to be the same with our *centrev*, importing a hundred *trevs* or *tribes.*]

1. A distinct body of the people as divided by family or fortune, or any other characteristick.

I ha' been writing all this night unto all the *tribes*
And centuries for their voices, to help Catiline
In his election. *Benj. Johnson's Cataline.*

If the heads of the *tribes* can be taken off, and the misled multitude will see their error, such extent of mercy is honourable. *Bacon's Advice to Villiers.*

Who now shall rear you to the sun, or rank
Your *tribes*, and water from th' ambrosial fount. *Milton.*

Straggling mountaineers, for publick good,
To rank in *tribes*, and quit the savage wood,
Houses to build. *Tate.*

I congratulate my country upon the increase of this happy *tribe* of men, since, by the present parliament, the race of freeholders is spreading into the remotest corners. *Addison.*

2. It is often used in contempt.

Folly and vice are easy to describe,
The common subjects of our scribbling *tribe.* *Roscommon.*

Tri'blet or **Tribo'ulet.** *n. s.* A goldsmith's tool for making rings. *Ains.*

Tribula'tion. *n. s.* [*tribulation*, Fr.] Persecution; distress; vexation; disturbance of life.

Tribulation being present causeth sorrow, and being imminent breedeth fear. *Hooker, b.* v.

The just shall dwell,
And after all their *tribulations* long,
See golden days, fruitful of golden deeds. *Milton.*

Death becomes
His final remedy; and after life
Try'd in sharp *tribulation*, and refin'd
By faith, and faithful works. *Milton's Par. Lost, b.* xi.

Our church taught us to pray, that God would, not only in all time of our *tribulation*, but in all time of our wealth, deliver us. *Atterbury's Sermons.*

Tribu'nal. *n. s.* [*tribunal*, Latin and French.]

1. The seat of a judge.

I' th' market-place, on a *tribunal* silver'd,
Cleopatra and himself in chairs of gold
Were publickly enthron'd. *Shakesp. Ant. and Cleopatra.*

He sees the room
Where the whole nation does for justice come,
Under whose large roof flourishes the gown,
And judges grave on high *tribunals* frown. *Waller.*

Here the *tribunal* stood. *Dryden's Æn.*

There is a necessity of standing at his *tribunal*, who is infinitely wise and just. *Grew's Cosmol. b.* iii.

2. A court of justice.

Summoning arch-angels to proclaim
Thy dread *tribunal.* *Milton.*

Tri'bune. *n. s.* [*tribun*, *tribunus*, Lat.]

1. An officer of Rome chosen by the people.

These are the *tribunes* of the people,
The tongues o' th' common mouth: I do despise them. *Shakespeare's Coriolanus.*

2. The commander of a Roman legion.

Tribuni'tial. } *adj.* [*tribunitius*, Lat.] Suiting a tribune;
Tribuni'tious. } relating to a tribune.

Let them not come in multitudes, or in a *tribunitious* manner; for that is to clamour counsels, not to inform. *Bacon.*

Oh happy ages of our ancestors,
Beneath the kings and *tribunitial* powers
One jail did all their criminals restrain. *Dryden's Juvenal.*

Tri'butary. *adj.* [*tributaire*, Fr. *tributarius*, Lat.]

1. Paying tribute as an acknowledgement of submission to a master.

Thenceforth this land was *tributary* made
T' ambitious Rome, and did their rule obey,
Till Arthur all that reckoning did defray:
Yet oft the Briton kings against them strongly sway'd. *Fairy Queen, b.* ii.

The two great empires of the world I know;
And since the earth none larger does afford,
This Charles is some poor *tributary* lord. *Dryden.*

Around his throne the sea-born brothers stood,
That swell with *tributary* urns his flood. *Pope.*

2. Subject; subordinate.

These he, to grace his *tributary* gods,
By course commits to several government,
And gives them leave to wear their saphire crowns,
And wield their little tridents. *Milton's Comus.*

O'er Judah's king ten thousand tyrants reign,
Legions of lust, and various pow'rs of ill
Insult the master's *tributary* will. *Prior.*

3. Paid in tribute.

Nor flatt'ry tunes these *tributary* lays. *Concanen.*

Tri'butary. *n. s.* [from *tribute.*] One who pays a stated sum in acknowledgement of subjection.

All the people therein shall be *tributaries* unto thee, and serve thee. *Deut.* xx. 11.

The Irish lords did only promise to become *tributaries* to king Henry the second: and such as only pay tribute, are not properly subjects but sovereigns. *Davies.*

TRI'BUTE. *n. s.* [*tribut*, Fr. *tributum*, Lat.] Payment made in acknowledgement; subjection.

The Lord's *tribute* of the sheep was six hundred. *Numb.*

They that received *tribute* money said, Doth not your master pay *tribute?* *Mat.* xvii. 2.

She receives
As *tribute* her warmth and light. *Milton.*

To acknowledge this was all he did exact;
Small *tribute*, where the will to pay was act. *Dryden.*

Tricoma'nes. *n. s.* A plant.

A branch of some capillary plant, resembling the common *trichomanes*, only the pinnæ are larger in a dusky grey slaty stone. *Woodward.*

Trice. *n. s.* [I believe this word comes from *trait*, Fr. corrupted by pronunciation.] A short time; an instant; a stroke.

If they get never so great spoil at any time, the same they waste in a *trice*, as naturally delighting in spoil, though it do themselves no good.

Just in the nick the cook knock'd thrice,
And all the waiters in a *trice*
His summons did obey:
Each serving man with dish in hand,
March'd boldly up like our train'd band,
Presented, and away. *Suckling.*

He

He could raise scruples dark and nice,
And after solve them in a *trice*. *Hudibras, p.* i.
So when the war had rais'd a storm,
I've seen a snake in human form,
All stain'd with infamy and vice,
Leap from the dunghil in a *trice*. *Swift.*

It seems incredible at first, that all the blood in our bodies should circulate in a *trice*, in a very few minutes; but it would be more surprising if we knew the short periods of the great circulation of water. *Bentley's Sermons.*

TRICHO'TOMY. *n. s.* Division into three parts.

Some disturb the order of nature by dichotomies, *trichotomies*, sevens, twelves: let the subject with the design you have in view determine the number of parts into which you divide it. *Watts.*

TRICK. *n. s.* [*treck*, Dutch.]

1. A sly fraud.

Sir Thomas Moor said, that a *trick* of law had no less power than the wheel of fortune, to lift men up, or cast them down. *Raleigh.*

A bantering droll took a journey to Delphos, to try if he could put a *trick* upon Apollo. *L'Estrange's Fables.*

Such a one thinks to find some shelter in my friendship, and I betray him: he comes to me for counsel and I shew him a *trick*. *South.*

He swore by Stix,
Whate'er she wou'd desire, to grant;
But wise Ardelia knew his *tricks*. *Swift.*

2. A dexterous artifice.

Gather the lowest and leaving the top,
Shall teach thee a *trick* for to double thy crop. *Tusser.*
And now, as oft in some distemper'd state,
On one nice *trick* depends the gen'ral fate. *Pope.*

3. A vicious practice.

Suspicion shall be stuck full of eyes:
For treason is but trusted like a fox,
Who ne'er so tame, so cherish'd and lock'd up,
Will have a wild *trick* of his ancestors. *Shakespeare.*

I entertain you with somewhat more worthy than the stale exploded *trick* of fulsom panegyricks. *Dryden.*

Some friends to vice pretend,
That I the *tricks* of youth too roughly blame. *Dryden.*

4. A juggle; an antick; any thing done to cheat jocosely, or to divert.

A rev'rend prelate stopp'd his coach and six,
To laugh a little at our Andrew's *tricks*. *Prior.*

5. An unexpected effect.

So fellest foes who broke their sleep,
To take the one the other, by some chance,
Some *trick* not worth an egg, shall grow dear friends. *Shakesp. Coriolanus.*

6. A practice; a manner; a habit.

I spoke it but according to the *trick*: if you'll hang me you may. *Shakespeare.*

The *trick* of that voice I well remember. *Shakespeare.*

Behold,
Although the print be little, the whole matter
And copy of the father; eye, nose, lip,
The *trick* of 's frown, his forehead. *Shak. Winter's Tale.*

7. A number of cards laid regularly up in play: as, *a* trick *of cards.*

To TRICK. *v. a.* [from the noun; *tricher*, Fr.]

1. To cheat; to impose on; to defraud.

It is impossible that the whole world should thus conspire to cheat themselves, to put a delusion on mankind, and *trick* themselves into belief. *Stephens's Sermons.*

2. To dress; to decorate; to adorn; properly to knot. [*trica*, in low Latin, signifies *a knot of hair*; *treccia*, Italian: hence *trace*. *Matt. Westmonasteriensis* says of *Godiva* of Coventry, that she rode *tricas capitis & crines dissolvens.*]

And *trick* them up in knotted curls anew. *Drayton.*

They turned the imposture upon the king, and gave out, that to defeat the true inheritor he had *tricked* up a boy in the likeness of Edward Plantagenet. *Bacon's Henry* VII.

Horridly *trickt*
With blood of fathers, mothers, daughters, sons,
Bak'd and impasted with the parching fires. *Shakesp.*

This pillar is but a medley, or a mass of all the precedent ornaments, making a new kind by stealth; and though the most richly *tricked*, yet the poorest in this, that he is a borrower of all his beauty. *Wotton's Architect.*

Their heads are *trickt* with tassels and flowers. *Sandys.*

Woful shepherds, weep no more,
For Lycidas, your sorrow, is not dead:
Sunk, though he be, beneath the wat'ry floor:
So sinks the Day-star in the ocean bed,
And yet anon repairs his drooping head,
And *tricks* his beams, and with new spangled ore,
Flames in the forehead of the morning sky. *Milton.*

A daw that had a mind to be sparkish, *tricked* himself up with all the gay feathers he could muster. *L'Estrange's Fab.*

Love is an airy good, opinion makes,
That *tricks* and dresses up the gawdy dream. *Dryden.*

People lavish it profusely in *tricking* up their children in fine cloaths, and yet starve their minds. *Locke.*

3. To perform by slight of hand, or with a light touch.

The colours and the ground prepare:
Dip in the rainbow, *trick* her off in air,
Chuse a firm cloud before it fall. *Pope.*

To TRICK. *v. n.* To live by fraud.

Thus they jog on, still *tricking*, never thriving,
And murd'ring plays, which they call reviving. *Dryden.*

TRI'CKER. *n. s.* [This is often written *trigger*; I know not which is right.] The catch which being pulled disengages the cock of the gun, that it may give fire.

Pulling aside the *tricker* we observed, that the force of the spring of the lock was not sensibly abated by the absence of the air. *Boyle.*

As a goose
In death contracts his talons close;
So did the knight, and with one claw
The *tricker* of his pistol draw. *Hudibras, p.* i.

TRI'CKING. *n. s.* [from *trick*.] Dress; ornament.

Get us properties and *tricking* for our fairies. *Shakespeare.*

TRI'CKISH. *adj.* [from *trick*.] Knavishly artful; fraudulently cunning; mischievously subtle.

All he says is in a loose, slippery, and *trickish* way of reasoning. *Pope.*

To TRI'CKLE. *v. n.* [Of this word I find no etymology that seems well authorised or probable.] To fall in drops; to rill in a slender stream.

He, prick'd with pride,
Forth spurred fast; adown his courser's side
The red blood *trickling*, stain'd the way. *Fa. Qu. b.* i.
Fast beside there *trickled* softly down
A gentle stream, whose murm'ring wave did play
Amongst the pumy stones, and made a sound
To lull him soft asleep that by it lay. *Fa. Qu. b.* ii.

Some noises help sleep; as, the blowing of the wind, and *trickling* of water, as moving in the spirits a gentle attention, which stilleth the discursive motion. *Bacon.*

He wakened by the *trickling* of his blood. *Wiseman.*

Beneath his ear the fast'ned arrow stood,
And from the wound appear'd the *trickling* blood. *Dryden.*
All at once his grief and rage appear'd,
And floods of tears ran *trickling* down his beard. *Dryden.*
He lay stretch'd along, his eyes fixt upward,
And ever and anon a silent tear
Stole down, and *trickled* from his hoary beard. *Dryden.*

The emblems of honour wrought on the front in the brittle materials above-mentioned, *trickled* away under the first impressions of the heat. *Addison's Freeholder*, N°. 28.

Imbrown'd with native bronze, lo! Henly stands,
Tuning his voice and balancing his hands:
How fluent nonsense *trickles* from his tongue!
How sweet the periods, neither said nor sung. *Pope.*
They empty heads console with empty sound.
No more, alas! the voice of fame they hear,
The balm of dulness *trickling* in their ear. *Pope's Dunciad.*
Subdu'd,
The frost resolves into a *trickling* thaw. *Thomson's Winter.*

TRI'CKSY. *adj.* [from *trick*.] Pretty. This is a word of endearment.

The fool hath planted in his memory
An army of good words; and I do know
A many fools that stand in better place,
Garnish'd like him, that for a *tricksy* word
Defy the matter. *Shakesp. Merchant of Venice.*
All this service have I done since I went.
——My *tricksy* spirit! *Shakespeare's Tempest.*

TRICO'RPORAL. *adj.* [*tricorpus*, Lat.] Having three bodies.

TRIDE. *adj.* [among hunters; *tride*, French.] Short and ready. *Bailey.*

TRI'DENT. *n. s.* [*trident*, Fr. *tridens*, Lat.] A three forked sceptre of Neptune.

His nature is too noble for the world:
He would not flatter Neptune for his *trident*. *Shakespeare.*
Can'st thou with fisgigs pierce him to the quick?
Or in his skull thy barbed *trident* stick? *Sandys on Job.*
He lets them wear their saphire crowns,
And wield their little *tridents*. *Milton.*

Several find a mystery in every tooth of Neptune's *trident*. *Addison on ancient Medals.*

TRI'DENT. *adj.* Having three teeth.

TRI'DING. *n. s.* [ꞇꞃiðinᵹa, Saxon.] The third part of a county or shire. *Bailey.*

TRIDUAN. *adj.* [from *triduum*, Lat.]

1. Lasting three days.
2. Happening every third day.

TRIE'NNIAL. *adj.* [*triennis*, Lat. *triennal*, Fr.]

1. Lasting three years.

I passed the bill for *triennial* parliaments. *King Charles.*

Richard the third, though he came in by blood, yet the ſhort time of his *triennial* reign he was without any, and proved one of my beſt lawgivers. *Howel's England's Tears.*

2. Happening every third year.

TRI'ER. *n. ſ.* [from *try.*]

1. One who tries experimentally.

The ingenious *triers* of the German experiment found, that their glaſs veſſel was lighter when the air had been drawn out than before by an ounce and very near a third. *Boyle.*

2. One who examines judicially.

Courts of juſtice are bound to take notice of acts of parliament, and whether they are truly pleaded or not; and therefore they are the *triers* of them. *Hale.*

There ſhould be certain *triers* or examiners appointed by the ſtate to inſpect the genius of every particular boy. *Spect.*

3. Teſt; one who brings to the teſt.

You were uſed
To ſay, extremity was the *trier* of ſpirits;
That common chances common men could bear. *Shakeſp.*

To TRI'FALLOW. *v. a.* [*tres*, Latin, and ꝼealᵹa, Saxon, a harrow.] To plow land the third time before ſowing. *Bailey.*

The beginning of Auguſt is the time of *trifallowing*, or laſt plowing, before they ſow their wheat. *Mortimer.*

TRI'FID. *adj.* [among botaniſts.] Cut or divided into three parts. *Bailey.*

TRIFI'STULARY. *adj.* [*tres* and *fiſtula*, Latin.] Having three pipes.

Many of that ſpecies whoſe *trifiſtulary* bill or crany we have beheld. *Brown's Vulgar Errours.*

To TRI'FLE. *v. n.* [*tryfelen*, Dutch.]

1. To act or talk without weight or dignity; to act with levity; to talk with folly.

When they ſaw that we ought to abrogate ſuch popiſh ceremonies as are unprofitable, or elſe might have other more profitable in their ſtead, they *trifle* and they beat the air about nothing which toucheth us, unleſs they mean that we ought to abrogate all popiſh ceremonies. *Hooker.*

2. To mock; to play the fool.

Do not believe,
That, from the ſenſe of all civility,
I thus would play and *trifle* with your reverence. *Shakeſp.*

3. To indulge light amuſement.

4. To be of no importance.

'Tis hard for every *trifling* debt of two ſhillings to be driven to law. *Spenſer.*

To TRI'FLE. *v. a.* To make of no importance. Not in uſe.

Threeſcore and ten I can remember well,
Within the volume of which time I've ſeen
Hours dreadful and things ſtrange; but this ſore night
Hath *trifled* former knowings. *Shakeſp. Macbeth.*

TRI'FLE. *n. ſ.* [from the noun.] A thing of no moment.

The inſtruments of darkneſs tell us truths;
Win us with honeſt *trifles*, to betray us
In deepeſt conſequence. *Shakeſp. Macbeth.*

Old Chaucer doth of Topas tell,
Mad Rabelais of Pantagruel,
A later third of Dowſabell,
With ſuch poor *trifles* playing:
Others the like have labour'd at,
Some of this thing, and ſome of that,
And many of they know not what,
But that they muſt be ſaying. *Drayton's Nymphid.*

The infinitely greateſt confeſſed good is neglected, to ſatisfy the ſucceſſive uneaſineſs of our deſires purſuing *trifles*. *Locke.*

TRI'FLER. *n. ſ.* [*trifelaar*, Dutch.] One who acts with levity; one that talks with folly.

A man cannot tell whether Apelles or Albert Durer were the more *triflers*, whereof the one would make a perſonage by geometrical proportions, the other by taking the beſt parts out of divers faces to make one excellent. *Bacon.*

Shall I, who can enchant the boiſt'rous deep,
Bid Boreas halt, make hills and foreſts move,
Shall I be baffled by this *trifler*, love. *Granville.*

As much as ſyſtematical learning is decried by ſome vain *triflers* of the age, it is the happieſt way to furniſh the mind with knowledge. *Watts.*

TRI'FLING. *adj.* [from *trifle.*] Wanting worth; unimportant; wanting weight.

To a ſoul ſupported with an aſſurance of the divine favour, the honours or afflictions of this life will be equally *trifling* and contemptible. *Rogers's Sermons.*

TRI'FLINGLY. *adv.* [from *trifling.*] Without weight; without dignity; without importance.

Thoſe who are carried away with the ſpontaneous current of their own thoughts, muſt never humour their minds in being thus *triflingly* buſy. *Locke.*

TRI'FORM. *adj.* [*triformis*, Lat.] Having a triple ſhape.

The moon her monthly round
Still ending, ſtill renewing through mid heav'n,
With borrow'd light her countenance *triform*
Hence fills, and empties, to enlighten th' earth. *Milton.*

TRI'GGER. *n. ſ.* [derived by *Junius* from *trigue*, Fr. from *intricare*, Lat.]

1. A catch to hold the wheel on ſteep ground.

2. The catch that being pulled looſes the cock of the gun.

The pulling the *trigger* of the gun with which the murder is committed, has no natural connection with thoſe ideas that make up the complex one, murder. *Locke.*

TRINGI'NTALS. *n. ſ.* [from *triginta*, Latin, *thirty.*]

Trentals or *tringintals* were a number of maſſes to the tale of thirty, inſtituted by Saint Gregory. *Ayliffe.*

TRI'GLYPH. *n. ſ.* [In architecture.] A member of the frize of the Dorick order ſet directly over every pillar, and in certain ſpaces in the intercolumnations. *Harris.*

The Dorick order has now and then a ſober garniſhment of lion's heads in the cornice, and of *triglyphs* and metopes always in the frize. *Wotton.*

TRI'GON. *n. ſ.* [*trigone*, Fr.] A triangle. A term in aſtrology.

The ordinary height of a man ninety-ſix digits, the ancient Egyptians eſtimated to be equal to that myſtical cubit among them ſtiled paſſus Ibidis, or the *trigon* that the Ibis makes at every ſtep, conſiſting of three latera, each thirty-two digits. *Hale's Origin of Mankind.*

TRI'GONAL. *adj.* [from *trigon.*] Triangular; having three corners.

A ſpar of a yellow hue ſhot into numerous *trigonal* pointed ſhoots of various ſizes, found growing to one ſide of a perpendicular fiſſure of a ſtratum of free-ſtone in digging. *Woodward on Foſſils.*

TRIGONO'METRY. *n. ſ.* [*trigonometrie*, Fr.]

Trigonometry is the art of meaſuring triangles, or of calculating the ſides of any triangle ſought, and this is plain or ſpherical. *Harris.*

On a diſcovery of Pythagoras all *trigonometry*, and conſequently all navigation, is founded. *Guardian.*

TRIGONOME'TRICAL. *adj.* [from *trigonometry.*] Pertaining to trigonometry.

TRILA'TERAL. *adj.* [*trilateral*, French; *tres* and *latus*, Lat.] Having three ſides.

TRILL. *n. ſ.* [*trillo*, Italian.] Quaver; tremulouſneſs of muſick.

Long has a race of heroes fill'd the ſtage,
That rant by note, and through the gamut rage,
In ſongs and airs expreſs their martial fire
Combat in *trills*, and in a fugue expire. *Addiſon.*

To TRILL. *v. a.* [from the noun.] To utter quavering.

Through the ſoft ſilence of the liſtening night
The ſober-ſuited ſongſtreſs *trills* her lay. *Thomſon.*

To TRILL. *v. n.*

1. To trickle; to fall in drops or ſlender ſtreams.

Did your letters pierce the queen to any demonſtration of grief?
I, ſhe took 'em; read 'em in my preſence;
And now and then an ample tear *trill'd* down
Her delicate cheek. *Shakeſp. King Lear.*

2. To play in tremulous vibrations of ſound.

Am I call'd upon the grave debate,
To judge of *trilling* notes and tripping feet. *Dryden.*

TRI'LLION. *n. ſ.* [A word invented by *Locke*: *trilion*, Fr.] A million of millions of millions; a million twice multiplied by a million.

TRILU'MINAR. } *adj.* [*triluminaris*, Latin.] Having three
TRILU'MINOUS. } lights. *Dict.*

TRIM. *adj.* [ᵹeꞇꞃẏmmeꝺ, Saxon, *completed.*] Nice; ſmug; dreſſed up.

Tone paine in cottage doth take,
When t'other *trim* bowers do make. *Tuſſer's Huſb.*

A *trim* exploit, a manly enterprize,
To conjure tears up in a poor maid's eyes
With your deriſion. *Shak. Midſummer Night's Dream.*

The Dorick order has, in compariſon of thoſe that follow, a more maſculine aſpect, and little *trimmer* than the Tuſcan that went before, ſave a ſober garniſhment now and then of lions heads in the cornice, and of triglyphs and metopes always in the frize. *Wotton's Architect.*

Doſt thou not bluſh to live ſo like a beaſt,
So *trim*, ſo diſſolute, ſo looſely dreſt. *Dryden's Perſius.*

To TRIM. *v. a.* [ꞇꞃẏmman, Saxon, *to build.*]

1. To fit out.

Malicious cenſurers ever,
As rav'nous fiſhes do a veſſel follow
That is new *trimm'd.* *Shakeſp. Henry VIII.*

2. To dreſs; to decorate.

Our youth got me to play the woman's part,
And I was *trim'd* in Julia's gown. *Shakeſpeare.*

Pennyroyal and orpin they uſe in the country to *trim* their houſes, binding it with a lath againſt a wall. *Bacon.*

Two arts attend architecture, like her principal gentlewomen, to dreſs and *trim* her, picture and ſculpture. *Wotton.*

The

The victim ox that was for altars prest,
Trimm'd with white ribbons and with garlands drest,
Sunk of himself. *Dryden's Georg.*

3. To shave; to clip.

Mephibosheth had neither dressed his feet, nor *trimmed* his beard. 2 *Sam.* xix. 24.

Clip and *trim* those tender strings like a beard. *Brown.*

The barber may *trim* religion as he pleases. *Howel.*

Trim off the small superfluous branches. *Mortimer.*

4. To make neat; to adjust.

I found her *trimming* up the diadem
On her dead mistress. *Shakesp. Ant. and Cleopatra.*

Go, sirrah, to my cell, as you look
To have my pardon, *trim* it handsomely. *Shakespeare.*

Yet are the men more loose than they!
More kemb'd, and bath'd, and rubb'd, and *trimm'd*
More sleek, more soft, and slacker limb'd. *Benj. Johnson.*

To blast the living, gave the dead their due,
And wreaths, herself had tainted, *trimm'd* anew. *Tickell.*

When workmen fit a piece into other work, they say they *trim* in a piece. *Moxon's Mech. Exercises.*

Each muse in Leo's golden days
Starts from her trance, and *trims* her wither'd bays. *Pope.*

5. To balance a vessel.

Sir Roger put his coachman to *trim* the boat. *Spectator.*

6. It has often *up* emphatical.

He gave you all the duties of a man,
Trimm'd up your praises with a princely tongue,
Spoke your deservings like a chronicle. *Shakespeare.*

To Trim. *v. n.* To balance; to fluctuate between two parties.

If such by *trimming* and time-serving, which are but two words for the same thing, betray the church by nauseating her pious orders, this will produce confusion. *South's Serm.*

For men to pretend that their will obeys that law, while all besides their will serves the faction; what is this but a gross, fulsome juggling with their duty, and a kind of *trimming* it between God and the devil. *South's Sermons.*

He who heard what ev'ry fool cou'd say,
Wou'd never fix his thought, but *trim* his time away.
Dryden's Hind and Panther.

Trim. *n. s.* Dress; geer; ornaments.

They come like sacrifices in their *trim*,
And to the five-ey'd maid of smoaky war,
All hot, and bleeding, will we offer them. *Shakespeare.*

Forget
Your laboursome and dainty *trims*, wherein
You made great Juno angry. *Shakesp. Cymbeline.*

The goodly London in her gallant *trim*,
The phœnix daughter of the vanquish'd old,
Like a rich bride does to the ocean swim,
And on her shadow rides in floating gold. *Dryden.*

Tri'mly. *adv.* [from *trim.*] Nicely; neatly.

Her yellow golden hair
Was *trimly* woven, and in tresses wrought. *Fairy Queen.*

The mother, if of the houshold of our lady, will have her son cunning and bold, in making him to live *trimly*. *Ascham.*

Tri'mmer. *n. s.* [from *trim.*] One who changes sides to balance parties; a turncoat.

The same bat taken after by a weazel begged for mercy: no, says the weazle, no mercy to a mouse: well, says t'other, but you may see by my wings that I am a bird; and so the bat 'scaped in both by playing the *trimmer*. *L'Estrange's Fab.*

To confound his hated coin,
All parties and religions join,
Whigs, tories, *trimmers*. *Swift.*

2. A piece of wood inserted.

Before they pin up the frame of ground-plates, they must fit in the summer and the girders, and all the joists and the *trimmers* for the stair-case. *Moxon's Mech. Exercise.*

Tri'mming. *n. s.* [from *trim.*] Ornamental appendages to a coat or gown.

Judgment without vivacity of imagination is too heavy, and like a dress without fancy; and the last without the first is too gay, and but all *trimming*. *Garth's Pref. to Ovid.*

Tri'nal. *adj.* [*trinus*, Lat.] Threefold.

Like many an angel's voice,
Singing before th' eternal majesty,
In their *trinal* triplicity on high. *Fa. Qu. b.* i.

That far-beaming blaze of majesty,
Wherewith he wont at heav'n's high council table
To sit the midst of *trinal* unity,
He laid aside. *Milton.*

Trine. *n. s.* [*trine*, Fr. *trinus*, Latin.] An aspect of planets placed in three angles of a trigon, in which they are supposed by astrologers to be eminently benign.

To th' other five,
Their planetary motions, and aspects,
In sextile, square, and *trine*, and opposite,
Of noxious efficacy. *Milton's Par. Lost, b.* x.

Now frequent *trines* the happier lights among,
And high-rais'd Jove from his dark prison freed,
Those weights took off that on his planet hung,
Will gloriously the new-laid works succeed. *Dryden.*

From Aries right-ways draw a line, to end
In the same round, and let that line subtend
An equal triangle; now since the lines
Must three times touch the round, and meet three signs,
Where'er they meet in angles those are *trines*. *Creech.*

To Trine. *v. a.* [from the noun.] To put in a trine aspect.

This advantage age from youth has won,
As not to be outridden, though outrun;
By fortune he was now to Venus *trin'd*,
And with stern Mars in Capricorn was join'd. *Dryden.*

TRI'NITY. *n. s.* [*trinitas*, Lat. *trinité*, Fr.] The incomprehensible union of the three persons in the Godhead.

Touching the picture of the *trinity*, I hold it blasphemous and utterly unlawful. *Peacham.*

In my whole essay there is not any thing like an objection against the *trinity*. *Locke.*

Tri'nket. *n. s.* [This *Skinner* derives somewhat harshly from *trinquet*, Fr. *trinchetto*, Ital. *a topsail.* I rather imagine it corrupted from *tricket*, some petty finery or decoration.]

1. Toys; ornaments of dress; superfluities of decoration.

Beauty and use can so well agree together, that of all the *trinkets* wherewith they are attired, there is not one but serves to some necessary purpose. *Sidney, b.* ii.

We'll see your *trinkets* here forthcoming all. *Shakesp.*

They throng who should buy first, as if my *trinkets* had been hallowed. *Shakesp. Winter's Tale.*

Let her but have three wrinkles in her face,
Soon will you hear the sawcy steward say,
Pack up with all your *trinkets* and away. *Dryden's Juv.*

She was not hung about with toys and *trinkets*, tweezer-cases, pocket-glasses. *Arbuthnot's Hist. of John Bull.*

How Johnny wheedl'd, threat'n'd, fawn'd,
Till Phyllis all her *trinkets* pawn'd. *Swift.*

2. Things of no great value; tackle; tools.

What husbandlie husbands except they be fooles,
But handsom have storehouse for *trinkets* and tooles. *Tuss.*

Go with all your servants and *trinkets* about you. *L'Estr.*

Trio'bolar. *adj.* [*triobolaris*, Latin.] Vile; mean; worthless.

Turn your libel into verse, and then it may pass current amongst the balladmongers for a *triobolar* ballad. *Cheynel.*

To Trip. *v. a.* [*treper*, Fr. *trippen*, Dutch.]

1. To supplant; to throw by striking the feet from the ground by a sudden motion.

He conjunct
Tripp'd me behind. *Shakespeare.*

Be you contented,
To have a son set your decrees at naught,
To *trip* the course of law, and blunt the sword
That guards the peace and safety of your person. *Shakesp.*

2. To strike the feet from under the body.

I *tript* up thy heels and beat thee. *Shakespeare.*

The words of Hobbes's defence *trip* up the heels of his cause; I had once resolved. To resolve presupposeth deliberation, but what deliberation can there be of that which is inevitably determined by causes without ourselves. *Bramhall.*

3. To catch; to detect.

These women
Can *trip* me, if I err; who, with wet cheeks,
Were present when she finish'd. *Shakesp. Cymbeline.*

To Trip. *v. n.*

1. To fall by losing the hold of the feet.

Virgil is so exact in every word, that none can be changed but for a worse: he pretends sometimes to *trip*, but it is to make you think him in danger when most secure. *Dryden.*

2. To fail; to err; to be deficient.

Saint Jerome, who pardons not over-easily his adversaries, if any where they chance to *trip*, presseth him as thereby making all sorts of men God's enemies. *Hooker, b.* v.

Many having used their utmost diligence to secure a retention of the things committed to the memory, cannot certainly know where it will *trip* and fail them. *South.*

Will shines in mixed company, making his real ignorance appear a seeming one: our club has caught him *tripping*, at which times they never spare him. *Addison's Spect.* N°. 105.

Several writers of uncommon erudition would expose my ignorance, if they caught me *tripping* in a matter of so great moment. *Addison's Spect.* N°. 228.

3. To stumble; to titubate.

I may have the idea of a man's drinking till his tongue *trips*, yet not know that it is called drunkenness. *Locke.*

4. To run lightly.

In silence sad,
Trip we after the night's shade. *Shakespeare.*

The old saying is, the third pays for all; the triplex, sir, is a good *tripping* measure. *Shakesp. Twelfth Night.*

He

He throws his arm, and with a long-drawn dash
Blends all together; then distinctly *trips*
From this to that; then quick returning skips
And snatches this again, and pauses there. *Crashaw.*

On old Lycæus or Cyllene hoar,
Trip no more in twilight ranks,
Though Erymanth your loss deplore,
A better soil shall give you thanks. *Milton's Arcades.*

She bounded by, and *tripp'd* so light,
They had not time to take a steady sight. *Dryden.*

To the garden walk she took her way,
To sport and *trip* along in cool of day. *Dryden.*

Stay, nymph, he cry'd, I follow not a foe;
Thus from the lion *trips* the trembling doe. *Dryden.*

Well thou dost to hide from common sight
Thy close intrigues, too bad to bear the light:
Nor doubt I, but the silver-footed dame
Tripping from sea on such an errand came. *Dryden.*

He'll make a pretty figure in a triumph,
And serve to *trip* before the victor's chariot. *Addison.*

The lower plaits of the drapery in antique figures in sculpture and painting, seem to have gathered the wind when the person is in a posture of *tripping* forward. *Addison.*

In Britain's isles, as Heylin notes,
The ladies *trip* in petticoats. *Prior.*

They gave me instructions how to slide down and *trip* up the steepest slopes. *Pope.*

5. To take a short voyage.

TRIP. *n. s.* [from the verb.]

1. A stroke or catch by which the wrestler supplants his antagonist.

O thou dissembling cub! what wilt thou be,
When time hath sow'd a grizzel on thy case?
Or will not else thy craft so quickly grow,
That thine own *trip* shall be thine overthrow? *Shakesp.*

He stript for wrestling, smears his limbs with oil,
And watches with a *trip* his foe to foil. *Dryden's Georg.*

It was a noble time when *trips* and Cornish hugs could make a man immortal. *Addison on ancient Medals.*

2. A stumble by which the foothold is lost.
3. A failure; a mistake.

He saw his way, but in so swift a pace,
To chuse the ground might be to lose the race:
They then, who of each *trip* th' advantage take,
Find but those faults which they want wit to make. *Dryd.*

4. A short voyage or journey.

I took a *trip* to London on the death of the queen. *Pope.*

TRI'PARTITE. *adj.* [*tripartite*, Fr. *tripartitus*, Latin.] Divided into three parts; having three correspondent copies.

Our indentures *tripartite* are drawn. *Shakesp. Henry* IV.

TRIPE. *n. s.* [*tripe*, Fr. *trippa*, Italian and Spanish.]

1. The intestines; the guts.

How say you to a fat *tripe* finely broil'd?
——I like it well. *Shakespeare.*

In private draw your poultry, clean your *tripe*. *King.*

2. It is used in ludicrous language for the human belly.

TIR'PEDAL. *adj.* [*tres* and *pes*, Lat.] Having three feet.

TRIPE'TALOUS. *adj.* [*tres* and πέταλον.] Having a flower consisting of three leaves.

TRI'PHTHONG. *n. s.* [*triphthongue*, Fr. *tres* and φθόγγη.] A coalition of three vowels to form one sound: as, *eau*; *eye*.

TRI'PLE. *adj.* [*triple*, Fr. *triplex*, *triplus*, Lat.]

1. Threefold; consisting of three conjoined.

See in him
The *triple* pillar of the world transform'd
Into a strumpet's stool. *Shakesp. Antony and Cleopatra.*

O night and shades,
How are ye join'd with hell in *triple* knot,
Against th' unarmed weakness of one virgin,
Alone and helpless! *Milton.*

Thrice happy pair! so near ally'd
In royal blood and virtue too:
Now love has you together ty'd,
May none this *triple* knot undo. *Waller.*

By thy *triple* shape as thou art seen
In heav'n, earth, hell, grant this. *Dryden.*

Strong Alcides, after he had slain
The *triple* Geryon, drove from conquer'd Spain
His captive herds. *Dryden's Æn.*

Out bounc'd the mastiff of the *triple* head;
Away the hare with double swiftness fled. *Swift.*

2. Treble; three times repeated.

We have taken this as a moderate measure betwixt the highest and lowest; but if we had taken only a *triple* proportion, it would have been sufficient. *Burnet.*

If then the atheist can have no imagination of more senses than five, why doth he suppose that a body is capable of more! If we had double or *triple* as many, there might still be the same suspicion for a greater number without end. *Bentley's Sermons.*

To TRI'PLE. *v. a.* [from the adjective.]

1. To treble; to make thrice as much, or as many.

To what purpose should words serve, when nature hath more to declare than groans and strong cries; more than streams of bloody sweat; more than his doubled and *tripled* prayers can express. *Hooker, b.* v.

If these halfpence should gain admittance, in no long space of time his limited quantity would be *tripled* upon us. *Swift.*

2. To make threefold.

Time, action, place, are so preserv'd by thee,
That e'en Corneille might with envy see
Th' alliance of his *tripled* unity. *Dryden.*

TRI'PLET. *n. s.* [from *triple.*]

1. Three of a kind.

There sit C—nts, D—ks, and Harrison,
How they swagger from their garrison;
Such a *triplet* could you tell
Where to find on this side hell. *Swift.*

2. Three verses rhyming together: as,

Waller was smooth, but Dryden taught to join
The varying verse, the full resounding line,
The long majestick march and energy divine. *Pope.*

Some wretched lines from this neglected hand
May find my Hero on the foreign strand,
Warm with new fires, and pleas'd with new command. *Prior.*

I frequently make use of *triplet* rhymes, because they bound the sense, making the last verse of the *triplet* a pindarick. *Dryden's Æn.*

TRI'PLICATE. *adj.* [from *triplex*, Lat.] Made thrice as much.

Triplicate ratio, in geometry, is the ratio of cubes to each other; which ought to be distinguish'd from triple. *Harris.*

All the parts, in height, length, and breadth, bear a duplicate or *triplicate* proportion one to another. *Grew.*

TRIPLICA'TION. *n. s.* [from *triplicate.*] The act of trebling or adding three together.

Since the margin of the visible horizon in the heavenly globe is parallel with that in the earthly, accounted but one hundred and twenty miles diameter; sense must needs measure the azimuths, or verticle circles, by *triplication* of the same diameter of one hundred and twenty. *Glanville's Sceps.*

TRIPLI'CITY. *n. s.* [*triplicité*, Fr. from *triplex*, Lat.] Trebleness; state of being threefold.

Like many an angel's voice,
Singing before th' eternal majesty,
In their trinal *triplicity* on high. *Fairy Qu. b.* i.

It was a dangerous *triplicity* to a monarchy, to have the arms of a foreigner, the discontents of subjects, and the title of a pretender to meet. *Bacon's Henry* VII.

Affect not duplicities nor *triplicities*, nor any certain number of parts in your division of things. *Watts's Logick.*

TRI'PMADAM. *n. s.* An herb.

Tripmadam is used in salads. *Mortimer's Husb.*

TRI'POD. *n. s.* [*tripus*, Latin.] A seat with three feet, such as that from which the priestess of Apollo delivered oracles.

Two *tripods* cast in antick mould,
With two great talents of the finest gold. *Dryden's Æn.*

TRI'POLY. *n. s.* [I suppose from the place whence it is brought.] A sharp cutting sand.

In polishing glass with sand, putty, or *tripoly*, it is not to be imagined that those substances can by grating and fretting the glass bring all its least particles to an accurate polish. *Newton's Opticks.*

TRI'POS. *n. s.* A tripod. See TRIPOD.

Welcome all that lead or follow,
To the oracle of Apollo;
Here he speaks out of his pottle,
Or the *tripos*, his tower bottle. *Benj. Johnson.*

Craz'd fool, who would'st be thought an oracle,
Come down from off the *tripos*, and speak plain. *Dryden.*

TRI'PPER. *n. s.* [from *trip.*] One who trips.

TRI'PPING. *adj.* [from *trip.*] Quick; nimble.

The clear sun of the fresh wave largely drew,
As after thirst; which made their flowing shrink
From standing lake, to *tripping* ebb; that stole
With soft foot tow'rds the deep. *Milton's Par. Lost.*

TRI'PPING. *n. s.* [from *trip.*] Light dance.

Back, shepherds, back, enough your play,
Here be without duck or nod,
Other *trippings* to be trod,
Of lighter toes. *Milton.*

TRI'PTOTE. *n. s.* [*triptoton*, Lat.]

Triptote is a noun used but in three cases. *Clark.*

TRIPU'DIARY. *adj.* [*tripudium*, Lat.] Performed by dancing.

Claudius Pulcher underwent the like success when he continued the *tripudiary* augurations. *Brown's Vulgar Errours.*

TRIPUDIA'TION. *n. s.* [*tripudium*, Lat.] Act of dancing.

TRI'PPINGLY. *adv.* [from *tripping.*] With agility; with swift motion.

This ditty after me
Sing, and dance it *trippingly*. *Shakespeare.*

Speak the speech *trippingly* on the tongue: but if you mouth it as many of our players do, I had as lieve the town-crier had spoke my lines. *Shakesp. Hamlet.*

Trire'me. *n. s.* [*triremis*, Lat.] A galley with three benches of oars on a side.

Trise'ction. *n. s.* [*tres* and *sectio*, Lat.] Division into three equal parts: the trisection of an angle is one of the desiderata of geometry.

Tri'stful. *adj.* [*tristis*, Lat.] Sad; melancholy; gloomy; sorrowful. A bad word.

Heav'n's face doth glow
With *tristful* visage; and, as 'gainst the doom,
I thought sick at the act. *Shakesp. Hamlet.*

Trisu'lc. *n. s.* [*trisulcus*, Lat.] A thing of three points.

Consider the threefold effect of Jupiter's *trisulc*, to burn, discuss, and terebrate. *Brown's Vulgar Errours.*

Trisylla'bical. *adj.* [*tresyllabe*, Fr. from *trisyllable.*] Consisting of three syllables.

TRISY'LLABLE. *n. s.* [*trisyllaba*, Latin.] A word consisting of three syllables.

TRITE. *adj.* [*tritus*, Latin.] Worn out; stale; common; not new.

These duties cannot but appear of infinite concern when we reflect how uncertain our time is: this may be thought so *trite* and obvious a reflection, that none can want to be reminded of it. *Rogers's Sermons.*

She gives her tongue no moment's rest,
In phrases batter'd, stale, and *trite*,
Which modern ladies call polite. *Swift.*

Tri'teness. *n. s.* [from *trite.*] Staleness; commonness.

Trithe'ism. *n. s.* [*tritheisme*, Fr. τρεῖς and Θεός.] The opinion which holds three distinct gods.

Tri'turable. *adj.* [*triturable*, Fr. from *triturate.*] Possible to be pounded or comminuted.

It is not only *triturable* and reducible to powder by contrition, but will not subsist in a violent fire. *Brown.*

Tritura'tion. *n. s.* [*trituration*, Fr. *trituro*, Lat.] Reduction of any substances to powder upon a stone with a muller, as colours are ground: it is also called levigation.

He affirmeth, that a pumice stone powdered is lighter than one entire; that abatement can hardly be avoided in *trituration.* *Brown's Vulgar Errours, b.* iv.

Tri'vet. *n. s.* [See Trevet.] Any thing supported by three feet.

The best at horse-race he ordain'd a lady for his prize,
Generally praiseful; fair and young, and skill'd in housewiferies,
Of all kind fitting; and withal a *trivet*, that enclos'd
Twenty-two measures. *Chapman's Iliad.*
The *trivet* table of a foot was lame,
A blot which prudent Baucis overcame,
Who thrusts beneath the limping leg a sherd. *Dryden.*

Tri'vial. *n. s.* [*trivial*, Fr. *trivialis*, Lat.]

1. Vile; worthless; vulgar; such as may be picked up in the highway.

Be subjects great, and worth a poet's voice,
For men of sense despise a *trivial* choice. *Roscommon.*

2. Light; trifling; unimportant; inconsiderable. This use is more frequent, though less just.

This argues conscience in your grace,
But the respects thereof are nice and *trivial*,
All circumstances well considered. *Shakesp. Rich.* III.
See yon mad fools, who, for some *trivial* right,
For love, or for mistaken honour, fight. *Dryden.*

Were they only some slight and *trivial* indiscretions, to which the example of the world exposed us, it might perhaps not much concern our religion. *Rogers's Serm.*

In ev'ry work regard the writer's end;
And if the means be just, the conduct true,
Applause, in spite of *trivial* faults, is due. *Pope.*

The ancient poets are like many modern ladies: let an action be never so *trivial* in itself, they always make it appear of the utmost importance. *Pope.*

Tri'vially. *adv.* [from *trivial.*]

1. Commonly; vulgarly.

Money is not the sinews of war, as is *trivially* said, where the sinews of mens arms, in effeminate people, fail. *Bacon.*

2. Lightly; inconsiderably.

Tri'vialness. *n. s.* [from *trivial.*]

1. Commonness; vulgarity.
2. Lightness; unimportance.

TRI'UMPH. *n. s.* [*triumphus*, Lat. *triomphe*, Fr.]

1. Pomp with which a victory is publickly celebrated.

Hence will I drag thee headlong by the heels
Unto a dunghil, which shall be thy grave;
And there cut off thy most ungracious head,
Which I will bear in *triumph* to the king. *Shakespeare.*

In ancient times the *triumphs* of the generals from victory, and the great donatives upon disbanding the armies, were things able to enflame all mens courage. *Bacon.*

2. State of being victorious.

Sublime with expectation when to see
In *triumph* issuing forth their glorious chief. *Milton.*
Hercules, from Spain,
Arriv'd in *triumph*, from Geryon slain. *Dryden's Æn.*

3. Victory; conquest.

Eros has
Packt cards with Cæsar, and false play'd my glory
Unto an enemy's *triumph.* *Shakesp. Ant. and Cleopatra.*
Each order bright
Sung *triumph*, and him sung victorious king. *Milton.*
Turn arcs of *triumph* to a garden-gate. *Pope.*
If fools admire, or whining coxcombs toast,
The vain coquets the trifling *triumphs* boast. *Logie.*

4. Joy for success.

Great *triumph* and rejoicing was in heav'n. *Milton.*

5. A conquering card now called trump. See Trump.

To Tri'umph. *v. n.* [*triumpho*, Lat. *triompher*, Fr. This word is always accented in prose on the first syllable, but in poetry sometimes on the last.]

1. To celebrate a victory with pomp; to rejoice for victory.

The *triumphing* of the wicked is short, and the joy of the hypocrite is but for a moment. *Job* xx. 5.

Your victory, alas, begets my fears;
Can you not then *triumph* without my tears. *Dryden.*

2. To obtain victory.

This great commander fought many times to persuade Solyman to forbear to use his forces any farther against the Christians, over whom he had sufficiently *triumphed*, and turn them upon the Persians. *Knolles's Hist. of the Turks.*

Then all this earthy grossness quit,
Attir'd with stars, we shall for ever sit,
Triumphing over death, and chance, and time. *Milton.*
There fix thy faith and *triumph* o'er the world;
For who can help, or who can save besides? *Rowe.*
While blooming youth and gay delight
Sit on thy rosey cheeks confest,
Thou hast, my dear, undoubted right
To *triumph* o'er this destin'd breast. *Prior.*

3. To insult upon an advantage gained.

How ill beseeming is it in thy sex
To *triumph*, like an Amazonian trull. *Shakespeare.*
Sorrow on all the pack of you,
That *triumph* thus upon my misery. *Shakespeare.*
Our grand foe,
Who now *triumphs*, and in th' excess of joy
Sole reigning, holds the tyranny of heav'n. *Milton.*

Triu'mphal. *adj.* [*triomphal*, Fr. *triumphalis*, Lat. from *triumph.*] Used in celebrating victory.

He left only *triumphal* garments to the general. *Bacon.*
Ye so near heav'n's door,
Triumphal with *triumphal* act have met. *Milton.*
Steel could the works of mortal pride confound,
And hew *triumphal* arches to the ground. *Pope.*
Lest we should for honour take
The drunken quarrel of a rake;
Or think it seated in a scar,
Or a proud *triumphal* car. *Swift.*

Triu'mphal. *n. s.* [*triumphalia*, Lat. triumphal ornaments.] A token of victory. Not in use.

He to his crew that sat consulting brought
Joyless *triumphals* of his hop'd success.
Milton's Paradise Regain'd.

Triu'mphant. *adj.* [*triumphans*, Lat. *triumphant*, Fr.]

1. Celebrating a victory.

Captives bound to a *triumphant* car. *Shakespeare.*

It was drawn as a *triumphant* chariot, which at the same time both follows and triumphs. *South's Sermons.*

2. Rejoicing as for victory.

Think you, but that I know our state secure,
I would be so *triumphant* as I am? *Shakesp. Rich.* III.
Off with the traitor's head;
And now to London with *triumphant* march,
There to be crowned. *Shakesp. Henry* VI. *p.* iii.
Successful beyond hope, to lead ye forth
Triumphant out of this infernal pit. *Milton.*

3. Victorious; graced with conquest.

He speedily through all the hierarchies
Intends to pass *triumphant*, and give laws. *Milton.*
Athena, war's *triumphant* maid,
The happy son will, as the father, aid. *Pope's Odyssey.*

Triu'mphantly. *adv.* [from *triumphant.*]

1. In a triumphant manner in token of victory; joyfully as for victory.

Victory with little loss doth play
Upon the dancing banners of the French;
Who are at hand *triumphantly* display'd. *Shakespeare.*
Through armed ranks *triumphantly* she drives,
And with one glance commands ten thousand lives. *Gran.*

2. Victoriously; with success.

Thou must, as a foreign recreant, be led
With manacles along our street; or else
Triumphantly tread on thy country's ruin,
And bear the palm. *Shakespeare's Coriolanus.*

3. With insolent exultation.

A mighty governing lye goes round the world, and has almost banished truth out of it; and so reigning *triumphantly* in in its stead, is the source of most of those confusions that plague the universe. *South's Sermons.*

TRIU'MPHER. *n. s.* [from *triumph.*] One who triumphs.

These words become your lips, as they pass through them,
And enter in our ears, like great *triumphers*,
In their applauding gates. *Shakesp. Timon of Athens.*

August was dedicated to Augustus by the senate, because in the same month he was the first time created consul, and thrice *triumpher* in Rome. *Peacham on Drawing.*

TRIU'MVIRATE. } *n. s.* [*triumviratus* or *triumviri*, Lat. *triumvirat*, Fr.] A coalition or concurrence of three men.
TRIUMVIRI.

Lepidus of the *triumvirate*
Should be depos'd. *Shakesp. Ant. and Cleopatra.*

The *triumviri*, the three corner cap of society. *Shakespeare.*

During that *triumvirate* of kings, Henry the eighth of England, Francis the first of France, and Charles the fifth emperor of Germany, none of the three could win a palm of ground but the other two would balance it. *Bacon's Essays.*

With these the Piercies them confederate,
And, as three heads conjoin in one intent,
And instituting a *triumvirate*,
Do part the land in triple government. *Daniel's Civil War.*

From distant regions fortune sends
An odd *triumvirate* of friends. *Swift.*

TRI'UNE. *adj.* [*tres* and *unus*, Lat.] At once three and one.

We read in scripture of a *triune* Deity, of God made flesh in the womb of a virgin, and crucified by the Jews. *Burnet.*

To TROAT. *v. a.* [with hunters.] To cry as a buck does at rutting time. *Dict.*

TRO'CAR. *n. s.* [*trocar* corrupted from *trois quart*, French.] A chirurgical instrument.

The handle of the *trocar* is of wood, the canula of silver, and the perforator of steel. *Sharp's Surgery.*

TROCHA'ICAL. *adj.* [*trochaïque*, Fr. *trochaicus*, Lat.] Consisting of trochees.

TROCHA'NTERS. *n. s.* [τροχαντῆρες.] Two processes of the thigh bone, called rotator major and minor, in which the tendons of many muscles terminate. *Dict.*

TRO'CHEE. *n. s.* [*trochæus*, Lat. *trochée*, Fr. τροχαῖος.] A foot used in Latin poetry, consisting of a long and short syllable.

TROCHI'LICKS. *n. s.* [τροχίλιον, τροχὸς, a wheel.] The science of rotatory motion.

There succeeded new inventions and horologies, composed by *trochilicks*, or the artifice of wheels, whereof some are kept in motion by weight, others without. *Brown.*

It is requisite that we rightly understand some principles in *trochilicks*, or the art of wheel instruments; as chiefly the relation betwixt the parts of a wheel and those of a balance, the several proportions in the semidiameter of a wheel being answerable to the sides of a balance. *Wilkins's Dædalus.*

TRO'CHINGS. *n. s.* The branches on a deer's head. *Ains.*

TROCHI'SCH. *n. s.* [τροχίσκος; *trochisque*, Fr. *trochiscus*, Latin.] A kind of tablet or lozenge.

The *trochisks* of vipers, so much magnified, and the flesh of snakes some ways condited and corrected. *Bacon.*

TRODE, the preterite of *tread.*

They *trode* the grapes and made merry. *Judges* ix. 27.

TRODE. *n. s.* [from *trode*, pret. of *tread.*] Footing.

The *trode* is not so tickle. *Spenser.*

They never set foot on that same *trode*,
But baulke their right way, and strain abroad. *Spenser.*

TROD. } participle passive of *tread.*
TRO'DDEN.

Jerusalem shall be *trodden* down of the Gentiles. *Luke* xxi.

Thou, infernal serpent, shalt not long
Rule in the clouds; like an autumnal star,
Or light'ning, thou shalt fall from heav'n *trod* down
Under his feet. *Milton's Par. Reg. b.* iv.

Ev'n the rough rocks with tender myrtle bloom,
And *trodden* weeds send out a rich perfume. *Addison.*

TRO'GLODYTE. *n. s.* [τρωγλοδύτης.] One who inhabits caves of the earth.

Procure me a *troglodyte* footman, who can catch a roe at his full speed. *Arbuth. and Pope's Mart. Scrib.*

To TROLL. *v. a.* [*trollen*, to roll, Dutch; perhaps from *trochlea*, Lat. a thing to turn round.] To move circularly; to drive about.

With the phant'sies of hey troll,
Troll about the bridal bowl,
And divide the broad-bread cake,
Round about the bride's stake. *Benj. Johnson's Underwoods.*

To TROLL. *v. n.*

1. To roll; to run round.

How pleasant on the banks of Styx
To *troll* it in a coach and six. *Swift.*

2. To fish for a pike with a rod which has a pulley towards the bottom, which I suppose gives occasion to the term.

Nor drain I ponds the golden carp to take,
Nor *trowle* for pikes, dispeoplers of the lake. *Gay.*

TRO'LLOP. *n. s.* [A low word, I know not whence derived.] A slatternly, loose woman.

TRO'LMYDAMES. *n. s.* [Of this word I know not the meaning.]

A fellow I have known to go about with *trolmydames*: I knew him once a servant of the prince. *Shak. Winter's Tale.*

TROOP. *n. s.* [*troupe*, Fr. *troppa*, Italian; *troope*, Dutch; *trop*, Swedish; *troppa*, low Latin.]

1. A company; a number of people collected together.

That which should accompany old age,
As honour, love, obedience, *troops* of friends,
I must not look to have. *Shakesp. Macbeth.*

Saw you not a blessed *troop*
Invite me to a banquet, whose bright faces
Cast thousand beams upon me like the sun. *Shakespeare.*

As the mind, by putting together the repeated ideas of unity, makes the collective mode of any number, as a score, or a gross; so by putting together several particular substances, it makes collective ideas of substances, as a *troop*, an army. *Locke.*

2. A body of soldiers.

Æneas seeks his absent foe,
And sends his slaughter'd *troops* to shades below. *Dryden.*

3. A small body of cavalry.

To TROOP. *v. n.* [from the noun.]

1. To march in a body.

I do not, as an enemy to peace,
Troop in the throngs of military men,
But rather shew a while like fearful war. *Shakespeare.*

They anon
With hundreds, and with thousands, *trooping* came,
Attended. *Milton's Par. Lost, b.* i.

Armies at the call of trumpet
Troop to their standard. *Milton's Par. Lost, b.* vii.

2. To march in haste.

Yonder shines Aurora's harbinger,
At whose approach ghosts, wand'ring here and there,
Troop home to churchyards. *Shakespeare.*

The dry streets flow'd with men,
That *troop'd* up to the king's capacious court. *Chapman.*

3. To march in company.

I do invest you jointly with my power,
Preheminence, and all the large effects
That *troop* with majesty. *Shakesp. King Lear.*

TRO'OPER. *n. s.* [from *troop.*] A horse soldier A trooper fights only on horseback; a dragoon marches on horseback, but fights either as a horseman or footman.

Custom makes us think well of any thing: what can be more indecent now than for any to wear boots but *troopers* and travellers? yet not many years since it was all the fashion. *Grew.*

TROPE. *n. s.* [τρόπος; *trope*, Fr. *tropus*, Lat.] A change of a word from its original signification; as, the clouds *foretel* rain for *foreshew.*

For rhetorick he could not ope
His mouth, but out there flew a *trope.* *Hudibras.*

If this licence be included in a single word, it admits of *tropes*; if in a sentence, of figures. *Dryden.*

TRO'PHIED. *adj.* [from *trophy.*] Adorned with trophies.

Some greedy minion, or imperious wife,
The *trophy'd* arches, story'd halls invade. *Pope.*

TRO'PHY. *n. s.* [*tropæum*, *trophæum*, Latin.] Something taken from an enemy, and shewn or treasured up in proof of victory.

What *trophy* then shall I most fit devise,
In which I may record the memory
Of my love's conquest, peerless beauty's prize
Adorn'd with honour, love, and chastity? *Spenser.*

To have borne
His bruised helmet and his bended sword,
Before him through the city, he forbids;
Giving all *trophy*, signal, and ostent,
Quite from himself to God. *Shakesp. Henry* V.

There lie thy bones,
Till we with *trophies* do adorn thy tomb. *Shakespeare.*

Twice will I not review the morning's rise,
Till I have torn that *trophy* from thy back,
And split thy heart for wearing it. *Shakespeare.*

In ancient times the *trophies* erected upon the place of the victory, the triumphs of the generals upon their return, the great donatives upon the disbanding of the armies, were things able to enflame all mens courage. *Bacon's Essays.*

Around the posts hung helmets, darts, and spears,
And captive chariots, axes, shields, and bars,
And broken beaks of ships, the *trophies* of their wars. *Dry.*

The tomb with manly arms and *trophies* grace,
To shew posterity Elpenor was. *Pope's Odyssey, b.* xi.

TRO'PICAL. *adj.* [from *trope.*]

1. Rhetorically changed from the original meaning.

A strict and literal acceptation of a loose and *tropical* expression was a second ground. *Brown's Vulgar Errours.*

The words are *tropical* or figurative, and import an hyperbole, which is a way of expressing things beyond what really and naturally they are in themselves. *South's Sermons.*

The

The foundation of all parables is, some analogy or similitude between the *tropical* or allusive part of the parable, and the thing intended by it. *South's Sermons.*

2. [From *tropick*.] Placed near the tropick; belonging to the tropick.

The pine apple is one of the *tropical* fruits. *Salmon.*

TRO'PICK. *n. s.* [*tropique*, Fr. *tropicus*, Lat.] The line at which the sun turns back, of which the North has the tropick of Cancer, and the South the tropick of Capricorn.

Under the *tropick* is our language spoke,
And part of Flanders hath receiv'd our yoke. *Waller.*
Since on ev'ry sea, on ev'ry coast,
Your men have been distress'd, your navy tost,
Sev'n times the sun has either *tropick* view'd,
The Winter banish'd, and the Spring renew'd. *Dryden.*

TROPOLO'GICAL. *n. s.* [*tropologique*, Fr. τρόπος and λόγος.] Varied by tropes; changed from the original import of the words.

TROPO'LOGY. *n. s.* [τρόπος and λόγος.] A rhetorical mode of speech including tropes, or a change of some word from the original meaning.

Not attaining the deuterology and second intention of words, they omit their superconsequences, coherences, figures, or *tropologies*, and are not persuaded beyond their literalities. *Brown's Vulgar Errours.*

TRO'SSERS. *n. s.* [*trousses*, Fr.] Breeches; hose. See TROUSE.

You rode like a kern of Ireland; your French hose off, and in your strait *trossers*. *Shakesp. Henry V.*

To TROT. *v. n.* [*trotter*, Fr. *trotten*, Dutch.]

1. To move with a high jolting pace.

Poor Tom, that hath made him proud of heart, to ride on a bay *trotting* horse, over four inch'd bridges, to course his own shadow for a traitor. *Shakesp. King Lear.*

Whom doth time *trot* withal?
—He *trots* hard with a young maid, between the contract of her marriage and the day it is solemniz'd: if the interim be but a sevennight time's pace, is so hard that it seems the length of seven years. *Shakesp. As you like it.*

Take a gentle *trotting* horse, and come up and see your old friends. *Dennis.*

2. To walk fast, in a ludicrous or contemptuous sense.

TROT. *n. s.* [*trot*, Fr. from the verb.]

1. The jolting high pace of a horse.

His honesty is not
So loose or easy, that a ruffling wind
Can blow away, or glitt'ring look it blind:
Who rides his sure and even *trot*,
While the world now rides by, now lags behind. *Herbert.*
Here lieth one who did most truly prove,
That he could never die while he could move;
So hung his destiny, never to rot
While he might still jog on and keep his *trot*. *Milton.*

The virtuoso's saddle will amble when the world is upon the hardest *trot*. *Dryden.*

2. An old woman. In contempt. I know not whence derived.

Give him gold enough, and marry him to an old *trot* with ne'er a tooth in her head: why, nothing comes amiss, so money comes withal. *Shak. Taming of the Shrew.*

How now bold-face, cries an old *trot*; sirrah, we eat our own hens, and what you eat you steal. *L'Estrange.*

TROTH. *n. s.* [*trouth*, old English; ꞇꞃeoƿ, Saxon.] Truth; faith; fidelity.

Saint Withold met the night-mare,
Bid her light and her *troth* plight. *Shakespeare.*
Stephen assails the realm, obtains the crown,
Such tumults raising as torment them both:
Th' afflicted state, divided in their *troth*
And partial faith, most miserable grown,
Endures the while. *Daniel's Civil War.*
In *troth*, thou'rt able to instruct grey hairs,
And teach the wily African deceit. *Addison's Cato.*

TRO'THLESS. *adj.* [from *troth*.] Faithless; treacherous.

Thrall to the faithless waves and *trothless* sky. *Fairfax.*

TRO'THPLIGHT. *adj.* [*troth* and *plight*.] Betrothed; affianced.

This, your son in law,
Is *trothplight* to your daughter. *Shakesp. Winter's Tale.*

To TRO'UBLE. *v. a.* [*troubler*, Fr.]

1. To disturb; to perplex.

An hour before the worshipp'd sun
Pear'd through the golden window of the East,
A *troubled* mind drew me to walk abroad. *Shakespeare.*
But think not here to *trouble* holy rest. *Milton.*

Never *trouble* yourself about those faults which age will cure. *Locke on Education.*

2. To afflict; to grieve.

It would not *trouble* me to be slain for thee, but much it torments me to be slain by thee. *Sidney, b. ii.*

They pertinaciously maintain that afflictions are no real evils, and therefore a wise man ought not to be *troubled* at them. *Tillotson's Sermons.*

Though it is in vain to be *troubled* for that which I cannot chuse, yet I cannot chuse but be afflicted. *Tillotson's Sermons.*

3. To distress; to make uneasy.

Be not dismay'd nor *troubled* at these tidings. *Milton.*
He was sore *troubled* in mind, and much distressed. *1 Mac.*

4. To busy; to engage overmuch.

Martha, thou art careful, and *troubled* about many things. *Luke x. 41.*

5. To give occasion of labour to. A word of civility or slight regard.

I will not *trouble* myself to prove that all terms are not definable, from that progress *in infinitum* which it will lead us into. *Locke.*

6. To teize; to vex.

The boy so *troubles* me;
'Tis past enduring. *Shakespeare.*

7. To disorder; to put into agitation or commotion.

A woman mov'd is like a fountain *troubled*;
Muddy, ill seeming, thick, bereft of beauty. *Shakespeare.*

An angel went down into the pool and *troubled* the water; whosoever first after the *troubling* stepped in was made whole. *John v. 4.*

God looking forth will *trouble* all his host. *Milton.*
Hear how she the ear employs;
Their office is the *troubled* air to take. *Davies.*
Seas are *troubled* when they do revoke
Their flowing waves into themselves again. *Davies.*

It is not bare agitation, but the sediment at the bottom that *troubles* and defiles the water. *South.*

The best law in our days is that which continues our judges during their good behaviour, without leaving them to the mercy of such who might, by an undue influence, *trouble* and pervert the course of justice. *Addison's Guard.* Nº. 99.

Thy force alone their fury can restrain,
And smooth the waves, or swell the *troubl'd* main. *Dryden.*

8. To mind with anxiety.

He had credit enough with his master to provide for his own interest, and *troubled* not himself for that of others. *Clar.*

9. [In low language.] To sue for a debt.

TRO'UBLE. *n. s.* [*trouble*, French.]

1. Disturbance; perplexity.

They all his host derided, while they stood
A while in *trouble*. *Milton.*

2. Affliction; calamity.

Double, double, toil and *trouble*,
Fire burn and cauldron bubble. *Shakesp. Macbeth.*

3. Molestation; obstruction; inconvenience.

Take to thee from among the cherubim
The choice of flaming warriours, lest the fiend
Some new *trouble* raise. *Milton.*

4. Uneasiness; vexation.

I have dream'd
Of much offence and *trouble*, which my mind
Knew never till this irksome night. *Milton.*

TRO'UBLE-STATE. *n. s.* [*trouble* and *state*.] Disturber of a community; publick makebate.

Those fair baits these *trouble-states* still use,
Pretence of common good, the king's ill course,
Must be cast forth. *Daniel's Civil War.*

TRO'UBLER. *n. s.* [from *trouble*.] Disturber; confounder.

Unhappy falls that hard necessity,
Quoth he, the *troubler* of my happy peace,
And vowed foe of my felicity. *Fairy Qu. b. i.*
Heav'ns hurl down their indignation
On thee, thou *troubler* of the poor world's peace! *Shak.*

The best temper of minds desireth good name and true honour; the lighter, popularity and applause; the more depraved, subjection and tyranny; as is seen in great conquerors and *troublers* of the world, and more in arch-hereticks. *Bac.*

Spain,
Whose chief support and sinews are of coin,
Our nation's solid virtue did oppose
To the rich *troublers* of the world's repose. *Waller.*

The sword justly drawn by us can scarce safely be sheathed, till the power of the great *troubler* of our peace be pared, as to be under no apprehensions for the future. *Atterbury.*

TRO'UBLESOME. *adj.* [from *trouble*.]

1. Full of molestation; vexatious; uneasy; afflictive.

Heav'n knows
By what bye-paths and indirect crooked ways
I met this crown; and I myself know well
How *troublesome* it sat upon my head:
To thee it shall descend with better quiet. *Shakespeare.*

He must be very wise that can forbear being troubled at things very *troublesome*. *Tillotson's Sermons.*

Though our passage through this world be rough and *troublesome*, yet the trouble will be but short, and the rest and contentment at the end will be an ample recompence. *Atterb.*

2. Burdensome; tiresome; wearisome.

My mother will never be *troublesome* to me. *Pope.*

3. Full of teizing business.

All this could not make us accuse her, though it made us almost pine away for spight, to lose any of our time in so *troublesome* an idleness. *Sidney.*

4. Slightly

4. Slightly harrassing.

They eas'd the putting off
These *troublesome* disguises which we wear. *Milton.*

Why doth the crown lie there upon his pillow,
Being so *troublesome* a bedfellow. *Shakesp. Henry* IV.

5. Unseasonably engaging; improperly importuning.

She of late is lightened of her womb,
That her to see should be but *troublesome.* *Fa. Qu. b.* i.

6. Importunate; teizing.

Two or three *troublesome* old nurses, never let me have a quiet night's rest with knocking me up. *Arbuthnot.*

TRO'UBLESOMELY. *adv.* [from *troublesome.*] Vexatiously; wearisomely; unseasonably; importunately.

Though men will not be so *troublesomely* critical as to correct others in the use of words; yet where truth is concerned, it can be no fault to desire their explication. *Locke.*

TRO'UBLESOMENESS. *n. s.* [from *troublesome.*]

1. Vexatiousness; uneasiness.

The lord treasurer, he complained of the *troublesomeness* of the place, for that the exchequer was so empty: the chancellor answered, be of good cheer, for now you shall see the bottom of your business at the first. *Bacon.*

2. Importunity; unseasonableness.

TRO'UBLOUS. *adj.* [from *trouble.*] Tumultuous; confused; disordered; put into commotion. An elegant word, but disused.

He along would fly
Upon the streaming rivers, sport to find;
And oft would dare tempt the *troublous* wind. *Spenser.*

Soon as they this mock king did espy,
Their *troublous* strife they stinted by and by. *Hubb. Tale.*

No other noise, nor people's *troublous* cries,
As still are wont t' annoy the walled town,
Might there be heard. *Fairy Queen, b.* i.

As a tall ship tossed in *troublous* seas,
Whom raging winds threaten to make the prey
Of the rough rocks. *Fairy Queen, b.* ii.

Then, masters, look to see a *troublous* world. *Shakesp.*

Only one supply
In four years *troublous* and expensive reign. *Daniel.*

TRO'VER. *n. s.* [*trouver*, French.] In the common law, is an action which a man hath against one that having found any of his goods refuseth to deliver them upon demand. *Cowel.*

TROUGH. *n. s.* [τροȝ, τροh, Saxon; *troch*, Dutch; *trou*, Danish; *traug*, Islandick; *truogo*, Italian.] Any thing hollowed and open longitudinally on the upper side.

The bloody boar
That spoil'd your summer fields and fruitful vines,
Swills your warm blood like wash, and makes his *trough*
In your embowel'd bosoms. *Shakesp. Rich.* III.

They had no ships but big *troughs*, which they call canoes. *Abbot's Description of the World.*

Where there is a good quick fall of rain water, lay a half *trough* of stone, of a good length, three foot deep, with one end upon the high ground, the other upon the low; cover the *trough* with brakes a good thickness, and cast sand upon the top of the brakes, the lower end of the *trough* will run like a spring of water. *Bacon's Nat. Hist.* N°. 29.

Some log, perhaps, upon the water swam,
An useless drift, which rudely cut within,
And hollow'd, first a floating *trough* became,
And cross some riv'let passage did begin. *Dryden.*

The water dissolves the particles of salt mixed in the stone, and is conveyed by long *troughs* and canals from the mines to Hall, where it is received in vast cisterns and boiled off. *Add.*

To TROUL. *v. n.* [*trollen*, to roll, Dutch.] See TROLL.

1. To move volubly.

Bred only, and completed, to the taste
Of lustful appetence; to sing, to dance,
To dress, and *troul* the tongue, and roll the eye. *Milton.*

2. To utter volubly.

Let us be jocund. Will you *troul* the catch
You taught me while-ere. *Shakespeare's Tempest.*

To TROUNCE. *v. a.* [derived by *Skinner* from *tronc* or *tronson*, French, a club.] To punish by an indictment or information.

More probable, and like to hold
Than hand, or seal, or breaking gold;
For which so many, that renounc'd
Their plighted contracts have been *trounc'd.* *Hudibras.*

If you talk of peaching, I'll peach first: I'll *trounce* you for offering to corrupt my honesty. *Dryden's Spanish Fryar.*

TROUSE. } *n. s.* [*trousse*, Fr. *truish*, Erse.] Breeches; hose.
TRO'USERS. } See TROSSERS.

The leather quilted jack serves under his shirt of mail, and to cover his *trouse* on horseback. *Spenser on Ireland.*

The unsightliness and pain in the leg may be helped by wearing a laced stocking; a laced *trouse* will do as much for -- thigh. *Wiseman's Surgery.*

[...] [τρuhτ, Saxon; *trocta*, *truta*, *trutta*, Lat.]
[...] spotted fish inhabiting brooks and quick streams.
[...]nd will keep *trout* and salmon in their seasonable
[...]t not in their reddish grain. *Carew.*

Worse than the anarchy at sea,
Where fishes on each other prey;
Where ev'ry *trout* can make as high rants
O'er his inferiours as our tyrants. *Swift.*

2. A familiar phrase for an honest, or perhaps for a silly fellow.

Here comes the *trout* that must be caught with tickling. *Shakespeare.*

To TROW. *v. n.* [τreoδian, Saxon; *troe*, Danish.] To think; to imagine; to conceive. A word now disused, and rarely used in ancient writers but in familiar language.

What handsomeness, *trow* you, can be observed in that speech, which is made one knows not to whom? *Sidney.*

Is there any reasonable man, *trow* you, but will judge it meeter that our ceremonies of Christian religion should be Popish than Turkish or Heathenish. *Hooker, b.* iv.

Lend less than thou owest,
Learn more than thou *trowest.* *Shakesp. King Lear.*

To-morrow next
We will for Ireland; and 'tis time, I *trow.* *Shakespeare.*

O rueful day! rueful indeed, I *trow.* *Gay.*

TROW. *interject.* [for *I trow*, or *trow you.*] An exclamation of enquiry.

Well, if you be not turn'd Turk, there is no more sailing by the star.
—What means the fool, *trow?* *Shakespeare.*

TRO'WEL. *n. s.* [*truelle*, Fr. *trulla*, Lat.]

A *trowel* is a tool to take up the mortar with, and spread it on the bricks; with which also they cut the bricks to such lengths as they have occasion, and also stop the joints. *Moxon.*

Fair princess, you have lost much good sport.
—Sport! of what colour?
—What colour, madam? how shall I answer you?
—As wit and fortune will.
—Or as the destinies decree.
—Well said, that was laid on with a *trowel.* *Shakespeare.*

This was dext'rous at his *trowel*,
That was bred to kill a cow well. *Swift.*

TROY-WE'IGHT. } *n. s.* [from *Troies*, Fr.] A kind of weight
TROY. } by which gold and bread are weighed, consisting of these denominations: a pound = 12 ounces; ounce = 20 pennyweights; pennyweight = 24 grains.

The English physicians make use of *troyweight* after the following manner.

Grains				
20	Scruple			
60	3	Drachm		
480	24	8	Ounce	
5760	288	96	12	Pound.

The Romans left their ounce in Britain, now our averdupois ounce, for our *troy* ounce we had elsewhere. *Arbuthnot.*

TRU'ANT. *n. s.* [*truand*, Old Fr. *treuwant*, Dutch, *a vagabond.*] An idler; one who wanders idly about, neglecting his duty or employment. To play the *truant* is, in schools, to stay from school without leave.

For my part I may speak it to my shame,
I have a *truant* been to chivalry. *Shakespeare.*

Though myself have been an idle *truant*,
Omitting the sweet benefit of time,
To cloath mine age with angel-like perfection;
Yet hath Sir Protheus made fair advantage of his days. *Shakesp. Two Gentlemen of Verona.*

Providence would only initiate mankind into the knowledge of her treasures, leaving the rest to our industry, that we might not live like idle loiterers and *truants.* *More.*

Our ships are laden with the Trojan store,
And you like *truants* come too late ashore. *Dryden's Æn.*

TRUANT. *adj.* Idle; wandering from business; lazy; loitering.

What keeps you from Wertemberg?
—A *truant* disposition, good my lord. *Shakesp. Hamlet.*

He made a blushing cital of himself,
And chid his *truant* youth with such a grace,
As if he master'd there a double spirit,
Of teaching, and of learning instantly. *Shakespeare.*

Where thou seest a single sheep remain
In shades aloof, or couch'd upon the plain,
Or late to lag behind with *truant* pace,
Revenge the crime, and take the traytor's head. *Dryden.*

To TRUANT. *v. n.* [*truander*, to beg about a country, French; *truwanten*, old German.] To idle at a distance from duty; to loiter; to be lazy.

'Tis double wrong to *truant* with your bed,
And let her read it in thy looks at board. *Shakespeare.*

TRU'ANTSHIP. *n. s.* [*trualté*, Old Fr. from *truant*; *truandise* in *Chaucer* is beggery.] Idleness; negligence; neglect of study or business.

The master should not chide with him if the child have done his diligence, and used no *truantship.* *Ascham.*

TRU'BTAIL. *n. s.* A short squat woman. *Ainsworth.*

TRUBS. *n. s.* [*tuber*, Lat.] A sort of herb. *Ains.*

TRUCE. *n. s.* [*truga*, low Lat. *tregua*, Italian; *truie*, old Fr.]

1. A temporary peace; a cessation of hostilities.

Leagues and *truces* made between superstitious persons, and such as serve God aright. *Hooker, b.* v.

They pray in vain to have sin pardoned, which seek not also to prevent sin by prayer, even every particularsin, by prayer against all sin, except men can name some transgression wherewith we ought to have *truce*. *Hooker.*

All this utter'd
With gentle breath, calm look, knees humbly bent,
Could not make *truce* with the unruly spleen
Of Tybalt, deaf to peace. *Shakespeare.*

This token serveth for a flag of *truce*
Betwixt ourselves, and all our followers. *Shakespeare.*

Men shall be lovers of their own selves, without natural affection, *truce* breakers. *2 Tim.* iii. 3.

Least the *truce* with treason should be mixt,
'Tis my concern to have the tree betwixt. *Dryden.*

Shadwel till death true dulness would maintain;
And in his father's right, and realm's defence,
Ne'er wou'd have peace with wit, nor *truce* with sense. *Dryd.*

2. Cessation; intermission; short quiet.

There he may find
Truce to his restless thoughts, and entertain
The irksome hours. *Milton.*

TRUCIDA'TION. *n. s.* [from *trucido*, Lat.] The act of killing.

To TRUCK. *v. n.* [*troquer*, Fr. *truccare*, Italian; *trocar*, Spanish; deduced by *Salmasius* from τρώγειν, *to get money.*] To traffick by exchange; to give one commodity for another.

To TRUCK. *v. a.* To give in exchange; to exchange.

The Indians *truck* gold for glasses. *L'Estrange.*

Go, miser! go; for lucre sell thy soul,
Truck wares for wares, and trudge from pole to pole;
That men may say, when thou art dead and gone,
See, what a vast estate he left his son. *Dryden.*

I see nothing left us, but to *truck* and barter our goods like the wild Indians, with each other. *Swift.*

TRUCK. *n. s.* [from the verb.]

1. Exchange; traffick by exchange.

It is no less requisite to maintain a *truck* in moral offices, than in the common business of commerce. *L'Estrange.*

Love is covetous; I must have all of you: heart for heart is an equal *truck*. *Dryden.*

2. [τροχὸς.] Wooden wheels for carriage of cannon. *Ains.*

TRU'CKLEBED, or *trundlebed. n. s.* [properly *troclebed*; from *trochlea*, Latin, or τροχὸς.] A bed that runs on wheels under a higher bed.

There's his chamber, his house, his castle, his standing bed and *trucklebed*. *Shakesp. Merry Wives of Windsor.*

If he that is in battle slain,
Be in the bed of honour lain;
He that is beaten may be said,
To lie in honour's *trucklebed*. *Hudibras, p.* i.

To TRU'CKLE. *v. n.* [This word is, I believe, derived from *trucklebed*, which is always under another bed.] To be in a state of subjection or inferiority; to yield; to creep.

Shall our nation be in bondage thus
Unto a land that *truckles* under us. *Cleaveland.*

For which so many a legal cuckold
Has been run down in courts and *truckl'd*. *Hudibras.*

Men may be stiff and obstinate upon a wrong ground, and ply and *truckle* too upon as false a foundation. *L'Estrange.*

Religion itself is forced to *truckle* to worldly policy. *Norris.*

His zeal was not to lash our crimes,
But discontent against the times:
For had we made him timely offers,
To raise his post or fill his coffers.
Perhaps he might have *truckled* down,
Like other brethren of his gown. *Swift.*

They were subdued and insulted by Alexander's captains, and continued under several revolutions, a small *truckling* state, of no name till they fell under the Romans. *Swift.*

TRU'CULENCE. *n. s.* [*truculentia*, Lat.]

1. Savageness of manners.

2. Terribleness of aspect.

TRUCULENT. *adj.* [*truculentus*, Lat.]

1. Savage; barbarous.

A barbarous Scythia where the savage and *truculent* inhabitants transfer themselves from place to place in waggons, as they can find pasture, and live upon milk, and flesh roasted in the sun at the pomels of their saddles. *Ray.*

2. Terrible of aspect.

3. Destructive; cruel.

Pestilential seminaries, according to their grossness or subtilty, cause more or less *truculent* plagues, some of such malignity, that they enecate in two hours. *Harvey on the Plague.*

To TRUDGE. *v. n.* [*truggiolare*, Italian.] To travel laboriously; to jog on; to march heavily on.

No man is secure, but night-walking heralds,
That *trudge* between the king and mistress Shore. *Shakesp.*

No sooner was he fit to *trudge*,
But both made ready to dislodge. *Hudibras, p.* iii.

Away they *trudged* together, and about midnight got to their journey's end. *L'Estrange's Fables.*

Go, miser! go; for lucre sell thy soul,
Truck wares for wares, and *trudge* from pole to pole;
That men may say, when thou art dead and gone,
See, what a vast estate he left his son! *Dryden.*

Once a poor rogue, 'tis true, I trod the street,
And *trudg'd* to Rome upon my naked feet:
Gold is the greatest god. *Dryden's Juvenal.*

He that will know the truth, must leave the beaten track, which none but servile minds *trudge* continually in. *Locke.*

TRUE. *adj.* [ꞇꞃeopa, ꞇꞃupa, Saxon.]

1. Not false; not erroneous; agreeing with fact, or with the nature of things.

Of those he chose he falsest two,
And fittest for to forge *true* seeming lies. *Fairy Qu. b.* i.

Teeth hadst thou in thy head when thou wast born,
And, if the rest be *true* which I have heard,
Thou cam'st into the world with thy legs forward. *Shak.*

A new commandment I write, which thing is *true* in him and in you. *1 John* ii. 8.

What you said had not been *true*,
If spoke by any else but you. *Cowley.*

2. Not false; agreeing with our own thoughts.

3. Pure from the crime of falsehood; veracious.

4. Genuine; not counterfeit.

The darkness is past, and the *true* light now shineth. *1 Joh.*

Among unequals what society
Can sort? What harmony or *true* delight? *Milton.*

Religion, as it is the most valuable thing in the world, so it gives the *truest* value to them who promote the practice of it by their example and authority. *Atterbury.*

5. Faithful; not perfidious; steady.

My revenge is now at Milford, would I had wings to follow it! come and be *true*. *Shakespeare's Cymbeline.*

So young and so untender?
——So young my lord, and *true*.
——Let it be so; thy truth then be thy dower. *Shakesp.*

Do not see
My fair rose wither; yet look up; behold,
That you in pity may dissolve to dew,
And wash him fresh again with *true* love tears. *Shakesp.*

The first great work
Is, that yourself may to yourself be *true*. *Roscommon.*

I'll rather die
Deserted, than oblige thee with a fact
Pernicious to thy peace, chiefly assur'd
Remarkably so late of thy so *true*,
So faithful, love unequal'd. *Milton's Par. Lost, b.* ix.

When this fire is kindled, both sides inflame it: all regard of merit is lost in persons employed, and these only chosen that are *true* to the party. *Temple.*

Smil'd Venus, to behold her own *true* knight
Obtain the conquest, though he lost the fight. *Dryden.*

True to the king her principles are found;
Oh that her practice were but half so found!
Stedfast in various turns of state she stood,
And seal'd her vow'd affection with her blood. *Dryden.*

The *truest* hearts for Voiture heav'd with sighs;
Voiture was wept by all the brightest eyes. *Pope.*

True to his charge the bard preserv'd her long
In honour's limits, such the pow'r of song. *Pope.*

6. Honest; not fraudulent.

The thieves have bound the *true* man: now could thou and I rob the thieves and go merrily to London, it would be argument for a week. *Shakesp. Henry* IV.

If king Edward be as *true* and just,
As I am subtle, false, and treacherous,
This day should Clarence closely be mew'd up. *Shakesp.*

7. Exact; truly conformable to a rule.

If all those great painters, who have left us such fair platforms, had rigorously observed it, they had made things more regularly *true*, but withal very unpleasing. *Dryden's Dufresnoy.*

He drew
A circle regularly *true*. *Prior.*

Tickel's first book does not want its merit; but I was disappointed in my expectation of a translation nicely *true* to the original; whereas in those parts where the greatest exactness seems to be demanded, he has been the least careful. *Arb.*

8. Rightful.

They seize the sceptre;
Then lose it to a stranger, that the *true*
Anointed King Messiah might be born
Bar'd of his right. *Milton.*

TRUEBO'RN. *n. s.* [*true* and *born.*] Having a right by birth.

Where'er I wander, boast of this I can,
Though banish'd, yet a *trueborn* Englishman. *Shakespeare.*

Let him that is a *trueborn* gentleman,
And stands upon the honour of his birth,
From off this briar pluck a white rose with me. *Shakesp.*

Truebre'd. *adj.* [*true* and *bred.*] Of a right breed.

Two of them I know to be as *truebred* cowards as ever turned back. *Shakespeare.*

Bauble do you call him? he's a substantial *truebred* beast, bravely forehanded. *Dryden's Don Sebastian.*

Truehe'arted. *n. s.* [*true* and *heart.*] Honest; faithful.

I have known no honester or *truerhearted* man: fare thee well. *Shakespeare.*

Tru'elove. *n. s.* An herb, called *herba Paris.*

Truelo'veknot. } *n. s.* [*true, love,* and *knot.*] Lines
Truelo'versknot. } drawn through each other with many involutions, considered as the emblem of interwoven affection.

I'll carve your name on barks of trees
With *trueloveknots*, and flourishes,
That shall infuse eternal spring. *Hudibras, p.* ii.

Tru'eness. *n. s.* [from *true.*] Sincerity; faithfulness.

The even carriage between two factions proceedeth not always of moderation, but of a *trueness* to a man's self, with end to make use of both. *Bacon's Essays.*

Truepe'nny. *n. s.* [*true* and *penny.*] A familiar phrase for an honest fellow.

Say'st thou so? art thou there, *truepenny?*
Come on. *Shakespeare.*

Tru'ffle. *n. s.* [*trufle, truffe,* French.]

In Italy, the usual method for the finding of *truffles*, or subterraneous mushrooms, called by the Italians tartufali, and in Latin tubera terræ, is by tying a cord to the hind leg of a pig, and driving him, observing where he begins to root. *Ray.*

Trug. *n. s.* A hod for mortar. *Ainsw.*

Trull. *n. s.* [*trulla,* Italian.]

1. A low whore; a vagrant strumpet.

I'm sure, I scar'd the dauphin and his *trull.* *Shakespeare.*
A *trull* who sits
By the town wall, and for her living knits. *Dryden.*

So Mævius, when he drain'd his skull,
To celebrate some suburb *trull*;
His similies in order set,
And ev'ry crambo he cou'd get;
Before he could his poem close,
The lovely nymph had lost her nose. *Swift.*

2. It seems to have had first at least a neutral sense: a girl; a lass; a wench.

Among the rest of all the route
A passing proper lasse,
A white-hair'd *trull*, of twenty years,
Or neere about there was:
In stature passing all the rest,
A gallant girl for hewe;
To be compar'd with townish nymphs,
So fair she was to viewe. *Turberville.*

Tru'ly. *adv.* [from *true.*]

1. According to truth; not falsely; faithfully; honestly.

They thought they might do it, not only willingly, because they loved him; and *truly*, because such indeed was the mind of the people; but safely, because she who ruled the king was agreed thereto. *Sidney, b.* ii.

No untruth can avail the patron long; for things most *truly* are most behoovefully spoken. *Hooker.*

Wisdom alone is *truly* fair. *Milton.*

2. Really; without fallacy.

3. Exactly; justly.

Right reason is nothing else but the mind of man judging of things *truly*, and as they are in themselves. *South.*

4. Indeed.

I have not undertaken it out of any wanton pleasure in mine own pen; nor *truly* without often pondering with myself beforehand what censures I might incur. *Wotton.*

TRUMP. *n. s.* [*trompe*, Dutch, and old Fr. *tromba,* Italian.]

1. A trumpet; an instrument of warlike musick.

Whilst any *trump* did sound, or drum struck up,
His sword did ne'er leave striking in the field. *Shakesp.*

Yet first to those ychain'd in sleep,
The wakeful *trump* of doom must thunder through the deep. *Milton.*

I heard
The neighing coursers and the soldiers cry,
And sounding *trumps* that seem'd to tear the sky. *Dryden.*

Beneath this tomb an infant lies,
To earth whose body lent,
Hereafter shall more glorious rise,
But not more innocent.
When the archangel's *trump* shall blow,
And souls to bodies join,
What crowds shall wish their lives below
Had been as short as thine. *Wesley.*

2. [Corrupted from *triumph. Latimer*, in a Christmas sermon, exhibited a game at cards, and made the ace of hearts *triumph. Fox.*] A winning card; a card that has particular privileges in a game.

Him Basto follow'd, but his fate more hard,
Gain'd but one *trump* and one plebeian card. *Pope.*

Now her heart with pleasure jumps,
She scarce remembers what is *trumps.* *Swift.*

3. *To put to* or *upon the* Trumps. To put to the last expedient.

We are now put *upon* our last *trump*; the fox is earth'd, but I shall send my two terriers in after him. *Dryden.*

To **Trump.** *v. a.* [from the noun.]

1. To win with a trump card.

2. *To* Trump *up.* [from *tromper*, Fr. to cheat.] To devise; to forge.

Tru'mpery. *n. s.* [*tromperie*, French, a cheat.]

1. Something fallaciously splendid; something of less value than it seems.

The *trumpery* in my house bring hither,
For state to catch these thieves. *Shakespeare's Tempest.*

2. Falsehood; empty talk.

Breaking into parts the story of the creation, and delivering it over in a mystical sense, wrapping it up mixed with other their own *trumpery*, they have sought to obscure the truth thereof. *Raleigh's Hist. of the World.*

3. Something of no value; trifles.

Embrio's and idiots, eremits and friars,
White, black, and grey, with all their *trumpery.* *Milton.*

Another cavity of the head was stuffed with billetdoux, pricked dances, and other *trumpery* of the same nature. *Addison.*

Tru'mpet. *n. s.* [*trompette*, French and Dutch.]

1. An instrument of martial musick sounded by the breath.

What's the business?
That such a hideous *trumpet* calls to parley
The sleepers of the house. *Shakespeare.*

If any man of quality will maintain upon Edmund earl of Glofter, that he is a manifold traitor, let him appear by the third sound of the *trumpet.* *Shakesp. King Lear.*

He blew
His *trumpet*, heard in Oreb since perhaps
When God descended, and perhaps once more
To sound at gen'ral doom. Th' angelick blast
Filled all the regions. *Milton.*

The last loud *trumpet*'s wond'rous sound
Shall through the rending tombs rebound,
And wake the nations under ground. *Roscommon.*

Things of deep sense we may in prose unfold,
But they move more in lofty numbers told;
By the loud *trumpet* which our courage aids,
We learn that sound, as well as sense, persuades. *Waller.*

The *trumpet*'s loud clangor
Excites us to arms,
With shrill notes of anger,
And mortal alarms. *Dryden.*

Every man is the maker of his own fortune, and must be in some measure the *trumpet* of his fame. *Tatler.*

No more the drum
Provokes to arms, or *trumpet*'s clangor shrill
Affrights the wives. *Philips.*

Let the loud *trumpet* sound,
Till the roofs all around,
The shrill echoes rebound. *Pope.*

2. In military stile, a trumpeter.

He wisely desired, that a *trumpet* might be first sent for a pass. *Clarendon, b.* viii.

Among our forefathers, the enemy, when there was a king in the field, demanded by a *trumpet* in what part he resided, that they might avoid firing upon the royal pavilion. *Addison.*

3. One who celebrates; one who praises.

Glorious followers, who make themselves as *trumpets* of the commendation of those they follow, taint business for want of secrecy, and export honour from a man, and make him a return in envy. *Bacon.*

That great politician was pleased to have the greatest wit of those times in his interests, and to be the *trumpet* of his praises. *Dryden.*

Trumpet-flower. *n. s.* [*bignonia*, Lat.] It hath a tubulous flower consisting of one leaf, which opens at top like two lips: these flowers are succeeded by pods, which are divided into two cells, and contain several winged seeds. *Miller.*

To **Tru'mpet.** *v. a.* [*trompetter*, Fr. from the noun.] To publish by sound of trumpet; to proclaim.

That I did love the Moor to live with him,
My downright violence to form my fortunes
May *trumpet* to the world. *Shakesp. Othello.*

Why so tart a favour
To *trumpet* such good tidings? *Shakespeare.*

They went with sound of trumpet; for they did nothing but publish and *trumpet* all the reproaches they could devise against the Irish. *Bacon's War with Spain.*

Tru'mpeter. *n. s.* [from *trumpet.*]

1. One who sounds a trumpet.

Trumpeters,
With brazen din blast you the city's ear,
Make mingle with our rattling tabourines. *Shakespeare.*

As they returned, a herald and *trumpeter* from the Scots overtook them. *Hayward.*

Their

Their men lie securely intrench'd in a cloud,
And a *trumpeter* hornet to battle sounds loud. *Dryden.*

An army of *trumpeters* would give as great a strength as this confederacy of tongue-warriors, who, like those military musicians, content themselves with animating their friends to battle. *Addison's Freeholder*, N°. 28.

2. One who proclaims, publishes, or denounces.

Where there is an opinion to be created of virtue or greatness, these men are good *trumpeters*. *Bacon's Essays.*

How came so many thousands to fight, and die in the same rebellion? why were they deceived into it by those spiritual *trumpeters*, who followed them with continual alarms of damnation if they did not venture life, fortune and all, in that which those impostors called the cause of God. *South.*

3. A fish. *Ainsw.*

TR'UMPET-TONGUED. *adj.* [*trumpet* and *tongue.*] Having tongues vociferous as a trumpet.

This Duncan's virtues
Will plead, like angels, *trumpet-tongu'd* against
The deep damnation of his taking off. *Shakesp Macbeth.*

To TRU'NCATE. *v. a.* [*trunco*, Lat.] To maim; to lop; to cut short.

TRUNCATION. *n. s.* [from *truncate.*] The act of lopping or maiming.

TRU'NCHEON. *n. s.* [*tronçon*, French.]

1. A short staff; a club; a cudgel.

With his *truncheon* he so rudely stroke
Cymocles twice, that twice him forc'd his foot revoke. *F. Q.*

Set limb to limb, and thou art far the lesser;
Thy hand is but a finger to my fist;
Thy leg is a stick compared with this *truncheon*. *Shakesp.*

The English slew divers of them with plummets of lead tied to a *truncheon* or staff by a cord. *Hayward.*

One with a broken *truncheon* deals his blows. *Dryden.*

2. A staff of command.

The hand of Mars
Beckon'd with fiery *truncheon* my retire. *Shakespeare.*

No ceremony that to great ones 'longs,
The marshal's *truncheon*, nor the judge's robe,
Become them with one half so good a grace,
As mercy does. *Shakesp. Measure for Measure.*

To TRU'NCHEON. *v. a.* [from the noun.] To beat with a truncheon.

Captain, thou abominable cheater! If captains were of my mind, they would *truncheon* you out of taking their names upon you before you earn'd them. *Shakespeare.*

TRUNCHEONEE'R. *n. s.* [from *truncheon.*] One armed with a truncheon.

I mist the meteor once, and hit that woman, who cried out, chibs! when I might see from far some forty *truncheoneers* draw to her succour. *Shakesp. Henry* VIII.

To TRU'NDLE. *v. n.* [*trondeler*, Picard French; ꞇꞃenꝺl, *a bowl*, Saxon.] To roll; to bowl along.

In the four first it is heaved up by several spondees intermixed with proper breathing places, and at last *trundles* down in a continued line of dactyls. *Addison's Spect.* N°. 253.

TRU'NDLE. *n. s.* [ꞇꞃenꝺl, Saxon.] Any round rolling thing.

TRU'NDLE-TAIL. *n. s.* Round tail.

Avaunt you curs!
Hound or spaniel, brache or hym,
Or bobtail tike, or *trundle-tail*. *Shakesp. King Lear.*

TRUNK. *n. s.* [*truncus*, Lat. *tronc*, Fr.]

1. The body of a tree.

He was
The ivy, which had hid my princely *trunk*,
And suckt my verdure out on't. *Shakespeare.*

About the mossy *trunk* I wound me soon;
For high from ground the branches would require
Thy utmost reach. *Milton's Par. Lost, b.* ix.

Creeping 'twixt 'em all, the mantling vine
Does round their *trunks* her purple clusters twine. *Dryden.*

Some of the largest trees have seeds no bigger than some diminutive plants, and yet every seed is a perfect plant with a *trunk*, branches, and leaves, inclosed in a shell. *Bentley.*

2. The body without the limbs of an animal.

The charm and venom which they drunk,
Their blood with secret filth infected hath,
Being diffused through the senseless *trunk*. *Fairy Qu. b.* ii.

Thou bring'st me happiness and peace, son John;
But health, alack, with youthful wings is flown
From this bare, wither'd *trunk*. *Shakesp. Henry* IV.

3. The main body of any thing.

The large *trunks* of the veins discharge the refluent blood into the next adjacent *trunk*, and so on to the heart. *Ray.*

4. [*Tronc*, French.] A chest for cloaths; a small chest commonly lined with paper.

Neither press, coffer, chest, *trunk*, well, vault, but he hath an abstract for the remembrance of such places. *Shak.*

Some odd fantastick lord would fain
Carry in *trunks*, and all my drudgery do. *Dryden.*

Where a young man learned to dance, there happened to stand an old *trunk* in the room, the idea of which had so mixed itself with the turns of all his dances, that, though he could dance excellently well, yet it was only whilst that *trunk* was there; nor could he perform well in any other place, unless that, or some such other *trunk*, had its due position in the room. *Locke.*

Your poem sunk,
And sent in quires to line a *trunk*:
If still you be dispos'd to rhyme,
Go try your hand a second time. *Swift.*

5. [*Trompe*, Fr.] The proboscis of an elephant, or other animal.

Leviathian that at his gills
Draws in, and at his *trunk* spouts out a sea. *Milton.*

When elephant 'gainst elephant did rear
His *trunk*, and castles justled in the air,
My sword thy way to victory had shown. *Dryden.*

6. A long tube through which pellets of clay are blown.

In rolls of parchment *trunks*, the mouth being laid to the one end and the ear to the other, the sound is heard much farther than in the open air. *Bacon's Nat. Hist.*

In a shooting *trunk*, the longer it is to a certain limit, the swifter and more forcibly the air drives the pellet. *Ray.*

To TRUNK. *v. a.* [*trunco*, Lat.] To truncate; to main; to lop. Obsolete.

Large streams of blood out of the *trunked* stock
Forth gushed, like water streams from riven rock. *Fairy Q.*

TRU'NKED. *adj.* [from *trunk*] Having a trunk.

She is thick set with strong and well *trunked* trees. *Howel.*

TRUNK-HOSE. *n. s.* [*trunk* and *hose.*] Large breeches formerly worn.

The short *trunk-hose* shall show thy foot and knee
Licentious, and to common eye-sight free;
And with a bolder stride, and looser air,
Mingl'd with men, a man thou must appear. *Prior.*

TRU'NNIONS. *n. s.* [*trognons*, Fr.] The knobs or bunchings of a gun, that bear it on the cheeks of a carriage. *Bailey.*

TRU'SION. *n. s.* [*trudo*, Lat.] The act of thrusting or pushing.

By attraction we do not understand drawing, pumping, sucking, which is really pulsion and *trusion*. *Bentley.*

TRUSS. *n. s.* [*trousse*, Fr.]

1. A bandage by which ruptures are restrained from lapsing.

A hernia would succeed, and the patient be put to the trouble of wearing a *truss*. *Wiseman's Surgery.*

2. Bundle; any thing thrust close together.

All as a poor pedler he did wend,
Bearing a *truss* of trifles at his back,
As belles and babies, and glasses in his packe. *Spenser.*

The rebels first won the plain at the hill's foot by assault, and then the even ground on the top, by carrying up great *trusses* of hay before them, to dead their shot. *Carew.*

An ass was wishing for a mouthful of fresh grass to knap upon, in exchange for a heartless *truss* of straw. *L'Estrange.*

The fair one devoured a *truss* of sallet, and drunk a full bottle to her share. *Addison's Spect.* N°. 410.

3. Trouse; breeches. Obsolete.

To TRUSS. *v. a.* [*trousser*, French.] To pack up close together.

What in most English writers useth to be loose and unright, in this author, is well grounded, finely framed, and strongly *trussed* up together. *Spenser.*

Some of them send the scriptures before, *truss* up bag and baggage, make themselves in a readiness, that they may fly from city to city. *Hooker, b.* ii.

You might have *trussed* him and all his apparel into an eelskin. *Shakespeare's Henry* IV. *p.* ii.

TRUST. *n. s.* [*traust*, Runick.]

1. Confidence; reliance on another.

What a fool is honesty! and *trust*, his sworn brother, a very simple gentleman. *Shakespeare.*

My misfortunes may be of use to credulous maids, never to put too much *trust* in deceitful men. *Swift.*

2. Charge received in confidence.

In my wretched case 'twill be more just
Not to have promis'd, than deceive your *trust*. *Dryden.*

His *trust* was with th' eternal to be deemed
Equal in strength. *Milton.*

3. Confident opinion of any event.

4. Credit given without examination.

Most take things upon *trust*, and misemploy their assent by lazily enslaving their minds to the dictates of others. *Locke.*

5. Credit without payment.

Ev'n such is time, who takes on *trust*
Our youth, our joys, our all we have,
And pays us but with age and dust. *Raleigh.*

6. Something committed to one's faith.

They cannot see all with their own eyes; they must commit many great *trusts* to their ministers. *Bacon.*

Thou the sooner
Temptation found'st, or over potent charms,
To violate the sacred *trust* of silence
Deposited within thee. *Milton's*

7. Deposit; something committed to charge, of ... count must be given.

Although the advantages one man posse... another, may be called his property with r... men, yet with respect to God they are only a ...

8. Fidelity; supposed honesty.
Behold, I commit my daughter unto thee of special *trust*; wherefore do not entreat her evil. *Tob.* x. 12.
9. State of him to whom something is entrusted.
I serve him truly, that will put me in *trust*. *Shak. King Lear.*
Being transplanted out of his cold barren diocese he was left in that great *trust* with the king. *Clarendon.*
Expect no more from servants than is just,
Reward them well if they observe their *trust*. *Denham.*

To TRUST. *v. a.* [from the noun.]
1. To place confidence in; to confide in.
I'd be torn in pieces ere I'd *trust* a woman
With wind. *Benj. Jonson.*
2. To believe; to credit.
Give me your hand: *trust* me you look well. *Shakesp.*
3. To admit in confidence to the power over any thing.
When you lie down, with a short prayer commit yourself into the hands of your faithful Creator; and when you have done, *trust* him with yourself as you must do when you are dying. *Taylor.*
4. To commit with confidence.
Give me good fame, ye pow'rs, and make me just,
This much the rogue to publick ears will *trust*:
In private then:——When wilt thou, mighty Jove,
My wealthy uncle from this world remove? *Dryden.*
Whom with your pow'r and fortune, Sir, you *trust*,
Now to suspect is vain. *Dryden.*
5. To venture confidently.
Fool'd by thee to *trust* thee from my side. *Milton.*
6. To sell upon credit.

To TRUST. *v. n.*
1. To be confident of something future.
I *trust* to come unto you, and speak face to face. 2 *John.*
From this grave, this dust,
My God shall raise me up I *trust*. *Raleigh.*
2. To have confidence; to rely; to depend without doubt.
The isles shall wait upon me, and on mine arm shall they *trust*. *Isa.* li. 5.
The Lord is a buckler to all that *trust* in him. 2 *Sam.* xxii.
Sin never shall hurt them more who rightly *trust*
In this his satisfaction. *Milton.*
3. To be credulous; to be won to confidence.
Well you may fear too far
——Safer than *trust* too far. *Shakespeare.*
4. To expect.
The simplicity of the goat shews us what an honest man is to *trust* to that keeps a knave company. *L'Estrange.*

TRUSTEE'. *n. s.* [from *trust.*]
1. One entrusted with any thing.
Having made choice of such a confessor that you may *trust* your soul with, sincerely open your heart to him, and look upon him only as he is a *trustee* from God, commissioned by him as his ministerial deputy, to hear, judge, and absolve you. *Taylor's Guide to a Penitent.*
2. One to whom something is committed for the use and behoof of another.
You are not the *trustees* of the publick liberty: and if you have not right to petition in a crowd, much less to intermeddle in the management of affairs. *Dryden.*

TRU'STER. *n. s.* [from *trust.*] One who trusts.
Nor shall you do mine ear that violence,
To make it *truster* of your own report
Against yourself. *Shakespeare's Hamlet.*

TRU'STINESS. *n. s.* [from *trusty.*] Honesty; fidelity; faithfulness.
If the good qualities which lie dispersed among other creatures, innocence in a sheep, *trustiness* in a dog, are singly so commendable, how excellent is the mind, which ennobles them into virtues. *Grew's Cosmol. b.* ii.

TRU'STLESS. *n. s.* [from *trust.*] Unfaithful; unconstant; not to be trusted. A word elegant, but out of use.
I beheld this fickle *trustless* state,
Of vain world's glory, flirting to and fro. *Spenser.*

TRU'STY. *adj.* [from *trust.*]
1. Honest; faithful; true; fit to be trusted.
This dastard, at the battle of Poictiers,
Before we met, or that a stroke was given,
Like to a *trusty* 'squire, did run away. *Shakespeare.*
This *trusty* servant
Shall pass between us. *Shakesp. King Lear.*
He removeth away the speech of the *trusty*, and taketh away the understanding of the aged. *Job* xii. 26.
Guyomar his *trusty* slave has sent. *Dryd. Indian Emperor.*
These prodigious treasures which flow'd in to him, he buried under-ground by the hands of his most *trusty* slaves. *Add.*
2. Strong; stout; such as will not fail.
When he saw no power might prevail,
His *trusty* sword he called to his aid. *Fairy Q.*
The neighing steeds are to the chariot ty'd,
The *trusty* weapon sits on ev'ry side. *Dryden's Æn.*

TRUTH. *n. s.* [ꞇɲeoꝑða, Saxon.]
1. The contrary to falsehood; conformity of notions to things.
Truth is the joining or separating of signs, as the things signified agree or disagree. *Locke.*
That men are pubescent at the year of twice seven is accounted a punctual *truth*. *Brown.*
Persuasive words, impregn'd
With reason to her seeming and with *truth*. *Milton.*
This clue leads them through the mizmaze of opinions and authors to *truth* and certainty. *Locke.*
2. Conformity of words to thoughts.
Shall *truth* fail to keep her word? *Milton.*
And lend a lie the confidence of *truth*. *Anonymous.*
3. Purity from falsehood.
So young and so untender?
——So young, my lord, and true.
——Let it be so, thy *truth* then be thy dower. *Shakesp.*
4. Fidelity; constancy.
The thoughts of past pleasure and *truth*,
The best of all blessings below. *Song.*
5. Honesty; virtue.
The money I tender for him in the court;
If this will not suffice, it must appear
That malice bears down *truth*. *Shakespeare.*
6. It is used sometimes by way of concession.
She said, *truth*, Lord: yet the dogs eat of the crumbs which fall. *Matth.* xv. 27.
7. Exactness; conformity to rule.
Ploughs to go true depend much upon the *truth* of the iron work. *Mortimer's Husbandry.*
8. Reality.
In *truth*, what should any prayer, framed to the minister's hand, require, but only so to be read as behoveth. *Hooker*
9. *Of a* TRUTH, or *in* TRUTH. In reality.
Of a truth, Lord, the kings of Assyria have destroyed the nations. 2 *Kings* xix. 17.

TRUTINA'TION. *n. s.* [*trutina*, Lat.] The act of weighing; examination by the scale.
Men may mistake if they distinguish not the sense of levity unto themselves, and in regard of the scale or decision of *trutination*. *Brown's Vulgar Errours, b.* iv.

To TRY. *v. a.* [*trier*, French.]
1. To examine; to make experiment of.
Some among you have beheld me fighting,
Come *try* upon yourselves what you have seen me. *Shak.*
He cannot be a perfect man,
Not being *tried* and tutor'd in the world. *Shakespeare.*
Doth not the ear *try* words, and the mouth taste meat? *Job.*
2. To experience; to assay; to have knowledge or experience of.
Thou know'st only good; but evil hast not *try'd*. *Milt.*
Some to far Oaxis shall be sold,
Or *try* the Libyan heat, or Scythian cold. *Dryden.*
With me the rocks of Scylla you have *try'd*,
Th' inhuman Cyclops, and his den defy'd;
What greater ills hereafter can you bear? *Dryden.*
3. To examine as a judge.
4. To bring before a judicial tribunal.
5. To bring to a decision, with *out* emphatical.
Nicanor hearing of their couragiousness to fight for their country, durst not *try* the matter by the sword. 2 *Mac.* xiv.
I'll *try* it *out*, and give no quarter. *Dryden's Don Sebastian.*
6. To act on as a test.
The fire sev'n times *tried* this;
Sev'n times *tried* that judgment is,
Which did never chuse amiss. *Shakespeare.*
7. To bring as to a test.
The *trying* of your faith worketh patience. *Jam.* i. 3.
They open to themselves at length the way
Up hither under long obedience *try'd*. *Milton.*
8. To essay; to attempt.
Let us *try* advent'rous work. *Milton.*
9. To purify; to refine.
After life
Try'd in sharp tribulation and refin'd
By faith and faithful works. *Milton.*

To TRY. *v. n.* To endeavour; to attempt.

TUB. *n. s.* [*tobbe*, *tubbe*, Dutch.]
1. A large open vessel of wood.
In the East Indies, if you set a *tub* of water open in a room where cloves are kept, it will be drawn dry in twenty-four hours. *Bacon's Nat. Hist.* N°. 78.
They fetch their precepts from the Cynick *tub*. *Milton.*
Skilful coopers hoop their *tubs*
With Lydian and with Phrygian dubs. *Hudibras.*
2. A state of salivation. I know not well why so called.
Season the slaves
For *tubs* and baths, bring down the rose-cheek'd youth
To th' *tub*-fast, and the diet. *Shakesp. Timon of Athens.*

TUBE. *n. s.* [*tube*, Fr. *tubus*, Lat.] A pipe; a siphon; a long body.
There bellowing engines with their fiery *tubes*
Dispers'd æthereal forms and down they fell. *Roscom.*
A spot like which astronomer
Trough his glaz'd optick *tube* yet never saw. *Milton.*
This bears up part of it out at the surface of the earth, the rest through the *tubes* and vessels of the vegetables thereon. *Woodward's Nat. Hist. p.* iii.

TU'BERCLE. *n. ſ.* [*tubercule*, Fr. from *tuberculum*, Latin.] A ſmall ſwelling or excreſcence on the body; a pimple.

A conſumption of the lungs, without an ulceration, arrives through a ſchirroſity, or a crude *tubercle*. *Harvey on Conſump.*

TUBE'ROSE. *n. ſ.* A flower.

The ſtalks of *tuberoſe* run up four foot high more or leſs, the common way of planting them is in pots in March, in good earth. *Mortimer's Huſbandry.*

Eternal ſpring, with ſmiling verdure here,
Warms the mild air, and crowns the youthful year,
The *tuberoſe* ever breathes and violets blow. *Garth's Diſpenſ.*

TU'BEROUS. *adj.* [*tubereux*, Fr. from *tuber*, Latin.] Having prominent knots or excreſcences.

Parts of *tuberous* hæmatitæ ſhew ſeveral varieties in the cruſts, ſtriature, and conſtitution of the body. *Woodward.*

TU'BULAR. *adj.* [from *tubus*, Lat.] Reſembling a pipe or trunk; conſiſting of a pipe; long and hollow; fiſtular.

He hath a *tubular* or pipe-like ſnout reſembling that of the hippocampus, or horſe-fiſh. *Grew's Muſeum.*

TU'BULE. *n. ſ.* [*tubulus*, Latin.] A ſmall pipe, or fiſtular body.

As the ludus Helmontii, and the other nodules have in them ſea-ſhells that were incorporated with them during the time of their formation at the deluge, ſo theſe ſtones had then incorporated with them teſtaceous *tubules*, related to the ſiphunculi or rather the vermiculi marini. *Woodw. on Foſſils.*

TU'BULATED. } *adj.* [from *tubulus*, Lat.] Fiſtular; longitu-
TU'BULOUS. } dinally hollow.

The teeth are *tubulated* for the conveyance of the poiſon into the wound they make; but their hollowneſs doth not reach to the top of the tooth. *Derham's Phyſico-Theol.*

TUCK. *n. ſ.* [*tweca* Welſh, a knife; *eſtoc*, French; *ſtocco*, Italian.]

1. A long narrow ſword.

If he by chance eſcape your venom'd *tuck*,
Our purpoſe may hold there. *Shakeſp. Hamlet.*

Theſe being prim'd, with force he labour'd
To free's ſword from retentive ſcabbard;
And after many a painful pluck,
From ruſty durance he bail'd *tuck*. *Hudibras, p.* i.

2. A kind of net.

The *tuck* is narrower meaſhed, and therefore ſcarce lawful with a long bunt in the midſt. *Carew.*

To TUCK. *v. n.* [from *trucken*, German.] To preſs. *Skinner.*

1. To cruſh together; to hinder from ſpreading.

She *tucked* up her veſtments, like a Spartan virgin, and marched directly forwards to the utmoſt ſummit of the promontory. *Addiſon.*

The ſex, at the ſame time they are letting down their ſtays, are *tucking* up their petticoats, which grow ſhorter and ſhorter every day. *Addiſon's Guardian.*

The following age of females firſt *tucked* up their garments to the elbows, and expoſed their arms to the air. *Addiſon.*

Dick adept! *tuck* back thy hair,
And I will pour into thy ear. *Prior.*

2. To incloſe, by tucking cloaths round.

Make his bed after different faſhions, that he may not feel every little change, who is not to have his maid always to lay all things in print and *tuck* him in warm. *Locke on Education.*

To TUCK. *v. n.* To contract. A bad word.

An ulcer diſcharging a naſty thin ichor, the edges *tuck* in, and growing ſkinned and hard, give it the name of a callous ulcer. *Sharp's Surgery.*

TU'CKER. *n. ſ.* A ſmall piece of linen that ſhades the breaſt of women.

A female ornament by ſome called a *tucker*, and by others the neck-piece, being a ſlip of fine linen or muſlin, uſed to run in a ſmall kind of ruffle round the uppermoſt verge of the ſtays. *Addiſon's Guardian.*

TU'CKETSONANCE. *n. ſ.* A word apparently derived from the French, but which I do not certainly underſtand; *tucquet* is a hat, and *toquer* is to ſtrike.

Let the trumpets ſound,
The *tuckſetſonance* and the note to mount. *Shakeſ. Hen.* V.

TU'EL. *n. ſ.* [*tuyeau*, French.] The anus. *Skinner.*

TU'ESDAY. *n. ſ.* [ꞇueꞅbæᵹ, Saxon; ꞇuv, Saxon, is Mars.] The third day of the week.

TU'FTAFFETY. *n. ſ.* [from *tufted* and *taffety*.] A villous kind of ſilk.

His cloaths were ſtrange, tho' coarſe, and black, tho' bare:
Sleeveleſs his jerkin was, and it had been
Velvet: but it was now, ſo much ground was ſeen,
Become *tufftaffaty*. *Donne.*

TUFT. *n. ſ.* [*tuffe*, French.]

1. A number of threads or ribbands, flowery leaves, or any ſmall bodies joined together.

Upon ſweet brier, a fine *tuft* or bruſh of moſs of divers colours, you ſhall ever find full of white worms. *Bacon.*

It is notorious for its goatiſh ſmell, and *tufts* not unlike the beard of that animal. *More's Antidote againſt Atheiſm.*

A *tuft* of daiſies on a flow'ry lay. *Dryden.*

Near a living ſtream their manſion place
Edg'd round with moſs and *tufts* of matted graſs. *Dryden.*

The male among birds often appears in a creſt, comb, a *tuft* of feathers, or a natural little plume, erected like a pinacle on the top of the head. *Addiſon's Spectator*, Nº 265.

2. A cluſter; a plump.

Going a little aſide into the wood, where many times before ſhe delighted to walk, her eyes were ſaluted with a *tuft* of trees ſo cloſe ſet together, as with the ſhade the moon gave through it, it might breed a fearful kind of devotion to look upon it. *Sidney.*

My houſe is at the *tuft* of olives hard by. *Shakeſpeare.*

With high woods the hills were crown'd;
With *tufts* the valleys, and each fountain ſide,
With borders long the rivers. *Milton's Par. Loſt.*

In bow'r and field he ſought, where any *tuft*
Of grove, or garden-plot more pleaſant,
Their tendance, or plantation for delight. *Milton's P. L.*

Under a *tuft* of ſhade, that on a green
Stood whiſp'ring ſoft, by a freſh fountain ſide
They ſat them down. *Milton's Par. Loſt, b.* iv.

To TUFT. *v. a.* To adorn with a tuft; a doubtful word, not authoriſed by any competent writer.

Sit beneath the ſhade
Of ſolemn oaks, that *tuft* the ſwelling mounts,
Thrown graceful round. *Thomſon.*

TU'FTED. *adj.* [from *tuft*.] Growing in tufts or cluſters.

There does a ſable cloud
Turn forth her ſilver lining on the night,
And caſt a gleam over this *tufted* grove. *Milton.*

Towers and battlements it ſees,
Boſom'd high in *tufted* trees,
Where perhaps ſome beauty lies
The cynoſure of neighbouring eyes. *Milton.*

'Midſt the deſert fruitful fields ariſe,
That crown'd with *tufted* trees and ſpringing corn,
Like verdant iſles the ſable waſte adorn. *Pope.*

TU'FTY. *adj.* [from *tuft*.] Adorned with tufts. A word of no authority.

Let me ſtrip thee of thy *tufty* coat,
Spread thy ambroſial ſtores. *Thomſon's Summer.*

To TUG. *v. a.* [ꞇiᵹan, ꞇeoᵹan, Saxon.]

1. To pull with ſtrength long continued in the utmoſt exertion; to draw.

No more *tug* one another thus, nor moil yourſelves; receive
Priſe equal; conqueſts crown ye both: the liſts to others leave. *Chapman's Iliads.*

Theſe two maſſy pillars
With horrible confuſion to and fro
He *tugg'd*, he ſhook, till down they came, and drew
Upon the heads of all that ſat beneath,
The whole roof after them, with burſt of thunder. *Milton.*

Take pains the genuine meaning to explore,
There ſweat, there ſtrain, *tug* the laborious oar. *Roſc.*

2. To pull; to pluck.

Prieſt, beware thy beard;
I mean to *tug* it, and to cuff you ſoundly. *Shak. Hen.* VI.

There leaving him to his repoſe
Secured from the purſuit of foes,
And wanting nothing but a ſong,
And a well tun'd theorbo hung
Upon a bough, to eaſe the pain
His *tugg'd* ears ſuffer'd, with a ſtrain. *Hudibras, p*

To TUG. *v. n.*

1. To pull; to draw.

The meaner ſort will *tug* luſtily at one oar. *Sa*

Lead your thoughts to the galleys, there thoſe wre captives are chained to the oars they *tug* at.

There is ſuch *tugging* and pulling this way and tha *More's Antidote againſt*

Thus galley-ſlaves *tug* willing at their oar,
Content to work in proſpect of the ſhore;
But would not work at all, if not conſtrained before

We have been *tugging* a great while againſt the ſ have almoſt weathered our point; a ſtretch or two do the work; but if inſtead of that we ſlacken ou drop our oars, we ſhall be hurried back to the whence we ſet out. *Addiſon on the*

2. To labour; to contend; to ſtruggle.

Caſt your good counſels
Upon his paſſion; let myſelf and fortune
Tug for the time to come. *Shakeſ*

His face is black and full of blood,
His hands abroad diſplay'd, as one that gr
And *tugg'd* for life. *Shake*

They long wreſtled and ſtrenuouſly *tugg'*
with a no leſs magnanimous than conſtant

Go now with ſome daring drug,
Bait thy diſeaſe, and while they *tug*,
Thou to maintain the cruel ſtriſe,
Spend the dear treaſure of thy liſe.

haw. TUG.

TUG. *n. s.* [from the verb.] Pull performed with the utmoſt effort.

Downward by the feet he drew
The trembling daſtard: at the *tug* he falls,
Vaſt ruins come along, rent from the ſmoking walls. *Dryd.*

TU'GGER. *n. s.* [from *tug.*] One that tugs or pulls hard.

TUI'TION. *n. s.* [*tuitio* from *tueor*, Lat.] Guardianſhip; ſuperintendent care; care of a guardian or tutor.

A folly for a man of wiſdom, to put himſelf under the *tuition* of a beaſt. *Sidney, b.* ii.

They forcibly endeavour to caſt the churches, under my care and *tution*, into the moulds they have faſhioned to their deſigns. *King Charles.*

If government depends upon religion, this ſhews the peſtilential deſign of thoſe that attempt to diſjoin the civil and eccleſiaſtical intereſts, ſetting the latter wholly out of the *tuition* of the former. *South's Sermons.*

When ſo much true life is put into them, freely talk with them about what moſt delights them, that they may perceive that thoſe under whoſe *tuition* they are, are not enemies to their ſatisfaction. *Locke.*

TU'LIP. *n. s.* [*tulipe*, Fr. *tulipa*, Lat.] A flower.

It hath a lilly flower, compoſed of ſix leaves, ſhaped ſomewhat like a pitcher; the pointal riſing in the middle of the flower is ſurrounded with ſtamina, and afterwards becomes an oblong fruit, which opens into three parts, and is divided into three cells, full of plain ſeeds, reſting upon one another in a double row. To theſe may be added a coated root, with fibres on the lower part. The properties of a good *tulip*, according to the characteriſticks of the beſt floriſts of the preſent age, are, 1. It ſhould have a tall ſtem. 2. The flower ſhould conſiſt of ſix leaves, three within, and three without, the former being larger than the latter. 3. Their bottom ſhould be proportioned to their top; their upper part ſhould be rounded off, and not terminate in a point. 4. The leaves when opened ſhould neither turn inward nor bend outward, but rather ſtand erect; the flower ſhould be of a middling ſize, neither over large nor too ſmall. 5. The ſtripes ſhould be ſmall and regular, ariſing quite from the bottom of the flower. The chives ſhould not be yellow, but of a brown colour. They are generally divided into three claſſes, viz. præcoces, or early flowers; media's, or middling flowers; and ſerotines, or late flowers. The early blowing *tulips* are not near ſo fair, nor riſe half ſo high as the late ones, but are chiefly valued for appearing ſo early in the ſpring. Their roots ſhould be taken up and ſpread upon mats in a ſhady place to dry; after which they ſhould be cleared from their filth, and put up in a dry place until the ſeaſon for planting. *Miller.*

The *tulip* opens with the riſing, and ſhuts with the ſetting ſun. *Hakewill.*

Why *tulips* of one colour produce ſome of another, and unning thro' all, ſtill eſcape a blue. *Brown's Vulgar Errours.*

IPTREE. A tree.

U'MBLE. *v. n.* [*tomber*, Fr. *tommelen*, Dutch; *tombo-* Italian.]

l; to come ſuddenly to the ground.

Though the treaſure
re's germins *tumble* all together,
ne. *Shakeſpeare.*

eat quantities tumultuouſly.

s come by the courſe of inheritance and teſta-
ne *tumbling* upon a man. *Bacon.*

walk, to riſe or *tumble*,
s motion jumble. *Prior.*

ſtone up the hill; which carried to the
mbles to the bottom. *Addiſon's Spectator.*

i.
ndys.
tched
Boyle.
way.
Atheiſm.
Dryd.
ream, and
more
arr

of one tree a gentleman bound with
d foot, ſo as well he might *tumble* and
Sidney, b. ii.

, and in falling ſtruck me
lows of the main. *Shakeſp. Rich.* III.

ious librations of the body.

, and teach the men t'obey;
tumbling, if you lead the way. *Rowe.*

w about by way of examination.

e ears of Maximilian, and *tumbling* it
oughts, that he ſhould at one blow be
ge of his daughter and his own, he loſt
Bacon's Henry VII.

is thoughts, and forming them into ex-
new fermentation, which works them
Collier on Pride.

2. To
their little quivers o'er,
Th
ſhafts. *Prior.*

den ide
r violence.
of their
itſelf on work in ſearch of ſome hid-
paſſions.
etimes they are rouzed and *tumbled* out
o open day-light by ſome turbulent
Locke's Works.

3. To throw down.

Wilt thou ſtill be hammering treachery,
To *tumble* down thy huſband and thyſelf,
From top of honour to diſgrace's feet? *Shakeſpeare.*

King Lycurgus, while he fought in vain,
His friend to free, was *tumbled* on the plain. *Dryden.*

If a greater force than his holds him faſt, or *tumbles* him down, he is no longer free. *Locke.*

TU'MBLE. *n. s.* [from the verb.] A fall.

A country-fellow got an unlucky *tumble* from a tree: why, ſays a paſſenger, I could have taught you a way to climb, and never hurt yourſelf with a fall. *L'Eſtrange.*

TU'MBLER. *n. s.* [from *tumble.*] One who ſhews poſtures by various contortions of body, or feats of activity.

What ſtrange agility and activeneſs do common *tumblers* and dancers on the rope attain to by continual exerciſe? *Wilkins's Math. Magick.*

Nic. bounced up with a ſpring equal to that of the nimbleſt *tumblers* or rope-dancers. *Arbuthnot.*

Never by *tumbler* thro' the hoops was ſhown,
Such ſkill in paſſing all, and touching none. *Pope.*

TU'MBREL. *n. s.* [*tombereau*, Freuch.] A dungcart.

Twifallow once ended, get *tumbrel* and man,
And compaſs that fallow as ſoon as ye can. *Tuſſ. Huſb.*

My corps is in a *tumbril* laid, among
The filth and ordure, and incloſ'd with dung;
That cart arreſt, and raiſe a common cry,
For ſacred hunger of my gold I die. *Dryden.*

What ſhall I do with this beaſtly *tumbril*? go lie down and ſleep, you ſot. *Congreve.*

To convince the preſent little race how unequal all their meaſures were to an antediluvian, in reſpect of the inſects which now appear for men, he ſometimes rode in an open *tumbril*. *Tatler.*

TUMEFA'CTION. *n. s.* [*tumefactio*, Latin.] Swelling.

The common ſigns and effects of weak fibres, are paleneſs, a weak pulſe, *tumefactions* in the whole body. *Arbuthnot.*

To TUME'FY. *v. a.* [*tumefacio*, Lat.] To ſwell; to make to ſwell.

I applied three ſmall cauſticks triangular about the *tumified* joint. *Wiſeman's Surgery.*

A fleſhy excreſcence, exceeding hard and *tumefied*, ſuppoſed to demand extirpation. *Sharp's Surgery.*

TU'MID. *adj.* [*tumidus*, Lat.]

1. Swelling; puffed up.
2. Protuberant; raiſed above the level.

So high as heav'd the *tumid* hills, ſo low
Down ſunk a hollow bottom broad and deep,
Capacious bed of waters. [*Milton.*

3. Pompous; boaſtful; puffy; falſely ſublime.

Though ſuch expreſſions may ſeem *tumid* and aſpiring; yet cannot I ſcruple to uſe ſeeming hyperboles in mentioning felicities, which make the higheſt hyperboles but ſeeming ones. *Boyle.*

TU'MOUR. *n. s.* [*tumor*, Latin.]

1. A morbid ſwelling.

Tumour is a diſeaſe, in which the parts recede from their natural ſtate by an undue encreaſe of their bigneſs. *Wiſeman.*

Having diſſected this ſwelling vice, and ſeen what it is that feeds the *tumour*, if the diſeaſe be founded in pride, the abating that is the moſt natural remedy. *Govern. of the Tongue.*

2. Affected pomp; falſe magnificence; puffy grandeur; ſwelling mien; unſubſtantial greatneſs.

His ſtile was rich of phraſe, but ſeldom in bold metaphors; and ſo far from the *tumour*, that it rather wants a little elevation. *Wotton.*

It is not the power of *tumour* and bold looks upon the paſſions of the multitude. *L'Eſtrange.*

TU'MOROUS. *adj.* [from *tumour.*]

1. Swelling; protuberant.

Who ever ſaw any cypreſs or pine, ſmall below and above, and *tumorous* in the middle, unleſs ſome diſeaſed plant. *Wotton.*

2. Faſtuous; vainly pompous; falſely magnificent.

According to their ſubject, theſe ſtiles vary; for that which is high and lofty, declaring excellent matter, becomes vaſt and *tumorous*, ſpeaking of petty and inferior things. *B. Johnſ.*

His limbs were rather ſturdy than dainty, ſublime and almoſt *tumorous* in his looks and geſtures. *Wotton.*

To TUMP, among gardeners, to fence trees about with earth.

To TU'MULATE. *v. n.* [*tumulo*, Latin.] To ſwell. This ſeems to be the ſenſe here, but I ſuſpect the word to be wrong.

Urinous ſpirits, or volatile alkalies, are ſuch enemies to acid, that as ſoon as they are put together, they *tumulate* and grow hot, and continue to fight till they have diſarmed or mortified each other. *Boyle.*

TU'MULOSE. *adj.* [*tumuloſus*, Lat.] Full of hills. *Bailey.*

TUMULO'SITY. *n. s.* [*tumulus*, Lat.] Hillineſs. *Bailey.*

TU'MULT. *n. s.* [*tumulte*, Fr. *tumultus*, Latin.]

1. A promiſcuous commotion in a multitude.

A *tumult* is improved into a rebellion, and a government overturned by it. *L'Eſtrange.*

With ireful taunts each other they oppoſe,
Till in loud *tumult* all the Greeks aroſe. *Pope.*

2. A

2. A multitude put into wild commotion.
3. A ftir; an irregular violence; a wild commotion.

What ftir is this? what *tumults* in the heav'ns?
Whence cometh this alarum and this noife? *Shakefpeare.*
Tumult and confufion all embroil'd. *Milton.*

This piece of poetry, what can be nobler than the idea it gives us of the fupreme Being thus raifing a *tumult* among the elements, and recovering them out of their confufion, thus troubling and becalming nature. *Addifon's Spectator.*

TUMU'LTUARILY. *adv.* [from *tumultuary.*] In a tumultuary manner.

TUMU'LTUARINESS. *n. f.* [from *tumultuary.*] Turbulence; inclination or difpofition to tumults or commotions.

The *tumultuarinefs* of the people, or the factioufnefs of prefbyters, gave occafion to invent new models. *K. Charles.*

TUMU'LTUARY. *adj.* [*tumultuaire*, Fr. from *tumult.*]

1. Diforderly; promifcuous; confufed.

Perkin had learned, that people under command ufed to confult, and after to march in order, and rebels contrariwife; and obferving their orderly, and not *tumultuary* arming, doubted the worft. *Bacon's Henry* VII.

My followers were at that time no way proportionable to hazard a *tumultuary* conflict. *K. Charles.*

Is it likely, that the divided atoms fhould keep the fame ranks in fuch a variety of *tumultuary* agitations in that liquid medium. *Glanv. Scep.*

2. Reftlefs; put into irregular commotion.

Men who live without religion, live always in a *tumultuary* and reftlefs ftate. *Atterbury's Sermons.*

To TUMU'LTUATE. *v. n.* [*tumultuor*, Lat.] To make a tumult.

TUMULTUA'TION. *n. f.* [from *tumultuate.*] Irregular and confufed agitation.

That in the found the contiguous air receives many ftrokes from the particles of the liquor, feems probable by the fudden and eager *tumultuation* of its parts. *Boyle's Works.*

TUMULTU'OUS. *adj.* [from *tumult*; *tumultueux*, Fr.]

1. Put into violent commotion; irregularly and confufedly agitated.

The ftrong rebuff of fome *tumultuous* cloud
Hurry'd him aloft. *Milton.*
His dire attempt; which nigh the birth
Now rowling, boils in his *tumultuous* breaft,
And like a devilifh engine back recoils
Upon himfelf. *Milton's Parad. Loft.*
The vital blood, that had forfook my heart,
Returns again in fuch *tumultuous* tides,
It quite o'ercomes me. *Addifon's Cato.*

2. Violently carried on by diforderly multitudes.

Many civil broils, and *tumultuous* rebellions, they fairly overcame, by reafon of the continual prefence of their King, whofe only perfon oftentimes contains the unruly people from a thoufand evil occafions. *Spenfer's State of Ireland.*

3. Turbulent; violent.

Nought refts for me in this *tumultuous* ftrife,
But to make open proclamation. *Shakefpeare.*

Furioufly running in upon him with *tumultuous* fpeech, he violently raught from his head his rich cap of fables. *Knolles.*

4. Full of tumults.

The winds began to fpeak louder, and as in a *tumultuous* kingdom, to think themfelves fitteft inftruments of commandment. *Sidney, b.* ii.

TUMU'LTUOUSLY. *adv.* [from *tumultuous.*] By act of the multitude; with confufion and violence.

It was done by edict, not *tumultuoufly*; the fword was not put into the people's hand. *Bacon's Holy War.*

TUN. *n. f.* [tunne, Sax. *tonne*, Dut. *tonne*, *tonneau*, Fr.]

1. A large cafk.

As when a fpark
Lights on a heap of powder, laid
Fit for the *tun*, fome magazine to ftore
Againft a rumour'd war. *Milton.*

2. A pipe; the meafure of two hogfheads.
3. Any large quantity proverbially.

I have ever follow'd thee with hate,
Drawn *tuns* of blood out of thy country's breaft. *Shakefp.*

4. A drunkard. In burlefque.

Here's a *tun* of midnight-work to come,
Og from a treafon-tavern rolling home. *Dryden.*

5. The weight of two thoufand pounds.
6. A cubick fpace in a fhip, fuppofed to contain a tun.
7. Dryden has ufed it for a perimetrical meafure, I believe without precedent or propriety.

A *tun* about was every pillar there;
A polifh'd mirrour fhone not half fo clear. *Dryden.*

To TUN. *v. a.* [from the noun.] To put into cafks; to barrel.

If in the muft, or wort, while it worketh, before it be *tunned*, the burrage ftay a time, and be often changed with frefh, it will make a fovereign drink for melancholy. *Bacon.*

The fame fermented juice degenerating into vinegar, yields an acid and corroding fpirit. The fame juice *tunned* up, arms itfelf with tartar. *Boyle's Works.*

TU'NABLE. *adj.* [from *tune.*] Harmonious; mufical.

A cry more *tunable*
Was never hallo'd to, nor cheer'd with horn. *Shakefp.*
Hard are the ways of truth, and rough to walk,
Smooth on the tongue difcours'd, pleafing to th' ear,
And *tunable* as fylvan pipe or fong. *Milton.*

All *tunable* founds, whereof human voice is one, are made by a regular vibration of the fonorous body, and undulation of the air, proportionable to the acutenefs or gravity of the tone. *Holder.*

Several lines in Virgil are not altogether *tunable* to a modern ear. *Garth's Pref. to Ovid.*

TU'NABLENESS. *n. f.* [from *tunable.*] Harmony; Melodioufnefs.

TU'NABLY. *adv.* [from *tunable.*] Harmonioufly; melodioufly.

TUNE. *n. f.* [*toon*, Dut. *ton*, Swed. *tuono*, Ital. *tone*, Fr. *tonus*, Lat.]

1. *Tune* is a diverfity of notes put together. *Locke.*

Came he to fing a raven's note,
Whofe difmal *tune* bereft my vital pow'rs. *Shakefp.*

Tunes and airs have in themfelves fome affinity with the affections; as merry *tunes*, doleful *tunes*, folemn *tunes*, *tunes* inclining mens minds to pity, warlike *tunes*; fo that *tunes* have a predifpofition to the motion of the fpirits. *Bacon.*

Keep unfteddy nature to her law,
And the low world in meafur'd motion draw
After the heav'nly *tune*, which none can hear
Of human mould with grofs unpurged ear. *Milton.*
That fweet fong you fung one ftarry night,
The *tune* I ftill retain, but not the words. *Dryden.*

The difpofition in the fiddle to play *tunes*. *Arb. & Pope.*

2. Sound; note.

Such a noife arofe
As the fhrouds make at fea in a ftiff tempeft,
As loud, and to as many *tunes*. *Shakefpeare.*

3. Harmony; order; concert of parts.

A continual parliament I thought would but keep the commonweal in *tune*, by preferving laws in their due execution and vigour. *K. Charles.*

4. State of giving the due founds, as *the fiddle is in tune*, or *out of tune.*
5. Proper ftate for ufe or application; right difpofition; fit temper; proper humour.

A child will learn three times as much when he is in *tune*, as he will with double the time and pains, when he goes aukwardly, or is dragged unwillingly to it. *Locke.*

6. State of any thing with refpect to order.

Diftreffed Lear, in his better *tune*, remembers what we are come about. *Shakefpeare.*

To TUNE. *v. a.* [from the noun.]

1. To put into fuch a ftate, as that the proper founds may be produced.

Their golden harps they took,
Harps ever *tun'd*, that glitter'd by their fide. *Milton.*
Tune your harps,
Ye angels, to that found; and thou, my heart,
Make room to entertain thy flowing joy. *Dryden.*

2. To fing harmonioufly.

Fountains, and ye that warble as ye flow,
Melodious murmurs, warbling *tune* his praife. *Milton.*
Rouze up, ye Thebans; *tune* your Io Pæans;
Your king returns, the Argians are o'ercome. *Dryden.*
Leave fuch to *tune* their own dull rhymes, and know
What's roundly fmooth, and languifhingly flow. *Pope.*

To TUNE. *v. n.*

1. To form one found to another.

The winds were hufh'd, no leaf fo fmall
At all was feen to ftir;
Whilft *tuning* to the waters fall,
The fmall birds fang to her. *Drayt. Q. of Cynthia.*
All founds on fret or ftop
Temper'd foft *tunings*, intermix'd with voice. *Milton.*

2. To utter with the voice inarticulate harmony.

TU'NEFUL. *adj.* [*tune* and *full.*] Mufical; harmonious.

I faw a pleafant grove,
With chant of *tuneful* birds refounding love. *Milton.*
Earth fmiles with flow'rs renewing, laughs the fky,
And birds to lays of love their *tuneful* notes apply. *Dryd.*
For thy own glory fing our fov'reign's praife,
God of verfes and of days?
Let all thy *tuneful* fons adorn
Their lafting works with William's name. *Prior.*
Poets themfelves muft fall, like thofe they fung,
Deaf the prais'd ear, and mute the *tuneful* tongue. *Pope.*

TU'NELESS. *adj.* [from *tune.*] Unharmonious; unmufical.

When in hand my *tunelefs* harp I take,
Then do I more augment my foes defpight. *Spenfer.*
Swallow, what doft thou
With thy *tunelefs* ferenade. *Cowley.*

TU'NER. *n. f.* [from *tune.*] One who tunes.

The pox of fuch antick, lifping, affected phantafies, thefe new *tuners* of accents. *Shakefpeare.*

TU'NICK. *n. s.* [*tunique*, Fr. *tunica*, Lat.]

1. Part of the Roman dress.

The *tunicks* of the Romans, which answer to our waistcoats, were without ornaments, and with very short sleeves. *Arbuthnot on Coins.*

2. Covering; integument; tunicle.

Lohocks and syrups abate and demulce the hoarseness of a cough, by mollifying the ruggedness of the intern *tunick* of the gullet. *Harvey on Conf.*

Their fruit is locked up all winter in their gems, and well fenced with neat and close *tunicks*. *Derham's Physico-Theology.*

The dropsy of the *tunica vaginalis* is owing to a preternatural discharge of that water continually separating on the internal surface of the *tunick*. *Sharp.*

TU'NICLE. *n. s.* [from *tunick*.] Cover; integument.

The humours and *tunicles* are purely transparent, to let in the light and colour unsoiled. *Ray.*

One single grain of wheat, barley, or rye, shall contain four or five distinct plants under one common *tunicle*; a very convincing argument of the providence of God. *Bentley.*

TU'NNAGE. *n. s.* [from *tun*.]

1. Content of a vessel measured by the tun.

The consideration of the riches of the ancients leads to that of their trade, and to enquire into the bulk and *tunnage* of their shipping. *Arbuthnot.*

2. Tax laid on a tun; as to levy *tunnage* and poundage.

TU'NNEL. *n. s.*

1. The shaft of a chimney; the passage for the smoke.

It was a vault ybuilt for great dispence,
With many ranges rear'd along the wall,
And one great chimney, whose long *tunnel* thence
The smoak forth threw. *Fairy Queen.*

The water being rarified, and by rarification resolved into wind, will force up the smoke, which otherwise might linger in the *tunnel*, and oftentimes reverse. *Wotton's Arch.*

2. A funnel; a pipe by which liquor is poured into vessels.

For the help of the hearing, make an instrument like a *tunnel*, the narrow part of the bigness of the hole of the ear, and the broader end much larger. *Bacon.*

3. A net wide at the mouth, and ending in a point, and so resembling a funnel or tunnel.

To TU'NNEL. *v. a.* [from the noun.]

1. To form like a tunnel.

The Phalænæ tribe inhabit the *tunnelled*, convolved leaves. *Derham's Physico-Theology.*

2. To catch in a net.

3. This word is used by Derham for to make net-work; to reticulate.

Some birds not only weave the fibrous parts of vegetables, and curiously *tunnel* them into nests, but artificially suspend them on the twigs of trees. *Derham.*

TU'NNY. *n. s.* [*tonnen*, Ital. *thynnus*, Lat.] A sea-fish.

Some fish are boiled and preserved fresh in vinegar, as *tonny* and turbot. *Carew.*

TUP. *n. s.* [I know not of what original.] A ram. This word is yet used in Staffordshire, and in other provinces.

To TUP. *v. n.* To but like a ram.

TU'RBAN. }
TUR'BANT. } *n. s.* [A Turkish word.] The cover worn by the Turks on their heads.
TU'RBAND. }

Gates of monarchs
Arch'd are so high, that giants may jet through,
And keep their impious *turbands* on, without
Good morrow to the sun. *Shakespeare.*

His hat was in the form of a *turban*, not so huge as the Turkish *turbans*. *Bacon.*

From utmost Indian isle, Taprobane,
Dusk faces with white silken *turbants* wreath'd. *Milton.*

I see the Turk nodding with his *turbant*. *Howel.*

Some for the pride of Turkish courts design'd,
For folded *turbants* finest Holland bear. *Dryden.*

TU'RBANED. *adj.* [from *turban*.] Wearing a turban.

A *turban'd* Turk
That beat a Venetian, and traduc'd the state,
I took by the throat. *Shakespeare.*

TU'RBARY. *n. s.* [*turbaria*, low Lat. from *turf*.] The right of digging turf. *Skinner.*

TU'RBID. *adj.* [*turbidus*, Latin.] Thick; muddy; not clear.

Though lees make the liquid *turbid*, yet they refine the spirits. *Bacon.*

The brazen instruments of death discharge
Horrible flames, and *turbid* streaming clouds
Of smoke sulphureous, intermix'd with these
Large globous irons fly. *Philips.*

The ordinary springs, which were before clear, fresh, and limpid, become thick and *turbid*, as long as the earthquake lasts. *Woodw. Nat. Hist.*

TU'RBIDNESS. *n. s.* [from *turbid*.] Muddiness; thickness.

TU'RBINATED. *adj.* [*turbinatus*, Latin.]

1. Twisted; spiral.

Let mechanism here produce a spiral and *turbinated* motion of the whole moved body without an external director. *Bentley.*

2. Among botanists plants are called *turbinated*, as some parts of them resemble, or are of a conical figure. *Dictionary.*

TURBINA'TION. *n. s.* [from *turbinated*.] The art of spinning like a top.

TU'RBITH. *n. s.* [*turpethus*, Latin.] Yellow precipitate.

I sent him twelve grains of *turbith* mineral, and purged it off with a bitter draught. I repeated the *turbith* once in three days; and the ulcers shell'd soon off. *Wiseman's Surgery.*

TU'RBOT. *n. s.* [*turbot*, French and Dutch.] A delicate fish.

Some fish are preserved fresh in vinegar, as *turbot*. *Carew.*

Of fishes you shall find in arms the whale, the salmon, the *turbot*. *Peacham.*

Nor oysters of the Lucrine lake
My sober appetite would wish,
Nor *turbot*. *Dryden.*

TU'RBULENCE. }
TU'RBULENCY. } *n. s.* [*turbulence*, Fr. *turbulentia*, Latin.]

1. Tumult; confusion.

I have dream'd
Of bloody *turbulence*; and this whole night
Hath nothing been but forms of slaughter. *Shakespeare.*

Oft-times noxious where they light
On man, beast, plant, wasteful and turbulent,
Like *turbulencies* in the affairs of men,
Over whose heads they roar, and seem to point:
They oft foresignify and threaten ill. *Milton.*

I come to calm thy *turbulence* of mind,
If reason will resume her sov'reign sway. *Dryden.*

2. Tumultuousness; liableness to confusion.

You think this *turbulence* of blood,
From stagnating preserves the flood,
Which thus fermenting by degrees,
Exalts the spirits, sinks the lees. *Swift.*

TU'RBULENT. *ad.* [*turbulentus*, Lat.]

1. Raising agitation; producing commotion.

From the clear milky juice allaying
Thirst, and refresh'd; nor envy'd them the grape,
Whose heads that *turbulent* liquor fills with fumes. *Milton.*

2. Exposed to commotion; liable to agitation.

Calm region once,
And full of peace; now tost, and *turbulent!* *Milton.*

3. Tumultuous; violent.

What wondrous sort of death has heav'n design'd
For so untam'd, so *turbulent* a mind? *Dryden.*

Nor need we tell what anxious cares attend
The *turbulent* mirth of wine, nor all the kinds
Of maladies that lead to death's grim cave,
Wrought by intemperance. *Dryden.*

Men of ambitious and *turbulent* spirits, that were dissatisfied with privacy, were allowed to engage in matters of state. *Bentl.*

TURBU'LENTLY. *adv.* [from *turbulent*.] Tumultuously; violently.

TU'RCISM. *n. s.* [*turcismus*, low Latin.] The religion of the Turks.

Methinks I am at Mecca, and hear a piece of *turcism* preached to me by one of Mahomet's priests. *Dr. Maine.*

He is condemned immediately, as preferring *Turcism* to Christianity. *Atterbury.*

TU'RCOIS. *n. s.* [*turcois*, Dutch.] A precious stone.

TURD. *n. s.* [tuꞃd, Saxon.] Excrement.

TURF. *n. s.* [tyꞃꝼ, Saxon; *torf*, Dutch; *torf*, Swedish.] A clod covered with grass; a part of the surface of the ground.

Where was this lane?
Close by the battle, ditch'd, and wall'd with *turf*. *Shakesp.*

Turf and peats are cheap fuels, and last long. *Bacon.*

Could that divide you from near ushering guides?
They left me weary on a grassy *turf*. *Milton.*

Then living *turfs* upon his body lay. *Dryden.*

Each place some monument of thee should bear;
I with green *turfs* would grateful altars raise. *Dryden.*

Their bucklers ring around,
Their trampling turns the *turf*, and shakes the solid ground. *Dryden's Æn.*

The ambassador every morning religiously saluted a *turf* of earth dug out of his own native soil, to remind him that all the day he was to think of his country. *Addison.*

His flock daily crops
Their verdant dinner from the mossy *turf*,
Sufficient. *Philips.*

Yet shall thy grave with rising flow'rs be drest,
And the green *turf* lie lightly on thy breast. *Pope.*

To TURF. *v. a.* [from the noun.] To cover with turfs.

The face of the bank next the sea is *turfed*. *Mortimer.*

TU'RFINESS. *n. s.* [from *turf*.] The state of abounding with turfs.

TU'RFY. *adj.* [from *turf*.] Full of turfs.

TU'RGENT. *adj.* [*turgens*, Lat.] Swelling; protuberant; tumid.

Where humours are *turgent*, it is necessary not only to purge them, but also to strengthen the infested parts. *Gov. Ton.*

The clusters clear,
White o'er the *turgent* film the living dew. *Thomson.*

TURGE'SCENCE. }
TURGE'SCENCY. } *n. ſ.* [*turgeſcens*, Lat.]

1. The act of ſwelling; the ſtate of being ſwollen.

The inſtant *turgeſcence* is not to be taken off, but by medicines of higher natures. *Brown's Vulgar Errours.*

TU'RGID. *adj.* [*turgidus*, Lat.]

1. Swelling; bloated; filling more room than before.

A bladder, moderately fill'd with air, and ſtrongly tied, held near the fire grew turgid and hard; and brought nearer, ſuddenly broke with a vehement noiſe. *Boyle.*

The ſpirits embroil'd with the malignity, and drowned in the blood *turgid* and tumified by the febril fermentation, are by phlebotomy relieved. *Harvey on Conſumptions.*

Diſburthen thou thy ſapleſs wood
Of its rich progeny; the *turgid* fruit
Abounds with mellow liquor. *Philips.*

Thoſe channels *turgid* with th' obſtructed tide
Stretch their ſmall holes and make their meſhes wide. *Bla.*

2. Pompous; tumid; faſtuous; vainly magnificent.

Some have a violent and *turgid* manner of talking and thinking; whatſoever they judge of is with a tincture of this vanity. *Watts's Logick.*

TURGI'DITY. *n. ſ.* [from *turgid.*] State of being ſwollen.

The fore-runners of an apoplexy are dulneſs, ſlowneſs of ſpeech, vertigos, weakneſs, wateryneſs, and *turgidity* of the eyes. *Arbuthnot on Diet.*

TU'RKEY. *n. ſ.* [*gallina turcica*, Lat.] A large domeſtick fowl brought from Turkey.

Here he comes ſwelling like a *turkey*-cock. *Shakeſp.*

The *turkey*-cock hath ſwelling gills, the hen leſs. *Bacon.*

So ſpeeds the wily fox,
Who lately filch'd the *turkey*'s callow care. *Gay.*

TU'RKOIS. *n. ſ.* [*turquoiſe*, French, from *turkey.*] A blue ſtone numbered among the meaner precious ſtones, now diſcovered to be a bone impregnated with cupreous particles.

Thoſe bony bodies found among copper-ores are tinged with green or blue: the *turcois* ſtone, as it is commonly ſtiled by lapidaries, is part of a bone ſo tinged. *Woodward.*

TU'RKSCAP. *n. ſ.* An herb. *Ainſ.*

TURM. *n. ſ.* [*turmæ*, Lat.] A troop. Not in uſe.

Legions and cohorts, *turms* of horſe and wings. *Milton.*

TURMERICK. *n. ſ.* [*turmerica*, Lat.] An Indian root which makes a yellow die.

TU'RMOIL. *n. ſ.* [derived by Skinner from *tremouille*, French, a mil-hopper, more probably derived from *moil*, to labour.] Trouble; diſturbance; harraſſing uneaſineſs; tumultuous moleſtation. Little in uſe.

He ſeeks, with torment and *turmoil*,
To force me live and will not let me die. *Spenſer.*

There I'll reſt, as after much *turmoil*
A bleſſed ſoul doth in elyſium. *Shakeſpeare.*

Blinded greatneſs ever in *turmoil*,
Still ſeeking happy life, makes life a toil. *Daniel.*

Happy when I, from this *turmoil* ſet free,
That peaceful and divine aſſemby ſee. *Denham.*

To TURMOI'L. *v. a.* [from the noun.]

1. To harraſs with commotion. Out of uſe.

That is not fault of will in thoſe godly fathers, but the troublous occaſions wherewith that wretched realm hath continually been *turmoiled.* *Spenſer.*

It is her fatal miſfortune above all othercountries, to be miſerably toſſed and *turmoiled* with theſeſtorms of affliction. *Spenſ.*

Haughty Juno, who with endleſs broil,
Did earth, and heav'n and Jove himſelf *turmoil*,
At length aton'd, her friendly pow'r ſhall join. *Dryden.*

2. To weary; to keep in unquietneſs.

Having newly left thoſe grammatic ſhallows, where they ſtuck unreaſonably to learn a few words, on the ſudden are tranſported to be toſt and *turmoil'd* with their unballaſted wits in fathomleſs aud unquiet deeps of controverſy. *Milton.*

To TURN. *v. a.* [ꞇuꞃnan, Sax. *tourner*, Fr. from *torno*, Lat.]

1. To put into a circular or vertiginous motion; to move round; to revolve.

She would have made Hercules *turn* the ſpit; yea and have cleft his club to make the fire too. *Shakeſp.*

He *turn'd* me about with his finger and thumb, as one would ſet up a top. *Shakeſpeare.*

Here's a knocking, indeed: if a man were porter of hell-gate he ſhould have old *turning* the key. *Shakeſp.*

They in numbers that compute
Days, months and years, towards his all-chearing lamp
Turn ſwift their various motions, or are *turn'd*
By his magnetic beam. *Milton's Par. Loſt.*

2. To put the upperſide downwards; to ſhift with regard to the ſides.

When the hen has laid her eggs ſo that ſhe can cover them, what care does ſhe take in *turning* them frequently, that all parts may partake of the vital warmth? *Addiſon.*

3. To change with reſpect to poſition.

Expert
When to advance, or ſtand, or *turn* the ſway
Of battle. *Milton.*

He bid his angels *turn* aſcanſe the poles. *Milton.*

4. To change the ſtate of the ballance.

You weigh equally, a feather will *turn* the ſcale. *Shakeſp.*

If I ſurvive, ſhall Troy the leſs prevail,
A ſingle ſoul's too light to *turn* the ſcale. *Dryden.*

5. To bring the inſide out.

He called me ſot;
And told me I had *turn'd* the wrong ſide out. *Shakeſp.*

The vaſt abyſs
Up from the bottom *turn'd* by furious winds. *Milton.*

6. To change as to the poſture of the body, or direction of the look.

His gentle dumb expreſſion *turn'd* at length
The eye of Eve to mark his play. *Milton.*

The rage of thirſt and hunger now ſuppreſt,
The monarch *turns* him to his royal gueſt. *Pope's Odyſſ.*

7. To form on a lathe by moving round. [*torno*, Lat.]

As the placing one foot of a pair of compaſſes on a plane, and moving about the other foot, deſcribes a circle with the moving point; ſo any ſubſtance, pitched ſteddy on two points, as on an axis, and moved about, alſo deſcribes a circle concentric to the axis: and an edge-tool ſet ſteddy to that part of the outſide of the ſubſtance, will in a circumvolution of that ſubſtance, cut off all the parts that lie farther off the axis, and make the outſide alſo concentric to the axis. This is the whole ſum of *turning.* *Moxon's Mech. Exer.*

The whole lathe is made ſtrong, becauſe the matter it *turns* being metal, is heavier than wood, and with forceable coming about, would, if the lathe were ſlight, make it tremble, and ſo ſpoil the work. *Moxon's Mech. Exer.*

8. To form; to ſhape.

His whole perſon is finely *turned*, and ſpeaks him a man of quality. *Tatler*, N° 75.

What nervous arms he boaſts, how firm his tread,
His limbs how *turn'd*, how broad his ſhoulders ſpread! *Pope.*

9. To transform, to metamorphoſe; to tranſmute.

My throat of war be *turn'd*
To the virgin's voice that babies lulls aſleep. *Shakeſp.*

This mock of his
Hath *turn'd* his balls to gunſtones. *Shakeſp. Hen.* V.

Turn the council of Ahitophel into fooliſhneſs. 2 *Sa.* xv.

Impatience *turns* an ague into a fever, a fever to the plague, fear into deſpair, anger into rage, loſs into madneſs, and ſorrow to amazement. *Taylor's Rule of living Holy.*

O goodneſs! that ſhall evil *turn* to good. *Milton.*

Of ſooty coal th' empirick alchemiſt
Can *turn*, or holds it poſſible to *turn*
Mettals of droſſieſt ore to perfect gold. *Milton.*

10. To make of another colour.

The choler of a hog *turned* ſyrup of violets green. *Floyer.*

11. To change; to alter.

Diſdain not me although I be not fair:
Doth beauty keep which never ſun can burn,
Nor ſtorms do *turn.* *Sidney.*

Some dear friend dead; elſe nothing in the world
Could *turn* ſo much the conſtitution
Of any conſtant man. *Shakeſp. Merch. of Venice.*

12. To make a reverſe of fortune.

Fortune confounds the wiſe,
And when they leaſt expect it, *turns* the dice. *Dryden.*

13. To tranſlate.

The bard whom pilfer'd paſtorals renown;
Who *turns* a Perſian tale for half a crown,
Juſt writes to make his barrenneſs appear. *Pope.*

14. To change to another opinion, or party, worſe or better; to convert; to pervert.

15. To change with regard to inclination or temper.

Turn thee unto me, and have mercy upon me. *Pſ.* xxv.

16. To alter from one effect or purpoſe to another.

That unreadineſs which they find in us, they *turn* it to the ſoothing up themſelves in that accurſed fancy. *Hooker.*

When a ſtorm of ſad miſchance beats upon our ſpirits, *turn* it into advantage, to ſerve religion or prudence. *Taylor.*

God will make theſe evils the occaſion of a greater good, by *turning* them to advantage in this world, or increaſe of our happineſs in the next. *Tillotſon.*

17. To betake.

Sheep, and great cattle, it ſeems indifferent which of theſe two were moſt *turned* to. *Temple.*

18. To transfer.

Theſe came to David to Hebron, to *turn* the kingdom of Saul to him. 1 *Chron.* xii. 23.

Turn ye not unto idols, nor make to yourſelves molten gods. *Lev.* xix. 4.

19. To fall upon.

The deſtruction of Demetrius, ſon to Philip II. of Macedon, *turned* upon the father, who died of repentance. *Bacon.*

20. To make to nauſeate.

This beaſtly line quite *turns* my ſtomach. *Pope.*

21. To make giddy.

Eaſtern prieſts in giddy circles run,
And *turn* their heads to imitate the ſun. *Pope.*

22. To infatuate; to make mad.

My aking head can scarce support the pain,
This cursed love will surely *turn* my brain:
Feel how it shoots. *Theocrit.*

Alas! she raves; her brain, I fear, is *turn'd*. *Rowe.*

23. To direct to, or from any point.

The sun
Was bid *turn* reins from th' equinoctial road. *Milton.*

A man, though he *turns* his eyes towards an object, yet he may chuse whether he will curiously survey it. *Locke.*

Unless he *turns* his thoughts that way, he will no more have clear and distinct ideas of the operations of his mind, than he will have of a clock, who will not *turn* his eyes to it. *Locke.*

They *turn* away their eyes from a beautiful prospect. *Add.*

24. To direct to a certain purpose or propension.

My thoughts are *turn'd* on peace.
Already have our quarrels fill'd the world
With widows and with orphans. *Addison's Cato.*

This *turns* the busiest spirits from the old notions of honour and liberty to the thoughts of traffick. *Addison.*

His natural magnanimity *turn'd* all his thoughts upon something more valuable than he had in view. *Addison.*

He *turn'd* his parts rather to books and conversation, than to politicks. *Prior.*

He is still to spring from one of a poetical disposition, from whom he might inherit a soul *turn'd* to poetry. *Pope.*

25. To double in.

Thus a wise taylor is not pinching,
But *turns* at ev'ry seam an inch in. *Swift.*

26. To revolve; to agitate in the mind.

Turn these ideas about in your mind, and take a view of them on all sides. *Watts.*

27. To drive from a perpendicular edge; to blunt.

Quick wits are more quick to enter speedily, than able to pierce far; like sharp tools whose edges be very soon *turn'd*. *Ascham.*

28. To drive by violence; to expel.

Rather *turn* this day out of the week;
This day of shame. *Shakespeare.*

They *turn'd* weak people and children unable for service, out of the city. *Knolles's Hist. of the Turks.*

He now was grown deform'd and poor,
And fit to be *turn'd* out of door. *Hudibras, p. iii.*

If I had taken to the church, I should have had more sense than to have *turn'd* myself out of my benefice by writing libels on my parishioners. *Dryden's Preface to Fables.*

'Twould be hard to imagine that God would *turn* him out of paradise, to till the ground, and at the same time advance him to a throne. *Locke.*

A great man in a peasant's house, finding his wife handsome, *turn'd* the good man out of his dwelling. *Addison.*

29. To apply.

They all the sacred mysteries of heaven
To their own vile advantages shall *turn*. *Milton.*

When the passage is open, land will be *turned* most to great cattle; when shut, to sheep. *Temple.*

30. To reverse; to repeal.

God will *turn* thy captivity, and have compassion upon thee. *Deut.* xxx.

31. To keep passing in a course of exchange or traffick.

These are certain commodities, and yield the readiest money of any that are *turn'd* in this kingdom, as they never fail of a price abroad. *Temple.*

A man must guard, if he intends to keep fair with the world, and *turn* the penny. *Collier of Popularity.*

32. To adapt the mind.

However improper he might have been for studies of a higher nature, he was perfectly well *turn'd* for trade. *Addison.*

33. To put towards another.

I will send my fear before thee, and make all thine enemies *turn* their backs unto thee. *Exod.* xxiii. 27.

34. To retort; to throw back.

Luther's conscience, by his instigations, *turns* these very reasonings upon him. *Atterbury.*

35. *To* TURN *away*. To dismiss from service; to discard.

She did nothing but turn up and down, as she had hoped to *turn away* the fancy that master'd her, and hid her face as if she could have hidden herself from her own fancies. *Sidney.*

Yet you will be hanged for being so long absent, or be *turn'd away*. *Shakesp. Twelfth Night.*

She *turn'd away* one servant for putting too much oil in her sallad. *Arbuthnot.*

36. *To* TURN *back*. To return to the hand from which it was received.

We *turn* not *back* the silks upon the merchant,
When we have spoil'd them. *Shak. Troilus and Cressida.*

37. *To* TURN *off*. To dismiss contemptuously.

Having brought our treasure
Then take we down his load, and *turn* him *off*,
Like to the empty ass, to shake his ears. *Shakespeare.*

The murmurer is *turn'd off*, to the company of those doleful creatures that inhabit the ruins of Babylon. *Gov. of Tong.*

He *turn'd off* his former wife to make room for this marriage. *Addison.*

38. *To* TURN *off*. To give over; to resign.

The most adverse chances are like the ploughing and breaking the ground, in order to a more plentiful harvest. And yet we are not so wholly *turned off* to that reversion, as to have no supplies for the present; for besides the comfort of so certain an expectation in another life, we have promises also for this. *Decay of Piety.*

39. *To* TURN *off*. To deflect.

The institution of sports was intended by all governments to *turn off* the thoughts of the people from busying themselves in matters of state. *Addison's Freeholder.*

40. *To* TURN *over*. To transfer.

Excusing himself and *turning over* the fault to fortune; then let it be your ill fortune too. *Sidney.*

41. *To* TURN *to*. To have recourse to a book.

He that has once acquired a prudential habit, doth not, in his business, *turn to* these rules. *Grew.*

Helvicus's tables may be *turn'd to* on all occasions. *Locke.*

42. *To be* TURNED *of*. To advance to an age beyond. An odd ungrammatical phrase.

Narcissus now his sixteenth year began,
Just *turned of* boy, and on the verge of man. *Ovid's Met.*

When *turned of* forty they determined to retire to the country. *Addison.*

Irus, though now *turned of* fifty, has not appeared in the world since five and twenty. *Addison.*

43. *To* TURN *over*. To refer.

After he had saluted Solyman, and was about to declare the cause of his coming, he was *turn'd over* to the Bassa's. *Knolles.*

'Tis well the debt no payment does demand,
You *turn* me *over* to another hand. *Dryden's Aurengzebe.*

44. *To* TURN *over*. To examine one leaf of a book after another.

Some conceive they have no more to do than to *turn over* a concordance. *Swift's Miscellanies.*

45. *To* TURN *over*. To throw off the ladder.

Criminals condemned to suffer
Are blinded first, and then *turn'd over*. *Butler.*

To TURN. *v. n.*

1. To move round; to have a circular or vertiginous motion.

Such a light and mettl'd dance
Saw you never;
And by lead-men for the nonce,
That *turn* round like grindlestones. *Ben. Johnson.*

The gate on golden hinges *turning*. *Milton.*

The cause of the imagination that things *turn* round, is, for that the spirits themselves *turn*, being compressed by the vapour of the wine; for every liquid body, upon compression, *turneth*, as we see in water: and it is all one to the sight, whether the visual spirits move, or the object moveth, or the medium moveth. And we see that long *turning* round breedeth the same imagination. *Bacon's Nat. Hist.*

2. To shew regard or anger, by directing the look towards any thing.

Pompey *turned* upon him and bad him be quiet. *Bacon.*

The understanding *turns* inwards on itself, and reflects on its own operations. *Locke.*

Turn, mighty monarch, *turn*, this way:
Do not refuse to hear. *Dryden.*

3. To move the body round.

Nature wrought so, that seeing me she *turn'd*. *Milton.*

He said, and *turning* short with speedy pace,
Casts back a scornful glance and quits the place. *Dryden.*

4. To move from its place.

The ancle-bone is apt to *turn* out on either side, by reason of relaxation of the tendons upon the least walking. *Wisem.*

5. To change posture.

If one with ten thousand dice, should throw five thousand sises once or twice, we might say he did it by chance; but if, with almost an infinite number he should, without failing, throw the same sises, we should certainly conclude he did it by art, or that these dice could *turn* upon no other side. *Cheyne.*

6. To have a tendency or direction.

There is not a more melancholy object than a man who has his head *turned* with religious enthusiasm. *Addison.*

His cares all *turn* upon Astyanax,
Whom he has lodg'd within the citadel. *A. Philips.*

7. To move the face to another quarter.

The night seems doubled with the fear she brings.
The morning, as mistaken, *turns* about,
And all her early fires again go out. *Dryden's Aurengzebe.*

8. To depart from the way; to deviate.

My lords *turn* in, into your servant's house. *Gen.* xix. 2.

Virgil, suppose in describing the fury of his heroe in a battle, when endeavouring to raise our concernment to the highest pitch, *turns* short on the sudden into some similitude, which diverts attention from the main subject. *Dryden.*

9. To alter; to be changed; to be transformed.

Your bodies may at last *turn* all to spirit. *Milton.*

A storm of sad mischance will *turn* into something that is good, if we list to make it so. *Taylor.*

This suspicion *turned* to jealousy, and jealousy to rage; then she disdains and threatens, and again is humble. *Dryd.*

Socrates meeting Alcibiades going to his devotions, and observing his eyes fixed with great seriousness, tells him that he had reason to be thoughtful, since a man might bring down evils by his prayers, and the things which the gods send him at his request might *turn* to his destruction. *Addison.*

For this I suffer'd Phoebus' steeds to stray,
And the mad ruler to misguide the day,
When the wide earth to heaps of ashes *turn'd*,
And heav'n itself the wand'ring chariot burn'd. *Pope.*

Rather than let a good fire be wanting, enliven it with the butter that happens to *turn* to oil. *Swift.*

10. To become by a change.

Cygnets from grey *turn* white; hawks from brown *turn* more white. *Bacon's Nat. Hist.*

Oil of vitriol and petroleum, a drachm of each, will *turn* into a mouldy substance. *Boyle.*

They *turn* viragos too; the wrestler's toil
They try. *Dryden's Juvenal.*

In this disease, the gall will *turn* of a blackish colour, and the blood verge towards a pitchy consistence. *Arbuthnot.*

11. To change sides.

I *turn'd*, and try'd each corner of my bed,
To find if sleep were there, but sleep was lost. *Dryden.*

As a man in a fever *turns* often, although without any hope of ease, so men in the extremest misery fly to the first appearance of relief, though never so vain. *Swift's Intellig.*

12. To change the mind, conduct, or determination.

Turn from thy fierce wrath. *Exod.* xxxii. 12.

Turn at my reproof: behold I will pour out my spirit. *Prov.*

He'll relent and *turn* from his displeasure. *Milton.*

13. To change to acid. Used of milk.

Has friendship such a faint and milky heart,
It *turns* in less than two nights? *Shak. Timon of Athens.*

Asses milk *turneth* not so easily as cows. *Bacon.*

14. To be brought eventually.

Let their vanity be flattered with things that will do them good; and let their pride set them on work on something which may *turn* to their advantage. *Locke on Education.*

Christianity directs our actions so, as every thing we do may *turn* to account at the great day. *Addison's Spect.*

For want of due improvement, these useful inventions have not *turned* to any great account. *Baker's Reflect. on Learning.*

15. To depend on, as the chief point.

When a man once perceives how far ideas agree or disagree, he will be able to judge of what other people say.

The question *turns* upon this point; when the presbyterians shall have got their share of employments, whether they ought not, by their own principles, to use the utmost of their power to reduce the whole kingdom to an uniformity. *Swift.*

Conditions of peace certainly *turn* upon events of war. *Sw.*

The first platform of the poem, which reduces into one important action all the particulars upon which it *turns*. *Pope.*

16. To grow giddy.

I'll look no more,
Lest my brain *turn*, and the deficient sight
Topple down headlong. *Shakespeare's King Lear.*

17. To have an unexpected consequence or tendency.

If we repent seriously, submit contentedly and serve him faithfully, afflictions shall *turn* to our advantage. *Wake.*

18. To TURN *away*. To deviate from a proper course.

The *turning away* of the simple shall slay him. *Prov.*

In some springs of water if you put wood, it will *turn* into the nature of stone. *Bacon.*

19. To return; to recoil.

His foul esteem
Sticks no dishonour on our front, but *turns*
Foul on himself. *Milton.*

20. To be directed to, or from any point.

Forthwith from dance to sweet repast they *turn*. *Milton.*

21. *To* TURN *off*. To divert one's course.

The peaceful banks which profound silence keep,
The little boat securely passes by
But where with noise the waters creep,
Turn off with care, for treacherous rocks are near. *Norris.*

TURN. *n. s.* [from the verb.]

1. The act of turning; gyration.

2. Meander; winding way.

Fear misled the youngest from his way;
But Nisus hit the *turns*. *Dryden.*

After a turbulent and noisy course among the rocks, the Teverne falls into the valley, and after many *turns* and windings glides peaceably into the Tiber. *Addison.*

3. A walk too and fro.

My good and gracious lord of Canterbury:
Come, you and I must walk a *turn* together. *Shakespeare.*

Nothing but the open air will do me good, I'll take a *turn* in your garden. *Dryden's Spanish Friar.*

Upon a bridge somewhat broader than the space a man takes up in walking, laid over a precipice, desire some eminent philosopher to take a *turn* or two upon it. *Collier.*

4. Change; vicissitude; alteration.

An admirable facility musick hath to express and represent to the mind, more inwardly than any other sensible mean, the very standing, rising, and falling; the very steps and inflections every way; the *turns* and varieties of all passions whereunto the mind is subject. *Hooker.*

Oh, world, thy slippery *turns!* friends now fast sworn,
On a dissension of a doit, break out
To bitterest enmity. *Shakespeare.*

The state of christendom might by this have a *turn*. *Bacon.*

The King with great nobleness and bounty, which virtues had their *turns* in his nature, restored Edward Stafford. *Bacon.*

This *turn* hath made amends! thou hast fulfill'd
Thy words, Creator bounteous. *Milton.*

This *turn*'s too quick to be without design;
I'll sound the bottom of 't ere I believe. *Dryden.*

Too well the *turns* of mortal chance I know,
And hate relentless of my heavenly foe. *Pope's Odyss.*

An English gentleman should be well versed in the history of England, that he may observe the several *turns* of state, and how produced. *Locke.*

5. Manner of proceeding; change from the original intention or first appearance.

The Athenians were offered liberty, but the wise *turn* they thought to give the matter, was a sacrifice of the author. *Swift.*

6. Chance; hap.

Every one has a fair *turn* to be as great as he pleases. *Col.*

7. Occasion; incidental opportunity.

An old dog, falling from his speed, was loaden at every *turn* with blows and reproaches. *L'Estrange.*

8. Time at which any thing is to be had or done.

Myself would be glad to take some breath, and desire that some of you would take your *turn* to speak. *Bacon.*

His *turn* will come to laugh at you again. *Denham.*

The spiteful stars have shed their venom down,
And now the peaceful planets take their *turn*. *Dryden.*

Though they held the power of the civil sword unlawful, whilst they were to be governed by it, yet they esteemed it very lawful when it came to their *turn* to govern. *Atterb.*

A saline constitution of the fluids is acid, alkaline, or muriatic: of these in their *turns*. *Arbuthnot.*

The nymph will have her *turn* to be
The tutor, and the pupil, he. *Swift.*

9. Actions of kindness or malice.

Lend this virgin aid,
Thanks are half lost when good *turns* are delay'd. *Fairfax.*

Some malicious natures place their delight in doing ill *turns*. *L'Estrange's Fab. b.* 102.

Shrewd *turns* strike deeper than ill words. *South.*

10. Reigning inclination.

This is not to be accomplished but by introducing religion to be the *turn* and fashion of the age. *Swift.*

11. A step off the ladder at the gallows.

They, by their skill in palmistry,
Will quickly read his destiny;
And make him glad to read his lesson,
Or take a *turn* for it at the session. *Butler.*

12. Convenience.

Diogenes' dish did never serve his master for more *turns*, notwithstanding that he made it his dish, cup, cap, measure, and water-pot, than a mantle doth an Irishman. *Spenser.*

They never found occasion for their *tourn*,
But almost starv'd did much lament and mourn. *Hubberd.*

His going I could frame to serve my *turn*;
Save him from danger, do him love and honour. *Shakesp.*

My daughter Catharine is not for your *turn*. *Shakespeare.*

To perform this murder was elect;
A base companion, few or none could miss,
Who first did serve their *turn*, and now serves his. *Dan.*

They tried their old friends of the city, who had served their *turns* so often, and set them to get a petition. *Clarendon.*

This philosophy may pass with the most sensual, while they pretend to be reasonable; but whenever they have a mind to be otherwise, to drink or to sleep, will serve the *turn*. *Temple's Miscellanies.*

13. The form; cast; shape; manner.

Our young men take up some cry'd up English poet, without knowing wherein his thoughts are improper to his subject, or his expressions unworthy of his thoughts, or the *turn* of both is unharmonious. *Dryden.*

Seldom any thing raises wonder in me, which does not give my thought a *turn* that makes my heart the better. *Addison.*

Female virtues are of a domestick *turn*. The family is the proper province for private women to shine in. *Addison.*

An agreeable *turn* appears in her sentiments upon the most ordinary affairs of life. *Addison.*

Wit doth not consist so much in advancing things new, as in giving things known an agreeable *turn*. *Addison's Spect.*

Before I made this remark, I wondered to see the Roman poets, in their description of a beautiful man, so often mention the *turn* of his neck and arms. *Addison.*

A young man of a sprightly *turn* in conversation, had an inordinate desire of appearing fashionable. *Spectator.*

Books give the same *turn* to our thoughts and reasoning, that good company does to our conversation. *Swift's Misc.*

The very *turn* of voice, the good pronunciation, and the alluring manner which some teachers have attained, will engage the attention. *Watts.*

14. The manner of adjusting the words of a sentence.

The *turn* of words, in which Ovid excells all poets, are sometimes a fault or sometimes a beauty, as they are used properly or improperly. *Dryden.*

The three first stanzas are rendered word for word with the original, not only with the same elegance, but the same short *turn* of expression peculiar to the sapphick ode. *Addison.*

The first coin being made of brass gave the denomination to money among the Romans, and the whole *turn* of their expressions is derived from it. *Arbuthnot.*

15. *By* TURNS. One after another.

They feel by *turns* the bitter change
Of fierce extremes; extremes by change more fierce. *Milt.*

The challenge to Dametas shall belong,
Menalcas shall sustain his under-song;
Each in his turn your tuneful numbers bring;
By turns the tuneful muses love to sing. *Dryden's Virg.*

By turns put on the suppliant, and the lord;
Threaten'd this moment, and the next implor'd. *Prior.*

TU'RNBENCH. *n. s.* [*turn* and *bench.*] A term of turners.

Small work in metal is turn'd in an iron lathe called a *turnbench*, which they screw in a vice, and having fitted their work upon a small iron axle, with a drill barrel, fitted upon a square shank, at the end of the axis, next the left-hand, they with a drill-bow, and drill-string, carry it about. *Moxon.*

TU'RNCOAT. *n. s.* [*turn* and *coat.*] One who forsakes his party or principles; a renegade;

Courtesy itself must turn to disdain, if you come in her presence—Then is courtesy a *turncoat*. *Shakesp.*

TU'RNER. *n. s.* [from *turn.*] One whose trade is to turn in a lathe.

Nor box, nor limes without their use are made,
Smooth-grain'd and proper for the *turner's* trade. *Dryden.*

Some *turners*, to shew their dexterity in turning, turn long and slender pieces of ivory, as small as an hay-stalk. *Moxon.*

TU'RNING. *v. a.* [from *turn.*] Flexure; winding; meander.

I ran with headlong haste
Thro' paths and *turnings* often trod by day. *Milton.*

TU'RNINGNESS. *n. s.* [from *turning.*] Quality of turning; tergiversation; subterfuge.

So nature formed him, to all *turningness* of sleights; that though no man had less goodness, no man could better find the places whence arguments might grow of goodness. *Sidn.*

TU'RNIP. *n. s.* A white esculent root.

The flower consists of four leaves, which are placed in form of a cross; out of the flower cup rises the pointal, which afterward turns to a pod, divided into two cells by an intermediate partition, to which the valves adhere on both sides, and are full of roundish seeds: a carneous and tuberose root. *Mil.*

November is drawn with bunches of parsnips and *turnips* in his right-hand. *Peacham on Drawing.*

The goddess rose amid the inmost round,
With wither'd *turnip*-tops her temples crown'd. *Gay.*

Turnips hide their swelling heads below. *Gay's Past.*

TURNPI'KE. *n. s.* [*turn* and *pike*, or *pique.*]

1. A cross of two bars armed with pikes at the end, and turning on a pin, fixed to hinder horses from entering.

2. Any gate by which the way is obstructed.

The gates are shut, and the *turnpikes* locked. *Arbuthnot.*

TU'RNSICK. *adj.* [*turn* and *sick.*] Vertiginous; giddy.

If a man see another turn swiftly and long; or if he look upon wheels that turn, himself waxeth *turnsick*. *Bacon.*

TURNSO'L. *n. s.* [*Heliotropium*, Lat.] A plant.

The flower consists of one leaf shaped like a funnel, having its centre wrinkled and folded, and its brim cut into ten segments alternately unequal: these flowers are collected into a long reflected spike, resembling a scorpion's tail; each flower is succeeded by four naked gibbose seeds. *Miller.*

TU'RNSPIT. *n. s.* [*turn* and *spit.*] He that anciently turned a spit, instead of which jacks are now generally used.

I give you joy of the report
That he's to have a place at court;
Yes, and a place he will grow rich in,
A *turnspit* in the royal kitchen. *Swift's Miscel.*

TU'RNSTILE. *n. s.* [*turn* and *stile.*] A turnpike.

A *turnstile* is more certain
Than, in events of war, dame Fortune. *Hudibras.*

Twirling *turnstiles* interrupt the way,
The thwarting passenger shall force them round. *Gay.*

TU'RPENTINE. *n. s.* [*turpentina*, Italian; *terebinthina*, Lat.] The gum exuded by the pine, the juniper, and other trees of that kind.

As the *turpentine* tree I stretched out my branches. *Ecclus.*

Vertgrease grinded with *turpentine*, put into a pot, and as you use it warm it. *Peacham on Drawing.*

TU'RQUOISE. *n. s.* See *Turkois.*

One shew'd me a ring, he had of your daughter for a monkey.—Out upon her! it was my *turquoise*, I had it when I was a bachelor. *Shakesp. Merchant of Venice.*

TU'RPITUDE. *n. s.* [*turpitude*, Fr. *turpitudo*, from *turpis*, Lat.] Essential deformity of words, thoughts or actions; inherent vileness; badness.

How would'st thou have paid
My better service, when my *turpitude*
Thou thus dost crown with gold. *Shakespeare.*

Decency imports a certain measure of one thing to another; the preservation of which is properly that rule by which every thing ought to act; and consequently the violation of it implies a *turpitude* or indecency. *South's Sermons.*

TU'RRET. *n. s.* [*turris*, Lat.] A small eminence raised above the rest of the building; a little tower.

Discourse I pr'y thee, on this *turret's* top. *Shakespeare.*

All things well ordered, he withdrew with speed
Up to a *turret* high, two ports between,
That so he might be near at every need,
And overlook the lands and furrows green. *Fairfax.*

Make Windsor hills in lofty numbers rise,
And lift her *turrets* nearer to the skies. *Pope. Winds. For.*

TU'RRETED. *adj.* [from *turret.*] Formed like a tower; rising like a tower.

Take a *turreted* lamp of tin, in the form of a square; the height of the turret being thrice as much as the length of the lower part, whereupon the lamp standeth. *Bacon's Nat. Hist.*

TU'RTLE.
TU'RTLEDOVE. } *n. s.* [turtle, Saxon; *tortorelle*, French; *tortarella*, Italian; *turtur*, Latin.]

1. A species of dove.

When shepherds pipe on oaten straws,
And merry larks are ploughmens clocks:
When *turtles* tread. *Shak. Love's Lab. Lost.*

We'll teach him to know *turtles* from jays. *Shak.*

Take me an heifer and a *turtle* dove. *Gen.* xv. 9.

Galen propos'd the blood of *turtles* dropt warm from their wings. *Wiseman.*

2. It is used among sailors and gluttons for a tortoise.

TUSH. *interj.* [Of this word I can find no credible etymology.] An expression of contempt.

Tush, say they, how should God perceive it: is there knowledge in the most high? *Psalm* lxxiii.

Sir Thomas Moor found fault with his lady's continual chiding, saying; the consideration of the time, for it was sent, should restrain her. *Tush, tush*, my lord, said she, look, here is one step to heaven-ward, shewing him a friar's girdle. I fear me, quoth Sir Thomas, this one step will not bring you up a step higher. *Camden's Remains.*

Tush never tell me, I take it much unkindly
That thou, Iago, who hast had my purse,
As if the strings were thine, should know of this. *Shak.*

TUSK. *n. s.* [tyxar, Saxon; *tosken*, old Frisick.] The long teeth of a pugnacious animal; the fang; the holding tooth.

Some creatures have over-long, or out-growing teeth, called fangs, or *tusks*; as boars and pikes. *Bacon.*

The boar depended upon his *tusks*. *L'Estrange.*

As two boars,
With rising bristles, and with frothy jaws,
Their adverse breasts with *tusks* oblique they wound. *Dryd.*

A monstrous boar
Whetting his *tusks*, and churning hideous foam. *Smith.*

TU'SKED.
TU'SKY. } *adj.* [from *tusk.*] furnished with tusks.

Into the naked woods he goes,
And seeks the *tusky* boar to tear. *Dryden.*

Of those beasts no one was horned and *tusked* too: the superfluous blood not sufficing to feed both. *Grew.*

TU'SSUCK. *n. s.* [diminitive of *tuzz.*] A tuft of grass or twigs.

The first is remarkable for the several *tussucks* or bunches of thorns, wherewith it is armed round. *Grew.*

TUT. *interj.* [This seems to be the same with *tush.*]

A particle noting contempt.

Tut, tut! grace me no grace, nor uncle me no uncle. *Shak.*

Tut, tut! here's a mannerly forbearance. *Shakesp.*

TUTANAG. *n. s.*

Tutanage is the Chinese name for spelter, which we erroneously apply to the metal of which canisters are made, that are brought over with the tea from China. It being a coarse pewter made with the lead carried from England and tin got in the kingdom of Quintang. *Woodward.*

TU'TELAGE. *n. s.* [*tutelle*, *tutelage*, Fr. *tutela*, Lat.] Guardianship; state of being under guardian.

If one in the possession of lands die, and leave a minor to succeed to him, his *tutelage* belongeth to the king. *Drummond.*

He accoupled the ambassage with an article in the nature of a request, that the French king might, according unto his right

right of ſeigniory or *tutelage*; diſpoſe of the marriage of the young ducheſs of Britany. *Bacon.*

TU'TELAR. } *adj.* [*tutela*, Lat.] Having the charge or guar-
TU'TELARY. } dianſhip of any perſon or thing; protecting; defenſive; guardian.

According to the traditions of the magicians the *tutelary* ſpirits, will not remove at common appellations, but at the proper names of things, whereunto they are protectors. *Brown.*

Temperance, that virtue without pride, and fortune without envy, that gives indolence of body, with an equality of mind; the beſt guardian of youth and ſupport of old age: the precept of reaſon, as well as religion, and phyſician of the ſoul as well as the body; the *tutelar* goddeſs of health, and univerſal medicine of life. *Temple.*

Theſe *tutelar* genii who preſided over the ſeveral people committed to their charge, were watchful over them. *Dryd.*

But you, O Grecian chiefs, reward my care,
Sure I may plead a little to your grace:
Enter'd the town; I then unbarr'd the gates,
When I remov'd the *tutelary* fates. *Dryden.*
Ye *tutelar* gods who guard this royal fabric. *Rowe.*

TUTOR. *n. ſ.* [*tutor*, Lat. *tuteur*, Fr.] One who has the care of another's learning and morals; a teacher or inſtructor.

When I am as I have been,
Approach me, and thou ſhalt be as thou waſt,
The *tutor* and the feeder of my riots;
Till then I baniſh thee on pain of death. *Shakeſp.*
Ah, *tutor*, look where bloody Clifford comes. *Shakeſp.*
When nobles are the tailors *tutors*;
No hereticks burnt but wenches ſuiters. *Butler.*

A primitive Chriſtian, that coming to a friend to teach him a pſalm, began, I ſaid I will look to my ways, that I offend not with my tongue; upon which he ſtop'd his *tutor*, ſaying, this is enough if I learn it. *Government of the Tongue.*

His body thus adorn'd, he next deſign'd
With lib'ral arts to cultivate his mind:
He ſought a *tutor* of his own accord,
And ſtudy'd leſſons he before abhorr'd. *Dryden.*

No ſcience is ſo ſpeedily learned by the nobleſt genius without a *tutor*. *Watts.*

To TUTOR. *v. a.* [from the noun.]

1. To inſtruct; to teach; to document.

This boy is foreſt born,
And hath been *tutor'd* in the rudiments
Of many deſperate ſtudies by his uncle. *Shakeſp.*
He cannot be a perfect man,
Not being tried and *tutor'd* in the world. *Shakeſp.*

The cock has his ſpurs, and he ſtrikes his feet inward with ſingular ſtrength and order; yet he does not this by any ſyllogiſtical method, but is merely *tutored* by inſtinct. *Hale.*

2. To treat with ſuperiority or ſeverity.

I hardly yet have learn'd
T'inſinuate, flatter, bow, and bend my knee:
Give ſorrow leave a while to *tutor* me
To this ſubmiſſion. *Shakeſp. Rich. II.*

I take a review of my little boys mounted upon hobby-horſes, and of little girls *tutoring* their babies. *Addiſon.*

TU'TORAGE. *n. ſ.* [from *tutor.*] The authority or ſolemnity of a tutor.

Children care not for the company of their parents or *tutors*, and men will care leſs for theirs, who would make them children by uſurping a *tutorage*. *Govern. of the Tongue.*

TU'TORESS. *n. ſ.* [from *tutor.*] Directreſs; inſtructreſs; governeſs.

Fidelia ſhall be your *tutoreſs*. *Moore's Foundling.*

TUTTY. *n. ſ.* [*tutia*, low Lat. *tuthie*, Fr.] A ſublimate of zinc or calamine collected in the furnace. *Ainſw.*

TU'TSAN, or *parkleaves*. *n. ſ.* [*androſæmum*, Lat.] A plant.

TUZ. *n. ſ.* [I know not whether it is not a word merely of cant.] A lock or tuft of hair.

With odorous oil thy head and hair are ſleek;
And then thou kemp'ſt the *tuzzes* on thy cheek;
Of theſe thy barbers take a coſtly care. *Dryden.*

TWAIN. *adj.* [ꞇpᵹen, baꞇpa, both twain, Saxon.] Two. An old word, not now uſed but ludicrouſly.

'Tis not the tryal of a woman's war,
The bitter clamour of two eager tongues,
Can arbitrate this cauſe betwixt us *twain*. *Shakeſp.*
Such ſmiling rogues as theſe,
Like rats, oft bite the holy cords in *twain*,
Too intricate t' unlooſe. *Shakeſp. King Lear.*
Of my condition take no care;
It fits not; thou and I long ſince are *twain*. *Milton.*
When old winter ſplit the rocks in *twain*;
He ſtrip'd the bears-foot of its leafy growth. *Dryden.*
The trembling widow, and her daughters *twain*,
This woeful cackling cry with horror heard. *Dryden.*

To TWANG. *v. n.* [A word formed from the ſound.] To ſound with a quick ſharp noiſe.

A thouſand *twanging* inſtruments
Will hum about mine ears. *Shakeſp. Tempeſt.*
His quiver o'er his ſhoulders Phœbus threw,
His bow *twang'd*, and his arrows rattled as they flew. *Dryd.*
With her thund'ring voice ſhe menac'd high;
And every accent *twang'd* with ſmarting ſorrow. *Dryden.*
The *twanging* bows
Send ſhowers of ſhafts, that on their barbed points
Alternate ruin bear. *Philips.*
Sounds the tough horn and *twangs* the quiv'ring ſtring. *Pope.*

To TWANG. *v. a.* To make to ſound ſharply.

A ſwaggering accent ſharply *twang'd* off, gives manhood approbation. *Shak. Twelfth Night.*

TWANG. *n. ſ.* [from the verb.]

1. A ſharp quick ſound.

They by the ſound and *twang* of noſe,
If all be ſound within, diſcloſe. *Butler's Hudibras.*
So ſwells each wind-pipe; aſs intones to aſs,
Harmonic *twang* of leather, horn and braſs. *Pope.*

2. An affected modulation of the voice.

If he be but a perſon in vogue with the multitude, he can make popular, rambling, incoherent ſtuff, ſeaſoned with *twang* and tautology, paſs for high rhetorick. *South's Sermons.*

He has ſuch a *twang* in his diſcourſe, and ungraceful way of ſpeaking thro' his noſe, that one can hardly underſtand him. *Arbuthnot.*

TWANG. *interj.* A word making a quick action, accompanied with a ſharp ſound. Little uſed, and little deſerving to be uſed.

There's one, the beſt in all my quiver,
Twang! thro' his very heart and liver. *Prior.*

TWA'NGLING. *adj.* [from *twang.*] Contemptibly noiſy.

She did call me raſcal, fidler,
And *twangling* jack, with twenty ſuch vile terms. *Shak.*

To TWANK. *v. n.* [Corrupted from *twang.*] To make to ſound.

A freeman of London has the privilege of diſturbing a whole ſtreet with *twanking* of a braſs kettle. *Addiſon.*

'TWAS. Contracted from *it was.*

If he aſks who bid thee, ſay *'twas* I. *Dryd.*

To TWA'TTLE. *v. n.* [ſchwatzen, German.] To prate; to gabble; to chatter.

It is not for every *twattling* goſſip to undertake. *L'Eſtrange.*

TWAY. For TWAIN.

Gyon's angry blade ſo fierce did play
On th' other's helmet, which as Titan ſhone,
That quit it clove his plumed creſt in *tway*. *Fairy Q.*

TWA'YBLADE. *n. ſ.* [*Ophris*, Lat.] It hath a polypetalous flower, conſiſting of ſix diſſimilar leaves, of which the five upper ones are ſo diſpoſed, as to repreſent in ſome meaſure an helmet, the under one being headed and ſhaped like a man. The empalement becomes a fruit, perforated with three windows, to which adhere valves, pregnant with very ſmall ſeeds like duſt. *Miller.*

To TWEAG. } *v. a.* [It is written *tweag* by Skinner, but *tweak*
To TWEAK. } by other writers; twacken, German.] To pinch; to ſqueeze betwixt the fingers.

Who calls me villain, breaks my pate acroſs,
Tweaks me by the noſe. *Shakeſp.*
To rouſe him from lethargick dump,
He *tweak'd* his noſe. *Butler.*
Look in their face, they *tweak'd* your noſe. *Swift.*

TWEAGUE. } *n. ſ.* [from the verb.] Perplexity; ludicrous
TWEAK. } diſtreſs. A low word.

This put the old fellow in a rare *tweague*. *Arbuthnot.*

To TWEE'DLE. *v. a.* [I know not whence deriv'd.] To handle lightly. It ſeems in the following paſſage miſprinted for *wheedle.*

A fidler brought in with him a body of luſty young fellows, whom he had *tweedled* into the ſervice. *Addiſon.*

TWEE'ZERS. *n. ſ.* [*etuy*, French.] Nippers, or ſmall pincers, to pluck off hairs.

There hero's wits are kept in pond'rous vaſes,
And beaus in ſnuff-boxes and *tweezer*-caſes. *Pope.*

TWELFTH. *adj.* ꞇpelꝼꞇa, Saxon.] Second after the tenth; the ordinal of twelve.

He found Eliſha plowing with twelve yoke of oxen, and he with the *twelfth*. *1 Kings.* xix. 9.

Suppoſing, according to the ſtandard, five ſhillings were to weigh an ounce, wanting about ſixteen grains, whereof one *twelfth* were copper, and eleven *twelfths* ſilver, it is plain here the quantity of ſilver gives the value. *Locke.*

TWE'LFTHTIDE. *n. ſ.* The twelfth day after Chriſtmas.

Plough-munday, next after that *twelfthtide*,
Bids out with the plough. *Tuſſ. Huſb.*

TWELVE. *adj.* [ꞇpelꝼ, Sax.] Two and ten; twice ſix.

Thou haſt beat me out *twelve* ſeveral times. *Shak. Coriolanus.*
Had we no quarrel elſe to Rome, but that
Thou art thence baniſh'd, we would muſter all,
From *twelve* to twenty. *Shak.*

What man talk'd with you yesternight
Out at your window betwixt *twelve* and one. *Shakespeare.*
On his left hand *twelve* reverend owls did fly:
So Romulus, 'tis sung, by Tyber's brook,
Presage of sway from twice six vultures, took. *Dryden.*

TWE'LVEMONTH. *n. s.* [*twelve* and *month.*] A year, as consisting of twelve months.

I shall laugh at this a *twelvemonth* hence. *Shakesp.*

This year or *twelvemonth*, by reason that the moon's months are shorter than those of the sun, is about eleven days shorter than the sun's year. *Holder.*

Taking the shoots of the past spring and pegging them down in very rich earth perfectly consumed, watering them upon all occasions, by this time *twelvemonth* they will be ready to remove. *Evelyn.*

In the space of about a *twelvemonth* I have run out of a whole thousand pound upon her. *Addison.*

Not twice a *twelvemonth* you appear in print. *Pope.*

TWE'LVEPENCE. *n. s.* [*twelve* and *pence.*] A shilling.

TWE'LVEPENNY. *adj.* [*twelve* and *penny.*] Sold for a shilling.

I would wish no other revenge, from this rhyming judge of the *twelvepenny* gallery. *Dryd.*

TWE'LVESCORE. *n. s.* [*twelve* and *score.*] Twelve times twenty; two hundred and forty.

Twelvescore virago's of the Spartan race. *Dryden.*

TWE'NTIETH. *adj.* [ꞇpenꞇeoᵹoða, Saxon.] Twice tenth; ordinal of twenty.

This year,
The *twentieth* from the firing the capitol,
As fatal too to Rome, by all predictions. *Ben. Johnson.*

The quantity of the fifteenth should be turned to a *twentieth.* *Bacon.*

Why was not I the *twentieth* by descent
From a long restive race of droning kings? *Dryden.*

This crown now must be raised, and coined one *twentieth* lighter; which is nothing but changing the denomination, calling that a crown now, which yesterday was but a part, *viz.* nineteen *twentieths.* *Locke.*

TWENTY. *adj.* [ꞇpenꞇiᵹ, Saxon.]

1. Twice ten.

At least nineteen in *twenty* of these perplexing words might be changed into easy ones. *Swift.*

2. A proverbial or indefinite number.

Maximilian, upon *twenty* respects, could not have been the man. *Bacon's Henry* VII.

TWI'BIL. *n. s.* [*twy* for *two* and *bill*, *bipennis*, Lat.] A halbert. *Ains.*

TWICE. *adv.* [ꞇpiᵹiꝺ, Saxon; *twees*, Dutch.]

1. Two times.

Upon his crest he struck him so,
That *twice* he reeled, ready *twice* to fall. *Fairy Q.*
He *twice* essay'd to cast his son in gold;
Twice from his hands he drop'd the forming mould. *Dryd.*

2. Doubly.

A little sum you mourn, while most have met
With *twice* the loss, and by as vile a cheat. *Dryden.*

3. It is often used in composition.

Life is tedious as a *twice* told tale,
Vexing the dull ear of a drowsy man. *Shakesp.*
Twice-born Bacchus burst the thund'rer's thigh,
And all the gods that wander thro' the sky. *Creech.*
Extol the strength of a *twice*-conquer'd race. *Dryden.*
And what so tedious as a *twice*-told tale. *Pope.*

To TWIDLE. *v. a.* [This is commonly written *tweedle.*] To touch lightly. A low word.

With my fingers upon the stupe, I pressed close upon it, and *twidled* it in, first one side, then the other. *Wiseman.*

TWIG. *n. s.* ꞇpiᵹ, ꞇpiᵹᵹa, Saxon; *twyg*, Dutch.] A small shoot of a branch; a switch tough and long.

The Britons had boats made of willow *twigs*, covered on the outside with hides, and so had the Venetians. *Raleigh.*

They chose the fig-tree, such as spread her arms,
Branching so broad and long, that in the ground
The bended *twigs* take root. *Milton.*
Can'st thou with a weak angle strike the whale,
His huge jaw with a *twig* or bulrush bore? *Sandys.*

If they cut the *twigs* at evening, a plentiful and pleasant juice comes out. *More.*

The tender *twig* shoots upwards to the skies. *Dryden.*
From parent bough
A cyon meetly sever: after force
A way into the crabstocks close wrought grain
By wedges, and within the living wound
Inclose the foster *twig*, around which spread
The binding clay. *Philips.*

TWI'GGEN. *adj.* [from *twig.*] Made of twigs.

I'll beat the knave with a *twiggen* bottle. *Shakesp.*

The sides and rim sewed together after the manner of *twiggen* work. *Grew.*

TWIGGY. *adj.* [from *twig.*] Full of twigs.

TWI'LIGHT. *n. s. tweelicht*, Dutch; ꞇpeoneleohꞇ, Saxon.] The dubious or faint light before sunrise, and after sunset; obscure light; uncertain view.

Her *twilights* were more clear than our mid-day. *Donne.*

Suspicions amongst thoughts, are like bats amongst birds, they ever fly by *twilight.* Certainly they are to be well guarded. *Bacon.*

A faint weak love of virtue, and of good,
Reflects from her on them, which understood
Her worth; and though she have shut in all day
The *twilight* of her memory doth stay. *Donne.*
He that saw hell in's melancholy dream,
And in the *twilight* of his phancy's theme
Scar'd from his sins, repented in a fright,
Had he view'd Scotland, had turn'd proselyte. *Cleveland.*
Ambrosial night, with clouds exhal'd
From that high mount of God, whence light and shade
Spring both, the face of brightest heav'n had chang'd
To grateful *twilight.* *Milton's Par. Lost.*
When the sun was down
They just arriv'd by *twilight* at a town. *Dryden.*

In the greatest part of our concernment he has afforded us only the *twilight* of probability, suitable to our state of mediocrity. *Locke.*

TWI'LIGHT. *adj.*

1. Not clearly or brightly illuminated; obscure; deeply shaded.

When the sun begins to fling
His flaring beams, me goddess bring
To arched walks of *twilight* groves. *Milton.*
O'er the *twilight* groves, and dusky caves,
Long-sounding isles, and intermingled graves,
Black melancholy sits, and round her throws
A death-like silence, and a dead repose. *Pope.*

2. Seen by *twilight.*

On old Lycæus or Cyllene hoar
Trip no more in *twilight* ranks. *Milton.*

TWIN. *n. s.* [ꞇpinn, Saxon; *tweelingen*, Dutch.]

1. Children born at a birth. It is therefore seldom used in the singular; though sometimes it is used for one of twins.

In this mystery of ill opinions, here's the *twin* brother of thy letter; but let thine inherit first, for mine never shall. *Sh.*

In bestowing
He was most princely: ever witness for him
Those *twins* of learning Ipswich and Oxford. *Shakesp.*

If that moment of the time of birth be of such moment, whence proceedeth the great difference of the constitutions of *twins*, which, tho' together born, have strange and contrary fortunes. *Drummond.*

The divided dam
Runs to the summons of her hungry lamb;
But when the *twin* cries halves, she quits the first. *Cleveland.*
They came *twins* from the womb, and still they live
As if they would go *twins* too to the grave. *Otway.*
Fair Leda's *twins*, in time to stars decreed,
One fought on foot, one curb'd the fiery steed. *Dryden.*

Had there been the same likeness in all men, as sometimes in *twins*, it would have given occasion to confusion. *Grew.*

2. Gemini, the sign of the zodiack.

This, when the sun retires,
First shines, and spreads black night with feeble fires,
Then parts the *twins* and crab. *Creech.*
When now no more, th' alternate *twins* are fir'd.
Short is the doubtful empire of the night. *Thomson.*

To TWIN. *v. n.* [from the noun.]

1. To be born at the same birth.

He that is approv'd in this offence,
Though he had *twinn'd* with me both at a birth,
Shall lose me. *Shakesp. Othello.*

2. To bring two at once.

Ewes yearly by *twinning* rich masters do make. *Tusser.*

3. To be paired; to be suited.

Hath nature given them eyes,
Which can distinguish 'twixt
The fiery orbs above and the *twinned* stones
Upon the humbl'd beach. *Shakesp.*
O how inscrutable! his equity
Twins with his power. *Sandys.*

TWINBO'RN. *adj.* [*twin* and *born.*] Born at the same birth.

Our sins lay on the King; he must bear all.
O hard condition and *twinborn* with greatness. *Shakesp.*

To TWINE. *v. a.* [ꞇpinan, Saxon; *twynan*, Dutch.]

1. To twist or complicate so as to unite, or form one body or substance out of two or more.

Thou shalt make an hanging of blue, and fine *twined* linen, wrought with needlework. *Exod.* xxvi. 36.

2. I know not whether this is from *twine* or *twin.*

By original lapse, true liberty
Is lost, which always with right reason dwells,
Twin'd, and from her hath no dividual being. *Milton.*

3. To unite itself.

Lumps of sugar lose themselves, and *twine*
Their subtile essence with the soul of wine. *Crashaw.*

To Twine. *v. n.*
1. To convolve itself; to wrap itself closely about.
Let wreaths of triumph now my temples *twine*,
The victor cry'd, the glorious prize is mine! *Pope.*
2. To unite by interposition of parts.
Friends now fast sworn, who *twine* in love
Unseparable, shall, within this hour,
On a dissension of a doit, break out
To bitterest enmity. *Shakespeare.*
3. To wind; to make flexures.
As rivers, though they bend and *twine*,
Still to the sea their course incline.
Or as philosophers who find
Some fav'rite system to their mind,
In ev'ry point to make it fit,
Will force all nature to submit. *Swift.*
The deer rustles thro' the *twining* brake. *Thomson.*

Twine. *n. s.* [from the verb.]
1. A twisted thread.
Not any damsel, which her vaunteth most
In skilful knitting of soft silken *twine*. *Spenser.*
A pointed sword hung threat'ning o'er his head,
Sustain'd but by a slender *twine* of thread. *Dryden.*
2. Twist; convolution.
Nor all the gods beside
Longer dare abide,
Not Typhon huge ending in snaky *twine*. *Milton.*
Welcome joy and feast,
Braid your locks with rosy *twine*.
Dropping odours, dropping wine. *Milton.*
3 Embrace; act of convolving itself round.
Everlasting hate
The vine to ivy bears, but with am'rous *twine*
Clasps the tall elm. *Philips.*

To Twinge. *v. a.* [*twingen*, German; *twinge*, Danish.]
1. To torment with sudden and short pain.
The gnat charg'd into the nostrils of the lion, and there *twing'd* him till he made him tear himself, and so master'd him. *L'Estrange.*
2. To pinch; to tweak.
When a man is past his sense,
There's no way to reduce him thence,
But *twinging* him by th' ears and nose,
Or laying on of heavy blows. *Hudibras.*

Twinge. *n. s.* [from the verb.]
1. Short sudden sharp pain.
The wickedness of this old villain startles me, and gives me a *twinge* for my own sin, though far short of his. *Dryd.*
2. A tweak; a pinch.
How can you fawn upon a master that gives you so many blows and *twinges* by the ears. *L'Estrange.*

Twink. *n. s.* [See Twinkle.] The motion of an eye; a moment. Not in use.
She hung about my neck, and kiss on kiss
She vied so fast, protesting oath on oath,
That in a *twink* she won me to her love. *Shakespeare.*

To Twi'nkle, *v. n.* [ꞇpinclian, Saxon.]
1. To sparkle; to flash irregularly; to shine with intermitted light; to shine faintly; to quiver.
At first I did adore a *twinkling* star,
But now I worship a celestial sun. *Shakespeare.*
As plays the sun upon the glassey streams,
Twinkling another counterfeited beam,
So seems this gorgeous beauty. *Shakespeare.*
Some their forked tails stretch forth on high,
And tear the *twinkling* stars from trembling sky. *Fairfax.*
God comprises all the goods we value in the creatures, as the sun doth the light that *twinkles* in the stars. *Boyle.*
The star of love,
That *twinkles* you to fair Almeyda's bed. *Dryden.*
Think you your new French proselytes are come
To starve abroad, because they starv'd at home,
Your benefices *twinkl'd* from afar. *Dryden.*
So weak your charms, that like a winter's night,
Twinkling with stars, they freeze me while they light. *Dryd.*
These stars do not *twinkle* when viewed through telescopes which have large apertures: for the rays of light which pass through divers parts of the aperture, tremble each of them apart; and by means of their various, and sometimes contrary tremors, fall at one and the same time upon different points in the bottom of the eye. *Newton.*
2. To open and shut the eye by turns.
The owl fell a moping and *twinkling*. *L'Estrange.*
3. To play irregularly.
His eyes will *twinkle*, and his tongue will roll,
As tho' he beck'ned, and call'd back his soul. *Donne.*

Twi'nkle. } *n. s.* [from the verb.]
Twi'nkling. }
1. A sparkling intermitting light; a motion of the eye.
Suddenly, with *twinkle* of her eye,
The damsel broke his misintended dart. *Spenser.*
I come, I come; the least *twinkle* had brought me to thee. *Dryden's Don Sebastian.*
2. A short space, such as is taken up by a motion of the eye.
Money can thy wants at will supply,
Shields, steeds, and arms, and all things for thee meet,
It can pourvey in *twinkling* of an eye. *Fairy Queen.*
These false beauties of the stage are no more lasting than a rainbow; when the actor gilds them no longer with his reflection, they vanish in a *twinkling*. *Dryden.*
The action, passion, and manners of so many persons in a picture, are to be discerned in the *twinkling* of an eye, if the sight could travel over so many different objects all at once. *Dryden.*

Twi'nling. *n. s.* [diminutive of *twin*.] A twin lamb; a lamb of two brought at a birth.
Twinlings increase bring. *Tusser's Husb.*

Twi'nner. *n. s.* [from *twin*.] A breeder of twins.
Ewes yeerely by twinning rich maisters do make,
The lambe of such *twinners* for breeders go take. *Tusser.*

To Twirl. *v. a.* [from *whirl*.] To turn round; to move by a quick rotation.
Wool and raw silk by moisture incorporate with other thread; especially if there be a little wreathing, as appeareth by the twisting and *twirling* about of spindles. *Bacon.*
Dextrous damsels *twirl* the sprinkling mop. *Gay.*
See ruddy maids,
Some taught with dextrous hand to *twirl* the wheel. *Dodsl.*

Twirl. *n. s.* [from the verb.]
1. Rotation; circular motion.
2. Twist; convolution.
The *twirl* on this is different from that of the others; this being an heterostropha, the *twirls* turning from the right-hand to the left. *Woodward on Fossils.*

To TWIST. *v. a.* [ᵹeꞇpıꞅꞇan, Saxon; *twisten*, Dutch.]
1. To form by complication; to form by convolution.
Do but despair,
And if thou want'st a cord, the smallest thread
That ever spider *twisted* from her womb,
Will strangle thee. *Shakespeare.*
To reprove discontent, the ancients feigned, that in hell stood a man *twisting* a rope of hay; and still he *twisted* on, suffering an ass to eat up all that was finished. *Taylor.*
Would Clotho wash her hands in milk,
And *twist* our thread with gold and silk;
Would she in friendship, peace, and plenty,
Spin out our years to four times twenty,
And should we both in this condition,
Have conquer'd love, and worse ambition,
Else these two passions by the way,
May chance to shew us scurvy play. *Prior.*
The task were harder to secure my own
Against the pow'r of those already known;
For well you *twist* the secret chains that bind
With gentle force the captivated mind. *Lyttleton.*
2. To contort; to writhe.
Either double it into a pyramidical, or *twist* it into a serpentine form. *Pope.*
3. To wreath; to wind; to encircle by something round about.
There are pillars of smoke *twisted* about with wreaths of flame. *Burnet's Theory of the Earth.*
4. To form; to weave.
If thou dost love fair Hero, cherish it,
And thou shalt have her: was't not to this end
That thou began'st to *twist* so fine a story? *Shakespeare.*
5. To unite by intertexture of parts.
All that know how prodigal
Of thy great soul thou art, longing to *twist*
Bays with that joy, which so early kist
Thy youthful temples, with what horror we
Think on the blind events of war. *Waller.*
6. To unite; to insinuate.
When avarice *twists* itself, not only with the practice of men, but the doctrines of the church; when ecclesiasticks dispute for money, the mischief seems fatal. *Decay of Piety.*

To Twist. *v. n.* To be contorted; to be convolved.
In an ileus, commonly called the *twisting* of the guts, is a circumvolution or insertion of one part of the gut within the other. *Arbuthnot on Aliments.*
Deep in her breast he plung'd the shining sword:
Th'Inachians view the slain with vast surprize,
Her *twisting* volumes, and her rolling eyes. *Pope.*

Twist. *n. s.* [from the verb.]
1. Any thing made by convolution, or winding two bodies together.
Minerva nurs'd him
Within a *twist* of twining osiers laid. *Addison.*

2. A single string of a cord.

Winding a thin string about the work, hazards its breaking by the fretting of the several *twists* against one another. *Maxon's Mech. Exer.*

3. A cord; a string.

Through these labyrinths, not my grov'ling wit,
But thy silk *twist*, let down from heav'n to me,
Did both conduct and teach me, how by it
To climb to thee. *Herbert.*

About his chin the *twist*
He ty'd, and soon the strangl'd soul dismiss'd. *Dryden.*

4. Contortion; writhe.

Not the least turn or *twist* in the fibres of any one animal, which does not render them more proper for that particular animal's way of life than any other cast or texture. *Addison.*

5. The manner of twisting.

Jack shrunk at first sight of it; he found fault with the length, the thickness, and the *twist*. *Arbuthnot.*

TWI'STER. *n. s.* [from *twist*.] One who twists; a ropemaker.

To this word I have annexed some remarkable lines, which explain twist in all its senses.

When a *twister* a-twisting will twist him a twist,
For the twisting of his twist, he three twines doth intwist;
But if one of the twines of the twist do untwist,
The twine that untwisteth untwisteth the twist.
Untwirling the twine that untwisteth between,
He twirls with his *twister* the two in a twine;
Then twice having twisted the twines of the twine,
He twitcheth the twine he had twined in twain.
The twain that in twining before in the twine,
As twins were intwisted, he now doth untwine,
'Twixt the twain intertwisting a twine more between,
He, twirling his *twister*, makes a twist of the twine. *Wallis.*

To TWIT. *v. a.* [eðpitan, Saxon.] To sneer; to flout; to reproach.

When approaching the stormy stowers,
We mought with our shoulders bear off the sharp showers,
And sooth to saine, nought seemeth sike strife,
That shepherds so *twiten* each other's life. *Spenser.*

When I protest true loyalty to her,
She *twits* me with my falshood to my friend. *Shakespeare.*

Æsop minds men of their errors without *twitting* them for what's amiss. *L'Estrange.*

This these scoffers *twitted* the Christians with. *Tillotson.*

Galen bled his patients, till by fainting they could bear no longer; for which he was *twitted* in his own time. *Baker.*

To TWITCH. *v. a.* [twiccian, Saxon.] To vellicate; to pluck with a quick motion; to snatch; to pluck with a hasty motion.

He rose, and *twitch'd* his mantle blue,
To-morrow to fresh woods, and pastures new. *Milton.*

Twitch'd by the sleeve he mouths it more and more. *Dryden's Juvenal.*

With a furious leap
She sprung from bed, disturbed in her mind,
And fear'd at ev'ry step a *twitching* spright behind. *Dryd.*

Thrice they *twitch'd* the diamond in her ear. *Pope.*

TWITCH. *n. s.* [from the verb.]

1. A quick pull; a sudden vellication.

But Hudibras give him a *twitch*,
As quick as light'ning in the breech. *Hudibras.*

The lion gave one hearty *twitch*, and got his feet out of the trap, but left his claws behind. *L'Estrange.*

2. A painful contraction of the fibres.

Other confed'rate pairs
Contract the fibres, and the *twitch* produce,
Which gently pushes on the grateful food
To the wide stomach, by its hollow road. *Blackmore.*

Mighty physical their fear is,
For soon as noise of combat near is,
Their heart descending to their breeches,
Must give their stomachs cruel *twitches*. *Prior.*

A fit of the stone is the cure, from the inflammation and pain occasioning convulsive *twitches*. *Sharp.*

TWI'TCHGRASS. *n. s.* A plant.

Twitch-grass is a weed that keeps some land loose, hollow, and draws away the virtue of the ground. *Mortimer.*

To TWI'TTER. *v. n.*

1. To make a sharp tremulous intermitted noise.

This must be done,
Swallows *twitter* on the chimney-tops. *Dryden.*

They *twitter* chearful, till the vernal months
Invite them back. *Thomson.*

2. To be suddenly moved with any inclination. A low word.

A widow which had a *twittering* toward a second husband, took a gossipping companion to manage the jobb. *L'Estr.*

TWI'TTER. *n. s.* Any motion or disorder of passion; such as a violent fit of laughing, or fit of fretting.

The ancient errant knights
Won all their ladies hearts in fights,
And cut whole giants into fritters,
To put them into amorous *twitters*. *Hudibras.*

The moon was in a heavy *twitter*, that her cloaths never fitted her. *L'Estrange.*

TWITTLETWA'TTLE. *n. s.* [A ludicrous reduplication of *twattle*.] Tattle; gabble. A vile word.

Insipid *twittletwatles*, frothy jests, and jingling witticisms, inure us to a misunderstanding of things. *L'Estrange.*

'TWIXT. A contraction of *betwixt*.

Twilight, short arbiter *'twixt* day and night. *Milton.*

TWO. *adj.* [*twai*, Gothick; τpu, Saxon.]

1. One and one.

Between *two* hawks, which flies the higher pitch;
Between *two* dogs, which hath the deeper mouth;
Between *two* blades, which bears the better temper;
Between *two* horses, which doth bear him best;
Between *two* girls, which hath the merriest eye,
I have some shallow spirit of judgment. *Shakespeare.*

Three words it will three times report, and then the *two* latter for some times. *Bacon's Nat. Hist.*

Fifteen chambers were to lodge us *two* and *two* together. *Bacon.*

They lay
By *two* and *two* across the common way. *Dryden.*

2. It is used in composition.

Next to the raven's age, the Pylian king
Was longest liv'd of any *two*-legg'd thing. *Dryden.*

A rational animal better described man's essence, than a *two*-legged animal, with broad nails, and without feathers. *Locke's Works.*

The *two*-shap'd Ericthonius had his birth
Without a mother, from the teeming earth. *Addison.*

Her register was a *two*-leaved book of record, one page containing the names of her living, and the other of her deceased members. *Ayliffe.*

TWO'EDGED. *adj.* [*two* and *edge*.] Having an edge on either side.

Clarissa drew, with tempting grace,
A *twoedg'd* weapon from her shining case. *Pope.*

TWO'FOLD. *adj.* [*two* and *fold*.] Double.

Our prayer against sudden death importeth a *twofold* desire, that death when it cometh may give us some convenient respite, or if that be denied us of God, yet we may have wisdom to provide always before hand. *Hooker.*

Through mirksom air her ready way she makes,
Her *twofold* team, of which two black as pitch,
And two were brown, yet each to each unlike,
Did softly swim away. *Fairy Queen.*

O thou! the earthly author of my blood,
Whose youthful spirit in me regenerate,
Doth now with *twofold* vigour lift me up,
To reach at victory above my head,
Add proof unto mine armour with thy prayers,
And with thy blessings steel my lance's point. *Shakesp.*

Our *twofold* seas wash either side. *Dryden.*

Time and place taken for distinguishable portions of space and duration, have each of them a *twofold* acceptation. *Locke.*

Ewes, that erst brought forth but single lambs,
Now dropp'd their *twofold* burdens. *Prior.*

Holiness may be taken in a *twofold* sense; for that external holiness, which belongs to persons or things, offered to God; or for those internal graces which sanctify our natures. *Atterb.*

TWO'FOLD. *adv.* Doubly.

A proselyte you make *twofold* more the child of hell than yourselves. *Matth.* xxiii. 15.

TWO'HANDED. *adj.* [*two* and *hand*.] Large; bulky; enormous of magnitude.

With huge *twohanded* sway,
Brandish'd aloft, the horrid edge came down,
Wide wasting. *Milton's Par. Lost.*

If little, then she's life and soul all o'er;
An Amazon, the large *twohanded* whore. *Dryden.*

TWO'PENCE. *n. s.* A small coin, valued at twice a penny.

You all shew like gilt *twopences* to me. *Shakespeare.*

To TYE. *v. a.* To bind. See TIE.

TYE. *n. s.* See TIE. A knot; a bond or obligation.

Lay your
Command upon me; to the which my duties
Are with a most indissoluble *tye*
For ever knit. *Shakespeare.*

I have no *tye* upon you to be true,
But that which loosen'd your's, my love to you. *Dryden.*

Honour's a sacred *tye*, the law of kings,
The noble mind's distinguishing perfection,
That aids and strengthens virtue where it meets her,
And imitates her actions where she is not. *Addis. Cato.*

It ought not to be sported with;
Lend me aid, I now conjure thee, lend,
By the soft *tye* and sacred name of friend. *Pope.*

TY'GER. *n. s.* See TIGER.

TYMBAL. *n. s.* [*tymbal*, French.] A kind of kettle-drum.

Yet gracious charity! indulgent guest!
Were not thy pow'r exerted in my breast;

Those

My speeches would send up unheeded pray'r:
The scorn of life would be but wild despair:
A *tymbal's* sound were better than my voice,
My faith were form, my eloquence were noise. *Prior.*

TYKE. *n. s.* [See TIKE.] Tyke in Scottish still denotes a dog, or one as contemptible and vile as a dog, and from thence perhaps comes *teague.*

Base *tyke,* call'st thou me host? now,
By this hand, I swear I scorn the term. *Shakespeare.*

TYMPANI'TES. *n. s.* [τυμπανίτης, from τυμπανίτω, to sound like a drum.] That particular sort of dropsy that swells the belly up like a drum, and is often cured by tapping.

TY'MPANUM. *n. s.* A drum; a part of the ear, so called from its resemblance to a drum.

The three little bones in meatu auditorio, by firming the *tympanum,* are a great help to the hearing. *Wiseman.*

TY'MPANY. *n. s.* [from *tympanum,* Lat.] A kind of obstructed flatulence that swells the body like a drum.

Hope, the christian grace, must be proportioned and attemperate to the promise; if it exceed that temper and proportion, it becomes a tumour and *tympany* of hope. *Hamm.*

He does not shew us Rome great suddenly,
As if the empire were a *tympany,*
But gives it natural growth, tells how and why
The little body grew so large and high. *Suckling.*

Others that affect
A lofty stile, swell to a *tympany.* *Roscommon.*

Pride is no more than an unnatural *tympany,* that rises in a bubble, and spends itself in a blast? *L'Estrange.*

Nor let thy mountain-belly make pretence
Of likeness; thine's a *tympany* of sense.
A tun of man in thy large bulk is writ,
But sure thou'rt but a kilderkin of wit. *Dryden.*

The air is so rarified in this kind of dropsical tumour as makes it hard and tight like a drum, and from thence it is called a *tympany.* *Arbuthnot.*

TYNY. *adj.* Small.

He that has a little *tyny* wit,
Must make content with his fortunes fit. *Shakespeare.*

TYPE. *n. s.* [*type,* Fr. *typus,* Lat. τύπος.]

1. Emblem; mark of something.

Clean renouncing
The faith they have in tennis, and tall stockings,
Short bolster'd breeches, and those *types* of travel,
And understanding again the honest men. *Shakespeare.*

Thy emblem, gracious queen, the British rose,
Type of sweet rule, and gentle majesty. *Prior.*

2. That by which something future is prefigured.

Informing them by *types*
And shadows of that destin'd seed to bruise
The serpent, by what means he shall atchieve
Mankind's deliverance. *Milton.*

The Apostle shews the Christian religion to be in truth and substance what the Jewish was only in *type* and shadow. *Tillotson's Sermons.*

3. A stamp; a mark not in use.

Thy father bears the *type* of King of Naples,
Yet not so wealthy as an English yeoman. *Shakespeare.*

What good is cover'd with the face of heav'n
To be discovered, that can do me good?
—Th'advancement of your children, gentle lady,
—Up to some scaffold, there to lose their heads;
—No, to the dignity and height of fortune,
The high imperial *type* of this earth's glory. *Shakespeare.*

4. A printing letter.

TY'PICK. } *n. s.* [*typique,* Fr. *typicus,* Lat.] Emblematical;
TY'PICAL. } figurative of something else.

The Levitical priesthood was only *typical* of the christian; which is so much more holy and honourable than that, as the institution of Christ is more excellent than that of Moses. *Atterbury.*

Hence that many coursers ran,
Hand-in-hand, a goodly train,
To bless the great Eliza's reign;
And in the *typic* glory show
What fuller bliss Maria shall bestow. *Prior.*

TY'PICALLY. *adv.* [from *typical.*] In a typical manner.

This excellent communicativeness of the divine nature is *typically* represented, and mysteriously exemplified by the Porphyrian scale of being. *Norris.*

TY'PICALNESS. *n. s.* [from *typical.*] The state of being typical.

To TY'PIFY. *v. a.* [from *type.*] To figure; to shew in emblem.

The resurrection of Christ hath the power of a pattern to us, and is so *typified* in baptism, as an engagement to rise to newness of life. *Hammond.*

Our Saviour was *typified* indeed by the goat that was slain; at the effusion of whose blood, not only the hard hearts of his enemies relented, but the stony rocks and vail of the temple were shattered. *Brown's Vulg. Errours.*

TYPO'GRAPHER. *ad.* [τύπος and γράφω.] A printer.

TYPOGRA'PHICAL. *adj.* [from *typography.*]

1. Emblematical; figurative.
2. Belonging to the printer's art.

TYPOGRA'PHICALLY. *adv.* [from *typographical.*]

1. Emblematically; figuratively.
2. After the manner of printers.

TYPO'GRAPHY. *n. s.* [*typographie,* Fr. *typographia,* Lat.]

1. Emblematical, figurative, or hieroglyphical representation.

Those diminutive and pamphlet treatises daily published amongst us, are pieces containing rather *typography* than verity. *Brown's Vulgar Errours.*

2. The art of printing.

TYRA'NNESS. *n. s.* [from *tyrant.*] A she tyrant.

They were by law of that proud *tyranness,*
Provok'd with wrath and envy's false surmise. *Fairy Qu.*

The *tyranness* doth joy to see
The huge massacres which her eyes do make. *Spenser.*

TYRA'NNICAL. } *n. s.* [*tyrannus,* Latin; *tyrannique,* French;
TYRA'NNICK. } τυραννικός.] Suiting a tyrant; acting like a tyrant; cruel; despotick; imperious.

Charge him home that affects
Tyrannic power. *Shakesp. Coriolanus.*

You have contriv'd to take
From Rome all season'd office, and to wind
Yourself into a power *tyrannical.* *Shakespeare.*

Domitian had been *tyrannical*; and in his time many noble houses were overthrown by false accusations. *Bacon.*

Our sects a more *tyrannick* power assume,
And would for scorpions change the rods of Rome. *Rosc.*

Subdue and quell, o'er all the earth,
Brute violence, and proud *tyrannick* pow'r. *Milton.*

If the spirit of a subject be rebellious, in a prince it will be *tyrannical* and intolerable. *Taylor.*

She hath recourse
To tears and prayers, again she feels the smart
Of a fresh wound from the *tyrannick* dart. *Denham.*

And by the nobles, by his commons curst,
Th' oppressor rul'd *tyrannick* where he durst;
Stretch'd o'er the poor and church his iron rod,
And treats alike his vassals and his God. *Pope.*

TYRA'NNICALLY. *adv.* [from *tyrannical.*] In manner of a tyrant.

TYRA'NNICIDE. *n. s.* [*tyrannus* and *cædo,* Latin.] The act of killing a tyrant.

To TY'RANNISE. *v. n.* [*tyraniser,* Fr. from *tyrant.*] To play the tyrant; to act with rigour and imperiousness.

While we trust in the mercy of God thro' Christ Jesus, fear will not be able to *tyrannise* over us. *Hooker.*

Then gan Carausius *tyrannise* anew,
And gainst the Romans bent their proper power,
And so Alectus treacherously slew,
And took on him the robe of Emperor. *Fairy Queen.*

I made thee miserable,
What time I threw the people's suffrages
On him, that thus doth *tyrannise* o'er me. *Shakespeare.*

A crew, whom like ambition joins
With him, or under him to *tyrannise.* *Milton.*

Beauty had crown'd you, and you must have been
The whole world's mistress, other than a queen;
All had been rivals, and you might have spar'd,
Or kill'd and *tyrannis'd* without a guard. *Waller.*

He does violence to his own faculties, *tyrannises* over his own mind, and usurps the prerogative that belongs to truth alone, which is to command assent by its own authority. *Locke's Works.*

TY'RANNOUS. *adj.* [from *tyrant.*] Tyrannical; despotick; arbitrary; severe; cruel; imperious. Not in use.

It is strange to see the unmanlike cruelty of mankind, who, not content with their *tyrannous* ambition, to have brought the others virtuous patience under them, think their masterhood nothing without doing injury to them. *Sidney.*

Lately grown into a loathing and detestation of the unjust and *tyrannous* rule of Harold an usurper. *Spenser.*

Betwixt two charming words, comes in my father,
And, like the *tyrannous* breathing of the north,
Shakes all our buds from blowing. *Shakespeare.*

Subjection to his empire *tyranous.* *Milton.*

'Tis excellent
To have a giant's strength; but it is *tyrannnous*
To use it like a giant. *Shakespeare.*

Fear you his *tyrannous* passion more, alas!
Than the queen's life. *Shakespeare.*

After the death of this *tyrannous* and ambitious king, these writings came abroad *Temple.*

TY'RANNY. *n. s.* [*tyrannis,* Latin; τυραννὶς; *tyrannie,* Fr.]

1. Absolute monarchy imperiously administered.

Our grand foe,
Who now triumphs, and, in th' excess of joy,
Sole reigning holds the *tyranny* of heav'n. *Milton.*

The

The cities fell often under *tyrannies*, which ſpring naturally out of popular governments. *Temple.*

2. Unreſiſted and cruel power

Boundleſs intemperance
In nature is a *tyranny*; it hath been
Th'untimely emptying of the happy throne,
And fall of many kings. *Shakeſpeare.*

3. Cruel government; rigorous command.

Bleed, bleed, poor country!
Great *tyranny* lay thou thy baſis ſure,
For goodneſs dares not check thee. *Shakeſpeare.*

Suſpicions diſpoſe kings to *tyranny*, and huſbands to jealouſy. *Bacon.*

God in judgment juſt,
Subjects him from without to violent lords;
Who oft as undeſervedly inthral
His outward freedom; *tyranny* muſt be. *Milton.*

4. Severity; rigour; inclemency.

The *tyranny* o' the open night's too rough
For nature to endure. *Shakeſpeare's King Lear.*

TYRA'NT. *n. ſ.* [τύραννος; *tyrannus*, Latin. Rowland contends that this word, with the correſpondent Greek and Latin, is derived from *tir*, Welch and Erſe, land, and *rhanner*, Welch, to ſhare, *q. d. tirhanner*, a ſharer, or divider of and among his vaſſals.]

1. An abſolute monarch governing imperiouſly.

2. A cruel deſpotick and ſevere maſter; an oppreſſor.

Love to a yielding heart is a king, but to a reſiſting is a *tyrant*. *Sidney, b.* i.

I would not be the villain that thou think'ſt,
For the whole ſpace that's in the *tyrant*'s graſp,
And the rich eaſt to boot. *Shakeſpeare's Macbeth.*

Diſſembling courteſy! how fine this *tyrant*
Can tickle where ſhe wounds! *Shakeſp. Cymb.*

The houſe of woe, and dungeon of our *tyrant*. *Milton.*

Conſider thoſe grand agents and lieutenants of the devil, by whom he ſcourges and plagues the world under him, to wit, *tyrants*; and was there ever any *tyrant* who was not alſo falſe and perfidious! *South's Sermons.*

Thou meant'ſt to kill a *tyrant*, not a king. *Dryden.*

When *tyrant* cuſtom had not ſhackl'd man,
But free to follow nature was the mode. *Thomſon.*

TYRE. *n. ſ.* [Properly *tire.*] See TIRE.

I have ſeen her beſet and bedecked all over with emeralds and pearls, ranged in rows about the *tyre* of her head. *Hakewill on Providence.*

TYRO. *n. ſ.* [Properly *tiro*, as in the Latin.] One yet not maſter of his art; one in his rudiments.

There ſtands a ſtructure on a riſing hill,
Where *tyro*'s take their freedom out to kill. *Garth's Diſp.*

V.

V, Has two powers, expressed in modern English by two characters, *V* consonant and *U* vowel, which ought to be considered as two letters; but as they were long confounded while the two uses were annexed to one form, the old custom still continues to be followed.

U, the vowel, has two sounds; one clear, expressed at other times by *eu*, as *obtuse*; the other close, and approaching to the Italian *u*, or English *oo*, as *obtund*.

V, the consonant, has a sound nearly approaching to those of *b* and *f*. With *b* it is by the Spaniards and Gascons always confounded, and in the Runick alphabet is expressed by the same character with *f*, distinguished only by a diacritical point. Its sound in English is uniform. It is never mute.

VA'CANCY. *n. s.* [from *vacant.*]

1. Empty space; vacuity.

How is't
That thus you bend your eye on *vacancy*,
And with th'incorporal air do hold discourse? *Sh. Hamlet.*

2. Chasm; space unfilled.

The reader finds a wide *vacancy*, and knows not how to transport his thoughts to the next particular, for want of some connecting idea. *Watts's Logick.*

3. [*Vacance*, Fr.] State of a post or employment when it is unsupplied.

In the *vacancy* of a bishop, the guardian of the spiritualities was summon'd to parliament in the bishop's room. *Ayliffe.*

4. [*Vacances*, Fr.] Time of leisure; relaxation; intermission; time unengaged.

If, sometimes, each other's eyes we meet,
Those little *vacancies* from toil are sweet. *Dryd. St. of In.*

The daily intervals of time and *vacancies* from necessary labour, together with the one day in seven in the christian world, allow sufficient time. *Watts.*

5. Listlesness; emptiness of thought.

When alone, or in company, they sit still without doing any thing, I like it worse; for all dispositions to idleness or *vacancy*, even before they are habits, are dangerous. *Wotton.*

VA'CANT. *adj.* [*vacant*, Fr. *vacans*, Latin.]

1. Empty; unfilled; void.

Why should the air so impetuously rush into the cavity of the receiver, if there were before no *vacant* room to receive it. *Boyle's Works.*

A better race to bring into their *vacant* room. *Milton.*

2. Free; unencumbered; uncrouded.

Religion is the interest of all; but philosophy of those only that are at leisure, and *vacant* from the affairs of the world. *More's Divine Dialogues.*

A very little part of our life is so *vacant* from uneasinesses, as to leave us free to the attraction of remoter good. *Locke.*

3. Not filled by an incumbent, or possessor.

Lest the fiend invade *vacant* possession. *Milton.*

Others when they allowed the throne *vacant*, thought the succession should immediately go to the next heir. *Swift.*

4. Being at leisure; disengaged.

They which have the government, scatter the army abroad, and place them in villages to take their victuals of them, at such *vacant* times as they lie not in camp. *Spenser.*

Sir John Berkley was the more *vacant* for that service, by the reduction of Barnstaple. *Clarendon.*

The memory relieves the mind in her *vacant* moments, and prevents any chasms of thought, by ideas of what is past. *Addison.*

5. Thoughtless; empty of thought; not busy.

The wretched slave,
Who, with a body fill'd, and *vacant* mind,
Gets him to rest, cramm'd with distressful bread. *Shakes.*

The duke had a pleasant and *vacant* face, proceeding from a singular assurance in his temper. *Wotton's Buck.*

Some vain amusement of a *vacant* soul. *Irene.*

To VA'CATE. *v. a.* [*vaco*, Latin.]

1. To annul; to make void; to make of no authority.

That after-act *vacating* the authority of the precedent, tells the world that some remorse touched even Strafford's most implacable enemies. *K. Charles.*

2. To make vacant; to quit possession of.

3. To defeat; to put an end to.

He *vacates* my revenge;
For while he trusts me, 'twere so base a part
To fawn, and yet betray. *Dryden.*

VACA'TION. *n. s.* [*vacation*, Fr. *vacatio*, Latin.]

1. Intermission of juridical proceedings, or any other stated employments; recess of courts or senates.

Vacation is all that time which passes between term and term, at London. *Cowel.*

As these clerks want not their full task of labour during the open term, so there is for them whereupon to be occupied in the *vacation* only. *Bacon Off. of Alienat.*

2. Leisure; freedom from trouble or perplexity.

Benefit of peace, quiet, and *vacation* for piety, have rendered it necessary in every christian commonwealth, by laws to secure propriety. *Hammond's Fundamentals.*

VA'CCARY. *n. s.* [*vacca*, Latin.] a cow-house; a cow-pasture. *Bailey.*

VACI'LLANCY. *n. s.* [*vacillans*, from *vacillo*, Lat. *vacillant*, Fr.] A state of wavering; fluctuation; inconstancy. Not much in use.

I deny that all mutability implies imperfection, though some does, as that *vacillancy* in human souls, and such mutations as are found in corporeal matter. *More's Divine Dialogues.*

VACILLA'TION. *n. s.* [*vacillatio*, from *vacillo*, Lat. *vacillation*, Fr.] The act or state of reeling or staggering.

The muscles keep the body upright, and prevent its falling, by readily assisting against every *vacillation*. *Derham.*

VA'CUIST. *n. s.* [from *vacuum.*] A philosopher that holds a *vacuum*: opposed to a *plenist*.

Those spaces, which the *vacuists* would have to be empty, because they are manifestly devoid of air, the plenists do not prove replenished with subtle matter. *Boyle.*

VACUA'TION. *n. s.* [*vacuus*, Latin.] The act of emptying. *Dict.*

VACU'ITY. *n. s.* [*vacuitas*, from *vacuus*, Lat. *vacuité*, Fr.]

1. Emptiness; State of being unfilled.

Hunger is such a state of *vacuity*, as to require a fresh supply of aliment. *Arbuthnot.*

2. Space unfilled; space unoccupied.

In filling up *vacuities*, turning out shadows and ceremonies, by explicit prescription of substantial duties, which those shadows did obscurely represent. *Hammond's Fund.*

He, that seat soon failing, meets
A vast *vacuity*. *Milton.*

Body and space are quite different things, and a *vacuity* is interspersed among the particles of matter. *Bentley.*

God, who alone can answer all our longings, and fill every *vacuity* of our soul, should intirely possess our heart. *Rogers.*

3. Inanity; want of reality.

The soul is seen, like other things, in the mirror of its effects: but if they'll run behind the glass to catch at it, their expectations will meet with *vacuity* and emptiness. *Glanv.*

VA'CUOUS. *adj.* [*vacuus*, Lat. *vacuë*, Fr.] Empty; unfilled.

Boundless the deep, because I AM who fill
Infinitude: nor *vacuous* the space. *Milton's Par. Lost.*

VA'CUUM. *n. s.* [Latin.] Space unoccupied by matter.

Our enquiries about *vacuum*, or space and atoms, will shew us some good practical lessons. *Watts.*

To VADE. *v. n.* [*vado*, Latin.] To vanish; to pass away. *Spenser.* A word useful in poetry, but not received.

Be ever gloried here thy sovereign name,
That thou may'st smile on all which thou hast made;
Whose frown alone can shake this earthly frame,
And at whose touch the hills in smoak shall *vade*. *Wotton.*

VA'GABOND. *adj.* [*vagabundus*, low Latin. *vagabond*, Fr.]

1. Wandering without any settled habitation; wanting a home.

Let them pronounce the steep Tarpeian death;
Vagabond exile: yet I wou'd not buy
Their mercy at the price of one fair word. *Shakesp. Cor.*

A *vagabond* debtor may be cited in whatever place or jurisdiction he is found. *Ayliffe's Parergon.*

2. Wandering; vagrant.

This common body,
Like to a *vagabond* flag upon the stream,
Goes to, and back, lacquying the varying tide. *Shakesp.*

Their prayers by envious winds
Blown *vagabond* or frustrate. *Milton.*

VA'GABOND. *n. s.* [from the *adj.*]

1. A vagrant; a wanderer, commonly, in a sense of reproach.

We call those people wanderers and *vagabonds*, that have no dwelling-place. *Raleigh's Hist. of the World.*

Reduced, like Hannibal, to seek relief
From court to court, and wander up and down
A *vagabond* in Afric. *Addison's Cato.*

2. One that wanders illegally, without a settled habitation.

Vagabond is a person without a home. *Watts.*

VAGA'RY. *n. s.* [from *vagus*, Latin.] A wild freak; a capricious frolick.

They chang'd their minds,
Flew off, and into strange *vagaries* fell,
As they wou'd dance. *Milton's Par. Lost. b.* vi. *l.* 613.

Would your son engage in some frolic, or take a *vagary*, were it not better he should do it with, than without your knowledge? *Locke on Education*, § 97.

VAGINOPE'NNOUS. *n. s.* [*vagina* and *penna*, Latin.] Sheath-winged; having the wings covered with hard cases.

VAGOUS. *adj.* [*vagus*, Lat. *vague*, Fr.] Wandering; unsettled. Not in use.

Such as were born and begot of a single woman, thro' a *vagous* lust, were called Sporii. *Ayliffe.*

VA'GRANCY. *n. s.* [from *vagrant.*] A state of wandering; unsettled condition.

VA'GRANT. *adj.* Wandering; unsettled; vagabond; unfixed in place.

Do not oppose popular mistakes and surmises, or *vagrant* and fictitious stories. *More's Divine Dialogues.*

Take good heed what men will think and say;
That beauteous Emma *vagrant* courses took,
Her father's house, and civil life forsook. *Prior.*

Her lips no living bard, I weet,
May say how red, how round, how sweet;
Old *Homer* only could indite
Their *vagrant* grace, and soft delight:
They stand recorded in his book,
When Helen smil'd, and Hebe spoke. *Prior.*

VA'GRANT. *n. s.* [*vagant*, Fr.] A sturdy beggar; wanderer; vagabond; man unsettled in habitation. In an ill sense.

Vagrants and outlaws shall offend thy view,
Train'd to assault, and disciplin'd to kill. *Prior.*

You'll not the progress of your atoms stay,
Nor to collect the *vagrants* find a way. *Blackmore.*

To relieve the helpless poor; to make sturdy *vagrants* relieve themselves; to hinder idle hands from being mischievous, are things of evident use. *F. Atterbury.*

Ye *vagrants* of the sky,
To right or left, unheeded, take your way. *Pope.*

VAGUE. *adj.* [*vague*, Fr. *vagus*, Latin.]

1. Wandering; vagrant; vagabond.

Gray encouraged his men to set upon the *vague* villains, good neither to live peaceably, nor to fight. *Hayward.*

2. Unfixed; unsettled; undetermined; indefinite.

The perception of being, or not being, belongs no more to these *vague* ideas, signified by the terms, whatsoever and thing, than it does to any other ideas. *Locke.*

VAIL. *n. s.* [*voile*, French. This word is now frequently written *veil*, from *velum*, Latin; and the verb *veil*, from the verb *velo*; but the old orthography commonly derived it, I believe rightly, from the French.]

1. A curtain; a cover thrown over any thing to be concealed.

While they supposed to lie hid in their secret sins, they were scattered under a dark *vail* of forgetfulness. *Wisdom.*

2. A part of female dress, by which the face and part of the shape is concealed.

3. Money given to servants. It is commonly used in the plural. See VALE.

To VAIL. *v. a.* To cover. See VEIL.

To VAIL. *v. a.* [*avaller le bonet*, French.]

1. To let fall; to suffer to descend.

They stifly refused to *vail* their bonnets, which is reckoned intollerable contempt by seafarers. *Carew.*

The virgin 'gan her beavoir *vale*,
And thank'd him first, and thus began her tale. *Fairfax.*

2. To let fall in token of respect.

Certain of the Turks gallies, which would not *vail* their top-sails, the Venetians fiercely assailed. *Knolles's Hist.*

They had not the ceremony of *veiling* the bonnet in salutations; for, in medals, they still have it on their heads. *Add.*

3. To fall; to let sink in fear, or for any other interest.

That furious Scot,
'Gan *vail* his stomach, and did grace the shame
Of those that turn'd their backs. *Shakespeare.*

To VAIL. *v. n.* To yield; to give place; to shew respect by yielding. In this sense, the modern writers have ignorantly written *veil*.

Thy convenience must *veil* to thy neighbour's necessity; and thy very necessities must yield to thy neighbour's extremity. *South.*

VAIN. *adj.* [*vain*, Fr. *vanus*, Latin.]

1. Fruitless; ineffectual.

Let no man speak again
To alter this; for counsel is but *vain*. *Shakespeare.*

Vain is the force of man,
To crush the pillars which the pile sustain. *Dryden.*

2. Empty; unreal; shadowy.

Before the passage horrid Hydra stands,
Gorgons, Geryon with his triple frame,
And *vain* chimera, vomits empty flame. *Dryden's Æn.*

Unmov'd his eyes, and wet his beard appears;
And shedding *vain*, but seeming real tears. *Dryden.*

3. Meanly proud; proud of petty things.

No folly like *vain* glory; nor any thing more ridiculous than for a *vain* man to be still boasting of himself. *L'Estran.*

He wav'd a torch aloft, and, madly *vain*,
Sought godlike worship from a servile train. *Dryden.*

The minstrels play'd on ev'ry side,
Vain of their art, and for the mastery vy'd. *Dryden.*

To be *vain* is rather a mark of humility than pride. *Vain* men delight in telling what honours have been done them, what great company they have kept, and the like; by which they plainly confess, that these honours were more than their due, and such as their friends would not believe, if they had not been told: whereas a man truly proud, thinks the honours below his merit, and scorns to boast. *Swift.*

Ah friend! to dazzle let the *vain* design;
To raise the thought, and touch the heart, be thine. *Pope.*

View this marble, and be *vain* no more. *Pope.*

4. Shewy; ostentatious.

Load some *vain* church with old theatrick state. *Pope.*

5. Idle; worthless; unimportant.

Both all things *vain*, and all who in *vain* things
Built their fond hopes of glory, or lasting fame,
Or happiness. *Milton's Paradise Lost.*

He heard a grave philosopher maintain,
That all the actions of our life were *vain*,
Which with our sense of pleasure not conspir'd. *Denham.*

To your *vain* answer will you have recourse,
And tell 'tis ingenite active force. *Blackmore.*

6. False; not true.

7. *In* VAIN. To no purpose; to no end; ineffectually; without effect.

He tempts in *vain*. *Milton.*

Providence and nature never did any thing *in vain*. *L'Estr.*

Strong Halys stands *in vain*; weak Phlegys flies. *Dryd.*

The philosophers of old did *in vain* enquire whether *summum bonum* consisted in riches, bodily delights, virtue, or contemplation. *Locke.*

If we hope for what we are not likely to possess, we act and think *in vain*, and make life a greater dream and shadow than it really is. *Addison's Spectator.*

If from this discourse one honest man shall receive satisfaction, I shall think that I have not written nor lived *in vain*. *West on the Resurrection.*

VAINGLO'RIOUS. *adj.* [*vanus* and *gloriosus*, Latin.] Boasting without performances; proud in disproportion to desert.

Vain-glorious man, when flutt'ring wind does blow,
In his light wings is lifted up to sky. *Fairy Queen.*

Strength to glory aspires
Vain-glorious, and through infamy seeks fame. *Milton.*

This his arrogant and *vain-glorious* expression witnesseth. *Hale.*

VAINGLO'RY. *n. s.* [*vana gloria*, Latin.] Pride above merit; empty pride; pride in little things.

He had nothing of *vain-glory*, but yet kept state and majesty to the height; being sensible, that majesty maketh the people bow, but *vain glory* boweth to them. *Bacon's Hen.* VII.

Expose every blast of *vain-glory*, every idle thought, to be chastened by the rod of spiritual discipline. *Taylor.*

This extraordinary person, out of his natural aversion to *vain-glory*, wrote several pieces, which he did not assume the honour of. *Addison.*

A monarch's sword, when mad *vain-glory* draws;
Not Waller's wreath can hide the nation's scar. *Pope.*

VAI'NLY. *adv.* [from *vain.*]

1. Without effect; to no purpose; in vain.

Our cannons malice *vainly* shall be spent
Against th' invulnerable clouds of heav'n. *Shakesp.*

In weak complaints you *vainly* waste your breath;
They are not tears that can revenge his death. *Dryden.*

2. Proudly; arrogantly.

My forepast proofs, howe'er the matter fall,

Shall

Shall tax my fears of little vanity,
Having *vainly* fear'd too little. *Shakespeare.*

Humility teaches us to think neither *vainly* nor vauntingly of ourselves. *Delany.*

3. Idly; foolishly.

Nor *vainly* hope to be invulnerable. *Milton.*

If Lentulus be ambitious, he shall be *vainly* credulous; presuming his advancement to be decreed by the Sybilline oracles. *Grew's Cosmol.*

VA'INNESS. *n. s.* [from *vain.*] The state of being vain. Pride; falshood; emptiness.

I hate ingratitude more in a man,
Than lying, *vainness*, babbling. *Shakespeare.*

VA'IVODE. *n. s.* [*waiwod*, a governor, Sclavonian.] A prince of the Dacian provinces.

VA'LANCE. *n. s.* [from *Valencia*, whence the use of them came. *Skinner.*] The fringes or drapery hanging round the tester and stead of a bed.

My house
Is richly furnished with plate and gold;
Valance of Venice, gold in needlework. *Shakspeare.*

Thrust the *valance* of the bed, that it may be full in sight. *Swift.*

To VALA'NCE. *v. a.* [from the noun.] To decorate with drapery. Not in use.

Old friend, thy face is *valanc'd* since
I saw thee last; com'st thou to beard me. *Shakes.*

VALE. *n. s.* [*val*, Fr. *vallis*, Latin.]

1. A low ground; a valley; a place between two hills. *Vale* is a poetical word.

In Ida *vale*: who knows not Ida *vale*?
An hundred shepherds woned. *Spenser.*
Met in the *vale* of Arde. *Shakesp. Hen.* VIII.
Anchises, in a flow'ry *vale*,
Review'd his muster'd race, and took the tale. *Dryden.*

2. [From *avail*, profit; or *vale*, farewell. If from *avail*, it must be written *vail*, as Dryden writes. If from *vale*, which I think is right, it must be *vale.*] Money given to servants.

Since our knights and senators account
To what their sordid, begging *vails* amount;
Judge what a wretched share the poor attends,
Whose whole subsistence on those alms depends. *Dryden.*

His revenue, besides *vales*, amounted to thirty pounds. *Swift.*

VALEDI'CTION. *n. s.* [*valedico*, Lat.] A farewel. *Ainsw.*

A *valediction* forbidding to weep. *Donne.*

VALEDI'CTORY. *adj.* [from *valedico*, Lat.] Bidding farewel.

VA'LENTINE. *n. s.* A sweetheart, chosen on Valentine's day.

Now all nature seem'd in love,
And birds had drawn their *valentines*. *Wotton.*

VALE'RIAN. *n. s.* [*valeriana*, Lat. *valerian*, Fr.] A plant.

The leaves grow by pairs opposite upon the stalks; the flower consists of one leaf, divided into five segments; these are succeeded by oblong flat seeds. *Miller.*

VA'LET. *n. s.* [*valet*, French.] A waiting servant.

Giving cast-clothes to be worn by *valets*, has a very ill effect upon little minds. *Addison.*

VALETUDINA'RIAN. } *adj.* [*valetudinaire*, Fr. *valetudo*, Lat.]
VALETU'DINARY. } Weakly; sickly; infirm of health.

Physic, by purging noxious humours, prevents sickness in the healthy, or recourse thereof in the *valetudinary*. *Browne.*

Shifting from the warmer vallies, to the colder hills, or from the hills to the vales, is a great benefit to the *valetudinarian*, feeble part of mankind. *Derham.*

Cold of winter, by stopping the pores of perspiration, keeps the warmth more within; whereby there is a greater quantity of spirits generated in healthful animals, for the case is quite otherwise in *valetudinary* ones. *Cheyne's Phil. Prin.*

Valetudinarians must live where they can command and scold. *Swift.*

VA'LIANCE. *n. s.* [from *valiant*; *vaillance*, Fr.] Valour; personal puissance; fierceness; bravery.

With stiff force he shook his mortal lance,
To let him weet his doughty *valiance*. *Spenser.*

VA'LIANT. *adj.* [*vaillant*, French.] Stout; personally puissant; brave.

Only be thou *valiant* for me, and fight the Lord's battles. 1 *Sam.* xviii. 17.

A son of Jesse, a mighty *valiant* man. 1 *Sam.* xvi. 18.

VA'LIANTLY. *adv.* [from *valiant.*] Stoutly; with personal strength; with personal bravery.

Farewel, kind lord; fight *valiantly* to-day:
Thou art fram'd of the firm truth of valour. *Shakes.*

It was the duty of a good soldier *valiantly* to withstand his enemies, and not to be troubled with any evil hap. *Knolles.*

VA'LIANTNESS. *n. s.* [from *valiant.*] Valour; personal bravery; puissance; fierceness; stoutness.

Thy *valiantness* was mine; thou suck'dst it from me. *Sh.*

Achimetes having won the top of the walls, by the *valiantness* of the defendants was forced to retire. *Knolles.*

Shew not thy *valiantness* in wine. *Ecclus*, xxxi. 25.

VA'LID. *adj.* [*valide*, Fr. *validus*, Latin.]

1. Strong; powerful; efficacious; prevalent.

Perhaps more *valid* arms,
Weapons more violent, when next we meet,
May serve to better us, and worse our foes. *Milton.*

2. Having force; prevalent; weighty; conclusive.

A difference in their sentiments as to particular questions, is no *valid* argument against the general truth believed by them, but rather a clearer and more solid proof of it. *Stephens.*

VALI'DITY. *n. s.* [*validité*. Fr. from *valid.*]

1. Force to convince; certainty.

You are persuaded of the *validity* of that famous verse,
'Tis expectation makes a blessing dear. *Pope.*

2. Value. A sense not used.

To thee and thine,
Remain this ample third of our fair kingdom;
No less in space, *validity*, and pleasure,
Than that conferr'd on Gonerill. *Shakespeare.*

VA'LLANCY. *n. s.* [from *valance.*] A large wig that shades the face.

But you, loud Sirs, who through your curls look big,
Criticks in plume and white *vallancy* wig. *Dryden.*

VA'LLEY. *n. s.* [*vallée*, Fr. *vallis*, Latin.] A low ground; a hollow between hills.

Live with me, and be my love,
And we will all the pleasure prove,
That hills and *vallies* yield. *Raleigh.*

Vallies are the intervals betwixt mountains. *Woodward.*

Sweet interchange of hill and *valley*. *Milton.*

VA'LOROUS. *adj.* [from *valour.*] Brave; stout; valiant.

The famous warriors of the antique world
Us'd trophies to erect in stately wise,
In which they would the records have enroll'd,
Of their great deeds and *valorous* emprise. *Spenser.*

Captain Jamy is a marvellous *valorous* gentleman. *Shakes.*

VA'LOUR. *n. s.* [*valeur*, Fr. *valor*, Latin. *Ainsw.*] Personal bravery; strength; prowess; puissance; stoutness.

That I may pour the spirits in thine ear,
And chastise, with the *valour* of my tongue,
All that impedes thee. *Shakespeare's Macbeth.*

Here I contest
As hotly and as nobly with thy love,
As ever in ambitious strength I did
Contend against thy *valour*. *Shakespeare's Coriolanus.*

When *valour* preys on reason,
It eats the sword it fights with. *Shakesp. Ant. and Cleo.*

An innate *valour* appeared in him, when he put himself upon the soldiers defence, as he received the mortal stab. *Howel.*

For contemplation he, and *valour* form'd;
For softness she, and sweet attractive grace. *Milton.*

Such were these giants; men of high renown!
For, in those days, might only shall be admir'd,
And *valour*, and heroic virtue, call'd. *Milton.*

Valour gives awe, and promises protection to those who want heart or strength to defend themselves. This makes the authority of men among women; and that of a master-buck in a numerous herd. *Temple's Miscel.*

VA'LUABLE. *adj.* [*valable*, Fr. from *value.*]

1. Precious; being of great price.

2. Worthy; deserving regard.

A just account of that *valuable* person, whose remains lie before us. *F. Atterbury's Serm.*

The value of several circumstances in story, lessens very much by distance of time; though some minute circumstances are very *valuable*. *Swift's Thoughts.*

VALUA'TION. *n. s.* [from *value.*]

1. Value set upon any thing.

No reason I, since of your lives you set
So slight a *valuation*, should reserve
My crack'd one to more care. *Shakesp. Cymbeline.*

Take out of men's minds false *valuations*, and it would leave the minds of a number of men, poor shrunken things. *Bacon.*

The writers expressed not the *valuation* of the denarius, without regard to its present *valuation*. *Arbuthnot on Coins.*

2. The act of setting a value; appraisement.

Humility in man consists not in denying any gift that is in him, but in a just *valuation* of it, rather thinking too meanly than too highly. *Ray on the Creation.*

VALUA'TOR. *n. s.* [from *value.*] An appraiser; one who sets upon any thing its price.

What *valuators* will the bishops make use of? *Swift.*

VA'LUE. *n. s.* [*value*, Fr. *valor*, Lat.]

1. Price; worth.

Ye are physicians of no *value*. *Job* xiii.

2. High rate.

Cæsar is well acquainted with your virtues,
And therefore sets this *value* on your life:
Let him but know the price of Cato's friendship,
And name your terms. *Addison's Cato.*

3. Rate; price equal to the worth of the thing bought.

He sent him money; it was with this obliging testimony, that his design was not to pay him the *value* of his pictures, because they were above any price. *Dryden.*

To

To VA'LUE. *v. a.* [*valoir*, Fr. from the noun.]
1. To rate at a certain price.
When the country grows better inhabited, the tithes and other obventions will be more augmented, and better *valued*. *Spenser.*
A mind *valuing* his reputation at the due price, will repute all dishonest gain much inferior thereunto. *Carew's Survey.*
God alone *values* right the good. *Milton.*
2. To rate highly; to have in high esteem.
Some of the finest treatises in dialogue, many very *valued* pieces of French, Italian, and English appear. *Addison.*
He *values* himself upon the compassion with which he relieved the afflicted. *Atterbury's Sermons.*
To him your orchard's early fruits are due,
A pleasing off'ring, when 'tis made by you;
He *values* these. *Pope.*
3. To appraise; to estimate.
If he be poorer than estimation, the priest shall *value* him. *Lev.* xxvii. 8.
4. To be worth; to be equal in worth to.
The peace between the French and us not *values*
The cost that did conclude it. *Shakespeare's Hen.* VIII.
5. To take account of.
If a man be in sickness, the time will seem longer without a clock than with; for the mind doth *value* every moment. *Bacon.*
6. To reckon at, with respect to number or power.
The queen is *valued* thirty thousand strong:
Her faction will be full as strong as ours. *Shakespeare*
7. To consider with respect to importance; to hold important.
The king must take it ill,
So slightly *valued* in his messenger. *Shakespear's K. Lear.*
Neither of them *valued* their promises, according to rules of honour or integrity. *Clarendon, b.* viii.
8. To equal in value; to countervail.
It cannot be *valued* with the gold of ophir. *Job.* xxviii. 16.
9. To raise to estimation.
She ordered all things, resisting the wisdom of the wisest, by making the possessor thereof miserable; *valuing* the folly of the most foolish, by making the success prosperous. *Sidney.*
Some *value* themselves to their country by jealousies of the crown. *Temple.*
Vanity, or a desire of *valuing* ourselves by shewing others faults. *Temple.*

VA'LUELESS. *adj.* [from *value.*] Being of no value.
A counterfeit
Resembling majesty; which, touch'd and tried,
Proves *valueless*. *Shakespeare's K. John.*

VA'LUER. *n. s.* [from *value.*] He that values.

VALVE. *n. s.* [*valva*, Latin.]
1. A folding door.
Swift through the *valves* the visionary fair
Repass'd. *Pope's Odyss. b.* IV.
2. Any thing that opens over the mouth of a vessel.
This air, by the opening of the *valve*, and forcing up of the sucker, may be driven out. *Boyle's Works.*
3. [In anatomy.] A kind of membrane, which opens in certain vessels to admit the blood, and shuts to prevent its regress.
The arteries, with a contractile force, drive the blood still forward; it being hindered from going backward by the *valves* of the heart. *Arbuthnot on Aliments.*

VA'LVULE. *n. s.* [*valvule*, Fr.] A small valve.

VAMP. *n. s.* The upper leather of a shoe. *Ainsworth.*

To VAMP. *v. a.* [This is supposed probably enough by *Skinner* to be derived from *avant*, Fr. *before*; and to mean laying on a new outside.] To piece an old thing with some new part.
You wish
To *vamp* a body with a dangerous physick,
That's sure of death without. *Shakesp. Coriolanus.*
This opinion hath been *vamped* up by Cardan. *Bentley.*
I had never much hopes of your *vampt* play. *Swift.*

VA'MPER. *n. s.* [from *vamp.*] One who pieces out an old thing with something new.

VAN. *n. s.* [from *avant*, French.]
1. The front of an army; the first line.
Before each *van* prick forth the airy knights. *Milton.*
The foe he had survey'd,
Arrang'd, as to him they did appear,
With *van*, main battle, wings and rear. *Hudibras.*
Van to *van* the foremost squadrons meet,
The midmost battles hast'ning up behind. *Dryden.*
2. [*van.* Fr. *vannus*, Latin.] Any thing spread wide by which a wind is raised; a fan.
The other token of their ignorance of the sea was an oar, they call it a corn-*van*. *Notes on Odyss.*
3. A wing with which the air is beaten.
His sail-broad *vans*
He spreads for flight, and in the surging smoke
Up-lifted, spurns the ground. *Milton's Par. Lost.*
A fiery globe
Of angels on full sail of wing drew nigh,
Who on their plumy *vans* receiv'd him soft
From his uneasy station, and upbore,
As on a floating couch, through the blithe air. *Milton.*
His disabled wing unstrung:
He wheel'd in air, and stretch'd his *vans* in vain;
His *vans* no longer could his flight sustain. *Dryden.*
The *vanes* are broad on one side, and narower on the other; both which minister to the progressive motion of the bird. *Derh.*

VA'NCOURIER. *n. s.* [*avantcourier.* French.] A harbinger; a precursor.

VANE. *n. s.* [*vaene*, Dutch.] A plate hung on a pin to turn with the wind.
A man she wou'd spell backward;
If tall, a lance ill-headed;
If speaking, why a *vane* blown with all winds. *Shakesp.*

VA'NGUARD. *n. s.* [*avant garde*, French.] The front, or first line of the army.
The king's *vant-guard* maintained fight against the whole power of the enemies. *Bacon.*
Vanguard to right and left the front unfold. *Milton.*

VANI'LLA. *n. s.* [*vanille*, French.] A plant. It hath an anomalous flower, consisting of six leaves, five of which are placed in a circular order, and the middle one is concave: the empalement becomes an horned, soft, fleshy fruit, filled with very small seeds. The fruit of those plants is used to scent chocolate. *Miller.*
When mixed with *vanillios*, or spices, it acquires the good and bad qualities of aromatic oils. *Arbuthnot on Aliments.*

To VA'NISH. *v. n.* [*vanesco*, Latin. *evanouir*, Fr.]
1. To lose perceptible existence.
High honour is not only gotten and born by pain and danger, but must be nursed by the like, or else *vanisheth* as soon as it appears to the world. *Sidney.*
Whither are they *vanish'd?*
—Into the air; and what seem'd corporal
Melted as breath into the wind. *Shakespeare.*
While fancy brings the *vanish'd* piles to view,
And builds imaginary Rome anew. *Pope.*
2. To pass away from the sight; to disappear
Now I have taken heart, thou *vanishest*. *Shakesp.*
He cut the cleaving sky,
And in a moment *vanish'd* from her eye. *Pope's Odyss.*
3. To pass away; to be lost.
All these delights will *vanish*. *Milton.*
That spirit of religion and seriousness, by which we had distinguished ourselves, *vanished* all at once, and a spirit of infidelity and prophaneness started up. *Atterbury.*

VA'NITY. *n. s.* [*vanitas*, Lat. *vanité*, Fr.]
1. Emptiness; uncertainty; inanity.
2. Fruitless desire; fruitless endeavour.
Vanity possesseth many, who are desirous to know the certainty of things to come. *Sidney.*
Thy pride,
And wand'ring *vanity*, when least was safe,
Rejected my forewarning. *Milton.*
3. Trifling labour.
To use long discourse against those things which are both against scripture and reason, might rightly be judged a *vanity* in the answerer, not much inferior to that of the inventor. *Raleigh's Hist. of the World.*
4. Falshood; untruth.
Here I may well shew the *vanity* of that which is reported In the story of Walsingham. *Sir J. Davies.*
5. Empty pleasure; vain pursuit; idle shew; unsubstantial enjoyment; petty object of pride.
Were it not strange if God should have made such store of glorious creatures on earth, and leave them all to be consumed in secular *vanity*, allowing none but the baser sort to be employed in his own service. *Hooker.*
I must
Bestow upon the eyes of this young couple
Some *vanity* of mine art. *Shakespeare's Tempest.*
Cast not her serious wit on idle things;
Maks her free will slave to *vanity*. *Davies.*
Sin, with *vanity*, had fill'd the works of men. *Milton.*
The eldest equal the youngest in the *vanity* of their dress; and no other reason can be given of it, but that they equal, if not surpass them, in the *vanity* of their desires. *South.*
Think not when woman's transient breath is fled,
That all her *vanities* at once are dead;
Succeeding *vanities* she still regards,
And though she plays no more, o'erlooks the cards. *Pope.*
6. Ostentation; arrogance.
The ground-work thereof is true, however they, through *vanity*, whilst they would not seem to be ignorant, do thereupon build many forged histories of their own antiquity. *Spenser.*
Whether it were out of the same *vanity*, which possessed all those learned philosophers and poets, that Plato also published, not under the right authors names, those things which he had read in the scriptures; or fearing the severity of the Areopagite, and the example of his master Socrates, I cannot judge. *Raleigh's Hist. of the World.*

Can

7. Petty pride; pride exerted upon slight grounds; pride operating on small occasions.

Can you add guilt to *vanity*, and take
A pride to hear the conquests which you make. *Dryden.*

'Tis an old maxim in the schools,
That *vanity*'s the food of fools;
Yet now and then your men of wit
Will condescend to take a bit. *Swift's Miscel.*

To VAN. *v. a.* [from *vannus*, Lat. *vanner*, Fr.] To fan; to winnow Not in use.

The corn, which in *vanning* lieth lowest is the best. *Bacon.*

To VA'NQUISH. *v. a.* [*vaincre*, French.]

1. To conquer; to overcome; to subdue.

Wert't not a shame, that, whilst you live at jar,
The fearful French, whom you late *vanquished*,
Should make a start o'er seas, and *vanquish* you? *Shakes.*

They subdued and *vanquished* the rebels in all encounters. *Clarendon, b.* viii.

The gods the victor, Cato the *vanquish'd* chose:
But you have done what Cato could not do,
To chuse the *vanquish'd*, and restore him too. *Dryden.*

2. To confute.

This bold assertion has been fully *vanquished* in a late reply to the bishop of Meaux's treatise. *F. Atterbury.*

VA'NQUISHER. *n. s.* [from *vanquish.*] Conqueror; subduer.

He would pawn his fortunes
To hopeless restitution, so he might
Be call'd your *vanquisher*. *Shakespeare.*

I shall rise victorious, and subdue
My *vanquisher*; spoil'd of his vaunted spoil. *Milton.*

Troy's *vanquisher*, and great Achilles' son. *A. Philips.*

VA'NTAGE. *n. s.* [from *advantage.*]

1. Gain; profit.

What great *vantage* do we get by the trade of a pastor? *Sydn.*

2. Superiority; state in which one had better means of action than another.

With the *vantage* of mine own excuse,
Hath he excepted most against my love. *Shakespeare.*

He had them at *vantage*, being tired and harrassed with a long march. *Bacon.*

The pardoned person must not think to stand upon the same *vantage* of ground with the innocent. *South.*

3. Opportunity; convenience.

Be assur'd, Madam, 'twill be done
With his next *vantage*. *Shakespeare's Cymbeline.*

To VA'NTAGE. *v. a.* [from *advantage.*] To profit.

We yet of present peril be afraid;
For needless fear did never *vantage* none. *Fairy Queen.*

VA'NTBRASS. *n. s.* [*avant bras*, Fr.] Armour for the arm.

I'll hide my silver beard in a gold beaver,
And in my *vantbrace* put this wither'd brawn. *Shakes.*

Put on *vantbrass*, and greves, and gauntlet. *Milton.*

VA'PID. *adj.* [*vapidus*, Latin.] Dead; having the spirit evaporated; spiritless; maukish; flat.

Thy wines let feed a-while
On the fat refuse; lest too soon disjoin'd,
From spritely it to sharp or *vapid* change. *Philips.*

The effects of a *vapid* and viscous constitution of blood, are stagnation, acrimony, and putrefaction. *Arbuthnot.*

VA'PIDNESS. *n. s.* [from *vapid.*] The state of being spiritless or maukish; maukishness.

VAPORA'TION. *n. s.* [*vaporation*, Fr. *vaporation*, Lat. from *vapour.*] The act of escaping in vapours.

VA'PORER. *n. s.* [from *vapour.*] A boaster; a braggart.

This shews these *vaporers*, to what scorn they expose themselves. *Government of the Tongue.*

VA'PORISH. *adj.* [from *vapour.*] Vaporous; Splenetick; humoursome.

Pallas grew *vap'rish* once and odd,
She would not do the least right thing. *Swift.*

VA'POROUS. *adj.* [*vaporeux*, Fr. from *vapour.*]

1. Full of vapours or exhalations; fumy.

The *vaporous* night approaches. *Shakespeare.*

It proceeded from the nature of the *vapourish* place. *Sandys.*

This shifting our abode from the warmer and more *vaporous* air of the vallies, to the colder and more subtile air of the hills, is a great benefit to the valetudinarian part. *Derham.*

2. Windy; flatulent.

If the mother eat much beans, or such *vaporous* food, it endangereth the child to become lunatick. *Bacon.*

Some more subtile corporeal element, may so equally bear against the parts of a little *vaporous* moisture, as to form it into round drops. *More's Antidote against Atheism.*

The food which is most *vaporous* and perspirable, is the most easily digested. *Arbuthnot.*

A little tube, jetting out from the extremity of an artery, may carry off these *vaporous* steams of the blood. *Cheyne.*

VA'POUR. *n. s.* [*vapeur*, Fr. *vapor*, Latin.]

1. Any thing exhalable; any thing that mingles with the air.

Vapour, and mist, and exhalation hot. *Milton.*

When first the sun too pow'rful beams displays,
It draws up *vapours* which obscure its rays:
But ev'n those clouds at last adorn its way,
Reflect new glories, and augment the day. *Pope.*

2. Wind; flatulence.

In the Thessalian witches, and the meetings of witches that have been recorded, great wonders they tell, of carrying in the air, transforming themselves into other bodies. These fables are the effects of imagination: for ointments, if laid on any thing thick, by stopping of the pores, shut in the *vapours*, and send them to the head extremely. *Bacon.*

3. Fume; steam.

The morning is the best, because the imagination is not clouded by the *vapours* of meat. *Dryden.*

In distilling hot spirits, if the head of the still be taken off, the *vapour* which ascends out of the still will take fire at the flame of a candle, and the flame will run along the *vapour* from the candle to the still. *Newton's Optics.*

For the imposthume, the *vapour* of vinegar, and any thing which creates a cough, are proper. *Arbuthnot on Diet.*

4. Mental fume; vain imagination; fancy unreal.

If his sorrow bring forth amendment, he hath the grace of hope, though it be clouded over with a melancholy *vapour*, that it be not discernible even to himself. *Hammond.*

5. [In the plural.] Diseases caused by flatulence, or by diseased nerves; hypochondriacal maladies; melancholy; spleen.

To this we must ascribe the spleen, so frequent in studious men, as well as the *vapours* to which the other sex are so often subject. *Addison's Spectator*, N°. 115.

To VA'POUR. *v. n.* [*vaporo*, Latin.]

1. To pass in a vapour, or fume; to emit fumes; to fly off in evaporations.

When thou from this world wilt go,
The whole world *vapours* in thy breath. *Donne.*

Swift running waters *vapour* not so much as standing waters. *Bacon's Nat. Hist.* N°. 767.

2. To bully; to brag;

Not true, quoth he? Howe'er you *vapour*,
I can what I affirm make appear. *Hudibras.*

These are all the mighty powers
You vainly boast, to cry down ours;
And what in real value's wanting,
Supply with *vapouring* and ranting. *Hudibras.*

That I might not be *vapour'd* down by insignificant testimonies, I used the name of your society to annihilate all such arguments. *Glanville's Pref. to Scep.*

Be you to us but kind;
Let Dutchmen *vapour*, Spaniards curse,
No sorrow we shall find. *E. Dorset's Song.*

To VA'POUR. *v. a.* To effuse, or scatter in fumes or vapour.

Break off this last lamenting kiss,
Which sucks two souls, and *vapours* both away. *Donne.*

He'd laugh to see one throw his heart away,
Another sighing *vapour* forth his soul,
A third to melt himself in tears. *B. Johnson.*

Opium loseth some of his poisonous quality, if *vapoured* out, and mingled with spirit of wine. *Bacon.*

It must be holpen by somewhat which may fix the silver, never to be restored, or *vapoured* away, when incorporated into such a mass of gold. *Bacon.*

VA'RIABLE. *adj.* [*variable*, Fr. *variabilis*, Latin.] Changeable; mutable; inconstant.

O swear not by th' inconstant moon,
That monthly changes in her circled orb;
Lest that thy love prove likewise *variable*. *Shakespeare.*

Haply countries different,
With *variable* objects, shall expel
This something settled matter in his heart. *Shakesp.*

By the lively image of other creatures, did those ancients represent the *variable* passions of mortals; as by serpents were signified deceivers. *Raleigh's Hist. of the World.*

His heart I know how *variable*, and vain,
Self-left. *Milton's Par. Lost, b.* xi. *l.* 92.

VA'RIABLENESS. *n. s.* [from *variable.*]

1. Changeableness; mutability.

You are not solicitous about the *variableness* of the weather, or the change of seasons. *Addison.*

2. Levity; inconstancy.

Censurers subject themselves to the charge of *variableness* in judgment. *Clarissa.*

VA'RIABLY. *adv.* [from *variable.*] Changeably; mutably; inconstantly; uncertainly.

VA'RIANCE. *n. s.* [from *vary.*] Discord; disagreement; dissention.

I am come to set a man at *variance* against his father. *Matth.*

A cause of law, by violent course,
Was, from a *variance*, now a war become. *Daniel's C. War.*

Not so as to set any one doctrine of the gospel at *variance* with others, which are all admirably consistent. *Sprat.*

She runs, but hopes she does not run unseen:
While a kind glance at her pursuer flies,
How much at *variance* are her feet and eyes? *Pope.*

If the learned would not sometimes submit to the ignorant; the old to the weaknesses of the young; there would be nothing but everlasting *variance* in the world. *Swift.*

Many bleed,
By shameful *variance* betwixt man and man. *Thomson.*

VARIA'TION. *n. s.* [*variatio*, Lat. *variation*, French.]

1. Change; mutation; difference from itself.

After much *variation* of opinions, the prisoner was acquitted of treason, but by most voices found guilty of felony. *Hayw.*

The operation of agents will easily admit of intention and remission, but the essences of things are conceived not capable of any such *variation*. *Locke.*

The fame of our writers is confined to these two islands, and it is hard it should be limited in time as much as place, by the perpetual *variations* of our speech. *Swift.*

There is but one common matter, which is diversified by accidents; and the same numerical quantity, by *variations* of texture, may constitute successively all kinds of body. *Bent.*

2. Difference; change from one to another.

In some other places are more females born than males; which, upon this *variation* of proportion, I recommend to the curious. *Graunt's Bills of Mortality.*

Each sea had its peculiar shells, and the same *variation* of soils; this tract affording such a terrestrial matter as is proper for the formation of one sort of shell-fish; that of another. *Woodward's Nat. Hist.*

3. Successive change.

Sir Walter Blunt,
Stain'd with the *variation* of each soil
Betwixt that Holmedon and this seat of ours. *Shakesp.*

4. [In grammar.] Change of termination of nouns.

The rules of grammar, and useful examples of the *variation* of words, and the peculiar form of speech, are often appointed to be repeated. *Watts's Improv. of the Mind.*

5. Change in natural phenomenons.

The duke run a long course of calm prosperity, without any visible eclipse or wane in himself, amidst divers *variations* in others. *Wotton's Life of Buckingham.*

6. Deviation.

If we admit a *variation* from the state of his creation, that *variation* must be necessarily after an eternal duration, and therefore within the compass of time. *Hale.*

I may seem sometimes to have varied from his sense; but the greatest *variations* may be fairly deduced from him. *Dryd.*

7. *Variation of the compass*; deviation of the magnetick needle from an exact parallel with the meridian.

VA'RICOUS. *adj.* [*varicosus*, Latin.] Diseased with dilation.

There are instances of one vein only being *varicous*, which may be destroyed by tying it above and below the dilatation. *Sharpe.*

To VA'RIEGATE. *v. a.* [*variegatus*, school Latin.] To diversify; to stain with different colours.

The shells are filled with a white spar, which *variegates* and adds to the beauty of the stone. *Woodward on Fossils.*

They had fountains of *variegated* marble in their rooms. *Arb.*

Ladies like *variegated* tulips show;
'Tis to the changes half the charms we owe:
Such happy spots the nice admirers take,
Fine by defect, and delicately weak. *Pope's Epist.*

VARIEGA'TION. *n. s.* [from *variegate*.] Diversity of colours.

Plant your choice tulips in natural earth, somewhat impoverished with very fine sand; else they will soon lose their *variegations*. *Evelyn's Kalend.*

VARI'ETY. *n. s.* [*varieté*, Fr. *varietas*, Latin.]

1. Change; succession of one thing to another; intermixture of one thing with another.

All sorts are here that all th' earth yields;
Variety without end. *Milton's Par. Lost.*

Variety is nothing else but a continued novelty. *South.*

If the sun's light consisted of but one sort of rays, there would be but one colour in the whole world, nor would it be possible to produce any new colour by reflections or refractions; and by consequence that the *variety* of colours depends upon the composition of light. *Newton's Opticks.*

2. One thing of many by which *variety* is made. In this sense it has a plural.

The inclosed warmth, which the earth hath in itself, stirred up by the heat of the sun, assisteth nature in the speedier procreation of those *varieties*, which the earth bringeth forth. *Raleigh's Hist. of the World.*

3. Difference; dissimilitude.

There is a *variety* in the tempers of good men, with relation to the different impressions they receive from different objects of charity. *F. Atterbury.*

4. Variation; deviation; change from a former state.

It were a great vanity to reject those reasons drawn from the nature of things, or to go about to answer those reasons by suppositions of a *variety* in things, from what they now appear. *Hale's Origin. of Mankind.*

VA'RIOUS. *adj.* [*varius*, Latin.]

1. Different; several; manifold.

Then were they known to men by *various* names,
And *various* idols, through the heathen world. *Milton.*

2. Changeable; uncertain; unfixed; unlike itself.

The names of mixed modes want standards in nature, whereby to adjust their signification; therefore they are very *various* and doubtful. *Locke.*

2. Unlike each other.

He in derision sets
Upon their tongues a *various* spirit,
To rase quite out their native language. *Milton.*

Vast crowds of vanquish'd nations march along,
Various in arms, in habit, and in tongue. *Dryden.*

Various of temper, as of face or frame,
Each individual: his great end the same. *Pope.*

So many and so *various* laws are given. *Milton.*

4. Variegated; diversified.

Herbs sudden flower'd,
Opening their *various* colours. *Milton.*

V'ARIOUSLY. *adv.* [from *various*.] In a various manner.

Having been *variously* tossed by fortune, directed his course to a safe harbour. *Bacon.*

Various objects from the sense,
Variously representing. *Milton.*

Those various squadrons, *variously* design'd,
Each vessel freighted with a several load;
Each squadron waiting for a several wind;
All find but one, to burn them in the road. *Dryden.*

Different aliments, while they repair the fluids and solids, act *variously* upon them according to their different natures. *Arbuth.*

VA'RIX. [Lat. *varice*, Fr.] A dilatation of the vein.

In ulcers of the legs, accompanied with *varices* or dilatations of the veins, the *varix* can only be assisted by the bandage. *Sharpe.*

VA'RLET. *n. s.* [*varlet*, old French, now *valet*.]

1. Anciently a servant or footman.

Such lords ill example do give,
Where *varlets* and drabs so may live. *Tusser's Husbandry.*

They spy'd
A *varlet* running towards them hastily. *Spenser.*

2. A scoundrel; a rascal. This word has deviated from its original meaning, as *fur* in Latin.

I am the veriest *varlet* that ever chew'd. *Shakesp. Hen. IV.*

Where didst thou leave these *varlets*? *Shakespeare.*

Thou, *varlet*, dost thy master's gains devour;
Thou milk'st his ewes, and often twice an hour. *Dryden.*

When the Roman legions were in a disposition to mutiny, an impudent *varlet*, who was a private centinel, resolved to try the power of his eloquence. *Addison.*

VA'RLETRY. *n. s.* [from *varlet*.] Rabble; croud; populace.

Shall they hoist me up,
And shew me to the shouting *varletry*
Of cens'ring Rome? *Shakesp. Ant. and Cleo.*

VA'RNISH. *n. s.* [*vernis*, Fr. *vernix*, Latin.]

1. A matter laid upon wood, metal, or other bodies, to make them shine.

We'll put on those shall praise your excellence,
And set a double *varnish* on the fame. *Shakesp.*

The fame of Cicero had not borne her age so well, if it had not been joined with some vanity? Like unto *varnish*, that makes cielings not only shine, but last. *Bacon.*

This the blue *varnish* that the green endears,
The sacred rust of twice ten hundred years. *Pope.*

2. Cover; palliation.

To VARNISH. *v. a.* [*vernisser*, *vernir*, Fr. from the noun.]

1. To cover with something shining.

O vanity!
To set a pearl in steel so meanly *varnished*. *Sidney.*

Clamber not you up to the casements,
Nor thrust your head into the publick street,
To gaze on christian fools with *varnish'd* faces. *Shakes.*

2. To cover; to conceal with something ornamental.

Specious deeds on earth, which glory excites;
Or close ambition *varnish'd* o'er with zeal. *Milton.*

His manly heart was still above
Dissembled hate, or *varnish'd* love. *Dryd.*

Men espouse the well-endow'd opinions in fashion, and then seek arguments to make good their beauty, or *varnish* over and cover their deformity. *Locke's Works.*

3. To palliate; to hide with colour of rhetorick.

To *varnish* all their errors, and secure
The ills they act, and all the world endure. *Denham.*

Cato's voice was ne'er employ'd
To clear the guilty, and to *varnish* crimes. *Addison.*

Speak the plain truth, and *varnish* not your crimes! *Philips.*

VA'RNISHER. *n. s.* [from *varnish*.]

1. One whose trade is to varnish.

An oil obtained of common oil, may probably be of good use to surgeons and *varnishers*. *Boyle's Works.*

2. A disguiser; an adorner.

Modest dulness lurks in thought's disguise;
Thou *varnisher* of fools, and cheat of all the wise. *Pope.*

VA'RVELS. *n. ſ.* [*vervelles*, Fr.] Silver rings about the leg of a hawk, on which the owner's name is engraved. *Dict.*

To VARY. *v. a.* [*vario*, Lat. *varier*, French.]

1. To change; to make unlike itſelf.

Let your ceaſeleſs change
Vary to our great creator ſtill new praiſe. *Milton.*

2. To change to ſomething elſe.

Gods that never change their ſtate,
Vary oft their love and hate. *Waller.*

We are to *vary* the cuſtoms, according to the time and country where the ſcene of action lies. *Dryden.*

The maſter's hand, which to the life can trace
The airs, the lines, and features of the face;
May, with a free and bolder ſtroke, expreſs
A *vary'd* poſture, or a flatt'ring dreſs. *Sir J. Denham.*

He *varies* ev'ry ſhape with eaſe,
And tries all forms that may Pomona pleaſe. *Pope.*

3. To make of different kinds.

God hath divided the genius of men according to the different affairs of the World; and *varied* their inclinations, according to the variety of actions to be performed. *Browne.*

4. To diverſify; to variegate.

God hath here
Vary'd his bounty ſo with new delights. *Milton.*

To VA'RY. *v n.*

1. To be changeable; to appear in different forms.

Darkling ſtands
The *varying* ſhore o'th' world. *Shakeſp. Ant. and Cleo.*

So *varied* he, and of his tortuous train
Curl'd many a wanton wreath. *Milton.*

2. To be unlike each other.

Thoſe who made laws, had their minds poliſhed above the vulgar: and yet unaccountably the public conſtitutions of nations *vary*. *Collier on Pride.*

3. To alter; to become unlike itſelf.

He had a ſtrange interchanging of large and inexpected pardons, with ſeveral executions; which could not be imputed to any inconſtancy, but to a principle he had ſet unto himſelf, that he would *vary* and try both ways in turn. *Bac.*

That each from other differs, firſt confeſs;
Next, that he *varies* from himſelf no leſs. *Pope's Epiſt.*

4. To deviate; to depart.

The crime conſiſts in violating the law, and *varying* from the right rule of reaſon. *Locke.*

5. To ſucceed each other.

While fear and anger, with alternate grace,
Pant in her breaſt, and *vary* in her face. *Addiſon's Cato.*

6. To diſagree; to be at variance.

In judgment of her ſubſtance thus they *vary*,
And *vary* thus in judgment of her ſeat;
For ſome her chair up to the brain do carry,
Some ſink it down into the ſtomach's heat. *Sir J. Davies.*

7. To ſhift colours.

Will the falcon ſtooping from above,
Smit with her *varying* plumage, ſpare the dove?
Admires the jay the inſect's gilded wings? *Pope.*

VA'RY, *n. ſ.* [from the verb.] Change; alteration. Not in uſe.

Such ſmiling rogues as theſe ſooth every paſſion;
Renege, affirm, and turn their halcyon beaks,
With every gale and *vary* of their maſters. *Shakeſpeare.*

VA'SCULAR. *adj.* [from *vaſculum*, Latin.]

1. Conſiſting of veſſels; full of veſſels.

Nutrition of the ſolids is performed by the circulating liquid in the ſmalleſt *vaſcular* ſolids. *Arbuthnot on Aliments.*

VASCULI'FEROUS. *adj.* [*vaſculum* and *fero*, Latin.] Such plants as have, beſides the common calyx, a peculiar veſſel to contain the ſeed, ſometimes divided into cells; and theſe have always a monopetalous flower, either uniform or difform. *Quincy.*

VA'SE. *n. ſ.* [*vaſe*, Fr. *vaſa*, Latin.] A veſſel; generally a veſſel rather for ſhow than uſe.

The toilet ſtands unveil'd,
Each ſilver *vaſe* in myſtick order laid. *Pope.*

VA'SSAL. *n. ſ.* [*vaſſal*, Fr. *vaſſallo*, Italian.]

1. One who holds by the will of a ſuperior lord.

Every petty prince, *vaſſal* to the emperor, can coin what money he pleaſeth. *Swift's ſhort View of Ireland.*

The *vaſſals* are invited to bring in their complaints to the viceroy, who impriſons and chaſtiſes their maſters. *Addiſon.*

2. A ſubject; a dependant.

She cannot content the lord with performance of his diſcipline, that hath at her ſide a *vaſſal*, whom Satan hath made his vicegerent, to croſs whatſoever the faithful ſhould do. *Hooker, b.* viii. §. 34.

Such as they thought fit for labour, they received as *vaſſals*; but imparted not the benefit of laws, but every one made his will a law unto his own *vaſſal*. *Spenſer's State of Ireland.*

The common people were free ſubjects to the king, not ſlaves a to their pretended lords. *Sir J. Davies.*

The m. not reaſon to remember, that paſſions ought to be not her maſters. *Raleigh.*

Vaſſals of his anger, when the ſcourge
Inexorable, and the torturing hour
Calls us to penance. *Milton.*

As all his *vaſſals* eagerly deſir'd;
With mind averſe, he rather underwent
His people's will, than gave his own conſent. *Dryden.*

He ſubjugated a king, and called him his *vaſſal*. *Baker.*

3. A ſervant; one who acts by the will of another.

I am his fortune's *vaſſal*, and I ſend him
The greatneſs he has got. *Shakeſp. Ant. and Cleop.*

4. A ſlave; a low wretch.

Thou ſwear'ſt thy Gods in vain
O *vaſſal!* miſcreant! *Shakeſp. K. Lear.*

VA'SSALAGE. *n. ſ.* [*vaſſelage*, Fr. from *vaſſal*.] The ſtate of a vaſſal; tenure at will; ſervitude; ſlavery; dependance.

He renounc'd the *vaſſalage*
Of Rome again. *Fairy Queen.*

All my pow'rs do their beſtowing loſe,
Like *vaſſalage* at unawares encountring
The eye of majeſty. *Shakeſpeare's Troilus and Creſſida.*

They wou'd have brought the Achæans from the condition of followers and dependents unto meer *vaſſalage*. *Raleigh.*

Let us not then purſue,
By force impoſſible, by leave obtain'd
Unacceptable, though in heav'n our ſtate
Of ſplendid *vaſſalage*. *Milton's Par. Loſt.*

Curs'd *vaſſalage*,
Firſt idoliz'd till love's hot fire be o'er;
Then ſlaves to thoſe who courted us before. *Dryden.*

VAST. *adj.* [*vaſte*, Fr. *vaſtus*, Latin.]

1. Large; great.

What the parliament meant to attempt with thoſe *vaſt* numbers of men, every day levied. *Clarendon, book* i.

That is an ample and capacious mind, which takes in *vaſt* and ſublime ideas without pain. *Watts.*

His open ſtores,
Though *vaſt*, were little to his ampler heart. *Thomſon.*

2. Viciouſly great; enormouſly extenſive or capacious.

The vicious language is *vaſt*, and gaping, ſwelling, and irregular; when it contends to be high, full of rock, mountain, and pointedneſs. *B. Johnſon.*

They view'd the *vaſt* unmeaſurable abyſs. *Milton.*

Others with *vaſt* Typhean rage more fell,
Rend up rocks. *Milton.*

VAST. *n. ſ.* [*vaſtum*, Latin.] An empty waſte.

They ſhook hands, as over a *vaſt*; and embrac'd, as from the ends of oppos'd winds. *Shakeſpeare.*

Through the *vaſt* of heav'n it ſounded. *Milton.*

The wat'ry *vaſt*,
Secure of ſtorms, your royal brother paſt. *Pope.*

VASTA'TION. *n. ſ.* [*vaſtatio*, from *vaſto*, Latin.] Waſte; depopulation.

This wild-fire made the ſaddeſt *vaſtations*, in the many fatal outrages which theſe eager contentions occaſion. *Decay of Piety.*

VASTI'DITY. *n. ſ.* [*vaſtitas*, Lat. from *vaſty*.] Wideneſs; immenſity. A barbarous word.

Perpetual durance,
Through all the world's *vaſtidity*. *Shakeſpeare.*

VA'STLY. *adv.* [from *vaſt*.] Greatly; to a great degree.

Holland's reſolving upon its own defence, without our ſhare in the war, would leave us to enjoy the trade of the world, and thereby grow *vaſtly* both in ſtrength and treaſures *Temple.*

It is *vaſtly* the concern of government, and of themſelves too, whether they be morally good or bad. *South.*

VA'STNESS. *n. ſ.* [from *vaſt*.] Immenſity; enormous greatneſs.

Behemoth, biggeſt born of earth, upheav'd
His *vaſtneſs*. *Milton's Par. Loſt.*

She by the rocks compell'd to ſtay behind,
Is by the *vaſtneſs* of her bulk confin'd. *Waller.*

When I compare this little performance with the *vaſtneſs* of my ſubject, methinks I have brought but a cockle-ſhell of water from the ocean. *Glanville.*

Arioſto obſerved not moderation in the *vaſtneſs* of his draught. *Dryden.*

Hence we may diſcover the cauſe of the *vaſtneſs* of the ocean. *Bentley's Sermons.*

VA'STY. *adj.* [from *vaſt*.] Large; enormouſly great.

I can call ſpirits from the *vaſty* deep. *Shakeſpeare.*

VAT. *n. ſ.* [*vat*, Dutch, ꝼat, Saxon.] A veſſel in which liquors are kept in the immature ſtate.

Plumpy Bacchus, with pink eyne,
In thy *vats* our cares be drown'd. *Shakeſp.*

Let him produce his *vats* and tubs in oppoſition to heaps of arms and ſtandards. *Addiſon.*

Wouldſt thou thy *vats* with gen'rous juice ſhould froth,
Reſpect thy orchats. *Philips.*

VA'TICIDE. *n. ſ.* [*vates* and *cædo*, Latin.] A murderer of poets.

The caitiff *vaticide* conceiv'd a prayer. *Pope's Dunciad.*

To VATI'CINATE. *v. n.* [*vaticinor*, Latin.] To propheſy; to practiſe prediction.

The moſt admired of all prophane prophets, whoſe predictions have been ſo much cried up, did *vaticinate* here. *Howel.*

VAVA'SOUR.

VA'VASOUR. *n. s.* [*vavasseur*, Fr.] One who himself holding of a superior lord, has others holding under him.

Names have been taken of civil honours, as king, knight, valvasor, or *vavasor*, squire. *Camden.*

VA'UDEVIL. *n. s.* [*vaudeville*, Fr.] A song common among the vulgar, and sung about the streets, *Trev.* A ballad; a trivial strain.

VAULT. *n. s.* [*voulte*, Fr. *volta*, Ital. *voluta*, low Latin.]

1. A continued arch.

O, you are men of stone:
Had I your tongues and eyes, I'd use them so
That heaven's *vault* should crack. *Shakesp. K. Lear.*

The word signifies an orb or sphere. And this shews us both the form of the Mosaical abyss, which was included within this *vault*: and the form of the habitable earth, which was the outward surface of this *vault*, or the cover of the abyss. *Burnet's Theory of the Earth.*

2. A cellar.

Creep into the kill-hole.
He will seek there; neither press, well, *vault*, but he hath an abstract for the remembrance of. *Shakesp.*

The wine of life is drawn, and the meer lees
Is left this *vault* to brag of. *Shakesp.*

Whether your fruitful fancy lies
To banish rats that haunt our *vault*. *Swift.*

3. A cave; a cavern.

The silent *vaults* of death, unknown to light,
And hell itself, lie naked to his sight. *Sandys.*

4. A repository for the dead.

Shall I not be stifled in the *vault*,
To whose foul mouth no healthsome air breathes in. *Shakes.*

To VAULT. *v. a.* [*voûter*, Fr. from the noun.]

To arch; to shape of a vault.

Hath nature given them eyes
To see this *vaulted* arch, and the rich cope
Of sea and land, which can distinguish 'twixt
The fiery orbs above, and the twinn'd stones
Upon th' humbl'd beach? *Shakesp. Cymbeline.*

2. To cover with an arch.

Over-head the dismal hiss
Of fiery darts in flaming vollies flew,
And flying *vaulted* either host with fire. *Milton*

To VAULT. *v. n. voltiger*, Fr. *volteggiare*, Italian.

1. To leap; to jump.

Vaulting ambition, which o'erleaps itself,
And falls on th' other. *Shakespear's Macbeth.*

The pretty *vaulting* sea refus'd to drown me,
Knowing that thou would'st have me drown'd on shore. *Sh.*

He is *vaulting* variable ramps
In your despite, upon your purse. *Shakesp.*

If I could win a lady by *vaulting* into my saddle with my armour on, I should quickly leap into a wife. *Shakesp.*

Leaning on his lance, he *vaulted* on a tree. *Dryden.*

If a man shou'd leap a garret, or *vault* down the monument, wou'd he leave the memory of a hero behind him? *Collier on Duelling.*

Lucan *vaulted* upon Pegasus with all the heat and intrepidity of youth. *Addison.*

2. To play the tumbler, or posture-master.

VAULT. *n. s.* [from the verb.] A leap; a jump.

VAU'LTAGE. *n. s.* [from *vault.*] Arched cellar. Not in use.

He'll call you to so hot an answer for it,
That caves and womby *vaultages* of France
Shall chide your trespass, and return your mock
In second accent to his ordnance. *Shakesp. Hen. V.*

VA'ULTED. *adj.* [from *vault.*] Arched; concave.

Restore the lock! she cries, and all around
Restore the lock! the *vaulted* roofs rebound. *Pope.*

VA'ULTER. *n. s.* [from *vault.*] A leaper; a jumper; a tumbler.

VA'ULTY. *adj.* [from *vault.*] Arched; concave. A bad word.

I will kiss thy detestable bones,
And put my eye-balls in thy *vaulty* brows,
And ring these fingers with thy houshold worms. *Shakesp.*

I'll say that is not the lark, whose notes do beat
The *vaulty* heav'ns so high above our heads. *Shakesp.*

VA'UNMURE. *n. s.* [*avant mur*, Fr.] A false wall; a work raised before the main wall.

With another engine named the warwolfe, he pierced with one stone, and cut, as even as a thread, two *vauntmures*. *Camden's Remains.*

This warlike captain, daily attempting the *vanmures*, in the end by force obtained the same; and so possessed of the place, desperately kept it 'till greater help came running in, who, with wonderful expedition, clapt up a strong covering betwixt the wall and the *vanmure*. *Knolles's Hist. of the Turks.*

To VAUNT. *v. a.* [*vanter*, Fr.] To boast; to display with ostentation.

Not that great champion
Whom famous poets verse so much doth *vaunt*;
And hath for twelve huge labours high extoll'd,
So many furies and sharp hits did haunt. *Fairy Queen.*

Not any damsel which her *vaunteth* most,
In skilful knitting of soft silken twine. *Spenser.*

My vanquisher spoil'd of his *vaunted* spoil. *Milton.*

To VAUNT. *v. n.*

1. To play the braggart; to talk with ostentation; to make vain show; to boast.

You say, you are a better soldier;
Let it appear so; make your *vaunting* true. *Shakesp.*

The illusions of magick were put down, and their *vaunting* in wisdom reproved with disgrace. *Wisdom* xvii. 7.

So spake th' apostate angel, though in pain;
Vaunting aloud, but rack'd with deep despair. *Milton.*

Pride which prompts a man to *vaunt* and overvalue what he is, does incline him to disvalue what he has. *Gov. of Tongue.*

2. I scarcely know in what sense Dryden has used this word, unless it be miswritten for *vaults*.

'Tis he: I feel him now in ev'ry part;
Like a new world he *vaunts* about my heart. *Dryden.*

VAUNT. *n. s.* [from the verb.] Brag; boast; vain ostentation.

Sir John Perrot bent his course not to that point, but rather quite contrary, in scorn, and in vain *vaunt* of his own counsels. *Spenser.*

Him I seduc'd with other promises and other *vaunts*. *Milton.*

Such *vaunts* who can with patience read,
Who thus describes his hero when he's dead?
In heat of action slain, he scorns to fall,
But still maintains the war, and fights at all. *Granville.*

VAUNT. *n. s.* [from *avant*, Fr.] The first part. Not used.

Our play
Leaps o'er the *vaunt* and firstlings. *Shakesp.*

VA'UNTER. *n. s.* [*vanteur*, Fr. from *vaunt.*] Boaster; braggart; man given to vain ostentation.

Some feign
To menage steeds, as did this *vaunter*; but in vain. *Spenser.*

Tongue-valiant hero, *vaunter* of thy might;
In threats the foremost, but the lag in fight. *Dryden.*

VA'UNTFUL. *adj.* [*vaunt* and *full.*] Boastful; ostentatious.

Whiles all the heavens on lower creatures smil'd,
Young Clarion, with *vauntful* lustihed,
After his guise did cast abroad to fare. *Spenser.*

VA'UNTINGLY. *adv.* [from *vaunting.*] Boastfully; ostentatiously.

I heard thee say, and *vauntingly* thou spak'st it,
That thou wert cause of noble Glo'ster's death. *Shakesp.*

VA'WARD. *n. s.* [*van* and *ward*] Fore part

Since we have the *vaward* of the day,
My love shall hear the music of my hounds. *Shakesp.*

Marcius,
Their bands i'th' *vaward* are the Antiates
Of their best trust. *Shakesp. Coriolanus.*

He desired nothing more than to have confirmed his authority in the minds of the vulgar, by the present and ready attendance of the *vayvod*. *Knolles's Hist. of the Turks.*

U'BERTY. *n. s.* [*ubertas*, Latin.] Abundance; fruitfulness.

UBICA'TION. } *n. s.* [from *ubi*, Latin.] Local relation; where-
UBI'ETY. } ness. A scholastick term.

Relations, *ubications*, duration, the vulgar philosophy admits to be something; and yet to enquire in what place they are, were gross. *Glanville.*

UBI'QUITARY. *adj.* [from *ubique*, Latin.] Existing every where.

For wealth and an *ubiquitary* commerce, none can exceed her. *How.*

UBI'QUITARY. *n. s.* [from *ubique*, Latin.] One that exists every where.

How far wide is Aquinas, which saith, by the same reason that an angel might be in two places, he might be in as many as you will? See now, either Xavier is every where, or else the carcass of a friar is more subtle than the nature of an angel. To conclude, either Aquinas is false, or the papists *ubiquitaries*. *Hall.*

UBI'QUITY. *n. s.* [from *ubique*, Latin.] Omnipresence; existence at the same time in all places.

In the one there is attributed to God death, whereof divine nature is not capable; in the other *ubiquity* unto man, which human nature admitteth not. *Hooker.*

Pem she hight,
A solemn wight,
As you should meet,
In any street,
In that *ubiquity*. *B. Johnson.*

Could they think that to be infinite and immense, the *ubiquity* of which they could thrust into a corner of their closet. *South.*

U'DDER. *n. s.* [uber, Saxon; *uder*, Dutch. *uber*, Lat.] The breast or dugs of a cow, or other large animal.

A lioness, with *udders* all drawn dry,
Lay couching head on ground. *Shakesp.*

Sithence the cow
Produc'd an ampler store of milk; the she-goat,
Not without pain, dragg'd her distended *udder*. *Prior.*

U'DDERED. *adj.* [from *udder.*] Furnished with udders.

Marian soft could stroke the *udder'd* cow. *Gay.*

VEAL.

Veal. *n. ſ.* [*veel*, a calf, *veeler*, *veſler*, to bring forth a calf, old French; *vitellus*, Latin.] The fleſh of a calf killed for the table.

Would'ſt thou with mighty beef augment thy meal?
Seek Leadenhall; St. James's ſends thee *veal*. *Gay.*

Ve'ction. }
Ve'ctitation. } *n. ſ.* [*vectio*, *vectito*, Latin.] The act of carrying, or being carried.

Enervated lords are ſoftly lolling in their chariots; a ſpecies of *vectitation* ſeldom uſed amongſt the antients. *Arbuthnot.*

Ve'cture. [*vectura*, Latin.] Carriage.

Three things one nation ſelleth unto another; the commodity as nature yieldeth it, the manufacture and the *vecture* or carriage. *Bacon's Eſſays.*

To Veer. *v. n.* [*virer*, French.] To turn about.

If a wild uncertainty prevail,
And turn your *veering* heart with ev'ry gale,
You loſe the fruit of all your former care,
For the ſad proſpect of a juſt deſpair. *Roſcommon.*

Nigh rivers mouth, where wind
Veers oft, as oft he ſteers and ſhifts her ſail. *Milton.*

I have no taſte of the noiſy praiſe
Of giddy crouds, as changeable as winds;
Servants to change, and blowing with the tide
Of ſwol'n ſucceſs; but *veering* with its ebb. *Dryden.*

A-head the maſter pilot ſteers
And as he leads, the following navy *veers*. *Dryden.*

It is a double misfortune to a nation given to change, when they have a ſovereign that is prone to fall in with all the turns and *veerings* of the people. *Addiſon's Freeholder.*

The wind *veered* about to north-weſt. *Derham.*

To Veer. *v. a.*

1. To let out.

As it is a great point of art, when our matter requires it, to enlarge and *veer* out all ſail; ſo to take it in and contract it, is of no leſs praiſe when the argument doth aſk it. *B. Johnſ.*

2. To turn; to change.

I ſee the haven nigh at hand,
To which I mean my weary courſe to bend;
Veer the main-ſheet, and bear up with the land. *Spenſer.*

Sailing farther, it *veers* its lilly to the weſt, and regardeth that quarter, wherein the land is nearer or greater. *Brown.*

Vegetabi'lity. *n. ſ.* [from *vegetable.*] Vegetable nature; the quality of growth without ſenſation.

The coagulating ſpirits of ſalts, and lapidifical juice of the ſea, entering the parts of the plant, overcomes its *vegetability*, and converts it unto a lapideous ſubſtance. *Browne.*

VE'GETABLE. *n. ſ.* [*vegetabilis*, ſchool Lat. *vegetabile*, Fr.] Any thing that has growth without ſenſation, as plants.

Vegetables are organized bodies conſiſting of various parts, containing veſſels furniſhed with different juices; and taking in their nouriſhment from without, uſually by means of a root, by which they are fixed to the earth, or to ſome other body, as in the generality of plants; ſometimes by means of pores diſtributed over the whole ſurface, as in ſub-marine plants. *Hill's Materia Medica.*

Let brutes and *vegetables* that cannot drink,
So far as drought and nature urges, think. *Waller.*

In *vegetables* it is the ſhape, and in bodies, not propagated by ſeed, it is the colour we moſt fix on. *Locke.*

Other animated ſubſtances are called *vegetables*, which have within themſelves the principle of another ſort of life and growth, and of various productions of leaves, flowers and fruit, ſuch as we ſee in plants, herbs, trees. *Watts.*

Ve'getable. *adj.* [*vegetabilis*, Latin.]

1. Belonging to a plant.

The *vegetable* world, each plant and tree,
From the fair cedar on the craggy brow,
To creeping moſs. *Prior.*

Both mechaniſms are equally curious, from one uniform juice to extract all the variety of *vegetable* juices; or from ſuch variety of food to make a fluid very near uniform to the blood of an animal. *Arbuthnot on Aliments.*

The well ſhower'd earth
Is deep enrich'd with *vegetable* life. *Thomſon.*

2. Having the nature of plants.

Amidſt them ſtood the tree of life,
High eminent, blooming ambroſial fruit
Of *vegetable* gold. *Milton's Par. Loſt.*

That vegetative terreſtrial hath been ever the ſtanding fund, out of which is derived the matter of all animal and *vegetable* bodies. *Woodward's Nat. Hiſt.*

To Ve'getate. *v. n.* [*vegeto*, Latin.] To grow as plants; to ſhoot out; to grow without ſenſation.

Rain-water may be endued with ſome *vegetating* or prolifick virtue, derived from ſome ſaline or oleoſe particles. *Ray.*

As long as the ſeeds remained lodged in a natural ſoil, they would ſoon *vegetate*, and ſend forth a new ſet of trees. *Woodward.*

See dying vegetables life ſuſtain;
See life diſſolving *vegetate* again. *Pope's Eſſay on Man.*

Vegeta'tion. *n. ſ.* [from *vegeto*, Latin.]

1. The power of producing the growth of plants.

The exterior ſurface conſiſted of a terreſtrial matter proper for the nouriſhment of plants, being little entangled with mere mineral matter, that was unfit for *vegetation*. *Woodward.*

The ſun, deep-darting to the dark retreat
Of *vegetation*, ſets the ſteaming power
At large. *Thomſon's Spring.*

Love warbles through the vocal groves,
And *vegetation* paints the plain. *Anonymous.*

2. The power of growth without ſenſation.

Plants, though beneath the excellency of creatures endued with ſenſe, yet exceed them in the faculty of *vegetation* and of fertility. *Hooker.*

Theſe pulſations I attribute to a plaſtick nature, or vital principle, as the *vegetation* of plants muſt alſo be. *Ray.*

Ve'getative. *adj.* [*vegetatif*, Fr. from *vegetate*.]

1. Having the quality of growing without life.

Creatures *vegetative* and growing, have their ſeeds in themſelves. *Raleigh's Hiſt. of the World.*

2. Having the power to produce growth in plants.

Homer makes deities of the *vegetative* faculties, and virtues of the field. *Broome's Notes on Odyſſ.*

Ve'getativeness. *n. ſ.* [from *vegetative.*] The quality of producing growth.

Vege'te. *adj.* [*vigetus*, Latin.] Vigorous; active; ſpritely.

The ſoul was *vegete*, quick and lively; full of the youthfulneſs and ſpritelineſs of youth. *South.*

The faculties in age muſt be leſs *vegete* and nimble than in youth. *Wallis.*

VE'GETIVE. *adj.* [from *vegeto*, Latin.] Vegetable; having the nature of plants.

Nor rent off, but cut off ripe bean with a knife,
For hindering ſtalke of hir *vegetive* life. *Tuſſ. Huſbandry.*

Ve'getive. *n. ſ.* [from the adjective.] A vegetable.

Hence *vegetives* receive their fragrant birth,
And clothe the naked boſom of the earth. *Sandys.*

The tree ſtill panted in th' unfiniſh'd part,
Not wholly *vegetive*; and heav'd her heart. *Dryden.*

Ve'hemence. }
Ve'hemency. } *n. ſ.* [*vehementia*, Latin.]

1. Violence; force.

Univerſal hubbub wild,
Of ſtunning ſounds and voices all confus'd,
Aſſaults his ear with loudeſt *vehemence*. *Milton.*

2. Ardour; mental violence; terrour.

Think ye are men; deem it not impoſſible for you to err: ſift impartially your own hearts, whether it be force of reaſon, or *vehemency* of affection, which hath bred, and ſtill doth feed theſe opinions in you. *Hooker's Pref.*

The beſt perſuaſions
Fail not to uſe; and with what *vehemency*
Th' occaſion ſhall inſtruct you. *Shakeſp. Hen.* VIII.

Would it apply well to the *vehemence* of your affection, that I ſhould win what you would enjoy? *Shakeſp.*

The extremity of the condition produced ſome earneſtneſs and *vehemency* of expreſſion more than ordinary. *Clarendon.*

This pure cauſe would kindle my rap'd ſpirits
To ſuch a flame of ſacred *vehemence*,
That dumb things wou'd be mov'd to ſympathize. *Milton.*

He hurries on his action with variety of events, and ends it in leſs compaſs than two months. This *vehemence* of his is moſt ſuitable to my temper. *Dryden.*

Marcus is over-warm; his fond complaints
Have ſo much earneſtneſs and paſſion in them,
I hear him with a ſecret kind of horror,
And tremble at his *vehemence* of temper. *Addiſon's Cato.*

VE'HEMENT. *adj.* [*vehement*, Fr. *vehemens*, Latin.]

1. Violent; forcible.

A ſtrong imagination hath more force upon light and ſubtile motions, than upon motions *vehement* or ponderous. *Bacon.*

Gold will endure a *vehement* fire for a long time, without any change. *Grew.*

2. Ardent; eager; fervent.

By their *vehement* inſtigation,
In this juſt ſuit come I to move your grace. *Shakeſp.*

I find
In all things elſe delight indeed; but ſuch,
As us'd or not, works in the mind no change,
Nor *vehement* deſire. *Milton's Par. Loſt.*

Ve'hemently. *adv.* [from *vehement.*]

1. Forcibly.

2. Pathetically; urgently.

The chriſtian religion inculcates kindneſs more *vehemently*, and forbids malice and hatred more ſtrictly than any religion did before. *Tillotſon.*

Ve'hicle. *n. ſ.* [*vehiculum*, Latin.]

1. That in which any thing is carried.

Evil ſpirits might very properly appear in *vehicles* of flame, to terrify and ſurprize. *Addiſon's Guardian.*

2. That part of a medicine which ſerves to make the principal ingredient potable.

That the meat deſcends by one paſſage; the drink, or moiſtening *vehicle* by another, is a popular tenent. *Brown.*

3. That by means of which any thing is conveyed.

The gaiety of a diverting word, ſerves as a *vehicle* to convey the force and meaning of a thing. *L'Eſtrange.*

To VEIL. *v. n.* [*velo*, Lat. See VAIL.]

1. To cover with a veil, or any thing which conceals the face.

Her face was *veil'd*; yet to my fancied ſight,
Love, ſweetneſs, goodneſs in her perſon ſhin'd. *Milton.*

It became the Jewiſh faſhion when they went to pray, to *veil* their heads and faces. *Boyle.*

2. To cover; to inveſt.

I deſcry,
From yonder blazing cloud that *veils* the hill,
One of the heav'nly hoſt. *Milton.*

3. To hide; to conceal.

Of darkneſs viſible ſo much be lent,
As half to ſhew, half *veil* the deep intent. *Pope's Dunciad.*

VEIL. *n. ſ.* [*velum*, Latin.]

1. A cover to conceal the face.

To feed his fiery luſtful eye,
He ſnatch'd the *veil* that hung her face before. *Fairy Queen.*

The Paphian queen from that fierce battle borne,
With gored hand, and *veil* ſo rudely torn,
Like terror did among the immortals breed. *Waller.*

The famous painter cou'd allow no place
For private ſorrow in a prince's face:
Yet, that his piece might not exceed belief,
He caſt a *veil* upon ſuppoſed grief. *Waller.*

As *veils* tranſparent cover, but not hide,
Such metaphors appear when right apply'd.
When through the phraſe we plainly ſee the ſenſe,
Truth with ſuch obvious meanings will diſpenſe. *Granville.*

She accepts the hero, and the dame
Wraps in her *vail*, and frees from ſenſe of ſhame. *Pope.*

2. A cover; a diſguiſe.

I will pluck the borrow'd *veil* of modeſty from the ſo ſeeming Mrs. Page; divulge Page himſelf for a ſecure and wilful Actæon. *Shakeſp. Merry Wives of Windſor.*

Knock on my heart; for thou haſt ſkill to find
If it ſound ſolid, or be fill'd with wind;
And thro' the *veil* of words thou view'ſt the naked mind. *Dry.*

The ill-natured man expoſes thoſe failings in human nature, which the other would caſt a *veil* over. *Addiſon.*

VEIN. *n. ſ.* [*veine*, Fr. *vena*, Latin.]

The veins are only a continuation of the extreme capillary arteries reflected back again towards the heart, and uniting their channels as they approach it, till at laſt they all form three large veins; the *cava deſcendens*, which brings the blood back from all the parts above the heart; the *cava aſcendens*, which brings the blood from all the parts below the heart; and the *porta*, which carries the blood to the liver. The coats of the veins are the ſame with thoſe of the arteries, only the muſcular coat is as thin in all the veins, as it is in the capillary arteries; the preſſure of the blood againſt the ſides of the veins being leſs than that againſt the ſides of the arteries. In the veins there is no pulſe, becauſe the blood is thrown into them with a continued ſtream, and becauſe it moves from a narrow channel to a wider. The capillary veins unite with one another, as the capillary arteries. In all the veins perpendicular to the horizon, excepting thoſe of the uterus and of the porta, are ſmall membranes or valves; like ſo many half thimbles ſtuck to the ſide of the veins, with their mouths towards the heart. In the motion of the blood towards the heart, they are preſſed cloſe to the ſide of the veins; but if blood ſhould fall back, it muſt fill the valves; and they being diſtended, ſtop up the channel, ſo that no blood can repaſs them. *Quincy.*

When I did firſt impart my love to you,
I freely told you all the wealth I had
Ran in my *veins*; I was a gentleman. *Shakeſpeare.*

Horror chill
Ran through his *veins*, and all his joints relax'd. *Milton.*

2. Hollow; cavity.

Found where caſual fire
Had waſted woods, on mountain, or in vale,
Down to the *veins* of earth. *Milton's Par. Loſt.*

Let the glaſs of the priſms be free from *veins*, and their ſides be accurately plane, and well poliſhed, without thoſe numberleſs waves or curls, which uſually ariſe from ſand-holes. *Newton's Opticks.*

3. Courſe of metal in the mine.

There is a *vein* for the ſilver. *Job* xxviii. 1.

Part hidden *veins* digg'd up, nor hath this earth
Entrails unlike, of mineral and ſtone. *Milton.*

It is in men as in ſoils, where ſometimes there is a *vein* of gold which the owner knows not of. *Swift's Thoughts.*

4. Tendency or turn of the mind or genius.

We ought to attempt no more than what is in the compaſs of our genius, and according to our *vein*. *Dryden.*

5. Favourable moment; time when any inclination is predominant.

Artizans have not only their growths and perfections, but likewiſe their *veins* and times. *Wotton's Architecture.*

6. Humour; temper.

I put your grace in mind
Of what you promis'd me.
I am not in the giving *vein* to-day. *Shakeſp. Rich.* III.

Certainly he that hath a ſatirical *vein*, as he maketh others afraid of his wit, ſo he had need to be afraid of others. *Bacon.*

They among themſelves in pleaſant *vein*
Stood ſcoffing. *Milton's Par. Loſt.*

Speak'ſt thou in earneſt or in jeſting *vein?* *Dryden.*

The currier ſtruck the uſurer upon the right *vein*. *L'Eſtra.*

7. Continued diſpoſition.

The *vein* I have had of running into ſpeculations of this kind, upon a greater ſcene of trade, have coſt me this preſent ſervice. *Temple.*

8. Current; continued production.

He can open a *vein* of true and noble thinking. *Swift.*

9. Strain; quality.

Now ſomewhat ſing, whoſe endleſs ſouvenance
Among the ſhepherds may aye remain;
Whether thee liſt, thy loved laſs advance,
Or honour Pan with higher hymns of praiſe. *Spenſer.*

10. Streak; variegation, as the veins of the marble

VE'INED. } *adj.* [*veineux*, Fr. from *vein*.]
VE'INY. }

1. Full of veins.

2. Streaked; variegated.

The root of an old white thorn will make very fine boxes and combs, and many of them are very finely *veined*. *Mortimer's Huſbandry.*

Effulgent, hence the *veiny* marble ſhines. *Thomſon.*

VELLE'ITY. *n. ſ.* [*velleïté*, Fr. *velleitas*, from *velle*, Latin.]

Velleity is the ſchool-term uſed to ſignify the loweſt degree of deſire. *Locke.*

The wiſhing of a thing is not properly the willing of it; but it is that which is called by the ſchools an imperfect *velleity*, and imports no more than an idle, un-operative complacency in, and deſire of the end, without any conſideration of the means. *South.*

To VE'LLICATE. *v. a.* [*vellico*, Latin.] To twitch; to pluck; to act by ſtimulation.

Thoſe ſmells are all ſtrong, and do pull and *vellicate* the ſenſe. *Bacon.*

Convulſions ariſing from ſomething *vellicating* a nerve in its extremity, are not very dangerous. *Arbuthnot.*

VELLICA'TION. *n. ſ.* [*vellicatio*, Lat.] Twitching; ſtimulation.

All purgers have a kind of twitching and *vellication*, beſides the griping, which cometh of wind. *Bacon.*

There muſt be a particular motion and *vellication* impreſt upon the nerves, elſe the ſenſation of heat will not be produced. *Watts's Improvement of the Mind.*

VE'LLUM. *n. ſ.* [*velin*, Fr. *ve'amen*, Latin; rather *vitulinum*, low Latin.] The ſkin of a calf dreſſed for the writer.

The ſkull was very thin, yielding to the leaſt preſſure of my finger, as a piece of *vellum*. *Wiſeman.*

VELO'CITY. *n. ſ.* [*velocité*, Fr. *velocitas*, Latin.] Speed; ſwiftneſs; quick motion.

Had the *velocities* of the ſeveral planets been greater or leſs than they are now, at the ſame diſtances from the ſun; or had their diſtances from the ſun, or the quantity of the ſun's matter, and conſequently his attractive power, been greater or leſs than they are now, with the ſame *velocities:* they would not have revolved in concentric circles, but moved in hyperbola's or parabola's, or in ellipſes very eccentric. *Bentley's Sermons.*

VE'LVET. *n. ſ.* [*veluto*, Ital. *villus*, Latin. *velours*, Fr.] Silk with a ſhort fur or pile upon it.

Clad in white *velvet* all their troop they led,
With each an oaken chaplet on his head. *Dryden.*

The different ranging the ſuperficial parts of bodies, as of *velvet*, watered ſilk, we think probably is nothing but the different refraction of their inſenſible parts. *Locke.*

VE'LVET. *adj.*

1. Made of velvet.

This was moulded on a porringer,
A *velvet* diſh. *Shakeſp. Taming of the Shrew.*

2. Soft; delicate.

Through the *velvet* leaves the wind,
All unſeen, 'gan paſſage find. *Shakeſ.*

Poor deer, quoth he, thou mak'ſt a teſtament
As worldlings do, giving thy ſum of more
To that which had too much. Then being alone
Left and abandon'd of his *velvet* friends;
'Tis right, quoth he; thus miſery doth part
The flux of company. *Shakeſp.*

To VE'LVET. *v. n.* To paint velvet.

Verditure, ground with a weak gum arabic water, is the paleſt green that is, but good to *velvet* upon black in any drapery. *Peacham on Drawing.*

VE'LURE. *n. ſ.* [*velours*, Fr.] Velvet. An old word.

His horſe with one girt, ſix times pieced, and a woman's crupper of *velure*, pieced with packthread. *Shakeſp.*

VE'NAL. *adj.* [*venal*, Fr. *venalis*, Latin.]

1. Mercenary; prostitute.

This verse be thine, my friend, nor thou refuse
This, from no *venal* or ungrateful muse. *Pope.*

2. [from *vein*.] Contained in the veins. A technical word.

It is unreasonable to affirm, that the cool *venal* blood should be heated so high in the interval of two pulses. *Ray.*

VENA'LITY. *n. s.* [*venalité*, Fr. from *venal*.] Mercenariness; prostitution.

VENA'TICK. *adj.* [*venaticus*, Latin.] Used in hunting.

VENA'TION. *n. s.* [*venatio*, Latin.] The act or practice of hunting.

The manner of their *venation* we shall find to be otherways than by sawing away of trees. *Brown's Vulgar Errours.*

To VEND. *v. a.* [*vendre*, Fr. *vendo*, Lat.] To sell; to offer to sale.

He had a great parcel of glasses packed up, which not having the occasion he expected to *vend*, and make use of, lay by him. *Boyle.*

VENDEE. *n. s.* [from *vend*.] One to whom any thing is sold.

If a vicar sows his glebe, or if he sells his corn, and the *vendee* cuts it, he must pay the tithes to the parson. *Ayliffe.*

VE'NDER. *n. s.* [*vendeur*, Fr. from *vend*.] A seller.

Where the consumption of commodity is, the *venders* seat themselves. *Graunt.*

Those make the most noise who have the least to sell, which is very observable in the *venders* of card-matches. *Addison.*

VE'NDIBLE. *adj.* [*vendibilis*, Latin.] Saleable; marketable.

Silence only is commendable
In a neat's tongue dried, and a maid not *vendible*. *Shakesp.*

This so profitable and *vendible* a merchandize, riseth not to a proportionable enhancement with other less beneficial commodities. *Carew.*

The ignorant mine-man, aiming only at the obtaining a quantity of such a metal as may be *vendible* under such a determinate name, has neither the design nor skill to make nice separations of the heterogeneous bodies. *Boyle.*

VE'NDIBLENESS. *n. s.* [from *vendible*.] The state of being saleable.

VENDITA'TION. *n. s.* [*venditatio*, from *vendito*, Latin.] Boastful display.

Some, by a cunning protestation against all reading, and *venditation* of their own naturals, think to divert the sagacity of their readers from themselves, and cool the scent of their own fox-like thefts; when yet they are so rank as a man may find whole pages together usurped from one author. *B. Johnson.*

VENDI'TION. *n. s.* [*venditio*, Fr. *vendition*, Latin.] Sale; the act of selling.

To VENE'ER. *v. a.* [among cabinet-makers.] To make a kind of marquetry or inlaid work, whereby several thin slices of fine woods of different sorts are fastened or glued on a ground of some common wood. *Bailey.*

VE'NEFICE. *n. s.* [*veneficium*, Latin.] The practice of poisoning.

VENEFI'CIAL. *adj.* from *veneficium*, Latin.] Acting by poison; bewitching.

The magical virtues of misselto, and conceived efficacy unto *veneficial* intentions, seemeth a Pagan relique derived from the antient Druides. *Brown's Vulgar Errours.*

VENEFI'CIOUSLY. *adv.* [from *veneficium*, Latin.] By poison or witchcraft.

Lest witches should draw or prick their names therein, and *veneficiously* mischief their persons, they broke the shell. *Brown's Vulgar Errours.*

VE'NEMOUS. *adj.* [from *venin*, Fr.] Poisonous. Commonly, though not better, *venomous.*

The barbarians saw the *venemous* beast hang on his hand. *Acts* xxviii. 4.

To VENE'NATE. *v. a.* [*veneno*, Latin.] To poison; to infect with poison.

These miasms entering the body, are not so energic, as to *venenate* the entire mass of blood in an instant. *Harvey.*

By giving this in fevers after calcination, whereby the *venenate* parts are carried off. *Woodward on Fossils.*

VENENA'TION. *n. s.* [from *venenate*.] Poison; venom.

This *venenation* shoots from the eye; and this way a basilisk may impoison. *Brown's Vulgar Errours.*

VENE'NE. } *adj.* [*veneneux*, Fr. from *venenum*, Latin.] Poisonous; venemous.
VENENO'SE. }

Dry air opens the surface of the earth to disincarcerate *venene* bodies, or to attract or evacate them hence. *Harvey.*

Malphigi, in his treatise of galls, under which he comprehends all preternatural and morbose tumours of plants, demonstrates that all such tumours, where any insects are found, are raised up by some *venenose* liquor, which, together with their eggs, such insects shed upon the leaves. *Ray.*

VE'NERABLE. *adj.* [*venerable*, Fr. *venerabilis*, Latin.] To be regarded with awe; to be treated with reverence.

As by the ministry of saints, it pleased God there to shew some rare effect of his power; or in regard of death, which those saints have suffered for the testimony of Jesus Christ, did thereby make the places where they died *venerable*. *Hooker.*

To make the passage easy, safe, and plain,
That leads us to this *venerable* wall. *Fairfax.*

Ye lamps of heav'n! he said, and lifted high
His hands, now free. Thou *venerable* sky!
Inviolable pow'rs, ador'd with dread,
Be all of you adjur'd. *Dryden's Æn.* II.

VE'NERABLY. *adj.* [from *venerable*.] In a manner that excites reverence.

The Palatine, proud Rome's imperial seat,
An awful pile! stands *venerably* great.
Thither the kingdoms and the nations come. *Addison.*

To VE'NERATE. *v. a.* [*venerer*, Fr. *veneror*, Latin.] To reverence; to treat with veneration; to regard with awe.

When baseness is exalted, do not bate
The place its honour for the person's sake:
The shrine is that which thou dost *venerate*,
And not the beast that bears it on its back. *Herbert.*

The lords and ladies here approaching paid
Their homage, with a low obeisance made;
And seem'd to *venerate* the sacred shade. *Dryden.*

A good clergyman must love and *venerate* the gospel that he teaches, and prefer it to all other learning. *Clarissa.*

VENERA'TION. *n. s.* [*veneration*, Fr. *veneratio*, Lat.] Reverend regard; awful respect.

Theology is the comprehension of all other knowledge, directed to its true end, *i. e.* the honour and *veneration* of the creator, and the happiness of mankind. *Locke.*

We find a secret awe and *veneration* for one who moves above us in a regular and illustrious course of virtue. *Addison.*

VENERA'TOR. *n. s.* [from *venerate*.] Reverencer.

If the state of things, as they now appear, involve a repugnancy to an eternal existence, the arguments must be conclusive to those great priests and *venerators* of nature. *Hale.*

VENE'REAL. *adj.* [*venereus*, Latin.]

1. Relating to love.

These are no *venereal* signs;
Vengeance is in my heart, death in my hand. *Shakes.*

Then swol'n with pride, into the snare I fell,
Of fair fallacious looks, *venereal* trains,
Soften'd with pleasure and voluptuous life. *Milton.*

They are averse to *venereal* pleasure. *Addison.*

2. Consisting of copper, called *venus* by chemists.

Blue vitriol, how *venereal* and unsophisticated soever, rubbed upon the whetted blade of a knife, will not impart its latent colour. *Boyle.*

VENE'REOUS. *adj.* [from *venery*.] Libidinous; lustful.

The male is lesser than the female, and very *venereous*. *Derh.*

VE'NERY. *n. s.* [*venerie*, from *vener*, Fr.]

1. The sport of hunting.

To the woods she goes to serve her turn,
And seek her spouse, that from her still does fly,
And follows other game and *venery*. *Fairy Queen.*

Describing beasts of *venery* and fishes, he hath sparingly inserted the vulgar conditions thereof. *Brown's Vulg. Errours.*

The Norman demolished many churches and chapels in New Forest, to make it fitter for his pleasure and *venery*. *Howel.*

2. [From *Venus*.] The pleasures of the bed.

Contentment, without the pleasure of lawful *venery*, is continence; of unlawful, chastity. *Grew's Cosmol.*

VE'NEY. *n. s.* A bout; a turn.

I bruis'd my shin with playing at sword and dagger, three *veneys* for a dish of stewed prunes. *Shakespeare.*

VENESE'CTION. *n. s.* [*vena* and *sectio*, Latin.] Blood-letting; the act of opening a vein; phlebotomy.

If the inflammation be sudden, after evacuation by lenient purgatives, or a clyster and *venesection*, have recourse to anodynes. *Wiseman's Surgery.*

To VENGE. *v. a.* [*venger*, French.] To avenge; to punish.

You are above,
You justices, that these our nether crimes,
So speedily can *venge*. *Shakes.*

VE'NGEABLE. *adj.* [from *venge*.] Revengeful; malicious.

A thrillant dart he threw,
Headed with ire, and *vengeable* despite. *Spenser.*

VE'NGEANCE. *n. s.* [*vengeance*, French.]

1. Punishment; penal retribution; avengement.

The right conceit which they had, that to perjury *vengeance* is due, was not without good effect as touching their lives, who feared the wilful violation of oaths. *Hooker.*

All the stor'd *vengeances* of heaven fall
On her ingrateful top! *Shakespeare's K. Lear.*

The souls of all that I had murder'd
Came to my tent, and every one did threat
To-morrow's *vengeance* on the head of Richard. *Shakesp.*

Let me see thy *vengeance* on them. *Jer.* xi. 20.

Resolutions of future reforming do not always satisfy thy justice, nor prevent thy *vengeance* for former miscarriages. *K. Charles.*

Jove's and Latona's son his wrath express'd,
In *vengeance* of his violated priest. *Dryden.*

The chorus interceeded with heaven for the innocent, and implored its *vengeance* on the criminal. *Addison's Spectator.*

2. It is uſed in familiar language. *To do with a vengeance*, is *to do with vehemence*; *what a vengeance*, emphatically what?

Till the day appear, of reſpiration to the juſt,
And *vengeance* to the wicked. *Milton.*

When the ſame king adventured to murmur, the pope could threaten to teach him his duty with a *vengeance*. *Raleigh.*

Aſmodeus the fiſhy fume
Drove, though enamour'd, from the ſpouſe
Of Tobit's ſon, and with a *vengeance* ſent
From Medea poſt to Egypt, there faſt bound. *Milton.*

But what a *vengeance* makes thee fly
From me too, as thine enemy? *Hudibras.*

VE'NGEFUL. *adj.* [from *vengeance* and *full.*] Vindictive; revengeful; retributive.

Doubt not but God
Hath wiſelier arm'd his *vengeful* ire. *Milton.*
Diſſembling for her ſake his riſing cares,
And with wiſe ſilence pond'ring *vengeful* wars. *Prior.*

VE'NIABLE. } *adj.* [*veniel*, Fr. from *venia*, Latin.]
VE'NIAL. }

1. Pardonable; ſuſceptive of pardon; excuſable.

If they do nothing 'tis a *venial* ſlip. *Shakeſpeare.*

More *veniable* is a dependence upon potable gold, whereof Paracelſus, who died himſelf at forty-ſeven, gloried that he could make other men immortal. *Brown's Vulgar Errours.*

What horror will invade the mind,
When the ſtrict judge, who would be kind,
Shall have few *venial* faults to find? *Roſcommon.*

While good men are in extirpating mortal ſins, I ſhould rally the world out of indecencies and *venial* tranſgreſſions. *Addiſon.*

2. Permitted; allowed.

No more of talk where God, or angel-gueſt,
With man, as with his friend, familiar us'd
To ſit indulgent, and with him partake
Rural repaſt; permitting him the while
Venial diſcourſe unblam'd. *Milton's Par. Loſt.*

VE'NIALNESS. *n. ſ.* [from *venial.*] State of being excuſable.

VENISON. *n. ſ.* [*venaiſon*, French.] Game; beaſt of chaſe; the fleſh of deer.

Shall we kill us *veniſon*?
And yet it irks me, the poor dappled fools
Shou'd have their round haunches gor'd. *Shakeſpeare.*

We have a hot *veniſon* paſty to dinner. *Shakeſpeare.*

In the records of Ireland, no mention is made of any park, though there be vert and *veniſon* within this land. *Davies's Hiſt. of Ireland.*

He for the feaſt prepar'd,
In equal portions with the *ven'ſon* ſhar'd. *Dryden.*

VENOM. *n. ſ.* [*venin*, French.] Poiſon.

Your eyes, which hitherto hath borne in them
The fatal balls of murthering baſiliſks:
The *venom* of ſuch looks we fairly hope
Have loſt their quality. *Shakeſp. Hen. V.*

Beware of yonder dog;
Look, when he fawns, he bites; and, when he bites,
His *venom* tooth will rankle to the death. *Shakeſ. Rich. III.*

Like ſome tall tree, the monſter of the wood,
O'erſhading all that under him would grow,
He ſheds his *venom* on the plants below. *Dryden.*

To **VENOM.** *v. a.* To infect with venom.

VE'NOMOUS. *adj.* [from *venom.*]

1. Poiſonous.

Thy tears are ſalter than a younger man's,
And *venomous* to thy eyes. *Shakeſp. Coriolanus.*

2. Malignant; miſchievous.

A poſterity not unlike their majority of miſchievous progenitors; a *venomous* and deſtructive progeny. *Brown.*

This falſity was broached by Cochleus, a *venomous* writer; one careleſs of truth or falſhood. *Addiſon.*

VE'NOMOUSLY. *adv.* [from *venomous.*] Poiſonouſly; miſchievouſly; malignantly.

His unkindneſs,
That ſtrip'd her from his benediction, turn'd her
To foreign caſualties. Theſe things ſting him
So *venomouſly*, that burning ſhame detains him
From his Cordelia. *Shakeſp. K. Lear.*

His praiſe of foes is *venomouſly* nice;
So touch'd, it turns a virtue to a vice. *Dryden.*

VE'NOMOUSNESS. *n. ſ.* [from *venomous.*] Poiſonouſneſs; malignity.

VENT. *n. ſ.* [*fente*, French.]

1. A ſmall aperture; a hole; a ſpiracle; paſſage at which any thing is let out.

On her breaſt
There is a *vent* of blood, and ſomething blown;
The like is on her arm. *Shakeſp. Ant. and Cleopatra.*

They at once their reeds
Put forth, and to a narrow *vent* apply'd
With niceſt touch. *Milton's Par. Loſt.*

Have near the bung-hole a little *vent*-hole ſtopped with a ſpile. *Mortimer's Huſbandry.*

Scarce any countries that are much annoyed with earthquakes, that have not one of theſe fiery *vents*, diſgorging that fire, whereby it gains an exit. *Woodward.*

To draw any drink, be not at the trouble of opening a *vent*; or if you take out the vent, ſtay not to put it in. *Swift.*

Full o'er their heads the ſwelling bag he rent,
And all the furies iſſued at the *vent*. *Pope.*

2. Paſſage out of ſecrecy to publick notice.

It failed by late ſetting-out, and ſome contrariety of weather, whereby the particular deſign took *vent* beforehand. *Wotton.*

3. The act of opening.

The farmer's cades mature,
Now call for *vent*; his lands exhauſt, permit
T' indulge a-while. *Philips.*

4. Emiſſion; paſſage.

The ſmother'd fondneſs burns within him;
When moſt it ſwells and labours for a *vent*,
The ſenſe of honour, and deſire of fame,
Drive the big paſſion back into his heart. *Addiſon's Cato.*

5. Diſcharge; means of diſcharge.

Had, like grief, been dew'd in tears,
Without the *vent* of words. *Milton.*

Land-floods are a great improvement of land, where a *vent* can be had. *Mortimer's Huſbandry.*

6. [*vente*, Fr. *venditio*, Lat.] Sale.

For the mart, it was alledged that the *vent* for Engliſh cloaths would hereby be open in all times of war. *Hayward.*

By this war there is no *vent* for any commodity but of wool. *Temple's Miſcellany.*

He drew off a thouſand copies of a treatiſe, which not one in threeſcore can underſtand, can hardly exceed the *vent* of that number. *Pope's Letters.*

To **VENT.** *v. a.* [*venter*, French, from the noun; *ſventare*, Italian.]

1. To let out at a ſmall aperture.

2. To let out; to give way to.

Hunger broke ſtone walls; that the gods ſent not
Corn for the rich men only: with theſe ſhreds
They *vented* their complainings. *Shakeſp. Coriolanus.*

When men are young, and have little elſe to do, they might *vent* the overflowings of their fancy that way. *Denham.*

Lab'ring ſtill, with endleſs diſcontent,
The queen of heav'n did thus her fury *vent*. *Dryden.*

3. To utter; to report.

Had it been *vented* and impoſed in ſome of the moſt learned ages, it might then, with ſome pretence of reaſon, have been ſaid to be the invention of ſome crafty ſtateſman. *Stephens.*

4. To emit; to pour out.

Revoke thy doom,
Or whilſt I can *vent* clamour from my throat,
I'll tell thee thou doſt evil. *Shakeſpear's K. Lear.*

5. To publiſh.

Their ſectators did greatly enrich their inventions, by *venting* the ſtolen treaſures of divine letters, alter'd by profane additions, and diſguiſed by poetical converſions. *Raleigh.*

6. To ſell; to carry to ſale.

This profitable merchandize not riſing to a proportionable enhancement with other leſs beneficial commodities, they impute to the owners not *venting* and venturing the ſame. *Carew.*

Therefore did thoſe nations *vent* ſuch ſpice, ſweet gums and pearls, as their own countries yielded. *Raleigh.*

To **VENT.** *v. n.* To ſnuff. As he *venteth* into the air. *Spenſer.*

VE'NTAIL. *n. ſ.* [from *vantail*, Fr.] That part of the helmet made to lift up. *Spenſer.*

VENTA'NNA. *n. ſ.* [Spaniſh.] A window.

What after paſs'd
Was far from the *ventanna*, when I ſate;
But you were near, and can the truth relate. *Dryden.*

VENTER. *n. ſ.* [Latin.]

1. Any cavity of the body, chiefly applied to the head, breaſt and abdomen, which are called by anatomiſts the three *venters*.

2. Womb; mother.

A has iſſue *B* a ſon, and *C* a daughter, by one *venter*; and *D* a ſon by another *venter*. If *B* purchaſes in fee, and dies without iſſue, it ſhall deſcend to the ſiſter, and not to the brother of the half blood. *Hale.*

VE'NTIDUCT. *n. ſ.* [*ventus* and *ductus*, Latin.] A paſſage for the wind.

Having been informed of divers *ventiducts*, I wiſh I had had the good fortune, when I was at Rome, to take notice of theſe organs. *Boyle.*

To **VENTILATE.** *v. a.* [*ventilo*, Latin.]

1. To fan with wind.

In cloſe, low, and dirty alleys, the air is penn'd up, and obſtructed from being *ventilated* by the winds. *Harvey.*

Miners, by perflations with large bellows, letting down tubes, and ſinking new ſhafts, give free paſſage to the air, which *ventilates* and cools the mines. *Woodward.*

2. To winnow; to fan.

3. To examine; to diſcuſs.

Nor is the right of the party, nor the judicial process in right of that party so far perempted; but that the same may be begun again, and *ventilated* de novo. *Ayliffe.*

VENTILATION. *n. s.* [*ventilatio*, Lat. from *ventilate.*]

1. The act of fanning; the state of being fanned.

The soul, worn with too frequent culture, must lie fallow, till it has recruited its exhausted salts, and again enriched itself by the *ventilations* of the air. *Addison.*

2. Vent; utterance. Not in use.

To his secretary Doctor Mason, whom he let lie in a pallet near him, for natural *ventilation* of his thoughts, he would break out into bitter eruptions. *Wotton's Buckingham.*

3. Refrigeration.

Procure the blood a free course, *ventilation* and transpiration by suitable and ecphractic purges. *Harvey.*

VENTILA'TOR. *n. s.* [from *ventilate.*] An instrument contrived by Dr. *Hale* to supply close places with fresh air.

VE'NTRICLE. *n. s.* [*ventricule*, Fr. *ventriculus*, Latin.]

1. The stomach.

Whether I will or not, while I live, my heart beats, and my *ventricle* digests what is in it. *Hale.*

2. Any small cavity in an animal body, particularly those of the heart.

Know'st thou how blood, which to the heart doth flow,
Doth from one *ventricle* to the other go? *Donne.*

The heart being a muscular part, the sides are composed of two orders of fibres running spirally from base to top, contrarily one to the other; and so being drawn or contracted, constringe the *ventricles*, and strongly force out the blood. *Ray.*

The mixture of blood and chyle, after its circulation through the lungs, being brought back into the left *ventricle* of the heart, is drove again by the heart into the aorta, through the whole arterial system. *Arbuthnot.*

VENTRI'LOQUIST. *n. s.* [*ventriloque*, Fr. *venter* and *loquor*, Lat.] One who speaks in such a manner as that the sound seems to issue from his belly.

VE'NTURE. *n. s.* [*avanture*, Fr.]

1. A hazard; an undertaking of chance and danger.

When he reads
Thy personal *venture* in the rebel's fight,
His wonders and his praises do contend
Which should be thine or his. *Shakesp. Macbeth.*

For a man to doubt whether there be any hell, and thereupon to live so as if absolutely there were none; but when he dies to find himself confuted in the flames, this must be the height of woe and disappointment, and a bitter conviction of an irrational *venture*, and absurd choice. *South.*

I, in this *venture*, double gains pursue,
And laid out all my stock to purchase you. *Dryden.*

When infinite happiness is put in one scale, against infinite misery in the other; if the worst that comes to the pious man, if he mistakes, be the best that the wicked can attain to, if he be in the right, who can, without madness, run the *venture?* *Locke.*

2. Chance; hap.

The king resolved with all speed to assail the rebels, and yet with that providence and surety, as should leave little to *venture* or fortune. *Bacon.*

3. The thing put to hazard; a stake.

My *ventures* are not in one bottom trusted,
Nor to one place. *Shakesp. Mer. of Venice.*

On such a full sea are we now a-float:
And we must take the current when it serves,
Or lose our *ventures*. *Shakesp. Julius Cæsar.*

Thrice happy you, that look as from the shore,
And have no *venture* in the wreck to see. *Daniel.*

4. *At a* VENTURE. At hazard; without much consideration; without any thing more than the hope of a lucky chance.

You have made but an estimate of those lands *at a venture*, so as it should be hard to build any certainty of charge upon it. *Spenser.*

A bargain *at a venture* made,
Between two partners in a trade. *Hudibras.*

A covetous and an envious man joined in a petition to Jupiter, who ordered Apollo to tell them that their desire should be granted *at a venture*. *L'Estrange.*

Here was no scampering away *at a venture*, without fear or wit. *L'Estrange.*

If Ahab be designed for death, though a soldier in the enemy's army draws a bow *at a venture*, yet the sure, unerring directions of providence shall carry it in a direct course to his heart. *South.*

To VE'NTURE. *v. n.* [from the noun.]

1. To dare.

A man were better rise in his suit; for he that would have *ventered* at first to have lost the suitor, will not in the conclusion lose both the suitor and his own former favour. *Bacon.*

Origen mentioning their being cast out of Jerusalem, *ventures* to assure them that they would never be re-established, since they had committed that horrid crime against the saviour of the world. *Addison on the Christian Religion.*

2. To run a hazard.

Nor is indeed that man less mad than these,
Who freights a ship to *venture* on the seas,
With one frail interposing plank to save
From certain death, roll'd on by ev'ry wave. *Dryden.*

I am so overjoy'd, I can scarce believe I am at liberty; like a bird that has often beaten her wing in vain against her cage, dare hardly *venture* out, though she see it open. *Dryden.*

3. *To* VE'NTURE *at.* / *To* VE'NTURE *on* or *upon.* } To engage in; or make attempts without any security of success, upon mere hope.

That slander is found a truth now; and held for certain,
The king will *venture at* it. *Shakespeare.*

It were a matter of great profit, save that it is too conjectural to *venture upon*, if one could discern what corn, herbs, or fruits are like to be in plenty and scarcity, by some signs in the beginning of the year. *Bacon.*

I never yet the tragic strain essay'd,
Deterr'd by that inimitable maid:
And when I *venture at* the comic stile,
Thy scornful lady seems to mock my toil. *Waller.*

Though they had ideas enough to distinguish gold from a stone, yet they but timorously *ventured on* such terms as aurietas and saxietas. *Locke.*

Turco-Papismus I would desire him to read, before he *ventures at* capping of characters. *Atterbury.*

To VE'NTURE. *v. a.*

1. To expose to hazard.

In my school-days, when I had lost one shaft,
I shot his fellow of the self-same flight;
By *vent'ring* both, I oft found both. *Shakesp.*

2. To put or send on a venture.

The fish *ventured* for France, they pack in staunch hogsheads, so as to keep them in their pickle. *Carew.*

VE'NTURER. *n. s.* [from *venture.*] He who ventures.

VE'NTUROUS. *adj.* [from *venture.*] Daring, bold, fearless; ready to run hazards.

Charles was guided by mean men, who would make it their master-piece of favour to give *venturous* counsels, which no great or wise man would. *Bacon.*

He paus'd not, but with *vent'rous* arm
He pluck'd, he tasted. *Milton's Par. Lost.*

The *vent'rous* humour of our mariners costs this island many brave lives every year. *Temple.*

Savage pirates seek through seas unknown,
The lives of others, *vent'rous* of their own. *Pope.*

VE'NTUROUSLY. *adv.* [from *venturous.*] Daringly; fearlesly; boldly.

Siege was laid to the fort by the Lord Gray, then deputy, with a smaller number than those were within the fort; *venturously* indeed; but haste was made to attack them before the rebels came in to them. *Bacon.*

VE'NTUROUSNESS. *n. s.* [from *venturous.*] Boldness; willingness to hazard.

Her coming into a place where the walls and cielings were whited over, much offended her sight, and made her repent her *vent'rousness*. *Boyle on Colours.*

VE'NUS' *basin.*
VE'NUS' *comb.*
VE'NUS' *hair.*
VE'NUS' *looking-glass.*
VE'NUS' *navel-wort.* } *n. s.* Plants.

VERA'CITY. *n. s.* [*verax*, Latin.]

1. Moral truth; honesty of report.

2. Physical truth; consistency of report with fact. Less proper.

When they submitted to the most ignominious and cruel deaths, rather than retract their testimony, there was no reason to doubt the *veracity* of those facts which they related. *Addison.*

VERA'CIOUS. *adj.* [*verax*, Latin.] Observant of truth.

VERB. *n. s.* [*verbe*, Fr. *verbum*, Lat.] A part of speech signifying existence, or some modification thereof, as action, passion. And withal some disposition or intention of the mind relating thereto, as of affirming, denying, interrogating, commanding. *Clarke's Latin Grammar.*

Men usually talk of a noun and a *verb*. *Shakes.*

VE'RBAL. *adj.* [*verbal*, Fr. *verbalis*, Latin.]

1. Spoken, not written.

2. Oral; uttered by mouth.

Made she no *verbal* quest? ——
——Yes; once or twice she heav'd the name of father
Pantingly forth, as if it prest her heart. *Shakespeare.*

3. Consisting in mere words.

If young African for fame,
His wasted country freed from Punick rage,
The deed becomes unprais'd, the man at least;
And loses, though but *verbal*, his reward. *Milton.*

Being at first out of the way to science, in the progress of their inquiries they must lose themselves, and the truth, in a *verbal* labyrinth. *Glanville.*

It was such a denial or confession of him as would appear in preaching: but this is managed in words and *verbal* profession. *South.*

4. Verbose; full of words. Out of use.

I am sorry
You put me to forget a lady's manners.
By being so *verbal*. *Shakesp.*

5. Minutely exact in words.
6. Literal, having word answering to word.

Neglect the rules each *verbal* critick lays,
For not to know some trifles is a praise. *Pope.*

Whosoever offers at *verbal* translation, shall have the misfortune of that young traveller, who lost his own language abroad, and brought home no other instead of it. *Denham.*

The *verbal* copier is incumber'd with so many difficulties at once, that he can never disentangle himself from all. *Dryden.*

7. [*verbal*, Fr. in grammar.] A *verbal* noun is a noun derived from a verb.

VERBA'LITY. *n. s.* [from *verbal.*] Mere bare words.

Sometimes he will seem to be charmed with words of holy scripture, and to fly from the letter and dead *verbality*, who must only start at the life and animated materials thereof. *Brown's Vulgar Errours.*

VE'RBALLY. *adv.* [from *verbal.*]

1. In words; orally.

The manner of our denying the deity of Christ here prohibited, was by words and oral expressions *verbally* to deny it. *South's Sermons.*

2. Word for word.

'Tis almost impossible to translate *verbally*, and well, at the same time. *Dryden.*

VERBATIM. *adv.* [Latin.] Word for word.

Think not, although in writing I preferr'd
The manner of thy vile outragious crimes,
That therefore I have forg'd, or am not able
Verbatim to rehearse the method of my pen. *Shakesp.*

See the transcripts of both charters *verbatim* in Mat. Paris. *Hale.*

To VE'RBERATE. *v. a.* [*verbero*, Lat.] To beat; to strike.

VERBERA'TION. *n. s.* [*verberation*, Fr. from *verberate.*] Blows; beating.

Riding or walking against great winds is a great exercise, the effects of which are redness and inflammation; all the effects of a soft press or *verberation*. *Arbuthnot.*

VERBO'SE. *adj.* [*verbosus*, Lat.] Exuberant in words; prolix; tedious by multiplicity of words.

Let envy
Ill-judging and *verbose*, from Lethe's lake,
Draw tuns unmeasurable. *Prior.*

They ought to be brief, and not too *verbose* in their way of speaking; and to propound the matter of their argument in a mild and gentle manner. *Ayliffe's Parergon.*

VERBO'SITY. *n. s.* [*verbosité*, Fr. from *verbose.*] Exuberance of words; much empty talk.

He draweth out the thread of his *verbosity*
Finer than the staple of his argument. *Shakesp.*

To give an hint more of the *verbosities* of this philosophy, a short view of a definition or two will be sufficient evidence. *Glanville.*

Homer is guilty of *verbosity*, and of a tedious prolix manner of speaking: he is the greatest talker of all antiquity. *Broome.*

VE'RDANT. *n. s.* [*verdoiant*, Fr. *viridans*, Lat.] Green. This word is so lately naturalized, that *Skinner* could find it only in a dictionary.

Each odorous bushy shrub
Fenc'd up the *verdant* wall. *Milton.*

VE'RDERER. *n. s.* [*verdier*, Fr. *viridarius*, low Lat.] An officer in the forest.

VE'RDICT. *n. s.* [*verum dictum*, Latin.]

1. The determination of the jury declared to the judge.

Before the jury go together, 'tis all to nothing what the *verdict* shall be. *Spenser.*

2. Declaration; decision; judgment; opinion.

Deceived greatly they are, who think that all they whose names are cited amongst the favourers of this cause, are on any such *verdict* agreed. *Hooker.*

These were enormities condemned by the most natural *verdict* of common humanity; and so very gross and foul, that no man could pretend ignorance avoided. *South.*

VE'RDIGRISE. *n. s.* The rust of brass, which in time being consumed and eaten with tallow, turneth into green; in Latin *ærugo*; in French *vert de gris*, or the hoary green. *Peacham.*

Brass turned into green, is called *verdigrise*. *Bacon.*

VE'RDITURE. *n. s.*

Verditure ground with a weak gum arabic water, is the faintest and palest green. *Peacham.*

VE'RDURE. *n. s.* [*verdure*, Fr.] Green; green colour.

Its *verdure* clad
Her universal face with pleasant green. *Milton.*

Let twisted olive bind those laurels fast,
Whose *verdure* must for ever last. *Prior.*

VE'RDUROUS. *adj.* [from *verdure.*] Green; covered with green; decked with green.

Higher than their tops
The *verd'rous* wall of paradise up-sprung;
Which to our general sire gave prospect large. *Milton.*

There the lowing herds chew *verd'rous* pasture. *Philips.*

VERECU'ND. *adj.* [*verecond*, old French; *verecundus*, Latin.] Modest; bashful. *Dict.*

VERGE. *n. s.* [*verge*, Fr. *virga*, Latin.]

1. A rod, or something in form of a rod, carried as an emblem of authority. The mace of a dean.

Suppose him now a dean compleat,
Devoutly lolling in his seat;
The silver *verge*, with decent pride,
Stuck underneath his cushion side. *Swift.*

2. [*vergo*, Latin.] The brink; the edge; the utmost border.

Would the inclusive *verge*
Of golden metal, that must round my brow,
Were red-hot steel to sear me to the brain. *Shakesp.*

I say, and will in battle prove,
Or here, or elsewhere, to the furthest *verge*,
That ever was survey'd by English eye. *Shakesp.*

You are old,
Nature in you stands on the very *verge*
Of her confine. *Shakesp. K. Lear.*

Serve they as a flow'ry *verge* to bind
The fluid skirts of that same watry cloud,
Lest it again dissolve and show'r the earth. *Milton.*

Let fortune empty her whole quiver on me,
I have a soul, that, like an ample shield,
Can take in all, and *verge* enough for more. *Dryden.*

Every thing great, within the *verge* of nature, or out of it, has a proper part assigned it in this poem. *Addison.*

Then let him chuse a damsel young and fair,
To bless his age, and bring a worthy heir,
To sooth his care, and, free from noise and strife,
Conduct him gently to the *verge* of life. *Pope.*

3. In law.

Verge is the compass about the king's court, bounding the jurisdiction of the lord steward of the king's houshold, and of the coroner of the king's house, and which seems to have been 12 miles round. *Verge* hath also another signification, and is used for a stick, or rod, whereby one is admitted tenant, and, holding it in his hand, sweareth fealty to the lord of a manor; who, for that reason, is called tenant by the *verge*. *Cowel.*

Fear not: whom we raise,
We will make fast within a hallow'd *verge*. *Shakesp.*

To VERGE. *v. n.* [*vergo*, Lat.] To tend; to bend downwards.

They serve indifferently for vowels in respect of the aperture, and for consonants in respect of the pene-appulse; and so much the more *verging* either way, according to the respective occasions. *Holder.*

The nearer I find myself *verging* to that period of life which is to be labour and sorrow, the more I prop myself upon those few supports that are left. *Swift.*

Such are indicated, when the juices of a human body *verge* to putrefaction. *Arbuthnot.*

Man,
Perhaps acts second to some sphere unknown;
Touches some wheel, or *verges* to some goal;
'Tis but a part we see, and not the whole. *Pope.*

VE'RGER. *n. s.* [from *verge.*] He that carries the mace before the dean.

I can tip the *verger* with half a crown, and get into the best seat. *Farquhar.*

VERI'DICAL. *adj.* [*veridicus*, Latin.] Telling truth. *Dict.*

VERIFICATION. *n. s.* [from *verify.*] Confirmation by argument or evidence.

In *verification* of this we will mention a phenomenon of our engine. *Boyle.*

To VE'RIFY. *v. n.* [*verifier*, Fr.] To justify against charge of falshood; to confirm; to prove true.

What seemeth to have been uttered concerning sermons, and their efficacy or necessity, in regard of divine matter, must consequently be *verified* in sundry other kinds of teaching, if the matter be the same in all. *Hooker.*

This is *verified* by a number of examples, that whatsoever is gained by an abusive treaty, ought to be restored. *Bacon.*

So shalt thou best fulfill, best *verify*
The prophets old, who sung thy endless reign. *Milton.*

So spake this oracle, then *verify'd*,
When Jesus, son of Mary, second Eve,
Saw Satan fall. *Milton's Par. Lost.*

Though you may mistake a year;
Though your prognosticks run too fast,
They must be *verify'd* at last. *Swift.*

Spain shall have three kings; which is now wonderfully *verified*; for besides the king of Portugal, there are now two rivals for Spain. *Swift's Merlin's Prophecy.*

VE'RILY. *adj.* [from *very.*]

1. In truth; certainly.

Verily 'tis better to be lowly born,
Than to be perk'd up in a glist'ring grief. *Shakespeare.*

2. With

2. With great confidence.

It was *verily* thought, that had it not been for four great disfavourers of that voyage, the enterprize had succeeded. *Bacon.*

By repealing the sacramental test, we are *verily* persuaded the consequence will be an entire alteration of religion among us. *Swift on the Sacramental Test.*

VERISI'MILAR. *adj.* [*verisimilis*, Latin.] Probable; likely.

VERISIMILITUDE. } *n. s.* [*verisimilitudo*, Latin.] Probability;
VERISIMI'LITY. } likelihood; resemblance of truth.

Touching the *verisimility* or probable truth of this relation, several reasons seem to overthrow it. *Brown.*

A noble nation, upon whom if not such verities, at least such *verisimilities* of fortitude were placed. *Brown's Vul. Er.*

Verisimilitude and opinion are an easy purchase; but true knowledge is dear and difficult. Like a point, it requires an acuteness to its discovery: while *verisimilitude*, like the expanded superficies, is obvious, sensible, and affords a large and easy field for loose enquiry. *Glanville.*

The plot, the wit, the characters, the passions, are exalted as high as the imagination of the poet can carry them, with proportion to *verisimility*. *Dryden's Essay on Dramatick Poetry.*

Though Horace gives permission to painters and poets to dare every thing, yet he encourages neither to make things out of nature and *verisimility*. *Dryden.*

VE'RITABLE. *adj.* [*veritable*, Fr.] True; agreeable to fact.

Indeed! is't true?
— Most *veritable*; therefore look to't well. *Shakesp.*

The presage of the year succeeding made from insects in oak-apples, is I doubt too indistinct, nor *veritable* from event. *Brown's Vulgar Errours.*

VERITY. *n. s.* [*verité*, Fr. *veritas*, Latin.]

1. Truth; consonance to the reality of things.

If any refuse to believe us disputing for the *verity* of religion established, let them believe God himself thus miraculously working for it. *Hooker.*

I saw their weapons drawn; there was a noise;
That's *verity*. *Shakespeare's Tempest.*

The precipitancy of disputation, and the stir and noise of passions that usually attend it, must needs be prejudicial to *verity*; its calm insinuations can no more be heard in such a bustle, than a whistle among a croud of sailors in a storm. *Glanville.*

It is a proposition of eternal *verity*, that none can govern while he is despised. We may as well imagine that there may be a king without majesty, a supreme without sovereignty. *South.*

2. A true assertion; a true tenet.

And that age, which my grey hairs make seem more than it is, hath not diminished in me the power to protect an undeniable *verity*. *Sidney.*

Wherefore should any man think, but that reading itself is one of the ordinary means, whereby it pleaseth God, of his gracious goodness, to instil that celestial *verity*, which being but so received, is nevertheless effectual to save souls. *Hooker.*

If there come truth from them,
Why by the *verities* on thee made good,
May they not be my oracles as well? *Shakesp.*

Must virtue be preserved by a lie?
Virtue and truth do ever best agree;
By this it seems to be a *verity*,
Since the effects so good and virtuous be. *Davies.*

3. Moral truth; agreement of the words with the thoughts.

VE'RJUICE. *n. s.* [*verjus*, French.] Acid liquor expressed from crab-apples. It is vulgarly pronounced *varges*.

Hang a dog upon a crab-tree, and he'll never love *verjuice*. *L'Estrange.*

The barley-pudding comes in place:
Then bids fall on; himself, for saving charges,
A peel'd slic'd onion eats, and tipples *verjuice*. *Dryden.*

The native *verjuice* of the crab, deriv'd
Through th' infix'd graff, a grateful mixture forms
Of tart and sweet. *Philips.*

VERMICE'LLI. n. s. [Italian.] A paste rolled and broken in the form of worms.

With oysters, eggs, and *vermicelli*,
She let him almost burst his belly. *Prior.*

VERMI'CULAR. *adj.* [*vermiculus*, Latin.] Acting like a worm; continued from one part to another of the same body.

By the *vermicular* motion of the intestines, the grosser parts are derived downwards, while the finer are squeez'd into the narrow orifices of the lacteal vessels. *Cheyne.*

To VERMI'CULATE. *v. a.* [*vermiculé*, Fr. *vermiculatus*, Lat.] To inlay; to work in chequer work, or pieces of divers colours. *Bailey.*

VERMICULA'TION. *n. s.* [from *vermiculate*.] Continuation of motion from one part to another.

My heart moves naturally by the motion of palpitation; my guts by the motion of *vermiculation*. *Hale.*

VE'RMICULE. *n. s.* [*vermiculus*, *vermis*, Latin.] A little grub, worm.

I saw the shining oak-ball ichneumon strike its terebra into an oak-apple, to lay its eggs therein: and hence are many *vermicules* seen towards the outside of these apples. *Derham.*

VERMI'CULOUS. *adj.* [*vermiculosus*, Lat.] Full of grubs.

VE'RMIFORM. *adj.* [*vermiforme*, Fr. *vermis* and *formo*, Lat.] Having the shape of a worm.

VE'RMIFUGE. *n. s.* [from *vermis* and *fugo*, Lat.] Any medicine that destroys or expels worms.

VE'RMIL. } *n. s.* [*vermeil*, *vermillon*, Fr.]
VERMI'LION. }

1. The cochineal; a grub of a particular plant.

2. Factitious or native cinnabar; sulphur mixed with mercury. This is the usual, though not primitive signification.

The imperfect metals are subject to rust, except mercury, which is made into *vermillion* by solution or calcination. *Bacon.*

The fairest and most principal red is *vermillion*, called in Latin *minium*. It is a poison, and found where great store of quicksilver is. *Peacham.*

3. Any beautiful red colour.

How the red roses flush up in her cheeks,
And the pure snow with goodly *vermil* stain,
Like crimson dy'd in grain. *Spenser.*

There grew a goodly tree him fair beside,
Loaden with fruit and apples rosie red,
As they in pure *vermillion* had been dy'd,
Whereof great virtues over all were read. *Fairy Queen.*

Simple colours are strong and sensible, though they are clear as *vermillion*. *Dryden's Dufresnoy.*

To VERMI'LION. *v. a.* [from the noun.] To die red.

A sprightly red *vermilions* all her face,
And her eyes languish with unusual grace. *Granville.*

VE'RMINE. *n. s.* [*vermine*, Fr. *vermis*, Latin.] Any noxious animal. Used commonly for small creatures.

What is your study? —
— How to prevent the fiend, and to kill *vermin*. *Shakesp.*

The head of a wolf, dried and hanged up in a dove-house, will scare away *vermin*, such as weazels and pole-cats. *Bacon.*

An idle person only lives to spend his time, and eat the fruits of the earth, like a *vermin* or a wolf. *Taylor.*

The stars determine
You are my prisoners, base *vermin*. *Hudibras.*

A weazle taken in a trap, was charg'd with misdemeanors, and the poor *vermin* stood much upon her innocence. *L'Estr.*

Great injuries these *vermin*, mice and rats, do in the field. *Mortimer's Husbandry.*

He that has so little wit
To nourish *vermin*, may be bit. *Swift.*

To VE'RMINATE. *v. n.* [from *vermin*.] To breed vermine.

VERMINA'TION. *n. s.* [from *verminate*.] Generation of vermine.

Redi discarding anomalous generation, tried experiments relating to the *vermination* of serpents and flesh. *Derham.*

VE'RMINOUS. *adj.* [from *vermine*.] Tending to vermine; disposed to breed vermine.

A wasting of childrens flesh depends upon some obstruction of the entrails, or *verminous* disposition of the body. *Harvey.*

VERMI'PAROUS. *adj.* [*vermis* and *pario*, Lat.] Producing worms.

Hereby they confound the generation of *vermiparous* animals with oviparous. *Brown's Vulgar Errours.*

VERNA'CULAR. *adj.* [*vernaculus*, Latin.] Native; of one's own country.

London weekly bills number deep in consumptions; the same likewise proving inseparable accidents to most other diseases; which instances do evidently bring a consumption under the notion of a *vernacular* disease to England. *Harvey.*

The histories of all our former wars are transmitted to us in our *vernacular* idiom. I do not find in any of our chronicles, that Edward the third ever reconnoiter'd the enemy, though he often discovered the posture of the French, and as often vanquished them. *Addison.*

VE'RNAL. *adj.* [*vernus*, Latin.] Belonging to the spring.

With the year
Seasons return; but not to me returns,
Or sight of *vernal* bloom, or summer's rose. *Milton.*

VE'RNANT. *n. s.* [*vernans*, Lat.] Flourishing as in the spring.

Else had the spring
Perpetual smil'd on earth, with *vernant* flow'rs,
Equal in days and nights. *Milton's Par. Lost.*

VERNI'LITY. *n. s.* [*verna*, Lat.] Servile carriage; the submissive fawning behaviour of a slave. *Bailey.*

VE'RREL. See FERRULE.

VERSABI'LITY. } *n. s.* [*versabilis*, Lat.] Aptness to be turn'd
VE'RSABLENESS. } or wound any way. *Dict.*

VE'RSAL. *adj.* [A cant word for *universal*.] Total; whole.

Some for brevity,
Have cast the *versal* world's nativity. *Hudibras.*

VE'RSATILE. *adj.* [*versatilis*, Lat.]

1. That may be turned round.

2 Changeable;

2. Changeable; variable.

One colour to us standing in one place, hath a contrary aspect in another; as in those *versatile* representations in the neck of a dove, and folds of scarlet. *Glanville.*

3. Easily applied to a new task.

VE'RSATILENESS. } *n. s.* [from *versatile.*] The quality of being versatile.
VERSATI'LITY. }

VERSE. *n. s.* [*vers*, Fr. *versus*, Latin.]

1. A line consisting of a certain succession of sounds, and number of syllables.

Thou hast by moonlight at her window sung,
With feigning voice, *verses* of feigning love. *Shakesp.*

2. [*verset*, Fr.] A section or paragraph of a book.

Thus far the questions proceed upon the construction of the first earth; in the following *verses* they proceed upon the demolition of that earth. *Burnet.*

3. Poetry; lays; metrical language.

Verse embalms virtue: and tombs and thrones of rhymes
Preserve frail transitory fame as much
As spice doth body from air's corrupt touch. *Donne.*

If envious eyes their hurtful rays have cast,
More pow'rful *verse* shall free thee from the blast. *Dryden.*

Whilst she did her various pow'r dispose;
Virtue was taught in *verse*, and Athens' glory rose. *Prior.*

You compose
In splay-foot *verse*, or hobbling prose. *Prior.*

4. A piece of poetry.

Let this *verse*, my friend, be thine. *Pope.*

To VERSE. *v. a.* [from the noun.] To tell in verse; to relate poetically.

In the shape of Corin sate all day,
Playing on pipes of corn, and *versing* love. *Shakesp.*

To be VE'RSED. *v. n.* [*versor*, Lat.] To be skilled in; to be acquainted with.

She might be ignorant of their nations, who was not *versed* in their names, as not being present at the general survey of animals, when Adam assigned unto every one a name concordant unto its nature. *Brown's Vulgar Errours.*

This, *vers'd* in death, th' infernal knight relates,
And then for proof fulfill'd their common fates. *Dryden.*

VE'RSEMAN. *n. s.* [*verse* and *man.*] A poet; a writer in *verse.*

The god of us *versemen*, you know, child, the sun. *Prior.*

VE'RSICLE. *n. s.* [*versiculus*, Lat.] A little verse.

VERSIFICA'TION. *n. s.* [*versification*, Fr. from *versify.*] The art or practice of making verses.]

Donne alone had your talent, but was not happy to arrive at your *versification.* *Dryden.*

Some object to his *versification*; which is in poetry, what colouring is in painting, a beautiful ornament. But if the proportions are just, though the colours should happen to be rough, the piece may be of inestimable value. *Granville.*

VERSIFICA'TOR. } *n. s.* [*versificateur*, Fr. *versificator*, Lat.]
VE'RSIFIER. } A versifier; a maker of verses with or without the spirit of poetry.

Statius, the best *versificator* next Virgil, knew not how to design after him. *Dryden.*

In Job and the Psalms we shall find more sublime ideas, more elevated language, than in any of the heathen *versifiers* of Greece or Rome. *Watts's Improvement of the Mind.*

To VE'RSIFY. *v. n.* [*versifier*, Fr. *versificor*, Latin.] To make verses.

You would wonder to hear how soon even children will begin to *versify.* *Sidney.*

To follow rather the Goths in rhyming, than the Greeks in true *versifying*, were even to eat acorns with swine, when we may freely eat wheat bread among men. *Ascham.*

I'll *versify* in spite, and do my best,
To make as much waste paper as the rest. *Dryden.*

To VE'RSIFY. *v. a.* To relate in verse.

Unintermix'd with fictious fantasies,
I'll *versify* the truth, not poetize. *Daniel.*

VE'RSION. *n. s.* [*version*, Fr. *versio*, Latin.]

1. Change; transformation.

Springs, the antients thought to be made by the *version* of air into water. *Bacon's Nat. Hist.*

2. Change of direction.

Comets are rather gazed upon, than wisely observed in their effects; that is, what kind of comet, for magnitude, colour, *version* of the beams, produceth what kind of effects. *Bacon.*

3. Translation.

This exact propriety of Virgil I particularly regarded; but must confess, that I have not been able to make him appear wholly like himself. For where the original is close, no *version* can reach it in the same compass. *Dryden.*

4. The act of translating.

VERT. *n. s. vert*, Fr.

Vert, in the laws of the forest, signifies every thing that grows, and bears a green leaf within the forest, that may cover and hide a deer. *Cowel.*

I find no mention in all the records of Ireland, of a park or free warren, notwithstanding the great plenty of *vert* and venison. *Sir J. Davies.*

VE'RTEBRAL. *adj.* [from *vertebræ*, Lat.] Relating to the joints of the spine.

The carotid, *vertebral*, and splenick arteries are not only variously contorted, but here and there dilated, to moderate the motion of the blood. *Ray on the Creation.*

VE'RTEBRE. *n. s.* [*vertebre*, Fr. *vertebra*, Latin.] A joint of the back.

The several *vertebres* are so elegantly compacted together, that they are as strong as if they were but one bone. *Ray.*

VE'RTEX *n. s.* [Latin.]

1. Zenith; the point over head.

These keep the *vertex*; but betwixt the bear
And shining zodiack, where the planets err,
A thousand figur'd constellations roll. *Creech.*

2. A top of a hill.

Mountains especially abound with different species of vegetables; every *vertex* or eminence affording new kinds. *Derham.*

VE'RTICAL. *adj.* [*vertical*, Fr. from *vertex.*]

1. Placed in the zenith.

'Tis raging noon; and *vertical* the sun
Darts on the head direct his forceful rays. *Thomson.*

2. Placed in a direction perpendicular to the horizon.

From these laws, all the rules of bodies ascending or descending in *vertical* lines may be deduced. *Cheyne.*

VERTICA'LITY. *n. s.* [from *vertical.*] The state of being in the zenith.

Unto them the sun is vertical twice a year; making two distinct summers in the different points of the *verticality.* *Brown's Vulgar Errours.*

VE'RTICALLY. *adv.* [from *vertical.*] In the zenith.

Although it be not vertical unto any part of Asia, yet it *vertically* passeth over Peru and Brasilia. *Brown.*

VERTICI'LLATE. *adj.* [from *verticillum*, Latin.]

Verticillate plants are such as have their flowers intermixt with small leaves growing in a kind of whirls about the joints of a stalk, as penny-royal, horehound, &c. *Quincy.*

VERTI'CITY. *n. s.* [from *vertex.*] The power of turning; circumvolution; rotation.

Those stars do not peculiarly glance on us, but carry a common regard unto all countries, unto whom their *verticity* is also common. *Brown's Vulgar Errours.*

We believe the *verticity* of the needle, without a certificate from the days of old. *Glanville.*

Whether they be globules, or whether they have a *verticity* about their own centers, that produce the idea of whiteness in us, the more particles of light are reflected from a body, the whiter does the body appear. *Locke.*

VE'RTIGINOUS. *adj.* [*vertiginosus*, Latin.]

1. Turning round; rotatory.

This *vertiginous* motion gives day and night successively over the whole earth, and makes it habitable all around. *Bentley.*

2. Giddy.

These extinguish candles, make the workmen faint and *vertiginous*; and, when very great, suffocates and kills them. *Woodward.*

VERTI'GO. *n. s.* [Latin.] A giddiness; a sense of turning in the head.

Vertigo is the appearance of visible objects that are without motion, as if they turned round, attended with a fear of falling, and a dimness of sight. *Quincy.*

The forerunners of an apoplexy are dulness, *vertigo's*, tremblings. *Arbuthnot.*

That old *vertigo* in his head,
Will never leave him till he's dead. *Swift.*

VE'RVAIN. } *n. s.* [*verveine*, Fr. *verbena*, Lat.] A plant.
VE'RVINE. }

It hath a labiated flower, consisting of one leaf, whose upper lip is upright, and commonly divided into two; but the under lip is cut into three parts; so that at first sight it appears like a flower with five leaves. These are succeeded by four naked seeds, which fill the calyx. The flowers generally grow in spikes, but not in whorles, round the stalks. *Miller.*

The night-shade strows to work him ill,
Therewith the *vervain*, and her dill,
That hindreth witches of their will. *Drayton.*

Some scatt'ring pot-herbs here and there he found,
Which cultivated with his daily care,
And bruis'd with *vervain*, were his frugal fare. *Dryden.*

VE'RVAIN *mallow. n. s.* A plant.

It hath the whole habit of the mallow or althæa; but differs from it in having its leaves deeply divided. *Miller.*

VE'RVELES. *n. s.* [*vervelle*, Fr.] Labels tied to a hawk. *Ains.*

VE'RY. *adj.* [*veray*, or *vrai*, French; whence *veray* in antient English.]

1. True; real.

Why do I pity him,
That with his *very* heart despiseth me. *Shakespeare.*
In *very* deed, as the Lord liveth. *1 Sam.* xxv. 34.

O that

O that in *very* deed we might behold it. *Dryd. and Lee.*

2. Having any qualities, commonly bad, in an eminent degree.

Those who had drunk of Circe's cup, were turned into *very* beasts. *Davies.*

There, where *very* desolation dwells,
By grots and caverns shagg'd with horrid shades,
She may pass on. *Milton.*

3. To note the things emphatically, or eminently.

'Tis an ill office for a gentleman;
Especially against his *very* friend. *Shakesp.*

Was not my love
The *verier* wag o'th' two? *Shakespeare.*

We can contain ourselves,
Were he the *veriest* antick in the world. *Shakesp.*

In a seeing age, the *very* knowledge of former times passes but for ignorance in a better dress. *South.*

The pictures of our great grandmothers in Queen Elizabeth's time, are cloathed down to the *very* wrists, and up to the *very* chin. *Addison's Guardian.*

4. Same.

Women are as roses, whose fair flower
Being once display'd, doth fall that *very* hour. *Shakesp.*

The cocks beat the partridge, which she laid to heart: but finding these *very* cocks cutting one another, she comforted herself. *L'Estrange.*

So catholick a grace is charity, that whatever time is the special opportunity of any other christian grace, that *very* time is also the special opportunity of charity. *Spratt.*

VE'RY. *adv.* In a great degree; in an eminent degree.

The Greek orator was so *very* famous for this, that his antagonist reading over the oration which had procured his banishment, asked them, if they were so much affected by the bare reading of it, how much more they would have been alarmed, had they heard him? *Addison.*

To VE'SICATE. *v. a.* [*vesica*, Latin.] To blister.

Celsus proposes, that in all these internal wounds, the external parts be *vesiccated*, to make more powerful revulsion from within. *Wiseman's Surgery.*

I saw the cuticula *vesicated*, and shining with a burning heat. *Wiseman.*

VESICA'TION. *n. s.* [from *vesicate*.] Blistering; separation of the cuticle.

I applied some vinegar prepared with litharge, defending the *vesication* with pledgets. *Wiseman's Surgery.*

VESI'CATORY. *n. s.* [*vesicatorium*, technical Latin.] A blistering medicine.

VE'SICLE. *n. s.* [*vesicula*, Latin.] A small cuticle, filled or inflated.

Nor is the humour contained in smaller veins, but in a *vesicle*, or little bladder. *Browne's Vulgar Errours.*

The lungs are made up of such air pipes and *vesicles* interwoven with blood-vessels, to purify, ferment, or supply the sanguineous mass with nitro-aerial particles. *Ray.*

VESI'CULAR. *adj.* [from *vesicula*, Lat.] Hollow; full of small interstices.

A muscle is a bundle of *vesicular* threads, or of solid filaments, involved in one common membrane. *Cheyne.*

VE'SPER. *n. s.* [Latin.] The evening star; the evening.

These signs are black *Vesper*'s pageants. *Shakesp.*

VE'SPERS *n. s.* [without the singular, from *vesperus*, Latin.] The evening service of the Romish church.

VE'SPERTINE. *adj.* [*vespertinus*, Latin.] Happening or coming in the evening; pertaining to the evening.

VE'SSEL. *n. s.* [*vassalle*, Fr. *vas*, Lat.]

1. Any thing in which liquids, or other things, are put.

For Banquo's issue have I fill'd my mind;
Put rancours in the *vessel* of my peace,
Only for them. *Shakesp. Macbeth.*

If you have two *vessel* to fill, and you empty one to fill the other, there still remains one *vessel* empty. *Burnet.*

2. The containing parts of an animal body.

Of these elements are constituted the smallest fibres; of those fibres the *vessels*; of those *vessels* the organs of the body. *Arbuthnot on Aliments.*

3. Any vehicle in which men or goods are carried on the water.

The sons and nephews of Noah, who peopled the isles, had *vessels* to transport themselves. *Raleigh's Essays.*

The *vessel* is represented as stranded. The figure before it seems to lift it off the shallows. *Addison on Medals.*

From storms of rage, and dangerous rocks of pride,
Let thy strong hand this little *vessel* guide;
It was thy hand that made it: through the tide
Impetuous of this life, let thy command
Direct my course, and bring me safe to land. *Prior.*

Now secure the painted *vessel* glides;
The sun-beams trembling on the floating tides. *Pope.*

4. Any capacity; any thing containing.

I have my fill
Of knowledge, what this *vessel* can contain. *Milton.*

To VE'SSEL. *v. a.* [from the noun.] To put into a vessel; to barrel.

Take earth, and *vessel* it; and in that set the seed. *Bacon*

VE'SSETS. *n. s.* A kind of cloth commonly made in Suffolk. *Bailey.*

VE'SSICNON. *n. s.* [among horsemen] A windgall, or soft swelling on the inside and outside of a horse's hoof. *Dict.*

VEST. *n. s.* [*vestris*, Lat.] An outer garment.

Over his lucid arms
A military *vest* of purple flow'd. *Milton's Par. Lost.*

When the queen in royal habit's drest,
Old mystick emblems grace th' imperial *vest*. *Smith.*

To VEST. *v. a.* [from the noun.]

1. To dress; to deck; to enrobe.

The verdant fields with those of heav'n may vie,
With ether *vested*, and a purple sky. *Dryden.*

Light! Nature's resplendent robe;
Without whose *vesting* beauty all were wrapt
In gloom. *Thomson.*

2. To dress in a long garment.

Just Simeon, and prophetic Anna spoke,
Before the altar and the *vested* priest. *Milton.*

3. To make possessor of; to invest with.

To settle men's consciences, 'tis necessary that they know the person, who by right is *vested* with power over them. *Locke.*

Had I been *vested* with the monarch's pow'r,
Thou must have sigh'd, unlucky youth! in vain. *Prior.*

4. To place in possession.

The militia their commissioners positively required to be entirely *vested* in the parliament. *Clarendon.*

Empire and dominion was *vested* in him, for the good and behoof of others. *Locke.*

VE'STAL. *n. s.* [*vestalis*, Latin.] A virgin consecrated to *Vesta*; a pure virgin.

Women are not
In their best fortunes strong; but want will perjure
The ne'er-touch'd *vestal*. *Shakespeare.*

How happy is the blameless *vestal*'s lot?
The world forgetting, by the world forgot. *Pope.*

VE'STAL. *adj.* [*vestalis*, Latin.] Denoting pure virginity.

Her *vestal* livery is but sick and green,
And none but fools do wear it. *Shakespeare.*

VE'STIBULE. *n. s.* [*vestibulum*, Lat.] The porch or first entrance of a house.

VE'STIGE. *n. s.* [*vestigium*, Lat.] Footstep; mark left behind in passing.

The truth passes so slightly through men's imaginations, that they must use great subtilty to track its *vestiges*. *Harvey.*

VE'STMENT. *n. s.* [*vestimentum*, Latin.] Garment; part of dress.

Were it not better that the love which men bear unto God, should make the least things that are employed in his service amiable, than that their over-scrupulous dislike of so mean a thing as a *vestment*, should from the very service of God withdraw their hearts and affections. *Hooker.*

Heaven then would seem thy image, and reflect
Those sable *vestments*, and that bright aspect. *Waller.*

The sculptors could not give *vestments* suitable to the quality of the persons represented. *Dryden.*

VE'STRY. *n. s.* [*vestiaire*, Fr. *vestiarium*, Latin.]

1. A room appendant to the church, in which the sacerdotal garments, and consecrated things are reposited.

Bold Amycus, from the robb'd *vestry* brings
The chalices of heav'n; and holy things
Of precious weight. *Dryden.*

2. A parochial assembly commonly convened in the vestry.

The common-council are chosen every year, so many for every parish, by the *vestry*, and common convention of the people of that parish. *Clarendon.*

Go with me where paltry constables will not summon us to *vestries*. *Blount to Pope.*

VE'STURE. *n. s.* [*vesture*, old Fr. *vestura*, Italian.]

1. Garment; robe.

Her breasts half hid, and half were laid to show;
Her envious *vesture* greedy sight repelling. *Fairfax.*

What, weep you when you but behold
Our Cæsar's *vesture* wounded? *Shakesp. Julius Cæsar.*

To bear my lady's train, lest the base earth
Should from her *vesture* chance to steal a kiss. *Shakesp.*

Here ruddy brass, and gold refulgent blaz'd;
There polish'd chests embroider'd *vestures* grac'd. *Pope.*

2. Dress; habit; external form.

There's not the smallest orb which thou behold'st,
But in his motion like an angel sings,
But this muddy *vesture* of decay
Doth grosly close us in, we cannot hear it. *Shakesp.*

Rocks, precipices, and gulfs, apparell'd with a *vesture* of plants, would resemble mountains and vallies. *Bentley.*

VETCH. *n. s.* [*vicia*, Lat.] A plant with a papilionaceous flower; from the empalement arises the pointal, which becomes a pod full of roundish or angular seeds: to which must be added, that the leaves grow by pairs on a middle rib, ending in a tendril.

Where

Where *vetches*, pulse, and tares have stood,
And stalks of lupines grew. *Dryden.*

An ervum is a sort of *vetch*, or small pea. *Arbuthnot.*

VE'TCHY. *n. s.* [from *vetch.*] Made of vetches; abounding in vetches; consisting of vetch or pease-straw.

If to my cottage thou wilt resort,
There may'st thou ligge in a *vetchy* bed,
'Till fairer fortune shew forth his head. *Spenser.*

VE'TERAN. *n. s.* [*veteranus*, Latin.] An old soldier; a man long practised in any thing.

We were forced to uncover, or be regarded as *veterans* in the beau monde. *Addison.*

The Arians, for the credit of their faction, took the eldest, the best experienced, the most wary, and the longest-practised *veterans* they had amongst them. *Hooker.*

If king Charles II. had made war upon France, he might have conquered it by the many *veterans*, which had been inured to service in the civil wars. *Addison.*

Ensigns that pierc'd the foe's remotest lines,
The hardy *veteran* with tears resigns. *Addison.*

VE'TERAN. *adj.* Long practised in war; long experienced.

There was a mighty strong army of land-forces, to the number of fifty thousand *veteran* soldiers *Bacon.*

The British youth shall hail thy wise command;
Thy temper'd ardour, and thy *veteran* skill. *Thomson.*

VETERINARIAN. *n. s.* [*veterinarius*, Lat.] One skilled in the diseases of cattle

That a horse has no gall, is not only swallowed by common farriers, but also receiv'd by good *veterinarians*, and some who have laudably discoursed upon horses. *Brown.*

To VEX. *v. a.* [*vexo*, Latin.]

1. To plague; to torment; to harrass.

Do you think
The king will suffer but the little finger
Of this man to be *vex'd?* *Shakesp. Hen.* VIII.

Do poor Tom some charity, whom the foul fiend *vexes*. *Shak.*

When she pressed him daily, so that his soul was *vexed* unto death, he told her all his heart. *Judges* xvi. 16.

Still may the dog the wand'ring troops constrain
Of airy ghosts, and *vex* the guilty train. *Dryden.*

You are the cause of all my care:
Your eyes ten thousand dangers dart;
Ten thousand torments *vex* my heart;
I love, and I despair. *Prior.*

2. To disturb; to disquiet.

Alack, 'tis he; why, he was met even now,
As mad as the *vext* sea; singing aloud. *Shakesp.*

Rang'd on the banks beneath our equal oars,
White curl the waves, and the *vex'd* ocean roars. *Pope.*

3. To trouble with slight provocations.

VEXA'TION. *n. s.* [from *vex.*]

1. The act of troubling.

O that husband,
My supreme crown of grief, and those repeated *vexations* of it. *Shakesp. Cymbeline.*

2. The state of being troubled; uneasiness; sorrow.

Vexation almost stops my breath,
That sundred friends greets in the hour of death. *Shakesp.*

Passions too violent, instead of heightening our pleasures, afford us nothing but *vexation* and pain. *Temple.*

3. The cause of trouble or uneasiness.

Your children were *vexation* to your youth;
But mine shall be a comfort to your age. *Shakesp.*

4. An act of harrassing by law.

Albeit the party grieved thereby, may have some reason to complain of an untrue charge, yet may he not well call it an unjust *vexation*. *Bacon.*

5. A slight teazing trouble.

VEXA'TIOUS. *adj.* [from *vexation.*]

1. Afflictive; troublesome; causing trouble.

Consider him maintaining his usurped title, by continual *vexatious* wars against the kings of Judah. *South.*

Vexatious thought still found my flying mind,
Nor bound by limits, nor to place confin'd;
Haunted my nights, and terrify'd my days;
Stalk'd through my gardens, and pursu'd my ways;
Nor shut from artful bow'r, nor lost in winding maze. *Prior.*

2. Full of trouble; full of uneasiness.

He leads a *vexatious* life, who in his noblest actions is so gored with scruples, that he dares not make a step without the authority of another. *Digby.*

3. Teazing; slightly troublesome.

VEXA'TIOUSLY. *adv.* [from *vexatious.*] Troublesomely; uneasily.

VEXA'TIOUSNESS. *n. s.* [from *vexatious.*] Troublesomeness; uneasiness.

VEXER. [from *vex.*] He who vexes.

U'GLILY. *adv.* [from *ugly.*] Filthily; with deformity; in such a manner as to raise dislike.

U'GLINESS. *n. s.* [from *ugly.*]

1. Deformity; contrariety to beauty.

All that else seem'd fair and fresh in sight,
Was turned now to dreadful *ugliness*. *Spenser.*

She takes her topicks from the advantages of old age and *ugliness*. *Dryden.*

2. Turpitude; loathsomeness; moral depravity.

Their dull ribaldry cannot but be very nauseous and offensive to any one, who does not, for the sake of the sin itself, pardon the *ugliness* of its circumstances. *South.*

U'GLY. *adj.* [This word was antiently written *ougly*; whence Mr. *Dier* ingeniously deduces it from *ouphlike*; that is, like an *ouph*, *elf*, or *goblin*. In Saxon oga is terrour; and in Gothic *ogan* is to fear.] Deformed; offensive to the sight; contrary to beautiful.

If Cassio do remain,
He hath a daily beauty in his life,
That makes me *ugly*. *Shakespeare.*

O, I have pass'd a miserable night,
So full of *ugly* sights, of ghastly dreams. *Shakesp.*

Was this the cottage, and the safe abode
Thou toldst me of? What grim aspects are these,
These *ugly*-headed monsters? *Milton.*

VI'AL. *n. s.* [φιαλή.] A small bottle.

Edward's seven sons
Were as sev'n *vials* of his sacred blood. *Shakesp.*

You Gods! look down,
And from your sacred *vials* pour your grace
Upon my daughter's head. *Shakesp.*

Take thou this *vial*, being then in bed,
And this distilled liquor drink thou off. *Shakesp.*

Another lamp burnt in an old marble sepulchre belonging to some of the antient Romans inclosed in a glass *vial*. *Wilkins.*

I placed a thin *vial*, well stopped up, within the smoke of the vapour, but nothing followed. *Addison.*

Chemical waters, that are each transparent, when separate, ferment into a thick troubled liquor, when mixed in the same *vial*. *Addison.*

To VI'AL. *v. a.* To inclose in a vial.

This she with precious *vial'd* liquors heals;
For which the shepherds at the festivals
Carol her goodness loud in rustick lays. *Milton.*

VI'AND. *n. s.* [*viande*, Fr. *vivanda*, Ital.] Food; meat dressed.

The belly only like a gulf remain'd,
I' th' midst of the body idle and unactive,
Still cupboarding the *viand*. *Shakesp.*

No matter, since
They've left their *viands* behind, for we have stomachs.
Wilt please you taste of what is here? *Shakesp.*

These are not fruits forbidden; no interdict
Defends the touching of these *viands* pure;
Their taste no knowledge works, at least of evil. *Milton.*

From some sorts of food less pleasant to the taste, persons in health, and in no necessity of using such *viands*, had better to abstain. *Ray.*

The tables in fair order spread;
Viands of various kinds allure the taste,
Of choicest sort and savour; rich repast! *Pope.*

VIA'TICUM. n. s. [Latin.]

1. Provision for a journey.

2. The last rites used to prepare the passing soul for its departure.

To VI'BRATE. *v. a.* [*vibro*, Latin.]

1. To brandish; to move to and fro with quick motion.

2. To make to quiver.

Breath vocalized, that is *vibrated* or undulated, may differently affect the lips, and impress a swift tremulous motion, which breath passing smooth doth not. *Holder.*

To VI'BRATE. *v. n.*

1. To play up and down, or to and fro.

The air, compressed by the fall and weight of the quicksilver, would repel it a little upwards, and make it *vibrate* a little up and down. *Boyle.*

Do not all fixed bodies, when heated beyond a certain degree, emit light, and shine? And is not this emission performed by the *vibrating* motions of their parts? *Newton.*

2. To quiver.

The whisper, that to greatness still too near,
Perhaps, yet *vibrates* on his sovereign's ear. *Pope.*

VIBRA'TION. *n. s.* [from *vibro*, Latin.] The act of moving, or being moved with quick reciprocations, or returns; the act of quivering.

It sparkled like the coal upon the altar, with the fervours of piety, the heats of devotion, and the sallies and *vibrations* of an harmless activity. *South.*

Do not the rays of light, in falling upon the bottom of the eye, excite *vibrations* in the tunica retina? Which *vibrations* being propagated along the solid fibres of the optick nerves into the brain, cause the sense of seeing. *Newton.*

Mild *vibrations* sooth the parted soul,
New to the dawning of celestial day. *Thomson.*

VI'CAR. *n. s.* [*vicarius*, Latin.]

1. The incumbent of an appropriated or impropriated benefice.

Procure the *vicar*
To stay for me at church, 'twixt twelve and one,
To give our hearts united ceremony. *Shakesp.*

Yours is the prize;
The *vicar* my defeat, and all the village fee. *Dryden.*

A landed youth, whom his mother would never suffer to look into a book for fear of spoiling his eyes, upon hearing the clergy decried, what a contempt must he entertain, not only for his *vicar* at home, but for the whole order. *Swift.*

2. One who performs the functions of another; a substitute.

An archbishop may not only excommunicate and interdict his suffragans, but his *vicar*-general may do the same. *Ayliffe.*

VI'CARAGE. *n. s.* [from *vicar.*] The benefice of a vicar.

This gentleman lived in his *vicarage* to a good old age, and having never deserted his flock, died vicar of Bray. *Swift.*

VICA'RIOUS. *adj.* [*vicarius*, Latin.] Deputed; delegated; acting in the place of another.

The soul in the body is but a subordinate efficient, and *vicarious* and instrumental in the hands of the Almighty, being but his substitute in this regiment of the body. *Hale.*

What can be more unnatural, than for a man to rebel against the *vicarious* power of God in his soul. *Norris.*

VI'CARSHIP. *n. s.* [from *vicar.*] The office of a vicar.

VICE. *n. s.* [*vitium*, Latin.]

1. The course of action opposite to virtue; depravity of manners; inordinate life.

No spirit more gross to love
Vice for itself. *Milton.*

The foundation of error will lie in wrong measures of probability; as the foundation of *vice* in wrong measures of good. *Locke.*

2. A fault; an offence. It is generally used for an habitual fault, not for a single enormity.

No *vice*, so simple, but assumes
Some mark of virtue on its outward parts. *Shakesp.*

Yet my poor country
Shall have more *vices* than it had before;
More suffer by him that shall succeed. *Shakesp.*

Ungovern'd appetite, a brutish *vice*. *Milton.*

I cannot blame him for inveighing so sharply against the *vices* of the clergy in his age. *Dryden.*

3. The fool, or punchinello of old shows.

I'll be with you again
In a trice, like to the old *vice*,
Your need to sustain;
Who with dagger of lath, in his rage and his wrath,
Cries, ah, ha! to the devil. *Shakespeare.*

His face made of brass, like a *vice* in a game. *Tusser.*

4. [*Vijs*, Dutch.] A kind of small iron press with screws, used by workmen.

He found that marbles taught him percussion; bottle-screws, the *vice*; whirligigs, the axis in peritrochio *Arbuth. and Pope.*

5. Gripe; grasp.

If I but fist him once; if he come but within my *vice*. *Shakespeare.*

6. [*Vice*, Latin.] It is used in composition for one, *qui vicem gerit*, who performs, in his stead, the office of a superiour, or who has the second rank in command: as *a* viceroy; vice-chancellor.

To VICE. *v. a.* [from the noun.] To draw.

With all confidence he swears,
As he had seen't, or been an instrument
To *vice* you to't, that you have touch'd his queen
Forbiddenly. *Shakespeare's Winter Tale.*

VI'CEADMIRAL. *n. s.* [*vice* and *admiral.*]

1. The second commander of a fleet.

The foremost of the fleet was the admiral: the rear-admiral was Cara Mahometes, an arch-pirate. The *vice*-admiral in the middle of the fleet with a great squadron of gallies, struck sail directly. *Knolles.*

2. A naval officer of the second rank.

VI'CEADMIRALTY. *n. s.* [from *vice-admiral.*] The office of a vice-admiral.

The *vice*-admiralty is exercised by Mr. Trenanion. *Carew.*

VICEA'GENT. *n. s.* [*vice* and *agent.*] One who acts in the place of another.

A vassal Satan hath made his *vice-agent*, to cross whatever the faithful ought to do. *Hooker.*

VI'CED. *adj.* [from *viced.*] Vitious; corrupt.

Be as a planetary plague, when Jove
Will o'er some high-*vic'd* city hang his poison
In the sick air. *Shakesp.*

VICEGE'RENT. *n. s.* [*vicem gerens*, Lat.] A lieutenant; one who is intrusted with the power of the superiour, by whom he is deputed.

All precepts concerning kings are comprehended in these; remember thou art a man; remember thou art God's *vicegerent*. *Bacon.*

Employ it in unfeigned piety towards God; in unshaken duty to his *vicegerent*; in hearty obedience to his church. *Sprat.*

Great Father of the gods, when for our crimes
Thou send'st some heavy judgment on the times;
Some tyrant king, the terrour of his age,
The type and true *vicegerent* of thy rage,
Thus punish. *Dryden.*

Thou great *vicegerent* of the king;
In all affairs thou sole director. *Swift.*

VICEGE'RENT. *adj.* [*vicegerens*, Lat.] Having a delegated power; acting by substitution.

Whom send I to judge thee? Whom but thee,
Vicegerent son! To thee I have transferr'd
All judgment, whether in heav'n, or earth, or hell. *Milton.*

VICEGE'RENCY. *n. s.* [from *vicegernt.*] The office of a vicegerent; lieutenancy; deputed power.

The authority of conscience stands founded upon its *vicegerency* and deputation under God. *South.*

VICECHA'NCELLOR. *n. s.* [*vicecancellarius*, Latin.] The second magistrate of the universities.

VI'CENARY. *adj.* [*vicenarius*, Lat.] Belonging to twenty. *Bailey.*

VI'CEROY. *n. s.* [*viceroi*, French.] He who governs in place of the king with regal authority.

Shall I, for lucre of the rest unvanquish'd,
Detract so much from that prerogative,
As to be call'd but *viceroy* of the whole? *Shakesp.*

Mendoza, *viceroy* of Peru, was wont to say, that the government of Peru was the best place the king of Spain gave, save that it was somewhat too near Madrid. *Bacon.*

We are so far from having a king, that even the *viceroy* is generally absent four fifths of his time. *Swift.*

VI'CEROYALTY. *n. s.* [from *viceroy.*] Dignity of a viceroy.

These parts furnish out *vice-royalties* for the grandees; but in war are incumbrances to the kingdom. *Addison.*

VI'CETY. *n. s.* [Of this word I know not well the meaning or original: a *nice* thing is now called in vulgar language, *point vice*, from the French perhaps, *point de vice*; whence the barbarous word *vicety* may be derived.] Nicety; exactness. A word not used.

Here is to the fruit of Pem,
Grafted upon Stub his stem;
With the peakish nicety,
And old Sherewood's *vicety*. *B. Johnson.*

VICI'NITY. *n. s.* [*vicinus*, Latin.]

1. Nearness; State of being near.

The position of things is such, that there is a *vicinity* between agents and patients, that the one incessantly invades the other. *Hale.*

The abundance and *vicinity* of country seats. *Swift.*

2. Neighbourhood.

He shall find out and recall the wandering particles home, and fix them in their old *vicinity*. *Rogers.*

Gravity alone must have carried them downwards to the *vicinity* of the sun. *Bentley.*

VI'CINAGE. *n. s.* [*vicinia*, Lat.] Neighbourhood; places adjoining.

VICI'NAL. } *adj.* [*vicinus*, Lat.] Near; neighbouring.
VICI'NE. }

Opening other *vicine* passages might obliterate any track; as the making of one hole in the yielding mud, defaces the print of another near it. *Glanville.*

VI'CIOUS. *adj* [from *vice.*] See VITIOUS. Devoted to vice; not addicted to virtue.

He heard this heavy curse,
Servants of servants on his *vicious* race. *Milton.*

VICI'SSITUDE. [*vicissitudo*, Latin.]

1. Regular change; return of the same things in the same succession.

It makes through heav'n
Grateful *vicissitude*, like day and night. *Milton.*

The rays of light are alternately disposed to be reflected or refracted for many *vicissitudes*. *Newton.*

This succession of things upon the earth, is the result of the *vicissitude* of seasons, and is as constant as is the cause of that *vicissitude*, the sun's declination. *Woodward.*

2. Revolution; change.

During the course of the war, did the *vicissitudes* of good and bad fortune affect us with humility or thankfulness. *Atterb.*

Verse sweetens toil, however rude the sound.
All at her work the village maiden sings;
Nor as she turns the giddy wheel around,
Revolves the sad *vicissitude* of things. *Giffard.*

VI'CONTIELS. In law *vicontiel* rents are certain farms, for which the sheriff pays a rent to the king, and makes what profit he can of them. *Vicontiel* writs are such writs as are triable in the county court, before the sheriff. *Bailey.*

VI'CTIM. *n. s.* [*victima*, Latin.]

1. A sacrifice; something slain for a sacrifice.

All that were authors of so black a deed,
Be sacrific'd as *victims* to his ghost. *Denham.*

And on the *victim* pour the ruddy wine. *Dryden.*

Clitumnus' waves, for triumphs after war,
The *victim* ox, and snowy sheep prepare. *Addison.*

2. Some-

2. Something destroyed.
Behold where age's wretched *victim* lies;
See his head trembling, and his half-clos'd eyes. *Prior.*

VI'CTOR. *n. s.* [*victor*, Lat.] Conqueror; vanquisher; he that gains the advantage in any contest. *Victor* is seldom used with a genitive, and never but with regard to some single action or person. We rarely say Alexander was *victor* of Darius, though we say he was *victor* at Arbela; but we never say he was *victor* of Persia.
This strange race more strange conceits did yield;
Who *victor* seem'd, was to his ruin brought;
Who seem'd o'erthrown, was mistress of the field. *Sidney.*
Some time the flood prevails, and then the wind,
Both tugging to be *victors*, breast to breast,
Yet neither conqueror, nor conquered. *Shakesp.*
Although the *victor*, we submit to Cæsar. *Shakesp.*
Say where and when
Their fight; what stroke shall bruise the *victor*'s heel. *Milt.*
Our Hebrew songs and harps in Babylon,
That pleas'd so well our *victors* ear, declare
That rather Greece from us these arts deriv'd. *Milton.*
Their hearts at last the vanquish'd re-assume,
And now the *victors* fall. *Denham.*
In love the *victors* from the vanquish'd fly;
They fly that wound, and they pursue that die. *Waller.*
Fortune's unjust; she ruins oft the brave,
And him who should be *victor*, makes the slave. *Dryden.*
Lose not a thought on me, I'm out of danger;
Heaven will not leave me in the *victor's* hand. *Addison.*

VICTO'RIOUS. *adj.* [*victorieux*, Fr.]
1. Conquering; having obtained conquest; superiour in contest.
Victory doth more often fall by errour of the vanquished, than by the valour of the *victorious*. *Hayward.*
The great son return'd *victorious* with his saints. *Milton.*
That happy sun, said he, will rise again,
Who twice *victorious* did our navy see:
And I alone must view him rise in vain,
Without one ray of all his star for me. *Dryden.*
2. Producing conquest.
Sudden these honours shall be snatch'd away,
And curs'd for ever this *victorious* day. *Pope.*
3. Betokening conquest.
Now are our brows bound with *victorious* wreaths;
Our bruised arms hung up for monuments. *Shakesp.*

VICTO'RIOUSLY. *adv.* [from *victorious.*] With conquest; successfully; triumphantly.
That grace will carry us, if we do not wilfully betray our succours, *victoriously* through all difficulties. *Hammond.*

VICTO'RIOUSNESS. *n. s.* [from *victorious.*] The state or quality of being victorious.

VI'CTORY. *n. s.* [*victoria*, Lat.] Conquest; success in contest; triumph.
At his nurse's tears
He whin'd and roar'd away your *victory*,
That pages blush'd at him. *Shakesp.*
Then to the heav'n of heav'ns he shall ascend
With *victory*, triumphing o'er his foes. *Milton.*
Obedience is a complicated act of virtue, and many graces are exercised in one act of obedience. It is an act of humility, of mortification and self-denial, of charity to God, of care of the publick, of order and charity to ourselves. It is a great instance of a *victory* over the most refractory passions. *Taylor.*

VI'CTRESS. *n. s.* [from *victor.*] A female that conquers.
I'll lead thy daughter to a conqueror's bed;
And she shall be sole *victress*; Cæsar's Cæsar. *Shakesp.*

VI'CTUAL. } *n. s.* [*victuailles*, Fr. *vittonaglia*, Ital.] Provision
VI'CTUALS. } of food; stores for the support of life; meat; sustenance.
He landed in these islands, to furnish himself with *victuals* and fresh water. *Abbot's Descrip. of the World.*
You had musty *victuals*, and he hath holp to eat it: he hath an excellent stomach. *Shakesp.*
He was not able to keep that place three days for lack of *victual*. *Knolles.*
They, unprovided of tackling and *victual*, are forced to sea by a storm. *K. Charles.*

To VI'CTUAL. *v. a.* [from the noun.] To store with provision for food.
Talbot, farewel;
I must go *victual* Orleans forthwith. *Shakes.*

VI'CTUALLER. *n. s.* [from *victuals.*] One who provides victuals.
They planted their artillery against the haven, to impeach supply of victuals; yet the English *victuallers* surceased not to bring all things necessary. *Hayward.*
Their conquest half is to the *victualler* due. *King.*

VIDE'LICET. adv. [Latin.] To wit; that is. This word is generally written *viz.*

VIDU'ITY. *n. s.* [from *viduus*, Lat.] Widowhood.

To VIE. *v. a.* [Of this word the etymology is very uncertain.]
1. To show, or practice in competition.
They *vie* power and expence with those that are too high. *L'Estrange.*
You *vie* happiness in a thousand easy and sweet diversions. *Evelyn.*
2. In this passage the meaning seems to be, to add; to accumulate.
She hung about my neck, and kiss on kiss
She *vied* so fast,
That in a twink she won me to her love. *Shakesp.*

To VIE. *v. n.* To contest; to contend; to strive for superiority.
In a trading nation, the younger sons may be placed in such a way of life, as may enable them to *vie* with the best of their family. *Addison.*
The wool, when shaded with Ancona's dye,
May with the proudest Tyrian purple *vie*. *Addison.*
Now voices over voices rise;
While each to be the loudest *vies*. *Swift.*

To VIEW. *v. a.* [*veu*, Fr. from *veoir*, or *voir.*]
1. To survey; to look on by way of examination.
Go, and *view* the country. *Jos.* vii. 2.
Th' almighty father bent down his eye,
His own works and their works at once to *view*. *Milton.*
View not this spire, by measures giv'n,
To buildings rais'd by common hands. *Prior.*
Whene'er we *view* some well-proportion'd dome;
No single parts unequally surprize;
All comes united to th' admiring eyes. *Pope.*
2. To see; to perceive by the eye.
With eyes aghast
View'd first their lamentable lot. *Milton.*
No more I hear, no more I *view*,
The phantom flies me, as unkind as you. *Pope.*

VIEW. *n. s.* [from the verb.]
1. Prospect.
You should tread a course
Pretty, and full of *view*; yea, haply, near
The residence of Posthumus. *Shakesp. Cymbeline.*
Vast and indefinite *views*, which drown all apprehensions of the uttermost objects, are condemned by good authors. *Wotton.*
The walls of Pluto's palace are in *view*. *Dryden.*
Cut wide *views* through mountains to the plain,
You'll wish your hill, or shelter'd hill again. *Pope.*
2. Sight; power of beholding.
Some safer resolution I've in *view*. *Milton.*
I go, to take for ever from your *view*,
Both the lov'd object, and the hated too. *Dryden.*
These things duly weigh'd, will give us a clear *view* into the state of human liberty. *Locke.*
Instruct me other joys to prize,
With other beauties charm my partial eyes;
Full in my *view* set all the bright abode,
And make my soul quit Abelard for God. *Pope.*
3. Act of seeing.
Th' unexpected sound
Of dogs and men, his wakeful ear does wound;
Rouz'd with the noise, he scarce believes his ear,
Willing to think th' illusions of his fear
Had giv'n this false alarm; but straight his *view*
Confirms that more than all he fears is true. *Denham.*
Objects near our *view* are thought greater than those of a larger size, that are more remote. *Locke.*
4. Sight; eye.
She was not much struck with those objects that now presented themselves to her *view*. *Female Quixote.*
5. Survey; examination by the eye.
Time never will renew,
While we too far the pleasing path pursue,
Surveying nature with too nice a *view*. *Dryden.*
6. Intellectual survey.
If the mind has made this inference by finding out the intermediate ideas, and taking a *view* of the connection of them, it has proceeded rationally. *Locke.*
7. Space that may be taken in by the eye; reach of sight.
The fame through all the neighb'ring nations flew,
When now the Trojan navy was in *view*. *Dryden.*
8. Appearance; show.
In that accomplish'd mind,
Helpt by the night, new graces find;
Which, by the splendour of her *view*,
Dazzl'd before we never knew. *Waller.*
9. Display; exhibition to the sight or mind.
To give a right *view* of this mistaken part of liberty, would any one be a changeling, because he is less determined by wise considerations than a wise man? *Locke.*
10 Prospect of interest.
No man sets himself about any thing, but upon some *view* or other, which serves him for a reason. *Locke.*
11. Intention; design.
He who sojourns in a foreign country, refers what he sees to the state of things at home; with that *view* he makes all his reflections. *Atterbury.*
With a *view* to commerce, in returning from his expedition against the Parthians, he passed through Egypt. *Arbuthnot.*

VI'EWLESS.

Vi'ewless. *adj.* [from *view.*] Unseen; not discernible by the sight.

To be imprison'd in the *viewless* winds,
And blown with restless violence about
The pendant world. *Shakesp.*

Each stair mysteriously was meant, nor stood
There always, but drawn up to heav'n sometimes
Viewless. *Milton's Par. Lost.*

Swift through the valves the visionary fair
Repass'd, and *viewless* mix'd with common air. *Pope.*

Light-bounding from the earth, at once they rise;
Their feet half *viewless* quiver in the skies. *Pope.*

Vigesima'tion. *n. s.* [*vegesimus*, Latin.] The act of putting to death every twentieth man. *Bailey.*

Vi'gil. *n. s.* [*vigilia*, Latin.]

1. Watch; devotions performed in the customary hours of rest.

So they in heaven their odes and *vigils* tun'd. *Milton.*

Shrines! where their *vigils* pale-ey'd virgins keep,
And pitying saints, whose statues learn to weep. *Pope.*

2. A fast kept before a holiday.

He that out-lives this day, and sees old age,
Will yearly on the *vigil* feast his neighbours,
And say to-morrow is St. Crispian. *Shakesp.*

3. Service used on the night before a holiday.

No altar is to be consecrated without reliques, which placed before the church door, the *vigils* are to be celebrated that night before them. *Stillingfleet.*

The rivals call my muse another way,
To sing their *vigils* for th' ensuing day. *Dryden.*

4. Watch; forbearance of sleep.

Though Venus and her son shou'd spare
Her rebel heart, and never teach her care;
Yet Hymen may perforce her *vigils* keep,
And for another's joy suspend her sleep. *Waller.*

Nothing wears out a fine face like the *vigils* of the card-table, and those cutting passions which attend them. *Addison.*

Vi'gilance. } *n. s.* [*vigilance*, Fr. *vigilantia*, Lat.]
Vi'gilancy. }

1. Forbearance of sleep.

Ulysses yielded unseasonably to sleep, and the strong passion for his country should have given him *vigilance*. *Broome.*

2. Watchfulness; circumspection; incessant care.

Shall Henry's conquest, Bedford's *vigilance*,
Your deeds of war, and all our counsel die? *Shakesp.*

No post is free, no place,
That guard and most unusual *vigilance*
Does not attend my taking. *Shakesp. K. Lear.*

In this their military care, there were few remarkable occasions under the duke, saving his continual *vigilancy*, and voluntary hazard of his person. *Wotton.*

Of these the *vigilance*
I dread; and to elude, thus wrapp'd in mist
Of midnight vapour, glide obscure. *Milton.*

We are enabled to subdue all other creatures; and use for our behoof the strength of the ox, the sagacity and *vigilancy* of the dog. *Ray.*

3 Guard; watch.

In at this gate none pass
The *vigilance* here plac'd, but such as come
Well known from heav'n. *Milton.*

VI'GILANT. *adj.* [*vigilans*, Latin.] Watchful; circumspect; diligent; attentive.

They have many prayers, but every of them very short, as if they were darts thrown out with a kind of sudden quickness; lest that *vigilant* and erect attention of mind, which in prayer is very necessary, should be wasted or dulled through continuance. *Hooker.*

Take your places, and be *vigilant*:
If any noise or soldier you perceive,
Let us have knowledge. *Shakespeare.*

The treasurer, as he was *vigilant* in such cases, had notice of the clerk's expiration so soon, that he procured the king to send a message to the master of the rolls. *Clarend.*

Vi'gilantly. *adv.* [from *vigilant.*] Watchfully; attentively; circumspectly.

Thus in peace, either of the kings so *vigilantly* observed every motion of the others, as if they had lived upon the alarm. *Hayward.*

Vi'gorous. *adj.* [from *vigor*, Latin.] Forcible; not weakened; full of strength and life.

Fam'd for his valour young;
At sea successful, *vigorous* and strong! *Waller.*

Their appetite is not dull'd by being gratified, but returns always fresh and *vigorous*. *Atterbury.*

Vi'gorously. *adv.* [from *vigour.*] With force; forcibly; without weakness.

The prince had two giant ships;
With his one so *vigorously* he press'd,
And flew so home, they could not rise again. *Dryden.*

If the fire burns bright and *vigorously*, it is no matter by what means it was at first kindled. *South.*

That prince whose cause you espouse so *vigorously*, is the principal in the war, and you but a second. *Swift.*

Vi'gorousness. *n. s.* [from *vigour.*] Force; strength.

He hath given excellent sufferance and *vigorousness* to the sufferers, arming them with strange courage, heroical fortitude, invincible resolution, and glorious patience. *Taylor.*

VI'GOUR *n. s.* [*vigor*, Lat.]

1. Force; strength.

Sometimes went and sometimes ran,
With supple joints, as lively *vigour* led. *Milton.*

Shame to be overcome,
Wou'd utmost *vigour* raise, and rais'd unite. *Milton.*

Pernicious fire wither'd all their strength,
And of their wonted *vigour* left them drain'd. *Milton.*

The mind and spirit remains
Invincible, and *vigour* soon returns. *Milton.*

No deep within her gulf can hold
Immortal *vigour*. *Milton.*

The *vigour* of this arm was never vain:
Witness these heaps of slaughter. *Dryden.*

2. Mental force; intellectual ability.

3. Energy; efficacy.

In the fruitful earth
His beams, unactive else, their *vigour* find. *Milton.*

How does Cartesius all his sinews strain,
The earth's attractive *vigour* to explain? *Blackmore.*

VILE. *adj.* [*vil*, Fr. *vilis*, Lat.] Base; mean; worthless; sordid; despicable.

Our case were miserable, if that wherewith we most endeavour to please God, were in his sight so *vile* and despicable as men's disdainful speech would make it. *Hooker.*

I disdaining scorn'd, and craved death,
Rather than I would be so *vile* esteem'd. *Shakesp.*

He to-day that sheds his blood with me,
Shall be my brother; be he ne'er so *vile*,
This day shall gentle his condition. *Shakesp.*

The inhabitants account gold but as a *vile* thing. *Abbot.*

That sinful creature man elected is,
And in our place the heavens possess he must;
Vile man, begot of clay, and born of dust. *Fairfax.*

A spontaneous production is against matter of fact; a thing without example not only in man, but the *vilest* of weeds. *Bentl.*

2. Morally impure; wicked.

Restor'd by thee, *vile* as I am, to place
Of new acceptance. *Milton.*

Vi'led. *adj.* [from *vile*, whence *revile.*] Abusive; scurrilous; defamatory.

He granted life to all except to one, who had used *vil'd* speeches against king Edward. *Hayward.*

Vi'lely. *adv.* [from *vile.*] Basely; meanly; shamefully.

The Volscians *vilely* yielded the town. *Shakesp.*

How can I
Forget my Hector, treated with dishonour,
Depriv'd of funeral rites, and *vilely* dragg'd,
A bloody corse, about the walls of Troy. *A. Philips.*

Vi'leness. *n. s.* [from *vile.*]

1. Baseness; meanness; despicableness.

His *vileness* us shall never awe:
But here our sports shall be:
Such as the golden world first saw,
Most innocent and free. *Drayton.*

Reflect on the essential *vileness* of matter, and its impotence to conserve its own being. *Creech.*

Considering the *vileness* of the clay, I wondered that no tribune of that age durst ever venture to ask the potter, what dost thou make? *Swift.*

2. Moral or intellectual baseness.

Then, *vileness* of mankind!
Could one, alas! repeat me good or great,
Wash my pale body, or bewail my fate? *Prior.*

To Vi'lify. *v. a.* [from *vile.*] To debase; to defame; to make contemptible.

Tomalin could not abide,
To hear his sovereign *vilify'd*. *Drayton.*

Their maker's image
Forsook them, when themselves they *vilify'd*
To serve ungovern'd appetite; and took
His image whom they serv'd. *Milton.*

The displeasure of their prince, those may expect, who would put in practice all methods to *vilify* his person. *Addison.*

Many passions dispose us to depress and *vilify* the merit of one rising in the esteem of mankind. *Addison.*

Vill. *n. s.* [*ville*, Fr. *villa*, Latin.] A village; a small collection of houses. Little in use.

This book gives an account of the manurable lands in every manor, town, or *vill*. *Hale.*

Vi'lla. *n. s.* [*villa*, Lat.] A country seat.

The antient Romans lay the foundations of their *villas* and palaces within the very borders of the sea. *Addison.*

All vast possessions; just the same the case,
Whether you call them *villa*, park, or chace. *Pope.*

VI'LLAGE. *n. s.* [*village*, Fr.] A small collection of houses in the country, less than a town.

Beggars, with roaring voices, from low farms,
Or pelting *villages*, sheep coats, and mills,
Inforce their charity. *Shakespeare.*

The early *village* cock
Hath twice done salutation to the morn. *Shakesp.*

You have many enemies, that know not
Why they are so; but, like the *village* curs,
Bark when their fellows do. *Shakespeare.*

The country *villages* were burnt down to the ground. *Knolles.*

Those *village*-words give us a mean idea of the thing. *Dryd.*

Seam'd o'er with wounds which his own sabre gave,
In the vile habit of a *village* slave. *Pope.*

VI'LLAGER. *n. s.* [from *village.*] An inhabitant of the village.

Brutus had rather be a *villager*,
Than to repute himself a son of Rome
Under such hard conditions. *Shakesp.*

When once her eye
Hath met the virtue of this magick dust,
I shall appear some harmless *villager*,
Whom thrift keeps up about his country geer. *Milton.*

If there are conveniencies of life, which common use reaches not, it is not reason to reject them, because every *villager* doth not know them. *Locke.*

VI'LLAGERY. *n. s.* [from *village.*] District of villages.

Robin Goodfellow, are you not he,
That fright the maidens of the *villagery?* *Shakesp.*

VI'LLAIN. *n. s.* [*vilain*, Fr. *villanus*, low Latin.]

1. One who held by a base tenure.

The Irish inhabiting the lands fully conquered, being in condition of slaves and *villains*, did render a greater revenue, than if they had been made the king's free subjects. *Davies.*

2. A wicked wretch.

We were prevented by a dozen armed knights, or rather *villains*, who, using this time of their extreme feebleness, all together set upon them.

O *villain! villain!* his very opinion in the letter. Abhorred *villain!* unnatural, detested, brutish *villain!* *Shakesp.*

What in the world,
That names me traitor, *villain*-like he lies. *Shakesp.*

He was stabbed to the heart by the hand of a *villain*, upon the mere impious pretence of his being odious to the parliament. *Clarendon.*

Calm thinking *villains*, whom no faith could fix;
Of crooked counsels, and dark politicks. *Pope.*

VI'LLANAGE. *n. s.* [from *villain.*]

1. The state of a villain; base servitude.

They exercise most bitter tyranny,
Upon the parts brought into their bondage:
No wretchedness is like to sinful *villanage*. *Fairy Queen.*

Upon every such surrender and grant, there was but one freeholder, which was the lord himself; all the rest were but tenants in *villanage*, and were not fit to be sworn in juries. *Davies.*

2. Baseness; infamy.

If in thy smoke it ends, their glories shine;
But infamy and *villanage* are thine. *Dryden.*

To VI'LLANIZE. *v. a.* [from *villain.*] To debase; to degrade; to defame.

Were virtue by descent, a noble name
Could never *villanize* his father's fame;
But, as the first, the last of all the line,
Would, like the sun, ev'n in descending shine. *Dryden.*

These are the fools, whose stolidity can baffle all arguments; whose glory is in their shame, in the debasing and *villanizing* of mankind to the condition of beasts. *Bentley.*

VI'LLANOUS. *adj.* [from *villain.*]

1. Base; vile; wicked.

2. Sorry.

Thou art my son; I have partly thy mother's word, partly my own opinion; but chiefly a *villanous* trick of thine eye doth warrant me. *Shakesp.*

3. It is used by *Shakespeare* to exaggerate any think detestable.

We shall lose our time,
And all be turn'd to barnacles or apes,
With foreheads *villanous* low. *Shakesp. Tempest.*

VI'LLANOUSLY. *adv.* [from *villainous.*] Wickedly; basely.

The wandering Numidian falsified his faith, and *villanously* slew Selymes the king, as he was bathing himself. *Knolles.*

VI'LLANOUSNESS. *n. s.* [from *villainous.*] Baseness; wickedness.

VILLANY. *n. s.* [from *villain*; *villonnie*, old French.]

1. Wickedness; baseness; depravity.

Trust not those cunning waters of his eyes;
For *villainy* is not without such a rheum:
And he, long traded in it, makes it seem
Like rivers of remorse and innocence. *Shakesp.*

He is the prince's jester; and the commendation is not in his wit, but in his *villany*. *Shakesp.*

2. A wicked action; a crime.

No *villany*, or flagitious action was ever yet committed; but a lie was first or last the principal engine to effect it. *South.*

Such *villainies* rous'd Horace into wrath;
And 'tis more noble to pursue his path,
Than an old tale. *Dryden.*

VILLA'TICK. *adj.* [*villaticus*, Lat.] Belonging to villages.

Evening dragon came,
Assailant on the perched roosts,
And nests in order rang'd,
Of tame *villatick* fowl. *Milton.*

VI'LLI. *n. s.* [Latin.]

In anatomy, are the same as fibres; and in botany, small hairs like the grain of plush or shag, with which, as a kind of excrescence, some trees do abound. *Quincy.*

VI'LLOUS. *adj.* [*villosus*, Lat.] Shaggy; rough.

The liquor of the stomach, which with fasting grows sharp, and the quick sensation of the inward *villous* coat of the stomach, seem to be the cause of the sense of hunger. *Arb.*

VIMI'NEOUS. *adj.* [*vimineus*, Latin.] Made of twigs.

As in the hive's *vimineous* dome,
Ten thousand bees enjoy their home;
Each does her studious action vary,
To go and come, to fetch and carry. *Prior.*

VI'NCIBLE. *adj.* [from *vinco*, Lat.] Conquerable; superable.

He not *vincible* in spirit, and well assured that shortness of provision would in a short time draw the seditious to shorter limits, drew his sword. *Hayward.*

Because 'twas absolutely in my power to have attended more heedfully, there was liberty in the principle, the mistake which influenced the action was *vincible*. *Norris.*

VI'NCIBLENESS. *n. s.* [from *vincible.*] Liableness to be overcome. *Dict.*

VI'NCTURE. *n. s.* [*vinctura*, Lat.] A binding. *Bailey.*

VINDE'MIAL. *adj.* [*vindemia*, Latin.] Belonging to a vintage.

To VINDE'MIATE. *v. n.* [*vindemia*, Latin.] To gather the vintage.

Now *vindemiate*, and take your bees towards the expiration of this month. *Evelyn.*

VINDEMIA'TION. *n. s.* [*vindemia*, Lat.] Grape-gathering. *Bailey.*

To VI'NDICATE. *v. a.* [*vindico*, Lat.]

1. To justify; to support; to maintain.

Where the respondent denies any proposition, the opponent must directly *vindicate* and confirm that proposition; *i. e.* he must make that proposition the conclusion of his next syllogism. *Watts's Improvement of the Mind.*

2. To revenge; to avenge.

We ought to have added, how far an holy war is to be pursued; whether to enforce a new belief, and to *vindicate* or punish infidelity? *Bacon.*

Man is not more inclinable to obey God than man; but God is more powerful to exact subjection, and to *vindicate* rebellion. *Pearson on the Creed.*

The more numerous the offenders are, the more his justice is concerned to *vindicate* the affront. *Tillotson.*

Assemble ours, and all the Theban race,
To *vindicate* on Athens thy disgrace. *Dryden.*

3. To assert; to claim with efficacy.

Never any touch'd upon this way, which our poet justly has *vindicated* to himself. *Dryden's Pref. to Ovid.*

The beauty of this town, without a fleet,
From all the world shall *vindicate* her trade. *Dryden.*

4. To clear; to protect.

God's ways of dealing with us, are by proposition of terrors and promises. To these is added the authority of the commander, *vindicated* from our neglect by the interposition of the greatest signs and wonders, in the hands of his prophets, and of his son. *Hammond.*

I may assert eternal providence,
And *vindicate* the ways of God to man. *Milton.*

VINDICA'TION. *n. s.* [*vindication*, Fr. from *vindicate.*] Defence; assertion; justification.

This is no *vindication* of her conduct. She still acts a mean part, and, through fear, becomes an accomplice, in endeavouring to betray the Greeks. *Broome.*

VI'NDICATIVE. *adj.* [from *vindicate.*] Revengeful; given to revenge.

He, in heat of action,
Is more *vindicative* than jealous love. *Shakesp.*

Publick revenges are for the most part fortunate; but in private revenges it is not so. *Vindicative* persons live the life of witches, who, as they are mischievous, so end they unfortunate. *Bacon.*

The fruits of adusted choler, and the evaporations of a *vindicative* spirit. *Howel.*

Do not too many believe no zeal to be spiritual, but what is censorious or *vindicative?* Whereas no zeal is spiritual, that is not also charitable. *Sprat's Sermons.*

Distinguish betwixt a passion purely *vindicative*, and those counsels where divine justice avenges the innocent. *L'Estrange.*

VINDICA'TOR. *n. s.* [from *vindicate.*] One who vindicates; an assertor.

He treats tyranny, and the vices attending it, with the utmost rigour; and consequently a noble soul is better pleas'd with a jealous *vindicator* of Roman liberty, than with a temporizing poet. *Dryden.*

VI'NDICATORY. *adj.* [from *vindicator.*]

1. Punitory; performing the office of vengeance.

The afflictions of Job were no *vindicatory* punishments to take vengeance of his sins, but probatory chastisements to make trial of his graces. *Bramhall's Answer to Hobbs.*

2. Defensory; justificatory.

VINDI'CTIVE. *adj.* [from *vindicta*, Latin.] Given to revenge; revengeful.

I am *vindictive* enough to repel force by force. *Dryden.*

Augustus was of a nature too *vindictive*, to have contented himself with so small a revenge. *Dryden.*

VINE. *n. s.* [*vinea*, Latin.] The plant that bears the grape.

The flower consists of many leaves placed in a regular order, and expanding in form of a rose: the ovary, which is situated in the bottom of the flower, becomes a round fruit, full of juice, and contains many small stones in each. The tree is climbing, sending forth claspers at the joints, by which it fastens itself to what plant stands near it, and the fruit is produced in bunches. The species are, 1. The wild vine, commonly called the claret grape. 2. The July grape. 3. The Corinth grape, vulgarly called the currant grape. 4. The parsley leav'd grape. 5. The miller's grape. This is called the Burgundy in England: the leaves of this sort are very much powdered with white in the spring, from whence it had the name of miller's grape. 6. Is what is called in Burgundy Pineau, and at Orleans, Auverna: it makes very good wine. 7. The white chasselas, or royal muscadine: it is a large white grape; the juice is very rich. 8. The black chasselas, or black muscadine; the juice is very rich. 9. The red chasselas, or red muscadine. 10 The burlake grape. 11. The white mustat, or white Frontiniac. 12. The red Frontiniac. 13. The black Frontiniac. 14. The damask grape. 15. The white sweet water. 16. The black sweet water. 17. The white muscadine. 18. The raisin grape. 19. The Greek grape. 20. The pearl grape. 21 The St. Peter's grape, or hesperian. 22. The malmsey grape. 23. The malmsey muscadine. 24. The red Hamburgh grape 25. The black Hamburgh, or warmer grape. 26. The Switzerland grape. 27. The white muscat, or Frontiniac of Alexandria; called also the Jerusalem muscat and gross muscat. 28. The red muscat, or Frontiniac of Alexandria. 29. The white melie grape. 30. The white morillon. 31. The Alicant grape. 32. The white Auvernat. 33. The grey Auvernat. 34. The raisin muscat. The late duke of Tuscany, who was very curious in collecting all the sorts of Italian and Greek grapes into his vineyards, was possessed of upwards of three hundred several varieties. *Miller.*

The *vine*-prop elm, the poplar never dry. *Fairy Queen.*

In her days every man shall eat in safety,
Under his own *vine*, what he plants. *Shakesp.*

The captain left of the poor to be *vine*-dressers. 2 *Kings* xxv.

Depending *vines* the shelving cavern screen,
With purple clusters blushing through the green. *Pope.*

VI'NEGAR. *n. s.* [*vinaigre*, Fr.]

1. Wine grown sour.

Vinegar is made by setting the vessel of wine against the hot sun; and therefore *vinegar* will not burn, much of the finer parts being exhaled. *Bacon.*

Heav'n's blest beam turns *vinegar* more sour. *Pope.*

2. Any thing really or metaphorically sour.

Some laugh like parrots at a bag-piper,
And others of such *vinegar* aspect,
That they'll not show their teeth in way of smile. *Shakesp.*

VI'NNEWED, or *Vinney. adj.* Mouldy. *Ainsworth.*

VI'NEYARD. *n. s.* [pingeapꝺ, Saxon.] A ground planted with vines.

Let us not live in France; let us quit all,
And give our *vineyards* to a barb'rous people. *Shakesp.*

Though some had so surfeited in the *vineyards*, and with the wines, that they had been left behind, the generosity of the Spaniards sent them all home again. *Clarendon.*

VI'NOUS. *adj.* [from *vinum*, Latin.] Having the qualities of wine; consisting of wine.

The motion of the oily drops may be in part due to some partial solution made by the *vinous* spirit. *Boyle.*

Water will imbibe
The small remains of spirit, and acquire
A *vinous* flavour. *Philips.*

VI'NTAGE. *n. s.* [*vinage*, Fr.] The produce of the vine for the year.

The best wines are in the driest *vintages*. *Bacon.*

Our first success in war make Bacchus crown,
And half the *vintage* of the year our own. *Waller.*

VI'NTAGER. *n. s.* [from *vintage.*] He who gathers the vintage. *Ainsworth.*

VI'NTNER. *n. s.* [from *vinum*, Lat.] One who sells wine.

The *vintner* may draw what religion he pleases. *Howel.*

The *vintner*, by mixing poison with his wines, destroys more lives than any malignant disease. *Swift.*

VI'NTRY. *n. s.* The place where wine is sold. *Ainsworth.*

VI'OL. *n. s.* [*violle*, Fr. *viola*, Ital.] A stringed instrument of musick.

My tongue's use is to me no more,
Than an unstringed *viol*, or a harp. *Shakesp.*

To strain a string, stop it with the finger, as in the necks of lutes and *viols*. *Bacon.*

Loud o'er the rest Cremona's trump doth sound;
Me softer airs besit, and softer strings
Of lute, or *viol*, still more apt for mournful things. *Milton.*

VI'OLABLE. *adj.* [from *violabilis*, Lat.] Such as may be violated or hurt.

VIOLA'CEOUS. *adj.* [from *viola*, Lat] Resembling violets.

To VIOLATE. *v. a.* [*violo*, Lat.]

1. To injure; to hurt.

I question thy bold entrance,
Employ'd to *violate* the sleep of those
Whose dwelling God hath planted here in bliss. *Milton.*

Kindness for man, and pity for his fate,
May mix with bliss, and yet not *violate*. *Dryden.*

Cease
To know what known will *violate* thy peace. *Pope.*

2. To infringe; to break any thing venerable.

Some of *violated* vows
'Twixt the souls of friend and friend. *Shakespeare.*

Those offences which are by their special qualities breaches of supernatural laws, do also, for that they are generally evil, *violate* in general that principle of reason, which willeth universally to fly from evil. *Hooker.*

3. To injure by irreverence.

I would *violate* my own arm rather than a church. *Brown.*

Forbid to *violate* the sacred fruit. *Milton.*

4. To ravish; to deflower.

The Sabines *violated* charms
Obscur'd the glory of his rising arms. *Prior.*

VIOLA'TION. *n. s.* [*violatio*, Lat.]

1. Infringement or injury of something sacred.

Their right conceit that to perjury vengeance is due, was not without good effect, as touching the course of their lives, who feared the wilful *violation* of oaths. *Hooker.*

Men, who had no other guide but their reason, considered the *violation* of an oath to be a great crime. *Addison.*

2. Rape; the act of deflowering.

If your pure maidens fall into the hand
Of hot and forcing *violation*. *Shakes.*

VIOLA'TOR. *n. s.* [*violator*, Lat.]

1. One who injures or infringes something sacred.

May such places, built for divine worship, derive a blessing upon the head of the builders, as lasting as the curse that never fails to rest upon the sacrilegious *violators* of them. *South.*

2. A ravisher.

Angelo is an adult'rous thief,
An hypocrite, a virgin *violator*. *Shakes.*

How does she subject herself to the *violator*'s upbraidings and insults. *Clarissa.*

VI'OLENCE. *n. s.* [*violentia*, Latin.]

1. Force; strength applied to any purpose.

To be imprison'd in the viewless wind,
And blown with restless *violence* about. *Shakesp.*

All the elements
At least had gone to wreck, disturb'd and torn
With *violence* of this conflict, had not soon
Th' eternal hung his golden scales. *Milton.*

2. An attack; an assault; a murder.

A noise did scare me from the tomb;
And she, too desperate, would not go with me:
But, as it seems, did *violence* on herself. *Shakesp.*

3. Outrage; unjust force.

Griev'd at his heart, when looking down he saw
The whole earth fill'd with *violence*; and all flesh
Corrupting each their way. *Milton's Par. Lost.*

4. Eagerness; vehemence.

That seal
You ask with such *violence*, the king
With his own hand gave me. *Shakesp.*

5. Injury; infringement.

We cannot, without offering *violence* to all records, divine and human, deny an universal deluge. *Burnet.*

6. Forcible defloration.

VI'OLENT. *adj.* [*violentus*, Lat.]

1. Forcible; acting with strength.

A *violent* cross wind blows. *Milton.*

2. Produced or continued by force.

The posture we find them in, according to his doctrine, must be look'd upon as unnatural and *violent*; and no *violent* state can be perpetual. *Burnet.*

3. Not natural, but brought by force.

Conqueror death discovers them scarce men;
Violent or shameful death their due reward. *Milton.*

4. Un-

4. Unjustly assailant; murderous.

Some *violent* hands were laid on Humphry's life. *Shakesp.*

A foe subtile or *violent*. *Milton.*

5. Unseasonably vehement.

We might be reckoned fierce and *violent*, to tear away that, which, if our mouths did condemn, our consciences would storm and repine thereat. *Hooker.*

The covetous extortioner should remember, that such *violents* shall not take heaven, but hell by force. *Decay of Piety.*

6. Extorted; not voluntary.

Vows made in pain, are *violent* and void. *Milton.*

VI'OLENTLY. *adv.* [from *violent*.] With force; forcibly; vehemently.

Temp'rately proceed to what you would
Thus *violently* redress. *Shakesp. Coriolanus.*

Flame burneth more *violently* towards the sides, than in the midst. *Bacon.*

Antient privileges must not, without great necessities, be revoked, nor forfeitures be exacted *violently*, nor penal laws urged rigorously. *Taylor's Rule of living holy.*

VI'OLET. *n. s.* [*violette*, Fr. *viola*, Lat.] A plant.

It hath a polypetalous anomalous flower, somewhat resembling the papilionaceous flower; for its two upper petals represent the standard, the two side ones the wings; but the lower one, which ends in a tail, resembles the iris. Out of the empalement arises the pointal, which becomes a three-cornered fruit opening into three parts, and full of roundish seeds. There are nine species. *Miller.*

When daisies pied, and *violets* blue,
Do paint the meadows much bedight. *Shakesp.*

Sweet echo, sweetest nymph that liv'st unseen,
By slow Meander's margent green,
And in the *violet*-embroider'd vale. *Milton.*

It alters not our simple idea, whether we think that blue be in the *violet* itself, or in our mind only; and only the power of producing it by the texture of its parts, to be in the *violet* itself. *Locke.*

VI'OLIN. *n. s.* [*violon*, Fr. from *viol*.] A fiddle; a stringed instrument of musick.

Praise with timbrels, organs, flutes;
Praise with *violins*, and lutes. *Sandys.*

Sharp *violins* proclaim
Their jealous pangs, and desperation,
For the fair disdainful dame. *Dryden.*

VI'OLIST. *n. s.* [from *viol*.] A player on the viol.

VIOLONCE'LLO. n. s. [Italian.] A stringed instrument of musick.

VI'PER. *n. s.* [*vipera*, Lat.]

1. A serpent of that species which brings its young alive, of which most are poisonous.

A *viper* came out of the heat, and fastened on his hand. *Acts* xxviii. 3.

He'll gall of asps with thirsty lips suck in;
The *viper*'s deadly teeth shall pierce his skin. *Sandys.*

Viper-catchers have a remedy, in which they place such great confidence, as to be no more afraid of the bite of a *viper*, than of a common puncture. This is no other than axungia viperina, presently rubbed into the wound. *Derham.*

2. Any thing mischievous.

Where is this *viper*,
That would depopulate the city, and
Be every man himself? *Shakesp. Coriolanus.*

VI'PERINE. *n. s.* [*viperinus*, Lat.] Belonging to a viper.

VI'PEROUS. *adj.* [*vipereus*, Lat. from *viper*.] Having the qualities of a *viper*.

My tender years can tell,
Civil dissention is a *vip'rous* worm,
That gnaws the bowels of the commonwealth. *Shakesp.*

We are peremptory to dispatch
This *viperous* traitor. *Shakesp.*

Some *vip'rous* critick may bereave
Th' opinion of thy worth for some defect. *Daniel's Musoph.*

VIPER's *bugloss*. *n. s.* [*echium*, Lat.] A plant.

The characters are, the cup of the flower is large, and divided into five long slender segments; the flower consists of one leaf, is shaped like a funnel, and somewhat inflected, having its upper part stretched, but in a greater length than the lower: the upper part, or galea of the flower, is divided into two; and the lower part, or beard, into three parts: in the middle of the flower are produced five stamina (or threads) which are reflexed. Each flower is succeeded by four seeds, which are in form of a viper's head. *Miller.*

VIPER's *grass*. *n. s.* [*scorzonera*, Lat.] A plant.

It hath a semi-flosculous flower, consisting of many half florets, which rest upon the embryoes, which are included in one common empalement, which is scaly: the embryoes afterwards become oblong seeds, which are furnished with down. *Miller.*

VIRA'GO. n. s. [Latin.]

1. A female warriour; a woman with the qualities of a man.

Melpomene represented like a *virago* or manly lady, with a majestick and grave countenance. *Peacham.*

To arms! to arms! the fierce *virago* cries,
And swift as lightening to the combat flies. *Pope.*

2. It is commonly used in detestation for an impudent turbulent woman.

VI'RELAY. *n. s.* [*virelay*, *virelai*, Fr.] A sort of little ancient French poem, that consisted only of two rhymes and short verses, with stops. *L'Acad.*

The mournful muse in mirth now list ne mask,
As she was wont in youngth and summer days;
But if thou algate lust like *virelays*,
And looser songs of love to undersong. *Spenser.*

The band of flutes began to play,
To which a lady sung a *virelay*:
And still at ev'ry close she would repeat
The burden of the song, the daisy is so sweet. *Dryden.*

VI'RENT. *adj.* [*virens*, Lat.] Green; not faded.

In these, yet fresh and *virent*, they carve out the figures of men and women. *Brown's Vulgar Errours.*

VI'RGE. *n. s.* [*virga*, Lat. better *verge*, from *verge*, French.] A dean's mace.

Suppose him now a dean compleat,
Devoutly lolling in his seat;
The silver *virge*, with decent pride,
Stuck underneath his cushion side. *Swift.*

VI'RGIN. *n. s.* [*vierge*, Fr. *virgo*, Lat.]

1. A maid; a woman unacquainted with men.

This aspect of mine hath fear'd the valiant;
The best regarded *virgins* of our clime
Have lov'd it too. *Shakesp.*

Senseless bauble!
Art thou a fœdary for this act, and look'st
So *virgin*-like without? *Shakesp. Cymbeline.*

The damsel was very fair, and a *virgin*. *Gen.* xxiv. 16.

Angelo is an adult'rous thief,
An hypocrite, a *virgin* violator. *Shakespeare.*

Much less can that have any place,
At which a *virgin* hides her face. *Cowley.*

2. A woman not a mother. Unusual.

Likest to Ceres in her prime,
Yet *virgin* of Proserpina from Jove. *Milton.*

3. Any thing untouched or unmingled.

Tapers of white wax, commonly called *virgin* wax, burn with less smoke than common yellow wax. *Boyle.*

I have found *virgin* earth in the peat-marshes of Cheshire. *Woodward.*

Below the upper was a deep bed of sand only, which I weighed, together with the *virgin*-mould. *Derham.*

4. The sign of the zodiack in which the sun is in August.

Thence down amain by Leo and the *Virgin*. *Milton.*

VI'RGIN. *adj.* Befitting a virgin; suitable to a virgin; maidenly.

Can you blame her then, being a maid, yet rosed over with the *virgin* crimson of modesty, if she deny the appearance of a naked blind boy. *Shakesp. Hen.* V.

What says the silver with her *virgin* hue? *Shakes.*

With ease a brother o'ercame
The formal decencies of *virgin*-shame. *Cowley.*

To VI'RGIN. *v. n.* [a cant word.] To play the virgin.

A kiss
Long as my exile, sweet as my revenge!
I carried from thee, my dear; and my true lip
Hath *virgin'd* it e'er since. *Shakespeare's Coriolanus.*

VI'RGINAL. *adj.* [from *virgin*.] Maiden; maidenly; pertaining to a virgin.

On the earth more fair was never seen,
Of chastity and honour *virginal*. *Fairy Queen.*

Tears *virginal*
Shall be to me even as the dew to fire;
And beauty, that the tyrant oft reclaims,
Shall to my flaming wrath be oil and flax. *Shakesp.*

Purity is a special part of this superstructure, restraining of all desires of the flesh within the known limits of conjugal or *virginal* chastity. *Hammond's Fundamentals.*

To VI'RGINAL. *v. n.* To pat; to strike as on the virginal. A cant word.

Still *virginalling* upon thy palm. *Shakesp.*

VI'RGINAL. *n. s.* [more usually *virginals*.] A musical instrument so called, because commonly used by young ladies.

The musician hath produced two means of straining strings. The one is stopping them with the finger, as in the necks of lutes and viols; the other is the shortness of the string, as in harps and *virginals*. *Bacon.*

VIRGI'NITY. *n. s.* [*virginitas*, Lat.] Maidenhead; unacquaintance with man.

You do impeach your modesty too much,
To trust the opportunity of night,
And the ill counsel of a desart place,
With the rich worth of your *virginity*. *Shakesp.*

Natural *virginity* of itself is not a state more acceptable to God; but that which is chosen in order to the conveniencies of religion, and separation from worldly incumbrances. *Taylor.*

VI'RILE. *n. s.* [*virilis*, Lat.] Belonging to man; not puerile; not feminine.

VIRI'LITY. *n. s.* [*virilité*, Fr. *virilitas*, Lat. from *virile.*]
1. Manhood; character of man.
The lady made generous advances to the borders of *virility.* *Rambler.*
2. Power of procreation.
The great climacterical was past, before they begat children, or gave any testimony of their *virility*; for none begat children before the age of sixty-five. *Brown.*

VIRMI'LION. *n. s.* Properly *vermilion.* A red colour.
Ægle, the fairest Nais of the flood,
With a *vermilion* dye his temples stain'd. *Roscommon.*

VI'RTUAL. *adj.* [*virtuel*, Fr. from *virtue.*] Having the efficacy without the sensible or material part.
Metalline waters have *virtual* cold in them. Put therefore wood into smith's water, and try whether it will not harden. *Bacon.*
Heat and cold have a *virtual* transition, without communication of substance. *Bacon.*
Love not the heav'nly spirits? And how their love
Express they? by looks only? or, do they mix
Irradiance? *virtual*, or immediate touch? *Milton.*
Every kind that lives,
Fomented by his *virtual* pow'r, and warm'd. *Milton.*
Neither an actual or *virtual* intention of the mind, but only that which may be gathered from the outward acts. *Stillingfleet.*

VIRTUA'LITY. *n. s.* [from *virtual.*] Efficacy.
In one grain of corn there lieth dormant a *virtuality* of many other, and from thence sometimes proceed an hundred ears. *Brown's Vulgar Errours.*

VI'RTUALLY. *adv.* [from *virtual.*] In effect, though not formally.
They are *virtually* contained in other words still continued. *Hammond's Fundamentals.*
Such is our constitution, that the bulk of the people *virtually* give their approbation to every thing they are bound to obey. *Addison.*

To VI'RTUATE. *v. a.* [from *virtue.*] To make efficacious.
Potable gold should be endued with a capacity of being assimilated to the innate heat, and radical moisture; or at least *virtuated* with a power of generating the said essentials. *Harvey.*

VI'RTUE. *n. s.* [*virtus*, Lat.]
1. Moral goodness.
Either I'm mistaken, or there is *virtue* in that Falstaff. *Shakes.*
If there's a power above us,
And that there is, all nature cries aloud
Through all her works, he must delight in *virtue*,
And that which he delights in must be happy. *Addison.*
Virtue only makes our bliss below. *Pope.*
The character of prince Henry is improved by Shakespear; and through the veil of his vices and irregularities, we see a dawn of greatness and *virtue.* *Shakesp. illustrated.*
2. A particular moral excellence.
In Belmont is a lady,
And she is fair, and, fairer than that word,
Of wond'rous *virtues.* *Shakesp. Merchant of Venice.*
Remember all his *virtues*,
And shew mankind that goodness is your care. *Addison.*
3. Medicinal quality.
All blest secrets,
All you unpublish'd *virtues* of the earth,
Be aidant and remediate. *Shakesp. K. Lear.*
The virtuous bezoar is taken from the beast that feedeth upon the mountains; and that without *virtue* from those that feed in the vallies. *Bacon.*
4. Medicinal efficacy.
An essay writer must practise the chymical method, and give the *virtue* of a full draught in a few drops. *Addison.*
5. Efficacy; power.
If neither words, nor herbs will do, I'll try stones; for there's a *virtue* in them. *L'Estrange.*
Where there is a full purpose to please God, there, what a man can do, shall, by *virtue* thereof, be accepted. *South.*
They are not sure, by *virtue* of syllogism, that the conclusion certainly follows from the premises. *Locke.*
This they shall attain, partly in *virtue* of the promise made by God; and partly in *virtue* of piety. *Atterbury.*
He used to travel through Greece, by *virtue* of this fable, which procured him reception in all the towns. *Addison.*
6. Acting power.
Jesus knowing that *virtue* had gone out of him, turned him about. *Mark* v. 30.
7. Secret agency; efficacy, without visible or material action.
She moves the body, which she doth possess;
Yet no part toucheth, but by *virtue*'s touch. *Davies.*
8. Bravery; valour.
Trust to thy single *virtue*; for thy soldiers
Took their discharge. *Shakesp. K. Lear.*
The conquest of Palestine, with singular *virtue* they performed, and held that kingdom some few generations. *Raleigh.*
9. Excellence; that which gives excellence.
In the Greek poets, as also in Plautus, the oeconomy of poems is better observed than in Terence; who thought the sole grace and *virtue* of their fable, the sticking in of sentences, as ours do the forcing in of jests. *B. Johnson.*
10. One of the orders of the celestial hierarchy.
Thrones, domination, princedoms, *virtues*, pow'rs. *Milt.*
A winged *virtue* through th' etherial sky,
From orb to orb unwearied dost thou fly. *Tickell.*

VI'RTUELESS. *adj.* [from *virtue.*]
1. Wanting virtue; deprived of virtue.
2. Not having efficacy; without operating qualities.
All second causes, together with nature herself, without that operative faculty which God gave them, would become altogether silent, *virtueless*, and dead. *Raleigh.*
Virtueless she wisht all herbs and charms,
Wherewith false men increase their patients harms. *Fairfax.*
Some would make those glorious creatures *virtueless.* *Hakewill.*

VIRTUO'SO. *n. s.* [Italian.] A man skilled in antique or natural curiosities; a man studious of painting, statuary, or architecture.
Methinks those generous *virtuosi* dwell in a higher region than other mortals. *Glanville.*
Virtuoso, the Italians call a man who loves the noble arts, and is a critick in them. And amongst our French painters, the word *vertueux* is understood in the same signification. *Dryd.*
This building was beheld with admiration by the *virtuosi* of that time. *Tatler*, N°. 52.
Showers of rain are now met with in every water-work; and the *virtuoso's* of France covered a little vault with artificial snow. *Addison.*

VI'RTUOUS. *adj.* [from *virtue.*]
1. Morally good.
If his occasion were not *virtuous*,
I should not urge it half so faithfully. *Shakespeare.*
Virtuous and holy, be thou conqueror. *Shakespeare.*
What she wills to do or say,
Is wisest, *virtuousest*, discreetest, best. *Milton.*
Favour'd of heav'n, who finds
One *virtuous* rarely found,
That in domestick good combines:
Happy that house! his way to peace is smooth. *Milton.*
2. [Applied to women.] Chaste.
Mistress Ford, the modest wife, the *virtuous* creature, that hath the jealous fool to her husband! *Shakesp.*
3. Done in consequence of moral goodness.
Nor love is always of a vicious kind,
But oft to *virtuous* acts inflames the mind. *Dryden.*
4. Efficacious; powerful.
With one *virtuous* touch, th' arch-chemic sun,
Produces, with terrestrial humour mix'd,
Here in the dark, so many precious things. *Milton.*
5. Having wonderful or eminent properties.
Out of his hand,
That *virtuous* steel he rudely snatch'd away. *Fairy Queen.*
Lifting up his *virtuous* staff on high,
He smote the sea, which calmed was with speed. *Spenser.*
He own'd that *virtuous* ring and glass. *Milton.*
6. Having medicinal qualities.
Some observe that there is a *virtuous* bezoar, and another without virtue; the *virtuous* is taken from the beast that feedeth where there are theriacal herbs; and that without virtue, from those that feed where no such herbs are. *Bacon.*
The ladies sought around
For *virtuous* herbs, which, gather'd from the ground,
They squeez'd the juice; and cooling ointment made. *Dryd.*

VI'RTUOUSLY. *adv.* [from *virtuous.*] In a virtuous manner; according to the rules of virtue.
The Gods are my witnesses, I desire to do *virtuously.* *Sidney.*
In sum, they taught the world no less *virtuously* how to die, than they had done before how to live. *Hooker.*
They that mean *virtuously*, and yet do so,
The devil their virtue tempts not, they tempt heav'n. *Shak.*
Not from grey hairs authority doth flow,
Nor from bald heads, nor from a wrinkled brow;
But our past life, when *virtuously* spent,
Must to our age those happy fruits present. *Denham.*
The coffeeman has a little daughter four years old, who has been *virtuously* educated. *Addison.*

VI'RTUOUSNESS. *n. s.* [from *virtuous.*] The state or character of being virtuous.
Many other adventures are intermeddled; as the love of Britomert, and *virtuousness* of Belphæbe; and the lasciviousness of Helenora. *Spenser.*

VI'RULENCE. } *n. s.* [from *virulent.*] Mental poison; malig-
VI'RULENCY. } nity; acrimony of temper; bitterness.
Disputes in religion are managed with *virulency* and bitterness. *Decay of Piety.*
It instils into their minds the utmost *virulence*, instead of that charity which is the perfection and ornament of religion. *Addison.*
The whigs might easily have maintained a majority among the clergy, if they had not too much encouraged this intemperance of speech, and *virulence* of pen, in the most prostitute of their party. *Swift.*

VI'RULENT. *adj.* [*virulent*, Fr. *virulentus*, Lat.]
1. Poisonous; venemous.
2. Poisoned in the mind; bitter; malignant.

VI'RULENTLY. *adv.* [from *virulent*.] Malignantly; with bitterness.

VI'SAGE. *n. s.* [*visage*, Fr. *visaggio*, Italian.] Face; countenance; look. It is now rarely used but with some ideas of dislike or horrour.

Phebe doth behold
Her silver *visage* in the watry glass,
Decking with liquid pearl the bladed grass. *Shakesp.*
When she shall hear this of thee, with her nails
She'll flea thy wolfish *visage*. *Shakesp. K. Lear.*
Whereto serves mercy,
But to confront the *visage* of offence. *Shakesp. Hamlet.*
With hostile frown,
And *visage* all inflam'd, first thus began. *Milton.*
By the rout, that made the hideous roar,
His goary *visage* down the stream was sent;
Down the swift Hebrus to the Lesbian shore. *Milton.*
Love and beauty still that *visage* grace;
Death cannot fright 'em from their wonted place. *Waller.*

To VI'SCERATE. *v. a.* [*viscera*, Latin.] To embowel; to exentrate.

VI'SCID. *adj.* [*viscidus*, Latin.] Glutinous; tenacious.

VISCI'DITY. *n. s.* [from *viscid*.]
1. Glutinousness; tenacity; ropiness.

This motion in some human creatures may be weak, in respect to the *viscidity* of what is taken, so as not to be able to propel it. *Arbuthnot.*

2. Glutinous concretion.

Catharticks of mercurials precipitate the *viscidities* by their stypticity. *Floyer.*

VISCO'SITY. *n. s.* [*viscosité*, Fr. from *viscous*.]
1. Glutinousness; tenacity.

The air being mixed with the animal fluids, determines their condition as to rarity, density, *viscosity*, tenuity. *Arbuth.*

2. A glutinous substance.

A tenuous emanation, or continued effluvium, after some distance, retracteth unto itself, as is observable in drops of syrups, and seminal *viscosities*. *Brown's Vulg. Errours.*

VI'SCOUNT. *n. s.* [*vicecomes*, Lat.]

Viscount signifies as much as sheriff; between which two words there is no other difference, but that the one comes from our conquerors the Normans, and the other from our ancestors the Saxons. *Viscount* also signifies a degree of nobility next to an earl, which is an old name of office, but a new one of dignity, never heard of amongst us, till Henry VI. his days. *Cowel.*

VISCOU'NTESS. *n. s.* [from *viscount*. *Viscount* and *viscountess* are pronounced *vicount* and *vicountess*.] The lady of a viscount; a peeress of the fourth order.

VI'SCOUS. *adj.* [*visqueux*, Fr. *viscosus*, Lat.] Glutinous; sticky; tenacious.

The cause of the scouring virtue of nitre is, that it hath a subtle spirit, which severeth and divideth any thing that is foul and *viscous*. *Bacon.*

Holly is of so *viscous* a juice as they make bird-lime of the bark. *Bacon.*

VISIBI'LITY. *n. s.* [*visibilité*, Fr. from *visible*.]
1. The state or quality of being perceptible by the eye.

The colours of outward objects brought into a darkened room, do much depend for their *visibility*, upon the dimness of the light they are beheld by. *Boyle.*

2. State of being apparent, or openly discoverable; conspicuousness.

They produced this as an instance against the perpetual *visibility* of the church, and he brings it to prove that it ceased to be a true church. *Stillingfleet.*

In these, the *visibility* and example of our virtues will chiefly consist. *Rogers's Sermons.*

VI'SIBLE. *n. s.* [*visible*, Fr. *visibilis*, Lat.]
1. Perceptible by the eye.

Visibles work upon a looking-glass, which is like the pupil of the eye; and audibles upon the places of echo, which resemble the cavern of the ear. *Bacon.*

On this mount he appeared; under this tree
Stood *visible*;
Here with him at this fountain talk'd. *Milton.*
Each thought was *visible*, that roll'd within,
As through a crystal case the figur'd hours are seen. *Dryden.*

A long series of ancestors shews the native lustre with great advantage; but if he degenerate from his line, the least spot is *visible* on ermine. *Dryden.*

2. Discovered to the eye.

If that the heavens do not their *visible* spirits
Send quickly down to tame the vile offences,
Humanity must perforce prey on itself,
Like monsters of the deep. *Shakesp. K. Lear.*

3. Apparent; open; conspicuous.

The factions at court were greater, or more *visible* than before. *Clarendon.*

4

VI'SIBLENESS. *n. s.* [from *visible*.] State or quality of being visible.

VI'SIBLY. *adv.* [from *visible*.] In a manner perceptible by the eye.

The day being *visibly* governed by the sun, is a little longer than the revolution of the equator; so much as is occasioned by the advance of the sun in his annual contrary motion along the ecliptick. *Holder.*

By the head we make known more *visibly* our supplications, our threatnings; enough to see the face, and to understand the mind at half a word. *Dryden.*

VI'SION. *n. s.* [*vision*, Fr. *visio*, Latin.]
1. Sight; the faculty of seeing.

Anatomists, when they have taken off from the bottom of the eye that outward and most thick coat called the dura mater, can then see through the thinner coats, the pictures of objects lively painted thereon. And these pictures, propagated by motion along the fibres of the optick nerves into the brain, are the cause of *vision*. *Newton's Opticks.*

These theorems being admitted into optics, there would be scope enough of handling that science voluminously, after a new manner; not only by teaching those things which tend to the perfection of *vision*, but also by determining mathematically all kinds of phenomena of colours which could be produced by refractions. *Newton's Opticks.*

2. The act of seeing.

Vision in the next life is the perfecting of faith in this; or faith here is turned into *vision* there, as hope into enjoying. *Hammond's Pract. Catechism.*

3. A supernatural appearance; a spectre; a phantom.

The day seems long, but night is odious;
No sleep, but dreams; no dreams, but *visions* strange. *Sidney.*
Last night the very gods shew'd me a *vision*. *Shakesp.*
God's mother deigned to appear to me;
And, in a *vision*, full of majesty,
Will'd me to leave my base vocation. *Shakesp. Hen. VI.*
Him God vouchsaf'd,
To call by *vision*, from his father's house,
Into a land which he will shew him. *Milton's Par. Lost.*

4. A dream; something shewn in a dream. A dream happens to a sleeping, a vision may happen to a waking man. A dream is supposed natural, a vision miraculous; but they are confounded.

His dream returns; his friend appears again:
The murd'rers come; now help, or I am slain!
'Twas but a *vision* still, and *visions* are but vain. *Dryden.*

The idea of any thing in our mind, no more proves the existence of that thing, than the *visions* of a dream make a true history. *Locke.*

VI'SIONARY. *adj.* [*visionnaire*, Fr. from *vision*.]
1. Affected by phantoms; disposed to receive impressions on the imagination.

No more these scenes my meditation aid,
Or lull to rest the *visionary* maid. *Pope's Eloisa to Abelard.*

2. Imaginary; not real; seen in a dream; perceived by the imagination only.

The hounds at nearer distance hoarsly bray'd;
The hunter close pursu'd the *visionary* maid. *Dryden.*

If you have any skill in dreams, let me know whether I have the same place in the real heart, that I had in the *visionary* one. *Addison.*

Our victories only led us to further *visionary* prospects; advantage was taken of the sanguine temper which success had wrought the nation up to. *Swift.*

VI'SIONARY. } *n. s.* [*visionaire*, Fr.] One whose imagination is
VI'SIONIST. } disturbed.

The lovely *visionary* gave him perpetual uneasiness. *Fem. Quix.*

To VI'SIT. *v. a.* [*visiter*, Fr. *visito*, Lat.]
1. To go to see.

You must go *visit* the lady that lies in.——I *visit* her with my prayers; but I cannot go thither. *Shakesp. Coriolanus.*

Virgins *visited* by angel pow'rs. *Pope.*

2. [In scriptural language.] To send good or evil judicially.

When God *visiteth*, what shall I answer him? *Job* xxxi. 14.
Thou shalt be *visited* of the Lord with thunder. *Isa.* xxix. 6.
When I *visit*, I will *visit* their sin upon them. *Ex.* xxxii. 34.
God *visit* thee in good things. *Judith* xiii. 20.

That venerable body is in little concern after what manner their mortal enemies intend to treat them, whenever God shall *visit* us with so fatal an event. *Swift.*

3. To salute with a present.

Samson *visited* his wife with a kid. *Judges* xv. 1.

4. To come to a survey, with judicial authority.

The bishop ought to *visit* his diocese every year in person. *Ayliffe.*

To VI'SIT. *v. n.* To keep up the intercourse of ceremonial salutations at the houses of each other.

VI'SIT. *n. s.* [*visite*, Fr. from the verb.] The act of going to see another.

In a designed or accidental *visit*, let some one take a book, which may be agreeable, and read in it. *Watts.*

VISI-

VI'SITABLE. *adj.* [from *visit.*] Liable to be visited.

All hospitals built since the reformation, are *visitable* by the king or lord chancellor. *Ayliffe's Parergon.*

VI'SITANT. *n. s.* [from *visit.*] One who goes to see another.

He alone
To find where Adam shelter'd, took his way,
Not unperceiv'd of Adam, who to Eve,
While the great *visitant* approach'd, thus spake. *Milton.*

One visit begins an acquaintance; and when the *visitant* comes again, he is no more a stranger. *South.*

Edward the first, who had been a *visitant* in Spain, upon action in the holy land, fixed both our pounds by the measures of the East. *Arbuthnot on Coins.*

Griev'd that a *visitant* so long shou'd wait
Unmark'd, unhonour'd, at a monarch's gate,
Instant he flew. *Pope's Odyssey. b.* i. l. 160.

VISITA'TION. *n. s.* [*visito*, Latin.]

1. The act of visiting.

He comes not
Like to his father's greatness; his approach,
So out of circumstance and sudden, tells us,
'Tis not a *visitation* fram'd, but forc'd
By need and accident. *Shakesp. Winter Tale.*

What would you with the princess?——
——Nothing but peace and gentle *visitation.* *Shakespeare.*

2. Object of visits.

O flow'rs,
My early *visitation*, and my last. *Milton's Par. Lost.*

3. [*Visitation*, Fr.] Judicial visit or perambulation.

The bishop ought to visit his diocese every year in person, unless he omits the same because he would not burthen his churches; and then ought to send his arch-deacon, which was the original of the arch-deacon's *visitation.* *Ayliffe.*

4. Judicial evil sent by God; state of suffering judicial evil.

That which thou dost not understand when thou readest, thou shalt understand in the day of thy *visitation.* For many secrets of religion are not perceived till they be felt, and are not felt but in the day of a great calamity. *Taylor.*

5. Communication of divine love.

The most comfortable *visitations* God hath sent men from above, have taken especially the times of prayer as their most natural opportunities. *Hooker.*

VISITATO'RIAL. *adj.* [from *visitor.*] Belonging to a judicial visitor.

Some will have it, that an archdeacon does of common right execute this *visitatorial* power in his archdeaconry: but others say that an archdeacon has a *visitatorial* power only of common right *per modum simplicis scrutinii*, as being bishop's vicar. *Ayliffe's Parergon.*

VI'SITER. *n. s.* [from *visit.*]

1. One who comes to see another.

Here's ado to lock up honesty and honour from the access of gentle *visitors.* *Shakespeare.*

You see this confluence, this great flood of *visiters.* *Shakes.*

Consumptives of this degree entertain their *visiters* with strange rambling discourses of their intent of going here and there. *Harvey.*

I have a large house, yet I should hardly prevail to find one *visiter*, if I were not able to hire him with a bottle of wine. *Swift to Gay.*

2. [*Visiteur*, Fr.] An occasional judge; one who regulates the disorders of any society.

The *visiters* expell'd the orthodox; they, without scruple or shame, possess'd themselves of their colleges. *Walton.*

To him you must your sickly state refer;
Your charter claims him as your *visiter.* *Garth.*

Whatever abuses have crept into the universities, might be reformed by strict injunctions to the *visitors* and heads of houses. *Swift's Project for the Advancement of Religion.*

VI'SNOMY. *n. s.* [corrupted from *physiognomy.*] Face; countenance. Not in use.

Twelve gods do sit around in royal state,
And Jove in midst with awful majesty,
To judge the strife between them stirred late:
Each of the gods by his like *visnomy*
Eath to be known, but Jove above them all,
By his great looks and pow'r imperial. *Spenser.*

VI'SIVE. *adj.* [*visif*, Fr. *visus*, Lat.] Formed in the act of seeing.

This happens when the axis of the *visive* cones, diffused from the object, fall not upon the same plane; but that which is conveyed into one eye is more depressed or elevated than that which enters the other. *Brown's Vulgar Errours.*

VI'SOR. *n. s.* [This word is variously written *visard*, *visar*, *visor*, *vizard*, *vizor*. I prefer *visor*, as nearest the Latin *visus*, and concurring with *visage*, a kindred word; *visiere*, French.] A mask used to disfigure and disguise.

I fear, indeed, the weakness of my government before, made you think such a mask would be grateful unto me; and my weaker government since, makes you pull off the *visor.* *Sidney.*

This loutish clown is such that you never saw so ill-favoured a *visar*; his behaviour such, that he is beyond the degree of ridiculous. *Sidney.*

By which deceit doth mask in *visor* fair,
And cast her colours dyed deep in grain,
To seem like truth, whose shape she well can fain. *Spenser.*

But that thy face is, *vizor*-like, unchanging,
Made impudent with use of evil deeds,
I wou'd essay, proud queen, to make thee blush. *Shakesp.*

One *visor* remains,
And that is Claudio; I know him by his bearing. *Shakesp.*

The Cyclops, a people of Sicily, remarkable for cruelty, might, perhaps, in their wars use a head-piece, or *vizor.* *Broome's Odyss. Notes.*

VI'SORED. *v. n.* [from *visor.*] Masked.

Hence with thy brew'd enchantments, foul deceiver!
Hast thou betray'd my credulous innocence
With *visor'd* falshood, and base forgery. *Milton.*

VI'STA. *n. s.* [Italian.] View; prospect through an avenue.

In St. Peter's, when a man stands under the dome, if he looks upwards, he is astonished at the spacious hollow of the cupola, that makes one of the beautifullest *vista's* that the eye can pass through. *Addison's Remarks on Italy.*

The finish'd garden to the view
Its *vista's* opens, and its alleys green. *Thomson's Spring.*

VI'SUAL. *adj.* [*visuel*, French.] Used in sight; exercising the power of sight; instrumental to sight.

An eye thrust forth so as it hangs a pretty distance by the *visual* nerve, hath been without any power of sight; and yet, after being replaced, recovered sight. *Bacon's Nat. Hist.*

The air,
No where so clear, sharpen'd his *visual* ray
To objects distant far. *Milton's Par. Lost.*

Then purg'd with euphrasy and rue
The *visual* nerve; for he had much to see. *Milton.*

Inward light, alas,
Puts forth no *visual* beam! *Milton's Agonistes.*

VI'TAL. *adj.* [*vitalis*, Latin.]

1. Contributing to life; necessary to life.

His heart, broken with unkindness and affliction, stretched so far beyond his limits with this excess of comfort, as it was able no longer to keep safe his *vital* spirits. *Sidney.*

All nature laughs, the groves are fresh and fair;
The sun's mild lustre warms the *vital* air. *Pope.*

2. Relating to life.

Let not Bardolph's *vital* thread be cut
With edge of penny cord, and vile reproach. *Shakespeare.*

On the rock a scanty measure place
Of *vital* flax, and turn the wheel a-pace. *Dryden.*

3. Containing life.

Spirits that live throughout;
Vital in every part; not as frail man,
In intrails, heart, or head, liver, or reins,
Cannot but by annihilating die. *Milton's Par. Lost.*

On the watry calm,
His brooding wings the spirit of God outspreads;
And *vital* virtue infus'd, and *vital* warmth
Throughout the fluid mass. *Milton's Par. Lost.*

4. Being the seat of life.

The dart flew on, and pierc'd a *vital* part. *Pope.*

5. So disposed as to live. Little used, and rather Latin than English.

Pythagoras and Hippocrates not only affirm the birth of the seventh month to be *vital*, that of the eighth mortal; but the progression thereto to be measured by rule. *Brown.*

6. Essential; chiefly necessary.

Know grief's *vital* part
Consists in nature, not in art. *Bp. Corbet.*

VITA'LITY. *n. s.* [from *vital.*] Power of subsisting in life.

Whether that motion, *vitality* and operation were by incubation, or how else, the manner is only known to God. *Raleigh's Hist. of the World.*

For the security of species produced only by seed, providence hath endued all seed with a lasting *vitality*, that if by any accident it happen not to germinate the first year, it will continue its fæcundity twenty or thirty years. *Ray.*

VI'TALLY. *adv.* [from *vital.*] In such a manner as to give life.

The organical structure of human bodies, whereby they are fitted to live and move, and be *vitally* informed by the soul, is the workmanship of a most wise, powerful, and beneficent maker. *Bentley.*

VI'TALS. *n. s.* [Without the singular.] Parts essential to life.

By fits my swelling grief appears,
In rising sighs, and falling tears,
That show too well the warm desires,
The silent, slow, consuming fires,
Which on my inmost *vitals* prey,
And melt my very soul away. *Phillips.*

VITE'LLARY. *n. s.* [from *vitellus*, Latin.] The place where the yolk of the egg swims in the white.

A greater

A greater difficulty in the doctrine of eggs is, how the sperm of the cock attaineth into every egg; since the *vitellary*, or place of the yolk, is very high. *Brown's Vulg. Errours.*

To VI'TIATE. *v. a.* [*vitio*, Latin.] To deprave; to spoil; to make less pure.

The sun in his garden gives him the purity of visible objects, and of true nature, before she was *vitiated* by luxury. *Evelyn's Kalend.*

The organs of speech are managed by so many muscles, that speech is not easily destroyed, though often somewhat *vitiated* as to some particular letters. *Holder.*

Spirits encountering foul bodies, and exciting a fermentation of those *vitiated* humours, precipitate into putrid fevers. *Harvey.*

This undistinguishing complaisance will *vitiate* the taste of the readers, and misguide many of them in their judgments, where to approve and where to censure. *Garth.*

A transposition of the order of the sacramental words, in some men's opinion, *vitiates* baptism. *Ayliffe's Parergon.*

VITIA'TION. *n. s.* [from *vitiate.*] Depravation; corruption.

The foresaid extenuation of the body is imputed to the blood's *vitiation* by malign, putrid vapours smoking throughout the vessels. *Harvey on Consumptions.*

To VITILI'TIGATE. *v. n.* [*vitiosus* and *litigo*, Lat.] To contend in law.

VITILITIGA'TION. *n. s.* [from *vitilitigate.*] Contention; cavillation.

I'll force you by right ratiocination,
To leave your *vitilitigation*. *Hudibras.*

VITIO'SITY. *n. s.* [from *vitiosus*, Lat.] Depravity; corruption.

He charges it wholly upon the corruption, perverseness, and *vitiosity* of man's will, as the only cause that rendered all the arguments his doctrine came cloathed with, unsuccessful. *South's Sermons.*

VI'TIOUS. *adj.* [*vicieux*, Fr. *vitiosus*, Latin.]

1. Corrupt; wicked; opposite to virtuous. It is rather applied to habitual faults, than criminal actions.

Make known
It is no *vitious* blot, murder, or foulness
That hath depriv'd me of your grace. *Shakesp. K. Lear.*

Witness th' irreverent son
Of him who built the ark; who, for the shame
Done to his father, heard his heavy curse,
'Servant of servants,' on his *vitious* race. *Milton.*

Wit's what the *vitious* fear, the virtuous shun;
By fools 'tis hated, and by knaves undone. *Pope.*

No troops abroad are so ill disciplin'd as the English; which cannot well be otherwise, while the common soldiers have before their eyes the *vitious* example of their leaders. *Swift.*

2. Corrupt; having physical ill qualities.

When *vitious* language contends to be high, it is full of rock, mountain, and pointedness. *B. Johnson.*

Here from the *vicious* air and sickly skies,
A plague did on the dumb creation rise. *Dryden.*

VI'TIOUSLY. *adv.* [from *vitious.*] Not virtuously; corruptly.

VI'TIOUSNESS. *n. s.* [from *vitious.*] Corruptness; state of being vitious.

When we in our *vitiousness* grow hard,
The wise gods seal our eyes. *Shakespeare.*

What makes a governor justly despised is *vitiousness* and ill morals. Virtue must tip the preacher's tongue, and the ruler's scepter with authority. *South.*

VI'TREOUS. *adj.* [*vitré*, Fr. *vitreus*, Lat.] Glassy; consisting of glass; resembling glass.

The hole answers to the pupil of the eye; the crystalline humour to the lenticular glass; the dark room to the cavity containing the *vitreous* humour, and the white paper to the retina. *Ray on the Creation.*

When the phlegm is too viscous, or separates into too great a quantity, it brings the blood into a morbid state: this viscous phlegm seems to be the *vitreous* petuite of the antients. *Arbuthnot on Aliments.*

VI'TREOUSNESS. *n. s.* [from *vitreous.*] Resemblance of glass.

VI'TRIFICABLE. *adj.* [from *vitrificate.*] Convertible into glass.

To VITRI'FICATE. *v. a.* [*vitrum* and *facio*, Lat.] To change into glass.

We have metals *vitrificated*, and other materials, besides those of which you make glass. *Bacon.*

VITRIFICA'TION. *n. s.* [*vitrification*, Fr. from *vitrificate.*] Production of glass; act of changing, or state of being changed into glass.

For *vitrification* likewise, what metals will endure it? Also, because *vitrification* is accounted a kind of death of metals, what *vitrification* will admit of turning back again, and what not? *Bacon's Physical Remarks.*

If the heat be more fierce, it maketh the grosser part itself run and melt; as in the making of ordinary glass; and in the *vitrification* of earth in the inner parts of furnaces; and in the *vitrification* of brick and metals. *Bacon's Nat. Hist.*

Upon the knowledge of the different ways of making minerals and metals capable of *vitrification*, depends the art of making counterfeit or fictitious gems. *Boyle on Colours.*

To VI'TRIFY. *v. a.* [*vitrifier*, Fr. *vitrum* and *facio*, Lat.] To change into glass.

Metals will vitrify; and perhaps some portion of the glass of metal *vitrified*, mixed in the pot of ordinary glass metal, will make the whole mass more tough. *Bacon.*

Iron-slag, *vitrified*, has in it cortices incompassing one another, like those in agats. *Woodward.*

To VI'TRIFY. *v. n.* To become glass; to be changed into glass.

Chymists make vessels of animal substances calcined, which will not *vitrify* in the fire; for all earth which hath any salt or oil in it, will turn to glass. *Arbuthnot on Aliments.*

VI'TRIOL. *n. s.* [*vitriol*, Fr. *vitriolum*, Lat.]

Vitriol is produced by addition of a metallick matter with the fossil acid salt. *Woodward.*

I rubbed it with the *vitriol*-stone. *Wiseman's Surgery.*

VI'TRIOLATE. } *adj.* [*vitriolé*, Fr. from *vitriolum*, Lat.] Impregnated with vitriol; consisting of vitriol.
VI'TRIOLATED. }

Iron may be dissolved by any tart, salt, or *vitriolated* water. *Bacon.*

The water having dissolved the imperfectly calcined body, the *vitriolate* corpuscles swimming in the liquor, by their occursions constituted little masses of vitriol, which gave the water they impregnated a fair *vitriolate* colour. *Boyle.*

VITRIO'LICK. } *adj.* [*vitriolique*, Fr. from *vitriolum*, Lat.] Resembling vitriol; containing vitriol.
VITRI'OLOUS. }

Copperose of Mars, by some called salt of steel, made by the spirits of vitriol or sulphur, will, after ablution, be attracted by the loadstone: and therefore whether those shooting salts partake but little of steel, and be not rather the *vitriolous* spirits fixed unto salt by the effluvium or odour of steel, is not without good question. *Brown's Vulg. Errours.*

These salts have somewhat of a nitrous taste, but mix'd with a smatch of a *vitriolick*. *Grew's Musæum.*

By over-fermentation, or long-keeping, wine becomes sharp as in hock, like the *vitriolick* acidity. *Floyer.*

VI'TULINE. *adj.* [*vitulinus*, Lat.] Belonging to a calf, or to veal. *Bailey.*

VITU'PERABLE. *adj.* [*vituperabilis*, Lat.] Blame worthy. *Ains.*

To VITU'PERATE. *v. a.* [*vituperer*, Fr. *vitupero*, Latin.] To blame; to censure.

VITUPERA'TION. *n. s.* [*vituperatio*, Lat.] Blame; censure.

Such a writing ought to be clean, and free from any cavil or *vituperation* of rasure. *Ayliffe's Parergon.*

VIVA'CIOUS. *adj.* [*vivax*, Lat.]

1. Long-lived.

Though we should allow them their perpetual calm and equability of heat, they will never be able to prove, that therefore men would be so *vivacious* as they would have us believe. *Bentley.*

2. Spritely; gay; active; lively.

VIVA'CIOUSNESS. } *n. s.* [*vivacité*, Fr. from *vivacious.*
VIVA'CITY. }

1. Liveliness; Spriteliness.

They are esteemed very hot in operation, and will, in a convenient air, survive some days the loss of their heads and hearts; so vigorous is their *vivacity*. *Boyle.*

He had a great *vivacity* in his countenance. *Dryden.*

2. Longævity; length of life.

Fables are rais'd concerning the *vivacity* of deer; for neither are their gestation nor increment such as may afford an argument of long life. *Brown's Vulgar Errours.*

VI'VARY. *n. s.* [*vivarium*, Lat.] A warren. *Ainsworth.*

VIVE. *adj.* [*vif*, Fr. *vivus*, Latin.] Lively; forcible; pressing.

By a *vive* and forcible perswasion, he mov'd him to a war upon Flanders. *Bacon.*

VI'VENCY. *n. s.* [*vivo*, Latin.] Manner of supporting or continuing life, or vegetation.

Although not in a distinct and indisputable way of *vivency*, or answering in all points the property of plants, yet in inferior and descending constitutions, they are determined by seminalities. *Brown's Vulgar Errours.*

VI'VES. *n. s.* A distemper among horses.

Vives is much like the strangles; and the chief difference is, that for the most part the strangles happen to colts and young horses while they are at grass, by feeding with their heads downwards; by which means the swelling inclines more to the jaws; but the *vives* happens to horses at any age and time, and is more particularly seated in the glands and kernels under the ears. *Farriers Dict.*

VI'VID. *adj.* [*vividus*, Latin.]

1. Lively; quick; striking.

The liquor, retaining its former *vivid* colour, was grown clear again. *Boyle.*

To make these experiments the more manifest, such bodies ought to be chosen as have the fullest and most *vivid* colours, and two of those bodies compared together. *Newton.*

Ah! what avail his glossy varying dyes?
The *vivid* green his shining plumes unfold,
His painted wings, and breast that flames with gold. *Pope.*

2. Spritely;

2. Spritely; active.

Body is a fit workhouſe for ſprightly, *vivid* faculties to exciſe and exert themſelves in. *South.*

Where the genius is bright, and the imagination *vivid*, the power of memory may loſe its improvement. *Watts.*

VI'VIDLY. *adv.* [from *vivid.*] With life; with quickneſs; with ſtrength.

In the moon we can with excellent teleſcopes diſcern many hills and vallies, whereof ſome are more, and ſome leſs *vividly* illuſtrated; and others have a fainter, others a deeper ſhade. *Boyle on Colours.*

Senſitive objects affect a man, in the ſtate of this preſent life, much more warmly and *vividly* than thoſe which affect only his nobler part, his mind. *South.*

VI'VIDNESS. *n. ſ.* [from *vivid.*] Life; vigour; quickneſs.

VIVI'FICAL. *adj.* [*vivificus*, Lat.] Giving life. *Bailey.*

To VIVI'FICATE. *v. a.* [*vivifico*, Lat.]

1. To make alive; to inform with life; to animate.

2. To recover from ſuch a change of form as ſeems to deſtroy the eſſential properties.

VIVIFICA'TION. *n. ſ.* [*vivification*, Fr. from *vivificate.*] The act of giving life.

If that motion be in a certain order, there followeth *vivification* and figuration. *Bacon.*

VIVI'FICK. *adj.* [*vivifique*, Fr. *vivificus*, Latin.] Giving life; making alive.

Without the ſun's ſalutary and *vivifick* beams, all motion would ceaſe, and nothing be left but darkneſs and death. *Ray.*

To VI'VIFY. *v. a.* [*vivifier*, Fr. *vivus* and *facio*, Lat.] To make alive; to animate; to endue with life.

It hath been obſerved by the antients, that there is a worm that breedeth in old ſnow, of a reddiſh colour, and dull of motion; which would ſhew, that ſnow hath in it a ſecret warmth, elſe it could hardly *vivify*. *Bacon.*

Sitting on eggs doth *vivify*, not nouriſh. *Bacon.*

Gut-worms, as ſoon as *vivified*, creep into the ſtomach for nutriment. *Harvey on Conſumptions.*

VIVI'PAROUS. *adj.* [*vivus* and *pario*, Lat.] Bringing the young alive; oppoſed to *oviparous*.

When we perceive that batts have teats, it is not unreaſonable to infer, they give ſuck; but whereas no other flying animals have theſe parts, we cannot from them infer a *viviparous* excluſion. *Brown's Vulgar Errours.*

Their ſpecies might continue, though they had been *viviparous*; yet it would have brought their individuals to very ſmall numbers. *More's Antidote againſt Atheiſm.*

If birds had been *viviparous*, the burthen of their womb had been ſo great and heavy, that their wings would have failed them. *Ray on the Creation.*

VI'XEN. *n. ſ.*

Vixen or *fixen* is the name of a ſhe-fox; otherwiſe applied to a woman whoſe nature and condition is thereby compared to a ſhe fox. *Verſtegan.*

O! when ſhe's angry, ſhe's keen and ſhrewd;
She was a *vixen*, when ſhe went to ſchool;
And though ſhe be but little, ſhe is fierce. *Shakeſp.*

See a pack of ſpaniels, called lovers, in a hot purſuit of a two-legg'd *vixen*, who only flies the whole loud pack, to be ſingled out by one. *Wycherly.*

VIZ. *n. ſ.* [This word is *videlicet*, written with a contraction.] To wit; that is. A barbarous form of an unneceſſary word.

That which ſo oft by ſundry writers
Has been apply'd t' almoſt all fighters,
More juſtly may b' aſcrib'd to this,
Than any other warrior, *viz.*
None ever acted both parts bolder,
Both of a chieftain and a ſoldier. *Hudibras.*

The chief of all ſigns which the Almighty endued man with, is humane voice, and the ſeveral modifications thereof by the organs of ſpeech, *viz.* the letters of the alphabet, form'd by the ſeveral motions of the mouth. *Holder.*

Let this be done relatively, *viz.* one thing greater or ſtronger, caſting the reſt behind, and rendering it leſs ſenſible by its oppoſition. *Dryden's Dufreſnoy.*

VI'ZARD. *n. ſ.* [*viſiere*, Fr. See VISOR.] A maſk uſed for diſguiſe.

Let the ſuits of the maſkers be graceful, and ſuch as become the perſon when the *vizards* are off. *Bacon.*

Æſchylus
Brought *vizards* in a civiler diſguiſe. *Roſcommon.*

A lye is like a *vizard*, that may cover the face indeed, but can never become it. *South.*

Ye ſhall know them by their fruits, not by their well or ill living; for they put on the *vizard* of ſeeming ſanctity. *Atterb.*

He miſtook it for a very whimſical ſort of maſk, but upon a nearer view he found, that ſhe held her *vizard* in her hand. *Addiſon.*

To VI'ZARD. *v. a.* [from the noun.] To maſk.

Degree being *vizarded*,
Th' unworthieſt ſhews as fairly in the maſk. *Shakeſp.*

VI'ZIER. *n. ſ.* [properly *Wazir.*] The prime miniſter of the Turkiſh empire.

He made him *vizier*, which is the chief of all the baſſa's. *Knolles's Hiſt. of the Turks.*

This grand *vizier* preſuming to inveſt
The chief imperial city of the weſt;
With the firſt charge compell'd in haſte to riſe,
His treaſure, tents and cannon left a prize. *Waller.*

U'LCER. *n. ſ.* [*ulcere*, Fr. *ulcus*, Latin.] A ſore of continuance; not a new wound.

Thou anſwer'ſt, ſhe is fair;
Pour'ſt in the open *ulcer* of my heart
Her eyes, her hair, her cheek, her gait, her voice! *Shakeſp.*

My *ulcers* ſwell,
Corrupt and ſmell. *Sandy's Paraphraſe.*

Inteſtine ſtone and *ulcer*, colick pangs. *Milton.*

While he was dreſſing that opening, other abſceſſes were raiſed, and from the ſeveral apoſtemations ſinuous *ulcers* were made. *Wiſeman's Surgery.*

To U'LCERATE. *v. a.* [*ulcerer*, Fr. *ulcero*, Latin.] To diſeaſe with ſores.

Some depend upon the intemperament of the part *ulcerated*; others upon the continual afflux of lacerative humours. *Harvey.*

An acrid and purulent matter mixeth with the blood, in ſuch as have their lungs *ulcerated*. *Arbuthnot on Aliments.*

ULCERA'TION. *n. ſ.* [*ulceration*, Fr. *ulceratio*, from *ulcero*, Lat.]

1. The act of breaking into ulcers.

2. Ulcer; ſore.

The effects of mercury on *ulcerations* are manifeſt. *Arbuth.*

U'LCEROUS. *adj.* [*ulceroſus*, Latin.] Afflicted with ſores.

Strangely viſited people,
All ſwoln and *ulc'rous* he cures. *Shakeſp. Macbeth.*

An *ulcerous* diſpoſition of the lungs, and an ulcer of the lungs, may be appoſitely termed cauſes of a pulmonique conſumption. *Harvey on Conſumptions.*

U'LCEROUSNESS. *n. ſ.* [from *ulcerous.*] The ſtate of being ulcerous.

U'LCERED. *adj.* [*ulceré*, Fr. from *ulcer.*] Grown by time from a hurt to an ulcer.

Æſculapius went about with a dog and a ſhe-goat; the firſt for licking *ulcered* wounds, and the goat's milk for the diſeaſes of the ſtomach. *Temple.*

ULI'GINOUS. *adj.* [*uliginoſus*, Latin.] Slimy; muddy.

The *uliginous* lacteous matter taken notice of in the coral fiſhings upon the coaſt of Italy, was only a collection of the corallin particles. *Woodward.*

U'LTIMATE. *adj.* [*ultimus*, Latin.] Intended in the laſt reſort; being the laſt in the train of conſequences.

I would be at the worſt; worſt is my port,
My harbour, and my *ultimate* repoſe. *Milton.*

Many actions apt to procure fame, are not conducive to this our *ultimate* happineſs. *Addiſon.*

The *ultimate* allotment of God to men, is really a conſequence of their own voluntary choice, in doing good or evil. *Rogers's Sermons.*

U'LTIMATELY. *adv.* [from *ultimate.*] In the laſt conſequence.

Charity is more extenſive than either of the two other graces, which center *ultimately* in ourſelves; for we believe, and we hope for our own ſakes: but love, which is a more diſintereſted principle, carries us out of ourſelves, into deſires and endeavours of promoting the intereſts of other beings. *Atterbury.*

Truſt in our own powers, *ultimately* terminates in the friendſhip of other men, which theſe advantages aſſure to us. *Rogers's Sermons.*

ULTI'MITY. *n. ſ.* [*ultimus*, Latin.] The laſt ſtage; the laſt conſequence. A word very convenient, but not in uſe.

Alteration of one body into another, from crudity to perfect concoction, is the *ultimity* of that proceſs. *Bacon.*

U'LTRAMARINE. *n. ſ.* [*ultra* and *marinus*, Latin.] One of the nobleſt blue colours uſed in painting, produced by calcination from the ſtone called lapis lazuli. *Hill.*

Others, notwithſtanding they are brown, ceaſe not to be ſoft and faint, as the blue of *ultramarine*. *Dryden.*

U'LTRAMARINE. *adj.* [*ultra marinus*, Lat.] Being beyond the ſea; foreign. *Ainſworth.*

ULTRAMO'NTANE. *adj.* [*ultramontain*, Fr. *ultra montanus*, Lat.] Being beyond the mountains.

ULTRAMU'NDANE. *adj.* [*ultra* and *mundus*, Lat.] Being beyond the world.

ULTRO'NEOUS. *adj.* [*ultro*, Lat.] Spontaneous; voluntary.

U'MBEL. *n. ſ.* In botany, the extremity of a ſtalk or branch divided into ſeveral pedicles or rays, beginning from the ſame point, and opening ſo as to form an inverted cone. *Dict.*

UMBE'LLATED. *adj.* In botany, is ſaid of flowers when many of them grow together in umbels. *Dict.*

UMBELLI'FEROUS. *adj.* [*umbel* and *fero*, Lat.] In botany, being a plant that bears many flowers, growing upon many footſtalks, proceeding from the ſame centre; and chiefly appropriated to ſuch plants whoſe flowers are compoſed of five leaves, as fennel and parſnip. *Dict.*

U'MBER. *n. ſ.*

1. *Umber* is a ſad colour; which grind with gum-water, and lighten it with a little ceruſe, and a ſhive of ſaffron. *Peacham.*

I'll put myself in poor and mean attire,
And with a kind of *umber* smirch my face. *Shakespeare.*

Umbre is very sensible and earthy; there is nothing but pure black which can dispute with it. *Dryden.*

The *umbres*, ochres, and minerals found in the fissures, are much finer than those found in the strata. *Woodward.*

2. A fish. [*thymallus*, Lat.]

The *umber* and grayling differ as the herring and pilcher do: but though they may do so in other nations, those in England differ nothing but in their names. *Walt. Angler.*

U'MBERED. *adj.* [from *umber* or *umbra*, Lat.] Shaded; clouded.

From camp to camp, through the foul womb of night,
Fire answers fire; and through their paly flames
Each battle sees the other's *umber'd* face. *Shakesp. Hen V.*

UMBI'LICAL. *adj.* [*umbilicale*, Fr. from *umbilicus*, Lat.] Belonging to the navel.

Birds are nourished by *umbilical* vessels, and the navel is manifest a day or two after exclusion. *Brown's Vulg. Errours.*

In a calf, the *umbilical* vessels terminate in certain bodies divided into a multitude of carneous papillæ, received into so many sockets of the cotyledons growing on the womb. *Ray.*

U'MBLES. *n. s.* [*umbles*, Fr.] A deer's entrails. *Dict.*

U'MBO. *n. s.* [Latin.] The point, or prominent part of a buckler.

Thy words together ty'd in small hanks,
Close as the Macedonian phalanx;
Or like the *umbo* of the Romans,
Which fiercest foes could break by no means. *Swift.*

U'MBRAGE. *n. s.* [*ombrage*, Fr.]

1. Shade; skreen of trees;

O, might I here
In solitude live savage; in some glade
Obscur'd, where highest woods, impenetrable
To star, or sun-light, spread their *umbrage* broad,
And brown as evening! *Milton's Par. Lost.*

Men swelt'ring run
To grotts and caves, and the cool *umbrage* seek
Of woven arborets. *Philips.*

2. Shadow; appearance.

The rest are *umbrages* quickly dispelled; the astrologer subjects liberty to the motions of heaven. *Bramh. against Hobbs.*

The opinion carries no shew of truth nor *umbrage* of reason on its side. *Woodward.*

Such a removal of the metal out of one part of the mass, and collecting of it in another, has misled some, and given *umbrage* to an opinion, that there is a growth of metal in ore exposed to the air. *Woodward on Fossils.*

3. Resentment; offence; suspicion of injury.

Although he went on with the war, yet it should be but with his sword in his hand, to bend the stiffness of the other party to accept of peace: and so the king should take no *umbrage* of his arming and prosecution. *Bacon.*

UMBRA'GEOUS. *adj.* [*ombragieux*, Fr.] Shady; yielding shade.

Umbrageous grots and caves of cool recess. *Milton.*

Walk daily in a pleasant, airy, and *umbrageous* garden. *Harvey.*

The stealing shower is scarce to patter heard,
Beneath th' *umbrageous* multitude of leaves. *Thomson.*

UMBRA'GEOUSNESS. *n. s.* [from *umbrageous*] Shadiness.

The exceeding *umbrageousness* of this tree, he compareth to the dark and shadowed life of man; through which the sun of justice being not able to pierce, we have all remained in the shadow of death, till it pleased Christ to climb the tree of the cross, for our enlight'ning and redemption. *Raleigh.*

UMBRA'TILE. *adj.* [*umbratilis*, Latin.] Being in the shade.

UMBRE'L. } *n. s.* [from *umbra*, Lat.] A skreen used in hot
UMBRE'LLA. } countries to keep off the sun, and in others to bear off the rain.

I can carry your *umbrella*, and fan your ladyship. *Dryden.*

Good housewives
Defended by th' *umbrella*'s oily shed,
Safe through the wet on clinking pattens tread. *Gay.*

UMBRIE'RE. *n. s.* The visor of the helmet. *Spenser.*

UMBRO'SITY. *n. s.* [*umbrosus*, Lat.] Shadiness; exclusion of light.

Oiled paper becometh more transparent, and admits the visible rays with much less *umbrosity*. *Brown's Vulg. Errours.*

U'MPIRAGE. *n. s.* [from *umpire.*] Arbitration; friendly decision of a controversy.

U'MPIRE. *n. s.* [This word *Minshew*, with great applause from *Skinner*, derives from *un pere*, Fr. a *father.*] An arbitrator; one who, as a common friend, decides disputes.

Give me some present counsel; or, behold,
'Twixt my extremes and me, this bloody knife
Shall play the *umpire*; arbitrating that,
Which the commission of thy years and art
Could to no issue of true honour bring. *Shakesp.*

Just death, kind *umpire* of men's miseries,
With sweet enlargement doth dismiss me hence. *Shakesp.*

The learned Sennertus, in that book, takes not upon him to play the advocate for the chymists, but the *umpire* betwixt them and the peripateticks. *Boyle.*

The vast distance that sin had put between the offending creature and the offended Creator, required the help of some great *umpire* and intercessor, to open him a new way of access to God; and this Christ did for us as mediator. *South.*

The jealous sects, that dare not trust their cause
So far from their own will as from the laws,
You for their *umpire* and their synod take. *Dryden.*

UN. A Saxon privative or negative particle answering to *in* of the Latins, and α of the Greeks, *on*, Dutch. It is placed almost at will before adjectives and adverbs. All the instances of this kind of composition cannot therefore be inserted; but I have collected a number sufficient, perhaps more than sufficient, to explain it.

UNABA'SHED. *adj.* [from *abashed.*] Not shamed; not confused by modesty.

Earless on high, stood *unabash'd* Defoe,
And Tutchin flagrant from the scourge below. *Pope.*

UNA'BLE. *adj.* [from *able.*]

1. Not having ability.

The Amalekites set on them, supposing that they had been weary, and unable to resist. *Raleigh's Hist. of the World.*

Zeal mov'd thee:
To please thy gods thou didst it; gods *unable*
T' acquit themselves, and prosecute their foes. *Milton.*

The prince *unable* to conceal his pain,
Gaz'd on the fair,
And sigh'd, and look'd, and sigh'd again. *Dryden.*

I intended to put it in practice, though far *unable* for the attempt of such a poem. *Dryden.*

Man, under the disadvantages of a weak and fallen nature, was *unable* even to form an idea of happiness worthy his reasonable ambition. *Rogers's Sermons.*

2. Weak; impotent.

A love that makes breath poor, and speech *unable*;
Beyond all manner of so much I love you. *Shakespeare.*

UNABO'LISHED. *adj.* [from *abolished.*] Not repealed; remaining in force.

The number of needless laws *unabolished*, doth weaken the force of them that are necessary. *Hooker.*

UNACCE'PTABLE. *adj.* [from *acceptable.*] Not pleasing; not such as is well received.

The marquis at that time was very *unacceptable* to his countrymen. *Clarendon.*

'Tis as indecent as *unacceptable*, and all men are willing to slink out of such company, the sober for the hazards, and jovial for the unpleasantness. *Government of the Tongue.*

Every method for deterring others from the like practices for the future, must be *unacceptable* and displeasing to the friends of the guilty. *Addison's Freeholder.*

If he shrinks from an *unacceptable* duty, there is a secret reserve of infidelity at the bottom. *Rogers's Sermons.*

UNACCE'PTABLENESS. *n. s.* [from *unacceptable.*] State of not pleasing.

This alteration arises from the *unacceptableness* of the subject I am upon. *Collier on Pride.*

UNACCE'PTED. *adj.* [from *accepted.*] Not accepted.

By turns put on the suppliant, and the Lord
Offer'd again the *unaccepted* wreath,
And choice of happy love, or instant death. *Prior.*

UNACCE'SSIBLENESS. *n. s.* [from *accessibleness.*] State of not being to be attained or approached.

Many excellent things are in nature, which, by reason of the remoteness from us, and *unaccessibleness* to them, are not within any of our faculties to apprehend. *Hale.*

UNACCO'MMODATED. *adj.* [from *accommodated.*] Unfurnished with external convenience.

Unaccommodated man is no more than such a poor, bare, forked animal as thou art. *Shakesp.*

UNACCO'MPANIED. *adj.* [from *accompanied.*] Not attended.

Seldom one accident, prosperous or adverse, cometh *unacccompanied* with the like. *Hayward.*

UNACCO'MPLISHED. *adj.* [from *accomplished.*] Unfinish'd; incomplete.

Beware of death, thou canst not die unperjur'd,
And leave an *unaccomplish'd* love behind.
Thy vows are mine. *Dryden.*

The gods dismay'd at his approach, withdrew,
Nor durst their *unaccomplish'd* crime pursue. *Dryden.*

UNACCO'UNTABLE. *adj.* [from *accountable.*]

1. Not explicable; not to be solved by reason; not reducible to rule.

I shall note difficulties, which are not usually observed, though *unaccountable.* *Glanville.*

The folly is so *unaccountable*, that enemies pass upon us for friend. *L'Estrange.*

There has been an *unaccountable* disposition of late, to fetch the fashion from the French. *Addison.*

What

What is yet more *unaccountable*, would he complain of their resisting his omnipotence. *Rogers's Sermons.*

The Chinese are an *unaccountable* people, strangely compounded of knowledge and ignorance. *Baker's Reflect. on Learn.*

The manner whereby the soul and body are united, and how they are distinguished, is wholly *unaccountable* to us. *Swift.*

2. Not subject; not controlled.

UNACCO'UNTABLY. *adv.* Strangely.

The boy proved to be the son of the merchant, whose heart had so *unaccountably* melted at the sight of him. *Addison.*

UNA'CCURATE. *adj.* [from *accurate.*] Not exact.

Galileo using an *unaccurate* way, defined the air to be in weight to water but as one to four hundred. *Boyle.*

UNA'CCURATENESS. *n. s.* [from *unaccurate.*] Want of exactness.

It may be much more probably maintained than hitherto, as against the *unaccurateness* and unconcludingness of the analytical experiments vulgarly to be relied on. *Boyle.*

UNACCU'STOMED. *adj.* [from *accustomed.*]

1. Not used; not habituated.

I was chastised as a bullock *unaccustomed* to the yoke. *Jer.* xxxi.

The necessity of air to the most of animals *unaccustomed* to the want of it, may best be judged of by the following experiments. *Boyle.*

2. New; not usual.

I'll send one to Mantua,
Where that same banish'd runagate doth live,
Shall give him such an *unaccustom'd* dram,
That he shall soon keep Tibalt company. *Shakesp.*

Their pristine worth
The Britons recollect, and gladly change
Sweet native home, for *unaccustom'd* air. *Philips.*

An old word ought never to be fixed to an *unaccustomed* idea, without just and evident necessity. *Watts's Logick.*

UNACKNO'WLEDGED. *adj.* [from *acknowledge.*] Not owned.

The fear of what was to come from an unknown, at least an *unacknowledged* successor to the crown, clouded much of that prosperity. *Clarendon.*

UNACQUA'INTANCE. *n. s.* [from *acquaintance.*] Want of familiarity; want of knowledge.

The first is an utter *unacquaintance* with his master's designs, in these words; the servant knoweth not what his master doth. *South.*

UNACQUA'INTED. *adj.* [from *acquainted.*]

1. Not known; unusual; not familiarly known.

She greatly grew amazed at the sight,
And th' *unacquainted* light began to fear. *Fairy Queen.*

2. Not having familiar knowledge.

Festus, an infidel, a Roman, one whose ears were *unacquainted* with such matter, heard him, but could not reach unto that whereof he spake. *Hooker.*

Where else
Shall I inform my *unacquainted* feet
In the blind mazes of this tangled world? *Milton.*

Art thou a courtier,
Or I a king? My ears are *unacquainted*
With such bold truths, especially from thee. *Denham.*

Youth, that with joys had *unacquainted* been,
Envy'd grey hairs, that once good days had seen. *Dryden.*

Let us live like those who expect to die, and then we shall find that we fear'd death only because we were *unacquainted* with it. *Wake's Preparation for Death.*

UNA'CTIVE. *adj.* [from *active.*]

1. Not brisk; not lively.

Silly people commend tame, *unactive* children, because they make no noise, nor give them any trouble. *Locke.*

2. Having no employment.

Man hath his daily work of body, or mind,
Appointed, which declares his dignity;
While other animals *unactive* range,
And of their doings God takes no account. *Milton.*

3. Not busy; not diligent.

His life,
Private, *unactive*, calm, contemplative;
Little suspicious to any king. *Paradise Regain'd.*

An homage which nature commands all understandings to pay to virtue; and yet it is but a faint, *unactive* thing; for in defiance of the judgment, the will may still remain as much a stranger to virtue as before. *South's Sermons.*

4. Having no efficacy.

In the fruitful earth
His beams, *unactive* else, their vigour find. *Milton.*

UNA'CTUATED. *adj.* Not actuated.

The peripatetick matter is a mere *unactuated* power. *Glanv.*

UNADMI'RED. *adj.* Not regarded with honour.

Oh! had I rather *unadmir'd* remain'd,
In some lone isle, or distant northern land;
Where the gilt chariot never marks the way. *Pope.*

UNADO'RED. *adj.* Not worshipped.

Nor was his name unheard, or *unador'd*
In antient Greece. *Milton.*

UNADO'RNED. *adj.* Not decorated; not embellished.

The earth, till then
Desert, and bare, unsightly, *unadorn'd*,
Brought forth the tender grass. *Milton's Par. Lost.*

But hoary winter, *unadorn'd* and bare,
Dwells in the dire retreat, and freezes there. *Addison.*

UNADVE'NTUROUS. *adj.* Not adventurous.

The wisest, unexperienc'd, will be ever
Timorous and loth, with novice modesty,
Irresolute, unhardy, *unadvent'rous.* *Milton's Par. Regain'd.*

UNADVI'SED. *adj.*

1. Imprudent; indiscreet.

Madam, I have *unadvis'd*
Deliver'd you a paper that I should not. *Shakesp.*

2. Done without due thought; rash.

This contract to-night
Is too rash, too *unadvis'd*, too sudden,
Too like the light'ning, which doth cease to be,
Ere one can say, it lightens. *Shakesp. Romeo and Juliet.*

These prosperous proceedings were turned back by the *unadvised* forwardness of divers chief counsellors, in making sudden and unreasonable alterations. *Hayward.*

Specifick conformities can be no *unadvised* productions; but are regulated by the immediate efficiency of some knowing agent. *Glanville.*

UNADVI'SEDLY. *adv.* Imprudently; rashly; indiscreetly.

A strange kind of speech unto christian ears; and such, as I hope they themselves do acknowledge *unadvisedly* uttered. *Hooker.*

What man's wit is there able to sound the depth of those dangerous and fearful evils, whereinto our weak and impotent nature is inclinable to sink itself, rather than to shew an acknowledgment of error in that which once we have *unadvisedly* taken upon us to defend, against the stream of a contrary publick resolution. *Hooker.*

What is done cannot be now amended;
Men shall deal *unadvisedly* sometimes,
Which after-hours give leisure to repent of. *Shakesp.*

A word *unadvisedly* spoken on the one side, or misunderstood on the other, has raised such an aversion to him, as in time has produced a perfect hatred of him. *South.*

UNADU'LTERATED. *adj.* Genuine; not spoiled by spurious mixtures.

I have only discovered one of those channels, by which the history of our Saviour might be conveyed pure and *unadulterated.* *Addison on the Christian Religion.*

UNAFFE'CTED. *n. s.*

1. Real; not hypocritical.

They bore the king
To lie in solemn state, a publick sight:
Groans, cries, and howlings fill the crouded place,
And *unaffected* sorrow sat on ev'ry face. *Dryden.*

2. Free from affectation; open; candid; sincere.

The maid improves her charms,
With inward greatness, *unaffected* wisdom,
And sanctity of manners. *Addison's Cato.*

Of softest manners, *unaffected* mind;
Lover of peace, and friend of human kind. *Pope's Epist.*

3. Not formed by too rigid observation of rules; not laboured.

Men divinely taught, and better teaching
The solid rules of civil government,
In their majestic, *unaffected* stile,
Than all the oratory of Greece and Rome. *Milton.*

4. Not moved; not touched.

UNAFFE'CTEDLY. *adv.* Really; without any attempt to produce false appearances.

He was always *unaffectedly* cheerful; no marks of any thing heavy at his heart broke from him. *Locke.*

UNAFFE'CTING. *adj.* Not pathetick; not moving the passions.

UNAFFLI'CTED. *adj.* Free from trouble.

My *unafflicted* mind doth feed
On no unholy thoughts for benefit. *Daniel's Musophilus.*

UNAGREE'ABLE. *adj.* Inconsistent; unsuitable.

Advent'rous work! yet to thy pow'r and mine,
Not *unagreeable*, to found a path
Over this main, from hell to that new world. *Milton.*

UNAGREE'ABLENESS. *n. s.* Unsuitableness to; inconsistency with.

Papias, a holy man, and scholar of St. John, having delivered the milennium, men chose rather to admit a doctrine, whose *unagreeableness* to the gospel oeconomy rendered it suspicious, than think an apostolick man could seduce them. *Decay of Piety.*

UNAI'DABLE. *adj.* Not to be helped.

The congregated college have concluded,
That labouring art can never ransom nature
From her *unaidable* estate. *Shakespeare.*

UNAI'DED. *adj.* Not assisted; not helped.

Their number, counting those th' *unaided* eye
Can see, or by invented tubes descry,
The widest stretch of human thought exceeds. *Blackmore.*

UNAI'MING. *adj.* Having no particular direction.

The noisy culverin, o'ercharg'd, lets fly,
And bursts, *unaiming*, in the rended sky:
Such frantick flights are like a madman's dream,
And nature suffers in the wild extreme. *Granville.*

UNA'KING *adj.* Not feeling or causing pain.

Shew them th' *unaking* scars which I would hide,
As if I had received them for the hire
Of their breath only. *Shakesp. Coriolanus.*

UNA'LIENABLE. *adj.* Not to be transferred.

Hereditary right should be kept sacred, not from any *unalienable* right in a particular family, but to avoid the consequences that usually attend the ambition of competitors. *Swift.*

UNALLA'YED. *adj.* Not impaired by bad mixtures.

Unallayed satisfactions are joys too heavenly to fall to many men's shares on earth. *Boyle.*

UNALLI'ED. *adj.*

1. Having no powerful relation.
2. Having no common nature; not congenial.

He is compounded of two very different ingredients, spirit and matter; but how such *unallied* and disproportioned substances should act upon each other, no man's learning yet could tell him. *Collier on Pride.*

UNA'LTERABLE. *adj.* Unchangeable; immutable.

The law of nature, consisting in a fixed, *unalterable* relation of one nature to another, is indispensable. *South.*

They fixt *unalterable* laws,
Settling the same effect on the same cause. *Creech.*

The truly upright man is inflexible in his uprightness, and *unalterable* in his purpose. *Atterbury.*

UNA'LTERABLENESS. *n. s.* Immutability; unchangeableness.

This happens from the *unalterableness* of the corpuscles, which constitute and compose those bodies. *Woodward.*

UNA'LTERABLY. *adv.* Unchangeably; immutably.

Retain *unalterably* firm his love intire. *Milton's Par. Lost.*

The day and year are standard measures, because they are *unalterably* constituted by those motions. *Holder on Time.*

UNA'LTERED. *adj.* Not changed; not changeable.

It was thought in him an unpardonable offence to alter any thing; in us intolerable that we suffer any thing to remain *unaltered*. *Hooker.*

To whom our Saviour, with *unalter'd* brow;
Thy coming hither, though I know thy scope,
I bid not, or forbid. *Paradise Regain'd.*

To shew the truth of my *unalter'd* breast,
Know that your life was giv'n at my request. *Dryden.*

Since these forms begin, and have their end,
On some *unalter'd* cause they sure depend. *Dryden.*

Grains and nuts pass often through animals *unalter'd*. *Arbuth.*

Amongst the shells that were fair, *unaltered*, and free from such mineral insinuations, there were some which could not be match'd by any species of shell-fish now found upon the sea shores. *Woodward's Nat. Hist.*

UNAMA'ZED. *adj.* Not astonished; free from astonishment.

Though at the voice much marvelling; at length
Not *unamaz'd*, she thus in answer spake. *Milton.*

UNAMBI'TIOUS. *adj.* Free from ambition.

My humble muse, in *unambitious* strains,
Paints the green forests, and the flow'ry plains. *Pope.*

I am one of those *unambitious* people, who will love you forty years hence. *Pope.*

UNAME'NDABLE. *adj.* [*inemendabilis*, Lat.] Not to be changed for the better.

He is the same man; so is every one here that you know: mankind is *unamendable*. *Pope to Swift.*

UNA'MIABLE. *adj.* Not raising love.

Those who represent religion in an *unamiable* light, are like the spies sent by Moses, to make a discovery of the land of promise, when, by their reports, they discouraged the people from entering upon it. *Addison's Spectator.*

These men are so well acquainted with the *unamiable* part of themselves, that they have not the confidence to think they are really beloved. *Addison's Spectator.*

Nor are the hills *unamiable*, whose tops
To heav'n aspire. *Philips.*

UNANALY'SED. *adj.* Not resolved into simple parts.

Some large crystals of refined and *unanalysed* nitre, appeared to have each of them six flat sides. *Boyle.*

UNA'NCHORED. *adj.* Not anchored.

A port there is, inclos'd on either side,
Where ships may rest, *unanchor'd*, and unty'd. *Pope.*

UNANE'LED. *adj.* [*un* and *knell.*] Without the bell rung. This sense I doubt.

Thus was I, sleeping, by a brother's hand
Cut off ev'n in the blossoms of my sin,
Unhousel'd, unanointed, *unanel'd*. *Shakesp. Hamlet.*

UNA'NIMATED. *adj.* Not enlivened; not vivified.

Look on those half lines as the imperfect products of a hasty muse: like the frogs in the Nile, part kindled into life, and part a lump of uninformed, *unanimated* matter. *Dryden.*

UNANI'MITY. *n. s.* [*unanimité*, Fr.] Agreement in design or opinion.

An honest party of men acting with *unanimity*, are of infinitely greater consequence, than the same party aiming at the same end by different views. *Addison.*

UNA'NIMOUS. *adj.* [*unanime*, Fr. *unanimis*, Lat] Being of one mind; agreeing in design or opinion.

They wont to meet
So oft in festivals of joy, and love
Unanimous, as sons of one great sire,
Hymning th' eternal father. *Milton's Par. Lost.*

With those which Minio's fields and Phyrgi gave,
All bred in arms, *unanimous* and brave. *Dryden.*

UNA'NIMOUSLY. *adv.* [from *unanimous.*] With one mind.

This particular is *unanimously* reported by all the antient christian authors. *Addison on the Christian Religion.*

UNANO'INTED. *adj.*

1. Not anointed.
2. Not prepared for death by extreme unction.

Thus was I, sleeping, by a brother's hand
Cut off ev'n in the blossoms of my sin,
Unhousel'd, *unanointed*, unanel'd. *Shakesp. Hamlet.*

UNA'NSWERABLE. *adj.* Not to be refuted.

This is a manifest and *unanswerable* argument. *Raleigh.*

I shall not conclude it false, though I think the emergent difficulties, which are its attendants, *unanswerable*. *Glanville.*

The pye's question was wisely let fall without a reply, to intimate that it was *unanswerable*. *L'Estrange.*

These speculations are strong intimations, not only of the excellency of a human soul, but of its independence on the body; and if they do not prove, do at least confirm, these two great points, which are established by many other reasons that are *unanswerable*. *Addison's Spectator.*

As to the excuse drawn from the demands of creditors, if it be real, it is *unanswerable*. *Atterbury's Sermons.*

UNA'NSWERABLY. *adv.* Beyond confutation.

It will put their little logick hard to it, to prove, that there can be any obedience, where there is no command. And therefore it *unanswerably* follows, that the abettors of the forementioned principle plead conscience in a direct and bare-faced contradiction to God's express command. *South.*

UNA'NSWERED. *adj.*

1. Not opposed by a reply.

Unanswer'd lest thou boast. *Milton's Par. Lost.*

Must I tamely bear
This arrogance *unanswer'd!* Thou'rt a traitor. *Addison.*

2. Not confuted.

All these reasons, they say, have been brought, and were hitherto never answer'd; besides a number of merriments and jests *unanswer'd* likewise. *Hooker.*

3. Not suitably returned.

Quench, Corydon, thy long *unanswer'd* fire;
Mind what the common wants of life require. *Dryden.*

UNAPPA'LLED. *adj.* Not daunted; not impress'd by fear.

If my memory must thus be thralled
To that strange stroke, which conquered all my senses;
Can thoughts still thinking so rest *unappalled?* *Sidney.*

Infernal ghosts
Environ'd thee; some howl'd, some yell'd, some shriek'd;
Some bent at thee their fiery darts; while thou
Sat'st *unappall'd* in calm and sinless peace. *Milton.*

As a lion, *unappall'd* with fear,
Springs on the toils, and rushes on the spear. *Dryden.*

Does this appear like guilt? When thus serene,
With eyes erect, and visage *unappall'd*,
Fixt on that awful face, I stand the charge;
Amaz'd, not fearing. *Smith's Phæd. and Hypolitus.*

UNAPPA'RRELLED. *adj.* Not dressed; not cloathed.

In Peru, though they were an *unapparelled* people, and had some customs very barbarous, yet the government of the Incas had many parts of civilty. *Bacon's Holy Wars.*

Till our souls be *unapparelled*
Of bodies, they from bliss are banished. *Donne.*

UNAPPA'RENT. *adj.* Obscure; not visible.

Thy potent voice he hears,
And longer will delay to hear thee tell
His generation, and the rising birth
Of nature, from the *unapparent* deep. *Milton.*

UNAPPEA'SABLE. *adj.* Not to be pacified; implacable.

The *unappeasable* rage of Hildebrand and his successors, never left persecuting him, by raising one rebellion upon another. *Raleigh's Essays.*

I see thou art implacable; more deaf
To pray'rs than winds to seas; yet winds to seas
Are reconcil'd at length, and seas to shore.
Thy anger, *unappeasable*, still rages,
Eternal tempest never to be calm'd. *Milton.*

UNAPPE'ASED. *adj.* Not pacified.

Sacrifice his flesh,
That so the shadows be not *unappeas'd*. *Shakesp.*

His son forgot, his empress *unappeas'd*;
How soon the tyrant with new love is seiz'd. *Dryden.*

UNAPPLI-

UNA'PPLICABLE. *adj.* [from *apply.*] Such as cannot be applied.

Gratitude, by being confined to the few, has a very narrow province to work on, being acknowledged to be *unapplicable*, and so consequently ineffectual to all others. *Hammond.*

Their beloved earl of Manchester appeared now as *unapplicable* to their purposes as the other. *Clarendon.*

The singling out, and laying in order those intermediate ideas, that demonstratively shew the equality or inequality of *unapplicable* quantities, has produced discoveries. *Locke.*

UNAPPREHE'NDED. *adj.* Not understood.

They of whom God is altogether *unapprehended*, are but few in number, and for grossness of wit such, that they hardly seem to hold the place of human being. *Hooker.*

UNAPPREHE'NSIVE. *adj.* [from *apprehend.*]

1. Not intelligent; not ready of conception.

The same temper of mind makes a man *unapprehensive* and insensible of any misery suffered by others. *South.*

2. Not suspecting.

UNAPPROA'CHED. *adj.* Inaccessible.

God is light,
And never but in *unapproached* light
Dwelt from eternity *Milton's Par. Lost.*

UNAPPRO'VED. *adj.* [from *approve.*] Not approved.

Evil into the mind
May come and go so *unapprov'd*, and leave
No spot behind. *Milton.*

UNA'PT. *adj.* [from *apt.*]

1. Dull; not apprehensive.

2. Not ready; not propense.

I am a soldier, and *unapt* to weep. *Shakesp.*
My blood hath been too cold and temperate,
Unapt to stir at these indignities. *Shakespeare.*

3. Unfit; not qualified.

Fear doth grow from an apprehension of deity indued with irresistible power to hurt; and is, of all affections (anger excepted) the *unaptest* to admit any conference with reason. *Hooker.*

A longing after sensual pleasures is a dissolution of the spirit of a man, and makes it loose, soft and wandering, *unapt* for noble, wise, or spiritual employments. *Taylor.*

4. Improper; unfit; unsuitable.

UNA'PTLY. *adv.* [from *unapt.*] Unfitly; improperly.

He swims on his back; and the shape of his back seems to favour it, being very like the bottom of a boat: nor do his hinder legs *unaptly* resemble a pair of oars. *Grew.*

UNA'PTNESS. *n. s.* [from *unapt.*]

1. Unfitness; unsuitableness.

Men's apparel is commonly made according to their conditions; and their conditions are often governed by their garments: for the person that is gowned, is by his gown put in mind of gravity, and also restrained from lightness by the very *unaptness* of his weed. *Spenser.*

2. Dulness; want of apprehension.

That *unaptness* made you minister
Thus to excuse yourself. *Shakesp. Timon of Athens.*

3. Unreadiness; disqualification; want of propension.

The mind, by being engaged in a task beyond its strength, like the body, strained by lifting at a weight too heavy, has often its force broken, and thereby gets an *unaptness*, or an aversion to any vigorous attempt ever after. *Locke.*

UNA'RGUED. *adj.* [from *argue.*]

1. Not disputed.

What thou bid'st,
Unargu'd I obey; so God ordains. *Milton's Par. Lost.*

2. Not censured.

Not that his work liv'd in the hands of foes,
Unargu'd then, and yet hath fame from those. *B. Johnson.*

To UNA'RM. *v. a.* [from *arm.*] To disarm; to strip of armour; to deprive of arms.

Unarm, unarm, and do not fight to-day. *Shakesp.*
Unarm me, Eros; the long day's task is done,
And we must sleep. *Shakesp. Ant. and Cleopatra.*

Galen would not leave unto the world too subtle a theory of poisons; *unarming* thereby the malice of venemous spirits. *Brown's Vulgar Errours.*

UNA'RMED. *adj.* [from *unarm.*] Having no armour; having no weapons.

On the western coast
Rideth a puissant navy: To our shores
Throng many doubtful, hollow-hearted friends,
Unarm'd, and unresolv'd to beat them back. *Shakesp.*
He all *unarm'd*
Shall chase thee with the terror of his voice
From thy demoniack holds, possession foul;
Thee and thy legions, yelling they shall fly,
And beg to hide them in a herd of swine. *Milton.*
Though *unarm'd* I am,
Here, without my sword or pointed lance,
Hope not, base man, unquestion'd hence to go. *Dryden.*

Whereas most other creatures are furnished with weapons for their defence; man is born altogether *unarmed*. *Grew.*

UNARRA'IGNED. *adj.* Not brought to a trial.

As lawful lord, and king by just descent,
Should here be judg'd, unheard, and *unarraign'd*. *Daniel.*

UNARRA'YED. *adj.* Not dressed.

As if this infant world yet *unarray'd*,
Naked and bare, in nature's lap were laid. *Dryden.*
Half *unarray'd*, he ran to his relief,
So hasty and so artless was his grief. *Dryden.*

UNA'RTFUL. *adj.*

1. Having no art, or cunning.

A chearful sweetness in his looks he has,
And innocence *unartful* in his face. *Dryden's Juvenal.*

2. Wanting skill.

How *unartful* would it have been to have set him in a corner, when he was to have given light and warmth to all the bodies round him? *Cheyne's Phil. Prin.*

UNA'RTFULLY. *adv.* In an unartful manner.

In the report, although it be not *unartfully* drawn, and is perfectly in the spirit of a pleader, there is no great skill required to detect the many mistakes. *Swift's Miscellany.*

UNARTIFI'CIALLY. *adv.* Contrarily to art.

Not a feather is *unartificially* made, misplaced, redundant, or defective. *Derham's Physico-Theology.*

UNA'SKED. *adj.* Not sought by solicitation.

With what eagerness, what circumstance
Unask'd, thou tak'st such pains to tell me only
My son's the better man. *Denham's Sophy.*
The bearded corn ensu'd
From earth *unask'd*, nor was that earth renew'd. *Dryden.*
How, or why
Shou'd all conspire to cheat us with a lye?
Unask'd their pains, ungrateful their advice;
Starving their gain, and martyrdom their price. *Dryden.*

UNASPI'RING. *adj.* Not ambitious.

To be modest and *unaspiring*, in honour preferring one another. *Rogers.*

UNASSA'ILED. *adj.* Not attacked; not assaulted.

As I intend, Clifford, to thrive to-day,
It grieves my soul to leave thee *unassail'd*. *Shakespeare.*
I believe
That he, the supreme good, t' whom all things ill
Are but as slavish officers of vengeance,
Would send a glist'ring guardian, if need were,
To keep my life and honour *unassail'd*. *Milton's Comus.*

UNASSA'ILABLE. *adj.* Exempt from assault.

In the number, I do but know one,
That *unassailable* holds on his rank,
Unshak'd of motion. *Shakesp. Julius Cæsar.*

UNASSA'YED. *adj.* Unattempted.

What is faith, love, virtue *unassay'd*
Alone, without exterior help sustain'd. *Milton.*

UNASSI'STED. *adj.* Not helped.

Its victories were the victories of reason, *unassisted* by the force of human power, and as gentle as the triumphs of light over darkness. *Addison's Freeholder.*

What *unassisted* reason could not discover, that God has set clearly before us in the revelation of the gospel: a felicity equal to our most enlarged desires; a state of immortal and unchangeable glory. *Rogers's Sermons.*

UNASSI'STING. *adj.* Giving no help.

With these I went, a brother of the war;
Nor idle stood, with *unassisting* hands,
When savage beasts, and men's more savage bands,
Their virtuous toil subdu'd: yet these I sway'd. *Dryden.*

UNASSU'MING. *adj.* Not arrogant.

Unassuming worth in secret liv'd,
And died neglected. *Thomson's Winter.*

UNASSU'RED. *adj.*

1. Not confident.

The ensuing treatise, with a timorous and *unassured* countenance, adventures into your presence. *Glanville.*

2. Not to be trusted.

The doubts and dangers, the delays and woes;
The feigned friends, the *unassured* foes,
Do make a lover's life a wretch's hell. *Spenser.*

UNATTA'INABLE. *adj.* Not to be gained or obtained; being out of reach.

Praise and prayer are God's due worship; which are *unattainable* by our discourse, simply considered, without the benefit of divine revelation. *Dryden's Religio Laici.*

I do not expect that men should be perfectly kept from error; that is more than human nature can, by any means, be advanced to: I aim at no such *unattainable* privilege; I only speak of what they should do. *Locke.*

UNATTA'INABLENESS. *n. s.* State of being out of reach.

Desire is stopped by the opinion of the impossibility, or *unattainableness* of the good proposed. *Locke.*

UNATTEMPTED. *adj.* Untried; not assayed.

He left no means *unattempted* of destroying his son. *Sidney.*
Not that I have the power to clutch my hand,
When his fair angels would salute my palm;
But that my hand, as *unattempted* yet,
Like a poor beggar, raileth on the rich. *Shakesp.*

It pursues
Things *unattempted* yet in prose or rhyme. *Milton.*
Leave nothing *unattempted* to destroy
That perjur'd race. *Denham.*

Shall we be discouraged from any attempt of doing good, by the possibility of our failing in it? How many of the best things would, at this rate, have been left *unattempted?* *Atterb.*

UNATTE'NDED. *adj.* Having no retinue, or attendants.
Your constancy
Hath left you *unattended.* *Shakesp. Macbeth.*
With goddess-like demeanor forth she went,
Not *unattended.* *Milton's Par. Lost.*

Such *unattended* generals can never make a revolution in Parnassus. *Dryden.*

UNATTE'NDING. *adj.* Not attending.
Ill is lost that praise,
That is address'd to *unattending* ears. *Milton.*
Ev'ry nymph of the flood, her tresses rending,
Throws off her armlet of pearl in the main;
Neptune in anguish his charge *unattending,*
Vessels are found'ring, and vows are in vain. *Dryden.*

UNATTE'NTIVE. *adj.* Not regarding.

Man's nature is so *unattentive* to good, that there can scarce be too many monitors. *Government of the Tongue.*

Such things are not accompanied with show, and therefore seldom draw the eyes of the *unattentive.* *Tatler,* N°. 55.

UNATTO'NED. *adj.* Not expiated.
Could you afford him such a bribe as that,
A brother's blood yet *unatton'd?* *Rowe.*

UNAVA'ILABLE. *adj.* Useless; vain with respect to any purpose.

When we have endeavoured to find out the strongest causes, wherefore they should imagine that reading is so *unavailable,* the most we can learn is, that sermons are the ordinance of God, the scriptures dark, and the labour of reading easy. *Hooker.*

UNAVA'ILING. *adj.* Useless; vain.
Since my inevitable death you know,
You safely *unavailing* pity show:
'Tis popular to mourn a dying foe. *Dryden's Aurengzebe.*
Supine he tumbles on the crimson sands,
Before his helpless friends and native bands,
And spreads for aid his *unavailing* hands. *Pope.*

UNAVOI'DABLE. *adj.*

1. Inevitable; not to be shunned.

Oppression on one side, and ambition on the other, are the *unavoidable* occasions of war. *Dryden.*

It is *unavoidable* to all, to have opinions, without certain proofs of their truth. *Locke.*

Single acts of transgression will, through weakness and surprize, be *unavoidable* to the best guarded. *Rogers.*

The merits of Christ will make up the *unavoidable* deficiencies of our service; will prevail for pardon to our sincere repentance. *Rogers.*

All sentiments of worldly grandeur vanish at that *unavoidable* moment, which decides the destiny of men. *Clarissa.*

2. Not to be missed in ratiocination.

That something is of itself, is self-evident, because we see things are; and the things that we see must either have had some first cause of their being, or have been always, and of themselves: one of them is *unavoidable.* *Tillotson.*

I think it *unavoidable* for every rational creature, that will examine his own or any other existence, to have the notion of an eternal, wise being, who had no beginning. *Locke.*

UNAVOI'DABLENESS. *n. s.* Inevitability.

How can we conceive it subject to material impressions? and yet the importunity of pain, and *unavoidableness* of sensations, strongly persuade that we are so. *Glanville.*

UNAVO'IDABLY. *adv.* Inevitably.

The most perfect administration must *unavoidably* produce opposition from multitudes who are made happy by it. *Addison.*

UNAVO'IDED. *adj.* Inevitable.
We see the very wreck that we must suffer;
And *unavoided* is the danger now. *Shakesp.*
Rare poems ask rare friends;
Yet satyrs, since the most of mankind be
Their *unavoided* subject, fewest see. *B. Johnson.*

UNAU'THORISED. *adj.* Not supported by authority; not properly commissioned.
To kiss in private?
An *unauthorized* kiss. *Shakespeare's Othello.*
It is for you to ravage seas and land,
Unauthoriz'd by my supreme command. *Dryden.*

UNAWA'RE. } *adv.* [from *aware,* or *wary.*]
UNAWA'RES. }

1. Without thought; without previous meditation.
It is my father's face,
Whom, in this conflict, I *unawares* have kill'd. *Shakesp.*
Firm we subsist; yet possible to swerve,
And fall into deception *unaware.* *Milton.*
A pleasant beverage he prepar'd before,
Of wine and honey mix'd; with added store
Of opium: to his keeper this he brought,
Who swallow'd *unawares* the sleepy draught,
And snor'd secure. *Dryden.*

'Tis a sensation like that of a limb lopp'd off; one is trying every minute *unawares* to use it, and finds it is not. *Pope.*

2. Unexpectedly; when it is not thought of; suddenly.

Take heed lest you fall *unawares* into that inconvenience you formerly found fault with. *Spenser.*

Lest destruction come upon him at *unawares,* and let his net that he hath hid, catch himself. *Psalm* xxxvi. 8.

My hand, *unawares* to me, was, by the force of that endeavour it just before employed to sustain the fallen weight, carried up with such violence, that I bruised it. *Boyle.*
He breaks at *unawares* upon our walks,
And, like a midnight wolf, invades the fold. *Dryden.*

Though we live never so long, we are still surprized: we put the evil day far from us, and then it catches us *unawares,* and we tremble at the prospect. *Wake.*

UNA'WED. *adj.* Unrestrained by fear or reverence.

The raging and fanatic distemper of the house of commons must be attributed to the want of such good ministers of the crown, as, being *unawed* by any guilt of their own, could have watched other mens. *Clarendon.*
Unforc'd by punishment, *unaw'd* by fear,
His words were simple, and his soul sincere. *Dryden.*

UNBA'CKED. *adj.*

1. Not tamed; not taught to bear the rider.
Then I beat my tabor;
At which, like *unback'd* colts, they prick'd their ears,
Advanc'd their eyelids, lifted up their noses,
As they smelt musick. *Shakesp. Tempest.*

A well wayed horse will safely convey thee to thy journey's end, when an *unbacked* filly may give thee a fall. *Suckling.*

They flinch like *unback'd* fillies. *Dennis's Letters.*

2. Not countenanced; not aided.
Let the weight of thine own infamy
Fall on thee unsupported, and *unback'd.* *Daniel's Civil War.*

UNBA'LANCED. *adj.* Not poised; not in equipoise.
Let earth *unbalanc'd* from her orbit fly,
Planets and suns run lawless through the sky. *Pope.*

UNBA'LLASTED. *adj.* Not kept steady by ballast; unsteady.

They having but newly left those grammatick flats, where they stuck unreasonably, to learn a few words with lamentable construction; and now on the sudden transported under another climate, to be tost and turmoiled with their *unballasted* wits, in fathomless and unquiet deeps of controversy, do, for the most part, grow into hatred of learning. *Milton.*
As at sea th' *unballast* vessel rides,
Cast to and fro, the sport of winds and tides:
So in the bounding chariot toss'd on high,
The youth is hurry'd headlong through the sky. *Addison.*

UNB'ANDED. *adj.* [from *band.*] Wanting a string, or band.

Your hose should be ungarter'd, your bonnet *unbanded,* and every thing demonstrating a careless desolation. *Shakesp.*

To UNB'AR. *v. a.* [from *bar.*] To open, by removing the bars; to unbolt.
'Tis not secure, this place or that to guard,
If any other entrance stand *unbarr'd.* *Denham.*
These rites the king refus'd,
Deaf to their cries; nor would the gates *unbar*
Of sacred peace, or loose th' imprison'd war. *Dryden.*

UNBA'RBED. *adj.* [*barba,* Lat.] Not shaven. Out of use.
Must I go shew them my *unbarbed* sconce?
Must my base tongue give to my noble heart
A lie? *Shakesp. Coriolanus.*

UNBA'RKED. *adj.* [from *bark.*] Decorticated; stripped of the bark.

A branch of a tree, *unbarked* some space at the bottom, and so set in the ground, hath grown. *Bacon.*

UNBA'SHFUL. *adj.* Impudent; shameless.
Nor did I with *unbashful* forehead wooe
The means of weakness and debility. *Shakespeare.*

UNBA'TED. *adj.* [from *bate.*] Not repressed; not blunted.
Where is the horse, that doth untread again
His tedious measures with th' *unbated* fire
That he did pace them first? *Shakesp. Merch. of Venice.*

UNBA'THED. *adj.* [from *bath.*] Not wet.
Fierce Pasimond, their passage to prevent,
Thrust full on Cymon's back in his descent;
The blade return'd *unbath'd,* and to the handle bent. *Dryd.*

UNBA'TTERED. *adj.* Not injured by blows.
I cannot strike at wretched kernes, whose arms
Are hir'd to bear their staves: or thou, Macbeth;
Or else my sword, with an *unbatter'd* edge,
I sheath again undeeded. *Shakespeare's Macbeth.*

UNBEA'RING. *adj.* Bringing no fruit.

Does

He with his pruning hook disjoins
Unbearing branches from their head,
And grafts more happy in their ſtead. *Dryden.*

To UNBA'Y. *v. a.* To ſet open; to free from the reſtraint of mounds.

I ought now to looſe the reins of my affections, to *unbay* the current of my paſſion, and love on without boundary or meaſure. *Norris's Miſcellany.*

UNBEA'TEN. *adj.*

1. Not treated with blows.

His mare was truer than his chronicle;
For ſhe had rode five miles unſpurr'd, *unbeaten*,
And then at laſt turn'd tail towards Neweaton. *Bp. Corbet.*

2. Not trodden.

We muſt tread *unbeaten* paths, and make a way where we do not find one; but it ſhall be always with a light in our hand. *Bacon.*

If your bold muſe dare tread *unbeaten* paths. *Roſcommon.*

Virtue, to crown her fav'rites, loves to try
Some new, *unbeaten* paſſage to the ſky. *Swift.*

UNBECO'MING. *adj.* Indecent; unſuitable; indecorous.

Here's our chief gueſt.——
——If he had been forgotten,
It had been as a gap in our great feaſt,
And all things *unbecoming*. *Shakeſpeare's Macbeth.*

No thought of flight,
None of retreat, no *unbecoming* deed
That argu'd fear. *Milton's Par. Loſt.*

I ſhould rather believe that the noſe was the ſeat of wrath in beaſts than in mankind; and that it was *unbecoming* of any but Pan, who had very much of the beaſt in him, to wrinkle up his noſe in anger. *Dryden.*

My grief lets *unbecoming* ſpeeches fall:
I ſhould have dy'd, and not complain'd at all. *Dryden.*

This petulancy in converſation prevails among ſome of that ſex, where it appears the moſt *unbecoming* and unnatural. *Addiſon's Freeholder.*

Men of wit, learning, and virtue, might ſtrike out every offenſive or *unbecoming* paſſage from plays. *Swift.*

Such proceed upon debates without *unbecoming* warmth. *Swift.*

UNBECO'MINGNESS. *n. ſ.* Indecency; indecorum.

If words are ſometimes to be uſed, they ought to be grave, kind and ſober, repreſenting the ill or *unbecomingneſs* of the fault. *Locke.*

To UNBE'D. *v. a.* To raiſe from a bed.

Eels *unbed* themſelves, and ſtir at the noiſe of thunder. *Walton's Angler.*

UNBEFI'TTING. *adj.* Not becoming; not ſuitable.

Love is full of *unbefitting* ſtrains,
All wanton as a child, ſkipping in vain. *Shakeſp.*

Far be it that I ſhould write thee ſin, or blame!
Or think thee *unbefitting* holieſt place. *Milton.*

He might ſeveral times have made peace with his diſcontented ſubjects upon terms not at all *unbefitting* his dignity or intereſt; but he rather choſe to ſacrifice the whole alliance to his private paſſion. *Swift.*

To UNBEGE'T. *v. n.* To deprive of exiſtence.

Wiſhes each minute he could *unbeget*
Thoſe rebel ſons, who dare t' uſurp his ſeat. *Dryden.*

UNBEGO'T.
UNBEGO'TTEN. } *adj.* [from *begot.*]

1. Eternal; without generation.

Why ſhould he attribute the ſame honour to matter, which is ſubject to corruption, as to the eternal, *unbegotten*, and immutable God? *Stillingfleet.*

2. Not yet generated.

God omnipotent, muſt'ring
Armies of peſtilence; and they ſhall ſtrike
Your children yet unborn, and *unbegot*. *Shakeſp.*

In thy pow'r
It lies yet, ere conception, to prevent
The race unbleſt, to being yet *unbegot*. *Milton's Par. Loſt.*

Where a child finds his own parents his perverters, better were it for him to have been unborn and *unbegot*, than aſk a bleſſing of thoſe whoſe converſation breathes nothing but a curſe. *South's Sermons.*

To UNBEGUI'LE. *v. a.* To undeceive; to ſet free from the influence of any deceit.

Then *unbeguile* thyſelf, and know with me,
That angels, though on earth employ'd they be,
Are ſtill in heav'n. *Donne.*

Their comelineſs *unbeguiled* the vulgar of the odd opinion the loyaliſts had formerly infuſed into them, by their concionatory invectives. *Howel's Vocal Foreſt.*

UNBEHE'LD. *adj.* Unſeen; not diſcoverable to the ſight.

Theſe then, though *unbeheld* in deep of night,
Shine not in vain. *Milton.*

UNBELI'EF. *n. ſ.*

1. Incredulity.

'Tis not vain or fabulous,
What the ſage poets, taught by th' heav'nly muſe,
Storied of old in high immortal verſe,
Of dire chimæra's, and enchanted iſles,
And rifted rocks, whoſe entrance leads to hell;
For ſuch there be, but *unbelief* is blind. *Milton.*

I'm juſtly plagu'd by this your *unbelief*,
And am myſelf the cauſe of my own grief. *Dryden.*

Such an univerſal acquaintance with things will keep you from an exceſs of credulity and *unbelief*; *i. e.* a readineſs to believe, or to deny every thing at firſt hearing. *Watts.*

2. Infidelity; irreligion.

Where profeſs'd *unbelief* is, there can be no viſible church of Chriſt; there may be where ſound belief wanteth. *Hooker.*

To UNBELIE'VE. *v. a.*

1. To diſcredit; not to truſt.

Heav'n ſhield your grace from woe,
As I, thus wrong'd, hence *unbelieved* go. *Shakeſp.*

So great a prince and favourite ſo ſuddenly metamorphoſed into travellers with no greater train, was enough to make any man *unbelieve* his five ſenſes. *Wotton's Buckingham.*

2. Not to think real or true.

Nor leſs than ſight and hearing could convince,
Of ſuch an unforeſeen and *unbeliev'd* offence. *Dryden.*

UNBELIE'VER. *n. ſ.* An infidel; one who believes not the ſcripture of God.

The antient fathers being often conſtrained to ſhew, what warrant they had ſo much to rely upon the ſcriptures, endeavoured ſtill to maintain the authority of the books of God, by arguments ſuch as *unbelievers* themſelves muſt needs think reaſonable, if they judged thereof as they ſhould. *Hooker.*

What endleſs war wou'd jealous nations tear,
If none above did witneſs what they ſwear?
Sad fate of *unbelievers*, and yet juſt,
Among themſelves to find ſo little truſt. *Waller.*

In the new teſtament, religion is uſually expreſſed by faith in God and Chriſt, and the love of them. Hence it is that true chriſtians are ſo frequently called believers; and wicked and ungodly men *unbelievers*. *Tillotſon.*

He pronounces the children of ſuch parents as were, one of them a chriſtian, and the other an *unbeliever*, holy, on account of the faith and holineſs of that one. *Atterbury.*

Men always grow vicious before they become *unbelievers*; but if you would once convince profligates by topicks drawn from the view of their own quiet, reputation, and health, their infidelity would ſoon drop off. *Swift's Miſcellanies.*

UNBELIE'VING. *adj.* Infidel.

No pauſe,
No ſtay of ſlaughter found his vigorous arm;
But th' *unbelieving* ſquadrons turn'd to flight,
Smote in the rear. *Phillips.*

This wrought the greateſt confuſion in the *unbelieving* Jews, and the greateſt conviction in the Gentiles. *Addiſon.*

In the days of the apoſtle, when all who profeſſed themſelves diſciples of Chriſt were converts of conſcience, this ſevere cenſure might be reſtrained to the *unbelieving* part of mankind. *Rogers's Sermons.*

UNBELO'VED. *adj.* Not loved.

Whoe'er you are, not *unbelov'd* by heav'n,
Since on our friendly ſhore your ſhips are driv'n. *Dryden.*

To UNBE'ND. *v. a.* To relax; to remit; to eaſe.

You *unbend* your noble ſtrength, to think
So brain-ſickly of things. *Shakeſpeare's Macbeth.*

It is lawful to relax and *unbend* our bow, but not to ſuffer it to be unready, or unſtrung. *Taylor's Holy Living.*

Here have I ſeen the king, when great affairs
Gave leave to ſlacken and *unbend* his cares,
Attended to the chace by all the flow'r of youth. *Denham.*

From thoſe great cares when eaſe your ſoul *unbends*,
Your pleaſures are deſign'd to noble ends. *Dryden.*

I muſt be in the battle; but I'll go
With empty quiver, and *unbended* bow. *Dryden.*

UNBE'NDING. *adj.*

1. Not ſuffering flexure.

Not ſo, when ſwift Camilla ſcours the plain,
Flies o'er th' *unbending* corn, and ſkims along the main. *Pope.*

2. Devoted to relaxation.

Since what was omitted in the acting is now kept in, I hope it may entertain your lordſhip at an *unbending* hour. *Rowe.*

UNBENE'VOLENT. *adj.* Not kind.

A religion which not only forbids, but by its natural influence ſweetens all bitterneſs and aſperity of temper, and corrects that ſelfiſh narrowneſs of ſpirit, which inclines men to a fierce, *unbenevolent* behaviour. *Rogers's Sermons.*

UNBE'NEFICED. *adj.* Not preferred to a benefice.

More vacant pulpits wou'd more converts make;
All wou'd have latitude enough to take:
The reſt *unbenefic'd* your ſects maintain. *Dryden.*

UNBENI'GHTED. *adj.* Never viſited by darkneſs.

Beyond the polar circles; to them day
Had *unbenighted* ſhone, while the low ſun,
To recompenſe his diſtance, in their ſight
Had rounded ſtill the horizon. *Milton's Par. Loſt.*

UNBENI'GN. *adj.* Malignant; malevolent.

To th' other five
Their planetary motions, and aspects,
In sextile, square, and trine, and opposite,
Of noxious efficacy; and when to join
In synod *unbenign.* *Milton's Par. Lost, b. x. l.* 661.

UNBE'NT. *adj.*

1. Not strained by the string.

Apollo heard, and conqu'ring his disdain,
Unbent his bow, and Greece inspir'd again. *Dryden.*

2. Having the bow unstrung.

Why hast thou gone so far,
To be *unbent* when thou hast ta'en thy stand,
Th' elected deer before thee? *Shakesp. Cymbeline.*

3. Not crushed; not subdued.

But thou, secure of soul, *unbent* with woes,
The more thy fortune frowns, the more oppose. *Dryden.*

4. Relaxed; not intent.

Be not always on affairs intent,
But let thy thoughts be easy and *unbent*:
When our mind's eyes are disengag'd and free,
They clearer, farther, and distinctly see. *Denham.*

UNBESEE'MING. *adj.* Unbecoming.

No emotion of passion transported me by the indignity of his carriage, to do or say any thing *unbeseeming* myself. *K. Charles.*

Far be the spirit of the chace from them;
Uncomely courage, *unbeseeming* skill. *Thomson.*

UNBESO'UGHT. *adj.* Not intreated.

Lest heat should injure us, his timely care
Hath, *unbesought*, provided; and his hands
Cloath'd us unworthy; pitying while he judg'd. *Milton.*

UNBESTO'WED. *adj.* Not given; not disposed of.

He had now but one son and one daughter *unbestowed. Bacon.*

UNBETRA'YED. *adj.* Not betrayed.

Many being privy to the fact,
How hard is it to keep it *unbetray'd*? *Daniel's Civil War.*

UNBEWA'ILED. *adj.* Not lamented.

Let determin'd things to destiny
Hold *unbewail'd* their way. *Shakesp. Ant. and Cleopatra.*

To UNBEWI'TCH. *v. a.* [from *witch.*] To free from fascination.

To UNBI'ASS. *v. a.* To free from any external motive; to disentangle from prejudice.

That our understandings may be free to examine, and reason *unbiassed* give its judgment; being that whereon a right direction of our conduct to true happiness depends; it is in this we should employ our chief care. *Locke.*

The standing evidences of the gospel, every time they are consider'd, gain upon sincere, *unbiass'd* minds. *Atterbury.*

The truest service a private man may do his country, is by *unbiassing* his mind, as much as possible, between the rival powers. *Swift.*

Where's the man who counsel can bestow,
Unbiass'd, or by favour, or by spite;
Not dully prepossess'd, nor blindly right. *Pope.*

UNBI'ASSEDLY. *adj.* Without external influence; without prejudice.

I have sought the true meaning; and have *unbiassedly* embraced what, upon a fair enquiry, appeared so to me. *Locke.*

UNBI'D. } *adj.*
UNBI'DDEN. }

1. Uninvited.

Unbidden guests
Are often welcomest when they are gone. *Shakesp.*

2. Uncommanded; spontaneous.

Thorns also and thistles it shall bring thee forth
Unbid. *Milton's Par. Lost, b. x. l.* 204.

Roses *unbid*, and ev'ry fragrant flow'r,
Flew from their stalks, to strow thy nuptial bow'r. *Dryden.*

Unbidden earth shall wreathing ivy bring,
And fragrant herbs the promises of spring. *Dryden.*

UNBI'GOTTED. *adj.* Free from bigotry.

Erasmus, who was an *unbigotted* Roman Catholick, was so much transported with this passage of Socrates, that he could scarce forbear looking upon him as a saint, and desiring him to pray for him. *Addison.*

To UNBI'ND. *v. a.* [from *bind.*] To loose; to untie.

His own woe's author, whoso bound it finds,
As did Pyrocles, and it willfully *unbinds.* *Fairy Queen.*

Ye Latian dames,
If there be here, who dare maintain
My right, nor think the name of mother vain,
Unbind your fillets, loose your flowing hair,
And orgies, and nocturnal rites prepare. *Dryden.*

On the sixth instant it was thought fit to *unbind* his head. *Tatler,* Nº. 55.

To UNBI'SHOP. *v. a.* [from *bishop.*] To deprive of episcopal orders.

I cannot look upon Titus as so far *unbishoped* yet, but that he still exhibits to us all the essentials of jurisdiction. *South.*

UNBI'TTED. *adj.* [from *bit.*] Unbridled; unrestrained.

We have reason to cool our raging motions, our carnal stings, our *unbitted* lusts; whereof I take this love to be a sect or cyon. *Shakesp. Othello.*

UNBLA'MABLE. *adj.* Not culpable; not to be charged with a fault.

Much more could I say concerning this *unblamable* inequality of fines and rates. *Bacon.*

He lov'd his people, him they idoliz'd;
And thence proceeds my mortal hatred to him;
That thus *unblamable* to all beside,
He err'd to me alone. *Dryden's Don Sebastian.*

UNBLAMABLY. *adv.* Without taint of fault.

Ye are witnesses, and God also, how holily, and justly, and *unblameably* we behaved ourselves. 1 *Thess.* ii. 10.

UNBLA'MED. *adj.* Blameless; free from fault.

Shall spend your days in joy *unblam'd*, and dwell
Long time in peace. *Milton's Par. Lost, b.* xii. *l.* 22.

Unblam'd, abundance crown'd the royal board,
What time this dome rever'd her prudent lord,
Who now is doom'd to mourn. *Pope's Odyssey.*

UNBLE'MISHED. *adj.* Free from turpitude; free from reproach; free from deformity.

O welcome, pure-ey'd faith, white-handed hope;
Thou hovering angel, girt with golden wings,
And thou *unblemish'd* form of chastity. *Milton's Comus.*

Under this stone lies virtue, youth,
Unblemish'd probity, and truth. *Waller.*

Is none worthy to be made a wife
In all this town? Suppose her free from strife,
Rich, fair, and fruitful; of *unblemish'd* life. *Dryden.*

They appointed, out of these new converts, men of the best sense, and of the most *unblemish'd* lives, to preside over these several assemblies. *Addison.*

UNBLE'NDED. *adj.* Not mingled.

None can boast a knowledge depurate from defilement, within this atmosphere of flesh; it dwells no where in *unblended* proportions on this side the empyreum. *Glanville.*

UNBLEN'CHED. *adj.* Not disgraced; not injured by any soil.

There, where very desolation dwells,
She may pass on with *unblench'd* majesty:
Be it not done in pride, or in presumption. *Milton.*

UNBLE'ST. *adj.*

1. Accursed; excluded from benediction.

It is a shameful and *unblessed* thing, to take the scum of people, and wicked, condemned men, to be the people with whom you plant. *Bacon.*

2. Wretched; unhappy.

In thy pow'r
It lies yet, ere conception, to prevent
The race *unblest*, to being yet unbegot. *Milton.*

What is true passion, if *unblest* it dies?
And where is Emma's joy, if Henry flies? *Prior.*

UNBLOO'DIED. *adj.* Not stained with blood.

Who finds the partridge in the puttock's nest,
But may imagine how the bird was dead,
Although the kite soar with *unbloodied* beak. *Shakesp.*

UNBLOO'DY. *adj.* Not cruel; not shedding blood; not stained with blood.

Under the ledge of Atlas lies a cave,
The venerable seat of holy hermits,
Who there, secure in separated cells,
From the purling streams, and savage fruits,
Have wholesome bev'rage, and *unbloody* feasts. *Dryden.*

UNBLO'WN. *adj.* Having the bud yet unexpanded.

Ah! my poor princes! Ah! my tender babes!
My *unblown* flowers, new-appearing sweets! *Shakesp.*

UNBLU'NTED. *adj.* Not becoming obtuse.

A sword, whose weight without a blow might slay;
Able, *unblunted*, to cut hosts away. *Cowley's Davideis.*

UNBO'DIED. *adj.*

1. Incorporeal; immaterial.

If we could conceive of things as angels and *unbodied* spirits do, without involving them in those clouds language throws upon them, we should seldom be in danger of such mistakes as are perpetually committed. *Watts's Logick.*

2. Freed from the body.

She hath the bonds broke of eternal night;
Her soul *unbodied* of the burdenous corpse. *Spenser.*

All things are but alter'd, nothing dies;
And here and there th' *unbody'd* spirit flies. *Dryden.*

UNBO'ILED. *ad.* Not sodden.

A quarter of a pint of rice *unboiled*, will arise to a pint boiled. *Bacon.*

To UNBO'LT. *v. a.* To set open; to unbar.

I'll call my uncle down;
He shall *unbolt* the gates. *Shakesp. Troilus and Cressida.*

UNBO'LTED. *adj.* Coarse; gross; not refined, as flour by bolting or sifting.

I will tread this *unbolted* villain into mortar, and daub the wall of a jakes with him. *Shakespeare's K. Lear.*

UNBO'NNETTED. *adj.* Wanting a hat or bonnet.

This night, wherein
The lion, and the belly-pinched wolf
Keep their fur dry; *unbonnetted* he runs,
And bids what will, take all. *Shakesp. K. Lear.*

UNBOO'KISH. *adj.*
1. Not studious of books.
2. Not cultivated by erudition.
As he shall smile, Othello shall go mad;
And his *unbookish* jealousy must construe
Poor Cassio's smiles, gestures, and light behaviour,
Quite in the wrong. *Shakespeare's Othello.*

UNBO'RN. *adj.* Not yet brought into life; future; being to come.
Some *unborn* sorrow, ripe in fortune's womb,
Is coming tow'rd me. *Shakesp. Richard* II.
The woes to come, the children yet *unborn*
Shall feel this day, as sharp to them as thorn. *Shakesp.*
Never so much as in a thought *unborn*,
Did I offend you. *Shakesp. As you like it.*
He on the wings of cherubim
Up-lifted, in paternal glory rode
Far into chaos, and the world *unborn*. *Milton's Par. Lost.*
To what wretched state reserv'd!
Better end here *unborn!* Why is life giv'n
To be thus wasted from us? *Milton's Par. Lost.*
A queen, from whom
The souls of kings *unborn* for bodies wait. *Dryden.*

UNBO'RROWED. *adj.* Genuine; native; one's own.
But the luxurious father of the fold,
With native purple, and *unborrow'd* gold,
Beneath his pompous fleece shall proudly sweat. *Dryden.*
In substances, especially those which the common and *unborrow'd* names of any language are applied to, some remarkable, sensible qualities, serve to distinguish one from another. *Locke.*

UNBO'TTOMED. *adj.*
1. Without bottom; bottomless.
The dark, *unbottom'd*, infinite abyss. *Milton.*
2. Having no solid foundation.
This is a special act of christian hope, to be thus *unbottomed* of ourselves, and fastened upon God, with a full reliance, trust, and dependance on his mercy. *Hammond.*

To UNBO'SOM. *v. a.*
1. To reveal in confidence.
I lov'd thee, as too well thou knew'st;
Too well, *unbosom'd* all my secrets to thee,
Not out of levity, but overpower'd
By thy request, who could deny thee nothing. *Milton.*
Do we *unbosom* all our secrets to him, and hide nothing that passeth in the depth of our hearts from him? *Atterbury.*
2. To open; to disclose.
Should I thence, hurried on viewless wing,
Take up a weeping on the mountains wild,
The gentle neighbourhood of grove and spring
Would soon *unbosom* all their echo's mild. *Milton.*

UNBO'UGHT. *adj.*
1. Obtained without money.
The *unbought* dainties of the poor. *Dryden's Horace.*
2. Not finding any purchaser.
The merchant will leave our native commodities *unbought* upon the hands of the farmer, rather than export them to a market, which will not afford him returns with profit. *Locke.*

UNBO'UND. *adj.*
1. Loose; not tied.
2. Wanting a cover.
He that has complex ideas, without particular names for them, would be in no better case than a bookseller, who had volumes that lay *unbound*, and without titles; which he could make known to others, only by shewing the loose sheets. *Locke.*
3. Preterite of *unbind*.
Some from their chains the faithful dogs *unbound*. *Dryden.*

UNBO'UNDED. *adj.*
1. Infinite; interminable.
Long were to tell what I have done;
I voyag'd the unreal, vast, *unbounded* deep
Of horrible confusion. *Milton.*
The wide, th' *unbounded* prospect lies before me;
But shadows, clouds, and darkness rest upon it. *Addison.*
2. Unlimitted; unrestrained.
He was a man
Of an *unbounded* stomach, ever ranking
Himself with princes. *Shakespeare.*
He had given his curiosity its full, *unbounded* range, and examin'd not only in contemplation, but by sensitive experiment, whatever could be good for the sons of men. *Decay of Piety.*

UNBOU'NDEDLY. *adv.* Without bounds; without limits.
So *unboundedly* mischievous is that petulant member, that heaven and earth are not wide enough for its range, but it will find work at home too. *Government of the Tongue.*

UNBOU'NDEDNESS. *n. s.* Exemption from limits.
Finitude, applied to created things, imports the proportions of the several properties of these things to one another. Infinitude, the *unboundedness* of these degrees of properties. *Cheyne.*

UNBO'WED. *adj.* Not bent.
He knits his brow, and shews an angry eye,
And passeth by with stiff, *unbowed* knee,
Disdaining duty that to us belongs. *Shakesp. Hen.* VI.

To UNBO'WEL. *v. n.* To exenterate; to eviscerate.
In this chapter I'll *unbowel* the state of the question. *Hakewill.*
It is now become a new species of divinity, to branch out with fond distinctions our holy faith, which the pious simplicity of the first christians received to practice; not to read upon as an anatomy, *unbowel* and dissect to try experiments. *Decay of Piety.*

To UNBRA'CE. *v. a.*
1. To loose; to relax.
With whose reproach and odious menace,
The knight emboiling in his haughty heart,
Knit all his forces, and gan soon *unbrace*
His grasping hold. *Fairy Queen, b. 2. c. 4. st. 9.*
Somewhat of mournful sure my ears does wound;
Drums *unbraced*, with soldiers broken cries. *Dryden.*
Nought shall the psaltry and the harp avail,
When the quick spirits their warm march forbear,
And numbing coldness has *unbrac'd* the ear. *Prior.*
Wasting years, that wither human race,
Exhaust thy spirits, and thy arms *unbrace*. *Pope's Iliad.*
2. To make the clothes loose.
Is it physical,
To walk *unbrac'd*, and suck up the humours
Of the dank morning? *Shakesp. Julius Cæsar.*
Hamlet, with his doublet all *unbrac'd*;
No hat upon his head, his stockings loose. *Shakesp.*

UNBRE'ATHED. *v. a.* Not exercised.
They now have toil'd their *unbreath'd* memories,
With this same play against our nuptials. *Shakesp.*

UNBRE'ATHING. *adj.* Unanimated.
They spake not a word;
But like dumb statues, or *unbreathing* stones,
Star'd each on other, and look'd deadly pale. *Shakesp.*

UNBRE'D. *adj.*
1. Not instructed in civility; ill educated.
Unbred minds must be a little sent abroad. *Gov. of Tongue.*
Children learn from *unbred* or debauched servants, untowardly tricks. *Locke on Education.*
Sure never any thing was so *unbred* as that odious man. *Congreve's Way of the World.*
2. Not taught.
A warriour dame,
Unbred to spinning, in the loom unskill'd. *Dryden.*

UNBREE'CHED. *adj.* Having no breeches.
Looking on my boy's face, methoughts I did recoil
Twenty-three years, and saw myself *unbreech'd*,
In my green velvet coat. *Shakespeare's Winter Tale.*

UNBRI'BED. *adj.* Not influenced by money or gifts; not hired.
The soul gave all:
Unbrib'd it gave; or, if a bribe appear,
No less than heav'n. *Dryden.*
To succour the distress'd;
Unbrib'd by love; unterrify'd by threats. *A. Phillips.*

UNBRI'DLED. *adj.* Licentious; not restrained.
This is not well, rash and *unbridled* boy,
To fly the favours of so good a king. *Shakesp.*
We have considered religious zeal, which transgresses in *unbridled* excess. *Spratt's Sermons.*
To what licence
Dares thy *unbridled* boldness run itself? *B. Johnson.*

UNBRO'KE. }
UNBRO'KEN. } *adj.* [from *break.*]
1. Not violated.
God pardon all oaths, that are broke to me;
God keep all vows *unbroke*, are made to thee. *Shakesp.*
Some married persons, even in their marriage, do please God, by preserving their faith *unbroken*. *Taylor.*
He first broke peace in heav'n, and faith, till then
Unbroken. *Milton.*
2. Not subdued; not weakened.
From his seat the Pylian prince arose:
Two centuries already he fulfill'd;
And now began the third, *unbroken* yet. *Dryden.*
How broad his shoulders spread! by age *unbroke!* *Pope.*
3. Not tamed.
A lonely cow,
Unworn with yokes, *unbroken* to the plow. *Addison.*

UNBR'OTHERLIKE. }
UNBRO'THERLY. } *adj.* Ill suiting with the character of a brother.
Victor's *unbrotherlike* heat towards the eastern churches, fomented that difference about Easter into a schism. *Decay of Piety.*

UNBRU'ISED. *adj* Not bruised; not hurt.
On Dardan plains,
The fresh, and yet *unbruised* Greeks do pitch
Their brave pavillions. *Shakesp.*
Thou'st years upon thee, and thou art too full
Of the war's surfeits, to go rove with one
That's yet *unbruis'd*. *Shakesp. Coriolanus.*
Care keeps his watch in ev'ry old man's eye:
And where care lodgeth, sleep will never lie;
But where *unbruised* youth, with unstuft brain,
Doth couch his limbs, there golden sleep doth reign. *Shakesp.*

To Unbu'ckle. *v. a.* To loose from buckles.

We have been down together in my sleep,
Unbuckling helms; fisting each other's throat,
And wak'd half dead with nothing. *Shakesp. Coriolanus.*

He that *unbuckles* this, till we do please
To doff't for our purpose, shall hear a storm. *Shakesp.*

His starry helm *unbuckled*, shew'd him prime
In manhood, where youth ended. *Milton's Par. Lost.*

All *unbuckling* the rich mail they wore,
Laid their bright arms along the sable shore. *Pope.*

To Unbuild. *v. a.* To raze; to destroy.

This is the way to kindle, not to quench;
T' *unbuild* the city, and to lay all flat. *Shakespeare.*

What will they then but *unbuild*
His living temples, built by faith to stand;
Their own faith, not another's? *Milton's Par. Lost.*

Unbui'lt. *adj.* Not yet erected.

Built walls you shun, *unbuilt* you see. *Dryden.*

Unbu'ried. *adj.* Not interred; not honoured with the rites of funeral.

Why suffer'st thou thy sons, *unburied* yet,
To hover on the dreadful shore of Styx? *Shakesp.*

The moss which groweth upon the skull of a dead man *unburied*, will stauch blood potently. *Bacon.*

The hardest ingredient to come by, is the moss upon the skull of a dead man *unburied*. *Bacon.*

Him double cares attend,
For his *unburied* soldiers, aud his friend. *Dryden.*

Breathless he lies; and his *unbury'd* ghost,
Depriv'd of funeral rites, pollutes your host. *Dryden.*

The wand'ring ghosts
Of king's *unbury'd* on the wasted coasts. *Pope's Statius.*

Unbu'rned. } *adj.*
Unbu'rnt. }

1. Not consumed; not wasted; not injured by fire.

Creon denies the rites of fun'ral fires to those,
Whose breathless bodies yet he calls his foes;
Unburn'd, unburied, on a heap they lie. *Dryden.*

2. Not heated with fire.

Burnt wine is more hard and astringent, than wine *unburnt*. *Bacon's Nat. Hist.* N. 898.

Unbu'rning. *adj.* Not consuming by heat.

What we have said of the *unburning* fire called light, streaming from the flame of a candle, may easily be applied to all other light deprived of sensible heat. *Digby.*

To Unbu'rthen. *v. a.*

1. To rid of a load.

We'll shake all cares and business from our age,
Conferring them on younger strengths; while we
Unburden'd crawl tow'rd death. *Shakesp. K. Lear.*

2. To throw off.

Sharp Buckingham *unburthens* with his tongue
The envious load that lies upon his heart. *Shakesp.*

3. To disclose what lies heavy on the mind.

From your love I have a warranty
T' *unburthen* all my plots and purposes,
How to get clear of all the debts I owe. *Shakesp.*

To Unbu'tton. *v. a.* To loose any thing buttoned.

Thou art fat-witted with drinking old sack, and *unbuttoning* thee after supper. *Shakesp. Hen.* IV.

Many catch cold on the breast, by leaving their doublets *unbuttoned*. *Harvey on Consumptions.*

His silk waistcoat was *unbuttoned* in several places. *Addison.*

Uncalci'ned. *adj.* Free from calcination.

A saline substance, subtler than sal ammoniack, carried up with it, *uncalcined* gold in the form of subtile exhalations. *Boyle.*

Unca'lled. *adj.* Not summoned; not sent for; not demanded.

Basilius had servants, who, though they came not *uncalled*, yet at call were ready. *Sidney.*

He, bolder now, *uncall'd* before her stood. *Milton.*

Mild Lucina came *uncall'd*, and stood
Beside the struggling boughs, and heard the groan,
Then reach'd her midwife hand to speed the throes. *Dryden.*

To Unca'lm. *adj.* To disturb.

What strange disquiet has *uncalm'd* your breast,
Inhuman fair, to rob the dead of rest? *Dryden.*

Unca'ncelled. *adj.* Not erased; not abrogated.

I only mourn my yet *uncancell'd* score;
You put me past the pow'r of paying more. *Dryden.*

Uncano'nical. *adj.* Not agreeable to the canons.

Unca'pable. *adj.* [*incapable*, Fr. *incapax*, Lat.] Not capable; not susceptible.

Thou art come to answer
A stony adversary, an inhuman wretch,
Uncapable of pity, void and empty
From any dram of mercy. *Shakesp. Mer. of Venice.*

He who believes himself *uncapable* of pardon, goes on without any care of reforming. *Hammond.*

This, whilst they are under the deceit of it, makes them *uncapable* of conviction; and they applaud themselves as zealous champions for truth, when indeed they are contending for error. *Locke.*

Unca'red *for*. *adj.* Not regarded; not attended to.

Their kings, to better their worldly estate, left their own and their people's ghostly condition *uncared for*.

Unca'rnate. *adj.* Not fleshly.

Nor need we be afraid to ascribe that to the incarnate son, which sometimes is attributed unto the *uncarnate* father. *Brown's Vulgar Errours.*

To Unca'se. *v. a.*

1. To disengage from any covering.

See Pompey is *uncasing* for the combat. *Shakesp.*

Thou shalt be master, Tranio, in my stead,
'Tis hatch'd, and shall be so: Tranio, at once
Uncase thee; take my colour'd hat and cloak. *Shakesp.*

Partly by his voice, and partly by his ears, was discover'd; and consequently *uncased*, well laughed at, and well cudgell'd. *L'Estrange.*

Uncase me, and do with me what you please. *Addison.*

2. To flay.

All men him *uncased* 'gan deride. *Hubberd's Tale.*

Unca'ught. *adj.* Not yet catched.

Let him fly far;
Not in this land shall he remain *uncaught*,
And found dispatch'd. *Shakesp. K. Lear.*

His bosom glows with treasures yet *uncaught*. *Gay.*

Unca'used. *adj.* Having no precedent cause.

Unca'utious. *adj.* Nat wary; heedless.

Unforeseen, they say, is unprepar'd:
Uncautious Arcite thought himself alone. *Dryden.*

Unce'lebrated. *adj.* Not solemnized.

Thus was the first day, ev'n and morn;
Nor pass'd *uncelebrated*, nor unsung
By the celestial choirs. *Milton's Par. Lost, b.* vii. *l.* 253.

Unce'nsured. *adj.* Exempt from publick reproach.

How difficult must it be for any ruler to live *uncensured*, where every one of the community is thus qualified for modelling the constitution? *Addison's Freeholder.*

Fear most to tax an honourable fool,
Whose right it is *uncensur'd* to be dull. *Pope.*

To be *uncensured*, and to be obscure, is the same thing. *Pope's Letters.*

Unce'rtain. *adj.* [*incertain*, Fr. *incertus*, Lat.]

1. Doubtful; not certainly known.

That sacred pile, so vast, so high,
That whether 'tis a part of earth or sky,
Uncertain seems; and may be thought a proud
Aspiring mountain, or descending cloud. *Denham.*

2. Doubtful; not having certain knowledge.

Man, without the protection of a superior being, is secure of nothing that he enjoys, and *uncertain* of every thing that he hopes for. *Tillotson.*

Condemned on Caucasus to lie,
Still to be dying, not to die;
With certain pain, *uncertain* of relief,
True emblem of a wretched lover's grief. *Granville.*

3. Not sure in the consequence.

I must be married to my brother's daughter,
Or else my kingdom stands on brittle glass:
Murther her brothers, and then marry her!
Uncertain way of gain! *Shakespeare's Richard* III.

Ascanius young, and eager of his game,
Soon bent his bow, *uncertain* in his aim:
But the dire fiend the fatal arrow guides,
Which pierc'd his bowels through his panting sides. *Dryden.*

In the bright air the fauchion shone,
Or whistling slings dismiss'd th' *uncertain* stone. *Gay.*

The search of our future being, is but a needless, anxious, and *uncertain* haste to be knowing, sooner than we can, what, without all this solicitude, we shall know a little later. *Pope.*

4. Unsettled; unregular.

As the form of our publick service is not voluntary, so neither are the parts thereof *uncertain*; but they are all set down in such order, and with such choice, as hath, in the wisdom of the church, seemed best. *Hooker.*

Unce'rtained. *adj.* Made uncertain. A word not used.

The diversity of seasons are not so *uncertained* by the sun and moon alone, who always keep one and the same course, but that the stars have also their working therein. *Raleigh.*

Unce'rtainly. *adv.* Not surely; not certainly.

They that are past all hope of good, are past
All fear of ill: and yet if he be dead,
Speak softly, or *uncertainly*. *Denham's Sophy.*

Go, mortals, now, and vex yourselves in vain
For wealth, which so *uncertainly* must come:
When what was brought so far, and with such pain,
Was only kept to lose it nearer home. *Dryden.*

Names must be of very unsteady meaning, if the ideas be referred to standards without us, that cannot be known at all, or but very imperfectly and *uncertainly*. *Locke.*

UNCE'RTAINTY. *n. f.*
1. Dubiousness; want of knowledge.
All great concernments must delays endure;
Rashness and haste make all things unsecure;
And if uncertain thy pretensions be,
Stay till fit time wear out *uncertainty*. *Denham.*
You common cry of curs, whose breath I hate,
Here then remain with your *uncertainty*;
Let ev'ry feeble rumour shake your hearts. *Shakesp.*
That which makes doubtfulness and *uncertainty* in the signification of some, more than other words, is the difference of ideas they stand for. *Locke.*
2. Contingency; want of certainty.
God's omniscience is a light shining into every dark corner, stedfastly grasping the greatest and most slippery *uncertainties*. *South's Sermons.*
3. Something unknown.
Our shepherd's case is every man's case, that quits a moral certainty for an *uncertainty*, and leaps from the honest business he was brought up to, into a trade he has no skill in. *L'Estrange.*

To UNCHA'IN. *v. a.* To free from chains.
Minerva thus to Perseus lent her shield,
Secure of conquest, sent him to the field:
The hero acted what the queen ordain'd;
So was his fame complete, and Andromede *unchain'd*. *Prior.*

UNCHA'NGEABLE. *adj.* Immutable; not subject to variation.
If the end for which a law provideth, be perpetually necessary; and the way whereby it provideth perpetually also most apt, no doubt but that every such law ought for ever to remain *unchangeable*. *Hooker, b.* iii. §. 10.

UNCHA'NGED. *adj.*
1. Not altered.
When our fortunes are violently changed, our spirits are *unchanged*. *Taylor's Rule of Holy Living.*
More safe I sing with mortal voice; *unchang'd*
To hoarse, or mute. *Milton's Par. Lost.*
2. Not alterable.
Dismiss thy fear,
And heav'n's *unchang'd* decrees attentive hear:
More pow'rful gods have torn thee from my side. *Dryden.*
Honour *unchang'd*, a principle profest,
Fixt to one side, but mod'rate to the rest. *Pope.*

UNCHA'NGEABLENESS. *n. f.* Immutability.
This *unchangeableness* of colour I am now to describe. *Newt.*

UNCHA'NGEABLY. *adv.* Immutably; without change.
All truth is *unchangeably* the same; that proposition, which is true at any time, being so for ever. *South.*
Her first order, disposition, frame,
Must then subsist *unchangeably* the same. *Blackmore.*

UNCHA'NGING. *adj.* Suffering no alteration.
But that thy face is, vizor-like, *unchanging*,
Made impudent with use of evil deeds,
I would essay, proud queen, to make thee blush. *Shakesp.*
True expression, like th' *unchanging* sun,
Clears and improves whate'er it shines upon:
It gilds all objects, but it alters none. *Pope.*

To UNCHA'RGE. *v. a.* To retract an accusation.
Even his mother shall *uncharge* the practice,
And call it accident. *Shakesp. Hamlet.*

UNCHA'RITABLE. *adj.* Contrary to charity; contrary to the universal love prescribed by christianity.
All the rich mines of learning ransack'd are
To furnish ammunition for this war;
Uncharitable zeal our reason whets,
And double edges on our passion sets. *Denham.*
This fills the minds of weak men with *uncharitable* interpretations of those actions of which they are not competent judges. *Addison's Freeholder*, N°. 37.

UNCHA'RITABLENESS. *n. f.* Want of charity.
The penitence of the criminal may have number'd him among the saints, when our unretracted *uncharitableness* may send us to unquenchable flames. *Govern. of the Tongue.*
Heaven and hell are the proper regions of mercy and *uncharitableness*. *Atterbury.*

UNCHA'RITABLY. *adv.* In a manner contrary to charity.
I did not mean the cutting off all that nation with the sword; which, far be it from me that I should ever think so desperately, or wish so *uncharitably*. *Spenser.*
Urge neither charity nor shame to me;
Uncharitably with me have you dealt,
And shamefully my hopes by you are butcher'd. *Shakesp.*
Men, imprudently and *uncharitably* often, employ their zeal for persons. *Sprat.*

UNCHA'RY. *adj.* Not wary; not cautious.
I've said too much unto a heart of stone,
And laid my honour too *unchary* out. *Shakespeare.*

UNCHA'STE. *adj.* Lewd; libidinous; not continent; not chaste; not pure.
One, that in divers places I had heard before blazed, as the most impudently *unchaste* woman of all Asia. *Sidney.*
In my master's garments,
Which he inforc'd from me, away he posts
With *unchaste* purpose, to violate
My lady's honour. *Shakesp. Cymbeline.*
He hath given her his monumental ring, and thinks himself made in the *unchaste* composition. *Shakespeare.*
Whosoever is *unchaste*, cannot reverence himself; and the reverence of a man's self is, next religion, the chiefest bridle of all vices. *Bacon.*
Lust, by *unchaste* looks,
Lets in defilement to the inward parts. *Milton.*
If she thinks to be separated by reason of her husband's *unchaste* life, then the man will be uncurably ruined. *Taylor.*

UNCHA'STITY. *n. f.* Lewdness; incontinence.
That generation was more particularly addicted to intemperance, sensuality, and *unchastity*. *Woodward.*
When the sun is among the horned signs, he may produce such a spirit of *unchastity*, as is dangerous to the honour of your worships families. *Arbuthnot.*

UNCHEE'RFULNESS. *n. f.* Melancholy; gloominess of temper.
Many, by a natural *uncheerfulness* of heart, love to indulge this uncomfortable way of life. *Addison's Spectator.*

UNCHE'CKED. *adj.* Unrestrained; not fluctuated.
What news on the Ryalto?
——Why, yet it lives there *uncheck'd*, that Anthonio hath a ship of rich lading wreck'd. *Shakesp. Mer. of Venice.*
Apt the mind, or fancy, is to rove
Uncheck'd, and of her roving is no end. *Milton.*
Thee on the wing thy *uncheck'd* vigour bore,
To wanton freely, or securely soar. *Smith to J. Phillips.*

UNCHE'WED. *adj.* Not masticated.
He fills his famish'd maw, his mouth runs o'er
With *unchew'd* morsels, while he churns the gore. *Dryden.*

To UNCHI'LD. *v. a.* To deprive of children.
He hath widow'd and *unchilded* many a one,
Which to this hour bewail the injury. *Shakesp.*

UNCHRI'STIAN. *adj.*
1. Contrary to the laws of christianity.
It's uncharitable, *unchristian*, and inhuman, to pass a peremptory sentence of condemnation upon a try'd friend, where there is any room left for a more favourable judgment. *L'Estrange.*
These *unchristian* fishers of men, are fatally caught in their own nets. *South.*
I cou'd dispense with the unphilosophicalness of this their hypothesis, were it not *unchristian*. *Norris.*
2. Unconverted; infidel.
Whereupon grew a question, whether a christian soldier might herein do as the *unchristian* did, and wear as they wore. *Hooker.*

UNCHRI'STIANNESS. *adj.* Contrariey to christianity.
The *unchristianness* of those denials might arise from a displeasure to see me prefer my own divines before their ministers. *K. Charles.*

UNCIRCUMCI'SED. *adj.* Not circumcised; not a Jew.
Th' *uncircumcis'd* smil'd grimly with disdain. *Cowley.*

UNCIRCUMCI'SION. *n f.* Omission of circumcision.
God, that gives the law that a Jew shall be circumcised, thereby constitutes *uncircumcision* an obliquity; which, had he not given that law, had never been such. *Hammond.*

UNCIRCUMSCRI'BED. *adj.* Unbounded; unlimited.
Though I, *uncircumscrib'd* myself, retire,
And put not forth my goodness. *Milton's Par. Lost.*
An arbitrary prince is the master of a non-resisting people; for where the power is *uncircumscribed*, the obedience ought to be unlimited. *Addison.*
The sovereign was flattered by a set of men into a persuasion, that the regal authority was unlimited and *uncircumscrib'd*. *Addison's Freeholder*, N°. 2.

UNCI'RCUMSPECT. *adj.* Not cautious; not vigilant.
Their *uncircumspect* simplicity had been used, especially in matters of religion. *Hayward.*

UNCIRCUMSTA'NTIAL. *adj.* Unimportant. A bad word.
The like particulars, although they seem *uncircumstantial*, are oft set down in holy scripture. *Browne's Vulgar Errours.*

UNCI'VIL. *adj.* [*incivil*, Fr. *incivilis*, Lat.] Unpolite; not agreeable to rules of elegance, or complaisance.
Your undutiful, *uncivil*, and uncharitable dealing in this your book, hath detected you. *Whitgift.*
They love me well, yet I have much to do,
To keep me from *uncivil* outrages. *Shakesp.*
My friends are so unreasonable, that they would have me be *uncivil* to him. *Spectator*, N°. 475.

UNCI'VILLY. *adv.* Unpolitely; not complaisantly.
Somewhat in it he would not have done, or desired undone, when he broke forth as desperately, as before he had done *uncivilly*. *Browne's Vulgar Errours.*

UNCI'VILIZED. *adj.*
1. Not reclaimed from barbarity.

But we, brave Britons, foreign laws despis'd,
And kept unconquer'd, and *uncivilized*:
Fierce for the liberties of wit, and bold,
We still defy'd the Romans, as of old. *Pope.*

2. Coarse; indecent.

Several, who have been polished in France, make use of the most coarse, *uncivilized* words in our language. *Addison.*

UNCLA'RIFIED. *adj.* Not purged; not purified.

One ounce of whey *unclarified*; one ounce of oil of vitriol, make no apparent alteration. *Bacon's Phys. Remarks.*

To UNCLA'SP. *v. a.* To open what is shut with clasps.

Thou know'st no less, but all: I have *unclasp'd*
To thee the book, ev'n of my secret soul. *Shakesp.*

Prayer can *unclasp* the girdles of the north, saying to a mountain of ice, be thou removed hence, and cast into the sea. *Taylor's Worthy Communicant.*

UNCLA'SSICK. Not classick.

Angel of dulness, sent to scatter round
Her magick charms o'er all *unclassick* ground. *Pope.*

U'NCLE. *n. s.* [*oncle*, Fr.] The father's or mother's brother.

Hamlet punishes his *uncle* rather for his own death, than the murther of his father. *Shakespeare Illustrated.*

UNCLEA'N. *n. s.*

1. Foul; dirty; filthy.

Charon,
A sordid god: down from his hoary chin
A length of beard descends, uncomb'd, *unclean*. *Dryden.*
Priests are patterns for the rest;
The gold of heav'n, who bear the God impress'd:
But when the precious coin is kept *unclean*,
The sov'reign's image is no longer seen.
If they be foul, on whom the people trust,
Well may the baser brass contract a rust. *Dryden.*

2. Not purified by ritual practices.

3. Foul with sin.

Besides how vile, contemptible, ridiculous,
What act more execrably *unclean*, profane? *Milton.*

What agonies must he endure? What difficulties overcome, before he can cleanse himself from the pollutions of sin, and be a fit inhabitant of that holy place, where no *unclean* thing shall enter? *Rogers's Sermons.*

4. Lewd; unchaste.

Let them all encircle him about,
And, fairy-like too, pinch the *unclean* knight,
And ask him, why that hour of fairy revel,
In their so sacred paths he dares to tread,
In shape profane. *Shakesp. Merry Wives of Windsor.*
Some tree, whose broad, smooth leaves together sow'd,
And girded on our loins, may cover round
Those middle parts; that this new comer, shame,
There sit not, and reproach us as *unclean*. *Milton.*

UNCLEA'NLINESS. *n. s.* Want of cleanliness.

This profane liberty and *uncleanliness*, the archbishop resolv'd to reform. *Clarendon.*

UNCLE'ANLY. *adj.*

1. Foul; filthy; nasty.

Civet is of a baser birth than tar;
The very *uncleanly* flux of a cat. *Shakespeare.*

2. Indecent; unchaste.

'Tis pity that these harmonious writers have ever indulged any thing *uncleanly* or impure to defile their paper. *Watts.*

UNCLEA'NNESS. *n. s.*

1. Lewdness; incontinence.

In St. Giles's I understood that most of the vilest and most miserable houses of *uncleanness* were. *Graunt's Bills of Mortality.*

2. Want of cleanliness; nastiness.

Be not curious nor careless in your habit; be not troublesome to thyself, or to others, by unhandsomeness, or *uncleanness*. *Taylor's Guide to Devotion.*

3. Sin; wickedness.

I will save you from all your *uncleannesses*. *Ez. xxxvi. 29.*

4. Want of ritual purity.

UNCLE'ANSED. *adj.* Not cleansed.

Pond earth is a good compost, if the pond have been long *uncleansed*: so the water be not too hungry. *Bacon's Nat. Hist.*

To UNCLE'W. *v. a.* [from *clew*.] To undo.

If I should pay you for't as 'tis extoll'd,
It would *unclew* me quite. *Shakesp. Timon of Athens.*

To UNCLE'NCH. *v. a.* To open the closed hand.

The hero so his enterprize recalls;
His fist *unclenches*, and the weapon falls. *Garth.*

UNCLI'PPED. *adj.* Whole; not cut.

As soon as there began a distinction between clipped and *unclipped* money, bullion arose. *Locke.*

To UNCLO'ATH. *v. a.* To strip; to make naked.

The boughs and branches are never *uncloathed* and left naked. *Raleigh's Hist. of the World.*

Poor orphans minds are left as *uncloath'd* and naked altogether, as their bodies. *Atterbury.*

Cover the couch over with thick woollen clothes, the warmth whereof will make it come presently; which once perceived, forthwith *uncloath* it. *Mortimer's Husbandry.*

To a distinct knowledge of things, we must *uncloath* them of all these mixtures, that we may contemplate them naked, and in their own nature. *Watts's Logick.*

To UNCLO'G. *v. a.*

1. To disencumber; to exonerate.

Could I meet 'em
But once a day, it would *unclog* my heart
Of what lies heavy to't. *Shakespeare.*

2. To set at liberty.

Then air, because *unclog'd* in empty space,
Flies after fire, and claims the second place. *Dryden.*

To UNCLOI'STER. *v. n.* To set at large.

Why did I not, *uncloister'd* from the womb,
Take my next lodging in a tomb? *Norris.*

To UNCLO'SE. *v. a.* To open.

Soon as thy letters trembling I *unclose*,
That well-known name awakens all my woes. *Pope.*

UNCLO'SED. *adj.* Not separated by inclosures.

The king's army would, through those *unclosed* parts, have done them little harm. *Clarendon.*

UNCLO'UDED. *adj.* Free from clouds; clear from obscurity; not darkened.

The father unfolding bright
Tow'rd the right hand his glory on the son
Blaz'd forth *unclouded* deity. *Milton's Par. Lost.*
True *virtues*, with *unclouded* light,
All great, all royal, shine divinely bright. *Roscommon.*
Blest with temper, whose *unclouded* ray,
Can make to-morrow cheerful as to-day. *Pope.*

UNCLO'UDEDNESS. *n. s.* Openness; freedom from gloom.

The love I would persuade, makes nothing more conducive to it, than the greatest *uncloudedness* of the eye, and the perfectest illustration of the object; which is such, that the clearest reason is the most advantageous light it can desire to be seen by. *Boyle.*

UNCLO'UDY *adj.* Free from a cloud.

Now night in silent state begins to rise,
And twinkling orbs bestrow th' *uncloudy* skies;
Her borrow'd lustre growing Cynthia lends. *Gay.*

To UNCLU'TCH. *v a.* To open.

If the terrors of the Lord could not melt his bowels, *unclutch* his griping hand, or disseize him of his prey; yet sure it must discourage him from grasping of heaven too. *Decay of Piety.*

To UNCOI'F. *v. a.* To pull the cap off.

Yonder are two apple-women scolding, and just ready to *uncoif* one another. *Arbuthnot and Pope.*

To UNCO'IL. *v. a.* [from *coil*.] To open from being coiled or wrapped one part upon another.

The spiral air-vessels are like threads of cobweb, a little *uncoiled*. *Derham's Physico-Theology.*

UNCOI'NED. *adj.* Not coined.

While thou liv'st, Kate, take a fellow of plain, *uncoined* constancy. *Shakespeare's Hen. V.*

An ounce of coined standard silver, must be of equal value to an ounce of *uncoined* standard silver. *Locke.*

UNCOLLE'CTED. *adj.* Not collected; not recollected.

Asham'd, confus'd, I started from my bed,
And to my soul yet *uncollected* said;
Into thyself, fond Solomon! return;
Reflect again, and thou again shalt mourn. *Prior.*

UNCO'LOURED. *adj.* Not stained with any colour, or die.

Out of things *uncoloured* and transparent, we can represent unto you all several colours. *Bacon.*

Whether to deck with clouds the *uncolour'd* sky,
Or wet the thirsty earth with falling show'rs;
Rising, or falling, still advance his praise. *Milton.*

UNCO'MBED. *adj.* Not parted or adjusted by the comb.

They might perceive his head
To be *unarmed*, and curled, *uncombed* hairs,
Upstarting stiff. *Fairy Queen, b. 1. c. 9. st. 22*
Their locks are beds of *uncomb'd* snakes, that wind
About their shady brows in wanton rings. *Crashaw.*
Thy locks *uncomb'd*, like a rough wood appear. *Dryden.*

UNCO'MEATABLE. *adj.* Inaccessible; unattainable. A low, corrupt word.

UNCO'MELINESS. *n. s.* Want of grace; want of beauty.

The ruined churches are so unhandsomely patched, and thatched, that men do even shun the places, for the *uncomeliness* thereof. *Spenser's Ireland.*

He prais'd women's modesty, and gave orderly, well-behaved reproof to all *uncomeliness*. *Shakesp.*

Those arches which the Tuscan writers call *di terzo*, and *di quarto acuto*, because they always concur in an acute angle, both for the natural imbecillity of the angle itself, and likewise for their very *uncomeliness*, ought to be exiled from judicious eyes. *Wotton's Architecture.*

Forgetting that duty of modest concealment which they owed to the father of their country, in case they had discovered any real *uncomeliness*. *K. Charles.*

The beauty or *uncomeliness* in good and ill breeding, will make deeper impressions on them, in the examples of others, than from any rules. *Locke.*

UNCO'MELY. *adj.* Not comely; wanting grace.

Though he thought inquisitiveness an *uncomely* guest, he could not but ask who she was. *Sidney.*

Neither is the same accounted an *uncomely* manner of riding: for great warriors say, they never saw a more comely man than the Irishman, nor that cometh on more bravely in his charge. *Spenser's Ireland.*

Many, who troubled them most in their counsels, durst not go thither, for fear of *uncomely* affronts. *Clarendon.*

Uncomely courage, unbeseeming skill. *Thomson's Autumn.*

UNCO'MFORTABLE. *adj.*

1. Affording no comfort; gloomy; dismal; miserable.

He much complaineth of his own *uncomfortable* exile, wherein he sustained many most grievous indignities, and endured the want of sundry, both pleasures and honours, before enjoyed. *Hooker.*

Christmass is in the most dead, *uncomfortable* time of the year, when the poor people would suffer very much, if they had not good cheer to support them. *Addison.*

Ours is melancholy and *uncomfortable* portion here below! A place, where not a day passes, but we eat our bread with sorrow and cares: the present troubles us, the future amazes; and even the past fills us with grief and anguish. *Wake.*

The sun ne'er views th' *uncomfortable* seats,
When radiant he advances or retreats. *Pope's Odyssey.*

2. Receiving no comfort; melancholy.

UNCO'MFORTABLENESS. *n. s.* Want of cheerfulness.

The want of just dispositions to the holy sacrament, may occasion this *uncomfortableness.* *Taylor's Worthy Communicant.*

UNCO'MFORTABLY. *adv.* Without cheerfulness.

UNCOMMA'NDED. *adj.* Not commanded.

It is easy to see what judgment is to be passed upon all those affected, *uncommanded,* absurd austerities of the Romish profession. *South.*

UNCO'MMON. *adj.* Not frequent; not often found or known.

Some of them are *uncommon,* but such as the reader must assent to, when he sees them explained. *Addison.*

UNCO'MMONLY. *adv.* Not frequently; to an uncommon degree.

UNCO'MMONNESS. *n. s.* Infrequency.

Our admiration of the antiquities about Naples and Rome, does not so much arise out of their greatness as *uncommonness.* *Addison.*

UNCOMPA'CT. *adj.* Not compact; not closely cohering.

These rivers were not streams of running matter; for how could a liquid, that lay hardening by degrees, settle in such a furrowed, *uncompact* surface? *Addison.*

UNCOMMU'NICATED. *adj.* Not communicated.

There is no such mutual infusion as really causeth the same natural operations or properties to be made common unto both substances; but whatsoever is natural to deity, the same remaineth in Christ *uncommunicated* unto his manhood; and whatsoever natural to manhood, his deity thereof is uncapable. *Hooker.*

UNCO'MPANIED. *adj.* Having no companion.

Thence she fled, *uncompanied,* unsought. *Fairfax.*

UNCOMPA'SSIONATE. *adj.* Having no pity.

Neither deep groans, nor silver-shedding tears,
Could penetrate her *uncompassionate* sire. *Shakesp.*

Hero and Leander were drowned in the *uncompassionate* surges. *Sandys's Journey.*

If thou in strength all mortals dost exceed;
In *uncompassionate* anger do not so. *Milton's Agonistes.*

UNCOMPE'LLED. *adj.* Free from compulsion.

The amorous needle, once joined to the loadstone, would never, *uncompelled,* forsake the inchanting mineral. *Boyle.*

Keep my voyage from the royal ear,
Nor, *uncompell'd,* the dangerous truth betray,
Till twice six times descends the lamp of day. *Pope.*

UNCOMPLAISA'NT. *adj.* Not civil; not obliging.

A natural roughness makes a man *uncomplaisant* to others, so that he has no deference for their inclinations. *Locke.*

UNCOMPLE'AT. *adj.* Not perfect; not finished.

Various incidents do not make different fables, but are only the *uncompleat* and unfinished parts of the same fable. *Pope.*

UNCOMPO'UNDED. *adj.*

1. Simple; not mixed.

Hardness may be reckoned the property of all *uncompounded* matter. *Newton's Opticks.*

Your *uncompounded* atoms, you
Figures in numbers infinite allow;
From which, by various combination, springs
This unconfin'd diversity of things. *Blackmore.*

2. Simple; not intricate.

The substance of the faith was comprised in that *uncompounded* style, but was afterwards prudently enlarged, for the repelling heretical invaders. *Hammond's Fundamentals.*

UNCOMPRE'SSED. *adj.* Free from compression.

We might be furnished with a reply, by setting down the differing weight of our receiver, when emptied, and when full of *uncompressed* air. *Boyle.*

UNCOMPREHE'NSIVE. *adj.*

1. Unable to comprehend.

2. In *Shakespeare* it seems to signify *incomprehensible.*

The providence, that's in a watchful state,
Knows almost every grain of Pluto's gold;
Finds bottom in th' *incomprehensive* deep. *Shakesp.*

UNCONCE'IVABLE. *adj.* Not to be understood; not to be comprehended by the mind.

In the communication of motion by impulse, we can have no other conception, but of the passing of motion out of one body into another; which is as obscure and *unconceivable,* as how our minds move or stop our bodies by thought. *Locke.*

Those atoms wond'rous small must be,
Small to an *unconceivable* degree;
Since though these radiant spoils dispers'd in air,
Do ne'er return, and ne'er the sun repair. *Blackmore.*

UNCONCE'IVABLENESS. *n. s.* Incomprehensibility.

The *unconceivableness* of something they find in one, throws men violently into the contrary hypothesis, though altogether as unintelligible. *Locke.*

UNCONCE'IVED. *adj.* Not thought; not imagined.

Vast is my theme, yet *unconceiv'd,* and brings
Untoward words, scarce loosen'd yet from things. *Creech.*

UNCONCE'RN. *n. s.* Negligence; want of interest; freedom from anxiety; freedom from perturbation.

Such things had been charged upon us by the malice of enemies, the want of judgment in friends, and the *unconcern* of indifferent persons. *Swift.*

UNCONCE'RNED. *adj.*

1. Having no interest.

An idle person is like one that is dead, *unconcerned* in the changes and necessities of the world. *Taylor.*

The earth's motion is to be admitted, notwithstanding the seeming contrary evidence of *unconcerned* senses. *Glanville.*

It seems a principle in human nature, to incline one way more than another, even in matters where we are wholly *unconcerned.* *Swift.*

2. Not anxious; not disturbed; not affected.

See the morn,
All *unconcern'd* with our unrest, begins
Her rosy progress smiling. *Milton's Par. Lost.*

You call'd me into all your joys, and gave me
An equal share; and in this depth of misery
Can I be *unconcerned?* *Denham's Sophy.*

The virgin from the ground
Upstarted fresh, already clos'd the wound;
And *unconcern'd* for all she felt before,
Precipitates her flight along the shore. *Dryden.*

Happy mortals, *unconcern'd* for more,
Confin'd their wishes to their native shore. *Dryden.*

We shall be easy and *unconcerned* at all the accidents of the way, and regard only the event of the journey. *Rogers.*

UNCONCE'RNEDLY. *adv.* Without interest or affection; without anxiety; without perturbation.

Not the most cruel of our conquering foes,
So *unconcern'dly* can relate our woes,
As not to lend a tear. *Denham.*

Death was denounc'd, that frightful sound,
Which ev'n the best can hardly bear:
He took the summons, void of fear,
And *unconcern'dly* cast his eyes around,
As if to find and dare the griesly challenger. *Dryden.*

Is heaven, with its pleasures for evermore, to be parted with so *unconcernedly?* Is an exceeding and eternal weight of glory too light in the balance against the hopeless death of the atheist, and utter extinction. *Bentley.*

UNCONCE'RNEDNESS. *n. s.* Freedom from anxiety, or perturbation.

No man, having done a kindness to another, would think himself justly dealt with, in a total neglect, and *unconcernedness* of the person who had received that kindness. *South.*

UNCONCE'RNING. *adj.* Not interesting; not affecting; not belonging to one.

Things impossible in their nature, or *unconcerning* to us, cannot beget it. *Decay of Piety.*

The science of medals, which is charged with so many *unconcerning* parts of knowledge, and built on such mean materials, appears ridiculous to those that have not examined it. *Addison on Antient Medals.*

UNCONCE'RNMENT. *n. s.* The state of having no share.

Being privileged by an happy *unconcernment* in those legal murders, you may take a sweeter relish of your own innocence. *South.*

UNCONCLU'DENT. } *adj.* Not decisive; inferring no plain or
UNCONCLU'DING. } certain conclusion or consequence.

Our arguments are inevident and *unconcludent.* *Hale.*

He makes his understanding only the warehouse of other mens false and *unconcluding* reasonings, rather than a repository of truth for his own use. *Locke.*

UNCONCLU'DINGNESS. *n. s.* Quality of being unconcluding.

 Either

Either may be much more probably maintained than hitherto, as against the unaccurateness and the *unconcludingness* of the analytical experiments vulgarly relied on. *Boyle.*

UNCONCO'CTED. *adj.* Not digested; not matured.

We swallow cherry-stones, but void them *unconcocted.* *Browne's Vulgar Errours.*

In theology, I put as great a difference between our new lights and antient truths, as between the sun and an *unconcocted*, evanid meteor. *Glanville.*

Did she extend the gloomy clouds on high,
Where all th' amazing fireworks of the sky,
In *unconcocted* seeds fermenting lie. *Blackmore.*

UNCONDE'MNED. *adj.* Not condemned.

It was a familiar and *uncondemned* practice amongst the Greeks and Romans, to expose, without pity, their innocent infants. *Locke.*

UNCONDI'TIONAL. *adj.* Absolute; not limited by any terms.

O pass not, Lord! an absolute decree,
Or bind thy sentence *unconditional*;
But in thy sentence our remorse foresee,
And, in that foresight, this thy doom recal. *Dryden.*

Our Saviour left a power in his church to absolve men from their sins; but this was not an absolute and *unconditional* power vested in any, but founded upon repentance, and on the penitent's belief in him alone. *Ayliffe's Parergon.*

UNCONFI'NED. *adj.*

1. Free from restraint.

I wonder at it.
That shews thou art *unconfin'd.* *Shakespeare.*

Chaucer has refined on Boccace, and has mended the stories he has borrowed: though prose allows more liberty of thought, and the expression is more easy when *unconfined* by numbers. Our countryman carries weight, and yet wins the race at disadvantage. *Dryden.*

Poets, a race long *unconfin'd* and free,
Still fond and proud of savage liberty,
Receiv'd his laws. *Pope's Essay on Criticism.*

2. Having no limits; unbounded.

If that which men esteem their happiness, were, like the light, the same sufficient and *unconfined* good, whether ten thousand enjoy the benefit of it, or but one, we should see men's good will and kind endeavours would be as universal. *Spectator,* N°. 601.

Blest with a taste exact, yet *unconfin'd*;
A knowledge both of books and human kind. *Pope.*

UNCONFI'NABLE. *adj.* Unbounded.

You rogue! you stand upon your honour! why, thou *unconfinable* baseness, it is as much as I can do to keep mine honour. *Shakespeare's Merry Wives of Windsor.*

UNCONFI'RMED. *adj.*

1. Not fortified by resolution; not strengthened; raw; weak.

The unexpected speech
The king had made upon the new-rais'd force,
In th' *unconfirm'd* troops, much fear did breed. *Daniel.*

2. Not strengthened by additional testimony.

He would have resign'd
To him his heav'nly office, nor was long
His witness *unconfirm'd.* *Milton's Par. Regain'd.*

3. Not settled in the church by the rite of confirmation.

UNCONFO'RM. *adj.* Unlike; dissimilar; not analagous.

Not *unconform* to other shining globes. *Milton.*

UNCONFO'RMABLE. *adj.* Inconsistent; not conforming.

Unto those general rules, they know we do not defend, that we may hold any thing *unconformable.* *Hooker.*

Moral good, is an action conformable to the rule of our duty. Moral evil, is an action *unconformable* to it, or a neglect to fulfil it. *Watts's Logick.*

UNCONFO'RMITY. *n. s.* Incongruity; inconsistency.

The moral goodness or evil of men's actions, which consist in their conformity or *unconformity* to right reason, must be eternal, necessary, and unchangeable. *South.*

UNCONFU'SED. *adj.* Distinct; free from confusion.

It is more distinct and *unconfused* than the sensitive memory. *Hale's Origin of Mankind.*

If in having our ideas in the memory ready at hand, consists quickness of parts; in this of having them *unconfused*, and being able nicely to distinguish one thing from another, consists the exactness of judgment. *Locke.*

UNCONFU'SEDLY. *adv.* Without confusion.

Every one finds that he knows, when any idea is in his understanding, and that, when more than one are there, he knows them, distinctly and *unconfusedly*, from one another. *Locke.*

UNCO'NFUTABLE. *adj.* Irrefragable; not to be convicted of errour.

One political argument they boasted of as *unconfutable*, that from the marriages of ecclesiasticks, would ensue poverty in many of the children, and thence a disgrace and burden to the church. *Sprat's Sermons.*

UNCONGE'ALED. *adj.* Not concreted by cold.

By exposing wine, after four months digestion in horse-dung, unto the extremity of cold, the aqueous parts will freeze, but the spirit retire, and be found *uncongealed* in the center. *Brown's Vulgar Errours.*

UNCO'NJUGAL. *adj.* Not consistent with matrimonial faith; not befitting a wife or husband.

My name
To all posterity may stand defam'd;
With malediction mention'd, and the blot
Of falshood most *unconjugal* traduc'd. *Milton's Agonistes.*

UNCONNE'CTED. *adj.* Not coherent; not joined by proper transitions or dependence of parts; lax; loose; vague.

Those who contemplate only the fragments broken off from any science, dispersed in short, *unconnected* discourses, can never survey an entire body of truth. *Watts.*

UNCONNI'VING. *adj.* Not forbearing penal notice.

To that hideous place not so confin'd,
By rigour *unconniving*; but that oft
Leaving my dolorous prison, I enjoy
Large liberty, to round this globe of earth. *Milton.*

UNCO'NQUERABLE. *adj.* Not to be subdued; insuperable; not to be overcome; invincible.

Louis was darting his thunder on the Alps, and causing his enemies to feel the force of his *unconquerable* arms. *Dryden.*

Spadillio, first *unconquerable* lord!
Led off two captive trumps, and swept the board. *Pope.*

UNCO'NQUERABLY. *adv.* Invincibly; insuperably.

The herds of Iphyclus, detain'd in wrong;
Wild, furious herds, *unconquerably* strong. *Pope.*

UNCO'NQUERED. *adj.*

1. Not subdued; not overcome.

To die so tamely,
O'ercome by passion and misfortune,
And still *unconquer'd* by my foes, sounds ill. *Denham.*

Unconquer'd yet, in that forlorn estate,
His manly courage overcame his fate. *Dryden.*

2. Insuperable; invincible.

These brothers had a-while served the king of Pontus; and in all his affairs, especially of war, whereunto they were only apt, they had shewed as *unconquered* courage, so rude a faithfulness. *Sidney.*

What was that snaky-headed gorgon shield,
That wise Minerva wore, *unconquer'd* virgin!
Wherewith she freez'd her foes to congeal'd stone,
But rigid looks, and chaste austerity,
And noble grace, that dash'd brute violence,
With sudden adoration and blank awe? *Milton.*

Unconquer'd lord of pleasure and of pain. *Johnson.*

UNCO'NSCIONABLE. *adj.*

1. Exceeding the limits of any just claim or expectation.

A man may oppose an *unconscionable* request for an unjustifiable reason. *L'Estrange.*

2. Forming unreasonable expectations.

You cannot be so *unconscionable* as to charge me for not subscribing of my name, for that would reflect too grossly upon your own party, who never dare it. *Dryden.*

3. Enormous; vast. A low word.

His giantship is gone somewhat crest-fall'n,
Stalking with less *unconscionable* strides,
And lower looks, but in a sultry chafe. *Milton's Agonistes.*

4. Not guided or influenced by conscience.

How infamous is the false, fraudulent, and *unconscionable*? hardly ever did any man of no conscience continue a man of any credit long. *South.*

UNCO'NSCIONABLENESS. *n. s.* Unreasonableness of hope or claim.

UNCO'NSCIONABLY. *adv.* Unreasonably.

Indeed 'tis pity you should miss
Th' arrears of all your services;
And for th' eternal obligation,
Y' have laid upon th' ungrateful nation,
Be used so *unconscionably* hard,
As not to find a just reward. *Hudibras, p.* ii. *cant.* 3.

This is a common vice; though all things here
Are sold, and sold *unconscionably* dear. *Dryden's Juvenal.*

UNCONSCIOUS. *adj.* Having no mental perception.

Unconscious causes only still impart
Their utmost skill, their utmost power exert;
Those which can freely chuse, discern, and know,
Can more or less of art and care bestow. *Blackmore.*

A yearling bullock to thy name shall smoke,
Untam'd, *unconscious* of the galling yoke. *Pope.*

UNCO'NSECRATED. *adj.* Not sacred; not dedicated; not devoted.

The sin of Israel had even *unconsecrated* and profaned that sacred edifice, and robbed it of its only defence. *South.*

UNCONSE'NTED. *adj.* Not yielded.

We should extend it even to the weaknesses of our natures, to our proneness to evil: for however these, *unconsented* to, will not be imputed to us, yet are they matter of sorrow. *Wake's Preparation for Death.*

UNCONSI'DERED. *adj.* Not considered; not attended to.

Love yourself; and in that love,
Not *unconsidered* leave your honour. *Shakespeare,*

It

It will not be *unconsidered*, that we find no open track in this labyrinth. *Brown's Vulgar Errours.*

UNCO'NSONANT. *adj.* Incongruous; unfit; inconsistent.

It seemeth a thing *unconsonant*, that the world should honour any other as the Saviour, but him whom it honoureth as the creator of the world. *Hooker.*

UNCO'NSTANT. *adj.* [*inconstant*, Fr. *inconstans*, Lat.] Fickle; not steady; changeable; mutable.

More *unconstant* than the wind; who woos
Ev'n now the frozen bosom of the north;
And, being anger'd, puffs away from thence,
Turning his face to the dew-dropping south. *Shakesp.*

Th' *unconstant* skies
Do change their course as sev'ral winds arise. *May's Virgil.*

UNCONSTRA'INED. *adj.* Free from compulsion.

Will you, with free and *unconstrained* soul,
Give me your daughter? *Shakespeare.*

These be the miseries which our first parents brought upon all mankind, unto whom God, in his creation, gave a free and *unconstrained* will. *Raleigh's Hist. of the World.*

Made for his use, yet he has form'd us so,
We *unconstrain'd*, what he commands us, do. *Dryden.*

His highness is return'd.——
And *unconstrain'd?* But with what change
Of countenance did he receive the message? *Denham.*

UNCONSTRA'INEDLY. *adv.* Without force suffered.

Such a patron has frankly, generously, and *unconstrainedly* relieved me. *South's Sermons.*

UNCONSTRA'INT. *n. s.* Freedom from constraint; ease.

Mr. Dryden writ more like a scholar; and though the greatest master of poetry, he wanted that easiness, that air of freedom and *unconstraint*, which is more sensibly to be perceived, than described. *Felton on the Classicks.*

UNCONSU'LTING. *adj.* [*inconsultus*, Lat.] Heady; rash; improvident; imprudent.

It was the fair Zelmane, Plexirtus's daughter, whom *unconsulting* affection, unfortunately born to mewards, had made borrow so much of her natural modesty, as to leave her more decent rayments. *Sidney.*

UNCONTE'STED. *adj.* Certain; past dispute.

UNCONSU'MED. *adj.* Not wasted; not destroyed by any wasting power.

Hope never comes,
That comes to all, but torture without end
Still urges, and a fiery deluge fed
With ever-burning sulphur *unconsum'd*. *Milton's Par. Lost.*

Fixedness, or a power to remain in the fire *unconsumed*, is an idea that always accompanies our complex idea, signified by the word gold. *Locke.*

UNCONSU'MMATE. *adj.* Not consummated.

Acron came to the fight,
Who left his spouse betroth'd, and *unconsummate* night. *Dryd.*

UNCONTE'MNED. *adj.* Not despised.

Which of the peers
Have *uncontemn'd* gone by him, or at least
Stood not neglected? *Shakesp. Hen.* VIII.

UNCONTE'NTED. *adj.* Not contented; not satisfied.

Permit me, chief,
To lead this *uncontented* gift away. *Dryden.*

UNCONTE'NTINGNESS. *n. s.* Want of power to satisfy.

The decreed *uncontentingness* of all other goods, is richly repaired by its being but an aptness to prove a rise to our love's settling in God. *Boyle.*

UNCONTE'STABLE. *adj.* Indisputable; not controvertible.

Where is the man that has *uncontestible* evidence of the truth of all that he holds, or of the falshood of all he condemns. *Locke.*

UNCONTE'STED. *adj.* Not disputed; evident.

'Tis by experience *uncontested* found,
Bodies orbicular, when whirling round,
Still shake off all things on their surface plac'd. *Blackmore.*

UNCONTRI'TE. *adj.* Not religiously penitent.

The priest, by absolving an *uncontrite* sinner, cannot make him contrite. *Hammond's Practical Catechism.*

UNCO'NTROVE'RTED. *adj.* Not disputed; not liable to debate.

One reason of the *uncontroverted* certainty of mathematical science is, because 'tis built upon clear and settled significations of names. *Glanville.*

UNCONTRO'ULABLE. *adj.*

1. Resistless; powerful beyond opposition.

Gaza mourns,
And all that band them to resist
His *uncontroulable* intent. *Milton.*

2. Indisputable; irrefragable.

The pension was granted, by reason of the king of England's *uncontroulable* title to England. *Hayward.*

This makes appear the error of those, who think it an *uncontroulable* maxim, that power is always safer lodged in many hands, than in one; those many are as capable of enslaving as a single person. *Swift.*

UNCONTRO'ULABLY. *adv.*

1. Without possibility of opposition.
2. Without danger of refutation.

Since this light was to rest within them, and the judgment of it wholly to remain in themselves, they might safely and *uncontroulably* pretend it greater or less. *South.*

Uncontroulably, and under general consent, many opinions are passant, which, upon due examination, admit of doubt. *Brown's Vulg. Errours.*

UNCONTRO'ULED. *adj.*

1. Unresisted; unopposed; not to be overruled.

Should I try the *uncontrouled* worth
Of this pure cause, 'twould kindle my rap'd spirits
To such a flame of sacred vehemence,
That dumb things would be mov'd to sympathize. *Milton.*

O'er barren mountains, o'er the flow'ry plain,
Extends thy *uncontroul'd* and boundless reign. *Dryden.*

The British navy, *uncontroul'd*,
Shall wave her double cross t' extremest clime
Terrific, and return with odorous spoils. *Phillips.*

2. Not convinced; not refuted.

That Julius Cæsar was so born, is an *uncontrouled* report. *Hayward.*

UNCONTRO'ULEDLY. *adv.* Without controul; without opposition.

Mankind avert killing, and being killed; but when the phantasm honour has once possessed the mind, no reluctance of humanity is able to make head against it; but it commands *uncontrouledly*. *Decay of Piety.*

UNCONVE'RSABLE. *adj.* Not suitable to conversation; not social.

Faith and devotion are traduced and ridiculed, as morose, *unconversable* qualities. *Rogers's Sermons.*

UNCONVE'RTED. *adj.* Not persuaded of the truth of christianity.

Salvation belongeth unto none, but such as call upon the name of our Lord Jesus Christ: which nations, as yet *unconverted*, neither do, nor possibly can do, till they believe. *Hooker.*

The *unconverted* heathens, who were pressed by the many authorities that confirmed our Saviour's miracles, accounted for them after the same manner. *Addison on the Christ. Relig.*

The apostle reminds the Ephesians of the guilt and misery of their former *unconverted* estate, when aliens from the commonwealth of Israel. *Rogers's Sermons.*

UNCONVI'NCED. *adj.* Not convinced.

A way not to be introduced into the seminaries of those, who are to propagate religion, or philosophy, amongst the ignorant and *unconvinced*. *Locke.*

To UNCO'RD. *v. a.* To loose a thing bound with cords.

UNCORRE'CTED. *adj.* Inaccurate; not polished to exactness.

I have written this too hastily and too loosely: it comes out from the first draught, and *uncorrected*. *Dryden.*

UNCORRU'PT. *adj.* Honest; upright; not tainted with wickedness; not influenced by iniquitous interest.

The pleasures of sin, and this world's vanities, are censured with *uncorrupt* judgment. *Hooker.*

Men alledge they can ne'er can find
Those beauties in a female mind,
Which raise a flame that will endure,
For ever *uncorrupt* and pure. *Swift.*

UNCORRU'PTED. *adj.* Not vitiated; not depraved.

Such a hero never springs,
But from the *uncorruped* blood of kings. *Roscommon.*

Man, yet new,
No rule but *uncorrupted* reason knew,
And with a native bent did good pursue. *Dryden.*

Nothing is more valuable than the records of antiquity: I wish we had more of them, aed more *uncorrupted*. *Locke.*

UNCORRU'PTNESS. *n. s.* Integrity; uprightness.

In doctrine, shew *uncorruptness*, gravity, sincerity. *Tit.* ii. 7.

To UNCO'VER. *v. a.*

1. To divest of a covering.

After you are up, *uncover* your bed, and open the curtains to air it. *Harvey.*

Seeing an object several millions of leagues, the very instant it is *uncovered*, may be shewn to be a mistake in matter of fact. *Locke.*

2. To deprive of cloaths.

Thou wert better in thy grave, than to answer, with thy *uncovered* body, this extremity of the skies. *Shakesp. K. Lear.*

3. To strip of the roof.

Porches and schools,
Uncover'd, and with scaffolds cumber'd stood. *Prior.*

4. To shew openly; to strip of a veil, or concealment.

He cover'd; but his robe
Uncover'd more: so rose the Danite strong,
Shorn of his strength. *Milton's Par. Lost.*

There will certainly come some day or other, to *uncover* every soul of us. *Pope's Letters.*

5. To bare the head, as in the presence of a superiour.

Rather let my head dance on a bloody pole,
Than stand *uncover'd* to the vulgar groom. *Shakesp.*

Unco'unsellable. *adj.* Not to be advised.

It would have been *uncounsellable* to have march'd to any distance, and have left such an enemy at their backs. *Clarendon.*

Unco'untable. *adj.* Innumerable.

Those *uncountable*, glorious bodies, were not set in the firmament for no other end than to adorn it. *Raleigh.*

Unco'unterfeit. *adj.* Genuine; not spurious.

True zeal is not any one single affection of the soul, but a strong mixture of many holy affections, filling the heart with all pious intentions; all, not only *uncounterfeit*, but most fervent. *Sprat's Sermons.*

To Unco'uple. *v. a.* To loose dogs from their couples.

Uncouple in the western valley, go;
Dispatch, I say, and find the forester. *Shaksp.*
The hunt is up, the morn is bright and gray;
The fields are fragrant, and the woods are green;
Uncouple here, and let us make a bay. *Shakesp.*
The land on which they fought, th' appointed place,
In which th' *uncoupled* hounds began the chace. *Dryden.*

Unco'urteous. *adj.* Uncivil; unpolite.

In behaviour some will say, ever sad, surely sober, and somewhat given to musing, but never *uncourteous*. *Sidney.*

Unco'urteously. *adv.* Uncivilly; unpolitely.

Though somewhat merrily, yet *uncourteously* he railed upon England, objecting extreme beggary, and mere barbarousness unto it. *Ascham's Schoolmaster.*

Unco'urtliness. *n. s.* Unsuitableness of manners to a court; inelegance.

The quakers presented an address, which, notwithstanding the *uncourtliness* of their phrases, the sense was very honest. *Addison.*

Unco'urtly. *adj.* Inelegant of manners; uncivil.

The lord treasurer not entering into those refinements of paying the publick money upon private considerations, hath been so *uncourtly* as to stop it. *Swift.*

Unco'uth. *adj.* [uncuð, Saxon.] Odd; strange; unusual.

A very *uncouth* sight was to behold,
How he did fashion his untoward pace;
For as he forward mov'd his footing old,
So backward still was turn'd his wrinkled face. *Fairy Queen.*
The lovers standing in this doleful wise,
A warrior bold unwares approached near,
Uncouth in arms yclad, and strange disguise. *Fairfax.*
I am surprized with an *uncouth* fear;
A chilling sweat o'erruns my trembling joints;
My heart suspects more than mine eye can see. *Shakesp.*
The trouble of thy thoughts this night
Affects me equally; nor can I like
This *uncouth* dream, of evil sprung, I fear. *Milton.*
Say on;
For I that day was absent, as befel,
Bound on a voyage *uncouth*, and obscure,
Far on excursion toward the gates of hell. *Milton.*

It was so *uncouth* a sight, for a fox to appear without a tail, that the very thought made him weary of his life. *L'Estrange.*

The secret ceremonies I conceal,
Uncouth, perhaps unlawful to reveal. *Dryden.*

I am more in danger to misunderstand his true meaning, than if I had come to him with a mind unpossessed by doctors of my sect, whose reasonings will of course make all chime that way, and make the genuine meaning of the author seem harsh, strained, and *uncouth* to me. *Locke.*

He made that a pleasant study, which, in the hands of Bartolus and Baldus, was *uncouth* and rugged. *Baker.*

Unco'uthly. *adv.* Oddly; strangely.

Venetians do not more *uncouthly* ride,
Than did their lubber state mankind bestride. *Dryden.*

Unco'uthness. *n. s.* Oddness; strangeness.

To deny himself in the lesser instances, that so when the greater come, they may not have the disadvantage of *uncouthness*, and perfect strangeness, to enhance their difficulty, must be acknowledged reasonable. *Decay of Piety.*

To Uncrea'te. *v. a.* To annihilate; to reduce to nothing; to deprive of existence.

Who created thee, lamenting learn;
Who can *uncreate* thee thou shalt know. *Milton.*
Light dies before her *uncreating* word.
Thus at her felt approach, and secret might,
Art after art goes out, and all is night. *Pope's Dunciad.*

Uncrea'ted. *adj.*

1. Not yet created.

How hast thou disturb'd
Heav'n's blessed peace, and into nature brought
Misery, *uncreated* till the crime
Of thy rebellion? *Milton.*

2. [*Incrée*, Fr.] Not produced by creation.

What cause within, or what without is found,
That can a being *uncreated* bound? *Blackmore.*

The next paragraph proves, that the idea we have of God is God himself; it being something, as he says, *uncreated*. *Locke.*

Uncre'ditableness. *n. s.* Want of reputation.

To all other disswasives, we may add this of the *uncreditableness*: the best that can be said is, that they use wit foolishly, whereof the one part devours the other. *Dec. of Piety.*

Uncro'pped. *adj.* Not cropped; not gathered.

Thy abundance wants
Partakers, and *uncropp'd* falls to the ground. *Milton.*

Uncro'ssed. *adj.* Uncancelled.

Such gain the cap of him, that makes them fine,
Yet keeps his book *uncross'd*. *Shakesp. Cymbeline.*

Uncro'uded. *adj.* Not straitened by want of room.

An amphitheatre,
On its publick shows, unpeopled Rome,
And held *uncrouded* nations in its womb. *Addison.*

To Uncro'wn. *v. a.* To deprive of a crown; to deprive of sovereignty.

He hath done me wrong;
And therefore I'll *uncrown* him ere't be long. *Shakesp.*
Ye pow'rs!
See a sacred king *uncrown'd*;
See your offspring, Albion, bound. *Dryden's Albion.*

U'nction. *n. s.* [*unction*, Fr.]

1. The act of anointing.

The *unction* of the tabernacle, the table, the laver, the altar of God, with all the instruments appertaining thereunto, made them for ever holy. *Hooker, b.* v. *s.* 20.

2. Unguent; ointment.

The king himself the sacred *unction* made;
As king by office, and as priest by trade. *Dryden.*

3. The act of anointing medically.

Such as are of hot constitutions, should use bathing in hot water, rather than *unctions*. *Arbuthnot on Aliments.*

4. Any thing softening, or lenitive.

Mother,
Lay not that flattering *unction* to your soul,
That not your trespass, but my madness speaks. *Shakesp.*

5. The rite of anointing in the last hours.

Their extreme *unction*, administered as the dying man's viaticum, which St. James mentioned as the ceremony of his recovery, may be added. *Hammond's Fundamentals.*

6. Any thing that excites piety and devotion.

Unctuo'sity. *n. s.* [from *unctuous*.] Fatness; oiliness.

Fuliginous exhalations contain an *unctuosity* in them, and arise from the matter of fuel. *Brown's Vulgar Errours.*

U'nctuous. *adj.* Fat; clammy; oily.

Dry up thy harrow'd veins, and plough-torn leas,
Whereof ingrateful man, with liqu'rish draughts,
And morsels *unctuous*, greases his pure mind,
That from it all consideration slips. *Shakespeare.*
A wand'ring fire,
Compact of *unctuous* vapour, which the night
Condenses, and the cold environs round,
Kindled through agitation to a flame. *Milton's Par. Lost.*
The trees were *unctuous* fir, and mountain ash. *Dryden.*
Whether they *unctuous* exhalations are,
Fir'd by the sun, or seeming so alone. *Dryden.*
Th' infernal winds,
Dilating, and with *unctuous* vapour fed,
Disdain'd their narrow cells. *Phlips.*

Camphire, oil-olive, linseed-oil, spirit of turpentine, and amber, are fat, sulphureous, *unctuous* bodies. *Newton.*

U'nctuousness. *n. s.* Fatness; oiliness; clamminess; greasiness.

A great degree of *unctuousness* is not necessary to the production of the like effects. *Boyle.*

Uncu'lled. *adj.* Not gathered.

A sweaty reaper from his tillage brought
First fruits, the green ear, and the yellow sheaf,
Uncull'd, as came to hand. *Milton's Par. Lost.*

Uncu'lpable. *adj.* Not blamable.

Those canons do bind, as they are edicts of nature; which the Jews observing as yet unwritten, and thereby framing such church orders, as in their law were not prescribed, are notwithstanding in that respect *unculpable*. *Hooker.*

Uncu'ckolded. *adj.* Not made a cuckold.

As it is a heart-breaking to see a handsome man loose-wiv'd, so it is a deadly sorrow to behold a foul knave *uncuckolded*. *Shakesp. Ant. and Cleopatra.*

Uncu'ltivated. *adj.* [*incultus*, Lat.]

1. Not cultivated; not improved by tillage.

Our isle, indeed, too fruitful was before;
But all *uncultivated* lay,
Out of the solar walk. *Dryden.*

God gave the world to men in common; but since he gave it for their benefit, it cannot be supposed he meant it should always remain common and *uncultivated*. *Locke.*

2. Not instructed; not civilized.

The first tragedians found that serious stile
Too grave for their *uncultivated* age. *Roscommon.*

These are instances of nations, where *uncultivated* nature has been left to itself, without the help of letters. *Locke.*

Uncu'mbered. *adj.* Not burthened; not embarrassed.

Lord of yourself, *uncumber'd* with a wife. *Dryden.*

Un-

UNCU'RBABLE. *adj.* That cannot be curbed, or checked.

So much *uncurbable* her garboiles, Cæsar,
Made out of her impatience, which not wanted
Shrewdness of policy. *Shakesp. Ant. and Cleopatra.*

UNCU'RBED. *adj.* Licentious; not restrained.

With frank, and with *uncurbed* plainness,
Tell us the Dauphin's mind. *Shakesp. Hen.* V.

To UNCU'RL. *v. a.* To loose from ringlets, or convolutions.

There stands a rock; the raging billows roar
Above his head in storms; but when 'tis clear,
Uncurl their ridgy backs, and at his feet appear. *Dryden.*
The lion's foe lies prostrate on the plain,
He sheaths his paws, *uncurls* his angry mane;
And, pleas'd with bloodless honours of the day,
Walks over, and disdains th' inglorious prey. *Dryden.*
The furies sink upon their iron beds,
And snakes *uncurl'd* hang list'ning round their heads. *Pope.*

To UNCU'RL. *v. n.* To fall from the ringlets.

My fleece of woolly hair now *uncurls*,
Even as an adder, when she doth unrowl
To do some fatal execution? *Shakesp. Titus Andronicus.*

UNCU'RLED. *adj.* Not collected into ringlets.

Alike in feature both, and garb appear;
With honest faces, though *uncurled* hair. *Dryden.*
But since, alas! frail beauty must decay;
Curl'd or *uncurl'd*, since locks will turn to grey;
What then remains, but well our pow'r to use,
And keep good humour still, whate'er we lose? *Pope.*

UNCU'RRENT. *adj.* Not current; not passing in common payment.

Your voice, like a piece of *uncurrent* gold, is not crack'd within the ring. *Shakesp. Hamlet.*

I can no other answer make but thanks;
And thanks, and ever thanks: and oft good turns
Are shuffled off with such *uncurrent* pay. *Shakespeare.*

To UNCU'RSE. *v. a.* To free from any execration.

Uncurse their souls; their peace is made
With head, and not with hands. *Shakesp. Richard* II.

UNCU'RST. *adj.* Not execrated.

Sir John Hotham unreproached, unthreatened, *uncursed* by any language or secret imprecation of mine, not long after pays his own and his eldest son's heads. *K. Charles.*

Heav'n sure has kept this spot of earth *uncurst*,
To shew how all things were created first. *Waller.*

UNCU'T. *adj.* Not cut.

We must resign! heav'n his great soul doth claim,
In storms as loud as his immortal fame:
His dying groans, his last breath shake our isle,
And trees *uncut* fall for his fun'ral pile. *Waller.*

To UNDA'M. *v. a.* To open; to free from the restraint of mounds.

When the fiery suns too fiercely play,
And shrivell'd herbs on with'ring stems decay;
The wary ploughman on the mountain's brow,
Undamms his watry stores. *Dryden's Georgicks.*

UNDA'MAGED. *adj.* Not made worse; not impaired.

Plants will frequent changes try,
Undamag'd, and their marriageable arms
Conjoin with others. *Philips.*

UNDA'UNTED. *adj.* Unsubdued by fear; not depressed.

Bring forth men children only;
For thy *undaunted* metal should compose
Nothing but males. *Shakesp. Macbeth.*
With him went
Harman, who did the twice fir'd Harry save,
And in his burning ship *undaunted* fought. *Dryden.*
Mirror of antient faith in early youth!
Undaunted worth, inviolable truth!
No foe unpunish'd in the fighting field,
Shall dare thee. *Dryden.*

UNDA'UNTEDNESS. *n. s.* Boldness; bravery; intrepidity.

Luther took up a brisker air of assurance, and shewed a particular *undauntedness* in the cause of truth, when it had so mighty an opposer. *Atterbury.*

The art of war, which they admired in him, and his *undauntedness* under dangers, were such virtues as these islanders were not used to. *Pope.*

UNDA'UNTEDLY. *adv.* Boldly; intrepidly; without fear.

It shall bid his soul go out of his body *undauntedly*, and lift up its head with confidence, before saints and angels. *South.*

UNDA'ZZLED. *adj.* Not dimmed, or confused by splendour.

Here matter new to gaze the devil met
Undazzled. *Milton's Par. Lost. b.* iii. *l.* 614.

As *undazzled* and untroubled eyes, as eagles can be supposed to cast on glow-worms, when they have been newly gazing on the sun. *Boyle.*

To UNDE'AF. *v. a.* To free from deafness.

Though Richard my life's counsel would not hear,
My death's sad tale may yet *undeaf* his ear. *Shakesp.*

UNDEBA'UCHED. *adj.* Not corrupted by debauchery.

When the world was bucksome, fresh and young,
Her sons were *undebauch'd*, and therefore strong. *Dryden.*

UNDE'CAGON. *n. s.* [from *undecim*, Lat. and γωνία, Gr.] A figure of eleven angles or sides.

UNDECA'YING. *adj.* Not suffering diminution or declension.

The fragrant myrtle, and the juicy vine,
Their parents *undecaying* strength declare,
Which with fresh labour, and unweary'd care,
Supplies new plants. *Blackmore on the Creation.*

UNDECA'YED. *adj.* Not liable to be diminished, or impaired.

How fierce in fight, with courage *undecay'd*!
Judge if such warriors want immortal aid. *Dryden.*
If in the melancholy shades below,
The flames of friends and lovers cease to glow;
Yet mine shall sacred last; mine *undecay'd*
Burn on through life, and animate my shade. *Pope.*

To UNDECE'IVE. *v. a.* To set free from the influence of a fallacy.

All men will try, and hope to write as well,
And, not without much pains, be *undeceiv'd*. *Roscommon.*
My muse enraged, from her urn,
Like ghosts of murder'd bodies does return
T' accuse the murderers, to right the stage,
And *undeceive* the long-abused age. *Denham.*

So far as truth gets ground in the world, so far sin loses it. Christ saves the world by *undeceiving* it. *South.*

Our coming judgments do in part *undeceive* us, and rectify the grosser errors. *Glanville.*

UNDECE'IVABLE. *adj.* Not liable to deceive.

It serves for more certain computation, by how much it is a larger and more comprehensive period, and under a more *undeceivable* calculation. *Holder on Time.*

UNDECE'IVED. *adj.* Not cheated; not imposed on.

All of a tenour was their after life;
No day discolour'd with domestick strife:
No jealousy, but mutual truth believ'd;
Secure repose, and kindness *undeceiv'd*. *Dryden.*

UNDECI'DED. *adj.* Not determined; not settled.

For one thing, which we have left to the order of the church, they had twenty which were *undecided* by the express word of God. *Hooker.*

To whose muse we owe that sort of verse,
Is *undecided* by the men of skill. *Roscommon.*
Aristotle has left *undecided* the duration of the action. *Dryd.*
When two adverse winds engage with horrid shock,
Levying their equal force with utmost rage,
Long *undecided* lasts the airy strife. *Philips.*

To UNDE'CK. *v. a.* To deprive of ornaments.

I find myself a traitor;
For I have given here my soul's consent,
T' *undeck* the pompous body of a king. *Shakespeare.*

UNDE'CKED. *adj.* Not adorned; not embellished.

Eve was *undeck'd*, save with herself. *Milton's Par. Lost.*

UNDECI'SIVE. *adj.* Not decisive; not conclusive.

Two nations differing about the antiquity of their language, made appeal to an *undecisive* experiment, when they agreed upon the trial of a child brought up among the wild inhabitants of the desert. *Glanville.*

UNDECLI'NED *adj.*

1. Not grammatically varied by termination.
2. Not deviating; not turned from the right way.

In his track my wary feet have stept;
His *undeclined* ways precisely kept. *Sandy's Paraphase.*

UNDE'DICATED. *adj.*

1. Not consecrated; not devoted.
2. Not inscribed to a patron.

I should let this book come forth *undedicated*, were it not that I look upon this dedication as a duty. *Boyle.*

UNDEE'DED. *adj.* Not signalized by action.

My sword, with an unbatter'd edge,
I sheath again *undeeded*. *Shakesp. Macbeth.*

UNDEFA'CED. *adj.* Not deprived of its form; not disfigured.

Those arms, which for nine centuries had brav'd
The wrath of time on antick stone engrav'd;
Now torn by mortars, stand yet *undefac'd*,
On nobler trophies by thy valour rais'd. *Granville.*

UNDEFE'ASIBLE. *adj.* Not defeasible; not to be vacated or annulled.

UNDEFI'LED. *adj.* Not polluted; not vitiated; not corrupted.

Virtue weareth a crown for ever, having gotten the victory, striving for *undefiled* rewards. *Wisdom* iv. 3.

Whose bed is *undefil'd*, and chaste, pronounc'd. *Milton.*
Her Arethusian stream remains unsoil'd,
Unmix'd with foreign filth, and *undefil'd*;
Her wit was more than man, her innocence a child. *Dryden.*

UNDEFI'NED. *adj.* Not circumscribed, or explained by a definition.

There is no such way to give defence to absurd doctrines, as to guard them round with legions of obscure, doubtful, *undefined* words. *Locke.*

UNDEFI'NABLE. *adj.* Not to be marked out, or circumscribed by a definition.

That which is indefinite, though it hath bounds, as not being infinite, yet those bounds to us are *undefinable*. *Grew.*

Why simple ideas are *undefinable* is, that the several terms of a definition, signifying several ideas, they can all, by no means, represent an idea, which has no composition at all. *Locke.*

UNDEFO'RMED. *adj.* Not deformed; not disfigured.

The sight of so many gallant fellows, with all the pomp and glare of war, yet *undeform'd* by battles, may possibly invite your curiosity. *Pope.*

UNDEFI'ED. *adj.* Not set at defiance; not challenged.

False traitor, thou broken hast
The law of arms, to strike foe *undefied*;
But thou thy treason's fruit, I hope, shalt taste
Right sour, and feel the law, the which thou hast defac'd. *Fairy Queen, b.* II. *c.* viii. *st.* 31.

Tarifa
Changed a blunt cane for a steel-pointed dart,
And meeting Ozmyn next,
Who wanting time for treason to provide,
He basely threw it at him, *undefy'd*. *Dryden.*

UNDELI'BERATED. *adj.* Not carefully considered.

The prince's *undeliberated* throwing himself into that engagement, transported him with passion. *Clarendon.*

UNDELI'GHTED. *adj.* Not pleased; not touched with pleasure.

The fiend
Saw *undelighted* all delight; all kind
Of living creatures, new to sight. *Milton's Par. Lost.*

UNDELI'GHTFUL. *adj.* Not giving pleasure.

He could not think of involving himself in the same *undelightful* condition of life. *Clarendon.*

UNDEMO'LISHED. *adj.* Not razed; not thrown down.

She *undemolish'd* stood, and ev'n 'till now
Perhaps had stood. *Philips.*

They stood by, and suffered Dunkirk to lie *undemolished*. *Swift.*

UNDEMO'NSTRABLE. *adj.* Not capable of fuller evidence.

Out of the precepts of the law of nature, as of certain, common, and *undemonstrable* principles, man's reason doth necessarily proceed unto certain more particular determinations: which particular determinations being found out according unto the reason of man, they have the names of human laws. *Hooker.*

UNDENI'ABLE. *adj.* Such as cannot be gainsaid.

That age which my grey hairs make seem more than it is, hath not diminished in me the power to protect an *undeniable* verity. *Sidney.*

Of those of the second class, we have a plain and *undeniable* certainty. *Woodward's Natural History.*

UNDENI'ABLY. *adv.* So plainly, as to admit no contradiction.

This account was differently related by the antients; that is, *undeniably* rejected by the moderns. *Brown's Vulg. Errours.*

I grant that nature all poets ought to study: but then this also *undeniably* follows, that those things which delight all ages, must have been an imitation of nature. *Dryden.*

UNDEPLO'RED. *adj.* Not lamented.

Rise, wretched widow! rise; nor *undeplor'd*
Permit my ghost to pass the Stygian ford;
But rise prepar'd to mourn thy perish'd lord. *Dryden.*

UNDEPRA'VED. *adj.* Not corrupted.

Knowledge dwelt in our *undepraved* natures, as light in the sun; it is now hidden in us like sparks in a flint. *Glanville.*

UNDEPRI'VED. *adj.* Not divested by authority; not stripped of any possession.

He, *undepriv'd*, his benefice forsook. *Dryden.*

U'NDER. *preposition.* [*undar*, Gothick; unðeꞃ, Saxon; *onder*, Dutch.]

1. In a state of subjection to.

When good Saturn, banish'd from above,
Was driven to hell, the world was *under* Jove. *Dryden.*

Every man is put under a necessity, by his constitution, as an intelligent being, to be determined by his own judgment, what is best for him to do; else he would be *under* the determination of some other than himself, which is want of liberty. *Locke.*

2. In the state of pupillage to.

To those that live
Under thy care, good rules and patterns give. *Denham.*

The princes respected Helim, and made such improvements *under* him, that they were instructed in learning. *Guardian.*

3. Beneath; so as to be covered, or hidden.

Fruit put in bottles, and the bottles let down into wells *under* water, will keep long. *Bacon's Nat. Hist.*

If it stood always under this form, it would have been *under* fire, if it had not been *under* water. *Burnet.*

Thy bees lodge *under* covert of the wind. *Dryden.*

Many a good poetick vein is buried *under* a trade, and never produces any thing for want of improvement. *Locke.*

4. Below in place; not above. This is the sense of *under sail*; that is, *having the sails* spread aloft.

As they went *under sail* by him, they held up their hands and made their prayers. *Sidney.*

By that fire that burn'd the Carthage queen,
When the false Trojan *under sail* was seen. *Shakespeare.*

Misseltoe hath been found to put forth *under* the boughs, and not only above the boughs; so it cannot be any thing that falleth upon the bough. *Bacon's Nat. Hist.*

Be gather'd now, ye waters, *under* heav'n. *Milton.*

5. In a less degree than.

Medicines take effect sometimes *under*, and sometimes above, the natural proportion of their virtue. *Hooker.*

If you write in your strength, you stand revealed at first; and should you write *under* it, you cannot avoid some peculiar graces. *Dryden's Dedication to Juvenal.*

6. For less than.

We are thrifty enough not to part with any thing serviceable to our bodies, *under* a good consideration; but make little account of what is most beneficial to our souls. *Ray.*

7. Less than; below.

Man, once fallen, was nothing but a total pollution, and not to be reformed by any thing *under* a new creation. *South.*

These men of forehead love to insure a cause, and seldom talk *under* certainty and demonstration. *Collier on Confidence.*

There are several hundred parishes in England *under* twenty pounds a year, and many *under* ten. *Swift.*

8. By the show of.

That which spites me more than all the wants,
He does it *under* name of perfect love. *Shakespeare.*

'Tis hard to bind any syllogism so close upon the mind, as not to be evaded *under* some plausible distinction. *Baker.*

9. With less than.

Several young men could never leave the pulpit *under* half a dozen conceits. *Swift.*

10. In the state of inferiority to; noting rank or order of precedence.

It was too great an honour for any man *under* a duke. *Addison's Spectator*, N°. 122.

11. In a state of being loaded with.

He shall but bear them, as the ass bears gold,
To groan and sweat *under* the business. *Shakespeare.*

He holds the people
Of no more soul, nor fitness for the world,
Than camels in their war; who have their provender
Only for bearing burthens, and sore blows
For sinking *under* them. *Shakesp. Coriolanus.*

12. In a state of oppression by, or subjection to.

After all, they have not been able to give any considerable comfort to the mind, *under* any of the great pressures of this life. *Tillotson's Sermons.*

At any rate we desire to be rid of the present evil, which we are apt to think nothing absent can equal; because, *under* the present pain, we find not ourselves capable of any, the least degree of happiness. *Locke.*

Women and childen did not shew the least signs of complaint, *under* the extremity of torture. *Collier.*

Illustrious parent! now some token give,
That I may Clymene's proud boast believe,
Nor longer *under* false reproaches grieve. *Addison.*

13. In a state in which one is seized or overborn.

The prince and princess must be *under* no less amazement. *Pope's Letters.*

14. In a state of being liable to, or limited by.

That which we move for our better instruction's sake, turneth unto choler in them; they answer fumingly. Yet in this their mood, they cast forth somewhat, wherewith, *under* pain of greater displeasure, we must rest contented. *Hooker.*

The greate part of mankind is slow of apprehension; and therefore, in many cases, *under* a necessity of seeing with other men's eyes. *South's Sermons.*

A generation sprung up amongst us, that flattered princes that they have a divine right to absolute power, let the laws and conditions *under* which they enter upon their authority, be what they will. *Locke.*

It is not strange to find a country half unpeopled, where so great a proportion of both sexes is tied *under* such vows of chastity. *Addison's Remarks on Italy.*

Things of another world are *under* the disadvantage of being distant, and therefore operate but faintly. *Atterbury.*

15. In a state of depression, or dejection by.

There is none but he,
Whose being I do fear; and, *under* him,
My genius is rebuk'd, as Antony's was by Cæsar. *Shakesp.*

16. In the state of bearing, or being known by.

This faction, *under* the name of Puritan, became very turbulent, during the reign of Elizabeth. *Swift.*

The raising of silver coin, has been only by coining it with less silver in it, *under* the same denomination. *Locke.*

17. In the state of.

If they can succeed without blood, as *under* the present disposition of things, it is very possible they may, it is to be hoped they will be satisfied. *Swift.*

18. Not having reached or arrived to; noting time.

Three sons he dying left *under* age;
By means whereof, their uncle Vortigern
Usurp'd the throne during their pupillage. *Fairy Queen.*

19. Represented by.

Morpheus is represented by the antient statuaries *under* the figure of a boy asleep, with a bundle of poppy in his hand. *Addison.*

20. In a state of protection.

Under favour, there are other materials for a commonwealth, besides stark love and kindness. *Collier.*

21. With respect to.

Mr. Duke may be mentioned *under* the double capacity of a poet and a divine. *Felton on the Classicks.*

22. Attested by.

Cato major, who had with great reputation borne all the great offices of the commonwealth, has left us an evidence, *under* his own hand, how much he was versed in country affairs. *Locke on Education.*

23. Subjected to; being the subject of.

To describe the revolutions of nature, will require a steady eye; especially so to connect the parts, and present them all *under* one view. *Burnet's Theory of the Earth.*

Memory is the storehouse of our ideas. For the narrow mind of man, not being capable of having many ideas *under* view at once, it was necessary to have a repository to lay them up. *Locke.*

The thing *under* proof is not capable of demonstration, and must be submitted to the trial of probabilities. *Locke.*

Distinct conceptions, that answer their verbal distinctions, serve to clear any thing in the subject *under* consideration. *Locke.*

I rather suspect my own judgment, than believe a fault to be in that poem, which lay so long *under* Virgil's correction, and had his last hand put to it. *Addison.*

24. In the next stage of subordination.

This is the only safe guard, *under* the spirit of God, that dictated these sacred writings, that can be relied on. *Locke.*

25. In a state of relation that claims protection.

U'NDER. *adv.*

1. In a state of subjection.

Ye purpose to keep *under* the children of Judah for bondmen and bond-women. 2 *Chron.* xxviii. 10.

2. Less: opposed to *over* or *more.*

He kept the main stock without alteration, *under* or over. *Addison's Spectator*, N°. 264.

3. It has a signification resembling that of an adjective; inferiour; subject; subordinate. But, perhaps, in this sense it should be considered as united to the following word.

I will fight
Against my canker'd country with the spleen
Of all the *under* fiends. *Shakesp. Coriolanus.*

4. It is much used in composition, in several senses, which the following examples will explain.

UNDERA'CTION. *n. s.* Subordinate action; action not essential to the main story.

The least episodes, or *underactions*, interwoven in it, are parts necessary, or convenient to carry on the main design. *Dryd.*

To UNDERBEA'R. *v. a.* [*under* and *bear.*]

1. To support; to endure.

What reverence he did throw away on slaves?
Wooing poor craftsmen with the craft of smiles,
And patient *underbearing* of his fortune. *Shakespeare.*

2. To line; to guard. Out of use.

The dutchess of Milan's gown; not like your cloth of gold, set with pearls, down-sleeves, side-sleeves, and skirts round, *underborne* with a bluish tinsel. *Shakesp. Much Ado about Noth.*

UNDERBEA'RER. *n. s.* [*under* and *bearer.*] In funerals, those that sustain the weight of the body, distinct from those who are bearers of ceremony, and only hold up the pall.

To UNDERBI'D. *v. a.* [*under* and *bid.*] To offer for any thing less than it is worth.

UNDERCLE'RK. *n. s.* [*under* and *clerk.*] A clerk subordinate to the principal clerk.

Coleby, one of his under-swearers, was tried for robbing the treasury, where he was an *underclerk*. *Swift.*

To UNDERDO'. *v. n.* [*under* and *do.*]

1. To act below ones abilities.

You overact, when you should *underdo*;
A little call yourself again, and think. *B. Johnson.*

2. To do less than is requisite.

Nature much oftener overdoes than *underdoes*: You shall find twenty eggs with two yolks, for one that hath none. *Grew.*

UNDERFA'CTION. *n. s.* [*under* and *faction.*] Subordnate faction; subdivision of a faction.

Christianity loses by contests of *underfactions*. *Decay of Piety.*

UNDERFE'LLOW. *n. s.* [*under* and *fellow.*] A mean man; a sorry wretch.

They carried him to a house of a principal officer, who with no more civility, though with much more business than those *underfellows* had shewed, in captious manner put interrogatories unto him. *Sidney.*

UNDERFI'LLING. *n. s.* [*under* and *fill.*] Lower part of an edifice.

To found our habitation firmly, first examine the bed of earth upon which we will build, and then the *underfillings*, or substruction, as the antients called it. *Wotton's Architecture.*

To UNDERFO'NG. *v. a.* [*under* and fangan, Saxon.] To take in hand.

Thou, Menalcas, that by thy treachery
Didst *underfong* my lady to wexe so light,
Shouldst well be known for such thy villainy. *Spenser.*

To UNDERF'URNISH. *v. a.* [*under* and *furnish.*] To supply with less than enough.

Can we suppose God would *underfurnish* man for the state he designed him, and not afford him a soul large enough to pursue his happiness? *Collier on Kindness.*

To UNDERGI'RD. *v. a.* [*under* and *gird.*] To bind below; to round the bottom.

When they had taken it up, they used helps, *undergirding* the ship. *Acts* xxvii. 17.

To U'NDERGO. *v. a.* [*under* and *go.*]

1. To suffer; to sustain; to endure evil.

With mind averse, he rather *underwent*
His people's will, than gave his own consent. *Dryden.*

2. To support; to hazard. Not in use.

I have mov'd certain Romans,
To *undergo* with me, an enterprize
Of honourable, dang'rous consequence. *Shakespeare.*

Such they were, who might presume t' have done
Much for the king, and honour of the state,
Having the chiefest actions *undergone*. *Daniel's Civil War.*

3. To sustain; to be the bearer of; to possess. Not in use.

Their virtues else, be they as pure as grace;
As infinite as man may *undergo*;
Shall, in the general censure, take corruption
From that particular fault. *Shakespeare's Hamlet.*

4. To sustain; to endure without fainting.

It rais'd in me
An *undergoing* stomach, to bear up
Against what should ensue. *Shakesp. Tempest.*

5. To pass through.

I carried on my enquiriess to try whether this rising world, when finish'd, would continue always the same; or what changes it would successively *undergo*, by the continued action of the same causes. *Burnet's Theory of tho Earth.*

Bread put into the stomach of a dying man, will *undergo* the alteration that is merely the effect of heat. *Arbuthnot.*

6. To be subject to.

Claudio *undergoes* my challenge, and either I must shortly hear from him, or I will subscribe him a coward. *Shakesp.*

UNDERGRO'UND. *n. s.* [*under* and *ground.*] Subterraneous space.

They have promised to shew your highness
A spirit rais'd from depth of *underground*. *Shakesp.*

Wash'd by streams
From *underground*, the liquid ore he drains
Into fit molds prepared. *Milton's Par. Lost.*

UNDERGRO'WTH. *n. s.* [*under* and *growth.*] That which grows under the tall wood.

So thick entwin'd,
As one continued brake, the *undergrowth*
Of shrubs, and tangling bushes, had perplex'd
All path of man, or beast, that pass'd that way. *Milton.*

UNDERHA'ND. *adv.* [*under* and *hand.*]

1. By means not apparent; secretly.

These multiplied petitions of worldly things in prayer, have, besides their direct use, a service, whereby the church *underhand*, through a kind of heavenly fraud, taketh therewith the souls of men, as with certain baits. *Hooker.*

2. Clandestinely; with fraudulent secrecy.

She *underhand* dealt with the principal men of that country, that they should persuade the king to make Plangus his associate. *Sidney.*

They, by their precedents of wit,
T' out-fast, out-loiter, and out-fit,
Can order matters *underhand*,
To put all business to a stand. *Hudibras.*

It looks, as if I had desired him *underhand* to write so ill against me; but I have not brib'd him to do me this service. *Dryden.*

Such mean revenge, committed *underhand*,
Has ruin'd many an acre of good land. *Dryden.*

Wood is still working *underhand* to force his halfpence upon us. *Swift.*

I'll hasten to my Roman soldiers,
Inflame the mutiny, and *underhand*
Blow up their discontents. *Addison's Cato.*

U'NDER-

UNDERHA'ND. *adj.* Secret; clandestine; sly.

I had notice of my brother's purpose, and have, by *underhand* means, laboured to dissuade him. *Shakespeare.*

I should take it as a very great favour from some of my *underhand* detractors, if they would break all measures with me. *Addison's Spectator*, N°. 262.

UNDERLA'BOURER. *n. s.* [*under* and *labourer.*] A subordinate workman.

About the carriage of one stone for Amasis, the distance of twenty days journey, for three years were employed two thousand chosen men, governors, besides many *underlabourers.* *Wilkins's Mathematical Magick.*

UNDERI'VED. *adj.* [from *derived.*] Not borrowed.

The ideas it is busied about should be, sometimes at least, those more congenial ones, which it had in itself, *underived* from the body. *Locke.*

To UNDERLA'Y. *v. a.* [*under* and *lay.*] To strengthen by something laid under.

UNDERLE'AF. *n. s.* [*under* and *leaf.*] A species of apple. *See* APPLE.

The *underleaf*, whose cyder is best at two years, is a plentiful bearer. *Mortimer's Art of Husbandry.*

To UNDERLI'NE. *v. a.* [*under* and *line.*] To mark with lines below the words.

By meer chance in appearance, though *underlined* with a providence, they had a full sight of the infanta. *Wotton.*

U'NDERLING. *n. s.* [from *under.*] An inferiour agent; a sorry, mean fellow.

The great men, by ambition never satisfied, grew factious; and the *underlings*, glad indeed to be *underlings* to them they hated least, to preserve them from such they hated most. *Sidney.*

Hereby the heads of the Septs are made stronger, whom it should be a most special policy to weaken, and to set up and strengthen divers of their *underlings* against them. *Spenser.*

The fault is not in our stars,
But in ourselves, that we are *underlings.* *Shakesp.*

O'er all his brethren he shall reign as king,
Yet every one shall make him *underling.* *Milton.*

They may print this letter, if the *underlings* at the post-office take a copy of it. *Pope and Swift.*

A sort of *underling* auxiliars to the difficulty of a work, are commentators and criticks, who frighten many by their number and bulk.

To UNDERMI'NE. *v. a.* [*under* and *mine.*]

1. To dig cavities under any thing, so that it may fall, or be blown up; to sap.

Though the foundation on a rock were laid,
The church was *undermin'd* and then betray'd. *Denham.*

An injudicious endeavour to exalt Virgil, is much the same, as if one should think to raise the superstructure by *undermining* the foundation. *Pope's Preface to the Iliad.*

2. To excavate under.

A vast rock *undermin'd* from one end to the other, and a highway running through it, as long and as broad as the mall. *Addison's Remarks on Italy.*

3. To injure by clandestine means.

Making the king's sword strike whom they hated, the king's purse reward whom they loved; and, which is worst of all, making the royal countenance serve to *undermine* the royal sovereignty. *Sidney.*

They, knowing Eleanor's aspiring humour,
Have hir'd me to *undermine* the dutchess. *Shakesp.*

The father secure,
Ventures his filial virtue,
Against whate'er may tempt, whate'er seduce,
Allure or terrify, or *undermine.* *Milton.*

The *undermining* smile becomes habitual; and the drift of his plausible conversation, is only to flatter one, that he may betray another. *Dryden.*

He should be warn'd who are like to *undermine* him, and who to serve him. *Locke on Education.*

UNDERMI'NER. *n. s.* [from *undermine.*]

1. He that saps; he that digs away the supports.

The enemies and *underminers* thereof are Romish Catholicks. *Bacon.*

2. A clandestine enemy.

When I perceiv'd all set on enmity,
As on my enemies, where-ever chanc'd,
I us'd hostility, and took their spoil,
To pay my *underminers* in their coin. *Milton's Agonistes.*

The most experienced disturbers and *underminers* of government, have always laid their first train in contempt, endeavouring to blow it up in the judgment and esteem of the subject. *South's Sermons.*

U'NDERMOST. *adj.* [This is a kind of superlative, anomalously formed from *under.*]

1. Lowest in place.

Using oil of almonds, we drew up with the *undermost* stone a much greater weight. *Boyle.*

2. Lowest in state or condition.

It happens well for the party that is *undermost*, when a work of this nature falls into the hands of those, who content themselves to attack their principles, without exposing their persons. *Addison's Freeholder*, N°. 19.

This opinion, taken up by other sectaries, was to last no longer than they were *undermost.* *Atterbury.*

UNDERNE'ATH. *adv.* [Compounded from *under* and *neath*; of which we still retain the comparative *nether*, but in adverbial sense use *beneath.*] In the lower place; below; under; beneath.

Forthwith up to the clouds
With him I flew, and *underneath* beheld
The earth outstretch'd immense, a prospect wide. *Milton.*

And as I awake, sweet musick breathe
Above, about, or *underneath*;
Sent by some spirit to mortals good. *Milton.*

Or sullen Mole that runneth *underneath*;
Or Severn swift, guilty of maidens death. *Milton.*

The monster caught in open day,
Inclos'd, and in despair to fly away,
Howls horrible from *underneath.* *Dryden.*

The slate did not lie flat upon it, but left a free passage *underneath.* *Addison.*

UNDERNE'ATH. *prep.* Under.

Fellows in arms,
Bruis'd *underneath* the yoke of tyranny,
Thus far into the bowels of the land
Have we march'd on. *Shakesp.*

Pray God, she prove not masculine ere long!
If *underneath* the standard of the French
She carry armour, as she hath begun. *Shakesp. Hen.* VI

Underneath this stone doth lie,
As much beauty as could die;
Which in life did harbour give,
To more virtue than could live. *B. Johnson.*

What is, hath been; what hath been shall ensue;
And nothing *underneath* the sun is new. *Sandys's Paraphrase.*

The north and south, and each contending blast,
Are *underneath* his wide dominion cast. *Dryden.*

UNDERO'FFICER. *n. s.* [*under* and *officer.*] An inferiour officer; one in subordinate authority.

This certificate of excommunication by bishops, of all others, is most in use; and would be more so, were it not for the manifold abuses about its execution committed by *underofficers.* *Ayliffe's Parergon.*

To U'NDERPIN. *v. a.* [*under* and *pin.*] To prop; to support.

Victors, to secure themselves against disputes of that kind, *underpin* their acquest *jure belli.* *Hale's Common Law.*

UNDE'ROGATORY. *adj.* Not derogatory.

Of our happiness the apostle gives a negative description; and to create in us apprehensions *underogatory* from what we shall possess, exalts them above all that we can fancy. *Boyle.*

U'NDERPART. *n. s.* [*under* and *part.*] Subordinate, or unessential part.

The English will not bear a thorough tragedy, but are pleased that it should be lightened wth *underparts* of mirth. *Dryden.*

UNDERPE'TTICOAT. *n. s.* [*uuder* and *petticoat.*] The petticoat worn next the body.

They go to bed as tired with doing nothing, as I after quilting a whole *under-petticoat.* *Spectator*, N°. 606.

U'NDERPLOT. *n. s.* [*under* and *plot.*]

1. A series of events proceeding collaterally with the main story of a play, and subservient to it.

In a tragi-comedy, there is to be but one main design; and though there be an *underplot*, yet it is subservient to the chief fable. *Dryden's Dedication to Juvenal.*

2. A clandestine scheme.

The husband is so misled by tricks, and so lost in a crooked intrigue, that he still suspects an *underplot.* *Addison.*

To UNDERPRA'ISE. *v. a.* [*under* and *praise.*] To praise below desert.

In *underpraising* thy deserts,
Here find the first deficience of our tongue. *Dryden.*

To UNDERPRI'ZE. *v. a.* [*under* and *prize.*] To value at less than the worth.

How far
The substance of my praise doth wrong this shadow
In *underprizing* it; so far this shadow
Doth limp behind the substance. *Shakespeare.*

To UNDERPRO'P. *v. a.* [*under* and *prop.*] To support; to sustain.

Here am I left to *underprop* the land,
Who, weak with age, cannot support myself. *Shakesp.*

There was made a shoring or *underproping* act for the benevolence; to make the sums not brought in, to be leviable by course of law. *Bacon's Hen.* VII.

Thou that art us'd t' attend the royal throne,
And *underprop* the head that bears the crown. *Fenton.*

UNDERPROPO'RTIONED. *adj.* [*under* and *proportion.*] Having too little proportion.

To be haughty, and to make scanty and *underproportioned* returns of civility, plainly tells people, they must be very mannerly. *Collier on Pride.*

UNDERPU´LLER. *n. ſ.* [*under* and *puller.*] Inferiour or ſubordinate puller.

The myſtery of ſeconds and thirds is ſuch a maſter-piece, that no deſcription can reach. Theſe *underpullers* in deſtruction are ſuch implicit mortals as are not to be matched. *Collier.*

To UNDERRA´TE. *v. a.* [*under* and *rate.*] To rate too low.

UNDERRA´TE. *n. ſ.* [from the verb.] A price leſs than is uſual.

The uſeleſs brute is from Newmarket brought,
And at an *underrate* in Smithfield bought,
To turn a mill. *Dryden.*

To UNDERSA´Y. *v. n.* [*under* and *ſay.*] To ſay by way of derogation. Not in uſe.

They ſay, they con to heaven the highway;
But I dare *underſay*,
They never ſet foot on that ſame trode,
But balke their right way, and ſtrain abroad. *Spenſer.*

UNDERSE´CRETARY. *n. ſ.* [*under* and *ſecretary.*] An inferiour or ſubordinate ſecretary.

The Jews have a tradition, that Elias ſits in heaven, and keeps a regiſter of all men's actions, good or bad. He hath his *under-ſecretaries* for the ſeveral nations, that takes minutes of all that paſſes. *Bacon's Theory of the Earth.*

To UNDERSE´LL. *v. a.* [*under* and *ſell.*] To defeat, by ſelling for leſs; to ſell cheaper than another.

Their ſtock being rated at ſix in the hundred, they may, with great gain, *underſell* us, our ſtock being rated at ten. *Child's Diſcourſe of Trade.*

UNDERSE´RVANT. *n. ſ.* [*under* and *ſervant.*] A ſervant of the lower claſs.

Beſides the nerves, the bones, as *underſervants*, with the muſcles, are employed to raiſe him up. *Grew's Coſmology.*

To U´NDERSET. *v. a.* [*under* and *ſet.*] To prop; to ſupport.

The merchant-adventurers, being a ſtrong company, and well *underſet* with rich men, and good order, held out bravely. *Bacon's Hen.* VII.

UNDERSE´TTER. *n. ſ.* [from *underſet.*] Prop; pedeſtal; ſupport.

The four corners thereof had *underſetters.* 1 *Kings* vii. 30.

UNDERSE´TTING. *n. ſ.* [from *underſet.*] Lower part; pedeſtal.

Their *underſettings*, or pedeſtals, are, in height, a third part of the column. *Wotton's Architecture.*

UNDERSHE´RIFF. *n. ſ.* [*under* and *ſheriff.*] The deputy of the ſheriff.

Since 'tis my doom, love's *underſhrieve*,
Why this reprieve?
Why doth my ſhe advowſon fly? *Cleveland's Poems.*

UNDERSHE´RIFFRY. *n. ſ.* [from *underſheriff.*] The buſineſs, or office of an *underſheriff.*

The cardinals of Rome call all temporal buſineſs, of wars and embaſſages, *ſhirreria*, which is *underſheriffries*; as if they were but matters for underſheriffs and catchpoles; though many times thoſe *underſheriffries* do more good than their high ſpeculations. *Bacon.*

UNDERSHOO´T. *part. adj.* [*under* and *ſhoot.*] Moved by water paſſing under it.

The impriſoned water payeth the ranſom of driving an *underſhoot* wheel for his enlargement. *Carew's Surv. of Cornwall.*

UNDERSO´NG. *n. ſ.* [*under* and *ſong.*] Chorus; burthen of a ſong.

So ended ſhe; and all the reſt around
To her redoubled that her *underſong.* *Spenſer.*
The challenge to Damætas ſhall belong;
Menalcas ſhall ſuſtain his *underſong*;
Each in his turn your tuneful numbers bring. *Dryden.*

To UNDERSTA´ND. *v. a.* preterite *underſtood.* [underſtan-dan, Saxon.]

1. To comprehend fully; to have knowledge of.

The Ulyſſes of Ovid upbraids his ignorance, that he *underſtood* not the ſhield for which he pleaded. *Dryden.*

2. To conceive.

His ſin might have been greater in that reſpect: but that it was not ſo to be *underſtood*, appears by the oppoſition. *Stillingfleet.*

The moſt learned interpreters *underſtood* the words of ſin, and not of Abel. *Locke.*

To UNDERSTA´ND. *v. n.*

1. To have uſe of the intellectual faculties; to be an intelligent or conſcious being.

I have given thee a wiſe and *underſtanding* heart. *Chronicles.*

2. To be informed.

I *underſtood* of the evil Eliaſhib did. *Neh.* xiii. 7.

I *underſtand* by Sanga, you have been
Solicited againſt the commonwealth
By one Umbrenus. *B. Johnſon's Cataline.*

All my ſoul be
Imparadis'd in you, in whom alone
I *underſtand*, and grow, and ſee. *Donne.*

UNDERSTA´NDING. *n. ſ.* [from *underſtand.*]

1. Intellectual powers; faculties of the mind, eſpecially thoſe of knowledge and judgment.

I ſpeak as my *underſtanding* inſtructs me, and as mine honeſty puts it to utterance. *Shakeſp. Winter Tale.*

Make him of quick *underſtanding* in the fear of the Lord. *Iſaiah.*

It maketh day-light *underſtanding*, out of darkneſs. *Bacon.*

When ſhe rates things, and moves from ground to ground,
The name of reaſon ſhe obtains by this:
But when by reaſon ſhe the truth hath found,
And ſtandeth fix'd, ſhe *underſtanding* is. *Davies.*

Life and ſenſe,
Fancy and *underſtanding*: whence the ſoul
Reaſon receives, and reaſon is her being. *Milton.*

God is to the *underſtanding* of man, as the light of the ſun is to our eyes, its firſt and moſt glorious object. *Tillotſon.*

2. Skill.

The *underſtandings* of a ſenate are often enſlaved by three or four leaders. *Swift.*

Right *underſtanding* conſiſts in the perception of the viſible or probable agreement or diſagreement of ideas. *Locke.*

Very mean people have raiſed their minds to a great ſenſe and *underſtanding* of religion. *Locke.*

3. Intelligence; terms of communication.

He hoped the loyalty of his ſubjects would concur with him in the preſerving of a good *underſtanding* between him and his people. *Clarendon.*

We have got into ſome *underſtanding* with the enemy, by means of Don Diego. *Arbuthnot.*

UNDERSTA´NDING. *adj.* Knowing; ſkilful.

The preſent phyſician is a very *underſtanding* man, and well read. *Addiſon's Remarks on Italy.*

UNDERSTA´NDINGLY. *adv.* [from *underſtand.*] With knowledge.

Sundays may be *underſtandingly* ſpent in theology. *Milton.*

UNDERSTOO´D. pret. and part. paſſive of *underſtand.*

UNDERSTRA´PPER. *n. ſ.* [*under* and *ſtrap.*] A petty fellow; an inferior agent.

Every *underſtrapper* perk'd up, and expected a regiment, or his ſon muſt be a major. *Swift.*

To UNDERTA´KE. *v. a.* preterite *undertook*; participle paſſive *undertaken.* [*underfangen*, German.]

1. To attempt; to engage in.

The taſk he *undertakes*
Is numbring ſands, and drinking oceans dry. *Shakeſp.*
Hence our gen'rous emulation came;
We *undertook*, and we perform'd the ſame. *Roſcommon.*
Fiercer than cannon, and than rocks more hard,
The Engliſh *undertake* th' unequal war. *Dryden.*
Of dangers *undertaken*, fame atchiev'd,
They talk by turns. *Dryden.*

2. To aſſume a character. Not in uſe.

His name and credit ſhall you *undertake*,
And in my houſe you ſhall be friendly lodg'd. *Shakeſp.*

3. To engage with; to attack.

It is not fit your lordſhip ſhould *undertake* every companion, that you give offence to. *Shakeſp. Cymbeline.*

You'll *undertake* her no more? *Shakeſpeare.*

4 To have the charge of.

To th' waterſide I muſt conduct your grace,
Then give my charge up to Sir Nicholas Vaux,
Who *undertakes* you to your end. *Shakeſp. Hen.* VIII.

To UNDERTA´KE. *v. n.*

1. To aſſume any buſineſs or province.

O Lord, I am oppreſſed, *undertake* for me. *Iſa.* xxxviii. 34.

I *undertook* alone to wing th' abyſs. *Mlilton.*

2. To venture; to hazard.

It is the cowiſh terror of his ſpirit,
That dare not *undertake.* *Shakeſp. K. Lear.*

3. To promiſe; to ſtand bound to ſome condition.

If the curious ſearch the hills after rains, I dare *undertake* they will not loſe their labour. *Woodward's Nat. Hiſt.*

UNDERTA´KEN. part. paſſive of *undertake.*

UNDERTA´KER. *n. ſ.* [from *undertake.*]

1. One who engages in projects and affairs.

Antrim was naturally a great *undertaker.* *Clarendon.*

Undertakers in Rome purchaſe the digging of fields, and arrive at great eſtates by it. *Addiſon.*

This ſerves to free the enquiry from the perplexities that ſome *undertakers* have encumber'd it with. *Woodward.*

Oblige thy fav'rite *undertakers*
To throw me in but twenty acres. *Prior.*

2. One who engages to build for another at a certain price.

Should they build as faſt as write,
'Twould ruin *undertakers* quite. *Swift's Miſcellany.*

3. One who manages funerals.

UNDERTA´KING. *n. ſ.* [from *undertake.*] Attempt; enterprize; engagement.

Mighty men they are called; which ſheweth a ſtrength ſurpaſſing others: and men of renown, that is, of great *undertaking* and adventurous actions. *Raleigh's Hiſt. of the World.*

If this ſeem too great an *undertaking* for the humour of our age, then ſuch a ſum of money ought to lie ready for taking off all ſuch pieces of cloth as ſhall be brought in. *Temple.*

UNDERTE'NANT. *n. s.* [*under* and *tenant.*] A secondary tenant; one who holds from him that holds from the owner.

Settle and secure the *undertenants*; to the end there may be a repose and establishment of every subject's estate, lord and tenant. *Davies's Hist. of Ireland.*

UNDERTOO'K. part. passive of *undertake.*

UNDERVALUA'TION. *n. s.* [*under* and *value.*] Rate not equal to the worth.

There is often failing by an *undervaluation*; for in divers children their ingenerate powers are of slow disclosure. *Wotton.*

To UNDERVA'LUE. *v. a.* [*under* and *value.*]

1. To rate low; to esteem lightly; to treat as of little worth.

Her name is Portia, nothing *undervalu'd*
To Cato's daughter. *Shakesp. Merchant of Venice.*

My chief delight lay in discharging the duties of my station; so that in comparison of it, I *undervalu'd* all ensigns of authority. *Atterbury.*

2. To depress; to make low in estimation; to despise.

I write not this with the least intention to *undervalue* the other parts of poetry. *Dryden.*

In a kingdom grown glorious by the reputation of a sovereign, multitudes lessen and *undervalue* it. *Addison.*

Schooling Luther is an *undervaluing* term, and would make one think that Erasmus had a mean opinion of him. *Atterbury.*

UNDERVA'LUE. *n. s.* [from the verb.] Low rate; vile price.

The unskilfulness, carelessness, or knavery of the traders, added much to the *undervalue* and discredit of these commodities abroad. *Temple.*

UNDERVA'LUER. *n. s.* [from *undervalue.*] One who esteems lightly.

An *undervaluer* of money was Sir Henry Wotton. *Walton.*

UNDERWE'NT. preterite of *undergo.*

U'NDERWOOD. *n. s.* [*under* and *wood.*] The low trees that grew among the timber.

When you fell *underwood*, sow haws and sloes. *Mortimer.*

U'NDERWORK. *n. s.* [*under* and *work.*] Subordinate business; petty affairs.

Those that are proper for war, fill up the laborious part of life, and carry on the *underwork* of the nation. *Addison.*

To UNDERWO'RK. *v. a.* preterite *underworked*, or *underwrought*; participle passive *underworked*, or *underwrought.*

1. To destroy by clandestine measures.

Thou from loving England art so far,
That thou hast *underwrought* its lawful king,
To cut off the sequence of posterity. *Shakespeare.*

2. To labour less than enough.

Apelles said of Protogenes, that he knew not when to give over. A work may be overwrought as well as *underwrought.* *Dryden.*

UNDERWO'RKMEN. *n. s.* [*under* and *workman.*] An inferiour, or subordinate labourer.

Underworkmen are expert enough at making a single wheel in a clock, but are utterly ignorant how to adjust the several parts. *Swift.*

To UNDERWRI'TE. *v. a.* [*under* and *write.*] To write under something else.

He began first with his pipe, and then with his voice, thus to challenge Dorus, and was by him answered in the *underwritten* sort. *Sidney.*

What addition and change I have made, I have here *underwritten.* *Sanderson.*

UNDERWRI'TER. *n. s.* [from *underwrite.*] An insurer; so called from writing his name under the conditions.

UNDESCRI'BED. *adj.* Not described.

They urge, that God left nothing in his word *undescribed*, whether it concerned the worship of God, or outward polity. *Hooker.*

This is such a singular practice, that I had rather leave it *undescribed*, than give it its proper character. *Collier on Pride.*

UNDESCRI'ED. *adj.* Not seen; unseen; undiscovered.

UNDESE'RVED. *adj.*

1. Not merited; not obtained by merit.

This victory, obtained with great, and truely not *undeserved*, honour to the two princes, the whole estates, with one consent, gave the crown to Musidorus. *Sidney, b.* ii.

2. Not incurred by fault.

The same virtue which gave him a disregard of fame, made him impatient of an *undeserved* reproach. *Addison.*

UNDESE'RVEDLY. *adv.* [from *undeserved.*] Without desert, whether of good or ill.

Our desire is to yield them a just reason, even of the least things, wherein *undeservedly* they have but as much as dreamed that we do amiss. *Hooker, b.* v. §. 7.

He which speaketh no more than edifieth, is *undeservedly* reprehended for much speaking. *Hooker, b.* v. §. 32.

These oft as *undeservedly* inthral
His outward freedom. *Milton's Par. Lost.*

Science distinguishes a man of honour from one of those athletick brutes, whom *undeservedly* we call heroes. *Dryden.*

UNDESE'RVER. *n. s.* One of no merit.

You see how men of merit are sought after; the *undeserver* may sleep, when the man of action is called on. *Shakesp.*

UNDESE'RVING. *adj.*

1. Not having merit; not having any worth.

It exerts itself promiscuously towards the deserving and the *undeserving*, if it relieves alike the idle and the indigent. *Addison.*

Shall we repine at a little misplaced charity, when an allwise being showers down every day his benefits on the unthankful and *undeserving.* *Atterbury.*

Who lose a length of *undeserving* days,
Would you usurp the lover's dear-bought praise? *Pope.*

2. Not meriting any particular advantage or hurt. With *of.*

I was carried to mislike, then to hate; lastly to destroy this son *undeserving* destruction. *Sidney.*

My felicity is in retaining the good opinion of honest men, who think me not quite *undeserving of* it. *Pope.*

UNDESI'GNED. *adj.* Not intended; not purposed.

Great effects by inconsiderable means are sometimes brought about; and those so wholly *undesigned* by such as are the immediate actors. *South.*

Where you conduct find,
Use and convenience; will you not agree,
That such effects could not be *undesign'd*,
Nor could proceed, but from a knowing mind? *Blackmore.*

UNDESI'GNING. *adj.*

1. Not acting with any set purpose.

Could atoms, which, with undirected flight,
Roam'd through the void, and rang'd the realms of night,
In order march, and to their posts advance,
Led by no guide, but *undesigning* chance? *Blackmore.*

2. Having no artful or fraudulent schemes; sincere.

He looks upon friendship, gratitude, and sense of honour, as terms to impose upon weak, *undesigning* minds. *South.*

UNDESI'RABLE. *adj.* Not to be wished; not pleasing.

To add what wants
In female sex, the more to draw his love,
And render me more equal; and perhaps,
A thing not *undesirable*, some time
Superior; for inferior, who is free? *Milton's Par. Lost.*

UNDESI'RED *adj.* Not wished; not solicited.

O goddess-mother, give me back to fate;
Your gift was *undesir'd*, and came too late. *Dryden.*

UNDESI'RING. *adj.* Negligent; not wishing.

The baits of gifts and money to despise,
And look on wealth with *undesiring* eyes:
When thou canst truly call these virtues thine,
Be wise, and free, by heav'n's consent and mine. *Dryden.*

UNDESTRO'YABLE. *adj.* Indestructible; not susceptive of destruction.

Common glass, once made, so far resists the violence of the fire, that most chymists think it a body more *undestroyable* than gold itself. *Boyle.*

UNDESTRO'YED. *adj.* Not destroyed.

The essences of those species are preserved whole and *undestroyed*, whatever changes happen to any, or all of the individuals. *Locke.*

UNDETE'RMINABLE. *adj.* Impossible to be decided.

On either side the fight was fierce, and surely *undeterminable* without the death of one of the chiefs. *Wotton.*

Rather an heir had no such right by divine institution, than that God should give such a right, but yet leave it doubtful and *undeterminable* who such heir is. *Locke.*

UNDETE'RMINATE. *adj.*

1. Not settled; not decided; contingent.

Surely the Son of God could not die by chance, nor the greatest thing that ever came to pass in nature, be left to an *undeterminate* event. *South.*

2. Not fixed.

Fluid, slippery, and *underminate* it is of itself. *More.*

UNDETE'RMINATENESS. } *n. s.* [from *undeterminate.*]
UNDETERMINA'TION. }

1. Uncertainty; indecision.

He is not left barely to the *undetermination*, incertainty and unsteadiness of the operation of his faculties, without a certain, secret, predisposition of them to what is right. *Hale.*

2. The state of not being fixed, or invincibly directed.

The idea of a free agent is *undeterminateness* to one part, before he has made choice. *More's Divine Dialogues.*

UNDETE'RMINED. *adj.*

1. Unsettled; undecided.

He has left his succession as *undetermined*, as if he had said nothing about it. *Locke.*

Extended wide
In circuit, *undetermin'd* square or round. *Milton.*

2. Not limited; not regulated.

It is difficult to conceive that any such thing should be as matter, *undetermined* by something called form. *Hale.*

UNDEVO'TED. *adj.* Not devoted.

The lords Say and Brooke, two popular men, and most *undevoted* to the church, positively refused to make any such protestation. *Clarendon, b.* ii.

Undia'phanous. *adj.* Not pellucid; not transparent.

When the materials of glass melted, with calcined tin, have composed a mass *undiaphanous* and white, this white enamel is the basis of all concretes, that goldsmiths employ in enamelling. *Boyle on Colours.*

Undi'd. the preterite of *undo.*

This so *undid* all I had done before:
I could attempt, and he endure no more. *Roscommon.*

Undige'sted. *adj.* Not concocted.

Ambition, the disease of virtue, bred
Like surfeits from an *undigested* fulness,
Meets death in that which is the means of life. *Denham.*

The glaring sun breaks in at ev'ry chink;
Yet plung'd in sloth we lie, and snore supine,
As fill'd with fumes of *undigested* wine. *Dryden.*

Meat remaining in the stomach *undigested*, dejection of appetite, wind coming upwards, are signs of a phlegmatick constitution. *Arbuthnot on Diet.*

Undi'ght. preterite *put off.* It is questionable whether it have a present tense.

From her fair head her fillets she *undight*,
And laid her stole aside. *Fairy Queen.*

Undi'nted. *adj.* Not impressed by a blow.

I must rid all the sea of pirates: this 'greed upon,
To part with unhackt edges, and bear back
Our barge *undinted.* *Shakesp. Ant. and Cleopatra.*

Undimi'nished. *adj.* Not impaired; not lessened.

I still accounted myself *undiminished* of my largest concessions. *K. Charles.*

Think not, revolted spirit! thy shape the same,
Or *undiminish'd* brightness, to be known
As when thou stood'st in heav'n, upright and pure. *Milton.*

Sergius, who a bad cause bravely try'd,
All of a piece, and *undiminish'd*, dy'd. *Dryden.*

The deathless muse, with *undiminish'd* rays,
Through distant times the lovely dame conveys. *Addison.*

When sacrilegious hands had rased the church, even to the foundation, these charities they suffered to stand *undiminish'd*, untouch'd. *Atterbury.*

Undi'pped. [*un* and *dip.*] Not dipped; not plunged.

I think thee
Impenetrably good; but, like Achilles,
Thou had'st a soft Egyptian heel *undip'd*,
And that has made thee mortal. *Dryden's Cleomenes.*

Undire'cted. *adj.* Not directed.

The realm was left, like a ship in a storm, amidst all the raging surges, unruled and *undirected* of any: for they to whom she was committed, fainted or forsook their charge. *Spenser.*

Could atoms, which, with *undirected* flight,
Roam'd through the void, and rang'd the realms of night,
Of reason destitute, without intent,
In order march. *Blackmore on the Creation.*

Undisce'rnible. *adj.* Not to be discerned; invisible.

I shou'd be guiltier than my guiltiness,
To think I should be *undiscernible*,
When I perceive your grace. *Shakespeare.*

The apostle knowing that the distinction of these characters was *undiscernible* by men in this life, admonishes those, who had the most comfortable assurances of God's favour, to be nevertheless apprehensive. *Rogers's Sermons.*

Undisce'rnibly. *adj.* Invisibly; imperceptibly.

Many secret indispositions will *undiscernibly* steal upon the soul, and it will require time and close application to recover it to the spiritualities of religion. *South's Sermons.*

Undisce'rned. *adj.* Not observed; not discovered; not descried.

Our profession, though it leadeth us into many truths *undiscerned* by others, yet doth disturb their communications. *Browne's Vulg. Errours.*

Broken they break, and rallying they renew,
In other forms, the military shew:
At last in order *undiscern'd* they join,
And march together in a friendly line. *Dryden.*

Undisce'rnedly. *adv.* So as to be undiscovered.

Some associated particles of salt-petre, by lurking *undiscernedly* in the fixed nitre, had escaped the analysing violence of the fire. *Boyle.*

Undisce'rning. *adj* Injudicious; incapable of making due distinction.

Undiscerning muse, which heart, which eyes,
In this new couple dost thou prize? *Donne.*

His long experience informed him well of the state of England; but of foreign transactions, he was entirely *undiscerning* and ignorant. *Clarendon.*

Thus her blind sister, fickle fortune, reigns,
And *undiscerning* scatters crowns and chains. *Pope.*

Undisco'rding. *adj.* Not disagreeing; not jarring in musick.

We on earth, with *undiscording* voice,
May rightly answer that melodious noise;
As once we did, 'till disproportion'd sin
Jarr'd against nature's chime. *Milton.*

Undi'sciplined. *adj.*

1. Not subdued to regularity and order.

To be dispensed withal is an argument of natural infirmity, if it be necessary; but if it be not, it signifies an *undisciplined* and unmortified spirit. *Taylor's Rule of Holy Living.*

Divided from those climes where art prevails;
Undisciplin'd by precepts of the wise;
Our inborn passions will not brook controul;
We follow nature. *Philips.*

2. Untaught; uninstructed.

A gallant man had rather fight to great disadvantages in the field, in an orderly way, than skuffle with an *undisciplin'd* rabble. *K. Charles.*

Dry is a man of a clear head, but few words; and gains the same advantage over Puzzle, that a small body of regular troops would gain over a numberless, *undisciplin'd* militia. *Spectator,* N°. 477.

Undisco'verable. *adj.* Not to be found out.

He was to make up his accounts, and by an easy, *undiscoverable* cheat, he could provide against the impending distress. *Rogers.*

Undisco'vered. *adj.* Not seen; not descried; not found out.

Coming into the falling of a way, which led us into a place, of each side whereof men might easily keep themselves *undiscovered*, I was encompassed suddenly by a great troop of enemies. *Sidney.*

When the griefs of Job were exceeding great, his words accordingly to open them were many: howbeit, still unto his seeming they were *undiscovered.* *Hooker.*

Time glides, with *undiscover'd* haste;
The future but a length behind the past. *Dryden.*

By your counsels we are brought to view
A rich and *undiscover'd* world in you. *Dryden.*

In such passages I discover'd some beauty yet *undiscover'd.* *Dryden.*

Undiscree't. *adj.* Not wise; imprudent.

If thou be among the *undiscreet*, observe the time. *Ecclus* xxvii.

Undisgui'sed. *adj.* Open; artless; plain; exposed to view.

If thou art Venus,
Disguis'd in habit, *undisguis'd* in shape;
O help us, captives, from our chains t'scape. *Dryden.*

If once they can dare to appear openly and *undisguised*, when they can turn the ridicule upon seriousness and piety, the contagion spreads like a pestilence. *Rogers's Sermons.*

Undisho'noured. *adj.* Not dishonoured.

Keep then fair league and truce with thy true bed:
I live distained, thou *undishonoured.* *Shakespeare.*

Undisma'yed. *adj.* Not discouraged; not depressed with fear.

He in the midst thus *undismay'd* began. *Milton's P. Lost.*

He aim'd a blow against his *undismay'd* adversary. *Arbuth.*

Though oft repuls'd, again
They rally *undismay'd.* *Philips.*

Undisobli'ging. *adj.* Inoffensive.

All this he would have expatiated upon, with connexions of the discourses, and the most easy, *undisobliging* transitions. *Broome's Notes on the Iliad.*

Undispe'rsed. *adj.* Not scattered.

We have all the redolence of the perfumes we burn upon his altars; the smoke doth vanish ere it can reach the sky; and whilst it is *undispersed*, it but clouds it. *Boyle.*

Undispo'sed. *adj.* Not bestowed.

The employments were left *undisposed* of, to keep alive the hopes of impatient candidates. *Swift.*

Undispu'ted. *adj.* Incontrovertible; evident.

You, by an *undisputed* title, are the king of poets. *Dryden.*

That virtue and vice tend to make these men happy, or miserable, who severally practise them, is a proposition of undoubted, and by me *undisputed*, truth. *Atterbury.*

Undisse'mbled. *adj.*

1. Openly declared.
2. Honest, not feigned.

Ye are the sons of a clergy, whose *undissembled* and unlimited veneration for the holy scriptures, hath not hindered them from paying an inferiour, but profound regard to the best interpreters of it, the primitive writers. *Atterbury.*

Undi'ssipated. *adj.* Not scattered; not dispersed.

Such little primary masses as our proposition mentions, may remain *undissipated.* *Boyle.*

Undisso'lving. *adj.* Never melting.

Not cold Scythia's *undissolving* snows,
Nor the parch'd Lybian sands thy husband bore,
But mild Parthenope. *Addison's Remarks on Italy.*

Undiste'mpered. *adj.*

1. Free from disease.
2. Free from perturbation.

Some such laws may be considered, in some parliament that shall be at leisure, from the urgency of more pressing affairs, and shall be cool and *undistempered.* *Temple.*

Un-

UNDISTI'NGUISHABLE. *adj.*

1. Not to be distinctly seen.

These things seem small and *undistinguishable*,
Like far off mountains turned into clouds. *Shakespeare.*

The quaint mazes in the wanton green,
For lack of tread, are *undistinguishable*. *Shakespeare.*

Its lineaments are destroy'd, and the materials mixt in an *undistinguishable* confusion. *Rogers.*

2. Not to be known by any peculiar property.

No idea can be *undistinguishable* from another, from which it ought to be different. *Locke.*

UNDISTI'NGUISHED. *adj.*

1. Not marked out by objects or intervals.

'Tis longer since the creation of angels than of the world, by seven hundred years: whereby we would mark out so much of that *undistinguish'd* duration, as we suppose would have admitted seven hundred annual revolutions of the sun. *Locke.*

2. Not seen, or not to be seen otherwise than confusedly; not separately and plainly descried.

'Tis like the milky way, all over bright;
But sown so thick with stars, 'tis *undistinguish'd* light. *Dryden.*

Wrinkles *undistinguish'd* pass,
For I'm asham'd to use a glass. *Swift.*

3. Admitting nothing between; having no intervenient space.

Oh *undistinguish'd* space of woman's will! *Shakespeare.*

The *undistinguish'd* seeds of good and ill,
Heav'n, in his bosom, from our knowledge hides. *Dryden.*

4. Not marked by any particular property.

Sleep to those empty lids
Is grown a stranger; and day and night,
As *undistinguish'd* by my sleep, as sight. *Denham.*

5. Not treated with any particular respect.

Sad chance of war! now destitute of aid,
Falls *undistinguish'd* by the victor spade. *Pope.*

UNDISTI'NGUISHING. *adj.* Making no difference.

The promiscuous and *undistinguishing* distribution of good and evil, which was necessary for carrying on the designs of providence in this life, will be rectified in another. *Addison.*

Undistinguishing complaisance will vitiate the taste of the readers. *Garth.*

2. Not to be plainly discerned.

UNDISTRA'CTED. *adj.* Not perplexed by contrariety of thoughts or desires.

When Enoch had walked with God, he was so far from being tired with that lasting assiduity, that he admitted him to a more immediate, and more *undistracted* communion with himself. *Boyle.*

UNDISTRA'CTEDLY. *adv.* Without disturbance from contrariety of sentiments.

St. Paul tells us, that there is difference betwixt married and single persons; the affections of the latter being at liberty to devote themselves more *undistractedly* to God. *Boyle.*

UNDISTRA'CTEDNESS. *n. s.* Freedom from interruption by different thoughts.

The strange confusions of this nation disturb that calmness of mind, and *undistractedness* of thoughts. *Boyle.*

UNDISTU'RBED. *adj.*

1. Free from perturbation; calm; tranquil.

To our high-rais'd phantasy present
That *undisturbed* song of pure content. *Milton.*

The peaceful cities of th' Ausonian shore,
Lull'd in their ease, and *undisturb'd* before,
Are all on fire. *Dryden.*

A state, where our imitation of God shall end in the *undisturbed* fruition of him to all eternity. *Atterbury.*

To be *undisturbed* in danger, sedately to consider what is fittest to be done, and to execute it steadily, is a complex idea of an action, which may exist. But to be *undisturbed* in danger, without using one's reason, is as real an idea as the other. *Locke.*

2. Not interrupted by any hindrance or molestation.

Nature stints our appetite,
And craves no more than *undisturb'd* delight;
Which minds, unmix'd with cares and fears, obtain;
A soul serene, a body void of pain. *Dryden.*

Unvex'd with quarrels, *undisturb'd* with noise,
The country king his peaceful realm enjoys. *Dryden.*
The English, *undisturb'd*, submiss obey. *Philips.*

3. Not agitated.

A good conscience is a port which is land-lock'd on every side, where no winds can possibly invade. There a man may not only see his own image, but that of his maker, clearly reflected from the *undisturb'd* and silent waters. *Dryden.*

UNDISTU'RBEDLY. *adv.* Calmly; peacefully.

Our minds are so weak, that they have need of all the assistances can be procured, to lay before them *undisturbedly* the thread and coherence of any discourse. *Locke.*

UNDIVI'DABLE. *adj.* Not separable; not susceptive of division.

The best actors in the world for tragedy, pastoral, scene *undividable*, or poem unlimited. *Shakesp. Hamlet.*

How comes it, husband,
That thou art thus estranged from thyself?
Thyself, I call it, being strange to me;
That *undividable*, incorporate,
Am better than thy dear self's better part. *Shakespeare.*

UNDIVI'DED. *adj.* Unbroken; whole; not parted.

Love is not divided between God and God's enemy: we must love God with all our heart; that is, give him a whole and *undivided* affection. *Taylor's Rule of Holy Living.*

He extends through all extent;
Spreads *undivided*, operates unspent. *Pope.*

UNDIVU'LGED. *adj.* Secret; not promulgated.

Let the great gods
Find out their enemies now. Tremble, thou wretch,
That hast within thee *undivulged* crimes,
Unwhipp'd of justice. *Shakesp. K. Lear.*

To UND'O. *v. a.* preterite *undid*; participle passive *undone*. [from *do*.]

1. To ruin; to bring to destruction.

As this immoderate favour of the multitude did him no good, so will it *undo* so many as shall trust unto it. *Hayward.*

Subdued, *undone*, they did at last obey,
And change their own for their invader's way. *Roscommon.*

Where, with like haste, though several ways they run,
Some to *undo*, and some to be *undone*. *Denham.*

Hither ye come, dislike, and so *undo*
The players, and disgrace the poet too. *Denham.*

When I behold the charming maid,
I'm ten times more *undone*; while hope and fear,
With variety of pain distract me. *Addison's Cato.*

2. To loose; to open what is shut or fastened; to unravel.

They false and fearful do their hands *undo*;
Brother, his brother; friend doth friend forsake. *Sidney.*

Pray *undo* this button. *Shakespeare's K. Lear.*

We implore thy powerful hand,
To *undo* the charmed band
Of true virgin here distress'd. *Milton.*

Were men so dull, they cou'd not see
That Lyce painted, should they flee,
Like simple birds, into a net,
So grossly woven and ill-set;
Her own teeth would *undo* the knot,
And let all go that she had got. *Waller.*

3. To change any thing done to its former state; to recall, or annul any action.

They may know, that we are far from presuming to think that men can better any thing which God hath done, even as we are from thinking, that men should presume to *undo* some things of men, which God doth know they cannot better. *Hooker.*

It was a torment
To lay upon the damn'd, which Sycorax
Could not again *undo*. *Shakespeare's Tempest.*

We seem ambitious God's whole work t' *undo*;
Of nothing he made us, and we strive too,
To bring ourselves to nothing back. *Donne.*

They make the Deity do and *undo*, go forward and backwards. *Burnet's Theory of the Earth.*

By granting me so soon,
He has the merit of the gift *undone*. *Dryden.*

Without this our repentance is not real, because we have not done what we can to *undo* our fault. *Tillotson.*

Now will this woman, with a single glance,
Undo what I've been labouring all this while. *Addison.*

When in time the martial maid
Found out the trick that Venus play'd,
She shakes her helm; she knits her brows,
And, fir'd with indignation, vows,
Tomorrow e'er the setting sun,
She'd all *undo*, that she had done. *Swift.*

UNDO'ING. *adj.* Ruining; destructive.

The great and *undoing* mischief which befalls men, is by their being misrepresented. *South.*

UNDO'ING. *n. s.* Ruin; destruction; fatal mischief.

To the utter *undoing* of some, many things by strictness of law may be done, which equity and honest meaning forbiddeth. *Hooker.*

False lustre could dazzle my poor daughter to her *undoing*. *Addison's Guardian.*

Fools that we are, we know that ye deceive us;
Yet act, as if the fraud was pleasing to us,
And our *undoing* joy. *Rowe's Royal Convert.*

UNDO'NE. *adj.* [from *undo*.]

1. Not done; not performed.

Do you smell a fault?
I cannot wish the fault *undone*, the
Issue of it being so proper. *Shakespeare's K. Lear.*

2. Ruined; brought to destruction.

Already is the work begun;
And we rest all *undone*, till all be done. *Daniel's Civ. War.*

There

There was no opportunity to call either of these two great persons to account for what they had done, or what they had left *undone*. *Clarendon.*

UNDO'UBTED. *adj.* Indubitable; indisputable; unquestionable.

His fact, till now, came not to an *undoubted* proof. *Shakesp.*

Thou, spirit, who ledst this glorious eremite
Into the desart, his victorious field,
Against the spiritual foe, and brought'st him thence,
By proof th' *undoubted* son of God, inspire. *Milton.*

The relations of your trials may be received as *undoubted* records of certain events, and as securely be depended on, as the propositions of Euclid. *Glanville.*

Made the world tremble with a num'rous host,
And of *undoubted* victory did boast. *Waller.*

Though none of these be strict demonstration, yet we have an *undoubted* assurance of them, when they are proved by the best arguments that the nature of the thing will bear. *Tillotson.*

UNDO'UBTEDLY. *adv.* Indubitably; without question; without doubt.

Some fault *undoubtedly* there is in the very resemblance of idolaters. *Hooker.*

This cardinal, *undoubtedly*
Was fashion'd to much honour. *Shakesp. Hen.* VIII.

Undoubtedly God will relent, and turn
From his displeasure. *Milton's Par. Lost.*

The original is *undoubtedly* one of the greatest this age has produced. *Dryden.*

He that believes the christian doctrine, if he adhere to it, and live accordingly, shall *undoubtedly* be saved. *Tillotson.*

UNDO'UBTING *adj.* Admitting no doubt.

They to whom all this is revealed, and received with an *undoubting* faith, if they do not presently set about so easy and so happy a task, must acknowledge themselves in the number of the blind. *Hammond.*

UNDRA'WN. *adj.* Not pulled by any external force.

Forth rush'd
The chariot of paternal deity *undrawn*,
Flashing thick flames, wheel within wheel;
Itself instinct with spirit, but convoy'd
By four cherubick shapes. *Milton's Par. Lost.*

UNDRE'ADED. *adj.* Not feared.

Better far,
Than still at hell's dark threshold t'have sat watch,
Unnam'd, *undreaded*, and thyself half starv'd. *Milton.*

UNDRE'AMED. *adj.* Not thought on.

A course more promising,
Than a wild dedication of yourselves
To unpath'd waters, *undream'd* shores; most certain
To miseries enough. *Shaksp. Winter Tale.*

To UNDRE'SS. *v. a.* [from *dress.*]

1. To divest of cloaths; to strip.

Undress you, and come now to bed. *Shakespeare.*

All were stol'n aside,
To counsel and *undress* the bride. *Suckling.*

Her fellows press'd,
And the reluctant nymph by force *undress'd*. *Addison's Ovid.*

2. To divest of ornaments, or the attire of ostentation.

Undress'd at evening, when she found
Their odours lost, their colours past,
She chang'd her look. *Prior.*

U'NDRESS. *n. s.* A loose or negligent dress.

Reform her into ease,
And put her in *undress* to make her please. *Dryden.*

UNDRE'SSED. *adj.*

1. Not regulated.

Thy vineyard lies half prun'd, and half *undress'd*. *Dryden.*

2. Not prepared for use.

The common country people wore perones, shoes of *undressed* leather. *Arbuthnot on Coins.*

UNDRI'ED. *adj* Not dried.

Their titles in the field were try'd:
Witness the fresh laments, and fun'ral tears *undry'd*. *Dryden.*

Four pounds of *undried* hops, thorough ripe, will make one of dry. *Mortimer's Husbandry.*

UNDRI'VEN. *adj.* Not impelled either way.

As wint'ry winds contending in the sky,
With equal force of lungs their titles try;
The doubtful rack of heav'n
Stands without motion, and the tide *undriv'n*. *Dryden.*

UNDRO'SSY. *adj.* Free from recrement.

When a noontide sun, with summer beams
Darts through a cloud, her watry skirts are edg'd
With lucid amber, or *undrossy* gold. *Philips.*

UNDU'BITABLE. *adj.* Not admitting doubt; unquestionable.

Let that principle, that all is matter, and that there is nothing else, be received for certain and *undubitable*, and it will be easy to be seen, what consequences it will lead us into. *Locke.*

UNDU'E. *adj.* [*indue*, Fr.]

1. Not right; not legal.

That proceeding being at that time taxed for rigorous and *undue*, in matter and manner, makes it very probable there was some greater matter against her. *Bacon.*

2. Not agreeable to duty.

He will not prostitute his power to mean and *undue* ends, nor stoop to little and low arts of courting the people. *Atterb.*

U'NDULARY. *adj.* [from *undulo*, Lat.] Playing like waves; playing with intermissions.

The blasts and *undulary* breaths thereof maintain no certainty in their course. *Browne's Vulgar Errours.*

To U'NDULATE. *v. a.* [from *undulo*, Lat.] To drive backward and forward; to make to play as waves.

Breath vocalized, *i. e.* vibrated and *undulated*, may in a different manner affect the lips, or tongue, or palate, and impress a swift, tremulous motion, which breath alone passing smooth doth not. *Holder's Elements of Speech.*

To U'NDULATE. *v. n.* To play as waves in curls.

Through *undulating* air the sounds are sent,
And spread o'er all the fluid element. *Pope.*

UNDULA'TION. *n. s.* [from *undulate.*] Waving motion.

Worms and leeches will move both ways; and so will most of those animals, whose bodies consist of round and annulary fibres, and move by *undulation*, that is, like the waves of the sea. *Browne's Vulgar Errours.*

All tuneable sounds are made by a regular vibration of the sonorous body, and *undulation* of the air, proportionable to the acuteness and gravity of the tone. *Holder.*

Two parallel walls beat the sound back on each other, till the *undulation* is quite worn out. *Addison.*

U'NDULATORY *adj.* [from *undulate.*] Moving in the manner of waves.

A constant *undulatory* motion is perceived by looking through telescopes. *Arbuthnot on Air.*

UNDU'LY. *adv.* Not properly; not according to duty.

Men *unduely* exercise their zeal against persons; not only against evil persons, but against those that are the most venerable. *Sprat's Sermons.*

UNDU'TEOUS. *adj.* Not performing duty; irreverent; disobedient.

She and I, long since contracted,
Are now so sure, that nothing can dissolve us.
And this deceit loses the name of craft,
Of disobedience, or *unduteous* title. *Shakesp.*

In Latium safe he lay,
From his *unduteous* son, and his usurping sway. *Dryden.*

UNDU'TIFUL. *adj.* Not obedient; not reverent.

England thinks it no good policy to have that realm planted with English, lest they should grow so *undutiful* as the Irish, and become more dangerous. *Spenser's Ireland.*

No man's reason did ever dictate to him, that it is fit for a creature not to love God; to be *undutiful* to his great sovereign, and ungrateful to his best benefactor. *Tillotson.*

UNDU'TIFULLY. *adv.* [from *undutiful.*] Not according to duty.

The fish had long in Cæsar's ponds been fed,
And from its lord *undutifully* fled. *Dryden's Juvenal.*

UNDU'TIFULNESS. *n. s.* Want of respect; irreverence; disobedience.

I would have thought they would rather have held in, and staid all the other from *undutifulness*, than need to be forced thereunto themselves. *Spenser's Ireland.*

Forbidding *undutifulness* to superiours, sedition and rebellion against magistracy. *Tillotson.*

UNDY'ING. *adj.* Not destroyed; not perishing.

Driven down
To chains of darkness, and th' *undying* worm. *Milton.*

UNEA'RNED. *adj.* Not obtained by labour or merit.

As I am honest Puck,
If we have *unearned* luck,
Now to 'scape the serpent's tongue,
We will make amends ere long. *Shakespeare.*

Our work is brought to little, though begun
Early, and th' hour of supper comes *unearn'd*. *Milton.*

Wilt thou rather chuse
To lie supinely, hoping heav'n will bless
Thy slighted fruits, and give thee bread *unearn'd*! *Philips.*

UNEA'RTHED. *adj.* Driven from the hold.

The mighty robber of the fold,
Is from his craggy, winding haunts *unearth'd*. *Thomson.*

UNEA'RTHLY. *adj.* Not terrestrial.

The sacrifice
How ceremonious, solemn, and *unearthly*
It was i' th' offering! *Shakesp. Winter Tale.*

UNE'ASILY. *adv.* Not without pain.

He lives *uneasily* under the burden. *L'Estrange.*

They make mankind their enemy by their unjust actions, and consequently live more *uneasily* in the world than other men. *Tillotson.*

UNE'ASINESS. *n. s.* Trouble; perplexity; state of disquiet.

Not a subject
Sits in heart-grief and *uneasiness*,
Under the sweet shade of your government. *Shakespeare.*

The same *uneasiness* which ev'ry thing
Gives to our nature, life must also bring. *Denham.*

We may be said to live like those who have their hope in another life, if we bear the *uneasinesses* that befall us here with constancy. *Atterbury.*

Men are dissatisfied with their station, and create to themselves all the *uneasiness* of want. They fancy themselves poor, and under this persuasion feel all the disquiet of real poverty. *Rogers's Sermons.*

His Majesty will maintain his just authority over them; and whatever *uneasiness* they may give themselves, they can create none in him. *Addison's Freeholder.*

The libels against his grandfather, that fly about his very court, give him *uneasiness.* *Swift.*

UNE'ASY. *adj.*

1. Painful; giving disturbance.

The wisest of the Gentiles forbad any libations to be made for dead infants, as believing they passed into happiness through the way of mortality, and for a few months wore an *uneasy* garment. *Taylor's Rule of Holy Living.*

On a tottering pinacle the standing is *uneasy*, and the fall deadly. *Decay of Piety.*

His present thoughts are *uneasy*, because his present state does not please him. *L'Estrange.*

Uneasy life to me,
Still watch'd and importun'd, but worse for thee. *Dryden.*

2. Disturbed; not at ease.

Happy low! lie down;
Uneasy lies the head that wears a crown. *Shakespeare.*

Uneasy justice upward flew,
And both the sisters to the stars withdrew. *Dryden.*

The passion and ill language proceeded from a gall'd and *uneasy* mind. *Tillotson.*

It is such a pleasure as makes a man restless and *uneasy*, exciting fresh desires. *Addison.*

One would wonder how any person should desire to be king of a country, in which the established religion is directly opposite to that he professes. Were it possible for such a one to accomplish his designs, his own reason might tell him, there could not be a more *uneasy* prince, nor a more unhappy people. *Addison's Freeholder.*

If we imagine ourselves intitled to any thing we have not, we shall be *uneasy* in the want of it; and that uneasiness will expose us to all the evil persuasions of poverty. *Rogers.*

The soul, *uneasy* and confin'd from home,
Rests and expatiates in a life to come. *Pope.*

3. Constraining; cramping.

Some servile imitators
Prescribe at first such strict, *uneasy* rules,
As they must ever slavishly observe. *Roscommon.*

4. Not unconstrained; not disengaged.

In conversation, a solicitous watchfulness about one's behaviour, instead of being mended, will be constrained, *uneasy*, and ungraceful. *Locke.*

5. Peevish; difficult to please.

A sour, untractable nature, makes him *uneasy* to those who approach him. *Addison's Spectator*, N°. 469.

6. Difficult. Out of use.

We will, not appearing what we are, have some question with the shepherd: from his simplicity, I think it not *uneasy* to get the cause of my son's resort thither. *Shakesp.*

This swift business
I must *uneasy* make; lest too light winning
Make the prize light. *Shakespeare's Tempest.*

Divers things, knowable by the bare light of nature, are yet so *uneasy* to be satisfactorily understood, that, let them be delivered in the clearest expressions, the notions themselves will appear obscure. *Boyle.*

UNEA'TEN. *adj.* Not devoured.

Though they had but two horses left *uneaten*, they had never suffered a summons to be sent to them. *Clarendon.*

UNE'ATH. *adv.* [from *eath*, eað, Saxon; easy.]

1. Not easily. Out of use.

Uneath may she endure the flinty street,
To tread them with her tender feeling feet. *Shakesp.*

2. It seems in *Spenser* to signify the same as *beneath.* Under; below.

A roaring, hideous sound,
That all the air with terror filled wide,
And seem'd *uneath* to shake the stedfast ground. *Fairy Queen.*

UNE'DIFYING. *adj.* Not improving in good life.

Our practical divinity is as sound and affecting, as that of our popish neighbours is flat and *unedifying.* *Atterbury.*

UNELE'CTED. *adj.* Not chosen.

Putting him to rage,
You should have ta'en th' advantage of his choler,
And pass'd him *unelected.* *Shakesp. Coriolanus.*

UNELI'GIBLE. *adj.* Not worthy to be chosen.

Both extremes, above or below the proportion of our character, are dangerous; and 'tis hard to determine which is most *uneligible.* *Rogers's Sermons.*

UNEMPLO'YED. *adj.*

1. Not busy; at leisure; idle.

Other creatures, all day long
Rove idle, *unemploy'd*, and less need rest. *Milton's Par. Lost.*

Wilt thou then serve Philistines with that gift,
Which was expresly given thee to annoy them?
Better at home lie bedrid, not only idle,
Inglorious, *unemploy'd*, with age out-worn. *Milton.*

Our wise creator has annexed to several objects, and to the ideas we receive of them, as also, to several of our thoughts, a concomitant pleasure, that those faculties which we are endowed with, might not remain idle and *unemployed.* *Locke.*

2. Not engaged in any particular work.

Pales unhonour'd, Ceres *unemploy'd*,
Were all forgot. *Dryden.*

Men, soured with poverty, and *unemploy'd*, easily give into any prospect of change. *Addison.*

UNE'MPTIABLE. *adj.* Not to be emptied; inexhaustible.

Whatsoever men or angels know, it is as a drop of that *unemptiable* fountain of wisdom, which hath diversly imparted her treasures. *Hooker.*

UNENDO'WED. *adj.* Not invested; not graced.

A man rather unadorned with any parts of quickness, and *unendowed* with any notable virtues, than notorious for any defect of understanding. *Clarendon.*

Aspiring, factious, fierce and loud,
With grace and learning *unendow'd.* *Swift.*

UNENGA'GED. *adj.* Not engaged; not appropriated.

When we have sunk the only *unengaged* revenues left, our incumbrances must remain perpetual. *Swift.*

UNENJOY'ED. *adj.* Not obtained; not possessed.

Each day's a mistress, *unenjoy'd* before;
Like travellers, we're pleas'd with seeing more. *Dryden.*

UNENJO'YING. *adj.* Not using; having no fruition.

The more we have, the meaner is our store;
Th' *unenjoying*, craving wretch is poor. *Creech.*

UNENLI'GHTENED. *adj.* Not illuminated.

Moral virtue natural reason, *unenlightened* by revelation, prescribes. *Atterbury.*

UNENLA'RGED. *adj.* Not enlarged; narrow, contracted.

Unenlarged souls are disgusted with the wonders which the microscope has discovered concerning the shape of little animals, which equal not a pepper-corn. *Watts.*

UNENSLA'VED. *adj.* Free; not enthralled.

By thee
She sits a sov'reign, *unenslav'd* and free. *Addison.*

UNENTERTA'INING. *adj.* Giving no delight; giving no entertainment.

It was not *unentertaining* to observe by what degrees I ceased to be a witty writer. *Pope.*

UNE'NVIED. *adj.* Exempt from envy.

The fortune, which no body sees, makes a man happy and *unenvied.* *Bacon.*

This loss
Thus far at least recover'd, hath much more
Establish'd in a safe, *unenvied* throne,
Yielded with full consent. *Milton's Par. Lost.*

These *unenvied* stand;
Since what they act, transcends what they command. *Denham.*

What health promotes, and gives *unenvy'd* peace,
Is all expenceless, and procur'd with ease. *Blackmore.*

Beneath our humble cottage let us haste,
And here, *unenvy'd*, rural dainties taste. *Pope's Odyssey.*

UNENTO'MBED. *adj.* Unburied; uninterred.

Think'st thou *unentomb'd* to cross the floods? *Dryden.*

UNE'QUABLE. *adj.* Different from itself; diverse.

March and September, the two equinoxes, are the most unsettled and *unequable* of seasons. *Bentley's Sermons.*

UNE'QUAL. *adj.* [*inæqualis*, Lat.]

1. Not even.

There sits deformity to mock my body;
To shape my legs of an *unequal* size. *Shakespeare.*

You have here more than one example of Chaucer's *unequal* numbers. *Dryden.*

2. Not equal; inferiour.

Among *unequals*, what society? *Milton.*

To bliss unknown my lofty soul aspires;
My lot *unequal* to my vast desires. *Arbuthnot.*

3. Partial; not bestowing on both the same advantages.

When to conditions of *unequal* peace,
He shall submit, then may he not possess
Kingdom nor life. *Denham.*

4. [*Inegal*, Fr.] Disproportionate; ill matched.

Unequal work we find,
Against *unequal* arms to fight in pain. *Milton.*

From his strong arm I saw his rival run,
And in a croud th' *unequal* combat shun. *Dryden.*

Fierce Belinda on the baron flies,
Nor fear'd the chief th' *unequal* fight to try. *Pope.*

5. Not regular; not uniform.

So strong, yet so *unequal* pulses beat. *Dryden.*

UN-

Une'qualable. *adj.* Not to be equalled; not to be paralelled.

Christ's love to God is filial and *unequalable*. *Boyle.*

Une'qualled. *adj.* Unparallelled; unrivalled in excellence.

By those *unequalled* and invaluable blessings, he manifested how much he hated sin, and how much he loved sinners. *Boyle.*

Dorinda came, divested of the scorn,
Which the *unequall'd* maid so long had worn. *Roscommon.*

Une'qually. *adv.* In different degrees; in disproportion one to the other.

When we view some well-proportion'd dome,
No single parts *unequally* surprize;
All comes united to th' admiring eyes. *Pope.*

Une'qualness. *n. s.* Inequality; state of being unequal.

Une'quitable. *adj.* Not impartial; not just.

We force him to stand to those measures which we think too *unequitable* to press upon a murderer. *Decay of Piety.*

Unequi'vocal. *adj.* Not equivocal.

This conceit is erroneous, making putrefactive generations correspondent unto seminal productions, and conceiving *unequivocal* effects, and univocal conformity unto the efficient. *Brown's Vulgar Errours.*

Une'rrableness. *n. s.* Incapacity of errour.

How much more than possible that has been, the many innovations of that church witness; and consequently the danger of presuming upon the *unerrableness* of a guide. *Decay of Piety.*

Une'rring. *adj.* [*inerrans*, Lat.]

1. Committing no mistake.

The irresistible infirmities of our nature, make a perfect and *unerring* obedience impossible. *Rogers's Sermons.*

Fast in chains constrain the various God;
Who bound obedient to superior force,
Unerring will prescribe your destin'd course. *Pope.*

His javelin threw,
Hissing in air th' *unerring* weapon flew. *Dryden.*

2. Incapable of failure; certain.

The king a mortal shaft lets fly
From his *unerring* hand. *Denham.*

Is this th' *unerring* power? the ghost reply'd;
Nor Phœbus flatter'd; nor his answers ly'd. *Dryden.*

Lovers of truth, for truth's sake; there is this one *unerring* mark, the not entertaining any proposition, with greater assurance than the proofs it is built upon will warrant. *Locke.*

Une'rringly. *adv.* Without mistake.

What those figures are, that should be mechanically adapted, to fall so *unerringly* into regular compositions, is beyond our faculties to conceive. *Glanville.*

Unesche'wable. *adj.* Inevitable; unavoidable; not to be escaped.

He gave the mayor sufficient warning to shift for safety, if an *uneschewable* destiny had not haltered him. *Carew.*

Unespi'ed. *adj.* Not seen; undiscovered; undescried.

Treachery, guile, and deceit, are things which may for a while, but do not long go *unespied*. *Hooker.*

From living eyes her open shame to hide,
And live in rocks and caves long *unespy'd*. *Fairy Queen.*

Nearer to view his prey, and *unespy'd*
To mark what of their state he more might learn. *Milton.*

The second shaft came swift and *unespy'd*;
And pierc'd his hand, and nail'd it to his side. *Dryden.*

Unesse'ntial. *adj.*

1. Not being of the last importance; not constituting essence.

Tillotson was moved rather with pity, than indignation, towards the persons of those who differed from him in the *unessential* parts of christianity. *Addison's Freeholder.*

2. Void of real being.

The void profound
Of *unessential* night receives him next. *Milton.*

Unesta'blished. *adj.* Not established.

From plain principles, doubt may be fairly solved, and not clapped up from petitionary foundations *unestablished*. *Brown.*

Une'ven. *adj.*

1. Not even; not level.

These high wild hills, and rough, *uneven* ways,
Draw out our miles, and make them wearisome. *Shakesp.*

Some said it was best to fight with the Turks in that *uneven*, mountain country, where the Turks chief strength consisting in the multitude of his horsemen, should stand him in small stead. *Knolles's Hist. of the Turks.*

They made the ground *uneven* about their nest, insomuch that the slate did not lie flat. *Addison.*

2. Not suiting each other; not equal.

The Hebrew verse consists of *uneven* feet. *Peacham.*

Une'venness. *n. s.*

1. Surface not level; inequality of surface.

This softness of the foot, which yields to the ruggedness and *unevenness* of the roads, renders the feet less capable of being worn, than if they were more solid. *Ray on the Creation.*

That motion which can continue long in one and the same part of the body, can be propagated a long way from one part to another, supposing the body homogeneal; so that the motion may not be reflected, refracted, interrupted or disordered by any *unevenness* of the body. *Newton.*

2. Turbulence; changeable state.

Edward II. though an unfortunate prince, and by reason of the troubles and *unevenness* of his reign, the very law itself had many interruptions; yet it held its current in that state his father had left it in. *Hale.*

3. Not smoothness.

Notwithstanding any such *unevenness* or indistinctness in the style of those places, concerning the origin and form of the earth. *Burnet's Theory of the Earth.*

Une'vitable. *adj.* [*inevitabilis*, Lat. *inevitable*, Fr.] Inevitable; not to be escaped.

So jealous is she of my love to her daughter, that I never yet begin to open my mouth to the *unevitable* Philoclea, but that her unwished presence gave my tale a conclusion, before it had a beginning. *Sidney.*

Unexa'cted. *adj.* Not exacted; not taken by force.

All was common, and the fruitful earth
Was free, to give her *unexacted* birth. *Dryden.*

Unexa'mined. *adj.* Not enquired; not tried; not discussed.

Yet within these five hours Hastings liv'd
Untainted, *unexamin'd*, free at liberty. *Shakespeare.*

They utter all they think, with a violence and indisposition, *unexamin'd*, without relation to person, place, or fitness. *B. Johnson.*

The most pompous seeming knowledge, that is built on the *unexamined* prejudices of sense, stands not. *Glanville.*

Unexa'mpled. *adj.* Not known by any precedent or example.

Charles returned with *unexampled* love from Algiers. *Raleigh.*

O *unexampl'd* love!
Love no where to be found less than divine. *Milton.*

God vouchsaf'd Enoch an *unexampled* exemption from death. *Boyle.*

Your twice-conquer'd vassals,
First, by your courage, then your clemency,
Here humbly vow to sacrifice their lives,
The gift of this your *unexampled* mercy,
To your command. *Denham's Sophy.*

I tune my pipe afresh, each night and day,
Thy *unexampled* goodness to extoll. *Philips.*

Unexce'ptionable. *adj.* Not liable to any objection.

Personal prejudices should not hinder us from pursuing, with joint hands and hearts, the *unexceptionable* design of this pious institution. *Atterbury.*

Unexco'gitable. *adj.* Not to be found out.

Wherein can man resemble his *unexcogitable* power and perfectness. *Raleigh's Hist. of the World.*

Une'xecuted. *adj.* Not performed; not done.

Leave *unexecuted* your own renowned knowledge. *Shakesp.*

Unexci'sed. *adj.* Not subject to the payment of excise.

Unexe'mplified. *adj.* Not made known by instance or example.

Those wonders a generation returned with so *unexemplified* an ingratitude, that it is not the least of his wonders, that he would vouchsafe to work any of them. *Boyle.*

This being a new, *unexemplify'd* kind of policy, must pass for the wisdom of this particular age, scorning the examples of all former ages. *South.*

Unexerci'sed. *adj.* Not practised; not experienced.

Messapus, with his ardour, warms
A heartless train, *unexercis'd* in arms. *Dryden.*

Abstract ideas are not so obvious to the yet *unexercised* mind, as particular ones. *Locke.*

Unexe'mpt. *adj.* Not free by peculiar privilege.

You invert the cov'nants of her trust,
And harshly deal like an ill borrower,
With that which you receiv'd on other terms,
Scorning the *unexempt* condition
By which all mortal frailty must subsist. *Milton.*

Unexhau'sted. *adj.* [*inexhaustus*, Lat.] Not spent; not drained to the bottom.

What avail her *unexhausted* stores?
While proud oppression in her vallies reigns. *Addison.*

Unexpa'nded. *adj.* Not spread out.

Every fœtus bears a secret hoard;
With sleeping, *unexpanded* issue stor'd. *Blackmore.*

Unexpe'cted. *adj.* Not thought on; sudden; not provided against.

Have wisdom to provide always beforehand, that those evils overtake us not, which death *unexpected* doth use to bring upon careless men; and although it be sudden in itself, nevertheless, in regard of our prepared minds, it may not be sudden. *Hooker, b. v. §. 46.*

Sith evils, great and *unexpected*, do cause oftentimes even them to think upon divine power with fearfullest suspicions, which have been otherwise the most sacred adorers thereof; how should we look for any constant resolution of mind in such cases, saving only where unfeigned affection to God, hath bred the most assured confidence to be assisted by his hand? *Hooker, b. v. §. 1.*

O an-

O *unexpected* stroke! worse than death!
Must I thus leave thee, paradise? *Milton's Par. Lost.*

Them *unexpected* joy surpriz'd,
When the great ensign of Messiah blaz'd. *Milton.*

Their *unexpected* loss and plaints out-breath'd. *Milton.*

Some amazement;
But such as sprung from wonder, not from fear,
It was so *unexpected*. *Denham's Sophy.*

To the pale foes they suddenly draw near,
And summon them to *unexpected* fight. *Dryden.*

Deep was the wound; he stagger'd with the blow,
And turn'd him to his *unexpected* foe. *Dryden.*

When Barcelona was taken by a most *unexpected* accident of a bomb lighting on the magazine, then the Catalonians revolted. *Swift.*

UNEXPE'CTEDLY. *adv.* Suddenly; at a time unthought of.

Oft he seems to hide his face,
But *unexpectedly* returns. *Milton's Agonistes.*

A most bountiful present, when I was most in want of it, came most seasonably and *unexpectedly* to my relief. *Dryden.*

If the concernment be poured in *unexpectedly* upon us, it overflows us. *Dryden.*

You have fairer warning than others, who are *unexpectedly* cut off. *Wake.*

My heart was filled with a deep melancholy, to see several dropping *unexpectedly* in the midst of mirth. *Addison.*

Though you went away so *unexpectedly*, yet we have informed ourselves of every thing that hath happened to you. *Gay.*

UNEXPE'CTEDNESS. *n. s.* Suddenness; unthought of time or manner.

He describes the *unexpectedness* of his appearance. *Watts.*

UNEXPE'RIENCED. *adj.* Not versed; not acquainted by trial or practice.

The wisest, *unexperienc'd*, will be ever
Timorous and loth, with novice modesty,
Irresolute, unhardy, unadvent'rous. *Milton.*

Long use may strengthen men against many such inconveniences, which, to *unexperienc'd* persons, may prove very hazardous. *Wilkins's Math. Magic.*

The pow'rs of Troy;
Not a raw and *unexperienc'd* train,
But a firm body of embattl'd men. *Dryden.*

These reproaches are the extravagant speeches of those *unexperienced* in the things they speak against. *Tillotson.*

Unexperienced young men, if unwarned, take one thing for another. *Locke.*

The smallest accident intervening, often produces such changes, that a wise man is just as much in doubt of events, as the most ignorant and *unexperienced*. *Swift.*

UNEXPE'DIENT. *adj.* Inconvenient; not fit.

The like would not be *unexpedient* after meat, to assist and cherish nature in her first concoction, and send their minds back to study in good tune. *Milton on Education.*

UNEXPE'RT. *adj.* [*inexpertus*, Lat.] Wanting skill or knowledge.

Receive the partner of my inmost soul:
Him you will find in letters, and in laws
Not *unexpert*. *Prior.*

UNEXPLO'RED. *adj.*

1. Not searched out.

Oh! say what stranger cause, yet *unexplor'd*,
Could make a gentle belle reject a lord? *Pope.*

2. Not tried; not known.

Under thy friendly conduct will I fly,
To regions *unexplor'd*. *Dryden.*

UNEXPO'SED. *adj.* Not laid open to censure.

They will endeavour to diminish the honour of the best treatise, rather than suffer the little mistakes of the author to pass *unexposed*. *Watts's Improvement of the Mind.*

UNEXPRE'SSIBLE. *adj.* Ineffable; not to be uttered.

What *unexpressible* comfort does overflow the pious soul, from a conscience of its own innocency. *Tillotson.*

UNEXPRE'SSIVE. *adj.*

1. Not having the power of uttering or expressing. This is the natural and analogical signification.

2. Inexpressible; unutterable; ineffable; not to be expressed. Improper, and out of use.

Run, run, Orlando, carve on every tree
The fair, the chaste, and *inexpressive* she. *Shakespeare.*

With nectar pure his ouzy locks he laves,
And hears the *unexpressive*, nuptial song,
In the blest kingdoms, meek, of joy and love. *Milton.*

The helmed cherubim,
And sworded seraphim,
Are seen in glitt'ring ranks, with wings display'd,
Harping in loud and solemn quire,
With *inexpressive* notes to heaven's new-born heir. *Milton.*

UNEXTE'NDED. *adj.* Occupying no assignable space; having no dimensions.

How inconceivable is it, that a spiritual, *i. e.* an *unextended* substance, should represent to the mind an extended one, as a triangle? *Locke.*

UNEXTI'NGUISHABLE. *adj.* [*inextinguible*, Fr.] Unquenchable; not to be put out.

Pain of *unextinguishable* fire
Must exercise us, without hope of end. *Milton.*

What native, *unextinguishable* beauty must be impressed through the whole, which the defœdation of so many parts by a bad printer, and a worse editor, could not hinder from shining forth? *Bentley.*

UNEXTI'NGUISHED. *adj.* [*inextinctus*, Lat.]

1. Not quenched; not put out.

The souls, whom that unhappy flame invades,
Make endless moans, and, pining with desire,
Lament too late their *unextinguish'd* fire. *Dryden.*

Ev'n o'er your cold, your ever-sacred urn,
His constant flame, shall *unextinguish'd* burn. *Lyttleton.*

2. Not extinguishable.

An ardent thirst of honour; a soul unsatisfied with all it has done, and an *unextinguish'd* desire of doing more. *Dryden.*

UNFA'DED. *adj.* Not withered.

A lovely flow'r,
Unfaded yet, but yet unfed below,
No more to mother earth, or the green stem shall owe. *Dryd.*

UNFA'DING. *adj.* Not liable to wither.

For her th' *unfading* rose of Eden blooms,
And wings of seraphs shed divine perfumes. *Pope.*

UNFA'ILING. *adj.* Certain; not missing.

Nothing the united voice of all history proclaims so loud, as the certain, *unfailing* curse, that has pursued and overtook sacrilege. *South's Sermons.*

Thou, secure of my *unfailing* word,
Compose thy swelling soul, and sheath the sword. *Dryden.*

UNFA'IR. *adj.* Disingenuous; subdolous; not honest.

You come, like an *unfair* merchant, to charge me with being in your debt. *Swift.*

UNFA'ITHFUL. *adj.*

1. Perfidious; treacherous.

If you break one jot of your promise, I will think you the most atheistical break-promise, and the most unworthy, that may be chosen out of the gross band of the *unfaithful*. *Shakespeare.*

My feet, through wine, *unfaithful* to their weight,
Betray'd me tumbling from a tow'ry height. *Pope.*

2. Impious; infidel.

Thence shall come
To judge th' *unfaithful* dead; but to reward
His faithful, and receive them into bliss. *Milton's Par. Lost.*

UNFA'ITHFULLY. *adv.* Treacherously; perfidiously.

There is danger of being *unfaithfully* counselled; and more for the good of them that counsel, than for him that is counselled. *Bacon.*

UNFA'ITHFULNESS. *n. s.* Treachery; perfidiousness.

As the obscurity of what some writers deliver, makes it very difficult to be understood; so the *unfaithfulness* of too many others, makes it unfit to be relied on. *Boyle.*

UNFA'LLOWED. *adj.* Not fallowed.

Th' *unfallow'd* glebe
Yearly o'ercomes the granaries with stores
Of golden wheat. *Phillips.*

UNFAMI'LIAR. *adj.* Unaccustomed; such as is not common.

The matters which we handle, seem, by reason of newness, dark, intricate, *unfamiliar*. *Hooker, b. i.*

Chaucer's uncouth, or rather *unfamiliar*, language, deters many readers. *Warton's Spenser.*

UNFA'SHIONABLE. *adj.* Not modish; not according to the reigning custom.

A man writes good sense, but he has not a happy manner of expression. Perhaps he uses obsolete and *unfashionable* language. *Watts's Logick.*

UNFA'SHIONABLENESS. *n. s.* Deviation from the mode.

Natural *unfashionableness* is much better than apish, affected postures. *Locke.*

UNFA'SHIONED. *adj.*

1. Not modified by art.

Mark but how terribly his eyes appear;
And yet there is something roughly noble there;
Which, in *unfashion'd* nature, looks divine,
And, like a gem, does in the quarry shine. *Dryden.*

2. Having no regular form.

A lifeless lump, *unfashion'd* and unfram'd,
Of jarring seeds, and justly chaos nam'd. *Dryden.*

UNFA'SHIONABLY. *adv.* [from *unfashionable*.]

1. Not according to the fashion.

2. Unartfully.

Deform'd, unfinish'd, sent before my time
Into this breathing world, scarce half made up;
And that so lamely and *unfashionably*,
That dogs bark at me. *Shakespeare's Rich. III.*

To UNFA'STEN. *v. a.* To loose; to unfix.

He had no sooner *unfastened* his hold, but that a wave forcibly spoiled his weaker hand of hold. *Sidney, b. ii.*

His

His foes are so enrooted with his friends,
That plucking to unfix an enemy,
He doth *unfasten* so, and shake a friend. *Shakespeare.*
Then in the key-hole turns
Th' intricate wards, and every bolt and bar
Of massy iron, or solid rock, with ease
Unfastens. *Milton's Par. Lost. b.* ii. *l.* 876.

UNFA'THERED. *adj.* Fatherless; having no father.
They do observe
Unfather'd heirs, and loathly births of nature. *Shakesp.*

UNFA'THOMABLE. *n. s.*
1. Not to be founded by a line.
In the midst of the plain a beautiful lake, which the inhabitants thereabouts pretend is *unfathomable.* *Addison.*
Beneath *unfathomable* depths they faint,
And secret in their gloomy caverns pant. *Addison's Ovid.*
2. That of which the end or extent cannot be found.
A thousand parts of our bodies may be diversified in all the dimensions of solid bodies; which overwhelms the fancy in a new abyss of *unfathomable* number. *Bentley's Sermons.*

UNFA'THOMABLY. *adv.* So as not to be founded.
Cover'd pits, *unfathomably* deep. *Thomson.*

UNFA'THOMED. *adj.* Not to be founded.
The Titan race
He sing'd with light'ning, rowl within the *unfathom'd* space. *Dryden.*

UNFATI'GUED. *adj.* Unwearied; untired.
Over dank, and dry,
They journey toilsome, *unfatigu'd* with length
Of march. *Phillips.*

UNFA'VOURABLY. *adv.*
1. Unkindly; unpropitiously.
2. So as not to countenance, or support.
Bacon speaks not *unfavourably* of this. *Glanville.*

UNFEA'RED. *adj.*
1. Not affrighted; intrepid; not terrified.
Just men
Though heaven should speak with all his wrath at once,
That with his breath the hinges of the world
Did crack, we should stand upright and *unfear'd.* *B. Johnson.*
2. Not dreaded; not regarded with terrour.

UNFE'ASIBLE. *adj.* Impracticable.

UNFE'ATHERED. *adj.* Implumous; naked of feathers.
The mother nightingale laments alone;
Whose nest some prying churl had found, and thence
By stealth convey'd th' *unfeather'd* innocence. *Dryden.*

UNFE'ATURED. *adj.* Deformed; wanting regularity of features.
Visage rough,
Deform'd, *unfeatur'd*, and a skin of buff. *Dryden.*

UNFE'D. *adj.* Not supplied with food.
Each bone might through his body well be read,
And every sinew seen through his long fast;
For nought he car'd, his carcass long *unfed.* *Fairy Queen.*
A grisly foaming wolf *unfed.* *Roscommon.*

UNFEE'D. *adj.* Unpaid.
It is like the breath of an *unfeed* lawyer; you gave me nothing for't. *Shakespeare's K. Lear.*

UNFEE'LING. *adj.* Insensible; void of mental sensibility.
Dull, *unfeeling*, barren ignorance,
Is made my goaler to attend on me. *Shakesp. Rich.* II.
Unlucky Welsted! thy *unfeeling* master,
The more thou ticklest, gripes his fist the faster. *Pope.*

UNFE'IGNED. *adj.* Not counterfeited; not hypocritical; real; sincere.
Here I take the like *unfeigned* oath,
Never to marry her. *Shakesp. Taming of the Shrew.*
Thousand decencies that daily flow
From all her words and actions, mix'd with love,
And sweet compliance, which declare *unfeigned*
Union of mind. *Milton's Par. Lost.*
Sorrow *unfeign'd*, and humiliation meek. *Milton.*
Employ it in *unfeigned* piety towards God. *Sprat.*

UNFE'IGNEDLY. *adv.* Really; sincerely; without hypocrisy.
He pardoneth all them that truly repent, and *unfeignedly* believe his holy gospel. *Common Prayer.*
How should they be *unfeignedly* just, whom religion doth not cause to be such; or they religious, which are not found such by the proof of their just actions? *Hooker.*
Prince dauphin, can you love this lady?——
——I love her most *unfeignedly.* *Shakesp. K. John.*
Thou hast brought me and my people *unfeignedly* to repent of the sins we have committed. *K. Charles.*

UNFE'LT. *adj.* Not felt; not perceived.
All my treasury
Is but yet *unfelt* thanks, which, more enrich'd,
Shall be your love and labour's recompence. *Shakespeare.*
Her looks, from that time infus'd
Sweetness into my heart, *unfelt* before. *Milton's Par. Lost.*
'Tis pleasant, safely to behold from shore
The rowling ships, and hear the tempest roar;
Not that another's pain is our delight,
But pains *unfelt* produce the pleasing sight. *Dryden.*

UNFE'NCED. *adj.*
1. Naked of fortification.
I'd play incessantly upon these jades;
Even till *unfenced* desolation
Leave them as naked as the vulgar air. *Shakespeare.*
2. Not surrounded by any inclosure.

UNFERME'NTED. *adj.* Not fermented.
All such vegetables must be *unfermented*; for fermentation changes their nature. *Arbuthnot on Aliments.*

UNFE'RTILE. *adj.* Not fruitful; not prolifick.
Peace is not such a dry tree, such a sapless, *unfertile* thing, but that it might fructify and increase. *Decay of Piety.*

To UNFE'TTER. *v. a.* To unchain; to free from shackles.
Unfetter me with speed,
I see you troubled that I bleed. *Dryden.*
This most useful principle may be *unfetter'd*, and restored to its native freedom of exercise. *Addison's Spectator.*
The soul in these instances is not entirely loose and *unfetter'd* from the body. *Addison's Spectator.*
Th' *unfetter'd* mind by thee sublim'd. *Thomson.*

UNFI'GURED. *adj.* Representing no animal form.
In *unfigured* paintings the noblest is the imitation of marbles, and of architecture, as arches, freezes. *Wotton.*

UNFI'LLED. *adj.* Not filled; not supplied.
Come not to table, but when thy need invites thee; and if thou beest in health, leave something of thy appetite *unfilled.* *Taylor's Rule of Living Holy.*
The air did not precisely fill up the vacuities of the vessel, since it left so many *unfilled.* *Boyle.*
The throne of my forefathers
Still stands *unfill'd.* *Addison's Cato.*

UNFI'RM. *adj.*
1. Weak; feeble.
Our fancies are more giddy and *unfirm*
Than women's are. *Shakesp. Twelfth Night.*
So is the *unfirm* king
In three divided; and his coffers found
With hollow poverty and emptiness. *Shakespeare.*
2. Not stable.
Take the time, while stagg'ring yet they stand,
With feet *unfirm*, and prepossess the strand. *Dryden.*

UNFI'LIAL. *adj.* Unsuitable to a son.
You offer him a wrong,
Something *unfilial.* *Shakespeare.*
Teach the people, that to hope for heaven is a mercenary, legal, and therefore *unfilial*, affection. *Boyle.*

UNFI'NISHED. *adj.* Incomplete; not brought to an end; not brought to perfection; imperfect; wanting the last hand.
It is for that such outward ornament
Was lavish'd on their sex, that inward gifts
Were left for haste *unfinish'd.* *Milton.*
I dedicate to you a very *unfinished* piece. *Dryden.*
His hasty hand left his pictures so *unfinished*, that the beauty in the picture faded sooner than in the person after whom it was drawn. *Spectator*, N°. 83.
This collection contains not only such pieces as come under our review, but many others, even *unfinished.* *Swift.*

UNFI'T. *adj.*
1. Improper; unsuitable.
They easily perceive how *unfit* that were for the present, which was for the first age convenient enough. *Hooker.*
Neither can I think you would impose upon me an *unfit* and over-ponderous argument. *Milton on Education.*
2. Unqualified.
Unfit he was for any worldly thing,
And eke unable once to stir or go. *Spenser.*
Old as I am, for ladies love *unfit*,
The pow'r of beauty I remember yet. *Dryden.*
A genius that can hardly take in the connection of three propositions, is utterly *unfit* for speculative studies. *Watts.*

To UNFI'T. *v. a.* To disqualify.
Those excellencies, as they qualified him for dominion, so they *unfitted* him for a satisfaction or acquiescence in his vassals. *Government of the Tongue.*

UNFITTING. *adj.* Not proper.
Although monosyllables, so rife in our tongue, are *unfitting* for verses, yet are they the most fit for expressing briefly the first conceits of the mind. *Camden.*

UNFI'TLY. *adv.* Not properly; not suitably.
Others, reading to the church those books which the apostles wrote, are neither untruly nor *unfitly* said to preach. *Hooker.*
The kingdom of France may be not *unfitly* compared to a body that hath all its blood drawn up into the arms, breast and back. *Howel.*

UNFI'TNESS. *n. s.*
1. Want of qualifications.
In setting down the form of common prayer, there was no need that the book should mention either the learning of a fit, or the *unfitness* of an ignorant minister. *Hooker.*

It is looked upon as a great weakneſs, and *unfitneſs* for buſineſs, for a man to be ſo open, as really to think not only what he ſays, but what he ſwears. *South.*

2. Want of propriety.

To UNFI'X. *v. a.*

1. To looſen; to make leſs faſt.

Plucking to *unfix* an enemy,
He doth unfaſten a friend. *Shakeſpeare's Hen.* IV.
Who can impreſs the foreſt, bid the tree
Unfix his earth-bound root? *Shakeſpeare's Macbeth.*

2. To make fluid.

Stiff with eternal ice, and hid in ſnow,
The mountain ſtands; nor can the riſing ſun
Unfix her froſts, and teach them how to run. *Dryden.*

UNFI'XED. *adj.*

1. Wandering; erratick; inconſtant; vagrant.

So vaſt the noiſe, as if not fleets did join;
But lands *unfix'd*, and floating nations ſtrove. *Dryden.*
Her lovely looks a ſprightly mind diſcloſe,
Quick as her eyes, and as *unfix'd* as thoſe. *Pope.*

2. Not determined.

Irreſolute on which ſhe ſhou'd rely:
At laſt *unfix'd* in all, is only fix'd to die. *Dryden.*

UNFLE'DGED. *adj.* That has not yet the full furniture of feathers; young; not completed by time; not having attained full growth.

The friends thou haſt, and their adoption try'd,
Grapple them to thy ſoul with hooks of ſteel:
But do not dull thy palm with entertainment
Of each new-hatch'd, *unfledg'd* comrade. *Shakeſpeare.*
In thoſe *unfledg'd* days was my wife a girl. *Shakeſpeare.*
Unfledg'd actors learn to laugh and cry. *Dryden.*

UNFLE'SHED. *adj.* Not fleſhed; not ſeaſoned to blood; raw.

Nature his limbs only for war made fit;
With ſome leſs foe thy *unfleſh'd* valour try. *Cowley.*
As a generous, *unfleſh'd* hound, that hears
From far the hunter's horn and chearful cry,
So will I haſte. *Dryden's Cleomenes.*

UNFO'ILED. *adj.* Unſubdued; not put to the worſt.

The uſurped powers thought themſelves ſecure in the ſtrength of an *unfoiled* army of ſixty thouſand men, and in a revenue proportionable. *Temple.*

To UNFO'LD. *v. a.*

1. To expand; to ſpread; to open.

I ſaw on him riſing
Out of the water, heav'n above the clouds
Unfold her cryſtal doors; thence on his head
A perfect dove deſcend. *Paradiſe Regain'd.*
Invade his hiſſing throat, and winding ſpires,
'Till ſtretch'd in length th' *unfolded* foe retires. *Dryden.*
Ah, what avail!
The vivid green his ſhining plumes *unfold.* *Pope.*
Sloth *unfolds* her arms, and wakes;
Liſt'ning envy drops her ſnakes. *Pope's St. Cecilia.*

2. To tell; to declare.

What tidings with our couſin Buckingham?——
—Such as my heart doth tremble to *unfold.* *Shakeſp.*
Unfold to me why you are heavy. *Shakeſpeare.*
Unfold the paſſion of my love;
Surprize her with diſcourſe of my dear faith. *Shakeſp.*
Helen, to you our minds we will *unfold.* *Shakeſpeare.*
How comes it thus? *Unfold*, celeſtial guide! *Milton.*
Things of deep ſenſe we may in proſe *unfold*;
But they move more, in lofty numbers told. *Roſcommon.*

3. To diſcover; to reveal.

Time ſhall *unfold* what plaited cunning hides,
Who covers faults, at laſt with ſhame derides. *Shakeſp.*

If the object be ſeen through two or more ſuch convex or concave glaſſes, every glaſs ſhall make a new image, and the object ſhall appear in the place, and of the bigneſs of the laſt image; which conſideration *unfolds* the theory of microſcopes and teleſcopes. *Newton's Opticks.*

4. To diſplay; to ſet to view.

We are the inhabitants of the earth, and endowed with underſtanding; doth it then properly belong to us, to examine and *unfold* the works of God? *Burnet.*

UNFO'LDING. *adj.* Directing to unfold.

The *unfolding* ſtar calls up the ſhepherd. *Shakeſpeare.*

To UNFOO'L. *v. a.* To reſtore from folly.

Have you any way to *unfool* me again? *Shakeſpeare.*

UNFORBI'D.
UNFORBI'DDEN. } *adj.* Not prohibited.

If *unforbid* thou may'ſt unfold
What we, not to explore the ſecrets, aſk
Of his eternal empire. *Milton's Par. Loſt.*

Theſe are the *unforbidden* trees; and here we may let looſe the reins, and indulge our thoughts. *Norris.*

A good man not only forbears thoſe gratifications, which are forbidden by reaſon and religion, but even reſtrains himſelf in *unforbidden* inſtances. *Atterbury.*

UNFORBI'DDENNESS. *n. ſ.* The ſtate of being unforbidden.

The bravery you are ſo ſevere to, is no where expreſsly prohibited in ſcripture; and this *unforbiddenneſs* they think ſufficient to evince, that the ſumptuouſneſs your condemn is not in its own nature ſinful. *Boyle.*

UNFO'RCED. *adj.*

1. Not compelled; not conſtrained.

This gentle and *unforc'd* accord of Hamlet
Sits ſmiling to my heart. *Shakeſpeare's Hamlet.*
Unforc'd by puniſhment, unaw'd by fear;
His words were ſimple, and his ſoul ſincere. *Dryden.*

2. Not impelled.

No more can impure man retain and move
In that pure region of a worthy love,
Than earthly ſubſtance can, *unforc'd*, aſpire,
And leave his nature to converſe with fire. *Donne.*

3. Not feigned.

Upon theſe tidings they broke forth into ſuch *unforced* and unfeigned paſſions, as it plainly appeared that good-nature did work in them. *Hayward.*

4. Not violent.

Windſor the next above the valley ſwells
Into my eye, and doth itſelf preſent
With ſuch an eaſy and *unforc'd* aſcent,
That no ſtupendous precipice denies
Acceſs, no horror turns away our eyes. *Denham.*

5. Not contrary to eaſe.

If one arm is ſtretched out, the body muſt be ſomewhat bow'd on the oppoſite ſide, in a ſituation which is *unforc'd. Dryd.*

UNFO'RCIBLE. *adj.* Wanting ſtrength.

The ſame reaſon which cauſeth to yield that they are of ſome force in the one, will conſtrain to acknowledge, that they are not in the other altogether *unforcible.* *Hooker.*

UNFOREBO'DING. *adj.* Giving no omens.

Unnumbered birds glide through th' aerial way,
Vagrants of air, and *unforeboding* ſtray. *Pope's Odyſſey.*

UNFOREKNOWN. *adj.* Not foreſeen by preſcience.

Which had no leſs prov'd certain, *unforeknown.* *Milton.*

UNFORESKIN'ED. *adj.* Circumciſed.

Won by a Philiſtine from the *unforeſkin'd* race. *Milton.*

UNFORESEE'N. *adj.* Not known before it happened.

Unforeſeen, they ſay, is unprepar'd. *Dryden.*

UNFORFEITED. *adj.* Not forfeited.

This was the antient, and is yet the *unforfeited* glory of our religion. *Rogers's Sermons.*

UNFORGO'TTEN. *adj.* Not loſt to memory.

The thankful remembrance of ſo great a benefit received, ſhall for ever remain *unforgotten.* *Knolles's Hiſt. of the Turks.*

UNFORGI'VING. *adj.* Relentleſs; implacable.

The ſow with her broad ſnout for rooting up
Th' intruſted ſeed, was judg'd to ſpoil the crop;
The covetous churl, of *unforgiving* kind,
Th' offender to the bloody prieſt reſign'd. *Dryden.*

UNFO'RMED. *adj.* Not modified into regular ſhape.

All putrefaction being a diſſolution of the firſt form, is a mere confuſion, and *unformed* mixture of the parts. *Bacon.*

The ſame boldneſs diſcovers itſelf in the ſeveral adventures he meets with during his paſſage through the regions of *unformed* matter. *Spectator*, Nº. 309.

UNFORSA'KEN. *adj.* Not deſerted.

They extend no farther to any ſort of ſins continued in or *unforſaken*, than as they are reconcileable with ſincere endeavours to forſake them. *Hammond's Fundamentals.*

UNFO'RTIFIED. *adj.*

1. Not ſecured by walls or bulwarks.

Their weak heads, like towns *unfortify'd*,
'Twixt ſenſe and nonſenſe daily change their ſide. *Pope.*

2. Not ſtrengthened; infirm; weak; feeble.

It ſhews a will moſt incorrect to heav'n;
A heart *unfortify'd*, a mind impatient;
An underſtanding ſimple, and unſchool'd. *Shakeſpeare.*

3. Wanting ſecurities.

They will not reſtrain a ſecret miſchief, which, conſidering the *unfortify'd* ſtate of mankind, is a great defect. *Collier.*

UNFO'RTUNATE. *adj.* Not ſucceſsful; unproſperous; wanting luck; unhappy.

All things religiouſly taken in hand, are proſperouſly ended; becauſe whether men in the end have that which religion did allow to deſire, or that which it teacheth them contentedly to ſuffer, they are in neither event *unfortunate.* *Hooker.*

Whoſoever will live altogether out of himſelf, and ſtudy other men's humours, ſhall never be *unfortunate.* *Raleigh.*

Vindictive perſons live the life of wicthes, who, as they are miſchievous, end *unfortunate.* *Bacon.*

He that would hunt a hare with an elephant, is not *unfortunate* for miſſing the mark, but fooliſh for chuſing ſuch an unapt inſtrument. *Taylor.*

The virgins ſhall on feaſtful days
Viſit his tomb with flowers, only bewailing
His lot *unfortunate* in nuptial choice,
From whence captivity and loſs of eyes. *Milton's Agoniſtes.*

UN-

UNFO'RTUNATELY *adv.* Unhappily; without good luck.

Unconsulting affection *unfortunately* born to mewards, made Zelmane borrow so much of her natural modesty, as to leave her more decent raiments. *Sidney.*

Most of these artists *unfortunately* miscarry'd, by falling down and breaking their arms. *Wilkins.*

She kept her countenance when the lid remov'd,
Disclos'd the heart, *unfortunately* lov'd. *Dryden.*

UNFO'RTUNATENESS. *adj.* [from *unfortunate.*] Ill luck. Not in use.

O me, the only subject of the destinies displeasure, whose greatest fortunateness is more unfortunate, than my sister's greatest *unfortunateness.* *Sidney.*

UNFO'UGHT. *adj.* [*un* and *fought.*] Not fought.

They used such diligence in taking the passages, that it was not possible they should escape *unfought* with. *Knolles.*

UNFOU'LED. *adj.* Unpolluted; uncorrupted; not soiled.

The humour and tunicles are purely transparent, to let in light *unfoul'd* and unsophisticated by any inward tincture. *More.*

UNFOU'ND. *adj.* Not found; not met with.

Somewhat in her excelling all her kind,
Excited a desire till then unknown;
Somewhat *unfound*, or found in her alone. *Dryden.*

UNFRA'MABLE. *adj.* Not to be moulded.

The cause of their disposition so *unframable* unto societies, wherein they live, is for that they discern not aright what force these laws ought to have. *Hooker.*

UNFRA'MED. *adj.* Not formed; not fashioned.

A lifeless lump, unfashion'd and *unfram'd*,
Of jarring seeds, and justly chaos nam'd. *Dryden.*

UNFRE'QUENT. *adj.* Uncommon; not happening often.

Part thereof is visible unto any situation; but being only discoverable in the night, and when the air is clear, it becomes *unfrequent.* *Browne's Vulgar Errours.*

To UNFREQUE'NT. *v. a.* To leave; to cease to frequent. A bad word.

Glad to shun his hostile gripe,
They quit their thefts, and *unfrequent* the fields. *Philips.*

UNFRE'QUENTED. *adj.* Rarely visited; rarely entered.

Many *unfrequented* plots there are,
Fitted by kind for rape and villainy. *Shakespeare.*

Retiring from the pop'lar noise, I seek
This *unfrequented* place to find some ease. *Milton.*

How well your cool and *unfrequented* shade
Suits with the chaste retirements of a maid? *Roscommon.*

Can he not pass an astronomick line,
Nor farther yet in liquid æther roll,
'Till he has gain'd some *unfrequented* place? *Blackmore.*

With what caution does the hen provide herself a nest in places *unfrequented*, and free from noise. *Addison.*

UNFREQUE'NTLY. *adj.* Not commonly.

They, like Judas, desire death, and not *unfrequently* pursue it. *Brown's Vulgar Errours.*

UNFRIE'NDED. *adj.* Wanting friends; uncountenanced; unsupported.

These parts to a stranger,
Unguided and *unfriended*, often prove
Rough and unhospitable. *Shakesp. Twelfth Night.*

Great acts require great means of enterprize;
Thou art unknown, *unfriended*, low of birth. *Milton.*

O God!
Who me *unfriended* brought'st, by wond'rous ways,
The kingdom of my fathers to possess. *Dryden.*

UNFRIE'NDLINESS. *n. s.* [from *unfriendly.*] Want of kindness; want of favour.

You might be apt to look upon such disappointments as the effects of an *unfriendliness* in nature or fortune to your particular attempts. *Boyle.*

UNFRIE'NDLY. *adj.* Not benevolent; not kind.

What signifies an *unfriendly* parent or brother? 'Tis friendship only that is the cement which effectively combines mankind. *Government of the Tongue.*

This fear is not that servile dread, which flies from God as an hostile, *unfriendly* being, delighting in the misery of his creatures. *Rogers's Sermons.*

UNFRO'ZEN. *adj.* Not congealed to ice.

Though the more aqueous parts will, by the loss of their motion, be turned into ice, yet the more subtile parts remain *unfrozen.* *Boyle.*

UNFRUI'TFUL. *adj.*

1. Not prolifick.

Ah! hopeless, lasting flames! like those that burn
To light the dead, and warm th' *unfruitful* urn. *Pope.*

2. Not fructiferous.

The naked rocks are not *unfruitful* there;
Their barren tops with luscious food abound. *Waller.*

3. Not fertile.

Lay down some general rules for the knowing of fruitful and *unfruitful* soils. *Mortimer's Husbandry.*

4. Not producing good effects.

UNFULFI'LLED. *adj.* Not fulfilled.

Fierce desire,
Still *unfulfilled* with pain of longing, pines. *Milton.*

To UNFU'RL. *v. a.* To expand; to unfold; to open.

The next motion is that of *unfurling* the fan, in which are several little flirts and vibrations. *Addison.*

Her ships anchor'd, and her sails *unfurl'd*
In either Indies. *Prior.*

His sails by Cupid's hand *unfurl'd*,
To keep the fair, he gave the world. *Prior.*

To UNFU'RNISH. *v. a.*

1. To deprive; to strip; to divest.

Thy speeches
Will bring me to consider that which may
Unfurnish me of reason. *Shakespeare's Winter Tale.*

2. To leave naked.

The Scot on his *unfurnish'd* kingdom
Came pouring like a tide into a breach. *Shakesp.*

UNFU'RNISHED. *adj.*

1. Not accommodated with utensils, or decorated with ornaments.

It derogates not more from the goodness of God, that he has given us minds *unfurnish'd* with those ideas of himself, than that he hath sent us into the world with bodies unclothed. *Locke.*

I live in the corner of a vast *unfurnish'd* house. *Swift.*

2. Unsupplied.

UNGA'IN. } *adj.* [unȝenȝ, Saxon.] Aukward; uncouth.
UNGA'INLY. }

An *ungainly* strut in their walk. *Swift.*

UNGA'LLED. *adj.* Unhurt; unwounded.

Let the stricken deer go weep,
The hart *ungalled* play;
For some must watch, while some must sleep;
So runs the world away. *Shakespeare's Hamlet.*

UNGA'RTERED. *adj.* Being without garters.

You chid at Sir Protheus, for going *ungartered.* *Shakesp.*

UNGA'THERED. *adj.* Not cropped; not picked.

We wonder'd why she kept her fruit so long:
For whom so late the *ungather'd* apples hung. *Dryden.*

UNGE'NERATED. *adj.* Unbegotten; having no beginning.

Millions of souls must have been *ungenerated*, and have had no being. *Raleigh's Hist. of the World.*

UNGENERA'TIVE. *adj.* Begetting nothing.

He is a motion *ungenerative*, that's infallible. *Shakespeare.*

UNGE'NEROUS. *adj.*

1. Not noble; not ingenuous; not liberal.

To look into letters already opened or dropped, is held an *ungenerous* act. *Pope.*

2. Ignominious.

The victor never will impose on Cato
Ungenerous terms. His enemies confess
The virtues of humanity are Cæsar's. *Addison.*

UNGE'NIAL. *adj.* Not kind or favourable to nature.

The northern shires have a more cloudy, *ungenial* air, than any part of Ireland. *Swift to Pope.*

Sullen seas wash th' *ungenial* pole. *Thomson.*

UNGE'NTLE. *adj.* Harsh; rude; rugged.

Smile, gentle heav'n! or strike, *ungentle* death!
For this world frowns, and Edward's sun is clouded. *Shakesp.*

He is
Vicious, *ungentle*, foolishly blunt, unkind. *Shakespeare.*

Love, to thee I sacrifice
All my *ungentle* thoughts. *Denham's Sophy.*

UNGE'NTLEMANLY. *adj.* Illiberal; not becoming a gentleman.

The demeanor of those under Waller, was much more *ungentlemanly* and barbarous. *Clarendon, b.* viii.

This he contradicts in the almanack published for the present year, and in an *ungentlemanly* manner. *Swift.*

UNGE'NTLENESS. *n. s.* Harshness; rudeness; severity.

Reward not thy sheepe, when ye take off his cote,
With twitches and patches as broad as a groat:
Let not such *ungentleness* happen to thine. *Tusser.*

UNGE'NTLY. *adv.* Harshly; rudely.

You've *ungently*, Brutus,
Stole from my bed. *Shakespeare's Julius Cæsar.*

Why speaks my father so *ungently*? *Shakesp. Tempest.*

Nor was it *ungently* received by Lindamira. *Arbuth. and Pope.*

UNGE'NTLENESS. *n. s.* Unkindness; incivility.

You have done me much *ungentleness*
To shew the letter that I writ to you. *Shakespeare.*

UNGEOME'TRICAL. *adj.* Not agreeable to the laws of geometry.

All the attempts before Sir Isaac Newton, to explain the regular appearances of nature, were *ungeometrical*, and all of them inconsistent and unintelligible. *Cheyne.*

UNGI'LDED. *adj.* Not overlaid with gold.

You, who each day can theatres behold,
Like Nero's palace, shining all with gold,
Our mean, *ungilded* stage will scorn. *Dryden.*

To

To UNGI'RD. *v. a.* To loose any thing bound with a girdle.
The man *ungirded* his camels, and gave them straw and provender. *Gen.* xxiv. 32.
The blest parent
Ungirt her spacious bosom, and discharg'd
The pond'rous birth. *Prior.*
UNGI'RT. *adj.* Loosely dressed.
One tender foot was bare, the other shod;
Her robe *ungirt.* *Waller.*
Mulciber assigns the proper place
For Carians, and th' *ungirt* Numidian race. *Dryden.*
UNGLO'RIFIED. *adj.* Not honoured; not exalted with praise and adoration.
Lest God should be any way *unglorified*, the greatest part of our daily service consisteth, according to the blessed apostle's own precise rule, in much variety of psalms and hymns; that out of so plentiful a treasure, there might be for every man's heart to chuse out for his own sacrifice. *Hooker.*
UNGLO'VED. *adj.* Having the hand naked.
When we were come near to his chair, he stood up, holding forth his hand *ungloved*, and in posture of blessing. *Bacon.*
UNGI'VING. *adj.* Not bringing gifts.
In vain at shrines th' *ungiving* suppliant stands:
This 'tis to make a vow with empty hands. *Dryden.*
To UNGLU'E. *v. a.* To loose any thing cemented.
Small rains relax and *unglue* the earth, to give vent to inflamed atoms. *Harvey on the Plague.*
She stretches, gapes, *unglues* her eyes,
And asks if it be time to rise. *Swift.*
To UNGO'D. *v. a.* To divest of divinity.
Were we wak'ned by this tyranny,
T' *ungod* this child again, it could not be
I should love her, who loves not me. *Donne.*
Thus men *ungodded* may to places rise,
And sects may be preferr'd without disguise *Dryden.*
UNGO'DLILY. *adv.* Impiously; wickedly.
'Tis but an ill essay of that godly fear, to use that very gospel so irreverently and *ungodlily*. *Government of the Tongue.*
UNGO'DLINESS. *n. s.* Impiety; wickedness; neglect of God.
How grossly do many of us contradict the plain precepts of the gospel by our *ungodliness* and worldly lusts? *Tillotson.*
UNGO'DLY. *adj.*
1. Wicked; negligent of God and his laws.
His just, avenging ire,
Had driven out th' *ungodly* from his sight,
And the habitations of the just. *Milton's Par. Lost.*
The sinner here intended is the *ungodly* sinner: he who forgets or defies his God. *Rogers.*
2. Polluted by wickedness.
Let not the hours of this *ungodly* day
Wear out in peace. *Shakespeare.*
UNGO'RED. *adj.* Unwounded; unhurt.
I stand aloof, and will no reconcilement;
'Till by some elder masters of known honour,
I have a voice and precedent of peace,
To keep my name *ungor'd.* *Shakesp. Hamlet.*
UNGO'RGED. *adj.* Not filled; not sated.
The hell-hounds, as *ungorged* with flesh and blood,
Pursue their prey. *Dryden.*
Oh *ungor'd* appetite! Oh ravenous thirst
Of a son's blood. *Smith's Phædra and Hippolytus.*
UNGO'VERNABLE. *adj.*
1. Not to be ruled; not to be restrained.
They'll judge every thing by models of their own; and thus are rendered unmanagable by any authority, and *ungovernable* by other laws, but those of the sword. *Glanville.*
2. Licentious; wild; unbridled.
So wild and *ungovernable* a poet, cannot be translated literally; his genius is too strong to bear a chain. *Dryden.*
He was free from any rough, *ungovernable* passions, which hurry men on to say and do very offensive things. *Atterbury.*
UNGO'VERNED. *adj.*
1. Being without government.
The estate is yet *ungovern'd.* *Shakesp. Rich.* III.
It pleaseth God above,
And all good men of this *ungovern'd* isle. *Shakespeare.*
2. Not regulated; unbridled; licentious.
Seek for him,
Lest his *ungovern'd* rage dissolve the life
That wants the means to lead it. *Shakesp. K. Lear.*
Themselves they vilify'd
To serve *ungovern'd* appetite. *Milton's Par. Lost.*
Nor what to bid, or what forbid, he knows;
Th' *ungovern'd* tempest to such fury grows. *Dryden.*
From her own back the burthen would remove,
And lays the load on his *ungovern'd* love. *Dryden.*
UNG'OT. *adj.*
1. Not gained; not acquired.
2. Not begotten.
He is as free from touch or soil with her,
As she from one *ungot.* *Shakesp. Measure for Measure.*
His loins yet full of *ungot* princes; all
His glory in the bud. *Waller.*
UNGRA'CEFUL. *adj.* Wanting elegance; wanting beauty.
Rophael answer'd heav'n,
Nor are thy lips *ungraceful*, sire of men. *Milton.*
A solicitous watchfulness about one's behaviour, instead of being mended, it will be constrained, uneasy, and *ungraceful.* *Locke.*
He enjoyed the greatest strength of good sense, and the most exquisite taste of politeness. Without the first learning is but an incumbrance; and without the last is *ungraceful.* *Addison.*
UNGRA'CEFULNESS. *n. s.* Inelegance; awkwardness.
To attempt the putting another genius upon him, will be labour in vain; and what is so plaistered on, will have always hanging to it the *ungracefulness* of constraint. *Locke.*
UNGRA'CIOUS. *adj.*
1. Wicked; odious; hateful.
He, catching hold of her *ungracious* tongue,
Thereon an iron lock did fasten firm and strong. *Spenser.*
I'll in the mature time,
With this *ungracious* paper strike the sight
Of the death-practis'd duke. *Shakesp. K. Lear.*
Do not, as some *ungracious* pastors do,
Shew me the steep and thorny way to heav'n;
Whilst he, a puft and reckless libertine,
Himself the primrose path of dalliance treads,
And recks not his own rede. *Shakesp. Hamlet.*
To the gods alone
Our future offspring, and our wives are known;
Th' audacious strumpet, and *ungracious* son. *Dryden.*
2. Offensive; unpleasing.
Show me no parts which are *ungracious* to the sight, as all pre-shortenings usually are. *Dryden.*
3. Unacceptable; not favoured.
They did not except against the persons of any, though several were most *ungracious* to them. *Clarendon.*
Any thing of grace towards the Irish rebels, was as *ungracious* at Oxford, as at London. *Clarendon.*
Neither is it rare to observe among excellent and learned divines, a certain *ungracious* manner, or an unhappy tone of voice, which they never have been able to shake off. *Swift.*
UNGRA'NTED. *adj.* Not given; not yielded; not bestowed.
This only from your goodness let me gain,
And this *ungranted*, all rewards are vain. *Dryden.*
UNGRA'TEFUL. *adj.*
1. Making no returns, or making ill returns for kindness.
No person is remarkably *ungrateful*, who was not also insufferably proud. *South.*
2. Making no returns for culture.
Most when driv'n by winds, the flaming storm
Of the long files destroys the beauteous form;
Nor will the wither'd stock be green again;
But the wild olive shoots, and shades th' *ungrateful* plain. *Dryd.*
3. Unpleasing; unacceptable.
It cannot be *ungrateful*, or without some pleasure to posterity, to see the most exact relation of an action so full of danger. *Clarendon.*
What is in itself harsh and *ungrateful*, must make harsh and *ungrateful* impressions upon us. *Atterbury.*
UNGRA'TEFULLY. *adv.*
1 With ingratitude.
When call'd to distant war,
His vanquish'd heart remain'd a victim here:
Oriana's eyes that glorious conquest made;
Nor was his love *ungratefully* repaid. *Granville.*
We often receive the benefit of our prayers, when yet we *ungratefully* charge heaven with denying our petitions. *Wake.*
2. Unacceptably; unpleasing.
UNGRA'TEFULNESS. *n. s.*
1. Ingratitude; ill return for good.
Can I, without the detestable stain of *ungratefulness*, abstain from loving him, who, far exceeding the beautifulness of his shape with the beautifulness of his mind, is content so to abase himself as to become Dametas's servant for my sake. *Sidn.*
2. Unacceptableness; unpleasing quality.
UNGRA'VELY. *adv.* Without seriousness.
His present portance
Gibingly, and *ungravely*, he did fashion. *Shakespeare.*
UNGROU'NDED. *adj.* Having no foundation.
Ignorance, with an indifferency for truth, is nearer to it than opinion with *ungrounded* inclination, which is the great source of errour. *Locke.*
This is a confidence the most *ungrounded* and irrational. For upon what ground can a man promise himself a future repentance, who cannot promise himself a futurity? *South.*
UNGRU'DGINGLY. *adv.* Without ill will; willingly; heartily; cheerfully.
If, when all his art and time is spent,
He say 'twill ne'er be found, yet be content;
Receive from him the doom *ungrudgingly*,
Because he is the mouth of destiny. *Donne.*

UNGUA'RDED.

UNGUA'RDED. *adj.*

1. Undefended.

Proud art thou met? Thy hope was to have reach'd
The throne of God *unguarded*, and his side
Abandon'd. *Milton's Par. Lost*, *b.* vi. *l.* 133.

All through th' *unguarded* gates with joy resort,
To see the slighted camp, the vacant port. *Denham.*

No door there was th' *unguarded* house to keep,
On creaking hinges turn'd, to break his sleep. *Dryden.*

2. Careless; negligent.

All the evils that proceed from an untied tongue, and an *unguarded*, unlimited will, we put upon the accounts of drunkenness. *Taylor.*

The spy, which does this treasure keep,
Does she ne'er say her pray'rs, nor sleep?
Or have not gold and flatt'ry pow'r,
To purchase one *unguarded* hour? *Prior.*

With an *unguarded* look she now devour'd
My nearer face; and now recall'd her eye,
And heav'd, and strove to hide a sudden sigh. *Prior.*

It was intended only to divert a few young ladies, of good sense and good humour enough to laugh not only at their sex's little *unguarded* follies, but at their own. *Pope.*

Are we not encompassed by multitudes, who watch every careless word, every *unguarded* action of our lives? *Rogers.*

UNGUI'DED. *adj.* Not directed; not regulated.

The blood weeps from my heart, when I do shape,
In forms imaginary, th' *unguided* days,
And rotten times that you shall look upon,
When I am sleeping with my ancestors. *Shakespeare.*

Can *unguided* matter keep itself to such exact conformities, as not in the least spot to vary from the species? *Glanville.*

They resolve all into the accidental, *unguided* motions of blind matter. *Locke.*

Nature, void of choice,
Does by *unguided* motion things produce,
Regardless of their order. *Blackmore on the Creation.*

U'NGUENT. *n. s.* [*unguentum*, Lat.] Ointment.

Pre-occupation of mind ever requireth preface of speech, like a fomentation to make the *unguent* enter. *Bacon.*

There is an intercourse between the magnetick *unguent* and the vulnerated body. *Glanville.*

With *unguents* smooth, the lucid marble shone. *Pope.*

UNGUE'SSED. *adj.* Not attained by conjecture.

He me sent, for cause to me *unguess'd*. *Fairy Queen.*

UNHA'BITABLE. *adj.* [*inhabitable*, Fr. *inhabitabilis*, Lat.] Not capable to support inhabitants; uninhabitable.

The night and day was always a natural day of twenty-four hours, in all places remote from the *unhabitable* poles of the world, and winter and summer always measured a year. *Holder.*

Though the course of the sun be curbed between the tropicks, yet are not those parts directly subject to his perpendicular beams, *unhabitable*, or extremely hot. *Ray.*

UNHA'CKED. *adj.* Not cut; not hewn; not notched with cuts.

With a blessed, and unvex'd retire,
With *unhack'd* swords, and helmets all unbruis'd,
We will bear home that lusty blood again. *Shakespeare.*

Part with *unhack'd* edges, and bear back
Our targe undinted. *Shakesp. Ant. and Cleopatra.*

To UNHA'LLOW. *v. a.* To deprive of holiness; to profane; to desecrate.

Perhaps the fact
Is not so heinous now, foretasted fruit;
Profan'd first by the serpent; by him first
Made common, and *unhallow'd*, ere our taste. *Milton.*

The vanity *unhallows* the virtue. *L'Estrange.*

This one use left such an indelible sacredness upon them, that the impiety of the design could be no sufficient reason to *unhallow* and degrade them to common use. *South.*

UNHA'LLOWED. *adj.* Unholy; profane.

Thy currish spirit
Govern'd a wolf, who hang'd for human slaughter:
Ev'n from the gallows did his fell soul fleet;
And while thou lay'st in thy *unhallow'd* dam
Infus'd itself in thee. *Shakesp. Merchant of Venice.*

I had not unlock'd my lips
In this *unhallow'd* air, but that this jugler
Would think to charm my judgment, as mine eyes,
Obtruding false rules, pranck'd in reason's garb. *Milton.*

Nor shall presume to violate these bands,
Or touch thy person with *unhallow'd* hands. *Dryden.*

Here cease thy flight, nor with *unhallow'd* lays
Touch the fair fame of Albion's golden days. *Pope.*

To UNHA'ND. *v. a.* To loose from the hand.

Still am I call'd. *Unhand* me, gentlemen. *Shakespeare.*

Unhand me, traitors. *Denham's Sophy.*

UNHA'NDLED. *adj.* Not handled; not touched.

A race of youthful and *unhandled* colts,
Fetching mad bounds. *Shakesp. Merch. of Venice.*

Cardinal Campeius
Hath left the cause o' th' king *unhandled. Shakesp. Hen.* VIII.

UNHA'NDSOME. *n. s.*

1. Ungraceful; not beautiful.

I was glad I had done so good a deed for a gentlewoman not *unhandsome*, whom before I had in like sort helped. *Sidney.*

She that so far the rest out-shin'd;
Silvia the fair, while she was kind,
Seems only not *unhandsome* now. *Waller.*

As I cannot admit that there is any thing *unhandsome* or irregular; so much less can I grant that there is any thing incommodious in the globe. *Woodward.*

2. Illiberal; disingenuous.

UNHA'NDSOMELY. *adv.* [from *unhandsome.*]

1. Inelegantly; ungracefully.

The ruined churches are so *unhandsomely* patched and thatched, that men do even shun the places for the uncomeliness thereof. *Spenser.*

2. Disingenuously; illiberally.

He raves, Sir; and to cover my disdain,
Unhandsomely would his denial feign. *Dryden.*

UNHA'NDSOMENESS. *n. s.* [from *unhandsome.*]

1. Want of beauty.

The sweetness of her countenance did give such a grace to what she did, that it did make handsome the *unhandsomeness* of it; and make the eye force the mind to believe, that there was a praise in that unskilfulness. *Sidney*, *b.* ii.

2 Want of elegance.

Be not troublesome to thyself, or to others, by *unhandsomeness* or uncleanness. *Taylor.*

3. Illiberalness; disingenuity.

UNHA'NDY. *adj.* Awkward; not dexterous.

UNHA'NGED. *adj.* Not put to death by the gallows.

There live not three good men *unhang'd* in England. *Shakes.*

UNHA'P. *n. s.* Missluck; ill fortune.

She visited that place, where first she was so happy as to see the cause of her *unhap*. *Sidney.*

UNHA'PPIED. [This word seems a participle from *unhappy*, which yet is never used as a verb.] Made unhappy.

You have misled a prince,
A happy gentleman in blood and lineament,
By you *unhappied*, and disfigur'd clean. *Shakespeare.*

UNHA'PPILY. *adv.* [from *unhappy.*] Miserably; unfortunately; wretchedly; calamitously.

You hold a fair assembly: you do well, lord.
You are a churchman, or I'll tell you, cardinal,
I should judge now most *unhappily*. *Shakespeare.*

He was *unhappily* too much used as a check upon the lord Coventry. *Clarendon.*

I unweeting have offended,
Unhappily deceiv'd! *Milton's Par. Lost.*

There is a day a coming, when all these witty fools shall be *unhappily* undeceived. *Tillotson's Sermons.*

UNHA'PPINESS. *n. s.*

1. Misery; infelicity.

If ever he have child, abortive be it,
Prodigious, and untimely brought to light,
And that be heir to his *unhappiness*. *Shakespeare.*

The real foundation of our *unhappiness* would be laid in our reason, and we should be more miserable than the beasts, by how much we have a quicker apprehension. *Tillotson.*

It is our great *unhappiness*, when any calamities fall upon us, that we are uneasy, and dissatisfied. *Wake.*

2. Calamity; distress.

She hath often dream'd of *unhappiness*, and waked herself with laughing. *Shakesp. Much Ado about Nothing.*

3. Misfortune; ill luck.

St. Austin hath laid down a rule to this purpose, though he had the *unhappiness* not to follow it always himself. *Burnet.*

UNHA'PPY. *adj.* Wretched; miserable; unfortunate; calamitous; distressed.

Desire of wand'ring this *unhappy* morn. *Milton.*

You know not, while you here attend,
Th' unworthy fate of your *unhappy* friend:
Breathless he lies, and his unbury'd ghost
Depriv'd of funeral rites. *Dryden.*

To UNHA'RBOUR. *v. a.* To drive from shelter.

UNHA'RBOURED. *adj.* Affording no shelter.

'Tis chastity:
She that has that is clad in complete steel;
And, like a quiver'd nymph, with arrows keen,
May trace huge forests, and *unharbour'd* heaths,
Infamous hills, and sandy perilous wilds. *Milton.*

UNHA'RDENED. *adj.* Not confirmed; not made hard.

Messengers
Of strong prevailment in *unharden'd* youth. *Shakespeare.*

UNHA'RDY. *adj.* Feeble; tender; timorous.

The wisest, unexperienc'd, will be ever
Tim'rous and loth, with novice modesty;
Irresolute, *unhardy*, undavent'rous. *Milton.*

UNHA'RMED. *adj.* Unhurt; not injured.

In strong proof of chastity well armed,
From love's weak, childish bow she lives *unharm'd. Shakesp.*

Though great light be insufferable to our eyes; yet the highest degree of darkness does not disease them, for causing no disorderly motion, it leaves that curious organ *unharmed. Locke.*

The Syrens once deluded, vainly charm'd;
Ty'd to the mast, Ulysses sail'd *unharm'd. Granville.*

UNHA'RMFUL. *adj.* Innoxious; innocent.

Themselves *unharmful*, let them live unharm'd;
Their jaws disabled, and their claws disarm'd. *Dryden.*

UNHARMO'NIOUS. *adj.*

1. Not symmetrical; disproportionate.

Those pure, immortal elements, that know
No gross, no *unharmonious* mixture foul,
Eject him, tainted now, and purge him off. *Milton.*

2. Unmusical; ill-sounding.

His thoughts are improper to his subject, his expressions unworthy of his thoughts, or the turn of both is *unharmonious. Dryden.*

That barbarous custom of abbreviating words, to fit them to the measure of verses, has formed harsh, *unharmonious* sounds. *Swift.*

To UNHA'RNESS. *v. a.*

1. To loose from the traces.

The sweating steers *unharness'd* from the yoke,
Bring back the crooked plough. *Dryden.*
The mules *unharness'd* range beside the main. *Pope.*

If there were six horses, the postillion always *unharnessed* four, and placed them on a table. *Swift.*

2. To disarm; to divest of armour.

UNHA'ZARDED. *adj.* Not adventured; not put in danger.

Here I shou'd still enjoy thee day and night
Whole to myself, *unhazarded* abroad,
Fearless at home. *Milton's Agonistes, l.* 807.

UNHA'TCHED. *adj.*

1. Not disclosed from the eggs.

2. Not brought to light.

Some *unhatch'd* practice
Hath puddled his clear spirit. *Shakespeare.*

UNHEA'LTHFUL. *adj.* Morbid; unwholesome.

The diseases which make years *unhealthful*, are spotted fevers; and the *unhealthful* season is the autumn. *Graunt.*

At every sentence set his life at stake,
Though the discourse were of no weightier things,
Than sultry summers, or *unhealthful* springs. *Dryden.*

UNHEA'LTHY. *adj.* Sickly; wanting health.

No body would have a child cramm'd at breakfast, who would not have him dull and *unhealthy. Locke on Education.*

He, intent on somewhat that may ease
Unhealthy mortals, and with curious search
Examines all the properties of herbs. *Philips.*

To UNHEA'RT. *v. a.* To discourage; to depress.

To bite his lip,
And hum at good Cominius, much *unhearts* me. *Shakesp.*

UNHEA'RD. *adj.*

1. Not perceived by the ear.

For the noise of drums and timbrels loud,
Their childrens cries *unheard. Milton's Par. Lost.*

2. Not vouchsafed an audience.

What pangs I feel, unpitied and *unheard! Dryden.*

3. Unknown in celebration.

Nor was his name *unheard*, or unador'd. *Milton.*

4. UNHEARD *of.* Obscure; not known by fame.

Free from hopes or fears, in humble ease,
Unheard of may I live and die in peace. *Granville.*

5. UNHEARD *of.* Unprecedented.

There is a foundation laid for the most *unheard of* confusion that ever was introduced into a nation. *Swift.*

UNHEA'TED. *adj.* Not made hot.

Neither salts, nor the distilled spirits of them can penetrate the narrow pores of *unheated* glass. *Boyle.*

UNHEE'DED. *adj.* Disregarded; not thought worthy of notice.

True experiments may, by reason of the easy mistake of some *unheeded* circumstance, be unsuccessfully tried. *Boyle.*

He of his fatal guile gave proof *unheeded. Milton.*

Her hair
In a simple knot was ty'd above;
Sweet negligence! *unheeded* bait of love. *Dryden.*

The triumph ceas'd—tears gush'd from ev'ry eye,
The world's great victor pass'd *unheeded* by. *Pope.*

UNHEE'DING. *adj.* Negligent; careless.

I have not often seen him; if I did,
He pass'd unmark'd by my *unheeding* eyes. *Dryden.*

UNHEE'DY. *adj.* Precipitate; sudden.

Learning his ship from those white rocks to save,
Which all along the southern sea-coast lay,
Threat'ning *unheedy* wreck, and rash decay,
He nam'd Albion. *Fairy Queen, b.* ii. *c.* 1.

Nor hath love's mind of any judgment taste;
Wings and no eyes, figure *unheedy* haste. *Shakesp.*

So have I seen some tender slip,
Sav'd with care from winter's nip;
The pride of her carnation train
Pluck'd up by some *unheedy* swain. *Milton.*

To UNHE'LE. *v. a.* To uncover; to expose to view. *Spenser.*

UNHE'LPED. *adj.* Unassisted; having no auxiliary; unsupported.

Unhelp'd I am, who pity'd the distress'd,
And none oppressing, am by all oppress'd. *Dryden.*

UNHE'LPFUL. *adj.* Giving no assistance.

I bewail good Glo'ster's case
With sad, *unhelpful* tears. *Shakesp. Hen.* VII.

UNHE'WN. *part. adj.* Not hewn.

In occasions of merriment, this rough-cast, *unhewn* poetry, was instead of stage plays. *Dryden's Dedication to Juvenal.*

UNHI'DEBOUND. *adj.* Lax of maw; capacious.

Though plenteous, all too little seems
To stuff this maw, this vast, *unhidebound* corps. *Milton.*

To UNHI'NGE. *v. a.*

1. To throw from the hinges.

2. To displace by violence.

For want of cement, ribs of rock disjoin'd
Without an earthquake, from their base would start,
And hills *unhing'd*, from their deep roots depart. *Blackmore.*

3. To disorder; to confuse.

Rather than not accomplish my revenge,
Just or unjust, I would the world *unhinge. Waller.*

If God's providence did not order it, cheats would not only justle private men out of their rights, but *unhinge* states, and run all into confusion. *Ray on the Creation.*

UNHO'LINESS. *n. s.* Impiety; profaneness; wickedness.

Too foul and manifest was the *unholiness* of obtruding upon men remission of sins for money. *Raleigh.*

UNHO'LY. *adj.*

1. Profane; not hallowed.

Doth it follow that all things now in the church are *unholy*, which the Lord hath not himself precisely instituted? *Hooker.*

2. Impious; wicked.

We think not ourselves the holier, because we use it; so neither should they with whom no such thing is in use, think us therefore *unholy*, because we submit ourselves unto that, which, in a matter so indifferent, the wisdom of authority and law have thought comely. *Hooker.*

From the paradise of God,
Without remorse, drive out the sinful pair,
From hallow'd ground th' *unholy. Milton's Par. Lost.*

Far other dreams my erring soul employ;
Far other raptures of *unholy* joy. *Pope.*

UNHO'NOURED. *adj.*

1. Not regarded with veneration; not celebrated.

Unhonour'd though I am, at least, said she,
Not unreveng'd that impious act shall be. *Dryden.*

Pales *unhonour'd*, Ceres unemploy'd,
Were all forgot. *Dryden.*

2. Not treated with respect.

Griev'd that a visitant so long shou'd wait,
Unmark'd, *unhonour'd*, at a monarch's gate. *Pope.*

To UNHOO'P. *v. a.* To divest of hoops.

Unhoop the fair sex, and cure this fashionable tympany got among them. *Addison's Spectator,* N°. 127.

UNHO'PED. / UNHO'PED *for.* } *adj.* Not expected; greater than hope had promised.

With *unhop'd* success
Th' embassadors return with promis'd peace. *Dryden.*

Heav'n has inspir'd with a sudden thought,
Whence your *unhop'd-for* safety may be wrought. *Dryden.*

UNHO'PEFUL. *adj.* Such as leaves no room to hope.

Benedict is not the *unhopefullest* husband that I know: thus far I can praise him; he is of approved valour. *Shakesp.*

I thought the rousing style I wrote in, might prove no *unhopeful* way to procure somewhat considerable from those great masters of chymical arcana. *Boyle.*

To UNHO'RSE. *v. a.* To beat from an horse; to throw from the saddle.

He would *unhorse* the lustiest challenger. *Shakespeare.*

The emperor rescued a noble gentleman, whom, *unhorsed* and sore wounded, the enemy was ready to have slain. *Knolles.*

On a fourth he flies, and him *unhorses* too. *Daniel.*

They are forc'd
To quit their boats, and fare like men *unhors'd. Waller.*

The knights *unhors'd* may rise from off the plain,
And fight on foot, their honour to regain. *Dryden.*

UNHO'SPITABLE. *adj.* [*inhospitalis*, Lat.] Affording no kindness or entertainment to strangers; cruel; barbarous.

The cruel nation, covetous of prey,
Stain'd with my blood th' *unhospitable* coast. *Dryden.*

UNHO'STILE. *adj.* Not belonging to an enemy.

The high-prancing steeds
Spurn their dismounted riders; they expire
Indignant, by *unhostile* wounds destroy'd. *Philips.*

To

To UNHOU'SE. *v. a.* To drive from the habitation.

Seek true religion: O where? Mirreus!
Thinking her *unhous'd* here, and fled from us,
Seek her at Rome. *Donne.*

Death unawares with his cold, kind embrace,
Unhous'd thy virgin soul from her fair biding place. *Milton.*

UNHOU'SED. *adj.*

1. Homeless; wanting a house.

Call the creatures,
Whose naked natures live in all the spight
Of wreakful heav'n; whose bare, *unhoused* trunks,
To the conflicting elements expos'd,
Answer meer nature. *Shakesp. Timon of Athens.*

2. Having no settled habitation.

But that I love the gentle Desdemona,
I would not my *unhoused*, free condition
Put into circumscription and confine. *Shakesp. Othello.*

Hear this,
You *unhous'd*, lawless, rambling libertines. *Southern.*

UNHOU'SELLED. *adj.* Having not the sacrament.

Thus was I sleeping, by a brother's hand,
Of life, of crown, of queen at once dispatch'd;
Cut off even in the blossoms of my sin,
Unhousell'd, unanointed, unanell'd. *Shakesp. Hamlet.*

UNHU'MBLED. *adj.* Not humbled; not touched with shame or confusion.

Should I of these the liberty regard,
Who, freed as to their antient patrimony,
Unhumbled, unrepented, unreformed,
Headlong would follow. *Milton's Par. Regain'd.*

UNHU'RT. *adj.* Free from harm.

Of fifteen hundred, eight hundred were slain in the field; and of the remaining seven hundred, two men only came off *unhurt*. *Bacon's War with Spain.*

I tread more lightly on the ground;
My nimble feet from *unhurt* flow'rs rebound;
I walk in air. *Dryden's State of Innocence.*

Supported by thy care,
Through burning climes I pass'd *unhurt*,
And breath'd in tainted air. *Addison's Spectator.*

The stars shall fade away;
But thou shalt flourish in immortal youth,
Unhurt, amidst the war of elements,
The wrecks of matter, and the crush of worlds. *Addison.*

UNHU'RTFUL. *adj.* Innoxious; harmless; doing no harm.

You hope the duke will return no more, or
You imagine me too *unhurtful* an opposite. *Shakespeare.*

Flames *unhurtful*, hovering, dance in air. *Blackmore.*

UNHU'RTFULLY. *adv.* Without harm; innoxiously.

We laugh at others as innocently and as *unhurtfully*, as at ourselves. *Pope to Swift.*

U'NICORN. *n. s.* [*unicornis*, *unus* and *cornu*, Lat.]

1. A beast, whether real or fabulous, that has only one horn.

Wert thou the *unicorn*, pride and wrath would confound thee. *Shakespeare's Timon of Athens.*

Unicorns may be betray'd with trees,
Bears with glasses, men with flatterers. *Shakespeare.*

Nature in cornigerous animals hath placed the horns inverted upwards, as in the rhinoceros, Indian ass, and *unicorn* beetles. *Brown's Vulgar Errours.*

It is not of consequence, that because Dioscorides hath made no mention of *unicorns* horn, there is therefore no such thing in nature. *Brown's Vulgar Errours.*

Some *unicorns* we will allow even among insects, as those nasicornous beetles described by Muffetus. *Brown.*

Will the fierce *unicorn* thy voice obey,
Stand at the crib, and feed upon the hay? *Sandys.*

2. A bird.

Of the *unicorn* bird, the principal marks are these; headed and footed like the dunghill cock, tailed like a goose, horned on his forehead, with some likeness, as the unicorn is pictured; spur'd on his wings, bigger than a swan. *Grew.*

U'NIFORM. *adj.* [*unus* and *forma*.]

1. Keeping its tenour; similar to itself.

Though when confusedly mingled, as in this stratum, it may put on a face never so *uniform* and alike, yet it is in reality very different. *Woodward.*

2. Conforming to one rule; acting in the same manner; agreeing with each other.

The only doubt is about the manner of their unity, how far churches are bound to be *uniform* in their ceremonies, and what way they ought to take for that purpose. *Hooker.*

Creatures of what condition soever, though each in different manner, yet all with *uniform* consent, admire her, as the mother of their peace and joy. *Hooker.*

Numbers, being neither *uniform* in their designs, nor direct in their views, neither could manage nor maintain the power they got. *Swift.*

UNIFO'RMITY. *n. s.* [*uniformité*, Fr.]

1. Resemblance to itself; even tenour.

There is no *uniformity* in the design of Spenser; he aims at the accomplishment of no one action. *Dryden.*

Queen Elizabeth was remarkable for that steadiness and *uniformity* which ran through all her actions. *Addison.*

2. Conformity to one pattern; resemblance of one to another.

The unity of that visible body and church of Christ, consisteth in that *uniformity*, which all the several persons thereunto belonging have, by reason of that one Lord, whose servants they all profess themselves; that one faith which they all acknowledge; that one baptism wherewith they are all initiated. *Hooker, b. iii.*

U'NIFORMLY. *adv.* [from *uniform*.]

1. Without variation; in an even tenour.

That faith received from the apostles, the church, though dispersed throughout the world, doth notwithstanding keep as safe, as if it dwelt within the walls of some one house, and as *uniformly* hold, as if it had but one only heart and soul. *Hooker, b. v.*

The capillamenta of the nerves are each of them solid and uniform; and the vibrating motion of the æthereal medium may be propagated along them from one end to the other *uniformly*, and without interruption. *Newton's Opticks.*

2. Without diversity of one from another.

UNIMA'GINABLE. *adj.* Not to be imagined by the fancy; not to be conceived.

Things to their thought
So *unimaginable*, as hate in heav'n. *Milton's Par. Lost.*

The skilful organist plies his grave-fancied descant in lofty fugues, or the whole symphony, with artful and *unimaginable* touches, adorns and graces the well-studied chords of some choice composer. *Milton on Education.*

An infinite succession of the generations of men, without any permanent foundation, is utterly *unimaginable*. *Tillotson.*

UNIMA'GINABLY. *adv.* To a degree not to be imagined.

Little commissures, where they adhere, may not be porous enough to be pervious to the *unimaginably* subtle corpuscles, that make up the beams of light. *Boyle.*

UNI'MITABLE. *adj.* [*inimitable*, Fr. *inimitabilis*, Lat.] Not to be imitated.

Both these are *unimitable*. *Burnet's Theory of the Earth.*

UNIMMO'RTAL *adj.* Not immortal; mortal.

They betook them several ways,
Both to destroy, or *unimmortal* make
All kinds. *Milton.*

UNIMPA'IRABLE. *adv.* Not liable to waste or diminution.

If the superior be *unimpairable*, it is a strong presumption, that the inferiors are likewise unimpaired. *Hakewill.*

UNIMPA'IRED. *adj.* Not diminished; not worn out.

Yet *unimpair'd* with labours, or with time,
Your age but seems to a new youth to climb. *Dryden.*

If our silver and gold diminishes, our publick credit continues *unimpaired*. *Addison on the State of the War.*

UNIMPLO'RED. *adj.* Not solicited.

If answerable stile I can obtain
Of my celestial patroness, who deigns
Her nightly visitation *unimplor'd*. *Milton's Par. Lost.*

UNIMPO'RTANT. *adj.* Assuming no airs of dignity.

A free, *unimportant*, natural, easy manner; diverting others just as we diverted ourselves. *Pope to Swift.*

UNIMPORTU'NED. *adj.* Net solicited; not teazed to compliance.

Who ever ran
To danger *unimportun'd*, he was then
No better than a sanguine, virtuous man. *Donne.*

UNIMPRO'VABLE. *adj.* Incapable of melioration.

UNIMPRO'VABLENESS. *n. s.* [from *unimprovable*.] Quality of not being improveable.

This must be imputed to their ignorance and *unimprovableness* in knowledge, being generally without literature. *Ham.*

UNIMPRO'VED. *adj.*

1. Not made more knowing.

Not a mask went *unimprov'd* away. *Pope.*

2. Not taught; not meliorated by instruction.

Young Fortinbrass,
Of *unimproved* mettle hot and full. *Shakesp. Hamlet*

Shallow, *unimproved* intellects, are confident pretenders to certainty. *Glanville*

UNINCREA'SABLE. *adj.* Admitting no increase.

That love, which ought to be appropriated to God, results chiefly from an altogether, or almost *unincreasable* elevation and vastness of affection. *Boyle.*

UNINDI'FFERENT. *adj.* Partial; leaning to a side.

His opinion touching the catholick church was as *unindifferent*, as, touching our church, the opinion of them that favour this pretended reformation is. *Hooker, b. iv.*

UNINDU'STRIOUS. *adj.* Not diligent; not laborious.

Pride we cannot think so sluggish or *unindustrious* an agent, as not to find out expedients for its purpose. *Decay of Piety.*

UNINFLA'MMABLE. *adj.* Not capable of being set on fire.

The *uninflammable* spirit of such concretes, may be pretended to be but a mixture of phlegm and salt. *Boyle.*

UNINLFLA'MED. *adj.* Not set on fire.

When weak bodies come to be inflamed, they gather a much greater heat than others have *uninflamed*. *Bacon.*

UNINFO'RMED. *adj.*

1. Untaught; uninstructed.

Nor *uninform'd*
Of nuptial sanctity, and marriage rites. *Milton's P. Lost.*

No *uninformed* minds can represent virtue so noble to us, that we necessarily add splendour to her. *Pope.*

2. Unanimated; not enlivened.

UNINGE'NUOUS. *adj.* Illiberal; disingenuous.

Did men know how to distinguish between reports and certainties, this stratagem would be as unskilful, as it is *uningenuous.* *Decay of Piety.*

UNINHA'BITABLE. *adj.* Unfit to be inhabited.

If there be any place upon earth of that nature that paradise had, the same must be found within that supposed *uninhabitable* burnt zone, or within the tropicks. *Raleigh.*

Had not the deep been form'd, that might contain
All the collected treasures of the main;
The earth had still o'erwhelm'd with water stood,
To man an *uninhabitable* flood. *Blackmore.*

UNINHA'BITABLENESS. *n. s.* Incapacity of being inhabited.

Divers radicated opinions, such as that of the *uninhabitableness* of the torrid zone, of the solidity of the celestial part of the world, are generally grown out of request. *Boyle.*

UNINHA'BITED. *adj.* Having no dwellers.

The whole island is now *uninhabited.* *Sandys.*

Uninhabited, untill'd, unsown
It lies, and breeds the bleating goat alone. *Pope.*

I cast anchor on the leeside of the island, which seemed to be *uninhabited.* *Gulliver's Travels.*

UNI'NJURED. *adj.* Unhurt; suffering no harm.

You may as well spread out the unsun'd heaps
Of misers treasure by an outlaw's den,
And tell me it is safe; as bid me hope
Danger will let a helpless maiden pass,
Uninjur'd in this wild, surrounding waste. *Milton.*

Then in full age, and hoary holiness
Retire, great teacher! to thy promis'd bliss:
Untouch'd thy tomb, *uninjur'd* be thy dust,
As thy own fame among the future just. *Prior.*

UNINSCRI'BED. *adj.* Having no inscription.

Make sacred Charles's tomb for ever known;
Obscure the place, and *uninscrib'd* the stone.
Oh fact accurst! *Pope.*

UNINSPI'RED. *adj.* Not having received any supernatural instruction or illumination.

Thus all the truths that men, *uninspired*, are enlightened with, came into their minds. *Locke.*

My pastoral muse her humble tribute brings,
And yet not wholly *uninspir'd* she sings. *Dryden.*

UNINSTRU'CTED. *adj.* Not taught; not helped by institution.

That fool intrudes, raw in this great affair,
And *uninstructed* how to stem the tide. *Dryden.*

It will be a prejudice to none but widows and orphans, and others *uninstructed* in the arts and management of more skilful men. *Locke.*

It is an unspeakable blessing to be born in those parts where wisdom flourishes; though there are even in these parts, several poor, *uninstructed* persons. *Addison.*

Though we find few amongst us, who profess themselves Anthropomorphites, yet we may find, amongst the ignorant and *uninstructed* christians, many of that opinion. *Locke.*

UNINSTRU'CTIVE. *adj.* Not conferring any improvement.

Were not men of abilities thus communicative, their wisdom would be in a great measure useless, and their experience *uninstructive.* *Addison.*

UNINTE'LLIGENT. *adj.* Not knowing; not skilful; not having any consciousness.

We will give you sleepy drinks, that your senses may be *unintelligent* of our insufficience. *Shakesp. Winter Tale.*

The visible creation is far otherwise apprehended by the philosophical enquirer, than the *unintelligent* vulgar. *Glanville.*

This conclusion, if men allow'd of, they would not destroy ill-formed productions. Ay, but these monsters. Let them be so; what will your drivelling, *unintelligent*, untractable changeling be? *Locke.*

Why then to works of nature is assign'd
An author *unintelligent* and blind;
When ours proceed from choice? *Blackmore.*

The obvious products of *unintelligent* nature. *Bentl.*

UNINTELLIGIBI'LITY. *n. s.* Quality of not being intelligible.

Credit the *unintelligibility* of this union and motion. *Glanville.*

If we have truly proved the *unintelligibility* of it in all other ways, this argumentation is undeniable. *Burnet.*

UNINTELLI'GIBLE. *adj.* [*inintelligible*, Fr.] Not such as can be understood

The Latin, three hundred years before Tully, was as *unintelligible* in his time, as the English and French of the same period are now. *Swift.*

Did Thetis
These arms thus labour'd for her son prepare;
For th[illegible] dul[illegible] soul to stare with stupid eyes,
On th[illegible]arn'd *unintelligible* prize! *Dryden.*

This notion must be despised as harmless, *unintelligible* enthusiasm. *Rogers's Sermons.*

UNINTE'LLIGIBLY. *adv.* In a manner not to be understood.

Sound is not *unintelligibly* explained by a vibrating motion communicated to the medium. *Locke.*

To talk of specifick differences in nature, without reference to general ideas, is to talk *unintelligibly.* *Locke.*

UNINTE'NTIONAL. *adj.* Not designed; happening without design.

Besides the *unintentional* deficiencies of my style, I have purposely transgressed the laws of oratory, in making my periods over-long *Boyle.*

UNI'NTERESSED. }
UNI'NTERESTED. } *adj.* Not having interest.

The greatest part of an audience is always *uninterested*, though seldom knowing. *Dryden.*

UNINTERMI'TTED. *adj.* Continued; not interrupted.

This motion of the heavenly bodies seems to be partly continued and *unintermitted*, as that motion of the first moveable partly interpolated and interrupted. *Hale's Origin.*

UNINTERMI'XED. *adj.* Not mingled.

Unintermix'd with fictious fantasies,
I verify the truth, not poetize. *Daniel's Civil War.*

UNINTERRU'PTED. *adj.* Not broken; not interrupted.

Thy constant quiet fills my peaceful breast
With unmixt joy, *uninterrupted* rest. *Roscommon.*

Governments so divided among themselves in matters of religion, maintain *uninterrupted* union and correspondence, that no one of them is for invading the rights of another. *Addis.*

The hills rise insensibly, and leave the eye a vast, *uninterrupted* prospect. *Addison.*

The *uninterrupted* stitch in superficial wounds, is rejected. *Sharp's Surgery.*

UNINTERRU'PTEDLY. *adv.* Without interruption.

The will thus determined, never lets the understanding lay by the object; but all the thoughts of the mind, and powers of the body are *uninterruptedly* employ'd. *Locke.*

[UN]INTRE'NCHED. *adj.* Not intrenched.

It had been cowardice in the Trojans, not to have attempted any thing against an army that lay unfortified and *unintrenched.* *Pope.*

UNINVE'STIGABLE. *adj.* Not to be searched out.

The number of the works of this visible world being *uninvestigable* by us, afford us a demonstrative proof of the unlimited extent of the creator's skill. *Ray.*

UNINVI'TED. *adj.* Not asked.

His honest friends, at thirsty hour of dusk,
Come *uninvited.* *Philips.*

UNJOI'NTED. *adj.*

1. Disjoined; separated.

I hear the sound of words; their sense the air
Dissolves *unjointed* ere it reach my ear. *Milton's Agonistes.*

2. Having no articulation.

They are all three immoveable or *unjointed*, of the thickness of a little pin. *Grew's Musæum.*

U'NION. *n. s.* [*unio*, Lat.]

1. The act of joining two or more, so as to make them one.

Adam, from whose dear side I boast me sprung,
And gladly of our *union* hear thee speak,
One heart, one soul in both! *Milton's Par. Lost.*

One kingdom, joy, and *union* without end. *Milton.*

2. Concord; conjunction of mind or interests.

The experience of those profitable emanations from God, most commonly are the first motive of our love; but when we once have tasted his goodness, we love the spring for its own excellency, passing from considering ourselves, to an *union* with God. *Taylor's Rule of Living Holy.*

3. A pearl. Not in use.

The king shall drink to Hamlet's better breath;
And in the cup an *union* shall he throw,
Richer than that which four successive kings
In Denmark's crown have worn. *Shakesp. Hamlet.*

4. [In law.] *Union* is a combining or consolidation of two churches in one, which is done by the consent of the bishop, the patron, and incumbent. And this is properly called an *union*: but there are two other sorts, as when one church is made subject to the other, and when one man is made prelate of both, and when a conventual is made cathedral. Touching *union* in the first signification, there was a statute, an. 37 Hen. VIII. chap. 21. that it should be lawful in two churches, whereof the value of the one is not above six pounds in the king's books, of the first fruits, and not above one mile distant from the other. *Union* in this signification is personal, and that is for the life of the incumbent; or real, that is, perpetual, whosoever is incumbent. *Cowel.*

UNI'PAROUS. *adj.* [*unus* and *pario.*] Bringing one at a birth.

Others make good the paucity of their breed with the duration of their days, whereof there want not examples in animals *uniparous.* *Brown's Vulgar Errours.*

U'NISON. *adj.* [*unus* and *sonus*, Lat.] Sounding alone.

Sounds intermix'd with voice
Choral, or *unison*. *Milton's Par. Lost*, *b.* vii.

U'NISON. *n. s.*

1. A string that has the same sound with another.

When moved matter meets with any thing like that, from which it received its primary impress, it will in like manner move it, as in musical strings tuned *unisons*. *Glanville.*

2. A single unvaried note.

Lost was the nation's sense, nor could be found,
While a long, solemn *unison* went round. *Dunciad*, *b.* iv.

U'NIT. *n. s.* [*unus*, *unitus*, Lat] One; the least number; or the root of numbers.

If any atom should be moved mechanically, without attraction, 'tis above a hundred million millions odds to an *unit*, that it would not strike upon any other atom, but glide through an empty interval without contact. *Bentley's Sermons.*

Units are the integral parts of any large number. *Watts.*

To UNI'TE. *v. a.* [*unitus*, Lat.]

1. To join two or more into one.

The force which wont in two to be dispersed,
In one alone right hand he now *unites*. *Fairy Queen.*

Whatever truths
Redeem'd from error, or from ignorance,
Thin in their authors, like rich veins of ore,
Your works *unite*, and still discover more. *Dryden.*

A proposition for *uniting* both kingdoms was begun. *Swift.*

2. To make to agree.

The king proposed nothing more than to *unite* his kingdom in one form of worship. *Clarendon.*

3. To make to adhere.

The peritonæum, which is a dry body, may be *united* with the musculous flesh. *Wiseman's Surgery.*

4. To join.

In the lawful name of marrying,
To give our hearts *united* ceremony. *Shakespeare.*

Let the ground of the picture be well *united* with colours of a friendly nature. *Dryden's Dufresnoy.*

5. To join in interest.

Unto their assembly, mine honour be not thou *united*. *Genesis.*

To UNI'TE. *v. n.*

1. To join in an act; to concur; to act in concert.

If you will now *unite* in your complaints,
And force them with a constancy, the cardinal
Cannot stand under them. *Shakesp. Hen.* VIII.

2. To coalesce; to be cemented; to be consolidated.

3. To grow into one.

UNI'TEDLY. *adv.* With union; so as to join.

The eyes, which are of a watry nature, ought to be much painted, and *unitedly* on their lower parts; but boldly touch'd above by the light and shadows. *Dryden's Dufresnoy.*

UNI'TER. *n. s.* The person or thing that unites.

Suppose an *uniter* of a middle constitution, that should partake of some of the qualities of both. *Glanville's Scept.*

UNI'TION. *n. s.* [*union*, Fr. from *unite.*] The act or power of uniting; conjunction; coalition. A word proper, but little used.

As long as any different substance keeps off the *unition*, hope not to cure a wound. *Wiseman's Surgery.*

U'NITIVE. *adj.* [from *unite.*] Having the power of uniting.

That can be nothing else but the *unitive* way of religion, which consists of the contemplation and love of God. *Norris.*

U'NITY. *n. s.* [*unitas*, Lat.]

1. The state of being one.

Those hereticks introduced a plurality of Gods; and so made the profession of the *unity* part of the symbolum, that should discriminate the orthodox from them. *Hammond.*

The production of one being the destruction of another, although they generate, they increase not; and must not be said to multiply, who do not transcend an *unity*. *Brown.*

Man is to beget
Like of his like; his image multiply'd:
In *unity* defective; which requires
Collateral love, and dearest amity. *Milton's Par. Lost.*

Whatever we can consider as one thing, suggests to the understanding the idea of *unity*. *Locke.*

2. Concord; conjunction.

That which you hear, you'll swear
You see, there is such *unity* in the proofs. *Shakespeare.*

We, of all christians, ought to promote *unity* among ourselves and others. *Sprat's Sermons.*

3. Agreement; uniformity.

To the avoiding of dissension, it availeth much, that there be amongst them an *unity*, as well in ceremonies as in doctrine. *Hooker*, *b.* iv.

4. Principle of dramatick writing, by which the tenour of the story, and propriety of representation is preserved.

The *unities* of time, place, and action, are exactly observed. *Dryden's Pref. to All for Love.*

Although in poetry it be absolutely necessary that the *unities* of time, place, and action should be thoroughly understood, there is still something more essential, that elevates and astonishes the fancy. *Addison.*

5. [In law.]

Unity of possession is a joint possession of two rights by several titles. For example, I take a lease of land from one upon a certain rent; afterwards I buy the fee-simple. This is an *unity* of possession, whereby the lease is extinguished; by reason that I, who had before the occupation only for my rent, am become lord of the same, and am to pay my rent to none. *Cowel.*

UNJU'DGED. *adj.* Not judicially determined.

Causes *unjudg'd* disgrace the loaded file,
And sleeping laws the king's neglect revile. *Prior.*

UNIVE'RSAL. *adj.* [*universalis*, Lat.]

1. General; extending to all.

All sorrowed: if all the world could have seen't, the woe had been *universal*. *Shakesp. Winter Tale.*

Appetite, an *universal* wolf,
So doubly seconded with will and power,
Must make perforce an *universal* prey,
And last eat up itself. *Shakesp. Troilus and Cressida.*

This excellent epistle, though, in the front of it, it bears a particular inscription, yet in the drift of it is *universal*, as designing to convince all mankind of the necessity of seeking for happiness in the gospel. *South.*

2. Total; whole.

From harmony, from heav'nly harmony,
This *universal* frame began. *Dryden.*

3. Not particular; comprising all particulars.

From things particular
She doth abstract the *universal* kinds. *Davies.*

An *universal* was the object of imagination, and there was no such thing in reality. *Arbuthnot and Pope.*

UNIVE'RSAL. *n. s.* The whole; the general system of the universe. Not in use.

To what end had the angel been set to keep the entrance into paradise after Adam's expulsion, if the *universal* had been paradise. *Raleigh's Hist. of the World.*

Plato calleth God the cause and original, the nature and reason of the *universal*. *Raleigh.*

UNIVERSA'LITY. *n. s.* [*universalitas*, school Lat.] Not particularity; generality; extension to the whole.

This catalogue of sin, is but of sin under a limitation; an *universality* of sin under a certain kind; that is, of all sins of direct and personal commission. *South's Sermons.*

The *universality* of the deluge I insist upon: and that marine bodies are found in all parts of the world. *Woodward.*

A special conclusion cannot be inferred from a moral *universality*, nor always from a physical one; though it may be always inferred from an *universality* that is metaphysical. *Watts.*

UNIVE'RSALLY. *adv.* [from *universal.*] Throughout the whole; without exception.

Those offences which are breaches of supernatural laws, violate in general that principle of reason which willeth *universally* to fly from evil. *Hooker.*

There best beheld, where *universally* admir'd. *Milton.*

What he borrows from the antients, he repays with usury of his own, in coin as good, and as *universally* valuable. *Dryd.*

This institution of charity-schools *universally* prevailed. *Addis.*

U'NIVERSE. *n. s.* [*univers*, Fr. *universum*, Lat.] The general system of things.

Creeping murmur, and the poring dark,
Fills the wide vessel of the *universe*. *Shakespeare.*

God here sums up all into man; the whole into a part; the *universe* into an individual. *South's Sermons.*

Father of heav'n!
Whose word call'd out this *universe* to birth. *Prior.*

UNIVE'RSITY. *n. s.* [*universitas*, Lat.] A school, where all the arts and faculties are taught and studied.

While I play the good husband at home, my son and servants spend all at the *university*. *Shakesp. Taming of the Shrew.*

The *universities*, especially Aberdeen, flourished under many excellent scholars, and very learned men. *Clarendon.*

UNI'VOCAL. *adj.* [*univocus*, Lat.]

1. Having one meaning.

Univocal words are such as signify but one idea, or but one sort of thing: equivocal words are such as signify two or more different ideas, or different sorts of objects. *Watts.*

2. Certain; regular; persuing always one tenour.

This conceit makes putrefactive generations correspondent unto seminal productions; and conceives inequivocal effects, and *univocal* conformity unto the efficient. *Brown.*

UNI'VOCALLY. *adv.* [from *univocal.*]

1. In one term; in one sense.

How is sin *univocally* distinguished into venial and mortal, if the venial be not sin? *Hall.*

It were too great presumption to think, that there is any thing in any created nature, that can bear any perfect resemblance of the incomprehensible perfection of the divine nature;

ture: very being itself does not predicate *univocally* touching God, and any created being, and intellect, and will, as we attribute them to him. *Hale.*

2. In one tenour.

All creatures are generated *univocally* by parents of their own kind; there is no such thing as spontaneous generation. *Ray.*

UNJO'YOUS. *adj.* Not gay; not cheerful.

Morn late rising o'er the drooping world,
Lifts her pale eye *unjoyous.* *Thomson's Winter.*

UNJU'ST. *adj.* [*injuste*, Fr. *injustus*, Lat.] Iniquitous; contrary to equity; contrary to justice. It is used both of persons and things.

I should forge
Quarrels *unjust* against the good and loyal,
Destroying them for wealth. *Shakesp. Macbeth.*

The Piercies,
Finding his usurpation most *unjust*,
Endeavour'd my advancement to the throne. *Shakesp.*

He that is *unjust* in the least, is *unjust* also in much. *Luke* xvi.

Succeeding kings just recovery of their right, from *unjust* usurpations and extortions, shall never be prejudiced by any act of mine. *K. Charles.*

Th' *unjust* the just hath slain. *Milton.*

He who was so *unjust* as to do his brother an injury, will scarce be so just to condemn himself for it. *Locke.*

UNJU'STIFIABLE. *adj.* Not to be defended; not to be justified.

If these reproaches, which aim only at ostentation of wit, be so *unjustifiable*, what shall we say to those that are drawn, that are founded in malice? *Government of the Tongue.*

In a just and honourable war we engaged; not out of ambition, or any other *unjustifiable* motive, but for the defence of all that was dear to us. *Atterbury.*

If we could look into effects, we might pronounce boldly: but for a man to give his opinion of what he sees but in part, is an *unjustifiable* piece of rashness. *Addison.*

UNJU'STIFIABLENESS. *n. s.* The quality of not being justifiable.

He wished them to consider of the illegality of all those commissions, and of the *unjustifiableness* of all the proceedings which had been by virtue of them. *Clarendon.*

UNJU'STIFIABLY. *adv.* In a manner not to be defended.

UNJU'STLY. *adj.* In a manner contrary to right.

If aught against my life
Thy country sought of thee, it sought *unjustly.* *Milton.*

Whom, but for voting peace, the Greeks pursue,
Accus'd *unjustly*, then *unjustly* slew. *Denham.*

Your choler does *unjustly* rise,
To see your friends pursue your enemies. *Dryden.*

Moderation the one side very justly disowns, and the other as *unjustly* pretends to. *Swift.*

UNKE'MPT. *adj.* Not combed. Obsolete.

Thenot, to that I chose thou dost me tempt;
But ah! too well I wot my humble vaine,
And how my rhimes been rugged and *unkempt.* *Spenser.*

To UNKE'NNEL. *v. a.*

1. To drive from his hole.

Search, seek, find out. I warrant we'll *unkennel* the fox.
Let me stop this way first. So, now uncape. *Shakespeare.*
I warrant you, colonel, we'll *unkennel* him. *Dryden.*

2. To rouse from its secrecy, or retreat.

If his occult guilt
Do not itself *unkennel* in one speech,
It is a damned ghost that we have seen. *Shakesp.*

UNKE'NT. *adj.* [*un* and *ken*, to know.] Unknown. Obsolete.

Go, little book, thyself present,
As child whose parent is *unkent*,
To him, that is the president
Of nobleness and chivalrie. *Spenser.*

UNKE'PT. *adj.*

1. Not kept; not retained.

2. Unobserved; unobeyed.

Many things kept generally heretofore, are now in like sort generally *unkept*, and abolished, every where. *Hooker.*

UNKI'ND. *adj.* Not favourable; not benevolent.

In nature there's no blemish but the mind;
None can be call'd deform'd, but the *unkind.* *Shakesp.*

To the noble mind
Rich gifts wax poor, when givers prove *unkind.* *Shakesp.*

To Nimrod our author seems a little *unkind*; and says, that he, against right, enlarged his empire. *Locke.*

A real joy I never knew,
Till I believ'd thy passion true;
A real grief I ne'er can find,
'Till thou prov'st perjur'd or *unkind.* *Prior.*

UNKI'NDLY. *adj.* [*un* and *kind.*]

1. Unnatural; contrary to nature.

They, with their filthiness,
Polluted this same gentle soil long time,
That their own mother loath'd their beastliness,
And 'gan abhor her brood's *unkindly* crime,
All were they born of her own native slime. *Fairy Queen.*

All works of nature,
Abortive, monstrous, or *unkindly* mix'd. *Milton.*

2. Malignant; unfavourable.

The goddess, that in rural shrine,
Dwell'st here with Pan, or Sylvan, by blest song
Forbidding every bleak, *unkindly* fog,
To touch the prosperous growth of this tall wood. *Milton.*

UNKI'NDLY. *adv.* Without kindness; without affection.

The herd, *unkindly* wise,
Or chaces him from thence, or from him flies. *Denham.*

If we *unkindly* part,
Will not the poor fond creature break her heart. *Dryden.*

UNKI'NDNESS. *n. s.* [from *unkind.*] Malignity; ill-will; want of affection.

Take no *unkindness* of his hasty words. *Shakespeare.*

His unjust *unkindness*, that in all reason should have quench'd her love, hath, like an impediment in the current, made it more violent and unruly. *Shakesp. Measure for Measure.*

After their return, the duke executed the same authority in conferring all favours, and in revenging himself upon those who had manifested any *unkindness* towards him. *Clarendon.*

Eve—As one who loves, and some *unkindness* meets,
With sweet, austere composure, thus reply'd. *Milton.*

Christ, who was the only person to have resented this *unkindness*, finds an extenuation of it. *South's Sermons.*

She sigh'd, she wept, she low'd; 'twas all she cou'd;
And with *unkindness* seem'd to tax the God. *Dryden.*

To UNKI'NG. *v. a.* To deprive of royalty.

God save king Henry, *unking'd* Richard says,
And send him many years of sunshine days. *Shakespeare.*

It takes the force of law: how then, my lord!
If as they would *unking* my father now,
To make you way. *Southern.*

UNKI'SSED. *adj.* Not kissed.

Foul words are but foul wind, and foul wind is but foul breath, and foul breath is noisome; therefore I will depart *unkist.* *Shakesp. Much Ado about Nothing.*

UNKNI'GHTLY. *adj.* Unbecoming a knight.

With six hours hard riding through wild places, I overgot them a little before night, near an old ill-favoured castle, the place where I perceived they meant to perform their *unknightly* errand. *Sidney, b.* ii.

To UNKNI'T. *v. a.*

1. To unweave; to separate.

Would he had continued to his country
As he began, and not *unknit* himself
The noble knot he made. *Shakesp. Coriolanus.*

2. To open.

Unknit that threat'ning, unkind brow,
And dart not scornful glances from those eyes. *Shakesp.*

U'NKLE. *v. a.* [*oncle*, French.] The brother of a father or mother. See UNCLE.

The English power is near, led on by Malcolm,
His uncle Siward, and the good Macduff. *Shakespeare.*

Give me good fame, ye pow'rs! and make me just:
Thus much the rogue to publick ears will trust:
In private then:—when wilt thou, mighty Jove!
My wealthy *uncle* from this world remove? *Dryden.*

To UNKNO'W. *v. a.* To cease to know.

It's already known;
Oh! can you keep it from yourselves, *unknow* it? *Smith.*

UNKNO'WABLE. *adj.* Not to be known.

Distinguish well between knowables and *unknowables.* *Watts.*

UNKNO'WING. *adj.*

1. Ignorant; not knowing.

Let me speak to th' yet *unknowing* world,
How these things came about *Shakesp. Hamlet.*

Though *unknowing* persons may accuse others, yet can they never the more absolve themselves. *Decay of Piety.*

Unknowing I prepar'd thy bridal bed;
With empty hopes of happy issue fed. *Dryden.*

Unknowing he requires it; and when known,
He thinks it his; and values it, 'tis gone. *Dryden.*

His hounds, *unknowing* of his change, pursue
The chace, and their mistaken master slew. *Dryden.*

Proteus, mounting from the hoary deep,
Surveys his charge, *unknowing* of deceit. *Pope.*

2. Not practised; not qualified.

So Lybian huntsmen, on some sandy plain,
From shady coverts rouz'd, the lion chace:
The kingly beast roars out with loud disdain,
And slowly moves, *unknowing* to give place. *Dryden.*

These were they, whose souls the furies steel'd,
And curs'd, with hearts *unknowing* how to yield. *Pope.*

UNKNO'WINGLY. *adv.* Ignorantly; without knowledge.

The beauty I behold has struck me dead:
Unknowingly she strikes, and kills by chance. *Dryden.*

They are like the Syrians, who were first smitten with blindness, and *unknowingly* led out of their way, into the capital of their enemy's country. *Addison's Freeholder.*

UNKNO'WN. *adj.*

1. Not known.

'Tis not *unknown* to you,
How much I have disabled my estate. *Shakespeare.*

Many are the trees of God, that grow
In paradise, and various, yet *unknown*
To us. *Milton's Paradise Lost.*

Here may I always on this downy grass,
Unknown, unseen, my easy minutes pass. *Roscommon.*

If any chance has hither brought the name
Of Palamedes, not *unknown* to fame,
Accus'd and sentenc'd for pretended crimes. *Dryden.*

Though incest is indeed a deadly crime,
You are not guilty, since *unknown* 'twas done,
And known, had been abhorr'd. *Dryden's Don Sebastian.*

At fear of death, that saddens all
With terrors round, can reason hold her throne?
Despise the known, nor tremble at th' *unknown.* *Pope.*

2. Greater than is imagined.

The planting of hemp and flax would be an *unknown* advantage to the kingdom. *Bacon.*

3. Not having cohabitation.

I am yet
Unknown to woman; never was forsworn. *Shakespeare.*

4. Without communication.

We stopped at a little inn, where the man of the house, formerly a servant in the knight's family, to do honour to his old master, had, *unknown* to Sir Roger, put him up in a sign-post. *Addison's Spectator*, N°. 122.

UNLA'BOURED. *adj.*

1. Not produced by labour.

Unlaboured harvests shall the fields adorn,
And cluster'd grapes shall blush on ev'ry thorn. *Dryden.*

2. Not cultivated by labour.

Not eastern monarchs on their nuptial day,
In dazzling gold and purple shine so gay,
As the bright natives of th' *unlabour'd* field,
Unvers'd in spinning, and in looms unskill'd. *Blackmore.*

3. Spontaneous; voluntary.

Their charms, if charms they have, the truth supplies,
And from the theme *unlabour'd* beauties rise. *Tickell.*

To UNLA'CE. *v. a.*

1. To loose any thing fastened with strings.

He could not endure so cruel case,
But thought his arms to leave, and helmet to *unlace.* *Spenser.*

A little river roll'd,
By which there sat a knight with helm *unlac'd*,
Himself refreshing with the liquid cold. *Fairy Queen, b.* i.

The helmet from my brow *unlac'd.* *Pope's Odyssey.*

2. To loose a lady's dress.

Can I forget, when they in prison placing her,
With swelling heart, in spite, and due disdainfulness,
She lay for dead, till I help'd with *unlacing* her. *Sidney.*

Unlace yourself, for that harmonious chime
Tells me from you that now it is bed-time. *Donne.*

3. To make loose; to put in danger of being lost. Not in use.

You *unlace* your reputation,
And spend your rich opinion for the name of a night-brawler. *Shakespeare's Othello.*

To UNLA'DE. *v. a.*

1. To remove from the vessel which carries.

He's a foolish seaman,
That, when his ship is sinking, will not
Unlade his hopes into another bottom. *Denham.*

2. To exonerate that which carries.

The vent'rous merchant, who design'd for far,
And touches on our hospitable shore,
Charm'd with the splendour of this northern star,
Shall here *unlade* him, and depart no more. *Dryden.*

3. To put out. Used of a vessel.

We landed at Tyre; for there the ship was to *unlade* her burden. *Acts* xxi. 3.

UNLA'ID. *adj.*

1. Not placed; not fixed.

Whatsoever we do behold now in this present world, it was inwrapped within the bowels of divine mercy, written in the book of eternal wisdom, and held in the hands of omnipotent power, the first foundations of the world being as yet *unlaid.* *Hooker, b.* v.

2. Not pacified; not stilled.

No evil thing that walks by night,
Blue, meagre hag, or stubborn *unlaid* ghost,
Hath hurtful pow'r o'er true virginity. *Milton.*

UNLAME'NTED. *adj.* Not deplored.

After six years spent in outward opulency, and inward murmur that it was not greater, he died *unlamented* by any. *Clarendon.*

Thus *unlamented* pass the proud away,
The pride of fools, and pageant of a day. *Pope.*

To UNLA'TCH. *v. a.* To open by lifting up the latch.

My worthy wife
The door *unlatch'd*; and, with repeated calls,
Invites her former lord within my walls. *Dryden.*

UNLA'WFUL. *adj.* Contrary to law; not permitted by the law.

Before I be convict by course of law,
To threaten me with death is most *unlawful.* *Shakesp.*

It is an *unlawful* thing for a Jew to come unto one of another nation. *Acts* x. 28.

Shew me when it is our duty, and when *unlawful* to take these courses, by some general rule of a perpetual, never-failing truth. *South.*

The secret ceremonies I conceal,
Uncouth, perhaps, *unlawful* to reveal. *Dryden.*

UNLA'WFULLY. *adv.*

1. In a manner contrary to law or right.

He that gains all that he can lawfully this year, next year will be tempted to gain something *unlawfully.* *Taylor.*

2. Illegitimately; not by marriage.

I had rather my brother die by the law, than my son should be *unlawfully* born. *Shakespeare.*

Give me your opinion, what part I, being *unlawfully* born, may claim of the man's affection, who begot me. *Addis.*

UNLA'WFULNESS. *n. s.* Contrariety to law; state of being not permitted.

If those alledged testimonies of scripture did indeed concern the matter to such effect as was pretended, that which they should infer were *unlawfulness.* *Hooker.*

The original reason of the *unlawfulness* of lying is, that it carries with it an act of injustice, and a violation of the right of him, to whom we were obliged to signify our minds. *South's Sermons.*

To UNLE'ARN. *v. a.* To forget, or disuse what has been learned.

Antisthenes, being asked of one, what learning was most necessary for man's life? answered, to *unlearn* that which is naught. *Bacon.*

This were to imply, that all books in being should be destroyed; and that all the age should take new pains to *unlearn* those habits which have cost them so much labour. *Holder.*

The government of the tongue is a piece of morality which sober nature dictates, which yet our greatest scholars have *unlearnt.* *Decay of Piety.*

Some cyders have by art, or age, *unlearn'd*
Their genuine relish, and of sundry wines
Assum'd the flavour. *Philips.*

What they thus learned from him in one way, they did not *unlearn* again in another. *Atterbury.*

A wicked man is not only obliged to learn to do well, but *unlearn* his former life. *Rogers's Sermons.*

UNLE'ARNED *adj.*

1. Ignorant; not informed; not instructed.

This selected piece, which you translate,
Foretells your studies may communicate,
From darker dialect of a strange land,
Wisdom that here th' *unlearn'd* shall understand. *D'avenant.*

And by succession of *unlearned* times,
As bards began, so monks rung on the chimes. *Roscommon.*

Some at the bar, with subtilty defend
The cause of an *unlearned*, noble friend. *Dryden.*

Though *unlearned* men well enough understood the words white and black, yet there were philosophers found, who had subtlety enough to prove that white was black. *Locke.*

2. Not gained by study; not known.

Mere words, or such things chiefly as were better *unlearned.* *Milton on Education.*

3. Not suitable to a learned man.

I will prove those verses to be very *unlearned*, neither savouring of poetry, wit, or invention. *Shakespeare.*

UNLE'ARNEDLY. Ignorantly; grossly.

He, in his epistle, plainly affirmeth, they think *unlearnedly*, who are of another belief. *Brown's Vulg. Errours.*

UNLEA'VENED. *adj.* Not fermented; not mixed with fermenting matter.

They baked *unleavened* cakes of the dough, for it was not leavened. *Exod.* ii. 39.

Purge out therefore the old leaven, that ye may be a new lump, as ye are *unleavened.* 1 *Cor.* v. 7.

UNLE'ISUREDNESS. *n. s.* Business; want of time; want of leisure. Not in use.

My essay touching the scripture having been written partly in England, partly in another kingdom, it were strange if there did not appear much unevenness, and if it did not betray the *unleisuredness* of the wandering author. *Boyle.*

UNLE'SS. *conjunct.* Except; if not; supposing that not.

Let us not say, we keep the commandments of the one, when we break the commandments of the other: for, *unless* we observe both, we obey neither. *Hooker.*

Unless I look on Sylvia in the day,
There is no day for me to look upon. *Shakespeare.*

What

What hidden ſtrength,
Unleſs the ſtrength of heav'n, if you mean that. *Milton.*
For ſure I am, *unleſs* I win in arms,
To ſtand excluded from Emilia's charms;
Nor can my ſtrength avail, *unleſs* by thee,
Endu'd with force, I gain the victory. *Dryden.*

The commendation of adverſaries is the greateſt triumph of a writer, becauſe it never comes *unleſs* extorted. *Dryden.*

No poet ever ſweetly ſung,
Unleſs he were, like Phœbus, young;
Nor ever nymph inſpir'd to rhyme,
Unleſs, like Venus, in her prime. *Swift.*

UNLE'SSONED. *adj.* Not taught.
The full ſum of me
Is an *unleſſon'd* girl, unſchool'd, unpractis'd;
Happy in this, ſhe is not yet ſo old
But ſhe may learn. *Shakeſpeare.*

UNLE'TTERED. *adj.* Unlearned; untaught.
When the apoſtles of our Lord were ordained to alter the laws of heatheniſh religion, St. Paul excepted, the reſt were unſchooled and *unlettered* men. *Hooker, b.* iv.

Such as the jocund flute, or gameſome pipe
Stirs up among the looſe, *unletter'd* hinds,
Who thank the gods amiſs. *Milton.*
Th' *unletter'd* chriſtian, who believes in groſs,
Plods on to heav'n, and ne'er is at a loſs. *Dryden.*

UNLE'VELLED. *adj.* Not cut even.
All *unlevell'd* the gay garden lies. *Tickell.*

UNLIBI'DINOUS. *adj.* Not luſtful.
In thoſe hearts
Love *unlibidinous* reign'd; nor jealouſy
Was underſtood, the injur'd lover's hell. *Milton.*

UNLI'CENSED. *adj.* Having no regular permiſſion.
Aſk what boldneſs brought him hither
Unlicenſed. *Milton's Par. Loſt, b.* iv.
Warn the thoughtleſs, ſelf-confiding train,
No more, *unlicens'd*, thus to brave the main. *Pope.*

UNLI'CKED. *adj* Shapeleſs; not formed: from the opinion that the bear licks her young to ſhape.
Shape my legs of an unequal ſize,
To diſproportion me in every part,
Like to a chaos, or *unlick'd* bear-whelp. *Shakeſpeare.*
Thoſe *unlickt* bear-whelps. *Donne.*
The bloody bear, an independent beaſt,
Unlick'd to form, in groans her hate expreſt. *Dryden.*

UNLI'GHTED. *adj.* Not kindled; not ſet on fire.
There lay a log *unlighted* on the earth:
For th' unborn chief the fatal ſiſters came,
And rais'd it up, and toſs'd it on the flame. *Dryden.*
The ſacred wood, which on the altar lay,
Untouch'd, *unlighted* glows. *Prior.*

UNLI'GHTSOME. *adj.* Dark; gloomy; wanting light.
Firſt the ſun,
A mighty ſphere! he fram'd, *unlightſome* firſt,
Though of æthereal mould. *Milton's Par. Loſt.*

UNLI'KE. *adj.*
1. Diſſimilar; having no reſemblance.
Where caſes are ſo *unlike* as theirs and ours, I ſee not how that which they did, ſhould induce, much leſs inforce us to the ſame practice. *Hooker, b.* v.

So the twins humours, in our Terence, are
Unlike; this harſh and rude, that ſmooth and fair. *Denham.*
Unlike the niceneſs of our modern dames;
Affected nymphs, with new affected names. *Dryden.*

Our ideas, whilſt we are awake, ſucceed one another, not much *unlike* the images in the inſide of a lanthorn. *Locke.*

Some ſhe diſgrac'd, and ſome with honours crown'd;
Unlike ſucceſſes equal merits found. *Pope.*

2. Improbable; unlikely; not likely.
Make not impoſſible that which but ſeems *unlike*. *Shakeſp.*
What befel the empire of Almaigne were not *unlike* to befal to Spain, if it ſhould break. *Bacon.*

UNLI'KELIHOOD.
UNLI'KELINESS. } [from *unlikely.*] Improbability.
The work was carried on, amidſt all the *unlikelihoods* and diſcouraging circumſtances imaginable; the builders holding the ſword in one hand, to defend the trowel working with the other. *South's Sermons.*

There are degrees herein, from the very neighbourhood of demonſtration, quite down to improbality and *unlikelineſs*, even to the confines of impoſſibility. *Locke.*

UNLI'KELY. *adj.*
1. Improbable; not ſuch as can be reaſonably expected.
Suſpicion Mopſa; for a very *unlikely* envy ſhe hath ſtumbled upon. *Sidney.*
2. Not promiſing any particular event.
My advice and actions both have met
Succeſs in things *unlikely*. *Denham's Sophy.*

This collection we thought not only *unlikely* to reach the future, but unworthy of the preſent age. *Swift.*

Effects are miraculous and ſtrange, when they grow by *unlikely* means. *Hooker.*

UNLI'KELY. *adv.* Improbably.
The pleaſures we are to enjoy in that converſation, not *unlikely* may proceed from the diſcoveries each ſhall communicate to another, of God and nature. *Pope.*

UNLI'KENESS. *n. ſ.* Diſſimilitude; want of reſemblance.
Imitation pleaſes, becauſe it affords matter for enquiring into the truth or falſhood of imitation, by comparing its likeneſs, or *unlikeneſs* with the original. *Dryden.*

UNLI'MITABLE. *adj.* Admitting no bounds.
He tells us 'tis unlimited and *unlimitable.* *Locke.*

UNLI'MITED. *adj.*
1. Having no bounds; having no limits.
So *unlimited* is our impotence to recompence or repay God's dilection, that it fetters our very wiſhes. *Boyle.*

It is ſome pleaſure to a finite underſtanding, to view *unlimited* excellencies, which have no bounds, though it cannot comprehend them. *Tillotſon.*

2. Undefined; not bounded by proper exceptions.
With groſs and popular capacities, nothing doth more prevail than *unlimited* generalities, becauſe of their plainneſs at the firſt ſight; nothing leſs, with men of exact judgment, becauſe ſuch rules are not ſafe to be truſted over far. *Hooker.*

3. Unconfined; not reſtrained.
All the evils that can proceed from an untied tongue, and an unguarded, *unlimited* will, we put upon the accounts of drunkenneſs. *Taylor.*

Aſcribe not unto God ſuch an *unlimited* exerciſe of mercy, as may deſtroy his juſtice. *Rogers's Sermons.*

Huſbands are counſelled not to truſt too much to their wives owning the doctrine of *unlimited* conjugal fidelity. *Arb.*

UNLI'MITEDLY. *adv.* Boundleſsly; without bounds.
Many aſcribe too *unlimitedly* to the force of a good meaning, to think that it is able to bear the ſtreſs of whatſoever commiſſions they ſhall lay upon it. *Decay of Piety.*

UNLI'NEAL. Not coming in the order of ſucceſſion.
They put a barren ſcepter in my gripe,
Thence to be wrench'd with an *unlineal* hand,
No ſon of mine ſucceeding. *Shakeſp. Macbeth.*

To UNLI'NK. *v. a.* To untwiſt; to open.
About his neck
A green and gilded ſnake had wreath'd itſelf;
Who with her head, nimble in threats, approach'd
The opening of his mouth; but ſuddenly
Seeing Orlando, it *unlink'd* itſelf. *Shakeſpeare.*

UNLI'QUIFIED. *adj.* Unmelted; undiſſolved.
Theſe huge, unwieldy lumps remained in the melted matter, rigid and *unliquified*, floating in it like cakes of ice in a river. *Addiſon's Remarks on Italy.*

To UNLO'AD. *v. a.*
1. To diſburden; to exonerate.
Like an aſs, whoſe back with ingots bows,
Thou bear'ſt thy heavy riches but a journey,
And death *unloadeth* thee. *Shakeſp. Meaſ. for Meaſure.*
Vain man forbear, of cares *unload* thy mind;
Forget thy hopes, and give thy fears to wind. *Creech.*
Some to *unload* the fertile branches run. *Pope.*

2. To put off any thing burdenſome.
To you duke Humphry muſt *unload* his grief. *Shakeſp.*
Nor can my tongue *unload* my heart's great burthen. *Shak.*

To UNLO'CK. *v. a.*
1. To open what is ſhut with a lock.
I have ſeen her *unlock* her cloſet, take forth paper. *Shakeſp.*
She ſprings a light,
Unlocks the door, and ent'ring out of breath,
The dying ſaw, and inſtruments of death. *Dryden.*

2. To open in general.
My purſe, my perſon, my extremeſt means,
Lie all *unlock'd* to your occaſions. *Shakeſp. Mer. of Venice.*
I had not thought to have *unlock'd* my lips
In this unhallow'd air, but that this jugler
Would think to charm my judgment, as mine eyes,
Obtruding falſe rules, pranck'd in reaſon's garb. *Milton.*
I yielded, and *unlock'd* her all my heart,
Who with a grain of manhood well reſolv'd,
Might eaſily have ſhook off all her ſnares. *Milton.*

Sand is an advantage to cold clays, in that it warms them, and *unlocks* their binding qualities. *Mortimer's Huſbandry.*

A lixivium of quick-lime *unlocks* the ſalts that are entangled in the viſcid juices of ſome ſcorbutick perſons. *Arbuthnot.*

Thy foreſts, Windſor! and thy green retreats
Invite my lays. Be preſent, ſylvan maids!
Unlock your ſprings, and open all your ſhades. *Pope.*

UNLO'CKED. *adj.* Not faſtened with a lock.

UNLOO'KED.
UNLOO'KED *for.* } *adj.* Unexpected; not foreſeen.
Yet perhaps had their number prevailed, if the king of Pontus had not come *unlook'd for* to their ſuccour. *Sidney.*
How much *unlook'd for* is this expedition! *Shakeſpeare.*
God, I pray him
That none of you may live your natural age,
But by ſome *unlook'd* accident cut off. *Shakeſpeare.*

Whatſoever

Whatsoever is new is *unlooked for*; and ever it mends some, and pares others. *Bacon.*

From that high hope, to what relapse
Unlook'd for are we fall'n. *Paradise Regain'd.*

Your affairs I have recommended to the king, but with *unlook'd* success. *Denham.*

Nor fame I slight, nor for her favours call;
She comes *unlook'd for*, if she comes at all. *Pope.*

UNLOO'SABLE. *adj.* [A word rarely used.] Not to be loosed.

Whatever may be said of the *unloosable* mobility of atoms, yet divers parts of matter may compose bodies, that need no other cement to unite them, than the juxta-position, and resting together of their parts, whereby the air, and other fluids that might dissipate them, are excluded. *Boyle.*

To UNLOO'SE. *v. a.* To loose. A word perhaps barbarous and ungrammatical, the particle prefixed implying negation; so that to *unloose*, is properly *to bind.*

York, *unloose* your long imprison'd thoughts,
And let thy tongue be equal with thy heart. *Shakespeare.*

The weak, wanton Cupid,
Shall from your neck *unloose* his am'rous fold;
And, like a dew-drop from the lion's mane,
Be shook to air. *Shakesp. Troilus and Cressida.*

Turn him to any cause of policy;
The gordian knot of it he will *unloose*,
Familiar as his garter. *Shakesp. Hen.* V.

It rested in you,
T' *unloose* this tied-up justice, when you pleas'd. *Shakesp.*

The latchet of his shoes I am not worthy to stoop down and *unloose*. *Mark* i. 7.

He that should spend all his time in tying inextricable knots, only to baffle the industry of those that should attempt to *unloose* them, would be thought not much to have served his generation. *Decay of Piety.*

To UNLOO'SE. *v. n.* To fall in pieces; to lose all union and connexion.

Without this virtue, the publick union must *unloose*; the strength decay; and the pleasure grow faint. *Collier.*

UNLO'VED. *adj.* Not loved.

As love does not always reflect itself, Zelmane, though reason there was to love Palladius, yet could not ever perswade her heart to yield with that pain to Palladius, as they feel, that feel *unloved* love. *Sidney, b.* ii.

What though I be not fortunate;
But miserable most to love *unlov'd!* *Shakespeare.*

He was generally *unloved*, as a proud and supercilious person. *Clarendon, b.* viii.

UNLO'VELINESS. *n. s.* Unamiableness; inability to create love.

The old man, growing only in age and affection, followed his suit with all means of unhonest servants, large promises, and each thing else that might help to countervail his own *unloveliness*. *Sidney, b.* ii.

UNLO'VELY. *adj.* That cannot excite love. There seems by this word generally more intended than barely negation. See UNLOVELINESS.

UNLO'VING. *adj.* Unkind; not fond.

Thou, blest with a goodly son,
Didst yield consent to disinherit him;
Which argu'd thee a most *unloving* father. *Shakespeare.*

UNLU'CKILY. *adv.* Unfortunately; by ill luck.

Things have fallen out so *unluckily*,
That we have had no time to move our daughter. *Shakesp.*

An ant dropt *unluckily* into the water. *L'Estrange.*

A fox *unluckily* crossing the road, drew off a considerable detachment. *Addison's Freeholder*, N° 3.

UNLU'CKY. *adj.*

1. Unfortunate; producing unhappiness. This word is generally used of accidents slightly vexatious.

You may make an experiment often, without meeting with any of those *unlucky* accidents which make such experiments miscarry. *Boyle.*

2. Unhappy; miserable; subject to frequent misfortunes.

Then shall I you recount a rueful case,
Said he; the which with this *unlucky* eye
I late beheld. *Fairy Queen, b.* i.

3. Slightly mischievous; mischievously waggish.

His friendship is counterfeit, seldome to trust;
His doings *unluckie*, and ever unjust. *Tusser.*

Why, cries an *unlucky* wag, a less bag might have served. *L'Estrange.*

A lad, th' *unluckiest* of his crew,
Was still contriving something bad, but new. *King.*

4. Ill-omen'd; inauspicious.

When I appear, see you avoid the place,
And haunt me not with that *unlucky* face. *Dryden.*

UNLU'STROUS. *adj.* Wanting splendour; wanting lustre.

Should I join gripes with hands
Made hard with hourly falshood, as with labour;
Then glad myself with peeping in an eye,
Base and *unlustrous* as the smoaky light
That's fed with stinking tallow. *Shakespeare.*

To UNLU'TE. *v. a.* To separate vessels closed with chymical cement.

Our antimony thus handled, affordeth us an ounce of sulphur, of so sulphureous a smell, that upon the *unluting* the vessels, it infected the room with a scarce supportable stink. *Boyle.*

UNMA'DE. *adj.*

1. Not yet formed; not created.

Thou wast begot in Demogorgon's hall,
And saw'st the secrets of the world *unmade*. *Fairy Queen.*

Then might'st thou tear thy hair,
And fall upon the ground as I do now,
Taking the measure of an *unmade* grave. *Shakespeare.*

2. Deprived of form or qualities.

The first earth was perfectly *unmade* again, taken all to pieces, and framed a-new. *Woodward's Nat. Hist.*

3 Omitted to be made.

You may the world of more defects upbraid,
That other works by nature are *unmade*;
That she did never at her own expence
A palace rear. *Blackmore.*

UNMA'IMED. *adj.* Not deprived of any essential part.

An interpreter should give his author entire and *unmaimed*; the diction and the versification only are his proper province. *Pope's Preface to the Iliad.*

UNMA'KABLE. *adj.* Not possible to be made.

If the principles of bodies are unalterable, they are also *unmakable* by any but a divine power. *Grew's Cosmology.*

To UNMA'KE. *v. a.* To deprive of former qualities before possessed. To deprive of form or being.

They've made themselves, and their fitness now
Does *unmake* you. *Shakesp. Macbeth.*

God does not make or *unmake* things, to try experiments. *Burnet's Theory of the Earth.*

Empire! thou poor and despicable thing,
When such as these make, or *unmake* a king. *Dryden.*

Bring this guide of the light within to the trial. God, when he makes the prophet, does not *unmake* the man. *Locke.*

To UNMA'N. *v. a.*

1. To deprive of the constituent qualities of a human being, as reason.

What, quite *unmann'd* in folly? *Shakesp. Macbeth.*

Gross errors *unman*, and strip them of the very principles of reason, and sober discourse. *South's Sermons.*

2. To emasculate.

3. To break into irresolution; to deject.

Her clamours pierce the Trojans ears,
Unman their courage, and augment their fears. *Dryden.*

Ulysses veil'd his pensive head;
Again *unman'd*, a shower of sorrows shed. *Pope.*

UNMA'NAGEABLE. *adj.*

1. Not manageable; not easily governed.

They'll judge every thing by models of their own, and thus are rendered *unmanageable* by any authority but that of absolute dominion. *Glanville.*

None can be concluded *unmanageable* by the milder methods of government, till they have been thoroughly tried upon him; and if they will not prevail, we make no excuses for the obstinate. *Locke.*

2. Not easily wielded.

UNMA'NAGED. *adj.*

1. Not broken by horsemanship.

Like colts, or *unmanaged* horses, we start at dead bones and lifeless blocks. *Taylor's Rule of Living Holy.*

2. Not tutored; not educated.

Savage princes flash out sometimes into an irregular greatness of thought, and betray, in their actions, an unguided force, and *unmanaged* virtue. *Felton on the Classicks.*

UNMA'NLIKE. } *adj.*
UNMA'NLY. }

1. Unbecoming a human being.

It is strange to see the *unmanlike* cruelty of mankind, who, not content with their tyrannous ambition, to have brought the others virtuous patience under them, think their masterhood nothing, without doing injury to them. *Sidney.*

Where the act is *unmanly*, or the expectation contradictious to the attributes of God, our hopes we ought never to entertain. *Collier against Despair.*

2. Unsuitable to a man; effeminate.

By the greatness of the cry, it was the voice of man; though it were a very *unmanlike* voice, so to cry. *Sidney.*

New customs,
Though never so ridiculous,
Nay, let them be *unmanly*, yet are follow'd. *Shakespeare.*

This is in thee a nature but affected;
A poor *unmanly* melancholy, sprung
From change of fortune. *Shakesp. Timon of Athens.*

My servitude, ignoble,
Unmanly, ignominious, infamous. *Milton's Agonistes.*

Think not thy friend can ever feel the soft
Unmanly warmth, and tenderness of love. *Addison.*

Unmanly dread invades the French astony'd,
And streight their useless arms they quit. *Philips.*

UNMA'NNERED. *adj.* Rude; brutal; uncivil.
You have a slanderous, beastly, unwash'd tongue,
In your rude mouth, and savouring yourself,
Unmanner'd lord. *B. Johnson's Catiline.*
If your barking dog disturb her ease,
Th' *unmanner'd* malefactor is arraign'd. *Dryden's Juvenal.*

UNMA'NNERLINESS. *n. s.* Breach of civility; ill behaviour.
A sort of *unmannerliness* is apt to grow up with young people, if not early restrain'd; and that is a forwardness to interrupt others speaking. *Locke on Education.*

UNMA'NNERLY. *adj.* Ill bred; not civil; not complaisant.
Sweetheart,
I were *unmannerly* to take you out,
And not to kiss you. *Shakesp. Hen. VIII.*
He call'd them untaught knaves, *unmannerly*,
To bring a slovenly, unhandsome coarse
Betwixt the wind and his nobility. *Shakesp. Hen. IV.*
He will prove the weeping philosoper, when he grows old, being so full of *unmannerly* sadness in his youth. *Shakespeare.*
Bare-faced ribaldry is both *unmannerly* in itself, and fulsome to the reader. *Dryden.*
A divine dares hardly shew his person among fine gentlemen; or, if he fall into such company, he is in continual apprehension that some pert man of pleasure should break an *unmannerly* jest, and render him ridiculous. *Swift.*

UNMA'NNERLY. *adv.* Uncivilly.
Forgive me,
If I have us'd myself *unmannerly*. *Shakespeare.*

UNMANU'RED. *adj.* Not cultivated.
The land,
In antique times was savage wilderness;
Unpeopl'd, *unmanur'd*, unprov'd, unprais'd. *Fairy Queen.*

UNMA'RKED. *adj.* Not observed; not regarded.
I got a time, *unmarked* by any, to steal away, I cared not whither, so I might escape them. *Sidney.*
This place *unmark'd*, though oft I walk'd the green,
In all my progress I had never seen. *Dryden.*
Entring at the gate, conceal'd in clouds,
He mix'd, *unmark'd*, among the busy throng,
Borne by the tide, and pass'd unseen along. *Dryden.*
Unmark'd, unhonour'd at a monarch's gate. *Pope.*

UNMA'RRIED. *adj.* Having no husband, or no wife.
Unmarried men are best friends, best masters, best servants, but not always best subjects, for they are light to run away. *Bacon.*
Husbands and wives, boys and *unmarry'd* maids. *Dryden.*

To UNMA'SK. *v. a.*
1. To strip of a mask.
2. To strip of any disguise.
With full cups they had *unmask'd* his soul. *Roscommon.*
Though in Greek or Latin they amuse us, yet a translation *unmasks* them, whereby the cheat is transparent. *Glanville.*

To UNMA'SK. *v. n.* To put off the mask.
My husband bids me; now I will *unmask*.
This is that face was worth the looking on. *Shakespeare.*

UNMA'SKED. *adj.* Naked; open to the view.
O I am yet to learn a statesman's art;
My kindness, and my hate *unmask'd* I wear,
For friends to trust, and enemies to fear. *Dryden.*

UNMA'STERABLE. *adj.* Unconquerable; not to be subdued.
The fœtor is *unmasterable* by the natural heat of man; not to be dulcified by concoction, beyond unsavoury condition. *Brown's Vulgar Errours.*

UNMA'STERED. *adj.*
1. Not subdued.
2. Not conquerable.
Weigh what loss your honour may sustain, if you
Or lose your heart, or your chaste treasure open
To his *unmaster'd* importunity. *Shakesp. Hamlet.*
He cannot his *unmaster'd* grief sustain,
But yields to rage, to madness and disdain. *Dryden.*

UNMA'TCHABLE. *adj.* Unparalelled; unequalled.
The soul of Christ, that saw in this life the face of God, was, through so visible presence of Deity, filled with all manner of graces and virtues in that *unmatchable* degree of perfection; for which, of him we read it written, that God with the oil of gladness anointed him. *Hooker, b. v.*
Most radiant, exquisite, and *unmatchable* beauty, tell me, if this be the lady of the house. *Shakespeare.*
England breeds very valiant creatures; their mastiffs are of *unmatchable* courage. *Shakesp. Hen. V.*

UNMA'TCHED. *adj.* Matchless; having no match, or equal.
That glorious day, which two such navies saw,
As each, *unmatch'd*, might to the world give law;
Neptune, yet doubtful whom he should obey,
Held to them both the trident of the sea. *Dryden.*

UNME'ANING. *adj.* Expressing no meaning.
With round, *unmeaning* face. *Pope.*

UNME'ANT. *adj.* Not intended.
The flying spear was after Ilus sent:
But Rhætus happen'd on a death *unmeant*. *Dryden.*

UNME'ASURABLE. *adj.* Boundless; unbounded.
Common mother! thou
Whose womb *unmeasurable*, and infinite breast
Teems and feeds all. *Shakesp. Timon of Athens.*
You preserved the lustre of that noble family, which the *unmeasurable* profusion of ancestors had eclipsed. *Swift.*

UNMEA'SURED. *adj.*
1. Immense; infinite.
Does the sun dread th' imaginary sign,
Nor farther yet in liquid æther roll,
'Till he has gain'd some unfrequented place,
Lost to the world, in vast, *unmeasur'd* space. *Blackmore.*
2. Not measured; plentiful.
From him all perfect good, *unmeasur'd* out, descends. *Milton.*

UNME'DITATED. *adj.* Not formed by previous thought.
Neither various style,
Nor holy rapture, wanted they, to praise
Their maker, in fit strains pronounc'd, or sung
Unmeditated. *Milton's Par. Lost, b. v.*

UNME'DLED *with. adj.* Not touched; not altered.
The flood-gate is opened and closed for six days, continuing other ten days *unmedled with.* *Carew.*

UNMEE'T. *adj.* Not fit; not proper; not worthy.
Madam was young, *unmeet* the rule of sway. *Spenser.*
I am *unmeet*;
For I cannot flatter thee in pride. *Shakespeare.*
O my father!
Prove you that any man with me convers'd
At hours *unmeet*, refuse me, hate me. *Shakespeare.*
Alack! my hand is sworn
Ne'er to pluck thee from thy thorn;
Vow, alack! for youth *unmeet*,
Youth so apt to pluck a sweet. *Shakespeare.*
Its fellowship *unmeet* for thee,
Good reason was thou freely should'st dislike. *Milton.*
That muse desires the last, the lowest place,
Who, though *unmeet*, yet touch'd the trembling string
For the fair fame of Anne. *Prior.*

UNME'LLOWED. *adj.* Not fully ripened.
His years but young, but his experience old;
His head *unmellow'd*, but his judgment ripe. *Shakespeare.*

UNME'LTED. *adj.* Undissolved by heat.
Snow on Ætna does *unmelted* lie,
Whence rowling flames, and scatter'd cinders fly. *Waller.*

UNME'NTIONED. *adj.* Not told; not named.
They left not any error in government *unmentioned* or unpressed, with the sharpest and most pathetical expressions. *Clar.*
Oh let me here sink down
Into my grave, *unmention'd* and unmourn'd! *Southern.*

UNME'RCHANTABLE. *adj.* Unsaleable; not vendible.
They feed on salt, *unmerchantable* pilchard. *Carew.*

UNME'RCIFUL. *adj.*
1. Cruel; severe; inclement.
For the humbling of this *unmerciful* pride in the eagle, providence has found out a way. *L'Estrange.*
The pleasant lustre of flame delights children at first; but when experience has convinced them, by the exquisite pain it has put them to, how cruel and *unmerciful* it is, they are afraid to touch it. *Locke.*
Whatsoever doctrine represents God as unjust and *unmerciful*, cannot be from God, because it subverts the very foundation of religion. *Rogers's Sermons.*
2. Unconscionable; exorbitant.
Not only the peace of the honest, unwriting subject was daily molested, but *unmerciful* demands were made of his applause. *Pope.*

UNME'RCIFULLY. *adv.* Without mercy; without tenderness.
A little warm fellow fell most *unmercifully* upon his Gallick majesty. *Addison.*

UNME'RCIFULNESS. *n. s.* Inclemency; cruelty; want of tenderness.
Consider the rules of friendship, lest justice turn into *unmercifulness*. *Taylor's Rule of Living Holy.*

UNME'RITED. *adj.* Not deserved; not obtained otherwise than by favour.
This day, in whom all nations shall be blest,
Favour *unmerited* by me, who sought
Forbidden knowledge by forbidden means. *Milton.*
A tottering pinnacle *unmerited* greatness is. *Gov. Tongue.*

UNME'RITABLE. *adj.* Having no desert. Not in use.
Your love deserves my thanks; but my desert
Unmeritable, shuns your high request. *Shakespeare.*

UNME'RITEDNESS. *n. s.* State of being undeserved.
As to the freeness or *unmeritedness* of God's love; we need but consider, that we so little could at first deserve his love, that he loved us even before we had a being. *Boyle.*

UNMI'LKED. *adj.* Not milked.
The ewes still folded, with distended thighs,
Unmilk'd, lay bleating in distressful cries. *Pope.*

UNMI'NDED. *adj.* Not heeded; not regarded.

He was
A poor, *unminded* outlaw, ſneaking home;
My father gave him welcome to the ſhore. *Shakeſpeare.*
He, after Eve ſeduc'd, *unminded*, ſlunk
Into the wood. *Milton.*

UNMI'NDFUL. *adj.* Not heedful; not regardful; negligent; inattentive.

Worldly wights in place
Leave off their work, *unmindful* of this law,
To gaze on them. *Fairy Queen.*

I ſhall let you ſee, that I am not *unmindful* of the things you would have me remember. *Boyle.*

Who now enjoys thee, credulous, all gold;
Who always vacant, always amiable,
Hopes thee; of flattering gales
Unmindful. *Milton.*

Unmindful of the crown that virtue gives,
After this mortal change, to her true ſervants,
Amongſt the enthroned gods on ſainted ſeats. *Milton.*

He, not *unmindful* of his uſual art,
Firſt in diſſembled fire attempts to part;
Then roaring beaſts he tries. *Dryden's Virgil.*

When thoſe who diſlike the conſtitution, are ſo very zealous in their offers for the ſervice of their country, they are not wholly *unmindful* of their party, or themſelves. *Swift.*

To UNMI'NGLE. *v. a.* To ſeparate things mixed.

It will *unmingle* the wine from the water; the wine aſcending, and the water deſcending. *Bacon's Nat. Hiſt.*

UNMI'NGLED. *adj.* Pure; not vitiated by any thing mingled.

As eaſy may'ſt thou fall
A drop of water in the breaking gulph,
And take *unmingled* thence your drop again,
Without addition or diminiſhing. *Shakeſpeare.*

Springs on high hills, are pure and *unmingled.* *Bacon.*

His cup is full of pure and *unmingled* ſorrow. *Taylor.*

Veſſels of *unmingled* wine,
Mellifluous, undecaying, and divine. *Pope.*

UNMI'NGLEABLE. *adj.* Not ſuſceptive of mixture. Not uſed.

The ſulphur of the concrete loſes by the fermentation, the property of oil being *unmingleable* with water. *Boyle.*

The *unmingleable* liquors retain their diſtinct ſurfaces. *Boyle.*

UNMI'RY. *adj.* Not fouled with dirt.

Paſs, with ſafe, *unmiry* feet,
Where the rais'd pavement leads athwart the ſtreet. *Gay.*

UNMI'TIGATED. *adj.* Not ſoftened.

With publick accuſation, uncovered ſlander, *unmitigated* rancour. *Shakeſpeare's Much Ado about Nothing.*

UNMI'XED. } *adj.* Not mingled with any thing; pure; not
UNMI'XT. } corrupted by additions.

Thy commandment all alone ſhall live
Within the book and volume of my brain,
Unmixt with baſer matter. *Shakeſpeare's Hamlet.*

It exhibits a mixture of new conceits and old; whereas the inſtauration gives the new, *unmixed* otherwiſe than with ſome little aſperſion of the old. *Bacon.*

Thy conſtant quiet fills my peaceful breaſt,
With *unmix'd* joy, uninterrupted reſt. *Roſcommon.*

What is glory but the blaze of fame,
The people's praiſe, if always praiſe *unmixt?* *Milton.*

Thy Arethuſan ſtream remains unſoil'd;
Unmixt with foreign filth, and *undefil'd.* *Dryden.*

Together out they fly,
Inſeparable now, the truth and lie:
And this or that *unmixt*, no mortal ear ſhall find. *Pope.*

UNMO'ANED. *adj.* Not lamented.

Fatherleſs diſtreſs was left *unmoan'd*;
Your widow dolours likewiſe be unwept. *Shakeſpeare.*

UNMOI'ST. *adj.* Not wet.

Volatile Hermes, fluid and *unmoiſt*,
Mounts on the wings of air. *Philips.*

UNMOI'STENED. *adj.* Not made wet.

The incident light that meets with a groſſer liquor, will have its beams more or leſs interruptedly reflected, than they would be if the body had been *unmoiſtened.* *Boyle.*

UNMOLE'STED. *adj.* Free from diſturbance; free from external troubles.

The fowls of the air, and the beaſts of the field, are ſupplied with every thing, *unmoleſted* by hopes or fears. *Rogers.*

Cleopatra was read o'er,
While Scot, and Wake, and twenty more,
That teach one to deny one'ſelf,
Stood *unmoleſted* on the ſhelf. *Prior.*

Safe on my ſhore each *unmoleſted* ſwain,
Shall tend the flocks, or reap the bearded grain. *Pope.*

To UNMOO'R. *v. a.*

1. To looſe from land, by taking up the anchors.

We with the riſing morn our ſhips *unmoor'd*,
And brought our captives, and our ſtores aboard. *Pope.*

2. Prior ſeems to have taken it for caſting anchor.

Soon as the Britiſh ſhips *unmoor*,
And jolly long-boat rows to ſhore. *Prior.*

UNMO'RALIZED. *adj.* Untutored by morality.

This is cenſured as the mark of a diſſolute and *unmoralized* temper. *Norris.*

UNMO'RTGAGED. *adj.* Not mortgaged.

Is there one God unſworn to my deſtruction?
The leaſt, *unmortgag'd* hope? for, if there be,
Methinks I cannot fall. *Dryden's All for Love.*

This he has repeated ſo often, that at preſent there is ſcarce a ſingle gabel *unmortgaged.* *Addiſon's Remarks on Italy.*

UNMO'RTIFIED. *adj.* Not ſubdued by ſorrow and ſeverities.

If our conſcience reproach us with *unmortified* ſin, our hope is the hope of an hypocrite. *Rogers's Sermons.*

UNMO'VEABLE. *adj.* Such as cannot be removed or altered.

Wherein conſiſts the preciſe and *unmoveable* boundaries of that ſpecies. *Locke.*

UNMO'VED. *adj.*

1. Not put out of one place into another.

Vipers that do fly
The light, oft under *unmov'd* ſtalls do lie. *May's Virgil.*
Nor winds, nor winter's rage o'erthrows
His bulky body, but *unmov'd* he grows. *Dryden.*

Cheſs-men, ſtanding on the ſame ſquares of the cheſs-board, we ſay they are all in the ſame place, or *unmoved*; though, perhaps, the cheſs-board hath been carried out of one room into another. *Locke.*

2. Not changed in reſolution.

Among innumerable falſe, *unmov'd*,
Unſhaken, unſeduc'd. *Milton.*

3. Not affected; not touched with any paſſion.

Cæſar, the world's great maſter and his own,
Unmov'd, ſuperior ſtill in ev'ry ſtate,
And ſcarce deteſted in his country's fate. *Pope.*

4. Unaltered by paſſion.

I meant to meet
My fate with face *unmov'd*, and eyes unwet. *Dryden.*

UNMO'VING. *adj.*

1. Having no motion.

The celeſtial bodies, without impulſe, had continued unactive, *unmoving* heaps of matter. *Cheyne's Phil. Prin.*

2. Having no power to raiſe the paſſions; unaffecting.

To UNMO'ULD. *v. a.* To change as to the form.

Its pleaſing poiſon
The viſage quite transforms of him that drinks,
And the inglorious likeneſs of a beaſt
Fixes inſtead, *unmoulding* reaſon's mintage,
Character'd in the face. *Milton.*

UNMO'URNED. *adj.* Not lamented; not deplored.

O let me here ſink down
Into my grave unmention'd and *unmourn'd.* *Southern.*

To UNMU'ZZLE. *v. a.* To looſe from a muzzle.

Now *unmuzzle* your wiſdom. *Shakeſpeare.*
Have you not ſet mine honour at the ſtake,
And baited it with all th' *unmuzzl'd* thoughts
Thy tyrannous heart can think? *Shakeſp. Twelfth Night.*

To UNMU'FFLE. *v. a.* To put off a covering from the face.

Unmuffle, ye faint ſtars! and thou, fair moon,
That wont'ſt to love the traveller's benizon,
Stoop thy pale viſage through an amber cloud,
And diſinherit chaos, that reigns here
In double night, of darkneſs and of ſhades. *Milton.*

UNMU'SICAL. *adj.* Not harmonious; not pleaſing by ſound.

Let argument bear no *unmuſical* ſound,
Nor jars interpoſe, ſacred friendſhip to grieve. *B. Johnſon.*

One man's ambition wants ſatisfaction, another's avarice, a third's ſpleen; and this diſcord makes up the very *unmuſical* harmony of our murmurs. *Decay of Piety.*

UNNA'MED. *adj.* Not mentioned.

Author of evil, unknown till thy revolt,
Unnam'd in heav'n. *Milton's Par. Loſt, b.* vi.

UNNA'TURAL. *adj.*

1. Contrary to the laws of nature; contrary to the common inſtincts.

Her offence
Muſt be of ſuch *unnatural* degree,
That monſters it. *Shakeſp. K. Lear.*

People of weak heads on the one hand, and vile affections on the other, have made an *unnatural* divorce between being wiſe and good. *Glanville's Sceps.*

'Tis irreverent and *unnatural*, to ſcoff at the infirmities of old age. *L'Eſtrange.*

2. Acting without the affections implanted by nature.

Rome, whoſe gratitude
Tow'rds her deſerving children, is enroll'd
In Jove's own book, like an *unnatural* dam,
Should now eat up her own. *Shakeſpeare's Coriolanus.*

If the tyrant were, to a ſon ſo noble, ſo *unnatural*,
What will he be to us? *Denham's Sophy.*

3. Forced;

3. Forced; not agreeable to the real state of persons or things.

They admire only glittering trifles, that in a serious poem are nauseous, because they are *unnatural.* Would any man, who is ready to die for love, describe his passion like Narcissus? *Dryden.*

In an heroic poem, two kinds of thoughts are carefully to be avoided; the first, are such as are affected and *unnatural*; the second, such as are mean and vulgar. *Addison.*

UNNA'TURALNESS. *n. s.* Contrariety to nature.

The God, which is the God of nature, doth never teach *unnaturalness.* *Sidney.*

UNNA'TURALLY. *adv.* In opposition to nature.

All the world have been frighted with an apparition of their own fancy, or they have most *unnaturally* conspired to cozen themselves. *Tillotson.*

UNNA'VIGABLE. *adj.* Not to be passed by vessels; not to be navigated.

Pindar's *unnavigable* song,
Like a swift stream from mountains pours along. *Cowley.*

Some who the depths of eloquence have found,
In that *unnavigable* stream were drown'd. *Dryden.*

Let wit her sails, her oars let wisdom lend;
The helm let politick experience guide:
Yet cease to hope thy short-liv'd bark shall ride
Down spreading fate's *unnavigable* tide. *Prior.*

The Indian seas were believ'd to be *unnavigable.* *Arbuthnot.*

UNNE'CESSARILY. *adv.* Without necessity; without need; needlessly.

To abrogate, without constraint of manifest harm thereby arising, had been to alter *unnecessarily*, in their judgment, the antient, received custom of the whole church. *Hooker.*

'Tis highly imprudent in the greatest of men, *unnecessarily* to provoke the meanest. *L'Estrange.*

These words come in without any connexion with the story, and consequently *unnecessarily.* *Broome.*

UNNE'CESSARINESS. *n. s.* Needlessness.

These are such extremes as afford no middle for industry to exist, hope being equally out-dated by the desperateness or *unnecessariness* of an undertaking. *Decay of Piety.*

UNNE'CESSARY. *adj.* Needless; not wanted; useless.

The doing of things *unnecessary*, is many times the cause why the most necessary are not done. *Hooker, b. v.*

Thou whoreson zed; thou *unnecessary* letter. *Shakespeare.*

Let brave spirits, fitted for command by sea or land, not be laid by, as persons *unnecessary* for the time. *Bacon.*

Lay that *unnecessary* fear aside;
Mine be the care new people to provide. *Dryden.*

Unnecessary coinage, as well as *unnecessary* revival of words, runs into affectation; a fault to be avoided on either hand. *Dryden.*

They did not only shun persecution, but affirmed, that it was *unnecessary* for their followers to bear their religion through such fiery trials. *Addison.*

The reader can easily discover how the plot will be unravelled at last; but the *unnecessary* intricacies in unravelling it, still remain to be accounted for. *Shakesp. Illustrated.*

UNNE'IGHBOURLY. *adj.* Not kind; not suitable to the duties of a neighbour.

Parnassus is but a barren mountain, and its inhabitants make it more so, by their *unneighbourly* deportment. *Garth.*

UNNE'IGHBOURLY. *adv.* In a manner not suitable to a neighbour; with malevolence; with mutual mischief.

These two christian armies might combine
The blood of malice in a vein of league,
And not to spend it so *unneighbourly.* *Shakespeare.*

UNNE'RVATE. *adj.* Weak; feeble. A bad word.

Scaliger calls them fine and lively in Musæus; but abject, *unnervate*, and unharmonious in Homer. *Broome.*

To UNNE'RVE. *v. a.* To weaken; to enfeeble.

The precepts are often so minute and full of circumstances, that they weaken and *unnerve* his verse. *Addison.*

UNNE'RVED. *adj.* Weak; feeble.

Pyrrhus at Priam drives, in rage strikes wide;
But with the whiff and wind of his fell sword,
Th' *unnerv'd* father falls. *Shakespeare's Hamlet.*

UNNE'TH. } UNNE'THES. } *adv.* [This is from un and eað, Saxon, *easy*; and ought therefore to be written *uneath.*] Scarcely; hardly; not without difficulty. Obsolete.

Diggon, I am so stiffe and stanke,
That *unneth* I may stand any more;
And how the western wind bloweth sore,
Beating the wither'd leaf from the tree. *Spenser.*

A shepherd's boy,
When winter's wasteful spight was almost spent,
Led forth his flocke, that had been long ypent;
So faint they waxe, and feeble in the fold,
That now *unnethes* their feet could 'em uphold. *Spenser.*

UNNO'BLE. *adj.* Mean; ignominious; ignoble.

I have offended reputation;
A most *unnoble* swerving. *Shakesp. Ant. and Cleopatra.*

UNNO'TED. *adj.* Not observed; not regarded; not heeded; not celebrated.

They may jest,
'Till their own scorn return to them *unnoted.* *Shakespeare.*

He drew his seat familiar to her side,
Far from the suitor train, a brutal crowd;
Where the free guest *unnoted* might relate,
If haply conscious of his father's fate. *Pope.*

A shameful fate now hides my hopeless head,
Unwept, *unnoted*, and for ever dead. *Pope's Odyssey.*

UNNU'MBERED. *adj.* Innumerable.

The skies are painted with *unnumber'd* sparks;
They are all fire, and every one doth shine. *Shakespeare.*

Our bodies are but the anvils of pain and diseases, and our minds the hives of *unnumbered* cares and passions. *Raleigh.*

Of various forms, *unnumber'd* spectres, more
Centaurs, and double shapes, besiege the door. *Dryden.*

Pitchy and dark the night sometimes appears;
Our joy and wonder sometimes she excites,
With stars *unnumber'd.* *Prior.*

UNOBSE'QUIOUSNESS. *n. s.* Incompliance; disobedience.

They make one man's particular failings, confining laws to others; and convey them, as such, to their succeeders, who are bold to misname all *unobsequiousness* to their incogitancy, presumption. *Brown's Vulgar Errours.*

UNOBE'YED. *adj.* Not obeyed.

Not leave
Unworshipp'd, *unobey'd*, the throne supreme. *Milton.*

UNOBJE'CTED. *adj.* Not charged as a fault, or contrary argument.

What will he leave *unobjected* to Luther, when he makes it his crime that he defied the devil. *Atterbury.*

UNOBNO'XIOUS. *adj.* Not liable; not exposed to any hurt.

So *unobnoxious* now, she hath buried both;
For none to death sins, that to sin is loth. *Donne.*

In fight they stood
Unwearied, *unobnoxious* to be pain'd. *Milton's Par. Lost.*

UNOBSE'RVABLE. *adj.* Not to be observed; not discoverable.

A piece of glass reduced to powder, the same which, when entire, freely transmitted the beams of light, acquiring by confusion, a multitude of minute surfaces, reflects, in a confused manner, little and singly *unobservable* images of the lucid body, that from a diaphanous, it degenerates into a white body. *Boyle on Colours.*

UNOBSE'RVANT. *adj.*

1. Not obsequious.
2. Not attentive.

The *unobservant* multitude may have some general, confused apprehensions of a beauty, that gilds the outside frame of the universe. *Glanville.*

UNOBSE'RVED. *adj.* Not regarded; not attended to; not heeded; not minded.

The motion in the minute parts of any solid body, which is the principal cause of violent motion, though *unobserved*, passeth without sound. *Bacon's Nat. Hist.*

They the son of God, our Saviour meek,
Sung victor; and from heav'nly feast refresh'd,
Brought on his way with joy; he, *unobserv'd*,
Home to his mother's house private return'd. *Milton.*

Every unwonted meteor is portentous, and the appearance of any *unobserved* star, some divine prognostick. *Glanville.*

Such was the Boyne, a poor, inglorious stream,
That in Hibernian vales obscurely stray'd,
And, *unobserv'd*, in wild meanders play'd. *Addison.*

Had I err'd in this case, it had been a well-meant mistake, and might have pass'd *unobserved.* *Atterbury.*

UNOBSE'RVING. *adj.* Inattentive; not heedful.

His similitudes are not placed, as our *unobserving* criticks tell us, in the heat of any action; but commonly in its declining. *Dryden.*

UNOBSTRU'CTED. *adj.* Not hindered; not stopped.

Unobstructed matter flies away,
Ranges the void, and knows not where to stay. *Blackmore.*

UNOBSTRU'CTIVE. *adj.* Not raising any obstacle.

Why should he halt at either station? why
Not forward run in *unobstructive* sky? *Blackmore.*

UNOBTA'INED. *adj.* Not gained; not acquired.

As the will doth now work upon that object by desire, which is motion towards the end, as yet *unobtained*: so likewise upon the same hereafter received, it shall work also by love. *Hooker.*

UNO'BVIOUS. *adj.* Not readily occurring.

Of all the metals, not any so constantly discloseth its *unobvious* colour, as copper. *Boyle on Colours.*

UNO'CCUPIED. *adj.* Unpossessed.

If we shall discover further to the north pole, we shall find all that tract not to be vain, useless, or *unoccupied.* *Ray.*

The fancy hath power to create them in the sensories, then *unoccupied* by external impressions. *Grew's Cosmology.*

UNO'FFERED. *adj.* Not proposed to acceptance.

For the sad business of Ireland, he could not express a greater sense, there being nothing left on his part *unoffered* or undone. *Clarendon.*

UNOFFE'NDING. *adj.*

1. Harmless; innocent.

Thy *unoffending* life I could not save;
Nor weeping could I follow to thy grave. *Dryden.*

2. Sinless; pure from fault.

If those holy and *unoffending* spirits, the angels, veil their faces before the throne of his majesty; with what awe should we, sinful dust and ashes, approach that infinite power we have so grievously offended. *Rogers's Sermons.*

To UNO'IL. *v. a.* To free from oil.

A tight maid, ere he for wine can ask,
Guesses his meaning, and *unoils* the flask. *Dryden.*

UNO'PENING. *adj.* Not opening.

Benighted wanderers, the forest o'er,
Curse the sav'd candle, and *unopening* door. *Pope.*

UNO'PERATIVE. *adj.* Producing no effects.

The wishing of a thing is not properly the willing of it; but an imperfect velleity, and imports no more than an idle, *unoperative* complacency in the end, with a direct abhorrence of the means. *South's Sermons.*

UNOPPO'SED. *adj.* Not encountered by any hostility or obstruction.

Proud, art thou met? thy hope was to have reach'd
The height of thy aspiring *unoppos'd*,
The throne of God unguarded. *Milton's Par. Lost.*

To every nobler portion of the town,
The curling billows roll their restless tide:
In parties now they struggle up and down,
As armies, *unoppos'd*, for prey divide. *Dryden.*

The people, like a headlong torrent go,
And ev'ry dam they break or overflow:
But *unoppos'd* they either lose their force,
Or wind in volumes to their former course. *Dryden.*

UNO'RDERLY. Disordered; irregular.

Since some ceremonies must be used, every man would have his own fashion; whereof what other would be the issue, but infinite distraction, and *unorderly* confusion in the church. *Sanderson.*

UNO'RDINARY. *adj.* Uncommon; unusual.

I do not know how they can be excused from murder, who kill monstrous births, because of an *unordinary* shape, without knowing whether they have a rational soul or no. *Locke.*

UNO'RGANIZED. *adj.* Having no parts instrumental to the nourishment of the rest.

It is impossible for any organ to regulate itself: much less may we refer this regulation to the animal spirits, an *unorganized* fluid. *Grew's Cosmology.*

UNORI'GINAL. } *adj.* Having no birth; ungenerated.
UNORI'GINATED. }

I toil'd out my uncouth passage, forc'd to ride
Th' untractable abyss, plung'd in the womb
Of *unoriginal* night, and chaos wild. *Milton's Par. Lost.*

In scripture, Jehovah signifies, that God is underived, *unoriginated*, and self-existent. *Stephens's Sermons.*

UNO'RTHODOX. *adj.* Not holding pure doctrine.

A fat benefice became a crime against its incumbent; and he was sure to be *unorthodox*, that was worth the plundering. *Decay of Piety.*

UNO'WED. *adj.* Having no owner.

England now is left
To tug and scramble, and to part by th' teeth
The *unowed* interest of proud, swelling state. *Shakespeare.*

UNO'WNED. *adj.*

1. Having no owner.

2. Not acknowledged.

Of night or loneliness it recks me not;
I fear the dread events that dog them both,
Least some ill-greeting touch attempt the person
Of our *unowned* sister. *Milton.*

Oh happy, *unown'd* youths! your limbs can bear
The scorching dog-star, and the winter's air;
While the rich infant, nurs'd with care and pain,
Thirsts with each heat, and coughs with ev'ry rain. *Gay.*

To UNPA'CK. *v. a.*

1. To disburden; to exonerate.

I, the son of a dear father murther'd,
Must, like a whore, *unpack* my heart with words. *Shakesp.*

2. To open any thing bound together.

He had a great parcel of glasses packed up, which, when he had *unpacked*, a great many cracked of themselves. *Boyle.*

UNPA'CKED. *adj.* Not collected by unlawful artifices.

The knight
Resolv'd to leave him to the fury
Of justice, and an *unpack'd* jury. *Hudibras.*

UNPA'ID. *adj.*

1. Not discharged.

Receive from us knee tribute not *unpaid*. *Milton.*

Nor hecatomb unslain, nor vows *unpaid*;
On Greeks, accurs'd, this dire confusion bring. *Dryden.*

What can atone, oh ever-injur'd shade!
Thy fate unpity'd, and thy rites *unpaid*? *Pope.*

2. Not receiving dues or debts.

How often are relations neglected, and tradesmen *unpaid*, for the support of this vanity? *Collier.*

Th' embroider'd suit, at least, he deem'd his prey;
That suit, an *unpaid* taylor snatch'd away. *Pope.*

3. UNPA'ID *for*. That for which the price is not yet given; taken on trust.

Richer, than doing nothing for a bauble;
Prouder, than rustling in *unpaid for* silk. *Shakespeare.*

UNPA'INED. *adj.* Suffering no pain.

Too unequal work we find,
Against unequal arms to fight in pain;
Against *unpain'd*, impassive. *Milton's Par. Lost.*

UNPA'INFUL. *adj.* Giving no pain.

That is generally called hard, which will put us to pain, sooner than change figure; and that soft, which changes the situation of its parts, upon an easy and *unpainful* touch. *Locke.*

UNPA'LATABLE. *adj.* Nauseous; disgusting.

The man who laugh'd but once to see an ass
Mumbling to make the cross-grain'd thistles pass,
Might laugh again to see a jury chaw
The prickles of *unpalatable* law. *Dryden.*

A good man will be no more disturbed at the methods of correction, than by seeing his friend take *unpalatable* physick. *Collier on Kindness.*

UNPA'RAGONED. *adj.* Unequalled; unmatched.

Either your *unparagon'd* mistress is dead, or she's out-priz'd by a trifle. *Shakespeare's Cymbeline.*

UNPARA'LLELED. *adj.* Not matched; not to be matched; having no equal.

I have been
The book of his good acts, whence men have read
His fame, *unparallelled*, haply amplified. *Shakespeare.*

Who had thought this clime had held
A deity so *unparallell'd*? *Milton's Arcades.*

The father burst out again in tears, upon receiving this instance of an *unparallelled* fidelity from one, who he thought had given herself up to the possession of another. *Addison.*

O fact *unparallell'd*! O Charles! O best of kings!
What stars their black, disastrous influence shed
On thy nativity? *Phillips.*

UNPA'RDONABLE. *adj.* [*impardonable*, Fr.] Irremissible.

It was thought in him an *unpardonable* offence to alter any thing: in us as intolerable, that we suffer any thing to remain unaltered. *Hooker.*

Oh, tis a fault too *unpardonable*. *Shakespeare.*

The kinder the master, the more *unpardonable* is the traitor. *L'Estrange.*

Consider how *unpardonable* the refusal of so much grace must render us. *Rogers's Sermons.*

UNPA'RDONABLY. *adv.* Beyond forgiveness.

Luther's conscience turns these reasonings upon him, and infers, that Luther must have been *unpardonably* wicked in using masses for fifteen years. *Atterbury.*

UNPA'RDONED. *adj.*

1. Not forgiven.

How know we that our souls shall not this night be required, laden with those *unpardoned* sins, for which we proposed to repent tomorrow. *Rogers's Sermons.*

2. Not discharged; cancelled by a legal pardon.

My returning into England *unpardoned*, hath destroyed that opinion. *Raleigh.*

UNPA'RDONING. *adj.* Not forgiving.

Curse on th' *unpard'ning* prince, whom tears can draw
To no remorse; who rules by lion's law;
And deaf to pray'rs, by no submission bow'd,
Rends all alike, the penitent and proud. *Dryden.*

UNPA'RLIAMENTARINESS. *n. s.* Contrariety to the usage or constitution of parliament.

Sensible he was of that disrespect; reprehending them for the *unparliamentariness* of their remonstrance in print. *Clar.*

UNPA'RLIAMENTARY. *adj.* Contrary to the rules of parliament.

The secret of all this unprecedented proceeding in their masters, they must not impute to their freedom in debate, but to that *unparliamentary* abuse of setting individuals upon their shoulders, who were hated by God and man. *Swift.*

UNPA'RTED. *adj.* Undivided; not separated.

Too little it eludes the dazzl'd sight,
Becomes mix'd blackness, or *unparted* light. *Prior.*

UNPA'RTIAL. *adj.* Equal; honest. Not in use.

Clear evidence of truth, after a serious and *unpartial* examination. *Sanderson.*

UNPA'RTIALLY. *adv.* Equally; indifferently.

Deem it not impossible for you to err; sift *unpartially* your own hearts, whether it be force of reason, or vehemency of affection, which hath bred these opinions in you. *Hooker.*

UNPA'SSABLE. *adj.* Admitting no paſſage.

Every country, which ſhall not do according to theſe things, ſhall be made not only *unpaſſable* for men, but moſt hateful to wild beaſts. *Eſth.* xvi 24.

They are vaſt and *unpaſſable* mountains, which the labour and curioſity of no mortal has ever yet known. *Temple.*

Making a new ſtandard for money, muſt make all money which is lighter than that ſtandard, *unpaſſable.* *Locke.*

You ſwell yourſelf as though you were a man of learning already; you are thereby building a moſt *unpaſſable* barrier againſt all improvement. *Watts's Improvement of the Mind.*

UNPA'SSIONATE. } *adj.* Free from paſſion; calm; impar-
UNPA'SSIONATED. } tial.

He attended the king into Scotland, and was ſworn a counſellor in that kingdom; where, as I have been inſtructed by *unpaſſionate* men, he did carry himſelf with ſingular ſweetneſs. *Wotton's Buckingham.*

More ſober heads have a ſet of miſconceits, which are as abſurd to an *unpaſſionated* reaſon, as thoſe to our unbiaſſed ſenſes. *Glanville's Sceps. c.* 13.

The rebukes, which their faults will make hardly to be avoided, ſhould not only be in ſober, grave, and *unpaſſionate* words, but alſo alone and in private. *Locke on Education.*

UNPA'SSIONATELY. *adv.* Without paſſion.

Make us *unpaſſionately* to ſee the light of reaſon and religion. *K. Charles.*

UNPA'THED. *adj.* Untracked; unmarked by paſſage.

A courſe more promiſing,
Than a wild dedication of yourſelves
To *unpath'd* waters, undream'd ſhores; moſt certain
To miſeries enough. *Shakeſp. Winter Tale.*

UNPA'WNED. *adj.* Not given to pledge.

He roll'd his eyes, that witneſs'd huge diſmay,
Where yet, *unpawn'd*, much learned lumber lay. *Pope.*

To UNPA'Y. *v. a.* To undo. A low ludicrous word.

Pay her the debt you owe her, and *unpay* the villainy you have done her: the one you may do with ſterling money, and the other with current repentance. *Shakeſpeare.*

UNPEA'CEABLE. *adj.* Quarrelſome; inclined to diſturb the tranquillity of others.

Lord, purge out of all hearts thoſe *unpeaceable*, rebellious, mutinous, and tyrannizing, cruel ſpirits; thoſe prides and haughtineſſes, judging and condemning, and deſpiſing of others. *Hammond's Fundamentals.*

The deſign is to reſtrain men from things, which make them miſerable to themſelves, *unpeaceable* and troubleſome to the world. *Tillotſon.*

To UNPE'G. *v. a.* To open any thing cloſed with a peg.

Unpeg the baſket on the houſe's top;
Let the birds fly. *Shakeſp. Hamlet.*

UNPE'NSIONED. *adj.* Not kept in dependance by a penſion.

Could penſion'd Boileau laſh in honeſt ſtrain
Flatt'rers and bigots, ev'n in Louis' reign;
And I not ſtrip the gilding off a knave,
Unplac'd, *unpenſion'd*, no man's heir or ſlave? *Pope.*

To UNPE'OPLE. *v. a.* To depopulate; to deprive of inhabitants.

The land
In antique times was ſavage wilderneſs,
Unpeopl'd, unmanur'd. *Fairy Queen.*

Shall war *unpeople* this my realm? *Shakeſpeare.*

To few unknown
Long after; now *unpeopl'd*, and untrod. *Milton.*

The lofty mountains feed the ſavage race,
Yet few, and ſtrangers in th' *unpeopl'd* place. *Dryden.*

He muſt be thirty-five years old, a doctor of the faculty, and eminent for his religion and honeſty; that his raſhneſs and ignorance may not *unpeople* the commonwealth. *Addiſon.*

UNPERCE'IVED. *adj.* Not obſerved; not heeded; not ſenſibly diſcovered; not known.

The aſhes, wind *unperceived* ſhakes off. *Bacon.*

He alone
To find where Adam ſhelter'd, took his way,
Not *unperceiv'd* of Adam. *Milton's Par. Loſt.*

Thus daily changing, by degrees I'd waſte,
Still quitting ground, by *unperceiv'd* decay,
And ſteal myſelf from life, and melt away. *Dryden.*

Unperceiv'd the heav'ns with ſtars were hung. *Dryden.*

Oft in pleaſing taſks we wear the day,
While ſummer ſuns roll *unperceiv'd* away. *Pope.*

UNPERCE'IVEDLY. *adv.* So as not to be perceived.

Some oleaginous particles, *unperceivedly*, aſſociated themſelves to it. *Boyle.*

UNPE'RFECT. *adj.* [*imparfait*, Fr. *imperfectus*, Lat.] Incomplete.

Apelles' picture of Alexander at Epheſus, and his Venus, which he left at his death *unperfect* in Chios, were the chiefeſt. *Peacham on Drawing.*

UNPE'RFECTNESS. *n. ſ.* Imperfection; incompleteneſs.

Virgil and Horace ſpying the *unperfectneſs* in Ennius and Plautus, by true imitation of Homer and Euripides, brought poetry to perfectneſs. *Aſcham's Schoolmaſter.*

UNPERFO'RMED. *adj.* Undone; not done.

A good law without execution, is like an *unperformed* promiſe. *Taylor's Rule of Holy Living.*

UNPE'RISHABLE. *adj.* Laſting to perpetuity; exempt from decay.

We are ſecured to reap in another world everlaſting, *unperiſhable* felicities. *Hammond's Fundamentals.*

UNPE'RJURED. *adj.* Free from perjury.

Beware of death; thou can'ſt not die *unperjur'd*,
And leave an unaccompliſh'd love behind.
Thy vows are mine. *Dryden.*

UNPERPLE'XED. *adj.* Diſentangled; not embarraſſed.

In learning, little ſhould be propoſed to the mind at once; and that being fully maſtered, proceed to the next adjoining part, yet unknown, ſimple, *unperplexed* propoſition. *Locke.*

UNPERSPI'RABLE. *adj.* Not to be emitted through the pores of the ſkin.

Bile is the moſt *unperſpirable* of animal fluids. *Arbuthnot.*

UNPERSUA'DABLE. *adj.* Inexorable; not to be perſuaded.

He, finding his ſiſter's *unperſuadable* melancholy, through the love of Amphialus, had for a time left her court. *Sidney.*

UNPE'TRIFIED. *adj.* Not turned to ſtone.

In many concreted plants, ſome parts remain *unpetrify'd*; that is, the quick and livelier parts remain as wood, and were never yet converted. *Brown's Vulgar Errours.*

UNPHILOSO'PHICAL. *adj.* Unſuitable to the rules of philoſophy, or right reaſon.

Your conceptions are *unphiloſophical.* You forget that the brain has a great many ſmall fibres in its texture; which, according to the different ſtrokes they receive from the animal ſpirits, awaken a correſpondent idea. *Collier.*

It became him who created them, to ſet them in order: and if he did ſo, it is *unphiloſophical* to ſeek for any other origin of the world, or to pretend that it might ariſe out of a chaos by the mere laws of nature. *Newton's Opticks.*

UNPHILOSO'PHICALLY. *adv.* In a manner contrary to the rules of right reaſon.

They forget that he is the firſt cauſe of all things, and diſcourſe moſt *unphiloſophically*, abſurdly, and unſuitably to the nature of an infinite being; whoſe influence muſt ſet the firſt wheel a-going. *South's Sermons.*

UNPHILOSO'PHICALNESS. *n. ſ.* Incongruity with philoſophy.

I could diſpenſe with the *unphiloſophicalneſs* of this their hypotheſis, were it not unchriſtian. *Norris.*

To UNPHILO'SOPHIZE. *v. a.* To degrade from the character of a philoſopher. A word made by *Pope.*

Our paſſions, our intereſts flow in upon us, and *unphiloſophize* us into mere mortals. *Pope.*

UNPIE'RCED. *adj.* Not penetrated; not pierced.

Th' *unpierc'd* ſhade imbrown'd the noontide bow'rs. *Milt.*

True Witney broad-cloth, with its ſhag unſhorn,
Unpierc'd, is in the laſting tempeſt worn. *Gay.*

UNPI'LLARED. *adj.* Diveſted of pillars.

See the cirque falls! th' *unpillar'd* temple nods!
Streets pav'd with heroes! Tiber choak'd with gods! *Pope.*

UNPI'LLOWED. *adj.* Wanting a pillow.

Perhaps ſome cold bank is her bolſter now,
Or 'gainſt the rugged bark of ſome broad elm,
Leans her *unpillow'd* head, fraught with ſad fears. *Milton.*

To UNPI'N. *v. a.* To open what is ſhut, or faſtened with a pin.

My love doth ſo approve him,
That even his ſtubbornneſs, his checks and frowns,
(Pr'ythee *unpin* me) have grace and favour in them. *Shakeſp.*

Unpin that ſpangled breaſt-plate which you wear,
That th' eyes of buſy fools may be ſtopt there. *Donne.*

Who is the honeſt man?
He that doth ſtill and ſtrongly good purſue,
To God, his neighbour, and himſelf moſt true:
Whom neither force, nor fawning can
Unpin, or wrench from giving all their due. *Herbert.*

UNPI'NKED. *adj.* Not marked with eyelet holes.

Gabriel's pumps were all *unpink'd* i' th' heel. *Shakeſpeare.*

UNPI'TIED. *adj.* Not compaſſionated; not regarded with ſympathetical ſorrow.

Richard yet lives; but at hand, at hand
Inſues his piteous and *unpitied* end. *Shakeſp. Rich.* III.

Rich in the world's opinion, and men's praiſe,
And full in all we cou'd deſire, but days:
He that is warn'd of this, and ſhall forbear
To vent a ſigh for him, or ſhed a tear;
May he live long ſcorn'd, and *unpity'd* fall,
And want a mourner at his funeral. *Bp. Corbet.*

But he whoſe words and fortunes diſagree,
Abſurd, *unpity'd*, grows a publick jeſt. *Roſcommon.*

He that does not ſecure himſelf of a ſtock of reputation in his greatneſs, ſhall moſt certainly fall *unpitied* in his adverſity. *L'Eſtrange.*

As the greateſt curſe that I can give,
Unpitied be depos'd, and after live. *Dryden's Aurenzebe.*

As some sad turtle his lost love deplores;
Thus, far from Delia, to the winds I mourn,
Alike unheard, *unpity'd*, and forlorn. *Pope.*
Passion *unpity'd*, and succesless love,
Plant daggers in my heart, and aggravate
My other griefs. *Addison's Cato.*

UNPI'TIFULLY. *adv.* Unmercifully; without mercy.
He beat him most pitifully.
—Nay, that he did not; he beat him most *unpitifully*. *Shakesp.*

UNPI'TYING. *adj.* Having no compassion.
To shame, to chains, or to a certain grave,
Lead on, *unpitying* guides, behold your slave. *Granville.*

UNPLA'CED. *adj.* Having no place of dependance.
Could pension'd Boileau lash in honest strain
Flatt'rers and bigots, ev'n in Louis' reign;
And I not strip the gilding off a knave,
Unplac'd, unpension'd? *Pope.*

UNPLA'GUED. *adj.* Not tormented.
Ladies, that have your feet
Unplagu'd with corns, we'll have a bout with you. *Shakesp.*

UNPLA'NTED. *adj.* Not planted; spontaneous.
Figs there *unplanted* through the fields do grow,
Such as fierce Cato did the Romans show. *Waller.*

UNPLA'USIBLE. *adj.* Not plausible; not such as has a fair appearance.

There was a mention of granting five subsidies; and that meeting being, upon very unpopular, and *unplausible* reasons, immediately dissolved, those five subsidies were exacted, as if an act had passed to that purpose. *Clarendon.*

I, under fair pretence of friendly ends,
And well-plac'd words of glosing courtesy,
Baited with reasons not *unplausible*,
Win me into the easy-hearted man,
And hug him into snares. *Milton.*

UNPLA'USIVE. *adj.* Not approving.
'Tis like he'll question me,
Why such *unplausive* eyes are bent on him. *Shakespeare.*

UNPLEA'SANT. *adj.* Not delighting; troublesome; uneasy.

Their skilful ears perceive certain harsh and *unpleasant* discords in the sound of our common prayer, such as the rules of divine harmony, such as the laws of God cannot bear. *Hooker.*

O sweet Portia!
Here are a few of the *unpleasant'st* words
That ever blotted paper. *Shakesp. Merch. of Venice.*

Wisdom is very *unpleasant* to the unlearned. *Ecclus.* v. 20.

Upon Adam's disobedience, God chased him out of paradise, the most delicious part of the earth, into some other, the most barren and *unpleasant*. *Woodward's Nat. Hist.*

UNPLEA'SANTLY. *adv.* Not delightfully; uneasily.

We cannot boast of good-breeding, and the art of life; but yet we don't live *unpleasantly* in primitive simplicity and good humour. *Pope.*

UNPLE'ASANTNESS. *n. s.* Want of qualities to give delight.

As for *unpleasantness* of sound, if it doth happen the good of men's souls doth deceive our ears, that we note it not, or arm them with patience to endure it. *Hooker.*

Many people cannot at all endure the air of London, not only for its *unpleasantness*, but for the suffocations which it causes. *Graunt's Bills of Mortality.*

All men are willing to skulk out of such company; the sober for the hazards, and the jovial for the *unpleasantness* of it. *Government of the Tongue.*

UNPLEA'SED. *adj.* Not pleased; not delighted.
Me rather had, my heart might feel your love,
Than my *unpleas'd* eye feel your courtesy. *Shakespeare.*
Condemn'd to live with subjects ever mute,
A salvage prince, *unpleas'd*, though absolute. *Dryden.*

UNPLEA'SING. *adj.* Offensive; disgusting; giving no delight.
Set to dress this garden:
How dares thy tongue sound this *unpleasing* news? *Shakesp.*

Hence the many mistakes, which have made learning so *unpleasing* and so unsuccessful. *Milton.*

If all those great painters, who have left us such fair platforms, had rigorously observed it in their figures, they had made things more regularly true, but withal very *unpleasing*. *Dryden's Dufresnoy.*

Howe'er *unpleasing* be the news you bring,
I blame not you, but your imperious king. *Dryden.*

UNPLI'ANT. *adj.* Not easily bent; not conforming to the will.

The chizel hath more glory than the pencil; that being so hard an instrument, and working upon so *unpliant* stuff, can yet leave strokes of so gentle appearance. *Wotton.*

UNPLO'WED. *adj.* Not plowed.

Good found land, that hath lain long *unplowed*. *Mortimer.*

To UNPLU'ME. *adj.* To strip of plumes; to degrade.

In the most ordinary phænomena in nature, we shall find enough to shame confidence, and *unplume* dogmatizing. *Glanv.*

UNPOE'TICAL. } *adj.* Not such as becomes a poet.
UNPOE'TICK. }

Nor for an epithet that fails,
Bite off your *unpoetick* nails.
Unjust! why you shou'd in such veins,
Reward your fingers for your brains? *Bp. Corbet.*

UNPO'LISHED. *adj.*

1. Not smoothed; not brightened by attrition.

Palladio, having noted in an old arch at Verona, some part of the materials cut in fine forms, and some *unpolished*, doth conclude, that the antients did leave the outward face of their marbles, or free-stone, without any sculpture, till they were laid in the body of the building. *Wotton.*

He affirms it to have been the antient custom of all the Greeks, to set up *unpolished* stones instead of images, to the honour of the gods. *Stillingfleet.*

2. Not civilized; not refined.

Finding new words,
Such as of old wise bards employ'd to make
Unpolish'd men their wild retreats forsake. *Waller.*
Those first *unpolish'd* matrons, big and bold,
Gave suck to infants of gigantick mould. *Dryden.*

UNPOLI'TE. *adj.* [*impoli*, Fr. *impolitus*, Lat.] Not elegant; not refined; not civil.

Discourses for the pulpit should be cast into a plain method, and the reasons ranged under the words, first, secondly, and thirdly; however they may be now fancied to sound *unpolite*, or unfashionable. *Watts's Improv. of the Mind.*

UNPOLLU'TED. *adj.* [*impollutus*, Lat.] Not corrupted; not defiled.

Lay her i' th' earth;
And from her fair and *unpolluted* flesh
May violets spring! *Shakespeare's Hamlet.*
'Till oft converse with heav'nly habitants
Begin to cast a beam on th' outward shape,
The *unpolluted* temple of the mind,
And turns it by degrees to the soul's essence,
'Till all be made immortal. *Milton.*
Though *unpolluted* yet with actual ill,
She half commits, who sins but in her will. *Dryden.*

UNPO'PULAR. *adj.* Not fitted to please the people.

The practices of these men, under the covert of feigned zeal, made the appearance of sincere devotion ridiculous and *unpopular*. *Addison's Freeholder*, Nº 37.

UNPO'RTABLE. *adj.* [*un* and *portable*.] Not to be carried.

Had their cables of iron chains had any great length, they had been *unportable*; and being short, the ships must have sunk at an anchor in any stream of weather or countertide. *Raleigh.*

UNPOSSE'SSED. *adj.* Not had; not obtained.

He claims the crown.——
—Is the chair empty? is the sword unsway'd?
Is the king dead? the empire *unpossess'd*? *Shakespeare.*
Such vast room in nature *unpossess'd*
By living soul, desert, and desolate,
Only to shine, yet scarce to contribute
Each orb a glimpse of light. *Milton.*
The cruel something *unpossess'd*,
Corrodes and leavens all the rest. *Prior.*

UNPOSSE'SSING. *adj.* Having no possession.
Thou *unpossessing* bastard, dost thou think,
That I would stand against thee? *Shakespeare.*

UNPRA'CTICABLE. *adj.* Not feasible.

I try'd such of the things that came into my thoughts, as were not in that place and time *unpracticable*. *Boyle.*

UNPRA'CTISED. *adj.* Not skilful by use and experience; raw; being in the state of a novice.

The full sum of me
Is an unlesson'd girl, unschool'd, *unpractis'd*. *Shakespeare.*
Unpractis'd, unprepar'd, and still to seek. *Milton.*
I am young, a novice in the trade;
The fool of love, *unpractis'd* to persuade,
And want the soothing arts. *Dryden.*
His tender eye, by too direct a ray,
Wounded, and flying from *unpractis'd* day. *Prior.*

UNPRAI'SED. *adj.* Not celebrated; not praised.

The land,
In antique times was salvage wilderness;
Unpeopl'd, unmanur'd, unprov'd, *unprais'd*. *Fairy Queen.*
If all the world
Sould in a pet of temperance feed on pulse,
Drink the clear stream, and nothing wear but frieze,
Th' all-giver would be unthank'd, wou'd be *unprais'd*. *Milt.*
If young African for fame
His wasted country freed from Punick rage,
The deed becomes *unprais'd*, the man at least,
And loses, though but verbal, his reward. *Milton.*
Nor pass *unprais'd* the vest and veil divine,
Which wand'ring foliage, and rich flow'rs entwine. *Dryden.*

UNPRECA'RIOUS. *adj.* Not dependent on another.

The stars, which grace the high expansion bright,
By their own beams, and *unprecarious* light,
At a vast distance from each other lie. *Blackmore.*

UNPRE'CEDENTED. *adj.* Not justifiable by any example.

The secret of all this *unprecedented* proceeding in their masters, they must not impute to freedom. *Swift.*

Fo

To Unpredi'ct. *v. a.* To retract prediction.
Means I must use, thou say'st prediction else
Will *unpredict*, and fail me of the throne. *Milton.*

Unprefe'rred. *adj.* Not advanced.
To make a scholar, keep him under, while he is young, or *unpreferred.* *Collier on Pride.*

Unpre'gnant. *adj.* Not prolifick.
This deed unshapes me quite, makes me *unpregnant*,
And dull to all proceedings. *Shakespeare.*

Unpreju'dicate. *adj.* Not prepossessed by any settled notions.
A pure mind in a chaste body, is the mother of wisdom, sincere principles, and *unprejudiciate* understanding. *Taylor.*

Unpre'judiced. *adj.* Free from prejudice; free from prepossession; not pre-occupied by opinion; void of preconceived notions.
The meaning of them may be so plain, as that any *unprejudiced* and reasonable man may certainly understand them. *Tillotson.*
Several, when they had informed themselves of our Saviour's history, and examined, with *unprejudiced* minds, the doctrines and manners of his disciples, were so struck, that they professed themselves of that sect. *Addison.*

Unprela'tical. Unsuitable to a prelate.
The archbishop of York, by such *unprelatical*, ignominious arguments, in plain terms advised him to pass that act. *Claren.*

Unpreme'ditated. *adj.* Not prepared in the mind beforehand.
Ask me what question thou canst possible,
And I will answer *unpremeditated.* *Shakesp. Hen.* VI.
He dictates to me slumb'ring; or inspires
Easy my *unpremeditated* verse. *Milton's Par. Lost.*
The flow of speech make *unpremeditated* harangues, or converse readily in languages that they are but little acquainted with. *Addison.*

Unprepa'red. *adj.*
1. Not fitted by previous measures.
Unpractis'd, *unprepar'd*, and still to seek. *Milton.*
To come *unprepar'd* before him, is an argument that we do not esteem God. *Duppa's Rules for Devotion.*
Fields are full of eyes, and woods have ears;
For this the wise are ever on their guard,
For, unforeseen, they say, is *unprepar'd.* *Dryden.*
2. Not made fit for the dreadful moment of departure.
I would not kill thy *unprepared* spirit;
No; heavens forefend *Shakesp. Othello.*
My *unprepar'd*, and unrepenting breath,
Was snatch'd away by the swift hand of death. *Roscommon.*

Unprepa'redness. *n. s.* State of being unprepared.
I believe my innocency and *unpreparedness* to assert my rights and honour, make me the most guilty in their esteem; who would not so easily have declared a war against me, if I had first assaulted them. *K. Charles.*

Unpreposse'ssed. Not prepossessed; not pre-occupied by notions.
The *unprepossessed* on the one hand, and the well-disposed on the other, are affected with a due fear of these things. *South.*
It finds the mind naked and *unprepossessed* with any former notions, and so easily and insensibly gains upon the assent. *South.*

Unpre'ssed. *adj.*
1. Not pressed.
Have I my pillow left *unpress'd* in Rome? *Shakespeare.*
In these soft shades, *unpress'd* by human feet,
Thy happy Phœnix keeps his balmy seat. *Tickell.*
2. Not inforced.
They left not any error in government unmentioned, or *unpressed*, with the sharpest and most pathetical expressions. *Clarendon.*

Unprete'nding. *adj.* Not claiming any distinctions.
Bad writers are not ridiculed, because ridicule ought to be a pleasure; but to undeceive and vindicate the honest and *unpretending* part of mankind from imposition. *Pope.*

Unpreva'iling. *adj.* Being of no force.
Throw to earth this *unprevailing* woe. *Shakesp. Hamlet.*

Unpreve'nted. *adj.*
1. Not previously hindered.
A pack of sorrows, which wou'd press you down,
If *unprevented*, to your timeless grave. *Shakespeare.*
1. Not preceded by any thing.
Thy grace
Comes *unprevented*, unimplor'd, unsought. *Milton.*

Unpri'ncely. *adj.* Unsuitable to a prince.
I could not have given my enemies greater advantages, than by so *unprincely* an inconstancy. *K. Charles.*

Unpri'nted. *adj.* Not printed.
Defer it, till you have finished these that are yet *unprinted.* *Pope.*

Unpri'ncipled. *adj.* Not settled in tenets or opinions.
I do not think my sister so to seek,
Or so *unprincipl'd* in virtue's book,
As that the single want of light and noise
Could stir the constant mood of her calm thoughts. *Milton.*
Others betake them to state affairs, with souls so *unprincipled* in virtue, and true generous breeding, that flattery, and court shifts, and tyrannous aphorisms, appear to them the highest points of wisdom. *Milton on Education.*

Unpri'sable. *adj.* Not valued; not of estimation.
A baubling vessel was he captain of,
For shallow draught and bulk *unprisable.* *Shakesp.*

Unprocla'imed. *adj.* Not notified by a publick declaration.
The Syrian king, who to surprize
One man, assassin-like, had levy'd war,
War *unproclaim'd* *Milton's Par. Lost, b.* xi.

Unpro'fitable. *adj.* Useless; serving no purpose.
The church being eased of *unprofitable* labours, needful offices may the better be attended. *Hooker.*
Should he reason with *unprofitable* talk? *Job* xv. 3.
My son Onesimus I have begotten in my bonds; which in time past was to thee *unprofitable*, but now profitable to thee and me. *Philemon* 11.
They receive aliment sufficient, and yet no more than they can well digest; and withal sweat out the coarsest and *unprofitablest* juice. *Bacon's Nat. Hist.*
It is better to fail honourably, than to survive in an *unprofitable* and unglorious life. *L'Estrange.*
Then they who brothers better claim disown,
Defraud their clients, and to lucre sold,
Sit brooding on *unprofitable* gold. *Dryden.*
With shame and sorrow fill'd,
For plotting an *unprofitable* crime. *Dryden.*
An ox that waits the coming blow,
Old and *unprofitable* to the plough. *Dryden.*
With tears so tender,
As any heart, but only her's, could move;
Trembling before her bolted doors he stood,
And there pour'd out th' *unprofitable* flood. *Dryden.*

Unpri'soned *adj.* Set free from confinement.
Several desires led parts away,
Water declin'd with earth, the air did stay;
Fire rose, and each from other but unty'd,
Themselves *unprison'd* were, and purify'd. *Donne.*

Unpri'zed. *adj.* Not valued.
Not all the dukes of wat'rish Burgundy,
Can buy this *unpriz'd*, precious maid of me. *Shakespeare.*

Unprofa'ned. *adj.* Not violated.
Unspoil'd shall be her arms, and *unprofan'd*
Her holy limbs with any human hand:
And in a marble tomb laid in her native land. *Dryden.*

Unpro'fitableness. *n. s.* Uselessness.
We are so persuaded of the *unprofitableness* of your science, that you can but leave us where you find us; but if you succeed, you increase the number of your party. *Addison.*

Unpro'fitably. *adv.* Uselessly; without advantage.
I shou'd not now *unprofitably* spend
Myself in words, or catch at empty hope,
By airy ways, for solid certainties. *B. Johnson.*
Our country's cause,
That drew our swords, now wrests 'em from our hands,
And bids us not delight in Roman blood
Unprofitably shed. *Addison's Cato.*

Unpro'fited. *adj.* Having no gain.
Be clamorous, and leap all civil bounds,
Rather than make *unprofited* return. *Shakespeare.*

Unproli'fick. *adj.* Barren; not productive.
Great rains drown many insects, and render their eggs *unprolifick*, or destroy them. *Hale.*

Unpro'mising. *adj.* Giving no promise of excellence; having no appearance of value.
If he be naturally listless and dreaming, this *unpromising* disposition is none of the easiest to be dealt with. *Locke.*
An attempt as difficult and *unpromising* of success, as if he should make the essay, to produce some new kinds of animals out of such senseless materials. *Bentley.*

Unprono'unced. *adj.* Not uttered; not spoken.
Mad'st imperfect words, with childish trips,
Half-pronounc'd, slide through my infant lips. *Milton.*

Unpro'per. *adj.* Not peculiar.
Millions nightly lie in those *unproper* beds,
Which they dare swear peculiar. *Shakesp. Othello.*

Unpro'perly. *adv.* Contrarily to propriety; improperly.
I kneel before thee, and *unproperly*
Shew duty as mistaken all the while
Between the child and parent. *Shakespeare's Coriolanus.*

Unpropi'tious. *adj.* Not favourable; inauspicious.
'Twas when the dog-star's *unpropitious* ray
Smote ev'ry brain, and wither'd ev'ry bay,
Sick was the sun. *Pope.*

Unpropo'rtioned. *adj.* Not suited to something else.
Give thy thoughts no tongue,
Nor any *unproportion'd* thought his act. *Shakespeare.*

Unpro'pped. *adj.* Not supported; not upheld.
He lives at random, carelessly diffus'd,
With languish'd head *unprop'd*,
As one past hope, abandon'd,
And by himself given over. *Milton's Agonistes.*

The

The fatal fang drove deep within his thigh,
And cut the nerves; the nerves no more sustain
The bulk; the bulk, *unpropp'd*, falls headlong on the plain. *Dryden.*

UNPROPO'SED. *adj.* Not proposed.
The means are *unpropos'd.* *Dryden.*

UNPRO'SPEROUS. *adj.* [*improsper*, Lat.] Unfortunate; not prosperous.
The winter had been very *unprosperous* and unsuccessful to the king. *Clarendon.*
Nought *unprosp'rous* shall thy ways attend,
Born with good omens, and with heav'n thy friend. *Pope.*

UNPRO'SPEROUSLY. *adj.* Unsuccessfully.
When a prince fights justly, and yet *unprosperously*, if he could see all those reasons for which God hath so ordered it, he would think it the most reasonable thing in the world. *Taylor.*

UNPROTE'CTED. *adj.* Not protected; not supported.
By woeful experience, thy both did learn, that to forsake the true God of heaven, is to fall into all such evils upon the face of the earth, as men, either destitute of grace divine, may commit, or *unprotected* from above, endure. *Hooker.*

UNPRO'VED. *adj.* Not evinced by arguments.
The land,
In antique times was savage wilderness,
Unpeopl'd, unmanur'd, *unproved*, unprais'd. *Spenser.*
There I found a fresh, *unproved* knight,
Whose manly hands, imbru'd in guilty blood,
Had never been. *Fairy Queen, b. i.*
There is much of what should be demonstrated, left *unproved* by those chymical experiments. *Boyle.*

To UNPROVI'DE. *v. a.* To divest of resolution or qualifications.
I'll not expostulate with her, lest
Her beauty *unprovide* my mind again. *Shakesp. Othello.*
Prosperity inviting every sense,
With various arts to *unprovide* my mind;
What but a Spartan spirit can sustain
The shock of such temptations? *Southern.*

UNPROVI'DED. *adj.*
1. Not secured or qualified by previous measures.
Where shall I find one that can steal well? O, for a fine thief of two and twenty, or thereabout; I am heinously *unprovided.* *Shakesp. Hen. IV.*
With his prepared sword he charges home
My *unprovided* body, lanc'd my arm. *Shakespeare.*
Tears, for a stroke foreseen, afford relief;
But *unprovided* for a sudden blow,
Like Niobe we marble grow,
And petrify with grief. *Dryden.*
2. Not furnished.
Those *unprovided* of tackling and victual, are forced to sea. *K. Charles.*
The seditious had neither weapons, order, nor counsel; but being in all things *unprovided*, were slain like beasts. *Hayward.*
Th' ambitious empress with her son is join'd,
And, in his brother's absence, has design'd
Th' *unprovided* town to take. *Dryden.*
True zeal is not a solitary, melancholy grace, as if only fit to dwell in mean minds; such as are utterly *unprovided* of all other natural, moral, or spiritual abilities. *Sprat.*
Courts are seldom *unprovided* of persons under this character, on whom most employments naturally fall. *Swift.*

UNPROVO'KED. *adj.* Not provoked.
The teeming earth, yet guiltless of the plough,
And *unprovok'd*, did fruitful stores allow. *Dryden.*
Let them forbear all open and secret methods of encouraging a rebellion so destructive, and so *unprovoked.* *Addison.*

UNPRU'NED. *adj.* Not cut; not lopped.
The whole land is full of weeds;
Her fruit trees all *unprun'd.* *Shakespeare.*

UNPU'NISHED. *adj.* [*impunis*, Lat.] Not punished; suffered to continue in impunity.
Bind not one sin upon another, for in one thou shalt not be *unpunished.* *Ecclus* vii. 8.
Divine justice will not let oppression go *unpunished.* *L'Estr.*
The vent'rous victor, march'd *unpunish'd* hence,
And seem'd to boast his fortunate offence. *Dryden.*

UNPU'RCHASED. *adj.* Unbought.
Unpurchas'd plenty our full tables loads,
And part of what they lent, return t'our gods. *Denham.*

UNPU'RGED. *adj.* Not purged.
Is Brutus sick?
And will he steal out of his wholesome bed,
To tempt the rheumy and *unpurged* air,
To add unto his sickness? *Shakesp. Julius Cæsar.*

UNPU'RPOSED. *adj.* Not designed.
Do it
Or thy precedent services are all
But accidents *unpurpos'd.* *Shakesp. Ant. and Cleopatra.*

UNPU'BLICK. *adj.* Private; not generally known.
Virgins must be retired and *unpublick*: for all freedom of society is a violence done to virginity, not in its natural, but in its moral capacity; that is, it loses part of its severity and strictness, by publishing that person, whose work is religion; whose thoughts must dwell in heaven. *Taylor.*

UNPU'BLISHED. *adj.*
1. Secret; unknown.
All blest secrets;
All you *unpublish'd* virtues of the earth,
Spring with my tears. *Shakesp. K. Lear.*
2. Not given to the publick.
Apply your care wholly to those which are *unpublish'd.* *Pope.*

UNPU'RGED. *adj.* Not purged; unpurified.
In her visage round those spots, *unpurg'd*
Vapours not yet into her substance turn'd. *Milton.*

UNPU'RIFIED. *adj.*
1. Not freed from recrement.
2. Not cleansed from sin.
Our sinful nation having been long in the furnace, is now come out, but *unpurified.* *Decay of Piety.*

UNPURSU'ED. *adj.* Not pursued.
All night the dreadless angel *unpursu'd*
Through heav'n's wide champain held his way. *Milton.*

UNPU'TRIFIED. *adj.* Not corrupted by rottenness.
Meat and drink last longer *unputrified*, or unsowered, in winter than in summer. *Bacon's Nat. Hist.*
No animal *unputrified*, being burnt, yields any alkaline salt, but putrified, yields a volatile alkali. *Arbuthnot.*

UNQUA'LIFIED. *adj.* Not fit.
'Till he has denudated himself of all these incumbrances, he is utterly *unqualified* for these agonies. *Decay of Piety.*
All the writers against christianity, since the revolution, have been of the lowest rank in regard to literature, wit, and sense; and upon that account wholly *unqualified* to propagate heresies, unless among a people already abandoned. *Sw.*
Tories are more hated by the zealous whigs, than the very papists, and as much *unqualified* for the smallest offices. *Sw.*

To UNQUA'LIFY. *v. a.* To disqualify; to divest of qualification.
Arbitrary power so diminishes the basis of the female figure, as to *unqualify* a woman for an evening walk. *Addison.*
Our private misfortunes may *unqualify* us for charity: but reflect, whether they may not have been inflicted by God, as a just punishment of our former unmercifulness. *Atterbury.*
Deafness *unqualifies* me for all company. *Swift.*

UNQUA'RRELLABLE. *adj.* Such as cannot be impugned.
There arise unto the examination such satisfactory and *unquarrelable* reasons, as may confirm the causes generally received. *Brown's Vulgar Errours.*

To UNQUEE'N. *v. a.* To divest of the dignity of queen.
Embalm me,
Then lay me forth; although *unqueen'd*, yet like
A queen, and daughter to a king, inter me. *Shakespeare.*

UNQUE'NCHABLE. *adj.* Unextinguishable.
We represent wildfires burning in water and *unquenchable.* *Bac.*
The people on their holidays,
Impetuous, insolent, *unquenchable.* *Milton's Agonistes.*
The criminal's penitence may have number'd him among the saints, when our unretracted uncharitableness may send us to *unquenchable* flames. *Government of the Tongue.*
Our love of God, our *unquenchable* desires to promote our well-grounded hopes to enjoy his glory, should take the chief place in our zeal. *Sprat's Sermons.*

UNQUE'NCHED. *adj.*
1. Not extinguished.
We have heats of dungs, and of lime *unquenched.* *Bacon.*
2. Not extinguishable.
Sadness, or great joy, equally dissipate the spirits, and immoderate exercise in hot air, with *unquenched* thirst. *Arbuth.*

UNQUE'NCHABLENESS. *n. s.* Unextinguishableness.
I was amazed to see the *unquenchableness* of this fire. *Hakewill.*

UNQUE'STIONABLE. *adj.*
1. Indubitable; not to be doubted.
The duke's carriage was surely noble throughout; of *unquestionable* courage in himself, and rather fearful of fame than danger. *Wotton.*
One reason that mathematical demonstrations are uncontroverted, is because interest hath no place in those *unquestionable* verities. *Glanville's Sceps.*
There is an *unquestionable* magnificence in every part of Paradise Lost. *Addison.*
2. Such as cannot bear to be questioned without impatience; this seems to be the meaning here.
What were his marks?——
——A lean cheek, which you have not; an *unquestionable* spirit, which you have not. *Shakespeare.*

UNQUE'STIONABLY. *adv.* Indubitably; without doubt.
If the fathers were *unquestionably* of the houshold of faith, and all to do good to them; then certainly their children cannot be strangers in this houshold. *Sprat.*
St. Austin was *unquestionably* a man of parts, but interposing in a controversy where his talent did not lie, shewed his zeal against the antipodes to very ill purpose. *Burnet.*

UNQUE'STIONED. *adj.*
1. Not doubted; passed without doubt.

Other relations in good authors, though we do not positively deny, yet have they not been *unquestioned* by some. *Brown.*

2. Indisputable; not to be opposed.

It did not please the gods, who instruct the people;
And their *unquestion'd* pleasures must be serv'd. *B. Johnson.*

3. Not interrogated; not examined.

Mutt'ring pray'rs as holy rites she meant,
Through the divided crowd *unquestion'd* went. *Dryden.*

UNQUI'CK. *adj.* Motionless.

His senses droop, his steady eyes *unquick*;
And much he ails, and yet he is not sick. *Daniel's Civ. War.*

UNQUI'CKENED. *adj.* Not animated; not ripened to vitality.

Every fœtus bears a secret hoard,
With sleeping, unexpanded issue stor'd;
Which num'rous, but *unquicken'd* progeny,
Clasp'd, and enwrapp'd, within each other lie. *Blackmore.*

UNQUI'ET. *adj.* [*inquiet*, Fr. *inquietus*, Lat.]

1. Moved with perpetual agitation; not calm; not still.

From grammatick flats and shallows, they are on the sudden transported to be tossed and turmoiled with their unballasted wits, in fathomless and *unquiet* depths of controversy. *Milton.*

2. Disturbed; full of perturbation; not at peace.

Go with me to church, and call me wife,
And then away to Venice to your friend;
For never shall you lie by Portia's side
With an *unquiet* soul. *Shakesp. Mer. of Venice.*

Thy love hopeful to regain,
From thee I will not hide
What thoughts in my *unquiet* breast are ris'n. *Milton.*

3. Restless; unsatisfied.

She glares in balls, front boxes, and the ring;
A vain, *unquiet*, glitt'ring, wretched thing. *Pope.*

Mirth from company is but a fluttering, *unquiet* motion, that beats about the breast for a few moments, and after leaves it empty. *Pope.*

UNQUI'ETLY. *adv.* Without rest.

Who's there besides foul weather?——
——One minded like the weather, most
Unquietly. *Shakesp. K. Lear.*

UNQUI'ETNESS. *n. s.*

1. Want of tranquillity.

Thou, like a violent noise, cam'st rushing in,
And mak'st them wake and start to new *unquietness.* *Denham.*

2. Want of peace.

It is most enemy to war, and most hateth *unquietness.* *Spens.*

3. Restlessness; turbulence.

What pleasure can there be in that estate,
Which your *unquietness* has made me hate? *Dryden.*

4. Perturbation; uneasiness.

Is my lord angry?——
—He went hence but now,
And certainly in strange *unquietness.* *Shakesp. Othello.*

From inordinate love, and vain fear, comes all *unquietness* of spirit, and distraction of our senses. *Taylor.*

UNRA'CKED. *adj.* Not poured from the lees.

Rack the one vessel from the lees, and pour the lees of the racked vessel into the *unracked* vessel. *Bacon's Nat. Hist.*

UNRA'KED. *adj.* Not thrown together and covered. Used only of fires.

Cricket, to Windsor chimnies shalt thou leap:
Where fires thou find'st *unrak'd*, and hearths unswept,
There pinch the maids. *Shakesp. Merry Wives of Windsor.*

UNRA'NSACKED. *adj.* Not pillaged.

He gave that rich city for a prey unto his soldiers, who left neither house, nor corner thereof *unransacked.* *Knolles.*

UNRA'NSOMED. *adj.* Not set free by payment for liberty.

Unransom'd here receive the spotless fair,
Accept the hecatomb the Greeks prepare. *Pope's Iliad.*

To UNRA'VEL. *v. a.*

1. To disentangle; to extricate; to clear.

There *unravel* all
This dark design, this mystery of fate. *Addison's Cato.*

With Machiavelian sagacity thou *unravell'dst* intrigues of state. *Arbuthnot.*

2. To disorder; to throw out of the present constitution.

How can any thing succeed well with people that are to be pleased with nothing, unless the ball of the universe may be *unravelled*, and the laws of providence reversed. *L'Estrange.*

O the traytor's name!
I'll know it; I will: art shall be conjur'd for it,
And nature all *unravell'd.* *Dryd. and Lee's Oedipus.*

So prophane and sceptical an age, takes a pride in *unravelling* all the received principles of reason and religion. *Tillotson.*

3. To clear up the intrigue of a play.

The solution, or *unravelling* of the intrigue, commences, when the reader begins to see the doubts cleared up. *Pope.*

Thus supernaturally is the plot brought to perfection; nor is the *unravelling* of it less happily imagined. *Shakesp. Illust.*

UNRA'ZORED. *adj.* Unshaven.

As smooth as Hebe's their *unrazor'd* lips. *Milton.*

UNRE'ACHED. *adj.* Not attained.

Labour with unequal force to climb
That lofty hill, *unreach'd* by former time. *Dryden.*

UNRE'AD. *adj.*

1. Not read; not publickly pronounced.

These books are safer and better to be left publickly *unread.* *Hooker, b. v.*

His muse had starv'd, had not a piece *unread*,
And by a player bought, supply'd her bread. *Dryden.*

2. Untaught; not learned in books.

Uncertain whose the narrower span,
The clown *unread*, or half-read gentleman. *Dryden.*

UNRE'ADINESS. *n. s.*

1. Want of readiness; want of promptness.

This impreparation and *unreadiness*, when they find in us, then turn it to the soothing up of themselves in that accursed fancy. *Hooker, b. v.*

2. Want of preparation.

Nothing is so great an enemy to tranquillity, and a contented spirit, as the amazement and confusions of *unreadiness* and inconsideration. *Taylor's Rule of Living Holy.*

UNRE'ADY. *adj.*

1. Not prepared; not fit.

The fairy knight
Departed thence, albe his wounds wide,
Not throughly heal'd, *unready* were to ride. *Fairy Queen.*

How now, my lords? what all *unready* so? *Shakespeare.*

2. Not prompt; not quick.

From a temperate inactivity, we are *unready* to put in execution the suggestions of reason; or by a content in every species of truth, we embrace the shadow thereof. *Brown.*

3. Awkward; ungain.

Young men, in the conduct of actions, use extreme remedies at first, and, that which doubleth all errors, will not acknowledge or retract them; like an *unready* horse, that will neither stop nor turn. *Bacon.*

UNRE'AL. *adj.* Unsubstantial.

Hence, terrible shadow!
Unreal mock'ry, hence! *Shakesp. Macbeth.*

I with pain
Voyag'd th' *unreal*, vast, unbounded deep
Of horrible confusion. *Milton's Par. Lost, b. x.*

UNRE'ASONABLE. *adj.*

1. Exorbitant; claiming, or insisting on more than is fit.

Since every language is so full of its own proprieties, that what is beautiful in one, is often barbarous in another, it would be *unreasonable* to limit a translator to the narrow compass of his author's words. *Dryden's Pref. to Ovid.*

My intention in prefixing your name, is not to desire your protection of the following papers, which I take to be a very *unreasonable* request; since, by being inscribed to you, you cannot recommend them without some suspicion of partiality. *Swift's Project for the Advancement of Religion.*

2. Not agreeable to reason.

No reason known to us; but that there is no reason thereof, I judge most *unreasonable* to imagine. *Hooker, b. i.*

It is *unreasonable* for men to be judges in their own cases; self-love will make men partial to themselves and their friends. *Locke.*

She entertained many *unreasonable* prejudices against him, before she was acquainted with his personal worth. *Addison.*

3. Greater than is fit; immoderate.

Those that place their hope in another world, have, in a great measure, conquer'd dread of death, and *unreasonable* love of life. *Atterbury.*

UNRE'ASONABLENESS. *n. s.*

1. Exorbitance; excessive demand.

The *unreasonableness* of propositions is not more evident, than that they are not the joint desires of their major number. *K. Charles.*

A young university disputant was complaining of the *unreasonableness* of a lady, with whom he was engaged in a point of controversy. *Addison's Freeholder, N° 32.*

2. Inconsistency with reason.

The *unreasonableness* and presumption of those that thus project, have not so much as a thought, all their lives long, to advance so far as attrition. *Hammond.*

UNRE'ASONABLY. *adv.*

1. In a manner contrary to reason.

2. More than enough.

I'll not over the threshold, till my lord return from the wars.—
—Fye! you confine yourself most *unreasonably.* *Shakespeare.*

To UNRE'AVE. *v. a.* [now *unravel*; from *un* and *reave*, or *ravel*; perhaps the same with *rive*, to tear, or break asunder.]

To unwind; to disentangle.

Penelope, for her Ulysses' sake,
Devis'd a web her woers to deceive;
In which the work that she all day did make,
The same at night she did *unreave.* *Spenser.*

UN-

UNREBA'TED. *adj.* Not blunted.

A number of fencers try it out with *unrebated* swords. *Hakew.*

UNREBU'KEABLE. *adj.* Obnoxious to no censure.

Keep this commandment without spot, *unrebukeable*, until the appearing of Christ. *1 Tim.* vi. 14.

UNRECE'IVED. *adj.* Not received.

Where the signs and sacraments of his grace are not, through contempt, *unreceived*, or received with contempt, they really give what they promise, and are what they signify. *Hooker.*

UNRECLA'IMED. *adj.*

1. Not turned.

A savageness of *unreclaimed* blood,
Of general assault. *Shakesp. Hamlet.*

2. Not reformed.

This is the most favourable treatment a sinner can hope for, who continues *unreclaimed* by the goodness of God. *Rogers.*

UNRECONCI'LEABLE. *adj.*

1. Not to be appeased; implacable.

He had many infirmities and sins, *unreconcileable* with perfect righteousness. *Hammond's Pract. Catechism.*

2. Not to be made consistent with.

Let me lament,
That our stars, *unreconcileable*, should have divided
Our equalness to this. *Shakesp. Ant. and Cleop.*

UNRE'CONCILED. *adj.* Not reconciled.

If you bethink yourself of any crime
Unreconcil'd as yet to heav'n and grace,
Solicit for it straight. *Shakesp. Othello.*

UNRECO'RDED. *adj.* Not kept in remembrance by publick monuments.

Unrecorded left through many an age,
Worthy t'have not remain'd so long unsung. *Milton.*
The great Antilocus! a name
Not *unrecorded* in the rolls of fame. *Pope's Odyssey.*

UNRECO'UNTED. *adj.* Not told; not related.

This is yet but young, and may be left
To some ears *unrecounted.* *Shakesp. Hen.* VIII.

UNRECRU'ITABLE. *adj.* Incapable of repairing the deficiencies of an army.

Empty and *unrecruitable* colonels of twenty men in a company. *Milton on Education.*

UNRECU'RING. *adj.* Irremediable.

I found her straying in the park,
Seeking to hide herself; as doth the deer,
That hath received some *unrecuring* wound. *Shakespeare.*

UNREDU'CED. *adj.* Not reduced.

The earl divided all the rest of the Irish countries *unreduced*, into shires. *Davies's Ireland.*

UNREFO'RMABLE. *adj.* Not to be put into a new form.

The rule of faith is alone unmoveable and *unreformable*; to wit, of believing in one only God omnipotent, creator of the world, and in his son Jesus Christ, born of the virgin Mary. *Hammond's Fundamentals.*

UNREFO'RMED. *adj.*

1. Not amended; not corrected.

This general revolt, when overcome, produced a general reformation of the Irishry, which ever before had been *unreformed.* *Davies's Ireland.*

We retain the Julian constitution of the year, *unreformed*, without consideration of the defective minutes. *Holder.*

2. Not brought to newness of life.

If he may believe that Christ died for him, as now he is, an *unreformed* christian, then what needs he reformation? *Hamm.*

Unhumbled, unrepentant, *unreform'd.* *Milton.*

UNREFRA'CTED. *adj.* Not refracted.

The sun's circular image is made by an *unrefracted* beam of light. *Newton's Opticks.*

UNREFRE'SHED. *adj.* Not cheared; not relieved.

Its symptoms are a spontaneous lassitude, being *unrefreshed* by sleep. *Arbuthnot.*

UNREGA'RDED. *adj.* Not heeded; not respected; neglected.

We, ever by his might,
Had thrown to ground the *unregarded* right. *Fairy Queen.*
Do'st see, how *unregarded* now
That piece of beauty passes?
There was a time when I did vow
To that alone;
But mark the fate of faces. *Suckling.*
On the cold earth lies th' *unregarded* king;
A headless carcass, and a nameless thing. *Denham.*
Me you have often counsell'd to remove
My vain pursuit of *unregarded* love. *Dryden.*

Laws against immorality have not been executed, and proclamations to inforce them, are wholly *unregarded.* *Swift.*

UNRE'GISTERED. *adj.* Not recorded.

Hotter hours,
Unregister'd in vulgar fame, you have
Luxuriously pick'd out. *Shakesp. Ant. and Cleopatra.*

UNREGE'NERATE. *adj.* Not brought to a new life.

This is not to be understood promiscuously of all men, *unregenerate* persons, as well us regenerate. *Stephens.*

UNRE'INED. *adj.* Not restrained by the bridle.

Lest from thy flying steed *unrein'd*, as once
Bellerophon, though from a lower clime
Dismounted, on th' Aleian field I fall. *Milton.*

UNRELE'NTING. *adj.* Hard; cruel; feeling no pity.

By many hands your father was subdu'd;
But only slaughter'd by the ireful arm
Of *unrelenting* Clifford. *Shakesp. Hen.* VI.
Place pitchy barrels on the fatal stake,
That so her torture may be shortened.
Will nothing turn your *unrelenting* hearts? *Shakesp.*
These are the realms of *unrelenting* fate;
And awful Rhadamanthus rules the state. *Dryden.*
False tears shall wet his *unrelenting* eyes,
And his glad heart with artful sighs shall heave. *Smith.*

UNRELIE'VABLE. *adj.* Admitting no succour.

As no degree of distress is *unrelievable* by his power, so no extremity of it is inconsistent with his compassion. *Boyle.*

UNRELI'EVED. *adj.*

1. Not succoured.

The goddess griev'd,
Her favour'd host shou'd perish *unreliev'd.* *Dryden.*

2. Not eased.

The uneasiness of *unrelieved* thirst is not lessened by continuance, but grows the more unsupportable. *Boyle.*

UNREMA'RKABLE. *adj.*

1. Not capable of being observed.

Our understanding, to make a complete notion, must add something else to this fleeting and *unremarkable* superficies, that may bring it to our acquaintance. *Digby.*

2. Not worthy of notice.

UNREME'DIABLE. *adj.* Admitting no remedy.

He so handled it, that it rather seemed he had more come into a defence of an *unremediable* mischief already committed, than that they had done it at first by his consent. *Sidney.*

UNREME'MBERING. *adj.* Having no memory.

That *unrememb'ring* of its former pain,
The soul may suffer mortal flesh again. *Dryden.*

UNREME'MBERED. *adj.* Not retained in the mind; not recollected.

I cannot pass *unremembered*, their manner of disguising the shafts of chimnies in various fashions, whereof the noblest is the pyramidal. *Wotton's Architecture.*

UNREME'MBRANCE. *n. s.* Forgetfulness; want of remembrance.

Some words are negative in their original language, but seem positive, because the negation is unknown; as amnesty, an *unremembrance*, or general pardon. *Watts's Logick.*

UNREMO'VEABLE. *adj.* Not to be taken away.

Never was there any woman, that with more *unremoveable* determination gave herself to love, after she had once set before her mind the worthiness of Amphialus. *Sidney, b.* ii.

You know the fiery quality of the duke,
How *unremoveable* and fixt he is
In his own course. *Shakespeare.*

UNREMO'VED. *adj.*

1. Not taken away.

It is impossible, where this opinion is imbibed and *unremoved*, to found any convincing argument. *Hammond.*

We could have had no certain prospect of his happiness, while the last obstacle was *unremoved.* *Dryden's Virgil.*

2. Not capable of being removed.

Like Teneriff or Atlas *unremov'd.* *Milton.*

UNREMO'VEABLY. *adv.* In a manner that admits no removal.

His discontents are *unremoveably* coupled to his nature. *Sha.*

UNREPA'ID. *adj.* Not recompensed; not compensated.

Hadst thou full pow'r
To measure out his torments by thy will;
Yet what could'st thou, tormentor, hope to gain?
Thy loss continues, *unrepaid* by pain. *Dryden.*

UNREPE'ALED. *adj.* Not revoked; not abrogated.

When you are pinched with any *unrepealed* act of parliament, you declare you will not be obliged by it. *Dryden.*

Nature's law, and *unrepeal'd* command,
That gives to lighter things the greatest height. *Blackmore.*

UNREPE'NTED. *adj.* Not regarded with penitential sorrow.

They are no fit supplicants to seek his mercy in the behalf of others, whose own *unrepented* sins provoked his just indignation. *Hooker, b.* v.

If I, vent'ring to displease
God for the fear of man, and man prefer,
Set God behind: which in his jealousy
Shall never, *unrepented*, find forgiveness. *Milton's Agonistes.*
As in *unrepented* sin she dy'd,
Doom'd to the same bad place, is punish'd for her pride. *Dryd.*

With what confusion will he hear all his *unrepented* sins produced before men and angels? *Rogers's Sermons.*

UNREPE'NTING. } *adj.* Not repenting; not penitent; not
UNREPENTANT. } sorrowful for sin.

Should

Should I of these the liberty regard,
Who freed, as to their antient patrimony,
Unhumbl'd, *unrepentant*, unreform'd,
Headlong would follow. *Milton's Par. Regain'd.*

My unprepar'd, and *unrepenting* breath,
Was snatch'd away by the swift hand of death. *Roscommon.*

All his arts reveal,
From the first moment of his vital breath,
To his last hour of *unrepenting* death. *Dryden.*

Nor tyrants fierce, that *unrepenting* die,
E'er felt such rage as thou. *Pope's Rape of the Lock.*

UNREPI'NING. *adj.* Not peevishly complaining.

Barefoot as she trod the flinty pavement,
Her footsteps all along were mark'd with blood;
Yet silent on she pass'd, and *unrepining.* *Rowe.*

UNREPLE'NISHED. *adj.* Not filled.

Some air retreated thither, kept the mercury out of the *unreplenished* space. *Boyle.*

UNREPRIE'VABLE. *adj.* Not to be respited from penal death.

Within me is a hell; and there the poison
Is, as a fiend, confin'd, to tyrannize
In *unreprievable* condemned blood. *Shakesp. K. John.*

UNREPRO'ACHED. *adj.* Not upbraided; not censured.

Sir John Hotham, *unreproached*, uncursed by any imprecation of mine, pays his head. *K. Charles.*

UNREPRO'VEABLE. *adj.* Not liable to blame.

You hath he reconciled, to present you holy, unblameable, and *unreproveable* in his sight. *Col.* i. 22.

UNREPRO'VED. *adj.*

1. Not censured.

Christians have their churches, and *unreproved* exercise of religion. *Sandys's Journey.*

2. Not liable to censure.

The antique world, in his first flow'ring youth,
With gladsome thanks, and *unreproved* truth,
The gifts of sov'reign bounty did embrace. *Fairy Queen.*

If I give thee honour due,
Mirth, admit me of thy crew,
To live with her, and live with thee,
In *unreproved* pleasures free. *Milton.*

UNREPU'GNANT. *adj.* Not opposite.

When scripture doth yield us natural laws, what particular order is thereunto most agreeable; when positive, which way to make laws *unrepugnant* unto them. *Hooker, b.* iii.

UNRE'PUTABLE. *adj.* Not creditable.

When we see wise men examples of duty, we are convinced that piety is no *unreputable* qualification, and that we are not to be ashamed of our virtue. *Rogers.*

UNREQUE'STED. *adj.* Not asked.

With what security can our embassadors go, *unrequested* of the Turkish emperor, without his safe conduct? *Knolles.*

UNREQUI'TABLE. *adj.* Not to be retaliated.

Some will have it that all mediocrity of folly is foolish, and because an *unrequitable* evil may ensue, an indifferent convenience must be omitted. *Brown's Vulg. Errours.*

So *unrequitable* is God's love, and so insolvent are we, that that love vastly improves the benefit, by which alone we might have pretended to some ability of retribution. *Boyle.*

UNRESE'NTED. *adj.* Not regarded with anger.

The failings of these holy persons, passed not *unresented* by God; and the same scripture which informs us of the sin, records the punishment. *Rogers.*

UNRESE'RVED. *adj.*

1. Not limited by any private convenience.

The piety our heavenly father will accept, must consist in an entire, *unreserved* obedience to his commands; since whosoever offends in one precept, is guilty of the whole law. *Rogers.*

2. Open; frank; concealing nothing.

UNRESE'RVEDNESS. *n. s.* Unlimitedness; frankness; largeness.

The tenderness and *unreservedness* of his love, made him think those his friends or enemies, that were so to God. *Boyle.*

UNRESE'RVEDLY. *adv.*

1. Without limitations.

I am not to embrace absolutely and *unreservedly* the opinion of Aristotle. *Boyle.*

2. Without concealment; openly.

I know your friendship to me is extensive; and it is what I owe to that friendship, to open my mind *unreservedly* to you. *Pope.*

UNRESE'RVEDNESS. *n. s.* Openness; frankness.

I write with more *unreservedness* than ever man wrote. *Pope.*

UNRESI'STED. *adj.*

1. Not opposed.

The ætherial spaces are perfectly fluid; they neither assist, nor retard, the planets, which roll through as free and *unresisted*, as if they moved in a vacuum. *Bentley's Sermons.*

2. Resistless; such as cannot be opposed.

Those gods! whose *unresisted* might
Have sent me to these regions void of light. *Dryden.*

What wonder then, thy hairs should feel
The conqu'ring force of *unresisted* steel? *Pope.*

UNRESI'STING. *adj* Not opposing; not making resistance.

What noise? that spirit's possess'd with haste,
That wounds th' *unresisting* postern with these strokes. *Sha.*

The sheep was sacrific'd on no pretence,
But meek and *unresisting* innocence:
A patient, useful creature. *Dryden.*

Since the planets move horizontally through the liquid and *unresisting* spaces of the heav'ns, where no bodies at all, or inconsiderable ones, occur, they may preserve the same velocity which the first impulse impress'd. *Bentley's Sermons.*

UNRESO'LVABLE. *adj.* Not to be solved; insoluble.

For a man to run headlong, while his ruin stares him in the face; still to press on to the embraces of sin, is a problem *unresolvable* upon any other ground, but that sin infatuates before it destroys. *South's Sermons.*

UNRESO'LVED. *adj.*

1. Not determined; having made no resolution.

On the western coast
Rideth a puissant navy: to our shores
Throng many doubtful, hollow-hearted friends,
Unarm'd, and *unresolv'd* to beat them back. *Shakesp.*

Turnus, *unresolv'd* of flight,
Moves tardy back, and just recedes from fight. *Dryden.*

2. Not solved; not cleared.

I do not so magnify this method, to think it will perfectly clear every hard place, and leave no doubt *unresolved.* *Locke.*

UNRESO'LVING. *adj.* Not resolving.

She her arms about her *unresolving* husband threw. *Dryd.*

UNRESPE'CTIVE. *adj.* Inattentive; taking little notice.

I will converse with iron-witted fools,
And *unrespective* boys; none are for me
That look into me with consid'rate eyes. *Shakespeare.*

UNRE'ST. *n. s.* Disquiet; want of tranquillity; unquietness.

Wise behest, those creeping flames by reason to subdue,
Before their rage grew to so great *unrest.* *Fairy Queen.*

Repose, sweet gold, for their *unrest*,
That have their alms out of the empress' chest. *Shakespeare.*

Dismay'd confusion all possess'd;
Th' afflicted troop, hearing their plot descry'd:
Then runs amaz'd distress, with sad *unrest*,
To this, to that; to fly, to stand, to hide. *Daniel.*

Silence, in truth, would speak my sorrows best;
For deepest wounds, can least their feelings tell;
Yet, let me borrow from mine own *unrest*,
But time to bid him, whom I lov'd, farewell. *Wotton.*

Up they rose,
As from *unrest*; and each the other viewing,
Soon found their eyes how open'd, and their minds
How darken'd! *Milton's Par. Lost, b.* ix.

UNRESTO'RED. *adj.*

1. Not restored.

2. Not cleared from an attainder.

The son of an *unrestored* traitor has no pretences to the quality of his ancestors. *Collier on Duelling.*

UNRESTRA'INED. *adj.*

1. Not confined; not hindered.

My tender age, in luxury was train'd,
With idle ease, and pageants entertain'd,
My hours my own, my pleasures *unrestrain'd.* *Dryden.*

2. Licentious; loose.

The taverns he daily doth frequent,
With *unrestrained*, loose companions. *Shakespeare.*

3. Not limited.

Were there in this aphorism an *unrestrained* truth, yet were it not reasonable to infer from a caution, a non-usance, or abolition. *Brown's Vulgar Errours.*

UNRETRA'CTED. *adj.* Not revoked; not recalled.

The penitence of the criminal may have numbered him amongst the saints, when our *unretracted* uncharitableness may send us to unquenchable flames. *Govern. of the Tongue.*

Nothing but plain malevolence can justify disunion. Malevolence shewn in a single, outward act, *unretracted*, or in habitual ill-nature. *Collier on Friendship.*

UNREVE'ALED. *adj.* Not told; not discovered.

Had ye once seen these her celestial treasures,
And *unrevealed* pleasures,
Then would ye wonder, and her praises sing. *Spenser.*

Dear, fatal name! rest ever *unreveal'd*;
Nor pass these lips, in holy silence seal'd. *Pope.*

UNREVE'NGED. *adj.* Not revenged.

So might we die, not envying them that live;
So would we die, not *unrevenged* all. *Fairfax.*

Unhonour'd though I am,
Not *unreveng'd* that impious act shall be. *Dryden.*

Great Pompey's shade complains that we are slow,
And Scipio's ghost walks *unreveng'd* amongst us. *Addison.*

UNRE'VEREND. *adj.* Irreverent; disrespectful.

See not your bride in these *unreverent* robes. *Shakespeare.*

Fie! *unreverend* tongue! to call her bad,
Whose sov'reignty so oft thou hast preferr'd,
With twenty thousand soul-confirming oaths. *Shakespeare.*

UN-

Unre'verently. *adv.* Disrespectfully.

I did *unreverently* blame the gods,
Who wake for thee, though thou snore for thyself. *B. Johns.*

Unreve'rsed. *adj.* Not revoked; not repealed.

She hath offer'd to the doom,
Which *unreversed* stands in effectual force,
A sea of melting tears. *Shakespeare.*

Unrevo'ked. *adj.* Not recalled.

Hear my decree, which *unrevok'd* shall stand. *Milton.*

Unrewa'rded. *adj.* Not rewarded; not recompensed.

Providence takes care that good offices may not pass *unrewarded.* *L'Estrange.*

Since for common good I yield the fair,
My private loss let grateful Greece repair;
Nor *unrewarded* let your prince complain,
That he alone has fought and bled in vain. *Pope.*

To Unri'ddle. *v. a.* To solve an enigma; to explain a problem.

Some kind power *unriddle* where it lies,
Whether my heart be faulty, or her eyes! *Suckling.*

The Platonick principles will not *unriddle* the doubt. *Glanv.*

A reverse often clears up the passage of an old poet, as the poet often serves to *unriddle* the reverse. *Addison.*

Unridi'culous. *adj.* Not ridiculous.

If an indifferent and *unridiculous* object could draw this austereness unto a smile, he hardly could with perpetuity resist proper motives thereof. *Brown's Vulgar Errours.*

To Unri'g. *v. a.* To strip of the tackle.

Rhodes is the sovereign of the sea no more;
Their ships *unrigg'd*, and spent their naval store. *Dryden.*

Unri'ght. Wrong. In *Spenser*, this word should perhaps be *untight.*

What in most English writers useth to be loose, and as it were *unright*, in this author is well grounded, timely framed, and strongly trussed up together. *Glossary to Spenser's Kal.*

Shew that thy judgment is not *unright.* *Wisdom* xii.

Unri'ghteous. *adj.* Unjust; wicked; sinful; bad.

Octavius here lept into his room,
And it usurped by *unrighteous* doom;
But he his title justify'd by might. *Fairy Queen, b.* ii.

Within a month!
Ere yet the salt of most *unrighteous* tears,
Had left the flushing in her galled eyes,
She married.—Oh most wicked speed! *Shakespeare.*

Let the wicked man forsake his way, and the *unrighteous* man his thoughts, and let him return unto the Lord. *Isa.* lv.

Unri'ghteously. *adv.* Unjustly; wickedly; sinfully.

For them
Their foes a deadly Shibboleth devise:
By which *unrighteously* it was decreed,
That none to trust, or profit should succeed,
Who would not swallow first a pois'nous wicked weed. *Dryd.*

A man may fall undeservedly under publick disgrace, or is *unrighteously* oppressed. *Collier on Pride.*

Unri'ghteousness. *n. s.* Wickedness; injustice.

Our Romanists can no more abide this proposition converted, than themselves. All sin, say they, is a transgression of the law; but every transgression of the law is not sin. The apostle, therefore, turns it for us: all *unrighteousness*, says he, is sin; but every transgression of the law is *unrighteousness*, saith Austin upon this place. *Hall.*

Some things have a natural deformity in them, as perjury, perfidiousness, *unrighteousness*, and ingratitude. *Tillotson.*

Unri'ghtful. *adj.* Not rightful; not just.

Thou, which know'st the way
To plant *unrightful* kings, wilt know again
To pluck him headlong from th' usurped throne. *Shakesp.*

To Unri'ng. *v. a.* To deprive of a ring.

Be forc'd to impeach a broken hedge,
And pigs *unring'd* at vis. franc. pledge. *Hudibras.*

To Unri'p. *v. a.* [This word is improper; there being no difference between *rip* and *unrip*; and the negative particle is therefore of no force; yet it is well authorised.] To cut open.

Like a traitor
Didst break that vow, and, with thy treach'rous blade,
Unrip'dst the bowels of thy sov'reign's son. *Shakespeare.*

He could not now, with his honour, so *unrip*, and put a lye upon all that he had said and done before, as to deliver him up. *Bacon's Hen.* VII.

We are angry with searchers, when they break open trunks, and *unrip* packs, and open sealed letters. *Taylor.*

Cato well observes, that friendship ought not to be *unripped*, but unstitched. *Collier.*

Unri'pe. *n. s.*

1. Immature; not fully concocted.

Purpose is of violent birth, but poor validity;
Which now, like fruits *unripe*, sticks on the tree,
But fall unshaken when they mellow be. *Shakespeare.*

In this northern tract our hoarser throats,
Utter *unripe* and ill-constrained notes. *Waller.*

He fix'd his *unripe* vengeance to defer,
Sought not the garden, but retir'd unseen,
To brood in secret on his gather'd spleen. *Dryden.*

2. Too early.

Who hath not heard of the valiant, wise, and just Dorilaus, whose *unripe* death doth yet, so many years since, draw tears from virtuous eyes? *Sidney, b.* ii.

Unri'pened. *adj.* Not matured.

Were you with these, you'd soon forget
The pale, *unripen'd* beauties of the north. *Addison's Cato.*

Unri'peness. *n. s.* Immaturity; want of ripeness.

The ripeness, or *unripeness*, of the occasion, must ever be well weighed; and generally it is good to commit the beginnings of all great actions to Argus, with his hundred eyes; and the ends to Briareus, with his hundred hands. *Bacon.*

Unri'valled. *adj.*

1. Having no competitor.

Honour forbid! at whose *unrival'd* shrine,
Ease, pleasure, virtue, all our sex resign. *Pope.*

2. Having no peer or equal.

To Unro'l. *v. a.* To open what is rolled or convolved.

O horror!
The queen of nations, from her antient seat,
Is sunk for ever in the dark abyss;
Time has *unroll'd* her glories to the last,
And now clos'd up the volume. *Dryden's All for Love.*

Unroma'ntick. *adj.* Contrary to romance.

It is a base, *unromantick* spirit not to wait on you. *Swift.*

To Unroo'f. *v. a.* To strip off the roof or covering of houses.

The rabble should have first *unroof'd* the city,
Ere so prevail'd with me. *Shakesp. Coriolanus.*

Unroo'sted. *adj.* Driven from the roost.

Thou dotard! thou art woman-tir'd, *unroosted*,
By thy old dame Partlet here. *Shakesp. Winter Tale.*

Unrough. *adj.* Smooth.

Siward's son,
And many *unrough* youths, that even now
Protest their first of manhood. *Shakesp. Macbeth.*

To Unroo't. *v. a.* To tear from the roots; to extirpate; to eradicate.

Since you've made the days and nights as one,
To wear your gentle limbs in my affairs,
Be bold; you do so grow in my requital,
That nothing can *unroot* you. *Shakespeare.*

Unroot the forest oaks and bear away
Flocks, folds, and trees, an undistinguish'd prey. *Dryden.*

Unro'unded. *adj.* Not shaped, not cut to a round.

Those unfil'd pistolets,
That more than cannon-shot avails or lets;
Which, negligently left *unrounded*, look
Like many-angled figures in the book
Of some dread conjurer. *Donne.*

Unro'yal. *adj.* Unprincely; not royal.

By the advice of his envious counsellors, he sent them with *unroyal* reproaches to Musidorus and Pyrocles, as if they had done traiterously. *Sidney.*

To Unru'ffle. *v. n.* To cease from commotion, or agitation.

Where'er he guides his finny coursers,
The waves *unruffle*, and the sea subsides. *Dryden.*

Unruffled. *adj.* Calm; tranquil; not tumultuous.

Vent all thy passion, and I'll stand its shock,
Calm and *unruffled* as a summer's sea,
When not a breath of wind flies o'er its surface. *Addison.*

Unru'led. *adj.* Not directed by any superiour power.

The realm was left, like a ship in a storm, amidst all the raging surges, *unruled* and undirected of any; for they to whom she was committed, fainted in their labour, or forsook their charge. *Spenser.*

Unru'liness. *n. s.* [from *unruly.*] Turbulence; tumultuousness; licentiousness.

By the negligence of some who were hardly to be commanded, and by the *unruliness* of others, who without leave were gone a-shore, so fair an occasion of victory was neglected. *Knol*

No care was had to curb the *unruliness* of anger, or the exorbitance of desire. Amongst all their sacrifices, they never sacrificed so much as one lust. *South's Sermons.*

Unru'ly. *adj.* Turbulent; ungovernable; licentious; tumultuous.

In sacred bands of wedlock ty'd
To Therion, a loose *unruly* swain;
Who had more joy to range the forest wide,
And chace the savage beast with busy pain. *Fairy Queen.*

Down I come, like glist'ring Phaeton,
Wanting the manage of *unruly* jades. *Shakesp. Rich.* II.

The best and soundest of his time hath been but rash; then must we look from his age, to receive but *unruly* waywardness. *Shakesp. K. Lear.*

The tongue is an *unruly* evil, full of deadly poison. *Ja.* iii.

Thou dost a better life, and nobler vigour give;
Dost each *unruly* appetite controul. *Roscommon.*

Love

Love insults, disguised in the cloud,
And welcome force of that *unruly* croud. *Waller.*

Passions kept their place, and transgressed not the boundaries of their proper natures; nor were the disorders begun, which are occasioned by the licence of *unruly* appetites. *Glanv.*

You must not go where you may dangers meet.
Th' *unruly* sword will no distinction make,
And beauty will not there give wounds, but take. *Dryden.*

UNSA'FE. *adj.* Not secure; hazardous; dangerous.

If they would not be drawn to seem his adversaries, yet others should be taught how *unsafe* it was to continue his friends. *Hooker, b.* v.

With speed retir'd
Where erst was thickest fight, th' angelick throng,
And left large field, *unsafe* within the wind
Of such commotion. *Milton's Par. Lost, b.* vi.

Uncertain ways *unsafest* are,
And doubt a greater mischief than despair. *Denham.*

Phlegyan robbers made *unsafe* the road. *Dryden.*

UNSA'FELY. *adv.* Not securely; dangerously.

Take it, while yet 'tis praise, before my rage,
Unsafely just, break loose on this bad age;
So bad, that thou thyself hadst no defence
From vice, but barely by departing hence. *Dryden.*

As no man can walk, so neither can he think, uneasily or *unsafely*; but in using, as his legs, so his thoughts amiss, which a virtuous man never doth. *Grew.*

UNSA'ID. *adj.* Not uttered; not mentioned.

Chanticleer shall wish his words *unsaid.* *Dryden.*

That I may leave nothing material *unsaid*, among the several ways of imitation, I shall place translation and paraphrase. *Felton's Classicks.*

UNSA'LTED. *adj.* Not pickled or seasoned with salt.

The muriatick scurvy, induced by two great quantity of sea-salt, and common among mariners, is cured by a diet of fresh *unsalted* things, and watery liquor acidulated. *Arbuthnot.*

UNSALU'TED. *adj.* [*insalutatus*, Lat.] Not saluted.

Gods! I prate;
And the most noble mother of the world
Leave *unsaluted.* *Shakesp. Coriolanus.*

UNSA'NCTIFIED. *adj* Unholy; not consecrated.

Her obsequies have been so far enlarged
As we have warrantry; her death was doubtful;
And but that great command o'ersways the order,
She should in ground *unsanctify'd* have lodg'd
'Till the last trump. *Shakespeare's Hamlet.*

UNSA'TIABLE. *adj.* [*insatiabilis*, Lat.] Not to be satisfied; greedy without bounds.

Unsatiable in their longing to do all manner of good to all the creatures of God, but especially men. *Hooker, b.* i.

Crassus the Roman, for his *unsatiable* greediness, was called the gulph of avarice. *Raleigh.*

UNSATISFA'CTORINESS. *n. s.* Failure of giving satisfaction.

That which most deters me from such trials, is their *unsatisfactoriness*, though they should succeed. *Boyle.*

UNSATISFA'CTORY. *adj.* Not giving satisfaction; not clearing the difficulty.

That speech of Adam, The woman thou gavest me to be with me, she gave me of the tree, and I did eat, is an *unsatisfactory* reply, and therein was involved a very impious error. *Brown's Vulg. Errours.*

Latria to the cross, is point blank against the definition of the council of Nice; and it is an *unsatisfactory* answer to say, they only were against latria given to images for themselves. *Stillingfleet.*

UNSA'TISFIEDNESS. *n. s.* [from *unsatisfied.*] The state of being not satisfied; want of fulness.

Between my own *unsatisfiedness* in conscience, and a necessity of satisfying the importunities of some, I was perswaded to chuse rather what was safe, than what seemed just. *K. Charles.*

That *unsatisfiedness* with transitory fruitions, that men deplore as the unhappiness of their nature, is indeed the privilege of it, as it is the prerogative of men not to be pleased with such fond toys as children doat upon. *Boyle.*

UNSA'TISFIED. *adj.*

1. Not contented; not pleased.

Q. Elizabeth being to resolve upon a great officer, and being by some put in some doubt of that person, whom she meant to advance, said, she was like one with a lanthorn seeking a man, and seemed *unsatisfied* in the choice of a man for that place. *Bacon.*

Flashy wits, who cannot fathom a large discourse, must be very much *unsatisfied* of me. *Digby.*

Concerning the analytical preparation of gold, they leave persons *unsatisfied.* *Boyle.*

2. Not filled; not gratified to the full.

Though he were *unsatisfied* in getting,
Yet in bestowing he was most princely. *Shakespeare.*

Whether shall I, by justly plaguing
Him whom I hate, be more unjustly cruel
To her I love? or, being kind to her,
Be cruel to myself, and leave *unsatisfied*
My anger and revenge? *Denham's Sophy.*

Eternity, human nature can't look into, without a religious awe: our thoughts are lost in the endless view, and return to us weary and *unsatisfied*, without finding bounds or place to fix on. *Rogers's Sermons.*

UNSA'TISFYING. *adj.* Unable to gratify to the full.

Nor is fame only *unsatisfying* in itself, but the desire of it lays us open to many accidental troubles. *Addison.*

UNSA'VOURINESS. *adj.* [from *unsavoury.*]

1. Bad taste.
2. Bad smell.

If we concede a national *unsavouriness* in any people, yet shall we find the Jews less subject hereto than any. *Brown.*

UNSA'VOURY. *adj.*

1. Tastless.

Can that which is *unsavoury* be eaten without salt? or is there any taste in the white of an egg? *Job* vi. 6.

2. Having a bad taste.

Unsavoury food, perhaps,
To spiritual natures. *Milton's Par. Lost.*

3. Having an ill smell; fetid.

Some may emit an *unsavoury* odour, which may happen from the quality of what they have taken. *Brown.*

4. Unpleasing; disgusting.

Things of so mean regard, although necessary to be ordered, are notwithstanding very *unsavoury*, when they come to be disputed of; because disputation pre-supposeth some difficulty in the matter. *Hooker, b.* v.

Unsavoury news; but how made he escape? *Shakesp.*

To UNSA'Y. *v. a.* To retract; to recant; to deny what has been said.

Call you me fair? that fair again *unsay*;
Demetrius loves you, fair. *Shakespeare.*

Say and *unsay*, feign, flatter, or abjure. *Milton.*

How soon
Would height recall high thoughts, how soon *unsay*
What feign'd submission swore. *Milton's Par. Lost.*

To say, and strait *unsay*, pretending first
To fly pain, professing next the spy,
Argues no leader, but a liar trac'd. *Milton.*

There is nothing said there, which you may have occasion to *unsay* hereafter. *Atterbury.*

UNSCA'LY. *adj.* Having no scales.

The jointed lobster, and *unscaly* soale. *Gay.*

UNSCA'RRED. *adj.* Not marked with wounds.

And must she die for this? O let her live;
So she may live *unscarr'd* from bleeding slaughter,
I will confess she was not Edward's daughter. *Shakespeare.*

UNSCHOLA'STICK. *adj.* Not bred to literature.

Notwithstanding these learned disputants, it was to the *unscholastick* statesman, that the world owed their peace and liberties. *Locke.*

UNSCHOO'LED. *adj.* Uneducated; not learned.

When the apostles were ordained to alter the laws of heathenish religion, they were, St. Paul excepted, *unschooled* and unlettered men. *Hooker, b.* iv.

UNSCO'RCHED. *adj.* Not touched by fire.

His hand,
Not sensible of fire, remain'd *unscorch'd.* *Shakespeare.*

UNSCO'URED. *adj.* Not cleaned by rubbing.

Th' enrolled penalties,
Which have, like *unscour'd* armour, hung by th' wall,
And none of them been worn. *Shakespeare.*

UNSCRA'TCHED. *adj.* Not torn.

I with much expedient march
Have brought a counter-check before your gates,
To save *unscratch'd* your city's threaten'd cheeks. *Shakesp.*

UNSCREE'NED. *adj.* Not covered; not protected.

Those balls of burnished brass, the tops of churches are adorned with, derive their glittering brightness from their being exposed, *unscreened*, to the sun's refulgent beams. *Boyle.*

UNSCRI'PTURAL. *adj.* Not defensible by scripture.

The doctrine delivered in my sermon was neither new nor *unscriptural*, nor in itself false. *Atterbury.*

To UNSE'AL. *v. a.* To open any thing sealed.

This new glare of light
Cast sudden on his face, *unseal'd* his sight. *Dryden.*

UNSE'ALED. *adj.*

1. Wanting a seal.

Your oaths
Are words, and poor conditions but *unseal'd.* *Shakespeare.*

2. Having the seal broken.

To UNSE'AM. *v. a.* To rip; to cut open.

He ne'er shook hands, nor bid farewel to him,
'Till he *unseam'd* him from the nape to th' chops,
And fix'd his head upon our battlements. *Shakespeare.*

Unsea'rchable. *adj.* Inscrutable; not to be explored.

All is best, though we often doubt
What th' *unsearchable* disposer
Of highest wisdom brings about,
And ever best found in the close. *Milton's Agonistes.*

Thou hast vouchsaf'd
This friendly condescension, to relate
Things else by me *unsearchable.* *Milton's Par. Lost.*

Job discourseth of the secrets of nature, and *unsearchable* perfections of the works of God *Tillotson.*

These counsels of God are to us *unsearchable*; neither has he left us in scripture any marks, by which we may infallibly conclude ourselves in that happy number he has chosen. *Rogers.*

It is a vast hindrance to the enrichment of our understandings, if we spend too much of our time among infinites and *unsearchables.* *Watts's Logick.*

Unse'archableness. *n. s.* Impossibility to be explored

The *unsearchableness* of God's ways should be a bridle to restrain presumption, and not a sanctuary for spirits of error. *Bramhall's Answ. to Hobbes.*

Unse'asonable. *adj.*

1. Not suitable to time or occasion; unfit; untimely; ill-timed.

Zeal, unless it be rightly guided, when it endeavours the most busily to please God, forceth upon him those *unseasonable* offices which please him not. *Hooker, b.* v.

Their counsel must seem very *unseasonable*, who advise men to suspect that wherewith the world hath had, by their own account, twelve hundred years acquaintance. *Hooker.*

It is then a very *unseasonable* time to plead law, when swords are in the hands of the vulgar. *Spenser's Ireland.*

The commissioners pulled down or defaced all images in churches, in such *unseasonable* fashion, as is done in hostility. *Hayward.*

This digression I conceived not *unseasonable* for this place, nor upon this occasion. *Clarendon.*

Haply mention may arise
Of something not *unseasonable* to ask. *Milton.*

Timothy lay out a-nights, and went abroad often at *unseasonable* hours. *Arbuthnot.*

2. Not agreeable to the time of the year.

Like an *unseasonable* stormy day,
Which makes the silver rivers drown their shores,
As if the world were all dissolv'd in tears. *Shakespeare.*

3. Late; as, unseasonable *time of night.*

Unse'asonableness. *n. s.* Disagreement with time or place.

The moral goodness, unfitness, and *unseasonableness* of moral or natural actions, falls not within the verge of a brutal faculty. *Hale's Origin of Mankind.*

Unse'asonably. *adv.* Not seasonably; not agreeably to time or occasion.

Some things it asketh *unseasonably*, when they need not to be prayed for, as deliverance from thunder and tempest, when no danger is nigh. *Hooker, b.* v.

Leave to fathom such high points as these,
Nor be ambitious, ere the time, to please;
Unseasonably wise, till age and cares
Have form'd thy soul to manage great affairs. *Dryden.*

By the methods prescribed, more good, and less mischief, will be done in acute distempers, than by medicines improperly and *unseasonably* applied. *Arbuthnot.*

Ulysses yielded *unseasonably*, and the strong passion for his country should have given him vigilance. *Broome.*

Unse'asoned. *adj.*

1. Unseasonable; untimely; ill-timed. Out of use.

Your majesty hath been this fortnight ill,
And these *unseason'd* hours perforce must add
Unto your sickness. *Shakesp. Hen.* IV.

I think myself in a better plight for a lender than you are; the which hath something emboldened me to this *unseasoned* intrusion. *Shakespeare.*

2. Unformed; not qualified by use.

'Tis an *unseason'd* courtier; advise him. *Shakespeare.*

3. Irregular; inordinate.

The commissioners pulled down or defaced all images in churches, in such unseasonable and *unseasoned* fashion, as if done in hostility. *Hayward.*

4. Not kept till fit for use.

5. Not salted; as, unseasoned *meat.*

Unse'conded. *adj.*

1. Not supported.

Him did you leave
Second to none, *unseconded* by you,
To look upon the hideous god of war
In disadvantage. *Shakesp. Hen.* IV.

2. Not exemplified a second time.

Strange and *unseconded* shapes of worms succeeded. *Brown.*

To Unse'cret. *v. a.* To disclose; to divulge.

He that consulteth what he should do, should not declare what he will do; but let princes beware, that the *unsecreting* of their affairs comes not from themselves. *Bacon.*

Unse'cret. *adj.* Not close; not trusty.

Who shall be true to us,
When we are so *unsecret* to ourselves? *Shakespeare.*

Unsecu're. *adj.* Not safe.

Love, though most sure,
Yet always to itself seems *unsecure.* *Denham.*

Unsedu'ced. *adj.* Not drawn to ill.

If she remain *unseduc'd*, you not making it appear otherwise; for your ill opinion, and th' assault you have made to her chastity, you shall answer me with your sword. *Shakesp.*

Among innumerable false, unmov'd,
Unshaken, *unseduc'd*, unterrify'd. *Milton's Paradise Lost.*

Unsee'ing. *adj.* Wanting the power of vision.

I shou'd have scratch'd out your *unseeing* eyes,
To make my master out of love with thee. *Shakespeare.*

To Unsee'm. *v. n.* Not to seem. Not in use.

You wrong the reputation of your name,
In so *unseeming* to confess receipt
Of that, which hath so faithfully been paid. *Shakespeare.*

Unsee'mliness. *n. s.* Indecency; indecorum; uncomeliness.

All as before his sight, whom we fear, and whose presence to offend with any the least *unseemliness*, we would be surely as loth as they, who most reprehend or deride that we do. *Hooker, b.* v.

Unsee'mly. *n. s.* Indecent; uncomely; unbecoming.

Contentions as yet were never able to prevent two evils; the one a mutual exchange of *unseemly* and unjust disgraces offered by men, whose tongues and passions are out of rule; the other a common hazard of both, to be made a prey by such as study how to work with most advantage in private. *Hooker.*

Let us now devise
What best may for the present serve to hide
The parts of each from other, that seem most
To shame obnoxious, and *unseemliest* seen. *Milton.*

Her gifts
Were such, as under government well seem'd;
Unseemly to bear rule. *Milton's Par. Lost.*

My sons, let your *unseemly* discord cease;
If not in friendship, live at least in peace. *Dryden.*

I wish every *unseemly* idea, and wanton expression had been banish'd from amongst them. *Watts.*

Unsee'mly. *adv.* Indecently; unbecomingly.

Charity doth not behave itself *unseemly*, seeketh not her own. 1 *Cor.* xiii. 5.

Unmanly dread invades the French astony'd;
Unseemly yelling; distant hills return
The hideous noise. *Philips.*

Unsee'n. *adj.*

1. Not seen; not discovered.

A jest *unseen*, inscrutable, invisible,
As a nose on a man's face, or a weathercock on a steeple. *Sh.*

Her father and myself
Will so dispose ourselves, that seeing, *unseen*,
We may of the encounter frankly judge. *Shakesp. Hamlet.*

A painter became a physician; whereupon one said to him, you have done well; for before the faults of your work were seen, but now they are *unseen.* *Bacon.*

Here may I always on this downy grass,
Unknown, *unseen*, my easy minutes pass. *Roscommon.*

Millions of spiritual creatures walk the earth
Unseen, both when we wake, and when we sleep. *Milton.*

At his birth a star
Unseen before in heaven, proclaims him come;
And guides the eastern sages who enquire
His place, to offer incense, myrrh, and gold. *Milton.*

He that on her his bold hand lays,
With Cupid's pointed arrows plays:
They with a touch, they are so keen,
Wound us unshot, and she *unseen.* *Waller.*

The footsteps of the deity he treads,
And secret moves along the crowded space,
Unseen of all the rude Phæacian race. *Pope's Odyssey.*

2. Invisible; undiscoverable.

The weeds of heresy being grown into ripeness, do, even in the very cutting down, scatter oftentimes those seeds which for a while lie *unseen* and buried in the earth; but afterward freshly spring up again no less pernicious than at the first. *Hooker.*

On she came,
Led by her heav'nly maker, though *unseen*
And guided by his voice. *Milton's Par. Lost.*

3. Unskilled; unexperienced.

He was not *unseen* in the affections of the court, but had not reputation enough to reform it. *Clarendon.*

Unse'lfish. *adj.* Not addicted to private interest.

The most interested cannot purpose any thing so much to their own advantage, notwithstanding which the inclination is nevertheless *unselfish.* *Spectator,* N° 588.

Unse'nt. *adj.*

1. Not sent.

2. Unsent *for*. Not called by letter or messenger.

If a physician should go from house to house *unsent for*, and enquire what woman hath a cancer, or what man a fistula, he would be as unwelcome as the disease itself. *Taylor.*

Somewhat of weighty consequence brings you here so often, and *unsent for*. *Dryden.*

Unse'parable. *adj.* Not to be parted; not to be divided.

Oh world, thy slippery turns! Friends now fast sworn,
Who twine as 'twere in love
Unseparable, shall, within this hour,
Break out to bitterest enmity. *Shakesp. Coriolanus.*

Unse'parated. *adj.* Not parted.

There seek the Theban bard;
To whom Persephone, entire and whole,
Gave to retain th' *unseparated* soul. *Pope's Odyssey.*

Unse'rviceable. *adj.* Useless; bringing no advantage or convenience.

The beast, impatient of his smarting wound,
Thought with his wings to fly above the ground;
But his late wounded wing *unserviceable* found. *Spenser.*

'Tis certainly demonstrated, that the condensation and expansion of any proportion of the air, is always proportional to the weight incumbent upon it: so that if the atmosphere had been much greater or less than it is, it would on the surface of the earth, have been *unserviceable* for vegetation and life. *Bentley's Sermons.*

It can be no *unserviceable* design to religion, to undeceive men in so important a point. *Rogers's Sermons.*

Unse'rviceably. *adj.* Without use; without advantage.

It does not enlarge the dimensions of the globe, or lie idly and *unserviceably* there, but part of it is introduced into the plants which grow thereon, and the rest either remounts again, with the ascending vapour, or is wash'd down into rivers. *Woodward's Nat. Hist.*

Unse't. *adj.* Not set; not placed.

They urge that God left nothing in his word undescribed, nothing *unset* down; and therefore charged them strictly to keep themselves into that without any alteration. *Hooker.*

To Unse'ttle. *v. a.*

1. To make uncertain.

Such a doctrine *unsettles* the titles to kingdoms and estates; for if the actions from which such settlements spring were illegal, all that is built upon them must be so too: but the last is absurd, therefore the first must be so likewise. *Arbuthnot.*

2. To move from a place.

As big as he was, did there need any great matter to *unsettle* him. *L'Estrange.*

3. To overthrow.

Unse'ttled. *adj.*

1. Not fixed in resolution; not determined; not steady.

Impartially judge, whether from the very first day that our religion was *unsettled*, and church government flung out of doors, the civil government has ever been able to fix upon a sure foundation. *South's Sermons.*

A solemn air, and the best comforter
To an *unsettled* fancy, cure thy brains. *Shakesp.*

Prepar'd I was not
For such a business; there am I found
So much *unsettled*. *Shakespeare.*

With them, a bastard of the king deceas'd,
And all th' *unsettl'd* humours of the land,
Rash, inconsiderate, fiery, voluntary. *Shakespeare.*

Uncertain and *unsettled* he remains
Deep vers'd in books, and shallow in himself. *Milton.*

A covetous man deliberated betwixt the qualms of a wambling stomach, and an *unsettled* mind. *L'Estrange.*

Unsettled virtue stormy may appear;
Honour, like mine, serenely is severe. *Dryden.*

2. Unequable; not regular; changeable.

March and September, the two equinoxes, are the most windy and tempestuous, the most *unsettl'd* and unequable seasons in most countries. *Bentley's Sermons.*

3. Not established.

My cruel fate,
And doubts attending an *unsettled* state,
Forc'd me to guard my coast. *Dryden.*

4. Not fixed in a place or abode.

David supposed that it could not stand with the duty which he owed unto God, to set himself in an house of cedar trees, and to behold the ark of the Lord's covenant *unsettled*. *Hooker.*

Unse'ttledness. *n. s.*

1. Irresolution; undetermined state of mind.

2. Uncertainty; fluctuation.

The *unsettledness* of my condition has hitherto put a stop to my thoughts concerning it. *Dryden.*

3. Want of fixity.

When the sun shines upon a river, though its waves roll this way and that by the wind, yet, for all their *unsettledness*, the sun strikes them with a direct and certain beam. *South.*

Unse'vered. *adj.* Not parted; not divided.

Honour and policy, like *unsever'd* friends,
I' th' war do grow together. *Shakesp. Coriolanus.*

Their bands, though slack, no dissolution fear;
Th' *unsever'd* parts the greatest pressure bear;
Though loose, and fit to flow, they still cohere. *Blackmore.*

To Unse'x. *v. a.* To make otherways than the sex commonly is.

All you spirits
That tend on mortal thoughts, *unsex* me here,
And fill me, from the crown to th' toe, top full
Of direct cruelty. *Shakesp. Macbeth.*

Unsha'dowed. *adj.* Not clouded; not darkened.

He alone sees all things with an *unshadowed*, comprehensive vision, who eminently is all. *Glanville.*

Unsha'keable. *adj.* Not subject to concussion. Not in use.

Your isle stands,
As Neptune's park, ribbed and paled in
With rocks *unshakeable*, and roaring waters. *Shakesp.*

Unsha'ked. *adj.* Not shaken. Not in use.

I know but one,
That unassailable holds on his rank,
Unshak'd of motion. *Shakesp. Jul. Cæsar.*

Unsha'ken. *adj.*

1. Not agitated; not moved.

Purpose is
Of violent birth, but poor validity;
Which now, like fruits unripe, sticks on the tree,
But fall *unshaken*, when they mellow be. *Shakespeare.*

The wicked's spite against God, is but like a madman's running his head against the wall, that leaves the wall *unshaken*, but dashes his own brains out. *Boyle.*

2. Not subject to concussion.

3. Not weakened in resolution; not moved.

Among innumerable false, unmov'd,
Unshaken, unseduc'd, unterrify'd. *Milton's Par. Lost.*

Ill wast thou shrouded then,
O patient son of God! yet only stood'st
Unshaken. *Milton's Par. Regain'd, b. iv.*

Employ it in unfeigned piety towards God, in *unshaken* duty to his vicegerent. *Sprat.*

His principles were founded in reason, and supported by virtue, and therefore did not lie at the mercy of ambition: his notions were no less steady and *unshaken*, than just and upright. *Addison.*

To Unsha'kle. *v. a.* To loose from bonds.

A laudable freedom of thought *unshackles* their minds from the narrow prejudices of education, and opens their eyes to a more extensive view of the publick good. *Addison.*

Unsha'med. *adj.* Not shamed.

The brave man seeks not popular applause;
Unsham'd, though foil'd, he does the best he can:
Force is of brutes, but honour is of man. *Dryden.*

Unsha'pen. *adj.* Misshapen; deformed.

This *unshapen* earth we now inhabit, is the form it was found in, when the waters had retired. *Burnet.*

Gasping for breath, th' *unshapen* Phocæ die,
And on the boiling wave extended lie. *Addison.*

Unsha'red. *adj.* Not partaken; not had in common.

Bliss, as thou hast part, to me is bliss;
Tedious *unshar'd* with thee, and odious soon. *Milton.*

To Unshe'ath. *v. a.* To draw from the scabbard.

Executioner, *unsheath* thy sword;
Clifford's manhood lies upon his tongue. *Shakespeare.*

Mowbray, the bishop Scroop, Hastings, and all
Are brought to the correction of your law:
There is not now a rebel's sword *unsheath'd*. *Shakespeare.*

Viewing the Trojan reliques, she *unsheath'd*
Æneas's sword. *Denham.*

Arcite, his sword *unsheath'd*. *Dryden.*

Far hence be souls profane!
Now, Trojan, take the way thy fates afford;
Assume thy courage, and *unsheath* thy sword. *Dryden.*

The Roman senate has resolv'd,
'Till time give better prospects, still to keep
The sword *unsheath'd*, and turn its edge on Cæsar. *Addison.*

Each chief his sev'nfold shield display'd,
And half *unsheath'd* the shining blade. *Pope.*

Unshe'd. *adj.* Not spilt.

To blood *unshed* the rivers must be turn'd. *Milton.*

Uhshe'ltered. *adj.* Wanting a screen; wanting protection.

He is breeding that worm, which will smite this gourd, and leave him *unsheltered* to that scorching wrath of God, which will make the improvement of Jonah's passionate wish, that God would take away his life, his most rational desire. *Decay of Piety.*

Unshi'elded. *adj.* Not guarded by the shield.

He try'd a tough, well-chosen spear!
Though Cygnus then did no defence provide,
But scornful offer'd his *unshielded* side. *Dryden.*

To Unshi'p. *v. a.* To take out of a ship.

At the cape we landed for fresh water; but discovering a leak, we *unshipped* our goods, and watered there. *Gulliver.*

UNSHO'CKED. *adj.* Not disgusted; not offended.

Thy spotless thoughts *unshock'd* the priest may hear. *Tickell.*

UNSHO'D. *adj.* [from *unshoed.*] Having no shoes.

Their feet *unshod*, their bodies wrapt in rags;
And both as swift on foot, as chased stags. *Fairy Queen.*

Withhold thy foot from being *unshod.* *Jer.* ii.

The king's army, naked and *unshod*, would, through those inclosed parts, have done them little harm. *Clarendon.*

UNSHOO'K. *part. adj.* Not shaken.

Pit, box, and gall'ry in convulsions hurl'd,
Thou stand'st *unshook* amidst a bursting world. *Pope.*

UNSHO'RN. *adj.* Not clipped.

This strength, diffus'd
No less through all my sinews, joints and bones,
Than thine, while I preserv'd these locks *unshorn*,
The pledge of my unviolated vow. *Milton's Agonistes.*

Straight as a line in beauteous order stood,
Of oaks *unshorn*, a venerable wood. *Dryden.*

UNSHO'T. *part. adj.* Not hit by shot.

He that on her his bold hand lays,
With Cupid's pointed arrow plays;
They, with a touch, they are so keen,
Wound us *unshot*, and she unseen. *Waller.*

To UNSHO'UT. *v. a.* To annihilate, or retract a shout.

Unshout the noise that banish'd Marcius;
Repeal him, with the welcome of his mother. *Shakespeare.*

UNSHO'WERED. *adj.* Not watered by showers.

Nor is Osiris seen
In Memphian grove or green,
Trampling th' *unshower'd* grass with lowings loud. *Milton.*

UNSHRI'NKING. *adj.* Not recoiling; not shunning danger or pain.

Your son, my lord, has paid a soldier's debt;
He only liv'd but till he was a man;
The which no sooner had his prowess confirm'd,
In the *unshrinking* station where he fought,
But, like a man, he died. *Shakesp. Macbeth.*

UNSHU'NNABLE. *adj.* Inevitable.

'Tis the plague of great ones,
Prerogativ'd are they less than the base;
'Tis destiny *unshunnable* like death. *Shakesp. Othello.*

UNSI'FTED. *adj.*

1. Not parted by a sieve.

The ground one year at rest, forget not thou
With richest dung to hearten it again,
Or with *unsifted* ashes. *May's Virgil.*

2. Not tried.

Affection! puh! you speak like a green girl,
Unsifted in such perilous circumstance. *Shakespeare.*

UNSI'GHT. *adj.* Not seeing. A low word, used only with *unseen*, as in the example following. Probably formed by corruption of *unsighted.*

They'll say our business to reform
The church and state is but a worm;
For to subscribe, *unsight*, unseen,
To an unknown church discipline. *Hudibras.*

UNSI'GHTED. *adj.* Invisible; not seen.

Beauties that from worth arise,
Are like the grace of deities,
Still present with us, though *unsighted.* *Suckling.*

UNSI'GHTLINESS. *n. s.* [from *unsightly.*] Deformity; disagreeableness to the eye.

The *unsightliness* in the legs, may be helped, by wearing a laced stocking. *Wiseman's Surgery.*

UNSI'GHTLY. *adj.* Disagreeable to the sight.

On my knees I beg,
That you'll vouchsafe me raiment, bed, and food.—
—Good Sir, no more: these are *unsightly* tricks. *Shakesp.*

Those blossoms also, and those dropping gums,
That lie bestrown, *unsightly*, and unsmooth,
Ask riddance, if we mean to tread with ease. *Milton.*

Amongst the rest, a small, *unsightly* root,
But of divine effect, he cull'd me out. *Milton.*

It must have been a fine genius for gardening, that could have formed such an *unsightly* hollow, into so beautiful an area. *Spectator*, Nº 477.

UNSINCE'RE. *adj.* [*insincerus*, Lat.]

1. Not hearty; not faithful.
2. Not genuine; impure; adulterated.

I have so often met with chymical preparations, which I have found *unsincere*, that I dare scarce trust any. *Boyle.*

3. Not sound; not solid.

Myrrha was joy'd the welcome news to hear;
But, clogg'd with guilt, the joy was *unsincere.* *Dryden.*

UNSINCE'RITY. *adj.* Adulteration; cheat.

A spirit of sea-salt may, without any *unsincerity*, be so prepared, as to dissolve crude gold. *Boyle.*

To UNSI'NEW. *v. a.* To deprive of strength.

Nor are the nerves of his compacted strength,
Stretch'd and dissolv'd into *unsinew'd* length. *Denham.*

Now toys and trifles from their Athens come,
And dates and pepper have *unsinew'd* Rome. *Dryden.*

The affected purity of the French has *unsinew'd* their heroick verse. The language of an epick poem is almost wholly figurative: yet are they so fearful of a metaphor, that no example of Virgil can encourage them to be bold with safety. *Dryden.*

UNSIN'GED. Not scorched; not touched by fire.

By the command of Domitian, when cast into a chaldron of burning oil, he came out *unsinged. Brown's Vulgar Errours.*

Three men passed through a fiery furnace, untouch'd, *unsinged.* *Stephens's Sermons.*

UNSI'NKING. *adj.* Not sinking.

Anxur feels the cool refreshing breeze
Blown off the sea, and all the dewy strand
Lies cover'd with a smooth, *unsinking* sand. *Addison.*

UNSI'NEWED. *adj.* Nerveless; weak.

Two special reasons
May to you, perhaps, seem much *unsinew'd*,
And yet to me are strong. *Shakespeare's Hamlet.*

UNSI'NNING. *adj.* Impeccable.

A perfect *unsinning* obedience, free from particular acts of transgression. *Rogers.*

UNSKA'NNED. *adj.* Not measured; not computed.

This tiger-footed rage, when it shall find
The harm of *unskann'd* swiftness will, too late,
Tie leaden pounds to's heels. *Shakesp. Coriolanus.*

UNSKI'LLED. *adj.* Wanting skill; wanting knowledge.

Unskill'd in Hellebore, if thou shouldst try
To mix it, and mistake the quantity,
The rules of physick would against thee cry. *Dryden.*

Unskill'd and young, yet something still I writ,
Of Ca'ndish beauty, join'd to Cecil's wit. *Prior.*

Not eastern monarchs on their nuptial day,
In dazzling gold and purple shine so gay,
As the bright natives of th' unlabour'd field,
Unvers'd in spinning, and in looms *unskill'd.* *Blackmore.*

Poets, like painters, thus *unskill'd* to trace
The naked nature, and the living grace,
With gold and jewels cover every part,
And hide with ornaments their want of art. *Pope.*

UNSKI'LFUL. *adj.* Wanting art; wanting knowledge.

This overdone, or come tardy off, though it make the *unskilful* laugh, cannot but make the judicious grieve. *Shakesp.*

Hear his sighs, though mute:
Unskilful with what words to pray, let me
Interpret for him. *Milton's Par. Lost.*

A man, *unskilful* in syllogism, could perceive the weakness and inconclusiveness of a long, artificial, and plausible discourse. *Locke.*

Using a man's words, according to the propriety of the language, though it be not always understood, leaves the blame on him, who is so *unskilful* in the language, as not to understand it, when used as it ought. *Locke.*

UNSKI'LFULLY. *adv.* Without knowledge; without art.

You speak *unskilfully*; or, if your knowledge be more, it is much darkened in your malice. *Shakespeare.*

UNSKI'LFULNESS. *n. s.* Want of art; want of knowledge.

The sweetness of her countenance did give such a grace to what she did, that it did make handsome the unhandsomeness, and make the eye force the mind to believe that there was a praise in that *unskilfulness.* *Sidney.*

Let no prices be heightened by the necessity or *unskilfulness* of the contractor. *Taylor's Rule of Living Holy.*

UNSLA'IN. *adj.* Not killed.

If there were any who felt a pity of so great a fall, and had yet any sparks of *unslain* duty left in them towards me, yet durst they not shew it. *Sidney, b.* iii.

Not hecatomb *unslain*, nor vows unpaid,
On Greeks accurs'd, this dire contagion bring. *Dryden.*

UNSLA'KED. *adj.* Not quenched.

Her desires new rous'd,
And yet *unslak'd*, will kindle in her fancy,
And make her eager to renew the feast. *Dryden.*

Wheat steep'd in brine, drawing the brine from it, they mix with *unslack'd* lime beat to powder, and so sow it. *Mortimer.*

UNSLEE'PING. *adj.* Ever wakeful.

And roseate dews dispos'd
All but th' *unsleeping* eyes of God to rest. *Milton's Par. Lost.*

UNSLI'PPING. *adj.* Not liable to slip; fast.

To knit your hearts
With an *unslipping* knot, take, Antony,
Octavia to wife. *Shakesp. Ant. and Cleopatra.*

UNSMI'RCHED. *adj.* Unpolluted; not stained.

That drop of blood that's calm proclaims me bastard;
Cries cuckold to my father; brands the harlot
Ev'n here, between the chaste and *unsmirch'd* brow
Of my true mother. *Shakesp. Hamlet.*

UNSMO'KED. *adj.* Not smoked.

His antient pipe in sable dy'd,
And half *unsmoak'd* lay by his side. *Swift.*

UNSMOO'TH. *adj.* Rough; not even; not level. Not used.

Those blossoms, and those dropping gums
That lie bestrown, unsightly, and *unsmooth*,
Ask riddance, if we mean to tread with ease. *Milton.*

UNSO'CIABLE. *adj.* [*insociabilis*, Lat.] Not kind; not communicative of good; not suitable to society.

By how much the more we are accompanied with plenty, by so much the more greedily is our end desired, whom when time hath made *unsociable* to others, we become a burden to ourselves. *Raleigh's Hist. of the World.*

Such a behaviour deters men from a religious life, by representing it as an *unsociable* state, that extinguishes all joy. *Addison's Spectator*, Nº 497.

UNSO'CIABLY. *adv.* Not kindly; without good-nature.

These are pleas'd with nothing that is not *unsociably* sour, ill-natur'd, and troublesome. *L'Estrange.*

UNSO'ILED. *adj.* Not polluted; not tainted; not stained.

Who will believe thee, Isabel?
My *unsoil'd* name, th' austereness of my life,
Will your accusation overweigh. *Shakespeare.*

The humours are transparent, to let in the light, *unsoiled* and unsophisticated by any inward tincture. *Ray.*

Her Arethusian stream remains *unsoil'd*,
Unmix'd with foreign filth, and undefil'd. *Dryden.*

UNSO'LD. *adj.* Not exchanged for money.

Mopsus the sage, who future things foretold,
And t'other seer, yet by his wife *unsold.* *Dryden.*

Adieu, my children! better thus expire
Unstall'd, *unsold*; thus glorious mount in fire. *Pope.*

UNSO'LDIERLIKE. *adj.* Unbecoming a soldier.

Perhaps they had sentinels waking while they slept; but even this would be *unsoldierlike* in our age. *Broome.*

UNSO'LID. *adj.* Fluid; not coherent.

The extension of body is nothing but the cohesion of solid, separable, moveable parts; and the extension of space, the continuity of *unsolid*, inseparable and unmoveable parts. *Locke.*

UNSOO'T. for *unsweet.* *Spenser.*

UNSOPHI'STICATED. *adj.* Not adulterated.

The humour and tunicles are purely transparent, to let in light and colours, unfouled and *unsophisticated* by any inward tincture. *More's Antidote against Atheism.*

Blue vitriol, how venereal and *unsophisticated* soever, rubb'd upon the whetted blade of a knife, will not impart its latent colour. *Boyle.*

If authors will not keep close to truth by unvaried terms, and plain, *unsophisticated* arguments; yet it concerns readers not to be imposed on, by fallacies. *Locke.*

UNSO'LVED. *adj.* Not explicated.

Why may not a sincere searcher of truth, by labour and prayer, find out the solution of those perplexities, which have hitherto been *unsolved?* *Watts.*

As Virgil propounds a riddle which he leaves *unsolved*; so I will give you another, and leave the exposition to your acute judgment. *Dryden.*

UNSO'RTED. *adj.* Not distributed by proper separation.

Their ideas, ever indifferent and repugnant, lie in the brain *unsorted*, and thrown together without order. *Watts.*

UNSO'UGHT. *adj.*

1. Had without seeking.

Mad man, that does seek
Occasion of wrath, and cause of strife;
She comes *unsought*; and shunned, follows eke. *Fairy Queen.*

Her virtue, and the conscience of her worth,
That would be woo'd, and not *unsought* be won. *Milton.*

They new hope resume,
To find whom at the first they found *unsought.* *Milton.*

The sea o'er-fraught would swell, and th' *unsought* diamonds
Would so emblaze the forehead of the deep. *Milton.*

Slumber, which forgot
When call'd before to come, now came *unsought.* *Milton.*

If some foreign and *unsought* ideas offer themselves, reject them, and keep them from taking off our minds from its present pursuit. *Locke.*

Thou that art ne'er from velvet slipper free,
Whence comes this *unsought* honour unto me? *Fenton.*

2. Not searched.

Hopeless to find, yet loth to leave *unsought*,
Or that, or any place that harbours men. *Shakespeare.*

UNSO'UND. *adj.*

1. Sickly; wanting health.

Intemp'rate youth
Ends in an age imperfect, and *unsound.* *Denham.*

An animal whose juices are *unsound*, can never be duly nourished; for *unsound* juices can never duly repair the fluids and solids. *Arbuthnot.*

2. Not free from cracks.

3. Rotten; corrupted.

4. Not orthodox.

These arguments being sound and good, it cannot be *unsound* or evil to hold still the same assertion. *Hooker.*

Eutyches of sound belief, as touching their true personal copulation, become *unsound*, by denying the difference which still continueth between the one and the other nature. *Hooker.*

5. Not honest; not upright.

Do not tempt my misery,
Lest it should make me so *unsound* a man,
As to upbraid you with those kindnesses
That I have done for you. *Shakespeare.*

6. Not true; not certain.

Their vain humours, fed
With fruitless follies and *unsound* delights. *Hubbard's Tale.*

7. Not fast; not calm.

The now sad king,
Toss'd here and there, his quiet to confound,
Feels sudden terror bring cold shivering;
Lifts not to eat; still muses; sleeps *unsound.* *Daniel.*

8. Not close; not compact.

Some lands make *unsound* cheese, notwithstanding all the care of the good housewife. *Mortimer's Husbandry.*

9. Not sincere; not faithful.

This Boobyclod soon drops upon the ground
A certain token that his love's *unsound*;
While Lubberkin sticks firmly. *Gay.*

10. Not solid; not material.

Of such subtle substance and *unsound*,
That like a ghost he seem'd, whose grave-cloaths are unbound. *Fairy Queen.*

11. Erroneous; wrong.

What fury, what conceit *unsound*,
Presenteth here to death so sweet a child? *Fairfax.*

His puissance, trusting in th' Almighty's aid,
I mean to try, whose reason I have try'd
Unsound and false. *Milton.*

12. Not fast under foot.

UNSO'UNDED. *adj.* Not tried by the plummet.

Glo'ster is
Unsounded yet, and full of deep deceit. *Shakesp. Hen.* VI.

Orpheus lute was strung with poets sinews,
Whose golden touch could soften steel and stones;
Make tygers tame, and huge leviathans
Forsake *unsounded* deeps to dance on sands. *Shakespeare.*

UNSO'UNDNESS. *n. s.*

1. Erroneousness of belief; want of orthodoxy.

If this be unsound, wherein doth the point of *unsoundness* lie? *Hooker, b.* iv.

2. Corruptness of any kind.

Neither is it to all men apparent, which complain of unsound parts, with what kind of *unsoundness* every such part is possessed. *Hooker, b.* iv.

3 Want of strength; want of solidity.

The *unsoundness* of this principle has been often expos'd, and is universally acknowledged. *Addison.*

UNSO'URED. *adj.*

1. Not made sour.

Meat and drink last longer unputrified and *unsour'd* in winter than in summer. *Bacon's Nat. Hist.*

2. Not made morose.

Secure these golden early joys,
That youth *unsour'd* with sorrow bears. *Dryden.*

UNSO'WN. *adj.* Not propagated by scattering seed.

Mushrooms come up hastily in a night, and yet are *unsown.* *Bacon.*

If the ground lie fallow and *unsown*, corn-flowers will not come. *Bacon's Nat. Hist.*

The flow'rs *unsown* in fields and meadows reign'd,
And western winds immortal spring maintain'd. *Dryden.*

UNSPA'RED. *adj.* Not spared.

Whatever thing
The scythe of time mows down, devour *unspared.* *Milton.*

UNSPA'RING. *adj.* Not sparing; not parsimonious.

She gathers tribute large, and on the board
Heaps with *unsparing* hand. *Milton.*

To UNSPE'AK. *v. a.* To retract; to recant.

I put myself to thy direction, and
Unspeak mine own detraction; here abjure
The taints and blames I laid upon myself. *Shakespeare.*

UNSPE'AKABLE. *adj.* Not to be expressed.

A thing, which uttered with true devotion and zeal of heart, affordeth to God himself that glory, that aid to the weakest sort of men, to the most perfect that solid comfort, which is *unspeakable.* *Hooker, b.* v.

A heavier task could not have been impos'd,
Than I to speak my grief *unspeakable.* *Shakespeare.*

Both addrest for fight
Unspeakable: for who, though with the tongue
Of angels, can relate? *Milton.*

The comfort it conveys is something bigger than the capacities of mortality; mighty, and *unspeakable*; and not to be understood, till it comes to be felt. *South's Sermons.*

This fills the minds of weak men with groundless fears, and *unspeakable* rage towards their fellow subjects. *Addison.*

UN-

Unspe'akably. *adv.* Inexpressibly; ineffably.

When nature is in her dissolution, and presents us with nothing but bleak and barren prospects, there is something *unspeakably* chearful in a spot of ground which is covered with trees, that smile amidst all the rigours of winter. *Spectator.*

Unspe'cified. *adj.* Not particularly mentioned.

Were it not requisite that it should be concealed, it had not passed *unspecified.* *Brown's Vulg. Errours.*

Unspe'culative. *adj.* Not theoretical.

Some *unspeculative* men may not have the skill to examine their assertions. *Government of the Tongue.*

Unspe'd. *adj.* Not dispatched; not performed.

Venutus withdraws,
Unsped the service of the common cause. *Garth.*

Unspe'nt. *adj.* Not wasted; not diminished; not weakened; not exhausted.

The sound inclosed within the sides of the bell, cometh forth at the holes *unspent* and more strong. *Bacon.*

Thy fame, not circumscrib'd with English ground,
Flies like the nimble journeys of the light,
And is, like that, *unspent* too in its flight. *Dryden.*

To Unsphe're. *v. a.* To remove from its orb.

You put me off with limber vows; but I,
Though you wou'd seek t' *unsphere* the stars with oaths,
Should yet say, Sir, no going. *Shakespeare.*

Let my lamp at midnight hour
Be seen in some high lonely tow'r,
Where I may oft out-watch the bear,
With thrice-great Hermes; or *unsphere*
The spirit of Plato, to unfold
What worlds, or what vast regions hold
Th' immortal mind. *Milton.*

Unspi'ed. *adj.* Not discovered; not seen.

With narrow search I must walk round
This garden, and no corner leave *unspy'd.* *Milton.*

Resolv'd to find some fault, before *unspy'd*;
And disappointed, if but satisfy'd. *Tickell.*

Unspi'lt. *adj.*

1. Not shed.

That blood which thou and thy great grandsire shed;
And all that since these sister nations bled,
Had been *unspilt,* had happy Edward known,
That all the blood he spilt had been his own. *Denham.*

2. Not spoiled; not marred.

To borrow to-daie, and to-morrow to mis,
For lender or borrower noiance it is;
Then have of thine owne, without lending *unspilt.* *Tusser.*

To Unspi'rit. *v. a.* To dispirit; to depress; to deject.

Denmark has continued ever since weak and *unspirited,* bent only upon safety. *Temple.*

Could it be in the power of any temporal loss, so much to discompose and *unspirit* my soul? *Norris.*

Unspo'iled. *adj.*

1. Not plundered; not pillaged.

All the way that they fled, for very despight, in their return they utterly wasted whatsoever they had before left *unspoiled.* *Spenser's State of Ireland.*

The English search'd the rivers in such sort, as they left few ships *unspoiled* or untaken. *Hayward.*

Unspoil'd shall be her arms, and unprofan'd
Her holy limbs. *Dryden.*

2. Not marred.

Unspo'tted. *adj.*

1. Not marked with any stain.

A milk-white hind,
Without *unspotted,* innocent within. *Dryden.*

Seven bullocks yet unyok'd for Phœbus chuse,
And for Diana seven *unspotted* ewes. *Dryden.*

2. Immaculate; not tainted with guilt.

Satyran bid him other business ply,
Than hunt the steps of pure, *unspotted* maid. *Fairy Queen.*

A heart *unspotted* is not easily daunted. *Shakesp. Hen. VI.*

There is no king, be his cause never so spotless, if it come to the arbitrement of swords, can try it out with all *unspotted* soldiers. *Shakesp. Hen. V.*

Pure religion and undefiled is this, to visit the fatherless and widows in their affliction, and to keep himself *unspotted* from the world. *James* i. 27.

Wisdom is the grey hair to men, and an *unspotted* life is old age. *Apocrypha.*

Make her his eternal bride;
And from her fair *unspotted* side
Two blissful twins are to be born. *Milton.*

Thou wilt not leave me in the loathsome grave
His prey, nor suffer my *unspotted* soul
For ever with corruption there to dwell. *Milton.*

Vindicate the honour of religion, by a pure and *unspotted* obedience to its precepts. *Rogers's Sermons.*

Unsqua'red. *adj.* Not formed; irregular.

When he speaks,
'Tis like a chime a mending, with terms *unsquar'd*;
Which, from the tongue of roaring Typhon dropt,
Would seem hyperboles. *Shakesp. Troilus and Cressida.*

Unsta'ble. *adj.* [*instabilis,* Lat.]

1. Not fixed; not fast.

Where gentry, title, wisdom,
Cannot conclude by the yea and no
Of gen'ral ignorance, it must omit
Real necessities, and give way the while
T' *unstable* slightness. *Shakespeare's Coriolanus.*

A popular state not founded on the general interests of the people, is of all others the most uncertain, *unstable,* and subject to the most easy changes. *Temple.*

Thus air was void of light, and earth *unstable.* *Dryden.*

See harness'd steeds desert the stony town,
And wander roads *unstable,* not their own. *Gay.*

2. Inconstant; irresolute.

A double-minded man is *unstable.* *James* i. 8.

Unsta'id. *adj.* Not cool; not prudent; not settled into discretion; not steady; mutable.

His *unstayed* youth had long wandered in the common labyrinth of love; in which time, to warn young people of his unfortunate folly, he compiled these twelve oeglogues. *Spenser.*

To the gay gardens his *unstaid* desire
Him wholly carried, to refresh his sprights. *Spenser.*

Will the king come, that I may breathe my last
In wholesome counsel to his *unstaid* youth. *Shakespeare.*

Tell me, how will the world repute me,
For undertaking so *unstaid* a journey?
I fear it will make me scandalized. *Shakespeare.*

Wo to that land,
Which gasps beneath a child's *unstaid* command. *Sandys.*

Vice leads
Vain *unstay'd* youth to beggary and shame. *Richards.*

Unsta'idness. *n. s.* Indiscretion; volatile mind.

The oft changing of his colour, with a kind of shaking *unstaidness* over all his body, he might see in his countenance some great determination mixed with fear. *Sidney.*

Unsta'ined. *adj.* Not stained; not died; not discoloured.

Pure and *unstained* religion ought to be the highest of all cares appertaining to public regimen. *Hooker, b.* v.

Ne let her waves with any filth be dy'd,
But ever, like herself, *unstained* hath been try'd. *Fa. Queen.*

I do commit into your hand
Th' *unstained* sword that you have us'd to bear,
With this remembrance, that you use the same
With a like bold, just, and impartial spirit,
As you have done 'gainst me. *Shakesp. Hen. IV.*

I will do it without fear or doubt,
To live an *unstain'd* wife to my sweet love. *Shakespeare.*

Your youth,
And the true blood which peeps forth faintly through it,
Do plainly give you out an *unstain'd* shepherd. *Shakespeare.*

The hooked chariot stood
Unstain'd with hostile blood. *Milton.*

That good earl, once president
Of England's council, and her treasury;
Who liv'd in both *unstain'd* with gold or fee,
And left them both, more in himself content. *Milton.*

Her people guiltless, and her fields *unstain'd.* *Roscommon.*

These, of the garter call'd, of faith *unstain'd,*
In fighting fields the laurel have obtain'd. *Dryden.*

To Unsta'te. *v. a.* To put out of state.

High-battled Cæsar will
Unstate his happiness, and be stag'd to th' shew
Against a sworder. *Shakesp. Ant. and Cleopatra.*

I wou'd *unstate* myself, to be in a due resolution. *Shakesp.*

Unsta'tutable. *adj.* Contrary to statute.

That plea did not avail, although the lease were notoriously *unstatutable,* the rent reserv'd, being not a seventh part of the real value. *Swift.*

Unsta'unched. *adj.* Not stopped; not stayed.

With the issuing blood
Stifle the villain, whose *unstaunched* thirst
York and young Rutland could not satisfy. *Shakespeare.*

Unste'adily. *adv.*

1. Without any certainty.

2. Inconstantly; not consistently.

He that uses his words loosely and *unsteadily,* will not be minded, or not understood. *Locke.*

Unste'adiness. *n. s.* Want of constancy; irresolution; mutability.

A prince of this character, will instruct us by his example, to fix the *unsteadiness* of our politicks. *Addison.*

In the result, we find the same spirit of cruelty, the same blindness, and obstinacy, and *unsteadiness.* *Swift.*

Unste'ady. *adj.*

1. Inconstant; irresolute.

And her *unsteady* hand hath often plac'd
Men in high pow'r, but seldom holds them fast. *Denham.*

No measures can be taken of an *unsteady* mind; still 'tis too much or too little. *L'Estrange.*

While

While choice remains, he will be ſtill *unſteady*,
And nothing but neceſſity can fix him. *Rowe.*

2. Mutable; variable; changeable.

If the motion of the ſun were as unequal as that of a ſhip driven by *unſteady* winds, it would not at all help us to meaſure time. *Locke.*

3. Not fixed; not ſettled.

UNSTE'ADFAST. *adj.* Not fixed; not faſt.

I'll read you matter,
As full of peril and advent'rous ſpirit,
As to o'erwalk a current, roaring loud,
On the *unſteadfaſt* footing of a ſpear. *Shakeſpeare.*

UNSTEE'PED. *adj.* Not ſoaked.

Other wheat was ſown *unſteeped*, but watered twice a day. *Bacon's Nat. Hiſt.*

To UNSTING. *v. a.* To diſarm of a ſting.

He has diſarmed his afflictions, *unſtung* his miſeries; and though he has not the proper happineſs of the world, yet he has the greateſt that is to be enjoyed in it. *South's Sermons.*

UNSTI'NTED. *adj.* Not limited.

In the works of nature is *unſtinted* goodneſs ſhewn us by their author. *Skelton.*

UNSTI'RRED. *adj.* Not ſtirred; not agitated.

Such ſeeming milks ſuffered to ſtand *unſtirred*, let fall to the bottom a reſinous ſubſtance. *Boyle on Colours.*

To UNSTI'TCH. *v. a.* To open by picking the ſtitches.

Cato well obſerves, though in the phraſe of a taylor, friendſhip ought not to be unripped, but *unſtiched*. *Collier.*

UNSTOO'PING. *adj.* Not bending; not yielding.

Such neighbour nearneſs to our ſacred blood
Should nothing priv'lege him, nor partialize
Th' *unſtooping* firmneſs of my upright ſoul. *Shakeſpeare.*

To UNSTO'P. *v. a.* To free from ſtop or obſtruction; to open.

Such white fumes have been afforded, by *unſtopping* a liquor diaphonous and red. *Boyle on Colours.*

The eyes of the blind ſhall be opened, and the ears of the deaf *unſtopped*. *Iſa.* xxxv. 5.

One would wonder to find ſuch a multitude of nitches *unſtopped*. *Addiſon's Remarks on Italy.*

UNSTO'PPED. *adj.* Meeting no reſiſtance.

The flame *unſtopp'd*, at firſt more fury gains,
And Vulcan rides at large with looſen'd reigns. *Dryden.*

UNSTRA'INED. *adj.* Eaſy; not forced.

By an eaſy and *unſtrained* derivation, it implies the breath of God. *Hakewill on Providence.*

UNSTRA'ITENED. *adj.* Not contracted.

The eternal wiſdom, from which we derive our beings, enriched us with all theſe ennoblements that were ſuitable to the meaſures of an *unſtraitened* goodneſs, and the capacity of ſuch a creature. *Glanville.*

UNSTRE'NGTHENED *adj.* Not ſupported; not aſſiſted.

The church of God is neither of capacity ſo weak, nor ſo *unſtrengthened* with authority from above, but that her laws may exact obedience at the hands of her own children. *Hooker.*

To UNSTRI'NG. *v. a.*

1. To relax any thing ſtrung; to deprive of ſtrings.

My tongue's uſe is to me no more,
Than an *unſtringed* viol or harp. *Shakeſp. Rich.* III.

Eternal ſtructures let them raiſe,
On William and Maria's praiſe;
Nor fear they can exhauſt the ſtore,
'Till nature's muſick lies *unſtrung*:
'Till thou, great God! ſhalt loſe thy double pow'r,
And touch thy lyre, and ſhoot thy beams no more. *Prior.*

His idle horn on fragrant myrtles hung;
His arrows ſcatter'd, and his bow *unſtrung*. *Smith.*

2. To looſe; to untie.

Invaded thus, for want of better bands,
His garland they *unſtring*, and bind his hands. *Dryden.*

UNSTRU'CK. *adj.* Not moved; not affected.

Over dank and dry,
They journey toilſome, unfatigu'd with length
Of march, *unſtruck* with horror at the ſight
Of Alpine ridges bleak. *Philips.*

UNSTU'DIED. *adj.* Not premeditated; not laboured.

In your converſation I cou'd obſerve a clearneſs of notion, expreſs'd in ready and *unſtudied* words. *Dryden.*

UNSTU'FFED. *adj.* Unfilled; unfurniſhed.

Care keeps his watch in every old man's eye;
And where care lodgeth, ſleep will never lie:
But where unbruiſed youth, with *unſtuft* brain,
Doth couch his limbs, there golden ſleep doth reign. *Shak.*

UNSUBSTA'NTIAL. *adj.*

1. Not ſolid; not palpable.

Welcome, thou *unſubſtantial* air that I embrace;
The wretch that thou haſt blown unto the worſt,
Owes nothing to thy blaſts. *Shakeſp. K. Lear.*

Darkneſs now roſe,
As daylight ſunk, and brought in low'ring night,
Her ſhadowy offspring, *unſubſtantial* both,
Privation mere of light and abſent day. *Milton.*

2. Not real.

If ſuch empty, *unſubſtantial* beings may be ever made uſe of on this occaſion, there were never any more nicely imagined and employed. *Addiſon.*

UNSUCCEE'DED. *adj.* Not ſucceeded.

Unjuſt equal o'er equals to let reign;
One over all, with *unſucceeded* power. *Milton.*

UNSUCCE'SSFUL. *adj.* Not having the wiſhed event; not fortunate; not well received.

O the ſad fate of *unſucceſsful* ſin!
You ſee yon heads without, there's worſe within. *Cleveland.*

Ye pow'rs return'd
From *unſucceſsful* charge! be not diſmay'd. *Milton.*

Hence appear the many miſtakes, which have made learning generally ſo unpleaſing and ſo *unſucceſsful*. *Milton.*

My counſels may be *unſucceſsful*, but my prayers
Shall wait on all your actions. *Denham.*

The corruption, perverſeneſs, and vitioſity of man's will, he charges as the only cauſe that rendered all the arguments his doctrine came cloathed with, *unſucceſsful*. *South.*

Had Portius been the *unſucceſsful* lover,
The ſame compaſſion would have fall'n on him. *Addiſon.*

Succeſsful authors do what they can to exclude a competitor, while the *unſucceſsful*, with as much eagerneſs, lay their claim to him as their brother. *Addiſon.*

Thoſe are generally more *unſucceſsful* in their purſuit after fame, who are more deſirous of obtaining it. *Addiſon.*

Leave dang'rous truths to *unſucceſsful* ſatire. *Pope.*

UNSUCCE'SSFULLY. *adv.* Unfortunately; without ſucceſs.

The humble and contented man pleaſes himſelf innocently; while the ambitious man attempts to pleaſe others ſinfully, and, perhaps, in the iſſue *unſucceſsfully* too. *South.*

UNSUCCE'SSFULNESS. *n. ſ.* Want of ſucceſs; event contrary to wiſh.

Admonitions, fraternal or paternal, then more publick reprehenſions, and upon the *unſucceſsfulneſs* of all theſe milder medicaments, the cenſures of the church. *Hammond.*

UNSUCCE'SSIVE. *adj.* Not proceeding by flux of parts.

We cannot ſum up the *unſucceſſive* and ſtable direction of God. *Brown's Vulgar Errours.*

The *unſucceſſive* duration of God with relation to himſelf, doth not communicate unto other created beings, the ſame manner of duration. *Hale.*

UNSU'CKED. *adj.* Not having the breaſts drawn.

Unſuck'd of lamb or kid, that tend their play. *Milton.*

UNSU'FFERABLE. *n. ſ.* Not ſupportable; intolerable; not to be endured.

The irkſome deformities, whereby through endleſs and ſenſeleſs effuſions of indigeſted prayers, they oftentimes diſgrace, in moſt *unſufferable* manner, the worthieſt part of chriſtian duty towards God. *Hooker, b.* v.

That glorious form, that light *unſufferable*,
And that far-beaming blaze of majeſty,
Wherewith he wont at heav'n's high council table
To ſit the midſt of trinal unity,
He laid aſide. *Milton.*

A ſtinking breath, and twenty ill ſmells beſides, are more *unſufferable* by her natural ſluttiſhneſs. *Swift.*

UNSUFFI'CIENCE. *n. ſ.* [*inſuffiſance*, Fr.] Inability to anſwer the end propoſed.

The error and *unſufficience* of the arguments, doth make it on the contrary ſide againſt them, a ſtrong preſumption that God hath not moved their hearts to think ſuch things as he hath not enabled them to prove. *Hooker, b.* v.

UNSUFFI'CIENT. *adj.* [*inſuffiſant*, Fr.] Unable; inadequate.

Malebranche having ſhewed the difficulties of the other ways, and how *unſufficient* they are, to give a ſatisfactory account of the ideas we have, erects this, of ſeeing all things in God, upon their ruin, as the true. *Locke.*

UNSU'GARED. *adj.* Not ſweetened with ſugar.

Try it with ſugar put into water formerly ſugared, and into other water *unſugared*. *Bacon's Nat. Hiſt.*

UNSU'ITABLE. *adj.* Not congruous; not equal; not proportionate.

Virginity, like an old courtier, wears her cap out of faſhion; richly ſuited, but *unſuitable*, juſt like the brooch and the tooth-pick, which we wear not now. *Shakeſpeare.*

He will ſmile upon her, which will now be ſo *unſuitable* to her diſpoſition, being addicted to a melancholy, that it cannot but turn him into contempt. *Shakeſp. Twelfth Night.*

That would likelieſt render contempt inſtead;
Hard recompence, *unſuitable* return
For ſo much good. *Milton's Par. Regain'd.*

All that heaven and happineſs ſignifies is *unſuitable* to a wicked man; and therefore could be no felicity to him. *Tillotſ.*

Conſider whether they be not unneceſſary expences; ſuch as are *unſuitable* to our circumſtances. *Atterbury.*

To enter into a party, as into an order of friars, with ſo reſigned an obedience to ſuperiours, is very *unſuitable* with the civil and religious liberties we ſo zealouſly aſſert. *Swift.*

UNSU'ITABLENESS. *n. ſ.* Incongruity; unfitneſs.

The *unſuitableneſs* of one man's aſpect to another man's fancy, has raiſed ſuch an averſion, as has produced a perfect hatred of him. *South.*

UNSU'ITING. *adj.* Not fitting; not becoming.

Whilst you were here, o'erwhelmed with your grief,
A passion most *unsuiting* such a man,
Cassio came hither. *Shakesp. Othello.*

Leave thy joys, *unsuiting* such an age,
To a fresh comer, and resign the stage. *Dryden.*

UNSU'LLIED. *adj.* Not fouled; not disgraced; pure.

My maiden honour yet is pure
As the *unsullied* lilly. *Shakespeare.*

To royal authority, a most dutiful observance has ever been the proper, *unsullied* honour of your church. *Sprat's Sermons.*

Rays which on Hough's *unsully'd* mitre shine. *Pope.*

These an altar raise:
An hecatomb of pure, *unsully'd* lays
That altar crowns. *Pope.*

UNSU'NG. *adj.* Not celebrated in verse; not recited in verse.

Thus was the first day ev'n and morn,
Nor pass'd uncelebrated, nor *unsung*
By the cœlestial choirs. *Milton's Par. Lost.*

Half yet remains *unsung*; but narrower bound
Within the visible diurnal sphere. *Milton's Par. Lost.*

Here the muse so oft her harp has strung,
That not a mountain rears its head *unsung*. *Addison.*

UNSU'NNED. *adj.* Not exposed to the sun.

I thought her as chaste as *unsunn'd* snow. *Shakespeare.*

You may as well spread out the *unsunn'd* heaps
Of misers treasure by an outlaw's den,
And tell me it is safe, as bid me hope
Danger will wink an opportunity,
And let a single, helpless maiden pass
Uninjur'd in this wild surrounding waste. *Milton.*

UNSUPE'RFLUOUS. *adj.* Not more than enough.

Nature's full blessings would be well dispens'd
In *unsuperfluous*, even proportion,
And she no whit encumber'd with her store. *Milton.*

UNSUPPLA'NTED. *adj.*

1. Not forced, or thrown from under that which supports it.

Gladsome they quaff, yet not encroach on night,
Season of rest; but well bedew'd repair
Each to his home with *unsupplanted* feet. *Philips.*

2. Not defeated by stratagem.

UNSUPPLI'ED. *adj.* Not supplied; not accommodated with something necessary.

Prodigal in ev'ry other grant,
Her sire left *unsupply'd* her only want. *Dryden.*

Every man who enjoys the possession of what he naturally wants, and is unmindful of the *unsupplied* distress of other men, betrays the same temper. *Spectator.*

UNSUPPO'RTABLE. *adj.* [*insupportable*, Fr.] Intolerable; such as cannot be endured.

The uneasiness of unrelieved thirst, by continuance grows the more *unsupportable*. *Boyle.*

The waters mounted up into the air, thicken and cool it; and by their interposition betwixt the earth and the sun, fence off the ardent heat, which would be otherwise *unsupportable*. *Woodward's Nat. Hist.*

UNSUPPO'RTABLY. *adv.* Intolerably.

For a man to do a thing, while his conscience assures him that he shall be infinitely, *unsupportably* miserable, is certainly unnatural. *South.*

UNSUPPO'RTED. *adj.*

1. Not sustained; not held up.

Them she up-stays
Gently with myrtle band; mindless the while
Herself, though fairest *unsupported* flow'r. *Milton.*

2. Not assisted.

Nor have our solitary attempts been so discouraged, as to despair of the favourable look of learning upon our single and *unsupported* endeavours. *Brown's Pref. to Vulgar Errours.*

UNSU'RE. Not fixed; not certain.

What is love? 'tis not hereafter:
Present mirth hath present laughter;
What's to come is still *unsure*. *Shakespeare.*

The men he prest but late,
To hard assays unfit, *unsure* at need,
Yet arm'd to point in well attempted plate. *Fairfax.*

The king, supposing his estate to be most safe, when indeed most *unsure*, advanced many to new honours. *Hayward.*

How vain that second life in others breath!
Th' estate which wits inherit after death!
Ease, health, and life, for this they must resign:
Unsure the tenure, but how vast the fine! *Pope.*

UNSURMO'UNTABLE. *adj.* [*insurmontable*, Fr.] Insuperable; not to be overcome.

What safety is it, for avoiding seeming absurdities, and *unsurmountable* rubs in one opinion, to take refuge in the contrary, which is built on something altogether as inexplicable? *Locke.*

UNSUSCE'PTIBLE. *adj.* Incapable; not liable to admit.

She a goddess died in grain,
Was *unsusceptible* of stain. *Swift.*

UNSUSPE'CT. } *adj.* Not considered as likely to do or mean
UNSUSPE'CTED. } ill.

Here is the head of that ignoble traitor,
The dangerous and *unsuspected* Hastings. *Shakesp. Rich. III.*

Author *unsuspect*,
Friendly to man, far from deceit or guile. *Milton.*

On the coast averse
From entrance, or cherubick watch, by stealth
Found *unsuspected* way. *Milton's Par. Lost.*

This day, my Persicus, thou shalt perceive,
Whether I keep myself those rules I give,
Or else an *unsuspected* glutton live. *Dryden.*

They are persons of unquestionable abilities, altogether *unsuspected* of avarice or corruption. *Swift.*

UNSUSPE'CTING. *adj.* Not imagining that any ill is designed.

When Albion sends her eager sons to war,
Pleas'd, in the gen'ral's sight, the host lie down
Sudden, before some *unsuspecting* town;
The captive race, one instant makes our prize,
And high in air Britannia's standard flies. *Pope.*

UNSUSPI'CIOUS. *adj.* Having no suspicion.

He his guide requested to let him lean
With both his arms on those two massy pillars,
That to the arched roof gave main support:
He *unsuspicious* led him. *Milton's Agonistes.*

The easy queen receiv'd my faint address,
With eager hope and *unsuspicious* faith. *Smith.*

UNSUSTA'INED. *adj.* Not supported; not held up.

Its head, though gay,
Hung drooping, *unsustain'd*. *Milton's Par. Lost.*

All *unsustain'd* between the wave and sky,
Beneath my feet the whirling billows fly. *Pope.*

To UNSWA'THE. *v. a.* To free from folds or convolutions of bandage.

In the morning an old woman came to *unswathe* me. *Addison.*

UNSWA'YABLE. *adj.* Not to be governed or influenced by another.

He bow'd his nature, never known before
But to be rough, *unswayable* and free. *Shakespeare.*

UNSWA'YED. *adj.* Not wielded; not held in the hand.

He makes for England, here to claim the crown.—
—Is the chair empty? is the sword *unsway'd*?
Is the king dead? the empire unpossess'd? *Shakespeare.*

To UNSWE'AR. *v. n.* Not to swear; to recant any thing sworn.

The ape was glade to end the strife so light,
And thereto swore; for who would not oft swear,
And oft *unswear*, a diadem to bear? *Hubbard's Tale.*

To UNSWE'AT. *v. a.* To ease after fatigue; to cool after exercise.

The interim of *unsweating* themselves regularly, and convenient rest before meat, may, with profit and delight, be taken up with solemn musick. *Milton on Education.*

UNSWE'ATING. *adj.* Not sweating.

In frost and snow, if you complain of heat,
They rub th' *unsweating* brow, and swear they sweat. *Dryd.*

UNSWEE'T. *adj.* Not sweet; disagreeable.

Long were to tell the troublous storms that toss
The private state, and make the life *unsweet*. *Fairy Queen.*

UNSWE'PT. *adj.* Not brushed away; not cleaned by sweeping.

What custom wills in all things, should we do't,
The dust of antique time would lie *unswept*. *Shakesp.*

UNSWO'RN. *adj.* Not bound by an oath.

You are not yet *unsworn*:
When you have vow'd, you must not speak with men. *Shak.*

UNTA'INTED. *adj.*

1. Not sullied; not polluted.

Sweet prince, th' *untainted* virtue of your years
Hath not yet div'd into the world's deceit. *Shakesp.*

What stronger breast-plate than a heart *untainted*? *Shak.*

Ireland's *untainted* loyalty remain'd. *Roscommon.*

Compare the ingenuous pliableness to virtuous counsels in youth, as it comes fresh and *untainted*, out of the hands of nature, with the confirmed obstinacy in an aged sinner. *South.*

This *untainted* year is all your own;
Your glories may, without our crimes, be shown. *Dryden.*

The most *untainted* credit of a witness will scarce be able to find belief. *Locke.*

Keep the air of the room *untainted* with fire, smoke, or the breaths of many people. *Arbuthnot.*

2. Not charged with any crime.

And yet within these five hours Hastings liv'd
Untainted, unexamin'd, free at liberty. *Shakespeare.*

3. Not corrupted by mixture.

The conscious walls conceal the fatal secret;
Th' *untainted* winds refuse th' infecting load. *Smith.*

UNTA'KEN. *adj.*

1. Not taken.

Until this day remaineth the vail *untaken* away. 2 *Cor.* iii.

The English searched the rivers in such sort, as they left few ships unspoiled or *untaken*. *Hayward.*

29 Z Dispose

Dispose already of th' *untaken* spoil. *Waller.*

Otherwise the whole business had miscarried, and Jerusalem remain'd *untaken*. *Dryden.*

A thousand schemes the monarch's mind employ;
Elate in thought, he sacks *untaken* Troy. *Pope.*

2. UNTAKEN *up*. Not filled.

The narrow limits of this discourse, will leave no more room *untaken up* by heaven. *Boyle.*

UNTA'LKED *of*. *adj*. Not mentioned in the world.

Spread thy close curtain, love-performing night,
That the runaway's eyes may wink, and Romeo
Leap to these arms, *untalk'd of* and unseen. *Shakespeare.*

No happiness can be, where is no rest;
Th' unknown, *untalk'd of* man is only blest. *Dryden.*

UNTA'MEABLE. *adj*. Not to be tamed; not to be subdued.

Gold is so *untameable* by the fire, that after many meltings and violent heats, it does scarce diminish. *Wilkins.*

He is swifter than any other bull, and *untameable*. *Grew.*

UNTA'MED. *adj*. Not subdued; not suppressed.

A people very stubborn and *untamed*; or, if ever tamed, yet lately have quite shooken off their yoke, and broken the bonds of their obedience. *Spenser's Ireland.*

What death has heav'n design'd,
For so *untam'd*, so turbulent a mind! *Dryden.*

Man alone acts more contrary to nature, than the wild and most *untamed* part of the creation. *Locke.*

To UNTA'NGLE. *v. a.* To loose from intricacy or convolution.

O time, thou must *untangle* this, not I;
It is too hard a knot for me t'untie. *Shakespeare.*

This is that very Mab,
That cakes the elflocks, in foul, sluttish hairs,
Which, once *untangl'd*, much misfortune bodes. *Shakesp.*

I'll give thee up my bow and dart;
Untangle but this cruel chain,
And freely let me fly again. *Prior.*

UNTA'STED. *adj*. Not tasted; not tried by the palate.

The tall stag resolves to try
The combat next; but if the cry
Invades again his trembling ear,
He straight resumes his wonted care;
Leaves the *untasted* spring behind,
And, wing'd with fear, outflies the wind. *Waller.*

If he chance to find
A new repast, or an *untasted* spring,
Blesses his stars, and thinks it luxury. *Addison's Cato.*

UNTA'STING. *adj*.

1. Not perceiving any taste.

Cydonian oil,
Whose balmy juice glides o'er th' *untasting* tongue. *Smith.*

2. Not trying by the palate.

UNTA'UGHT. *adj*.

1. Uninstructed; uneducated; ignorant; unlettered.

A lie is continually in the mouth of the *untaught*. *Ecclus.* xx.

Taught, or *untaught*, the dunce is still the same;
Yet still the wretched master bears the blame. *Dryden.*

On ev'ry thorn delightful wisdom grows,
In ev'ry stream a sweet instruction flows;
But some *untaught* o'erhear the whisp'ring rill,
In spite of sacred leisure, blockheads still. *Young.*

2. Debarr'd from instruction.

He, that from a child *untaught*, or a wild inhabitant of the woods, will expect principles of sciences, will find himself mistaken. *Locke.*

3. Unskilled; new; not having use or practice.

Suffolk's imperial tongue is stern and rough,
Us'd to command, *untaught* to plead for favour. *Shakespeare.*

To UNTE'ACH. *v. a.* To make to quit, or forget what has been inculcated.

That elder berries are poison, as we are taught by tradition, experience will *unteach* us. *Brown's Vulgar Errours.*

Their customs are by nature wrought;
But we, by art, *unteach* what nature taught. *Dryden.*

UNTE'MPERED. *adj*. Not tempered.

One built up a wall, and others daubed it with *untempered* mortar. *Ezek.* xiii. 10.

UNTE'MPTED. *adj*.

1. Not embarrassed by temptation.

In temptation dispute not, but rely upon God, and contend not with him but in prayer, and with the help of a prudent *untempted* guide. *Taylor's Rule of Living Holy.*

2. Not invited by any thing alluring.

Untempted, or by wager or by price,
He would attempt to climb the precipice. *Cotton on the Peak.*

UNTE'NABLE. *adj*.

1. Not to be held in possession.

2. Not capable of defence.

He produced a warrant, that the town being *untenable*, he should retire. *Clarendon, b.* viii.

Casaubon abandons a post that was *untenable*. *Dryden.*

UNTE'NANTED. *adj*. Having no tenant.

The country seems to be full stock'd with cattle, no ground being *untenanted*. *Temple.*

UNTE'NDED. *adj*. Not having any attendance.

They fall, unblest, *untended*, and unmourn'd. *Thomson.*

UNTE'NDER. *adj*. Wanting softness; wanting affection.

Goes thy heart with this?—
—Aye, my lord ——
—So young, and so *untender*?—
—So young, my lord, and true. *Shakespeare.*

UNTE'NDERED. *adj*. Not offered.

Cassibelan granted Rome a tribute,
Yearly three thousand pounds; which by thee lately
Is left *untender'd*. *Shakespeare's Cymbeline.*

To UNTE'NT. *v. a.* To bring out of a tent.

Will he not, upon our fair request,
Untent his person, and share the air with us? *Shakespeare.*

UNTE'NTED. *adj*. [from *tent.*] Having no medicaments applied.

Blasts and fogs upon thee!
Th' *untented* woundings of a father's curse
Pierce every fence about thee! *Shakespeare's K. Lear.*

UNTE'RRIFIED. *adj*. Not affrighted; not struck with fear.

Among innumerable false, unmov'd,
Unshaken, unseduc'd, *unterrify'd*. *Milton.*

To succour the distrest; to give help
To an afflicted mother,
Unbrib'd by love, *unterrify'd* by threats;
These are exploits worthy Achilles' son. *A. Philips.*

UNTHA'NKED. *adj*.

1. Not repaid with acknowledgment of a kindness.

If all the world
Should in a pet of temperance feed on pulse,
Drink the clear stream, and nothing wear but freeze,
Th' all-giver wou'd be *unthank'd*, wou'd be unprais'd. *Milt.*

Their batter'd admiral too soon withdrew,
Unthank'd by ours for his unfinish'd fight. *Dryden.*

2. Not received with thankfulness.

Forc'd from her presence, and condemn'd to live:
Unwelcome freedom, and *unthank'd* reprieve. *Dryden.*

UNTHA'NKFUL. *adj*. Ungrateful; returning no acknowledgment for good received.

The casting away of things profitable for sustenance, is an *unthankful* abuse of the fruits. *Hooker.*

He is kind to the *unthankful*. *Luke* vi. 35.

They which he created, were *unthankful* unto him which prepared life for them. 2 *Esdr.* viii.

If you reckon that for evil, you are *unthankful* for the blessing. *Taylor's Rule of Holy Living.*

The bare supposal of one petty loss, makes us *unthankful* for all that's left. *L'Estrange.*

UNTHA'NKFULLY. *adv*. Without thanks; without gratitude.

I judged it requisite to say something, to prevent my being thought to have *unthankfully* taken one of the chief passages of my discourse from a book, to which I was utterly a stranger. *Boyle.*

UNTHA'NKFULNESS. *n. s.* Neglect or omission of acknowledgement for good received; want of sense of benefits; ingratitude.

Thou diest in thine *unthankfulness*; and thine ignorance makes thee away. *Shakespeare.*

Immoderate favours breed first *unthankfulness*, and afterwards hate. *Hayward.*

The unthankful stand reckoned among the most enormous sinners, which evinces the virtue opposite to *unthankfulness*, to bear the same place in the rank of duties. *South's Sermons.*

UNTHA'WED. *adj*. Not dissolved after frost.

Your wine lock'd up,
Or fish deny'd, the river yet *unthaw'd*. *Pope.*

To UNTHI'NK. *v. a.* To recal, or dismiss a thought.

Unthink your speaking, and say so no more. *Shakesp.*

UNTHI'NKING. *adj*. Thoughtless; not given to reflection.

Grey-headed infant! and in vain grown old;
Art thou to learn, that in another's gold
Lie charms resistless! that all laugh to find
Unthinking plainness so o'erspread thy mind. *Dryden.*

An effectual remedy for the wandering of thoughts whoever shall propose, would do great service to the studious, and perhaps help *unthinking* men to become thinking. *Locke.*

The *unthinking* part contract an unreasonable aversion to that ecclesiastical constitution. *Addison.*

With earnest eyes, and round *unthinking* face,
He first the snuff-box open'd, then the case. *Pope.*

UNTHO'RNY. *adj*. Not obstructed by prickles.

It were some extenuation of the curse, if *in sudore vultus tui* were confinable unto corporal exercitations, and there still remained a paradise, or *unthorny* place of knowledge. *Brown.*

UNTHO'UGHT *of*. *adj*. Not regarded; not heeded.

That shall be the day, whene'er it lights,
This gallant Hotspur, this all-praised knight,
And your *unthought of* Harry chance to meet. *Shakespeare.*

To

To UNTHREA'D. *v. a.* To loose.

He with his bare wand can *unthread* thy joints,
And crumble all thy sinews. *Milton.*

UNTHRE'ATENED. *adj.* Not menaced.

Sir John Hotham was unreproached, and *unthreatened*, by any language of mine. *K. Charles.*

UNTHRI'FT. *n. s.* An extravagant; a prodigal.

My rights and royalties
Pluckt from my arms perforce, and giv'n away
To upstart *unthrifts*. *Shakespeare.*

The curious *unthrift* makes his cloaths too wide,
And spares himself, but would his taylor chide. *Herbert.*

Yet nothing still; then poor and naked come;
Thy father will receive his *unthrift* home,
And thy blest Saviour's blood discharge the mighty sum. *Dryd.*

UNTHRI'FT. *adj.* Profuse; wasteful; prodigal; extravagant.

In such a night,
Did Jessica steal from the wealthy Jew,
And, with an *unthrift* love, did run from Venice. *Shakesp.*

UNTHRI'FTILY. *adv.* Without frugality.

Our attainments cannot be overlarge, and yet we manage a narrow fortune very *unthriftily*. *Collier.*

UNTHRI'FTINESS. *n. s.* Waste; prodigality; profusion.

The third sort are the poor by idleness or *unthriftiness*, as riotous spenders, vagabonds, loiterers. *Hayward.*

The more they have hitherto embezzled their parts, the more should they endeavour to expiate that *unthriftiness*, by a more careful managery for the future. *Govern. of the Tongue.*

UNTHRI'FTY. *adj.*

1. Prodigal; profuse; lavish; wasteful.

The castle I found of good strength, having a great mote round about it; the work of a noble gentleman, of whose *unthrifty* son he had bought it. *Sidney, b.* ii.

Can no man tell me of my *unthrifty* son? *Shakespeare.*

Our absence makes us *unthrifty* to our knowledge. *Shakesp.*

2. Not easily made to thrive or fatten. A low word.

Grains given to a hide-bound or *unthrifty* horse, recover him. *Mortimer's Husbandry.*

UNTHRI'VING. *adj.* Not thriving; not prospering; not growing rich.

Let all who thus unhappily employ their inventive faculty, consider, how *unthriving* a trade it is finally like to prove, that their false accusations of others will rebound in true ones on themselves. *Government of the Tongue.*

To UNTHRO'NE. *v. a.* To pull down from a throne.

Him to *unthrone*, we then
May hope, when everlasting fate shall yield
To fickle chance, and chaos judge the strife. *Milton.*

To UNTI'E. *v. a.*

1. To unbind; to free from bonds.

Though you *untie* the winds, and let them fight
Against the churches; though the yesty waves
Confound and swallow navigation up. *Shakesp. Macbeth.*

2. To loosen from convolution or knot.

All that of myself is mine,
Lovely Amoret, is thine;
Sacharissa's captive fain
Would *untie* his iron chain;
And those scorching beams to shun,
To thy gentle shadow run. *Waller.*

The chain I'll in return *untie*,
And freely thou again shalt fly. *Prior.*

The fury heard; while on Cocytus' brink,
Her snakes *untied*, sulphureous waters drink. *Pope.*

3. To set free from any obstruction.

All the evils of an *untied* tongue, we put upon the accounts of drunkenness. *Taylor.*

4. To resolve; to clear.

They quicken sloth, perplexities *untie*;
Make roughness smooth, and hardness mollifie. *Denham.*

A little more study will solve those difficulties, *untie* the knot, and make your doubts vanish. *Watts.*

UNTI'ED. *adj.*

1. Not bound; not gathered in a knot.

Her hair
Unty'd, and ignorant of artful aid,
A-down her shoulders loosely lay display'd. *Prior.*

2. Not fastened by any binding, or knot.

Your hose should be ungartered, your shoe *untied*, and every thing about you demonstrating a careless desolation. *Shakespeare.*

UNTI'L. *adv.*

1. To the time that.

Treasons are acted,
As soon as thought; though they are never believ'd
Until they come to act. *Denham.*

2. To the place that.

In open prospect nothing bounds our eye,
Until the earth seems join'd unto the sky. *Dryden.*

UNTI'L. *prep.* To. Used of time. The other use is obsolete.

So soon as he from far descry'd
Those glist'ring arms, that heaven with light did fill,
He rous'd himself full blithe, and hasten'd them *until.* *Spenser.*

UNTI'LLED. *adj.* Not cultivated.

The glebe *untill'd*, might plenteous crops have born;
Rich fruits and flow'rs, without the gard'ner's pains,
Might ev'ry hill have crown'd, have honour'd all the plains. *Blackmore on the Creation.*

Lands lain long *untill'd*, contract a sour juice, which causes the land to run to unprofitable trumpery. *Mortimer.*

The soil *untill'd*, a ready harvest yields;
With wheat and barley wave the golden fields. *Pope.*

UNTI'MBERED. *adj.* Not furnished with timber; weak.

Where's then the saucy boat,
Whose weak *untimber'd* sides but even now
Co-rival'd greatness? or to harbour fled,
Or made a toast for Neptune? *Shakespeare.*

UNTI'MELY. *adj.* Happening before the natural time.

Boundless intemp'rance hath been
Th' *untimely* emptying of the happy throne. *Shakespeare.*

Matrons and maids
With tears lament the knight's *untimely* fate. *Dryden.*

Such were the notes thy once-lov'd poet sung,
'Till death *untimely* stopp'd his tuneful tongue.
Oh just beheld and lost! *Pope.*

UNTI'MELY. *adv.* Before the natural time.

He only fair, and what he fair hath made;
All other fair, like flowers *untimely* fade. *Spenser.*

If ever he have child, abortive be it;
Prodigious and *untimely* brought to light. *Shakespeare.*

Butchers, and villains!
How sweet a plant have you *untimely* cropt? *Shakespeare.*

Call up our friends,
And let them know what we mean to do,
And what's *untimely* done. *Shakesp. Hamlet.*

Why came I so *untimely* forth
Into a world, which, wanting thee,
Cou'd entertain us with no worth? *Waller.*

UNTI'NGED. *adj.*

1. Not stained; not discoloured.

It appears what beams are *untinged*, and which paint the primary, or secondary iris. *Boyle on Colours.*

2. Not infected.

Your inattention I cannot pardon; Pope has the same defect, neither is Bolingbroke *untinged* with it. *Swift to Gay.*

UNTI'RABLE. *adj.* Indefatigable; unwearied.

A most incomparable man, breath'd as it were
To an *untirable* and continuate goodness. *Shakespeare.*

UNTI'RED. *adj.* Not made weary.

Hath he so long held out with me *untir'd*,
And stops he now for breath? *Shakesp. Rich.* III.

See great Marcellus! how *untir'd* in toils,
He moves with manly grace, how rich with regal spoils! *Dry.*

UNTI'TLED. *adj.* [*un* and *title.*] Having no title.

O nation miserable!
With an *untitled* tyrant, bloody scepter'd;
When shalt thou see thy wholesome days again? *Shakesp.*

U'NTO. *prep.* [It was the old word for *to*; now obsolete.] To.

O continue thy loving kindness *unto* them. *Ps.* xxxvi.

It was their hurt untruly to attribute such great power *unto* false gods. *Hooker.*

She, by her wicked arts, and wily skill,
Unawares me wrought *unto* her wicked will. *Spenser.*

The use of the navel is to continue the infant *unto* the mother, and by the vessels thereof convey its sustentation. *Brown.*

Children permitted the freedom of both hands, often confine *unto* the left. *Brown.*

Me, when the cold Digentian stream revives,
What does my friend believe I think or ask?
Let me yet less possess, so I may live,
Whate'er of life remains *unto* myself. *Temple.*

UNTO'LD. *adj.*

1. Not related.

Better a thousand such as I,
Their grief *untold*, should pine and die;
Than her bright morning, overcast
With sullen clouds, should be defac'd. *Waller.*

2. Not revealed.

Characters where obscene words are very indecent to be heard: for that reason, such a tale shall be left *untold* by me. *Dryden.*

UNTO'UCHED. *adj.*

1. Not touched; not reached.

Achilles, though dipt in Styx, yet having his heel *untouched* by that water, was slain in that part. *Brown's Vulg. Errours.*

Three men passed through a fiery furnace *untouched*, unsinged. *Stephens's Sermons.*

2. Not moved; not affected.

They, like persons wholly *untouched* with his agonies, and unmoved with his passionate intreaties, sleep away all concern for him or themselves. *Sidney.*

3. Not meddled with.

We muſt purſue the ſylvan lands;
Th' abode of nymphs, *untouch'd* by former hands. *Dryden.*

Several very antient trees grow upon the ſpot, from whence they conclude, that theſe particular tracts muſt have lain *untouch'd* for ſome ages. *Addiſon.*

UNTO'WARD. *adj.*

1. Froward; perverſe; vexatious; not eaſily guided, or taught.

Have to my window; and if ſhe be froward,
Then haſt thou taught Hortenſio to be *untoward.* *Shakeſp.*

The ladies prove averſe,
And more *untoward* to be won,
Than by Caligula the moon. *Hudibras.*

The rabbins write, when any Jew
Did make to God or man a vow,
Which afterwards he found *untoward,*
Or ſtubborn to be kept, or too hard;
Any three other Jews o' th' nation,
Might free him from the obligation. *Hudibras.*

They were a croſs, odd, *untoward* people. *South.*

Some men have made a very *untoward* uſe of this, and ſuch as he never intended they ſhould. *Woodward.*

2. Aukward; ungraceful.

Vaſt is my theme, yet unconceiv'd, and brings
Untoward words, ſcarce looſen'd from the things. *Creech.*

Some clergymen hold down their heads within an inch of the cuſhion; which, beſides the *untoward* manner, hinders them from making the beſt advantage of their voice. *Swift.*

UNTO'WARDLY. *adj.* Aukward; perverſe; froward.

They learn, from unbred or debauched ſervants, *untowardly* tricks and vices. *Locke on Education.*

UNTO'WARDLY. *adv.* Aukwardly; ungainly; perverſely.

He that provides for this ſhort life, but takes no care for eternity, acts as *untowardly* and as croſsly to the reaſon of things, as can be. *Tillotſon.*

He explained them very *untowardly.* *Tillotſon.*

UNTRA'CEABLE. *adj.* Not to be traced.

The workings of providence are ſecret and *untraceable,* by which it diſpoſes of the lives of men. *South's Sermons.*

UNTRA'CED. *adj.* Not marked by any footſteps.

Nor wonder, if advantag'd in my flight,
By taking wing from thy auſpicious height,
Through *untrac'd* ways, and airy paths I fly,
More boundleſs in my fancy than my eye. *Denham.*

UNTRA'CTABLE. *adj.* [*intraitable,* Fr. *intractabilis,* Lat.]

1. Not yielding to common meaſures and management; not governable; ſtubborn.

The French, ſuppoſing that they had advantage over the Engliſh, began to be ſtiff, and almoſt *untractable,* ſharply preſſing for ſpeedy reſolutions and ſhort meetings. *Haywerd.*

If any father have a ſon thus perverſe and *untractable,* I know not what more he can do but pray for him. *Locke.*

Ulcers *untractable* in the legs, with a gangrenous appearance in the ſkin. *Arbuthnot on Diet.*

2. Rough; difficult.

I forc'd to ride th' *untractable* abyſs. *Milton.*

UNTRA'CTABLENESS. *n. ſ.* Unwillingneſs, or unfitneſs to be regulated or managed; ſtubbornneſs.

The great difference in mens intellectuals ariſes from a defect in the organs of the body, particularly adapted to think; or in the dulneſs or *untractableneſs* of thoſe faculties, for want of uſe. *Locke.*

UNTRA'DING. *adj.* Not engaged in commerce.

Men leave eſtates to their children in land, as not ſo liable to caſualties as money, in *untrading* and unſkilful hands. *Locke.*

UNTRA'INED. *adj.*

1. Not educated; not inſtructed; not diſciplined.

My wit *untrain'd* in any kind of art. *Shakeſpeare.*

The king's forces charged lively, and they again as ſtoutly received the charge; but being an *untrained* multitude, without any ſoldier or guide, they were ſoon put to flight. *Hayw.*

Life,
To noble and ignoble, is more ſweet
Untrain'd in arms, where raſhneſs leads not on. *Milton.*

No expert general will bring a company of raw, *untrained* men into the field; but will, by little bloodleſs ſkirmiſhes, inſtruct them in the manner of the fight. *Decay of Piety.*

2. Irregular; ungovernable.

Gad not abroad at ev'ry queſt and call
Of an *untrained* hope or paſſion:
To court each place of fortune that doth fall,
Is wantonneſs in contemplation. *Herbert.*

UNTRANSFE'RRABLE. *adj.* Incapable of being given from one to another.

In parliament there is a rare co-ordination of power, though the ſovereignty remain ſtill entire and *untransferable,* in the prince. *Howel's Pre-eminence of Parliament.*

UNTRANSPA'RENT. *adj.* Not diaphanous; opaque.

Though held againſt the light they appear'd of a tranſparent yellow, yet looked on with one's back turn'd to the light, they exhibited an *untranſparent* blue. *Boyle on Colours.*

UNTRA'VELLED. *adj.*

1. Never trodden by paſſengers.

We find no open track, or conſtant manuduction in this labyrinth, but are oft times fain to wander in America, and *untravelled* parts. *Brown's Pref. to Vulgar Errours.*

Long *untravell'd* heaths. *Thomſon.*

2. Having never ſeen foreign countries.

An *untravelled* Engliſhman cannot reliſh all the beauties of Italian pictures; becauſe the poſtures expreſſed in them are often ſuch as are peculiar to that country. *Addiſon.*

To UNTRE'AD. *v. a.* To tread back; to go back in the ſame ſteps.

We will *untread* the ſteps of damned flight,
And, like a bated and retired flood,
Leaving our rankneſs and irregular courſe,
Stoop low within thoſe bounds we have o'erlook'd. *Shakeſp.*

UNTRE'ASURED. *adj.* Not laid up; not repoſited.

Her attendants
Saw her a-bed, and in the morning early
They found the bed *untreaſur'd* of their miſtreſs. *Shakeſp.*

UNTRE'ATABLE. *adj.* Not treatable; not practicable.

Men are of ſo *untreatable* a temper, that nothing can be obtained of them. *Decay of Piety.*

UNTRI'ED. *adj.*

1. Not yet attempted.

It behoves,
From hard eſſays, and ill ſucceſſes paſt,
A faithful leader, not to hazard all
Through ways of danger, by himſelf *untry'd.* *Milton.*

That ſhe no ways nor means may leave *untry'd,*
Thus to her ſiſter ſhe herſelf apply'd. *Denham.*

2. Not yet experienced.

Never more
Mean I to try, what raſh *untry'd* I ſought,
The pain of abſence from thy ſight. *Milton's Par. Loſt.*

The happieſt of mankind overlooking thoſe ſolid bleſſings which they already have, ſet their hearts upon ſomewhat which they want; ſome *untry'd* pleaſure, which, if they could but taſte, they ſhould then be compleatly bleſt. *Atterbury.*

Self-preſervation, the long acquaintance of ſoul and body, the *untry'd* condition of a ſeparation, are ſufficient reaſons not to turn our backs upon life, out of an humour. *Collier.*

Eternity! thou pleaſing, dreadful thought!
Through what variety of *untry'd* being,
Through what new ſcenes and changes muſt we paſs? *Addiſ.*

3. Not having paſſed trial.

The father ſecure,
Ventures his filial virtue, though *untry'd,*
Againſt whate'er may tempt. *Milton's Par. Regain'd.*

UNTRIU'MPHABLE. *adj.* Which allows no triumph.

What towns, what garriſons might you,
With hazard of this blood ſubdue;
Which now y'are bent to throw away
In vain, *untriumphable* fray? *Hudibras.*

UNTRO'D. }
UNTRO'DDEN. } *adj.* Not paſſed; not marked by the foot.

The way he came, not having mark'd, return
Was difficult, by human ſteps *untrod.* *Paradiſe Regain'd.*

Now while the heav'n by the ſun's team *untrod,*
Hath took no print of the approaching light,
And all the ſpangled hoſt keep watch. *Milton.*

A garland made of ſuch new bays,
And ſought in ſuch *untrodden* ways,
As no man's temples e'er did crown. *Waller.*

Who was the firſt to explore th' *untrodden* path,
When life was hazarded in ev'ry ſtep? *Addiſon's Cato.*

UNTRO'LLED. *adj.* Not bowled; not rolled along.

Hard fate! *untroll'd* is now the charming dye;
The playhouſe and the parks unviſited muſt lie. *Dryden.*

UNTRO'UBLED. *adj.*

1. Not diſturbed by care, ſorrow, or guilt.

Quiet *untroubled* ſoul, awake! awake!
Arm, fight and conquer, for fair England's ſake. *Shakeſp.*

2. Not agitated; not confuſed.

Our Saviour meek, and with *untroubled* mind,
After his airy jaunt, though hurry'd ſore,
Hungry and cold, betook him to his reſt. *Milton.*

3. Not interrupted in the natural courſe.

Would they think with how ſmall allowance
Untroubled nature doth herſelf ſuffice,
Such ſuperfluities they would deſpiſe. *Fairy Queen.*

4. Tranſparent; clear.

The equal diſtribution of the ſpirits in the liquor with the tangible parts, ever repreſenteth bodies clear and *untroubled.* *Bacon.*

UNTRU'E. *adj.*

1. Falſe; contrary to reality.

By what conſtruction ſhall any man make thoſe compariſons true, holding that diſtinction *untrue.* *Hooker.*

That a veſſel filled with aſhes, will receive the like quantity of water, that it would have done if it had been empty, is utterly *untrue,* for the water will not go in by a fifth part. *Bacon.*

2. Falſe;

2. False; not faithful.

I cannot break so sweet a bond,
Unless I prove *untrue*;
Nor can I ever be so fond,
To prove *untrue* for you. *Suckling.*

Flora commands those nymphs and knights,
Who liv'd in slothful ease, and loose delights:
Who never acts of honour durst pursue,
The men inglorious knights, the ladies all *untrue.* *Dryden.*

UNTRU'LY. *adv.* Falsely; not according to truth.

It was their hurt *untruly* to attribute so great power unto false gods. *Hooker, b.* v.

On these mountains it is generally received that the ark rested, but *untruly.* *Raleigh's Hist. of the World.*

UNTRU'STINESS. *n. s.* Unfaithfulness.

Secretary Peter, under pretence of gravity, covered much *untrustiness* of heart. *Hayward.*

UNTRU'TH. *n. s.*

1. Falsehood; contrariety to reality.
2. Moral falsehood; not veracity.

He who is perfect, and abhors *untruth*,
With heavenly influence inspires my youth. *Sandys.*

3. Treachery; want of fidelity.

I would,
So my *untruth* had not provok'd him to it,
The king had cut off my head with my brother's. *Shakesp.*

4. False assertion.

In matter of speculation or practice, no *untruth* can possibly avail the patron and defender long; and things most truly, are likewise most behovefully spoken. *Hooker, b.* iii.

There is little hope for common justice in this dispute, from a man, who lays the foundations of his reasonings in so notorious an *untruth.* *Atterbury.*

UNTU'NABLE. *adj.* Unharmonious; not musical.

My news in dumb silence will I bury,
For they are harsh, *untunable*, and bad. *Shakespeare.*

A lutestring, merely unequal in its parts, giveth a harsh and *untunable* sound; which strings we call false. *Bacon.*

His harsh *untunable* pipe is no more fit than a raven's, to join with the musick of a choir. *Tatler,* N° 54.

To UNTU'NE. *v. a.*

1. To make incapable of harmony.

Take but degree away, *untune* that string,
And hark what discord follows. *Shakespeare.*

When the last and dreadful hour,
This crumbling pageant shall devour,
The trumpet shall be heard on high,
The dead shall live, the living die,
And musick shall *untune* the sky. *Dryden.*

The captives, as their tyrant shall require,
That they should breathe the song, and touch the lyre,
Shall say; can Jacob's servile race rejoice,
Untun'd the musick, and disus'd the voice? *Prior.*

2. To disorder.

O you kind gods!
Cure this great breach in his abused nature;
Th' *untuned* and jarring senses, O wind up
Of this child-changed father. *Shakesp. K. Lear.*

UNTU'RNED. *adj.* Not turned.

New crimes invented, left *unturn'd* no stone,
To make my guilt appear, and hide his own. *Dryden.*

So eager hath the inquisitive part of mankind been to bring this matter to a fair issue, that no stone hath been left *unturned*, no way, whereby these things could have been brought forth of the sea, but one or other hath pitch'd upon. *Woodward.*

UNTU'TORED. *adj.* Uninstructed; untaught.

Thy mother took into her blameful bed
Some stern *untutor'd* churl; and noble stock
Was graft with crab-tree slip, whose fruit thou art. *Shakesp.*

Thy even thoughts with so much plainness flow,
Their sense *untutor'd* infancy may know:
Yet to such height is all that plainness wrought,
Wit may admire, and letter'd pride be taught. *Prior.*

To UNTWI'NE. *v. a.*

1. To open what is held together by convolution.

But since the sisters did so soon *untwine*
So fair a thread, I'll strive to piece the line. *Waller.*

2. To open what is wrapped on itself.

It turns finely and softly three or four turns, caused by the *untwining* of the beard by the moisture. *Bacon.*

3. To separate that which clasps round any thing.

Divers worthy gentlemen of England, all the Syren songs of Italy could never *untwine* from the mast of God's word. *Ascham.*

To UNTWI'ST. *v. a.* To separate any things involved in each other, or wrapped up on themselves.

Untwisting his deceitful clew,
He 'gan to weave a web of wicked guile. *Fairy Queen.*

The interest of prince and people is so enfolded in a mutual embrace, that they cannot be *untwisted* without pulling a limb off. *Taylor's Rule of Living Holy.*

Untwisting all the chains that tie
The hidden soul of harmony. *Milton.*

No, I'll *untwist* you;
I have occasion for your stay on earth. *Dryden.*

Tarred hempen ropes cut small and *untwisted*, are beneficial for lands. *Mortimer's Husbandry.*

Untwist a wire, and from her gums
A set of teeth completely comes. *Swift.*

To UNTY'. *v. a.* [See UNTIE.] To loose.

O time! thou must untangle this, not I:
It is too hard a knot for me t' *unty.* *Shakespeare.*

To UNVA'IL. *v. a.* To uncover; to strip of a veil. This word is *unvail*, or *unveil*, according to its etymology. See VAIL, and VEIL.

Troy reviv'd, her mourning face *unvail'd.* *Denham.*

Now *unveil'd*, the toilet stands display'd,
Each silver vase in mystick order laid. *Pope.*

UNVA'LUABLE. *adj.* Inestimable; being above price.

Secure the innocence of children, by imparting to them the *unvaluable* blessing of a virtuous and pious education. *Atterb.*

UNVA'LUED. *adj.*

1. Not prized; neglected.

He may not, as *unvalued* persons do,
Carve for himself; for on his choice depends
The safety and the health of the whole state. *Shakesp.*

2. Inestimable; above price.

I thought I saw a thousand fearful wrecks;
Inestimable stones, *unvalu'd* jewels. *Shakespeare.*

UNVA'NQUISHED. Not conquered; not overcome.

Shall I for lucre of the rest *unvanquish'd*,
Detract so much from that prerogative,
As to be called but viceroy of the whole? *Shakespeare.*

Victory doth more often fall by error of the *unvanquished*, than by the valour of the victorious. *Hayward.*

They rise *unvanquish'd* *Milton's Par. Lost, b.* vi.

UNVA'RIABLE. *adj.* [*invariable*, Fr.] Not changeable; not mutable.

The two great hinges of morality stand fixt and *unvariable* as the two poles: whatever is naturally conducive to the common interest, is good; and whatever has a contrary influence, is evil. *Norris.*

UNVA'RIED. *adj.* Not changed; not diversified.

If authors cannot be prevailed with to keep close to truth and instruction, by *unvaried* terms, and plain, unsophisticated arguments; yet it concerns readers not to be imposed on. *Locke.*

They ring round the same *unvaried* chimes,
With sure returns of still-expected rhymes. *Pope.*

UNVA'RNISHED. *adj.*

1. Not overlaid with varnish.
2. Not adorned; not decorated.

I will a round, *unvarnish'd* tale deliver,
Of my whole course of love; what drugs, what charms
I won his daughter with. *Shakesp. Othello.*

UNVA'RYING. *adj.* Not liable to change.

We cannot keep by us any standing, *unvarying* measure of duration, which consists in a constant fleeting succession, as we can of certain lengths of extension, as inches marked out in permanent parcels of matter. *Locke.*

To UNVE'IL. *v. a.* [See VEIL and VAIL.]

1. To uncover; to divest of a veil.

The moon,
Apparent queen, *unveil'd* her peerless light. *Milton.*

To the limpid stream direct thy way,
When the gay morn *unveils* her smiling ray. *Pope.*

2. To disclose; to show.

The providence, that's in a watchful state,
Knows almost every grain of Pluto's gold;
Does ev'n our thoughts *unveil* in their dumb cradles. *Shak.*

UNVE'ILEDLY. *adv.* Plainly; without disguise.

Not knowing what use you will make of what has been *unveiledly* communicated to you, I was unwilling that some things, which had cost me pains, should fall into any man's hands, that scorns to purchase knowledge with pains. *Boyle.*

UNVE'NTILATED. *adj.* Not fanned by the wind.

This animals, to succour life, demand;
Nor should the air *unventilated* stand;
The idle deep corrupted would contain
Blue deaths. *Blackmore's Creation.*

UNVE'RITABLE. *adj.* Not true.

All these proceeded upon *unveritable* grounds. *Brown.*

UNVE'RSED. *adj.* Unacquainted; unskilled.

Not eastern monarchs, on their nuptial day,
In dazzling gold and purple shine so gay,
As the bright natives of th' unlabour'd field,
Unvers'd in spinning, and in looms unskill'd. *Blackmore.*

UNVE'XED. *adj.* Untroubled; undisturbed.

With a blest and *unvext* retire,
With unhack'd swords, and helmets all unbruis'd,
We will bear home that lusty blood again. *Shakespeare.*

Unvex'd with thought of wants which may betide;
Or for to-morrow's dinner to provide. *Dryden's Juvenal.*

UNVI'OLATED. *adj.* Not injured; not broken.

Herein you war against your reputation,
And draw within the compass of suspect
Th' *unviolated* honour of your wife. *Shakespeare.*

He, with singular constancy, preserved his duty and fidelity to his majesty *unviolated.* *Clarendon.*

This strength diffus'd
No less through all my sinews, joints, and bones,
Than thine, while I preserv'd these locks unshorn,
The pledge of my *unviolated* vow. *Milton.*

UNVI'RTUOUS. *adj.* Wanting virtue.

If they can find in their hearts that the poor, *unvirtuous,* fat knight shall be any further afflicted, we two will be the ministers. *Shakesp. Merry Wives of Windsor.*

UNVI'SITED. *adj.* Not resorted to.

In some wild zone
Dwell, not *unvisited* of heav'n's fair light,
Secure. *Milton's Par. Lost, b.* ii.

The playhouse and the park *unvisited* must lie. *Dryden.*

UNU'NIFORM. *adj.* Wanting uniformity.

Such an *ununiform* piety is in many so exactly apportioned to Satan's interest, that he has no cause to wish the change of his tenure. *Decay of Piety.*

UNVO'YAGEABLE. *adj.* Not to be passed over or voyaged.

Not this *unvoyageable* gulph obscure,
Detain from following thy illustrious track. *Milton.*

UNU'RGED. *adj.* Not incited; not pressed.

The time was once, when thou *unurg'd* would'st vow,
That never words were musick to thine ear,
Unless I spake. *Shakesp. Comedy of Errours.*

UNU'SED. *adj.*

1. Not put to use; unemployed.

She, whose husband about that time died, forgetting the absent Plangus, or, at least, not hoping of him to attain so aspiring a purpose, left no art *unused,* which might keep the line from breaking, whereat the fish was already taken. *Sidney.*

Sure he that made us with such large discourse,
Looking before and after, gave us not
That capability and godlike reason,
To rust in us *unus'd.* *Shakespeare's Hamlet.*

2. Not accustomed.

He, *unused* to such entertainment, did shortly and plainly answer what he was. *Sidney, b.* ii.

One, whose eyes,
Albeit *unused* to the melting mood,
Dropt tears as fast as the Arabian trees
Their medicinal gum. *Shakesp. Othello.*

What art thou?
Not from above: no, thy wan looks betray
Diminish'd light, and eyes *unus'd* to day. *Dryden.*

UNU'SEFUL. *adj.* Useless; serving no purpose.

I was persuaded, by experience, that it might not be *unuseful* in the capacities it was intended for. *Glanville.*

Birds flutter with their wings, when there is but a little down upon them, and they are as yet utterly *unuseful* for flying. *More's Antidote against Atheism.*

As when the building gains a surer stay,
We take th' *unuseful* scaffolding away. *Dryden.*

Pleas'd to find his age
Declining, not *unuseful* to his lord. *Philips.*

UNU'SUAL. *adj.* Not common; not frequent; rare.

With this *unusual* and strange course they went on, till God, in whose heaviest worldly judgments I nothing doubt but that there may lie hidden mercy, gave them over to their own inventions. *Hooker.*

You gain your point, if your industrious art
Can make *unusual* words easy and plain. *Roscommon.*

A sprightly red vermilions all her face;
And her eyes languish with *unusual* grace. *Granville.*

That peculiar turn, that the words should appear new, yet not *unusual,* but very proper to his auditors. *Felton.*

The river flows redundant, and attacks
The ling'ring remnant with *unusual* tide. *Philips.*

UNU'SUALNESS. *n. s.* Uncommonness; infrequency.

It is the *unusualness* of the time, not the appearance, that surprizes Alcinous. *Broome.*

UNU'TTERABLE. *adj.* Ineffable; inexpressible.

Sighs now breath'd
Unutterable; which the spirit of pray'r
Inspir'd, and wing'd for heav'n with speedier flight
Than loudest oratory. *Milton's Par. Lost, b.* xi.

It wounds my soul
To think of your *unutterable* sorrows,
When you shall find Hippolitus was guiltless. *Smith.*

UNVU'LNERABLE. *adj.* Exempt from wound: not vulnerable.

The god of soldiers inform
Thy thoughts with nobleness, that thou may'st prove
To shame *unvulnerable,* and stick i' th' wars
Like a great sea mark, standing every flaw. *Shakespeare.*

UNWA'KENED. *adj.* Not roused from sleep.

The more
His wonder was, to find *unwaken'd* Eve
With tresses discompos'd. *Milton's P. Lost, b.* v.

UNWA'LLED. *adj.* Having no walls.

He came to Tauris, a great and rich city, but *unwalled,* and of no strength. *Knolles's Hist. of the Turks.*

UNWA'RES. *adv.* Unexpectedly; before any caution, or expectation.

She, by her wicked arts,
Too false and strong for earthly skill or might,
Unwares me wrought unto her wicked will. *Fairy Queen.*

His loving mother came upon a day
Unto the woods, to see her little son,
And chanc'd *unwares* to meet him in the way,
After his sports and cruel pastime done. *Fairfax, b.* i.

Still we sail, while prosperous blows the wind,
Till on some secret rock *unwares* we light. *Fairfax.*

UNWA'RILY. *adv.* Without caution; carelessly.

The best part of my powers
Were in the washes all *unwarily*
Devour'd by the unexpected flood. *Shakespeare.*

If I had not *unwarily* engaged myself for the present publishing it, I should have kept it till I had look'd over it. *Digby.*

By such principles, they renounce their legal claim to liberty and property, and *unwarily* submit to what they really abhor. *Freeholder,* N° 10.

UNWARINESS. *n. s.* [from *unwary.*] Want of caution; carelessness.

The same temper which inclines us to a desire of fame, naturally betrays us into such slips and *unwarinesses,* as are not incident to men of a contrary disposition. *Spectator,* N° 256.

UNWA'RLIKE. *adj.* Not fit for war; not used to war; not military.

He safely might old troops to battle lead,
Against th' *unwarlike* Persian, and the Mede;
Whose hasty flight did from a bloodless field,
More spoils than honour to the victor yield. *Waller.*

Avert *unwarlike* Indians from his Rome,
Triumph abroad, secure our peace at home. *Dryden.*

UNWA'RNED. *adj.* Not cautioned; not made wary.

Unexperienced young men, if *unwarn'd,* take one thing for another, and judge by the outside. *Locke.*

May hypocrites,
That slyly speak one thing, another think,
Drink on *unwarn'd,* till by inchanting cups
Infatuate, they their wily thoughts disclose. *Philips.*

UNWA'RRANTABLE. *adj.* Not defensible; not to be justified; not allowed.

At very distant removes an extemporary intercourse is feasible, and may be compassed without *unwarrantable* correspondence with the people of the air. *Glanville.*

He who does an *unwarrantable* action through a false information, which he ought not to have believed, cannot in reason make the guilt of one sin the excuse of another. *South.*

UNWA'RRANTABLY. *adv.* Not justifiably; not defensibly.

A true and humble sense of your own unworthiness, will not suffer you to rise up to that confidence, which some men *unwarrantably* pretend to, nay, *unwarrantably* require of others. *Wake's Preparation for Death.*

UNWA'RRANTED. *adj.* Not ascertained; uncertain.

The subjects of this kingdom believe it is not legal for them to be enforced to go beyond the seas, without their own consent, upon hope of an *unwarranted* conquest; but to resist an invading enemy, the subject must be commanded out of the counties where they inhabit. *Bacon.*

UNWA'RY. *adj.*

1. Wanting caution; imprudent; hasty; precipitate.

Nor think me so *unwary,*
To bring my feet again into the snare
Where once I have been caught. *Milton's Agonistes.*

So spake the false archangel, and infus'd
Bad influence into th' *unwary* breast. *Milton.*

So talk'd the spirited sly snake; and Eve,
Yet more amaz'd, *unwary* thus reply'd. *Milton.*

Turning short, he struck with all his might
Full on the helmet of th' *unwary* knight:
Deep was the wound. *Dryden.*

Propositions about religion are insinuated into the *unwary,* as well as unbiassed understandings of children, and riveted there by long custom. *Locke.*

2. Unexpected. Obsolete.

All in the open hall amazed stood,
At suddenness of that *unwary* sight,
And wonder'd at his breathless hasty mood. *Fairy Queen.*

UNWA'SHED.
UNWA'SHEN. } *adj.* Not washed; not cleansed by washing.

Another lean *unwash'd* artificer
Cuts off his tale, and talks of Arthur's death. *Shakesp.*

To eat with *unwashen* hands defileth not a man. *Matth.* xv.

He accepts of no unclean, no *unwashed* sacrifice; and if repentance usher not in, prayer will never find admittance. *Duppa.*

When the fleece is shorn, if sweat remains
Unwash'd, it soaks into their empty veins. *Dryden.*

UNWA'STED. *adj.* Not consumed; not diminished.

Why have those rocks so long *unwasted* stood,
Since, lavish of their stock, they through the flood
Have, ages past, their melting crystal spread,
And with their spoils the liquid regions fed? *Blackmore.*

UNWA'STING. *adj.* Not growing less; not decaying.

Purest love's *unwasting* treasure;
Constant faith, fair hope, long leisure;
Sacred Hymen! these are thine. *Pope.*

UNWA'YED. *adj.* Not used to travel; not seasoned in the road.

Beasts, that have been rid off their legs, are as much for a man's use, as colts that are *unwayed*, and will not goat all. *Suckl.*

UNWE'AKENED. *adj.* Not weakened.

By reason of the exsuction of some air out of the glass, the elastical power of the remaining air was very much debilitated, in comparison of the *unweakened* pressure of the external air. *Boyle.*

UNWE'APONED. *adj.* Not furnished with offensive arms.

As the beasts are armed with fierce teeth, paws, horns, and other bodily instruments of much advantage against *unweaponed* men; so hath reason taught man to strengthen his hand with such offensive arms, as no creature else can well avoid. *Raleigh.*

UNWE'ARIABLE. *adj.* Not to be tired.

Desire to resemble him in goodness, maketh them *unweariable*. *Hooker, b.* i.

UNWE'ARIED. *adj.*

1. Not tired; not fatigued.

The Creator from his work
Desisting, though *unwearied*, up return'd. *Milton.*
Their bloody task *unweary'd*, still they ply. *Waller.*
Still th' *unweary'd* sire pursues the tuneful strain. *Dryden.*

2. Indefatigable; continual; not to be spent; not sinking under fatigue.

Joy'd to range abroad in fresh attire,
Through the wide compass of the airy coast,
And with *unwearied* limbs each part t' enquire. *Spenser.*
Godlike his *unweary'd* bounty flows;
First loves to do, then loves the good he does. *Denham.*
A winged virtue through th' etherial sky,
From orb to orb *unweary'd* dost thou fly. *Tickell.*

An *unwearied* devotion in the service of God, recommended the gospel to the world. *Rogers's Sermons.*

The righteous shall certainly be saved, but then the christian character of a righteous man implies a constant, *unwearied* perseverance in many painful instances of duty. *Rogers.*

To UNWE'ARY. *v. a.* To refresh after weariness.

It *unwearies*, and refreshes more than any thing, after too great labour. *Temple.*

UNWE'D. *adj.* Unmarried.

This servitude makes you to keep *unwed*. *Shakesp.*

UNWE'DGEABLE. *adj.* Not to be cloven.

Merciful heav'n!
Thou rather with thy sharp and sulph'rous bolt
Split'st the *unwedgeable* and gnarled oak,
Than the soft myrtle. *Shakesp. Measure for Measure.*

UNWEE'DED. *adj.* Not cleared from weeds.

Fie! 'tis an *unweeded* garden,
That grows to seed; things rank, and gross in nature,
Possess it merely. *Shakespeare's Hamlet.*

UNWEE'PED. *adj.* Not lamented. Now *unwept*.

He must not float upon his watry bier
Unweept, and welter to the parching wind,
Without the meed of some melodious tear. *Milton.*

UNWEE'TING. *adj.* Ignorant; unknowing.

Her seeming dead he found with feigned fear,
As all *unweeting* of that well she knew;
And pained himself with busy care to rear
Her out of careless swoon. *Fairy Queen, b.* i.
But contrary, *unweeting* he fulfilled
The purpos'd counsel, pre-ordain'd and fix'd
Of the most high. *Paradise Regain'd.*

UNWE'IGHED. *adj.*

1. Not examined by the balance.

Solomon left all the vessels *unweighed*, because they were exceeding many. 1 *Kings* vii.

2. Not considered; negligent.

What *unweighed* behaviour hath this Flemish drunkard pickt out of my conversation, that he dares in this manner essay me? why he hath not been thrice in my company. *Shakesp.*

Daughter, what words have pass'd thy lips *unweigh'd*,
Deem not unjustly by my doom opprest,
Of human race the wisest, and the best. *Pope's Odyssey.*

UNWE'IGHING. *adj.* Inconsiderate; thoughtless.

Wise? why, no question but he was—a very superficial, ignorant, *unweighing* fellow. *Shakespeare.*

UNWE'LCOME. *adj.* Not pleasing; not grateful; not well received.

Such welcome and *unwelcome* things at once,
'Tis hard to reconcile. *Shakesp. Macbeth.*
Soon as th' *unwelcome* news
From earth arriv'd at heaven-gate, displeas'd
All were who heard. *Milton's Par. Lost, b.* x.
Though he that brings *unwelcome* news
Has but a losing office, yet he that shews
Your danger first, and then your way to safety,
May heal that wound he made. *Denham's Sophy.*
Forc'd from her presence, and condemn'd to live;
Unwelcome freedom, and unthank'd reprieve. *Dryden.*

From the very first instances of perception, some things are grateful, and others *unwelcome* to them; some things that they incline to, and others that they fly. *Locke.*

Such hasty nights as these, would give very *unwelcome* interruptions to our labours. *Bentley's Sermons.*

UNWE'PT. *adj.* Not lamented; not bemoaned.

Our fatherless distress was left unmoan'd;
Your widow dolours likewise be *unwept*. *Shakesp. Rich.* III.
We, but the slaves that mount you to the throne:
A base, ignoble crowd, without a name;
Unwept, unworthy of the fun'ral flame;
By duty bound to forfeit each his life. *Dryden.*

UNWE'T. *adj.* Not moist.

Once I meant to meet
My fate with face unmov'd, and eyes *unwet*;
Yet since I have thee here in narrow room,
My tears shall set thee first afloat within thy tomb. *Dryden.*

UNWHI'PT. *adj.* Not punished; not corrected with the rod.

Tremble, thou wretch,
That hast within thee undivulged crimes,
Unwhipt of justice. *Shakesp. K. Lear.*
Once I caught him in a lie;
And then, *unwhipt*, he had the grace to cry. *Pope.*

UNWHO'LESOME. *adj.*

1. Insalubrious; mischievous to health.

The discovery of the disposition of the air, is good for the prognosticks of wholesome and *unwholesome* years. *Bacon.*

There I a prisoner chain'd, scarce freely draw
The air imprison'd also, close and damp,
Unwholesome draught; but here I find amends,
The breath of heav'n fresh-blowing, pure and sweet,
With day-spring born; here leave me to respire. *Milton.*

How can any one be assured, that his meat and drink are not poisoned, and made *unwholesome* before they are brought to him? *South.*

Rome is never fuller of nobility than in summer; for the country towns are so infested with *unwholesome* vapours, that they dare not trust themselves in them, while the heats last. *Addison on Italy.*

Children born healthy, often contract diseases from an *unwholesome* nurse. *Arbuthnot on Diet.*

2. Corrupt; tainted.

We'll use this *unwholesome* humidity; this gross, watry pumpion: we'll teach him to know turtles from jays. *Shakesp.*

UNWI'ELDILY. *adv.* Heavily; with difficult motion.

Unwieldily they wallow first in ooze;
Then in the shady covert seek repose. *Dryden.*

UNWI'ELDINESS. *n. s.* Heaviness; difficulty to move, or be moved.

To what a cumbersome *unwieldiness*,
And burdenous corpulence my love had grown,
But that I made it feed upon
That which love worst endures, discretion. *Donne.*

The supposed *unwieldiness* of its massy bulk, grounded upon our experience of the inaptitude of great and heavy bodies to motion, is a mere imposture of our senses. *Glanville.*

UNWI'ELDY. *adj.* Unmanageable; not easily moving or moved; bulky; weighty; ponderous.

An ague, meeting many humours in a fat, *unwieldy* body of fifty-eight years old, in four or five fits, carried him out of the world. *Clarendon.*

Part, huge of bulk!
Wallowing *unwieldy*, enormous in their gait,
Tempest the ocean. *Milton's Par. Lost, b.* vii.
Unwieldy sums of wealth, which higher mount,
Than files of marshal'd figures can account. *Dryden.*
Nothing here th' *unwieldy* rock avails,
Rebounding harmless from the plaited scales,
That, firmly join'd, preserv'd him from a wound,
With native armour crusted all around. *Addison's Ovid.*

What carriage can bear away all the rude and *unwieldy* loppings of a branchy tree at once? *Watts's Impr. of the Mind.*

UNWI'LLING. *adj.* Loath; not contented; not inclined; not complying by inclination.

The nature of man is *unwilling* to continue doing that wherein it shall always condemn itself. *Hooker, b.* v.

If thou dost find him tractable,
Encourage him, and tell him all our reasons.
If he be leaden, icy, cold, *unwilling*,
Be thou so too. *Shakespeare's Rich.* III.

If

If the sun rise *unwilling* to his race,
Clouds on his brows, and spots upon his face,
Suspect a drizzling day. *Dryden.*
Heav'n's unchang'd decrees attentive hear;
More pow'rful gods have torn thee from my side,
Unwilling to resign, and doom'd a bride. *Dryden.*

UNWI'LLINGLY. *adv.* Not with good-will; not without loathness.
The whining school-boy, with his satchel,
And shining morning face, creeping like snail
Unwillingly to school. *Shakesp. As You Like It.*
A feast the people hold to Dagon, and forbid
Laborious works, *unwillingly* this rest
Their superstition yields. *Milton's Agonistes.*
Still dismay'd
By seas or skies, *unwillingly* they stay'd. *Denham.*
These men were once the prince's foes, and then
Unwillingly they made him great: but now,
Being his friends, shall willingly undo him. *Denham.*
The dire contagion spreads so fast,
That where it seizes, all relief is vain;
And therefore must *unwillingly* lay waste
That country, which would else the foe maintain. *Dryden.*

UNWI'LLINGNESS. *n. s.* Loathness; disinclination.
Obedience, with professed *unwillingness* to obey, is no better than manifest disobedience. *Hooker, b.* v.
What moved the man to yield to her persuasions? Even the same cause that hath moved all men since, an *unwillingness* to grieve her, and make her sad, lest she should pine, and be overcome with sorrow. *Raleigh's Hist. of the World.*
I see with what *unwillingness*
You lay upon me this command, and through your fears
Discern your love, and therefore must obey you. *Denham.*
There is in most people a reluctance and *unwillingness* to be forgotten. We observe, even among the vulgar, how fond they are to have an inscription over their grave. *Swift.*

To UNWI'ND. *v. a.* pret. and part. passive *unwound.*
1. To separate any thing convolved; to untwist; to untwine.
All his subjects having by some years learned, so to hope for good and fear harm, only from her, that it should have needed a stronger virtue than his, to have *unwound* so deeply an entered vice. *Sidney, b.* ii.
Empirick politicians use deceit:
You boldly shew that skill which they pretend,
And work by means as noble as your end;
Which should you veil, we might *unwind* the clue,
As men do nature, till we came to you. *Dryden.*
2. To disentangle; to loose from entanglement.
Desiring to serve God as they ought; but being not so skillful as in every point to *unwind* themselves, where the snares of glosing speech lie to entangle them, are in mind not a little troubled, when they hear so bitter invectives against that, which this church hath taught them to reverence as holy. *Hooker, b.* v.
As you *unwind* her love from him,
Lest it should ravel, and be good to none,
Bottom it on me. *Shakesp. Two Gentlemen of Verona.*

To UNWI'ND. *v. n.* To admit evolution.
Put the bottoms into clean scalding water, and they will easily *unwind.* *Mortimer's Husbandry.*

UNWI'PED. *adj.* Not cleared.
Their hands and faces were all badg'd with blood,
So were their daggers, which *unwip'd* we found
Upon their pillows. *Shakesp. Macbeth.*

UNWI'SE. *adj.* Weak; defective in wisdom.
O good, but most *unwise* patricians! why,
You grave, but reckless senators, have you thus
Giv'n Hydra here to chuse an officer? *Shakesp. Coriolanus.*
Be not ta'en tardy by *unwise* delay. *Shakespeare.*
He who of those delights can judge, and spare
To interpose them oft, is not *unwise.* *Milton.*
This the Greeks say, this the barbarians; the wise and the *unwise.* *Tillotson.*
When kings grow stubborn, slothful, or *unwise*,
Each private man for publick good should rise. *Dryden.*
When the balance of power is duly fixt in a state, nothing is more dangerous or *unwise*, than to give way to the first steps of popular encroachments. *Swift.*

UNWI'SELY. *adv.* Weakly; not prudently; not wisely.
Lady Zelmane, like some, *unwisely* liberal, that more delight to give presents than pay debts, chose rather to bestow her love upon me, than to recompense him. *Sidney.*
Unwisely we the wiser East
Pity, supposing them oppress'd
With tyrant's force. *Waller.*

To UNWISH. *v. a.* To wish that which is, not to be.
My liege, would you and I alone,
Without more help, could fight this royal battle.——
——Why now thou hast *unwish'd* five thousand men;
Which likes me better than to wish us one. *Shakespeare.*

To desire there were no God, were plainly to *unwish* their own being, which must be annihilated in the substraction of that essence, which substantially supporteth them. *Brown.*

UNWI'SHED. *adj.* Not sought; not desired.
So jealous is she of my love to her daughter, that I never yet begin to open my mouth to the unevitable Philoclea, but that her *unwished* presence gave my tale a conclusion, before it had a beginning. *Sidney.*
To his *unwished* yoke
My soul consents not to give sov'reignty. *Shakespeare.*
While heaping *unwish'd* wealth I distant roam;
The best of brothers at his natal home
By the dire fury of a traitress wife,
Ends the sad evening of a stormy life. *Pope.*

UNWI'ST. *adj.* Unthought of; not known. *Spenser.*

To UNWI'T. *v. a.* To deprive of understanding. Not used.
Friends all but now; even now
In quarter, and in terms like bride and groom
Divesting them for bed; and then, but now,
As if some planet had *unwitted* men,
Swords out, and tilting one at other's breasts *Shakespeare.*

UNWITHDRA'WING. *adj.* Continually liberal.
Wherefore did nature pour her bounties forth,
With such a full and *unwithdrawing* hand,
Covering the earth with odours, fruits, and flocks? *Milton.*

UNWITHSTOO'D. *adj.* Not opposed.
Cressy plains,
And Agincourt, deep ting'd with blood, confess
What the Silures vigour *unwithstood*,
Cou'd do in rigid fight. *Philips.*

UNWI'TNESSED. *adj.* Wanting evidence; wanting notice.
Least their zeal to the cause should any way be *unwitnessed.* *Hooker.*

UNWI'TTINGLY. *adv.* [Properly *unweetingly*, from *unweeting.*] Without knowledge; without consciousness.
In these fatal things it falls out, that the high-working powers make second causes *unwittingly* accessary to their determinations. *Sidney.*
Those things are termed most properly natural agents, which keep the law of their kind *unwittingly*, as the heavens and elements of the world, which can do no otherwise than they do. *Hooker, b.* i.
Atheists repudiate all title to heaven, merely for present pleasure; besides the extreme madness of running such a desperate hazard after death, they *unwittingly* deprive themselves here of that tranquillity they seek for. *Bentley.*

UNWO'NTED. *adj.*
1. Uncommon; unusual; rare; infrequent.
His sad, dull eyes, sunk deep in hollow pits,
Could not endure th' *unwonted* sun to view. *Fairy Queen.*
My father's of a better nature
Than he appears by speech; this is *unwonted*
Which now came from him. *Shakespeare.*
Every *unwonted* meteor is portentous, and some divine prognostick. *Glanville.*
Thick breath, quick pulse, and heaving of my heart,
All signs of some *unwonted* change appear. *Dryden.*
2. Unaccustomed; unused.
Philoclea, who blushing, and withal smiling, making shamefastness pleasant, and pleasure shamefast, tenderly moved her feet, *unwonted* to feel the naked ground. *Sidney, b.* ii.
Sea calves *unwonted* to fresh waters fly. *May.*
O how oft shall he
On faith and changed gods complain; and seas
Rough with black winds and storms,
Unwonted shall admire. *Milton.*

UNWOR'KING. *adj.* Living without labour.
Lazy and *unworking* shopkeepers in this being worse than gamesters, do not only keep so much of the money of a country in their hands, but make the publick pay them for it. *Locke.*

UNWO'RSHIPPED. *adj.* Not adored.
He resolv'd to leave
Unworshipp'd, unobey'd the throne supreme. *Milton.*

UNWO'RTHILY. *adv.* Not according to desert; either above or below merit.
I vow'd, base knight,
To tear the garter from thy craven leg,
Which I have done, because *unworthily*
Thou wast installed. *Shakesp. Hen.* VI.
Fearing lest my jealous aim might err,
And so *unworthily* disgrace the man,
I gave him gentle looks. *Shakespeare.*
If we look upon the Odyssey as all a fiction, we consider it *unworthily.* It ought to be read as a story founded upon truth, adorned with embellishments of poetry. *Broome.*

UNWO'RTHINESS. *n. s.* Want of worth; want of merit.
A mind fearing the *unworthiness* of every word that should be presented to her ears, at length brought it forth in this manner. *Sidney, b.* ii.

O let not an excellent ſpirit do itſelf ſuch wrong, as to think where it is placed, embraced, and loved, there can be any *unworthineſs*; ſince the weakeſt miſt is not eaſilier driven away by the ſun, than that is chaſed away with ſo high thoughts. *Sidney.*

Every night he comes with ſongs compos'd
To her *unworthineſs*: it nothing ſteads us
To chide him from our eaves, for he perſiſts. *Shakeſpeare.*

I fear'd to find you in another place;
But, ſince you're here, my jealouſy grows leſs:
You will be kind to my *unworthineſs*. *Dryden.*

Have a true and humble ſenſe of your own *unworthineſs*, which will not ſuffer you to riſe to a confidence unwarrantably pretended to by ſome. *Wake on Death.*

UNWO'RTHY. *adj.*

1. Not deſerving.

The Athanaſian creed and doxology ſhould remain in uſe, the one as a moſt divine explication of the chiefeſt articles of our chriſtian belief; the other as an heavenly acclamation of joyful applauſe to his praiſes, in whom we believe: neither the one nor the other *unworthy* to be heard ſounding, as they are in the church of Chriſt. *Hooker.*

Every particular accident, not *unworthy* the remembrance, for brevity I wittingly paſs over. *Knolles.*

2. Wanting merit.

Degree being vizarded,
Th' *unworthieſt* ſhews as fairly in the maſk. *Shakeſpeare.*

Are there *unworthy* men choſen to offices? *Whitgifte.*

So may I, blind fortune leading me,
Miſs that which one *unworthier* may attain;
And die with grieving. *Shakeſp. Merch. of Venice.*

3. Mean.

Tell me, Philoclea, did you ever ſee ſuch a ſhepherd? did you ever hear of ſuch a prince? and then tell me if a ſmall or *unworthy* aſſault have conquered me? *Sidney.*

4. Not ſuitable; not adequate.

I laid at her feet a work, which was *unworthy* her, but which I hope ſhe will forgive. *Dryden.*

Our friend's papers are in my hands, and I will take care to ſuppreſs things *unworthy* of him. *Pope to Swift.*

Care is taken to interſperſe additions in ſuch a manner, that ſcarce any book can be bought, without purchaſing ſomething *unworthy* of the author. *Swift.*

5. Unbecoming; vile.

The brutal action rous'd his manly mind:
Mov'd with *unworthy* uſage of the maid,
He, though unarm'd, reſolv'd to give her aid. *Dryden.*

UNWO'UND. part. paſſ. and pret. of *unwind.* Untwiſted.

Thatchers tie with withs, but old pitch'd ropes *unwound* are more laſting. *Mortimer's Huſbandry.*

UNWO'UNDED. *adj.*

1. Not wounded.

We may offend
Our yet *unwounded* enemies. *Milton's Par. Loſt, b.* vi.

2. Not hurt.

Oh! bleſt with temper:
She who can love a ſiſter's charms, or hear
Sighs for a daughter with *unwounded* ear. *Pope.*

To UNWRE'ATH. *v. a.* To untwine.

The beards of wild oats, and of divers other wild plants, continually wreath and *unwreath* themſelves, according to the temperature of the ambient air. *Boyle.*

UNWRI'TING. *adj.* Not aſſuming the character of an author.

The peace of the honeſt *unwriting* ſubject was daily moleſted. *Arbuthnot.*

UNWRI'TTEN. *adj.* Not conveyed by writing; oral; traditional.

A rule of right *unwritten*, but delivered by tradition from one to another. *Spenſer's State of Ireland.*

As to his underſtanding, they bring him in void of all notion, a rude, *unwritten* blank; making him to be created as much an infant, as others are born. *South's Sermons.*

The laws of England may be divided into the written law, and the *unwritten*. *Hale.*

UNWRO'UGHT. *adj.* Not laboured; not manufactured.

Or prove at leaſt to all of wiſer thought,
Their hearts were fertile land, although *unwrought*. *Fairfax.*

Yet thy moiſt clay is pliant to command;
Unwrought and eaſy to the potter's hand:
Now take the mold, now bend thy mind to feel
The firſt ſharp motions of the forming wheel. *Dryden.*

UNWRU'NG. *adj.* Not pinched.

We that have free ſouls, it touches us not; let the galled jade winch, our withers are *unwrung*. *Shakeſp. Hamlet.*

UNYIELDED. *adj.* Not given up.

O'erpower'd at length, they force him to the ground,
Unyielded as he was, and to the pillar bound. *Dryden.*

To UNYO'KE. *v. a.*

1. To looſe from the yoke.

Our army is diſpers'd already:
Like youthful ſteers *unyok'd*, they took their courſe
Eaſt, weſt, north, ſouth. *Shakeſp. Hen.* IV.

Homer calls them like gods, and yet gives them the employment of ſlaves; they *unyoke* the mules. *Broome.*

2. To part; to diſjoin.

Shall theſe hands, ſo lately purg'd of blood,
So join'd in love, ſo ſtrong in both,
Unyoke this ſeizure, and this kind regret. *Shakeſpeare.*

UNYO'KED. *adj.*

1. Having never worn a yoke.

Sev'n bullocks yet *unyok'd* for Phœbus chuſe,
And for Diana ſev'n unſpotted ewes. *Dryden.*

2. Licentious; unreſtrained.

I will a-while uphold
The *unyok'd* humour of your idleneſs. *Shakeſp. Hen.* IV.

UNZO'NED. *adj.* Not bound with a girdle.

Eaſy her motion ſeem'd, ſerene her air;
Full, though *unzon'd*, her boſom. *Prior.*

VOCA'BULARY. *n. ſ.* [*vocabularium*, Lat. *vocabulaire*, Fr.] A dictionary; a lexicon; a word-book.

Some have delivered the polity of ſpirits, and that they ſtand in awe of conjurations, which ſignify nothing, not only in the dictionary of man, but in the ſubtiler *vocabulary* of Satan. *Brown's Vulg. Errours.*

Among other books, we ſhould be furniſhed with *vocabularies* and dictionaries of ſeveral ſorts. *Watts.*

VO'CAL. *adj.* [*vocal*, Fr. *vocalis*, Lat.]

1. Having a voice.

Eyes are *vocal*, tears have tongues;
And there be words not made with lungs;
Sententious ſhow'rs! O let them fall,
Their cadence is rhetorical. *Craſhaw.*

Witneſs if I be ſilent, morn or even,
To hill, or valley, fountain, or freſh ſhade,
Made *vocal* by my ſong, and taught his praiſe. *Milton.*

Smooth-ſliding Mincius, crown'd with *vocal* reeds,
That ſtrain I heard was of a higher mood. *Milton.*

None can animate the lyre,
And the mute ſtrings with *vocal* ſouls inſpire,
As Helen, in whoſe eyes ten thouſand Cupids dwell. *Dryden.*

Memnon, though ſtone, was counted *vocal*;
But 'twas the god, mean while, that ſpoke all.
Rome oft has heard a croſs haranguing,
With prompting prieſt behind the hanging. *Prior.*

2. Uttered or modulated by the voice.

They which, under pretence of the law ceremonial being abrogated, require the abrogation of inſtrumental muſick, approving nevertheleſs the uſe of *vocal* melody to remain, muſt ſhew ſome reaſon wherefore the one ſhou'd be thought a legal ceremony, and not the other. *Hooker.*

And join'd their *vocal* worſhip to the choir
Of creatures wanting voice. *Milton's Par. Loſt.*

VOCA'LITY. *n. ſ.* [*vocalitas*, Lat. from *vocal.*] Power of utterance; quality of being utterable by the voice.

L and R being in extremes, one of roughneſs, the other of ſmoothneſs and freeneſs of *vocality*, are not eaſy in tract of vocal ſpeech to be pronounced ſpiritually. *Holder.*

To VO'CALIZE. *v. a.* [from *vocal.*] To form into voice.

It is one thing to give an impulſe to breath alone; another thing to *vocalize* that breath, *i. e.* in its paſſage through the larynx, to give it the ſound of human voice. *Holder.*

VO'CALLY. *adv.* [from *vocal.*] In words; articulately.

Although it is as natural to mankind, to expreſs their deſires *vocally*, as it is for brutes to uſe their natural vocal ſigns; yet the forming of languages into this or that faſhion, is a buſineſs of inſtitution. *Hale's Origin of Mankind.*

VOCA'TION. *n. ſ.* [*vocation*, Fr. *vocatio*, Lat.]

1. Calling by the will of God.

Neither doth that which St. Paul, or other apoſtles, teach, enforce the utter diſability of any other men's *vocation* thought requiſite in this church for the ſaving of ſouls. *Hooker, b.* v.

They which thus were in God eternally by their intended admiſſion to life, have, by *vocation* or adoption, God actually now in them. *Hooker, b.* v.

2. Summons.

What can be urged for them who not having the *vocation* of poverty to ſcribble, out of meer wantonneſs make themſelves ridiculous? *Dryden.*

3. Trade; employment.

He would think his ſervice greatly rewarded, if he might obtain by that means to live in the ſight of his prince, and yet practiſe his own choſen *vocation*. *Sidney, b.* i.

God's mother, in a viſion full of majeſty,
Will'd me to leave my baſe *vocation*. *Shakeſp. Hen.* VI.

God has furniſhed men with faculties ſufficient to direct them in the way they ſhould take, if they will ſeriouſly employ them, when their ordinary *vocations* allow them the leiſure. *Locke.*

A whore in her *vocation*,
Keeps punctual to an aſſignation. *Swift.*

VO'CATIVE. *n. ſ.* [*vocatif*, Fr. *vocativus*, Lat.] The grammatical caſe uſed in calling or ſpeaking to.

Vocifera'tion. *n. s.* [*vociferatio*, *vocifero*, Lat.] Clamour; outcry.

The lungs, kept too long upon the ſtretch by *vociferation*, or loud ſinging, may produce the ſame effect. *Arbuthnot.*

Voci'ferous. *adj.* [*vocifero*, Lat.] Clamorous; noiſy.

Several templars, and others of the more *vociferous* kind of critics, went with a reſolution to hiſs, and confeſs'd they were forced to laugh. *Pope.*

VOGUE. *n. s.* [*vogue*, Fr. from *voguer*, to float, or fly at large.] Faſhion; mode.

It is not more abſurd to undertake to tell the name of an unknown perſon by his looks, than to vouch a man's ſaintſhip from the *vogue* of the world. *South.*

Uſe may revive the obſoleteſt words,
And baniſh thoſe that now are moſt in *vogue*. *Roſcommon.*

What factions th' have, and what they drive at
In publick *vogue*, or what in private. *Hudibras.*

In the *vogue* of the world, it paſſes for an exploit of honour, for kings to run away with whole countries that they have no pretence to. *L'Eſtrange.*

No periodical writer, who always maintains his gravity, and does not ſometimes ſacrifice to the graces, muſt expect to keep in *vogue* for any time. *Addiſon.*

At one time they keep their patients ſo cloſe and warm, as almoſt to ſtifle them; and all on a ſudden the cold regimen is in *vogue*. *Baker's Reflections on Learning.*

VOICE, *n. s.* [*voix*, Fr. *vocis*, Lat.]

1. Sound emitted by the mouth.
2. Sound of the mouth, as diſtinguiſhed from that uttered by another mouth.

Air in ſounds that are not tones, which are all equal, admitteth much variety, as in the *voices* of living creatures, and in the *voices* of ſeveral men; for we can diſcern ſeveral men by their *voices*. *Bacon's Nat. Hiſt.*

3. Any ſound made by breath.

O Marcus, I am warm'd; my heart
Leaps at the trumpet's *voice*, and burns for glory. *Addiſon.*

4. Vote; ſuffrage; opinion expreſſed.

Are you all reſolved to give your *voices*?
But that's no matter, the greater part carries it. *Shakeſp.*

I've no words;
My *voice* is in my ſword! thou bloodier villain
Than terms can give thee out. *Shakeſp. Macbeth.*

The ſtate was betrayed by the multitude and corruption of *voices*, and muſt ſhortly periſh, if not committed to the grave judgment of ſome few; for two hundred gave *voices*, reducing that multitude to fifty, who, for their experience, were holden for men of greateſt gravity. *Knolles.*

Some laws ordain, and ſome attend the choice
Of holy ſenates, and elect by *voice*. *Dryden.*

To Voice. *v. a.* [from the noun.]

1. To rumour; to report. Out of uſe.

Is this th' Athenian minion, whom the world
Voic'd ſo regardfully? *Shakeſp. Timon of Athens.*

It was *voiced* that the king purpoſed to put to death Edward Plantagenet, priſoner in the tower; whereat there was great murmur. *Bacon's Hen. VII.*

Many ſought to feed
The eaſy creditors of novelties,
By *voicing* him alive. *Daniel's Civil War.*

2. To vote.

Your minds, pre-occupied with what
You rather muſt do, than what you ſhould do,
Made you, againſt the grain, to *voice* him conſul. *Shakeſp.*

To Voice. *v. n.* To clamour; to make outcries. Obſolete.

Stir not queſtions of juriſdiction; and rather aſſume thy right in ſilence, than *voice* it with claims. *Bacon.*

It is not the gift of every perſon to harangue the multitude, to *voice* it loud and high. *South's Sermons.*

Vo'iced. *adj.* [from the noun.] Furniſhed with a voice.

That's Erythæa,
Or ſome angel *voic'd* like her. 'Tis ſhe! my ſtruggling ſoul
Would fain go out to meet and welcome her! *Denham.*

VOID. *adj.* [*vuide*, Fr.]

1. Empty; vacant.

The earth was without form and *void*, and darkneſs was upon the face of the deep. *Geneſis* i. 2.

I'll get me to a place more *void*, and there
Speak to great Cæſar as he comes along. *Shakeſpeare.*

2. Vain; ineffectual; null; vacated.

If it be *void*, and to no purpoſe, that the names of men are ſo frequent in their books, what did move them to bring them in? *Hooker.*

My word ſhall not return *void*, but accompliſh that which I pleaſe. *Iſa.* lv. 11.

This cuſtom made their whole government *void*, as an engine built againſt human ſociety, worthy to be fired and pulled down. *Bacon.*

Though the wiſdom of a future parliament may find cauſe to declare this, or that act of parliament *void*, yet there will be the ſame temper requiſite to repeal it. *Clarendon.*

The two houſes declared, that nothing which ſhould from that time paſs under the great ſeal, ſhould be good and valid, but *void* and null. *Clarendon, b.* viii.

Some kind of ſubjection is due from every man to every man, which cannot be made *void* by any power whatſoever. *Swift.*

3. Unſupplied; unoccupied.

Queen Elizabeth, importuned much to ſupply divers great offices that had been long *void*, anſwered nothing to the matter, but roſe up on the ſudden, and ſaid, I am ſure my office will not be long *void*. *Camden.*

4. Wanting; unfurniſhed; empty.

If ſome be admitted into the miniſtry, *void* of learning, or lewd in life, are all the reſt to be condemned? *Whitgifte.*

How *void* of reaſon are our hopes and fears! *Dryden.*

Being *void* of all friendſhip and enmity, they never complain. *Swift.*

5. Unſubſtantial; unreal.

Senſeleſs, lifeleſs idol, *void* and vain. *Pope.*

Void. *n. s.* [from the adject.] An empty ſpace; vacuum; vacancy.

Pride, where wit fails, ſteps in to our defence,
And fills up all the mighty *void* of ſenſe. *Pope.*

With what power
Were firſt th' unwieldy planets launch'd along
Th' illimitable *void*? *Thomſon.*

To Void. *v. a.* [from the adjective; *vuider*, Fr.]

1. To quit; to leave empty.

If they will fight with us, bid them come down,
Or *void* the field. *Shakeſp. Hen.* V.

How in our *voiding* lobby haſt thou ſtood,
And duly waited for my coming forth? *Shakeſp. Hen.* VI.

Towards this paſſage, ſomewhat darker than the chamber which he *voided*, this aſſaſſinate gave him, with a back blow, a deep wound into his left ſide. *Wotton's Buckingham.*

2. To emit; to pour out.

The aſcending water is vented by fits, every circumvolution *voiding* only ſo much as is contained in one helix. *Wilkins.*

3. To emit as excrement.

Excrements ſmell ill to the ſame creature that *voideth* them; and the cat burieth what ſhe *voideth*. *Bacon.*

Believ'd the heav'ns were made of ſtone,
Becauſe the ſun had *voided* one. *Hudibras.*

By the uſe of emulſions, and frequent emollient injections, his urine *voided* more eaſily. *Wiſeman's Surgery.*

Fleſhy filaments, or matter *voided* by urine, are ſuſpicious ſymptoms of a ſtone in the kidnies, eſpecially if the patient has been ſubject to *voiding* of gravel. *Arbuthnot.*

4. To vacate; to nullify; to annul.

It was become a practice, upon any ſpecious pretences, to *void* the ſecurity that was at any time given for money ſo borrowed. *Clarendon.*

Vo'idable. *adj.* [from *void.*] Such as may be annulled.

If the metropolitan, pretending the party deceaſed had *bona notabilia* in divers dioceſes, grants letters of adminiſtration, ſuch adminiſtration is not void, but *voidable* by a ſentence. *Ayl.*

Vo'ider. *n. s.* [from *void.*] A baſket, in which broken meat is carried from the table.

A *voider* for the nonce,
I wrong the devil ſhould I pick their bones. *Cleaveland.*

Vo'idness. *n. s.* [from *void.*]

1. Emptineſs; vacuity.
2. Nullity; inefficacy.
3. Want of ſubſtantiality.

If thereby you underſtand their nakedneſs and *voidneſs* of all mixt bodies, good divines are of opinion, that the work of the creation was not in itſelf diſtinguiſhed by days. *Hakew.*

VOITURE. *n. s.* [French.] Carriage; tranſportation by carriage. Not in uſe.

They ought to uſe exerciſe by *voiture* or carriage. *Arbuthnot.*

Vo'lant. *adj.* [*volans*, Lat. *volant*, Fr.]

1. Flying; paſſing through the air.

The *volant*, or flying automata, are ſuch mechanical contrivances as have a ſelf-motion, whereby they are carried aloft in the air, like birds. *Wilkins's Math. Magick.*

2. Nimble; active.

His *volant* touch
Inſtinct through all proportions, low, and high,
Fled, and purſu'd tranſverſe the reſonant fugue. *Milton.*

Blind Britiſh bards, with *volant* touch,
Traverſe loquacious ſtrings, whoſe ſolemn notes
Provoke to harmleſs revels. *Philips.*

Vo'latile. *adj.* [*volatilis*, Lat.]

1. Flying; paſſing through the air.

The caterpillar towards the end of ſummer waxeth *volatile*, and turneth to a butterfly. *Bacon's Nat. Hiſt.*

There is no creature only *volatile*, or no flying animal but hath feet as well as wings; becauſe there is not ſufficient food for them always in the air. *Ray on the Creation.*

2. [*Volatile*, Fr.] Having the power to paſs off by ſpontaneous evaporation.

In vain, though by their pow'rful art they bind
Volatile Hermes. *Milton's Paradiſe Loſt, b.* iii.

When

When arsenick with soap gives a regulus, and with mercury sublimate a *volatile* fusible salt, like butter of antimony; doth not this shew that arsenick, which is a substance totally *volatile*, is compounded of fix'd and *volatile* parts, strongly cohering by a mutual attraction; so that the *volatile* will not ascend without carrying up the fixed? *Newton.*

3. Lively; fickle; changeable of mind; full of spirit.

Active spirits, who are ever skimming over the surface of things with a *volatile* temper, will fix nothing in their mind. *Watts's Improvement of the Mind.*

You are as giddy and *volatile* as ever, just the reverse of Mr. Pope, who hath always loved a domestick life. *Swift.*

VO'LATILE. *n. s.* [*volatile*, Fr.] A winged animal.

The air conveys the heat of the sun, maintains fires, and serves for the flight of *volatiles.* *Brown's Vulgar Errours.*

VO'LATILENESS. } VOLATI'LITY. } *n. s.* [*volatilité*, Fr. from *volatile.*]

1. The quality of flying away by evaporation; not fixity.

Upon the compound body, chiefly observe the colour, fragility, or pliantness, the *volatility* or fixation, compared with simple bodies. *Bacon.*

Of *volatility*, the utmost degree is, when it will fly away without returning. *Bacon.*

Heat causeth the spirits to search some issue out of the body, as in the *volatility* of metals. *Bacon.*

The animal spirits cannot, by reason of their subtilty and *volatileness*, be discovered to the sense. *Hale.*

The *volatility* of mercury argues that they are not much bigger; nor may they be much less, lest they lose their opacity. *Newton's Opticks.*

By the spirit of a plant, we understand that pure, elaborated oil, which, by reason of its extreme *volatility*, exhales spontaneously, in which the odour or smell consists. *Arbuthnot.*

2. Mutability of mind.

VOLATILIZA'TION. *n. s.* [from *volatilize.*] The act of making volatile.

Chemists have, by a variety of ways, attempted in vain the *volatilization* of the salt of tartar. *Boyle.*

To VO'LATILIZE. *v. a.* [*volatiliser*, Fr. from *volatile*] To make volatile; to subtilize to the highest degree.

Spirit of wine has a refractive power, in a middle degree between those of water and oily substances, and accordingly seems to be composed of both, united by fermentation: the water, by means of some saline spirits with which it is impregnated, dissolving the oil, and *volatilizing* it by the action. *Newton's Opticks.*

Spirituous liquors are so far from attenuating, *volatilizing*, and rend'ring perspirable the animal fluids, that it rather condenseth them. *Arbuthnot on Aliments.*

VOLE. *n. s.* [*vole*, Fr.] A deal at cards, that draws the whole tricks.

Past six, and not a living soul!
I might by this have won a *vole.* *Swift.*

VOLCA'NO. *n. s.* [Italian, from *Vulcan.*] A burning mountain.

Navigators tell us there is a burning mountain in an island, and many *volcano's* and fiery hills. *Brown.*

When the Cyclops o'er their anvils sweat,
From the *volcano's* gross eruptions rise,
And curling sheets of smoke obscure the skies. *Garth.*

Subterraneous minerals ferment, and cause earthquakes, and cause furious eruptions of *volcano's*, and tumble down broken rocks. *Bentley's Sermons.*

VO'LERY. *n. s.* [*volerie*, Fr.] A flight of birds.

An old boy, at his first appearance, is sure to draw on him the eyes and chirping of the whole town *volery*; amongst which, there will not be wanting some birds of prey, that will presently be on the wing for him. *Locke.*

VOLITA'TION. *n. s.* [*volito*, Lat.] The act or power of flying.

Birds and flying animals are almost erect, advancing the head and breast in their progression, and only prone in the act of *volitation.* *Brown's Vulgar Errours.*

VOLI'TION. *n. s.* [*volitio*, Lat.] The act of willing; the power of choice exerted.

There is as much difference between the approbation of the judgment, and the actual *volitions* of the will, as between a man's viewing a desirable thing with his eye, and reaching after it with his hand. *South's Sermons.*

Volition is the actual exercise of the power the mind has to order the consideration of any idea, or the forbearing to consider it; or to prefer the motion of any part of the body to its rest, by directing any particular action, or its forbearance. *Locke.*

VO'LITIVE. *adj.* Having the power to will.

They not only perfect the intellectual faculty, but the *volitive*; making the man not only more knowing, but more wise and better. *Hale.*

VO'LLEY. *n. s.* [*volée*, Fr.]

1. A flight of shot.

From the wood a *volley* of shot flew two of his company. *Raleigh's Apology.*

More on his guns relies, than on his sword,
From whence a fatal *volley* we receiv'd. *Waller.*

2. A burst; an emission of many at once.

A fine *volley* of words, gentlemen, and quickly shot off. *Shakespeare.*

Distrustful sense with modest caution speaks;
It still looks home, and short excursions makes;
But rattling nonsense in full *vollies* breaks. *Pope.*

To VO'LLEY. *v. n.* To throw out.

The holding every man shall beat as loud
As his strong sides can *volley.* *Shakesp. Ant. and Cleopatra.*

VO'LLIED. *adj.* [from *volley.*] Disploded; discharged with a volley.

I stood
Thy fiercest, when in battle to thy aid
The blasting *volley'd* thunder made all speed. *Milton.*

The Gallick navy, impotent to bear
His *volley'd* thunder, torn, dissever'd, scud. *Philips.*

VOLT. *n. s.* [*volte*, Fr.] *Volt* signifies a round or a circular tread; a gate of two treads made by a horse going sideways round a center; so that these two treads make parallel tracts, the one which is made by the fore feet larger, and the other by the hinder feet smaller; the shoulders bearing outwards, and the croupe approaching towards the center. *Farrier's Dict.*

VOLUBI'LITY. *n. s.* [*volubilité*, Fr. *volubilitas*, from *volubilis*, Lat.]

1. The act or power of rolling.

Volubility, or aptness to roll, is the property of a bowl, and is derived from its roundness. *Watts's Logick.*

Then cælestial spheres should forget their wonted motions, and by irregular *volubility*, turn themselves any way, as it might happen. *Hooker, b. i.*

2. Activity of tongue; fluency of speech.

Say she be mute, and will not speak a word,
Then I'll commend her *volubility.* *Shakespeare.*

He express'd himself with great *volubility* of words, natural and proper. *Clarendon.*

He had all the French assurance, cunning, and *volubility* of tongue. *Addison.*

She ran over the catalogue of diversions with such a *volubility* of tongue, as drew a gentle reprimand from her father. *Female Quixote.*

3. Mutability; liableness to revolution.

He that's a victor this moment, may be a slave the next: and this *volubility* of human affairs, is the judgment of providence, in the punishment of oppression. *L'Estrange.*

VO'LUBLE. *adj.* [*volubilis*, Lat.]

1. Formed so as to roll easily; formed so as to be easily put in motion.

Neither the weight of the matter of which a cylinder is made, nor its round *voluble* form, which, meeting with a precipice, do necessarily continue the motion of it, are any more imputable to that dead, choiceless creature in its first motion. *Hammond.*

The adventitious corpuscles may produce stability in the matter they pervade, by expelling thence those *voluble* particles, which, whilst they continued, did by their shape unfit for cohesion, or, by their motion, oppose coalition. *Boyle.*

2. Rolling; having quick motion.

This less *voluble* earth,
By shorter flight to th' east, had left him there. *Milton.*

Then *voluble*, and bold; now hid, now seen,
Among thick-woven arborets. *Milton's Par. Lost, b. iv.*

3. Nimble; active. Applied to the tongue.

A friend promised to dissect a woman's tongue, and examine whether there may not be in it certain juices, which render it so wonderfully *voluble* and flippant. *Addison.*

These with a *voluble* and flippant tongue, become mere echo's. *Watts's Improvement of the Mind.*

4. Fluent of words. It is applied to the speech, or the speaker.

Cassio, a knave very *voluble*; no further conscionable, than in putting on the meer form of civil and humane seeming, for the better compassing of his loose affection. *Shakesp.*

If *voluble* and sharp discourse be marr'd,
Unkindness blunts it more than marble hard. *Shakespeare.*

VO'LUME. *n. s.* [*volumen*, Lat.]

1. Something rolled, or convolved.

2. As much as seems convolved at once; as a fold of a serpent, a wave of water.

Threescore and ten I can remember well;
Within the *volume* of which time I've seen
Hours dreadful, and things strange. *Shakesp. Macbeth.*

Unoppos'd they either lose their force,
Or wind in *volumes* to their former course. *Dryden.*

Behind the gen'ral mends his weary pace,
And silently to his revenge he sails:
So glides some trodden serpent on the grass,
And long behind his wounded *volume* trails. *Dryden.*

Thames' fruitful tides,
Slow through the vale in silver *volumes* play. *Fenton.*

By the insinuations of these crystals, the *volumes* of air are driven out of the watery particles, and many of them uniting, form larger *volumes*, which thereby have a greater force to expand themselves. *Cheyne.*

3. [*Volume*, Fr.] A book; so called, because books were antiently rolled upon a staff.

Guyon all this while his book did read,
Ne yet has ended; for it was a great
And ample *volume*, that doth far exceed
My leisure, so long leaves here to repeat. *Fairy Queen.*

Calmly, I do beseech you.——
Aye, as an hostler, that for the poorest piece
Will bear the knave by th' *volume*. *Shakespeare.*

I shall not now enlarge on the wrong judgments whereby men mislead themselves. This would make a *volume*. *Locke.*

If one short *volume* cou'd comprize
All that was witty, learn'd and wise:
How wou'd it be esteem'd and read? *Swift.*

VOLU'MINOUS. *adj.* [from *volume*.]

1. Consisting of many complications.

The serpent roll'd *voluminous* and vast. *Milton.*

2. Consisting in many volumes, or books.

If heav'n write aught of fate, by what the stars
Voluminous, or single characters
In their conjunction met, give me to spell. *Milton.*

There is pleasure in doing something new, though never so little, without pestering the world with *voluminous* transcriptions. *Graunt's Bills of Mortality.*

3. Copious; diffusive.

He did not bear contradiction without much passion, and was too *voluminous* in discourse. *Clarendon.*

The most severe reader makes allowances for many rests and nodding-places in a *voluminous* writer. *Spectator*, Nº 124.

VOLU'MINOUSLY. *adv.* [from *voluminous*.] In many volumes or books.

The controversies are hotly managed by the divided schools, and *voluminously* every where handled. *Granville.*

VO'LUNTARILY. *adv.* [*volontiers*, Fr. from *voluntary*.] Spontaneously; of one's own accord; without compulsion.

Sith there is no likelihood that ever *voluntarily* they will seek instruction at our hands, it remaineth that unless we will suffer them to perish, salvation itself must seek them. *Hooker.*

To be agents *voluntarily* in our own destruction, is against God and nature. *Hooker*, *b.* v.

Self-preservation will oblige a man *voluntarily*, and by choice, to undergo any less evil, to secure himself but from the probability of an evil incomparably greater. *South.*

VO'LUNTARY. *adj.* [*volontaire*, Fr. *voluntarius*, Lat.]

1. Acting without compulsion; acting by choice.

God did not work as a necessary, but a *voluntary* agent; intending before-hand, and decreeing with himself, that which did outwardly proceed from him. *Hooker*, *b.* i.

The lottery of my destiny
Bars me the right of *voluntary* chusing. *Shakespeare.*

2. Willing; acting with willingness.

Then virtue was no more, her guard away,
She fell to lust a *voluntary* prey. *Pope's Odyssey.*

3. Done without compulsion.

Voluntary forbearance denotes the forbearance of an action, consequent to an order of the mind. *Locke.*

The old duke is banished; the new duke, and three or four loving lords, have put themselves into *voluntary* exile with him. *Shakesp. As You Like It.*

They must have recourse to abstinence, which is but *voluntary* fasting, and to exercise, which is but *voluntary* labour. *Seed's Sermon.*

4. Acting of its own accord; spontaneous.

The publick prayers of the people of God in churches thoroughly settled, did never use to be *voluntary* dictates, proceeding from any man's extemporal wit. *Hooker*, *b.* v.

Thoughts which *voluntary* move
Harmonious numbers. *Milton.*

VO'LUNTARY. *n. s.* [from the adjective.]

1. A volunteer; one who engages in any affair of his own accord.

All th' unsettled humours of the land;
Rash, inconsid'rate, fiery *voluntaries*. *Shakespeare.*

Ajax was here the *voluntary*, and you as under an impress. *Shakespeare.*

The bordering wars were made altogether by *voluntaries*, upon their own head. *Davies's Ireland.*

Aids came in partly upon missives, and partly *voluntaries* from all parts. *Bacon.*

2. A piece of musick play'd at will, without any settled rule.

Whistling winds, like organs, play'd,
Until their *voluntaries* made
The waken'd earth in odours rise,
To be her morning sacrifice. *Cleaveland.*

By a *voluntary* before the first lesson, we are prepar'd for admission of those divine truths, which we are shortly to receive. *Spectator*, Nº 630.

VOLUNTEE'R. *n. s.* [*voluntaire*, Fr.] A soldier who enters into the service of his own accord.

Congreve, and the author of the Relapse, being the principals in the dispute, I satisfy them; as for the *volunteers*, they will find themselves affected with the misfortune of their friends. *Collier.*

All Asia now was by the ears;
And Gods beat up for *volunteers*
To Greece and Troy. *Prior.*

To VOLUNTEE'R. *v. n.* To go for a soldier. A cant word.

Leave off these wagers, for in conscience speaking,
The city needs not your new tricks for breaking:
And if you gallants lose, to all appearing,
You'll want an equipage for *volunteering*. *Dryden.*

VOLU'PTUARY. *n. s.* [*voluptuaire*, Fr. *voluptuarius*, Lat.] A man given up to pleasure and luxury.

Does not the *voluptuary* understand in all the liberties of a loose and a lewd conversation, that he runs the risk of body and soul? *L'Estrange.*

The parable was intended against the *voluptuaries*; men who liv'd like heathens, dissolutely, without regarding any of the restraints of religion. *Atterbury.*

VOLU'PTUOUS. *n. s.* [*voluptuosus*, Lat. *voluptueux*, Fr.] Given to excess of pleasure; luxurious.

He them deceives; deceiv'd in his deceit;
Made drunk with drugs of dear *voluptuous* receipt. *Spenser.*

If a new sect have not two properties, it will not spread. The one is the supplanting, or the opposing of authority established; the other is the giving license to pleasures, and a *voluptuous* life. *Bacon.*

Thou wilt bring me soon
To that new world of light and bliss, among
The gods, who live at ease, where I shall reign
At thy right hand *voluptuous*, without end. *Milton.*

Then swol'n with pride, into the snare I fell
Of fair fallacious looks; venereal trains,
Soft'ned with pleasure, and *voluptuous* life. *Milton.*

Speculative atheism subsists only in our speculation; whereas really human nature cannot be guilty of the crime. Indeed a few sensual and *voluptuous* persons may for a season eclipse this native light of the soul, but can never wholly smother and extinguish it. *Bentley's Sermons.*

VOLU'PTUOUSLY. *adv.* [from *voluptuous*.] Luxuriously; with indulgence of excessive pleasure.

Had I a dozen sons, I had rather eleven died nobly for their country, than one *voluptuously* surfeit out of action. *Shak.*

This cannot be done, if my will be so worldly or *voluptuously* disposed, as never to suffer me to think of them; but perpetually to carry away, and apply my mind to other things. *South.*

VOLU'PTUOUSNESS. *n. s.* [from *voluptuous*.] Luxuriousness; addictedness to excess of pleasure.

There's no bottom
In my *voluptuousness*: your wives, your daughters,
Your matrons, and your maids, could not fill up
The cistern of my lust. *Shakesp. Macbeth.*

If he fill'd his vacancy with his *voluptuousness*,
Full surfeits, and the dryness of his bones
Call on him for't. *Shakesp. Ant. and Cleopatra.*

Here where still ev'ning is, not noon nor night;
Where no *voluptuousness*, yet all delight. *Donne.*

These sons of Epicurus, for *voluptuousness* and irreligion, must pass for the only wits of the age. *South.*

You may be free, unless
Your other lord forbids, *voluptuousness*. *Dryden.*

VOLU'TE. *n. s.* [*volute*, Fr.] A member of a column.

That part of the capitals of the Ionick, Corinthian, and Composite orders, which is supposed to represent the bark of trees twisted and turned into spiral lines, or, according to others, the head-dresses of virgins in their long hair. According to Vitruvius, those that appear above the stems in the Corinthian order, are sixteen in every capital, four in the Ionick, and eight in the Composite. These *volutes* are more especially remarkable in the Ionick capital, representing a pillow or cushion laid between the abacus and echinus: whence that antient architect calls the *voluta* pulvinus. *Harris.*

It is said there is an Ionick pillar in the Santa Maria Transtevere, where the marks of the compass are still to be seen on the *volute*; and that Palladio learnt from thence the working of that difficult problem. *Addison.*

VO'MICA. *n. s.* [Latin.] An encysted humour in the lungs.

If the ulcer is not broke, it is commonly called a *vomica*, attended with the same symptoms as an empyema; because the *vomica* communicating with the vessels of the lungs, must necessarily void some of the putrid matter, and taint the blood. *Arbuthnot on Diet.*

VO'MICK NUT. *n. s.*

Vomick nut is the nucleus of a fruit of an East-Indian tree, the wood of which is the lignum colubrinum, or snakewood of the shops. It is flat, compressed, and round, of the breadth of a shilling, and about the thickness of a crown-piece. It is certain poison to quadrupeds and birds; and taken

taken internally, in small doses, it disturbs the whole human frame, and brings on convulsions. *Hill's Mat. Medica.*

To VOMIT. *v. n.* [*vomo*, Latin.]

1. To cast up the contents of the stomach.

The dog, when he is sick at the stomach, knows his cure, falls to his grass, *vomits*, and is well. *More.*

To VO'MIT. *v. a.* [*vomir*, Fr.]

1. To throw up from the stomach.

Hast thou found honey? eat so much as is sufficient, lest thou be filled therewith, and *vomit* it. *Prov.* xxv. 16.

The fish *vomited* out Jonah upon the dry land. *Jonah* ii.

Vomiting is of use, when the foulness of the stomach requires it. *Wiseman's Surgery.*

Weak stomachs *vomit* up the wine that they drink in too great quantities, in the form of vinegar. *Arbuthnot.*

2. To throw up with violence from any hollow.

VO'MIT. *n. s.* [from the verb.]

1. The matter thrown up from the stomach.

He shall cast up the wealth by him devour'd,
Like *vomit* from his yawning entrails pour'd. *Sandys.*

2. An emetick medicine; a medicine that causes vomit.

Whether a *vomit* may be safely given, must be judged by the circumstances; if there be any symptoms of an inflammation of the stomach, a *vomit* is extremely dangerous. *Arbuth.*

VOMI'TION. *n. s.* [from *vomo*, Lat.] The act or power of vomiting.

How many have saved their lives, by spewing up their debauch? Whereas, if the stomach had wanted the faculty of *vomition*, they had inevitably died. *Grew's Cosmology.*

VO'MITIVE. *adj.* [*vomitif*, Fr.] Emetick; causing vomits.

From this vitriolous quality, mercurius dulcis, and vitriol *vomitive*, occasion black ejections. *Brown's Vulg. Errours.*

VO'MITORY. *adj.* [*vomitoire*, Fr. *vomitorius*, Lat.] Procuring vomits; emetick.

Since regulus of stibium, or glass of antimony, will communicate to water or wine a purging or *vomitory* operation, yet the body itself, after iterated infusions, abates not virtue or weight. *Brown's Vulgar Errours.*

Some have vomited up such bodies as these, namely, thick, short, blunt pins, which, by straining, they vomit up again, or by taking *vomitories* privately. *Harvey on Consumptions.*

VORA'CIOUS, *adj.* [*vorace*, Fr. *vorax*, Lat.]

1. Greedy to eat; ravenous; edacious.

So *voracious* is this humour grown, that it draws in every thing to feed it. *Government of the Tongue.*

VORA'CIOUSLY. *adv.* [from *voracious*.] Greedily; ravenously.

VORA'CIOUSNESS. } *n. s.* [*voracité*, Fr. *voracitas*, Lat. from *vo-*
VORA'CITY. } *racious*.] Greediness; ravine; ravenousness.

He is as well contented with this, as those that with the rarities of the earth pamper their *voracities*. *Sandys.*

Creatures by their *voracity* pernicious, have commonly fewer young. *Derham's Physico-Theology.*

VO'RTEX. *n. s.* In the plural *vortices*. [Latin.] Any thing whirled round.

If many contiguous *vortices* of molten pitch were each of them as large as those which some suppose to revolve about the sun and fix'd stars; yet these, and all their parts would, by their tenacity and stiffness, communicate their motion to one another. *Newton's Opticks.*

Nothing else could impel it, unless the etherial matter be supposed to be carried about the sun, like a *vortex*, or whirlpool, as a vehicle to convey it and the rest of the planets. *Bentley's Sermons.*

The gath'ring number, as it moves along,
Involves a vast involuntary throng;
Who gently drawn, and struggling less and less,
Roll in her *vortex*, and her power confess. *Pope.*

VO'RTICAL. *adj.* [from *vortex*.] Having a whirling motion.

If three equal round vessels be filled, the one with cold water, the other with oil, the third with molten pitch, and the liquors be stirred about alike, to give them a *vortical* motion; the pitch, by its tenacity, will lose its motion quickly; the oil, being less tenacious, will keep it longer; and the water being still less tenacious, will keep it longest, but yet will lose it in a short time. *Newton's Opticks.*

It is not a magnetical power, nor the effect of a *vortical* motion; those common attempts towards the explication of gravity. *Bentley's Sermons.*

VO'TARIST. *n. s.* [*devotus*, Lat.] One devoted to any person or thing; one given up by a vow to any service or worship; votary.

I wish a more strict restraint
Upon the sisterhood, the *votarists* of St. Clare. *Shakespeare.*

Earth, yield me roots! What is here?
Gold! yellow, glittering, precious gold!
No, gods, I am no idle *votarist*. *Shakespeare.*

The grey-hooded ev'n,
Like a sad *votarist* in palmer's weed,
Rose from the hindmost wheels of Phœbus' wain. *Milton.*

VO'TARY. *n. s.* One devoted, as by a vow, to any particular service, worship, study, or state of life.

Wherefore waste I time to counsel thee?
Thou art a *votary* to fond desire. *Shakespeare.*

Thou, faint god of sleep! forget that I
Was ever known to be thy *votary*.
No more my pillow shall thine altar be,
Nor will I offer any more to thee,
Myself a melting sacrifice. *Crashaw.*

By these means, men worship the idols have been set up in their minds, and stamp the characters of divinity upon absurdities and errors, become zealous *votaries* to bulls and monkies. *Locke.*

The enemy of our happiness has his servants and *votaries*, among those who are called by the name of the son of God. *Rogers's Sermons.*

How can heav'nly wisdom prove
An instrument to earthly love?
Know'st thou not yet, that men commence
Thy *votaries* for want of sense. *Swift.*

VO'TARY. *adj.* Consequent to a vow.

Superstition is now so well advanced, that men of the first blood are as firm as butchers by occupation; and *votary* resolution is made equipollent to custom, even in matter of blood. *Bac.*

VO'TARESS. *n. s.* [female of *votary*.] A woman devoted to any worship or state.

The imperial *vot'ress* passed on,
In maiden meditation, fancy free. *Shakespeare.*

His mother was a *vot'ress* of my order;
And, in the spiced Indian air by night,
Full often she hath gossip'd by my side. *Shakespeare.*

No rosary this *vot'ress* needs,
Her very syllables are beads. *Cleaveland.*

Thy *vot'ress* from my tender years I am;
And love, like thee, the woods and sylvan game. *Dryden.*

What force have pious vows? the queen of love
His sister sends, her *vot'ress* from above. *Pope.*

VOTE *n. s.* [*votum*, Lat.] Suffrage; voice given and numbered.

He that joins instruction with delight,
Profit with pleasure, carries all the *votes*. *Roscommon.*

How many have no other ground for their tenets, than the supposed honesty or learning of those of the same profession? as if truth were to be established by the *vote* of the multitude. *Locke.*

The final determination arises from the majority of opinions or *votes* in the assembly, because they ought to be sway'd by the superior weight of reason. *Watts.*

To VOTE. *v. a.*

1. To chuse by suffrage; to determine by suffrage.

You are not only in the eye and ear of your master; but you are also a favourite, the favourite of the time, and so are in his bosom also; the world hath also *voted* you, and doth so esteem of you. *Bacon.*

2. To give by vote.

The parliament *voted* them one hundred thousand pounds by way of recompence for their sufferings. *Swift.*

VO'TER. *n. s.* [from *vote*.] One who has the right of giving his voice or suffrage.

Elections growing chargeable, the *voters*, that is, the bulk of the common people, have been universally seduced into bribery, perjury, drunkenness, malice, and slander. *Swift.*

He hates an action base;
Can sometimes drop a *voter's* claim,
And give up party to his fame. *Swift.*

VO'TIVE. *adj.* [*votivus*, Lat.] Given by vow.

Such in Isis' temple you may find,
On *votive* tablets to the life pourtray'd. *Dryden.*

Venus! take my *votive* glass;
Since I am not what I was,
What from this day I shall be,
Venus! let me never see. *Prior.*

To VOUCH. *v. a.* [*voucher*, Norman French.]

1. To call to witness; to obtest.

The sun and day are witnesses for me;
Let him who fights unseen relate his own,
And *vouch* the silent stars and conscious moon. *Dryden.*

2. To attest; to warrant; to maintain.

You do not give the cheer; the feast is sold
That is not often *vouched*, while 'tis making
'Tis given with welcome. *Shakesp. Macbeth.*

The consistency of the discourse, and the pertinency of it to the design he is upon, *vouches* it worthy of our great apostle. *Locke.*

They made him ashamed to *vouch* the truth of the relation, and afterwards to credit it. *Atterbury.*

To VOUCH. *v. n.* To bear witness; to appear as a witness; to give testimony.

He declares he will not believe her, until the elector of Hanover shall *vouch* for the truth of what she hath so solemnly affirmed. *Swift.*

VOUCH. *n. s.* [from the verb.] Warrant; atteſtation.

What praiſe couldſt thou beſtow on a deſerving woman indeed? one that in the authority of her merit, did juſtly put on the *vouch* of very malice itſelf? *Shakeſp. Othello.*

VO'UCHER. *n. s.* [from *vouch.*] One who gives witneſs to any thing.

Better to ſtarve,
Than crave the hire which firſt we do deſerve:
Why in this wolviſh gown ſhould I ſtand here,
To beg of Hob and Dick, that do appear,
Their needleſs *voucher?* *Shakeſp. Coriolanus.*

The ſtamp is a mark, and a public *voucher*, that a piece of ſuch denomination is of ſuch a weight, and of ſuch a fineneſs, *i. e.* has ſo much ſilver in it. *Locke.*

All the great writers of that age ſtand up together as *vouchers* for one another's reputation. *Spectator,* N°. 253.

I have added nothing to the malice or abſurdity of them, which it behoves me to declare, ſince the *vouchers* themſelves will be ſo ſoon loſt. *Pope.*

To VOUCHSA'FE. *v. a.* [*vouch* and *ſafe.*]

1. To permit any thing to be done without danger.

2. To condeſcend to grant.

He grew content to mark their ſpeeches, then marvel at ſuch wit in ſhepherds, after to like their company, and laſtly to *vouchſafe* conference. *Sidney.*

Shall I *vouchſafe* your worſhip a word or two?——
—Two thouſand, fair woman, and I'll
Vouchſafe thee hearing. *Shakeſpeare.*

But if the ſenſe of touch ſeem ſuch delight
Beyond all other, think the ſame *vouchſaf'd*
To cattle and each beaſt. *Milton.*

It is not ſaid by the apoſtle, that God *vouchſafed* to the heathens the means of ſalvation; and yet I will not affirm that God will ſave none of thoſe, to whom the ſound of the goſpel never reached. *South's Sermons.*

To VOUCHSA'FE. *v. n.* To deign; to condeſcend; to yield.

Do I not ſee Zelmane, who does not think a thought which is not firſt weigh'd by wiſdom and virtue? doth not ſhe *vouchſafe* to love me with like ardour? *Sidney, b.* ii.

Vouchſafe, divine perfection of a woman,
Of theſe ſuppoſed crimes to give me leave
By circumſtance but to acquit myſelf. *Shakeſp. Rich.* III.

Vouchſafe, illuſtrious Ormond, to behold
What pow'r the charms of beauty had of old. *Dryden.*

VOUCHSA'FEMENT. *n. s.* [from *vouchſafe.*] Grant; condeſcenſion.

The infinite ſuperiority of God's nature, places a vaſt diſparity betwixt his greateſt communicated *vouchſafements*, and his boundleſs, and therefore to his creatures incommunicable perfections. *Boyle.*

VOW. *n. s.* [*vœu*, Fr. *votum*, Lat.]

1. Any promiſe made to a divine power; an act of devotion, by which ſome part of life, or ſome part of poſſeſſions is conſecrated to a particular purpoſe.

The gods are deaf to hot and peeviſh *vows*;
They are polluted offerings. *Shakeſpeare.*

If you take that *vow* and that wiſh to be all one, you are miſtaken; a wiſh is a far lower degree than a *vow. Hammond.*

She *vows* for his return, with vain devotion, pays. *Dryd.*

2. A ſolemn promiſe, commonly uſed for a promiſe of love or matrimony.

By all the *vows* that ever men have broke,
In number more than ever women ſpoke. *Shakeſpeare.*

Thoſe who wear the woodbine on their brow,
Were knights of love, who never broke their *vow*;
Firm to their plighted faith. *Dryden.*

To VOW. *v. a.* [*vouer*, Fr. *voveo*, Lat.] To conſecrate by a ſolemn dedication; to give to a divine power.

David often *voweth* unto God the ſacrifice of praiſe and thankſgiving in the congregation. *Hooker.*

To Maſter Harvey, upon ſome ſpecial conſideration, I have *vowed* this my labour. *Spenſer.*

Vow and pay unto the Lord. *Pſ.* lxxvi.

When we have not only *vowed*, but delivered them over into the poſſeſſion of Almighty God, for the maintenance of his publick worſhip, and the miniſters thereof, they are not now arbitrable, nor to be revoked. *Spelman.*

Whoever ſees theſe irreligious men,
With burden of a ſickneſs, weak and faint,
But hears them talking of religion then,
And *vowing* of their ſoul to ev'ry ſaint. *Davies.*

This plant Latinus, when his town he wall'd,
Then found, and from the tree Laurentum call'd:
And laſt, in honour of his new abode,
He *vow'd* the laurel to the laurel's god. *Dryden.*

To VOW. *v. n.* To make vows or ſolemn promiſes.

Doſt ſee how unregarded now
That piece of beauty paſſes?
There was a time, when I did *vow*
To that alone: but mark the fate of faces. *Suckling.*

VO'WEL. *n. s.* [*voyelle*, Fr. *vocalis*, Lat.] A letter which can be uttered by itſelf.

I diſtinguiſh letters into *vowels* and conſonants, yet not wholly upon their reaſon, that a *vowel* may be ſounded alone, a conſonant not without a *vowel*; which will not be found all true; for many of the conſonants may be ſounded alone, and ſome joined together without a vowel, as bl. ſt. and as we pronounce the latter ſyllable of people, riffle. *Holder.*

Virgil makes the two *vowels* meet without an eliſion. *Broome.*

VOWFE'LLOW. *n. s.* [*vow* and *fellow.*] One bound by the ſame vow.

Who are the votaries,
That are *vowfellows* with this virtuous king? *Shakeſp.*

VO'YAGE. *n. s.* [*voyage*, Fr.]

1. A travel by ſea.

Guyon forward 'gan his *voyage* make,
With his black palmer, that him guided ſtill. *Fairy Queen.*

Our ſhips went ſundry *voyages*, as well to the pillars of Hercules, as to other parts in the Atlantick and Mediterranean ſeas. *Bacon.*

This great man acted like an able pilot in a long *voyage*; contented to ſit in the cabin when the winds were allay'd, but ready to reſume the helm when the ſtorm aroſe. *Prior.*

2. Courſe; attempt; undertaking. A low phraſe.

If he ſhou'd intend his *voyage* towards my wife, I wou'd turn her looſe to him; and what he gets more of her than ſharp words, let it lie on my head. *Shakeſpeare.*

If you make your *voyage* upon her, and prevail, I am no further your enemy. *Shakeſp. Cymbeline.*

3. The practice of travelling.

All nations have interknowledge of one another, by *voyage* into foreign parts, or ſtrangers that come to them. *Bacon.*

To VO'YAGE. *v. n.* [*voyager*, Fr. from the noun.] To travel by ſea.

For *voyaging* to learn the direful art,
To taint with deadly drugs the barbed dart;
Ilus refus'd t'impart the baneful truſt. *Pope's Odyſſey.*

To VO'YAGE. *v. a.* To travel; to paſs over.

I with pain
Voyag'd th' unreal, vaſt, unbounded deep
Of horrible confuſion. *Milton's Par. Loſt.*

VO'YAGER. *n. s.* [*voyageur*, Fr. from *voyage.*] One who travels by ſea.

Diſdain not in thy conſtant travelling
To do as other *voyagers*, and make
Some turns into leſs creeks, and wiſely take
Freſh water at the Heliconian ſpring. *Donne.*

How comfortable this is, *voyagers* can beſt tell. *Cheyne.*

Deny your veſſels, ye deny in vain;
A private *voyager* I paſs the main. *Pope's Odyſſey.*

UP. *adv.* [up, Saxon; *op*, Dutch and Daniſh.]

1. Aloft; on high; not down.

From thoſe two Mytilene brethren, admire the wonderful changes of worldly things, now *up* now down, as if the life of man were not of much more certainty than a ſtage play. *Knolles's Hiſt. of the Turks.*

Thither his courſe he bends; but *up* or down,
By center, or eccentrick, hard to tell,
Or longitude. *Milton.*

2. Out of bed; in the ſtate of being riſen from reſt.

Helen was not *up?* was ſhe? *Shakeſpeare.*

His chamber being commonly ſtived with ſuiters, when he was *up*, he gave his legs, arms, and breaſt to his ſervants to dreſs him; his eyes to his letters, and ears to petitioners. *Wotton.*

3. In the ſtate of being riſen from a ſeat.

Upon his firſt riſing, a general whiſper ran among the country people, that Sir Roger was *up*. *Addiſon.*

4. From a ſtate of decumbiture or concealment.

Now morn with roſy light had ſtreak'd the ſky,
Up roſe the ſun, and *up* roſe Emily;
Addreſs'd her early ſteps to Cynthia's fane. *Dryden.*

5. In a ſtate of being built.

Up with my tent; here will I lie to-night;
But where to-morrow?—well, all's one for that. *Shakeſp.*

6. Above the horizon.

As ſoon as the ſun is *up*, ſet upon the city. *Judges* ix.

7. To a ſtate of advancement.

Till we have wrought ourſelves *up* into this degree of chriſtian indifference, we are in bondage. *Atterbury.*

8. In a ſtate of exaltation.

Thoſe that were *up* themſelves, kept others low;
Thoſe that were low themſelves held others hard,
Ne ſuffered them to riſe, or greater grow. *Fairy Queen.*

Henry the fifth is crown'd; *up* vanity!
Down royal ſtate! all you ſage counſellors hence. *Shakeſp.*

9. In a ſtate of climbing.

10. In a ſtate of inſurrection.

The gentle archbiſhop of York is *up*
With well-appointed powers. *Shakeſp. Hen.* IV.

Rebels there are *up*,
And put the Engliſhmen unto the ſword. *Shakeſpeare.*

Thou

Thou hast fir'd me; my soul's *up* in arms,
And mans each part about me. *Dryden.*

11. In a state of being increased, or raised.

Grief and passion are like floods raised in little brooks by a sudden rain; they are quickly *up*, and if the concernment be pour'd unexpectedly in upon us, it overflows us. *Dryden.*

12. From a remoter place, coming to any person or place.

As a boar was whetting his teeth, *up* comes a fox to him. *L'Estrange.*

13. From younger to elder years.

I am ready to die from my youth *up*. *Ps.* lxxxviii.

14. Up *and down.* Dispersedly; here and there.

Abundance of them are seen scattered *up and down* like so many little islands when the tide is low. *Addison.*

15. Up *and down.* Backward and forward.

Our desire is, in this present controversy, not to be carried *up and down* with the waves of uncertain arguments, but rather positively to lead on the minds of the simpler sort by plain and easy degrees, till the very nature of the thing itself do make manifest what is truth. *Hooker, b.* v.

The skipping king he rambled *up and down*,
With shallow jesters. *Shakespeare.*

Up and down he traverses his ground;
Now wards a felling blow, now strikes again:
Then nimbly shifts a thrust, then lends a wound;
Now back he gives, then rushes on amain. *Daniel.*

Thou and death
Shall dwell at ease, and *up and down* unseen
Wing silently the buxom air. *Milton.*

On this windy sea of land, the fiend
Walk'd *up and down* alone, bent on his prey. *Milton.*

What a miserable life dost thou lead, says a dog to a lion, to run starving *up and down* thus in woods. *L'Estrange.*

—She moves! life wanders *up and down*
Through all her face, and lights up every charm. *Addison.*

16. Up *to.* To an equal height with.

Tantalus was punished with the rage of an eternal thirst, and set *up to* the chin in water, that fled from his lips whenever he attempted to drink it. *Addison.*

17. Up *to* Adequately to.

The wisest men in all ages have lived *up to* the religion of their country, when they saw nothing in it opposite to morality. *Addison.*

They are determined to live *up to* the holy rule, by which they have obliged themselves to walk. *Atterbury.*

We must not only mortify all these passions that solicit us, but we must learn to do well, and act *up to* the positive precepts of our duty. *Rogers's Sermons.*

18. Up *with.* A phrase that signifies the act of raising any thing to give a blow.

She, quick and proud, and who did Pas despise,
Up with her fist, and took him on the face;
Another time, quoth she, become more wise:
Thus Pas did kiss her hand with little grace. *Sidney.*

19. It is added to verbs, implying some accumulation, or increase.

If we could number *up* those prodigious swarms that settled in every part of the Campania of old Rome, they would amount to more than can be found in any six parts of Europe of the same extent. *Addison's Remarks on Italy.*

20. Up, interject.

21. A word exhorting to rise from bed.

Up, up! cries gluttony, 'tis break of day;
Go drive the deer, and drag the finny prey. *Pope.*

22. A word of exhortation, exciting or rousing to action.

Up then, Melpomene, the mournful muse of nine;
Such cause of mourning never hadst afore.
Up, grisly ghosts; and *up* my rueful rime;
Matter of mirth now shalt thou have no more. *Spenser.*

But *up*, and enter now into full bliss. *Milton.*

Up, up, for honour's sake; twelve legions wait you,
And long to call you chief. *Dryden.*

Up. prep. From a lower to a higher part; not down.

In going *up* a hill, the knees will be most weary; in going down, the thighs: for that in lifting the feet, when a man goeth *up* the hill, the weight of the body beareth most upon the knees, and in going down, upon the thighs. *Bacon.*

To Upbe'ar. *v. a.* preter. *upbore*; part. pass. *upborn.* [*up* and *bear.*]

1. To sustain aloft; to support in elevation.

Upborn with indefatigable wings. *Milton.*

Rang'd in a line the ready racers stand,
Start from the goal, and vanish o'er the strand:
Swift as on wings of wind, *upborn* they fly,
And drifts of rising dust involve the sky. *Pope.*

2. To raise aloft.

This with pray'r,
Or one short sigh of human breath, *upborn*,
Ev'n to the seat of God. *Milton's Par. Lost.*

A monstrous wave *upbore*
The chief, and dash'd him on the craggy shore. *Pope.*

3. To support from falling.

Vital pow'rs 'gan wax both weak and wan,
For want of food and sleep; which two *upbear*,
Like weighty pillars, this frail life of man. *Fairy Queen.*

To Upbra'id. *v. a.* [upȝebꞃœban, upȝebꞃeban, Saxon.]

1. To charge contemptuously with any thing disgraceful.

The fathers, when they were *upbraided* with that defect, comforted themselves with the meditation of God's most gracious nature, who did not therefore the less accept of their hearty affection. *Hooker, b.* v.

It seem'd in me
But as an honour snatch'd with boist'rous hand,
And I had many living to *upbraid*
My gain of it by their assistances,
Which daily grew to quarrel. *Shakesp. Hen.* IV.

If you refuse your aid, yet do not
Upbraid us with our distress. *Shakesp. Coriolanus.*

Vain man! how long wilt thou thy God *upbraid?*
And, like the roaring of a furious wind,
Thus vent the vile distemper of thy mind? *Sandys.*

How cunningly the sorceress displays
Her own transgressions, to *upbraid* me mine. *Milton.*

'Tis a general complaint against you, and I must *upbraid* you with it, that because you need not write, you will not. *Dryden.*

You may the world of more defects *upbraid*,
That other works by nature are unmade;
That she did never at her own expence
A palace rear. *Blackmore.*

2. To object as matter of reproach.

Those that have been bred together, are more apt to envy their equals when raised: for it doth *upbraid* unto them their own fortunes, and pointeth at them. *Bacon.*

Any of these, without regarding the pains of churchmen, grudge or *upbraid* to them those small remains of antient piety, which the rapacity of some ages has scarce left. *Sprat.*

May they not justly to our climes *upbraid*,
Shortness of night, and penury of shade. *Prior.*

3. To urge with reproach.

I have too long born
Your blunt *upbraidings*, and your bitter scoffs. *Shakesp.*

He that knowingly commits an ill, has the *upbraidings* of his own conscience. *Decay of Piety.*

4. To reproach on account of a benefit received from the reproacher.

Ev'ry hour
He flashes into one gross crime or other;
His knights grow riotous, and he himself *upbraids* us
On ev'ry trifle. *Shakesp. K. Lear.*

If any lack wisdom, let him ask of God, that giveth liberally, and *upbraideth* not. *Ja.* i. 5.

Be ashamed of *upbraiding* speeches before friends: and after thou hast given *upbraid* not. *Ecclus.* xli. 22.

5. To bring reproach upon; to shew faults by being in a state of comparison.

Ah, my son, how evil fits it me to have such a son, and how much doth thy kindness *upbraid* my wickedness? *Sidney.*

The counsel which I cannot take,
Instead of healing, but *upbraids* my weakness. *Addison.*

6. To treat with contempt. Not in use.

There also was that mighty monarch laid,
Low under all, yet above all in pride;
That name of native sire did foul *upbraid*,
And would, as Ammon's son, be magnify'd. *Fairy Queen.*

Upbra'idingly. *adv.* By way of reproach.

The time was, when men would learn and study good things, not envy those that had them. Then men were had in price for learning; now letters only make men vile. He is *upbraidingly* called a poet, as if it were a contemptible nickname. *B. Johnson.*

To Upbra'y. *v. a.* [A word formed from *upbraid* by Spenser, for the sake of a rhyming termination.] To shame.

Vile knight,
That knights and knighthood dost with shame *upbray*,
And shew'st th' ensample of thy childish might,
With silly, weak, old women thus to fight. *Spenser.*

Upbro'ught. part. pass. of *upbring.* Educated; nurtured.

Divinely wrought,
And of the brood of angels, heav'nly born,
And with the crew of blessed saints *upbrought*,
Each of which did her with her gifts adorn. *Spenser.*

Upha'nd. *adj.* [*up* and *hand.*] Lifted by the hand.

The *uphand* sledge is used by underworkmen, when the work is not of the largest, yet requires help to batter. They use it with both their hands before them, and seldom lift their hammer higher than their head. *Moxon's Mech. Exer.*

U'pcast. [Participle from to *cast up*. The verb to *upcast* is not in use.] Thrown upwards.

Beasts with *upcast* eyes forsake their shade,
And gaze, as if I were to be obey'd. *Dryden.*

Old Saturn, here with *upcast* eyes,
Beheld his abdicated skies. *Addison.*

U'PCAST. *n. s.* A term of bowling; a throw; a cast.

Was there ever man had such luck? when I kiss'd the jack, upon an *upcast* to be hit away! *Shakesp. Cymbeline.*

To UPGA'THER. *v. a.* [*up* and *gather.*] To contract.

Himself he close *upgather'd* more and more
Into his den, that his deceitful train,
By his there being might not be bewraid,
Ne any noise, ne any question made. *Spenser.*

UPHE'LD. pret. and part. pass. of *uphold.* Maintained; sustained.

He who reigns
Monarch in heav'n, 'till then, as one secure,
Sat on his throne, *upheld* by old repute. *Milton.*

UPHI'LL. *adj.* [*up* and *hill.*] Difficult; like the labour of climbing an hill.

What an *uphill* labour must it be to a learner, who has those first rudiments to master at twenty years of age, which others are taught at ten. *Clarissa.*

To UPHO'ARD. *v. a.* [*up* and *hoard.*] To treasure; to store; to accumulate in private places.

Heaps of huge words *uphoarded* hideously
With horrid sound, though having little sense,
They think to be chief praise of poetry;
And thereby wanting due intelligence,
Have marr'd the face of goodly poesie,
And made a monster of their fantasie. *Spenser.*

If thou hast *uphoarded* in thy life
Extorted treasure, in the womb of earth,
Speak of it. *Shakespeare.*

To UPHO'LD. *v. a.* preter. *upheld*; and part. pass. *upheld*, and *upholden.* [*up* and *hold.*]

1. To lift on high.

The mournful train with groans and hands *upheld*,
Besought his pity. *Dryden.*

2. To support; to sustain; to keep from falling.

While life *upholds* this arm,
This arm *upholds* the house of Lancaster. *Shakesp.*

This great man found no means to continue and *uphold* his ill-purchased greatness, but by rejecting the English law, and assuming, in lieu thereof, the barbarous customs of the Irish. *Davies's Ireland.*

Poetry and painting were *upheld* by the strength of imagination. *Dryden's Dufresnoy.*

3. To keep from declension.

There is due from the judge to the advocate some commendation, where causes are fair pleaded; for that *upholds* in the client the reputation of his council, and beats down in him the conceit of his cause. *Bacon.*

Never was a time, when the interposition of the magistrate was more necessary, to secure the honour of religion, and *uphold* the authority of those great principles, by which his own authority is best *upheld.* *Atterbury.*

4. To support in any state of life.

Many younger brothers have neither lands nor means to *uphold* themselves. *Raleigh.*

5. To continue; to keep from defeat.

Divers, although peradventure not willing to be yoked with elderships, yet were contented to *uphold* opposition against bishops, not without greater hurt to the course of their whole proceedings. *Hooker.*

6. To keep from being lost.

Faulconbridge,
In spite of spite, alone *upholds* the day. *Shakespeare.*

7. To continue without failing.

A deaf person, by observing the motions of another man's mouth, knows what he says, and *upholds* a current communication of discourse with him. *Holder.*

8. To continue in being.

As Nebuchodnosor liveth, who hath sent thee for the *upholding* of every living thing. *Judith* xi. 7.

A due proportion is held betwixt the parts, as well in the natural body of man, as the body politick of the state, for the *upholding* of the whole. *Hakewill.*

UPHO'LDER. *n. s.* [from *uphold.*]

1. A supporter.

Suppose then Atlas ne'er so wise:
Yet when the weight of kingdoms lies
Too long upon his single shoulders,
Sink down he must, or find *upholders.* *Swift.*

2. A sustainer in being.

The knowledge thereof is so many manuductions to the knowledge and admiration of the infinite wisdom of the creator and *upholder* of them. *Hale.*

3. An undertaker; one who provides for funerals.

The company of *upholders* have a right upon the bodies of the subjects. *Arbuthnot.*

Where the brass knocker wrapt in flannel band,
Forbids the thunder of the footman's hand;
Th' *upholder*, rueful harbinger of death,
Waits with impatience for the dying breath. *Gay.*

UPHO'LSTERER. *n. s.* [A corruption of *upholder.*] One who furnishes houses; one who fits up apartments with beds and furniture.

If a corner of the hanging wants a single nail, send for the *upholsterer.* *Swift.*

Mere wax as yet, you fashion him with ease,
Your barber, cook, *upholsterer.* *Pope.*

U'PLAND. *n. s.* [*up* and *land.*] Higher ground.

Men at first, after the flood, liv'd in the *uplands* and sides of the mountains, and by degrees sunk into the plains. *Burnet.*

U'PLAND. *adj.* Higher in situation.

Those in Cornwall do no more by nature than others elsewhere by choice, conceive themselves an estranged society from the *upland* dwellers, and carry an emulation against them. *Carew's Survey of Cornwall.*

Sometimes with secure delight,
The *upland* Hamlets will invite. *Milton.*

UPLA'NDISH. *adj.* [from *upland.*] Mountainous; inhabiting mountains.

Lion-like, *uplandish*, and mere wild,
Slave to his pride; and all his nerves being naturally compil'd
Of eminent strength; stalks out and preys upon a silly sheep. *Chapman's Iliads.*

To UPLA'Y. *v. a.* [*up* and *lay.*] To hoard; to lay up.

We are but farmers of ourselves; yet may,
If we can stock ourselves and thrive, *uplay*
Much, much good treasure for the great rent-day. *Donne.*

To UPLI'FT. *v. a.* [*up* and *lift.*] To raise aloft.

Mechanick slaves,
With greasy aprons, rules, and hammers, shall
Uplift us to the view. *Shakesp. Ant. and Cleopatra.*

The banish'd Bolingbroke repeals himself,
And, with *uplifted* arms, is safe arriv'd
At Ravenspurg. *Shakesp. Rich.* II.

Together both, with next t' almighty arm
Uplifted imminent, one stroke they aim'd. *Milton.*

Satan talking to his nearest mate,
With head *uplift* above the wave, and eyes
That sparkling blaz'd. *Milton's Par. Lost, b.* i.

When by just vengeance guilty mortals perish,
The gods behold their punishment with pleasure,
And lay th' *uplifted* thunder-bolt aside. *Addison's Cato.*

Songs, sonnets, epigrams, the winds *uplift*,
And whisk them back to Evans, Young and Swift. *Pope.*

U'PMOST. *adj.* [an irregular superlative formed from *up.*] Highest; topmost.

Away! ye skum,
That still rise *upmost* when the nation boils;
That have but just enough of sense to know
The master's voice, when rated to depart. *Dryden.*

UPO'N. *prep.* [*up* and *on.*]

1. Not under; noting being on the top or outside.

As I did stand my watch *upon* the hill,
I look'd toward Birnam; and anon methought
The wood began to move. *Shakesp. Macbeth.*

2. Thrown over the body, as cloaths.

I have seen her rise from her bed, throw her night-gown *upon* her. *Shakesp. Macbeth.*

3. By way of imprecation or infliction.

Hard-hearted Clifford! take me from the world;
My soul to heav'n, my blood *upon* your heads. *Shakespeare.*

4. It expresses obtestation, or protestation.

How? that I should murder her?
Upon the love, and truth, and vows, which I
Have made to thy command!—I, her!—her blood! *Shak.*

5. It is used to express any hardship or mischief.

If we would neither impose *upon* ourselves, nor others, we must lay aside that fallacious method of censuring by the lump. *Burnet.*

6. In consequence of. Now little in use.

Let me not find you before me again *upon* any complaint whatsoever. *Shakesp. Measure for Measure.*

Then the princes of Germany had but a dull fear of the greatness of Spain, *upon* a general apprehension of the ambitious designs of that nation. *Bacon.*

They were entertained with the greatest magnificence that could be, *upon* no greater warning. *Bacon.*

I wish it may not be concluded, lest, *upon* second cogitations, there should be cause to alter. *Bacon.*

These forces took hold of divers; in some *upon* discontent, in some *upon* ambition, in some *upon* levity, and desire of change, and in some few *upon* conscience and belief, but in most *upon* simplicity; and in divers out of dependance upon some of the better sort, who did in secret favour these bruits. *Bacon.*

He made a great difference between people that did rebel *upon* wantonness, and them that did rebel *upon* want. *Bacon.*

Upon pity they were taken away, *upon* ignorance they are again demanded. *Hayward.*

Promises can be of no force, unless they be believed to be conditional, and unless that duty proposed to be inforced by them, be acknowledged to be part of that condition, *upon* performance of which those promises do, and *upon* the neglect of which those promises shall not belong to any. *Hammond.*

The earl of Cleveland, a man of signal courage, and an excellent officer *upon* any bold enterprise, advanced. *Clarendon.*

The king had no kindness for him *upon* an old account, as remembering the part he had acted against the earl of Strafford. *Clarendon, b. viii.*

Though sin offers itself in never so pleasing and alluring a dress at first, yet the remorse and inward regrets of the soul, *upon* the commission of it, infinitely overbalance those faint and transient gratifications. *South's Sermons.*

The common corruption of human nature, *upon* the bare stock of its original depravation, does not usually proceed so far. *South's Sermons.*

When we make judgments *upon* general presumptions, they are made rather from the temper of our own spirit, than from reason. *Burnet.*

'Tis not the thing that is done, but the intention in doing it, that makes good or evil. There's a great difference betwixt what we do *upon* force, and what *upon* inclination. *L'Estrange.*

The determination of the will *upon* enquiry, is following the direction of that guide. *Locke.*

There broke out an irreparable quarrel between their parents; the one valuing himself too much *upon* his birth, and the other *upon* his possessions. *Spectator*, N° 164.

The design was discovered by a person, as much noted for his skill in gaming, as in politicks, *upon* the base, mercenary end of getting money by wagers. *Swift.*

6. In immediate consequence of.

Waller should not make advantage *upon* that enterprize, to find the way open to him to march into the west. *Clarendon.*

A louder kind of sound was produced by the impetuous eruptions of the halituous flames of the salt-petre, *upon* casting a live coal thereon. *Boyle.*

So far from taking little advantages against us for every failing, that he is willing to pardon our most wilful miscarriages, *upon* our repentance and amendment. *Tillotson.*

Upon lessening interest to four *per cent.* you fall the price of your native commodities, or lessen your trade. *Locke.*

The mind, *upon* the suggestion of any new notion, runs immediately after similies, to make it the clearer. *Locke.*

If, *upon* the perusal of such writings, he does not find himself delighted; or if, *upon* reading the admired passages in such authors, he finds a coldness and indifference in his thoughts, he ought to conclude, that he wants the faculty of discovering them. *Spectator*, N° 409.

This advantage we lost *upon* the invention of fire-arms. *Addis.*

7. In a state of view.

Is it *upon* record? or else reported
Successively, from age to age? *Shakesp. Rich. III.*

The next heroes we meet with *upon* record were Romulus Numa. *Temple.*

The atheists taken notice of among the antients, are left branded *upon* the records of history. *Locke.*

8. Supposing a thing granted.

If you say necessity is the mother of arts and inventions, and there was no necessity before, and therefore these things were slowly invented, this is a good answer *upon* our supposition. *Burnet's Theory of the Earth.*

9. Relating to a subject.

Ambitious Constance would not cease,
'Till she had kindled France, and all the world,
Upon the right and party of her son. *Shakesp. K. John.*

Yet when we can intreat an hour to serve,
Would spend it in some words *upon* that business,
If you would grant the time. *Shakesp. Macbeth.*

Upon this, I remember a strain of refined civility, that when any woman went to see another of equal birth, she worked at her own work in the other's house. *Temple.*

10. With respect to.

The king's servants, who were sent for, were examined *upon* all questions proposed to them. *Dryden.*

11. In consideration of.

Upon the whole matter, and humanly speaking, I doubt there was a fault somewhere. *Dryden.*

Upon the whole, it will be necessary to avoid that perpetual repetition of the same epithets which we find in Homer. *Pope.*

12. In noting a particular day.

Constantia he looked upon as given away to his rival, *upon* the day on which their marriage was to be solemnized. *Addison.*

13. Noting reliance or trust.

We now may boldly spend *upon* the hope
Of what is to come in. *Shakesp. Hen. IV.*

God commands us, by our dependance *upon* his truth and his holy word, to believe a fact that we do not understand: and this is no more than what we do every day in the works of nature, *upon* the credit of men of learning. *Swift.*

14. Near to; noting situation.

The enemy lodged themselves at Aldermaston, and those from Newberry and Reading, in two other villages *upon* the river Kennet, over which he was to pass. *Clarendon.*

The Lucquese plead prescription for hunting in one of the duke's forests, that lies *upon* their frontiers. *Addison.*

15. On pain of.

To such a ridiculous degree of trusting her she had brought him, that she caused him send us word, that *upon* our lives we should do whatsoever she commanded us. *Sidney, b. ii.*

16. At the time of; on occasion of.

Impartially examine the merits and conduct of the presbyterians *upon* these two great events, and the pretensions to favour which they challenge upon them. *Swift.*

17. By inference from.

Without it, all discourses of government and obedience, *upon* his principles, would be to no purpose. *Locke.*

18. Noting attention.

He presently lost the sight of what he was *upon*; his mind was filled with disorder and confusion. *Locke.*

19. Noting particular pace.

Provide ourselves of the virtuoso's saddle, which will be sure to amble, when the world is *upon* the hardest trot. *Dryden.*

20. Exactly; according to.

In goodly form comes on the enemy;
And by the ground they hide, I judge the number
Upon or near the rate of thirty thousand. *Shakespeare.*

21. By; noting the means of support.

Upon a closer inspection of these bodies, the shells are affixed to the surfaces of them in such a manner, as bodies, lying on the sea-shores, *upon* which they live. *Woodward.*

U'PPER. *adj.* [a comparative from *up.*]

1. Superiour in place; higher.

Give the forehead a majestick grace, the mouth smiling; which you shall do by making a thin *upper* lip, and shadowing the mouth line a little at the corners. *Peacham.*

Our knight did bear no less a pack
Of his own buttocks on his back;
Which now had almost got the *upper*
Hand of his head, for want of crupper. *Hudibras.*

The understanding was then clear, and the soul's *upper* region lofty and serene, free from the vapours of the inferior affections. *South's Sermons.*

With speed to night repair:
For not the gods, nor angry Jove will bear
Thy lawless wand'ring walks in *upper* air. *Dryden.*

Deep as the dark infernal waters lie,
From the bright regions of the chearful sky;
So far the proud ascending rocks invade
Heav'n's *upper* realms, and cast a dreadful shade. *Addison.*

2. Higher in power.

The like corrupt and unreasonable custom prevailed far, and got the *upper*-hand of right reason with the greatest part. *Hooker, b. i.*

U'PPERMOST. *adj.* [superlative from *upper.*]

1. Highest in place.

The waters, called the waters above the heavens, are but the clouds, and waters engendered in the *uppermost* air. *Raleigh.*

In all things follow nature, not painting clouds in the bottom of your piece, and waters in the *uppermost* parts. *Dryden.*

2. Highest in power or authority.

The lower powers are gotten *uppermost*, and we see like men on our heads, as Plato observed of old, that on the right hand, which is indeed on our left. *Glanville.*

'Tis all one to the common people who's *uppermost*. *L'Estr.*

This species of discretion will carry a man safe through all parties, so far, that whatever faction happens to be *uppermost*, his claim is allowed for a share. *Swift.*

3. Predominant; most powerful.

As in perfumes compos'd with art and cost,
'Tis hard to say what scent is *uppermost*;
Nor this part musk or civet can we call,
Or amber, but a rich result of all;
So she was all a sweet. *Dryden.*

U'PPISH. *adj.* [from *up.*] Proud; arrogant. A low word.

To UPRA'ISE. *v. a.* [*up* and *raise.*] To raise up; to exalt.

This would interrupt his joy
In our confusion, and our joy *upraise*
In his disturbance. *Milton's Par. Lost, b. ii.*

To UPRE'AR, *v. a.* [*up* and *rear.*] To rear on high.

Heav'n-born charity! thy blessings shed;
Bid meagre want *uprear* her sickly head. *Gay.*

UPRI'GHT. *adj.* [*up* and *right.* This word, with its derivatives, is in prose accented on the first syllable; but in poetry seems to be accented indifferently on the first or second.]

1. Straight up; perpendicularly erect.

Comb down his hair; look! look! it stands *upright*. *Sha.*

They are *upright* as the palm-tree. *Jer* x.

In the morning, taking of somewhat of easy digestion, as milk, furthers nourishment: but this would be done sitting *upright*, that the milk may pass more speedily to the stomach. *Bacon's Nat. Hist.*

A tree at first setting, should not be shaken; and therefore put two little forks about the bottom of your trees, to keep them *upright*. *Bacon's Nat. Hist.*

Circe, the daughter of the sun; whose charms
Whoever tasted lost his *upright* shape,
And downward fell into a grov'ling swine. *Milton.*

Forthwith *upright* he rears from off the pool
His mighty stature. *Milton's Par. Lost, b.* i.

You have the orthography, or *upright* of this ground-plat, and the explanation thereof, with a scale of feet and inches. *Moxon's Mech. Exer.*

2. Erected; pricked up.

All have their ears *upright*, waiting when the watchword shall come, that they should all arise unto rebellion. *Spenser.*

Stood Theodore surpriz'd in deadly fright,
With chatt'ring teeth, and bristling hair *upright*. *Dryden.*

3. Honest; not declining from the right.

Such neighbour nearness shou'd not partialize
Th' unstooping firmness of my *upright* soul. *Shakespeare.*

How hast thou instill'd
Thy malice into thousands, once *upright*
And faithful, now prov'd false! *Milton's Par. Lost.*

The most *upright* of mortal men was he;
The most sincere, and holy woman, she. *Dryden.*

U'PRIGHTLY. *adv.* [from *upright.*]

1. Perpendicularly to the horizon.
2. Honestly; without deviation from the right.

Men by nature apter to rage than deceit; not greatly ambitious, more than to be well and *uprightly* dealt with. *Sidney.*

Princes in judgment, and their delegate judges, must judge the causes of all persons *uprightly* and impartially, without any personal consideration. *Taylor.*

To live *uprightly* then is sure the best,
To save ourselves, and not to damn the rest. *Dryden.*

U'PRIGHTNESS. *n. s.* [from *upright.*]

1. Perpendicular erection.

So the fair tree, which still preserves
Her fruit and state, while no wind blows,
In storms from that *uprightness* swerves,
And the glad earth about her strows
With treasure from her yielding boughs. *Waller.*

2. Honesty; integrity.

The hypocrite bends his principles and practice to the fashion of a corrupt world: but the truly upright man is inflexible in his *uprightness*, and unalterable in his purpose. *Atterbury.*

To UPRI'SE. *v. n.* [*up* and *rise.*]

1. To rise from decumbiture.

Early, before the morn with crimson ray,
The windows of bright heaven opened had,
Through which into the world the dawning day
Might look, that maketh every creature glad,
Uprose Sir Gyon. *Fairy Queen, b.* ii.

Thou knowest my down-sitting and mine *uprising*. *Ps.* cxxxix.

Uprose the virgin with the morning light,
Obedient to the vision of the night. *Pope.*

2. To rise from below the horizon.

Uprose the sun. *Cowley.*

3. To rise with acclivity.

Was that the king that spurr'd his horse so hard
Against the steep *uprising* of the hill? *Shakespeare.*

UPRI'SE *n. s.* Appearance above the horizon.

Did ever raven sing so like a lark,
That gives sweet tidings of the sun's *uprise*? *Shakespeare.*

U'PROAR. *n. s.* [*oproer*, Dutch. This word likewise is accented on the first syllable in prose; in verse, indifferently on either.] Tumult; bustle; disturbance; confusion.

The Jews which believed not, set all the city on an *uproar*. *Acts* xvii. 5.

It were well if his holiness had not set the world in an *uproar*, by nourishing of war. *Raleigh.*

He levied forces in a disorder'd *uproar*, albeit the treason rested in him and some other his complices. *Hayward.*

Others with vast Typhæan rage more fell,
Rend up both rocks and hills, and ride the air
In whirlwind: hell scarce holds the wild *uproar*. *Milton.*

Horror thus prevail'd,
And wild *uproar*! ah, who at length will end
This long pernicious fray? *Philips.*

The impiety of this sentiment set the audience in an *uproar*; and made Socrates, though an intimate friend of the poet, go out of the theatre with indignation. *Addison.*

To U'PROAR. *v. a.* [from the noun.] To throw into confusion. Not in use.

Had I power, I should
Pour the sweet milk of concord into hell,
Uproar the universal peace, confound
All unity on earth. *Shakespeare's Macbeth.*

To U'PROOT. *v. a.* [*up* and *root.*] To tear up by the root.

Orpheus could lead the savage race,
And trees *uprooted* left their place,
Sequacious of the lyre:
But bright Cecilia rais'd the wonder higher,
When to her organ vocal breath was giv'n,
An angel heard, and straight appear'd,
Mistaking earth for heav'n. *Dryden.*

To UPRO'USE. *v. a.* [*up* and *rouse.*] To waken from sleep; to excite to action.

Thou art *uprous'd* by some distemperature. *Shakespeare.*

U'PSHOT. *n. s.* [*up* and *shot.*] Conclusion; end; last amount; final event.

With this he kindleth his ambitious spighte
To like desire and praise of noble fame,
The only *upshot*, whereto he doth aim. *Hubbard's Tale.*

I cannot pursue with any safety this sport to the *upshot*. *Shak.*

In this *upshot*, purposes mistook
Fall on th' inventor's heads. *Shakespeare's Hamlet.*

Every leading demonstration to the main *upshot* of all, which is the proportion betwixt the sphere and cylinder, is a pledge of the wit and reason of that mathematician. *More.*

Upon the *upshot*, afflictions are but the methods of a merciful providence, to force us upon the only means of setting matters right. *L'Estrange.*

Here is an end of the matter, says the prophet: here is the *upshot* and result of all; here terminate both the prophecies of Daniel and St. John. *Burnet's Theory of the Earth.*

Let's now make an end of matters peaceably, as we shall quickly come to the *upshot* of our affair. *Arbuthnot.*

At the *upshot*, after a life of perpetual application, to reflect that you have been doing nothing for yourself, and that the same or less industry might have gained you a friendship that can never deceive or end; a glory, which, though not to be had till after death, yet shall be felt and enjoy'd to eternity. *Pope.*

U'PSIDE *down.* [an adverbial form of speech.] With total reversement; in complete disorder; with the lower part above the higher.

In his lap a mass of coin he told,
And turned *upside down* to feed his eye,
And covetous desire, with his huge treasure. *Fairy Queen.*

The flood did not so turn *upside down* the face of the earth, as thereby it was made past knowledge, after the waters were decreased. *Raleigh's Hist. of the World.*

The severe notions of christianity turned all this *upside down*, filling all with surprize and amazement. They came upon the world, like light darting full upon the face of a man asleep, who had a mind not to be disturbed. *South.*

U'PSPRING. *n. s.* [*up* and *spring.*] This word seems to signify upstart; a man suddenly exalted.

The king doth wake to-night, and takes his rouse;
Keeps wassel, and the swagg'ring *upspring* reels. *Shakesp.*

To UPSTA'ND. *v. n.* [*up* and *stand.*] To be erected.

Sea calves unwonted to fresh rivers fly;
The water snakes with scales *upstanding* die. *May.*

To UPSTA'Y. *v. a.* [*up* and *stay.*] To sustain; to support.

Them she *upstays*
Gently with myrtle band; mindless the while
Herself, though fairest unsupported flow'r. *Milton.*

To UPSTA'RT. *v. n.* [*up* and *start.*] To spring up suddenly.

He *upstarted* brave
Out of the well, wherein he drenched lay,
As eagle fresh out of the ocean wave. *Spenser.*

Thus having spoke, he sat; thus answer'd then,
Upstarting from his throne, the king of men,
His breast with fury fill'd. *Dryden.*

U'PSTART. *n. s.* [*up* and *start.*] One suddenly raised to wealth power, or honour; what suddenly rises and appears.

Two hundred in a place will be enough for the safeguard of that country, and keeping under all sudden *upstarts*, that shall seek to trouble the peace thereof. *Spenser's Ireland.*

My rights and royalties
Pluckt from my arms perforce, and given away
To *upstart* unthrifts. *Shakespeare.*

Mushrooms have two strange properties; the one, that they yield so delicious a meat; the other, that they come up so hastily, even in a night, and yet they are unsown: and therefore such as are *upstarts* in state, they call in reproach mushrooms. *Bacon's Nat. Hist.*

The king did not neglect Ireland, the soil where these mushrooms and *upstart* weeds, that spring up in a night, did chiefly prosper. *Bacon.*

A place of bliss
In the purlieus of heav'n, and therein plac'd
A race of *upstart* creatures, to supply
Perhaps our vacant room. *Milton's Par. Lost, b.* ii.

Inordinate desires,
And *upstart* passions, catch the government
From reason. *Milton's Par. Lost.*

Mean *upstarts*, when they come once to be preferred, forget their fathers. *L'Estrange.*

Trade,

Trade, he said, carried from us the commodities of our country, and made a parcel of *upstarts*, as rich as men of the most antient families. *Addison's Freeholder*, N° 22.

To UPSWA'RM. *v. a.* [*up* and *swarm.*] To raise in a swarm. Out of use.

You've taken up the subjects of my father;
And both against the voice of heav'n and him
Have here *upswarm'd* them. *Shakesp. Hen.* IV.

To UPTA'KE. *v. a.* [*up* and *take.*] To take into the hands.

He hearkned to his reason, and the child
Uptaking, to the palmer gave to bear. *Fairy Queen.*

To UPTRA'IN. *v. a.* [*up* and *train.*] To bring up; to educate. Not used.

King Lear in happy peace long reign'd,
But had no issue male him to succeed,
But three fair daughters, which were well *uptrain'd*
In all that seem'd fit for kingly seed. *Fairy Queen.*

To UPTU'RN. *v. a.* [*up* and *turn.*] To throw up; to furrow.

So scented the grim feature, and *upturn'd*
His nostrils wide into the murky air. *Milton.*
Beyond all marks, with many a giddy round
Down rushing, it *upturns* a hill of ground. *Pope.*

U'PWARD. *adj.* [*up* and peaꞃꝺ, Saxon.] Directed to a higher part.

Spread upon a lake, with *upward* eye,
A plump of fowl behold their foe on high. *Dryden.*
The angel said,
With *upward* speed his agile wings he spread. *Prior.*

U'PWARD. *n. s.* The top. Out of use.

From th' extreamest *upward* of thy head,
To the descent and dust below thy foot,
A most toad-spotted traitor. *Shakesp. K. Lear.*

U'PWARD.
U'PWARDS. } *adv.* [*up* and peaꞃꝺ.]

1. Towards a higher place.

I thought
To smooth your passage, and to soften death:
For I would have you, when you *upward* move,
Speak kindly of me to our friends above. *Dryden.*
In sheets of rain the sky descends,
And ocean swell'd with waters *upwards* tends;
One rising, falling one; the heav'ns and sea
Meet at their confines, in the middle way. *Dryden.*

A man on a cliff, is at liberty to leap twenty yards downwards into the sea, not because he has power to do the contrary action, which is to leap twenty yards *upwards*, for that he cannot do; but he is therefore free, because he has a power to leap, or not to leap. *Locke.*

2. Towards heav'n and God.

Looking inward, we are stricken dumb; looking *upward*, we speak and prevail. *Hooker, b.* v.

3. With respect to the higher part.

Dagon, sea-monster! *upward* man,
And downward fish. *Milton's Par. Lost, b.* i.

4. More than; with tendency to a higher or greater number.

Their counsel must seem very unseasonable, who advise men now to suspect that, wherewith the world hath had, by their own account, twelve hundred years acquaintance and *upwards*, enough to take away suspicion. *Hooker, b.* v.

I have been your wife in this obedience
Upward of twenty years; and have been blest
With many children by you. *Shakesp. Hen.* VIII.

5. Towards the source.

Be Homer's works your study;
Thence form your judgment, thence your notions bring,
And trace the muses *upward* to their spring. *Pope.*

To UPWI'ND. *v. a.* pret. and pass. *upwound.* [*up* and *wind.*] To convolve.

As she lay upon the dirty ground,
Her huge long tail her den all overspread;
Yet was in knots and many boughts *upwound*. *Fa. Queen.*

URBA'NITY. *n. s.* [*urbanité*, Fr. *urbanitas*, Lat.] Civility; elegance; politeness; merriment; facetiousness.

A rustical severity banishes all *urbanity*, whose harmless condition is consistent with religion. *Brown's Vulg. Errours.*

Raillery is the sauce of civil entertainment; and without some such tincture of *urbanity*, good humour falters. *L'Estr.*

Moral doctrine, and *urbanity*, or well-mannered wit, constitute the Roman satire. *Dryden.*

U'RCHIN. *n. s.* [*heureuchin*, Armorick; *erinaceus*, Lat.]

1. A hedge-hog.

Urchins shall, for that vast of night that they may work,
All exercise on thee. *Shakespeare's Tempest.*
A thousand fiends, a thousand hissing snakes,
Ten thousand swelling toads, as many *urchins*,
Would make such fearful and confused cries,
As any mortal body, hearing it,
Would straight fall mad. *Shakesp. Titus Andronicus.*

That nature designs the preservation of the more infirm creatures, by the defensive armour it hath given them, is demonstrable in the common hedge-hog, or *urchin*. *Ray.*

2. A name of slight anger to a child.

Pleas'd Cupid heard, and check'd his mother's pride:
And who's blind now, mamma? the *urchin* cry'd.
'Tis Cloe's eye, and cheek, and lip, and breast:
Friend Howard's genius fancy'd all the rest. *Prior.*

URE. *n. s.* Practice; use; habit. Obsolete.

Is the warrant sufficient for any man's conscience to build such proceedings upon, as are and have been put in *ure* for the establishment of that cause? *Hooker.*

He would keep his hand in *ure* with somewhat of greater value, till he was brought to justice. *L'Estrange.*

U'RETER. *n. s.* [*uretere*, Fr.] *Ureters* are two long and small canals from the bason of the kidnies, one on each side. They lie between the doubling of the peritonæum, and descending in the form of an S, pierce the bladder near its neck, where they run first some space betwixt its coats, and then they open in its cavity. Their use is to carry the urine from the kidnies to the bladder. *Quincy.*

The kidnies and *ureters* serve for expurgation. *Wiseman.*

U'RETHRA. *n. s.* [*uretre*, Fr.] The passage of the urine.

Caruncles are loose flesh, arising in the *urethra*. *Wiseman.*

To URGE. *v. a.* [*urgeo*, Lat.]

1. To incite; to push.

You do mistake your business: my brother
Did *urge* me in his act. *Shakesp. Ant. and Cleopatra.*
He pleaded still not guilty;
The king's attorney, on the contrary,
Urg'd on examinations, proofs, confessions,
Of divers witnesses. *Shakesp. Hen.* VIII.
What I have done my safety *urg'd* me to. *Shakespeare.*
This *urges* me to fight, and fires my mind. *Dryden.*
High Epidaurus *urges* on my speed,
Fam'd for his hills, and for his horses breed. *Dryden.*

The heathens had but uncertain apprehensions of what *urges* men most powerfully to forsake their sins. *Tillotson.*

He, seiz'd with horror, in the shades of night,
Through the thick desarts headlong *urg'd* his flight. *Pope.*

2. To provoke; to exasperate.

Urge not my father's anger, Eglamour,
But think upon my grief. *Shakespeare.*

3. To follow close, so as to impell.

Man? and for ever? wretch! what wouldst thou have?
Heir *urges* heir, like wave impelling wave. *Pope.*

4. To labour vehemently.

5. To press; to enforce.

The enemy's in view; draw up your powers;
Your haste is now *urg'd* on you. *Shakespeare.*
Urge your petitions in the street. *Shakesp. Jul. Cæsar.*
And great Achilles *urge* the Trojan fate. *Dryden.*

6. To press as an argument.

Urge the necessity and state of times,
And be not peevish. *Shakespeare's Rich.* III.

7. To importune; to solicit.

He *urged* sore,
With piercing words and pitiful implore,
Him hasty to arise. *Fairy Queen, b.* ii.

8. To press in opposition, by way of objection.

Though every man have a right in dispute to *urge* a false religion, with all its absurd consequences; yet it is barbarous incivility scurrilously to sport with that which others account religion. *Tillotson.*

To URGE. *v. n.* To press forward.

A palace, when 'tis that which it should be,
Stands such, or else decays:
But he which dwells there is not so; for he
Strives to *urge* upward, and his fortune raise. *Donne.*

U'RGENCY. *n. s.* [from *urgent.*] Pressure of difficulty or necessity.

Being for some hours extremely pressed by the necessities of nature, I was under great difficulties between *urgency* and shame. *Gulliver's Travels.*

U'RGENT. *adj.* [*urgent*, Fr. *urgens*, Lat.]

1. Cogent; pressing; violent.

Things so ordained are to be kept; howbeit not necessarily, any longer than till there grow some *urgent* cause to ordain the contrary. *Hooker, b.* iv.

Not alone
The death of Fulvia, but more *urgent* touches,
Do strongly speak t' us. *Shakesp. Ant. and Cleopatra.*

This ever hath been that true cause of more wars, than upon all other occasions, though it least partakes of the *urgent* necessity of state. *Raleigh.*

Let a father seldom strike, but upon very *urgent* necessity, and as the last remedy. *Locke on Education.*

2. Importunate; vehement in solicitation.

The Egyptians were *urgent* upon the people, that they might send them out in haste. *Exod.* xii. 33.

U'RGENTLY. *adv.* [from *urgent.*] Cogently; violently; vehemently; importunately.

Acrimony in their blood, and afflux of humours to their lungs, *urgently* indicate phlebotomy. *Harvey.*

U'RGER. *n. ſ.* [from *urge.*] One who preſſes; importuner.

I wiſh Pope were as great an *urger* as I. *Swift.*

U'RGEWONDER. *n. ſ.* A ſort of grain.

This barley is called by ſome *urgewonder.* *Mortimer.*

U'RIM. *n. ſ.*

Urim and thummim were ſomething in Aaron's breaſt-plate; but what, criticks and commentators are by no means agreed. The word *urim* ſignifies light, and thummim perfection. It is moſt probable that they were only names given to ſignify the clearneſs and certainty of the divine anſwers which were obtained by the high prieſt conſulting God with his breaſt-plate on, in contradiſtinction to the obſcure, enigmatical, uncertain, and imperfect anſwers of the heathen oracles. *Newton's Notes on Milton.*

He in cœleſtial panoply, all arm'd
Of radiant *urim*, work divinely wrought. *Milton.*

U'RINAL. *n. ſ.* [*urinal*, Fr. from *urine.*] A bottle, in which water is kept for inſpection.

Theſe follies ſhine through you, like the water in an *urinal.* *Shakeſpeare's Two Gentlemen of Verona.*

A candle out of a muſket will pierce through an inch board, or an *urinal* force a nail though a plank. *Brown.*

This hand, when glory calls,
Can brandiſh arms, as well as *urinals.* *Garth.*

Some with ſcymitars in their hands, and others with *urinals*, ran to and fro. *Spectator*, Nº 159.

U'RINARY, *adj.* [from *urine.*] Relating to the urine.

The urachos or ligamentous paſſage is derived from the bottom of the bladder, whereby it diſchargeth the wateriſh and *urinary* part of its contents. *Brown's Vulg. Errours.*

Diureticks that relax the *urinary* paſſages, ſhould be tried before ſuch as ſtimulate. *Arbuthnot on Aliments.*

U'RINATIVE. *adj.* Working by urine; provoking urine.

Medicines *urinative* do not work by rejection and indigeſtion, as ſolutive do. *Bacon's Nat. Hiſt.*

URINA'TOR. *n. ſ.* [*urinateur*, Fr. *urinator*, Lat.] A diver; one who ſearches under water.

The precious things that grow there, as pearl, may be much more eaſily fetched up by the help of this, than by any other way of the *urinators.* *Wilkins's Math. Magic.*

Thoſe relations of *urinators* belong only to thoſe places where they have dived, which are always rocky. *Ray.*

U'RINE. *n. ſ.* [*urine*, Fr. *urina*, Lat.] Animal water.

Drink, Sir, is a great provoker of noſe-painting, ſleep, and *urine.* *Shakeſpeare.*

As though there were a ſeminality in *urine*, or that, like the ſeed, it carried with it the idea of every part, they fooliſhly believe we can viſibly behold therein the anatomy of every particle. *Brown's Vulgar Errours.*

The chyle cannot paſs by *urine* nor ſweat. *Arbuthnot.*

To U'RINE. *v. n.* [*uriner*, Fr. from the noun.] To make water.

Places where men *urine* commonly, have ſome ſmell of violets. *Bacon's Nat. Hiſt.*

No oviparous animal, which ſpawn or lay eggs, doth *urine*, except the tortoiſe. *Brown's Vulg. Errours.*

U'RINOUS. *adj.* [from *urine.*] Partaking of urine.

The putrid matter being diſtilled, affords a water impregnated with an *urinous* ſpirit, like that obtainable from animal ſubſtances. *Arbuthnot on Aliments.*

URN. *n. ſ.* [*urne*, Fr. *urna*, Lat.]

1. Any veſſel, of which the mouth is narrower than the body.

Minos, the ſtrict inquiſitor,
Lives, and crimes, with his aſſeſſors, hears;
Round, in his *urn*, the blended balls he rolls;
Abſolves the juſt, and dooms the guilty ſouls. *Dryden.*

2. A water pot; particularly that in the ſign of Aquarius.

The fiſh oppoſe the maid, the watry *urn*
With adverſe fires ſees raging Leo burn. *Creech.*

3. The veſſel in which the remains of burnt bodies were put.

Or lay theſe bones in an unworthy *urn*,
Tombleſs, with no remembrance over them. *Shakeſpeare.*

A ruſtick digging in the ground by Padua, found an *urn*, or earthen pot, in which there was another *urn*; and in this leſſer, a lamp clearly burning. *Wilkins.*

His ſcatter'd limbs with my dead body burn;
And once more join us in the pious *urn.* *Dryden.*

URO'SCOPY. *n. ſ.* [οὖρον and σκέπτω.] Inſpection of urine.

In this work, attempts will exceed performances; it being compoſed by ſnatches of time, as medical vacations, and *uroſcopy* would permit. *Brown's Vulg. Errours.*

U'RRY. *n. ſ.* A mineral.

In the coal-mines they dig a blue or black clay, that lies near the coal, commonly called *urry*, which is an unripe coal, and is very proper for hot lands, eſpecially paſture-ground. *Mortimer's Huſbandry.*

US. the oblique caſe of *we.*

The lord made not this covenant with our fathers, but with *us*, even *us*, who are all of us here alive this day. *Deut.* v.

Many, O Lord, are thy wonderful works, and thy thoughts which are to *us* ward. *Pſ.* xl. 5.

U'SAGE. *n. ſ.* [*uſage*, Fr.]

1. Treatment.

Which way
Might'ſt thou deſerve, or they impoſe this *uſage*,
Coming from us? *Shakeſp. K. Lear.*

The luſtre in your eye, heav'n in your cheek,
Plead you fair *uſage.* *Shakeſp. Troil. and Creſſida.*

My brother
Is priſ'ner to the biſhop, at whoſe hands
He hath good *uſage*, and great liberty. *Shakeſp. Hen. VI.*

What *uſage* have I met with from this adverſary, who paſſes by the very words I tranſlated, and produces other paſſages; and then hectors and cries out of my diſingenuity. *Stil.*

Are not hawks brought to the hand, and to the lure; and lions reclaimed by good *uſage?* *L'Eſtrange.*

Neptune took unkindly to be bound,
And Eurus never ſuch hard *uſage* found
In his Æolian priſon. *Dryden.*

2. Cuſtom; practice long continued.

Of things once received and confirmed by uſe, long *uſage* is a law ſufficient. In civil affairs, when there is no other law, cuſtom itſelf doth ſtand for law. *Hooker*, *b.* ii.

3. Manners; behaviour. Obſolete.

A gentle nymph was found,
Hight Aſtery, excelling all the crew,
In courteous *uſage*, and unſtained hue. *Spenſer.*

U'SAGER. *n. ſ.* [*uſager*, Fr. from *uſage.*] One who has the uſe of any thing in truſt for another.

He conſum'd the common treaſury;
Whereof he being the ſimple *uſager*
But for the ſtate, not in propriety,
Did alien t' his minions. *Daniel's Civil War.*

U'SANCE. *n. ſ.* [*uſance*, Fr.]

1. Uſe; proper employment.

What art thou,
That here in deſert haſt thine habitance,
And theſe rich heaps of wealth doſt hide apart
From the world's eye, and from her right *uſance?* *Spenſer.*

2. Uſury; intereſt paid for money.

He lends out money gratis, and brings down
The rate of *uſance.* *Shakeſp. Merch. of Venice.*

USE. [*uſus*, Lat.]

1. The act of employing any thing to any purpoſe.

The fat of the beaſt that dieth of itſelf, may be uſed in any other *uſe.* *Lev.* vii. 24.

Number, the mind makes *uſe* of in meaſuring all things by us meaſurable. *Locke.*

Conſider the hiſtory, with what *uſe* our author makes of it. *Loc.*

2. Qualities that make a thing proper for any purpoſe.

Rice is of excellent *uſe* for illneſſes of the ſtomach, that proceed from cold or moiſt humours; a great digeſter and reſtorer of appetite. *Temple.*

3. Need of; occaſion on which a thing can be employed.

This will ſecure a father to my child;
That done, I have no father *uſe* for life. *A. Philips.*

4. Advantage received; power of receiving advantage.

More figures in a picture than are neceſſary, our author calls figures to be let; becauſe the picture has no *uſe* for them. *Dryden's Dufreſnoy.*

5. Convenience; help.

Diſtinct growth in knowledge, carries its own light in every ſtep of its progreſſion; than which nothing is of more *uſe* to the underſtanding. *Locke.*

Nothing would be of greater *uſe* towards the improvement of knowledge and politeneſs, than ſome effectual method for correcting, enlarging, and aſcertaining our language. *Swift.*

When will my friendſhip be of *uſe* to thee? *A. Philips.*

6. Uſage; cuſtomary act.

That which thoſe nations did uſe, having been alſo in *uſe* with others, the antient Roman laws do forbid. *Hooker*, *b.* iv.

He, that firſt brought the word ſham, wheedle, or banter in *uſe*, put together, as he thought fit, thoſe ideas he made it ſtand for. *Locke.*

7. Practice; habit.

Sweetneſs, truth, and ev'ry grace,
Which time and *uſe* are wont to teach,
The eye may in a moment reach,
And read diſtinctly in her face. *Waller.*

8. Cuſtom; common occurrence.

O Cæſar! theſe things are beyond all *uſe*,
And I do fear them. *Shakeſp. Julius Cæſar.*

9. Intereſt; money paid for the uſe of money.

If it be good, thou haſt received it from God, and then thou art more obliged to pay duty and tribute, *uſe*, and principal to him. *Taylor's Rule of Holy Living.*

Moſt of the learned, both heathen and chriſtian, aſſert the taking of *uſe* to be utterly unlawful; yet the divines of the reformed church beyond the ſeas, do generally affirm it to be lawful. *South's Sermons.*

To Use. *v. a.* [*user*, Fr. *usus*, Lat.]

1. To employ to any purpose.

You're welcome,
Most learned rev'rend Sir, into our kingdom;
Use us and it. *Shakesp. Hen.* VIII.

They could *use* both the right hand and the left, in hurling stones and shooting arrows. 1 *Chr.* xii. 2.

Two trumpets of silver, that thou mayest *use* for the calling of the assembly. *Num.* x. 2.

He was unhappily too much *used* as a check upon the Lord Coventry; and when that lord perplexed their counsels with inconvenient objections, the authority of the Lord Manchester was still called upon. *Clarendon.*

These words of God to Cain, are, by many interpreters, understood in a quite different sense than what our author *uses* them in. *Locke.*

That prince was *using* all his endeavours to introduce popery, which he openly professed. *Swift.*

2. To accustom; to habituate.

He that intends to gain th' Olympick prize,
Must *use* himself to hunger, heat and cold. *Roscommon.*

Those who think only of the matter, *use* themselves only to speak extempore. *Locke on Education.*

I've hitherto been *used* to think
A blind officious zeal to serve my king,
The ruling principle. *Addison's Cato.*

A people long *used* to hardships, lose by degrees the very notions of liberty; they look upon themselves as at mercy. *Sw.*

3. To treat.

Why dost thou *use* me thus? I know thee not. *Shakesp.*

When he came to ask leave of Solyman that he might depart, he was courteously *used* of him. *Knolles.*

I know
My Aurengzebe would ne'er have *us'd* me so. *Dryden.*

If Virgil or Ovid be thus *used*, 'tis no longer to be called their work, when neither the thoughts nor words are drawn from the original. *Dryden.*

I love to *use* people according to their own sense of good-breeding. *Tatler*, N° 86.

Cato has *us'd* me ill; he has refus'd
His daughter Marcia to my ardent vows. *Addison's Cato.*

Gay is *used* as the friends of tories are by whigs, and generally by tories too. *Pope to Swift.*

4. To practise.

Use hospitality one to another, without grudging. 1 *Pet.* iv.

5. To behave. Out of use.

Pray forgive me, if I have *us'd* myself unmannerly. *Shakesp.*

To Use. *v. n.*

1. To be accustomed; to practise customarily.

They *use* to place him that shall be their captain upon a stone, always reserved for that purpose, and placed commonly upon a hill. *Spenser's State of Ireland.*

In polling of trees, many do *use* to leave a bough or two on the top, to help to draw up the sap. *Bacon.*

A prudent governor, to advance religion, will not consider men's duty but their practice; not what they ought to do, but what they *use* to do. *South's Sermons.*

2. To be customarily in any manner; to be wont.

Fears *use* to be represented in such an imaginary fashion, as they rather dazzle men's eyes, than open them. *Bacon.*

Snakes that *use* within the house for shade,
Securely lurk, and, like a plague, invade
Thy cattle with venom. *May's Virgil.*

The waters going and returning as the waves and great commotions of the sea *use* to do, retired leisurely. *Burnet.*

Conduct me well
In these strange ways, where never foot did *use*. *Spenser.*

3. To frequent. Obsolete.

Ye vallies low, where the mild whispers *use*
Of shades, and wanton winds, and gushing brooks. *Milton.*

U'seful. *adj.* [*use* and *full.*] Convenient; profitable to any end; conducive or helpful to any purpose.

Providence would only enter mankind into the *useful* knowledge of her treasures, leaving the rest to employ our industry. *More's Antidote.*

Gold and silver being little *useful* to the life of man, in proportion to food, raiment, and carriage, has its value only from the consent of men. *Locke.*

That the legislature should have power to change the succession, is very *useful* towards preserving our religion and liberty. *Swift.*

Deliver a particular account of the great and *useful* things already performed. *Swift.*

U'sefully. *adv.* [from *useful.*] In such a manner as to help forward some end.

In this account they must constitute two at least, male and female, in every species; which chance could not have made so very nearly alike, without copying, nor so *usefully* differing, without contrivance. *Bentley's Sermons.*

U'sefulness. *n. s.* Conduciveness or helpfulness to some end.

The grandeur of the commonwealth shows itself chiefly in works that were necessary or convenient. On the contrary, the magnificence of Rome, under the emperors, was rather for ostentation, than any real *usefulness*. *Addison.*

U'selessly. *adv.* [from *useless.*] Without the quality of answering any purpose.

In a sauntering humour, some, out of custom, let a good part of their lives run uselesly away, without business or recreation. *Locke.*

U'selessness. *n. s.* [from *useless.*] Unfitness to any end.

He made a learned discourse on the trouble, *uselesness*, and indecency of foxes wearing tails. *L'Estrange.*

He would convince them of the vanity and *uselessness* of that learning, which makes not the possessor a better man. *South.*

U'seless. *adj.* [from *use.*] Answering no purpose; having no end.

So have I seen the lost clouds pour
Into the sea an *useless* show'r;
And the vext sailors curse the rain,
For which poor shepherds pray'd in vain. *Waller.*

The hurtful teeth of vipers are *useless* to us, and yet are parts of their bodies. *Boyle.*

His friend, on whose assistance he most relied, either proves false and forsakes him, or looks on with an *useless* pity, and cannot help him. *Rogers's Sermons.*

The waterman forlorn along the shore,
Pensive reclines upon his *useless* oar. *Gay.*

U'ser. *n. s.* [from *use.*] One who uses.

Such things, which, by imparting the delight to others, makes the *user* thereof welcome, as musick, dancing, hunting, feasting, riding. *Sidney.*

My lord received from the countess of Warwick, a lady powerful in the court, and indeed a virtuous *user* of her power, the best advice that was ever given. *Wotton.*

U'SHER. *n. s.* [*huissier*, Fr.]

1. One whose business is to introduce strangers, or walk before a person of high rank.

The wife of Antony
Should have an army for an *usher*, and
The neighs of horse to tell her approach
Long ere she did appear. *Shakesp. Ant. and Cleopatra.*

You make guards and *ushers* march before, and then enters your prince. *Tatlers*, N° 53.

Gay paid his courtship with the croud,
As far as modest pride allow'd;
Rejects a servile *usher's* place,
And leaves St. James's in disgrace. *Swift.*

2. An under-teacher; one who introduces young scholars to higher learning.

Though grammar profits less than rhetorick's,
Yet ev'n in those his *usher* claims a share. *Dryden.*

To U'sher. *v. a.* [from the noun.] To introduce as a forerunner or harbinger; to forerun.

No sun shall ever *usher* forth my honours,
Or gild again the noble troops that waited
Upon my smiles. *Shakespeare's Hen.* VIII.

The sun,
Declin'd, was hasting now with prone career
To th' ocean isles, and in th' ascending scale
Of heav'n, the stars, that *usher* evening, rose. *Milton.*

As the deluge is represented a disruption of the abyss, so the future combustion of the earth is to be *usher'd* in, and accompanied with violent impressions upon nature, and the chief will be earthquakes. *Burnet's Theory of the Earth.*

With songs and dance we celebrate the day,
And with due honours *usher* in the May. *Dryden.*

The Examiner was *usher'd* into the world by a letter, setting forth the great genius of the author. *Addison.*

Oh name for ever sad! for ever dear!
Still breath'd in sighs, still *usher'd* with a tear. *Pope.*

Usqueba'ugh. *n. s.* [An Irish and Erse word, which signifies the water of life.] It is a compounded distilled spirit, being drawn on aromaticks; and the Irish sort is particularly distinguished for its pleasant and mild flavour. The Highland sort is somewhat hotter; and, by corruption, in Scottish they call it *whisky*.

U'stion. *n. s.* [*ustion*, Fr. *ustus*, Lat.] The act of burning; the state of being burned.

Usto'rious. *adj.* [*ustum*, Latin.] Having the quality of burning.

The power of a burning glass is by an *ustorious* quality in the mirror or glass, arising from a certain unknown substantial form. *Watts.*

U'sual. *adj.* [*usuel*, Fr.] Common; frequent; customary; frequently occurring.

Consultation with oracles was a thing very *usual* and frequent in their times. *Hooker, b.* i.

Could I the care of Providence deserve,
Heav'n must destroy me, if it would preserve:
And that's my fate, or sure it would have sent
Some *usual* evil for my punishment. *Dryden.*

U'SUALLY. *adv.* [from *usual.*] Commonly; frequently; customarily.

If men's desires are *usually* as large as their abilities, what course we took to allure the former, by that we might engage the latter. *South's Sermons.*

Where men err against this method, it is *usually* on purpose, and to shew their learning. *Swift.*

U'SUALNESS. *n. s.* [from *usual.*] Commonness; frequency.

USUCA'PTION. *n. s.* [*usus* and *capio*, Lat.] In the civil law, the acquisition of the property of a thing, by possession and enjoyment thereof for a certain term of years prescribed by law. *Dict.*

USUFRU'CT. *n. s.* [*usufruit*, Fr. *usus* and *fructus*, Lat.] The temporary use; enjoyment of the profits, without power to alienate.

The persons receiving the same, have only the *usufruct* thereof, and not any fee or inheritance therein. *Ayliffe.*

USUFRU'CTUARY. *n. s.* [*usufructuaire*, Fr. *usufructuarius*, Lat.] One that has the use and temporary profit, not the property of a thing.

The parsons of parishes are not in law accounted proprietors, but only *usufructuaries*, as having no right of fee simple vested in them. *Ayliffe's Parergon.*

To U'SURE. *n. s.* [*usura*, Lat.] To practice usury; to take interest for money.

Is this the balsam that the *usuring* senate
Pours into captains wounds? *Shakesp. Timon of Athens.*

U'SURER. *n. s.* [*usurier*, Fr. *usura*, Lat.] One who puts money out at interest. Commonly used for one that takes exorbitant interest.

Fie; thou sham'st thy shape, thy love, thy wit;
Which, like an *usurer*, abound'st in all,
And usest none in that true use indeed,
Which should bedeck thy shape, thy love, thy wit. *Shak.*
When *usurers* tell their gold i' th' field,
And bawds and whores do churches build. *Shakespeare.*

If thou lend money to any that is poor, thou shalt not be to him as an *usurer*, nor lay upon him usury. *Ex.* xxii. 25.

There may be no commutative injustice, while each retains a mutual benefit, the *usurer* for his money, the borrower for his industry. *Child on Trade.*

The asses usuræ occasioned great tumults among the people; yet he that took it was not reckoned to transgress any law; and there were some greedy *usurers* that exacted double, triple. *Arbuthnot on Coins.*

USU'RIOUS. *adj.* [*usuaire*, Fr. from *usury.*] Given to the practise of usury; exorbitantly greedy of profit.

For every hour that thou wilt spare me now,
I will allow,
Usurious god of love, twenty to thee,
When with my brown my grey hairs equal be. *Donne.*

To USU'RP. *v. a.* [*usuper*, Fr. *uusurpo*, Lat.] To possess by force or intrusion; to seize, or possess without right.

So ugly a darkness, as if it would prevent the night's coming, *usurped* the day's right. *Sidney, b.* ii.

Not having the natural superiority of fathers, their power must be *usurped*, and then unlawful; or if lawful, then granted or consented unto by them over whom they exercise the same, or else given them extraordinarily from God. *Hooker.*

In as much as the due estimation of heavenly truth dependeth wholly upon the known and approved authority of those famous oracles of God, it greatly behoveth the church to have always most special care, humane inventions *usurp* the room and title of divine worship. *Hooker, b.* v.

Victorious prince of York!
Before I see thee seated in that throne,
Which now the house of Lancaster *usurps*,
These eyes shall never close. *Shakesp. Hen.* VI.
What art thou, that *usurp'st* this time of night,
Together with that fair and warlike form? *Shakesp.*

Their fox-like thefts are so rank, as a man may find whole pages *usurp'd* from one author. *B. Johnson.*

So he dies,
But soon revives; death over him no pow'r
Shall long *usurp*: ere the third dawning light
Return, the stars of morn shall see him rise
Out of his grave. *Milton's Par. Lost, b.* xii.
All fountains of the deep
Broke up, shall heave the ocean to *usurp*
Beyond all bounds, 'till inundation rise
Above the highest hills. *Milton.*
Farewell court,
Where vice not only hath *usurpt* the place,
But the reward, and even the name of virtue. *Denham.*
Your care about your banks infers a fear
Of threat'ning floods and inundations near:
If so, a just reprize would only be
Of what the land *usurp'd* upon the sea. *Dryden.*
Who next *usurps*, will a just prince appear,
So much your ruin will his reign endear. *Dryden.*
Struggling in vain, impatient of her load,
And lab'ring underneath the pond'rous God;
The more she strove to shake him from her breast,
With more and far superior force he press'd,
Commands his entrance, and, without controul,
Usurps her organs, and inspires her soul. *Dryden.*
Who's this, that dares *usurp*
The guards and habit of Numidia's prince? *Addison's Cato.*

USURPA'TION. [*usurpation*, Fr. from *usurp.*] Forcible, unjust, illegal seizure or possession.

The Piercies,
Finding his *usurpation* most unjust,
Endeavour'd my advancement to the throne. *Shakespeare.*

Succeeding kings recovery of their right from unjust *usurpations*, shall never be prejudiced by any act of mine. *K. Char.*

To raise a tempest on the sea was *usurpation* on the prerogative of Neptune, who had given him no leave. *Dryden.*

O baseness to support a tyrant throne,
And crush your freeborn brethren of the world!
Nay, to become a part of *usurpation*,
T' espouse the tyrant's person and her crimes. *Dryden.*

Whatever opposition was made to the *usurpations* of K. James, proceeded altogether from the church of England. *Swift.*

USU'RPER. *n. s.* [from *usurp.*] One who seizes or possesses that to which he has no right. It is generally used of one who excludes the right heir from the throne.

Ever sithence he hath continued his first usurped power, and now exacteth upon all men what he list: so that now to subdue or expel an *usurper*, should be no unjust enterprize, but a restitution of antient right unto the crown. *Spneser.*

Richard duke of York,
Was rightful heir unto the English crown;
And that your majesty was an *usurper*. *Shakespeare.*
But this *usurper*, his encroachment proud,
Stays not on man; to God his tow'r intends
Siege and defiance. *Milton.*
Few *usurpers* to the shades descend
By a dry death, or with a quiet end. *Dryden.*
He griev'd, the land he freed should be oppress'd,
And he less for it than *usurpers* do. *Dryden.*

USU'RPINGLY. *adv.* [from *usurp.*] Without just claim.

Lay aside the sword,
Which sways *usurpingly* these several titles,
And put the same into young Arthur's hand,
Thy right royal sovereign. *Shakespeare's K. John.*

U'SURY. [*usuré*, Fr. *usura*, Lat.]

1. Money paid for the use of money; interest.

He that high does sit, and all things see,
With equal eyes, their merits to restore;
Behold, what ye this day have done for me,
And what I cannot quit, requite with *usury*. *Fairy Queen.*
The wished day is come at last,
That shall, for all the pains and sorrows past,
Pay to her *usury* of long delight. *Spenser.*

Our angles are like money put to *usury*; they may thrive, though we sit still and do nothing. *Walton's Angler.*

What he borrows from the antients, he repays with *usury* of his own; in coin as good, and almost as universally valuable. *Dryden's Dedication to Juvenal.*

2. The practice of taking interest. It is commonly used with some reproach.

Usury bringeth the treasure of a realm into few hands: for the usurer being at certainties, and others at uncertainties, at the end, most of the money will be in the box. *Bacon.*

U'TENSIL. *n. s.* [*utensile*, Fr. *utensile*, low Lat.] An instrument for any use, such as the vessels of the kitchen, or tools of a trade.

Burn but his books; he has brave utensils,
Which, when he has a house, he'll deck withal. *Shakesp.*
Mules after these, camels and dromedaries,
And waggons fraught with *utensils* of war. *Milton.*

Tithes and lands given to God are never; and plate, vestments, and other sacred *utensils*, are seldom consecrated. *South.*

The springs of life their former vigour feel;
Such zeal he had for that vile *utensil*. *Garth's Dispensary.*

U'TERINE. *adj.* [*uterin*, Fr. *uterinus*, Lat.] Belonging to the womb.

In hot climates, and where the *uterine* parts exceed in heat, by the coldness of some simple, they may be reduced unto a conceptive constitution. *Brown's Vulgar Errours.*

The vessels of the interior glandulous substance of the womb, are contorted with turnings and meanders, that they might accommodate themselves without danger of rupture to the necessary extension of the *uterine* substance. *Ray.*

UTERUS. *n. s.* [Latin.] The womb.

UTI'LITY. *n. s.* [*utilité*, Fr. *utilitas*, Lat.] Usefulness; profit; convenience; advantageousness.

Those things which have long gone together, are confederate; whereas new things piece not so well; but though they help by their *utility*, yet they trouble by their inconformity. *Bacon's Nat. Hist.*

Should

Should we blindly obey the restraints of physicians and astrologers, we should confine the *utility* of physick unto a very few days. *Brown's Vulgar Errours.*

M. Zulichem desired me that I would give a relation of the cure of the gout, that might be made publick, as a thing which might prove of common *utility* to so great numbers as were subject to that disease. *Temple.*

U'TIS. *n. s.* A word which probably is corrupted, at least, is not now understood.

Then here will be old *utis*: it will be an excellent stratagem. *Shakespeare's Hen.* IV.

U'TMOST. *adj.* [utmœst, Saxon; from utter.]

1. Extreme; placed at the extremity.

Much like a subtile spider, which doth sit
In middle of her web, which spreadeth wide;
If ought do touch the *utmost* thread of it,
She feels it instantly on ev'ry side. *Davies.*

As far remov'd from God and light of heav'n,
As from the center thrice to th' *utmost* pole. *Milton.*

I went
To view the *utmost* limits of the land. *Dryden.*

2. Being in the highest degree.

I'll undertake to bring him,
Where he shall answer by a lawful form,
In peace, to his *utmost* peril. *Shakesp. Coriolanus.*

U'TMOST. *n. s.* The most that can be; the greatest power; the highest degree.

What miscarries,
Shall be the general's fault, though he perform
To the *utmost* of a man. *Shakesp. Coriolanus.*

I will be free,
Even to the *utmost* as I please in words. *Shakespeare.*

Such a conscience, as has employed the *utmost* of its ability to give itself the best information, and clearest knowledge of its duty, that it can, is a rational ground for a man to build such an hope upon. *South.*

Try your fortune.——
—I have to the *utmost*. Dost thou think me desperate
Without just cause? *Dryden's All for Love.*

A man, having carefully enquired into all the grounds of probability and unlikeliness, and done his *utmost* to inform himself in all particulars, may come to acknowledge on which side the probability rests. *Locke.*

The enemy thinks of raising threescore thousand men: let us perform our *utmost*, and we shall overwhelm them with our multitudes. *Addison.*

U'TTER. *adj.* [utter, Saxon.]

1. Situate on the outside, or remote from the center.

In my flight
Through *utter* and through middle darkness borne,
I sung of chaos, and eternal night. *Milton's P. Lost, b.* iii.

2. Placed without any compass; out of any place.

Pursue these sons of darkness; drive them out
From all heav'n's bounds, into the *utter* deep. *Milton.*

3. Extreme; excessive; utmost. This seems to be Milton's meaning here.

Such place eternal justice had prepar'd
For those rebellious; here their prison ordain'd
In *utter* darkness; and their portion set
As far remov'd from God, and light of heav'n,
As from the center thrice to th' utmost pole. *Milton.*

4. Complete; irrevocable.

The parliament thought the *utter* taking it away, absolutely necessary for the preservation of the kingdom. *Clarendon.*

There could not be any other estimate made of the loss, than by the *utter* refusal of the auxiliary regiments of London and Kent to march farther. *Clarendon, b.* viii.

They feel fewer corporal pains, and are *utter* strangers to all those anxious thoughts which disquiet mankind. *Atterbury.*

To U'TTER. *v. a.* [from the adjective; to make publick, or *let out*; *palam facere.*]

1. To speak; to pronounce; to express.

Men spake not with the instruments of writing, neither writ with the instruments of speech; and yet things recorded with the one, and *uttered* with the other, may be preached well enough with both. *Hooker.*

These very words I've heard him *utter.* *Shakespeare.*

There's more gold: but, sirrah,
We say the dead are well. Bring it to that,
The gold I give thee will I melt, aad pour
Down thy ill-*uttering* throat. *Shakespeare.*

Conceiving and *uttering* from the heart words of falsehood. *Isa.* lix. 13.

Shall not they teach thee and tell thee, and *utter* words out of their heart? *Job* viii. 10.

Who knows but his poor, bleeding heart,
Amidst its agonies, remember'd Marcia,
And the last words he *utter'd*, call'd me cruel! *Addison.*

2. To disclose; to discover; to publish.

When do partial and sinister affections more *utter* themselves, than when an election is committed to many? *Whitg.*

Were it folly to be modest in *uttering* what is known to all the world? *Raleigh.*

I meant my words should not reach your ears; but what
I *utter'd* was most true. *Dryden's All for Love.*

3. To sell; to vend.

Such mortal drugs I have, but Mantua's law
Is death to any he that *utters* them. *Shakesp. Rom. and Juliet.*

They bring it home, and *utter* it commonly by the name of Newfoundland fish. *Abbot's Descrip. of the World.*

The Devonshire and Somersetshire grasiers feed yearly great droves of cattle in the north quarter of Cornwall, and *utter* them at home. *Carew's Survey of Cornwall.*

4. To disperse; to emit at large.

To preserve us from ruin, the whole kingdom should continue in a firm resolution never to receive or *utter* this fatal coin. *Swift.*

U'TTERABLE. *adj.* [from *utter.*] Expressible; such as may be uttered.

U'TTERANCE. *n. s.* [from *utter.*]

1. Pronunciation; manner of speaking.

He, with *utt'rance* grave, and countenance sad,
From point to point discours'd his voyage. *Fa. Queen.*

2. [*Outrance*, Fr.] Extremity; terms of extreme hostility.

Of him I gather'd honour;
Which he to seek of me again perforce,
Behoves me keep at *utterance.* *Shakesp. Cymbeline.*

Mine eternal jewel
Giv'n the common enemy of man,
To make them kings; the seed of Banquo kings!
Rather than so, come, fate, into the list,
And champion me to th' *utterance.* *Shakesp. Macbeth.*

3. Vocal expression; emission from the mouth.

'Till Adam, though no less than Eve abash'd,
At length gave *utterance* to these words constrain'd. *Milton.*

Speaking is a sensible expression of the notions of the mind, by several discriminations of *utterance* of voice, used as signs, having by consent several determinate significancies. *Holder.*

There have been some inventions, which have been able for the *utterance* of articulate sounds, as the speaking of certain words. *Wilkins's Math. Magick.*

Many a man thinks admirably well, who has a poor *utterance*; while others have a charming manner of speech, but their thoughts are trifling. *Watts.*

U'TTERER. *n. s.* [from *utter.*]

1. One who pronounces.

2. A divulger; a discloser.

Utterers of secrets he from thence debarr'd;
Babblers of folly, and blazers of crime. *Fa. Queen.*

3. A seller; a vender.

U'TTERLY. *adv.* [from *utter.*] Fully; completely; perfectly. For the most part, in an ill sense.

God, whose property is to shew his mercies then greatest, when they are nearest to be *utterly* despaired. *Hooker, b.* iv.

Arguments taken from the authority of men, may not only so far forth as hath been declared, but further also be of some force in human sciences; which force, be it never so small, doth shew that they are not *utterly* naught. *Hooker, b.* ii.

All your int'rest in those territories
Is *utterly* bereft you; all is lost. *Shakesp. Hen.* VI.

He was so *utterly* tired with an employment so contrary to his humour, that he did not consider the means that would lead him out of it. *Clarendon, b.* viii.

While in the flesh we cannot be *utterly* insensible of the afflictions that befal us. *Atterbury.*

U'TTERMOST. *adj.* [from *utter.*]

1. Extreme; being in the highest degree.

Bereave me not,
Whereon I live! thy gentle looks, thy aid,
Thy counsel, in this *uttermost* distress. *Milton.*

2. Most remote.

The land, from the *uttermost* end of the straits on Peru side, did go towards the south. *Abbot's Descrip. of the World.*

U'TTERMOST. *n. s.* The greatest degree.

There needed neither promise nor persuasion to make her do her *uttermost* for her father's service. *Sidney, b.* ii.

He cannot have sufficient honour done unto him; but the *uttermost* we can do, we must. *Hooker, b.* i.

UVE'OUS. *adj.* [from *uva*, Lat.]

The *uveous* coat, or iris of the eye, hath a musculous power, and can dilate and contract that round hole in it, called the pupil. *Ray on the Creation.*

VULCA'NO. n. s. [Italian.] A burning mountain; volcano.

Earth calcin'd, flies off into the air; the ashes of burning mountains, in *vulcano's*, will be carried to great distances. *Arb.*

VU'LGAR. *adj.* [*vulgaire*, Fr. *vulgaris*, Lat.]

1. Plebeian; suiting to the common people; practised among the common people.

Men

Men who have passed all their time in low and *vulgar* life, cannot have a suitable idea of the several beauties and blemishes in the actions of great men. *Addison.*

2. Mean; low; being of the common rate.

It requiring too great a sagacity for *vulgar* minds to draw the line between virtue and vice, no wonder if most men attempt not a laborious scrutiny into things themselves, but only take names and words, and so rest in them. *South.*

Now wasting years my former strength confound,
And added woes have bow'd me to the ground:
Yet by the stubble you may guess the grain,
And mark the ruins of no *vulgar* man. *Broome.*

3. Publick; commonly bruited.

Do you hear aught of a battle toward?——
—Most sure, and *vulgar*; every one hears that. *Shakesp.*

VU'LGAR. *n. s.* [*vulgaire*, Fr.] The common people.

I'll about;
Drive away the *vulgar* from the streets. *Shakespeare.*

Those men, and their adherents, were then looked upon by the affrighted *vulgar*, as greater protectors of their laws and liberties than myself. *K. Charles.*

The *vulgar* imagine the pretender to have been a child imposed upon the nation by the fraudulent zeal of his parents, and their bigotted counsellors. *Swift.*

VULGA'RITY. *n. s.* [from *vulgar*.]

1. Meanness; state of the lowest people.

Although their condition may place them many spheres above the multitude; yet are they still within the line of *vulgarity* and democratical enemies to truth. *Brown.*

True it is, and I hope I shall not offend their *vulgarities*, if I say they are daily mocked into error by devisers. *Brown.*

2. Particular instance or specimen of meanness.

Is the grand sophos of Persius, and the sublimity of Juvenal to be circumscribed with the meanness of words, and *vulgarity* of expression? *Dryden's Dedication to Juvenal.*

VU'LGARLY. *adv.* [from *vulgar*.] Commonly; in the ordinary manner; among the common people.

He was, which people much respect
In princes, and which pleases *vulgarly*,
Of goodly pers'nage, and of sweet aspect. *Daniel.*

He, that believes himself uncapable of pardon, goes on without thought of reforming; such an one we call *vulgarly* a desperate person. *Hammond's Practical Catechism.*

As it is *vulgarly* understood, that he cut a passage for his army through these mighty mountains, it may seem incredible. *Brown's Vulgar Errours.*

VU'LNERABLE. *adj.* [*vulnerable*, Fr. *vulnerabilis*, Lat.] Susceptive of wounds; liable to external injuries.

Let fall thy blade on *vulnerable* crests;
I bear a charmed life, which must not yield
To one of woman born. *Shakesp. Macbeth*

Achilles though dipt in Styx, yet having his heel untouche by that water, although he were fortified elsewhere, he w slain in that part, as only *vulnerable* in the inferior and brut part. *Brown's Vulgar Errour*

VU'LNERARY. *adj.* [*vulneraire*, Fr. *vulnerarius*, Lat.] Usef in the cure of wounds.

Try whether the same effect will not ensue, by commo *vulnerary* plaisters. *Brown's Vulgar Errour*

I kept the orifice open, and prescribed him *vulneraries*. *Wiseman's Surger*

To VU'LNERATE. *v. a.* [*vulnero*, Lat.] To wound; to hur

De facto there is such an intercourse between the magnetic unguent and the *vulnerated* body. *Glanvill's Scep*

VU'LPINE. *adj.* [*vulpinus*, Lat.] Belonging to a fox.

VU'LTURE. *n. s.* [*vultur*, Lat.] A large bird of prey remark able for voracity.

Nor the night raven, that still deadly yells,
Nor griesly *vultures* make us once affear'd. *Spense*

We've willing dames enough, there cannot be
That *vulture* in you to devour so many,
As will to greatness dedicate themselves. *Shakes*

A rav'nous *vulture* in his open'd side,
Her crooked beak and cruel talons try'd. *Dryde*

VU'LTURINE. *adj.* [*vulturinus*, Lat.] Belonging to a vultur

UVU'LA. *n. s.* [*uvula*, Lat.] In anatomy, a round soft spon geous body, suspended from the palate near the foramina the nostrils over the glottis. *Dic*

By an instrument bended up at one end, I got up behin the *uvula*. *Wiseman's Surge*

UXO'RIOUS. *adj.* [*uxorius*, Lat.] Submissively fond of wife; infected with connubial dotage.

Towards his queen he was nothing *uxorious*, nor scarce in dulgent; but companionable and respective. *Baco*

That *uxorious* king, whose heart, though large,
Beguil'd by fair idolatresses, fell
To idols foul. *Milton's Paradise Lo*

How would'st thou insult,
When I must live *uxorious* to thy will
In perfect thraldom, how again betray me? *Milto*

UXO'RIOUSLY. *adv.* [from *uxorious*.] With fond submission to a wif

If thou art thus *uxoriously* inclin'd
To bear thy bondage with a willing mind,
Prepare thy neck. *Dryden's Juvena*

UXO'RIOUSNESS. *n. s.* [from *uxorious*.] Connubial dotage fond submission to a wife.

W.

W.

W, Is a letter of which the form is not to be found in the alphabets of the learned languages; though it is not improbable that by our *w* is expressed the sound of the Roman *v*, and the Eolick *f*. Both the form and sound are excluded from the languages derived from the Latin.

W is sometimes improperly used in diphthongs as a vowel, for *u*, *view*; *strew*: the sound of *w* consonant is uniform.

To WA'BBLE. *v. n.* [A low, barbarous word.] To shake; to move from side to side.

If in your work you find it *wabble*; that is, that one side of the flat inclines to the right or left hand, with soft blows of an hammer set it to rights, and then screw it hard up. *Moxon.*

WAD. *n. s.* [peob hay, Saxon.]

1. A bundle of straw thrust close together.

2. *Wadd*, or black lead, is a mineral of great use and value. *Woodward.*

WA'DDING. *n. s.* [from *wad*, *vad*, Islandick.] A kind of soft stuff loosely woven, with which the skirts of coats are stuffed out.

To WA'DDLE. *v. n.* [*wagghelen*, Dutch, to *waggle*; whence, by a casual corruption, *waddle*.] To shake, in walking from side to side; to deviate in motion from a right line.

She could have run and *waddled* all about. *Shakesp.*

The strutting petticoat smooths and levels all distinctions; while I cannot but be troubled to see so many well-shaped, innocent virgins bloated up, and *waddling* up and down like big-bellied women. *Spectator*, N° 127.

The farmer's goose,
Grown fat with corn and sitting still,
Can scarce get o'er the barn-door sill,
And hardly *waddles* forth to cool
Her belly in the neighb'ring pool. *Swift.*

A dabchick *waddles* through the copse
On feet and wings, and flies, and wades, and hops. *Pope.*

Dulness, of business the directing soul,
To human heads like biass to the bowl;
Which, as more pond'rous, makes their aim more true,
Obliquely *waddling* to the mark in view. *Pope.*

To WADE. *v. n.* [from *vadum*, Lat. pronounced *wadum*.]

1. To walk through the waters; to pass water without swimming.

We'll *wade* to the market-place in Frenchmen's blood. *Sha.*

She *waded* through the dirt to pluck him off. *Shakespeare.*

I am in blood
Stept in so far, that, should I *wade* no more,
Returning were as tedious as go o'er. *Shakesp. Macbeth.*

He staid seven days at the Crassus, until a bridge was made for the transporting of his army, for that the river was not to be *waded* over. *Knolles's Hist. of the Turks.*

Then since fortune's favours fade;
You that in her arms do sleep,
Learn to swim, and not to *wade*,
For the hearts of kings are deep. *Wotton's Poems.*

With head, hands, wings, or feet pursues his way,
And swims, or sinks, or *wades*, or creeps, or flies. *Milton.*

It is hard to *wade* deep in baths where springs arise. *Brown.*

Fowls that frequent waters, and only *wade*, have as well long legs as long necks; and those that are made for swimming have feet like oars. *More's Divine Dialogues.*

Those birds only *wade* in the water, and do not swim. *More.*

As when a dabchick waddles through the copse
On feet and wings, he flies, and *wades*, and hops. *Pope.*

2. To pass difficultly and laboriously.

They were not permitted to enter unto war, nor conclude any league of peace, nor to *wade* through any act of moment between them and foreign states, unless the oracle of God, or his prophets, were first consulted with. *Hooker*, *b.* iii.

I have *waded* through the whole cause, searching the truth by the causes of truth. *Hooker.*

The substance of those controversies whereunto we have begun to *wade*, be rather of outward things appertaining to the church, than of any thing wherein the being of the church consisteth. *Hooker*, *b.* iii.

Virtue gives herself light, through darkness for to *wade*. *Fairy Queen*, *b.* i.

I should chuse rather with spitting and scorn to be tumbled into the dust in blood, bearing witness to any known truth of our Lord; than, by a denial of those truths, through blood and perjury *wade* to a sceptre, and lord it in a throne. *South.*

'Tis not to my purpose to *wade* into those bottomless controversies, which, like a gulph, have swallowed up so much time of learned men. *Decay of Piety.*

The dame
Now try'd the stairs, and *wading* through the night,
Search'd all the deep recess, and issu'd into light. *Dryden.*

The wrathful God then plunges from above,
And where in thickest waves the sparkles drove,
There lights, and *wades* through fumes, and gropes his way,
Half-sing'd, half-stifl'd. *Dryden.*

Simonides, the more he contemplated the nature of the Deity, found that he *waded* but the more out of his depth, and that he lost himself in the thought. *Addison.*

WA'FER. *n. s.* [*wafel*, Dutch.]

1. A thin cake.

Wife, make us a dinner; spare flesh, neither corn;
Make *wafers* and cakes, for our sheepe must be shorne. *Tusser.*

Poor Sancho they persuaded that he enjoyed a great dominion, and then gave him nothing to subsist upon but *wafers* and marmalade. *Pope.*

2. The bread given in the eucharist by the Romanists.

That the same body of Christ should be in a thousand places at once; that the whole body should lie hid in a little thin *wafer*; yet so, that the members thereof should not one run into another, but continue distinct, and have an order agreeable to a man's body, it doth exceed reason. *Hall.*

3. Paste made to close letters.

To WAFT. *v. a.* [probably from *wave*.]

1. To carry through the air, or on the water.

A braver choice of dauntless spirits,
Than now the English bottoms have *waft* o'er,
Did never float upon the swelling tide. *Shakespeare.*

Our high admiral
Shall *waft* them over with our royal fleet. *Shakespeare.*

Whether cripples, who have lost their thighs, will not sink but float; their lungs being able to *waft* up their bodies, which are in others overpoised by the hinder legs, we have not made experiment. *Brown's Vulgar Errours.*

Nor dares his transport-vessel cross the waves,
With such whose bones are not compos'd in graves:
A hundred years they wander on the shore;
At length, their penance done, are *wafted* o'er. *Dryden.*

Lend to this wretch your hand, and *waft* him o'er
To the sweet banks of yon forbidden shore. *Dryden.*

From hence might first spring that opinion of the vehicles of spirits; the vulgar conceiving that the breath was that wherein the soul was *wafted* and carried away. *Ray.*

They before *wafted* over their troops into Sicily in open vessels. *Arbuthnot on Coins.*

In vain you tell your parting lover,
You wish fair winds may *waft* him over:
Alas! what winds can happy prove,
That bear me far from what I love? *Prior.*

Speed the soft intercourse from soul to soul,
And *waft* a sigh from Indus to the pole. *Pope.*

2. To beckon; to inform by a sign of any thing moving.

To WAFT. *v. n.* To float.

It *wafted* nearer yet, and then she knew,
That what before she but surmis'd, was true. *Dryden.*

Those trumpets his triumphant entry tell,
And now the shouts *waft* near the citadel. *Dryden.*

WAFT. *n. s.* [from the verb.]

1. A floating body.

From the bellowing east oft the whirlwind's wing
Sweeps up the burthen of whole wintry plains,
In one wide *waft*. *Thomson's Winter.*

2. Motion of a streamer. Used as a token or mean of information at sea.

WA'FTAGE. *n. s.* [from *waft.*] Carriage by water or air. Not in use.

What ship of Epidamnum stays for me?——
—A ship you sent me to, to hire *waftage*. *Shakespeare.*

I stalk about her door,
Like a strange soul upon the Stygian banks,
Staying for *waftage*. *Shakesp. Troilus and Cressida.*

WA'FTER. *n. s.* [from *waft.*] A passage boat. *Ainsworth.*

WA'FTURE. *n. s.* [from *waft.*] The act of waving. Not in use.

You answer'd not;
But with an angry *wafture* of your hand
Gave sign for me to leave you. *Shakesp. Julius Cæsar.*

To WAG. *v. a.* [ƿagian, Saxon; *waggen*, Dutch.] To move lightly; to shake slightly.

I can counterfeit the deep tragedian;
Tremble and start at *wagging* of a straw. *Shakespeare.*

You may as well forbid the mountain pines
To *wag* their high tops, and to make a noise,
When they are fretted with the gusts of heav'n. *Shakesp.*

All that pass, hiss and *wag* their head at thee. *La.* ii. 15.

Thou canst not *wag* thy finger, or begin
The least light motion, but it tends to sin. *Dryden.*

So have I seen in black and white,
A prating thing, a magpye hight,
Majestically stalk;
A stately, worthless animal,
That plies the tongue, and *wags* the tail,
All flutter, pride, and talk. *Swift.*

To WAG. *v. n.*

1. To be in quick or ludicrous motion.

Be merry, my wife has all;
For women are shrews, both short and tall;
'Tis merry in hall, where beards *wag* all. *Shakesp.*

I will fight with him upon this theme,
Until my eyelids will no longer *wag*. *Shakesp. Hamlet.*

2. To go; to be moved.

I will provoke him to't, or let him *wag*. *Shakespeare.*

Her charms she mutter'd o'er;
And yet the resty sieve *wagg'd* ne'er the more:
I wept for woe. *Dryden's Theocritus.*

WAG. *n. s.* [ƿæᵹan, Saxon, to cheat.] Any one ludicrously mischievous; a merry droll.

Cupid the *wag*, that lately conquer'd had
Wise counsellors, stout captains puissant;
And ty'd them fast to lead his triumphs bad,
Glutted with them, now plays with meanest things. *Sidney.*

Was not my lord the verier *wag* o' th' two? *Shakesp.*

We wink at *wags*, when they offend,
And spare the boy, in hopes the man may mend. *Dryden.*

A counsellor never pleaded without a piece of packthread in his hand, which he used to twist about a finger all the while he was speaking: the *wags* used to call it the thread of his discourse. *Addison.*

WAGE. *n. s.* the plural *wages* is now only used. [*wegen*, or *wagen*, German; *gages*, Fr.]

1. Pay given for service.

All friends shall taste
The *wages* of their virtue, and all foes
The cup of their deservings. *Shakesp. K. Lear.*

The last petition is for my men; they are the poorest,
But poverty could never draw them from me;
That they may have their *wages* duly paid them,
And something over to remember me. *Shakespeare.*

By Tom Thumb, a fairy page;
He sent it, and doth him engage,
By promise of a mighty *wage*,
It secretly to carry. *Drayton's Nymphid.*

The thing itself is not only our duty, but our glory: and he who hath done this work, has, in the very work, partly received his *wages*. *South.*

2. Gage; pledge. *Ainsw.*

To WAGE. *v. a.* [The origination of this word, which is now only used in the phrase *to wage war*, is not easily discovered: *waegen*, in German, is to attempt any thing dangerous.]

1. To attempt; to venture.

We must not think the Turk is so unskilful,
Neglecting an attempt of ease and gain,
To wake and *wage* a danger profitless. *Shakespeare.*

2. To make; to carry on. Applied to war.

Return to her, and fifty men dismiss'd!
No; rather I abjure all roofs, and chuse
To *wage* against the enmity o' th' air,
To be a comrade with the wolf. *Shakesp. K. Lear.*

Your reputation *wages war* with the enemies of your royal family, even within their trenches. *Dryden.*

He ponder'd, which of all his sons was fit
To reign, and *wage* immortal *war* with wit. *Dryden.*

3. [From *wage, wages.*] To set to hire.

Thou must *wage*
Thy works for wealth, and life for gold engage. *F. Queen.*

4. To take to hire; to hire for pay; to hold in pay; to employ for wages.

I seem'd his follower, not partner; and
He *wag'd* me with his countenance, as if
I had been mercenary. *Shakespeare's Coriolanus.*

The officers of the admiralty having places of so good benefit, it is their parts, being well *waged* and rewarded, exactly to look into the sound building of ships. *Raleigh.*

The king had erected his courts of ordinary resort, and was at the charge not only to *wage* justice and their ministers, but also to appoint the safe custody of records. *Bacon.*

This great lord came not over with any great number of *waged* soldiers. *Davies's Ireland.*

5. [In law.]

When an action of debt is brought against one, as for money or chattles, left or lent the defendant, the defendant may *wage* his law; that is, swear, and certain persons with him, that he owes nothing to the plaintiff in manner as he hath declared. The offer to make the oath is called *wager* of law: and when it is accomplished, it is called the making or doing of law. *Blount.*

WA'GER. *n. s.* [from *wage*, to venture.]

1. A bett; any thing pledged upon a chance or performance.

Love and mischief made a *wager*, which should have most power in me. *Sidney.*

The sea strove with the winds which should be louder; and the shrouds of the ship, with a ghastful noise to them that were in it, witnessed that their ruin was the *wager* of the other's contention. *Sidney, b.* ii.

Full fast she fled, ne ever look'd behind;
As if her life upon the *wager* lay. *Fairy Queen.*

Besides these plates for horse-races, the *wagers* may be as the persons please. *Temple.*

Factious, and fav'ring this or t'other side,
Their *wagers* back their wishes. *Dryden.*

If any atheist can stake his soul for a *wager*, against such an inexhaustible disproportion; let him never hereafter accuse others of credulity. *Bentley's Sermons.*

2. [In law.] An offer to make oath. See to wage in law.

Multiplication of actions upon the case were rare formerly, and there by *wager* of law ousted, which discouraged many suits. *Hale.*

To WA'GER. *v. a.* [from the noun.] To lay; to pledge as a bett; to pledge upon some casualty or performance.

'Twas merry, when you *wager'd* on your angling. *Shakesp.*

He that will lay much to stake upon every flying story, may as well *wager* his estate which way the wind will sit next morning. *Government of the Tongue.*

I feed my father's flock;
What can I *wager* from the common stock? *Dryden.*

WA'GES. *n. s.* See WAGE.

WA'GGERY. *n. s.* [from *wag.*] Mischievous merriment; roguish trick; sarcastical gaiety.

'Tis not the *waggeries* or cheats practised among schoolboys, that make an able man; but the principles of justice, generosity, and sobriety. *Locke.*

WA'GGISH. *adj.* [from *wag.*] Knavishly merry; merrily mischievous; frolicksome.

Change fear and niceness,
The handmaids of all women, or, more truly,
Woman its pretty self, to *waggish* courage. *Shakespeare.*

This new conceit is the *waggish* suggestion of some sly and sculking atheists. *More's Divine Dialogues.*

A company of *waggish* boys watching of frogs at the side of a pond, still as any of them put up their heads, they would be pelting them down with stones. Children, says one of the frogs, you never consider, that though this may be play to you, 'tis death to us. *L'Estrange.*

As boys, on holidays let loose to play,
Lay *waggish* traps for girls that pass that way;
Then shout to see in dirt and deep distress
Some silly cit. *Dryden.*

WA'GGISHNESS. *n. s.* [from *waggish.*] Merry mischief.

A christian boy in Constantinople had like to have been stoned for gagging, in a *waggishness*, a long billed fowl. *Bacon.*

To WA'GGLE. *v. n.* [*wagghelen*, German.] To waddle; to move from side to side.

The sport Basilius would shew to Zelmane, was the mounting of his hawk at a heron, which getting up on his *waggling* wings with pain, as though the air next to the earth were not fit for his great body to fly through, was now grown to diminish the sight of himself. *Sidney.*

Why do you go nodding and *waggling* so, as if hip-shot? says the goose to her gosseling. *L'Estrange.*

WA'GON. *n. s.* [ƿæᵹen, Sax. *waeghens*, Dutch; *vagn*, Islandick.]

1. A heavy carriage for burthens.

The Hungarian tents, were enclosed round with *waggons*, one chained to another. *Knolles's Hist. of the Turks.*

Waggons fraught with utensils of war. *Milton.*

2. A chariot. Not in use.

Now fair Phœbus 'gan decline in haste,
His weary *waggon* to the western vale. *Spenser.*

Then to her *waggon* ſhe betakes,
And with her bears the witch. *Spenser.*

O Proſerpina,
For the flowers now that frighted thou let'ſt fall
From Dis's *waggon.* *Shakeſpeare.*

Her *waggon* ſpokes made of long ſpinners legs;
The cover, of the wings of graſshoppers. *Shakeſpeare.*

WA'GONNER. *n. ſ.* [from *wagon.*] One who drives a wagon.

By this, the northern *waggoner* had ſet
His ſevenfold team behind the ſtedfaſt ſtar,
That was in ocean waves yet never wet. *Fairy Queen, b.* i.

Gallop apace, you fi'ry-footed ſteeds,
Tow'rd Phœbus' manſion! ſuch a *waggoner*
As Phaeton would whip you to the weſt. *Shakeſpeare.*

A *waggoner* took notice upon the creaking of a wheel, that it was the worſt wheel that made moſt noiſe. *L'Eſtrange.*

The *waggoners* that curſe their ſtanding teams,
Wou'd wake e'en drowſy Druſus from his dreams. *Dryden.*

I deſcribed to him the uſe and the nature of it; and the next day the *waggoners* arrived with it. *Gulliver's Travels.*

WA'GTAIL. *n. ſ.* A bird. *Ainſw.*

WAID. *v. a.* [I ſuppoſe for *weighed.*] Cruſhed.

His horſe *waid* in the back, and ſhoulder ſhotten. *Shakeſp.*

WAIF. *n. ſ.* [*wavium, waivium,* law Lat. from *wave.*] Goods found, but claim'd by no body; that of which every one waves the claim. Commonly written *weif.* *Ainſw.*

To WAIL. *v. a.* [*gualare,* Italian.] To moan; to lament; to bewail.

Wiſe men ne'er *wail* their preſent woes,
But preſently prevent the ways to *wail.* *Shakeſpeare.*

Say, if my ſpouſe maintains her royal truſt?
Or if no more her abſent lord ſhe *wails,*
But the falſe woman o'er the wife prevails? *Pope.*

To WAIL. *v. n.* To grieve audibly; to expreſs ſorrow.

Son of man *wail* for the multitude. *Ez.* xxxii. 18.

I will *wail* and howl. *Mic.* i. 8.

WAIL. *n. ſ.* Audible ſorrow.

Around the woods
She ſighs her ſong, which with her *wail* reſound. *Thomſon.*

WA'ILING. *n. ſ.* [from *wail.*] Lamentation; moan; audible ſorrow.

The camp filled with lamentation and mourning, which would be increaſed by the weeping and *wailing* of them, which ſhould never ſee their brethren. *Knolles.*

Other cries amongſt the Iriſh, ſavour of the Scythian barbariſm; as the lamentations of their burials, with deſpairful outcries, and immoderate *wailings.* *Spenſer's Ireland.*

Take up *wailing* for us, that our eyes may run down with tears. *Jer.* ix. 18.

The *wailings* of a maiden I recite. *Gay.*

WA'ILFUL. *adj.* [from *wail* and *full.*] Sorrowful; mournful.

Lay lime to tangle her deſires
By *wailful* ſonnets, whoſe compoſed rhimes
Should be full fraught with ſerviceable vows. *Shakeſpeare.*

WAIN. *n. ſ.* [contracted from *wagon.*] A carriage.

There antient night arriving, did alight
From her high weary *wain.* *Spenſer.*

Yours be the harveſt; 'tis the beggar's gain,
To glean the fallings of the loaded *wain.* *Dryden.*

WA'INROPE. *n. ſ.* [*wain* and *rope.*] A large cord, with which the load is tied on the wagon.

Oxen and *wainropes* cannot hale them together. *Shakeſp.*

WA'INSCOT. *n. ſ.* [*wageſchot,* Dutch.] The inner wooden covering of a wall.

Some have the veins more varied and chambletted; as oak, whereof *wainſcot* is made. *Bacon.*

She never could part with plain *wainſcot* and clean hangings. *Arbuthnot.*

A rat your utmoſt rage defies,
That ſafe behind the *wainſcot* lies. *Swift.*

To WA'INSCOT. *v. a.* [*waegenſchotten,* Dutch.]

1. To line walls with boards.

Muſick ſoundeth better in chambers *wainſcotted,* than hanged. *Bacon.*

2. To line in general.

It is moſt curiouſly lined, or *wainſcotted,* with a white teſtaceous cruſt, of the ſame ſubſtance and thickneſs with the *tubuli marini.* *Grew.*

One ſide commands a view of the garden, and the other is *wainſcotted* with looking-glaſs. *Addiſon's Guardian.*

WAIR. *n. ſ.* [In carpentry.] A piece of timber two yards long, and a foot broad. *Bailey.*

WAIST. *n. ſ.* [*gwaſe,* Welſh from the verb *gwaſen,* to preſs or bind.]

1. The ſmalleſt part of the body; the part below the ribs.

The one ſeem'd woman to the *waiſt,* and fair,
But ended foul in many a ſcaly fold,
Voluminous and vaſt. *Milton's Par. Loſt, b.* ii.

She, as a veil, down to her ſlender *waiſt,*
Her unadorned golden treſſes wore,
Diſhevel'd. *Milton's Par. Loſt, b.* iv.

They ſeiz'd, and with entangling folds embrac'd,
His neck twice compaſſing, and twice his *waiſt.* *Denham.*

Stiff ſtays conſtrain her ſlender *waiſt.* *Gay.*

2. The middle deck, or floor of a ſhip.

Sheets of water from the clouds are ſent,
Which hiſſing through the planks, the flames prevent,
And ſtop the fiery peſt: four ſhips alone
Burn to the *waiſt,* and for the fleet atone *Dryden.*

To WAIT. *v. a.* [*wachten,* Dutch.]

1. To expect; to ſtay for.

Bid them prepare within;
I am to blame to be thus *waited* for. *Shakeſpeare.*

Aw'd with theſe words, in camps they ſtill abide,
And *wait* with longing looks their promis'd guide. *Dryden.*

Such courage did the antient heroes ſhow,
Who, when they might prevent, would *wait* the blow. *Dry.*

2. To attend; to accompany with ſubmiſſion or reſpect.

He choſe a thouſand horſe, the flow'r of all
His warlike troops, to *wait* the funeral. *Dryden.*

3. To attend as a conſequence of ſomething.

Remorſe and heavineſs of heart ſhall *wait* thee,
And everlaſting anguiſh be thy portion. *Rowe.*

4. To watch as an enemy.

He is *waited* for of the ſword. *Job* xv. 22.

To WAIT. *v. n.*

1. To expect; to ſtay in expectation.

All the days of my appointed time will I *wait* till my change come. *Job* xiv. 14.

The poultry ſtand
Waiting upon her charitable hand. *Gay.*

2. To pay ſervile or ſubmiſſive attendance.

Though Syrinx your Pan's miſtreſs were,
Yet Syrinx well might *wait* on her. *Milton's Arcades.*

One morning *waiting* on him at Cauſham, ſmiling upon me, he ſaid, he could tell me ſome news of myſelf. *Denham.*

Fortune and victory he did purſue,
To bring them, as his ſlaves, to *wait* on you. *Dryden.*

A parcel of ſoldiers robbed a farmer of his poultry, and then made him *wait* at table. *Swift.*

3. To attend. A phraſe of ceremony.

The dinner is on the table; my father deſires your worſhip's company.—
—I will *wait* on him. *Shakeſp. Merry Wives of Windſor.*

4. To ſtay; not to depart from.

How ſhall we know when to *wait* for, when to decline perſecution. *South's Sermons.*

With Vulcan's rage the riſing winds conſpire,
And near our palace rolls the flood of fire:
Haſte, my dear father, 'tis no time to *wait,*
And load my ſhoulders with a willing freight. *Dryden.*

I know, if I am deprived of you, I die:
But oh! I die, if I *wait* longer for you. *A. Philips.*

5. To ſtay by reaſon of ſome hindrance.

6. To look watchfully.

It is a point of cunning to *wait* upon him, with whom you ſpeak, with your eye, as the Jeſuits give it in precept. *Bacon.*

7. To lie in ambuſh as an enemy.

Such ambuſh *waited* to intercept thy way. *Milton.*

8. To follow as a conſequence.

It will import thoſe men who dwell careleſs, to enter into ſerious conſultation how they may avert that ruin, which *waits* on ſuch a ſupine temper. *Decay of Piety.*

WAIT. *n. ſ.* Ambuſh; inſidious and ſecret attempts.

If he hurl at him by laying of *wait,* that he die; he that ſmote him ſhall be put to death. *Num.* xxxv. 20.

Why ſat'ſt thou like an enemy in *wait?* *Milton.*

WA'ITER. *n. ſ.* [from *wait.*] An attendant; one who attends for the accommodation of others.

Let the drawers be ready with wine and freſh glaſſes,
Let the *waiters* have eyes, though their tongues muſt be ty'd. *B. Johnſon's Tavern Academy.*

The leaſt tart or pie,
By any *waiter* there ſtolen and ſet by. *Bp. Corbet.*

A man of fire is a general enemy to all the *waiters* where you drink. *Tatler,* Nº. 61.

The *waiters* ſtand in ranks; the yeomen cry,
Make room. *Swift.*

WA'ITING *gentlewoman.*
WA'ITING *maid.*
WA'ITING *woman.* } *n. ſ.* [from *wait.*] An upper ſervant, who attends on a lady in her chamber.

He made me mad,
To talk ſo like a *waiting-gentlewoman,*
Of guns, and drums, and wounds. *Shakeſp. Hen.* IV.

Flibbertigibbet, prince of mopping and mowing, ſince poſſeſſes chamber-maids and *waiting-women.* *Shakeſp. K. Lear.*

The *waiting-woman* might be converſant in romances. *Swift.*

The *waiting-maid* hopes to ingratiate herſelf. *Swift.*

To

To WAKE. *v. n.* [*wakan*, Gothick; pacian, Saxon; *waecken*, Dutch.]

1. To watch; not to sleep.

All night she watch'd, ne once a-down would lay
Her dainty limbs in her sad dreriment,
But praying still did *wake*, and *waking* did lament. *Spenser.*

The father *waketh* for the daughter, and the care for her taketh away sleep. *Ecclus.* xlii. 9.

Thou holdest mine eyes *waking*. *Ps.* lxxvii. 4.

In the valley of Jehoshaphat,
The judging God shall close the book of fate;
And there the last assizes keep,
For those who *wake*, and those who sleep. *Dryden.*

I cannot think any time, *waking* or sleeping, without being sensible of it. *Locke.*

Though wisdom *wakes*, suspicion sleeps. *Milton.*

2. To be roused from sleep.

Each tree stirr'd appetite, whereat I *wak'd*. *Milton.*

3. To cease to sleep.

The sisters awaked from dreams, which flattered them with more comfort, than their *waking* would consent to. *Sidney.*

Come, thou powerful God,
And thy leaden charming rod,
Dipt in the Lethean lake,
O'er his watchful temples shake,
Lest he should sleep, and never *wake*. *Denham.*

4. To be put in action; to be excited.

Gentle airs to fan the earth now *wak'd*. *Milton.*

To WAKE. *v. a.* [peccian, Saxon; *wecken*, Dutch.]

1. To rouse from sleep.

They *wak'd* each other, and I stood and heard them. *Sha.*

The waggoners that curse their standing teams,
Wou'd *wake* e'en drowsy Drusus from his dreams. *Dryden.*

Shock, who thought she slept too long,
Leap'd up, and *wak'd* his mistress with his tongue. *Pope.*

2. To excite; to put in motion, or action.

Prepare war, *wake* up the mighty men; let them come up. *Joel* iii. 9.

Thine, like Amphion's hand, had *wak'd* the stone,
And from destruction call'd the rising town;
Nor could he burn so fast, as thou couldst build. *Prior.*

What you've said,
Has *wak'd* a thought in me, which may be lucky. *Rowe.*

To *wake* the soul by tender strokes of art,
To raise the genius, and to mend the heart. *Prol. to Cato.*

3. To bring to life again, as if from the sleep of death.

To second life,
Wak'd in the renovation of the just. *Milton.*

WAKE. *n. s.* [from the verb.]

1. The feast of the dedication of the church, formerly kept by watching all night.

Fill oven ful of flawnes, Ginnie passe not for sleepe,
Tomorrow thy father his *wake*-daie will keepe. *Tusser.*

The droiling peasant scarce thinks there is any world beyond his village, nor gaiety beyond that of a *wake*. *Gov. of Tongue.*

Putting all the Grecian actors down,
And winning at a *wake* their parsley crown. *Dryden.*

Sometimes the vulgar will of mirth partake,
And have excessive doings at their *wake*. *King's Art of Cook.*

2. Vigils; state of forbearing sleep.

By dimpled brook, and fountain brim,
The wood-nymphs deckt with daisies trim,
Their merry *wakes* and pastimes keep:
What hath night to do with sleep? *Milton.*

WA'KEFUL. *adj.* [*wake* and *full.*] Not sleeping; vigilant.

Before her gate high God did sweat ordain,
And *wakeful* watches ever to abide. *Spenser.*

Why dost thou shake thy leaden sceptre? go,
Bestow thy poppy upon *wakeful* woe,
Sickness and sorrow, whose pale lids ne'er know
Thy downy finger; dwell upon their eyes,
Shut in their tears; shut out their miseries. *Crashaw.*

All thy fears,
Thy *wakeful* terrors, affrighting dreams,
Have now their full reward. *Denham's Sophy.*

Dissembling sleep, but *wakeful* with the fright,
The day takes off the pleasure of the night. *Dryden.*

WA'KEFULNESS. *n. s.* [from *wakeful.*]

1. Want of sleep.

Other perfumes are fit to be used in burning agues, consumptions, and too much *wakefulness*. *Bacon's Nat. Hist.*

2. Forbearance of sleep.

To WA'KEN. *v. n.* [from *wake.*] To wake; to cease from sleep; to be roused from sleep.

Early Turnus *wak'ning* with the light,
All clad in armour, calls his troops to fight. *Dryden.*

To WA'KEN. *v. a.*

1. To rouse from sleep.

When he was *waken'd* with the noise,
And saw the beast so small;
What's this, quoth he, that gives so weak a voice,
That *wakens* men withal? *Spenser.*

A man that is *wakened* out of sleep. *Zech.* iv. 1.

We make no longer stay; go, *waken* Eve. *Milton.*

2. To excite to action.

Then Homer's and Tyrtæus' martial muse
Waken'd the world, and sounded loud alarms. *Roscommon.*

3. To produce; to bring forth.

They introduce
Their sacred song, and *waken* raptures high. *Milton.*

WA'KEROBIN. *n. s.* [A plant.] The leaves are entire, long, and triangular at the base: the flower consists of one leaf, shaped like an ass's eye: from the bottom of the flower rises the pointal, with embryo's, each of which becomes a roundish berry, containing seeds. *Miller.*

WALE. *n. s.* [pell, Saxon; a web.] A rising part in the surface of cloth.

To WALK. *v. a.* [*walen*, German; pealcan, Saxon, to roll.]

1. To move by leisurely steps, so that one foot is set down, befor the other is taken up.

What mean you, Cæsar? think you to *walk* forth? *Sha.*

A man was seen *walking* before the door very composedly. *Cla.*

2. It is used in the ceremonious language of invitation, for *come* or *go*.

Sir, *walk* in.——
—I had rather *walk* here, I thank you. *Shakespeare.*

3. To move for exercise or amusement.

These bow'rs as wide as we need *walk*. *Milton.*

4. To move the slowest pace. Not to trot, gallop, or amble. Applied to a horse.

5. To appear as a spectre.

The spirits of the dead
May *walk* again; if such thing be, thy mother
Appear'd to me last night. *Shakesp. Winter's Tale.*

It then draws near the season
Wherein the spirit is wont to *walk*. *Shakesp. Hamlet.*

There were *walking* spirits of the house of York, as well in Ireland as in England. *Davies's Ireland.*

Some say no evil thing that *walks* by night,
In fog, or fire, by lake, or moorish fen,
Blue meagre hag, or stubborn unlaid ghost,
That breaks his magick chains at curfew time;
No goblin, or swart fairy of the mine,
Hath hurtful pow'r o'er true virginity. *Milton.*

6. To act on any occasion.

Do you think I'd *walk* in any plot,
Where Madam Sempronia should take place of me,
And Fulvia come i' th' rear? *B. Johnson.*

7. To be in motion. Applied to a clamorous or abusive female tongue; and is still in low language retain'd.

As she went, her tongue did *walk*
In foul reproach, and terms of vile despight;
Provoking him by her outragious talk,

8. To act in sleep.

When was it she last *walk'd*?——
——I have seen her rise from her bed, unlock her closet, take forth paper, fold it, write upon't, read it, and return to bed; yet all this while in a most fast sleep. *Shakesp. Macbeth.*

9. To range; to move about.

Affairs that *walk*,
As they say spirits do at midnight, have
In them a milder nature, than the business
That seeks dispatch by day. *Shakesp. Hen.* VIII.

10. To move off.

When he comes forth, he will make their cows and garrans to *walk*, if he doth no other harm to their persons. *Spens.*

11. To act in any particular manner.

Do justly, love mercy, and *walk* humbly with thy God. *Mic.*

If thou forget the Lord, and *walk* after other gods, ye shall surely perish. *Deut.* viii. 19.

I'll love with fear the only God, and *walk*
As in his presence. *Milton.*

12. To travel.

The Lord hath blessed thee; he knoweth thy *walking* through this wilderness. *Deut.* ii. 7.

To WALK. *v. a.*

1. To pass through.

I do not without danger *walk* these streets. *Shakespeare.*

No rich or noble knave,
Shall *walk* the world in credit to his grave. *Pope.*

2. To lead out, for the sake of air or exercise.

WALK. *n. s.* [from the verb.]

1. Act of walking for air or exercise.

Not *walk* by moon without thee, is sweet. *Milton.*

Her keeper by her side,
To watch her *walks*, his hundred eyes applied. *Dryden.*

Philander used to take a *walk* in a neighbouring wood. *Addis.*

I long to renew our old intercourse, our morning conferences, and our evening *walks*. *Pope.*

2. Gait; step; manner of moving.

Morpheus, of all his numerous train, express'd
The shape of man, and imitated best;
The *walk*, the words, the gesture could supply,
The habit mimick, and the mien supply. *Dryden.*

3. A

3. A length of ſpace, or circuit through which one walks.

He uſually from hence to th' palace gate
Makes it his *walk*. *Shakeſp. Macbeth.*

If that way be your *walk*, you have not far. *Milton.*

She would never miſs one day,
A *walk* ſo fine, a ſight ſo gay. *Prior.*

4. An avenue ſet with trees.

He hath left you all his *walks*,
His private harbours, and new-planted orchards,
On that ſide the Tiber. *Shakeſpeare's Julius Cæſar.*

Goodlieſt trees planted with *walks* and bow'rs. *Milton.*

5. Way; road; range; place of wandering.

The mountains are his *walks*, who wand'ring feeds
On ſlowly-ſpringing herbs. *Sandys's Paraphraſe.*

Set women in his eye, and in his *walk*,
Among daughters of men the faireſt found. *Milton.*

Our ſouls, for want of that acquaintance here,
May wander in the ſtarry *walks* above. *Dryden.*

That bright companion of the ſun,
Whoſe glorious aſpect ſeal'd our new-born king;
And now a round of greater years begun,
New influence from his *walks* of light did bring. *Dryden.*

Wanting an ampler ſphere to expatiate in, he open'd a boundleſs *walk* for his imagination. *Pope.*

6. [*Turbo*, Lat.] A fiſh. *Ainſw.*

7. *Walk* is the ſloweſt or leaſt raiſed pace, or going of a horſe. In a *walk*, a horſe lifts two legs of a ſide, one after the other, beginning with the hind leg firſt; as ſuppoſe that he leads with the legs on his right ſide, then he lifts his far hind foot firſt; and in the time that he is ſetting it down, which in a ſtep is always ſhort of the tread of his fore foot upon the ſame ſide, he lifts his far fore foot, and ſets it down before his near foot, and juſt as he lifts up his near hind foot, and ſets it down again juſt ſhort of his near fore foot, and juſt as he is ſetting it down, he lifts his near fore foot, and ſets it down juſt before his far fore foot. *Farrier's Dict.*

WA'LKER. *n. ſ.* [from *walk*.] One that walks.

I ride and walk, and am reputed the beſt *walker* in this town. *Swift to Gay.*

May no ſuch vicious *walkers* croud the ſtreet. *Gay.*

WA'LKINGSTAFF. *n. ſ.* A ſtick which a man holds to ſupport him in walking.

The club which a man of an ordinary ſize could not lift, was but a *walkingſtaff* for Hercules. *Glanville.*

WALL. *n. ſ.* [*wal*, Welſh; *vallum*, Lat. pall, Saxon; *walle*, Dutch.]

1. A ſeries of brick or ſtone carried upwards, and cemented with mortar; the ſides of a building.

Poor Tom! that eats the *wall*-newt and the water-newt. *Shakeſp. K. Lear.*

Where though I mourn my matchleſs loſs alone,
And none between my weakneſs judge and me;
Yet ev'n theſe gentle *walls* allow my moan,
Whoſe doleful echo's with my plaints agree. *Wotton.*

Part riſe in cryſtal *wall* or ridge direct. *Milton.*

2. Fortification; works built for defence. In this ſenſe it is commonly uſed plurally.

With love's light wings did I o'erperch theſe *walls*;
For ſtony limits cannot hold out love. *Shakeſpeare.*

General, the *walls* are thine:
Witneſs the world, that I create thee here
My lord and maſter. *Shakeſpeare's K. Lear.*

A prey
To that proud city, whoſe high *walls* thou ſaw'ſt
Left in confuſion. *Milton's Par. Loſt, b.* xii.

I ruſh undaunted to defend the *walls*. *Dryden.*

3. *To take the wall.* To take the upper place; not to give place.

I will *take the wall* of any man or maid of Montague's. *Shakeſpeare's Romeo and Juliet.*

When once the poet's honour ceaſes,
From reaſon far his tranſports rove:
And Boileau, for eight hundred pieces,
Makes Louis *take the wall* of Jove. *Prior.*

To WALL. *v. a.* [from the noun.]

1. To incloſe with walls.

There bought a piece of ground, which Birſa call'd,
From the bull's hide they firſt inclos'd and *wall'd*. *Dryden.*

2. To defend by walls.

The *walled* towns do work my greater woe:
The foreſt wide is fitter to reſound
The hollow echo of my careful cries. *Spenſer.*

His council adviſed him to make himſelf maſter of ſome good *walled* town. *Bacon's Hen.* VII.

The Spaniards caſt themſelves continually into roundels, their ſtrongeſt ſhips *walling* in the reſt. *Bacon's War with Spain.*

And terror of his name, that *walls* us in
From danger. *Denham's Sophy.*

WALLCREE'PER. *n. ſ.* A bird. *Ainſw.*

WA'LLET. *n. ſ.* [peallian, to travel, Saxon.]

1. A bag, in which the neceſſaries of a traveller are put; a knapſack.

Having entered into a long gallery, he laid down his *wallet*, and ſpread his carpet, in order to repoſe himſelf upon it. *Add.*

2. Any thing protuberant and ſwagging.

Who would believe, that there were mountaineers
Dew-lapt like bulls, whoſe throats had hanging at them
Wallets of fleſh. *Shakeſpeare.*

WALLE'YED. *adj.* [*wall* and *eye*.] Having white eyes.

Wall-eyed ſlave! whither wouldſt thou convey
This growing image of thy fiend-like face? *Shakeſpeare.*

WA'LLFLOWER. *n. ſ.* See STOCKGILLIFLOWER, of which it is a ſpecies.

Wallflowers are of ſeveral ſorts; as the common ones, the great ſingle ones, the great double ones, the ſingle white, the double white, the double red, and the pale yellow; all which flower about the end of March, and in May or April. *Mortimer's Huſbandry.*

WA'LLFRUIT. *n. ſ.* Fruit, which to be ripened, muſt be planted againſt a wall.

To *wallfruit* and garden-plants, there cannot be a worſe enemy than ſnails. *Mortimer's Huſbandry.*

To WA'LLOP. *v. n.* [pealan, to boil, Saxon.] To boil.

WA'LLOUSE. *n. ſ.* [*cimex*, Lat.] An inſect. *Ainſw.*

To WALLOW. *v. n.* [*walugan*, Gothick; palpian, Saxon.]

1. To move heavily and clumſily.

Part, huge of bulk!
Wallowing unwieldy, enormous in their gait,
Tempeſt the ocean. *Milton's Par. Loſt, b.* vii.

2. To roll himſelf in mire, or any thing filthy.

Gird thee with ſackcloth, and *wallow* thyſelf in aſhes. *Jer.* vi.

Dead bodies, in all places of the camp, *wallowed* in their own blood. *Knolles's Hiſt. of the Turks.*

A boar was *wallowing* in the water, when a horſe was going to drink. *L'Eſtrange.*

3. To live in any ſtate of filth or groſs vice.

God ſees a man *wallowing* in his native impurity, delivered over as an abſolute captive to ſin, polluted with its guilt, and enſlaved by its power; and in this moſt loathſome condition, fixes upon him as an object of his diſtinguiſhing mercy. *South.*

A WA'LLOW. *n. ſ.* [from the verb.] A kind of rolling walk.

One taught the toſs, and one the French new *wallow*;
His ſword-knot this, his cravat that deſign'd. *Dryden.*

WALLRU'E. *n. ſ.* An herb. *Ainſw.*

WA'LLWORT. *n. ſ.* A plant, the ſame with dwarf-elder, or danewort. See ELDER.

WA'LNUT. *n. ſ.* [palþ hnuta, Saxon. *nux juglans*.] The characters are; it hath male flowers, or katkins, which are produced at remote diſtances from the fruit on the ſame tree; the outer cover of the fruit is very thick and green, under which is a rough hard ſhell, in which the fruit is incloſed, ſurrounded with a thin ſkin: the kernel is deeply divided into four lobes; and the leaves of the tree are pinnated or winged. The ſpecies are, 1. The common walnut. 2. The large French walnut. 3. The thin-ſhell'd walnut. 4. The double walnut. 5. The late-ripe walnut. 6. The hard-ſhell'd walnut. 7. The Virginian black walnut. 8. Virginian black walnut, with a long furrowed fruit. 9. The hickery, or white Virginian walnut. 10. The ſmall hickery, or white Virginian walnut. *Miller.*

'Tis a cockle, or a *walnut*-ſhell;
A knack, a toy. *Shakeſp. Taming of the Shrew.*

Help to ſearch my houſe this one time; if I find not what I ſeek, let them ſay of me, as jealous as Ford, that ſearcheth a hollow *walnut* for his wife's leman. *Shakeſpeare.*

Some woods have the veins ſmooth as fir and *walnut*. *Bacon.*

WA'LLPEPPER. *n. ſ.* See HOUSELEEK, of which it is a ſpecies.

WA'LTRON. *n. ſ.*

The morſe, or *waltron*, is called the ſea-horſe. *Woodward.*

To WA'MBLE. *v. n.* [*wemmelen*, Dutch.] To roll with nauſea and ſickneſs. It is uſed of the ſtomach.

A covetous man deliberated betwixt the qualms of a *wambling* ſtomach, and an unſettled mind. *L'Eſtrange.*

WAN. *adj.* [pann, Saxon; *gwan*, weakly, Welſh.] Pale, as with ſickneſs; languid of look.

Sad to view his viſage pale and *wane*,
Who erſt in flowers of freſheſt youth was clad. *Fa. Queen.*

All the charms of love,
Salt Cleopatra, ſoften thy *wan* lip!
Let witchcraft join with beauty. *Shakeſp. Ant. and Cleopatra.*

Why ſo pale and *wan*, fond lover?
Pr'ythee, why ſo pale?
Will, when looking well can't move her,
Looking ill prevail? *Suckling.*

Their courſe through thickeſt conſtellations held,
Spreading their bane; the blaſted ſtars look'd *wan*. *Milton.*

How chang'd from him,
Companion of my arms! how *wan*! how dim!
How faded all thy glories! *Dryden.*

WAN. for *won*; the old pret. of *win*.

And thoſe with which th' Eubean young man *wan*
Swift Atalanta, when through craft he her outran. *Spenſer.*

He *wan* the king with secrecy and diligence; but chiefly because he was his old servant in his less fortunes. *Bacon.*

WAND. *n. s.* [*vaand*, Danish.]

1. A small stick, or twig; a long rod.

The skilful shepherd peel'd me certain *wands*. *Shakesp.*

With a whip or *wand*, if you strike the air, the sharper and quicker you strike it, the louder sound it giveth. *Bacon.*

His spear, to equal which the tallest pine
Hewn on Norwegian hills, to be the mast
Of some great admiral, were but a *wand*. *Milton.*

A child runs away laughing, with good smart blows of a *wand* on his back, who would have cried for an unkind word. *Locke on Education.*

2. Any staff of authority, or use.

Though he had both spurs and *wand*, they seemed rather marks of sovereignty, than instruments of punishment. *Sidney.*

He held before his decent steps a silver *wand*. *Milton.*

3. A charming rod.

Nay, lady, sit; if I but wave this *wand*,
Your nerves are all chain'd up in alabaster. *Milton.*

Picus bore a buckler in his hand;
His other wav'd a long divining *wand*. *Dryden.*

To WA'NDER. *v. n.* [ƿandrian, Saxon; *wandelen*, Dutch.]

1. To rove; to ramble here and there; to go, without any certain course. It has always an ill sense.

I have no will to *wander* forth of doors. *Shakespeare.*

I will go lose myself,
And *wander* up and down to view the city. *Shakespeare.*

The old duke is banish'd; four loving lords have put themselves into exile with him, whose revenues enrich the new duke; therefore he gives them good leave to *wander*. *Shakesp.*

Then came *wand'ring* by
A shadow like an angel, with bright hair
Dabbled in blood, and he shriek'd out aloud. *Shakespeare.*

They *wandered* about in sheeps and goats skins. *Heb.* xi.

Let them *wander* up and down for meat. *Ps.* lix.

From this nuptial bow'r,
How shall I part, and whither *wander* down
Into a lower world? *Milton's Par. Lost, b.* xi.

Here should my wonder dwell, and here my praise;
But my fixt thoughts my *wand'ring* eye betrays. *Denham.*

A hundred years they *wander* on the shore. *Dryden.*

Virgil introduces his Æneas in Carthage, before he brings him to Laurentum; and even after that, he *wanders* to the kingdom of Evander. *Dryden's Dufresnoy.*

2. To deviate; to go astray.

— O let me not *wander* from thy commandments. *Ps.* cxix.

They give the reins to *wand'ring* thoughts,
'Till by their own perplexities involv'd,
They ravel more. *Milton.*

To WA'NDER. *v. a.* To travel over, without a certain course.

The nether flood
Runs diverse, *wand'ring* many a famous realm. *Milton.*

Those few escap'd
Famine and anguish, will at last consume,
Wand'ring that wat'ry desart. *Milton's Par. Lost, b.* ix.

See harness'd steeds desert the stony town,
And *wander* roads unstable, not their own. *Gay.*

WA'NDERER. *n. s.* [from *wander*.] Rover; rambler.

Nor for my peace will I go far,
As *wanderers* that still do roam;
But make my strengths such as they are,
Here in my bosom, and at home. *B. Johnson.*

He here to every thirsty *wanderer*,
By sly enticement, gives his baneful cup. *Milton.*

The whole people is a race of such merchants as are *wanderers* by profession, and at the same time are in all places incapable of lands or offices. *Spectator*, N° 495.

Taste, that eternal *wanderer*, which flies,
From head to ears, and now from ears to eyes. *Pope.*

WA'NDERING. *n. s.* [from *wander*.]

1. Uncertain peregrination.

He asks the god, what new appointed home
Should end his *wand'rings*, and his toils relieve? *Addison.*

2. Aberration; mistaken way.

If any man's eagerness of glory has made him oversee the way to it, let him now recover his *wanderings*. *Decay of Piety.*

3. Incertainty; want of being fixed.

A proper remedy for this *wandering* of thoughts, would do great service to the studious. *Locke.*

To WANE. *v. n.* [ƿanian, to grow less, Saxon.]

1. To grow less; to decrease. Applied to the moon.

The husbandman, in sowing and setting, upon good reason observes the waxing and *waining* of the moon. *Hakewill.*

Waining moons their settled periods keep,
To swell the billows, and ferment the deep. *Addison.*

2. To decline; to sink.

A lady far more beautiful
Than any woman in this *waining* age. *Shakespeare.*

I will interchange
My *wained* state for Henry's regal crown. *Shakesp.*

Your father were a fool
To give thee all; and in his *waining* age
Set foot under thy table. *Shakespeare.*

In these confines slily have I lurk'd,
To watch the *waining* of mine enemies. *Shakesp. Rich.* III.

Nothing more jealous than a favourite, towards the *waining* time, and suspect of satiety. *Wotton.*

I'm *waining* in his favour, yet I love him. *Dryden.*

You saw but sorrow in its *waining* form,
A working sea remaining from a storm;
When the now weary waves roll o'er the deep,
And faintly murmur, ere they fall asleep. *Dryden.*

Land and trade ever will wax and *wane* together. *Child.*

Her *waining* form no longer shall incite
Envy in woman, or desire in man. *Rowe's Jane Shore.*

WANE. *n. s.* [from the verb.]

1. Decrease of the moon.

The sowing at the *wane* of the moon, is thought to make the corn sound. *Bacon.*

Young cattle, that are brought forth in the full of the moon, are stronger and larger than those that are brought forth in the *wane*. *Bacon.*

This is fair Diana's case;
For all astrologers maintain,
Each night a bit drops off her face,
When mortals say she's in her *wane*. *Swift.*

2. Decline; diminution; declension.

You're cast upon an age, in which the church is in its *wane*. *South.*

WA'NNED. *adj.* [from *wan*.] Turned pale and faint coloured.

Is it not monstrous that this player here,
But in a fiction, in a dream of passion,
Could force his soul so to his own conceit,
That, from her working, all his visage *wann'd*. *Shakesp.*

WA'NNESS. *n. s.* [from *wan*.] Paleness; languor.

To WANT. *v. a.* [ƿana, Saxon.]

1. To be without something fit or necessary.

Want no money, Sir John; you shall *want* none. *Shakesp.*

A man to whom God hath given riches, so that he *wanteth* nothing for his soul of all that he desireth, yet God giveth him not power to eat thereof. *Eccl.* vi. 2.

2. To be defective in something.

Smells do most of them *want* names. *Locke.*

Nor can this be,
But by fulfilling that which thou didst *want*,
Obedience to the law. *Milton.*

3. To fall short of; not to contain.

Nor think, though men were none,
That heav'n wou'd want spectators, God *want* praise. *Milt.*

4. To be without; not to have.

By descending from the thrones above,
Those happy places, thou hast deign'd a-while
To *want*, and honour these. *Milton's Par. Lost.*

How loth I am to have recourse to rites
So full of horror, that I once rejoice
I *want* the use of sight. *Dryden and Lee's Oedipus.*

The unhappy never *want* enemies. *Clarissa.*

5. To need; to have need of; to lack.

It hath caused a great irregularity in our calendar, and *wants* to be reformed, and the equinox to be rightly computed. *Holder.*

God, who sees all things intuitively, does not *want* helps; he neither stands in need of logick, nor uses it. *Baker.*

6. To wish for; to long for.

Down I come, like glist'ring Phaeton,
Wanting the manage of unruly jades. *Shakespeare.*

The sylvans to their shades retire,
Those very shades and streams new shades and streams require,
And *want* a cooling breeze of wind to fan the raging fire. *Dry.*

What *wants* my son? for know
My son thou art, and I must call thee so. *Addison's Ovid.*

Men who *want* to get a woman into their power, seldom scruple the means. *Clarissa.*

To WANT. *v. n.*

1. To be wanted; to be improperly absent; not to be in sufficient quantity.

Nor did there *want* cornice or freeze. *Milton.*

Finds wealth where 'tis, bestows it where it *wants*;
Cities in desarts, woods in cities plants. *Denham.*

We have the means in our hands, and nothing but the application of them is *wanting*. *Addison.*

As in bodies, thus in souls, we find
What *wants* in blood and spirits, swell'd with wind. *Pope.*

The design, the disposition, the manners, and the thoughts, are all before it; where any of those are *wanting*, or imperfect, so much *wants* in the imitation of human life. *Dryden.*

2. To fail; to be deficient.

Nor shall I to the work thou enterprisest
Be *wanting*, but afford thee equal aid. *Milton.*

Though England is not *wanting* in a learned nobility, yet unhappy circumſtances have confined me to a narrow choice. *Dryden's Dedication to Lord Clifford.*

Whatever fortune, good or bad betide,
No time ſhall find me *wanting* to my truth. *Dryden.*

Religion will never be without enemies, nor thoſe enemies be *wanting* in endeavours to expoſe it to the contempt of mankind. *Rogers's Sermons.*

Several are againſt his ſevere uſage of you, and would be glad of an occaſion to convince the reſt of their error, if you will not be *wanting* to yourſelf. *Swift.*

3. To be miſſed; to be not had.

Twelve, *wanting* one, he ſlew,
My brethren: I alone ſurviv'd. *Dryden.*

Granivorous animals have a long colon and cæcum, which in carnivorous are *wanting*. *Arbuthnot on Aliments.*

WANT. *n. ſ.*

1. Need.

It infers the good
By thee communicated, and our *want*. *Milton.*

Parents ſhould diſtinguiſh between the *wants* of fancy, and thoſe of nature. *Locke.*

2. Deficiency.

This proceeded not from any *want* of knowledge, but of judgment. *Dryden.*

One objection to Civita Vecchia, is, that the air is not wholeſome: this proceeds from *want* of inhabitants. *Addiſon.*

The blood flows through the veſſels, by the exceſs of the force of the heart above the incumbent preſſure, which in fat people is exceſſive; and as *want* of a due quantity of motion of the fluids increaſeth fat, the diſeaſe is the cauſe of itſelf. *Arbuthnot on Aliments.*

3. The ſtate of not having.

You ſhall have no reaſon to complain of me, for *want* of a generous diſdain of this world. *Pope.*

4. Poverty; penury; indigence.

Nothing is ſo hard for thoſe who abound in riches, as to conceive how others can be in *want*. *Swift.*

5. [ƿand, Saxon.] A mole.

WA'NTON. *n. ſ.* [This word is derived by *Minſhew* from *want one*, a man or woman that wants a companion. This etymology, however odd, *Junius* ſilently adopts. *Skinner*, who had more acuteneſs, cannot forbear to doubt it, but offers nothing better.]

1. Laſcivious; libidinous; letcherous; luſtful.

Thou art froward by nature, enemy to peace,
Laſcivious, *wanton*; more than well beſeems
A man of thy profeſſion. *Shakeſp. Hen.* VI.

Entic'd to do him *wanton* rites. *Milton.*

2. Licentious; diſſolute.

My plenteous joys,
Wanton in fulneſs, ſeek to hide themſelves
In drops of ſorrow. *Shakeſp. Macbeth.*

Men grown *wanton* by proſperity,
Study'd new arts of luxury and eaſe. *Roſcommon.*

3. Frolickſome; gay; ſportive; airy.

As flies to *wanton* boys, we are to th' gods:
They kill us for their ſport. *Shakeſp. K. Lear.*

Note a wild and *wanton* herd,
Or race of youthful and unhandled colts,
Fetching mad bounds. *Shakeſp. Merch. of Venice.*

Time drives the flocks from field to fold;
The flow'rs do fade, and *wanton* fields
To wayward winter reckoning yields. *Raleigh.*

How eagerly ye follow my diſgrace,
As if it fed ye; and how ſleek and *wanton*
Y' appear, in every thing may bring my ruin. *Shakeſpeare.*

4. Looſe; unreſtrained.

How does your tongue grow *wanton* in her praiſe! *Addiſ.*

5. Quick, and irregular of motion.

6. Luxuriant; ſuperfluous.

What we by day lop overgrown,
One night or two, with *wanton* growth derides,
Tending to wild. *Milton.*

Women richly gay in gems and *wanton* dreſs. *Milton.*

7. Not regular; turned fortuitouſly.

The quaint mazes in the *wanton* green,
For want of tread are undiſtinguiſhable. *Milton.*

WA'NTON. *n. ſ.*

1. A laſcivious perſon; a ſtrumpet; a whoremonger.

An old *wanton* will be doating upon women, when he can ſcarce ſee without ſpectacles. *South's Sermons.*

To lip a *wanton* in a ſecure couch,
And to ſuppoſe her chaſte. *Shakeſp. Othello.*

2. A trifler; an inſignificant flutterer.

Shall a beardleſs boy,
A cocker'd, ſilken *wanton* brave your fields,
Mocking the air with colours idly ſpread,
And find no check? *Shakeſpeare's K. John.*

Paſs with your beſt violence;
I am afraid you make a *wanton* of me. *Shakepeare's Hamlet.*

3. A word of ſlight endearment.

Peace, my *wantons*; he will do,
More than you can aim unto. *B. Johnſon.*

To WA'NTON. *v. n.* [from the noun.]

1. To play laſciviouſly.

He from his guards and midnight tent,
Diſguis'd o'er hills and vallies went,
To *wanton* with the ſprightly dame,
And in his pleaſure loſt his fame. *Prior.*

2. To revel; to play.

Oh! I heard him *wanton* in his praiſe;
Speak things of him might charm the ears. *Otway.*

Nature here
Wanton'd as in her prime, and play'd at will
Her virgin fancies. *Milton.*

O ye muſes! deign your bleſt retreat,
Where Horace *wantons* at your ſpring,
And Pindar ſweeps a bolder ſtring. *Fenton.*

3. To move nimbly, and irregularly.

WA'NTONLY. *adv.* [from *wanton.*] Laſciviouſly; frolickſomely; gayly; ſportively; careleſly.

Thou doſt but try how far I can forbear,
Nor art that monſter which thou wouldſt appear:
But do not *wantonly* my paſſion move,
I pardon nothing that relates to love. *Dryden.*

WA'NTONNESS. *n. ſ.* [from *wanton.*]

1. Laſciviouſneſs; letchery.

The ſpirit of *wantonneſs* is ſcar'd out of him. *Shakeſp.*

Bulls and goats bled apace; but neither the violence of the one, nor the *wantonneſs* of the other, ever died a victim at any of their altars. *South.*

2. Sportiveneſs; frolick; humour.

When I was in France,
Young would be as ſad as night,
Only for *wantonneſs*. *Shakeſp. K. John.*

Love, rais'd on beauty, will like that decay;
Our hearts may bear its ſlender chain a day:
As flow'ry bands in *wantonneſs* are worn,
A morning's pleaſure, and at evening torn. *Pope.*

3. Licentiouſneſs; negligence of reſtraint.

The tumults threatened to abuſe all acts of grace, and turn them into *wantonneſs*. *K. Charles.*

'Till *wantonneſs* and pride
Raiſe out of friendſhip hoſtile deeds in peace. *Milton.*

WA'NTWIT. *n. ſ.* [*want* and *wit.*] A fool; an idiot.

Such a *wantwit* ſadneſs makes of me,
That I have much ado to know myſelf. *Shakeſpeare.*

WA'NTY. *n. ſ.* [I know not whence derived.] A broad girth of leather, by which the load is bound upon the horſe.

A panel and *wanty*, pack-ſaddle and ped,
With line to fetch litter. *Tuſſer.*

WA'PED. *adj.* [Of this word I know not the original, except that to *whape*, to ſhock, or deject, is found in Spenſer; from which the meaning may be gathered.] Dejected; cruſhed by miſery.

This makes the *waped* widow wed again. *Shakeſpeare.*

WA'PENTAKE. *n. ſ.* [from wœpun, Saxon, and *take*, *wapentakium*, *wapentagium*, low Latin.]

Wapentake is all one with what we call a hundred: as upon a meeting for that purpoſe, they touched each other's weapons, in token of their fidelity and allegiance. *Cowel.*

Hundred ſignifieth a hundred pledges, which were under the command and aſſurance of their alderman; which, as I ſuppoſe, was alſo called a *wapentake*, ſo named, of touching the weapon or ſpear of their alderman, and ſwearing to follow him faithfully, and ſerve their prince truly. But others think, that a *wapentake* was ten hundreds, or boroughs. *Spenſer.*

WAR. *n. ſ.* [*werre*, old Dutch; *guerre*, Fr.]

War may be defined the exerciſe of violence under ſovereign command againſt withſtanders; force, authority, and reſiſtance being the eſſential parts thereof. Violence, limited by authority, is ſufficiently diſtinguiſhed from robbery, and the like outrages; yet conſiſting in relation towards others, it neceſſarily requires a ſuppoſition of reſiſtance, whereby the force of *war* becomes different from the violence inflicted upon ſlaves or yielding malefactors. *Raleigh.*

On, you nobleſt Engliſh,
Whoſe blood is fetcht from fathers of *war* proof. *Shakeſp.*

After a denunciation or indiction of *war*, the *war* is no more confined to the place of the quarrel, but left at large. *Bacon.*

I ſaw the figure and armour of him, that headed the peaſants in the *war* upon Bern, with the ſeveral weapons found on his followers. *Addiſon.*

2. The inſtruments of war, in poetical language.

The god of love inhabits there,
With all his rage, and dread, and grief, and care;
His complement of ſtores, and total *war*. *Prior.*

3. Forces; army. Poetically.

On th' embattled ranks the waves return,
And overwhelm the *war*. *Milton's Par. Loſt, b.* xii.

4. The profeſſion of arms.

Thine

Thine almighty word leapt down from heaven, as a fierce man of *war* into the midst of a land of destruction. *Wisdom.*

5. Hostility; state of opposition; act of opposition.

Duncan's horses
Turn'd wild in nature, broke their stalls, flung out,
Contending 'gainst obedience, as they would
Make *war* with man. *Shakespeare's Macbeth.*

To WAR. *v. n.* [from the noun] To make war; to be in a state of hostility.

Was this a face,
To be expos'd against the *warring* winds? *Shakesp.*
Why should I *war* without the walls of Troy,
That find such cruel battle here within? *Shakespeare.*
Make peace with God, for you must die, my lord.—
—Have you that holy feeling in your soul,
To counsel me to make my peace with God,
And are you yet to your own soul's so blind,
That you will *war* with God, by murd'ring me? *Shakesp.*

He teacheth my hands to *war*. *2 Sam.* xxii.

This charge I commit unto thee, son Timothy, that thou by them mightest *war* a good warfare. *1 Tim.* i. 18.

He limited his forces, to proceed in aid of the Britons, but in no wise to *war* upon the French. *Bacon's Hen.* VII.

We seem ambitious God's whole work t' undo;
With new diseases on ourselves we *war*,
And with new physick, a worse engine far. *Donne.*

His next design
Was all the Theban race in arms to join,
And *war* on Theseus. *Dryden.*

To the island of Delos, by being reckoned a sacred place, nations *warring* with one another resorted with their goods, and traded as in a neutral country. *Arbuthnot on Coins.*

To WAR. *v. a.* To make war upon. A word not any longer used.

And them long time before great Nimrod was,
That first the world with sword and fire *warred*. *Spenser.*
To them the same was render'd, to the end,
To *war* the Scot, and borders to defend. *Daniel's Civ. War.*

To WA'RBLE. *v. a.* [*werben*, old Teutonick; *wervelen*, German; to twirl, or turn round.]

1. To quaver any sound.

2. To cause to quaver.

Follow me as I sing,
And touch the *warbled* string. *Milton.*

3. To utter musically.

She can thaw the numbing spell,
If she be right invok'd with *warbled* song. *Milton.*

To WA'RBLE. *v. n.*

1. To be quavered.

Such strains ne'er *warble* in the linnet's throat. *Gay.*

2. To be uttered melodiously.

A plaining song, plain-singing voice requires,
For *warbling* notes from inward cheering flow. *Sidney.*
There birds resort, and in their kind, thy praise
Among the branches chant in *warbling* lays. *Wotton.*

3. To sing.

Creatures that liv'd and mov'd, and walk'd, or flew;
Birds on the branches *warbling*; all things smil'd. *Milton.*
She *warbled* in her throat,
And tun'd her voice to many a merry note,
But indistinct. *Dryden.*
A bard amid the joyous circle sings
High airs attemper'd to the vocal strings;
Whilst *warbling* to the varied strain advance,
Two sprightly youths to form the bounding dance. *Pope.*

WA'RBLER. *n. s.* [from *warble.*] A singer; a songster.

Hark! on ev'ry bough,
In lulling strains the feather'd *warblers* woo. *Tickell.*

WARD. A syllable much used as an affix in composition, as *heavenward*, with tendency to heaven; *hitherward*, this way; from peapδ, Saxon

Before she could come to the arbour, she saw walking from her-*ward*, a man in shepherdish apparel. *Sidney.*

To WARD. *v. a.* [peaplian, Saxon; *waren*, Dutch; *garder*, French.]

1. To guard; to watch.

He marched forth towards the castle wall,
Whose gates he found fast shut, ne living wight
To *ward* the same, nor answer comer's call. *Fairy Queen.*

2. To defend; to protect.

Tell him it was a hand that *warded* him
From thousand dangers, bid him bury it. *Shakespeare.*

3. To fence off; to obstruct, or turn aside any thing mischievous.

Not once the baron lift his armed hand
To strike the maid, but gazing on her eyes,
Where lordly Cupid seem'd in arms to stand,
No way to *ward* or shun her blows he tries. *Fairfax.*
Up and down he traverses his ground;
Now *wards* a felling blow, now strikes again. *Daniel.*
Toxeus amaz'd, and with amazement slow,
Or to revenge, or *ward* the coming blow,
Stood doubting; and while doubting thus he stood,
Receiv'd the steel bath'd in his brother's blood. *Dryden.*
The pointed javelin *warded* off his rage. *Addison.*

The provision of bread for food; cloathing to *ward* off the inclemency of the air, were to be first look'd after. *Woodw.*

It instructs the scholar in the various methods of *warding* off the force of objections, and of discovering and repelling the subtle tricks of sophisters. *Watts's Improv. of the Mind.*

To WARD. *v. n.*

1. To be vigilant; to keep guard.

2. To act upon the defensive with a weapon.

So redoubling her blows, drove the stranger to no other shift than to *ward* and go back. *Sidney, b.* ii.

Short crooked swords in closer fight they wear,
And on their *warding* arms light bucklers bear. *Dryden.*

WARD. *n. s.* [from the verb.]

1. Watch; act of guarding.

Still when she slept, he kept both watch and *ward*. *Spenser.*
Sublime on these a tow'r of steel is rear'd;
And dire Tisiphone there keeps the *ward*.
Girt in her sanguine gown, by night and day,
Observant of the souls that pass the downward way. *Dryden*

2. Garrison; those who are intrusted to keep a place.

By reason of these two forts, though there be but small *wards* left in them, there are two good towns now grown, which are the greatest stay of both those two countries. *Spenser*

Th' assieged castles *ward*
Their stedfast stonds did mightily maintain. *Spenser*

3. Guard made by a weapon in fencing.

Thou know'st my old *ward*; here I lay, and thus I bore my point. *Shakesp. Hen.* IV

Come from thy *ward*,
For I can here disarm thee with this stick. *Shakesp. Tempest*
Now, by proof it shall appear,
Whether thy horns are sharper, or my spear.
At this, I threw: for want of other *ward*,
He lifted up his hand, his front to guard. *Dryden*

4. Fortress; strong hold.

She dwells securely on the excellency of her honour. Now could I come to her with any detection in my hand, I could drive her from the *ward* of her purity, her reputation, and thousand other her defences, which now are too too strongly embattled against me. *Shakesp. Merry Wives of Windsor*

5. [*Warda*, law Lat.] District of a town.

Throughout the trembling city plac'd a guard,
Dealing an equal share to every *ward*. *Dryden*

6. Custody; confinement.

That wretched creature being deprehended in that impiety was held in *ward*. *Hooker*

Stopt there was his too veh'ment speech with speed,
And he sent close to *ward* from where he stood. *Daniel*

7. The part of a lock, which, corresponding to the proper key, hinders any other from opening it.

In the key-hole turns
Th' intricate *wards*, and ev'ry bolt and bar. *Milton*

As there are locks for several purposes, so are there several inventions in the making and contriving their *wards*, or guards. *Moxon's Mech. Exer*

The keys, as well as the locks, were fitted *ward* to *ward* by the same wisdom. *Grew's Cosmology.*

8. One in the hands of a guardian.

The king causeth bring up his *wards*, but bestoweth no more of their rents upon them than is useful. *Drummond*

You know our father's *ward*,
The fair Monimia: is your heart at peace?
Is it so guarded that you could not love her? *Otway.*
Thy Violante's heart was ever thine,
Compell'd to wed, before she was my *ward*. *Dryden*
When stern as tutors, and as uncles hard,
We lash the pupil, and defraud the *ward*. *Dryden*

Titles of honour and privileges, the rich and the great can never deserve, unless they employ them for the protection of these, the true *wards* and children of God. *Sprat*

9. The state of a child under a guardian.

I must attend his majesty's command, to whom I am now in *ward*, evermore in subjection. *Shakespeare*

Lewis the eleventh of France having much abated the greatness and power of the peers, would say, that he had brought the crown out of *ward*. *Bacon*

10. Guardianship; right over orphans.

It is also inconvenient in Ireland, that the *wards* and marriages of gentlemen's children should be in the disposal of any of those lords. *Spenser*

WA'RDEN. *n. s.* [*waerden*, Dutch.]

1. A keeper; a guardian.

2. A head officer.

The *warden* of apothecaries hall. *Garth*

A magi

3. Warden of the cinque ports.

A magistrate that has the jurisdiction of those havens in the east part of England, commonly called the cinque ports, or five havens, who has there all that jurisdiction which the admiral of England has in places not exempt. The reason why one magistrate should be assigned to these havens seems to be, because in respect of their situation, they formerly required a more vigilant care than other havens, being in greater danger of invasion by our enemies. *Cowel.*

4. [*Pyrum volemum*, Lat. I know not whence denominated.] A large pear.

Nor must all shoots of pears alike be set,
Crustumian, Syrian pears, and *wardens* great. *May's Virg.*
Ox-cheek when hot, and *wardens* bak'd some cry. *King.*

WA'RDER. *n. s.* [from *ward.*]

1. A keeper; a guard.

Upon those gates with force he fiercely flew,
And rending them in pieces, felly slew
Those *warders* strange, and all that else he met. *Hubberd.*
Where be these *warders*, that they wait not here?
Open the gates. *Shakespeare's Henry VI.*
Though bladed corn be lodg'd and trees blown down,
Though castles topple on their *warders* heads. *Shakespeare.*
The *warders* of the gate but scarce maintain
Th' unequal combat, and resist in vain. *Dryden.*

2. A truncheon by which an officer of arms forbade fight.

Sound trumpets, and set forward combatants.
—But stay, the king hath thrown his *warder* down. *Shakespeare.*
Then, then, when there was nothing could have staid
My father from the breast of Bolingbroke,
O, when the king did throw his *warder* down,
His own life hung upon the staff he threw. *Shakespeare.*

WA'RDMOTE. *n. s.* [peaɲo and mot, or gemot, Saxon; *wardemotus*, low Lat.] A meeting; a court held in each ward or district in London for the direction of their affairs.

WA'RDROBE. *n. s.* [*garderobe*, French; *garderoba*, low Lat.] A room where cloaths are kept.

The third had of their *wardrobe* custody,
In which were not rich tires nor garments gay,
The plumes of pride, and wings of vanity,
But cloaths meet to keep keen cold away. *Fairy Queen.*
I will kill all his coats,
I'll murder all his *wardrobe* piece by piece
Until I meet the king. *Shakespeare's Henry IV.*
Behold!
What from his *wardrobe* her belov'd allows,
To deck the wedding-day of his unspotted spouse. *Dryden.*

It would not be an impertinent design to make a kind of an old Roman *wardrobe*, where you should see toga's and tunica's, the chlamys and trabea, and all the different vests and ornaments so often mentioned in the Greek and Roman authors. *Addison.*

WA'RDSHIP *n. s.* [from *ward.*]

1. Guardianship.

By reason of the tenures in chief revived, the sums for respect of homage be encreased, and the profits of *wardships* cannot but be much advanced. *Bacon.*

2. Pupillage; state of being under ward.

The houses sued out their livery, and redeemed themselves from the *wardship* of tumults. *King Charles.*

WARE. The preterite of *wear*, more frequently *wore.*

A certain man *ware* no cloaths. *Luke* viii. 27.

WARE. *adj* [For this we commonly say *aware.*]

1. Being in expectation of; being provided against.

The lord of that servant shall come in a day when he looketh not for him, and in an hour that he is not *ware* of him. *Matth.* xxiv. 50.

2. Cautious; wary.

What man so wise, what earthly wit so *ware*,
As to descry the crafty cunning train
By which deceit doth mask in Vizor fair. *Fairy Queen.*
Bid her well be *ware* and still erect. *Milton.*

To WARE. *v. n.* To take heed of; to beware.

A shuffled, sullen, and uncertain light
That dances through the clouds, and shuts again,
Then *ware* a rising tempest on the main. *Dryden.*

WARE. *n. s.* [paɲn, Saxon; *waere*, Dutch; *wara*, Swedish.] Commonly something to be sold.

Let us, like merchants, shew our foulest *wares*,
And think, perchance, they'll sell. *Shakespeare.*

If the people bring *ware* or any victuals to sell, that we would not buy it. *Nehem.* x. 31.

I know thou whole art but a shop
Of toys and trifles, traps and snares,
To take the weak, and make them stop;
Yet art thou falser than thy *wares*. *Ben. Johnson.*
Why should my black thy love impair?
Let the dark shop commend the *ware*. *Cleaveland.*

He turns himself to other *wares* which he finds your markets take off. *Locke.*

WA'REFUL. *adj.* [*ware* and *full.*] Cautious; timorously prudent.

WA'REFULNESS. *n. s.* [from *wareful.*] Cautiousness. Obsolete.

With pretence from Strephon her to guard,
He met her full; but full of *warefulness*. *Sidney.*

WA'REHOUSE. *n. s.* [*ware* and *house.*] A storehouse of merchandise.

His understanding is only the *warehouse* of other mens lumber, I mean false and unconcluding reasonings rather than a repository of truth for his own use. *Locke.*

She had never more ships at sea, greater quantities of merchandise in her *warehouses* than at present. *Addison.*

She the big *warehouse* built,
Rais'd the strong crane. *Thomson's Autumn.*

WA'RELESS. *adj.* [from *ware.*] Uncautious; unwary. *Spens.*

WA'RELY. *adv.* [from *ware.*] Warily; cautiously; timorously.

They bound him hand and foot with iron chains,
And with continual watch did *warely* keep. *Fairy Queen.*

WA'RFARE. *n. s.* [*war* and *fare.*] Military service; military life.

In the wilderness
He shall first lay down the rudiments
Of his great *warfare*, ere I send him forth
To conquer sin and death. *Milton's Paradise Regained.*
Faithful hath been your *warfare*, and of God
Accepted, fearless in his righteous cause. *Milton.*

Tully, when he read the Tactics, was thinking on the bar which was his field of battle: the knowledge of *warfare* is thrown away on a general who does not make use of what he knows. *Dryden.*

The state of Christians, even when they are not actually persecuted, is a perpetual state of *warfare* and voluntary sufferings. *Atterbury's Sermons.*

The scripture has directed us to refer these miscarriages in our Christian *warfare* to the power of three enemies. *Rogers.*

To WA'REFARE. *v. n.* [from the noun.] To lead a military life.

That was the only amulet in that credulous *warfaring* age to escape dangers in battles. *Camden's Remains.*

WA'RHABLE. *adj.* [*war* and *hable*, from *habilis*, Lat. or *able.*] Military; fit for war.

The weary Britons, whose *warhable* youth
Was by Maximilian lately led away,
With wretched miseries and woeful ruth,
Were to those pagans made an open prey. *Fairy Queen.*

WA'RILY. *adv.* [from *wary.*] Cautiously; with timorous prudence; with wise forethought.

The charge thereof unto a courteous sp'rit
Commended was, who thereby did attend,
And *warily* awaited day and night,
From other covetous fiends it to defend. *Fairy Queen.*

The change of laws, especially concerning matters of religion, must be *warily* proceeded in. *Hooker.*

It will concern a man to treat conscience awfully and *warily*, by still observing what it commands, but especially what it forbids. *South's Sermons.*

They searched diligently and concluded *warily*. *Sprat.*

WA'RINESS. *n. s.* [from *wary.*] Caution; prudent forethought; timorous scrupulousness.

For your own conscience he gives innocence,
But for your fame a discreet *wariness*. *Donne.*

To determine what are little things in religion, great *wariness* is to be used. *Sprat's Sermons.*

The path was so very slippery, the shade so exceeding gloomy, and the whole wood so full of echoes, that they were forced to march with the greatest *wariness*, circumspection and silence. *Addison's Freeholder.*

Most men have so much of ill nature, or of *wariness*, as not to sooth the vanity of the ambitious man. *Addison.*

I look upon it to be a most clear truth; and expressed it with more *wariness* and reserve than was necessary. *Atterbury.*

WARK. *n. s.* [Anciently used for *work*; whence *bulwark.*] Building.

Thou findest fault where any's to be found,
And buildest strong *wark* upon a weak ground. *Spenser.*

WA'RLIKE. *n. s.* [*war* and *like.*]

1. Fit for war; disposed to war.

She using so strange, and yet so well succeeding a temper, made her people by peace *warlike*. *Sidney.*

Old Siward with ten thousand *warlike* men,
All ready at appoint, was setting forth. *Shakespeare's Macbeth.*

When a *warlike* state grows soft and effeminate, they may be sure of a war. *Bacon.*

O imprudent Gauls,
Relying on false hopes, thus to incense
The *warlike* English. *Philips.*

2. Military; relating to war.

The great arch-angel from his *warlike* toil
Surceas'd. *Milton's Paradise Lost.*

WAR'LING. *n. s.* [from *war.*] This word is I believe only found in the following adage, and seems to mean, one often quarrelled with.

Better be an old man's darling than a young man's *warling*. *Camden's Remains.*

WA'RLOCK. } *n. ſ.* [*vardlookr*, Iſlandick, a charm; peꞃlog,
WA'RLUCK. } Saxon, an evil ſpirit. This etymology was communicated by Mr. *Wiſe.*] A male witch; a wizzard.

Warluck in Scotland is applied to a man whom the vulgar ſuppoſe to be converſant with ſpirits, as a woman who carries on the ſame commerce is called a witch: he is ſuppoſed to have the invulnerable quality which *Dryden* mentions, who did not underſtand the word.

He was no *warluck*, as the Scots commonly call ſuch men, who they ſay are iron free or lead free. *Dryden.*

WARM. *adj.* [*warm*, Gothick; peaꞃm, Sax. *warm*, Dutch.]

1. Not cold, though not hot; heated to a ſmall degree.

He ſtretched himſelf upon the child, and the fleſh of the child waxed *warm.* *2 Kings* iv. 34.

Main ocean flow'd, not idle, but with *warm*
Prolifick humour, ſoft'ning all her globe. *Milton.*

2. Zealous; ardent.

I never thought myſelf ſo *warm* in any party's cauſe as to deſerve their money. *Pope.*

Scaliger in his poetics is very *warm* againſt it. *Broome's Notes on the Odyſſey.*

3. Violent; furious; vehement.

Welcome day-light; we ſhall have *warm* work on't:
The Moor will 'gage
His utmoſt forces on his next aſſault,
To win a queen and kingdom. *Dryden's Spaniſh Friar.*

4. Buſy in action.

I hate the ling'ring ſummons to attend,
Death all at once would be a nobler end;
Fate is unkind: methinks a general
Should *warm*, and at the head of armies fall. *Dryden.*

5. Fanciful; enthuſiaſtick.

If there be a ſober and a wiſe man, what difference will there be between his knowledge and that of the moſt extravagant fancy in the world? If there be any difference between them, the advantage will be on the *warm*-headed man's ſide, as having the more ideas, and the more lively. *Locke.*

To WARM. *v. a.* [from the adjective.]

1. To free from cold; to heat in a gentle degree.

It ſhall be for a man to burn, for he ſhall take thereof and *warm* himſelf. *Iſa.* xliv. 15.

There ſhall not be a coal to *warm* at, nor fire to ſit before it. *Iſa.* xlvii. 14.

The mounted ſun
Shot down direct his fervid rays to *warm*
Earth's inmoſt womb. *Milton.*

Theſe ſoft fires with kindly heat
Of various influence, foment and *warm.* *Milton.*

2. To heat mentally; to make vehement.

The action of Homer being more full of vigour than that of Virgil, is more pleaſing to the reader: one *warms* you by degrees, the other ſets you on fire all at once, and never intermits his heat. *Dryden.*

WA'RMINGPAN. *n. ſ.* [*warm* and *pan.*] A covered braſs pan for warming a bed by means of hot coals.

WA'RMINGSTONE. *n. ſ.* [*warm* and *ſtone.*] To theſe uſeful ſtones add the *warming*-ſtone, digged in Cornwall, which being once well heated at the fire retains its warmth a great while, and hath been found to give eaſe in the internal hæmorrhoids. *Ray on the Creation.*

WA'RMLY. *adv.* [from *warm.*]

1. With gentle heat.

There the warming ſun firſt *warmly* ſmote
The open field. *Milton.*

2. Eagerly; ardently.

Now I have two right honeſt wives
One to Atrides I will ſend,
And t'other to my Trojan friend;
Each prince ſhall thus with honour have
What both ſo *warmly* ſeem to crave. *Prior.*

The ancients expect you ſhould do them right in the account you intend to write of their characters: I hope you think more *warmly* than ever of that deſign. *Pope.*

WA'RMNESS. } *n. ſ.* [from *warm.*]
WARMTH. }

1. Gentle heat.

Then am I the priſoner, and his bed my goal; from the loathed *warmth* whereof deliver me. *Shakeſpeare's King Lear.*

Cold plants have a quicker perception of the heat of the ſun encreaſing than the hot herbs have; as a cold hand will ſooner find a little *warmth* than an hot. *Bacon's Natural Hiſtory.*

He vital virtue infuſ'd, and vital *warmth*
Throughout the fluid maſs. *Milton.*

Here kindly *warmth* their mounting juice ferments
To nobler taſtes, and more exalted ſcents. *Addiſon.*

2. Zeal; paſſion; fervour of mind.

What *warmth* is there in your affection towards any of theſe princely ſuitors that are already come? *Shakeſpeare.*

Our duties towards God and man, we ſhould perform with that unfeigned integrity which belongs to Chriſtian piety; with that temper and ſobriety which becomes Chriſtian prudence and charity; with that *warmth* and affection which agrees with Chriſtian zeal. *Sprat's Sermons.*

Your opinion that it is entirely to be neglected, would have been my own, had it been my own caſe; but I felt more *warmth* here than I did when firſt I ſaw his book againſt myſelf. *Pope.*

3. Fancifulneſs; enthuſiaſm.

The ſame *warmth* of head diſpoſes men to both. *Temple.*

To WARN. *v. a.* [pæꞃnian, Saxon; *waernen*, Dutch; *warna*, Swediſh; *varna*, Iſlandick.]

1. To caution againſt any fault or danger; to give previous notice of ill.

What do'ſt thou ſcorn me for my gentle counſel?
And ſooth the devil that I *warn* thee from? *Shakeſpeare.*

Our firſt parents had been *warn'd*
The coming of their ſecret foe, and 'ſcap'd
His mortal ſnare. *Milton's Paradiſe Loſt.*

The hand can hardly lift up itſelf high enough to ſtrike, but it muſt be ſeen; ſo that it *warns* while it threatens; but a falſe inſidious tongue may whiſper a lie ſo cloſe and low, that though you have ears to hear yet you ſhall not hear. *South.*

Juturna *warns* the Daunian chief,
Of Lauſus' danger, urging ſwift relief. *Dryden.*

If we conſider the miſtakes in mens diſputes and notions, how great a part is owing to words, and their uncertain or miſtaken ſignifications; this we are the more carefully to be *warned* of, becauſe the arts of improving it have been made the buſineſs of mens ſtudy. *Locke.*

The father, whilſt he *warn'd* his erring ſon,
The ſad examples which he ought to ſhun
Deſcrib'd. *Prior.*

When firſt young Maro ſung of kings and wars,
Ere *warning* Phœbus touch'd his trembling ears,
Perhaps he ſeem'd above the critick's law,
And but from nature's fountains ſcorn'd to draw. *Pope.*

2. To admoniſh of any duty to be performed, or practice or place to be avoided or forſaken.

Cornelius was *warned* from God by an holy angel to ſend for thee. *Acts* x. 22.

He had chidden the rebellious winds for obeying the command of their uſurping maſter: he had *warned* them from the ſeas; he had beaten down the billows. *Dryden.*

3. To notify previouſly good or bad.

He wonders to what end you have aſſembled
Such troops of citizens to come to him,
His grace not being *warn'd* thereof before. *Shakeſpeare.*

He charg'd the ſoldiers with preventing care,
Their flags to follow, and their arms prepare,
Warn'd of the enſuing fight, and bade 'em hope the war. *Dryden's Æneid.*

Man, who knows not hearts, ſhould make examples,
Which like a *warning*-piece muſt be ſhot off,
To fright the reſt from crimes. *Dryden's Spaniſh Friar.*

WA'RNING. *n. ſ.* [from *warn.*]

1. Caution againſt faults or dangers; previous notice of ill.

I will thank the Lord for giving me *warning* in the night. *Pſ.*

He groaning from the bottom of his breaſt,
This *warning* in theſe mournful words expreſt. *Dryden.*

Here wretched Phlegias warns the world with cries,
Could *warning* make the world more juſt or wiſe. *Dryden.*

You have fairer *warning* than others who are unexpectedly cut off, and ſo have a better opportunity, as well as greater engagements to provide for your latter end. *Wake.*

A true and plain relation of my misfortunes may be of uſe and *warning* to credulous maids, never to put too much truſt in deceitful men. *Swift's Story of the Injured Lady.*

2. Previous notice: in a ſenſe indifferent.

Death called up an old man, and bade him come; the man excuſed himſelf, that it was a great journey to take upon ſo ſhort a *warning.* *L'Eſtrange.*

I ſaw with ſome diſdain, more nonſenſe than either I or as bad a poet could have crammed into it at a month's *warning*; in which time it was wholly written. *Dryden.*

WARP. *n. ſ.* [peaꞃp, Saxon; *werp*, Dutch.] That order of thread in a thing woven that croſſes the woof.

The fourteenth is the placing of the tangible parts in length or tranſverſe, as it is in the *warp* and the woof of texture, more inward or more outward. *Bacon's Natural Hiſtory.*

To WARP. *v. n.* [peoꞃpan, Saxon; *werpen*, Dutch, to throw; whence we ſometimes ſay, *the work caſts.*] To change from the true ſituation by inteſtine motion; to change the poſition of one part to another.

This fellow will but join you together as they join wainſcot, then one of you will prove a ſhrunk-pannel, and like green timber *warp.* *Shakeſpeare's As you like it.*

They clamp one piece of wood to the end of another piece, to keep it from caſting or *warping.* *Moxon's Mech. Exerciſe.*

2. To lose its proper course or direction.

There's our commission
From which we would not have you *warp*. *Shakesp.*
This is strange! methinks
My favour here begins to *warp*. *Shakespeare.*

All attest this doctrine, that the pope can give away the right of any sovereign, if he shall never so little *warp*. *Dryden.*

This we should do as directly as may be, with as little *warping* and declension towards the creature as is possible. *Norris.*

3. To turn.

The potent rod
Of Amram's son in Egypt's evil day
Wav'd round the coast, up call'd a pitchy cloud
Of locusts, *warping* on the eastern wind,
That o'er the realm of impious Pharaoh hung
Like night. *Milton's Paradise Lost.*

To WARP. *v. a.*

1. To contract; to shrivel.
2. To turn aside from the true direction.

This first avow'd, nor folly *warp'd* my mind;
Nor the frail texture of the female kind
Betray'd my virtue. *Dryden.*
Not foreign or domestick treachery
Could *warp* thy soul to their unjust decree. *Dryden.*

A great argument of the goodness of his cause, which required in its defender zeal, to a degree of warmth able to *warp* the sacred rule of the word of God. *Locke.*

I have no private considerations to *warp* me in this controversy, since my first entering upon it. *Addison.*

Not *warp'd* by passion, aw'd by rumour,
Not grave through pride, or gay through folly;
An equal mixture of good humour,
And sensible soft melancholy. *Swift.*

A constant watchfulness against all those prejudices that might *warp* the judgment aside from truth. *Watts.*

3. It is used by *Shakespeare* to express the effect of frost.

Freeze, freeze, thou bitter sky,
Thou do'st not bite so nigh
As benefits forgot:
Though thou the waters *warp*,
Thy sting is not so sharp
As friends remember'd not. *Shak. As you like it.*

To WA'RRANT. *v. n.* [*garantir*, French.]

1. To support or maintain; to attest.

She needed not disdain any service, though never so mean, which was *warranted* by the sacred name of father. *Sidney.*

He that readeth unto us the Scriptures delivereth all the mysteries of faith, and not any thing amongst them all more than the mouth of the Lord doth *warrant*. *Hooker.*

If this internal light be conformable to the principles of reason, or to the word of God, which is attested revelation, reason *warrants* it, and we may safely receive it for true. *Locke.*

2. To give authority.

Now we'll together, and the chance of goodness
Be like our *warranted* quarrel. *Shakes. Macbeth.*

3. To justify.

How can any one *warrant* himself in the use of those things against such suspicions, but in the trust he has in the common honesty and truth of men in general? *South.*

True fortitude is seen in great exploits,
That justice *warrants* and that wisdom guides;
All else is tow'ring frenzy and distraction. *Addison.*

4. To exempt; to privilege; to secure.

If my coming, whom, she said, he feared, as soon as he knew me by the armour, had not *warranted* her from that near approaching cruelty. *Sidney.*

These thoughts cannot, in this your loneliness, *warrant* you from suspicion in others, nor defend you from melancholy in yourself. *Sidney.*

I'll *warrant* him from drowning. *Shakesp. Tempest.*

In a place
Less *warranted* than this, or less secure,
I cannot be, that I should fear to change it. *Milton.*

5. To declare upon surety.

What a galled neck have we here! Look ye, mine's as smooth as silk, I *warrant* ye. *L'Estrange.*

The Moors king
Is safe enough, I *warrant* him for one. *Dryd. Span. Fryar.*

WA'RRANT. *n. s.* [from the verb.]

1. A writ conferring some right or authority.

Are you now going to dispatch this deed?
—We are, my lord, and come to have the *warrant*,
That we may be admitted where he is. *Shak. Rich. III.*

He sent him a *warrant* for one thousand pounds a year pension for his life. *Clarendon.*

2. A writ giving the officer of justice the power of caption.

There was a damn'd design, cries one, no doubt;
For *warrants* are already issued out. *Dryden's Juvenal.*

3. A justificatory commission or testimony.

His promise is our plain *warrant*, that in his name what we ask we shall receive. *Hooker.*

Is this a *warrant* sufficient for any man's conscience to build such proceedings upon, as have been and are put in use for the establishment of that cause? *Hooker.*

The place of Paradise might be seen unto Moses, and unto the prophets which succeeded him; both which I take for my *warrant* to guide me in this discovery. *Raleigh.*

His *warrant* does the Christian faith defend;
On that relying, all their quarrels end. *Waller.*

The Jewish religion was yet in possession; and therefore, that this might so enter as not to intrude, it was to bring its *warrant* from the same hand of Omnipotence. *South's Sermons.*

4. Right; legality. Obsolete.

I attach thee
For an abuser of the world, a practicer
Of arts inhibited and out of *warrant*. *Shakes. Othello.*
Therefore to horse,
And let us not be dainty of leave-taking,
But shift away: there's *warrant* in that theft,
Which steals itself when there's no mercy left. *Shakesp.*

WA'RRANTABLE. *adj.* [from *warrant.*] Justifiable; defensible.

To purchase a clear and *warrantable* body of truth, we must forget and part with much we know. *Brown.*

His meals are coarse and short, his employment *warrantable*, his sleep certain and refreshing. *South.*

If I can mend my condition by any *warrantable* industry, the way is fair and open; and that's a privilege every reasonable creature has in his commission. *L'Estrange.*

WA'RRANTABLENESS. *n. s.* [from *warrantable.*] Justifiableness.

By the foil thereof you may see the nobleness of my desire to you, and the *warrantableness* of your favour to me. *Sidney.*

WA'RRANTABLY. *adv.* [from *warrantable.*] Justifiably.

The faith which God requires is only this, that he will certainly reward all those that believe in him, and obey his commandments; but for the particular application of this faith to ourselves, that deserves no more of our assent, nor can indeed *warrantably* have it, than what is founded upon the serious consideration of our own performances. *Wake.*

WA'RRANTER. *n. s.* [from *warrant.*]

1. One who gives authority.
2. One who gives security.

WA'RRANTISE. *n. s.* [*warrantiso*, law Latin; from *warrant.*] Authority; security.

There's none protector of the realm but I:
Break up the gates, I'll be your *warrantize*. *Shakes. H. VI.*

WA'RRANTY. *n. s.* [*warrantia*, law Latin; *garantie*, *garant*, French.]

1. [In the common law.] A promise made in a deed by one man unto another for himself and his heirs, to secure him and his heirs against all men, for the enjoying of any thing agreed of between them. *Cowel.*

2. Authority; justificatory mandate.

Her obsequies have been so far enlarg'd
As we have *warranty*: her death was doubtful;
And but that great command o'ersways the order,
She should in ground unsanctify'd have lodg'd
'Till the last trump. *Shakespeare.*

In the use of those epithets we have the *warranty* and consent of all the churches, since they ever had a liturgy. *Taylor.*

3. Security.

Every one cannot distinguish between fine and mixed silver: those who have had the care and government of politick societies, introduced coinage as a remedy: the stamp was a *warranty* of the publick, that under such a denomination they should receive a piece of such a weight and fineness. *Locke.*

To WARRA'Y. *v. a.* [from *war.*] To make war upon.

But Ebranc salved both their infancies
With noble deeds, and *warrayd* on Brunchild
In Hainault, where yet of his victories
Brave monuments remain, which yet that land envys. *F. Q.*
Of these a mighty people shortly grew,
And puissant kings, which all the world *warraid*,
And to themselves all nations did subdue. *Fairy Queen.*
This continual, cruel, civil war,
The which myself against myself do make,
Whilst my weak powers of passions *warraid* are,
No skill can stint, nor reason can aslake. *Spenser.*
Six years were run since first in martial guise
The Christian lords *warraid* the eastren land. *Fairfax.*

WARRE. *adj.* [ƿœꞃꞃ, Saxon.] Worse. Obsolete.

They say the world is *warre* than it wont,
All for her shepherds is beastly and bloont:
Others saine, but how truly I note,
All for they holden shame of their cote. *Spenser's Past.*

WA'RREN. *n. s.* [*waerande*, Dutch; *guerenne*, French.] A kind of park for rabits.

I found him here, as melancholy as a lodge in a *warren*. *Shakesp. Much Ado about Nothing.*

The coney convenes a whole *warren*, tells her story, and advises upon a revenge. *L'Estrange.*

Men

Men ſhould ſet ſnares in their *warrens* to catch polcats and foxes. *Dryden's Spaniſh Fryar.*

WA'RRENER. *n. ſ.* [from *warren.*] The keeper of a warren.

WA'RRIOUR. *n. ſ.* [from *war.*] A ſoldier; a military man.

I came from Corinth,
Brought to this town by that moſt famous *warrior*,
Duke Menaphon. *Shakeſp. Comedy of Errours.*

Fierce fiery *warriors* fight upon the clouds,
In ranks and ſquadrons and right form of war,
Which drizzled blood upon the Capitol. *Shakeſp. Jul. Cæſ.*

I ſing the *warriour* and his mighty deeds. *Lauderdale.*

The *warriour* horſes ty'd in order fed. *Dryden's Æn.*

The mute walls relate the *warriour*'s fame,
And Trojan chiefs the Tyrians pity claim. *Dryden's Æn.*

Camilla led her troops, a *warriour* dame;
Unbred to ſpinning, in the loom unſkill'd,
She choſe the nobler Pallas of the field. *Dryden's Æn.*

WART. *n. ſ.* [peaꞃꞇ, Saxon; *werte*, Dutch.] A corneous excreſcence; a ſmall protuberance on the fleſh.

If thou prate of mountains, let them throw
Millions of acres on us, 'till our ground,
Singeing his pate againſt the burning ſun,
Make Oſſa like a *wart.* *Shak. Hamlet.*

In old ſtatues of ſtone, which have been put in cellars, the feet of them being bound with leaden bands, there it appeared the lead did ſwell, inſomuch as it hanged upon the ſtone like *warts.* *Bacon's Natural Hiſtory.*

Like vile ſtones lying in ſaffron'd tin,
Or *warts*, or weals, it hangs upon her ſkin. *Donne.*

In painting, the *warts* and moles, adding a likeneſs to the face, are not to be omitted. *Dryden's Dufreſnoy.*

He is taken with thoſe *warts* and moles, and hard features, by thoſe who repreſent him on the ſtage, or he is no more Achilles. *Dryden.*

Malpighi, in his treatiſe of galls, under which he comprehends all preternatural and morboſe tumours of plants, doth demonſtrate that all ſuch *warts*, tumours and excreſcences, where any inſects are found, are excited or raiſed up by ſome venenoſe liquors, which with their eggs ſuch inſects ſhed; or boring with their terebræ, inſtil into the very pulp of ſuch buds. *Ray on the Creation.*

WA'RTWORT. *n. ſ.* [*wart* and *wort.*] Spurge.

WA'RTY. *adj.* [from *wart.*] Grown over with warts.

WA'RWORN. *adj.* [*war* and *worn.*] Worn with war.

Their geſture ſad,
Inveſt in lank lean cheeks and *warworn* coats,
Preſented them unto the gazing moon
So many horrid ghoſts. *Shakeſ. Henry* V.

WA'RY. *adj.* [pœꞃ, Saxon.] Cautious; ſcrupulous; timorouſly prudent.

He is above, and we upon earth; and therefore it behoveth our words to be *wary* and few. *Hooker.*

Leontius, their biſhop, although an enemy to the better part, yet *wary* and ſubtle, as all the heads of the Arrians faction were, could at no time be plainly heard to uſe either form. *Hooker.*

Good cauſe he had to haſten thence away;
For on a day his *wary* dwarf had ſpy'd,
Where in a dungeon deep huge numbers lay,
Of captive wretched thrals that wailed night and day. *F. Q.*

Each thing feigned ought more *wary* be. *Hubb. Tale.*

Each warns a *warier* carriage in the thing,
Leſt blind preſumption work their ruining. *Daniel.*

Others grow *wary* in their praiſes of one, who ſets too great a value on them, leſt they ſhould raiſe him too high in his own imagination. *Addiſon's Spectator.*

WAS. The preterite of *To* BE.

Enoch walked with God, and *was* not; for God took him. *Gen.* v. 24.

To WASH. *v. a.* [ƿaꞅcan, Saxon; *waſſchen*, Dutch.]

1. To cleanſe by ablution.

How fain, like Pilate, would I *waſh* my hands
Of this moſt grievous guilty murther done! *Shakeſ. R.* III.

Look, how ſhe rubs her hands.
——It is an accuſtom'd action with her to ſeem thus *waſhing* her hands. *Shakeſp. Macbeth.*

Waſh me throughly from mine iniquity, and cleanſe me from my ſin. *Pſ.* li. 2.

Thou didſt *waſh* thyſelf. *Ez.* xxiii. 40.

Shall he that gives fire to the train pretend to *waſh* his hands of the hurt that is done by the playing of the mine? *L'Eſtrange's Fables.*

2. To moiſten.

3. To affect by ablution.

Be baptized, and *waſh* away thy ſins. *Acts* xxii. 16.

Sins of irreligion muſt ſtill be ſo accounted for as to crave pardon, and be *waſhed* off by repentance. *Taylor.*

Recollect the things you have heard, that they may not be *waſhed* all away from the mind by a torrent of other engagements. *Watts's Improvement of the Mind.*

4. To colour by waſhing.

To *waſh* over a coarſe or inſignificant meaning, is to counterfeit nature's coin. *Collier of the Aſpect.*

To WASH. *v. n.*

1. To perform the act of ablution.

I will go *waſh*;
And when my face is fair, you ſhall perceive
Whether I bluſh or no. *Shakeſp. Coriolanus.*

Waſh and be clean. *2 Kings* v. 13.

Are not the rivers of Damaſcus better than all the waters of Iſrael? May I not *waſh* in them? *2 Kings* v. 12.

Let each becalm his troubled breaſt,
Waſh and partake ſerene the friendly feaſt. *Pope's Odyſſey.*

2. To cleanſe cloaths.

She can *waſh* and ſcour.
—A ſpecial virtue; for then ſhe need not be *waſhed* and ſcoured. *Shak. Two Gentlemen of Verona.*

WASH. *n. ſ.* [from the verb.]

1. Alluvion; any thing collected by water.

The *waſh* of paſtures, fields, commons, and roads, where rain-water hath a long time ſettled, is of great advantage to all land. *Mortimer's Huſbandry.*

2. A bog; a marſh; a fen; a quagmire.

Full thirty times hath Phœbus car gone round
Neptune's ſalt *waſh*, and Tellus' orb'd ground. *Shakeſpeare.*

The beſt part of my power
Were in the *waſhes* all unwarily
Devoured by the unexpected flood. *Shakeſp. King John.*

4. A medical or coſmetick lotion.

Try whether children may not have ſome *waſh* to make their teeth better and ſtronger. *Bacon's Natural Hiſtory.*

They paint and patch their imperfections
Of intellectual complections,
And daub their tempers o'er with *waſhes*,
As artificial as their faces. *Hudibras.*

He tried all manner of *waſhes* to bring him to a better complexion; but there was no good to be done. *L'Eſtrange.*

None are welcome to ſuch, but thoſe who ſpeak paint and *waſh*; for that is the thing they love; and no wonder, ſince it is the thing they need. *South's Sermons.*

To ſteal from rainbows, ere they drop in ſhow'rs,
A brighter *waſh.* *Pope's Rape of the Lock.*

Here gallypots and vials plac'd,
Some fill'd with *waſhes*, ſome with paſte. *Swift.*

5. A ſuperficial ſtain or colour.

Imagination ſtamps ſignification upon his face, and tells the people he is to go for ſo much, who oftentimes, being deceived by the *waſh*, never examine the metal, but take him upon content. *Collier.*

6. The feed of hogs gathered from waſhed diſhes.

The wretched, bloody, and uſurping boar,
That ſpoil'd your ſummer-fields and fruitful vines,
Swills your warm blood like *waſh*, and makes his trough
In your embowell'd boſoms. *Shakeſp. Richard* III.

7. The act of waſhing the cloaths of a family; the linen waſhed at once.

WA'SHBALL. *n. ſ.* [*waſh* and *ball.*] Ball made of ſoap.

I aſked a poor man how he did; he ſaid he was like a *waſhball*, always in decay. *Swift.*

WA'SHER. *n. ſ.* [from *waſh.*] One that waſhes.

Quickly is his laundreſs, his *waſher*, and his wringer. *Shak.*

WA'SHY. *adj.* [from *waſh.*]

1. Watry; damp.

On the *waſhy* ouze deep channels wore,
Eaſy, ere God had bid the ground be dry. *Milton.*

2. Weak; not ſolid.

A poliſh of clearneſs, evenly and ſmoothly ſpread, not overthin and *waſhy*, but of a pretty ſolid conſiſtence. *Wotton.*

WASP. *n. ſ.* [ƿæꞅp, Saxon; *veſpa*, Latin; *gueſpe*, French.] A briſk ſtinging inſect, in form reſembling a bee.

More *waſps*, that buz about his noſe,
Will make this ſting the ſooner. *Shakeſpeare's Henry* VIII.

Encount'ring with a *waſp*,
He in his arms the fly doth claſp. *Drayton.*

Why, what a *waſp*-tongu'd and impatient
Art thou, to break into this woman's mood,
Tying thine ear to no tongue but thine own? *Shak. H.* IV.

WA'SPISH. *adj.* [from *waſp.*] Peeviſh; malignant; irritable; iraſcible.

I'll uſe you for my laughter,
When you are *waſpiſh.* *Shakeſp. Julius Cæſar.*

Come, you waſp, you are too angry.
—If I be *waſpiſh*, beſt beware my ſting. *Shakeſpeare.*

By the ſtern brow and *waſpiſh* action,
Which ſhe did uſe as ſhe was writing of it,
It bears an angry tenour. *Shak. As you like it.*

The taylor's wife was only a good hearty ſhrew, under the impotency of an unruly *waſpiſh* humour: ſhe would have her will. *L'Eſtrange.*

Upon this groſs miſtake the poor *waſpiſh* creature runs on for many leaves. *Stillingfleet.*

Much

Much do I ſuffer, much, to keep in peace
This jealous, *waſpiſh*, wrong-head, rhiming race. *Pope.*

WA'SPISHLY. *adv.* [from *waſpiſh.*] Peeviſhly.

WA'SPISHNESS. *n. ſ.* [from *waſpiſh.*] Peeviſhneſs; irritability.

WA'SSAIL. *n. ſ.* [from pær ƿœl, your health, Saxon.]

1. A liquour made of apples, ſugar, and ale, anciently much uſed by Engliſh goodfellows.

2. A drunken bout.

The king doth wake to-night, and takes his rouſe,
Keeps *waſſail*, and the ſwagg'ring upſpring reels. *Shakeſp.*

WA'SSAILER. *n. ſ.* [from *waſſail.*] A toper; a drunkard.

I'm loth to meet the rudeneſs, and ſwill'd inſolence
Of ſuch late *waſſailers*. *Milton.*

WAST. The ſecond perſon of *was*, from *To be*.

To WASTE. *v. a.* [aperτan, Saxon; *woeſten*, Dutch; *guaſtare*, Italian; *vaſtare*, Latin.]

1. To diminiſh.

The fire that mounts the liquor 'till't run o'er,
Seeming t' augment it, *waſtes* it. *Shakeſp. H.* VIII.

Firſt vegetive, then feels, and reaſons laſt;
Rich of three ſouls, and lives all three to *waſte*. *Dryden.*

Could ſighs furniſh new breath, or draw life and ſpirits from the *waſting* of your's, your friends would encourage your paſſion. *Temple.*

2. To deſtroy wantonly and luxuriouſly; to ſquander.

The people's praying after the miniſter, they ſay, *waſteth* time. *Hooker.*

There muſt be providence uſed, that our ſhip-timber be not *waſted*. *Bacon.*

No ways and means their cabinet employ,
But their dark hours they *waſte* in barren joy. *Garth.*

3. To deſtroy; to deſolate.

He only their proviſions *waſtes* and burns. *Daniel.*
Peace to corrupt, no leſs than war to *waſte*. *Milton.*

The Tyber
Inſults our walls, and *waſtes* our fruitful grounds. *Dryden.*

Now *waſting* years my former ſtrength confound,
And added woes have bow'd me to the ground;
Yet by the ſtubble you may gueſs the grain,
And mark the ruins of no vulgar man. *Broome.*

4. To wear out.

Here condemn'd
To *waſte* eternal days in woe and pain. *Milton.*

5. To ſpend; to conſume.

O were I able
To *waſte* it all myſelf, and leave you none. *Milton.*

To WASTE. *v. n.* To dwindle; to be in a ſtate of conſumption.

Man dieth and *waſteth* away. *Job* xiv. 10.

Their thoughts are thoughts of iniquity; *waſting* and deſtruction are in their paths. *Iſ.* lix. 7.

The latter watch of *waſting* night,
And ſetting ſtars to kindly ſleep invite. *Dryden.*

WASTE. *adj.* [from the verb.]

1. Deſtroyed; ruined.

Sophi leaves all *waſte* in his retreat. *Milton.*

The multiplication and obſtinacy of diſputes, which have ſo laid *waſte* the intellectual world, is owing to nothing more than to the ill uſe of words. *Locke.*

When thus the gather'd ſtorms of wretched love,
In my ſwoln boſom, with long war had ſtrove,
Laid all the civil bonds of manhood *waſte*,
And ſcatter'd ruin as the torrent paſt. *Prior.*

2. Deſolate; uncultivated.

There be very *waſte* countries and wilderneſſes; but we find not mention whether any do inhabit there. *Abbot.*

He found him in a deſert land, and in the *waſte* howling wilderneſs. *Deut.* xxxii. 10.

3. Superfluous; exuberant; loſt for want of occupiers.

Quite ſurcharg'd with her own weight,
And ſtrangl'd with her *waſte* fertility. *Milton.*

4. Worthleſs; that of which none but vile uſes can be made.

5. That of which no account is taken, or value found.

It may be publiſhed as well as printed, that ſo much ſkill in Hebrew derivations may not lie for *waſte* paper. *Dryden.*

WASTE. *n. ſ.* [from the verb.]

1. Wanton or luxurious deſtruction; the act of ſquandering; conſumption; loſs.

Reaſons induce us to think it a good work, which they, in their care for well beſtowing of time, account *waſte*. *Hooker.*

Thin air is better pierced, but thick air preſerveth the ſound better from *waſte*. *Bacon's Natural Hiſtory.*

Freedom who loves, muſt firſt be wiſe and good;
But from that mark how far they rove we ſee,
For all this *waſte* of wealth, and loſs of blood. *Milton.*

It was providently deſigned to repair the *waſte* daily made by the frequent attrition in maſtication. *Ray on the Creation.*

So fooliſh and laviſh are we, that too often we uſe ſome words in mere *waſte*, and have no ideas for them. *Watts.*

2. Uſeleſs expence.

But youth, the periſhing good, runs on too faſt,
And unenjoy'd it ſpends itſelf to *waſte*;
Few know the uſe of life before 'tis paſt. *Dryden.*

Secure the workings of your ſoul from running to *waſte*, and even your looſer moments will turn to happy account. *Watts.*

3. Deſolate or uncultivated ground.

Land that is left wholly to nature, that hath no improvement of paſturage, tillage, or planting, is called *waſte*. *Locke.*

Lifted aloft he 'gan to mount up higher,
And, like freſh eagle, made his hardy flight
Thro' all that great wide *waſte*, yet wanting light. *Spenſer.*

4. Ground, place, or ſpace unoccupied.

Theſe gentlemen, on their watch,
In the dead *waſte* and middle of the night,
Had been thus encountred. *Shakeſp. Hamlet.*

Forty days Elijah, without food,
Wander'd this barren *waſte*. *Milton's Paradiſe Regain'd.*

Lords of the world's great *waſte*, the ocean, we
Whole foreſts ſend to reign upon the ſea. *Waller.*

From that dire deluge, through the wat'ry *waſte*,
Such length of years, ſuch various perils paſt. *Dryden.*

Thee I purſue, oh great ill-fated youth!
Through the diſmal *waſte* of gloomy death. *Smith.*

See the man who ſpacious regions gave,
A *waſte* for beaſts, himſelf deny'd a grave. *Pope.*

5. Region ruined and deſerted.

All the leafy nation ſinks at laſt,
And Vulcan rides in triumph o'er the *waſte*. *Dryden's Æn.*

6. Miſchief; deſtruction.

The ſpirit of wantonneſs is ſure ſcarce out of him: if the devil have him not in fee-ſimple, he will never, I think, in the way of *waſte*, attempt us again. *Shakeſ.*

WA'STEFUL. *adj.* [*waſte* and *full.*]

1. Deſtructive; ruinous.

The folly of man
Let in theſe *waſteful* furies. *Milton's Paradiſe Loſt.*

2. Wantonly or diſſolutely conſumptive.

To ſmooth the ice, or add another hue
Unto the rainbow, or with taper light
To ſeek the beauteous eye of heav'n to garniſh,
Is *waſteful* and ridiculous exceſs. *Shakeſp. K. John.*

In ſuch caſes they ſet them off more with wit and activity, than with coſtly and *waſteful* expences. *Bacon.*

3. Laviſh; prodigal; luxuriantly liberal.

How has kind heav'n adorn'd the happy land,
And ſcatter'd bleſſings with a *waſteful* hand! *Addiſon.*

4. Deſolate; uncultivated; unoccupied.

In wilderneſs and *waſteful* deſarts ſtray'd,
To ſeek her knight. *Fairy Queen.*

Outrageous as a ſea, dark, *waſteful*, wild. *Milton.*

WA'STEFULLY. *adv.* [from *waſteful.*] With vain and diſſolute conſumption.

Never any man would think our labour miſ-ſpent, or the time *waſtefully* conſumed. *Hooker.*

To her new-made favourite, Morat,
Her laviſh hand is *waſtefully* profuſe. *Dryden's Aurengz.*

WA'STEFULNESS. *n. ſ.* [from *waſteful.*] Prodigality.

WA'STENESS. *n. ſ.* [from *waſte.*] Deſolation; ſolitude.

She, of nought afraid,
Through woods and *waſteneſs* wide him daily ſought. *Spenſ.*

That day is a day of wrath, a day of *waſteneſs*. *Zeph.* i. 15.

WA'STER. *n. ſ.* [from *waſte.*] One that conſumes diſſolutely and extravagantly; a ſquanderer; vain conſumer.

Divers Roman knights,
The profuſe *waſters* of their patrimonies,
So threatned with their debts, as they will now
Run any deſperate fortune. *Ben. Johnſon's Catiline.*

Plenty, in their own keeping, makes them wanton and careleſs, and teaches them to be ſquanderers and *waſters*. *Locke.*

Upon cards and dice never learn any play, and ſo be incapacitated for thoſe encroaching *waſters* of uſeful time. *Locke.*

Sconces are great *waſters* of candles. *Swift.*

WASTREL. *n. ſ.* [from *waſte.*]

Their works, both ſtream and load, lie in ſeveral, or in *waſtrell*, that is, in incloſed grounds, or in commons. *Carew.*

WATCH. *n. ſ.* [pæcce, Saxon.]

1. Forbearance of ſleep.

2. Attendance without ſleep.

All the long night their mournful *watch* they keep,
And all the day ſtand round the tomb and weep. *Addiſon.*

3. Attention; cloſe obſervation.

In my ſchool-days, when I had loſt one ſhaft,
I ſhot his fellow, of the ſelf-ſame flight,
The ſelf-ſame way, with more adviſed *watch*,
To find the other forth; by vent'ring both,
I oft found both. *Shakeſp. Merchant of Venice.*

4. Guard; vigilant keep.

Still, when ſhe ſlept, he kept both *watch* and ward. *F. Q.*

Hie thee to thy charge;
Uſe careful *watch*, chuſe truſty centinels. *Shakeſp. R.* III.

Love can find entrance not only into an open heart, but alſo into a heart well fortified, if *watch* be not well kept. *Bacon.*

5. Watchman; men ſet to guard. It is uſed in a collective ſenſe.

Before her gate, high God did ſweat ordain,
And wakeful *watches* ever to abide. *Fairy Queen.*

Such ſtand in narrow lanes,
And beat our *watch*, and rob our paſſengers. *Shakeſpeare.*

The ports he did ſhut up, or at leaſt kept a *watch* on them, that none ſhould paſs to or fro that was ſuſpected. *Bacon.*

The tow'rs of heav'n are fill'd
With armed *watch*, that render all acceſs
Impregnable. *Milton's Paradiſe Loſt.*

An abſurdity our Saviour accounted it for the blind to lead the blind, and to put him that cannot ſee to the office of a *watch*. *South's Sermons.*

6. Place where a guard is ſet.

He upbraids Iago, that he made him
Brave me upon the *watch*. *Shakeſp. Othello.*

7. Poſt or office of a watchman.

As I did ſtand my *watch* upon the hill,
I look'd toward Birnam, and anon methought
The wood began to move. *Shakeſp. Macbeth.*

8. A period of the night.

Your fair daughter,
At this odd, even, and dull *watch* o' th' night,
Is now tranſported with a gondalier,
To the groſs claſps of a laſcivious Moor. *Shak. Othello.*

All night he will purſue; but his approach
Darkneſs defends between, 'till morning *watch*. *Milton.*

The latter *watch* of waſting night,
And ſetting ſtars, to kindly ſleep invite. *Dryden's Æn.*

9. A pocket-clock; a ſmall clock moved by a ſpring.

A *watch*, beſides the hour of the day, gives the day of the month, and the place of the ſun in the zodiack. *Hale.*

On the theatre we are confined to time; and though we talk not by the hour-glaſs, yet the *watch* often drawn out of the pocket warns the actors that their audience is weary. *Dryd.*

That Cloe may be ſerv'd in ſtate,
The hours muſt at her toilet wait;
Whilſt all the reaſoning fools below
Wonder their *watches* go ſo ſlow. *Prior.*

To WATCH. *v. n.* [pacian, Saxon.]

1. Not to ſleep; to wake.

I have two nights *watch'd* with you; but can perceive no truth in your report. *Shakeſp. Macbeth.*

Watching care will not let a man ſlumber, as a ſore diſeaſe breaketh ſleep. *Ecclus* xxxi. 2.

Sleep, liſt'ning to thee, will *watch*. *Milton.*

2. To keep guard.

I will *watch* over them for evil, and not for good. *Jer.* xliv.

In our *watching* we have *watched* for a nation that could not ſave us. *Lam.* iv. 17.

He gave ſignal to the miniſter that *watch'd*. *Milton.*

3. To look with expectation.

My ſoul waiteth for the Lord, more than they that *watch* for the morning. *Pſ.* cxxx. 6.

4. To be attentive; to be vigilant.

Watch thou in all things, endure afflictions. 2 *Tim.* iv. 5.

5. To be cautiouſly obſervant.

Watch over thyſelf, counſel thyſelf, judge thyſelf impartially. *Taylor.*

6. To be inſidiouſly attentive.

He ſomewhere nigh at hand
Watches, no doubt, with greedy hope to find
His wiſh, and beſt advantage us aſunder,
Hopeleſs to circumvent us join'd. *Milton.*

To WATCH. *v. a.*

1. To guard; to have in keep.

Flaming miniſters *watch* and tend their charge. *Milton.*

2. To obſerve in ambuſh.

Saul ſent meſſengers unto David's houſe to *watch* him, and to ſlay him. 1 *Sa.* xix. 11.

He is bold, and lies near the top of the water, *watching* the motion of any water-rat that ſwims betwixt him and the ſky. *Walton.*

They under rocks their food
In jointed armour *watch*. *Milton.*

3. To tend.

Paris *watched* the flocks in the groves of Ida. *Broome.*

4. To obſerve in order to detect or prevent.

WA'TCHER. *n. ſ.* [from *watch.*]

1. One who watches.

Get on your night-gown, leſt occaſion call us,
And ſhew us to be *watchers*. *Shak. Macbeth.*

Love hath chac'd ſleep from my enthralled eyes,
And made them *watchers* of mine own heart's ſorrow. *Shak.*

2. Diligent overlooker or obſerver.

It is obſerved, by thoſe that are more attentive *watchers* of the works of nature. *More.*

WA'TCHET. *adj.* [pæceð, Saxon, weak. *Skinner.*] Blue; pale blue.

Whom 'midſt the Alps do hanging throats ſurpriſe?
Who ſtares in Germany at *watchet* eyes? *Dryden's Juven.*

WA'TCHFUL. *adj.* [*watch* and *full.*] Vigilant; attentive; cautious; nicely obſervant.

Call home our exil'd friends,
That fled the ſnares of *watchful* tyranny. *Shak. Macbeth.*

Be *watchful*, and ſtrengthen the things ready to die. *Rev.* iii.

Nodding a while, and *watchful* of his blow,
He fell; and falling cruſh'd th' ungrateful nymph below. *Dry.*

Readers ſhould not lay by that caution which becomes a ſincere purſuit of truth, and ſhould make them always *watchful* againſt whatever might conceal or miſrepreſent it. *Locke.*

WA'TCHFULLY. *adv.* [from *watchful.*] Vigilantly; cautiouſly; attentively; with cautious obſervation; heedfully.

If this experiment were very *watchfully* tried in veſſels of ſeveral ſizes, ſome ſuch things may be diſcovered. *Boyle.*

WA'TCHFULNESS. *n. ſ.* [from *watchful.*]

1. Vigilance; heed; ſuſpicious attention; cautious regard; diligent obſervation.

The experience of our own frailties, and the conſideration of the *watchfulneſs* of the tempter, diſcourage us. *Hammond.*

Love, fantaſtick pow'r! that is afraid
To ſtir abroad 'till *watchfulneſs* be laid;
Undaunted then o'er cliffs and valleys ſtrays,
And leads his vot'ries ſafe through pathleſs ways. *Prior.*

Huſbands are counſelled not to truſt too much to their wives owning the doctrine of unlimited conjugal fidelity, and ſo to neglect a due *watchfulneſs* over their manners. *Arbuthnot.*

Prejudices are cured by a conſtant jealouſy and *watchfulneſs* over our paſſions, that they may never interpoſe when we are called to paſs a judgment. *Watts.*

By a ſolicitous *watchfulneſs* about one's behaviour, inſtead of being mended, it will be conſtrained. *Locke.*

2. Inability to ſleep.

Watchfulneſs, ſometimes called a coma vigil, often precedes too great ſleepineſs. *Arbuthnot on Diet.*

WA'TCHHOUSE. *n. ſ.* [*watch* and *houſe.*] Place where the watch is ſet.

Where ſtatues breath'd, the works of Phidias' hands,
A wooden pump or lonely *watchhouſe* ſtands. *Gay.*

WA'TCHING. *n. ſ.* [from *watch.*] Inability to ſleep.

The bullet, not having been extracted, occaſioned great pain and *watchings*. *Wiſeman's Surgery.*

WA'TCHMAKER. *n. ſ.* [*watch* and *maker.*] One whoſe trade is to make watches, or pocket-clocks.

Smithing comprehends all trades which uſe forge or file, from the anchorſmith to the *watchmaker*; they all uſing the ſame tools, though of ſeveral ſizes. *Moxon.*

WA'TCHMAN. *n. ſ.* [*watch* and *man.*] Guard; ſentinel; one ſet to keep ward.

On the top of all I do eſpy
The *watchman* waiting, tydings glad to hear. *Fa. Queen.*

Turn him into London-ſtreets, that the *watchmen* might carry him before a juſtice. *Bacon.*

Drunkenneſs calls off the *watchmen* from their towers; and then all evils that proceed from a looſe heart, an untied tongue, and a diſſolute ſpirit, we put upon its account. *Taylor.*

Our *watchmen* from the tow'rs, with longing eyes,
Expect his ſwift arrival. *Dryden's Spaniſh Fryar.*

The melancholy tone of a *watchman* at midnight. *Swift.*

WA'TCHTOWER. *n. ſ.* [*watch* and *tower.*] Tower on which a centinel was placed for the ſake of proſpect.

In the day-time ſhe ſitteth in a *watchtower*, and flieth moſt by night. *Bacon.*

Up unto the *watchtower* get,
And ſee all things deſpoil'd of fallacies. *Donne.*

To hear the lark begin his flight,
And ſinging ſtartle the dull night
From his *watchtower* in the ſkies,
'Till the dappled dawn doth riſe. *Milton.*

The ſenſes in the head, as ſentinels in a *watchtower*, convey to the ſoul the impreſſions of external objects. *Ray.*

WA'TCHWORD. *n. ſ.* [*watch* and *word.*] The word given to the centinels to know their friends.

All have their ears upright, waiting when the *watchword* ſhall come, that they ſhould all ariſe into rebellion. *Spenſer.*

We have heard the chimes at midnight, maſter Shallow.
—That we have, ſir John: our *watchword*, hem, boys. *Shak.*

A *watchword* every minute of the night goeth about the walls, to teſtify their vigilancy. *Sandys.*

WA'TER. *n. ſ.* [*waeter*, Dutch; pæteꞃ, Saxon.]

1. Sir Iſaac Newton defines *water*, when pure, to be a very fluid ſalt, volatile, and void of all ſavour or taſte; and it ſeems to conſiſt of ſmall, ſmooth, hard, porous, ſpherical particles, of equal diameters, and of equal ſpecifick gravities, as Dr. Cheyne obſerves; and alſo that there are between them ſpaces ſo large, and ranged in ſuch a manner, as to be pervious on all ſides. Their ſmoothneſs accounts for their ſliding eaſily over one another's ſurfaces: their ſphericity keeps them alſo from touching one another in more points than one; and by both theſe their frictions in ſliding over one another, is rendered the leaſt poſſible. Their hardneſs accounts for the incompreſſibility of water, when it is free from the intermixture of air. The poroſity of water is ſo very great, that there is at leaſt forty times as much ſpace as matter in it; for water is nineteen times ſpecifically lighter than gold, and conſequently rarer in the ſame proportion. *Quincy.*

My mildneſs hath allay'd their ſwelling griefs,
My mercy dry'd their *water*-flowing tears. *Shak. H.* VI.

Your *water* is a ſore decayer of your whorſon dead body. *Shakeſpeare's Hamlet.*

The ſweet manner of it forc'd
Thoſe *waters* from me, which I would have ſtopp'd,
But I had not ſo much of man in me;
But all my mother came into mine eyes,
And gave me up to tears. *Shakeſ. Henry* V.

Men's evil manners live in braſs, their virtues
We write in *water*. *Shakeſp. Henry* VIII.

Thoſe healths will make thee and thy ſtate look ill, Timon: here's that which is too weak to be a ſinner, honeſt *water*, which ne'er left man i' th' mire. *Shakeſpeare's Timon.*

Water is the chief ingredient in all the animal fluids and ſolids; for a dry bone, diſtilled, affords a great quantity of inſipid *water*: therefore *water* ſeems to be proper drink for every animal. *Arbuthnot on Aliments.*

2. The ſea.

Travel by land or by *water*. *Common Prayer.*

By *water* they found the ſea, weſtward from Peru, always very calm. *Abbot's Deſcription of the World.*

3. Urine.

If thou could'ſt, doctor, caſt
The *water* of my land, find her diſeaſe,
And purge it to a ſound and priſtine health,
I would applaud thee. *Shak. Macbeth.*

Go to bed, after you have made *water*. *Swift.*

4. *To hold* WATER. To be ſound; to be tight. From a veſſel that will not leak.

A good Chriſtian and an honeſt man muſt be all of a piece, and inequalities of proceeding will never *hold water*. *L'Eſtr.*

5. It is uſed for the luſtre of a diamond.

'Tis a good form,
And rich: here is a *water*, look ye. *Shakeſp. Timon.*

6. WATER is much uſed in compoſition for things made with *water*, being in *water*, or growing in *water*.

She might ſee the ſame *water*-ſpaniel, which before had hunted, come and fetch away one of Philoclea's gloves, whoſe fine proportion ſhewed well what a dainty gueſt was wont there to be lodged. *Sidney.*

Oh that I were a mockery king of ſnow,
Standing before the ſun of Bolingbroke,
And melt myſelf away in *water*-drops. *Shakeſpeare.*

Poor Tom eats the wall-newt, and the *water*-newt. *Shakeſ.*

Touch me with noble anger!
O let not women's weapons, *water*-drops,
Stain my man's cheeks. *Shak. King Lear.*

Let not the *water*-flood overflow me. *Pſ.* lxix. 15.

They ſhall ſpring up as among the graſs, as willows by the *water*-courſes. *Iſ.* xliv. 4.

As the hart panteth after the *water*-brook, ſo panteth my ſoul after thee, O God. *Pſalms.*

Deep calleth unto deep, at the noiſe of thy *water*-ſpouts. *Pſ.* xlii. 7.

He turneth rivers into a wilderneſs, and the *water*-ſprings into dry ground. *Pſ.* cvii. 33.

There were ſet ſix *water*-pots of ſtone. *Jo.* ii. 6.

Hercules's page, Hylas, went with a *water*-pot to fill it at a pleaſant fountain that was near. *Bacon's Natural Hiſtory.*

As the carp is accounted the *water*-fox for his cunning, ſo the roach is accounted the *water* ſheep. *Walton's Angler.*

Sea-calves unwonted to freſh rivers fly;
The *water*-ſnakes with ſcales upſtanding die *May's Virgil.*

By making the *water*-wheels larger, the motion will be ſo ſlow, that the ſcrew will not be able to ſupply the outward ſtreams. *Wilkins's Dædalus.*

Rain carried away apples, together with a dunghill that lay in the *water*-courſe. *L'Eſtrange.*

Oh help, in this extremeſt need,
If *water*-gods are deities indeed. *Dryden.*

The *water*-ſnake, whom fiſh and paddocks fed,
With ſtaring ſcales lies poiſon'd in his bed. *Dryd. Virgil.*

Becauſe the outermoſt coat of the eye might be pricked, and this humour let out, therefore nature hath made proviſion to repair it by the help of certain *water*-pipes, or lymphæducts, inſerted into the bulb of the eye, proceeding from glandules that ſeparate this water from the blood. *Ray on the Creation.*

The *lacerta aquatica*, or *water*-newt, when young, hath four neat ramified fins, two on one ſide, growing out a little above its forelegs, to poiſe and keep its body upright, which fall off when the legs are grown. *Derham's Phyſico-Theology.*

Other mortar uſed in making *water*-courſes, ciſterns, and fiſhponds, is very hard and durable. *Moxon.*

The moſt brittle *water*-carriage was uſed among the Egyptians, who, as Strabo faith, would ſail ſometimes in boats made of earthen ware. *Arbuthnot.*

A gentleman watered St. foin in dry weather at new ſowing, and, when it came up, with a *water*-cart, carrying his water in a caſk, to which there was a tap at the end, which lets the water run into a long trough full of ſmall holes. *Mort.*

In Hampſhire they ſell *water*-trefoil as dear as hops. *Mort.*

To WA'TER. *v. a.* [from the noun.]

1. To irrigate; to ſupply with moiſture.

A river went out of Eden to *water* the garden. *Gen.* ii. 10.

A man's nature runs to herbs or weeds; therefore let him ſeaſonably *water* the one, and deſtroy the other. *Bacon.*

Chaſte moral writing we may learn from hence,
Neglect of which no wit can recompenſe;
The fountain which from Helicon proceeds,
That ſacred ſtream, ſhould never *water* weeds. *Waller.*

Could tears *water* the lovely plant, ſo as to make it grow again after once 'tis cut down, your friends would be ſo far from accuſing your paſſion, that they would encourage it, and ſhare it. *Temple.*

You may *water* the lower land when you will. *Mortimer.*

2. To ſupply with water for drink.

Now 'gan the golden Phœbus for to ſteep
His fiery face in billows of the weſt,
And his faint ſteeds *water'd* in ocean deep,
Whilſt from their journal labours they did reſt. *Fa. Queen.*

Doth not each on the ſabbath looſe his ox from the ſtall, and lead him away to *watering*? *Lu.* xiii. 15.

His horſemen kept them in ſo ſtrait, that no man could, without great danger, go to *water* his horſe. *Knolles.*

Water him, and, drinking what he can,
Encourage him to thirſt again with bran. *Dryden.*

3. To fertilize or accommodate with ſtreams.

Mountains, that run from one extremity of Italy to the other, give riſe to an incredible variety of rivers that *water* it. *Addiſon on Italy.*

4. To diverſify as with waves.

The different ranging the ſuperficial parts of velvet and *watered* ſilk, does the like. *Locke.*

To WA'TER. *v. n.*

1. To ſhed moiſture.

I ſtain'd this napkin with the blood,
That valiant Clifford with his rapier's point
Made iſſue from the boſom of the boy;
And if thine eyes can *water* for his death,
I give thee this to dry thy cheeks withal. *Shak. Henry* VI.

Mine eyes,
Seeing thoſe beads of ſorrow ſtand in thine,
Began to *water*. *Shakeſp. Julius Cæſar.*

The tickling of the noſtrils within, doth draw the moiſture to the noſtrils, and to the eyes by conſent; for they alſo will *water*. *Bacon's Natural Hiſtory.*

How troubleſome is the leaſt mote, or duſt falling into the eye! and how quickly does it weep, and *water* upon the leaſt grievance! *South's Sermons.*

2. To get or take in water; to be uſed in ſupplying water.

He ſet the rods he had pulled before the flocks in the gutters in the *watering* troughs. *Gen.* xxx. 38.

Mahomet ſent many ſmall boats, manned with harquebuſiers and ſmall ordnance, into the lake near unto the camp, to keep the Chriſtians from *watering* there. *Knolles.*

3. *The mouth* WATERS. The man longs; there is a vehement deſire. From dogs who drop their ſlaver when they ſee meat which they cannot get.

Cardinal Wolſey's *teeth watering* at the biſhoprick of Wincheſter, ſent one unto biſhop Fox, who had advanced him, for to move him to reſign the biſhoprick, becauſe extreme age had made him blind; which motion Fox did take in ſo ill part, that he willed the meſſenger to tell the cardinal, that, although now I am blind, I have eſpied his malicious unthankfulneſs. *Camden's Remains.*

Theſe reaſons made his *mouth* to *water*,
With amorous longings to be at her. *Hudibras.*

Thoſe who contend for 4 *per cent.* have ſet men's *mouths a-watering* for money at that rate. *Locke.*

WATERCO'LOURS. *n. ſ.* [*water* and *colour.*]

Painters make colours into a ſoft conſiſtence with water or oil; thoſe they call *watercolours*, and theſe they term oilcolours. *Boyle on Colours.*

Leſs ſhould I dawb it o'er with tranſitory praiſe,
And *watercolours* of theſe days:
Theſe days! where e'en th' extravagance of poetry
Is at a loſs for figures to expreſs
Men's folly, whimſies, and inconſtancy. *Swift.*

WA'TERCRESSES. *n. ſ.* [*ſiſymbrium*, Latin.] A plant.

It hath a flower compoſed of four leaves, which are placed in form of a croſs, out of whoſe empalement riſes the pointal, which afterward becomes a fruit or pod, which is divided into two cells by an intermediate partition, to which the valves adhere on both ſides, and furniſhed with ſeeds which are roundiſh. To theſe marks muſt be added, that the whole appearance of the plant is peculiar to the ſpecies of this genus. There are five ſpecies. *Miller.*

The nymphs of floods are made very beautiful; upon their heads are garlands of *watercreſſes*. *Peacham on Drawing.*

WA'TERER. *n. ſ.* [from *water.*] One who waters.

This ill weed, rather cut off by the ground than plucked up by the root, twice or thrice grew forth again; but yet, maugre the warmers and *waterers*, hath been ever parched up. *Carew.*

WA'TERFAL. *n. s.* [*water* and *fall.*] Cataract; cascade.

I have seen in the Indies far greater *waterfalls* than those of Nilus. *Raleigh.*

Not Lacedæmon charms me more,
Than high Albana's airy walls,
Resounding with her *waterfalls.* *Addison.*

WATERFOWL. *n. s.* Fowl that live, or get their food in water.

Waterfowl joy most in that air, which is likest water. *Bacon.*

Waterfowls supply the weariness of a long flight by taking water, and numbers of them are found in islands, and in the main ocean. *Hale's Origin of Mankind.*

Fish and *waterfowl*, who feed of turbid and mudy slimy water, are accounted the cause of phlegm. *Floyer.*

The stomachs of *waterfowl* that live upon fish, are human. *Arbuthnot on Aliments.*

WATERGRU'EL. *n. s.* [*water* and *gruel.*] Food made with oatmeal and water.

For breakfast milk, milk-pottage, *watergruel*, and flummery, are very fit to make for children. *Locke.*

The aliment ought to be slender, as *watergruel* acidulated. *Arbuthnot on Diet.*

WA'TERINESS. *n. s.* [from *watery.*] Humidity; moisture.

The forerunners of an apoplexy are dulness, night-mares, weakness, *waterynefs*, and turgidity of the eyes. *Arbuthnot.*

WA'TERISH. *adj.* [from *water.*]

1. Resembling water.

Where the principles are only phlegm, what can be expected from the *waterish* matter, but an insipid manhood, and a stupid old infancy? *Dryden.*

2. Moist; insipid.

Some parts of the earth grow moorish or *waterish*, others dry. *Hale's Origin of Mankind.*

WA'TERISHNESS. *n. s.* [from *waterish.*] Thinness; resemblance of water.

A pendulous sliminess answers a pituitous state, or an acerbity, which resembles the tartar of our humours, or *waterishness*, which is like the serosity of our blood. *Floyer.*

WA'TERLEAF. *n. s.* A plant. It hath a bell-shaped flower, consisting of one leaf, and cut into several segments: from the bottom part of the flower arises the pointal, which afterward becomes a fruit, opening in two parts, inclosing seeds of the same shape as the vessel. *Miller.*

WA'TERLILLY. *n. s.* [*nymphæa*, Lat.] A plant. The characters are; the flower consists of several leaves, which expand in form of a rose; out of the flower cup arises the pointal, which afterwards becomes an almost globular fruit, consisting of many cells, filled with seeds, which are for the most part oblong. *Miller.*

Let them lie dry twelve months, to kill the water-weeds, as *waterlillies* and bull-rushes. *Walton's Angler.*

WA'TERMAN. *n. s.* [*water* and *man.*] A ferryman; a boatman.

Having blocked up the passage to Greenwich, they ordered the *watermen* to let fall their oars more gently. *Dryden.*

Bubbles of air working upward from the very bottom of the lake, the *watermen* told us that they are observed always to rise in the same places. *Addison on Italy.*

The *waterman* forlorn, along the shore,
Pensive reclines upon his useless oar. *Gay.*

WA'TERMARK. *n. s.* [*water* and *mark.*] The utmost limit of the rise of the flood.

Men and beasts
Were borne above the tops of trees that grew
On th' utmost margin of the *watermark.* *Dryden.*

WA'TERMELON. *n. s.* A plant. It hath trailing branches, as the cucumber or melon, and is distinguished from other cucurbitaceous plants, by its leaf deeply cut and jagged, and by its producing uneatable fruit. *Miller.*

WA'TERMIL. *n. s.* Mill turned by water.

Forth flowed fresh
A gushing river of black gory blood,
That drowned all the land whereon he stood:
The stream thereof would drive a *watermill.* *Fairy Queen.*

The picture may be set forth with farm houses and *watermills.* *Peacham on Drawing.*

Corn ground by windmills, erected on hills, or in the plains where the *watermills* stood. *Mortimer's Husbandry.*

WA'TERMINT. *n. s.* A plant.

WA'TERRADISH. *n. s.* A species of water-cresses, which see.

WA'TERRAT. *n. s.* A rat that makes holes in banks.

There be land-rats and *water-rats.* *Shakespeare.*

The pike is bold, and lies near the top of the water, watching the motion of any frog, or *water-rat*, or mouse. *Walton.*

WATERRO'CKET. *n. s.* A species of water-cresses.

WA'TERVIOLET. *n. s.* [*hottonia*, Lat.] A plant. It hath a rose-shaped flower, consisting of one leaf, which is divided into two parts, almost to the bottom: in the center of the flower arises the pointal, which afterwards becomes a cylindrical fruit, in which are contained spherical seeds. *Miller.*

WATERSA'PPHIRE. *n. s.* A sort of stone.

Watersapphire is the occidental sapphire, and is neither of so bright a blue, nor so hard as the oriental. *Woodward.*

WA'TERWITH. *n. s.* [*water* and *with.*] A plant.

The *waterwith* of Jamaica growing on dry hills, in the woods, where no water is to be met with, its trunk, if cut into pieces two or three yards long, and held by either end to the mouth, affords so plentifully a limpid, innocent, and refreshing water, or sap, as gives new life to the droughty traveller or hunter. *Derham's Physico-Theology.*

WA'TERWORK. *n. s.* [*water* and *work.*] Play of fountains; artificial spouts of water; any hydraulick performance.

Engines invented for mines and *waterworks* often fail in the performance. *Wilkins's Math. Magic.*

The French took from the Italians the first plans of their gardens, as well as *waterworks.* *Addison.*

WA'TERY. *adj.* [from *water.*]

1. Thin; liquid; like water.

Quicksilver, which is a most crude and *watery* body, heated, and pent in, hath the like force with gunpowder. *Bacon.*

The bile, by its saponaceous quality, mixeth the oily and *watery* parts of the aliment together. *Arbuthnot on Aliments.*

2. Tastless; insipid; vapid; spiritless.

We'll use this unwholesome humidity, this gross, *watery* pumpion. *Shakespeare's Merry Wives of Windsor.*

No heterogeneous mixture use, as some
With *watry* turneps have debas'd their wines. *Philips.*

3. Wet; abounding with water.

When the big lip, and *wat'ry* eye
Tell me, the rising storm is nigh:
'Tis then thou art yon angry main,
Deform'd by winds, and dash'd by rain. *Prior.*

4. Relating to the water.

On the brims her sire, the *wat'ry* god,
Roll'd from a silver urn his crystal flood. *Dryden.*

5. Consisting of water.

The *wat'ry* kingdom is no bar
To stop the foreign spirits; but they come,
As o'er a brook, to see fair Portia. *Shakespeare.*

Those few escap'd
Famine, and anguish, will at last consume,
Wand'ring that *wat'ry* desart. *Milton's Par. Lost, b.* xi.

Betwixt us and you wide oceans flow,
And *wat'ry* desarts. *Dryden's Indian Emperor.*

Together to the *wat'ry* camp they haste. *Dryden.*

Perhaps you'll say,
That the attracted *wat'ry* vapours rise
From lakes and seas, and fill the lower skies. *Blackmore.*

WA'TTLE. *n. s.* [from *waghelen*, to shake, German. *Skinner.*]

1. The barbs, or loose red flesh that hangs below the cock's bill.

The loach is of the shape of an eel, and has a beard of *wattels* like a barbel. *Walton.*

The barbel is so called, by reason of his barb, or *wattels*, at his mouth, which is under his nose or chops. *Walton.*

His comb and *wattels* are an ornament becoming his martial spirit. *More's Antidote against Atheism.*

2. A hurdle. *Ainsw.*

To WA'TTLE. *v. a.* [ƿatelas, Saxon, *twigs.*] To bind with twigs; to form, by platting twigs one within another.

Might we but hear
The folded flocks penn'd in their *wattled* cotes,
Or sound of pastoral reed with oaten stops. *Milton.*

A plough was found in a very deep bog, and a hedge *wattled* standing. *Mortimer's Husbandry.*

WAVE. *n. s.* [ƿæge, Saxon; *waegh*, Dutch; *vague*, French.]

1. Water raised above the level of the surface; billow; water driven into inequalities.

The shore, that o'er his *wave*-worn basis bow'd. *Shakesp.*

The *waves* that rise would drown the highest hill;
But at thy check they flee, and when they hear
Thy thund'ring voice, they post to do thy will. *Wotton.*

Amidst these toils succeeds the balmy night;
Now hissing waters the quench'd guns restore;
And weary *waves* withdrawing from the fight,
Are lull'd, and pant upon the silent shore. *Dryden.*

The *wave* behind impels the *wave* before. *Pope.*

Luxuriant on the *wave*-worn bank he lay
Stretch'd forth, and panting in the sunny ray. *Pope.*

2. Unevenness; inequality.

Thus it happens, if the glass of the prisms be free from veins, and their sides be accurately plane and well polished, without those numberless *waves*, or curls, which usually arise from sand-holes a little smoothed in polishing with putty. *Newton.*

To WAVE. *v. n.* [from the noun.]

1. To play loosely; to float.

I may find
Your warlike ensigns *waving* in the wind. *Dryden.*

Messapus' helm
He laces on, and wears the *waving* crest. *Dryden.*

2. To be moved as a ſignal.

A bloody arm it is, that holds a pine
Lighted, above the capitol, and now
It *waves* unto us. *B. Johnſon's Catiline.*

3. To be in an unſettled ſtate; to fluctuate.

They *wave* in and out, no way ſufficiently grounded, no way reſolved, what to think, ſpeak, or write, more than only that becauſe they have taken it upon them, they muſt be oppoſite. *Hooker, b.* v.

If he did not care whether he had their love or no, he *wav'd* indifferently 'twixt doing them neither good nor harm. *Shakeſp. Coriolanus.*

To Wave. *v. a.* [from the noun.]

1. To raiſe into inequalities of ſurface.

He had a thouſand noſes,
Horns welk'd and *wav'd* like the enridged ſea. *Shakeſpeare.*

2. To move looſely.

They *wav'd* their fiery ſwords, and in the air
Made horrid circles. *Milton.*

Æneas *wav'd* his fatal ſword
High o'er his head. *Dryden.*

He beckoned to me, and, by the *waving* of his hand, directed me to approach the place where he ſat. *Addiſon.*

3. To waft; to remove any thing floating.

Some men never conceive how the motion of the earth below ſhould *wave* one from a knock perpendicularly directed from a body in the air above. *Brown's Vulg. Errours.*

4. To beckon; to direct by a waft or motion of any thing.

Look with what courteous action
It *waves* you to a more removed ground:
But do not go with it. *Shakeſpeare.*

5. [*Gueſver*, Fr. *Skinner.*] To put off.

He reſolved not to *wave* his way upon this reaſon, that if he ſhould but once, by ſuch a diverſion, make his enemy believe he were afraid of danger, he ſhould never live without. *Wotton's Life of the Duke of Buckingham.*

Theſe, *waving* plots, found out a better way;
Some god deſcended, and preſerv'd the play. *Dryden.*

6. To put aſide for the preſent.

I have *wav'd* the ſubject of your greatneſs, to reſign myſelf to the contemplation of what is more peculiarly yours. *Dryden.*

Since ſhe her intereſt for the nation's *wav'd*,
Then I who ſav'd the king, the nation ſav'd. *Dryden.*

To Wa'ver. *v. n.* [paꝑian, Saxon.]

1. To play to and fro; to move looſely.

I took two triangular glaſſes, and one of them being kept fixt in the ſame poſture, that the Iris it projected on the floor might not *waver*, I caſt on the ſame floor another Iris, with another priſm, moving it to and fro. *Boyle.*

The whitening ſhower deſcends,
At firſt then *wavering*. *Thomſon's Winter.*

2. To be unſettled; to be uncertain, or inconſtant; to fluctuate; not to be determined.

In which amazement, when the miſcreant
Perceived him to *waver*, weak and frail,
Whilſt trembling horror did his conſcience daunt,
And helliſh anguiſh did his ſoul aſſail. *Fairy Queen.*

Remember where we are;
In France, among a fickle, *wavering* nation. *Shakeſpeare.*

Thou almoſt mak'ſt me *waver* in my faith,
To hold opinion with Pythagoras,
That ſouls of animals infuſe themſelves
Into the trunks of men. *Shakeſpeare.*

Hold faſt the faith without *wavering*. *Heb.* x.

The *wav'ring* faith of people vain and light. *Daniel.*

Faith as abſolutely determines our minds, and as perfectly excludes all *wavering*, as our knowledge itſelf; and we may as well doubt of our own being, as we can, whether any revelation from God be true. *Locke.*

What if Hoſpinian ſhould have ſaid, that Luther *waver'd* in the point of the ſacrament? does it follow that he really did ſo? *Atterbury.*

They, who at this diſtance from the firſt riſe of the goſpel, after weighing the ſeveral evidences of it, *waver* in their faith, would have *waver'd*, though they had ſeen the firſt promulgers work wonders. *Atterbury.*

Wa'verer. *n. ſ.* [from *waver.*] One unſettled and irreſolute.

Come, young *waverer*, come, and go with me;
In one reſpect I'll thy aſſiſtant be. *Shakeſpeare.*

Wa'vy. *adj.* [from *wave.*]

1. Riſing in waves.

For thee the ocean ſmiles, and ſmooths her *wavy* breaſt;
And heav'n itſelf with more ſerene and purer light is bleſt. *Dryden.*

2. Playing to and fro, as in undulations.

Where full-ear'd ſheaves of rye
Grow *wavy* on the tilth, that ſoil ſelect
For apples. *Philips.*

Let her glad vallies ſmile with *wavy* corn;
Let fleecy flocks her riſing hills adorn. *Prior.*

Wawes, or *waes. n. ſ.* A word uſed by *Spenſer*, according to the Saxon pronunciation.

1. For waves.

Another did the dying brands repair
With iron tongs, and ſprinkled oft the ſame
With liquid *waes*. *Fairy Queen.*

2. In the following paſſage it ſeems to be for woes [pa, Saxon.]

Whilſt they fly that gulf's devouring jaws,
They on this rock are rent, and ſunk in helpleſs *wawes*. *Spenſ.*

To Wawl. *v. n.* [pa, *grief*, Saxon.] To cry; to howl.

The firſt time that we ſmell the air,
We *wawle* and cry. *Shakeſpeare's K. Lear.*

WAX. *n. ſ.* [pæxe, Saxon; *wex*, Daniſh; *wacks*, Dutch.]

1. The thick tenacious matter gathered by the bee, and formed into cells for the reception of the honey.

Wax conſiſts of an acid ſpirit, of a nauſeous taſte, and an oil or butter, which is emollient, laxative, and anodyne. *Arb.*

They give us food which may with nectar vie,
And *wax*, that does the abſent ſun ſupply. *Roſcommon.*

All the magiſtrates, every new or full moon, give honour to Confucius with bowings, *wax* candles, and incenſe. *Stillin.*

While viſits ſhall be paid on ſolemn days,
When num'rous *wax* lights in bright order blaze;
So long my honour, name, and praiſe ſhall live. *Pope.*

2. Any tenacious maſs, ſuch as is uſed to faſten letters.

We ſoften the *wax*, before we ſet on the ſeal. *More.*

3. A kind of concretion in the fleſh.

A fontanel in her neck was much inflamed, and many *wax*-kernels about it. *Wiſeman's Surgery.*

To Wax. *v. a.* [from the noun.] To ſmear; to join with wax.

He form'd the reeds, proportion'd as they are;
Unequal in their length, and *wax'd* with care,
They ſtill retain the name of his ungrateful fair. *Dryden.*

To Wax. *v. n.* pret. *wox, waxed*, part. paſſ. *waxed, waxen.* [peaxan, Saxon; *wachſen*, German.]

1. To grow; to increaſe; to become bigger, or more. Uſed of the moon, in oppoſition to *wane*, and figuratively of things which grow by turns bigger and leſs.

The huſbandman in ſowing and ſetting, upon good reaſon, obſerves the *waxing* and waning of the moon. *Hakewill.*

Land and trade are twins, they *wax* and wane together. *Child.*

2. To paſs into any ſtate; to become; to grow. It is in either ſenſe now almoſt diſuſed.

Where things have been inſtituted, which being convenient and good at the firſt, do afterward in proceſs of time *wax* otherwiſe, we make no doubt but they may be altered, yea, though councils or cuſtoms general have received them. *Hooker.*

Careleſs the man ſoon *wox*, and his wit weak
Was overcome of things that did him pleaſe. *Fairy Queen.*

Art thou like the adder *waxen* deaf? *Shakeſpeare.*

We will deſtroy this place; becauſe the cry of them is *waxen* great before the Lord. *Gen.* xix. 13.

Flowers removed *wax* greater, becauſe the nouriſhment is more eaſily come by in the looſe earth. *Bacon.*

This anſwer given, Argantes wild drew near,
Trembling for ire, and *waxing* pale for rage;
Nor could he hold. *Fairfax, b.* ii.

If I *wax* but cold in my deſire,
Think heav'n hath motion loſt, and the world fire. *Donne.*

Their manners *wax* more and more corrupt, in proportion as their bleſſings abound. *Atterbury.*

Wa'xen. *n. ſ.* [from *wax.*] Made of wax.

Swarming next appear'd
The female bee, that feeds her huſband drone
Delicioully, and builds her *waxen* cells
With honey ſtor'd. *Milton's Paradiſe Loſt, b.* vii.

I can yet ſhoot beams, whoſe heat can melt
The *waxen* wings of this ambitious boy. *Denham.*

So weary bees in little cells repoſe;
But if night-robbers lift the well-ſtor'd hive,
An humming through their *waxen* city grows,
And out upon each other's wings they drive. *Dryden.*

Others with ſweets the *waxen* cells diſtend. *Gay.*

Way. *n. ſ.* [pœᵹ, Saxon; *weigh*, Dutch.]

1. The road in which one travels.

I am amaz'd, and loſe my *way*,
Among the thorns and dangers of this world. *Shakeſpeare.*

You cannot ſee your *way*.—
—I have no *way*, and therefore want no eyes:
I ſtumbled when I ſaw. *Shakeſp. K. Lear.*

To God's eternal houſe direct the *way*,
A broad and ample road. *Milton.*

Flutt'ring the god, and weeping ſaid,
Pity poor Cupid, generous maid!
Who happen'd, being blind, to ſtray,
And on thy boſom loſt his *way*. *Prior.*

2. Broad road made for paſſengers.

Know'ſt thou the *way* to Dover?—
—Both ſtile and gate, horſe-*way*, and foot-path. *Shakeſp.*

3. A length of journey.

An old man that had travelled a great *way* under a huge burden, found himſelf ſo weary, that he called upon death to deliver him. *L'Eſtrange.*

4. Courſe

4. Course; direction of motion.

I now go toward him, therefore follow me,
And mark what *way* I make. *Shakesp. Winter Tale.*

He stood in the gate, and ask'd of ev'ry one,
Which *way* she took, and whither she was gone. *Dryden.*

Attending long in vain, I took the *way*,
Which through a path, but scarcely printed, lay *Dryden.*

With downward force he took his *way*,
And roll'd his yellow billows to the sea. *Dryden.*

My seven brave brothers, in one fatal day,
To death's dark mansions took the mournful *way*. *Dryden.*

To observe every the least difference that is in things, keeps the understanding steady and right in its *way* to knowledge. *Locke.*

5. Advance in life.

The boy was to know his father's circumstances, and that he was to make his *way* by his own industry. *Spectator*, N° 123.

6. Passage; power of progression made or given.

Back do I toss these treasons to thy head:
This sword of mine shall give them instant *way*,
Where they shall rest for ever. *Shakesp. K. Lear.*

Th' angelick choirs,
On each hand parting, to his speed gave *way*,
Through all th' empyreal road. *Milton's Par. Lost*, *b.* v.

Youth and vain confidence thy life betray:
Through armies this has made Melantius' *way*. *Waller.*

The reason may be, that men seldom come into those posts, till after forty; about which time the natural heat beginning to decay, makes *way* for those distempers. *Temple.*

The air could not readily get out of those prisons, but by degrees, as the earth and water above would give *way*. *Burnet.*

As a soldier, foremost in the fight,
Makes *way* for others. *Dryden.*

Some make themselves *way*, and are suggested to the mind by all the ways of sensation and reflection. *Locke.*

7. Vacancy made by timorous or respectful recession.

There would be left no difference between truth and falsehood, if what we certainly know, give *way* to what we may possibly be mistaken in. *Locke.*

Nor was he satisfy'd, unless he made the pure profession of the gospel give *way* to superstition and idolatry, wherever he had power to expel the one, and establish the other. *Atterbury.*

I would give *way* to others, who might argue very well upon the same subject. *Swift.*

8. Local tendency.

Come a little nearer this *way*,
I warrant thee no body hears. *Shakesp. Mer. Wives of Wind.*

9. Course; regular progression.

But give me leave to seize my destin'd prey,
And let eternal justice take the *way*. *Dryden.*

10. Situation where a thing may probably be found.

These inquisitions are never without baseness, and very often useless to the curious inquirer. For men stand upon their guards against them, laying all their counsels and secrets out of their *way*. *Taylor's Rule of Living Holy.*

11. A situation or course obstructive and obviating.

The imagination being naturally tumultuous, interposeth itself without asking leave, casting thoughts in our *way*, and forcing the understanding to reflect upon them. *Duppa.*

12. Tendency to any meaning, or act.

There is nothing in the words that sounds that *way*, or points particularly at persecution. *Atterbury.*

13. Access; means of admittance.

Being once at liberty, 'twas said, having made my *way* with some foreign prince, I would turn pirate. *Raleigh.*

14. Sphere of observation.

The general officers, and the publick ministers that fell in my *way*, were generally subject to the gout. *Temple.*

15. Means; mediate instrument; intermediate step.

By noble *ways* we conquest will prepare;
First offer peace, and that refus'd, make war. *Dryden.*

What conceivable *ways* are there, whereby we should come to be assured that there is such a being as God? *Tillotson.*

A child his mother so well instructed this *way* in geography, that he knew the limits of the four parts of the world. *Locke.*

It is not impossible to God to make a creature with more *ways* to convey into the understanding the notice of corporeal things, than those five he has given to man. *Locke.*

16. Method; scheme of management.

He durst not take open *way* against them, and as hard it was to take a secret, they being so continually followed by the best, and every way ablest of that region. *Sidney*, *b.* ii.

Will not my yielded crown redeem my breath?
Still am I fear'd? is there no *way* but death? *Daniel.*

As by calling evil good, a man is misrepresented to himself in the *way* of flattery; so by calling good evil, he is misrepresented to others, in the *way* of slander. *South's Sermons.*

Now what impious *ways* my wishes took?
How they the monarch, and the man forsook? *Prior.*

The senate, forced to yield to the tribunes of the people, thought it their wisest course to give *way* also to the time. *Swift.*

17. Private determination.

He was of an high mind, and loved his own will and his *way*, as one that revered himself, and would reign indeed. *Bacon.*

If I had my *way*,
He had mew'd in flames at home, not i' th' senate;
I had sing'd his furs by this time. *B. Johnson's Catiline.*

18. Manner; mode.

She with a calm carelessness let every thing slide, as we do by their speeches, who neither in matter nor person do any *way* belong unto us. *Sidney.*

God hath so many times and *ways* spoken to men. *Hooker.*

Few writers make an extraordinary figure, who have not something in their *way* of thinking or expressing, that is entirely their own. *Spectator*, N° 160.

His *way* of expressing and applying them, not his invention of them, is what we admire. *Addison.*

19. Method; manner of practice.

Having lost the *way* of nobleness, he strove to climb to the height of terribleness. *Sidney.*

Matter of mirth,
She could devise, and thousand *ways* invent,
To feed her foolish humour, and vain jolliment. *Spenser.*

Taught
To live th' easiest *way*, not with perplexing thoughts. *Milton.*

20. Method or plan of life, conduct, or action.

A physician, unacquainted with your body, may put you in a *way* for a present cure, but overthroweth your health in some other kind. *Bacon.*

To attain
The height and depth of thy eternal *ways*,
All human thought comes short. *Milton.*

When a man sees the prodigious expence our forefathers have been at in these barbarous buildings, one cannot but fancy what miracles they would have left us, had they only been instructed in the right *way*. *Addison on Italy.*

21. Right method to act or know.

We are quite out of the *way*, when we think that things contain within themselves the qualities that appear to us in them. *Lo.*

They are more in danger to go out of the *way*, who are marching under the conduct of a guide that will mislead them, than he that has not yet taken a step, and is likelier to enquire after the right *way*. *Locke.*

By me, they offer all that you can ask,
And point an easy *way* to happiness. *Rowe.*

22. General scheme of acting.

Men who go out of the *way* to hint free things, must be guilty of absurdity, or rudeness. *Clarissa.*

23. *By the way.* Without any necessary connection with the main design; *en passant.*

Note, *by the way*, that unity of continuance is easier to procure, than unity of species. *Bacon's Nat. Hist.*

Will. Honeycomb, now on the verge of threescore, asked me, in his most serious look, whether I would advise him to marry lady Betty Single, who, *by the way*, is one of the greatest fortunes about town. *Spectator*, N° 475.

24. *To go* or *come one's way*, *or ways*; to come along, or depart. A familiar phrase.

Nay, *come your ways*;
This is his majesty, say your mind to him. *Shakespeare.*

To a boy fast asleep upon the brink of a river, fortune came and wak'd him; prithee get up, and *go thy ways*, thou'lt tumble in and be drown'd else. *L'Estrange.*

25. *Way* and *ways*, are now often used corruptly for *wise*.

But if he shall any *ways* make them void after he hath heard them, then he shall bear her iniquity. *Numb.* xxx. 15.

They erect conclusions no *way* inferible from their premises. *Brown's Vulgar Errours.*

Being sent to reduce Paros, he mistook a great fire at a distance for the fleet, and being no *ways* a match for them, set sail for Athens. *Swift.*

'Tis no *way* the interest even of priesthood. *Pope.*

Waybread. *n. s.* A plant. *Ainsw.*

Wayfa'rer. *n. s.* [*way* and *fare*, to go.] Passenger; traveller.

Howsoever, many *wayfarers* make themselves glee, by putting the inhabitants in mind of this privilege; who again, especially the women, forslow not to bain them. *Carew.*

Wayfaring. *adj.* Travelling; passing; being on a journey.

They to whom all this is revealed, if they will not be directed into a path so plained and smoothed, that the *wayfaring* men, though fools, shall not err therein, must needs acknowledge themselves in the number of the blind, that will not enter into God's rest. *Hammond's Fundamentals.*

Way'faringtree. *n. s.* [*viburnum*, Lat.] A plant.

The flower consists of one leaf, which is divided into five parts, and expands in a circular order; these are collected into the form of an umbrella: the ovary, which is placed on the upper part of the flower, becomes a soft berry, full of juice, which contains one stony compressed furrowed seed. *Miller.*

To Wayla'y. *v. a.* [*way* and *lay.*] To watch insidiously in the way; to beset by ambush.

I will

I will *waylay* thee going home, where if it be thy chance to kill me,—thou kill'ſt me like a rogue and a villain. *Shakeſp.*

The employment of money is chiefly merchandizing or purchaſing; and uſury *waylays* both: it dulls and damps all induſtries. *Bacon.*

How thou lurk'ſt
In valley or green meadow to *waylay*
Some beauty rare. *Milton's Paradiſe Regained.*

Now on their coaſts our conquering navy rides,
Waylays their merchants, and their land beſets,
Each day new wealth without their care provides,
They lay aſleep with prizes in their nets. *Dryden.*

Like hunted caſtors, conſcious of their ſtore,
Their *waylaid* wealth to Norway's coaſts they bring. *Dryd.*

WAYLA'YER. *n. ſ.* [from *waylay.*] One who waits in ambuſh for another.

WAY'LESS. *adj.* [from *way.*] Pathleſs; untracked.

When on upon my *wayleſs* walk,
As my deſires me draw,
I, like a madman fell to talk
With every thing I ſaw. *Drayton's Queen of Cynthia.*

WAY'MARK. *n. ſ.* [*way* and *mark.*] Mark to guide in travelling.

Set thee up *waymarks*, make thee high heaps. *Jer.* xxxi. 21.

To WAY'MENT. *v. a.* [ʒa, Saxon.] To lament, or grieve. Obſolete.

What boots it to weep and to *wayment*,
When ill is chanc'd, but doth the ill increaſe,
And the weak mind with double woe torment. *Fairy Queen.*

WAY'WARD. *adj.* ꝥa woe, and ꝥeaꞃꝺ, Saxon.] Froward; peeviſh; moroſe; vexatious.

That night the elder it was, the more *wayward* it ſhewed itſelf towards them. *Sidney.*

How *wayward* is this fooliſh love,
That, like a teſty babe, will ſcratch the nurſe,
And preſently all humbled, kiſs the rod. *Shakeſpeare.*

Wayward beauty doth not fancy move,
A frown forbids, a ſmile engendreth love. *Fairfax.*

To miſchief bent,
He ſeldom does a good with good intent;
Wayward, but wiſe; by long experience taught
To pleaſe both parties, for ill ends he ſought. *Dryden.*

WAY'WARDLY. *adv.* [from *wayward.*] Frowardly; perverſely.

Waywardly proud; and therefore bold: becauſe extremely faulty. *Sidney.*

Howſoever, ſome will ſtill be *waywardly* diſpoſed; yet if ſuch as be in authority will do their duties, they may by convenient diſcipline be kept within the bounds of modeſty, or elſe removed. *Whitegifte.*

WAY'WARDNESS. *n. ſ.* [from *wayward.*] Frowardneſs; perverſeneſs.

Such the behaviour of ladies, as builded their chaſtity not upon *waywardneſs*, but choice of worthineſs. *Sidney.*

The beſt of his time hath been but raſh; then muſt we look from his age to receive not alone the imperfections of long engrafted condition; but the unruly *waywardneſs* that infirm and cholerick years bring. *Shakeſpeare.*

A child will have as much wit as he hath *waywardneſs*. *Wotton on Education.*

WE. *pronoun.* [See I.]

1. The plural of *I.*

Retire *we* to our chamber,
A little water clears us of this deed. *Shakeſpeare.*

Fair and noble hoſteſs,
We are your gueſts to night. *Shakeſpeare's Macbeth.*

Notwithſtanding animals had nothing like the uſe of reaſon, *we* find in them all the lower parts of our nature, in the greateſt ſtrength. *Addiſon.*

2. Improperly and ungrammatically for the oblique caſe, *us.*

To poor *we*,
Thine enmity's moſt capital. *Shakeſpeare.*

WEAK. *adj.* [ꝥæc, Saxon; *week*, Dutch.]

1. Feeble; not ſtrong.

He is weary and *weak* handed. 2 *Sam.* xvii. 2.

Here only *weak*,
Againſt the charm of beauty's powerful glance. *Milton.*

Wer't thou not *weak* with hunger, mad with love,
My hand ſhould force thee. *Dryden.*

Fame and reputation are *weak* ties: many have not the leaſt ſenſe of them: powerful men are only awed by them as they conduce to their intereſt. *Dryden.*

Children, being by the courſe of nature born *weak*, and unable to provide for themſelves, they have, by the appointment of God, a right to be maintained by their parents. *Locke.*

2. Infirm; not healthy.

Here I ſtand your brave,
A poor, infirm, *weak*, and deſpis'd old man. *Shakeſpeare.*

3. Soft; pliant; not ſtiff.

4. Low of ſound.

A voice not ſoft, *weak*, piping and womaniſh; but audible, ſtrong and manlike. *Aſcham.*

5. Feeble of mind; wanting ſpirit; wanting diſcernment.

As the caſe ſtands with this preſent age, full of tongue and *weak* of brain, we yield to the ſtream thereof. *Hooker.*

This murder'd prince, though *weak* he was,
He was not ill, nor yet ſo *weak*, but that
He ſhew'd much martial valour in his place. *Daniel.*

She firſt his *weak* indulgence will accuſe. *Milton.*

That Portugal hath yet no more than a ſuſpenſion of arms, they may thank the Whigs, whoſe falſe repreſentations they were ſo *weak* to believe. *Swift.*

6. Not much impregnated with any ingredient: as a *weak* tincture, *weak* beer.

7. Not powerful; not potent.

I muſt make fair weather yet a while,
Till Henry be more *weak* and I more ſtrong. *Shakeſpeare.*

The *weak*, by thinking themſelves ſtrong, are induced to venture and proclaim war againſt that which ruins them; and the ſtrong, by conceiting themſelves *weak*, are thereby rendered unactive and uſeleſs. *South's Sermons.*

If the poor found the rich diſpoſed to ſupply their wants, or if the *weak* might always find protection from the mighty, they could none of them lament their own condition. *Swift.*

8. Not well ſupported by argument.

A caſe ſo *weak* and feeble hath been much perſiſted in. *Hook.*

9. Unfortified.

To quell the tyrant love, and guard thy heart
On this *weak* ſide, where moſt our nature fails,
Would be a conqueſt worthy Cato's ſon. *Addiſon's Cato.*

To WEA'KEN. *v. a.* To debilitate; to enfeeble; to deprive of ſtrength.

The firſt which *weakened* them was their ſecurity. *Hooker.*

Their hands ſhall be *weakened* from the work that it be not done. *Neh.* vi. 9.

Inteſtine broils,
Weakening the ſcepter of old night. *Milton.*

Every violence offered to the body *weakens* and impairs it, and renders it leſs durable. *Ray on the Creation.*

Let us not *weaken* ſtill the weaker ſide
By our diviſions. *Addiſon's Cato.*

Solemn impreſſions that ſeem to *weaken* the mind, may, by proper reflection, be made to ſtrengthen it. *Clariſſa.*

WEA'KLING. *n. ſ.* [from *weak.*] A feeble creature.

Thou art no Atlas for ſo great a weight;
And, *weakling*, Warwick takes his gift again,
And Henry is my king, Warwick his ſubject. *Shakeſpeare.*

Æſop begged his companions not to overcharge him; they found him a *weakling*, and bade him pleaſe himſelf. *L'Eſtrange.*

WEA'KLY. *adv.* [from *weak.*]

1. Feebly; with want of ſtrength.

The motion of gravity worketh *weakly*, both far from the earth, and alſo within the earth. *Bacon.*

Was plighted faith ſo *weakly* ſeal'd above,
That for one error, I muſt loſe your love? *Dryden.*

2. Indiſcreetly; injudiciouſly; timorouſly; with feebleneſs of mind.

This high gift of ſtrength committed to me,
Under the ſeal of ſilence could not keep,
But *weakly* to a woman muſt reveal it. *Milton.*

Tancred, I neither am diſpos'd to make
Requeſt for life, nor offer'd life to take:
Much leſs deny the deed; but leaſt of all
Beneath pretended juſtice *weakly* fall. *Dryden's Fables.*

WEA'KLY. *adj.* [from *weak.*] Not ſtrong; not healthy.

Being old and *weakly*, twenty years in priſon, it was ten to one that ever I ſhould have returned. *Raleigh.*

WEA'KNESS. *n. ſ.* [from *weak.*]

1. Want of ſtrength; want of force; feebleneſs.

Troy in our *weakneſs* lives, not in her ſtrength. *Shakeſp.*

Argument
Of human *weakneſs* rather than of ſtrength. *Milton.*

The General's force, as kept alive by fight,
Now, not oppos'd, no longer can purſue:
Laſting till heav'n had done his courage right,
When he had conquer'd, he his *weakneſs* knew. *Dryden.*

New graces yearly like thy works diſplay,
Soft without *weakneſs*, without glaring gay. *Pope.*

By ſuch a review we ſhall diſcern and ſtrengthen our *weakneſſes* with good reſolution, and ſo order our future converſation as may render us leaſt expoſed to falling. *Rogers's Sermons.*

2. Infirmity; unhealthineſs.

Perſons in thoſe poſts derive a *weakneſs* of conſtitution from the eaſe and luxury of their anceſtors, and the delicacy of their own education. *Temple.*

3. Want of cogency.

She ſeems to be conſcious of the *weakneſs* of thoſe teſtimonies. *Tillotſon.*

4. Want of judgment; want of reſolution; fooliſhneſs of mind.

Weakneſs is thy excuſe,
And I believe it; *weakneſs* to reſiſt
Philiſtian gold: if *weakneſs* may excuſe,
What murderer, what traitor, parricide,
Inceſtuous, ſacrilegious, but may plead it?
All wickedneſs is *weakneſs*. *Milton.*

5. Defect;

5. Defect; failing.

If you will work on any man, you must know his nature, and so lead him; or his *weaknesses* and disadvantages, and so awe him. *Bacon.*

Many find a pleasure in contradicting the common reports of fame, and in spreading abroad the *weaknesses* of an exalted character. *Addison's Spectator.*

WEA'KSIDE. *n. s.* [*weak* and *side.*] Foible; deficience; infirmity.

This dog would have fought for his master in any other case; but the love of mutton was his *weakside.* *L'Estrange.*

Their application to trade has increased their shipping, which they found to be their *weakside* in their last attempts. *Temple.*

WEAL. *n. s.* [pelan, Saxon; *wealust*, Dutch.]

1. Happiness; prosperity; flourishing state.

Our *weal* on you depending,
Counts it your *weal*, that he have liberty. *Shakespeare.*

As we love the *weal* of our souls and bodies, let us so behave ourselves as we may be at peace with God. *Bacon.*

Thine, and of all thy sons,
The *weal* or woe in thee is plac'd; beware! *Milton.*

Ireland ought to be considered, not only in its own interest, but likewise in relation to England, upon whose *weal* in the main, that of this kingdom depends. *Temple.*

2. Republick; state; publick interest.

Blood hath been shed
Ere human statute purg'd the gen'ral *weal.* *Shakespeare.*

How shall the muse, from such a monarch steal
An hour, and not defraud the publick *weal.* *Pope.*

WEAL. *n. s.* [palan, Saxon.] The mark of a stripe.

Like warts or *weals* it hangs upon her skin. *Donne.*

WEAL *away. interj.* Alas. Obsolete. *Spenser.*

WEALD, *Wald, Walt.* Whether singly or jointly signify a wood or grove, from the Saxon peald. *Gibson.*

WEALTH. *n. s.* [paleð, rich, Saxon.] Riches; money, or precious goods.

In desart hast thine habitance,
And these rich heaps of *wealth* doth hide apart
From the world's eye and from her right usance. *Fa. Queen.*

I should forge
Quarrels unjust against the good and loyal,
Destroying them for *wealth.* *Shakespeare's Macbeth.*

I wish thee, Vin, above all *wealth*,
Both bodily and ghostly health:
Not too much wit or *wealth* come to thee;
For much of either may undo thee. *Bishop Corbet.*

Each day new *wealth* without their care provides,
They lie asleep with prizes in their nets. *Dryden.*

WEA'LTHILY. *adv.* [from *wealthy.*] Richly.

I come to wive it *wealthily* in Padua,
If *wealthily*, then happily in Padua. *Shakespeare.*

WEA'LTHINESS. *n. s.* [from *wealthy.*] Richness.

WEA'LTHY. *adj.* [from *wealth.*] Rich; opulent; abundant.

If a gentleman, or any *wealthy* yeoman, have any children, the eldest shall be kept in some order, but all the rest shall shift and fall to this occupation of stealing. *Spenser.*

I will be married to a *wealthy* widow,
Ere three days pass. *Shakesp. Taming of the Shrew.*

My speculations, when sold single, like cherries upon the stick, are delights for the rich and *wealthy*; after some time they come to market in great quantities, and are every ordinary man's money. *Addison's Spectator.*

Not Neptune's self from all his floods receives
A *wealthier* tribute than to thine he gives. *Pope.*

To WEAN. *v. a.* [penan, Saxon.]

1. To put from the breast; to ablactate.

She was *weaned* when it did taste the wormwood on the nipple; pretty fool to see it fall out with the dug. *Shakespeare.*

I have behaved as a child that is *weaned* of his mother. *Ps.*

In *weaning* young creatures, the best way is never to let them suck the paps at all; for then they will drink up milk without any difficulty. *Ray on the Creation.*

A fortnight before you *wean* calves from milk, let water be mixed with it. *Mortimer's Husbandry.*

2. To withdraw from any habit or desire.

Here the place whose pleasant sight,
From other shades have *wean'd* my wand'ring mind;
Tell me what wants me here. *Spenser.*

I the rather *wean* me from despair,
For love of Edward's offspring in my womb. *Shakespeare.*

Seriously reflect on the happy state he shall most certainly arrive to, if he but *wean* himself from these worldly impediments here that clog his soul's flight. *Digby.*

Children newly *weaned* from their parents, put out their hands towards them in their dreams, as if they were still present. *Stillingfleet.*

There the coarse cake, and homely husks of beans,
From pamp'ring riot the young stomach *weans.* *Dryden.*

They were intended by the Author of our being, to *wean* us gradually from our fondness of life, the nearer we approach to the end of it. *Swift.*

WEA'NEL. } *n. s.* [from *wean.*]
WEA'NLING. }

1. An animal newly weaned.

Though when as Lowder was far away,
This wolfish sheep would catchen his prey;
A lamb, or a kid, or a *weanel* wast,
With that to the wood would he speed haste. *Spenser.*

To gorge the flesh of lambs and *weanling* kids,
On hills where flocks are fed, flies tow'rd the springs
Of Ganges or Hydaspes. *Milton's Parad. Lost.*

2. A child newly weaned.

WEA'PON. *n. s.* [peapon, Saxon.] Instrument of offence; something with which one is armed to hurt another.

The giant
Down let fall his arm, and soft withdrew
His *weapon* huge, that heaved was on high,
For to have slain the man that on the ground did ly. *Fa. Q.*

The cry of Talbot serves me for a sword;
For I have loaden me with many spoils,
Using no other *weapon* but his name. *Shakesp. Henry VI.*

Take this *weapon*
Which I have here recover'd from the Moor. *Shakes. Othello.*

Touch me with noble anger;
O let not womens *weapons*, water drops,
Stain my man's cheeks. *Shakespeare's King Lear.*

His foes, who came to bring him death,
Bring him a *weapon* that before had none. *Daniel.*

With his full force he whirl'd it first around,
Imperial Juno turn'd the course before;
And fix'd the wand'ring *weapon* in the door. *Dryden's Æn.*

WEA'PONED. *adj.* [from *weapon.*] Armed for offence; furnished with arms.

In what sort, so ill *weaponed*, could you atchieve this enterprize? *Sidney.*

Both the combatants entered, apparelled only in their doublets and hoses, and *weaponed* with sword, buckler, and dagger. *Hayward.*

WEA'PONLESS. *adj.* [from *weapon.*] Having no weapon; unarmed.

Ran on embattl'd armies, clad in iron,
And *weaponless* himself,
Made arms ridiculous, useless the forgery
Of brazen shield and spear, the hammer'd cuirass,
Chalybean temper'd steel, and frock of mail,
Adamantean proof. *Milton.*

WEA'PONSALVE. *n. s.* [*weapon* and *salve.*] A salve which was supposed to cure the wound, being applied to the weapon that made it.

That the sympathetick powder and the *weaponsalve* constantly perform what is promised of them, I leave others to believe. *Boyle.*

To WEAR. *v. a.* Preterite *wore*, participle *worn.* [penan, Sax.

1. To waste with use or time.

O wicked world! one that is well nigh *worn* to pieces with age, to show himself a young gallant. *Shakespeare.*

Protogenes could lay his colours so artificially, that one being *worn* off, a fresh should succeed to the number of five. *Peacham.*

Waters *wear* the stones. *Job* xiv. 19.

An hasty word, or an indiscreet action does not presently dissolve the bond, but that friendship may be still found at heart; and so outgrow and *wear* off these little distempers. *South's Sermons.*

They have had all advantages to the making them wise unto salvation, yet suffer their manhood to *wear* out and obliterate all those rudiments of their youth. *Decay of Piety.*

'Tis time must *wear* it off; but I must go. *Dryden.*

No differences of age, tempers, or education can *wear* it out, and set any considerable number of men free from it. *Tillotson's Sermons.*

Theodosius exerted himself to animate his penitent in the course of life she was entering upon, and *wear* out of her mind groundless fears. *Addison's Spectator.*

2. To consume tediously.

What masks, what dances,
To *wear* away this long age of three hours. *Shakespeare.*

In most places, their toil is so extreme as they cannot endure it above four hours; the residue they *wear* out at coites and kayles. *Carew's Survey of Cornwall.*

Wisest and best men full oft beguil'd,
With goodness principl'd, not to reject
The penitent, but ever to forgive,
Are drawn to *wear* out miserable days. *Milton.*

To his name inscrib'd, their tears they pay,
Till years and kisses *wear* his name away. *Dryden.*

Kings titles commonly begin by force,
Which time *wears* off and mellows into right. *Dryden.*

3. To carry appendant to the body.

This pale and angry rose
Will I for ever *wear.* *Shakespeare's Henry VI.*

Why

Why art thou angry?—
That such a slave as this should *wear* a sword,
Who *wears* not honesty. *Shakespeare's King Lear.*
What is this
That *wears* upon his baby brow the round
And top of sovereignty. *Shakespeare's Macbeth.*
I am the first-born son of him, that last
Wore the imperial diadem of Rome. *Shakespeare.*

Their adorning, let it not be that outward adorning of plaiting the hair, and of *wearing* of gold. 1 *Pet.* iii. 3.

Eas'd the putting off
These troublesome disguises which we *wear*. *Milton.*
He ask'd what arms the swarthy Memnon *wore*;
What troops he landed. *Dryden's Virg. Æneid.*

This is unconscionable dealing, to be made a slave, and not know whose livery I *wear*. *Dryden's Spanish Friar.*

On her white breast a sparkling cross she *wore*. *Pope.*

4. To exhibit in appearance.

Such an infectious face her sorrow *wears*,
I can bear death, but not Cydaria's tears. *Dryden.*

5. To affect by degrees.

Trials *wear* us into a liking of what possibly, in the first essay, displeased us. *Locke.*

A man who has any relish for true writing, from the masterly strokes of a great author every time he peruses him, *wears* himself into the same manner. *Addison's Spectator.*

6. *To* WEAR *out*. To harrass.

He shall *wear out* the saints. *Dan.* vii. 25.

7. *To* WEAR *out*. To waste or destroy by use.

This very rev'rent letcher, quite *worn out*
With rheumatisms, and crippled with his gout. *Dryden.*

To WEAR. *v. n.*

1. To be wasted with use or time.

Thou wilt surely *wear* away. *Exod.* xviii. 18.

In those who have lost their sight when young, in whom the ideas of colours having been but slightly taken notice of, and ceasing to be repeated, do quite *wear* out. *Locke.*

2. To be tediously spent.

Thus *wore* out night, and now the herald lark
Left his ground-nest, high tow'ring to descry
The Morn's approach, and greet her with his song. *Milton.*

3. To pass by degrees.

If passion causes a present terror, yet it soon *wears* off; and inclination will easily learn to slight such scarecrows. *Locke.*

The difficulty will every day grow less and *wear* off, and obedience become easy and familiar. *Rogers's Sermons.*

WEAR. *n. s.* [from the verb.]

1. The act of wearing; the thing worn.

It was th' inchantment of her riches
That made m' apply t' your crony witches;
That in return would pay th' expence,
The *wear* and tear of conscience. *Hudibras.*

2. [pær, Saxon, a fen; *wâr*, German, a mound.] A dam to shut up and raise the water; often written *weir* or *wier*.

They will force themselves through flood gates, or over *wears*, hedges or stops in the water. *Walton's Angler.*

WEARD. *n. s. Weard*, whether initial or final, signifies watchfulness or care, from the Saxon peaрban, to ward or keep. *Gib.*

WEA'RER. *n. s.* [from *wear*.] One who has any thing appendant to his person.

The celestial habits, and the reverence
Of the grave *wearers*. *Shakespeare's Winter's Tale.*
Were I the *wearer* of Antonio's beard,
I would not shave't to-day. *Shakesp. Ant. and Cleopatra.*
Cowls, hoods and habits with their *wearers* tost,
And flutter'd into rags. *Milton.*

Armour bears off insults, and preserves the *wearer* in the day of battle; but the danger once repelled, it is laid aside, as being too rough for civil conversation. *Dryden.*

We ought to leave room for the humour of the artist or *wearer*. *Addison on Italy.*

WEA'RING. *n. s.* [from *wear*.] Cloaths.

It was his bidding;
Give me my nightly *wearing* and adieu. *Shakespeare.*

WEA'RINESS. *n. s.* [from *weary*.]

1. Lassitude; state of being spent with labour.

Come, our stomachs
Will make what's homely savoury; *weariness*
Can snore upon the flint, when resty sloth
Finds the down pillow hard. *Shakesp. Cymbeline.*

Water-fowls supply the *weariness* of a long flight by taking water. *Hale.*

Heaven, when the creature lies prostrate in the weakness of sleep and *weariness*, spreads the covering of night and darkness to conceal it. *South's Sermons.*

To full bowls each other they provoke;
At length, with *weariness* and wine oppress'd,
They rise from table, and withdraw to rest. *Dryden.*

2. Fatigue; cause of lassitude.

The more remained out of the *weariness* and fatigue of their late marches. *Clarendon.*

3. Impatience of any thing.

4. Tediousness.

WEA'RISH. *adj.* [I believe from pæр, Saxon, a quagmire.] Boggy; watery.

A garment over-rich and wide for many of their *wearish* and ill disposed bodies. *Carew's Survey of Cornwall.*

WEA'RISOME. *adj.* [from *weary*.] Troublesome; tedious; causing weariness.

The soul preferreth rest in ignorance before *wearisome* labour to know. *Hooker.*

These high wild hills, and rough uneven ways
Draw out our miles, and make them *wearisome*. *Shakesp.*

Troops came to the army the day before, harassed with a long and *wearisome* march. *Bacon.*

Costly I reckon not them alone which charge the purse, but which are *wearisome* and importune in suits. *Bacon.*

Shrinking up, or stretching out are *wearisome* positions, and such as perturb the quiet of those parts. *Brown.*

This must be our task
In heav'n, this our delight; how *wearisome*
Eternity so spent, in worship paid
To whom we hate. *Milton's Paradise Lost.*
Satiety from all things else doth come,
Then life must to itself grow *wearisome*. *Denham.*

WEA'RISOMELY. *adv.* [from *wearisome*.] Tediously; so as to cause weariness.

As of Nimrod, so are the opinions of writers different touching Assur, and the beginning of that great state of Assyria; a controversy *wearisomely* disputed without any direct proof or certainty. *Raleigh.*

WEA'RISOMENESS. *n. s.* [from *wearisome*.]

1. The quality of tiring.

2. The state of being easily tired.

A wit, quick without lightness, sharp without brittleness, desirous of good things without newfangleness, diligent in painful things without *wearisomeness*. *Ascham's Schoolmaster.*

To WEARY. *v. a.* [from the adjective.]

1. To tire; to fatigue; to harrass; to subdue by labour.

Better that the enemy seek us;
So shall he waste his means, *weary* his soldiers,
Doing himself offence. *Shakespeare's Julius Cæsar.*

The people labour in the very fire, *weary* themselves for very vanity. *Hab.* ii. 13.

Dewy sleep oppress'd them *weary'd*. *Milton.*
Sea would be pools without the brushing air,
To curl the waves; and sure some little care
Should *weary* nature so, to make her want repose. *Dryden.*
You have already *weary'd* fortune so,
She cannot farther be your friend or foe,
But sits all breathless. *Dryden.*

It would not be difficult to continue a paper by resuming the same subjects, and *wearying* out the reader with the same thoughts in a different phrase. *Addison's Freeholder.*

2. To make impatient of continuance.

I stay too long by thee, I *weary* thee. *Shakesp. Henry* V.

Should the government be *wearied* out of its present patience, what is to be expected by such turbulent men? *Addis.*

3. To subdue or harrass by any thing irksome.

Must'ring all her wiles,
With blandish'd parleys, feminine assaults,
Tongue-batteries; she surceas'd not day nor night
To storm me over-watch'd and *weary'd* out. *Milton.*

WEARY. *adj.* [pepiᵹ, Saxon; *waeren*, to be tired, Dutch]

1. Subdued by fatigue; tired with labour.

Fair Phœbus 'gan decline, in haste,
His *weary* waggon to the western vale. *Spenser.*
Gentle Warwick,
Let me embrace thee in my *weary* arms,
I, that did never weep, now melt with woe. *Shakespeare.*
I am *weary*, yea, my memory is tir'd:
Have we no wine here? *Shakespeare.*
An old man broken with the storms of state,
Is come to lay his *weary* bones among ye:
Give him a little earth for charity. *Shakespeare.*

Let us not be *weary* in well-doing. *Gal.* vi. 9.

Our swords so wholly did the fates employ,
That they at length grew *weary* to destroy;
Refus'd the work we brought, and out of breath,
Made sorrow and despair attend for death. *Dryden.*

2. Impatient of the continuance of any thing painful or irksome.

The king was as *weary* of Scotland, as he had been impatient to go thither, finding all things proposed to him without consideration of his honour or interest. *Clarendon.*

My hopes all flat, nature within me seems,
In all her functions, *weary* of herself. *Milton.*

3. Desirous to discontinue.

See the revolution of the times,
Make mountains level, and the continent
Weary of solid firmness, melt itself
Into the seas. *Shakespeare's Henry* IV.

4. Weary;

4. Cauſing wearineſs; tireſome.

Their gates to all were open evermore
That by the *weary* way were travelling,
And one ſat waiting ever them before
To call in comers by that needy were and poor. *Fa. Queen.*

The *wearieſt* and moſt lothed life
That age, ach, penury, impriſonment,
Can lay on nature, is a paradiſe
To what we fear of death. *Shakeſpeare.*

Put on what *weary* negligence you pleaſe,
You and your fellows; I'd have it come to queſtion. *Shak.*

WEA'SEL. *n. ſ.* [peſel, Saxon; *weſel*, Dutch; *muſtela*, Latin.] A ſmall animal that eats corn and kills mice.

Ready in gybes, quick-anſwer'd, ſaucy, and
As quarrelſome as the *weaſel*. *Shakeſpeare's Cymbeline.*

A *weaſel* once made ſhift to ſlink
In at a corn loft through a chink. *Pope.*

WE'SAND. *n. ſ.* [paſen, Saxon. This word is is very variouſly written; but this orthography is neareſt to the original word.] The windpipe; the paſſage through which the breath is drawn and emitted.

Marry Diggon, what ſhould him affray,
To take his own where-ever it lay;
For had his *weaſand* been a little wider,
He would have devoured both hidder and ſhidder. *Spenſer.*

Cut his *wezand* with thy knife. *Shakeſpeare's Tempeſt.*

Matter to be diſcharged by expectoration muſt firſt paſs into the lungs, then into the aſpera arteria, or *weaſand*, and from thence be coughed up and ſpit out by the mouth. *Wiſem.*

The ſhaft that ſlightly was impreſs'd,
Now from his heavy fall with weight encreas'd,
Drove through his neck aſlant; he ſpurns the ground,
And the ſoul iſſues through the *weazon*'s wound. *Dryden.*

The unerring ſteel deſcended while he ſpoke,
Pierc'd his wide mouth, and through his *weazon* broke. *Dryden.*

WEA'THER. *n. ſ.* [peðeɲ, Saxon.]

1. State of air, reſpecting either cold or heat, wet or drineſs.

Who's there, beſides foul *weather*?—One mended like the *weather*, moſt unquietly. *Shakeſp. King Lear.*

I am far better born than is the king;
But I muſt make fair *weather* yet a while,
Till Henry be more weak and I more ſtrong. *Shakeſpeare.*

Men muſt content themſelves to travel in all *weathers*, and through all difficulties. *L'Eſtrange.*

The ſun
Foretells the change of *weather* in the ſkies,
Through miſts he ſhoots his ſullen beams,
Suſpect a driſling day. *Dryden.*

2. The change of the ſtate of the air.

It is a reverend thing to ſee an ancient caſtle not in decay; how much more to behold an ancient family, which have ſtood againſt the waves and *weathers* of time? *Bacon.*

3. Tempeſt; ſtorm.

What guſts of *weather* from that gath'ring cloud,
My thoughts preſage. *Dryden's Virgil.*

To WEA'THER. *v. a* [from the noun.]

1. To expoſe to the air.

He perch'd on ſome branch thereby,
To *weather* him and his moiſt wings to dry. *Spenſer.*

Muſtard-ſeed gather for being too ripe,
And *weather* it wel, yer ye give it a ſtripe. *Tuſſer.*

2. To paſs with difficulty.

He *weather'd* fell Charibdis; but ere long,
The ſkies were darkened, and the tempeſts ſtrong. *Garth.*

Could they *weather* and ſtand the ſhock of an eternal duration, and yet be at any time ſubject to a diſſolution. *Hale.*

3. *To* WEATHER *a point.* To gain a point againſt the wind; to accompliſh againſt oppoſition.

We have been tugging a great while againſt the ſtream, and have almoſt *weather'd our point*; a ſtretch or two more will do the work. *Addiſon.*

4. *To* WEA'THER *out.* To endure.

When we have paſs'd theſe gloomy hours,
And *weather'd out* the ſtorm that beats upon us. *Addiſon.*

WEA'THERBEATEN. *adj.* Haraſſed and ſeaſoned by hard weather.

They perceived an aged man and a young, both poorly arrayed, extremely *weatherbeaten*; the old man blind, the young man leading him. *Sidney.*

She enjoys ſure peace for evermore,
As *weatherbeaten* ſhip arrived on happy ſhore. *Fairy Queen.*

Thrice from the banks of Wye,
And ſandy bottom'd Severn, have I ſent
Him bootleſs home, and *weatherbeaten* back. *Shak. H. IV.*

I hope when you know the worſt, you will at once leap into the river, and ſwim through handſomely, and not *weatherbeaten* with the divers blaſts of irreſolution, ſtand ſhivering upon the brink. *Suckling.*

A *weatherbeaten* veſſel holds
Gladly the port. *Milton.*

Dido received his *weatherbeaten* troops. *Dryden's Virgil.*

The old *weatherbeaten* ſoldier carries in his hand the Roman eagle. *Addiſon.*

WEA'THERBOARD, *or Weatherbow. n. ſ.* In the ſea language, that ſide of a ſhip that is to the windward. *Dict.*

WEA'THERCOCK. *n. ſ.* [*weather* and *cock.*]

1. An artificial cock ſet on the top of a ſpire, which by turning ſhows the point from which the wind blows.

But alas! the ſun keeps his light, though thy faith be darkened; the rocks ſtand ſtill, though thou change like a *weathercock.* *Sidney.*

A kingfiſher hanged by the bill, converting the breaſt to that point of the horizon from whence the wind doth blow, is a very ſtrange introducing of natural *weathercocks.* *Brown.*

2. Any thing fickle and inconſtant.

Where had you this pretty *weathercock*?——I cannot tell what his name is my huſband had him of. *Shakeſpeare.*

He break my promiſe and abſolve my vow!
The word which I have given ſhall ſtand like fate,
Not like the king's that *weathercock* of ſtate. *Dryden.*

WEA'THERDRIVEN. *part.* Forced by ſtorms or contrary winds.

Philip, during his voyage towards Spain, was *weatherdriven* into Weymouth. *Carew's Survey of Cornwall.*

WEATHERGA'GE. *n. ſ.* [*weather* and *gage.*] Any thing that ſhews the weather.

To vere and tack, and ſteer a cauſe,
Againſt the *weathergage* of laws. *Hudibras.*

WEA'THERGLASS. *n. ſ.* [*weather* and *glaſs.*] A barometer.

As in ſome *weatherglaſs* my love I hold,
Which falls or riſes with the heat or cold,
I will be conſtant yet. *Dryden.*

John's temper depended very much upon the air; his ſpirits roſe and fell with the *weatherglaſs.* *Arbuthnot.*

We ſhall hardly wiſh for a perpetual equinox to ſave the charges of *weatherglaſſes*; for the two equinoxes of our year are the moſt windy and tempeſtuous. *Bentley's Sermons.*

WEATHERSPY'. *n. ſ.* [*weather* and *ſpy.*] A ſtar-gazer; an aſtrologer; one that foretels the weather.

And ſooner may a gulling *weatherſpy*,
By drawing forth heav'n's ſcheme tell certainly,
What faſhion'd hats or ruffs, or ſuits next year,
Our giddy-headed antick youth will wear. *Donne.*

WEA'THERWISE. *adj.* [*weather* and *wiſe.*] Skillful in foretelling the weather.

WEA'THERWISER. *n. ſ.* [*weather* and *wiſen*, Dutch; to ſhow.] Any thing that foreſhows the weather.

Moſt vegetables expand their flowers and down in warm ſun ſhiny weather, and again cloſe them toward the evening, or in rain, as is in the flowers of pimpernel, the opening and ſhutting of which are the countryman's *weatherwiſer.* *Derham's Phyſico-Theology.*

To WEAVE. *v. a.* Preterite *wove*, *weaved*, part. paſſ. *woven*, *weaved*; [pefan, Saxon; *weven*, Dutch.]

1. To form by texture; to form by inſerting one part of the materials within another.

Here in her hairs
The painter plays the ſpider, and hath *woven*
A golden meſh to intrap the hearts of men,
Faſter than gnats in cobwebs. *Shakeſpeare.*

The women *wove* hangings for the grove. 2 *Kings* xxiii. 7.

White ſeem'd her robes, yet *woven* ſo they were,
As ſnow and gold together had been wrought. *Dryden.*

Theſe purple veſts were *weav'd* by Dardan dames. *Dryden.*

Dan Pope for thy misfortune griev'd,
With kind concern and ſkill has *weav'd*
A ſilken web; and ne'er ſhall fade
Its colours; gently has he laid
The mantle o'er thy ſad diſtreſs:
And Venus ſhall the texture bleſs. *Prior.*

2. To unite by intermixture.

When religion was *woven* into the civil government, and flouriſhed under the protection of the emperors, mens thoughts and diſcourſes were full of ſecular affairs; but in the three firſt centuries of chriſtianity, men who embraced this religion had given up all their intereſts in this world, and lived in a perpetual preparation for the next. *Addiſon.*

3. To interpoſe; to inſert.

The duke be here to-night! the better! beſt!
This *weaves* itſelf perforce into my buſineſs. *Shakeſpeare.*

To WEAVE. *v. n.* To work with a loom.

WEA'VER. *n. ſ.* [from *weave.*] One who makes threads into cloth.

Upon theſe taxations,
The clothiers all not able to maintain,
The many to them 'longing, have put off
The ſpinſters, carders, fullers, *weavers.* *Shak. Hen. VIII.*

My days are ſwifter than a *weaver*'s ſhuttle, and are ſpent without hope. *Job* vii. 6.

The *weaver* may cast religion upon what loom he please. *How.*

Her flag aloft spreads ruffling to the wind,
And sanguine streamers seem the flood to fire:
The *weaver* charm'd with what his loom design'd,
Goes on to see, and knows not to retire. *Dryden.*

WEA'VERFISH. *n. s.* [*araneus piscis*, Latin.] A fish. *Ainsworth.*

WEB. *n. s.* [pebba, Saxon.]

1. Texture; any thing woven.

Penelope, for her Ulysses' sake,
Devis'd a *web* her wooers to deceive;
In which the work that she all day did make,
The same at night she did again unreave. *Spenser.*

Spiders touch'd, seek their *web's* inmost part. *Davies.*

By day the *web* and loom,
And homely houshold task shall be her doom. *Dryden.*

The fates, when they this happy *web* have spun,
Shall bless the sacred clue and bid it smoothly run. *Dryden.*

Dan Pope with skill hath weav'd
A silken *web*; and ne'er shall fade
Its colours. *Prior.*

2. Some part of a sword. Obsolete.

The sword, whereof the *web* was steel;
Pommel, rich stone; hilt, gold, approv'd by touch. *Fairf.*

3. A kind of dusky film that hinders the sight; suffusion.

This is the foul flibertigibbet; he gives the *web* and the pin, squints the eye, and makes the hairlip. *Shakespeare.*

WE'BBED. *adj.* [from *web.*] Joined by a film.

Such as are whole-footed, or whose toes are *webbed* together, their legs are generally short, the most convenient size for swimming. *Derham's Physico-Theology.*

WE'BFOOTED. *adj.* [*web* and *foot.*] Palmipedous; having films between the toes.

Webfooted fowls do not live constantly upon the land, nor fear to enter the water. *Ray on the Creation.*

WE'BSTER. *n. s.* [pebꞅꞇꞃe, Saxon; a woman-weaver.] A weaver. Obsolete.

After local names, the most in number have been derived from occupations; as Taylor, *Webster*, Wheeler. *Camden.*

To WED. *v. a.* [pedian, Saxon.]

1. To marry; to take for husband or wife.

If one by one you *wedded* all the world,
Or, from the all that are, took something good
To make a perfect woman; she you kill'd
Would be unparalell'd. *Shakespeare.*

Never did thy beauty, since the day
I saw thee first, and *wedded* thee, adorn'd
With all perfection, so inflame my senses. *Milton.*

Cloe, blind to wit and worth,
Weds the rich dullness of some son of earth. *Pope.*

2. To join in marriage.

In Syracusa was I born, and *wed*
Unto a woman happy but for me. *Shakespeare.*

Then I shall be no more;
And Adam, *wedded* to another Eve,
Shall live with her. *Mtlion's Paradise Lost.*

The woman in us still prosecutes a deceit like that begun in the garden; and our understandings are *wedded* to an Eve, as fatal as the mother of their miseries. *Glanville.*

3. To unite for ever.

Affliction is enamour'd of thy parts,
And thou art *wedded* to calamity. *Shakesp. Rom. and Jul.*

4. To take for ever.

Though the principal men of the house of commons were again elected to serve in this parliament, yet they were far from *wedding* the war, or taking themselves to be concerned to make good any declaration made by the former. *Clarendon.*

They positively and concernedly *wedded* his cause. *Clarendon.*

5. To unite by love or fondness.

Men are *wedded* to their lusts, and resolved upon a wicked course; and so it becomes their interest to wish there were no God. *Tillotson's Sermons.*

To WED. *v. n.* To contract matrimony.

When I shall *wed*,
That lord whose hand shall take my plight, shall carry
Half my love with him, half my care and duty. *Shakespeare.*

To love, to *wed*,
For Hymen's rites, and for the marriage bed
You were ordain'd. *Suckling.*

Nor took I Guiscard, by blind fancy led,
Or hasty choice as many women *wed*;
But with deliberate care. *Dryden.*

WE'DDING. *n. s.* [from *wed.*] Marriage; nuptials; the nuptial ceremony.

Come, away!
For you shall hence upon your *wedding*-day. *Shakespeare.*

I will dance and eat plums at your *wedding*. *Shakespeare.*

Let her beauty be her *wedding* dower;
For me and my possessions she esteems not. *Shakespeare.*

When my son was entered into his *wedding*-chamber, he fell down and died. *2 Esdr. x. 1.*

These three country bills agree, that each *wedding* produces four children. *Graunt's Bills of Mortality.*

His friends were invited to come and make merry with him, and this was to be the *wedding*-feast. *L'Estrange.*

If she affirmed herself to be a virgin, she must on her *wedding*-day, and in her *wedding* cloaths perform the ceremony of going alone into the den, and stay an hour with the lion. *Swift.*

A woman seldom asks advice before she has bought her *wedding*-cloaths. *Spectator.*

WEDGE. *n. s.* [*vegge*, Danish; *wegge*, Dutch.]

1. A body, which having a sharp edge, continually growing thicker, is used to cleave timber; one of the mechanical powers.

A barbarous troop of clownish fone,
The honour of these noble bows down threw;
Under the *wedge* I heard the trunk to groan. *Spenser.*

The fifth mechanical faculty is the *wedge* used in the cleaving of wood. *Wilkins's Mathematical Magick.*

He left his *wedge* within the cloven oak
To whet their courage. *Dryden's Æneid.*

The oak let many a heavy groan, when he was cleft with a *wedge* of his own timber. *Arbuthnot's Hist. of John Bull.*

2. A mass of metal.

As sparkles from the anvil used to fly,
When heavy hammers on the *wedge* are swaid. *Fa. Qu.*

When I saw a goodly Babylonish garment, and a *wedge* of gold of fifty shekels weight, then I coveted them. *Josh.* vii.

3. Any thing in the form of a wedge.

In warlike musters they appear,
In rhombs and *wedges* and half-moons and wings. *Milton.*

To WEDGE. *v. a.* [from the noun.] To fasten with wedges; to straiten with wedges; to cleave with wedges; to stop; to obstruct.

My heart,
As *wedged* with a sigh would rive in twain,
Lest Hector, or my father, should perceive me. *Shakesp.*

Where have you been broiling?—
—Among the crowd i' the abbey, where a finger
Could not be *wedg'd* in more. *Shakespeare's Henry* VIII.

Your wit will not so soon out as another man's will; it is strongly *wedged* up in a blockhead. *Shakespeare.*

Part
In common, rang'd in figure *wedge* their way;
Intelligent of seasons. *Milton's Paradise Lost.*

Sergesthus in the centaur, soon he pass'd,
Wedg'd in the rocky shoals and sticking fast. *Dryden.*

Wedge on the keenest scythes,
And give us steeds that snort against the foe. *A. Philips.*

What impulse can be propagated from one particle, entomb'd and *wedged* in the very center of the earth, to another in the center of Saturn. *Bentley's Sermons.*

WE'DLOCK. *n. s.* [peð and *lac*, Sax. marriage and gift.] Marriage; matrimony.

She doth stray about
By holy crosses, where she kneels and prays
For happy *wedlock* hours. *Shakespeare.*

Sirrah, your brother is legitimate;
Your father's wife did after *wedlock* bear him:
And if she did play false, the fault was her's. *Shakesp.*

Can *wedlock* know so great a curse,
As putting husbands out to nurse. *Cleaveland.*

He his happiest choice too late,
Shall meet already link'd, and *wedlock*-bound
To a fell adversary. *Milton's Paradise Lost.*

May not a prison or a grave,
Like *wedlock*, honour's title have? *Denham.*

One thought the sex's prime felicity
Was from the bonds of *wedlock* to be free:
And uncontroll'd to give account to none. *Dryden.*

A man determined about the fiftieth year of his age to enter upon *wedlock*. *Addison.*

WE'DNESDAY. *n. s.* [podenꞅbæg, Saxon; *odensday*, Swedish; *woensday*, Dutch; *wensday*, Islandick.] The fourth day of the week, so named by the Gothick nations from *Woden* or *Odin*.

Where is the honour of him that died on *wednesday*. *Shak.*

WEE. *adj.* [A Saxon word of the same root with *weeing*, Dutch; *wenig*, German.] Little; small: whence the word *weasel* or *weesel* is used for little; as a *weesel* face. In *Scotland* it denotes small or little; as *wee* ane, a little one, or child; a *wee* bit, a little bit.

Does he not wear a great round beard, like a glover's paring knife?—No, forsooth; he hath but a little *wee* face with a little yellow beard. *Shakesp. Merry Wives of Windsor.*

WEECHELM. *n. s.* [This is often written *witch elm.*] A species of elm.

A cion of a *weechelm* grafted upon an ordinary elm, will put forth leaves as broad as the brim of a hat. *Bacon.*

WEED. *n. s.* [peoð, Saxon, tares.]

1. An herb noxious or useless.

If he had an immoderate ambition; which is a *weed*, if it be a *weed*, apt to grow in the best soils, it doth not appear that it was in his nature. *Clarendon.*

He wand'ring feeds
On ſlowly growing herbs and ranker *weeds*. *Sandys.*

Too much manuring fill'd that field with *weeds*,
While ſects, like locuſts, did deſtroy the ſeeds. *Denham.*

Stinking *weeds* and poiſonous plants have their uſe. *More.*

When they are cut, let them lie, if weedy, to kill the *weeds*. *Mortimer's Husbandry.*

Their virtue, like their Tyber's flood
Rolling, its courſe deſign'd the country's good;
But oft the torrent's too impetuous ſpeed,
From the low earth tore ſome polluting *weed*;
And with the blood of Jove there always ran
Some viler part, ſome tincture of the man. *Prior.*

2. [Wœda, Saxon; *waed*, Dutch.] A garment; cloaths; habit; dreſs. Now ſcarce in uſe, except in *widow's weeds*, the mourning dreſs of a widow.

My mind for *weeds* your virtue's livery wears. *Sidney.*

Neither is it any man's buſineſs to cloath all his ſervants with one *weed*; nor theirs to cloath themſelves ſo, if left to their own judgments. *Hooker.*

They meet upon the way
An aged ſire, in long black *weeds* yclad;
His feet all bare, his beard all hoary gray,
And by his belt his book he hanging had. *Fairy Queen.*

Livery is alſo called the upper *weed* which a ſerving man wears, ſo called as it was delivered and taken from him at pleaſure. *Spenſer.*

The ſnake throws her enamelled ſkin,
Weed wide enough to wrap a fairy in. *Shakeſpeare.*

Throngs of knights and barons bold,
In *weeds* of peace high triumphs hold,
With ſtore of ladies. *Milton.*

Lately your fair hand in woman's *weed*
Wrapp'd my glad head. *Waller.*

To Weed. *v. a.* [from the noun.]

1. To rid of noxious plants.

When you ſow the berries of bays, *weed* not the borders for the firſt half year; for the weed giveth them ſhade. *Bacon.*

Your ſeedlings having ſtood 'till June, beſtow a *weeding* or a ſlight howing upon them. *Mortimer.*

2. To take away noxious plants.

Oh Marcius,
Each word thou'ſt ſpoke hath *weeded* from my heart
A root of ancient envy. *Shakeſp. Coriolanus.*

3. To free from any thing hurtful or offenſive.

He *weeded* the kingdom of ſuch as were devoted to Elaiana, and manumized it from that moſt dangerous confederacy. *Howel's Vocal Foreſt.*

Sarcaſms, contumelies, and invectives, fill ſo many pages of our controverſial writings, that, were thoſe *weeded* out, many volumes would be reduced to a more moderate bulk and temper. *Decay of Piety.*

4. To root out vice.

Wiſe fathers be not as well aware in *weeding* from their children ill things, as they were before in grafting in them learning. *Aſcham's Schoolmaſter.*

One by one, as they appeared, they might all be *weeded* out, without any ſigns that ever they had been there. *Locke.*

We'eder. *n. ſ.* [from *weed.*] One that takes away any thing noxious.

A *weeder* out of his proud adverſaries,
A liberal rewarder of his friends. *Shakeſp. Richard* III.

We'edhook. *n. ſ.* [*weed* and *hook.*] A hook by which weeds are cut away or extirpated.

In May get a *weedhook*, a crotch, and a glove,
And weed out ſuch weeds as the corn doth not love. *Tuſſer.*

We'edless. *adj.* [from *weed.*] Free from weeds; free from any thing uſeleſs or noxious.

So many *weedleſs* paradiſes be,
Which of themſelves produce no venomous ſin. *Donne.*

A cryſtal brook,
When troubled moſt it does the bottom ſhow;
'Tis *weedleſs* all above, and rockleſs all below. *Dryden.*

We'edy. *adj.* [from *weed.*]

1. Conſiſting of weeds.

There on the pendant boughs, her coronet weed
Clamb'ring to hang, an envious ſliver broke,
When down her *weedy* trophies and herſelf
Fell in the weeping brook. *Shakeſ. Hamlet.*

2. Abounding with weeds.

Hid in a *weedy* lake all night I lay,
Secure of ſafety. *Dryden's Æn.*

If it is *weedy*, let it lie upon the ground. *Mortimer.*

Week. *n. ſ.* [peoc, Saxon; *weke*, Dutch; *wecka*, Swediſh.] The ſpace of ſeven days.

Fulfill her *week*, and we will give thee this alſo. *Gen.* xxix.

We'ekday. *n. ſ.* [*week* and *day.*] Any day not Sunday.

One ſolid diſh his *weekday* meal affords,
An added pudding ſolemniz'd the Lord's. *Pope.*

We'ekly. *adj.* [from *week.*] Happening, produced, or done once a week; hebdomadary.

The Jews had always their *weekly* readings of the law of Moſes. *Hooker.*

So liv'd our ſires, ere doctors learn'd to kill,
And multiply'd with heirs their *weekly* bill. *Dryden.*

Nothing more frequent in their *weekly* papers, than affecting to confound the terms of clergy and high-church, and then loading the latter with calumny. *Swift.*

We'ekly. *adv.* [from *week.*] Once a week; by hebdomadal periods.

Theſe are obliged to perform divine worſhip in their turns *weekly*, and are ſometimes called hebdomadal canons. *Ayliffe.*

Weel. *n. ſ.* [pœl, Saxon.]

1. A whirlpool.

2. A twiggen ſnare or trap for fiſh, [perhaps from *willow.*]

To Ween. *v. n.* [penan, Saxon; *waenen*, Dutch.] To think; to imagine; to form a notion; to fancy. Obſolete.

Ah lady dear, quoth then the gentle knight,
Well may I *ween* your grief is wond'rous great. *Spenſer.*

So well it her beſeems, that ye would *ween*
Some angel ſhe had been. *Spenſer's Epithalamium.*

When *weening* to return, whence they did ſtray,
They cannot find that path which firſt was ſhown;
But wander to and fro in ways unknown,
Furtheſt from end then, when they neareſt *ween*. *Fa. Queen.*

Thy father, in pity of my hard diſtreſs,
Levy'd an army, *weening* to redeem
And reinſtal me in the diadem. *Shakeſp. Henry* VI.

Ween you of better luck,
I mean, in perjur'd witneſs, than your maſter,
Whoſe miniſter you are, while here he liv'd
Upon this naughty earth. *Shak. Henry* VIII.

They *ween'd*
That ſelf-ſame day, by fight or by ſurprize,
To win the mount of God; and on his throne
To ſet the envier of his ſtate, the proud
Aſpirer; but their thoughts prov'd fond and vain. *Milton.*

To Weep. *v. n.* preter. and part. paſſ. *wept*, *weeped*. [peopan, Saxon.]

1. To ſhow ſorrow by tears.

In that ſad time
My manly eyes did ſcorn an humble tear;
And what theſe ſorrows could not hence exhale,
That beauty hath, and made them blind with *weeping*. *Shak.*

I fear he will prove the *weeping* philoſopher when he grows old, being ſo full of unmannerly ſadneſs in his youth. *Shakeſp.*

The days of *weeping* and mourning for Moſes were ended. *Deutr.* xxxiv. 8.

Have you *wept* for your ſin, ſo that you were indeed ſorrowful in your ſpirit? Are you ſo ſorrowful that you hate it? Do you ſo hate it that you have left it? *Taylor.*

Away, with women *weep*, and leave me here,
Fix'd, like a man, to die without a tear,
Or ſave, or ſlay us both. *Dryden.*

A corps it was, but whoſe it was, unknown;
Yet mov'd, howe'er, ſhe made the caſe her own;
Took the bad omen of a ſhipwreck'd man,
As for a ſtranger *wept*. *Dryden.*

When Darius *wept* over his army, that within a ſingle age not a man of all that conflu︎ence would be left alive, Artabanus improved his meditation by adding, that yet all of them ſhould meet with ſo many evils, that every one ſhould wiſh himſelf dead long before. *Wake's Preparation for Death.*

This lovely *weeping* fair cannot be dearer to thee,
Than thou art to thy faithful Seofrid. *Rowe.*

2. To ſhed tears from any paſſion.

Then they for ſudden joy did *weep*,
And I for ſorrow ſung,
That ſuch a king ſhould play bo-peep,
And go the fools among. *Shakeſp. King Lear.*

3. To lament; to complain.

They *weep* unto me, ſaying, give us fleſh that we may eat. *Num.*

To Weep. *v. a.*

1. To lament with tears; to bewail; to bemoan.

If thou wilt *weep* my fortunes, take my eyes. *Shakeſpeare.*

Nor was I near to cloſe his dying eyes,
To waſh his wounds, to *weep* his obſequies. *Dryden.*

We wand'ring go
Through dreary waſtes, and *weep* each other's woe. *Pope.*

2. To ſhed moiſture.

Thus was this place
A happy rural ſeat of various view,
Groves whoſe rich trees *wept* od'rous gums and balm. *Milt.*

Let India boaſt her plants, nor envy we
The *weeping* amber or the balmy tree,
While by our oaks the precious loads are borne,
And realms commanded which thoſe trees adorn. *Pope.*

3. To abound with wet.

Rey-graſs grows on clayey and *weeping* grounds. *Mortimer.*

We'eper. *n. ſ.* [from *weep.*]

1. One who ſheds tears; a lamenter; a bewailer; a mourner.

If you have ſerved God in a holy life, ſend away the women and the *weepers*: tell them it is as much intemperance to weep too much as to laugh too much: if thou art alone, or with fitting company, die as thou should'st; but do not die impatiently, and like a fox catched in a trap. *Taylor.*

Laughter is easy; but the wonder lies,
What store of brine supply'd the *weeper*'s eyes. *Dryden.*

2. A white border on the sleeve of a mourning coat.

WE'ERISH. *adj.* [See WEARISH.] This old word is used by *Ascham* in a sense which the lexicographers seem not to have known. Applied to tastes, it means insipid; applied to the body, weak and washy: here it seems to mean sour; surly.

A voice not soft, weak, piping, womanish; but audible, strong, and manlike: a countenance not *weerish* and crabbed, but fair and comely. *Ascham's Schoolmaster.*

To WEET. *v. n.* preterite *wot*, or *wote*. [pitan, Saxon; *weten*, Dutch.] To know; to be informed; to have knowledge. Obsolete.

Him the prince with gentle court did board;
Sir knight, mought I of you this court'sy read,
To *weet* why on your shield, so goodly scor'd,
Bear ye the picture of that lady's head? *Spenser.*

I bind,
On pain of punishment, the world to *weet*
We stand up peerless. *Shakesp. Ant. and Cleopatra.*

But well I *weet* thy cruel wrong
Adorns a nobler poet's song. *Prior.*

WE'ETLESS. *adj.* [from *weet.*] Unknowing. *Spenser.*

WE'EVIL. *n. s.* [pifel, Saxon; *vevel*, Dutch.] A grub.

A worm called a *weevil*, bred under ground, feedeth upon roots; as parsnips and carrots. *Bacon's Natural History.*

Corn is so innocent from breeding of mice, that it doth not produce the very *weevils* that live in it and consume it. *Bentley.*

WE'EZEL *n. s.* [See WEASEL.]

I suck melancholy out of a song, as a *weazel* sucks eggs. *Shak.*

The corn-devouring *weezel* here abides,
And the wise ant. *Dryden's Georg.*

WEFT. The old preterite and part. pass. from *To wave. Spens.*

WEFT. *n. s.* [*guaive*, French; *vosa*, to wander, Islandick; *vagus*, Latin.]

1. That of which the claim is generally waved; any thing wandering without an owner, and seized by the lord of the manour.

His horse, it is the herald's *weft*;
No, 'tis a mare. *Ben. Johnson's Underwoods.*

2. It is in *Bacon* for *waft*, a gentle blast.

The smell of violets exceedeth in sweetness that of spices, and the strongest sort of smells are best in a *weft* afar off. *Bac.*

WEFT. *n. s.* [pepta, Saxon.] The woof of cloth.

WE'FTAGE. *n. s.* [from *weft.*] Texture.

The whole muscles, as they lie upon the bones, might be truly tanned; whereby the *weftage* of the fibres might more easily be observed. *Grew's Musæum.*

To WEIGH. *v. a.* [pægan, Saxon; *weyhen*, Dutch.]

1. To examine by the balance.

Earth taken from land adjoining to the Nile, and preserved, so as not to be wet nor wasted, and *weighed* daily, will not alter weight until the seventeenth of June, when the river beginneth to rise; and then it will grow more and more ponderous, 'till the river cometh to its height. *Bacon's Natural History.*

Th' Eternal hung forth his golden scales,
Wherein all things created first he *weigh'd*. *Milton.*

2. To be equivalent to in weight.

By the exsuction of the air out of a glass-vessel, it made that vessel take up, or suck up, to speak in the common language, a body *weighing* divers ounces. *Boyle.*

3. To pay, allot, or take by weight.

They that must *weigh* out my afflictions,
They that my trust must grow to, live not here;
They are, as all my comforts are, far hence. *Shakespeare.*

They *weighed* for my price thirty pieces of silver. *Zech.* xi.

4. To raise; to take up the anchor.

Barbarossa, using this exceeding cheerfulness of his soldiers, *weighed* up the fourteen gallies he had sunk. *Knolles.*

Here he left me, ling'ring here delay'd
His parting kiss, and there his anchor *weigh'd*. *Dryden.*

5. To examine; to balance in the mind.

Regard not who it is which speaketh, but *weigh* only what is spoken. *Hooker.*

I have in equal balance justly *weigh'd*
What wrongs our arms may do, what wrongs we suffer,
And find our griefs heavier than our offences. *Shak. H.* IV.

The ripeness or unripeness of the occasion must ever be well *weighed*. *Bacon.*

His majesty's speedy march left that design to be better *weighed* and digested. *Clarendon.*

You chose a retreat, and not 'till you had maturely *weighed* the advantages of rising higher, with the hazards of the fall. *Dryden.*

All grant him prudent; prudence interest *weighs*,
And interest bids him seek your love and praise. *Dryden.*

The mind, having the power to suspend the satisfaction of any of its desires, is at liberty to examine them on all sides, and *weigh* them with others. *Locke.*

He is the only proper judge of our perfections, who *weighs* the goodness of our actions by the sincerity of our intentions. *Addison's Spectator.*

6. *To* WEIGH *down.* To overballance.

Fear *weighs down* faith with shame. *Daniel's Civ. War.*

7. *To* WEIGH *down.* To overburden; to oppress with weight; to depress.

The Indian fig boweth so low, as it taketh root again; the plenty of the sap, and the softness of the stalk, making the bough, being overloaden, *weigh down*. *Bacon.*

In thy blood will reign
A melancholy damp of cold and dry,
To *weigh* thy spirits *down*. *Milton.*

Her father's crimes
Sit heavy on her, and *weigh down* her prayers;
A crown usurp'd, a lawful king depos'd,
His children murder'd. *Dryden's Spanish Fryar.*

My soul is quite *weigh'd down* with care, and asks
The soft refreshment of a moment's sleep. *Addison's Cato.*

Excellent persons, *weighed down* by this habitual sorrow of heart, rather deserve our compassion than reproach. *Addison.*

To WEIGH. *v. n.*

1. To have weight.

Exactly weighing and strangling a chicken in the scales, upon an immediate ponderation, we could discover no difference in weight; but suffering it to lie eight or ten hours, until it grew perfectly cold, it *weighed* most sensibly lighter. *Brown.*

2. To be considered as important; to have weight in the intellectual ballance.

This objection ought to *weigh* with those, whose reading is designed for much talk and little knowledge. *Locke.*

A wise man is then best satisfied, when he finds that the same argument which *weighs* with him has *weighed* with thousands before him, and is such as hath born down all opposition. *Addis.*

3. To raise the anchor.

When gath'ring clouds o'ershadow all the skies,
And shoot quick lightnings, *weigh*, my boys, he cries. *Dry.*

4. To bear heavily; to press hard.

Can'st thou not minister to a mind diseas'd,
And with some sweet oblivious antidote
Cleanse the stuff'd bosom of that perilous stuff
Which *weighs* upon the heart? *Shakesp. Macbeth.*

WEIGHED. *adj.* [from *weigh.*] Experienced.

In an embassy of weight, choice was made of some sad person of known experience, and not of a young man, not *weighed* in state matters. *Bacon.*

WE'IGHER. *n. s.* [from *weigh.*] He who weighs.

WEIGHT. *n. s.* [piht, Saxon.]

1. Quantity measured by the ballance.

Tobacco cut and weighed, and then dried by the fire, loseth *weight*; and, after being laid in the open air, recovereth *weight* again. *Bacon's Natural History.*

Fain would I chuse a middle course to steer;
Nature's too kind, and justice too severe:
Speak for us both, and to the balance bring,
On either side, the father and the king:
Heav'n knows my heart is bent to favour thee;
Make it but scanty *weight*, and leave the rest to me. *Dryd.*

Boerhaave fed a sparrow with bread four days, in which time it eat more than its own *weight*; and yet there was no acid found in its body. *Arbuthnot on Aliments.*

2. A mass by which, as the standard, other bodies are examined.

Just balances, just *weights* shall ye have. *Lev.* xix. 36.

Undoubtedly there were such *weights* which the physicians used, who, though they might reckon according to the *weight* of the money, they did not weigh their drugs with pieces of money. *Arbuthnot on Coins.*

When the balance is intirely broke, by mighty *weights* fallen into either scale, the power will never continue long in equal division, but run intirely into one. *Swift.*

3. Ponderous mass.

A man leapeth better with *weights* in his hands than without; for that the *weight*, if proportionable, strengtheneth the sinews by contracting them; otherwise, where no contraction is needful, *weight* hindereth: as we see in horseraces, men are curious to foresee that there be not the least *weight* upon the one horse more than upon the other. In leaping with *weights*, the arms are first cast backwards, and then forwards, with so much the greater force. *Bacon's Natural History.*

Wolsey, who from his own great store might have
A palace or a college for his grave,
Lies here interr'd:
Nothing but earth to earth, no pond'rous *weight*
Upon him, but a pebble or a quoit:
If thus thou lie'st neglected, what must we
Hope after death, who are but shreds of thee? *Bp. Corbet.*

All their confidence
Under the *weight* of mountains bury'd deep. *Milton.*

Pride, like a gulf, swallows us up; our very virtues, when so leavened, becoming *weights* and plummets to sink us to the deeper ruin. *Government of the Tongue.*

Then shun the ill; and know, my dear,
Kindness and constancy will prove
The only pillars fit to bear
So vast a *weight* as that of love. *Prior.*

4. Gravity; heaviness; tendency to the center.

Heaviness or *weight* is not here considered as being such a natural quality, whereby condensed bodies do of themselves tend downwards; but rather as being an affection, whereby they may be measured. *Wilkins.*

The shaft that slightly was impress'd,
Now from his heavy fall with *weight* increas'd,
Drove through his neck. *Dryden.*

What natural agent impel them so strongly with a transverse side blow against that tremendous *weight* and rapidity, when whole worlds are falling? *Bentley.*

5. Pressure; burthen; overwhelming power.

Thou art no Atlas for so great a *weight*. *Shakespeare.*

So shall the world go on,
To good malignant, to bad men benign,
Under her own *weight* groaning. *Milton.*

We must those, who groan beneath the *weight*
Of age, disease, or want, commiserate. *Denham.*

The prince may carry the plough, but the *weight* lies upon the people. *L'Estrange.*

Possession's load was grown so great,
He sunk beneath the cumb'rous *weight*. *Swift.*

6. Importance; power; influence; efficacy.

How to make ye suddenly an answer,
In such a point of *weight*, so near mine honour,
In truth I know not. *Shakesp. Henry VIII.*

If this right of heir carry any *weight* with it, if it be the ordinance of God, must not all be subject to it. *Locke.*

To make the sense of esteem or disgrace sink the deeper, and be of the more *weight*, other agreeable or disagreeable things should constantly accompany these different states. *Locke.*

An author's arguments lose their *weight*, when we are persuaded that he only writes for argument's sake. *Addison.*

See, Lord, the sorrows of my heart,
Ere yet it be too late;
And hear my Saviour's dying groans,
To give those sorrows *weight*. *Addison's Spectator.*

The solemnities that encompass the magistrate add dignity to all his actions, and *weight* to all his words. *Atterbury.*

WE'IGHTILY. *adv.* [from *weighty.*]

1. Heavily; ponderously.
2. Solidly; importantly.

Is his poetry the worse, because he makes his agents speak *weightily* and sententiously? *Broome's Notes on the Odyssey.*

WE'IGHTINESS. *n. s.* [from *weighty.*]

1. Ponderosity; gravity; heaviness.
2. Solidity; force.

I fear I have dwelt longer on this passage than the *weightiness* of any argument in it requires. *Locke.*

3. Importance.

The apparent defect of her judgment, joined to the *weightiness* of the adventure, caused many to marvel. *Hayward.*

WE'IGHTLESS. *adj* [from *weight.*]

1. Light; having no gravity.

How by him balanc'd in the *weightless* air?
Can'st thou the wisdom of his works declare? *Sandys.*

2. Not possible to be weighed. Improper.

It must both *weightless* and immortal prove,
Because the centre of it is above. *Dryden.*

WE'IGHTY. *adj.* [from *weight.*]

1. Heavy; ponderous.

You have already weary'd fortune so,
She cannot farther be your friend or foe;
But sits all breathless, and admires to feel
A fate so *weighty*, that it stops her wheel. *Dryden.*

2. Important; momentous; efficacious.

I to your assistance do make love,
Masking the business from the common eye
For sundry *weighty* reasons. *Shakesp. Macbeth.*

No fool Pythagoras was thought:
Whilst he his *weighty* doctrines taught,
He made his list'ning scholars stand,
Their mouth still cover'd with their hand:
Else, may-be, some odd-thinking youth,
Less friend to doctrine than to truth,
Might have refus'd to let his ears
Attend the musick of the spheres. *Prior.*

Thus spoke to my lady the knight full of care,
Let me have your advice in a *weighty* affair. *Swift.*

3. Rigorous; severe. Not in use.

If, after two days shine, Athens contains thee,
Attend our *weightier* judgment. *Shakes. Timon.*

WE'LAWAY. *interj.* [This I once believed a corruption of *weal away*, that is, *happiness is gone*: so *Junius* explained it; but the Saxon exclamation is palapa, *woe on woe*: from *welaway*, is formed by corruption *weladay.*] Alas.

Harrow now out, and *wealaway*, he cried,
What dismal day hath sent this cursed light! *Spenser.*

Ah, *welaway*! most noble lords, how can
Your cruel eyes endure so piteous sight? *Fairy Queen.*

Welaway, the while I was so fond,
To leave the good that I had in hond. *Spenser.*

WE'LCOME. *adj.* [*bien venu*, French; pilcume, Saxon; *welkom*, Dutch.]

1. Received with gladness; admitted willingly to any place or enjoyment; grateful; pleasing.

I serve you, madam:
Your graces are right *welcome*. *Shakesp. King Lear.*

He, though not of the plot, will like it,
And wish it should proceed; for, unto men
Prest with their wants, all change is ever *welcome*. *B. Johns.*

Here let me earn my bread,
'Till oft invocated death
Hasten the *welcome* end of all my pains. *Milton.*

He that knows how to make those he converses with easy, has found the true art of living, and being *welcome* and valued every where. *Locke.*

2. *To bid* WELCOME. To receive with professions of kindness.

Some stood in a row in so civil a fashion, as if to *welcome* us; and divers put their arms a little abroad, which is their gesture when they *bid* any *welcome*. *Bacon.*

WE'LCOME. *interj.* A form of salutation used to a new comer, elliptically used for *you are welcome.*

Welcome, he said,
O long expected to my dear embrace. *Dryden.*

Welcome, great monarch, to your own. *Dryden.*

WE'LCOME. *n. s.*

1. Salutation of a new comer.

Welcome ever smiles, and farewel goes out sighing. *Shakesp.*

Leontes opening his free arms, and weeping
His *welcome* forth. *Shak. Winter's Tale.*

2. Kind reception of a new comer.

I should be free from injuries, and abound as much in the true causes of *welcomes*, as I should find want of the effects thereof. *Sidney.*

I look'd not for you yet, nor am provided
For your fit *welcome*. *Shakes. King Lear.*

Madam, new years may well expect to find
Welcome from you, to whom they are so kind:
Still as they pass they court and smile on you,
And make your beauty as themselves seem new. *Waller.*

Where diligence opens the door of the understanding, and impartiality keeps it, truth finds an entrance and a *welcome* too. *South's Sermons.*

To WE'LCOME. *v. a.* To salute a new comer with kindness.

I know no cause
Why I should *welcome* such a guest as grief,
Save bidding farewel to so sweet a guest
As my sweet Richard. *Shakesp. Richard II.*

They stood in a row in so civil a fashion, as if to *welcome* us. *Bacon.*

Thus we salute thee with our early song,
And *welcome* thee, and wish thee long. *Milton.*

To *welcome* home
His warlike brother, is Pirithous come *Dryden.*

The lark and linnet strain their warbling throats,
To *welcome* in the Spring. *Dryden.*

WE'LCOME *to our House* *n. s.* An herb. *Ainsworth.*

WE'LCOMENESS. *n. s.* [from *welcome.*] Gratefulness.

Our joys, after some centuries of years, may seem to have grown elder, by having been enjoyed so many ages; yet will they really still continue new, not only upon the scores of their *welcomeness*, but by their perpetually equal, because infinite, distance from a period. *Boyle.*

WE'LCOMER. *n. s.* [from *welcome.*] The saluter or receiver of a new comer.

Farewel, thou woful *welcomer* of glory. *Shakespeare.*

WELD, or *Would.* *n. s.* [*luteola*, Latin.] Yellow weed, or dyers weed.

Its leaves are oblong and intire: it has an anomalous flower, consisting of many dissimilar leaves: the fruit is globular, hollow, and divided into three parts. The dyers use it for dying bright yellows and lemon colours; and this is by some supposed to be the plant used by the ancient Picts in painting their bodies. *Miller.*

To WELD, for *To wield.* *Spenser.*

To WELD. *v. a.* To beat one mass into another, so as to incorporate them.

Sparkling or *welding* heat is used when you double up your iron to make it thick enough, and so *weld* or work in the doubling into one another. *Moxon's Mech. Exer.*

WE'LDER. *n. s.* A term perhaps merely Irish; though it may be derived from *To wield*, to *turn* or *manage*: whence *wielder*, welder.

Such immediate tenants have others under them, and so a third and fourth in subordination, 'till it comes to the *welder*, as they call him, who sits at a rack-rent, and lives miserably. *Swift.*

WE'LFARE. *n. s.* [*well* and *fare.*] Happiness; success; prosperity.

If friends to a government forbear their assistance, they put it it in the power of a few desperate men to ruin the *welfare* of those who are superiour to them in strength and interest. *Add.*

Discretion is the perfection of reason: cunning is a kind of instinct that only looks out after our immediate interest and *welfare*. *Addison's Spectator.*

To WELK. *v. a.* [Of this word in *Spenser* I know not well the meaning: pealcan, in Saxon, is to *roll*; *wolken*, in German, and pelcen, in Saxon, are clouds; whence I suppose *welk*, *welk*, or *whilk* is an undulation or corrugation, or corrugated or convolved body. *Whilk* is used for a small shell-fish.] To cloud; to obscure.

Now sad Winter *welked* hath the day,
And Phœbus, weary of his yearly task,
Established hath his steeds in lowly lay,
And taken up his inn in fishes hask. *Spenser.*

As gentle shepherd in sweet eventide,
When ruddy Phœbus 'gins to *welk* in West,
Marks which do bite their hasty supper best. *Fairy Queen.*

The *welked* Phœbus 'gan avale
His weary wain. *Spenser.*

WE'LKED. *adj.* Wrinkled; wreathed.

Methought his eyes
Were two full moons: he had a thousand noses,
Horns *welk'd* and wav'd like the enridged sea. *Shakespeare.*

WE'LKIN. *n. s.* [from pealcan, to roll, or pelcen, clouds, Sax.]

1. The visible regions of the air. Out of use, except in poetry.

Ne in all the *welkin* was no cloud. *Chaucer.*

He leaves the *welkin* way most beaten plain,
And rapt with whirling wheels inflames the skyen,
With fire not made to burn, but fairly for to shine. *Fa. Qu.*

The swallow peeps out of her nest,
And cloudy *welkin* cleareth. *Spenser's Pastorals.*

Spur your proud horses hard, and ride in blood:
Amaze the *welkin* with your broken staves. *Shak. R.* III.

With feats of arms
From either end of heav'n the *welkin* burns. *Milton.*

Now my task is smoothly done,
I can fly, or I can run
Quickly to the green earth's end,
Where the bow'd *welkin* slow doth bend. *Milton.*

Their hideous yells
Rend the dark *welkin*. *Philips.*

2. WELKIN *Eye*, is, I suppose, blue eye; skycoloured eye.

Yet were it true
To say this boy were like me! Come, sir page,
Look on me with your *welkin eye*, sweet villain. *Shakespeare.*

WELL. *n. s.* [pelle, pœll, Saxon.]

1. A spring; a fountain; a source.

Begin then, sisters of the sacred *well*,
That from beneath the seat of Jove doth spring. *Milton.*

As the root and branch are but one tree,
And *well* and stream do but one river make;
So if the root and *well* corrupted be,
The stream and branch the same corruption take. *Davies.*

2. A deep narrow pit of water.

The muscles are so many *well*-buckets: when one of them acts and draws, 'tis necessary that the other must obey. *Dryden.*

3. The cavity in which stairs are placed.

Hollow newelled stairs are made about a square hollow newel: suppose the *well*-hole to be eleven foot long, and six foot wide, and we would bring up a pair of stairs from the first floor eleven foot high, it being intended a sky-light shall fall through the hollow newel. *Moxon's Mech. Exer.*

To WELL. *v. n.* [peallan, Saxon.] To spring; to issue as from a spring.

Thereby a crystal stream did gently play,
Which from a sacred fountain *welled* forth alway. *Fa. Qu.*
The bubbling wave did ever freshly *well*. *Fairy Queen.*

A dreary corse,
All wallow'd in his own yet lukewarm blood,
That from his wound yet *welled* fresh, alas! *Spenser.*

Himself assists to lift him from the ground,
With clotted locks, and blood that *well'd* from out the wound. *Dryden's Æn.*

From his two springs,
Pure *welling* out, he through the lucid lake
Of fair Dambea rolls his infant stream. *Thomson's Summer.*

To WELL. *v. a.* To pour any thing forth.

To her people wealth they forth do *well*,
And health to every foreign nation. *Fairy Queen.*

WELL. *adj.* [*Well* seems to be sometimes an adjective, though it is not always easy to determine its relations.]

1. Not sick; not unhappy.

Mark, we use
To say the dead are *well*. *Shakesp. Ant. and Cleopatra.*

Lady, I am not *well*, else I should answer
From a full flowing stomach. *Shakesp. King Lear.*

In poison there is physick; and this news,
That would, had I been *well*, have made me sick,
Being sick, hath in some measure made me *well*. *Shakesp.*

While thou art *well*, thou mayest do much good; but when thou art sick, thou can'st not tell what thou shalt be able to do: it is not very much nor very good. Few men mend with sickness, as there are but few who by travel and a wandering life become devout. *Taylor's Guide to Devotion.*

Men under irregular appetites never think themselves *well*, so long as they fancy they might be better; then from better they must rise to best. *L'Estrange.*

'Tis easy for any, when *wel'*, to give advice to them that are not. *Wake's Preparation for Death.*

2. Convenient; happy.

Holdings were so plentiful, and holders so scarce, as *well* was the landlord, who could get one to be his tenant. *Carew.*

Charity is made the constant companion and perfection of all virtues; and *well* it is for that virtue where it most enters, and longest stays. *Sprat's Sermons.*

This exactness is necessary, and it would be *well* too, if it extended itself to common conversation. *Locke.*

It would have been *well* for Genoa, if she had followed the example of Venice, in not permitting her nobles to make any purchase of lands in the dominions of a foreign prince. *Ad.*

3. Being in favour.

He followed the fortunes of that family; and was *well* with Henry the fourth. *Dryden.*

4. Recovered from any sickness or misfortune.

I am sorry
For your displeasure; but all will sure be *well*. *Shakespeare.*

Just thoughts, and modest expectations are easily satisfied. If we don't over-rate our pretensions, all will be *well*. *Collier.*

WELL. *adv.* [*will*, Gothick; pell, Saxon; *wel*, Dutch; *vel*, Islandick.]

1. Not ill; not unhappily.

Some sense, and more estate, kind heav'n
To this *well*-lotted peer has given:
What then? he must have rule and sway;
Else all is wrong till he's in play. *Prior.*

2. Not ill; not wickedly.

My bargains, and *well*-won thrift he calls int'rest. *Shak.*

Thou one bad act with many deeds *well* done
May'st cover. *Milton.*

3. Skilfully; properly.

A private caution I know not *well* how to sort, unless I should call it political, by no means to build too near a great neighbour. *Wotton.*

Beware and govern *well* thy appetite. *Milton.*

Whether the learn'd Minerva be her theme,
Or chaste Diana bathing in the stream;
None can record their heavenly praise so *well*. *Dryden.*

What poet would not mourn to see
His brother write as *well* as he? *Swift.*

4. Not amiss; not unsuccessfully; not erroneously.

Solyman commended them for a plot so *well* by them laid, more than he did the victory of others got by good fortune, not grounded upon any good reason. *Knolles.*

The soldier that philosopher *well* blam'd,
Who long and loudly in the schools declaim'd. *Denham.*

'Tis almost impossible to translate verbally and *well*. *Dryden.*

5. Not insufficiently; not defectively.

The plain of Jordan was *well* watered every where. *Genesis.*

We are *well* able to overcome it. *Num.* xiii. 30.

The merchant adventurers being a strong company, and *well* underset with rich men, held out bravely. *Bacon.*

6. To a degree that gives pleasure.

I like *well*, in some places, fair columns upon frames of carpenters work. *Bacon.*

7. With praise; favourably.

All the world speaks *well* of you. *Pope.*

8. Well is sometimes like the French *bien*, a term of concession.

The knot might *well* be cut, but untied it could not be. *Sidney.*

To know
In measure what the mind can *well* contain. *Milton.*

9. It is a word by which something is admitted as the ground for a conclusion.

Well, let's away, and say how much is done. *Shakespeare.*

Well, by this author's confession, a number superior are for the succession in the house of Hanover. *Swift.*

10. *As well as.* Together with; not less than.

Coptos was the magazine of all the trade from Æthiopia, by the Nile, *as well as* of those commodities that came from the west by Alexandria. *Arbuthnot on Coins.*

11. *Well is him or me*; *bene est*, he is happy.

Well is him that dwelleth with a wife of understanding, and that hath not slipped with his tongue. *Ecclus.* xxv. 8.

12. *Well nigh.* Nearly; almost.

I freed *well nigh* half th' angelick name. *Milton.*

13. It is used much in composition, to express any thing right, laudable, or not defective.

Antiochus understanding him not be *well* affected to his affairs, provided for his own safety. 2 *Mac.* iv. 21.

There may be safety to the *well*-affected Persians; but to those which do conspire against us, a memorial of destruction. *Esth.* xvi. 23.

Should a whole host at once discharge the bow,
My *well*-aim'd shaft with death prevents the foe. *Pope.*

What

What *well*-appointed leader fronts us here? *Shakesp.*

Well-apparel'd April on the heel
Of limping winter treads. *Shakesp. Romeo and Juliet.*

The pow'r of wisdom march'd before,
And ere the sacrificing throng he join'd,
Admonish'd thus his *well*-attending mind. *Pope.*

Such musick
Before was never made,
But when of old the sons of morning sung,
Whilst the Creator great
His constellations set,
And the *well*-balanc'd world on hinges hung. *Milton.*

Learners must at first be believers, and their master's rules having been once made axioms to them, they mislead those who think it sufficient to excuse them, if they go out of their way in a *well*-beaten track. *Locke.*

He chose a thousand horse, the flow'r of all
His warlike troops, to wait the funeral:
To bear him back, and share Evander's grief;
A *well*-becoming, but a weak relief. *Dryden.*

Those opposed files,
Which lately met in the intestine shock,
And furious close of civil butchery,
Shall now, in mutual *well*-beseeming rank,
March all one way. *Shakesp. Hen. IV.*

O'er the Elean plains, thy *well*-breath'd horse
Impels the flying car, and wins the course. *Dryden.*

More dismal than the loud disploded roar
Of brazen enginry, that ceaseless storms
The bastion of a *well*-built city. *Philips.*

He conducted his course among the same *well*-chosen friendships and alliances with which he began it. *Addison.*

My son corrupts a *well*-derived nature
With his inducement. *Shakespeare.*

If good accrue, 'tis conferr'd most commonly on the base and infamous; and only happening sometimes to *well*-deservers. *Dryden.*

It grieves me he should desperately adventure the loss of his *well*-deserving life. *Sidney, b.* ii.

What a pleasure is *well*-directed study in the search of truth! *Locke.*

A certain spark of honour, which rose in her *well*-disposed mind, made her fear to be alone with him, with whom alone she desired to be. *Sidney, b.* ii.

The unprepossessed, the *well*-disposed, who both together make much the major part of the world, are affected with a due fear of these things. *South's Sermons.*

A clear idea is that, whereof the mind hath such a full and evident perception, as it does receive from an outward object, operating duly on a *well*-disposed organ. *Locke.*

Amid the main, two mighty fleets engage;
Actium surveys the *well*-disputed prize. *Dryden.*

The ways of *well*-doing are in number even as many, as are the kinds of voluntary actions: so that whatsoever we do in this world, and may do it ill, we shew ourselves therein by *well*-doing to be wise. *Hooker, b.* ii.

The conscience of *well*-doing may pass for a recompence. *L'Estrange.*

God will judge every man according to his works; to them, who by patient continuance in *well*-doing, endure through the heat and burden of the day, he will give the reward of their labour. *Rogers's Sermons.*

As far the spear I throw,
As flies an arrow from the *well*-drawn bow. *Pope.*

Fair nymphs and *well*-dress'd youths around her shone,
But ev'ry eye was fixt on her alone. *Pope.*

Such a doctrine in St. James's air,
Shou'd chance to make the *well*-drest rabble stare. *Pope.*

The desire of esteem, riches, or power, makes men espouse the *well*-endowed opinions in fashion. *Locke.*

We ought to stand firm in *well*-established principles, and not be tempted to change for every difficulty. *Watts.*

Echenus sage, a venerable man!
Whose *well*-taught mind the present age surpass'd. *Pope.*

Some reliques of the true antiquity, though disguised, a *well*-eyed man may happily discover. *Spenser on Ireland.*

How sweet the products of a peaceful reign?
The heaven-taught poet, and enchanting strain:
The *well*-fill'd palace, the perpetual feast;
A land rejoicing, and a people blest. *Pope.*

Turkish blood did his young hands imbrue.
From thence returning with deserv'd applause,
Against the Moors his *well*-flesh'd sword he draws. *Dryden.*

Fairest piece of *well*-form'd earth,
Urge not thus your haughty birth. *Waller.*

A rational soul can be no more discerned in a *well*-formed, than ill-shaped infant. *Locke.*

A *well*-formed proposition is sufficient to communicate the knowledge of a subject. *Watts.*

Oh! that I'd dy'd before the *well*-fought wall!
Had some distinguish'd day renown'd my fall,
All Greece had paid my solemn funerals. *Pope.*

Good men have a *well*-grounded hope in another life; and are as certain of a future recompence, as of the being of God. *Atterbury.*

Let firm, *well*-hammer'd soles protect thy feet
Through freezing snows. *Gay's Trivia.*

The camp of the heathen was strong, and *well*-harnessed, and compassed round with horsemen. 1 *Mic.* iv. 7.

Among the Romans, those who saved the life of a citizen, were dressed in an oaken garland; but among us, this has been a mark of such *well*-intentioned persons as would betray their country. *Addison.*

He, full of fraudful arts,
This *well*-invented tale for truth imparts. *Dryden.*

He, by enquiry, got to the *well*-known house of Kalander. *Sidney.*

Soon as thy letters trembling I unclose,
That *well*-known name awakens all my woes. *Pope.*

Where proud Athens rears her tow'ry head,
With opening streets, and shining structures spread,
She past, delighted, with the *well*-known seats. *Pope.*

From a confin'd *well*-manag'd store,
You both employ and feed the poor. *Waller.*

A noble soul is better pleas'd with a zealous vindicator of liberty, than with a temporizing poet, or *well*-manner'd court-slave, and one who is ever decent, because he is naturally servile. *Dryden's Dedication to Juvenal.*

Well-meaners think no harm; but for the rest,
Things sacred they pervert, and silence is the best. *Dryden.*

By craft they may prevail on the weakness of some *well*-meaning men to engage in their designs. *Rogers's Sermons.*

He examines that *well*-meant, but unfortunate, lie of the conquest of France. *Arbuthnot.*

A critick supposes he has done his part, if he proves a writer to have fail'd in an expression; and can it be wonder'd at, if the poets seem resolved not to own themselves in any error? for as long as one side despises a *well*-meant endeavour, the other will not be satisfied with a moderate approbation. *Pope's Preface to his Works.*

Many sober, *well*-minded men, who were real lovers of the peace of the kingdom, were imposed upon. *Clarendon.*

Jarring int'rests of themselves create
Th' according musick of a *well*-mix'd state. *Pope.*

When the blast of winter blows,
Into the naked wood he goes;
And seeks the tusky boar to rear,
With *well*-mouth'd hounds, and pointed spear. *Dryden.*

The applause that other people's reason gives to virtuous and *well*-ordered actions, is the proper guide of children, till they grow able to judge for themselves. *Locke.*

The fruits of unity, next unto the *well*-pleasing of God, which is all in all, are towards those that are without the church; the other toward those that are within. *Bacon.*

The exercise of the offices of charity is always *well*-pleasing to God, and honourable among men. *Atterbury.*

My voice shall sound, as you do prompt mine ear;
And I will stoop, and humble my intents
To your *well*-practis'd wise directions. *Shakesp. Hen. VI.*

The *well*-proportion'd shape, and beauteous face,
Shall never more be seen by mortal eyes. *Dryden.*

'Twas not the hasty product of a day,
But the *well*-ripen'd fruit of wise delay. *Dryden.*

Procure those that are fresh gathered, strait, smooth, and *well*-rooted. *Mortimer's Husbandry.*

If I should instruct them to make *well*-running verses, they want genius to give them strength. *Dryden.*

The eating of a *well*-seasoned dish, suited to a man's palate, may move the mind, by the delight itself that accompanies the eating, without reference to any other end. *Locke.*

Instead of *well*-set hair, baldness. *Isa.* iii. 24.

Abraham and Sarah were old, and *well*-stricken in age. *Genesis.*

Many *well*-shaped innocent virgins are waddling like big-bellied women. *Spectator,* N° 127.

We never see beautiful and *well*-tasted fruits from a tree choaked with thorns and briars. *Dryden's Dufresnoy.*

The *well*-tim'd oars
With sounding strokes divide the sparkling waves. *Smith.*

Wisdom's triumph is *well*-tim'd retreat,
As hard a science to the fair as great. *Pope.*

Mean time we thank you for your *well*-took labour.
Go to your rest. *Shakesp. Hamlet.*

Oh you are *well*-tun'd now; but I'll let down the pegs that make this musick. *Shakesp. Othello.*

Her *well*-turn'd neck he view'd,
And on her shoulders her dishevel'd hair. *Dryden.*

A *well*-weighed judicious poem, which at first gains no more upon the world than to be just received, insinuates itself by insensible degrees into the liking of the reader. *Dryden.*

He rails
On me, my bargains, and my *well*-won thrift,
Which he calls interest. *Shakesp. Merch. of Venice.*

Each by turns the other's bound invade,
As, in some *well*-wrought picture, light and shade. *Pope.*

WE'LLADAY. *interject.* [This is a corruption of *welaway.* See WELAWAY.] Alas.

O *well*-

O *welladay*, miſtreſs Ford, having an honeſt man to your huſband, to give him ſuch cauſe of ſuſpicion. *Shakeſpeare.*

Ah, *welladay!* I'm ſhent with baneful ſmart. *Gay.*

WELLBE'ING. *n. ſ.* [*well* and *be.*] Happineſs; proſperity.

Man is not to depend upon the uncertain diſpoſitions of men for his *wellbeing*, but only on God and his own ſpirit. *Taylor's Rule of Living Holy.*

For whoſe *wellbeing*
So amply, and with hands ſo liberal,
Thou haſt provided all things. *Milton's Par. Loſt, b.* viii.

The moſt ſacred ties of duty are founded upon gratitude: ſuch as the duties of a child to his parent, and of a ſubject to his ſovereign. From the former there is required love and honour, in recompence of being; and from the latter obedience and ſubjection, in recompence of protection and *wellbeing*. *South's Sermons.*

All things are ſubſervient to the beauty, order, and *wellbeing* of the whole. *L'Eſtrange.*

He who does not co-operate with this holy ſpirit, receives none of thoſe advantages which are perfecting of his nature, and neceſſary to his *wellbeing*. *Spectator*, Nº. 571.

WELLBO'RN. *n. ſ.* Not meanly deſcended.

One whoſe extraction from an antient line,
Gives hope again that *wellborn* men may ſhine. *Waller.*

Heav'n, that *wellborn* ſouls inſpires,
Prompts me, through lifted ſwords, and riſing fires,
To ruſh undaunted to defend the walls. *Dryden.*

WELLBRE'D. *adj.* [*well* and *bred.*] Elegant of manners; polite.

None have been with admiration read,
But who, beſides their learning, were *wellbred*. *Roſcom.*

Both the poets were *wellbred* and well-natur'd. *Dryden.*

Wellbred ſpaniels civilly delight,
In mumbling of the game they dare not bite. *Pope.*

WELLNA'TURED. *adj.* [*well* and *nature.*] Good-natured; kind.

WELLDO'NE. *interject.* A word of praiſe.

Welldone, thou good and faithful ſervant. *Matt.* xxv. 21.

WELLFA'VOURED. *adj.* [*well* and *favour.*] Beautiful; pleaſing to the eye.

His wife ſeems to be *wellfavoured*. I will uſe her as the key of the cuckoldy rogue's coffer. *Shakeſpeare.*

WELLME'T. *interj.* [*well* and *meet.*] A term of ſalutation.

Once more to-day *wellmet*, diſtemper'd lords;
The king by me requeſts your preſence ſtraight. *Shakeſp.*

On their life no grievous burthen lies,
Who are *wellnatur'd*, temperate and wiſe:
But an inhuman and ill-temper'd mind,
Not any eaſy part in life can find. *Denham.*

The manners of the poets were not unlike; both of them were well-bred, *wellnatured*, amorous, and libertine at leaſt in their writings; it may be alſo in their lives. *Dryden.*

Still with eſteem no leſs convers'd than read;
With wit *wellnatur'd*, and with books well-bred. *Pope.*

WELLNI'GH. *adv.* [*well* and *nigh.*] Almoſt.

The ſame ſo ſore annoyed has the knight,
That *wellnigh* choaked with the deadly ſtink,
His forces fail. *Fairy Queen, b.* i.

My feet were almoſt gone: my ſteps had *wellnigh* ſlipt. *Pſ.*

England was *wellnigh* ruined by the rebellion of the barons, and Ireland utterly neglected. *Davies.*

Whoever ſhall read over St. Paul's enumeration of the duties incumbent upon it, might conclude, that *wellnigh* the whole of chriſtianity is laid on the ſhoulders of charity alone. *Sprat's Sermons.*

Notwithſtanding a ſmall diverſity of poſitions, the whole aggregate of matter, as long as it retained the nature of a chaos, would retain *wellnigh* an uniform tenuity of texture. *Bentley.*

WELLSPE'NT. *adj.* Paſſed with virtue.

They are to lie down without any thing to ſupport them in their age, but the conſcience of a *wellſpent* youth. *L'Eſtrange.*

What a refreſhment then will it be to look back upon a *wellſpent* life? *Calamy's Sermons.*

The conſtant tenour of their *wellſpent* days,
No leſs deſerv'd a juſt return of praiſe. *Pope.*

WE'LLSPRING. *n. ſ.* [pœllȝeſpꞃıŋȝ, Saxon.] Fountain; ſource.

The fountain and *wellſpring* of impiety, is a reſolved purpoſe of mind to reap in this world, what ſenſual profit or ſenſual pleaſure ſoever the world yieldeth. *Hooker.*

Underſtanding is a *wellſpring* of life. *Prov.* xvi. 22.

WELLWI'LLER. *n. ſ.* [*well* and *willer.*] One who means kindly.

Diſarming all his own countrymen, that no man might ſhew himſelf a *wellwiller* of mine. *Sidney, b.* ii.

There are fit occaſions miniſtred for men to purchaſe to themſelves *wellwillers* by the colour, under which they oftentimes proſecute quarrels of envy. *Hooker.*

WELLWI'SH. *n. ſ.* [*well* and *wiſh.*] A wiſh of happineſs.

Let it not enter into the heart of any one that hath a *wellwiſh* for his friends or poſterity, to think of a peace with France, till the Spaniſh monarchy be entirely torn from it. *Add.*

WELLWI'SHER. *n. ſ.* [from *wellwiſh.*] One who wiſhes the good of another.

The actual traitor is guilty of perjury in the eye of the law; the ſecret *wellwiſher* of the cauſe is ſo before the tribunal of conſcience. *Addiſon's Freeholder*, Nº. 6.

Betray not any of your *wellwiſhers* into the like inconveniencies. *Spectator*, Nº. 271.

No man is more your ſincere *wellwiſher* than myſelf, or more the ſincere *wellwiſher* of your family. *Pope.*

WELT. *n. ſ.* A border; a guard; an edging.

Little low hedges made round like *welts*, with ſome pretty pyramids, I like well. *Bacon.*

Certain ſcioli, or ſmatterers, are buſy in the ſkirts and outſides of learning, and have ſcarce any thing of ſolid literature to recommend them. They may have ſome edging or trimming of a ſcholar, a *welt*, or ſo; but no more. *B. Johnſon.*

To WELT. *v. a.* [from the noun.] To ſew any thing with a border.

To WE'LTER. *v. n.* [ꝩealtan, Saxon; *welteren*, Dutch; *volutari*, Lat.]

1. To roll in water or mire.

He muſt not float upon his watry bier
Unweep'd, nor *welter* to the parching winds. *Milton.*

The companions of his fall o'erwhelm'd
He ſoon diſcerns; and *welt'ring* by his ſide
The next himſelf. *Milton's Par. Loſt, b.* i.

The gaſping head flies off; a purple flood
Flows from the trunk, that *welters* in the blood. *Dryden.*

He ſung Darius, great and good,
By too ſevere a fate,
Fallen from his high eſtate,
And *welt'ring* in his blood. *Dryden's St. Cecilia.*

2. To roll voluntarily; to wallow.

If a man inglut himſelf with vanity, or *welter* in filthineſs like a ſwine, all learning, all goodneſs is ſoon forgotten. *Aſcham.*

WEMM. *n. ſ.* [ꝩem, Saxon.] A ſpot; a ſcar.

Although the wound be healed, yet the *wemme* or ſcar ſtill remaineth. *Brerewood on Languages.*

WEN. *n. ſ.* [ꝩen, Saxon.] A fleſhy or callous excreſcence, or protuberance.

Warts are ſaid to be deſtroy'd by the rubbing them with a green elder ſtick, and then burying the ſtick to rot in muck. It would be tried with corns and *wens*, and ſuch other excreſcences. *Bacon's Nat. Hiſt.*

Mountains ſeem but ſo many *wens* and unnatural protuberances upon the face of the earth. *More.*

The poet rejects all incidents which are foreign to his poem: they are *wens* and other excreſcences, which belong not to the body. *Dryden's Dufreſnoy.*

A promontory *wen* with grieſly grace,
Stood high upon the handle of his face. *Dryden.*

WENCH. *n. ſ.* [ꝩencle, Saxon.]

1. A young woman.

What do I, ſilly *wench*, know what love hath prepared for me? *Sidney, b.* ii.

Now—how doſt thou look now? Oh ill-ſtarr'd *wench!*
Pale as thy ſmock! when we ſhall meet at compt,
This look of thine will hurl my ſoul from heav'n,
And fiends will ſnatch at it. Cold, cold, my girl,
Ev'n like thy chaſtity. *Shakeſp. Othello.*

Thou wouldſt perſwade her to a worſe offence
Than that, whereof thou didſt accuſe her *wench*. *Donne.*

2. A young woman in contempt; a ſtrumpet.

But the rude *wench* her anſwer'd nought at all. *Spenſer.*

Do not play in *wench*-like words with that
Which is ſo ſerious. *Shakeſp. Cymbeline.*

Men have theſe ambitious fancies,
And wanton *wenches* read romances. *Prior.*

3. A ſtrumpet.

It is not a digreſſion to talk of bawds in a diſcourſe upon *wenches*. *Spectator*, Nº 266.

WE'NCHER. *n. ſ.* [from *wench.*] A fornicator.

He muſt be no great eater, drinker, or ſleeper; no gameſter, *wencher*, or fop. *Grew's Coſmology.*

To WEND. *v. n.* [ꝩendan, Saxon.]

1. To go; to paſs to or from. This word is now obſolete, but its preterite *went*, is ſtill in uſe.

Back to Athens ſhall the lovers *wend*
With league, whoſe date till death ſhall never end. *Shakeſp.*

They *went* on, and inferred, that if the world were a living creature, it had a ſoul. *Bacon's Nat. Hiſt.*

Then Rome ſhall *wend* to Benevento;
Great feats ſhall he atchieve! *Arbuthnot.*

2. To turn round. It ſeems to be an old ſea term.

A ſhip of 600 tons will carry as good ordnance as a ſhip of 1200 tons; and though the greater have double the number, the leſſer will turn her broadſides twice, before the greater can *wend* once. *Raleigh.*

WE'NNEL. *n. ſ.* [a corrupted word for *weanling.*] An animal newly taken from the dam.

Pinch never thy *wennels* of water or meat,
If ever ye hope for to have them good neat. *Tuſſer.*

WE'NNY. *adj.* [from *wen.*] Having the nature of a wen.

Some perſons, ſo deformed with theſe, have ſuſpected them to be *wenny*. *Wiſeman's Surgery.*

Went. *pret.* See Wend and Go.

Wept. pret. and part. of *weep*.

She for joy tenderly *wept*. *Milton.*

Were. of the verb to *be*.

To give our sister to one uncircumcised, *were* a reproach unto us. *Gen.* xxxiv. 14.

In infusions in things that are of too high a spirit, you *were* better pour off the first infusion, and use the latter. *Bacon.*

Henry divided, as it *were*,
The person of himself into four parts. *Daniel's Civil War.*

As though there *were* any feriation in nature, or *justitium*'s imaginable in professions, this season is termed the physicians vacation. *Brown's Vulgar Errours.*

He had been well assur'd that art
And conduct *were* of war the better part. *Dryden.*

Were. *n. s.* A dam. See Wear.

O river! let thy bed be turned from fine gravel to weeds and mud; let some unjust niggards make *weres* to spoil thy beauty. *Sid.*

Wert. the second person singular of the preterite of to *be*.

Thou *wert* heard *B. Johnson.*

O that thou *wert* as my brother. *Cant.* viii. 1.

All join'd, and thou of many *wert* but one. *Dryden.*

Werth. *weorth, wyrth. n. s.* Whether initial or final in the names of places, signify a farm, court, or village, from the Saxon peoꞃðiꝫ, used by them in the same sense. *Gibson's Cam.*

We'sil. *n. s.* See Wesand.

The *wesil*, or windpipe, we call aspera arteria. *Bacon.*

West. *n. s.* [ꝥeꞅꞇ, Saxon; *west*, Dutch.] The region where the sun goes below the horizon at the equinoxes.

The *west* yet glimmers with some streaks of day:
Now spurs the lated traveller apace,
To gain the timely inn. *Shakesp. Macbeth.*

The moon in level'd *west* was set. *Milton.*

All bright Phœbus views in early morn,
Or when his evening beams the *west* adorn. *Pope.*

West. *adj.* Being towards, or coming from, the region of the setting sun.

A mighty strong *west* wind took away the locusts. *Ex.* x.

This shall be your *west* border. *Num.* xxxiv. 6.

The Phenicians had great fleets; so had the Carthaginians, which is yet farther *west*. *Bacon.*

West. *adv.* To the west of any place.

West of this forest,
In goodly form comes on the enemy. *Shakespeare.*

What earth yields in India east or *west*. *Milton.*

West from Orontes to the ocean. *Milton.*

We'stering. *adj.* Passing to the west.

The star that rose at evening bright,
Toward heav'ns descent had slop'd his *westering* wheel. *Milt.*

We'sterly. *adj.* [from *west*.] Tending or being towards the west.

These bills give us a view of the most easterly, southerly, and *westerly* parts of England. *Graunt's Bills of Mortality.*

We'stern. *adj.* [from *west*.] Being in the west, or toward the part where the sun sets.

Now fair Phœbus 'gan decline in haste
His weary waggon to the *western* vale. *Spenser.*

The *western* part is a continued rock. *Addison.*

We'stward. *adv.* [ꝥeꞅꞇeaꞃð, Saxon.] Towards the west.

By water they found the sea *westward* from Peru, which is always very calm. *Abbot's Description of the World.*

The grove of sycamore,
That *westward* rooteth from the city side. *Shakespeare.*

When *westward* like the sun you took your way,
And from benighted Britain bore the day. *Dryden.*

The storm flies,
From *westward*, when the show'ry kids arise. *Addison.*

At home then stay,
Nor *westward* curious take thy way. *Prior.*

We'stwardly. *adv.* [from *westward*.] With tendency to the west.

If our loves faint, and *westwardly* decline;
To me thou falsely thine,
And I to thee mine actions shall disguise. *Donne.*

Wet. *adj.* [ꝥæꞇ, Saxon; *waed*, Danish.]

1. Humid; having some moisture adhering.

They are *wet* with the show'rs of the mountains. *Job.* xxiv.

The soals of the feet have great affinity with the head, and the mouth of the stomach; as going *wet*-shod to those that use it not, affecteth both. *Bacon's Nat. Hist.*

2. Rainy; watery.

Wet weather seldom hurts the most unwise. *Dryden.*

Wet. *n. s.* Water; humidity; moisture; rainy weather.

Plants appearing weather'd, stubby, and curled, is the effect of immoderate *wet*. *Bacon.*

Now the sun, with more effectual beams,
Had cheer'd the face of the earth, and dry'd the *wet*
From drooping plant. *Milton's Par. Regain'd.*

Tuberoses will not endure the *wet*; therefore set your pots into the conserve, and keep them dry. *Evelyn.*

Your master's riding-coat turn inside out, to preserve the outside from *wet*. *Swift.*

To Wet. *v. a.* [from the noun.]

1. To humectate; to moisten; to make to have moisture adherent.

Better learn of him, that learned be,
And han been watered at the muses well;
The kindly dew drops from the higher tree,
And *wets* the little plants, that lowly dwell. *Spenser.*

A drop of water running swiftly over straw, *wetteth* not. *Bac.*

Wet the thirsty earth with falling show'rs. *Milton.*

2. To drench with drink.

Let's drink the other cup to *wet* our whistles, and so sing away all sad thoughts. *Walton's Angler.*

We'ther. *n. s.* [ꝥeðeꞃ, Saxon; *weder*, Dutch.] A ram castrated.

I am a tainted *wether* of the flock,
Meetest for death. *Shakesp. Merch. of Venice.*

He doth not apprehend how the tail of an African *weather* outweigheth the body of a good calf, that is, an hundred pound. *Brown's Vulg. Errours.*

Although there be naturally of horses, bulls, or rams, more males than females; yet artificially, that is, by making geldings, oxen, and *weathers*, there are fewer. *Graunt.*

When Blowzelind expir'd, the *weather*'s bell
Before the drooping flock toll'd forth her knell. *Gay.*

It is much more difficult to find a fat *weather*, than if half that species were fairly knock'd on the head. *Swift.*

We'tness. [from *wet*.] The state of being wet; moisture; humidity.

The *wetness* of these bottoms often spoils them for corn. *Mortimer's Husbandry.*

To Wex. *v. a.* [corrupted from *wax* by Spenser, for a rhyme, and imitated by Dryden.] To grow; to increase.

She first taught men a woman to obey;
But when her son to man's estate did *wex*,
She it surrender'd. *Fairy Queen, b.* ii.

She trod a *wexing* moon, that soon wou'd wane,
And drinking borrow'd light, be fill'd again. *Dryden.*

Counting sev'n from noon,
'Tis Venus' hour, and in the *wexing* moon. *Dryden.*

We'zand. *n. s.* [see *wesand*.] The windpipe.

Air is ingustible, and by the rough artery, or *wezand*, conducted into the lungs. *Brown's Vulgar Errours.*

Whale. *n. s.* [hꝥale, Saxon.] The largest of fish; the largest of the animals that inhabit this globe.

God created the great *whales*. *Genesis.*

Barr'd up with ribs of *whale*-bone, she did leese
None of the *whale*'s length, for it reach'd her knees. *Bp. Corbet.*

The greatest *whale* that swims the sea,
Does instantly my pow'r obey. *Swift.*

Whame. *n. s.*

The *whame*, or burrel-fly, is vexatious to horses in summer, not by stinging, but by their bombylious noise, or tickling them in sticking their nits on the hair. *Derham.*

Wha'ly. *adj.* [See *weal*.] Marked in streaks.

A bearded goat, whose rugged hair,
And *whaly* eyes, the sign of jealousy,
Was like the person's self, whom he did bear. *Fa. Queen.*

Wharf. *n. s.* [*warf*, Swedish; *werf*, Dutch.] A perpendicular bank or mole, raised for the convenience of lading or emptying vessels.

Duller should'st thou be, than the fat weed,
That roots itself in ease on Lethe's *wharf*,
Would'st thou not stir in this. *Shakesp. Hamlet.*

There were not in London used so many *wharfs*, or keys, for the landing of merchants goods. *Child on Trade.*

Wha'rfage. *n. s.* [from *wharf*.] Dues for landing at a wharf.

Wha'rfinger. *n. s.* [from *wharf*.] One who attends a wharf.

To Whurr. *v. n.* To pronounce the letter *r* with too much force. *Dict.*

What. *pronoun.* [hꝥæꞇ, Saxon; *wat*, Dutch.]

1. That which.

What you can make her do,
I am content to look on; *what* to speak,
I am content to hear. *Shakesp. Winter Tale.*

In these cases we examine the why, the *what*, and the how of things. *L'Estrange.*

He's with a superstitious fear not aw'd,
For *what* befals at home, or *what* abroad. *Dryden.*

A satire on one of the common stamp, never meets with that approbation, as *what* is aimed at a person whose merit places him upon an eminence. *Addison.*

Mark *what* it is his mind aims at in the question, and not what words he expresses. *Locke.*

If any thing be stated in a different manner from *what* you like, tell me freely. *Pope to Swift.*

Whatever commodities lie under the greatest discouragements from England, those are *what* they are most industrious in cultivating. *Swift.*

2. Which part.

If we rightly estimate things, *what* in them is purely owing to nature, and *what* to labour, we shall find ninety-nine parts of a hundred are wholly to be put on the account of labour. *Locke.*

3. Some-

3. Something that is in one's mind indefinitely.

I tell thee *what*, corporal, I could tear her. *Shakespeare.*

4. Which of several.

Whether it were the shortness of his foresight, the strength of his will, or the dazling of his suspicions, or *what* it was, certain it is, that the perpetual troubles of his fortunes could not have been without some main errors in his nature. *Bacon.*

Comets are rather gazed upon than wisely observed; that is, *what* kind of comet for magnitude, colour, placing in the heaven, or lasting, produceth *what* kind of effect. *Bacon.*

See *what* natures accompany *what* colours; for by that you shall induce colours by producing those natures. *Bacon.*

Shew *what* aliment is proper for that intention, and *what* intention is proper to be pursued in such a constitution. *Arbuth.*

5. An interjection by way of surprise or question.

What! canst thou not forbear me half an hour,
Then get thee gone, and dig my grave thyself? *Shakespeare.*

What if I advance an invention of my own to supply the defect of our new writers. *Dryden's Juvenal.*

6. What *Though*. *What* imports it *though?* notwithstanding. An elliptical mode of speech.

What though a child may be able to read; there is no doubt but the meanest among the people under the law had been as able as the priests themselves were to offer sacrifice, did this make sacrifice of no effect? *Hooker.*

What though none live my innocence to tell,
I know it; truth may own a generous pride,
I clear myself, and care for none beside. *Dryden.*

7. What *Time*, *What Day*. At the time when; on the day when.

What day the genial angel to our sire
Brought her, more lovely than Pandora. *Milton.*

Then balmy sleep had charm'd my eyes to rest,
What time the morn mysterious visions brings,
While purer slumbers spread their golden wings. *Pope.*

Me sole the daughter of the deep address'd;
What time with hunger pin'd, my absent mates
Roam'd the wild isle in search of rural cates. *Pope.*

8. [Pronoun interrogative.] Which of many? interrogatively.

What art thou,
That here in desart hast thy habitance? *Fairy Queen.*

What is't to thee if he neglect thy urn,
Or without spices lets thy body burn? *Dryden.*

Whate'er I begg'd, thou like a dotard speak'st
More than is requisite; and *what* of this?
Why is it mention'd now. *Dryden.*

What one of an hundred of the zealous bigots in all parties ever examined the tenets he is so stiff in? *Locke.*

When any new thing comes in their way, children ask the common question of a stranger, *what* is it? *Locke.*

9. To how great a degree, used either interrogatively or demonstratively.

Am I so much deform'd?
What partial judges are our love and hate? *Dryden.*

10. It is used adverbially for partly; in part.

The enemy having his country wasted, *what* by himself, and *what* by the soldiers, findeth succour in no place. *Spenser.*

Thus, *what* with the war, *what* with the sweat, *what* with the gallows, and *what* with poverty, I am custom shrunk. *Sha.*

The year before, he had so used the matter, that *what* by force, *what* by policy, he had taken from the Christians above thirty small castles. *Knolles's Hist. of the Turks.*

When they come to cast up the profit and loss, *what* betwixt force, interest, or good manners, the adventurer escapes well, if he can but get off. *L'Estrange.*

What with carrying apples, grapes, and fewel, he finds himself in a hurry. *L'Estrange.*

What with the benefit of their situation, the art and parsimony of their people, they have grown so considerable, that they have treated upon an equal foot with great princes. *Tem.*

They live a popular life, and then *what* for business, pleasures, company, there's scarce room for a morning's reflexion. *Norris.*

If these halfpence should gain admittance, in no long space of time, *what* by the clandestine practices of the coiner, *what* by his own counterfeits and those of others, his limited quantity would be tripled. *Swift.*

11. What *Ho*. An interjection of calling.

What ho, thou genius of the clime, *what ho*,
Ly'st thou asleep beneath these hills of snow?
Stretch out thy lazy limbs. *Dryden.*

Wha'tever. }
Wha'tso. } *pronouns.* [from *what* and *soever*. *Whatso* is
Wha'tsoever. } not now in use.

1. Having one nature or another; being one or another either generically, specifically or numerically.

To forfeit all your goods, lands, tenements,
Castles, and *whatsoever*, and to be
Out of the king's protection. *Shakespeare's Henry* VIII.

If thence he 'scape into *whatever* world. *Milton.*

In *whatsoever* shape he lurk I'll know. *Milton.*

Wisely restoring *whatsoever* grace
It lost by change of times, or tongues or place. *Denham.*

Holy writ abounds in accounts of this nature, as much as any other history *whatsoever*. *Addison's Freeholder.*

No contrivance, no prudence *whatsoever* can deviate from his scheme, without leaving us worse than it found us. *Atterbury.*

Thus *whatever* successive duration shall be bounded at one end, and be all past and present, must come infinitely short of infinity. *Bentley's Sermons.*

Whatever is read differs as much from what is repeated without book, as a copy does from an original. *Swift.*

2. Any thing, be it what it will.

Whatsoever our liturgy hath more than theirs, they cut it off. *Hooker.*

Whatever thing
The scythe of time mows down, devour. *Milton.*

3. The same, be it this or that.

Be *whate'er* Vitruvius was before. *Pope.*

4. All that; the whole that; all particulars that.

From hence he views with his black lidded eye,
Whatso the heaven in his wide vault contains. *Spenser.*

Whate'er the ocean pales or sky inclips
Is thine. *Shakespeare.*

At once came forth *whatever* creeps. *Milton.*

Wheal. *n. s.* [See Weal] A pustule; a small swelling filled with matter.

The humour cannot transpire, whereupon it corrupts and raises little *wheals* or blisters. *Wiseman's Surgery.*

WHEAT. *n. s.* [ƿheate, Saxon; *weyde*, Dutch; *triticum*, Lat.] The grain of which bread is chiefly made.

It hath an apetalous flower, disposed into spikes; each of them consists of many stamina which are included in a squamose flower-cup, having awns: the pointal rises in the center, which afterwards becomes an oblong seed, convex on one side, but furrowed on the other: it is farinaceous, and inclosed by a coat which before was the flower-cup: these are produced singly, and collected in a close spike, being affixed to an indented axis. The species are; 1. White or red *wheat*, without awn. 2. Red *wheat*, in some places called Kentish *wheat*. 3. White *wheat*. 4. Red-eared bearded *wheat*. 5. Cone *wheat*. 6. Grey *wheat*, and in some places duck-bill *wheat* and grey pollard. 7. Polonian *wheat*. 8. Many eared *wheat*. 9. Summer *wheat*. 10. Naked barley. 11. Long grained *wheat*. 12. Six rowed *wheat*. 13. White eared *wheat* with long awns: Of all these sorts cultivated in this country, the cone *wheat* is chiefly preserved, as it has a larger ear and a fuller grain than any other; but the seeds of all should be annually changed; for if they are sown on the same farm, they will not succeed so well as when the seed is brought from a distant country. *Miller.*

He mildews the white *wheat*, and hurts the poor creature of the earth. *Shakespeare's King Lear.*

Reuben went in the days of *wheat*-harvest. *Gen.* xxx.

August shall bear the form of a young man of a fierce aspect; upon his head a garland of *wheat* and rie. *Peacham.*

Next to rice is *wheat*; the bran of which is highly acescent. *Arbuthnot on Aliments.*

The damsels laughing fly: the giddy clown
Again upon a *wheat*-sheaf drops a down. *Gay.*

Whea'ten. *adj.* [from *wheat*.] Made of wheat.

Of *wheaten* flour shalt thou make them. *Exod* xxix.

Here summer in her *wheaten* garland crown'd. *Addison.*

The assize of *wheaten* bread is in London. *Arbuth.*

His task it was the *wheaten* loaves to lay,
And from the banquet take the bowls away. *Pope.*

There is a project on foot for transporting our best *wheaten* straw to Dunstable, and obliging us by law to take off yearly so many tun of the straw hats. *Swift.*

Whea'tear. *n. s.* A small bird very delicate.

What cook would lose her time in picking larks, *wheatears*, and other small birds. *Swift.*

Whea'tplum. *n. s.* A sort of plum. *Ainsworth.*

To Wheedle. *v. a.* [Of this word I can find no etymology, though used by good writers, and *Locke* seems to mention it as a cant word.] To entice by soft words; to flatter; to persuade by kind words.

His bus'ness was to pump and *wheedle*,
And men with their own keys unriddle,
To make them to themselves give answers,
For which they pay the necromancers. *Hudibras.*

A fox stood licking of his lips at the cock, and *wheedling* him to get him down. *L'Estrange.*

His sire,
From Mars his forge sent to Minerva's schools
To learn the unlucky art of *wheedling* fools. *Dryden.*

He that first brought the word sham, or *wheedle*, in use, put together as he thought fit, ideas he made it stand for. *Locke.*

A laughing, toying, *wheedling*, whimp'ring she,
Shall make him amble on a gossip's message. *Rowe.*

The world has never been prepared for these trifles by prefaces, *wheedled* or troubled with excuses. *Pope.*

Johnny *wheedl'd*, threaten'd, fawn'd,
Till Phillis all her trinkets pawn'd. *Swift.*

WHEEL. *n. ſ.* [ƿeol, Saxon; *wiel*, Dutch; *hioel*, Iſlandick.]

1. A circular body that turns round upon an axis.

Carnality within raiſes all the combuſtions without: this is the great *wheel* to which the clock owes its motion. *Dec. P.*

The gaſping charioteer beneath the *wheel*
Of his own car. *Dryden.*

Fortune ſits all breathleſs, and admires to feel
A fate ſo weighty, that it ſtops her *wheel.* *Dryden.*

Some watches are made with four *wheels*, others with five. *Locke.*

A *wheel*-plough is one of the beſt and eaſieſt draughts. *Mortimer's Huſbandry.*

2. A circular body.

Let go thy hold when a great *wheel* runs down a hill, leſt it break thy neck with following it. *Shakeſpeare's King Lear.*

3. A carriage that runs upon wheels.

The ſtar that roſe at ev'ning bright,
Towards heav'n's deſcent had ſtopt his weſtering *wheel.* *Milton.*

Through the proud ſtreet ſhe moves the publick gaze,
The turning *wheel* before the palace ſtays. *Pope.*

4. An inſtrument on which criminals are tortured.

Let them pull all about mine ears, preſent me
Death on the *wheel*, or at wild horſes heels. *Shakeſpeare.*

Thou art a ſoul in bliſs, but I am bound
Upon a *wheel* of fire. *Shakeſp. King Lear.*

For all the torments of her *wheel*
May you as many pleaſures ſhare. *Waller.*

His examination is like that which is made by the rack and *wheel.* *Addiſon.*

5. The inſtrument of ſpinning.

Verſe ſweetens care, however rude the ſound,
All at her work the village maiden ſings;
Nor as ſhe turns the giddy *wheel* around,
Revolves the ſad viciſſitudes of things. *Giffard.*

6. Rotation; revolution.

Look not too long upon theſe turning *wheels* of viciſſitude, leſt we become giddy. *Bacon.*

According to the common viciſſitude and *wheel* of things, the proud and the inſolent, after long trampling upon others, come at length to be trampled upon themſelves. *South's Sermons.*

7. A compaſs about; a tract approaching to circularity.

He throws his flight in many an airy *wheel.* *Milton.*

To WHEEL. *v. n.* [from the noun.]

1. To move on wheels.

2. To turn on an axis.

The moon carried about the earth always ſhews the ſame face to us, not once *wheeling* upon her own center. *Bentley.*

3. To revolve; to have a rotatory motion.

4. To turn; to have viciſſitudes.

5. To fetch a compaſs.

Spies
Held me in chace, that I was forc'd to *wheel*
Three or four miles about. *Shakeſpeare's Coriolanus.*

You my Myrmidons,
Mark what I ſay, attend me where I *wheel.* *Shakeſpeare.*

Continually *wheeling* about, he kept them in ſo ſtrait, that no man could, without great danger, go to water his horſe. *Knol.*

He at hand provokes
His rage, and plies him with redoubled ſtrokes;
Wheels as he *wheels.* *Dryden.*

Half theſe draw off, and coaſt the ſouth
With ſtricteſt watch: theſe other *wheel* the north:
Our circuit meets full weſt: as flame they part,
Half *wheeling* to the ſhield, half to the ſpear. *Milton.*

Now ſmoothly ſteers through air his rapid flight,
Then *wheeling* down the ſteep of heav'n he flies
And draws a radiant circle o'er the ſkies. *Pope.*

6. To roll forward.

The courſe of juſtice *wheel'd* about,
And left thee but a very prey to time. *Shakeſpeare.*

Thunder
Muſt *wheel* on the earth, devouring where it rolls. *Milton.*

To WHEEL. *v. a.* To put into a rotatory motion; to make to whirl round.

Heav'n rowl'd
Her motions, as the great firſt Mover's hand
Firſt *wheels* their courſe. *Milton's Paradiſe Loſt.*

WHEE'LBARROW. *n. ſ.* [*wheel* and *barrow.*] A carriage driven forward on one wheel.

Carry bottles in a *wheelbarrow* upon rough ground, but not filled full, but leave ſome air. *Bacon.*

Pippins did in *wheelbarrows* abound *King.*

WHEE'LER. *n. ſ.* [from *wheel.*] A maker of wheels.

After local names, the moſt have been derived from occupations, as Potter, Smith, Braſier, *Wheeler*, Wright. *Camden.*

WHEE'LWRIGHT. *n. ſ.* [*wheel* and *wright.*] A maker of wheel-carriages.

It is a tough wood, and all heart, being good for the *wheelwrights.* *Mortimer.*

WHEE'LY. *adj.* [from *wheel.*] Circular; ſuitable to rotation.

Hinds exerciſe the pointed ſteel
On the hard rock, and give a *wheely* form
To the expected grinder. *Philips.*

To WHEEZE. *v. n.* [ƿeoſon, Saxon.] To breath with noiſe.

The conſtriction of the trachæa ſtreightens the paſſage of the air, and produces the *wheezing* in the aſthma. *Floyer.*

It is eaſy to run into ridicule the beſt deſcriptions, when once a man is in the humour of laughing, till he *wheezes* at his own dull jeſt. *Dryden.*

The fawning dog runs mad; the *wheezing* ſwine
With coughs is choak'd. *Dryden's Virgil.*

Prepare balſamick cups, to *wheezing* lungs
Medicinal, and ſhort-breath'd. *Philips.*

Wheezing aſthma loth to ſtir. *Swift.*

WHELK. *n. ſ.* [See to WELK.]

1. An inequality; a protuberance.

His face is all bubuckles, and *whelks*, and knobs, and flames of fire. *Shakeſpeare's Henry V.*

2. A puſtule. [See WEAL.]

To WHELM. *v. a.* [apƿilſan, Saxon; *wilma*, Iſlandick.]

1. To cover with ſomething not to be thrown off; to bury.

Grievous miſchiefs which a wicked fay
Had wrought, and many *whelm'd* in deadly pain. *Fa. Qu.*

This pink is my prize, or ocean *whelm* them all. *Shak.*

So the ſad offence deſerves,
Plung'd in the deep for ever let me lye,
Whelm'd under ſeas. *Addiſon.*

Diſcharge the load of earth that lies on you, like one of the mountains under which the poets ſay, the giants and men of the earth are *whelmed.* *Pope.*

Deplore
The *whelming* billow and the faithleſs oar. *Gay.*

2. To throw upon ſomething ſo as to cover or bury it.

On thoſe curſed engines triple row,
They ſaw them *whelm'd*, and all their confidence
Under the weight of mountains bury'd deep. *Milton.*

Whelm ſome things over them and keep them there. *Mortim.*

WHELP. *n. ſ.* [*welp*, Dutch; *huolpar*, Iſlandick; *hwalp*, Swediſh.]

1. The young of a dog; a puppy.

They call'd us, for our fierceneſs, Engliſh dogs,
Now, like their *whelps*, we crying run away. *Shakeſpeare.*

Whelps come to their growth within three quarters of a year. *Bacon's Natural Hiſtory.*

Whelps are blind nine days, and then begin to ſee as generally believed; but as we have elſewhere declared, it is rare that their eye-lids open until the twelfth day. *Brown.*

2. The young of any beaſt of prey.

The lion's *whelp* ſhall be to himſelf unknown. *Shakeſpeare.*

Thoſe unlickt bear *whelps.* *Donne.*

3. A ſon. In contempt.

The young *whelp* of Talbot's raging brood
Did fleſh his puny ſword in Frenchmens blood. *Shakeſpeare.*

4. A young man. In contempt.

Slave, I will ſtrike your ſoul out with my foot,
Let me but find you again with ſuch a face:
You *whelp.* *Ben. Johnſon's Catiline.*

That aukward *whelp*, with his money-bags, would have made his entrance. *Addiſon's Guardian.*

To WHELP. *v. n.* To bring young. Applied to beaſts, generally beaſts of prey.

A lioneſs hath *whelped* in the ſtreets,
And graves have yawn'd. *Shakeſpeare's Julius Cæſar.*

In a bitch ready to *whelp*, we found four puppies. *Boyle.*

In their palaces,
Where luxury late reign'd, ſea-monſters *whelp'd*
And ſtabled. *Milton's Paradiſe Loſt.*

WHEN. *adv.* [*whan*, Gothick; ƿænne, Sax. *wanneer*, Dutch.]

1. At the time that.

Divers curious men judged that one Theodoſius ſhould ſucceed, *when* indeed Theodoſius did. *Camden.*

One who died ſeveral ages ago, raiſes a ſecret fondneſs and benevolence for him in our minds, *when* we read his ſtory. *Add.*

2. At what time?

When was it ſhe laſt walk'd?—
—Since his majeſty went into the field. *Shakeſp. Macbeth.*

If there's a pow'r above us,
And that there is all nature cries aloud,
Through all her works; he muſt delight in virtue,
And that which he delights in muſt be happy.
But *when?* or where? *Addiſon.*

3. Which time.

I was adopted heir by his conſent;
Since *when*, his oath is broke. *Shakeſpeare's Henry VI.*

4. At which time.

By this the bloody troops were at the door,
When as a ſudden and a ſtrange diſmay,
Enforc'd them ſtrain who ſhould go in before. *Daniel.*

5. After the time that.

When I have once handed a report to another, how know I how he may improve it? *Government of the Tongue.*

5. At what time.

Kings may
Take their advantage *when* and how they list. *Daniel.*

6. At what particular time.

His seed, *when* is not set, shall bruise my head. *Milton.*

7. WHEN *as.* At the time when; what time.

This *when as* Guyon saw, he 'gan enquire
What meant that preace about that lady's throne. *Fa. Queen.*
When as sacred light began to dawn
In Eden on the humid flow'rs, that breath'd
Their morning incense, came the human pair. *Milton.*

WHENCE. *adv.* [Formed from *where* by the same analogy with *hence* from *here.*]

1. From what place.
2. From what person.

Whence, feeble nature! shall we summon aid,
If by our pity and our pride betray'd? *Prior.*

3. From which premises.

Their practice was to look no farther before them than the next line; *whence* it will follow, that they can drive to no certain point. *Dryden.*

4. From which place or person.

Grateful to acknowledge *whence* his good descends. *Milt.*

5. For which cause.

Recent urine, distilled with a fixed alkali, is turned into an alkaline nature; *whence* alkaline salts, taken into a human body, have the power of turning its benign salts into fiery and volatile. *Arbuthnot on Aliments.*

6. From what source.

I have shewn *whence* the understanding may get all the ideas it has. *Locke.*

7. *From* WHENCE. A vitious mode of speech.

From whence he views, with his black-lidded eye,
Whatso the heaven in his wide vault contains. *Spenser.*
To leave his wife, to leave his babes,
His mansion, and his titles, in a place
From whence himself does fly. *Shakesp. Macbeth.*

8. *Of* WHENCE. Another barbarism.

He ask'd his guide,
What and *of whence* was he who press'd the hero's side? *Dryden's Æn.*

WHE'NCESOEVER. *adv.* [*whence* and *ever.*] From what place soever.

Any idea, *whencesoever* we have it, contains in it all the properties it has. *Locke.*

Wretched name, or arbitrary thing!
Whence ever I thy cruel essence bring,
I own thy influence; for I feel thy sting. *Prior.*

WHE'NEVER. } *adv.* [*when* and *ever*, or *soever.*] At whatso-
WHE'NSOEVER. } ever time.

O welcome hour *whenever!* Why delays
His hand to execute? *Milt. Paradise Lost.*

Men grow first acquainted with many of these self-evident truths, upon their being proposed; not because innate, but because the consideration of the nature of the things, contained in those words, would not suffer him to think otherwise, how or *whensoever* he is brought to reflection. *Locke.*

Our religion, *whenever* it is truly received into the heart, will appear in justice, friendship, and charity. *Rogers.*

WHERE. *adv.* [hpœr, Saxon; *waer*, Dutch.]

1. At which place or places.

She visited that place, *where* first she was so happy as to see the cause of her unhap. *Sidney.*

God doth in publick prayer respect the solemnity of places, *where* his name should be called on amongst his people. *Hooker.*

In every land we have a larger space,
Where we with green adorn our fairy bow'rs. *Dryden.*
In Lydia born,
Where plenteous harvests the fat fields adorn. *Dryden.*

2. At what place.

Ah! *where* was Eloise? *Pope.*

3. At the place in which.

Where I thought the remnant of mine age
Should have been cherish'd by her child-like duty,
I now am full resolv'd to take a wife. *Shakespeare.*

4. *Any* WHERE. At any place.

Those subterraneous waters were universal, as a dissolution of the exterior earth could not be made *any where* but it would fall into waters. *Burnet's Theory of the Earth.*

5. WHERE, like *here*, has in composition a kind of pronominal signification: as, *whereof*, of which.

6. It has the nature of a noun. Not now in use.

He shall find no *where* safe to hide himself. *Spenser.*
Bid them farewel, Cordelia, though unkind:
Thou losest here, a better *where* to find. *Shakesp. K. Lear.*

WHE'REABOUT. *adv.* [*where* and *about.*]

1. Near what place.
2. Near which place.

Thou firm set earth,
Hear not my steps, which way they walk, for fear
Thy very stones prate of my *whereabout.* *Shakespeare's Macbeth.*

3. Concerning which.

The greatness of all actions is measured by the worthiness of the subject from which they proceed, and the object *whereabout* they are conversant: we must of necessity, in both respects, acknowledge that this present world affordeth not any thing comparable unto the duties of religion. *Hooker.*

WHEREA'S. *adv.* [*where* and *as.*]

1. When on the contrary.

Are not those found to be the greatest zealots who are most notoriously ignorant? *whereas* true zeal should always begin with true knowledge. *Sprat's Sermons.*

The aliment of plants is nearly one uniform juice; *whereas* animals live upon very different sorts of substances. *Arbuthnot.*

2. At which place. Obsolete.

They came to fiery flood of Phlegeton,
Whereas the damned ghosts in torments fry. *Fa. Queen.*
Prepare to ride unto St. Alban's,
Whereas the king and queen do mean to hawk. *Shak. H. VI.*

3. The thing being so that. Always referred to something different.

Whereas we read so many of them so much commended, some for their mild and merciful disposition, some for their virtuous severity, some for integrity of life; all these were the fruits of true and infallible principles delivered unto us in the word of God. *Hooker.*

Whereas all bodies seem to work by the communication of their natures, and impressions of their motions; the diffusion of species visible seemeth to participate more of the former, and the species audible of the latter. *Bacon.*

Whereas wars are generally causes of poverty, the special nature of this war with Spain, if made by sea, is like to be a lucrative war. *Bacon.*

Whereas seeing requires light, a free medium, and a right line to the objects, we can hear in the dark, immured, and by curve lines. *Holder's Elements of Speech.*

Whereas at first we had only three of these principles, their number is already swoln to five. *Baker on Learning.*

One imagines that the terrestrial matter, which is showered down with rain, enlarges the bulk of the earth: another fancies that the earth will ere long all be washed away by rains, and the waters of the ocean turned forth to overwhelm the dry land: *whereas*, by this distribution of matter, continual provision is every where made for the supply of bodies. *Woodward.*

WHEREA'T. *adv.* [*where* and *at.*] At which.

This he thought would be the fittest resting place, 'till we might go further from his mother's fury; *whereat* he was no less angry, and ashamed, than desirous to obey Zelmane. *Sidn.*

This is in man's conversion unto God, the first stage *whereat* his race towards heaven beginneth. *Hooker.*

Whereat I wak'd, and found
Before mine eyes all real, as the dream
Had lively shadow'd. *Milton's Paradise Lost.*

WHEREBY'. *adv.* [*where* and *by.*] By which.

But even that, you must confess, you have received of her, and so are rather gratefully to thank her, than to press any further, 'till you bring something of your own, *whereby* to claim it. *Sidney.*

Prevent those evils *whereby* the hearts of men are lost. *Hook.*

You take my life,
When you do take the means *whereby* I live. *Shakespeare.*

If an enemy hath taken all that from a prince *whereby* he was a king, he may refresh himself by considering all that is left him, *whereby* he is a man. *Taylor.*

This is the most rational and most profitable way of learning languages, and *whereby* we may best hope to give account to God of our youth spent herein. *Milton.*

This delight they take in doing of mischief, *whereby* I mean the pleasure they take to put any thing in pain that is capable of it, is no other than a foreign and introduced disposition. *Locke.*

WHERE'VER. *adv.* [*where* and *ever.*] At whatsoever place.

Which to avenge on him they dearly vow'd,
Wherever that on ground they mought him find. *Fa. Queen.*
Him serve, and fear!
Of other creatures, as him pleases best,
Wherever plac'd, let him dispose. *Milton's Paradise Lost.*
Not only to the sons of Abraham's loins
Salvation shall be preach'd; but to the sons
Of Abraham's faith, *wherever* through the world. *Milton.*
Where-e'er thy navy spreads her canvas wings,
Homage to thee, and peace to all she brings. *Waller.*

The climate, about thirty degrees, may pass for the Hesperides of our age, whatever or *where-ever* the other was. *Temp.*

He cannot but love virtue, *wherever* it is. *F. Atterbury.*

Wherever he hath receded from the Mosaick account of the earth, he hath receded from nature and matter of fact. *Woodw.*

Wherever Shakespeare has invented, he is greatly below the novelist; since the incidents he has added are neither necessary nor probable. *Shakespeare Illustrated.*

WHE'REFORE. *adv.* [*where* and *for.*]

1. For which reason.

The ox and the ass desire their food, neither purpose they unto themselves any end *wherefore.* *Hooker.*

There

There is no cause *wherefore* we should think God more desirous to manifest his favour by temporal blessings towards them than towards us. *Hooker.*

Can ye alledge any just cause *wherefore* absolutely ye should not condescend, in this controversy, to have your judgment over-ruled by some such definitive sentence? *Hooker.*

Shall I tell you why?
——Ay, sir, and *wherefore*; for, they say, every why hath a *wherefore*. *Shak. Comedy of Errours.*

2. For what reason?

Wherefore gaze this goodly company,
As if they saw some wond'rous monument? *Shakespeare.*
O *wherefore* was my birth from heav'n foretold
Twice by an angel? *Milton's Agonistes.*

WHEREI'N. *adv.* [*where* and *in*.] In which.

Whenever yet was your appeal denied?
Wherein have you been galled by the king? *Shakes. H.* VI.

Try waters by weight, wherein you may find some difference, and the lighter account the better. *Bacon.*

Heav'n
Is as the book of God before thee set,
Wherein to read his wond'rous works. *Milton.*
Too soon for us the circling hours
This dreaded time have compast, *wherein* we
Must bide the stroke of that long threaten'd wound. *Milton.*
This the happy morn
Wherein the son of heav'n's eternal king,
Our great redemption from above did bring! *Milton.*

Had they been treated with more kindness, and their questions answered, they would have taken more pleasure in improving their knowledge, *wherein* there would be still newness. *Locke.*

There are times *wherein* a man ought to be cautious as well as innocent. *Swift.*

WHEREI'NTO. *adv.* [*where* and *into*.] Into which.

Where's the palace, *whereinto* foul things
Sometimes intrude not? *Shakesp. Othello.*

Another disease is the putting forth of wild oats, *whereinto* corn oftentimes degenerates. *Bacon's Natural History.*

My subject does not oblige me to point forth the place *whereinto* this water is now retreated. *Woodward.*

Their treaty was finished, *wherein* I did them several good offices, by the credit I now had at court, and they made me a visit. *Gulliver's Travels.*

WHE'RENESS. *n. s.* [from *where*.] Ubiety.

A point hath no dimensions, but only a *whereness*, and is next to nothing. *Grew's Cosmol.*

WHEREO'F. *adv.* [*where* and *of*.] Of which.

A thing *whereof* the church hath, ever sithence the first beginning, reaped singular commodity. *Hooker.*

How this world, when and *whereof* created. *Milton.*

I do not find the certain numbers *whereof* their armies did consist. *Davies on Ireland.*

'Tis not very probable that I should succeed in such a project, *whereof* I have not had the least hint from any of my predecessors, the poets. *Dryden.*

WHEREO'N. *adv.* [*where* and *on*.] On which.

As for those things *whereon*, or else wherewith, superstition worketh, polluted they are by such abuse. *Hooker.*

Infected be the air *whereon* they ride. *Shakesp. Macbeth.*
So looks the strand, *whereon* th' imperious flood
Hath left a witness'd usurpation. *Shakesp. Henry* IV.
He lik'd the ground *whereon* she trod. *Milton.*

WHE'RESO. } *adv.* [*where* and *soever*.] In what place
WHERESOE'VER. } soever.

That short revenge the man may overtake,
Whereso he be, and soon upon him light. *Fairy Queen.*
Poor naked wretches, *wheresoe'er* you are,
That bide the pelting of this pitiless storm,
How shall your houseless heads defend you
From seasons such as these? *Shak. King Lear.*
He oft
Frequented their assemblies, *whereso* met. *Milt. Parad. Lost.*
Can misery no place of safety know?
The noise pursues me *wheresoe'er* I go. *Dryden.*

WHERETO'. } *adv.* [*where* and *to*, or *unto*.] To which.
WHEREUNTO'. }

She bringeth forth no kind of creature, *whereto* she is wanting in that which is needful. *Hooker.*

What Scripture doth plainly deliver, to that the first place both of credit and obedience is due; the next *whereunto* is whatsoever any man can necessarily conclude by force of reason: after these, the voice of the church succeedeth. *Hooker.*

I hold an old accustom'd feast,
Whereto I have invited many a guest. *Shak. Rom. and Jul.*
Whereto th' Almighty answer'd, not displeas'd. *Milton.*

WHEREUPO'N. *n. s.* [*where* and *upon*.] Upon which.

The townsmen mutinied, and sent to Essex; *whereupon* he came thither. *Clarendon.*

Whereupon there had risen a general war betwixt them, if the earl of Desmond had not been sent into England. *Davies on Ireland.*

WHEREWI'TH. } *adv.* [*where* and *with*, or *withal*.] With
WHEREWITHA'L. } which.

As for those things *wherewith* superstition worketh, polluted they are. *Hooker.*

Her bliss is all in pleasure and delight,
Wherewith she makes her lovers drunken. *Fairy Queen.*
Northumberland, thou ladder *wherewithal*
The mounting Bolingbroke ascends my throne. *Shakesp.*

In regard of the troubles *wherewith* this king was distressed in England, this army was not of sufficient strength to make an entire conquest of Ireland. *Davies on Ireland.*

The builders of Babel, still with vain design,
New Babels, had they *wherewithal*, would build. *Milton.*

You will have patience with a debtor, who has an inclination to pay you his obligations, if he had *wherewithal* ready about him. *Wycherley.*

The frequency, warmth and affection, *wherewith* they are proposed. *Rogers's Sermons.*

But it is impossible for a man, who openly declares against religion, to give any reasonable security that he will not be false and cruel, whenever a temptation offers, which he values more than he does the power *wherewith* he was trusted? *Swift.*

To WHE'RRET. *v. a.* [Corrupted, I suppose, from *ferret*.]

1. To hurry; to trouble; to teaze. A low colloquial word.
2. To give a box on the ear. *Ainsworth.*

WHE'RRY. *n. s.* [Of uncertain derivation.] A light boat used on rivers.

And falling down into a lake,
Which him up to the neck doth take,
His fury somewhat it doth slake,
He calleth for a ferry;
What was his club he made his boat,
And in his oaken cup doth float,
As safe as in a *wherry*. *Drayton's Nymphid.*
Let the vessel split on shelves,
With the freight enrich themselves:
Safe within my little *wherry*,
All their madness makes me merry. *Swift.*

To WHET. *v. a.* [ƿhettan, Saxon; *wetten*, Dutch.]

1. To sharpen by attrition.

Fool, thou *whet'st* a knife to kill thyself. *Shakesp. R.* III.
Thou hid'st a thousand daggers in thy thoughts,
Which thou hast *whetted* on thy stony heart,
To stab at half an hour of my frail life. *Shakes. H.* IV.
This visitation
Is but to *whet* thy almost blunted purpose. *Shak. Hamlet.*

Unsophisticated vitriol, rubbed on the *whetted* blade of a knife, will not impart its colour. *Boyle.*

There is the Roman slave *whetting* his knife, and listening. *Addison on Italy.*

Eloquence, smooth and cutting, is like a razor *whetted* with oil. *Swift.*

2. To edge; to make angry or acrimonious.

Peace, good queen;
O *whet* not on these too too furious peers;
For blessed are the peace-makers. *Shakesp. H.* VI.
Since Cassius first did *whet* me against Cæsar,
I have not slept. *Shakesp. Julius Cæsar.*
I will *whet* on the king. *Shak. King John.*

He favoured the Christian merchants; and the more to *whet* him forwards, the bassa had cunningly insinuated into his acquaintance one Mulearabe. *Knolles.*

Let not thy deep bitterness beget
Careless despair in me; for that will *whet*
My mind to scorn. *Donne.*

The cause why onions, salt, and pepper, in baked meats, move appetite, is by vellication of those nerves; for motion *whetteth*. *Bacon's Natural History.*

A disposition in the king began to be discovered, which, nourished and *whetted* on by bad counsellors, proved the blot of his times; which was the crushing treasure out of his subjects purses, by penal laws. *Bacon's Henry* VII.

'Tis a sad contemplation, that we should sacrifice the church's peace to the *whetting* and inflaming of a little vain curiosity. *Decay of Piety.*

Great contemporaries *whet* and cultivate each other. *Dryd.*

Himself invented first the shining share,
And *whetted* human industry by care;
Nor suffer'd sloth to rust his active reign. *Dryden's Georg.*

WHET. *n. s.* [from the verb.]

1. The act of sharpening.
2. Any thing that makes hungry, as a dram.

An iv'ry table is a certain *whet*;
You would not think how heartily he'll eat. *Dryden.*

He assisted at four hundred bowls of punch, not to mention sips, drams, and *whets*. *Spectator.*

WHE'THER. *adv.* [ƿhæðer, Saxon.] A particle expressing one part of a disjunctive question in opposition to the other.

As they, so we have likewise a publick form, how to serve God both morning and evening, *whether* sermons may be had or no. *Hooker.*

Resolve *whether* you will or no. *Shakesp. Rich.* III.

Perkins's

Perkins's three counsellors registered themselves sanctuary-men; and *whether* upon pardon obtained, or continuance within the privilege, they were not proceeded with. *Bacon.*

If we adjoin to the lords, *whether* they prevail or not, we engulph ourselves into assured danger. *Hayward.*

Then did'st thou found that order, *whether* love
Or victory thy royal thoughts did move,
Each was a noble cause. *Denham.*

Epictetus forbids a man, on such an occasion, to consult with the oracle *whether* he should do it or no, it being necessary to be done. *Decay of Piety.*

Whether by health or sickness, life or death, mercy is still contriving and carrying on the spiritual good of all who love God. *South's Sermons.*

This assistance is only offered to men, and not forced upon them, *whether* they will or no. *Tillotson.*

When our foreign trade exceeds our exportation of commodities, our money must go to pay our debts, *whether* melted or not. *Locke.*

Whether it be that the richest of these discoveries fall not into the pope's hands, or for some other reason, the prince of Farnese will keep this seat from being turned up, 'till one of his own family is in the chair. *Addison on Italy.*

WHE'THER. *pronoun.* Which of two.

Whither when they came, they fell at words
Whether of them should be the lord of lords. *Hubberd's Tale.*
Whether of them twain did the will of his father? *Mat.* xxi.

Whether is more beneficial, that we should have the same yearly quantity of heat distributed equally, or a greater share in Summer, and in Winter a less? *Bentley.*

Let them take *whether* they will: if they deduce all animals from single pairs, even to make the second of a pair, is to write after a copy. *Bentley.*

WHE'TSTONE. *n. s.* [*whet* and *stone.*] Stone on which any thing is whetted, or rubbed to make it sharp.

The minds of the afflicted do never think they have fully conceived the weight or measure of their own woe: they use their affection as a *whetstone* both to wit and memory. *Hooker.*

What avail'd her resolution chaste,
Whose soberest looks were *whetstones* to desire? *Fairfax.*

Whom the *whetstone* sharps to eat,
And cry, milstones are good meat. *Ben. Johnson.*

Diligence is to the understanding as the *whetstone* to the razor; but the will is the hand, that must apply the one to the other. *South.*

A *whetstone* is not an instrument to carve with; but it sharpens those that do. *Shakespeare Illustrated.*

WHE'TTER. *n. s.* [from *whet.*] One that whets or sharpens.

Love and enmity are notable *whetters* and quickeners of the spirit of life in all animals. *More.*

WHEY. *n. s.* [hpæᵹ, Saxon; *wey*, Dutch.]

1. The thin or serous part of milk, from which the oleose or grumous part is separated.

I'll make you feed on curds and *whey.* *Shakespeare.*

Milk is nothing but blood turned white, by being diluted with a greater quantity of serum or *whey* in the glandules of the breast. *Harvey on Consumptions.*

2. It is used of any thing white and thin.

Those linnen cheeks of thine
Are counsellors to fear. What, soldiers *whey* face! *Shakes.*

WHE'YEY. } *adj.* [from *whey.*] Partaking of whey; resem-
WHE'YISH. } bling whey.

Those medicines, being opening and piercing, fortify the operation of the liver, in sending down the *wheyey* part of the blood to the reins. *Bacon's Natural History.*

He that quaffs
Such *wheyish* liquors, oft with cholick pangs
He'll roar. *Philips.*

WHICH. *pron.* [hpilc, Saxon; *welk*, Dutch.]

1. The pronoun relative; relating to things.

The apostles term it the pledge of our heavenly inheritance, sometimes the handsel or earnest of that *which* is to come. *Hooker*, *b.* v.

Do they not blaspheme that worthy name, by the *which* ye are called? *Ja.* ii. 7.

In destructions by deluge, the remnant *which* hap to be reserved are ignorant. *Bacon.*

To *which* their want of judging abilities, add also their want of opportunity to apply to such a serious consideration as may let them into the true goodness and evil of things, *which* are qualities *which* seldom display themselves to the first view. *South's Sermons.*

The queen of furies by their side is set,
And snatches from their mouths th' untasted meat,
Which, if they touch, her hissing snakes she rears. *Dryden.*

After the several earths, consider the parts of the surface of this globe *which* is barren, as sand and rocks. *Locke.*

2. It formerly was used for *who*, and related likewise to persons: as in the first words of the Lord's prayer.

The Almighty, *which* giveth wisdom to whomsoever it pleaseth him, did, for the good of his church, stay those eager affections. *Hooker.*

Do you hear, sir, of a battle?
——Every one hears that,
Which can distinguish sound. *Shakesp. King Lear.*

Had I been there, *which* am a silly woman,
The soldiers should have toss'd me on their pikes,
Before I would have granted to that act. *Shakesp. H.* VI.

3. The genitive of *which*, as well as of *who*, is *whose*; but *whose*, as derived from *which*, is scarcely used but in poetry.

Of man's first disobedience, and the fruit
Of that forbidden tree, *whose* mortal taste. *Milton.*

4. It is sometimes a demonstrative: as, take *which* you will.

What is the night?
—Almost at odds with morning, *which* is *which.* *Shakesp.*

5. It is sometimes an interrogative: as, *which* is the man.

Two fair twins,
The puzzled strangers *which* is *which* enquire. *Tickel.*

WHI'CHSOEVER. *pron.* [*which* and *soever.*] Whether one or the other.

Whichsoever of these he takes, and how often soever he doubles it, he finds that he is not one jot nearer the end of such addition than at first setting out. *Locke.*

WHIFF. *n s.* [*chwyth*, Welsh.] A blast; a puff of wind.

Pyrrhus at Priam drives, in rage strikes wide;
But with the *whiff* and wind of his fell sword,
Th' unnerved father falls. *Shakesp. Hamlet.*

Who,
If some unsav'ry *whiff* betray the crime,
Invents a quarrel straight. *Dryden.*

Three pipes after dinner he constantly smokes,
And seasons his *whiffs* with impertinent jokes. *Prior.*

Nick pulled out a boatswain's whistle: upon the first *whiff* the tradesmen came jumping in. *Arbuthnot.*

To WHI'FFLE. *v. n.* [from *whiff.*] To move inconstantly, as if driven by a puff of wind.

Nothing is more familiar than for a *whiffling* fop, that has not one grain of the sense of a man of honour, to play the hero. *L'Estrange.*

A person of a *whiffling* and unsteady turn of mind cannot keep close to a point of controversy, but wanders from it perpetually. *Watts.*

Was our reason given, to be thus puff'd about,
Like a dry leaf, an idle straw, a feather,
The sport of ev'ry *whiffling* blast that blows? *Rowe.*

WHI'FFLER. *n. s.* [from *whiffle.*]

1. One that blows strongly.

The beach
Pales in the flood with men, with wives and boys,
Whose shouts and claps out-voice the deep-mouth'd sea,
Which, like a mighty *whiffler* 'fore the king,
Seems to prepare his way. *Shak. Henry* V.

2. One of no consequence; one moved with a whiff or puff.

Our fine young ladies retain in their service a great number of supernumerary and insignificant fellows, which they use like *whifflers*, and commonly call shoeing-horns. *Spectator.*

Every *whiffler* in a laced coat, who frequents the chocolate-house, shall talk of the constitution. *Swift.*

WHIG. *n. s.* [hpæᵹ, Saxon.]

1. Whey.

2. The name of a faction.

The southwest counties of Scotland have seldom corn enough to serve them round the year; and the northern parts producing more than they need, those in the west come in the Summer to buy at Leith the stores that come from the north; and from a word, whiggam, used in driving their horses, all that drove were called the whiggamors, and shorter the whiggs. Now in that year before the news came down of duke Hamilton's defeat, the ministers animated their people to rise and march to Edinburgh; and they came up marching on the head of their parishes with an unheard-of fury, praying and preaching all the way as they came. The marquis of Argyle and his party came and headed them, they being about six thousand. This was called the whiggamor's inroad; and ever after that, all that opposed the court came in contempt to be called *whigs:* and from Scotland the word was brought into England, where it is now one of our unhappy terms of disunion. *Burnet.*

Whoever has a true value for church and state, should avoid the extremes of *whig* for the sake of the former, and the extremes of tory on the account of the latter. *Swift.*

WHI'GGISH. *adj.* [from *whig.*] Relating to the whigs.

She'll prove herself a tory plain,
From principles the whigs maintain;
And, to defend the *whiggish* cause,
Her topicks from the tories draws. *Swift.*

WHI'GGISM. *n. s.* [from *whig.*] The notions of a whig.

I could quote passages from fifty pamphlets, wholly made up of *whiggism* and atheism. *Swift.*

WHILE. *n s.* [*weil*, German; hpile, Saxon.] Time; space of time.

If my beauty be any thing, then let it obtain this much of you, that you will remain some *while* in this company, to ease your own travel and our solitariness. *Sidney.*

I have seen her rise from her bed, and again return to bed; yet all this *while* in a most fast sleep. *Shakesp. Macbeth.*

One *while* we thought him innocent,
And then w' accus'd the consul. *Ben. Johnson's Catiline.*

I hope all ingenuous persons will advertise me fairly, if they think it worth their *while*, of what they dislike in it. *Digby.*

Pausing a *while*, thus to herself she mus'd. *Milton.*

How couldst thou look for other, but that God should condemn thee for the doing of those things for which thine own conscience did condemn thee, all the *while* thou wast doing of them? *Tillotson.*

That which I have all this *while* been endeavouring to convince men to, is no other but what God himself doth particularly recommend. *Tillotson.*

Few, without the hope of another life, would think it worth their *while* to live above the allurements of sense. *Atterb.*

What fate has disposed of the papers, 'tis not worth *while* to tell. *Locke.*

WHILE. }
WHILES. } *adv.* [ƿhile, Saxon. *Whiles* is now out of use.]
WHILST. }

1. During the time that.

Whiles I was protector,
Pity was all the fault that was in me. *Shakes. Henry* VI.

What we have, we prize not to the worth,
Whiles we enjoy it; but being lackt and lost,
Why, then we rack the value. *Shakespeare.*

Repeated, *while* the sedentary earth
Attains her end. *Milton.*

2. As long as.

Use your memory, and you will sensibly experience a gradual improvement, *while* you take care not to over-load it. *Watts's Logick.*

3. At the same time that.

Whiles by the experiment of this ministration they glorify God, for your professed subjection unto the Gospel. 2 *Cor.* ix.

Can he imagine that God sends forth an irresistible strength against some sins, *whilst* in others he permits men a power of repelling his grace? *Decay of Piety.*

To WHILE. *v. n.* [from the noun.] To loiter.

Men guilty this way never have observed that the *whiling* time, the gathering together, and waiting a little before dinner, is the most aukwardly passed away of any. *Spectator.*

WHI'LERE. *adv.* [*while* and *ere*, or *before.*] A little while ago.

That cursed wight, from whom I 'scap'd *whilere*,
A man of hell, that calls himself despair. *Fairy Queen.*

Let us be jocund: will you troul the catch
You taught me but *while-ere?* *Shakespeare.*

Here lies Hobbinol, our shepherd *whilere.* *Raleigh.*

He who, with all heav'n's heraldry, *whilere*
Enter'd the world, now bleeds to give us ease. *Milton.*

WHI'LOM. *adv.* [ƿhilom, Saxon, that is, *once on a time.*] Formerly; once; of old.

Where now the studious lawyers have their bowers,
There *whilom* wont the Templar knights abide,
'Till they decayed through pride. *Spenser.*

In northern clime a val'rous knight
Did *whilom* kill his bear in fight,
And wound a fiddler. *Hudibras.*

Yet art thou not inglorious in thy fate;
For so Apollo, with unweeting hand,
Whilom did slay his dearly loved mate. *Milton.*

WHIM. *n. s.* [This word is derived by *Skinner* from a thing turning round; nor can I find any etymology more probable.] A freak; an odd fancy; a caprice; an irregular motion of desire.

All the superfluous *whims* relate,
That fill a female gamester's pate. *Swift.*

To WHI'MPER. *v. n.* [*wimmeren*, German.] To cry without any loud noise.

The father by his authority should always stop this sort of crying, and silence their *whimpering.* *Locke.*

A laughing, toying, wheedling, *whimp'ring* she,
Shall make him amble on a gossip's message. *Rowe.*

In peals of thunder now she roars, and now
She gently *whimpers* like a lowing cow. *Swift.*

WHI'MPLED. *adj.* [I suppose from *whimper.*] This word seems to mean distorted with crying.

This *whimpled*, whining, purblind, wayward boy,
This signior Junio's giant dwarf, Dan Cupid,
Regent of love-rhimes, lord of folded arms,
Th' anointed sovereign of sighs and groans. *Shakespeare.*

WHI'MSEY. *n. s.* [Only another form of the word *whim.*] A freak; a caprice; an odd fancy; a whim.

At this rate a pretended freak or *whimsey* may be palliated. *L'Estrange.*

All the ridiculous and extravagant shapes that can be imagined, all the fancies and *whimsies* of poets and painters, and Egyptian idolaters, if so be they are consistent with life and propagation, would be now actually in being, if our atheists notion were true. *Ray on the Creation.*

So now, as health or temper changes,
In larger compass Alma ranges;
This day below, the next above,
As light or solid *whimseys* move. *Prior.*

What I speak, my fair Cloe, and what I write, shows
The difference there is betwixt nature and art;
I court others in verse, but I love thee in prose;
And they have my *whimsies*, but thou hast my heart. *Prior.*

Oranges in *whimsey*-boards went round. *King.*

Less should I dawb it o'er with transitory praise,
And water-colours of these days;
These days! where e'en th' extravagance of poetry
Is at a loss for figures to express
Men's folly, *whimsies*, and inconstancy. *Swift.*

WHI'MSICAL. *adj.* [from *whimsey.*] Freakish; capricious; oddly fanciful.

Another circumstance in which I am very particular, or, as my neighbours call me, *whimsical:* as my garden invites into it all the birds, I do not suffer any one to destroy their nests. *Addison's Spectator.*

WHIN. *n. s.* [*chwyn*, Welsh; *genista spinosa*, Latin.] A weed; furze.

With *whins* or with furzes thy hovel renew. *Tusser.*

Plants that have prickles in their leaf are holly, juniper, *whin*-bush, and thistle. *Bacon.*

To WHINE. *v. n.* [ƿanian, Saxon; *weenen*, Dutch; *cwyno*, Welsh.] To lament in low murmurs; to make a plaintive noise; to moan meanly and effeminately.

They came to the wood, where the hounds were in couples staying their coming, but with a *whining* accent craving liberty. *Sidney.*

At his nurse's tears
He *whin'd* and roar'd away your victory,
That pages blush'd at him. *Shakes. Coriolanus.*

Twice and once the hedge-pig *whin'd.* *Shakes. Macbeth.*

Whip him,
'Till, like a boy, you see him cringe his face,
And *whine* aloud for mercy. *Shakesp. Ant. and Cleopatra.*

All the common people have a *whining* tone and accent in their speech, as if they did still smart or suffer some oppression. *Davies on Ireland.*

Then, if we *whine*, look pale,
And tell our tale,
Men are in pain
For us again;
So, neither speaking, doth become
The lover's state, nor being dumb. *Suckling.*

He made a viler noise than swine
In windy weather, when they *whine.* *Hudibras.*

Some, under sheeps cloathing, had the properties of wolves, that is, they could *whine* and howl as well as bite and devour. *South's Sermons.*

I was not born so base to flatter crouds,
And move your pity by a *whining* tale. *Dryd. Don Sebast.*

Laughing at their *whining* may perhaps be the proper method. *Locke.*

Life was given for noble purposes; and therefore it must not be sacrificed to a quarrel, nor *whined* away in love. *Collier.*

Upon a general mourning, mercers and woollen-drapers would in four and twenty hours raise their cloths and silks to above a double price; and, if the mourning continued long, then *whining* with petitions to the court, that they were ready to starve. *Swift.*

WHINE. *n. s.* [from the verb.] Plaintive noise; mean or affected complaint.

The favourable opinion of men comes oftentimes by a few demure looks and affected *whines*, set off with some odd devotional postures and grimaces. *South.*

Thy hateful *whine* of woe
Breaks in upon my sorrows, and distracts
My jarring senses with thy beggar's cry. *Rowe's J. Shore.*

To WHI'NNY. *v. n.* [*hinnio*, Lat. from the sound.] To make a noise like a horse or colt.

WHI'NYARD. *n. s.* [ƿinnan and aȝe, to gain honour, Saxon, *Skinner.* I know not whether this word was ever used seriously, and therefore perhaps it might be denominated in contempt from *whin*, a tool to cut *whins.*] A sword, in contempt.

He snatch'd his *whinyard* up, that fled
When he was falling off his steed. *Hudibras.*

To WHIP. *v. a.* [ƿheopan, Saxon; *wippen*, Dutch.]

1. To strike with any thing tough and flexible.

He took
The harness'd steeds, that still with horror shook,
And plies them with the lash, and *whips* 'em on;
And, as he *whips*, upbraids 'em with his son. *Addison.*

2. To sew slightly.

In half *whipt* muslin needles useless lie. *Gay.*

3. To

3. To drive with laſhes.

This unbeard ſawcineſs, and boyiſh troops,
The king doth ſmile at; and is well prepar'd
To *whip* this dwarfiſh war, theſe pigmy arms,
From out the circle of his territories. *Shak. King John.*

Let's *whip* theſe ſtragglers o'er the ſeas again;
Laſh hence theſe over-weening rags of France,
Theſe famiſh'd beggars. *Shakeſp. Richard* III.

Since I pluckt geeſe, play'd truant, and *whipt* top, I knew not what 'twas to be beaten 'till lately. *Shakeſpeare.*

If ordered every day to *whip* his top, ſo long as to make him weary, he will wiſh for his book, if you promiſe it him as a reward of having *whipt* his top luſtily quite out. *Locke.*

4. To correct with laſhes.

I'll leave you to the hearing of the cauſe,
Hoping you'll find good cauſe to *whip* them all. *Shakeſpeare.*

Reaſon with the fellow,
Before you puniſh him, where he heard this,
Leſt you ſhould chance to *whip* your information. *Shakeſp.*

Hourly we ſee ſome raw pin-feather'd thing
Attempt to mount, and fights and heroes ſing,
Who for falſe quantities was *whipt* at ſchool
But t'other day, and breaking grammar-rule. *Dryden.*

How did he return this haughty brave,
Who *whipt* the winds, and made the ſea his ſlave? *Dryden.*

This requires more than ſetting children a taſk, and *whipping* them without any more ado, if it be not done to our fancy. *Locke.*

Oh chain me! *whip* me! let me be the ſcorn
Of ſordid rabbles and inſulting crowds!
Give me but life. *Smith's Phædra and Hippol.*

Heirs to titles and large eſtates have a weakneſs in their eyes, and are not able to bear the pain and indignity of *whipping.* *Swift.*

5. To laſh with ſarcaſm.

They would *whip* me with their fine wits, 'till I was as creſt fallen as a dried pear. *Shak. Merry Wives of Windſor.*

6. To inwrap.

Its ſtring hath both ends neatly lapt over with another about three inches in length, and ſo is firmly *whipt* about with ſmall gut, that it may the eaſier move in the edge of the rowler. *Moxon's Mech. Exer.*

To Whip. *v. a.* To take any thing nimbly.

In his lawleſs fit,
Behind the arras hearing ſomething ſtir,
He *whips* his rapier out, and cries a rat!
And in this brainiſh apprehenſion kills
The unſeen good old man. *Shak. Hamlet.*

She in a hurry *whips* up her darling under her arm. *L'Eſtr.*

Raiſe yourſelf upon your hinder legs, and then ſtretch out your head: I can eaſily *whip* up to your horns, and ſo out of the well. *L'Eſtrange.*

Briſk Suſan *whips* her linnen from the rope,
Whilſt the firſt drizzling ſhow'r is born aſlope. *Swift.*

Thus diſpoſed, it lies ready for you to *whip* it out in a moment. *Swift.*

To Whip. *v. n.* To move nimbly.

Two friends travelling together met a bear upon the way: the one *whips* up a tree, and the other throws himſelf flat upon the ground. *L'Eſtrange.*

The ſimple 'ſquire made a ſudden ſtart to follow; but the juſtice of the quorum *whipped* between. *Tatler.*

WHIP. *n. ſ.* [hpeop, Saxon.] An inſtrument of correction tough and pliant.

There ſat infernal pain,
And faſt beſide him ſat tumultuous ſtrife;
The one in hand an iron *whip* did ſtrain,
The other brandiſhed a bloody knife. *Fairy Queen.*

Put in ev'ry honeſt hand a *whip*,
To laſh the raſcal naked through the world. *Shak. Othello.*

Love is merely madneſs, and deſerves as well a dark-houſe and a *whip* as madmen do. *Shakeſpeare.*

A *whip* for the horſe, a bridle for the aſs. *Prov.* xxvi. 3.

High on her head ſhe rears two twiſted ſnakes;
Her chain ſhe rattles, and her *whip* ſhe ſhakes. *Dryden.*

In his right hand he holds the *whip*, with which he is ſuppoſed to drive the horſes of the ſun. *Addiſon.*

Each ſtaunch polemick
Came *whip* and ſpur, and daſh'd thro' thin and thick. *Dunc.*

Whi'pcord. *n. ſ.* [*whip* and *cord.*] Cord of which laſhes are made.

In Raphael's firſt works are many ſmall foldings, often repeated, which look like ſo many *whipcords.* *Dryden.*

Whi'pgrafting. *n. ſ.* [In gardening.]

Whipgrafting is done two ways: firſt, cut off the head of the ſtock, and ſmooth it; then cut the graft from a knot or bud on one ſide ſloping, about an inch and a half long, with a ſhoulder, but not deep, that it may reſt on the top of the ſtock: the graft muſt be cut from the ſhouldering ſmooth and even, ſloping by degrees, that the lower end be thin: place the ſhoulder on the head of the ſtock, and mark the length of the cut part of the graft, and with your knife cut away ſo much of the ſtock as the graft did cover, but not any of the wood of the ſtock: place both together, that the cut part of both may join, and the ſap unite the one to the other; and bind them cloſe together, and defend them from the rain with tempered clay or wax, as before. The other way of *whipgrafting* is, where the grafts and the ſtocks are of an equal ſize: the ſtock muſt be cut ſloping upwards from one ſide to the other, and the graft after the ſame manner from the ſhoulder downwards, that the graft may exactly join with the ſtock in every part, and ſo bind, and clay or wax them as before. *Mortimer's Husbandry.*

Whi'phand. *n. ſ.* [*whip* and *hand.*] Advantage over.

The archangel, when diſcord was reſtive and would not be drawn from her beloved monaſtry with fair words, has the *whiphand* of her, and drags her out with many ſtripes. *Dryd.*

Whi'plash. *n. ſ.* The laſh or ſmall end of a whip.

Have *whiplaſh* wel knotted and cartrope inough. *Tuſſer.*

Whi'pper. *n. ſ.* [from *whip.*] One who puniſhes with whipping.

Love is meerly a madneſs, and deſerves as well a dark-houſe and a whip as madmen do; and the reaſon why they are not ſo puniſhed is, that the *whippers* are in love too. *Shakeſpeare.*

Whi'ppingpost. *n. ſ.* [*whip* and *poſt.*] A pillar to which criminals are bound when they are laſhed.

Could not the *whippingpoſt* prevail,
With all its rhet'rick, nor the jail,
To keep from flaying ſcourge thy ſkin,
And ankle free from iron gin? *Hudibras.*

Whi'psaw. *n. ſ.* [*whip* and *ſaw.*]

The *whipſaw* is uſed by joiners to ſaw ſuch great pieces of ſtuff that the handſaw will not eaſily reach through. *Moxon.*

Whi'pstaff. *n. ſ.* [On ſhipboard.] A piece of wood faſtened to the helm, which the ſteerſman holds in his hand to move the helm and turn the ſhip. *Bailey.*

Whi'pster. *n. ſ.* [from *whip.*] A nimble fellow.

I am not valiant neither;
But ev'ry puny *whipſter* gets my ſword. *Shakeſp. Othello.*

Give that *whipſter* but his errand,
He takes my lord chief juſtice' warrant. *Prior.*

Whipt, for *whipped.*

In Bridewel a number be ſtript,
Leſſe worthie than theeſe to be *whipt.* *Tuſſer.*

To WHIRL. *v. a.* [hpýnpan, Saxon; *wirbelen*, Dutch.] To turn round rapidly.

Five moons were ſeen to-night,
Four fixed, and the fifth did *whirl* about
The other four in wond'rous motion. *Shakeſ. K. John.*

My thoughts are *whirled* like a potter's wheel:
I know not where I am, nor what I do. *Shakeſ. Henry* VI.

He *whirls* his ſword around without delay,
And hews through adverſe foes an ample way. *Dryden.*

With his full force he *whirl'd* it firſt around;
But the ſoft yielding air receiv'd the wound. *Dryden.*

With what a *whirling* force his lance he toſs'd!
Heav'ns what a ſpring was in his arm to throw! *Dryden.*

The Stygian flood,
Falling from on high, with bellowing ſound,
Whirls the black waves and rattling ſtones around. *Addiſon.*

With impetuous motion *whirl'd* apace,
This magick wheel ſtill moves, yet keeps its place. *Granv.*

They have ever been taught by their ſenſes, that the ſun, with all the planets and the fixed ſtars, are *whirled* round this little globe. *Watts's Improvement of the Mind.*

To Whirl. *v. n.* To run round rapidly.

He, rapt with *whirling* wheels, inflames the ſkyen,
With fire not made to burn, but fairly for to ſhine. *Spenſer.*

As young ſtriplings whip the top for ſport
On the ſmooth pavement of an empty court,
The wooden engine flies and *whirls* about,
Admir'd with clamours of the beardleſs rout. *Dryden.*

She what he ſwears regards no more
Than the deaf rocks when the loud billows roar;
But *whirl'd* away, to ſhun his hateful ſight,
Hid in the foreſt. *Dryden's Æn.*

Wild and diſtracted with their fears,
They juſtling plunge amidſt the ſounding deeps;
The flood away, the ſtruggling ſquadron ſweeps,
And men and arms, and horſes *whirling* bears. *Smith.*

Whirl. *n. ſ.* [from the verb.]

1. Gyration; quick rotation; circular motion; rapid circumvolution.

'Twere well your judgments but in plays did range;
But ev'n your follies and debauches change
With ſuch a *whirl*, the poets of your age
Are tir'd, and cannot ſcore them on the ſtage. *Dryden.*

Wings raiſe my feet; I'm pleas'd to mount on high,
Trace all the mazes of the liquid ſky;
Their various turnings and their *whirls* declare,
And live in the vaſt regions of the air. *Creech's Manilius.*

Nor *whirl* of time, nor flight of years can waste. *Creech.*

I have been watching what thoughts came up in the *whirl* of fancy, that were worth communicating. *Pope.*

How the car rattles, how its kindling wheels
Smoke in the *whirl*: the circling sand ascends,
And in the noble dust the chariot's lost. *Smith.*

2. Any thing moved with rapid rotation.

Though in dreadful *whirls* we hung
High on the broken wave,
I knew thou wert not slow to hear,
Nor impotent to save. *Addison's Spectator.*

WHI'RLBAT. *n. s.* [*whirl* and *bat.*] Any thing moved rapidly round to give a blow. It is frequently used by the poets for the ancient cestus.

At *whirlbat* he had slain many, and was now himself slain by Pollux. *L'Estrange.*

The *whirlbat's* falling blow they nimbly shun,
And win the race e're they begin to run. *Creech's Manil.*

The guardian angels of kingdoms he rejected, as Dares did the *whirlbats* of Eryx, when they were thrown before him by Entellus. *Dryden.*

The *whirlbat* and the rapid race shall be
Reserv'd for Cæsar, and ordain'd by me. *Dryden's Virgil.*

WHI'RLBONE. *n. s.* The patella. *Ainsworth.*

WHI'RLIGIG. *n. s.* [*whirl* and *gig.*] A toy which children spin round.

He found that marbles taught him percussion, and *whirligigs* the axis in peritrochio. *Arbuthn. and Pope's Mart. Scribl.*

That since they gave things their beginning,
And set this *whirligig* a spinning. *Prior.*

WHI'RLPIT. } *n. s.* [hpýnꝑpole, Saxon.] A place where the
WHI'RLPOOL. } water moves circularly, and draws whatever comes within the circle towards its center; a vortex.

Poor Tom! whom the foul fiend hath led through ford and *whirlpool*, o'er bog and quagmire. *Shak. King Lear.*

In the fathomless profound
Down sunk they, like a falling stone,
By raging *whirlpits* overthrown. *Sandys.*

This calm of heaven, this mermaid's melody,
Into an unseen *whirlpool* draws you fast,
And in a moment sinks you. *Dryden's Spanish Fryar.*

Send forth, ye wise! send forth your lab'ring thought:
Let it return with empty notions fraught,
Of airy columns every moment broke,
Of circling *whirlpools*, and of spheres of smoke. *Prior.*

There might arise some vertiginous motions or *whirlpools* in the matter of the chaos, whereby the atoms must be thrust and crowded to the middle of those *whirlpools*, and there constipate one another into great solid bodies. *Bentley.*

WHI'RLWIND. *n. s.* [*werbelwind*, German.] A stormy wind moving circularly.

In the very torrent and *whirlwind* of your passion, beget a temperance that may give it smoothness. *Shakesp. Hamlet.*

With *whirlwinds* from beneath she toss'd the ship,
And bare expos'd the bosom of the deep. *Dryden's Æn.*

WHI'RRING. *adj.* A word formed in imitation of the sound expressed by it.

From the brake the *whirring* pheasant springs,
And mounts exulting on triumphant wings. *Pope.*

WHISK. *n. s.* [*wischen*, to wipe, German.]

1. A small besom, or brush.

The white of an egg, though in part transparent, yet, being long agitated with a *whisk* or spoon, loses its transparency. *Boyle.*

If you break any china with the top of the *whisk* on the mantle-tree, gather up the fragments. *Swift.*

2. A part of a woman's dress.

An easy means to prevent being one farthing the worse for the abatement of interest, is wearing a lawn *whisk* instead of a point de Venice. *Child of Trade.*

To WHISK. *v. a.* [*wischen*, to wipe, German.]

1. To sweep with a small besom.

2. To move nimbly, as when one sweeps.

Cardan believ'd great states depend
Upon the tip o' th' bear's tail's end;
That as she *whisk'd* it t'wards the sun,
Strow'd mighty empires up and down. *Hudibras.*

WHI'SKER. *n. s.* [from *whisk.*] The hair growing on the cheek unshaven; the mustachio.

A sacrifice to fall of state,
Whose thread of life the fatal sisters
Did twist together with its *whiskers*. *Hudibras.*

Behold four kings in majesty rever'd,
With hoary *whiskers* and a forky beard. *Pope.*

A painter added a pair of *whiskers* to the face. *Addison.*

To WHI'SPER. *v. n.* [*wisperen*, Dutch.] To speak with a low voice, so as not to be heard but by the ear close to the speaker.

He sometime with fearful countenance would desire the king to look to himself; for that all the court and city were full of *whisperings* and expectation of some sudden change. *Sidney.*

All that hate me *whisper* together against me. *Ps.* xli. 7.

In speech of man, the *whispering* or susurrus, whether louder or softer, is an interiour sound; but the speaking out is an exteriour sound, and therefore you can never make a tone, nor sing in *whispering*; but in speech you may. *Bacon.*

The king Acestis calls;
Then softly *whisper'd* in her faithful ear,
And bade his daughters at the rites appear. *Pope.*

It is as offensive to speak wit in a fool's company, as it would be ill manners to *whisper* in it: he is displeased at both, because he is ignorant of what is said. *Pope.*

He comes and *whispers* in his ear. *Swift.*

The hollow *whisp'ring* breeze, the pliant rills
Purle down amid' the twisted roots. *Thomson.*

To WHI'SPER. *v. a.*

1. To address in a low voice.

When they talk of him they shake their heads,
And *whisper* one another in the ear. *Shak. King John.*

Give sorrow words; the grief that does not speak,
Whispers the o'erfraught heart, and bids it break. *Shakesp.*

He first *whispers* the man in the ear, that such a man should think such a card. *Bacon's Natural History.*

The steward *whispered* the young Templer, that's true to my knowledge. *Tatler.*

2. To utter in a low voice.

You have heard of the news abroad, I mean the *whisper'd* ones; for they are yet but ear-kissing arguments. *Shakespeare.*

They might buzz and *whisper* it one to another, and, tacitly withdrawing from the apostles, noise it about the city. *Bent.*

3. To prompt secretly.

Charles the emperor,
Under pretence to see the queen his aunt,
For 'twas indeed his colour, but he came
To *whisper* Wolsey, here makes visitation. *Shak. H. VIII.*

WHI'SPER. *n. s.* [from the verb.] A low soft voice.

The extension is more in tones than in speech; therefore the inward voice or *whisper* cannot give a tone. *Bacon.*

Strictly observe the first hints and *whispers* of good and evil that pass in the heart, and this will keep conscience quick and vigilant. *South.*

Soft *whispers* through th' assembly went. *Dryden.*

He uncall'd, his patron to controul,
Divulg'd the secret *whispers* of his soul. *Dryden.*

WHI'SPERER. *n. s.* [from *whisper.*]

1. One that speaks low.

2. A private talker.

Kings trust in eunuchs hath rather been as to good spials and good *whisperers* than good magistrates. *Bacon.*

WHIST. [This word is called by *Skinner*, who seldom errs, an interjection commanding silence, and so it is commonly used; but *Shakespeare* uses it as a verb, and *Milton* as an adjective.]

1. Are silent.

Come unto these yellow sands,
And then take hands;
Curt'sied when you have, and kist,
The wild waves *whist*. *Shakespeare's Tempest.*

2. Still; silent.

The winds, with wonder *whist*,
Smoothly the waters kiss'd,
Whispering new joys to the mild ocean. *Milton.*

3. Be still.

WHIST. *n. s.* A game at cards, requiring close attention and silence.

The clergyman used to play at *whist* and swobbers. *Swift.*

Whist awhile
Walks his grave round, beneath a cloud of smoke,
Wreath'd fragrant from the pipe. *Thomson's Autumn.*

To WHI'STLE. *v. n.* [hpıꝩꞇlan, Saxon; *fistulo*, Latin.]

1. To form a kind of musical sound by an inarticulate modulation of the breath.

I've watch'd and travell'd hard:
Some time I shall sleep out, the rest I'll *whistle*. *Shakesp.*

His big manly voice
Changing again toward childish treble pipes,
He *whistles* in his sound. *Shakespeare.*

Let one *whistle* at the one end of a trunk, and hold your ear at the other, and the sound shall strike so sharp as you can scarce endure it. *Bacon's Natural History.*

While the plowman near at hand
Whistles o'er the furrow'd land. *Milton.*

Should Bertran sound his trumpets,
And Torrismond but *whistle* through his fingers,
He draws his army off. *Dryden's Spanish Fryar.*

He *whistl'd* as he went for want of thought. *Dryden.*

The ploughman leaves the task of day,
And trudging homeward *whistles* on the way. *Gay.*

2. To make a sound with a small wind instrument.

3. To sound shrill.

Soft whispers run along the leafy woods,
And mountains *whistle* to the murm'ring floods. *Dryden.*

Rhætus

Rhætus from the hearth a burning brand
Selects, and whirling waves; 'till from his hand
The fire took flame, then dash'd it from the right
On fair Charaxus' temples, near the sight
Then *whistling* past came on. *Dryden.*

When winged deaths in *whistling* arrows fly,
Wilt thou, though wounded, yet undaunted stay,
Perform thy part, and share the dangerous day? *Prior.*

The wild winds *whistle*, and the billows roar,
The splitting raft the furious tempest tore. *Pope.*

To WHISTLE. *v. a.* To call by a whistle.

Whistle them backwards and forwards, 'till he is weary. *South's Sermons.*

He chanced to miss his dog: we stood still 'till he had *whistled* him up. *Addison.*

When simple pride for flatt'ry makes demands,
May dunce by dunce be *whistled* off my hands! *Pope.*

WHI'STLE. *n. s.* [hpiꞅꞇle, Saxon.]

1. Sound made by the modulation of the breath in the mouth.

My sire in caves constrains the wind,
Can with a breath their clam'rous rage appease;
They fear his *whistle*, and forsake the seas. *Dryden.*

2. A sound made by a small wind instrument.

3. The mouth; the organ of whistling.

Let's drink the other cup to wet our *whistles*, and so sing away all sad thoughts. *Walton's Angler.*

4. A small wind instrument.

The masters and pilots were so astonished that they knew not how to direct; and if they knew, they could scarcely, when they directed, hear their own *whistle*. *Sidney.*

Behold,
Upon the hempen tackle shipboys climbing;
Hear the shrill *whistle*, which doth order give
To sounds confus'd. *Shakesp. Henry V.*

Small *whistles*, or shepherds oaten pipes, give a sound, because of their extreme slenderness, whereby the air is more pent than in a wider pipe. *Bacon's Natural History.*

Her infant grandame's *whistle* next it grew,
The bells she gingl'd, and the *whistle* blew. *Pope.*

5. The noise of winds.

6. A call, such as sportsmen use to their dogs.

Madam, here comes my lord.
—I have been worth the *whistle*. *Shakesp. King Lear.*

The knight, pursuing this epistle,
Believ'd he'd brought her to his *whistle*. *Hudibras.*

WHI'STLER. *n. s.* [from *whistle*.] One who whistles.

The prize was a guinea to be conferred upon the ablest *whistler*, who could whistle clearest, and go through his tune without laughing. *Addison.*

WHIT. *n. s.* [pihꞇ, a thing; apihꞇ, any thing, Saxon.] A point; a jot.

We love, and are no *whit* regarded. *Sidney.*

The motive cause of doing it is not in ourselves, but carrieth us as if the wind should drive a feather in the air; we no *whit* furthering that whereby we are driven. *Hooker.*

Her sacred book with blood ywrit,
That none could read, except she did him teach;
She unto him disclosed every *whit*,
And heavenly documents thereout did preach. *Fairy Queen.*

Although the lord became the king's tenant, his country was no *whit* reformed thereby, but remained in the former barbarism. *Davies on Ireland.*

Nature's full blessings would be well dispens'd
In unsuperfluous, even proportion,
And she no *whit* encumber'd with her store. *Milton.*

In account of ancient times it ought to satisfy any enquirer, if they can be brought any *whit* near one another. *Tillotson.*

It is every *whit* as honourable to assist a good minister, as to oppose a bad one. *Addison's Freeholder*, N°. 48.

WHITE. *adj.* [hpiꞇ, Saxon; *wit*, Dutch.]

1. Having such an appearance as arises from the mixture of all colours; snowy.

When the paper was held nearer to any colour than to the rest, it appeared of that colour to which it approached nearest; but when it was equally, or almost equally distant from all the colours, so that it might be equally illuminated by them all, it appeared *white*. *Newton's Opticks.*

Why round our coaches crowd the *white*-glov'd beaus? *Pope.*

Ulysses cut a piece from the chine of the *white*-tooth'd boar, round which there was much fat. *Broome.*

2. Having the colour of fear; pale.

My hand will
That multitudinous sea incarnadine,
Making the green one red.——
—My hands are of your colour, but I shame
To wear a heart so *white*. *Shakesp Macbeth.*

3. Having the colour appropriated to happiness and innocence.

Welcome, pure-ey'd faith, *white*-handed hope;
Thou hovering angel girt with golden wings,
And thou unblemish'd form of chastity. *Milton.*

Wert thou that sweet-smiling youth?
Or that crown'd matron, sage, *white*-robed truth? *Milton.*

Let this auspicious morning be exprest
With a *white* stone, distinguish'd from the rest;
White as thy fame, and as thy honour clear,
And let new joys attend on thy new-added year. *Dryden.*

To feastful mirth be this *white* hour assign'd,
And sweet discourse, the banquet of the mind. *Pope.*

Peace o'er the world her olive-wand extend,
And *white*-rob'd innocence from heav'n descend. *Pope.*

4. Grey with age.

I call you servile ministers,
That have with two pernicious daughters join'd,
Your high-engender'd battles 'gainst a head
So old and *white* as this. *Shakespeare's K. Lear.*

So minutes, hours, and days, weeks, months and years
Past over, to the end they were created,
Would bring *white* hairs unto a quiet grave. *Shakespeare.*

5. Pure; unblemished.

Unhappy Dryden! in all Charles's days,
Roscommon only boasts unspotted lays:
And in our own, excuse some courtly stains,
No *whiter* page than Addison's remains. *Pope.*

WHITE. *n. s.*

1. Whiteness; any thing white; white colour.

A friend coming to visit me, I stopp'd him at the door, and before I told him what the colours were, or what I was doing, I asked him which of the two *whites* were the best, and wherein they differed? and after he had at that distance view'd them well, he answer'd, that they were both good *whites*, and that he could not say which was best, nor wherein their colours differ'd. *Newton's Opticks.*

My Nan shall be the queen of all the fairies,
Finely attired in a robe of *white*. *Shakespeare.*

2. The mark at which an arrow is shot.

If a mark be set up for an archer at a great distance, let him aim as exactly as he can, the least wind shall take his arrow, and divert it from the *white*. *Dryden.*

Remove him then, and all your plots fly sure
Point blank, and level to the very *white*
Of your designs. *Southern.*

3 The albugineous part of eggs.

I'll fetch some flax and *whites* of eggs
T' apply to's bleeding face. *Shakespeare.*

The strongest repellents are the *whites* of new-laid eggs beaten to a froth, with alum. *Wiseman's Surgery.*

What principle manages the *white* and yolk of an egg into such a variety of textures, as is requisite to fashion a chick? *Boyle.*

The two in most regions represent the yolk and the membrane that lies next above it; so the exterior region of the earth is as the shell of the egg, and the abyss under it as the *white* that lies under the shell. *Burnet's Theory of the Earth.*

4. The white part of the eye.

Our general himself
Sanctifies himself with's hands,
And turns up the *white* o' th' eye to his discourse. *Shakesp.*

The horny or pellucid coat of the eye, doth not lie in the same superficies with the *white* of the eye, but riseth up as a hillock, above its convexity. *Ray.*

To WHITE. *v. a.* [from the adjective.] To make white; to dealbate.

His raiment became shining, exceeding white as snow; so as no fuller on earth can *white* them. *Mar.* ix. 3.

Like unto *whited* sepulchres, which appear beautiful outward, but are within full of dead men's bones. *Matt.* xxiii.

WHITELE'AD. *n. s.*

White lead is made by taking sheet-lead, and having cut it into long and narrow slips, they make it up into rolls, but so that a small distance may remain between every spiral revolution. These rolls are put into earthen pots, so ordered that the lead may not sink down above half way, or some small matter more in them: these pots have each of them very sharp vinegar in the bottom, so full as almost to touch the lead. When the vinegar and lead have both been put into the pot, it is covered up close, and so left for a certain time; in which space the corrosive fumes of the vinegar will reduce the surface of the lead into a more white coal, which they separate by knocking it with a hammer. There are two sorts of this sold at the colour shops, the one called ceruse, which is the most pure part, and the other is called white lead. *Quincy.*

WHI'TELY. *adj.* [from *white*.] Coming near to white.

A *whitely* wanton, with a velvet brow,
With two pitch-balls stuck in her face for eyes. *Shakesp.*

Now, governor, I see I must blush
Quite through this vail of night a *whitely* shame,
To think I could design to make those free,
Who were by nature slaves. *Southern's Oroonoko.*

WHI'TEMEAT. *n. s.* [*white* and *meat.*] Food made of milk.
Much saltness in *whitemeat* is ill for the stone. *Tusser.*
The Irish banished into the mountains, lived only upon *whitemeats.* *Spenser.*

To WHI'TEN. *v. a.* [from *white.*] To make white.
The smoke of sulphur will not black a paper, and is commonly used by women to *whiten* tiffanies. *Brown.*
Flax, the soil and climate are proper for *whitening*, by the frequency of brooks, and also of winds. *Temple.*
Women of my complexion ought to be more modest, especially since our faces debar us from all artificial *whitenings.* *Guardian*, N°. 61.

Striking her cliff, the storm confirms her pow'r;
The waves but *whiten* her triumphant shore. *Prior.*

Whether the darken'd room to muse invite,
Or *whiten'd* wall provoke the skew'r to write;
In durance, exile, Bedlam, or the mint,
Like Lee or Budgell, I will rhyme and print. *Pope.*

To WHI'TEN. *v. n.* To grow white.
The bark expects its freight;
The loosen'd canvas trembles with the wind,
And the sea *whitens* with auspicious gales. *Smith.*

WHI'TENER. *n. s.* [from *whiten.*] One who makes any thing white.

WHI'TENESS. *n. s.* [from *white.*]
1. The state of being white; freedom from colour.
This doth lead me to her hand,
Of my first love the fatal band,
Where *whiteness* doth for ever sit;
Nature herself enamell'd it. *Sidney*, *b.* ii.
Whiteness is a mean between all colours, having disposed itself indifferently to them all, so as with equal facility to be tinged with any of them. *Newton's Opticks.*
2. Paleness.
Thou tremblest, and the *whiteness* of thy cheek,
Is apter than thy tongue to tell thy errand. *Shakespeare.*
3. Purity; cleanness.
The least spot is visible on ermine; but to preserve this *whiteness* in its original purity, you have, like that ermine, forsaken the common track of business, which is not always clean. *Dryden.*

WHI'TEPOT. *n. s.* A kind of food.
Cornwall squab-pye, and Devon *whitepot* brings. *King.*

WHITES. *n. s.* [*fluor albus.*] It arises from a laxness of the glands of the uterus, and a cold pituitous blood. *Quincy.*

WHITETHO'RN. *n. s.* A species of thorn.
As little as a *whitethorn* and a pear-tree seem of kin, a cion of the latter will sometimes prosper well, being grafted upon a stock of the former. *Boyle.*

WHI'TEWASH. *n. s.* [*white* and *wash.*] A wash to make the skin seen fair.
The clergy, during Cromwell's usurpation, were very much taken up in reforming the female world; I have heard a whole sermon against a *whitewash.* *Addison.*

WHI'TEWINE. *n. s.* [*white* and *wine.*] A species of wine produced from the white grapes.
The seeds and roots are to be cut, beaten, and infused in *whitewine.* *Wiseman's Surgery.*

WHI'THER. *adv.* [hpyðer, Saxon.]
1. To what place? interrogatively.
Sister, well met; *whither* away so fast?—
—No farther than the Tower. *Shakesp. Rich.* III.
The common people swarm like summer flies;
And *whither* fly the gnats, but to the sun? *Shakespeare.*
Ah! *whither* am I hurry'd? ah! forgive,
Ye shades, and let your sister's issue live. *Dryden.*
2. To what place? Absolutely.
I stray'd I knew not *whither.* *Milton.*
3. To which place; relatively.
Whither, when as they came, they fell at words,
Whether of them should be the lord of lords. *Spenser.*
At Canterbury, *whither* some voice was run on before, the mayor seized on them, as they were taking fresh horses. *Wotton.*
That lord advanced to Winchester, *whither* Sir John Berkley brought him two regiments more of foot. *Clarendon.*
4. To what degree? Obsolete; perhaps never in use.
Whither at length wilt thou abuse our patience?
Still shall thy fury mock us? *B. Johnson.*

WHITHERSOE'VER. *adv.* [*whither* and *soever.*] To whatsoever place.
For whatever end faith is designed, and *whithersoever* the nature and intention of the grace does drive us, thither we must go, and to that end we must direct all our actions. *Taylor.*

WHI'TING. *n. s.* [*wittingh*, Dutch; *alburnus*, Lat.]
1. A small seafish.
Some fish are gutted, split, and kept in pickle, as *whiting* and mackerel. *Carew's Survey of Cornwall.*
The muscular fibres of fishes are more tender than those of terrestrial animals, and their whole substance more watery. Some fishes, as *whitings*, can be almost entirely dissolved into water. *Arbuthnot on Aliments.*
2. A soft chalk. [from *white.*]
That this impregnated liquor may be improved, they pour it upon *whiting*, which is a white chalk, or clay finely powdered, cleansed, and made up into balls. *Boyle.*
When you clean your plate, leave the *whiting* plainly to be seen in all the chinks. *Swift.*

WHI'TISH. *n. s.* [from *white.*] Somewhat white.
The same aqua-fortis, that will quickly change the redness of red lead into a darker colour, will, being put upon crude lead, produce a *whitish* substance, as with copper it did a bluish. *Boyle.*

WHI'TISHNESS. *n. s.* [from *whitish.*] The quality of being somewhat white.
Take good venereal vitriol of a deep blue, and compare with some of the entire crystals, purposely reserved, some of the subtile powder of the same salt, which will exhibit a very considerable degree of *whitishness.* *Boyle on Colours.*

WHI'TLEATHER. *n. s.* [*white* and *leather.*] Leather dressed with alum, remarkable for toughness.
Whole bridle and saddle, *whitlether* and nal,
With collars and harneis. *Tusser's Husbandry.*
He bor'd the nerves through, from the heel to th' ankle, and then knit
Both to his chariot, with a thong of *whitleather.* *Chapman.*
Nor do I care much, if her pretty snout
Meet with her furrow'd chin, and both together
Hem in her lips, as dry as good *whitleather.* *Suckling.*

WHI'TLOW. *n. s.* [hpıτ, Saxon, and *loup*, a wolf. *Skinner.* hpıτ, Saxon, and *low*, a flame. *M. Lye.*] A swelling between the cuticle and cutis, called the mild whitlow, or between the periosteum and the bone, called the malignant whitlow.
Paronychia is a small swelling about the nails and ends of the fingers, by the vulgar people generally called *whitflaw.* *Wisem.*

WHI'TSOUR. *n. s.* A kind of apple. See APPLE.

WHI'TSTER, or *whiter. n. s.* [from *white.*] A whitener.
Carry it among the *whitsters* in Datchet mead. *Shakespeare.*

WHI'TSUL. *n. s.* A provincial word.
Their meat was *whitsul*, as they call it, namely, milk, sour milk, cheese, curds, butter. *Carew.*

WHI'TSUNTIDE. *n. s.* [*white* and *Sunday*; because the converts newly baptized, appeared from Easter to Whitsuntide in white. *Skinner.*] The feast of Pentecost.
Strephon, with leafy twigs of laurel tree,
A garland made on temples for to wear;
For he then chosen was the dignity
Of village lord that *Whitsontide* to bear. *Sidney.*
This they employ in brewing and baking against *Whitsontide.* *Carew's Survey of Cornwall.*
And let us do it with no shew of fear;
Nor with no more than if we heard that England
Were busied with a *Whitson* morrice dance. *Shakespeare.*

WHI'TTENTREE. *n. s.* A sort of tree. *Ainsworth.*

WHI'TTLE. *n. s.* [hpýτel, Saxon.]
1. A white dress for a woman. Not in use.
2. [hpýτel, Saxon.] A knife.
There's not a *whittle* in th' unruly camp,
But I do prize it at my love, before
The reverend'st throat in Athens. *Shakespeare.*
A dagger hanging at his belt he had,
Made of an antient sword's well-temper'd blade;
He wore a Sheffield *whittle* in his hose. *Betterton's Miller.*

To WHI'TTLE. *v. a.* [from the noun.] To cut with a knife; to edge; to sharpen. Not in use.
When they are come to that once, and are thoroughly *whittled*, then shall you have them cast their wanton eyes upon men's wives. *Hakewill on Providence.*

To WHIZ. *v. n.* [from the sound that it expresses.] To make a loud humming noise.
The exhalations, *whizzing* in the air,
Give so much light, that I may read by them. *Shakespeare.*
Turn him about,
I know him, he'll but *whiz*, and strait go out. *Dryden.*
Soon all with vigour bend their trusty bows,
And from the quiver each his arrow chose:
Hippocoon's was the first; with forceful sway
It flew, and *whizzing* cut the liquid way. *Dryden.*

WHO. *pronoun.* [hpa, Saxon; *wie*, Dutch.]
1. A pronoun relative, applied to persons.
We have no perfect description of it, nor any knowledge how, or by *whom* it is inhabited. *Abbot.*
Oft have I seen a timely-parted ghost,
Of ashy semblance, meagre, pale, and bloodless,
Being all descended to the lab'ring heart,
Who, in the conflict that it holds with death,
Attracts the same for aidance 'gainst the enemy. *Shakesp.*
Were the grac'd person of our Banquo present,
Whom I may rather challenge for unkindness,
Than pity for mischance. *Shakesp. Macbeth.*
The son of Duncan,
From *whom* this tyrant holds the due of birth,
Lives in the English court. *Shakesp. Macbeth.*
A man can never be obliged to submit to any power, unless he can be satisfied, *who* is the person *who* has a right to exercise it. *Locke.*

Tell who loves *who*; what favours some partake,
And who is jilted. *Dryden.*

We are still as much at a loss, *who* civil power belongs to. *Locke.*

2. *As who should say*, elliptically for *as one who should say*.

Hope throws a generous contempt upon ill usage, and looks like a handsome defiance of a misfortune: *as who should say*, you are somewhat troublesome now, but I shall conquer you. *Collier against Despair.*

3. *Whose* is the genitive of *which*, as well as of *who*, and is applied to things.

Whose soever sins ye remit, they are remitted; and *whose* soever sins ye retain, they are retained. *John* xx. 23.

The question *whose* solution I require,
Is what the sex of women most desire. *Dryden.*

Is there any other doctrine, *whose* followers are punished? *Add.*

4. It has sometimes a disjunctive sense.

There thou tell'st of kings, and *who* aspire;
Who fall, *who* rise, *who* triumphs, *who* do moan. *Daniel.*

WHOE'VER. *pronoun.* [*who* and *ever.*] Any one, without limitation or exception.

Whoever doth to temperance apply
His stedfast life, and all his actions frame,
Trust me, shall find no greater enemy,
Than stubborn perturbation to the same. *Fairy Queen.*

I think myself beholden, *whoever* shews me my mistakes. *Loc.*

Whoe'er thou art, that fortune brings to keep
The rights of Neptune, monarch of the deep;
Thee first it fits, O stranger, to prepare
The due libation, and the solemn prayer. *Pope.*

Whoever is really brave, has always this comfort when he is oppress'd, that he knows himself to be superior to those who injure him, by forgiving it. *Pope.*

WHOLE. *adj.* [palȝ, Saxon; *heal*, Dutch.]

1. All; total; containing all.

Burn the *whole* ram upon the altar. *Ex.* xxix. 18.

All the *whole* army stood agaz'd at him. *Shakespeare.*

Fierce extremes,
Contiguous might distemper the *whole* frame. *Milton.*

2. Uninjured; unimpaired.

Anguish is come upon me, because my life is yet *whole* in me. 2 *Sa.* i. 9.

3. Well of any hurt or sickness.

When they had done circumcising all the people, they abode in the camp, till they were *whole*. *Jos* v. 8.

WHOLE. *n. s.* The totality; no part omitted; the complex of all the parts.

Fear God, and keep his commandments, for this is the *whole* of man. *Ecclesiastes.*

Begin with sense, of ev'ry art the soul;
Parts answering parts, shall slide into a *whole*. *Pope.*

It contained the *whole* of religion amongst the antients; and made philosophy more agreeable. *Broome.*

There is a metaphysical *whole*, when the essence of a thing is said to consist of two parts, the genus and the difference, *i. e.* the general and the special nature, which, being joined together, make up a definition. *Watts's Logick.*

WHO'LESALE. *n. s.* [*whole* and *sale.*] Sale in the lump, not in separate small parcels.

These are *wholesale* chapmen to Satan, that do not truck and barter one crime for another, but take the whole herd. *Government of the Tongue.*

This cost me at the *wholesale* merchant's a hundred drachma's;
I make two hundred by selling it in retail. *Addison.*

Some from vanity, or envy, despise a valuable book, and throw contempt upon it by *wholesale*. *Watts.*

WHO'LESOME. *adj.* [*heelsam*, Dutch; *heylsam*, Teutonick; both from þæl, Saxon, *health.*]

1. Sound. Contrary to unsound in doctrine.

They suffer us to famish, repeal daily any *wholesome* act established against the rich, and provide more piercing statutes to chain up the poor. *Shakesp. Coriolanus.*

'Tis no less
To govern justly, make your empire flourish,
With *wholesome* laws, in riches, peace, and plenty;
Than, by the expence of wealth and blood, to make
New acquisitions. *Denham's Sophy.*

So the doctrine contain'd be but *wholesome* and edifying, a want of exactness in speaking may be overlook'd. *Atterbury.*

2. Contributing to health.

Night not now, as ere man fell,
Wholsome and cool and mild; but with black air
Accompany'd, with damps and dreadful gloom. *Milton.*

Besides the *wholesome* luxury which that place abounds with, a kitchen garden is a more pleasant sight than the finest orangery. *Addison.*

She held it *wholesomer* by much,
To rest a little on the couch. *Prior.*

3. Preserving; salutary. Obsolete.

The Lord helpeth his anointed, and will hear him from his holy heaven; even with the *wholesome* strength of his right hand. *Psalm* xx. 6.

4. Kindly; pleasing. A burlesque use.

I cannot make you a *wholesome* answer; my wit's diseased. *Shakesp. Hamlet.*

To wail friends lost,
Is not by much so *wholesome*, profitable,
As to rejoice at friends but newly found. *Shakespeare.*

WHO'LESOMELY. *adv.* [from *wholesome.*] Salubriously; salutiferously.

WHO'LESOMENESS. *n. s.* [from *wholesome.*]

1. Quality of conducing to health; salubrity.

We made a standard of the healthfulness of the air, from the proportion of acute and epidemical diseases, and of the *wholesomeness* of the food from that of the chronical. *Graunt.*

At Tonon they shewed us a great fountain of water, that is in great esteem for its *wholesomeness*; weighing two ounces in a pound less than the same measure of the lake water. *Add.*

2. Salutariness; conduciveness to good.

WHO'LLY. *adv.* [from *whole.*]

1. Completely; perfectly.

The thrust was so strong, that he could not so *wholly* beat it away, but that it met with his thigh, through which it ran. *Sidney, b.* ii.

Nor *wholly* lost we so deserv'd a prey;
For storms repenting part of it restor'd. *Dryden.*

Thus equal deaths are dealt with equal chance;
By turns they quit their ground, by turns advance:
Victors, and vanquish'd in the various field,
Nor *wholly* overcome, nor *wholly* yield. *Dryden.*

This story was written before Boccace; but its author being *wholly* lost, Chaucer is now become an original. *Dryden.*

They employ'd themselves *wholly* in domestick life; and provided a woman could keep her house in order, she never troubled herself about regulating the commonwealth. *Addison.*

2. Totally; in all the parts or kinds.

Metals are *wholly* subterrany. *Bacon.*

WHOM. the accusative of *who*, singular and plural.

There be men in the world, *whom* you had rather have your son be with five hundred pounds, than some other with five thousands. *Locke on Education.*

WHOMSOE'VER. *pron.* [*who* and *soever.*] Any without exception.

With *whomsoever* thou findest thy goods, let him not live. *Gen.* xxxi. 32.

Nature has bestowed mines on several parts; but their riches are only for the industrious and frugal. *Whomsoever* else they visit, 'tis with the diligent and sober only they stay. *Locke.*

WHOO'BUB. *n. s.* Hubbub. See HUBBUB.

In this time of lethargy, I pick'd and cut most of their festival purses: and had not the old man come in with a *whoobub* against his daughter, and scar'd my choughs from the chaff, I had not left a purse in the whole army. *Shakesp.*

WHOOP. *n. s.* [See *hoop.*]

1. A shout of pursuit.

Let them breathe a-while, and then
Cry *whoop*, and set them on again. *Hudibras.*

A fox crossing the road, drew off a considerable detachment, who clapp'd spurs to their horses, and pursued him with *whoops* and hallows. *Addison.*

2. [*Upupa*, Latin.] A bird. *Dict.*

To WHOOP. *v. n.* [from the noun.] To shout with malignity.

Treason and murder ever kept together,
As two yoke devils sworn to either's purpose:
Working so grosly in a nat'ral cause,
That admiration did not *whoop* at them. *Shakespeare.*

To WHOOP. *v. a.* To insult with shouts.

While he trusts me, 'twere so base a part
To fawn, and yet betray; I shou'd be hiss'd
And *whoop'd* in hell for that ingratitude. *Dryden.*

WHORE. *n. s.* [hon, Saxon; *hoere*, Dutch.]

1. A woman who converses unlawfully with men; a fornicatress; an adultress; a strumpet.

To put out the word *whore*, thou dost me wo,
Throughout my book; troth, put out woman too. *B. Johns.*

2. A prostitute; a woman who receives men for money.

Orontes
Conveys his wealth to Tiber's hungry shores,
And fattens Italy with foreign *whores*. *Dryden.*

We weary'd should lie down in death:
This cheat of life would take no more;
If you thought fame but empty breath;
Your Phyllis but a perjur'd *whore*. *Prior.*

To WHORE. *v. n.* [from the noun.] To converse unlawfully with the other sex.

'Tis a noble general's prudent part,
To cherish valour, and reward desert:
Let him be daub'd with lace, live high, and *whore*;
Sometimes be lousy, but be never poor. *Dryden.*

To WHO'RE. *v. a.* To corrupt with regard to chastity.

WHO'REDOM. *n. s.* [from *whore.*] Fornication.

Some let go *whoredom* as an indifferent matter, which yet strive for an holy-day, as for their life. *Hall.*

Nor can that person who accounts it his recreation to see one man wallowing in his filthy revels, and another infamous by his sensuality, be so impudent as to allege, that all the enormous draughts of the one can leave the least relish upon the tip of his tongue; or that all the fornications and *whoredoms* of the other can quench his own lust. *South's Sermons.*

WHOREMA'STER. } *n. s.* [*whore* and *master* or *monger.*] One
WHOREMO'NGER. } who keeps whores, or converses with a fornicatress.

What is a *whoremaster*, fool? a fool in good cloaths and something like thee. *Shakespeare.*

As if we were drunkards, by a planetary influence; an admirable evasion of *whoremaster* man, to lay his goatish disposition on the change of a star. *Shakespeare's King Lear.*

Art thou fully persuaded that no *whoremonger* nor adulterer shall have any inheritance in the kingdom of God? and dost thou continue to practise these vices? *Tillotson's Sermons.*

A rank notorious *whoremaster*, to choose,
To thrust his neck into the marriage noose. *Dryden.*

If he were jealous, he might clip his wife's wings; but what would this avail, when there were flocks of *whoremasters* perpetually hovering over his house. *Addison's Guardian.*

WHO'RESON. *n. s.* [*whore* and *son.*] A bastard. It is generally used in a ludicrous dislike.

Whoreson, mad compound of majesty, thou art welcome. *Shakespeare's Henry* IV.

Thou *whoreson* Zed! thou unnecessary letter. *Shakespeare.*

How now, you *whoreson* peasant,
Where have you been these two days loitering? *Shakesp.*

Frog was a cunning, sly *whoreson*, quite the reverse of John. *Arbuthnot's History of John Bull.*

WHO'RISH. *adj.* [from *whore.*] Unchast; incontinent.

You, like a letcher, out of *whorish* loins
Breed out your inheritors. *Shakesp. Troilus and Cressida.*

By means of a *whorish* woman a man is brought to a piece of bread. *Prov.* vi. 26.

WHO'RTLEBERRY. *n. s.* [ƿeoꞃꞇbeꞃian, Saxon.] Bilberry. A plant.

The flower consists of one leaf, shaped like a pitcher; from whose empalement arises the pointal, fixed like a nail in the upper part of the flower, which becomes a soft umbilicated fruit or berry full of juice, in which are inclosed seeds, for the most part small. *Miller.*

WHOSE. *n. s.*

1. Genitive of *who.*

Though I could
With barefac'd power sweep him from my sight,
And bid my will avouch it, yet I must not;
For certain friends that are both his and mine,
Whose loves I may not drop. *Shakespeare's Macbeth.*

2. Genitive of which.

Thy name afrights me, in *whose* sound is death. *Shakesp.*

Those darts *whose* points make gods adore
His might, and deprecate his power. *Prior.*

WHO'SO. } *pronoun.* [*who* and *soever.*] Any, without re-
WHOSOE'VER. } striction.

Whoso is out of hope to attain to another's virtue, will seek to come at even hand, by depressing another's fortune. *Bacon.*

Let there be persons licensed to lend upon usury; let the rate be somewhat more easy for the merchant than that he formerly payed; for all borrowers shall have some ease, be he merchant or *whosoever.* *Bacon.*

He inclos'd
Knowledge of good, and evil, in this tree,
That *whoso* eats thereof, forthwith attains
Wisdom. *Milton's Paradise Lost.*

Whosoever hath Christ for his friend, shall be sure of counsel, and *whosoever* is his own friend will be sure to obey it. *South's Sermons.*

WHURT. *n. s.* A whortleberry; a bilberry.

For fruits, both wild, as *whurts*, strawberries, pears and plums, though the meaner sort come short, the gentlemen step not far behind those of other parts. *Carew.*

WHY. *adv.* [ƿpi, ꝼoꞃƿpi, Saxon.]

1. For what reason? Interrogatively.

They both deal justly with you; *why?* not from any regard they have for justice, but because their fortune depends on their credit. *Swift.*

2. For which reason. Relatively.

Mortar will not have attained its utmost compactness till fourscore years after it has been employed; and this is one reason *why*, in demolishing ancient fabricks, it is more easy to break the stone than the mortar. *Boyle.*

No ground of enmity
Why he should mean me ill. *Milton.*

Such, whose sole bliss is eating; who can give
But that one brutal reason, *why* they live. *Dryden.*

3. For what reason. Relatively.

Shall I tell you *why*:—
—Ay, sir, and wherefore; for they say,
Every *why* hath a wherefore. *Shakespeare.*

I was dispatch'd for their defence and guard;
And listen *why*, for I will tell you now. *Milton.*

We examine the *why*, the what and the how of things. *L'Estrange.*

Turn the discourse; I have a reason *why*
I would not have you speak so tenderly. *Dryden.*

4. It is sometimes used emphatically.

Ninus' tomb, man; *why*, you must not speak that yet: that you answer to Pyram. *Shakespeare.*

You have not been a-bed then?
Why, no; the day had broke before we parted. *Shakespeare.*

Whence is this? *why:* from that essential suitableness which obedience has to the relation which is between a rational creature and his Creator. *South's Sermons.*

WHYNO'T. *adv.* A cant word for violent or peremptory procedure.

Capoch'd your rabbins of the synod,
And snap'd their canons with a *whynot.* *Hudibras.*

WI. [Sax.] Holy. Thus *wimund*, holy peace; *wibert*, eminent for sanctity; *alwi*, altogether holy, as Hierocles, Hieronymus, Hosius, &c. *Gibson's Camden.*

WIC, *Wich.* Comes from the Saxon pic, which according to the different nature and condition of places, hath a threefold signification; implying either a village, or a bay made by the winding banks of a river, or a castle. *Gibson's Camden.*

WICK. *n. s.* [peoce, Saxon; *wiecke*, Dutch.] The substance round which is applied the wax or tallow of a torch or candle.

But true it is, that when the oil is spent,
The light goes out, and *wick* is thrown away;
So, when he had resign'd his regiment,
His daughter 'gan despise his drooping day. *Fa. Queen.*

There lives within the very flame of love
A kind of *wick* or snuff that will abate it. *Shakespeare.*

Bodies are inflamed wholly and immediately, without any *wick* to help the inflammation. *Bacon's Natural History.*

Little atoms of oil or melted wax continually ascend apace up the *wick* of a burning candle. *Digby.*

The fungous parcels about the *wicks* of candles only signifieth a moist and pulvious air about them. *Brown's Vulgar Err.*

WI'CKED. *adj.* [Of this common word the etymology is very obscure: picca, is *an enchanter*; pæccan, is *to oppress*; piꞃian, *to curse*; piccꝺ, is *crooked:* all these however *Skinner* rejects for *vitiatus*, Latin. Perhaps it is a compound of pic, *vile*, *bad*, and *head*, *malum caput.*]

1. Given to vice; not good; flagitious; morally bad.

The dwelling place of the *wicked* shall come to nought. *Job.*

And as the better spirit, when she doth bear
A scorn of death, doth shew she cannot die;
So when the *wicked* soul death's face doth fear,
Ev'n then she proves her own eternity. *Davies.*

He of their *wicked* ways shall them admonish. *Milton.*

But since thy veins paternal virtue fires,
Go and succeed! the rivals aims despise;
For never, never *wicked* man was wise. *Pope's Odyssey.*

2. It is a word of ludicrous or slight blame.

That same *wicked* bastard of Venus, that blind rascally boy, that abuses every one's eyes because his own are out, let him be judge how deep I am in love. *Shakespeare.*

3. Cursed; baneful; pernicious; bad in effect.

The *wicked* weed which there the fox did lay,
From underneath his head he took away. *Hubberd.*

As *wicked* dew as e'er my mother brush'd,
With raven's feather from unwholsome fen,
Drop on you both. *Shakespeare's Tempest.*

WI'CKEDLY. *adv.* [from *wicked.*] Criminally; corruptly; badly.

I would now send him where they all should see,
Clear as the light his heart shine; where no man
Could be so *wickedly* or fondly stupid,
But should cry out, he saw, touch'd, felt wickedness,
And grasp'd it. *Ben. Johnson.*

He behaved himself with great modesty and wonderful repentance; being convinced in his conscience that he had done *wickedly.* *Clarendon.*

That thou may'st the better bring about
Thy wishes, thou art *wickedly* devout. *Dryden.*

'Tis phrase absurd to call a villain great:
Who *wickedly* is wise, or madly brave,
Is but the more a fool, the more a knave. *Pope.*

WI'CKEDNESS. *n. s.* [from *wicked.*] Corruption of manners; guilt; moral ill.

It is not good that children should know any *wickedness*; old folks have discretion and know the world. *Shakespeare.*

These tents thou saw'st so pleasant, were the tents
Of *wickedness*; wherein shall dwell his race
Who slew his brother. *Milton's Paradise Lost.*

WI'CKER. *adj.* [*vigre*, a twig, Danish; *twiggen*, Dutch.] Made of small sticks.

Each one a little *wicker* basket had
Made of fine twigs, entrailed curiously;
In which they gather'd flow'rs. *Spenser.*

The

The long broad ſhields, made up of *wicker* rods, which are commonly uſed among the northern Iriſh, but eſpecially among the Scots, are brought from the Scythians. *Spenſer.*

If your influence be quite damm'd up
With black uſurping miſts, ſome gentle taper,
Though a ruſh candle from the *wicker* hole
Of ſome clay habitation, viſit us
With thy long-levell'd rule of ſtreaming light. *Milton.*

A fooliſh painter drew January ſitting in a *wicker* chair, with four nightcaps on by the fire, and without doors green trees, as if it had been in the midſt of July. *Peacham.*

WI'CKET. *n. ſ.* [*wicked*, Welſh; *guighet*, Fr. *wicket*, Dutch.] A ſmall gate.

When none yielded, her unruly page,
With his rude claws the *wicket* open rent,
And let her in. *Fairy Queen.*

Theſe *wickets* of the ſoul are plac'd on high,
Becauſe all ſounds do lightly mount aloft. *Davies.*

Now St. Peter at heav'ns *wicket* ſeems
To wait them with his keys. *Milton.*

The cave was now a common way,
The *wicket*, often open'd, knew the key. *Dryden.*

The chaffering with diſſenters, and dodging about this or the other ceremony, is like opening a few *wickets*, by which no more than one can get in at a time. *Swift.*

WIDE. *adj.* [pıde, Saxon; *wijd*, Dutch.]

1. Broad; extended far each way.

They found fat paſture, and the land was *wide* and quiet. 1 *Chron.* iv. 40.

He wand'ring long a *wider* circle made,
And many-languag'd nations he ſurvey'd. *Pope.*

2. Broad to a certain degree: as *three inches* wide.

3. Deviating; remote.

Many of the fathers were far *wide* from the underſtanding of this place *Raleigh.*

Conſider the abſurdities of that diſtinction betwixt the act and the obliquity, and the contrary being ſo *wide* from the truth of ſcripture and the attributes of God, and ſo noxious to good life, we may certainly conclude, that to the perpetration of whatſoever ſin, there is not at all any predeſtination of God. *Hammond's Fundamentals.*

To move
His laughter at their quaint opinions *wide*. *Milton.*

Oft *wide* of nature muſt he act a part,
Make love in tropes, in bombaſt break his heart. *Tickell.*

WIDE. *adv.*

1. At a diſtance. In this ſenſe *wide* ſeems to be ſometimes an adverb.

A little *wide*,
There was a holy chapel edify'd,
Wherein the hermit wont to ſay
His holy things each morn and even tide. *Fairy Queen.*

Of this I have heard more from others who lived much among the Chineſe; a people whoſe way of thinking ſeems to lie as *wide* of ours in Europe as their country does. *Temple.*

2. With great extent.

Of all theſe bounds rich'd
With plenteous rivers, and *wide* ſkirted meads,
We make thee lady. *Shakeſpeare's King Lear.*

On the eaſt-ſide of the garden place,
Cherubic watch; and of a ſword the flame
Wide-waving; all approach far off to fright. *Milton.*

With huge two-handed ſway,
Brandiſh'd aloft, the horrid edge came down,
Wide waſting *Milton.*

The ſouth wind roſe, and with black wings.
Wide hovering all the clouds together drove
From under heav'n. *Millton's Paradiſe Loſt.*

Stretch'd at eaſe the panting lady lies,
To ſhun the fervor of meridian ſkies;
While ſweating ſlaves catch ev'ry breeze of air,
And with *wide*-ſpreading fans refreſh the fair. *Gay.*

Yet *wide* was ſpread their fame in ages paſt,
And poets once had promis'd they ſhould laſt. *Pope.*

WI'DELY. *adv.* [from *wide.*]

1. With great extent each way.

Any that conſiders how immenſe the intervals of the chaos are, in proportion to the bulk of the atoms, will hardly induce himſelf to believe, that particles ſo *widely* diſſeminated could ever throng one another to a compact texture. *Bentley.*

2. Remotely; far.

Let him exerciſe the freedom of his reaſon, and his mind will be ſtrengthned, and the light which the remote parts of truth will give to one another, will ſo aſſiſt his judgment, that he will ſeldom be *widely* out. *Locke.*

To WI'DEN. *v. a.* [from *wide.*] To make wide; to extend.

So now the gates are ope; now prove good ſeconds;
'Tis for the followers, fortune *widens* them,
Not for the flyers. *Shakeſpeare's Coriolanus.*

Theſe accidents when they firſt happen, ſeem but ſmall and contemptible; but by degrees they branch out and *widen* themſelves into a numerous train of miſchievous conſequences. *South.*

He was accuſtomed to ſleep with a peaceable noſe, ſoftning in his ſlumbers the wrinkles of it, and the anger which commonly mounted to that part; but now his noſtrils were *widened* to the laſt degree of fury. *Dryden's Dufreſnoy.*

To WI'DEN. *v. n.* To grow wide; to extend itſelf.

It is in this that the ſpecies of brutes are diſcriminated from man, and that proper difference, wherein they are wholly ſeparated, and which at laſt *widens* to ſo vaſt a diſtance. *Locke.*

With her the temple ev'ry moment grew,
Upward the columns ſhoot, the roofs aſcend,
And arches *widen*, and long iſles extend. *Pope.*

WI'DENESS. *n. ſ.* [from *wide.*]

1. Breadth; large extent each way.

The rugged hair began to fall away;
The ſweetneſs of her eyes did only ſtay,
Though not ſo large; her crooked horns decreaſe;
The *wideneſs* of her jaws and noſtrils ceaſe. *Dryden.*

2. Comparative breadth.

Within the ſame annual time, the center of the earth is carried above fifty times as far round the orbis magnus, whoſe *wideneſs* we now aſſume to be twenty thouſand terreſtrial diameters. *Bentley's Sermons.*

WI'DGEON. A water-fowl not unlike a wild duck, but not ſo large.

Among the firſt ſort we reckon creyſers, curlews, and *widgeon.* *Carew.*

WI'DOW. *n. ſ.* [pıdpa, Sax. *weduwe*, Dutch; *weddw*, Welſh; *vidua*, Latin.] A woman whoſe huſband is dead.

To take the *widow*,
Exaſperates, makes mad her ſiſter Gonerill. *Shakeſpeare.*

Catharine no more
Shall be call'd queen; but princeſs dowager,
And *widow* to prince Arthur. *Shakeſpeare's Hen.* VIII.

Our fatherleſs diſtreſs was left unmoan'd,
Your *widow*-dolours likewiſe be unwept. *Shak. Richard* III.

And will ſhe yet debaſe her eyes on me,
That cropt the golden prime of this ſweet prince,
And made her *widow* to a woeful bed. *Shakeſpeare.*

The barren they more miſerable make,
And from the *widow* all her comfort take. *Saudys.*

He warns the *widow*, and her houſhold gods
To ſeek a refuge in remote abodes. *Dryden.*

Who has the paternal power whilſt the *widow*-queen is with child. *Locke.*

To WI'DOW. *v. a.* [from *widow.*]

1. To deprive of a huſband.

In this city he
Hath *widow'd* and unchilded many a one,
Which to this hour bewail the injury. *Shak. Coriolanus.*

Poor ropes you are beguil'd;
Both you and I; for Romeo is exil'd:
He made you for a high way to my bed,
But I, a maid, die maiden *widowed.* *Shakeſpeare.*

Thy little care to mend my *widow'd* nights,
Has forc'd me to recourſe of marriage rites,
To fill an empty ſide. *Dryden.*

2. To endow with a widow-right.

For his poſſeſſions,
Although by confiſcation they are ours,
We do inſtate and *widow* you withal,
To buy you a better huſband. *Shakeſpeare.*

3. To ſtrip of any thing good.

The *widow'd* iſle in mourning
Dries up her tears. *Dryden.*

For him you waſte in tears your *widow'd* hours. *Dryden.*

Inclement weather and froſty blaſts deface
The blithſome year, trees of their ſhrivel'd fruits
Are *widow'd*, dreary ſtorms o'er all prevail. *Philips.*

WI'DOWER. *n. ſ.* [from *widow.*] One who has loſt his wife.

The king, ſealing up all thoughts of love under the image of her memory, remained a *widower* many years after. *Sidney.*

The main conſents are had, and here we'll ſtay
To ſee our *widower*'s ſecond marriage-day. *Shakeſpeare.*

They that marry, as they that ſhall get no children; and they that marry not, as the *widowers.* 2 *Eſdr.* xvi. 44.

WI'DOWHOOD. *n. ſ.* [from *widow.*] The ſtate of a widow.

Cecropia, having in her *widowhood* taken this young Arteſia into her charge, had taught her to think that there is no wiſdom but in including both heaven and earth in one's ſelf. *Sidney.*

Ne ween my right with ſtrength adown to tread,
Through weakneſs of my *widowhood* or woe,
For truth is ſtrong. *Fairy Queen.*

She employed her laſt *widowhood* to works no leſs bountiful than charitable. *Carew's Survey of Cornwall.*

It is of greater merit wholly to abſtain from things deſireable, than after fruition to be content to leave them; as they who magnify ſingle life prefer virginity much before *widowhood.* *Wotton.*

Cherish thy hasten'd *widowhood* with the gold
Of matrimonial treason: so farewell. *Milton.*

2. Estate settled on a widow. Not in use.

For that dow'ry, I'll assure her of
Her *widowhood*, be it that she survives me,
In all my lands. *Shakesp. Taming of the Shrew.*

WIDOWHU'NTER. *n. s.* [*widow* and *hunter.*] One who courts widows for a jointure.

The *widowhunters* about town often afford them great diversion. *Addison's Spectator.*

WIDOWMA'KER. *n. s.* [*widow* and *maker.*] One who deprives women of their husbands.

It grieves my soul
That I must draw this metal from my side
To be a *widowmaker*. *Shakesp. King John.*

WI'DOW-WAIL. *n. s.* [*widow* and *wail*] A plant.

It hath a flower consisting of one leaf, which is deeply divided into three parts: the cup of the flower is also of one leaf, divided into three segments; the fruit consists of three hard berries closely joined together; in each of which is contained one oblong seed; to which may be added, it hath the appearance of a shrub, and the leaves are small and oblong. *Miller.*

WIDTH. *n. s.* [from *wide.*] Breadth; wideness. A low word.

For the *width* of the mortess gage this side, then for the tennant, gage on that end of the quarter you intend the tennant shall be made. *Moxon.*

Let thy vines in intervals be set,
Indulge their *width*, and add a roomy space,
That their extremest lines may scarce embrace. *Dryden.*

To WIELD. *v. a.* [pealdan, Saxon; to manage in the hand.] To use with full command, as a thing not too heavy for the holder.

Base Hungarian wight, wilt thou the spigot *wield*. *Shakesp.*

His looks are full of peaceful majesty,
His head by nature fram'd to wear a crown,
His hand to *wield* a scepter, and himself
Likely in time to bless a regal throne. *Shakespeare.*

There is that hand bolden'd to blood and war,
That must the sword in wond'rous actions *wield*. *Daniel.*

They are in the dark before they are aware; and then they make a noise only with terms; which, like too heavy weapons that they cannot *wield*, carry their strokes beyond their aim. *Digby on Bodies.*

The least of whom could *wield*
These elements, and arm him with the force
Of all their regions. *Milton's Paradise Lost.*

Part *wield* their arms, part curb the foaming steed. *Milton.*

If Rome's great senate could not *wield* that sword,
Which of the conquer'd world had made them lord;
What hope had ours, while yet their pow'r was new,
To rule victorious armies, but by you? *Waller.*

He worthiest, after him, his sword to *wield*,
Or wear his armour, or sustain his shield. *Dryden.*

WI'ELDY. *adj.* [from *wield.*] Manageable.

WI'ERY. *adj.* [from *wire.*]

1. Made of wire: it were better written *wiry*.

Your gown going off, such beauteous state reveals,
As when through flow'ry meads th' hill's shadow steals;
Off with that *wiry* coronet, and shew
The hairy diadem which on your head doth grow. *Donne.*

2. Drawn into wire.

Polymnia shall be drawn with her hair hanging loose about her shoulders, resembling *wiery* gold. *Peacham on Drawing.*

3. [From pæn, a pool.] Wet; wearish; moist. Obsolete.

Where but by chance a silver drop hath fall'n,
Ev'n to that drop ten thousand *wiery* friends
Do glew themselves in sociable grief. *Shakespeare.*

WIFE. *n. s.* Plural *wives* [piꝼ, Saxon; *wiff*, Dutch.]

A woman that has a husband.

Your claim, fair sister,
I bar it in the interest of my *wife*. *Shakespeare's King Lear.*

There's no bottom, none
In my voluptuousness: your *wives*, your daughters,
Your matrons and your maids could not fill up
The cistern of my lust. *Shakespeare's Macbeth.*

Why saidst thou, she is my sister? so I might have taken her to me to *wife*. *Gen.* xii. 19.

The *wife*, where danger or dishonour lurks,
Safest and seemliest by her husband stays. *Milton.*

The *wife* her husband murders, he the *wife*. *Dryden.*

Fond of his friend, and civil to his *wife*. *Pope.*

2. It is used for a woman of low employment.

Strawberry *wives* lay two or three great strawberries at the mouth of their pot, and all the rest are little ones. *Bacon.*

WIG. *n. s.* *Wig* being a termination in the names of men signifies war, or else a heroe, from piga, a word of that signification. *Gibson's Camden.*

WIG. *n. s.* [Contracted from *periwig.*]

1. False hair worn on the head.

Triumphing Tories and desponding Whigs
Forget their feuds, and join to save their *wigs*. *Swift.*

2. A sort of cake. *Ainsworth.*

WIGHT. *n. s.* [piht, Saxon.] A person; a being. Obsolete.

Beshrew the witch! with venomous *wights* she stays,
Tedious as hell; but flies the grasps of love,
With wings more momentary swift than thought. *Shakesp.*

This world below did need one *wight*,
Which might thereof distinguish ev'ry part. *Davies.*

This meaner *wights*, of trust and credit bare,
Not so respected, could not look t'effect. *Daniel.*

A *wight* he was, whose very sight wou'd
Entitle him mirror of knighthood. *Hudibras.*

The water flies all taste of living *wight*. *Milton.*

How could'st thou suffer thy devoted knight,
On thy own day, to fall by foe oppress'd,
The *wight* of all the world who lov'd thee best. *Dryden.*

His station he yielded up to a *wight* as disagreeable as himself. *Addison's Guardian.*

WIGHT. *adj.* Swift; nimble. Out of use.

He was so wimble and so *wight*,
From bough to bough he leaped light,
And oft the pumies latched. *Spenser's Pastorals.*

WI'GHTLY. *adv.* [from *wight.*] Swiftly; nimbly.

Her was her, while it was day-light,
But now her is a most wretched wight;
For day that was is *wightly* past,
And now at last the night doth hast. *Spenser.*

WIHT. An initial in the names of men, signifies strong; nimble; lusty; being purely Saxon. *Gibson's Camden.*

WILD. *adj.* [pilo, Saxon; *wild*, Dutch.]

1. Not tame; not domestick.

For I am he am born to tame you, Kate,
And bring you from a *wild* cat to a kate,
Conformable as other houshold kates. *Shakespeare.*

Winter's not gone yet, if the *wild* geese fly that way. *Shak.*

All beasts of the earth since *wild*. *Milton.*

2. Propagated by nature; not cultivated.

Whatsoever will make a *wild* tree a garden tree, will make a garden tree to have less core or stone. *Bacon's Natural History.*

Goose grass or *wild* tansy is a weed that strong clays are very subject to. *Mortimer's Husbandry.*

The *wild* bee breeds in the stocks of old willows, in which they first bore a canal, and furnish afterwards with hangings, made of rose leaves: and to finish their work divide the whole into several rooms or nests. *Grew's Musæum.*

3. Desart; uninhabited.

The wild beast where he wons in forest *wild*. *Milton.*

4. Savage; uncivilized.

Affairs that walk,
As they say spirits do, at midnight, have
In them a *wilder* nature, than the business
That seeks dispatch by day. *Shakespeare's Henry* VIII.

Though the inundation destroyed man and beast generally, yet some few *wild* inhabitants of the woods escaped. *Bacon.*

When they might not converse with any civil men without peril of their lives, whither should they fly but into the woods and mountains, and there live in a *wild* and barbarous manner. *Davies on Ireland.*

May those already curst Essexian plains,
Where hasty death and pining sickness reigns,
Prove as a desart, and none there make stay,
But savage beasts, or men as *wild* as they. *Waller.*

5. Turbulent; tempestuous; irregular.

His passions and his virtues lie confus'd,
And mixt together in so *wild* a tumult,
That the whole man is quite disfigur'd in him. *Addison.*

6. Licentious; ungoverned.

That *wild* rout that tore the Thracian bard. *Milton.*

Valour grown *wild* by pride, and pow'r by rage,
Did the true charms of majesty impair:
Rome by degrees advancing more in age,
Show'd sad remains of what had once been fair. *Prior.*

7. Inconstant; mutable; fickle.

In the ruling passion, there alone,
The *wild* are constant, and the cunning known. *Pope.*

8. Inordinate; loose.

Other bars he lays before me,
My riots past, my *wild* societies. *Shakespeare.*

Besides, thou art a beau; what's that my child?
A fop well-drest, extravagant and *wild*:
She that cries herbs has less impertinence,
And in her calling, more of common sense. *Dryden.*

9. Uncouth; strange.

What are these,
So wither'd, and so *wild* in their attire,
That look not like th' inhabitants o' the earth,
And yet are on't. *Shakespeare's Macbeth.*

10. Done or made without any consistent order or plan.

With mountains, as with weapons, arm'd; they make
Wild work in heav'n. *Milton's Paradise Lost.*

The sea was very necessary to the ends of providence, and would have been a very *wild* world had it been without. *Woodward's Natural History.*

11. Meerly imaginary.

As universal as these appear to be, an effectual remedy might be applied: I am not at present upon a *wild* speculative project, but such a one as may be easily put in execution. *Swift.*

WILD, *n. s.* [from the adjective.] A desart; a tract uncultivated and uninhabited.

We sometimes
Who dwell this *wild*, constrain'd by want come forth
To town or village nigh. *Milton's Paradise Regained.*

This gentle knight
Forsook his easy couch at early day,
And to the wood and *wilds* pursu'd his way. *Dryden.*

Then Libya first, of all her moisture drain'd,
Became a barren waste, a *wild* of sand. *Addison.*

Is there a nation in the *wilds* of Afric,
Amidst the barren rocks and burning sands
That does not tremble at the Roman name? *Addison.*

You rais'd these hallow'd walls; the desart smil'd,
And paradise was open'd in the *wild.* *Pope.*

WILD *Basil. n. s.* [*acinus*, Lat.] A plant.

It hath leaves like those of the lesser basil; the cup of the flower is oblong and furrowed; the flowers are produced in bunches on the top of little footstalks, which arise from between the footstalk of the leaf and the stalk of the plants in which it differs from serpyllum. *Miller.*

WILD *Cucumber. n. s.* [*elaterium*, Latin.] A plant.

The branches are somewhat like those of the cucumber, but have no tendrils; the fruit is prickly, and when ripe bursts with great elasticity, and abounds with fetid juice. *Miller.*

WILD *Olive. n. s.* [*eleagnus*, Latin, from ἐλαία, an olive, and ἄγνος *vitex*;] This plant hath leaves like those of the chaste tree, and a fruit like an olive. *Miller.*

WILDSE'RVICE. *n. s.* [*cratægus*, Lat.] A plant.

The leaves are single; the flower consists of five leaves, which expand in form of a rose. The fruit is small, and shaped like a pear, in which are many hard seeds. *Miller.*

To WI'LDER. *v. a.* [from *wild.*] To loose or puzzle in an unknown or pathless tract.

The little courtiers, who ne'er come to know
The depth of factions, as in mazes go,
Where interests meet, and cross so oft, that they
With too much care are *wilder'd* in the way. *Dryden.*

Oh thou! who free'st me from my doubtful state,
Long lost and *wilder'd* in the maze of fate,
Be present still. *Pope.*

WI'LDERNESS. *n. s.* [from *wild.*]

1. A desert; a tract of solitude and savageness.

He travell'd through wide wasteful ground,
That nought but desert *wilderness* shew'd all around. *F. Qu.*

When as the land she saw no more appear,
But a wild *wilderness* of waters deep,
Then 'gan she greatly to lament and weep. *Spenser.*

O my poor kingdom, sick with civil blows!
When that my care could not with-hold thy riots,
What wilt thou do when riot is thy care?
O, thou wilt be a *wilderness* again,
Peopled with wolves, thy old inhabitants. *Shakespeare.*

But who can always on the billows lie?
The wat'ry *wilderness* yields no supply. *Waller.*

All those animals have been obliged to change their woods and *wildernesses* for lodgings in cities. *Arbuth. & Pope.*

2. The state of being wild or disorderly. Not in use.

The paths and bow'rs, doubt not, but our joint hands
Will keep from *wilderness* with ease. *Milton.*

WI'LDFIRE. *n. s.* [*wild* and *fire.*] A composition of inflammable materials, easy to take fire, and hard to be extinguished.

When thou rann'st up Gadshill in the night to catch my horse, I did think thou had'st been an ignis fatuus, or a ball of *wildfire.* *Shakespeare.*

Though brimstone, pitch, *wildfire*, burn equally, and are hard to quench, yet they make no such firy wind as gunpowder. *Bacon's Nat. Hist.*

Yet shall it in his boiling stomach turn
To bitter poison, and like *wildfire* burn;
He shall cast up the wealth by him devour'd. *Sandys.*

No matter in the world so proper to write with as *wildfire*, as no characters can be more legible than those which are read by their own light. *Addis. Guard.*

In flames, like Semele's, be brought to bed,
While opening hell spouts *wildfire* at your head. *Pope.*

WILDGO'OSECHASE. *n. s.* A pursuit of something as unlikely to be caught as the wildgoose.

If our wits run the *wildgoosechace*, I have done; for thou hast more of the *wildgoose* in one of thy wits, than I have in my whole five. *Shakespeare.*

Let a man consider the time, money, and vexation, that this *wildgoosechace* has cost him, and then say what have I gotten to answer all this expence, but loose, giddy frolick? *L'Estrange.*

WI'LDING. *n. s.* [*wildelinghe*, Dut.] A wild sour apple.

Ten ruddy *wildings* in the wood I found,
And stood on tip-toes, reaching from the ground. *Dryd.*

The red streak, of all cyder fruit, hath obtained the preference, being but a kind of *wilding*, never pleasing to the palate. *Mortimer.*

The *wilding*'s fibres are contriv'd
To draw th' earth's purest spirit, and resist
Its feculence. *Phillips.*

WI'LDLY. *adv.* [from *wild.*]

1. Without cultivation.

That which grows *wildly* of itself, is worth nothing. *More.*

2. With disorder; with perturbation or distraction.

Put your discourse into some frame, and start not so *wildly* from my affair. *Shakespear.*

Mrs. Page, at the door, sweating, blowing, and looking *wildly*, would needs speak with you. *Shakespeare.*

Young mothers *wildly* stare with fear opprest,
And strain their helpless infants to their breast. *Dryden.*

His fever being come to a height, he grew delirious, and talked very *wildly.* *Female Quixote.*

3. Without attention; without judgment.

As th'unthought accident is guilty
Of what we *wildly* do, so we profess
Ourselves to be the slaves of chance, and flies
Of every wind that blows. *Shakespeare.*

4. Irregularly.

She, *wildly* wanton, wears by night away
The sign of all our labours done by day. *Dryden.*

WI'LDNESS. *n. s.* [from *wild.*]

1. Rudeness; disorder like that of uncultivated ground.

The heath, which was the third part of our plot, I wish to be framed, as much as may be, to a natural *wildness.* *Bac.*

2. Inordinate vivacity; irregularity of manners.

This same starved justice hath done nothing but prated to me of the *wildness* of his youth, and the feats he hath done about Turnbal-street; and every third word a lie. *Shakesp.*

He is giv'n
To sports, to *wildness*, and much company. *Shakespeare.*

3. Savageness; brutality.

He came in like a wild man; but such a *wildness* as shewed his eye-sight had tamed him, full of withered leaves; which though they fell not, still threatened falling. *Sidney.*

Vainly thou tell'st me, what the woman's care
Shall in the *wildness* of the wood prepare. *Prior.*

4. Uncultivated state.

Their *wildness* lose, and quitting nature's part,
Obey the rules and discipline of art. *Dryden.*

5. Deviation from a settled course; irregularity.

A delirium is but a short *wildness* of the imagination; and a settled irregularity of fancy is distraction and madness. *Watts's Log.*

6. Alienation of mind.

Ophelia, I wish
That your good beauties be the happy cause
Of Hamlet's *wildness*; so shall I hope your virtues
May bring him to his wonted way again. *Shakesp.*

WILE. *n. s.* [pile, Saxon; *wiel*, Islandick.] A deceit; a fraud; a trick; a stratagem; a practice artful, sly, and insidious.

Their leader by his *wiles* had much obtain'd,
And done much mischief on the English state. *Daniel.*

My sentence is for open war; of *wiles*
More unexpert, I boast not; them let those
Contrive who need. *Milton.*

Life essay'd the surest *wile*,
Gilding itself with Laura's smile. *Roscommon.*

So Sforza, curs'd with a too fertile brain,
Lost by his *wiles* the pow'r his wit did gain. *Dryd.*

The heart of man is so full of *wiles*, artifices, and deceit, that there is no guessing at what he is from his speeches. *Addison's Guardian.*

Wisdom's above suspecting *wiles*,
The queen of learning gravely smiles. *Swift.*

WI'LFUL. *adj.* [*will* and *full.*]

1. Stubborn; contumacious; perverse; inflexible.

2. Done or suffered by design.

Sthenobœa herself did choak
With *wilful* cord, for wanting of her will. *Fairy Queen.*

Thou to me
Art all things under heav'n, all places thou,
Who for my *wilful* crime art banish'd hence. *Milton.*

The silent stranger stood amaz'd to see
Contempt of wealth, and *wilful* poverty. *Dryden.*

WI'LFULLY. *adv.* [from *wilful.*]

1. Obstinately; stubbornly.

The mother, who being determinately, least I should say of a great lady *wilfully*, bent to marry her to Demagoras, tried all ways which a witty and hard-hearted mother could devise. *Sidney.*

Evil could she conceal her fire, and *wilfully* persevered she in it. *Sidney.*

Religion is matter of our freest choice; and if men will obstinately and *wilfully* set themselves against it, there is no remedy. *Tillotson's Serm.*

2. By design; on purpose.

That will carry us, if we do not *wilfully* betray our succours, through all difficulties. *Hammond.*

If you do not *wilfully* pass over any of your greater offences, but confess particularly, and repent seriously of them, God will more easily pass by your lesser infirmities. *Bp Tayl.*

This let him know;
Lest, *willfully* offending, he pretend
Surprisal. *Milton.*

Wi'lfulness. *n. s.* [from *wilful.*] Obstinacy; stubbornness; perverseness.

So full of *wilfulness* and self-liking is our nature, that without some definitive sentence, which being given, may stand, small hope there is that strifes will end. *Hooker.*

Thy causeless ruth repress;
He that his sorrow sought through *wilfulness*,
And his foe fetter'd would release again,
Deserves to taste his folly's fruit. *Fairy Queen.*

Never hydra-headed *wilfulness*
So soon did lose his seat, and all at once,
As in this king. *Shakespeare.*

A stiff and stubborn obstinacy, is not so much firmness and resolution, as *wilfulness*. *L'Estrange.*

That is not hastily to be interpreted obstinacy or *wilfulness*, which is the natural product of their age. *Locke.*

Wi'lily. *adv.* [from *wily.*] By stratagem; fraudulently.

They did work *wilily*, and went and made as if they had been ambassadors. *Jos.*

Wili'ness. *n. s.* [from *wily.*] Cunning; guile.

The ungodly, for his own lust, doth persecute the poor: let them be taken in the crafty *wiliness* that they have imagined. *Psalm* x. 2.

She supplied the weakness of force by *wiliness* of art, and advantage of treaty. *How. Voc. Forest.*

WILL. *n. s.* [pilla, Saxon; *wille*, Dutch.]

1. Choice; arbitrary determination.

Will is the power, which the mind has to order the consideration of any idea, or the forbearing to consider it, or to prefer the motion of any part of the body to its rest, and vice versa. *Locke's Works.*

Two principal fountains there are of human actions, knowledge and *will*; which *will*, in things tending towards any end, is termed choice. *Hooker, b.* i.

Is it her nature, or is it her *will*,
To be so cruel to an humble foe?
If nature, then she may it mend with skill;
If *will*, then she at *will* may *will* forego. *Spenser.*

These things have a shew of wisdom in *will* worship and humility. *Col.* ii. 23.

Will holds the sceptre in the soul,
And on the passions of the heart doth reign. *Sir J. Dav.*

The truth is, such a man understands by his *will*, and believes a thing true or false, merely as it agrees or disagrees with a violent inclination; and therefore, whilst that inclination lasts in its strength, he discovers nothing of the different degrees of evidence. *Atterbury.*

2. Discretion; choice.

Go then the guilty at thy *will* chastize. *Pope.*

3. Command; direction.

At his first sight the mountains are shaken, and at his *will* the south wind bloweth. *Eccles.* xliii. 16.

4. Disposition; inclination; desire.

I make bold to press upon you with so little preparation.
Your welcome; what's your *will?* *Shakespeare.*

He hath a *will*, he hath a power to perform. *Drummond.*

He said, and with so good a *will* to die,
Did to his breast the fatal point apply,
It found his heart. *Dryden.*

5. Power; government.

Deliver me not over unto the *will* of mine enemies *Psal.*

He had the *will* of his maid before he could go; he had the mastery of his parents ever since he could prattle; and why, now he is grown up, must he be restrained? *Locke.*

6. Divine determination.

I would give a thousand furlongs of sea for an acre of barren ground. The *wills* above be done; but I would fain die a dry death. *Shakespeare.*

7. Testament; disposition of a dying man's effects.

Another branch of their revenue still
Remains, beyond their boundless right to kill,
Their father yet alive, impower'd to make a *will*. *Dryd.*

Do men make their last *wills* by word of mouth only? *Stephen's Sermons.*

8. Good-*will*. Favour; kindness.

I'll to the doctor, he hath my *good-will*,
And none but he to marry with Nan Page. *Shakesp.*

9. Good-*will*. Right intention.

Some preach Christ of envy, and some of good *will*. *Phil.* i. 15.

10. Ill-*will*. Malice; malignity.

11. [Contracted from *William.*] *Will* with a wisp, Jack with a lanthorn.

Will with the wisp is of a round figure, in bigness like the flame of a candle; but sometimes broader, and like a bundle of twigs set on fire. It sometimes gives a brighter light than that of a wax-candle; at other times more obscure, and of a purple colour. When viewed near at hand, it shines less than at a distance. They wander about in the air, not far from the surface of the earth; and are more frequent in places that are unctuous, mouldy, marshy, and abounding with reeds. They haunt burying places, places of execution, dunghills. They commonly appear in summer, and at the beginning of autumn, and are generally at the height of about six feet from the ground. Now they dilate themselves, and now contract. Now they go on like waves, and rain as it were sparks of fire; but they burn nothing. They follow those that run away, and fly from those that follow them. Some that have been catched were observed to consist of a shining, viscous, and gelatinous matter, like the spawn of frogs, not hot or burning, but only shining; so that the matter seems to be phosphorus, prepared and raised from putrified plants or carcasses by the heat of the sun; which is condensed by the cold of the evening, and then shines. *Musch.*

Will-a-wisp misleads night-faring clowns,
O'er hills and sinking bogs. *Gay.*

To Will. *v. a.* [*wilgan*, Gothick; pillan, Saxon; *willen*, Dutch.]

1. To desire that any thing should be, or be done.

To *will*, is to bend our souls to the having or doing of that which they see to be good. *Hooker.*

Let Richard be restored to his blood,
As *will* the rest; so *willeth* Winchester. *Shakespeare.*

I speak not of God's determining his own will, but his predetermining the acts of our will. There is as great difference betwixt these two, as betwixt my *willing* a lawful thing myself, and my inducing another man to do that which is unlawful. *Hammond on Fundamentals.*

Whosoever *wills* the doing of a thing, if the doing of it be in his power, he will certainly do it; and whosoever does not do that thing, which he has in his power to do, does not properly *will* it. *South.*

A man that sits still, is said to be at liberty, because he can walk if he *wills* it. *Locke.*

2. To be inclined or resolved to have.

She's too rough for me;
There, there, Hortensio, *will* you any wife? *Shakesp.*

3. To command; to direct.

St. Paul did *will* them of Corinth, every man to lay up somewhat on the Sunday, and to reserve it in store for the church of Jerusalem, for the relief of the poor there. *Hooker.*

How rarely does it meet with this time's guise,
When man was *willed* to love his enemies. *Shakesp.*

Our battle is more full of names than yours,
Our men more perfect in the use of arms,
Our armours all as strong, our cause the best;
Then reason *wills* our hearts should be as good. *Shakesp.*

He *willed* him to be of good comfort, promising to bestow upon him whatsoever he should win. *Knolles.*

If they had any business, his Majesty *willed* that they should attend. *Clarendon.*

'Tis your's, O queen! to *will*
The work, which duty binds me to fulfil. *Dryden.*

4. It has a loose and slight signification.

Let the circumstances of life be what, or where they *will*, a man should never neglect improvement. *Watts.*

5. It is one of the signs of the future tense; of which it is difficult to show or limit the signification.

I will come. I am determined to come; importing choice.

Thou wilt come. It must be so that thou must come; importing necessity.

Wilt thou come? Hast thou determined to come? importing choice.

He will come. He is resolved to come; or it must be that he must come, importing either choice or necessity.

It will come. It must so be that it must come; importing necessity.

The plural follows the analogy of the singular.

Wi'lli and *Vili*, among the English Saxons, as *viele* at this day among the Germans, signified many. So *willielmus* is the defender of many: *wilfred*, peace to many; which are answered in sense and signification by Polymachus, Polycrates, and Polyphilus. *Gib. Camd.*

Wi'lling. *adj.* [from *will.*]

1. Inclined to any thing.

He *willing* to please one in authority, forced all his skill to make the resemblance of the best fashion. *Wisd.*

Some other able, and as *willing*, pays
The rigid satisfaction. *Milton.*

Can any man trust a better support under affliction, than the friendship of Omnipotence, who is both able and *willing*, and knows how to relieve him? *Bentley.*

2. Pleased;

2. Pleafed; defirous.
3. Favourable; well difpofed to any thing.
As many as were *willing* hearted brought bracelets and ear-rings. *Ex.* xxxv. 22.
4. Ready; complying.
Religion hath force to qualify all forts of men, to make governors the apter to rule with confcience, inferiors for confcience fake the *willinger* to obey. *Hooker.*
We've *willing* dames enough. *Shakefpeare.*
He ftoop'd with weary wings and *willing* feet. *Milt.*
5. Chofen.
They're held with his melodious harmony,
In *willing* chains, and fweet captivity. *Milton.*
6. Spontaneous.
Forbear, if thou haft pity,
Thefe groans proceed not from a fenfelefs plant,
No fpouts of blood run *willing* from a tree. *Dryden.*
7. Confenting.
How can hearts not free ferve *willing.* *Milton.*

WI'LLINGLY. *adv.* [from *will.*]
1. With one's own confent; without diflike; without reluctance.
That prefervation of peace and unity amongft Chriftian churches fhould be by all good means procured, we join moft *willingly* and gladly with them. *Hooker.*
I dare not make myfelf fo guilty,
To give up *willingly* that noble title
Your mafter wed me to. *Shakefpeare.*
This ranfom, if my whole inheritance
May compafs, it fhall *willingly* be paid. *Milton.*
2. By one's own defire.
The condition of that people is not fo much to be envied as fome would *willingly* reprefent it. *Addifon.*

WI'LLINGNESS. *n. f.* [from *willing.*] Confent; freedom from reluctance; ready compliance.
We praife the things we hear with much more *willingnefs*, than thofe we fee; becaufe we envy the prefent, and reverence the paft; thinking ourfelves inftructed by the one, and overlaid by the other. *Ben. Johnfon.*
It is not doing good after that fame wonderful manner, that Chrift's example obligeth us unto, but to a like *willingnefs* and readinefs to do good as far as our power reacheth. *Calamy.*
Force never yet a generous mind did gain;
We yield on parley; but are ftorm'd in vain;
Conftraint, in all things, makes the pleafure lefs,
Sweet is the love which comes with *willingnefs.* *Dryden.*

WILLOW. *n. f.* [ƿelie, Saxon, *falix*, Lat. *gwilou*, Welfh.] A tree worn by forlorn lovers.
It hath amentaceous flowers confifting of feveral ftamina, which are collected into a fpike but are barren. The embryoes are produced upon different trees from the male flowers, and afterwards become a fruit or hufk, fhaped like a cone, opening in two parts, and containing downy feeds. *Mil.*
I offered him my company to a *willow* tree, to make him a garland, as being forfaken, to bind him up a rod, as being worthy to be whipt. *Shakefp.*
In fuch a night
Stood Dido with a *willow* in her hand
Upon the wild fea banks. *Shakefp.*
Tell him, in hope he'll prove a widower fhortly,
I wear the *willow* garland for his fake. *Shakefpeare.*
When heaven's burning eye the fields invades,
To marfhes he refcrts, obfcur'd with reeds,
And hoary *willows*, which the moifture feeds. *Sandy.*
Afflicted Ifrael fhall fit weeping down,
Their harps upon the neighb'ring *willows* hung,
Nor joyous hymn encouraging their tongue. *Prior.*

WI'LLOWISH. *adj.* [*willow.*] Refembling the colour of willow.
Make his body with greenifh coloured crewel, or *willowifh* colour. *Walton.*

WI'LLOWWORT. *n. f.* A plant.
The flower confifts of feveral leaves, produced from the inclofures of the flower-cup, placed circularly, and expanded like a rofe; from the centre of the flower-cup rifes the pointal, which becomes a fruit of two cells, full of fmall feeds, wrapped up in the flower-cup. *Miller.*

WI'LY. *adj.* [from *wile.*] Cunning; fly; full of ftratagem; fraudulent.
They are fo cautelous and *wily* headed, efpecially being men of fmall practice in law matters, that you would wonder whence they borrow fuch fubtilities and fhifts. *Spenfer.*
In the *wily* fnake
Whatever flights, none would fufpicions mark
As from his wit, and native fubtilty
Proceeding. *Milton's Par. Loft.*
Since this falfe, *wily*, doubling difpofition of mind, is fo intolerably mifchievous to fociety, God is fometimes pleafed, in mere compaffion to men, to give them warning of it, by fetting fome odd mark upon fuch Cains. *South's Serm.*
My *wily* nurfe by long experience found,
And firft difcover'd to my foul its wound;
'Tis love faid fhe *Dryden.*

WI'MBLE. *n. f.* [*wimpel*, old Dutch, from *wemelen*, to bore.] An inftrument with which holes are bored.
At harveft-home, trembling to approach
The little barrel, which he fears to broach:
He 'fays the *wimble*, often draws it back,
And deals to thirfty fervants but a fmack. *Dryd.*
As when a fhipwright ftands his workmen o'er,
Who plye the *wimble* fome huge beam to bore;
Urg'd on all hands it nimbly fpins about,
The grain deep-piercing till it fcoops it out. *Pope.*
The trepan is like a *wimble*, ufed by joiners. *Sharp.*

WI'MBLE. *adj.* Active; nimble; fhifting to and fro. Such feems to be the meaning here.
He was fo *wimble* and fo wight,
From bough to bough he leaped light,
And oft the pumies latched:
Therewith afraid I ran away;
But he that earft feem'd but to play,
A fhaft in earneft fnatched. *Spenfer.*

WI'MPLE. *n. f.* [*guimple*, Fr.] A hood; a veil. It is printed in *Spenfer* perhaps by miftake *wimble.*
So fair and frefh, as faireft flower in May,
For fhe had laid her mournful ftole afide,
And widow-like fad *wimble* thrown away. *Fairy Q.*
The Lord will take away the changeable fuits of apparel, and the *wimples*, and the crifping-pins. *Ifrael* ii. 22.

To WIMPLE. *v. a.* To draw down as a hood or veil.
The fame did hide,
Under a veil that *wimbled* was full low. *Fairy Q.*

WIN. Whether initial or final in the names of men, may either denote a mafculine temper, from pin, which fignifies in Saxon, war, ftrength, &c. or elfe the general love and efteem he hath among the people; from the Saxon pine, *i. e.* dear, beloved. In the name of places it implies a battle fought there. *Gibf.*

To WIN. *v. a.* [Pret. *wan* and *won*; part. paf. *won*, pinna, Saxon; *winnen*, Dutch.]
1. To gain by conqueft.
The town of Gaza where the enemy lay encamped, was not fo ftrong but it might be *won.* *Knolles.*
His whole defcent, who thus fhall Canaan *win.* *Milton.*
Follow chearful to the trembling town;
Prefs but an entrance, and prefume it *won.* *Dryden.*
2. To gain the victory in a conteft.
Loyalty is ftill the fame
Whether it *win* or lofe the game:
True as the dial to the fun,
Altho' it be not fhin'd upon. *Hudibras, b.* iii.
I five years at Tarentum *wan*
The queftorfhip, and then our love began. *Denham.*
Thy well breath'd horfe
Impels the flying car and *wins* the courfe. *Drrd.*
3. To gain fomething withheld.
Refolv'd to *win*, he meditates the way,
By force to ravifh, or by fraud betray. *Pope.*
4. To obtain.
Thy virtue *wan* me; with virtue preferve me. Doft thou love me? Keep me then ftill worthy to be beloved. *Sidney.*
When you fee my fon, tell him, that his fword can never *win* the honour that he lofes. *Shakefpeare.*
Devilifh Macbeth
By many of thefe trains hath fought to *win* me. *Shak.*
5. To gain by play.
He had given a difagreeable vote in parliament, for which reafon not a man would have fo much correfpondence with him as to *win* his money. *Addifon.*
6. To gain by perfuafion.
They *win* great numbers to receive
With joy the tidings brought from heav'n. *Milton.*
7. To gain by courtfhip.
She's beautiful; and therefore to be woo'd:
She is a woman, therefore to be *won.* *Shakefp.*
That flood witnefs'd his inconftant flame,
When thus he fwore, and *won* the yielding dame. *Gay.*

To WIN. *v. n.*
1. To gain the victory.
Nor is it ought but juft,
That he who in debate of truth hath *won*,
Should *win* in arms. *Milton.*
2. To gain influence or favour.
You exprefs yourfelf very defirous to *win* upon the judgment of your mafter, and not upon his affections only. *Bacon.*
You have a foftnefs and beneficence *winning* on the hearts of others. *Dryden.*
Thy words like mufick every breaft controul;
Steal thro' the air, and *win* upon the foul. *Pope.*
3. To gain ground.
The rabble will in time *win* upon power. *Shakefp.*
4. To be conqueror or gainer at play.
Charles I will play no more to night;
My mind's not on't, you are too hard for me.
— Sir, I did never *win* of you before.
—But little, Charles;
Nor fhall not when my fancy's on my play. *Shak.*

To

To WINCE. *v. n.* [*gwingo*, Welsh.] To kick as impatient of a rider, or of pain.

I will sit as quiet as a lamb,
I will not stir, nor wince, nor speak a word. *Shakesp.*
Room, room, for my horse will *wince*,
If he came within so many yards of a prince. *B. Johns.*
The angry beast did straight resent
The wrong done to his fundament,
Began to kick, and fling, and *wince*,
As if h'had been beside his sense. *Hudibras.*

WINCH. *n. s.* [*guincher*, French, to twist.] A windlace; something held in the hand by which a wheel or cylinder is turned.

Put a *winch* with the wheel. *Mortimer.*

To WINCH. *v. a.* [The same with *wince*, or perhaps from *guincher*, French, to *twist*; *winch* signifying sometimes to writhe or contort the body.] To kick with impatience; to shrink from any uneasiness.

We who have free souls,
It touches not, let the gall'd jade *winch*;
Our withers are unwrung. *Shakesp. Hamlet.*
Have these bones rattled, and this head
So often in thy quarrel bled!
Nor did I ever *winch* or grudge it. *Hudibras.*
This last allusion gaul'd the panther more;
Yet seem'd she not to *winch*, tho' shrewdly pain'd. *Dryd.*

Their consciences are gall'd, and this makes them *winch* and fling, as if they had some mettle. *Tillotson.*

WI'NCOPIPE. *n. s.*

There is a small red flower in the stubble-fields, which country people call the *wincopipe*; which if it open in the morning, you may be sure, a fair day will follow. *Bacon.*

WIND. *n. s.* [pinð, Saxon; *wind*, Dutch; *gwynt*, Welsh.]

1. Wind is when any tract of air moves from the place it is in, to any other, with an impetus that is sensible to us, wherefore it was not ill called by the antients, a swifter course of air; a flowing wave of air; a flux, effusion, or stream of air. *Muschenbroek.*

The worthy fellow is our general. He's the rock, the oak not to be *wind* shaken. *Shak. Coriolanus.*

Love's heralds should be thoughts,
Which ten times faster glides than the sun beams,
Driving back shadows over low'ring hills.
Therefore do nimble-pinion'd doves draw love;
And therefore hath the *wind*-swift Cupid wings. *Shak.*

Falmouth lieth farther out in the trade way, and so offereth a sooner opportunity to *wind*-driven ships than Plymouth. *Carew.*

Wind is nothing but a violent motion of the air, produced by its rarefaction, more in one place than another, by the sun-beams, the attractions of the moon, and the combinations of the earth's motions. *Cheyne.*

2. Direction of the blast from a particular point. As eastward; westward.

I'll give thee a *wind*.
I myself have all the other,
And the very points they blow;
All the quarters that they know
T' th' shipman's card. *Shakesp. Macbeth.*

3. Breath; power or act of respiration.

If my *wind* were but long enough to say my prayers, I would repent. *Shakesp.*

His *wind* he never took whilst the cup was at his mouth, but justly observ'd the rule of drinking with one breath. *Hake.*

The perfume of the flowers, and their virtues to cure shortness of *wind* in pursy old men, seems to agree most with the orange. *Temple.*

It stop'd at once the passage of his *wind*,
And the free soul to flitting air resign'd. *Dryden.*

4. Air caused by any action.

On each side her
Stood pretty dimpled boys, like smiling Cupids
With divers colour'd fans, whose *wind* did seem
To glow the delicate cheeks which they did cool. *Shakesp.*
In an organ, from one blast of *wind*,
To many a row of pipes the sound-board breathes. *Milt.*

5. Breath modulated by an instrument.

Where the air is pent, there breath or other blowing, which carries but a gentle percussion, suffices to create sound; as in pipes and *wind* instruments. *Bacon.*

Their instruments were various in their kind,
Some for the bow, and some for breathing *wind*. *Dryden.*

6. Air impregnated with scent.

A hare had long escap'd pursuing hounds,
By often shifting into distant grounds,
Till finding all his artifices vain,
To save his life, he leap'd into the main.
But there, alas! he could no safety find,
A pack of dog-fish had him in the *wind*. *Swift.*

7. Flatulence; windiness.

It turns
Wisdom to folly, as nourishment to *wind*. *Milton.*

8. Any thing insignificant or light as wind.

Think not with *wind* of airy threats to awe. *Milton.*

9. *Down the* WIND. To decay.

A man that had a great veneration for an image in his house, found that the more he prayed to it to prosper him in the world, the more he went *down the wind* still. *L'Estrange.*

10. *To take or have the* WIND. To gain or have the upper-hand.

Let a king in council beware how he opens his own inclinations too much, for else counsellors will but take the *wind* of him; instead of giving free counsel. *Bacon.*

To WIND. *v. a.* [pinðan, Sax. *winden*, Dutch. from the noun.]

1. To blow; to sound by inflation.

The squire 'gan nigher to approach,
And *wind* his horn under the castle wall,
That with the noise it shook as it would fall. *F. Q.*
Every Triton's horn is *winding*,
Welcome to the wat'ry plain. *Dryden.*
Ye vig'rous swains! while youth ferments your blood,
Wind the shrill horn, or spread the waving net. *Pope.*

2. To turn round; to twist.

Nero could touch and time the harp well; but in government sometimes he used to *wind* the pins too high, and sometimes let them down too low. *Bacon.*

The figure of a sturdy woman done by Michael Angelo, washing and *winding* of linen cloaths, in which act she wrings out the water that made the fountain. *Wotton.*

Wind the wood-bine round this arbour. *Milton.*

3. To regulate in action.

He vaulted with such ease into his seat,
As if an angel dropt down from the clouds,
To turn and *wind* a firy pegasus,
And witch the world with noble horsemanship. *Shak.*
In a commonwealth or realm,
The government is call'd the helm;
With which, like vessels under sail,
They're turn'd and *winded* by the tail. *Hudibras.*

4. To nose; to follow by scent.

5. To turn by shifts or expedients.

Whence turning of religion's made
The means to turn and *wind* a trade. *Hudibras.*

6. To introduce by insinuation.

You have contriv'd to take
From Rome all season'd offices, and to *wind*
Yourself into a power tyrannical. *Shakes. Coriolanus.*

Edmund, seek him out, *wind* me into him, frame the business after your own wisdom. *Shakes. King Lear.*

Little arts and dexterities they have to *wind* in such things into discourse. *Government of the Tongue.*

7. To change.

Were our legislature vested in the prince, he might *wind* and turn our constitution at his pleasure, and shape our government to his fancy. *Addison.*

8. To entwist; to enfold; to encircle.

Sleep thou and I will *wind* thee in my arms. *Shak.*
You know me well, and herein spend but time
To *wind* about my love with circumstance. *Shakesp.*
Sometime am I
All *wound* with adders who with cloven tongues
Do hiss me into madness. *Shakesp.*

9. *To* WIND *out*. To extricate.

When he found himself dangerously embarked he bethought himself of all possible ways to disentangle himself, and *to wind* himself *out* of the labyrinth he was in. *Clarendon.*

10. *To* WIND *up*. To bring to a small compass, as a bottom of thread.

Without solemnly *winding up* one argument, and intimating that he began another, he lets his thoughts, which were fully possessed of the matter, run in one continued strain. *Locke.*

11. *To* WIND *up*. [Used of a watch] To convolve the spring; to put in order to a certain end.

I frown the while, and perchance *wind up* my watch, or play with some rich jewel. *Shakesp.*

Fate seemed to *wind* him *up* for fourscore years,
Yet freshly ran he on, ten winters more:
Till like a clock worn out with calling time,
The wheels of weary life at last stood still. *Dryd.*

Will not the author of the universe, having made an automaton, which can *wind up* itself, see whether it hath stood still, or gone true. *Grew.*

12. *To* WIND *up*. To raise by degrees.

These he did so *wind up* to his purpose that they withdrew from the court. *Hayward.*

When they could not coolly convince him, they railed, and called him an heretick: thus they *wound* up his temper to a pitch, and treacherously made use of that infirmity. *Ater.*

13. *To* WIND *up*. To straiten a string by turning that on which it is rolled; to put in tune.

Hylas! why sit we mute,
Now that each bird saluteth the spring?
Wind up the slacken'd strings of thy lute,
Never canst thou want matter to sing. *Waller.*

Your lute may *wind* its strings but little higher
To tune their notes to that immortal quire. *Prior.*

15. *To* WIND *up.* To put in order for regular action: from a watch.

O you kind gods!
Cure this great breach of his abused nature;
Th' untun'd and jarring senses, O, *wind up*,
Of this child changed father. *Shakesp.*

The weyrd sisters, hand in hand,
Posters of the sea and land,
Thus do go about, about,
Thrice to thine, and thrice to mine,
And thrice again to make up nine:
Peace, the charm's *wound up.* *Shakesp. Macbeth.*

To WIND. *v. n.*

1. To turn; to change.

So swift your judgments turn and *wind*,
You cast our fleetest wits a mile behind. *Dryden.*

2. To turn; to be convolved.

Some plants can support themselves, and some others creep along the ground, or *wind* about other trees, and cannot support themselves. *Bacon's Natural History.*

Stairs of a solid newel spread only upon one small newel, as the several folds of fans spread about their center; but these, because they sometimes *wind*, and sometimes fly off from that *winding*, take more room up in the stair-case. *Moxon.*

3. To move round.

If aught obstruct thy course, yet stand not still,
But *wind* about, 'till thou hast topp'd the hill. *Denham.*

4. To proceed in flexures.

It shall not *wind* with such a deep indent,
As rob me of so rich a bottom here. *Shakespeare.*

He *winds* with ease
Through the pure marble air his oblique way,
Amongst innumerable stars. *Milton's Paradise Lost.*

It was a rock *winding* with one ascent. *Milton.*

The silver Thames, her own domestick flood,
Shall bear her vessels, like a sweeping train;
And often *wind*, as of his mistress proud,
With longing eyes to meet her face again. *Dryden.*

You that can search those many corner'd minds,
Where woman's crooked fancy turns and *winds.* *Dryden.*

Still fix thy eyes intent upon the throng,
And, as the passes open, *wind* along. *Gay.*

Swift ascending from the azure wave,
He took the path that *winded* to the cave. *Pope.*

5. To be extricated; to be disentangled.

Long lab'ring underneath, ere they could *wind*
Out of such prison. *Milton.*

WI'NDBOUND. *adj.* [*wind* and *bound.*] Confined by contrary winds.

Yet not for this the *windbound* navy weigh'd;
Slack were their sails, and Neptune disobey'd. *Dryden.*

When I bestir myself, it is high sea in his house; and when I sit still, his affairs forsooth are *windbound.* *Addison's Spectat.*

Is it reasonable that our English fleet, which used to be the terror of the ocean, should be *windbound?* *Spectator.*

WI'NDEGG. *n. s.* An egg not impregnated; an egg that does not contain the principles of life.

Sound eggs sink, and such as are addled swim; as do also those termed hypenemia, or *windeggs.* *Brown's Vulgar Errours.*

WI'NDER. *n. s.* [from *wind.*]

1. An instrument or person by which any thing is turned round.

To keep troublesome servants out of the kitchen, leave the *winder* sticking on the jack to fall on their heads. *Swift.*

2. A plant that twists itself round others.

Plants that put forth their sap hastily, have their bodies not proportionable to their length; and therefore they are *winders* and creepers, as ivy and bryony. *Bacon's Natural History.*

WI'NDFALL. *n. s.* [*wind* and *fall.*] Fruit blown down from the tree.

Gather now, if ripe, your Winter fruits, as apples, to prevent their falling by the great winds; also gather your *windfalls.* *Evelyn's Kalendar.*

WI'NDFLOWER. *n. s.* The anemone. A flower.

WI'NDGALL. *n. s.* [*wind* and *gall.*]

Windgalls are soft, yielding, flatulent tumours or bladders, full of corrupt jelly, which grow upon each side of the fetlock joints, and are so painful in hot weather and hard ways, that they make a horse to halt. They are caused by violent straining, or by a horse's standing on a sloping floor, or from extreme labour and heat, or by blows. *Farrier's Dict.*

His horse infected with the fashions, full of *windgalls*, and sped with spavins. *Shakesp. Taming of the Shrew.*

WI'NDGUN. *n. s.* [*wind* and *gun.*] Gun which discharges the bullet by means of wind compressed.

The *windgun* is charged by the forcible compression of air, being injected through a syringe; the strife and distention of the imprisoned air serving, by the help of little falls or shuts within, to stop and keep close the vents by which it was admitted. *Wilkins's Math. Magick.*

Forc'd from *windguns*, lead itself can fly,
And wond'rous slugs cut swiftly through the sky. *Pope.*

WI'NDINESS. *n. s.* [from *windy.*]

1. Fulness of wind; flatulence.

A *windiness* and puffing up of your stomach after dinner, and in the morning. *Harvey on Consumptions.*

Orifices are prepared for the letting forth of the rarefied spirits in ructus, or *windiness*, the common effects of all fermented liquors. *Floyer on the Humours.*

2. Tendency to generate wind.

Sena loseth somewhat of its *windiness* by decocting; and, generally, subtile or windy spirits are taken off by incension or evaporation. *Bacon's Natural History.*

3. Tumour; puffiness.

From this his modest and humble charity, virtues which rarely cohabit with the swelling *windiness* of much knowledge, issued this. *Brerewood on Languages.*

WI'NDING. *n. s.* [from *wind.*] Flexure; meander.

It was the pleasantest voyage in the world to follow the *windings* of this river Inn, through such a variety of pleasing scenes as the course of it naturally led us. *Addison on Italy.*

The ways of heav'n are dark and intricate;
Our understanding traces them in vain,
Nor sees with how much art the *windings* run,
Nor where the regular confusion ends. *Addison's Cato.*

WI'NDINGSHEET. *n. s.* [*wind* and *sheet.*] A sheet in which the dead are enwrapped.

These arms of mine shall be thy *windingsheet*;
My heart, sweet boy, shall be thy sepulchre;
For from my heart thine image ne'er shall go. *Shak H. VI.*

The great *windingsheets*, that bury all things in oblivion, are deluges and earthquakes. *Bacon.*

The chaste Penelope, having, as she thought, lost Ulysses at sea, employed her time in preparing a *windingsheet* for Laertes, the father of her husband. *Spectator.*

WI'NDLASS. *n. s.* [*wind* and *lace.*]

1. A handle by which a rope or lace is wrapped together round a cylinder.

2. A handle by which any thing is turned.

Thus do we of wisdom and of reach,
With *windlasses*, and with assays of byas,
By indirections find directions out. *Shakesp. Hamlet.*

WI'NDLE. *n. s.* [from *To wind.*] A spindle. *Ainsworth.*

WI'NDMILL. *n. s.* [*wind* and *mill.*] A mill turned by the wind.

We like Don Quixote do advance
Against a *windmill* our vain lance. *Waller.*

Such a sailing chariot might be more conveniently framed with moveable sails, whose force may be impressed from their motion, equivalent to those in a *windmill.* *Wilkins.*

Windmills grind twice the quantity in an hour that watermills do. *Mortimer's Husbandry.*

His fancy has made a giant of a *windmill*, and he's now engaging it. *F. Atterbury.*

WI'NDOW. *n. s.* [*vindue*, Danish. *Skinner* thinks it originally *wind-door.*]

1. An aperture in a building by which air and light are intromitted.

Being one day at my *window* all alone,
Many strange things happened me to see. *Spenser.*

A fair view her *window* yields,
The town, the river, and the fields. *Waller.*

He through a little *window* cast his sight,
Though thick of bars that gave a scanty light;
But ev'n that glimmering serv'd him to descry
Th' inevitable charms of Emily. *Dryden.*

When you leave the *windows* open for air, leave books on the *window*-seat, that they may get air too. *Swift.*

2. The frame of glass or any other materials that covers the aperture.

To thee I do commend my watchful soul,
Ere I let fall the *windows* of mine eyes:
Sleeping or waking, oh defend me still! *Shakesp. R. III.*

In the sun's light, let into my darkened chamber through a small round hole in my *window*-shutter, at about ten or twelve feet from the *window*, I placed a lens. *Newton's Opt.*

3. Lines crossing each other.

The fav'rite, that just begins to prattle,
Is very humorsome, and makes great clutter,
'Till he has *windows* on his bread and butter. *King.*

4. An aperture resembling a window.

To WI'NDOW. *v. a.* [from the noun.]

1. To furnish with windows.

Between these half columns above, the whole room was *windowed* round. *Wotton's Architecture.*

With pert flat eyes she *window'd* well its head,
A brain of feathers, and a heart of lead. *Pope's Dunciad.*

2. To place at a window.

Would'st thou be *window'd* in great Rome, and see
Thy master thus with pleacht arms, bending down
His corrigible neck, his face subdu'd
To penetrative shame? *Shakes. Ant. and Cleopatra.*

3. To

3. To break into openings.

Poor naked wretches, wherefoe'er you are,
That bide the pelting of this pitilefs ftorm,
How fhall your houfelefs heads, and unfed fides,
Your loop'd and *window'd* raggednefs, defend you
From feafons fuch as thefe? *Shak. King Lear.*

WI'NDPIPE. *n. f.* [*wind* and *pipe*.] The paffage for the breath; the *afpera arteria*.

Let gallows gape for dogs, let man go free,
And let not hemp his *windpipe* fuffocate. *Shakef. H. V.*

The wezzon, rough artery, or *windpipe*, is a part infervient to voice and refpiration: thereby the air defcendeth unto the lungs, and is communicated unto the heart. *Brown.*

The quacks of government, who fat
At th' unregarded helm of ftate,
Confider'd timely how t' withdraw,
And fave their *windpipes* from the law. *Hudibras.*

Becaufe continual refpiration is neceffary for the fupport of our lives, the *windpipe* is made with annulary cartilages. *Ray.*

The *windpipe* divides itfelf into a great number of branches, called bronchia: thefe end in fmall air-bladders, capable to be inflated by the admiffion of air, and to fubfide at the expulfion of it. *Arbuthnot on Aliments.*

WI'NDWARD. *adv.* [from *wind*.] Towards the wind.

WI'NDY. *adj.* [from *wind*.]

1. Confifting of wind.

See what fhowers arife,
Blown with the *windy* tempeft of my foul
Upon thy wounds, that kill mine eyes and heart. *Shakefp.*

Subtile or *windy* fpirits are taken off by incenfion or evaporation. *Bacon.*

2. Next the wind.

Lady, you have a merry heart.
——Yes, my lord, I thank it, poor fool,
It keeps on the *windy* fide of care. *Shakefpeare.*

3. Empty; airy.

Why fhould calamity be full of words?
——*Windy* attorneys to their client woes,
Poor breathing orators of miferies. *Shak. Rich. III.*

What *windy* joy this day had I conceiv'd,
Hopeful of his deliv'ry, which now proves
Abortive as the firft-born bloom of Spring,
Nipt with the lagging rear of Winter's froft. *Milton.*

Look, here's that *windy* applaufe, that poor tranfitory pleafure, for which I was difhonoured. *South.*

Of ev'ry nation, each illuftrious name
Such toys as thefe have cheated into fame,
Exchanging folid quiet to obtain
The *windy* fatisfaction of the brain. *Dryden's Juvenal.*

4. Tempeftuous; molefted with wind.

On this *windy* fea of land the fiend
Walk'd up and down. *Milton.*

It is not bare agitation, but the fediment at the bottom, that troubles and defiles the water; and when we fee it *windy* and dufty, the wind does not make but only raife duft. *South.*

5. Puffy; flatulent.

In fuch a *windy* colic, water is the beft remedy after a furfeit of fruit. *Arbuthnot on Aliments.*

WINE. *n. f.* [pın, Saxon; *vinn*, Dutch.]

1. The fermented juice of the grape.

The *wine* of life is drawn, and the meer lees
Is left this vault to brag of. *Shakefp. Macbeth.*

Do not fall in love with me;
For I am falfer than vows made in *wine*. *Shakef.*

The increafe of the vineyards for the *wine*-cellars. *Chron.*

Be not amongft *wine*-bibbers, amongft riotous eaters. *Prov.*

Thy garments like him that treadeth in the *wine*-fat. *If.*

They took old facks upon their affes, and *wine*-bottles old and rent, and bound up. *Jof.* ix. 4.

Where the *wine*-prefs is hard wrought, it yields a harfh *wine* that taftes of the grape-ftone. *Bacon.*

His troops on my ftrong youth like torrents rufht;
As in a *wine*-prefs, Judah's daughter crufht. *Sandys.*

With large *wine*-offerings pour'd, and facred feaft. *Milt.*

Shall I, to pleafe another *wine*-fprung mind,
Lofe all mine own? God hath giv'n me a meafure,
Short of his canne and body: muft I find
A pain in that, wherein he finds a pleafure? *Herbert.*

The firftlings of the flock are doom'd to die;
Rich fragrant *wines* the cheering bowl fupply. *Pope.*

If the hogfhead falls fhort, the *wine*-cooper had not filled it in proper time. *Swift's Directions to the Butler.*

2. Preparations of vegetables by fermentations, called by the general name of *wines*, have quite different qualities from the plant; for no fruit, taken crude, has the intoxicating quality of *wine*. *Arbuthnot.*

WING. *n. f.* ȝehpınȝ, Saxon; *winge*, Danifh.]

1. The limb of a bird by which fhe flies.

As Venus' bird, the white fwift lovely dove,
Doth on her *wings* her utmoft fwiftnefs prove,
Finding the gripe of falcon fierce not fur. *Sidney.*

Ignorance is the curfe of God,
Knowledge the *wing* wherewith we fly to heav'n. *Shakefp.*

An eagle ftirreth up her neft, fpreadeth abroad her *wings*, taketh them, and beareth them on her *wings*. *Deut.* xxxii.

A fpleenlefs wind fo ftretcht
Her *wings* to waft us, and fo urg'd our keel. *Chapman.*

The prince of augurs, Helitherfes, rofe;
Prefcient he view'd th' aerial tracts, and drew
A fure prefage from ev'ry *wing* that flew. *Pope's Odyffey.*

2. A fan to winnow.

Wing, cartnave, and bufhel, peck, ready at hand. *Tuffer.*

3. Flight; paffage by the wing.

Light thickens, and the crow
Makes *wing* to th' rooky wood:
Good things of day begin to droop and drowze,
While night's black agents to their prey do rouze. *Shak.*

Thy affections hold a *wing*
Quite from the flight of all thy anceftors. *Shakefp. H. IV.*

I have purfued her as love hath purfued me, on the *wing* of all occafions. *Shakefp. Merry Wives of Windfor.*

While paffion is upon the *wing*, and the man fully engaged in the profecution of fome unlawful object, no remedy or controul is to be expected from his reafon. *South.*

You are too young your power to underftand;
Lovers take *wing* upon the leaft command. *Dryden.*

And ftraight, with in-born vigour, on the *wing*,
Like mounting larks, to the new morning fing. *Dryden.*

Then life is on the *wing*; then moft fhe finks,
When moft fhe feems reviv'd. *Smith's Phædra and Hippol.*

4. The motive of flight.

Fearful commenting
Is leaden fervitor to dull delay;
Delay leads impotent and fnail-pac'd beggary:
Then fiery expedition be my *wing*,
Jove's Mercury, and herald for a king. *Shakefp. R. III.*

5. The fide bodies of an army.

The footmen were Germans, to whom were joined as *wings* certain companies of Italians. *Knolles's Hift. of the Turks.*

The left *wing* put to flight,
The chiefs o'erborn, he rufhes on the right. *Dryden.*

6. Any fide piece.

The plough moft proper for ftiff black clays is long, large, and broad, with a deep head and a fquare earth-board, the coulter long and very little bending, with a very large *wing*. *Mortimer's Hufbandry.*

To WING. *v. a.* [from the noun.]

1. To furnifh with wings; to enable to fly.

The fpeed of gods
Time counts not, tho' with fwifteft minutes *wing'd*. *Milt.*

Who knows but he, whofe hand the lightning forms,
Who heaves old ocean, and who *wings* the ftorms,
Pours fierce ambition in a Cæfar's mind,
Or turns young Ammon loofe to fcourge mankind. *Pope.*

2. To fupply with fide bodies.

We ourfelf will follow
In the main battle, which on either fide
Shall be well *winged* with our chiefeft horfe. *Shakef. R. III.*

To WING. *v. n.* To pafs by flight.

I, an old turtle,
Will *wing* me to fome wither'd bough, and there
My mate, that's never to be found again,
Lament 'till I am loft. *Shakefpeare's Winter's Tale.*

Warm'd with more particles of heav'nly flame,
He *wing'd* his upward flight, and foar'd to fame;
The reft remain'd below, a crowd without a name. *Dryd.*

Struck with the horrour of the fight,
She turns her head, and *wings* her flight. *Prior.*

From the Meotis to the northern fea,
The goddefs *wings* her defp'rate way. *Prior.*

WI'NGED. *adj.* [from *wing*.] Furnifhed with wings; flying; fwift; rapid.

Now we bear the king
Tow'rd Calais: grant him there, and there being feen,
Heave him away upon your *winged* thoughts
Athwart the fea. *Shakefpeare's Henry V.*

Hie, good fir Michael, bear this fealed brief
With *winged* hafte to the lord marfhal. *Shakef. H. IV.*

And fhall grace not find means, that finds her way,
The fpeedieft of thy *winged* meffengers,
To vifit all thy creatures? *Milton's Paradife Loft.*

We can fear no force
But *winged* troops, or Pegafean horfe. *Waller.*

The *winged* lion's not fo fierce in fight,
As Lib'ri's hand prefents him to our fight. *Waller.*

The cockney is furprifed at many actions of the quadruped and *winged* animals in the fields. *Watts.*

WINGEDPEA'. *n. f.* [*ochrus*, Latin.] A plant.

It hath a papilionaceous flower, out of whofe empalement rifes the pointal, which afterwards becomes a pod, for the moft part round and cylindrical, filled with roundifh feeds. *Miller.*

Wi'ngshell. *n. s.* [*wing* and *shell.*] The shell that covers the wing of insects.

The long-shelled goat-chaffer is above an inch long, and the *wingshells* of themselves an inch, and half an inch broad; so deep as to come down below the belly on both sides. *Grew.*

Wi'ngy. *adj.* [from *wing.*] Having wings.

They spring together out, and swiftly bear
The flying youth through clouds and yielding air;
With *wingy* speed out-strip the eastern wind,
And leave the breezes of the morn behind. *Addison.*

To WINK. *v. n.* [pinctan, Saxon; *wincken*, Dutch.]

1. To shut the eyes.

Let's see thine eyes; *wink* now, now open them:
In my opinion, yet, thou see'st not well. *Shak. Hen.* VI.

They're fairies; he that speaks to them shall die:
I'll *wink* and couch; no man their sports must eye. *Shak.*

His false cunning
Taught him to face me out of his acquaintance,
And grew a twenty years removed thing,
While one would *wink*. *Shakes. Twelfth Night.*

He with great imagination,
Proper to madmen, led his pow'rs to death,
And, *winking*, leap'd into destruction. *Shakes. H.* IV.

In despite of all this, he runs foolishly into his sin and ruin, merely because he *winks* hard, and rushes violently like a horse into the battle. *Taylor.*

The Scripture represents wicked men as without understanding; not that they are destitute of the natural faculty: they are not blind, but they *wink*. *Tillotson.*

If any about them should make them think there is any difference between being in the dark and *winking*, get it out of their minds. *Locke.*

2. To hint, or direct by the motion of the eyelids.

You saw my master *wink* and laugh upon you. *Shakesp.*

Send him a spoon when he wants a knife: *wink* at the footman to leave him without a plate. *Swift.*

3. To close and exclude the light.

While Hermes pip'd and sung, and told his tale,
The keeper's *winking* eyes began to fail,
And drowsy slumber on the lids to creep,
'Till all the watchman was at length asleep. *Dryden.*

When you shoot, and shut one eye,
You cannot think he would deny
To lend the t'other friendly aid,
Or *wink*, as coward, and afraid. *Prior.*

4. To connive; to seem not to see; to tolerate.

They be better content with one that will *wink* at their faults, than with him that will reprove them. *Whitgifte.*

I, for *winking* at your discords too,
Have lost a brace of kinsmen. *Shak. Romeo and Juliet.*

Let not night see my black and deep desires;
The eye *wink* at the hand! *Shakesp. Macbeth.*

The king gave him great gifts, and *winked* at the great spoil of Bosworth-field, which came almost wholly to this man's hands. *Bacon's Henry* VII.

Let us not write at a loose rambling rate,
In hope the world will *wink* at all our faults. *Roscommon.*

Some faults of course with childhood end;
We therefore *wink* at wags, when they offend,
And spare the boy, in hopes the man may mend. *Dryden.*

Obstinacy cannot be *winked* at, but must be subdued. *Locke.*

Cato is stern, and awful as a god:
He knows not how to *wink* at human frailty,
Or pardon weakness that he never felt. *Addison's Cato.*

5. To be dim.

The sullen tyrant slept not all the night,
But, lonely walking by a *winking* light,
Sobb'd, wept and groan'd, and beat his wither'd breast. *Dry.*

Wink. *n. s.* [from the verb.]

1. Act of closing the eye.

You doing thus,
To the perpetual *wink* for ay might put
This ancient moral. *Shakespeare's Tempest.*

At every *wink* of an eye some new grace will be born. *Shak.*

Since I receiv'd command to do this business,
I have not slept one *wink*. *Shakes. Cymbeline.*

The beams so reverend and strong,
Do'st thou not think
I could eclipse and cloud them with a *wink*,
But that I would not lose her sight so long? *Donne.*

It raged so all night, that I could not sleep a *wink*. *Temple.*

Not write! but then I think;
And for my soul I cannot sleep a *wink*. *Pope.*

2. A hint given by motion of the eye.

Her *wink* each bold attempt forbids. *Sidney.*

The stockjobber thus from 'Change-alley goes down,
And tips you the freeman a *wink*;
Let me have but your vote to serve for the town,
And here is a guinea to drink. *Swift.*

Wi'nker. *n. s.* [from *wink.*] One who winks.

A set of nodders, *winkers*, and whisperers, whose business is to strangle all others offspring of wit in their birth. *Pope.*

Wi'nkingly. *adv.* [from *winking.*] With the eye almost closed.

If one beholdeth the light, he vieweth it *winkingly*, as those do that are purblind; but if any thing that is black, he looketh upon it with a broad and full eye. *Peacham on Drawing.*

Wi'nner. *n. s.* [from *win.*] One who wins.

A gamester, having lost all, borroweth of his next fellow-gamester somewhat to maintain play; wnich he setting unto him again, shortly thereby winneth all from the *winner*. *Spenser.*

Go together,
You precious *winners* all; your exultation
Partake to every one. *Shakes. Winter's Tale.*

Beshrew the *winners*; for they play'd me false. *Shakesp.*

Whether the *winner* laughs or no, the loser will complain; and rather than quarrel with his own skill, will do it at the dice. *Temple.*

Wi'nning. *participial adj.* [from *win.*] Attractive; charming.

Yet less fair,
Less *winning* soft, less amiably mild,
Than that smooth wat'ry image. *Milton's Paradise Lost.*

On her, as queen,
A pomp of *winning* graces waited still;
And from about her shot darts of desire
Into all eyes, to wish her still in sight. *Milt. Parad. Lost.*

Cato's soul
Shines out in every thing she acts or speaks,
While *winning* mildness and attractive smiles
Dwell in her looks, and with becoming grace
Soften the rigour of her father's virtues. *Addison's Cato.*

Wi'nning. *n. s.* [from *win.*] The sum won.

A simile in one of Congreve's prologues compares a writer to a buttering gamester, that stakes all his *winnings* upon every cast; so that if he loses the last throw, he is sure to be undone. *Addison's Freeholder.*

To Wi'nnow. *v. a.* [pindpian, Saxon; *evanno*, Latin.]

1. To separate by means of the wind; to part the grain from the chaff.

Were our royal faith martyrs in love,
We shall be *winnow'd* with so rough a wind,
That even our corn shall seem as light as chaff,
And good from bad find no partition. *Shakesp. Hen.* IV.

In the sun your golden grain display,
And thrash it out and *winnow* it by day. *Dryden's Virgil.*

2. To fan; to beat as with wings.

Now on the polar winds, then with quick fan
Winnows the buxom air. *Milton's Paradise Lost.*

3. To sift; to examine.

Winnow well this thought, and you shall find
'Tis light as chaff that flies before the wind. *Dryden.*

4. To separate; to part.

Bitter torture shall
Winnow the truth from falshood. *Shakesp. Cymbeline.*

To Wi'nnow. *v. n.* To part corn from chaff.

Winnow not with every wind, and go not into every way. *Ecclus* v. 9.

Wi'nnower. *n s.* [from *winnow.*] He who winnows.

WI'NTER. *n. s.* [pinter, Saxon; *winter*, Danish, German, and Dutch.] The cold season of the year.

Though he were already stept into the *winter* of his age, he found himself warm in those desires, which were in his son far more excuseable. *Sidney.*

After Summer evermore succeeds
The barren *Winter* with his nipping cold. *Shak. Hen.* VI.

Those flaws and starts
Impostors brow to fear, would well become
A woman's story at a *Winter's* fire. *Shakesp. Macbeth.*

He hath bought a pair of cast lips of Diana: a nun of *Winter's* sisterhood kisses not more religiously; the very ice of chastity is in them. *Shakesp. As you like it.*

The two beneath the distant poles complain
Of endless *Winter* and perpetual rain. *Dryden.*

Liest thou asleep beneath those hills of snow?
Stretch out thy lazy limbs; awake, awake,
And *Winter* from thy furry mantle shake. *Dryden.*

Suppose our poet was your foe before,
Yet now, the bus'ness of the field is o'er,
'Tis time to let your civil wars alone,
When troops are into *Winter*-quarters gone. *Dryden.*

He that makes no reflections on what he reads, only loads his mind wlth a rhapsody of tales, fit in *Winter*-nights for the entertainment of others. *Locke.*

The republick have sent to prince Eugene to desire the emperor's protection, with an offer of *Winter*-quarters for four thousand Germans. *Addison on Italy.*

Stern *Winter* smiles on that auspicious clime,
The fields are florid with unfading prime. *Pope.*

To define *Winter*, I consider first wherein it agrees with Summer, Spring, Autumn, and I find they are all seasons of the year; therefore a season of the year is a genus: then I observe wherein it differs from these, and that is in the shortness of the days; therefore this may be called its special nature, or difference:

difference: then, by joining these together, I make a definition. *Winter* is that season of the year wherein the days are shortest. *Watts's Logick.*

To WI'NTER. *v. n.* [from the noun.] To pass the Winter.

The fowls shall summer upon them, and all the beasts of the earth shall *winter* upon them. *Is.* xviii. 6.

Because the haven was not commodious to *winter* in, the more part advised to depart. *Acts* xxvii. 12.

To WI'NTER. *v. a.* To feed or manage in the Winter.

The cattle generally sold for slaughter within, or exportation abroad, had never been handled or *wintered* at handmeat. *Temple.*

Young lean cattle may by their growth pay for their *wintering*, and so be ready to fat next Summer. *Mortimer.*

WINTER is often used in composition.

The king sat in the *winter*-house, and there was a fire burning before him. *Jer.* xxxvi. 22.

If in November and December they fallow, 'tis called a *winter*-fallowing. *Mortimer.*

Shred it very small with thyme, sweet margarome, and a little *winter*-savoury. *Walton's Angler.*

WI'NTERBEATEN. *adj.* [*Winter* and *beat.*] Harrassed by severe weather.

He compareth his careful case to the sad season of the year, to the frosty ground, to the frozen trees, and to his own *winterbeaten* flocke. *Spenser.*

WI'NTERCHERRY. *n. s.* [*alkekenge.*] A plant.

The fruit is about the bigness of a cherry, and inclosed in the cup of the flower, which swells over it in form of a bladder. *Miller.*

WI'NTERCITRON. *n. s.* A sort of PEAR, which see.

WI'NTERGREEN. *n. s.* [*pyrola*, Latin.] A plant.

It hath a rose-shaped flower, consisting of several leaves, which are placed circularly; out of whose cup arises the pointal, ending in a proboscis, which afterwards turns to a roundish fruit, which is channelled, generally umbellated, and consisting of five cells, which are commonly full of small seeds. *Miller.*

WI'NTERLY. *adj.* [*Winter* and *like.*] Such as is suitable to Winter; of a wintry kind.

If't be Summer news,
Smile to't before; if *winterly*, thou need'st
But keep that count'nance still. *Shakesp. Cymbeline.*

WI'NTRY. *adj.* [from *Winter.*] Brumal; hyemal.

He saw the Trojan fleet dispers'd, distress'd
By stormy winds, and *wintry* heav'n oppress'd. *Dryden.*

WI'NY. *adj.* [from *wine.*] Having the taste or qualities of wine.

Set cucumbers here and there among muskmelons, and see whether the melons will not be more *winy*, and better tasted. *Bacon's Natural History.*

To WIPE. *v. a.* [pipan, Saxon.]

1. To cleanse by rubbing with something soft.

Such a handkerchief,
I'm sure it was your wife's, did I to-day
See Cassio *wipe* his beard with. *Shak. Othello.*

She a gentle tear let fall
From either eye, and *wip'd* them with her hair. *Milton.*

Then with her vest the wound she *wipes* and dries. *Denh.*

2. To take away by tersion.

Calumniate stoutly; for though we *wipe* away with never so much care the dirt thrown at us, there will be left some sulliage behind. *Decay of Piety.*

3. To strike off gently.

Let me *wipe* off this honourable dew,
That silverly doth progress on thy cheeks. *Shakespeare.*

Some natural tears they dropp'd, but *wip'd* them soon. *Milton's Paradise Lost.*

A young man, having suffered many tortures, escaped with life, and told his fellow Christians, that the pain of them had been rendered tolerable by the presence of an angel, who stood by him and *wiped* off the tears and sweat. *Addison.*

4. To clear away.

Macduff, this noble passion,
Child of integrity, hath from my soul
Wip'd the black scruples; reconcil'd my thoughts
To thy good truth and honour. *Shakes. Macbeth.*

5. To cheat; to defraud.

The next bordering lords commonly incroach one upon another, as one is stronger, or lie still in wait to *wipe* them out of their lands. *Spenser on Ireland.*

6. *To* WIPE *out.* To efface.

This blot, that they object against your house,
Shall be *wip'd out* in the next parliament. *Shak. Hen.* VI.

As thou lov'st me, Camillo, *wipe* not *out* the rest of thy services by leaving me now. *Shakesp. Winter's Tale.*

Take one in whom decrepid old age has blotted out the memory of his past knowledge, and clearly *wiped out* the ideas his mind was formerly stored with, and stopped up all the passages for new ones to enter; or if there be some of the inlets yet left open, the impressions made are scarce perceived. *Locke.*

WIPE. *n. s.* [from the verb.]

1. An act of cleansing.

2. A blow; a stroke; a jeer; a gybe; a sarcasm.

To statesmen would you give a *wipe*,
You print it in Italick type:
When letters are in vulgar shapes,
'Tis ten to one the wit escapes;
But when in capitals exprest,
The dullest reader smoaks the jest. *Swift.*

3. A bird. *Ainsworth.*

WI'PER. *n. s.* [from *wipe.*] An instrument or person by which any thing is wiped.

The maids and their makes,
At dancing and wakes,
Had their napkins and posies,
And the *wipers* for their noses. *Ben. Johnson.*

WIRE. *n. s.* [*virer*, French, to draw round. *Skinner.*] Metal drawn into slender threads.

Tane was the damsel; and without remorse
The king condemn'd her, guiltless, to the fire:
Her vail and mantle pluckt they off by force,
And bound her tender arms in twisted *wire.* *Fairfax.*

Thou shalt be whipt with *wire*, and stew'd in brine,
Smarting in ling'ring pickle. *Shakesp. Ant. and Cleopatra.*

The soldier, that man of iron,
Whom ribs of horror all environ,
That's strong with *wire* instead of veins,
In whose embraces you're in chains. *Beaumont and Fletcher.*

And the cherubick host, in thousand quires,
Touch their immortal harps of golden *wires.* *Milton.*

Some roll a mighty stone, some laid along,
And, bound with burning *wires*, on spokes of wheels are hung. *Dryden's Æn.*

To WI'REDRAW. *v. a.* [*wire* and *draw.*]

1. To spin into wire.

2. To draw out into length.

A fluid moving through a flexible canal, when small, by its friction will naturally lengthen, and *wiredraw* the sides of the canal, according to the direction of its axis. *Arbuthnot.*

3. To draw by art or violence.

I have been wrongfully accused, and my sense *wiredrawn* into blasphemy. *Dryden.*

WI'REDRAWER. *n. s.* [*wire* and *draw.*] One who spins wire.

Those who have need of unmixed silver, as gilders and *wiredrawers*, must, besides an equal weight of silver mixed with other metals, give an overplus to reward the refiner's skill. *Locke.*

To WIS. *v. a.* pret. and part. pass. *wist.* [*wissen*, German; *wysen*, Dutch.] To know. Obsolete.

Thus proud and fierce, unto the hearts he stept
Of them poor souls; and cutting reason's reins,
Made them his own before they had it *wist.* *Sidney.*

There be fools alive, I *wis*,
Silver'd o'er; and so was this. *Shakespeare.*

This book, advisedly read and diligently followed but one year at home, would do a young gentleman more good, I *wis*, than three years travel abroad. *Ascham's Schoolmaster.*

When Mammon saw his purpose mist,
Him to entrap unwares, another's way he *wist.* *Fa. Queen.*

Marry with a king,
A batchelor, a handsome stripling too,
I *wis* your grandam had a worser match. *Shakesp. R.* III.

When for more worlds the Macedonian cry'd,
He *wist* not Thetys in her lap did hide
Another yet, a world reserv'd for you,
To make more great than that he did subdue. *Waller.*

WI'SDOM. *n. s.* [piꞅdom, Saxon; *wiisdom*, Danish.] Sapience; the power of judging rightly.

That which moveth God to work is goodness, and that which ordereth his work is *wisdom*, and that which perfecteth his work is power. *Hooker.*

'Tis much he dares,
And to that dauntless temper of his mind,
He hath a *wisdom* that doth guide his valour
To act in safety. *Shakesp. Macbeth.*

Wisdom and fortune combating together,
If that the former dare but what it can,
No chance may shake it. *Shakes. Ant. and Cleopatra.*

As from senses reason's work doth spring,
So many reasons understanding gain,
And many understandings knowledge bring,
And by much knowledge *wisdom* we obtain. *Davies.*

Wisdom is that which makes men judge what are the best ends, and what the best means to attain them, and gives a man advantage of counsel and direction. *Temple.*

As science is properly that knowledge which relateth to the essences of things, so *wisdom* to their operations. *Grew's Cosm.*

WISE. *adj.* [piꞅ, Saxon; *wiis*, Dutch and Danish.]

1. Sapient; judging rightly, particularly of matters of life; having practical knowledge.

I would have you *wise* unto that which is good, and simple concerning evil. *Rom.* xvi. 19.

Heav'n is for thee too high; be lowly *wise*. *Milton.*

All their writings were composed in verse, which were called runes, or viises, and from thence the term of *wise* came. *Temp.*

Since the floods demand
For their descent a prone and sinking land:
Does not this due declivity declare,
A *wise* director's providential care? *Blackmore.*

The *wisest* and best men in all ages, have lived up to the religion of their country, when they saw nothing in it opposite to morality. *Addison.*

2. Skilful; dextrous.

Speak unto all that are *wise*-hearted, whom I have filled with the spirit of wisdom, that they may make Aaron's garments. *Ex.* xxviii. 3.

Do we count him a *wise* man, who is *wise* in any thing but his own proper profession and employment, and *wise* for every body but himself? *Tillotson.*

They are *wise* to do evil, but to do good they have no knowledge. *Jer.* iv. 22.

3. Skilled in hidden arts.

There was an old fat woman even now with me.——
—Pray, was't not the *wise* woman of Brainford? *Shakesp.*

4. Grave; becoming a wise man.

One eminent in *wise* deport spake much. *Milton.*

WISE. *n. s.* [pıre, Saxon; *wyse*, Dutch; *weise*, German; *guise*, Fr. *guisa*, Italian.] Manner; way of being or acting. This word, in the modern dialect, is often corrupted into *ways.*

This song she sings in most commanding *wise*;
Come, shepherd's boy, let now thy heart be bow'd
To make itself to my least look a slave. *Sidney.*

Ere we farther pass, I will devise
A passport for us both, in fittest *wise*. *Hubberd's Tale.*
On this *wise* ye shall bless Israel. *Numb.* vi. 23.

The lovers standing in this doleful *wise*,
A warrior bold approached. *Fairfax.*

With foam upon thy lips, and sparkling eyes,
Thou say'st and do'st in such outrageous *wise*,
That mad Orestes, if he saw the show,
Wou'd swear thou wert the madder of the two. *Dryden.*

'Tis in no *wise* strange that such a one should believe, that things were blindly shuffled. *Woodward.*

WISEA'CRE *n. s.* [It was antiently written *wisesegger*, as the Dutch *wiseggher*, a soothsayer.]

1. A wise, or sententious man. Obsolete.

2. A fool; a dunce.

Why, says a *wiseacre* that sat by him, were I as the king of France, I would scorn to take part with footmen. *Addison.*

WI'SELY. *adv.* [from *wise.*] Judiciously; prudently.

If thou covet death, as utmost end
Of misery; so thinking to evade
The penalty pronounc'd; doubt not God
Hath *wiselier* arm'd his vengeful ire. *Milton's Par. Lost.*

He sits like discontented Damocles,
When by the sportive tyrant *wisely* shown.
The dangerous pleasure of a flatter'd throne. *Dryden.*

Admitting their principles to be true, they act *wisely*: they keep their end, evil as it is, steadily in view. *Rogers.*

The doctors, tender of their fame,
Wisely on me lay all the blame:
We must confess his case was nice,
But he wou'd never take advice. *Swift.*

WI'SENESS. *n. s.* [from *wise.*] Wisdom; sapience. Obsolete.

No less deserveth his wittiness in devising, his pithiness in uttering, his pastoral rudeness, and his moral *wiseness*. *Spenser.*

To WISH. *v. n.* [pıscıan, Saxon.]

1. To have strong desire; to long.

The sun beat upon the head of Jonah, that he fainted, and *wished* in himself to die. *Jonah* iv. 8.

That Noah or Janus understood navigation, may be very well supported by his image found upon the first Roman coins. One side was stampt with a Janus bifrons, and the other with a rostrum, or prow of a ship. This is as good an argument as an antiquary could *wish* for. *Arbuthnot on Coins.*

2. To be disposed, or inclined.

Those potentates, who do not *wish* well to his affairs, have shewn respect to his personal character. *Addison.*

3. It has a slight signification of hope.

I *wish* it may not prove some ominous foretoken of misfortune, to have met with such a miser as I am. *Sidney.*

To WISH. *v. a.*

1. To desire; to long for.

He was fain to pull him out by the heels, and shew him the beast as dead as he could *wish* it. *Sidney, b.* i.

If all the year were playing holidays,
To sport would be as tedious as to work;
But when they seldom come, they *wisht* for come. *Shakesp.*
They have more than heart could *wish*. *Ps.* lxxiii. 7.

There are ships prepar'd by my command,
That shall convey you to the *wisht*-for port. *Addison's Cato.*

2. To recommend by wishing.

Had I as many sons as I have hairs,
I would not *wish* them to a fairer death. *Shakesp. Macbeth.*

3. To imprecate.

If heavens have any grievous plague in store,
Exceeding those that I can *wish* upon thee;
O let them keep it till thy sins be ripe,
And then hurl down their indignation. *Shakesp. Rich.* III.

4. To ask.

Digby should find the best way to make Antrim communicate the affair to him, and to *wish* his assistance. *Clarendon.*

WISH. *n. s.* [from the verb.]

1. Longing desire.

To his *wish*,
Beyond his hope, Eve separate he spies. *Milton.*

A *wish* is properly the desire of a man sitting or lying still; but an act of the will, is a man of business vigorously going about his work. *South's Sermons.*

2. Thing desired.

What next I bring shall please thee; be assur'd,
Thy likeness, thy fit help, thy other self,
Thy *wish*, exactly to thy heart's desire. *Milton's Par. Lost.*

3. Desire expressed.

Shame come to Romeo!——
—Blister'd be thy tongue
For such a *wish*. *Shakespeare's Romeo and Juliet.*

I admire your whig-principles of resistance in the spirit of the Barcelonians: I join in your *wish* for them. *Pope.*

WI'SHEDLY. *adv.* [from *wished.*] According to desire. Not used.

What could have happened unto him more *wishedly*, than with his great honour to keep the town still. *Knolles.*

WI'SHER. *n. s.* [from *wish.*]

1. One who longs.

2. One who expresses wishes.

With half that wish, the *wisher's* eyes be press'd. *Shakesp.*

WI'SHFUL. *adj.* [from *wish* and *full.*] Longing; showing desire.

From Scotland am I stol'n ev'n of pure love,
To greet mine own land with my *wishful* sight. *Shakespeare.*

WI'SHFULLY. *adv.* [from *wishful.*] Earnestly; with longing.

WI'SKET. *n. s.* A basket. *Ainsworth.*

WISP. *n. s.* [*wisp*, Swedish, and old Dutch.] A small bundle, as of hay or straw.

A gentleman would fast five days, without meat, bread, or drink; but the same used to have continually a great *wisp* of herbs that he smelled on: and amongst those, some esculent herbs of strong scent, as onions. *Bacon's Nat. Hist.*

Jews, who their whole wealth can lay
In a small basket, on a *wisp* of hay. *Dryden.*

WIST. pret. and part. of *wis.*

WI'STFUL. *adj.*

1. Attentive; earnest; full of thought.

Why, Grubbinel, dost thou so *wistful* seem?
There's sorrow in thy look. *Gay's Pastorals.*

2. It is used by Swift, as it seems, for *wishful.*

Lifting up one of my sashes, I cast many a *wistful* melancholy look towards the sea. *Gulliver's Travels.*

WI'STFULLY. *adv.* [from *wistful.*] Attentively; earnestly.

With that he fell again to pry
Through perspective more *wistfully*. *Hudibras.*

WI'STLY. *adv.* [from *wis.*] Attentively; earnestly.

Speaking it, he *wistly* look'd on me;
As who shall say,—I would thou wert the man. *Shakesp.*

To WIT. *v. n.* [pıtan, Saxon.] To know. This word is now only used in the phrase *to wit*; that is to say.

There is an officer, to *wit*, the sheriff of the shire, whose office it is, to walk up and down his bailiwick. *Spenser.*

Yet are these feet, whose strengthless stay is numb,
Unable to support this lump of clay,
Swift-winged with desire to get a grave;
As *witting*, I no other comfort have. *Shakesp. Hen.* VI.

WIT. *n. s.* [ʒepıt, Saxon; from pıtan, to know.]

1. The powers of the mind; the mental faculties; the intellects. This is the original signification.

Who would set his *wit* to so foolish a bird? *Shakespeare.*

The king your father was reputed for
A prince most prudent, of an excellent
And unmatch'd *wit* and judgment. *Shakesp. Hen.* VIII.

Will puts in practice what the *wit* deviseth:
Will ever acts, and *wit* contemplates still:
And as from *wit* the power of wisdom riseth,
All other virtues daughters are of will.
Will is the prince, and *wit* the counsellor,
Which doth for common good in council sit;
And when *wit* is resolv'd, will lends her power
To execute what is advis'd by *wit*. *Davies's Ireland.*

For *wit* and pow'r, their last endeavours bend
T' outshine each other. *Dryden.*

2. Imagination; quickness of fancy.

They never meet, but there's a skirmish of *wit* between them.—
—Alas, in our last conflict four of his five *wits* went halting off, and now is the whole man govern'd by one. *Shakesp.*

Lewd, shallow, hair-brain'd huffs, make atheism and contempt of religion, the only badge and character of *wit*. *South.*

And though a tun in thy large bulk be writ,
Yet thou art but a kilderkin of *wit*. *Dryden.*

Wit lying most in the assemblage of ideas, and putting those together with quickness and variety, wherein can be found any resemblance, or congruity, thereby to make up pleasant pictures in the fancy. Judgment, on the contrary, lies in separating carefully one from another, ideas, wherein can be found the least difference, thereby to avoid being misled by similitude. *Locke.*

Cou'd any but a knowing prudent cause
Begin such motions, and assign such laws?
If the great mind had form'd a different frame,
Might not your wanton *wit* the system blame? *Blackmore.*

3. Sentiments produced by quickness of fancy.

All sorts of men take a pleasure to gird at me. The brain of this foolish compounded clay, man, is not able to invent any thing that tends more to laughter, than what I invent, and is invented on me. I am not only witty in myself, but the cause that *wit* is in other men. *Shakespeare.*

His works become the frippery of *wit.* *B. Johnson.*

The Romans made those times the standard of their *wit*, when they subdu'd the world. *Sprat.*

The definition of *wit* is only this; that it is a propriety of thoughts and words; or, in other terms, thoughts and words elegantly adapted to the subject. *Dryden.*

Let a lord once but own the happy lines;
How the *wit* brightens, and the style refines! *Pope.*

4. A man of fancy.

Intemperate *wits* will spare neither friend nor foe; and make themselves the common enemies of mankind. *L'Estr.*

A poet, being too witty himself, could draw nothing but *wits* in a comedy: even his fools were infected with the disease of their author. *Dryden.*

To tell them wou'd a hundred tongues require;
Or one vain *wit's*, that might a hundred tire. *Pope.*

5. A man of genius.

Searching *wits*, of more mechanick parts;
Who grac'd their age with new-invented arts:
Those who to worth their bounty did extend,
And those who knew that bounty to commend. *Dryden.*

How vain that second life in others breath?
Th' estate which *wits* inherit after death;
Ease, health, and life, for this they must resign,
Unsure the tenure, but how vast the fine!
The great man's curse, without the gain endure;
Be envy'd, wretched; and be flatter'd, poor. *Pope.*

6. Sense; judgment.

Strong was their plot,
Their practice close, their faith suspected not;
Their states far off, and they of wary *wit.* *Daniel.*

Come, leave the loathed stage,
And this more loathsome age;
Where pride and impudence in faction knit,
Usurp the chair of *wit.* *B. Johnson.*

Though his youthful blood be fir'd with wine,
He wants not *wit* the danger to decline. *Dryden.*

7. In the plural. Sound mind; intellect not crazed.

If our *wits* run the wild-goose chace, I have done: for thou hast more of the wild-goose in one of thy *wits*, than I have in my whole five. *Shakesp. Romeo and Juliet.*

I had a son,
Now outlaw'd from my blood; he sought my life:
The grief hath craz'd my *wits.* *Shakesp. K. Lear.*

Are his *wits* safe? is he not light of brain? *Shakespeare.*

Sound sleep cometh of moderate eating; he riseth early, and his *wits* are with him: but the pain of watching, and choler, and pangs of the belly, are with an unsatiable man. *Ecclus.* xxxi. 20.

Wickedness is voluntary frenzy, and every sinner does more extravagant things than any man that is crazed, and out of his *wits*, only that he knows better what he does. *Tillotson.*

No man in his *wits* can seriously think that his own soul hath existed from all eternity. *Bentley.*

8. Contrivance; stratagem; power of expedients.

How can it chuse but bring the simple to their *wits* end? how can it chuse but vex and amaze them? *Hooker.*

I was like to be apprehended for the witch of Brainford; but that my admirable dexterity of *wit*, counterfeiting the action of an old woman, delivered me. *Shakespeare.*

Sleights from his *wit* and subtlety proceed. *Milton.*

The neighbourhood were at their *wits* end, to consider what would be the issue. *L'Estrange.*

WI'TCRAFT. *n.s.* [*wit* and *craft.*] Contrivance; invention. Obsolete.

He was no body that could not hammer out of his name an invention by this *witcraft*, and picture it accordingly. *Camden's Remains.*

WI'TCRACKER. *n.s.* [*wit* and *cracker.*] A joker; one who breaks a jest.

A college of *witcrackers* cannot flout me out of my humour; dost thou think I care for a satire or an epigram? *Shak.*

WI'TWORM. *n.s.* [*wit* and *worm.*] One that feeds on wit; a canker of wit.

Thus to come forth so suddenly a *witworm.* *B. Johnson.*

WITCH. *n.s.* [picce, Saxon.]

1. A woman given to unlawful arts.

Wise judges have prescribed, that men may not rashly believe the confessions of *witches*, nor the evidence against them. For the *witches* themselves are imaginative; and people are credulous, and ready to impute accidents to witchcraft. *Bacon's Nat. Hist.*

The night-hag comes to dance
With Lapland *witches*, while the lab'ring moon
Eclipses at their charms. *Milton.*

When I consider whether there are such persons as *witches*, my mind is divided: I believe in general that there is such a thing as witchcraft, but can give no credit to any particular instance of it. *Addison's Spectator*, Nº 117.

2. [From pic, Saxon.] A winding sinuous bank.

Leave me those hills where harbrough nis to see;
Nor holy bush, nor briar, nor winding *witch.* *Spenser.*

To WITCH. *v.a.* [from the noun.] To bewitch; to enchant.

'Tis now the very *witching* time of night,
When churchyards yawn. *Shakesp. Hamlet.*

Me ill befits, that in der-doing arms,
And honour's suit my vowed days do spend,
Unto thy bounteous baits, and pleasing charms,
With which weak men thou *witchest* to attend. *Spenser.*

I'll *witch* sweet ladies with my words and looks. *Shakesp.*

Sit and *witch* me? *Shakesp Hen.* VI.

WI'TCHCRAFT. *n.s.* [*witch* and *craft.*] The practices of witches.

Urania name, whose force he knew so well,
He quickly knew what *witchcraft* gave the blow. *Sidney.*

If you cannot
Bar his access to the king, never attempt
Any thing on him, for he hath a *witchcraft*
Over the king in's tongue. *Shakesp. Hen.* VIII.

People are credulous, and ready to impute accidents and natural operations to *witchcraft.* *Bacon's Nat. Hist.*

What subtile *witchcraft* man constrains,
To change his pleasure into pains. *Denham.*

WI'TCHERY. *n.s.* [from *witch.*] Enchantment.

Another kind of petty *witchery*, if it be not altogether deceit, they call charming of beasts and birds. *Raleigh.*

Great Comus!
Deep-skill'd in all his mother's *witcheries.* *Milton.*

To WITE. *v.a.* [pitan, Saxon.] To blame; to reproach.

The palmer 'gan most bitterly
Her to rebuke, for being loose and light;
Which not abiding, but more scornfully
Scoffing at him, that did her justly *wite*,
She turn'd her boat about. *Fairy Queen, c.* xii.

WITE. *n.s.* [from the verb.] Blame; reproach. *Spenser.*

WITH. *preposit.* [pið, Saxon.]

1. By. Noting the cause.

Truth, tir'd *with* iteration,
As true as steel, as plantage to the moon. *Shakespeare.*

With ev'ry stab her bleeding heart was torn,
With wounds much harder to be seen than born. *Rowe.*

2. Noting the means.

Rude and unpolished are all operations of the soul in their beginnings, before they are cultivated *with* art and study. *Dryd.*

3. Noting the instrument.

Boreas through the lazy vapour flies,
And sweeps, *with* healthy wings, the rank polluted skies. *Rowe.*

By perflations *with* large bellows, miners give motion to the air. *Woodward.*

4. On the side of; for.

O madness of discourse!
That cause sets up *with*, and against thyself! *Shakespeare.*

5. In opposition to; in competition or contest.

I do contest as hotly and as nobly *with* thy love,
As ever against thy valour. *Shakesp. Coriolanus.*

He shall lie *with* any friar in Spain. *Dryden's Spanish Friar.*

6. Noting comparison.

Can blazing carbuncles *with* her compare? *Sandys.*

7. In society.

God gave man a soul that should live for ever, although the body be destroyed; and those who were good should be *with* him. *Stillingfleet.*

In all thy humours, whether grave or mellow,
Thou'rt such a touchy, testy, pleasing fellow;
Hast so much wit, and mirth, and spleen about thee,
There is no living *with* thee, nor without thee. *Tatler.*

8. In company of.

At the instant that your messenger came, in loving visitation was *with* me, a young doctor from Rome. *Shakespeare.*

9. In appendage; noting consequence, or concomitance.

Men might know the persons who had a right to regal power, and *with* it to their obedience. *Locke.*

10. In mutual dealing.

I will buy *with* you, sell *with* you, talk *with* you, walk *with* you, and so following; but I will not eat *with* you, drink *with* you, nor pray *with* you. *Shakespeare.*

11. Noting

11. Noting confidence; as *I trust you with all my secrets*; or, *I trust all my secrets with you.*

12. In partnership.

Though Jove himself no less content would be,
To part his throne, and share his heaven *with* thee. *Pope.*

13. Noting connection.

Pity your own, or pity our estate,
Nor twist our fortunes *with* your sinking fate. *Dryden.*

14. Immediately after.

With that she told me, that, though she spake of her father Cremes, she would hide no truth from me. *Sidney, b.* ii.

With that, he crawled out of his nest,
Forth creeping on his caitiff hands and thighs. *Fairy Queen.*

In falling, both an equal fortune try'd;
Wou'd fortune for my fall so well provide!
With this he pointed to his face, and show'd
His hands, and all his habit smear'd with blood. *Dryden.*

With that, the God his darling phantom calls,
And from his falt'ring lips this message falls. *Garth.*

15. Amongst.

Jasper Duke of Bedford, whom the king used to employ *with* the first in his wars, was then sick. *Bacon.*

Tragedy was originally *with* the antients, a piece of religious worship. *Rymer's Tragedies of last Age.*

Immortal powers the term of conscience know,
But interest is her name *with* men below. *Dryden.*

16. Upon.

Such arguments had invincible force *with* those Pagan philosophers, who became Christians. *Addison.*

17. In consent. Noting parity of state.

See! where on earth the flow'ry glories lie:
With her they flourish'd, and *with* her they die. *Pope.*

18. *With* in composition signifies opposition, or privation.

WI'THAL. *adv.* [*with* and *all.*]

1. Along with the rest; likewise; at the same time.

Yet it must be *withal* considered, that the greatest part of the world are they which be farthest from perfection. *Hooker.*

How well supply'd with noble counsellors?
How modest in exception, and *withal*
How terrible in constant resolution? *Shakesp. Hen.* V.

The one contains my picture, prince;
If you chuse that, then I am yours *withal.* *Shakespeare.*

This that prince did not transmit as a power, to make conquest, but as a retinue for his son, and *withal* to enable him to recover some part of Ulster. *Davies's Ireland.*

God, when he gave me strength, to shew *withal*
How slight the gift was, hung it in my hair. *Milton.*

Christ had not only an infinite power to work miracles, but also an equal wisdom to know the just force and measure of every argument, to persuade, and *withal* to look through and through all the dark corners of the soul of man, and to discern what prevails upon them, and what does not. *South.*

I cannot, cannot bear; 'tis past; 'tis done:
Perish this impious, this detested son!
Perish his sire, and perish I *withal*,
And let the house's heir, and the hop'd kingdom fall. *Dryd.*

2. It is sometimes used by writers where we now use *with.*

Time brings means to furnish him *withal*;
Let him but wait th' occasions as they fall. *Daniel.*

It is to know what God loves and delights in, and is pleased *withal*, and would have us do in order to our happiness. *Tillotson.*

We owe to christianity the discovery of the most perfect rule of life, that ever the world was acquainted *withal.* *Tillotson.*

To WITHDRA'W. *v. a.* [*with* and *draw*; from pið, or piðeꞃ, Saxon, *against*, and *draw.*]

1. To take back; to deprive of.

It is not possible they should observe the one, who from the other *withdraw* unnecessarily obedience. *Hooker, b.* v.

Impossible it is that God should *withdraw* his presence from any thing, because the very substance of God is infinite. *Hooker.*

2. To call away; to make to retire.

Nausicaa is *withdrawn*, and a whole nation introduced, for a more general praise of Ulysses. *Broome.*

To WITHDRA'W. *v. n.* To retire; to retreat.

She from her husband soft *withdrew.* *Milton.*

At this excess of courage all amaz'd,
The foremost of his foes a-while *withdraw:*
With such respect in enter'd Rome they gaz'd,
Who on high chairs the godlike fathers saw. *Dryden.*

Duumvir has pass'd the noon of life; but cannot *withdraw* from entertainments, which are pardonable only before that stage of our being. *Tatler,* N° 54.

WITHDRA'WINGROOM. *n. s.* [*withdraw* and *room.*] Room behind another room for retirement.

For an ordinary gentleman, a hall, a great parlour, with a *withdrawingroom*, with a kitchen, butteries, and other conveniencies, is sufficient. *Mortimer's Husbandry.*

WI'THE. *n. s.*

1. A willow twig.

An Irish rebel put up a petition, that he might be hanged in a *with*, and not a halter, because it had been so used with former rebels. *Bacon.*

2. A band, properly a band of twigs; [piðe signifies a band.]

These cords and *wythes* will hold men's consciences, when force attends and twists them. *K. Charles.*

Birch is of use for ox-yoaks, hoops, screws, *wythes* for faggots. *Mortimer's Husbandry.*

To WI'THER. *v. n.* [ʒepiðeꞃoð, Saxon, dry, faded.]

1. To fade; to grow sapless; to dry up.

That which is of God we defend, to the uttermost of that ability which he hath given: that which is otherwise, let it *wither* even in the root from whence it hath sprung. *Hooker.*

When I have pluck'd thy rose,
I cannot give it vital growth again;
It needs must *wither.* *Shakesp. Othello.*

It shall *wither* in all the leaves of her spring. *Ezek.* xvii. 9.

The soul may sooner leave off to subsist, than to love; and like the vine, it *withers* and dies, if it has nothing to embrace. *South's Sermons.*

2. To waste, or pine away.

Are there so many left of your own family, that you should desire wholly to reduce it, by suffering the last branch of it to *wither* away before its time. *Temple.*

3. To lose, or want animal moisture.

Vain men, how vanishing a bliss we crave,
Now warm in love, now *with'ring* in the grave. *Dryden.*

To WI'THER. *v. a.*

1. To make to fade.

The sun is no sooner risen with a burning heat, but it *withereth* the grass, and the flower thereof falleth. *Ja.* i. 11.

2. To make to shrink, decay, or wrinkle, for want of animal moisture.

Age cannot *wither* her, nor custom stale her infinite variety. *Shakespeare's Ant. and Cleopatra.*

Look how I am bewitch'd; behold, mine arm
Is, like a blasted sapling, *withered* up. *Shakespeare.*

What are these,
So *wither'd*, and so wild in their attire,
That look not like th' inhabitants o' th' earth,
And yet are on't? *Shakespeare's Macbeth.*

Thy youth, thy strength, thy beauty, which will change
To *wither'd*, weak, and grey. *Milton.*

In Spain our springs, like old men's children be,
Decay'd and *wither'd*, from their infancy:
No kindly showers fall on our barren earth,
To hatch the seasons in a timely birth. *Dryden.*

WI'THEREDNESS. *n. s.* [from *withered.*] The state of being withered; marcidity.

Water them as soon as set, 'till they have recovered their *witheredness.* *Mortimer's Husbandry.*

WI'THERBAND. *n. s.* A piece of iron, which is laid under a saddle, about four fingers above the horse's *withers*, to keep the two pieces of wood tight, that form the bow. *Farrier's Dict.*

WI'THERS. *n. s.* Is the joining of the shoulder-bones at the bottom of the neck and mane, towards the upper part of the shoulder. *Farrier's Dict.*

Let the gall'd beast wince;
We are unwrung in the *withers.* *Shakespeare.*

Rather than let your master take long journies, contrive that the saddle may pinch the beast in his *withers.* *Swift.*

WI'THERRUNG. *n. s.* *Witherrung* sometimes is caused by a bite of a horse, or by a saddle being unfit, especially when the bows are too wide; for when they are so, they bruise the flesh against the spines of the second and third vertebræ of the back, which forms that prominence that rises above their shoulders. *Farrier's Dict.*

To WITHHO'LD. *v. a.* [*with* and *hold.*] *Withheld*, or *withholden*, pret. and part.

1. To restrain; to keep from action; to hold back.

That hand, which as no kind of imminent danger could cause at first to *withhold* itself, so neither have any practices, so many, so bloody, following since, been ever able to make weary. *Hooker, b.* iv.

Sith mine he is, or free or bound;
Withhold, O sovereign prince, your hasty hand
From knitting league with him. *Spenser.*

The prince
Would fain have come with me to meet your grace;
And by his mother was perforce *withheld.* *Shakespeare.*

Be careful to *withhold*
Your talons from the wretched and the bold:
Tempt not the brave and needy to despair;
For though your violence should leave them bare
Of gold and silver, swords and darts remain. *Dryden.*

Volition is an act of the mind, knowingly exerting that dominion it takes itself to have over any part of man, by employing it in, or *withholding* it from any particular action. *Locke.*

2. To

2. To keep back; to refuse.

What difficulties there are, which as yet *withhold* our assent, till we be further and better satisfied, I hope no indifferent amongst them will scorn or refuse to hear. *Hooker.*

Soon as Titan 'gan his head exault,
And soon again as he his light *withhault*,
Their wicked engines they against it bent. *Fairy Queen.*

WITHHO'LDEN. *part. pass.* of *withhold.*

The word keep back, sheweth, that it was a thing formerly due unto God; for we cannot say that any thing is kept back, or *withholden*, that was not due before. *Spelman.*

WITHHOLDER. *n. s.* [from *withhold*] e who withholds.

WITHI'N. *prep.* [piðinnan, Saxon.]

1. In the inner part of.

Who then shall blame
His pester'd senses to recoil and start,
When all that is *within* him does condemn
Itself for being there. *Shakesp. Macbeth.*

By this means, not only many helpless persons will be provided for, but a generation of men will be bred up, *within* ourselves, not perverted by any other hopes. *Sprat.*

'Till this be cur'd by religion, it is as impossible for a man to be happy, that is, pleased and contented *within* himself, as it is for a sick man to be at ease. *Tillotson.*

The river is afterwards wholly lost *within* the waters of the lake, that one discovers nothing like a stream, till within about a quarter of a mile from Geneva. *Addison.*

2. In the compass of; not beyond; used both of place and time.

Next day we saw, *within* a kenning before us, thick clouds, which put us in hope of land. *Bacon.*

A beet-root, and a radish root, which had all their leaves cut close to the roots, *within* six weeks had fair leaves. *Bacon.*

Most birds come to their growth *within* a fortnight. *Bacon.*

Within some while the king had taken up such liking of his person, that he resolved to make him a masterpiece. *Wotton.*

The invention of arts necessary or useful to human life, hath been *within* the knowledge of men. *Burnet.*

As to infinite space, a man can no more have a positive idea of the greatest, than he has of the least space. For in this latter, which is more *within* our comprehension, we are capable only of a comparative idea of smallness, which will always be less than any one, whereof we have the positive idea. *Lo.*

Were every action concluded *within* itself, and drew no consequences after it, we should undoubtedly never err in our choice of good. *Locke.*

This, with the green hills and naked rocks *within* the neighbourhood, makes the most agreeable confusion. *Addison.*

Bounding desires *within* the line, which birth and fortune have marked out, is an indispensable duty. *Atterbury.*

3. Not longer ago than.

Within these five hours Hastings liv'd
Untainted, unexamin'd, free at liberty. *Shakespeare.*

Within these three hours, Tullus,
Alone I fought in your Corioli walls,
And made what work I pleas'd. *Shakesp. Coriolanus.*

4. Into the reach of.

When on the brink the foaming boar I met,
The desp'rate savage rush'd *within* my force,
And bore me headlong with him down the rock. *Otway.*

5. In the reach of.

Secure of outward force, within himself
The danger lies, yet lies *within* his pow'r;
Against his will he can receive no harm. *Milton.*

I have suffer'd in your woe;
Nor shall be wanting ought *within* my pow'r
For your relief. *Dryden.*

Though Aurengzebe return a conqueror,
Both he and she are still *within* my power. *Dryden.*

6. Into the heart or confidence of.

When by such insinuations they have once got *within* him, and are able to drive him on from one lewdness to another, no wonder if they rejoice to see him guilty of all villainy. *South.*

7. Not exceeding.

Be inform'd how much your husband's revenue amounts to, and be so good a computer, as to keep *within* it. *Swift.*

8. In the inclosure of.

No interwoven reeds a garland made,
To hide his brows *within* the vulgar shade;
But poplar wreaths around his temples spread. *Addison.*

Sedentary and *within*-door arts, and delicate manufactures, that require rather the finger than the arm, have a contrariety to a military disposition. *Bacon's Nat. Hist.*

WITHI'N. *adv.*

1. In the inner parts; inwardly; internally.

This is yet the outward, fairest side
Of our design. *Within* rests more of fear,
More dread of sad event yet undescry'd. *Daniel.*

Death thou hast seen
In his first shape on man; but many shapes
Of death, and many are the ways that lead
To his grim cave; all dismal! yet to sense
More terrible at th' entrance, than *within.* *Milton.*

2. In the mind.

Language seems too low a thing to express your excellence, and our souls are speaking so much *within*, that they despise all foreign conversation. *Dryden's State of Innocence.*

These, as thy guards from outward harms, are sent;
Ills from *within* thy reason must prevent. *Dryden.*

WITHI'NSIDE. *adv.* [*within* and *side.*] In the interiour parts.

The forceps for extracting the stone is represented a little open, that the teeth may be better seen *withinside.* *Sharp.*

WITHO'UT. *prep.* [piðutan, Saxon.]

1. Not with.

Many there are, whose destinies have prevented their desires, and made their good motives the wards of their executors, not *without* miserable success. *Hall.*

2. In a state of absence from.

Hast so much wit, and mirth, and spleen about thee,
There is no living with thee, nor *without* thee. *Tatler.*

3. In the state of not having.

The virtuous bezoar is taken from the beast that feedeth upon the mountains; and that *without* virtue, from those that feed in the vallies. *Bacon.*

Infallibility and inerrableness are assumed and inclosed by the Romish church, *without* any inerrable ground to hold it on. *Ham.*

If the ideas be not innate, there was a time, when the mind was *without* those principles; and then they will not be innate, but be derived from some other original. *Locke.*

4. Beyond; not within the compass of.

Eternity, before the world and after, is *without* our reach: but that little spot of ground that lies betwixt those two great oceans, this we are to cultivate. *Burnet's Theory of the Earth.*

5. In the negation, or omission of.

Without the separation of the two monarchies, the most advantageous terms from the French, must end in our destruction. *Addison.*

6. Not by; not by the use of; not by the help of.

Excess of diet in costly meats and drinks fetched from beyond the seas, would be avoided: wise men will do it *without* a law; I would there might be a law to restrain fools. *Bacon.*

7. On the outside of.

Without the gate
Some drive the cars, and some the coursers rein. *Dryden.*

8. Not within.

When the weather hinders me from taking my diversions *without* doors, I frequently make a little party with select friends. *Ad.*

9. With exemption from.

The great lords of Ireland informed the king, that the Irishry might not be naturalized *without* damage to themselves or the crown. *Davies's Ireland.*

Happiness under this view, ev'ry one constantly pursues. Other things acknowledged to be good, he can look upon *without* desire, pass by, and be content without. *Locke.*

WITHO'UT. *adv.*

1. Not on the inside.

Forming trees and shrubs into sundry shapes, is done by moulding them within, and cutting them *without.* *Bacon.*

Wise men use studies; for they teach not their own use; but that is a wisdom *without* them, and above them, won by observation. *Bacon.*

These were from *without* the growing miseries. *Milton.*

Having gone as far as they could *without*, they began to observe them within. *Grew.*

2. Out of doors.

The reception of light into the body of the building, was very prompt from *without*, and from within. *Wotton.*

Their doors are barr'd against a bitter flout;
Snarl, if you please, but you shall snarl *without.* *Dryden.*

3. Externally; not in the mind.

WITHO'UT. *conjunct.* Unless; if not; except. Not in use.

I find my love shall be proved no love, *without* I leave to love, being too unfit a vessel in whom so high thoughts should be engraved. *Sidney, b.* ii.

You will never live to my age, *without* you keep yourselves in breath with exercise, and in heart with joyfulness. *Sidney.*

WITHOU'TEN. *prep.* [piðutan, Saxon.] Without. Obsolete.

Her face so fair, as flesh it seemed not,
But heavenly pourtrait of bright angel's hue,
Clear as the sky, *withouten* blame or blot,
Through goodly mixture of complexion's dew. *Spenser.*

To WITHSTA'ND. *v. a.* [*with* and *stand.*] To gainstand; to oppose; to resist.

The violence of sorrow is not at the first to be striven withal, being like a mighty beast, sooner tamed with following, than overthrown by *withstanding.* *Sidney.*

The wonderful zeal and fervour wherewith ye have *withstood* the received orders of this church, was the first thing which caused me to enter unto consideration, whether every christian man fearing God, stand bound to join with you. *Hooker.*

It is our frailty that in many things we all do amiss, but a virtue that we would do amiss in nothing, and a testimony of that virtue, that when we pray that what occasion of sin soever do offer itself, we may be strengthened from above to *withstand* it. *Hooker, b.* v.

They

They soon set sail; nor now the fates *withstand*;
Their forces trusted with a foreign hand. *Dryden.*

When Elymas withstood Paul and Barnabas, and when Paul says of Alexander, he hath greatly *withstood* our words, do we think the *withstanding* there was without speaking? *Atterb.*

WITHSTA'NDER. *n. s.* [from *withstand.*] An opponent; resisting power.

War may be defined the exercise of violence under sovereign command against *withstanders*; force, authority, and resistance being the essential parts thereof. *Raleigh.*

WI'THY. *n. s.* [ϸiðiꝫ, Saxon.] Willow. A tree.

WI'TLESS. *adj.* [from *wit.*] Wanting understanding.

Why then should *witless* man so much misween
That nothing is but that which he hath seen? *Fairy Queen.*

I have ever lov'd the life remov'd;
And held in idle price to haunt assemblies,
Where youth, and cost, and *witless* brav'ry keeps. *Shakesp.*

So't pleas'd my destiny,
Guilty of my sin of going, to think me
As vain, as *witless*, and as false as they
Which dwell in court. *Donne.*

He kept us slaves, by which we fitly prove
That *witless* pity breedeth fruitless love. *Fairfax.*

The apple's outward form
Delectable, the *witless* swain beguiles,
'Till with a writhen mouth and spattering noise
He tastes the bitter morsel and rejects. *Philips.*

WI'TLING. *n. s.* [Diminutive of *wit.*] A pretender to wit; a man of petty smartness.

You have taken off the senseless ridicule, which for many years the *witlings* of the town have turned upon their fathers and mothers. *Addison's Spectator.*

Those half-learn'd *witlings* num'rous in our isle,
As half-form'd insects on the banks of Nile. *Pope.*

A beau and *witling* perish'd in the throng,
One dy'd in metaphor, and one in song. *Pope.*

WI'TNESS. *n. s.* [ϸitneꝼꝼe, Saxon.]

1. Testimony; attestation.

The devil can cite scripture for his purpose;
An evil soul producing holy *witness*,
Is like a villain with a smiling cheek;
A goodly apple rotten at the heart. *Shakespeare.*

May we, with the warrant of womanhood, and the *witness* of a good conscience, pursue him any further revenge? *Shak.*

If I bear *witness* of myself, my *witness* is not true. *John.*

The spirit beareth *witness* with our spirit that we are the children of God. *Rom.* viii. 16.

Many bare false *witness*, but their *witness* agreed not. *Mar.*

Nor was long his *witness* unconfirmed. *Milton.*

Ye moon and stars bear *witness* to the truth!
His only crime, if friendship can offend,
Is too much love to his unhappy friend. *Dryden's Æneid.*

Our senses bear *witness* to the truth of each others report, concerning the existence of sensible things. *Locke.*

2. One who gives testimony.

The king's attorney
Urg'd on examinations, proofs, confessions
Of divers *witnesses*. *Shakespeare's Henry* VIII.

God is *witness* betwixt me and thee. *Gen.* xxxi. 50.

Thy trial choose
With me, best *witness* of thy virtue try'd. *Milton.*

A fat benefice became a crime, and *witness* too against its incumbent. *Decay of Piety.*

Nor need I speak my deeds, for these you see;
The sun and day are *witnesses* for me. *Dryden.*

3. *With a* WITNESS. Effectually; to a great degree, so as to leave some lasting mark or testimony behind. A low phrase.

Here was a blessing handed out with the first pairs of animals at their creation; and it had effect *with a witness*. *Wood.*

Now gall is bitter *with a witness*;
And love is all delight and sweetness. *Prior.*

To WI'TNESS. *v. a.* [from the noun.] To attest.

There ran a rumour
Of many worthy fellows that were out,
Which was to my belief *witness'd* the rather,
For that I saw the tyrant's power a-foot. *Shakespeare.*

Hearest thou not how many things they *witness* against thee? *John* xxvii. 13.

Though by the father he were hir'd to this,
He ne'er could *witness* any touch or kiss. *Donne.*

These be those discourses of God, whose effects those that live *witness* in themselves; the sensible in their sensible natures, the reasonable in their reasonable souls. *Raleigh.*

To WI'TNESS. *v. n.* To bear testimony.

The sea strave with the winds which should be louder, and the shrouds of the ship with a ghastly noise to them that were in it, *witnessed* that their ruin was the wager of the others contention. *Sidney.*

Mine eye doth his effigies *witness*,
Most truly limn'd and living in your face. *Shakespeare.*

Witness you ever-burning lights above!
You elements that clip us round about!
Witness that here Iago now doth give
The execution of his wit, hands and heart,
To Othello's service. *Shakespeare's Othello.*

Lorenzo
Shall *witness* I set forth as soon as you,
And even but now return'd. *Shakespeare.*

I *witness* to
The times that brought them in. *Shakespeare.*

Another beareth witness of me, and I know that the witness which he *witnesseth* of me is true. *John* v. 32.

The Americans do acknowledge and speak of the deluge in their continent, as Acosta *witnesseth*, and Laet in the histories of them. *Burnet's Theory of the Earth.*

Witness, ye heav'ns! I live not by my fault,
I strove to have deserv'd the death I sought. *Dryden's Æneid.*

Lord Falkland *witnesses* for me, that in a book there were many subjects that I had thought on for the stage. *Dryden.*

Witness for me ye awful gods,
I took not arms till urg'd by self-defence,
The eldest law of nature. *Rowe.*

WI'TNESS. *interj.* An exclamation signifying that person or thing may attest it.

For want of words, or lack of breath,
Witness, when I was worried with thy peels. *Milton.*

WITSNA'PPER. *n. s.* [*wit* and *snap.*] One who affects repartee.

Go in, sirrah; bid them prepare for dinner.—
—That is done, sir; they have all stomachs.——
—What a *witsnapper* are you! *Shakespeare.*

WI'TTED. *adj.* [from *wit.*] Having wit: as a quick *witted* boy.

WI'TTICISM. *n. s.* [from *witty.*] A mean attempt at wit.

We have a libertine fooling even in his last agonies, with a *witticism* between his teeth, without any regard to sobriety and conscience. *L'Estrange.*

He is full of conceptions, points of epigram and *witticisms*, all which are below the dignity of heroick verse. *Addison.*

WI'TTILY. *adv.* [from *witty.*]

1. Ingeniously; cunningly; artfully.

But is there any other beast that lives,
Who his own harm so *wittily* contrives? *Dryden.*

2. With flight of imagination.

In conversation *wittily* pleasant, pleasantly gamesome. *Sidney.*

The old hermit, that never saw pen and ink, very *wittily* said to a niece of king Gordobuck, that that is, is. *Shakesp.*

The obstinate contemners of all helps and arts, such as presuming on their own natural parts, dare deride all diligence, and seem to mock at the terms when they understand not the things; think that way to get off *wittily* with their ignorance. *Ben. Johnson.*

WI'TTINESS. *n. s.* [from *witty.*] The quality of being witty.

No less deserveth his *wittiness* in devising, his pithiness in uttering, his pastoral rudeness and his moral wiseness. *Spenser.*

WI'TTINGLY. *adv.* [from *witting*, knowing; ϸitan, Saxon, to weet or know.] Knowingly; not ignorantly; with knowledge; by design.

Whatsoever we work as men, the same we do *wittingly* work and freely; neither are we, according to the manner of natural agents any way so tied, but that it is in our power to leave things we do undone. *Hooker.*

Withhold revenge, 'tis not my fault,
Nor *wittingly* have I infring'd my vow. *Shak. Henry* VI.

During that dreadful siege, every particular accident for brevity I *wittingly* pass over. *Knolles's Hist. of the Turks.*

He knowingly and *wittingly* brought evil into the world. *More*

No forger of lies willingly and *wittingly* furnished out the means of his own detection. *West on the Resurrection.*

WI'TTOL. *n. s.* [ϸittol, Sax.] A man who knows the falsehood of his wife and seems contented; a tame cuckold.

O Mars, for what doth serve thy armed ax?
To let that *witold* beast consume in flames
Thy Venus child. *Sidney.*

Amaimon sounds well; Lucifer well; yet they are the names of fiends: but cuckold, *wittol*, the devil himself hath not such a name. *Shakespeare's Merry Wives of Windsor.*

The Theban *wittal*, when he once descries
Jove is his rival, falls to sacrifice. *Cleaveland.*

WI'TTOLLY. *adj.* [from *wittol.*] Cuckoldly.

The jealous *wittolly* knave hath masses of money. *Shakesp.*

WI'TTY. *adj.* [from *wit.*]

1. Judicious; ingenious.

The deep-revolving, *witty* Buckingham
No more shall be the neighbour to my counsels. *Shakesp.*

Thou art beautiful in thy countenance, and *witty* in thy words. *Judith* xi. 23.

2. Full of imagination.

Histories make men wise, poets *witty*, the mathematick subtile. *Bacon.*

Where there is a real stock of wit, yet the *wittiest* sayings will be found in a great measure the issues of chance. *South.*

In gentle verse the *witty* told their flame,
And grac'd their choicest songs with Emma's name. *Prior.*

3. Sarcastick; full of taunts.

Honeycomb, who was so unmercifully *witty* upon the women, has given the ladies ample satisfaction by marrying a farmer's daughter. *Addison' Spectator.*

WI'TWAL. *n. s.* A bird. *Ainsworth.*

To WIVE. *v. n.* [from *wife.*] To marry; to take a wife.

Were she as rough
As are the swelling Adriatick seas,
I come to *wive* it wealthily in Padua. *Shakespeare.*

The ancient saying is no heresy,
Hanging and *wiving* goes by destiny. *Shakespeare.*

A shop of all qualities that man loves woman for; besides that hook of *wiving*, fairness, which strikes the eye. *Shakesp.*

Design or chance makes others *wive*,
But nature did this match contrive. *Waller.*

To WIVE. *v. a.*

1. To match to a wife.

She dying gave it me;
And bid me, when my fate would have me *wiv'd*,
To give it her. *Shakespeare's Othello.*

2. To take for a wife.

If he have the condition of a saint, and the complexion of a devil, I had rather he should shrive me than *wive* me. *Shakesp.*

WI'VELY. *adv.* [from *wives.*] Belonging to a wife.

Basilius could not abstain from praising Parthenia, as the perfect picture of a womanly virtue, and *wively* faithfulness. *Sid.*

WIVES. *n. s.* The plural of wife.

A man of his learning should not so lightly have been carried away with old *wives* tales, from approvance of his own reason. *Spenser's Ireland.*

WI'ZARD. *n. s.* [from *wise.*] A conjurer; an inchanter; a he-witch. It had probably at first a laudable meaning.

Patience, good lady; *wizards* know their times. *Shakesp.*

He hearkens after prophecies and dreams,
And from the cross-row plucks the letter G;
And says, a *wizard* told him that by G
His issue disinherited should be. *Shakesp. Richard* III.

That damn'd *wizard*, hid in sly disguise,
For so by certain signs I knew, had met
Already, ere my best speed could prevent
The aidless innocent lady his wish'd prey. *Milton.*

The prophecies of *wizards* old
Increas'd her terror, and her fall foretold. *Waller.*

The wily *wizard* must be caught,
For, unconstrain'd, he nothing tells for nought. *Dryden.*

WO. *n. s.* [pa, Saxon.]

1. Grief; sorrow; misery; calamity.

The king is mad: how stiff is my vile sense,
That I stand up and have ingenious feeling
Of my huge sorrows! better I were distract;
So should my thoughts be sever'd from my griefs;
And *woes* by wrong imaginations, lose
The knowledge of themselves. *Shakespeare's King Lear.*

So many miseries have craz'd my voice,
That my *woe* weary'd tongue is still. *Shakespeare.*

Her rash hand in evil hour,
Forth reaching to the fruit, Eve pluck'd, she eat:
Earth felt the wound; and nature from her seat
Sighing through all her works, gave signs of *woe*
That all was lost. *Milton's Paradise Lost.*

O'er dreary wastes, they weep each other's *wo.* *Pope.*

2. It is often used in denunciations, *wo be*; or in exclamations of sorrow *wo is*; anciently *wo wurth*; pa purp, Saxon.

All is but lip wisdom which wants experience: I now, *wo is* me, do try what love can do. *Sidney.*

Wo is my heart;
That poor soldier, that so richly fought,
Whose rags sham'd gilded arms; whose naked breast
Stept before shields of proof, cannot be found. *Shakespeare.*

Many of our princes, *woe* the while!
Lie drown'd and soak'd in mercenary blood. *Shakespeare.*

Happy are they which have been my friends; and *woe* to my lord chief-justice. *Shakespeare's Henry* IV.

Howl ye, *wo worth* the day. *Ezek.* xxx. 2.

Wo be to the shepherds of Israel that do feed themselves. *Ez.*

Wo is me for my hurt, my wound is grievous. *Jer.* x. 19.

If God be such a being as I have described, *wo* to the world if it were without him: this would be a thousand times greater loss to mankind than the extinguishing of the sun. *Tillotson.*

Woe to the vanquish'd, *woe!* *Dryden's Albion.*

3. A denunciation of calamity; a curse.

Can there be a *wo* or curse in all the stores of vengeance equal to the malignity of such a practice; of which one single instance could involve all mankind in one universal confusion. *South's Sermons.*

4. Wo seems in phrases of denunciation or imprecation to be a substantive, and in exclamation an adjective, as particularly in the following lines.

Woe are we, sir! you may not live to wear
All your true followers out. *Shak. Antony and Cleopatra.*

5. Wo is used by *Shakespeare* for a stop or cessation; from the particle *wo* pronounced by carters to their horses when they would have them stop.

Love's a mighty lord;
And hath so humbled me as, I confess,
There is no *wo* to his correction. *Shakespeare.*

WOAD. *n. s.* [pad, Saxon.] A plant.

The flower consists of four leaves, which are disposed in form of a cross; out of whose flower cup rises the pointal, which afterwards turns to a fruit in the shape of a tongue, flat at the edge, gaping two ways, having but one cell, in which is contained for the most part one oblong seed; is cultivated in England for the use of dyers, who use it for laying the foundation of many colours. *Miller.*

In times of old, when British nymphs were known
To love no foreign fashions like their own;
When dress was monstrous, and fig-leaves the mode,
And quality put on no paint but *woad.* *Garth.*

WO'BEGONE. *n. s.* [*wo* and *begone.*] Lost in wo; distracted in wo; overwhelmed with sorrow.

Such a man,
So dull, so dead in look, so *woebegone*,
Drew Priam's curtain in the dead of night,
And would have told him half his Troy was burn'd;
But Priam found the fire, ere he his tongue. *Shakespeare.*

Tancred he saw his life's joy set at nought,
So *woebegone* was he with pains of love. *Fairfax.*

WOFT. The obsolete participle passive from To WAFT.

A braver choice of dauntless spirits
Than now the English bottoms have *woft*,
Did never float upon the swelling tide. *Shakespeare.*

WO'FUL. *adj.* [*wo* and *full*]

1. Sorrowful; afflicted; mourning.

The *woful* Gynecia, to whom rest was no ease, had left her lothed lodging, and gotten herself into the solitary places those desarts were full of. *Sidney.*

How many *woful* widows left to bow
To sad disgrace! *Daniel's Civil War.*

In a tow'r, and never to be loos'd,
The *woful* captive kinsmen are inclos'd. *Dryden.*

2. Calamitous; afflictive.

3. Wretched; paltry; sorry.

What *woful* stuff this madrigal would be,
In some starv'd hackney-sonneteer, or me?
But let a lord once own the happy lines,
How the wit brightens! how the style refines! *Pope.*

WO'FULLY. *adv.* [from *woful.*]

1. Sorrowfully; mournfully.

2. Wretchedly; in a sense of contempt.

He who would pass such a judgment upon his condition, as shall be confirmed at that great tribunal, from which there lies no appeal, will find himself *wofully* deceived, if he judges of his spiritual estate by any of these measures. *South.*

WOLD. *n. s.* *Wold*, whether singly or jointly, in the names of places, signifies a plain open country; from the Saxon pold, a plain and a place without wood. *Gibson's Camden.*

Wold and *wald* with the Saxons signified a ruler or governour; from whence *bertwold* is a famous governour; *æthelwold* a noble governour: *herwald*, and by inversion *waldher*, a general of an army. *Gibson's Camden.*

WO'LF. [palp, Saxon; *wolf*, Dutch.]

1. A kind of wild dog that devours sheep.

Advance our waving colours on the walls,
Rescu'd is Orleans from the English *wolves.* *Shakespeare.*

No, rather I abjure all roofs, and chuse
To be a com'rade with the *wolf* and owl,
Necessity's sharp pinch. *Shakespeare's King Lear.*

If *wolves* had at thy gate howl'd that stern time,
Thou should'st have said, go, porter, turn the key,
All cruels else subscrib'd. *Shakesp. King Lear.*

2. An eating ulcer.

How dangerous it is in sensible things to use metaphorical expressions; and what absurd conceits the vulgar will swallow in the literals, an example we have in our profession, who having called an eating ulcer by the name of *wolf*, common apprehension conceives a reality therein. *Brown's Vulgar Errours.*

WO'LFDOG. *n. s.* [*wolf* and *dog.*]

1. A dog of a very large breed kept to guard sheep.

The luckless prey, how treach'rous tumblers gain,
And dauntless *wolfdogs* shake the lion's mane. *Tickell.*

2. A dog bred between a dog and wolf.

WO'LFISH. *adj.* [from *wolf.*] Resembling a wolf in qualities or form.

Thy desires
Are *wolfish*, bloody, starv'd, and ravenous. *Shakespeare.*

I have another daughter,
Who, I am sure, is kind and comfortable;
When she shall hear this of thee, with her nails
Shall flea thy *wolfish* visage. *Shakespeare's King Lear.*

Nothing more common than those *wolfish* back-friends in all our pretensions. *L'Estrange.*

A pre-

A pretence of kindneſs is the univerſal ſtale to all baſe projects: all *wolfiſh* deſigns walk under ſheeps cloathing. *Gov. Ton.*

WOLFSBA'NE. *n. ſ.* [*wolf* and *bane.*] A poiſonous plant; aconite.

It hath circumſcribed roundiſh divided leaves; the flower conſiſts of four leaves, ſhaped like a monkey's hood: each of theſe flowers are ſucceeded by three or more pods which contain ſeveral rough ſeeds: the moſt part of theſe ſpecies are deadly poiſon. *Miller.*

Wolfsbane is an early flower. *Mortimer's Huſbandry.*

WO'LFSMILK. *n. ſ.* An herb. *Ainſworth.*

WO'LVISH. *adj.* [from *wolves*, of *wolf*; *wolfiſh* is more proper.] Reſembling a wolf.

Why in this *wolviſh* gown do I ſtand here,
To beg of Hob and Dick. *Shakeſp. Coriolanus.*

My people are grown half wild, they would not worry one another ſo in that *wolviſh* belluine manner elſe. *Howell.*

There is a baſe *wolviſh* principle within that is gratified with another's miſery. *South's Sermons.*

WO'MAN. [ƿiƿman, ƿimman, Saxon; whence we yet pronounce *women* in the plural, *wimmen*, *Skinner.*]

1. The female of the human race.

That man who hath a tongue is no man,
If with his tongue he cannot win a *woman.* *Shakeſpeare.*

Thou dotard, thou art *woman*-tir'd, unrooſted
By thy dame Parlet here. *Shakeſpeare's Winter's Tale.*

Women are ſoft, mild, pitiful and flexible;
Thou ſtern, obdurate, flinty, rough, remorſeleſs. *Shakeſp.*

And Abimelech took men-ſervants and *women* ſervants. *Gen.*

O *woman*, lovely *woman*, nature form'd thee
To temper man: we had been brutes without thee. *Otway.*

Ceneus a *woman* once and once a man;
But ending in the ſex ſhe firſt began. *Dryden's Æn.*

Women are made as they themſelves would chooſe,
Too proud to aſk, too humble to refuſe. *Garth.*

Women in their nature are much more gay and joyous than men; whether it be that their blood is more refined, their fibres more delicate, and their animal ſpirits more light; vivacity is the gift of *women*, gravity that of men. *Addiſon.*

2. A female attendant on a perſon of rank.

I could not perſonally deliver to her
What you commanded me; but by her *woman*
I ſent your meſſage. *Shakeſpeare's Henry VIII.*

To WO'MAN. *v. a.* [from the noun.] To make pliant like a woman.

I've felt ſuch quirks of joy and grief,
That the firſt face of neither on the ſtart
Can *woman* me unto't. *Shakeſpeare.*

WO'MANED. *adj.* [from *woman.*] Accompanied; united with a woman.

I do attend here on the general,
And think it no addition, nor my wiſh,
To have him ſee me *woman'd.* *Shakeſpeare's Othello.*

WOMANHA'TER. *n. ſ.* [*woman* and *hater.*] One that has an averſion from the female ſex.

How could it come into your mind,
To pitch on me of all mankind,
Againſt the ſex to write a ſatyr;
And brand me for a *womanhater.* *Swift.*

WO'MANHOOD. } *n. ſ.* [from *woman.*] The character and col-
WO'MANHEAD. } lective qualities of a woman. Obſolete.

Ne in her ſpeech, ne in her haviour,
Was lightneſs ſeen, or looſer vanity,
But gracious *womanhood* and gravity. *Fairy Queen.*

There dwells ſweet love and conſtant chaſtity,
Unſpotted faith, and comely *womanhood*,
Regard of honour, and mild modeſty. *Spenſer.*

'Tis preſent death I beg; and one thing more,
That *womanhood* denies my tongue to tell:
O keep me from their worſe than killing luſt. *Shakeſpeare.*

When my grave is broke up again,
Some ſecond gueſt to entertain;
For graves have learn'd that *womanhead*
To be to more than one a bed. *Donne.*

WO'MANISH. *adj.* [from *woman.*] Suitable to a woman.

Neither doubt you, becauſe I wear a woman's apparel, I will be the more *womaniſh*; ſince I aſſure you there is nothing I deſire more than fully to prove myſelf a man. *Sidney.*

Zelmane making a *womaniſh* habit to be the armour of her boldneſs, giving up her life to the lips of Philoclea, humbly beſought her to keep her ſpeech a while within the paradiſe of her mind. *Sidney.*

A voice not ſoft, weak, piping, and *womaniſh*, but audible, ſtrong, and manlike. *Aſcham.*

She then to him theſe *womaniſh* words 'gan ſay,
For love of me, leave off. *Fairy Queen.*

Our fathers minds are dead,
And we are govern'd with our mothers ſpirits;
Our yoke and ſuff'rance ſhew us *womaniſh.* *Shakeſpeare.*

I do not think he fears death;
He never was ſo *womaniſh.* *Shakeſpeare.*

During his baniſhment, he was ſo ſoftened and dejected, as he wrote nothing but a few *womaniſh* epiſtles. *Bacon.*

In a ſad look or *womaniſh* complaint. *Denham.*

I melt to *womaniſh* tears, and if I ſtay,
I find my love my courage will betray. *Dryden.*

The godlike hero, in his breaſt
Diſdain'd, or was aſham'd to ſhow
So weak, ſo *womaniſh* a woe. *Dryden.*

To WO'MANISE. *v. a.* [from *woman.*] To emaſculate; to effeminate; to ſoften. Proper, but not uſed.

This effeminate love of a woman doth *womanize* a man. *Sid.*

WOMANKI'ND. *n. ſ.* [*woman* and *kind.*] The female ſex; the race of women.

Muſidorus had over bitterly glanced againſt the reputation of *womankind.* *Sidney.*

So eaſy is t'appeaſe the ſtormy wind
Of malice, in the calm of pleaſant *womankind. Fairy Queen.*

Becauſe thou doat'ſt on *womankind*, admiring
Their ſhape, their colour, and attractive grace,
None are, thou think'ſt, but taken with ſuch toys. *Milton.*

Each inconvenience makes their virtue cold;
But *womankind* in ills is ever bold. *Dryden's Juvenal.*

Juba might make the proudeſt of our ſex,
Any of *womankind*, but Marcia, happy. *Addiſon's Cato.*

She advanc'd, that *womankind*
Would by her model form their mind. *Swift.*

WO'MANLY. *adj.* [from *woman.*]

1. Becoming a woman; ſuiting a woman; feminine; not maſculine.

I'm in this earthly world, where to do harm
Is often laudable; to do good ſometime
Accounted dangerous folly: why then, alas!
Do I put up that *womanly* defence,
To ſay I'd done no harm. *Shakeſpeare.*

She brings your froward wives
As priſoners, to her *womanly* perſuaſion. *Shakeſpeare.*

All will ſpy in thy face
A bluſhing *womanly* diſcovering grace. *Donne.*

Rage choaks my words; 'tis *womanly* to weep. *Dryden.*

Let him be taught to put off all thoſe tender airs, affected ſmiles, and all the enchanting *womanly* behaviour that has made him the object of his own admiration. *Arbuthnot and Pope.*

2. Not childiſh; not girliſh.

Young perſons, under a *womanly* age, are often troubled with ſome of the ſame ſymptoms. *Arbuthnot on Diet.*

WO'MANLY. *adv.* [from *woman.*] In the manner of a woman; effeminately.

WOMB. *n. ſ.* [*wamba*, Goth. ƿamb, Sax. *wamb*, Iſlandick.]

1. The place of the fætus in the mother.

When yet he was but tender bodied, and the only ſon of my *womb.* *Shakeſpeare's Coriolanus.*

New-born children bring not many ideas into the world, bating ſome faint ideas of hunger and thirſt which they may have felt in the *womb.* *Locke.*

Conceiving, as ſhe ſlept, her fruitful *womb*
Swell'd with the founder of immortal Rome. *Addiſon.*

2. The place whence any thing is produced.

The earth was form'd, but in the *womb* as yet
Of waters, embryon immature involv'd,
Appear'd not. *Milton.*

The *womb* of earth the genial ſeed receives. *Dryden.*

To WOMB. *v. a.* [from the noun.] To incloſe; to breed in ſecret.

Not for all the ſun ſees, or
The cloſe earth *wombs*, will I break my oath
To this my fair belov'd. *Shakeſpeare's Winter's Tale.*

WO'MBY. *adj.* [from *womb.*] Capacious.

He'll call you to ſo hot an anſwer for it,
That caves and *womby* vaultages of France
Shall chide your treſpaſs, and return your mock,
In ſecond accent to his ordnance. *Shakeſp. Henry V.*

WO'MEN. Plural of woman.

Thus it ſhall befal
Him who to worth in *women* over-truſts. *Milton.*

WON. The preterite and participle paſſive of *win.*

All theſe the Parthian,
From the luxurious kings of Antioch *won.* *Milton.*

Againſt myſelf I victorious have *won*,
And by my fatal abſence am undone. *Dryden.*

My mother is *won* over to my ſide, but dares not mention me to my father, for fear of provoking him. *Addiſon's Spectat.*

To WON. *v. n.* [ƿunian, Saxon; *wonen*, German.] To dwell; to live; to have abode. Not in uſe.

Him fortuned
To come where vile Acraſia does *wonn.* *Fairy Queen.*

Out of the ground uproſe
As from his lair, the wild beaſt where he *wons*
In foreſt wild. *Milton's Paradiſe Loſt.*

A people near the northern pole that *won*;
Whom Ireland ſent from loughes and foreſts hore. *Fairf.*

WON. *n. ſ.* [from the verb.] Dwelling; habitation. Obſolete.

What ſecret place, quoth he, can ſafely hold
So huge a maſs, and hid from heaven's eye;
Or where haſt thou thy *won*, that ſo much gold
Thou can'ſt preſerve from wrong and robbery. *Fairy Queen.*

To

To WO'NDER. *v. n.* [ƿunꝺꞃian, Saxon; *wonder*, Dutch.] To be ſtruck with admiration; to be pleaſed or ſurpriſed ſo as to be aſtoniſhed.

The want of theſe magazines of victuals I have oftentimes complained of in England, and *wondered* at in other countries. *Spenſer's Ireland.*

His deadly wound was healed: and all the world *wondered* after the beaſt. *Rev.* xiii. 3.

No wonder to us, who have converſed with too many ſtrange unparallel'd actions, now to *wonder* at any thing: wonder is from ſurpriſe, and ſurpriſe ceaſes upon experience. *South's Sermons.*

King Turnus *wonder'd* at the fight renew'd. *Dryden.*

Who can *wonder* that all the ſciences have been ſo overcharged with inſignificant and doubtful expreſſions, capable to make the moſt quick-ſighted very little the more knowing. *Locke.*

I could not ſufficiently *wonder* at the intrepidity of theſe diminutive mortals, who durſt venture to mount and walk upon my body. *Swift.*

WO'NDER. *n. ſ.* [ƿunꝺoꞃ, Saxon; *wonder*, Dutch.]

1. Admiration; aſtoniſhment; amazement; ſurpriſe cauſed by ſomething unuſual or unexpected.

What is he, whoſe griefs
Bear ſuch an emphaſis? whoſe phraſe or ſorrow
Conjure the wand'ring ſtars, and makes them ſtand
Like *wonder*-wounded hearers. *Shakeſpeare's Hamlet.*

Wonder cauſeth aſtoniſhment, or an immoveable poſture of the body; for in *wonder* the ſpirits fly not as in fear, but only ſettle. *Bacon's Natural Hiſtory.*

2. Cauſe of wonder; a ſtrange thing; ſomething more or greater than can be expected.

The Corniſh *wonder*-gatherer deſcribeth the ſame. *Carew.*

Great effects come of induſtry in civil buſineſs; and to try things oft, and never to give over, doth *wonders*. *Bacon.*

Lo, a *wonder* ſtrange!
Of every beaſt, and bird, and inſect ſmall
Came ſevens, and pairs. *Milton's Paradiſe Loſt.*

What woman will you find,
Though of this age the *wonder* and the fame,
On whom his leiſure will vouchſafe an eye
Of fond deſire? *Milton's Paradiſe Regained.*

No *wonder* ſleep from careful lovers flies,
To bathe himſelf in Sachariſſa's eyes;
As fair Aſtrea once from earth to heav'n,
By ſtrife and loud impiety was driven. *Waller.*

Drawn for your prince, that ſword could *wonders* do:
The better cauſe makes mine the ſharper now. *Waller.*

3. Any thing mentioned with wonder.

There Babylon the *wonder* of all tongues. *Milton.*

Ample ſouls among mankind have arrived at that prodigious extent of knowledge which renders them the *wonder* and glory of the nation where they live. *Watts.*

WO'NDERFUL. *adj.* [*wonder* and *full*] Admirable; ſtrange; aſtoniſhing.

I uttered that which I underſtood not, things too *wonderful* for me which I knew not. *Job* xlii. 3.

Strange
Hath been the cauſe, and *wonderful* to hear. *Milton.*

All this is very *wonderful*, Shakeſpeare multiplies miracle upon miracle to bring about the ſame event in the play, which chance with more propriety performs in the novel. *Shak. Illuſt.*

WO'NDERFUL. *adv.* To a wonderful degree. Improperly uſed.

The houſe which I am about to build ſhall be *wonderful* great. 2 *Chron.* ii. 9.

WO'NDERFULLY. *adv.* [from *wonderful.*] In a wonderful manner; to a wonderful degree.

He was much made on by the pope, who knowing himſelf to be unprofitable to the Chriſtian world, was *wonderfully* glad to hear that there were ſuch echoes of him ſounding in remote parts. *Bacon's Henry* VII.

There is ſomething *wonderfully* divine in the airs of this picture. *Addiſon's Italy.*

WO'NDERMENT. *n. ſ.* [from *wonder.*] Aſtoniſhment; amazement. Not in uſe, except in low language.

When my pen would write her titles true,
It raviſh'd is with fancy's *wonderment*. *Spenſer.*

Thoſe things which I here ſet down, do naturally take the ſenſe, and not reſpect petty *wonderments*. *Bacon.*

The neighbours made a *wonderment* of it, and aſked him what he meant. *L'Eſtrange.*

WO'NDERSTRUCK. *adj.* [*wonder* and *ſtrike.*] Amazed.

Aſcanius, *wonderſtruck* to ſee
That image of his filial piety. *Dryden's Æneid.*

WO'NDROUS. *adj.* [This is contracted from *wonderous*, of *wonder.*]

1. Admirable; marvellous; ſtrange; ſurpriſing.

The credit of whoſe virtue reſt with thee;
Wondrous indeed, if cauſe of ſuch effects. *Milton.*

In ſuch charities ſhe paſs'd the day;
'Twas *wond'rous* how ſhe found an hour to pray. *Dryden.*

Reſearches into the ſprings of natural bodies, and their motions, ſhould awaken us to admire the *wondrous* wiſdom of our Creator in all the works of nature. *Watts.*

2. [*Wondrous* is barbarouſly uſed for an adverb.] In a ſtrange degree.

From that part where Moſes remembereth the giants, begotten by the ſons of good men upon the daughters of the wicked; did they ſteal thoſe *wondrous* great acts of their ancient kings and powerful giants. *Raleigh.*

To ſhun th' allurement is not hard
To minds reſolv'd, forewarn'd and well-prepar'd;
But *wond'rous* difficult, when once beſet,
To ſtruggle through the ſtraits, and break th' involving net. *Dryden.*

You are ſo beautiful,
So *wondrous* fair, you juſtify rebellion. *Dryden.*

Sylphs, yet mindful of their ancient race,
Are, as when women, *wond'rous* fond of place. *Pope.*

WO'NDROUSLY. *adv.* [from *wondrous.*] To a ſtrange degree.

My lord led *wondrouſly* to diſcontent. *Shakeſpeare.*

This made Proſerpina
Make to them the greater ſpeed,
For fear that they too much ſhould bleed,
Which *wondrouſly* her troubled. *Drayton.*

Such doctrines in the pigeon houſe were taught:
You need not aſk how *wondrouſly* they wrought. *Dryden.*

Of injur'd fame, and mighty wrongs receiv'd,
Cloe complains, and *wondrouſly*'s aggriev'd. *Granville.*

To WONT. } *v. n.* [Preterite and participle *wont*; ƿunian,
To be WONT. } Saxon; *gewoonen*, Dutch.] To be accuſtomed; to uſe; to be uſed.

A yearly ſolemn feaſt ſhe *wont* to make
The day that firſt doth lead the year around. *Fairy Queen.*

Through power of that, his cunning thieveries
He *wonts* to work, that none the ſame eſpies. *Hubberd.*

Jaſon the Theſſalian was *wont* to ſay, that ſome things muſt be done unjuſtly, that many things may be done juſtly. *Bacon.*

I this night have dream'd;
If dream'd, not as I oft am *wont*, of thee,
But of offence and trouble. *Milton's Paradiſe Loſt.*

The eagle's fate and mine are one,
Which on the ſhaft that made him die
Eſpy'd a feather of his own,
Wherewith he *wont* to ſoar ſo high. *Waller.*

A mother was *wont* always to indulge her daughters, when any of them deſired ſquirrels or birds, but then they muſt keep them well. *Locke.*

Another ſort of ſophiſm is *wont* to be called an imperfect enumeration or falſe induction, when from a few experiments men infer general theorems. *Watts's Logick.*

WONT. *n. ſ.* [from the verb] Cuſtom; habit; uſe. Out of uſe.

Paſſing their time according to their *wont*, they waited for the coming of Phalantus. *Sidney.*

Things natural in that regard forget their ordinary natural *wont*, that which is heavy mounting ſometime upwards of its own accord. *Hooker.*

'Tis not his *wont* to be the hindmoſt man,
Whate'er occaſion keeps him from us now. *Shakeſpeare.*

They are by ſudden alarm or watchword to be called out to their military motions under ſky or covert, according to the ſeaſon, as was the Roman *wont*. *Milton.*

WONT. A contraction of will not.

WO'NTED. *part. adj.* [from the verb.] Accuſtomed; uſed; uſual.

Her champion ſtout, to aid his friend,
Again his *wonted* weapon proved. *Fairy Queen.*

So pray'd they, innocent, and to their thoughts
Firm peace recover'd ſoon and *wonted* calm. *Milton.*

The pond-frog would fain have gotten the other frog over; but ſhe was *wonted* to the place, and would not remove. *L'Eſt.*

Who have no houſe, ſit round where once it was,
And with full eyes each *wonted* room require;
Haunting the yet warm aſhes of the place,
As murther'd men walk where they did expire. *Dryden.*

WO'NTEDNESS. *n. ſ.* [from *wonted.*] State of being accuſtomed to. Not in uſe.

Did I ſee any thing more of Chriſt in thoſe that pretend to other modes of government, I might ſuſpect my judgment biaſſed with prejudice or *wontedneſs* of opinion. *King Charles.*

WO'NTLESS. *adj.* [from *wont.*] Unaccuſtomed; unuſual.

Whither, love, wilt thou now carry me?
What *wontleſs* fury do'ſt thou now inſpire
Into my feeble breaſt, when full of thee? *Spenſer.*

To WOO. *v. a.* [ꞷoꝺoꝺ, courted, Saxon.] To court; to ſue to for love.

We cannot fight for love, as men may do;
We ſhould be *woo'd*, and were not made to *woo*. *Shakeſpeare.*

Some lay in dead mens ſkulls; and in thoſe holes
Where eyes did once inhabit, there were crept,
As 'twere in ſcorn of eyes, reflecting gems;
That *woo'd* to the ſlimy bottom of the deep,
And mock'd the dead bones that lay ſcatter'd by. *Shakeſpeare.*

Fancie.

Fancies and notions he purſues,
Which ne'er had being but in thought:
Each like the Grecian artiſt *woos*
The image he himſelf has wrought. *Prior.*

My proud rival *woos*
Another partner to his throne and bed.
Philips's Diſtreſt Mother.

Oh, ſtretch thy reign, fair peace! from ſhore to ſhore,
Till conqueſt ceaſe, and ſlav'ry be no more;
Till the freed Indians in their native groves
Reap their own fruits, and *woo* their ſable loves. *Pope.*

2. To court ſolicitouſly; to invite with importunity.

Yet can ſhe love a foreign emperor,
Whom of great worth and pow'r ſhe hears to be;
If ſhe be woo'd but by ambaſſador,
Or but his letters or his pictures ſee:
So while the virgin ſoul on earth doth ſtay,
She *woo'd* and tempted is ten thouſand ways
By theſe great pow'rs, which on the earth bear ſway,
The wiſdom of the world, wealth, pleaſure, praiſe.
Davies.

Sweet bird that ſhun'ſt the noiſe of folly,
Moſt muſical, moſt melancholy!
Thee, chauntreſs oft the woods among,
I *woo* to hear thy even-ſong. *Milton.*

To Woo. *v. n.* To court; to make love.

With pomp, and trains, and in a crowd they *woo*,
When true felicity is but in two. *Dryden.*

WOOD. *adj.* [*wods*, Gothick; pod, Saxon; *woed*, Dutch.] Mad; furious; raging. Obſolete.

Winds do rage, as winds were *wood*,
And cauſe ſpring tides to raiſe great flood. *Tuſſer.*

Coal-black ſteeds yborn of helliſh brood,
That on their ruſty bits did champ as they were *wood*.
Fairy Queen.

Calm the tempeſt of his paſſion *wood*;
The banks are overflown, when ſtopped is the flood. *Fa. Q.*

Wood. *n. ſ.* [pube, Saxon; *woud*, Dutch.]

1. A large and thick plantation of trees.

The *wood*-born people fall before her flat,
And worſhip her as goddeſs of the *wood*. *Fairy Queen.*

St. Valentine is paſt:
Begin theſe *wood*-birds but to couple now? *Shakeſpeare.*

The *woods* are ruthleſs, dreadful, deaf and dull:
There ſpeak and ſtrike. *Shakeſpeare's Titus and Andronicus.*

Light thickens, and the crow
Makes wing to the rooky *wood*. *Shakeſpeare's Macbeth.*

Hecate, when ſhe gave to rule the *woods*,
Then led me trembling through thoſe dire abodes. *Dryden.*

2. The ſubſtance of trees; timber.

Balm his foul head with warm diſtilled waters,
And burn ſweet *wood* to make the lodging ſweet. *Shakeſp.*

The cavity of the tin plate was filled with a melted cement, made of pitch, roſin, and *wood*-aſhes, well incorporated.
Boyle.

Having filled it about five inches with throughly kindled *wood*-coals, we let it down into the glaſs. *Boyle.*

Of long growth there ſtood
A laurel's trunk, a venerable *wood*. *Dryden's Æneid.*

The ſoft *wood* turners uſe commonly. *Moxon.*

The ſize of faggots and *wood*-ſtacks differs in moſt countries.
Mortimer's Huſbandry.

Herrings muſt be ſmoked with *wood*. *Child.*

Wooda'nemone. *n. ſ.* A plant.

Woo'dbind. } *n. ſ.* [pubbinð, Saxon.] Honeyſuckle.
Woo'dbine. }

Beatrice, e'en now
Couch'd in the *woodbind* coverture. *Shakeſpeare.*

The nymphs of the mountains would be drawn, upon their heads garlands of *woodbine* and wild roſes. *Peacham.*

Woo'dcock. *n. ſ.* [pobucoc, Saxon.] A bird of paſſage with a long bill; his food is not known. It is a word ludicrouſly uſed for a dunce.

He hath bid me to a calve's head and a capon; ſhall I not find a *woodcock* too. *Shakeſpeare.*

Soon as in doubtful day the *woodcock* flies,
Her cleanly pail the pretty houſewife bears. *Gay.*

Woo'ded. *adj.* [from *wood.*] Supplied with wood.

The lord Strutts have been poſſeſſed of a very great landed eſtate, well-conditioned, *wooded* and watered. *Arbuthnot.*

Woo'ddrink. *n. ſ.* Decoction or infuſion of medicinal woods, as ſaſſafras.

The drinking elder-wine or *wooddrinks* are very uſeful.
Floyer on the Humours.

Woo'den. *adj.* [from *wood.*]

1. Ligneous; made of wood; timber.

Like a ſtrutting player, whoſe conceit
Lies in his hamſtring, he doth think it rich
To hear the *wooden* dialogue and ſound
'Twixt his ſtretch'd footing and the ſcaffoldage. *Shakeſpeare.*

They uſed to vault or leap up; and therefore they had *wooden* horſes in their houſes and abroad. *Brown's Vulgar Errours.*

Preſs'd with the burden, Cæneus pants for breath;
And on his ſhoulders bears the *wooden* death. *Dryden.*

The haberdaſher ſtole off his hat that hung upon a *wooden* peg. *Addiſon's Spectator.*

2. Clumſy; awkward.

I'll win this lady Margaret: for whom?
Why, for my king: tuſh, that's a *wooden* thing. *Shakeſpeare.*

When a bold man is out of countenance, he makes a very *wooden* figure on it. *Collier of Confidence.*

Woodfre'tter. *n. ſ.* [*teres*, Lat.] An inſect; a Woodworm.
Ainſworth.

Woo'dhole. *n. ſ.* [*wood* and *hole.*] Place where wood is laid up.

What ſhould I do? or whither turn? amaz'd,
Confounded to the dark receſs I fly,
Of *woodhole*. *Philips.*

Woo'dland. *n. ſ.* [*wood* and *land.*] Woods; ground covered with woods.

This houſhold beaſt, that us'd the *woodland* grounds,
Was view'd at firſt by the young hero's hounds,
As down the ſtream he ſwam. *Dryden's Æneid.*

He that rides poſt through a country, may, from the tranſient view, tell how in general the parts lie; here a moraſs, and there a river, *woodland* in one part, and ſavanas in another.
Locke.

By her awak'd, the *woodland* choir
To hail the common god prepares;
And tempts me to reſume the lyre,
Soft warbling to the vernal airs.
Fenton's Ode to Lord Gower.

Here hills and vales, the *woodland* and the plain,
Here earth and water ſeems to ſtrive again. *Pope.*

Woodla'rk. *n. ſ.* A melodious ſort of wild lark.

Woo'dlouse. *n. ſ.* [*wood* and *louſe.*] An Inſect.

The millepes or *woodlouſe* is a ſmall inſect of an oblong figure, about half an inch in length, and a fifth of an inch in breadth; of a dark blueiſh or livid grey colour, and having its back convex or rounded: notwithſtanding the appellation of millepes, it has only fourteen pair of ſhort legs; it is a very ſwift runner, but it can occaſionally roll itſelf up into the form of a ball, which it frequently does, and ſuffers itſelf to be taken. They are found in great plenty under old logs of wood or large ſtones, or between the bark and wood of decayed trees. Millepedes are aperient, attenuant, and detergent; and the beſt way of taking them is ſwallowing them alive, which is eaſily and conveniently done; and they are immediately deſtroyed on falling into the ſtomach. *Hill's Materia Medica.*

Wrap thyſelf up like a *woodlouſe*, and dream revenge.
Congreve.

There is an inſect they call a *woodlouſe*,
That folds up itſelf in itſelf, for a houſe,
As round as a ball, without head, without tail,
Incloſ'd cap-a-pe in a ſtrong coat of mail. *Swift.*

Woo'dman. *n. ſ.* [*wood* and *man.*] A ſportſman; a hunter.

Their cry being compoſed of ſo well ſorted mouths, that any man would perceive therein ſome kind of proportion, but the ſkilful *woodmen* did find a muſick. *Sidney.*

The duke is a better *woodman* than thou takeſt him for.
Shakeſpeare.

This is ſome one like us night-foundered here,
Or elſe ſome neighbour *woodman*. *Milton.*

So when the *woodman's* toil her cave ſurrounds,
And with the hunter's cry the grove reſounds,
With grief and rage the mother-lion ſtung,
Fearleſs herſelf, yet trembles for her young. *Pope.*

Woo'dmonger. *n. ſ.* [*wood* and *monger.*] A woodſeller.

Woo'dnote. *n. ſ.* Wild muſick.

Then to the well-trod ſtage anon,
If Johnſon's learned ſock be on,
Or ſweeteſt Shakeſpear, fancy's child,
Warble his native *woodnotes* wild. *Milton.*

Woodny'mph. [*wood* and *nymph.*] Dryad.

Soft ſhe withdrew, and like a *woodnymph* light,
Oread, or Dryad, or of Delia's train,
Betook her to the groves. *Milton's Paradiſe Loſt.*

By dimpled brook and fountain brim,
The *woodnymphs*, deck'd with daiſies trim,
Their merry wakes and paſtimes keep. *Milton.*

Woodo'ffering. *n. ſ.* Wood burnt on the altar.

We caſt the lots for the *woodoffering*. *Neh.* x. 34.

Woo'dpecker. *n. ſ.* [*wood* and *peck*; *picus martius*, Lat.] A bird.

The ſtructure of the tongue of the *woodpecker* is very ſingular, whether we look at its great length, its bones and muſcles, its incompaſſing parts of the neck and head, the better to exert itſelf in length, and, again, to retract it into its cell; and laſtly, whether we look at its ſharp, horny, bearded point, and the gluey matter at the end of it, the better to ſtab and draw little maggots out of wood. *Derham's Phyſico-theology.*

Woodpi'geon *or Woodculver*. *n. ſ.* A wild pigeon.

Woodroo'f. *n. ſ.* An herb. *Ainſworth.*

Wo'odsare. *n. s.*
The froth called *woodsare*, being like a kind of spittle, is found upon herbs, as lavender and sage. *Bacon.*
Wo'odseere. *n. s.* [*wood* and *sere.*] The time when there is no sap in the tree.
From May to October leave cropping, for why,
In *woodseere*, whatsoever thou croppest shall die. *Tusser.*
Wo'odsorrel. *n. s.* [*oxys*, Latin.] A plant.
The characters are: it hath a bell-shaped flower, consisting of one leaf, having its brim wide expanded, and cut into several divisions: the pointal, which rises from the flowercup, becomes an oblong membranous fruit, divided into seminal cells, opening outward from the base to the top, and inclosing seeds, which often start from their lodges, by reason of the elastick force of the membrane which involves them. *Miller.*
Woo'dward. *n. s.* [*wood* and *ward.*] A forester.
Wo'ody. *adj.* [from *wood.*]
1. Abounding with wood.
Thou hast led me up
A *woody* mountain, whose high top was plain. *Milton.*
Oft in glimmering bow'rs and glades
He met her, and in secret shades
Of *woody* Ida's inmost grove. *Milton.*
Four times ten days I've pass'd
Wand'ring this *woody* maze, and human food
Nor tasted, nor had appetite. *Milton's Paradise Regain'd.*
Diana's *woody* realms he next invades,
And, crosses through the consecrated shades, *Addison.*
2. Ligneous; consisting of wood.
In the *woody* parts of plants, which are their bones, the principles are so compounded as to make them flexible without joints, and also elastick. *Grew.*
Herbs are those plants whose stalks are soft, and have nothing *woody* in them, as grass and hemlock. *Locke.*
3. Relating to woods.
With the *woody* nymphs when she did play. *Fairy Queen.*
All the satyrs scorn their *woody* kind,
And henceforth nothing fair but her on earth they find. *Fairy Queen.*
Woo'er. *n. s.* [from *woo.*] One who courts a woman.
The *wooers* most are toucht in this ostent,
To whom are dangers great and imminent. *Chapman.*
Aristippus said, that those that studied particular sciences, and neglected philosophy, were like Penelope's *wooers*, that made love to the waiting woman. *Bacon's Apophthegms.*
Usurping *wooers* felt his thund'ring sword,
And willing nations knew their native lord. *Creech.*
Woof. *n. s.* [from *wove.*]
1. The set of threads that crosses the warp; the weft.
The placing of the tangible parts in length or transverse, as in the warp and the *woof* of textile, is more inward or more outward. *Bacon's Natural History.*
2. Texture; cloath.
A vest of purple flow'd,
Iris had dipp'd the *woof*. *Milton's Paradise Lost.*
I must put off
These my sky-robes, spun out of Iris' *woof*. *Milton.*
To spread the pall beneath the regal chair,
Of softest *woof*, is bright Alcippe's care. *Pope's Odyssey.*
Woo'ingly. *adv.* [from *wooing.*] Pleasingly; so as to invite stay.
The temple-haunting martlet does approve,
By his lov'd mansionry, that heaven's breath
Smells *wooingly* here. *Shakes. King Lear.*
WOOL. *n. s.* [pul, Saxon; *wollen*, Dutch.]
1. The fleece of sheep; that which is woven into cloath.
Base-minded wretches, for respect of gain, some paultry *wool* may yield you, to let so much time pass without knowing perfectly her estate. *Sidney.*
A gown made of the finest *wool*,
Which from our pretty lambs we pull;
Fair lined slippers for the cold,
With buckles of the purest gold. *Raleigh.*
Concerning their complaint for price of *wool*, he would give order that his commissioners should cause clothiers to take *wool*, paying only two parts of the price. *Hayward.*
Struthium is a root used by the *wool*-dressers. *Arbuthnot.*
2. Any short thick hair.
In the cauldron boil and bake;
Wool of batt and tongue of dog. *Shakesp. Macbeth.*
Wo'olfel. *n. s.* [*wool* and *fell.*] Skin not stripped of the wool.
Wool and *woolfels* were ever of little value in this kingdom. *Davies on Ireland.*
Wo'ollen. *adj.* [from *wool.*] Made of wool not finely dressed, and thence used likewise for any thing coarse.
I was wont
To call them *woollen* vassals, things created
To buy and sell with groats. *Shakesp. Coriolanus.*
I could not endure a husband with a beard on his face: I had rather lye in *woollen*. *Shakesp. Much Ado about Nothing.*
Woollen cloth will tenter, linen scarcely. *Bacon.*
At dawn of day our general cleft his pate,
Spite of his *woollen* night-cap. *Dryden.*
Woo'llen. *n. s.* Cloath made of wool.
His breeches were of rugged *woollen*,
And had been at the siege of Bullen. *Hudibras.*
Odious! in *woollen!* 'twould a saint provoke!
No, let a charming chintz and Brussels lace
Wrap my cold limbs and shade my lifeless face. *Pope.*
He is a bel-esprit and a *woollen* draper. *Swift.*
Wo'olpack. } **Wo'olsack.** } *n. s.* [*wool*, *pack*, and *sack.*]
1. A bag of wool; a bundle of wool.
2. The seat of the judges in the house of lords.
At bar abusive, on the bench unable,
Knave on the *woolsack*, fop at council-table. *Dryden.*
3. Any thing bulky without weight.
Chaos of presbyt'ry, where laymen guide
With the tame *woolpack* clergy by their side. *Cleaveland.*
Wo'olward. *adv.* [*wool* and *ward.*] In wool. Not used.
I have no shirt: I go *woolward* for penance. *Shakespeare.*
Wo'olly. *adj.* [from *wool.*]
1. Consisting of wool; cloathed with wool.
When the work of generation was
Between these *woolly* breeders,
The skilful shepherd peel'd me certain wands. *Shakespeare.*
Some few, by temp'rance taught, approaching slow,
To distant fate by easy journeys go:
Gently they lay 'em down, as ev'ning sheep
On their own *woolly* fleeces softly sleep. *Dryden.*
2. Resembling wool.
What signifies
My fleece of *woolly* hair, that now uncurls? *Shakespeare.*
Nothing profits more
Than frequent snows: O may'st thou often see
Thy furrows whiten'd by the *woolly* rain,
Nutritious! *J. Philips.*
WORD. *n. s.* [popd, Saxon; *woord*, Dutch.]
1. A single part of speech.
If you speak three *words*, it will three times report you the three *words*. *Bacon.*
As conceptions are the images of things to the mind within itself, so are *words* or names the marks of those conceptions to the minds of them we converse with. *South's Sermons.*
Amongst men who confound their ideas with *words*, there must be endless disputes, wrangling, and jargon. *Locke.*
Each wight who reads not, and but scans and spells,
Each *word* catcher that lives on syllables. *Pope.*
2. A short discourse.
Shall I vouchsafe your worship a *word* or two?
—Two thousand, and I'll vouchsafe thee the hearing. *Shak.*
A *word*, Lucilius,
How he receiv'd you. *Shakesp. Julius Cæsar.*
A friend who shall own thee in thy lowest condition, answer all thy wants, and, in a *word*, never leave thee. *South.*
In a *word*, the Gospel describes God to us in all respects such a one as we would wish him to be. *Tillotson.*
3. Talk; discourse.
Why should calamity be full of *words*?
—Windy attorneys to their client woes!
Let them have scope, though what they do impart
Help nothing else, yet they do ease the heart. *Shak. R.* III.
If you dislike the play,
Pray make no *words* on't 'till the second day,
Or third be past; for we would have you know it,
The loss will fall on us, not on the poet. *Denham.*
Cease this contention: be thy *words* severe,
Sharp as he merits; but the sword forbear. *Dryden.*
If *words* are sometimes to be used, they ought to be grave, kind, and sober, representing the ill, or unbecomingness of the faults. *Locke.*
If I appear a little *word*-bound in my first solutions, I hope it will be imputed to the long disuse of speech. *Spectator.*
4. Dispute; verbal contention.
In argument upon a case,
Some *words* there grew 'twixt Somerset and me. *Shakesp.*
5. Language.
Found you no displeasure by *word* or countenance? *Shakesp.*
I'll write thee a challenge, or I'll deliver thy indignation to him by *word* of mouth. *Shakes. Twelfth Night.*
He commanded the men to be ranged in battalions, and rid to every squadron, giving them such *words* as were proper to the occasion. *Clarendon.*
An easy way, by *word* of mouth communicated to me. *Boyle.*
6. Promise.
Obey thy parents, keep thy *word* justly, swear not. *Shakes.*
I take your princely *word* for these redresses.
—I give it you, and will maintain my *word*. *Shak. H.* IV.
The duke shall wield his conqu'ring sword,
The king shall pass his honest *word*. *Dryden.*
7. Signal; token.
Every soldier, kill his prisoners;
Give the *word* through. *Shak. Henry* V.

8. Account; tydings; meſſage.

Bring me *word* thither
How the world goes, that to the pace of it
I may ſpur on my journey. *Shakeſp. Coriolanus.*

Why ſhould ſhe write to Edmund? Might not you
Tranſport her purpoſes by *word*? *Shakeſp. King Lear.*

Two optick nerves ſhe ties,
Like ſpectacles acroſs the eyes;
By which the ſpirits bring her *word*,
Whene'er the balls are fix'd or ſtirr'd. *Prior.*

9. Declaration.

I know you brave, and take you at your *word*;
That preſent ſervice which you vaunt, afford. *Dryden.*

10. Affirmation.

Every perſon has enough to do to work out his own ſalvation; which, if we will take the apoſtle's *word*, is to be done with fear and trembling. *Decay of Piety.*

I deſire not the reader ſhould take my *word*, and therefore I will ſet two of their diſcourſes in the ſame light for every man to judge. *Dryden.*

11. Scripture; word of God.

They ſay this church of England neither hath the *word* purely preached, nor the ſacraments ſincerely miniſtred. *Whitg.*

12. The ſecond perſon of the ever adorable Trinity. A ſcripture term.

Thou my *Word*, begotten ſon, by thee
This I perform. *Milton.*

To Word. *v. n.* [from the noun.] To diſpute.

He that deſcends not to *word* it with a ſhrew, does worſe than beat her. *L'Eſtrange.*

To Word. *v. a.* To expreſs in proper words.

Let us blacken him what we can, ſaid Harriſon of the bleſſed king, upon the *wording* and drawing up his charge againſt approaching trial. *South's Sermons.*

Whether I have improved theſe fables or no, in the *wording* or meaning of them, the book muſt ſtand or fall to itſelf. *L'Eſt.*

The apology for the king is the ſame, but *worded* with greater deference to that great prince. *Addiſon.*

Wo'rdy. *adj.* [from *word.*] Verboſe; full of words.

Phocion, beholding a *wordy* orator, while he was making a magnificent ſpeech full of vain promiſes, ſaid, I now fix my eyes upon a cypreſs-tree: it has all the pomp imaginable in its branches, leaves, and height; but it bears no fruit. *Spectat.*

We need not laviſh hours in *wordy* periods,
As do the Romans, ere they dare to fight. *Philips's Briton.*

Intemp'rate rage, a *wordy* war, began. *Pope.*

Wore. The preterite of *wear.*

This on his helmet *wore* a lady's glove,
And that a ſleeve embroider'd by his love. *Dryden.*

My wife, the kindeſt, deareſt, and the trueſt
That ever *wore* the name. *Rowe's Royal Convert.*

To WORK. *v. n.* pret. *worked*, or *wrought.* [peoɲcan, Saxon; *werken*, Dutch.]

1. To labour; to travail; to toil.

Good Kent, how ſhall I live and *work*
To match thy goodneſs? life will be too ſhort. *Shakeſp.*

Go and *work*; for no ſtraw ſhall be given you. *Ex.* v. 18.

Whether we *work* or play, or ſleep or wake,
Our life doth paſs, and with time's wings doth fly. *Davies.*

2. To be in action; to be in motion.

Glory grows guilty of deteſted crimes,
When for fame's ſake
We bend to that the *working* of the heart. *Shakeſpeare.*

In Morat your hopes a crown deſign'd,
And all the woman *work'd* within your mind. *Dryden.*

3. To act; to carry on operations.

May be the Lord will *work* for us. 1 *Sa.* xiv. 6.

Our better part remains
To *work* in cloſe deſign. *Milton.*

4. To act as a manufacturer.

They that *work* in fine flax. *Iſ.* xix. 9.

5. To ferment.

Into wine and ſtrong beer put ſome like ſubſtances, while they *work*, which may make them fume and inflame leſs. *Bac.*

Try the force of imagination upon ſtaying the *working* of beer, when the barm is put in. *Bacon.*

If in the wort of beer, while it *worketh*, before it be tunned, the burrage be often changed with freſh, it will make a ſovereign drink for melancholy. *Bacon's Natural Hiſtory.*

6. To operate; to have effect.

With ſome other buſineſs put the king
From theſe ſad thoughts that *work* too much upon him. *Shak.*

All things *work* together for good to them that love God. *Rom.* viii. 28.

Gravity *worketh* weakly, both far from the earth, and alſo within the earth. *Bacon.*

Although the ſame tribute laid by conſent, or by impoſing, be all one to the purſe, yet it *works* diverſely on the courage: no people overcharged with tribute is fit for empire. *Bacon.*

Theſe poſitive undertakings *wrought* upon many to think that this opportunity ſhould not be loſt. *Clarendon.*

Nor number, nor example with him *wrought*
To ſwerve from truth, or change his conſtant mind. *Milton.*

We ſee the *workings* of gratitude in the Iſraelites. *South.*

Objects of pity, when the cauſe is new,
Would *work* too fiercely on the giddy crowd. *Dryden.*

Poiſon will *work* againſt the ſtars: beware,
For ev'ry meal an antidote prepare. *Dryd. jun. Juvenal.*

When this reverence begins to *work* in him, next conſider his temper of mind. *Locke.*

This ſo *wrought* upon the child, that afterwards he deſired to be taught. *Locke.*

Humours and manners *work* more in the meaner ſort than with the nobility. *Addiſon on Italy.*

The ibibaboca is a foot round, and three yards and a half long: his colours are white, black, and red: of all ſerpents his bite is the moſt pernicious, yet *worketh* the ſloweſt. *Grew.*

7. To obtain by diligence.

Without the king's aſſent
You *wrought* to be a legate. *Shakeſp Henry* VIII.

He hath *wrought* with God this day. 1 *Sa.* xiv. 45.

8. To act internally; to operate as a purge, or other phyſick.

Work on,
My medicine, *work!* thus credulous fools are caught. *Shak.*

I ſhould have doubted the operations of antimony, where ſuch a potion could not *work.* *Brown's Vulgar Errours.*

It is benign, nor far from the nature of aliment, into which, upon defect of *working*, it is oft times converted. *Brown.*

Moſt purges heat a little; and all of them *work* beſt, that is, cauſe the blood ſo to do, as do fermenting liquors, in warm weather, or in a warm room. *Grew's Coſmol.*

9. To act as on an object.

Let it be pain of body, or diſtreſs of mind, there's matter yet left for philoſophy and conſtancy to *work* upon. *L'Eſtr.*

Natural philoſophy has ſenſible objects to *work* upon; but then it often puzzles the reader with the intricacy of its notions. *Addiſon.*

The predictions Bickerſtaff publiſhed, relating to his death, too much affected and *worked* on his imagination. *Swift.*

10. To make way.

Body ſhall up to ſpirit *work.* *Milton.*

Who would truſt chance, ſince all men have the ſeeds
Of good and ill, which ſhould *work* upward firſt? *Dryden.*

11. To be toſſed or agitated.

Vex'd by wint'ry ſtorms, Benacus raves,
Confuſ'd with *working* ſands and rolling waves. *Addiſon.*

To Work. *v. a.*

1. To make by degrees.

Sidelong he *works* his way. *Milton.*

Through winds, and waves, and ſtorms he *works* his way,
Impatient for the battle: one day more
Will ſet the victor thundering at our gates. *Addiſon.*

2. To labour; to manufacture.

He could have told them of two or three gold mines, and a ſilver mine, and given the reaſon why they forbare to *work* them at that time, and when they left off from *working* them. *Raleigh's Apology.*

The chaos, by the Divine Power, was *wrought* from one form into another, 'till it ſettled into an habitable earth. *Burn.*

This mint is to *work* off part of the metals found in the neighbouring mountains. *Addiſon.*

The young men acknowledged in love-letters, ſealed with a particular wax, with certain enchanting words *wrought* upon the ſeals, that they died for her. *Tatler.*

They now begin to *work* the wond'rous frame,
To ſhape the parts, and raiſe the vital flame. *Blackmore.*

The induſtry of the people *works* up all their native commodities to the laſt degree of manufacture. *Swift.*

3. To bring by action into any ſtate.

So the pure limpid ſtream, when foul with ſtains
Of ruſhing torrents and deſcending rains,
Works itſelf clear, and, as it runs, refines,
'Till by degrees the floating mirrour ſhines. *Addiſon's Cato.*

4. To influence by ſucceſſive impulſes.

If you would *work* any man, know his nature and faſhions, and ſo lead him. *Bacon.*

To haſten his deſtruction, come yourſelf,
And *work* your royal father to his ruin. *A. Philips.*

5. To produce; to effect.

Fly the dreadful war,
That in thyſelf thy leſſer parts do move,
Outrageous anger, and woe-*working* jar. *Fairy Queen.*

Love *worketh* no ill to his neighbour. *Rom.* xiii. 10.

Our light affliction for a moment *worketh* for us a far more eternal weight of glory. 2 *Cor.* iv. 18.

We might *work* any effect, not holpen by the co-operation of ſpirits, but only by the unity of nature. *Bacon.*

Moiſture, although it doth not paſs through bodies without communication of ſome ſubſtance, as heat and cold do, yet it *worketh* effects by qualifying of the heat and cold. *Bacon.*

Such power, being above all that the underſtanding of man can conceive, may well *work* ſuch wonders. *Drummond.*

God, only wise, to punish pride of wit,
Among mens wits hath this confusion *wrought*;
As the proud tow'r, whose points the clouds did hit,
By tongues confusion was to ruin brought. *Davies.*

Of the tree,
Which, tasted, *works* knowledge of good and evil,
Thou may'st not: in the day thou eat'st, thou dy'st. *Milton.*

6. To manage.

Mere personal valour could not supply want of knowledge in building and *working* ships. *Arbuthnot.*

7. To put to labour; to exert.

Now, Marcus, thy virtue's on the proof;
Put forth thy utmost strength, *work* every nerve,
And call up all thy father in thy soul. *Addison's Cato.*

8. To embroider with a needle.

9. *To* Work *out.* To effect by toil.

Not only every society, but every single person has enough to do to *work out* his own salvation. *Decay of Piety.*

The mind takes the hint from the poet, and *works out* the rest by the strength of her own faculties. *Addison.*

10. *To* Work *out.* To eraze; to efface.

Tears of joy for your returning spilt,
Work out and expiate our former guilt. *Dryden.*

11. *To* Work *up.* To raise.

That which is wanting to *work up* the pity to a greater height, was not afforded me by the story. *Dryden.*

This lake resembles a sea, when *worked up* by storms. *Addis.*

The sun, that rolls his chariot o'er their heads,
Works up more fire and colour in their cheeks. *Addis. Cato.*

We should inure ourselves to such thoughts, 'till they have *worked up* our souls into filial awe and love of him. *Atterbury.*

Work. *n. s.* [peopc, Saxon; *werk*, Dutch.]

1. Toil; labour; employment.

Bread, correction, and *work* for a servant. *Ecclus.* xxxiii.

In the bottom of some mines in Germany there grow vegetables, which the *work*-folks say have magical virtue. *Bac.*

The ground, unbid, gives more than we can ask;
But *work* is pleasure, when we chuse our task. *Dryden.*

2. A state of labour.

All the world is perpetually at *work*, only that our poor mortal lives should pass the happier for that little time we possess them, or else end the better when we lose them: upon this occasion riches came to be coveted, honours esteemed, friendship pursued, and virtues admired. *Temple.*

3. Bungling attempt.

It is pleasant to see what *work* our adversaries make with this innocent canon: sometimes 'tis a mere forgery of hereticks, and sometimes the bishops that met there were not so wise as they should have been. *Stillingfleet.*

4. Flowers or embroidery of the needle.

Round her *work* she did empale,
With a fair border wrought of sundry flowers,
Inwoven with an ivy-winding trail. *Spenser.*

That handkerchief, you gave me: I must take out the *work*: a likely piece of work, that you should find it in your chamber, and know not who left it there. This is some minx's token, and I must take out the *work*? There, give it your hobbyhorse: wheresoever you had it, I'll take out no *work* on't. *Shakesp. Othello.*

5. Any fabrick or compages of art.

Nor was the *work* impair'd by storms alone,
But felt th' approaches of too warm a sun. *Pope.*

6. Action; feat; deed.

The instrumentalness of riches to *works* of charity, have rendered it necessary in every Christian commonwealth by laws to secure propriety. *Hammond.*

As to the composition or dissolution of mixt bodies, which is the chief *work* of elements, and requires an intire application of the agents, water hath the principality and excess over earth. *Digby.*

Nothing lovelier can be found in woman,
Than good *works* in her husband to promote. *Milton.*

While as the *works* of bloody Mars employ'd,
The wanton youth inglorious peace enjoy'd. *Pope.*

7. Any thing made.

Where is that holy fire, which verse is said
To have? Is that enchanting force decay'd?
Verse, that draws nature's *works* from nature's law,
Thee, her best *work*, to her *work* cannot draw. *Donne.*

O fairest of creation! last and best
Of all God's *works*! creature, in whom excels
Whatever can to sight or thought be form'd;
Holy, divine, good, amiable, or sweet,
How art thou lost! *Milton's Paradise Lost.*

8. Management; treatment.

Let him alone; I'll go another way to *work* with him. *Shak.*

9. *To set on* Work. To employ; to engage.

It *setteth* those wits *on work* in better things, which would be else employed in worse. *Hooker.*

Wo'rker *n. s.* [from *work.*] One that works.

Ye fair nymphs, which oftentimes have loved
The cruel *worker* of your kindly smarts,
Prepare yourselves, and open wide your hearts. *Spenser.*

His father was a *worker* in brass. *1 Kings* vii. 14.

You spoke me fair; but even then betrayed me: depart from me, you professors of holiness, but *workers* of iniquity. *South's Sermons.*

Wo'rkfellow. *n. s.* [*work* and *fellow.*] One engaged in the same work with another.

Timotheus, my *workfellow*, and Lucius, salute you. *Rom.*

Wo'rkhouse. }
Wo'rkinghouse. } *n. s.* [from *work* and *house.*]

1. A place in which any manufacture is carried on.

The quick forge and *workinghouse* of thought. *Shak. H. V.*

Protogenes had his *workhouse* in a garden out of town, where he was daily finishing those pieces he begun. *Dryden.*

2. A place where idlers and vagabonds are condemned to labour.

Hast thou suffered at any time by vagabonds and pilferers? Esteem and promote those useful charities which remove such pests into prisons and *workhouses*. *Atterbury.*

Wo'rkingday. *n. s.* [*work* and *day.*] Day on which labour is permitted; not the sabbath.

How full of briars is this *workingday* world? *Shakespeare.*

Will you have me, lady?
——No, my lord, unless I might have another for *workingdays*; your grace is too costly to wear every day. *Shakesp.*

Wo'rkman. *n. s.* [*work* and *man.*] An artificer; a maker of any thing.

When *workmen* strive to do better than well,
They do confound their skill in covetousness. *Shakesp.*

If prudence works, who is a more cunning *workman*? *Wisd.*

There was no other cause preceding than his own will, no other matter than his own power, no other *workman* than his own word, and no other consideration than his own infinite goodness. *Raleigh.*

They have inscribed the pedestal, to shew their value for the *workman*. *Addison on Italy.*

Wo'rkmanly. *adj.* [from *workman.*] Skilful; well performed; workmanlike.

Wo'rkmanly. *adv.* Skilfully; in a manner becoming a workman.

In having but fortie foot *workmanly* dight,
Take saffron enough for a lord and a knight. *Tusser.*

We will fetch thee straight
Daphne roaming through a thorny wood,
Scratching her legs, that one shall swear she bleeds,
And at that sight shall sad Apollo weep,
So *workmanly* the blood and tears are drawn. *Shakespeare.*

Wo'rkmanship. *n. s.* [from *workman.*]

1. Manufacture; something made by any one.

Nor any skill'd in *workmanship* emboss'd,
Nor any skill'd in loops of fing'ring fine,
Might in their diverse cunning ever dare
With this so curious network to compare. *Spenser.*

By how much Adam exceeded all men in perfection, by being the immediate *workmanship* of God, by so much did that chosen garden exceed all parts of the world. *Raleigh.*

He moulded him to his own idea, delighting in the choice of the materials; and afterwards, as great architects use to do, in the *workmanship* of his regal hand. *Wotton.*

What more reasonable than to think, that if we be God's *workmanship*, he shall set this mark of himself upon all reasonable creatures? *Tillotson.*

2. The skill of a worker; the degree of skill discovered in any manufacture.

The Tritonian goddess having heard
Her blazed fame, which all the world had fill'd,
Came down to prove the truth, and due reward
For her praise-worthy *workmanship* to yield. *Spenser.*

3. The art of working.

If there were no metals, 'tis a mystery to me how Tubal-cain could ever have taught the *workmanship* and use of them. *Woodward's Natural History.*

Wo'rkmaster. *n. s.* [*work* and *master.*] The performer of any work.

What time this world's great *workmaster* did cast
To make all things, such as we now behold,
It seems that he before his eyes had plac'd
A goodly pattern, to whose perfect mould
He fashion'd them so comely. *Spenser.*

Every carpenter and *workmaster* that laboureth. *Eccl.* xxxviii.

Desire, which tends to know
The works of God, thereby to glorify
The great *workmaster*, leads to no excess. *Milt. Parad. Lost.*

Wo'rkwoman. *n. s.* [*work* and *woman.*]

1. A woman skilled in needle-work.

The most fine-fingred *workwoman* on ground,
Arachne, by his means was vanquished. *Spenser.*

2. A woman that works for hire.

Wo'rkyday. *n. s.* [Corrupted from *workingday.*] The day not the sabbath.

Tell her but a *workyday* fortune. *Shakespeare.*

The other days, and thou
Make up one man; whose face thou art,
The *workydays* are the back part;
The burden of the week lies there. *Herbert.*

Holydays.

Holydays, if haply she were gone,
Like *workydays*, I wish would soon be done: *Gay.*

WORLD. *n. s.* [ponlb, Saxon; *wereld*, Dutch.]

1. *World* is the great collective idea of all bodies whatever. *Loc.*

2. System of beings.

Begotten before all *worlds*. *Nicene Creed.*

God hath in these last days spoken unto us by his son, by whom he made the *worlds*. *Hebr.* i. 2.

Know how this *world*
Of heav'n and earth conspicuous first began. *Milton.*

3. The earth; the terraqueous globe.

He the *world*
Built on circumfluous waters. *Milton's Paradise Lost.*

4. Present state of existence.

I'm in this earthly *world*, where to do harm
Is often laudable; to do good sometime
Accounted dangerous folly. *Shakesp. Macbeth.*

I was not come into the *world* then. *L'Estrange.*

He wittingly brought evil into the *world*. *More.*

Christian fortitude consists in suffering for the love of God, whatever hardships can befal in the *world*. *Dryden.*

5. A secular life.

Happy is she that from the *world* retires,
And carries with her what the *world* admires.
Thrice happy she, whose young thoughts fixt above,
While she is lovely, does to heav'n make love;
I need not urge your promise, ere you find
An entrance here, to leave the *world* behind? *Waller.*

By the *world*, we sometimes understand the things of this *world*; the variety of pleasures and interests which steal away our affections from God. Sometimes we are to understand the men of the *world*, with whose solicitations we are so apt to comply. *Rogers's Sermons.*

6. Publick life.

Hence banished, is banish'd from the *world*;
And *world* exil'd is death. *Shakesp. Romeo and Juliet.*

7. Business of life; trouble of life.

Here I'll set up my everlasting rest,
And shake the yoke of man's suspicious stars
From this *world*-wearied flesh. *Shakesp. Romeo and Juliet.*

8. Great multitude.

You a *world* of curses undergo,
Being the agents, or base second means. *Shakespeare.*

Nor doth this wood lack *worlds* of company;
For you in my respect are all the world. *Shakespeare.*

I leave to speak of a *world* of other attempts furnished by kings. *Raleigh's Apology.*

What a *world* of contradictions would follow upon the contrary opinion, and what a *world* of confusions upon the contrary practice. *Bp. Sanderson.*

Just so romances are, for what else
Is in them all, but love and battles?
O' th' first of these we have no great matter
To treat of, but a *world* o' th' latter. *Hudibras.*

It brought into this world a *world* of woe. *Milton.*

There were a *world* of paintings, and among the rest the picture of a lion. *L'Estrange.*

Marriage draws a *world* of business on our hands, subjects us to law-suits, and loads us with domestick cares. *Dryden.*

From thy corporeal poison freed,
Soon hast thou reach'd the goal with mended pace;
A *world* of woes dispatch'd in little space. *Dryden.*

Why will you fight against so sweet a passion,
And steel your heart to such a *world* of charms? *Addison.*

9. Mankind; an hyperbolical expression for many.

This hath bred high terms of separation between such and the rest of the *world*, whereby the one sort are named the brethren, the godly; the other worldlings, time-servers, pleasers of men more than of God. *Hooker.*

'Tis the duke's pleasure,
Whose disposition, all the *world* well knows,
Will not be rubb'd nor stopp'd. *Shakesp. K. Lear.*

Why dost thou shew me thus to th' *world*?
Bear me to prison. *Shakesp. Measure for Measure.*

He was willing to declare to all the *world*, that, as he had been brought up in that religion established in the church of England, so he could maintain the same by unanswerable reasons. *Clarendon.*

10. Course of life.

Persons of conscience will be afraid to begin the *world* unjustly. *Clarissa.*

11. Universal empire.

Rome was to sway the *world*. *Milton.*

This through the east just vengeance hurl'd,
And lost poor Antony the *world*. *Prior.*

12. The manners of men.

Children should not know any wickedness. Old folks have discretion, and know the *world*. *Shakespeare.*

What start at this! when sixty years have spread
Their grey experience o'er thy hoary head?
Is this the all observing age could gain?
Or hast thou known the *world* so long in vain? *Dryden.*

If knowledge of the *world* makes man perfidious,
May Juba ever live in ignorance. *Addison's Cato.*

The girl might pass, if we could get her
To know the *world* a little better;
To know the *world*! a modern phrase
For visits, ombre, balls and plays. *Swift.*

13. A collection of wonders; a wonder. Obsolete.

The bassa having recommended Barbarussa, it was a *world* to see, how the court was changed upon him. *Knolles.*

14. Time. A sense originally Saxon; now only used in *World without end.*

15. *In the world.* In Possibility.

All the precautions *in the world* were taken for the marriage of his younger brother. *Addison.*

16. *For all the world.* Exactly. A ludicrous sense; now little used.

He had a pair of horns like a bull, his feet cloven, as many eyes upon his body as my grey mare hath dapples, and *for all the world* so placed. *Sidney, b.* ii.

WO'RLDLINESS. *n. s.* [from *worldly*.] Covetousness; addictedness to gain.

WO'RLDLING. *n. s.* [from *world*.] A mortal set upon profit.

Baseminded wretches! are your thoughts so deeply bemired in the trade of ordinary *worldlings*, as for respect of gain to let so much time pass. *Sidney.*

The one sort are nam'd the brethren, the godly; the other *worldlings*, timeservers, and pleasers of men more than pleasers of God. *Hooker.*

God of the world and *worldlings*,
Great Mammon! greatest god below the sky. *Fa. Queen.*

For his weeping in the needless stream;
Poor deer, quoth he, thou mak'st a testament
As *worldings* do, giving thy sum of more
To that which had too much. *Shakesp. As You Like It.*

That other on his friends his thoughts bestows:
The covetous *worldling*, in his anxious mind,
Thinks only on the wealth he left behind. *Dryden.*

If we consider the expectations of futurity, the *worldling* gives up the argument. *Rogers.*

WO'RLDLY. *adj.* [from *world*.]

1. Secular; relating to this life, in contradistinction to the life to come.

He is divinely bent to meditation;
And in no *worldly* suits would he be moved,
To draw him from his holy exercise. *Shakesp. Rich.* III.

Hast thou not *worldly* pleasure at command? *Shakesp.*

Tell me, ye toad-swol'n, flinty Pharaoh's, tell;
Can *worldly* pleasures equal pains of hell? *N. Richards.*

The fortitude of a christian consists in patience, not in enterprizes which the poets call heroic, and which are commonly the effects of interest, pride, and *worldly* honour. *Dryden.*

Compare the happiness of men and beasts no farther than it results from *worldly* advantages. *Atterbury.*

2. Bent upon this world; not attentive to a future state.

They'll practise how to live secure,
Worldly or dissolute, on that their lords
Shall leave them to enjoy. *Milton's Par. Lost, b.* xi.

3. Human; common; belonging to the world.

Many years it hath continued, standing by no other *worldly* mean, but that one only hand which erected it. *Hooker.*

Times and places are approved witnesses of *worldly* actions. *Raleigh's Hist. of the World.*

WO'RLDLY. *adv.* [from *world*.] With relation to the present life.

It is a token of a *worldly* wise man, not to contend in vain against the nature of times wherein he liveth. *Raleigh.*

Subverting *worldly* strong and *worldly* wise,
By simply meek. *Milton's Par. Lost, b.* xii.

This cannot be done, if my will be *worldly*, or voluptuously disposed. *South's Sermons.*

Since your mind is *worldly* bent,
Therefore of the two gifts in my dispose,
Think ere you speak, I grant you leave to choose. *Dryden.*

WORM. *n. s.* [pýpm, Saxon; *worm*, Dutch; *vermis*, Lat.]

1. A small harmless serpent that lives in the earth.

Both the princes
Thy broken faith hath made a prey to *worms*. *Shakespeare.*

Help me into some house,
Or I shall faint; — a plague o' both your houses!
They have made *worms* meat of me. *Shakespeare.*

Though *worms* devour me, though I turn to mold,
Yet in my flesh I shall his face behold:
I from my marble monument shall rise
Again intire, and see him with these eyes. *Sandy's Par.*

At once came forth whatever creeps the ground,
Insect or *worm*. *Milton.*

2. A poisonous serpent.

The mortal *worm*. *Shakespeare.*

3. Animal bred in the body.

Physicians observe these *worms* engendered within the body of man. *Harvey on Consumptions.*

4. The animal that spins silk.

Thou owest the *worm* no silk, the sheep no wool. *Shakesp.*

5. Grubs that gnaw wood and furniture.
'Tis no awkward claim,
Pick'd from the *worm*-holes of long vanish'd days,
Nor from the dust of old oblivion rak'd. *Shakesp. Hen.* V.
6. Something tormenting.
The *worm* of conscience still begnaw thy soul. *Shakesp.*
The chains of darkness, and th' undying *worm. Milton.*
7. Any thing vermiculated, or turned round; any thing spiral.
The threads of screws, when bigger than can be made in screw-plates, are called *worms*. The length of a *worm* begins at the one end of the spindle, and ends at the other; the breadth of the *worm* is contained between any two grooves on the spindle; the depth of the *worm* is cut into the diameter of the spindle, *viz.* the depth between the outside of the *worm*, and the bottom of the groove. *Moxon.*

To Worm. *v. n.* [from the noun.] To work slowly, secretly, and gradually.
When debates and fretting jealousy,
Did *worm* and work within you more and more,
Your colour faded. *Herbert.*

To Worm. *v. a.*
1. To drive by slow and secret means.
They find themselves *wormed* out of all power, by a new spawn of independents, sprung from your own bowels. *Swift.*
2. To deprive a dog of something, nobody knows what, under his tongue, which is said to prevent him, nobody knows why, from running mad.
Every one that keepeth a dog, should have him *wormed. Mort.*

Wo'rmeaten. *adj.* [[*worm* and *eaten.*]
1. Gnawed by worms.
For his verity in love, I do think him as concave as a covered goblet, or a *wormeaten* nut. *Shakespeare.*
2. Old; worthless.
His chamber all was hanged about with rolls,
And old records from antient times deriv'd;
Some made in books, some in long parchment scrolls.
That were all *wormeaten*, and full of canker holes. *Spenser.*
Things among the Greeks, which antiquity had worn out of knowledge, were called ogygia, which we call *wormeaten*, or of defaced date. *Raleigh's Hist. of the World.*
Thine's like *wormeaten* trunks cloath'd in seal's skin;
Or grave, that's dust without, and stink within. *Donne.*

Wo'rmwood. *n. s.* [from its virtue to kill worms in the body.]
Wormwood hath an indeterminate stalk, branching out into many small shoots, with spikes of naked flowers hanging downward; the leaves are hoary and bitter. Of this plant there are thirty-two species, one of which, the common *wormwood*, grows in the roads; but it is also planted in gardens for common use. Great variety of sea *wormwoods* are found in the salt marshes of England, and sold in the markets for the true Roman *wormwood*, though they differ greatly. *Mill.*
She was wean'd; I had then laid
Wormwood to my dug. *Shakesp. Romeo and Juliet.*
Pituitous Cacochymia must be corrected by bitters, as *wormwood* wine. *Floyer on the Humours.*
I ask whether one be not invincibly conscious to himself of a different perception, when he actually tastes *wormwood*, or only thinks on that favour. *Locke.*

Wo'rmy. *adj.* [from *worm.*] Full of worms.
Spirits that in crossways and floods have burial,
Already to their *wormy* beds are gone. *Shakespeare.*
Yet can I not persuade me thou art dead,
Or that thy corse corrupts in earth's dark womb,
Or that thy beauties lie in *wormy* bed. *Milton.*

Worn. part. pass. of *wear.*
His is a maiden shield,
Guiltless of fight: mine batter'd, hew'd and bor'd,
Worn out of service, must forsake his lord. *Dryden.*
What I now offer, is the wretched remainder of a sickly age, *worn* out with study, and oppress'd by fortune. *Dryden.*
The greatest part of mankind are given up to labour, whose lives are *worn* out only in the provisions for living. *Locke.*
Your cold hypocrisy's a stale device,
A *worn*-out trick; would'st thou be thought in earnest,
Cloath thy feign'd zeal in rage, in fire, in fury. *Addison.*

Wo'rnil. *n. s.*
In the backs of cows in the summer, are maggots generated, which in Essex we call *wornils*, being first only a small knot in the skin. *Derham's Physico-Theology.*

To Wo'rry. *v. a.* [ꝩoꝛiᵹen, Saxon: whence probably the word *warray.*]
1. To tear, or mangle, as a beast tears its prey.
If we with thrice such powers left at home,
Cannot defend our own doors from the dog,
Let us be *worried.* *Shakesp. Hen.* V.
The fury of the tumults might fly so high as to *worry* and tear those in pieces, whom as yet they but play'd with in their paws. *K. Charles.*
'Tis no new thing for the dogs that are to keep the wolves from *worrying* the sheep, to be deliver'd up to the enemy, for fear the sheep should *worry* the wolves. *L'Estrange.*
This revives and imitates that inhuman barbarity of the old heathen persecutors, wrapping up christians in the skins of wild beasts, that so they might be *worried* and torn in pieces by dogs. *South's Sermons.*
2. To harrass, or persecute brutally.
Then embraces his son-in-law; then again *worries* he his daughter with clipping her. *Shakesp. Winter's Tale.*
For want of words, or lack of breath,
Witness when I was *worried* with thy peals. *Milton.*
It has pleased Providence at length to give us righteousness instead of exaction, and hopes of religion to a church *worried* with reformation. *South's Sermons.*
All his care
Was to preserve me from the barbarous rage,
Which *worried* him only for being mine. *Southern.*
I shall not suffer him to *worry* any man's reputation, nor indeed fall on any person whatsoever. *Addison.*
Let them rail,
And then *worry* one another at their pleasure. *Rowe.*
Madam, contrive and invent,
And *worry* him out, 'till he gives his consent. *Swift.*

Worse. *adj.* The comparative of *bad: bad, worse, worst.* [ꝩiꝛꝛ, Saxon.] More bad; more ill.
Why should he see your faces *worse* liking than the children of your sort? *Daniel* i. 10.
Whether this or *worse*, love not the faithful side. *Milton.*
In happiness and misery, the question still remains, how men come often to prefer the *worse* to the better, and to chuse that, which, by their own confession, has made them miserable. *Locke.*

Worse. *adv.* In a manner more bad.
The more one sickens, the *worse* at ease he is. *Shakesp.*

The Worse. *n. s.* [from the adjective.]
1. The loss; not the advantage; not the better.
Was never man, who most conquests atchiev'd,
But sometimes had *the worse*, and lost by war. *Spenser.*
Judah was put to *the worse* before Israel; and they fled to their tents. 2 *Kings* xiv. 12.
2. Something less good.
A man, whatever are his professions, always thinks *the worse* of a woman, who forgives him for making an attempt on her virtue. *Clarissa.*

To Worse. *v. a.* [from the adjective.] To put to disadvantage. This word, though analogical enough, is not now used.
Perhaps more valid arms,
Weapons more violent, when next we meet,
May serve to better us, and *worse* our foes. *Milton.*

Wo'rser. *adj.* A barbarous word, formed by corrupting *worse* with the usual comparative termination.
Gods! take my breath from me;
Let not my *worser* spirit tempt me again
To die before you please. *Shakespeare.*
A dreadful quiet felt, and *worser* far
Than arms, a sullen interval of war. *Dryden.*

Wo'rship. *n. s.* [ꝩeoꝛðꞅcyꝑe, Saxon.]
1. Dignity; eminence; excellence.
Thou madest him lower than the angels, to crown him with glory and *worship.* *Ps.* viii. 5.
Elfin born of noble state,
And muckle *worship* in his native land,
Well could he tourney, and in lists debate. *Fairy Queen.*
My train are men of choice, and rarest parts,
That all particulars of duty know;
And in the most exact regard support
The *worship* of their names. *Shakespeare's King Lear.*
2. A character of honour.
I belong to *worship*, and affect
In honour, honesty. *Shakespeare's Hen.* VIII.
Dinner is on table; my father desires your *worship's* company. *Shakesp. Merry Wives of Windsor.*
The old Romans freedom did bestow,
Our princes *worship* with a blow. *Hudibras.*
What lands and lordships for their owner know
My quondam barber, but his *worship* now. *Dryden.*
3. A term of ironical respect.
Against your *worship*, when had S—k writ?
Or P—ge pour'd forth the torrent of his wit? *Pope.*
4. Adoration; religious act of reverence.
They join their vocal *worship* to the quire
Of creatures wanting voice. *Milton.*
He wav'd a torch aloft, and, madly vain,
Sought godlike *worship* from a servile train. *Dryden.*
The *worship* of God is an eminent part of religion, and prayer is a chief part of religious *worship*: hence religion is described by seeking God. *Tillotson.*
There were several inroads into Germany, particularly a voyage of the Egyptians under Osiris up the Danube; from them the Suevi had their *worship* of Isis. *Arbuthnot.*
5. Honour; respect; civil deference.
The humble guest shall have *worship* in the presence of those who sit at meat with him. *Luke* xiv. 10.

Since

Since God hath appointed government among men, it is plain that his intention was, that some kind of *worship* should be given from some to others; for where there is a power to punish and reward, there is a foundation of *worship* in those who are under that power; which *worship* lies in expressing a due regard to that power, by a care not to provoke it, and an endeavour to obtain the favour of it, which, among mankind, is called civil *worship*. *Stillingfleet.*

6. Idolatry of lovers.

'Tis not your inky brows, your black silk hair,
Your bugle eyeballs, nor your cheek of cream
That can entame my spirits to your *worship*. *Shakespeare.*

To Wo'rship. *v. a.* [from the noun.]

1. To adore; to honour or venerate with religious rites.

Thou shalt *worship* no other God. *Exod.* xxxiv. 14.

Let no man beguile you of your reward, in a voluntary humility and *worshipping* of angels. *Col.* ii. 18.

Adore and *worship* God Supreme. *Milton.*

First *worship* God; he that forgets to pray,
Bids not himself good-morrow nor good-day. *T. Randolph.*

On the smooth rind the passenger shall see
Thy name engrav'd, and *worship* Helen's tree. *Dryden.*

2. To respect; to honour; to treat with civil reverence.

Our grave,
Like Turkish mute, shall have a tongueless mouth,
Not *worshipp'd* with a waxen epitaph. *Shakesp. Henry* V.

To Wo'rship. *v. n.* To perform acts of adoration.

I and the lad will go yonder and *worship*. *Gen.* xxii. 5.

The people went to *worship* before the golden calf. 1 *Kings.*

Wo'rshipful. *adj.* [*worship* and *full.*]

1. Claiming respect by any character or dignity.

This is *worshipful* society,
And fits the mounting spirit like myself. *Shakespeare.*

When old age comes upon him, it comes alone, bringing no other evil with it; but when it comes to wait upon a great and *worshipful* sinner, who for many years has ate well and done ill, it is attended with a long train of rheums. *South.*

2. A term of ironical respect.

Every man would think me an hypocrite indeed; and what excites your most *worshipful* thought to think so? *Shakespeare.*

Suppose this *worshipful* idol be made, yet still it wants sense and motion. *Stillingfleet.*

Wo'rshipfully. *adv.* [from *worshipful.*] Respectfully.

Hastings will lose his head, ere give consent,
His master's son, as *worshipfully* he terms it,
Shall lose the royalty of England's throne. *Shakespeare.*

Wo'rshipper. *n. s.* [from *worship.*] Adorer; one that worships.

What art thou, thou idol ceremony?
What kind of god art thou that suffer'st more
Of mortal griefs, than do thy *worshippers*. *Shakes. Henry* V.

Those places did not confine the immensity of God, nor give his *worshippers* a nearer approach to heaven by their height. *South's Sermons.*

If posterity takes its notions of us from our medals, they must fancy one of our kings paid a great devotion to Minerva, that another was a professed *worshipper* of Apollo. *Addison.*

Worst. *adj.* The superlative of *bad*, formed from *worse*: *bad, worse, worst.*] Most bad; most ill.

If thou hadst not been born the *worst* of men,
Thou hadst been knave and flatterer. *Shakespeare.*

The pain that any one actually feels is still of all other the *worst*; and it is with anguish they cry out. *Locke.*

Worst. *n. s.* The most calamitous or wicked state; the utmost height or degree of any thing ill.

Who is't can say, I'm at the *worst*?
I'm worse than e'er I was,
And worse I may be yet: the *worst* is not,
So long as we can say, this is the *worst*. *Shakespeare.*

That you may be armed against the *worst* in this unhappy state of affairs in our distressed country, I send you these considerations on the nature and immortality of the soul. *Digby.*

Happy the man, and happy he alone,
He, who can call to-day his own:
He who secure within can say,
To morrow do thy *worst*, for I have liv'd to day. *Dryden.*

Sir Roger gets into the frontiers of his estate, before he beats about in search of a hare, on purpose to spare his own fields, where he is always sure of finding diversion when the *worst* comes to the *worst*. *Addison's Spectator.*

To Worst. *v. a.* [from the adjective.] To defeat; to overthrow.

The case will be no worse than where two duellists enter the field, where the *worsted* party hath his sword given him again without further hurt. *Suckling.*

The bear was in a greater fright,
Beat down and *worsted* by the knight. *Hudibras.*

It is downright madness to contend where we are sure to be *worsted*. *L'Estrange.*

The victorious Philistines were *worsted* by the captivated ark, which foraged their country more than a conquering army. *South's Sermons.*

She could have brought the chariot again, when she saw her brother *worsted* in the duel. *Dryden's Dedicat.*

Wo'rsted. *n. s.* [from *Worsted*, a town in Norfolk famous for the woolen manufacture.] Woolen yarn; wool spun.

A base, proud, shallow, beggarly three suited, hundred pound, filthy *worsted*-stocking knave. *Shakespeare's King Lear.*

There Ridpath, Roper cudgel'd might ye view;
The very *worsted* still look'd black and blue. *Pope.*

Wort. *n. s.* [ƿyrt, Saxon; *wort*, Dutch.]

1. Originally a general name for an herb; whence it still continues in many, as *liverwort, spleenwort.*

2. A plant of the cabbage kind.

3. [ƿyrt, Saxon.] New beer either unfermented, or in the act of fermentation.

If in the *wort* of beer, while it worketh, before it be tunned, the burrage be often changed with fresh, it will make a sovereign drink for melancholy. *Bacon's Natural History.*

Worth, or *Wurth. v. n.* [ƿeorðan, Saxon.] To be. This word is only now retained in *wo worth*, or *wurth*; *wo* be.

Wo *worth* the man
That first did teach the cursed steel to bite
In his own flesh, and make way to the living sp'rit. *F. Q.*

Worth. In the termination of the names of places comes from ƿorð, a court or farm, or ƿorðiᵹ, a street or road. *Gibson.*

WORTH. *n. s.* [ƿeorð, Saxon.]

1. Price; value.

Your clemency will take in good *worth* the offer of these my simple and mean labours. *Hooker.*

What is *worth* in any thing,
But so much money as 'twill bring? *Hudibras.*

A common marcasite shall have the colour of gold exactly; and yet upon trial yield nothing of *worth* but vitriol and sulphur. *Woodward's Natural History.*

2. Excellence; virtue.

How can you him unworthy then decree;
In whose chief part your *worths* implanted be. *Sidney.*

Is there any man of *worth* and virtue, although not instructed in the school of Christ, that had not rather end the days of this transitory life as Cyrus, than to sink down with them of whom Elihu hath said, *momento moriuntur*. *Hooker.*

Having from these suck'd all they had of *worth*,
And brought home that faith which you carried forth,
I throughly love. *Donne.*

Her virtue, and the conscience of her *worth*
That would be woo'd. *Milton.*

A nymph of your own train
Gives us your character in such a strain,
As none but she, who in that court did dwell,
Could know such *worth*, or *worth* describe so well. *Waller.*

3. Importance; valuable quality.

Peradventure those things whereupon so much time was then well spent, have sithence that lost their dignity and *worth*. *Hooker.*

Take a man possessed with a strong desire of any thing, and the *worth* and excellency of that thing appears much greater than when that desire is quite extinguished. *South's Ser.*

Worth. *adj.*

1. Equal in price to, equal in value to.

Women will love her that she is a woman,
More *worth* than any man: men that she is
The rarest of all women. *Shakespeare's Winter's Tale.*

Your son and daughter found this trespass *worth*
The shame which here it suffers. *Shakespeare.*

You have not thought it *worth* your labour to enter a professed dissent against a philosophy, which the greatest part of the virtuosi of Europe have deserted, as a mere maze of words. *Glanville's Sceptick.*

As if 'tis nothing *worth* that lies conceal'd;
And science is not science till reveal'd? *Dryden.*

At Geneva are merchants reckoned *worth* twenty hundred thousand crowns. *Addison's Italy.*

It is *worth* while to consider how admirably he has turned the course of his narration, and made his husbandman concerned even in what relates to the battle. *Addison.*

2. Deserving of.

The castle appeared to be a place *worth* the keeping, and capable to be made secure against a good army. *Clarendon.*

Here we may reign secure, and, in my choice,
To reign is *worth* ambition, though in hell. *Milton.*

Haste hither Eve, and *worth* thy sight behold,
Eastward among those trees, what glorious shape
Comes this way moving. *Milton's Paradise Lost.*

Whatsoever
Is worthy of their love is *worth* their anger. *Denham.*

This is life indeed; life *worth* preserving;
Such life as Juba never felt till now. *Addison's Cato.*

I have long had it in my thoughts to trouble you with a letter; but was discouraged for want of something that I could think *worth* sending fifteen hundred miles. *Berkley to Pope.*

Many

Many things are *worth* enquiry to one man, which are not so to another. *Watts's Improvement of the Mind.*

3. Equal in possessions to.

Dang'rous rocks,
Which touching but my gentle vessel's side,
Would scatter all the spices on the stream,
Enrobe the roaring waters with my silks;
And in a word, but even now *worth* this,
And now *worth* nothing. *Shakesp Merchant of Venice.*

Although *worth* nothing, he shall be proffered in marriage the best endowed, and most beautiful virgin of their island. *Sandys's Journey.*

WO'RTHILY. *adv.* [from *worthy.*]

1. Suitably; not below the rate of.

The divine original of our souls hath little influence upon us to engage us to walk *worthily* of our extraction, and to do nothing that is base. *Ray.*

2. Deservedly.

They are betray'd
While they pervert pure nature's healthful rules
To loathsome sickness, *worthily*, since they
God's image did not reverence in themselves. *Milton.*

You *worthily* succeed, not only to the honours of your ancestors, but also to their virtues. *Dryden.*

3. Justly; not without cause.

Christian men having, besides the common light of all men, so great help of heavenly direction from above, together with the lamps of so bright examples as the church of God doth yield, it cannot but *worthily* seem reproachful for us to leave both the one and the other. *Hooker.*

The king is present; if 't be known to him
That I gainsay my deed, how may he wound,
And *worthily*, my falshood. *Shakesp. Henry VIII.*

A Christian cannot lawfully hate any one; and yet I affirm that some may very *worthily* deserve to be hated; and of all, the deceiver deserves it most. *South's Sermons.*

WO'RTHINESS. *n. s.* [from *worthy.*]

1. Desert.

The prayers which our Saviour made were for his own *worthiness* accepted, ours God accepteth not, but with this condition, if they be joined with a belief in Christ. *Hooker.*

2. Excellence; dignity; virtue.

Determining never to marry but him, whom she thought worthy of her; and that was one in whom all *worthinesses* were harboured. *Sidney.*

He that is at all times good, must hold his virtue to you, whose *worthiness* would stir it up where it wanted, rather than slack it where there is such abundance. *Shakespeare.*

Who is sure he hath a soul, unless
It see and judge, and follow *worthiness*,
And by deeds praise it? he who doth not this,
May lodge an inmate soul, but 'tis not his. *Donne.*

What set my thoughts on work was the *worthiness* and curiosity of the subject in itself. *Holder.*

3. State of being worthy; quality of deserving.

She is not worthy to be loved, that hath not some feeling of her own *worthiness*. *Sidney.*

WO'RTHLESS, *adj.* [from *worth.*]

1. Having no virtues, dignity, or excellence.

You, his false hopes, the trust of England's honour,
Keep off aloof with *worthless* emulation. *Shakespeare.*

A little time will melt her frozen thoughts,
And *worthless* Valentine shall be forgot. *Shakespeare.*

On Laura's lap you lay,
Chiding the *worthless* crowd away. *Roscommon.*

2. Having no value.

My anxious pains we all the day,
In search of what we like, employ:
Scorning at night the *worthless* prey,
We find the labour gave the joy. *Prior.*

Am I then doom'd to fall
By a boy's hand? and for a *worthless* woman? *Addison.*

WO'RTHLESSNESS. *n. s.* [from *worthless.*] Want of excellence; want of dignity; want of value.

But that mine own *worthlessness* spoils the conceit, I could think our company parallel to the seven wise men of Greece. *More's Divine Dialogues.*

A notable account is given us by the apostle of this windy insignificant charity of the will, and of the *worthlessness* of it, not enlivened by deeds. *South's Sermons.*

WO'RTHY. *adj.* [from *worth.*]

1. Deserving; such as merits: with *of* before the thing deserved.

She determined never to marry any but him, whom she thought *worthy of* her, and that was one in whom all worthinesses were harboured. *Sidney.*

Further, I will not flatter you,
That all I see in you is *worthy* love,
Than this; that nothing do I see in you
That should merit hate. *Shakespeare's King John.*

Thou art *worthy of* the sway,
To whom the heav'ns in thy nativity
Adjudg'd an olive branch and laurel crown. *Shakespeare.*

2. Valuable; noble; illustrious; having excellence or dignity.

If the best things have the perfectest and best operations, it will follow, that seeing man is the *worthiest* creature on earth, and every society of men more *worthy* than any man, and of society that is the most excellent which we call the church. *Hooker.*

He now on Pompey's basis lies along,
No *worthier* than the dust? *Shakespeare's Julius Cæsar.*

A war upon the Turks is more *worthy* than upon any other Gentiles in point of religion and honour; though hope of success might invite some other choice. *Bacon.*

Think of her worth, and think that God did mean,
This *worthy* mind should *worthy* things embrace:
Blot not her beauties with thy thoughts unclean,
Nor her dishonour with thy passion base. *Davies.*

Happier thou may'st be, *worthier* canst not be. *Milton.*

3. Having worth; having virtue.

The doctor is well money'd, and his friends
Potent at court; he, none but he, shall have her;
Though twenty thousand *worthier* come to crave her. *Shak.*

The matter I handle is the most important within the whole extent of human nature, for a *worthy* person to employ himself about. *Digby on the Soul.*

We see, though order'd for the best,
Permitted laurels grace the lawless brow,
Th' unworthy rais'd, the *worthy* cast below. *Dryden.*

4. Not good. A term of ironical celebration.

My *worthy* wife our arms mislaid,
And from beneath my head my sword convey'd;
The door unlatch'd; and with repeated calls
Invites her former lord within my walls. *Dryden.*

5. Suitable for any quality good or bad; equal in value; equal in dignity.

Flowers *worthy* of paradise. *Milton.*

Thou, Drances, art below a death from me:
Let that vile soul in that vile body rest,
The lodging is well *worthy* of the guest. *Dryden.*

My suff'rings for you make your heart my due;
Be *worthy* me, as I am *worthy* you. *Dryden.*

6. Suitable to any thing bad.

The merciless Macdonald,
Worthy to be a rebel; for to that
The multiplying villanies of nature
Do swarm upon him. *Shakespeare's Macbeth.*

7. Deserving of ill.

What has he done to Rome that's *worthy* death. *Shakesp.*

If the wicked man be *worthy* to be beaten, the judge shall cause him to be beaten. *Deut.* xxv. 2.

WO'RTHY. *n. s.* [from the adjective.] A man laudable for any eminent quality, particularly for valour.

Such as are constellated unto knowledge come short of themselves if they go not beyond others, and must not sit down under the degree of *worthies*. *Brown's Vulgar Errours.*

What do these *worthies*
But rob and spoil, burn, slaughter, and enslave
Peaceable nations. *Milton's Paradise Regained.*

No *worthies* form'd by any muse but thine
Could purchase robes, to make themselves so fine. *Waller.*

For this day's palm, and for thy former acts,
Thou Arthur hast acquir'd a future fame,
And of three Christian *worthies* art the first. *Dryden.*

The next *worthy* came in with a retinue of historians. *Tatler.*

To WO'RTHY. *v. a.* [from the adjective.] To render worthy; to aggrandise; to exalt. Not used.

He conjunct, trip'd me behind;
And put upon him such a deal of man,
That *worthied* him; got praises of the king,
For him attempting, who was self-subdu'd. *Shakespeare.*

To WOT. *v. n.* [pitan, Saxon; whence *weet*, to know; of which the preterite was *wot*, knew; which by degrees was mistaken for the present tense.] To know; to be aware. Obsolete.

The salve of reformation they mightily call for, but where, and what the sores are which need it, as they *wot* full little, so they think not greatly material to search. *Hooker.*

Well I *wot*, compar'd to all the rest
Of each degree, that beggar's life is best. *Hubberd.*

More water glideth by the mill
Than *wots* the miller of. *Shakespeare.*

Wot you, what I found?
Forsooth, an inventory, thus importing. *Shakespeare.*

WOVE. The preterite and participle passive of *weave.*

Adam, waiting her return, had *wove*
Of choicest flow'rs, a garland. *Milton.*

WO'VEN. The participle passive of *weave.*

WOULD. The preterite of *will.*

1. It is generally used as an auxiliary verb with an infinitive, to which it gives the force of the subjunctive mood.

If God's providence did not so order it, cheats *would* daily be committed, which would justle private men out of their rights, and unhinge states. *Ray.*

2. *I* Would *do it.* My reſolution is that it ſhould be done by me.
Thou Wou'ldest *do it.* Such muſt be the conſequence to thee.
He Would or *it would.* This muſt be the conſequence to *him* or *it.*
3. The plural as the ſingular.

He by the rules of his own mind, could conſtrue no other end of mens doings but ſelf-ſeeking, ſuddenly feared what they could do, and as ſuddenly ſuſpected what they *would* do, and as ſuddenly hated them, as having both might and mind ſo to do. *Sidney.*

4. Was or am reſolved; wiſh or wiſhed to.

She *would* give her a leſſon for walking ſo late, that ſhould make her keep within doors for one fortnight. *Sidney.*

Jealous Philoclea, that was even jealous of herſelf; for Zelmane *would* needs have her glove. *Sidney.*

You *would* be ſatisfied?—
Would? nay, and will. *Shakeſpeare's Othello.*

They know not what they are, nor what they *would* be, any further than that they *would* not be what they are. *L'Eſtr.*

It will be needleſs to enumerate all the ſimple ideas belonging to each ſenſe: nor indeed is it poſſible if we *would*; there being a great many more of them belonging to moſt of the ſenſes than we have names for. *Locke.*

By pleaſure and pain I *would* be underſtood to ſignify, whatſoever delights or moleſts us, whether from the thoughts of our minds, or any thing operating on our bodies. *Locke.*

5. It is a familiar term for *wiſh to do,* or *to have.*

What *would'ſt* thou with us? *Shakeſpeare's King Lear.*
Mr. Slender, what *would* you with me?—
—I *Would* little or nothing with you. *Shakeſpeare.*

6. Should wiſh.

Celia! if you apprehend
The muſe of your incenſed friend;
Nor *would* that he record your blame,
And make it live; repeat the ſame;
Again deceive him, and again,
And then he ſwears he'll not complain. *Waller.*

7. It is uſed in old authours for *ſhould.*

The exceſs of diet *would* be avoided. *Bacon.*

As for percolation, which belongeth to ſeparation, trial *would* be made by clarifying by adheſion, with milk put into new beer and ſtirred with it. *Bacon's Natural Hiſtory.*

8. It has the ſignification of I wiſh, or I pray; this, I believe, is improper; and formed by a gradual corruption of the phraſe, *would God;* which originally imported, *that God would, might God will, might God decree;* from this phraſe ill underſtood came, *would to God;* thence, *I would to God:* And thence *I would,* or elliptically, *would* come to ſignify, *I wiſh:* and ſo it is uſed even in good authours, but ought not to be imitated.

I would my father look'd but with my eyes. *Shakeſpeare.*
I would this muſick would come. *Shakeſpeare.*
I, this ſound I better know:

Wiſe men will do it without a law; I *would* there might be a law to reſtrain fools. *Bacon's Advice to Villiers.*

Liſt! *I would* I could hear mo. *Ben. Johnſon.*

This is yet the outward, faireſt ſide
Of our deſign: within reſts more of fear
Than my moſt worthy lords, *I would* there were. *Daniel.*
Would thou hadſt hearken'd to my words, and ſtay'd
With me, as I beſought thee, when that ſtrange
Deſire of wand'ring, this unhappy morn,
Poſſeſs'd thee. *Milton's Paradiſe Loſt.*

Would God we might prevent the need of ſuch unkindly expedients, and by a thankful ſenſe of what we have, provide to conſerve it. *Decay of Piety.*

I ſcarce am pleas'd, I tamely mount the throne,
Would Aurengzebe had all their ſouls in one. *Dryden.*
And *would* to heav'n the ſtorm you felt, would bring
On Carthaginian coaſts your wand'ring king. *Dryden.*

Wou'lding. *n. ſ.* [from *would.*] Motion of deſire; diſpoſition to any thing; propenſion; inclination; incipient purpoſe.

It will be every man's intereſt to join good performances to ſpiritual purpoſes, to ſubdue the exorbitancies of the fleſh, as well as to continue the *wouldings* of the ſpirit. *Hammond.*

Wound. *n. ſ.* [punꝺ, Saxon; *wonde,* Dutch.] A hurt given by violence.

I am faint; my gaſhes cry for help.—
—So well thy words become thee as thy *wounds,*
They ſmack of honour both. *Shakepeare's Macbeth.*
Now ſhew the *wound* mine eyes have made in thee;
Scratch thee but with a pin, and there remains
Some ſcar of it. *Shakeſpeare.*
He ſtooping, open'd my left ſide, and took
From thence a rib: wide was the *wound,*
But ſuddenly fill'd up and heal'd. *Milton.*

The aliment of ſuch as have freſh *wounds* ſhould be mild without ſtimulating or ſaline ſubſtances. *Arbuthnot on Aliments.*

They feel the ſmart and ſee the ſcar of their former *wounds;* and know that they muſt be made a ſacrifice to the leaſt attempt towards a change. *Swift.*

To Wound. *v. a.* [from the noun] To hurt by violence.

Th' untented *woundings* of a father's curſe
Pierce ev'ry ſence about thee. *Shakeſpeare's King Lear.*
I kill, and I make alive; I *wound,* and I heal. *Deut.*

The battle went ſore againſt Saul, and the archers hit him, and he was ſore *wounded.* 1 *Sam.* xxxi. 3.

God ſhall *wound* the head of his enemies. *Pſalm* lxviii. 21.

He was *wounded* for our tranſgreſſions, he was bruiſed for our iniquities. *Iſa.* liii. 5.

When ye ſin ſo againſt the brethren, and *wound* their weak conſcience, ye ſin againſt Chriſt. 1 *Cor.* viii. 12.

Adonis from his native rock
Ran purple to the ſea, ſuppos'd with blood
Of Thammuz, yearly *wounded.* *Milton.*
Heroes of old, when *wounded* ſhelter ſought. *Dryden.*

The ſavages *wounded* Atkins, and ſlew his followers. *Robinſon Cruſoe.*

Wound. The preterite and participle paſſive of *wind.*

They took the body of Jeſus and *wound* it in linen cloaths, with the ſpices. *John.* xix. 40.

All will be but like bottoms of thread cloſe *wound* up. *Bacon.*

The young men *wound* him up, and buried him. *Acts* v.

Theſe mathematical engines cannot be ſo eaſily and ſpeedily *wound* up, and ſo certainly levelled as the other. *Wilkins.*

The parliament being called here, and the main ſettlement of Ireland *wound* up in England, and put into the Duke of Ormond's hands to paſs here into an act, all perſons came over in a ſhoal. *Temple.*

Wou'ndless. *adj.* [from *wound.*] Exempt from wounds.

Wou'ndwort. *n. ſ.* [*vulneraria,* Latin.] A plant.

It hath a papilionaceous flower, out of whoſe tubular and turgid empalement ariſes the pointal, which afterward becomes a ſhort pod, filled with roundiſh ſeeds: the pod is encloſ'd in a membranous bladder was before the empalement. *Miller.*

Wou'ndy. *adj.* Exceſſive. A low bad word.

We have a world of holydays; that 'tis a *woundy* hindrance to a poor man that lives by his labour. *L'Eſtrange.*

Theſe ſtockings of Suſan's coſt a *woundy* deal of pains the pulling on. *Gay.*

Wox. }
Woxe. } The preterite of *wax.* Became. Obſolete.

The ape in wond'rous ſtomach *wox,*
Strongly encourag'd by the crafty fox. *Hubberd.*
Not one puff of wind there did appear,
That all the three the great *wox* much afraid. *Spenſer.*

Wo'xen. The participle of *to wax.* Obſolete. *Spenſer.*

Wrack. *n. ſ.* [*wrack,* Dutch; ꝑræcce, Saxon, a wretch; the poets uſe *wrack* or *wreck* indifferently as rhyme requires, the later writers of proſe commonly *wreck.* See Wreck.]

1. Deſtruction of a ſhip by winds or rocks.

Now, with full ſails into the port I move,
And ſafely can unlade my breaſt of love;
Quiet and calm: why ſhould I then go back,
To tempt the ſecond hazard of a *wrack.* *Dryden.*

2. Ruin; deſtruction. This is the true Saxon meaning.

With uſe of evil, growing more and more evil, they took delight in ſlaughter, and pleaſed themſelves in making others *wrack* the effect of their power. *Sidney.*

A world devote to univerſal *wrack.* *Milton.*

To Wrack. *v. a.* [from the noun.]

1. To deſtroy in the water; to wreck. [See Wreck.]
2. It ſeems in *Milton* to mean to *rock,* to ſhake.

Each on his rock transfix'd, the ſport and prey
Of *wracking* whirlwinds. *Milton.*

3. To torture, to torment. This is commonly written *rack;* and the inſtrument of torture, always *rack.*

Merab rejoic'd in her *wrack'd* lover's pain,
And fortify'd her virtue with diſdain. *Cowley.*

Pharaoh's and Joſeph's dreams are oftentimes *wracked* beyond their ſymbolization. *Brown's Vulgar Errours.*

To Wra'ngle. *v. n.* [from *wrangheſeur,* Dutch. *Minſhew. wrong, Skinner.*] To diſpute peeviſhly; to quarrel perverſely; to altercate; to ſquabble.

Yes, for a ſcore of kingdoms you ſhould *wrangle,*
And I would call it fair play. *Shakeſpeare's Tempeſt.*
Some unhatch'd practice
Hath puddled his clear ſpirit; and in ſuch caſes,
Men's natures *wrangle* with inferiour things,
Though great ones are their object. *Shakeſpeare's Othello.*

How wounding a ſpectacle is it to ſee thoſe who were by Chriſt deſigned for fiſhers of men, picking up ſhells on the ſhore, and unmanly *wrangling* about them too. *Decay of P.*

In incompleat ideas we impoſe on ourſelves, and *wrangle* with others. *Locke.*

Amongſt unthinking men, who examine not ſcrupulouſly ideas, but confound them with words, there muſt be endleſs diſpute and *wrangling.* *Locke.*

His great application to the law had not infected his temper with any thing litigious; he did not know what it was to *wrangle* on indifferent points. *Addiſon's Freeholder.*

Fill'd with the sense of age, the fire of youth,
A scorn of *wrangling*, yet a zeal for truth. *Pope.*
And all the question, *wrangle* e'er so long,
Is only this, if God has plac'd him wrong. *Pope.*

WRA'NGLE. *n. s.* [from the verb.] A quarrel; a perverse dispute.

The giving the priest a right to the tithe would produce law-suits and *wrangles*. *Swift.*

WRA'NGLER. *n. s.* [from *wrangle.*] A perverse, peevish, disputative man.

Tell him h'ath made a match with such a *wrangler*,
That all the courts of France will be disturb'd
With chases. *Shakespeare's Henry* V.
Lord, the house and family are thine,
Though some of them repine;
Turn out these *wranglers*, which defile thy seat:
For where thou dwellest all is neat. *Herbert.*

You should be free in every answer, rather like well-bred gentlemen in polite conversation, than like noisy and contentious *wranglers*. *Watts's Improvement of the Mind.*

To WRAP. *v. a.* [ƿꞃeopꞃian, Saxon, to turn; *wreffler*, Danish.]

1. To roll together; to complicate.

Peter seeth the napkin that was about his head *wrapped* together by itself. *John* xx. 7.
This said, he took his mantle's foremost part,
He 'gan the same together fold and *wrap*. *Fairfax.*

2. To involve; to cover with something rolled or thrown round.

Nilus opens wide
His arms, and ample bosom to the tide,
And spreads his mantle o'er the winding coast:
In which he *wraps* his queen and hides the flying host. *Dryden.*

The sword made bright is *wrapt* up for the slaughter. *Ezek.*
Their vigilance to elude, I *wrapt* in mist
Of midnight vapour glide obscure. *Milton.*

Wrap candles up in paper. *Swift's Directions to the Butler.*

3. To comprise; to contain.

Leontine's young wife, in whom all his happiness was *wrapt* up, died in a few days after the death of her daughter. *Addison.*

4. *To* WRAP *up.* To involve totally.

Some dear cause
Will in concealment *wrap* me *up* a while;
When I am known aright, you shall not grieve
Lending me this acquaintance. *Shakespeare's King Lear.*

King John fled to Lascus, who was careful how to comfort him, *wrapt up* in so many calamities, after the loss of his kingdom. *Knolles's History of the Turks.*

Things reflected on, in gross and transiently, carry the shew of nothing but difficulty in them, and are thought to be *wrapped up* in impenetrable obscurity. *Locke.*

5. [It is often corruptly written for *rap* or *rapt*, from *rapio*, Latin.] To snatch up miraculously.

Whatever things were discovered to St. Paul, when he was *wrapped* up into the third heaven, all the description he makes is, that there are such things as eye hath not seen, ear heard, nor hath it entered into the heart of man to conceive. *Locke.*

6. To transport; to put in ecstasy.

Much more the reverent sire prepar'd to say,
Wrap'd with his joy; how the two armies lay. *Cowley.*

7. [Perhaps the following passage should properly be *rap'd*; though *wrapped* is now frequently used in this sense.]

Wrapt up in silent fear he lies. *Waller.*
Wrap'd in amaze the matrons wildly stare. *Dryden.*

WRA'PPER. *n. s.* [from *wrap.*]

1. One that wraps.

2. That in which any thing is wrapped.

My arms were pressed to my sides, and my legs closed together by so many *wrappers*, that I looked like an Egyptian mummy. *Addison's Spectator.*

WRATH. *n. s.* [ƿꞃað, Saxon; *wrede*, Danish; *wreed*, cruel, Dutch.] Anger; fury; rage.

Thou dost the prayers of the righteous seed
Present before the majesty divine,
And his avenging *wrath* to clemency incline. *Fairy Queen.*
With one fool's head I came to *woo*,
But I go away with two:
Sweet, adieu! I'll keep my oath,
Patiently to bear my *wrath*. *Shak. Merch. of Venice.*

I fear,—lest there be debates, envyings, *wraths*, strifes. *Cor.*
He hop'd not to escape, but shun
The present, fearing guilty what his *wrath*
Might suddenly inflict. *Milton.*

WRA'THFUL. *adj.* [*wrath* and *full.*] Angry; furious; raging.

He cry'd, as raging seas are wont to roar,
When wintry storm his *wrathful* wreck doth threat. *Fairy Queen.*
Fly from wrath:
Sad be the fights, and bitter fruits of war,
And thousand furies wait on *wrathful* swords. *Fa. Queen.*
How now, your *wrathful* weapons drawn. *Shakespeare.*

The true evangelical zeal should abound more in the mild and good natured affections, than the vehement and *wrathful* passions. *Sprat's Sermons.*

WRA'THFULLY. *adv.* [from *wrathful.*] Furiously; passionately.

———Gentle friends,
Let's kill him boldly, but not *wrathfully*. *Shakespeare.*

WRA'THLESS. *adj.* [from *wrath.*] Free from anger.

Before his feet, so sheep and lions lay,
Fearless and *wrathless*, while they heard him play. *Waller.*

To WREAK. *v. a.* Old preterite and part. pass. of *wroke*. [ƿꞃæcan, Saxon; *wrecken*, Dutch; *recken*, German.]

1. To revenge.

In an ill hour thy foes thee hither sent,
Another's wrongs to *wreak* upon thy self. *Fairy Queen.*
Him all that while occasion did provoke
Against Pyrocles, and new matter fram'd
Upon the old, him stirring to be *wroke*
Of his late wrongs. *Fairy Queen.*
Pale death our valiant leader hath opprest,
Come *wreak* his loss, whom bootless ye complain. *Fairfax.*

2. To execute any violent design. This is the sense in which it is now used.

On me let death *wreak* all his rage. *Milton.*
He left the dame,
Resolv'd to spare her life, and save her shame,
But that detested object to remove,
To *wreck* his vengeance, and to cure her love. *Dryden.*
Think how you drove him hence, a wand'ring exile,
To distant climes, then think what certain vengeance
His rage may *wreak* on your unhappy orphan. *Smith.*
Her husband scour'd away,
To *wreak* his hunger on the destin'd prey. *Pope.*

3. It is corruptly written for *reck*, to heed; to care.

My master is of churlish disposition,
And little *wreaks* to find the way to heav'n
By doing deeds of hospitality. *Shak. As you like it.*

WREAK. *n. s.* [from the verb.]

1. Revenge; vengeance.

Fortune, mine avowed foe,
Her wrathful *wreaks* themselves do now allay. *Fa. Queen.*
Join with the Goths, and with revengeful war
Take *wreak* on Rome for this ingratitude,
And vengeance on the traitor Saturnine. *Shakes. Tit. Andr.*

2. Passion; furious fit.

What and if
His sorrows have so overwhelm'd his wits,
Shall we be thus afflicted in his *wreaks*,
His fits, his frenzy, and his bitterness? *Shakesp. Tit. Andr.*

WRE'AKFUL. *adj.* [from *wreak.*] Revengeful; angry.

Call the creatures,
Whose naked natures live in all the spite
Of *wreakful* heaven. *Shakespeare.*
She in Olympus' top
Must visit Vulcan for new arms, to serve her *wreakful* son. *Chapman's Iliad.*

WRE'AKLESS. *adj.* [I know not whether this word be miswritten for *reckless*, careless; or comes from *wreak*, revenge, and means unrevenging.]

So flies the *wreakless* shepherd from the wolf;
So first the harmless flock doth yield his fleece,
And next his throat unto the butcher's knife. *Shakes. H.* VI.

WREATH. *n. s.* [ƿꞃeoð, Saxon.]

1. Any thing curled or twisted.

The *wreath* of three was made a *wreath* of five: to these three first titles of the two houses, were added the authorities parliamentary and papal. *Bacon's Henry* VII.

Clouds began
To darken all the hill, and smoke to roll
In dusky *wreaths* reluctant flames. *Milton's Par. Lost.*
He of his tortuous train
Curl'd many a wanton *wreath*. *Milton.*
Let altars smoak,
And richest gums, and spice, and incense roll
Their fragrant *wreaths* to heav'n. *Smith's Phæd. and Hip.*

2. A garland; a chaplet.

Now are our brows bound with victorious *wreaths*,
Our bruised arms hung up for monuments. *Shakesp. R.* III.
Dropp'd from his head, a *wreath* lay on the ground. *Roscommon.*
The boughs of Lotos, form'd into a *wreath*,
This monument, thy maiden beauty's due,
High on a plane-tree shall be hung to view. *Dryden.*
When for thy head the garland I prepare,
A second *wreath* shall bind Aminta's hair;
And when my choicest songs thy worth proclaim,
Alternate verse shall bless Aminta's name. *Prior.*

To prince Henry the laurels of his rival are transferred, with the additional *wreath* of having conquered that rival. *Shakespeare Illustrated.*

To WREATH. *v. a.* preterite *wreathed*; part. paſſ. *wreathed*, *wreathen*. [from the noun.]

1. To curl; to twiſt; to convolve.

Longaville
Did never ſonnet for her ſake compile,
Nor never laid his *wreathed* arms athwart
His loving boſom, to keep down his heart. *Shakeſpeare.*

About his neck
A green and gilded ſnake had *wreath'd* itſelf,
Who, with her head, nimble in threats approach'd
The opening of his mouth; but ſuddenly,
Seeing Orlando, it unlink'd itſelf,
And with indented glides did ſlip away. *Shak. As you like it.*

The beard of an oat is *wreathed* at the bottom, and one ſmooth entire ſtraw at the top: they take only the part that is *wreathed*, and cut off the other. *Bacon.*

2. It is here uſed for to *writhe*.

Impatient of the wound,
He rolls and *wreaths* his ſhining body round;
Then headlong ſhoots beneath the daſhing tide. *Gay.*

3. To interweave; to entwine one in another.

Two chains of pure gold of *wreathen* work ſhalt thou make them, and faſten the *wreathen* chains to the ouches. *Ex.* xxviii.

As ſnakes breed in dunghills not ſingly, but in knots; ſo in ſuch baſe noiſome hearts you ſhall ever ſee pride and ingratitude indiviſibly *wreathed* and twiſted together. *South.*

Here, where the labourer's hands have form'd a bow'r
Of *wreathing* trees, in ſinging waſte an hour. *Dryden.*

4. To encircle as a garland.

In the flow'rs that *wreath* the ſparkling bowl,
Fell adders hiſs, and pois'nous ſerpents rowl. *Prior.*

5. To encircle as with a garland.

For thee ſhe feeds her hair,
And with thy winding ivy *wreathes* her lance. *Dryden.*

The ſoldier, from ſucceſsful camps returning,
With laurel *wreath'd*, and rich with hoſtile ſpoil,
Severs the bull to Mars. *Prior.*

WRE'ATHY. *adj.* [from *wreath*] Spiral; curled; twiſted.

That which is preſerved at St. Dennis, near Paris, hath *wreathy* ſpires, and cochleary turnings about, which agreeth with the deſcription of an unicorn's horn in Ælian. *Brown.*

WRECK. *n. ſ.* [ƿꞃæcce, Saxon, a miſerable perſon; *wracke*, Dutch, a ſhip broken.]

1. Deſtruction by being driven on rocks or ſhallows at ſea; deſtruction by ſea.

Fair be ye ſure; but hard and obſtinate,
As is a rock amidſt the raging floods;
'Gainſt which a ſhip, of ſuccour deſolate,
Doth ſuffer *wreck* both of herſelf and goods. *Spenſer.*

Like thoſe that ſee their *wreck*
Ev'n on the rocks of death; and yet they ſtrain,
That death may not them idly find t' attend
To their uncertain taſk, but work to meet their end. *Daniel.*

Think not that flying fame reports my fate;
I preſent, I appear, and my own *wreck* relate. *Dryden.*

2. Diſſolution by violence.

Not only Paradiſe,
In this commotion, but the ſtarry cope
Had gone to *wreck*. *Milton's Paradiſe Loſt.*

3. Ruin; deſtruction.

Whether he was
Combin'd with Norway, or did line the rebel
With hidden help and vantage; or that with both
He labour'd in his country's *wreck*, I know not. *Shakeſp.*

4. It is miſprinted here for *wreak*.

He cry'd as raging ſeas are wont to roar,
When wintry ſtorm his wrathful *wreck* doth threat. *Spenſer.*

To WRECK. *v. a.* [from the noun.]

1. To deſtroy by daſhing on rocks or ſands.

Have there been any more ſuch tempeſts, wherein ſhe hath wretchedly been *wrecked?* *Spenſer on Ireland.*

A pilot's thumb,
Wreck'd as homeward he did come. *Shakeſ. Macbeth.*

The coral found growing upon *wrecked* ſhips and loſt anchors, that are daily dragged up out of the ſea, demonſtrates that coral continues to be formed to this day. *Woodward.*

2. To ruin.

Weak and envy'd, if they ſhould conſpire,
They *wreck* themſelves, and he hath his deſire. *Daniel.*

3. In the following paſſages it is ignorantly uſed for *wreak*, in its different ſenſes of *revenge* and *execute*.

Eighty odd years of ſorrow have I ſeen,
And each hour's joy *wreck'd* with a week of teen. *Shakeſp.*

I faint! I die! the goddeſs cry'd:
O cruel, could'ſt thou find none other
To *wreck* thy ſpleen on? Parricide!
Like Nero, thou haſt ſlain thy mother. *Prior.*

To WRECK. *v. n.* To ſuffer wreck.

With manlier objects we muſt try
His conſtancy, with ſuch as have more ſhew
Of worth, of honour, glory, and popular praiſe,
Rocks whereon greateſt men have often *wreck'd*. *Milton.*

WREN. *n. ſ.* [ƿꞃenna, Saxon.] A ſmall bird.

The poor *wren*,
The moſt diminutive of birds, will fight,
Her young ones in her neſt, againſt the owl. *Shakeſp. Macb.*

All ages have conceived that the *wren* is the leaſt of birds, yet the diſcoveries of America have ſhewed us one far leſs, the hum-bird not much exceeding a beetle. *Brown's Vulgar Errours.*

To WRENCH. *v. a.* [ƿꞃingan, Saxon; *wrenghen*, Dutch.]

1. To pull by violence; to wreſt; to force.

Wrench his ſword from him. *Shakeſ. Othello.*

Oh form!
How often do'ſt thou with thy caſe, thy habit,
Wrench awe from fools, and tie the wiſer ſouls
To thy falſe ſeeming! *Shak. Meaſure for Meaſure.*

Give me that mattock and the *wrenching* iron. *Shakeſp.*

Cæſar's army, wanting ſomething, demanded a miſſion or diſcharge, though with no intention it ſhould be granted; but thought by that means to *wrench* him to their other deſires. *Bacon.*

Sing the Parthian, when transfix'd he lies,
Wrenching the Roman jav'lin from his thighs. *Dryden.*

Achilles *wrench'd* it out, and ſent again
The hoſtile gift. *Dryden.*

Struggling to get looſe, I broke the ſtrings, and *wrenched* out the pegs that faſtened my arm to the ground. *Gull. Travels.*

2. To ſprain; to diſtort.

O moſt ſmall fault!
How ugly didſt thou in Cordelia ſhow?
Which, like an engine, *wrencht* my frame of nature
From the fix'd place; drew from my heart all love,
And added to the gall. *Shakeſp. King Lear.*

You *wrenched* your foot againſt a ſtone, and were forced to ſtay. *Swift.*

WRENCH. *n. ſ.* [from the verb.]

1. A violent pull or twiſt.

2. A ſprain.

Some ſmall part of the foot being injured by a *wrench*, the whole leg thereby loſes its ſtrength. *Locke.*

3. WRENCHES, in *Chaucer*, ſignifies means, ſleights, ſubtilties; which is, I believe, the ſenſe here.

He reſolved to make his profit of this buſineſs of Britain, as a quarrel for war; and that of Naples as a *wrench* and mean for peace. *Bacon's Henry* VII.

To WREST. *v. a.* [ƿꞃæſtan, Saxon.]

1. To twiſt by violence; to extort by writhing or force.

To wring this ſentence, to *wreſt* thereby out of men's hands the knowledge of God's doctrine, is without all reaſon. *Aſcham.*

To what wretched ſtate reſerv'd,
Better end here unborn! Why is life giv'n,
To be thus *wreſted* from us? *Milton's Paradiſe Loſt.*

Where you charged in perſon, you were a conqueror: the rebels afterwards recovered ſtrength, and *wreſted* that victory from others that they had loſt to you. *Dryden.*

Our country's cauſe,
That drew our ſwords, now *wreſts* 'em from our hand,
And bids us not delight in Roman blood,
Unprofitably ſhed. *Addiſon's Cato.*

O prince, I bluſh to think what I have ſaid;
But fate has *wreſted* the confeſſion from me. *Addiſon.*

2. To diſtort; to writhe; to force.

So far to extend their ſpeeches, is to *wreſt* them againſt their meaning. *Hooker.*

My father's purpoſes have been miſtook,
And ſome about him have too laviſhly
Wreſted his meaning and authority. *Shakeſp. Henry* IV.

Wreſt once the law to your authority;
To do a great right, do a little wrong. *Shakeſpeare.*

WREST. *n. ſ.* [from the verb.]

1. Diſtortion; violence.

Whereas it is concluded, out of thoſe ſo weak premiſes, that the retaining of divers things in the church of England, which other reformed churches have caſt out, muſt needs argue that we do not well, unleſs we can ſhew that they have done ill: what needed this *wreſt*, to draw out from us an accuſation of foreign churches? *Hooker.*

2. It is uſed in *Spenſer* and *Shakeſpeare* for an active or moving power: I ſuppoſe, from the force of a tilter acting with his lance in his reſt.

Adown he keſt it with ſo puiſſant *wreſt*,
That back again it did aloft rebound,
And gave againſt his mother earth a groneful ſound. *F. Q.*

Antenor is ſuch a *wreſt* in their affairs,
That their negotiations all muſt ſlack'n,
Wanting his manage. *Shakeſ. Troilus and Creſſida.*

WRESTER. *n. ſ.* [from *wreſt*.] He who wreſts.

To WRE'STLE. *v. n.* [from *wreſt*.]

1. To contend who ſhall throw the other down.

You have loſt the ſight of good *wreſtling*. *Shakeſpeare.*

If ever he goes alone again, I'll never *wreſtle* for prize more. *Shakeſ. As you like it.*

Another, by a fall in *wreſtling*, ſtarted the end of the clavicle from the ſternon. *Wiſeman's Surgery.*

To play or *wreſtle* well, it ſhould be uſed with thoſe that do it better. *Temple.*

None in the leap ſpring with ſo ſtrong a bound,
Or firmer in the *wreſtling* preſs the ground. *Pope.*

2. To ſtruggle; to contend.

I perſuaded them, if they lov'd Benedick,
To wiſh him *wreſtle* with affection,
And never to let Beatrice know of it. *Shakeſpeare.*

He knew not how to *wreſtle* with deſperate contingencies, and ſo abhorred to be entangled in ſuch. *Clarendon.*

WRE'STLER. *n. ſ.* [from *wreſtle.*]

1. One who wreſtles; one who profeſſes the athletick art.

Was not Charles, the duke's *wreſtler*, here? *Shakeſp.*

When the young *wreſtlers* at their ſport grew warm,
Old Milo wept, to ſee his naked arm. *Denham.*

'Tis not from whom, but where we live;
The place does oft thoſe graces give:
Great Julius, on the mountains bred,
A flock perhaps, or herd, had led;
He that the world ſubdu'd, had been
But the beſt *wreſtler* on the green. *Waller.*

2. One who contends in wreſtling.

So earneſt with thy God, can no new care,
No ſenſe of danger, interrupt thy prayer?
The ſacred *wreſtler*, 'till a bleſſing giv'n,
Quits not his hold, but halting conquers heav'n. *Waller.*

Two *wreſtlers* help to pull each other down. *Dryden.*

WRETCH. *n. ſ.* [ƿꞃecca, Saxon.]

1. A miſerable mortal.

When I loved, I was a *wretch.* *Accidence.*

She weeps, and ſays her Henry is depos'd;
He ſmiles, and ſays his Edward is inſtall'd;
That ſhe, poor *wretch*, for grief can ſpeak no more. *Shak.*

The butcher takes away the calf,
And binds the *wretch*, and beats it when it ſtrives. *Shakeſp.*

Illuſtrious *wretch!* repine not, nor reply:
View not what heav'n ordains, with reaſon's eye;
For bright the object is, the diſtance is too high. *Prior.*

2. A worthleſs ſorry creature.

Baſe-minded *wretches*, are your thoughts ſo deeply bemired in the trade of ordinary worldlings, as for reſpect of gain ſome paultry wool may yield you, to let ſo much time paſs without knowing perfectly her eſtate? *Sidney.*

He now
Has theſe poor men in queſtion: never ſaw I
Wretches ſo quake; they kneel, they kiſs the earth,
Forſwear themſelves as often as they ſpeak. *Shakeſpeare.*

Title of honour, worth and virtue's right,
Should not be given to a *wretch* ſo vile. *Daniel's Civil War.*

When they are gone, a company of ſtarved hungry *wretches* ſhall take their places. *L'Eſtrange.*

3. It is uſed by way of ſlight, or ironical pity, or contempt.

When ſoon away the waſp doth go;
Poor *wretch* was never frighted ſo:
He thought his wings were much too ſlow,
O'erjoy'd they ſo were parted. *Drayton's Nymphid.*

Then, if the ſpider find him faſt beſet,
She iſſues forth, and runs along her loom:
She joys to touch the captive in her net,
And drags the little *wretch* in triumph home. *Dryden.*

4. It is ſometimes a word of tenderneſs, as we now ſay *poor thing.*

Chaſtened but thus, and thus his leſſon taught,
The happy *wretch* ſhe put into her breaſt. *Sidney.*

WRE'TCHED. *adj.* [from *wretch.*]

1. Miſerable; unhappy.

Theſe we ſhould judge to be moſt miſerable, but that a *wretcheder* ſort there are, on whom, whereas nature hath beſtowed ripe capacity, their evil diſpoſition ſeriouſly goeth about therewith to apprehend God, as being not God. *Hooker.*

O cruel death! to thoſe you are more kind,
Than to the *wretched* mortals left behind. *Waller.*

Why do'ſt thou drive me
To range all o'er a waſte and barren place,
To find a friend? The *wretched* have no friends. *Dryden.*

2. Calamitous; afflictive.

3. Sorry; pitiful; paltry; worthleſs.

When God was ſerved with legal ſacrifices, ſuch was the miſerable and *wretched* condition of ſome mens minds, that the beſt of every thing they had, being culled out for themſelves, if there were in their flocks any poor, ſtarved, or diſeaſed thing not worth the keeping, they thought it good enough for the altar of God. *Hooker.*

Affected noiſe is the moſt *wretched* thing,
That to contempt can empty ſcribblers bring. *Roſcommon.*

Forgive the many failings of thoſe who, with their *wretched* art, cannot arrive to thoſe heights that you poſſeſs. *Dryden.*

4. Deſpicable; hatefully contemptible.

An adventure worthy to be remembered for the unuſed examples therein, as well of true natural goodneſs as of *wretched* ungratefulneſs. *Sidney.*

WRE'TCHEDLY. *adv.* [from *wretched.*]

1. Miſerably; unhappily.

From theſe two wars, ſo *wretchedly* entered into, the duke's ruin took its date. *Clarendon.*

2. Meanly; deſpicably.

When ſuch little ſhuffling arts come once to be ripped up, and laid open, how poorly and *wretchedly* muſt that man ſneak, who finds himſelf guilty and baffled too? *South.*

WRE'TCHEDNESS. *n. ſ.* [from *wretched.*]

1. Miſery; unhappineſs; afflicted ſtate.

My miſery cannot be greater than it is: fear not the danger of my blind ſteps, I cannot fall worſe than I am, and do not obſtinately continue to infect thee with my *wretchedneſs.* *Sidn.*

He 'gan inquire
What hard miſhap him brought to ſuch diſtreſs,
And made that caitif's thrall the thrall of *wretchedneſs.* *F. Q.*

Clarion did at laſt decline
To loweſt *wretchedneſs*; and is there then
Such rancor in the hearts of mighty men? *Spenſer.*

When they are weary of wars, and brought down to extreme *wretchedneſs*, then they creep a little, and ſue for grace, 'till they have recovered their ſtrength again. *Spenſer.*

I love not to ſee *wretchedneſs* o'ercharg'd,
And duty in his ſervice periſhing. *Shakeſpeare.*

We have with the feeling loſt the very memory of ſuch *wretchedneſs* as our forefathers endured by thoſe wars, of all others the moſt cruel. *Raleigh.*

2. Pitifulneſs; deſpicableneſs.

WRE'TCHLESS. *n. ſ.* [This is, by I know not whoſe corruption, written for *reckleſs.*] Careleſs; mindleſs; heedleſs.

For any man to put off his preſent repentance, on contemplation of a poſſibility that his latter repentance may ſerve the turn, is the moſt *wretchleſs* preſumption, and hath no promiſe of mercy annexed to it. *Hammond.*

If perſons of ſo circumſpect a piety have been thus overtaken, what ſecurity can there be for our *wretchleſs* oſcitancy? *Government of the Tongue.*

To WRI'GGLE. *v. n.* [ƿꞃigan, Saxon; *ruggelen*, Dutch.] To move to and fro with ſhort motions.

If ſheep or thy lamb fall a *wrigling* with tail,
Go by and by ſearch it, whiles help may prevail. *Tuſſer.*

The buſy importunities of theſe extenſional phantaſms I look upon as contemptuouſly, as upon the quick *wrigglings* up and down of piſmires. *More.*

The excellency of ſawing is to keep kerf exactly in the line marked to be ſawn, without *wriggling* on either ſide. *Moxon's Mech. Exer.*

To bed went the bridegroom and the bride:
Was never ſuch an ill-pair'd couple ty'd;
Reſtleſs he toſs'd, and tumbled to and fro,
And roll'd and *wriggled* farther off for woe. *Dryden.*

How wildly will ambition ſteer!
A vermin *wriggling* in th' uſurper's ear. *Dryden.*

And both he and his ſucceſſors would often *wriggle* in their ſeats as long as the cuſhion laſted. *Swift.*

To WRI'GGLE. *v. a.* To put in a quick reciprocating motion; to introduce by ſhifting motion.

Ralpho was mounted now, and gotten
O'erthwart his beaſt with active vaulting,
Wriggling his body to recover
His ſeat, and caſt his right leg over. *Hudibras.*

A ſlim thin-gutted fox made a hard ſhift to *wriggle* his body into a hen-rooſt. *L'Eſtrange.*

WRI'GGLETAIL. *n. ſ.* For *wrigglingtail.* See WRIGGLE.

My ragged ronts all ſhiver and ſhake;
They wont in the wind, wagg their *wriggletails*,
Peark as a peacoke, but nought it avails. *Spenſer.*

WRIGHT. *n. ſ.* [ƿꞃihta, ƿẏꞃhta, Saxon.] A workman; an artificer; a maker; a manufacturer.

It is impoſſible duly to conſider theſe things, without being rapt into admiration of the infinite wiſdom of the Divine Architect, and contemning the arrogant pretences of the world and animal *wrights*, and much more the productions of chance. *Cheyne.*

The verb To write has the ſame ſound with *wright*, a workman, right or equity, and rite or ceremony; but ſpelled very differently. *Watts's Logick.*

To WRING. *v a.* preter. and part. paſſ. *wringed* and *wrung.* [ƿꞃingan, Saxon.]

1. To twiſt; to turn round with violence.

The prieſt ſhall *wring* off his head, and burn it on the altar. *Lev.* i. 15.

2. To force out of any body by contortion.

He thruſt the fleece together, and *wringed* the dew out of it, a bowl full of water. *Judg.* vi. 38.

The dregs all the wicked ſhall *wring* out and drink. *Pſ.* lxxv.

The figure of a ſturdy woman, done by Michael Angelo, waſhing and winding of linen cloths; in which act ſhe *wrings* out the water that made the fountain. *Wotton.*

2

Apply

Apply mild detergents on pledgets of lint over it, with a compreſs *wrung* out. *Wiſeman.*

3. To ſqueeze; to preſs.

In ſleep I heard him ſay, ſweet Deſdemona,
Let us be wary, let us hide our loves!
And then, ſir, would he gripe and *wring* my hand. *Shakeſ.*

4. To writhe.

The ſilly owner of the goods
Weeps over them, and *wrings* his hapleſs hands. *Shakeſp.*

5. To pinch.

The king began to find where his ſhoe did *wring* him, and that it was his depreſſing the houſe of York that did rankle and feſter the affections of his people. *Bacon's Henry* VII.

If he had not been too much grieved, and *wrung* by an uneaſy and ſtreight fortune, he would have been an excellent man of buſineſs. *Clarendon.*

6. To force by violence; to extort.

I had rather coin my heart,
And drop my blood for drachma's, than to *wring*
From the hard hands of peaſants their vile traſh
By any indirection. *Shak. Julius Cæſar.*

Who can be bound by any ſolemn vow
To *wring* the widow from her cuſtom'd right,
And have no other reaſon for his wrong,
But that he was bound by a ſolemn oath? *Shak. Hen.* VI.

That which I muſt ſpeak,
Muſt either puniſh me, not being believ'd,
Or *wring* redreſs from you. *Shak. Meaſ. for Meaſure.*

Thirty ſpies,
Threatening cruel death, conſtrain'd the bride
To *wring* from me, and tell to them my ſecret. *Milton.*

7. To harraſs; to diſtreſs; to torture.

He dives into the king's ſoul, and there ſcatters
Doubts, dangers, *wringing* of the conſcience,
Fear and deſpair, and all theſe for his marriage. *Shakeſp.*

Pleaſure enchants, impetuous rage tranſports,
And grief dejects and *wrings* the tortur'd ſoul. *Roſcommon.*

Did'ſt thou taſte but half the griefs
That *wring* my ſoul, thou couldſt not talk thus coldly. *Add.*

8. To diſtort; to turn to a wrong purpoſe.

To *wring* this ſentence, to wreſt thereby out of men's hands the knowledge of God's doctrine, is without all reaſon. *Aſcham's Schoolmaſter.*

Lord, how dare theſe men thus *wring* the ſcriptures? *Whitg.*

9. To perſecute with extortion.

The merchant-adventurers have been often wronged and *wringed* to the quick; but were never quick and lively in thanks to thoſe by whoſe endeavours they were freed. *Hayw.*

To Wring. *v. n.* To writhe with anguiſh.

'Tis all men's office to ſpeak patience
To thoſe that *wring* under the load of ſorrow;
But no man's virtue nor ſufficiency,
To be ſo moral, when he ſhall endure
The like himſelf. *Shak. Much Ado about Nothing.*

Wri'nger. *n. ſ.* [from *wring.*] One who ſqueezes the water out of cloaths.

One Mrs. Quickly is in the manner of his nurſe, his laundreſs, his waſher, and his *wringer.* *Shakeſpeare.*

Wri'nkle. *n. ſ.* [ƿꞃıncle, Saxon; *wrinkel*, Dutch.]

1. Corrugation or furrow of the ſkin or the face.

Give me that glaſs, and therein will I read:
No deeper *wrinkles* yet? Hath ſorrow ſtruck
So many blows upon this face of mine,
And made no deeper wounds? *Shakeſp. Richard* II.

She hath continued a virgin without any viſible token, or leaſt *wrinkle* of old age. *Howel's Vocal Foreſt.*

To ſee a beggar's brat in riches flow,
Adds not a *wrinkle* to my even brow. *Dryden.*

Though you and all your ſenſeleſs tribe,
Could art, or time, or nature bribe,
To make you look like beauty's queen,
And hold for ever at fifteen;
No bloom of youth can ever blind
The cracks and *wrinkles* of your mind:
All men of ſenſe will paſs your door,
And croud to Stella's at fourſcore. *Swift.*

2. Any roughneſs.

Our Britiſh heav'n was all ſerene;
No threatning cloud was nigh,
Not the leaſt *wrinkle* to deform the ſky. *Dryden.*

To Wri'nkle. *v. a.* [ƿꞃınclian, Saxon.]

1. To corrugate; to contract into furrows.

It is ſtill fortune's uſe
To let the wretched man outlive his wealth,
To view with hollow eye and *wrinkled* brow
An age of poverty. *Shakeſ. Merchant of Venice.*

Scorn makes us *wrinkle* up the noſe, and ſtretch the noſtrils alſo, at the ſame time drawing up the upper lip. *Bacon.*

Here ſteams aſcend,
That in mixt fumes the *wrinkled* noſe offend. *Gay.*

Here ſtood ill-nature, like an ancient maid,
Her *wrinkled* form in black and white array'd. *Pope.*

2. To make rough or uneven.

A keen north-wind, blowing dry,
Wrinkled the face of deluge, as decay'd. *Milton.*

WRIST. *n. ſ.* [ƿꞃıſꞇ, Saxon.] The joint by which the hand is joined to the arm.

He took me by the *wriſt*, and held me hard. *Shakeſp.*

The brawn of the arm muſt appear full, ſhadowed on one ſide; then ſhew the *wriſt*-bone thereof. *Peacham.*

The axillary artery, below the cubit, divideth unto two parts; the one running along the radius, and paſſing by the *wriſt*, or place of the pulſe, is at the fingers ſubdivided unto three branches. *Brown's Vulgar Errours.*

Wri'stband. *n. ſ.* [*wriſt* and *band.*] The faſtening of the ſhirt at the hand.

Writ. *n. ſ.* [from *write.*]

1. Any thing written; ſcripture. This ſenſe is now chiefly uſed in ſpeaking of the Bible.

The church, as a witneſs, preacheth his mere revealed truth, by reading publickly the ſacred Scripture; ſo that a ſecond kind of preaching is the reading of holy *writ.* *Hooker.*

Divine Eliza, ſacred empreſs,
Live ſhe for ever, and her royal places
Be fill'd with praiſes of divineſt wits,
That her eternize with their heavenly *writs.* *Spenſer.*

Bagdat riſes out of the ruins of the old city of Babylon, ſo much ſpoken of in holy *writ.* *Knolles's Hiſt. of the Turks.*

Others famous after known,
Although in holy *writ* not nam'd. *Paradiſe Regain'd.*

He cannot keep his fingers from meddling with holy *writ.* *More's Divine Dialogues.*

Sacred *writ* our reaſon does exceed. *Waller.*

His ſtory, filled with ſo many ſurpriſing incidents, bears ſo cloſe an analogy with what is delivered in holy *writ*, that it is capable of pleaſing the moſt delicate reader, without giving offence to the moſt ſcrupulous. *Addiſon's Spectator.*

Of ancient *writ* unlocks the learned ſtore,
Conſults the dead, and lives paſt ages o'er. *Pope.*

2. A judicial proceſs.

Hold up your head: hold up your hand,
Wou'd it were not my lot to ſhew ye
This cruel *writ*, wherein you ſtand
Indicted by the name of Cloe. *Prior.*

3. A legal inſtrument.

The king is fled to London,
To call a preſent court of parliament:
Let us purſue him, ere the *writs* go forth. *Shak. Hen.* VI.

I folded the *writ* up in form of th' other,
Subſcrib'd it, gave the impreſſion, plac'd it ſafely,
The changeling never known. *Shakeſpeare.*

For every *writ* of entry, whereupon a common recovery is to be ſuffered, the queen's fine is to be rated upon the *writ* original, if the lands compriſed therein be held. *Ayliffe.*

Writ. The preterite of *write.*

When Sappho *writ*,
By their applauſe the criticks ſhow'd their wit. *Prior.*

Wri'tative. A word of *Pope*'s coining: not to be imitated.

Increaſe of years makes men more talkative, but leſs *writative*; to that degree, that I now write no letters but of plain how d'ye's. *Pope to Swift.*

To WRITE. *v. a.* preterite *writ* or *wrote*; part. paſſ. *written*, *writ*, or *wrote.* [ƿꞃıꞇan, aƿꞃıꞇan, Saxon; *ad rita*, Iſlandick; *wreta*, a letter, Gothick.]

1. To expreſs by means of letters.

I'll *write* you down,
The which ſhall point you forth, at every ſitting,
What you muſt ſay. *Shakeſpeare.*

Men's evil manners live in braſs, their virtues we *write* in water. *Shakeſ. Henry* VIII.

When a man hath taken a wife, and ſhe find no favour in his eyes, then let him *write* her a bill of divorcement. *Deut.*

Write ye this ſong for you, and teach it Iſrael. *Deut.* xxxi.

David *wrote* a letter to Joab, and ſent it by Uriah. 2 *Sa.* xi.

The time, the place, the manner how to meet,
Were all in punctual order plainly *writ.* *Dryden.*

2. To engrave; to impreſs.

Cain was ſo fully convinced that every one had a right to deſtroy ſuch a criminal, that he cries out, every one that findeth me ſhall ſlay me; ſo plain was it *writ* in the hearts of all mankind. *Locke.*

3. To produce as an author.

When more indulgent to the writer's eaſe,
You are ſo good, to be ſo hard to pleaſe;
No ſuch convulſive pangs it will require
To *write*—the pretty things that you admire. *Granville.*

4. To tell by letter.

I choſe to *write* the thing I durſt not ſpeak
To her I lov'd. *Prior.*

To Write. *v. n.*

1. To perform the act of writing.

I have ſeen her riſe from her bed, take forth paper, fold it, and *write* upon't. *Shakeſp. Macbeth.*

Baſſanio gave his ring away
Unto the judge that begg'd it; and his clerk,
That took ſome pains in *writing*, he begg'd mine. *Shakeſp.*

2. To play the authour.
Hearts, tongues, figures, ſcribes, bards, poets, cannot
Think, ſpeak, caſt, *write*, ſing, number
His love to Antony. *Shakeſ. Ant. and Cleopatra.*

There is not a more melancholy object in the learned world than a man who has *written* himſelf down. *Addiſon.*

3. To tell in books.
I paſt the melancholy flood,
With that grim ferryman which poets *write* of. *Shak. R.* III.

4. To ſend letters.
He *wrote* for all the Jews, concerning their freedom. 1 *Eſdr.*

5. To call one's ſelf; to be entitled; to uſe the ſtile of.
About it, and *write* happy when thou'ſt done. *Shakeſp.*
Let it not your wonder move,
Leſs your laughter that I love;
Though I now *write* fifty years,
I have had, and have my peers. *Ben. Johnſon.*

He *writes* himſelf *divina providentia*, whereas other biſhops only uſe *divina permiſſione*. *Ayliffe.*

6. To compoſe; to form compoſitions.
Chaſte moral *writing* we may learn from hence,
Neglect of which no wit can recompence;
The fountain which from Helicon proceeds,
That ſacred ſtream, ſhould never water weeds. *Waller.*

They can *write* up to the dignity and character of their authors. *Felton on the Claſſicks.*

WRI'TER. *n. ſ.* [from *write.*]
1. One who practiſes the art of writing.
2. An authour.

All three were ruined by juſtice and ſentence, as delinquents; and all three famous *writers*. *Bacon.*

Peaceable times are the beſt to live in, though not ſo proper to furniſh materials for a *writer*. *Addiſon's Freeholder.*

Writers are often more influenced by a deſire of fame, than a regard to the publick good. *Addiſon's Freeholder.*

Would a *writer* know how to behave himſelf with relation to poſterity, let him conſider in old books what he finds that he is glad to know, and what omiſſions he moſt laments. *Swift.*

To WRITHE. *v. a.* [ƿꞃıðan, Saxon.]
1. To diſtort; to deform with diſtortion.
It cannot be this weak and *writhed* ſhrimp
Should ſtrike ſuch terror in his enemies. *Shakeſ. Henry* VI.
Hatefulleſt diſreliſh *writh'd* their jaws
With ſoot and cinders. *Milton.*
Her mouth ſhe *writh'd*, her forehead taught to frown,
Her eyes to ſparkle fires to love unknown:
Her ſallow cheeks her envious mind did ſhew,
And ev'ry feature ſpoke aloud the curſtneſs of a ſhrew. *Dry.*

2. To twiſt with violence.
Then Satan firſt knew pain,
And *writh'd* him to and fro convolv'd. *Milton's Parad. Loſt.*
Amid' the plaited ſcales it took its courſe,
And in the ſpinal marrow ſpent its force;
The monſter hiſs'd aloud, and rag'd in vain,
And *writh'd* his body to and fro with pain;
He bit the dart. *Addiſon.*

3. To wreſt; to force by violence.
The reaſon which he yieldeth, ſheweth the leaſt part of his meaning to be that whereunto his words are *writhed*. *Hook.*

4. To twiſt.
The king of heav'n
Bar'd his red arm, and launching from the ſky
His *writhen* bolt, not ſhaking empty ſmoke,
Down to the deep abyſs the flaming felon ſtrook. *Dryden.*

To WRITHE. *v. n.* To be convolved with agony or torture.
Let each be broken on the rack;
Then, with what life remains, impaled, and left
To *writhe* at leiſure round the bloody ſtake. *Addiſon.*

To WRI'THLE. *v. a.* [from *writhe.*] To wrinkle; to corrugate.
Her *writhled* ſkin, as rough as maple rind,
So ſcabby was, that would have loathed all womankind. *Spenſ.*

WRI'TING. *n. ſ.* [from *writ.*]
1. A legal inſtrument.
2. A compoſure; a book.

They thought no other *writings* in the world ſhould be ſtudied, inſomuch as one of their great prophets exhorting them to caſt away all reſpects unto human *writings*, to his motion they condeſcended. *Hooker.*

Such arguments had an invincible force with thoſe pagan philoſophers, who became Chriſtians, as we find in moſt of their *writings*. *Addiſon.*

3. A written paper of any kind.
In at his windows throw
Writings, all tending to the great opinion
That Rome holds of his name. *Shakeſ. Julius Cæſar.*

WRI'TINGMASTER. *n. ſ.* One who teaches to write.
The facility of which I ſpoke conſiſts not in bold ſtrokes, if it makes not a great effect at a diſtance: that ſort of freedom belongs rather to a *writingmaſter* than a painter. *Dryden.*

WRI'TTEN. The participle paſſive of *write.*
Their doctrine and their ſtory *written* left,
They die. *Milton.*

Language is a connexion of audible ſigns, the moſt apt in nature for communication of our thoughts: *written* language is a deſcription of the ſaid audible ſigns, by ſigns viſible. *Holder.*

WRO'KEN. The part. paſſ. of *To wreak.* *Spenſer.*

WRONG. *n. ſ.* [ƿꞃanᵹe, Saxon.]
1. An injury; a deſigned or known detriment.

It is a harm, and no *wrong* which he hath received. *Sidney.*

She reſolved to ſpend all her years, which her youth promiſed ſhould be many, in bewailing the *wrong*, and yet praying for the wrongdoer. *Sidney.*

If he may not command them, then that law doth *wrong* that bindeth him to bring them forth to be juſtified. *Spenſer.*
They ever do pretend
To have receiv'd a *wrong*, who *wrong* intend. *Daniel.*

Imitation of an author is the moſt advantageous way for a tranſlator to ſhew himſelf, but the greateſt *wrong* which can be done to the reputation of the dead. *Dryden.*

Cowley preferred a garden and a friend, to thoſe whom in our own *wrong* we call the great. *Dryden.*
Expecting more in my own *wrong*,
Protracting life, I've liv'd a day too long. *Dryden.*

2. Errour; not right.
Be not blindly guided by the throng,
The multitude is always in the *wrong*. *Roſcommon.*
One ſpake much of right and *wrong*. *Milton.*
Proceed: quoth Dick, ſir, I aver
You have already gone too far;
When people once are in the *wrong*,
Each line they add is much too long:
Who faſteſt walks, but walks aſtray,
Is only fartheſt from his way. *Prior.*

In the judgment of right and *wrong*, every man has a ſelf. *Watts's Logick.*

WRONG. *adj.* [from the noun.]
1. Not morally right; not agreeable to propriety or truth.

I find you are an invincible Amazon, ſince you will overcome, though in a *wrong* matter. *Sidney.*

We never think of the main buſineſs of life, 'till a vain repentance minds us of it at the *wrong* end. *L'Eſtrange.*

When the dictates of honour are contrary to thoſe of religion and equity, they give *wrong*, ambitious, and falſe ideas of what is good and laudable. *Addiſon's Spectator.*

2. Not phyſically right; unfit; unſuitable.
Of Glo'ſter's treachery,
And of the loyal ſervice of his ſon,
When I inform'd him, then he call'd me ſot,
And told me I had turn'd the *wrong* ſide out. *Shak. K. Lear.*

Dividing a living of five hundred pounds a year into ten parts, is a contrivance, the meaning whereof hath got on the *wrong* ſide of my comprehenſion. *Swift.*

Singularity ſhews ſomething *wrong* in the mind. *Clariſſa.*

WRONG. *adv.* Not rightly; amiſs.
If he go *wrong*, ſhe will give him over to his own ruin. *Eccl.*

A thouſand odd capricio's, men's minds are acted by, may make one man quote another man's words *wrong*. *Locke.*
Ten cenſure *wrong*, for one that writes amiſs. *Pope.*

To WRONG. *v. a.* [from the noun.] To injure; to uſe unjuſtly.

So worthy a part of divine ſervice we ſhould greatly *wrong*, if we did not eſteem preaching as the bleſſed ordinance of God. *Hooker.*
For fear the ſtones her tender foot ſhould *wrong*,
Be ſtrewed with fragrant flowers all along. *Spenſer.*
Judge me, you gods! *wrong* I mine enemy? *Shakeſpeare.*
Thank him who puts me loath to this revenge
On you, who *wrong* me not, for him who *wrong'd*. *Milton.*
Once more farewel!
And know thou *wrong'ſt* me, if thou think'ſt
Ever was love or ever grief like mine. *Addiſon.*

WRONGDO'ER. *n. ſ.* [*wrong* and *doer.*] An injurious perſon.

She reſolved to ſpend all her years in bewailing the wrong, and yet praying for the *wrongdoer*. *Sidney.*

If any ſeat be taken away by a ſtranger, the churchwarden may have action againſt the *wrongdoer*. *Ayliffe.*

WRO'NGER. *n. ſ.* [from *wrong.*] He that injures; he that does wrong.
Jealouſy is a green-ey'd monſter, which doth make
The meat it feeds on: that cuckold lives in bliſs,
Who, certain of his fate, loves not his *wronger*. *Shak. Oth.*

Many times a prince is driven to ſpend far more of his treaſure in puniſhing by war the *wrongers* of his people, than the loſs of his people did amount unto. *Raleigh.*

WRO'NGFUL. *adj.* [*wrong* and *full.*] Injurious; unjuſt.
I am ſo far from granting thy requeſt,
That I deſpiſe thee for thy *wrongful* ſuit. *Shakeſpeare.*

He that hath wronged ſo in daily trade, that he knows not in what meaſure he hath done it, muſt redeem his fault by alms, according to the value of his *wrongful* dealing. *Taylor.*

Those whom forms of laws
Condemn'd to die, when traitors judg'd their cause,
Nor want they lots, nor judges to review
The *wrongful* sentence, and award a new. *Dryden.*

WRO'NGFULLY. *adv.* [from *wrongful.*] Unjustly.

Dorus, said Pamela, you blame your fortune very *wrongfully*, since the fault is not in fortune, but in you, that cannot frame yourself to your fortune; and as *wrongfully* do require Mopsa to so great a disparagement as to her father's servant. *Sidney.*

This poor fellow,
He had thought to murder *wrongfully.* *Shakesp.*

Salius then, exclaiming loud,
Urges his cause may in the court be heard,
And pleads, the prize is *wrongfully* conferr'd. *Dryden.*

I cry thee mercy, for suspecting a friar of the least good-nature; what, would you accuse him *wrongfully.* *Dryden.*

He who suffers *wrongfully* in a man's opinion, resolves to give him reason for his suspicion. *Spectator*, N°. 170.

WRO'NGHEAD. } *adj.* [*wrong* and *head.*] Having a per-
WRONGHE'ADED. } verse understanding.

Much do I suffer, much to keep in peace
This jealous, waspish, *wronghead*, rhyming race. *Pope.*

WRO'NGLY. *adv.* [from *wrong.*] Unjustly; amiss.

What thou would'st highly
That would'st thou holily; would'st not play false,
And yet would'st *wrongly* win. *Shakesp. Macbeth.*

Madmen having joined together some ideas very *wrongly*, err, as men do that argue right from wrong principles. *Locke.*

WRO'NGLESSLY. *adv.* [from *wrongless.*] Without injury to any.

Dearly esteemed of her for his exceeding good parts, being honourably courteous, and *wronglessly* valiant, considerately pleasant in conversation, and an excellent courtier, without unfaithfulness. *Sidney.*

WROTE. pret. and part. of *write.*

No man has the estate of his soul drawn upon his face, nor the decree of his election *wrote* upon his forehead. He who would know a man thoroughly, must follow him into the closet of his heart; the inspection of which is only the prerogative of omniscience. *South.*

WROTH. *adj.* [ƿraþ, Sax. *vrod*, Danish.] Angry. Out of use.

The Lord said unto Cain, why art thou *wroth?* *Gen.* iv.

Thou hast rejected us; thou art very *wroth* against us. *La.*

WROUGHT. [ƿroȝt, Saxon. The pret. and part. pass. as it seems, of *work*; as the Dutch *wercken*, makes *gerocht.*]

1. Effected; performed.

Why trouble ye the woman? for she hath *wrought* a good work upon me. *Matt.* xxvi. 10.

He that doeth truth, cometh to the light, that his deeds may be made manifest, that they are *wrought* in God. *John* iii.

The Jews wanted not power and ability to have convinced the world of the falshood of these miracles, had they never been *wrought.* *Stephens's Sermons.*

2. Influenced; prevailed on.

Had I thought the sight of my poor image
Would thus have *wrought* you, for the stone is mine,
I'd not have shewed it. *Shakespeare.*

Nor number, nor example with him *wrought*
To swerve from truth. *Milton.*

Do not I know him? could his brutal mind
Be *wrought* upon? could he be just or kind? *Dryden.*

This Artemisa, by her charms,
And all her sex's cunning, *wrought* the king. *Rowe.*

3. Produced; caused.

All his good prov'd ill in me,
And *wrought* but malice. *Milton.*

They *wrought* by their faithfulness the publick safety. *Dryd.*

This *wrought* the greatest confusion in the unbelieving Jews, and the greatest conviction in the Gentiles, who every where speak with astonishment of these truths they met with in this new magazine of learning, which was opened. *Addison.*

4. Worked; laboured.

They that *wrought* in silver, and whose works are unsearchable, are gone down to the grave. *Bar.* iii. 18.

Moses and Eleazar took the gold, even all *wrought* jewels. *Num.* xvi. 22.

What might be *wrought*
Fusil, or graven in metal. *Milton.*

5. Gained; attained.

We ventur'd on such dang'rous seas,
That if we *wrought* out life, 'twas ten to one. *Shakespeare.*

6. Operated.

Such another field
They dreaded worse than hell: so much the fear
Of thunder, and the sword of Michael,
Wrought still within them. *Milton.*

His too eager love
Has made him busy to his own destruction.
His threats have *wrought* this change of mind in Pyrrhus.
Philips's Distrest Mother.

7. Worked.

Take an heifer which hath not been *wrought* with, and which hath not drawn in the yoke. *Deut.* xxi. 3.

As infection from body to body is received many times by the body passive, yet is it by the good disposition thereof repulsed and *wrought* out, before it be formed in a disease. *Bacon.*

8. Actuated.

Vain Morat, by his own rashness *wrought*,
Too soon discover'd his ambitious thought;
Believ'd me his, before I spoke him fair,
And pitch'd his head into the ready snare. *Dryden.*

9. Manufactured.

It had been no less a breach of peace to have *wrought* any mine of his, than it is now a breach of peace, to take a town of his in Guiana, and burn it. *Raleigh.*

Celestial panoply, divinely *wrought.* *Milton.*

10. Formed.

He that hath *wrought* us for the same thing, is God. 2 *Cor.*

11. Excited by degrees.

The two friends had *wrought* themselves to such an habitual tenderness for the children under their direction, that each of them had the real passion of a father. *Addison.*

Advantage was taken of the sanguine temper which so many successes had *wrought* the nation up to. *Swift.*

12. Guided; managed.

A ship by skilful steersman *wrought.* *Milton.*

13. Agitated; disturbed.

We stay upon your leisure.——
—Give me your favour: my dull brain was *wrought*
With things forgot. *Shakesp. Macbeth.*

WRUNG. The preter. and part. passive of *wring.*

No mortal was ever so much at ease, but his shoe *wrung* him somewhere. *L'Estrange.*

Mix'd with the tender anguish nature shoots
Through the *wrung* bosom of the dying man. *Thomson.*

WRY. *adj.* [from *writhe.*]

1. Crooked; deviating from the right direction.

Sometimes to her news of myself to tell
I go about, but then is all my best
Wry words, and stamm'ring, or else doltish dumb;
Say then, can this but of enchantment come? *Sidney.*

Cutting the *wry* neck is never to be practised, but when the disorder is a contraction of the mastoideus muscle. *Sharp.*

2. Distorted.

It is but a kick with thy heels, and a *wry* mouth, and Sir Roger will be with thee. *Arbuthnot.*

Instructive work! whose *wry*-mouth'd portraiture
Display'd the fates her confessors endure. *Pope.*

3. Wrung; perverted; wrested.

He mangles and puts a *wry* sense upon protestant writers. *Att.*

To WRY. *v. n.* [from the adjective.] To be contorted and writhed; to deviate from the right direction.

These *wry* too much on the right hand, ascribing to the holy scripture such kind of perfection as it cannot have. *Sand.*

To WRY. *v. a.* [from the adjective.] To make to deviate; to distort.

To what pass are our minds brought, that from the right line of virtue are *wryed* to these crooked shifts? *Sidney.*

X.

X Is a letter, which, though found in Saxon words, begins no word in the English language.

Y.

Y, At the beginning of words, is a consonant; at the end, and when it follows a consonant, is a vowel, and has the sound of *i*. It is used at the end of words, and whenever two *i i*'s would come together; and in words derived from the Greek, to express the *v*. *Y* was much used by the Saxons, whence *y* is found for *i* in the old English writers.

YACHT. *n. s.* A small ship for carrying passengers.

YARD. *n. s.* [ᵹeaꞃᵭ, Saxon.]

1. Inclosed ground adjoining to an house.

One of the lions leaped down into a neighbour's *yard*, where, nothing regarding the crowing of the cocks, he eat them up. *Brown's Vulgar Errours.*

Xanthus one day sent Æsop into the *yard*, and bade him look well about him. *L'Estrange.*

His wanton kids with budding horns prepar'd,
Fight harmless battles in his homely *yard*. *Dryden.*

2. [ᵹeꞃᵭ, Saxon.] A measure of three feet.

A peer, a counsellor, and a judge, are not to be measured by the common *yard*, but by the pole of special grace. *Bacon.*

The arms, spread cross in a straight line, and measured from one end of the long finger on one hand, to that of the other; made a measure equal to the stature, and is named a fathom. Half of that, *viz.* from the end of the long finger of either arm, so spread, to the middle of the breast is, with us, called a *yard*. *Holder on Time.*

An aqueduct of a Gothick structure, that conveys water from mount St. Francis to Spoletto, from the foundation of the lowest arch to the top, is two hundred and thirty *yards*. *Add.*

3. The supports of the sails.

A breeze from shore began to blow;
The sailors ship their oars, and cease to row;
Then hoist their *yards* a-trip, and all their sails
Let fall to court the wind. *Dryden.*

YA'RDWAND. *n. s.* [*yard* and *wand.*] A measure of a yard.

All the revolutions in nature can give it nothing more than different degrees of dimensions. What affinity has thinking with such attributes? no more than there is between a syllogism and a *yardwand*. *Collier.*

YARE. *adj.* [ᵹeaꞃpe, Saxon.] Ready; dextrous; eager.

Yare, *yare*, good Iros, quick;—methinks I hear
Antony call. *Shakesp. Ant. and Cleopatra.*

I do desire to learn, Sir; and I hope, if you have occasion to use me for your turn, you shall find me *yare*. *Shakespeare.*

YA'RELY. *adv.* [from *yare.*] Dextrously; skilfully.

The silken tackles,
Swell with the touches of those flower-soft hands
That *yarely* frame the office. *Shakesp. Ant. and Cleop.*

YARN. *n. s.* [ᵹeaꞃn, Saxon.] Spun wool; woollen thread.

You would be another Penelope; yet they say, all the *yarn* she spun in Ulysses's absence, did but fill Ithaca full of moths. *Shakesp. Coriolanus.*

The web of our life is of a mingled *yarn*, good and ill together; our virtues would be proud, if our faults whipt them not; and our crimes would despair, if they were not cherish'd by our virtues. *Shakespeare.*

Yarn is a commodity very proper to this country, which of all others ought to be most encouraged. *Temple.*

It may be useful for the reeling of *yarn*. *Wilkins.*

The fates but only spin the coarser clue,
The finest of the wool is left for you.
Spare me but one small portion of the twine,
And let the sisters cut below your line:
The rest among the rubbish may they sweep,
Or add it to the *yarn* of some old miser's heap. *Dryden.*

To YARR. *v. n.* [from the sound, *hirrio*, Lat.] To growl, or snarl like a dog. *Ainsworth.*

YA'RROW. *n. s.* A plant which grows wild on the dry banks, and is used in medicine.

YAWL. *n. s.* A little vessel belonging to a ship, for convenience of passing to and from it.

To YAWN. *v. n.* [ᵹeonan, Saxon.]

1. To gape; to oscitate; to have the mouth opened involuntarily by fumes, as in sleepiness.

The sad-ey'd justice, with his surly hum,
Delivering o'er to executors pale
The lazy, *yawning* drone. *Shakesp. Hen. V.*

In *yawning*, the inner parchment of the ear is extended. When a man *yawneth*, he cannot hear so well. *Bacon.*

At length shook off himself, and ask'd the dame;
And asking *yawn'd*, for what intent she came? *Dryden.*

To whom the *yawning* pilot fast asleep,
Me didst thou bid, to trust the treacherous deep? *Dryden.*

2. To open wide.

The gashes,
That bloodily did *yawn* upon his face. *Shakespeare.*

'Tis now the very witching time of night,
When churchyards *yawn*. *Shakesp. Hamlet.*

Now will I dam up this thy *yawning* mouth,
For swallowing up the treasure of the realm. *Shakesp.*

He shall cast up the wealth by him devour'd,
Like vomit, from his *yawning* entrails pour'd. *Sandys.*

Hell at last
Yawning receiv'd them whole, and on them clos'd. *Milton.*

The sword pierc'd his tender sides;
Down fell the beauteous youth; the *yawning* wound
Gush'd out a purple stream. *Dryden.*

High she rear'd her arm, and with her sceptre struck
The *yawning* cliff: from its disparted height
Adown the mount the gushing torrent ran. *Prior.*

3. To express desire by yawning.

The chiefest thing at which lay-reformers *yawn*, is, that the clergy may, through conformity in condition, be poor as the apostles were. In which one circumstance, if they imagine so great perfection, they must think that church which hath such store of mendicant friars, a church in that respect most happy. *Hooker.*

YAWN. *n. s.* [from the verb.] Oscitation.

Thee, Paridel, she mark'd thee, there
Stretch'd on the rack of a too easy chair;
And heard thy everlasting *yawn* confess
The pains and penalties of idleness. *Pope's Dunciad.*

2. Gape; hiatus.

Hence to the borders of the marsh they go,
That mingles with the baleful streams below;
And sometimes with a mighty *yawn*, 'tis said,
Opens a dismal passage to the dead,
Who, pale with fear, the rending earth survey,
And startle at the sudden flash of day. *Addison.*

YA'WNING. *adj.* [from *yawn.*] Sleepy; slumbering.

Ere to black Hecat's summons
The shard-born beetle, with his drowsy hums,
Hath rung night's *yawning* peal, there shall be done
A deed of dreadful note. *Shakesp. Macbeth.*

Y'CLAD. part. for *clad.* Cloathed.

Her sight did ravish, but her grace in speech,
Her words *yclad* with wisdom's majesty,
Make me from wond'ring fall to weeping joys. *Shakesp.*

Y'CLEPED. [The participle passive of *clepe*, to call; clepan, Saxon; with the increasing particle *y*, which was used in the old English in the preterites and participles, from the Saxon ᵹe.] Called; termed; named.

But come, thou goddess, fair and free,
In heav'n *yclep'd* Euphrosine,
And by men, heart-easing mirth. *Milton.*

YDRA'D. The old pret. of *to dread.* *Spenser.*

YE. The nominative plural of *thou.*

Ye are they which justify yourselves. *Luke* xvi. 15.

YEA. *adv.* [ea, or ᵹea, Saxon; *ja*, Danish, German, and Dutch.] Yes. A particle of affirmation.

I am weary; *yea*, my memory is tir'd. *Shakespeare.*

A rascally, *yea*, forsooth, knave, to bear a gentleman in hand, and then stand upon security. *Shakespeare.*

From

From theſe Philippinæ are brought coſtly ſpices, *yea*, and gold too? *Abbot's Deſcription of the World.*

Yea, hath God ſaid, ye ſhall not eat of every tree in the garden. *Gen.* iii. 1.

Let your converſation be *yea*, *yea*; nay, nay. *Matth.* v.

All the promiſes of God are *yea*, and amen; that is, are verified, which is the importance of *yea*, and confirmed, which is meant by amen, into an immutability. *Hammond.*

They durſt abide
Jehovah thund'ring out of Sion, thron'd
Between the cherubim; *yea*, often plac'd
Within his ſanctuary itſelf their ſhrines. *Milton.*

Why do diſputes in wrangling ſpend the day?
Whilſt one ſays only *yea*, and t'other nay. *Denham.*

Notwithſtanding this great proximity of man to himſelf; *yea*, and notwithſtanding the obſervations made in all ages, we ſtill remain ignorant of many things concerning ourſelves. *Hale.*

To Yead, *or* Yede. *v. n.* preterite *yode.* [This word ſeems to have been corruptly formed from ȝeoδ, the Saxon preterite of ȝan.] To go; to march. Obſolete.

They wander at will, and ſtay at pleaſure,
And to their folds *yeade* at their own leiſure. *Spenſer.*

Then bad the knight this lady *yede* aloof,
And to an hill herſelf withdraw aſide,
From whence ſhe might behold that battle's proof,
And eke be ſafe from danger far deſcry'd. *Fairy Queen.*

Yet for ſhe *yode* thereat half aghaſt,
And Kiddy the door ſparred after her faſt. *Spenſer.*

That ſame mighty man of God,
That bloud red billows like a walled front,
On either ſide diſparted with his rod,
'Till that his army dry-foot through them *yod.* *Spenſer.*

To Yean. *v. n.* [eaman, Saxon.] To bring young. Uſed of ſheep.

The ſkilful ſhepherd peel'd me certain wands;
He ſtruck them up before the fulſome ewes,
Who, then conceiving, did in *yeaning* time
Fole party-colour'd lambs. *Shakeſpeare.*

So many days my ewes have been with young:
So many weeks, ere the poor fools will *yean.* *Shakeſpeare.*

This I ſcarcely drag along,
Who *yeaning* on the rocks has left her young. *Dryden.*

Ewes *yean* the polled lamb with the leaſt danger. *Mortimer.*

Yea'nling. *n. ſ.* [from *yean.*] The young of ſheep.

All the *yeanlings* which were ſtreak'd and pied,
Should fall as Jacob's hire. *Shakeſpeare.*

Year. *n. ſ.* [ȝeaꞃ, Saxon.]

If one by the word *year* mean twelve months of thirty days each, *i. e.* three hundred and ſixty days; another intend a ſolar *year* of three hundred ſixty-five days; and a third mean a lunar *year*, or twelve lunar months, *i. e.* three hundred fifty-four days, there will be a great variation and error in their account of things, unleſs they are well apprized of each other's meaning. *Watts's Logick.*

See the minutes, how they run:
How many makes the hour full compleat,
How many hours bring about the day,
How many days will finiſh up the *year*,
How many *years* a mortal man may live. *Shakeſpeare.*

With the *year*
Seaſons return, but not to me returns
Day, or the ſweet approach of morn. *Milton.*

Oviparous creatures have eggs enough at firſt conceived in them, to ſerve them for many *years* laying, allowing ſuch a proportion for every *year*, as will ſerve for one or two incubations. *Ray on the Creation.*

He accepted a curacy of thirty pounds a *year*. *Swift.*

2. It it often uſed plurally, without a plural termination.

I fight not once in forty *year*. *Shakeſpeare.*

3. In the plural old age.

Some mumble-news,
That ſmiles his cheek in *years*, and knows the trick
To make my lady laugh when ſhe's diſpos'd,
Told our intents. *Shakeſp. Love's Labour Loſt.*

There died alſo Cecile, mother to king Edward IV. being of extreme *years*, and who had lived to ſee three princes of her body crowned, and four murthered. *Bacon's Hen.* VII.

He look'd in *years*, yet in his *years* were ſeen,
A youthful vigour, and autumnal green. *Dryden.*

Ye'arling. *adj.* [from *year.*] Being a year old.

A *yearling* bullock to thy name ſhall ſmoke;
Untam'd, unconſcious of the galling yoke. *Pope.*

Ye'arly. *adj.* [from *year.*] Annual; happening every year; laſting a year.

The *yearly* courſe that brings this day about,
Shall never ſee it but a holiday. *Shakeſp. K. John.*

Why the changing oak ſhould ſhed
The *yearly* honour of his ſtately head;
Whilſt the diſtinguiſh'd yew is ever ſeen,
Unchang'd his branch, and permanent his green. *Prior.*

Ye'arly. *adv.* Annually; once a year.

He that outlives this day, and ſees old age,
Will *yearly* on the vigil feaſt his neighbours,
And ſay, tomorrow is Saint Criſpian. *Shakeſp. Hen.* V.

For numerous bleſſings *yearly* ſhower'd,
And property with plenty crown'd;
For freedom ſtill maintain'd alive;
For theſe, and more, accept our pious praiſe. *Dryden.*

To Yearn. *v. n.* [eaꞃnan, Saxon.] To feel great internal uneaſineſs. In *Spenſer* it is ſometimes *earn.*

He deſpis'd to tread in due degree,
But chaff'd, and foam'd, with courage fierce and ſtern,
And to be eas'd of that baſe burden ſtill did *yearn.* *Spenſer.*

Make the libbard ſtern
Leave roaring, when in rage he for revenge did *yearn.* *Spenſ.*

Though peeping cloſe into the thick,
Might ſee the moving of ſome quick:
But were it fairy, fiend, or ſnake,
My courage *earned* it to wake,
And manfully thereat ſhot. *Spenſer.*

Falſtaff, he is dead,
And we muſt *yern* therefore. *Shakeſpeare's Hen.* V.

Joſeph made haſte; for his bowels did *yern* upon his brother: and he ſought where to weep, and he enter'd into his chamber. *Gen.* xliii. 30.

When the fair Leucothoe he ſpy'd,
To check his ſteeds, impatient Phœbus *yearn'd*,
Though all the world was in his courſe concern'd. *Waller.*

Yet for all the *yearning* pain
Y' have ſuffer'd for their loves, in vain,
I fear they'll prove ſo nice and coy,
To have, and t' hold, and to enjoy. *Hudibras.*

Where our heart does but relent, his melts; where our eye pities, his bowels *yearn.* *South's Sermons.*

At beholding the miſeries of others, they find ſuch *yearnings* in their bowels, and ſuch ſenſible commotions raiſed in their breaſts, as they can by no means ſatisfy. *Calamy.*

Your mother's heart *yearns* towards you. *Addiſon.*

Unmov'd the mind of Ithacus remain'd;
But Anticlus, unable to controul,
Spoke loud the language of his *yearning* ſoul. *Pope.*

To Yearn. *v. a.* To grieve; to vex.

She laments for it, that it would
Yern your heart to ſee it. *Shakeſpeare.*

Yest. *n. ſ.* [ȝeſt, Saxon.]

1. The foam, ſpume, or flower of beer in fermentation; barm.

Yeaſt and outward means do fail,
And have no power to work on ale. *Hudibras.*

When drays bound high, they never croſs behind,
Where bubbling *yeaſt* is blown by guſts of wind. *Gay.*

2. The ſpume on a troubled ſea.

Now the ſhip boring the moon with her main-maſt, and anon ſwallow'd with *yeaſt* and froth, as you'd thruſt a cork into a hogſhead. *Shakeſp. Winter's Tale.*

Ye'sty. *adj.* [from *yeſt.*] Frothy; ſpumy.

Though you untie the winds, and let them fight
Againſt the churches; though the *yeſty* waves
Confound and ſwallow navigation up. *Shakeſp. Macbeth.*

Yelk. *n. ſ.* [from ȝealepe, *yellow*, Saxon.] The yellow part of the egg. It is commonly pronounced, and often written *yolk.*

The *yolk* of the egg conduceth little to the generation of the bird, but only to the nouriſhment of the ſame: for if a chicken be opened, when it is new hatched, you ſhall find much of the *yolk* remaining. *Bacon's Nat. Hiſt.*

That a chicken is formed out of the *yelk* of an egg, with ſome antient philoſophers the people ſtill opinion. *Brown.*

All the feather'd kind,
From th' included *yolk*, not ambient white aroſe. *Dryden.*

To YELL. *v. n.* To cry out with horrour and agony.

Nor the night raven, that ſtill deadly *yells*;
Nor griſly vultures make us once affeared. *Spenſer.*

Each new morn,
New widows howl, new orphans cry; new ſorrows
Strike heav'n on the face, that it reſounds,
As if it felt with Scotland, and *yell'd* out
Like ſyllables of dolour. *Shakeſp. Macbeth.*

Now worſe than e'er he was before,
Poor Puck doth *yell*, poor Puck doth roar,
That wak'd queen Mab, who doubted ſore
Some treaſon had been wrought her. *Drayton's Nymphiad.*

Yelling monſters, that with ceaſeleſs cry
Surround me. *Milton.*

Night-ſtruck fancy dreams the *yelling* ghoſt. *Thomſon.*

Yell. *n. ſ.* [from the verb.] A cry of horrour.

With like tim'rous accent and dire *yell*,
As when, by night and negligence, the fire
Is ſpread in populous cities. *Shakeſpeare's Othello.*

Hence are heard the groans of ghoſts, the pains
Of ſounding laſhes, and of dragging chains.
The Trojan flood aſtoniſh'd at their cries,
And aſk'd his guide from whence thoſe *yells* ariſe. *Dryden.*

Others in frantick mood
Run howling through the streets; their hideous *yells*
Rend the dark welkin. *Philips.*

YE'LLOW. *adj.* [yealepe, Saxon; *gheleuwe*, Dutch; *giallo*, Italian.] Being of a bright glaring colour, as gold.

Only they that come to see a fellow
In a long motley coat, guarded with *yellow*,
Will be deceiv'd. *Shakesp. Henry* VIII. *Prologue.*

He brought the green ear and the *yellow* sheaf. *Milton.*

After a lively orange, followed an intense bright and copious *yellow*, which was also the best of all the *yellows*. *Newton.*

Negligent of food,
Scarce seen, he wades among the *yellow* broom. *Thomson.*

YE'LLOWBOY. *n. s.* A gold coin. A very low word.

John did not starve the cause; there wanted not *yellowboys* to see council. *Arbuthnot's John Bull.*

YE'LLOWHAMMER. *n. s.* A bird.

YE'LLOWISH. *adj.* [from *yellow.*] Approaching to yellow.

Although amber be commonly of a *yellowish* colour, yet there is found of it also black, white, brown, green, blue, and purple. *Woodward's Natural History.*

YE'LLOWISHNESS. *n. s.* [from *yellowish.*] The quality of approaching to yellow.

Bruised madder, being drenched with the like alcalizate solution, exchanged its *yellowishness* for a redness. *Boyle.*

YE'LLOWNESS. *n. s.* [from *yellow.*]

1. The quality of being yellow.

Apples, covered in lime and ashes, were well matured, as appeared in the *yellowness* and sweetness. *Bacon's Natural Hist.*

Yellowness of the skin and eyes, and a saffron-coloured urine, are signs of an inflammatory disposition of the liver. *Arbuthn.*

2. It is used in *Shakespeare* for jealousy.

Ford I will possess with *yellowness*. *Shakespeare.*

YE'LLOWS. *n. s.* A disease in horses. It owes its original to obstructions in the gall-pipe, which are caused by slimy or gritty matter; or to the stoppage of the roots of those little ducts opening into that pipe, by the like matter; or to a compression of them by a fulness and plenitude of the blood-vessels that lie near them. When the gall-pipe, or the roots rather of the common ducts of that pipe, are any wise stopped up, that matter which should be turned into gall is taken up by the vein, and carried back again into the mass of blood, and tinctures it yellow; so that the eyes, inside of the lips, slaver, and all the parts of the horse, that are capable of shewing the colour, appear yellow. *Farrier's Dict.*

His horse sped with spavins, and raied with the *yellows*. *Shakespeare's Taming of the Shrew.*

To YELP. *v. n.* [ʒealpan, Saxon.] To bark as a beagle-hound after his prey.

A little herd of England's tim'rous deer,
Maz'd with a *yelping* kennel of French curs. *Shak. H.* VI.

YE'OMAN. *n. s.* [Of this word the original is much doubted: the true etymology seems to be that of *Junius*, who derives it from *geman*, Frisick, a villager.]

1. A man of a small estate in land; a farmer; a gentleman farmer.

Gentlemen should use their children as the honest farmers and substantial *yeomen* do theirs. *Locke.*

He that has a spaniel by his side is a *yeoman* of about one hundred pounds a year, an honest man: he is just qualified to kill an hare. *Addison.*

2. It seems to have been anciently a kind of ceremonious title given to soldiers: whence we have still *yeomen* of the guard.

Tall *yeomen* seemed they, and of great might,
And were enranged ready still for fight. *Fairy Queen.*

You, good *yeomen*,
Whose limbs were made in England, shew us here
The mettle of your pasture. *Shakesp. Henry* V.

He instituted, for the security of his person, a band of fifty archers, under a captain, to attend him, by the name of *yeomen* of his guard. *Bacon's Henry* VII.

Th' appointment for th' ensuing night he heard;
And therefore in the cavern had prepar'd
Two brawny *yeomen* of his trusty guard. *Dryden.*

At Windsor St. John whispers me i' th' ear;
The waiters stand in ranks, the *yeomen* cry
Make way for the dean, as if a duke pass'd by. *Swift.*

3. It was probably a freeholder not advanced to the rank of a gentleman.

His grandfather was Lyonel duke of Clarence,
Third son to the third Edward king of England:
Spring crestless *yeomen* from so deep a root? *Shak. H.* VI.

4. It seems to have had likewise the notion of a gentleman servant.

A jolly *yeoman*, marshal of the hall,
Whose name was appetite, he did bestow
Both guests and meats. *Spenser.*

YE'OMANRY. *n. s.* [from *yeoman.*] The collective body of yeomen.

This did amortize a great part of the lands of the kingdom unto the hold and occupation of the *yeomanry*, or middle people, of a condition between gentlemen and cottagers. *Bacon.*

To YERK. *v. a.* [Of unknown etymology.] To throw out or move with a spring.

A leaping horse is said to *yerk*, or strike out his hind legs, when he flings and kicks with his whole hind quarters, stretching out the two hinder legs near together, and even, to their full extent. *Farrier's Dict.*

Their wounded steeds
Fret fetlock deep in gore, and with wild rage
Yerk out their armed heels at their dead masters. *Shakesp.*

YERK. *n. s.* [from the verb.] A quick motion.

To YERN. *v. a.* See YEARN.

I am not covetous of gold;
It *yerns* me not, if men my garments wear. *Shak. H.* V.

YES. *adv.* [ʒiſe, Saxon.] A term of affirmation; the affirmative particle opposed to *no.*

This were a fit speech for a general in the head of an army, when going to battle: *yes*, and it is no less fit speech in the head of a council, upon a deliberation of entrance into a war. *Bacon.*

Yes, you despise the man to books confin'd,
Who from his study rails at human kind,
Though what he learns he speaks. *Pope.*

YE'STER. *adj.* [*ghister*, Dutch; *hesternus*, Latin.] Being next before the present day. It is not often used but in composition with another word, as *day* or *night.*

Love might as well be sow'd upon our sands,
As in a breast so barren:
To love an enemy, the only one
Remaining too, whom *yester* sun beheld
Must'ring her charms. *Dryden's Don Sebastian.*

YE'STERDAY. *n. s.* [ʒiſtanbæʒ, Saxon.] The day last past; the day next before to-day.

To-morrow, and to-morrow, and to-morrow,
Creeps in this petty pace from day to day,
To the last syllable of recorded time;
And all our *yesterdays* have lighted fools
The way to dusty death. *Shakes. Macbeth.*

We are but of *yesterday*, and know nothing, because our days upon earth are a shadow. *Job* viii. 9.

You are both fluid, chang'd since *yesterday*;
Next day repairs but ill last day's decay;
Nor are, although the river keep the name,
Yesterday's waters and to-day's the same. *Donne.*

If *yesterday* could be recall'd again,
Ev'n now would I conclude my happy reign. *Dryden.*

Yesterday was set apart as a day of publick thanksgiving for the late extraordinary successes. *Addison.*

Mrs. Simper sends complaint in your *yesterday's* Spectator. *Addison's Spectator.*

Naked from the womb
We *yesterday* came forth; and in the tomb
Naked again we must to-morrow lie:
Born to lament, to labour, and to die. *Prior.*

YE'STERDAY. *adv.* On the day last past.

Martius gave us *yesterday* a representation of the empire of the Turks, with no small vigour of words. *Bacon.*

YE'STERNIGHT. *n. s.* The night before this night.

YE'STERNIGHT. *adv.* On the night last past.

Eleven hours I've spent to write it over;
For *yesternight* by Catesby was it sent me. *Shakesp. R.* III.

The distribution of this conference was made by Eupolis *yesternight*. *Bacon.*

YET. *conjunct.* [ʒẏt, ʒet, ʒeta, Saxon.] Nevertheless; notwithstanding; however.

They had a king was more than him before;
But *yet* a king, where they were nought the more. *Daniel.*

Though such men have lived never so much upon the reserve; *yet* if they be observed to have a particular fondness for persons noted for any sin, it is ten to one but there was a communication in the sin, before there was so in affection. *South.*

The heathens would never suffer their gods to be reviled, which *yet* were no gods; and shall it be allowed to any man to make a mock of him that made heaven and earth? *Tillots.*

He is somewhat arrogant at his first entrance, and is too inquisitive through the whole tragedy; *yet* these imperfections being balanced by great virtues, they hinder not our compassion for his miseries. *Dryden's Dufresnoy.*

Let virtuoso's in five years be writ,
Yet not one thought accuse thy toil of wit. *Dryden.*

YET. *adv.*

1. Beside; over and above.

This furnishes us with *yet* one more reason, why our Saviour lays such a particular stress on acts of mercy. *Atterbury.*

2. Still; the state still remaining the same.

They attest facts they had heard while they were *yet* heathens; and had they not found reason to believe them, they would still have continued heathens, and made no mention of them in their writings. *Addison.*

3. Once again.

Yet, *yet* a moment, one dim ray of light,
Indulge, dread chaos and eternal night. *Pope's Dunciad.*

4. At this time; so soon; hitherto: with a negative before it.
Thales being asked when a man should marry, said, young men not *yet*; old men, not at all. *Bacon.*

5. At least; at all. Noting uncertainty or indetermination.
A man that would form a comparison betwixt Quintilian's declamations, if *yet* they be Quintilian's, and the orations of Tully, would be in danger of forfeiting his discretion. *Baker.*

6. It notes increase or extension of the sense of the words to which it is joined.
Shake not his hour-glass, when his hasty sand
Is ebbing to the last:
A little longer, *yet* a little longer,
And nature drops him down without your sin,
Like mellow fruit without a winter storm. *Dryden.*
Yet a few days, and those which now appear
In youth and beauty like the blooming year,
In life's swift scene shall change. *Dryden.*

7. Still; in a new degree.
He that takes from a thief, that which the thief took from an honest man, and keeps it to himself, is the wickeder thief of the two, by how much the rapine is made *yet* blacker by the pretence of piety and justice. *L'Estrange.*

8. Even; after all. A kind of emphatical addition to a negative.
If any man neglect his duty, his fault must not be ascribed to the rule appointed, neither *yet* to the whole church. *Whitg.*
Men may not too rashly believe the confessions of witches, nor *yet* the evidence against them; for the witches themselves are imaginative, and people are credulous, and ready to impute accidents and natural operations to witchcraft. *Bacon.*
Nor *yet* amidst this joy and brightest morn
Was absent, after all his mischief done,
The prince of darkness. *Milton's Paradise Regain'd.*

9. Hitherto.
Hope beginning here, with a trembling expectation of things far removed, and as *yet* but only heard of, endeth with real and actual fruition of that which no tongue can express. *Hook.*

YE'VEN, for *given.*
Wants not a fourth grace to make the dance even?
Let that room to my lady be *yeven*;
She shall be a grace,
To fill the fourth place,
And reign with the rest in heaven. *Spenser.*

YEW. *n. s.* [ıp, Saxon; *yw*, Welsh. This is often written *eugh*; but the former orthography is at once nearer to the sound and the derivation. See EUGH.] A tree of tough wood.
It hath amentaceous flowers, which consist of many apices, for the most part shaped like a mushroom, and are barren; but the embryoes, which are produced at remote distances on the same tree, do afterward become hollow bell-shaped berries, which are full of juice, and include seeds somewhat like acorns, having, as it were, a little cup to each. *Miller.*
The shooter *eugh*, the broad-leav'd sycamore,
The barren plantane, and the walnut found;
The myrrhe, that her foul sin doth still deplore,
Alder the owner of all waterish ground. *Fairfax.*
Slips of *yew*,
Shiver'd in the moon's eclipse. *Shakesp. Macbeth.*
They would bind me here
Unto the body of a dismal *yew*. *Shakesp. Titus Andronicus.*
He drew,
And almost join'd the horns of the tough *yew*. *Dryden.*
The distinguish'd *yew* is ever seen,
Unchang'd his branch, and permanent his green. *Prior.*

YE'WEN. *adj.* [from *yew*] Made of the wood of yew.
His stiff arms to stretch with *eughen* bow,
And manly legs still passing to and fro. *Hubberd's Tale.*

YFE'RE. *adv.* [ʒfepe, Saxon.] Together. *Spenser.*

To YIELD. *v. a.* [ʒelban, Saxon, to pay.]
1. To produce; to give in return for cultivation or labour.
When thou tillest the ground, it shall not henceforth *yield* unto thee her strength. *Gen.* iv. 12.
Strabo tells us the mines at Carthagena *yielded* the Romans, *per diem*, to the value of twenty-five thousand drachms, eight hundred and seven pounds five shillings and ten pence. *Arbuth.*
2. To produce in general.
He makes milch kine *yield* blood. *Shakespeare.*
The wilderness *yieldeth* food for them. *Job* xxiv. 5.
All the substances of an animal, fed even with acescent substances, *yield* by fire nothing but alkaline salts. *Arbuthnot.*
3. To afford; to exhibit.
Philoclea would needs have her glove, and not without so mighty a lour as that face could *yield*. *Sidney.*
The mind of man desireth evermore to know the truth, according to the most infallible certainty which the nature of things can *yield*. *Hooker.*
If you take the idea of white, which one parcel of snow *yielded* yesterday to your sight, and another idea of white from another parcel of snow you see to-day, and put them together in your mind, they run into one, and the idea of white- *Locke.*
4. To give as claimed of right.
I the praise
Yield thee, so well thou hast this day purvey'd. *Milton.*
5. To allow; to permit.
I *yield* it just, said Adam, and submit. *Milton.*
Life is but air,
That *yields* a passage to the whistling sword,
And closes when 'tis gone. *Dryden's Don Sebastian.*
6. To emit; to expire.
Often did I strive
To *yield* the ghost; but still the envious flood
Kept in my soul, and would not let it forth
To find the empty, vast and wand'ring air. *Shak. Rich.* III.
He gathered up his feet into the bed, and *yielded* up the ghost. *Gen.* xlix. 33.
7. To resign; to give up.
He not *yielding* over to old age his country delights, especially of hawking, was at that time, following a merlin, brought to see this injury offered unto us. *Sidney.*
Thus I have *yielded* up into your hand
The circle of my glory. *Shakesp. King John.*
She to realities *yields* all her shows. *Milton.*
'Tis the pride of man which is the spring of this evil, and an unwillingness to *yield* up their own opinions. *Watts.*
8. To surrender.
The enemies sometimes offered unto the soldiers, upon the walls, great rewards, if they would *yield* up the city, and sometimes threatened them as fast. *Knolles.*
They laugh, as if to them I had quitted all,
At random *yielded* up to their misrule. *Milton.*

To YIELD. *v. n.*
1. To give up the conquest; to submit.
He *yields* not in his fall;
But fighting dies, and dying kills withal. *Daniel.*
All is not lost: immortal hate,
And courage never to submit or *yield*. *Milton.*
If the inspiring and expiring organ of any animal be stopt, it suddenly *yields* to nature, and dies. *Walton's Angler.*
There he saw the fainting Grecians *yield*,
And here the trembling Trojans quit the field,
Pursu'd by fierce Achilles. *Dryden.*
2. To comply with any person.
Considering this present age so full of tongue, and weak of brain, behold we *yield* to the stream thereof. *Hooker.*
I see a *yielding* in the looks of France:
Mark, how they whisper. *Shakesp. King John.*
This supernatural soliciting, if ill,
Why hath it given me earnest of success?
If good, why do I *yield* to that suggestion,
Whose horrid image doth upfix my hair? *Shakesp. K. Lear.*
With her much fair speech she caused him to *yield*. *Prov.*
The Jews have agreed to desire thee that thou wouldst bring down Paul; but do not thou *yield* unto them. *Acts* xxiii. 21.
3. To comply with things.
There could be no secure peace, except the Lacedemonians *yielded* to those things, which being granted, it would be no longer in their power to hurt the Athenians. *Bacon.*
If much converse
Thee satiate, to short absence I could *yield*. *Milton.*
4. To concede; to admit; to allow; not to deny.
If we *yield* that there is a God, and that this God is almighty and just, it cannot be avoided but that, after this life ended, he administers justice unto men. *Hakewill.*
5. To give place as inferiour in excellence or any other quality.
The fight of Achilles and Cygnus, and the fray betwixt the Lapithæ and Centaurs, *yield* to no other part of this poet. *Dry.*
Tell me in what more happy fields
The thistle springs, to which the lily *yields*? *Pope.*

YIE'LDER. *n. s.* [from *yield.*] One who yields.
Briars and thorns at their apparel snatch,
Some sleeves, some hats; from *yielders* all things catch. *Shak.*
Some guard these traitors to the block of death,
Treason's true bed, and *yielder* up of breath. *Shak. Hen.* IV.

YOKE. *n. s.* [ʒeoc, Sax. *jock*, Dutch; *jugum*, Lat. *joug*, Fr.]
1. The bandage placed on the neck of draught oxen.
Bring a red heifer, wherein is no blemish, and upon which never came *yoke*. *Numb.* xix. 2.
A yearling bullock to thy name shall smoke,
Untam'd, unconscious of the galling *yoke*. *Pope.*
2. A mark of servitude; slavery.
Our country sinks beneath the *yoke*;
It weeps, it bleeds. *Shakespeare's Macbeth.*
In bands of iron fetter'd you shall be;
An easier *yoke* than what you put on me. *Dryd. Aurengz.*
3. A chain; a link; a bond.
This *yoke* of marriage from us both remove,
Where two are bound to draw, though neither love. *Dry.*
4. A couple; two; a pair.
Those that accuse him in his intent towards our wives, a *yoke* of his discarded men. *Shakespear.*
His lands a hundred *yoke* of oxen till'd. *Dryden's Æ.*

A y

A *yoke* of mules outgoes a *yoke* of oxen, when set to work at the same time; for mules are swifter. *Broome.*

To Yoke. *v. a.* [from the noun.]

1. To bind by a yoke to a carriage.

This Stetes promised to do, if he alone would *yoak* together two brazen-hoofed bulls, and, plowing the ground, sow dragons teeth. *L'Estrange.*

Four milk-white bulls, the Thracian use of old,
Were *yok'd* to draw his car of burnish'd gold. *Dryden.*

2. To join or couple with another.

My name
Be *yok'd* with his that did betray the best. *Shakespeare.*

Cassius, you are *yoked* with a lamb,
That carries anger as the flint bears fire. *Shak. Jul. Cæsar.*

Seek not in Latian bands to *yoke*
Our fair Lavinia. *Dryden's Æn.*

3. To enslave; to subdue.

These are the arms
With which he *yoketh* your rebellious necks,
Razeth your cities. *Shakespeare.*

4. To restrain; to confine.

Men marry not; but chuse rather a libertine single life, than to be *yoked* in marriage. *Bacon.*

The words and promises, that *yoke*
The conqueror, are quickly broke. *Hudibras.*

Xerxes, the liberty of Greece to *yoke*,
Over Hellespont bridg'd his way. *Milton.*

Yo'ke-elm. *n. s.* A tree. *Ainsworth.*

Yo'kefellow. } *n. s.* [*yoke* and *fellow*, or *mate*.]
Yo'kemate. }

1. Companion in labour.

Yokefellows in arms,
Let us to France. *Shakespeare's Henry* V.

2. Mate; fellow.

You cannot think me fit
To be th' *yokefellow* of your wit,
Nor take one of so mean deserts
To be the part'ner of your parts. *Hudibras.*

Before Toulon thy *yokemate* lies,
Where all the live-long night he sighs. *Stepney.*

Those who have most distinguished themselves by railing at the sex, very often chuse one of the most worthless for a companion and *yokefellow*. *Addison's Spectator.*

Yold, for *yielded.* Obsolete. *Spenser.*

Yolk. *n. s.* [See Yelk.] The yellow part of an egg.

Nature hath provided a large *yolk* in every egg, a great part whereof remaineth after the chicken is hatched; and, by a channel made on purpose, serves instead of milk to nourish the chick for a considerable time. *Ray on the Creation.*

Yon. } *adj.* [ȝeonδ, Saxon.] Being at a distance within view.
Yond. }
Yo'nder. }

Madam, *yond* young fellow swears he will speak with you. *Shakespeare's Twelfth Night.*

Good mother, do not marry me to *yon* fool. *Shakespeare.*

Would you not laugh to meet a great counsellor of state in a flat cap, his gloves under his girdle, and *yond* haberdasher in a velvet gown furred with sables? *Ben. Johnson's Discoveries.*

Tigranes, being encamped upon a hill with four hundred thousand men, discovered the army of the Romans, being not above fourteen thousand, marching towards him: he made himself merry with it, and said, *yonder* men are too many for an ambassage, and too few for a fight. *Bacon's Natural History.*

For proof look up,
And read thy lot in *yon* celestial sign. *Milton's Parad. Lost.*

Yon flow'ry arbors, *yonder* allies green. *Milton.*

Let other swains attend the rural care,
But nigh *yon* mountain let me tune my lays. *Pope.*

Yon. } *adv.* At a distance within view. It is used when we direct the eye from another thing to the object.
Yond. }
Yo'nder. }

The fringed curtains of thine eyes advance,
And say what thou see'st *yond.* *Shakesp. Tempest.*

First, and chiefest, with thee bring
Him that *yon* soars on golden wing,
Guiding the fiery-wheeled throne,
The cherub, contemplation. *Milton.*

Yonder are two apple-women scolding. *Arbuthn and Pope.*

Yond. *adj.* [I know not whence derived.] Mad; furious: perhaps transported with rage; under alienation of mind, in which sense it concurs with the rest.

Then like a lion, which hath long time fought
His robbed whelps, and at the last them found
Amongst the shepherd swains, then waxeth wood and *yond*;
So fierce he laid about him. *Fairy Queen.*

Nor those three brethren, Lombards, fierce and *yond.* *Fairf.*

Yore, or *of Yore. adv.* [ȝeoȝaɲa, Saxon]

1. Long.

Witness the burning altars, which he swore,
And, guilty, heavens of his bold perjury;
Which though he hath polluted oft and *yore*,
Yet I to them for judgment just do fly. *Fairy Queen.*

2. Of old time; long ago.

Thee bright-ey'd Vesta long *of yore*
To solitary Saturn bore. *Milton.*

There liv'd, as authors tell, in days *of yore*,
A widow somewhat old, and very poor. *Dryden.*

In times *of yore* an ancient baron liv'd;
Great gifts bestow'd, and great respect receiv'd. *Prior.*

The dev'l was piqu'd such saintship to behold,
And long'd to tempt him, like good Job of old;
But Satan now is wiser than *of yore*,
And tempts by making rich, not making poor. *Pope.*

You. *pron.* [eop, iuh, Saxon: the accusative of ȝe, ye.]

1. The oblique case of *ye.*

Ye have heard of the dispensation of the grace of God, which is given me to *you* ward. *Eph.* iii. 2.

I thought to show *you*
How easy 'twas to die, by my example,
And hansel fate before *you.* *Dryden's Cleomenes.*

2. It is used in the nominative; and though first introduced by corruption, is now established.

You nimble lightnings, dart your blinding flames
Into her scornful eyes. *Shakesp. King Lear.*

3. It is the ceremonial word for the second person singular, and is always used, except in solemn language.

Madam, the fates withstand, and *you*
Are destin'd Hymen's willing victim too. *Pope.*

4. It is used indefinitively, as the French *on.*

We passed by what was one of those rivers of burning matter: this looks, at a distance, like a new-plowed land; but as *you* come near it, *you* see nothing but a long heap of heavy disjointed clods. *Addison on Italy.*

YOUNG. *adj.* [ıonȝ, ȝeonȝ, Saxon; *jong*, Dutch.]

1. Being in the first part of life; not old.

Guests should be interlarded, after the Persian custom, by ages *young* and old. *Carew's Survey of Cornwall.*

He woos both high and low, both rich and poor,
Both *young* and old. *Shakespeare.*

There's not the smallest orb which thou behold'st,
But in his motion like an angel sings,
Still quiring to the *young*-ey'd cherubims. *Shakespeare.*

I firmly am resolv'd
Not to bestow my *youngest* daughter,
Before I have a husband for the elder. *Shakespeare.*

Thou old and true Menenius,
Thy tears are salter than a *younger* man's,
And venomous to thine eyes. *Shakespeare's Coriolanus.*

He ordain'd a lady for his prize,
Generally praiseful, fair and *young*, and skill'd in housewiferies. *Chapman.*

In timorous deer he hansels his *young* paws,
And leaves the rugged bear for firmer claws. *Cowley.*

Nor need'st by thy daughter to be told,
Though now thy sprity blood with age be cold,
Thou hast been *young.* *Dryden.*

When we say a man is *young*, we mean that his age is yet but a small part of that which usually men attain to: and when we denominate him old, we mean that his duration is run out almost to the end of that which men do not usually exceed. *Locke.*

It will be but an ill example to prove, that dominion, by God's ordination, belonged to the eldest son; because Jacob the *youngest* here had it. *Locke.*

From earth they rear him struggling now with death,
And Nestor's *youngest* stops the vents of breath. *Pope.*

2. Ignorant; weak.

Come, elder brother, thou art too *young* in this. *Shakesp.*

3. It is sometimes applied to vegetable life.

There be trees that bear best when they begin to be old, as almonds; the cause is, for that all trees that bear must have an oily fruit; and *young* trees have a more watry juice, and less concocted. *Bacon.*

Young. *n. s.* The offspring of animals collectively.

The hedge-sparrow fed the cuckoo so long,
That it had its head bit off by its *young.* *Shakesp. King Lear.*

So many days my ewes have been with *young*;
So many weeks ere the poor fools will yean. *Shakespeare.*

The eggs disclos'd their callow *young.* *Milton.*

The reason why birds are oviparous, and lay eggs, but do not bring forth their young alive, is because there might be more plenty. *More's Antidote against Atheism.*

Not so her *young*; for their unequal line
Was heroes make, half human, half divine;
Their earthly mold obnoxious was to fate,
Th' immortal part assum'd immortal state. *Dryden.*

Those insects, for whose *young* nature hath not made provision of sufficient sustenance, do themselves gather and lay up in store for them. *Ray on the Creation.*

You'ngish. *adj.* [from *young.*] Somewhat young.

She let her second room to a very genteel *youngish* man. *Tat.*

You'ngling. *n. s.* [from *young*; ȝeonȝlınȝ, Saxon.] Any creature in the first part of life.

More dear unto their God, than *younglings* to their dam. *Fairy Queen.*

Youngling, thou canst not love so dear as I.—
—Grey beard, thy love doth freeze. *Shakespeare.*

When we perceive that bats have teats, it is not unreasonable to infer, they suckle their *younglings* with milk. *Brown.*

Encourag'd thus she brought her *younglings* nigh. *Dryden.*

The stately beast the two Tyrrheidæ bred,
Snatch'd from his dam, and the tame *youngling* fed. *Dryden.*

YOU'NGLY. *adv.* [from *young.*]

1. Early in life.

Say we read lectures to you,
How *youngly* he began to serve his country,
How long continu'd, and what stock he springs of. *Shakesp.*

2. Ignorantly; weakly.

YOU'NGSTER. } [from *young.*] A young person. In con-
YOU'NKER. } tempt.

How like a *younker* or a prodigal
The skarfed bark parts from her native bay,
Hugg'd and embraced by the strumpet wind. *Shakespeare.*

What, will you make a *younker* of me? shall I not take mine ease in mine inn, but I shall so have my pocket pick'd. *Shakespeare's Henry IV.*

See how the morning opes her golden gates,
And takes her farewel of the glorious sun:
How well resembles it the prime of youth,
Trimm'd like a *yonker* prancing to his love. *Shakespeare.*

Fame tells, by age fame reverend grown,
That Phœbus gave his chariot to his son;
And whilst the *youngster* from the path declines,
Admiring the strange beauty of the signs,
Proud of his charge, he drove the fiery horse,
And would outdo his father in his course. *Creech.*

The *youngster*, who at nine and three,
Drinks with his sisters milk and tea,
From breakfast reads till twelve o'clock,
Burnet and Heylin, Hobbes and Locke. *Prior.*

YOUNGTH. *n. s.* [from *young.*] Youth. Obsolete.

The mournful muse in mirth now list ne mask,
As she was wont in *youngth* and summer days. *Spenser.*

YOUR. *pronoun.* [eoper, Saxon.]

1. Belonging to you. It is used properly when we speak to more than one, and ceremoniously and customarily when to only one.

Either *your* unparagoned mistress is dead, or she's outprized by a trifle. *Shakespeare.*

2. YOUR is used in an indeterminate sense.

Every true man's apparel fits *your* thief: if it be too little for *your* thief, *your* true man thinks it big enough. If it be too big for *your* thief, *your* thief thinks it little enough; so every true man's apparel fits *your* thief. *Shakespeare.*

There is a great affinity between coins and poetry, and *your* medallist and critick are much nearer related than the world imagine. *Addison on ancient Medals.*

A disagreement between these seldom happens, but among *your* antiquaries and schoolmen. *Felton on the Classicks.*

3. YOURS is used when the substantive goes before or is understood; as this is *your* book, this book is *yours*.

Pray for this man and for his issue,
Whose heavy hand hath bow'd you to the grave,
And beggar'd *yours* for ever. *Shakespeare's Macbeth.*

That done, our day of marriage shall be *yours*,
One feast, one house, one mutual happiness. *Shakespeare.*

This kiss, if it durst speak,
Would stretch thy spirits up into the air:
Conceive and fare thee well.—
—*Yours* in the ranks of death.—— *Shakespeare's King Lear.*

He is forsworn, if e'er those eyes of *yours*
Behold another day break in the east. *Shakespeare.*

While the sword this monarchy secures,
'Tis manag'd by an abler hand than *yours*. *Dryden.*
My wealth, my city and myself are *yours*. *Dryden.*

It is my employment to revive the old of past ages to the present, as it is *yours* to transmit the young of the present to the future. *Pope.*

YOURSE'LF. *n. s.* [*your* and *self*] You, even you; ye, not others.

If it stand as you *yourself* still do,
Within the eye of honour; be assur'd,
My purse, my person, my extremest means,
Lie all unlock'd to your occasions. *Shakespeare.*

O heav'ns!
If you do love old men, if your sweet sway
Allow obedience, if *yourselves* are old,
Make it your cause. *Shakespeare's King Lear.*

YOUTH. *n. s.* [ȝeoȝuð, Saxon.]

1. The part of life succeeding to childhood and adolescence; the time from fourteen to twenty eight.

But could *youth* last, and love still breed,
Had joys no date, and age no need;
Then these delights my mind might move,
To live with thee, and be thy love. *Shakespeare.*

See how the morning opes her golden gates,
And takes her farewel of the glorious sun;
How well resembles it the prime of *youth*,
Trim'd like a yonker, prancing to his love. *Shakesp.*

His starry helm unbuckled show'd him prime
In manhood, where *youth* ended. *Milton.*

The solidity, quantity, and strength of the aliment is to be proportioned to the labour or quantity of muscular motion, which in *youth* is greater than any other age. *Arbuthnot.*

2. A young man.

Siward's son,
And many unrough *youths* even now,
Protest their first of manhood. *Shakespeare's Macbeth.*

If this were seen,
The happiest *youth* viewing his progress through,
What perils past, what crosses to ensue,
Would shut the book and sit him down and die. *Shakesp.*

About him exercis'd heroick games
Th' unarmed *youth* of heav'n. *Milton.*

O'er the lofty gate his art emboss'd
Androgeos' death, and off'rings to his ghost;
Sev'n *youths* from Athens yearly sent, to meet
The fate appointed by revengeful Crete. *Dryden.*

The pious chief
A hundred *youths* from all his train elects,
And to the Latian court their course directs. *Dryden.*

3. Young men. Collectively.

As it is fit to read the best authors to *youth* first, so let them be of the openest and clearest; as Livy before Sallust, Sidney before Donne. *Ben. Johnson.*

The graces put not more exactly on
Th' attire of Venus, when the ball she won,
Than that young beauty by thy care is drest,
When all your *youth* prefers her to the rest. *Waller.*

YOU'THFUL. *adj.* [*youth* and *full.*]

1. Young.

Our army is dispers'd already:
Like *youthful* steers unyok'd they took their course,
East, west, north, south. *Shakespeare's Henry IV.*

There, in a heap of slain, among the rest,
Two *youthful* knights they found beneath a load opprest
Of slaughter'd foes. *Dryden.*

2. Suitable to the first part of life.

Here be all the pleasures
That fancy can beget on *youthful* thoughts,
When the fresh blood grows lively, and returns
Brisk as the April buds in primrose season. *Milton.*

In his years were seen,
A *youthful* vigour and autumnal green. *Dryden.*

The nymph surveys him, and beholds the grace
Of charming features, and a *youthful* face. *Pope.*

3. Vigorous as in youth.

How is a good Christian animated by a stedfast belief of an everlasting enjoyment of perfect felicity, such as, after millions of millions of ages is still *youthful* and flourishing, and inviting as at the first? no wrinkles in the face, no grey hairs on the head of eternity. *Bentley.*

YOU'THFULLY. *adv.* [from *youthful.*] In a youthful manner.

YOU'THLY. *adj.* [from *youth.*] Young; early in life. Obsolete.

True be thy words, and worthy of thy praise,
That warlike feats dost highest glorify,
Therein have I spent all my *youthly* days,
And many battles fought and many frays. *Fairy Queen.*

YOU'THY. *adj.* [from *youth.*] Young; youthful. A bad word.

The scribler had not genius to turn my age, as indeed I am an old maid, into raillery, for affecting a *youthier* turn than is consistent with my time of day. *Spectator.*

YPI'GHT. *part.* [*y* and *pight*, from *pitch.*] Fixed.

That same wicked wight
His dwelling has low in an hollow cave,
Far underneath a craggy clift *ypight*,
Dark, doleful, dreary, like a greedy grave. *Spenser.*

YUCK. *n. s.* [*jocken*, Dutch.] Itch.

YULE. *n. s.* [ȝeol, ȝeol, ȝehul, Saxon.] The time of Christmas.

YUX. *n. s.* [ȝeox, Saxon.] The hiccough.

Z.

Z, Is found in the Saxon alphabets, ſet down by Grammarians, but is read in no word originally Teutonick: its ſound is uniformly that of an hard S.

ZA'FFAR. }
ZA'FFIR. } *n. ſ.*

Powder the calx of cobalt, very fine, and mix it with three times its weight of powdered flints, this being wetted with common water, the whole concretes into a ſolid maſs called *zaffre*, which from its hardneſs has been miſtaken for a native mineral. *Hill on Foſſils.*

Cobalt being ſublimed, the flowers are of a blue colour; theſe, German mineraliſts call *zaffir.* *Woodward.*

The artificers in glaſs tinge their glaſs blue with that dark mineral *zaphara.* *Boyle on Colours.*

ZA'NY. *n. ſ.* [Probably of *zanei.*] The contraction of Giovanni or ſanna, a ſcoff, according to *Skinner.*] One employed to raiſe laughter by his geſtures, actions and ſpeeches; a merry Andrew; a buffoon.

Some carrytale, ſome pleaſeman, ſome ſlight *zany*,
Some mumblenews, ſome trencher knight, ſome Dick,
Told our intents before. *Shakeſpeare.*

Then write that I may follow, and ſo be
Thy echo, thy debtor, thy foil, thy *zany*,
I ſhall be thought, if mine like thine I ſhape,
All the world's lion, though I be thy ape. *Donne.*

Oh, great reſtorer of the good old ſtage,
Preacher at once, and *zany* of thy age. *Pope's Dunciad.*

ZA'RNICH. *n. ſ.* *Zarnich* is a ſolid ſubſtance in which orpiment is frequently found; and it approaches to the nature of orpiment, but without its luſtre and foliated texture. The common kinds of *zarnich* are green and yellow; and to this we owe the diſtinction of orpiment into theſe colours, though there is no ſuch ſubſtance as green orpiment. *Zarnich* contains a large quantity of arſenick in it. *Hill's Materia Medica.*

ZEAL. *n. ſ.* [ζῆλος, *zelus*, Latin.] Paſſionate ardour for any perſon or cauſe.

This preſent age, wherein *zeal* hath drowned charity and ſkill; meekneſs will not now ſuffer any man to marvel, whatſoever he ſhall hear reproved by whomſoever. *Hooker*

If I had had time to have made new liveries, I would have beſtowed the thouſand pound I borrowed of you: but it is no matter, this poor ſhow doth better; this doth infer the *zeal* I had to ſee him. *Shakeſpeare's Henry IV.*

O Cromwell, Cromwell!
Had I but ſerv'd my God with half the *zeal*
I ſerv'd my king, he would not in mine age
Have left me naked to mine enemies. *Shakeſpeare.*

Among the ſeraphims
Abdiel, than whom none with more *zeal* ador'd
The Deity, and divine commands obey'd,
Stood up, and in a flame of *zeal* ſevere,
The current of his fury thus oppos'd. *Milton's Parad. Loſt.*

Zeal, the blind conductor of the will. *Dryden.*

She with ſuch a *zeal* the cauſe embrac'd,
As women, where they will, are all in haſte;
The father, mother, and the kin beſide,
Were overborne by the fury of the tide. *Dryden.*

The princes applaud with a furious joy,
And the king ſeiz'd a flambeau with *zeal* to deſtroy. *Dryden.*

Seriouſneſs and *zeal* in religion is natural to the Engliſh. *Tillotſon's Sermons.*

Good men often blemiſh the reputation of their piety by over-acting ſome things in their religion; by an indiſcreet *zeal* about things wherein religion is not concerned. *Tillotſon.*

True *zeal* ſeems not to be any one ſingle affection of the ſoul; but rather a ſtrong mixture of many holy affections; rather a gracious conſtitution of the whole mind, than any one particular grace, ſwaying a devout heart, and filling it with all pious intentions; all not only uncounterfeit, but moſt fervent. *Sprat's Sermons.*

When the ſins of a nation have provoked God to forſake it, he ſuffers thoſe to concur in the moſt pernicious counſels for enſlaving conſcience, who pretend to the greateſt *zeal* for the liberty of it. *Stillingfleet.*

This rebellion has diſcovered to his majeſty, who have eſpouſed his intereſts with *zeal* or indifference. *Addiſon's Freeh.*

A ſcorn of flattery and a *zeal* for truth. *Pope.*

ZEA'LOT. *n. ſ.* [*zeloteur*, French; ζηλωτης.] One paſſionately ardent in any cauſe. Generally uſed in diſpraiſe.

The fury of *zealots*, inteſtine bitterneſs and diviſion were the greateſt occaſion of the laſt fatal deſtruction of Jeruſalem. *King Charles.*

Are not thoſe men too often the greateſt *zealots* who are moſt notoriouſly ignorant? true zeal ſhould always begin with true knowledge, and thence proceed to an unwearied paſſion, for what it once knows to be worthy of ſuch paſſion. *Sprat.*

No wonder that ſo many of theſe deluded *zealots* have been engaged in a cauſe which they at firſt abhorred, and have wiſhed or acted for the ſucceſs of an enterprize, that might have ended in the extirpation of the proteſtant religion. *Addiſon.*

ZEA'LOUS. *adj.* [from *zeal.*] Ardently paſſionate in any cauſe.

Our hearts are right with God, and our intentions pious, if we act our temporal affairs with a deſire no greater than our neceſſity, and in actions of religion we be *zealous*, active, and operative, ſo far as prudence will permit. *Taylor.*

This day, at height of noon, came to my ſphere,
A ſpirit, *zealous*, as he ſeem'd to know
More of the Almighty's works. *Milton's Paradiſe Loſt.*

We ſhould be not only devout towards God, but *zealous* towards men; endeavouring by all prudent means to recover them out of thoſe ſnares of the devil, whereby they are taken captive. *Decay of Piety.*

It is not at all good to be *zealous* againſt any perſon, but only againſt their crimes. It is better to be *zealous* for things than for perſons: but then it ſhould be only for good things; a rule that does certainly exclude all manner of zeal for ill things, all manner of zeal for little things. *Sprat's Sermons.*

Being inſtructed only in the general, and *zealous* in the main deſign; and as finite beings, not admitted into the ſecrets of government, the laſt reſorts of providence, or capable of diſcovering the final purpoſes of God, they muſt be ſometimes ignorant of the means conducing to thoſe ends in which alone they can oppoſe each other. *Dryden.*

ZEA'LOUSLY. *adv.* [from *zealous.*] With paſſionate ardour.

Thy care is fixt, and *zealouſly* attends,
To fill thy odorous lamp with deeds of light,
And hope that reaps not ſhame. *Milton.*

To enter into a party as into an order of friars, with ſo reſigned an obedience to ſuperiors, is very unſuitable with the civil and religious liberties we ſo *zealouſly* aſſert. *Swift.*

ZEA'LOUSNESS. *n. ſ.* [from *zealous.*] The quality of being zealous.

ZE'CHIN. *n. ſ.* [So named from *zecha*, a place in Venice where the mint is ſettled for coinage.] A gold coin worth about nine ſhillings ſterling.

ZEDO'ARY. *n. ſ.* [*zedoaire*, French.] A ſpicy plant, ſomewhat like ginger in its leaves, but of a ſweet ſcent.

ZED. *n. ſ.* The name of the letter z.

Thou whoreſon *zed*, thou unneceſſary letter. *Shakeſpeare.*

ZE'NITH. *n. ſ.* [Arabick.] The point over head oppoſite to the nadir.

Fond men! if we believe that men do live
Under the *zenith* of both frozen poles,
Though none come thence, advertiſement to give,
Why bear we not the like faith of our ſouls? *Davies.*

Theſe ſeaſons are deſigned by the motions of the ſun, when that approaches neareſt our *zenith*, or vertical point, we call it ſummer. *Brown's Vulgar Errours.*

ZE'PHYR. } *n. s.* [*zephyrus*, Latin.] The west wind; and
ZE'PHYRUS. } poetically any calm soft wind.

They are as gentle
As zephyrs blowing below the violet. *Shakespeare's Cymbeline.*

Zephyr, you shall see a youth with a merry countenance, holding in his hand a swan with wings displayed, as about to sing. *Peacham on Drawing.*

Forth rush the levent and the ponent winds,
Eurus and *Zephyr*. *Milton.*

Mild as when *Zephyrus* on Flora breathes. *Milton.*

Their every musick wakes,
Whence blending all the sweeten'd *zephyr* springs. *Thomson.*

ZEST. *n. s.*

1. The peel of an orange squeezed into wine.
2. A relish; a taste added.

To ZEST. *v. a.* To heighten by an additional relish.

ZETE'TICK. *adj.* [from ζητέω.] Proceeding by enquiry.

ZEU'GMA. *n. s.* [from ζεῦγμα.] A figure in Grammar, when a verb agreeing with divers nouns, or an adjective with divers substantives, is referred to one expresly, and to the other by supplement, as lust overcame shame, boldness fear, and madness reason.

ZOC'LE. *n. s.* [In architecture.] A small sort of stand or pedestal, being a low square piece or member, serving to support a busto, statue, or the like, that needs to be raised; also a low square member serving to support a column, instead of a pedestal, base, or plinth. *Dict.*

ZO'DIACK. *n. s.* [*zodiaque*, French; ζωδιακὸς, ἐκ τῶν ζώων, the living creatures, the figures of which are painted on it in globes.] The track of the sun through the twelve signs; a great circle of the sphere, containing the twelve signs.

The golden sun salutes the morn,
And having gilt the ocean with his beams,
Gallops the *zodiack* in his glist'ring coach. *Shakespeare.*

Years he number'd scarce thirteen,
When fates turn'd cruel;
Yet three fill'd *zodiacks* had he been
The stage's jewel. *Ben. Johnson.*

By his side,
As in a glist'ring *zodiack* hung the sword,
Satan's dire dread; and in his hand the spear. *Milton.*

It exceeds even their absurdity to suppose the *zodiack* and planets to be efficient of, and antecedent to themselves, or to exert any influences before they were in being. *Bentley.*

Here in a shrine that cast a dazling light,
Sat fixt in thought the mighty Stagyrite;
His sacred head a radiant *zodiack* crown'd,
And various animals his sides surround. *Pope.*

ZONE. *n. s.* [ζωνὴ; *zona*, Latin.]

1. A girdle.

The middle part
Girt like a starry *zone* his waist, and round
Skirted his loins, and thighs, with downy gold
And colours dipp'd in heav'n. *Milton's Paradise Lost.*

An embroider'd *zone* surrounds her waist. *Dryden.*

Thy statues, Venus, though by Phidias' hands
Design'd immortal, yet no longer stands;
The magick of thy shining *zone* is past,
But Salisbury's garter shall for ever last. *Granville.*

Scarce could the goddess from her nymph be known,
But by the crescent and the golden *zone*. *Pope.*

2. A division of the earth.

The whole surface of the earth is divided into five *zones*: the first is contained between the two tropicks, and is called the torrid *zone*. There are two temperate *zones*, and two frigid *zones*. The northern temperate *zone* is terminated by the tropick of Cancer and the artick polar circle: the southern temperate *zone* is contained between the tropick of Capricorn and the polar circle: the frigid *zones* are circumscribed by the polar circles, and the poles are in their centers.

True love is still the same: the torrid *zones*,
And those more frigid ones,
It must not know:
For love grown cold or hot,
Is lust or friendship, not
The thing we show;
For that's a flame would die,
Held down or up too high:
Then think I love more than I can express,
And would love more, could I but love thee less. *Suckling.*

As five *zones* th' etherial regions bind,
Five correspondent are to earth assign'd:
The sun, with rays directly darting down,
Fires all beneath, and fries the middle *zone*. *Dryden.*

3. Circuit; circumference.

Scarce the sun
Hath finish'd half his journey, and scarce begins
His other half in the great *zone* of heav'n. *Milton.*

ZOO'GRAPHER. *n. s.* [ζωὴ and γράφω.] One who describes the nature, properties, and forms of animals.

One kind of locust stands not prone, or a little inclining upward; but a large erectness, elevating the two fore legs, and sustaining itself in the middle of the other four, by *zoographers* called the prophet and praying locust. *Brown's Vulgar Errours.*

ZOO'GRAPHY. *n. s.* [of ζωὴ and γράφω.] A description of the forms, natures, and properties of animals.

If we contemplate the end of the effect, its principal final cause being the glory of its maker, this leads us into divinity; and for its subordinate, as it is designed for alimental sustenance to living creatures, and medicinal uses to man, we are thereby conducted into *zoography*. *Glanv. Sceps.*

ZOO'LOGY. *n. s.* [of ζῶον and λόγος.] A treatise concerning living creatures.

ZOO'PHYTE. *n. s.* [ζωόφυτον, of ζῶος and φυτὸν.] Certain vegetables or substances which partake of the nature both of vegetables and animals.

ZOOPHO'RICK *Column. n. s.* [In architecture.] A statuary column, or a column which bears or supports the figure of an animal. *Dict.*

ZOO'PHORUS. *n. s.* [ζωοφορος.] A part between the architraves and cornice, so called on account of the ornaments carved on it, among which were the figures of animals. *Dict.*

ZOO'TOMIST. *n. s.* [of ζωοτομία.] A dissector of the bodies of brute beasts.

ZOO'TOMY. *n. s.* [ζωτομία, of ζῶον and τεμνω.] Dissection of the bodies of beasts.

F I N I S.